WITHDRAWN

THE PUBLISHER'S PAGE

We call this book a directory but it's really a guide – a guide to the best practitioners in all the main areas of business law.

Our recommendations are based on thousands of interviews. Researchers talk to clients and attorneys throughout America, asking them about the lawyers they see in action. Comments that sum up the general opinion are quoted in the text. From this research, we compile our ratings – the tables that rank the leading law firms and individuals.

The recommendations, therefore, are objective, unbiased. No-one can 'buy their way in'. If the research doesn't justify a place in the tables, names are not included. We value our reputation for independence and objectivity.

Every year we improve our research. If you tell us we have overlooked someone who deserves to be mentioned, we take note in researching next year's edition. We aim to give you rankings and commentary you can rely on – a guide you can trust.

Michael Chambers

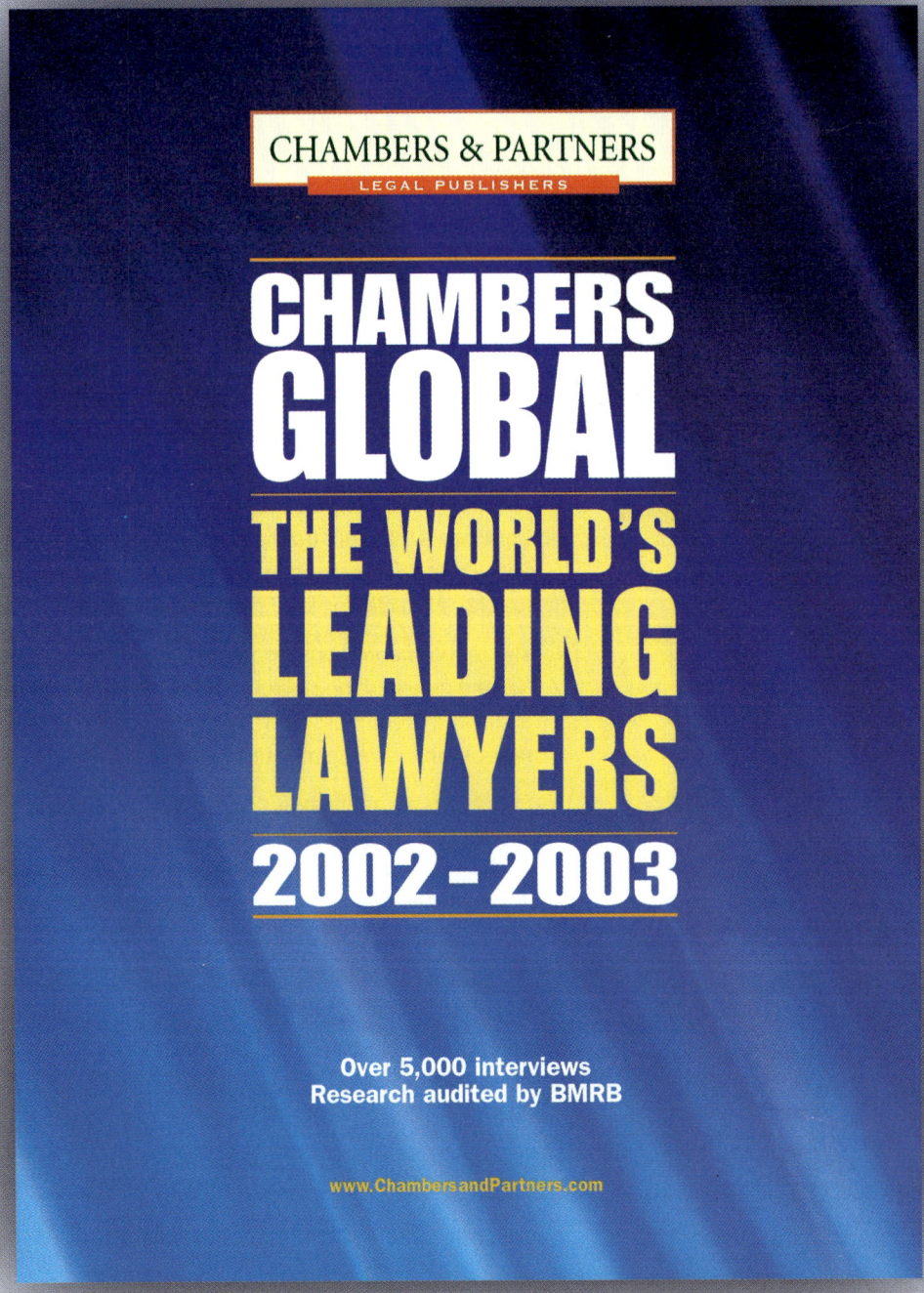

CONTENTS

OVERVIEWS

The research team	IV
The next Marty Lipton?	VI
Practice area overviews	VII
Law firms with the most ranked individuals	XXVI
Law firm mergers	XXX
Abbreviations used	XXXII

RANKINGS & COMMENTARY

Alabama	1		Montana	394
Alaska	9		Nebraska	400
Arizona	16		Nevada	406
Arkansas	23		New Hampshire	415
California	28		New Jersey	424
Colorado	75		New Mexico	433
Connecticut	87		New York	439
Delaware	94		North Carolina	544
District of Columbia	102		North Dakota	554
Florida	150		Ohio	558
Georgia	180		Oklahoma	580
Hawaii	212		Oregon	587
Idaho	219		Pennsylvania	595
Illinois	223		Rhode Island	620
Indiana	277		South Carolina	624
Iowa	286		South Dakota	630
Kansas	294		Tennessee	635
Kentucky	300		Texas	643
Louisiana	307		Utah	684
Maine	319		Vermont	692
Maryland	327		Virginia	698
Massachusetts	336		Washington	706
Michigan	360		West Virginia	714
Minnesota	368		Wisconsin	723
Mississippi	378		Wyoming	730
Missouri	385			

LAW FIRM PROFILES 759

OTHER RECOMMENDED FIRMS 911

GENERAL COUNSEL TO THE FORTUNE 500	739	**INDEX TO INDIVIDUAL LAWYERS**	975
INDEX TO ALL LAW FIRMS	957		

Published by **Chambers & Partners Publishing**
(a division of Orbach & Chambers Ltd)
Saville House, 23 Long Lane, London EC1A 9HL
Tel 011 44 207 606 1300
Fax 011 44 207 600 3191

Publisher Michael Chambers
Editors Rieta Ghosh, Paula Wasley
Assistant Editor Catherine Willberg
Editorial Assistant Joanne Grote
Profiles Editors Richard Pettet, Alex Ballantine
Profiles Assistants Charlotte Rankin, Hayley Whiting
Production Team Jasper John, Paul Cummings

Business Development Manager Brad Sirott
Distribution Marli Enslin
Orders to: Chambers & Partners Publishing
Printed in England by Polestar Wheatons Ltd

ISBN 0-5514-420-3
Copyright © 2003 Michael Chambers and Orbach and Chambers Ltd

THE RESEARCH TEAM 2002-2003

- **Paula Wasley**
Read English at Princeton University and took a Diploma in French at the Sorbonne. Subsequently a bilingual assistant at a top Paris Hotel and a research assistant to a correspondent at the Paris office of a major news agency.

- **James Lloyd**
Read Philosophy at UCL followed by a Masters in Comparative Politics at the University of York. Has also written for Chambers Student Guide.

- **Susana Claudio**
Degree in Journalism (1994-1998) at University of Seville, Spain. Correspondent to Spanish Television during national elections, writer in Spanish newspaper Diario de Andalucia. One year in Rome working as a communications consultant. Fluent in Spanish, Italian and French.

- **Penuel Burchall**
Read English Language and Literature at St Hugh's College, Oxford. Worked in the editorial department of a reference publishing house before receiving an MA with Distinction from the University of Durham.

- **Julian Segal**
Read Business Studies at Manchester University. Trained with London West End firm for two years specialising in property and employment law. Subsequently worked as a sports broadcast journalist.

- **Sophia Digas**
Studied political and social sciences at Lund University and the Universiteit Van Amsterdam. Completed an MA at Loughborough University, and International Journalism Diploma from Washington DC with internship at the Washington Times. Fluent in Swedish, Greek and English.

- **Isabel Tonge**
Graduated from Manchester University with a First in English Language and Literature. Undertook an internship with the European Commission and has worked as an English teacher in South America.

- **Anna Saunders**
Read English Literature & Language at Pembroke College, Oxford before training and working as a Fine Art Auctioneer.

- **Thao Hua**
Read history at the University of North Texas and later completed a one-year law research fellowship for journalists at the University of Michigan. Worked as a legal affairs writer for a top US newspaper.

- **Alexandra Quilici**
Read Politics at the American University in Paris. Completed a Masters in Modern History and a Masters in Political and Social Communications at Université Paris 1 Panthéon-Sorbonne. Has worked in business research, advertising sales and financial information. Bilingual.

- **Cristina Dominguez**
Admitted to the Florida State Bar. JD, cum laude, University of Miami School of Law. BA, The American University majoring in International Relations. Fluent in Spanish and Italian.

- **Catherine Rodgers**
Graduated from King's College London with a first in English Language and Literature. Completed two mini-pupillages with sets of barristers, gaining experience in aspects of criminal law.

- **Mark Knowles**
Read classics followed by management studies at Downing College, Cambridge. Worked as a preparatory school teacher, sports journalist with a published book on the 2002 FIFA World Cup and a headhunter.

- **Richard James**
Read English Literature at the University of Wales, Cardiff. Former paralegal and recently published author.

- **Kerrie Taylor**
Solicitor. Read Spanish at University of St Andrews and University of Salamanca, Spain. Trained with leading Inns of Court law firm in London.

INTRODUCTION

This guide – like *Chambers UK* and *Chambers Global* – is designed to reflect market opinion.

Entry in the guide is based solely on market recommendation. Our researchers spent a year canvassing clients and lawyers across the US to obtain a consistent market view of which firms and attorneys are considered leaders in their field. Over 4500 telephone interviews were conducted, from Maine to Hawaii. Tens of thousands of comments were collected. These are the results.

We accept that there is ultimately no strict scientific basis on which to compare the value and quality of lawyers. What appeals to one client may not appeal to another. But by interviewing enough sources, a ranking does emerge – a ranking created by the market. Not everyone will agree with it, but clients will be interested to see if their own preferences are shared by others.

● Lloyd Pearson
Read Politics at University of Leeds. Worked as a political researcher for a government minister. Subsequently took up graduate scheme in publishing and worked as researcher for a travel organisation.

● Naomi Lawson
Read German at Lady Margaret Hall, Oxford. Worked in Germany for a year as an English teaching assistant before gaining experience in various areas of publishing.

● Marco di Palma
Read French and English at King's College, London. M.Litt (Magdalen College, Oxford) and Ph.D (University College, London). Has worked in public broadcasting, teaching and as a legal translator/writer for a multinational corporation in Turin, Italy. Fluent in French and Italian.

● Joanne O'Connor
Read law at the University of New South Wales, Sydney, Australia. Graduated with a first in postgraduate study in English Literature. Worked as a researcher for a leading Sydney law firm.

● Tanja Roug
Lawyer. Read law at Copenhagen University, Denmark. Subsequently gained an LLM with distinction at Southampton University. Worked as a lawyer in a boutique patent and trademark firm in London. Speaks fluent Danish and German.

● Sonya Sceats
Graduated from the Australian National University with first class Honours and the University Medal in Political Science, followed by a Bachelor of Laws. Experience working as an academic researcher and paralegal in a number of city London and Sydney firms.

● Lee Saunders
Read French and History at University of Leeds. Worked as an English teacher in Paris, France and subsequently as a research analyst in London for an American media company.

● Kathryn Duke
Read Classical Civilisation at Kent University. Previous experience includes both book and magazine publishing and extensive freelance journalism.

● Gemma Westacott
Degree in Journalism, Queensland University of Technology (Australia). Senior court reporter for Australian newspaper. Last worked for UK business trade magazine.

● Eleni Chalkidou
MA in Journalism from Westminster University. Worked as a journalist for BBC News Online, International Financial Law Review and Corporate Finance magazine. Fluent in Greek, German, Spanish and Krio (spoken in Sierra Leone).

● Katharine Skorupska
Read Philosophy and French at New College, Oxford; MA with distinction in Renaissance French from New College, Oxford. Has taught English in Paris, and worked as an Academic Advisor for American visiting students to Oxford.

● William Cummins
Lawyer. Read law at the University of Sussex. LLM at School of Oriental & African Studies, University of London in public international law. Trained at a City law firm. Applying for admission as an attorney in New York following successful bar examination.

● Ben Tendler
Graduated from the University of Bristol with a First in English Literature. Previously worked as a freelance market researcher.

● Michael Leigh
Gained a First in Philosophy from Bristol University, where he also completed a doctorate in modern social contract theory. Has taught ethics and political philosophy and undertaken freelance satire for local newspapers.

THE NEXT MARTY LIPTON?

Martin Lipton, founder of Wachtell Lipton Rosen & Katz and "inventor of M&A"

Richard Beattie, Simpson Thacher & Bartlett

Allen Finkelson, Cravath, Swaine & Moore

David Katz, Wachtell, Lipton, Rosen & Katz

To be hailed a "legend" in one's lifetime is an honor that few can boast. But Martin Lipton has always been exceptional. The famous founding partner of New York's elite Wachtell Lipton Rosen & Katz reached the pinnacle of his career during the 80's era of hostile takeovers and, in the view of many, has remained there ever since. Together with Skadden Arps founder Joseph Flom, Lipton is credited with "inventing M&A" and is still celebrated for his development of the 'poison-pill' defense technique.

Described by peers as a "phenomenon like no other," Lipton has created an enormous legacy, both in terms of the corporate powerhouse firm he created and in the enormous contributions he has made to the US legal market. At 71, he shows no signs of slowing down. Sources report "you can't keep him out of the office" and in the past year alone Lipton has put his names to such deals as South African Breweries' $5.6 billion merger with Philip Morris' Miller Brewing and Publicis' merger with BCom3. Nevertheless, market observers have already begun debating whether there is anyone in New York with the star quality to fill Marty's shoes.

In an effort to answer this engaging question, Chambers' researchers surveyed a collection of Fortune 500 clients and leading New York lawyers, asking them: "Who is the next Martin Lipton?"

Although opinion in the market was very much divided, a few select names consistently rose to the top of Chambers' findings. To determine the point, we thought we'd ask the mighty man himself, and presented our list of finalists to Martin Lipton for his comment.

The shortlist of potential successors, as identified by interviewees, spanned many generations and several firms. Among those recommended were: Richard Beattie, 64, of Simpson Thacher & Bartlett; Allen Finkelson, 57, of Cravath, Swaine & Moore; and David Katz, 39, of Wachtell, Lipton, Rosen & Katz.

Simpson Thacher chairman Richard Beattie was lauded by many for his "magnificent reputation" and ability to advise on complex matters ranging from crisis management to corporate governance. While closer to Lipton's own generation, Beattie scored highest with clients, who consider him both a valued "rainmaker" and "the engine of the firm." Praise was also forthcoming from Lipton, who asserted: "He is certainly a frontrunner and is well recognized worldwide for his tremendous skills."

Allen Finkelson at Cravaths was admired by competitors and clients for his "flair" for complex M&A transactions. This deeply experienced attorney "has seen it all before." Particularly well-regarded in the media and technology sectors, Finkelson acts as principal counsel to IBM in its acquisition and joint venture activities. Beloved for his "bright and witty demeanor," Finkelson received credit from Lipton who acknowledged his talent and listed him "among the very best."

At Lipton's own firm, David Katz emerged as the most likely heir apparent to the Wachtell legacy. At 39, Katz is young in comparison with his illustrious colleagues and was referred to as "the only truly emerging one" by Martin Lipton, who was, unsurprisingly, emphatic in his endorsement. Roundly praised as a star in the making, Katz was identified as the attorney within the next generation of New York attorneys who most displayed the "get-up-and-go" that made Lipton's career. Commentators applauded his "everlasting energy," his involvement in the toughest deals, and the "passion" with which he approaches difficult negotiations. Lipton himself modestly described Katz as "the best M&A lawyer in the world."

Practice Area Overviews

Antitrust	VII	Environment	XVI
Arbitration	VII	Insurance	XVII
Banking & Finance	VIII	Intellectual Property	XVIII
Bankruptcy	IX	Litigation	XIX
Capital Markets	X	Media & Entertainment	XXI
Construction	X	Private Equity	XXIII
Communications	XI	Project Finance	XXIII
Corporate/M&A	XII	Real Estate	XXIV
Employment	XV	Shipping	XXV
Energy & Natural Resources	XVI	Tax	XXV

ANTITRUST

Antitrust law has enjoyed an upswing in public discussion following press coverage of the US monopoly case against Microsoft. The software giant faces further monopoly claims in Europe. In New York, **Cravath Swaine & Moore** led AOL Time Warner in an antitrust suit against Microsoft, alleging the PC operating systems provider attempted to force AOL's Netscape from the market. Evan Chesler was lead partner in the case. Meanwhile Harry Reasoner from **Vinson & Elkins** in Texas represented Sun Microsystems in urging the US Department of Justice to commence antitrust proceedings against Microsoft. The firm's antitrust group is supported by a strong regulatory practice in Washington DC. Other notable cases include defending Blockbuster in pricing conspiracy allegations brought by independent video retailers.

Covering the gamut of antitrust law, **Arnold & Porter** has recently tackled some of the most complex antitrust litigation in Washington DC. Particularly well-versed in IP matters, the firm defended Xerox in challenges to its refusal to sell patented parts and copyrighted software. Heavy hitters within the team include Bill Baer, Michael Sohn and Donna Patterson.

Bingham McCutchen stood out in the Massachusetts market for partner Daniel Goldberg's work in drafting the Massachusetts Antitrust Act. The group also offers expertise in relation to government enforcement issues, compliance programs and monopolizations. Renowned partner John 'Jack' Curtin has recently acted in international price-fixing cartel matters in the graphite and carbon fiber industries.

In Pennsylvania, interviewees consistently recommended **Dechert** as the market leader. Drawing on resources from as far away as London and Brussels, the team has handled high-profile cases including government investigations of such heavyweights as GlaxoSmithKline. Joseph Tate focuses on the defense of blue-chip clients in class action suits. Colleague George Gordon successfully defended American Airlines in a case alleging conspiracy to fix and reduce commissions for travel agents abroad.

Kenny Nachwalter Seymour Arnold Critchlow & Spector is a key player in Florida, especially for representing plaintiffs who opt out of antitrust class actions, largely in Sherman Act conspiracy cases. Bill Blechman won renown for appearing for the plaintiffs in DC's District Court in the vitamins antitrust litigation against Takeda Vitamin & Food USA.

In Georgia, **King & Spalding** earns respect for its solutions-oriented advice on all aspects of trade regulation and competition law. The firm is also admired for handling complex antitrust investigations and litigation. Jeff Cashdan was cocounsel for Coca-Cola in a claim brought by PepsiCo alleging monopolization in the fountain beverage segment.

Several firms dominate the Illinois market, including **Kirkland & Ellis**, which is known for its trial-readiness. Tefft Smith was lead defense counsel to Kraft in a nationwide cheese price-fixing case, while Andrew Langan defended Abbott Laboratories in a brand name prescription drugs case. Competitor **Mayer Brown Rowe & Maw**'s robust antitrust advisory practice is said to bolster its strength in litigation. The group was also recommended for pre-merger notifications and advice on franchise agreements. Key partner Lee Abrams was lead trial lawyer for Ford in the ChoiceParts antitrust litigation.

The Californian market is dominated by **Gibson Dunn & Crutcher**. Complemented by a strong regulatory team in DC, the firm covers the gamut of antitrust counseling and litigation, including private treble damages, preliminary injunction litigation and class action defense, for an international clientele. Most notably Bob Cooper has recently acted on the Hewlett-Packard dispute involving Intel.

ARBITRATION

The two main centers for international arbitration remain New York and Washington DC. There are a number of major law firms across the US that possess a high level of experience in arbitrations before the AAA, ICC and ICSID, but such teams often combine this speciality with complex commercial litigation.

In New York, the field is dominated by **Debevoise & Plimpton**. Here, Donald Donavan and David Rivkin handle international arbitrations in the energy, construction and insurance fields. The firm has acted on a multibillion AAA arbitration between a US and a European company arising from a venture in Latin America.

White & Case remains the key player in the DC market, where it can draw on complementary strength offered by its New York-based attorneys. Carolyn Lamm and Abby Cohen Smutny are respected for their work in ICSID proceedings and arbitrations before other bodies, on behalf of sovereign bodies and foreign corporate clients. Any discussion of DC arbitration specialists would not be complete without mention of John Townsend of **Hughes Hubbard & Reed**. He was described by observers as "the archetypal Washington insider," and is famed for his expertise in AAA and ICC arbitrations.

PRACTICE OVERVIEWS

BANKING & FINANCE

Top ten US loans

Borrower	Loan Package $billions	Principal Amount $bn	Bookrunner(s)	Lawyers Borrowers	Lawyers Lenders
General Electric Capital	16.03	7.25	JPM/CITIBANK(JB)	n/a	Simpson Thacher & Bartlett
Comcast	12.825	7.0	JPMCH/BOA(JB)	Davis Polk & Wardwell	Simpson Thacher & Bartlett
AOL Time Warner	10.0	6.0	JPMCH/BOA(JB)	Cravath Swaine & Moore	Simpson Thacher & Bartlett
Weyerhaeuser	8.0	4.0	JPM/MS-SENIORFUND(JB)	n/a	n/a
General Motors Acceptance	7.35	7.35	JPM/BOA(JB)	n/a	n/a
Verizon Communications	7.0	7.0	JPM	In-house	Cravath Swaine & Moore
American Express	7.0	5.95	JPM	n/a	n/a
Morgan Stanley Dean Witter	5.5	5.5	JPM	Shearman & Sterling	Cravath Swaine & Moore
EchoStar Communications	5.5	2.75	DEUTSCHE-NY/CSFB(JB)	n/a	White & Case
Household Finance	5.385	4.485	JPM/BOA(JB)	n/a	n/a

Source: Loan Information – Thomson Financial; Law firms – Chambers & Partners

As our table indicates, the market for massive syndicated loans remains the dominion of the Wall Street firms. **Cravath Swaine & Moore** continues to enjoy strong ties to JPMorgan Chase, tackling the toughest multi-currency loans. The practice neatly dovetails expertise in acquisition financing and restructuring – led by Rob Kiessling – with its highly specialist work in LBO financings, conducted under the guidance of Allen Parker. **David Polk & Wardwell** has witnessed the mergers of its key clients DLJ (with CSFB) and JPMorgan (with Chase Manhattan), emerging relatively unscathed. Here, Brad Smith and his team have acted on Comcast's financing to acquire AT&T Broadband. At **Simpson Thacher & Bartlett**, smooth negotiator Frank Huck acted for JPMorgan Chase on the largest syndicated loan of the year, made to GE Capital. The firm's prowess in the private equity market has also ensured the banking group a strong profile for leveraged financing.

In Massachusetts, the 2002 merger between Bingham Dana and McCutchen Doyle has created the highly respected asset-based and acquisition financing practice of **Bingham McCutchen**. An historical relationship with the Bank of Boston and extensive dealings with Fleet Bank has placed the firm at the forefront of the market. It shares the limelight with Boston-based **Goodwin Procter**, an extensive practice best known for its regulatory expertise and its representation of community banks. In Philadelphia, **Blank Rome** operates a nationally respected practice that has advised American Business Financial Services in issuing more than a billion dollars in pass-through certificates.

Shutts & Bowen's banking team, operating from offices in Orlando and Miami, is lauded as the preeminent banking regulatory specialist in Florida, attracting both domestic and foreign banks, including the principal player in Latin America. In Georgia, the banking practice of **Alston & Bird** is synonymous with megadeals, and transactions with an international element. The team has advised on the restructuring of banks in Indonesia, Russia and most recently Afghanistan. For regulatory issues, and the representation of community banks, **Powell Goldstein Frazer & Murphy** has carved out a first-class reputation. The group has guided financial institutions on their privatization strategies. In North Carolina, the Charlotte firm **Moore & Van Allen** was singled out by clients for its experience of secured and unsecured financings and bond issuance both in the state and across state borders.

Outside of New York, Illinois remains a key market for sophisticated multi-jurisdictional financings. **Mayer Brown Rowe & Maw** fields a team of great depth and talent. Market sources spoke especially of its structured finance expertise and its involvement in strategic restructurings. Robert Baptista is the firm's leading light, and brings to the table his abilities as a practical deal-closer. **Sidley Austin Brown & Wood** has a long roster of high-quality practitioners. The group, under the guidance of senior statesman Bruce Bernstein, enjoys a national profile in syndicated loans and acquisition finance for such clients as Bank of America, Bank One and Citibank. In the securitization arena, this group can often be found at the cutting edge of new product development.

Two other firms in the Midwest stood out during our research.

PRACTICE OVERVIEWS

Jones Day is one of the most respected national firms in the US. From its office in Cleveland, the banking and finance practice draws on extensive national and global resources, successfully integrating 25 offices. This multidisciplinary group acts on capital markets, private equity and bankruptcy-related transactions. **Squire Sanders & Dempsey** has established strong connections with an admired client base of major financial institutions. The group's understanding of public finance, particularly bond issuance, combines well with its multinational syndicated loans practice.

On the West coast, **Gibson Dunn & Crutcher**'s Los Angeles-based finance group was commended for its breadth of practice. It has a national reputation for acquisition financing on behalf of hi-tech corporates and private equity funds. **O'Melveny & Myers** splits its department into two groups: financial institutions and financing. These groups cooperate with the firm's overseas offices on cross-border transactions, and have developed strong ties to developers and lenders in the media sector.

BANKRUPTCY OVERVIEW

Top ten bankruptcies

	Company	bankruptcy date	Total Assets (prebankruptcy) $bn	Company Lawyers	Lawyer to the Unsecured Creditors' Committee
1	WorldCom	7/21/02	$103.9	Weil Gotshal & Manges	Akin Gump Strauss Hauer & Feld
2	Conseco	12/18/02	$61.392	Kirkland & Ellis	Fried Frank Harris Shriver & Jacobson
3	Global Crossing	1/28/02	$30.185	Weil Gotshal & Manges	Brown Rudnick Berlack Israel
4	UAL Corporation	12/9/02	$25.197	Kirkland & Ellis	Sonnenschein Nath & Rosenthal
5	Adelphia	6/25/02	$21.499	Willkie Farr & Gallagher	Kasowitz Benson Torres & Friedman
6	Kmart Corporation	1/22/02	$14.63	Skadden Arps Slate Meagher & Flom	Otterbourg Steindler Houston & Rosen
7	NTL .	5/8/02	$13.026	Skadden Arps Slate Meagher & Flom	Fried Frank Harris Shriver & Jacobson
8	US Airways, .	11/8/02	$7.941	Skadden Arps Slate Meagher & Flom	Otterbourg Steindler Houston & Rosen
9	XO Communications	17/6/02	$7.93	Willkie Farr & Gallagher	Akin Gump Strauss Hauer & Feld
10	Williams Comms	22/4/02	$5.992	White & Case	Kirkland & Ellis

Corporate uncertainty and the generally troubled state of the US economy have produced a wealth of restructuring and Chapter 11 work. Insolvency departments around the US are reaping the benefits.

The past year saw America's largest bankruptcy filing to date: WorldCom's $104 billion Chapter 11 filing. The lead role in the case was snapped up by New York's **Weil Gotshal & Manges**, seen by many to be the nation's preeminent debtors' practice. The firm has an historic focus on corporate restructuring and has had a tremendously successful year, acting as debtors' counsel in two of 2002's top ten bankruptcies. Accomplished attorney Marcia Goldstein led the firm's representation of WorldCom, while colleague Martin Bienenstock cemented his reputation in the field through his role as Chapter 11 counsel to Enron, which filed for Chapter 11 in December 2001.

At a national level, Weil Gotshal competes with **Skadden Arps Slate Meagher & Flom** for the largest cases. Boasting an enormous national team, Skadden Arps has significant strength and depth and undertakes major work from practices in New York, Chicago, Wilmington and Los Angeles. The powerhouse firm also fares well in our table of top ten bankruptcies, appearing as debtors' counsel in the Chapter 11 proceedings for Kmart, NTL and US Airways. The firm has the resources to coordinate large matters between offices across the US. And the presence of Chicago-based bankruptcy superstar John (Jack) Butler adds to its profile in the market.

Also strongest in Chicago, **Kirkland & Ellis** was identified as a market leader for its breadth of practice. This nationally renowned practice features major player Jamie Sprayregen who acted in the bankruptcies of Conseco, United Airlines and Williams Communications.

Debtor-oriented **Willkie Farr & Gallagher** also made headlines with its representation of Adelphia Communications and XO Communications in bankruptcy proceedings. On the creditors' side, firms such as **Milbank Tweed Hadley & McCloy** and **Fried Frank Harris Shriver & Jacobson** are recognized as top names in the area, while **Akin Gump Strauss Hauer & Feld** and **Brown Rudnick Berlack Israels** have niches in bondholder work.

Along the eastern seaboard, Boston-based firms **Goodwin Procter** and **Hale and Dorr** were rated for broad experience of both debtor and creditor representation while, in Pennsylvania, **Blank Rome,**

PRACTICE OVERVIEWS

Duane Morris and Reed Smith all share top band rankings. **Wilmer Cutler & Pickering** has acted on a string of notable cases, including PSINet, Iridium and ANC Rental and ranks in DC alongside **Swidler Berlin Shereff Friedman**.

Delaware has traditionally been a hub for Chapter 11 activity, thanks to the state's bankruptcy courts' traditionally favorable stance toward debtors. Here, **Young Conaway Stargatt & Taylor**, featuring Jim Patton, emerged as a premier name for reorganizations, prepackaged bankruptcies and out-of-court workouts.

In the South, Atlanta-based **Alston & Bird** has a heavy marketshare of debtors' work, advising the likes of Einstein Brothers Bagels and the Atlanta Gas Light Company in corporate restructuring and troubled company acquisition. **Berger Singerman** is prominent in Florida acting for creditors, debtors and creditors' committees and shares pole position in the state with full-service firm **Greenberg Traurig**. **Haynes and Boone** was a clear leader in Texas where respected attorneys Robin Phelan and Bob Albergotti have led the team to success in international workouts and business reorganizations.

The California market has been dominated by a never-ending flow of technology bankruptcies. Insolvency boutique **Klee Tuchin Bogdanoff & Stern** owes its rise in the market in part to this steady stream of work. The 15-attorney firm advised on the debt restructuring of Anacomp and represented Frederick's of Hollywood in its Chapter 11. Rival **Pachulski Stang Ziehl Young Jones & Weintraub** boasts California's largest bankruptcy team and has been visible acting for the likes of Gencor Industries in reorganization matters.

CAPITAL MARKETS

The capital markets remain quiet as the slowdown in equity issuances continues. The drop in IPO activity, most noticeable within the foundering telecom sector, has brought bond work to the fore, and many of the larger Wall Street firms are increasing their emphasis on debt offerings and bond refinancing. In the current economic climate, it is primarily those firms with historic depth in the field and long-standing ties to the major investment banks that have been able to maintain stable practices. Market sources also cite international reach as an important factor in a firm's success, as those practices with developed worldwide networks have greater access to work in both the US and European and Asian exchanges and are best able to perform in an increasingly globalized marketplace.

Top-tier practice **Davis Polk & Wardwell** scores well on all counts, boasting both close ties to JPMorgan Chase and Morgan Stanley and a large team of capital markets specialists across offices in New York, London, Paris, Frankfurt, Tokyo and Hong Kong that is consistently praised for high standards of quality. Even the famously US-centric **Cravath Swaine & Moore** has strength at the international level with practitioners in London and Hong Kong providing support to an accomplished New York team on global offerings. Cravaths has benefited from the perceived 'flight to quality;' its brand name cachet has brought in some of the larger IPOs of the year such as Alcon Laboratories $2.2 billion flotation.

New York's two primary high yield debt practices **Cahill Gordon & Reindel** and **Latham & Watkins** have lately been involved in debt restructuring activities. **Sullivan & Cromwell** fares particularly well in *Chambers*' tables, earning top-band rankings for both debt & equity work and derivatives. Here, names such as securities lawyer Bill Williams and commodities expert Ken Raisler are considered particular assets. In derivatives, the firm shares pole position with **Cleary Gottlieb Steen & Hamilton**. Hailed by interviewees as "a premier Wall Street practice" Cleary Gottlieb has been active both in regulatory matters and industry initiatives as well as in the development of novel products and growth areas such as credit derivatives.

Growth in synthetic and hybrid products has seen closer cooperation between firms' derivatives and securitization lawyers. Some, such as **Sidley Austin Brown & Wood** have taken steps to formally integrate the two practice areas.

Orrick Herrington & Sutcliffe is considered a market leader in the securitization of all asset classes. The California-headquartered firm secures a top-band ranking in New York, thanks to Ed de Sear and Cam Cowan's stellar market reputations. **Skadden Arps Slate Meagher & Flom** enjoys national renown for its capital markets capacities. The firm features highly in the New York securitization tables for its work in traditional securitizations and novel CDO and restructuring transactions.

In California, Skadden Arps emerged as the joint market leader with **Wilson Sonsini Goodrich & Rosati**. The Skadden Arps LA team is known for its links to CSFB and strength in debt and high yield finance while Bay Area firm Wilson Sonsini has built up respected debt & equity and derivatives practices off the back of its famed technology-sector focus.

CONSTRUCTION

Within construction law, national specialist firm **Thelen Reid & Priest** dominates the market by dint of its strength and breadth throughout the country. The firm secures top-band rankings in the field for its core Los Angeles, San Francisco, New York and DC offices. The product of a 1998 bicoastal merger between two historically renowned market leaders, the firm enjoys an outstanding national reputation that has attracted such valued clients as Bechtel and Bovis Lend Lease in New York and Swinerton Builders, Kajima and DPR Construction in California. The group advises on all aspects of construction law, with particular expertise in large infrastructure and development projects. Seen recently representing Ebasco against Exxon, John Clark in Los Angeles was saluted as an icon of construction litigation while San Francisco partner Stephen O'Neal earned high marks for his involvement in many of San Francisco's most significant construction disputes.

If the firm reigns supreme in California it faces tough competition from **Peckar & Abramson** and **Postner & Rubin** in New York. Headquartered in New Jersey, Peckar & Abramson is the founding member of the International Construction Law Alliance and has been involved in the largest construction issues. Name partner Robert Peckar, is particularly active in national and international arbitration proceedings. Eight-lawyer boutique Postner & Rubin is heavily involved in highway construction, marine, healthcare, industrial and housing facilities. Firm founders Bill Postner and Bob Rubin were both recognized for their experience in the field.

Operating from offices in Miami, Orlando and Tampa, **Carlton Fields** undertakes all aspects of construction law and dominates the Florida market. Areas covered range from transactional to litigious matters: the firm is particularly noted for its work on public/private development projects. George Meyer was identified as one of the firm's chief assets. This highly respected lawyer has advised on some of the region's most publicized projects. The firm's clients include well-known names such as Kellogg Brown & Root, Lucent Technologies and Fairfield Resorts. Its closest competitor is 12-attorney Fort Lauderdale boutique **Leiby Taylor Stearns Linkhorst & Roberts**, which acts for a variety of developers, owners, designers and contractors. Star attorney Larry Leiby is the founder of the Florida Bar construction law committee and was widely recommended as a deeply experienced practitioner. Leiby is regularly involved in sophisticated transactions and most notably represented Dooley & Mack Constructors against the Florida Board of Education in payment disputes. In Virginia, **Watt Tieder Hoffar & Fitzgerald** impressed researchers with its talented team, featuring leading attorneys Jules Hoffar and John Tieder. The firm has a heavy focus on contentious work.

Full service firm **Schiff Hardin & Waite** and construction boutique **Stein Ray & Harris** share pole position in the Illinois construction rankings. Stein Ray & Harris represents contractors and owners and is currently acting for the University of Chicago in its large construction program. Schiff Hardin & Waite, which advised on the Chicago Bears' $632 million renovation of their Soldier Field stadium, is especially recognized for its outstanding attorneys Paul Lurie and Mark Friedlander. The latter is particularly renowned for his groundbreaking work on design-build agreements. In Ohio, **Thompson Hine** was acknowledged as among the Midwest's leading construction practices. The firm acts predominantly for Ohio-based clients and receives praise for its activities on public and state entities and athletics projects.

The 13-lawyer Texan firm **Canterbury Stuber Elder Gooch & Surratt** rates highly for its contentious proficiency. Under the leadership of top-band attorney, Joe Canterbury, the firm represents contractors and subcontractors in complicated transactional matters.

COMMUNICATIONS

Due to the federal government's control over the communications sector, Washington DC remains a focal point for regulation. Considered in the big league for regulatory matters, **Wiley Rein & Fielding** is currently representing the Newspaper Association of America, CBS-Viacom and Gannett, while working on media ownership rules changes. The firm's position is reinforced by its concentration of attorneys with experience either at the FCC or on Capitol Hill. These include former chairman of the FCC, Dick Wiley. Competitor **Kellogg Huber Hansen Todd & Evans** also focuses on trials and appeals before federal and state courts and federal agencies. Michael Kellogg was commended for his track record in the US Supreme Court and appellate litigation in the telecom field.

Numerous other major firms across the US possess extensive experience in communications law and related technology and e-commerce issues. Dominating the New York market, **Milbank Tweed Hadley & McCloy** is admired for expertise in IT, space & satellites, telecom and corporate finance transactions and enjoys an excellent reputation in the market for outsourcing deals. The firm's profile was boosted by John Halvey's return from Safeguard Scientifics. Researchers were also directed towards preeminent space lawyer Peter Nesgos, who recently represented the underwriters in the Intelsat bond offering and proposed IPO.

Interviewees identified **Mayer Brown Rowe & Maw** as the dominant player for telecommunications in Illinois. The firm's long-standing advice to Ameritech secures its position, with renowned rainmaker Theodore Livingston serving as the company's lead external counsel. The practice is also admired for its transactional IT experience with Brad Peterson noted for his representation of CNA Financial Corporation on technology transactions.

Communications expertise at **Baker Botts**, the leading communications firm in Texas, is inextricably linked with the firm's lauded IP group. Head of the firm's IP group, Jerry Mills, boasts an impressive resumé which includes licensing and transactional work for Microelectronics Computer Technology. Also noted as a market leader, Charles Szalkowski heads Baker Bott's technology and emerging growth companies group and recently advised on the funding of Questia Media.

In California, the key firm is **Wilson Sonsini Goodrich & Rosati**. Thought to dominate Silicon Valley as much as his firm, Larry Sonsini was singled out to researchers for his enormous reputation in the field. Respected for his work in M&A, Sonsini led the team that advised Hewlett-Packard on its $19 billion merger with Compaq. Jeff Saper also received widespread market commendation.

CORPORATE/M&A — Top ten US M&A deals 2002

Date Announced	Date Effective	Target Name	Acquirer Name	Value of Deal ($bn)	Target Advisers
07/15/2002		Pharmacia	Pfizer	61.341	Goldman Sachs & Co Carnegie International
11/14/2002		Household International	HSBC Holdings (HSBC)	15.294	Goldman Sachs & Co Keefe Bruyette & Woods
02/22/2002	11/12/2002	TRW	Northrop Grumman	11.958	Goldman Sachs & Co Credit Suisse First Boston
04/16/2002		NTL	Bondholders	10.6	Credit Suisse First Boston Morgan Stanley JPMorgan Salomon Smith Barney Rothschild
05/21/2002	07/11/2002	Golden State Bancorp	Citigroup	5.882	Goldman Sachs & Co
05/30/2002	09/07/2002	Miller Brewing (Philip Morris)	South African Breweries	5.573	Dresdner Kleinwort Wasserstein Lehman Brothers
01/14/2002	03/05/2002	Rodamco-Real Estate Assets	Investor Group	5.337	JPMorgan ING Barings
11/17/2002		TRW - Automotive Parts	Blackstone Group	4.725	Salomon Smith Barney Stephens Financial Group Goldman Sachs & Co Credit Suisse First Boston
08/20/2002		Qwest Commun Intl - QwestDex	Investor Group	4.3	Lehman Brothers Merrill Lynch & Co
12/17/2002		Pfizer - Adams	Cadbury Schweppes	4.2	Merrill Lynch & Co Lazard

Top ten US M&A deals 2002

CORPORATE/M&A

Acquirer Advisers	Target Legal Adviser	Acquirer Legal Adviser
Bear Stearns & Co Lazard	Mannheimer Swartling Advokatbyra Sullivan & Cromwell Skadden Arps Slate Meagher & Flom	Gibson Dunn & Crutcher Jones Day Linklaters Arnold & Porter Clifford Chance Cadwalader Wickersham & Taft
Morgan Stanley HSBC Investment Banking Rohatyn Associates Cazenove & Co	Norton Rose Wachtell Lipton Rosen & Katz Simpson Thacher & Bartlett	Cleary Gottlieb Steen & Hamilton
Salomon Smith Barney Stephens Financial Group	Skadden Arps Slate Meagher & Flom Sullivan & Cromwell	King & Spalding Gibson Dunn & Crutcher Cleary Gottlieb Steen & Hamilton Hahn Loeser & Parks Minter Ellison Freshfields Bruckhaus Deringer
UBS Warburg	Clifford Chance	Shearman & Sterling
Salomon Smith Barney	Fried Frank Harris Shriver & Jacobson Wachtell Lipton Rosen & Katz	Skadden Arps Slate Meagher & Flom
JPMorgan Cazenove & Co	Wachtell Lipton Rosen & Katz Clifford Chance Webber Wentzel Bowens Sutherland Asbill & Brennan	Cleary Gottlieb Steen & Hamilton Lovells Linklaters Weil Gotshal & Manges
UBS Warburg Merrill Lynch & Co Deutsche Bank Banc of America Securities Goldman Sachs & Co ABN AMRO Bank Salomon Smith Barney	Freshfields Bruckhaus Deringer Winston & Strawn De Brauw Blackstone Westbroek Davis Polk & Wardwell Simpson Thacher & Bartlett	Skadden Arps Slate Meagher & Flom Willkie Farr & Gallagher Fried Frank Harris Shriver & Jacobson Allen & Overy Arnold & Porter Debevoise & Plimpton Stibbe Minter Ellison
Merrill Lynch & Co JPMorgan Lehman Brothers	Gibson Dunn & Crutcher	Simpson Thacher & Bartlett Osler Hoskin & Harcourt
JPMorgan Bank of America International Wachovia Securities Deutsche Bank	Debevoise & Plimpton	Latham & Watkins
Credit Suisse First Boston Hoare Govett	Cadwalader Wickersham & Taft Jones Day Arnold & Porter Dewey Ballantine Clifford Chance	Shearman & Sterling Slaughter and May

PRACTICE OVERVIEWS

CORPORATE/M&A

M&A activity continues to be sporadic throughout the US, with billion dollar megamergers few and far between. As our table of top M&A deals demonstrates, the market remains dominated by the major Wall Street firms. Chief among these is **Wachtell Lipton Rosen & Katz**, famous for its clear-cut focus on headline public company deals. Felt by commentators to be in a league of its own, the firm houses market giants such as Martin Lipton and Richard Katcher and has appeared on such transactions as HSBC's $15.3 billion acquisition of Household International and the $5.6 billion merger of Miller Brewing and South African Breweries. Corporate giant **Skadden Arps Slate Meagher & Flom** isn't far behind. Continuing the traditions of excellence set by firm founder Joseph Flom, the firm is unrivaled in its depth and resources. In addition to its large New York base, the firm maintains highly-rated corporate practices in its Chicago, LA, Palo Alto, San Francisco, Boston and Wilmington offices. Skadden Arps attorneys acted for TRW in its $12 billion acquisition by Northrop Grumman and represented the financial advisers in connection with Pfizer's acquisition of Pharmacia.

Outside New York, DC-based **Hogan & Hartson** wins acclaim for its depth of expertise in corporate finance and real estate. Warren Gorrell in particular was identified by interviewees as a world-class lawyer with Wall Street capabilities. Old-line Pennsylvania practices **Dechert** and **Morgan Lewis & Bockius** also earned recognition for broad-based corporate practices with international capacity. Dechert has particular strength in M&A transactions involving investment funds and financial services, while Morgan Lewis, the largest firm in the state, is involved in ongoing work for 3-Dimensional Pharmaceuticals in connection with Johnson & Johnson's proposed $130 million acquisition.

Three firms emerged at the top in Massachusetts. **Ropes & Gray** earns plaudits for its traditional focus on M&A, private equity and high yield debt and has close connections with a number of local Boston funds. **Hale and Dorr** is heavily involved in venture capital financing and commands tremendous loyalty among Massachusetts biotech, telecom and technology clients. **Goodwin Procter** is well known in the market for an outstanding REIT practice and for all-round expertise in M&A, joint ventures and fund formation.

In Atlanta, **King & Spalding** towers over competitors, commanding an extensive portfolio of blue-ribbon clients and a deep bench of talented corporate specialists. Under the leadership of Michael Egan, the practice acts for the likes of Coca-Cola and Sprint and is currently acting for SunTrust Banks in its $130 million acquisition of Lighthouse Financial Services. Florida firm **Akerman Senterfitt** has been steadily improving its profile in the market and boasts a dynamic practice across the state. It competes directly with full-service firm **Greenberg Traurig**, which earns respect for its large share of cross-border Latin American deals. The Texas market centers around the oil and gas industry and thus favors energy heavyweights **Baker Botts** and **Vinson & Elkins**. Stephen Massad at Baker Botts was named by clients as among the best corporate lawyers in the country. He and his team have acted on such deals as Petroleum Geo-Services' merger with Veritas DGC. Despite its ties to major client Enron, Vinson & Elkins continues to thrive in energy M&A. The team acted in the $2.9 billion sale of Triton Energy to Amerada Hess and advised Mitchell Energy & Development on its $3.5 billion acquisition by Devon Energy.

Within the Midwest, Chicago remains the nerve center for corporate transactions. Here, **Sidley Austin Brown & Wood** and **Mayer Brown Rowe & Maw** vie for the largest public company deals. Classic Chicago firm Mayer Brown boasts leading market figure Bob Helman, international capabilities and key relationships with clients such as Northern Trust. Sidley Austin Brown & Wood was recommended for its collegial group of attorneys, led by managing partner Tom Cole. The firm advised Lucent Technologies in connection with its $300 million acquisition by CSG Systems. Nationally respected **Kirkland & Ellis** is the top name in town for private equity transactions. Benefiting from the considerable market reputation of Jack Levin, the firm handles a volume of LBO activity for clients such as Madison Dearborn Partners and Bain Capital. Enormous national firm **Jones Day** retains a large Cleveland base, renowned for its excellent international corporate practice. A US-wide M&A practice, headed by Lyle Ganske, is advising Ameren on a pending $1.4 billion acquisition of CILCORP from AES. Also in Cleveland, full-service firm **Squire Sanders & Dempsey** has an outstanding national profile in public finance. Mary Ann Jorgenson heads the firm's international business practice, advising on M&A and corporate control issues. Elsewhere, firms such as Minneapolis practices **Dorsey & Whitney** and **Faegre & Benson** and Missouri-based **Bryan Cave** receive significant shares of the Midwestern transactional market.

Despite the marked drop-off in technology transactions, the California corporate market still revolves primarily around the native telecom, IT and biotech industries, with additional work driven by the entertainment, venture capital and defense sectors. Northrop Grumman's $11.9 billion acquisition of TRW was handled by **Gibson Dunn & Crutcher**'s Andy Bogen. This widely admired practice benefits from close ties to blue-chip corporates and the firm's highly developed antitrust capacities in undertaking big-ticket deals. Larry Sonsini's firm **Wilson Sonsini Goodrich & Rosati** leads the market for hi-tech M&A and venture capital. LA-based **Latham & Watkins** boasts a superb international network and is thought to be California's broadest practice. The firm's national M&A team, cochaired by Paul Tosetti, advised a consortium of private equity investors on the $4.3 billion acquisition of QwestDex. Outside California, Seattle-headquartered **Perkins Coie** and Portland firm **Stoel Rives** handle a volume of M&A, joint venture and venture capital transactions from their respective West Coast office networks.

PRACTICE OVERVIEWS

EMPLOYMENT

Employment law forms a crucial area of expertise for many corporations in their day-to-day governance, and is a key factor in mergers. Discrimination litigation arising from race, sex and disability claims has taken center stage following the slowdown in labor law and union-related litigation and arbitration.

MAINLY DEFENDANT FIRMS:

Proskauer Rose stands at the forefront of the New York market for its work defending marquee clients such as Citibank, Donna Karan International and Spin Magazine against discrimination claims. Its attorneys are deal-focused, but were also commended by clients for their ability to "add the human element." **Morgan Lewis & Bockius** has perhaps the greater spread of dedicated attorneys, with nationally respected employment groups in Pennsylvania, New York and Washington DC. In the DC market the team has advised on collective bargaining issues in the trucking industry, while in New York it acted for Merrill Lynch in a discrimination class action.

Jones Day also has a strong national presence with the support of overseas offices. The group in DC has represented Wal-Mart in a large sex discrimination class action and provided labor law advice on issues arising from LTV's bankruptcy. Its attorneys were recommended to *Chambers*' researchers as strategic thinkers who combine excellent litigation skills with an understanding of business needs. The other DC leader is **Paul Hastings Janofsky & Walker**. Its substantial resources have attracted a number of Fortune 100 clients. The firm has recently advised Boeing on gender and race discrimination class actions and represented Northwest Airlines in union-related issues.

Boston-based **Ropes & Gray** was singled out by the market for its experience in complex litigation before government agencies. This group represented a Fortune 100 financial institution in a challenge to its retirement plan. In Pittsburgh, **Reed Smith** shares the top spot in *Chambers*' ranking with Morgan Lewis & Bockius. Reed Smith has carved out a similar national reputation for its powerful practice, endorsed both for its historic focus on traditional labor law matters, and its litigation prowess. The firm's multi-state client base includes manufacturers as well as healthcare, law and accountancy firms.

Chicago's **Seyfarth Shaw** is respected for its pragmatic approach. Attorneys here defended a national restaurant chain following EEOC claims that it discriminates in favor of female servers. **Franczek Sullivan** is the state's most prominent employment boutique, despite its relative youth – the firm was founded in 1994. It has acted in contract negotiations and arbitration proceedings for the City of Chicago. **Vedder Price Kaufman & Kammholz** also boasts a high-profile employment group. Sources described its attorneys as consistently impressive in a broad spectrum of disciplines such as OSHA, ADA class actions and EEOC proceedings.

In Cleveland two firms share the top spot in *Chambers*' USA. **Baker & Hostetler** acts for the East Cleveland School Board, as well as newspaper clients such as Scripps-Howard and the New York Post. **Duvin Cahn & Hutton** also boasts a national reputation for labor and employment litigation and counseling. Here, Robert Duvin is credited by peers as being the driving force behind the firm's outstanding profile in labor law issues. In Minnesota, two of the state's major international law firms shone. Both **Dorsey & Whitney**, with its 22 offices in the US, Canada, Europe and Asia, and **Faegre & Benson** with its team of over 30 attorneys, are respected for their labor relations and discrimination litigation prowess. In Missouri, **Blackwell Sanders Peper Martin** was recommended to researchers for its professionalism and experience.

In the Texan market, three firms received particular endorsement. **Baker Botts** impressed clients in, among others, the telecom and energy sectors, with its attorneys' detailed knowledge of both labor and employment law. The group has represented Exxon Chemical Company (now ExxonMobil) in race discrimination cases. **Fulbright & Jaworski** benefits from its large litigation capacity. It advises on discrimination claims, wage and hour and ERISA issues for clients such as Motorola. The attorneys at **Vinson & Elkins** were also widely endorsed for their expertise in discrimination defense, civil rights counseling and traditional labor law issues.

Ford & Harrison dominates the Florida market. It is a nationally prominent boutique that, market observers agree, achieves high standards throughout the firm. Civil rights, discrimination and union-related issues form the staple diet here, for clients of the caliber of Walt Disney World. In Georgia, **Kilpatrick Stockton** combines respected strength in general counseling and employment litigation, with defining expertise in labor law. Market observers also pointed to **King & Spalding**'s fine handling of high-profile class actions and its success in attracting a glittering client portfolio. The team recently secured a summary judgment in an age discrimination class action in favor of Gerber Products.

Alongside its outstanding DC practice, **Paul Hastings Janofsky & Walker** has won the respect of market observers for the skills of its Atlanta office in handling the defense to Title VII claims. Other areas of specialism include OSHA and ADA litigation. In Los Angeles too, it has a superb profile, and dominates *Chambers*' rankings following widespread endorsement as "the best in California." The group here has acted for Microsoft in a nationwide race and gender class action.

In Seattle, **Davis Wright Tremaine** fields a team that includes a former regional attorney to the EEOC. Labor law is also an area of strength, and the team has assisted AT&T Broadband in labor contract negotiations across California. **Perkins Coie** is well known for its representation of Boeing. It also serves telecom and technology clients alongside a healthy roster of forestry and maritime interests. Sources identified **Barran Liebman** as a powerful force in the Portland market. This boutique is built around a core of seasoned veterans, active in headline discrimination cases and complex labor negotiations.

MAINLY PLAINTIFF FIRMS:

New York's **Outten & Golden** is famed in the market for its successful advice on class actions. Discrimination claims, and wage and hour issues form just a portion of the cases it undertakes against corporate giants like MetLife and Wal-Mart. Wayne Outten is a conscientious and practical attorney, respected for his litigation skills. **Vladeck Waldman Elias & Engelhard** was recommended to researchers for its experience of landmark cases. Judith Vladeck was described by sources as a genuine pioneer in the field. In the Washington DC plaintiffs' market, **Bredhoff & Kaiser** stands out as the clear leader for its depth of talent. It won particular praise for its preeminent unions practice.

Abrahamson Vorachek & Mikva of Chicago is renowned for its highly professional approach. **Miner Barnhill & Galland** too has enjoyed success in representing large groups of plaintiffs in sexual harassment and race discrimination claims. Pittsburgh's **Rothman Gordon** impressed market observers with its strong negotiation skills before boards such as the NLRB, EEOC and the US Department of Labor. **Willig Williams & Davidson** particularly stands out for its labor law practice. The team advises over 150 unions throughout the East Coast and won plaudits for its effective handling of complex issues.

Two dedicated plaintiff firms share the top slot in our Texas rankings. **Gregg M Rosenberg & Associates** is no stranger to key discrimination cases and brings a wealth of courtroom experience to each case. **Mandell & Wright** is home to Eliot Tucker, one of the highest-profile attorneys in the state. He and the group advise unions and

PRACTICE OVERVIEWS

individuals on Title VII cases and contract actions. San Francisco-based **McGuinn Hillsman & Palefsky** has won acclaim for its handling of civil rights and employment litigation, under the guidance of Cliff Palefsky. The group is respected, not only for its litigation skills, but also for its understanding of mediation and arbitration as effective tools to resolve disputes. The team at **Rudy Exelrod & Zieff** was commended to researchers for its deep knowledge and ability to tackle the most complex pieces of litigation. It recently represented over 2,400 employees in an overtime class action, obtaining a judgment in excess of $124 million.

ENERGY & NATURAL RESOURCES

Texas is the hub for energy and natural resources activities in the US. Researchers found that **Vinson & Elkins** – despite its close ties to Enron – sits at the forefront of electricity and oil and gas matters. This international firm dominates the region and other parts of the world, developing a special focus on Latin America and Asia. Bruce Bilger, the force behind the firm's expansion, is regarded by observers as the market's leading transactional player. The group represented Duke Energy on its $8.5 billion acquisition of Westcoast Energy. The biggest challenge to Vinson & Elkins is **Baker Botts**, which represents national and international clients in oil and gas and electricity matters with a focus on LNG projects. Sources agreed that David Asmus has the technical knowledge to deal with the most complex oil and gas transactions. ExxonMobil, ChevronTexaco and Mobil Argentina are just a few of the clients represented by what seemed to be the fastest-growing firm in Texas: **King & Spalding**. The firm has doubled its size in the past two years and owes much of its success to star attorney, John Cogan.

In New York, substantial M&A transactions dominate the gas and oil-producing market. Here, **LeBoeuf Lamb Greene & MacRae** was highly recommended to researchers for its comprehensive understanding of the Public Utility Holding Company Act of 1935 and its regulatory prowess. In Washington DC, two firms stood out for their electricity regulatory expertise. **Steptoe & Johnson** is best known for a high-quality team, headed by Lon Bouknight. Its skills in handling FERC actions have impressed many. **Skadden Arps Slate Meagher & Flom** enjoys an unrivaled presence in the region for its work in the electricity field and for oil and gas matters. The team here benefits from the skills of attorney Clifford (Mike) Naeve.

Georgia-based **Sutherland Asbill & Brennan** and **Troutman Sanders** have the two most active energy practice groups in the South. The former is respected for its work in landmark litigations and the development of power plants. The latter is heavily involved in transactional and regulatory issues and has defended Mirant, a major electricity generation and distribution company.

The Chicago headquarters of international firm, **Mayer Brown Rowe & Maw** is a key player in the energy and natural resources sector. Litigation and regulatory proceedings are an area of strength, and the group advised Nicor Gas on its 'Customer Select' proceedings before the Illinois Commerce Commission (ICC). **Foley & Lardner** is rated highly for state regulatory work and its smooth handling of complex matters for clients such as Commonwealth Edison. The firm's merger with Hopkins & Sutter over a year ago has bolstered this practice across the board.

Los Angeles-based **Milbank Tweed Hadley & McCloy** has been active in the tendering for state power contracts following the California power crisis and acts as counsel to official creditors on the PG&E Corp committee. **Orrick Herrington & Sutcliffe** was commended to researchers as a particularly influential player in public finance. It has been linked closely with the restructuring of the utility industry.

ENVIRONMENT

Our New York environmental table features firms that advise their blue-chip client base on key environmental issues, adding real value as part of a full-service offering. **Cravath Swaine & Moore** has handled environmental matters for Bristol-Myers Squibb on its acquisition of DuPont's pharmaceutical business and acted for Conoco on its merger with Phillips Petroleum. Its fellow Wall Street firm, **Davis Polk & Wardwell** advises clients on environmental liability in the chemical, petroleum, paper and real estate industries. Boutique firm **Sive Paget & Riesel** is one of the few firms to concentrate entirely on environmental law. Attorneys here act for clients such as Duracell, Cooper Industries, Kraft Foods and Goodyear. At **Arnold & Porter**, Mike Gerrard was widely endorsed by market sources for his work in transactional and contentious matters.

On the East Coast, Boston-based firm **Foley Hoag** advises on complex matters relating to hazardous waste and air regulations, representing clients such as the City of Boston, Invensys Systems and Emerson College. The firm is one of the most respected in the region, with concentration on land use, development projects and environmental compliance. Its attorneys represented USGen New England in air regulation and energy-related matters. **Goodwin Procter**'s experience ranges from compliance counseling to litigation for clients such as Cisco Systems, Polaroid and Entergy. Pittsburgh-based **Babst Calland Clements and Zomnir** has the biggest environmental practice in Pennsylvania. Sources indicated that it dominates the western part of the state, fielding attorneys with strong industrial experience and technical knowledge. Bala Cynwyd boutique **Manko Gold Katcher & Fox** stands out for its experience in Superfund matters, transactional and regulatory work. One niche that distinguishes the firm is its expertise in bioterrorism. The dominant firm in DC is **Sidley Austin Brown & Wood**. Attorneys here are widely respected for their advice on environmental enforcement issues for clients of the caliber of GE and American Electric Power.

Sidley Austin Brown & Wood also scored well in our research into the Illinois market. It was one of the first to develop a dedicated environmental practice with core skills in regulatory and statutory issues supported by its esteemed litigation practice. **Mayer Brown Rowe & Maw** also secured a place in the top spot of our table. Researchers identified fields such as oil and chemical industries as areas of focus. The team is particularly visible advising on permit negotiations before state and federal agencies. Columbus-based **Porter Wright Morris & Arthur** was commended to researchers for its vast expertise in air and water pollution issues. Complex litigation lies at the heart of the **Vorys Sater Seymour & Pease** environmental practice. The group acts for Allied Waste Industries, Honda of America Mfg and Siemens. Cleveland firm **Squire Sanders & Dempsey** was singled out during *Chambers*' research for first-class representation of local government authorities on air and water pollution, Superfund and state action cases. **Thompson Hine**'s litigation prowess has ensured that the firm has a strong profile for defense against criminal and civil environmental regulation enforcement proceedings.

Georgia's **Alston & Bird** has acted for Dow Chemical in some of the country's biggest asbestos claims. Meanwhile **King & Spalding** has impressed market observers with its success in attracting such clients as GE, Honeywell and Brown & Williamson Tobacco. Tallahassee environmental and regulatory boutique **Hopping Green & Sams** made an impact on the research team for its distinctive statewide practice. Its knowledge of air pollution matters is second to none in the state.

There are two market leaders for environmental law in Texas. **Baker Botts** in Austin took a prominent role in revisions to the Clean Air Plan for the Houston-Galveston area. It has on its client roster Shell and Dow Chemical. The firm came top for complex environmental matters and shone on issues surrounding environmental regulatory matters. It also has a niche in air quality regulatory affairs. The other outstanding firm in this market is **Vinson & Elkins**. Power utilities, aerospace and pesticide manufacturing companies have all used the firm for their regulatory and contentious environmental issues. The firm handles a global workload, which reaches into South America and eastern Europe.

National firm **Dorsey & Whitney** has been successful in attracting criminal cases to its office in Anchorage, complementing its regular flow of litigation and transactional environmental work, which includes toxic tort, international compliance and Superfund matters. Its recent caseload has included advice to a sponsor of the Natro-Gas pipeline on the Foothills project. Researchers were also drawn to two other leading environmental practices in Alaska. **Foster Pepper Rubini & Reeves**, with its widely recognized attorney Susan Reeves, wins the respect of peers for its transactional expertise. **Perkins Coie** has a focus on oil spill contingency planning and has acted for the cleanups of both the Thorne Bay landfills site and the industrial property and marine sediments at Ward Cove.

Two California environmental law practices should share the top rank of our table. **Bingham McCutchen** has the largest environmental team, highly regarded for its extensive statewide reach. Attorneys here have advised on a chemical plant acquisition by Zeneca and Valero Energy's divestiture of its oil refinery and service stations worth $1.1 billion. **Latham & Watkins** is widely recognized for its depth of knowledge of water and air quality cases. It also advises on the conduct of substantial transactions and environmental compliance issues.

INSURANCE

While environmental and health matters remain the central concerns of the insurance sector, the industry has also recently found itself preoccupied with the issues raised by the 9/11 terrorist attacks. The Terrorism Risk Insurance Act of 2002 provides a temporary federal program for sharing the risk of loss from foreign terrorist attacks between the Government and the insurance industry.

California remains prominent in the area of environmental coverage. Acclaimed firms include **Howrey Simon Arnold & White**, whose respected insurance coverage practice received the boost of 28 extra coverage lawyers from Troop Steuber Pasich, Reddick & Tobey in 2001. In addition to the traditional areas of environmental and asbestos litigation, the firm also handles advertising liabilities, computer viruses and natural disaster losses. Kirk Pasich is regarded as the market leader for policyholder representation in California, while Dave Steuber represented PepsiAmericas in coverage litigation for claims of environmental contamination, property damage, personal injury and toxic tort. Powered by its connections in London, **Hancock Rothert & Bunshoft** is acclaimed for its work on environmental and asbestos coverage matters. The firm's heavy-hitting partners include Philip Matthews, Rick Seabolt and Pat Cathcart. They have worked on matters including the Aerojet and Shell Oil-Rocky Mountain Arsenal cases.

In Washington DC, policyholder firm **Covington & Burling** has been busy with complex high-value coverage litigation. In a number of notable cases involving both asbestos and breast implant-related litigation, the firm has obtained more than $1 billion in coverage cases for clients such as Owens Corning, Dow Corning and 3M. The widely esteemed Robert Sayler continues to train the next generation of coverage litigation lawyers. Meanwhile Mitchell Dolin acted in litigation relating to first-party property coverage relating to the destruction of the World Trade Center.

The top name in New York's insurance market is undoubtedly **LeBoeuf Lamb Greene & MacRae**. Historically renowned for regulatory work, the group's far-ranging expertise also covers such areas as insurance litigation and industry-specific transactions. The group has maintained its long-standing relationship with Lloyd's as US counsel, and its strong bench of insurance specialists includes Alex Dye and Don Henderson.

Fowler White Boggs Banker's broad insurance practice leads Florida's market. The group is especially commended for its dedicated casualty department, which is experienced in litigating products liability and healthcare insurance claims.

Dominating coverage litigation and transactional matters in Illinois is **Lord Bissell & Brook**. Best known for its representation of the London market, the firm undertakes toxic tort and products liability matters. Mark Goodman advises on new consumer privacy rules, supporting the firm's large non-contentious insurance practice.

Texan specialist insurance group **Thompson Coe Cousins & Irons** was also rated as strong in litigation and noncontentious counseling. The firm represented International Insurance Company and United States Fire Insurance Company in a coverage dispute arising from claims for environmental damages and bodily injuries against RSR Corporation. Richard Geiger and Jay Thompson are highly respected for representing the insurance industry before state and federal regulatory bodies.

INTELLECTUAL PROPERTY

In an increasingly knowledge-driven economy, intellectual property is a key consideration in business decisions. New products, brands and creative designs appear almost daily, while fast-developing technologies and the internet burden the market further. However, one of the hottest topics of contention is the balance between the patent system and access to drugs and healthcare.

In Washington DC, **Finnegan Henderson Farabow Garrett & Dunner** provides a broad range of IP services. Donald Dunner was particularly noted for his representation of GlaxoSmithKline against several manufacturers of generic pharmaceuticals. His partner Ford Farabow also represents large pharmaceutical manufacturers and scientific instrument and cosmetic companies in both enforcing and defending patent suits.

New York's **Fish & Neave** covers the entire spectrum of IP law including patents, trademarks, copyright and trade secrets. Albert Fey represented Microsoft in a declaratory judgment action for non-infringement and invalidity of patents in the data communications industry.

Hale and Dorr's litigation prowess makes it a leader in the Massachusetts IP market. The team offers comprehensive IP services and recently defended Dynatech and Whistler against Cincinnati Microwave in a patent infringement dispute over radar detectors. Bill Lee is the group's leading light, focusing predominantly on patent disputes, although he is also experienced in trademark and trade secret cases.

Despite some recent defections, **Woodcock Washburn** continues to dominate the market in Pennsylvania. Supported by the firm's satellite office in Seattle, which handles IP work for Microsoft, the group is particularly well known for its expertise in biotech, medical devices and electronics. Key names at the firm include John Donohue and Dale Heist. Highly recommended for patent litigation, the firm successfully defended nutritional supplement manufacturer Rexall Sundown in a patent infringement action.

Ohio's **Jones Day** represents substantial cases for national blue-chip clients. The freestanding practice excels in patent cases involving complex technological issues and benefits from the firm's large base of institutional corporate clients. Kenneth Adamo is the key name here, and considered something of a celebrity.

Georgia also offers several top-tier IP groups, such as the long-standing team at **Kilpatrick Stockton**. Bolstered by a recent merger with local IP boutique Jones & Askew, the group offers a wealth of contentious and noncontentious knowledge across the range of trademark, copyright and patent law. Jim Johnson often advises on the IP issues related to financings for start-ups and midlevel biotech companies. Other heavy hitters are Joseph Beck, Miles Alexander and Tony Askew. Another strong Georgia practice is **Needle & Rosenberg**. Offering particular strength in patent prosecution, the group's expertise serves many of the top 50 US chemical and pharmaceutical companies. Bill Needle's particular prowess in the area was affirmed by his appointment by US District Court judges to serve as a Special Master in patent infringement cases.

Researchers were impressed by IP boutique **Brinks Hofer Gilson & Lione** domination of the Illinois market. Holding long-standing links to traditional Midwest manufacturing companies, the team handles all areas of contentious, prosecution and transactional IP work. Roy Hofer heads the firm's IP litigation team and was particularly noted for his experience in patent, trade secrets and unfair competition litigation. Competitor **Kirkland & Ellis** is the premier group among the general practice firms. Offering depth of contentious expertise, the team was particularly highly regarded for its strong trademark litigation skills.

The formidable team at **Baker Botts** lead the Texas market. Endorsed for expertise in patent prosecution and litigation, the team is especially noted for its representation of the electronics industry. Jerry Mills heads the well-balanced group, which also undertakes client counseling. Competitor **Fulbright & Jaworski** offers particular expertise in biotech patent prosecution and litigation. Notable cases include Lou Pirkey's representation of ExxonMobil in its high-profile 'cartoon tiger' dispute with Kellogg.

Covering all areas of IP law, **Irell & Manella** tops the California rankings for broad experience of patent infringement, trademark, copyright, trade secrets and antitrust litigation. The team is also highly regarded for its transactional expertise and often advises clients from the hi-tech and entertainment sectors on high-premium deals.

PRACTICE OVERVIEWS

LITIGATION OVERVIEW

Securities Litigation

Investment banks	Aggregate fine ($ millions)	Law firms	Lawyers
Salomon Smith Barney	400	Wilmer Cutler & Pickering	Robert McCaw Lewis Liman Brent Gurney Harry Weiss
Merrill Lynch	200	Fried Frank Harris Shriver & Jacobson Morvillo Abramowitz Grand Iason & Silberberg	Audrey Strauss (lead council) Bob Morvillo Rudolph Giuliani advice
CSFB	200	Davis Polk & Wardwell	Carey Dunne Susan Merrill
Morgan Stanley	125	Kirkland & Ellis	Peter Doyle Alex Dimitrief Maria Ginzburg
Goldman Sachs	110	Sullivan & Cromwell	David Braff
UBS Warburg	105	Cleary Gottlieb Steen & Hamilton	Max Gitter Mitchell Lowenthal
JPMorgan Chase	80	Simpson Thacher & Bartlett	Mark Cunha
Bear Stearns	80	Cadwalader Wickersham & Taft	Dennis Block
Lehman Brothers	80	Paul Weiss Rifkind Wharton & Garrison	Mark Pomerantz
Citigroup	n/a	Wachtell Lipton Rosen & Katz	n/a
Deutsche Bank	80	n/a	n/a

To qualify for a place in *Chambers'* litigation rankings, firms have to demonstrate the capacity to represent corporate clients across a range of disciplines. Examples might include commercial disputes, securities, banking, civil fraud and real estate litigation.

New York's key litigation practices have kept busy with a stream of highly-publicized securities investigations and litigation for major Wall Street banks. Leading firms **Paul Weiss Rifkind Wharton & Garrison**, **Simpson Thacher & Bartlett**, **Wachtell Lipton Rosen & Katz** and **Davis Polk & Wardwell** have all been involved, acting respectively for investment banks Lehman Brothers, JPMorgan Chase, Citigroup and CSFB. Here, names such as Martin London, Roy Reardon, Herb Wachtell and Bob Fiske regularly attract headlines for their involvement in major cases.

Litigation boutiques like **Boies Schiller & Flexner** also play a key role in the market. Dominated by the tremendous personality, David Boies, the firm is renowned for its representation of Al Gore in litigation arising from the Florida vote count during the 2000 Presidential election. **Williams & Connolly** enjoys an illustrious reputation as DC's premier litigation firm. Star litigator Brendan Sullivan is particularly well known for his representation of the nine dissenting states in the Microsoft antitrust litigation.

Recommended for its aggressive approach to litigation, Boston-based **Hale and Dorr** has specialized expertise in IP and securities litigation and undertakes significant cases for a loyal base of biotech, IT and telecom clients. It shares a top band ranking in Massachusetts with **Ropes & Gray**. The latter notably defended Goldman Sachs and Deutsche Bank against antitrust claims relating to gold and gold derivatives.

Other respected litigation practices in the Northeast include Philadelphia's **Dechert**, said to rise above the Pennsylvania competition for its international reach and sophistication. The practice, chaired by Robert Heim, has been representing Philip Morris in individual cases and class action disputes throughout the eastern US.

The Midwest boasts a number of nationally reputed litigation practices. Foremost among these is Ohio's **Jones Day**, which rates highest for its large and uniformly impressive teams in Cleveland and Columbus. The firm has acted extensively for the US tobacco industry and has a long-standing relationship with RJ Reynolds. John Strauch coordinates a national litigation practice that comprises some of the country's leading commercial litigators. In Chicago, **Kirkland & Ellis** enjoys a similarly high profile for involvement in some of the US's largest and most prominent cases. This consistently excellent practice

PRACTICE OVERVIEWS

LITIGATION (continued)

is known for its tough, aggressive approach to litigation. Sophisticated courtroom performer David Bernick was particularly noted for his role as national trial counsel to Brown & Williamson in tobacco litigation. At **Winston & Strawn,** Dan Webb is admired for a track record of winning unwinnable cases and for his representation of Microsoft in antitrust matters.

As the numbers of complex multi-jurisdictional commercial disputes continue to rise, the role of local counsel becomes increasingly more important. This development has benefited the likes of Minneapolis' **Anthony Ostlund & Baer** and **Robins Kaplan Miller & Ciresi** and Kansas City's **Berkowitz Stanton Brandt Williams & Shaw** and **Blackwell Sanders Peper Martin** which assist in coordinating national cases for major corporates.

In the South, boutiques such as Miami-based **Podhurst Orseck Josefsberg Eaton Meadow Olin & Perwin** and Jacksonville practice **Bedell Dittmar DeVault Pillans & Coxe** occupy similar roles as Florida counsel in multi-state litigation and appellate matters. In Atlanta, **Alston & Bird** earned a top band rating thanks to its focus on client service and experience of complex national and international business disputes. It shares pole position in Georgia with **King & Spalding**, which was commended as a sophisticated practice with strength in products liability, personal injury defense, contract disputes and toxic and environmental torts.

Houston-based boutiques **Gibbs & Bruns** and **Susman Godfrey** were acknowledged as Texas' leading litigation outfits. Twenty-four attorney Gibbs & Brun has a growing reputation in the market for its team of superb and experienced litigators, while Susman Godfrey has lately been involved in a number of major securities suits on behalf of shareholders of multinational companies. Together, the two firms provide stiff competition to full-service **Vinson & Elkins,** which boasts Texas' largest litigation practice and close ties to the state's major oil and gas companies.

In California, the market is dominated by the state's major full-service firms, many of which have a particular focus on IP litigation. Of these, **Morrison & Foerster** is considered a major force in the Bay Area with broad expertise in IP, securities litigation and financial services disputes. The firm's standout attorney, James Brosnahan, attracted considerable attention through his representation of accused Taliban supporter, the American John Walker Lindh. Recognized as a hi-tech powerhouse, **Wilson Sonsini Goodrich & Rosati** enjoys a large marketshare among Silicon Valley clients and is said to excel in IP, securities and employment litigation. Operating from five California locations, **Gibson Dunn & Crutcher** has strength in depth across a range of specialist practice areas. The firm's highly regarded appellate practice secured a Supreme Court victory for George W Bush, while the firm's commercial litigators have won major cases for the likes of Dow Jones and DaimlerChrysler. Among California's niche practices, boutique **Keker & Van Nest** stands out for its focus on big-ticket IP litigation, while **Milberg Weiss Bershad Hynes & Lerach** is nationally recognized for its representation of plaintiffs in securities class actions.

Outside of California, Seattle-based **Byrnes & Keller** and Portland's **Stoel Rives** were identified as two of the Northwest's most influential litigation practices. Boutique firm Byrnes & Keller has a commercial bias and experience representing pharmaceutical manufacturers against class action suits and products liability cases. Both the firm's founding partners Peter Byrnes and Brad Keller were recommended as leading trial attorneys in the state. Full-service Stoel Rives has a broad-based litigation practice that complements its highly rated transactional strength. The team, featuring Barnes Ellis, represents a diverse portfolio of clients ranging from pharmaceutical interests and timber companies to government contractors and Native American tribes.

High-profile media/celebrity cases 2002 — MEDIA & ENTERTAINMENT

Case	Attorneys for the plaintiff	Attorneys for the defendant	Description
Marcel Avram v **Michael Jackson**	Louis R. Miller, Ed Lara, Mila Livitz; Christensen, Miller, Fink, Jacobs, Glaser, Weil & Shapiro, Los Angeles (www.chrismill.com)	Steve Cochrane & Zia Modabar; Katten Muchin, Zavis Rosenman, Los Angeles	$21 million breach-of-contract lawsuit brought by concert promoter over two cancelled millennium concerts. Case ongoing at time of press.
Steven Slesinger Inc v **Walt Disney Corp**	Bert Fields & Bonnie Eskanazi; Greenberg Glusker Fields Claman Machtinger & Kinsella, Los Angeles (www.ggfirm.com)	Daniel M. Petrocelli; O'Melveny & Myers, Los Angeles (www.omm.com)	Ongoing litigation regarding the rights to Winnie the Pooh and related characters, which were licensed to Disney by SSI and also involving a dispute over the amount of royalties paid. Expected to go to trial September 2003, filed 1991, Los Angeles Superior Court.
Anna Kournikova v **General Media Communications**	Randy M. Mastro, William E. Wegner, Ethan D. Dettmer; Gibson, Dunn & Crutcher LLP (www.gibsondunn.com)	Victor Kovner; Davis Wright Tremaine, NY	Case brought by Anna Kournikova against General Media Communications regarding photographs published in Penthouse magazine, which claimed to be of her but were in fact of Judith Soltesz-Benetton. Demand for jury trial filed in May 2002, US District Court Central District of California, Western Division. As a result of the case, GMC were also sued by Judith Soltesz-Benetton (represented by Judd Burstein, Burstein & Fass LLP), the woman in the photographs. The case settled in May 2002. A class action was also brought by lawyer Reed Stomberg of Miami, Florida on behalf of himself and all the purchasers of the magazine.
Newmark v **Turner Broadcasting & ors**	Fred von Lohmann, Electronic Frontier Foundation (www.eff.org) & Ira Rothken of Rothken Law Firm	Andrew M. White; White O'Connor Curry Gatti & Avanzado LLP (for Viacom, Disney & NBC) Robert M. Schwartz; O'Melveny & Myers LLP (for Time Warner – Turner Broadcasting is a subsidiary of Time Warner) Scott P. Cooper; Proskauer Rose LLP (for MGM, Fox & Universal) Robert H. Rotstein; McDermott Will & Emery (for Columbia)	ReplayTV customers are suing the entertainment industry to protect their rights to skip over commercials and record television programmes for later viewing using digital video recorders (June 2002). In 2001, dozens of Hollywood movie and TV studios sued ReplayTV for making and distributing the PVRs.
US v **Elcomsoft**		Joseph M. Burton, Duane Morris LLP	Elcomsoft was charged with violating the Digital Millenium Copyright Act (DMCA) by selling a product it developed called Adobe eBook Processor. The software allowed users to disable security settings on Adobe Systems Inc's e-book files so they could be printed, shared and viewed on various computing devices. It was cleared of all charges in December 2002, the jury having been instructed to find ElcomSoft guilty if it agreed that the company developed and sold its product with knowledge and intent of violating the DMCA.
Sherwood 48 Associates v **Sony Corporation of America**	Daniel J. Warren and Carrie A. Hanlon; Sutherland, Asbill & Brennan, Atlanta (www.sablaw.com) Anthony J. Constantini and Gregory P. Gulia; Duane Morris LLP, New York (www.duanemorris.com)	Bruce Keller; Debevoise & Plimpton	Spiderman case: owners of Times Square buildings and billboards sued Sony for superimposing advertisements on billboards as they appear in the 2002 Spiderman movie, alleging trademark violations and unfair competition. Case was dismissed by the judge, ruling that the digitally remodeled Times Square was entitled to First Amendment protection.

MEDIA & ENTERTAINMENT
High-profile media/celebrity cases 2002

Case	Attorneys for the plaintiff	Attorneys for the defendant	Description
Kasky v **Nike**	Counsel for Kasky are Paul R. Hoeber & Alan M. Caplan; Bushnell, Caplan & Fielding LLP William S. Lerach; Milberg, Weiss, Bershad, Hynes & Lerach	Walter Dellinger; O'Melveny & Myers and Laurence Tribe, Harvard Law Professor	Statutory false advertising and consumer deception claim allowed to proceed against Nike based on press releases, OpEds and letters to the editor defending its manufacturing practices in less developed countries. Important decision by the California Supreme Court on the definition of "commercial speech" that receives less legal protection. It will be decided by the US Supreme Court this year.
Gennifer Flowers v **James Carville, George Stephanopoulos & Sen. Hillary Clinton**	Larry Klayman	Laura Handman; Davis Wright Tremain LLP (for George Stephanopoulos) David Kendall; Williams & Connolly (for Hillary Clinton) William McDaniel Jr.; McDaniel, Bennett & Griffin	Ninth Circuit reinstated libel and false light claims by women who claimed to have a relationship with former President based on statement made in book by George Stephanapoulos.
Global Relief Foundation v **New York Times et al**	Roger Simmons; Gordon & Simmons.	David Schulz; Clifford Chance LLP (for Associated Press) David Sanders; Jenner & Block (for ABC) Michael Conway; Foley & Lardner (for New York Times, Boston Globe, and Daily News) Roger Myers; Steinhart & Falconer (for San Francisco Chronicle).	Lawsuit in Northern District of Illinois by Islamic charity that claims it was defamed by several news organizations that reported on Government's suspicion that it was funneling money to terrorists.
CBS v **ABC**	Leslie Gordon Fagen; Paul, Weiss, Rifkind, Wharton & Garrison	Thomas A. Smart; Kaye Scholer LLP	Litigation over the alleged copying of the reality TV show 'Survivor' by look-alike show 'Get me Out of Here…I'm a Celebrity.' Ruling on 13th January in favour of ABC that both shows "combine well-known and frequently used elements of earlier works" and therefore it would be hard for CSB to prove the format of Celebrity was copied from Survivor.

MEDIA & ENTERTAINMENT

Media and entertainment law expertise is largely split between the First Amendment talent in Washington DC and New York, and California's preeminent representation of motion picture companies and individual artists.

In DC, boutique firm **Levine Sullivan & Koch** dominates content-related litigation including libel, invasion of privacy and First Amendment work. Lee Levine has most notably represented media defendants in the Bartnicki v Vopper press freedom case. **Williams & Connolly** is also commended for its groundbreaking defense strategies in media litigation. Kevin Baine is said to know First Amendment law intimately and has successfully defended more than 100 libel cases. The firm's high-profile clients include The National Enquirer and The Washington Post.

Dominating the New York market, **Davis Wright Tremaine** is a leading choice for First Amendment, defamation, privacy and copyright matters. Recommended practitioner Victor Kovner represented General Media Communications in the claim brought by Anna Kournikova regarding photos published in Penthouse magazine.

California's boutique firm **Gang Tyre Ramer & Brown** represents a raft of top artists, producers and other talents in the motion picture and music industries. These include Steven Spielberg, Clint Eastwood and REM. Partner Bruce Ramer is commended for his entertainment law knowledge, while Don Passman specializes in the music business. Competitor **Ziffren Brittenham Branca Fischer Gilbert-Lurie & Stiffelman** is also extolled for its expertise in the motion picture, television, music and multimedia industries. Ken Ziffren focuses on representing individuals in the motion picture and television sectors. His envied client roster includes Harrison Ford, Bruce Willis and Liberty Media Group.

Meanwhile, Illinois-based **Winston & Strawn** is considered to hold a dominating position in advertising and promotional law. Stephen Durchslag was particularly singled out as preeminent in advertising law. He recently represented Energizer Holdings in a false advertising and unfair competition suit brought against Duracell and parent company Gillette.

PRACTICE OVERVIEWS

PRIVATE EQUITY

The current private equity market is proving a challenge not only for fund formation attorneys but also for those involved in secondary financing and exits. The downturn in M&A, liquidity difficulties and the distressed nature of some funds, have seen restructuring and refinancing placed high on the agenda.

We have looked in detail at two of the key markets: New York and Boston, but the corporate departments of many major firms are heavily experienced in the field. For instance, in Chicago, **Kirkland & Ellis**'s private equity group is national in scope and operation. No other Midwest firm comes close to rivaling its dominance. Here, Jack Levin remains a legendary figure, whose name is synonymous with the LBO movement. His firm has recently acted for Madison Dearborn Partners on its acquisition of Jefferson Smurfit, one of the largest LBOs in European history.

In our New York section, **Simpson Thacher & Bartlett** stands at the forefront of the market securing the loyalty of key clients such as KKR, The Blackstone Group and The Carlyle Group. Dick Beattie, chairman of the firm, has spent much of this career developing strong ties to KKR, a role now continued by Casey Cogut. The group has recently acted for the sponsors on the $1.7 billion LBO of Houghton Mifflin from Vivendi Universal. The firm is equally respected for its funds structuring prowess, advising on both offshore and cross-border structures. **Debevoise & Plimpton** possesses the combined firepower of Woody Campbell and Michael Harrell in its advice on funds structuring in the US, Europe and the Far East. This group has attracted sophisticated clients such as Clayton, Dubilier & Rice, for structuring, investment and buyout work.

Testa Hurwitz & Thibeault was recommended as the leader in the Boston market. Its clients are drawn from the emerging technology and healthcare markets, with its recent activities focused on buyout clubs and the internal restructuring of funds. **Ropes & Gray** was also singled out for its tax-efficient structuring of funds originated by its marquee clients such as Goldman Sachs and Harvard University.

PROJECT FINANCE

US top ten deals in project finance for 2002

Project	Borrower	Legal Adviser	Amount $m	Sector	Financial close date
Orion Power MidWest Assets Refinancing	Orion Power MidWest LP	Lender : McGuire, Woods, Battle & Booth Consortium : Thelen Reid & Priest	1,049	Power	10/29/2002
Kern River Expansion II	Kern River Transmission Co	Lender : Skadden Arps Slate Meagher & Flom Consortium : Willkie, Farr & Gallagher	875	Gas Pipeline	06/21/2002
Bethlehem Commerce Center Power Plant	Conectiv Bethlehem	Lender : Latham & Watkins Consortium : Skadden Arps Slate Meagher & Flom	700	Power	05/22/2002
Southern Co Portfolio I	Southern Power Co	Lender : Dewey Ballantine Consortium : Balch & Bingham"	575	Power	05/18/2002
Tenaska Fluvanna Power Plant	Tenaska Virginia Partners	Lender : Skadden Arps Slate Meagher & Flom Consortium : Pillsbury Winthrop	552	Power	07/08/2002
Lyondell-Citgo Refining Refinancing III	Lyondell-Citgo Refining LP	Lender : Bracewell & Patterson Consortium : Andrews & Kurth	520	Oil Refinery	12/10/2002
Rhode Island State Energy Partners Project	FPL Risep	Lender : Chadbourne & Parke Consortium : Steel Hector Davis	450	Power	06/28/2002
Progress Genco Portfolio Financing	Progress Genco Ventures LLC	Lender : Milbank Tweed Hadley & McCloy Consortium : Skadden Arps Slate Meagher & Flom	440	Power	15/05/2002
Jackson Power Project	AlphaGen LLC	Lender : Milbank Tweed Hadley & Mc Cloy Consortium : Winston & Strawn	364	Power	05/14/2002
Red Hills Generating Sale Lease Back	Choctaw Generation LP	Lender : Latham & Watkins Consortium : McGuire, Woods, Battle & Booth	360	Power	12/20/2002

Source: Dealogic ProjectWare

PRACTICE OVERVIEWS

The table overleaf shows a broad spread of US-based projects including both power and infrastructure initiatives. While the domestic power market has been relatively quiet, Latin America has proved to be active in the construction of power plants and LNG generating facilities. The Californian power crisis has encouraged power selling operations designed to restructure the state's energy market.

Nationally, **Latham & Watkins** was described by sources as being in a league of its own. It has successfully diversified from its traditional strength in power projects into oil and gas, telecom and infrastructure projects. From New York, Dave Gordon and Bill Voge regularly act on complex international projects in Latin America and the Middle East. Andy Singer divides his time between both New York and San Diego, ensuring the firm's dominance on the West Coast. In a quiet domestic market, the firm acted for the arrangers on the $2.8 billion TECO Energy and Panda Energy International financing of generating facilities in Arkansas and Arizona.

Milbank Tweed Hadley & McCloy makes a similarly strong showing on both the East and West Coasts, and is supported by a string of overseas offices. The firm has played an integral role in the $3.2 billion Barracuda oil platform project in Brazil, and has advised on power selling transactions designed to restructure the Californian energy markets.

Vinson & Elkins' sizable and dynamic projects practice has withstood the collapse of key client Enron. Researchers found that the Texan giant's global reach and power expertise has provided a steady stream of big-ticket work for Bruce Bilger's team. Power clients such as East Coast Power and Duke Energy combine with financial institutions of the caliber of JPMorgan Chase to make Vinson & Elkins' client roster the envy of many.

Washington DC remains the center for activities on behalf of multilateral agencies, and home to regulatory attorneys with experience in the FERC. The DC office of **Chadbourne & Parke** works closely with its New York counterpart, and the group is commended for its knowledge of the domestic power market. Peter Fitzgerald's problem-solving and non-confrontational style has made him a popular choice within multilateral agencies and those seeking political risk insurance advice. In New York, Chaim Wachsberger continues to be lauded by observers as a veteran of the sector.

White & Case has attracted a broad client base, which features export credit agencies, sponsors and lenders, with much of its activity found in the oil and gas sector. Researchers found that the firm's profile is greatest in cross border transactions such as Art Scavone's work for US Ex-Im Bank in the financing of the Shin satellite project in Thailand. From the DC office, Victor DeSantis' negotiation skills were noted in his work with the Inter-American Development Bank on a power project in Brazil.

REAL ESTATE

Investment in the real estate market has stood up well, due in part to low interest rates and the poor performance of equities. The global activities of mega-REITs and other tax-driven investment vehicles continue to drive many major US real estate practices.

In New York, corporate leasing remains a key strength of **Fried, Frank Harris Shriver & Jacobson**'s real estate practice, while its tax and restructuring expertise are a lure to major clients such as Tishman Speyer Properties and Lazard Frères Real Estate Investors. Department chair Jonathan Mechanic is one of the market's 'go-to' attorneys. He and the team have recently secured a marquee client in Jack Resnick & Sons. **Paul Hastings Janofsky & Walker** boasts a nationally respected group. Many sources placed Marty Edelman in a class of his own for high-profile work. **Skadden Arps Slate Meagher & Flom**, with rainmaker Ben Needell, has developed a massive department, active on the full spectrum of real estate matters. It was particularly praised for its transactional work, which it carries out for such high-profile clients as IBM and Deutsche Banc Alex Brown.

In Washington DC, **Arnold & Porter**'s workload has included advice to The JBG Companies as developer of a new $500 million headquarters for the US Department of Transportation. This broad-based practice fields attorneys with specialist knowledge of financing, development and litigation. **Holland & Knight** stands out for its niche expertise in the hospitality industry. The team has recently secured approval for a 1.5 million sq ft project in DC for the SEC.

Boston-based **Goulston & Storrs** has an historic focus on real estate work. Almost half of its attorneys are focused on the sector. Its respected developer/sponsor client base includes Massachusetts General Hospital, which the firm advised on the leasing and construction of its research facility at Charles River Plaza. In Pennsylvania, a trio of law firms share the limelight. **Ballard Spahr Andrews & Ingersoll** was endorsed by clients for its diverse spread of experience. It advised on the lease for the new home of the Philadelphia Orchestra, and on the construction of The Phillies' new baseball stadium. **Blank Rome**'s attorneys are renowned for their polished negotiating skills. Clients say that each transaction is smoothly executed. At **Wolf Block Schorr and Solis-Cohen**, a sizable Philadelphia-based team acts on national transactions such as Liberty Property Trust's $400 million development of a new office tower. Its real estate structured finance group is involved in complex securitizations.

Chicago's **Katten Muchin Zavis Rosenman** is felt by commentators to excel in mortgage financing, leasing and development work for REITs and developers, such as The Palladium Company project in West Palm Beach. **Mayer Brown Rowe and Maw** was singled out by clients for its uniformly high-quality attorneys. Sources highlighted its work on gritty local matters, as well as its knowledge of sophisticated financing techniques.

Thompson Hine's Cleveland office forms the hub of its real estate practice, pooling talented attorneys from its three other offices in the state. This firm has an international client base. For example, it advised a multinational chemical company on a $1 billion joint venture transaction involving multiple properties in the US and Canada. Clients praised the depth of **Vorys Sater Seymour & Pease**'s practice, and its ability to handle anything that comes its way. The firm's statewide reach has seen it act on multiparty transactions, particularly in relation to public facilities. In Minneapolis, **Dorsey & Whitney**'s strong tradition in the real estate sector has attracted Fortune 500 companies on high caliber transactions. **Faegre & Benson** rivals Dorsey & Whitney for the quality of its hard-working attorneys. Their first-class negotiating skills have attracted clients like Norwest Bank and Niketown.

Winstead Sechrest & Minick has dramatically enhanced its real estate capacity in Texas, having merged with two boutiques in 2001. The group has advised on the development of a stadium for a new NFL franchise in Texas. **Haynes and Boone** has seven offices across the state and enjoys a national reputation for its work with institutional lenders. M&A and complex financing structures are what **Jenkens & Gilchrist** is best known for. **Vinson & Elkins** combines its profile in energy and infrastructure projects with real estate and construction strength.

King & Spalding is a key player in the Georgia real estate market. Its understanding of equity investment and secured financings makes it a popular choice for institutional investors. The group has assisted Kimco Realty Opportunity Portfolio in acquiring $1 billion worth of real estate. National firm **Greenberg Traurig** stands at the forefront of the Florida market with a substantial presence in transactional matters. The client roster here features such giants as The Trump Group.

On the West Coast, **Allen Matkins Leck Gamble & Mallory** is a real estate boutique that many sources placed at the cutting edge of the sector. The firm's entrepreneurial attorneys represented Catellus Development in the sale of land at the Kaiser Commerce Center. Interviewees praised international firm **Paul Hastings Janofsky & Walker** for marshaling the resources to handle any deal. Its work has included assisting GE Capital on the financing of non-performing loan portfolios in Asia.

Seattle-based **Foster Pepper & Shefelman** employs a multi-disciplinary approach to real estate issues, boasting strength in litigation, structured finance and regulatory law. Public projects such as the new Seattle Seahawks Stadium have provided a huge boost to its profile. It shares a top band ranking in Washington with **Preston Gates & Ellis**, which is well known for a high-profile clientele that includes Microsoft. It has recently advised on the acquisition of property in downtown Seattle for the development of a public sculpture park, and acted for a microchip manufacturing company in the acquisition of a facility in Puyallup. Market sources felt that the lion's share of Portland's developer and institutional clients belongs to **Ball Janik**. The firm's great deal-maker, Stephen Janik, has represented Oregon Health & Science University in a $600 million expansion project.

SHIPPING

New York is the center of the US shipping industry and has all the leading shipping law firms.

Esteemed admiralty firm **Healy & Baillie** is the front-runner for all aspects of maritime law. Expertise ranges from shipping finance and shipping-related bankruptcies to litigation and arbitration. Star attorney John Kimball was celebrated for his work in charter party disputes and litigation and is widely respected by clients such as Ocean Rig, Premier Product Tankers and protection and indemnity clubs.

Although Healy & Baillie was acknowledged as a clear leader in New York, its dominance in the market is challenged by such leading firms as **Hill Rivkins & Hayden**, as well as **Holland & Knight** and **Seward & Kissel,** which all rate highly for their maritime practices.

Hill Rivkins & Hayden, which recently strengthened its shipping practice through the acquisition of four lawyers from Kirlin, Campbell & Keating, is especially commended for experience in ship finance and bankruptcy. The firm is led by Ray Hayden, the current president of The Maritime Law Association of the United States. Admiralty litigation, ship finance and contracts are among the strengths and skills of **Holland & Knight**. The highly respected team includes salvage experts and former mariners among its ranks. Larry Rutkowski at **Seward & Kissel** was recognized by interviewees as a key player in shipping finance. He led the firm's representation of JPMorgan Chase/Den norske Bank/Nordea/Hamburgische Landesbank on a $350 million credit facility for Overseas Shipholding Group.

TAX

Tax issues have become increasingly central to the deal-making process. Many of the largest cross-border acquisitions and financings are now driven by complicated tax structures. The trend toward increased sophistication and specialization is particularly evident within the financial products arena where tax lawyers have taken a leading role in the creation of innovative and cutting-edge financing structures.

New York's **Cleary Gottlieb Steen & Hamilton** is acknowledged as a clear leader in this area, with superstar lawyers Ed Kleinbard and Jim Peaslee widely recognized for their financial products work on behalf of blue-chip financial institution clients. By contrast, **Cravath Swaine & Moore** is far more focused on transactional corporate matters and boasts an elite team of talented attorneys providing quality tax support for the firm's steady volume of high-end M&A deals.

Ropes & Gray houses the largest tax team in Massachusetts, with some 45 attorneys acting on corporate tax, compensation issues, partnerships, and international tax planning. The firm is applauded for its creative approach to transactions and ranks in the top band alongside Boston competitors **Hale and Dorr** and **Goodwin Procter**.

The focus of the DC firms is largely on regulatory matters and many compete directly with the accounting firms in offering advice and representation to corporate clients on IRS and Treasury Department investigations. The traditional dominance of established DC tax boutiques, such as **Caplin & Drysdale**, is now facing challenges from more aggressive start-up operations such as **McKee Nelson**, which has made headlines both through its rapid expansion and strategic focus on accounting matters and tax controversy work.

Sutherland Asbill & Brennan commands an army of tax lawyers, distributed between its Atlanta and DC offices. The 50-lawyer team was particularly recommended for expertise in complex tax litigation. Also in Atlanta, **Alston & Bird** enjoys a national reputation for excellence in transactional matters and international tax planning. **Dean Mead Egerton Bloodworth Capouano & Bozarth** is considered by many to be among the best in the state in Florida, and offers serious competition to the larger full-service firms **Greenberg Traurig**, **Holland & Knight** and **Steel Hector & Davis**.

With its heavy emphasis on energy sector transactions, **Vinson & Elkins** emerged top in the Texas tax rankings with lead partner Ed Osterberg singled out for experience in cross-border deals and partnership taxation.

In Chicago, **Kirkland & Ellis** possesses a dynamic practice, heavily focused on restructuring work and the tax aspects of private equity transactions. Here, Jack Levin was recognized for his superlative reputation in both tax and LBO matters. The firm shares a top band rating with corporate-focused **Mayer Brown Rowe & Maw.**

Famed for its strength in IP, California firm Irell & Manella is a popular choice for tax advice among the state's major technology and communications companies. Its LA competitor, **Latham & Watkins,** is more visible on national and international M&A, representing numerous investment funds and clients such as Amgen and AOL TimeWarner.

Firms with the most big-hitters nationwide

This table (Table A) ranks firms according to the number of lawyers recommended in *Chambers USA*. It naturally favors the larger full-service firms with strong presences in a number of regions. For instance, international giant **Skadden Arps Slate Meagher & Flom** easily secures a top band placement with 77 attorneys ranked. Similarly, **Latham & Watkins**, which has individuals ranked in California, New York, Illinois, DC and New Jersey appears high on the table. By contrast, **Cravath Swaine & Moore**, acting solely from New York, does particularly well to secure so many individual rankings. Many see this as proof of the firm's exceptional quality. The table also shows a bias toward firms with a strong regional dominance, which accounts in part for **Kilpatrick Stockton**'s particularly high ranking.

TABLE A: Number of ranked individuals

Firm	Ranked Individuals	Ranked Offices in bold
Skadden, Arps, Slate, Meagher & Flom LLP & Affiliates	77	**Boston**, **Chicago**, **Houston**, **Los Angeles**, **Newark**, **New York**, **Palo Alto**, Reston, **San Francisco**, **Washington, DC**, **Wilmington**
Mayer, Brown, Rowe & Maw	56	Charlotte, **Chicago**, **Houston**, **Los Angeles**, **New York**, Palo Alto, **Washington, DC**
Latham & Watkins LLP	44	Boston, **Chicago**, Costa Mesa, **Los Angeles**, **Menlo Park**, **New York**, Newark, Reston, **San Diego**, San Francisco, **Washington, DC**
Sidley Austin Brown & Wood	44	**Chicago**, **Dallas**, **Los Angeles**, **New York**, San Francisco, **Washington, DC**
King & Spalding LLP	43	**Atlanta**, **Houston**, New York, Washington, DC
Davis Polk & Wardwell	38	**Menlo Park**, **New York**, Washington, DC
Simpson Thacher & Bartlett	38	Los Angeles, **New York**, Palo Alto
Jones Day	36	Atlanta, **Chicago**, Cleveland, Columbus, **Dallas**, Houston, Irvine, Los Angeles, Menlo Park, **New York**, Pittsburgh, **Washington, DC**
Holland & Knight LLP	34	Annapolis, Atlanta, Bethesda, Boston, Bradenton, **Chicago**, Fort Lauderdale, Jacksonville, **Lakeland**, Los Angeles, McLean, **Miami**, **New York**, Oakbrook Terrace, Orlando, Portland, **Providence**, San Antonio, San Francisco, Seattle, St Petersburg, Tallahassee, Tampa, **Washington, DC**, West Palm Beach
Sullivan & Cromwell LLP	34	**Los Angeles**, **New York**, Palo Alto, Washington, DC
Weil, Gotshal & Manges LLP	34	Austin, **Boston**, **Dallas**, Houston, Miami, **New York**, **Redwood Shores**, Washington, DC
Vinson & Elkins LLP	33	**Austin**, **Dallas**, **Houston**, New York, **Washington, DC**
Alston & Bird LLP	32	**Atlanta**, Charlotte, New York, Raleigh, Washington, DC
Kirkland & Ellis	29	**Chicago**, **Los Angeles**, **New York**, San Francisco, **Washington, DC**
Piper Rudnick LLP	28	Baltimore, Boston, Chicago, Dallas, Easton, Edison, **Las Vegas**, Los Angeles, New York, Philadelphia, Reston, Tampa, **Washington, DC**
Morgan, Lewis & Bockius LLP	27	Harrisburg, Irvine, **Los Angeles**, McLean, **Miami**, **New York**, Palo Alto, **Philadelphia**, Pittsburgh, Princeton, San Francisco, **Washington, DC**
Kilpatrick Stockton LLP	26	**Atlanta**, Augusta, **Charlotte**, Raleigh, Washington, DC, **Winston-Salem**
Shearman & Sterling	25	Menlo Park, **New York**, San Francisco, **Washington, DC**
Baker Botts LLP	24	**Austin**, **Dallas**, **Houston**, New York, **Washington, DC**
Cravath, Swaine & Moore	24	**New York**
Foley & Lardner	24	**Chicago**, Denver, Detroit, **Jacksonville**, Los Angeles, **Madison**, **Milwaukee**, Orlando, Sacramento, San Diego, San Francisco, Tallahassee, **Tampa**, Washington, DC, West Palm Beach
Stoel Rives LLP	24	**Boise**, **Portland**, **Salt Lake City**, Sacramento, San Francisco, **Seattle**, Tahoe City
Wachtell, Lipton, Rosen & Katz	24	**New York**
Gibson, Dunn & Crutcher LLP	23	Dallas, Denver, Irvine, **Los Angeles**, New York, **Palo Alto**, San Francisco, **Washington, DC**
Ballard Spahr Andrews & Ingersoll LLP	22	Baltimore, Denver, Philadelphia, **Salt Lake City**, **Voorhees**, Washington, DC, Wilmington
Debevoise & Plimpton	21	**New York**, Washington, DC
Goodwin Procter LLP	21	**Boston**, New York, Roseland, Washington, DC
Hunton & Williams	21	Atlanta, Austin, Charlotte, Dallas, Knoxville, McLean, **Miami**, New York, Norfolk, Raleigh, **Richmond**, **Washington, DC**

TABLE A: Number of ranked individuals continued

Firm	Ranked Individuals	Ranked Offices in bold
Winston & Strawn	21	**Chicago,** Los Angeles, New York, San Francisco, Washington, DC
Arnold & Porter	20	Century City, **Denver,** Los Angeles, McLean, **New York, Washington, DC**
Hale and Dorr	20	**Boston, New York, Princeton, Reston,** Washington, DC, Waltham
Hogan & Hartson LLP	20	**Baltimore,** Boulder, Colorado Springs, **Denver,** Los Angeles, McLean, Miami, **New York, Washington, DC**
Troutman Sanders LLP	20	Atlanta, McLean, Norfolk, Raleigh, **Richmond,** Virginia Beach, **Washington, DC**
Akin Gump Strauss Hauer & Feld LLP	19	**Austin,** Dallas, Denver, **Houston,** Los Angeles, McLean, **New York,** Philadelphia, San Antonio, **Washington, DC**
Frost Brown Todd LLC	19	Cincinnati, Columbus, Lexington, **Louisville,** Middletown, Nashville, New Albany
Fulbright & Jaworski LLP	19	Austin, Dallas, **Houston,** Los Angeles, Minneapolis, New York, **San Antonio, Washington, DC**
Davis Wright Tremaine LLP	18	Anchorage, Bellevue, Honolulu, **Los Angeles,** New York, Portland, **San Francisco, Seattle,** Washington, DC
Perkins Coie LLP	18	**Anchorage,** Bellevue, Boise, Chicago, Denver, Los Angeles, Menlo Park, Olympia, Portland, San Francisco, **Seattle,** Washington, DC
White & Case LLP	18	**Los Angeles, Miami, New York,** Palo Alto, San Francisco, **Washington, DC**
Greenberg Traurig LLP	17	Atlanta, Boca Raton, Boston, Chicago, Denver, Florham Park, **Fort Lauderdale,** McLean, **Miami,** New York, **Orlando,** Philadelphia, **Phoenix,** Santa Monica, Tallahassee, Washington, DC, **West Palm Beach,** Wilmington
McDermott, Will & Emery	17	**Boston, Chicago,** Irvine, **Los Angeles,** Miami, New York, **Palo Alto, Washington, DC**
Morrison & Foerster LLP	17	Century City, Denver, Irvine, **Los Angeles,** McLean, **New York, Palo Alto,** Sacramento, San Diego, **San Francisco, Walnut Creek, Washington, DC**
O'Melveny & Myers LLP	17	Century City, Irvine, **Los Angeles,** McLean, Menlo Park, **New York,** Newport Beach, **San Francisco, Washington, DC**
Sonnenschein Nath & Rosenthal	17	**Chicago, Kansas City,** Los Angeles, New York, **San Francisco,** Short Hills, St Louis, Washington, DC, West Palm Beach
Squire, Sanders & Dempsey LLP	17	Cincinnati, **Cleveland, Columbus,** Houston, Los Angeles, Miami, New York, Palo Alto, **Phoenix,** San Francisco, Tampa, Tysons Corner, Washington, DC
Sutherland Asbill & Brennan LLP	17	Atlanta, Austin, Houston, New York, Tallahassee, **Washington, DC**
Wilson Sonsini Goodrich & Rosati	17	Austin, Kirkland, New York, **Palo Alto,** Reston, **Salt Lake City, San Francisco**
Cleary Gottlieb Steen & Hamilton	16	**New York, Washington, DC**
Dorsey & Whitney LLP	16	Anchorage, Costa Mesa, Denver, Des Moines, **Fargo, Great Falls, Minneapolis, Missoula,** New York, Palo Alto, **Salt Lake City,** San Francisco, Seattle, Washington, DC
Holland & Hart LLP	16	Aspen, **Billings, Boise,** Boulder, **Cheyenne,** Colorado Springs, **Denver,** Greenwood Village, **Jackson, Salt Lake City,** Santa Fe, Washington, DC
Milbank, Tweed, Hadley & McCloy	16	**Los Angeles, New York, Palo Alto,** Washington, DC
Paul, Hastings, Janofsky & Walker LLP	16	Atlanta, Costa Mesa, **Los Angeles, New York,** San Francisco, Stamford, **Washington, DC**
Reed Smith LLP	16	Century City, Falls Church, Harrisburg, Leesburg, Los Angeles, Newark, New York, Oakland, **Philadelphia, Pittsburgh,** Princeton, Richmond, San Francisco, Washington, DC, Westlake Village, Wilmington
Ropes & Gray	16	**Boston,** New York, Providence, San Francisco, Washington, DC
Bingham McCutchen LLP	15	**Boston, Hartford,** Los Angeles, **New York,** East Palo Alto, **San Francisco,** Walnut Creek, **Washington, DC**
Faegre & Benson LLP	15	Boulder, **Denver,** Des Moines, **Minneapolis**
Quarles Brady LLP and Affiliates	15	Boca Raton, Chicago, Madison, **Milwaukee,** Naples, **Phoenix, Tucson**
Venable LLP	15	**Baltimore,** Rockville, Towson, **Vienna, Washington, DC**

Firms with star lawyers nationwide

This table (Table B) shows those firms with the greatest number of individuals appearing in the star category or band one of *Chambers USA* rankings. Although large national firms such as **Skadden Arps Slate Meagher & Flom** and **Jones Day** have a natural advantage, the table also gives prominence to firms with big-name attorneys.

Here, the recognized high quality of firms such as **Cravath Swaine & Moore** shines through. Firms that tend to dominate the market within a particular city or region also fare well. This would apply to practices such as **Faegre & Benson** (Denver & Minneapolis) and **Alston & Bird** (Atlanta).

TABLE B: Number of 'star' and 'band one' individuals ranked

Firm	Ranked Individuals	Ranked Offices in bold
Skadden, Arps, Slate, Meagher & Flom LLP & Affiliates	17	**Boston, Chicago, Houston, Los Angeles,** Newark, **New York, Palo Alto,** Reston, **San Francisco, Washington, DC, Wilmington**
Dorsey & Whitney LLP	12	**Anchorage,** Costa Mesa, Denver, Des Moines, **Fargo, Great Falls, Minneapolis, Missoula,** New York, Palo Alto, **Salt Lake City,** San Francisco, Seattle, Washington, DC
Mayer, Brown, Rowe & Maw	11	Charlotte, **Chicago, Houston, Los Angeles, New York,** Palo Alto, **Washington, DC**
Sidley Austin Brown & Wood	10	**Chicago, Dallas, Los Angeles, New York,** San Francisco, **Washington, DC**
Simpson Thacher & Bartlett	10	Los Angeles, **New York, Palo Alto**
Cravath, Swaine & Moore	9	**New York**
Davis Polk & Wardwell	9	**Menlo Park, New York,** Washington, DC
Latham & Watkins LLP	9	Boston, **Chicago,** Costa Mesa, **Los Angeles, Menlo Park, New York,** Newark, Reston, **San Diego,** San Francisco, **Washington, DC**
Baker Botts LLP	8	**Austin, Dallas, Houston, New York, Washington, DC**
Faegre & Benson LLP	8	Boulder, **Denver,** Des Moines, **Minneapolis**
Holland & Knight LLP	8	Annapolis, Atlanta, Bethesda, Boston, Bradenton, **Chicago,** Fort Lauderdale, **Jacksonville, Lakeland,** Los Angeles, McLean, **Miami, New York,** Oakbrook Terrace, **Orlando,** Portland, **Providence,** San Antonio, San Francisco, Seattle, St Petersburg, **Tallahassee, Tampa, Washington, DC,** West Palm Beach
Jones Day	8	Atlanta, **Chicago, Cleveland,** Columbus, **Dallas,** Houston, Irvine, Los Angeles, Menlo Park, **New York,** Pittsburgh, **Washington, DC**
King & Spalding LLP	8	**Atlanta, Houston,** New York, Washington, DC
Piper Rudnick LLP	8	**Baltimore, Boston, Chicago,** Dallas, Easton, Edison, **Las Vegas,** Los Angeles, New York, Philadelphia, Reston, Tampa, **Washington, DC**
Sullivan & Cromwell LLP	8	**Los Angeles, New York,** Palo Alto, Washington, DC
Alston & Bird LLP	6	**Atlanta,** Charlotte, New York, Raleigh, Washington, DC
Bradley Arant Rose & White LLP	6	**Birmingham,** Huntsville, **Jackson,** Montgomery, Washington, DC
Drinker Biddle & Shanley LLP/ Drinker Biddle & Reath LLP	6	**Berwyn, Florham Park,** Los Angeles, New York, **Philadelphia,** Princeton, San Francisco, Washington, DC, Wilmington
Hale and Dorr	6	**Boston, New York, Princeton, Reston,** Washington, DC, Waltham
Hunton & Williams	6	Atlanta, Austin, Charlotte, Dallas, Knoxville, McLean, **Miami,** New York, Norfolk, Raleigh, **Richmond, Washington, DC**
Kirkland & Ellis	6	**Chicago, Los Angeles, New York,** San Francisco, **Washington, DC**
Thelen Reid & Priest LLP	6	**Los Angeles,** Morristown, **New York, San Francisco,** San Jose, **Washington, DC**
Wachtell, Lipton, Rosen & Katz	6	**New York**
Ballard Spahr Andrews & Ingersoll LLP	5	**Baltimore, Denver, Philadelphia, Salt Lake City, Voorhees,** Washington, DC, Wilmington

TABLE B: Number of 'star' and 'band one' individuals ranked continued

Firm	Ranked Individuals	Ranked Offices in bold
Belin Lamson McCormick Zumbach Flynn, PC	5	**Des Moines**
Bingham McCutchen LLP	5	**Boston, Hartford, Los Angeles, New York,** East Palo Alto, **San Francisco,** Walnut Creek, **Washington, DC**
Davenport, Evans, Hurwitz & Smith LLP	5	**Sioux Falls**
Debevoise & Plimpton	5	**New York,** Washington, DC
Foley & Lardner	5	**Chicago,** Denver, Detroit, **Jacksonville,** Los Angeles, **Madison, Milwaukee,** Orlando, Sacramento, San Diego, San Francisco, Tallahassee, **Tampa,** Washington, DC, West Palm Beach
Haynes and Boone, LLP	5	**Austin, Dallas,** Fort Worth, **Houston,** Richardson, **San Antonio,** Washington, DC
McLane, Graf, Raulerson & Middleton PA	5	Concord, **Manchester,** Nashua, Portsmouth
Robinson, Bradshaw & Hinson, P.A.	5	**Charlotte,** Rock Hill
Stinson Morrison Hecker LLP	5	**Kansas City,** Omaha, **Overland Park,** Phoenix, St Louis, Washington, DC, Wichita
Vinson & Elkins LLP	5	**Austin, Dallas, Houston,** New York, **Washington, DC**
White & Case LLP	5	**Los Angeles, Miami, New York,** Palo Alto, San Francisco, **Washington, DC**
Williams & Connolly LLP	5	**Washington, DC**
Blackwell Sanders Peper Martin LLP	4	Edwardsville, **Kansas City, Omaha, Overland Park,** Springfield, St Louis, Washington, DC
Milbank, Tweed, Hadley & McCloy	4	**Los Angeles, New York, Palo Alto,** Washington, DC

US Law Firm mergers 2002-2003

New Firm Name	Merger partners	Date	Number of Attorneys Worldwide (figures are approximate)
Jones Day / Jones Day Gouldens (London)	Jones Day (National) and Gouldens (London)	February 8, 2003	2000
Jones Day Showa (Tokyo)	Jones Day (National) and Showa Law Office (Tokyo)	January 1, 2002	1850
Mayer Brown Rowe & Mawe	Mayer Brown & Platt (National) and Rowe & Maw (London)	February 1, 2002	1300
Holland & Knight LLP	Holland & Knight (Tampa) and McBride Baker & Coles (Chicago)	August 14, 2002	1273
Morgan Lewis & Bockius LLP	Morgan Lewis & Bockius (National) and Hopgood Calimafde Judlowe & Mondolino (New York)	January 1, 2002	1300
Weil Gotshal & Manges LLP	Weil Gotshal & Manges (New York) and Serra Leavy & Cazals (Paris)	January 1, 2003	1000
Reed Smith Crosby Heafey (California only) Reed Smith LLP (US) Reed Smith (UK)	Reed Smith (Pittsburgh) and Crosby Heafey Roach & May (California)	January 1, 2003	1000
Reed Smith LLP (US) Reed Smith (UK)	Reed Smith LLP (Pittsburgh) and Parker Duryee Rosoff & Haft (New York)	January 1, 2002	1000
Hogan & Hartson LLP	Hogan & Hartson (Washington DC) and Squadron Ellenoff Plesent & Sheinfeld (New York and Los Angeles)	March 1, 2002	900
Piper Rudnick	Piper Rudnick (National) and Verner Liipfert Bernhard McPherson and Hand (Washington DC)	October 1, 2002	900
O'Melveny & Myers LLP	O'Melveny & Myers (Los Angeles) and O'Sullivan (New York)	September 16, 2002	850
Hunton & Williams	Hunton & Williams (Richmond) and Worsham Forsythe & Wooldridge (Texas)	January 1, 2002	850
Fulbright & Jaworski LLP	Fulbright & Jaworski (Houston) and Owen & Davis (New York)		825
Bryan Cave LLP (Globally) Bryan Cave/Robinson Silverman (New York)	Bryan Cave (St Louis) and Robinson Silverman Pearce Aronsohn & Berman (New York)	July 1, 2002	800
Bingham McCutchen LLP	Bingham Dana (National) and McCutchen Doyle Brown & Enersen (San Francisco)	July 1, 2002	800
Paul Hastings Janofsky & Walker LLP (Globally) Koo and Partners, in association with Paul Hastings (in Hong Kong for the next three years)	Paul Hastings Janofsky & Walker (National) and Koo and Partners (Hong Kong)	April 30, 2002	800
Dorsey & Whitney LLP	Dorsey & Whitney (Minneapolis) and Flehr Hohbach Test Albritton & Herbert (San Francisco and Palo Alto)	May 2, 2002	750
Sonnenschein Nath & Rosenthal	Sonnenschein Nath & Rosenthal (Chicago) and RubinBaum (New York)	June 1, 2002	600

US Law Firm mergers 2002-2003

New Firm Name	Merger partners	Date	Number of Attorneys Worldwide (figures are approximate)
Shook Hardy & Bacon International LLP (London) Shook Hardy & Bacon LLP (Globally)	Shook Hardy & Bacon (Kansas City) and Arnander Irvine & Zietman (London)	July 1, 2002	600
Katten Muchin Zavis Rosenman (KMZ Rosenman)	Katten Muchin Zavis (Chicago) and Rosenman & Colin (New York)	March 27, 2002	600
Nixon Peabody LLP	Nixon Peabody (National) and Hutchins Wheeler & Dittmar (Boston)	February 1, 2003	600
Willkie Farr & Gallagher	Willkie Farr & Gallagher (New York) and Dieux & Associes (Belgium)	March 1, 2002	540
Gray Cary Ware & Freidenrich LLP	Gray Cary Ware & Freidenrich (Palo Alto) and Blumenfeld & Cohen (Washington DC)	January 31, 2002	480
Faegre Benson Hobson Audley LLP	Hobson Audley (London) and Faegre & Benson LLP (Minneapolis)	January 2, 2003	475
Womble Carlyle Sandridge & Rice PLLC	Womble Carlyle Sandridge & Rice (Winston-Salem) and Pepper & Corazzini (Washington DC)	March 1, 2002	450
McKenna Long & Aldridge LLP	Long Aldridge & Norman (Atlanta) and McKenna & Cuneo	June 1, 2002	376
Thompson Hine LLP	Gould & Wilkie (New York) and Thompson Hine (Cleveland)	May 1, 2002	373
Stinson Morrison Hecker LLP	Morrison & Hecker (Kansas City) and Stinson Mag & Fizzell (Kansas City)	May 1, 2002	335
Manatt Phelps & Phillips LLP	Manatt Phelps Phillips (Los Angeles) and Kalkines Arky Zall & Bernstein (New York)	January 1, 2003	272
Withers LLP (UK and globally) Withers Bergman LLP (US only)	Withers (London) and Bergman Horowitz & Reynolds (New Haven)	January 1, 2002	226
Brown Rudnick Berlack Israels LLP	Brown Rudnick Freed & Gesmer (Boston) and Berlack Israels & Liberman (New York)	February 1, 2002	200
Fisher & Philips LLP	Fisher & Philips (Atlanta) and Gordon & Meneghello (Oregon)	September 1, 2002	170
Gibbons Del Deo Dolan Griffinger & Vecchione PC	Gibbons Del Deo Dolan Griffinger & Vecchione (New Jersey) and Cobrin & Gittes (New York)	April 1, 2002	160

Abbreviations used

AAA	American Arbitration Association
ABA	American Bar Association
ADA	Americans with Disabilities Act
ACREL	American College of Real Estate Lawyers
ADEA	Age Discrimination in Employment Act
AMA	American Medical Association
CAA	Clean Air Act
CERCLA	The Comprehensive Environmental Response, Compensation, and Liability Act
CRM	Customer Relationship Management
CWA	Clean Water Act
DMCA	Digital Millennium Copyright Act
EEOC	Equal Employment Opportunity Commission
ERISA	Employee Retirement Income Security Act of 1974
FCC	Federal Communications Commission
FERC	Federal Energy Regulatory Commission
FLSA	Fair Labor Standards Act
FMLA	Family and Medical Leave Act
FTC	Federal Trade Commission
ICC	International Criminal Court
ICSID	International Centre for Settlement of Investment Disputes
IFA	International Fiscal Association
IPL	Intellectual Property Law
ITC	International Trade Commission
LCIA	London Court of International Arbitration
MSHA	Mine Safety and Health Administration
NAFTA	North American Free Trade Agreement
NLRA	National Labor Relations Act
NLRB	National Labor Relations Board
OFCCP	Office of Federal Contract Compliance Programs
OSHA	Occupational Safety and Health Act/Administration
RCRA	Resource Conservation and Recovery Act
RICO	Racketeer-Influenced and Corrupt Organizations Act
RIC	Regulated Investment Companies
SLAPPs	Strategic Lawsuits against Public Participation
UNCITRAL	United Nations Commission on International Trade Law
WIPO	World Intellectual Property Organization

RANKINGS AND COMMENTARY

CHAMBERS
USA
2003–2004

CORPORATE/M&A

ALABAMA

CONTENTS: Corporate/M&A p.1; Employment: Mainly Plaintiff p.2; Mainly Defendant p.3; Litigation: General Commercial p.4; Real Estate p.6; Individuals' Profiles p.7.

ALABAMA'S TOP FOUR
1. Bradley Arant Rose & White
2. Balch & Bingham
3. Burr & Forman
4. Maynard, Cooper & Gale

Ranking based on Chambers' research within the state.

All quotes in the text are from interviews with clients and competitors.

OVERVIEW: Top-ranking **Bradley Arant Rose & White** is also the largest firm in the state. Its reputation is chiefly based on litigation work, but its corporate skills are highly praised. The firm is widely used for employment discrimination class actions, and has also been called "the first point of call" for institutional financing in the real estate sector. John Morrow, who specializes in commercial and personal injury defense cases, is highly rated by clients. Thomas Carruthers is known as the dean of the corporate bar. Clients include Chubb, Coca-Cola and Hyundai.

Balch & Bingham has been recommended for real estate and corporate work. The firm is best known for its utility client, Southern Company. It also has one of the largest public finance practices in the state, and is well known for litigation cases defending securities class actions and financial disputes. Real estate lawyer Hampton Boles has gained a reputation for working for banks, while Jim Hughey is a leading figure in corporate issues. Other clients include UBS PaineWebber.

Manufacturing industry clients are key to **Burr & Forman**. The firm's corporate group is also active on the banking scene. It has a distinguished list of real estate clients and is well known for its lending practice, as well as having a high reputation for traditional labor law. Corporate lawyer Lee Thuston acts for major clients Mercedes-Benz and Honda, and Fred Powell is a high-profile member of the real estate team.

Maynard, Cooper & Gale is smaller than the other firms ranked here. But its strength is its real estate lending department. It acts for local lenders, real estate investment trusts (REITs) and private investors. In common with numerous other Alabama law firms, it also has an active corporate practice with many banking clients. It has niche expertise in bond issuance. Robert Sexton is seen as a key lawyer in the real estate department, while Mark Drew is widely known for his work on corporate securities and tax. Clients include Bank of America and the Alabama Teachers' Retirement System.

CORPORATE/M&A

ALABAMA
Leading firms (Corporate/M&A)
1. **BRADLEY ARANT ROSE & WHITE LLP** Birmingham
2. **BALCH & BINGHAM** Birmingham
   BURR & FORMAN Birmingham
   MAYNARD, COOPER & GALE PC Birmingham
3. **BERKOWITZ LEFKOVITS ISOM** Birmingham
   SIROTE & PERMUTT PC Birmingham

Leading individuals (Corporate/M&A)
1. **CARRUTHERS Thomas** Bradley Arant Rose, Birmingham
   HUGHEY James Balch & Bingham, Birmingham
2. **GRENIER John** Bradley Arant Rose & White, Birmingham
   KUSHNER Harold Berkowitz Lefkovits, Birmingham
   THUSTON Lee Burr & Forman, Birmingham
3. **COOPER John** Sirote & Permutt PC, Birmingham
   DREW Mark Maynard, Cooper & Gale PC, Birmingham
   PRICE Gene Burr & Forman, Birmingham

Firms and individuals are listed alphabetically in each band.

Bradley Arant Rose & White LLP
The Firm: Interviewees spoke of the firm's "*tremendous reputation*" among its corporate clients. Highlights include acting for Hyundai in the development of its $1 billion Montgomery plant. The firm also advised Retirement Systems of Alabama in its development of the Robert Trent Jones Golf Trail. On the business bankruptcy side, the firm acted as lead counsel for Birmingham Steel in its Delaware bankruptcy filing.

The Lawyers: Peers and clients commended **Thomas Carruthers** as the "*dean*" of the Alabama corporate bar. Peers also singled out **John (Beau) Grenier** as a "*rising star*" of the team.

The Clients: A separate banking group undertakes work for local banks including SouthTrust Bank. Hyundai and The University of Alabama are also clients.

Balch & Bingham
see firm details p.768

The Firm: Best known for its work with electric utility Southern Company. The team advises on mergers, acquisitions, securities and public debt offerings. It boasts one of the largest public finance practices in the state. An office in Washington DC provides lobbying, legislative and regulatory support for the firm's electric utilities clients.

The Lawyers: The lead player here is **Jim Hughey**. Active in acquisitions and dispositions, he also advises closely held companies on corporate planning matters. Hughey represented Stockham Valves & Fittings in the sale of its valve business to Crane, and advised Vesta Insurance Group in its $25 million acquisition of American Founders Financial.

The Clients: The group acts for utility clients Alabama Power, Southern Nuclear and Mississippi Power alongside significant financial institutions and insurance companies such as Alabama Bankers Association and Montgomery Mutual Insurance. Systems provider Intergraph is also an active client.

Burr & Forman
The Firm: The firm maintains its reputation for manufacturing industry expertise with high-profile clients such as Mercedes-Benz US International, USX and Vulcan Engineering. In addition, a growing finance practice advises corporate and banking clients. The corporate group is involved in the formation, acquisition and sale of corporates, commercial banks and savings and loan institutions.

The Lawyers: "*Clear leader*" **Lee Thuston** is respected by peers for his work with Mercedes-Benz. He acted for Mercedes-Benz US International and American Honda Motor Company in the implementation of incentives packages in the State of Alabama. **Gene Price** was extolled as a specialist in the healthcare industry, advising on corporate, IP, M&A and securities law.

The Clients: Mercedes-Benz US International; USX; Vulcan Engineering and Honda.

Maynard, Cooper & Gale PC
The Firm: Busy corporate practice advising public and private companies on securities law compliance, M&A and venture capital work. The group advised on the $50 million IPO of

ALABAMA

EMPLOYMENT & LABOR LAW

healthcare IT company, Computer Programs & Systems. Active in public financings, the group has niche expertise in bond issuance. The firm's restructuring practice is thriving; it completed the $10 million capital restructuring of Offshore Tool & Energy, for example.

The Lawyers: **Mark Drew** is esteemed by peers for his work in corporate securities and tax.

The Clients: The firm serves issuers, trustees, credit enhancers and financial advisers. Clients include Drummond Company, Source Medical Solutions, Bank of America and Torchmark.

Berkowitz Lefkovits Isom & Kushner

The Firm: Bolstered by the expertise of the *"truly preeminent"* **Harold Kushner** (see p.7). The firm advises on M&A and securities matters. Particularly recommended for its representation of closely held companies. Practice highlights include acting for the former shareholders of Parisian in their $130 million reacquisition of the company from Hooker Corporation. It also advised Atrion in the $40 million sale of its natural gas business to Midcoast Energy Resources.

The Clients: SouthTrust Bank; Hibbett Sporting Goods; Hanna Steel and The Colonial Company.

Sirote & Permutt PC

The Firm: While the firm's corporate profile has diminished, its tax expertise won strong endorsement. The group provides strategic and legal advice for corporate clients. Handles M&A, corporate restructurings and joint venture and strategic alliance transactions alongside public and private offerings for closely held and public company clients.

The Lawyers: Chief executive **John Cooper** is the group's main name. Noted for his expertise in securities and tax. Advises clients on structuring acquisitions and dispositions and tax planning issues. Cooper is experienced in public and private offerings of technology-based companies, where he counsels issuers and investors in securities offerings.

EMPLOYMENT & LABOR LAW

MAINLY PLAINTIFF

ALABAMA
Leading firms
(Employment: Mainly Plaintiff)

1. **GORDON, SILBERMAN, WIGGINS** Birmingham
2. **WHATLEY DRAKE, LLC** Birmingham
3. **MEELHEIM, WILKINSON & MEELHEIM** Birmingham
   NAKAMURA, QUINN & WALLS Birmingham

Leading individuals
(Employment: Mainly Plaintiff)

1. **QUINN Michael** *Gordon, Silberman*, Birmingham
2. **WIGGINS Robert** *Gordon, Silberman*, Birmingham
3. **CHILDS Robert** *Gordon, Silberman*, Birmingham
   ROBERTSON Ann *Gordon, Silberman*, Birmingham
   WHATLEY Joe *Whatley Drake, LLC*, Birmingham
4. **ALLEN Andrew** *Whatley Drake, LLC*, Birmingham
   ARENDALL David *Sole Practitioner*, Birmingham
   DRAKE Jack *Whatley Drake, LLC*, Birmingham
   MEELHEIM Richard *Meelheim, Wilkinson*, Birmingham
   SAXON John *Sole Practitioner*, Birmingham
   WILKINSON Cynthia *Meelheim, Wilkinson*, Birmingham

Firms and individuals are listed alphabetically in each band.

Gordon, Silberman, Wiggins & Childs

The Firm: In terms of size, quality and scope, the firm is an undisputed leader in Alabama. Although the group represents plaintiffs in a wide array of matters, employment law is an acknowledged strength and it has a strong stable of hard-hitting and tenacious players.

The Lawyers: **Mike Quinn** was overwhelmingly endorsed as *"an outstanding trial lawyer who is great with juries."* Commentators attributed his success to his flair for *"getting to the essence of something and communicating it to ordinary people."* **Bob Wiggins** also stood out as a *"highly skilled and technically astute"* attorney who is well known for class action cases. Following a string of victories in sexual harassment and sex discrimination cases, **Ann Robertson** has established a reputation as a *"strong and aggressive"* attorney. **Bob Childs** was also recommended as a *"dedicated and innovative"* lawyer who was seen to possess the ability to handle big cases.

The Clients: The group acts for individuals and groups of plaintiffs. Alongside other firms, it has reached a settlement in a large race discrimination class action. It has also represented the plaintiffs in a case relating to discrimination in overtime pay and promotion.

Whatley Drake, LLC

The Firm: Although the firm has branched out into numerous other areas of plaintiff work, interviewees insisted that *"they're a choice firm for employment law."* With the resources to take on a variety of cases, including class actions, the firm has expertise in employment and labor law and continues to represent United Steelworkers. Recent work has included securing a $102,000 verdict against Wal-Mart in an ADA case and, on the labor front, convincing an arbitration panel in Alabama that temporary workers were entitled to the protection of a collective bargaining agreement.

The Lawyers: **Joe Whatley** is *"the standout name"* and was lauded by defense attorneys for the depth of his experience and his ability to think on his feet. **Jack Drake** was also recommended as a *"tenacious and talented"* litigator who is particularly well known for his success in a range of class actions. Although not of the same prominence as the name partners, **Andrew Allen** was also endorsed as *"a bright guy who understands the facts and knows how to apply them."*

Meelheim, Wilkinson & Meelheim

The Firm: An office of four lawyers concentrates its efforts almost exclusively on the representation of plaintiffs in a wide range of employment issues including the FMLA and breaches of contract. Defense attorneys praised them for being *"reasonable and realistic,"* but they are also recognized as competent and thorough attorneys who *"do a great job for their clients."*

The Lawyers: **Rick Meelheim** was warmly mentioned as a larger-than-life character who has a *"low-key but effective"* courtroom style. His colleague **Cynthia Wilkinson** was also recognized as an easy-to-deal-with and respected attorney.

Nakamura, Quinn & Walls

The Firm: The firm's caseload is strongly focused on union representation where commentators saw it as *"a standout practice."* With a second office in Decatur, Georgia, interviewees insisted that the practice extends beyond the confines of Alabama and that it has connections with unions nationwide. The lawyers, headed by Pat Nakamura, are respected for being *"tenacious but understated"* advocates for their clients.

Other Notable Practitioners

Sole practitioner **David Arendall** was recommended as an experienced employment litigator who acts for clients with regard to violations of the FLSA and the FLMA, and in a variety of discrimination cases. He has recently acted for the plaintiff in a wage and hour case brought against Osmose. **John Saxon**, also a sole practitioner, was described as *"a fine lawyer who knows the law inside out."* As well as handling a full spectrum of discrimination matters, he also represents executives and has on occasion advised small businesses.

EMPLOYMENT & LABOR LAW — ALABAMA

MAINLY DEFENDANT

ALABAMA
Leading firms
(Employment: Mainly Defendant)

[1]
- BRADLEY ARANT ROSE & WHITE LLP Birmingham

[2]
- BURR & FORMAN Birmingham
- CONSTANGY, BROOKS & SMITH, LLC Birmingham
- LEHR MIDDLEBROOKS PRICE Birmingham

[3]
- CABANISS, JOHNSTON, GARDNER Birmingham

[4]
- JOHNSTON BARTON PROCTOR Birmingham
- MAYNARD, COOPER & GALE PC Birmingham
- OGLETREE, DEAKINS, NASH, SMOAK Birmingham

Leading individuals
(Employment: Mainly Defendant)

[1]
- ALEXANDER James Bradley Arant Rose, Birmingham
- GARDNER William Cabaniss, Johnston, Birmingham

[2]
- INGRAM Fred Burr & Forman, Birmingham
- MIDDLEBROOKS David Lehr Middlebrooks, Birmingham
- POWELL Charles Johnston Barton Proctor, Birmingham

[3]
- COLEMAN John Burr & Forman, Birmingham
- FRAZIER Sydney Cabaniss, Johnston, Birmingham
- LACY Peyton Ogletree, Deakins, Nash, Birmingham
- LEE Jeffrey Maynard, Cooper & Gale PC, Birmingham
- MAY James Bradley Arant Rose & White, Birmingham
- NELSON Carol Sue Constangy, Brooks, Birmingham
- PROCTOR David Lehr Middlebrooks Price, Birmingham

[4]
- BROWN Stephen Maynard, Cooper, Birmingham
- FREDERICK Barry Lehr Middlebrooks, Birmingham

Firms and individuals are listed alphabetically in each band.

Bradley Arant Rose & White LLP

The Firm: Research confirmed the view that this was one of the *"classiest groups in the market."* One of the largest employment and labor departments in the state, comprising 20 lawyers in a number of offices, it was described by commentators as *"thoroughly professional and easy to deal with."* Traditional labor issues are an important component of the firm's broad repertoire but its standing is particularly high for employment discrimination class actions.
The Lawyers: Although interviewees commented on the uniformly high quality of the team's attorneys, **Jim Alexander** emerged as the clear leader of the pack. A 30-year veteran of the sector, he is known primarily as an aggressive employment litigator, and was endorsed to researchers as a *"bright, insightful attorney with excellent technical knowledge."* He defeated a proposed national class action suit, based on alleged gender discrimination in a sales position for a major national manufacturer. Although slightly overshadowed by his colleague, **Jim May** is also a respected employment lawyer who regularly defends OFCCP proceedings and represents clients before the EEOC.
The Clients: Clients include: Boy Scouts of America; Brasfield & Gorrie; Capital Vial of Alabama; Chubb; Coca-Cola Bottling Company United; Federal Reserve Bank of Atlanta; Goodyear; Marriott International; UPS; City of Birmingham; United Technologies and Vulcan Materials Company.

Burr & Forman

The Firm: An *"energetic"* group of 15 lawyers from this old-line corporate firm has acknowledged expertise in a full range of labor and employment issues. It is in traditional labor law, however, that its market reputation rides highest.
The Lawyers: Famed as one of the state's experts in this area, **Fred Ingram** has extensive experience in labor negotiations, unfair labor practices, arbitrations and strike injunctions. One of his most important cases has included the representation of PPG Industries and Teamsters Local 402 before the NLRB. Focusing more on employment law, the *"studious"* **John Coleman** defends individual and class discrimination claims and also dedicates a proportion of his caseload to OSHA and FLSA matters. In a recent case for 3M, he successfully obtained summary judgment, dismissing race and retaliation claims.
The Clients: Clients include: US Steel; Mercedes-Benz; Honda Manufacturing of Alabama; American Honda Motor Company; Sears Roebuck; Cingular Wireless and MeadWestvaco.

Constangy, Brooks & Smith, LLC

The Firm: The Birmingham office of this small employment boutique was recommended by rivals for the depth of its local knowledge and its *"excellent technical competence."* Although it regularly defends employers against a full gamut of discrimination claims and offers labor law expertise, clients emphasized the weight given to preventative advice and policy development.
The Lawyers: Leading litigator **Carol Sue Nelson** is considered to be the department's outstanding figure, and was rated by opponents as an *"excellent communicator"* with judges and juries.
The Clients: Clients include major national corporates, including BellSouth, Boeing and Sara Lee.

Lehr Middlebrooks Price & Proctor

The Firm: Originally formed from the employment group of a corporate firm, the team has an established reputation as a *"top-quality boutique."* Preventative counseling is at the heart of the practice, but a team of 13 lawyers also litigates a range of employment and labor matters as well as issues connected with OSHA and employee benefits.
The Lawyers: **David Middlebrooks** is renowned for his in-depth practical experience in both labor and employment matters, notably on discrimination cases, and won approval from clients as a *"genuine and down-to-earth guy."* In a race discrimination case involving Media General, he secured summary judgment and was successful in a counterclaim against one of the plaintiffs related to the breach of her employment contract. **David Proctor**'s style is said by observers to be *"forthright,"* and he has earned himself a market reputation as a *"terrific litigator"* who frequently represents clients before the EEOC and OFCCP. **Barry Frederick** was also singled out to researchers as a *"thorough attorney with a great courtroom style."*
The Clients: Clients include: Xerox; Colonial BancGroup; Willis North America; GKN Westland Aerospace; Circuit City Stores; JVC America and BP Amoco.

Cabaniss, Johnston, Gardner, Dumas & O'Neal

The Firm: Although it is respected for its Title VII defense expertise, the firm's reputation in the employment and labor sphere is widely held to rest on the shoulders of *"the dean of the defense bar"* **Bill Gardner**. He commands the respect of both clients and competitors, and was endorsed for his *"knack of spotting the key issues from the start."* Commentators also pointed to his *"meticulous"* approach to a case and *"excellent writing style."* **Sydney Frazier** may be seen less frequently than Gardner but he appeals to rivals as a *"straight-shooting"* labor lawyer with particular expertise in workers' compensation.
The Clients: Clients include major national corporates.

Johnston Barton Proctor & Powell LLP

The Firm: A *"seasoned"* group of lawyers from this full-service corporate firm covers an array of labor and employment issues including union-organizing campaigns, wage and hour issues and discrimination cases.
The Lawyers: **Charles Powell** is one of the senior members of the defense bar. He devotes a proportion of his time to employment matters and represents clients before the EEOC, but received particular endorsement for his traditional labor practice. In two separate matters before the NLRB, he has represented Coors Brewing Co in relation to a union-organizing campaign. He has also prevented the issuance of a complaint connected to Wal-Mart's conversion of its traditional supermarket meat-cutting operations to an alternative meat distribution program.
The Clients: Baptist Health Systems, Delphi Automotive Systems, Coors Brewing Co; Rock and O'Charley's are clients.

Maynard, Cooper & Gale PC

The Firm: Although the firm does not have the profile of some of its competitors, it is regarded by experienced observers as *"a professional and reliable group."* Employment law is the focus of a

ALABAMA

LITIGATION

workload that typically includes defending cases brought under Title VII, ADA and ADEA in state and federal courts and before federal agencies.
The Lawyers: Heading up the ten-strong team is **Steve Brown** who was recommended to researchers as an *"accomplished trial lawyer."* His colleague, rising star **Jeff Lee**, is seen by rivals as *"one of the most promising younger lawyers in the state."* He has successfully defended an aviation company against claims of breach of contract and fraud, brought by a substantial group of former employees.

The Clients: Clients include manufacturing and financial institutions, national retailers and healthcare providers.

Ogletree, Deakins, Nash, Smoak & Stewart, PC
The Firm: A *"definite player"* in the Alabama market, this national boutique won recognition for its multifaceted employment practice, which includes employee benefits and immigration issues. Its broad practice also covers traditional labor issues where it has extensive experience in union-organizing campaigns involving airlines and hospitals.
The Lawyers: Former NLRB attorney **Peyton Lacy** is one of the key figures at the firm. Although he is best known for the labor sphere of his practice, competitors highlighted his *"disarming style in discrimination cases."*
The Clients: The group acts a range of clients including national corporations and local enterprises.

LITIGATION

ALABAMA
Leading firms
(Litigation: General Commercial)

1 BRADLEY ARANT ROSE & WHITE LLP *Birmingham*
LIGHTFOOT, FRANKLIN & WHITE *Birmingham*
2 STARNES & ATCHISON LLP *Birmingham*
3 CUNNINGHAM, BOUNDS, YANCE *Mobile*
HARE, WYNN, NEWELL & NEWTON *Birmingham*
RUSHTON, STAKELY, JOHNSTON *Montgomery*
4 BALCH & BINGHAM *Birmingham*
BEASLEY, ALLEN, CROW, METHVIN *Montgomery*
CHRISTIAN & SMALL LLP *Birmingham*
HELMSING, LEACH, HERLONG, NEWMAN *Mobile*
MAYNARD, COOPER & GALE PC *Birmingham*

Leading individuals
(Litigation: General Commercial)

1 FRANKLIN Samuel *Lightfoot, Franklin, Birmingham*
GEWIN James *Bradley Arant Rose, Birmingham*
LIGHTFOOT Warren *Lightfoot, Franklin, Birmingham*
MORROW John *Bradley Arant Rose, Birmingham*
2 ASHFORD Leon *Hare, Wynn, Newell, Birmingham*
CUNNINGHAM Robert *Cunningham, Bounds, Mobile*
EDWARDS Michael *Balch & Bingham, Birmingham*
KEENE Thomas *Rushton, Stakely, Johnston, Montgomery*
MCWHORTER Hobart *Bradley Arant Rose, Birmingham*
STARNES Stancil *Starnes & Atchison, Birmingham*
WHITE Jere *Lightfoot, Franklin & White, Birmingham*
3 ATCHISON Michael *Starnes & Atchison, Birmingham*
BEASLEY Jere *Beasley, Allen, Crow, Montgomery*
CHRISTIAN Tom *Christian & Small LLP, Birmingham*
HELMSING Fredrick *Helmsing, Leach, Herlong, Mobile*
MCGIVAREN Crawford *Cabaniss, Johnston, Birmingham*
YANCE Jim *Cunningham, Bounds, Yance, Mobile*

Firms and individuals are listed alphabetically in each band.

Bradley Arant Rose & White LLP
The Firm: A typical comment we heard was that the firm has *"experience and expertise in just about everything,"* and this, the biggest litigation team in Alabama, was consistently deemed to be *"top of the heap."* A group of 60 attorneys feature prominently on complex commercial litigation and appellate work, representing a range of clients in shareholders' and securities class actions, products liability defense, environment and construction cases and insurance coverage. The firm advised a class of some 18,000 out-of-state companies alleging the unconstitutionality of the Alabama state franchise tax and seeking refunds for taxes already paid.
The Lawyers: The *"number-one choice"* for many clients, **John Morrow** is active in commercial and personal injury defense work, and is currently occupied as chief defense counsel for Pittsburgh and Midway Coal Mining Company in surface subsidence claims brought by homeowners. Rivals and clients continue to endorse his accessibility and *"down-to-earth"* courtroom persona. **James Gewin** is acknowledged by peers as a *"superb trial lawyer."* Having cut his teeth in construction litigation, he now defends national pharmaceutical and healthcare companies in products liability and other complex cases. He is also noted for his expertise in securities, including derivatives, suits. *"Birmingham legend"* **Hobart McWhorter** also gained consistent market approval as an attorney who *"can still scare the opposition."*
The Clients: Other clients include Dryvit Systems and Russell Corporation.

Lightfoot, Franklin & White, LLC
The Firm: This litigation boutique was universally recognized to be *"practicing at the highest level, "* and handling the full spectrum of commercial litigation defense. In addition to business litigation, the group of 45 lawyers is also active in personal injury, products liability, class actions

GENERAL COMMERCIAL

and antitrust defense. Notable recent cases have included the defense of Monsanto/Solutia in class action litigation concerning PCB contamination in Anniston, Alabama.
The Lawyers: **Sam Franklin** won overwhelming endorsement as a defense litigator. Boasting *"a wealth of trial experience,"* he is acting for ExxonMobil on its appeal against a high-stakes oil royalties ruling. **Warren Lightfoot** continues to enjoy the praise of peers and clients, who describe him as *"savvy, confident and tough-minded."* He is best known for products liability defense in the automotive field, and acts for a heavyweight client base, including GM, Ford, DaimlerChrysler, Yamaha and Volkswagen. **Jere White** was also recommended to researchers as a *"top-flight trial lawyer."* He is active in trademark, unfair competition, business tort and environmental litigation, both for plaintiffs and defendants, and has also undertaken substantial insurance coverage litigation.
The Clients: Clients include : DuPont; Georgia-Pacific; Chevron; Kimberly-Clark; GE; Boeing and Auburn University.

Starnes & Atchison LLP
see firm details p.883
The Firm: This respected litigation boutique focuses on medical malpractice defense work, although it is also active in commercial, securities and general civil litigation. Commentators described the group of close to 50 lawyers as *"first rate at everything they do."* The firm acted for a director in the Just For Feet securities litigation and is defending a national bank in pending Enron litigation in Alabama.
The Lawyers: The *"personal favorite"* of many, firm cofounder **Stan Starnes** was widely endorsed. Active in medical malpractice defense, he is said to *"exude polish"* in court, where he has represented The University of Alabama in Title IX sex discrimination litigation. His colleague **Mike Atchison** received a

LITIGATION

ALABAMA

healthy share of market approval for his work on behalf of clients such as Honda and Protective Life Insurance Company.

The Clients: Clients include: The University of Alabama; Aetna Insurance Company; Allstate; GlaxoSmithKline and HealthSouth.

Cunningham, Bounds, Yance, Crowder & Brown, LLC

The Firm: The group is famed for its representation of the State of Alabama in the recent high-profile oil royalties cases, and has also been active on a range of plaintiffs' litigation. This has included national and state plaintiffs' class actions in antitrust, products liability and consumer fraud. Rivals said of these *"worthy adversaries"* that they *"work hard, are well prepared and have the ear of the courts."*

The Lawyers: Name partners **Robert Cunningham** and **Jim Yance** stand out. Both lawyers were active in the Exxon, Hunt Petroleum and Shell Oil cases, where they cemented their reputations as *"premier lawyers"* in Alabama.

The Clients: Clients include the State of Alabama Department of Conservation and Natural Resources.

Hare, Wynn, Newell & Newton LLP

see firm details p.812

The Firm: The oldest of the successful plaintiff firms was widely commended to researchers as *"the best in its field."* A team of 15 attorneys is active in the full spectrum of torts, including plaintiffs' business, environmental, personal injury and wrongful death litigation. The group also litigates a range of business cases from antitrust and IP to securities fraud and Qui Tam actions.

The Lawyers: Leon Ashford (see p.7) is the leading light. A prominent performer in plaintiff class actions and whistle-blower litigation, he is appreciated by clients as an attorney who *"understands how to move the ball,"* and who refuses to be *"bogged down by distractions."* The group acted for whistle-blower employees of Atlantic Richfield Company in the high-profile oil royalties litigation against major oil companies, which returned $437 million to the US Treasury. In addition, it has represented whistle-blowers in private attorney general litigation against Southern Ohio Fabricators, alleging failure to comply with naval standards in the manufacture of generators for US Navy destroyers.

The Clients: Other clients include employees and private individuals.

Rushton, Stakely, Johnston & Garrett

The Firm: The litigation group at this full-service Montgomery firm was especially noted to researchers for its top-flight medical defense practice. However, a *"well-established and qualified"* team handles the full range of litigation defense work for business clients, including personal injury, insurance defense, professional malpractice, shareholder disputes, products liability and environment cases.

The Lawyers: *"Low-key but thorough"* trial attorney **Tommy Keene** represents local doctors and hospitals in healthcare disputes, counting medical liability, antitrusts and employment disputes among his specialtys.

The Clients: Hospitals; hospital authorities; nursing homes and health insurers.

Balch & Bingham

see firm details p.768

The Firm: Enjoying a steady stream of work from high-profile utility and finance clients, the firm is said to shine in defending securities class actions and financial disputes. Clients commended the team's *"professionalism"* and ability to handle *"large, complex matters."* This facility was underlined by the firm's advice to Deloitte & Touche in connection with its audits of the financial statements of Just For Feet. Elsewhere, the group has acted for a number of corporate clients on antitrust litigation.

The Lawyers: *"In a class of his own at the firm"*, **Mike Edwards** was singled out for his work defending financial institutions on a range of securities cases. Interviewees applauded him as an *"outstanding advocate"* with *"real business sensitivity."*

The Clients: Clients include: Compass Bank; Am South Bank; South Trust Bank; Alabama Power; Archer Daniels Midland Company and UBS PaineWebber.

Beasley, Allen, Crow, Methvin, Portis & Miles, PC

The Firm: With close to 50 attorneys, the largest plaintiff firm in Alabama dwarfs its competitors. The group is said to *"own south Alabama"* and dominates the plaintiff market in its Montgomery backyard. Rivals noted the firm's consistent success in mass toxic tort, products liability and securities litigation.

The Lawyers: The brightest star here is said to be **Jere Beasley**. Although his forceful style of litigation is not to everyone's taste, he remains respected for his courtroom acumen. The firm has acted for plaintiffs against Ford and Firestone in the high-profile rollover lawsuits, as well as acting against GM in wrongful death suits arising from defectively designed seatbelts in its Buick Skylark model.

The Clients: Clients include plaintiff groups and individuals.

Christian & Small LLP

The Firm: A full-service Birmingham firm launched in July 2000, the group is said to be causing a splash in the litigation sector in Alabama.

The Lawyers: Making most of the waves is firm cofounder and *"fine trial lawyer"* **Tom Christian**. His practice often involves the defense of physicians and hospitals in medical malpractice litigation, although he also appears on behalf of pharmaceutical companies.

The Clients: Clients include: St. Vincent's Hospital; Community Health Systems; Medical Assurance; AIG Aviation and Caremark.

Helmsing, Leach, Herlong, Newman & Rouse, PC

see firm details p.816

The Firm: An *"impressive"* boutique litigation group of nine lawyers that is active in aviation defense work, products liability, securities and general business litigation.

The Lawyers: Fred Helmsing (see p.7) won general praise for his trial expertise. He defended Hunt Petroleum in oil royalties litigation brought by the State of Alabama, and acted for Montgomery Aviation against claims arising from a fatal plane crash.

Maynard, Cooper & Gale PC

The Firm: Clients gave the seal of approval to this full-service Birmingham-based firm, which handles a range of commercial litigation, including environmental torts, products liability, insurance, consumer finance and medical malpractice defense matters. The team, whose leading figures are Boots Gale and Lee Bains, is prominent in bad faith defense cases on behalf of well-known insurance company clients.

The Clients: Clients include: Aetna Life and Casualty Company; Am South Bank; Waste Management; University of Alabama at Birmingham; Travelers and New York Life and Met Life.

Other Notable Practitioners

Crawford McGivaren Jr stands out at Cabaniss, Johnston, Gardner, Dumas & O'Neal. Although he covers the full range of business litigation, he is best-known for his appearances on tax controversy cases.

ALABAMA

REAL ESTATE

REAL ESTATE

ALABAMA
Leading firms (Real Estate)

1
- BALCH & BINGHAM *Birmingham*
- BRADLEY ARANT ROSE & WHITE LLP *Birmingham*
- BURR & FORMAN *Birmingham*

2
- MAYNARD, COOPER & GALE PC *Birmingham*

3
- BERKOWITZ LEFKOVITS ISOM *Birmingham*
- LEITMAN, SIEGAL & PAYNE, PC *Birmingham*

Leading individuals (Real Estate)

1
- BOLES Hampton *Balch & Bingham*, Birmingham
- HAGEFSTRATION John *Bradley Arant*, Birmingham
- POWELL Fred *Burr & Forman*, Birmingham

2
- BEAVERS Charles *Bradley Arant Rose*, Birmingham
- LANIER Randolph *Balch & Bingham*, Birmingham

3
- MONK Stephen *Bradley Arant Rose*, Birmingham
- SEXTON Robert *Maynard, Cooper & Gale*, Birmingham
- SMITH Felton *Balch & Bingham*, Birmingham

4
- HELD Jerry *Sirote & Permutt PC*, Birmingham
- ISOM Chervis *Berkowitz Lefkovits Isom*, Birmingham
- MIXSON Dwight *Burr & Forman*, Birmingham
- SIEGAL Bradley *Leitman, Siegal & Payne*, Birmingham
- SIEGAL Don *Leitman, Siegal & Payne*, Birmingham

Firms and individuals are listed alphabetically in each band.

Balch & Bingham
see firm details p.768
The Firm: The team is principally associated with its work on behalf of Alabama Power, but it is also active in representing developers, investors and utility clients on a wide range of real estate transactions. These include financing, development, land use and zoning work, as well as eminent domain proceedings and substantial real estate lending.
The Lawyers: Peers singled out top lenders' lawyer **Hampton Boles** for his *"tremendous work for banks."* A *"bright and methodical"* attorney, he is now active in regulatory work for bank clients, where he appears regularly before the Alabama Banking Department and the Alabama Insurance Department. **Randy Lanier** also won praise from rivals for his work in commercial real estate development and for his land use expertise, often put to use for utility clients in right of way matters. Completing a formidable lineup is rising star **Felton Smith**. He has advised extensively on acquisitions, sales, operations and managing and leasing transactions.
The Clients: The group recently advised a developer on the large-scale residential and commercial community Riverchase, and represented Jefferson County Economic & Industrial Development Authority on mixed-use developments.

Bradley Arant Rose & White LLP
The Firm: The largest firm in Alabama is known for handling sophisticated and complex real estate transactions. A group of 12 attorneys was commended by clients as *"our first point of call,"* notably for institutional financing work, where the team is widely rated as the market leader.
The Lawyers: Some interviewees considered **John Hagefstration** to be *"the best real estate lawyer in Alabama."* Clients were enthusiastic about his *"can-do attitude"* on contract negotiations and his drafting of loan documents and tax-deferred exchanges. **Charlie Beavers** also won praise as a respected attorney with niche land use and zoning expertise, while **Stephen Monk** was endorsed to researchers for his active developer practice.
The Clients: The group represented Hyundai in the billion dollar development of its first US plant in Alabama, and advised EBSCO Properties on the land use, zoning, financing, construction and leasing of the mixed-use Tattersall Park Lifestyle Center in north Shelby County. Other clients include EBSCO Properties, SouthTrust Bank and State Employees' Retirement System.

Burr & Forman
The Firm: A real estate team producing *"superior quality"* work advises a stable of clients that reads like a who's who of local banks and institutional lenders. In addition to its renowned lending practice, the group also represents a number of the region's major developers.
The Lawyers: **Fred Powell** is said to *"evince a passion for everything he does,"* and rivals admire his ability to *"cut to the chase"* in a deal. He forged his reputation in commercial lending transactions, and now acts for buyers and sellers in the timber industry, recently advising on the acquisition of timber tracts in Maine. Also recommended to researchers was the respected **Dwight Mixson** who represents local developers, lenders and realty companies.
The Clients: The group excels in real estate financing work for clients including the Colonial, Regents and SouthTrust Banks, as well as JPMorgan Chase and CSFB Mortgage Capital. Other clients include: AIG Baker; Lawrence-Arendall-Humphries Real Estate and RealtySouth.

Maynard, Cooper & Gale PC
The Firm: Real estate lending is this department's principal forte, where it acts for local institutional lenders, REITs and private investors. Competitors admired the *"youth and enthusiasm"* of this 15-strong group, which is currently advising on the sale and redevelopment of the Fort McClellan Army Base.
The Lawyers: **Robert Sexton** was highlighted to researchers as a *"tenacious and professional"* attorney. He has an active developer practice, as well as advising on substantial lending work, and is acting with state agencies on the much-anticipated development of the Hyundai car plant in Montgomery.
The Clients: Clients include AmSouth Bank and Alabama Teachers' Retirement System.

Berkowitz Lefkovits Isom & Kushner
The Firm: Commentators paid tribute to the *"hot"* developer practice at this full-service outfit. The team of seven attorneys is said to be a *"key player"* in *"cutting-edge"* shopping center and retail development, in which it acts on a range of transactions. These include financings, land use and zoning matters, ground leases, shop leases and out-parcel sales for a largely entrepreneurial developer clientele.
The Lawyers: **Chervis Isom** (see p.7) is recognized as an expert in the retail sector, and advised Bayer Properties on The Summit retail development, which includes the first Saks department store in Alabama.
The Clients: Other clients include Bayer Properties; Colonial Properties Trust; AmSouth Leasing and Cavalier Homes.

Leitman, Siegal & Payne, PC
The Firm: Although smaller than many of its leading rivals, the firm's real estate department is said to boast *"an abundance of depth and talent,"* most strongly associated with its high-profile development work. The firm is most active in mixed-use and office developments, advising on acquisitions, financings, leasings and dispositions for its developer and investor clientele.
The Lawyers: **Bradley Siegal** and **Don Siegal** both received consistent market plaudits, largely for their work on behalf of REIT client Colonial Properties Trust. Here, the group recently advised on a $100 million office building acquisition in Orlando, Florida.
The Clients: The firm's development expertise spread internationally when it advised the joint Finnish/US enterprise, Polar-BEK International, on the development of the $42 million Daugava Hotel in Riga, Latvia.

Other Notable Practitioners
Jerry Held of Sirote & Permutt PC is thought to be the dominant figure in his department and is well known for his expertise in foreclosure matters.

ALABAMA

Leaders in Alabama

ALEXANDER, James
Bradley Arant Rose & White LLP,
Birmingham 205 521 8000
Recommended in Employment

ALLEN, Andrew
Whatley Drake, LLC, Birmingham
205 328 9576
Recommended in Employment

ARENDALL, David
David R Arendall - Sole Practitioner,
Birmingham 205 252 1550
Recommended in Employment

ASHFORD, Leon
Hare, Wynn, Newell & Newton LLP,
Birmingham 205 328 5330
leon@hwnn.com
Recommended in Litigation
Specialization: Medical malpractice, construction and industrial accidents, truck and automobile accidents, negligence/fraud, complex litigation - personal injury, wrongful death.
Prof. Memberships: Bar Admission: 1973, Alabama State Bar. Association of Trial Lawyers of America, American Board of Trial Advocates, American Bar Association, Birmingham Bar, Alabama State Bar, Alabama Trial Lawyers Association, American College of Trial Lawyers. Licenses include US District Courts of Alabama, US Courts of Appeals for 5th and 11th Circuits, Alabama Supreme Court.
Career: Previous positions: Assistant Attorney General, 1973; Associate Professor, Cumberland School of Law, 1982.
Personal: Education: University of Alabama, Member of 'A' Club. Law School: J.D., University of Alabama School of Law, Member of Phi Delta Phi, Member of Bench & Bar. Frequent CLE Speaker; Disciplinary Hearing Officer, Alabama Bar Association; Executive Committee, Birmingham Bar Association, 1982-85; President, Young Lawyers Section, 1980; Executive Committee, Young Lawyers Section, Alabama State Bar, 1979; Executive Committee, Young Lawyers Section of The Birmingham Bar Association, 1976-79; ABICLE - Walter P Gewin Award, 1994; Member, Canterbury United Methodist Church.

ATCHISON, W Michael
Starnes & Atchison LLP, Birmingham
205 868 6000
Recommended in Litigation

BEASLEY, Jere
Beasley, Allen, Crow, Methvin, Portis & Miles, PC, Montgomery 334 269 2343
Recommended in Litigation

BEAVERS, Charles
Bradley Arant Rose & White LLP, Birmingham 205 521 8000
Recommended in Real Estate

BOLES, Hampton
Balch & Bingham, Birmingham
205 251 8100
Recommended in Real Estate

BROWN, Stephen
Maynard, Cooper & Gale PC,
Birmingham 205 254 1000
Recommended in Employment

CARRUTHERS, Thomas
Bradley Arant Rose & White LLP,
Birmingham 205 521 8000
Recommended in Corporate/M&A

CHILDS, Robert
Gordon, Silberman, Wiggins & Childs,
Birmingham 205 328 0640
Recommended in Employment

CHRISTIAN, Tom
Christian & Small LLP, Birmingham
205 795 6588
Recommended in Litigation

COLEMAN, John
Burr & Forman LLP, Birmingham
205 251 3000
Recommended in Employment

COOPER, John
Sirote & Permutt PC, Birmingham
205 930 5100
Recommended in Corporate/M&A

CUNNINGHAM, Robert
Cunningham, Bounds, Yance, Crowder & Brown, LLC, Mobile 251 471 6191
Recommended in Litigation

DRAKE, Jack
Whatley Drake, LLC, Birmingham
205 328 9576
Recommended in Employment

DREW, Mark
Maynard, Cooper & Gale PC,
Birmingham 205 254 1000
Recommended in Corporate/M&A

EDWARDS, Michael
Balch & Bingham, Birmingham
205 251 8100
Recommended in Litigation

FRANKLIN, Samuel
Lightfoot, Franklin & White, LLC,
Birmingham 205 581 0700
Recommended in Litigation

FRAZIER, Sydney
Cabaniss, Johnston, Gardner, Dumas & O'Neal, Birmingham 205 716 5200
Recommended in Employment

FREDERICK, Barry
Lehr Middlebrooks Price & Proctor,
Birmingham 205 326 3002
Recommended in Employment

GARDNER, William
Cabaniss, Johnston, Gardner, Dumas & O'Neal, Birmingham 205 716 5200
Recommended in Employment

GEWIN, James
Bradley Arant Rose & White LLP,
Birmingham 205 521 8000
Recommended in Litigation

GRENIER, John
Bradley Arant Rose & White LLP,
Birmingham 205 521 8000
Recommended in Corporate/M&A

HAGEFSTRATION, John
Bradley Arant Rose & White LLP,
Birmingham 205 521 8000
Recommended in Real Estate

HELD, Jerry
Sirote & Permutt PC, Birmingham
205 930 5100
Recommended in Real Estate

HELMSING, Frederick G
Helmsing, Leach, Herlong, Newman & Rouse, PC, Mobile 251 432 5521
fgh@helmsinglaw.com
Recommended in Litigation
Specialization: Handles a variety of cases, including matters involving defense of white collar criminal cases with an emphasis on charges of criminal tax fraud and related financial crimes and civil cases involving civil fraud, contract disputes and insurance defense. He has served as a faculty member or panelist at American Bar Association sponsored educational programs aimed at lawyers throughout the United States and covering subjects such as white collar crime, criminal tax fraud and money laundering, and criminal liability of attorneys. He is frequently listed in several leading legal publications.
Prof. Memberships: He is a member of the American, Alabama and Mobile Bar associations, the Florida Bar Association, and the Escambia and Santa Rose County Bar Association. He is also a Fellow in the American College of Trial Lawyers.
Career: Received his undergraduate degree in accounting in 1963. After a brief period of private accounting practice in Mobile, he attended the University of Alabama School of Law where he received his law degree in 1965. He then attended New York University from which he received an LLM in Taxation in 1967. He has been in the private practice of law in Mobile with *Helmsing, Leach,*

Herlong, Newman & Rouse since his return from post-graduate studies in New York.
Personal: Born in Mobile, Alabama, in 1940. Grew up in Mobile and attended Spring Hill College.

HUGHEY JR, James F
Balch & Bingham, Birmingham
205 251 8100
Recommended in Corporate/M&A

INGRAM, Fred
Burr & Forman LLP, Birmingham
205 251 3000
Recommended in Employment

ISOM, Chervis
Berkowitz Lefkovits Isom & Kushner,
Birmingham 205 250 8302
cisom@blik.com
Recommended in Real Estate
Specialization: Shareholder. Real estate (including acquisition of land, assemblage, development, construction financing and leasing), capital finance, commercial lending and finance. Chairman of the firm's real estate section.
Prof. Memberships: Admitted to Alabama Bar, 1967. Listed in The Best Lawyers in America. Associate Member, International Council of Shopping Centers; Member, American College of Mortgage Attorneys; Member, American Bar Association; Member, Birmingham Bar Association.
Personal: B.A., Birmingham-Southern College, 1962. J.D., Cumberland School of Law of Samford University, 1967. Member, Curia Honoris.

KEENE, Thomas
Rushton, Stakely, Johnston & Garrett,
Montgomery 334 834 8480
Recommended in Litigation

KUSHNER, Harold B
Berkowitz Lefkovits Isom & Kushner,
Birmingham 205 250 8303
hkushner@blik.com
Recommended in Corporate/M&A
Specialization: Shareholder. Practice is concentrated in tax and corporate law including mergers and acquisitions, securities, estate and trust planning and employer resources. Represents clients in diverse industries including steel, manufacturing, retail, technology and software, real estate development and health care.
Career: Admitted to the Louisiana Bar in 1971 and the Alabama Bar in 1975. Listed in The Best Lawyers in America. Chairman, Alabama Securities Commission. Member, American Bar Association and its Personal Services Organizations Committee. Representative of the Alabama

ALABAMA

Bar Association on the Internal Revenue Service Practitioner's Council. Member, Birmingham Bar Association. Former Chairman, The Entrepreneurial Center. Board Member, Birmingham Jewish Federation. Board Member, National Committee for Community and Justice.
Personal: B.A., University of Alabama, 1968. J.D., Tulane University, 1971. Member, Tulane Law Review. LL.M., in Taxation, New York University, 1974.

LACY, Peyton
Ogletree, Deakins, Nash, Smoak & Stewart, PC, Birmingham 205 328 1900
Recommended in Employment

LANIER, Randolph
Balch & Bingham, Birmingham
205 251 8100
Recommended in Real Estate

LEE, Jeffrey
Maynard, Cooper & Gale PC, Birmingham 205 254 1000
Recommended in Employment

LIGHTFOOT, Warren
Lightfoot, Franklin & White, LLC, Birmingham 205 581 0700
Recommended in Litigation

MAY, James
Bradley Arant Rose & White LLP, Birmingham 205 521 8000
Recommended in Employment

MCGIVAREN JNR, Crawford
Cabaniss, Johnston, Gardner, Dumas & O'Neal, Birmingham 205 716 5200
Recommended in Litigation

MCWHORTER, Hobart
Bradley Arant Rose & White LLP, Birmingham 205 521 8000
Recommended in Litigation

MEELHEIM, Richard
Meelheim, Wilkinson & Meelheim, Birmingham 205 252 2500
Recommended in Employment

MIDDLEBROOKS, David
Lehr Middlebrooks Price & Proctor, Birmingham 205 326 3002
Recommended in Employment

MIXSON, Dwight
Burr & Forman LLP, Birmingham
205 251 3000
Recommended in Real Estate

MONK, Stephen
Bradley Arant Rose & White LLP, Birmingham 205 521 8000
Recommended in Real Estate

MORROW, John
Bradley Arant Rose & White LLP, Birmingham 205 521 8000
Recommended in Litigation

NELSON, Carol Sue
Constangy, Brooks & Smith, LLC, Birmingham 205 323 7676
Recommended in Employment

POWELL, Charles
Johnston Barton Proctor & Powell LLP, Birmingham 205 458 9400
Recommended in Employment

POWELL, Fred
Burr & Forman LLP, Birmingham
205 251 3000
Recommended in Real Estate

PRICE, Gene
Burr & Forman LLP, Birmingham
205 251 3000
Recommended in Corporate/M&A

PROCTOR, David
Lehr Middlebrooks Price & Proctor, Birmingham 205 326 3002
Recommended in Employment

QUINN, Michael
Gordon, Silberman, Wiggins & Childs, Birmingham 205 328 0640
Recommended in Employment

ROBERTSON, Ann
Gordon, Silberman, Wiggins & Childs, Birmingham 205 328 0640
Recommended in Employment

SAXON, John
John D Saxon - Sole Practitioner, Birmingham 205 324 0223
Recommended in Employment

SEXTON, Robert
Maynard, Cooper & Gale PC, Birmingham 205 254 1000
Recommended in Real Estate

SIEGAL, Bradley
Leitman, Siegal & Payne, PC, Birmingham 205 251 5900
Recommended in Real Estate

SIEGAL, Don
Leitman, Siegal & Payne, PC, Birmingham 205 251 5900
Recommended in Real Estate

SMITH, Felton
Balch & Bingham, Birmingham
205 251 8100
Recommended in Real Estate

STARNES, Stancil
Starnes & Atchison LLP, Birmingham
205 868 6000
Recommended in Litigation

THUSTON, Lee
Burr & Forman LLP, Birmingham
205 251 3000
Recommended in Corporate/M&A

WHATLEY, Joe
Whatley Drake, LLC, Birmingham
205 328 9576
Recommended in Employment

WHITE, Jere
Lightfoot, Franklin & White, LLC, Birmingham 205 581 0700
Recommended in Litigation

WIGGINS, Robert
Gordon, Silberman, Wiggins & Childs, Birmingham 205 328 0640
Recommended in Employment

WILKINSON, Cynthia
Meelheim, Wilkinson & Meelheim, Birmingham 205 252 2500
Recommended in Employment

YANCE, Jim
Cunningham, Bounds, Yance, Crowder & Brown, LLC, Mobile 251 471 6191
Recommended in Litigation

ALASKA

CORPORATE/M&A

CONTENTS: Corporate/M&A p.9; Employment: Mainly Plaintiff p.10; Mainly Defendant p.11; Environment p.11; Litigation: General Commercial p.12; Real Estate p.13; Individuals' Profiles p.14.

ALASKA'S TOP THREE
1. Dorsey & Whitney
2. Davis Wright Tremaine
3. Ashburn & Mason

Ranking based on Chambers' research within the state.

All quotes in the text are from interviews with clients and competitors.

OVERVIEW: Dorsey & Whitney is highly thought of for its work on local issues, particularly in the overlapping areas of real estate and environment. It is also prominent in corporate work, with backup from teams across the US and in Canada, Europe and Asia. Among this firm's lawyers, James Reeves is respected for his real estate expertise and Richard Rosston for corporate counseling. Clients include Safeway and Fred Meyer.

Davis Wright Tremaine is one of the largest firms in the state and a major player nationwide. The firm has a strong reputation for employment law, with its Anchorage team working particularly closely with their highly rated Seattle colleagues. It is also becoming increasingly known for corporate work, particularly in the IP field. The real estate practice attracts respected lawyers, who are known for their leasing documentation and environmental expertise. Parry Grover is singled out for his employment law skills, and Barbara Kraft for her work on corporate deals. Clients include Bank of America and Shell Oil Products US.

Ashburn & Mason is a smaller firm with a local feel. Operating in a different market from national firms, it tends to act for smaller, Alaska-based clients. The firm is highly rated for its real estate practice, particularly its high-quality documentation and skills in real estate finance. Practitioners were also noted for high ethical standards in litigation work and received particular praise for their work with public utilities. Donald McClintock in the real estate department has been described as "first class" and is noted for his litigation work.

CORPORATE/M&A

ALASKA
Leading firms (Corporate/M&A)
1. BIRCH, HORTON, BITTNER & CHEROT Anchorage
   DORSEY & WHITNEY LLP Anchorage
2. DAVIS WRIGHT TREMAINE LLP Anchorage
3. HUGHES THORSNESS POWELL Anchorage
   PRESTON GATES & ELLIS LLP Anchorage

Leading individuals (Corporate/M&A)
1. DURRELL Brian Durrell Law Group, PC, Anchorage
   ROSSTON Richard Dorsey & Whitney LLP, Anchorage
2. BLACK Kathryn Birch, Horton, Bittner, Anchorage
   DAWSON Jon Davis Wright Tremaine LLP, Anchorage
   KRAFT Barbara Davis Wright Tremaine, Anchorage
   ODSEN Frederick Hughes Thorsness Powell, Anchorage

Firms and individuals are listed alphabetically in each band.

Birch, Horton, Bittner & Cherot

The Firm: An established corporate practice, seen to be growing in size and strength. The *"well-connected"* four-strong team was said to wield *"political sway,"* a vital asset in the eyes of local clients. Peers praised this group of *"strong personalities"* for their *"thoroughness and attention to detail."* Specialist attorneys advise on M&A, bond financings, banking issues and real estate development. Recent undertakings include advising on bond financings for several boroughs and counseling a major commercial oil company on the purchase and sale of oil and gas interests.

The Lawyers: Banking specialist **Kathryn Black** enjoys a loyal following among financial institutions who she counsels in relation to bankruptcies, repossessions, commercial loans, secured transactions and real estate financings. Black recently represented Northwest Farm Credit Services on a multimillion dollar loan backed by Alaskan timber assets.

The Clients: KeyBank National Association; Alaska Industrial Development and Export Authority; Alaska Railroad; Encore Credit Corporation and Seward Association for the Advancement of Marine Science.

Dorsey & Whitney LLP

The Firm: Alaska's *"top choice"* for national and international clients, the firm is rated highly for its *"depth of resources"* and *"tremendous backup"* provided by corporate teams across the US, Canada, Europe and Asia. In addition to a national reputation for handling significant M&A transactions, the group is highly regarded for its *"sound perspectives"* on local Alaskan issues and advises several Alaska Native Corporations on corporate governance, proxy statements and real estate ventures.

The Lawyers: *"Impressive"* **Richard Rosston** wins client loyalty for general corporate counseling and expertise in real estate-related commercial issues. This *"cordial"* attorney *"produces results"* on M&A transactions and was commended for his *"realistic approach"* to lease negotiations, financings and licensing matters. Recent work includes restructuring a Taiwanese investment in an Alaskan seafood marketing venture.

The Clients: Safeway; Denali Foods (doing business as Taco Bell of Alaska); Limited; Merrill Lynch Business Financial Services; Nissho Iwai Energy Development and Central Investments Holdings.

Davis Wright Tremaine LLP
see firm details p.787

The Firm: The Anchorage practice draws on the firm's *"significant national resources"* and earns respect from peers and clients for the extensive experience of its *"high-quality lawyers."* The firm is a major player nationwide and handles sizable commercial transactions from offices in New York, DC, California, Washington, Oregon, Hawaii and China. Attorneys advise local and national clients on complex transactions, business disputes, acquisitions and dispositions. The firm is also developing a reputation for IP work, particularly internet and e-commerce issues.

The Lawyers: *"Fair-minded and reasonable,"* **Barbara Kraft** (see p.15) stands out for her *"understanding of the tax implications"* of corporate deals. Much of her work involves advising nonprofit organizations in the state on regulatory compliance and structuring and documenting commercial transactions. **Jon Dawson**'s (see p.14) practice emphasizes litigious matters and the representation of businesses and financial institutions in complex commercial disputes. Also pioneering the firm's IP and internet law practice, Dawson prepares licensing and distribution agreements and advises on trademark and copyright issues.

The Clients: Alaska Native Tribal Health Consortium; Yukon Fuel Company; Alaska Industrial Resources; Secure Asset Reporting Services and Hope Community Resources.

Hughes Thorsness Powell Huddleston & Bauman LLC

The Firm: This *"strong local firm"* is highly regarded by peers for its *"good stable of attorneys"* and emphasis on Alaskan business concerns.

ALASKA
EMPLOYMENT & LABOR LAW

Practitioners advise on the purchase and sale of local corporations, assets and real estate and provides general corporate counseling to smaller publicly and privately held companies. Four corporate attorneys also offer litigation skills and expertise in bankruptcy and workout proceedings.

The Lawyers: Fred Odsen brings a *"thoughtful approach"* and *"commercial outlook"* to secured lending transactions and bankruptcy-related property dispositions within the oil and gas industry.

The Clients: Financial institutions and major corporates.

Preston Gates & Ellis LLP
The Firm: The Anchorage office of this national firm attracts comment for its *"competitive local rates"* and *"familiarity with Alaskan corporate culture."* The group handles an array of commercial transactions, including M&A, capital raising, financings, joint ventures and public offerings. Peers describe the team's attorneys as *"realistic about bringing a deal together."* The corporate practice has a large real estate component, with attorneys advising on sales and purchases, commercial building leases and development projects. Practitioners act for local clients in the oil and gas, timber, fishing and minerals industries and have particular expertise in relation to natural resources transactions.

The Lawyers: Douglas Parker is managing partner of the firm's Anchorage office.

The Clients: The Williams Companies; Calista; Wells Fargo and Gunderboom.

Other Notable Practitioners
"Levelheaded" **Brian Durrell** of Durrell Law Group, PC was identified for expertise in transactions, tax issues and the representation of smaller and family corporations. His CPA background is thought to be an asset in tax-driven financings. Durrell recently helped to structure a joint venture for the development and operation of a satellite launching site.

EMPLOYMENT & LABOR LAW — MAINLY PLAINTIFF

ALASKA
Leading firms
(Employment: Mainly Plaintiff)

1. **CLAPP PETERSON & STOWERS LLC** Anchorage
2. **JERMAIN, DUNNAGAN & OWENS PC** Anchorage
   TINDALL BENNETT & SHOUP PC Anchorage
3. **WINFREE LAW OFFICE** Fairbanks

Leading individuals
(Employment: Mainly Plaintiff)

1. **HOLEN Lee** Lee Holen Law Office, Anchorage
   SCHENDEL William Winfree Law Office, Fairbanks
2. **PETUMENOS Timothy** Birch, Horton, Anchorage
   SHOUP David Tindall Bennett & Shoup PC, Anchorage
   VAN FLEIN Thomas Clapp Peterson, Anchorage

Firms and individuals are listed alphabetically in each band.

Clapp Peterson & Stowers LLC
The Firm: This high-quality plaintiffs' practice attracts an increasing share of commercial business disputes involving wrongful termination. Described as having *"the wherewithal to take on cases that sole practitioners can't,"* the firm attracts frequent referrals from top defense firms. Highlights include attaining a $500,000 settlement in Herrman v ARI and a confidential settlement in Garuba v Lockheed Martin. The firm handles a host of plaintiffs' claims including products liability matters, appellate work, healthcare and insurance cases, personal injury and wrongful death claims.

The Lawyers: Tom Van Flein (see p.15) was recognized as a *"sharp lawyer who sorts the wheat from the chaff."* He earns particular praise from peers for his *"reasonable"* negotiation style.

The Clients: Multiple Risk Managers; Fireman's Fund; CNA; Alaska Dental Society; Medical Insurance Exchange of California and NovaGold Resources.

Jermain, Dunnagan & Owens PC
The Firm: The firm maintains a solid reputation in the field based on 25 years of experience handling sexual harassment and discrimination cases, and wage claims. Practitioners also advise on the development and review of personnel policies and pension issues. With expertise in both the defense and plaintiff side, the firm commands respect from peers for its representation of unions. A seven-strong group of *"really solid attorneys"* were said to know the *"ins and outs"* of employment law.

The Lawyers: Bill Jermain is the leading practice attorney in the employment department.

The Clients: The firm represents private individuals, public sector employers and employees, and businesses involved in collective bargaining or private employment contracts.

Tindall Bennett & Shoup PC
The Firm: A civil and trial *"boutique"* with a strong profile for plaintiffs' employment work. The firm deals equally with traditional contract issues, management labor law and ADA and EEOC work. Practitioners also handle a significant amount of tort activity.

The Lawyers: David Shoup was mentioned as a strong trial attorney. Described as a *"terrierlike"* litigator, Shoup's aggressive court performances make him a valuable asset to the firm.

The Clients: Practitioners typically represent plaintiffs in the healthcare, shipping, banking and construction industries, and utilities.

Winfree Law Office
The Firm: This small Fairbanks firm's employment practice has until recently had a largely defense-work orientation. The recruitment of William Schendel, however, has altered the group's plaintiff/defendant balance. Typical work includes handling EEOC plaintiffs' complaints, defending union stewards in sexual harassment claims and mediating on hostile work environment issues.

The Lawyers: Recent addition **William Schendel** brings a strong plaintiffs' practice to the firm. Admired by peers statewide for *"knowing the exact degree to which the law is on his side,"* Schendel is said to do *"more employment law than anyone else"* in Alaska. Praised as a *"tough but highly ethical"* opponent, he handles a volume of wage and hour disputes and age, sex and race discrimination cases. Schendel works frequently with the University of Alaska and recently appeared in the Alaska Supreme Court in a case determining a municipality's right to grant employment preference to native Americans.

The Clients: Fairbanks North Star Borough School District; Doyon, Plumbers & Steamfitters Union Local 375; Alaska Riverways ('Riverboat Discovery'); City of Fairbanks and Fairbanks Resource Agency.

Other Notable Practitioners
The reputation of sole practitioner **Lee Holen** is among the highest in Alaska for plaintiffs' work. She specializes exclusively in employment law, including wrongful discharge, ADA, labor disputes and wage and hour claims. This *"outstanding individual"* is well liked for her *"low-key"* manner and *"direct"* approach to employment cases. She acts for state and federal employees as well as private individuals, and undertakes sexual harassment investigations for employers. Experienced trial attorney **Tim Petumenos** of Birch, Horton, Bittner & Cherot has an active contingent fee plaintiffs' practice. Interviewees remarked on his *"strong, aggressive and effective"* courtroom appearances.

EMPLOYMENT & LABOR LAW — ALASKA

MAINLY DEFENDANT

ALASKA
Leading firms
(Employment: Mainly Defendant)
1. PERKINS COIE LLP *Anchorage*
2. DAVIS WRIGHT TREMAINE LLP *Anchorage*
   PRESTON GATES & ELLIS LLP *Anchorage*
3. OWENS & TURNER, PC *Anchorage*

Leading individuals
(Employment: Mainly Defendant)
1. DANIEL Thomas *Perkins Coie LLP, Anchorage*
2. GROVER Parry *Davis Wright Tremaine LLP, Anchorage*
   PARKER Douglas *Preston Gates & Ellis LLP, Anchorage*
3. ROHLF Joan *Guess & Rudd PC, Anchorage*

Up-and-coming individuals
HALL Helena *Perkins Coie LLP, Anchorage*

Firms and individuals are listed alphabetically in each band.

Perkins Coie LLP
The Firm: An extensive client portfolio sees the practice advising on the biggest cases in Alaska's employment sector. Three specialist attorneys cover a range of employment issues, including contracts and manuals, wrongful discharge and civil rights claims. Practitioners are recommended both for *"outstanding work"* and staying current with employment issues. Clients remark that they *"wouldn't know where to start without Perkins Coie."* The firm has broad experience in public sector employment matters involving municipal and state governments. Recent defense work includes a whistle-blower case brought against a a major newspaper and an age discrimination case against a high-profile oil company. The firm also argued a union arbitration case in the Alaska Supreme Court on behalf of the University of Alaska.

The Lawyers: Office managing partner **Thomas Daniel** was identified by peers and clients as *"in a league of his own."* This *"model lawyer"* commands respect through his extensive trial experience, and was commended for *"getting right to the nitty-gritty of a case."* He has a *"strong second lieutenant"* in up-and-coming **Helena Hall**. Identified as a *"future leader in the community,"* Hall was recommended for her thorough and professional approach to employment matters.

The Clients: BP; NANA Regional; Alaska Airlines; Delta Air Lines; Kiewit Construction and UPS.

Davis Wright Tremaine LLP
see firm details p.787

The Firm: Four dedicated attorneys *"cover the gamut of employment law,"* appearing on both sides of the fence in employment litigation. The group delivers *"quality performances"* and has a strong track record in defense work. The firm represents management on collective bargaining issues, employment discrimination and wrongful discharge litigation, and defends employers in both district and state courts. Labor relations work includes unfair labor practice claims, arbitration and wage and hour cases. The firm has offices all along the West Coast and the Anchorage office receives support from the firm's highly rated Seattle employment practice.

The Lawyers: Peers praise **Parry Grover** (see p.14) as an *"excellent writer-thinker"* who *"looks for solutions rather than ways of billing the heck out of a case."* He focuses exclusively on employment law and *"keeps one step ahead"* of developments in the field.

The Clients: Chugach Electric Association, GCI Telecommunications and Alaska Regional Hospital.

Preston Gates & Ellis LLP
The Firm: The group is backed by the *"depth and resources of an international firm."* The team focuses on management/labor relations and defends a broad range of employment claims, including wrongful discharge, FMLA, wage and hour and ERISA matters. In recent years the firm has handled an increasing number of sexual abuse and disability claims. The development of a new benefits practice further enhances the firm's employment capabilities.

The Lawyers: The recruitment in 2000 of **Douglas Parker** brought the firm's employment law practice into the spotlight. Managing partner of the Anchorage office, Parker was praised as a hard-working and *"effective"* attorney with a *"strong courtroom presence."* Clients particularly admire his *"sensitivity to local issues."* Highlights include defending against FMLA and wrongful termination claims in Button v Alaska Petroleum Contractors. More recently, Parker has defended negligence cases against both a church and a drug treatment program, entailing allegations of negligent hiring and multiple claims of sexual abuse.

The Clients: ConocoPhillips Alaska; Williams Alaska Petroleum; Era Aviation; Akeela Treatment Services; Natchiq and Cook Inlet Region, Inc.

Owens & Turner, PC
The Firm: A *"traditional"* Alaskan employment practice with a long-standing reputation in the field and a team of *"really solid attorneys."* Issues covered include wrongful discharge, discrimination, wage and hour claims and general employee management counseling.

The group earns particular recognition for its union work and has experience advising on union-organizing drives, elections and collective bargaining matters. Historically, the firm has been involved in the negotiation of many of the labor agreements that govern Alaskan union/employer relations and continues to advise employers on their interpretation and application.

The Lawyers: The team is reputed to know the *"ins and outs"* of employment law. Thomas Owens Jr is the contact partner for the practice.

The Clients: Alaska Pacific University; First National Bank of Anchorage; Municipality of Anchorage; BP Exploration (Alaska); Nabors Alaska Drilling; Alaska Railroad and Northern Air Cargo.

Other Notable Practitioners
Up-and-coming practitioner **Joan Rohlf** of Guess & Rudd PC was named as one of the *"next generation"* of Alaskan employment lawyers. Said to have a *"good head on her shoulders,"* Rohlf undertakes substantial harassment and discrimination litigation.

ENVIRONMENT

Dorsey & Whitney LLP
The Firm: Peers respect this national firm for the diversity of its expertise and the high-caliber advice given by its lawyers. The recent recruitment of a former chair of the US Attorney General's environmental issues committee has attracted criminal cases to the firm, supplementing its litigation and transactional work. The portfolio includes air law, hazardous waste and Superfund matters. The firm also advises on insurance coverage, toxic torts, criminal enforcement and international environmental compliance. The group's recent highlights include acting for freighter operators with regard to MARPOL 73/78 (the International Convention for the Prevention of Pollution from Ships) violations. The team also advised a sponsor of the Natro-Gas pipeline on the Foothills project, and regularly advises foreign fishing companies regarding federal and international regulatory issues.

The Lawyers: Interviewees reported that **Jim Reeves** *"attracts the finest work."* Described as *"extraordinarily articulate,"* Reeves combines

ALASKA

ENVIRONMENT

ALASKA
Leading firms (Environment)
1. DORSEY & WHITNEY LLP *Anchorage*
   FOSTER PEPPER RUBINI & REEVES *Anchorage*
   PERKINS COIE LLP *Anchorage*
2. GUESS & RUDD PC *Anchorage*
   HARTIG RHODES HOGE & LEKISCH PC *Anchorage*

Leading individuals (Environment)
1. REEVES Susan *Foster Pepper Rubini, Anchorage*
2. FJELSTAD Eric *Perkins Coie LLP, Anchorage*
   REEVES James *Dorsey & Whitney LLP, Anchorage*
3. HARTIG Lawrence *Hartig Rhodes Hoge, Anchorage*
   LYLE George *Guess & Rudd PC, Anchorage*
   REGES Robert *Ruddy, Bradley, Kolkhorst, Juneau*

Firms and individuals are listed alphabetically in each band.

litigation prowess with an acute knowledge of environmental and natural resources law.
The Clients: BP; Phillips Petroleum Company; Gateway Forest Products; Oswego; Boyang Maritime; Foothills Pipe Lines and NM Rothschild & Sons.

Foster Pepper Rubini & Reeves PLLC
The Firm: Respected by peers for its specialty in environmental law. The firm is experienced in corporate and real estate transactional matters, and advises on compliance with federal and state laws. Attorneys negotiate permits and authorizations, and advise on disputes arising from the allocation of liability. Highlights include permitting and authorization matters before the Alaska Industrial Development and Export Authority in relation to the Heally Clean Coal Plant.
The Lawyers: The firm owes much of its reputation to **Susan Reeves**. *"Probably as good as they get,"* claim peers. Reeves impresses with her transactional experience, sound judgment and *"low-key"* style. A skilled litigator, she also acts on administrative law and planning matters. She assesses compliance with federal and state environmental laws, and has worked extensively with the Alaska Department of Environmental Conservation and the EPA.

The Clients: Crowley Marine Services; Municipality of Anchorage; North Slope Borough; Anadarko Petroleum; Yukon Pacific Company; Marathon Oil and Unocal.

Perkins Coie LLP
The Firm: Regarded as a key player by market commentators, the firm focuses largely on oil spill contingency planning. The group's experience in federal matters and its diverse practice are the keys to its high profile. Recent work has included advising on compliance issues and contaminated sites. For example, it represented a natural resources company in negotiations with state and federal authorities for the cleanup of 15 sites located on federal property.
Issues arising from the EPA's suspension and debarment program and the sale of property to federal agencies are also on the agenda. Active in the defense of potentially responsible parties in CERCLA operations, the team has advised on the cleanups of both the Thorne Bay landfills site and the industrial property and marine sediments at Ward Cove.
The Lawyers: The group's high profile in the environmental arena is broadly attributed to **Eric Fjelstad**. He is commended for his negotiation skills, depth of knowledge and results-oriented attitude.
The Clients: The group acts for North Slope oil and gas producers; cruise ship companies; local government bodies and mining, construction and aviation companies.

Guess & Rudd PC
The Firm: Noted by interviewees for its expertise in natural resources law, the firm is active in environment-related administrative and enforcement work. Much of the workload is derived from environmental cleanups and insurance work; in the latter, the firm is skilled in matters arising from contaminated properties. The team undertakes extensive permitting work in the mining and oil and gas industries, and advises corporate and real estate clients on environmental cleanups of abandoned sites.

The Lawyers: **George Lyle** is respected for his insurance defense work in relation to contaminated properties. He possesses a strong science background and broad experience. His sound judgment and confidence earn him praise as *"a credible, trustworthy attorney."*
The Clients: Oil and gas companies; Alaska Native Corporations; mining companies and property owners.

Hartig Rhodes Hoge & Lekisch PC
The Firm: Stands out for permitting, land use and resource development issues. The firm also handles title and natural resources-related matters in its environmental law practice. Attorneys were commended to researchers for both their litigation skills and understanding of enforcement issues. On the transactional side, the team advises on the drafting of environmental provisions in sale, loan and leasing agreements. It also provides guidance on the investigation and cleanup of contaminated sites.
The Lawyers: **Lawrence Hartig** was endorsed to researchers for his work in permitting and compliance issues. His expertise in water and air permitting earned him high regard as a *"preeminent lawyer"* in the field. The firm has been actively involved in the development of the Red Dog Mine in northwestern Alaska and a mine in Juneau.
The Clients: Financial institutions; private developers; mining companies; fish processors; timber companies; municipalities and Alaska Native Corporations.

Other Notable Practitioners
Robert Reges of Ruddy, Bradley, Kolkhorst & Reges in Juneau is respected by peers for his in-depth knowledge and experience of EPA and state regulations. Peers agree that he *"picks up on the right issues,"* while clients single him out for his work in air quality issues, permitting and contaminated sites litigation. He has assisted BP Exploration (Alaska) in amending an air permit for the North Star and Badami facilities.

LITIGATION

GENERAL COMMERCIAL

ALASKA
Leading firms
(Litigation: General Commercial)
1. FELDMAN & ORLANSKY *Anchorage*
   FRIEDMAN, RUBIN & WHITE *Anchorage*
2. ASHBURN & MASON, PC *Anchorage*
3. ATKINSON, CONWAY & GAGNON *Anchorage*
   BURR, PEASE & KURTZ, PC *Anchorage*

Firms are listed alphabetically in each band.

Feldman & Orlansky
The Firm: Possessing an *"unparalleled reputation,"* the firm was singled out by peers for its *"top-notch quality work."* Its emphasis lies in complex civil and criminal trials, including appellate work. It has counseled a US fish processor in a large antitrust case involving allegations of a price-fixing conspiracy.
The group was applauded by peers for its successful handling of both defendant and plaintiff matters, and described as highly academic in its approach. It fields *"terrific trial attorneys"* with a strong team ethos. Recent highlights include advising the Alaska Native Interest Intervenors in redistricting cases. The firm also defended cruise lines and oil and timber companies in alleged violations of pollution laws.
The Lawyers: *"Highly ethical"* **Jeff Feldman** concentrates on complex civil and criminal litigation, undertaking a high volume of trial work.

LITIGATION

ALASKA

ALASKA
Leading individuals
(Litigation: General Commercial)

1 FELDMAN Jeff *Feldman & Orlansky*, Anchorage
 FRIEDMAN Richard *Friedman, Rubin*, Anchorage
2 ASHBURN Mark *Ashburn & Mason, PC*, Anchorage
 PETUMENOS Timothy *Birch, Horton*, Anchorage
3 BANKSTON William *Bankston, Gronning*, Anchorage
 OESTING David *Davis Wright Tremaine*, Anchorage

Individuals are listed alphabetically in each band.

He is admired for his outstanding appellate work and his ability to move with ease between the plaintiff and defendant worlds. Clients praise his ability to *"express complex legal issues in a straightforward style"* and commend his writing skills, which are *"second to none."*
The Clients: BP Exploration (Alaska); Daimler-Chrysler; Royal Caribbean Cruises; Purdue Pharma and Trident Seafoods.

Friedman, Rubin & White
The Firm: *"Far and away the top firm in the state,"* interviewees pointed to its impressive track record in obtaining successful jury results. Bad faith insurance litigation forms the bulk of the workload, which also includes medical malpractice work, commercial litigation, consumer protection matters and civil rights enforcement. The practice is increasingly becoming national in focus. It has been active in high-stakes litigation such as defamation, fraud and police use of excessive force cases.
The Lawyers: *"Absolutely outstanding,"* **Rick Friedman** enjoys the support of *"a good team behind him."* Active in bad faith insurance litigation, he was recommended to researchers for his intelligent, persuasive style, which makes him popular with juries: *"He knows what it takes to present a winning case."* He acted on Bellott v State Farm in which a State Farm agent was awarded $152 million.
The Clients: The firm recently represented a homeowners' association in an earthquake claim, achieving a $20 million settlement before the punitive phase of the trial.

Ashburn & Mason, PC
The Firm: The group was respected by peers for its high ethical standards of practice and excellent technical skills. Public utilities work is an area in which the group displays *"thorough knowledge."* The eight-strong team works extensively on both the plaintiff and defendant sides, particularly in employment, antitrust and real estate matters. The group advised the University of Alaska in arbitrations of labor disputes with unions, and litigated contract disputes and tort claims in the Alaska Superior Court and Alaska District Court.
The Lawyers: **Mark Ashburn** is respected for expertise in employment litigation and administrative law. *"A quintessentially objective professional,"* he is regarded as an aggressive trial attorney, winning acclaim for his attention to detail. He is a key figure at the firm for both his experience and caseload; recent highlights include representing Japanese importer Okaya in an antitrust case involving Bristol Bay salmon.
The Clients: University of Alaska; AT&T; Enstar; Alaska Marine Pilots; Miller Brewing Company; Okaya and Orca Oil Company.

Atkinson, Conway & Gagnon
The Firm: This well-established group is respected by peers for its wealth of experience and high quality of work. The firm enjoys a diverse commercial practice, which sees it advising on issues arising from Alaska Native Corporations, state taxation, malpractice claims and professional liability. Commentators also recommend the firm for construction litigation and insurance defense.
The Lawyers: The firm is home to a team of experienced attorneys, with top-quality standards of practice; rivals suggest: *"You wouldn't be able to find a bad lawyer in the firm if you tried."* Patrick Gilmore is the leading attorney for litigation here.

Burr, Pease & Kurtz, PC
The Firm: Enjoys a long-established reputation for insurance defense litigation. Observers point to the group's high degree of integrity, and, though some find its approach aggressive, all commended the quality of advice given. The team acts on both the defendant and plaintiff sides, and has a track record in products liability and negligence defense cases. It also embraces the issues most relevant to Alaskan industry, including air transport, timber and mineral extraction and oil and gas work. Other areas of experience include employment, professional malpractice, bankruptcy and construction law.
The Lawyers: Attorneys are commended for their respected trial performance and *"gentlemanly approach."* Nelson Page was identified as the contact partner.

Other Notable Practitioners
Peers endorsed **William Bankston** of Bankston, Gronning, O'Hara, Sedor, Mills & Heaphey, PC for his analytical and writing skills, and aggressive approach to commercial litigation. His work encompasses bankruptcy, construction, real estate, education and securities disputes. **David Oesting** (see p.15) at Davis Wright Tremaine LLP is celebrated as the court-appointed lead counsel for 30,000 plaintiffs, in connection with the 'Exxon Valdez' suits. Statewide rivals describe Oesting as an *"outstanding litigator."* Former prosecutor **Tim Petumenos** at Birch, Horton, Bittner & Cherot earns high regard across the board for his high level of experience. Active on both the plaintiff and defendant sides, he has been involved in medical malpractice and professional liability cases.

REAL ESTATE

ALASKA
Leading firms (Real Estate)

1 ASHBURN & MASON, PC *Anchorage*
2 ATKINSON, CONWAY & GAGNON *Anchorage*
 DAVIS WRIGHT TREMAINE LLP *Anchorage*
 DORSEY & WHITNEY LLP *Anchorage*
3 STANLEY & SCHADT *Anchorage*

Firms are listed alphabetically in each band.

Ashburn & Mason, PC
The Firm: This small firm wins acclaim from clients for its top-quality documentation and skill in real estate finance. The group is active in collateralized securities, credit-based lending and the use of conduits. On the corporate front, it advises on the sale and purchase of land and commercial property. Peers respect the group's strong litigation practice, which includes extensive eminent domain work.
Highlights include building and leaseback projects at the Alaska Regional Hospital and the acquisition, financing and leaseback of Anchorage City Hall. Residential development projects advised on include Southport and Eagle Crossing – two substantial undertakings in Anchorage, together involving over 2000 dwelling units.
The Lawyers: **Donald McClintock** conducts all the firm's transactional real estate matters to a standard that peers say is *"always first class."* Clients recommend his *"get-the-deal-done attitude."* An *"extremely sharp attorney,"* he has a reputation for being thorough and practical and possesses *"probably the best credentials in Alaska for public land takings and acquisitions."* Clients also pointed to his litigation prowess.
The Clients: Carr Gottstein GP and Koonce Pfeffer & Bettis are clients of the firm.

ALASKA — REAL ESTATE

ALASKA
Leading individuals (Real Estate)

1 MCCLINTOCK Donald *Ashburn & Mason*, Anchorage
2 GAGNON Bruce *Atkinson, Conway & Gagnon*, Anchorage
MCCOLLUM James *Sole Practitioner*, Anchorage
REECE Joseph *Davis Wright Tremaine LLP*, Anchorage
REEVES James *Dorsey & Whitney LLP*, Anchorage
3 SCHADT Gordon *Stanley & Schadt*, Anchorage
STANLEY Jim *Stanley & Schadt*, Anchorage

Individuals are listed alphabetically in each band.

Atkinson, Conway & Gagnon
The Firm: Recommended by peers, the local firm of Atkinson, Conway & Gagnon is one of the smaller contenders in the field. Its real estate practice is largely tied to the firm's general commercial and litigation work. Acquisition, sale and financing of commercial, industrial and residential developments in Alaska forms the bulk of the workload. The group works beyond the state's borders, actively participating in commercial property acquisitions for Alaska Native Corporations and Alaskan residents seeking investment diversity.
The Lawyers: Bruce Gagnon was endorsed by interviewees for his integrity in transactions and high-quality advice. He also handles litigation matters.
The Clients: The group is especially active in the timber industry.

Davis Wright Tremaine LLP
see firm details p.787
The Firm: Nationwide, the firm has the capacity to cover the gamut of real estate issues. The Alaskan practice is closely tied to the group's litigation and financing expertise and is often seen acting for lenders. Leasing documentation and environmental issues are also key strengths. Highlights include a complex transaction involving the sale of an office building in Anchorage, and the sale of a radio station.
The Lawyers: Peers noticed that the firm attracts *"so many good people."* **Joseph Reece** (see p.15) stands out among these, particularly for his levels of client service. Clients praised him for acting as a *"buffer,"* and keeping them *"appraised and on-track."* Reece combines his real estate practice work with litigation and corporate matters. He represented the seller in the sale of a large tract of land for residential development and acted for a lender in a foreclosure action on a shopping center.
The Clients: Weyerhaeuser; Bank of America; Shell Oil Products US; Alaska Broadcasting Corporation; Rite Aid and Matanuska-Susitna Borough.

Dorsey & Whitney LLP
The Firm: Adjudged by peers as a *"fine firm with high standards."* This relatively new Anchorage-based team has made its mark with a broad-ranging real estate practice covering title disputes, permitting and zoning. Landlords and tenants seek the group's advice on alcohol permitting and land use matters. Recent highlights on the transactional side include a complex sale and financing for the owner of multiple ground leases. It has also advised the owners of restaurant franchises on leasing, purchasing and franchising matters.
The Lawyers: James Reeves draws on his experience in real estate matters, litigation and natural resources law. This *"sharp"* attorney advises on litigation arising from government permits and zoning matters and councels corporate clients on financings. He represented a mining project acquiring the right of way for a mining venture, and acted in a dispute involving real estate owned by a corporate subsidiary of an Alaska Native Corporation.
The Clients: Waipono; Denali Foods; Pci Commercial; Safeway; Fred Meyer and Merrill Lynch Business Financial Services.

Stanley & Schadt
The Firm: A smaller, local partnership recommended by peers for its depth of knowledge and experience. It was endorsed for its conscientious handling of small to mid-sized transactions. These attorneys have a clear, deal-oriented perspective on the market due to *"the high frequency of their transactions."*
The Lawyers: Gordon Schadt was commended to researchers for his expertise in title issues. *"Bright"* Jim Stanley is said to *"know real estate law inside out,"* and his profile benefits from the representation of larger out-of-state clients.
The Clients: Many of the clients are local businesses, but the firm also caters for larger entities outside Alaska.

Other Notable Practitioners
Sole practitioner **James McCollum**'s real estate practice encompasses transactions for both local and out-of-state entities on title issues. He advises on the planning of communities and condominium developments, representing local builders and developers and national corporations.

Leaders in Alaska

ASHBURN, Mark
Ashburn & Mason, PC, Anchorage
907 276 4331
Recommended in Litigation

BANKSTON, William
Bankston, Gronning, O'Hara, Sedor, Mills & Heaphey, PC, Anchorage
907 276 1711
Recommended in Litigation

BLACK, Kathryn
Birch, Horton, Bittner & Cherot, Anchorage 907 276 1550
Recommended in Corporate/M&A

DANIEL, Thomas
Perkins Coie LLP, Anchorage
907 279 8561
Recommended in Employment

DAWSON, Jon S
Davis Wright Tremaine LLP, Anchorage
907 257 5300
jondawson@dwt.com
Recommended in Corporate/M&A
Specialization: Partner in litigation, intellectual property and commercial law. Experience representing businesses and financial institutions in complex commercial disputes and transactions; in real estate disputes and transactions; in maritime litigation; as creditors in bankruptcy proceedings; in IP transactions and disputes; and in defense of wrongful discharge and discrimination suits.
Prof. Memberships: American/Alaska State Bar Associations.
Career: Admitted Alaska Bar (1984), Washington State Bar (inactive) (1983). Joined *DWT*, 1983; named partner, 1989.
Publications: Frequently lectures on IP and commercial law issues.

Personal: JD, University of California at Berkeley, 1983 (Order of the Coif). BA, (Highest Distinction), University of Kansas, 1980.

DURRELL, Brian
Durrell Law Group, PC, Anchorage
907 258 3224
Recommended in Corporate/M&A

FELDMAN, Jeff
Feldman & Orlansky, Anchorage
907 272 3538
Recommended in Litigation

FJELSTAD, Eric
Perkins Coie LLP, Anchorage
907 279 8561
Recommended in Environment

FRIEDMAN, Richard
Friedman, Rubin & White, Anchorage
907 258 0704
Recommended in Litigation

GAGNON, Bruce
Atkinson, Conway & Gagnon, Anchorage
907 276 1700
Recommended in Real Estate

GROVER, Parry
Davis Wright Tremaine LLP, Anchorage
907 257 5341
parrygrover@dwt.com
Recommended in Employment
Specialization: Partner, Employment and Labor Law Department. Experience representing management in employment discrimination and wrongful discharge litigation; and labor relations matters including representation, unfair labor practices, collective bargaining, arbitration and wage/hour cases.
Prof. Memberships: Alaska State Bar Association. Board Member, Eagle Glacier Nordic Training Center (1993-2000). Commissioner, Anchorage Parks & Recreation Commission (1994-2000).

ALASKA

Career: Admitted to Alaska Bar (1980). Joined *DWT*, 1976; became partner, 1984.
Publications: Co-author/editor, 'Alaska Employment Law Deskbook'. Frequent speaker on employment law and labor relations matters.
Personal: JD, with honors, University of Washington, 1976 (Order of the Coif). BA, (magna cum laude), University of Washington, 1969.

HALL, Helena
Perkins Coie LLP, Anchorage
907 279 8561
Recommended in Employment

HARTIG, Lawrence
Hartig Rhodes Hoge & Lekisch PC, Anchorage 907 276 1592
Recommended in Environment

HOLEN, Lee
Lee Holen Law Office, Anchorage
907 278 0298
Recommended in Employment

KRAFT, Barbara Simpson
Davis Wright Tremaine LLP, Anchorage
907 257 5324
barbarasimpsonkraft@dwt.com
Recommended in Corporate/M&A

Specialization: Partner in Corporate Law Department. Practice includes advising Alaska entities on their complex transactions, including issues relating to real estate, financing options and structure of acquisition.
Prof. Memberships: Alaska Bar Association; Anchorage Bar Association.
Career: Admitted to Alaska Bar (1988). Joined *DWT* in 1988 and became a partner effective 1998.
Publications: 'The State and Local Tax Lawyer' (ABA), 'State and Local Tax Important Developments' (1995-2000).
Personal: JD, University of Washington School of Law, 1988 (Order of the Coif). BA, with honors, Oregon State University, 1982. Sits on the Board of Directors for Anchorage Historic Properties, Inc and Alaska Dance Theatre.

LYLE, George
Guess & Rudd PC, Anchorage
907 793 2200
Recommended in Environment

MCCLINTOCK, Donald
Ashburn & Mason, PC, Anchorage
907 276 4331
Recommended in Real Estate

MCCOLLUM, James
James McCollum - Sole Practitioner, Anchorage 907 770 7773
Recommended in Real Estate

ODSEN, Frederick
Hughes Thorsness Powell Huddleston & Bauman LLC, Anchorage 907 274 7522
Recommended in Corporate/M&A

OESTING, David W
Davis Wright Tremaine LLP, Anchorage
907 257 5323
daveoesting@dwt.com
Recommended in Litigation

Specialization: Partner, litigation, bankruptcy, commercial transactions departments. Focuses practice primarily on commercial and maritime litigation. Court-appointed lead counsel in the Exxon Valdez oil spill litigation for the roughly 32,000 plaintiffs, which include fishermen, communities, Alaska Natives, businesses and landowners.
Career: Admitted to the Washington State Bar (1970) and Alaska Bar (1981). Joined firm 1970; partner, 1976. Partner-in-charge of the firm's Anchorage office since 1980.
Personal: JD, with honors, Washington University School of Law, 1970, (Order of the Coif). BA, Earlham College, 1967. Member, Board of Directors for the Alaska Native Heritage Center.

PARKER, Douglas
Preston Gates & Ellis LLP, Anchorage
907 276 1969
Recommended in Employment

PETUMENOS, Timothy
Birch, Horton, Bittner & Cherot, Anchorage 907 276 1550
Recommended in Employment, Litigation

REECE, Joseph
Davis Wright Tremaine LLP, Anchorage
907 257 5325
josephreece@dwt.com
Recommended in Real Estate

Specialization: Partner in *DWT's* real property and land use department. Focuses practice on real estate transactions, including financing, purchases and sales, leasing, commercial and residential development, loan participation and environmental issues.
Prof. Memberships: American Bar Association; Alaska State Bar Association; Anchorage Bar Association.
Career: Admitted to the Alaska Bar in 1981. Joined *DWT* in 1987 and became a partner in 1990.
Publications: Frequent lecturer at CLE seminars on commercial and real estate law.
Personal: JD, (cum laude), Gonzaga University School of Law, 1981. BA, (magna cum laude), Loyola University, New Orleans, 1970.

REEVES, James
Dorsey & Whitney LLP, Anchorage
907 276 4557
Recommended in Environment, Real Estate

REEVES, Susan
Foster Pepper Rubini & Reeves PLLC, Anchorage 907 222 7100
Recommended in Environment

REGES, Robert
Ruddy, Bradley, Kolkhorst & Reges, Juneau 907 789 0047
Recommended in Environment

ROHLF, Joan
Guess & Rudd PC, Anchorage
907 793 2200
Recommended in Employment

ROSSTON, Richard
Dorsey & Whitney LLP, Anchorage
907 276 4557
Recommended in Corporate/M&A

SCHADT, Gordon
Stanley & Schadt, Anchorage
907 376 4979
Recommended in Real Estate

SCHENDEL, William
Winfree Law Office, Fairbanks
907 451 6500
Recommended in Employment

SHOUP, David H
Tindall Bennett & Shoup PC, Anchorage
907 278 8533
Recommended in Employment

STANLEY, Jim
Stanley & Schadt, Anchorag
907 376 4979
Recommended in Real Estate

VAN FLEIN, Thomas V
Clapp Peterson & Stowers LLC, Anchorage 907 272 9272
tvanflein@cpsattorneys.com
Recommended in Employment

Specialization: Focusing on employment law, commerical litigation, product liability and professional liability, with extensive civil trial and civil practice experience in both state and federal courts.
Prof. Memberships: President, Anchorage Inn of Court (2002-2003); Editor-in-Chief, Alaska Bar Rag (official publication of the Alaska Bar Association) (2000-present); Alaska Bar Association (active); California Bar Association (inactive)
Career: Admitted to Alaska Bar (1990); California Bar (1990); Law Clerk, Alaska Supreme Court (1989-1990); *Paul, Hastings, Janofsky & Walker* (LA) (1990-1993); *Charlston, Revich & Williams* (LA) (1993-1995); Member, *Clapp, Peterson & Stowers* (1995-present).
Publications: Allocation of Fault and Products Liability: A Comment on Safety Products and Human Error, 19 Alaska Law Review 141 (2002); Prospective Application of the Restatement Third of Torts: Product Liability in Alaska, 17 Alaska Law Review 1 (2000); Standards of Proof Under INS v. Fonseca: Separate Tests for Withholding of Deportation and Grants of Asylum, 5 Arizona Journal of International Law 259 (1988)

ARIZONA

CORPORATE/M&A

CONTENTS: Corporate/M&A p.16; Employment: Mainly Plaintiff p.17; Mainly Defendant p.18; Litigation: General Commercial p.19; Real estate p.20; Individuals' profiles p.21.

ARIZONA'S TOP SIX
1. Fennemore & Craig
2. Snell & Wilmer
3. Quarles & Brady Streich Lang
4. Lewis & Roca
5. Bryan Cave
5. Osborn Maledon

Ranking based on Chambers' research within the state.

All quotes in the text are from interviews with clients and competitors.

OVERVIEW: The top firm to emerge from our research in Arizona is **Fennemore Craig**. Although not the biggest, it is recognized as one of the leading law firms in the Southwest. The firm has a strong local presence, and is particularly known for its real estate work. However, it is also making a mark in the corporate sector.

Karen McConnell is described as an excellent M&A lawyer, while Bob Hackett was singled out for his corporate, securities and banking work. The firm represents many clients in the sports sector, including the Arizona Tourism and Sports Authority.

One of the largest law firms in the state, **Snell & Wilmer**, is ranked second. This 360-strong firm has been operating in the state for more than 100 years, and derives a lot of its business - particularly in the corporate sector - from its entrenched position. Peers singled out Steve Pidgeon as one of the state's foremost corporate and securities lawyers. Clients include a large number of public companies, among them Hypercom.

Quarles & Brady Streich Lang, ranked third, became the second largest law firm in the state following a merger in 2000. Peers said the firm was progressing in the corporate arena in particular. M&A and securities lawyer Bob Moya was singled out for enhancing the firm's reputation. AT&T and Bank One Arizona are among its clients.

Lewis and Roca, ranked fourth, is noted for its corporate counsel and transactional experience. It is also gaining recognition for its work on behalf of e-commerce, hi-tech and emerging companies.

Bryan Cave is ranked fifth. Like many Arizona law firms, it is noted for its real estate work. Since merging with a New York-based law firm in 2002, the firm has more than 800 lawyers in an international network of offices. This global reach gives it expertise in cross-border corporate work.

Boutique firm **Osborn Maledon**, described as a force in the local market, is ranked joint fifth. It was singled out for its role in venture finance matters. The firm assists emerging growth and hi-tech companies and represented Interact Commerce in its recent sale to The Sage Group.

CORPORATE/M&A

ARIZONA
Leading firms (Corporate/M&A)

1
- SNELL & WILMER LLP *Phoenix*
- SQUIRE, SANDERS & DEMPSEY LLP *Phoenix*

2
- BRYAN CAVE LLP *Phoenix*
- FENNEMORE CRAIG *Phoenix*
- OSBORN MALEDON, PA *Phoenix*
- QUARLES & BRADY STREICH LANG LLP *Phoenix*

3
- GREENBERG TRAURIG *Phoenix*

4
- JENNINGS, STROUSS & SALMON, PLC *Phoenix*
- LEWIS AND ROCA *Phoenix*

Leading individuals (Corporate/M&A)

1
- JOHNSON Christopher *Squire, Sanders, Phoenix*
- PIDGEON Steve *Snell & Wilmer LLP, Phoenix*
- RICHARDSON Joseph *Bryan Cave LLP, Phoenix*

2
- COHEN Jon *Snell & Wilmer LLP, Phoenix*
- CURZON Thomas *Osborn Maledon, PA, Phoenix*
- FEENEY Matthew *Snell & Wilmer LLP, Phoenix*
- KANT Bob *Greenberg Traurig, Phoenix*
- MCCONNELL Karen *Fennemore Craig, Phoenix*
- MOYA Bob *Quarles & Brady Streich Lang LLP, Phoenix*
- PLACENTI Frank *Bryan Cave LLP, Phoenix*

3
- CRABB Joseph *Squire, Sanders, Phoenix*
- DEWALD Scott *Lewis and Roca, Phoenix*
- HACKETT Bob *Fennemore Craig, Phoenix*
- HOFFMANN Christian *Quarles & Brady, Phoenix*

Firms and individuals are listed alphabetically in each band.

Snell & Wilmer LLP
The Firm: Researchers found a widespread admiration for the firm, which was referred to by one lawyer as *"the 800 pound gorilla in the state."* Its position in the Arizona corporate market is well entrenched, and the group is backed by the resources of 360 lawyers in six offices.

The Lawyers: The *"incredibly bright"* **Steve Pidgeon** was considered by peers to be *"one of the preeminent corporate and security lawyers in the state."* *"Tremendously hard-working,"* he undertakes venture capital investment as well as M&A and securities work for public traded companies. Pidgeon has *"years of experience"* to draw upon and was lauded for his *"practical"* approach and his *"excellent reputation statewide."* The firm has represented Burr-Brown, a Tucson-based semiconductor chip manufacturer, in its sale to Texas Instruments for $7.6 billion. Pidgeon led a team involved in the $300 million merger of Swift Transportation and MS Carriers to form the largest public truckload carrier in the US. **Jon Cohen** was acclaimed by peers as *"one of the smartest guys around"* and a top securities and M&A lawyer, who impresses with his *"tremendous 30-year career span."* **Matt Feeney** has a *"strong general corporate practice,"* with a leaning toward securities. He represents public companies and has proved a popular choice for large utility companies. His clients include Pinnacle West and Arizona Public Service.

The Clients: Operating out of Phoenix and Tucson, the firm represents a large number of public companies across a range of industries, including names such as Hypercom.

Squire, Sanders & Dempsey LLP
The Firm: The firm operates one of the largest corporate groups in the state, which can draw on the support of more than 750 lawyers in 26 offices worldwide. The Phoenix office was described to researchers as *"respected for its corporate and securities practice."* This 15-strong corporate team has *"particular skill"* in M&A and private equity, restructuring and real estate.

The Lawyers: Chris Johnson has a long-standing practice that has *"seen it all,"* following his *"tremendous experience"* in securities and corporate restructuring matters. Armed with *"a terrific understanding of the issues,"* Johnson is a *"business-oriented lawyer and an excellent strategic adviser."* He has impressed clients and peers with his work with troubled companies, displaying *"a knack of turning them around."* One of Johnson's key lieutenants is **Joe Crabb**, who has *"considerable experience of transactions"* in the venture capital and private equity arena.

Bryan Cave LLP
The Firm: An international network of offices gives this firm an advantage in cross-border corporate transactions. In July 2002, Bryan Cave

CORPORATE/M&A

ARIZONA

continued its expansion through a merger with New York-based Robinson Silverman Pearce Aronsohn & Berman. The firm now numbers over 800 attorneys. The Phoenix office fields a ten-strong corporate team that can draw on the support of the firm's tax attorneys.

The Lawyers: Peers agree that the team boasts *"two excellent deal lawyers"* in **Joe Richardson** and **Frank Placenti**. Placenti is head of the corporate finance and transaction practice group. Described by peers as *"smart and influential,"* he was endorsed as a *"boardroom strategist"* equipped with *"a strong business sense."* He has developed an understanding of the *"sophistication of public companies"* through his experience in corporate governance, M&A and securities matters. Richardson is endowed with a *"vast knowledge of securities law, in theory and practice."* His practice includes the representation of issuers in IPOs, and he has recently been active in aircraft leasing matters.

Fennemore Craig

The Firm: With a reputation as a *"high-quality firm,"* it operates from three Arizona offices and fields over 150 lawyers. Although known predominantly for real estate, the firm has been identified by peers for the *"push in the corporate area"* made by its team of over 20 attorneys.

The Lawyers: The *"practical"* **Karen McConnell** was described to researchers as an *"excellent M&A lawyer and a pleasure to work with"* across a range of specialties, including corporate reorganizations and venture capital finance. Her clients include Arizona-based public companies, and she has acted as corporate counsel for Allied Waste Industries. *"Highly experienced"* **Bob Hackett** provides *"committed client service"* across the gamut of corporate, securities and banking law. His practice focuses on pre-IPO technology and manufacturing companies.

The Clients: Clients include Arizona Tourism and Sports Authority, Phelps Dodge, PETsMART, and Allied Waste Industries.

Osborn Maledon, PA

The Firm: Based in Phoenix, the firm is considered a *"force in the local market."* Its 12-strong team was endorsed for its role as counsel to hi-tech and emerging growth companies facing the early rounds of financing. Much of the firm's advice to these entities encompasses M&A and securities matters.

The Lawyers: Leading light **Tom Curzon** was consistently applauded as *"a pragmatic lawyer."* Peers agree that he has won a *"great deal of respect in the business community."*

The Clients: The firm represented SalesLogix (now Interact Commerce), a Scottsdale CRM software company, in three venture capital financings, two acquisitions, its IPO and acquisition of the ACT! product line, and its recent sale for $264 million to The Sage Group. Other leading clients include Viasoft and Cox Communications.

Quarles & Brady Streich Lang LLP

The Firm: In June 2000 Quarles & Brady and Streich Lang merged and can now draw upon more than 150 attorneys in the Phoenix and Tucson offices. These form part of a national network of seven offices. Peers acknowledged that the firm is *"no longer limited by size,"* commending its success in *"moving up through the gears"* in the corporate arena.

The Lawyers: The *"practical judgment and breadth of experience"* belonging to **Bob Moya** has *"considerably bolstered"* the firm's reputation in M&A and securities law. Much of his practice focuses on midmarket entrepreneurial or high-growth companies in public and private offerings. **Chris Hoffman** has represented many clients in public and private securities financings. A *"talented"* corporate lawyer, he was commended for his advice to brokerage clients.

The Clients: AT&T; Bank One Arizona; Lucent Technologies and Wells Fargo.

Greenberg Traurig

see firm details p.808

The Firm: The Phoenix office has operated since 1999, bolstered by 30 attorneys from O'Connor, Cavanagh, Anderson, Killingsworth & Beshears. Part of a national network across 17 cities, this corporate practice numbers 40 attorneys. It advises on a range of public and private company M&A, corporate governance and public offerings.

The Lawyers: Much of the group's profile rests on the shoulders of **Bob Kant**. Primarily a securities lawyer, he was commended to researchers as a *"highly experienced attorney,"* who enjoys *"considerable connections"* within the corporate market. He advises issuers of equity and debt securities sold through major investment banks across the US.

The Clients: The firm represents national, regional and local investment banks, Fortune 500 corporates and emerging growth companies.

Jennings, Strouss & Salmon, PLC

The Firm: Operating with four offices across Arizona, the corporate practice comprises over a dozen attorneys. Peers endorsed this *"talented"* team for its *"reasonable approach"* to negotiations. A full-service practice, it was particularly recommended for its expertise in venture capital financings.

The Lawyers: Keith Overholt is chair of the firm's commercial law department.

The Clients: A broad range of clients includes some of the state's largest institutions and also smaller entrepreneurs from manufacturing, finance, technology, healthcare and agribusiness. Valley National Bank is a leading client.

Lewis and Roca

The Firm: Although perhaps better known for its litigation prowess, this 50-year-old firm is respected for its corporate counsel and transactional experience. It advises local and out-of-state companies on securities offerings, M&A, restructuring and venture capital and bank finance.

The Lawyers: Scott DeWald, a former Quarles & Brady Streich Lang attorney, was singled out by peers as a *"fine all-rounder"* who possesses *"strong technical skills."* His practice is closely identified with e-commerce, hi-tech and emerging growth companies.

The Clients: The firm advises manufacturers, financial institutions and hi-tech companies. Fortune 500 entities and smaller local businesses also use the firm.

EMPLOYMENT & LABOR LAW

MAINLY PLAINTIFF

ARIZONA
Leading firms
(Employment: Mainly Plaintiff)

[1] **GÓMEZ & PETITTI, PC** Phoenix
SCHLEIER, JELLISON & SCHLEIER Phoenix
[2] **LANGERMAN LAW OFFICES** Phoenix

Firms are listed alphabetically in each band.

Gómez & Petitti, PC

The Firm: A niche firm that earned most praise for its plaintiff work, it has also appeared on a substantial number of defendant cases.

The Lawyers: The team's reputation rests on the shoulders of the *"supremely talented"* **David Gómez**, who is respected by peers for his ability to *"deal with the most complex cases."* Although best known as an outstanding litigator, he also offers his clients strategic counseling services.

Schleier, Jellison & Schleier

The Firm: Founded in 1999, the firm has acted in a number of high-profile cases in a relatively short time. Competitors report that they are *"impressed by the quality and depth of their work."*

The Lawyers: Tod Schleier is known nationally as *"one of the best plaintiff lawyers in Arizona."* Noted for his aggressive style of litigation, this prominent practitioner received endorsement for his expertise in discrimination and sexual

ARIZONA — EMPLOYMENT & LABOR LAW

ARIZONA
Leading individuals
(Employment: Mainly Plaintiff)

1. **GÓMEZ David** *Gómez & Petitti, PC* Phoenix
   SCHLEIER Tod *Schleier, Jellison & Schleier,* Phoenix
2. **LANGERMAN Amy** *Langerman Law Offices,* Phoenix

Individuals are listed alphabetically in each band.

harassment cases. He also handles substantial mediation work.

Langerman Law Offices
The Firm: *"Doing superb work for employees,"* Amy Langerman occupies a high rank in public estimation. She was praised to researchers as a *"hard-working litigator with a wonderful ability to think strategically,"* and is primarily renowned for her expertise in wrongful discharge litigation, protection of whistle-blowers and constitutional law. Among her recent successes, several high-profile sexual harassment and retaliation cases against national and international corporations have featured strongly.

EMPLOYMENT & LABOR LAW — MAINLY DEFENDANT

ARIZONA
Leading firms
(Employment: Mainly Defendant)

1. **BRYAN CAVE LLP** Phoenix
   SNELL & WILMER LLP Phoenix
   STEPTOE & JOHNSON LLP Phoenix
2. **FENNEMORE CRAIG** Phoenix
   LEWIS AND ROCA Phoenix
   QUARLES & BRADY STREICH LANG LLP Phoenix

Leading individuals
(Employment: Mainly Defendant)

1. **KATZ Lawrence** *Steptoe & Johnson LLP,* Phoenix
2. **CLEES Joseph** *Bryan Cave LLP,* Phoenix
   WILLIAMS Lonnie *Snell & Wilmer LLP,* Phoenix
3. **COHEN Richard** *Lewis and Roca,* Phoenix
   PETTIBONE Jon *Quarles & Brady,* Phoenix
   STOLKIN Ronald *Fennemore Craig,* Phoenix

Firms and Individuals are listed alphabetically in each band.

Bryan Cave LLP
The Firm: Peers consider this firm, headquartered in St Louis, Missouri, to be *"one of the first ports of call"* for employment and labor law in Arizona. *"Excellent at handling sophisticated stuff,"* according to competitors, the 14 partners in the Phoenix office cover all aspects of employment law, with particular emphasis on employment litigation in federal and state courts, preventative work and employee benefits. The team has also appeared on a number of high-profile cases for wrongful termination, discrimination and sexual harassment, while union avoidance cases are another area of niche expertise.
The Lawyers: Singled out to researchers for *"his integrity and common sense,"* **Joseph Clees** heads the national practice and is universally admired as *"a brilliant intellectual resource"* who is perceived to have much to do with the group's *"pragmatic style."*
The Clients: A powerful client base includes manufacturing, public utility and technology entities and international and national corporates.

Snell & Wilmer LLP
The Firm: Offices in Phoenix and Tucson give this *"outstanding"* group coverage across the state. Handles all aspects of employment and traditional labor law, and is considered to be particularly strong in trial cases and for corporate-related employment work.
The Lawyers: Many commentators rate the *"absolutely brilliant"* **Lonnie Williams** as *"the leading employment trial lawyer in Arizona."* Initially focused on medical malpractice, he currently divides his time between mediation and discrimination cases, and is universally regarded as *"a winner in court."*
The Clients: Clients include leading national and international corporates.

Steptoe & Johnson LLP
The Firm: Described to researchers as *"a respected firm with a good client core,"* this Washington DC-based firm handles large-scale employment litigation cases, especially those involving discrimination claims. The group's caseload also includes counseling, arbitration and mediation, and the group is applauded by peers for its ERISA litigation work.
The Lawyers: Rivals see the firm's leading practitioner to be **Larry Katz**, who was described to our researchers as *"the key name for employment law in the state."* He specializes in employment litigation cases, labor relation issues and wrongful discharge litigation.
The Clients: Clients come from the healthcare, manufacturing and retail industries and include national and international corporates.

Fennemore Craig
The Firm: The oldest firm in Arizona, with 25 employment attorneys in its Phoenix and Tucson offices, it acts for leading US employers. The firm's caseload includes union avoidance, workers' and unemployment compensation, day-to-day counseling work and employment-related immigration issues. It is also prominent on discrimination claims.
The Lawyers: There is *"enormous admiration"* for **Ronald Stolkin** who is regarded by contemporaries as *"one of the most complete employment lawyers around."* His practice covers employment litigation cases, as well as a wide range of employment issues before government agencies such as the EEOC and the Arizona Civil Rights Division.
The Clients: Clients include leading national corporates.

Lewis and Roca
The Firm: The firm has a strong client roster of famous national companies. Discrimination, unfair labor practice, wage and hour, and health matters are undertaken. Members of the firm are also responsible for writing the Arizona Employment Law Letter.
The Lawyers: **Rick Cohen** has nearly 30 years of experience in employment issues and has written widely on the subject. Described to researchers as an *"effective technician,"* he is renowned for employment discrimination cases at appellate level.
The Clients: Clients include many leading national corporates.

Quarles & Brady Streich Lang LLP
The Firm: The group is noted for its *"good coverage of Arizona"* and has reinforced its reputation for traditional labor advice since its 2000 merger. Also handles employment litigation, workers' compensation, mediation and employee benefits. The team successfully represented an international manufacturer in a whistle-blower case. It also appeared on a successful mediation of five discrimination charges before the EEOC, and successfully acted for a national software manufacturer in a charge brought by the EEOC alleging sex discrimination.
The Lawyers: **Jon Pettibone**, the most visible partner in this team, has an established name for traditional labor matters and was especially singled out for his NLRB and EEOC practice.
The Clients: The team serves a wide range of local, national and international employers from industries such as transportation, healthcare, retail and manufacturing. Clients include: UPS; CTS; Peoria Unified School District; Safeway and Chancellor Beacon Academies.

LITIGATION — ARIZONA

LITIGATION

ARIZONA
Leading firms
(Litigation: General Commercial)

1
- BROWN & BAIN, PA *Phoenix*
- FENNEMORE CRAIG *Phoenix*
- LEWIS AND ROCA *Phoenix*
- OSBORN MALEDON, PA *Phoenix*

2
- HARALSON, MILLER, PITT & MCANALLY *Tucson*
- QUARLES & BRADY STREICH LANG LLP *Tucson*
- SNELL & WILMER LLP *Phoenix*

3
- MEYER, HENDRICKS & BIVENS *Phoenix*
- RUSING & LOPEZ, PLLC *Tucson*

Leading individuals
(Litigation: General Commercial)

1
- BAIRD Peter *Lewis and Roca*, Phoenix
- ECKSTEIN Paul *Brown & Bain, PA*, Phoenix
- MALEDON William *Osborn Maledon, PA*, Phoenix

2
- GREEN Jordan *Fennemore Craig*, Phoenix
- HURWITZ Andrew *Osborn Maledon, PA*, Phoenix
- MALTZ Gerald *Haralson, Miller*, Tucson
- MEEHAN Michael *Quarles & Brady Streich*, Tucson

3
- RUSING Michael *Rusing & Lopez, PLLC*, Tucson
- SHERK Kenneth *Fennemore Craig*, Phoenix

Firms and Individuals are listed alphabetically in each band.

Brown & Bain, PA
see firm details p.775

The Firm: A litigation practice with an abundance of quality practitioners. *"Right on top of things,"* in the opinion of clients. One commented that the team combines *"responsiveness with a deep understanding of our business needs."* The IP/IT unit is central to the litigation practice, and contributes significantly to the firm's strength. The firm has expertise in the semiconductor, microchip and computer software industries. Acted for Cypress Semiconductor in a patent infringement case brought by EMI North America. Defended Intel in litigation brought by the Lemelson Partnership. Also specializes in media, antitrust and securities litigation, and regularly handles US Supreme Court cases. The firm currently represents a prominent construction company, challenging the tourism and sports authority over a major new development.

The Lawyers: **Paul Eckstein** (see p.21) has a wealth of experience in Arizona and beyond. Regarded as one of the state's most versatile trial lawyers, with a specialty in technology disputes and also in constitutional and election litigation.

The Clients: Clients include: Maxim; Microchip Technology; United Technologies; Pennzoil; PwC; Apple; IBM and the Arizona Daily Star.

Fennemore Craig
The Firm: Arizona's oldest firm with a traditional, conservative image. Known for its consistently high-quality litigation focusing in particular on white-collar crime, insurance defense and legal malpractice, the firm also has a respected appellate practice.

The Lawyers: **Jordan Green** acts mainly in white-collar criminal defense cases, on behalf of individuals and corporations. Also handles other commercial litigation and antitrust work. Peers describe him as a *"real trial lawyer who has amassed stacks of courtroom experience."* **Ken Sherk** is noted for his extensive case resumé and *"fine courtroom judgment."* Lawyers' malpractice defense forms the main thrust of his practice. Recent cases include acting for: Fortune 500 company in multi-state antitrust investigation; officer of regional utility company investigated for false statements to the Government; hospital in a federal prosecution.

The Clients: Clients include: Fortune 500 companies; Indian tribes; home builders; utilities; hospitals and law firms.

Lewis and Roca
The Firm: A major litigation force in Phoenix, said to have made *"great inroads into the Tucson market."* Traditionally a full-service generalist practice with experience of cases in numerous business sectors. Has combined commercial litigation with criminal work – the firm boasts some notable US Supreme Court white-collar wins. Other strengths include professional malpractice (largely for major law firms), IP, labor, securities and real estate.

The Lawyers: Top of everyone's list is **Peter Baird** – *"the cream of the crop,"* say fellow Arizona lawyers. Said to have developed a *"genuinely national practice,"* he gets work referred by other US law firms, and takes on corporate and professional liability cases for domestic and foreign clients. Recently, he defended British Gas in a director liability arbitration, and represented a major Phoenix law firm in a negligence trial.

The Clients: Clients include: Kabuto Arizona Properties; AutoNation; CNA Insurance; Household International and Wells Fargo.

Osborn Maledon, PA
The Firm: Clients praised this *"incredibly responsive and cost-effective"* litigation unit, which *"doesn't get bogged down in bureaucracy."* The main thrust of the workload here is large, complex commercial litigation, antitrust and securities cases.

The Lawyers: Of the Phoenix firm's 30 litigators, **Bill Maledon** was singled out to researchers as a *"first-class trial lawyer."* His litigation practice focuses on antitrust, trade regulation, products liability and sports law. **Andrew Hurwitz** appeals to clients as a *"top-drawer lawyer, ideal for heavy-duty litigation where we really need the right advice."* He is also nationally renowned for his appellate practice, and has featured prominently at the US Supreme Court. Other partners are acknowledged for expertise in environmental litigation, white-collar crime and malpractice (accountancy and legal). Cases handled include a large antitrust case on behalf of the PGA Golf Tour, the defense of products liability claims brought against Philip Morris, and an antitrust case against WL Gore & Associates.

The Clients: Clients include Honeywell, AT&T, PwC and Arizona Public Service.

GENERAL COMMERCIAL

Haralson, Miller, Pitt & McAnally
The Firm: Offers an unusual mix of business litigation and plaintiff personal injury work in large catastrophe cases, acting for both companies and individuals. Represented a commercial property landowner in a high-profile planning dispute. Recent malpractice suits included a case against a surgeon for a neurological injury.

The Lawyers: **Gerald Maltz** is the most recognizable name of a group that is said to be *"full of crackerjack litigators."* Peers warm to his unruffled style, which is employed in cases ranging from patents (often for plaintiffs) and legal malpractice to personal injury.

The Clients: Clients include: Arizona Independent Redistricting Commission; Farmers Investment Company; Campus Research Corporations; The University of Arizona and the Phoenix Suns basketball team.

Quarles & Brady Streich Lang LLP
The Firm: With offices in Phoenix and Tucson, this merged Midwest firm has established itself as a litigation force right across the state. A number of litigators were recommended to *Chambers'* researchers, practicing in areas such as insurance, bankruptcy and construction.

The Lawyers: Most often mentioned was **Michael Meehan**, an experienced Tucson lawyer who joined the firm in 2001 from Meehan & Associates. He was widely recommended for his technically thorough, and at times robust, approach. Fellow lawyers praised the range of his litigation skills – he acts for both defendants and plaintiffs, and has experience in the appeals courts.

Snell & Wilmer LLP
The Firm: Arizona's largest firm has a sizable litigation team – 50 in Phoenix and 12 in Tucson – that handles the full range of disciplines. Notable strengths exist in insurance, antitrust and zoning.

ARIZONA

REAL ESTATE

The team acted for Rockwell Collins in a major antitrust case, and is currently involved in a multiple patent infringement case involving Microsoft.
The Lawyers: John Bouma is the litigator in charge of the Phoenix office; Jeffrey Willis is the contact partner in Tucson.
The Clients: Other clients include: Del Webb; Edelson Technology Partners; Perini Building Company; Arizona Public Service Company; Pinnacle West Capital; American General Assurance Company; Meredith; DMG-MAXIMUS; Prudential Real Estate and Bank of America.

Meyer, Hendricks & Bivens
The Firm: Formed in 1995 as a spin-off from Osborn Maledon. 90% of the firm's activity centers around commercial litigation, with the rest comprising plaintiff work, medical malpractice and personal injury. Partners have particular niches in IP, technology and securities.
The Lawyers: Headed by Don Bivens, the head of the Arizona Bar Association, a comparatively small team (four partners, 11 associates) manages to *"appear on everybody's shortlist,"* and pulls in clients of the caliber of Southern California Edison.
The Clients: The firm acted for the bondholders (in tandem with Weil, Gotshal & Manges) in a dispute with Motorola, and defended OSRAM SYLVANIA in a battle over rights to the Timex 'Indiglo' watch patent. MetLife is another leading client.

Rusing & Lopez, PLLC
The Firm: Highly respected in its local market, this Tucson firm's trump card is considered to be **Mick Rusing**, who specializes in business and injury litigation, both plaintiff and defense, and has handled disputes concerning construction, real estate and the environment. Recent examples of work include a major fraud case for Cary Marmis relating to the sale of Tucson General Hospital, a $5.5 million class action settlement by electricity customers against Citizens Utilities and the successful defense of beryllium manufacturer Brush Wellman in a multiple-party toxic tort case.
The Clients: Clients include: City of Tucson; Fairfield Homes; Gates Learjet; Bank of America; The University of Arizona; Cox Communications and ServiceMaster.

REAL ESTATE

ARIZONA
Leading firms (Real Estate)

1
- BRYAN CAVE LLP *Phoenix*
- FENNEMORE CRAIG *Phoenix*
- MARISCAL, WEEKS, MCINTYRE, *Phoenix*
- SQUIRE, SANDERS & DEMPSEY LLP *Phoenix*

2
- GALLAGHER & KENNEDY, PA *Phoenix*
- QUARLES & BRADY STREICH LANG LLP *Phoenix*
- SNELL & WILMER LLP *Phoenix*

3
- LEWIS AND ROCA *Phoenix*

Leading individuals (Real Estate)

1
- LANSKY David *Mariscal, Weeks, McIntyre,* Phoenix
- LISKER Steven *Bryan Cave LLP,* Phoenix
- MAST Greg *Gallagher & Kennedy, PA,* Phoenix

2
- HENDERSON Scott *Squire Sanders,* Phoenix
- KRAMER Jay *Fennemore Craig,* Phoenix
- MAY Bruce *Quarles & Brady Streich Lang LLP,* Phoenix
- ROBINSON Bob *Fennemore Craig,* Phoenix
- VAN WINKLE Kenneth *Lewis and Roca,* Phoenix

3
- BATES Bob *Snell & Wilmer LLP,* Phoenix
- MORROW James *Quarles & Brady,* Phoenix
- POKORSKI Jody *Snell & Wilmer LLP,* Phoenix
- SAVAGE Stephen *Fennemore Craig,* Phoenix
- WILEY Jay *Snell & Wilmer LLP,* Phoenix
- WINKLER Peter *Mariscal, Weeks,* Phoenix
- WRIGHT Joyce *Snell & Wilmer LLP,* Phoenix

Firms and individuals are listed alphabetically in each band.

Bryan Cave LLP
The Firm: The firm's excellent reputation for real estate is widely expected to be consolidated by the July 2002 merger with respected New York firm Robinson Silverman Pearce Aronsohn & Berman. The new firm will have more than 800 lawyers. Of the 75 in the Phoenix office, 12 lawyers will focus on traditional real estate, notably on the development of residential homes, inner city redevelopment and the commercial development of shopping malls, sports and entertainment facilities.
The Lawyers: The star of the show here is **Steve Lisker**, whose prominence in the big-ticket residential market was unanimously recognized in our research. He was described as a *"top-drawer performer,"* with *"a vast experience"* of advising home builders on land acquisition and the whole development process.
The Clients: Clients include: Post Properties; Camden Property Trust; Lincoln Properties Group, Suncrown Development and The Rouse Company.

Fennemore Craig
The Firm: Competitors recognize the firm as one of the real estate market leaders in the Southwest. Three offices in Arizona contain around 25 real estate practitioners. The workload ranges from acquisition, sales and leasing to finance and development (a particularly strong area of practice).
The Lawyers: The firm's muscle in real estate finance is attributed by our respondents to **Bob Robinson** and **Jay Kramer**. Licensed in accountancy, the *"methodical and thoughtful"* Robinson has over 30 years' experience and is considered to have a *"sound grasp of complex financial deals."* His practice emphasizes asset-based and real estate finance, workouts of troubled loans and the acquisition, development and sale of real estate. Kramer, whose workload is divided between master-planned communities and real estate finance, is respected by clients for his *"attention to detail"* and his *"practical approach to problem-solving."* Also recommended was **Steve Savage**, a *"consummate professional,"* who has a traditional real estate practice.
The Clients: The group has represented the Arizona Tourism and Sports Authority in the development of a new stadium for the NFL team, Arizona Cardinals, and is working on a new stadium for the NHL team, the Phoenix Coyotes. Clients include: Allied Waste Industries; Apple; The Lyle Anderson Company and the Phoenix Suns.

Mariscal, Weeks, McIntyre & Friedlander, PA
The Firm: The 54-lawyer Phoenix-based firm is acknowledged by rivals to be *"major competition"* in the real estate market.
The Lawyers: It thrives on what was characterized to researchers as *"the Lansky factor."* **David Lansky** is viewed as a *"strong and aggressive"* attorney, who has a niche in the retail development sector and represents Vestar, one of the leading privately held real estate companies in the western US. This relationship provides substantial work in the development of open-air retail centers and the management of retail, office and industrial properties. The *"bright, thoughtful and skillful"* **Peter Winkler** also gained consistent plaudits from contemporaries.
The Clients: Clients include Vestar, Arizona Electric Power Cooperative, Lincoln Property Company and Northern Trust Bank of Arizona.

Squire, Sanders & Dempsey LLP
The Firm: With around 20 full-time real estate attorneys in its Phoenix office, the firm has become increasingly influential in the local real estate market. Its strength is perceived to lie on the development side, and the group's client portfolio has an international flavor.
The Lawyers: **Scott Henderson** is widely recognized as an *"extremely talented attorney,"* notably in the area of multi-family housing. His *"vivacious*

REAL ESTATE

ARIZONA

personality" and *"excellent skills at the negotiating table"* have thrust him to the head of the local pack of real estate lawyers.

The Clients: The firm advised Laguna Beach Resorts on the purchase of The Laguna Beach Colony, a 30-acre resort and residential project, from Marriott International.

Gallagher & Kennedy, PA

The Firm: This young, full-service firm maintains a sound reputation for real estate in spite of defections such as that of Scott Henderson to Squire, Sanders & Dempsey. Particularly strong on the development and environment side of real estate, the team also has an established name for transactional work.

The Lawyers: This transactional strength is generally attributed to the presence of **Greg Mast**, who was endorsed to researchers as *"a thoughtful guy with an excellent bedside manner."* He has advised the developers on a variety of mixed office-retail and industrial developments, including the Camelback Esplanade and Scottsdale Spectrum, and continues to act for the developers on the 2.5 million sq ft office, retail and hotel buildings at the Collier Center in downtown Phoenix.

The Clients: Clients include Opus West, Motorola, Arizona Cardinals and Arizona Diamondbacks, and AirTouch Communications.

Quarles & Brady Streich Lang LLP

The Firm: Since the October 2000 merger between Quarles & Brady and Streich Lang PA, the new firm (the second largest in Arizona) has greater strength in real estate. Its Arizona offices have a real estate group of around 15 lawyers acknowledged for an expertise in real estate finance.

The Lawyers: A member of ACREL, **Jim Morrow** is admired by opponents as *"one of the world's hardest workers,"* and has a substantial finance-based practice. Also in the Phoenix office, and known for his development work, **Bruce May** was recommended to researchers as *"knowledgeable, diligent and noncombative,"* and has carried out purchase, sale and leasing agreements for the broker/dealer Charles Schwab.

Snell & Wilmer LLP

The Firm: The firm has 14 real estate attorneys in Arizona. The emphasis of their practice is on real estate finance, representing major financial institutions, local developers and master planners.

The Lawyers: Among a respected group of lawyers with *"uniform quality,"* **Bob Bates** is *"one of the best generalists around,"* and advises on leasing, public-private partnerships and sports facility developments. **Jody Pokorski**'s development expertise for institutional clients received due praise, while *"real good grafter"* **Jay Wiley**'s *"attention to detail"* in the development sector also gained market approval. **Joyce Wright**'s diverse practice was noted for its emphasis on the hospitality industry, and she was recommended to researchers as a *"businesslike attorney, who is easy to work with."* She represented MONY Life Insurance Company in connection with the Pointe South Mountain Resort in Phoenix, and advised the City of Mesa on the development of a multipurpose stadium to be used for NFL football games, concerts and cultural events.

The Clients: Clients include Starwood Hotels and Reliant Energy.

Lewis and Roca

The Firm: Best known for its expertise in the contentious aspects of real estate law, the firm is also building a reputation for real estate lending. The Tucson office is noted for providing support in land use and zoning matters.

The Lawyers: The *"highly intelligent"* and *"personable"* **Ken Van Winkle** is the leading figure here. His practice embraces real estate M&A, equity and debt financing and leasing, and he represents a variety of lenders, REITs and insurance companies.

The Clients: Clients include financial institutions and REITs.

Leaders in Arizona

BAIRD, Peter
Lewis and Roca, Phoenix
602 262 5311
Recommended in Litigation

BATES, Bob
Snell & Wilmer LLP, Phoenix
602 382 6000
Recommended in Real Estate

CLEES, Joseph
Bryan Cave LLP, Phoenix
602 364 7000
Recommended in Employment

COHEN, Jon
Snell & Wilmer LLP, Phoenix
602 382 6000
Recommended in Corporate/M&A

COHEN, Richard
Lewis and Roca, Phoenix
602 262 5311
Recommended in Employment

CRABB, Joseph
Squire, Sanders & Dempsey LLP,
Phoenix 602 528 4000
Recommended in Corporate/M&A

CURZON, Thomas
Osborn Maledon, PA, Phoenix
602 640 9000
Recommended in Corporate/M&A

DEWALD, Scott
Lewis and Roca, Phoenix
602 262 5311
Recommended in Corporate/M&A

ECKSTEIN, Paul F
Brown & Bain, P.A., Phoenix
602 351 8222
eckstein@brownbain.com
Recommended in Litigation
Specialization: Civil litigation matters with an emphasis on contract, tort, antitrust, intellectual property, constitutional, election and media law issues at both the trial and appellate levels. Since 1995 he has spent an increasing amount of time as a private arbitrator and mediator.
Prof. Memberships: American Bar Association; State Bar of Arizona; Maricopa County Bar Association; Committee on Court Reform in Arizona; Arizona Center for Law in the Public Interest.
Career: Admitted in Arizona 1965.

Joined *Brown & Bain* in 1965; Member since 1970; Managing Director, 1987-95; Chairman, 2000-present. Other bar memberships: United States District Court for the District of Arizona; Supreme Court of the United States; United States Court of Appeals for the Ninth Circuit; United States District Court for the Northern District of California. Served as co-prosecutor in the impeachment trial of Governor Evan Mecham.
Personal: Born 6 September 1940. Educated at Pomona College, BA, cum laude, Phi Beta Kappa, and Harvard Law School. Married with two children. Member of Board of Directors of Phoenix Children's Hospital (1983-present, Chair of the Board 1995-97); Board of Trustees of Pomona College (1983-present, Chair of Presidential Search Committee, 1990-91 and 2002-03); Vice-Chair of the Board 1992-2002); Board of Directors of the Arizona State University Law Society (1978-present, President 1991-92); Chair, Arizona Selection Committee for the Rhodes Scholarships (1989-95), Member (1998-present); Chair, District VIII Selection Committee for the Rhodes Scholarships (1996-97); Lawyer Representative, Ninth Circuit Judicial Conference (1999-2002); National Board of Directors, Lawyers Committee for Civil Rights Under Law (2000-present).

FEENEY, Matthew
Snell & Wilmer LLP, Phoenix
602 382 6000
Recommended in Corporate/M&A

GÓMEZ, David
Gómez & Petitti, PC Phoenix
602 957 8686
Recommended in Employment

GREEN, Jordan
Fennemore Craig, Phoenix
602 916 5000
Recommended in Litigation

HACKETT, Bob
Fennemore Craig, Phoenix
602 916 5000
Recommended in Corporate/M&A

ARIZONA LEADERS

HENDERSON, Scott
Squire, Sanders & Dempsey LLP, Phoenix 602 528 4000
Recommended in Real Estate

HOFFMANN, Christian
Quarles & Brady Streich Lang LLP, Phoenix 602 229 5200
Recommended in Corporate/M&A

HURWITZ, Andrew
Osborn Maledon, PA, Phoenix
602 640 9000
Recommended in Litigation

JOHNSON, Christopher
Squire, Sanders & Dempsey LLP, Phoenix 602 528 4000
Recommended in Corporate/M&A

KANT, Bob
Greenberg Traurig LLP, Phoenix
602 445 8000
Recommended in Corporate/M&A

KATZ, Lawrence
Steptoe & Johnson LLP, Phoenix
602 257 5200
Recommended in Employment

KRAMER, Jay
Fennemore Craig, Phoenix
602 916 5000
Recommended in Real Estate

LANGERMAN, Amy
Langerman Law Offices, Phoenix
602 240 5525
Recommended in Employment

LANSKY, David
Mariscal, Weeks, McIntyre & Friedlander, PA, Phoenix 602 285 5000
Recommended in Real Estate

LISKER, Steven
Bryan Cave LLP, Phoenix
602 364 7000
Recommended in Real Estate

MALEDON, William
Osborn Maledon, PA, Phoenix
602 640 9000
Recommended in Litigation

MALTZ, Gerald
Haralson, Miller, Pitt & McAnally, Tucson
520 792 3836
Recommended in Litigation

MAST, Greg
Gallagher & Kennedy, PA, Phoenix
602 530 8000
Recommended in Real Estate

MAY, Bruce
Quarles & Brady Streich Lang LLP, Phoenix 602 229 5200
Recommended in Real Estate

MCCONNELL, Karen
Fennemore Craig, Phoenix
602 916 5000
Recommended in Corporate/M&A

MEEHAN, Michael
Quarles & Brady Streich Lang LLP, Tucson 520 770 8700
Recommended in Litigation

MORROW, James
Quarles & Brady Streich Lang LLP, Phoenix 602 229 5200
Recommended in Real Estate

MOYA, Bob
Quarles & Brady Streich Lang LLP, Phoenix 602 229 5200
Recommended in Corporate/M&A

PETTIBONE, Jon
Quarles & Brady Streich Lang LLP, Phoenix 602 229 5200
Recommended in Employment

PIDGEON, Steve
Snell & Wilmer LLP, Phoenix
602 382 6000
Recommended in Corporate/M&A

PLACENTI, Frank
Bryan Cave LLP, Phoenix
602 364 7000
Recommended in Corporate/M&A

POKORSKI, Jody
Snell & Wilmer LLP, Phoenix
602 382 6000
Recommended in Real Estate

RICHARDSON, Joseph
Bryan Cave LLP, Phoenix
602 364 7000
Recommended in Corporate/M&A

ROBINSON, Bob
Fennemore Craig, Phoenix
602 916 5000
Recommended in Real Estate

RUSING, Michael
Rusing & Lopez, PLLC, Tucson
520 792 4800
Recommended in Litigation

SAVAGE, Stephen
Fennemore Craig, Phoenix
602 916 5000
Recommended in Real Estate

SCHLEIER, Tod
Schleier, Jellison & Schleier, Phoenix
602 277 0157
Recommended in Employment

SHERK, Kenneth
Fennemore Craig, Phoenix
602 916 5000
Recommended in Litigation

STOLKIN, Ronald
Fennemore Craig, Phoenix
602 916 5000
Recommended in Employment

VAN WINKLE, Kenneth
Lewis and Roca, Phoenix
602 262 5311
Recommended in Real Estate

WILEY, Jay
Snell & Wilmer LLP, Phoenix
602 382 6000
Recommended in Real Estate

WILLIAMS, Lonnie
Snell & Wilmer LLP, Phoenix
602 382 6000
Recommended in Employment

WINKLER, Peter
Mariscal, Weeks, McIntyre & Friedlander, PA, Phoenix 602 285 5000
Recommended in Employment

WRIGHT, Joyce
Snell & Wilmer LLP, Phoenix
602 382 6000
Recommended in Real Estate

ARKANSAS

CORPORATE/M&A

CONTENTS: Corporate/M&A p.23; Employment: Mainly Plaintiff p.24; Mainly Defendant p.24; Litigation: General Commercial p.25; Real Estate p.26; Individuals' Profiles p.27.

ARKANSAS' TOP THREE
1. Wright, Lindsey & Jennings
2. Mitchell Williams Selig Gates Woodyard
3. Friday, Eldredge & Clark

Ranking based on Chambers' research within the state.

All quotes in the text are from interviews with clients and competitors.

OVERVIEW: Now in its hundredth year, **Wright, Lindsey & Jennings** offers a full service from its offices in Fayetteville and Little Rock. It was enthusiastically recommended as an "extremely reputable" and "honorable" firm. Interviewees commended the more than 60 lawyer complement for its strength in corporate/M&A, real estate, general commercial litigation and employment law. Key clients include Wal-Mart and Bank of America. Another full-service firm, **Mitchell Williams Selig Gates Woodyard**, attracts plaudits for consistently high-quality attorneys. Its leading real estate practice was proclaimed "the best in Arkansas" for its varied transactional workload. The firm notably represented the seller in the largest ever transfer of privately held real estate assets in the state. Commentators also identified niche strengths in securities litigation, insurance defense disputes and environmental matters and singled out litigator Allan Gates for his role in developing one of Arkansas' first environmental law practices. The firm acts for 3M and Weyerhaeuser.

Friday, Eldredge & Clark is one of the largest firms in the state. Sources consider the practice to be "ahead of the competition" in litigation, where the firm tends to dominate Arkansas' larger cases.

Clients include Ernst & Young and Hewlett-Packard.

CORPORATE/M&A

ARKANSAS
Leading firms (Corporate/M&A)
1. **KUTAK ROCK LLP** Little Rock
   WRIGHT, LINDSEY & JENNINGS LLP Little Rock
2. **FRIDAY, ELDREDGE & CLARK** Little Rock
   MITCHELL WILLIAMS SELIG Little Rock

Leading individuals (Corporate/M&A)
1. **BENHAM Paul** *Friday, Eldredge & Clark,* Little Rock
   BUFORD Douglas *Wright, Lindsey* Little Rock
   SELIG John *Mitchell Williams,* Little Rock

Firms and Individuals are listed alphabetically in each band.

Kutak Rock LLP
The Firm: Lawyers in Little Rock and Fayetteville enjoy the support of a network of offices across the US. In Arkansas, eight attorneys are dedicated to corporate matters. Clients from a range of industries are attracted to the firm's advice on capital-raising transactions and M&A. The group is also skilled in regulatory matters and especially in relation to securities law. Despite the unfavorable economic climate, the firm has continued to advise ALLTEL on a number of matters, including the pending acquisition of the wireless operations of CenturyTel. It has also represented Pinnacle Bancshares in its acquisition by Bancorp South.
The Lawyers: Although no one individual stood out during our research, David Smith is a key player in commercial transactions. Much of his profile is based on his tax advice.
The Clients: The firm acts for a number of clients in the region, including those from the healthcare, telecom, financial, commercial banking and manufacturing industries.

Wright, Lindsey & Jennings LLP
The Firm: *Chambers'* interviewees praised the firm, not only for the quality of its corporate department but also for the support offered by its adjoining groups. The firm advises on a wide array of commercial transactions, business planning and regulatory matters. Peers highlighted its expertise on public company transactions as a key strength. Other strong suits include its advice pertaining to bankruptcies and securities offerings.
The Lawyers: In keeping with the firm's reputation, **Doug Buford** was endorsed for his securities-related work. He was also respected for his sound judgment on corporate transactional matters and tax structuring.
The Clients: The firm acts for a number of multinational corporations that have bases in Arkansas, as well as local and regional entities.

Friday, Eldredge & Clark
The Firm: Peers commend the practice for its *"full complement of experience."* It is active both within Arkansas as well as outside the state. Municipal bond work has provided the group with much of its workload, and it advises clients on M&A, joint venture transactions and various financings. The firm has also assisted on regulatory compliance matters. The small group of lawyers has advised on the construction of independent power projects, and works closely with colleagues in the real estate, tax, litigation and employment groups to provide a seamless client service.
The Lawyers: Paul Benham was commended by interviewees as a seasoned lawyer, well versed in securities law. His practice also extends to advising clients on corporate finance matters.
The Clients: Public utilities, retail companies and financial institutions are among the firm's client base.

Mitchell Williams Selig Gates Woodyard, PLLC
The Firm: A diverse practice sees the firm advising clients on a broad spectrum of corporate matters and transactions. A core group of corporate law specialists works in close conjunction with colleagues from the tax, real estate and insurance groups. It has been especially active in the representation of institutional lenders. Some of its key engagements have included counseling clients on bank acquisitions and securities offerings. In light of the economic situation, bankruptcy proceedings and Chapter 11 filings have also proved to be an active area.
The Lawyers: John Selig was identified by competitors as the firm's standout practitioner from among a group of 15 lawyers. His experience spans advice on M&A transactions, financings and the representation of issuers and underwriters in securities offerings. He has also built up a niche practice acting for electrical cooperatives.
The Clients: Core clients of the firm include banks and other financial institutions, and a broad range of corporations, both based in Arkansas and further afield.

ARKANSAS

EMPLOYMENT & LABOR LAW

MAINLY PLAINTIFF

ARKANSAS
Leading firms
(Employment: Mainly Plaintiff)
1. **LAVEY & BURNETT** Little Rock
2. **EUBANKS, WELCH, BAKER & SCHULZE** Little Rock
   HARRILL & SUTTER PLLC Little Rock

Leading individuals
(Employment: Mainly Plaintiff)
1. **LAVEY Jack** Lavey & Burnett, Little Rock
2. **HARMON Melva**, Sole Practitioner, Little Rock
   WALKER John John Walker, Little Rock
   WELCH Morgan Eubanks, Welch, Little Rock
3. **BURNETT John** Lavey & Burnett, Little Rock
   HUNT Eugene Hunt Law Firm, Pine Bluff
   SUTTER Luther Harrill & Sutter PLLC, Little Rock

Firms and Individuals are listed alphabetically in each band.

Lavey & Burnett
The Firm: The firm was heavily endorsed for its representation of unions, but is also experienced in employment law and undertakes civil rights cases from time to time. In the field of labor law, the group is most frequently involved in arbitrations while age, race and sex discrimination cases are the staple fare of the employment practice.
The Lawyers: Jack Lavey is a senior member of the bar and was warmly endorsed as a *"consistently excellent"* attorney. He won particular approval from defense lawyers who saw him as someone who is *"outgoing, friendly and reasonable to deal with."* Although sometimes overshadowed by his colleague, John Burnett also earned the respect of peers for his labor practice. Among his clients are communications and electrical unions.

Eubanks, Welch, Baker & Schulze
The Firm: Founded in 2000, this small group of attorneys is well known for its litigation capabilities and has an active practice in medical negligence and personal injury matters. In the employment field, the group was recognized for its representation of individuals in age, sex and race discrimination cases.
The Lawyers: Morgan (Chip) Welch is the individual with the highest profile here and was described to researchers as a *"strong and self-confident attorney."* A string of successful results have given him a reputation among competitors as a particularly effective advocate on jury trials.

Harrill & Sutter PLLC
The Firm: Recommended primarily for its work in the employment field, the firm has handled several high-profile matters and has an especially strong reputation for ADA and FMLA cases.
The Lawyers: Luther Sutter may *"ruffle a few feathers"* in some quarters but is generally regarded as an attorney who *"is fair and sensitive to his clients."*

Other Notable Practitioners
Two sole practitioners are considered to stand out in Little Rock. **Melva Harmon** is well known for representing the Teamsters union, and won rave reviews from market commentators who see her as an *"easygoing and ethical"* lawyer. *"The dean of Title VII"* cases is **John Walker**, who was recommended by one interviewee as *"better on his feet than anyone else I know."* In Pine Bluff, **Eugene Hunt** of the Hunt Law Firm has a solid reputation for his detailed preparation of discrimination cases.

EMPLOYMENT & LABOR LAW

MAINLY DEFENDANT

ARKANSAS
Leading firms
(Employment: Mainly Defendant)
1. **CROSS, GUNTER, WITHERSPOON** Little Rock
   WRIGHT, LINDSEY & JENNINGS LLP Little Rock
2. **FRIDAY, ELDREDGE & CLARK** Little Rock
3. **MITCHELL WILLIAMS SELIG GATES** Little Rock
   ROSE LAW FIRM Little Rock

Leading individuals
(Employment: Mainly Defendant)
1. **BOE Tim** Rose Law Firm, Little Rock
   GRAVES Kathlyn Wright Lindsey, Little Rock
2. **DAVIS Oscar** Friday, Eldredge & Clark, Little Rock
   GUNTER Russell Cross, Gunter, Little Rock
   MOORE Michael Friday, Eldredge & Clark, Little Rock
   ROBINSON Spencer Ramsay, Bridgforth, Pine Bluff
3. **FREELAND Byron** Mitchell Williams Selig, Little Rock
   WITHERSPOON Carolyn Cross, Gunter, Little Rock

Firms Individuals are listed alphabetically in each band.

Cross, Gunter, Witherspoon & Galchus, PC
The Firm: The firm's lengthy experience in the sector, coupled with an ability to bring substantial resources to bear, has helped to establish it as one of the premier employment shops in the market. Although various individuals were singled out, peers felt that this was a strong team combining several young up-and-coming lawyers with a number of respected senior practitioners.
The Lawyers: Russell Gunter, who has 25 years' experience in the field, was recommended for his labor management relations practice, while Carolyn Witherspoon was tipped to researchers as a talented employment litigator. Much of the firm's work is devoted to counseling employers on the avoidance of employment-related disputes and representing them in a variety of union negotiations. The team also litigates in state and federal courts; it succeeded in reaching a settlement of a race discrimination case and achieved summary judgment in an ADA case brought against a bank.
The Clients: Clients include: US Bank; Beverly Enterprises; ABF Freight System and Reliant.

Wright, Lindsey & Jennings LLP
The Firm: Enthusiastically recommended by Chambers' interviewees as an *"extremely reputable"* operation, the group is most active in the employment sphere. Its six lawyers have experience in defending employment discrimination claims including ADA, Title VII and the FMLA but have also advised clients on union organizing campaigns and contract negotiations. Plaintiffs' attorneys acknowledged that *"they provide a good service to their clients and know when it's best to settle."*
The Lawyers: Kathy Graves is the group's most prominent individual and was universally endorsed for her *"attention to detail."* Her practice has a heavy litigation emphasis and she has defended age and race discrimination cases for public and private employers.
The Clients: Clients include Weyerhaeuser and Lion Oil.

Friday, Eldredge & Clark
The Firm: A compact group of lawyers from one of the largest firms in the state, it is well known for its varied practice and provides advice on the full spectrum of labor and employment matters. The team's workload combines defense of employment discrimination claims under a number of statutes with the representation of employers in union-organizing campaigns and elections.
The Lawyers: Oscar Davis is a former attorney at the NLRB and continues to practice in the labor field although peers also recognized him as

LITIGATION — ARKANSAS

a leading light in OSHA matters. His colleague **Michael Moore** was also admired as an attorney with *"lots of ability and good judgment."*
The Clients: Clients include leading national corporates.

Mitchell Williams Selig Gates Woodyard, PLLC
The Firm: Although it does not have the high profile of some of its principal competitors, the firm has acknowledged experience in the field, and was particularly rated for employment law advice. Here, it has represented management in a host of lawsuits arising from claims of discrimination, defamation and wrongful termination. It also has labor law capability and, as an adjunct to the practice, a small group of lawyers is on hand to advise on ERISA issues.
The Lawyers: Known primarily for his defense of discrimination cases, **Byron Freeland** was identified to researchers as the group's key individual. He was described as a *"reliable guy,"* and has represented one of the largest hospital systems in Arkansas in a Title VII defense.
The Clients: Clients include major national corporates.

Rose Law Firm
The Firm: The firm's workload includes assisting clients on the defense of lawsuits under Title VII, ADA, ADEA, FMLA and OSHA. It also has experience in state and federal courts, and has represented clients before both the EEOC and the NLRB.
The Lawyers: With only a couple of other individuals specializing in this area at the firm, the group's profile is owed almost exclusively to **Tim Boe**. Recommended for the depth of his experience, he is known as a *"determined and thorough"* lawyer who is knowledgeable in both labor and employment fields.
The Clients: Clients include leading national corporates.

Other Notable Practitioners
Based in Pine Bluff, **Spencer Robinson** of Ramsay, Bridgforth, Harrelson & Starling was commended to researchers as a *"hard-working and personable"* attorney. His broad practice has seen him negotiate contracts with steelworkers and he frequently appears on NLRA proceedings.

LITIGATION — GENERAL COMMERCIAL

ARKANSAS
Leading firms
(Litigation: General Commercial)
1. **FRIDAY, ELDREDGE & CLARK** Little Rock
2. **MITCHELL WILLIAMS SELIG GATES** Little Rock
3. **QUATTLEBAUM, GROOMS** Little Rock
   WRIGHT, LINDSEY & JENNINGS LLP Little Rock
4. **ROSE LAW FIRM** Little Rock
   WILLIAMS & ANDERSON LLP Little Rock

Leading individuals
(Litigation: General Commercial)
1. **QUATTLEBAUM Steven** Quattlebaum, Little Rock
   SHEMIN Ken Shemin Law Firm, Fayetteville
   SUTTON William Friday, Eldredge & Clark, Little Rock
2. **CRASS Kevin** Friday, Eldredge & Clark, Little Rock
   GATES Allan Mitchell Williams Selig Gates, Little Rock
   KAPLAN Philip Kaplan, Brewer, Maxey, Little Rock
3. **BEARD Richard** Mitchell Williams Selig Gates, Little Rock
   DONOVAN Richard Rose Law Firm, Little Rock
   KUMPE Peter Williams & Anderson LLP, Little Rock
   NESTRUD Charles Chisenhall Nestrud, Little Rock
   POWELL David Wright Lindsey, Little Rock

Firms and individuals are listed alphabetically in each band.

Friday, Eldredge & Clark
The Firm: Commentators were adamant that the firm *"is well in advance of others in Arkansas for litigation."* Rivals commended both the breadth of the firm's practice and the size of its resources, which allow the group to *"dominate"* big-ticket cases.
The Lawyers: Managing partner **William Sutton**, whose *"mastery"* in the courtroom is said to *"exceed that of anyone in town,"* emerges as the firm's leading attorney. Described to researchers as *"formidable,"* he handles numerous defense cases in the business tort and contract fields. He was general attorney for Union Pacific Railroad and represented Brunswick in an antitrust case as primary appellate lawyer. **Kevin Crass** also received his share of market commendation as an *"accomplished and experienced"* litigator. Several peers endorsed his *"impressive"* judgment, adding that *"he knows exactly what he's doing in court."* He has undertaken defense work in class actions brought by consumers and accounting clients, and was also instructed by Arkansas brokers in a dispute involving securities claims.
The Clients: Clients include: Ernst & Young; Hewlett-Packard; Regions Bank; ALLTEL; St. Paul; Entergy Arkansas and Oaklawn Jockey Club.

Mitchell Williams Selig Gates Woodyard, PLLC
The Firm: The firm continues to enjoy a large stake in major commercial litigation work and its attorneys attract plaudits for their *"consistently high quality."* Securities litigation prowess accompanies other niche strengths in environment and insurance defense disputes.
The Lawyers: **Allan Gates** is a *"capable and highly experienced"* litigator who was one of the first in Arkansas to develop an environmental practice. He was instructed to represent a regional group of cities involving 400,000 citizens in an interstate dispute over water quality standards in Oklahoma. He was also lead counsel for Raytheon in an air quality and hazardous waste lawsuit involving the incineration of chemical weapons at the Pine Bluff Arsenal. **Richard Beard** also elicits enthusiastic backing for his *"courtroom presence."*
The Clients: Clients include 3M and Weyerhaeuser.

Quattlebaum, Grooms, Tull & Burrow PLLC
see firm details p.868
The Firm: The firm was created by defections from Williams & Anderson in mid-2000 and competes favorably with established competitors. One interviewee remarked that the group includes *"quality attorneys across the board"* who counsel a portfolio of substantial clients. The firm has developed considerable experience in the toxic tort and environment arena, and also undertakes a high volume of complex commercial work in antitrust and breach of fiduciary duty cases.
The Lawyers: Spearheading the business litigation group is the *"poised and effective"* **Steve Quattlebaum** (see p.27). A *"high-grade"* trial lawyer, he is renowned for toxic tort (particularly Superfund cases) and products liability disputes. He served as co-counsel for Mercedes-Benz in a case brought against the manufacturer's air bags.
The Clients: Clients include: Merck & Co; Schering-Plough; Nissan; Wal-Mart; Johnson & Johnson; Union Carbide; BASF; Koppers Industries; Shell Oil; Texaco and Uniroyal Chemical.

Wright, Lindsey & Jennings LLP
The Firm: A respected and *"honorable"* firm, its strengths in this field lie in corporate, tax and insurance litigation. Its client base among insurance companies is particularly healthy, while tort defense litigation is another area of expertise, especially on products liability cases. Attorneys defended BPS in lawsuits brought against the manufacturer's agricultural chemicals.
The Lawyers: The respected **David Powell** is the headline commercial litigator at the firm. *"Older and wiser than most,"* he impresses peers with his *"consummate"* judgment.
The Clients: Clients include: CAN Insurance;

ARKANSAS

REAL ESTATE

Scottsdale Insurance; Ohio Casualty Group; Nationwide Insurance; Prudential Life; Highland and Bank of America.

Rose Law Firm
The Firm: Some recent personnel defections have not reduced the standing of this respected litigation group. Research confirms that the group's size, wide litigation capabilities and strong client base guarantee it a sizable slice of major local commercial work. The business litigation team represented Volvo's truck division in an antitrust case, and the team was also instructed by GM and Firestone in defense of two multi-state consumer fraud cases.
The Lawyers: **Richard Donovan** consistently received praise as a *"thoroughly admirable"* litigator.
The Clients: Clients include Stephens Group, Ford, Volvo, Firestone and GMAC.

Williams & Anderson LLP
see firm details p.898
The Firm: This *"solid"* firm offers a generalist litigation practice with particular expertise in antitrust defense and as appellate counsel for insurance companies. The team has been instructed by local media and news-gathering organizations in trade regulation and libel cases, and has also advised banking clients on lender liability issues.
The Lawyers: **Peter Kumpe** received warm endorsement as a *"successful appellate lawyer"* and has undertaken a number of high-profile cases. He represented Miller Brewing in a distributor dispute before the regulatory board, and acted on a dispute with Arkansas tobacco wholesalers in a pricing issue under the fair trade statute.
The Clients: Clients include: Camden News Publishing; Arkansas-Democrat Gazette; Wal-Mart and GE.

Other Notable Practitioners
Fayetteville-based sole practitioner **Ken Shemin** is regarded as the *"finest attorney of his kind."* An alumnus of Rose Law Firm, he specializes in trade secrets, intellectual property and corporate securities. As trial lawyers go, peers confirm that there are *"none brighter"* than **Philip Kaplan** of Kaplan, Brewer, Maxey & Haralson. He is said to run an *"exceedingly vibrant practice,"* specializing in complex business cases. **Charles Nestrud** of Chisenhall, Nestrud & Julian, PA is highly regarded by contemporaries and has a reputation as an expert on environment disputes.

REAL ESTATE

ARKANSAS
Leading firms (Real Estate)
1. MITCHELL WILLIAMS SELIG GATES *Little Rock*
   WRIGHT, LINDSEY & JENNINGS LLP *Little Rock*
2. DOVER DIXON HORNE *Little Rock*
   QUATTLEBAUM, GROOMS *Little Rock*
3. HANKINS & HICKS *Little Rock*
   KUTAK ROCK LLP *Little Rock*

Leading individuals (Real Estate)
1. BARRIER Christopher *Mitchell William, Little Rock*
   DOVER Darrell *Dover Dixon Horne, Little Rock*
   GROOMS Tim *Quattlebaum, Grooms, Little Rock*
   SPIVEY John *Wright, Lindsey & Jennings, Little Rock*
2. MITCHELL Maurice *Mitchell Williams, Little Rock*
3. HANKINS Stuart *Hankins & Hicks, Little Rock*
   SCHALLHORN Scott *Kutak Rock LLP, Little Rock*

Firms and individuals are listed alphabetically in each band.

Mitchell Williams Selig Gates Woodyard, PLLC
The Firm: Widely proclaimed as *"the best in Arkansas,"* the real estate department of this large full-service outfit acts in a broad range of real estate transactions. A group of nine lawyers undertakes acquisitions, dispositions, leasing, financing, construction contract negotiation, tax-deferred exchanges and low income housing tax credits for a corporate, retail and family client base. The group represented the seller in the largest transfer of privately held real estate assets in the state's history.
The Lawyers: Researchers were told that **Chris Barrier** has been at *"the top of the profession for many years."* He is chiefly distinguished by his track record in lending work. **Maurice Mitchell** was also singled out by interviewees as an *"ethical and professional"* transactional lawyer.
The Clients: Clients include major national corporates and financial institutions.

Wright, Lindsey & Jennings LLP
The Firm: This old-time Arkansas firm, now in its hundredth year, is acknowledged by rivals as *"a clear leader"* for real estate advice. Around 12 lawyers practice in a range of commercial real estate transactions, including development, acquisitions, zoning, land use, leasing and financing.
The Lawyers: Leading figure **John Spivey** won universal praise from peers as a *"capable and likable"* practitioner.
The Clients: Clients include Wal-Mart.

Dover Dixon Horne
The Firm: In addition to an active lending practice, the firm also performs substantial transactional real estate work for commercial realtors.
The Lawyers: Its reputation in this sphere, however, is inextricably linked with that of founding partner and *"true gentleman"* **Darrell Dover**. Principally devoted to real estate financing transactions, he is general counsel to the Arkansas Teacher Retirement System (ATRS), for whom he undertakes loans, equity purchases and investments in limited liability companies. He represented ATRS on the formation of a joint venture with Cooper Realty Investments for the $75 million purchase of office buildings in Nashville, Tennessee.
The Clients: Clients include corporates.

Quattlebaum, Grooms, Tull & Burrow PLLC
see firm details p.868
The Firm: This relative newcomer to the Arkansas landscape has made a big impression in the real estate arena. Considered to have taken the *"cream of the crop"* from Williams & Anderson, the firm now boasts a *"solid bedrock"* of experienced transactional lawyers. The group represents regional and national developers, lenders and brokers on a full range of real estate transactions.
The Lawyers: Commentators say that **Tim Grooms** (see p.27) *"does his homework"* on large loan deals, and he was strongly endorsed as an *"aggressive but experienced"* practitioner.
The Clients: Clients include: Arkansas REALTORS Association; Arkansas Home Builder's Association; Waste Management and Arkansas Community Bankers Association.

Hankins & Hicks
The Firm: A small group of three attorneys owe much of their real estate presence to a large developer client in North Little Rock. Although lacking the resources of the larger firms, the group nonetheless won praise from peers for its *"uniform quality."*
The Lawyers: Rivals are happy to refer work to **Stuart Hankins**.
The Clients: Clients include developers.

Kutak Rock LLP
The Firm: The Little Rock office of this national firm undertakes primarily transactional real estate work for its corporate client base. It also acts for a number of developer clients on the financing and development of projects around Little Rock and

ARKANSAS

northwest Arkansas, and undertakes work on low income housing tax credits.
The Lawyers: Peers and clients all endorsed Scott Schallhorn as *"knowledgeable and easy to work with."* His is a broad practice, covering acquisitions and disposals of commercial real estate, and financing for a largely developer client base.
The Clients: Clients include Tyson Foods.

Leaders in Arkansas

BARRIER, Christopher
Mitchell Williams Selig Gates Woodyard, PLLC, Little Rock 501 688 8800
Recommended in Real Estate

BEARD, Richard
Mitchell Williams Selig Gates Woodyard, PLLC, Little Rock 501 688 8800
Recommended in Litigation

BENHAM, Paul
Friday, Eldredge & Clark, Little Rock
501 376 2011
Recommended in Corporate/M&A

BOE, Tim
Rose Law Firm, Little Rock
501 375 9131
Recommended in Employment

BUFORD, Douglas
Wright, Lindsey & Jennings LLP, Little Rock 501 371 0808
Recommended in Corporate/M&A

BURNETT, John
Lavey & Burnett, Little Rock
501 376 2269
Recommended in Employment

CRASS, Kevin
Friday, Eldredge & Clark, Little Rock
501 376 2011
Recommended in Litigation

DAVIS, Oscar
Friday, Eldredge & Clark, Little Rock
501 376 2011
Recommended in Employment

DONOVAN, Richard
Rose Law Firm, Little Rock
501 375 9131
Recommended in Litigation

DOVER, Darrell
Dover Dixon Horne, Little Rock
501 375 9151
Recommended in Real Estate

FREELAND, Byron
Mitchell Williams Selig Gates Woodyard, PLLC, Little Rock 501 688 8800
Recommended in Employment

GATES, Allan
Mitchell Williams Selig Gates Woodyard, PLLC, Little Rock 501 688 8800
Recommended in Litigation

GRAVES, Kathlyn
Wright, Lindsey & Jennings LLP, Little Rock 501 371 0808
Recommended in Employment

GROOMS, Timothy
Quattlebaum, Grooms, Tull & Burrow PLLC, Little Rock 501 379 1713
tgrooms@qgtb.com
Recommended in Real Estate
Specialization: Primary areas of practice are banking law, real estate, acquisitions and financing, and he serves as General Counsel to the Arkansas REALTORS Association, Arkansas Homebuilders Association and the Arkansas Community Bankers.
Prof. Memberships: American, Arkansas and Pulaski County Bar Associations.
Career: Admitted to the Arkansas Bar (1984). A founding partner of *Quattlebaum, Grooms, Tull & Burrow PLLC.* Licensed real estate broker, Arkansas, 1979.
Personal: Received a JD (with high honors) from the University of Arkansas at Little Rock Law School in 1984 and a BBA (magna cum laude) from the University of Arkansas at Little Rock in 1981.

GUNTER, Russell
Cross, Gunter, Witherspoon & Galchus, PC, Little Rock 501 371 9999
Recommended in Employment

HANKINS, Stuart
Hankins & Hicks, Little Rock
501 371 9226
Recommended in Real Estate

HARMON, Melva
Melva Harmon - Sole Practitioner, Little Rock 501 372 1133
Recommended in Employment

HUNT, Eugene
Hunt Law Firm, Pine Bluff
870 535 4967
Recommended in Employment

KAPLAN, Philip
Kaplan, Brewer, Maxey & Haralson, Little Rock 501 372 0500
Recommended in Litigation

KUMPE, Peter
Williams & Anderson LLP, Little Rock
501 372 0800
Recommended in Litigation

LAVEY, Jack
Lavey & Burnett, Little Rock
501 376 2269
Recommended in Employment

MITCHELL, Maurice
Mitchell Williams Selig Gates Woodyard, PLLC, Little Rock 501 688 8800
Recommended in Real Estate

MOORE, Michael
Friday, Eldredge & Clark, Little Rock
501 376 2011
Recommended in Employment

NESTRUD, Charles
Chisenhall, Nestrud & Julian, PA, Little Rock 501 372 5800
Recommended in Litigation

POWELL, David
Wright, Lindsey & Jennings LLP, Little Rock 501 371 0808
Recommended in Litigation

QUATTLEBAUM, Steven
Quattlebaum, Grooms, Tull & Burrow PLLC, Little Rock 501 379 1707
quattlebaum@qgtb.com
Recommended in Litigation
Specialization: Primary areas of practice include business, products liability, environmental and toxic tort litigation.
Prof. Memberships: American Board of Trial Advocates, Products Liability Advisory Council, William R Overton Inn of Court.
Career: Admitted to the Arkansas Bar (1984). A founding partner of *Quattlebaum, Grooms, Tull & Burrow PLLC.*
Publications: Defending the Institution of Trial by Jury, Voire Dire, Fall 2001; Effective Video Presentations at Trial, Arkansas Lawyer, Spring and Summer 1993.
Personal: Received a JD from the University of Arkansas at Fayetteville 1983 and a BA from Western State College of Colorado in 1981.

ROBINSON, Spencer
Ramsay, Bridgforth, Harrelson & Starling LLP, Pine Bluff 870 535 9000
Recommended in Employment

SCHALLHORN, Scott
Kutak Rock LLP, Little Rock
501 975 3000
Recommended in Real Estate

SELIG, John
Mitchell Williams Selig Gates Woodyard, PLLC, Little Rock 501 688 8800
Recommended in Corporate/M&A

SHEMIN, Ken
Shemin Law Firm, Fayetteville
479 973 4442
Recommended in Litigation

SPIVEY, John
Wright, Lindsey & Jennings LLP, Little Rock 501 371 0808
Recommended in Real Estate

SUTTER, Luther
Harrill & Sutter PLLC, Little Rock
501 224 1050
Recommended in Employment

SUTTON, William
Friday, Eldredge & Clark, Little Rock
501 376 2011
Recommended in Litigation

WALKER, John
John Walker - Sole Practitioner, Little Rock 501 374 3758
Recommended in Employment

WELCH, Morgan
Eubanks, Welch, Baker & Schulze, Little Rock 501 537 1000
Recommended in Employment

WITHERSPOON, Carolyn
Cross, Gunter, Witherspoon & Galchus, PC, Little Rock 501 371 9999
Recommended in Employment

CALIFORNIA

OVERVIEW

CONTENTS: Antitrust p.29; Banking p.30; Capital Markets p.32; Communications p.34; Construction p.36; Corporate/M&A p.37; Employment p.39; Energy & Natural Resources p.41; Environment p.42; Insolvency p.44; Insurance p.46; Intellectual Property p.47; Litigation: General Commercial p.49; Media & Entertainment p53; Projects p.55; Real Estate p.56; Tax p.58; Individuals' Profiles p.60.

CALIFORNIA'S TOP NINE
1. Latham & Watkins
2. Gibson, Dunn & Crutcher
3. O'Melveny & Myers
4. Morrison & Foerster
5. Wilson Sonsini Goodrich & Rosati
6. Skadden, Arps, Slate, Meagher & Flom
7. Orrick, Herrington & Sutcliffe
8. Cooley Godward
9. Milbank, Tweed, Hadley & McCloy

Ranking based on Chambers' research within the state.

All quotes in the text are from interviews with clients and competitors.

OVERVIEW: Latham & Watkins boasts 21 offices worldwide. It comfortably beat its West Coast rivals in the most recent fee income tables. So, it is appropriate that it should emerge from Chambers' research as the strongest and broadest practice in California. It does well in almost every table, topping four: corporate; environment; projects and tax. In project finance it is the center of gravity for West Coast financings, acting in such deals as the $3.5 billion Calpine Construction Finance Corporation I & II power projects. The tax team, meanwhile, is said to have achieved dominance in M&A tax law. In M&A itself, Paul Tosetti remains "second to none," while the combination of Christopher (Kit) Kaufman and Alan Mendelson is largely responsible for the firm's growing profile in IT and life sciences, and in the Bay Area generally.

The next two firms to emerge from our research are also large, traditional, LA-centered operations, with superb links to blue-chip corporates. **Gibson, Dunn & Crutcher** tops the tables in corporate, banking, litigation and antitrust. Antitrust, in particular, is a strong suit of the practice. It works well with its DC office and boasts, in Bob Cooper, a candidate for the premier antitrust litigator in the country. Litigation generally is a strength, the firm's top-tier practice having won major cases for George W Bush, Dow Jones and DaimlerChrysler. Meanwhile "star of the show" Andy Bogan ensures the firm's M&A profile remains high.

It shares top banking honors with **O'Melveny & Myers**. The firm, with structured finance guru Jim De Meules, won praise for its impressive lender client base and formidable track record in a range of financings. It is less of a player in M&A, but its banking expertise gives it prominence in areas such as insolvency and real estate finance. Its litigation department too is said to have no weak links. It is the only full-service corporate firm to have made a big impression in LA's entertainment industry, where its clients include The Anschutz Entertainment Group, EMI, Warner Bros. and Yahoo!

The northern Californian market, which is more dependent on hi-tech start-ups and equity financing, has been quieter than the southern part of the state. The lower showing of the leading San Francisco firms in Chambers' tables perhaps reflects this. **Morrison & Foerster** "jumps out of the pack" for its litigation expertise. Its large team boasts, in James Brosnahan, arguably the state's highest profile litigator. IP is another area of strength. Its full-service IP practice won plaudits for quality in depth. The firm is also gaining a growing reputation for its international profile in its core areas.

Wilson Sonsini Goodrich & Rosati has led the field for equity capital markets for some time, with an enormous share of the state's IPOs. This work has obviously been quieter, but the firm is making strides in high yield debt and derivatives. Many interviewees still rate it "in a class of its own." It also retains its traditional dominance of the communications field. Bay Area guru and miracle worker Larry Sonsini is acknowledged to have built the Valley and ensures the firm's continuing hegemony, especially of hi-tech M&A and venture capital. In the litigation arena, the firm excels in IP, employment and, especially, securities class action defense. It represented Hewlett-Packard in the high-profile litigation surrounding its $19 million merger with Compaq.

The fourth of the big, LA-focused corporate specialists is **Skadden, Arps, Slate, Meagher & Flom.** The Wall Street giant was one of the first East coast firms to move into California, in 1983. Commentators say that it has adapted well, most notably in the more mid-sized corporate market. The firm is smaller than some of its rivals, but highly focused. It only features in five tables, but reaches the top band of two. Its stylish capital markets practice, in particular, is a major presence. It is known for all forms of debt and high yield finance and has superb links to investment banks, notably CSFB.

Orrick, Herrington & Sutcliffe is an institution in San Francisco, with a broad practice. It is known, for example, for its expertise in bank regulatory work and structured finance. It also has a high profile for employment defense work, and a reputation for quality over quantity. It is in the troubled energy sector, however, that its reputation is highest. The firm played a leading role in the formation of Pacific Gas & Electric and, following its insolvency, is assisting it in the divestiture of assets.

Cooley Godward acted opposite Wilson Sonsini in the long-running battle over the Hewlett-Packard/Compaq merger, winning praise for its advice. However, this powerhouse in the hi-tech sphere is best known for its corporate activity. For example, it represented COR Therapeutics on its acquisition by Millennium Pharmaceuticals, in a deal valued at around $2 billion.

Milbank, Tweed, Hadley & McCloy is the only firm to combine a top name in both the energy and insolvency fields. So it is no surprise to find it playing a major role in the PG&E case, one of the largest ever insolvencies in the state, where Paul Aronzon is representing the committee of unsecured creditors. On the transactional side, Edwin Feo is the state's "Mr Energy." The firm also has a top international name for project financing, and has acted in deals such as the $3.2 billion Barracuda oil platform project in Brazil.

ANTITRUST

CALIFORNIA

ANTITRUST

CALIFORNIA
Leading firms (Antitrust)
1. GIBSON, DUNN & CRUTCHER LLP *Los Angeles*
2. LATHAM & WATKINS *Los Angeles*
3. HELLER EHRMAN WHITE LLP *San Francisco*
4. HOWREY SIMON ARNOLD & WHITE *Los Angeles*
   O'MELVENY & MYERS LLP *Los Angeles*
5. BINGHAM MCCUTCHEN LLP *San Francisco*
   BLECHER & COLLINS *Los Angeles*
   MORRISON & FOERSTER LLP *San Francisco*

Leading individuals (Antitrust)
1. COOPER Robert *Gibson, Dunn & Crutcher*, Los Angeles
2. ROSCH Tom *Latham & Watkins*, San Francisco
   WALL Daniel *Latham & Watkins*, San Francisco
3. BLECHER Maxwell *Blecher & Collins*, Los Angeles
   BOMSE Stephen *Heller Ehrman*, San Francisco
   LYNCH Patrick *O'Melveny & Myers LLP*, Los Angeles
   POPOFSKY Laurence *Heller Ehrman*, San Francisco
   SPRATLING Gary *Gibson, Dunn & Crutcher*, San Francisco
4. COMPTON Charles *Wilson Sonsini Goodrich*, Palo Alto
   GOLDMAN Melvin *Morrison & Foerster*, San Francisco
   HOCKETT Chris *Bingham McCutchen*, San Francisco
   NOLAN Tom *Howrey Simon Arnold & White*, Los Angeles
   PICKETT Donn *Bingham McCutchen LLP*, San Francisco
   PREOVOLOS Penelope *Morrison & Foerster*, San Francisco
   ROSENFELD Robert *Heller Ehrman*, San Francisco
   SWANSON Daniel *Gibson Dunn*, Los Angeles
   TAYLOR Robert *Howrey Simon Arnold*, Menlo Park

Firms and individuals are listed alphabetically in each band.

Gibson, Dunn & Crutcher LLP

The Firm: Antitrust has long been a hallmark of the firm and its strong regulatory practice in Washington DC is complemented by trial expertise in Los Angeles. Regarded by peers as a *"dynamo"* in California, this diverse group is active in a range of antitrust counseling and litigation, including private treble damages, preliminary injunction litigation and class action defense for an international clientele.

The Lawyers: Among a formidable team, **Bob Cooper** shines. Revered by contemporaries as a *"marvelous oral advocate,"* his courtroom manner was described to researchers as *"highly persuasive, charming and genuine,"* with clients commending his ability to *"connect with all audiences."* He has recently acted on the Hewlett-Packard dispute involving Intel, where he has cemented his reputation as *"the premier antitrust litigator in the country."* The group's international and criminal practice has been bolstered with last year's recruitment of **Gary Spratling**. Formerly with the antitrust division of the US Department of Justice, he was strongly endorsed as a *"guru"* in civil and criminal antitrust litigation, and is particularly known for his work in international criminal enforcement and merger activities. He appeared for Akzo Nobel on a recent anti-cartel investigation. Also active in the group's international practice is **Dan Swanson**. Rivals commended him as an *"extremely analytical"* and *"highly talented"* antitrust practitioner. He represented CVC in the appeal over its proposed acquisition of Austrian fibers manufacturer Lenzing.

The Clients: Elsewhere, the group celebrated a notable victory, now subject to appeal, for American Airlines against smaller operators in a case alleging predatory pricing activities. Honeywell, Akzo Nobel and CVC are all active clients.

Latham & Watkins
see firm details p.835

The Firm: As well as acting for a diverse base of Fortune 500 clients on regulatory matters, class action and treble damages defense, the group undertakes a wide range of merger control work. With the opening of its Brussels office in 2001, it is now considered by rivals to be a presence in the global as well as domestic antitrust markets. Clients paid tribute to the *"genuine expertise"* of the department's lawyers, singling out the quality of their written work for particularly high praise.

The Lawyers: A *"sophisticated old warhorse of the antitrust bar,"* **Tom Rosch** (see p.71) leads the group. He handles both regulatory and merger control work and was commended to researchers as *"a classic gentleman with a robust practice." "Capable and assertive litigator"* **Dan Wall** (see p.74) *"loves to get his teeth into cases."* Clients described him as *"responsive and hard-working"* and appreciate his *"clear, direct and forceful"* style. Best known for his hi-tech work, he recently advised on the proposed $16 billion acquisition of biotech company Immunex by Amgen.

The Clients: The group has been involved in the high-profile California Wholesale Electricity class actions, which were brought by customers and government bodies following electricity price increases in 2000. Intel, Gillette, Mars and DaimlerChrysler are clients.

Heller Ehrman White & McAuliffe LLP

The Firm: Principally known for its litigation prowess, the firm's antitrust group was frequently lauded by clients as a *"first-rate"* operation. It has been prominent in a number of high-profile appeals, acting as principal antitrust counsel to long-standing client Visa, and advising Microsoft on litigation arising from its hotly contested dispute with the US Department of Justice.

The Lawyers: Peers endorsed practice cochair **Steve Bomse** for his *"academically rigorous"* litigation style. He was commended to researchers as *"the brains behind the outfit and a brilliant brief writer,"* although commentators singled out other members of the team for their courtroom flair. **Larry Popofsky** is renowned as an appellate specialist. He is said to have *"practically defined the field in California,"* playing an instrumental role in many prominent US Supreme Court cases. The group is acting for Visa in the high-profile 'merchant' case brought by a class of around four million retailers, including Wal-Mart, Safeway and Sears Roebuck, and worth around $100 billion, as well as advising on the New York consumer class action concerning Visa's fees for foreign currency conversion. **Bob Rosenfeld** completes a strong lineup, and is principally known for his work managing the Microsoft antitrust wars. The caseload has included advising on the defense to damages claims filed by individual consumers, arising from a US Department of Justice antitrust ruling.

The Clients: Microsoft, 3M and Visa are among the firm's respected clients.

Howrey Simon Arnold & White

The Firm: A growing force in both the domestic and international antitrust markets, the firm is said to have *"splashed headlong into the pool"* with the opening in 2002 of a Brussels office. Supported by a large DC office, a smaller group of about ten dedicated antitrust lawyers in California is chiefly recognized for its litigation expertise.

The Lawyers: Although now heavily involved in IP law, **Bob Taylor** is still considered to be a leading antitrust player at the firm. Clients consider him to be *"at the top of his game,"* and he advises on a wide range of antitrust work for entities such as semiconductor manufacturer Tokyo Seimitsu and a range of biotech and IT companies. **Tom Nolan** was strongly endorsed for his *"careful, high-quality"* expertise in a number of *"titanic"* cases. Rivals ruefully conceded that *"he has been a real thorn in our side,"* and his victory on behalf of ring laser gyroscope manufacturer Litton Systems over Honeywell resulted in one of the largest settlements in the history of The Sherman Act – some $440 million. He is also acting for hair products manufacturer and Wella subsidiary Sebastian International in antitrust litigation brought by grocery chain Albertson's.

The Clients: Intel; Litton Systems; American Airlines and Sebastian International.

O'Melveny & Myers LLP

The Firm: The firm's antitrust team in California is sometimes felt to be overshadowed by its DC group. However, peers nonetheless commended this litigation-focused group as a *"player of significance"* in its Los Angeles homeland.

The Lawyers: At the center of the team is *"bigname"* **Pat Lynch**. He was consistently endorsed by peers for his ability to *"combine technical expertise with the ability to reach juries,"* and is known for his work on a number of high-profile matters, including representing software company Bristol Technologies in its antitrust action against Microsoft. He has recently acted for Gemstar-TV

CALIFORNIA — ANTITRUST

Guide International in its patent infringement litigation against EchoStar, Pioneer and Scientific-Atlanta taken up to the ITC.
The Clients: The firm has a respected client base, which features Gemstar-TV Guide International.

Bingham McCutchen LLP
The Firm: The group maintains its reputation as an *"excellent litigation shop,"* a reputation that should be reinforced following the firm's long-awaited decision to merge with Boston-based Bingham Dana. In addition to a range of antitrust litigation, the firm also undertakes merger control, joint venture and licensing advice across a range of industries including telecommunications, software and transport.
The Lawyers: *"Rainmaker"* **Donn Pickett** is said to stand out. Currently acting for luxury goods manufacturer LVMH in the consumer antitrust class action against cosmetic industry defendants, he was also involved in the Kodak and uranium cartel cases. The team's *"rising star"* is felt to be **Chris Hockett**. Commentators believe that he is *"well received by juries."* He acted in the high-profile *San Francisco Chronicle* case against Hearst, as well as defending a Japanese importing company accused of price-fixing in the Alaskan salmon market.
The Clients: LVMH; Microsoft; AT&T Wireless; AT&T and Covad Communications.

Blecher & Collins
The Firm: The firm's name is inextricably linked with that of its star plaintiff lawyer **Max Blecher**. Universally applauded as a *"spectacular trial lawyer,"* his accessible courtroom manner and *"man of the people"* persona is said to *"charm the socks off jurors."* He is best known for his high-profile victory for independent service operators over Kodak, and is a ubiquitous presence in consumer class action antitrust litigation. Here, he wins substantial peer commendation as a *"formidable foe"* and a lawyer of *"enormous integrity."*
The Clients: Handgards and ABC International Traders are clients.

Morrison & Foerster LLP
see firm details p.854
The Firm: Market observers generally associate the firm with its hi-tech antitrust practice, where it acts on a range of litigation and counseling, from distribution, advertising and monopoly cases to class action defense and criminal investigations.
The Lawyers: Noted for his work on antitrust cases in the pharmaceutical industry, **Mel Goldman** (see p.64) received plaudits as an *"incredibly thorough and thoughtful"* litigator. **Penelope Preovolos** (see p.70) stands out for her prolific writing and scholarship. Described to researchers as *"five feet of dynamite,"* she is said to be an *"effective and persuasive"* speaker, best known for her work with major client Apple. In addition to Robinson-Patman Act litigation, she also counsels a variety of hi-tech clients on resale price maintenance and exclusive dealing issues. She is currently defending Chanel in a consumer class action alleging conspiracy to engage in resale price maintenance.
The Clients: The firm advises, among others, Apple and Chanel.

Other Notable Practitioners
Charles Compton of Wilson Sonsini Goodrich & Rosati plies his trade at a firm that is not usually heralded for its antitrust prowess. However, he is regarded as a *"hugely competent"* antitrust generalist, typically to be found counselling clients from the hi-tech world.

BANKING & FINANCE

CALIFORNIA
Leading firms (Banking & Finance)

1. GIBSON, DUNN & CRUTCHER LLP *Los Angeles*
   O'MELVENY & MYERS LLP *Los Angeles*
2. LATHAM & WATKINS *Los Angeles*
   ORRICK, HERRINGTON *Los Angeles, San Francisco*
3. MORRISON & FOERSTER LLP *Los Angeles*
   PILLSBURY WINTHROP *Los Angeles, San Francisco*
   SHEPPARD, MULLIN, RICHTER *Los Angeles*

Leading individuals (Banking & Finance)

1. DE MEULES James *O'Melveny & Myers*, Los Angeles
2. KILB Brian *Gibson, Dunn & Crutcher LLP*, Los Angeles
   KIRBY Matthew *O'Melveny & Myers LLP*, Los Angeles
3. FARRAR Stanley *Sullivan & Cromwell LLP*, Los Angeles
   FIELDS Henry *Morrison & Foerster LLP*, Los Angeles
   HILSON John *Paul, Hastings, Janofsky*, Los Angeles
   PECK Rodney *Pillsbury Winthrop LLP*, San Francisco
4. BENJAMIN Alan *Orrick, Herrington*, Los Angeles
   BERCHILD John *Sheppard, Mullin, Richter*, Los Angeles
   COLEMAN Thomas *Orrick, Herrington*, San Francisco

Firms and individuals are listed alphabetically in each band.

Gibson, Dunn & Crutcher LLP
The Firm: Considered by commentators to have a broader finance practice than many of its Californian rivals, the firm was especially commended to researchers for its work on the lenders' side. Its national reputation for M&A work translates into a substantial volume of acquisition finance, refinancing and restructuring, on which the group frequently advises in association with offices in New York, London and Paris. Team members also handle debt and structured financing, high yield bond offerings, project finance and securitizations for a range of hi-tech corporates, sponsored equity funds and international banks. Real estate finance is also recognized to be a niche area of expertise for the firm.
The Lawyers: *"Excellent communicator"* **Brian Kilb** has a general commercial practice in secured and unsecured lending, banking and corporate finance. Described by peers as *"a well-balanced practitioner,"* he is also respected for his bank regulatory work.
The Clients: Clients include Wells Fargo, Intel and Gap.

O'Melveny & Myers LLP
The Firm: The firm is recognized to have *"a formidable track record"* on behalf of local financial institutions, who it has advised on acquisition financings, restructurings and securitizations. The department is split into two groups, financial institutions and financing, both concentrated primarily in the Los Angeles office. They frequently work with offices in London, Hong Kong, Shanghai and Tokyo on cross-border financing transactions, as well as arranging financing for local borrowers, notably in the media sector.
The Lawyers: **Jim De Meules** has a stellar reputation for advice on credit facilities and structured financing. Described to researchers as *"one of the finest lawyers in California,"* he represents both major lenders and borrowers such as insurance companies. Interviewees also recommended the vastly experienced **Matthew Kirby**, whose practice focuses on restructuring finance and acquisition financing.
The Clients: Together with the London and New York teams, the firm represented Dole Food Company in the disposition of its controlling interest in the Honduran beverage company, Cervecería Hondureña. Other clients include: CIGNA; Salomon Smith Barney; CSFB; BNP Paribas; Wells Fargo and Trust Company of the West.

BANKING & FINANCE — CALIFORNIA

Latham & Watkins
see firm details p.835

The Firm: Although it is not generally felt to have the individual stars of some of its principal competitors, the firm's size and international reach are recognized by peers to be *"powerful weapons for getting finance work."* The firm is most associated with project finance, but also offers expertise in complex structured products, syndicated loans and real estate finance.

The Lawyers: The team, which features Victoria Marmorstein, represented the underwriters (Merrill Lynch, Thomas Weisel Partners, Wells Fargo Securities and JPMorgan Chase) in the sale of shares in SangStat Medical, a medical manufacturer.

The Clients: The group represented American Express Asset Management in numerous collateralized debt obligations and structured finance products. Also acted for AOL Time Warner in structured finance transactions including the sale of receivables of various AOL Time Warner affiliates (Time, New Line Cinema and Turner Broadcasting). Other clients include: AIG Sun America; Citibank; Citicorp North America; Congress Financial; CSFB; Deutsche Bank; Dresdner Bank; First Nationwide Bank; GE Capital; National Bank of Canada; Royal Bank of Canada; The First National Bank of Chicago and Wells Fargo.

Orrick, Herrington & Sutcliffe
see firm details p.859

The Firm: Chambers' researchers were left in no doubt that the firm occupies a respected position in the finance sector, notably for bank regulatory and structured finance work. Present in San Francisco, Los Angeles and Sacramento, attorneys in California work closely with respected teams in New York and Washington DC, often acting on behalf of leading lenders. Restructuring, refinancing and workouts have also provided the team with major recent sources of instruction. The firm advised the agent bank in a $675 million syndicated credit facility to a leading owner and operator of riverboat and related entertainment in the Midwest and southern US. It also acted for the agent on a $2.5 billion syndicated credit facility for the US financing arm of a large automotive company. Active in the insurance sector, the team represented a group of insurance companies in an out-of-court restructuring of the debts of a leading construction company.

The Lawyers: Formerly counsel at California First Bank (now Union Bank of California), the *"hard-working and practical"* **Tom Coleman** (see p.62) represents major US financial institutions in syndicated and synthetic leasing work. Clients respect him for *"getting the deal done."* **Alan Benjamin** (see p.60) is primarily associated with his advice to Wells Fargo, and is said to have *"a practical approach"* to syndicated credits and restructurings.

The Clients: Clients include: Bank of America; ABN AMRO; Société Générale; Principal Life Insurance Company; CIGNA; CIT Group; Guaranty Business Credit and Fleet Capital.

Morrison & Foerster LLP
see firm details p.854

The Firm: The firm has an integrated global finance practice across Asia and Europe, and about 50 lawyers advise on a high volume of structured financing and securitizations. Known primarily for undertaking medium-ticket work for banks and credit card companies, the team is also noted for its experience of banking M&A and regulatory matters.

The Lawyers: In a large team, **Henry Fields** (see p.64) is considered to stand out from the pack. He represents major international banks in Asia, Europe and the US, and is especially highly regarded for banking M&A and regulatory advice. Representing both banks, he acted on the merger of Sanwa Bank California and The Tokai Bank of California, which resulted in the formation of United California Bank. He represented United California Bank on its $2.4 billion sale to Bank of the West (BNP Paribas) and acted for The Bank of East Asia (Hong Kong) on its acquisition of Grand National Bank.

The Clients: Clients include: Visa; MasterCard; United California Bank; Star Systems and Bank SinoPac.

Pillsbury Winthrop LLP
see firm details p.866

The Firm: *"Certainly players in the market,"* the team has a solid reputation for regulatory advice, transactional work and acquisition finance. Its client portfolio continues to include a number of the country's most respected financial institutions.

The Lawyers: *"One of the most experienced lawyers on the scene"* is **Rodney Peck** (see p.70). Although particularly commended to researchers for his regulatory expertise, he also has wide experience of securities transactions, credit facilities and syndicated loans.

The Clients: NatWest Securities; Montgomery Securities; Bank of the West; Western Bank; BNP Paribas; Bank of America and Federal Home Loan Bank of San Francisco.

Sheppard, Mullin, Richter & Hampton LLP

The Firm: The firm's strength in this area is thought to lie in asset lending, real estate finance and bankruptcy-related work. Although it focuses exclusively on the Californian market and is smaller than its main rivals, the 20-attorney team has an enviable reputation for *"quality finance work"* on behalf of local financial institutions. The firm has represented bank syndicates on numerous secured lending transactions, and has wide experience of refinancing and workouts of defaulted bonds. The group acted for Northrop Grumman on the sale of debentures via a Rule 144A offering, which was a deal valued at $1.5 billion. It also represented Bank of Los Altos on its merger with Heritage Bank of Commerce.

The Lawyers: The leading light here is **John Berchild**, who rivals acknowledge as *"an accomplished finance specialist."*

The Clients: Clients include: Bank of America; Citicorp North America; Union Bank of California; Wells Fargo; Nissan Credit and California Bank & Trust.

Other Notable Practitioners

Stanley Farrar is the dominant personality of the banking team at the Los Angeles office of Sullivan & Cromwell. Market commentators recommended this versatile commercial lawyer for a broad practice that successfully combines M&A, securitizations and bank regulatory expertise. **John Hilson** was commended to researchers for his assest-based lending expertise. Peers saluted *"an outstanding all-around finance attorney,"* whose practice also covers workouts and debt financings. Following the dissolution of Brobeck, Phleger & Harrison LLP, Hilson has now joined the Los Angeles office of Paul, Hastings, Janofsky & Walker LLP.

CALIFORNIA

CAPITAL MARKETS

CALIFORNIA
Leading firms (Capital Markets)

1 SKADDEN, ARPS *Los Angeles*
WILSON SONSINI GOODRICH & ROSATI *Palo Alto*
2 DAVIS POLK & WARDWELL *Menlo Park*
LATHAM & WATKINS *Los Angeles*
3 COOLEY GODWARD LLP *San Francisco*
SIMPSON THACHER & BARTLETT *Palo Alto*
SULLIVAN & CROMWELL LLP *Los Angeles*
4 GIBSON, DUNN & CRUTCHER LLP *Los Angeles*
MILBANK, TWEED, HADLEY & McCLOY *Palo Alto*

Leading individuals (Capital Markets)

1 DALLAS Bruce *Davis Polk & Wardwell,* Menlo Park
SAGGESE Nicholas *Skadden, Arps, Slate,* Los Angeles
SONSINI Larry *Wilson Sonsini Goodrich,* Palo Alto
2 FORE John *Wilson Sonsini Goodrich,* Palo Alto
HINMAN William *Simpson Thacher,* Palo Alto
KING Kenton *Skadden, Arps, Slate, Meagher,* Palo Alto
RESSLER Alison *Sullivan & Cromwell LLP,* Los Angeles
3 BARONSKY Kenneth *Milbank, Tweed,* Los Angeles
BELLAH MAGUIRE Jennifer *Gibson, Dunn,* Los Angeles
LAZAROW Warren *O'Melveny & Myers LLP,* Menlo Park

Firms and individuals are listed alphabetically in each band.

Skadden, Arps, Slate, Meagher & Flom LLP & Affiliates
see firm details p.878

The Firm: Peers acknowledge that the New York firm has *"stylishly graced the market"* since opening in Los Angeles in 1983. Its capital markets practice competes directly with indigenous rivals and is recognized as the leading out-of-state presence in California. The success of the debt practice stems from links forged with the Los Angeles investment banking community, notably the erstwhile Drexel Burnham Lambert (later Donaldson, Lufkin & Jenrette), and CSFB. Clients praised the team's ability to advise on any form of debt and high yield finance, saying: *"It stands alone from New York, and has built up a great skill set of its own."*

The Lawyers: Los Angeles stalwart **Nick Saggese** (see p.71) was commended by financial institutions for his grasp of complex underwriting detail, and admired by corporates and buyout funds for his expertise in innovative leveraged finance structures. *"He's a businessman first, then a lawyer; he doesn't create problems just to be the hero who solves them."* In the younger Palo Alto office, respected all-rounder **Kenton King** (see p.66) was endorsed to researchers for an equity practice that straddles capital markets and M&A. Among a raft of high-profile equity deals, he was involved in McAfee.com's $880 million acquisition by Network Associates and acted for Compaq on its $18 billion purchase by Hewlett-Packard.

The Clients: The LA team represented Deutsche Bank Alex. Brown and Bear Stearns in Sun International's $200 million senior sub note issue, acted for CSFB on Liberty Media's $237 million note issue and advised PETCO Animal Supplies on its $200 million note issue. Other clients of the firm include: UBS Warburg; Goldman Sachs; Texas Pacific Group; Colony Capital; Leonard Green & Partners; Compaq; Yahoo!; Ascend Communications; AltaVista; DSP Communications; Robertson Stephens; Banc of America Securities; Chase H&Q; Lehman Brothers; Merrill Lynch; Salomon Smith Barney; Thomas Weisel Partners; Willamette Industries and Exodus Communications.

Wilson Sonsini Goodrich & Rosati

The Firm: Acknowledged to be *"in a class of its own,"* by some interviewees. For deal flow and slice of market share, it remains the one to beat. This legal technology powerhouse has an equity practice – up to half the firm's lawyer count – that outnumbers its smaller debt team.

The Lawyers: A group of senior partners, led by Bay Area guru **Larry Sonsini**, is said to run *"enormous public companies' practices,"* acting for a mix of telecom, IT, semiconductor and software businesses. The 30-lawyer debt team, headed by the respected **John Fore**, is said to have made great strides on high yield debt finance and derivatives transactions. Likened to a SWAT team, it is routinely called in to assist on the most thorny and complex of transactions. The group recently advised Goldman Sachs on a multibillion dollar derivatives-related offering for Albertson's, the second largest grocery chain in the US.

The Clients: Other deals include acting as financial advisers to Deutsche Bank Securities on the $1.3 billion merger of Ameritrade and Datek. The firm's client roster includes: Goldman Sachs; Morgan Stanley; Micron; Network Associates; InfoGation; Avanex and 3Dlabs.

Davis Polk & Wardwell

The Firm: Established in California in 1999, the group offers a powerful range of debt, securities and derivatives advice from offices in Menlo Park. Rival firms particularly acknowledge its success in the local bank underwriting market. The team has strong ties to Morgan Stanley and Salomon Smith Barney, and financial institutions confirmed the popularity of the practice as a *"creative sounding board for new securities products."* A notable derivatives practice offers expertise in pre- and post-paid equity forward transactions, and has handled a number of 'pipes' – equity private placements for a publicly traded company.

The Lawyers: Clients acclaimed **Bruce Dallas** to researchers for *"quarterbacking everything to the highest standard."* His practice encompasses equity derivatives, tech-related public offerings and IPOs. In 2002, his team acted for lead manager Salomon Smith Barney on the PayPal IPO. As issuer's counsel, the team also advised Comcast on a $1.5 billion offering of 'phones' convertible debentures. This tax-driven deal allowed the Philadelphia-based broadband cable company to monetize Comcast's ownership in Sprint's stock.

The Clients: Morgan Stanley; Salomon Smith Barney; E*TRADE and Comcast.

Latham & Watkins
see firm details p.835

The Firm: Everyone we spoke to commended the size and breadth of Latham's capital markets practice. One lawyer from a rival firm claimed that the team stood *"a cut above most local firms"* and was *"the closest I've seen to New York quality."* The range of debt and equity work undertaken, including a prolific high yield practice and a strong private equity team, gives some protection from market volatility. On the debt side, the team acted for Safeway on offerings totaling over $2 billion, advised Amgen on a Rule 144A $3.5 billion debt offering of liquid yield option notes (due 2032) and acted for Owens-Brockway in $1 billion of senior secured notes, due 2009. Equity matters include representing PETCO Animal Supplies on its $279 million IPO, advising Lehman Brothers as underwriter to ZymoGenetics' $120 million IPO, and acting for Merrill Lynch as co-underwriter of SangStat Medical's $89 million public equity offering of 4.5 million shares.

The Lawyers: Tracy Edmonson heads the Bay Area capital markets group, a unit handling complex high yield debt transactions and IPOs. The greatest concentration of partners, however, is in LA and includes the national corporate chair Tom Sadler and M&A lawyer Paul Tosetti, both of whom can move into capital markets territory.

The Clients: Safeway; Amgen; Owens-Brockway; PETCO Animal Supplies; Nike; Fleming Companies; Advanced Micro Devices; BRE Properties; Aderis Pharmaceuticals; ViaSat; Mission Energy Holding Company; JPMorgan; Merrill Lynch; Deutsche Bank; CSFB; Lehman Brothers; Bank of America; US Bancorp Piper Jaffray; Goldman Sachs; Adaptec and Aviron.

Cooley Godward LLP

The Firm: Despite the Valley's recent difficulties, the firm remains a leading force in the equity capital markets.

The Lawyers: Joseph Scherer (debt securities) and Kenneth Guernsey (corporate/venture capital) in San Francisco, and Mark Tanoury in Palo

CAPITAL MARKETS — CALIFORNIA

Alto, who heads the firm's 'business' department, are among the practice's major names.
The Clients: Applied Materials, Adobe Systems and LSI Logic are clients.

Simpson Thacher & Bartlett
The Firm: The team advises a mixture of issuers and underwriters in capital-raising transactions, with emphasis on public and private financings and IPOs. Activity is centered around business sectors such as e-commerce, healthcare and pharmaceuticals. Members of the team have expertise in derivatives, and also act for prominent private equity and venture capital firms such as Accel-KKR, Babcock & Brown and Blum Capital Partners. Transactions recently handled by the team include counseling Agilent Technologies on its $1 billion convertible debt offering, advising Abgenix in connection with its $200 million convertible debt offering, and representing Seagate Technology in a high yield bond offering and related refinancing. The firm also acted for Goldman Sachs and Morgan Stanley as underwriters on the IPO for Loudcloud.
The Lawyers: Bill Hinman is considered to be the driving force behind the push into California's capital markets. Fellow lawyers agree that his arrival from Shearman & Sterling in 2000 was *"something of a coup,"* which has enhanced the credibility of the Palo Alto unit.
The Clients: Seagate Technology; Agilent Technologies; drugstore.com; Morgan Stanley Dean Witter; Goldman Sachs; CSFB; Merrill Lynch; Apple; AirTouch Communications; Adobe Systems; MIPS Technologies; Silicon Graphics; Abgenix; Accenture; AOL Time Warner; Celera Genomics Group; Gemstar-TV Guide International; Global Crossing; GE Capital and Timogen Systems.

Sullivan & Cromwell
see firm details p.8117
The Firm: The firm's policy of exporting native New York talent to its other offices is felt to have reaped rewards in California. Both the 50-lawyer Los Angeles office (established in 1983) and the more recently opened premises in Palo Alto (17 lawyers) are felt to offer *"consistently high New York-style quality levels."* The offices work in tandem on the debt and equity capital markets, advising domestic and international issuers and investment banks. The workload also includes IPOs, secondary offerings, shelf registrations and securitized real estate transactions. Strong links to Goldman Sachs are reinforced by advice to heavyweight names such as UBS Warburg and CSFB. The firm represented underwriter Goldman Sachs in an $800 million high yield bond deal for Mission Energy Holding – an offering of senior secured notes under Rule 144A and Regulation S, and $385 million of borrowings under a new term loan facility. A team from Palo Alto led for the underwriters in three debt securities offerings by Gap during 2001 and 2002, and advised Nokia on the completion of a $440 million share exchange with Amber Networks.
The Lawyers: Financial clients and fellow lawyers praised LA-based **Alison Ressler** (see p.71) for her *"hands-on and energetic style."*
The Clients: Goldman Sachs; UBS Warburg; CSFB; NTT DoCoMo; SDL; Tenet Healthcare; Perlegen Sciences; The PMI Group; Nokia; Vodafone; Airborne; Amylin Pharmaceuticals; Catena Networks; Chiron; First Community Bancorp; Knight Ridder and OmniSky.

Gibson, Dunn & Crutcher LLP
The Firm: The firm's solid corporate clientele and transactional skills are said to support a successful, if understated, capital markets practice. Clients drew attention to the versatility of a unit that offers services across the debt and equity spectrum, although equity is said to be the stronger suit.
The Lawyers: Chambers' researchers picked up positive recommendations for corporate generalist **Jennifer Bellah Maguire**. Her *"resourcefulness"* is considered to be her chief asset, as she moves among equity capital markets, private equity fund formation and M&A.
The Clients: The firm advised Leonard Green & Partners in the formation of GCP California Fund and represented Magnetek on the $100 million divestiture of its lighting division. Other clients include: Aurora Capital Partners; Gryphon Partners; Global Innovations Partners; Investcorp and Robertson Stephens.

Milbank, Tweed, Hadley & McCloy
The Firm: Considered by interviewees to be a growing force on the West Coast, the Californian practice of this New York firm was widely recommended. The team represents leading financial institutions in Los Angeles, as well as public and private companies throughout the western US. It has represented underwriters in high yield and equity offerings, including deals for Stater Bros. Markets, a Southern California-based supermarket chain, Oregon-based automobile dealership Lithia Motors, and Embarcadero Technologies, a San Francisco-based software company.
The Lawyers: Clients attribute the increasing profile of the unit to **Ken Baronsky**, a fixture at the LA office since it opened in the 1980's. He handles a mixture of debt and equity work and is felt to be well connected in Southern California banking circles.
The Clients: QUALCOMM; Station Casinos; Pacific Aerospace & Electronics; Gordon Biersch; Trust Company of the West; SunAmerica; Oaktree Capital Management; Banc of America Securities; UBS Warburg; DrKW; Jefferies & Co; Libra Securities; Houlihan Lokey Howard & Zukin; Salem Communications; Isle of Capri; SRS Labs and Neff.

Other Notable Practitioners
The *"energetic"* **Warren Lazarow** was recommended to researchers for his expertise in the public and private markets, and venture capital work, with sector emphasis residing in communications, software and semiconductors. Formerly a member of the now defunct Brobeck, Phleger & Harrison LLP, Lazarow has joined the Menlo Park office of O'Melveny & Myers LLP. The move strengthens the group's resources in Northern California and bolsters its national and international reputation.

CALIFORNIA

COMMUNICATIONS/TECHNOLOGY

CALIFORNIA
Leading firms (Communications: IT)

1. **WILSON SONSINI GOODRICH & ROSATI** Palo Alto
2. **COOLEY GODWARD LLP** Palo Alto
3. **FENWICK & WEST** Palo Alto
   LATHAM & WATKINS Menlo Park
4. **GRAY CARY WARE & FREIDENRICH LLP** Palo Alto
5. **GUNDERSON DETTMER STOUGH** Menlo Park
   SKADDEN, ARPS Palo Alto
   VENTURE LAW GROUP Menlo Park
6. **MORRISON & FOERSTER LLP** Palo Alto
   PILLSBURY WINTHROP LLP Palo Alto

Leading individuals
(Communications: IT)

★ **SONSINI Larry** Wilson Sonsini Goodrich, Palo Alto

1. **DAVIDSON Gordon** Fenwick & West, Palo Alto
   GUNDERSON Bob Gunderson Dettmer, Menlo Park
   JOHNSON Craig Venture Law Group, Menlo Park
   MENDELSON Alan Latham & Watkins, Menlo Park
   SAPER Jeff Wilson Sonsini Goodrich, Palo Alto
2. **CLIMAN Richard** Cooley Godward LLP, Palo Alto
   DEL CALVO Jorge Pillsbury Winthrop LLP, Palo Alto
   GALLO Greg Gray Cary Ware & Freidenrich, Palo Alto
   KAUFMAN Christopher Latham & Watkins, Menlo Park
   TANOURY Mark Cooley Godward LLP, Palo Alto
3. **DETTMER Scott** Gunderson Dettmer, Menlo Park
   GREEN Josh Venture Law Group, Menlo Park
   KENNEDY Mike Wilson Sonsini Goodrich, San Francisco
   KING Kenton Skadden, Arps, Slate, Meagher, Palo Alto
4. **BOCHNER Steven** Wilson Sonsini Goodrich, Palo Alto
   KORMAN Marty Wilson Sonsini Goodrich, Palo Alto
   SIMONS Laird Fenwick & West, Palo Alto
   SMITH Greg Skadden, Arps, Slate, Meagher, Palo Alto
5. **BERTELSEN Mark** Wilson Sonsini Goodrich, Palo Alto
   CAMAHORT Steve Wilson Sonsini Goodrich, Palo Alto
   FLAUM Keith Cooley Godward LLP, Palo Alto
   KELLER Don Venture Law Group, Menlo Park
   LAZAROW Warren O'Melveny & Myers LLP, Menlo Park
   MUTO Fred Cooley Godward LLP, San Diego
   ROSATI Mario Wilson Sonsini Goodrich, Palo Alto
   SPECTOR Scott Fenwick & West, Palo Alto
   TONSFELDT Steve Venture Law Group, Menlo Park
   VETTER Jeff Fenwick & West, Palo Alto

Firms and individuals are listed alphabetically in each band.

Wilson Sonsini Goodrich & Rosati
The Firm: The firm is acknowledged by competitors on the West Coast to *"stand by itself as a brand."* Representing national and international technology companies, and specializing in the most sophisticated transactions, the firm houses specialists in all areas, including M&A, venture capital, corporate finance, securities, litigation, tax and IP.

The Lawyers: *"Miracle worker"* **Larry Sonsini** was continually singled out to researchers as unique; he retains a flawless reputation, especially for M&A. By common consent, he dominates Silicon Valley as much as his own firm: *"There is no one to take his place; he built the Valley."* However, this firm is far from a one-man band. The *"smart and aggressive"* **Jeff Saper** is viewed by peers as Sonsini's *"second-in-command,"* and receives widespread admiration for his large practice in public and private offerings and M&A. The esteemed **Mike Kennedy**, head of the M&A group, has in the past year represented a number of major players, including NBC Internet on its acquisition by NBC. **Steve Bochner**'s work in venture capital financings has gained him substantial recognition, with competitors paying tribute to his *"great business judgment and understanding."* **Marty Korman**'s reputation with clients is as a business lawyer who *"cuts to the chase."* As well as work with Hewlett-Packard, he advised Simplex Solutions on its $300 million merger with Cadence Design Systems. Contemporaries agree that **Steve Camahort** *"has definitely arrived."* His M&A caseload has included advising Deutsche Bank Securities on the $1.3 billion merger of Ameritrade and Datek. **Mark Bertelsen** still gains a decent share of market endorsement for the *"diversity"* of his practice, while **Mario Rosati** has a long-standing reputation as an influential client-getter.

The Clients: The firm, led by Larry Sonsini, successfully squared up against rivals Cooley Godward in court, as part of its advice to Hewlett-Packard on its $19 billion merger with Compaq. It also acted for Network Associates on its proposed acquisition of McAfee.com. Clients include: NBC Internet; Hewlett-Packard; Simplex Solutions; Network Associates; Deutsche Bank Securities; Solectron; Avanex; Viant; SmartForce; Proxim and OpenTV.

Cooley Godward LLP
The Firm: Admired for its *"decisive action"* in response to the collapse in the US dot.com and venture capital market, the firm remains a key competitor, notably through its immense M&A practice. A number of specialist practice groups provide a full service to a clientele that ranges from telecom to biotech companies. Rivals concede that this *"diversified and broader practice has served the firm well"* in recent months.

The Lawyers: **Rick Climan** was consistently commended to researchers as a *"strong leader"* of the firm's M&A group. The experienced **Mark Tanoury** also gained strong market endorsement as a corporate attorney who is *"able to overlay his business sense and interpersonal skills with mastery of the legal issues."* **Keith Flaum** is thought to be *"making a name for himself"* with his M&A-led practice, while in the San Diego office all-rounder **Fred Muto** was described as *"a really decent attorney."*

The Clients: The firm recently played a leading role in the long-running saga of the merger between Hewlett-Packard and Compaq, winning many plaudits for its advice on behalf of Walter Hewlett. Elsewhere, it acted for LSI Logic when it acquired C-Cube Microsystems in a stock-for-stock deal valued at about $878 million, one of the first so-called 'two-step' deals. Other work includes acting for Conexant Systems in a joint venture with The Carlyle Group to form a specialty foundry company.

Fenwick & West
The Firm: In common with a number of its rivals, the team has endured something of a roller coaster year in the sector. However, with competitors and clients commenting on the firm's *"excellent quality of work"* and a reported 7% increase in revenues for the last financial year, the group remains in comparatively good health.

The Lawyers: **Gordy Davidson** is by far the name most associated with the firm – *"he has been there since the very start of Silicon Valley and has done every kind of transaction there is"* – and retains an enviable reputation for business-getting ability and technical strength. *"Sound attorney"* **Laird Simons** was singled out to researchers for his commercial acumen, while **Jeff Vetter** was recommended for his work in technology-related M&A; recently, he led a team representing Digeo in its merger with Moxi Digital. **Scott Spector**, an expert in the employee benefits aspects of the hi-tech industry, was one of a number of the group's lawyers involved in advising Talarian on its $115 million acquisition by TIBCO Software.

The Clients: The firm represented Elantec Semiconductor on its $1.4 billion merger with Intersil, and also advised VeriSign on its acquisition of Illuminet Holdings (a provider of telecom network and signaling services) – a deal valued at approximately $1.2 billion. Other clients include Digeo, Talarian, Intuit and HNC Software.

Latham & Watkins
see firm details p.835

The Firm: This international giant is much admired for the foothold it has gained in the Silicon Valley market since its establishment there in 1997. Researchers often heard from competitors that the firm has *"clearly been beefing up"* its technology practice, and that, in a climate where many firms are suffering, this is one that is *"a much bigger force, heading in the right direction."*

COMMUNICATIONS/TECHNOLOGY

CALIFORNIA

The Lawyers: A key figure in this expansion is *"strong personality"* **Alan Mendelson** (see p.68), who is credited by clients with *"an incredible wealth of experience that no one can match, together with great business sense."* His practice now includes work for both life sciences and IT companies. He acted for Amgen in its $16.7 billion acquisition of Immunex, and for Mellanox Technologies, an Israel-based semiconductor company, in raising approximately $56 million in venture financing. Respected by interviewees for his innovation and dedication, **Christopher (Kit) Kaufman** (see p.66) is considered by peers to be one of the firm's *"greatest assets."* He has recently made a specialty of hostile takeovers in the hi-tech industry, and advised Mentor Graphics on its hostile bid for IKOS Systems.

The Clients: The firm recently represented Integrated Device Technology in its acquisition of Newave Semiconductor, whose operations are based in China. Also on the roster are: Amgen; Mellanox Technologies; Mentor Graphics; Integrated Device Technology; Alliant Partners; NorthPoint Communications; Mayfield Fund and Coral Ventures.

Gray Cary Ware & Freidenrich LLP
see firm details p.806

The Lawyers: Described to researchers as *"the heart and soul of Gray Cary,"* **Greg Gallo** has by far the highest profile here, and acts for a client portfolio that includes Agile Software.

The Clients: Agile Software; IKOS Systems; Schlumberger Technology; Emusic.com; Finisar; Extreme Networks; Extricity Software; Launch Media; Lara Networks and TAB Products.

Gunderson Dettmer Stough Villeneuve Franklin & Hachigian

The Firm: Focused on catering to the needs of fast-growing tech companies, the business model of firms such as Gunderson Dettmer has been hit by the economic downturn that has affected the tech industry. Despite this, the caliber of lawyers at the firm is still impressive.

The Lawyers: Peers urged researchers *"never to lose sight of"* **Bob Gunderson**, who is seen as a *"dynamic player"* in the industry. He is nationally recognized for his expertise in venture capital, and the public and private financing of hi-tech companies. Fellow founding partner **Scott Dettmer** is currently engaged in restructurings and 'down-round' financings, and is admired by contemporaries for his ability to *"plug legal issues into the business side of a deal."*

The Clients: The firm represented AccessLan Communications on its sale to Advanced Fibre Communications, and acted for Ashford.com, which was acquired for $14.5 million by Global Sports.

Skadden, Arps, Slate, Meagher & Flom LLP & Affiliates
see firm details p.878

The Firm: The team remains reputed for its firmwide strength in M&A, which has given the group *"some noteworthy successes"* in recent months. Since opening the Palo Alto office in 1998, the firm is generally considered to be *"a more visible force than they once were."* The firm represented Compaq in its much-contested merger with Hewlett-Packard (valued at $19 billion) and advised Yahoo! on its acquisition of HotJobs.com for $436 million. Other matters have included acting for the special committee of the board of directors of McAfee.com (valued at $880 million) on its unsolicited proposed acquisition by Network Associates.

The Lawyers: *"A gentleman and a bright technology thinker,"* **Kenton King** (see p.66) impresses peers with his high-visibility M&A work. **Greg Smith** (see p.72) is known for his impressive range of experience and *"full book of business."*

The Clients: Compaq; Yahoo!; McAfee.com; CSFB; Exodus Communications and West STEAG Partners.

Venture Law Group

The Firm: *"Probably the most creative and aggressive during the wild internet days,"* according to interviewees, the firm is now considered to be in transition. The decision to shed some personnel has mirrored that of many firms in the sector, however, and peers remain upbeat about the continued high caliber of the group's attorneys whose focus has historically been on start-ups.

The Lawyers: The *"visionary"* **Craig Johnson**'s intellect is much admired in the industry and his stature as a founding partner of the firm is unquestioned. **Josh Green** was commended to researchers for his corporate expertise and has advised clients such as Yahoo! on a number of recent acquisitions. The respected **Don Keller**'s practice embraces corporate governance, securities and M&A, while **Steve Tonsfeldt**'s transactional expertise was also acknowledged by contemporaries.

The Clients: The firm represented CrossWorlds in its $129 million acquisition by IBM. Clients here also include: TIBCO Software; Creative Technologies; Yahoo!; Ramp Networks; Seattle Genetics and Rosetta Inpharmatics.

Morrison & Foerster LLP
see firm details p.854

The Firm: The firm's national and international presence earn market respect. Comprising a large group of attorneys with considerable experience of technology matters, the firm's coverage of the industry includes litigation, licensing and commercial transactions. The San Francisco office was one of a multi-office team that represented DSP Group on the merger of its semiconductor unit with Parthus Technologies, an Irish competitor, to form ParthusCeva. It also helped to represent Hitachi on a joint venture with IBM to combine the two companies' disk drive operations. In Palo Alto, the firm recently closed a preferred stock financing for Cavium Networks, and completed a $26 million third-round financing on behalf of Sonics.

The Lawyers: Bill Sherman is the dominant name in the Palo Alto office, while Billy Schwartz is the leading figure in San Francisco.

The Clients: DSP Group; Hitachi; Cavium Networks; Sonics and Thomson multimedia.

Pillsbury Winthrop LLP
see firm details p.866

The Firm: The firm, which is *"building a good practice,"* is reported to be *"trying to make a splash"* in Silicon Valley. Its M&A deals include advice to Advanced Fibre Communications on its acquisition of AccessLan Communications, and the representation of the target in Chordiant Software's $13 million stock purchase of OnDemand.

The Lawyers: Causing most of the waves is **Jorge del Calvo** (see p.63), whose expertise is in securities offerings and venture capital transactions, largely in the telecom arena. Recently, he took public Magma Design Automation, an IPO valued at $63 million, which was one of the first technology public offerings to take place post-9/11. Another such IPO was that of LogicVision, valued at about $40 million.

The Clients: Magma Design Automation and LogicVision are clients of the firm.

Other Notable Practitioners

Warren Lazarow is the former head of the business and technology group at Brobeck, Phleger & Harrison LLP in Northern California. He has now joined the Menlo Park office of O'Melveny & Myers LLP, following Brobeck's dissolution. Lazarow was cited by interviewees for his venture capital expertise; he also works on debt and equity offerings and M&A.

CALIFORNIA — CONSTRUCTION

CONSTRUCTION

CALIFORNIA
Leading firms (Construction)

1. **THELEN REID & PRIEST** Los Angeles, San Francisco
2. **FARELLA BRAUN & MARTEL LLP** San Francisco
   GIBBS, GIDEN, LOCHER & TURNER Los Angeles
3. **COX CASTLE & NICHOLSON LLP** Los Angeles
   MONTELEONE & MCCRORY, LLP Los Angeles
4. **BINGHAM MCCUTCHEN LLP** San Francisco
   HUNT, ORTMANN, BLASCO, PALFFY Pasedena
   WATT, TIEDER, HOFFAR & FITZGERALD Irvine

Leading individuals (Construction)

1. **CLARK John** Thelen Reid & Priest LLP, Los Angeles
   GIBBS Kenneth Gibbs, Giden, Locher, Los Angeles
   HARRIS Alan Farella Braun & Martel LLP, San Francisco
   O'NEAL Stephen Thelen Reid & Priest, San Francisco
   SINK Charles Farella Braun & Martel, San Francisco
2. **BALLATI Deborah** Farella Braun & Martel, San Francisco
   BUONCRISTIANI David Thelen Reid, San Francisco
   MINCHELLA Mike Monteleone & McCrory, Los Angeles
   TEPLIN Lawrence Cox Castle & Nicholson, Los Angeles
   THUM Robert Thelen Reid & Priest LLP, Los Angeles
3. **BENNETT Fred** Quinn Emanuel Urquhart, Los Angeles
   HUGHES Frank Miller, Morton, Caillat, San Jose
   TRUAX Tim Cox Castle & Nicholson LLP, Los Angeles
4. **HUNT Gordon** Hunt, Ortmann, Blasco, Palffy, Pasedena
   O'BRIEN Harry Coblentz, Patch, Duffy, San Francisco
   ORTMANN Dale Hunt, Ortmann, Blasco, Pasedena
   ZOVICKIAN Stephen Bingham McCutchen, San Francisco

Firms and individuals are listed alphabetically in each band.

Thelen Reid & Priest LLP
see firm details p.888
The Firm: Rivals paid tribute to the omnipotence of *"a superstar firm of construction law."* A national force in this sector, the firm is reckoned to have the largest construction group in North America. It has a historical reputation for dealing with 'bricks and mortar' industries and infrastructure work, which dates right back to the construction of the Hoover Dam and the Golden Gate Bridge.
The Lawyers: **John Clark** (see p.62) is regarded as an icon of construction litigation. Renowned for his *"thoroughness and depth of experience,"* he appeals to clients as *"an extraordinarily hard-working guy; he is a gentleman who wins cases."* His recent track record has included appearing on a $32 million claim for Ebasco against Exxon. No less popular with market observers was **Steve O'Neal** (see p.69), who was endorsed to researchers as *"one of the best around."* O'Neal, who also specializes in litigation and alternative dispute resolution (ADR), has recently worked on some of the largest construction disputes in San Francisco: one in connection with the Sony Metreon and another concerning a mixed-use project in which he represented the San Francisco State University Foundation. *"Top-rank professional"* **David Buoncristiani** (see p.61) is another highly regarded construction litigator, who also frequently turns his hand to mediation, while the respected **Rob Thum**'s (see p.73) contentious practice focuses on engineering/construction and government contract work. Contemporaries acknowledge him as *"a talented and successful practitioner."*
The Clients: Now covering both contentious and noncontentious cases, the group is regarded as the key representative of some enormous contractors, and is particularly associated with its advice to Bechtel, Swinerton Builders, Kajima and DPR Construction.

Farella Braun & Martel LLP
The Firm: *"Construction is a crucial part of their practice,"* observed one commentator of this 40-year-old Californian law firm, which is credited by rivals with possessing *"honest attorneys of the highest caliber."* Although it handles all aspects of construction law advice, the firm is best known for its outstanding litigation and mediation capacity. The construction group advises a blue-chip clientele on high-premium disputes, and is universally acknowledged to be *"well equipped to deal with big cases."*
The Lawyers: **Charles Sink**'s reputation as *"a great attorney and a true construction expert"* is uncontested. One of the construction sector's preeminent litigators, his recent cases have included advising on a $100 million set of claims against construction giant Kvaerner. The versatile **Alan Harris** acts as a litigator, mediator and arbitrator, and was endorsed to researchers as *"an outstanding construction lawyer who knows his stuff thoroughly."* Transactionally, he has advised on a wide range of construction contracts in a career that has spanned 30 years. **Deborah Ballati** is regarded by peers as *"a hard-working attorney who gets good results."* Her caseload has included matters for clients such as Walsh Construction and The Regents of the University of California.
The Clients: Kvaerner; Walsh Construction Co; CH2M HILL and the City and County of San Francisco.

Gibbs, Giden, Locher & Turner
The Firm: Operating from offices in Los Angeles and Las Vegas, Nevada, the firm, founded in 1978, has grown to about 50 attorneys and is said by peers to enjoy a *"fantastic status"* in its local market. The caseload here includes litigation, arbitration, mediation and transactional work.
The Lawyers: Much of the group's reputation is attributed to senior partner and construction law guru **Kenneth Gibbs**, who was originally a litigator, but is now principally associated with ADR. A prolific writer, he is a legendary name among his fellow attorneys, one of whom admitted: *"He teaches the rest of us guys how it's done."* Over the past year, he has counseled the University of Southern California over construction issues.
The Clients: The team is renowned for its advice to a wide range of owner clients, and gained sustained market commendation for its municipal government work and supplier representation. The firm is instructed by Swinerton, Fluor and Centex.

Cox Castle & Nicholson LLP
The Firm: Although it is most noted for its outstanding real estate practice, the firm's construction department also came in for consistent market plaudits. Clients were especially warm in their praise for the group's niche ability in construction defect-related cases.
The Lawyers: *"Key figure"* **Lawrence Teplin** has a broad contentious practice, in which construction disputes play a significant role. The head of the firm's litigation department, he was endorsed to researchers for his expertise in construction defect and delay claims, and has recently been involved in one such claim for a large resort development. **Tim Truax** impresses his peers with his *"capable and polished style."* His caseload covers a wide range of issues, from contract drafting to litigation, mediation and arbitration.
The Clients: It handles both transactional and contentious work, and is most noted for its advice to owners and lenders.

Monteleone & McCrory, LLP
see firm details p.852
The Firm: One of the oldest construction law firms in the state, it received consistent market support for its *"excellent command of public contracting matters in Southern California."* Although well versed in transactional matters, the firm's main thrust is in litigation, contract disputes, negotiations and ADR.
The Lawyers: The department's outstanding figure is considered to be **Mike Minchella** (see p.69), who was regularly endorsed by contemporaries: *"He has bags of experience, good practical sense and excels at the key thing – simplifying complex matters."* He represented Obayashi in claims worth $100 million, relating to the LA Metro Red Line subway, and advised Kiewit Pacific on matters arising from the construction of the Hyperion Treatment Facility.
The Clients: Large contractor companies constitute a substantial proportion of the client portfolio. Obayashi and JF Shea Co use the firm.

CORPORATE/M&A — CALIFORNIA

Bingham McCutchen LLP
The Firm: Market commentators are in no doubt where the firm's focus lies: *"They are renowned for their litigation practice, so they have some great construction litigators."* Transactional matters are generally handled by attorneys from the firm's real estate department, although it remains to be seen whether its recent merger will shift the firm's emphasis on the construction sector.
The Lawyers: **Stephen Zovickian** is regarded as the team's leading light, and has handled major claims for Catellus Development and Louisiana-Pacific, as well as covering plenty of healthcare industry work. Peers acknowledge that he has a *"well-earned reputation and doesn't pull his punches."*
The Clients: Catellus Development and Louisiana-Pacific.

Hunt, Ortmann, Blasco, Palffy & Rossell Inc
The Firm: Observers regard this traditional construction boutique as *"a solid group with a couple of excellent senior partners."* Advising on both transactional and contentious aspects of the law, the firm is now home to about 25 attorneys.
The Lawyers: **Gordon Hunt** is one of the *"old guard"* of the sector, and, according to peers, *"has been doing this stuff since before it was fashionable."* His practice focuses on contentious work, and his client portfolio includes names such as the City of Los Angeles and Saint John's Health Center. **Dale Ortmann** also enjoys a high standing among his fellow professionals, who regard him as *"a fine litigator who is good at grasping the important details."*
The Clients: WE O'Neil Construction Co; City of Los Angeles; Charles Pankow Builders and City of Oxnard.

Watt, Tieder, Hoffar & Fitzgerald
The Firm: Another of the respected construction boutiques operating in California, it has a reputation as *"a sound practice with some good specialists."* Work undertaken is wide-ranging, and includes representing general and government contractors, subcontractors, architects, engineers, owners and developers.
The Lawyers: Although no individual attorney here was considered to stand out, clients spoke warmly of the firm's *"super team ethos."*
The Clients: The firm advises contractors, subcontractors, architects and engineers.

Other Notable Practitioners
Fred Bennett (see p.60), who works from the Los Angeles office of Quinn Emanuel Urquhart Oliver & Hedges LLP, *"is a true professional,"* according to peers. Known both for contract drafting and for his litigation prowess, he has advised on the Walt Disney Concert Hall development in Los Angeles. **Frank Hughes** is a senior partner at Miller, Morton, Caillat & Nevis in San José. Much of his recent work has focused on the fallout from the dot.com crash, and he represented Hathaway Dinwiddie Construction Company in a $29 million litigation against AboveNet. One opponent viewed him as *"an experienced litigator with some fine results to his credit."* **Harry O'Brien** of Coblentz, Patch, Duffy & Bass LLP is a transactional lawyer with a real estate background, who also negotiates and drafts construction contracts. Researchers were impressed by the warmth of commendation for this popular practitioner, who *"can always diffuse difficult situations."* He lists The Roman Catholic Archdiocese of San Francisco and Gap retailers among his clientele.

CORPORATE/M&A

CALIFORNIA
Leading firms (Corporate/M&A)

1
- GIBSON, DUNN & CRUTCHER Los Angeles, Palo Alto
- LATHAM & WATKINS Los Angeles, Menlo Park
- SKADDEN, ARPS Los Angeles, Palo Alto, San Francisco
- WILSON SONSINI GOODRICH Palo Alto, San Francisco

2
- COOLEY GODWARD LLP Palo Alto, San Francisco

3
- O'MELVENY & MYERS LLP Los Angeles

Leading individuals (Corporate/M&A)

1
- BOGEN Andy Gibson, Dunn & Crutcher, Los Angeles
- SONSINI Larry Wilson Sonsini Goodrich, Palo Alto
- TOSETTI Paul Latham & Watkins, Los Angeles

2
- COBEN Jerome Skadden, Arps, Slate, Los Angeles
- KAUFMAN Christopher Latham & Watkins, Menlo Park
- KING Kenton Skadden, Arps, Slate, Meagher, Palo Alto

3
- KENNEDY Mike Wilson Sonsini Goodrich, San Francisco
- MENDELSON Alan Latham & Watkins, Menlo Park
- SAGGESE Nicholas Skadden, Arps, Slate, Los Angeles

4
- CALOF Lawrence Gibson, Dunn & Crutcher, Palo Alto
- CLIMAN Richard Cooley Godward LLP, Palo Alto
- DAVIDSON Gordon Fenwick & West, Palo Alto
- GIUNTA Joseph Skadden, Arps, Slate, Los Angeles
- LARSON John Morgan, Lewis, San Francisco
- LESSER Henry Gray Cary Ware, Palo Alto
- OLSON Gary Latham & Watkins, Los Angeles
- SAPER Jeff Wilson Sonsini Goodrich, Palo Alto

Firms and individuals are listed alphabetically in each band.

Gibson, Dunn & Crutcher LLP
The Firm: Considered *"a terrific team with an excellent presence on big-ticket deals,"* the firm is acknowledged for its enviable clientele roster and the quality of its comparatively young attorneys. The team specializes in cross-border M&A, acting for buyers and targets, and it has also been active during the past year on a number of public offerings.
The Lawyers: Both clients and major rivals pay tribute to **Andy Bogen**, described to researchers as *"California's biggest expert for public company M&A deals."* His 36 years of practice and *"an innate talent to deal easily with the most complex transactions"* are often cited as reasons why his legendary name remains *"the star of the show."* Based at the Palo Alto office, the *"versatile and smart"* **Larry Calof** also gained high marks this year.
The Clients: The firm represented Cadence Design Systems in its acquisition of two private EDA companies, Silicon Perspective and Plato Design Systems, and on its merger with Simplex Solutions, a deal valued at $300 million. It also acted for Northrop Grumman on its hostile $11 billion tender offer to acquire TRW. Elsewhere, the firm represented Amazon.com on its sale of shares to AOL Time Warner. Other clients include Intel; Northrop Grumman; Amazon.com; Cadence Design Systems; DR Horton.

Latham & Watkins
see firm details p.835
The Firm: The firm is seen to benefit from its superb international network to be one of the clear leaders in the Californian corporate market. Los Angeles remains the hub of the firm's activity, although it is also felt to have increased its presence in the Bay Area. Undertaking a broad range of instructions for private and public companies, the team concentrates its transactional work on IT, life sciences and service industries. Clients agree that the firm's major strengths lie in *"superb people and massive resources."*
The Lawyers: Cochair of the M&A practice **Paul Tosetti** (see p.73) maintains his reputation as the firm's most visible corporate figure. His transactional acumen was declared by a number of commentators to be *"second to none."* The firm is frequently called on to advise the buyer on hostile takeovers. Here **Christopher (Kit) Kaufman** (see p.66) gained consistent peer recommendation as *"a proactive, business-oriented attorney."* He acted for Mentor Graphics on its hostile bid for IKOS Systems. Newly ranked **Alan Mendelson** (see p.68), who focuses on venture capital matters in the technology sector, is seen by clients as an *"able lawyer who gives sensible advice,"* while the understated **Gary Olson** (see p.69) also received strong market approval. Together with Tosetti and Mendelson, he

CALIFORNIA
CORPORATE/M&A

represented Amgen on the Californian aspects of the $16 billion acquisition of Seattle rival Immunex.
The Clients: Other matters for the firm include acting for V3 Semiconductor, a Canadian-based semiconductor company, on its sale to QuickLogic. Among its clients are: Integrated Device Technology; NorthPoint Communications; Amgen; V3 Semiconductor; Mentor Graphics.

Skadden, Arps, Slate, Meagher & Flom LLP & Affiliates
see firm details p.878
The Firm: This international giant clearly ranks as a leading competitor in California's domestic market, and is also naturally acclaimed for the *"excellent development of its international strategy."* Packed with market-leading names, the M&A group carries out cross-border and domestic transactional work both for private clients and high-profile public companies. Notable strengths exist in the gaming, healthcare, multi-media and sports industries.
The Lawyers: A familiar name on high-profile transactions, **Jerry Coben** (see p.62) received widespread endorsement for *"his great dedication to his clients' needs."* The respected **Nick Saggese** (see p.71) maintains a broad generalist practice, divided between M&A transactions, securities offerings and corporate restructurings. **Joe Giunta** is also esteemed by contemporaries as *"a fine technician,"* while hi-tech expert **Kenton King** (see p.66) attracted the attention of Silicon Valley interviewees for *"his huge appetite for complex work."* He acted for Yahoo! in its $436 million unsolicited takeover proposal for HotJobs.com.
The Clients: The firm also represented CSFB on the acquisition by United Global Com of European assets from Liberty Media. The firm also works for Colony Capital Investors III; Leonard Green & Partners; Texas Pacific Group; Del Webb; Zacky Farms; Ascend Communications and Compaq; Yahoo!

Wilson Sonsini Goodrich & Rosati
The Firm: Maintaining its reputation as the *"preeminent M&A practice in the hi-tech world,"* this Silicon Valley firm's capacity for big-ticket deals is beyond dispute. In spite of the lack of an international network comparable to its major rivals in the state, it is *"almost always the first choice"* of blue-chip bidders, targets and financial advisors for transactions with a hi-tech slant.
The Lawyers: **Larry Sonsini** maintains his legendary reputation as *"the father of the practice, with the most successful career in the state."* Interviewees acknowledge the unique status of this ubiquitous practitioner, paying particular homage to his *"impressive business acumen."* Chairman of the M&A group **Mike Kennedy** is regarded by contemporaries as *"an attorney of great resource and transactional skill."* He represented NBC Internet on its acquisition by NBC. Versatile hi-tech lawyer **Jeff Saper** also gained recognition from peers for his contribution to a number of major transactions.
The Clients: The firm represented Apple Computer on the purchase of Zayante and acted for Navarro Networks on its sale to Cisco Systems. Other highlights include acting for Simplex Solutions on its merger with Cadence Design Systems – a transaction valued at $300 million – and representing OpenTV on its $185 million sale to Liberty Media. The firm also acts for: Apple Computer; Viant; Solectron; Avanex; Network Associates; SmartForce; Proxim; 3Dlabs; RapidStream; Annuncio Software; Simplex Solutions; OpenTV; NBC Internet; Hewlett-Packard.

Cooley Godward LLP
The Firm: Considered *"a powerhouse in the hi-tech sphere,"* the M&A group continues to attract its share of market support. Twenty partners cover all aspects of corporate matters for technology, life sciences and biotech companies, as well as venture capital groups and other financial institutions.
The Lawyers: **Richard Climan** was endorsed to researchers as *"an outstanding professional with a winning style of negotiation."* His department represented COR Therapeutics on its acquisition by Millennium Pharmaceuticals, valued at around $2 billion, and acted for Gilead Sciences in the sale of its oncology operations to OCI Pharmaceuticals. The M&A group joined the litigation group in advising Walter Hewlett on his well-publicized proxy objection to the Hewlett-Packard/Compaq merger.
The Clients: Applied Materials; Siebel Systems; eBay; LSI Logic; Adobe Systems; Wind River Systems; Borland Software; Conexant Systems.

O'Melveny & Myers LLP
The Firm: A new entrant to the M&A tables for the West Coast, this international full-service firm is respected for its statewide coverage, and prominence on national and cross-border mergers, tender offers and joint ventures.
The Lawyers: Led by Jim Levin, the group has expertise in industries as diverse as telecoms, health maintenance, utilities, gaming and entertainment. The team represented Univision Communications, the largest Spanish-language television broadcaster in the US, on its acquisition of 13 television stations throughout the country from USA Networks. It also acted for a major shopping center REIT on a joint venture to acquire and develop a 45-acre site in Southern California.
The Clients: The firm advises national and international corporates such as Univision Communications.

Other Notable Practitioners
A leading name in the Bay Area, **Henry Lesser** (see p.67) of Gray Cary Ware & Freidenrich received widespread client commendation for his *"long experience and impressive skills"* in the M&A sphere of the biotech, hi-tech, semiconductor and software industries. During the past 12 months, he represented NetRatings on its agreement to acquire Jupiter Media Metrix and its separate acquisition of the portion of ACNielsen eRatings.com not already owned by it. **Gordon Davidson** of Fenwick & West is a prominent figure in the Silicon Valley marketplace. Best known as a peerless technology lawyer, he has also earned the respect of rivals for his *"wonderful transactional brain,"* which he has applied to a number of big-ticket deals. Following the dissolution of Brobeck, Phleger & Harrison LLP, **John Larson** has joined Morgan, Lewis & Bockius, giving the firm a presence in the San Francisco market. Larson appeals to contemporaries as a *"smart counselor who has a clear, thorough understanding of the way finance works."* he brings with him a wealth of experience in M&A corporate finance and venture capital matters.

CALIFORNIA

EMPLOYMENT & LABOR LAW — MAINLY PLAINTIFF

CALIFORNIA
Leading firms
(Employment: Mainly Plaintiff)

1 MCGUINN, HILLSMAN & PALEFSKY *San Francisco*
RUDY, EXELROD & ZIEFF, LLP *San Francisco*
2 BORNN & SURLS *Marina Del Rey*
HADSELL & STORMER *Pasadena*

Leading individuals
(Employment: Mainly Plaintiff)

1 PALEFSKY Cliff *McGuinn, Hillsman*, San Francisco
RUDY Mark *Rudy, Exelrod & Zieff, LLP*, San Francisco
2 BORNN Nancy *Bornn & Surls*, Marina Del Rey
EXELROD Alan *Rudy, Exelrod & Zieff*, San Francisco
STORMER Dan *Hadsell & Stormer*, Pasadena

Firms and individuals are listed alphabetically in each band.

McGuinn, Hillsman & Palefsky
The Firm: Described by some defense firms as *"the best plaintiff team in California,"* this boutique was unanimously acclaimed for its work on civil rights and employment litigation cases.

Many attribute the group's preeminence to the presence of **Cliff Palefsky**. He was singled out to researchers as *"the first choice for employees,"* and has earned market plaudits as *"one of the most gifted litigators of his time."* Cofounder of the National Employment Lawyers Association, this respected advocate has vast experience of arbitration, mediation and executive termination cases.

Rudy, Exelrod & Zieff, LLP
The Firm: An automatic choice of market commentators, the firm is renowned among peers for *"high-quality technicians who turn out successful results."* Wrongful termination, discrimination and wage and hours class actions are key elements of the firm's workload. The spotlight here falls on **Mark Rudy**, commended to researchers as a lawyer with *"an extraordinary ability to solve difficult cases with ease."* He receives strong support from **Alan Exelrod**, who has an established name for his work in sexual harassment suits. The team recently obtained a judgment in excess of $124 million in Bell v Farmers Insurance Exchange, an overtime class action in which the firm represented more than 2400 employees.

Bornn & Surls
The Firm: This niche team is considered to have been formed in the image of its high-profile leader, **Nancy Bornn**, *"a notable lawyer, who will turn her hand to most projects."* Working for a wide variety of employees, the firm has a particularly sound reputation for advice on discrimination, human rights and executive severances.

Hadsell & Stormer
The Firm: Dan Stormer is the big name that underpins this Pasadena-based boutique. Admired by fellow lawyers for his expertise in civil rights, constitutional law and litigation, this *"smart lawyer"* is said to be *"a knowledgeable guy with a great capacity to argue his case."* He appeared against Unocal in the California Superior Court in a case relating to alleged abuses of employment rights during Unocal's Yadana pipeline project in Burma.

EMPLOYMENT & LABOR LAW — MAINLY DEFENDANT

CALIFORNIA
Leading firms
(Employment: Mainly Defendant)

1 PAUL, HASTINGS, JANOFSKY *Los Angeles*
2 GIBSON, DUNN & CRUTCHER LLP *Los Angeles*
ORRICK, HERRINGTON & SUTCLIFFE *Los Angeles*
3 LITTLER MENDELSON PC *San Francisco*
MORRISON & FOERSTER LLP *Los Angeles*
O'MELVENY & MYERS LLP *Los Angeles*
SEYFARTH SHAW *Los Angeles*
4 LATHAM & WATKINS *Los Angeles*
MORGAN, LEWIS & BOCKIUS LLP *Los Angeles*
SHEPPARD, MULLIN, RICHTER *Los Angeles*
5 HELLER EHRMAN WHITE *Los Angeles, San Francisco*
WILSON SONSINI GOODRICH *San Francisco*

Firms are listed alphabetically in each band.

Paul, Hastings, Janofsky & Walker LLP
see firm details p.861
The Firm: Highly respected by rival firms, this national employment team has been described to researchers as *"the best in California without question."* Covering the spectrum of labor and employment work, the group serves an enviable list of financial institutions and companies from the oil, manufacturing and entertainment sectors.

The Lawyers: Chambers' researchers were left in no doubt that **Paul Grossman** (see p.65) is one of the employment world's *"giants."* A national figure, his prominence is recognized well beyond the confines of California. In spite of his position as chairman of the firm, he has been seen in recent California Supreme Court action in Lane v Hughes, where the jury awarded a record $89.5 million in a discrimination case. **Nancy Abell** (see p.60) boasts a strong reputation for her class action expertise, and represents a number of America's most prestigious blue-chips. Clients applaud her ability *"to see the practical side of the things."* She acted as lead counsel to Microsoft in a nationwide race and gender class action (Donaldson v Microsoft). A leading name in San Francisco, **Paul Cane** (see p.61), has been warmly recommended by peers who rate him as *"a tried and tested trial lawyer."* Together with Grossman, Cane represented the defendant in the Guz v Bechtel discrimination case. In the same city, **Kirby Wilcox** (see p.74) was endorsed to researchers as a *"first-rate practitioner who handles complex deals with efficiency."* He is another to receive strong market endorsement for his experience of class actions.
The Clients: Clients include Sempra Energy, WellPoint and Microsoft.

Gibson, Dunn & Crutcher LLP
The Firm: Consistently involved in high-profile cases, the firm's employment department continues to be perceived by competitors as a successful player across the West Coast, in spite of some staff departures. The employment group works closely with the firm's top-class litigation department, and has acknowledged expertise in labor issues, employment litigation and corporate-related advice.
The Lawyers: Discrimination expert **David Cathcart** was unanimously commended to researchers as *"a star practitioner who exercises iron control over his cases."* Peers also rated **Pamela Hemminger** as *"a fine orator,"* and pointed to her heavyweight client portfolio. The group serves clients from both public and private sectors, and has particular strength in the telecom and health industries.
The Clients: The team represented an aerospace company in its defense against a whistle-blower claim by an associate general counsel – this case was recently the subject of an opinion by the California Supreme Court. It also acted for an insurance company in successfully defeating one of the few class actions based on wrongful termination in California.

CALIFORNIA

EMPLOYMENT & LABOR LAW

CALIFORNIA
Leading individuals
(Employment: Mainly Defendant)

[1]
- **CATHCART David** *Gibson, Dunn,* Los Angeles
- **GROSSMAN Paul** *Paul, Hastings, Janofsky,* Los Angeles

[2]
- **ABELL Nancy** *Paul, Hastings, Janofsky,* Los Angeles
- **SINISCALCO Gary** *Orrick, Herrington,* San Francisco
- **WILCOX Kirby** *Paul, Hastings, Janofsky,* San Francisco

[3]
- **ALVAREZ Fred** *Wilson Sonsini Goodrich,* Palo Alto
- **CANE Paul** *Paul, Hastings, Janofsky,* San Francisco
- **MATHIASON Garry** *Littler Mendelson PC,* San Francisco
- **PFISTER Thomas** *Latham & Watkins,* Los Angeles

[4]
- **HAGEN Catherine** *O'Melveny & Myers,* Newport Beach
- **HEMMINGER Pamela** *Gibson, Dunn,* Los Angeles
- **KADUE David** *Seyfarth Shaw,* Los Angeles
- **PEPE Stephen** *O'Melveny & Myers,* Newport Beach
- **WHEELER Raymond** *Morrison & Foerster,* Palo Alto

Individuals are listed alphabetically in each band.

Orrick, Herrington & Sutcliffe
see firm details p.859
The Firm: Another member of the pack chasing Paul Hastings, the firm earned repeated client endorsement for its *"devotion to quality over quantity."* The team is renowned for its litigation capacity, and advises a high-powered clientele that ranges from traditional industries to new tech companies. The firm appeared on a recent case for a division of GE.
The Lawyers: Researchers received recommendations for the uniform quality of the team, but standing out from the pack is **Gary Siniscalco** (see p.72), cochair of the employment group. Both clients and competitors pay tribute to this prominent lawyer for his *"brilliant work"* in complex litigation cases, class actions and counseling. During the past year, he has advised American Airlines, Northwest Airlines and Salomon Smith Barney on a range of employment litigation and arbitration cases.
The Clients: American Lawyer Media; AT&T; Apple; Bayer; Bell Atlantic; Blockbuster Videos; Burlington Coat Factory Stores; Citigroup; Delta Air Lines; GE; Hilton Hotels; IBM; Informix; Marriott International; Merrill Lynch and Service America.

Littler Mendelson PC
The Firm: Clients commend the group for its *"businesslike approach,"* and the largest team in California services an impressive list of mid-sized employers from all industries. Market sources recommended the resources and sheer size of the group spread over 12 offices. It advises on the full range of employment and labor matters including disability benefits, unfair labor practice and workers' compensation. Practitioners are also respected for their litigation abilities.
The Lawyers: The group's star is **Garry Mathiason**, whose *"great depth of knowledge"* commands widespread respect. His track record includes discrimination litigation, wrongful termination cases, unfair labor practice and representational proceedings. Based between the San Francisco and San Jose offices, he has a specialty representing technology and start-ups companies.
The Clients: The client roster ranges from Fortune 500 companies to small businesses.

Morrison & Foerster LLP
see firm details p.854
The Firm: Traditionally strong in labor law, the firm is regarded by peers as *"a serious competitor with deep resources."* In addition to outstanding expertise in union/employer relations, the firm handles a variety of employment matters including counseling, employment litigation and immigration issues.
The Lawyers: In Palo Alto, the respected **Raymond Wheeler** (see p.74) is said to *"bring a wealth of experience"* to the team. He is renowned for advising hi-tech companies on labor and employment issues.
The Clients: JDS Uniphase; Novellus Systems; Seagate Technology; Aetna; UPS and Ralph's Groceries.

O'Melveny & Myers LLP
The Firm: Of the firm's five Californian offices, Los Angeles has the most recognized name for employment work in the state. Endorsed to researchers for its depth, the team offers a full range of employment services, from preventative work to dispute resolution.
The Lawyers: Based in Newport Beach, **Stephen Pepe** heads the department, and is generally considered to be *"a local mover and shaker."* In **Catherine Hagen**, the firm possesses a *"wonderful lawyer for discrimination and sexual harassment issues."*
The Clients: California Institute of Technology; Columbia Pictures; Ford; Lockheed Martin; Sony; US Airways and Verizon.

Seyfarth Shaw
The Firm: This prominent national employment player boasts strong ties to a number of Fortune 100 companies, and was consistently mentioned to our researchers as *"one of the most active teams on the management side."* The group covers all aspects of union issues, employment contracts, counseling and employment litigation.
The Lawyers: In the opinion of competitors, **David Kadue** is the outstanding name at the firm for workplace harassment and wrongful termination claims. A number of food and service companies are to be found on his client roster, which also comprises financial institutions, airlines and hi-tech corporations.
The Clients: Fortune 500 companies.

Latham & Watkins
see firm details p.835
The Firm: Operating from the litigation department, this national colossus is principally admired for its corporate-related employment practice, although the workload here also encompasses discrimination, class actions, sexual harassment and overtime claims. Unusually for a firm of this ilk, it also handles some plaintiff work.
The Lawyers: Researchers were impressed by the levels of market support for **Tom Pfister** (see p.70), who was described by clients as *"a real intellectual and a joy to work with."* He boasts a wide-ranging experience representing employers in major class action employment cases, particularly in discrimination and overtime compensation matters.
The Clients: The firm represented Denny's in resolving nationwide class action public accommodation discrimination lawsuits, and defended Southern California Edison in class action claims of employment discrimination. Another highlight includes acting for Toyota Motor Sales in alleged class action discrimination claims in California and New Jersey. Other clients include: Detroit Edison; Mitsubishi; Blue Shield; Xerox; Nissan Motor; Covenant Care Technicolor; Illinois State University; Harrah's Entertainment; National Semiconductor and Toyota Logistics.

Morgan, Lewis & Bockius LLP
The Firm: Although its profile is perhaps stronger on the East Coast, the firm's Californian employment team is reckoned to produce *"a consistently high standard of work."* The Los Angeles office acts for a sizable number of employers in areas as diverse as securities, manufacturing, entertainment and technology.
The Lawyers: Over the past 12 months, the group's focus has been on discrimination cases and corporate support work.
The Clients: Fortune 500 companies.

Sheppard, Mullin, Richter & Hampton LLP
The Firm: Employment law is one of the firm's main specializations, and Chambers' research uncovered *"a decent practice with a lot of years in the game."* The team acts exclusively for employers, ranging from small businesses to Fortune 100 companies. Areas of niche expertise include the manufacturing, healthcare, technology and hospitality industries. Over the past year, the team has been especially active on employment litigation claims concerning wage and hours matters, class actions and union/management relations. It has recently advised a number of healthcare organizations on a variety of negotiations with unions.
The Lawyers: The team, which includes Douglas Farmer, boasts a number of attorneys who

ENERGY & NATURAL RESOURCES — CALIFORNIA

are highly regarded in fields such as wage and hour regulations.
The Clients: Frito-Lay; Northrop; State Farm; Victoria's Secret; Liberty Mutual; Nordstrom; Bank of America; Wells Fargo and State Compensation Insurance Fund.

Heller Ehrman White & McAuliffe LLP
The Firm: A small but respected department, which has taken a leading role across the West Coast in wrongful discharge litigation, discrimination cases and counseling. The firm is generally considered to be more prominent on contentious matters than on labor and employment counseling, but has still undertaken substantial corporate support work and employment agreements on behalf of its blue-chip client base.
The Lawyers: Patricia Gillette is cochair of the national practice group.
The Clients: Bank of America; Microsoft; LifeSpan BioSciences; Northwest Chamber Orchestra; TeraBeam Networks; Toolfarm.com; WorldCom; PwC; SeaWorld and Sprint Spectrum.

Wilson Sonsini Goodrich & Rosati
The Firm: Dominating the hi-tech sector, the firm's employment group is especially renowned for its handling of sexual harassment, disability discrimination and wage and hour matters as they affect that industry. The team recently obtained a favorable court ruling in a case relating to employers' liability for harassment by a supervisor.
The Lawyers: According to interviewees, the presence of employment litigator **Fred Alvarez** since 1997 has reinforced the firm's status in this area of practice. Peers describe him as *"a practical, results-oriented lawyer."* As well as his advice on class actions, this renowned practitioner is recommended for his experience in labor and employment issues in a number of government bodies.
The Clients: Sun Microsystems; KLA-Tencor; Intertel and Bamboo.com.

ENERGY & NATURAL RESOURCES

CALIFORNIA
Leading firms
(Energy & Natural Resources)

1. MILBANK, TWEED, HADLEY *Los Angeles*
   ORRICK, HERRINGTON & SUTCLIFFE *San Francisco*
2. LATHAM & WATKINS *San Diego*
   WHITE & CASE LLP *Los Angeles*
3. MORRISON & FOERSTER LLP *Walnut Creek*
4. DAVIS WRIGHT TREMAINE LLP *San Francisco*
   GOODIN MACBRIDE SQUERI RITCHIE *San Francisco*

Leading individuals
(Energy & Natural Resources)

1. BLOOM Jerry *White & Case LLP, Los Angeles*
   FEO Edwin *Milbank, Tweed, Hadley, Los Angeles*
2. MALKIN Joseph *Orrick, Herrington, San Francisco*
3. BOOTH William *Sole Practitioner, Walnut Creek*
   ELLISON Christopher *Ellison Schneider, Sacramento*
   HANSCHEN Peter *Morrison & Foerster, Walnut Creek*
4. DAY Michael *Goodin MacBride Squeri, San Francisco*
   GREENWALD Steve *Davis Wright, San Francisco*
   MACBRIDE Thomas *Goodin MacBride, San Francisco*

Firms and individuals are listed alphabetically in each band.

Milbank, Tweed, Hadley & McCloy
The Firm: Operating from its Los Angeles office, the firm's power and energy group possesses an acknowledged international dimension, and is regarded as the premier team for worldwide energy project financings. On the domestic front, the group has a distinguished presence in independent power transactions, working with developers and lenders for new production, refining and generation facilities. Responding to California's electricity problems, the firm represents companies tendering for state power contracts, and its attorneys are counsel to official creditors on the PG&E Corp committee.
The Lawyers: The department brings together a large group of specialists in both power and upstream oil and gas issues to advise on cross-border transactions, but the leading individual here is unquestionably *"Mr Energy,"* **Edwin Feo**. Renowned for his transactional prowess, notably on the financing side, he has an enviable developer clientele.
The Clients: The firm advised on the structuring and negotiating of a $325 million deal to develop the Tuxpan-II power plant in Veracruz, Mexico, and the $359.5 million financing of the Brazos Valley Project to build a gas-fired power plant in Fort Bend, Texas. Its clients include: Ameresco; Mitsubishi; Kyushu Electric Power Co. and Sempra Energy Resources.

Orrick, Herrington & Sutcliffe
see firm details p.859
The Firm: Described to researchers as *"something of an institution"* in San Francisco, the firm's energy department has deep historical roots in the north of the state. It had a pivotal role in the formation of the PG&E Co and continues to work with municipal and investor-owned utilities, as well as independent power producers. Following the energy crisis, the firm has been closely associated with the restructuring of the utility industry, working with PG&E Co in the divestiture of its generation assets, and helping to establish the Power Exchange and Independent System Operator. Competitors regard the firm's strengths to lie particularly in public finance and regulatory work, especially for the City of San Francisco.
The Lawyers: Since the arrival of **Joseph Malkin** (see p.68) from O'Melveny & Myers in mid-2000, the global energy, communications and infrastructure group of which he is cochair has *"gained significant strength,"* in the opinion of clients. Those who have seen him in action on behalf of public power producers say that he is *"good at everything that he turns his attention to."*
The Clients: Clients include: PG&E Generating Co; Sempra Energy; AES; Qwest and Williams Energy.

Latham & Watkins
see firm details p.835
The Firm: Two areas were identified to researchers as the team's particular strong suits. Its electricity work was regarded as *"the best"* by one direct competitor, while the firm's vast general commercial depth helps the energy department to be regarded as *"one of the most successful in California for transactions."* The firm has advised on a number of cross-border deals involving power development, redevelopment and expansion. On the development side, it acted on a 700MW power plant project in San Bernardino County, and the redevelopment and expansion of a plant in the Bay Area for Mirant. It is also engaged in the development of two plants approved by the Governor's emergency executive order for power expansion in San Diego and Palm Springs.
The Lawyers: Clients were impressed by the collective strength of the group's attorneys, suggesting that such overall quality compensated for a generally perceived absence of individual stars. Robert Dahlquist is a key member of this team.
The Clients: Among its highlights, the firm advised Sempra Energy on its undertaking to transmit power from Mexico to California, and acted for MidAmerican Energy in connection

CALIFORNIA
ENERGY & NATURAL RESOURCES

with its establishment of a geothermal plant in Imperial Valley (San Diego). Other clients include: Calpine; PG&E Corp; Mirant; Constellation Power; InterGen; Congentrix Energy and San Diego Gas & Electric.

White & Case LLP
The Firm: Ever since six attorneys left Morrison & Foerster to join White & Case in the late 1990's, the latter's energy finance practice has concentrated on sponsoring and developing energy projects. The practice is a leading player in the independent power production industry and has an active regulatory and litigation group. As with other energy practices across California, the state's energy tribulations have provided an ample supply of business. At the height of the crisis, attorneys from White & Case joined a summit meeting in Washington at the behest of the Clinton Administration, acting as lead advocate for negotiations in Sacramento's qualifying facilities; these represent up to a third of the total power generation in California. Fallout from market deregulation also continues to furnish opportunities in bankruptcy settlements and litigation. The firm serves as counsel to the official committee for creditors of PG&E Co, and advised Southern California Edison on the qualifying facilities issue.
The Lawyers: Group leader **Jerry Bloom** enjoys a prominent public profile as a *"knowledgeable, experienced and diligent attorney,"* and is especially respected by peers for his regulatory work.
The Clients: Clients include: AES; Calpine; Inland Paperboard and Packaging; Sithe Energies; Delta Power Company; PE-Berkeley; Mirant and Southern California Edison.

Morrison & Foerster LLP
see firm details p.854
The Firm: Several observers identified the energy group's strengths in development and litigation matters, and much of the workload here centers on the deregulation and restructuring of the electricity and gas industries. On the contentious side, the group has had particular success in suing public utilities, representing various clients in proceedings before federal and state agencies.
The Lawyers: For development matters, **Peter Hanschen** (see p.65) emerged as the team's outstanding attorney. Said to *"understand the electricity industry profoundly,"* he has across-the-board experience in regulation, restructuring and expansion, including alternative energy projects in the Far East.
The Clients: The firm has been counsel to El Paso in class actions concerning unfair business practices and is currently counsel for creditors in the PG&E Co bankruptcy. It also receives instructions from such heavy-hitters as: AES; New West Energy; Agricultural Energy Consumers Association; Sierra Pacific Power Company; Kern River Gas Transmission Company; Pacific Pipeline System and Electricity Generating Authority of Thailand.

Davis Wright Tremaine LLP
see firm details p.787
The Firm: A comparative newcomer among California's leading energy groups, the firm has rapidly established a strong profile for its public utilities practice in San Francisco. Competitors rate the group as a *"substantial opponent,"* and also acknowledge its appearances before a number of state and federal regulatory agencies. The firm customarily acts as regulatory counsel for merchant energy plant developers and lenders.
The Lawyers: **Steven Greenwald** (see p.65) was commended to researchers for his *"solid regulatory practice."* He advised Calpine on its acquisition and financing of Unocal's Geysers geothermal facilities in northern California.
The Clients: Clients include: Calpine, PG&E Corp and El Paso Natural Gas Company.

Goodin MacBride Squeri Ritchie & Day LLP
The Firm: The reputation of this firmly established boutique firm rests principally with its *"visible presence"* before the California Public Utilities Commission (CPUC). Its energy practice represents a number of utility clients affected by CPUC's decisions, including those involved in the selling, transmission and storage of energy and natural gas. The firm recently secured a favorable resolution at the CPUC for the restructuring of the natural gas market in southern California.
The Lawyers: The team includes registered lobbyists conducting extensive legislative work in Sacramento. One such, and a key contributor to the creation of the deregulated energy market in California, is **Michael Day**, assessed by opponents as a *"superb regulatory lawyer."* **Thomas MacBride Jr** is a respected name in the public utilities field.
The Clients: Clients include: Enron; Dynegy; Duke Energy; Questar; Caithness Energy; CMS Energy and Alberta Energy Company.

Other Notable Practitioners
Operating from offices in Walnut Creek, near San Francisco, sole practitioner **William Booth** enters the Chambers' rankings. Considered a *"great energy person,"* his experience of the industry is said to *"put him up there with the best."* Long-standing experience and knowledge of the California Energy Commission earns Sacramento-based **Christopher Ellison** of Ellison Schneider & Harrison a major reputation among his fellow regulatory lawyers.

ENVIRONMENT

CALIFORNIA
Leading firms (Environment)

1. BINGHAM MCCUTCHEN Los Angeles, San Francisco
   LATHAM & WATKINS Los Angeles
2. MORRISON & FOERSTER LLP San Francisco
3. PILLSBURY WINTHROP LLP San Francisco
4. GIBSON, DUNN & CRUTCHER LLP Los Angeles
   WESTON BENSHOOF ROCHEFORT Los Angeles

Firms are listed alphabetically in each band.

Bingham McCutchen LLP
The Firm: One of the original Californian players, the firm covers virtually every area of environmental and land use law in both Los Angeles and San Francisco. Clients acknowledged its *"incredibly responsive"* work ethic. Competitors conceded that the group has the strongest bench of environment practitioners with the largest statewide reach.
The Lawyers: In the wake of some high-profile departures (Barry Goode to the Governor's Office as Secretary of Legal Affairs and David Andrews to PepsiCo, for example), some interviewees said that the team had few individual stars. An exception is **Patricia Shanks**, highly regarded for her transactional acumen.
The Clients: Transactions have included the sale of oil refineries worth $895 million for ExxonMobil, a chemical plant acquisition by Zeneca and Valero Energy's divestiture of its oil refinery and service stations worth $1.1 billion. Its clients include: Stanford University; National Semiconductor; Intel; Kaiser Aluminum & Chemical; BFGoodrich; Applera; Hitachi; Mitsui and Siemens.

ENVIRONMENT — CALIFORNIA

CALIFORNIA
Leading individuals (Environment)

1 WYMAN Robert *Latham & Watkins*, Los Angeles
2 BARR Michael *Pillsbury Winthrop LLP*, San Francisco
CORASH Michèle *Morrison & Foerster*, San Francisco
KIRWAN BJ *Latham & Watkins*, Los Angeles
3 LUCERO Gene *Latham & Watkins*, Los Angeles
RUBALCAVA Sharon *Weston Benshoof*, Los Angeles
WEINER Peter *Paul, Hastings, Janofsky*, San Francisco
4 HERNANDEZ Jennifer *Beveridge & Diamond PC*, San Francisco
SCHMALL Deborah *Farella Braun & Martel*, San Francisco
SHANKS Patricia *Bingham McCutchen*, Los Angeles
STEEL Michael *Pillsbury Winthrop LLP*, San Francisco
ZISCHKE Michael *Morrison & Foerster*, San Francisco

Individuals are listed alphabetically in each band.

Latham & Watkins
see firm details p.835

The Firm: Rivals acknowledge its *"ubiquitous presence"* in California across the spectrum of environmental issues. In particular, the group's work on water and air quality cases is said to be *"among the finest"* in the state. The workload includes substantial transactional experience, environmental compliance work and obtaining land use approvals for, eg: the Playa Vista project, the STAPLES Center and the Sea Launch *"base project"* at Long Beach for Boeing. The firm also won permission for the conversion of military bases in Sacramento and the construction of power plants in San Bernardino County.

The Lawyers: The team was recently bolstered by the arrival of former Deputy Secretary of the Interior, David Hayes – resident in Washington DC but active in California – who has been appointed chairman of the firm's global environmental department. He joins *"guru of the field"* **Robert Wyman Jr** (see p.74). Regarded as the state's number one expert on Californian air pollution control, Wyman was recommended to researchers for combining a *"philosophical and academic appreciation"* of law with *"sensitivity towards his clients."* **BJ Kirwan** (see p.66) is noted for her long-standing air quality practice and experience of hazardous waste. A *"terrifically capable lawyer"* in the opinion of contemporaries, she has also gained prominence in the Proposition 65 arena. **Gene Lucero** (see p.67), recommended for his work on water quality and land contamination, also received substantial market endorsement.

The Clients: Hughes; Boeing Commercial/Space; Los Angeles Sports and Entertainment District and PSEG Nuclear.

Morrison & Foerster LLP
see firm details p.854

The Firm: Although it is not felt to pack quite the statewide punch of the two market leaders, the firm nevertheless possesses an infrastructure that gives it among the most significant environment practices in California. Its powerhouse lies in the north of the state, where it receives recognition for both national and international land use and Proposition 65 advice.

The Lawyers: Much of the commentary about the firm was inextricably linked to **Michèle Corash** (see p.62), who is said by some to *"dominate"* the land use and environment law group. Her reputation rests on work for Superfund private cost and recovery actions and Proposition 65 on which she is widely regarded as an expert with a *"significant following in the US."* She receives support from the respected **Michael Zischke** (see p.74), who has a leading reputation for land use and compliance advice.

The Clients: Recent projects for the team have included gaining clearance for the widening of the San Francisco airport's runway, and development work and housing approval for the University of California. Other clients include Rio Tinto (US Borax), US and global real estate developers, and petrochemical industries.

Pillsbury Winthrop LLP
see firm details p.866

The Firm: Increased market competition has meant that this historical heavyweight can no longer be considered the preeminent environment force in California. However, the firm retains a powerful presence in Northern California, where it is assessed by clients as *"an excellent team with a diverse repertoire."*

The Lawyers: Two San Francisco-based attorneys received recognition for their contributions. *"A former guru of the federal Clean Air Act (CAA) and air quality regulation,"* **Michael Barr** (see p.60) has a reputation as one of California's top lawyers in this area. Barr has represented Chevron and Sempra Energy on regulatory matters. **Michael Steel** (see p.73), meanwhile, is regarded as among the best lawyers for environmental regulatory compliance, and was described to researchers as a *"capable and knowledgeable Proposition 65 specialist."* Steel's clients have included the pharmaceutical and biotech companies DNAX, Schering-Plough and Medtronic.

The Clients: 3M; Imation; NEO; Affymetrix; American Airlines; Chevron; Association of American Railroads; TXI; Sempra Energy; Golden Gate National Parks Association; DNAX; Schering-Plough and Medtronic.

Gibson, Dunn & Crutcher LLP

The Firm: A *"vibrant"* team of 30 years' standing represents a mixture of national and international clients. Acknowledged for its litigation expertise, the environment and natural resources practice group also maintains a decent profile in compliance and regulatory counseling. The group's work frequently dovetails with that of the real estate, and international trade and customs practice groups.

The Lawyers: A multidisciplinary team headed by Patrick Dennis in Los Angeles undertakes work in cost recovery, enforcement, regulation and toxic tort matters. Dennis has advised clients on environmental issues relating to buying and selling power plant facilities and petroleum refineries.

The Clients: The firm advises major corporations in the banking, electronic, chemical, and oil and gas industries.

Weston Benshoof Rochefort Rubalcava MacCuish LLP

The Firm: Despite some recent partner departures – three left to join Morgan, Lewis & Bockius in 2002 – this boutique practice is rated among the market leaders for air quality control. The firm also possesses recognized strengths in land use and real estate law. Research identified an emphasis on work with public sector clients, and the group advised on clearance for the construction of the Alameda Corridor Project between Los Angeles and Long Beach.

The Lawyers: Described as *"someone who knows where all the skeletons are buried,"* **Sharon Rubalcava** was nominated to researchers for her air quality expertise and her work with the Air Resources Board (ARB).

The Clients: The firm advises companies from the petroleum, mining, aerospace and manufacturing industries. Its clients include the Alameda Corridor Transportation Authority.

Other Notable Practitioners

"Tirelessly involved in environmental law," **Jennifer Hernandez** (see p.65) of Beveridge & Diamond PC has built an extensive network among regulatory agencies. Her forthright style does not appeal to all commentators but it *"usually works with the agencies."* **Deborah Schmall** at Farella Braun & Martel is a *"bright and capable compliance lawyer"* with an agency background, who is rated by clients for her *"ability to secure favorable results."* **Peter Weiner** (see p.74) of Paul, Hastings, Janofsky & Walker LLP specializes in hazardous waste and brownfield remediation. More than an environmental lawyer, peers say he is also a *"highly capable"* business lawyer.

CALIFORNIA

INSOLVENCY/CORPORATE RECOVERY

CALIFORNIA
Leading firms
(Insolvency/Corporate Recovery)

1 KLEE, TUCHIN, BOGDANOFF *Los Angeles*
MILBANK, TWEED, HADLEY & MCCLOY *Los Angeles*
PACHULSKI, STANG, ZIEHL, YOUNG *Los Angeles*
2 STUTMAN, TREISTER & GLATT PC *Los Angeles*
3 LATHAM & WATKINS *Los Angeles*
MURPHY SHENEMAN JULIAN *San Francisco*
O'MELVENY & MYERS LLP *Los Angeles*
SKADDEN, ARPS, SLATE, MEAGHER *Los Angeles*
4 HOWARD, RICE, NEMEROVSKI *San Francisco*
SHEPPARD, MULLIN, RICHTER *San Francisco*
SIDLEY AUSTIN BROWN & WOOD *Los Angeles*

Leading individuals
(Insolvency/Corporate Recovery)

1 ARONZON Paul *Milbank, Tweed, Hadley,* Los Angeles
KLEE Kenneth *Klee, Tuchin, Bogdanoff,* Los Angeles
2 LUREY Michael *Latham & Watkins,* Los Angeles
MOORE Robert *Milbank, Tweed, Hadley,* Los Angeles
MURPHY Patrick *Murphy Sheneman,* San Francisco
PACHULSKI Richard *Pachulski, Stang,* Los Angeles
WHITE Robert *O'Melveny & Myers,* Los Angeles
3 GREENFIELD Robert *Stutman, Treister,* Los Angeles
LOGAN Ben *O'Melveny & Myers,* Los Angeles
TUCHIN Michael *Klee, Tuchin, Bogdanoff,* Los Angeles
4 BENVENUTTI Peter *Heller Ehrman White,* San Francisco
BOGDANOFF Lee *Klee, Tuchin, Bogdanoff,* Los Angeles
HAVEL Richard *Sidley Austin Brown,* Los Angeles
HOLDEN Frederick *Orrick, Herrington,* San Francisco
LOPES James *Howard, Rice, Nemerovski,* San Francisco
PACHULSKI Isaac *Stutman, Treister,* Los Angeles
PATTERSON Tom *Klee, Tuchin, Bogdanoff,* Los Angeles

Firms and individuals are listed alphabetically in each band.

Klee, Tuchin, Bogdanoff & Stern LLP
see firm details p.831

The Firm: Founded in 1999 by three partners from Stutman, Treister & Glatt, this one-office, 15-attorney firm is exclusively an insolvency boutique and handles a large proportion of debtors' work. The prevailing market feeling about this firm is one of potential – competitors consider it to be an *"up-and-coming"* group, with an *"impressive"* depth of practice.
The Lawyers: **Ken Klee** (see p.66), a co-author of the US Bankruptcy Code, was commended to researchers for his *"intellectual weight."* Although a professor at UCLA, he still manages to provide *"first-rate quality,"* both as an expert witness and in his counseling work. He receives sound support from the *"effective"* **Michael Tuchin** (see p.73) and **Lee Bogdanoff** (see p.61), who are both noted for the breadth of their practices, representing debtors, creditors and acquirers.

Tom Patterson (see p.70), who joined from Sidley Austin in January 2002 and has a focus on regulated industries and insurance is considered by peers to be *"a loss for Sidley Austin but a gain for Klee Tuchin."*
The Clients: On the debtors' side, the firm's work includes advising Frederick's of Hollywood, a national clothing retailer, in its Chapter 11 case. Representative creditor clients include CBS and Paramount Studios/Viacom, for whom the firm has acted in cases of bankruptcy filings of film exhibitors. The firm has also advised Anacomp, an information storage and retrieval company, which emerged from Chapter 11 debt restructuring on 31 December 2001. Other clients include Outsource International and Boston Chicken Plan Trust.

Milbank, Tweed, Hadley & McCloy
The Firm: The financial restructuring group at this multinational firm was singled out to researchers for its high-quality committee work on major cases.
The Lawyers: Its leading figure is the *"aggressive and energetic"* **Paul Aronzon**, who this year received universal commendation for his work on the Pacific Gas and Electric Company case, in which the firm represented the whole committee of creditors. Regarded by rivals as the group's *"chief deal-maker,"* Aronzon also comes recommended for his work with bondholders. The *"smart and creative"* **Bob Moore** also received consistently favorable market feedback from contemporaries who appreciate his reliability: *"If he gives his word, you can trust it."*
The Clients: The firm represents the official committee of unsecured creditors in the Enron case, and the agent for the secured lenders in the Global Crossing case. Other clients include debtors, creditors' committees and lenders' agents.

Pachulski, Stang, Ziehl, Young, Jones & Weintraub PC
see firm details p.860

The Firm: An established insolvency boutique with national scope, it boasts easily the largest team in the state and is acknowledged by competitors to get *"absolutely top-class work."* The firm's presence in the insolvency judicial center of Delaware is also frequently cited as a contributor to the firm's work on a number of prominent litigation cases and out-of-court workouts. The firm has experience in the representation of debtors in Chapter 11 cases, and in creditors' committee work. Recent matters include the completion of an equity plan of reorganization on behalf of Gencor Industries.
The Lawyers: **Richard Pachulski** is *"certainly the driving force"* of the team and has long experience, both in and out of court, representing

debtors and creditors. He is supported by *"probably as many bankruptcy lawyers as in many national firms."*
The Clients: Bondholders, debtors and creditors figure in its client base.

Stutman, Treister & Glatt PC
see firm details p.885

The Firm: A mid-sized firm, with one office and 33 attorneys, this bankruptcy boutique represents both debtors and creditors. In spite of the departure of Messrs Klee, Tuchin and Bogdanoff in 1999 to found their own boutique, the firm's *"reputation for quality from top to bottom"* persists. Clients in particular found the firm to be *"focused and creative."*
The Lawyers: **Bob Greenfield** is considered to be *"a particularly effective attorney,"* while the respected **Isaac Pachulski** was singled out for his experience of appellate matters.
The Clients: The firm acted as lead Chapter 11 counsel for Mariner Post-Acute Network and Mariner Health Group, and for AMC Entertainment in its acquisition of General Cinemas in the latter's Chapter 11 case. The firm also represented the chemical corporation Huntsman in out-of-court restructurings, and, in the Enron case, is acting for Baupost Group and Racepoint Partners. Other clients include: Southern California Edison; Edwards Theaters Circuit; Level 3; US Airways; FINOVA Capital and Georgia-Pacific.

Latham & Watkins
see firm details p.835

The Firm: This strong practice, which regularly represents banks and other financial instititutions in creditors' work, also has a significant reputation for debtor and bankruptcy M&A representation. The firm has acted as one of the special counsel for Pacific Gas and Electric Company, the utility involved in Chapter 11 reorganization proceedings in San Francisco. It also represented the company in a motion to consolidate multiple claims for personal injury into a single proceeding. Its Chapter 11 representation includes acting for NorthPoint Communications, which involved obtaining Bankruptcy Court approval to conclude the sale of its assets to AT&T for approximately $140 million. Further Chapter 11 representation includes Consolidated Freightways and certain of its affiliates. Creditors' committee work has included the cases of MedPartners Provider Network and Superior National Insurance Group. On the bankruptcy M&A side, the firm represented Schottenstein Stores in its purchase of Bugle Boy, an acquisition totaling approximately $68 million.
The Lawyers: The *"exceptionally talented"* **Mike Lurey** (see p.68) is the most prominent lawyer of the group; he is supported by a number of *"highly skilled"* attorneys.

INSOLVENCY/CORPORATE RECOVERY — CALIFORNIA

The Clients: Other clients include CSFB and Sizzler Restaurants International.

Murphy Sheneman Julian & Rogers
see firm details p.856

The Firm: Considered by some commentators to be *"one of the strongest boutiques around,"* this mid-sized firm has offices in San Francisco and Los Angeles. It represents both creditors and debtors, and is recognized by rivals to have *"significant expertise"* in litigation and business reorganizations.

The Lawyers: Leading name **Pat Murphy** was commended to researchers for his *"unique combination of encyclopedic knowledge and a great sense of humor."*

The Clients: Clients include creditors' committees, debtors and corporate clients.

O'Melveny & Myers LLP

The Firm: A national firm with a *"good, strong bankruptcy presence"* in California, it acts for bank groups and agents in restructurings and bankruptcies as well as providing debtors', creditors' committee and workout representation. The firm is active in entertainment and healthcare bankruptcies and workouts and has represented bank groups or agents for bank groups in certain Chapter 11 reorganizations including those of WorldCom, Sun Healthcare Group and Condor Systems. The firm advised the exit lender in the Chapter 11 case of United Artists Theaters and the exit lender and debtor-in-possession lenders in the case of AEI Resources, among others. Representative debtors' work includes the Chapter 11 cases of At Home, Phar-Mor and Mega Foods. The firm also represents many bank groups in out-of-court restructurings.

The Lawyers: Both the *"fabulous knowledge"* of **Bob White** and the *"first-rate"* work of **Ben Logan** were regularly endorsed to Chambers' researchers.

The Clients: Clients include Deutsche Bank; Bank of America; CIBC; Wachovia Bank; Wells Fargo; BNP Paribas; Angelo, Gordon & Co and CIGNA.

Skadden, Arps, Slate, Meagher & Flom LLP & Affiliates
see firm details p.878

The Firm: The firm's LA-based corporate restructuring group may be smaller than some of the market leaders but is nevertheless acknowledged by peers as a *"major practice that does sophisticated and complex work."* Emphasizing transactional rather than contentious work, the group, which includes noted writer Richard Levin, is generally seen advising corporate debtors. The firm negotiated a prepackaged Chapter 11 for ZiLOG, a semiconductor manufacturer with a $280 million total debt, and recently acted for Prandium in a prepackaged Chapter 11 restructuring, covering $225 million in bond debt. Representative out-of-court restructuring clients include Crown Pacific, for whom the firm reorganized $700 million in bank and insurance company debt.

The Clients: Additional clients include Sierra Pacific Resources, Owens Corning, Fedco and Wilshire Center Marketplace.

Howard, Rice, Nemerovski, Canady, Falk & Rabkin

The Firm: A full-service firm based in San Francisco, the bankruptcy practice here is described by competitors as *"significant,"* not least because of its high-profile representation of Pacific Gas and Electric Company, California's enormous utility which filed its Chapter 11 in April 2001. Other examples of Chapter 11 cases for the firm include those of Imaginarium and Paradigm Technology. The firm also represents entities seeking to acquire assets from a Chapter 11 estate, or to take control of a debtor-in-possession. An example of work in this area came with the group's advice to Cold Spring Management. This New York fund acquired a claim in the Chapter 11 case of Geothermal Resources International, and confirmed a plan of reorganization that preserved for the debtor approximately $60 million in net loss to be carried forward. Work for lenders has included advising a consortium of eight venture funds in the Chapter 11 case of Portable Energy Products.

The Lawyers: **James Lopes**, the lead counsel to Pacific Gas and Electric Company, won high market praise for his work on this – *"undoubtedly the biggest bankruptcy case pending on the West Coast."* He advised on both the Chapter 11 filing and the subsequent reorganization plan.

The Clients: Clients include: Pacific Gas and Electric Company; Imaginarium; Paradigm Technology; Cold Spring Management and Good Samaritan Hospital.

Sheppard, Mullin, Richter & Hampton LLP

The Firm: Bankruptcy work is seen by rivals to be a *"significant component"* of this California-based, full-service firm's workload. The bankruptcy and financial restructuring group offers experience in all types of insolvency matters and is reputed to be *"particularly strong"* when acting on the creditors' side.

The Lawyers: Chair of the finance and bankruptcy practice group is Richard Brunette, a specialist in commercial litigation and business bankruptcies.

The Clients: Creditors' work includes representation of GE Capital in a large, single asset real estate case. The firm also acted on behalf of the unofficial committee of lessors of equipment in At Home's Chapter 11 case. On the debtors' side, the firm has acted for speciality gift retailer Natural Wonders in its Chapter 11 proceedings. The firm regularly acts for banking clients, including Bank of America, Union Bank of California, Wells Fargo and Comerica.

Sidley Austin Brown & Wood
see firm details p.877

The Firm: A *"deep bench of lawyers with any number of first-rate people,"* the practice is particularly admired for its creditors' representation, although it also offers a full range of advice to debtors, committees of bondholders, trustees, acquirers and troubled companies. The firm has had recent involvement in the Kmart Chapter 11 case, acting for Noritsu America (a subsidiary of Japan-based Noritsu Koki), supplier of on-site photo processing equipment. It also advised Northwind Aladdin in adversary proceedings with Aladdin Hotel & Casino, which had filed for Chapter 11 protection.

The Lawyers: **Rich Havel** was often mentioned to researchers as a reliable destination for client referrals. Recently, he has focused his practice on large corporates involved in out-of-court or Chapter 11 restructurings, working with both creditors and financially distressed companies.

The Clients: Other clients include the Healthcare Association of Southern California, Warnaco Group, Thurston Group, ACI Telecommunications and CIBC.

Other Notable Practitioners

Peter Benvenutti, head of the bankruptcy practice at Heller Ehrman White & McAuliffe LLP, was commended to researchers for his substantial experience in complex business restructurings, as well as for his courtroom expertise. **Fred Holden** was noted to researchers for his *"excellent judgment."* A former member of the now dissolved Brobeck, Phleger & Harrison, he has joined the San Francisco office of Orrick, Herrington & Sutcliffe LLP. He has a client portfolio comprising debtors, creditors and creditors' committees, and is also renowned for his advice on government receiverships. His highlights include serving as general counsel to a trustee of BCCI and representing Philippine Airlines in a $2.5 billion reorganization and workout of aircraft financing. He has also been active in the preparation to file a Chapter 11 case expected to resolve over $5 billion of asbestos claims.

CALIFORNIA — INSURANCE

INSURANCE

CALIFORNIA
Leading firms (Insurance)

1
- HANCOCK ROTHERT *Los Angeles, San Francisco*
- HELLER EHRMAN WHITE *Los Angeles, San Francisco*
- HOWREY SIMON ARNOLD & WHITE *Los Angeles*

2
- O'MELVENY & MYERS LLP *San Francisco*

3
- BARGER & WOLEN *Los Angeles*
- LATHAM & WATKINS *Los Angeles*
- MUNGER, TOLLES & OLSON *Los Angeles*
- SONNENSCHEIN NATH & ROSENTHAL *San Francisco*

Leading individuals (Insurance)

1
- BROWN Donald *Covington & Burling, San Francisco*
- GOODWIN David *Heller Ehrman White, San Francisco*
- MATTHEWS Philip *Hancock, Rothert, San Francisco*
- PASICH Kirk *Howrey Simon Arnold, Los Angeles*

2
- CATHCART Patrick *Hancock, Rothert, San Francisco*
- GOLDBERG Stephen *Heller Ehrman White, Los Angeles*
- SEABOLT Richard *Hancock, Rothert, San Francisco*
- STEUBER David *Howrey Simon Arnold, Los Angeles*

3
- BABBE David *Morrison & Foerster LLP, Los Angeles*
- CHECOV Martin *O'Melveny & Myers, San Francisco*
- COHEN Nancy *Heller Ehrman White, Los Angeles*
- GLAD Paul *Sonnenschein Nath, San Francisco*
- HOBEL Lawrence *Heller Ehrman White, San Francisco*
- LEVIN Barry *Heller Ehrman White, San Francisco*
- OAKES Royal *Barger & Wolen, Los Angeles*

4
- CRANE Steven *Berkes Crane Robinson, Los Angeles*
- LERMAN Cary *Munger, Tolles & Olson, Los Angeles*
- LUNDBERG Andrew *Latham & Watkins, Los Angeles*
- ROSEN Peter *Mayer, Brown, Rowe & Maw, Los Angeles*

Firms and individuals are listed alphabetically in each band.

Hancock Rothert & Bunshoft LLP
see firm details p.811
The Firm: Powered by its connections with the London Market, this *"aggressive"* insurer group won market approval from all quarters. Clients were particularly vocal in their praise, with one describing the firm's heavy-hitting partners as *"the most impressive carriers' counsel I've met."* Having been instrumental in major environmental and asbestos coverage matters, including the Aerojet and Shell Oil-Rocky Mountain Arsenal cases, the group continues to enjoy an active practice representing insurers in coverage disputes with policyholders.
The Lawyers: The *"diplomatic"* **Philip Matthews** (see p.68) commands universal respect. A *"reasonable and ethical"* lawyer who *"doesn't pound his fists,"* he was applauded by rivals as a *"worthy adversary"* with whom *"you can negotiate and get a deal done."* General litigator **Rick Seabolt** (see p.72) was also strongly endorsed by peers for his *"integrity and reliability,"* and for the *"superior quality"* of his written work and advocacy. He is currently acting in litigation involving Raytheon, a large defense contractor in Massachusetts. **Pat Cathcart** (see p.62) also came to the attention of researchers. Described as a *"knowledgeable, reasonable and effective"* attorney, he received consistent market support for the quality of his appellate work.
The Clients: The group recently celebrated a major victory on behalf of underwriters at Lloyd's in the landmark Powerine case. It also advised on an insurance coverage matter pending in Indiana, involving Kraft.

Heller Ehrman White & McAuliffe LLP
The Firm: Having cut its teeth with Johns Manville on asbestos coverage matters in the 1980's, the group has since diversified and now enjoys a particularly renowned name for business interruption claims. The firm's insurance coverage practice, bolstered by a strong litigation group, also retains its *"top-notch"* reputation among policyholder firms in California.
The Lawyers: In a formidably deep team, **David Goodwin** shines as an attorney who is *"preeminent as a scholar and a tactician."* A specialist in Supreme Court of California appellate work, he is renowned among peers for his *"perfect judgment"* and *"quiet intelligence."* As a counselor, clients praised his *"efficiency"* and *"encyclopedic knowledge of insurance law."* He is presently acting for British Petroleum against insurers in a $500 million business interruption claim, arising from the June 1999 explosion of the Olympic pipeline in Bellingham, Washington. *"Exceptional"* and *"highly experienced"* coverage litigators **Steve Goldberg** and **Nancy Cohen** were recommended to researchers for their highly publicized work for GMAC, the principal lender to Larry Silverstein, in the pending multibillion dollar coverage litigation against Swiss Re. **Barry Levin** also won peer endorsement as an *"effective"* trial lawyer, in which capacity he has most recently acted for major pharmaceutical company Syntex in an insurance coverage dispute involving the cleanup of dioxin contamination in Times Beach, Missouri. *"Smart and determined"* **Lawrence Hobel** also impressed rivals, who pointed to his work on behalf of clients such as Kaiser Aluminium.
The Clients: Other clients include: Texaco, Pacific Gas & Electric Company and Alcoa.

Howrey Simon Arnold & White
The Firm: With the arrival of 28 coverage lawyers from Troop Steuber Pasich, Reddick & Tobey in January 2001, the firm's insurance coverage practice has enjoyed a growth that is unsurpassed in California. Now 50 strong, the team is renowned among rivals for its *"adversarial"* representation of a broad client base of policyholders in coverage litigation. Several commentators proclaimed the group to be *"the best in California."* In addition to the traditional areas of environmental and asbestos coverage litigation, the team handles matters regarding coverage for advertising liabilities, business interruption, computer viruses, copyright infringement, employee fidelity claims, directors' and officers' liabilities, and natural disaster losses.
The Lawyers: **Kirk Pasich** is esteemed by rivals as a *"passionate"* and *"highly effective"* trial lawyer, although his *"aggressive"* courtroom manner does not meet with universal approval. However, he is regarded as the market leader for policyholder representation in California, and has carved out a particular niche in the area of entertainment industry recovery, where he has one of the largest practices in the US. Clients include ABC, Sony Pictures, Walt Disney, Universal Studios, Miramax and 20thCentury Fox. Practice area coleader **Dave Steuber** was firmly endorsed as a *"superb and credible"* trial lawyer, and is admired by opponents for his *"good working relationships with insurers."* He represented PepsiAmericas against major insurers in coverage litigation for claims of environmental contamination, property damage, personal injury and toxic tort. In addition, he acted for Union Pacific in coverage disputes arising from environmental liabilities incurred by Southern Pacific at sites across North America.
The Clients: Coca-Cola; Lucasfilm; Sony Pictures; Walt Disney; PepsiAmericas and Union Pacific.

O'Melveny & Myers LLP
The Firm: The group gained particularly strong market support for its representation of insurers in California. A team of more than 50 attorneys nationally handles a broad range of matters for its insurance company clients, including coverage and bad faith litigation, appellate work, reinsurance coverage arbitrations, consumer and class action defense and insolvency proceedings.
The Lawyers: **Martin Checov** was firmly endorsed to researchers as an *"aggressive but fair attorney"* who *"knows the law."* Clients appreciated his *"integrity and business acumen."* He represented insurance company clients in the defense of California Business & Professions Code Section 17200 (unfair competition claims). In a consultative role, he has also assisted insurer clients with the drafting of policy language.
The Clients: CIGNA Companies; Lloyd's and London Market insurers; Reliance Insurance Company; State Farm.

Barger & Wolen
The Firm: Conceived as an insurance regulatory, corporate and litigation firm, this 30-year-old boutique won praise from peers as a *"smart and talented"* team with a notable insurance compa-

INSURANCE — CALIFORNIA

ny clientele. In addition to regulatory work, the firm also acts for insurance companies in class actions, bad faith and punitive damages claims, reinsurance contract disputes, life insurance and disability claims.
The Lawyers: Royal Oakes gained consistent recommendation from contemporaries. As well as acting for clients including UnumProvident and MetLife, he is also known for his high-profile work as general counsel to the Radio and Television News Association of Southern California.
The Clients: Other clients include: Travelers, AXA and Farmers.

Latham & Watkins
see firm details p.835
The Firm: This *"solid"* insurance practice of about 40 lawyers was noted to researchers for its *"bright attorneys"* and occasional appearances on major cases, although not all commentators appreciated the firm's *"highly adversarial"* approach to litigation. Having built its practice on CERCLA litigation, the group now advises on a broad range of insurance matters, including business interruption cases, insurance matters in the entertainment industry and policy drafting.
The Lawyers: Clients and rivals commended the *"sharp and analytical"* Andy Lundberg (see p.68) for the *"energy and creativity"* he brings to his work. He acted for a Silicon Valley bank in the Motion Picture Gap Financing Insurance litigation against major insurers, including AIG.
The Clients: Other work includes representing America West Airlines against Zurich in a business interruption claim arising from the failure of its primary computer system over a holiday weekend in 2000. Pepperdine University is also a client of the firm.

Munger, Tolles & Olson
The Firm: Bolstered by a *"vigorous"* litigation practice, a smaller group focuses on insurance coverage litigation for corporate policyholders in a range of disputes. These flow from general liability policies, directors and officers and errors and omissions coverage, and fidelity bonds, as well as asbestos and environmental matters. The firm also undertakes analysis and consultancy work and negotiates on behalf of policyholder clients to maximize policy coverage. It recently concluded a coverage matter for Stauffer Chemical Company (now Aventis CropScience USA). This concerned environmental liabilities relating to pollution from an acid mine on Iron Mountain.
The Lawyers: Cary Lerman won endorsement from peers, who respect him for his *"excellent standard"* of work. He acted for a major oil company against its insurers in a coverage dispute relating to wrongful death actions following environmental exposure.
The Clients: Other clients include: Allstate and National Medical Enterprises.

Sonnenschein Nath & Rosenthal
see firm details p.882
The Firm: The group undertakes a broad range of work for insurance company clients including entity formation, insurance regulatory work, enforcement intervention, reinsurance and risk transfer work. This sits alongside insolvency, bankruptcy and workout matters, securities work and insurance coverage, class action, bad faith and antitrust litigation.
The Lawyers: Paul Glad (see p.64) heads the practice, and was commended to researchers as a *"voluble but well-informed and highly visible"* appellate specialist. He is particularly recognized by clients for his ability to *"turn cases around."*
The Clients: Clients include: Travelers; Fireman's Fund; Allstate and AIG Companies.

Other Notable Practitioners
Peter Rosen (see p.71) of Mayer, Brown, Rowe & Maw is now regarded by peers as having *"graduated to the big time,"* with his advice to Westfield in the high-profile World Trade Center coverage litigation against Swiss Re. Morrison & Foerster LLP's **David Babbe** (see p.60) was firmly commended by peers as a *"top-drawer strategist."* Clients appreciate that he is *"really good at making sure that the client knows what's going on all the time."* Major clients include Hartford and Travelers, for whom he is currently acting in a coverage dispute with a telecommunications company. Having recently formed Berkes Crane Robinson & Seal LLP, **Steven Crane** won praise from peers as a *"superb analyst,"* with commentators describing him as *"a creative leader in major cases – a lawyer who advances the ball."* He was involved in the high-profile Aerojet case and continues to have a profile for complex litigation, insurance coverage, bad faith, environmental law, toxic tort and mediation matters. **Don Brown** is regarded by peers and clients as *"among the best"* in California. A leading light at the now dissolved firm, Brobeck, Phleger & Harrison LLP, he has taken residence at the San Francisco office of Covington & Burling. He is a *"bright and creative"* policyholder lawyer, noted for his fluent courtroom manner, and appeals to clients as *"a responsive, logical attorney who's easy to talk to."* he acted as lead counsel for ExxonMobil in its high-profile $3 billion dollar lawsuit against 300 insurers over coverage for environmental cleanup liabilities across North America. He has also advised Fortune 100 policyholder companies in the latest wave of asbestos disputes, involving coverage for product and premises liability

INTELLECTUAL PROPERTY

CALIFORNIA
Leading firms (Intellectual Property)

1. IRELL & MANELLA LLP *Los Angeles*
2. MORRISON & FOERSTER *Palo Alto, San Francisco*
   WEIL, GOTSHAL & MANGES LLP *Redwood Shores*
3. FENWICK & WEST *Palo Alto*
   FINNEGAN HENDERSON FARABOW *Palo Alto*
   FISH & NEAVE *Palo Alto*
4. CHRISTIE, PARKER & HALE, LLP *Pasadena*
   DAY CASEBEER MADRID & BATCHELDER *Cupertino*
   KEKER & VAN NEST LLP *San Francisco*
   KIRKLAND & ELLIS *Los Angeles*
   KNOBBE MARTENS OLSON & BEAR *San Francisco*
   MCDERMOTT, WILL & EMERY *Palo Alto*
   SKADDEN, ARPS *Palo Alto*
   TOWNSEND AND TOWNSEND *San Francisco*

Firms are listed alphabetically in each band.

Irell & Manella LLP
The Firm: *"Full of brilliant people who know what there is to know,"* the firm's IP groups continue to stand above the competition. The litigation department is said by interviewees to have an *"outstanding track record"* and covers all areas of relevant law, including patent infringement, trademark, copyright, trade secrets and antitrust issues. Although the firm's transactional expertise is sometimes overshadowed, it features prominently on a number of high-premium deals, often advising clients from the hi-tech and entertainment sectors.
The Lawyers: Endorsed to researchers as *"one of the greats of the profession,"* **Morgan Chu** is regarded by peers as a *"courageous and tenacious"* litigator who will *"take on anything and everyone."* Clients especially appreciate his ability to *"communicate the most complex subject matter in a simple manner."*
The Clients: Clients come from an enormous range of industries, including software, semiconductor, biotech, pharmaceutical and telecom. They include: Hewlett-Packard; Affymetrix; Elan; Novellus Systems; AT&T; Western Digital; Intel and Broadcom.

Morrison & Foerster LLP
see firm details p.854
The Firm: A full-service IP practice group, respected by peers for its *"quality in depth,"* advises on the spectrum of transactional and contentious matters. The team's patent work concerns industries such as biotech, pharmaceutical, mechanical engineering, software and telecommunications, while the firm also represents clients on a range of copyright, trade secrets and trademark-related issues. It successfully rep-

CALIFORNIA

INTELLECTUAL PROPERTY

CALIFORNIA
Leading individuals
(Intellectual Property)

★ **CHU Morgan** *Irell & Manella LLP,* Los Angeles

1
- **McMAHON Terry** *McDermott, Will & Emery,* Palo Alto
- **POWERS Matthew** *Weil, Gotshal,* Redwood Shores

2
- **DAY Lloyd (Rusty)** *Day Casebeer Madrid,* Cupertino
- **HAYES David** *Fenwick & West,* Palo Alto
- **JACOBS Michael** *Morrison & Foerster,* San Francisco
- **KRUPKA Robert** *Kirkland & Ellis,* Los Angeles
- **MARTENS Don** *Knobbe Martens Olson & Bear,* Irvine
- **PRETTY Laurence** *Christie, Parker & Hale,* Pasadena

3
- **ABEL Sally** *Fenwick & West,* Palo Alto
- **KEKER John** *Keker & Van Nest LLP,* San Francisco
- **LAURIE Ronald** *Skadden, Arps, Slate, Meagher,* Palo Alto
- **STREETER Jon** *Keker & Van Nest LLP,* San Francisco

4
- **BRIDGES Andrew** *Wilson Sonsini Goodrich,* Palo Alto
- **DODSON Gerald** *Morrison & Foerster LLP,* Palo Alto
- **McELHINNY Harold** *Morrison & Foerster,* San Francisco
- **SMITH Neil** *Howard, Rice, Nemerovski,* San Francisco

Up-and-coming individuals
- **JOHNSON Daniel** *Fenwick & West,* San Francisco

Individuals are listed alphabetically in each band.

---

resented Festo in a landmark case against Shoketsu Kinzoku Kogyo Kabushiki – a patent infringement case involving the availability of the 'doctrine of equivalents' to amended claims.
The Lawyers: *"Sensible and straightforward"* **Michael Jacobs** (see p.66) is the group's leading name; he focuses on litigating patents, copyright and trade secrets cases. He is most associated with expertise in life sciences, where he has represented Chiron in a number of patent disputes. Esteemed patent litigator **Gerald Dodson** (see p.63) appears on a variety of complex cases and represented the Universtiy of Rochester Medical Center in a major patent infringement against Pharmacia, GD Searle, Pfizer and Monsanto, involving the drug Celebrex. He also won a unanimous jury verdict for Silicon Genesis in a patent infrngement brought by Soitec. **Harold McElhinny** (see p.68) was also recommended to researchers; he is a trial lawyer with a general federal and state court litigation practice, including various IP matters.
The Clients: Other clients include Affymetrix, Intel, Yahoo! and Fujitsu.

Weil, Gotshal & Manges LLP
see firm details p.897
The Firm: The firm's IP practice group in California has expertise in all areas of IP law, but is especially known for its technology litigation group, which focuses on patents relating to semiconductor devices, DNA sequencing, medical devices and telecommunications. The team recently represented PerkinElmer's Applied Biosystems Division in a major patent infringement action involving DNA sequencing technology.
The Lawyers: *"Creative"* **Matt Powers** (see p.70) is recognized as a major player in Silicon Valley. He tries patent and trade secrets cases in a wide range of technology areas, including semiconductor services, manufacturing equipment and processes, DNA sequencing, medical devices and other biotech matters. His client portfolio includes Micron, for whom he was lead counsel in a multi-jurisdictional patent action, involving DRAM technology. He also represented Alcatel on its patent infringement suits against Cisco Systems.
The Clients: Clients include: Intel; Oracle; National Semiconductor; Pfizer and SmithKline Beecham.

Fenwick & West
The Firm: *"We see these guys pretty regularly,"* say competitors of this highly rated IP group, which is equally renowned for transactional and contentious work. The firm was singled out to researchers for its deep bench of talented individual practitioners.
The Lawyers: Head of the IP group **David Hayes** is viewed by peers as a *"brilliant"* practitioner who *"really pays attention to detail."* His practice concentrates on IP litigation as well as counseling and advice on technology transfers, distribution and licensing. He has appeared on the Napster litigation, which raised a number of copyright law issues, and also represented T-Netix in its patent suit against MCI WorldCom regarding automated phone services to prisons. *"Excellent"* trademark attorney **Sally Abel** focuses on counseling and the management of international trademarks, and on trademark rights in cyberspace. She is a panelist at WIPO and has been involved in a number of high-profile domain name disputes. **Daniel Johnson** remains regarded as an up-and-coming name in this area and is an expert in copyright and hi-tech patent litigation and licensing issues. He is currently representing ONI in a patent dispute involving fiber-optic networks, and, on the copyright side, has appeared for Compuware against IBM in a software dispute.
The Clients: Clients include: Sun Microsystems; Apple; Cisco Systems; NetScreen; Asyst Technology and Logitech.

Finnegan Henderson Farabow Garrett & Dunner LLP
The Firm: While it is better known for its unparalleled strength in Washington DC, the firm's IP offering in Palo Alto is acknowledged by competitors as a *"pretty successful"* branch of the national operation. Here, the team offers counseling, planning and transactional and litigation services, although it is most recognized for its patent prosecution and litigation expertise. Recent successes include defending Home Diagnostics against LifeScan, and ICSI against Winbond in patent infringement disputes.
The Clients: The firm's clientele, as on the East Coast, extends to some of the biggest global names from technology and industry: Hewlett-Packard; Agilent Technologies; Sun Microsystems; Amgen; Immunex; Mattel; Applied Biosystems; Eli Lilly; GlaxoSmithKline; 3M; American Home Products; Head Sports and Boeing, among others.

Fish & Neave
The Firm: *"At the upper end of the scale"* according to rivals, the firm's West Coast IP capacity continues to earn widespread respect, although its peerless New York office is still far better known. Servicing a predominantly hi-tech clientele, the team handles all aspects of IP law but is most often linked with high-profile patent litigation cases.
The Clients: The firm represented Compaq in a patent lawsuit against eMachines, and acted for Purdue Pharma in a suit against Endo Pharmaceuticals. Other clients include Lucent Technologies, LSI Logic, Harrah's Entertainment and VIA Technologies.

Christie, Parker & Hale, LLP
The Firm: This boutique earned high market commendation for the *"great breadth of its practice"* and the *"sheer consistency"* of its attorneys. The group advises on patents, trademark, copyright, plant variety protection, litigation and IP matters.
The Clients: Other notable clients include Durel and Teleflora.

Day Casebeer Madrid & Batchelder LLP
The Firm: The firm continues to be respected by lawyers and clients alike and owes its reputation principally to the efforts of an *"outstanding"* IP litigation group. The team advised Sun Microsystems in its antitrust, copyright and unfair competition suit against Microsoft, and appeared for Amgen in its dispute against Hoechst Marion Roussel.
The Lawyers: Led by flagship partner **Rusty Day**, the firm represents a powerful hi-tech clientele on the prosecution, enforcement and defense of IP rights worldwide.
The Clients: Notable in its client roster are PerkinElmer, Genentech, Geron, ICOS, National Semiconductor, QUALCOMM and Raytheon.

Keker & Van Nest LLP
The Firm: The firm has a wonderful reputation for general business litigation, and although not generally characterized as IP specialists, its attor-

INTELLECTUAL PROPERTY — CALIFORNIA

neys have made numerous courtroom appearances on patent trade secret and copyright infringement disputes.

The Lawyers: *"One of the best trial lawyers in the business,"* **John Keker**'s IP expertise is but one strand of his contentious practice. In this field, he frequently appears at appellate level for clients from the technology industry and has represented Harris Corporation in various patent infringement disputes and acted on a patent dispute for Tegal against Tokyo Electron. **Jon Streeter** *"shows up wherever you look."* This *"splendid"* litigator has a burgeoning reputation for complex patent disputes.

The Clients: Clients include Tegal and Harris Corporation.

Kirkland & Ellis
see firm details p.830

The Firm: The firm's IP practice group specializes in litigation, transactional, counseling and administrative matters involving patent, design, trademark, copyright and IT-related issues. The group's contentious expertise came in for particularly high praise; it recently represented Honeywell against Hamilton Sundstrand in a patent dispute concerning aircraft auxiliary power systems.

The Lawyers: A trial lawyer with *"great personality and insight,"* **Bob Krupka** (see p.66) was commended to researchers as the principal reason for the firm's prominence in this sector. He specializes in patent, copyright, trademark and trade secrets litigation for clients from various industries. Highlights include representing Schering-Plough in a patent dispute connected with antihistamines.

The Clients: Pioneer Electronics is another notable client.

Knobbe Martens Olson & Bear

The Firm: Another notable West Coast IP specialist, the firm advises a broad client base on the full spectrum of relevant law.

The Lawyers: Much of its profile is ascribed to the vision of leading light **Don Martens**, endorsed to researchers as an attorney who has *"passed the test of time and succeeded."* He is a renowned patent litigator, with acknowledged expertise in the biotech and hi-tech sectors.

The Clients: The firm has represented major clients such as Callaway Golf and American Airlines on patent disputes.

McDermott, Will & Emery
see firm details p.846

The Firm: The firm has a substantial IP practice that services clients on prosecution, counseling and litigation. Its litigation group was recently successful in obtaining a trademark injunction for EMC against Hewlett-Packard to change the name and designation of a product line.

The Lawyers: Interviewees focused their attention on *"one of the biggest names in the Valley,"* **Terry McMahon** (see p.68). A high-profile litigator, he primarily deals with patent disputes, but has also been involved in trademark, copyright and trade secrets cases. He successfully represented Broadcom in a jury trial relating to digital video processing and computer network technology.

The Clients: Other clients include: Seagate Technology; Logitech; Motorola; Advanced Micro Devices; Microsoft and Lucasfilm.

Skadden, Arps, Slate, Meagher & Flom LLP & Affiliates
see firm details p.878

The Firm: The IP and technology group offers expertise in litigation, counseling, technology transfer and licensing agreements, patents, trademark and copyright prosecution, and strategic planning and portfolio analysis. In addition, the firm's vast corporate client base provides the department with a wealth of transactional opportunities.

The Lawyers: *"An excellent strategist,"* **Ronald Laurie** (see p.67) was roundly endorsed by clients for his versatile practice, which includes transactional work, patent prosecution and litigation.

The Clients: AlliedSignal, Anheuser-Busch, Estée Lauder, Gillette, Pfizer, Reuters America, Sun Microsystems and US Airways are some notable client names.

Townsend and Townsend and Crew LLP

The Firm: This boutique provides all IP-related services including transactions, patent litigation and prosecution, trademark and copyright advice. A number of peers commented that they would be *"delighted"* to refer clients to this *"outstandingly competent"* firm. The group is acknowledged to have an excellent track record in patent cases relating to the medical sector. It also secured a substantial settlement for Bath & Beyond in a trademark infringement case against Bed Bath & Beyond.

The Clients: Clients include: Oracle; Flextronics; Microsoft; Hyundai Electronics and MIPS Technologies.

Other Notable Practitioners

Neil Smith of Howard, Rice, Nemerovski, Canady, Falk & Rabkin was commended to researchers as *"a local favorite among trademark practitioners."* He received strong market endorsement for his strength as a courtroom performer. **Andrew Bridges** of Wilson Sonsini Goodrich & Rosati also came in for sustained approval as a *"smart and streetwise"* expert on trademark law. Recently recruited from Christie, Parker & Hale to Hogan & Hartson, patent litigator **Laurence Pretty** impresses opponents with his courtroom presence and is noted by clients for his ability to *"break complex matters down to their essentials."* He has litigated on a range of patent disputes, appearing on a significant breast implant patent infringement case on behalf of 3M and representing Bausch & Lomb in its suit against Barnes-Hind/Hydrocurve over patented contact lenses.

LITIGATION — GENERAL COMMERCIAL

Gibson, Dunn & Crutcher LLP

The Firm: One of California's largest litigation groups. Operates from five Californian offices. Recommended by peers for its quality and strength in depth. The department is split into groups dedicated to antitrust, legal malpractice, insurance and securities. In addition, the firm possesses a top-tier appellate practice, which famously secured a Supreme Court victory for George W Bush, and, in the commercial sphere, won major cases for DaimlerChrysler and Dow Jones.

The Lawyers: Eminent litigator Robert Warren is one of the firm's long-standing members. Now over 70 years of age, he is not actively seeking new cases. **Bob Cooper**, a popular figure in Californian legal circles, is said to be one of the finest trial lawyers around. Juries are said to warm to his *"smooth, polished"* style, most typically in antitrust matters. He secured a win for American Airlines in a Department of Justice action, alleging monopolization of the slots at Dallas-Fort Worth Airport. Legal malpractice defense cases also feature in his caseload, such as a recent high-profile matter for O'Melveny & Myers.

The Clients: The firm acts for a number of heavyweight clients including: American Airlines; Intel; Hewlett-Packard; Northrop; Tenet Healthcare; AMR and DaimlerChrysler.

Morrison & Foerster LLP
see firm details p.854

The Firm: A major force in the Bay Area, the litigation team received sustained market endorsement as a group that *"instantly and impressively jumps out of the pack."* Of the firm's 350 litigators, 150 work from the San Francisco office, with

CALIFORNIA — LITIGATION

CALIFORNIA
Leading firms
(Litigation: General Commercial)

Band 1
- GIBSON, DUNN & CRUTCHER LLP *Los Angeles*
- MORRISON & FOERSTER LLP *San Francisco*
- WILSON SONSINI GOODRICH & ROSATI *Palo Alto*

Band 2
- ALSCHULER GROSSMAN STEIN *Los Angeles*
- HELLER EHRMAN WHITE & McAULIFFE *Los Angeles*
- KEKER & VAN NEST LLP *San Francisco*
- LATHAM & WATKINS LLP *Los Angeles*
- MILBERG WEISS BERSHAD HYNES *San Diego*
- MUNGER, TOLLES & OLSON *Los Angeles*
- O'MELVENY & MYERS LLP *Los Angeles*

Band 3
- BINGHAM MCCUTCHEN LLP *Los Angeles*
- BLECHER & COLLINS *Los Angeles*
- CLIFFORD CHANCE US LLP *San Francisco*
- COTCHETT, PITRE, SIMON *Burlingame*
- FARELLA BRAUN & MARTEL LLP *San Francisco*
- FOGEL, FELDMAN, OSTROV *Santa Monica*
- GREENE, BROILLET, TAYLOR *Santa Monica*
- HENNIGAN, BENNETT & DORMAN *Los Angeles*
- O'DONNELL & SHAEFFER *Los Angeles*
- QUINN EMANUEL URQUHART OLIVER *Los Angeles*

Leading individuals
(Litigation: General Commercial)

Band 1
- BROSNAHAN James *Morrison*, San Francisco
- GROSSMAN Marshall *Alschuler Grossman*, Los Angeles
- KEKER John *Keker & Van Nest LLP*, San Francisco
- LERACH William *Milberg Weiss Bershad*, San Diego

Band 2
- BLECHER Maxwell *Blecher & Collins*, Los Angeles
- BRIAN Brad *Munger, Tolles & Olson*, Los Angeles
- COOPER Robert *Gibson, Dunn & Crutcher*, Los Angeles
- COTCHETT Joseph *Cotchett, Pitre, Simon*, Burlingame
- FELDMAN Robert *Wilson Sonsini Goodrich*, Palo Alto
- GOLDMAN Melvin *Morrison*, San Francisco
- O'DONNELL Pierce *O'Donnell & Shaeffer*, Los Angeles
- OLSON Ronald *Munger, Tolles & Olson*, Los Angeles
- VANYO Bruce *Wilson Sonsini Goodrich & Rosati*, Palo Alto

Band 3
- ARONSON Seth *O'Melveny & Myers LLP*, Los Angeles
- DAWES Paul *Latham & Watkins LLP*, Menlo Park
- FELDMAN Boris *Wilson Sonsini Goodrich*, Palo Alto
- FELDMAN Larry *Fogel, Feldman, Ostrov*, Santa Monica
- GREENE Browne *Greene, Broillet, Taylor*, Santa Monica
- HENNIGAN Mike *Hennigan, Bennett*, Los Angeles
- LONG Robert *Latham & Watkins LLP*, Los Angeles
- LYNCH Patrick *O'Melveny & Myers LLP*, Los Angeles
- POPOFSKY Laurence *Heller Ehrman*, San Francisco
- QUINN John *Quinn Emanuel Urquhart, LLP*, Los Angeles
- RUBY Allen *Ruby & Schofield*, San José
- SCHWAB Douglas *Heller Ehrman White*, San Francisco
- SNOW Tower *Clifford Chance US LLP*, San Francisco
- YOUNG Doug *Farella Braun & Martel*, San Francisco

Firms and individuals are listed alphabetically in each band.

---

securities class actions, financial services disputes and IP litigation forming the major focus of the practice. A further seven offices in California give the firm statewide coverage.

The Lawyers: Perhaps the highest profile among Californian lawyers belongs to **James Brosnahan** (see p.61). In 2002, he represented John Walker Lindh, the American accused of supporting the Taliban, yet his versatility and advocacy skills have seen him score trial victories in several areas of practice - complex commercial, patent and criminal. In 2001, Brosnahan successfully defended Altera in a patent case concerning reprogrammable computer chips. Also based in San Francisco is **Mel Goldman** (see p.64), a securities class action defense expert. One peer conceded that losing an audition to him was *"bearable - he's a dazzling lawyer with a fantastic courtroom presence."*

The Clients: The firm recently represented DoubleClick in a series of class actions concerning internet privacy. Other clients include: Nestlé; Bank of America; Apple and Chevron.

Wilson Sonsini Goodrich & Rosati

The Firm: Although this hi-tech powerhouse is felt to lack the breadth of some of its nearest rivals, it is acknowledged to excel in three core areas - securities, IP and employment litigation. All senior litigators specialize in one of these fields. Securities litigation is the group's forte, where it secured many of the most lucrative class action defense cases. Large and highly leveraged teams are equipped to handle a high volume of cases, with values ranging from $200-300 million to $10 billion.

The Lawyers: Chambers' researchers encountered strong market approval for **Robert Feldman** as a commercial litigation generalist, although his patent litigation practice received special attention. On the securities front, two names stand out: the architect of the practice, **Bruce Vanyo**; and fellow partner, **Boris Feldman**. Both were singled out for the strength of their hi-tech practices. They represent public companies, their directors and officers in securities litigation, shareholder class actions, derivative lawsuits and SEC enforcement proceedings. Bruce Vanyo has notched up about 120 securities class actions, while Boris Feldman has been lead counsel in over 70.

The Clients: Clients include: Autodesk; Genentech; Hewlett-Packard; 3Com; Palm; Boeing; Dell; Fluor; America West; Seagate Technology; Silicon Graphics; Sun Microsystems; Sybase; Mirage Resorts; Banc of America Securities and Goldman Sachs.

Alschuler Grossman Stein & Kahan LLP
see firm details p.762

The Firm: An independent, LA-based firm specializing in complex business litigation, it has close relationships with prominent firms in the US and overseas. With over 80 attorneys, the group is known for its insurance and professional liability expertise, and acts for top names in the entertainment industry.

The Lawyers: Marshall Grossman (see p.65) is the firm's outstanding practitioner, and is regarded in LA circles as a forceful and robust litigator with a track record of trial successes. His team represented Arthur Andersen in a $1.2 billion securities class action - the first securities fraud case to go to trial in ten years. He also advised US and international insurance companies, such as Royal & SunAlliance.

The Clients: In the entertainment sector, partners at this firm have helped to negotiate Mariah Carey's multimillion contractual settlement with EMI. Other clients include DreamWorks SKG and Tommy Hilfiger.

Heller Ehrman White & McAuliffe LLP

The Firm: A growing force in the Californian litigation market, with litigation dominating the firm's workload (accounting for half its revenue, with the biotech and life sciences sector proving a major source of work). A strong antitrust litigation department handles a sizable chunk of work for Microsoft.

The Lawyers: Leading individuals are concentrated in San Francisco, although three other offices in California bring the firm's total strength in the state to about 250 litigators. Several partners were recommended to researchers, but two names stood out. **Laurence Popofsky** is a senior litigator, who is often seen on major cases in antitrust, security fraud, intellectual property and personal injury. He represented 3M in its appeal over a $68 million adverse jury verdict in Philadelphia, and acted for Visa in suits against the US Department of Justice and Wal-Mart. **Doug Schwab**, rated as a *"brilliant and hardworking lawyer,"* is a popular figure among peers, and is active in securities litigation and accountants' liability.

The Clients: Other clients include: Hawaii Medical Association; Philip Morris; Pacific Gas and Electric; McDonald's; Apple; Teledyne; Ernst & Young; Levi Strauss; Coca-Cola; LVMH; WorldCom and Bank of America.

Keker & Van Nest LLP

The Firm: Big-ticket IP litigation now accounts for a large chunk of the firm's activity. Acted for Xilinx, a semiconductor company, in its multibillion dollar patent infringement case against Altera.

The Lawyers: Founding partner **John Keker** is one of California's most prolific trial heavyweights. Respected for his criminal defense and business litigation practice. *"He's as good as it gets in California,"* and *"you can go to the bank on his word,"* say observers of a man noted for his fearsome courtroom presence and ruthless cross-

LITIGATION

CALIFORNIA

examination. Fellow lawyers praise his honesty and integrity – *"you don't need to put everything in writing when you're dealing with him."* Famous for prosecuting Oliver North in the 1987 Iran-Contra scandal, Keker has since turned his hand to a range of criminal and civil disputes, acting for both plaintiffs and defendants.

The Clients: On a pro bono basis, John Keker represented Russian software programmer Dmitry Sklyarov, who was charged by the US with violating the Digital Millennium Copyright Act (DMCA). Other clients include: Cadence Design Systems; Intel; Coherent; Clorox; Ventritex; JDS Uniphase; Genentech and InterTrust Technologies.

Latham & Watkins LLP
see firm details p.835

The Firm: Vast resources and a national string of offices are thought by market commentators to place the firm at the *"top of most large companies' lists."* LA is the focal point of a network that advises on everything from IP, antitrust and securities to insurance and employment litigation. All the 'big 5' accountancy firms are clients, and the malpractice team represents a handful of Andersen directors in the Enron case.

The Lawyers: Bob Long (see p.67) is a prominent senior litigator, and has returned to fee-earning in legal and accountancy malpractice cases after a period as managing partner. He won a jury verdict for client Micron in a case against Stefano, and, on behalf of Amgen, obtained a $28 million summary judgment in a contractual dispute arising from Amgen's sale of two biotech divisions to Techne Corp.

Clients respect Silicon Valley-based **Paul Dawes** (see p.63) for the *"absolute clarity and business sense"* that he brings to complex business litigation and securities. He represented Ford in the Ford Explorer/Firestone tire recall case, and acted for hospital company HCA in class action securities and derivative litigation.

The Clients: Elsewhere, the practice secured the reversal of a $253 million jury verdict in a federal appeal on behalf of Nintendo. Other clients here include: Hughes; Lockheed; Northrop; Arthur Andersen; Ernst & Young; 3M; Brown University; Chrysler; Fisher-Price; Mars; Xerox; Southern California Edison; LACERA; Genentech; Sprint; drkoop.com; SRI and Beverly Enterprises.

Milberg Weiss Bershad Hynes & Lerach LLP

The Firm: The nation's largest and best-known securities plaintiff class action firm has three offices in California alongside its headquarters in New York.

The Lawyers: Bill Lerach (see p.67) is widely acknowledged as the king of consumer and investor class actions. Feared by corporate America, there is no escaping the number of his successes. 2002's highlight saw Lerach take center stage in the Enron bankruptcy saga. He served as lead counsel for the principal plaintiff, the University of California, which lost $145 million on its Enron investment.

The Clients: Institutional shareholders, private investors and consumers all feature among the firm's client base.

Munger, Tolles & Olson

The Firm: Once a litigation boutique, the firm has expanded from its 1960's roots to house over 150 lawyers, and is now considered to be a serious challenger to the larger Los Angeles commercial firms. The team received glowing reports from peers and clients, for both its *"vigorous commitment to the litigation field"* and large pool of *"skillful, persuasive litigators."*

The Lawyers: Brad Brian is *"right at the top of everyone's list"* for his extensive jury trial experience and *"smooth courtroom manner."* His expertise centers on white-collar criminal defense and complex commercial litigation. **Ron Olson** received credit for his role in turning an embryonic litigation team into a *"real force."* Peers drew researchers' attention to his courtroom style, which is said to be *"packed full of ideas and arguments."*

The Clients: Highlights for the firm include representing Shell in a $220 million appeal over alleged failure to disclose environmental conditions in the sale of oil field property and acting for California Steel Industries in a $26 million action brought by a Panamanian shipping company. Before juries, the team secured a positive outcome in a discrimination case for Delta Air Lines. Clients also include: Berisford Capital; California Pizza Kitchen; Docenave; Coldwell Banker; MCA Records; Mission Power Engineering; Northrop Grumman; Republic of the Philippines; Rolls-Royce; Southern California Edison; TRW; Unocal; ABC; Far East National Bank and Guardsmark.

O'Melveny & Myers LLP

The Firm: The firm is a powerhouse in its Los Angeles backyard, but has also penetrated the Northern California market with some success. Around 180 litigators are distributed among six Californian offices, offering expertise in the full range of commercial litigation. Clients insisted that there are *"no weak links"* in a team praised for its consistent quality. It handles, inter alia, IP, insurance, white-collar criminal defense and employment cases.

The Lawyers: Special market plaudits were bestowed on securities specialist **Seth Aronson**, who heads up the LA office, and **Pat Lynch**, a commercial litigator with particular skills in the IP and antitrust field. He has appeared on a number of complex trials for clients such as IBM (software piracy), and was involved in the Gemstar/ITC case.

The Clients: The firm has long-established connections to the Hollywood entertainment industry, and has forged close ties with key client Ford, who it regularly represents in class actions. Apple also appears on the client roster.

Bingham McCutchen LLP

The Firm: Newly merged with Boston firm Bingham Dana. A respected litigation player, present on big-ticket cases. The team acted for Covad Communications in a major piece of litigation against Pacific Bell, which ended in a $750 million settlement. Was engaged in a battle with Bell-South. Acted for Amazon.com in a patent dispute against Barnes & Noble, while Balabanian represents the Fang family, owner of The San Francisco Examiner.

The Lawyers: The cochairs of the litigation practice are Alfred Pfeiffer (communications, antitrust, IP) and David Balabanian (complex commercial litigation), who head a team of 150 litigators (half the firm) in four Californian offices.

The Clients: Other clients include: Louisiana-Pacific; Pacific Exchange; Hyundai; AT&T; Eastman Kodak; Orckit Communications; Reliant; Mitsui and JPMorgan Chase.

Blecher & Collins

The Firm: Prominent cases include representing ABC International Traders in an unfair competition case against Matsushita and acting for Handgards, a Nebraskan manufacturer, in a successful antitrust action against Johnson & Johnson.

The Lawyers: Maxwell Blecher, an *"outstanding plaintiff antitrust lawyer,"* received substantial market endorsement. Although now 70, he is regarded as one of the West Coast's *"classic trial all-rounders,"* and has helped lead his small niche firm to the forefront in cutting-edge antitrust and general commercial litigation.

The Clients: Other clients include Syufy Enterprises and Los Angeles Memorial Coliseum Commission.

Clifford Chance US LLP
see firm details p.783

The Firm: The global giant staged one of the most publicized coups of the year by poaching 17 partners and 30 associates from Brobeck, Phleger & Harrison, with most drawn from the latter's highly rated securities litigation practice. The firm has recently opened four Californian offices in San Francisco, Palo Alto, Los Angeles and San Diego. The new practice is recommended highest for securities expertise, although the group also commands strength in antitrust, IP and general commercial litigation. Onlookers consider the move a *"major step"* for the firm and are waiting to see how the practice will make its mark locally.

The Lawyers: A *"man with a vision,"* **Tower**

CALIFORNIA

Snow (see p.73) is the *"charismatic leader"* responsible for the exodus of Brobeck Phleger attorneys to form Clifford Chance's new West Coast practice. He possesses broad experience of complex litigation matters and particular expertise in securities matters. Commentators report that this *"big-picture man"* has already had notable success in attracting a number of major communications and telecom clients to the practice.
The Clients: Cisco Systems; Broadcom; Intel and Sun Microsystems.

Cotchett, Pitre, Simon & McCarthy
The Firm: A small and well-respected Bay Area litigation boutique, it has earned a reputation for taking on plaintiff cases with a strong social justice element. The team acts for individuals, corporations, public entities and banks in a range of business sectors.
The Lawyers: Joseph Cotchett is widely known as a *"flamboyant and politically active lawyer,"* whose trial experience is said to make him an ideal choice for the more *"crusading cases."* He rose to prominence in the 1980's by winning large settlements for investors in white-collar fraud cases, and, in the 1990's, was lead trial lawyer in the Lincoln Savings and Loan Association/American Continental scandal. More recently, he led for the Consumers Union, defending it from Isuzu's $242 million defamation claim.
The firm also filed a securities suit on behalf of Toronto-based Silvercreek Management against the banks Salomon Smith Barney, Goldman Sachs and Bank of America over their marketing of Enron investments.
The Clients: E. & J. Gallo Winery; Consumers Union of America; University of California and Silvercreek Management.

Farella Braun & Martel LLP
The Firm: Areas of contentious expertise at the firm include white-collar crime, energy, IP, antitrust securities, environment, construction and insurance.
The Lawyers: Doug Young is considered the standout lawyer in this 125-lawyer San Francisco firm. His advocacy skills and *"wonderfully smooth delivery"* gained approval right across the state. Young acted for the University of California and California State University in a 2001 case concerning Enron's obligations to supply 'direct access' electric power to campuses. He also represented Visa USA and seven individuals accused in Milwaukee State Court of theft of trade secrets, and Australian oil company BHP in a multi-defendant gasoline price-fixing action filed by the Attorney General of Hawaii.
The Clients: Other clients include: The Limited, Lane Bryant and American Booksellers Association.

Fogel, Feldman, Ostrov, Ringler & Klevens
The Firm: This small Santa Monica firm is known to draw attractive, big-ticket work, notably in the fields of civil litigation, labor and personal injury.
The Lawyers: Larry Feldman is widely respected by the legal community in Southern California for his ability to pull in *"interesting and complex litigation."* He focuses on personal injury and business litigation.

Greene, Broillet, Taylor, Wheeler & Panish
The Firm: A leading plaintiffs' trial firm with a string of successful results to its credit, it represents clients in the full range of mass torts, including aviation, asbestos and tobacco litigation.
The Lawyers: Name partner **Browne Greene** has a strong reputation in the personal injury field, and is admired by contemporaries for his *"winning way with juries."*
The Clients: The firm's most famous win came on behalf of victims of the 'exploding gas tank', a landmark $4.9 billion judgment against GM delivered in July 1999. More recently, the team has represented clients in the 'Diet Drug Fen-Phen' litigation, and has acted for the County of Los Angeles in its challenge to tobacco companies.

Hennigan, Bennett & Dorman
The Firm: A contentious firm of 25 lawyers, it is recommended for both defense and plaintiff litigation in areas such as insolvency, antitrust and securities.
The Lawyers: Mike Hennigan is widely recognized in LA as a leading trial exponent, and is particularly praised for his skillful handling of securities class actions.

O'Donnell & Shaeffer
The Firm: Formed in 1996, this youthful firm has quickly established itself in the LA legal market. It represents plaintiffs and defendants in a variety of litigious areas - IP, entertainment, products liability and new media.
The Lawyers: Pierce O'Donnell is *"quite a name"* in Southern California, and is praised for his *"hard work, thorough preparation and effectiveness."* He is best known for his entertainment industry expertise, notably his successful representation of Art Buchwald against Paramount Pictures in the famous 'Coming to America' case. More recently, he secured a victory for Lockheed Martin against 3200 toxic tort claims, and acted for GoTo.com in a $21 million trademark infringement win against Walt Disney.
The Clients: Other clients include: Firestone; Pfizer; Kidder, Peabody & Co; NBC; Reebok International; Metro-Goldwyn-Mayer; Texaco; Miramax Films; New Line Cinema; Republic of France; City of Los Angeles; Sony; Faye Dunaway; Phillips Petroleum and DreamWorks SKG.

Quinn Emanuel Urquhart Oliver & Hedges LLP
see firm details p.869
The Firm: Prominent Californian litigation firm known for its impressive record of trial wins, lengthy case resume and high courtroom visibility. General counsel at large corporations spoke of it as *"more than just a litigation firm."* The practice represents companies across the industry spectrum, but IP litigation accounts for the lion's share of practice activity.
The Lawyers: John Quinn (see p.71) is credited for his role in developing the firm to its current standing at over 150 lawyers and five Californian offices. He's also in demand from leading corporates, who believe the blend of a *"scholarly approach with creative, jury-friendly advocacy"* is ideal for big-ticket litigation. In 2002, Quinn was part of a team that was successful in $80 million proceedings in Cleveland on behalf of office supplies company Avery Dennison.
The Clients: A group of the firm's attorneys also secured a verdict for clients Zurich Group and Bancorp Services in a $118 million trade secrets case in St.Louis. Among its other clients can be found: IBM; Mattel; Hughes Electronics; DIRECTV; AOL; Trust Company of the West; CSFB; Computer Sciences; Teledyne Technologies; GM; Walt Disney; Toyota; TRW and Waste Management.

Other Notable Practitioners
Chambers' researchers were told that San Jose-based **Allen Ruby** of Ruby & Schofield is held in *"the highest esteem by everybody."* His boutique firm practices civil and criminal litigation in areas such as IP, personal injury negligence and products liability.

MEDIA & ENTERTAINMENT

CALIFORNIA

MEDIA & ENTERTAINMENT

CALIFORNIA
Leading firms (Media & Entertainment)

1 GANG TYRE RAMER & BROWN *Beverly Hills*
ZIFFREN BRITTENHAM BRANCA *Los Angeles*

2 GREENBERG GLUSKER FIELDS *Los Angeles*

3 DAVIS WRIGHT TREMAINE LLP *Los Angeles*
MANATT, PHELPS & PHILLIPS, LLP *Los Angeles*
O'MELVENY & MYERS LLP *Los Angeles*

4 AKIN GUMP STRAUSS HAUER *Los Angeles*
ARMSTRONG HIRSCH JACKOWAY *Los Angeles*

5 LEVY, RAM & OLSON *San Francisco*
RIEGELS CAMPOS & KENYON *Sacramento*
WEISSMANN, WOLFF, BERGMAN *Beverly Hills*
WINN & ALEXANDER LLP *Capitola*

Leading individuals
(Media & Entertainment)

1 RAMER Bruce *Gang Tyre Ramer & Brown*, Beverly Hills
SAGER Kelli *Davis Wright Tremaine LLP*, Los Angeles
ZIFFREN Kenneth *Ziffren Brittenham*, Los Angeles

2 HEINKE Rex *Akin Gump Strauss Hauer*, Los Angeles
PHILLIPS Lee *Manatt, Phelps & Phillips*, Los Angeles

3 FIELDS Bertram *Greenberg Glusker Fields*, Los Angeles
KENYON Charity *Riegels Campos*, Sacramento
OLSON Karl *Levy Ram & Olson*, San Francisco

4 ALEXANDER Judith *Winn & Alexander LLP*, Capitola
BURKE Thomas *Davis Wright Tremaine*, San Francisco
HIRSCH Barry *Armstrong Hirsch*, Los Angeles
PASSMAN Donald *Gang Tyre Ramer*, Beverly Hills
WEISSMANN Eric *Weissmann, Wolff*, Beverly Hills

Firms and individuals are listed alphabetically in each band.

Gang Tyre Ramer & Brown
The Firm: Peers acknowledge that this boutique has been around since the *"dawn of motion pictures,"* and is considered to be the premier operation in its field. It represents major artists, producers and other talents in the motion picture and music industries across the full spectrum of entertainment and media law. The team was especially commended to researchers for its range of industry contacts, and is thought to house *"a group of true experts."*
The Lawyers: Foremost among these experts is *"first-rate"* **Bruce Ramer**, an entertainment law specialist, who advises a raft of top individual talent, and who comes endorsed as an *"ethical and knowledgeable guy."* *"Strong negotiator"* **Don Passman** specializes in the music business, and negotiates contracts and deals for a client base that includes major entertainers, publishers, record companies, managers, producers and individual artists.
The Clients: The firm advises producers, publishers, record companies and movie companies. Its roster includes: Steven Spielberg; Clint Eastwood; REM; Janet Jackson; Quincy Jones; Tina Turner and Green Day.

Ziffren Brittenham Branca Fischer Gilbert-Lurie & Stiffelman LLP
The Firm: Extolled to researchers as a group that is *"as good as they come,"* the firm represents major talents, producers and top companies in the motion picture, television, music and multimedia industries. The firm's attorneys appeal to contemporaries as a *"businesslike and knowledgeable bunch."*
The Lawyers: **Kenneth Ziffren** focuses on representing high-profile individuals in the motion picture and television industries. One industry observer confided to researchers that *"when he speaks, you listen."*
The Clients: Bruce Willis; Eddie Murphy; Harrison Ford; Matt Damon; Ben Affleck; Liberty Media Group; DreamWorks SKG and DIRECTV.

Greenberg Glusker Fields Claman Machtinger & Kinsella LLP
see firm details p.807
The Firm: A substantial entertainment practice provides both transactional and litigation services for production companies and various talents such as actors, musicians, writers and producers. Transactional services include negotiations of talent agreements and contracts for the financing, development and production of motion pictures.
The Lawyers: *"Tough and experienced litigator"* **Bertram Fields** (see p.64) is noted for the breadth of his practice, and provides both transactional and litigation advice to a diverse clientele. On the litigation side, he recently defended Tom Cruise in an action for defamation, and represented Steven Slesinger, Inc. in its Winnie the Pooh royalty dispute with Disney.
The Clients: Tom Cruise; Mike Nichols; James Cameron; Joel Silver; Jonathan Demme; Dustin Hoffman and Warren Beatty.

Davis Wright Tremaine LLP
see firm details p.787
The Firm: The firm can lay claim to expertise in a number of areas of media law, and represents firms and individuals in the television, radio, print media and motion picture industries at trial and appellate levels. Recent successful cases include advising the New York Times in a libel claim and acting for MTV in a defamation dispute.
The Lawyers: Interviewees described **Kelli Sager** (see p.71) as *"a true friend of the media business."* She was singled out for her First Amendment and access litigation work, and won plaudits from peers for her courtroom manner. Her caseload has included advising E! Entertainment Television on a theft of idea claim, and representing the Los Angeles Times against a restraining order vetoing the publication of an article. A *"sharp"* attorney, **Thomas Burke** (see p.61) has particular expertise in new media law, often advising on IT content liability and conducting web site legal reviews. Recent work includes appearing for Bay Guardian Publishing in a dispute involving alleged theft of proprietary business information by a former employee, and an appeal case for a San Francisco radio station involving libel, invasion of privacy and First Amendment issues.
The Clients: The New York Times Company; Los Angeles Times; CBS Broadcasting; E! Entertainment Television; Paramount Pictures; Condé Nast Publications; Courtroom Television Network; MTV Networks; Univision Television Group; Warner Bros.; Alameda Newspaper Group; Association of Alternative Newsweeklies; CNN; The Bakersfield Californian and Bay Guardian Publishing.

Manatt, Phelps & Phillips, LLP
The Firm: This full-service firm is home to both a television and motion picture group and a music department; the latter was especially recommended to Chambers' researchers. Advising both companies and individual talent, the firm was involved in the creation and negotiation of contracts in connection with the establishment of Musicnet. The team also acted for The Eagles in negotiating agreements relating to its 2002 tour.
The Lawyers: *"Preeminent music law guru"* **Lee Phillips** focuses on contract negotiations and the provision of legal advice for major musicians, composers and record companies. He recently concluded a major deal for Carly Simon for her songwriting and recording services with The Walt Disney Company's production of films of the Winnie the Pooh character as well as finalizing a deal for Dionne Warwick's upcoming album.
The Clients: Carly Simon; The Eagles; Musicnet; Barbra Streisand; Dionne Warwick; Brian Wilson; Neil Young; Burt Bacharach; Don Henley; Glenn Frey; Tracy Chapman and Kenny Loggins.

O'Melveny & Myers LLP
The Firm: The only full-service commercial firm to have made a serious impression on market consciousness in this sector, it is acknowledged for the *"uniform quality"* of its media and entertainment attorneys. Cross-border work is a key element of the workload. Transactional matters have included advising The Anschutz Entertainment Group on a joint venture for live stage presentations, acting for Ted Turner Pictures on a production and distribution agreement, and advising Qwest on the renegotiation of sports sponsorship arrangements.
The Lawyers: Clients paid tribute to the group's

CALIFORNIA — MEDIA & ENTERTAINMENT

deal-making abilities, and the team has recognized expertise in contract negotiations and transactions involving the production, financing and distribution of motion pictures and television programs. The leader of the entertainment and media department is Christopher Murray.

The Clients: The Anschutz Entertainment Group; Big Idea Productions; EMI; Enron Broadband Services; Warner Bros.; Yahoo!; Ted Turner Pictures and Qwest.

Akin, Gump, Strauss, Hauer & Feld LLP
see firm details p.761

The Firm: A substantial media and entertainment group that advises on a wide range of work, including contract negotiations and documentation, and financing transactions for internationally renowned entertainment and media companies. The group represented Walt Disney in a suit brought by the writer of the book on which the movie 'Who Framed Roger Rabbit?' was based, and acted for Sony on the settlement of a dispute with John Travolta.

The Lawyers: Praised by clients as a *"fantastically experienced"* litigator, **Rex Heinke** represents an array of print media and online publishers, television networks, motion picture studios and entertainment production and distribution companies. He specializes in First Amendment, entertainment, media and IT disputes, and has an established track record in libel and invasion of privacy cases. A recent highlight came with his successful defense of MGM in an invasion of privacy suit concerning the contents of a 'real-life' television show.

The Clients: Disney; Paramount Pictures; Newsweek; Freedom Communications; McClatchy Newspapers; Los Angeles Times; Sony Pictures and MGM.

Armstrong Hirsch Jackoway Tyerman & Wertheimer

The Firm: Described to researchers as *"a notable player in the Californian market,"* the firm's media and entertainment practice group is its primary focus. It provides both transactional and litigation services for writers, directors, producers, talent agents and individual talent, and was particularly endorsed for its abilities in contract drafting and negotiation.

The Lawyers: **Barry Hirsch** provides transactional services to individual talents and is known to peers as a *"positive and aggressive"* deal-maker.

The Clients: The firm advises managers, studios and production companies. Francis Ford Coppola, Robert Redford and Julia Roberts use the firm.

Levy Ram Olson & Rossi

The Firm: Highly regarded for its media and First Amendment law services, the firm's media group has a notable regional and national newspaper clientele. Its workload includes advice on reporter's shield law, invasion of privacy, access to public court records and defamation litigation. The firm also handles pre-publication and pre-broadcasting reviews.

The Lawyers: Clients appreciate the talents of the *"accomplished and bright"* **Karl Olson**, who specializes in defending news media clients and individuals against defamation and SLAPPs (Strategic Lawsuits Against Public Participation). He also advises on public and press access issues and pre-publication and pre-broadcast counseling. One of his successes involved the settlement of a dispute between nine newspaper publishing companies and the City of San Francisco.

The Clients: Los Angeles Times; California Newspaper Publishers Association and Contra Costa Times.

Riegels Campos & Kenyon

The Firm: An experienced department, principally associated with its work in the contentious areas of media law. It has represented newspapers, television stations and magazines in seeking access to courts, public records and meetings and in defense of defamation and other tort actions.

The Lawyers: **Charity Kenyon** wins the admiration of contemporaries for her ability *"to get the right results."* A First Amendment expert, she also acted for The Sacramento Bee in a Ninth Circuit Court of Appeals case, involving access to court documents.

The Clients: McClatchy Newspapers; Time Magazine; Los Angeles Times, and CBS, ABC and FOX affiliate television stations.

Weissmann, Wolff, Bergman, Coleman, Silverman & Holmes, LLP

The Firm: Peers regard this boutique as *"a good home for good lawyers."* It advises an impressive clientele on both transactional and litigation matters. Fielding attorneys who are *"media savvy,"* the firm is respected for its involvment in high-profile privacy and defamation cases.

The Lawyers: *"Smart and people-oriented"* **Eric Weissmann** represents both individuals and entities on a variety of entertainment law issues, and has also performed agent work for a number of motion picture directors.

The Clients: Warner Bros, Gene Wilder and Michael Cimino feature on the firm's client roster.

Winn & Alexander LLP

The Firm: The firm's media and First Amendment practice group handles a broad range of pre-publication and pre-broadcast review work, and is also respected for its experience of defense of defamation, invasion of privacy and commercial misappropriation claims.

The Lawyers: Said to be *"in touch with the latest ideas and issues,"* **Judy Alexander** represents newspapers, magazines, journalists and TV documentary producers in all aspects of media law. Clients were impressed by her *"outstanding speed of response."*

The Clients: The firm advised on the negotiation of television coproduction agreements between the Center for Investigative Reporting and the producers of 'FRONTLINE'. Other clients include: San Jose Mercury News; Los Angeles Times; The Sacramento Bee; Monterey County Herald; Santa Cruz Sentinel; Good Times; Stanford Daily; Capital Cities/ABC; NBC and Fox Television.

PROJECTS — CALIFORNIA

CALIFORNIA
Leading firms (Projects)
1. **LATHAM & WATKINS** Los Angeles, San Diego
   MILBANK, TWEED, HADLEY & MCCLOY Los Angeles
2. **ORRICK, HERRINGTON** Los Angeles, San Francisco
3. **MORGAN, LEWIS & BOCKIUS LLP** Los Angeles
   THELEN REID & PRIEST LLP San Francisco

Leading individuals (Projects)
1. **FEO Edwin** Milbank, Tweed, Hadley, Los Angeles
2. **SHORTZ Richard** Morgan, Lewis & Bockius, Los Angeles
   SPIELBERG David Stoel Rives LLP, San Francisco
3. **SINGER Andrew** Latham & Watkins, San Diego
   WEITZEL Mark Thelen Reid & Priest, San Francisco

Firms and individuals are listed alphabetically in each band.

Latham & Watkins
see firm details p.835

The Firm: The project finance group, spearheaded from San Diego and Los Angeles, mirrors the firm's national and international reputation for projects work. Rivals acknowledge it as *"the center of gravity"* for project finance on the West Coast, identifying the firm's extensive resources in land use, permitting and environmental expertise as integral to its success. The firm continues to advise on a range of massive transactions, both at home and overseas. It advised Bank of Nova Scotia and CSFB as lead arrangers of the $3.5 billion Calpine Construction Finance Corporation I & II revolving portfolio financings to construct power plants throughout the US. Abroad, the firm has mediated between lenders and agencies engaged in energy projects in Morocco, Indonesia, Colombia, the Philippines and Pakistan.

The Lawyers: Although his practice is perhaps even better known in New York, **Andrew Singer** (see p.72) is also regarded by the Californian market as an *"effective and results-oriented"* attorney. He represented lead coordinating arrangers Citibank and Société Générale in connection with the $2.8 billion TECO-Panda financing of natural gas-fired generating facilities in Arkansas and Arizona.

The Clients: The team represents lenders and developers in equal measure. Its client roster includes: MidAmerican Energy; Cogentrix Energy; Citibank; Société Générale; CSFB; ING Barings; BNP Paribas; Bank of America; ABN AMRO; PSEG Global; TECO Energy; Panda Energy and Calpine.

Milbank, Tweed, Hadley & McCloy

The Firm: A *"superior"* project finance group, based in Los Angeles, is home to a core group of *"abundantly experienced"* lawyers, who are primarily geared to developer projects. The international magnitude of the firm's expertise – particularly in Latin America and Asia – spans the telecom, energy and transportation arenas. In Mexico, the firm orchestrated QUALCOMM's recent financing of Pegaso Telecomunicaciones, and as developer and lessee counsel, it has played a crucial role in the $3.2 billion Barracuda oil platform project and Caratinga oil and gas fields developments in Brazil. Closer to home, a rapid growth in permitting, triggered by California's energy crisis, has seen the firm active in power selling transactions and operations designed to restructure the state's energy market.

The Lawyers: A renowned energy specialist and managing partner of the Los Angeles office, **Edwin Feo** gained unanimous approval as the market leader in California. An *"experienced, fair-minded and constructive opponent,"* he has represented various parties on a number of power, infrastructure and environmental financings.

The Clients: Other clients include: Enron; Texaco; Sempra Energy; American Electric Power; Edison Mission Energy; Mitsubishi; SeaWest WindPower; Ameresco; ABN AMRO; Société Générale and Bank of America.

Orrick, Herrington & Sutcliffe
see firm details p.859

The Firm: At state and municipal level, this local *"pillar"* of a firm has a historical reputation. The firm's California-based transportation finance group has advised on the financing of facilities for San Francisco International Airport and the Bay Area Rapid Transit system. Reforms to the state's energy markets, meanwhile, have seen the firm increasingly active on behalf of investor-owned utilities and independent power producers to construct new generating facilities nationwide. In a recent private venture, the firm advised Banc of America Securities as underwriter to the refinancing of debt issued in a leveraged lease financing of the Panther Creek waste coal power plant.

The Lawyers: Projects work is handled by attorneys from the global energy, communications and infrastructure, transportation finance, public finance and private finance groups. It largely concentrates on the domestic front, where Mary Neale heads the Los Angeles office and Roger Davis leads the team in San Francisco.

The Clients: Sponsors and developers both figure prominently in the firm's client portfolio. It has secured instructions from: San Francisco International Airport; Banc of America Securities; ABN AMRO; Tomen and Union Bank of California.

Morgan, Lewis & Bockius LLP

The Firm: Operations conducted from the firm's Californian offices focus on the domestic market, typically financing projects for independent power producers and developers. The firm recently served as counsel for Black Hills Power to build a total of four power plants, three in Colorado and one in Las Vegas. In energy financing, attorneys advised Reliant Resources on its acquisition of Orion Power Holdings, a transaction worth $2.9 billion.

The Lawyers: The bulk of the firm's project attorneys are recruited from its business finance group in Los Angeles. Managing partner of the group and co-chairman of the energy and infrastructure finance section, **Richard Shortz** is regarded as the firm's leading light in this area. *"Senior, smooth and a favorite with clients,"* he enjoys an established reputation for domestic and international power projects.

The Clients: Other clients include: Mitsubishi; TEPCO; Texaco; Pennsylvania Power; Duke Energy; Sempra Energy; Edison and Reliant Resources.

Thelen Reid & Priest LLP
see firm details p.888

The Firm: A strong player in the domestic power sector, the firm is known for its active developer practice in San Francisco, hub of its project development and asset financings offering. Attorneys here are acknowledged to possess *"broad, long-term experience"* in financing and refinancing transactions for power facilities across California and Texas.

The Lawyers: The *"superb"* **Mark Weitzel** (see p.74) is regarded as the firm's number-one asset in this area. Peers drew the attention of researchers to his *"constructive negotiating style,"* while clients endorsed his *"keen, analytical eye"* and *"flair for the economics of a deal."*

The Clients: The firm represented Calpine in the development and sale and leaseback of a partial merchant plant in Texas, and, in Mexico, acted for the Inter-American Development Bank as lender in a $647 million loan to the Samalayuca II power project. Its roster includes: Calpine; GE; Bechtel; TXU; MDU Resources Group and Inter-American Development Bank.

Other Notable Practitioners
At home with both development and lender project finance, clients acknowledge **David Spielberg**'s *"thorough knowledge of non-recourse financing."* A partner at Stoel Rives in San Francisco, and the first attorney to negotiate power contracts with the State of California, he represented Calpine on the financing of two revolving construction facilities worth $3.5 billion.

CALIFORNIA

REAL ESTATE

REAL ESTATE

CALIFORNIA
Leading firms (Real Estate)

1 ALLEN, MATKINS, LECK, GAMBLE *Los Angeles*
PAUL, HASTINGS, JANOFSKY *Los Angeles*

2 COX CASTLE & NICHOLSON LLP *Los Angeles*
GIBSON, DUNN & CRUTCHER LLP *Los Angeles*
MORRISON & FOERSTER LLP *San Francisco*

3 DEWEY BALLANTINE LLP *Los Angeles*
PILLSBURY WINTHROP LLP *Los Angeles*
PIRCHER, NICHOLS & MEEKS *Los Angeles*

4 LATHAM & WATKINS *Los Angeles*
MAYER, BROWN, ROWE & MAW *Los Angeles*
O'MELVENY & MYERS LLP *Los Angeles*
ORRICK, HERRINGTON & SUTCLIFFE *San Francisco*

5 COBLENTZ, PATCH, DUFFY & BASS *San Francisco*
ELLMAN, BURKE, HOFFMAN *San Francisco*
SHEPPARD, MULLIN, RICHTER *San Francisco*

Leading individuals (Real Estate)

1 WALKER Paul *Dewey Ballantine LLP,* Los Angeles

2 MATKINS Michael *Allen, Matkins, Leck,* Los Angeles
MEYER Michael *Pillsbury Winthrop LLP,* Los Angeles

3 EATMAN Louis *Mayer, Brown, Rowe,* Los Angeles
FEDER Philip *Paul, Hastings, Janofsky,* Los Angeles
MIHLSTEN George *Latham & Watkins,* Los Angeles
NELLIS Noel *Orrick, Herrington,* San Francisco
NICHOLS Phillip *Pircher, Nichols & Meeks,* Los Angeles
NICHOLSON Phillip *Cox Castle,* Los Angeles
SENEKER Carl (Kim) *Morrison & Foerster,* San Francisco

4 DUFFY Pamela *Coblentz, Patch, Duffy,* San Francisco
ELLMAN Howard *Ellman, Burke, Hoffman,* San Francisco
FILETI Thomas *Morrison & Foerster LLP,* Los Angeles
MALLORY Rick *Allen, Matkins, Leck,* San Francisco
NATSIS Tony *Allen, Matkins, Leck, Gamble,* Los Angeles
SHARF Jesse *Gibson, Dunn & Crutcher,* Los Angeles
THOMPSON Robert *Sheppard, Mullin,* San Francisco

5 ARNOLD Dennis *Gibson, Dunn & Crutcher,* Los Angeles
CAREY Stevens *Pircher, Nichols & Meeks,* Los Angeles
PIRCHER Leo *Pircher, Nichols & Meeks,* Los Angeles
THORNTON Charles *Paul, Hastings,* San Francisco

Firms and Individuals are listed alphabetically in each band.

Allen, Matkins, Leck, Gamble & Mallory LLP

The Firm: *"More significant than many large firms,"* according to some commentators, this is a real estate boutique that is acknowledged by rivals to work *"at the cutting edge"* of the sector. Its leasing and developing advice is widely considered to be among the best in the US, while the team's individual attorneys are also characterized by clients as *"a superb, entrepreneurial group."*

The Lawyers: At the head of the team is *"business-oriented"* founding partner **Michael Matkins**, who maintains a diverse practice that includes both traditional real estate transactions and complex investment work. One of the youngest of the Californian market leaders, **Tony Natsis** has a reputation as an *"aggressive business-getter,"* and is a leasing specialist, while **Rick Mallory** was also recommended to researchers as *"a formidable competitor."*

The Clients: Highlights for the firm include representing Catellus Development in transactions such as the sale of land at Kaiser Commerce Center and in warehouse lease deals with Ford. Clients include developers, investors, lenders, borrowers and landlords.

Paul, Hastings, Janofsky & Walker LLP
see firm details p.861

The Firm: *"So large, they can cover any deal,"* the real estate group is admired for its *"massive, institutional"* status. Although some interviewees contend that the loss of a number of the firm's leaders, notably Paul Walker to Dewey Ballantine in 1999, has lessened its real estate profile, the majority still place the group at the top of the tree, with one even referring to it as *"the only significant real estate practice in LA."* The firm represented GE Capital in financing non-performing loan portfolios in Asia, and acted for Colony Capital in its purchase of a $900 million portfolio of non-performing loans from an affiliate of the Korean Government. Closer to home, the group advised the Los Angeles Unified School District in negotiations concerning the Ambassador Hotel site in Los Angeles.

The Lawyers: **Phil Feder** (see p.64) is head of department, and appeals to clients as *"a dynamic guy who knows how to bring on younger attorneys."* **Charlie Thornton** (see p.73), who earned widespread praise for his *"professionalism,"* is a respected all-rounder, advising on acquisitions, financing, investment structures and real estate development.

The Clients: GE Capital; Colony Capital; Los Angeles Unified School District; Lehman Brothers; Carlyle and Oaktree Capital Management.

Cox Castle & Nicholson LLP

The Firm: Researchers frequently had their attention drawn to this powerful boutique's *"tremendous familiarity"* with the needs of the industry. Although typically associated with development work, the firm offers the full range of real estate advice, including sales and acquisitions, reciprocal easement agreements and leasing.

The Lawyers: A group of *"highly competitive attorneys"* is personified by **Phil Nicholson**, who was described by peers as a *"savvy operator"* with a prominent client base.

The Clients: The firm advises developers, landowners, business institutions, and healthcare organizations, among others.

Gibson, Dunn & Crutcher LLP

The Firm: Strength on the financing side of real estate transactions is this department's ace, and commentators paid regular tribute to its *"breadth of experience and depth of resources."* Clients agree that the firm *"hires first-rate lawyers,"* and the team advises an imposing portfolio of institutional lenders and private investors on a range of sale and leaseback transactions, joint ventures and mezzanine financings. The group is also noted for expertise on the development side and in the restructuring of troubled loans.

The Lawyers: Los Angeles-based team leader **Jesse Sharf** was endorsed to researchers as a *"smart and impressive generalist,"* while **Dennis Arnold** is highly rated for his loan work, and maintains a diverse practice that extends to project finance, debt restructuring and energy issues.

The Clients: The firm represented Pacific Coast Capital Partners in the structuring, acquisition, development and sale of a two million sq ft industrial property, and acted for Westbrook Partners in the acquisition of land in Hawaii for exclusive golf/residential complexes. Blackacre Capital and Lehman Brothers are also clients of the firm.

Morrison & Foerster LLP
see firm details p.854

The Firm: The firm is considered to have bucked the often-identified trend for large, international firms to de-emphasize their real estate practice group, and is said by clients to provide *"absolutely first-rate advice."* While it advises on all areas of real estate law, the firm's reputation lies principally in real estate financing and the sale and acquisition of assets. It represents major REITs and other public and private companies, and has an acknowledged niche in the hotel and resort sector.

The Lawyers: **Kim Seneker** (see p.72), who until 2000 was cochair of the firm's real estate practice, is noted by rivals as much for his leadership as for his technical expertise: *"He has held the fort there, and still maintains an excellent personal practice."* A veteran of complex property finance transactions, he appeals to clients for his *"ability to see the big picture."* **Tom Fileti**'s (see p.64) star is in the ascendant, and he was consistently recommended to researchers as *"a master at off-balance sheet financing"* who *"closes every loophole."*

The Clients: Recent work includes representation of Deutsche Bank as agent, in the financing (revolving credit, term and interim facilities), aggregating more than $1 billion, provided to The Macerich Company in its acquisition of a portfolio of shopping centers. Also representing Deutsche Bank as agent, the firm acted on a $250 million financing provided to Westfield America Trust in its acquisition of a portion of the US

REAL ESTATE

CALIFORNIA

shopping center portfolio of Rodamco North America. In transactional matters, the firm has acted for AMB Property on its acquisition of the eight-building, 850,000 sq ft Ford Distribution Center, California. Further clients include: Novellus Systems; Lennar Mare Island; Lennar Partners; Union Dominion Realty Trust; Classic Residence by Hyatt; UBS Realty Investors and Genentech.

Dewey Ballantine LLP
see firm details p.790
The Firm: Market appraisal of this team is implicitly bound up with the reputation of its undisputed star, **Paul Walker** (see p.74), who joined the firm in February 1999 from Paul, Hastings, Janofsky & Walker. The firm was especially commended to researchers for its strength in workouts, loans and real estate securitization – all areas in which Walker excels. His reputation is built on client focus: *"He understands what his client wants to achieve, and devotes himself to that without ego or scorekeeping."*
The Clients: Walker and his team represented GE Capital in a leveraged leaseback transaction, covering five states and worth $98 million, while the firm also acted for CSFB in a $350 million workout of a franchise securitization. The client base also includes: Pacific Coast Capital Partners; Lehman Brothers; DRA Advisors; GE Pension Trust and Wells Fargo.

Pillsbury Winthrop LLP
see firm details p.866
The Firm: Particularly recommended for commercial leasing, the firm's real estate department represents a number of large institutional clients, as well as smaller entities, in transactions of varying size and degree.
The Lawyers: Leading light **Michael Meyer** (see p.69) spends most of his time on leasing, and has a reputation among some observers as *"the number-one leasing lawyer"* in the state. His client roster includes such major names as Nestlé, MGM, Merrill Lynch and Ticketmaster.
The Clients: The firm was selected to represent the Los Angeles Unified School District to negotiate for the completion of a new high school complex for 4600 students, and has advised the County of Sacramento on the sale of McClellan Air Force Base. The firm also receives instructions from: County of Sacramento; International Lease Finance; Key3Media; Princess Cruises; Sterling Software; Shorenstein Company and Gap.

Pircher, Nichols & Meeks
The Firm: Generally regarded as the nearest challenger to Allen Matkins as California's top real estate boutique, the firm can call on the services of a number of respected attorneys, and covers, inter alia, loan and portfolio acquisitions, substantial leasing expertise and long-term ground leases and sale and leasebacks.
The Lawyers: The *"enthusiastic"* **Phil Nichols** is admired by competitors for his *"good instinct"* for the financing side of real estate, and is acknowledged to have *"the inside track with developers and borrowers."* **Stevens Carey** and **Leo Pircher** also received substantial market endorsement.
The Clients: Since 1996, the firm has been involved in the Playa Vista project, a 1087-acre mixed-use development located in the Los Angeles metropolitan area, representing the owners and affiliates in purchases and sales, financing, development and leasing transactions. Other clients include Urban Shopping Centers and Waterton Residential Property Fund VI.

Latham & Watkins
see firm details p.835
The Firm: Its enormous corporate clientele provides the firm with readily available material for its respected real estate department. However, the group has not quite established a reputation for stand-alone commercial property work to equal the market leaders in California.
The Lawyers: Rivals acknowledge the presence of *"a number of highly regarded lawyers,"* with particular expertise in land use, zoning and permit work. Foremost among these is **George Mihlsten** (see p.69), who is widely envied for his *"wonderful contacts in LA."* He has recently been advising on the new Disney resort in Anaheim, California, and on the 20,000-seat STAPLES Center sports arena.
The Clients: Since 1995, the firm has represented LandGrant Development in the Las Americas redevelopment project at the border of San Diego and Tijuana, Mexico, and has acted for the San Diego Padres in the construction of a new baseball park. Clients also include: Disney; JMI Realty; Price Legacy and Goldman Sachs.

Mayer, Brown, Rowe & Maw
see firm details p.843
The Firm: Despite the firm's enormous size, particularly following its recent merger, clients were pleased with its *"responsiveness"* and *"personal"* representation, and endorsed the group's ability to *"get to the heart of the matter."*
The Lawyers: The real estate team earns highest marks for its transactional prowess, headed by **Lou Eatman** (see p.63), who was regularly commended to researchers as a *"straight-up guy."* Clients were loud in their praise for his ability to *"handle the most complex strategic transactions."*
The Clients: The firm advised TIAA-CREF on a complex restructuring of about $200 million in mortgage debt on the Pacific Design Center, West Hollywood. It acted for CB Richard Ellis Strategic Partners in a mezzanine financing transaction for the new Quaker Oats high-rise headquarters building in Chicago. The firm also acts for The Bank of Nova Scotia and CIBC.

O'Melveny & Myers LLP
The Firm: Renowned for its work in financing and development, the firm represents Kennecott Development in the Salt Lake City area, advising on the Sunrise Project, a 4500-acre mixed-use development. It also acted for US Airways on the financing of new terminals at Philadelphia International Airport.
The Lawyers: Some recent departures from the real estate department have led to the market perception that, although respectable, the group lacks the star quality of a few years ago. Nevertheless, clients remain enthusiastic about a department where the levels of service were described to researchers as: *"outstanding; the turnaround time is excellent."*
The Clients: Kennecott Development; US Airways; Nationwide Health Properties; Duke Energy International; SunAmerica; Continental Airlines; Prudential Real Estate Investors; Delta Air Lines and BPAmoco.

Orrick, Herrington & Sutcliffe
see firm details p.859
The Firm: Interviewees indicated to researchers that this was a *"high-quality,"* transactionally focused practice that works locally, nationally and internationally. The firm's largest transaction of 2001 was a $2.2 billion acquisition by CalWest Industrial Properties of Cabot Industrial Properties Trust, a publicly traded REIT and its operating partnership. Other highlights have included representing Catellus Development in financing a $200 million loan and a $140 million construction loan for an office development located in San Francisco.
The Lawyers: Competitors admired a team of *"skilled and broadly experienced"* lawyers, of whom **Noel Nellis** (see p.69), chair of the firm's real estate group, is the most prominent. He was commended by peers and clients alike for his technical expertise.
The Clients: CalWest Industrial Properties; Catellus Development; SSR Realty Advisors; Alecta Investments; LACERA; RREEF; Layton-Belling & Associates; Newcastle Partners and University of California.

Coblentz, Patch, Duffy & Bass LLP
The Firm: The department is highly recommended for its land use practice, and received substantial endorsement for its work in public-private enterprises, as well as handling leasings, acquisitions and disposals. The key client in the firm's portfolio remains Catellus Development, the developers of the 300-acre mixed-use Mission Bay project, Northern California.
The Lawyers: *"The leader of the pack"* here is

CALIFORNIA   TAX

Pam Duffy, whose *"intellectual strength"* marks her out to contemporaries as one of the leading zoning lawyers in the state. The firm has been involved in the development of a 500,000 sq ft corporate headquarters for Gap, the new ballpark for the San Francisco Giants and a 1.3 million sq ft San Francisco retail and hotel complex for Forest City Development.

The Clients: Catellus Development; Gap; San Francisco Giants; Forest City Development; Citicorp Center and PG&E.

Ellman, Burke, Hoffman & Johnson

The Firm: A smaller boutique firm, it is considered by competitors to be *"well up to handling complex transactions."* The firm acted on the financing of a 750,000 sq ft building in San Francisco, worth approximately $360 million, and organized conservation easements for an 18,000-acre ranch, owned by Parrott Investment Company.

The Lawyers: Much of the firm's reputation is attributed to founding partner **Howard Ellman**, whose *"experience and intellectual capacity"* particularly impresses his peers. The focus of his practice is largely on development, conservation and water law.

The Clients: Hines; Parrott Investment Company; AT&T; Spieker Properties and US Home.

Sheppard, Mullin, Richter & Hampton LLP

The Firm: A full-service law firm with seven offices, all in California, its real estate department is commended for its *"local knowledge."* Competitors speak of the firm's *"experience and breadth,"* but the practice is best known for its work in redevelopment. The firm represented AMB Property, which won the right to develop Pier One, the first major site in the area, representing more than 100,000 sq ft of space. It also acted as land use counsel for the San Francisco Ferry Building and as project counsel for Lend Lease Development in connection with the proposed $270 million Bryant Street Pier project.

The Lawyers: The popular and *"affable"* **Bob Thompson** has a respected all-around practice, although his involvement in the development of the San Francisco waterfront is his principal claim to fame.

The Clients: AMB Property; Lend Lease Development; University of California, San Francisco; Presidio Trust; Boston Properties; Bloomingdale's; Lennar Homes and City and County of San Francisco.

TAX

CALIFORNIA
Leading firms (Tax)

1 IRELL & MANELLA LLP *Los Angeles*
LATHAM & WATKINS *Los Angeles*

2 FENWICK & WEST *Palo Alto*
GIBSON, DUNN & CRUTCHER LLP *Los Angeles*

3 BAKER & MCKENZIE *Palo Alto*
MORRISON & FOERSTER LLP *San Francisco*
O'MELVENY & MYERS LLP *Los Angeles*

4 COOLEY GODWARD LLP *Palo Alto*
MCDERMOTT, WILL *Los Angeles, Palo Alto*
ORRICK, HERRINGTON & SUTCLIFFE *San Francisco*
PILLSBURY WINTHROP LLP *San Francisco*

Leading individuals (Tax)

1 CLAIR John *Latham & Watkins, Los Angeles*
FULLER James *Fenwick & West, Palo Alto*
KOHL Glen *Cooley Godward LLP, Palo Alto*
OFFER Stuart *Morrison & Foerster LLP, San Francisco*

2 BEHNIA Hatef *Gibson, Dunn & Crutcher, Los Angeles*
BRYAN Karen *Latham & Watkins, Los Angeles*
CUFF Terence *Loeb & Loeb LLP, Los Angeles*
DIVOLA Julie *Pillsbury Winthrop LLP, San Francisco*
FREIER Elliot *Irell & Manella LLP, Los Angeles*
HYMAN Milt *Irell & Manella LLP, Los Angeles*
SAX Paul *Orrick, Herrington & Sutcliffe, San Francisco*

3 BLASHEK Robert *O'Melveny & Myers LLP, Los Angeles*
CHILTON Fred *McDermott, Will & Emery, Palo Alto*
HUMPHREYS Ivan *Wilson Sonsini Goodrich, Palo Alto*
IREDALE Nancy *Paul, Hastings, Janofsky, Los Angeles*
PHILLIP James *Gibson, Dunn & Crutcher, Los Angeles*
RABINOWITZ Joel *Irell & Manella LLP, Los Angeles*

Firms and individuals are listed alphabetically in each band.

Irell & Manella LLP

The Firm: Although it is famed for its IP proficiency, the firm was founded with tax law as one of its primary concerns, and retains a reputation among clients and peers for fielding *"an extremely strong clutch of tax lawyers."* Operating from two offices in California, the firm covers the entire spectrum of tax law and advises a number of huge US corporate clients.

The Lawyers: **Milt Hyman** was described to researchers as *"a guy who is at the top of the profession and who has been there forever."* His wide-ranging practice encompasses bankruptcy tax matters, on which he has published a definitive text, and tax controversy work. **Elliot Freier** appeals to clients as *"one of the best tax lawyers that I have seen."* He is another attorney with a profound knowledge of bankruptcy law and his clientele has included Charter Communications, Paul Allen and Vulcan. **Joel Rabinowitz** is primarily involved in international taxation. He is renowned for his deep, theoretical knowledge of the law, and has niche expertise in tax advice relating to the gaming and hospitality industries.

The Clients: Mirage Resorts; Mirage Bellagio; Teledyne; Charter Communications and Vulcan.

Latham & Watkins
see firm details p.835

The Firm: Now regarded as one of the preeminent authorities on tax law in the US, the firm is considered to have few weaknesses in this area. Peers spoke of the Californian team's *"dominance in M&A tax law,"* while other interviewees drew the attention of researchers to *"the firm's historical excellence in the field."*

The Lawyers: **John Clair** (see p.62) was universally endorsed to researchers as a *"thoughtful, decent, insightful and imaginative attorney."* He advised on the tax aspects of the $25 billion acquisition of a biotech company, and has represented a variety of public utilities on their attempts to finance their way clear of California's recent energy crisis. *"Down-to-earth"* **Karen Bryan** (see p.61) also elicited high praise for her *"creativity and intelligence."* She advised Fortune 500 pharmaceutical company Amgen on various transactions, most notably the $16 billion acquisition of Immunex.

The Clients: In addition to an outstanding corporate client base, the group represents a number of the country's principal investment funds. Amgen and AOL TimeWarner also feature on the client roster.

Fenwick & West

The Firm: Rivals regard the firm as *"a Goliath of international tax,"* which it mainly handles from its Palo Alto office. Clients include large organizations from the electronics, oil, automobile and pharmaceutical industries. The firm is renowned for its transactional work and also offers advice on tax planning and litigation.

The Lawyers: *"Think of tax in California and you think of "* **Jim Fuller**, was the market consensus. He was recommended to researchers as *"a hardworker, a prodigious writer and one whose name you see everywhere."*

The Clients: Among an array of federal tax court cases, the firm advised on Chrysler v Commissioner and Illinois Tool Works v Commissioner. Other clients include: HNC Software; Netopia; Elantec Semiconductor; ONI Systems and VeriSign.

TAX — CALIFORNIA

Gibson, Dunn & Crutcher LLP
The Firm: Although not traditionally regarded as tax specialists, the firm has an enormous flow of corporate transactions for its compact group of corporate tax and estate planning lawyers in Los Angeles. Competitors recognize that the firm has established *"a solid team with some notable attorneys"* who specialize in domestic and international transactional work and tax litigation.
The Lawyers: **Hatef Behnia** was selected as one of the firm's stellar tax practitioners. His expertise is spread across a wide area of corporate and business transactional tax issues and contemporaries regard him as *"one of the crème de la crème."* The popular **Jim Phillipp** appeals to clients as *"an exemplary tax attorney,"* and has substantial experience of state and federal tax litigation as well as cross-border transfer pricing.
The Clients: Multinational corporations, entrepreneurs and start-up companies all form part of the firm's client roster.

Baker & McKenzie
see firm details p.767
The Firm: The firm's presence all over the globe helps to give it what one leading competitor described as *"an international tax practice to match any firm on the West Coast."* Although the tax work covered by the firm is diverse, it is the tax implications of large cross-border M&A and joint ventures in which its attorneys are felt to excel, notably at the Palo Alto office.
The Lawyers: Head of the global tax practice group, John Peterson is said to preside over a *"host of consistently good attorneys"* whose strong team ethic particularly caught the eye of interviewees.
The Clients: The client roster here features major corporations and financial institutions.

Morrison & Foerster LLP
see firm details p.854
The Firm: Eight offices throughout California advise on the full spectrum of tax law, although the firm received markedly strong recommendation for its state and local taxation expertise. The group is a veteran of a number of cases before California Supreme Court.
The Lawyers: Among a respected team, the *"dedicated"* **Stu Offer** (see p.69) clearly stands out for his contemporaries, who extolled his *"good grasp of the minutiae."* He has represented JDS Uniphase on a number of recent acquisitions, and was involved in the multibillion dollar acquisition of Technicolor, part of Carlton Communications, by Thomson multimedia. His practice also embraces tax planning and international tax advice.
The Clients: JDS Uniphase and Thomson multimedia are among the firm's clients.

O'Melveny & Myers LLP
The Firm: While it possesses an active transactional tax group, the firm has a substantially lower profile for tax controversy work. Compensation comes through strong employee benefits and estate planning practice groups, as well as niche expertise in municipal bond work.
The Lawyers: The team in the firm's Los Angeles office attracted high market praise. Clients were particularly emphatic in their endorsement of *"solid performer"* **Rob Blashek**. His practice focuses on corporate and business transactional tax matters and workouts. He has represented the Spanish-language media company Univision Communications on a host of acquisitions, and acted for Clarity Partners, a venture capital group with an investment fund approaching $1 billion.
The Clients: Univision Communications; Marriott Hotels; California Institute of Technology and Clarity Partners.

Cooley Godward LLP
The Firm: The firm's Palo Alto tax group gained great impetus with the arrival of the much-traveled **Glen Kohl**. Peers regard him as *"an obvious standout. He's a brilliant and creative lawyer with a good business background and top government contacts."* He served in the US Treasury during the Clinton administration, and also spent time in-house with a tech company. He has regularly structured transactions for some of the largest tech companies in the US and recently represented COR Therapeutics on its $2 billion acquisition by Millennium Pharmaceuticals.
The Clients: COR Therapeutics is a key name on the firm's client roster.

McDermott, Will & Emery
see firm details p.846
The Firm: Founded as a tax law firm, the firm's acknowledged national and international capability in this area includes a respected team in California. Here the group has been augmented by the recent hire of five attorneys from local rival Fenwick & West. International taxation issues are the firm's forte, and the team has a sound reputation for transactional work, tax planning, transfer pricing and tax litigation.
The Lawyers: **Fred Chilton** (see p.62) currently heads the firm's tax practice in California, having recently arrived from Fenwick & West. He was described to researchers as a *"first-rate attorney who knows his stuff."* On the tax controversy side, he has advised clients on their defense to the transfer of intangibles, and has been active in the area of advanced pricing agreements.
The Clients: Hi-tech, banking and retail companies are all to be found in the firm's client base.

Orrick, Herrington & Sutcliffe
see firm details p.859
The Firm: Other firms may *"spring more readily to mind"* for tax advice, but Orrick's public finance tax group came in for repeated market endorsement: *"They are the premier practice for tax-exempt bonds,"* admitted one rival. Municipal finance, which accounts for about 18% of the firm's tax work, is the area in which the group is held to have no peer in California. Elsewhere, the firm advises extensively on the tax aspects of asset securitizations.
The Lawyers: **Paul Sax** (see p.72) is a recognized expert in tax litigation and also counsels clients on tax planning. Researchers were impressed by the depth of approval for this *"experienced and excellent controversy lawyer."*
The Clients: AOL Time Warner; Bear Stearns; Chase Manhattan; CSFB; Bank of America; Merrill Lynch; United Artists and E & J Gallo Winery.

Pillsbury Winthrop LLP
see firm details p.866
The Firm: *"One or two extremely talented individuals"* are considered to be the major selling point of this diverse Californian tax practice. The firm handles a range of state and local taxation issues, and is felt to benefit from the presence of a number of former government personnel.
The Lawyers: **Julie Divola** (see p.63) heads the firm's San Francisco tax group. She focuses on M&A, joint ventures and partnership matters, and is also respected for her experience of REIT and RIC work. Clients *"can't speak highly enough of her,"* with one adding that *"she certainly tops my list."* She came to prominence with her advice to AirTouch on its acquisition by Vodafone, and also represents various hi-tech, biotech, and healthcare companies.
The Clients: Vodafone AirTouch and Chevron USA are two of this firm's high-profile clients.

Other Notable Practitioners
Terry Cuff of Loeb & Loeb LLP in Los Angeles was commended to researchers for his *"profound knowledge of partnership tax."* He also has extensive experience of real estate taxation issues. **Ivan Humphreys** works out of Palo Alto for Wilson Sonsini Goodrich & Rosati. He has recently represented Sun Microsystems on numerous transactions, as well as acting for Hewlett-Packard and Palm, and impresses peers with his *"incredible breadth of knowledge."* At the Los Angeles office of Paul, Hastings, Janofsky & Walker LLP, former IRS attorney **Nancy Iredale** (see p.66) is esteemed for her tax controversy work, where she is said to *"know her way around the procedures."* She advised on an advanced pricing agreement for a large electronics company, and has appeared at an appeal for a petrochemical company.

CALIFORNIA LEADERS

Leaders in California

ABEL, Sally
Fenwick & West, Palo Alto
650 494 0600
Recommended in Intellectual Property

ABELL, Nancy
Paul, Hastings, Janofsky & Walker LLP,
Los Angeles 213 683 6162
nancyabell@paulhastings.com
Recommended in Employment
Specialization: Chair of Employment Law Department. Represents employers in matters including wrongful discharge, discrimination, sexual harassment, whistle blower, and labor-management litigation; OFCCP class actions and affirmative action compliance reviews; unfair labor practice charges; organizing campaigns; labor negotiations; arbitrations; and EEOC proceedings.
Publications: 'An Employer's Guide for Preparing Affirmative Action Programs'; 'An Employer's Guide to the Americans with Disabilities Act (1991)'; Author of 'Federal Contractor Affirmative Action Compliance chapter of Employment Discrimination Law'.
Personal: Graduated first in her class - Pitzer College of the Claremont Colleges - 1972; graduated Order of the Coif and Order of the Barristers - The UCLA School of Law -1979.

ALEXANDER, Judith
Winn & Alexander LLP, Capitola
831 479 3490
Recommended in Media & Entertainment

ALVAREZ, Fred
Wilson Sonsini Goodrich & Rosati,
Palo Alto 650 493 9300
Recommended in Employment

ARNOLD, Dennis
Gibson, Dunn & Crutcher LLP,
Los Angeles 213 229 7000
Recommended in Real Estate

ARONSON, Seth
O'Melveny & Myers LLP, Los Angeles
213 430 6000
Recommended in Litigation

ARONZON, Paul
Milbank, Tweed, Hadley & McCloy,
Los Angeles 213 892 4000
Recommended in Insolvency

BABBE, David B
Morrison & Foerster LLP, Los Angeles
213 892 5549
dbabbe@mofo.com
Recommended in Insurance
Specialization: Partner focusing on insurance coverage, professional liability and banking litigation within a general business litigation practice. Has handled an array of insurance coverage litigation in both state and federal courts as well as served as liaison counsel in a multi-billion dollar environmental coverage action.
Prof. Memberships: Member, Litigation Section, American Bar Association. Member, Association of Business Trial Lawyers.
Career: Admitted to practice in California. Currently Managing Partner of *Morrison & Foerster's* Los Angeles office.
Personal: BA degree, magna cum laude, University of California, Irvine, 1978; JD degree, second in class, University of California, Los Angeles School of Law, 1981, Order of the Coif; Member, Moot Court Honors Board.

BALLATI, Deborah
Farella Braun & Martel LLP,
San Francisco 415 954 4400
Recommended in Construction

BARONSKY, Kenneth
Milbank, Tweed, Hadley & McCloy,
Los Angeles 213 892 4000
Recommended in Capital Markets

BARR, Michael R
Pillsbury Winthrop LLP, San Francisco
415 983 1151
mbarr@pillsburywinthrop.com
Recommended in Environment
Specialization: Partner in the environment, land use and natural resources; global energy; and land use areas. Practices in the commercial and administrative law fields and has extensive experience assisting established and emerging companies in the transportation, communications, computer, chemical, food products, energy, mining and manufacturing industries. He focuses on emerging issues and innovative solutions to complex commercial and regulatory matters. Has assisted public and privately held companies, associations, trade groups and other entities on many matters of first impression, such as development rights creation, banking and trading. He has served on many advisory and trade groups. He speaks often on emerging development, commercial and administrative issues to round tables, associations and foundations on subjects as diverse as space commercialization, rubber manufacturing and hard rock mining. He has participated in and led many teams involved in business planning, venture startup, financing, project development, strategic reorganization, long term joint ventures and many other innovative activities.
Career: Admitted to practice: State of California.
Personal: JD, Harvard University, 1973; BS, University of Washington at Seattle, 1970.

BEHNIA, Hatef
Gibson, Dunn & Crutcher LLP,
Los Angeles 213 229 7000
Recommended in Tax

BELLAH MAGUIRE, Jennifer
Gibson, Dunn & Crutcher LLP,
Los Angeles 213 229 7000
Recommended in Capital Markets

BENJAMIN, Alan
Orrick, Herrington & Sutcliffe,
Los Angeles 213 612 2431
abenjamin@orrick.com
Recommended in Banking & Finance
Specialization: Focuses on complex financial transactions, including secured and unsecured loan transactions, project financings, leveraged buyouts, lease transactions, debt restructurings. Significant experience in large syndicated financings and intercreditor arrangements. Recent experience includes loans and bonds to Native American tribes.
Career: *Orrick, Herrington & Sutcliffe LLP;* Partner, 1994-present; Managing Director, 2001; Executive Committee Member, 1997-2001; Private Finance Group Chair, 1996-2000. *Morrison & Foerster LLP,* partner, 1983-94; associate 1977-83.
Personal: UCLA Law School, JD 1997, Order of the Coif; UCLA School of Management, MBA 1997, Beta Gamma Sigma; UCLA, 1974 AB, Phi Beta Kappa.

BENNETT, Fred G
Quinn Emanuel Urquhart Oliver & Hedges, LLP, Los Angeles
213 624 7707
fredbennett@quinnemanuel.com
Recommended in Construction
Specialization: Senior partner. Specializes in business litigation, international and domestic arbitration. Extensive experience in technical disputes, including satellite/aerospace litigation, construction, engineering and architectural disputes; commercial disputes; intellectual property disputes; corporate partnership disputes and dissolutions; and general business litigation. Has tried or arbitrated as lead counsel, domestically and internationally, over 25 major disputes to verdict or award.
Prof. Memberships: Member, California State Bar (1974-); US District Court, District of California (1974-); US Court of Appeals, Second, Fifth, Ninth and Tenth Circuits. US Council of International Business (National Committee and Arbitration, Western Subcommittee Chair; Institute for Transactional Arbitration (Advisory Board); American Arbitration Association (member of Commercial and Construction Large Complex Case Panels); Chairman and Large Complex Case Panel Continuing Education Committee (California); Los Angeles County Bar Association; International Bar Association; American Bar Association; Inter-American Bar Association; Brigham Young University (Board of Visitors, emeritus); Claremont College (Board of Visitors, 1994-99).
Career: Senior Partner at *Quinn Emanuel Urquhart Oliver & Hedges, LLP,* 1998-; Senior Partner, Partner (Trial Department, Chairman of Technical and ADR Groups) and Associate, *Gibson, Dunn & Crutcher, LLP,* 1973-98.
Publications: 'Dispositive Motions', LCCP Continuing Education Program, American Arbitration Association (October 1996); 'Discovery', LCCP Continuing Education Program, American Arbitration Association (May 1996); 'Award and Appeal', LCCP Continuing Education Program, American Arbitration Association (October 1997); 'Handling Tough Evidentiary Objections', LCCP Continuing Education Education Program, American Arbitration Association (April 1998); 'Drafting Arbitration Clauses', Business Litigation Report (Newsletter of *Quinn Emanuel Urquhart Oliver & Hedges, LLP*), February 1998. 'Characteristics of ICC Arbitrations', ICC National Seminar, San Francisco, California (April 17, 1998); 'Obtaining the Injunctive Relief You Need When You Need it in Arbitration', Business Litigation Report, February 1999; 'Role of the Panel Chair and Conducting a Preliminary Hearing', AAA National Neutrals Conference, Orlando, Florida 1998; 'Guidelines for Preparing Reasoned Arbitration Awards', AAA Continuing Education Program (September 2000); 'Enforcing Arbitration Awards Worldwide', Quinn Emanuel Annual Arbitration Seminar (October 2001); 'Beyond the Rules: Winning International Arbitration Strategies from The Viewpoints of Arbitrators, Administrators & Advocates', Quinn Emanuel Annual Arbitration Seminar (November 2002); 'Disclosure Rules for Arbitrators', AAA Continuing Education Program (November 2002).
Personal: Honours BA degree, University of Utah 1970 (magna cum laude, Phi Beta Kappa). JD, UCLA Law Review.

BENVENUTTI, Peter
Heller Ehrman White & McAuliffe LLP,
San Francisco 415 772 6000
Recommended in Insolvency

BERCHILD, John
Sheppard, Mullin, Richter & Hampton LLP, Los Angeles 213 620 1780
Recommended in Banking & Finance

LEADERS CALIFORNIA

BERTELSEN, Mark
Wilson Sonsini Goodrich & Rosati,
Palo Alto 650 493 9300
Recommended in Communications

BLASHEK, Robert
O'Melveny & Myers LLP, Los Angeles
310 553 6700
Recommended in Tax

BLECHER, Maxwell
Blecher & Collins, Los Angeles
213 622 4222
Recommended in Antitrust, Litigation

BLOOM, Jerry
White & Case LLP, Los Angeles
213 620 7700
Recommended in Energy

BOCHNER, Steven
Wilson Sonsini Goodrich & Rosati,
Palo Alto 650 493 9300
Recommended in Communications

BOGDANOFF, Lee R
Klee, Tuchin, Bogdanoff & Stern LLP,
Los Angeles 310 407 4070
lbogdanoff@ktbslaw.com
Recommended in Insolvency
Specialization: Is a member and co-manager of *Klee, Tuchin, Bogdanoff & Stern LLP*. He has represented debtors in and out-of-court, often in very large and complex cases, as well as parties interested in acquiring assets from debtors. He has also represented creditors' committees, including serving as special counsel to the creditors' committee in the Iridium companies cases (holders of unsecured claims in a failed satellite enterprise involving over $3 billion in debt) and numerous out-of-court committees. Has served as lead counsel in some of the largest chapter 11 cases pending at the time. Has represented many acquirers, including Twentieth Century Fox, in connection with a variety of acquisitions (including the purchase of assets from Carolco and Marvel) and the GAP.

BOGEN, Andy
Gibson, Dunn & Crutcher LLP,
Los Angeles 213 229 7000
Recommended in Corporate/M&A

BOMSE, Stephen
Heller Ehrman White & McAuliffe LLP,
San Francisco 415 772 6000
Recommended in Antitrust

BOOTH, William
Sole Practitioner, Walnut Creek,
925 296 2460
Recommended in Energy

BORNN, Nancy
Born & Surls, Marina Del Rey
310 577 8112
Recommended in Employment

BRIAN, Brad
Munger, Tolles & Olson, Los Angeles
213 683 9100
Recommended in Litigation

BRIDGES, Andrew
Wilson Sonsini Goodrich & Rosati,
Palo Alto 650 493 9300
Recommended in Intellectual Property

BROSNAHAN, James
Morrison & Foerster LLP, San Francisco
415 268 7189
jbrosnahan@mofo.com
Recommended in Litigation
Specialization: Partner engaged in civil and criminal trials. Has tried more than 130 jury cases and argued both civil and criminal appeals in state and federal court, including two cases in the United States Supreme Court.
Prof. Memberships: American College of Trial Lawyers, the American Board of Trial Advocates, the International Academy of Trial Lawyers, the International Society of Barristers, the American Law Institute, and the American Board of Criminal Lawyers Association, the American Bar Association Foundation, Fellow; Master Advocate on the faculty and member of the Board of Trustees of the National Institute for Trial Advocacy; Lawyers Club of San Francisco; World Affairs Council of Northern California; Association of Business Trial Lawyers, Northern California; Edward J McFetridge American Inn of Court; United States Supreme Court Historical Society; American Lawyer Newspapers Group, Inc., National Board of Contributors; Libel Defense Center, Defense Counsel Section; and the National Council of the Lawyers Committee for Human Rights.
Career: Admitted to practice in Arizona and California. Practiced five years as Assistant United States Attorney prosecuting federal cases in Phoenix, Arizona and San Francisco, California. Joined firm in 1975 as partner. Was associate member of Office of Independent Counsel: Iran-Contra. Lead prosecutor in US v Caspar Weinberger (October-December 1992). Inducted into The State Bar of California's 'Trial Lawyers Hall of Fame' in 1996; received 'Samuel E Gates Award' by the American College of Trial Lawyers in October 2000; named 'Trial Lawyer of the Year'; by American Board of Trial Advocates, 2001; awarded 'Legend of the Law'; award by Lawyers' Club of San Francisco and named one of the 'Top 100 Most Influential Attorneys' by California legal press, 'Daily Journal' in 2002.
Publications: Chapter: 'Corporate Criminal Liability', White Collar Crimes, ALI-ABA, 1980, with Samuel Miller and Ron Foy; Author, Trial Handbook for California Lawyers, Bancroft-Whitney, 1974 and Trial Advocacy Text [publication forthcoming].
Personal: BSBA, Boston College, 1956; LLB, Harvard Law School, 1959.

BROWN, Donald W
Covington & Burling, San Francisco
415 591 6000
Recommended in Insurance

BRYAN, Karen
Latham & Watkins LLP, Los Angeles
213 891 8176
karen.bryan@lw.com
Recommended in Tax
Specialization: Partner, Tax Department. Focuses on corporate and general income taxation, with emphasis on the tax aspects and structuring of mergers, acquisitions, divestitures, reorganizations of business entities and consolidated groups, debt and equity restructurings and financings, IRS audits, appeals and tax litigation. Handles tax controversies from examination through appellate levels. Has coordinated responses to major IRS discovery initiatives.
Prof. Memberships: Member, ABA's Corporate Tax Committee and Individual Income Tax Committee. Member, Planning Committee, USC Institute.
Personal: JD, University of Southern California, 1979. MA, University of California, Los Angeles, 1973. AB, Bryn Mawr College, 1972.

BUONCRISTIANI, David
Thelen Reid & Priest LLP, San Francisco
415 369 7227
dbuoncristiani@thelenreid.com
Recommended in Construction
Specialization: More than 30 years of commercial litigation experience with primary emphasis on national and international construction industry related disputes, including all facets of public and private construction works of improvement; representation of contractors in bid protest disputes arising under competitively-bid contracts; claim preparation and claim evaluation; prosecution and defense of contractor claims before both State and Federal courts and before arbitration tribunals and governmental administrative panels, such as the Board of Contract Appeals. Experienced in all phases of discovery and pre-trial/pre-hearing procedures and adversarial hearings and the preparation and use of both manual and computerized document/information indexing and retrieval systems and computer-generated graphics and evidence. Extensive experience with mediation and other forms of alternative dispute resolution.
Prof. Memberships: Fellow: American College of Construction Lawyers. American Bar Association, Forum on the Construction Industry and Public Contracts and Litigation Sections. Associated General Contractors Legal Advisory Committee, 1984-2002. Bar Association of San Francisco; State Bar of California (1972).
Career: Admitted to practice before all California Courts; US Claims Court, 1976; Martindale Hubbell rating: 'a v.' Representative Speaking Engagements: Speaker, Construction Law Superconference, 1985-2001; Speaker, B Warren Hart Memorial Lecture Series on Construction Law, 1983; Guest Lecturer on Construction Law, University of California, Berkeley and Boalt Hall Law School 1989-95; Speaker, Prentice Hall 'Trying a Complex Construction Case', 1994; Speaker, Project Management Institute's Annual Conference, 1996.
Publications: Contributing Editor, 'Construction Litigation: Representing the Contractor' Wiley Publications (1992 and 2001). Contributing Editor, 'Proving and Pricing Construction Claims', Wiley Publications (1996). Contributing Editor, 'Construction Litigation Formbook', First Edition, Wiley Publications (1990).
Personal: Law degree from Univeristy of California, Hastings College of the Law, (1971). Member, Thurston Honor Society and the Order of the Coif; Managing Editor of the 'Hastings Law Journal'. BA from University of San Francisco (1968).

BURKE, Thomas
Davis Wright Tremaine LLP,
San Francisco 415 276 6552
thomasburke@dwt.com
Recommended in Media & Entertainment
Specialization: Partner in Communications/Media Law Department. Instrumental in establishing *DWT's* internet/e-commerce practice. Represents publishers/broadcasters in defamation, invasion of privacy, right of publicity, copyright, false advertising and other content-related litigation. Experienced pre-publication counselor and advisor on obtaining access to public records and proceedings.
Prof. Memberships: Adjunct Professor of Media Law, Graduate School of Journalism, University of California at Berkeley.
Career: Joined firm, 1996; became partner, 1998.
Publications: Co-Editor, 'Reporter's Handbook on Media Law' (CNPA 1999); Co-Author, 'Internet Law and Practice' (West 2002).
Personal: JD, (magna cum laude), University of San Francisco School of Law, 1989. BS, (magna cum laude), Arizona State University, 1984.

CALOF, Lawrence
Gibson, Dunn & Crutcher LLP, Palo Alto
650 849 5300
Recommended in Corporate/M&A

CAMAHORT, Steve
Wilson Sonsini Goodrich & Rosati,
Palo Alto 650 493 9300
Recommended in Communications

CANE, Paul
Paul, Hastings, Janofsky & Walker LLP,
San Francisco 415 856 7014
paulcane@paulhastings.com
Recommended in Employment
Specialization: Chair of Appellate Practice Group. Argued and/or briefed cases including Guz v Bechtel National, Inc., Turner v Anheuser Busch, Inc., Rochlis v Walt Disney Co., Foley v Interactive Data Corp., Armendariz v Foundation Health

CALIFORNIA LEADERS

Psychcare Services, Inc., and Cotran v Rollins Hudig Hall International, Inc. **Publications:** Co-author of 'An Employer's Guide to the Americans with Disabilities Act' (1991); Editor in chief of Lindemann & Grossman's 'Employment Discrimination Law' (3d ed 1996), the American Bar Association's official, two-volume treatise in the field. **Personal:** Dartmouth College (1976) summa cum laude; Boalt Hall School of Law at the University of California at Berkeley (1979).

CAREY, Stevens
Pircher, Nichols & Meeks, Los Angeles
310 201 8900
Recommended in Real Estate

CATHCART, David
Gibson, Dunn & Crutcher LLP,
Los Angeles 213 229 7000
Recommended in Employment

CATHCART, Patrick
Hancock, Rothert & Bunshoft LLP,
San Francisco 213 623 7777
pcathcart@hrblaw.com
Recommended in Insurance

Specialization: Partner and co-chair of business litigation practice group. Concentrates on complex business litigation, with an emphasis on multi-party insurance coverage litigation and professional liability matters. Has been lead defense counsel, or trial counsel, in the following cases: Pintlar v Aetna (the Bunker Hill litigation) (US District Court, Idaho); Martin Marietta et al v Aetna Casualty & Surety Co (Los Angeles) (two jury trials); FMC Corporation v Liberty Mutual, et al (San Jose, California) (three month jury trial); Rockwell International Corporation v Aetna Cas. & Surety Co., et al (Los Angeles); Southern California Gas Co. v AEGIS, Ltd., et al (Los Angeles); McColl-Frontenac Inc. v Adriatic Insurance Company et al (Los Angeles); Armstrong v Aetna (six week arbitration in 1998, before retired US District Judge Nicholas Bua, Chicago, Illinois); Golden Eagle v Associated International Ins. Co., et al (Los Angeles) Highlands Ins. Co. v Powerine Oil Company and related cross actions (Los Angeles); Fuller-Austin v Fireman's Fund (Los Angeles). Is involved in litigation on behalf of clients against Del Monte Corporation (litigation pending in Hawaii), I C Industries, Southern Pacific Transportation Company. Has represented clients before appellate courts on a variety of issues (see Certain Underwriters at Lloyd's, London v Superior Court 24 Cal 4th 945 (2001)). Has litigated intellectual property disputes, beginning with litigation between 'PC Magazine' and 'PC World Magazine' over trade name infringement in 1983. Has represented a major contractor in two arbitrations in the Hague, Netherlands, in connection with construction disputes involving pipeline and pumping station contracts with the government of Iran; a major contractor in litigation against the United States government and several insurance companies over liability for the failure of a large dam in eastern Idaho, and motion picture producers in with Village Roadshow Pictures (an Australian motion picture production, distribution and exhibition company). Extensive experience in handling professional liability claims against lawyers and law firms. **Prof. Memberships:** American Bar Association; State Bar of California; Association of Business Trial Lawyers (member of Board of Governors, currently Treasurer); Los Angeles County Bar Association. **Career:** Admitted to California Bar (1975). Partner at *Hancock Rothert & Bunshoft LLP* (1982), and founded the firm's Los Angeles office in 1989. **Personal:** JD from University of California Hastings College of Law (1975); AB from Stanford University (1968); graduate, Phillips Academy, Andover (1964). Member, US Peace Corps/Iran (1969-71).

CHECOV, Martin
O'Melveny & Myers LLP, San Francisco
415 984 8700
Recommended in Insurance

CHILTON, Fred
McDermott, Will & Emery, Palo Alto
650 813 5121
fchilton@mwe.com
Recommended in Tax

Specialization: Partner in the firm's Tax Department. Focuses on the representation of high-technology and other companies on complex tax matters. **Career:** Adjunct Professor in the Golden Gate University Masters in Tax program. Law clerk for Judge Leo H Irwin, US Tax Court and a Tax Law Specialist in the Foreign Rulings Group of the Internal Revenue Service. Often speaks and serves as chair for seminars on behalf of the World Trade Institute, Practicing Law Institute and the Tax Executives Institute. Has written a number of articles on a variety of federal income tax issues. **Personal:** Received BA in 1967 from Fresno State College. Atttended Hastings College of Law, and received JD in 1971. Earned LLM in Taxation from New York University in 1973.

CHU, Morgan
Irell & Manella LLP, Los Angeles
310 277 1010
Recommended in Intellectual Property

CLAIR, John
Latham & Watkins LLP, Los Angeles
213 485 1234
john.clair@lw.com
Recommended in Tax

Specialization: Partner, Tax Department. Extensive experience in corporate taxation. Advises clients on tax issues involved in mergers, acquisitions, divestitures, financial products and services, and administrative and judicial tax controversies. **Prof. Memberships:** Los Angeles County, State of California and American Bar Associations. **Publications:** Contributor for Practising Law Institute, Tax Executives Institute, New York University Tax Institute, University of Chicago Federal Tax Institute. **Personal:** JD, University of Pennsylvania, 1972. AB, Brown University, 1968.

CLARK, John
Thelen Reid & Priest LLP, Los Angeles
213 576 8040
jbclark@thelenreid.com
Recommended in Construction

Specialization: His practice areas of specialty include construction, commercial litigation, government contracts and ADR. **Prof. Memberships:** American Bar Association, Public Contract Law Section, Forum Committee on the Construction Industry; Fellow, American College of Construction Lawyers; Board of Editors, Stanford Law Review. **Career:** Admitted to Bar: 1966, California; 1962, New York; 1991, Colorado. **Publications:** 'The AGCC Handbook of California Construction Law' (Associated General Contractors of California), 1992; 'California Construction Law' (Federal Publications) 1980-present; 'Understanding the Government Procurement Process' (Engineering News Record); 'Claims and the Project Schedule' (Federal Publications), 1983. **Personal:** Received LLB from Stanford University in 1961 and a BS in General Engineering from Stanford University in 1958.

CLIMAN, Richard
Cooley Godward LLP, Palo Alto
650 843 5000
Recommended in Communications, Corporate/M&A

COBEN, Jerome L
Skadden, Arps, Slate, Meagher & Flom LLP, Los Angeles 213 687 5010
jcoben@skadden.com
Recommended in Corporate/M&A

Specialization: Leader of *Skadden's* West Coast Corporate Practice. Has a broad-based corporate and securities law practice, representing both issuers and investment banks in a wide variety of corporate finance, mergers and acquisition and general corporate matters. **Prof. Memberships:** Member, American and Los Angeles County Bar associations. **Career:** JD, New York University School of Law, 1966-69 (Root-Tilden Scholar); AB, Brown University 1962-66 (cum laude). **Publications:** Co-author, 'Types of Securities' in 'Start up & Emerging Companies: Planning, Financing & Operating the Successful Business' (Law Journal Seminars-Press 2000).

COHEN, Nancy
Heller Ehrman White & McAuliffe LLP,
Los Angeles 213 689 0200
Recommended in Insurance

COLEMAN, Thomas
Orrick, Herrington & Sutcliffe,
San Francisco 415 773 5870
tycoleman@orrick.com
Recommended in Banking & Finance

Specialization: Represents banks and other financial institutions in a variety of transactions, including syndicated and single-lender credit agreements, both secured and unsecured; project financings; public finance transactions; and synthetic and other lease arrangements. **Career:** *Morrison & Foerster LLP*, associate, 1976-79; California First Bank (now Union Bank of California), Vice President and Counsel, 1979-85; *Clifford-Turner* (now *Clifford Chance*), Solicitors, visiting attorney, 1984; *Orrick, Herrington & Sutcliffe LLP*, partner, 1985-date. Currently, Chair of Professional Development Committee and General Counsel of Orrick. **Personal:** University of Virginia, BA 1971, JD 1975.

COMPTON, Charles
Wilson Sonsini Goodrich & Rosati,
Palo Alto 650 493 9300
Recommended in Antitrust

COOPER, Robert
Gibson, Dunn & Crutcher LLP,
Los Angeles 213 229 7000
Recommended in Antitrust, Litigation

CORASH, Michèle B
Morrison & Foerster LLP, San Francisco
415 268 7124
mcorash@mofo.com
Recommended in Environment

Specialization: Partner specializing in environmental law and in defense of enforcement actions and class actions relating to consumer products. **Prof. Memberships:** Board of Directors, California Council on Environmental and Economic Balance; Member-Blue Ribbon Commission-California EPA Unified Environmental Statute; Member, American Bar Association Standing Committee on Environmental Law; Board of Advisors, 'Ecology Law Quarterly'; Board of Advisors, 'Hastings West-Northwest Journal of Environmental Law and Policy.' **Career:** Admitted to practice in California and the District of Columbia. Joined *Morrison & Foerster* in 1988 after serving as General Counsel of the United States Environmental Protection Agency. Was also a member of Vice President Bush's Regulatory Reform Task Force. Environmental Section of the Inter-Pacific Bar Association. Recently honored as one of the 'Top 30 Women Litigators in California' and as a 'Top 100 Most Influential Lawyers in California' by Los Angeles and San Francisco Daily Journals. **Publications:** Editor, 'Prop 65 News.'

Personal: BA, Economics, Mount Holyoke College, 1967; JD, cum laude, New York University School of Law, 1970.

COTCHETT, Joseph
Cotchett, Pitre, Simon & McCarthy, Burlingame 650 697 6000
Recommended in Litigation

CRANE, Steven
Berkes Crane Robinson & Seal, LLP, Los Angeles 213 955 1150
Recommended in Insurance

CUFF, Terence
Loeb & Loeb LLP, Los Angeles
310 282 2000
Recommended in Tax

DALLAS, Bruce
Davis Polk & Wardwell, Menlo Park
650 752 2000
Recommended in Capital Markets

DAVIDSON, Gordon
Fenwick & West, Palo Alto
650 494 0600
Recommended in Communications, Corporate/M&A

DAWES, Paul
Latham & Watkins LLP, Menlo Park
650 463 2626
paul.dawes@lw.com
Recommended in Litigation
Specialization: Partner, Litigation Department. Focuses on complex business litigation and providing advice to boards of directors and committees of publicly owned corporations, involving securities matters, intellectual property disputes and regulatory authority investigations.
Prof. Memberships: American Law Institute, 1987-present.
Career: Former National Chair, Litigation Department. Council, ABA's Litigation Section, 1989-92. Chair, Committee on Securities Litigation, BASF, 1998-99. Co-chair, ABA's Litigation Section Committee on Business Torts, 1994-97 and co-chair, Corporate Counsel, 1986-89.
Publications: Co-editor, 'Corporate Compliance Services', 1993. Co-author, 'Business and Commercial Litigation in the Federal Courts', 1998.
Personal: JD, University of Wisconsin, 1970. BA, University of Michigan, 1967.

DAY, Lloyd (Rusty)
Day Casebeer Madrid & Batchelder LLP, Cupertino 408 255 3255
Recommended in Intellectual Property

DAY, Michael
Goodin MacBride Squeri Ritchie & Day LLP, San Francisco 415 392 7900
Recommended in Energy

DE MEULES, James
O'Melveny & Myers LLP, Los Angeles
213 430 6000
Recommended in Banking & Finance

DEL CALVO, Jorge
Pillsbury Winthrop LLP, Palo Alto
650 233 4537
jorge@pillsburywinthrop.com
Recommended in Communications
Specialization: His practice focuses primarily on representation of technology companies in securities and venture capital transactions, including public offerings, private placements, mergers and acquisitions and joint ventures. He has represented issuers and underwriters in hundreds of private and public offerings of equity securities, including initial public offerings, and merger and acquisition transactions, representing sellers and purchasers. He represented Network Solutions in its IPO as well as its $2.2 billion follow-on public offering – the largest internet follow-on public equity offering in history. His representation of investment bankers includes work with such clients as Goldman Sachs & Co., Deutsche Banc Alex. Brown, Lehman Brothers Inc. and Needham & Company, Inc. on a number of public offerings, private placements, spinoffs and other transactions.
Career: Admitted to practice: State of California. Member: American Bar Association. Visiting Lecturer at Stanford Law School, teaching corporate law courses.
Publications: Coordinating Editor of the 'Venture Capital and Public Offering Negotiation', a two-volume treatise for lawyers.
Personal: JD, Harvard Law School (cum laude), 1981. MA, Harvard University (public policy), 1981. MA, University of California at Los Angeles (Latin American History), 1978. BA, Stanford University (Phi Beta Kappa, with distinction), 1977. ND, University of the Philippines, 1982.

DETTMER, Scott
Gunderson Dettmer Stough Villeneuve Franklin & Hachigian, Menlo Park
650 321 2400
Recommended in Communications

DIVOLA, Julie
Pillsbury Winthrop LLP, San Francisco
415 983 7446
julie.divola@pillsburywinthrop.com
Recommended in Tax
Specialization: Partner in the tax and private equity funds practice areas, chair of the San Francisco Tax Practice. Experienced in federal income tax planning for business and financial transactions. Her practice focuses on corporate and partnership taxation with particular emphasis on structuring mergers, acquisitions, divestitures and reorganizations; counseling with regard to the formation and restructuring of partnerships and joint ventures; advice in connection with project finance transactions; and tax controversy matters. She has experience in structuring and advising specialized entities such as real estate investment trusts (REITs) and regulated investment companies (RICs). Has worked extensively with a variety of industries.
Prof. Memberships: American Bar Association (Tax Section) Corporate Tax Committee (Chair, Corporate Tax Subcommittee on Taxable Acquisitions); California Bar Association (Tax Section) Corporate Tax Committee (Chair, Corporate Tax Committee); Bar Association of San Francisco, San Francisco Tax Club.
Career: Admitted to practice: State of California.
Personal: JD, University of San Francisco School of Law, 1986, summa cum laude; BA, University of California at Santa Barbara, 1980.

DODSON, Gerald
Morrison & Foerster LLP, Palo Alto
650 813 5983
gdodson@mofo.com
Recommended in Intellectual Property
Specialization: Partner specializing in complex patent litigation. Lead trial and appellate counsel for the University of Rochester Medical Center in a patent infringement action against Pharmacia, G.D. Searle, Pfizer, and Monsanto involving the drug, Celebrex, a 'super aspirin' that is the fastest selling new drug in history. In September 2001, won a unanimous 12-0 jury verdict for Clorox Corporation over Procter & Gamble involving a patent dispute over the fluid mechanics in the Brita water treatment pitcher used to purify tap water. Recently, was lead trial and appellate counsel for the Regents of the University of California in patent litigation against Genentech over a human growth hormone biotechnology patent. Case settled for $200 million, one of the largest settlements in the history of patent law, largest ever in biotechnology. Also represents companies on pioneering patent cases covering medical devices, optical and electronic hardware and software fields.
Career: Admitted to the California State Bar and to the US Patent & Trademark Office. Before private practice, served as Chief Counsel for Health and Environmental Subcommittee, US House of Representatives, and with Solicitor's Office, US Department of the Interior. Headed the congressional investigation of Union Carbide's pesticide plant disaster in Bhopal.
Personal: BSME, Lafayette College, 1969; JD, University of Maryland Law School, 1972; LLM, George Washington University Law School, 1977.

DUFFY, Pamela
Coblentz, Patch, Duffy & Bass LLP, San Francisco 415 391 4800
Recommended in Real Estate

EATMAN, Louis P
Mayer, Brown, Rowe & Maw, Los Angeles 213 229 5144
leatman@mayerbrownrowe.com
Recommended in Real Estate
Specialization: Advises on real estate finance, acquisitions and sales, workouts and restructures, foreclosures and deeds in lieu of foreclosure. Represents commercial banks, savings banks, life insurance companies, pension funds and their advisors, investment banks, real estate investment trusts, portfolio asset managers, other institutional mortgage lenders and investors, commercial property landlords and tenants.
Prof. Memberships: American College of Real Estate Lawyers. International Council of Shopping Centers. Pension Real Estate Association. Board of Directors, Constitutional Rights Foundation (President-elect; Chair, Board Nominating Committee). California Mortgage Bankers Association.
Career: Joined *Mayer, Brown, Rowe & Maw*, as partner, 1994. Firm Practice Leader, Real Estate Group. Partner-in-Charge of Los Angeles Office. Formerly with *Loeb & Loeb*.
Publications: Speaker and panelist on real estate financing and workout issues. Faculty Member for the 1995 ALI-ABA Advanced Course of Study on 'Real Estate Defaults, Workouts, and Reorganizations' (1995). Speaker on 'Shopping Center Financing,' 1996 International Council of Shopping Centers Annual Law Conference (October 1996).
Personal: Born 16 November 1948. Stanford Law School, JD, 1974. Stanford Graduate Business School, MBA, 1974. Georgetown University School of Foreign Service, B.S.F.S., cum laude, 1970; Phi Beta Kappa.

ELLISON, Christopher
Ellison Schneider & Harrison, Sacramento 916 447 2166
Recommended in Energy

ELLMAN, Howard
Ellman, Burke, Hoffman & Johnson, San Francisco 415 777 2727
Recommended in Real Estate

EXELROD, Alan
Rudy, Exelrod & Zieff, LLP, San Francisco
415 434 9800
Recommended in Employment

FARRAR, Stanley
Sullivan & Cromwell, Los Angeles
310 712 6600
farrars@sullcrom.com
Recommended in Banking & Finance
Specialization: Has extensive experience in representing financial institutions in mergers and acquisitions, securities offerings, commercial transactions, corporate governance and bank regulatory matters. Clients include some of the largest US commercial banks and leading financial institutions in Europe, Japan, Australia and Latin America. Actively involved in corporate finance and securities law matters.
Prof. Memberships: American Bar Association (former Chair, Subcommittees on Bank Holding and Letters of Credit); Cali-

CALIFORNIA LEADERS

fornia State Bar Association (former Chairman, Financial Institutions Committee); Los Angeles County Bar Association.
Career: Joined *Sullivan & Cromwell* in 1968. Partner since 1984.
Publications: Writes and lectures on financial institutions, including the Gramm-Leach-Bliley Act. Member, Banking Law Advisory Board, Practicing Law Institute.
Personal: Born in 1943. Boalt Hall School of Law (JD, 1967); University of California, Berkeley (BS, 1964).

FEDER, Philip
Paul, Hastings, Janofsky & Walker LLP, Los Angeles 213 683 6298
philipfeder@paulhastings.com
Recommended in Real Estate
Specialization: Chairman of *Paul, Hastings, Janofsky & Walker's* Real Estate Department; concentrates his practice in real estate transactions, both domestic and international, with emphasis in finance, acquisitions and dispositions, and real estate loan workouts. Regularly represents investors on transactions in Asia and in Europe.
Career: Frequent speaker to both real estate attorneys and other real estate professionals; elected as a member of the American College of Real Estate Lawyers.
Personal: AB degree in Economics, with honors in 1976 from Stanford University; JD degree from Columbia University Law School in 1979, where he was a Harlan Fiske Stone Scholar.

FELDMAN, Boris
Wilson Sonsini Goodrich & Rosati, Palo Alto 650 493 9300
Recommended in Litigation

FELDMAN, Larry
Fogel, Feldman, Ostrov, Ringler & Klevens, Santa Monica 310 453 6711
Recommended in Litigation

FELDMAN, Robert
Wilson Sonsini Goodrich & Rosati, Palo Alto 650 493 9300
Recommended in Litigation

FEO, Edwin
Milbank, Tweed, Hadley & McCloy, Los Angeles 213 892 4000
Recommended in Energy, Projects

FIELDS, Bertram
Greenberg Glusker Fields Claman Machtinger & Kinsella LLP, Los Angeles 310 553 3610
bfields@ggfirm.com
Recommended in Media & Entertainment
Specialization: For over 30 years, has represented major entertainment clients, including Twentieth Century Fox, MGM and Paramount. He represented Jeffrey Katzenberg in landmark action against Disney. He currently represents Tom Cruise and Dustin Hoffman.
Prof. Memberships: Beverly Hills, Los Angeles County and American Bar Associations; The State Bar of California.
Career: California Bar, New York Bar; US District Court, Central District of California and District of Hawaii; US Court of Appeals, Ninth Circuit; US Supreme Court.
Publications: Has authored two published novels and is the subject of profiles in numerous publications.
Personal: UCLA and Harvard Law School.

FIELDS, Henry
Morrison & Foerster LLP, Los Angeles 213 892 5275
hfields@mofo.com
Recommended in Banking & Finance
Specialization: Partner who has advised on banking issues for more than 30 years. Frequently consults on strategic opportunities for banking and non-banking activities, investments and acquisitions, and has represented banks before federal and state bank regulatory agencies on a broad variety of applications and other issues. His representation includes mergers and acquisitions, capital market transactions and bank securities activities. He has represented domestic and international banks and thrift institutions in a number of significant mergers and acquisitions. Also engages in a general corporate and commercial law practice.
Prof. Memberships: Member, Board of Directors, International Financial Institutions Association of California; Member (and former Chair), Board of Directors, Institute for Corporate Counsel; and Member, Board of Directors, Starbright Foundation.
Career: Admitted to practice in California, New Jersey, and New York. Joined *Morrison & Foerster LLP* in 1980. Named one of the world's leading banking lawyers by the International Financial Law Review. He is one of only four attorneys in California to receive the highest individual rating in banking and finance by 'Global Counsel 3000' (7th edition).
Personal: BA, Harvard College, 1968, Phi Beta Kappa; JD, Yale Law School, 1972, Managing Editor, Yale Law Journal; Federal Clerkship, 1972-73, Honorable Leonard I Garth.

FILETI, Thomas
Morrison & Foerster LLP, Los Angeles 213 892 5276
tfileti@mofo.com
Recommended in Real Estate
Specialization: Partner representing clients in connection with investments in and the financing, operation and disposition of real estate assets. Has particular expertise in area of financing of corporate real estate facilities. Practice also emphasizes real estate financings and purchase and sale transactions of all types, including credit leases, lease financings and other complex tax and accounting driven finance transactions, including REITS.
Prof. Memberships: Member, American Bar Association; Member, Los Angeles County Bar Association.
Career: Admitted to practice in California. Joined *Morrison & Foerster* in 1984, Partner since 1987. Head of firm's Real Estate Practice Group in Los Angeles office.
Personal: AB degree, distinction all subjects, Cornell University, 1978; JD, cum laude, University of Pennsylvania Law School, 1981.

FLAUM, Keith
Cooley Godward LLP, Palo Alto 650 843 5000
Recommended in Communications

FORE, John
Wilson Sonsini Goodrich & Rosati, Palo Alto 650 493 9300
Recommended in Capital Markets

FREIER, Elliot
Irell & Manella LLP, Los Angeles 310 277 1010
Recommended in Tax

FULLER, James
Fenwick & West, Palo Alto 650 494 0600
Recommended in Tax

GALLO, Greg
Gray Cary Ware & Freidenrich LLP, Palo Alto 650 833 2000
Recommended in Communications

GIBBS, Kenneth
Gibbs, Giden, Locher & Turner, Los Angeles 310 552 3400
Recommended in Construction

GIUNTA, Joseph J
Skadden, Arps, Slate, Meagher & Flom LLP, Los Angeles 213 687 5040
jgiunta@skadden.com
Recommended in Corporate/M&A
Specialization: Partner, Los Angeles. Handles all types of merger and acquisition transactions, both friendly and hostile. He is experienced in proxy contests, tender offers, restructurings, recapitalizations and leveraged buyouts. Has represented purchasers, sellers and their financial advisors in a wide variety of merger, acquisition and disposition transactions. Among others, he has represented Zenith National Insurance, Inc.; Del Webb Corporation; Plum Creek Timber Co.; Baxter International, Inc. and its spun-off public company, Edwards Lifesciences Corporation; Merisel Inc.; CEMEX, S.A.; Fedco Inc.; Farmers Insurance Group of Companies and affiliates; Cobra Golf Inc.; Earth Technology Corporation; Costco Wholesale Corporation; and Sapiens International Corp.
Career: JD, American University, Washington College of Law, 1976 (magna cum laude; Associate Editor, American University Law Review); BS, Stanford University, 1972.

GLAD, Paul E B
Sonnenschein Nath & Rosenthal, San Francisco 415 882 5001
pglad@sonnenschein.com
Recommended in Insurance
Specialization: Partner and Chair of the Insurance Practice Group, head of the San Fransisco Office. He represents major insurance industry clients in every legal capacity, from handling coverage issues to bad-faith claims, from combating class action lawsuits to regulatory challenges. He is a co-author of Bancroft-Whitney's California 'Insurance Laws' annotated and is an editor of and frequent contributor to a number of major insurance industry publications, including 'Underwriters' Report' and 'Insurance Litigation Reporter'.
Career: Director, San Fransisco Bar Association 1995-96; Chairman, San Fransisco Bar Association Insurance Law Section 1993-95; Chairman, Endowment of San Fransisco 1993-98; Director, 1992-; Faculty, Environmental Law Institute; Faculty, Business Insurance Law Institute. Chairman, National Seminar on Advertising Injury Insurance Coverage Issues, New York (1991); Chairman, Bad Faith Claims and Trends, New York (1994, 1996) and Orlando (1995); Presenter, significant issues in California Insurance Law, California Appellate Judicial Conference (1997, 1998, 1999, 2000); and regular seminar presenter for PLI, Executive Enterprises, ACI, Rutter Group and CEB. Law Clerk to Justice James A Cobey, California Court of Appeal (2nd Appellate District), 1977-78. Extern to Judge William M Byrne, US District Court, Central District of California, 1976.
Personal: UCLA Law School JD, 1977, Stanford University, 1972, with Distinction.

GOLDBERG, Stephen
Heller Ehrman White & McAuliffe LLP, Los Angeles 213 689 0200
Recommended in Insurance

GOLDMAN, Melvin
Morrison & Foerster LLP, San Francisco 415 268 7311
mgoldman@mofo.com
Recommended in Antitrust, Litigation
Specialization: One of the nation's leading civil litigators, specializing in the defense of antitrust and securities litigation representing a wide range of companies, financial institutions, and their directors and officers in defense of class and derivative litigation and SEC actions involving a variety of accounting and financial disclosure issues. Lectures widely on securities litigation topics.
Career: Admitted to practice in California and Illinois. Joined *Morrison & Foerster* in 1965.
Personal: BA, DePaul University, 1958; JD, Northwestern University School of Law, 1961, Order of the Coif; Managing Editor, 'Law Review'; MSL, Stanford University School of Law, 1963.

LEADERS

CALIFORNIA

GOODWIN, David
Heller Ehrman White & McAuliffe LLP, San Francisco 415 772 6000
Recommended in Insurance

GREEN, Josh
Venture Law Group, Menlo Park
650 854 4488
Recommended in Communications

GREENE, Browne
Greene, Broillet, Taylor, Wheeler & Panish, Santa Monica 310 576 1200
Recommended in Litigation

GREENFIELD, Robert
Stutman, Treister & Glatt PC,
Los Angeles 213 251 5100
Recommended in Insolvency

GREENWALD, Steven
Davis Wright Tremaine LLP, San Francisco 415 276 6528
stevegreenwald@dwt.com
Recommended in Energy
Specialization: Partner, energy law. Representation includes independent power projects and financing parties in public and private debt, equity financing and purchasing and selling generation assets; independent power producers and marketers in state and federal regulatory proceedings; and independent electric generators and power marketers in contractual negotiations/disputes with purchasing utilities.
Prof. Memberships: California Bar Association. Board of Directors, Power Association of Northern California.
Career: Admitted to California Bar (1975). Joined as partner, 1993.
Publications: Frequent speaker/commentator on all issues related to the energy business.
Personal: JD, (summa cum laude), University of Michigan, 1973 (Order of the Coif). BA, University of Pennsylvania, 1970.

GROSSMAN, Marshall
Alschuler Grossman Stein & Kahan LLP,
Los Angeles 310 255 9118
mgrossman@agsk.com
Recommended in Litigation
Specialization: During career, has both prosecuted and defended major commercial litigation. Served as lead counsel for the plaintiff classes in the Equity Funding Securities Litigation and represented the owners of Guess? Jeans in their successful litigation against the owners of Jordache. He has represented Apple Computer, Inc. and Packard Bell NEC, Inc. in the defense of patent infringement and Lanham Act litigation, including the highly publicized battle between Compaq and Packard Bell. In 1999, led Arthur Andersen's trial team to a defense jury verdict in a $1 billion dollar action securities fraud lawsuit. At this time, represents several of the largest public accounting firms in complex federal securities litigation and related federal investigations.
Prof. Memberships: American, Beverly Hills (Chair, Civil Practice and Procedure Committee, 1969-70; Member, Board of Governors, 1970-76), Century City, and Los Angeles County Bar Associations; State Bar of California; Beverly Hills Barristers (President, 1972-73); Association of Business Trial Lawyers (Member, Board of Governors, 1973-75).
Career: A partner of *Alschuler Grossman Stein & Kahan LLP*. Has practiced with the firm since 1964. Lecturer in Law, University of Southern California Law Center, 1966-69. Lawyer Representative, Ninth Circuit. In 1989 and again in 1999, was recognized by a leading US law journal as among the 'Best Trial Lawyers in America'. Referred to by former Mayor Richard J. Riordan of Los Angeles as the 'toughest litigator in Los Angeles'. Is listed in a publication of the best lawyers in America. Has long been active in community affairs, having served as a Commissioner on the California Coastal Commission and on the boards of Public Counsel, and the United Way. Currently serves as a member of the State of California Commission on Judicial Performance, on the boards of Bet Tzedek Legal Services, Jewish Big Brothers and on the national board of the American Jewish Committee.
Personal: University of California at Los Angeles; University of Southern California (BSL and LLB, 1964). Order of the Coif; Phi Alpha Delta. Production Editor, Southern California Law Review, 1963-64.

GROSSMAN, Paul
Paul, Hastings, Janofsky & Walker LLP,
Los Angeles 213 683 6203
paulgrossman@paulhastings.com
Recommended in Employment
Specialization: Represents major private employers in all aspects of employment law, including class actions, wage/hour, wrongful discharge (with an emphasis on significant jury trials), discrimination, sexual harassment, whistleblower, and labor-management litigation.
Prof. Memberships: American Bar Association Labor and Employment Law Section and its Equal Employment Opportunity Committee.
Publications: Co-author of Lindemann & Grossman, 'Employment Discrimination Law' (Bureau of National Affairs, 1996 and 1998), the official book of the American Bar Association in its field.
Personal: BA degree in 1961 from Amherst College; JD degree in 1964 from Yale Law School; Member of the Board of Editors of the Yale Law Journal.

GUNDERSON, Bob
Gunderson Dettmer Stough Villeneuve Franklin & Hachigian, Menlo Park
650 321 2400
Recommended in Communications

HAGEN, Catherine
O'Melveny & Myers LLP, Newport Beach
949 760 9600
Recommended in Employment

HANSCHEN, Peter
Morrison & Foerster LLP, Walnut Creek
925 295 3450
phanschen@mofo.com
Recommended in Energy
Specialization: Partner advising in all aspects of energy matters, including state and federal energy regulations, energy related transactions, energy project financing and energy related arbitrations. Has been in the forefront of electric regulation matters for last quarter century. Member of firm's domestic and international project finance practice groups.
Career: Admitted to practice in California. Joined *Morrison & Foerster LLP* in 1999 from law firm of *Graham and James*. Began career in the legal department of Pacific Gas and Electric Company, eventually becoming their general counsel. During the last five years with PG&E, he handled all of the company's regulatory matters before California Public Utilities Commission and other state and federal regulatory agencies.
Personal: BA, magna cum laude, San Francisco State University, 1967; JD, University of California, Berkeley, Boalt Hall, 1971.

HARRIS, Alan
Farella Braun & Martel LLP,
San Francisco 415 954 4400
Recommended in Construction

HAVEL, Richard
Sidley Austin Brown & Wood,
Los Angeles 213 896 6000
Recommended in Insolvency

HAYES, David
Fenwick & West, Palo Alto
650 494 0600
Recommended in Intellectual Property

HEINKE, Rex
Akin Gump Strauss Hauer & Feld LLP,
Los Angeles 310 229 1000
Recommended in Media & Entertainment

HEMMINGER, Pamela
Gibson, Dunn & Crutcher LLP,
Los Angeles 213 229 7000
Recommended in Employment

HENNIGAN, Mike
Hennigan, Bennett & Dorman,
Los Angeles 213 694 1200
Recommended in Litigation

HERNANDEZ, Jennifer
Beveridge & Diamond, P.C.,
San Francisco 415 262 4001
jhernandez@bdlaw.com
Recommended in Environment
Specialization: Practices environmental and land use law in California and other Western States focusing on resolving federal, state and local approvals for complex development projects. Achieved national prominence in work on Brownfield redevelopment, wetlands and endangered species development projects, advising buyers, sellers, investors, local agencies and developers. Represents a diverse group of industries on compliance, enforcement and audit issues relating to air and water quality, hazardous materials and waste, Proposition 65 and other regulatory issues.
Prof. Memberships: Presidio Trust Board Member (appointed by President Clinton) charged with managing to financial self-sufficiency the Presidio National Park in San Francisco. Board Member of the California League of Conservation Voters, California Center for Land Recycling, and Sustainable Conservation. Advisory Committee Member of California Environmental Redevelopment Fund, which created and is managing California's first pooled loan program for private sector Brownfields equity and debt placements. Founded the Environmental Law Forum in San Francisco and founding member of the California State Bar's Environmental Law Section.
Career: Admitted to California Bar (1984). Director of *Beveridge & Diamond, P.C.* since joining firm in 1993. Taught environmental and land use law at Stanford Law School, the University of California, the California Environmental Law Institute, and other venues. Co-founder and Chairman of Board (1994-97) for LandBank, Inc., a national Brownfields redevelopment company.
Publications: Has written two books and more than 30 articles on environmental, redevelopment and land use law issues.
Personal: JD from Stanford University (1984) and AB (with honors) from Harvard University (1981).

HILSON, John
Paul, Hastings, Janofsky & Walker LLP,
Los Angeles 213 683 6000
Recommended in Banking & Finance

HINMAN, William
Simpson Thacher & Bartlett, Palo Alto
650 251 5000
Recommended in Capital Markets

HIRSCH, Barry
Armstrong Hirsch Jackoway Tyerman & Wertheimer, Los Angeles 310 553 0305
Recommended in Media & Entertainment

HOBEL, Lawrence
Heller Ehrman White & McAuliffe LLP,
San Francisco 415 772 6000
Recommended in Insurance

HOCKETT, Christopher
Bingham McCutchen LLP, San Francisco
415 393 2000
Recommended in Antitrust

CALIFORNIA

LEADERS

HOLDEN, JR, Frederick W
Orrick, Herrington & Sutcliffe,
San Francisco 415 392 1122
Recommended in Insolvency

HUGHES, Frank
Miller, Morton, Caillat & Nevis, San Jose
408 292 1765
Recommended in Construction

HUMPHREYS, Ivan
Wilson Sonsini Goodrich & Rosati,
Palo Alto 650 493 9300
Recommended in Tax

HUNT, Gordon
Hunt, Ortmann, Blasco, Palffy & Rossell
Inc, Pasedena 626 440 5200
Recommended in Construction

HYMAN, Milt
Irell & Manella LLP, Los Angeles
310 277 1010
Recommended in Tax

IREDALE, Nancy L
Paul, Hastings, Janofsky & Walker LLP,
Los Angeles 213 683 6232
nancyiredale@paulhastings.com
Recommended in Tax
Specialization: Partner specializing in tax controversy. Provides tax advice to international and domestic clients and has tried and/or settled federal and California civil and criminal tax cases. Named outstanding California tax lawyer by the California State Bar, appointed by the IRS Commissioner to his 'Advisory Group'. Cited by the Los Angeles Business Journal as one of the most powerful women in Los Angeles law.
Prof. Memberships: Elected as the only woman president of the 107 year+ Jonathan Club.
Personal: Graduated first in her class from the School of Foreign Service of Georgetown University; received her law degree from Yale Law School.

JACOBS, Michael A
Morrison & Foerster LLP, San Francisco
415 268 7455
mjacobs@mofo.com
Recommended in Intellectual Property
Specialization: Partner concentrating on high technology and intellectual property litigation matters. Most recently, has represented clients in biotechnology and information technology disputes. Has helped to shape laws governing the emerging information and entertainment technologies, and managed a litigation team in the On Command Video case, which established that video 'on demand' performances must be licensed under the copyright public performance right. Led the technical team representing Fujitsu Ltd. in its landmark operating system software arbitration with IBM. Served as a member of the editorial board of the Association of Business Trial lawyers, Northern California, and wrote a periodic column on intellectual property litigation.

Career: Admitted to the California State Bar in 1993. Became Partner in the San Francisco office of *Morrison & Foerster* in 1990. Co-head of the firm's 140 person Intellectual Property Group; served as the firm's Managing Partner for Operations from 1995 to 1997.
Publications: Co-author, with Prof. Donald Chisum, of 'World Intellectual Property Guidebook', United States (1992, Matthew Bender & Company, New York).
Personal: BA History, Stanford University, 1977, Phi Beta Kappa with honors; United States Foreign Service, assignments in Kingston, Jamaica, and Washington, DC; JD, Yale Law School, 1983.

JOHNSON, Craig
Venture Law Group, Menlo Park
650 854 4488
Recommended in Communications

JOHNSON, Daniel
Fenwick & West, San Francisco
415 875 2300
Recommended in Intellectual Property

KADUE, David
Seyfarth Shaw, Los Angeles
310 277 7200
Recommended in Employment

KAUFMAN, Christopher (Kit)
Latham & Watkins LLP, Menlo Park
650 463 2606
christopher.kaufman@lw.com
Recommended in Communications, Corporate/M&A
Specialization: Specialises in mergers and acquisitions, securities offerings, venture capital and start-up companies and general corporate work. Principal focus is on high-technology companies. Represents companies in hostile takeovers and proxy contests, as well as consensual acquisitions. Worked on over 400 private offerings for high-tech start-up companies, representing either issuer or investors. Venture capital clients include Mayfield Fund. Extensive experience in corporate governance and fiduciary duty responsibilities, particularly in conflict of interest situations where a publicly held corporation is controlled by another corporation.
Personal: JD, Harvard University, 1970 (magna cum laude). BA, Amherst College, 1967.

KEKER, John
Keker & Van Nest LLP, San Francisco
415 391 5400
Recommended in Intellectual Property, Litigation

KELLER, Don
Venture Law Group, Menlo Park 650 854 4488
Recommended in Communications

KENNEDY, Mike
Wilson Sonsini Goodrich & Rosati, San Francisco 415 947 2000
Recommended in Communications, Corporate/M&A

KENYON, Charity
Riegels Campos & Kenyon, Sacramento
916 779 7114
Recommended in Media & Entertainment

KILB, Brian
Gibson, Dunn & Crutcher LLP, Los Angeles 213 229 7000
Recommended in Banking & Finance

KING, Kenton
Skadden, Arps, Slate, Meagher & Flom LLP, Palo Alto 650 470 4530
kking@skadden.com
Recommended in Capital Markets, Communications, Corporate/M&A
Specialization: Head of *Skadden's* Palo Alto and San Francisco offices and corporate group in the Bay Area. Has extensive experience in a broad range of corporate and securities law matters, including US and cross-border M&A, joint ventures, investment and capital markets transactions, and restructurings. Also represents clients in licensing and strategic partnering transactions in the IT and biotechnology sectors. Has worked on several high-profile transactions, including representing Compaq Computer Corporation in its $25 billion merger with Hewlett-Packard Company; Ascend Communications, Inc. in its $20 billion acquisition by Lucent Technologies, Inc.; and Yahoo! Inc. in its $436 million unsolicited takeover proposal for HotJobs.com, Ltd.
Career: Law Clerk to the Honorable Kenneth W Starr, US Court of Appeals for the District of Columbia Circuit (1987-88); JD, Boalt Hall School of Law at the University of California at Berkeley, 1987; BA, Stanford University, 1977.
Publications: 'Representing the Public Company in an LBO Transaction: Recent Developments' Practising Law Institute (1989); 'Exon-Florio Update: Final Regulations Are Released,' M&A Review (1992); 'Venture Capital in Focus - Warning: Rescue May Raise Risks,' The National Law Journal (1997).

KIRBY, Matthew
O'Melveny & Myers LLP, Los Angeles
213 430 6000
Recommended in Banking & Finance

KIRWAN, BJ
Latham & Watkins LLP, Los Angeles
213 485 1234
bj.kirwan@lw.com
Recommended in Environment
Specialization: Partner, Environment, Land and Resources Department. Focuses on air pollution and air toxic counseling, Proposition 65 counseling and environmental permitting, administrative variances and litigation. Substantial experience in hazardous waste, recycling, cogeneration, landfill and soil and groundwater remediation.
Prof. Memberships: Board Member and Chair, Air and Waste Committee, California Chamber of Commerce.
Career: Past Member, ABA Standing Committee on Environmental Law; Past Chair, ABA Environmental Controls Committee of the Business Law Section; Vice Chair, Air Quality Committee and Chair, Environmental Quality Committee of the ABA Natural Resources Section. Past President, Boalt Hall Alumni Association. Past Member, Governor's Environmental Law Reform Committee.
Publications: Various articles on air pollution and emissions trading and on Proposition 65.
Personal: JD, University of California, Boalt Hall School of Law, 1971. AB, University of California, Berkeley, 1968.

KLEE, Kenneth N
Klee, Tuchin, Bogdanoff & Stern LLP,
Los Angeles 310 407 4080
kklee@ktbslaw.com
Recommended in Insolvency
Specialization: Is a founding Member of *Klee, Tuchin, Bogdanoff & Stern LLP*, specializing in corporate reorganization, insolvency, and bankruptcy law. He joined the UCLA Law faculty in July 1997 after teaching bankruptcy and reorganization law as a visiting lecturer since 1979. From 1974 to 1977, was associate counsel to the House Judiciary Committee, where he was one of the principal draftsmen of the 1978 Bankruptcy Code. Currently serves as a lawyer delegate to the Ninth Circuit Judicial Conference. He also served as an adviser to the American Law Institute's Transnational Insolvency Project.

KOHL, Glen
Cooley Godward LLP, Palo Alto
650 843 5000
Recommended in Tax

KORMAN, Marty
Wilson Sonsini Goodrich & Rosati,
Palo Alto 650 493 9300
Recommended in Communications

KRUPKA, Robert G
Kirkland & Ellis, Los Angeles 213 680-8456
bob_krupka@kirkland.com
Recommended in Intellectual Property
Specialization: Specialist in patent, trade secret, copyright, trademark, advertising, marketing, unfair competition, internet and antitrust litigation and counseling. Extensive experience in contested intellectual property matters, trials involving technologically complex subject matter, obtaining expedited remedies, and proceedings before the International Trade Commission. Tried over 50 cases to judgment. Tried eight jury trials to verdict, all victorious. Obtained verdicts totaling over $175 million; negotiated settlements

resulting in over $1 billion. Handled over two dozen expedited remedy hearings (TRO's, preliminary injunctions, temporary exclusion orders) and 20 Markman (claim interpretation) hearings.
Personal: Georgetown University, BS, 1971. University of Chicago Law School, JD, 1974.

LARSON, John
Morgan, Lewis & Bockius LLP, San Francisco 415 442 0900
Recommended in Corporate/M&A

LAURIE, Ronald
Skadden, Arps, Slate, Meagher & Flom LLP, Palo Alto 650 470 4510
rlaurie@skadden.com
Recommended in Intellectual Property
Specialization: Founding Partner, Palo Alto. Co-Chair: Information Technology Practice. Advises clients in the computer, communications, media and financial services industries on intellectual property strategy, with a primary focus on the strategic use of IP assets in complex business transactions including mergers and acquisitions, technology divestitures, joint ventures and strategic alliances. Has been an advisor to the USPTO, the US copyright office, and WIPO, among others, and is a permanent faculty member of the World Law Institute.
Career: JD, University of San Francisco, 1968; BSIE, University of California at Berkeley, 1964; has taught at Stanford and Boalt (UC-Berkeley) law schools; worked in Silicon Valley for 43 years, as a computer programmer and software engineer prior to becoming a lawyer.
Publications: Contributing editor to 'The Computer Lawyer and the Journal of Internet Law'; co-editor of the two-volume treatise 'International Intellectual Property'.
Personal: Born, San Francisco, CA 1942; Married 19 years to Mina Laurie.

LAZAROW, Warren
O'Melveny & Myers LLP, Menlo Park 650 473 2600
Recommended in Capital Markets

LERACH, William
Milberg Weiss Bershad Hynes & Lerach LLP, San Diego 619 231 1058
Recommended in Litigation
Specialization: Widely recognised as one of the leading securities lawyers in the United States. Has headed up the prosecution of hundreds of securities class and stockholder derivative actions that have resulted in recoveries for defrauded shareholders and victimised corporations amounting to billions of dollars. The subject of considerable media attention and a frequent commentator on securities and corporate law, as well as a frequent lecturer. Represents numerous Public and Taft-Hartley pension plans in corporate securities matters. Testified before federal and state legislative committees concerning corporate governance and securities matters and frequently quoted in the national media regarding corporate issues. Honoured by President Clinton and appointed a member of the United States Holocaust Memorial Council.
Prof. Memberships: Member of the American Bar Association Litigation Section's Committee on Class Actions and Derivative Skills and has been involved in many of the largest and highest profile securities class action and corporate derivative suits in recent years, including Enron, Dynegy, Qwest and WorldCom. Listed in a leading US legal publication and a Master of the American Inns of Court. President of the National Association of Securities and Commercial Lawyers (NASCAT), a national group of attorneys specialising in commercial and securities litigation. Member of the Editorial Board of 'Class Action Report' and frequently lectures on class and derivative actions, accountants' liability, and attorneys' fees. Guest lecturer at Stanford University, University of California at Los Angeles and at San Diego, University of Pittsburgh, San Diego State University and at the Council of Institutional Investors and the International Corporate Governance Network. Also a member of the American Law Institute faculty on Federal and State Class Action Litigation.
Publications: Published numerous articles and op-ed pieces, including 'Achieving Corporate Governance Enhancements Through Litigation', keynote address to Council of Institutional Investors spring meeting, Mar. 27, 2001; 'Why Insiders Get Rich, and the Little Guy Loses', 'L.A. Times', Jan. 20, 2002; 'The Alarming Decline in The Quality of Financial Reporting' and 'The Chickens Have Come Home to Roost: How Wall Street, the Big Accounting Firms and Corporate Interests Chloroformed Congress and Cost America's Investors Trillions'.

LERMAN, Cary
Munger, Tolles & Olson, Los Angeles 213 683 9100
Recommended in Insurance

LESSER, Henry
Gray Cary Ware & Freidenrich LLP, Palo Alto 650 833 2425
HLesser@graycary.com
Recommended in Corporate/M&A
Specialization: Has been continuously involved in corporate securities practice, with a particular focus on corporate acquisitions, corporate governance and restructuring matters, since 1977. Over the course of his career, he has been involved in all aspects of merger and acquisition work involving public and private companies, including hostile tender offers, proxy contests, friendly mergers, leveraged buyouts, stock acquisitions and asset sales. His clients have included a wide variety of bidders, targets, stockholders and financial advisors. Has been involved in a number of the largest friendly and contested takeovers of recent years, including the Unocal and Unitrin matters that resulted in seminal decisions of the Delaware Supreme Court and Wells Fargo's acquisition of First Interstate. Since moving to Silicon Valley in 1997, he has represented buyers and sellers in a broad range of technology and life sciences transactions.
Prof. Memberships: American Law Institute; Former vice chair of the California State Bar's Business Law Section, and former chair of the Section's Corporations Committee and Opinions Committee; ABA Business Law Section's Negotiated Acquisitions and Corporate Governance Committees (co-chair of its subcommittee on Corporate Governance Guidelines).
Career: Admitted to practice in California (1984), New York (1977), and England and Wales (1969). Partner - *Wachtell, Lipton, Rosen and Katz*, New York, 1980-83; Partner - various major law firms in Los Angeles, 1983-97; partner - *Heller Ehrman White & McAuliffe LLP*, Palo Alto, 1997-2000. Joined *Gray Cary Ware & Freidenrich LLP* in 2000 and is a partner in the firm's Corporate Securities Group. Serves as co-chair of the M&A Group and chair of the Global Steering Committee.
Publications: Author, Some Practical Suggestions for the M&A Due Diligence Process, 'The Practical Lawyer' (September and October 2000). Editor Emeritus (and original Editor in Chief), 'The Corporate Governance Advisor', Aspen Law & Business, and contributor of numerous articles thereto. Co-author of 'Takeover Defense', 4th Edition, Aspen Law & Business. Author of three chapters on the Williams Act, 'Securities Law Techniques,' Matthew Bender & Co. Co-author of the 1990 Update to Fleischer, Responses to 'Takeover Bids: Corporate SEC Tactical and Fiduciary Considerations,' BNA Corporate Practice Series 6-2nd. Named contributing writer for Lipton and Steinberger, 'Takeovers and Freezeouts,' (first edition and supplements), Law Journal Seminars-Press. Co-author, Boards Adopt Governance Guidelines, 'The National Law Journal' (June 1999). Author, Do Courts Swallow the Poison Pill? 'Legal Times' (June 1999). Co-author, Shareholder By-Law Amendments: The Looming Battle, 'The M & A Lawyer,' Vol. 1, No. 8 (January 1998). Co-author, Formulating Governance Standards, 'The National Law Journal' (June 1998).
Personal: BA - Cambridge University (1968); MA- Cambridge University (Squire Law Scholar, First Class Honors in Law with distinction for work of special merit, 1972); LLM- Harvard University School of Law (Harkness Fellow of the Commonwealth Fund of New York, 1973).

LEVIN, Barry
Heller Ehrman White & McAuliffe LLP, San Francisco 415 772 6000
Recommended in Insurance

LOGAN, Ben
O'Melveny & Myers LLP, Los Angeles 310 553 6700
Recommended in Insolvency

LONG, Robert
Latham & Watkins LLP, Los Angeles 213 891 8130
bob.long@lw.com
Recommended in Litigation
Specialization: Partner, Litigation Department. Focuses on complex business litigation and trial practice, with a range of experience that includes defense of professional liability cases against lawyers and accountants, partnership disputes, defense of securities law cases, general commercial disputes and other complex business litigation.
Prof. Memberships: Fellow, American College of Trial Lawyers.
Career: Former Managing Partner, Los Angeles office. Former chair, Professional Liability Practice Group.
Personal: JD, Indiana University School of Law, 1971 (summa cum laude). BA, Economics, Indiana University, 1968.

LOPES, James
Howard, Rice, Nemerovski, Canady, Falk & Rabkin, San Francisco 415 434 1600
Recommended in Insolvency

LUCERO, Gene
Latham & Watkins LLP, Los Angeles 213 891 8475
gene.lucero@lw.com
Recommended in Environment
Specialization: Chair, Los Angeles Environment, Land & Resources Department. Practice focuses on environmental issues that affect land use and development, including Superfund, hazardous waste regulation, water quality and supply laws and air quality requirements, including complex environmental cases brought by federal or state governments. Also experienced in assessment of environmental liabilities in business transactions and mediation/litigation of disputes arising in such matters.
Career: Director, Office of Waste Programs Enforcement, EPA, Washington, DC, 1982-88. Deputy Regional Administrator, EPA, Region VIII, 1980-82. Assistant Attorney General, Colorado, 1975-78.
Publications: 'CERCLA Rights and Liabilities - Annual Update', The Impact of Environmental Law on Real Estate and Other Commercial Transactions, ALI-ABA 2002.
Personal: JD, University of California Boalt Hall School of Law, 1972. BA, Stanford University, 1970.

CALIFORNIA LEADERS

LUNDBERG, Andrew
Latham & Watkins LLP, Los Angeles
213 891 8248
andy.lundberg@lw.com
Recommended in Insurance
Specialization: Chair, Los Angeles Litigation Department and head of *Latham's* firmwide Insurance Coverage Practice Group. Represents policyholders in major insurance coverage litigation involving all insurance lines. Clients include Ford Motor Company; Montrose Chemical; America West Airlines; GlaxoSmithKline; Silicon Valley Bank; Odwalla, Inc; City of Hope; the University of Southern California; Pepperdine University; and World Cup USA 1994. Also advises on novel business litigation matters, including representing the LA Dodgers in ticketholder class actions relating to the cancellation of the 1994 season.
Personal: JD, Harvard Law School, 1981. AB, Stanford University, 1978. Director, Outward Bound School West.

LUREY, Michael
Latham & Watkins LLP, Los Angeles
213 891 8304
michael.lurey@lw.com
Recommended in Insolvency
Specialization: Co-chair, Global Insolvency Practice Group. Represents debtors, lenders, creditors' committees, borrowers and other parties in all aspects of insolvency matters, including chapter 11 cases and out of court restructurings. Represents Consolidated Freightways in its chapter 11 case. Represented NorthPoint Communications Group as debtor in possession in its chapter 11. Represented creditors' committee in chapter 11 cases of Superior National Insurance and MedPartners Provider Network.
Prof. Memberships: Member, American College of Bankruptcy. Member, Committee on Business Bankruptcy and the Corporation, Banking and Business Law Section, American Bar Association.
Personal: JD, Harvard Law School, 1970. BS, Northwestern University, 1967.

LYNCH, Patrick
O'Melveny & Myers LLP, Los Angeles
310 553 6700
Recommended in Antitrust, Litigation

MACBRIDE, Thomas
Goodin MacBride Squeri Ritchie & Day LLP, San Francisco 415 392 7900
Recommended in Energy

MALKIN, Joseph
Orrick, Herrington & Sutcliffe,
San Francisco 415 773 5505
jmalkin@orrick.com
Recommended in Energy
Specialization: Energy and telecommunications regulatory and transactional practice focuses on industry restructuring, mergers, asset dispositions, and acquisitions. Recent projects include representation of PG&E Corporation in connection with financings, utility bankruptcy, generation sales, and proceedings before the California Public Utilities Commission (CPUC) investigating holding company-utility relations; representation of Sempra Energy's San Diego Gas & Electric Company unit in CPUC proceedings concerning electric rates, industry restructuring, and procurement practices; and representation of Qwest Communications in various regulatory matters. Co-chair of *Orrick's* Global Energy, Communications, and Infrastructure Group.
Personal: Yale Law School, JD, 1972. Claremont McKenna College, BA, 1968.

MALLORY, Rick
Allen, Matkins, Leck, Gamble & Mallory LLP, San Francisco 415 837 1515
Recommended in Real Estate

MARTENS, Don
Knobbe Martens Olson & Bear, Irvine
949 760 0404
Recommended in Intellectual Property

MATHIASON, Garry
Littler Mendelson PC, San Francisco
415 433 1940
Recommended in Employment

MATKINS, Michael
Allen, Matkins, Leck, Gamble & Mallory LLP, Los Angeles 213 622 5555
Recommended in Real Estate

MATTHEWS, Philip
Hancock, Rothert & Bunshoft LLP,
San Francisco 415 981 5550
pmatthews@hrblaw.com
Recommended in Insurance
Specialization: Partner in the San Francisco office. His practice focuses on general civil litigation and insurance counseling and litigation, with an emphasis on complex cases. He has been involved in some of the largest trials and appeals in California, including the trial and appeal of Shell Oil Co. vs. Accident and Casualty Co. of Winterthur (Rocky Mountain Arsenal case) and In Re Coordinated Asbestos Litigation (Manville, Fibreboard, Armstrong and GAF Coverage cases.) He also has been liaison and trial counsel in numerous complex cases such as Shell Oil Co. vs. Accident and Casualty Co. of Winterthur (Rocky Mountain Arsenal case), In Re Coordinated Asbestos Litigation, Flintkote v. American Mutual, Four Star Oil & Gas Co. vs. Allianz (Texaco Environmental Coverage Litigation), Texaco Refining & Marketing, Inc. vs. Fireman's Fund Insurance Co. (Texaco Toxic Tort), Exxon vs. Insurance Company of North America (Exxon Environmental Coverage Litigation) and Kaiser Aluminum & Chemical Corporation vs. Certain Underwriters at Lloyds. He also has experience in bankruptcy law and litigation and corporate transactions. Has spoken at a number of forums on a variety of topics relating to complex litigation, including Mealey's Conference Re Settling Complex Insurance Coverage Cases, Mealey's Conference on Tobacco Litigation, the American Bar Association Insurance Coverage Litigation Section on Allocation Issues in California and Mealey's Allocation Conference. He co-chaired Mealey's 2001 California Insurance Law Conference.
Prof. Memberships: American Bar Association, Bar Association of San Francisco, Chairperson of the Board of the Episcopal Charities of the Diocese of California, and is director of Project Concern International. Is active in non-profit and religious organizations.
Career: Admitted to California Bar (1978). A partner of *Hancock Rothert & Bunshoft LLP* since 1985. On the Management Committee of *Hancock Rothert & Bunshoft LLP* during 1989-94 and 1996-99, serving as Managing Partner of the firm's San Francisco office during several of those years.
Personal: George Washington University (BA, 1974). University of California, Hastings College of the Law (JD, 1977).

MCELHINNY, Harold
Morrison & Foerster LLP, San Francisco
415 268 7265
hmcelhinny@mofo.com
Recommended in Intellectual Property
Specialization: Partner concentrating on a federal and state court, intellectual property litigation practice. Also advises airlines and airport proprietors on regulatory and nuisance liability issues. Represented Chiron Corporation in a protracted dispute with Genentech over a method for inducing baker's yeast to secrete human insulin-like growth factor. After a two week court trial, and two appellate decisions, the Federal Circuit confirmed Chiron inventors were entitled to priority. Currently serves as lead counsel to EchoStar Communications Corp in patent litigation against Gemstar-TV.
Prof. Memberships: Member, American Bar Association; Member, Intellectual Property Law section of the State Bar of California; Member, American Intellectual Property Law Association. Served as President of the Northern California Association of Business Trial Lawyers from 1996-97.
Career: Admitted to California State Bar in 1976. Became partner in San Francisco office of *Morrison & Foerster* in 1981. From 1996 to 1999, served as Firmwide Chair of the Litigation Department.
Personal: BA, University of Santa Clara, 1970; Peace Corps, North Africa; JD, Boalt Hall School of Law, UC Berkeley, 1975, Order of the Coif; Law Clerk, Honorable M Joseph Blumenfeld, US District Court, Connecticut, 1975 to 1976.

MCMAHON, Terry
McDermott, Will & Emery, Palo Alto
650 813 5010
tmcmahon@mwe.com
Recommended in Intellectual Property
Specialization: Partner and head of West Coast intellectual property practice. Focuses on patent, copyright, trade secrets, trade dress, trademark and high stakes litigation. Has 25 years of litigation experience successfully representing hi-tech heavyweights on 'bet the company' cases. Acted in Airtouch v Pacbell (client); Storage Technology v EMC Corporation (client); Creative Technology Ltd. v Aureal Semiconductor, Inc.(client); Reifflin v Microsoft (client); Sun Microsystems v Microsoft (client) and Intel v Broadcom (client). Lead counsel in the representation of Advanced Micro Devices (AMD) in its extensive arbitration against Intel, and as lead counsel in AMD's victory over Intel in federal court jury trial on the right to use Intel's copyright microcode.
Prof. Memberships: Member, Santa Clara Bar Association, the American Bar Association, the Association of Defense Counsel of Northern California, and the California Trial Lawyers Association.
Career: Admitted to practice in California, the US Court of Appeals for the Ninth and Federal Circuits, the California Supreme Court and various district courts in California, Colorado and Virginia.
Personal: Received JD cum laude and BA from the University of Santa Clara. Serves as adjunct professor teaching Intellectual Property Litigation Techniques at Santa Clara University's Law School.

MENDELSON, Alan C
Latham & Watkins LLP, Menlo Park
650 463 4693
alan.mendelson@lw.com
Recommended in Communications, Corporate/M&A
Specialization: Co-chair of *Latham's* Venture and Technology Practice Group. Represents emerging and public growth companies, venture capital firms and investment banks. Handles venture capital, private and public financings, mergers and acquisitions and strategic collaborations. Experienced in counseling management teams and boards of directors and serves as the corporate secretary for many public and private companies. Also serves on the board of directors of several biotechnology and software companies. Served as Acting General Counsel of Cadence Design Systems and Amgen.
Personal: JD, Harvard University, 1973 (cum laude). AB, University of California, Berkeley, 1969 (Phi Beta Kappa).

MEYER, Michael
Pillsbury Winthrop LLP, Los Angeles
213 488 7310
mmeyer@pillsburywinthrop.com
Recommended in Real Estate
Specialization: Co-managing partner of Pillsbury Winthrop's Los Angeles office, has a national reputation as one of the preeminent leasing attorneys in the United

LEADERS

CALIFORNIA

States. He represents many American financial institutions, accounting firms and law firms with major lease transactions, and has represented the governments of Japan, Australia, Malaysia and Canada on leases for their respective Consulates. He is considered one of the country's leading authorities on the establishment of Fair Market Rental Rates pursuant to arbitrations, the Assignment and Subleasing Provision, and the Inter-Relationships between the Tenant Improvement Agreement and the Rent Commencement Date.
Prof. Memberships: American Bar Association, Los Angeles County Bar Association; University of Chicago Law School Alumni Association of Southern California - President (1980-82), Board of Trustees Los Angeles County Bar Association, Board of Directors Los Angeles County Bar Foundation, Board of Directors New Otani America Corporation, Board of Directors Building Owners and Managers Association, Board of Directors Public Counsel, Board of Directors Boy Scouts of America (Greater Los Angeles), Board of Directors United Way 1992-95, Board of Directors Los Angeles Sports & Entertainment Commission.
Career: Admitted to practice: State of California.
Personal: JD, University of Chicago, 1967; BS, University of Wisconsin, 1964.

MIHLSTEN, George
Latham & Watkins LLP, Los Angeles
213 891 8196
george.mihlsten@lw.com
Recommended in Real Estate
Specialization: Partner, Environment, Land and Resources Department. Substantial experience in real estate transactions and in securing regulatory approvals for large-scale development and transportation projects. Projects include studios, resorts, office complexes, mixed use projects, hospitals, high-rise condominium projects, shopping centers, residential projects, master plan approvals and transportation plan. Specific projects include Staples Center arena and Disney's California Adventure Theme Park. Served on task forces dealing with issues such as housing policies, transportation policies, permit streamlining and environmental review processes.
Prof. Memberships: Los Angeles, California and American Bar Associations.
Personal: JD, University of Southern California, 1980; MBA, 1980; BS, 1977.

MINCHELLA, Michael F
Monteleone & McCrory, LLP,
Los Angeles 213 612 9900
minchella@mmlawyers.com
Recommended in Construction
Specialization: Senior partner practicing business and commercial litigation with emphasis on construction industry matters, including contracting, engineering, architecture, and related services in public and private contracts. He has represented a variety of clients including contractors, owners, and professionals, in many venues, in major and complex disputes involving highways, tunnels, dams, bridges, pipelines, treatment plants, high rise buildings, sports arenas, and schools. In addition his practice includes negotiation and dispute resolution regarding commerical contracts such as sales and leases of real property and business interests. He also serves as an arbitrator and mediator.
Prof. Memberships: Member of the State Bar of California; the American Bar Association, Public Contract and Labor Law sections; and Los Angeles County Bar Association.
Career: Admitted to practice in California, 1970. Also admitted to practice in several US District Courts and the US Court of Claims. Managing partner of *Monteleone & McCrory, LLP* (joined in 1974).
Personal: Received BS from Loyola University of Los Angeles (now Loyola Marymount University) in 1966, and JD from Loyola Law School in 1969.

MOORE, Robert
Milbank, Tweed, Hadley & McCloy,
Los Angeles 213 892 4000
Recommended in Insolvency

MURPHY, Patrick
Murphy Sheneman Julian & Rogers,
San Francisco 415 398 4700
Recommended in Insolvency

MUTO, Fred
Cooley Godward LLP, San Diego
858 550 6000
Recommended in Communications

NATSIS, Tony
Allen, Matkins, Leck, Gamble & Mallory LLP, Los Angeles 310 788 2400
Recommended in Real Estate

NELLIS, Noel
Orrick, Herrington & Sutcliffe,
San Francisco 415 773 5806
nnellis@orrick.com
Recommended in Real Estate
Specialization: Practice focuses on negotiating and documenting transactions in the areas of financing (including construction and long-term lending, ground leasing, and sale-leaseback transactions), leasing, development, construction, and operation of real property. Responsible for the legal aspects of numerous large-scale land development projects such as high-rise office buildings, shopping centers, hotel and resort properties, and industrial buildings. Chair of Orrick's Real Estate Group.
Personal: University of California, Berkeley, Boalt Hall, JD, 1966. University of California, Berkeley, BA, 1963.

NICHOLS, Phillip
Pircher, Nichols & Meeks, Los Angeles
310 201 8900
Recommended in Real Estate

NICHOLSON, Phillip
Cox Castle & Nicholson LLP, Los Angeles
310 277 4222
Recommended in Real Estate

NOLAN, Tom
Howrey Simon Arnold & White,
Los Angeles 213 892 1800
Recommended in Antitrust

OAKES, Royal
Barger & Wolen, Los Angeles
213 680 2800
Recommended in Insurance

O'BRIEN, Harry
Coblentz, Patch, Duffy & Bass LLP,
San Francisco 415 391 4800
Recommended in Construction

O'DONNELL, Pierce
O'Donnell & Shaeffer, Los Angeles
213 532 2000
Recommended in Litigation

OFFER, Stuart
Morrison & Foerster LLP, San Francisco
415 268 7052 soffer@mofo.com
Recommended in Tax
Specialization: Partner concentrating on tax aspects of mergers, acquisitions and divestitures, specialized financings, general corporate transactions, and tax intensive corporate transactions. International practice involves tax planning for US based companies with foreign operations as well as advising foreign corporation with respect to the US tax aspects of their operations and investments in the United States.
Prof. Memberships: American Bar Association Section of Taxation (Chair, Sarbanes-Oxley Task Force; Former Vice Chair, Former Chair, Corporate Tax Committee) Trustee, American Tax Policy Institute; Advisory Board, NYU Institute on Federal Taxation and 'Mergers and Acquisitions' magazine; Member, International Fiscal Association; Fellow, American College of Tax Counsel.
Career: Admitted to practice in California and Washington, DC. Joined firm in 1972, became Partner in 1976. Chair of the firm's Corporate and International Tax Practice Groups.
Personal: BA, University of Washington, 1964; LLB, Columbia University School of Law, 1967; Managing Editor, 'Columbia Law Review'. Law Clerk (1967-68), Judge Featherston, United States Tax Court. Active Duty, US Army Judge Advocate General's Corps (1968-72).

OLSON, Gary
Latham & Watkins LLP, Los Angeles
213 891 8366
gary.olson@lw.com
Recommended in Corporate/M&A
Specialization: Partner in Corporate Department. Extensive experience in mergers and acquisitions. Represents issuers and underwriters in corporate finance transactions, such as Amgen's US $3.5 billion zero coupon convertible offering. Represented independent directors of WellPoint Health Networks in a US$1.5 billion recapitalisation transaction. Recent clients include 'Fortune 500' companies, such as AutoZone, Amgen, Hughes Electronics and Sempra Energy.
Prof. Memberships: Member, 1933 Act Subcommittee of the ABA's Business Law Section.
Career: Chair of the firm's Corporate Department, 1989-96.
Personal: JD, University of Kansas, 1968 (Order of the Coif, editor-in-chief of law review). BS, Kansas State College, 1965.

OLSON, Karl
Levy, Ram & Olson, San Francisco
415 433 4949
Recommended in Media & Entertainment

OLSON, Ronald
Munger, Tolles & Olson, Los Angeles
213 683 9100
Recommended in Litigation

O'NEAL, Stephen V
Thelen Reid & Priest LLP, San Francisco
415 369 7222
svoneal@thelenreid.com
Recommended in Construction
Specialization: Practices in the areas of construction, real estate and complex business litigation, ADR. He has extensive experience in representing owners, contractors, material suppliers and sureties on private and public construction projects, including negotiating and drafting construction contracts and bid documents, handling bid protests, managing contractor terminations, and handling litigation in federal and state courts in both bench and jury trials, before arbitration panels and mediators relating to claims, contract disputes and construction defects. He has lead bench, jury trial and ADR representation of clients in complex civil litigation matters in the technology industry in state and federal courts and before arbitration tribunals. His practice also includes handling real estate litigation matters in state and federal courts, including bench and jury trials, ranging from land use and permit issues through commercial landlord-tenant problems, retail center purchase and sale litigation, owner-anchor tenant disputes, judicial foreclosure litigation, and substantial workout experience. He maintains an active mechanic's lien practice as well and served for two years as General Counsel to a California commercial developer. Successfully represented clients in some of the largest government contracts disputes in California, focusing on practice under the Acquisition of Electronic Data-Processing and Telecommunications Goods and Services provisions of the California Public Contract Code.
Prof. Memberships: Member, California Bar, Real Property Law Section; American

CALIFORNIA LEADERS

Bar Association, Section of Litigation and the Forum Committee on the Construction Industry; Bar Association of San Francisco; Construction Industry Panel of Arbitrators, American Arbitration Association; Special Master, US District Court Northern District of California.
Career: Admitted to practice in the United States District Courts for the Northern and Eastern Districts of California and pro hac vice in the United States District Courts for the Eastern District of Missouri, Northern District of Georgia, and the District of Guam.
Publications: Author: 'Accrual of Statutes of Limitations: California's Discovery Exceptions Swallow the Rule, 68 Cal. L. Rev. 106' (1980). Use of Mechanic's Liens, Payment Bonds, Miller Act to Protect Rights, Contractor, February 1988.
Personal: Received JD (1980) from the University of California, Berkeley, Boalt Hall School of Law, where he was Associate Editor, 'California Law Review' and received AB (1975) from the University of California, Los Angeles.

ORTMANN, Dale
Hunt, Ortmann, Blasco, Palffy & Rossell Inc, Pasadena 626 440 5200
Recommended in Construction

PACHULSKI, Isaac
Stutman, Treister & Glatt PC, Los Angeles 213 251 5100
Recommended in Insolvency

PACHULSKI, Richard
Pachulski, Stang, Ziehl, Young, Jones & Weintraub PC, Los Angeles 310 277 6910
Recommended in Insolvency

PALEFSKY, Cliff
McGuinn, Hillsman & Palefsky, San Francisco 415 421 9292
Recommended in Employment

PASICH, Kirk
Howrey Simon Arnold & White, Los Angeles 310 712 1000
Recommended in Insurance

PASSMAN, Donald
Gang Tyre Ramer & Brown, Beverly Hills 310 777 4800
Recommended in Media & Entertainment

PATTERSON, Tom
Klee, Tuchin, Bogdanoff & Stern LLP, Los Angeles 310 407 4035
tpatterson@ktbslaw.com
Recommended in Insolvency
Specialization: Is a member of *Klee, Tuchin, Bogdanoff & Stern LLP*. He has represented both debtors and creditors' committees in complex chapter 11 and out-of-court proceedings. He has represented hospital provider groups in most of the recent HMO insolvencies pending in California (including MedPartners Provider Network, Maxicare, Wattshealth, and Lifeguard) and has also been involved in most of the significant insurer insolvencies in California in the past ten years, including, most recently, Superior National, where he represented the acquirer of the on-going insurance business, and Golden Eagle, where he currently represents the liquidating trustees. Is a frequent speaker on bankruptcy and insolvency related topics.

PECK, Rodney
Pillsbury Winthrop LLP, San Francisco 415 983 1516
rpeck@pillsburywinthrop.com
Recommended in Banking & Finance
Specialization: Partner in corporate, securities, finance and banking law areas, including representing buyers and sellers in mergers and acquisitions, bank transactional and regulatory matters, corporate and securities transactions and structured finance transactions. His practice focuses on financial services, energy and telecommunications industries. He advised Chevron Corporation in its merger with Texaco Inc., a $36 billion transaction. He has represented major commercial bank lenders in complex syndicated and other loan transactions.
Prof. Memberships: Board of Trustees, Dominican University of California, San Rafael, California; Financial Institutions Committee of the State Bar of California; Committee on Banking Law of the Section of Corporation, Banking and Business Law of the American Bar Association; member of the Ad Hoc Committee of the State Bar of California (1978) which advised the California Superintendent of Banks on revisions to the California Banking Law.
Career: Admitted to practice: State of California. Joined Pillsbury 1970, partner since 1978. Senior partner and co-head of firm's Financial Institutions Practice Group; member of Managing Board since 1988. He has served the firm as Managing Partner-Financial Planning and Policy and as chair of the Finance Committee.
Publications: 'Representing the Target Bank or Bank Holding Company in a Negotiated Acquisition', in New Banks and New Bankers 1981; 'The Non-Bank Bank Phenomenon: Recent Developments and Implications for Interstate Banking', in New Banks and New Bankers 1984; 'Swaps Programmes for Banks', International Financial Law Review (December 1985); 'Collateralisation of Swap Transactions', in Swap Finance (Euromoney Publications 1986); 'Events of Default Under Swap Contracts', in Euromoney Swap Finance Service Update I (1987); 'The Federal Home Loan Banks and the Home Finance System', in the 'Business Lawyer' (May 1988); and 'FIRREA and the New Federal Home Loan Bank System', in the 'Santa Clara University Law Review' (1992).
Personal: JD, Columbia University School of Law, 1970. AB, Stanford University, 1967

PEPE, Stephen
O'Melveny & Myers LLP, Newport Beach 949 760 9600
Recommended in Employment

PFISTER, Thomas
Latham & Watkins LLP, Los Angeles 213 891 7992
tom.pfister@lw.com
Recommended in Employment
Specialization: Partner in the Litigation Department, focusing on employment litigation on behalf of management. Represents employers in a broad range of state and federal lawsuits, including defense and resolution of major class-action discrimination cases.
Prof. Memberships: Fellow, American College of Labor and Employment Lawyers.
Career: Previously served on the Executive Committee; headed the firm's Employment Law Group; served as Los Angeles Office Managing Partner.
Publications: Chapters on class actions, Lindemann & Grossman's 'Employment Discrimination Law'; numerous papers presented at national seminars on developments in employment law and class action litigation.
Personal: JD, Harvard Law School, 1974. BA, Stanford University, 1970.

PHILLIPP, James
Gibson, Dunn & Crutcher LLP, Los Angeles 213 229 7000
Recommended in Tax

PHILLIPS, Lee
Manatt, Phelps & Phillips, LLP, Los Angeles 310 312 4000
Recommended in Media & Entertainment

PICKETT, Donn
Bingham McCutchen LLP, San Francisco 415 393 2000
Recommended in Antitrust

PIRCHER, Leo
Pircher, Nichols & Meeks, Los Angeles 310 201 8900
Recommended in Real Estate

POPOFSKY, Laurence
Heller Ehrman White & McAuliffe LLP, San Francisco 415 772 6000
Recommended in Antitrust, Litigation

POWERS, Matthew D
Weil, Gotshal & Manges LLP, Redwood Shores 650 802 3200
matthew.powers@weil.com
Recommended in Intellectual Property
Specialization: Managing Partner of the firm's Silicon Valley office and serves on the Management Committee of the firm as a whole. Specialises in intellectual property litigation and counselling worldwide, and is recognised as one of the world's leading trial lawyers for intellectual property disputes. Regularly participates in the largest, most significant patent litigations in several industries, including semiconductors, software, medical devices and biotechnology. Was lead counsel for Cisco Systems in the patent litigation initiated by Lucent (involving over 20 patents), is lead counsel for Perkin Elmer's Applied Biosystems Division and Celera in several patent litigations involving DNA sequencing technology, is lead counsel for Intel in several patent matters and for Micron Technology in the patent litigation initiated by Lucent (involving over 10 semiconductor and telecommunications patents), and Micron Technology against Rambus, as well as several parties in internet/software patent litigations. Was lead trial counsel for Applied Materials in its patent litigations against ASM International, NV and Novellus Systems, which resulted in payments to Applied Materials of well over $150 million. Regularly advises clients in Europe and Asia and often directs litigation outside the United States.
Personal: JD, Harvard Law School (1982), BS, Northwestern University (1979).

PREOVOLOS, Penelope A
Morrison & Foerster LLP, San Francisco 415 268 7187
ppreovolos@mofo.com
Recommended in Antitrust
Specialization: Partner with extensive experience in antitrust, false advertising/unfair trade practice and consumer class action litigation and counseling, particularly involving computer and other high technology companies. Has served as lead counsel in a number of major California state cases as well as representing defendants in federal antitrust cases.
Prof. Memberships: Chair, 1994-95, and Secretary, 1993-94, of the California State Bar Antitrust Section. Member, Litigation and Antitrust Sections, American Bar Association.
Career: Admitted to practice in California. Joined the firm in 1980, became partner in 1985. Co-chair, *Morrison & Foerster* Antitrust, Marketing and Distribution Practice Group since 1990.
Personal: AB, greatest distinction, University of California, Berkeley, 1976, Phi Beta Kappa, University Medal, English Departmental Citation; JD, cum laude, Harvard Law School, 1979, Executive Editor, Harvard Civil Right - 'Civil Liberties Law Review', 1978-79. Law Clerk, Honorable Charles M Merrill, US Court of Appeals, Ninth Circuit (1979-80).

PRETTY, Laurence
Christie, Parker & Hale, LLP, Pasadena 626 795 9900
Recommended in Intellectual Property

QUINN, John B
Quinn Emanuel Urquhart Oliver & Hedges, LLP, Los Angeles 213 624 7707
johnquinn@quinnemanuel.com
Recommended in Litigation

Specialization: Managing Partner, *Quinn Emanuel Urquhart Oliver & Hedges, LLP*. Practice areas include general trial practice, intellectual property litigation, antirust and unfair competition litigation, banking and financial institution litigation, real estate litigation, entertainment litigation, securities and class action litigation. Practices in all areas of business litigation. Notable litigation resolutions: lead trial lawyer for General Motors in its lawsuit in federal court in Detroit against Volkswagen arising out of the departure of Ignacio Lopez. General Motors received $1.1 billion in settlement. Won an $80 million verdict on behalf of Avery Dennison in theft of trade secrets and RICO case in federal court in Cleveland. Won a defense verdict after a three-month jury trial in action arising out of the sale of a subsidiary of a major defense contractor in which $20 million was at issue. Obtained a defense verdict after a two-month jury trial on behalf of a Fortune 200 company in a trade secret and unfair competition action brought by its major competitor. Obtained a jury verdict for a hospital management company in a race discrimination suit in what was the longest employment trial in California history after plaintiff rejected a $1 million settlement offer. Obtained a defense verdict for an aerospace company in a whistleblower suit after a two-month jury trial. Obtained a defense verdict for an entertainment company in a highly publicized sexual harassment suit. Was successful lead defense trial lawyer for an aerospace company in the retrial of a tortious interference suit in which the plaintiff had won $15 million in the previous trial and had rejected a $1 million settlement offer before the second trial. Obtained summary judgment on behalf of an aerospace company in an action for breach of an alleged joint venture agreement.
Prof. Memberships: J Reuben Clark School of Law, Brigham Young University, 1977. Lecturer on Federal Practice, California Continuing Education of the Bar. Member, Los Angeles County Bar Association. Member, Federal Courts and Practices Committee. Member, American Bar Association. Member, Forum Committees on: Health Law; Construction Industry. Member, Sections on: Corporations; Public Contract Law; Banking and Business Law; Litigation; Patent, Trademark and Copyright Law. Member, The State Bar of California. Member, Committee on Federal Courts. Member, The State Bar of New York. Member, Million Dollar Advocates Forum. Director, Rose Bowl Operating Company. General Counsel, Academy of Motion Picture Arts and Sciences, 1987-present.
Publications: Editor, 'Harvard Law Review', 1974-76.
Personal: Harvard Law School (JD, cum laude, 1976). Knox Fellow, Harvard University, 1977, Claremont Men's College (BA, magna cum laude, 1973). Since 1987, he has been General Counsel of the Academy of Motion Picture Arts and Sciences. Finisher, Ironman Triathlon World Championship, Kailua Kona, Hawaii, 1999.

RABINOWITZ, Joel
Irell & Manella LLP, Los Angeles
310 277 1010
Recommended in Tax

RAMER, Bruce
Gang Tyre Ramer & Brown, Beverly Hills
310 777 4800
Recommended in Media & Entertainment

RESSLER, Alison
Sullivan & Cromwell, Los Angeles
resslera@sullcrom.com
310 712 6600
Recommended in Capital Markets
Specialization: Has broad experience in corporate finance, mergers and acquisitions, and private equity investments in a variety of regulated and unregulated industries. Has worked on IPOs for diverse range of companies, including Asia Global Crossing, Exelixis, Tibco Software, Korn/Ferry International, Microsoft and Spieker Properties. Additional corporate finance experience includes complex transactions involving both equity and debt securities on a secured and unsecured basis, such as principal equity investments, acquisition financing, offerings of equity and debt securities for real estate investment trusts, rights offerings, and offerings of convertible and exchangeable securities.
Prof. Memberships: American Bar Association; California State Bar Association; Los Angeles County Bar Association.
Career: Joined *Sullivan & Cromwell* in 1984. Partner since 1991.
Personal: Born in 1958. Columbia Law School, (JD, 1983); Brown University, (BA, 1980).

ROSATI, Mario
Wilson Sonsini Goodrich & Rosati, Palo Alto 650 493 9300
Recommended in Communications

ROSCH, Tom
Latham & Watkins LLP, San Francisco
415 395 8148
tom.rosch@lw.com
Recommended in Antitrust
Specialization: Partner, Litigation Department. Preeminent practitioner with 35 years' experience in antitrust and trade regulation law. Lead counsel in more than one hundred federal and state antitrust cases.
Prof. Memberships: Fellow, American College of Trial Lawyers.
Career: Director, Federal Trade Commission's Bureau of Consumer Protection, 1973-75. Former managing Partner of the San Francisco office. Chair, ABA's Antitrust Section, 1990.
Publications: Numerous publications, including 'Developments in the Law of Vertical Restraints', PLI, 1999, and 'Manual of Federal Trade Commission Practice', BNA, 1992.
Personal: LLB, Harvard University, 1965 (cum laude). Knox Fellow, Cambridge University, 1962. BA, Harvard University, 1961 (magna cum laude).

ROSEN, Peter K
Mayer, Brown, Rowe & Maw, Los Angeles 213 229 5172
prosen@mayerbrownrowe.com
Recommended in Insurance
Specialization: Securities litigation, private securities disputes, broker-dealer matters, special investigations. Property disputes, professional liability, directors and officers' liability, commercial general liability policies, insurance coverage. Advising Boards of Directors and Senior Management on directors' and officers' litigation, compensation and benefits agreements, employment practices, insurance strategies, indemnification, and bylaws and agreements.
Career: Joined *Mayer, Brown, Rowe & Maw* as partner, 1997. Formerly with *Weisman & Rosen*, Los Angeles, 1989-97; *Boren, Sloan & Rosen*, Los Angeles, 1986-89; *Paul, Hastings, Janofsky & Walker*, Los Angeles, 1980-86; *Ball, Hunt, Hart, Brown & Baerwitz*, Los Angeles, 1978-80.
Publications: Author: 'Sharing the Database - How Contentious Parties Saved Time and Money by Building a Joint Document Database', California Lawyer, September 1994. 'Confessions of a PC Junkie', California Lawyer, October 1990. 'Legal Works '97, The Technology Show,' Price Waterhouse's LegalTech, Los Angeles ABA TechShow '97.
Personal: University of Southern California, JD, 1978; Law Review. University of Southern California, MPA, 1978. Occidental College, University of California at Los Angeles, BA, 1975.

ROSENFELD, Robert
Heller Ehrman White & McAuliffe LLP, San Francisco 415 772 6000
Recommended in Antitrust

RUBALCAVA, Sharon
Weston Benshoof Rochefort Rubalcava MacCuish LLP, Los Angeles
213 576 1000
Recommended in Environment

RUBY, Allen
Ruby & Schofield, San José 408 998 8500
Recommended in Litigation

RUDY, Mark
Rudy, Exelrod & Zieff, LLP, San Francisco
415 434 9800
Recommended in Employment

SAGER, Kelli
Davis Wright Tremaine LLP, Los Angeles
213 633 6821
kellisager@dwt.com
Recommended in Media & Entertainment
Specialization: Partner, media, entertainment, and First Amendment law, including defamation, privacy, copyright, access, shield laws. 17 years litigation experience representing television networks, radio stations, studios, newspapers, authors, publishers and national magazines. Clients include 'New York Times', 'Los Angeles Times', E! Entertainment Television, Paramount Pictures, MTV Networks. Represented media in high profile trials, including OJ Simpson and Winona Ryder trials.
Career: Among 'Top 50 Women Litigators', 'National Law Journal' (December 2001). Among '100 Most Influential Lawyers in California', 'Los Angeles Daily Journal' (1998-2002). Joined as partner, 1994.
Personal: JD, (cum laude), Utah School of Law, 1985. BA, West Georgia College, 1981.

SAGGESE, Nicholas P
Skadden, Arps, Slate, Meagher & Flom LLP, Los Angeles 213 687 5550
nsaggese@skadden.com
Recommended in Capital Markets, Corporate/M&A
Specialization: Has been involved with numerous mergers and acquisitions, debt and equity offerings, and corporate restructurings. Examples of recent transactions include: the acquisition of Herbalife International by affiliates of Whitney & Co. and Golden Gate Private Equity, Inc.; the acquisition of international cable assets from Liberty Media Corporation by UnitedGlobalCom, Inc.; the leveraged recapitalization of PETCO Animal Supplies, Inc. by affiliates of Leonard Green & Partners, LP and Texas Pacific Group; the purchase and subsequent sale of Harveys Casino Resorts by an affiliate of Colony Capital, Inc.; the acquisition of International Media Group, Inc. by affiliates of Leonard Green & Partners, LP; the acquisition of AboveNet Communications by Metromedia Fiber Network, Inc.; and bond offerings for Hilton Hotels Corp., Host Marriott, LP, Liberty Media Corporation, Regal Cinemas Corporation, Solectron Corporation, and Kerzner International Limited (formerly Sun International Hotels Limited) among others. Also advised on the recent IPOs of PETCO Animal Supplies, Inc. and Regal Entertainment Group.
Prof. Memberships: Board member of non-profit organizations including Los Angeles Regional Foodbank and LA County Bar Foundation and member of Board of Visitors of Loyola Law School.

Career: JD, Loyola Law School of Los Angeles, 1980 (cum laude; Member, Loyola Law Review, St. Thomas More Law Honour Society); MBA, University of California at Los Angeles, 1973 (Beta Gamma Sigma Honour Society); BA, University of California at Los Angeles, 1969; co-editor and principal author of treatise on corporate and securities law aspects of corporate restructurings.

SAPER, Jeff
Wilson Sonsini Goodrich & Rosati, Palo Alto 650 493 9300
Recommended in Communications, Corporate/M&A

SAX, Paul
Orrick, Herrington & Sutcliffe, San Francisco 415 773 5949
pjsax@orrick.com
Recommended in Tax

Specialization: Tax controversies and litigation. Tax planning for domestic and multinational corporations. Also planning for large family-owned businesses, California taxation, and nonprofit organizations. Chair of Orrick's Tax Department.
Prof. Memberships: Chair (1999-2000), American Bar Association, Section of Taxation; Fellow, American College of Tax Counsel; Life Fellow, American Bar Foundation; Trustee, American Tax Policy Institute; Tax Section Delegate, American Bar Association House of Delegates.

SCHMALL, Deborah
Farella Braun & Martel LLP, San Francisco 415 954 4400
Recommended in Environment

SCHWAB, Douglas
Heller Ehrman White & McAuliffe LLP, San Francisco 415 772 6000
Recommended in Litigation

SEABOLT, Richard
Hancock, Rothert & Bunshoft LLP, San Francisco 415 981 5550
rlseabolt@hrblaw.com
Recommended in Insurance

Specialization: Partner in the San Francisco office, co-chair of the firm's Business Litigation Practice Group. Extensive experience in complex trials and appeals arising from commercial disputes, including commercial, construction, and insurance contracts, and business torts. Has tried a number of significant cases to defense verdicts, including three cases where the plaintiffs' financial losses were between $20 million and $500 million. He was lead defense counsel in Aerojet-General Corp. v Transport, a ten-month, four-phase trial (two jury phases) conducted in a specially constructed, converted auditorium courtroom involving more than thirty other law firms. After three months of trial, the jury returned a unanimous defense verdict, rejecting Aerojet's claim for pollution cleanup costs estimated at between $500 million to $1 billion. 'The National Law Journal' and the 'California Daily Journal' highlighted the case as among the largest jury trials tried to a defense verdict in 1992. The California Supreme Court later affirmed the defense verdict, which resulted in a Court of Appeal opinion that quoted from his closing argument. See, Aerojet-General Corp. v American Excess, 97 Cal.App.4th 387, 412 (Feb. 2002). Other trial and arbitration successes include: an arbitration before a three judge panel involving the dissolution of a financial services joint venture that resulted in recovery of attorneys' fees; an arbitration involving a national accounting firm's partnership noncompete clause; a defense jury verdict in FMC's $20 million claim for environmental cleanup at its Mouat site, and the successful defense of the first named defendant in a $30 million construction delay case involving an advanced wastewater treatment plant. Other complex civil disputes include an International Chamber of Commerce arbitration involving construction of an Indonesian cement plant, a construction contract claim arising from the Trans-Panama Pipeline, computerized engraving system trade secret claim, and a claim arising from the breach of a semiconductor fabrication contract. Frequently speaks on civil litigation topics.
Prof. Memberships: Member of the Executive Committee of the Litigation Section of the State Bar of California, and chair of its Jury Instructions Committee. Member of the ABTL (Association of Business Trial Lawyers) Annual Program Committee, and a Commercial Arbitration Panelist - American Arbitration Association.
Career: Admitted in California (1975). Partner since 1982, after joining the firm in 1975.
Personal: University of Michigan (BGS, with distinction 1971). University of California, Hastings College of the Law (JD, 1975).

SENEKER, Carl (Kim)
Morrison & Foerster LLP, San Francisco 415 268 6619
cseneker@mofo.com
Recommended in Real Estate

Specialization: Partner practicing in commercial real estate transactions, secured debt restructuring and creditors' rights, and environmental law, zoning, and land use regulation. Extensive experience in all matters involving acquisition, financing, development, leasing and operation of commercial and residential real estate projects. Financing work includes construction lending, permanent finance and securitized loans, convertible and participating debt, sale-leasebacks and high credit leases, and syndicated lending. Land use entitlement experience includes many large-scale commercial, residential and industrial projects, as well as advice and counsel on compliance with environmental requirements applicable to real estate development.
Prof. Memberships: Member and Past President, American College of Real Estate Lawyers, Member, American College of Mortgage Attorneys, Anglo-American Real Property Institute, and Lambda Alpha National Land Economics Society.
Career: Admitted to practice in California. Joined *Morrison & Foerster* in 1971; became partner in 1975.
Personal: AB, Stanford University, 1964; JD, University of California, Berkeley, Boalt Hall, 1967; Editor in Chief, 'California Law Review'. Law Clerk, Associate Justice William O Douglas, United States Supreme Court, (1967-68).

SHANKS, Patricia
Bingham McCutchen LLP, Los Angeles 213 680 4600
Recommended in Environment

SHARF, Jesse
Gibson, Dunn & Crutcher LLP, Los Angeles 213 229 7000
Recommended in Real Estate

SHORTZ, Richard
Morgan, Lewis & Bockius LLP, Los Angeles 213 612 2500
Recommended in Projects

SIMONS, Laird
Fenwick & West, Palo Alto 650 494 0600
Recommended in Communications

SINGER, Andrew
Latham & Watkins LLP, San Diego 619 238 2869
andrew.singer@lw.com
Recommended in Projects

Specialization: Partner in and practice group leader of Latham's Project Finance Group. Substantial experience representing lenders, utilities and owner/developers in project financings around the world in power, oil and gas, and undersea cable sectors. Experience includes the structuring, documentation and negotiation of financing arrangements and the preparation and negotiation of project contracts. Also handles the coordination of the work and input of other project specialists, including investment bankers, insurance consultants, independent engineers, environmental consultants and technical consultants.
Prof. Memberships: New York, California and American Bar Associations.
Personal: JD, Harvard University, 1987. BS, Cornell University, 1984.

SINISCALCO, Gary
Orrick, Herrington & Sutcliffe, San Francisco 415 773 5833
grsiniscalco@orrick.com
Recommended in Employment

Specialization: Practice focuses on class action and complex litigation defense. Extensive expertise in EEO, affirmative action, wrongful discharge, and wage-and-hour matters. Has litigated class actions and individual employment cases before federal and state courts and administrative agencies for leading industrial and technology companies in the US. Founding member, National Employment Law Institute & American Employment Law Counsel.
Career: Georgetown University Law Center, JD, 1969. LeMoyne College, BA, 1965.

SINK, Charles
Farella Braun & Martel LLP, San Francisco 415 954 4400
Recommended in Construction

SMITH, Greg
Skadden, Arps, Slate, Meagher & Flom LLP, Palo Alto 650 470 4590
grsmith@skadden.com
Recommended in Communications

Specialization: Partner, Palo Alto & San Francisco. Experience in the areas of corporate finance, including public offerings and private placements of debt and equity, mergers and acquisitions, licensing and related transactions, and corporate restructurings. Represents emerging growth technology and life science companies in all stages of development, including incorporation, venture capital financings, initial public offerings and mergers and acquisitions; also complex finance transactions, including high-yield and convertible debt securities offerings pursuant to Rule 144A and otherwise; represents underwriters, financial advisors and placement agents with technology and other transactions as well as foreign and international companies with both domestic and foreign transactions. Transactions include the representation of Credit Suisse First Boston; Bear, Stearns; Merrill Lynch; Morgan Stanley; SangStat Medical Corporation; Tumbleweed Communications Co.; McKesson Corporation; NP Test, Inc. (Schlumberger Limited); Niku Corporation; and Salesforce.com Inc.
Career: JD, Columbia Law School, 1988 (Harlan Fiske Stone Scholar); BA, Stanford University, 1985 (with distinction; Phi Beta Kappa).
Personal: Chairman of the Board, Friends of Music at Stanford University.

SMITH, Neil
Howard, Rice, Nemerovski, Canady, Falk & Rabkin, San Francisco 415 434 1600
Recommended in Intellectual Property

SNOW JR, Tower C
Clifford Chance US LLP, San Francisco 415 778 4702
tower.snow@cliffordchance.com
Recommended in Litigation

Specialization: Serves on Clifford Chance's Americas Management Group and has extensive experience in all types of litigation involving the Sarbanes-Oxley Act of 2002, Securities Litigation Uniform Standards Act of 1998, the Private Securities Litigation Reform Act of 1995, the Securities Act of 1933, the Securities Exchange Act of 1934 and Foreign Corrupt Practices Act. He has authored over 200 articles on securities litigation issues. He is listed by numerous publications as one of the most influential lawyers in the world and has served as advisor for the Securities and Exchange Commission Report to the President.

SONSINI, Larry
Wilson Sonsini Goodrich & Rosati, Palo Alto 650 493 9300
Recommended in Capital Markets, Communications, Corporate/M&A

SPECTOR, Scott
Fenwick & West, Palo Alto
650 494 0600
Recommended in Communications

SPIELBERG, David
Stoel Rives LLP, San Francisco
415 617 8900 *Recommended in Projects*

SPRATLING, Gary
Gibson, Dunn & Crutcher LLP, San Francisco 415 393 8200
Recommended in Antitrust

STEEL, Michael J
Pillsbury Winthrop LLP, San Francisco
415 983 7320
msteel@pillsburywinthrop.com
Recommended in Environment
Specialization: Partner in the environment, land use and natural resources; global energy; litigation areas. His practice focuses on federal, state and local regulatory compliance issues, and the defense of Unfair Practices Act, Proposition 65 and other enforcement actions. He has appeared before the US Environmental Protection Agency, the State Department of Toxic Substances Control and the California Regional Water Quality Control Boards, and state and federal OSHA. He advises a variety of industrial companies regarding hazardous substance handling, air quality and employee safety. Has provided compliance counseling to a number of pharmaceutical, biotech, food service and grocery companies and defended multi-defendant unfair practices actions alleging misrepresentation of product characteristics.
Career: Admitted to practice: State of California.
Personal: JD, University of California, Hastings College of the Law, 1982; BA, University of California at Davis, 1977.

STEUBER, David
Howrey Simon Arnold & White, Los Angeles 213 892 1800
Recommended in Insurance

STORMER, Dan
Hadsell & Stormer, Pasadena
818 585 9600
Recommended in Employment

STREETER, Jon
Keker & Van Nest LLP, San Francisco
415 391 5400
Recommended in Intellectual Property

SWANSON, Daniel
Gibson, Dunn & Crutcher LLP, Los Angeles 213 229 7430
dswanson@gibsondunn.com
Recommended in Antitrust
Specialization: Litigation partner in *Gibson, Dunn & Crutcher's* Los Angeles office and co-chair of the firm's Antitrust Practice Group. He has substantial trial and appellate experience, co-chairs the ABA Antitrust Section's International Antitrust Committee and frequently represents international clients. He also has extensive IP expertise and regularly represents clients in the entertainment, communications, and high-technology sectors. He has lectured widely on antitrust, contributed to leading antitrust treatises, testified in the 2002 DOJ-FTC Joint Hearings regarding Competition and IP Policy and serves on the Antitrust Report Editorial Board.
Personal: Graduated magna cum laude from Harvard Law School and has PhD and masters degrees in Economics from Harvard University, where he was a Harvard Teaching Fellow.

TANOURY, Mark
Cooley Godward LLP, Palo Alto
650 843 5000
Recommended in Communications

TAYLOR, Robert
Howrey Simon Arnold & White, Menlo Park 650 463 8100
Recommended in Antitrust

TEPLIN, Lawrence
Cox Castle & Nicholson LLP, Los Angeles
310 277 4222
Recommended in Construction

THOMPSON, Robert
Sheppard, Mullin, Richter & Hampton LLP, San Francisco 415 434 9100
Recommended in Real Estate

THORNTON, Charles
Paul, Hastings, Janofsky & Walker LLP, San Francisco 415 856 7000
charlesthornton@paulhastings.com
Recommended in Real Estate
Specialization: Concentrates his practice in real estate and related corporate matters, including joint ventures, the acquisition, leasing and financing of real estate and real estate development; Represents real estate owners, developers and investors.
Prof. Memberships: Authored several articles on corporate and real estate matters. Member - Lambda Alpha; Director - YMCA of San Francisco.
Career: Chair of the Real Estate Department in the firm's San Francisco office; Former chair of the San Francisco and Los Angeles offices.
Personal: AB degree - Cornell University; JD degree - the University of Michigan Law School (1967); Assistant editor of the 'Michigan Law Review'.

THUM, Robert
Thelen Reid & Priest LLP, Los Angeles
213 576 8014
rthum@thelenreid.com
Recommended in Construction
Specialization: Primary areas of legal practice include engineering/construction disputes, arbitration and litigation and government contracts disputes and litigation.
Prof. Memberships: Arbitrator, National Panel of Construction Arbitrators, American Arbitration Association Arbitrator, Public Construction Arbitration Program, CA Office of Administrative Hearings, American Bar Association: Forum Committee on the Construction Industry, Public Contract Law and Litigation Sections California State Bar Association: Construction, Real Estate and Litigation Sections.
Career: Admitted to bar: Ohio, 1970; US Court of Military Appeals, 1971; California, 1974; US Supreme Court, 1975.
Publications: 'California Construction Law' (Federal Publications 2001); 'Guide to Construction Contracts and Disputes' (3d ed., California CEB 2000); 'Practical Construction Law' (Federal Publications 1999); 'The Authority to Issue Changes', in 'Changes' (Wiley Law 1994); 'Handbook of California Construction Law' (AGCof California 1993); 'Bid Guarantees', in 'Construction Bidding Law' (Wiley Law 1991); 'Changes', in 'Construction Subcontracting: Legal Guide' (Wiley Law 1990); 'Liability of Designers and Contractors to the End-User' (ABA Forum Committee 1985); 'Claims and Project Schedule' in 'Scheduling and Proof of Claims' (Fed. Publications 1985); 'The Owner's Warranty of Plans and Specifications' 14 Public Contract L.J. 240 (1984); 'Interpretation of Plans and Specifications', in 'Government Construction Contracting' (Federal Publications 1982).
Personal: Law degree from the Cornell Law School, 1970, where was Editor of the 'Cornell Law Review'. Received AB cum laude from Princeton University, 1967. Served as Captain, US Marine Corps J.A.G., 1971-73.

TONSFELDT, Steve
Venture Law Group, Menlo Park
650 854 4488
Recommended in Communications

TOSETTI, Paul
Latham & Watkins LLP, Los Angeles
213 485 1234
paul.tosetti@lw.com
Recommended in Corporate/M&A
Specialization: Partner in the Corporate Department and Co-chair of the firm's global Mergers and Acquisitions Group. Specializes in the acquisition and disposition of public and private companies, on both a solicited and unsolicited basis. Extensive experience with leveraged buy-outs.
Prof. Memberships: American Bar Association, California State Bar Association, Los Angeles Bar Association.
Publications: Editor, 'Corporate Governance Advisor', regular speaker at Practicing Law Institute and academic events.
Personal: JD, Harvard University, 1981 (cum laude, Supreme Court Editor of 'Harvard Law Review'). MA, Oxford University, 1979 (First Class Honours from Magdelen College). BA, Harvard University, 1976 (cum laude).

TRUAX, Tim
Cox Castle & Nicholson LLP, Los Angeles
310 277 4222
Recommended in Construction

TUCHIN, Michael L
Klee, Tuchin, Bogdanoff & Stern LLP, Los Angeles 310 407 4040
mtuchin@ktbslaw.com
Recommended in Insolvency
Specialization: Is a member and co-manager of *Klee, Tuchin, Bogdanoff & Stern LLP*. On the debtor side, he currently represents Fountain View, Inc. (which operates 49 skilled care nursing and assisted care living facilities, and pharmacy and therapy businesses) and Frederick's of Hollywood, Inc (a world-renowned retailer of innovative specialty apparel operating more than 150 stores, a catalogue, and an internet business). Out of court, he has led successful restructurings of the Lusk Company (a large California homebuilder with close to $1 billion in debts), an international giftware manufacturer, an international manufacturer of computer accessories, a national express delivery business, and LA Kings, Ltd. (the then-owner of the Los Angeles Kings hockey franchise). Currently represents, and has represented, creditors in numerous Chapter 11 cases, including American Rice (filed in Corpus Christi, Texas), Ameriserve (filed in Delaware), Carmike Theatres (filed in Delaware), Catapult Entertainment (filed in San Jose, California), Edwards Theatres (filed in Orange County, California). Has represented numerous purchasers of assets (including Viacom, Paramount Pictures, and The Gap). Currently serves as the President of the Financial Lawyers Conference of Los Angeles and as Vice President of the Los Angeles Bankruptcy Forum.

VANYO, Bruce
Wilson Sonsini Goodrich & Rosati, Palo Alto 650 493 9300
Recommended in Litigation

VETTER, Jeff
Fenwick & West, Palo Alto 650 494 0600
Recommended in Communications

CALIFORNIA LEADERS

WALKER, Paul
Dewey Ballantine LLP, Los Angeles
213 621 6200
pwalker@deweyballantine.com
Recommended in Real Estate
Specialization: Real estate lending, workout, capital markets, creditors' rights, development and leasing, representing domestic and foreign lenders, liquidating banks and opportunity funds, and major real estate developers.
Career: Co-Chair of Real Estate Practice Group and Managing Partner, *Dewey Ballantine LLP*, Los Angeles.
Personal: BA, University of Notre Dame, 1966. LLB, University of Pennsylvania, 1969.

WALL, Daniel
Latham & Watkins LLP, San Francisco
415 395 8240
dan.wall@lw.com
Recommended in Antitrust
Specialization: Co-chair, Global Antitrust and Competition Practice. Represents companies in antitrust litigation and government investigations. Concentrates in high technology antitrust matters, including standard setting, technological tying and the exploitation of intellectual property. Extensive experience in monopolization litigation.
Prof. Memberships: ABA Antitrust Section; numerous leadership positions.
Career: Antitrust Division, Justice Department, 1980-82; *Skadden, Arps*, 1982-84; *McCutchen, Doyle, Brown & Enersen*, 1984-99; *Latham & Watkins*, 1999-present.
Publications: Numerous articles on the application of economic theory to antitrust issues and high technology antitrust.
Personal: JD, University of Santa Clara, 1980 (magna cum laude). BA, University of California, Davis, 1977 (cum laude).

WEINER, Peter
Paul, Hastings, Janofsky & Walker LLP, San Francisco 415 856 7010
peterweiner@paulhastings.com
Recommended in Environment
Specialization: Heads West Coast environmental practice. Represents manufacturers, property owners and developers, and other businesses, in federal, state, and local environmental, energy, and OSHA regulatory matters, litigation and legislation. Areas include 'brownfields' development, hazardous waste management, property clean-up, water supply issues, air and water quality, OSHA, California Environmental Quality Act, pesticide registration, Proposition 65, environmental insurance, and California energy law. Registered lobbyist for California government.
Personal: BA, Harvard, 1966 (magna cum laude, phi beta kappa). LLB, Yale, 1970, (member, Yale Law Journal). MSc Econ, 1967, London School of Economics. Admissions: California Bar, various federal courts in California and the US Supreme Court.

WEISSMANN, Eric
Weissmann, Wolff, Bergman, Coleman, Silverman & Holmes, LLP, Beverly Hills
310 858 7888
Recommended in Media & Entertainment

WEITZEL, Mark P
Thelen Reid & Priest LLP, San Francisco
415 369 7007
mweitzel@thelenreid.com
Recommended in Projects
Specialization: Specializes in project finance, energy and infrastructure matters, with over 20 years' experience in the acquisition, development, financing and operation of infrastructure projects and companies. Particular specialties in equipment and project lease transactions, US and foreign tax matters, the negotiation of investment, acquisition and shareholder agreements, and the structuring of complex equity and debt investments.
Prof. Memberships: World's Leading Project Finance Lawyers, Euromoney 2001. American Bar Association. Member, Sections on Taxation and Business Law. Member, Committees on Capital Recovery and Leasing, and Partnerships. California Bar Association. Member, Sections on Taxation and Business Law
Career: Co-Chair of Thelen Reid's Energy, Utility and Infrastructure Practice Group, and Project and Asset Finance Department.
Publications: 'New Strategies for Financing Power Projects, Forbes Infrastructure Conference', 2002; 'Leasing of Power Projects, Energy Notes', 2001; 'Worldwide Infrastructure Conference', 1997; 'High Speed Rail Conference', 1997; 'Water and Wastewater Summit', 1997; 'Project Finance, American College of Real Estate Counsel', 1997.
Personal: Law degree and Masters in Business Administration degree (Finance Concentration) in 1980 from UCLA. A member of the UCLA Law Review and Order of the Coif at UCLA Law School, and National Business Honor Society at the UCLA Graduate School of Management. Undergraduate degree in 1976 from Stanford University, With Distinction.

WHEELER, Raymond
Morrison & Foerster LLP, Palo Alto
650 813 5656
rwheeler@mofo.com
Recommended in Employment
Specialization: Partner advising on all aspects of labor and employment law, including litigation before the federal and state courts and administrative agencies, such as the NLRB and the EEOC. Has extensive experience representing major corporations in collective bargaining, union organizing and decertification efforts and labor arbitrations. Has handled several employment discrimination class actions, and has represented companies in hundreds of arbitrations, injunctive actions, wrongful discharge suits, and administrative proceedings.
Prof. Memberships: Charter Fellow, College of Labor and Employment Lawyers; Management Member, Council of the Labor and Employment Law section, American Bar Association; National Advisory Board, Berkeley Journal of Employment and Labor Law.
Career: Admitted to practice in California. Joined *Morrison & Foerster* in 1971, became partner in 1976. Presently Chair of the Labor and Employment Law Department. Named among the 'Best Lawyers in America' in the publication of Naifeh and Smith.
Publications: Numerous publications including Senior Editor, 'The Developing Labor Law.' 'Mergers, Acquisitions and Takeovers: Labor Relations Consequences of Corporate Transactions', 'The Labor Lawyer, 1991; 'Federal Preemption of State Wrongful Discharge Actions'; published in both The Labor Lawyer, 1985, and The Industrial Relations Law Journal, 1986.
Personal: BA, University of Texas at Austin, 1967; JD, Harvard Law School, 1970, Executive Editor, Harvard Law Review (1969-70); Law Clerk (1970-71), Honorable Irving L. Goldberg, US Court of Appeals, Fifth Circuit.

WHITE, Robert
O'Melveny & Myers LLP, Los Angeles
310 553 6700
Recommended in Insolvency

WILCOX, Kirby
Paul, Hastings, Janofsky & Walker LLP, San Francisco 415 856 7002
kirbywilcox@paulhastings.com
Recommended in Employment
Specialization: Practice involves all aspects of employment litigation and counseling for corporations.
Publications: Chief editorial consultant for the Matthew Bender treatise entitled 'California Employment Law', editorial consultant for the Matthew Bender treatise entitled 'California Guide to Employee Handbooks and Personnel Policy Manuals', and employer consultant for the Matthew Bender legal developments service entitled 'California Employment Law Reporter'.
Personal: BA, 1970 - Harvard University (cum laude); MS, 1971 - the London School of Economics; JD, 1977 - Hastings College of Law; Executive Editor of the Hastings Law Journal and externed for Federal District Judge William O Orrick.

WYMAN JR, Robert
Latham & Watkins LLP, Los Angeles
213 891 8346
robert.wyman@lw.com
Recommended in Environment
Specialization: Partner, Environment, Land and Resources Department. Firm's lead Clean Air Act counsel. Represents businesses on matters involving air quality, energy and transportation. Designed several market-based programs, including the South Coast Regional Clean Air Incentives Market. Advises clients on emissions trades, including greenhouse gas transactions and risk management. Civil and criminal defense of enforcement claims.
Prof. Memberships: Member, Clean Air Act Advisory Committee, US EPA. Board of Directors, Environmental Law Institute.
Personal: JD, University of Virginia, 1980. AB, Princeton University, 1976.

YOUNG, Doug
Farella Braun & Martel LLP,
San Francisco 415 954 4400
Recommended in Litigation

ZIFFREN, Kenneth
Ziffren Brittenham Branca Fischer Gilbert-Lurie & Stiffelman LLP,
Los Angeles 310 552 3388
Recommended in Media & Entertainment

ZISCHKE, Michael H
Morrison & Foerster LLP, San Francisco
415 268 6718
mzischke@mofo.com
Recommended in Environment
Specialization: Partner specializing in the California Environment Quality Act (CEQA) and land use litigation and compliance, covering a range of environmental impact and land use issues. Advises, counsels, and litigates on behalf of public agencies, businesses, industry developers, and lenders and investors.
Prof. Memberships: Advisor, Environmental Law Section, California State Bar; Member, Association of Environmental Professionals, California Building Industry Association, Select Committee on Industry Litigation, and the Construction Materials Association of California.
Career: Admitted to practice in California. Joined *Morrison & Foerster* in 2000 from law firm of *Landels Ripley & Diamond LLP*, where he served as Chair of the CEQA and Land Use Practice Group.
Publications: Co-author, 'Practice Under the California Environmental Quality Act' (California Continuing Education of the Bar, two volumes, 1993 supplemented annually); co-author, 'Land Use Initiatives and Referenda in California' (Solano Press, 1990).
Personal: BA, magna cum laude, Dartmouth College, 1977; JD, University of California, Berkeley, Boalt Hall, 1982.

ZOVICKIAN, Stephen
Bingham McCutchen LLP, San Francisco
415 393 2000
Recommended in Construction

CORPORATE/M&A │ COLORADO

CONTENTS: Corporate/M&A p.75; Employment: Mainly Plaintiff p.77; Mainly Defendant p.78; Litigation: General Commercial p.79; Real Estate p.81; Individuals' Profiles p.83.

COLORADO'S TOP FIVE
1. Holme Roberts & Owen
2. Holland & Hart
3. Davis Graham & Stubbs
4. Bartlit Beck Herman Palenchar & Scott
5. Brownstein Hyatt & Farber

Ranking based on Chambers' research within the state.

All quotes in the text are from interviews with clients and competitors.

OVERVIEW: Holme Roberts & Owen has one of the strongest corporate departments in the state, with work ranging from sports and entertainment to telecommunications and natural resources. It is also respected for class action employment work and is noted for its trial experience. Corporate lawyer Dean Salter is admired for his work with start-up companies. Clients include IBM and Lockheed Martin.

Colorado's largest law firm, **Holland & Hart**, has well-established roots in the state. It has been praised for its employment expertise, and has a high profile in litigation work. The firm has experienced a resurgence since the bursting of the dot.com bubble, with many local clients now tending to favor more traditional firms. Scott Barker in the litigation department is highly respected. The firm has acted for such names as AT&T and Time Warner Cable.

Davis Graham & Stubbs boasts a strong corporate practice focused on private equity and M&A. It also has an aggressive employment group. Within litigation, it is known for antitrust and trade matters. A key member of the firm is corporate lawyer Ronald Levine, credited with reshaping the firm in recent years. Clients include Union Bankshares and Microsoft.

Chicago-based **Bartlit Beck Herman Palenchar & Scott** maintains a large second office in Denver. It has one of the most respected litigation departments in the country and a high-profile national clientele. Star litigator Fred Bartlit numbers George W Bush, who used the firm during the 2000 election, among his clients. The firm also acts for Shell and Marriott International.

Brownstein Hyatt & Farber is well known as an aggressive, politically well-connected firm. Its strength lies on the corporate side, where it has several major clients. The firm also helps emerging and hi-tech companies in capital-raising efforts. It has the largest real estate group in the state, and the practice's chair Ed Barad is seen as one of the best in his field. Corporate department head Steven Siegel is described as superb. Clients include First Data and United Airlines.

CORPORATE/M&A

COLORADO
Leading firms (Corporate/M&A)

1. BROWNSTEIN HYATT & FARBER PC *Denver*
   COOLEY GODWARD LLP *Broomfield*
   HOGAN & HARTSON LLP *Denver*
   HOLME ROBERTS & OWEN LLP *Denver*
2. BARTLIT BECK HERMAN PALENCHAR *Denver*
   DAVIS GRAHAM & STUBBS LLP *Denver*
3. ARNOLD & PORTER *Denver*
   FAEGRE & BENSON LLP *Denver*
   HOLLAND & HART LLP *Denver*
   SHERMAN & HOWARD LLC *Denver*

Leading individuals (Corporate/M&A)

1. HILTON Paul *Hogan & Hartson LLP, Denver*
   LEVINE Ronald *Davis Graham & Stubbs LLP, Denver*
   LINFIELD James *Cooley Godward LLP, Broomfield*
   PALENCHAR James *Bartlit Beck Herman, Denver*
   SALTER Dean *Holme Roberts & Owen LLP, Denver*
2. HOLMES Whitney *Hogan & Hartson LLP, Denver*
   LEVY Mark *Holland & Hart LLP, Denver*
   PLUMRIDGE Richard *Holme Roberts & Owen, Denver*
   SIEGEL Steven *Brownstein Hyatt & Farber, PC, Denver*
   WHEELER Francis *Cooley Godward LLP, Broomfield*
3. BLAIR Andrew *Sherman & Howard LLC, Denver*
   FITZGERALD John *Arnold & Porter, Denver*
   STOCKS Bruce *Perkins Coie LLP, Denver*
   WRIGHT Doug *Faegre & Benson LLP, Denver*

Firms and individuals are listed alphabetically in each band.

Brownstein Hyatt & Farber, PC
The Firm: Synonymous with its deep-rooted political connections, the firm is the *"big winner on the local front."* Clients appreciated the group's ability to get things done *"without too many headaches."* Its expertise spans both public and private company M&A, leveraged buyouts, and the issue of debt and equity securities. The firm has also assisted emerging growth and hi-tech entities from seed capital through the various rounds of financing.

The Lawyers: Heading the firm's corporate department is **Steven Siegel** (see p.85), who represented Vail Resorts in its acquisition of the Heavenly ski resort in Lake Tahoe. The $100 million deal involved issues spanning two states – Nevada and California – and included water rights, land use and environmental concerns. Clients pointed to his *"superb"* legal knowledge, and endorsed his ability to combine this with practical sensibilities.

The Clients: First Data, Qwest Level 3 Communications, TeleTech Holdings and United Airlines are clients of the firm.

Cooley Godward LLP
The Firm: Taking a cue from the firm's Palo Alto headquarters, the Broomfield office concentrates on high-growth information technology and life sciences companies, as well as advising the investors and financial institutions that fund them. Though many agree that they *"have great contacts in the venture community and enjoy a substantial track record,"* the firm has, like many others, had to layoff people since the burst of dot.com bubble.

The Lawyers: Leading the Colorado operation is **James Linfield**, described by peers as *"sharp and extremely credible."* His practice centers on emerging companies and venture capital funds, in transactions involving corporate finance, strategic alliances, and M&A. He represented the underwriters in a $30 million IPO of HealtheTech in 2002. Another *"terrific"* practitioner is **Francis Wheeler**, who handled an $86 million IPO for SignalSoft and represented EFTC Corporation, now Suntron, in a private equity and tender offer transaction totaling $90 million.

The Clients: Recent transactions include an agreement between SOFTBANK and The Body Shop to develop an online business. Other clients of the firm include: UnitedGlobalCom; CH2M Hill Companies; Raindance Communications; Allos Therapeutics; Sequel Partners and The Centennial Funds.

Hogan & Hartson LLP
see firm details p.818

The Firm: Clients acknowledge *"a high degree of confidence"* in the firm's Denver office. It is one of the few remaining national firms that set up shop in Colorado during the economic boom of the early 1990's. Though focused on venture capital, the group also established a sizable bricks-and-mortar clientele, and it has benefited from

COLORADO

CORPORATE/M&A

strong ties to its operation in Washington DC. While rivals pointed to the relative youth of the group, clients proclaimed that Hogan & Hartson's attorneys have *"held their ground against the best."*
The Lawyers: **Whitney Holmes** (see p.84) was considered by one client to be *"as technically knowledgeable as anybody in Colorado."* He has advised such companies as CoorsTek on corporate and securities matters, including a $33 million public offering. He also led a $400 million IPO of Regal Entertainment Group, one of the largest movie theater chains in the US. Holmes was joined in early 2003 by **Paul Hilton**, formerly the managing partner of the Broomfield office of Brobeck, Phleger & Harrison. Rivals admired Hilton for his *"strong business sense."* He has handled a variety of complex transactional matters, including counseling boards of directors.
The Clients: The firm counseled TeleTech Holdings on a $60 million private placement transaction. Adolph Coors, CH2M Hill Companies, The Anschutz Company and AT&T Broadband also use the firm.

Holme Roberts & Owen LLP

The Firm: Interviewees agreed that this is one of the strongest corporate practices among Colorado's homegrown firms. The group was described as *"terrific,"* especially in matters relating to sports and entertainment, telecommunications and natural resources. For example, the firm represented The Anschutz Entertainment Group in a proposed redevelopment of the Millennium Dome in London as a 20,000-seat sports and entertainment arena in addition to offices and shops.
The Lawyers: **Dean Salter** has earned a loyal following among entrepreneurial pioneers, *"with a combination of intelligence and experience that sets him apart."* He primarily represents telecom and technology companies, and has also advised a cable television company in connection with its European business activities. Respected as a successful business developer, Salter has recently stepped down as chair of the firm's executive committee. **Richard Plumridge** was described to researchers as the *"brand name"* behind the now defunct Brobeck, Phleger & Harrison. He joined Holme Roberts in early 2003. His competitors credited Plumridge with an uncanny understanding of his clients' businesses, and singled out his his sound judgement as one of his most valuable legal assets.
The Clients: Adolph Coors; Qwest; United GlobalCom; TV Guide Magazine Group and Wild Oats Markets.

Bartlit Beck Herman Palenchar & Scott

The Firm: Though the firm is thought to have a more dazzling profile in litigation, it remains for many interviewees *"one of the go-to corporate practices in town."* The group successfully defended Colorado MEDtech from a hostile takeover attempt by HEI, and advised the Rocky Mountain Mezzanine Fund II in a senior debt and warrant transaction.
The Lawyers: **James Palenchar** was described as an *"exceptional"* transactional partner, and *"aggressive in all the right ways."* He represented Shell Oil in a hostile takeover bid valued at about $1.8 billion for Barrett Resources, a Denver oil and natural gas company. Palenchar specializes in M&A, securities regulation and corporate finance. He also advises on governance matters and compliance with the federal securities laws.
The Clients: The group advises Liberty Media, Gaiam, and the Public Employees' Retirement Association of Colorado.

Davis Graham & Stubbs LLP

The Firm: Peers believe that a corporate makeover in recent years can largely be attributed to one *"very skilled lawyer"* by the name of **Ronald Levine**. He led a $1.8 billion sale of HS Resources to Kerr-McGee, in a transaction that closed within *"a tight timeline so as not to miss a strategic window in the oil and gas industry."* Levine also advised Jones Intercable in its sale to Comcast, one of the largest US cable television companies, and acted for an interstate bakery in a secondary offering. Levine is said to have *"reshaped"* the firm's practice to focus on private equity and M&A.
The Clients: M2P Capital, Union Bankshares and Ultimate Electronics use the firm.

Arnold & Porter

see firm details p.765
The Firm: Experiencing *"a rise in their stock,"* the Denver office has in recent years extended its corporate practice, particularly on the private equity side. The firm combines its international reputation with regional contacts and experience, winning clients such as financial institutions, recreation and resort companies, and developers.
The Lawyers: Leading the pack is **John Fitzgerald** (see p.83), who represented such firms as Kohlberg & Co and Madison Dearborn Partners in transactions that included leveraged buyouts and venture capital financings ranging from $20 million to $1 billion. Competitors described him as *"strong"* and *"national in scope."*
The Clients: Continental Illinois Venture Corporation, American Industrial Partners and The Centennial Funds are clients of the firm.

Faegre & Benson LLP

The Firm: Attracting a list of statewide heavyweights that include McDATA, Encoda Systems and Time Warner Telecom, the corporate practice at Faegre & Benson's Denver office expanded while others were shrinking. Clients found the *"well-qualified"* team to be *"reasonable"* in its pricing structure, while competitors said the firm was one of the most effective on the local corporate front.
The Lawyers: **Doug Wright** was singled out as one of the highly skilled generalists in the market. He handed a $350 million Rule 144A transaction for Mail-Well, and acted on an acquisition of a public transportation contract for FirstGroup America.
The Clients: CH2M Hill Companies, MACTEC and Time Warner Telecom feature in the firm's client roster.

Holland & Hart LLP

see firm details p.819
The Firm: A *"fabulous"* Colorado full-service firm, it is an experienced all-rounder with established roots that branch out regionally. The team has handled such deals as a $300 million project financing transaction involving an electrical power plant and a $20 million venture capital financing project for IQNavigator.
The Lawyers: *"Adept in the technical areas,"* **Mark Levy** (see p.84) represented Crown Media Holdings in an $820 million purchase of a film library. He also completed a complex re-incorporation of the National Cattlemen's Beef Association, the marketing organization and trade association for one million cattle farmers and ranchers in the US.
The Clients: Time Warner Cable; AT&T; Aegis Analytical and Centennial Ventures are leading clients of the firm.

Sherman & Howard LLC

The Firm: Peers noted that the group has *"retooled itself for the better,"* with a clearer business strategy and additional resources. It is active in a wide variety of deals that include purchases and sales, mergers, tax-free reorganizations and leveraged buyouts. Furthermore, the firm is able to draw on other specializations such as tax, real estate, natural resources and environmental law to complement its corporate practice.
The Lawyers: One of the group's top attorneys, **Andrew Blair** has a *"broader practice than most."* He has extensive experience in handling transactions for public and private corporations, as well as partnerships and limited liability companies. Said to be *"highly knowledgeable and extremely pleasant,"* Blair is a point of contact for general corporate counsel at several large operations, including Liberty Media.
The Clients: The group advises AT&T Broadband, JD Edwards and Hathaway.

EMPLOYMENT & LABOR LAW — COLORADO

Other Notable Practitioners
"*A qualitatively good lawyer,*" **Bruce Stocks** of Morrison & Foerster LLP was praised by peers as both a skilled draftsman and a sophisticated negotiator. He closed a $400 million transaction for MACTEC, involving debt and equity issues, and advised on a number of acquisitions for Newmont Mining. Clients credited his effective representation to an ability to understand "*issues that are important from a commercial perspective.*"

EMPLOYMENT & LABOR LAW — MAINLY PLAINTIFF

COLORADO
Leading firms
(Employment: Mainly Plaintiff)

1. KILLMER & LANE *Denver*
   TRUHLAR & TRUHLAR *Littleton*
2. BERENBAUM, WEINSHIENK & EASON *Denver*
   BRAUER, BUESCHER, GOLDHAMMER *Denver*
   KING & GREISEN *Denver*
   MCNAMARA & MARTINEZ *Denver*
3. COLLISON & BECHTOLD *Denver*
   ROSEMAN & KAZMIERSKI *Denver*

Leading individuals
(Employment: Mainly Plaintiff)

1. KILLMER Darold *Killmer & Lane*, Denver
   TRUHLAR Robert *Truhlar & Truhlar*, Littleton
2. BRAUER Walter *Brauer, Buescher*, Denver
   BUCKLEY Martin *Berenbaum*, Denver
   KING Diane *King & Greisen*, Denver
   MCNAMARA Todd *McNamara & Martinez*, Denver
3. COLLISON Madeline *Collison & Bechtold*, Denver
   FEIGER Lynn *Lohf, Shaiman, Jacobs & Hyman*, Denver
   ROSEMAN Barry *Roseman & Kazmierski*, Denver

Up-and-coming individuals
CULVER John *Benezra & Culver*, Lakewood

Firms and Individuals are listed alphabetically in each band.

Killmer & Lane
The Firm: **Darold Killmer** got top billing at a firm that focuses on employment discrimination and other civil rights issues. In a 2002 published opinion in the Tenth Circuit Court of Appeals, he represented an immigrant from Ethiopia in a discrimination lawsuit. A "*knowledgeable and aggressive*" attorney, he is praised by opponents for his ability to take "*a good case and turn it into a great one.*"

Truhlar & Truhlar
The Firm: The firm has an impressive history of "*big trial*" verdicts, and has won some of the highest settlement figures in Colorado's labor and employment sector. Leading the practice is **Robert Truhlar**, who is known among peers as a "*sought-after*" and "*tireless worker*" who is "*really good at getting money out of the defendants.*" Those who have been on the other side of his legal expertise describe him as "*clearly a force,*" especially for breach of contract and discrimination claims.

Berenbaum, Weinshienk & Eason
The Firm: Renowned for its breadth and experience in labor and employment litigation, the firm has successfully prosecuted and defended age, sex, race and other discrimination matters, as well as retaliation claims and ERISA disputes. The group also advised such high-profile unions as the Teamsters, and has regularly handled labor/management issues such as contract agreements.
The Lawyers: Leading the firm's labor and employment law department is **Martin Buckley**, a former trial attorney for the US Department of Justice who has extensive experience in matters including trade secrets agreements, OSHA compliance and wrongful termination. He was commended to researchers as an "*unbelievably detail-oriented*" litigator.

Brauer, Buescher, Goldhammer, Kelman & Eckert
The Firm: One of Colorado's preeminent firms for union representation, it is known for its "*classic*" representation of unions statewide. The firm advised the International Brotherhood of Electrical Workers in a case involving bargaining issues against a public utility company. In a separate ERISA-related suit, the group represented Qwest employees who accused the company and its directors of failing to disclose the true nature of the company's financial conditions to 401(k) participants. The case is one of many class action suits filed in the wake of the collapse of Enron.
The Lawyers: **Walter Brauer** was recommended to researchers for his ability "*to recognize not only the labor side of things, but also the management side of things.*"

King & Greisen
The Firm: Cast as "*exceptional advocates,*" the team won two seven-figure verdicts within several months of each other, earning a reputation of having "*that 1% of inspiration to go with the 99% of perspiration.*" The firm has advised on cases such as an age and sex discrimination allegation involving a female superintendent of a Colorado school district. The superintendent was compensated in an undisclosed settlement.
The Lawyers: **Diane King**, the firm's "*go-getter,*" led a jury trial that resulted in a $1.5 million verdict for a female prison guard in a sexual discrimination and retaliation case.

McNamara & Martinez
The Firm: This is the firm behind some of the biggest class action verdicts in Colorado's labor and employment law sector. Leading this boutique firm is **Todd McNamara** (see p.84). He won a $2.2 million verdict in an ERISA case, the largest of its kind at the time, and later settled another similar case for $5 million. Described by competitors both as a "*sophisticated*" jurist and a "*driven*" advocate, he is respected by peers for his knowledge of the law, his ability to think on his feet and his "*pure courtroom instincts.*"

Collison & Bechtold
The Firm: Winning more than her fair share of cases involving labor and employment disputes in Colorado, **Madeline Collison** is regarded as "*the brains*" behind a number of courtroom victories. She represented 33 women truck drivers, loaders and package sorters against a national trucking company in a sex discrimination and sexual harassment case. In a separate lawsuit against the Department of Veterans Affairs, Collison argued that a developmentally disabled woman with an IQ of 72 was harassed by two individuals, one of whom was a supervisor. The woman later received compensation of $100,000.

Roseman & Kazmierski
The Firm: A firm with one eye on the public employment arena, it is said to have "*seasoned, talented lawyers*" dedicated to such issues as age discrimination, retaliation and wrongful discharge. **Barry Roseman**, "*a scholar*" of his field, is said to have built a notable practice representing employees against such government agencies as the Department of the Interior and the Department of Defense.

COLORADO

EMPLOYMENT & LABOR LAW

Other Notable Practitioners
The dean of Colorado's labor and employment law, **Lynn Feiger** of Lohf, Shaiman, Jacobs & Hyman has probably *"trained more lawyers than anybody else in the state."* Her strength is in fighting wrongful terminations and sexual harassment violations, and she has established a reputation for *"putting some bite"* into her courtroom appearances. *"A savvy guy who knows how to try cases,"* competitors singled out **John Culver** of Benezra & Culver for his impressive string of courtroom victories. He has built his reputation on multi-party and class action litigation, especially cases involving constitutional civil rights matters. He helped a client to prevail against a Colorado school district in a failure to hire case under the ADA and the Rehabilitation Act.

EMPLOYMENT & LABOR LAW

MAINLY DEFENDANT

COLORADO
Leading firms
(Employment: Mainly Defendant)

1. HOLLAND & HART LLP *Denver*
2. SHERMAN & HOWARD LLC *Denver*
3. FAEGRE & BENSON LLP *Denver*
   HOLME ROBERTS & OWEN LLP *Denver*
4. BROWNSTEIN HYATT & FARBER, PC *Denver*
   DAVIS GRAHAM & STUBBS LLP *Denver*
   HOGAN & HARTSON LLP *Denver*

Leading individuals
(Employment: Mainly Defendant)

1. HUSBAND John *Holland & Hart LLP, Denver*
   SATTLER Bruce *Faegre & Benson LLP, Denver*
2. DEENY Ray *Sherman & Howard LLC, Colorado Springs*
   EURICH Gregory *Holland & Hart LLP, Denver*
   OADE Preston *Holme Roberts & Owen LLP, Denver*
3. ARO Edwin *Hogan & Hartson LLP, Denver*
   POWELL David *Brownstein Hyatt & Farber, Denver*
   STACY David *Elzi Pringle Gurr & Stacy, Denver*
4. NEWCOM Charles *Sherman & Howard LLC, Denver*
   SATRIANA Dan *Hall & Evans, LLC, Denver*
   SIEBERT Bernie *Sherman & Howard LLC, Denver*

Individuals are listed alphabetically in each band.

Holland & Hart LLP
see firm details p.819
The Firm: Described to researchers as a management-side labor and employment *"powerhouse,"* the firm is driven by a *"definitive collection of high-caliber attorneys"* with a revered name in Colorado for combining legal *"book smarts"* with no-nonsense *"practicalities."* The group won praise from clients and competitors for its traditional labor expertise, and is still considered to have *"real depth and scope,"* despite the recent loss to Brownstein Hyatt & Farber of David Powell.
The Lawyers: **John Husband** (see p.84) is regarded as a *"precedent-setting"* attorney whose cases dealing with wrongful discharge and employment torts have earned him a reputation for linking intellectual sophistication with commercial sense. He successfully defended two recent major class action lawsuits, the first for UPS and the second, in a claim totaling more than $200 million, for one of the world's biggest oil companies. Class certification was denied in both cases. **Gregory Eurich** (see p.83) *"is just about as good as they get,"* according to contemporaries. His forte is in labor disputes litigation and he has defended a variety of employers against claims of race, sex and age discrimination. Besides his solid grip on the law, peers and clients noted the *"oomph"* in his personality, which is particularly perceived to appeal to juries.
The Clients: Clients include: AT&T; Storage Technology; Agilent Technologies and Albertson's.

Sherman & Howard LLC
The Firm: The only major firm in Colorado to represent employers alone, it boasts one of the most comprehensive labor and employment practices in the Rocky Mountain region, including a separate group focusing on employee benefits and other administrative matters. The firm's courtroom victories include defending a large insurance firm and an aerospace company in sexual harassment claims as well as a disability discrimination lawsuit in which an employee's contract was terminated following an on-the-job injury. The group also has a number of specialists in areas such as OSHA/MSHA and is perceived to be *"at the forefront"* of the ERISA market.
The Lawyers: **Ray Deeny**, cited to researchers as *"probably the firm's best labor and employment lawyer,"* is known for his *"bulldog toughness"* in the courtroom. In one employment defamation trial in which Deeny represented one of the largest US grocery chains, the jury returned a defense verdict after 15 minutes of deliberation. In addition, he has been successful in throwing out dozens of claims relating to the ADA. **Charles Newcom**'s main focus is on wrongful discharge, but he has also developed a highly regarded practice deciphering MSHA regulations. His *"sophisticated"* approach to investigations into on-the-job fatalities and other safety-related matters has earned him a reputation among clients for being *"good at finding business solutions to a problem."* **Bernie Siebert** has *"considerable experience"* of labor defense, successfully negotiating contracts for clients such as the United Steelworkers. He also defended a top Colorado employer against discrimination and unfair labor charges.
The Clients: Other clients include Hertz, Liberty Media, Wal-Mart, Newmont Mining and Eastman Kodak.

Faegre & Benson LLP
The Firm: The Denver branch of the Minneapolis-based firm is powered by *"a strong presence in intellectual property"* and such personalities as Charles Weese, a former senior attorney for Qwest's labor and employment group before he joined the firm as special counsel. The group represented an established software company in a trademark dispute involving two former programmers who went to work for a competitor.
The Lawyers: **Bruce Sattler** is *"all over the map"* of Colorado's employment defense sector. A noted generalist who is at home in the courtroom and as a mediator, he is said to have the *"ability to resolve a case in the best interest of his clients."* In addition to a staple of ADA and wrongful discharge claims, he handled a workplace violence matter in which an employee turned up for a termination meeting with a handgun.
The Clients: Clients include Qwest, University of Denver and Xcel Energy.

Holme Roberts & Owen LLP
The Firm: One of the most experienced in taking on class action employment matters, the firm is felt by competitors to stand out for its trial experience. The team has also handled labor matters such as contract administration, disputes and collective bargaining negotiations for a variety of clients, including professional sports teams.
The Lawyers: Heading the firm's employment practice is *"great fighter"* **Preston Oade**, who has more than 100 trials to his credit. Defending CoorsTek, a manufacturer of semiconductor components, he defeated an attempt to certify a class action suit claiming sexual discrimination, harassment and retaliation. One of the five plaintiffs' cases was thrown out and the company settled with the other four for about $5,000 each. His ability *"to see at an early point how a case will play out"* earned widespread client plaudits.
The Clients: Clients include Lockheed Martin, IBM and The Denver Post.

Brownstein Hyatt & Farber, PC
The Firm: Not traditionally a strong presence in Colorado's employment law sector, the firm benefits from a strong corporate clientele and became *"a force to be reckoned with"* after hiring one of Holland & Hart's best employment lawyers,

LITIGATION — COLORADO

David Powell (see p.85).

The Lawyers: Powell is regarded by peers as *"one of the most down-to-earth defense attorneys in Denver,"* he focuses on the employer-employee relationship, including wrongful discharge, disability, sexual harassment, and discrimination. In one sexual harassment claim, he was not only successful in defending an insurance company, but also won a breach of contract counter claim in which a jury awarded the company more than $20,000.

The Clients: The firm successfully defended United Airlines in a race discrimination case, and has niche expertise in contract-related issues. Other clients include Level 3 Communications and Xcel.

Davis Graham & Stubbs LLP

The Firm: An excellent corporate client base and a solid team including the respected Janet Savage have contributed to the employment reputation of a firm that was characterized to researchers as *"aggressive to the nth degree."* The team is devoted to trial work and counseling, often assisting clients to devise employee handbooks, drug- and alcohol-testing programs and personnel policies.

The Clients: The firm has defended companies against wrongful termination claims and represents employers in various labor issues, including NLRB proceedings.

Hogan & Hartson LLP
see firm details p.818

The Firm: The firm's employment group in Denver is felt to have grown into a *"good healthy practice"* since the arrival of the esteemed **Ed Aro** (see p.83) and an accompanying raft of heavyweight clients. The team has enjoyed a string of victories in defending companies against discrimination claims, one of which involved a high-level executive at WorldCom who quit after he was demoted for poor performance, alleging that he suffered unduly harsh disciplinary retaliation because of his age.

The Lawyers: Aro, who is one of six directors of the firm's international labor and employment practice, won a defense verdict in the WorldCom case. He also has considerable experience in intellectual property issues and does substantial work in areas relating to non-competition agreements.

The Clients: Clients include National Renewable Energy Laboratory, Janus Capital and Sun Microsystems.

Other Notable Practitioners

Elzi Pringle & Gurr's **David Stacy** (see p.85) is noted by peers for his *"good instincts."* Described to researchers as *"a natural litigator,"* he won two defense verdicts for Qwest within a period of 18 months, one involving race discrimination and the other a sexual-orientation discrimination case. **Dan Satriana** of Hall & Evans LLC was commended to researchers as a top employment trial lawyer who can take on *"any case and win it."* He has defended employers in claims of wrongful discharge, discrimination, FLSA and Colorado Wage Act violations, as well as covenants not to compete and constitutional torts.

LITIGATION — GENERAL COMMERCIAL

COLORADO
Leading firms
(Litigation: General Commercial)

1. DAVIS GRAHAM & STUBBS LLP *Denver*
   HOLLAND & HART LLP *Denver*
   JACOBS, CHASE, FRICK, KLEINKOPF *Denver*
2. BARTLIT BECK HERMAN PALENCHAR *Denver*
   HILL & ROBBINS *Denver*
   HOLME ROBERTS & OWEN LLP *Denver*
   ROTHGERBER JOHNSON & LYONS LLP *Denver*
3. FAEGRE & BENSON LLP *Denver*
   HOFFMAN REILLY POZNER *Denver*
   KELLY HAGLUND GARNSEY & KAHN *Denver*

Leading individuals
(Litigation: General Commercial)

1. CHASE Jeffrey *Jacobs, Chase, Frick, Kleinkopf, Denver*
   HILL Robert *Hill & Robbins, Denver*
   LYONS James *Rothgerber Johnson, Denver*
2. BARTLIT Fred *Bartlit Beck Herman, Denver*
   BLACK Bruce *Holme Roberts & Owen LLP, Denver*
   CERIANI Gary *Davis & Ceriani, Denver*
3. HARRIS Dale *Davis Graham & Stubbs LLP, Denver*
   REILLY Daniel *Hoffman Reilly Pozner, Denver*
   THOMASCH Roger *Ballard Spahr Andrews, Denver*
4. BARKER Scott *Holland & Hart LLP, Denver*
   GARNSEY Walter *Kelly Haglund Garnsey, Denver*
   MCCARTHY Michael *Faegre & Benson LLP, Denver*
   MILLER Gale *Davis Graham & Stubbs LLP, Denver*

Firms and individuals are listed alphabetically in each band.

Davis Graham & Stubbs LLP

The Firm: Within this broad-based practice, our researchers identified specializations that include conflicts arising from internal corporate investigations and derivative actions. One of the firm's main attractions is its antitrust and trade group, which is home to two of the top antitrust litigators in the state. It also has *"excellent support from mid-level and junior partners."*

The Lawyers: Headlining the antitrust practice is **Dale Harris**, a *"prince of a lawyer,"* who is said to possess a remarkable ability to stake out winning positions. He has represented major corporates such as Goodyear, and has also argued for a small rock concert promoter in a federal suit which alleged that a major communications company was using its radio ownership to attain a commercial advantage. Harris has *"the presence and the gravitas"* for major trials. **Gale Miller** is a *"go-to lawyer; particularly strong on the paper aspects of a case."* He has gained broad experience from his time at the FTC. Among his recent highlights, Miller defended Microsoft in an antitrust class action involving Colorado consumers.

The Clients: Qwest; Microsoft; Goodyear; Johns Manville and The Trane Company.

Holland & Hart LLP
see firm details p.819

The Firm: Cutting-edge technology and *"great coverage"* in legal expertise were the two main attributes cited by interviewees who ranked the firm at the top of its field. It is adept at handling high-profile plaintiffs' cases, and boasts a host of specialist practice areas, including a department dedicated to the natural resources sector. Attorneys have tackled issues as esoteric as Native American fishing rights, while the firm's high-stakes litigation includes interstate water rights. The firm is considered a force in intellectual property law, claiming one of the largest jury verdicts in US history in a computer software piracy case. The department employs a full-time trial consultant and has its own graphics studio and multimedia center for creating courtroom exhibits. The firm is also praised for its handling of a business dispute, winning a $125 million verdict in a case involving fraud, fraudulent conveyances and breach of contract claims in Webb County, Texas.

The Lawyers: **Scott Barker** (see p.83) was recommended for being *"just as smart as can be."* He has argued a water rights dispute for ARCO, and also led a $50 million environmental insurance coverage case involving five wood treatment plants.

The Clients: Among others, the firm advises: AT&T; ICG Telecom Group; Lockheed Martin Idaho Technologies and the Nez Pierce Tribe.

Jacobs, Chase, Frick, Kleinkopf & Kelley

The Firm: Both peers and clients acknowledge that the firm punches above its weight, providing a *"top-notch"* service. Diligent litigators who *"turn over every rock,"* the group of ten focuses on commercial litigation, with a strong track record on defense matters.

COLORADO

LITIGATION

The Lawyers: One of the luminaries is **Jeff Chase**, who was described to researchers as a *"number one stand-up comedian, in addition to being a brilliant trial lawyer."* Chase has argued heated issues such as international breach of contract, the theft of trade secrets and intellectual property rights. He is said to be able to take the cases that others consider *"a bit of a reach"* and achieve *"amazing"* results. The group also includes a former Denver deputy district attorney and a former court-appointed attorney who helped defend Terry Lynn Nichols in the Oklahoma Bombing case.
The Clients: Qwest, US West and Colorado Rockies are leading clients of the firm.

Bartlit Beck Herman Palenchar & Scott
The Firm: One of the nation's most dynamic litigation boutiques, the Chicago-based firm's second home in Denver benefits from the reflected glory. It brings a senior partner-led approach to its cases and was endorsed for producing litigators steeped with trial experience.
The Lawyers: The star of the firm, **Fred Bartlit**, splits his time between Chicago and Denver and serves a national clientele, including George W Bush in the 2000 election contest. Besides Bartlit's impressive client list and potent trial skills, opponents admire his ability to focus on the endgame. When he takes to the courtroom, it's like *"a lone gunman coming into the city at high noon."* While some expressed reservations that he's *"not quite as homespun as I would want in a Denver courtroom,"* he was overwhelmingly voted as one of the best for the bet-your-company variety of commercial disputes. He successfully represented MediaOne Group in a contract dispute against US West in front of a three-member arbitration panel, and defended United Technologies in an antitrust case.
The Clients: GM, Hughes Aircraft, Shell and Marriott International are leading clients of the firm.

Hill & Robbins
The Firm: A gem in complex commercial litigation, the seven-strong team specializes in court battles that require strategic solutions. With three attorneys concentrating solely on water laws, the firm is known for venturing into such high-profile disputes as a water rights conflict between the States of Colorado and Kansas over the Arkansas River.
The Lawyers: The firm represented Black Hawk, a historic mining town, in a court battle with its neighbor in a case to decide whether to permit gambling. The lead counsel in that case, **Robert Hill**, is said to be not only *"extraordinary"* in the courtroom, but also *"able to diffuse a dispute before it goes to trial."* A *"first-rate lawyer,"* he has successfully handled several securities fraud matters and was involved in a high-profile pension suit affecting about 3,500 employees, which concerned age discrimination in a cash balance plan.
The Clients: The firm advises Lloyd's and the State of Colorado.

Holme Roberts & Owen LLP
The Firm: Particularly recommended for its work in the oil and gas field, the practice has acted on an array of commercial litigation matters, including antitrust regulations, securities fraud and derivative actions.
The Lawyers: Among the strongest of the group is **Bruce Black**, who formerly worked in the antitrust division of the US Department of Justice. A *"first-rate litigator,"* he is respected for his experience in antitrust, securities and mail fraud. Black has *"great judgment"* and *"the ability to weed out what should, and should not, be put in front of a jury."*
The Clients: The firm advises financial institutions, underwriters, broker-dealers, public and private companies.

Rothgerber Johnson & Lyons LLP
The Firm: Principally recommended because of its star litigator **James Lyons** (see p.84), the firm is known for its representation of *"heavyweights"* in cases *"when it's more than a zero-sum game."*
The Lawyers: James Lyons won a $25 million jury verdict in a case against Goodyear involving a defective product, and successfully defended Denver International Airport in several class action lawsuits involving bond issues. He has also represented Triple Peaks, a ski resort company based in Vermont, in a breach of purchase agreement. Rivals pointed to his well-established connections to prominent politicians, including former President Bill Clinton, in addition to his courtroom abilities. He is known for multiparty litigation in which there's *"a lot to be done behind the scenes."*
The Clients: GE and Anthem Blue Cross and Blue Shield of Colorado are examples of the firm's clientele.

Faegre & Benson LLP
The Firm: This *"thriving"* office derives an advantage from a strong regional supporting network. Although it offers a broad range of litigious experience, the group has also established a niche in hi-tech matters. It acted on such issues as a trade secret dispute involving two computer programmers who left one software company to work for a competitor.
The Lawyers: A key figure at the firm, **Michael McCarthy** was described as *"aggressive, with a keen sense of what to expect from a jury."* He was lead counsel for the Colorado Rockies baseball team in a number of matters, including a bankruptcy court fraudulent transfer claim involving valuation of the Rockies franchise. He also advised a prominent cable television company in a federal class action suit, asserting securities fraud and breach of fiduciary duty claims.
The Clients: State Farm Insurance, Colorado Rockies and the Vail Valley Foundation are clients of the firm.

Hoffman Reilly Pozner & Williamson
The Firm: One of the most *"aggressive"* and respected boutiques for commercial litigation, it is lead counsel to plaintiffs in a series of class action suits against Qwest involving delays in the installation of telephone services. The firm's 12-strong group also defended Lockheed Martin in an age discrimination allegation, and represented NFL ticket holders in a class action suit against the franchise.
The Lawyers: Among the firm's crème de la crème, peers identified **Daniel Reilly** as an *"absolutely meticulous"* litigator. He was lead plaintiffs' counsel in a multi-state fraud lawsuit against a stock brokerage firm. The case involved four jury trials and resulted in a global settlement of more than $30 million.
The Clients: The firm acts for GE, Shell Chemicals and The Gates Corporation.

Kelly Haglund Garnsey & Kahn
see firm details p.828

The Firm: A litigation boutique that routinely handles *"a mixed bag of things,"* its experience runs the gamut, including election redistricting cases, Indian tribal land disputes and First Amendment matters. For instance, the firm defended a software manufacturer against allegations that one of the company's computer games had led to criminal behavior among teenagers who were exposed to the violent scenarios.
The Lawyers: The firm's expertise varies widely and includes a former Sierra Club Defense Fund lawyer, a First Amendment specialist and an attorney experienced in representing the American Civil Liberties Union. Adjudged by peers *"the firm's best lawyer,"* **Walter Garnsey** (see p.83) acted on behalf of Indian tribe officials in a suit against an oil company, which involved gasoline pipeline construction on tribal land. The case settled for about $2.5 million in addition to a substantial commitment by the oil company to restore some land. Garnsey also counseled a national bank in a pension-related matter alleging breach of fiduciary duties.
The Clients: Novartis and the New England Patriots Football Club are examples of the firm's clients.

Other Notable Practitioners
Gary Ceriani of Davis & Ceriani has been described to researchers as a *"piranha with a sense of humor"* and *"a lone practitioner with a lot of intestinal fortitude."* He won high praise for his

REAL ESTATE — COLORADO

powers of persuasion in front of a jury. Ceriani led a federal breach of fiduciary contest that resulted in an $8.5 million jury verdict for his clients, and successfully tried a case against a stock brokerage company and its underwriter for statutory and negligent misrepresentation claims. An Oklahoma jury awarded two mutual fund companies more than $22 million in that case. *"There aren't too many curveballs he hasn't seen,"* a client said. **Roger Thomasch**, leader of the litigation section of Ballard Spahr Andrews & Ingersoll, gained a respected following among *"out-of-town clients."* They cited his *"feel for juries"* and *"great judgments"* as the reason he was used for complex litigation. He defended Goodyear in products liability trials, one of which involved a product used in heating systems. He also represented the University of Colorado in a patent dispute.

REAL ESTATE

COLORADO
Leading firms (Real Estate)

1. OTTEN, JOHNSON, ROBINSON, NEFF *Denver*
2. BROWNSTEIN HYATT & FARBER PC *Denver*
   SHERMAN & HOWARD LLC *Denver*
3. HOLME ROBERTS & OWEN LLP *Denver*
   ISAACSON, ROSENBAUM, WOODS *Denver*
4. BALLARD SPAHR ANDREWS *Denver*
   FAEGRE & BENSON LLP *Denver*
   JACOBS, CHASE, FRICK, KLEINKOPF *Denver*
   STEINER DARLING & HUTCHINSON LLP *Denver*

Leading individuals (Real Estate)

1. BROWN Robert *Sherman & Howard LLC, Denver*
   ROBINSON Frank *Otten, Johnson, Robinson Denver*
2. BARAD Edward *Brownstein Hyatt & Farber, PC, Denver*
   CARPENTER Willis *Carpenter & Klatskin, Denver*
   STEINER Beat *Steiner Darling, Denver*
   STERNBERG John *Otten, Johnson, Robinson, Denver*
3. BACH Robert *Holme Roberts & Owen LLP, Denver*
   LOTTNER Alan *Lottner Rubin Fishman, Denver*
   PERMUT Barry *Isaacson, Rosenbaum, Denver*
   SENN Mark *Senn Lewis & Visciano, Denver*
4. CALVIN Charles *Faegre & Benson LLP, Denver*
   CULHANE James *Davis Graham, Denver*
   FIELDS Leslie *Faegre & Benson LLP, Denver*
   JACOBS Paul *Jacobs, Chase, Frick, Kleinkopf, Denver*
   QUAIL Beverly *Ballard Spahr Andrews, Denver*
   RAGONETTI Thomas *Otten, Johnson, Denver*
   SAMUELS JONES Karen *Gorsuch Kirgis, Denver*

Firms and individuals are listed alphabetically in each band.

Otten, Johnson, Robinson, Neff & Ragonetti, PC

The Firm: A firm that *"lives and breathes real estate,"* it was said to be a pitch above its competitors with its breadth of practice and depth of expertise. The 26-member group includes a civil engineer, a city and regional planning academic and a specialist in the representation of institutional lenders. The firm has advised on the financing of hotels, office buildings, raw land acquisitions and bond issues. Representative deals included a $100 million acquisition of a low-income housing tax credit business, and a $250 million construction credit line led by KeyBank National Association. The group also advised on a 711-unit apartment project financed through a $54 million bond issue by the State of Oregon Health, Housing, Educational and Cultural Facilities Authority. Interviewees agreed: *"They're good business lawyers and also excellent technicians."*

The Lawyers: The team's primary deal-maker is **Frank Robinson**, whose *"engineering and surveying background really shows."* A registered land surveyor, his expertise spans *"financing, to dispositions, to almost anything anybody has ever done."* **John Sternberg** is counsel to some of the nation's largest developers. He advised on several redevelopments in downtown Albuquerque, Minneapolis, Phoenix and San Francisco. A *"favorite"* among the real estate bar, Sternberg's *"acute eye for that crucial issue that others will miss"* has been a fulcrum for his success in areas such as site acquisition, leasing, construction financing and disposition work. **Thomas Ragonetti** is the firm's intellectual authority on land use law, and was endorsed as the point man for getting governmental approvals. Though rivals warned that he can be more assertive than necessary, they credited him with *"a clear knowledge of the local community."*

The Clients: Frontier Airlines; GE Capital; Bank of America Commercial Finance and US Bank National Association.

Brownstein Hyatt & Farber, PC

The Firm: Hailed by the competition as the most politically connected firm in Colorado, it *"is organized to do terrific things"* for its much-envied clientele, which includes Vail Associates, Trammell Crow Company and Shea Homes of Colorado. The 35-strong group – the largest in the state – boasts a host of specialists, in fields that include zoning and land use, water rights and matters pertaining to mineral resources.

The Lawyers: Peers pointed to **Ed Barad** (see p.83) as one of the most knowledgeable attorneys on the state's real estate bar. Chair of the real estate group, he led the disposition of AT&T Broadband's headquarters and a $50 million 80-acre land acquisition near Oakland, California. Sources agreed: *"Ed is smart, thoughtful and clients love him."*

The Clients: The firm acts for: SunAmerica; Bank One; US WEST; CSFB and Wells Fargo Realty Advisors.

Sherman & Howard LLC

The Firm: Regarded as one of the pillars of the real estate bar in Colorado, the firm's reputation spans the gamut, including acquisitions, sales and lending matters. The group is respected for its work on resort developments and multi-state transactions. For instance, the firm represented ski areas in connection with permitting requirements before the USDA Forest Service. It also advised a Cleveland bank with respect to loans to Colorado developers.

The Lawyers: One of the firm's top-flight attorneys is **Robert Brown**, *"who not only knows the substance of the law, but also the business."* This ability to analyze risks in terms of market forces has enhanced his profile in matters such as defaulted loans, workouts, foreclosures and receiverships. He advises both financial institutions and corporates, and has a specialization in advising franchisers and franchisees. Brown is handling the development of a 70-acre medical facility, which includes a 150-bed hospital and offices for Kaiser Permanente in Denver.

The Clients: Exempla Heathcare, MassMutual and Ohio Savings Bank are leading clients of the firm.

Holme Roberts & Owen LLP

The Firm: This solid group of accomplished practitioners has a full-service reputation, which is firmly grounded in the Rocky Mountain region. Peers acknowledge that the firm fields *"lawyers who know their stuff."* The group represented developers in projects such as two public-private partnerships to build student apartments at the University of Colorado in Denver and the University of Northern Colorado in Greeley. The firm counseled Stapleton Development in the rezoning of the Stapleton Airport site, formerly the city's main airport, prior to the opening of Denver International Airport.

The Lawyers: Straddling both real estate and banking law, **Robert Bach** was singled out by rivals as a good generalist, whose *"gentle personality"* makes him an effective negotiator. A forte of his is financing, and he has advised on a $40 million syndicated credit facility to a restaurant operator, and a $52.5 million syndicated credit facility for the construction of a timeshare, retail and condominium project.

COLORADO

REAL ESTATE

The Clients: The firm acts for Amgen, Silver Creek Holding Co. and Southern Pacific Transportation Company.

Isaacson, Rosenbaum, Woods & Levy, PC
The Firm: Rooted in real estate ever since its conception, the firm is linked to some of the biggest transactions in Colorado. Projects included the University of Colorado at Boulder Research Park, a four-building downtown complex in Denver and the Hyatt Regency Denver. Clients described the 15-lawyer group as providing *"more bang for the buck."* They appreciated its diversity, which includes niche practices in municipal real estate law, land conservation and preservation of open space.
The Lawyers: Heading the real estate department is **Barry Permut** who was endorsed for his ability to *"quickly distill a transaction into important highlights – he doesn't get caught up in the unnecessary details."* He was the lead attorney in a $25 million sale, which included a substantial roll-up provision, and has counseled the construction lender in the Hudson Bay Center and Tabor Center. He also represented the developer of Colorado Sporting Clubs. *"He doesn't let his ego come into play. He's just smart, knows what's right and gets things done,"* one competitor said.
The Clients: Bank of America, University of Colorado, Miller Global Properties and the Colorado Coalition of Land Trusts use the firm.

Ballard Spahr Andrews & Ingersoll
see firm details p.769
The Firm: Though it is a full-service real estate practice, the group attracts accolades for its tackling of complex financing transactions. In recent years, the firm served as underwriters' counsel in dozens of bond issues totaling more than $13 billion for the construction and refinancing of Denver International Airport. Interviewees commended it as *"a stronghold in terms of volume of deals and exposure in the community."* The group also handled the $600 million tax-exempt financing for public improvement of a 4700-acre site that was formerly the city's airport. Other deals include a $54 million bond issue for a 500,000 sq ft World Port cargo facility, and $78 million worth of bonds for the development of car rental facilities.
The Lawyers: **Beverly Quail** is credited with being *"responsible for the progress of the real estate practice."* She is respected for her development and financing work and peers described her as *"creative – she makes a deal work."* She is active in some of the firm's most high-profile transactions, including mixed-use projects in Denver.
The Clients: Stapleton Development and the City of Denver are among the firm's clients.

Faegre & Benson LLP
The Firm: With an eminent domain and land use practice that *"shines,"* the firm's Denver branch represented the City of Black Hawk in the acquisition of large tracts of land for the construction of water treatment facilities. In other transactions, the firm counseled a UK affiliate of a Canadian bank in a $140 million construction loan for a downtown Denver office building. It also advised an electronics manufacturer in the development and resale of a 160-acre training campus.
The Lawyers: **Leslie Fields** is *"the first choice for eminent domain,"* according to peers and clients. He heads a group of four lawyers who focus on the niche area, in addition to eight others in the department. Fields, who won land, mineral and water rights for the Denver International Airport, also represented private landowners both in prosecuting and defending the condemnation of properties. Competitors also singled out **Charles Calvin** as *"one of the most knowledgeable, smartest real estate lawyers in Colorado"* whose intellectual capabilities can sometimes overshadow a practical solution. Calvin juggles both real estate and banking transactions, with a specialty in dealing with complex problems such as attaining a difficult easement that allowed a condominium developer to use a portion of a neighboring property. He's also counseling a non-profit organization on a hospital proposal costing an estimated $250 million.
The Clients: The group advised such companies as Xcel Energy, VoiceStream and Telluride Real Estate Corporation

Jacobs, Chase, Frick, Kleinkopf & Kelley
The Firm: This is a versatile boutique with a bumper crop of high-profile clients. It fields a group of specialists who *"can handle any kind of transaction."* The firm advised Intrawest on the development of ski resorts in Colorado and golf courses in Arizona, and acted for a national biotech company with its corporate campus in Arapahoe County, Colorado. The group attracted clients who were impressed with the firm's *"superior level of competence."* The team includes an attorney who focuses on transportation and utility issues, such as joint-use agreements.
The Lawyers: The firm's managing partner, **Paul Jacobs**, advises on stadium developments and other high-profile matters. He also has experience in development projects such as resorts, industrial parks, shopping centers and hotels. He clinched a deal to build a new baseball stadium in San Diego, and represented the City of Denver in the redevelopment of Union Station. Jacobs is respected as a *"mentor"* to many of the 14 lawyers in the real estate group.
The Clients: Qwest, Union Pacific, Sage Hospitality Resources and Destination Hotels & Resorts are leading clients of the firm.

Steiner Darling & Hutchinson
The Firm: Admired for keeping even the most *"demanding clients"* happy, the five-attorney group attracts *"complex transactions that have unusual aspects to them."* For instance, the firm handled the 22,000-acre planned residential community development of Highlands Ranch, and advised on another project consisting of 21 multimillion dollar homes set near the Telluride ski resort.
The Lawyers: **Beat Steiner** was praised by peers as a creative craftsman for tackling groundbreaking issues. He succeeded in drafting a 25-year vested rights agreement allowing IBM to have its own powerhouse on a $2.5 million campus in Boulder, a city known for its antidevelopment stance. *"Head and shoulders above the rest,"* according to one client, Steiner also advised on the Buffalo Run housing development, a Whole Foods Market grocery store and the headquarters of Frontier Airlines at Denver International Airport.
The Clients: Shea Homes and Wells Fargo use the firm.

Other Notable Practitioners
The first and last word in title matters, **Willis Carpenter** of Carpenter & Klatskin was commended by peers as *"extremely good on the technical side."* He was also referred to as the beacon of the Colorado real estate bar and the definitive source for matters relating to farms and ranches. **James Culhane** *"is strongest in the home-building area,"* and was deemed the point of reference for projects that are *"inherently complicated."* Culhane, of Davis Graham & Stubbs LLP, handled the acquisition and development of a Broomfield corporate campus, the sale of the Pepsi Center sports arena and a $350 million property lease. **Alan Lottner** of Lottner Rubin Fishman Brown & Saul PC has carved a name for himself in commercial acquisition, disposition and leasing work. Though peers believe *"his strong personality doesn't necessarily fit everybody,"* they conceded that his *"intense"* intellect benefits clients in the long run. Lottner has closed deals involving apartment complexes, office buildings and shopping centers in various states, including Colorado, Texas, California and Arizona. **Karen Samuels Jones** of Gorsuch Kirgis LLP was classified by peers as *"a hard worker who knows the business well"* and is reasonable in negotiations. Proficient in real estate lending, she represented Wells Fargo, Bank One and Allstate in loans for projects such as shopping centers, condominiums and office buildings. **Mark Senn** of Senn Lewis & Visciano *"wrote the book"* on leasing matters. He has a *"tremendous international grasp of the issues that come up in leasing,"* and has secured hundreds of leasing deals all over the country, involving office complexes, shopping centers and other commercial establishments. *"He's the best tenant lawyer I've ever come across,"* claimed one rival.

COLORADO

Leaders in Colorado

ARO, Edwin
Hogan & Hartson LLP, Denver
303 899 7389
eparo@hhlaw.com
Recommended in Employment
Specialization: Partner in the firm's Litigation Group, and a Practice Group Director of its Labor and Employment Group. A trial lawyer who represents businesses in employment, intellectual property and commercial litigation matters.
Career: Law Clerk to the Hon Richard Matsch, United States District Court for the District of Colorado. Joined *Hogan & Hartson LLP* in 1998, after nine years with *Holme Roberts & Owen LLP*. Adjunct Law Professor at the University of Denver since 1994.
Personal: Born 20 July 1964, in Colorado Springs, Colorado. BA University of Denver. JD, magna cum laude, Boston University School of Law. Member and Editor, 'Boston University Law Review'.

BACH, Robert
Holme Roberts & Owen LLP, Denver
303 861 7000
Recommended in Real Estate

BARAD, Edward N
Brownstein Hyatt & Farber, PC, Denver
303 223 1108
ebarad@bhf-law.com
Recommended in Real Estate
Specialization: Practices real estate law with emphasis on commercial development and finance and co-chairs the firm's Real Estate Group. Extensive experience representing developers and lenders in commercial real estate transactions. Representative clients include: Wyndham International, Inc., US West Real Estate, Inc., Forest City Development, Cherokee Partners, SIMEON Commercial Properties, Credit Suisse First Boston, Shea Homes of Colorado, AT&T/Comcast, Ellman Companies, Pacifica Holding Company, HealthONE.
Prof. Memberships: Elected Member Board of Governors, American College of Real Estate Lawyers, Colorado & American Bar Association, Sections of Real Property Law; Chairman, Legislative, Speaker's Bureau Committees; Co-Chairman, Opinion Letter Standards Committee, Colorado Bar Real Estate Section; Chairman, Rules Subcommittee, Colorado Bar Ethics Committee; Hearing Examiner, Supreme Court Grievance Committee; Vice-Chairman, Opinion Letter Subcommittee University of Colorado Real Estate Council.
Career: A shareholder at *Brownstein Hyatt & Farber*. Wrote the rules Colorado Bar Ethics Committee. Former chairman and principal draftsman for the committee that published the Colorado Standards for Mortgage Loan Opinion Letters.
Personal: Received a JD from the University of Colorado School of Law, 1973, and a BS from the University of Colorado, 1969.

BARKER, Scott
Holland & Hart LLP, Denver
303 295 8513
sbarker@hollandhart.com
Recommended in Litigation
Specialization: Partner practicing in complex civil litigation, with experience in more than 60 trials, one third of which were to juries. Cases tried in Colorado, Wyoming, Idaho, New Mexico, California and Washington. Extensive experience in complex litigation, including class actions.
Prof. Memberships: American College of Trial Lawyers (Fellow), International Association of Defense Counsel, American Bar Association, Colorado Bar Association, Denver Bar Association, American and Colorado Bar Foundations.
Career: Admitted to Colorado Bar (1981). Past Chair of *Holland & Hart's* Management Committee.
Personal: Received a JD from Harvard University (1981) and a BA from the US Air Force Academy (1970). Rhodes Scholar.

BARTLIT, Fred
Bartlit Beck Herman Palenchar & Scott, Denver 303 592 3100
Recommended in Litigation

BLACK, Bruce
Holme Roberts & Owen LLP, Denver
303 861 7000
Recommended in Litigation

BLAIR, Andrew
Sherman & Howard LLC, Denver
303 297 2900
Recommended in Corporate/M&A

BRAUER, Walter
Brauer, Buescher, Goldhammer, Kelman & Eckert, Denver 303 333 7751
Recommended in Employment

BROWN, Robert
Sherman & Howard LLC, Denver
303 297 2900
Recommended in Real Estate

BUCKLEY, Martin
Berenbaum, Weinshienk & Eason, Denver 303 825 0800
Recommended in Employment

CALVIN, Charles
Faegre & Benson LLP, Denver
303 592 9000
Recommended in Real Estate

CARPENTER, Willis
Carpenter & Klatskin, Denver
303 534 6315
Recommended in Real Estate

CERIANI, Gary
Davis & Ceriani, Denver 303 534 9000
Recommended in Litigation

CHASE, Jeffrey
Jacobs, Chase, Frick, Kleinkopf & Kelley, Denver 303 685 4800
Recommended in Litigation

COLLISON, Madeline
Collison & Bechtold, Denver
303 388 4551
Recommended in Employment

CULHANE, James
Davis Graham & Stubbs LLP, Denver
303 892 9400
Recommended in Real Estate

CULVER, John
Benezra & Culver, Lakewood
303 716 0254
Recommended in Employment

DEENY, Ray
Sherman & Howard LLC, Colorado Springs 719 475 2440
Recommended in Employment

EURICH, Gregory
Holland & Hart LLP, Denver
303 295 8166
geurich@hollandhart.com
Recommended in Employment
Specialization: Partner practicing in labor law, with particular emphasis on litigation of labor disputes. Work has included defending major clients against claims of race, sex, age, disability and national origin discrimination, actions involving collective bargaining agreements, and wrongful discharge claims in lawsuits before state and federal trial and appellate courts in much of the Western United States. Lead trial counsel in nearly 100 trials, a substantial portion of which have been jury trials. Lead trial counsel in a successful challenge to constitutionality of amendment to Colorado's constitution prohibiting civil rights to gays and lesbians known as Evans v. Romer, 516 US 620 (1996).
Prof. Memberships: Colorado Supreme Court Committee on Pattern Jury Instructions (1997-present), Colorado Pledge to Diversity Law Firm Group (Co-Chair), Colorado Trial Lawyers Association, The Association of Trial Lawyers of America, Defense Research Institute, Colorado Defense Lawyers Association.
Career: Admitted to the Colorado and US District Court, District of Colorado (1973), US Court of Appeals, Tenth Circuit (1977) and US Supreme Court.
Personal: Received JD from the University of Michigan (Magna Cum Laude, Order of the Coif) in 1973 and a BA from the University of Michigan (Cum Laude, Phi Beta Kappa) in 1970.

FEIGER, Lynn
Lohf, Shaiman, Jacobs & Hyman, Denver 303 753 9000
Recommended in Employment

FIELDS, Leslie
Faegre & Benson LLP, Denver
303 592 9000
Recommended in Real Estate

FITZGERALD, John
Arnold & Porter, Denver 303 863 2331
John_Fitzgerald@aporter.com
Recommended in Corporate/M&A
Specialization: Corporate and transactional attorney. He practices in the areas of venture capital, leveraged buyouts, mergers and acquisitions, and corporate finance matters. He is a partner in the Washington, DC and Denver offices of *Arnold & Porter*. In the private equity area (both venture capital and leveraged buyouts). Advises clients on a full range of legal matters, including fund formation, acquisition structuring, and acquisition financing, as well as tax and regulatory issues implicated by these matters. Other significant private equity practice components involve leveraged 'buildups' or 'roll-ups' which are, in effect, consolidations of companies in a certain industry, and structuring private equity transactions that minimize any adverse tax impact and maximize tax deferral of portfolio company investments. His practice also involves assisting clients with general merger and acquisition legal work, for both private and public companies. More than 40 of these transactions have involved financial institutions (banks, thrifts, mortgage companies, and consumer finance firms).

GARNSEY, JR, Walter W
Kelly Haglund Garnsey + Kahn, Denver
303 296 9412
wgarnsey@khgk.com
Recommended in Litigation
Specialization: Member of *Kelly Haglund Garnsey + Kahn LLC* specializing in complex commercial litigation in federal and state courts, administrative agencies, and arbitration tribunals. Commercial litigation emphasis on the law of contracts, business entities (eg corporations, limited liability companies, and partnerships), financial institutions, securities, construction, and real estate. Additional emphasis on employment litigation and land use matters under federal Indian law. One of only 1880 United States attorneys listed in all editions of a

COLORADO — LEADERS

leading legal publication since initial publication in 1983.
Prof. Memberships: Fellow, American College of Trial Lawyers; Member, American, Colorado, and Denver Bar Associations.
Career: Associate, *Holland & Hart* (Denver, Colorado): 1971-73; Trial Attorney, Denver Regional Litigation Center, Equal Employment Opportunity Commission: 1973-1974; Member, *Kelly Haglund Garnsey + Kahn LLC*: 1974-present.
Personal: Born April 1, 1945; Stanford University Law School, JD 1971; Yale University, BA (cum laude) 1967.

HARRIS, Dale
Davis Graham & Stubbs LLP, Denver
303 892 9400
Recommended in Litigation

HILL, Robert
Hill & Robbins, Denver 303 296 8100
Recommended in Litigation

HILTON, Paul
Hogan & Hartson, Denver
303 899 7389
Recommended in Corporate/M&A

HOLMES, Whitney
Hogan & Hartson LLP, Denver
303 454 2420
wholmes@hhlaw.com
Recommended in Corporate/M&A

Specialization: Partner in the Denver office of *Hogan & Hartson LLP*, specializing in public and private securities and corporate finance, mergers and acquisitions. Represents a broad spectrum of companies in venture capital financings, initial public offerings, secondary offerings, and private placements of equity and debt securities, as wells as all aspects of friendly and hostile acquisitions, asset acquisitions, mergers, leveraged buyouts, joint ventures, and proxy contests. He frequently represents public and private companies in financing transactions, including bank credit financing and public and private placements of debt securities, reporting obligations under federal securities laws and general corporate governance matters.
Prof. Memberships: American Bar Association. Colorado Bar Association. Chairman, Securities Law Subsection of the Business Law Section of the Colorado Bar Association, September 2002 to present.
Career: Practiced for 12 years, including eight for *Willkie Farr & Gallagher* in New York City, before joining *Hogan & Hartson* in 1999.
Publications: A frequent speaker on SEC, corporate governance, mergers and acquisitions and corporate finance issues.
Personal: Received his law degree, magna cum laude, from Cornell Law School in 1987 and served as note editor of the 'Cornell International Law Journal'. Received undergraduate degree in English Literature from Pomona College in 1984.

HUSBAND, John
Holland & Hart LLP, Denver
303 295 8228
jhusband@hollandhart.com
Recommended in Employment

Specialization: Partner practicing in labor and employment law. He has been involved in hundreds of cases, has extensive judicial and administrative experience, has tried cases in 20 states and been lead trial counsel in over 250 adversarial proceedings, trials, major arbitrations or administrative actions that have been tried to conclusion. He advises on a range of employment matters, including class action lawsuits, wrongful discharge, equal employment opportunity, trade secrets and covenants not to compete, wage and hour, privacy, disability, occupational safety, affirmative action and the law involving collective action, strikes, unions and collective bargaining.
Prof. Memberships: Fellow to the College of Labor and Employment Lawyers, American Bar Association (Employee Rights and Responsibilities Committee, Management Advisory Committee, Co-Chair Publications Sub-Committee, Editor of ER&R Committee Newsletter), The Colorado Lawyer (column editor), Colorado Employment Law Letter (Editor),The Colorado Safety Association (Director and Officer), National Labor Relations Board (Practices and Procedures Committee for Region 27), University of Toledo, College of Law (Board of Governors), Leadership Denver Association.
Career: Admitted to Ohio Bar (1977) and Colorado (1978).
Personal: Received a JD from University of Toledo (1977) and a BS from Ohio State University (1974).

JACOBS, Paul
Jacobs, Chase, Frick, Kleinkopf & Kelley, Denver 303 685 4800
Recommended in Real Estate

KILLMER, Darold
Killmer & Lane, Denver 303 571 1000
Recommended in Employment

KING, Diane
King & Greisen, Denver 303 298 9878
Recommended in Employment

LEVINE, Ronald
Davis Graham & Stubbs LLP, Denver
303 892 9400
Recommended in Corporate/M&A

LEVY, Mark
Holland & Hart LLP, Denver
303 295 8073
mlevy@hollandhart.com
Recommended in Corporate/M&A

Specialization: Has substantial experience with securities laws. Assists public companies with ongoing compliance with securities laws, including periodic reports, proxy statements, press releases, Section 16 requirements, Rule 144 sales, fiduciary duties and other matters. Also works on public and private offerings. Substantial experience in the acquisitions and dispositions of a variety of small and large businesses, bank loans and other private financings, the formation and operation of corporations and general business agreements.
Prof. Memberships: Member, Federal Regulation of Securities and Law and Accounting Committees of the Section of Business Law, American Bar Association (1995-present); Chairperson (1999-2000) and member, Colorado Bar Association Convention Committee (1998-2001); Member, Article 8 of the Uniform Commercial Code Committee, Colorado Bar Association (1995-1996); Co-chairman, Colorado Bar Association's Securities Law Review Committee (prepared the Colorado Securities Act enacted in 1990); Member, chairperson (1994-95), the Alumni Board of Directors for the University of Colorado Law School (1992-96); Member, Rockies Venture Club; and Member, American Society of Corporate Secretaries.
Career: Admitted to Colorado Bar (1972).
Personal: Received a JD from University of Colorado (1972, Order of the Coif) and a BA from the University of Colorado (1968).

LINFIELD, James
Cooley Godward LLP, Broomfield
720 566 4000
Recommended in Corporate/M&A

LOTTNER, Alan
Lottner Rubin Fishman Brown & Saul, PC, Denver 303 292 1200
Recommended in Real Estate

LYONS, James M
Rothgerber Johnson & Lyons LLP,
Denver 303 628 9546
jlyons@rothgerber.com
Recommended in Litigation

Specialization: Specializes in complex business litigation and arbitration of all types, recently including corporate, environmental, and securities law. He has more than 30 years of courtroom and jury trial experience in state and federal courts. He also has extensive government relations and international trade experience from his work in Ireland and the United Kingdom. Recent clients include The Anschutz Corporation, Bell Canada Enterprises, the City and County of Denver, General Electric, HealthOne, Rocky Mountain Health Care (Blue Cross and Blue Shield of Colorado and New Mexico), and Triple Peaks Ski Corporation.
Prof. Memberships: Fellow, American College of Trial Lawyers; Fellow, International Academy of Trial Lawyers; Named to Best Lawyers in America (Business Litigation); Master Barrister, Doyle's Inn Chapter of the American Inns of Court; Member of the Colorado, Denver, and Illinois Bar Associations.
Career: Admitted to Colorado, Illinois, US District Court, District of Colorado, US District Court, Northern District of Illinois, US Court of Appeals, Seventh and Tenth Circuits and US Supreme Court. He is Senior Trial Partner with the law firm of *Rothgerber Johnson & Lyons LLP*, where he has been associated since 1971. He is an instructor with the University of Denver College of Law, the University of Colorado School of Law, and the National Institute of Trial Advocacy. Recently completed his service as Special Advisor to the President of the United States and the Secretary of State for Economic Initiatives in Ireland, 1997-2001. Prior to this role, President Clinton appointed him as United States Observer, International Fund for Ireland, 1993-2001. He served as general counsel for the Office of President-Elect William Jefferson Clinton from November 1992 to January 1993.
Personal: Honorary Doctor of Laws (LLD) in 2002 from the University of Ulster, Belfast, Northern Ireland. Received a JD from DePaul University College of Law in 1971 where he was associate editor of the DePaul Law Review. Received a BA from the College of the Holy Cross in 1968.

MCCARTHY, Michael
Faegre & Benson LLP, Denver
303 592 9000
Recommended in Litigation

MCNAMARA, Todd
McNamara & Martinez LLP, Denver
303 333 8700
tjm@mcmarlaw.com
Recommended in Employment

Specialization: The shareholder in charge of a mid-sized firm's employment law section for approximately 10 years. Opened own firm, 1995, and limits practice exclusively to employment law matters. Was lead class counsel in Wilkerson et al v Martin Marietta, the largest age discrimination claim brought within the state of Colorado. The case settled for a reported $7.6 million. In LaSalle v PSCo., secured one of the largest ERISA judgments in the state on behalf of 90 plaintiffs. That claim, as well as the companion 151 plaintiff ERISA case, ultimately settled. Soon thereafter, secured the first race discrimination case verdict in the United States against a real estate franchise for failure to award a sales agency to an African-American in Tyler v Remax. Was co-counsel in Vaszlavik v StorageTek, a 400+ plaintiff age discrimination class action which settled in 2000 for $5 million. This year, served as counsel in another landmark ERISA class action, Piet et al v Lontine, et al, which settled for $4.8 million. Has consistently secured the

COLORADO

largest, or among the largest, class action and multi-plaintiff judgments and settlements in Colorado over the past five years. Lectures frequently both within Colorado and nationally on a variety of employment law issues. Reported cases include: Tyler v Remax, 232 F.3d 808 (10th Cir. 2000); Fuller, et al v Pep Boys, 888 F Supp 2d 1158 (D. Colo. 2000); Jandro v Foster, 53 F. Supp. 2d 1058 (D. Colo. 1999); LaSelle, et al v Public Service, 988 F.Supp. 1348 (D. Colo. 1997); Vaszlavik, et al v Storage Tech. Corp., 175 F.R.D. 672 (D. Colo. 1997); Wilkerson, et al v Martin-Marietta Corp., 875 F.Supp. 1456 (D. Colo. 1995), 171 F.R.D. 273 (D. Colo. 1997); Bronk v US West, 943 F.Supp. 1317 (D. Colo. 1996), 140 F.3d 1335 (10th Cir. 1998); Antonelli, et al v. Public Service, 24 BPR 2274 (1998).
Prof. Memberships: Panel of Arbitrators, American Arbitration Association; Panel of Mediators, American Arbitration Association; American Bar Association; Colorado Bar Association; Federal Bar Association; Association of Trial Lawyers of America; National Employment Lawyers Association; Plaintiff's Employment Lawyers Association (Board of Directors).
Career: Admitted to the Colorado and New York Bar Associations (1980); admitted to the US District Court, District of Colorado and Southern District of New York; US Court of Appeals, 10th Circuit.
Publications: Co-Author: 'Federal Employment Jury Instructions - Supplement' (James Publishing, 2002, 2001 and 2000); 'Federal Employment Jury Instructions' (James Publishing, 1999); 'EEOC Procedures Regarding Timely Issuance of Notices of Right to Sue' (Colorado Lawyer, 2000); 'Go the Distance - Maximizing Your Recovery of Attorneys Fees and Costs' (Trial Talk, 1998).
Personal: Received a JD (cum laude) from St. John's University School of Law in 1979 and a BA (magnum cum laude) from Chaminade College in 1974.

MILLER, Gale
Davis Graham & Stubbs LLP, Denver
303 892 9400
Recommended in Litigation

NEWCOM, Charles
Sherman & Howard LLC, Denver
303 297 2900
Recommended in Employment

OADE, Preston
Holme Roberts & Owen LLP, Denver
303 861 7000
Recommended in Employment

PALENCHAR, James
Bartlit Beck Herman Palenchar & Scott, Denver 303 592 3100
Recommended in Corporate/M&A

PERMUT, Barry
Isaacson, Rosenbaum, Woods & Levy, PC, Denver 303 292 5656
bpermut@irwl.com
Recommended in Real Estate

PLUMRIDGE, Richard
Holme Roberts & Owen LLP, Denver
303 861 7000
Recommended in Corporate/M&A

POWELL JR, David D
Brownstein Hyatt & Farber, PC, Denver
303 223 1157
dpowell@bhf-law.com
Recommended in Employment
Specialization: Co-chair of the Employment Group at *Brownstein Hyatt & Farber*, specializing in the counsel and defense of employers on a variety of matters arising from the employer-employee relationship, including wrongful discharge, disability and family leave issues, sexual harassment and discrimination based on race, national origin, gender and age. Has handled significant litigation matters on behalf of employers in both state and federal courts. A frequent lecturer and a former editor of the 'Colorado Employment Law letter'. Past recipient of the Richard Marden Davis Award.
Prof. Memberships: Member, American Bar Association; Member, Colorado Bar Association; Editor, Colorado Employment Law Letter; Board Member, Faculty of Federal Advocates; Member, National Bar Association; Member, Sam Cary Bar Association; Member, Community Advisory Board, Rocky Mountain Public Broadcasting System; Former Member, Board of Trustees, Colorado School of Mines; Frequent lecturer at seminars on employment-related topics.
Career: A shareholder at *Brownstein Hyatt & Farber*. Served as a Deputy District Attorney for over three years in the Denver District Attorney's Office before joining the Denver office of *Holland & Hart, LLP* as a partner.
Personal: Received a JD from UCLA Law School in 1983, while serving as one of the Managing Editors of the UCLA Law Review. Acquired a BA from the University of Santa Clara in 1980.

QUAIL, Beverly
Ballard Spahr Andrews & Ingersoll LLP, Denver 303 292 2400
Recommended in Real Estate

RAGONETTI, Thomas
Otten, Johnson, Robinson, Neff & Ragonetti, PC, Denver 303 825 8400
Recommended in Real Estate

REILLY, Daniel
Hoffman Reilly Pozner & Williamson, Denver 303 893 6100
Recommended in Litigation

ROBINSON, Frank
Otten, Johnson, Robinson, Neff & Ragonetti, PC, Denver 303 825 8400
Recommended in Real Estate

ROSEMAN, Barry
Roseman & Kazmierski, Denver
303 839 1771
Recommended in Employment

SALTER, Dean
Holme Roberts & Owen LLP, Denver
303 861 7000
Recommended in Corporate/M&A

SAMUELS JONES, Karen
Gorsuch Kirgis LLP, Denver
303 376 5000
Recommended in Real Estate

SATRIANA, Dan
Hall & Evans, LLC, Denver
303 628 3300
Recommended in Employment

SATTLER, Bruce
Faegre & Benson LLP, Denver
303 592 9000
Recommended in Employment

SENN, Mark
Senn Lewis & Visciano, Denver
303 298 1122
Recommended in Real Estate

SIEBERT, Bernie
Sherman & Howard LLC, Denver
303 297 2900
Recommended in Employment

SIEGEL, Steven
Brownstein Hyatt & Farber, PC, Denver
303 223 1150
sssiegel@bhf-law.com
Recommended in Corporate/M&A
Specialization: Head of the firm's Corporate & Securities Group, concentrating on mergers and acquisitions, leveraged buy-outs, public and private securities offerings, senior and subordinated debt financings, restructurings and general corporate advice for both public and private entities, including start-ups. Successfully completed multiple transactions with a variety of clients, including Vail Associates, Starwood Hotels, Apollo Real Estate Advisors, Gart Sports Company, Greenspun, Inc., Kohlberg & Company, KRG Capital Partners, Celerity Partners, The Wellbridge Company, Corporate Express, Inc., and Ascent Corporation.
Prof. Memberships: Member, American Bar Association; Member, New York Bar Association; Member, State Bar of Colorado; Member, Colorado Association of Corporate Counsel.
Career: Practicing at *Brownstein Hyatt & Farber* since 1995. Shareholder and member of the firm's Management Committee. Prior to joining the firm, partner at the New York office of *Kirkland & Ellis*.
Personal: Received a JD from The University of Chicago Law School, 1987, and a BS, magna cum laude, from the Wharton School of the University of Pennsylvania, 1984, Benjamin Franklin Scholar.

STACY, David
Elzi Pringle Gurr & Stacy, Denver
303 623 9111
dstacy@elzigurr.com
Recommended in Employment
Specialisation: Management labor and employment law, litigation and trials. Is a trial lawyer whose practice for the past 25 years has focused on labor and employment law, the protection of confidential and proprietary business information, and commercial litigation. Has tried in excess of 30 jury cases and numerous court trials and arbitrations, many on behalf of the largest corporations in the United States. Regularly defends claims of race, gender, age, religious and sexual orientation discrimination, workplace harassment, wrongful discharge and breach of contract before state and federal trial and appellate courts. He also counsels employers concerning performance management, investigations, employee health issues, discipline, reductions in force, and other aspects of the employment relationship. Has represented litigants in matters relating to trade secrets, the misappropriation of confidential business information, unfair competition, and the enforcement of noncompetition and nonsolicitation agreements and other legal rights relating to unfair business practices. Has presented numerous seminars on employment law and trial tactics to lawyers, law students, clients and industry groups.
Prof. Memberships: Colorado Bar Association (Labor & Employment Section, Co-Chair 1998-2000); (Litigation Section, 1992 Civil Litigator of the Year); Denver Bar Association; Faculty of Federal Advocates; Fellow, Colorado Bar Foundation.
Career: *Elberger, Stacy, Smith & Martin* (1979-1996); *Parcel, Mauro, Hultin & Spaanstra* (1996-1998); *Freeborn & Peters* (1998-2000); *Davis, Graham & Stubbs* (2000-2001); *Elzi, Pringle, Gurr & Stacy* (2001-Present).
Publications: Contributing editor, 'Federal Employment Jury Instructions', James Publishing, Inc., 1999; chapter author, 'Litigation of Employment Cases', The Practitioner's Guide to Colorado Employment Law, Continuing Education in Colorado, Inc., 1998; 'Edmondson: Dramatic Changes in the Use of Peremptory Challenges,' Colorado Lawyer, 1991.
Personal: Married to Meredith Moore Stacy, September 12, 1981; son, Michael David Stacy, DOB: September 27, 1982.

COLORADO
LEADERS

STEINER, Beat
Steiner Darling & Hutchinson LLP, Denver
303 837 2380
Recommended in Real Estate

STERNBERG, John
Otten, Johnson, Robinson, Neff & Ragonetti, PC, Denver 303 825 8400
Recommended in Real Estate

STOCKS, Bruce
Perkins Coie LLP, Denver
303 291 2322
Recommended in Corporate/M&A

THOMASCH, Roger
Ballard Spahr Andrews & Ingersoll LLP, Denver 303 292 2400
Recommended in Litigation

TRUHLAR, Robert
Truhlar & Truhlar, Littleton
303 794 2404
Recommended in Employment

WHEELER, Francis
Cooley Godward LLP, Broomfield
720 566 4000
Recommended in Corporate/M&A

WRIGHT, Doug
Faegre & Benson LLP, Denver
303 592 9000
Recommended in Corporate/M&A

CORPORATE/M&A

CONNECTICUT

CONTENTS: Corporate/M&A p.87; Employment: Mainly Plaintiff p.88; Mainly Defendant p.88;
Litigation: General Commercial p.89; Real Estate p.91; Individuals' Profiles p.92.

CONNECTICUT'S TOP FOUR
1. Day Berry & Howard
2. Robinson & Cole
3. Wiggin & Dana
4. Cummings & Lockwood

Ranking based on Chambers' research within the state.

All quotes in the text are from interviews with clients and competitors.

OVERVIEW: Top-ranking **Day Berry & Howard** is Connecticut's biggest and most visible firm. It receives a high volume of business and appears as counsel in many of the largest cases tried in the state. Historically litigation-driven and very aggressive, the firm has the bodies and the resources for big, expensive cases. Within labor and employment, the firm boasts some highly regarded litigators. The firm has been given an opportunity to display its depth in real estate following the retirement of some respected individuals. The firm is also noted for being strong on corporate governance and SEC compliance. In commercial litigation, Thomas Groark is described as a superb litigator. Clients include ITT Industries and CSFB.

Robinson & Cole, a sophisticated and highly esteemed firm, ranks second. The firm is undisputed leader in real estate where it is recommended for size and across-the-board quality. On the corporate side, the practice is strong in midmarket transactions and particularly active within the manufacturing and financial services sectors. Dwight Merriam is a key expert on the real estate team, while Alan Spier is respected for his venture capital advice. Clients include United Technologies and Pfizer.

Traditional Connecticut firm **Wiggin & Dana** rates highly for depth and full-service capacities. The commercial litigation practice is recommended for franchise and antitrust work, while the firm's employment team is said to offer high-quality advice. Commercial litigator William Doyle is much admired, as is Peter Lefeber in the employment group. Clients include GE Capital and Arthur Andersen.

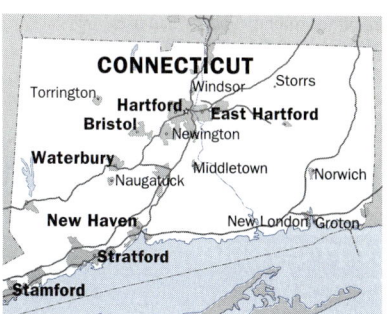

Cummings & Lockwood enjoys a first-class reputation for transactional corporate work. The practice handles a large volume of midmarket transactions but also works on larger corporate financings. The litigation department is growing steadily in size and strength. M&A practice chair James Lotstein is highly praised, while employment team leader Richard Voigt is considered probably the best OSHA lawyer in the state. Clients include Aetna and GE.

CORPORATE/M&A

CONNECTICUT
Leading firms (Corporate/M&A)
1. FINN DIXON & HERLING LLP *Stamford*
2. CUMMINGS & LOCKWOOD *Hartford*
   ROBINSON & COLE LLP *Hartford*
3. DAY, BERRY & HOWARD LLP *Hartford*

Leading individuals (Corporate/M&A)
1. FINN Harold *Finn Dixon & Herling LLP, Stamford*
2. LOTSTEIN James *Cummings & Lockwood, Hartford*
   MARCO Frank *Mintz Levin Cohn Ferris, New Haven*
   SPIER Alan *Robinson & Cole LLP, Hartford*

Firms and individuals are listed alphabetically in each band.

Finn Dixon & Herling LLP
see firm details p.794
The Firm: This *"corporate boutique"* has strengthened its M&A capabilities through the recruitment of Jon Hirschoff from Tyler Cooper & Alcorn LLP. Commentators agree that it leads the market in M&A, corporate finance and securities, operating from under the umbrella of the firm's business practice. A *"terrific"* stable of prestigious national corporate clients in part accounts for its *"first-tier status."*
The Lawyers: A *"cutting-edge"* corporate team is headed by name partner **Harold Finn** (see p.93). Rivals are fulsome in their praise for this *"New York veteran;"* they regard him as *"among the best in the business."*
The Clients: National private equity houses, multinationals and privately held midmarket corporations use the firm.

Cummings & Lockwood
The Firm: This *"high-quality"* Hartford firm receives general commendation as one of Connecticut's leading corporate practices. The team attracts particular mention for handling a volume of mid-market transactions, but has also proven itself in larger corporate financings. Attorneys advised on the Travelers' spin-off from Citigroup in a $4 billion IPO of 23% common equity – one of the largest domestic IPOs in the insurance sector.
The Lawyers: Practice chair **James Lotstein** is esteemed as a *"gifted"* corporate generalist. Particularly praised for his analytical and leadership skills, Lotstein was said to *"facilitate complex statewide transactions."* He represented Neschen in its purchase of Hunt Corporation's graphics division, and advised Gerber Scientific in the sale of Stereo Optical to Essilor International.
The Clients: The department counseled Aetna in the sale of its healthcare business to ING Group. Other clients include: CUNO; GE; Gerber Scientific; Travelers and The Thomson Corporation.

Robinson & Cole LLP
The Firm: A traditional Connecticut heavyweight with acknowledged muscle in midmarket transactions. The firm enjoys a constant diet of M&A, routinely closing between five and ten deals a year in the $15-100 million bracket. A substantial share of the Hartford practice involves transactions within the manufacturing and financial services sectors. Attorneys were recommended to researchers as *"savvy deal-makers."*
The Lawyers: At the forefront of the team is **Alan Spier**, well regarded for his advice to venture capital-financed companies. Peers described Spier as a *"smart"* corporate specialist who *"knows how to move a transaction forward."*
The Clients: MedSpan used the firm for its $18 million sell-off to Oxford Health Plans. Attorneys also counseled a pharmaceutical company in a complex venture capital financing. Other clients include: The Stop & Shop Supermarket Company; Pfizer; United Technologies; The TJX Companies and Boehringer Ingleheim.

Day, Berry & Howard LLP
The Firm: A *"top business firm"* with noteworthy strength in corporate governance and SEC compliance. The Greenwich branch is well known for a focus on investor and hedge fund clients. However, the firm handles a range of transactional work from offices in Greenwich, Hartford and Stamford.
The Lawyers: Paula Lacey Herman chairs the mergers and acquisitions group from the Hartford office.
The Clients: Attorneys advised Northeast Utilities and its affiliates in multibillion dollar financings and Rule 144A issues. The firm is also counsel for ITT Industries' acquisitions, and advises EDO, a manufacturer of electronic equip-

CONNECTICUT

EMPLOYMENT & LABOR LAW

ment for military and civilian use.
Other Notable Practitioners
Frank Marco of Mintz Levin Cohn Ferris Glovsky & Popeo PC is a venture capital specialist. He represents investors and emerging growth companies in capital formation and is especially renowned for his work with technology clients. Transactional advice includes CiDRA's sale of its divisions to Halliburton for $130 million.

EMPLOYMENT & LABOR LAW — MAINLY PLAINTIFF

CONNECTICUT
Leading firms
(Employment: Mainly Plaintiff)
1. GARRISON, LEVIN-EPSTEIN CHIMES *New Haven*
   LIVINGSTON ADLER PULDA MEIKELJOHN *Hartford*

Leading individuals
(Employment: Mainly Plaintiff)
1. GARRISON Joseph *Garrison, Levin-Epstein*, New Haven
2. ADLER Gregg *Livingston Adler Pulda Meikeljohn*, Hartford
   DE TOLEDO Victoria *Casper & de Toledo*, Stamford
   ELDERGILL Kathleen *Beck & Eldergill*, Manchester
3. GOLUB David *Silver Golub & Teitell LLP*, Stamford
   LIVINGSTON Daniel *Livingston Adler Pulda*, Hartford

Firms and Individuals are listed alphabetically in each band.

Garrison, Levin-Epstein Chimes & Richardson PC
The Firm: This specialist boutique firm was recommended to researchers as *"one of the best firms in the state"* for employment law matters. Attorneys handle trial and appellate cases in both the state and federal courts. Non-litigation matters also form part of the workload.
The Lawyers: *"Outstanding"* **Joseph Garrison** is considered a *"class act"* among plaintiff attorneys. An *"educator"* as well as a lawyer, Garrison *"fights hard for his clients, but also brings a practical nous"* to his cases. His practice includes private arbitration work for executives involving contract interpretation and age discrimination matters. Past cases include discrimination at work (Heller v Champion International) and a review of a jury verdict centered on standards for granting a motion for a new trial (Farrior v Town of Waterford).

Livingston Adler Pulda Meikeljohn & Kelly PC
The Firm: This boutique practice confines itself to labor law, and can often be found representing labor unions. Its reputation for defending minority and progressive groups is recognized on a national level.
The Lawyers: **Gregg Adler** is well known among rivals as a *"terrific opponent"* whose *"laid-back approach"* has secured a wide following. **Daniel Livingston** is equally respected as a *"forceful and clever advocate."*
The Clients: Connecticut Women's Education & Legal Fund, Connecticut Citizen's Action Group and labor unions.

Other Notable Practitioners
The *"aggressive but compassionate"* **Victoria de Toledo** of Casper & de Toledo LLC received plaudits for her trial work on behalf of employees and organizations. **Kathleen Eldergill** (see p.92) of Beck & Eldergill PC *"understands the law inside out"* and is a *"persuasive and compelling"* trial lawyer. She takes a special interest in government employees and claims brought under the Civil Rights Act or the First Amendment. *"Knowledgeable and creative"* **David Golub** at Silver Golub & Teitell LLP represents plaintiffs in discrimination, ERISA and other employment-related actions in state and federal courts.

EMPLOYMENT & LABOR LAW — MAINLY DEFENDANT

CONNECTICUT
Leading firms
(Employment: Mainly Defendant)
1. DAY, BERRY & HOWARD LLP *Hartford, Stamford*
2. SHIPMAN & GOODWIN LLP *Hartford*
   WIGGIN & DANA LLP *New Haven*
3. DURANT, NICHOLS, HOUSTON HODSON *Bridgeport*
   JACKSON LEWIS *Stamford*
4. CUMMINGS & LOCKWOOD *Hartford*
   SIEGEL, O'CONNOR, ZANGARI *Hartford*

Firms are listed alphabetically in each band.

Day, Berry & Howard LLP
The Firm: Adjudged by peers to be *"litigation-oriented,"* the firm is found by some commentators to be *"aggressive"* in its approach. The firm boasts one of the largest labor practices in the state and has a strong following within the Connecticut hi-tech market. Senior attorneys are supported by a *"great back-up team"* and routinely advise management clients on restrictive covenants and employee discrimination suits. Class actions involving claims of discrimination and ERISA violations feature prominently in the group's workload. The firm is experienced in alternative dispute resolution (ADR), and tries labor cases in its thriving educational practice.
The Lawyers: Felix Springer was described to researchers as the *"reflex choice"* for clients. Chair of the employment department, he has argued in state and federal appellate courts, and counsels management on the use of ADR. Peers regard **Albert Zakarian** as *"an honorable opponent,"* with a *"sterling reputation"* in employment law. He was highly recommended for his trial skills. **Daniel Schwartz** was singled out for his *"depth of knowledge,"* particularly in the telecom, manufacturing and insurance markets.
The Clients: United Technologies; Northeast Utilities; Aetna US Healthcare; A&P Supermarkets and Verizon.

Shipman & Goodwin LLP
The Firm: Although smaller than competitors, this boutique practice rates highly for its record in labor defense matters. A broad spectrum of labor experts make up an *"extremely strong"* practice. The team is well known for its work on collective bargaining issues for a large base of public employers, both in and out of state. Research found that healthcare institutions frequently consult attorneys here on matters regarding benefits for state employees. The firm also provides counsel on non-litigious labor relations. Attorneys represent the state in connection with unionization of the judicial branch of local government.
The Lawyers: A *"first-tier"* management labor lawyer, **Brian Clemow** enjoys much public exposure for his media profile as a legal expert. Peers describe him as an *"accomplished"* attorney whose work in union relations spans both the public sector and manufacturers. Clemow defended a lawsuit brought against Governor Rowland involving the replacement of 4000 striking nursing home employees.
The Clients: Trinity College; University of Hartford; Hartford Hospital; education boards; schools and colleges; manufacturers; banks; insurance companies; healthcare providers and utilities.

EMPLOYMENT & LABOR LAW — CONNECTICUT

CONNECTICUT
Leading individuals
(Employment: Mainly Defendant)

1
- SPRINGER Felix *Day, Berry & Howard LLP,* Hartford
- ZAKARIAN Albert *Day, Berry & Howard LLP,* Hartford

2
- CLEMOW Brian *Shipman & Goodwin LLP,* Hartford
- DURANT Terry *Durant, Nichols, Houston,* Bridgeport

3
- CLOHERTY Thomas *Murtha Cullina LLP,* Hartford
- O'BRIEN George *Tyler Cooper & Alcorn LLP,* New Haven

4
- KEE Conrad *Jackson Lewis,* Stamford
- LEFEBER Peter *Wiggin & Dana LLP,* New Haven
- SCHWARTZ Daniel *Day, Berry & Howard,* Stamford
- VOIGT Richard *Cummings & Lockwood,* Hartford
- ZANDY John *Wiggin & Dana LLP,* New Haven

Individuals are listed alphabetically in each band.

Wiggin & Dana LLP
The Firm: Interviewees recommend the firm for *"consistently high-quality advice."* The practice advises on all aspects of labor and employment matters, including ADR, discrimination, labor relations, OSHA, wage and hour compliance, compensation and harassment.

The Lawyers: **Peter Lefeber** was commended to researchers as one of the *"leading lights"* of the practice. His clients include manufacturers, insurance companies, utilities and healthcare organizations. The *"no-nonsense"* **John Zandy** chairs the employment and benefits department. He acts for employers in the healthcare, technology and service industries, specializing in contract negotiations and terminations. Zandy arbitrated during a month-long strike by unions at a local university, in a case that went to the Second Circuit Court of Appeals.

The Clients: Clients are also drawn from the biotech, construction, financial services, retail, cable television, publishing and education industries.

Durant, Nichols, Houston Hodson & Cortese-Costa PC
The Firm: This *"well-thought-of boutique"* represents clients from the manufacturing, construction and financial services industries as well as healthcare institutions, educational facilities and municipalities. The team was noted for a focus on traditional labor defense, in both union and non-union environments.

The Lawyers: Senior figure **Terry Durant** was described to researchers as *"a class act and a gentleman."* A former chairman of the Connecticut Bar Association, he is commended for his *"astute advice and regulatory wisdom."*

The Clients: Norwalk Hospital; AIG; City of New Haven; New Haven Housing Authority; Chubb Specialty Insurance; United Aluminum; Southern Connecticut Gas; Town of Oxford; Roncalli Health Care System; Scasco Energy and St. Vincent's Medical Center.

Jackson Lewis
The Firm: Known for a *"combative and litigious style,"* the firm is widely considered an employment law *"heavyweight."* A statewide reputation has attracted both national clients and a large share of Connecticut insurance companies. Attorneys possess experience in a variety of discrimination and breach of contract claims and appear in jury and bench trials at state and federal levels. The team also advises companies on collective bargaining issues.

The Lawyers: **Conrad Kee** practices from the firm's Stamford office. Commentators particularly remarked on the *"quality"* of his management defense work.

The Clients: The firm represents public and private businesses and nonprofit institutions.

Cummings & Lockwood
The Firm: Offers the full range of litigation services in addition to consultation and preventative strategies for business clients. Attorneys mediate in unfair labor practice proceedings before the NLRB and have experience in contractual arbitration proceedings. Other areas of expertise include advising on state and federal court injunctive actions, wrongful discharge and discrimination cases.

The Lawyers: *"Outstanding"* attorney **Richard Voigt** leads the team from the Hartford office. A former US Department of Labor official, Voigt was judged by peers to be *"probably the best OSHA lawyer in the state."*

The Clients: The firm has advised GE, Northeast Utilities and Pitney Bowes on employment matters.

Siegel, O'Connor, Zangari, O'Donnell & Beck PC
The Firm: This *"well-established"* labor boutique was commended for its representation of employers before the Connecticut Commission on Human Rights and Opportunities, and the EEOC. Lawyers advise on union-organizing drives, NLRB representation hearings, unfair labor practices and collective bargaining negotiations. Jury and bench trial successes include Kondrat v International Paper Company, Vasquez v New Britain General Hospital and Toroh v Bairnco.

The Lawyers: Richard O'Connor is the firm's managing partner for labor and employment matters.

The Clients: Kollmorgen; Fordham Distributors; Eaton; Grange Investments; State of Connecticut Department of Higher Education; Town of Southington; Town of Vernon; New Britain General Hospital and various boards of education.

Other Notable Practitioners
Thomas Cloherty at Murtha Cullina LLP brings *"vast experience"* to his labor defense practice. Cloherty, who hails from the NLRB, arbitrated in the two-year strike of nursing home employees at Avery Heights. Peers point to his *"unmistakable confidence"* in labor conflicts. **George O'Brien** is chair of the labor and employment practice group at Tyler Cooper & Alcorn LLP and *"always impresses"* as a management expert. As chief labor negotiator for a hospital, he reached two multi-year contract settlements with a New York City union.

LITIGATION — GENERAL COMMERCIAL

Day, Berry & Howard LLP
The Firm: Historically litigation-driven, this firm has *"the bodies and the resources for big, expensive cases."* Market commentators identified the *"high quality and experience"* of the firm's seasoned litigators, who have *"track records in major cases."* Attorneys are commended for their pre-litigation negotiations and skills as trial lawyers: *"their lawyers really work hard to get the result."* Franchise and distributorship matters figure prominently. The group is active in manufacturers' and distributors' disputes, particularly in the oil industry. It represented a major petroleum company and its franchisees during the sale of gas stations across Connecticut. In a separate franchise dispute, attorneys represented a large distributor of gasoline in New England.

The Lawyers: Observers endorsed **James Sicilian** for his sound judgment and courtroom presence. He is the local lawyer for a US software company in its antitrust cases. **Thomas Groark** is credited with an *"effective and smooth style"* that makes him a *"superb litigator."* **James Stapleton** a former judge who has returned to practice, brings a wider perspective to his cases. **Steve Greenspan**'s court performances are judged by rivals to be *"a hit"* with juries and witnesses alike.

The Clients: Data communications, computer software and manufacturing companies, and firms in the petrochemical and publicly traded energy industries.

CONNECTICUT

LITIGATION

CONNECTICUT
Leading firms
(Litigation: General Commercial)

1. **DAY, BERRY & HOWARD LLP** Hartford
2. **WIGGIN & DANA LLP** New Haven
3. **CUMMINGS & LOCKWOOD** Hartford
   ROBINSON & COLE LLP Hartford
4. **MURTHA CULLINA LLP** Hartford
   SHIPMAN & GOODWIN LLP Hartford

Leading individuals
(Litigation: General Commercial)

1. **BRADY Francis** *Murtha Cullina LLP*, Hartford
   FITZGERALD Anthony *Carmody & Torrance*, New Haven
   SICILIAN James *Day, Berry & Howard*, Hartford
2. **DOYLE William** *Wiggin & Dana*, New Haven
   FOGARTY James *Fogarty, Cohen, Selby*, Greenwich
   WADE James *Robinson & Cole LLP*, Hartford
3. **BRIGHT William** *Cummings & Lockwood*, Hartford
   GROARK Thomas *Day, Berry & Howard LLP*, Hartford
   STAPLETON James *Day, Berry & Howard*, Hartford
   SULLIVAN Shaun *Wiggin & Dana LLP*, New Haven
4. **BELT David** *Jacobs, Grudberg, Belt & Dow*, New Haven
   DUNHAM Edward *Wiggin & Dana LLP*, New Haven
   GREENSPAN Steve *Day, Berry & Howard*, Hartford
   SAGARIN Daniel *Hurwitz & Sagarin LLC*, Milford
   SANSON Paul *Shipman & Goodwin LLP*, Hartford
   WYLD Robert *Shipman & Goodwin LLP*, Hartford

Firms and Individuals are listed alphabetically in each band.

Wiggin & Dana LLP

The Firm: New England counsel to Cendant franchise brands and national litigation counsel for Subway. The group is also general counsel to the country's largest wine importer, Banfi Vintners. For franchise and antitrust work, competitors declared the commercial litigation practice to be an *"excellent choice."* Attorneys have secured a high profile with their representation of Connecticut's educational institutions, and with their trial advocacy for Arthur Andersen in Houston, Texas.

The Lawyers: **William Doyle** was described to *Chambers'* researchers as *"a competitive but fair fighter."* He has *"a smooth and persuasive approach."* Doyle represented Yale University in a patent dispute. Chair of the practice **Shaun Sullivan** attracts commendation as *"a clever attorney who's always going to outwork the opposition."* He acted as lead trial counsel to a consortium of ten New England electric utilities in asserting claims in excess of $200 million arising from the failed Millstone 3 nuclear power plant in Waterford. Sullivan also advised Olin on an IP suit against a large Japanese manufacturer of copper alloys. Completing the elite team at the firm is **Edward Dunham**, who impresses with his *"quick, clear and creative mind."* His practice focuses on franchise, distributors' and dealers' disputes.

The Clients: Olin; Yale University; University of New Haven; The United Illuminating Company; GE Capital; Arthur Andersen; Schlotzsky's; Subway; Bandag; Cendant; Banfi Vintners; American Home-School Publishing and Westbrook Technology.

Cummings & Lockwood

The Firm: Peers agree that the stature of this firm's litigation practice is *"steadily growing"* in Connecticut. The *"well-balanced"* commercial litigation team is active in breach of contract, trade secrets and partnership disputes. The firm attracted particular praise for its strength in IP matters.

The Lawyers: Department chair **William Bright** focuses on business torts, antitrust, and franchise and distributors' litigation, with particular experience within the retail and energy industries. Bright represented a quasi-public statewide solid waste management authority in a contract matter relating to the supply of services.

The Clients: Connecticut Resources Recovery Authority (CRRA); CUNO; IBM; ChevronTexaco; Xerox; Cendant and International Paper Company.

Robinson & Cole LLP

The Firm: A *"sophisticated outfit,"* possessing one of the largest trial and appellate sections in the state. A large base of blue-chip clients consult the firm for a range of litigious matters. Attorneys have obtained settlements for several insurance companies in Hartford, and have acted in contract interpretation and defense of product delivery for United Technologies.

The Lawyers: *"Accomplished"* **James Wade** is a *"first-class advocate"* and the foremost attorney of the litigation team. He acts in civil and criminal trials relating to securities and banking violations. On the commercial side, he represented a chemical company involved in claims of environmental pollution, and acted as private counsel for an explosives manufacturer.

The Clients: United Technologies; IBM; GE; Pitney Bowes; Xerox and Pfizer.

Murtha Cullina LLP

The Firm: The firm possesses a recognized strong suit in enforcing policy coverage rights for corporate policyholders. Insurance coverage attorneys act for corporations suing insurance companies to recover their costs in complex, multi-state litigations.

The Lawyers: Much of the group's profile lies with leading insurance coverage expert **Francis Brady**. Researchers were left in no doubt: he *"combines the virtues of a great fighter and a skillful conciliator."* In the 13-year case, Reichhold Chemicals v Hartford Accident and Indemnity Company, Brady successfully represented the plaintiff who sued insurers for the reimbursement of cleanup costs.

The Clients: The firm advises manufacturing, banking, construction, utilities and healthcare companies and the dot.com sector.

Shipman & Goodwin LLP

The Firm: Interviewees affirm the complex business practice group contains *"pockets of true excellence,"* pointing specifically to expertise in complex business disputes arising from franchising, antitrust and trade regulation matters. Practitioners have represented major oil companies, national corporations, super-regional banks and national and regional franchisers.

The Lawyers: Co-chair of the practice **Paul Sanson** is recommended by peers as *"capable and trustworthy."* He was lead attorney for an energy company in a contract dispute involving a $12 million claim, tried before a jury at a Connecticut state court – a judgment notwithstanding the verdict (JNOV) motion subsequently reduced the claim to $1. Also acted for a toy manufacturer in a FTC investigation involving an alleged vertical boycott, preventing competitors from selling toys at a lower price. **Robert Wyld** specializes in complex business litigation, intra-corporate disputes and insurance litigation. According to peers, he has *"an extraordinary gift for detail and strong presentation in court."*

The Clients: Leading manufacturers and energy companies are typical clients of the firm.

Other Notable Practitioners

Anthony Fitzgerald at Carmody & Torrance LLP hails from the *"old school of superb generalists."* Best known for his work with Northeast Utilities. Also hired to defend top Connecticut law firms against claims of malpractice. **James Fogarty** of Fogarty, Cohen, Selby & Nemiroff LLC was recommended to *Chambers'* researchers for his skills as a trial lawyer. **David Belt** of Jacobs, Grudberg, Belt & Dow is an antitrust specialist whose expertise is *"second to none."* **Daniel Sagarin** of Hurwitz & Sagarin LLC was recommended for his expertise in securities and antitrust cases.

REAL ESTATE | CONNECTICUT

REAL ESTATE

CONNECTICUT
Leading firms (Real Estate)

1 ROBINSON & COLE LLP *Hartford*
2 BINGHAM MCCUTCHEN LLP *Hartford*
SHIPMAN & GOODWIN LLP *Hartford, Stamford*
3 BROWN RUDNICK BERLACK ISRAELS *Hartford*
DAY, BERRY & HOWARD LLP *Stamford*
DECHERT *Hartford*
4 SUSMAN, DUFFY & SEGALOFF PC *New Haven*
WIGGIN & DANA LLP *New Haven*

Leading individuals (Real Estate)

1 HAWKINS Barry *Shipman & Goodwin LLP,* Hartford
MERRIAM Dwight *Robinson & Cole LLP,* Hartford
OLAND Mark *Bingham McCutchen LLP,* Hartford
2 ASMAR Mark *Brown Rudnick Berlack Israels,* Hartford
BUCK Gurdon *Robinson & Cole LLP,* Hartford
KRASOW Herbert *Krasow, Garlick & Hadley,* Hartford
LUBIN Andrew *Susman, Duffy & Segaloff,* New Haven
3 APPICELLI Frank *Bingham McCutchen LLP,* Hartford
BERKMAN Jerome *Day, Berry & Howard,* Stamford
GILLIES John *Dechert,* Hartford
SVONKIN Mark *Sole Practitioner,* West Hartford

Firms and individuals are listed alphabetically in each band.

Robinson & Cole LLP
The Firm: A substantial real estate department commended by peers for its *"concentration of dedicated lawyers."* The practice integrates real estate, land use, environment, construction management and utilities law. It has expertise in the leasing and finance arena, and is home to certified community planners. The group has acted as environmental counsel for United Technologies and local government in Honolulu and Reno.
The Lawyers: Peers agree that **Dwight Merriam** stands out as the *"premier"* expert in zoning matters with notable experience in land use issues and large-scale developments both in Connecticut and nationally. Merriam advised on the permitting and environmental work for Pfizer's world research center in New London, a several hundred million dollar deal. **Gurdon Buck** devotes the largest share of his land use practice to common covenant and common interest community matters. His work for condominium development projects is rated as *"second to none."*
The Clients: Attorneys completed a 1.4 million sq ft mall expansion for Taubman Centers. The group acted for the Kiawah Island Resorts in South Carolina in the development of 7500 residential units and several golf courses. Also advised on a shopping center tract in Huntsville, Alabama, with airspace units sold and financed separately. Other clients include: The TJX Companies; The Stop & Shop Supermarket Company; United Technologies; Pfizer; City of Bridgeport and Equity Office.

Bingham McCutchen LLP
The Firm: The group acts across three main sectors: restructuring and workouts; equity and leasing; and zoning work. The bulk of the workload relates to private and publicly owned commercial and residential properties. Rivals acknowledge the firm's *"superbly talented"* practitioners and depth of experience. The team is further distinguished by a concentration of young attorneys predicted to be *"the future of real estate."*
The Lawyers: Clients and peers alike endorsed **Mark Oland** as a *"sophisticated and well-grounded attorney."* He represented the New England Patriots in a $400 million financing, equity infusion and zoning of a stadium in Massachusetts. Oland also acted for a financial institution in the mortgaging of 6000 properties in 17 states belonging to a US coal producer, securing a $900 million loan. The firm's *"triple-strength team"* includes **Frank Appicelli**. He has represented commercial banks and debt and equity providers in a variety of mortgage loan transactions.
The Clients: The firm advises REITs, pension funds, insurance companies and banking institutions. Other clients include: Boston Properties; Aetna Life Insurance Company; John Hancock; Principle Life Insurance Company; FleetBoston Financial; UBS Realty; UBS AG; Lend Lease; Harvard University; University of Connecticut – Stamford; First Union National Bank and City of Bristol.

Shipman & Goodwin LLP
The Firm: Combines commercial leasing, development and finance, and environmental and land use practices. Interviewees commended the team's activities in the public sector, acting for government entities such as the City of Waterbury. Its work for common-interest communities also elicited strong recommendations. Beyond the public sector, attorneys have advised on offshore pension investments in Connecticut real estate.
The Lawyers: According to interviewees, **Barry Hawkins** *"has a great head on his shoulders."* He combines real estate litigation – typically land use appeals and foreclosures – with transactional work.
The Clients: The team counselled the State of Connecticut in the redevelopment of the former G Fox department store building in Hartford for the Capital Community College. Other clients include: Gartner; People's Bank; Webster Bank; Fleet Bank; Hartford Hospital and the City of Waterbury.

Brown Rudnick Berlack Israels
The Firm: Commended as a *"highly proficient"* unit, the firm primarily represents developers and has a profile in low-income and affordable housing transactions. Practitioners are also skilled in complex multi-state commercial transactions. The Hartford-based attorneys represented the developers in the conversion of a downtown department store (800,000 sq ft) into a community college, office and retail complex. The firm additionally advised the lead lender in a syndicated loan funding for the Adriaen's Landing convention and science center, and acted for a private developer of a project featuring a 600-car garage and 100 units of housing in Bushel Park.
The Lawyers: Gaining plaudits all round was the *"practical and smart"* **Mark Asmar**. He was described by peers as a *"deal-closer"* and commended for his negotiation skills.
The Clients: Community Renewal Team; Hartford Downtown Revival; Ginsburg Development LLC; Trumbull on the Park; People's Bank; Aetna Life Insurance Company and Milano Realty.

Day, Berry & Howard LLP
The Firm: Commercial leasings and developments are seen to drive the real estate operation. Rivals noted the group's experience in transactional real estate matters and strong following among institutional investors. On the development side, the firm acted for the sponsor of the $750 million project, Adriaen's Landing – a mixed-use urban redevelopment on the Connecticut River in Hartford. Also advised on the development of Rentschler Field – a 650-acre master-planned development project comprising almost 2.5 million sq ft of R&D, office and light industrial space in East Hartford.
The Lawyers: **Jerome Berkman** was judged by peers to be an *"outstanding player"* in commercial real estate. He has represented urban renewal redevelopers in Stamford, acted for landlords and tenants in commercial leases, and advised borrowers in construction and long-term loans secured by mortgages.
The Clients: CSFB; Global Petroleum; Accor; Cheslock, Bakker & Associates and MassMutual.

Dechert
see firm details p.789
The Firm: A ten-strong team of *"results-oriented lawyers"* was recommended for *"detailed advice"* on property matters. *"Extremely skilled"* attorneys feature in national transactions, and are a popular choice for out-of-state clients. Hartford practitioners act together with attorneys in offices across the US and in the UK as part of an integrated real estate practice. The bulk of work is finance-driven, with real estate investment and mortgage lending featuring prominently.

CONNECTICUT LEADERS

The Lawyers: Interviewees singled out **John Gillies** as a real estate specialist with extensive experience acting for institutional investors. Gillies represented Landmark Partners in raising $300 million from pension fund investors.

The Clients: Attorneys represent Wall Street financial institutions, banks, insurance companies and advisers to pension funds, plus a small cadre of developers, buyers and sellers. Typical clients include: GMAC; CSFB; Starwood Capital Group; Landmark Partners; Aetna; The Hartford and Citigroup.

Susman, Duffy & Segaloff PC

The Firm: Sources claim that the commercial real estate practice has New Haven *"sewn up."* It acts on a *"steady stream"* of acquisitions and purchase contracts, as well as permitting, financing, construction and leasing matters. The firm has represented six Class A office buildings in Connecticut, and advised an international retailer on 300,000 sq ft of property. Golf course developments and hotel financings are a feature of the practice, while subsidized multi-family housing also provides a sizable share of work. Attorneys have represented developers for six US Department of Housing and Urban Development (HUD) projects in New Haven.

The Lawyers: Peers rate **Andrew Lubin** as *"among the best in negotiating transactions."* Lubin concentrates on acquisition and finance and was responsible for closing an $18 million multi-state land deal involving almost a dozen borrowers.

The Clients: US Department of Housing and Urban Development (HUD); Wachovia Bank; Citizens Bank; Webster Bank; Fleet Bank; New Haven Savings Bank and Carabetta Enterprises.

Wiggin & Dana LLP

The Firm: Market leaders acknowledge the *"substantial experience"* of the team. The combined real estate, environmental and land use department is headed by Susan Bryson from the firm's New Haven office. A real estate finance and development group represents developers, institutions, underwriters and investors.

The Clients: Attorneys represented McCormack Baron & Associates in the development of mixed-income and urban redevelopment projects. They also represented Lubert-Adler Partners in its acquisition and redevelopment of the Chapel Square Mall and Office Tower in New Haven. Other clients include: People's Bank; Mack-Cali Realty; New London Development; Williams Jackson Ewing and ING Realty Partners.

Other Notable Practitioners

Peers recommend the *"brilliant"* **Herbert Krasow** at Krasow, Garlick & Hadley LLC for complex transactions and commercial leasing matters. He *"can spot all the issues a mile away."* Sole practitioner **Mark Svonkin** drew commendation for his work with developers. One interviewee described him as a *"practical deal-maker who won't let any detail escape him."*

Leaders in Connecticut

ADLER, Gregg
Livingston Adler Pulda Meikeljohn & Kelly PC, Hartford   860 233 9821
Recommended in Employment

APPICELLI, Frank
Bingham McCutchen LLP, Hartford
860 240 2700
Recommended in Real Estate

ASMAR, Mark
Brown Rudnick Berlack Israels, Hartford
860 509 6524
Recommended in Real Estate

BELT, David
Jacobs, Grudberg, Belt & Dow PC, New Haven   203 772 3100
Recommended in Litigation

BERKMAN, Jerome
Day, Berry & Howard LLP, Stamford
203 977 7300
Recommended in Real Estate

BRADY, Francis
Murtha Cullina LLP, Hartford
860 240 6000
Recommended in Litigation

BRIGHT, William
Cummings & Lockwood, Hartford
860 275 6700
Recommended in Litigation

BUCK, Gurdon
Robinson & Cole LLP, Hartford
860 275 8200
Recommended in Real Estate

CLEMOW, Brian
Shipman & Goodwin LLP, Hartford
860 251 5000
Recommended in Employment

CLOHERTY, Thomas
Murtha Cullina LLP, Hartford
860 240 6000
Recommended in Employment

DE TOLEDO, Victoria
Casper & de Toledo LLC, Stamford
203 325 8600
Recommended in Employment

DOYLE, William
Wiggin & Dana, New Haven
203 498 4400
Recommended in Litigation

DUNHAM, Edward Wood
Wiggin & Dana, New Haven
203 498 4400
Recommended in Litigation

DURANT, Terry
Durant, Nichols, Houston Hodson & Cortese-Costa PC, Bridgeport
203 366 3438
Recommended in Employment

ELDERGILL, Kathleen
Beck & Eldergill, PC, Manchester
860 646 5606
firm@beckeldergill.com
Recommended in Employment
Specialization: Principal in the Manchester, Connecticut law firm of *Beck & Eldergill, P.C.*, a general practice firm of nine lawyers. She practices primarily in the area of plaintiffs' employment litigation, and particularly enjoys litigating against government employers. Practice areas include: employment; civil rights; civil litigation; consumer law; environmental law. Reported cases: Williams v. CHRO on Human Rights & CHRO 257 Conn. 258 (2001)(amicus); Meyers v. Cornwell Quality Tools, Inc., 41 Conn. App. 19 (1996); Starr v. Commissioner of Environment Protection, 236 Conn. 722 (1996); Sadloski v. Manchester, 235 Conn. 637 (1995); Schnabel v. Tyler, 230 Conn. 735 (1994); Tyler v. Schnabel, 34 Conn. App. 216 (1994); Sadloski v. Manchester, 228 Conn. 79 (1993); Schnabel v. Tyler, 32 Conn. App. 704 (1993); State v. Ball, 226 Conn. 265 (1993); Starr v. Commissioner of Environmental Protection, 226 Conn. 358 (1993); Lester v. Resort Camplands International, Inc. 27 Conn. App. 59 (1992); Killingly v. Connecticut Siting Council, 220 Conn. 516 (1991); Double 1 Ltd. Partnership v. Plan & Zoning Comm. 218 Conn. 65 (1991); Preston v. Department of Environmental Protection, 218 Conn. 821 (1991); Concerned Citizens of Sterling v. Ct. Siting CNCl., 215 Conn. 474 (1990); Preston v. Connecticut Siting Council, 21 Conn. App. 85 (1990); Lewin v. United States Surgical Corporation, 21 Conn. App. 629 (1990); Preston v. Connecticut Siting Council, 20 Conn. App. 474 (1990); Zinker v. Doty, 907 F.2d 357 (2d Cir. 1990) and 637 F. Supp. 138 (D. Conn. 1986); Connecticut Light & Power Co. v. Dept., Pub. UTIL., 210 Conn. 349 (1989); Dorman v. Satti, 862 F.2d 432 (2d Cir. 1988) and 678 F. Supp. 375 (D. Conn. 1988); Brady v. Town of Colchester, 863 F.2d 205 (2d Cir. 1988); Frost v. Chromalloy Aero. Tech. Corp., 697 F. Supp. 82 (D. Conn. 1988); Sadlowski v. Manchester, 206 Conn. 579 (1988); United States v. Rosario, 820 F. 2d 584 (2d Cir. 1987); Concerned Citizens of Sterling v. Town of Sterling, 204 Conn. 551 (1987); Mumford Cove Assn., Inc. v. Town of Groton 786 F. 2d 530 (2d Cir. 1986); State v. Ostroski, 201 Conn. 534 (1986); State v. Shifflett, 199, Conn. 718 (1986); Coollick v. Windham, 7 Conn. App. 142 (1986); State v. Stanley, 197 Conn. 309 (1985); State v. Pelletier, 196 Conn. 32 (1985); Acheson v. White, 195 Conn. 211 (1985); State v. McCulley 5 Conn. App. 612 (1985); Southland Corp. v. Vernon, 1 Conn. App. 439 (1984).
Prof. Memberships: Manchester Bar Association; Association of Trial Lawyers of America; Connecticut Trial Lawyers Association; Connecticut Employment Lawyers Association; National Employment Lawyers Association; Small Claims Commissioner State of Connecticut. Special Master, United States District Court for the District of Connecticut. Fellow: American College of Trial Lawyers; Connecticut Bar Foundation, James W. Cooper Fellows Program. (Certified in Civil Trial Advocacy by the National Board of Trial Advocacy).
Career: Admitted 1981, Connecticut and US District Court, District of Connecti-

cut; 1983, US Court of Appeals, Second Circuit; 1988, US Supreme Court.
Personal: Law School: University of Connecticut, JD, with high honors, 1981. College: University of Connecticut, BA, highest honors, Phi Beta Kappa, 1975.

FINN III, Harold B
Finn Dixon & Herling LLP, Stamford
203 325 5000
hfinn@fdh.com
Recommended in Corporate/M&A
Specialization: Concentrates practice in the law relating to business organizations and financial transactions, including corporate governance, mergers and acquisitions, the public and private offering of securities, banking and lending, and related litigation. Represents both publicly-held corporations and private companies, including pooled investment vehicles in the form of partnerships, limited liability companies and trusts.
Prof. Memberships: Admitted to the bars of the States of Connecticut and New York. Member of the Council of the Business Law Section of the American Bar Association and former Chair of such Section's Banking Law Committee. Chairman of the Securities Advisory Committee to the Banking Commissioner of the State of Connecticut. Past Co-Chair of Task Force on the Revision of the Connecticut Business Corporation Act. Former Chair of the Business Law Section of the Connecticut Bar Association. Elected Member of the American Law Institute.
Personal: Received undergraduate degree from Yale University in 1960 and received law degree, magna cum laude, from Columbia University in 1966, where was articles editor of the Columbia Law Review. Following law school, he served as a law clerk to the late Chief Justice Earl Warren and the late Associate Justice Stanley F Reed.

FITZGERALD, Anthony
Carmody & Torrance LLP, New Haven
203 777 5501
Recommended in Litigation

FOGARTY, James
Fogarty, Cohen, Selby & Nemiroff LLC, Greenwich 203 661 1000
Recommended in Litigation

GARRISON, Joseph
Garrison, Levin-Epstein Chimes & Richardson PC, New Haven
203 777 4425
Recommended in Employment

GILLIES, John
Dechert, Hartford 860 524 3999
Recommended in Real Estate

GOLUB, David
Silver Golub & Teitell LLP, Stamford
203 325 4491
Recommended in Employment

GREENSPAN, Steve
Day, Berry & Howard LLP, Hartford
860 275 0100
Recommended in Litigation

GROARK, Thomas
Day, Berry & Howard LLP, Hartford
860 275 0100
Recommended in Litigation

HAWKINS, Barry
Shipman & Goodwin LLP, Hartford
860 251 5000
Recommended in Real Estate

KEE, Conrad
Jackson Lewis, Stamford
203 961 0404
Recommended in Employment

KRASOW, Herbert
Krasow, Garlick & Hadley LLC, Hartford
860 549 7100
Recommended in Real Estate

LEFEBER, Peter
Wiggin & Dana LLP, New Haven
203 498 4400
Recommended in Employment

LIVINGSTON, Daniel
Livingston Adler Pulda Meikeljohn & Kelly PC, Hartford 860 233 9821
Recommended in Employment

LOTSTEIN, James
Cummings & Lockwood, Hartford
860 275 6700
Recommended in Corporate/M&A

LUBIN, Andrew
Susman, Duffy & Segaloff P.C., New Haven 203 624 9830
Recommended in Real Estate

MARCO, Frank
Mintz Levin Cohn Ferris Glovsky and Popeo PC, New Haven 203 777 8200
Recommended in Corporate/M&A

MERRIAM, Dwight
Robinson & Cole LLP, Hartford
860 275 8200
Recommended in Real Estate

O'BRIEN, George
Tyler Cooper & Alcorn LLP, New Haven
203 784 8200
Recommended in Employment

OLAND, Mark
Bingham McCutchen LLP, Hartford
860 240 2700
Recommended in Real Estate

SAGARIN, Daniel
Hurwitz & Sagarin LLC, Milford
203 877 8000
Recommended in Litigation

SANSON, Paul
Shipman & Goodwin LLP, Hartford
860 251 5000
Recommended in Litigation

SCHWARTZ, Daniel L
Day, Berry & Howard LLP, Stamford
203 977 7300
Recommended in Employment

SICILIAN, James
Day, Berry & Howard LLP, Hartford
860 275 0100
Recommended in Litigation

SPIER, Alan
Robinson & Cole LLP, Hartford
860 275 8200
Recommended in Corporate/M&A

SPRINGER, Felix
Day, Berry & Howard LLP, Hartford
860 275 0100
Recommended in Employment

STAPLETON, James
Day, Berry & Howard LLP, Hartford
860 275 0100
Recommended in Litigation

SULLIVAN, Shaun
Wiggin & Dana LLP, New Haven
203 498 4400
Recommended in Litigation

SVONKIN, Mark
The Law Office of Mark J. Svonkin P.C., West Hartford 860 521 2811
Recommended in Real Estate

VOIGT, Richard
Cummings & Lockwood, Hartford
860 275 6700
Recommended in Employment

WADE, James
Robinson & Cole LLP, Hartford
860 275 8200
Recommended in Litigation

WYLD, Robert
Shipman & Goodwin LLP, Hartford
860 251 5000
Recommended in Litigation

ZAKARIAN, Albert
Day, Berry & Howard LLP, Hartford
860 275 0100
Recommended in Employment

ZANDY, John
Wiggin & Dana LLP, New Haven
203 498 4400
Recommended in Employment

DELAWARE

CORPORATE/M&A

CONTENTS: Corporate/M&A p.94; Employment Mainly Plaintiff p.95; Mainly Defendant p.95; Insolvency p.96; Litigation: General Commercial p97; Real Estate p.99; Individuals' Profiles p.99.

DELAWARE'S TOP FIVE
1. Young Conaway Stargatt & Taylor
1. Richards Layton & Finger
1. Morris, Nichols, Arsht & Tunnell
2. Potter Anderson & Corroon
3. Skadden, Arps, Slate, Meagher & Flom

Ranking based on Chambers' research within the state.

All quotes in the text are from interviews with clients and competitors.

OVERVIEW: The battle for top place in Delaware has been a tough one, with the performance of three firms so closely matched that they rank joint first.

Young Conaway Stargatt & Taylor acts largely as special Delaware counsel for out-of-state lawyers on corporate transactions. The same is true of most of the local law firms. This firm earns national recognition for its bankruptcy practice, although employment and real estate are also significant areas of specialization. Chairman of the firm Jim Patton is highly rated for Chapter 11 reorganisations, while Sheldon Sandler is a high-profile employment lawyer. Clients include ING DIRECT and AstraZeneca.

Richards Layton & Finger has a friendly rivalry with the third firm at the top, **Morris, Nichols, Arsht & Tunnell**. Richards Layton is the larger of the two, and receives the lion's share of Delaware corporate matters. Rated for its insolvency work, the firm is also strong in real estate. Insolvency practice chair Mark Collins is seen as the first choice for banks in the state. Robert Krapf was mentioned as the leading real estate attorney in Delaware. Clients include JPMorgan and Citibank.

Morris, Nichols, Arsht & Tunnell is strong in corporate counseling, transactions and litigation. Although its bankruptcy practice is not as established as some of the other main firms, it is fast earning a reputation in this field. Bill Sudell is reckoned to be the driving force here, while transactions expert Frederick (Rick) Alexander is also highly praised. Clients include Sony Electronics and JPMorgan Chase.

Potter Anderson & Corroon ranks second. It has a solid reputation for transactions and corporate counseling, and is also admired for employment and insolvency work. Senior litigator Michael Goldman is prominent, while Laurie Selber Silverstein is a top creditors' lawyer. Clients include DuPont and Southwestern Bell Telephone Company.

Skadden, Arps, Slate, Meagher & Flom ranks third. It is unique in Delaware, receiving business from its own national network. Not considered a local player, it gives support to the firm's other offices. Gregg Galardi is prominent within a large insolvency team. Clients include Polaroid and The Williams Companies.

CORPORATE/M&A

DELAWARE
Leading firms (Corporate/M&A)
1. **MORRIS, NICHOLS, ARSHT** Wilmington
   RICHARDS LAYTON & FINGER Wilmington
2. **POTTER ANDERSON & CORROON LLP** Wilmington
3. **SKADDEN, ARPS** Wilmington
   YOUNG CONAWAY STARGATT Wilmington

Leading individuals (Corporate/M&A)
1. **ALEXANDER Frederick** Morris, Nichols, Wilmington
   BUSSARD Donald Richards Layton & Finger, Wilmington
2. **BALOTTI Frank** Richards Layton & Finger, Wilmington
   BLACK Lewis Morris, Nichols, Arsht, Wilmington
   SPARKS Gilchrist Morris, Nichols, Arsht, Wilmington
3. **EASTON Richard** Skadden, Arps, Wilmington
   GOLDMAN Michael Potter Anderson, Wilmington

Firms and individuals are listed alphabetically in each band.

Morris, Nichols, Arsht & Tunnell
The Firm: While smaller than main rival Richards Layton & Finger, the group was nonetheless lauded as a *"quality outfit,"* active in corporate counseling, transactions and litigation. Commentators observed that these two leading firms have the Delaware market *"stitched-up,"* with some describing the market for corporate legal services as *"a two-horse race."* Despite the softening of the M&A market, the team's expertise in fiduciary duties and corporate governance makes it a frequent point of reference for special committees and out-of-state law firms acting on major corporate transactions.

The Lawyers: Transactions expert **Frederick (Rick) Alexander** elicited high praise as a *"bright and hard-working"* younger attorney. Said to be *"fast becoming a leading light,"* he acted for the special committee of America Online Latin America on a $160 million financing by major stockholder AOL Time Warner, and also advised on the joint venture between USA Networks and Vivendi Universal. *"Senior and experienced"* **Lewis Black** receives endorsement for his transactional and advisory work. He acted for Ford in a recapitalization that involved the acquisition of part of rental car company Hertz. *"Supremely versatile"* **Gil Sparks** is thought to complete this strong corporate lineup with his preeminent litigation skills.
The Clients: Sony Electronics; Viacom; Philadelphia Stock Exchange; Vencor and AstraZeneca.

Richards Layton & Finger
The Firm: Together with friendly rival Morris, Nichols, Arsht & Tunnell, the firm receives the lion's share of Delaware corporate work. It has pursued a full-service model and is now perceived to have gained an edge in terms of *"capacity and numbers of bodies."* Practitioners chiefly advise national law firms on matters of Delaware corporate law. A large practice counseling non-incorporated partnerships is unrivaled in the state.
The Lawyers: A popular choice for referrals, **Donald Bussard** was singled out as the *"real star"* of the corporate practice. Having earned his stripes as a litigator, Bussard now enjoys prominence for corporate governance and transactional work, where clients value his *"practical, no-nonsense advice."* Consulting with Cravath, Swaine & Moore, he served as Delaware counsel to Vivendi Universal in its acquisition of USA Networks' studio operations. Corporate litigator **Frank Balotti** also won praise for his advisory work.
The Clients: The group acted alongside Latham & Watkins for Nestlé in its takeover of Dreyer's Grand Ice Cream, and worked with O'Melveny & Myers for Univision Communications in a takeover of Hispanic Broadcasting Corp. Other highlights include acting as special Delaware counsel to Reader's Digest.

Potter Anderson & Corroon LLP
The Firm: An established Delaware firm with long experience of transactional matters and general corporate counseling. Practitioners routinely advise on risk management, partnership agreements, fiduciary obligations and securities issues. Transactional highlights include acting for Warner-Lambert in its 2000 merger with Pfizer, and representing Morton's Restaurant Group in a merger with affiliates of investment company Castle Harlan.

EMPLOYMENT & LABOR LAW — DELAWARE

The Lawyers: Senior litigator **Michael Goldman** is the group's prominent face, advising company directors and alternative entities on issues of corporate governance and fiduciary duties. Displaying the *"versatility"* that characterizes *"old-school"* Delaware attorneys, he has successfully acted for premier client DuPont against Conoco, and advised energy company Aquila in its merger with UtiliCorp United. He also provided advice and litigation expertise to Northrop Grumman against General Dynamics in its successful bid for Newport News Shipbuilding.

The Clients: Morton's Restaurant Group; DuPont; Warner-Lambert and major law firms.

Skadden, Arps, Slate, Meagher & Flom LLP & Affiliates
see firm details p.878

The Firm: Unique in the Delaware market, the practice receives a *"constant stream of work"* through Skadden Arp's national network, contrasting with local firms that operate primarily as referral practices. Twenty attorneys are said to work *"hand in glove"* with the firm's other offices, both providing support and taking the lead on acquisitions, sales and corporate advisory matters. Recent highlights include acting for NCS HealthCare on its acquisition by Genesis Health Ventures and advising CitiGroup on its acquisition of Golden State Bancorp. The group has also acted for USX, now Marathon Oil, in the separation of its steel and energy businesses.

The Lawyers: Rich Easton (see p.100) was commended to researchers as a *"prominent"* attorney, active in high-profile corporate transactions.

The Clients: Citigroup; Milton Hershey Trust; Rite Aid; USX; The Williams Companies and NCS HealthCare.

Young Conaway Stargatt & Taylor, LLP
see firm details p.907

The Firm: Like most local firms, the group acts largely as special Delaware counsel to out-of-state lawyers on corporate transactions. Its reputation here has benefited from the national profile of its preeminent bankruptcy practice. Although lacking the individual star players of its major corporate rivals, the firm nonetheless won peer endorsement for a *"healthy"* corporate counseling and transactional practice.

The Lawyers: While the *"terrific"* Bruce Stargatt is less active in practice, market commentators continued to extol the *"knowledgeable and practical"* advice of the firm's other corporate lawyers. These attorneys are seen to *"work well with outside counsel and are tough when they need to be."* William Johnston is the contact partner for the corporate and business litigation and counseling practice.

The Clients: Recent highlights include acting for Hughes in its spin-off from GM and subsequent merger with EchoStar and advising women's cable channel Oxygen Media on corporate and commercial matters. Additionally, the group advised on USA Interactive's proposed buyout of Ticketmaster and attendant litigation.

EMPLOYMENT & LABOR LAW — MAINLY PLAINTIFF

DELAWARE
Leading firms
(Employment: Mainly Plaintiff)
1. **HEIMAN, ABER, GOLDLUST & BAKER** Wilmington

Leading individuals
(Employment: Mainly Plaintiff)
1. **WIER Richard** Sole Practitioner, Wilmington
2. **NEUBERGER Thomas** Sole Practitioner, Wilmington
3. **ABER Gary** Heiman, Aber, Goldlust & Baker, Wilmington

Firms and individuals are listed alphabetically in each band.

Heiman, Aber, Goldlust & Baker

The Firm: Hailed as a *"true believer"* in fighting the employee's corner, **Gary Aber** is a ubiquitous presence in Delaware employment litigation. A *"nuisance"* to employers and a *"hero"* to employees, he has celebrated some significant victories for his clients, including a $4 million jury damages award against Pathmark Stores under the ADA. Aber has also contributed to substantive law on the subject, working to establish the covenant of good faith and fair dealing as an exception to the at-will employment doctrine in wrongful discharge matters.

The Lawyers: Much of the firm's reputation is tied to ranked practitioner Gary Aber. However, his partner, Perry Goldlust, was also recommended to researchers as one of the few Delaware attorneys who represents unions.

The Clients: The firm represents employee plaintiffs at all levels in cases of race, sex and disability discrimination as well as unfair dismissal and sexual harassment claims.

Other Notable Practitioners

"Discriminating in the cases he takes on," sole practitioner **Richard Wier** is widely considered to have the edge over rivals for plaintiffs' work. One of Delaware's few employment specialists, he has *"thrown his hat into the ring;"* researchers found that he commands the respect of rivals, peers and the courts. A former state attorney general, Wier combines *"significant trial experience"* with a *"low-key"* negotiating style, and acts for a national and international clientele in discrimination litigation and severance and benefits negotiations. He also advises small employers on contract and manual drafting. *"An obvious choice for public sector matters,"* **Thomas Neuberger**, another sole practitioner, enjoys a high profile in First Amendment whistle-blower claims. Rivals concede him to be an *"able and persuasive adversary"* with a string of notable victories to his name. Neuberger has handled successful employment claims against DuPont and acted as cocounsel to a US Air Force pilot who challenged restrictions placed on female service members on tour in Saudi Arabia.

EMPLOYMENT & LABOR LAW — MAINLY DEFENDANT

DELAWARE
Leading firms
(Employment: Mainly Defendant)
1. **YOUNG CONAWAY STARGATT** Wilmington
2. **POTTER ANDERSON & CORROON LLP** Wilmington
3. **MORRIS, JAMES, HITCHENS** Wilmington

Individuals are listed alphabetically in each band.

Young Conaway Stargatt & Taylor, LLP
see firm details p.907

The Firm: Employment is one of the firm's core areas, and researchers were told that the firm demonstrates a *"real commitment to employment law."* Despite the encroachment of Philadelphia firms into the Delaware market, this homegrown outfit continues to enjoy preeminence in the area. As *"undisputed leader,"* it covers the gamut of employment and labor law transactions, providing advice and litigation to a prestigious selection of management clientele. Eight attorneys also advise clients on pension and benefits schemes, union avoidance and employment issues arising out of bankruptcies.

The Lawyers: The acknowledged dean of the

DELAWARE

INSOLVENCY/CORPORATE RECOVERY

DELAWARE
Leading individuals
(Employment: Mainly Defendant)

1. **SANDLER Sheldon** *Young Conaway*, Wilmington
2. **WILLOUGHBY Barry** *Young Conaway*, Wilmington
3. **MCDONOUGH Kathleen** *Potter Anderson*, Wilmington
   WILLIAMS David *Morris, James, Hitchens*, Wilmington

Firms and individuals are listed alphabetically in each band.

Delaware employment bar, **Sheldon Sandler** (see p.101), leads the way with an *"established"* practice focused largely on private sector discrimination litigation and arbitration. His clients include AstraZeneca and Wilmington Trust. He is currently representing MBNA America Bank in a disabilities case arising from the employer's withdrawal of an accommodation. Commentators felt that Sandler's *"academic"* style was perfectly complemented by the *"pragmatism and business savvy"* of labor law specialist **Barry Willoughby** (see p.101). Willoughby appears before the NLRB and advises employer clients on union issues, Title VII and wrongful discharge claims. He recently defended a school district against a claim of whistle-blower retaliation, resulting in a limited claim and denial of punitive damages. He also successfully defended Procter & Gamble in a race discrimination claim.
The Clients: Wilmington Trust; MBNA America Bank; ICI; ING DIRECT and AstraZeneca.

Potter Anderson & Corroon LLP
The Firm: A prominent employment law practice devoted to counseling and litigation in relation to work force reductions, drug testing, sexual harassment and discrimination. A broad clientele ranges from leading nonprofit organizations to established Delaware employers and start-ups. On the labor front, the group also handles union negotiations, avoidance, grievances and NLRB arbitrations.
The Lawyers: Practice head **Kathleen McDonough** was identified as the firm's *"standout"* practitioner. A *"terrific and levelheaded"* attorney, she is best known for her work with major client DuPont. She has defended clients in ADA, Title VII and ADEA litigation, and counsels employers in connection with corporate downsizings.
The Clients: DuPont; Winterthur Museum, Garden & Library; private companies and non-profit organizations.

Morris, James, Hitchens & Williams, LLP
The Firm: This smaller practice emphasizes litigation and counseling for a public sector client base which includes 11 school districts and the State of Delaware. Commentators perceive the group to be well supported by management and other departments and offered particular praise for the group's leading individuals.
The Lawyers: Star player **David Williams** is credited with making the team a *"definite force"* in Delaware employment law. In addition to defense work on discrimination, disability and sexual harassment claims, Williams also acts as lead negotiator in collective bargaining agreements and as expert witness on Delaware employment law. He defended the State of Delaware against a US Department of Justice action challenging the legality of cognitive tests administered to the police. Elsewhere, he successfully represented the Delaware Department of Justice in a sex discrimination claim relating to a promotion decision.
The Clients: The firm acts for school districts, the State of Delaware and other public sector clients.

INSOLVENCY/CORPORATE RECOVERY

DELAWARE
Leading firms
(Insolvency/Corporate Recovery)

1. **SKADDEN, ARPS** Wilmington
   YOUNG CONAWAY STARGATT Wilmington
2. **RICHARDS LAYTON & FINGER** Wilmington
   SAUL EWING LLP Wilmington
3. **MORRIS, NICHOLS, ARSHT & TUNNELL** Wilmington
   PACHULSKI, STANG, ZIEHL, YOUNG Wilmington
   POTTER ANDERSON & CORROON LLP Wilmington

Leading individuals
(Insolvency/Corporate Recovery)

1. **PATTON James** *Young Conaway Stargatt*, Wilmington
2. **COLLINS Mark** *Richards Layton & Finger*, Wilmington
   GALARDI Gregg *Skadden, Arps*, Wilmington
   PERNICK Norman *Saul Ewing LLP*, Wilmington
3. **JONES Laura** *Pachulski, Stang, Ziehl*, Wilmington
   SELBER SILVERSTEIN Laurie *Potter Anderson*, Wilmington
   SUDELL William *Morris, Nichols, Arsht*, Wilmington
4. **BRADY Robert** *Young Conaway Stargatt*, Wilmington
   CHEHI Mark *Skadden, Arps*, Wilmington
   CLARK Anthony *Skadden, Arps*, Wilmington
5. **GLASSMAN Neil** *The Bayard Firm*, Wilmington
   SHANNON Brendan *Young Conaway Stargatt*, Wilmington
   STRATTON David *Pepper Hamilton LLP*, Wilmington

Firms and individuals are listed alphabetically in each band.

Skadden, Arps, Slate, Meagher & Flom LLP & Affiliates
see firm details p.878
The Firm: The Wilmington office of this *"vast international juggernaut"* draws on the *"horsepower and resources of its other offices,"* particularly the firm's *"fast-growing"* Chicago and New York debtor practices. The 25-strong group acts regularly for debtors and acquirers in *"mega"* Chapter 11 filings and has won particular renown for its work on Polaroid's restructuring.
The Lawyers: This *"large, skilled team"* boasts a wealth of talent. Peers extol **Gregg Galardi** (see p.100) as a *"tenacious and erudite"* attorney who combines *"trial savvy"* with a *"dogged and skillful"* negotiation style. Galardi has represented debtors in a range of matters, including the Stone & Webster, Safety-Kleen and Montgomery Ward bankruptcies. Commentators say his *"aggressive"* style is complemented by the *"consensus-driven"* approach of *"peacemaker"* **Mark Chehi** (see p.100). Chehi is best known for his work on the Exodus Communications bankruptcy, and has also represented AMP Life, the largest creditor in the WCI Group bankruptcy, in Portland, Oregon. Although a self-described *"pure litigator,"* **Tony Clark** (see p.100) has been called a *"dean"* of the Delaware bankruptcy bar, and is widely credited with *"nurturing Skadden Arps' practice"* in the state. He represented large automotive and truck wheel manufacturer, Hayes Lemmerz International, on its $1 billion voluntary debt restructuring under Chapter 11.
The Clients: Polaroid, Hayes Lemmerz International and Exodus Communications.

Young Conaway Stargatt & Taylor, LLP
see firm details p.907
The Firm: Delaware's original bankruptcy practice retains its reputation as a *"sophisticated and professional"* debtor outfit. This *"deep and talented"* young team is celebrated for its Chapter 11 reorganizations, pre-packaged bankruptcies, out-of-court workouts and restructurings.
The Lawyers: Firm chairman **Jim Patton** (see p.101) enjoys a national reputation for Chapter 11 reorganizations, in which his experience and *"creative, big-picture thinking"* consistently earn him the title of *"best in the state."* He has appeared as lead and cocounsel for debtors in key Delaware bankruptcies, including Continental Airlines and United Merchants and Manufacturing, helping to cement his reputation as the *"founding father"* of the Delaware bankruptcy bar. He also acts for future asbestos claimants in the Owens Corning, Armstrong World Industries and Babcock & Wilcox asbestos bankruptcies. His colleague, **Bob Brady** (see p.99), is *"making a real name for himself"* for his representation of both creditors' committees and debtors. Also prominent is *"standout"* practitioner **Brendan Shannon** (see p.101). He represented the official committee of

INSOLVENCY/CORPORATE RECOVERY — DELAWARE

unsecured creditors in the reorganization of Alamo Rent-A-Car and National Car Rental, and advised Globalstar in its financial restructuring of a $4 million debt.
The Clients: Globalstar, Alamo Rent-A-Car and National Car Rental.

Richards Layton & Finger
The Firm: The firm's reputation for secured creditors' work is unsurpassed in Delaware, with rivals and clients proclaiming it the *"number-one creditors' shop in the state."* This *"thriving"* practice is nationally recognized for its representation of banks and financial institutions in Chapter 11 reorganizations, although it also acts as lead and local counsel for creditors' committees and debtors.
The Lawyers: Practice chair **Mark Collins** was endorsed to researchers as the *"counsel of choice for banks in Delaware."* He received particular praise for his negotiation skills, where he demonstrates a *"gift for making people reach compromises."* Alongside institutional creditor clients such as JP Morgan and Citibank, he has also acted for debtors in major bankruptcies including Nextel and Teleglobe Communications.
The Clients: Teleglobe Communications; JPMorgan; Citibank and FINOVA Group.

Saul Ewing LLP
The Firm: This important bankruptcy practice has taken the lead role in *"significant engagements,"* most notably its representation of Owens Corning in its enormous Chapter 11 reorganization.
The Lawyers: The firm's reputation for bankruptcy work is inextricably linked with that of its founder and star individual, the *"sharp and practical"* **Norman Pernick**. A *"superior strategist,"* Pernick was lauded by peers for his *"solid client relationships"* and ability to *"drive a deal."* In addition to his work as lead counsel to Owens Corn-

ing, he has undertaken major debtor and creditors' committee representations.
The Clients: The practice has acted in the Owens Corning and Kellstrom Industries bankruptcies.

Morris, Nichols, Arsht & Tunnell
The Firm: The *"developing"* bankruptcy practice of this established Delaware corporate firm is speedily earning a reputation for quality creditors' and creditors' committee work. The group advises on out-of-court workouts and restructurings, but is primarily involved in Chapter 11 proceedings.
The Lawyers: **Bill Sudell** is felt to be the driving force behind the team's growth. A *"sophisticated attorney with a sophisticated practice,"* Sudell was highly recommended for representation of creditors. Recent highlights include serving as committee counsel in the Owens Corning bankruptcy, as well as acting as bank counsel in the Polaroid restructuring.
The Clients: JPMorgan Chase and Net 2000.

Pachulski, Stang, Ziehl, Young, Jones & Weintraub PC
see firm details p.860
The Firm: Now in its second year, the Delaware office of this established Californian boutique is considered an *"emerging force"* in the debtor and committee arena. Although its reputation is strongest in the representation of debtors, the 13-lawyer group also undertakes work for creditors' committees, bank groups and acquirers in Chapter 11 and out-of-court workouts.
The Lawyers: *"Well-connected"* **Laura Davis Jones** is universally credited with the group's rapid rise in Delaware. She enjoys *"legendary status"* for her work on the Continental Airlines case, and has since acted for such high-profile debtors as Trans World Airlines and Zenith Electronics.
The Clients: The team has represented clients American Tissue and Trans World Airlines.

Potter Anderson & Corroon LLP
The Firm: A smaller bankruptcy practice, esteemed by rivals for its representation of creditors in Chapter 11 proceedings. Eight attorneys act almost exclusively for nondebtor entities, including creditors, creditors' committees and purchasers, although it is in its work with unsecured creditors that the group is felt really to shine.
The Lawyers: *"Smart and aggressive"* **Laurie Selber Silverstein** was named as *"one of the best creditors' lawyers in town."* The *"first point of call for unsecured creditors,"* she was counsel to the unsecured creditors' committee in the Epic Capital case.
The Clients: The group has been involved in most of the telecom bankruptcies filed in Delaware and has acted for SBC affiliates Southwestern Bell Telephone Company and Pacific Bell Telephone Company in the prepackaged Metrocall and Winstar Communications bankruptcies.

Other Notable Practitioners
"Energetic" **Neil Glassman** of The Bayard Firm attracts attention for his representation of creditors' committees. Glassman acted for the creditors' committee in the Winstar Communications Chapter 11 reorganization and was creditors' counsel for Dictaphone. A *"prominent"* attorney doing *"more and more debtor work,"* he restructured the restaurant company FRD Acquisition Co. *"Excellent in substantive law,"* **David Stratton** of Philadelphia-based firm Pepper Hamilton LLP is also visible as creditors' committee counsel. Among notable creditors' representations, he has acted for committees in the Fruit of the Loom and Hechinger Investment Company bankruptcies. On the debtors' side, his firm has appeared in hi-tech bankruptcies, including Sega.com's Chapter 11 proceedings, and advised on VecTour's business reorganization. Stratton also acted for music company complainants against the proposed purchase of Napster by German media conglomerate Bertelsmann.

LITIGATION

DELAWARE
Leading firms
(Litigation: General Commercial)

1. MORRIS, NICHOLS, ARSHT Wilmington
   RICHARDS LAYTON & FINGER Wilmington
2. POTTER ANDERSON & CORROON LLP Wilmington
   YOUNG CONAWAY STARGATT & TAYLOR Wilmington
3. ASHBY & GEDDES Wilmington
   SKADDEN, ARPS Wilmington
4. GRANT & EISENHOFER PA Wilmington
   ROSENTHAL, MONHAIT, GROSS Wilmington

Firms are listed alphabetically in each band.

Morris, Nichols, Arsht & Tunnell
The Firm: Peers identified the firm as a *"big-name"* local defense counsel in corporate and commercial litigation. Class and derivatives actions, shareholders' suits and takeovers feature in the group's workload. The firm also acts as local counsel in patent litigation. A *"powerful"* group of 50 attorneys handles a *"large volume of litigation with consistent quality"* for corporate boards in the Delaware Court of Chancery.
The Lawyers: Standing *"head and shoulders"* above his peers is the universally respected **Gil Sparks**. Clients and colleagues share *"great confidence in his judgment and skill,"* while rivals applaud his *"ability to relate to any number of*

GENERAL COMMERCIAL

people." He forged his *"towering"* reputation in high-profile cases such as the Unocal and Revlon matters, and is now acting for Ford in shareholders' actions arising out of the Firestone tire recall. He is also representing Viacom in shareholders' litigation stemming from of its 1999 merger with CBS. **Ken Nachbar** is esteemed by rivals, particularly for his *"outstanding"* trial skills. **Bill Lafferty** is cementing his reputation among peers as a *"likable attorney – in the ascendant."* **Alan Stone** acts largely for defendants in corporate disputes in the Delaware Court of Chancery. Recent highlights include successfully defending the credit card bank Juniper against an application for an injunction against further

DELAWARE

LITIGATION

DELAWARE
Leading individuals
(Litigation: General Commercial)

[1] SPARKS Gilchrist *Morris, Nichols, Arsht*, Wilmington
[2] ASHBY Lawrence *Ashby & Geddes*, Wilmington
BALOTTI Frank *Richards Layton & Finger*, Wilmington
FINKELSTEIN Jesse *Richards Layton*, Wilmington
MCBRIDE David *Young Conaway Stargatt*, Wilmington
PAYSON Robert *Potter Anderson*, Wilmington
WOLFE Donald *Potter Anderson*, Wilmington
[3] GOLDMAN Michael *Potter Anderson*, Wilmington
NACHBAR Kenneth *Morris, Nichols, Arsht*, Wilmington
RICHARDS Charlie *Richards Layton & Finger*, Wilmington
[4] ABRAMS Kevin *Richards Layton & Finger*, Wilmington
LAFFERTY William *Morris, Nichols, Arsht*, Wilmington
STONE Alan *Morris, Nichols, Arsht*, Wilmington
WALSH Peter *Potter Anderson & Corroon*, Wilmington

Individuals are listed alphabetically in each band.

financing, which was taken out by its venture capital partner, Benchmark Capital. He also acted for Unocal in matters involving a short-form merger.
The Clients: The group is representing ARCO Chemical Company in litigation arising out of its 1998 acquisition by Lyondell. It is also respected for its work on behalf of major, national law firms. Other clients include Unocal and Juniper.

Richards Layton & Finger
The Firm: Delaware's largest firm boasts a broad, deep litigation practice, esteemed for its local counsel work for corporate defendants in the Delaware Court of Chancery. Twenty-five lawyers are also active as lead and local counsel in general commercial, IP and bankruptcy litigation.
The Lawyers: Of the "*old school*" Delaware bar, **Frank Balotti** undertakes both corporate advice and litigation work, in addition to his prolific publishing and lecturing. He continues to command respect as a "*class act*" in litigation, having featured in many of Delaware's key corporate cases. An international reputation for corporate defense work makes **Jesse Finkelstein** one of the firm's "*best assets.*" "*Outstanding – terrific and thorough,*" he was recently successful in defending Hilton Hotels against a challenge to a rights plan drafted by its directors. A "*senior figure*" in the firm's lineup, **Charlie Richards** also enjoys a strong reputation, particularly for his work with oil companies. He has acted in major oil company takeovers, including the Marathon Oil Company/Pennaco Energy acquisition. Elsewhere, he represented Donna Karan International when it was taken over by French luxury goods company LVMH. He advised Conoco in litigation arising out of its merger with Phillips Petroleum Company, including against DuPont. Completing a "*stellar*" lineup, **Kevin Abrams** stands out as a corporate litigator.
The Clients: The group acts for Conoco and AOL Time Warner.

Potter Anderson & Corroon LLP
The Firm: One of Delaware's oldest litigation practices. Although smaller than its chief rivals, it is said to be staffed with "*excellent attorneys.*" The group is active in corporate, employment and creditors' rights litigation.
The Lawyers: "*Sound in judgment,*" **Bob Payson** was a popular figure among opponents. He is an "*efficient and trustworthy adversary,*" and has acted as Delaware counsel for Hewlett-Packard in its dispute with Walter Hewlett. Also advised the WWF in its dispute with Barry Diller. **Don Wolfe** was commended by interviewees as a "*player of significance*" in Delaware. His practice centers on litigation in the Delaware Court of Chancery and on corporate counseling for boards of directors and special board committees. He has featured in many of the major Delaware cases, including Hewlett-Packard and TriStar Pictures. Also advised boards of directors and special committees for Pharmacia, Levi Strauss and Hewlett-Packard. **Mike Goldman**, chairman of the firm, enjoyed a recent victory for client DuPont against Conoco. He acted for Franklin Mutual Advisers LLC in a control dispute over ICN Pharmaceuticals. **Peter Walsh** has successfully defended shareholder class actions, and won an appeal for New Castle County in an insurance coverage dispute.
The Clients: The group acts for DuPont, Franklin Mutual Advisers LLC and Hewlett-Packard.

Young Conaway Stargatt & Taylor, LLP
see firm details p.907
The Firm: The firm was founded on plaintiffs' personal injury work. Its litigation practice now encompasses local counsel work in large-scale disputes and bankruptcy matters. Described to researchers as an "*eclectic*" group. It is active in the defense of class and derivative actions and plaintiff work in minority shareholders' valuation actions. The group also enjoys expertise in tobacco-related disputes, where it acted for the American Legacy Foundation, which was seeking a declaration of contractual independence from the tobacco company, Lorillard.
The Lawyers: Although **David McBride**'s (see p.100) "*aggressive*" style did not meet with universal approval, he commands widespread respect among peers. He acts in the defense of class and derivative actions in the Delaware Court of Chancery. Recent highlights include representing IBP in its successful bid to force Tyson Foods to consummate their agreed merger. He also acted for CIBC – an equity holder – against privately held internet banking company Juniper Financial.
The Clients: Harvard University, CIBC, American Legacy Foundation and IBP use the firm.

Ashby & Geddes
The Firm: This boutique's reputation in litigation is inextricably linked with that of its name partner **Larry Ashby**. A "*well-connected*" attorney, he was acclaimed a "*class act*" by rivals and clients. He recently acted with Cooley Godward on behalf of Walter Hewlett in his high-profile dispute with Hewlett-Packard.

Skadden, Arps, Slate, Meagher & Flom LLP & Affiliates
see firm details p.878
The Firm: Interviewees agree that a "*tremendous client base*" and "*outstanding local lawyers*" make the Delaware office of this New York giant a "*prominent force*" in litigation. It acts as lead counsel in national corporate litigation, and supports Skadden Arps' other offices.
The Clients: The group, which includes Steven Rothschild, is acting for The Williams Companies and certain of its directors in connection with federal securities litigation pending in Oklahoma.

Grant & Eisenhofer PA
The Firm: Commended by peers as an "*emerging force*" in Delaware. This litigation boutique was founded in 1997 by former partners of Skadden Arps. It commands respect for its representation of institutional investors in shareholders' and derivatives actions, federal securities fraud litigation and IP disputes.
The Clients: Debtors and institutional investors use the group for bankruptcy matters. It represented the principal in a battle for control over auto parts retailer Dart Group. Also represented an Australian client in a $30 million RICO and securities fraud litigation involving two publicly held companies.

Rosenthal, Monhait, Gross & Goddess, PA
The Firm: Peers reported that a "*huge volume*" of work, undertaken by a "*deeply talented team*" ensures that the group stands out among plaintiff firms in Delaware. The team, which includes Joe Rosenthal, appears primarily as local counsel for plaintiffs in corporate, securities and commercial litigation.
The Clients: Recent practice highlights include acting with Milberg Weiss Bershad Hynes & Lerach for shareholder Kathleen Rooney against payment company PayPal and online auctioneer eBay – challenging the takeover deal struck between the two companies. The group also acted for plaintiffs against DaimlerChrysler, alleging violations of the Securities Exchange Act.

REAL ESTATE — DELAWARE

DELAWARE
Leading firms (Real Estate)
1. YOUNG CONAWAY STARGATT *Wilmington*
2. RICHARDS LAYTON & FINGER *Wilmington*
3. SAUL EWING LLP *Wilmington*
4. MORRIS, JAMES, HITCHENS *Wilmington*

Leading individuals (Real Estate)
1. **KRAPF Robert** Richards Layton & Finger, *Wilmington*
2. **DIPRINZIO Eugene** Young Conaway Stargatt, *Wilmington*
   ISKEN Donald Morris, Nichols, Arsht, *Wilmington*
   LEVINE Richard Young Conaway Stargatt, *Wilmington*
3. **KRISTOL Daniel** Richards Layton & Finger, *Wilmington*
   LISICKY Joseph Morris, James, Hitchens, *Wilmington*
   STABLER Wendie Saul Ewing LLP, *Wilmington*

Firms and individuals are listed alphabetically in each band.

Young Conaway Stargatt & Taylor, LLP
see firm details p.907
The Firm: Interviewees agreed that the firm has "*all the bases covered*" with this "*large, well-balanced*" commercial real estate practice. Ten lawyers advise on land use transactions for local and national institutional and entrepreneurial developers. Residential, retail and warehouse developments form part of the workload. The group also acts for financial institutions and REITs on real estate lending, and works for national title insurers in multi-state transactions.
The Lawyers: Eugene DiPrinzio (see p.100) was strongly endorsed to researchers as "*one of the best in Delaware,*" largely for his work for developers. Among a large roster of clients, he represents PREIT-Rubin, the REIT that owns the Christiana Mall project in Newark, Delaware, and acts for national home builders such as Ryan Homes. Rivals commended **Richard Levine** (see p.100) for his representation of lenders, including MBNA America Bank.
The Clients: PREIT-Rubin, Ryan Homes and MBNA America Bank are typical of the firm's client base.

Richards Layton & Finger
The Firm: Peers agree that "*sheer numbers*" and a stable of clients that reads like a local who's who ensure the firm's prominence in real estate. Six dedicated real estate attorneys advise investors and local developers on residential and commercial development transactions.
The Lawyers: Robert Krapf was singled out by rivals who widely proclaimed him to be the "*leading real estate attorney in the state.*" An experienced practitioner, he is thought to enjoy a "*broad, sophisticated practice.*" **Dan Kristol** wins endorsement from peers for his work in the zoning, development and leasing of space to retailers and restaurants. Past work has included developments for home improvement stores Lowe's and Home Depot, restaurants Waffle House and Applebee's International, and Eckerd's drugstores.
The Clients: Local developers and investors make up a large proportion of the group's client list.

Saul Ewing LLP
The Firm: Controlling a "*good book of business,*" this Philadelphia-based firm has a solid foothold on the East Coast. It won praise for its representation of institutional investors, REITs and developers in commercial real estate transactions. The group is active in financings, zoning approvals, acquisitions, sales and leasings.
The Lawyers: "*Hot*" zoning and land use attorney **Wendie Stabler** was recommended to researchers. She represents colleges, nonprofit organizations, developers and major telecom carriers in zoning and land use proceedings before state and county agencies. She is best known for her work with major client AstraZeneca, and acted as lead land use counsel in the expansion of its US headquarters in Wilmington, Delaware.
The Clients: AstraZeneca; AT&T Wireless; Conectiv; The Welfare Foundation and Wilmington College.

Morris, James, Hitchens & Williams, LLP
The Firm: This local full-service outfit won consistent peer and client endorsement for its "*depth of knowledge.*" A team of six attorneys acts for local developers and investors in the acquisitions and sales, and financing and leasing of commercial real estate. It has also been active in office buildings and warehousing facilities.
The Lawyers: Among a "*deep bench,*" **Joe Lisicky** was singled out to researchers as a "*major player,*" particularly for his work in the development field. His recent practice highlights include acting for the purchaser of two office towers in Wilmington city center.
The Clients: The firm acts for investors and developers.

Other Notable Practitioners
"*Experienced and highly skilled,*" **Don Isken** is Morris, Nichols, Arsht & Tunnell's sole real estate partner – the "*whole show.*" While he acts in a range of real estate matters for both lender and developer clients, he is renowned for his representation of large national developer clients in sophisticated transactions. Recent practice highlights include acting for the purchaser of the $82 million Chase Manhattan Center in downtown Wilmington, one of the state's tallest buildings. Locally, he acts for The Delaware River & Bay Authority and for The Port of Wilmington on leasing matters. Other clients include GE Capital.

Leaders in Delaware

ABER, Gary
Heiman, Aber, Goldlust & Baker, Wilmington 302 658 1800
Recommended in Employment

ABRAMS, Kevin
Richards Layton & Finger, Wilmington 302 658 6541
Recommended in Litigation

ALEXANDER, Frederick
Morris, Nichols, Arsht & Tunnell, Wilmington 302 658 9200
Recommended in Corporate/M&A

ASHBY, Lawrence
Ashby & Geddes, Wilmington 302 654 1888
Recommended in Litigation

BALOTTI, Frank
Richards Layton & Finger, Wilmington 302 658 6541
Recommended in Corporate/M&A, Litigation

BLACK, Lewis
Morris, Nichols, Arsht & Tunnell, Wilmington 302 658 9200
Recommended in Corporate/M&A

BRADY, Robert S
Young Conaway Stargatt & Taylor, LLP, Wilmington 302 571 6690
rbrady@ycst.com
Recommended in Insolvency
Specialization: Partner in the business reorganisation and restructuring department. Bankruptcy clients have included, among others, Continental Airlines, Columbia Gas, Integrated Health Services, Budget Rent-a-Car and Golden Books.
Prof. Memberships: Member: Delaware State (Member, Sections on: General Corporation Law; Litigation) and American (Member, Sections on: Business Law; Litigation) Bar Associations; American Bankruptcy Institute.
Career: Admitted to Delaware bar (1990).
Personal: Born Salem, New Jersey, November 20, 1964. Education: Virginia Polytechnic Institute and State University (BS, 1987); Dickinson School of Law (JD, cum laude, 1990). Member, Woolsack Honor Society, a law school honorary society limited to graduates in the top 10% of their class. Recipient, American Jurisprudence Awards in Torts and Constitutional Law. Member, Dickinson Law Review, 1989/1990.

DELAWARE   LEADERS

BUSSARD, Donald
Richards Layton & Finger, Wilmington
302 658 6541
Recommended in Corporate/M&A

CHEHI, Mark S
Skadden, Arps, Slate, Meagher & Flom LLP, Wilmington 302 651 3160
mchehi@skadden.com
Recommended in Insolvency
Specialization: Has extensive experience in major corporate restructurings, workouts and Chapter 11 cases in Delaware and other jurisdictions - and handles complex bankruptcy, corporate and commercial litigation matters. Has represented debtors, creditors, lenders, committees and acquirers in a wide variety of situations. Also represents and advises other clients in non-bankruptcy corporate, transactional, commercial and litigation matters.
Career: JD, The Law School, The University of Chicago, 1990. BA, Haverford College, 1980.

CLARK, Anthony W
Skadden, Arps, Slate, Meagher & Flom LLP, Wilmington 302 651 3080
tclark@skadden.com
Recommended in Insolvency
Specialization: Heads the firm's corporate restructuring and bankruptcy litigation practice in Wilmington. Also handles complex corporate, securities and general litigation matters. Has extensive experience representing debtors, creditors and acquirors in major corporate reorganization cases in Delaware and elsewhere. Significant Chapter 11 debtor representations include Hayes Lemmerz International, Inc., Mid-American Waste Systems, Inc., UDC Homes, United Merchants and Manufacturers Inc., Wang Laboratories, Inc., and Cardinal Industries Inc.
Personal: JD, Temple University School of Law, 1979; BA, State University of New York at Cortland, 1973.

COLLINS, Mark
Richards Layton & Finger, Wilmington
302 658 6541
Recommended in Insolvency

DIPRINZIO, Eugene A
Young Conaway Stargatt & Taylor, LLP, Wilmington 302 571 6664
ediprinzio@ycst.com
Recommended in Real Estate
Specialization: Partner; Chair of the Real Estate Section. His practice emphasizes the handling of complex commercial real estate transactions and the representation of financial institutions and other lenders involving commercial mortgage loans and asset-based lending. In addition, he has represented numerous property developers and borrowers in connection with their overall activities and has more than twenty years experience in closing real estate transactions on a primary basis. He has been engaged in many substantial leasing transactions on behalf of landlords and tenants and has successfully represented building owners in prosecuting their property tax assessment appeals. He is counsel to title insurers and assists with the closing of multi-state transactions.
Prof. Memberships: He is a Fellow and Delaware State Chair of the American College of Mortgage Attorneys and a frequent lecturer on a variety of real estate topics.
Career: Admitted to practice law in both Pennsylvania and Delaware.

EASTON, Richard L
Skadden, Arps, Slate, Meagher & Flom LLP, Wilmington 302 651 3040
reaston@skadden.com
Recommended in Corporate/M&A
Specialization: Has as a wide-ranging corporate practice, concentrating in mergers and acquisitions, securities and Delaware corporate law matters. Advises other lawyers in the firm and its affiliates on the Delaware law aspects of their transactions and leads the firm's representation in other transactions. Has represented many corporate, investment banking and individual clients in a variety of transactions, including negotiated acquisitions, contested takeovers, proxy contests, and going-private, leveraged buyout and restructuring transactions. Has also represented both issuers and underwriters in public offerings of debt and equity securities. Provides general corporate and securities law advice to a number of corporate clients and regularly deals with disclosure, fiduciary duty and corporate governance-related matters.
Prof. Memberships: Member, New York and Delaware bar associations.
Career: JD, Georgetown, 1975; BA, Wesleyan University, 1972 (cum laude).

FINKELSTEIN, Jesse
Richards Layton & Finger, Wilmington
302 658 6541
Recommended in Litigation

GALARDI, Gregg M
Skadden, Arps, Slate, Meagher & Flom LLP, Wilmington 302 651 3150
ggalardi@skadden.com
Recommended in Insolvency
Specialization: Represents major corporations in business reorganizations, restructurings, acquisitions and divestitures. Clients have included debtors, creditors, creditors' committees, bank groups, investors, acquirors and financial advisors in all stages of complex restructuring transactions, from Chapter 11 reorganizations to out-of-court negotiations and workouts. Has recently served as lead or co-lead counsel on several high-profile Chapter 11 matters in and outside of the US.
Career: American Bankruptcy Institute; Turnaround Management Association; International Federation of Insolvency Practitioners; Local Rules Committee, Delaware Banruptcy Bar; Litigation Section of the Delaware Bar Association. University of Pennsylvania: JD, 1990; PhD., Philosophy, 1990; MA, Economics, 1985; BA, 1979.

GLASSMAN, Neil
The Bayard Firm, Wilmington
302 655 5000
Recommended in Insolvency

GOLDMAN, Michael
Potter Anderson & Corroon LLP, Wilmington 302 984 6000
Recommended in Corporate/M&A, Litigation

ISKEN, Donald
Morris, Nichols, Arsht & Tunnell, Wilmington 302 658 9200
Recommended in Real Estate

JONES, Laura Davis
Pachulski, Stang, Ziehl, Young, Jones & Weintraub, Wilmington 302 652 4100
Recommended in Insolvency

KRAPF, Robert
Richards Layton & Finger, Wilmington
302 658 6541
Recommended in Real Estate

KRISTOL, Daniel
Richards Layton & Finger, Wilmington
302 658 6541
Recommended in Real Estate

LAFFERTY, William
Morris, Nichols, Arsht & Tunnell, Wilmington 302 658 9200
Recommended in Litigation

LEVINE, Richard A
Young Conaway Stargatt & Taylor, LLP, Wilmington 302 571 6640
rlevine@ycst.com
Recommended in Real Estate
Specialization: Administrative Partner; practices in the areas of real estate, commercial transactions and banking law. In the real estate area, he has substantial experience representing purchasers and sellers of commercial real estate, including shopping centers, office buildings and industrial properties. His work in this area includes land development, construction, leasing and financing. He has also represented lenders with respect to construction and permanent financing. His practice outside of real estate includes the representation of banks and financial institutions with respect to Delaware law and the representation of buyers and sellers of business entities, whether structured as equity or asset sales. These transactions have varied from local 'mom and pop' businesses to participation as local counsel in transactions of national scope. In particular, his practice frequently involves rendering opinions of Delaware law with respect to local, national and international business and financial transactions. He has also assisted in the sale of several entities involved in reorganization proceedings.

LISICKY, Joseph
Morris, James, Hitchens & Williams, LLP, Wilmington 302 888 6800
Recommended in Real Estate

MCBRIDE, David
Young Conaway Stargatt & Taylor, LLP, Wilmington 302 571 6639
dmcbride@ycst.com
Recommended in Litigation
Specialization: Partner; his practice is concentrated in the area of corporate law and corporate and commercial litigation. He has been involved in a plethora of Delaware corporate law cases, particularly in the area of mergers and acquisitions, including Paramount Communications Inc. v. QVC Network, Inc., Paramount Communications Inc. v. Time Inc., Revlon Inc. v. MacAndrews & Forbes Holding Inc., In re First Boston Inc. Shareholders Litig., In re Resorts Int'l. Shareholders Litig., Freedman v. Restaurant Associates Indus., Inc., Robert M. Bass Group, Inc. v. Evans (Macmillan, Inc.), Shamrock Holdings Inc. v. Polaroid Corp., In re RJR Nabisco, Inc. Shareholders Litigation, Henley Group v. Santa Fe Southern Pacific Corp., Pennzoil Co. v. Getty Oil Co., and Edelman v. Phillips Petroleum.
Prof. Memberships: Member of the American Law Institute, the Corporate Council of the Corporate Law Section of the Delaware State Bar Association, the Rules Committee of the Delaware Court of Chancery, the Board of Editors of the Delaware Lawyer, a director of the Historical Society for the Court of Chancery, and has authored several articles and CLE outlines in the area of corporate law.
Career: A graduate of the Georgetown University School of Foreign Service in 1971, and the Emory University School of Law in 1975, he began private practice in 1975.

MCDONOUGH, Kathleen
Potter Anderson & Corroon LLP, Wilmington 302 984 6000
Recommended in Employment

NACHBAR, Kenneth
Morris, Nichols, Arsht & Tunnell, Wilmington 302 658 9200
Recommended in Litigation

NEUBERGER, Thomas Stephen
Law Office of Thomas S. Neuberger P.A., Wilmington 302 655 0582
Recommended in Employment

LEADERS   DELAWARE

PATTON, JR, James L
Young Conaway Stargatt & Taylor, LLP,
Wilmington 302 571 6684
jpatton@ycst.com
Recommended in Insolvency
Specialization: Corporate restructurings and mass tort related insolvencies. Clients have included, among many others, Continental Airlines, Inc., Columbia Gas Systems, Inc., Days Inns of America, Inc., MEI Diversified, Inc., Simmons Upholstered Furniture, Inc., Lomas Financial Corporation, Fuller-Austin Insulation Company; Florida Coast Paper Company, Alterra Healthcare Corporation, the Asbestos Future Claims Representative in connection with The Celotex Corporation, Babcock & Wilcox Company, Owens-Corning, Armstrong World Industries, Inc., Federal-Mogul Global Inc., USG Corporation, Pittsburgh Corning Corporation, Kaiser Group International, Inc., Narco, and Halliburton Company, as well as debtors in over 40 prepackaged bankruptcy cases.
Prof. Memberships: Member, Delaware State Bar Association, Chairman, Bankruptcy Law Subcommittee, Commercial Law Section (1986-); Member, American Bar Association, Business Law Section, Business Bankruptcy Committee, Claims Trading Subcommittee (Vice Chair, 2002-); Member, Association of Trial Lawyers of America; Member, American Bankruptcy Institute; Member of Board of Contributors, Fletcher Corporate Bankruptcy, Reorganization and Dissolution, Clark, Boardman, Callaghan (1992); Participant on Judge Scirica's Working Group on Mass Torts in connection with the Report of the Advisory Committee on Civil Rules and the Working Group on Mass Torts to the Chief Justice of the United States and to the Judicial Conference of the United States (1999); Fellow, American College of Bankruptcy.
Career: Chairman, *Young Conaway Stargatt & Taylor, LLP*; joined firm in 1983 and became partner in 1989.
Publications: Co-author, 'Effects of Bankruptcy on Director & Officer Liability' and 'Directors & Officer Liability Insurance Presented at Third Circuit Judicial Conference', 2002; Co-author, 'Futures Representative's Informational Brief', Mealey's 'Asbestos Bankruptcy Conference', 2001; Co-author, 'Dancing with Scylla and Charybdis: the Tough Job of Directors of a Troubled Company', presented at the American Bar Association, Section of Business Law, Spring Meeting, 2000.

PAYSON, Robert
Potter Anderson & Corroon LLP,
Wilmington 302 984 6000
Recommended in Litigation

PERNICK, Norman
Saul Ewing LLP, Wilmington
302 421 6800
Recommended in Insolvency

RICHARDS, Charlie
Richards Layton & Finger, Wilmington
302 658 6541
Recommended in Litigation

SANDLER, Sheldon N
Young Conaway Stargatt & Taylor, LLP,
Wilmington 302 571 6673
ssandler@ycst.com
Recommended in Employment
Specialization: Partner and Chairman of the Employment Law Department of *Young Conaway Stargatt & Taylor, LLP*. He also serves on the firm's Management Committee.
Prof. Memberships: Founding Chairman of the Delaware State Bar Association's Labor and Employment Law Section, has chaired the Lawyers' Advisory Committee to the Court of Appeals for the Third Circuit, served as President of the Delaware Chapter of the Federal Bar Association, served on the Delaware Court of Chancery Rules Committee, and has taught Legal Aspects of Human Resource Management in Widener University's MBA program.
Publications: Author of the chapter on employment law in 'The Delaware Supreme Court: The First Fifty Year's', a book commissioned by the Delaware Supreme Court in commemoration of its first half-century as Delaware's highest court. In surveys of Delaware lawyers published in Delaware Today Magazine in 1996, 1999 and 2001, he was named one of Delaware's leading labor lawyers.
Personal: He is a graduate of the University of Michigan (1962) and the University of Pennsylvania Law School (1965), and holds a degree of Master of Laws in Labor Law from Temple University (1978).

SELBER SILVERSTEIN, Laurie
Potter Anderson & Corroon LLP,
Wilmington 302 984 6000
Recommended in Insolvency

SHANNON, Brendan Linehan
Young Conaway Stargatt & Taylor, LLP,
Wilmington 302 571 6696
bshannon@ycst.com
Recommended in Insolvency
Specialization: Partner; specializing in the representation of chapter 11 debtors-in-possession and official committees appointed in chapter 11 corporate reorganizations.
Prof. Memberships: Member of the Delaware and Pennsylvania Bars, and a member of the Delaware Chapter of the Federal Bar Association and the American Bankruptcy Institute.
Personal: Graduate of Princeton University and Marshall-Wythe School of Law at the College of William and Mary.

SPARKS, Gilchrist
Morris, Nichols, Arsht & Tunnell,
Wilmington 302 658 9200
Recommended in Corporate/M&A, Litigation

STABLER, Wendie
Saul Ewing LLP, Wilmington
302 421 6800
Recommended in Real Estate

STONE, Alan
Morris, Nichols, Arsht & Tunnell,
Wilmington 302 658 9200
Recommended in Litigation

STRATTON, David
Pepper Hamilton LLP, Wilmington
302 777 6500
Recommended in Insolvency

SUDELL, William
Morris, Nichols, Arsht & Tunnell,
Wilmington 302 658 9200
Recommended in Insolvency

WALSH, Peter
Potter Anderson & Corroon LLP,
Wilmington 302 984 6000
Recommended in Litigation

WIER, Richard
Richard R. Wier, Jr.,P.A., Wilmington
302 888 3222
Recommended in Employment

WILLIAMS, David
Morris, James, Hitchens & Williams, LLP,
Wilmington 302 888 6800
Recommended in Employment

WILLOUGHBY, Barry
Young Conaway Stargatt & Taylor, LLP,
Wilmington 302 571 6666
bwilloughby@ycst.com
Recommended in Employment
Specialization: Partner; Employment Law Department of *Young Conaway Stargatt & Taylor, LLP*. His practice is primarily limited to representation of employers in claims of employment discrimination, retaliation, and 'wrongful discharge' under federal and state law, including defense of charges of racial and sexual harassment. He also defends public employers in First Amendment 'whistleblower' cases and other constitutional law allegations such as asserted violations of due process or equal protection. He also represents employers in union related conflicts, including representation in organizing campaigns, unfair labor practice proceedings, and grievance/arbitration hearings.
Prof. Memberships: Community and civic activities include pro bono service as Counsel and ex-officio Board Member of the United Way of Delaware, Inc. and General Counsel and Corporate Secretary of Junior Achievement of Delaware, Inc.
Publications: In surveys of Delaware lawyers published by Delaware Today magazine, he was named one of Delaware's leading labor lawyers.
Personal: Graduated from the University of Delaware in 1976 with High Honors and with Distinction. In 1979, he graduated cum laude from the Dickinson School of Law where he was a member of the Law Review and Woolsack Society, a law school honor society limited to graduates in the top ten percent of their class.

WOLFE JR, Donald
Potter Anderson & Corroon LLP,
Wilmington 302 984 6000
Recommended in Litigation

DISTRICT OF COLUMBIA

OVERVIEW

CONTENTS: Antitrust p.103 Arbitration p.106; Communications p.106; Construction p.110; Corporate/M&A p.111; Employment: p.112; Energy p.113; Environment p.117; Insolvency p.119; Insurance p.120; Intellectual Property p.121; Litigation p.122; Media p.125; Projects p.126; Real Estate p.127; Tax p.129; Individuals' Profiles p.131.

DC'S TOP TEN
1. Hogan & Hartson
2. Arnold & Porter
3. Wilmer, Cutler & Pickering
4. Skadden, Arps. Slate, Meagher & Flom
5. Latham & Watkins
6. Covington & Burling
6. Gibson, Dunn & Crutcher
7. Jones Day
8. Sidley Austin Brown & Wood
9. Williams & Connolly

Ranking based on Chambers' research within the state.

All quotes in the text are from interviews with clients and competitors.

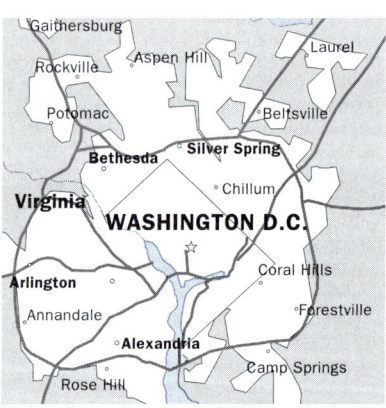

OVERVIEW: Washington DC is a hard market to break into: experience and contacts are vital for success in regulatory and legislative work. Traditionally, many national firms have been happy to leave this work to local players. That is changing, as the Sarbanes-Oxley and Patriot Acts increase the importance of regulatory expertise. However, perhaps unsurprisingly, the three firms that head *Chambers'* tables are indigenous to DC.

All of them have strong presences in litigation and regulatory work. However, **Hogan & Hartson** noses ahead in the rankings because it also possesses the most depth and capacity for corporate work. Under world-class Warren Gorrell, the team has developed the premier REITs practice. It acts in deals like Equity Office Properties Trust's $7.2 billion acquisition of Spieker Properties. The firm has also shown itself to be among the keenest of the DC outfits to expand, boasting a network of foreign offices. This has aided it in international antitrust work, such as Carnival's hostile tender for P&O Princess Cruises, which it counseled through challenges from the FTC and European Commission. The firm's reputation for handling big-league communications work received a boost from its March 2002 merger with New York-based Squadron Ellenoff Plesent & Sheinfeld.

Arnold & Porter is best known for its elite antitrust practice. Star player Bill Baer leads a team of about 50 lawyers say peers. The acknowledged antitrust leader, it specializes in complex litigation. This includes acting in the high-profile case alleging a cartel in the vitamin industry. It has also shepherded some enormous deals through both domestic and EU controls. Many of its other noteworthy practices, including communications and litigation, have a strong antitrust flavor. However, the firm also possesses transactional expertise. It assisted SBC Communications in its acquisitions of Pacific Bell and Ameritech, and boasts a superior real estate practice with broad experience.

Wilmer, Cutler & Pickering is perhaps best known for its insolvency profile. It has acted as debtors' counsel in many notable Chapter 11 cases, including PSINet and Iridium. The icing was recently added to the cake when it was appointed as one of the six firms handling the WorldCom investigations of the company's accounting practices. Its profile for general litigation is also high, with former US Solicitor General Seth Waxman among the country's premier Supreme Court advocates. Overall, this is a firm on the rise. Its practical and focused corporate department is bulking up and pulling in some big deals, while an improving antitrust team has been successfully clearing huge transactions like Bestfoods' $60 billion merger with Unilever.

The Wall Street firms have not yet invested heavily in DC. **Skadden, Arps, Slate, Meagher & Flom** is an exception. Its tremendous client base in the energy and projects spheres relies upon the top-class regulatory services that the group supplies. Unlike many DC practices, however, its transactional focus is also strong. A premier-league tax department, for example, has a great profile for advising on M&A and structured finance. This has been exhibited in such deals as IBM's acquisition of PwC Consulting. International tax coordination is another strength, with Paul Oosterhuis able to navigate the tax laws of any country.

The national firms have been quicker to stake a claim in the DC market. So far, according to *Chambers'* tables, the most successful of these has been **Latham & Watkins**. The firm's strength in communications and projects makes a DC presence essential. In communications, the firm has an increasingly global profile and a strong mix of transactional and corporate expertise. It has handled such deals as DIRECTV's merger with EchoStar, valued at $30 billion. The projects team, with John Sachs has great experience in Latin America and a growing domestic profile. The firm also boasts one of the best environmental practices in town.

Another indigenous DC firm that is doing well is **Covington & Burling**. It enjoys a long-standing tradition of insurance work, where it has an unrivaled reputation for complex coverage litigation. It benefits greatly from the kudos of dean of the insurance bar Robert Sayler. Sayler's stellar reputation extends to general commercial litigation, where the firm enjoys a name for technical expertise. In the communications sector, its broad practice includes strength in media and broadcasting. It acts for the likes of Microsoft, The Washington Post Company and affiliates of NBC.

A strong thread of litigation expertise unites **Gibson, Dunn & Crutcher**'s DC practice groups. Its environmental and antitrust practices, for example, are built around high-quality litigation teams.

As a West Coast firm, technology is also important, and many of its groups, including the impressive employment department, are known for their hi-tech, biotech and healthcare focuses. In litigation itself, the firm has a fine appellate practice, built up by Theodore Olson, the current US Solicitor General.

National firm **Jones Day** has also done well in DC. It is respected for antitrust work, with a particularly good profile in the telecommunication and pharmaceutical markets. Masterful strategist Joe Sims has represented Aventis in the vitamin cartel case and acted in the antitrust review of the AOL Time Warner merger. The firm also boasts outstanding lawyers in the employment field and a high-profile energy practice with a particular name for electricity regulatory advice.

Sidley Austin Brown & Wood also has a noteworthy energy practice, with a strong regulatory presence at the FERC. In litigation too, the firm fields a superior team headed by Carter Phillips, a former Assistant to the US Solicitor General. It is in environmental law, however, that the office really stands out. The jewel in the crown of a superb national practice, it has expertise across multiple disciplines, but is particularly commended for its environmental enforcement capabilities. Angus Macbeth and Dave Buente are major players in this arena.

"If you think of litigation in DC you think of **Williams & Connolly**," according to market sources. Its mixed practice encompasses high-profile criminal and commercial work, which it handles with a characteristically pugnacious style. In Brendan Sullivan, it boasts an excellent tactician with no weaknesses in court. He represented the nine dissenting states in the well-publicized Microsoft antitrust litigation. The firm has a particular tradition of media litigation, representing such clients as The Washington Post, The National Enquirer, Newsweek, CNN and NBC.

ANTITRUST — DISTRICT OF COLUMBIA

DISTRICT OF COLUMBIA
Leading firms (Antitrust)

1 ARNOLD & PORTER
2 JONES DAY
3 CLEARY GOTTLIEB STEEN & HAMILTON
    CLIFFORD CHANCE US LLP
4 GIBSON, DUNN & CRUTCHER LLP
    HOGAN & HARTSON LLP
    HOWREY SIMON ARNOLD & WHITE
    O'MELVENY & MYERS LLP
5 BOIES, SCHILLER & FLEXNER
    FRIED, FRANK, HARRIS, SHRIVER & JACOBSON
    WILMER, CUTLER & PICKERING
6 CROWELL & MORING LLP
    MORGAN, LEWIS & BOCKIUS LLP
    SHEARMAN & STERLING

Leading individuals (Antitrust)

1 BAER Bill *Arnold & Porter,*
    LEDDY Mark *Cleary Gottlieb Steen & Hamilton,*
    SIMS Joe *Jones Day,*
2 CARY George *Cleary Gottlieb Steen & Hamilton,*
    McDAVID Janet *Hogan & Hartson LLP,*
    MELAMED Doug *Wilmer, Cutler & Pickering,*
    NEWBORN Steve *Clifford Chance US LLP,*
    PROGER Phillip *Jones Day,*
    RILL James *Howrey Simon Arnold & White,*
    RULE Charles (Rick) *Fried, Frank, Harris, Shriver*
    SOHN Michael *Arnold & Porter,*
3 FLEXNER Donald *Boies, Schiller & Flexner,*
    KATTAN Joseph *Gibson, Dunn & Crutcher LLP,*
    LOFTIS James *Gibson, Dunn & Crutcher LLP,*
    PARKER Richard *O'Melveny & Myers LLP,*
    ROSEN Richard *Arnold & Porter,*
4 KLAWITER Donald *Morgan, Lewis & Bockius LLP,*
    PATTERSON Donna *Arnold & Porter,*
    SCHECHTER Mark *Howrey Simon Arnold & White,*
    SCHILDKRAUT Marc *Howrey Simon Arnold & White,*
    SMITH Randolph *Crowell & Moring LLP,*
    SUNSHINE Steven *Shearman & Sterling,*
5 BLUMENTHAL William *King & Spalding LLP,*
    DENGER Michael *Gibson, Dunn & Crutcher LLP,*
    EGAN James *Clifford Chance US LLP,*
    FEINSTEIN Deborah *Arnold & Porter,*
    LETZLER Kenneth *Arnold & Porter,*
    VALENTINE Debra *O'Melveny & Myers LLP,*
    VARNEY Christine *Hogan & Hartson LLP,*
    WALD Douglas *Arnold & Porter,*
    YDE Paul *Freshfields Bruckhaus Deringer LLP,*

Firms and Individuals are listed alphabetically in each band.

Arnold & Porter
see firm details p.765

The Firm: This *"elite"* group of 48 DC antitrust specialists was deemed to be *"perfectly placed"* at the top of the market. Recommended as *"covering the gamut,"* the team of distinguished practitioners has tackled some of the most complex antitrust litigation in DC over the past 12 months, with a growing number of cases involving IP. The firm defended Xerox, for example, in challenges to its refusal to sell patented parts and licensed copyrighted software. Attorneys also negotiated settlements in one of the largest criminal antitrust cases in the country, which alleged price-fixing in the vitamin industry, and piloted some of the largest M&A ever proposed through the EC investigation process.

The Lawyers: Said to *"know the agencies backward and forward,"* department head **Bill Baer** (see p.132) leads a *"heck of a team."* Baer steered global giant Pfizer through its acquisition of Pharmacia. He also advised Micron in a DOJ investigation and defended Wyeth against alleged monopolization in the estrogen replacement therapy market. Firm chairman **Michael Sohn** (see p.146) is considered a formidable combatant who is *"quite hard to beat when he gets involved."* His practice focuses on antitrust clearance of M&A and treble damage class action suits. **Richard Rosen** (see p.144), a *"smart analyst and litigator,"* was esteemed by sources for his expertise in technology-related matters. **Donna Patterson**'s (see p.142) experience as former DOJ Deputy Assistant Attorney General of the Antitrust Division was felt to give her a significant *"edge"* in the market. She has supervised the investigations of such high-stakes M&A as GE's bid for Honeywell. Also leader of the firm's healthcare task force, Patterson counseled the likes of Aetna in antitrust matters. **Deborah Feinstein** (see p.135), described by peers as a *"bright"* and *"effective"* advocate, handled GE's acquisition of Bently Nevada, one of the largest suppliers of products and services for maintaining industrial equipment in the US. She has also advised Genzyme in its acquisition of Novazyme Pharmaceuticals, a manufacturer of enzyme replacement therapy. *"Terrifically talented"* **Kenneth Letzler** (see p.138) is the firm's lead attorney for Monsanto on antitrust matters. An expert in issues such as distribution, licensing and pricing in the consumer products and pharmaceutical industries, Letzler counseled clients in the music industry on piracy issues, particularly those involving the internet. **Doug Wald** (see p.148) was rated by peers as a *"capable, quiet and careful"* attorney. He successfully defended Philip Morris against an antitrust challenge arising from the company's nationwide settlement.

The Clients: GlaxoSmithKline; Philip Morris; Unilever; USA Interactive; Kroger; Boston Scientific and Kraft.

Jones Day
see firm details p.823

The Firm: *"Enjoying the confidence of a substantial client base,"* the firm advises blue-chip companies on a full range of antitrust matters, particularly those involving new technology markets such as telecommunications and pharmaceuticals. With specialists in 13 countries, the team's cross-border reach was thought to clear the way for *"getting some of the most difficult deals through."* The practice suffered a disappointment when Charles James chose to accept a position at ChevronTexaco instead of returning to the firm following a stint as DOJ's Assistant Attorney General in charge of the Antitrust Division. However, this is not felt to affect the firm's standing in the field.

The Lawyers: *"A masterful strategist,"* **Joe Sims** (see p.145) was reported to have *"one of the best practices around."* He continues to represent Aventis in the vitamin cartel case and helped steer the AOL Time Warner merger through antitrust review. Chair of the firm's antitrust and technology practices, Sims is a *"fearless"* advocate, widely admired for his willingness to *"dig his heels in."* **Phillip Proger** (see p.143) received kudos from peers for being a *"fantastic"* advocate whose easygoing style provides a *"good counterbalance to Sims."* He stands out among competitors for his *"strategic precision"* and *"effective people skills."* Commanding *"a high degree of respect"* among peers and government agency officials alike, Proger represented Bayer in the antitrust case involving Cipro, the anti-anthrax drug. He also advised Pernod Ricard in its sale of Orangina and defended Federated Department Stores against a patent infringement allegation.

The Clients: Abbott Laboratories; British Telecommunications; France Télécom; Ernst & Young; Nextel Communications; Procter & Gamble and Ultramar Diamond Shamrock.

Cleary Gottlieb Steen & Hamilton
see firm details p.782

The Firm: The firm boasts a number of *"high-profile partners"* with long-standing experience in international competition. The DC partners work closely with strong teams in Brussels, Paris, Rome and Frankfurt, making the firm the *"top choice for EU clearance work."* Practitioners were said to enjoy a *"high degree of trust among regulators"* and were particularly noted for their skill in international cartel and price-fixing matters. The DC group benefits from a *"good flow of business"* from the firm's New York office and acts on *"more than its fair share of megadeals."* For example, the team acted as worldwide antitrust counsel to Conoco in its merger with Phillips Petroleum Company, which created one of the largest integrated energy companies in the US.

DISTRICT OF COLUMBIA — ANTITRUST

The Lawyers: Mark Leddy is a *"complete-package lawyer"* whose *"formidable courtroom abilities,"* peers say, would *"scare absolutely anybody."* Leddy brings *"a great deal of integrity"* to the table in deals such as GE's proposed takeover of Honeywell, representing United Technologies in opposing the bid. Focusing largely on antitrust regulatory matters, **George Cary** was commended by rivals for having *"a lot of weapons in his armory."* They added that he *"treats every issue as a do-or-die situation."* Cary defended GlaxoSmithKline in a class action antitrust lawsuit involving pharmaceutical patents and handled an investigation involving digital music for AOL Time Warner. He also advised BrokerTec Global in the $240 million sale of its US and UK trading operations to ICAP.
The Clients: United Technologies; Dow Chemical and Cable & Wireless.

Clifford Chance US LLP
see firm details p.783
The Firm: The 40-lawyer team received tremendous accolades for *"smoothing the way,"* attaining government clearance in some of the most difficult M&A deals. In navigating Shell Oil through its $1.8 billion acquisition of Pennzoil-Quaker State Company, the firm convinced regulators that the deal was in the interest of consumers, despite it making Shell a leader in both the US and global lubricants markets. While the recent departure of Kevin Arquit to Simpson Thacher & Bartlett is considered a significant setback, the firm's DC antitrust practice remains strong.
The Lawyers: The DC practice was said to revolve around its star, **Steve Newborn** (see p.141), who was endorsed by competitors and clients alike for his *"ability to hit on exactly the right arguments."* He led Siemens' strategic alliance with Atecs Mannesmann, a division of Mannesmann AG. Clients endorsed Newborn as an *"astute generalist"* with a *"feisty"* approach to antitrust cases. He advised Bergen Brunswig in its merger with AmeriSource Health, a deal that was more difficult because a similar transaction had failed about two years ago following a government challenge. Praised by peers as a *"low-key, strategic thinker,"* **James Egan** (see p.135) has defended blue-chip clients in matters involving price-fixing, mergers, joint ventures, and other horizontal and vertical restraints of trade. Egan counseled Biovail on an FTC challenge to an agreement with Elan involving an anti-hypertension drug.
The Clients: MasterCard; DuPont; Hoffman-La Roche; Johnson & Johnson and Kinder Morgan.

Gibson, Dunn & Crutcher LLP
The Firm: The practice is felt to *"punch above its weight"* in antitrust litigation. A DC team of about a dozen attorneys earns high marks among interviewees for *"consistently serving clients well."* The firm is well known for its focus on the technology sector and receives support on international matters from practitioners in LA, London and Paris. The team won a consent decree for Premdor in its acquisition of Masonite from International Paper.
The Lawyers: Joseph Kattan, rated by competitors as a *"shrewd analyst,"* guided Intel through litigation involving the EC in its quest to invoke a US statute involving discovery proceedings. He is also involved in the DOJ's investigation of online music and distribution issues in California. *"Smarter than the average bear,"* **Jim Loftis** was said to be among *"the best in the country."* He represented Northrop Grumman in its acquisition of TRW and served as lead counsel in a civil price-fixing case involving high-pressure laminate. He also litigated a criminal price-fixing case relating to the carbon fiber industry. Cochair of the firm's antitrust and trade regulation practice is **Michael Denger**, who defended Daiichi Pharmaceutical in the vitamin antitrust case. He was also involved in the European rail pass multi-district litigation and advised Ralston Purina Company on its acquisition by Nestlé.
The Clients: Koch Industries; Pitney Bowes; Conexant Systems; Cadence Design Systems and Ticketmaster.

Hogan & Hartson LLP
see firm details p.818
The Firm: *"Major players"* in the field, the team has benefited from the firm's efforts to expand its European antitrust capacities. The 28-strong group works with fellow practitioners in Brussels and Berlin, offering *"expert"* cross-border advice on mergers, government investigations, antitrust litigation and consumer protection issues. Sources report that the group is *"extremely good at satisfying clients' demands"* and has taken on some of the most challenging antitrust matters of 2002. The firm represented Carnival in a hostile tender for P&O Princess Cruises, which was also considering a proposed friendly alliance with Royal Caribbean Cruises. According to competitors, the team saw the merger through despite difficulties and challenges from both the FTC and EC.
The Lawyers: Rivals commend the firm's star, **Janet McDavid** (see p.139), as a *"tough advocate"* who *"works like a demon for her clients."* McDavid led the Carnival review and won an anticompetitive case for American Express. She also represented EMI in a DOJ investigation concerning online music distribution. **Christine Varney** (see p.147), said by peers to be *"well connected, energetic and a political mover and shaker,"* concentrated on antitrust issues relating to IP and other e-commerce areas. She handled the antitrust reviews of both Synopsys' merger with Avant! and eBay's acquisition of PayPal.
The Clients: Twentieth Century Fox; General Dynamics; International Paper; Liberty Alliance Project; EMI; IBM; Mercedes-Benz and Cytyc.

Howrey Simon Arnold & White
The Firm: The firm *"prides itself on its litigation strength"* and, with about 150 attorneys practicing in DC, boasts one of the largest antitrust groups in the capital. A healthy showing of former FTC and DOJ officials makes this firm a *"tried and true"* choice for almost any complex antitrust matter. Moreover, the firm has widened its sphere of influence in Europe by launching a transatlantic cartel team. The firm advised two clients in opposing GE's bid for Honeywell, which was blocked by the EC, and steered Nestlé through European and Canadian antitrust reviews of its $10.3 billion acquisition of Ralston Purina Company.
The Lawyers: Researchers were told that cochair of the antitrust practice **James Rill** *"knows the game inside out."* He represented Univision Communications in its purchase of Hispanic Broadcasting Corporation (HBC). A *"polished"* advocate with *"tough-minded aggressiveness,"* **Marc Schildkraut** was dubbed an *"effective analyst"* who can ably take a case from counseling through to litigation. He defended Intel against IP-related monopolization claims and represented Schering-Plough in a FTC case involving a generic drug patent dispute. With 18 years of experience at the DOJ, **Mark Schechter** has *"seen it all, from the other side."* He has represented American Airlines in its proposed alliance with British Airways and has advised blue-chip companies ICI Americas, CSX and Bertelsmann.
The Clients: HJ Heinz; ExxonMobil; Verizon; Anheuser-Busch; Caterpillar; 3M and Dana.

O'Melveny & Myers LLP
The Firm: With a substantial number of victories in antitrust disputes, the team *"hasn't missed a step,"* competitors said. The recent addition of Michael Antalics, former Deputy Director of the FTC's Bureau of Competition, was thought to be a significant step forward in the team's attempts to expand the practice. The firm represented International Game Technology in an FTC investigation into its acquisition of Anchor Gaming, forming the largest casino gaming supplier in the country.
The Lawyers: Richard Parker, cochair of the antitrust practice, was recommended as a strategic thinker with a *"litigator's eye."* He represented Avant! in a $750 million merger with semiconductor products supplier, Synopsys, and has acted for Quest Diagnostics in its merger with Unilab. Univision Communications also retained him in connection with its acquisition of HBC. **Debra Valentine**, who colleagues described as *"strong, smart and effective,"* has a more international

ANTITRUST — DISTRICT OF COLUMBIA

practice. She advised Honeywell on many of its deals, which included antitrust clearance in as many as six countries, and defended antitrust allegations for Orbitz, a travel web site owned by five major airlines.
The Clients: ExxonMobil; Christie's; Sotheby's; HCA; Hertz; Degussa; AMD and Brooks Automation.

Boies, Schiller & Flexner
The Firm: This renowned general litigation boutique represents both plaintiffs and defendants in antitrust disputes. Commentators reported that the firm has *"come into the market effectively and aggressively,"* and has earned a reputation for a *"dogged"* approach to antitrust disputes.
The Lawyers: Although the group's reputation was firmly established on the courtroom skills of David Boies in New York, **Don Flexner** has helped tip the balance toward regulatory work. He represented EchoStar in its proposed merger with Hughes, owner of DIRECTV. Also deemed by rivals as *"a terrific litigator who has a good knowledge of civil antitrust law,"* Flexner defended Northwest Airlines against a DOJ antitrust lawsuit.
The Clients: EchoStar; Adelphia Communications; Florida Power & Light and Tyco International.

Fried, Frank, Harris, Shriver & Jacobson
see firm details p.797
The Firm: Transactional work is the practice's bread and butter, and the antitrust team benefits from the firm's strong corporate base and market presence in both DC and New York in attracting headline M&A. This *"talented group"* was praised by interviewees for its successful record in representing clients before regulatory agencies.
The Lawyers: As chair of the firm's antitrust practice, **Charles (Rick) Rule** (see p.144) is a *"creative professional and fine analyst"* with experience of acting on some of the highest profile mergers. He ushered NYNEX through its merger with Bell Atlantic (now known as Verizon). This *"intelligent and principled"* attorney also helped convince the Government to block a previously negotiated agreement by General Dynamics to acquire Newport News Shipbuilding. Officials subsequently approved a hostile bid by Rule's client, Northrop Grumman.
The Clients: Microsoft; DTM Corporation; PRI Automation; Invensys; Bacardi; MGM; Schering-Plough; US Airways and Goldman Sachs.

Wilmer, Cutler & Pickering
see firm details p.901
The Firm: Researchers were told that the firm's profile was *"on the rise"* following recent notable successes. It secured, for example, antitrust clearance before both the FTC and EC for Bestfoods' $60 billion merger with Unilever. The return of William Kolasky in late 2002 following his tenure as DOJ's Deputy Assistant Attorney General in charge of international antitrust and policy enforcement for the Antitrust Division is likely to provide another leg up for the practice.
The Lawyers: Cochair of the antitrust and competition practice group is *"top-quality"* attorney **Doug Melamed** (see p.140), whose analytical skills and *"understated"* manner win him peer endorsement. He advised Bayer in its $8 billion acquisition of Aventis CropScience. Litigation-related matters included defending memory chipmaker Rambus in a case concerning allegations that the company may have violated antitrust rules by failing to disclose information on future patents.
The Clients: Disney; The Anschutz Corporation; Commerce One; PepsiCo; Bal Harbour Shops and American Home Products.

Crowell & Moring LLP
The Firm: A *"practice that seems to be in harvest mode,"* rivals said; the team was viewed as having a strong leadership but lacking *"younger, up-and-coming types."* The group advised Northwest Airlines and Continental Airlines in a consumer class action lawsuit alleging collusive practices through computer reservation systems by eight major airlines. In a separate matter, it represented a group of 23 indirect copper buyers, including some telecom companies, in arguing that a copper broker had illegally manipulated prices worldwide.
The Lawyers: Chair of the antitrust practice **Randy Smith** is valued by clients for his *"tremendous experience"* in the field. Praised as a *"quick study,"* Smith enjoys a loyal following among blue-chip clients. He handled a DOJ inquiry into a teaming agreement for a significant US Air Force program and an EC investigation into airline alliances.
The Clients: DuPont; United Technologies; Alcoa; CSX Transportation and SBC Communications.

Morgan, Lewis & Bockius LLP
The Firm: Competitors describe the Philadelphia-based firm as a solid group that *"knows the agencies and does a good job on the transactional side."* The DC team advised Svedala Industri in its acquisition by Metso and Dow Chemical in a number of acquisitions.
The Lawyers: *"Industrious and conscientious"* **Donald Klawiter** is widely revered for his work involving criminal cartels. He defended Degussa against price-fixing allegations and a separate class action lawsuit involving an animal feed additive. Klawiter has also represented a Swiss company in a case involving price-fixing of citric acid. Hailed as *"the man to call if you have a cartel problem,"* Klawiter has experience serving as lead counsel in investigations held simultaneously in several countries, including Canada, Japan, Australia and Europe.
The Clients: Cadbury Schweppes, Bombardier and Vail Resorts.

Shearman & Sterling
see firm details p.874
The Firm: The DC antitrust group is viewed as a strong link in the firm's respected global practice, and therefore a worthy contender in cross-border transactions. The group has advised GlaxoSmithKline and other international companies in antitrust reviews both in the US and abroad.
The Lawyers: Commentators report that **Steven Sunshine** *"breaks through roadblocks like a sledgehammer."* He successfully represented Watson Pharmaceuticals in a multi-district antitrust case against Bristol-Myers Squibb concerning the latter's alleged attempt to block the approval of a generic antianxiety drug. A *"strong analyst,"* Sunshine also advised De Beers in the restructuring of its diamond distribution channels.
The Clients: Waste Management, Fiat and Siemens are clients.

Other Notable Practitioners
Described by peers as a *"first-rate analyst with significant experience,"* **William Blumenthal** (see p.133) of King & Spalding LLP primarily advises on M&A and joint ventures. However, this *"sound antitrust theorist"* also represents clients in matters involving distribution restraints, cartel behavior and marketing practices. In its launching of a US antitrust practice, international law firm Freshfields Bruckhaus Deringer LLP hired from Vinson & Elkins LLP the *"young and ambitious"* **Paul Yde**. One rival predicted Yde would be in the top tier *"in ten years, maybe a lot sooner."* Cast as an *"analytically sound"* advocate, he advises clients in matters relating to antitrust reviews, investigations and litigation brought by the DOJ and FTC.

DISTRICT OF COLUMBIA

ARBITRATION — INTERNATIONAL

DISTRICT OF COLUMBIA
Leading firms (Arbitration (International))
1. WHITE & CASE LLP
2. HUGHES HUBBARD & REED LLP
3. BOIES, SCHILLER & FLEXNER
   WILMER, CUTLER & PICKERING

Leading individuals (Arbitration (International))
1. TOWNSEND John *Hughes Hubbard & Reed LLP*
2. LAMM Carolyn *White & Case LLP*
3. SMUTNY Abby Cohen *White & Case LLP*
4. GOODMAN Ronald *White & Case LLP*
   SCHILLER Jonathan *Boies, Schiller & Flexner*
   VOLLMER Andrew *Wilmer, Cutler & Pickering*

Firms and Individuals are listed alphabetically in each band.

White & Case LLP
The Firm: The firm complements its highly rated New York office with an arbitration group in the capital that is universally acclaimed as *"clearly the best in the business."* In DC, the firm is best known for ICSID arbitration work, but is now increasingly representing clients under ICC arbitration rules. It is involved in two Chilean ICC arbitrations and also represented a major US power developer in an ICSID arbitration of a dispute with Turkey.
The Lawyers: **Carolyn Lamm** is primarily involved with advising foreign corporate clients and sovereigns and also sits as an arbitrator. Renowned for her personality and professional skills, she is said by contemporaries to be *"a delight to work with."* She counseled the Indonesian Government on enforcement proceedings in the US, Hong Kong and Singapore following a UNCITRAL arbitration award, and represented the US in a NAFTA arbitration under ICSID rules. **Abby Cohen Smutny** is rated by peers as an *"outstandingly thorough attorney."* ICSID proceedings are her particular forte, where she acted for Hungary in a dispute arising under the Energy Charter Treaty and a bilateral investment treaty relating to power purchase agreements. She also represented a Czech bank in a dispute with Slovakia involving claims of over $750 million. **Ronald Goodman** recently joined the DC group following stints in Paris and South Africa, and is highly rated for his knowledge of ICSID and ICC rules. He is currently involved in a Bolivian construction dispute at the ICC arbitration board.

Hughes Hubbard & Reed LLP
The Firm: This team advises on a variety of international arbitrations, and has experience of most of the major arbitral boards. Most notably it is currently representing a leading pharmaceutical company against a European opponent in ICC arbitrations.
The Lawyers: Commentators agree that the group is dominated by the *"commercially minded"* **John Townsend**, *"the archetypal Washington insider,"* who focuses on AAA, ICC and ad hoc arbitrations, as well as counseling clients on contract arbitration clauses. He has recently appeared on an AAA arbitration that raised questions about the scope of arbitration immunity.

Boies, Schiller & Flexner
The Firm: The firm's arbitration lawyers have experience in all major arbitral settings, including ICC, LCIA, UNCITRAL, ICSID, AAA, NASD and ad hoc arbitrations. Highlights have included advising Worldspan against Abacus before an ICC tribunal in London, which resulted in an award of $40 million in damages and costs.
The Lawyers: Managing partner **Jonathan Schiller** *"should be on everyone's list,"* according to peers. He represents clients under all rules, including ad hoc settings, advising sovereign nations and companies on commercial disputes arising from construction projects, joint ventures and distribution, and also serving as arbitrator. He recently represented a Kuwaiti oil company in a LCIA arbitration against a UK oil company.

Wilmer, Cutler & Pickering
see firm details p.901
The Firm: Although the firm's international arbitration practice is centered in London, its DC office has nevertheless received substantial market recognition. The team handles disputes under most international arbitration rules and also has substantial experience of ad hoc arbitrations.
The Lawyers: **Andrew Vollmer** (see p.148) is described to researchers as *"a great source of knowledge."* His practice is split between arbitration and litigation. In addition to representing clients in arbitral settings, he counsels on the drafting of arbitration clauses.

COMMUNICATIONS/TECHNOLOGY

Kellogg, Huber, Hansen, Todd & Evans PLLC
The Firm: *"Doing extraordinarily effective work at the moment,"* according to informed figures in DC. The firm's status in the industry and its lawyers' all-around expertise were frequently noted by Chambers' interviewees. The group focuses on trials and appeals before federal and state courts and federal agencies, and has wide appellate experience. Clients described the firm as *"a high-oxygen place with lawyers smarter than the rest of us."* The firm is outside counsel for the Bell companies acting on long-distance relief, the application of the 1996 Telecom Act and antitrust litigation.
The Lawyers: **Michael Kellogg** is *"certainly the most prominent"* at the practice, and has a track record in US Supreme Court and appellate litigation in the telecom field that *"leaves others standing."* **Mark Evans** *"argues a lot of cases"* and received consistent endorsement from contemporaries.
The Clients: Recent action has been for Verizon, SBC Communications and BellSouth. Other commercial clients include GE and the United States Telecom Association.

Wiley Rein & Fielding LLP
The Firm: *"One of the strongest competitors in this area,"* the firm offers a full service in the communications and technology sectors. Its work on behalf of the Bell companies gives the team a substantial profile in the sector, but the firm is also a significant force in general broadcast (including digital television), cable, satellite, internet and wireless industries. *"In the big league"* for regulatory matters, the firm has a reputation for being well connected politically, reinforced by personnel with experience at the FCC or on Capitol Hill. The firm is currently working on media ownership rule changes, in which it represents, among others, the Newspaper Association of America, CBS-Viacom, Gannett, Clear Channel, Belo and Emmis.
The Lawyers: **Dick Wiley** was endorsed to researchers as a *"unique communications attorney."* This former general counsel, commissioner and chairman of the FCC earned universal acclaim for his *"enormous energy and involvement in all the big issues."*
The Clients: The firm has appeared at the FCC and Supreme Court on a variety of spectrum issues for Verizon Wireless, AT&T Wireless and Motorola, as well as acting for Zenith and CBS-Viacom on digital television transition issues. Other clients include: Cable & Wireless; Intelsat; Ibiquity; Sirius and Time Domain.

COMMUNICATIONS/TECHNOLOGY — DISTRICT OF COLUMBIA

DISTRICT OF COLUMBIA
Leading firms (Communications)

1
- KELLOGG, HUBER, HANSEN, TODD & EVANS
- WILEY REIN & FIELDING LLP

2
- COVINGTON & BURLING
- HARRIS, WILTSHIRE & GRANNIS LLP
- HOGAN & HARTSON LLP
- LATHAM & WATKINS LLP
- LAWLER METZGER & MILKMAN LLC
- WILLKIE FARR & GALLAGHER
- WILMER, CUTLER & PICKERING

3
- LEVINE, BLASZAK, BLOCK & BOOTHBY LLP
- MAYER, BROWN, ROWE & MAW
- MINTZ LEVIN COHN FERRIS GLOVSKY AND POPEO
- SHAW PITTMAN
- SIDLEY AUSTIN BROWN & WOOD
- SWIDLER BERLIN SHEREFF FRIEDMAN LLP

4
- ARNOLD & PORTER
- MORRISON & FOERSTER LLP
- PAUL, WEISS, RIFKIND, WHARTON & GARRISON
- PRESTON GATES ELLIS & ROUVELAS MEEDS LLP
- SKADDEN, ARPS, SLATE, MEAGHER & FLOM LLP

Leading individuals (Communications)

★ **WILEY** Richard *Wiley Rein & Fielding LLP*

1
- **KELLOGG** Michael *Kellogg, Huber, Hansen, Todd*
- **VERVEER** Philip *Willkie Farr & Gallagher*

2
- **BLAKE** Jonathan *Covington & Burling*
- **EPSTEIN** Gary *Latham & Watkins LLP*
- **METZGER** Richard *Lawler Metzger LLC & Milkman*
- **ROHRBACH** Peter *Hogan & Hartson LLP*
- **SYMONS** Howard *Mintz Levin Cohn Ferris Glovsky*

3
- **GERSTELL** Glenn *Milbank, Tweed, Hadley & McCloy*
- **LAKE** William *Wilmer, Cutler & Pickering*
- **LIPMAN** Andy *Swidler Berlin Shereff Friedman LLP*
- **MASUR** Daniel *Mayer, Brown, Rowe & Maw*
- **NAKAHATA** John *Harris, Wiltshire & Grannis LLP*
- **SPECTOR** Phillip *Paul, Weiss, Rifkind, Wharton*
- **ZAHLER** Robert *Shaw Pittman*

4
- **BOOTHBY** Colleen *Levine, Blaszak, Block & Boothby*
- **FERRIS** Charles *Mintz Levin Cohn Ferris Glovsky*
- **HARRIS** Scott *Harris, Wiltshire & Grannis LLP*
- **LEVINE** Henry *Levine, Blaszak, Block & Boothby LLP*
- **TRITT** Cheryl *Morrison & Foerster LLP*

5
- **BLASZAK** James *Levine, Blaszak, Block & Boothby*
- **EVANS** Mark *Kellogg, Huber, Hansen, Todd & Evans*
- **MILKMAN** Ruth *Lawler Metzger & Milkman*
- **QUALE** John *Skadden, Arps, Slate, Meagher & Flom*
- **WADLOW** Clark *Sidley Austin Brown & Wood*

Firms and Individuals are listed alphabetically in each band.

Covington & Burling
see firm details p.786

The Firm: The firm is known for its long-standing tradition in media work, particularly on broadcasting issues, and continues its involvement in legislation and regulatory and judicial procedures in areas including broadband and spectrum. In addition, the firm offers expertise in telecom, satellite, internet and personal communications services/cellular work.

The firm represented the independent directors of Adelphia Communications on lawsuits, FCC and congressional matters and advised Microsoft on broadband issues. It also acted as counsel to Microsoft in its recent agreement with the FTC to a consent order related to Microsoft's Passport online authentication service.

The Lawyers: Jonathan Blake (see p.132) has a *"first-rate"* reputation among peers, and clients commended his *"technical expertise and ability to see the overall picture, bringing things to the table that I wouldn't even have thought of."*

The Clients: Other clients include: CBS affiliates; NBC affiliates; The Washington Post Company and New Skies.

Harris, Wiltshire & Grannis LLP

The Firm: Considered to be an *"up-and-coming"* boutique, the firm is lauded for its *"cadre of very smart people who have come onto the scene and attracted a good client base."* Expertise is in a wide range of communications and IT matters, with commentators praising in particular the firm's specialties in *"almost quirky new age areas and international issues."* Clients also remarked to researchers on the firm's ability *"to get matters through"* with speed and expertise, which they attributed to its firsthand knowledge of the FCC.

The Lawyers: A former FCC Chief of Staff, the *"unflappable"* John Nakahata is thought to be an *"expert on the Hill and the FCC."* His profile is in common carrier issues and he recently represented coalitions in lobbying for changes in universal service and access. Scott Harris has experience on international and spectrum wireless issues, and he is particularly valued for his FCC experience. Recently he represented News Corporation on its satellite-related interests in the US, and advised Cisco Systems on advanced wireless issues.

The Clients: Other clients include: Voicestream (T-Mobile); Microsoft; Intel; Apple; Z-Tel; Level 3; New Skies and SDR Forum.

Hogan & Hartson LLP
see firm details p.818

The Firm: *"One of the best broad practices"* is rated highly for its *"big-league"* regulatory work. It also offers regulatory and legislative advice to local and national wireless, telecom, broadcasting and internet clients.

Following the firm's merger with New York firm Squadron Ellenoff Plesent & Sheinfeld in March 2002, it has further expanded its representation of News Corporation, and has advised the media conglomerate on its European direct-to-home satellite activities and investments, and on acquisitions of new TV stations in the US. Internationally, the firm acted for BT in its breakup with AT&T.

The Lawyers: *"The real star"* is seen to be **Peter Rohrbach** (see p.144), codirector of the communications practice group. He has been heavily involved in long-distance entry activity on behalf of Qwest, as well as acting for them in M&A matters and regulatory litigation. It also played a part in the NextWave Telecom bankruptcy and in wireless work for operators, manufacturers and users, including action regarding policies for new ultra-wideband services and work for a coalition of major automobile companies on telematics issues.

The Clients: Other clients include: Clear Channel; BT; Cable & Wireless and AOL Time Warner.

Latham & Watkins LLP
see firm details p.835

The Firm: The firm's multinational network contributes to a communications practice that is becoming more global in scope. The DC office proffers advice on regulatory matters, but is also reportedly becoming more involved in national and international transactional matters in the industry, supported by a full-service corporate practice. Competitors remarked that the firm has *"built up a substantial communications practice with quality backup."*

Work for the firm includes action for Singapore Technologies Telemedia on its acquisition of Global Crossing and for Leap Wireless on wireless spectrum auctions. It has also acted for large radio broadcasting companies such as Entercom and Beasley in M&A and regulatory matters.

The Lawyers: **Gary Epstein** (see p.135), head of the firm's global telecommunications practice, was often listed among rivals' most admired lawyers. He acted for Telmex in its entry into the US market and for DIRECTV in connection with its merger with EchoStar, a deal valued at $30 billion.

The Clients: Other clients include: Hughes; Century Telecommunications; Inmarsat; TELUS and Hughes Network Systems.

Lawler Metzger & Milkman

The Firm: Soaring in the estimation of peers and clients, this telecom boutique is considered to be one of a *"new age of firms"* which is *"picking up lots of business and really coming up the ranks."* Competitors routinely praised the caliber of lawyers at the firm, many of whom have FCC and Capitol Hill experience and thus give the firm substantial telecommunications regulatory and legislative capability. Satellite, cable, common carrier, wireless and mass media issues are all elements of the firm's caseload.

The Lawyers: *"One of the brightest in the city,"* **Richard Metzger** is admired for his private and government experience: *"He really knows the nuts and bolts of the FCC practice."* Also highly

DISTRICT OF COLUMBIA
COMMUNICATIONS/TECHNOLOGY

regarded for her FCC and industry knowledge is **Ruth Milkman**, who won glowing reports from clients.

The Clients: The firm remains WorldCom's lead FCC counsel and also maintains its reputation for *"attracting the best new entrants to the sector."* The firm is assisting Comcast in seeking FCC approval of its merger with AT&T Broadband, and represented Nextel Communications before the FCC on wireless regulatory matters.

Willkie Farr & Gallagher
see firm details p.900

The Firm: The DC office, particularly rated for its *"extremely able"* bench of lawyers, specializes in regulatory matters, and is an influential player in cable and telecom issues, with experience before the FCC, FTC and US Department of Justice. Among its clients are entities from the cable, telecom, wireless, software, satellite and broadcast industries.

The firm advised AT&T in connection with the acquisition of AT&T Broadband by Comcast, and acted for IDT in its purchase of Winstar's assets. In bankruptcy proceedings, the firm has acted for 360networks and XO Communications, and is restructuring counsel for Adelphia Cable. Involvement in the wireless industry includes advising TruePosition on location services, and the firm serves as outside counsel for the Cellular Telecommunications & Internet Association.

The Lawyers: *"Certainly the leader there"* is **Phil Verveer** (see p.147), who will, according to one competitor, *"give his efforts body and soul - there are not many to match him."*

The Clients: Clients: Sprint; Time Warner Telecom; Motorola; Microsoft; Allegiance Telecom.

Wilmer, Cutler & Pickering
see firm details p.901

The Firm: *"Still highly prominent,"* the firm's solid reputation in the telecom field is supported by a wealth of expertise in areas including common carriage, wireless, internet and cyber law, content provision and broadcasting.

The firm's involvement in a landmark FCC arbitration for Verizon against AT&T and WorldCom continued in 2002, and work in bankruptcy cases increased; representative debtor clients in this area include Iridium and PSINet. The group represented Verizon as a creditor in telecom bankruptcies, and acted for Qwest in a US Supreme Court case concerning the prices at which large telecom companies must share their facilities with competitors.

The Lawyers: *"There are a lot of extremely capable people there,"* researchers heard, and the group is cochaired by **Bill Lake** (see p.138), a specialist in regulatory and appellate litigation. He earned praise, not only for his technical skills, but also for his ability to introduce *"really fabulous new people into his team."* He advised Verizon in the NextWave Telecom litigation, which is simultaneously before several federal courts.

The Clients: Other clients include: Fox; Disney; ABC; NBC and AOL Time Warner.

Levine, Blaszak, Block & Boothby LLP
see firm details p.840

The Firm: Advising corporate users of telecom and IT services, the firm is endorsed as *"a leader in its field,"* which involves the negotiation of network-related agreements with telecom companies and advising on disputes arising from them. Clients, who include big-name corporates from the cable, TV, radio, telecom and IT industries, praised the firm's *"confidence and insight into the communications industry - they have their finger on the pulse of what is really being negotiated in technology agreements, including the regulatory and legislative perspective."* The firm acted for United Airlines in an agreement with AT&T, was counsel to DaimlerChrysler in negotiations with WorldCom and represented Merrill Lynch in global outsourcing agreements with AT&T.

The Lawyers: *"Flamboyant and dramatic"* **Hank Levine** (see p.138) is *"a tenacious negotiator who can be quite charming."* His colleague **Jim Blaszak** (see p.133) is appreciated as an attorney who *"inspires our confidence,"* while **Colleen Boothby** (see p.133) is respected for her regulatory knowledge and acts for users and users' committees before the FCC.

The Clients: Other clients include: Ad Hoc Telecommunications Users Committee; Information Technology Industry Council; Washington Mutual; UBS Warburg; ChevronTexaco; New Zealand Dairy Board; Visa; Morgan Stanley and IBM.

Mayer, Brown, Rowe & Maw
see firm details p.843

The Firm: Competitors are impressed with the firm's transactional expertise in the technology and communications industries, and the group is rated as *"a national player"* for outsourcing deals in IT, telecommunications and managed networks.

The firm acted for medical/surgical supplies distributor Owens & Minor in a renegotiation of an existing agreement with Perot Systems, and has been working on two transactions for global pharmaceutical company Pharmacia. It has also advised on several large matters on behalf of MetLife and MetLife Bank, which include the termination of the latter's outsourcing arrangement, the negotiation of a new arrangement with an alternative provider and the negotiation of a custody/trust services outsourcing arrangement.

The Lawyers: Dan Masur (see p.139) is considered to be *"one of the most prominent lawyers in IT outsourcing"* and researchers heard constant praise for his *"good business manner."*

The Clients: Other clients include: Marathon Oil; Weyerhaeuser; Solutia; Cinergy and Clarion Partners.

Mintz Levin Cohn Ferris Glovsky and Popeo PC

The Firm: *"Thriving and active,"* the firm is noted for work in telecom, cable, mass media and wireless issues, advising on regulatory and legislative matters.

The firm recently represented Comcast before regulatory authorities in connection with its acquisition of AT&T Broadband.

The Lawyers: *"Some well-respected attorneys"* make up the Mintz Levin group: **Howard Symons** is seen to be *"well connected"* in the industry; while veteran practitioner **Charles Ferris** is recognized as the *"father of the practice."*

The Clients: Clients include wire and wireless carriers, cable operators and program networks, and trade associations representing the cable and wireless industries. Representative clients include: AT&T, AT&T Wireless and Cablevision Systems.

Shaw Pittman

The Firm: The core of the firm's practice in DC is its representation of large users of technology in complex outsourcing transactions. In IT and business process outsourcing, the firm is described by competitors as *"top-notch,"* and clients commend the *"comprehensive"* nature of the service, which includes input from non-legal consultants. In addition to its reputation in global outsourcing, the firm's expertise ranges from procurement to systems integration and regulatory matters.

The firm's track record includes representing Empire BlueCross BlueShield on the development of a state-of-the-art claims processing system supplied by IBM, and advising American Express on the creation of a global technology services partnership with IBM, a $4 billion, seven-year relationship. Elsewhere, the firm acted for Equant on a $6.6 billion strategic alliance for network services involving SITA and France Telecom.

The Lawyers: Bob Zahler, seen as *"the majordomo"* at the DC office, is acknowledged to have shaped the technology practice.

The Clients: Other clients include: JPMorgan Chase; Merrill Lynch; Air Canada and AstraZeneca.

Sidley Austin Brown & Wood
see firm details p.877

The Firm: *"A fine firm,"* its communications and IT group has a regulatory and transactional practice representing clients across the telecom and broadcast industries. Handling regulatory issues, the firm has experience before the FCC and other federal agencies, and advises clients on issues such as news/broadcasting cross-ownership and television companies' transition to digital.

COMMUNICATIONS/TECHNOLOGY — DISTRICT OF COLUMBIA

The Lawyers: Head of the 21-partner group is **Clark Wadlow**, who has been practicing in the DC communications bar since 1972. Frequently involved in continuing legal education programs, he is acknowledged by competitors as an expert in the field.

The Clients: Competitors recognize that the firm handles major matters for AT&T, *"one of the biggest players in this area;"* this includes advising on the communications issues in conjunction with its merger with Comcast. Another important client is Tribune Company, for which Clark Wadlow recently acted as lead on the regulatory aspects of Tribune's acquisition of The Times Mirror Company, a deal that has raised cross-ownership issues. The firm has also advised Tribune, along with other broadcast companies, on the transition to digital television, and also acted on Tribune's acquisition of two TV stations in Indianapolis. On the telecom side, clients include Iridium, which the firm advises on its global satellite/cell phone system.

Swidler Berlin Shereff Friedman LLP

The Firm: The high quality of work at the firm was often recommended to researchers, and the firm continues its representation of telecom carrier companies, wire and wireless clients, ISPs, equipment manufacturers and telecom users, advising on regulatory, legislative and corporate matters. Interviewees often commented on the team's international experience: it is active in the telecom sectors in Latin America, Europe and Asia, and also advises on industry-specific bankruptcy and M&A matters.

The Lawyers: The *"tremendously knowledgeable"* **Andy Lipman** wins praise from clients for his work in telecom competition cases.

The Clients: Clients include: Allegiance; Level 3; Global Crossing; Network Plus; Winstar; Adelphia; RCN; Focal; US LEC; El Paso and Cantor Fitzgerald.

Arnold & Porter
see firm details p.765

The Firm: Admired for its work in the regulatory, transactional and legislative fields, the firm has a substantial clientele from the telecom industry. Its expertise in the antitrust field frequently gave rise to favorable comment, and clients agreed that the group, headed by Norman Sinel, is *"extremely knowledgeable."* The firm's major client is SBC Communications, which it advises on strategic planning as well as regulatory and transactional matters. Recent deals included advising SBC on its acquisitions of Pacific Bell, Ameritech and Southern New England Telephone Company. The team also advised Cingular, a joint venture of SBC and BellSouth providing wireless operations throughout the country.

The Clients: Other clients include: Verizon, NBC and AOL.

Morrison & Foerster LLP
see firm details p.854

The Firm: The firm advises on a wide range of regulatory and transactional matters, but its strength on the regulatory side was particularly commended to researchers.

The Lawyers: Former chief of the FCC Common Carrier Bureau and cohead of the firm's communications practice group, **Cheryl Tritt** (see p.147) was described by peers as *"top of the line for intellectual ability,"* and as *"the lawyer I would recommend when conflicted out."*

The Clients: Satellite clients include ICO Global Communications, a UK-authorized mobile satellite company, which the firm has advised on licensing and strategic planning and has represented before the FCC. In the wireless industry, the firm has counseled VoiceStream (T-Mobile) on regulatory and transactional matters, and in the internet area, the firm counsels Genuity. Wire and multimedia, and wireless start-up companies represented by the firm include Space Data and Monet Mobile. Further clients include: ALLTEL, NTT and Sprint.

Paul, Weiss, Rifkind, Wharton & Garrison
see firm details p.862

The Firm: The firm is rated as a competitor in the field, and its particular areas of specialization include satellite, wireless, cable and fibre-optic projects. The international focus of the practice was noted to researchers; the firm's offices in Asia and Europe enable it to represent international clients on their US interests. The team acted for Hutchison Whampoa on its intended purchase of Global Crossing, following the latter's bankruptcy proceedings.
The firm has represented SES AMERICOM in regulatory matters, including AMERICOM2Home, a major direct-to-home satellite project, and acts for AOL Time Warner in FCC and court matters, including cable television issues.

The Lawyers: The experience and skill of the *"highly plugged-in"* **Phil Spector** are particularly well regarded by competitors.

The Clients: Other clients include: SES GLOBAL, FLAG Telecom and Iridium Satellite.

Preston Gates Ellis & Rouvelas Meeds LLP

The Firm: *"Knowledgeable and well connected,"* the firm's telecommunications practice group advises on matters including regulatory, commercial, litigation and public policy.

The Clients: Clients include local, national and international carriers, utilities and service providers. The team is particularly noted for its connections with federal and state government entities.

Skadden, Arps, Slate, Meagher & Flom LLP & Affiliates
see firm details p.878

The Firm: The firm is acknowledged to have been actively recruiting in this area, and has assembled a group of attorneys with wide-ranging Hill and FCC experience. Its M&A focus extends into its work in the communications and technology industries, and the DC office is best known for its regulatory advice on transactional matters.
The group advised on News Corporation's transfer from analog to digital, digital rights management issues and legislative matters. It also represented Gray Communications, a US broadcaster and publisher, in connection with its $500 million acquisition of Benedek Broadcasting, and Price Wireless on regulatory matters in its $1.7 billion merger with Verizon Wireless. International work handled from DC includes advice on national telephone networks in South Africa and Western Africa.

The Lawyers: **John Quale** (see p.143) is well thought of for his regulatory expertise in the context of transactions and spectrum allocation.

The Clients: Other clients include: Celsat; National Association of Broadcasters; SBC Communications; Apollo Advisors; Lockheed Martin and Telecom New Zealand.

Other Notable Practitioners

Glenn Gerstell, managing partner of Milbank, Tweed, Hadley & McCloy LLP's DC office and head of the firm's global communications practice, maintains his reputation among peers as a solid transactional lawyer in the communications sector.

DISTRICT OF COLUMBIA — CONSTRUCTION

CONSTRUCTION

DISTRICT OF COLUMBIA
Leading firms (Construction)
1. THELEN REID & PRIEST LLP
2. MCMANUS SCHOR ASMAR & DARDEN LLP
3. BASTIANELLI, BROWN & KELLEY
4. JENKENS & GILCHRIST
   PIPER RUDNICK LLP

Leading individuals (Construction)
- ★ NESS Andrew *Thelen Reid & Priest LLP*
- 1. HARRIS Larry *Piper Rudnick LLP*
     PATIN Douglas *Spriggs & Hollingsworth*
     WEST Joseph *Arnold & Porter*
- 2. BASTIANELLI Adrian *Bastianelli, Brown & Kelley*
     GOLDBERG Howard *Goldberg, Pike & Besche*
     KRAFTSON Daniel *Jenkens & Gilchrist*
     SCHOR Laurence *McManus Schor Asmar & Darden*
- 3. JAFFE Michael *Thelen Reid & Priest LLP*
     MCMANUS Joseph *McManus Schor Asmar & Darden*

Firms and Individuals are listed alphabetically in each band.

Thelen Reid & Priest LLP
see firm details p.888
The Firm: This sizable firm has a national reputation for construction law. Thirteen DC attorneys work in tandem with practices in New York, LA, San Francisco, Silicon Valley and New Jersey, advising on large development and infrastructure projects. Competitors consistently commended the team as *"right at the very top"* for its concentration of *"first-rate lawyers."* The group covers every aspect of construction law from the transactional to the contentious for a broad base of owner and contractor clients.
The Lawyers: DC practice head **Andy Ness** (see p.141) was described by peers as *"one of the brightest guys around."* A *"great lawyer with a fantastic reputation,"* Ness recently acted in an international arbitration involving a dispute between a contractor and the owner of a power plant in Pakistan. Other work includes the development of a $500 million clinical research center at the National Institutes of Health in Bethesda, MD, and a dispute among a contractor, subcontractor and owner of a Venezuelan steel plant. The recent arrival of **Michael Jaffe** and a small team from Arent Fox has further boosted the firm's profile in the field. This *"Grade A"* lawyer is well known for his work for Clark Construction Group, which he recently represented in claims against a subcontractor and its surety in connection with a FBI center in Quantico, VA. He also acted for Clark in litigation surrounding renovations to the US Botanic Garden in DC. Elsewhere, he represented Centex Construction Group in litigation concerning the alleged wrongful death of a child in the Atlantis resort in The Bahamas.
The Clients: Bechtel; The Clark Construction Group; Centex Construction Group and Raytheon.

McManus Schor Asmar & Darden LLP
The Firm: Regarded as an *"outstanding practice with some prominent national clients,"* this construction boutique has grown to 17 attorneys since its formation in 1997. The group provides cradle-to-grave services, offering expertise in government contracts, airport, hotel and hospital construction projects and insurance and surety issues. The client base has shifted from mainly contractor representation to an even split with owner and developer clients.
The Lawyers: Name partner **Larry Schor** was mentioned as a *"superlative"* attorney with noteworthy experience in government contracts matters. He serves as head of the firm's government contracts group and recently completed a term as president of The American College of Construction Lawyers. Recent work includes counseling, litigation and mediation for St. Louis-based McCarthy Building Companies on major government contracts.
Cofounder **Joe McManus** heads the contract documents and special projects practice groups. This *"talented, problem-solving"* individual is frequently called upon to act as arbitrator. He acted for Peebles Atlantic Development in a dispute with a contractor and advises Osprey Developers Company, a general contractor in The Bahamas.
The Clients: McCarthy Building Companies, Osprey Developers Company and Peebles Atlantic Development.

Bastianelli, Brown & Kelley
The Firm: This construction boutique of about a dozen lawyers was highly recommended for dispute resolution matters, in which it has a reputation for *"neutrality and integrity."* The team regularly features in mediations, arbitrations, structured negotiations and dispute review boards. Attorneys are adept at project development and financing, contract administration and bid protests, and regulatory compliance matters.
The Lawyers: Commentators singled out **Adrian Bastianelli** as a *"knowledgeable and even-tempered"* practitioner with *"top-drawer"* mediation skills. He has served as an arbitrator or mediator on over 80 construction cases and acted as chair of five dispute review boards in Boston on the Central Artery/Tunnel Project and two on the Dalles Rapid Transit project.
The Clients: A diverse client base includes contractors, subcontractors, engineers, sureties, architects, developers, financiers and owners.

Jenkens & Gilchrist
The Firm: Headquartered in Dallas, this national full-service firm maintains a five-attorney construction group in its DC office. The group advises contractors, state and local governments, and private parties on all aspects of construction from the initial project design to litigation and resolution.
The Lawyers: **Dan Kraftson** attracts widespread praise for his success in construction litigation on behalf of Fairfax County, VA. He represents clients in a variety of state and federal courts, arbitration proceedings, administrative hearings and other dispute resolution mechanisms. On the transactional side, Kraftson focuses on counseling contractors and owners on the drafting and negotiation of contract terms. Projects that he has worked on include waste water treatment facilities, chemical processing plants, highways, and nuclear and fossil power plants.
The Clients: Kellogg Brown & Root, contractors, state and local governments, and private parties.

Piper Rudnick LLP
see firm details p.867
The Firm: Five DC partners and one of counsel attorney work as part of a national team, receiving and referring substantial construction matters to practices in Chicago, Baltimore, New York, Philadelphia and Tampa. The group primarily represents owners, developers and contractors and occasionally undertakes matters on behalf of large subcontractors. Clients appreciate the team's *"reliable, clear-sighted"* advice on project development.
The Lawyers: Head of the national construction group **Larry Harris** is admired by peers as a *"fabulous human being with loads of experience."* He has been involved in counseling for Essex Construction and represented Westbank as a lender to the Mandarin Oriental Hotel Group. Harris also acted in an arbitration for Marubeni in relation to a power plant operation in Cali, Colombia.
The Clients: Architects; engineers; developers; lenders; sureties; governmental entities; contractors; design professionals; construction managers; design builders; subcontractors; suppliers and manufacturers.

Other Notable Practitioners
"Professional" **Doug Patin** heads the construction group at Spriggs & Hollingsworth. His litigation-based practice includes traditional construction and government contracts disputes. He also possesses expertise on matters such as builder's risk and liability insurance disputes, bid protests, bond claims, jury trials and complex litigation involving fiduciary duty claims.
Peers praised **Joe West** (see p.148) at Arnold &

CORPORATE/M&A — DISTRICT OF COLUMBIA

Porter as *"a dean of the bar."* He heads the firm's government contracts department and is experienced in counseling contractors, owners and buyers both prior to and during litigation. **Howard Goldberg**, founding partner of Baltimore construction boutique, Goldberg Pike & Besche, rates highly for his representation of architects and engineers. He is visible in the DC market as frequent adviser to The American Institute of Architects.

CORPORATE/M&A

DISTRICT OF COLUMBIA
Leading firms (Corporate/M&A)
1. HOGAN & HARTSON LLP
2. GIBSON, DUNN & CRUTCHER LLP
   LATHAM & WATKINS LLP
3. SHAW PITTMAN
   WILMER, CUTLER & PICKERING

Leading individuals (Corporate/M&A)
1. GORRELL Warren *Hogan & Hartson LLP*
2. ADLER Howard *Gibson, Dunn & Crutcher LLP*
   HUBER John *Latham & Watkins LLP*
3. GLOVER Stephen *Gibson, Dunn & Crutcher LLP*
   LENNON Daniel *Latham & Watkins LLP*
   MAZO Mark *Hogan & Hartson LLP*

Firms and Individuals are listed alphabetically in each band.

Hogan & Hartson LLP
see firm details p.818
The Firm: Clearly the most prominent practice in DC, observers believe that the firm has *"by far the most depth and capacity for corporate work."* A popular choice within the local business community, its strength lies in corporate finance and real estate. Peers applaud a team built on *"gentlemen of integrity."*
The Lawyers: Chairman of the firm **Warren Gorrell** wins acclaim as a *"top-flight corporate lawyer."* He represents investment banks and public and private corporations. He stands out in DC as a *"world-class lawyer with Wall Street capabilities."* Peers describe him as a rainmaker for the firm, particularly in the REITs area, where he represented Equity Office Properties Trust in its $7.2 billion acquisition of Spieker Properties. He also represented Merrill Lynch in the $450 million IPO of Heritage Property Investment Trust.
Mark Mazo (see p.139) is a *"true cross-border lawyer with a sophisticated practice."* Commentators described him as a *"remarkably professional attorney"* with a *"calm but forceful"* style. Focused on joint ventures, and strategic and financial investments. He is often found representing investors, notably from the French aerospace industry, into the US. He advised a major international media organization, and a Saudi Arabian prince on investments into Europe.
The Clients: News Corporation; Host Marriott; Havas; Equity Office Properties Trust; Sithe Energies; Orbital Sciences; CIENA; E*TRADE and LabCorp.

Gibson, Dunn & Crutcher LLP
The Firm: The DC office of this Californian firm has established a *"significant practice"* in the area according to peers. Its *"outstanding corporate group"* is skilled in both transactional and counseling work. John Olson is a senior figure at the firm, although he is no longer active in transactional work. He remains a valuable source of advice on corporate governance and policy issues.
The Lawyers: Peers believe that **Howard Adler**'s practice is deeply rooted in the local business community: he is *"known throughout town."* He divides his time between M&A and IPOs. Adler is a respected figure in the northern Virginia hi-tech market. **Stephen Glover** has a national practice in M&A and corporate finance. He is an expert in the government contracts sectors. Clients enthused about his *"calm negotiating skills and sound judgment."*
The Clients: Corporations, investment banks and financial institutions.

Latham & Watkins LLP
see firm details p.835
The Firm: A Californian firm that peers agree has *"definitely established a capability in DC."* Tipped for its work in securities, telecommunications and corporate finance, the group is said to have developed strong relationships with investment banks. However, the real driving force of this *"thriving"* practice is its historical role as primary counsel to The Carlyle Group for M&A matters.
The Lawyers: A key figure in The Carlyle Group work is the *"tenacious"* **Daniel Lennon** (see p.138). Clients report that he is a *"practical"* lawyer and is *"quick to see the real issues."* In addition to several acquisitions for The Carlyle Group, he worked on the $401 million IPO of United Defense Industries. **John Huber** (see p.137) is *"an outstanding corporate lawyer,"* and former director of the SEC's division of corporation finance. He provides regulatory expertise for the firm's vast international corporate practice and works on public offerings, private placements, Rule 144A and M&A transactions. Huber has recently been active in the telecom and healthcare sectors.
The Clients: The Carlyle Group is one of the firm's key clients.

Shaw Pittman
The Firm: This midmarket practice is said by peers to have strong links to the local business community. The group, which features Robert Robbins, focuses on the real estate and technology markets. Its REIT practice has seen over $1 billion of debt offerings in 2002, and the firm is distinguished as one of the leading IT outsourcing practices in the US. The DC group works closely with the northern Virginia office in dealings with emerging growth companies. The corporate group also represents media and sports entities.
The Clients: Crescent Real Estate Equities is a key client of the firm.

Wilmer, Cutler & Pickering
see firm details p.901
The Firm: The firm is perceived to have been *"bulking up its resources"* in recent times. Although peers could not identify a single 'star' lawyer, they enthused about the firm's *"well-rounded corporate department."* The group engages in the full range of M&A, corporate finance and private equity work. Strong regulatory and securities law practices ensure the team, which features Russell Bruemmer, can supply a breadth of expertise. Clients identified a *"collegial"* group of lawyers particularly attuned to the deal-making process: *"Practical and focused, they are good at coalition building."*
The Clients: Recent highlights include representing Danaher in its acquisitions of Fuke ($625 million) and Pacific Scientific ($460 million). The group advised Aether Systems in its purchase of IFX, Mobeo and LocusOne. The sports industry is an active source of work, particularly in the buying and selling of teams and stadiums. The firm has also represented Fannie Mae in the issuance of both equity and debt securities in the US and foreign markets. Educational Testing Service and Sears Roebuck are typical clients of the firm.

DISTRICT OF COLUMBIA — EMPLOYMENT & LABOR LAW

EMPLOYMENT & LABOR LAW — MAINLY PLAINTIFF

DISTRICT OF COLUMBIA
Leading firms (Employment: Mainly Plaintiff)

1. BREDHOFF & KAISER
2. KALIJARVI, CHUZI & NEWMAN PC
   SPRENGER & LANG PLLC
3. BAPTISTE & WILDER

Leading individuals (Employment: Mainly Plaintiff)

1. COHEN George — *Bredhoff & Kaiser*
2. CHUZI George — *Kalijarvi, Chuzi & Newman PC*
   FITZPATRICK Robert — *Fitzpatrick & Associates*
   LANG Jane — *Sprenger & Lang PLLC*
3. BAPTISTE Robert — *Baptiste & Wilder*
   SELLERS Joseph — *Cohen, Milstein, Hausfeld & Toll*

Firms and Individuals are listed alphabetically in each band.

Bredhoff & Kaiser
The Firm: Peers applauded the firm as *"clear leaders"* in the DC plaintiffs' market and the *"pre-eminent"* group for union-related issues. This 32-attorney practice has *"considerable depth"* and acts for clients across the US. It remains best known for its work on traditional labor law and has built up a profile for civil rights and constitutional issues. The group has represented plaintiffs in worker protection cases before the US Supreme Court, and has negotiated collective bargaining agreements for international and local unions.

The Lawyers: Defendant counsel singled out **George Cohen** as *"a long-time adversary and a quick-witted expert"* on union matters.

Kalijarvi, Chuzi & Newman PC
The Firm: This well-regarded firm practices across a broad range of race, gender and age discrimination disputes and labor relations and wrongful discharge matters. The group is experienced in standing before federal and state courts, and agencies such as the Federal Labor Relations Authority and the EEOC.

The Lawyers: Interviewees commended **George Chuzi** as *"an attentive and smart"* attorney who has a long-standing profile in the field. He was particularly recommended for his expertise in sexual harassment cases.

Sprenger & Lang PLLC
The Firm: Much of the firm's profile lies with its eponymous partner, **Jane Lang**. A track record of *"tremendous litigation successes"* has placed Lang at the forefront of the market. Defendant attorneys agree that the firm is a *"popular choice for major class actions,"* particularly in race and sex discrimination litigation. They also pointed to the next generation of attorneys at the firm who are *"carrying its reputation forward."* In recent years the firm has developed an employee benefits class action practice, arising out of alleged ERISA violations.

Baptiste & Wilder
The Firm: Commended by interviewees for its *"expertise in traditional labor"* matters, the firm is best known for its representation of labor unions. Both the airline and railroad industries have been a source of activity in recent years for unfair practices, union relations and issues arising from bankruptcy and restructuring. The firm has represented mechanics, flight attendants and fleet service employees in hearings before the National Mediation Board (NMB). Typical clients of the group include the airline division of the Teamsters union and the Brotherhood of Locomotive Engineers.

The Lawyers: Peers warmly recommended **Robert Baptiste** for his work before the NMB. He is a skilled labor relations attorney, handling NLRA matters and disputes arising from ERISA claims.

Other Notable Practitioners
Joseph Sellers of Cohen, Milstein, Hausfeld & Toll, PLLC was recommended to researchers as a *"thoughtful attorney with great judgment."* He was respected for his work on civil rights class actions and race, age, disability and gender discrimination matters. Peers described **Robert Fitzpatrick** of Fitzpatrick & Associates as a *"mighty attorney"* who has carved out a profile in employment-related disputes. He is also respected as a speaker on the employment market.

EMPLOYMENT & LABOR LAW — MAINLY DEFENDANT

DISTRICT OF COLUMBIA
Leading firms (Employment: Mainly Defendant)

1. JONES DAY
   MORGAN, LEWIS & BOCKIUS LLP
   PAUL, HASTINGS, JANOFSKY & WALKER LLP
2. AKIN GUMP STRAUSS HAUER & FELD LLP
   GIBSON, DUNN & CRUTCHER LLP
   SEYFARTH SHAW
3. OGLETREE, DEAKINS, NASH, SMOAK & STEWART

Leading individuals (Employment: Mainly Defendant)

1. BROWN Barbara — *Paul, Hastings, Janofsky & Walker*
2. CHATILOVICZ Peter — *Seyfarth Shaw*
   SALEM George — *Akin Gump Strauss Hauer & Feld LLP*
3. BABSON Marshall — *Jones Day*
   GOLDSMITH Willis — *Jones Day*
   KILBERG William — *Gibson, Dunn & Crutcher LLP*

Firms and Individuals are listed alphabetically in each band.

Jones Day
see firm details p.823

The Firm: An integrated labor and employment group can draw on the resources of its offices across the US and overseas. In DC, a team of 14 advises on discrimination and wrongful discharge disputes, while its traditional labor relations experience includes collective bargaining, strike-related matters and OSHA work. Peers commend the firm as home to *"outstanding lawyers with a diversified practice."*

The group has a focus on litigation and has been involved in major class actions in recent years. Adept at handling high-profile cases, the group is representing Wal-Mart in a large sex discrimination class action. In the labor sphere, it acted for steel company LTV on issues arising from its bankruptcy. This type of experience has also proved useful in counseling other clients facing restructuring or insolvency in the volatile communications sector.

The Lawyers: Clients endorsed **Willis Goldsmith** (see p.136) as an *"excellent litigator and an important source of strategic guidance."* Chair of the labor and employment group, Goldsmith's practice encompasses statewide and international cases, particularly in OSHA matters. **Marshall Babson** (see p.132) was described as *"a walking encyclopedia"* on traditional labor law. Peers pointed to his deep knowledge of NLRA issues as typical of his *"experience and sound judgment."*

The Clients: Verizon, The Washington Post and Bridgestone/Firestone.

Morgan, Lewis & Bockius LLP
The Firm: Competitors acknowledged that the firm has *"a deep practice in DC with a substantial national presence."* Much of the firm's work involves counseling across state borders and on an international level, where its network of offices provides a distinct advantage. Our interviewees described them as a *"knowledgeable team of great depth"* with the capacity to act on complex cases. The group advises on collective bargaining and

EMPLOYMENT & LABOR LAW — DISTRICT OF COLUMBIA

union issues, and discrimination disputes. It has also witnessed an increase in employment matters arising from bankruptcies. Recent highlights include the negotiation of collective bargaining agreements in the trucking industry and counseling on labor law issues arising from corporate mergers.

The Lawyers: Based in DC, Robert Dufek is the national practice group manager of the labor and employment law practice.

The Clients: The firm advises clients across a broad range of sectors such as financial services, pharmaceuticals and entertainment, often drawn from the Fortune 500 list.

Paul, Hastings, Janofsky & Walker LLP
see firm details p.861

The Firm: Peers acknowledge that class action defense is a great strength of the group, which benefits from *"long experience and substantial resources."* For instance, the DC team worked with colleagues in Los Angeles on the defense of a class action litigation for Microsoft. The group has represented Ford in a class action based on its management evaluation system and advised Boeing on race and gender discrimination class actions. It also has a focus on OSHA compliance. On the traditional labor front, attorneys advise on collective bargaining, NLRA and union-organizing campaigns. In DC, the Railways Labor Act practice has represented Northwest Airlines in presidential emergency board proceedings with the Aircraft Mechanics Fraternal Association (flight attendants) and acted for United Airlines in proceedings with the International Association of Machinists & Aerospace Workers (mechanics).

The Lawyers: Peers acclaimed **Barbara Brown** (see p.133) as a *"pioneer in discrimination matters"* and a *"brilliant litigator."* Her practice consists of litigation and counseling on issues arising from sexual harassment and ADA compliance. Brown has also developed a niche in the representation of law firms.

The Clients: Typically clients are drawn from the Fortune 100 list and local corporate base. Ford, GE, Boeing, Amtrak and FMC use the firm.

Akin Gump Strauss Hauer & Feld LLP
see firm details p.701

The Firm: Well respected for its work in traditional labor law, the firm has a broad practice in collective bargaining, union issues and unfair labor practices. The firm's commitment to employment law as a key practice area has ensured its prominence in cutting-edge matters such as class action, wage and hour and equal employment opportunities litigation, and bankruptcy-related issues. A network of ten US offices, providing advice on cross-border matters and European Union legislation, is supported by attorneys based in London and Brussels. The group has advised on the scope of management rights in the railroad industry before the US Supreme Court.

The Lawyers: George Salem is respected as an *"attorney with integrity"* who has won a following with his *"sensible approach to cases."* He remains respected for his experience gained as chief legal officer in the US Department of Labor during the second Reagan Administration.

The Clients: The firm has advised clients in the airline, grocery and food industries on employment issues arising from restructuring. It also advised a grocery chain on race discrimination claims. Clients are drawn from the Fortune 500 and smaller local corporates.

Gibson, Dunn & Crutcher LLP

The Firm: A *"substantial presence"* in DC is undoubtedly bolstered by the firm's West Coast practice. The group has attorneys in seven offices across the US, providing counseling on nationwide class actions. A healthy balance in its workload has been struck among union and NLRA matters, wage and hour class actions, and OSHA and employment discrimination litigation. The firm is also skilled in transaction-related advice such as corporate mergers or issues arising from restructuring and insolvency.

The Lawyers: William Kilberg was recommended to researchers for his *"impeccable judgment"* and *"first-rate litigation skills."* He has appeared in the US Supreme Court and US Courts of Appeals. He recently advised on an ERISA case on appeal from the Washington State Supreme Court, and advised UPS on a reading of the ADA.

The Clients: The hi-tech, biotech and healthcare sectors are an ongoing source of clients for the labor and employment group. The firm also advises Fortune 500 and middle-market employers in the finance, real estate and manufacturing industries.

Seyfarth Shaw

The Firm: *"Nationally recognized,"* according to peers, the group is best known for its experience in union relationships. The group has attorneys in nine offices across the US, who coordinate national class actions in the fields of race and gender discrimination, ADA, affirmative action and collective bargaining.

The Lawyers: Peter Chatilovicz was deemed *"a highly skilled"* traditional labor law attorney. He is managing partner of the DC office and head of the labor and employment group. He specializes in collective bargaining negotiations, NLRA and ADA issues, and wage and hour disputes.

The Clients: The firm's wealth of experience has ensured that it attracts clients from both the local business community and larger national corporates.

Ogletree, Deakins, Nash, Smoak & Stewart PC

The Firm: Peers endorsed the firm as *"specialists"* in labor and employment issues across the US. The group is active in both traditional union issues, including collective bargaining, and discrimination disputes. Its attorneys are experienced in arbitration, and offer advice on pensions and other employee benefits; they are also active in litigation and practice general counseling. The firm has advised on issues relating to the Human Genome Project and the use of DNA testing to identify employees' potential risk of illness.

The Lawyers: Harold Coxson is a key member of the group.

The Clients: The firm represents many of the Fortune 100 companies and trade associations such as Printing Industries of America and the Society for Human Resources Management.

ENERGY — OIL & GAS/ELECTRICITY

Skadden, Arps, Slate, Meagher & Flom LLP & Affiliates
see firm details p.878

The Firm: This impressive group, which has its headquarters in DC, continues to be recommended as a top-class operation. Interviewees identified its *"tremendous client base"* and pool of talented attorneys as two winning features. The substantial team won recognition for its regulatory expertise in the oil, gas and electricity markets. Electricity, in particular, has been one of its most dynamic areas of practice owing to the Californian crisis and the process of deregulation. For example, the team acted as principal regulatory counsel to Dynegy in relation to Californian restructuring issues and consequent FERC litigation. Other key matters included acting for Florida Power & Light in the formation of GridFlorida RTO (regional transmission organization), and advising PPL on its development of three greenfield 'peaker' electricity-generating facilities on Long Island. The group also enjoys a preeminent position in oil and gas work. Typical matters involve advising on the purchase and sale of pipelines, refineries and chemical plants, as well as on purchase and transport agreements. The firm's activities in shaping legislation also won praise from interviewees.

DISTRICT OF COLUMBIA — ENERGY

DISTRICT OF COLUMBIA
Leading firms (Energy: Oil & Gas)

1. SKADDEN, ARPS, SLATE, MEAGHER & FLOM LLP
2. LEBOEUF, LAMB, GREENE & MACRAE LLP
   VINSON & ELKINS LLP
3. BAKER BOTTS LLP
   SIDLEY AUSTIN BROWN & WOOD
   STEPTOE & JOHNSON LLP
4. ANDREWS & KURTH LLP
   CROWELL & MORING LLP
   FULBRIGHT & JAWORSKI LLP
   LATHAM & WATKINS LLP
5. HUNTON & WILLIAMS
   JONES DAY

Leading firms (Energy: Electricity)

1. SKADDEN, ARPS, SLATE, MEAGHER & FLOM LLP
   STEPTOE & JOHNSON LLP
2. JONES DAY
   LEBOEUF, LAMB, GREENE & MACRAE LLP
3. BAKER BOTTS LLP
   CHADBOURNE & PARKE LLP
   HUNTON & WILLIAMS
   VINSON & ELKINS LLP
4. DEWEY BALLANTINE LLP
   DICKSTEIN SHAPIRO MORIN & OSHINSKY LLP
   MORGAN, LEWIS & BOCKIUS LLP
   TROUTMAN SANDERS LLP
   VAN NESS FELDMAN

Firms are listed alphabetically in each band.

The Lawyers: Clifford (Mike) Naeve (see p.141) is undoubtedly one of the firm's main draws. Sources described him as an *"incredibly sophisticated lawyer"* who combines political acumen, people skills and common sense. His stint as a FERC commissioner has also lent him a *"big-picture perspective."* Bill Scherman (see p.145), who has appeared in a number of high-profile cases, was also seen as a key individual. Although his style wasn't to everyone's taste, interviewees saw him as a *"pragmatic"* lawyer who *"serves his clients well."* Lynn Coleman (see p.134) is a senior member of the group, who is respected for his regulatory knowledge. On the junior side, John Estes (see p.135) enters the rankings this year. He was tipped as a *"fine young lawyer."* His colleague Martin Klepper (see p.138) maintains an eclectic practice combining expertise in project finance with experience in a range of energy transactions.

The Clients: The firm's top-class client base includes Florida Power & Light; Entergy; Progress Energy; El Paso; NRG Energy; PPL and PG&E.

LeBoeuf, Lamb, Greene & MacRae LLP
see firm details p.838

The Firm: The firm enjoys a formidable reputation in this area, thanks to the depth of its experience and its *"terrific lawyers."* It advises on a variety of transactions for oil and gas producers, distributors and publicly owned utilities. The firm maintains particularly strong relationships with pipeline operators. Highlights have included acting for National Grid Group on its acquisition of Niagara Mohawk. The group is also respected for its ability to provide a broad range of regulatory advice, particularly in relation to The Public Utility Holding Company Act of 1935 (PUHCA) matters. In the international arena, it has acted as US regulatory counsel for German power company E.ON in its proposed acquisition of a majority interest in Ruhrgas. However, much of the past year's work was in the evolving electricity sphere, where it is developing a *"first-rate"* reputation.

The Lawyers: Lawrence Acker (see p.131) is principally involved in administrative litigation. Interviewees saw him as a skilled attorney *"with the personality to deal with all sorts of people."* He has been heavily involved in Californian refund proceedings, where he has acted for IDACORP Energy and represented a group of 25 marketers and utilities. Brian O'Neill (see p.141) heads the practice in DC and continues to be an active figure in the gas industry. Sources regard him as a low-key but impressive individual.

The Clients: The firm acts for a range of energy companies, including MidAmerican Energy Company; E.ON; Westar Energy; National Grid Group and PEPCO.

Vinson & Elkins LLP
see firm details p.891

The Firm: This Texan energy powerhouse continues to elicit warm praise from peers, despite a difficult year following the demise of Enron. Although noted for its diverse practice, the bulk of its recommendations were won in the oil and gas sphere. Here, its regulatory group has been involved in certificate and rate proceedings before the FERC. It has also represented two Duke Energy affiliates, Maritimes & Northeast Pipeline and Algonquin Gas Transmission Company, in winning approvals for the expansion of a natural gas pipeline. The group is recognized as a force in transactional work, for which it can also draw upon the firm's antitrust expertise. It has obtained FERC and PUHCA approval for Duke Energy's acquisition of Canadian company Westcoast Energy. The firm remains active internationally, and has been involved in Latin American LNG business. Its electricity practice lacks the profile of its oil and gas complement and has suffered a setback through the departure of Adam Wenner to Chadbourne & Parke in late 2002. However it continues to advise a range of clients including electric utilities, RTOs and independent power developers.

The Lawyers: The key individual here is David Andril (see p.131), who was recommended to researchers as an *"energetic and practical"* lawyer. He is best known for his natural gas work, in which he frequently advises on pipeline expansions and gas imports.

The Clients: The firm's enviable client base includes: Duke Energy; Energy East; British Gas; Algonquin Gas Transmission Company; PSEG Global and Inter-American Development Bank.

Baker Botts LLP

The Firm: Although this firm is considered to be stronger in its Texan homeland, the DC office won plaudits for its broad range of experience, encompassing the transactional, regulatory and litigious aspects of energy law. In particular, it stood out for the quality of its gas practice, which peers considered to be among the leaders. While its staple diet includes contractual pipeline matters, it also has experience of securing regulatory approvals for the development of natural gas pipelines and LNG-receiving terminals.

The Lawyers: Tom Eastment is described as a *"choice individual"* for gas pipeline work, with a pragmatic approach. He successfully won a summary judgement for major producers, including ExxonMobil, BP Amoco and Texaco Natural Gas, in a challenge to a FERC order that had imposed onerous reporting requirements on the plaintiffs in relation to their offshore operations. Bruce Kiely is active on the natural gas scene, but is also a key figure in the firm's lesser-known electricity practice. He has been involved in the restructuring of the electricity industry and litigation arising from the Californian energy crisis.

The Clients: The firm represented AES Ocean Express in its proposed construction of an interstate pipeline. Other important clients include: Dynegy; ExxonMobil; Reliant Energy; Entergy and Mirant.

Sidley Austin Brown & Wood
see firm details p.877

The Firm: Peers identify this firm as one of the few to disrupt the dominion of Texan firms in the area of oil and gas, and praise it for the depth of its bench. Much of its profile is due to its regulatory presence at the FERC, although industry sources acknowledge that it is also a player in transactional matters. These have included acting as lead counsel on the $700 million Millennium Pipeline project from eastern Canada to New York. It is also active in litigation. Here it secured a new trial for ExxonMobil in a natural gas royalties case, in which a jury previously awarded $3.5 billion in damages. The group's other areas of

ENERGY
DISTRICT OF COLUMBIA

DISTRICT OF COLUMBIA
Leading individuals
(Energy & Natural Resources)

★ **NAEVE** Clifford *Skadden, Arps, Slate, Meagher & Flom*

1
BOUKNIGHT Lon *Steptoe & Johnson LLP*
SCHERMAN William *Skadden, Arps, Slate, Meagher*

2
ACKER Lawrence *LeBoeuf, Lamb, Greene & MacRae*
DOWNS Clark *Jones Day*
EASTMENT Thomas *Baker Botts LLP*
ELROD Eugene *Sidley Austin Brown & Wood*
O'NEILL Brian *LeBoeuf, Lamb, Greene & MacRae*

3
ANDRIL David *Vinson & Elkins LLP*
BALIS Stanley *Miller, Balis & O'Neil PC*
BOWE JR James *Dewey Ballantine LLP*
BROSE Steve *Steptoe & Johnson LLP*
GREEN Douglas *Steptoe & Johnson LLP*
KLEPPER Martin *Skadden, Arps, Slate, Meagher & Flom*
WILLIAMS William *Fulbright & Jaworski LLP*

4
COLEMAN Lynn *Skadden, Arps, Slate, Meagher & Flom*
CONTRATTO Dana *Crowell & Moring LLP*
FREMUTH Michael *Andrews & Kurth LLP*
REED Steve *Steptoe & Johnson LLP*
WATERS Jennifer *Crowell & Moring LLP*

5
BERNER Frederic *Sidley Austin Brown & Wood*
EISENSTAT Larry *Dickstein Shapiro Morin & Oshinsky*
ESTES John *Skadden, Arps, Slate, Meagher & Flom*
GENTILE Carmen *Bruder Gentile & Marcoux LLP*
JAFFE Kenneth *Swidler Berlin Shereff Friedman LLP*
KIELY Bruce *Baker Botts LLP*
MCGRANE John *Morgan, Lewis & Bockius LLP*
NORTON Floyd *Morgan, Lewis & Bockius LLP*
O'DONNELL Earle *Dewey Ballantine LLP*
O'SULLIVAN John *Chadbourne & Parke LLP*
ROBERTS Richard *Steptoe & Johnson LLP*
SCHWARTZ David *Latham & Watkins LLP*
WENNER Adam *Chadbourne & Parke LLP*

Individuals are listed alphabetically in each band.

specialization include the regulation of natural gas pipelines and the electric power industry. This expertise has led to its participation in refund proceedings in California.
The Lawyers: **Gene Elrod**'s practice spans the oil, gas and electricity industries. Sources admired his *"excellent judgment"* and *"sensible and balanced advice."* **Fred Berner** is best known for his litigation of energy issues, particularly those relating to competitive and antitrust matters in the deregulated markets.
The Clients: Millennium Pipeline; Colonial Pipeline; BP; Idaho Power; Columbia Gas Transmission; Shell; Longhorn Pipeline; TEPPCO Partners; CMS Energy and DTE Energy.

Steptoe & Johnson LLP
The Firm: This compact group of lawyers is renowned for its strong regulatory capabilities in both electricity and oil. Peers felt that the firm's success in the former was due in part to its detailed knowledge of utilities, and pointed to an especially strong profile in the establishment of RTOs. Although it is best known for its representation of clients in FERC proceedings, its ability to combine regulatory and antitrust expertise with transactional experience has seen it act for E.ON on its acquisition of Powergen. The firm also fields one of the premier oil groups in town, which has been active recently on major pipeline cases before regulatory agencies. Most importantly, the team has acted as co-lead counsel for the owners of the Trans-Alaskan Pipeline in the defense of a proceeding before the Regulatory Commission of Alaska challenging the rates set for the transportation of petroleum.
The Lawyers: *"Top-tier"* **Lon Bouknight** heads the group. He was recommended to researchers as one of the preeminent practitioners in the electric power industry. Sources praised his antitrust and litigation skills, saying that when he is involved in a case, *"people see him and pay attention."* *"Practical and focused"* **Doug Green** has represented American Electric Power in connection with its corporate restructuring. Described as *"one of the toughest regulatory lawyers around,"* **Steve Brose** won high marks for the extent of his knowledge of oil pipeline matters, while **Steve Reed** was endorsed as a *"strong oral advocate and excellent writer."* Interviewees also drew researchers' attention to **Rick Roberts**, who is establishing a reputation as a *"top-notch FERC litigator."*
The Clients: American Electric Power; Southern California Edison; Con Edison; Northeast Utilities; Trans-Alaskan Pipeline System; Colonial Pipeline; ExxonMobil Pipeline Company and Alpine Transportation.

Andrews & Kurth LLP
see firm details p.764
The Firm: The group is chiefly known for its natural gas expertise. It represents clients in administrative litigation matters and has a sterling reputation for regulatory advice before various agencies. Its workload extends to counseling energy companies on the regulatory aspects of their acquisitions, financings and restructuring arrangements. In the past year the firm has represented The Williams Companies in two cases before the FERC, including a precedent-setting case brought by Shell Oil regarding natural gas gathering and transmission rates.
The Lawyers: Clients endorse **Mike Fremuth** (see p.135) as a *"hands-on team player,"* while competitors praise him as *"one of the finest gas litigators in the business."*
The Clients: Although no longer acting for El Paso, the team continues to represent natural gas and oil pipeline owners, gathering companies, oil and gas producers and users, and energy marketing companies. In particular, it advises The Williams Companies and Anadarko Petroleum.

Crowell & Moring LLP
The Firm: Although some interviewees felt that the firm's profile has diminished slightly over the past few years, it continues to be a force in the market. Sources repeatedly praised its natural gas practice, which boasts an enviable client roster heavy with utilities. The group has represented Kansas Gas Service, a division of ONEOK, in pipeline supplier rate and delivery proceedings at the FERC. It also maintains an active practice focusing on international work, particularly in Latin America. A ten-lawyer group, for example, continues to advise Yacimientos Petroliferos Fiscales Bolivianos on the Bolivia-Brazil Pipeline project.
The Lawyers: **Dana Contratto** is noted for his legislative work on Capitol Hill. Clients recommend him as a *"tenacious and intelligent"* lawyer. **Jennifer Waters** also captured the attention of our interviewees for being *"especially good at appellate work and oral arguments."*
The Clients: ONEOK; Baltimore Gas and Electric Company; Memphis Gas, Water & Light; Knoxville Utilities Board and PG&E.

Fulbright & Jaworski LLP
see firm details p.799
The Firm: The firm's reputation rests principally on its pipeline expertise, in which it ranks as an important player. The practice, which is ably supported by a team in Texas, undertakes work in the natural gas, LNG and oil areas but also has knowledge of the electricity industry. Wide-ranging regulatory matters form a large portion of the firm's workload. It has been involved in some notable cross-border transactions and the development of LNG projects. It is also an active force in litigation, often representing clients in rule-makings and contested issues before a variety of agencies. Its expertise in royalty issues has won it particular market commendation.
The Lawyers: **Bill Williams** (see p.149) was described as a *"terrific natural gas lawyer,"* and recommended to researchers as *"a good advocate with a laser-sharp focus."*
The Clients: The firm represents a mix of clients with gas, LNG, oil and electricity interests.

Latham & Watkins LLP
see firm details p.835
The Firm: This up-and-coming group of talented lawyers is buoyed by the firm's impressive project finance practice. They work closely with projects colleagues in New York and DC to counsel on the regulatory aspects of transactions, and are heavily involved in West Coast energy markets. The group has recently represented a number of clients, before the FERC and state and federal courts, in relation to investigations into so-called 'Enron trading strategies'.
The Lawyers: Although the firm's profile might

DISTRICT OF COLUMBIA ENERGY

be greater in the oil and gas sectors, one of its most respected lawyers, **David Schwartz** (see p.145), is best known for representing electric utilities. He acted for Sithe Energies in its successful opposition to attempts by both the New York independent system operator, NYISO, and New York transmission owners to impose charges on Sithe's pre-existing transmission contract.
The Clients: Sempra Energy Resources; Mirant Americas Energy Marketing; Sithe Energies and AES.

Hunton & Williams
The Firm: Hunton & William's reputation in project finance is thought to be key to its profile in the energy arena. However, its multifaceted practice also has expertise in M&A, restructuring and debt and equity finance. The group is active in the oil and gas sector, although it is felt to be at its strongest in the electricity market where it has been active in the restructuring and deregulation of wholesale and retail energy markets. The regulation of natural gas pipelines and the setting of market-based rates are key features of its gas practice.
The Lawyers: The team has suffered a loss through the untimely death in late 2002 of the hugely popular Mike Barr. Dallas-based Robert Fillmore coordinates the regulated utilities team, while Arnold Quint is also active in this field.
The Clients: The group represents traditional investor-owned electric utilities and energy marketing and trading companies and a number of independent transmission system operators in New York and the northeastern US. TXU, PG&E, InterGen and AES are clients.

Jones Day
see firm details p.823
The Firm: This *"fantastic"* energy group maintains a prominent position in the market. Sources herald it as one of the strongest outfits in the electricity industry, providing *"high-quality"* regulatory advice. It has assisted several companies in FERC investigations into the Californian power market and is also engaged in winning approval for utility transactions, including Ameren's acquisition of Cilcorp. Its profile is lower in oil and gas-related work, though it was nonetheless credited with an active pipeline practice.
The Lawyers: *"Great strategist"* **Clark Downs** (see p.134) was described as an *"accomplished regulatory lawyer,"* renowned for his *"creativity"* and *"pure IQ."*
The Clients: The firm's stable of clients includes cogeneration companies, hydroelectric developers, independent power producers and power marketers. These include FirstEnergy; Exelon; The Dayton Power & Light Company; Central and South West Corporation; Allegheny Energy and Edison Mission Energy.

Chadbourne & Parke LLP
see firm details p.781
The Firm: The group's experience in project finance was seen as key to its profile in the energy arena. The team is well versed in gaining approvals for M&A and acquisitions before regulatory agencies; peers felt, however, that its reputation was greatest in the financing sphere. The electricity sector was identified as an area of particular strength, though the firm also has oil and gas capabilities. In 2002, the group advised Cleco on its acquisition of Mirant's interest in the Perryville project, a 750MW natural gas-fired generating plant. It was also involved in litigation relating to the Californian energy crisis.
The Lawyers: John O'Sullivan was recommended for his broad and up-to-date expertise. His wide experience includes work on natural gas pipeline projects. The group has been further strengthened by the arrival of **Adam Wenner** from Vinson & Elkins, who is admired for his *"familiarity with sophisticated regulatory issues."* He frequently represents clients before the FERC, the SEC and state utility commissions, and is experienced in obtaining merger approvals.
The Clients: The firm has advised industrial and developer clients on the rules of cogeneration and independent power production. It continues to represent owners and developers as well as lenders to independent power producers (IPPs). Clients include Cleco, Perryville Energy Partners and Sithe Energies subsidiary, EF Oxnard.

Dewey Ballantine LLP
see firm details p.790
The Firm: The firm won high praise for its electricity practice, which was formed ten years ago through the recruitment of a core of electricity regulatory attorneys. Since then its profile has gradually increased as it advises electric utilities, power marketers, project operators and independent power sellers on a variety of matters including regional transmission organization (RTO) developments, market-based rates and transmission issues.
The Lawyers: Earle O'Donnell (see p.141) was described by market sources as a *"smart and practical attorney who lives for this type of thing."* **Jim Bowe** (see p.133) also elicited praise from interviewees, for both his legal knowledge and his keen business sense. He is best known as a natural gas lawyer, and has advised Louisville Gas & Electric Company on federal regulatory matters. He also represented the lenders in the non-recourse financing of InterGen's La Rosita natural gas-fired electricity-generating facilities.
The Clients: The firm's client roster includes PG&E and Louisville Gas & Electric Company.

Dickstein Shapiro Morin & Oshinsky LLP
The Firm: Industry sources recommend this group for both a blue-chip client base and experience of regulatory and litigation issues. Its knowledge of electricity regulation was felt to be its trump card and it regularly counsels clients on power supply and transmission issues, and acts in administrative and rulemaking proceedings. The transactional side of the practice was not felt to have the profile of its regulatory counterpart, but attorneys there are nonetheless experienced in restructurings, divestitures and mergers.
The Lawyers: Larry Eisenstat was recommended to researchers as a *"strong and aggressive advocate"* with extensive FERC experience.
The Clients: The firm regularly advises utilities, marketers and independent power producers.

Morgan, Lewis & Bockius LLP
The Firm: A group of about 12 lawyers comprise what was described to researchers as a *"significant"* force in the electricity industry. Its varied practice includes advising on M&A transactions and restructurings as well as negotiating power contracts and transmission rates and services. The firm also has a smaller gas practice and is well known for its robust nuclear practice group.
The Lawyers: John McGrane has a reputation as a *"levelheaded"* attorney, who is adept at collaborating with a range of people, while his colleague, **Floyd Norton**, was seen as a noteworthy player at the FERC.
The Clients: The firm represents electric utilities, power pools, RTOs and power marketers.

Troutman Sanders LLP
The Firm: The firm's growing reputation in this field is rooted firmly in its electricity expertise, although the practice also has a natural gas component. Having recently made efforts to expand, the team, now numbering approximately 15 lawyers, is *"making strides"* and was identified as a force to watch in the future. Interviewees found that attorneys here were particularly strong in electricity transmission matters, especially with regard to independent system operators, but had also been involved in restructuring and the California n energy situation.
The Lawyers: The team has suffered a setback due to Donald Santa's departure to the Interstate Natural Gas Association of America in January 2003. However, an able team includes Lisanne Crowley, who is experienced in representing gas and electric utilities in proceedings before the FERC.
The Clients: The firm continues to act for a range of clients with electricity interests, including the Southern Company.

Van Ness Feldman
The Firm: This DC firm, which has a Seattle regional office, focuses on energy, environmental

ENVIRONMENT — DISTRICT OF COLUMBIA

and natural resources law. It received market commendation for its *"top-notch"* FERC operations. Peers also praised it for the quality of its advice on complicated federal cases. Clients are counseled on transactions, the structuring of projects, and state and federal regulatory matters, as well as on legislative initiatives, in which the team was felt to have particular expertise.

The Lawyers: Margaret (Peg) Moore features among a knowledgeable team of over 50 lawyers.

The Clients: Typical clients of the group include regulated electric utilities, independent power project developers and power marketers.

Other Notable Practitioners

Stanley Balis of Miller, Balis & O'Neil PA stood out as one of the few practitioners to specialize in representing cooperative and municipal gas and electricity utilities. He was recommended as a *"tremendously talented lawyer."* **Ken Jaffe** has emerged as the key individual at Swidler Berlin Shereff Friedman LLP following Ed Berlin's withdrawal from 'front-line' work. Although he lacks the standing of Berlin, Jaffe was endorsed as a *"promising"* regulatory lawyer. At Bruder Gentile & Marcoux LLP, **Carmen Gentile** was described as a *"well-regarded electricity lawyer"* with a wealth of experience behind him.

ENVIRONMENT

DISTRICT OF COLUMBIA
Leading firms (Environment)

1 SIDLEY AUSTIN BROWN & WOOD
2 HUNTON & WILLIAMS
   LATHAM & WATKINS LLP
3 MORGAN, LEWIS & BOCKIUS LLP
4 ARNOLD & PORTER
   BEVERIDGE & DIAMOND PC
   COVINGTON & BURLING
5 GIBSON, DUNN & CRUTCHER LLP
   MCKENNA LONG & ALDRIDGE
   SWIDLER BERLIN SHEREFF FRIEDMAN LLP
   VENABLE LLP

Leading individuals (Environment)

1 BUENTE David *Sidley Austin Brown & Wood*
   HAYES David *Latham & Watkins LLP*
   MACBETH Angus *Sidley Austin Brown & Wood*
2 GARRETT Theodore *Covington & Burling*
   MILCH Thomas *Arnold & Porter*
   QUARLES John *Morgan, Lewis & Bockius LLP*
3 FIELD Andrea *Hunton & Williams*
   LEWIS William *Morgan, Lewis & Bockius LLP*
   NICKEL Henry *Hunton & Williams*
   STEINBERG Michael *Morgan, Lewis & Bockius LLP*
4 BROWNELL William *Hunton & Williams*
   GAYNOR Kevin *Vinson & Elkins LLP*
   KNAUSS Charles *Swidler Berlin Shereff Friedman*
   LUDWISZEWSKI Raymond *Gibson, Dunn & Crutcher*
   SMITH Turner *Hunton & Williams*
   STOLL Richard *Foley & Lardner*
   SUSSMAN Robert *Latham & Watkins LLP*
5 BIEKE James *Shea & Gardner*
   BUCKLEY Christopher *Gibson, Dunn & Crutcher LLP*
   HAGEN Paul *Beveridge & Diamond PC*
   MENOTTI David *Shaw Pittman*
   RAHER Patrick *Hogan & Hartson LLP*
   STARR Judson *Venable LLP*
   WEINSTEIN Ken *Latham & Watkins LLP*

Firms and Individuals are listed alphabetically in each band.

Sidley Austin Brown & Wood
see firm details p.877

The Firm: The firm possesses a string of highly respected environmental departments in cities such as New York and Chicago. However, the DC office stands out for most commentators as the jewel in the crown. The office provides expertise in virtually all areas of environmental law but won the highest accolades for its advice pertaining to environmental enforcement issues, where a team of 13 *"outstanding practitioners"* includes several alumni from government agencies.

The Lawyers: Previously at the US Department of Justice, **Dave Buente** is recognized as one of the biggest players for enforcement and criminal matters. He has *"his finger on the pulse"* of governmental developments and was applauded to researchers for his in-depth knowledge of both statutes and case law. He negotiated a settlement for GE concerning waste remediation and natural resources damage claims for contamination of the Housatonic River in New England. Heading the group is one of the city's senior figures, **Angus Macbeth**, who was endorsed as an undisputed *"star."* He covers a plethora of environmental matters, and peers remarked on his *"understanding of the technical issues"* and *"thoughtful"* approach to cases. His resumé has included appearing for GE in a dispute with the EPA regarding the possible dredging of the Hudson River.

The Clients: The team has represented Transcontinental Gas Pipeline in a settlement with the EPA of claims under three separate statutes at more than 30 stations along the pipeline. Other clients include GE, American Electric Power, Consolidated Edison and Cummins.

Hunton & Williams

The Firm: A *"strong and active"* group of lawyers from this firm, which is headquartered in Virginia, was recognized by competitors as a *"major player"* for DC regulatory matters. Although the workload encompasses an assortment of environmental statutes, including the CWA, the Superfund Program and wetlands-related issues, it was the firm's expertise in CAA matters that won the greatest market recognition. In this area, fortified by a strong electric utility client base, the firm was acknowledged as a national leader.

The Lawyers: In a strong team, **Andrea Bear Field** was recommended to researchers for her varied experience in the sector. She has been engaged in the CAA's New Source Review matters, and also has a name for other clean air work. Another *"pretty good choice"* for clean air work is the vastly experienced **Henry Nickel**. He is regarded by contemporaries as a key player in the CAA field, and is frequently involved in litigation at appellate level. Specializing in the defense of enforcement actions, **Bill Brownell** was described by peers as a *"patient"* attorney who is *"not easily rattled."* His caseload has included acting for the Tennessee Valley Authority in challenging the EPA's reinterpretation of CAA regulations. The respected **Turner Smith** is active in the international sphere, in which he is involved in litigation, transactional and policy work.

The Clients: Other clients include the Tennessee Valley Authority and American Trucking Associations.

Latham & Watkins LLP
see firm details p.835

The Firm: Widely acclaimed by interviewees as *"one of the strongest"* environmental groups in the market, the firm continues to represent clients from the chemical, pesticide, paper and semiconductor industries. Although the group undertakes a percentage of overseas work, it was especially lauded for its national strength, notably on transactional matters. In the regulatory sphere, a broad practice attracted particular praise for its toxic substances work, in which it is generally viewed as the leading authority.

The Lawyers: Formerly Deputy Secretary of the Interior in the Clinton Administration, **David Hayes** (see p.137) is clearly the group's outstanding practitioner. Peers recognized him as a *"personable and hard-working"* attorney with

DISTRICT OF COLUMBIA — ENVIRONMENT

excellent connections. Experienced in a range of areas, he has advised a German-based company in buyout negotiations, and negotiated a major settlement with a US electronics company in connection with a large Superfund remediation matter in Arizona.

Chairing the group in DC, **Bob Sussman** (see p.146) is respected by the market for a practice that is centered on air quality control matters. His recent engagements have included acting for Tampa Electric in a settlement of an EPA enforcement action against electric utilities. **Ken Weinstein** (see p.148) is best known for his pesticides and chemical regulation practice. Here, he has represented CropLife America in challenges to EPA policies on the review of pesticide tolerances and the use of human data in pesticide registrations.

The Clients: Notable clients include: 3M; BASF; Siemens; Ford; PG&E National Energy Group; American Forest & Paper Association and The Business Roundtable.

Morgan, Lewis & Bockius LLP

The Firm: The firm has a long history in this practice area, and possesses acknowledged niche expertise in CAA and hazardous waste cases. Despite a perceived lack of high-profile environment attorneys in the junior ranks, the group can lay claim to a number of DC's most notable individuals.

The Lawyers: **John Quarles** was described to researchers as a *"distinguished veteran"* of the local environment bar. Credited with building the firm's practice in the sector, his experience extends into a number of areas, although commentators particularly rated his Superfund expertise. **Mike Steinberg** was endorsed as one of the *"choice"* practitioners for contaminated properties and hazardous waste matters. He represented the US chemical industry in its court challenge to an EPA rule under RCRA. **Bill Lewis** heads the firm's CAA practice, although many interviewees felt that his expertise reaches well beyond this. He has defended clients against enforcement actions in which the EPA alleged violations of the CAA's New Source Review permitting requirements.

The Clients: Clients include: American Airlines; Sequa; FAG Bearings; JPMorgan Chase; Apollo Group and Citicorp Venture Capital.

Arnold & Porter
see firm details p.765

The Firm: Clients and competitors were united in their endorsement of a firm that is ably supported by another notable environmental practice in New York. Although it is not generally felt to equal the depth of the market leaders in DC, the group has the resources to handle transactional, regulatory and contentious aspects of environmental law. Areas of particular expertise were identified as the cleanup of contaminated properties and CAA matters.

The Lawyers: The group's star attorney is **Tom Milch** (see p.140) whose caseload includes enforcement defense and compliance issues. He was recommended by peers as a *"terrific problem solver."* He defended Safety-Kleen in claims involving the Pinewood hazardous waste landfill site in South Carolina. The group has also advised BP on matters involving historical property contamination across the US, including the defense of a lawsuit in the State of New York regarding PCB (polychlorinated biphenyls) contamination in the Hudson River.

The Clients: Other clients include IMC Global, Sappi Fine Paper North America and Detroit Diesel.

Beveridge & Diamond PC
see firm details p.771

The Firm: This firm was championed by interviewees as a *"preeminent regulatory group,"* and is one of the few remaining environmental boutiques in DC. Its depth is such that it is able to assemble subspecialized teams for a full spectrum of environmental matters, including pollution control work and chemical and pesticide regulation. The team has litigation experience before both state and federal agencies and also maintains offices in San Francisco, New York and Baltimore. In an office of about 50 lawyers, the firm's team ethos is generally regarded as its strong point.

The Lawyers: **Paul Hagen** (see p.136) won individual recognition for his international practice. He represents US industries in treaty negotiations, and advises on the environmental aspects of overseas infrastructure projects.

The Clients: Clients include the American Chemistry Council and the Electronic Industries Alliance.

Covington & Burling
see firm details p.786

The Firm: Highly respected by the market for its long history in this area, the firm continues to be regarded as a *"serious competitor."* Superfund and enforcement issues are a rich source of work for the group. It also advises clients on day-to-day regulatory and permitting matters, and maintains an active practice covering issues under the Federal Insecticide, Fungicide, and Rodenticide Act (FIFRA). The 15-lawyer group also successfully represented a metals recycler in a joint criminal investigation by the US Attorney's office and the EPA into alleged RCRA violations, and participated in the United Nations Environment Programme global treaty negotiations on persistent organic pollutants.

The Lawyers: Much of the credit for the group's current standing is ascribed to **Ted Garrett**, who was commended to researchers as a *"luminary"* of the bar. His diverse practice incorporates Superfund and air and water legislation. Garrett acted for a group of utilities in a successful challenge to the EPA's CAA ozone transport regulations.

The Clients: Clients include: Kerr-McGee; Pechiney; Vulcan Materials; Nestlé; Solutia; Northrop Grumman; Boeing and Kansas City Power & Light.

Gibson, Dunn & Crutcher LLP

The Firm: Attorneys at this comparatively small group frequently assist on the environmental aspects of transactions, as well as advising on all the major substantive areas, including air, ground and surface water, and solid, hazardous and radioactive waste. Commentators identified the group's litigation practice, however, as a particular sphere of quality.

The Lawyers: Formerly at the EPA and the US Department of Justice, **Ray Ludwiszewski** is renowned for his *"in-depth knowledge of policy and substance."* His colleague, **Chris Buckley**, was described to researchers as a *"litigator at heart"* with extensive experience of environmental and toxic tort suits.

The Clients: The firm appeared in defense of paper companies in litigation initiated by the federal government relating to the New Source Review provisions of the CAA. It also advised Cincinnati and Hamilton County, Ohio, in an action under the CWA. Other clients include ARCO, Occidental Chemical, Lockheed Martin and California Farm Bureau Federation.

McKenna Long & Aldridge

The Firm: This firm, which merged in 2002, concentrates its practice on chemical and pesticide regulation under state and federal laws. Rivals concede that its practice concerning FIFRA matters is one of the largest and most respected in the DC market. Work in these areas has included representing Aventis in relation to the manufacture of a genetically engineered corn product. Charles O'Connor heads the team, which now comprises about 12 lawyers.

The Clients: Other clients include SC Johnson, 3M, Dow Chemical and Sumitomo Chemical.

Swidler Berlin Shereff Friedman LLP

The Firm: A team of *"young and aggressive"* attorneys was identified by commentators as one of the *"up-and-coming practices"* in the city. Although smaller than many other groups, it is a respected force for regulatory matters and is well known for its legislative work.

The Lawyers: **Chuck Knauss** is known to have *"superbly detailed knowledge"* of environmental laws, and was involved in the rewriting of the CAA. Much of the group's workload has centered on the CAA's New Source Review requirements

INSOLVENCY/CORPORATE RECOVERY — DISTRICT OF COLUMBIA

in which it has assisted with the acquisition of permits for new facilities and with major modifications at existing sites.
The Clients: Clients include: GM; GE; Ford; International Paper; Georgia-Pacific and ExxonMobil.

Venable LLP
The Firm: Although the firm is well versed in day-to-day environmental law and has experience in Superfund and hazardous waste matters, its stature within the market owes most to its reputation for environmental criminal defense work. Acting for a diverse group of clients, a team of 13 lawyers assists large corporations, small companies and individuals under investigation for possible violations of environmental statutes.
The Lawyers: **Judson Starr** is one of two former chiefs of the US Department of Justice's environmental crimes section currently at the firm. Endorsed to researchers as *"a talented litigator,"* he also advises a range of clients on environmental compliance.
The Clients: Leading national corporates feature in its client list.

Other Notable Practitioners
A familiar face at the EPA, **Dick Stoll** of Foley & Lardner was described by competitors as *"superb"* for hazardous waste issues. At Vinson & Elkins LLP, **Kevin Gaynor** (see p.136) applies a *"problem-solving approach"* to good effect in his enforcement defense practice. He recently represented a utility in a case brought by the EPA, claiming violations of the New Source Review requirements under the CAA.
Devoting a substantial portion of his practice to Superfund matters, **Jim Bieke** of Shea & Gardner has advised GE in connection with several locations, including the Pittsfield/Housatonic PCB site. **Dave Menotti** of Shaw Pittman elicited peer praise for his *"first-rate"* advice on chemical regulation. **Pat Raher** (see p.143) of Hogan & Hartson LLP *"knows his stuff"* on the CAA, and acts for a broad client base, including utilities and car manufacturers.

INSOLVENCY/CORPORATE RECOVERY

DISTRICT OF COLUMBIA
Leading firms (Insolvency/Corporate Recovery)

1
- SWIDLER BERLIN SHEREFF FRIEDMAN LLP
- WILMER, CUTLER & PICKERING

2
- AKIN GUMP STRAUSS HAUER & FELD LLP
- ARNOLD & PORTER

Leading individuals (Insolvency/Corporate Recovery)

1
- FRANKEL Roger *Swidler Berlin Shereff Friedman LLP*
- LEWIS Daniel *Arnold & Porter*
- PERLSTEIN William *Wilmer, Cutler & Pickering*

2
- SAMORAJCZYK Stanley *Akin Gump Strauss Hauer*

3
- BAXTER Michael St Patrick *Covington & Burling*
- KUNEY David *Sidley Austin Brown & Wood*
- LITT Daniel *Dickstein Shapiro Morin & Oshinsky LLP*
- WYRON Richard *Swidler Berlin Shereff Friedman LLP*

Firms and Individuals are listed alphabetically in each band.

Swidler Berlin Shereff Friedman LLP
The Firm: Peers believe that this DC-based firm has developed its profile through *"major cases"* and can now lay claim to performing on a *"national stage."* It is experienced in acting for midmarket public companies, purchasers of assets and secured creditors. Benefiting from the growth in insolvency matters, the firm has had a role in recent bankruptcies in the telecom industry, such as Ardent Communications and Zephion Networks.
The Lawyers: Much admiration for the firm emanates from **Roger Frankel**, *"one of the most experienced around."* He heads the bankruptcy group and has broad experience in debtors' and creditors' work. Interviewees described him as *"straight-shooting,"* and the highlight of a group of *"bright"* supporting players whose principal strength is *"deal-making."* Among them, **Richard Wyron** stood out as bringing *"good judgment"* and a balanced approach to his cases. A *"smart lawyer who gets the best deal for his client,"* Wyron has a broad practice that includes real estate developers, owners and managers.

Wilmer, Cutler & Pickering
see firm details p.901
The Firm: This national practice is known for its skill in handling *"major, complex engagements."* It is equally at home in both a transactional or litigation setting. The practice is also distinguished by the firm's expertise in regulatory law. It has acted as debtors' counsel on a string of notable Chapter 11 cases, for instance, PSINet, US Office Products Company and Iridium. Creditors' work includes the Chapter 11 of ANC Rental, and advising the ad hoc committee of noteholders in Glasstech Holdings.
The Lawyers: Researchers were left in no doubt that the firm can field a team of high-quality insolvency attorneys. The stellar profile of managing partner **William Perlstein** (see p.142) attracted the most acclaim. He typically represents large public company debtors and was recommended as a *"quick thinker"* with a *"low-key"* approach. He represented Verizon in an agreement with NextWave Telecom to settle disputes with the federal government regarding spectrum licenses.

Akin Gump Strauss Hauer & Feld LLP
see firm details p.701
The Firm: Bolstered by a respected New York team, this DC practice focuses on complex restructurings, often featuring a cross-border element. It has recently witnessed a surge of activity in telecommunications, and has developed through work in the healthcare, financial services, retailing and real estate industries.
The Lawyers: Head of the DC group is **Stanley Samorajczyk**, a *"gentleman and a pleasure to deal with".* Peers agree he has the *"experience to see the real issues."* He has acted on the restructuring of a major healthcare provider, and advised corporate clients on their relationships with troubled companies.
The Clients: The group's highlights include the insolvencies of Boston Chicken, Toshoku America, and the reorganization of Criimi Mae.

Arnold & Porter
see firm details p.765
The Firm: Adjudged to field a talented bench of attorneys in insolvency work. The group is predominantly found representing creditors and creditors' committees. Also involved in asset-purchaser work.
The Lawyers: *"Extremely smart"* **Daniel Lewis** (see p.138) is thought by peers to be a safe pair of hands for complex work. He practices nationally, acting for creditors and purchasers of assets out of bankruptcy. Telecom, energy, airline and financial services industries have provided a steady stream of work. Interviewees were impressed with Lewis' *"enormous integrity"*, and his representation of creditors in the high-profile bankruptcy of Criimi Mae.

DISTRICT OF COLUMBIA — INSURANCE

The Clients: The firm acted for the creditors' committee in the Chapter 11 of Covanta Energy.

Other Notable Practitioners
"Thoughtful and smart," **Michael St Patrick Baxter** (see p.132) of Covington & Burling is most often found representing creditors. **David Kuney** of Sidley Austin Brown & Wood's DC office was described to researchers as an *"excellent bankruptcy litigator"* with a *"strident"* style. Kuney made his name in real estate bankruptcies, and has a client list that includes investment banks and Fortune 500 companies. **Daniel Litt** of Dickstein Shapiro Morin & Oshinsky LLP is a *"forceful, hard-working"* attorney, mostly found acting

INSURANCE

DISTRICT OF COLUMBIA
Leading firms (Insurance)

1
- COVINGTON & BURLING

2
- GILBERT HEINTZ & RANDOLPH
- HOGAN & HARTSON LLP

3
- BAACH ROBINSON & LEWIS
- DICKSTEIN SHAPIRO MORIN & OSHINSKY LLP
- HOWREY SIMON ARNOLD & WHITE
- STEPTOE & JOHNSON LLP
- WILEY REIN & FIELDING LLP

Leading individuals (Insurance)

1
- HEINTZ John *Gilbert Heintz & Randolph*
- OSHINSKY Jerold *Dickstein Shapiro Morin & Oshinsky*
- SAYLER Robert *Covington & Burling*
- WARIN Roger *Steptoe & Johnson LLP*

2
- BOWMAN William *Hogan & Hartson LLP*
- DOLIN Mitchell *Covington & Burling*
- GILBERT Scott *Gilbert Heintz & Randolph*
- SHULMAN Robert *Howrey Simon Arnold & White*

3
- BAACH Martin *Baach Robinson & Lewis*
- BRUNNER Thomas *Wiley Rein & Fielding LLP*
- BUCHANAN John *Covington & Burling*
- FOGGAN Laura *Wiley Rein & Fielding LLP*
- GREANEY William *Covington & Burling*
- ROCAP James *Baker Botts LLP*
- SKINNER William *Covington & Burling*

Firms and ndividuals are listed alphabetically in each band.

Covington & Burling
see firm details p.786

The Firm: This *"top-notch"* policyholder firm has an enduring position as *"the most prominent practice"* in DC. Such is its long-standing profile and historically deep bench that a number of leading coverage litigators at other firms can trace their lineage to the firm. The team is renowned for representing large corporations in complex high-value coverage litigation. It came to prominence in a number of notable cases involving both asbestos and breast implant-related litigation, obtaining more than $1 billion in coverage cases for clients such as Owens Corning, Dow Corning and 3M. It was also involved in the first case that secured coverage for a firearms manufacturer named in government lawsuits against the firearms industry, and in the first case that secured asbestos coverage in the railroad industry. Recent work has included representing a major US pharmaceutical company in London-based arbitration concerning products liability coverage.

The Lawyers: *"Dean of the insurance bar"* **Robert Sayler** (see p.145) fills the senior statesman role and is credited with training a generation of lawyers in coverage litigation. Having worked on some of the largest disputes in the insurance industry, he has broadened his practice in recent years, but remains revered by clients from the largest corporations. Described to researchers as a *"skillful, polished"* attorney, **Mitchell Dolin** (see p.134) has worked on some of the firm's most high-profile cases on behalf of corporate policyholders, and also undertakes alternative dispute resolution work. He acted in litigation relating to first-party property coverage relating to the destruction of the World Trade Center (WTC). **John Buchanan** (see p.134) represents corporate policyholders in complex insurance coverage disputes, including litigation, settlement negotiation and alternative dispute resolution. A *"tough negotiator,"* he continues to work on asbestos environmental litigation, as well as WTC matters.

The respected **William Greaney** focuses on insurance claims for products liability and environmental exposure, and has represented corporate policyholders and state governments in asbestos, toxic tort, IP, construction defects and crime/fidelity coverage litigation. Also noted by contemporaries was **William Skinner** (see p.145), who has an insurance coverage litigation and captive insurance practice, and is renowned for his advice on the creation and representation of offshore and domestic group captive insurance companies.

The Clients: The firm's client base includes AK Steel; American Chemistry Council; Armstrong; Conrail; Dow Corning; ExxonMobil; NFL; NCR; Norfolk Southern; Owens Corning; PPL; SIGARMS; 3M and UBS Warburg Real Estate.

Gilbert Heintz & Randolph

The Firm: A young policyholder boutique, it has rapidly acquired an enviable brand name as a firm at the forefront of the coverage litigation market. Interviewees noted that this *"go-getting"* firm has distinguished itself as a leader in innovative dispute settlement techniques.

The Lawyers: **John Heintz** focuses on large-scale corporate liabilities and insurance recovery. *"Obviously a leading name,"* he has acted for several WTC clients, and is a veteran of numerous asbestos and lead paint-related cases. **Scott Gilbert**'s practice is devoted to strategic counseling, and he has applied his expertise in alternative dispute resolution techniques to a wide variety of coverage disputes. By common consent one of the leading practitioners in this area, he was the primary policyholder negotiator and drafter of the Wellington Agreement, one of the largest insurance settlements in US history, and has extensive experience of AAA arbitrations.

The Clients: The team services a client base that extends from corporations to plaintiff committees and individuals, and the majority of the workload relates to mass tort disputes. Cases often involve asbestos, silica, IUDs, breast implants, heart valves, pharmaceuticals, lead paint, and environmental contamination. Clients include AOL; Armstrong World Industries; ArvinMeritor; CertainTeed; Dana Environmental Services; Dow Corning; Equal Rights Center; Federal-Mogul; Host Marriott; JM Family Enterprises; The Lefrak Organization; Millennium Chemicals; National Fair Housing Alliance; National Service Industries; Pfizer; Schlumberger; SEPCO and Verizon.

Hogan & Hartson LLP
see firm details p.818

The Firm: *"Definitely on the shortlist,"* according to rivals, the firm is widely accepted to be among the leading practices representing insurance carriers. It has recently served as national coordinating counsel to a major insurer in asbestos coverage litigation, and also appeared in a case to decide whether insurance coverage applies to environmental claims filed against multinational corporations.

The Lawyers: Acknowledged as the group's premier individual for coverage disputes, the *"fabulous"* **William Bowman** (see p.133) was acclaimed to researchers as a *"major player in this area."* His trial and appellate practice has seen him active in federal and state courts.

The Clients: The firm acts for major corporations, including Hartford Financial.

INSURANCE — DISTRICT OF COLUMBIA

Baach Robinson & Lewis
The Firm: Peers described this boutique as *"the most significant London-related practice in DC."* The firm advises on a range of matters including pollution, asbestos, health hazards, pharmaceutical claims, workers' compensation and reinsurance.
The Lawyers: The attorney highlighted to researchers was **Martin Baach**, who has acted as US counsel for the London insurance market, and advised other domestic and international insurers and reinsurers. Focusing on complex coverage matters, products and professional liability, and international and domestic arbitration, he is found by contemporaries to be a *"careful, creative and hard-working lawyer."*
The Clients: The firm represents underwriters at Lloyd's, London market insurance companies and domestic insurers.

Dickstein Shapiro Morin & Oshinsky LLP
The Firm: A leading policyholder practice with a wealth of national experience, it has been involved in high-profile mass tort work, including a breast implant case that remains one of the largest class actions in US history.
The Lawyers: The group's preeminent practitioner, **Jerold Oshinsky**, received endorsements from across the market. *"Prominent in this area for many years,"* he was commended to researchers as an *"insurance attorney at the top of the profession."* He is a veteran of complex multi-party cases going back to the 1980's, and has a profile that is felt to eclipse that of his firm. Recently, he has been particularly busy with products liability, professional liability, 9/11 disputes and environmental coverage litigation.
The Clients: The firm acts for major corporations.

Howrey Simon Arnold & White
The Firm: The *"highly visible"* policyholder practice covers the full gamut of insurance coverage litigation work including toxic torts, products liability, construction defects, and business interruption claims.
The Lawyers: Although its depth of resources in this field is not generally perceived to equal that of the market leaders, the firm still generates a substantial profile through the efforts of the *"excellent"* **Robert Shulman**. As cochair of the insurance recovery practice, he has wide experience in coverage matters, and has managed class actions through litigation and alternative dispute resolution.
The Clients: Major corporations form the bulk of the firm's insurance client base.

Steptoe & Johnson LLP
The Firm: A broad practice representing insurance companies, it has undertaken matters involving asbestos, environmental and hazardous waste claims, as well as reinsurance cases involving coverage, good faith, fraud, RICO and breach of fiduciary duty.
The Lawyers: *"One of the top people for insurer coverage in town,"* **Roger Warin** is thought to overshadow the rest of his group, and has worked on cases involving asbestos, toxic substances and environmental claims.
The Clients: The firm acts for major insurance companies.

Wiley Rein & Fielding LLP
The Firm: Judged by peers to have a *"significant role representing insurance groups,"* the firm has undertaken some notable work in property insurance and computer failure cases.
The Lawyers: The group is distinguished by the presence of a pair of attorneys who are recognized as *"two of the top people in their field."* The respected **Laura Foggan** has a practice in insurance coverage cases that includes claims under general, products, property and professional liability policies. She also has experience of more than 200 appellate cases. Head of the practice **Thomas Brunner** was commended to researchers as *"a consummate diplomat in the settlement context."* He has experience of asbestos and hazardous waste cases, and has recently been representing Zurich in coverage disputes following the events of 9/11.
The Clients: An impressive client roster includes Aegis Insurance Services; BCS Insurance Company; Blue Cross and Blue Shield Association; Chubb Executive Risk; CNA Insurance Companies; GE Financial Assurance; Genesis Professional Liability Managers; Kemper Insurance Companies; Liberty Mutual Insurance Company; Mutual of Omaha Insurance Company; OneBeacon Insurance; Swiss Re America; Travelers and Zurich-American Insurance Group.

Other Notable Practitioners
James Rocap of Baker Botts was judged by interviewees to be a *"terrifically able"* practitioner. He has regularly acted for Travelers, including a recent success in the Supreme Court of Delaware, where he advised the company on a coverage case filed by Liggett Group.

INTELLECTUAL PROPERTY

DISTRICT OF COLUMBIA
Leading firms (Intellectual Property)
1. FINNEGAN HENDERSON FARABOW GARRETT
2. HOWREY SIMON ARNOLD & WHITE
3. BANNER & WITCOFF LTD
   STERNE KESSLER GOLDSTEIN & FOX
4. MCDERMOTT, WILL & EMERY

Firms are listed alphabetically in each band.

Finnegan Henderson Farabow Garrett & Dunner LLP
The Firm: Peers believe that this boutique is home to *"the best lawyers currently active in IPL."* It provides a broad range of IP services and its litigation group continues to be highly recommended by interviewees.
The Lawyers: Appellate lawyer **Donald Dunner** (see p.134) impresses with his high-profile caseload and in-depth knowledge of the law. He litigates patent disputes, predominantly at appellate level. His clients are drawn from the pharmaceutical, hi-tech and biotech industries. He represented Rhone-Poulenc Rorer against Bristol-Myers Squibb over a cancer drug and acted for GlaxoSmithKline against a number of manufacturers of generic pharmaceuticals. Also acted for Xerox against Palm involving a dispute over PalmPilot software licensing.
"Leading litigator" **Ford Farabow** (see p.135) represents large pharmaceutical manufacturers and scientific instrument and cosmetic companies in both enforcing and defending patent suits. He is currently working on a number of cases for GlaxoSmithKline. **Charles Lipsey** (see p.139) focuses on patent infringement litigation for clients in the mechanical, chemical and electrical technologies.
The Clients: Hi-tech, biotech, chemical and pharmaceutical manufacturers.

Howrey Simon Arnold & White
The Firm: This large IP group provides services for strategy, litigation and counseling as well as being active in handling procurement and portfolio management. It also covers trademarks, trade secrets, copyright and IT matters. This seven-office US operation is supported by attorneys in Brussels and London.
The Lawyers: *"Excellent litigator"* **James Davis** has been noted for his high-profile caseload. He specializes in patent law and litigates in the federal courts and at the ITC. Davis is also experienced in alternative dispute resolution and mediation.
The Clients: Fortune 500 companies.

DISTRICT OF COLUMBIA | LITIGATION

DISTRICT OF COLUMBIA
Leading individuals (Intellectual Property)

1 DUNNER Donald *Finnegan Henderson Farabow Garrett*
2 DAVIS James *Howrey Simon Arnold & White*
   FARABOW Ford *Finnegan Henderson Farabow Garrett*
   LIPSEY Charles *Finnegan Henderson Farabow Garrett*
   LUPO Raphael *McDermott, Will & Emery*
3 BAUMGARTEN Jon *Proskauer Rose*
   POTENZA Joseph *Banner & Witcoff Ltd*
   STERNE Robert *Sterne Kessler Goldstein & Fox*

Individuals are listed alphabetically in each band.

Banner & Witcoff Ltd
The Firm: This boutique firm provides all IP-related services, including patents, trademarks, trade secrets and copyright matters. The group has an active litigation department and also advises on franchise disputes and unfair competition.
The Lawyers: **Joseph Potenza** is noted as *"bright and talented."* He concentrates on litigation, but is also known for his licensing and patent counseling work.
The Clients: Hi-tech companies and pharmaceutical manufacturers

Sterne Kessler Goldstein & Fox
The Firm: Primarily recognized for its transactional work. This boutique firm is viewed by peers as one of the fastest growing firms in DC. It contains practice groups covering all aspects of IP and related laws, including litigation.
The Lawyers: **Robert Sterne** is the *"driving force of the firm."* He specializes in the electronic, telecom, internet and e-commerce sectors. He offers patent protection and patent enforcement services and provides distribution strategies.

McDermott, Will & Emery
see firm details p.846
The Firm: Its IP and litigation practice groups provide comprehensive services in patents, trademarks and transactional matters. Especially known for its litigation work, it practices in federal district courts throughout the US, before the US Patent and Trademark Office (USPTO) and in the US Courts of Appeals. Much of its workload is derived from the technology, pharmaceutical and manufacturing industries.
The Lawyers: *"Terrific and talented"* **Raphael Lupo** (see p.139) is a highly regarded patent litigator. Peers believe that much of the firm's profile in this area originates with him. He focuses on patent, trademarks, copyright and trade secrets litigation and associated counseling.
The Clients: Fortune 500 and technology companies and nonprofit trade associations.

Other Notable Practitioners
The *"brilliant"* **Jon Baumgarten** of Proskauer Rose LLP is recommended as a leading copyright lawyer in DC. He has a number of high-profile clients.

LITIGATION | GENERAL COMMERCIAL

DISTRICT OF COLUMBIA
Leading firms
(Litigation: General Commercial)

1 WILLIAMS & CONNOLLY LLP
2 ARNOLD & PORTER
   COVINGTON & BURLING
   HOGAN & HARTSON LLP
   WILMER, CUTLER & PICKERING
3 KIRKLAND & ELLIS
4 BAKER BOTTS LLP
   GIBSON, DUNN & CRUTCHER LLP
   MAYER, BROWN, ROWE & MAW
   SHEA & GARDNER
   SIDLEY AUSTIN BROWN & WOOD

Firms are listed alphabetically in each band.

Williams & Connolly LLP
see firm details p.899
The Firm: *"An outstanding firm"* for contentious matters, it fields a huge bench of trial attorneys, and is widely regarded by market observers as *"the best pure litigation firm in DC."* Competitors admit that *"they are on everyone's shortlist,"* acknowledging: *"If you think of litigation in DC, you think of them."*
While the group's reputation for high-profile criminal cases is long established, its varied commercial caseload now includes contracts, securities, IP and appellate, banking, regulatory and insurance matters, as well as substantial mass tort defense cases.
The department's in-house style causes some to wince. Peers described the firm's approach as *"fighting the battle at every trench and multiplying the number of trenches."* Other echoed the sentiment: *"They contest cases all the way, and don't mind if they tread on a few toes while they do it."* However, no one doubts the deep well of talent available to the firm, and clients spoke enthusiastically of a *"consistently excellent group"* who *"work like Trojans."*
The Lawyers: The attorney most often picked out is the *"wonderful"* **Brendan Sullivan** (see p.146). *"A sharp, smart and cerebral"* attorney, he was endorsed by researchers as an *"excellent tactician"* who shows *"no weaknesses"* in court. A stellar practice has recently been highlighted by his representation of the nine dissenting states in the Microsoft antitrust litigation. Clients paid tribute to *"one tough hombre"* who will *"provide you with the best case you can get."* *"Premier trial lawyer"* **John Vardaman** (see p.147) has litigated throughout state and federal courts. His practice has been characterized by class action work, involving toxic torts and products liability in the pharmaceutical and railroad industries. An *"intelligent and confident"* attorney, he has also been involved in the firm's work in several mass disaster cases.
As a leading legal malpractice defense lawyer and outside counsel to a major insurer of law firms, **John Villa** (see p.147) is a high-profile attorney who also focuses on financial and securities-related litigation. Described by one client as *"the most tenacious lawyer I have ever met,"* **Paul Wolff** (see p.149) *"goes for the jugular,"* and is an expert on litigation relating to complex financial transactions. He acts for banks and the audit committees of publicly traded companies, has advised on a dispute between a hotel management company and the owners of one of its managed properties, and has worked with a large Dutch pension fund on a real estate dispute. Clients appreciate his ability to *"understand the most complicated things quickly"* and his *"tough as nails"* approach; they report that *"he never wants you to give up."*
William McDaniels (see p.139) is said to be *"a bright guy who understands what is important."* As well as running an active media and employment practice, he has undertaken substantial products liability work related to the medical manufacturing sector. The *"extremely sound"* **Aubrey Daniel** (see p.134) and **David Kendall** (see p.137), who has a civil practice incorporating copyright, trademarks and unfair competition, also gained consistent market approval.
The Clients: Clients include Archer Daniels Midland; GE; AOL Time Warner; 3M; Marriott International and Lockheed Martin.

Arnold & Porter
see firm details p.765
The Firm: Rivals concede that the firm has one of the leading litigation groups in DC, citing its *"broad and institutional"* capacity, notably in products liability, financial services, securities and, above all, antitrust cases. A massive team is able to staff the largest cases, and the group possesses lawyers who can *"litigate with the toughest of them."*
The Lawyers: Three individuals gained sustained market recognition. **Stephen Sacks** (see p.144) is renowned for securities litigation,

LITIGATION

DISTRICT OF COLUMBIA

DISTRICT OF COLUMBIA
Leading individuals
(Litigation: General Commercial)

★ **SAYLER Robert** Covington & Burling
SULLIVAN Brendan Williams & Connolly LLP
WAXMAN Seth Wilmer, Cutler & Pickering

[1] **DELLINGER Walter** O'Melveny & Myers LLP
JEFFRESS William Baker Botts LLP
PHILLIPS Carter Sidley Austin Brown & Wood
ROBERTS John Hogan & Hartson LLP
VARDAMAN John Williams & Connolly LLP
YANNUCCI Thomas Kirkland & Ellis

[2] **ALDOCK John** Shea & Gardner
BRAY John King & Spalding LLP
DANIEL Aubrey Williams & Connolly LLP
HENSLER David Hogan & Hartson LLP
KENDALL David Williams & Connolly LLP
SACKS Stephen Arnold & Porter
STARR Kenneth Kirkland & Ellis
TARANTO Richard Farr & Taranto
VERRILLI Donald Jenner & Block
VILLA John Williams & Connolly LLP
WOLFF Paul Williams & Connolly LLP

[3] **BENNETT Robert** Skadden, Arps, Slate, Meagher & Flom
BLEAKLEY Peter Arnold & Porter
BOWMAN William Hogan & Hartson LLP
GELLER Kenneth Mayer, Brown, Rowe & Maw
HUNGAR Thomas Gibson, Dunn & Crutcher LLP
KLEIN Michael Wilmer, Cutler & Pickering
MCDANIELS William Williams & Connolly LLP
MCLUCAS William Wilmer, Cutler & Pickering
NATHAN Irvin Arnold & Porter
SILBERT Earl Piper Rudnick LLP

Individuals are listed alphabetically in each band.

including fraud cases, although his practice also embraces such matters as breach of contract work. Clients commended his *"great sense of how to unravel financial transactions."* **Peter Bleakley** (see p.133) is respected by peers as *"a fine trial lawyer,"* and is best known for products liability cases, which he undertakes for a high-profile clientele including Philip Morris and names from the pharmaceutical industry. Antitrust and IP litigation also constitute substantial elements of his caseload. Products liability is also regarded as the forte of **Irvin Nathan** (see p.141), who is considered by contemporaries to be *"one of the best at what he does."*

Covington & Burling
see firm details p.786

The Firm: Perceived to have gained its contentious experience in a regulatory setting, the firm is not generally associated with the trial lawyer tradition of some of its principal rivals. However, researchers encountered unanimous agreement with the judgment that *"they are such a fine firm that they handle litigation as competently as everything else."* The firm's strength is considered to lie in *"the highly technical areas of law,"* and it has acknowledged expertise in areas such as regulatory law, products liability, antitrust, insurance and work for pharmaceutical companies.

The Lawyers: Robert Sayler (see p.145) gained massive endorsement from all quarters. He is known as a national guru of the insurance bar, but as a general commercial litigator he is also regarded as *"a lawyer's lawyer."* His active trial practice involves representing corporations in high-value insurance coverage disputes, which he has recently combined with a raft of IP disputes, many in the farm products industry. Clients commended this *"professional and smart"* attorney for his *"wonderful manner as a trial lawyer."*

The Clients: Clients include: Armstrong World Industries; Boeing; The Pittston Company; Dow Corning; 3M; Monsanto; ExxonMobil; Procter & Gamble; ITT Industries; National Medical Enterprises and the NFL.

Hogan & Hartson LLP
see firm details p.818

The Firm: This local powerhouse has a well-established contentious practice, and is said by peers to field a *"bunch of strong litigators."* Acknowledged to have *"a large and solid trial department,"* the firm has strengths in the insurance, healthcare and real estate industries.

The Lawyers: The firm's appellate group is headed by former US Deputy Solicitor General **John Roberts** (see p.144), *"a superb lawyer at the very top of the profession."* He has represented an array of blue-chip clients on matters including insurance regulation, land use and labor, admiralty and administrative law. Another standout practitioner at the firm is the *"highly persuasive"* **David Hensler** (see p.137), whose practice includes contract, bankruptcy, civil RICO and ERISA work. *"A steady and well-prepared"* attorney with *"a great demeanor,"* Hensler recently handled a large RICO civil action involving ten shopping malls. He has also appeared on a recent pair of civil antitrust class actions, and represented two major insurance carriers in litigation throughout the US. The respected **William Bowman** (see p.133) has a versatile practice that encompasses commercial, insurance coverage, environmental, antitrust, contract, trade regulation and products liability litigation.

The Clients: Clients include: DaimlerChrysler; American Red Cross; Hughes Network Systems; National Geographic Society; Mylan Pharmaceuticals and Chubb.

Wilmer, Cutler & Pickering
see firm details p.901

The Firm: Described to researchers as a *"monolith,"* this respected commercial litigation department was most often applauded for its strength in securities, antitrust and communications cases. Observers were quick to underline both the eminence of the team's top-rated practitioners and the quality of the team as a whole.

The Lawyers: The firm's appellate reputation is centered around former US Solicitor General **Seth Waxman** (see p.148), universally acclaimed as *"one of the premier Supreme Court advocates."* Commentators agree that *"he understands not only law, but the strategy of appellate practice, and how it fits into the dispute resolution process in this country."* Although his practice concentrates on US Supreme Court and appellate litigation, he also undertakes strategic litigation consultations for large corporate clients. Recent cases include a commercial class action and securities litigation for several large banks, a commercial contract dispute involving engineering and pollution issues, and a case involving patents and licenses for an agricultural company. Researchers discovered a courtroom advocate who is *"enormously quick on his feet"* and has an *"incredible ability to hit all the right grace notes, and to parry all the questions from the bench."*

The respected **Michael Klein** (see p.137) combines experience in corporate litigation with a strong track record in a range of transactional and counseling roles to publicly and privately held companies. Interviewees attributed much of the firm's strength in securities litigation to **William McLucas** (see p.140), a former director of enforcement at the SEC, whose practice emphasizes securities enforcement and regulation. He was recently retained by WorldCom to conduct an internal inquiry in connection with admitted accounting irregularities, and led a similar investigation into the collapse of Enron.

The Clients: The firm has an enviable client portfolio. It has acted as outside counsel to American Home Products on products liability litigation, while banking clients have included Citibank, Bank One, PNC Bank and CoreStates Bank.

Kirkland & Ellis
see firm details p.830

The Firm: As the DC office of a premier national practice based in Chicago, it does not have a high profile locally. Peers acknowledged, however, that the compact group of excellent attorneys has particular depth in First Amendment, competition, products liability and appellate work.

The Lawyers: Renowned for his media expertise, flagship partner **Thomas Yannucci** (see p.149) is a *"fabulous lawyer with outstanding judgment,"* and is regularly on call to a portfolio of Fortune 500 clients. *"Measured but not timid,"* Yannucci's style is thought to be excellent for *"listening and bringing people together."* His highly diversified practice includes antitrust, contract,

DISTRICT OF COLUMBIA LITIGATION

class action and SEC work, and recent specific cases have also encompassed trade secrets and trademark matters. Clients report that he is *"well suited for a company keen to present an enlightened and responsive image."*

The firm's appellate practice benefits from the presence of former US Solicitor General **Kenneth Starr** (see p.146), who has returned to private practice and is a *"respected attorney with a heavyweight name."*

Baker Botts LLP
The Firm: The firm is generally considered to have enhanced its local capability following the 2001 merger with leading DC boutique Miller, Cassidy, Larroca & Lewin. Now perceived by peers to have a *"sound and consistent"* litigation group, it combines traditional strength in energy and technology disputes with regulatory experience in DC.

The Lawyers: The best-known litigator is **William Jeffress**, who was endorsed to researchers for his *"superb coverage of just about any contentious subject you care to mention."* Although he also undertakes a substantial volume of criminal work, this top-flight trial attorney was resoundingly recommended for his commercial work. Recent matters include a false claims action in Tennessee in the healthcare sector, an alien tort claims action, trade secrets disputes and a breach of contract defense in Florida. Professional negligence and libel matters round out his caseload.

Gibson, Dunn & Crutcher LLP
The Firm: The California-based giant has established a fine reputation for its appellate practice in DC, and rivals concede that *"for an out-of-town firm, they have done well."* While the appellate practice is the mainstay of the group's reputation, it also advises an international client base on a range of labor and antitrust disputes.

The Lawyers: The appellate team's name was made under the aegis of the present US Solicitor General Theodore Olson. The key individual now is felt to be *"Olson's protégé,"* **Thomas Hungar**, an *"accomplished and persuasive attorney."* His appellate practice focuses on commercial and constitutional matters, and has embraced administrative law, products liability, and telecom and employment cases.

Mayer, Brown, Rowe & Maw
see firm details p.843

The Firm: Principally recommended for its *"outstanding appellate practice,"* the firm has the oldest and largest such group in the US. Its reputation for premier punitive cases is uncontested.

The Lawyers: The firm can field a total of four former US Deputy Solicitor Generals among its attorneys. One of these is the respected **Kenneth Geller** (see p.136), who has argued about 40 cases in the US Supreme Court. Geller has particular appellate experience in products liability work, especially on behalf of large automobile manufacturers.

Shea & Gardner
The Firm: A single-office boutique trial shop, it has *"first-rate"* lawyers practicing a wide range of litigation, including class actions, ERISA, toxic torts, transport, arbitration, bankruptcy, antitrust, appellate, insurance and environmental matters. The firm is often retained as an alternative to 'big-firm' counsel and clients report that *"their papers are well written and well thought out."*

The Lawyers: *"Top-notch"* **John Aldock** concentrates on complex commercial litigation, with an emphasis on insurance, class actions and products liability. Tipped for his international experience, he has recently represented several companies in asbestos liability disputes, and is described by clients as *"extremely responsive"* and capable of a *"sophisticated analysis of complex problems."*

Sidley Austin Brown & Wood
see firm details p.877

The Firm: Competitors concede that this Chicago leader has a *"significant"* contentious practice in DC, which is involved in *"major matters."* Representing clients in corporate and criminal investigations is a particular forte, and the firm is acknowledged to possess some *"outstanding"* appellate lawyers.

The Lawyers: Former Assistant to the US Solicitor General and managing partner of the DC office, **Carter Phillips** was universally commended as an appellate attorney, having argued 25 cases before the US Supreme Court while at the firm. He undertakes plaintiff and defense work for a predominantly commercial clientele, recently representing a large petroleum company, an insurance client, and a large corporation in a matter against the EPA. Observers singled out his *"mastery of the case"* and *"direct, focused"* courtroom manner.

Other Notable Practitioners
Former US Assistant Attorney General in the Clinton Administration, **Walter Dellinger** of O'Melveny & Myers LLP is widely regarded as a key US Supreme Court attorney. Possessing a *"deep historical knowledge of Supreme Court jurisprudence"* that is judged the equal of *"anyone else in the courtroom, including the justices on the bench,"* Dellinger is regarded by peers as *"a captivating speaker."* He has acted for large corporations on matters including mass tort cases.

Top DC trial lawyer **John Bray** (see p.13643) of King & Spalding is renowned as a civil litigator. Recently active in a breach of contract over medical products and a breach of a joint venture agreement, he was also recommended to researchers for his work in tax and insurance coverage litigation. Clients thought that his *"engaging personality"* ensures *"a great rapport with the jury."*

Richard Taranto of boutique appellate firm Farr & Taranto is rated by contemporaries as *"one of the finest lawyers of his type."* Interviewees paid tribute to his *"clear and direct"* style, both in court and on paper.

Don Verrilli (see p.147) of Jenner & Block is another appellate lawyer with substantial experience of large commercial matters before the federal courts and US Supreme Court. He has recently been active in the telecom industry, arguing in the US Supreme Court on behalf of a client seeking to break into the local market, and advising another client in connection with the reclaiming of licenses.

Outstanding criminal lawyer **Robert Bennett** (see p.132) of Skadden, Arps, Slate, Meagher & Flom LLP is also respected for his commercial practice, and is conceded to be a *"marquee"* individual. In a similar position at Piper Rudnick LLP is **Earl Silbert** (see p.145), who was highly rated by commentators for his *"serious"* commercial cases.

MEDIA & ENTERTAINMENT

DISTRICT OF COLUMBIA

MEDIA & ENTERTAINMENT

DISTRICT OF COLUMBIA
Leading firms (Media & Entertainment)
1. LEVINE SULLIVAN & KOCH LLP
   WILLIAMS & CONNOLLY LLP
2. BAKER & HOSTETLER LLP
   JENNER & BLOCK
   KIRKLAND & ELLIS

Leading individuals (Media & Entertainment)
1. BAINE Kevin *Williams & Connolly LLP*
   KENDALL David *Williams & Connolly LLP*
   LEVINE Lee *Levine Sullivan & Koch LLP*
   SANFORD Bruce *Baker & Hostetler LLP*
   SMITH Paul *Jenner & Block*
   YANNUCCI Thomas *Kirkland & Ellis*
   ZWEIFACH Gerson *Williams & Connolly LLP*

Firms and individuals are listed alphabetically in each band.

Levine Sullivan & Koch LLP

The Firm: A boutique media litigation practice with a seven-partner team of *"top-notch attorneys."* The firm regularly serves as outside counsel to publishers and broadcasters in connection with content-related litigation, including libel, invasion of privacy, IP and First Amendment issues. Practitioners also provide pre-broadcast and pre-publication review services to assist media clients in risk management.

The Lawyers: The *"eloquent"* **Lee Levine** enjoys a far-reaching reputation in First Amendment work. Described by peers as *"a real star,"* he won acclaim representing media defendants in the US Supreme Court case of Bartnicki v Vopper, one of the most significant press freedom cases of recent years. Clients appreciate his *"great practical advice"* and particularly noted his skill in drafting *"clear and well-written"* briefs.

The Clients: The firm is First Amendment counsel to CBS, and represented a coalition of news media organizations in rights of access to judicial proceedings, including the Microsoft antitrust proceedings.

Williams & Connolly LLP
see firm details p.899

The Firm: The firm retains its historic reputation as a premier media litigation firm with a *"deep bench"* of star attorneys. *"Extremely bright and creative"* lawyers were commended for developing groundbreaking defense strategies. The firm is synonymous with its portfolio of high-profile media clients, which includes The Washington Post and The National Enquirer.

The Lawyers: **Kevin Baine** (see p.132) is said to know First Amendment law *"backward and forward."* Recommended by peers for media representation *"at any level,"* he has considerable appellate experience and has successfully defended more than 100 libel cases. He recently acted in a series of multi-district libel suits, defended a television news organization's use of hidden cameras, and represented the owner of The Salt Lake Tribune in a dispute over the management and future ownership of the newspaper. His partner, **David Kendall** (see p.137), handles cases relating to the First Amendment, libel, privacy and copyright for clients such as Newsweek, The National Enquirer and the Motion Picture Association of America. This *"wise and accomplished"* attorney has been advising copyright holders in piracy suits against several internet music services and represented content providers in litigation against satellite, cable and broadcast copyright piracy. *"Talented"* **Gerson Zweifach** (see p.149) has proven himself with *"significant successes"* in difficult cases. He has defended movie studios, book publishers, tabloids and television networks against a wide variety of high-profile claims.

The Clients: The Washington Post; Newsweek; CNN; NBC; Disney; News Corporation; Fox Television; ABC; CBS; The National Enquirer and Playboy.

Baker & Hostetler LLP

The Firm: This substantial practice is a *"definite presence"* in the area. A dedicated media and First Amendment department advises television, radio and cable broadcasters, newspapers, publishers and individual journalists. As long-standing counsel to the Society of Professional Journalists, the firm has also been involved in lobbying on First Amendment and right of access legislative initiatives.

The Lawyers: A lawyer with an *"enormous reputation,"* **Bruce Sanford** is general counsel to a major organization of journalists. He has represented many leading national news media and book publishers in more than 1000 libel, IP and First Amendment cases.

The Clients: ABC; NBC; Fox Television; The EW Scripps Company; AOL Time Warner; Random House; Simon & Schuster and Bertelsmann.

Jenner & Block
see firm details p.822

The Firm: Seen primarily in an appellate context, the firm brings to bear *"superb people and considerable facilities"* on First Amendment matters. Attorneys specialize in new media constitutional issues relating to free speech, but also undertake more traditional engagements.

The Lawyers: Practice cochair **Paul Smith** (see p.145) focuses on the appellate aspects of First Amendment work, with a particular emphasis on technology and internet-related issues. Recommended as an *"impressive advocate,"* Smith recently represented the American Library Association in a challenge to the constitutionality of the Children's Internet Protection Act.

The Clients: The firm represented Forbes Magazine in a libel and invasion of privacy action. It has also been defending companies in the video games industry against negligence charges brought following the 1999 Columbine High School shootings.

Kirkland & Ellis
see firm details p.830

The Firm: On the other side of the fence, this firm is well regarded for a *"hard-hitting"* plaintiffs' media practice. The firm's reputation in the area rests almost entirely on leading litigator **Thomas Yannucci** (see p.149). Felt to be *"at the top of the profession,"* Yannucci represents large corporate clients in libel and defamation claims. He distinguished himself in cases such as Chiquita Brands International's claims against Gannett Company and The Cincinnati Enquirer, concerning the right to anonymity of a journalist's confidential source.

DISTRICT OF COLUMBIA — PROJECTS

PROJECTS

DISTRICT OF COLUMBIA
Leading firms (Projects)

1 CHADBOURNE & PARKE LLP
　WHITE & CASE LLP
2 LATHAM & WATKINS LLP
　SKADDEN, ARPS, SLATE, MEAGHER & FLOM LLP
3 HUNTON & WILLIAMS

Leading individuals (Projects)

1 DESANTIS Victor *White & Case LLP*
2 FITZGERALD Peter *Chadbourne & Parke LLP*
　KLEPPER Martin *Skadden, Arps, Slate, Meagher & Flom*
　SACHS John *Latham & Watkins LLP*
　WARD Erica *Skadden, Arps, Slate, Meagher & Flom*
3 MACHLIN Barry *Mayer, Brown, Rowe & Mawe*
　MARTIN Keith *Chadbourne & Parke LLP*
　MCISAAC Christopher *Winston & Strawn*
　NEAHER Edward *White & Case LLP*

Firms and Individuals are listed alphabetically in each band.

Chadbourne & Parke LLP
see firm details p.781

The Firm: This well-established and *"thriving"* practice was frequently described as the first port of call for project finance in DC. A talented team of lawyers won sustained market approval for being *"uniformly good to work with."* The group, which cooperates closely with the New York office, won praise for its steady stream of high-caliber work. It is felt to be particularly active on behalf of multilateral agencies. Best known for its power industry expertise, the group nonetheless maintains a profile in oil and gas, telecommunications and petrochemical projects. It is especially visible in Latin America and in emerging markets. The firm also derives strength from a number of energy regulatory lawyers with experience before FERC. One of the key representations has advised The Overseas Private Investment Corporation (OPIC) on the AES Tietê project financing in Brazil.

The Lawyers: Interviewees point to *"fantastically good"* **Peter Fitzgerald** as the leading light of the group. Clients spoke of his cost-conscious, punctual service and *"problem-solving and non-confrontational"* style. Fitzgerald's sustained involvement on the international stage has lent him experience in a broad spectrum of matters. His advice to multilateral agencies and expertise in political risk insurance was particularly recommended. **Keith Martin** operates in a niche area; peers said he is a leading figure for advice on the tax aspects of project finance deals.

The Clients: The firm boasts a top-notch client base, including OPIC; International Finance Corporation (IFC); EBRD; CSFB; AES; El Paso and Duke Energy.

White & Case LLP

The Firm: This *"world-class"* group has built up one of the largest projects practices in the city and regularly acts for a host of premier league clients. In particular, it has nurtured relationships with multilateral agencies, export credit agencies and international lenders, although its experience also extends to sponsor representation. The firm's profile is said by peers to be greatest in cross-border transactions. For example, it recently acted for a consortium of lenders, including Barclays Capital, Crédit Lyonnais, Société Générale and IFC, in the Association of European Development Finance Institutions Suez Gulf and Port Said power projects in Egypt. The size of the group leaves it vulnerable to claims of uneven quality lower down the ranks. However, clients praised the group for its solutions-oriented *"take charge approach: it takes away your headaches and understands the issues."*

The Lawyers: **Victor DeSantis** spearheads the group in DC. He won rave reviews from interviewees for his international lender-based practice. Clients identified his *"meticulous"* approach and ability to foresee problems ahead of time as key strengths. Peers also praised him as a *"terrific"* deal-maker whose nonconfrontational style makes him a popular figure in negotiations. One of his key engagements has been representing Inter-American Development Bank (IDB) in the Termobahia power project in Brazil. **Edward Neaher** is an *"impressive and commercial"* practitioner. A former attorney at the IFC, the majority of his work is undertaken on behalf of investors and lenders in infrastructure projects.

The Clients: Important clients of the firm include Société Générale; Deutsche Bank; Crédit Lyonnais; Citibank; HSBC; Barclays Bank; OPIC; Japanese Bank for International Cooperation (JBIC); IDB and IFC.

Latham & Watkins LLP
see firm details p.835

The Firm: The combined strength of the New York and DC offices makes this one of the most prominent and respected groups on the East Coast. In previous years, Latin America has been an area of especial activity. Recently, however, the DC group has turned more toward the domestic market. Attorneys from the projects group frequently team up with colleagues specializing in energy regulatory advice on power, and oil and gas projects. While the group is adept at advising lenders, a large percentage of its work is dedicated to representing sponsors. Here it has assisted a projects company, owned by Marubeni Corporation and Petrobras, in the development and financing of a 440MW gas-fired cogeneration project in Brazil.

The Lawyers: Interviewees repeatedly praised a group of attorneys that is *"terrifically good and excellent to deal with."* The team won most plaudits for its practical and pragmatic approach to transactions, and its ability to *"identify the big issues and get the deals done quickly."* **John Sachs** (see p.144) emerged as the most prominent individual from a group of ten attorneys. He was recommended to researchers as *"one of the best people in the city."* He has accumulated a wealth of experience acting for developers and lenders and has also been involved in a number of acquisitions and divestitures in the energy sector.

The Clients: Typical clients include Marubeni Power; PG&E National Energy Group; PPL Global; Tractebel; IDB; Corporación Andino de Formento and Abbey National Bank.

Skadden, Arps, Slate, Meagher & Flom LLP & Affiliates
see firm details p.878

The Firm: The combination of a stellar reputation with some *"top-notch lawyers"* makes this a firm that is *"always on the projects shortlist."* The group is regarded as one of the leading players in both the domestic and international markets. Peers consider it a particularly prominent force in power generation and oil and gas transactions. Its extensive experience in this area has seen it act for institutional lenders, underwriters and developers on financings, including public and private debt offerings, equity placements, syndications and securities issuances. The group has advised NRG Energy in its $2 billion construction and acquisition credit facility, and in the financing of three projects under it. The current market downturn has also resulted in a number of restructurings.

The Lawyers: Although based in Detroit, **Erica Ward** (see p.148) also maintains an office in DC where she is frequently found advising a range of participants on electric power projects. She is one of the founding members of the firm's energy and project finance group and was praised by peers for her attention to detail and an *"ability to garner resources"* in transactions. **Marty Klepper** (see p.138) was acknowledged for his broad experience in the energy sector, where he has been involved in financings, acquisitions and divestitures. He was described as an *"aggressive advocate,"* adept at representing both lenders and developers.

The Clients: The firm's impressive client roster includes names like NRG Energy; Lehman Brothers; CSFB and Goldman Sachs.

Hunton & Williams

The Firm: This firm, which is tipped as an up-and-coming practice, lays claim to a diverse client base and is involved in a range of project financings. It is engaged in developing power and

REAL ESTATE — DISTRICT OF COLUMBIA

natural gas pipelines for lenders, sponsors and equity investors, and has experience of a variety of infrastructure projects including water, telecommunications and transportation. Much of the firm's activity has been in Latin America, where it represented InterGen as the developer in the $532 million project financing of the 1060MW greenfield La Rosita power project in Mexico. The team also assisted PG&E National Energy Group in connection with the $348 million leveraged lease financing of the Attala power project in Mississippi.

The Lawyers: The untimely death of Mike Barr has deprived the firm of one of the most highly respected practitioners in the business. The team in DC continues to be supported by a network of offices in the Far East and London. It includes Jeff Schroeder, who is active in North America and Mexico.

The Clients: Typical clients include Detroit Edison; IDB; PG&E National Energy Group; Progress Energy; TXU Group; AES; Tractebel and Philip Morris Capital.

Other Notable Practitioners

Barry Machlin at Mayer, Brown, Rowe & Maw divides his time between the firm's DC and Chicago offices. He was felt by peers to be especially expert in representing multilaterals and export credit agencies, and to have a *"thorough understanding of what his clients want."* **Christopher McIsaac** (see p.140) of Winston & Strawn is an *"active"* lawyer, involved most commonly for lenders. His portfolio of deals includes acting for US Ex-Im Bank in connection with the project financing of the $1.1 billion Rio Polimeros integrated ethylene and polyethelene complex in Brazil.

REAL ESTATE

DISTRICT OF COLUMBIA
Leading firms (Real Estate)

1
- ARNOLD & PORTER
- HOLLAND & KNIGHT LLP
- PIPER RUDNICK LLP

2
- ARENT FOX
- HOGAN & HARTSON LLP
- SHAW PITTMAN

3
- AKIN GUMP STRAUSS HAUER & FELD LLP
- BINGHAM MCCUTCHEN LLP
- MAYER, BROWN, ROWE & MAW
- VENABLE LLP

Leading individuals (Real Estate)

1
- EPSTIEN Jay *Piper Rudnick LLP*
- QUIN Whayne *Holland & Knight LLP*

2
- FRIES Joseph *Arent Fox*
- KLEIN Frederick *Piper Rudnick LLP*

3
- BEYDA Richard *Grossberg Yochelson Fox & Beyda*
- GOODWIN Michael *Arnold & Porter*
- HOROWITZ Philip *Arter & Hadden LLP*
- HUMES Gary *Arnold & Porter*
- OSNOS David *Arent Fox*
- PORTER Stephen *Arnold & Porter*
- ROSENTHAL Barry *Bingham McCutchen LLP*
- SEGAL Earl *Akin Gump Strauss Hauer & Feld LLP*
- WEISEL Sheldon *Shaw Pittman*
- WILLNER Keith *Mayer, Brown, Rowe & Maw*

4
- DWYER Jeffry *Greenberg Traurig LLP*
- ENGEL John *Shaw Pittman*
- GLASGOW Norman *Holland & Knight LLP*
- GREENSTEIN Abraham *Greenstein Delorme*
- KAHN David *Holland & Knight LLP*
- NEWMAN Richard *Arent Fox*
- PARMLEY Bruce *Hogan & Hartson LLP*
- RUBIN Blake *Arnold & Porter*
- TUCKER Stefan *Venable LLP*
- VOLLMANN Alan *Holland & Knight LLP*

Firms and Individuals are listed alphabetically in each band.

Arnold & Porter
see firm details p.765

The Firm: A *"superior"* real estate practice, commended by clients for a large number of *"impressive"* attorneys. Expertise ranges from land use and development to real estate financing, tax, leasing, securities, acquisition and disposition, and bankruptcy.

The Lawyers: Interviewees *"put their money on"* **Michael Goodwin** (see p.136), a general real estate lawyer with a focus on representing owners and developers. Tipped as a *"future star"* by clients and competitors, Goodwin recently represented long-standing development client The Kaempfer Company and Forest City Enterprises in their involvement in the redevelopment of the Waterside Mall in southwest Washington. *"Effective"* **Gary Humes** (see p.137) specializes in build-to-suit transactions for large corporates and in public-private partnerships, often involving the federal government. This *"balanced"* practitioner recently acted for The JBG Companies, the developer of a new 1.3 million sq ft, $500 million headquarters for the US Department of Transportation, and for Computer Associates on build-to-suit, sale and leaseback and other real estate matters. *"Statesmanlike"* **Stephen Porter** (see p.142) has wide experience encompassing real estate tax, corporate, leasing and finance work. Notable recent work includes obtaining government tax financing for the International Spy Museum in DC, in which the firm represented the developers, The Malrite Company.

Blake Rubin (see p.144) is admired for his expertise in real estate and partnership taxation. Real estate owners and developers believe him to be *"one of the best at tax structuring."*

The Clients: Highlights include representing the Kimpton Hotel & Restaurant Group as developers in the renovation and hotel-conversion of the government-owned Tariff building in DC. Additional clients include BAA McArthur Glen Europe and Host Marriott.

Holland & Knight LLP
see firm details p.820

The Firm: This *"comprehensive"* real estate practice was felt to have *"strength in numbers."* A 43-strong group offers expert advice in most traditional areas of real estate and real estate finance. The firm has niche expertise in the hospitality industry, with practitioners advising on a volume of timeshare properties.

The Lawyers: Competitors consider **Whayne Quin** (see p.143) to be the *"king of the mountain"* for zoning issues. His work also includes land use, preservation, urban planning and building code matters. Recent work includes securing approval for Louis Dreyfus Property Group, developers of a 1.5 million sq ft project in DC for the SEC. Clients praise **Norman Glasgow**'s (see p.136) *"excellence"* in zoning, building code and historic preservation work. Leader of the group is **David Kahn** (see p.137), whom peers credit with having *"built the department."* Kahn specializes in commercial real estate finance, development and leasing. **Al Vollman** (see p.147) is a transactional and leasing specialist, commended for his *"high level of legal acumen."* He recently advised Lehman Brothers on the completion of the 2.5 million sq ft US Patent and Trademark Office complex in Alexandria.

The Clients: Kahn and his team recently acted for Lincoln Property Company on Maritime Plaza, a multi-phase 12-acre office park/hotel project. Additional clients include: John Hancock Life Insurance; Goldman Sachs; Marriott International; Fairmont Hotels & Resorts; CSFB; Apollo Real Estate Advisors; The John Akridge Companies; ING and The Praedium Group.

Piper Rudnick LLP
see firm details p.867

The Firm: *"A terrific group,"* considered by leaders in the field to be *"one of the strongest real estate practices in the country."* Diverse and broad, the team commands expertise in all areas of real estate and real estate finance.

DISTRICT OF COLUMBIA — REAL ESTATE

The Lawyers: The team is bolstered by the presence of **Jay Epstien** (see p.135), a specialist in leasing, developments and acquisitions. Considered *"dynamic and influential,"* Epstien's *"superstar"* status is accepted by competitors and clients alike. Clients declare him their lawyer of choice and competitors concede that he is *"the master of leasing."* Another *"major competitor"* in the real estate bar is **Frederick Klein** (see p.137), who handles real estate finance, tax, acquisitions and dispositions.

The Clients: Attorneys act for owners and developers from all market segments (including multi-family, apartment and retail properties), for financial institutions and banks such as Fleet-Boston Financial and HypoVereinsbank, as well as for underwriters and retail tenants such as Target and Polo Ralph Lauren.

The group has advised in connection with several prominent new building projects in DC. These include counseling on the joint venture ownership of The Investment Building, now owned by The Kaempfer Company, KanAm/Westwind and SITQ Immobilier, and acting for Lawrence Ruben Company on the development, financing and leasing of Lincoln Square office building. The firm also represented the United Brotherhood of Carpenters and Joiners of America on leasing and development matters.

Arent Fox

The Firm: A full-service transactional practice, handling a range of real estate-related corporate, securities, tax, litigation and bankruptcy work. Peers credit the firm with producing *"good, experienced real estate specialists"* who *"know their way around the district."*

The Lawyers: Commentators believe **Joseph Fries** *"can't be beaten"* for traditional real estate matters. Acclaimed as *"deep and learned,"* Fries has noteworthy expertise in transactional planning, structuring, negotiating and documenting. An *"absolute expert,"* **David Osnos** is respected by peers for his long-standing practice and his business sense. **Richard Newman**'s emphasis on public finance, especially in multi-family projects and in the securitization of government leases, earns him the reputation of being a *"wise head."* His recent work includes the acquisition and financing of the headquarters for the AARP (American Association of Retired Persons) using taxable bonds.

The Clients: The firm represented the owner-operator and major league basketball (NBA) and ice hockey (NHL) teams in connection with the acquisition, construction and financing of the MCI Center, a multipurpose sports and entertainment arena in DC. Practitioners also represent Goldman Sachs on acquisitions, sales and financings, and advise major REITs on securities, corporate, tax and transactional matters. Clients include AIG and Marriott International.

Hogan & Hartson LLP
see firm details p.818

The Firm: A traditional real estate practice recommended for its *"depth and quality."* A preeminent corporate practice contributes to the firm's reputation for transactional real estate matters. Expertise exists in relation to acquisitions and dispositions, joint ventures, financings, leasings, developments and workouts. The firm is well known for its premier REITs and securities practice and handles significant work for a large base of major hospitality industry clients. Competitors note that the firm is *"a big player in REIT and corporate real estate work,"* while pointing out that this focus is *"a move away from local real estate issues."*

The Lawyers: A team of *"extremely capable lawyers"* was recommended by competitors, with particular mention of *"key leader"* **Bruce Parmley** (see p.142). Parmley is a transactional lawyer with a focus on hotels and the hospitality industry, both nationally and internationally.

The Clients: The team acted for Thayer Lodging Group in its $600 million acquisition and development of the Grande Lakes Orlando resort, and represented Charles E Smith Residential Realty in its $3.6 billion merger in 2001 with Archstone Communities to form Archstone-Smith. Additional clients include: Host Marriott; Four Seasons; Sithe Energies; Charles E Smith Commercial Realty and Equity Office Properties Trust.

Shaw Pittman

The Firm: A large practice commended by market leaders for its *"substantial breadth and depth."* The team is considered particularly strong in its representation of REITs and is admired for expert leasing, zoning and bankruptcy/corporate recovery work for real estate clients. Attorneys act for both local and national clients, who praise the group for its *"dedication"* and hard-working ethos.

The Lawyers: Practice founder **Sheldon Weisel** is *"very detail-oriented;"* competitors believe he is *"a great lawyer who will never make a mistake."* A widely experienced transactional lawyer, Weisel has been involved in financings, acquisitions and dispositions. He acted for Mack-Cali Realty on the $70 million sale of a large DC office building. Interviewees recommend practice chair **John Engel** for his *"spectacular"* approach to transactions. He recently acted on behalf of a joint venture between Lincoln Property Company and Clark Realty Capital in a public-private partnership with the US Navy to develop and manage housing for military personnel in San Diego.

The Clients: The team acts as land use and zoning counsel for The George Washington University. On the financing side, Fannie Mae is a major longtime client for investment capital work. BF Saul and Boston Properties are additional clients.

Akin Gump Strauss Hauer & Feld LLP
see firm details p.701

The Firm: This *"versatile"* practice handles real estate transactions, financings, litigation and regulatory matters on behalf of owners, developers and investors. The team has particular experience in mixed-use development projects. An active corporate practice has the group acting on REIT mergers and related property transactions.

The Lawyers: **Earl Segal** was mentioned as a *"significant figure"* in the real estate community. He maintains a transactional practice, acting on a range of sales and acquisitions, and leasing transactions as well as retail, office and mixed-use development projects.

The Clients: The firm acts for national and multi-national institutions. A significant hospitality practice includes a number of large hotels and hotel REITs as clients. Retail clients include supermarkets.

Bingham McCutchen LLP

The Firm: The national real estate practice has expanded following the July 2002 merger between Bingham Dana and West Coast firm McCutchen Doyle Brown & Enersen. In DC, core practice areas include acquisitions, sales, financings and joint ventures. Project experience extends to office, family, industrial and retail developments. The group has noteworthy expertise in military base reuse projects in which it draws on specialists in real estate, environmental and land use issues.

The Lawyers: Practice cochair **Barry Rosenthal** acts for a base of real estate operators, developers and financial institutions, including insurance companies, banks, REITs and pension fund advisers. Competitors regard him as a *"highly prominent lenders' lawyer."*

The Clients: The group represented Wells Fargo in connection with an acquisition financing for a portfolio of multi-family properties valued in excess of $150 million. Members also acted for The JBG Companies in connection with the development and sale and leaseback bond financing of a $75 million project, fully leased to the National Institutes of Health. Additional clients include US Bancorp, TA Associates Realty and Paradigm Development Company.

Mayer, Brown, Rowe & Maw
see firm details p.843

The Firm: The Chicago-based firm is considered a *"giant"* on its home turf; the DC real estate practice, however, is relatively small. The group principally represents capital providers and developers in transactions ranging from financings, ventures and leasings to acquisitions and dispositions. The group acts for a significant base of national insurance companies such as MetLife and New York Life in large mortgage-lending transactions. Internationally, the firm represents inbound and outbound European and Asian investors.

TAX | DISTRICT OF COLUMBIA

The Lawyers: Partner **Keith Willner** (see p.149) is described by peers as a *"very talented lawyer but a bit of a lone star in the office."* Clients praised his *"even-keeled legal sense."*

The Clients: The practice represents major REITs, pension funds, opportunity funds and other institutional investors in the acquisitions, developments, sales, dispositions and leasings of all types of commercial real estate. The firm acts as regular counsel to Lend Lease on hotel acquisitions, dispositions and financing work. Practitioners are also visible advising landlords and tenants in major office leasing transactions.

Venable LLP

The Firm: Competitors especially rate the group for real estate tax matters, although the practice also offers a full range of transactional expertise including acquisitions, financings and developments. Clients are drawn from a broad cross section of local real estate owners, including entrepreneurs and REITs.

The Lawyers: *"Extraordinarily talented"* **Stefan Tucker** is renowned for his real estate tax expertise, advising on both federal and local aspects. His practice includes structuring ownership vehicles for real estate acquisitions and developments, advising on the tax consequences regarding dispositions of real estate, and counseling on the long-term capital gains treatment of taxable sales. The firm has further boosted its capacities in the field through its recruitment of **Philip Horowitz** from Arter & Hadden. Identified as *"one of the great real estate lawyers in town,"* Horowitz represents owners, developers and corporate and governmental users of real estate in connection with purchases, sales and leasing and financing transactions.

The Clients: The firm represents national and international owners, developers and financial institutions.

Other Notable Practitioners

Richard Beyda of Grossberg Yochelson Fox & Beyda is considered a *"giant"* whose *"word is his bond."* The real estate boutique is one of the oldest firms in DC and has a particularly good reputation among competitors for development work. **Jeff Dwyer** of Greenberg Traurig LLP is known for his excellent work in financial transactions, of which a sizable proportion is on behalf of REITs. Recent matters include the $55 million sale of all the assets of ILM Senior Living, a REIT that owned assisted-living facilities in six states. **Abraham Greenstein**, managing partner of Greenstein Delorme & Luchs, was said to offer *"terrific, great-value"* representation in real estate matters including commercial leasings, financings, acquisitions and developments.

TAX

DISTRICT OF COLUMBIA
Leading firms (Tax)

1
- CAPLIN & DRYSDALE
- MCKEE NELSON LLP
- SKADDEN, ARPS, SLATE, MEAGHER & FLOM LLP

2
- BAKER & MCKENZIE
- IVINS, PHILLIPS & BARKER
- MCDERMOTT, WILL & EMERY
- MILLER & CHEVALIER

3
- STEPTOE & JOHNSON LLP
- SUTHERLAND ASBILL & BRENNAN LLP

Firms are listed alphabetically in each band.

Caplin & Drysdale

The Firm: Considered DC's *"premier tax boutique,"* it is one of the few felt to *"compete directly with the Big Four accounting firms."* 35 of the 50 attorneys focus on tax matters ranging from international planning, corporate acquisitions and partnership issues to state and local tax, employee benefits and white-collar fraud. This *"versatile"* group was recommended for its *"across the board excellence."* Less active on transactional work, the firm's greatest expertise lies in general advice and tax planning. Particularly recommended for international matters, the firm offers *"expert advice"* on international exempt organizations, transfer pricing and foreign tax credits. The practice is known for attracting *"top-quality talent"* from the IRS and Treasury Department, and thus retains a *"useful insight into the workings of government agencies."* This is thought to give the group an edge on controversy work involving appearances before the IRS appeals office. The firm's other attorneys specialize in civil litigation, focusing largely on asbestos liability matters and related bankruptcy litigation.

The Lawyers: The firm is thought to owe its profile in international tax planning and controversy work to the presence of **David Rosenbloom**, who receives widespread accolades as the *"dean of the international tax bar."* A former Treasury Department official, Rosenbloom is particularly noted for his knowledge of tax treaty matters. This *"superb"* practitioner advises US and foreign corporations and financial institutions on inbound and outbound investments, transfer pricing, foreign tax credits and multi-treaty tax issues.

The Clients: US and foreign corporations and financial institutions.

McKee Nelson LLP
see firm details p.848

The Firm: The firm has grown *"in leaps and bounds"* since its 1999 inception, and has quickly established itself as one of DC's *"go-to"* firms for tax advice. This specialist tax and capital markets firm now has offices in both DC and New York, and was congratulated for having recruited *"supremely talented"* attorneys to the practice. An alliance with Ernst & Young is thought to provide a steady flow of cross-referral work. The group is best known for its *"vigorous"* tax controversy practice and represents both US and foreign taxpayers in IRS audits and appeals, competent authority matters and trial and appellate litigation. Practitioners acted for AT&T in an interest recovery action under the Tucker Act and represented Merrill Lynch before the Commissioner in determining whether a Section 304 redemption and subsequent sale should be collapsed under the step transaction doctrine. The current practice consists of 19 DC and one NY attorney, who cover a range of tax accounting matters, criminal and civil tax litigation and the tax aspects of acquisitions and structured finance transactions.

The Lawyers: A leading partnerships tax lawyer, **Bill McKee** (see p.140) was mentioned by clients as *"the first person we'd consult on a legislative change."* He and fellow founding partner **William Nelson** (see p.141) are coauthors of a standard treatise on partnership taxation. Both were noted for their *"impressive intellect"* and *"businesslike"* approach to tax matters. Partner **John Magee** (see p.139) has an established reputation as a leading tax litigator. Described as a *"client magnet,"* Magee covers all aspects of tax controversy and international tax, including transfer pricing. He is currently acting for Dow Chemical in a reported case concerning corporate-owned life insurance and the deductibility of interest and administrative fees.

The Clients: GE; GlaxoSmithKline Holdings; Boeing; AT&T; Dow Chemical; Merrill Lynch; Lehman Brothers and Sears Roebuck.

Skadden, Arps, Slate, Meagher & Flom LLP
see firm details p.878

The Firm: In contrast to other DC practices, the group focuses heavily on transactional work, advising US and multinational corporates on M&A, tax-based structured finance and financial products. The six DC-based partners form part of a *"well-integrated"* national practice, working closely with larger practices in New York, LA and

DISTRICT OF COLUMBIA

TAX

DISTRICT OF COLUMBIA
Leading individuals (Tax)

1 OOSTERHUIS Paul *Skadden, Arps, Slate, Meagher*
ROSENBLOOM David *Caplin & Drysdale*

2 GOLDBERG Fred *Skadden, Arps, Slate, Meagher & Flom*
LIBIN Jerome *Sutherland Asbill & Brennan LLP*
MCKEE Bill *McKee Nelson LLP*
SCHNEIDER Leslie *Ivins, Phillips & Barker*
TERR Leonard *Baker & McKenzie*

3 MAGEE John *McKee Nelson LLP*
MAY Gregory *Freshfields Bruckhaus Deringer LLP*
MOORE Robert *Miller & Chevalier*
NELSON William *McKee Nelson LLP*
SILVERMAN Mark *Steptoe & Johnson LLP*
SWENSON David *Baker & McKenzie*

4 BENNETT Mary *Baker & McKenzie*
CULBERTSON Robert *King & Spalding LLP*
GIBBS Lawrence *Miller & Chevalier*
PARI Joseph *Dewey Ballantine LLP*
RIEDY James *McDermott, Will & Emery*
RUDNICK Robert *Shearman & Sterling*
WELLEN Robert *Ivins, Phillips & Barker*
WIACEK Raymond *Jones Day*

Individuals are listed alphabetically in each band.

Chicago. The DC group is particularly distinguished by its international tax capacity, and practitioners frequently coordinate tax advice with partners in Paris and London on major cross-border acquisitions. The firm recently acted for IBM in its acquisition of PwC Consulting. A strong project finance practice sees the group advising on a number of joint ventures, financings and partnership agreements for clients in the oil, utilities and gas sectors. The firm also offers non-transactional tax planning advice and undertakes controversy work for a large number of blue-chip corporations.

The Lawyers: **Paul Oosterhuis** (see p.142) coordinates the firm's international tax practice and was said to have at his command a *"wealth of experience"* in multi-jurisdictional transactions. He inspires a loyal client following for his *"sheer talent and intellect"* and his ability to *"navigate the tax laws of any country."* Oosterhuis recently advised Affiliated Computer Services on the proposed acquisition of a division of Proctor & Gamble and is representing Aventis in the negotiation of a joint venture with Bayer. A former IRS Commissioner and Treasury Department Assistant Secretary, **Fred Goldberg** (see p.136) is reported to wield *"plenty of clout"* within the agencies. He was recommended as a *"hard-nosed"* litigator and a *"solutions-driven"* attorney. Goldberg advises clients on controversy matters, IRS administrative and regulatory proceedings and tax legislation. His practice spans transfer pricing, tax-exempt organizations, post-INDOPCO capitalization issues, insurance contracts and IRS criminal investigations.

The Clients: United Airlines; Alcoa; Levi Strauss; Johnson & Johnson; IBM; Aventis; Schering-Plough; Hewlett-Packard; GlaxoSmithKline and Pfizer.

Baker & McKenzie
see firm details p.767

The Firm: A major international firm that *"operates like a boutique"* at local level. The firm's highly developed global franchise lends itself to international work, while DC's 25-lawyer team acts as *"one atom of a molecule,"* receiving referrals from some 300 local law specialists in the Baker & McKenzie network. The group advises on multi-jurisdictional tax planning matters, cross-border acquisitions, intercompany pricing cases and international tax treaty matters. In tax controversy, the firm has filed an amicus curiae brief in the Supreme Court on behalf of a consortium of seven companies in a suit against Boeing relating to global trade issues.

The Lawyers: Particularly recommended for international litigation and foreign tax treaty work, **Leonard Terr** (see p.146) was described as a *"high-caliber"* attorney with a *"wide perspective"* on the market. A tax generalist, Terr advises on international tax planning, controversy and transactional matters. His lobbying efforts on treaty reform have made him a *"key figure"* in DC. Partner **David Swenson** (see p.146) is highly visible on tax litigation and in the transfer pricing group. Peers regard him as a *"rainmaker"* for his ability to attract clients. **Mary Bennett** (see p.132) was praised for her *"astute"* advice on inbound investments. She is also active in lobbying work relating to the airline industry.

The Clients: AOL; Boeing; BP Amoco; Lucent Technologies; Marriott International; MetLife; Microsoft; 3M; Nissan and Zurich.

Ivins, Phillips & Barker

The Firm: This traditional DC boutique is thought to be *"unusual"* in its emphasis on transactional-based corporate tax work. The 33-lawyer firm focuses exclusively on tax and employee benefits, offering expertise in corporate acquisitions and tax-driven financings, tax controversy, international tax matters, pensions and executive compensation.

While the practice has suffered setbacks in the form of recent partner departures, the firm remains a *"first-rate operation"* characterized by *"the highest standards of quality."*

The group retains its small-firm culture, emphasizing close client relationships and a high level of partner involvement. It is envied for a *"terrific stable"* of Fortune 500 clients, with a particular concentration in the manufacturing, defense, oil and chemical industries. The firm's largest client is Northrop Grumman - a small team in California handles a large proportion of the defense contractor's tax issues. Notable work includes winning a significant US Supreme Court case on behalf of United Dominion Industries involving net operating loss carrybacks.

The Lawyers: **Les Schneider** has been hailed as *"the country's expert on accounting methods."* He has written the leading treatise on inventory accounting, but advises on all aspects of tax accounting. An *"outstanding corporate adviser,"* **Robert Wellen** concentrates on transactional M&A, restructuring and spin-off work. He and his team have been representing HJ Heinz in the spinoff of the StarKist seafood and pet food business and the subsequent acquisition by Del Monte Foods. He also handled tax issues in connection with the merger of real estate interests Equity Office Properties Trust and Spieker Properties.

The Clients: Northrop Grumman; Visa; GenCorp; Boeing; GE; Fidelity Investments; Exxon-Mobil; CITGO; Burlington Industries and HJ Heinz.

McDermott, Will & Emery
see firm details p.846

The Firm: This *"comprehensive"* tax practice receives greatest attention for its work on international transactions. Twenty DC lawyers work in tandem with attorneys in the Chicago, NY, LA and London offices in advising on cross-border M&A and finance matters. The firm has recruited from the IRS and the tax division of the DOJ, enhancing the group's reputation for regulatory expertise. The group has a loyal following among the tax directors and chief financial officers of Fortune 500 companies, who praise its members for their *"keen analytical skills"* and *"business-minded approach."* Interviewees also commented on the firm's strength in matters relating to tax-exempt healthcare organizations. The firm is currently acting as tax adviser to Georgia-Pacific in connection with a pending multibillion dollar tax-free spin-off of its consumer products and packaging business.

The Lawyers: Most visible in the team is **James Riedy** (see p.143), who rates highly for his *"breadth of knowledge and experience"* in international tax matters. He maintains a broad-based practice incorporating tax consulting and planning, transactional matters and transfer pricing issues. Clients praise his *"deep understanding of technical issues."*

The Clients: The firm advises major public companies and US multinationals such as Georgia-Pacific on transactional matters. Attorneys have handled tax cases and audits on behalf of Boca Investerings Partnership; American Pacesetter; ChevronTexaco; Boise Cascade and Indeck Energy Services.

TAX | **DISTRICT OF COLUMBIA**

Miller & Chevalier

The Firm: A *"fixture"* in the DC market, the firm is built on a *"traditional model"* with tax at its core. Fifty lawyers focus on tax planning, controversy and consulting work with some overlap with the large litigation and trade law practices. The group earns greatest recommendation for tax-related litigation, in which it is seen to handle *"major cases for major clients."* Practitioners regularly advise large US and multinational corporates before the US Tax Court, the US Court of Federal Claims and federal district courts. Notable industry strength exists in the energy, finance, chemical, retail and pharmaceutical sectors. The firm recently advised a US corporation in developing a structure for an attempted takeover of a Canadian corporation.

The Lawyers: Tax department chair **Robert Moore** was extolled by peers as an *"extraordinary litigator."* A *"man of many talents,"* he focuses on tax controversy work and continues to act as lead counsel to Exxon in IRS and Treasury Department challenges.

His partner, **Lawrence Gibbs**, was named as a *"distinguished statesman and diplomat of the tax bar."* A former IRS Commissioner, Gibbs maintains a broad practice, encompassing tax planning, compliance, controversy and administrative and legislative matters.

The Clients: The firm acts for major corporations in the energy, transport, finance, retail and pharmaceutical industries, as well as for tax-exempt and charitable organizations.

Steptoe & Johnson LLP

The Firm: The diverse practice is commended for its *"industrious"* attorneys and *"broad coverage"* of corporate tax issues. Practitioners advise on tax controversy, compliance, transactional, planning and policy matters. The firm attracted particular comment for its well-developed insurance tax practice; attorneys are visible representing leveraged corporate-owned and bank-owned life insurance policyholders in audits and IRS challenges. Other areas of strength include multi-state tax planning and tax exempt organization and ERISA matters.

The Lawyers: *"Everybody likes"* practice head **Mark Silverman**. This *"personable"* individual maintains a high profile at the bar through extensive writing and public speaking. Known in DC as a *"strong Sub C guy,"* he is said to possess an *"encyclopedic knowledge of US corporate taxation."* He maintains an active tax policy practice and has been involved in discussions with Congress and the Treasury Department on proposed tax initiatives. Silverman specializes in planning and transactional matters and is highly regarded for his expertise in relation to troubled businesses. The practice has received an additional boost with the return of international tax specialist Philip West from Arthur Andersen.

The Clients: The team advises public corporations, venture capital groups and tax-exempt organizations.

Sutherland Asbill & Brennan LLP

see firm details p.887

The Firm: A large and well-respected tax practice is split between the Atlanta and DC offices. The firm retains a historic reputation for specialization in the field, and now boasts one of the largest tax groups in the city. The 50-lawyer team rates highest for general tax counseling, but also handles a range of transactional work, including corporate acquisitions, dispositions, restructurings and financings. A niche strength is insurance tax, on which the group advises foreign mutual funds and financial institutions such as Goldman Sachs and CSFB on matters specific to the property and casualty insurance industries.

The Lawyers: Praised as a *"brilliant lawyer and generalist,"* **Jerome Libin** (see p.138) is well known for his *"old-school practice that cuts across many dimensions."* His practice covers a mix of transactional work, tax planning and controversy matters. As current president of the IFA, Libin enjoys a high profile in the international taxation field. This *"classy"* practitioner was recommended both because of his involvement in significant federal tax cases and for his knowledge of tax treaty law.

The Clients: Philip Morris; Proctor & Gamble; Goldman Sachs; CSFB; GM and Fannie Mae.

Other Notable Practitioners

Gregory May of Freshfields Bruckhaus Deringer LLP is said to have *"distinguished himself beautifully in the financial transactions area."* This *"world-class practitioner"* displays *"sound judgment"* and a *"deep understanding of the law."* He frequently advises CSFB, CIBC and JPMorgan Chase on securitizations and new financial products.

"First-rate" attorney **Robert Culbertson** (see p.134) at King & Spalding specializes in international tax planning and controversy. A former IRS official, Culbertson is said to keep *"tentacles deep in government."* He is a member of both the firm's Islamic finance and Latin American practice groups and rates highly for *"technical excellence."*

At Dewey Ballantine, young partner **Joseph Pari** (see p.142) maintains a general M&A and advisory practice. Praised as *"hard-working and able,"* Pari was said to have particular expertise in Subchapter C corporations. *"Bright and effective"* **Raymond Wiacek** (see p.148) coordinates the tax practice at Jones Day. Competitors singled him out for his skill in transfer pricing matters. **Robert Rudnick** of Sherman & Sterling divides his time between the DC and New York offices. *"Excellent at putting together structures,"* Rudnick enjoys a widespread reputation for financial products work. He serves as principal outside counsel to Freddie Mac and earns praise for his expertise in securitization transactions.

Leaders in DC

ACKER, Lawrence G
LeBoeuf, Lamb, Greene & MacRae, LLP, Washington, DC 202 986 8016
lacker@llgm.com
Recommended in Energy
Specialization: Concentrates on major complex litigation before administrative agencies considering refund, rate, tariff and merger matters, and advises senior company officials respecting competition affecting formerly regulated industries. Assists clients in preparing every phase of administrative litigation from strategic planning and initiation to witness examination through appeals.
Prof. Memberships: Energy Bar Association.
Career: Joined *LeBoeuf* in 1984; *Bracewell & Patterson* (1981-84); Federal Energy Regulatory Commission (1978-81); *Acker & Mansfield*, Arlington, Virginia (1976-78); Arlington Legal Aid Society (1974-76).
Personal: Born 1950; Georgetown University (JD) 1974; Syracuse University (BA) 1971.

ADLER, Howard
Gibson, Dunn & Crutcher LLP, Washington, DC 202 955 8500
Recommended in Corporate/M&A

ALDOCK, John
Shea & Gardner, Washington, DC
202 828 2000
Recommended in Litigation

ANDRIL, David
Vinson & Elkins LLP, Washington, DC
202 639 6542
dandril@velaw.com
Recommended in Energy
Specialization: Practice concentrates on natural gas sales and transportation contracting, and regulation of the natural gas industry in the United States and overseas.
Prof. Memberships: Member: Federal Energy Bar Association.
Career: Admitted to District of Columbia Bar in 1980. Came to the firm in 1980 and was admitted to the partnership in January 1989.

DISTRICT OF COLUMBIA — LEADERS

ARNHOLZ, John
McKee Nelson LLP, Washington, DC 202 775 4138
jarnholz@mckeenelson.com
Recommended in Capital Markets
Specialization: Securitization and structured finance, corporate/securities. Represents issuers and underwriters in securitization transactions with a significant emphasis on cross-border and global offerings. Works with a broad range of financial assets, including residential mortgage loans, debt obligations, home equity loans, auto loans, franchise loans, and high LTV loans. Has been active in structured finance transactions in international markets. Has represented underwriters and issuers in many significant securitization programmes.
Career: Prior to joining *McKee Nelson* in May 2001, was a partner in the Washington, DC office of *Sidley Austin Brown & Wood LLP*. Recieved a JD from the Georgetown University Law Center in 1985.

BAACH, Martin
Baach Robinson & Lewis, Washington, DC 202 833 8900
Recommended in Insurance

BABSON, Marshall
Jones Day, Washington,DC
202 879 3644
mbabson@jonesday.com
Recommended in Employment
Specialization: Labour law practice representing employers in all aspects of labour relations, including litigation and counseling, NLRB, EEOC, OSHA, collective bargaining, and arbitration. Clients include Albertion's, General Electric, Washington Post, SAIC and Yale University.
Prof. Memberships: Member, Practice and Procedure Committee of the Labor and Employment Law Section, American Bar Association and Employment Lawyers Advisory Committee of the National Association of Manufacturers. Member, board of directors of the National Chamber Litigation Center. Serves as one of only ten US lawyers on the Litigation Center's Labor Law Advisory Committee.
Career: Prior to joining *Jones Day*, was senior partner of the Washington, DC office of *Ogletree, Deakins, Nash, Smoak & Stewart*.
Publications: Author of numerous articles regarding labor and employment law. Regularly appears in national symposiums to discuss new developments in employment law. In 1994, testified before President Clinton's Dunlop Commission regarding the status of US labor laws and more recently, testified before Congress regarding proposed employment legislation.

BAER, Bill
Arnold & Porter, Washington, DC
202 942 5936
William_Baer@aporter.com
Recommended in Antitrust
Specialization: Heads *Arnold & Porter's* highly regarded antitrust practice.
Career: Prior to rejoining the firm in January 2000, he served as Director of the Federal Trade Commission's Bureau of Competition for five years. Among other matters he oversaw the Commission's successful court challenges to the Staples/Office Depot and drug wholesaler mergers, review of Time Warner's acquisition of Turner Broadcasting System and the Ciba-Geigy/Sandoz merger, as well as challenges to exclusionary tactics of Toys-R-Us, Intel and Mylan Laboratories. Currently represents clients in high stakes antitrust litigation and provides antitrust counsel on a wide range of issues, including mergers and joint ventures in the high-tech, pharmaceutical and communications sectors, antitrust and intellectual property and criminal investigations by DOJ's Antitrust Division. Practiced law at *Arnold & Porter* from 1980 to 1995, where he helped secure the 1994 acquittal of the General Electric Company on criminal price fixing charges. He also served at the Federal Trade Commission from 1975 to 1980, where he held a number of positions, including Attorney Advisor to the Chairman, and Assistant General Counsel and Director of Congressional Relations.

BAINE, Kevin T
Williams & Connolly LLP, Washington, DC 202 434 5010
kbaine@wc.com
Recommended in Media & Entertainment
Specialization: With almost 30 years of experience, he devotes a majority of his practice to First Amendment and media litigation. He has successfully defended over 100 libel cases and litigated a variety of cases raising issues of freedom of speech, freedom of the press, and freedom of religion. He has also handled a broad range of civil litigation at trial and appellate level - including copyright, trademark, employment discrimination, education, tort, contract, and general commercial cases. He has also represented universities in cases involving academic tenure and student discipline, and religious organizations in church governance and discipline issues.

BALIS, Stanley
Miller, Balis & O'Neil, PC, Washington, DC 202 296 2960
Recommended in Energy

BAPTISTE, Robert
Baptiste & Wilder, Washington, DC
202 223 0723
Recommended in Employment

BASTIANELLI, Adrian
Bastianelli, Brown & Kelley, Washington, DC 202 293 8815
Recommended in Construction

BAUMGARTEN, Jon
Proskauer Rose, Washington, DC
202 416 6899
Recommended in Intellectual Property

BAXTER, Michael St Patrick
Covington & Burling, Washington, DC
202 662 5164
MBaxter@cov.com
Recommended in Insolvency
Specialization: Co-chair of the firm's insolvency practice. Practice includes representing companies in bankruptcy, advising creditors of companies in bankruptcy, advising on the structuring of transactions involving financially troubled companies, counseling companies in workouts and debt restructurings, representing official committees in bankruptcy cases, and acting as Chapter 11 bankruptcy trustee.
Prof. Memberships: American Law Institute; International Insolvency Institute; Chair, ABA Chapter 11 Subcommittee; Select Advisory Committee on Bankruptcy Reorganization; Law Society of Upper Canada.
Career: *Covington & Burling*, 1983 to present.
Publications: Contributing editor, 'Norton Bankruptcy Law and Practice 2D'. Contributing author, 1999 'Annual Survey of Letter of Credit Law & Practice'. He has published extensively in the insolvency area and is a frequent speaker at professional programs.
Personal: LLM, Harvard Law School, 1983; LLB, University of Western Ontario, 1979. Law clerk to the Chief Justice of Ontario, 1981-82.

BENNETT, Mary
Baker & McKenzie, Washington, DC
202 452 7045
mary.c.bennett@bakernet.com
Recommended in Tax
Specialization: Specializing in US tax planning and controversies for multinational corporations (eg withholding taxes, cross-border financings, foreign tax credits, controlled foreign corporations, and tax treaties). Deals regularly with IRS to obtain letter rulings, competent authority determinations, and regulatory relief, and represents companies on tax policy matters before US Treasury and Congress. Adjunct Professor of Advanced International Tax, Georgetown University.
Prof. Memberships: International Fiscal Association, ABA Tax Section.
Publications: A Commentary on the US - Netherlands Income Tax Convention (1995).
Personal: AB, cum laude, Harvard University, 1976; Universite de Paris, 1974-75; JD, Columbia Law School, 1979; LLM, Tax, Boston University, 1985.

BENNETT, Robert
Skadden, Arps, Slate, Meagher & Flom LLP, Washington, DC 202 371 7180
rbennett@skadden.com
Recommended in Litigation
Specialization: Heads *Skadden's* international government enforcement group. Leads civil and criminal litigation practice in the Washington, DC, office. Has tried a number of high-profile cases. Represents corporations, directors and officers in criminal, civil and SEC enforcement matters. Advises management and boards on preventive and remedial measures. Assists boards and audit committees in conducting internal investigations. Represents corporations and officers and directors in complex civil and criminal matters and qui tam actions. Has extensive experience representing clients before Congressional committees.
Prof. Memberships: Fellow of the American College of Trial Lawyers.
Career: Member of defense bar since 1971. Law Clerk to the Honorable Howard F. Corcoran, United States District Court for the District of Columbia; Assistant United States Attorney for the District of Columbia (1967-70); Special Counsel, United States Senate Select Committee on Ethics in several major investigations; Special Counsel, District of Columbia Commission on Judicial Disabilities and Tenure (1976-82); LLM, Harvard Law School, 1965; LLB, Georgetown Law Center, 1964; University of Virginia Law School, 1961-62; BA Georgetown University, 1961; Judge, The Court of Arbitration for Sport (2002 - present).

BERNER, Frederic
Sidley Austin Brown & Wood, Washington, DC 202736 8000
Recommended in Energy

BEYDA, Richard
Grossberg Yochelson Fox & Beyda, Washington, DC 202 296 9696
Recommended in Real Estate

BIEKE, James
Shea & Gardner, Washington, DC
202 828 2000
Recommended in Environment

BLAKE, Jonathan D
Covington & Burling, Washington, DC
202 662 5506
jblake@cov.com
Recommended in Communications
Specialization: Communications (television, cable, wireless PCS, satellites, broadband, new technologies), media, internet, licensing, deals, international, legislation, litigation, and corporate governance. Highlights: represented first cellular and PCS systems in US; helped launch digital television beginning 20 years ago; helped launch two-way wireless strategy.
Prof. Memberships: American Bar Association - Chair, 1993-present, International Telecommunications Committee;

LEADERS — DISTRICT OF COLUMBIA

Federal Communications Bar Association - President, 1984-85.
Career: Head of the firm's Technology, Media and Communications group; senior communications partner; named one of the top 100 most powerful lawyers by a leading legal publication, 1997-2002.
Publications: Numerous publications and speeches.
Personal: Yale University (LLB, 1964; BA 1960); Oxford University (MA in Law); Phi Beta Kappa, Rhodes Scholar; Yale Law Journal. Married to Elizabeth Shriver. Five children.

BLASZAK, James
Levine, Blaszak, Block & Boothby LLP, Washington, DC 202 857 2550
jblaszak@lb3law.com
Recommended in Communications
Specialization: Specialization is evaluating, negotiating and documenting telecommunications service contracts for buyers of such services. He has advised purchasers in connection with scores of those agreements, as well as customized agreements for cellular, frame relay, and satellite services. Among the clients he has assisted are numerous Fortune 100 companies. Also has participated in complex rate and regulatory cases, and has prosecuted applications for radio licenses and operating authority and satellite system authorizations. He has counseled clients on a wide range of matters implicating federal and state telecommunications laws. He is counsel to the Ad Hoc Telecommunications Users Committee, whose members are among the largest purchasers of communications services.
Prof. Memberships: Member of the District of Columbia Bar and the Federal Communications Bar Association.
Career: Partner at *Gardner, Carton and Douglas* before joining *Levine, Blaszak, Block & Boothby* as a partner. Before entering private practice, he served in a variety of positions at the Federal Communications Commission, including Chief of the Domestic Facilities and Satellite Branch and Legal Advisor to the Chief, Common Carrier Bureau. Graduated from the University of Texas School of Law.

BLEAKLEY, Peter
Arnold & Porter, Washington, DC
202 942 5888
Peter_Bleakley@aporter.com
Recommended in Litigation
Specialization: Has tried nearly 100 civil and criminal cases. These cases are principally in the areas of antitrust, intellectual property, product liability and business fraud. Most recently, he has represented Xerox Corporation in a decade-long litigation involving both antitrust and intellectual property issues, as well as the Recording Industry Association of America in a high-profile intellectual property case. He also has been trial counsel in product liability cases for Philip Morris Companies, the American Red Cross, Wyeth and Motorola, and in various securities and business fraud cases. Over the years, he has also represented The Southland Corporation (7-Eleven Inc.), Tandy Corporation, Xerox, Wyeth, and Philip Morris, among others, in various trials in federal and state courts throughout the country.

BLUMENTHAL, William
King & Spalding LLP, Washington, DC
202 626 2625
wblumenthal@kslaw.com
Recommended in Antitrust
Specialization: Partner responsible for competition law aspects of domestic and multijurisdictional mergers, acquisitions, and joint ventures. Also represents clients in matters involving distribution restraints, cartel behavior, and advertising and marketing practices.
Prof. Memberships: Include ABA Antitrust Section (former Vice Chair); Business & Industry Advisory Committee to OECD; US Chamber of Commerce Antitrust Council.
Career: Admitted to District of Columbia Bar (1980). Partner in *King & Spalding LLP* since 1995.
Publications: Articles in: 'George Washington Law Review', 'California Law Review', 'Antitrust Law Journal', 'Antitrust Bulletin', 'Antitrust Report' and other publications.
Personal: JD, Harvard Law School, 1980. BA and MA, Brown University, 1977.

BOOTHBY, Colleen
Levine, Blaszak, Block & Boothby LLP, Washington, DC 202 857 2550
cboothby@lb3law.com
Recommended in Communications
Specialization: Represents telecommunications users, IT companies, and associations (including IBM, Microsoft, GE Capital Communication Services, the Ad Hoc Telecommunications Users Committee, the High Tech Broadband Coalition, the Information Technology Industry Council, and the New York Clearinghouse Association) before the US Federal Communications Commission and courts. Provides strategic counsel on a broad range of subjects, including the regulation of telecommunications networks, IT products, the internet and public/private intranets; customer privacy and proprietary network information; inside wire and building access; and the pricing of local exchange and interexchange services. Frequent speaker before such groups as the Communications Managers Association, ACUTA, and the National Centrex Users Group.
Prof. Memberships: Federal Communications Bar Association (Co-Chair, Common Carrier Practice Committee, 1998-99). District of Columbia Bar Association (Steering Committee, Administrative Law and Agency Practice Committee, 2000-date).
Career: Admitted to District of Columbia Bar in 1980. Federal Communications Commission (Deputy and Associate Chief, Tariff Division; Legal Assistant to the Bureau Chief, Common Carrier Bureau; Senior Supervising Attorney, International and Tariff Divisions), 1983-93.
Personal: AB, Pomona College, 1977. JD, Boalt Hall School of Law (Associate Editor, California Law Review), 1980.

BOUKNIGHT, Lon
Steptoe & Johnson LLP, Washington, DC
202 429 3000
Recommended in Energy

BOWE JR, James F
Dewey Ballantine LLP, Washington, DC
202 429 1444
jbowe@deweyballantine.com
Recommended in Energy
Specialization: Energy (including energy project development, energy regulatory matters, energy company M&A). Project finance (US, North America, Latin America). Oil and gas law.
Prof. Memberships: Energy Bar Association. American Bar Association. Member of the Bar of the District of Columbia and the bars of several federal courts.
Career: Admitted to practice 1982, District of Columbia. Private practice since 1982. Partner, *Dewey Ballantine LLP*, July 1994-present. Adjunct Professor, Oil and Gas Law, Georgetown University Law Center, 1990-95.
Personal: Born May 17, 1955. BA, Williams College, 1977. JD, Northwestern University School of Law, 1982.

BOWMAN, William
Hogan & Hartson LLP, Washington, DC
202 637 6434
wjbowman@hhlaw.com
Recommended in Insurance, Litigation
Specialization: Partner in the Litigation Group and resident in *Hogan & Hartson LLP's* Washington, DC office. Practice is principally in the area of litigation, including trial and appellate practice involving commercial, insurance coverage, environmental, antitrust, contract, trade regulation, and product liability litigation. Has practiced actively in federal and state courts, the District of Columbia, Virginia, Maryland, and many other parts of the country.
Career: Served as a law clerk to The Honorable Thomas A Flannery of the United States District Court for the District of Columbia following graduation from law school. From 1977 to 1983, was an Assistant United States Attorney for the District of Columbia, handling an active criminal trial and appellate practice and serving for two and a half years as Chief of the Career Criminal Unit. Spent a year as Chief Counsel to the US Senate Judiciary Committee Subcommittee on Juvenile Justice. Joined *Hogan & Hartson* in 1984.
Personal: Received undergraduate degree from Harvard College in 1973 and JD from Georgetown University Law Center in 1976.

BRAY, John
King & Spalding LLP, Washington, DC
202 737 0500
jbray@kslaw.com
Recommended in Litigation
Specialization: Over 35 years experience in civil and criminal litigation in federal district courts including: asbestos liability, federal tax, environmental, defense procurement, insurance coverage, antitrust cases, and cases presenting a host of business, financial and government regulatory issues. Has also been involved in numerous historic criminal conspiracy cases and trials throughout the US dealing with complex issues in: tax, antitrust claims, international investigations, fraudulent conveyances, environmental issues and insurance coverage.
Prof. Memberships: Fellow of the American College of Trial Lawyers.
Personal: Undergraduate degree from St. Louis University and JD degree from St. Louis University School of Law.

BROSE, Steve
Steptoe & Johnson LLP, Washington, DC
202 429 3000
Recommended in Energy

BROWN, Barbara
Paul, Hastings, Janofsky & Walker LLP, Washington, DC 202 508 9551
barbarabrown@paulhastings.com
Recommended in Employment
Specialization: Represents employers in entire range of employment law matters, particularly employment discrimination class actions.
Prof. Memberships: Past co-chair of the EEO Committee of the American Bar Association's Labor and Employment Law Section; Member of the governing Council of the Section.
Publications: Co-author: 'Equal Employment Law Update' (BNA 7th ed., Fall 1999), a comprehensive treatment of recent appellate authority across the field of employment law and litigation, and of 'The Legal Guide to Human Resources' (Warren, Gorham & Lamont, 3d Rev. Ed. 1996, Supp. 2002).
Personal: BA - Harvard University (magna cum laude, Phi Beta Kappa); JD - Yale Law School.

BROWNELL, William
Hunton & Williams, Washington, DC
202 955 1500
Recommended in Environment

DISTRICT OF COLUMBIA

LEADERS

BRUNNER, Thomas
Wiley Rein & Fielding LLP, Washington, DC 202 719 7000
Recommended in Insurance

BUCHANAN, John
Covington & Burling, Washington, DC 202 662 5366
JBuchanan@cov.com
Recommended in Insurance
Specialization: Represents policy holders in complex insurance coverage disputes and transactions. Experience covers wide range of property/casualty claims, including environmental, asbestos and other GL claims; media liability, IP- and competition-related claims; D&O, Software E&O, and fidelity claims; product tampering, time-element, marine, satellite in-orbit, and other first-party claims. Helped clients recover over $400 million during recent one-year period.
Prof. Memberships: American Law Institute; American Bar Association, Litigation Section, Insurance Coverage Litigation Committee (current Subcommittee Co-Chair; past Task Force Co-Chair).
Career: Partner since 1986. Firm's first Insurance Practice Group Coordinator, 1987-97. Admitted DC Bar, 1979. Law Clerk, 3d Circuit US Court of Appeals, 1978-79.
Publications: Frequent speaker and writer on insurance topics, including chapters in 'Law & Practice of Insurance Coverage Litigation'(West 2000); 'Manual for Complex Insurance Coverage Litigation' (Prentice Hall 1995).
Personal: JD, Harvard, 1978; Honours BA (1st Class), Oxford, 1974; AB (Phi Beta Kappa), Princeton, 1972.

BUCKLEY, Christopher
Gibson, Dunn & Crutcher LLP, Washington, DC 202 955 8500
Recommended in Environment

BUENTE, David
Sidley Austin Brown & Wood, Washington, DC 202 736 8000
Recommended in Environment

CARY, George
Cleary Gottlieb Steen & Hamilton, Washington, DC 202 974 1500
Recommended in Antitrust
See New York chapter for profile

CHATILOVICZ, Peter
Seyfarth Shaw, Washington, DC 202 463 2400
Recommended in Employment

CHUZI, George
Kalijarvi, Chuzi & Newman PC, Washington, DC 202 331 9260
Recommended in Employment

COHEN, George
Bredhoff & Kaiser, Washington, DC 202 842 2600
Recommended in Employment

COLEMAN, Lynn R
Skadden, Arps, Slate, Meagher & Flom LLP, Washington, DC 202 371 7600
lcoleman@skadden.com
Recommended in Energy
Specialization: Partner, Washington DC domestic and international energy practice and co-ordinates the legislative and public policy practice. Handles a wide variety of energy transactions, regulatory proceedings and complex litigation; deals with oil, gas, electric, coal and nuclear energy issues. Represents clients on issues of government policy, and has worked extensively on government regulation of energy projects and transactions; also represents clients on issues of government policy, including legislation in Congress and executive branch initiatives.
Prof. Memberships: Admitted in the Districts of Columbia and Texas. Member, Administrative Conference of United States (1979-81); Chair, President's Task Force on Coal Exports (1980-81); Special Committee on Energy Law, American Bar Association (1980-85).
Career: LLB, University of Texas, 1964 (Ed., Texas Law Review; Order of the Coif; Chancellor); BA, Abilene Christian College, 1961; Law clerk to the Hon. John R. Brown, US Court of Appeals, Fifth Circuit (1964-65); General Counsel and Deputy Secretary, US Department of Energy (1978-81).

CONTRATTO, Dana
Crowell & Moring LLP, Washington, DC 202 624 2500
Recommended in Energy

COWAN, Cameron
Orrick, Herrington & Sutcliffe, Washington, DC 202 339 8488
ccowan@orrick.com
Recommended in Capital Markets
Specialization: Represents financial institutions, investment banks, and companies with particular expertise in the structuring, issuance, and purchase of asset-backed, mortgage-backed, and derivative products.
Career: Prior to Orrick, *Milbank, Tweed, Hadley, & McCloy*, Washington DC, partner, 1990-93. Managing Director of *Orrick*'s finance practices and member of *Orrick*'s Executive Committee. Member of Executive Committee and Management Committee and Chair of Legal Subcommittee of American Securitization Forum.
Publications: Co-author of 'Mortgage-Backed Securities: Developments and Trends in the Secondary Mortgage Market'.
Personal: University of Virginia School of Law, JD, 1981. Columbia University Graduate School of Business, MBA. Syracuse University, BS magna cum laude.

CULBERTSON, Robert
King & Spalding LLP, Washington, DC 202 626 2642
rculbertson@kslaw.com
Recommended in Tax
Specialization: Over 20 years' experience in international taxation, both the public and private sectors, specializing in international tax planning/controversy resolution.
Career: Prior to joining *King & Spalding* he was leader of the Washington international tax services office of PricewaterhouseCoopers. Began his career with the IRS drafting regulations. Joined staff of the Joint Committee on Taxation working on international provisions of the Tax Reform Act of 1986. Rejoined IRS in 1986, then served as Associate Chief Counsel International 1991-95, responsible for international tax regulations, rulings, and litigation policy.
Personal: BA, Yale College and graduate of Harvard Law School.

DANIEL, Aubrey
Williams & Connolly LLP, Washington, DC 202 434 5116
adaniel@wc.com
Recommended in Litigation
Specialization: As one of the firm's most experienced trial lawyers, his practice is concentrated in complex, high stakes litigation involving white-collar criminal defense, commercial disputes, antitrust, insurance coverage, and products liability defense and prosecution. He has tried numerous criminal and civil cases, in federal and state courts all over the country, and won significant victories, including the 1979 acquittal of a state's attorney on bribery and public corruption charges to the multitude of civil and criminal actions arising out of the allegations of the FBI's notorious undercover operative Mark Whitacre.

DAVIS, James
Howrey Simon Arnold & White, Washington, DC 202 783 0800
Recommended in Intellectual Property

DELLINGER, Walter
O'Melveny & Myers LLP, Washington, DC 202 383 5300
Recommended in Litigation

DENGER, Michael
Gibson, Dunn & Crutcher LLP, Washington, DC 202 955 8500
Recommended in Antitrust

DESANTIS, Victor
White & Case LLP, Washington, DC 202 626 3600
Recommended in Projects

DOLIN, Mitchell F
Covington & Burling, Washington, DC 202 662 5210
mdolin@cov.com
Recommended in Insurance
Specialization: Practice concentrated on the litigation, arbitration, and mediation of insurance disputes concerning asbestos and mass torts, directors and officers, first party property, and other large loss situations. Aside from appearing as an advocate in numerous domestic and international insurance arbitrations, he has been named an arbitrator and expert in such proceedings.
Prof. Memberships: American Arbitration Association (National Roster of Neutrals); American Judicature Society (Board of Directors); American Law Institute (Member); London Court of International Arbitration (Member).
Career: Law clerk, Chief Judge Charles Clark, US Court of Appeals, Fifth Circuit (1981-82). With *Covington & Burling* since 1982, becoming a partner in 1989.
Publications: Author of book chapters and articles on insurance and arbitration topics; has spoken on these topics at conferences of the ABA, ALI-ABA, CPR, and other organziations.
Personal: Tufts University, BA, 1978; New York University School of Law, JD, 1981.

DOWNS, Clark Evans
Jones Day, Washington, DC 202 879 3883
cedowns@jonesday.com
Recommended in Energy
Specialization: Has represented (for over 25 years) electric utilities and investment bankers before state commissions and the Federal Energy Regulatory Commission in rate and other regulatory proceedings. Practice has frequently been involved in the regulation of financial matters under the Public Utility Holding Company Act of 1935 and the Atomic Energy Act, the acquisition and disposition of substantial utility assets, in consultation on electric utility business strategy, and in legislative matters, including the Energy Policy Act of 1992.
Prof. Memberships: Previously served as member of the board of directors of the Energy Bar Association and as its delegate to the ABA House of Delegates. Member of the American Bar Association (Administrative Law and Regulatory Practice and Public Utility Law Sections) and the District of Columbia Bar. Frequent speaker on electric utility matters and active in community affairs. Fellow of the American Bar Foundation. Listed in a number of leading American legal publications.

DUNNER, Donald
Finnegan Henderson Farabow Garrett & Dunner LLP, Washington, DC 202 408 4000
don.dunner@finnegan.com
Recommended in Intellectual Property
Specialization: Partner. Handles all areas of patent law including prosecution, licensing, litigation, validity and infringement studies, and counseling. Has tech-

nical expertise in the areas of chemical engineering, chemistry, biotechnology and pharmaceuticals. Has litigated numerous cases in the federal district courts, but is best known for appellate practice before the United States Court of Appeals for the Federal Circuit.
Career: Admitted in 1958, District of Columbia; 1963, US Supreme Court; 1982, US Court of Appeals for the Federal Circuit; registered to practice before US Patent and Trademark Office.
Publications: Co-Author: 'Court Review of Patent Office Decisions', 1969, 1973; Co-Author: 'Patent Law Perspectives', 1970-1988; Co-Author: 'Court of Appeals for the Federal Circuit Practice and Procedure', 1985.
Personal: Born May 12, 1931. Purdue University (BSChE, 1953); Georgetown University Law Center (JD, 1958).

DWYER, Jeffry
Greenberg Traurig LLP, Washington, DC 202 331 3100
Recommended in Real Estate

EASTMENT, Thomas
Baker Botts LLP, Washington, DC 202 639 7700
Recommended in Energy

EGAN, James
Clifford Chance US LLP, Washington, DC 212 878 8000
jim.egan@cliffordchance.com
Recommended in Antitrust
Specialization: Represents a wide range of clients in private antitrust actions in federal and state courts, and in investigations and cases brought by the Department of Justice, the Federal Trade Commission and the Securities and Exchange Commission. He also counsels clients on antitrust compliance issues. From 1990 to 1994, he served as Director for Litigation of the Bureau of Competition of the FTC, and previous to that as assistant director for litigation, and assistant director for mergers and joint ventures.

EISENSTAT, Larry
Dickstein Shapiro Morin & Oshinsky LLP, Washington, DC 202 785 9700
Recommended in Energy

ELROD, Eugene
Sidley Austin Brown & Wood, Washington, DC 202 736 8000
Recommended in Energy

ENGEL, John
Shaw Pittman, Washington, DC 202 663 8000
Recommended in Real Estate

EPSTEIN, Gary
Latham & Watkins LLP, Washington, DC 202 637 2249
gary.epstein@lw.com
Recommended in Communications
Specialization: Partner in charge of the telecommunications practice. Advises telecommunications and satellite companies on domestic and international regulation; US regulatory counsel for DIRECTV and TelMex. Counsels foreign and foreign-owned companies on US international policies, including ownership restrictions and authorisations for international services. Directly involved in privatization or other restructuring of telecommunications sectors in many countries.
Career: Chief, Common Carrier Bureau of the Federal Communications Commission, 1981-83; Chairman, FCC's Industry Advisory Committee on Implementation of Reduced Orbital Spacing Between Domestic Fixed Satellites, 1984-86; Chairman, FCC's Industry Advisory Committee for 1995 WRC.
Personal: JD, Harvard University, 1971 (cum laude).

EPSTIEN, Jay
Piper Rudnick LLP, Washington, DC 202 861 3850
jay.epstien@piperrudnick.com
Recommended in Real Estate
Specialization: Real estate, real estate finance.
Career: Represents local and national owners, developers and users in all aspects of real estate transactions involving urban office buildings, suburban office and industrial parks, shopping centers, and multifamily residential projects. The lead lawyer on many of the largest downtown office leases in Washington, DC representing both landlords and tenants, including numerous law firms that have sought his counsel. Lectures frequently on commercial real estate issues and is listed in a leading US legal publication.
Personal: JD, Cornell University; BS, Case Western Reserve University.

ESTES, III, John N
Skadden, Arps, Slate, Meagher & Flom LLP, Washington, DC 202 371 7950
jestes@skadden.com
Recommended in Energy
Specialization: Practice focuses on energy-related matters, with a particular emphasis on electric utilities and gas pipelines. He has worked on a variety of issues arising in regulatory, litigation and transactional settings, including restructuring activities and mergers and acquisitions in the electric utility industry. Prior to joining *Skadden*, he spent five years at the Commission briefing and arguing cases in various federal courts of appeal.
Career: JD, Louisiana State University,1983; BA, Tulane University, 1979.

EVANS, Mark
Kellogg, Huber, Hansen, Todd & Evans PLLC, Washington, DC 202 326 7900
Recommended in Communications

FARABOW, Ford
Finnegan Henderson Farabow Garrett & Dunner LLP, Washington, DC 202 408 4000
ford.farabow@finnegan.com
Recommended in Intellectual Property
Specialization: Partner. Litigates jury and non-jury patent infringement cases. Patent, trade secret, and licensing disputes practice focuses on the technical fields of chemistry, pharmaceuticals, chemical engineering, and materials science. Has litigated in federal district and state trial courts throughout the US, domestic and foreign arbitration trials. At the appellate level, has handled numerous cases in the Federal Circuit Court of Appeals and in other circuits.
Career: Admitted in 1963, South Carolina; 1965, District of Columbia; 1981, US Supreme Court; 1982, US Court of Appeals for the Federal Circuit; registered to practice before US Patent and Trademark Office.
Personal: Born January 6, 1938. Clemson University (BSChE, 1959); The George Washington University National Law Center (JD, with honors, 1963).

FEINSTEIN, Deborah
Arnold & Porter, Washington, DC 202 942 5015
Deborah_Feinstein@aporter.com
Recommended in Antitrust
Specialization: Has concentrated on antitrust and trade regulation matters since joining the firm. From 1989 to 1991, she served as a special assistant to the Director of the Bureau of Competition of the Federal Trade Commission and attorney advisor to Commissioner Dennis Yao. She represented The Kroger Co. in its acquisition of Fred Meyer, the largest grocery store transaction ever completed. She represented Philip Morris and Kraft in connection with their acquisition of Nabisco. She also represents General Electric in transactions involving a variety of its business units.
Personal: Was recently named by Chambers & Partners' 2002-2003 and 2001-2002 'Chambers Global' (a survey of the world's leading lawyers), as one of the top 25 antitrust attorneys in Washington, DC.

FERRIS, Charles
Mintz Levin Cohn Ferris Glovsky and Popeo PC, Washington, DC 202 434 7300
Recommended in Communications

FIELD, Andrea Bear
Hunton & Williams, Washington, DC 202 955 1500
Recommended in Environment

FITZGERALD, Peter
Chadbourne & Parke LLP, Washington, DC 202 974 5600
Recommended in Projects

FITZPATRICK, Robert
Fitzpatrick & Associates, Washington, DC 202 588 5300
Recommended in Employment

FLEXNER, Donald
Boies, Schiller & Flexner, Washington, DC 202 237 2727
Recommended in Antitrust

FOGGAN, Laura
Wiley Rein & Fielding LLP, Washington, DC 202 719 7000
Recommended in Insurance

FRANKEL, Roger
Swidler Berlin Shereff Friedman LLP, Washington, DC 202 424 7500
Recommended in Insolvency

FREMUTH, Michael
Andrews & Kurth LLP, Washington, DC 202 662 2700
mfremuth@akllp.com
Recommended in Energy
Specialization: Involvement with all aspects of federal regulation of the natural gas industry and has been a speaker at several conferences on natural gas industry issues. Lead regulatory counsel for Transcontinental Gas Pipeline Corporation from 1991 through its purchase by the Williams Companies and now is lead outside counsel for regulatory matters for Tennessee Gas Pipeline Company. Has argued numerous cases before the Federal Energy Regulatory Commission and before the federal circuit courts. Advises natural gas companies on all regulated aspects of their businesses and on antitrust issues.
Prof. Memberships: Federal Energy (Chairman, Antitrust Committee, 1984-85). Bar Associations: State Bar of California, District of Columbia Bar.
Career: Partner in the Energy Section of the Washington, DC office. Has been with *Andrews & Kurth* since 1982 and has been a partner since 1988. Practised for six years as an antitrust attorney at *Morgan, Lewis & Bockius* law firm.
Personal: Received undergraduate degree summa cum laude and Phi Beta Kappa from Princeton University in 1969 and law degree with honors from Stanford University in 1976. Prior to attending law school, was a professional pitcher with the Detroit Tigers and Philadelphia Phillies organisations.

FRIES, Joseph
Arent Fox, Washington, DC 202 857 6000
Recommended in Real Estate

GARRETT, Theodore
Covington & Burling, Washington, DC 202 662 6000
Recommended in Environment

DISTRICT OF COLUMBIA

GAYNOR, Kevin
Vinson & Elkins LLP, Washington, DC
202 639 6688
kgaynor@velaw.com
Recommended in Environment
Specialization: Heads the firm's Washington office environmental practice.
Prof. Memberships: Co-Chair: Environment, Energy, and Natural Resources Steering Committee, DC Bar. Member: Environment and Litigation Sections, American Bar Association.
Career: Admitted to Connecticut Bar in 1973, District of Columbia Bar in 1978, and Maryland Bar in 1991. Joined the firm as a partner in 1993.
Publications: Environmental Enforcement: Industry Should Not Be Complacent, 'The Environmental Law Reporter', News and Analysis, April 2002. Criminal Enforcement of Environmental Law, 'Colorado Journal of International Environmental Law and Policy', Volume 10, Number 1, Winter 1999.

GELLER, Kenneth S
Mayer, Brown, Rowe & Maw, Washington, DC 202 263 3225
kgeller@mayerbrownrowe.com
Recommended in Litigation
Specialization: Appellate litigation, specializing in Supreme Court and appellate practice. Wrote or edited some 300 briefs and certiorari petitions in the Supreme Court. Argued some 40 cases in the Supreme Court.
Career: Joined *Mayer, Brown, Rowe & Maw* as partner, 1986. Partner in Charge of Washington, DC, office and member of firm management committee. Former Deputy Solicitor General, US Department of Justice, 1979-86; Assistant to the Solicitor General, United States Department of Justice, 1975-79; Assistant Special Prosecutor, Watergate Special Prosecution Force, 1973-75; Nickerson, Kramer, Lowenstein, Nessen and Kamin, New York, 1972-73; Law Clerk to The Honorable Walter R Mansfield, US Court of Appeals for the Second Circuit, 1971-72.
Publications: Co-Author: 'Supreme Court Practice', 8th ed., 2002; 7th ed., BNA (1993). Contributing Author: 'Business and Commercial Litigation In Federal Courts', Robert L Haig, ed., West Group & ABA (1998).
Personal: Born 22 September 1947. Harvard University, JD magna cum laude, 1971; Editor, Law Review. City College of New York, BA magna cum laude, 1968. Presidential Award for Distinguished Service, 1983.

GENTILE, Carmen
Bruder Gentile & Marcoux LLP, Washington, DC 202 783 1350
Recommended in Energy

GERSTELL, Glenn
Milbank, Tweed, Hadley & McCloy, Washington, DC 202 835 7500
Recommended in Communications

GIBBS, Lawrence
Miller & Chevalier, Washington, DC
202 626 5800
Recommended in Tax

GILBERT, Scott
Gilbert Heintz & Randolph, Washington, DC 202 772 2200
Recommended in Insurance

GLASGOW, Norman
Holland & Knight LLP, Washington, DC
202 955 3000
nglasgow@hklaw.com
Recommended in Real Estate
Specialization: Partner in the Real Estate Department, representing real estate developers in zoning, building code and historic preservation law matters, before the Board of Zoning Adjustment, Zoning Commission, State Historic Review Board and Commission of Fine Arts. He also represents clients in street and alley closings, and in that regard, has substantial contact with members of the District of Columbia City Council and has appeared as a witness in many Council hearings involving land use matters. He has handled numerous cases before the Board of Zoning Adjustment and has handled and participated in many major Zoning Commission cases. He is active in civic affairs; addressing the area's affordable housing crisis by working extensively with a number of non-profit affordable housing providers and community development corporations.

GLOVER, Stephen
Gibson, Dunn & Crutcher LLP, Washington, DC 202 955 8500
Recommended in Corporate/M&A

GOLDBERG, Fred
Skadden, Arps, Slate, Meagher & Flom LLP, Washington, DC 202 371 7110
fgoldber@skadden.com
Recommended in Tax
Specialization: Partner, Washington, DC. Focuses practice in the areas of tax controversy, tax administration and tax legislation. Advises clients as special counsel on a wide range of sensitive matters; tax opinion work and advice regarding novel tax administration issues; compliance, oversight and management reviews on behalf of senior management and boards of directors of various companies; counsel on legislative matters, including various capital market proposals, various foreign tax provisions and tax reform; all phases of civil audit, administrative appeals and litigation; IRS collection matters, clients subject to third-party IRS discovery proceedings and clients involved in IRS criminal investigations.
Career: JD, Yale University, 1973; BA, Yale University, 1969; Assistant Secretary for Tax Policy, Department of the Treasury(1992); Commissioner, Internal Revenue Service (1989-92); Chief Counsel, Internal Revenue Service (1984-86).

GOLDSMITH, Willis J
Jones Day, Washington, DC
202 879 3920
wgoldsmith@jonesday.com
Recommended in Employment
Specialization: Chairs the firm's Labor and Employment practice. Experience includes practice before state and federal trial and appellate courts in matters under the National Labour Relations Act, the Occupational Safety and Health Act, the Employee Retirement Income Security Act, Title VII of the Civil Rights Act of 1964, Section 301 of the Taft-Hartley Act, Section 1113 of the Bankruptcy Code and in injunction, breach of contract and employment cases. Admitted to practice before federal district courts and courts of appeal as well as the United States Supreme Court.
Prof. Memberships: Member, ABA. Member, the editorial advisory board of the Benefits Law Journal, 1990-2002. Author of various articles and participated in many conferences focusing on employment law. Listed in several leading American legal publications. Fellow of the College of Labour and Employment Lawyers. Member, the advisory board of the New York University School of Law Center for Labor and Employment Law.

GOODMAN, Ronald
White & Case LLP, Washington, DC
202 626 3600
Recommended in Arbitration

GOODWIN, Michael
Arnold & Porter, Washington, DC
202 942 5558
Michael_Goodwin@aporter.com
Recommended in Real Estate
Specialization: Practice encompasses all facets of commercial real estate, with special focus on development, hospitality, financing and public/private partnership transactions. He represents developers in land assemblage, debt and equity financing, leasing and sales. He also represents hotel owners and operators in the acquisition, development, operation and sale of the full spectrum of hospitality products nationwide, including full service hotels, convention center hotels, and resorts. Has been heavily involved in negotiating public incentives for real estate development, in the form of TIF, PILOTs, tax abatement and other subsidies. He is a graduate of Harvard Law School.

GREANEY, William
Covington & Burling, Washington, DC
202 662 6000
Recommended in Insurance

GREEN, Douglas
Steptoe & Johnson LLP, Washington, DC
202 429 3000
Recommended in Energy

GREENSTEIN, Abraham
Greenstein Delorme & Luchs, Washington, DC 202 452 1400
Recommended in Real Estate

HAGEN, Paul
Beveridge & Diamond PC, Washington, DC
202 789 6022
phagen@bdlaw.com
Recommended in Environment
Specialization: As Chair of the firm's International Environmental Practice Section, he counsels multinational corporations, trade associations and leading non-profit organizations on the negotiation and implementation of regional and global environmental agreements. Works extensively with clients in the chemicals, electronics and biotechnology sectors. His work includes representing clients on a wide range of product stewardship legislation and on issues arising under numerous international agreements, including the Basel Convention, the Biosafety Protocol, the Whaling Convention, the Kyoto Protocol, the Rotterdam Prior Informed Consent Convention, and the Stockholm Convention on Persistent Organic Pollutants. Advises clients on the environmental and social guidelines of the World Bank and IFC and on the environmental aspects of trade and investment agreements, including matters arising under the NAFTA and WTO. His domestic practice includes counseling on environmental compliance and enforcement matters.
Prof. Memberships: Currently serves on the Board of Directors of the Environmental Law Institute (ELI) and the American Bird Conservancy. Appointed to the ABA's Standing Committee on Environmental Law. Member of the IUCN Commission on Environmental Law.
Career: Admitted to Maryland (1990) and District of Columbia (1992) bars. Director of Beveridge & Diamond, P.C. Adjunct professor of law, Washington College of Law at American University. Served on U.S.I.A. delegation to South Africa to advise government on the drafting of environmental laws and advisor to the People's Republic of China on its implementation of new land use and natural resource legislation.
Personal: Received BA, Providence College (1986) and JD, Washington College of Law at American University (1990).

HARRIS, Larry
Piper Rudnick LLP, Washington, DC
202 371 6000
Recommended in Construction

HARRIS, Scott
Harris, Wiltshire & Grannis LLP, Washington, DC 202 730 1300
Recommended in Communications

DISTRICT OF COLUMBIA

HAYES, David
Latham & Watkins LLP, Washington, DC
202 637 2204
david.hayes@lw.com
Recommended in Environment
Specialization: Global Chair, Environment, Land and Resources Department. Focuses on counseling, litigation and transactions involving environmental, energy and natural resources matters. Experience in EPA-related regulatory matters, including contaminated sites, chemical regulation, air and water pollution issues. Experience with natural resource-related matters, including water rights and allocation, endangered species act implementation, energy project permitting, land conservation projects and Indian-related matters.
Prof. Memberships: Energy and environmental advisor, Hewlett Foundation. Environmental advisory committee, PacifiCorp. Board member, American Rivers. Council member, ABA's Environment, Energy and Resources Section.
Career: Deputy Secretary, US Department of the Interior, 1997-99.
Personal: JD, Stanford Law School, 1978. AB, University of Notre Dame, 1975 (summa cum laude).

HEINTZ, John
Gilbert Heintz & Randolph, Washington, DC 202 772 2200
Recommended in Insurance

HENSLER, David
Hogan & Hartson LLP, Washington, DC
202 637 5630
djhensler@hhlaw.com
Recommended in Litigation
Specialization: Partner in the Washington, DC office of *Hogan & Hartson LLP*. and director of the Litigation Group. Practice involves complex commercial litigation with a focus on securities fraud, D&O insurance coverage disputes, RICO actions, aviation and noise impact litigation, antitrust litigation and intellectual property disputes.
Prof. Memberships: Is a Fellow of the American College of Trial Lawyers and a member of the District of Columbia Bar. Also admitted to practice before many federal district and appellate courts and the United States Supreme Court.
Career: Was in the General Counsel's Office of the Securities and Exchange Commission, handling securities fraud litigation, prior to joining *Hogan & Hartson* in 1968. Was an adjunct professor at Georgetown University Law Center for eight years where he taught Law and Economics.
Publications: Co-author of several articles on asset valuation in the context of corporate takeovers and divestitures.

HOROWITZ, Philip
Arter & Hadden LLP, Washington, DC
202 775 7100
Recommended in Real Estate

HUBER, John
Latham & Watkins LLP, Washington, DC
202 637 2242
john.huber@lw.com
Recommended in Corporate/M&A
Specialization: Corporate partner specializing in public offerings, private placements of debt and equity securities as well as tender offers and mergers. Specializes in matters involving accounting issues and Sarbanes-Oxley Act, including financial statement matters and accounting issues.
Prof. Memberships: Member, NASDR's Corporate Financing Committee. Former Chairman, ABA's Task Force on Regulation FD. Former Chairman, ABA's Subcommittee on Securities Registration. Former member, Legal Advisory Board of NASD.
Career: Worked at SEC, 1975-86; Director and Deputy Director, SEC's Division of Corporation Finance, 1981-86.
Personal: LLM, Georgetown University, 1978. JD, University of Wisconsin, 1974 (cum laude). BA, University of Wisconsin, 1968 (with honors).

HUMES, Gary
Arnold & Porter, Washington, DC
202 942 5001
Gary_Humes@aporter.com
Recommended in Real Estate
Specialization: Practices primarily in the areas of build-to-suit transactions and large-scale office leases, public-private partnerships and other complex transactions involving the Federal Government, and real estate development and financing. His clients include Fortune 500 companies, non-profit organizations, large law firms, hotel owners and operators, and real estate developers. He structures and negotiates ground and space leases, joint ventures, purchase agreements, design and construction contracts, brokerage and development management agreements, and tax-exempt and taxable financings.
Personal: Education: received his JD from Cornell Law School (1981), his SM from the University of Chicago (1974), was a PhD candidate in Theoretical Physics (1974-76), and he received his BA from Wesleyan University (1972).

HUNGAR, Thomas
Gibson, Dunn & Crutcher LLP, Washington, DC 202 955 8500
Recommended in Litigation

JAFFE, Kenneth
Swidler Berlin Shereff Friedman LLP, Washington, DC 202 424 7500
Recommended in Energy

JAFFE, Michael
Thelen Reid & Priest LLP, Washington, DC 202 508 4000
Recommended in Construction

JEFFRESS, William
Baker Botts LLP, Washington, DC
202 639 7700
Recommended in Litigation

KAHN, David
Holland & Knight LLP, Washington, DC
202 955 3000
dkahn@hklaw.com
Recommended in Real Estate
Specialization: Leader of the Washington DC office quotes 50-lawyer real estate practice group. Practices in the areas of commercial real estate development and finance and commercial leasing. Represents numerous real estate developers, as well as institutional owners, investors and lenders, including domestic and foreign insurance companies, pension funds and national banks, in connection with their real estate development/investment activities throughout the United States. This representation includes the negotiation and documentation of purchase and sale agreements, development agreements, construction and permanent loan agreements, deeds of trust, ground leases, loan and equity participations, joint venture agreements, construction contracts and office and retail leases.

KATTAN, Joseph
Gibson, Dunn & Crutcher LLP, Washington, DC 202 955 8500
Recommended in Antitrust

KELLOGG, Michael
Kellogg, Huber, Hansen, Todd & Evans PLLC, Washington, DC 202 326 7900
Recommended in Communications

KENDALL, David
Williams & Connolly LLP, Washington, DC 202 434 5145
dkendall@wc.com
Recommended in Litigation, Media & Entertainment
Specialization: Litigates a variety of civil and criminal cases and has represented a variety of criminal defendants charged with 'white collar' offenses. In civil litigation, he has represented accounting firms, including Arthur Andersen in the University Savings case and McGladrey & Pullen in the A.H. Robins bankruptcy proceedings stemming from the Dalkon Shield litigation. In commercial arbitration, he recently won for the Baltimore Orioles $10 million and naming rights to the Camden Yards ballpark. He represented the Clintons in a variety of matters, including the 1998-99 impeachment proceedings and represented a number of copyright holders in anti-piracy suits.

KIELY, Bruce
Baker Botts LLP, Washington, DC
202 639 7700
Recommended in Energy

KILBERG, William
Gibson, Dunn & Crutcher LLP, Washington, DC 202 955 8500
Recommended in Employment

KLAWITER, Donald
Morgan, Lewis & Bockius LLP, Washington, DC 202 739 3000
Recommended in Antitrust

KLEIN, Frederick
Piper Rudnick LLP, Washington, DC
202 861 6668
frederick.klein@piperrudnick.com
Recommended in Real Estate
Specialization: Real estate; real estate finance.
Career: He practices in all areas of commercial real estate law, representing construction and permanent lenders, domestic and foreign banks, life insurance companies, local and national developers, and owners and developers of office buildings, multifamily projects, shopping centers, urban office buildings and suburban office and industrial parks. Has handled the acquisition and disposition of commercial projects in the mid-Atlantic region and elsewhere throughout the United States.
Publications: Co-author, 'American Bar Association's Real Property Tax Deskbook' chapter on District of Columbia real property taxation.
Personal: JD, University of Miami; AB, Duke University.

KLEIN, Michael
Wilmer, Cutler & Pickering, Washington, DC 202 663 6620
Michael.Klein@wilmer.com
Recommended in Litigation
Specialization: Partner in firm's corporate, litigation, and securities law sections. Wide-ranging practice, including experience in wide array of corporate and securities transactions and related litigation. Experiences, both as lawyer and businessman, as founder, active investor, executive and director of public and private businesses, creating and sustaining ventures, taking companies public and private, and representing and counseling them, their executives and/or directors in various circumstances. This is brought to bear in board rooms and courtrooms, as lawyer and 'Special Counsel' to boards of directors and special committees in various settings, including negotiated and litigated control contests, reviews of internal controls and accounting issues, inquiries into questioned executive and corporate conduct, and on a variety of other matters related to corporate governance. Has counseled and litigated successfully in a number of high stakes and well publicized engagements across a broad spectrum of issues involving both private parties and in opposition to federal agencies.
Prof. Memberships: American Law Institute; Editorial Board, 'Insights', (cor-

porate and securities law journal).
Career: Admitted to Florida (1966) and District of Columbia (1969) bars. Joined firm as associate in 1969, became partner in 1974.
Personal: Graduate of the University of Miami (BBA 1963; JD 1966) and Harvard University (LLM 1967).

KLEPPER, Martin
Skadden, Arps, Slate, Meagher & Flom LLP, Washington, DC 202 371 7120
mklepper@skadden.com
Recommended in Energy, Projects
Specialization: Development, financing and acquisition of energy, transportation and other large infrastructure projects throughout the world. Also handled major transactions related to privatization and restructurings within the electric and gas industry, and has extensive experience in financing sports stadiums and arenas. Has been the lead lawyer representing developers of power plants and gas pipelines, contractors, banks, underwriters and equity investors in connection with acquisitions, joint ventures and project financings (over 100 major transactions in more than 24 countries) totalling more than $10 billion and including some of the most complex transactions in recent years. Frequent guest speaker, chairman of programs, and lecturer at project and international financing conferences. Has written and edited numerous publications, including more than 20 articles.
Prof. Memberships: Board of Directors, National Independent Energy Producers (1993-95); Member, Co-ordinating Group on Energy Law, American Bar Association (1985-89); Chairman, Energy Law Committee, Real Property Probate and Trust Section, American Bar Association (1980-86).
Career: JD, Rutgers Law School, 1973 (Articles Editor, Rutgers Law Review); BA, University of Pennsylvania, Wharton School, 1969; Adjunct Professor, Georgetown Law School, 2002 - present.

KNAUSS, Charles
Swidler Berlin Shereff Friedman LLP, Washington, DC 202 424 7500
Recommended in Environment

KRAFTSON, Daniel
Jenkens & Gilchrist, Washington, DC 202 326 1500
Recommended in Construction

KUNEY, David
Sidley Austin Brown & Wood, Washington, DC 202 736 8000
Recommended in Insolvency

LAKE, William T
Wilmer, Cutler & Pickering, Washington, DC 202 663 6725
William.Lake@wilmer.com
Recommended in Communications
Specialization: Partner and member of the firm's Management Committee. Also co-chairs the firm's Communications and E-Commerce Practice Group. Practice focuses on US and EU telecommunications, competition, data protection, and intellectual property. Represents major US and European telecommunications operators (wireline and wireless) in regulatory matters and transactions. In collaboration with the firm's European offices, assists companies in obtaining regulatory and competition clearances for transnational mergers and acquisitions in the telecommunications industry.
Prof. Memberships: American Bar Association Forum Committee on Communications, Section of International Law and Practice, Section of Science and Technology, and Section of Patent, Trademark, and Copyright Law; Federal Communications Bar Association; US Council for International Business.
Career: Law clerk to Justice John M Harlan, US Supreme Court, 1969-70, and to Judge Henry J Friendly, US Court of Appeals for the Second Circuit, 1968-69. Joined firm in 1973 and became partner in 1977. Served as Principal Deputy Legal Adviser at the US Department of State from 1980-81. Writes and speaks frequently on telecommunications topics.
Personal: Graduate of Yale University (BA 1965, summa cum laude, Economics) and Stanford University (LLB 1968, first in class).

LAMM, Carolyn
White & Case LLP, Washington, DC 202 626 3600
Recommended in Arbitration

LANG, Jane
Sprenger & Lang, PLLC, Washington, DC 202 265 8010
Recommended in Employment

LEDDY, Mark
Cleary Gottlieb Steen & Hamilton, Washington, DC 202 974 1500
Recommended in Antitrust
See New York chapter for profile

LENNON, Daniel
Latham & Watkins LLP, Washington, DC 202 637 2347
dan.lennon@lw.com
Recommended in Corporate/M&A
Specialization: Partner, Corporate Department. Significant experience in mergers and acquisitions, venture capital financings, and private and public securities offerings. Particular expertise in acquisition and financing transactions on behalf of leveraged buyout sponsors and other private equity firms. Clients include The Carlyle Group, Arlington Capital Partners, The Halifax Group and United Defense Industries. Represented The Carlyle Group in its $915 million leveraged acquisition of Rexnord Corporation and its $850 million leveraged acquisition of United Defense and represents United Defense in its IPO.
Personal: JD, Catholic University of America, 1990. BA, University of Notre Dame, 1987.

LETZLER, Kenneth
Arnold & Porter, Washington, DC 202 942 5000
Kenneth_Letzler@aporter.com
Recommended in Antitrust
Specialization: Specializes in antitrust and trade regulation with an emphasis on firms involved in the pharmaceutical business and biotechnology, such as GlaxoSmithKline, Hoffmann-LaRoche Inc. and Monsanto. He has advised on antitrust aspects of international joint ventures and has negotiated collaborative research and development arrangements between US pharmaceutical companies and a European pharmaceutical research firm. He has served as counsel before the Federal Trade Commission and the Department of Justice in numerous merger cases, including cases where the principal assets involved were patent, know-how, and other intellectual property rights. He also clerked for the US Court of Appeals, District of Columbia Circuit. Is admitted to the District of Columbia Bar and is admitted to practice in front of the US Supreme Court.
Personal: Education: holds a JD from Harvard Law School (1968) and a BA from Columbia University (1965).

LEVINE, Henry D
Levine, Blaszak, Block & Boothby LLP, Washington, DC 202 857 2550
hlevine@lb3law.com
Recommended in Communications
Specialization: Specializing in the representation of large telecommunications users in transactions and disputes with carriers, he has negotiated contracts and resolved disputes on behalf of such Fortune 100 Companies as Merrill Lynch, General Motors, IBM, Marriott, Lockheed Martin, the Securities Industry Association, and Visa.
Prof. Memberships: The District of Columbia Bar, the ABA Forum Committee on Communications Law, and the Federal Communications Bar Association.
Career: Admitted to the Bars of New York, the District of Columbia, and Federal courts including the United States Supreme Court. From 1983 through 1992, he was a partner in the Washington, DC office of *Morrison & Foerster*, where he founded and chaired the firm's Communications Group. He has been a partner in *Levine, Blaszak, Block & Boothby, LLP* since the firm was founded in 1993. In 1996, Network World named him one of the 25 most powerful people in networking, citing his "unique experience, knowledge and savvy" in "dealing with the pricing, terms and conditions that shape custom network contracts."
Personal: BA (magna cum laude) from Yale in 1972; JD (magna cum laude) from Harvard Law School in 1976; Master's Degree in Public Policy from Harvard's Kennedy School of Government in 1976.

LEVINE, Lee
Levine Sullivan & Koch LLP, Washington, DC 202 508 1100
Recommended in Media & Entertainment

LEWIS, Daniel
Arnold & Porter, Washington, DC 202 942 5661
Daniel_Lewis@aporter.com
Recommended in Insolvency
Specialization: Specializes in bankruptcy law. Currently head of *Arnold & Porter's* bankruptcy practice group, he has served as counsel to such clients as Braniff Airways, Inc., the Equity Security Holders Committee in the Global Marine bankruptcy, and the State of Maryland in the EPIC real estate organization. He also has handled real estate workout and bankruptcy matters for The Boston Company and New York Life Insurance Company. He has handled numerous real estate workout and bankruptcy matters from Lennar Partners. Has also represented a major creditor in the Mission Insurance receivership proceedings, the second largest insurance receivership in the US, and has counseled Baker Hughes Corporation in the resolution of its $200 million patent infringement claim.

LEWIS, William
Morgan, Lewis & Bockius LLP, Washington, DC 202 739 3000
Recommended in Environment

LIBIN, Jerome
Sutherland Asbill & Brennan LLP, Washington, DC 202 383 0145
jlibin@sablaw.com
Recommended in Tax
Specialization: Firmwide Chair of Tax Practice Group, handles broad range of domestic and international tax matters for US and foreign clients. Principal areas of concentration are corporate acquisitions, dispositions and restructurings, financial transactions and transfer pricing. Works extensively in both tax planning and tax controversy, including tax litigation. Advises multinational corporations such as General Motors, Philip Morris, Honeywell International, Hershey Foods and Hallmark Cards.
Prof. Memberships: President of International Fiscal Association (IFA), largest professional organization in world devoted exclusively to study of international

LEADERS — DISTRICT OF COLUMBIA

tax matters. Member of American Bar Association Tax Section (former Council Member) and District of Columbia Bar Taxation Division (former Chair). Also Fellow, American College of Tax Counsel.
Career: Joined *Sutherland Asbill & Brennan* in 1961, following year of service as law clerk to US Supreme Court Justice Charles Whittaker.
Publications: Author or co-author of numerous articles in various tax publications.
Personal: University of Michigan Law School (editor-in-chief of Law Review); Northwestern University.

LIPMAN, Andy
Swidler Berlin Shereff Friedman LLP, Washington, DC 202 424 7500
Recommended in Communications

LIPSEY, Charles
Finnegan Henderson Farabow Garrett & Dunner LLP, Washington, DC
202 408 4000
charles.lipsey@finnegan.com
Recommended in Intellectual Property
Specialization: Partner. Concentrates on intellectual property litigation, particularly patent infringement litigation, in the district courts, the Federal Circuit, and the US Supreme. Has handled cases involving mechanical, chemical, and electrical technologies, with emphasis on biotechnology and pharmaceutical chemistry. Has extensive experience in patent infringement litigation, patent arbitration proceedings, and patent interferences.
Career: Admitted in 1977, Virginia; 1979, District of Columbia; US Court of Appeals for the Federal Circuit; registered to practice before US Patent and Trademark Office.
Publications: Co-Author of 'Patent Law Perspectives', Matthew Bender & Co. 1982-88.
Personal: Born November 27, 1950. Georgia Institute of Technology (BSChE, 1972); The George Washington University National Law Center (JD, with high honors, 1977) (LLM, Patent and Trademark Regulation Law with high honors, 1981).

LITT, Daniel
Dickstein Shapiro Morin & Oshinsky LLP, Washington, DC 202 785 9700
Recommended in Insolvency

LOFTIS, James
Gibson, Dunn & Crutcher LLP, Washington, DC 202 955 8500
Recommended in Antitrust

LONARDO, Joseph
Vorys, Sater, Seymour and Pease, Washington, DC 202 467 8811
Recommended in Environment

LUDWISZEWSKI, Raymond
Gibson, Dunn & Crutcher LLP, Washington, DC 202 955 8500
Recommended in Environment

LUPO, Raphael
McDermott, Will & Emery, Washington, DC 202 756 8366
rlupo@mwe.com
Recommended in Intellectual Property
Specialization: Partner in the Intellectual Property Department. Focuses on patent, trademark, copyright and trade secrets litigation and counseling. Has extensive experience as lead counsel in federal district courts and before International Trade Commission. Has presented and argued over 100 appeals before Court of Appeals for the Federal Circuit and its predecessor(CCPA). Has represented clients in complex technology areas involving computers and computer-related technologies, including integrated circuit cases involving DRAMs, SRAMs, EPROMs, ASICs, flash memories, microprocessors and other semiconductor configurations.
Prof. Memberships: Former President of the Giles S Rich American Inn of Court, 1995. Former member of the Amicus Committee of the AIPLA and the Amicus Committee of the American Bar Association Patent, Trademark and Copyright Section.
Career: US patent examiner, 1964-69. Associate Solicitor, US Patent Office, 1969-77 and acting member, Board of Patent Interferences and director, Patent Planning Staff. Deputy assistant general counsel for patents, Department of Energy, 1977. Went into private practice in 1980.
Personal: Received BSEE and JD from the George Washington University. Admitted to Virginia, District of Columbia, US Supreme Court, the Court of Appeals for the Federal Circuit, the District Court for the District of Columbia, and the District Court for the Eastern District of Virginia.

MACBETH, Angus
Sidley Austin Brown & Wood, Washington, DC 202 736 8000
Recommended in Environment

MAGEE, John B
McKee Nelson LLP, Washington, DC 202 775 8671
jmagee@mckeenelson.com
Recommended in Tax
Specialization: Taxation, tax controversy, international tax, transfer pricing. Has extensive experience in all aspects of income tax planning, IRS administrative proceedings and tax litigation.
Career: Prior to joining *McKee Nelson* in January 2000, was chair of the tax practice department at the Washington DC law firm of *Miller & Chevalier*. Also served as a member of the firm's executive committee. Is a frequent lecturer at the Practicing Law Institute, the Tax Executives Institute, the Federal Bar Association and other forums.
Personal: Received an LLM in Taxation from Georgetown University Law Center in 1977 and a JD in 1972 from the University of Washington School of Law, where he served on the law review and received the Order of the Coif distinction.

MARTIN, Keith
Chadbourne & Parke LLP, Washington, DC 202 974 5600
Recommended in Projects

MASUR, Daniel A
Mayer, Brown, Rowe & Maw, Washington, DC 202 263 3226
dmasur@mayerbrownrowe.com
Recommended in Communications
Specialization: Partner in the Corporate, Information Technology, Telecommunications and Outsourcing Practices. Formerly Vice President and General Counsel of I-NET, Inc., a rapidly growing provider of information technology, network and outsourcing services. Represents major international firms in a broad range of information technology, communications and outsourcing transactions. Representative transactions include the outsourcing of business processes and functions, information technology services and support, application development and maintenance, telecommunications services, network management and support, e-commerce transaction processing and support, and leasing/procurement. Representative transactions also include software and systems development and implementation, software licensing, systems integration, and strategic alliances/joint ventures. Representative clients include established and emerging firms in banking, real estate, pharmaceuticals, consumer products, electronic commerce, financial services, insurance, health care, distribution, manufacturing, health care, forestry products, telecommunications, aerospace, defense contracting, chemicals, chemicals, life sciences and electric power.
Prof. Memberships: Admitted to practice in the District of Columbia (1977).
Career: Joined *Mayer, Brown, Rowe & Maw* as a partner in 1997. Prior to that, served as a partner with *Reed, Smith, Shaw & McClay* 1994-97 and as Vice President and General Counsel for I-NET, Inc. (1994-97).
Personal: Earned JD from Georgetown University in 1977, (Editor of the Georgetown Law Journal), and BA from Marquette University in 1974.

MAY, Gregory
Freshfields Bruckhaus Deringer LLP, Washington, DC 202 777/969 4500
Recommended in Tax

MAZO, Mark
Hogan & Hartson LLP, Washington, DC 202 637 5673
memazo@hhlaw.com
Recommended in Corporate/M&A
Specialization: Senior partner in *Hogan & Hartson LLP*'s International Business Transactions practice, representing international investors and European and US companies in cross-border M&A, strategic investments, and joint ventures in Europe and the US. Principal clients include the European Aeronautic Defence and Space Company (EADS) and its business units (including Eurocopter and EADS SOGERMA), HRH Prince Alwaleed Bin Talal Bin Abdulaziz al Saud, Alcatel Space, the News Corporation and the Titan Corporation.
Publications: Numerous publications on foreign investment into the United States. Lectured extensively on international joint ventures.
Personal: Born 12 January 1950. Education: Princeton University (AB,1971, magna cum laude, Phi Beta Kappa, Distinguished Military Graduate-US Army); Harvard Law School (JD, 1974, cum laude). Listed in 'Who's Who In America', 'Who's Who In the World', and 'Who's Who In American Law'.

MCDANIELS, William
Williams & Connolly LLP, Washington, DC 202 434 5055
wmcdaniels@wc.com
Recommended in Litigation
Specialization: For more than 35 years, he has been actively engaged in civil and criminal trial work, including first amendment and media work, contract, products liability, medical malpractice, intellectual property, employment, administrative law, antitrust, business torts, general commercial litigation, Qui Tam defense, and homicide. His civil practice has included numerous cases involving challenges under the Administrative Procedure Act to actions of various federal agencies. In white collar criminal defense, he has successfully defended cases involving allegations of bank fraud, healthcare fraud, sports bribery, gambling offenses, money laundering, environmental crimes, and violations of the Economic Espionage Act.

MCDAVID, Janet L
Hogan & Hartson LLP, Washington, DC 212 637 8780
jlmcdavid@hhlaw.com
Recommended in Antitrust
Specialization: Partner in the Washington, DC office of *Hogan & Hartson LLP*, specializing in antitrust, with a particular emphasis on government investigations and litigation. Has served as counsel in a number of significant antitrust matters, including for Carnival Corporation in its proposed merger with P&O Princess Cruises; for DaimlerChrysler, Ford, and GM in several joint ventures; for American Express in the US Justice Department investigation of and litigation with Visa and MasterCard; for General Dynamics in several defence industry transactions; and for Mobil in its merger with Exxon.

Prof. Memberships: Former chair of the Section of Antitrust Law of the American Bar Association (ABA) (1999-2000). Also previously served as chair-elect (1998-99), vice-chair (1997-98), and program officer of the ABA Antitrust Section (1994-97); a member of the Antitrust Section Council (1991-94); and chair or vice-chair of the Antitrust Section's Committees on Franchising, Section 2 of the Sherman Act, and Civil Practice and Procedure (1985-97). She was a member of the Governing Committee of the ABA Forum on Franchising (1991-97) and chair of the 1993 Annual Forum on Franchising. She is also a member of the Antitrust Council of the US Chamber of Commerce and the US Council for International Business.
Career: Member of the Advisory Team to the Transition Team of the Federal Trade Commission (FTC) for the Bush Administration in 2000 and was a member of the FTC Transition Team for the Clinton Administration in 1992. Also served as co-chair of the ABA Antitrust Section's Task Force on Competition Policy, which provided advice on antitrust issues to the Clinton Administration. Also served on two US Department of Defense (DoD) Antitrust Task Forces (1993-94 and 1996-97) appointed by the Secretary and General Counsel of the DoD to advise on antitrust issues involved in defence industry mergers and joint ventures, and on vertical integration and supplier decisions among defence contractors.
Publications: Author/co-author of many books and articles involving antitrust law, including: 'Mergers & Acquisitions', 'The Antitrust Evidence Handbook', 'Antitrust and Health Care', and 'Antitrust & Trade Associations Practice Guide' (all published by the ABA Antitrust Section); 'Proposed Reform of the EU Merger Regulation: A US Perspective'; 'Global Merger Review Regimes'; 'EU Merger Regulation'; 'How to Avoid Negotiations on Second Requests'; 'What's the FTC Up To'; 'Globalization and the EU'; 'Globalization of Premerger Notification and Review: Practical Problems and Solutions'; 'Antitrust Intersection with IP'; 'The Revival of Franchise Antitrust Claims'; 'The Defense of Mergers in the Defense Industry'; 'Antitrust Issues in Health Care Reform'; and 'The 1992 Horizontal Merger Guidelines: A Practitioner's View of Key Issues in Defending a Merger'. A frequent speaker on antitrust issues.
Personal: Received her JD from Georgetown University Law Center in 1974, where she was an editor of the Georgetown Law Journal, and BA with honors from Northwestern University in 1971. Joined *Hogan & Hartson LLP* in 1974. Current member of the District of Columbia Bar, and is admitted to practice before the United States Supreme Court and several other federal courts.

MCGRANE, John
Morgan, Lewis & Bockius LLP, Washington, DC 202 739 3000
Recommended in Energy

MCISAAC, Christopher
Winston & Strawn, Washington, DC 202 371 5971
cmcisaac@winston.com
Recommended in Projects
Specialization: International and domestic project financings, cross-border lease financings, secured lending.
Career: Member of the Executive Committee. Joined firm as partner, 1995. Associate, *Milbank, Tweed, Hadley & McCloy*, 1985-95, Washington, DC, Singapore, and Tokyo.
Publications: 'Leveraged Leasing of Power Facilities', 'Equipment Leasing - Leveraged Leasing, Practising Law Institute', 1999.
Personal: University of North Carolina, BA, with highest honors, Phi Beta Kappa, 1982, Morehead Scholar; University of Virginia School of Law, JD, 1985, Dillard Fellow.

MCKEE, Bill
McKee Nelson LLP, Washington, DC 202 775 8580
bmckee@mckeenelson.com
Recommended in Tax
Specialization: Practice Areas: taxation. Practice encompasses all areas of federal taxation, with a special emphasis on partnership taxation.
Career: Prior to founding the firm in November 1999, was a tax partner in the DC office of *King & Spalding*. Joined *King & Spalding* in 1983. Served as Tax Legislative Counsel at the US Treasury Department from 1981-83. Is a member of the American Law Institute, the American College of Tax Counsel, and the National Institute for Tax Professionals. Was a law professor at the University of Virginia School of Law from 1969-81. Also a visiting professor in the Graduate Tax Programme at the New York University School of Law from 1975-77. Frequent speaker at seminars around the country on the subject of partnership taxation.
Publications: Co-author of the treatise 'Federal Taxation of Partnerships and Partners' (Warren, Gorham & Lamont, 3rd edition, 1997), and also co-authored 'Federal Taxation of Partnerships and Partners: Structuring and Drafting Agreements' (Warren, Gorham & Lamont, 2nd edition, 1993).
Personal: A 1966 cum laude graduate of Yale University, received a JD, magna cum laude, in 1969 from the Harvard Law School, and was an editor of the 'Harvard Law Review'.

MCLUCAS, William
Wilmer, Cutler & Pickering, Washington, DC 202 663 6622
William.McLucas@wilmer.com
Recommended in Litigation
Specialization: Partner in firm's securities section, with a practice that focuses on securities enforcement, regulation, and litigation matters.
Career: Admitted to Pennsylvania (1975), District of Columbia (1998), and New York (1999) bars. Has been a partner of the firm since joining in 1998. Formerly with the US Securities and Exchange Commission's Division of Enforcement, where he served as Director of Enforcement for eight years. While at the SEC, received the National Public Service Award, the Tom C Clark Outstanding Lawyer Award, and the President's Award for Distinguished Executive Service. Named one of the One Hundred Most Influential Attorneys in America by a leading US law journal.
Personal: Graduate of Pennsylvania State University (BA 1972, Phi Beta Kappa) and Temple University (JD 1975).

MCMANUS, Joseph
McManus Schor Asmar & Darden LLP, Washington, DC 202 296 9260
Recommended in Construction

MELAMED, Doug
Wilmer, Cutler & Pickering, Washington, DC 202 663 6090
Douglas.Melamed@wilmer.com
Recommended in Antitrust
Specialization: Leading authority on antitrust law, who has held senior government antitrust positions, has had extensive experience in private practice, and has written and lectured widely on antitrust and competition issues. Practice includes counseling businesses about antitrust issues related to licensing, distribution and other competitive strategies, joint ventures, mergers and other transactions and representing businesses in private and government antitrust litigation, in government investigations and in the merger clearance process. Recent major matters have included the Bayer/Aventis CropScience, Aramark/Service Master, and Anschutz/Regal mergers and the FTC administrative case against Rambus, Inc.
Prof. Memberships: American Bar Association, Antitrust Section; American Law Institute.
Career: Partner, *Wilmer, Cutler & Pickering*; co-chair of firm's Antitrust and Competition Practice Group and member of firm's Policy Committee. Acting Assistant Attorney General, Antitrust Division, US Department of Justice (September 2000-January 20, 2001) and Principal Deputy Assistant Attorney General, Antitrust Division, US Department of Justice (October 1996-September 2000). Distinguished Visitor from Practice (1992-93) and Adjunct Professor (1993-94) at Georgetown University Law Center.
Personal: Harvard Law School (JD 1970, cum laude); Yale College (BA 1967, Political Science and Economics, Phi Beta Kappa and other academic honorary societies, magna cum laude, Honors with Exceptional Distinction in Political Science and Economics).

MENOTTI, David
Shaw Pittman, Washington, DC 202 663 8000
Recommended in Environment

METZGER, Richard
Lawler Metzger & Milkman LLC, Washington, DC 202 777 7700
Recommended in Communications

MILCH, Thomas
Arnold & Porter, Washington, DC 202 942 5030
Thomas_Milch@aporter.com
Recommended in Environment
Specialization: A partner in Washington, DC, he directs the firm's environmental practice. His practice principally includes federal enforcement and private party litigation under US environmental law, counseling national and multinational companies on environmental compliance issues, and addressing environmental issues that arise in complex corporate and real estate transactions. He has served as lead counsel on major Superfund cleanups and in contaminated property litigation for Fortune 100 companies. He has particular expertise in parent/subsidiary and successor liability, natural resources damages, sediment cleanups, and environmental toxic tort litigation.
Prof. Memberships: He has served as a member of the ABA's Standing Committee on Environmental Law (1996-1998), and was Chairman of the ABA's Special Committee on Environmental Litigation Techniques (SONREEL) (1991-1994). From 1992 to 1998, he also served on the Board of Directors and Executive Committee of the Environmental Law Institute. He presently serves on the Board of RESOLVE, Inc., a nonprofit organization committed to alternative dispute resolution in the environmental field, and Wildlife Trust International, an international conservation group committed to biodiversity protection.
Personal: Education: he is a graduate of Yale College summa cum laude and Yale Law School, where he served as an officer of the 'Yale Law Journal'.

MILKMAN, Ruth
Lawler Metzger & Milkman LLC, Washington, DC 202 777 7700
Recommended in Communications

MOORE, Robert
Miller & Chevalier, Washington, DC 202 626 5800
Recommended in Tax

DISTRICT OF COLUMBIA
LEADERS

NAEVE, Clifford M
Skadden, Arps, Slate, Meagher & Flom LLP, Washington, DC 202 371 7070
mnaeve@skadden.com
Recommended in Energy

Specialization: Partner, Washington, DC Involved in energy policy and regulatory matters such as the restructuring of the electric power industry, having represented clients in a variety of federal and state regulatory proceedings and restructuring transactions. Has represented numerous utilities before the FERC in merger proceedings and has been involved in several friendly and unsolicited merger transactions. Has worked with a variety of utilities on innovative electric transmission cases, wholesale rate proceedings and retail access experiments. Has represented major oil and gas producers, natural gas pipelines, electric co-operatives and financial institutions in a variety of commercial and regulatory matters. Also represents clients before Congress on issues ranging from energy and environmental matters to taxes and tender offer reforms.
Career: JD, George Washington University, 1984 (Highest Honors; Order of the Coif); MPA, LBJ School of Public Affairs, The University of Texas at Austin, 1972; BS, Mechanical Engineering, The University of Texas at Austin, 1970; Legislative Director, Office of US Senator Lloyd Bentsen (1978-80); Commissioner, Federal Energy Regulatory Commission (1985-88); Member, Electricity Advisory Board to the Secretary of Energy (2002 - present).

NAKAHATA, John
Harris, Wiltshire & Grannis LLP, Washington, DC 202 730 1300
Recommended in Communications

NATHAN, Irvin
Arnold & Porter, Washington, DC 202 942 5070
Irvin_Nathan@aporter.com
Recommended in Litigation

Specialization: A senior litigation partner who regularly represents corporations, and their officers, directors and employees, in criminal and complex civil litigations, including securities fraud, civil RICO, and corporate compliance matters. He is a Fellow of the American College of Trial Lawyers, a member of the American Law Institute and a Fellow of the American Bar Foundation. He is listed in a leading legal review. He has tried many jury and bench trials and emergency injunctive hearings in federal and state courts.
Career: In addition to his practice at *Arnold & Porter*, he has served as Principal Associate Deputy Attorney General at the US Department of Justice under Attorney General Janet Reno (1993-94); Deputy Assistant Attorney General for Enforcement in the Criminal Division under Attorneys General Griffin Bell and Benjamin Civiletti (1979-81); Special Minority Counsel to the United States Senate Intelligence Committee (1981) and Chairman of the White Collar Crime Committee of the Criminal Justice Section of the American Bar Association (1982-84).

NEAHER, Edward
White & Case LLP, Washington, DC 202 626 3600
Recommended in Projects

NELSON, William F
McKee Nelson LLP, Washington, DC 202 775 8582
wnelson@mckeenelson.com
Recommended in Tax

Specialization: Taxation, tax controversy. Practice encompasses all areas of federal taxation, with a special emphasis on partnership taxation and controversy matters.
Prof. Memberships: Prior to founding the firm in November 1999, was a tax partner in *King & Spalding's* Atlanta office, joining the firm in 1972. From 1986-88, served as Chief Counsel for the Internal Revenue Service, returning to *King & Spalding* at the end of his appointment. Received a JD from the University of Virginia School of Law in 1972, where he was editor in chief of the 'Virginia Law Review' and was named to the Order of the Coif.
Publications: Co-author of the treatise 'Federal Taxation of Partnerships and Partners' (Warren, Gorham & Lamont, 3rd edition, 1997), and also co-authored 'Federal Taxation of Partnerships and Partners: Structuring and Drafting Agreements' (Warren, Gorham & Lamont, 2nd edition, 1993). Has written articles on tax law for numerous journals, including 'The Tax Law Review', 'Taxes', and the 'Virginia Law Review'. Frequent lecturer at various tax institutes.

NESS, Andrew D
Thelen Reid & Priest LLP, Washington, DC 202 508 4368
adness@thelenreid.com
Recommended in Construction

Specialization: Has concentrated on dispute resolution and counseling with respect to construction and engineering-related matters and government contracts since 1979, and has represented many major contractors, owners/developers and engineering firms. Lead counsel for numerous major construction disputes on complex projects, including the Quetta Power Project (Pakistan), Petrotrin and Slovnaft Refineries (Trinidad & Slovakia), Marriott Hotels (Virginia), TVA Cumberland FGD Retrofit (Tennessee), Great Lakes Pulp & Fibre (Michigan), Great Mall of the Bay Area (California) and NIH Clinical Research Center (Maryland). In addition to litigation in federal and state courts and both domestic and international arbitrations, has extensive experience in the use of mediation and other alternative dispute resolution techniques. Also engaged regularly in drafting and negotiation of design and construction contracts.
Prof. Memberships: American Bar Association Forum on the Construction Industry (past Chair of Division 10, Legislation and Environment). ABA Public Contract Law Section (Vice-Chair, Construction Division). Charter Member of the Advisory Board for bi-weekly publication 'The Government Contractor.'
Career: Managing Partner of *Thelen Reid & Priest LLP's* Washington, DC Office. Admitted to practice in the District of Columbia, Virginia and California, the US Court of Federal Claims, and five US District Courts.
Publications: Co-editor of Federal Government Construction Contracts (ABA Forum on Construction Industry 2003), and authored chapters in 2002 Construction Law Update (Aspen 2002), Construction Law Handbook (Aspen 1999) and Construction Subcontracting: A Guide for Industry Professionals (John Wiley & Sons 1991). Authored numerous articles in The Construction Lawyer, Construction Briefings and other industry publications.
Personal: Graduate of Harvard Law School, JD (1977), magna cum laude, served as Articles Editor of the Harvard Journal on Legislation. BS (1974) from Stanford University, with distinction, majoring in Electrical Engineering. Served as Law Clerk to the Hon. Robert F Peckham, Chief Judge, US District Court for Northern District of California.

NEWBORN, Steve A
Clifford Chance US LLP, Washington, DC 202 912 5005
steve.newborn@cliffordchance.com
Recommended in Antitrust

Specialization: Serves as global head of the *Clifford Chance US* antitrust practice. He was the director of litigation at the Federal Trade Commission's Bureau of Competition where he headed its merger enforcement program and was awarded the Brandeis Award as the commission's finest litigator. He continues to conduct major litigation but specializes in mergers and acquisitions, obtaining approvals for well over a hundred transactions. Chambers 2002-03 reported that some commentators rated Newborn as 'someone you'll turn to on a life and death merger transaction.' He was a major contributor to the 1992 Federal Merger Guidelines.

NEWMAN, Richard
Arent Fox, Washington, DC 202 857 6000
Recommended in Real Estate

NICKEL, Henry
Hunton & Williams, Washington, DC 202 955 1500
Recommended in Environment

NORTON, Floyd
Morgan, Lewis & Bockius LLP, Washington, DC 202 739 3000
Recommended in Energy

O'DONNELL, Earle
Dewey Ballantine LLP, Washington, DC 202 429 2327
eodonnell@deweyballantine.com
Recommended in Energy

Specialization: Energy (including trial and appellate litigation, energy project development, energy company M&A, and federal energy compliance).
Prof. Memberships: Energy Bar Association; Member of the United States Supreme Court Bar and the Bars of many courts of appeal; Member of Maryland and District of Columbia Bars; Secretary Foundation of the Energy Law Journal; Member, Board of Directors, Charitable Foundation of the Energy Bar Association.
Career: Chair of Energy Practice Group, *Dewey Ballantine LLP*; private practice since 1975.
Publications: Consulting Editor and Co-Author of 'Global Overview' and United States Chapters, Electricity Regulation 2003, published by Global Competition Review (2002); Co-Author of 'The Challenge of Contracting In A Retail Open Access Environment,' Competitive Utility, December (1999); Co-Author of 'Acquiring Ownership of Distressed Assets: A Golden Opportunity,' Competitive Utility, December (1998).
Personal: Born February 2, 1949; JD with honors, George Washington University National Law Center (Law Review, Order of the Coif), 1975.

O'NEILL, Brian
LeBoeuf, Lamb, Greene & MacRae, LLP, Washington, DC 202 986 8012
boneill@llgm.com
Recommended in Energy

Specialization: Provides advice to international clients as to energy privatization and regulatory matters. Clients include electric utilities, several major interstate natural gas pipelines and one of the largest domestic oil pipelines. Has litigated regulatory proceedings involving complex ratemaking issues, new multi-million dollar construction projects, transportation and supply contract matters.
Prof. Memberships: District of Columbia Bar; Florida Bar; Federal Energy Bar Association; American Bar Association.
Career: Joined *LeBoeuf* in 1980. *Farmer, Shibley, McGuinn & Flood* (1975-80); Federal Power Commission, Trial Attorney (1972-75); Military Service: US Air Force (1971-72).
Personal: Florida State University (JD) 1971; and Florida State University (BA) 1968.

OOSTERHUIS, Paul
Skadden, Arps, Slate, Meagher & Flom LLP, Washington, DC 202 371 7130
poosterh@skadden.com
Recommended in Tax

Specialization: Partner, Washington, DC. International and corporate lax law. Represents clients on a wide range of international and domestic tax matters with experience in international acquisitions, dispositions and joint venture transactions. Also represents US and non-US multinational companies in cross-border financing arrangements and non-transactional international tax planning, in cross-border acquisitions. Represented IBM Corporation in its acquisition of the PwC Consulting firms, American General Corporation, Daimler-Benz, and MCI (now MCI WorldCom), among others. In recent years, has also represented numerous clients in post-acquisition integration efforts, including: Hewlett Packard and Compaq Computer Corporation. Has represented various clients with respect to the international aspects of public spin-off transactions. Apart from specific transactions, regularly represents clients on international tax planning matters generally, including transfer pricing matters. Represents clients before the US Department of Treasury and the Congress on tax policy matters and technical issues. Frequent lecturer before the Tax Executives Institute and the American Bar Association, and writes on a variety of tax-related topics for professional publications.
Career: JD, Harvard University, 1973 (cum laude); BA, Brown University, 1969 (magna cum laude); Legislation Attorney, Joint Committee on Taxation, US Congress (1973-76); Legislation Counsel, Joint Committee on Taxation, US Congress (1977-78); taught international tax as an Adjunct Professor of Law, Georgetown University Law Center (1977-83).

OSHINSKY, Jerold
Dickstein Shapiro Morin & Oshinsky LLP, Washington, DC 202 785 9700
Recommended in Insurance

OSNOS, David
Arent Fox, Washington, DC
202 857 6000
Recommended in Real Estate

O'SULLIVAN, John
Chadbourne & Parke LLP, Washington, DC 202 974 5600
Recommended in Energy

PARI, Joseph
Dewey Ballantine LLP, Washington, DC
202 862 1000
jpari@deweyballantine.com
Recommended in Tax

Specialization: Has represented numerous acquirers, targets, debtors, creditors' committees, investment banks, investors, and distributing and controlled corporations in acquisitive and divisive transactions. Practice relates to the federal income taxation of mergers, acquisitions, spin-offs, other divisive strategies, restructurings, workouts in and out of bankruptcy and acquisition financing, with a particular emphasis on corporate tax planning, the preservation and utilisation of favorable tax attributes such as net operating losses, and consolidated return matters, and also to the use of pass-through entities in acquisitive and divisive transactions and certain complex financial products.
Prof. Memberships: American Bar Association: Council Director for Corporate Tax Committee, Committee on Affiliated and Related Corporations, and Bankruptcy Task Force; Former Chair of the Committee on Affiliated and Related Corporations; Former Chair of the Subcommittee on Consolidated Returns of the Committee on Affiliated and Related Corporations; Co-Chair of the 1998-2002 IRS-Federal Bar Association Domestic Corporate Tax Symposia; Advisory Board of the New York University Institute on Federal Taxation; Editorial Advisory Boards of the Journal of Corporate Taxation and the Mergers and Acquisitions tax journal; Advisory Board of the Federal Bar Association; and Advisory Board of the National Foreign Trade Council, Inc.
Career: Partner, *Dewey Ballantine LLP*, since 1996; and adjunct faculty member at the Georgetown University Law Center.
Publications: Published works include 'Anti-Freeze' - Consolidated Return Anti-Avoidance, Anti-Stuffing, and Anti-Stripping Rules Designed to Chill Tax Planning (with Gordon E. Warnke); An Issue Spotter's Guide to Certain Consolidated Return and Related Issues in Connection with Subsidiary Acquisitions and Dispositions; Corporate Distributions Under Section 355 (with Thomas F. Wessel, M. Todd Prewett and Richard D'Avino); and Two-Step Stock Acquisitions and Reverse Subsidiary Mergers (with Robert G. Lorndale, Jr).
Personal: LLM, 1988, Taxation, New York University School of Law; JD, 1987, Boston College Law School (magna cum laude); BS, 1984, Biology, Providence College (cum laude). Lives in Arlington, Virginia with wife Brigitta and son Michael.

PARKER, Richard G
O'Melveny & Myers LLP, Washington, DC
202 383 5300
Recommended in Antitrust

PARMLEY, Bruce
Hogan & Hartson LLP, Washington, DC
202 637 5644
BEParmley@HHLAW.com
Recommended in Real Estate

Specialization: Co-Director of *Hogan & Hartson LLP*'s Real Estate Group; twice elected to firm's Executive Committee since 1995. Extensive practice in real estate and related matters for 25 years, particularly hotel projects and portfolio transactions, including hotel and office investment, business structuring, equity and debt capital markets, bank and institutional financings, and all aspects of acquisitions, capital structures, sale, development, leasing, management and operations. Substantial domestic and international hotel transactional experience. Experience and techniques of the real estate, hotel, REIT, tax and related groups have been acquired during the course of two decades involving the full range of representation on projects. Provide specialized, high quality legal services in a timely, responsible and 'value added' cost effective manner. Admitted in the District of Columbia since 1976. Joined *Hogan & Hartson LLP* in 1988.

PATIN, Douglas
Spriggs & Hollingsworth, Washington, DC 202 898 5800
Recommended in Construction

PATTERSON, Donna
Arnold & Porter, Washington, DC
202 942 5000
Donna_Patterson@aporter.com
Recommended in Antitrust

Specialization: A partner in the Antitrust and Litigation Practice Groups. She joined the firm in 1988 and has represented numerous clients in FTC and Antitrust Division investigations of proposed mergers and acquisitions, in state and federal court antitrust and complex commercial litigation, and as an antitrust counselor.
Career: She was lead US antitrust counsel for General Electric in its proposed acquisition of Honeywell in 2001 and successfully represented Nucor Corp. in its acquisition of Birmingham Steel in 2002. She successfully litigated one of the rare full trials on the merits of a merger case, State of New York v. Kraft General Foods, Inc. From 1997 until August 2000, she was Deputy Assistant Attorney General in the Antitrust Division of the United States Department of Justice with primary responsibility for merger investigations. During that time she supervised the investigations and litigation of dozens of proposed transactions including US v Lockheed, US v Primestar, and US v Aetna.
Personal: Was recently named by Chambers & Partners 'Chambers Global' 2002-2003 and 2001-2002 as one of the top 25 antitrust attorneys in Washington, DC.

PERLSTEIN, William J
Wilmer, Cutler & Pickering, Washington, DC 202 663 6274
William.Perlstein@wilmer.com
Recommended in Insolvency

Specialization: Partner of the firm and Chairman of the Management Committee. Also heads the firm's bankruptcy and workout practice. Practice has included significant representations of creditor's committees, bank groups, debtors, trustees, and claims acquirers in many bankruptcy and workout cases throughout the United States. In addition, has had significant roles in the drafting of bankruptcy and bank receivership legislation including amendments affecting repurchase and swap agreements. Has testified before committees of both Houses of Congress and presented a paper on bank insolvencies before the Organisation for Economic and Co-operative Development in Paris. Major engagements have included LTV Corporation, Orange County, General Development Corp., Lomas Financial, Iridium, PSI Net, and Spectravision cases.
Prof. Memberships: Board of Directors of the American Bankruptcy Institute; Fellow and Counsel to the American College of Bankruptcy; American Law Institute; American Bar Association Business Bankruptcy Committee, and Chair of the Subcommittee on Legislation.
Career: Admitted to Connecticut (1974), District of Columbia (1976), and New York (2000) bars. Joined firm in 1975 and became partner in 1982.
Personal: Attended The London School of Economics (1969-70) and is a graduate of Union College (BA, 1971) and Yale Law School (JD, 1974).

PHILLIPS, Carter
Sidley Austin Brown & Wood, Washington, DC 202 736 8000
Recommended in Litigation

PORTER, Stephen
Arnold & Porter, Washington, DC
202 942 5004
Stephen_Porter@aporter.com
Recommended in Real Estate

Specialization: Has practiced in the real estate, tax, and corporate areas for more than 35 years. In 1974, he was a founding partner of *Dunnells, Duvall & Porter*. His practice principally involves large-scale, complex real estate transactions, corporate and real estate financing, leasing, and general business counseling. He has counseled a number of major corporations, non-profit organizations, and professional firms seeking to relocate their offices, as well as developers of hotels, marinas, and office buildings.
Prof. Memberships: He has also served as a member of the Advisory Board of the Center for Strategic & International Studies; Chairman of the Board of the Washington Performing Arts Society; Chairman of the Board of the Forum for Psychiatry and the Humanities; and as a member of the Board of Directors of the Washington School of Psychiatry. He is currently a member of the Board of Trustees of the Federal City Council and a

LEADERS — DISTRICT OF COLUMBIA

member of the Boards of both the Greater Washington Board of Trade and the District of Columbia Chamber of Commerce.

POTENZA, Joseph
Banner & Witcoff, Ltd, Washington, DC
202 508 9100
Recommended in Intellectual Property

PROGER, Phillip A
Jones Day, Washington, DC
202 879 4668
paproger@jonesday.com
Recommended in Antitrust

Specialization: Coordinator of the firm's Government Regulation Group which includes, among other practices, the Antitrust & Competition Law Practice. Focuses on the representation of clients in government antitrust investigations in the US and internationally, as well as government and private antitrust litigation. Work involves investigations concerning mergers, acquisitions and joint ventures, particularly in the healthcare, retail, chemical, automotive, telecommunication and industrial products industries. Clients for whom representation is publicly known include Aetna, Alcan Aluminum Corporation, American Greetings, Bayer, CIGNA, Clear Channel Communications, Diebold, Federated Department Stores, Louisiana-Pacific, Rite Aid, and Valero.
Prof. Memberships: Member, The American Law Institute, ABA, IBA, Ohio State Bar Association, District of Columbia Bar and the Advisory Board of BNA Antitrust and Trade Regulation Report and the editorial board of 'The M&A Lawyer';. Fellow, The American Bar Foundation.
Career: Chaired the ABA's Section of Antitrust Law from 1998-99 and is past chair of that Section's Merger Committee. Has testified before the United States Congress, the Federal Trade Commission, the Department of Justice's International Competition Policy Advisory Committee and the Organization for Economic Cooperation and Development.
Publications: Regularly writes and speaks on antitrust topics. Speaker at seminars sponsored by the American Bar Association, The American Law Institute, The Conference Board, The New England Antitrust Conference, and The Ohio Intensified Antitrust Conference.
Personal: Received JD from University of Maryland School of Law in 1973, graduating with honors and serving on the law review.

QUALE, John
Skadden, Arps, Slate, Meagher & Flom LLP, Washington, DC 202 371 7200
jquale@skadden.com
Recommended in Communications
Specialization: Partner, Washington, DC. Represents companies with respect to broad range of communications law issues arising in regulatory, legislative and transactional matters. Clients include broadcast, cable, satellite and wireless companies and a major trade association. Also represents venture capital and investment firms and commercial banks in communications matters. Served as corporate and regulatory counsel in numerous transactions involving regulated communications companies. Counseled clients on structuring transactions and assisted in negotiating and documenting purchases and sales of media properties. Also advised clients concerning FCC multiple and alien ownership regulations, providing guidance as to compliance, and assisted them in rule waivers to permit market entry. In connection with these transactions, has obtained FCC approval of license transfers in large number of contested cases. In addition to his work on transactional matters, has represented clients seeking authorizations for satellite systems and other new communications technologies. Has been frequent participant in industry and association forums and the author of several articles on federal communications regulation.
Prof. Memberships: Member, Federal Communications Bar Association (Member, Executive Committee, 1993-99; Treasurer, 1982-83, 1998-99; Co-Chair, Professional Responsibility Committee, 1989-90).
Personal: JD, Harvard Law School, 1971 (cum laude); AB, Harvard College, 1968 (cum laude).

QUARLES, John
Morgan, Lewis & Bockius LLP, Washington, DC 202 739 3000
Recommended in Environment

QUIN, Whayne
Holland & Knight LLP, Washington, DC
202 955 3000
wquin@hklaw.com
Recommended in Real Estate
Specialization: Partner in the Real Estate Department, practicing in the area of municipal law with special focus on land use, zoning, urban planning, building and housing codes, historic preservation, environmental, transportation, urban and related real estate matters. His clients have included educational institutions, nonprofit organizations, builders, developers, financial institutions, chanceries, international and national agencies, and property owners. Nationally, he has been a consultant to the private sector in the fields of land use, historic preservation, housing and building-related matters. As an urban strategist, he has advised clients on the requirements and procedures necessary to accomplish residential, commercial and industrial development. He has experience in over 3,000 cases ranging from additions to single family dwellings to large commercial and mixed-use developments throughout the District of Columbia.

RAHER, Patrick
Hogan & Hartson LLP, Washington, DC
202 637 5682
pmraher@hhlaw.com
Recommended in Environment
Specialization: Partner in the Washington, DC office of *Hogan & Hartson LLP* and Director of the firm's Environmental Practice Group. Practices principally in the environmental and transportation law areas with an emphasis on legislative, rulemaking and judicial matters relating to highly complex technical and engineering situations that affect the clients with whom he works. Works closely with trade associations, in-house legal staff and engineering and scientific support personnel within the offices of corporate clients. Helps clients vigorously pursue objectives by presenting their positions on scientific, engineering and health issues to legislative committees, governmental agencies, departments and courts in a form that is compatible with relevant environmental goals. For example, on behalf of the Snack Food Association, led the effort to have the Environmental Protection Agency (EPA) classify various production emissions as non-volatile organic compounds (VOC) to limit the need for Clean Air Act (CAA) Permitting. Is lead counsel in defending one of the nation's largest coal burning utilities against allegations that operations at over thirty-two power generating units violates CAA permitting requirements. In a matter for the pharmaceutical industry, used expert testimony to revise a proposed Clean Water Act (CWA) standard to eliminate VOC controls for water treatment and consider the issue under more favorable provisions of the CAA. In the area of Clean Air Permitting, assisted auto manufacturers, oil refiners and electric utilities in permit proceedings designed to streamline and expedite construction and operating permits to obtain pre-approval of plant changes without protracted permitting proceedings. In the area of litigation, headed up the defense of two of the largest criminal environmental investigations and spearheaded the effective settlement of two of EPA's electric utility New Source Review cases.
Prof. Memberships: Served on numerous committees from 1976-present; most recently Co-Chairperson, US EPA Subcommittee for Ozone, PM, and Regional Haze (1995-97); Member, US EPA Clean Air Act Advisory Committee (1994-present); Member, US EPA Mobile Source Advisory Committee (1994-present); and Co-Chairperson, US EPA New Source Review Subcommittee (1992-present).
Career: An appointed member of the US Environmental Protection Agency Clean Air Act Advisory Committee since 1992.
Publications: Author/co-author of many books and articles involving environmental law, including: 'Lead in Office Building Drinking Water: A Key Environmental Analysis Issue for the 1990's'; 'Hidden Pitfalls in Groundwater Cleanup Rules'; 'Gualtney' and its Progeny: The Current Status of Citizen's Suits Under the Clean Water Act'; 'Being Aware of 18 U.S.C. 1001 and the EPA Regulatory Thicket'; 'What Might the Supreme Court Say on Officer and Director Liability if US v. Park Applies to Environmental Statutes?'; 'How to Get Things Done At the EPA'; and 'Economic Internationalism vs. National Parochialism: Barcelona Traction: Journal of Law and Policy in International Business'.
Personal: Received his JD from Georgetown University Law Center in 1972, and BBA with highest honors from the University of Notre Dame in 1969. Joined *Hogan & Hartson LLP* in 1973. Current member of the Bars of District of Columbia and Maryland.

REED, Steve
Steptoe & Johnson LLP, Washington, DC
202 429 3000
Recommended in Energy

RIEDY, James
McDermott, Will & Emery, Washington, DC 202 756 8314
jriedy@mwe.com
Recommended in Tax
Specialization: Partner in Tax Department. Main area of work includes US federal income tax law applicable to cross-border transactions and investments. Practice encompasses both US multinational investments outside the US and non-US, multinational investments in the US. Practice includes consulting on technical tax matters, advising on major corporate acquisitions, corporate internal restructuring and transfer pricing.
Prof. Memberships: Member of Tax Section of the American Bar Association and International Fiscal Association.
Career: Admitted to the Kansas Bar in 1977; District of Columbia, 1981; and US Supreme Court, 1982. Joined the tax division, appellate section of the US Department of Justice in 1977; Lee, Toomey & Kent from 1981 to 1993; McDermott, Will & Emery to the present.
Publications: Frequent commentator and lecturer on US international tax issues.
Personal: Born 25th July 1952; juris doctor degree in 1977 from the University of Kansas; master of laws degree in taxation from Georgetown University in 1981.

RILL, James F
Howrey Simon Arnold & White, Washington, DC 202 783 0800
Recommended in Antitrust

DISTRICT OF COLUMBIA

ROBERTS, John
Hogan & Hartson LLP, Washington, DC
202 637 5810
jgroberts@hhlaw.com
Recommended in Litigation
Specialization: Head of the *Hogan & Hartson LLP*'s Appellate Practice Group.
Prof. Memberships: Member of the American Law Institute and the American Academy of Appellate Lawyers, and has also received the Edmund J Randolph Award for outstanding service to the Department of Justice. He is a member of the Bars of the District of Columbia, the United States Supreme Court, and various federal courts of appeals.
Career: Following law school graduation, clerked for The Honorable Henry J Friendly of the United States Court of Appeals for the Second Circuit, and the following year for then-Associate Justice William H Rehnquist. Following his clerkship experience, served as Special Assistant to United States Attorney General William French Smith. In 1982 President Reagan appointed him to the White House Staff as Associate Counsel to the President, a position in which he served until joining *Hogan & Hartson LLP* in 1986. His responsibilities as Associate Counsel to the President included counseling on the President's constitutional powers and responsibilities, as well as other legal issues affecting the executive branch. At *Hogan & Hartson*, has developed a civil litigation practice, with an emphasis on appellate matters. He personally argued before the United States Supreme Court and the lower federal courts, participating in a wide variety of matters on behalf of corporate clients, trade associations, governments, and individuals. Left the firm in 1989 to accept appointment as Principal Deputy Solicitor General of the United States, a position in which he served until returning to the firm in 1993. In that capacity he personally argued before the Supreme Court and the federal courts of appeals on behalf of the United States, and participated in formulating the litigation position of the government and determining when the government would appeal adverse decisions. Had general substantive responsibility within the Office of the Solicitor General for cases arising from the Civil and Civil Rights Divisions of the Justice Department, as well as from a variety of independent agencies, including the FDIC, RTC, Federal Reserve Board, EEOC, FCC, SEC, CFTC, and SBA. He also participated in the judicial selection process. He has presented oral arguments before the Supreme Court in more than thirty cases, covering the full range of the Court's jurisdiction, including admiralty, antitrust, arbitration, environmental law, First Amendment, health care law, Indian law, bankruptcy, tax, regulation of financial institutions, administrative law, labor law, federal jurisdiction and procedure, interstate commerce, civil rights, and criminal law.
Personal: Graduated from Harvard College, summa cum laude, in 1976, and received his law degree, magna cum laude, in 1979 from the Harvard Law School, where he was managing editor of the 'Harvard Law Review'.

ROBERTS, Richard
Steptoe & Johnson LLP, Washington, DC
202 429 3000
Recommended in Energy

ROCAP, James
Baker Botts LLP, Washington, DC
202 639 7700
Recommended in Insurance

ROHRBACH, Peter
Hogan & Hartson LLP, Washington, DC
202 637 8631
parohrbach@hhlaw.com
Recommended in Communications
Specialization: Partner in the Washington, DC office of *Hogan & Hartson LLP* and co-director of the firm's Communications Practice Group. Handles many different regulatory matters before the Federal Communications Commission and state public utility commissions. Specialized experience in mergers, acquisitions and bankruptcy matters. Large practice in the telecommunications area, with particular emphasis on telephone industry regulation, satellite communications and information services. Clients include major national and international carriers, as well as newer companies that are growing in response to opportunities created by the Telecommunications Act of 1996, the Internet and related developments. Also handles broadcast law matters, with a particular emphasis on radio companies. Assists video programming distributors on regulatory issues affecting their businesses.
Career: Joined *Hogan & Hartson* in 1979 and became a partner in 1987.
Personal: Received his JD from Stanford University Law School in 1979, where he was a senior notes editor of the 'Stanford Law Review', and BA, magna cum laude, from Yale University in 1975. Current member of the Bar of the District of Columbia, and is admitted to practice before the United States District Court and Court of Appeals for the District of Columbia Circuit. Has taught a seminar in communications law at the American University Law School, and participates in various industry organizations.

ROSEN, Richard L
Arnold & Porter, Washington, DC
202 942 5000
Richard_Rosen@aporter.com
Recommended in Antitrust
Specialization: Represents clients before the federal antitrust agencies in merger and acquisitions and other matters and in general antitrust counselling and litigation. His practice focuses on clients in the information technology and telecommunications fields, including Computer Associates International, VeriSign, Micron Technology, SBC Communications and Cingular Wireless.
Career: Prior to joining *Arnold & Porter*, served as Chief of the Communications and Finance Section of the US Department of Justice Antitrust Division, Assistant Director of the Federal Trade Commission's Bureau of Competition and as Attorney Advisor to the Chairman of the Federal Trade Commission.
Personal: He is admitted to the New York and the District of Columbia Bars and is admitted to practice in front of the US Supreme Court.

ROSENBLOOM, H David
Caplin & Drysdale, Washington, DC 202 862 5000
Recommended in Tax

ROSENTHAL, Barry
Bingham McCutchen LLP, Washington, DC 202 778 6150
Recommended in Real Estate

RUBIN, Blake D
Arnold & Porter, Washington, DC
202 942 5828
Blake_Rubin@aporter.com
Recommended in Real Estate
Specialization: Practices in the area of federal taxation, with particular emphasis on matters relating to real estate and partnership taxation. His practice includes planning, policy, and controversy matters. He has extensive experience structuring large partnership and real estate transactions, and regularly represents several of the nation's 20 largest real estate developers and owners in transactional matters. He serves as principal outside tax counsel to several of the country's largest REITs, representing them both in transactional matters and with respect to issues relating to their tax qualification. He has also served as tax counsel in connection with the formation and operation of numerous corporate joint ventures. In the policy area, he represents clients before Congress, the Treasury Department, and the Internal Revenue Service. In the controversy area, he has handled major cases before the Internal Revenue Service and in the courts.
Personal: He is listed in a leading US publication as one of the best lawyers in America. He is also the founder and President of the Washington, DC Center for Public Interest Tax Law, a not-for-profit corporation that provides pro bono representation to low income taxpayers before the US Tax Court.

RUDNICK, Robert
Shearman & Sterling, Washington, DC
202 508 8000
Recommended in Tax

RULE, Charles F (Rick)
Fried, Frank, Harris, Shriver & Jacobson, Washington, DC 202 639 7300
Rick.Rule@FriedFrank.com
Recommended in Antitrust
Specialization: Chair of antitrust department. Focuses practice on US and international antitrust and economic regulation.
Prof. Memberships: Member, Advisory Board of BNA's Antitrust & Trade Regulation Report; Member, Advisory Board of the Washington Legal Foundation and of the Landmark Legal Foundation. Former Chair, Economics Committee of the American Bar Association Antitrust Section; Former Chair, Corporations, Securities and Antitrust Practice Group of the Federalist Society.
Career: Admitted District of Columbia. Joined firm as a partner in 2001. Partner, *Covington & Burling* (1989-2001). Assistant Attorney General, Antitrust Division of the Justice Department (1986-89), Deputy Assistant Attorney (1984-86) and Special Assistant to the Assistant Attorney General (1982-84).
Personal: Born 1955. Received JD from the University of Chicago Law School in 1981 and BA from Vanderbilt University in 1978.

SACHS, John
Latham & Watkins LLP, Washington, DC
202 637 2264
john.sachs@lw.com
Recommended in Projects
Specialization: Chair of the Washington Project Finance Practice. Represents sponsors, lenders, governments and national utilities in all phases of the development and financing of domestic and foreign infrastructure projects, including electricity, oil and gas, water and transportation projects. Particular experience in the development and project financing of private power projects and the acquisition of existing assets in the power sector. Handles all aspects of competitive bids, structuring of projects and negotiation of project agreements and loan documentation.
Prof. Memberships: Federal Energy Bar Association.
Personal: JD, Harvard Law School, 1980. BA, Yale University, 1976 (magna cum laude).

SACKS, Stephen
Arnold & Porter, Washington, DC
202 942 5681
Stephen_Sacks@aporter.com
Recommended in Litigation
Specialization: Specializes in litigation, with particular emphasis on securities fraud and commercial disputes. He has also represented a number of corporate and accounting firm clients in investigations conducted by the SEC and in class actions alleging securities law violations. Representative clients include Fannie

Mae, Motorola, Rhodia, PricewaterhouseCoopers, Deloitte & Touche, the PGA, and Bear Stearns.

SALEM, George
Akin Gump Strauss Hauer & Feld LLP, Washington, DC 202 887 4000
Recommended in Employment

SAMORAJCZYK, Stanley
Akin Gump Strauss Hauer & Feld LLP, Washington, DC 202 887 4000
Recommended in Insolvency

SANFORD, Bruce
Baker & Hostetler LLP, Washington, DC 202 861 1621
Recommended in Media & Entertainment

SAYLER, Robert
Covington & Burling, Washington, DC 202 662 6000
RSayler@cov.com
Recommended in Insurance, Litigation
Specialization: Partner who has been lead counsel for successful insurance policy holders in billion dollar-plus insurance coverage disputes for asbestos, DES, environmental clean-up, and breast implant liabilities; acting for Armstrong World Industries, Boeing, Pittston, Dow Corning, 3M, Monsanto, Exxon, Procter & Gamble, ITT, National Medical Enterprises and the National Football League.
Prof. Memberships: Chair, Litigation Section, of the American Bar Association; Fellow of the American College of Trial Lawyers and the American Bar Foundation; CPR DC Panel of Distinguished Arbitration Neutrals; and the CPR Commission on the Future of Arbitration.
Career: 1965-present, *Covington & Burling*.
Publications: Author of dozens of articles and book chapters on insurance coverage issues, ADR, civility, trial strategies and oral advocacy skills.
Personal: Received an LLB from Harvard University and an AB from Stanford University.

SCHECHTER, Mark
Howrey Simon Arnold & White, Washington, DC 202 783 8000
Recommended in Antitrust

SCHERMAN, William S
Skadden, Arps, Slate, Meagher & Flom LLP, Washington, DC 202 371 7060
wscherma@skadden.com
Recommended in Energy
Specialization: Partner, Washington, DC. Specializes in energy law and litigation. Provides litigation, strategic, commercial, regulatory, and legislative advice to clients regarding both the US and international energy markets. Played a key role in a number of major pro-competitive policy initiatives. For example, helped guide the Commission's efforts to foster greater competition in the electric utility industry. In this connection, contributed to the development of the Energy Policy Act of 1992 and testified before Congress on numerous occasions with regard to legislation and other energy policy-related matters. Also played a major role in developing Order No. 636, reforming the natural gas pipeline industry.
Career: JD, University of Louisville School of Law, 1984 (Articles Editor, Law Review); BA, George Washington University, 1980; Chief of Staff and Senior Legal and Policy Advisor for the FERC (1987); general counsel for the Federal Energy Regulatory Commission.

SCHILDKRAUT, Marc
Howrey Simon Arnold & White, Washington, DC 202 783 0800
Recommended in Antitrust

SCHILLER, Jonathan
Boies, Schiller & Flexner, Washington, DC 202 237 2727
Recommended in Arbitration

SCHNEIDER, Leslie
Ivins, Phillips & Barker, Washington, DC 202 393 7600
Recommended in Tax

SCHOR, Laurence
McManus Schor Asmar & Darden LLP, Washington, DC 202 296 9260
Recommended in Construction

SCHWARTZ, David
Latham & Watkins LLP, Washington, DC 202 637 2125
david.schwartz@lw.com
Recommended in Energy
Specialization: Partner, Electric Restructuring Group. Extensive experience representing market participants in the electric industry, including electric utilities, independent power producers, power marketers, as well as foreign governments and financial institutions on a variety of supply-side and demand-side energy matters. Advises clients on project development, restructuring contracts, M&A, transmission issues and other contract, rate and policy matters. Involved in drafting legislation, advising foreign governments on energy regulations, efficiency, pricing and privatization, and regulatory matters.
Prof. Memberships: Federal Energy Bar Association; American Bar Association; International Bar Association.
Personal: JD, The American University, 1989. BA, Bowdoin College, 1986.

SEGAL, Earl
Akin Gump Strauss Hauer & Feld LLP, Washington, DC 202 887 4000
Recommended in Real Estate

SELLERS, Joseph
Cohen, Milstein, Hausfeld & Toll, PLLC, Washington, DC 202 408 4600
Recommended in Employment

SHULMAN, Robert
Howrey Simon Arnold & White, Washington, DC 202 783 0800
Recommended in Insurance

SILBERT, Earl
Piper Rudnick LLP, Washington, DC 202 861 6250
earl.silbert@piperrudnick.com
Recommended in Litigation
Specialization: Litigation; professional liability and ethics; white collar.
Prof. Memberships: President, American College of Trial Lawyers, 2000-01; Master of Bench, American Inn of Court.
Career: He had a distinguished career in public service before entering private practice, including five years in the US Department of Justice, service as the first Watergate prosecutor, and five years as the US Attorney for the District of Columbia. He has lectured and authored numerous articles on evidence, the attorney-client and work product privileges, RICO and representations in grand jury investigations.
Personal: LLB, Harvard Law School; BA, Harvard University.

SILVERMAN, Mark
Steptoe & Johnson LLP, Washington, DC 202 429 3000
Recommended in Tax

SIMS, Joe
Jones Day, Washington, DC 202 879 3863
jsims@jonesday.com
Recommended in Antitrust
Specialization: Chairs *Jones Day's* Antitrust and Competition Law Practice. Provides antitrust counsel for such companies as America Online (for which he advised on the acquisition of Netscape and the combination with Time Warner, among a range of matters), CBS (which he has represented for over two decades, including its predecessor firm Westinghouse Electric, and recently represented in its combination with Viacom Inc., to form one of the world's largest media companies), Liberty Media Corp., Proctor & Gamble, Abbottt Laboratories, Campbell Soup, American Tower Corp, Gencorp, Inc., and Textron Inc. Represents Aventis in the various vitamins matters in the United States and other jurisdictions, and RJ Reynolds Tobacco Co. in a series of private treble damage actions alleging price fixing in cigarettes. Primary outside counsel for the organisers of the Internet Corporation for Assigned Names and Numbers (ICANN), the global non-profit private sector body that is gradually assuming the administrative and technical management of the infrastructure of the Internet from the United States Government.
Prof. Memberships: Member of the American Law Institute.
Career: Also chairs the Technology Issues Practice of *Jones Day*, which is the internal structure charged with co-ordinating the delivery of technology-related legal services by *Jones Day*. Joined the Antitrust Division of the Department of Justice as a trial attorney in 1970, became Special Assistant to the Assistant Attorney General in 1973, and was appointed Deputy Assistant Attorney General, the second highest rank in the Division, in 1975. Joined *Jones Day* in 1978 to establish a Washington antitrust capacity.
Personal: Admitted to practice in the United States Supreme Court and a majority of the United States Courts of Appeal. Received JD from the College of Law at Arizona State University in 1970, graduating magna cum laude and serving as a law review editor.

SKINNER, William
Covington & Burling, Washington, DC 202 662 5470
wskinner@cov.com
Recommended in Insurance
Specialization: Principal areas of practice include insurance coverage litigation, insurance advice, group captive insurers and general litigation. His insurance litigation experience includes the Armstrong Non-Products ADR, the 3M Breast Implant Litigation, the Dow Corning Breast Implant Litigation, the PSE&G environmental coverage case and the Coordinated California Asbestos Coverage Cases.
Publications: Recent publications include 'Non-Products Coverage For Asbestos-Related Bodily Injury Claims' Eurolegal Conference (May, 2002); 'Allocation Between Claims-Made and Occurrence Policies' in Vol. 10, No. 1 Coverage (ABA 2000); and 'The Mother of All Battles - The Quest For Asbestos Insurance Coverage' by Robert N Sayler and William P Skinner, in Vol. 27, No. 1 Litigation (ABA 2000).
Personal: JD, Harvard Law School, 1975, magna cum laude; BA, Harvard College, 1972.

SMITH, Paul
Jenner & Block, Washington, DC 202 639 6060
psmith@jenner.com
Recommended in Media & Entertainment
Specialization: Co-chairs appellate and Supreme Court, and media and First Amendment practices. Has argued seven cases before US Supreme Court. Has worked on First Amendment cases including Rubin v Coors, Reno v ACLU, United States v American Library Association and Food Lion v ABC.
Prof. Memberships: District of Columbia Bar Board of Governors and Washington Council of Lawyers board member (President, 1990-91).
Career: Admitted to District of Columbia Bar (1981) and Maryland (1988). Clerked for Supreme Court Justice Powell, 1980-81, and Second Circuit Judge

Oakes, 1979-80.
Personal: Received a JD from Yale in 1979; Editor in Chief, Yale Law Journal.

SMITH, Turner
Hunton & Williams, Washington, DC
202 955 1500
Recommended in Environment

SMITH, Wm Randolph
Crowell & Moring LLP, Washington, DC
202 624 2500
Recommended in Antitrust

SMUTNY, Abby Cohen
White & Case LLP, Washington, DC
202 626 3600
Recommended in Arbitration

SOHN, Michael N
Arnold & Porter, Washington, DC
202 942 5000
Michael_Sohn@aporter.com
Recommended in Antitrust

Specialization: Chairman of *Arnold & Porter*, he served as General Counsel of the Federal Trade Commission from 1977 to 1980. His practice encompasses a broad range of antitrust and consumer protection matters, with a particular focus on the antitrust aspects of mergers and acquisitions where FTC or Justice Department review is involved, and treble damage class-action litigation. His clients include Boston Scientific Corporation, General Electric Company, Intel Corporation, Merck & Co Inc, Occidental Petroleum Corporation, PepsiCo, Rhodia, and Wyeth.
Career: During his tenure as General Counsel of the FTC, he was designated a council member of the Administrative Conference of the United States and a member of the Executive Committee of the Regulatory Council of the United States.
Publications: He is a contributing author to 'The Ernst & Young Management Guide to Mergers and Acquisitions'.
Personal: He has been listed as a leading lawyer in the field of antitrust by a top legal publication, and Chambers & Partners' 2002-2003 and 2001-2002 editions of 'Chambers Global' named him as one of the five top-ranked antitrust attorneys in Washington, DC.

SPECTOR, Phillip
Paul, Weiss, Rifkind, Wharton & Garrison, Washington, DC 202 223 7300
Recommended in Communications
See New York chapter for profile

STARR, Judson
Venable LLP, Washington, DC
202 962 4800
Recommended in Environment

STARR, Kenneth
Kirkland & Ellis, Washington, DC
202 879 5130
Kenneth_Starr@dc.kirkland.com
Recommended in Litigation
Specialization: Joined *Kirkland & Ellis* in February 1993. In August 1994, he was appointed Independent Counsel on the Whitewater matter and served until October 1999. From May 27, 1989 to January 20, 1993, he served as Solicitor General of the United States, where he argued 25 cases before the Supreme Court involving a wide range of governmental regulatory and constitutional issues of commercial importance. Prior to that, he served as a United States Circuit Judge appointed on October 11, 1983.
Personal: Brown University, AM, 1969. George Washington University, AB, 1968. Duke Law School, JD 1973.

STEINBERG, Michael
Morgan, Lewis & Bockius LLP, Washington, DC 202 739 3000
Recommended in Environment

STERNE, Robert
Sterne Kessler Goldstein & Fox, Washington, DC 202 371 2600
Recommended in Intellectual Property

STOLL, Richard
Foley & Lardner, Washington, DC
202 672 5300
Recommended in Environment

SULLIVAN, Brendan V
Williams & Connolly LLP, Washington, DC 202 434 5800
bsullivan@wc.com
Recommended in Litigation
Specialization: Described by The Washington Post as a 'world class lawyer,' he is recognized as one of the best known and respected trial lawyers in America, with an extraordinary record of successes. His principal practice areas include all types of complex commercial litigation, including securities, antitrust, banking, RICO, and license disputes; the defense of major law firms in malpractice cases and the defense of accounting firms; products liability; mass tort; and high-profile criminal litigation. In a recent survey of 500 leading lawyers in Washington, he ranked 'Number One' and was regarded as 'unmatched in preparation, quick-wittedness and aggressiveness.'

SUNSHINE, Steven C
Shearman & Sterling, Washington, DC
202 508 8000
Recommended in Antitrust

SUSSMAN, Robert
Latham & Watkins LLP, Washington, DC
202 637 2183
bob.sussman@lw.com
Recommended in Environment
Specialization: Chair, Washington, DC Environment, Land and Resources Department. Focuses on air quality control, energy and transportation policy, environmental management reform, enforcement and toxic substances. Represents clients in utility, chemical, transportation and manufacturing industries.
Prof. Memberships: Vice Chair, Second Generation Committee, ABA Section on Natural Resources Energy and Environmental Law; Board on Chemical Sciences and Technology, National Academy of Sciences.
Career: Deputy Administrator, Environmental Protection Agency, 1993-94.
Publications: Numerous articles on environmental policy and legislation, Environmental Forum, 'Environmental Law Reporter', other publications.
Personal: LLD, Yale University, 1973 (editor, 'Yale Law Jounal'). BA, Yale University, 1969 (magna cum laude, Phi Beta Kappa).

SWENSON, C David
Baker & McKenzie, Washington, DC
202 452 7011
c.david.swenson@bakernet.com
Recommended in Tax
Specialization: Domestic and international taxation of multinational corporations. Practice involves corporate tax planning and tax controversies relating to domestic and international transactions, with focus on: organization of multinational corporate structures, including joint ventures, mergers, acquisitions, and divestitures; intercompany pricing; international tax planning involving Subpart F, Foreign Tax Credit, hybrid entities, derivative financial products, insurance matters, PFICs, foreign currency issues; competent authority matters; tax controversies; Advance Pricing Agreements; and implementation of global tax minimization strategies.
Personal: BA with honours, University of Mississippi. LLM, Taxation, Georgetown University Law Center, where he is currently an Adjunct Professor, having taught international tax since 1986.

SYMONS, Howard J
Mintz Levin Cohn Ferris Glovsky and Popeo PC, Washington, DC
202 434 7300
Recommended in Communications

TARANTO, Richard
Farr & Taranto, Washington, DC
202 775 0184
Recommended in Litigation

TERR, Leonard
Baker & McKenzie, Washington, DC
202 452 7087
leonard.b.terr@bakernet.com
Recommended in Tax
Specialization: Partner, Washington, DC office. Over 20 years experience representing US based and foreign based multinationals, foreign governments, international organizations and trade associations in all phases of international tax practice. Representative client matters include planning, obtaining rulings on and implementing multi-country restructurings, mergers and acquisitions, divestitures and joint ventures involving companies in the automobile, aerospace, consumer products, electronics, insurance, natural resources, pharmaceutical, services, telecommunications and other industries; securing bilateral and multilateral Advance Pricing Agreements; interacting with tax treaty negotiators to obtain favorable provisions in pending new treaties and protocols on behalf of companies and industry groups; testifying on proposed international tax regulations; achieving favorable settlements of tax cases involving tax shelter and other issues; and obtaining favorable Competent Authority agreements in tax controversies involving most European, Asia-Pacific, Latin and North American treaty jurisdictions.
Prof. Memberships: Consultant, American Law Institute project on Tax Treaties; current or former editorial board member, Tax Notes International, Tax Management International Journal, The Journal of Corporate Taxation, Hartford Institute on Insurance Taxation; member, former US National Reporter, International Fiscal Association; former Chair, ABA, Tax Section Foreign Activities of US Taxpayers Committee, Section 367 Subcommittee, Source Subcommittee; member, Task Force on Global Tax Policy; Chair, Washington International Tax Study Group. Has lectured and published widely on international tax matters.
Personal: JD, Cornell University (1975); PhD (1971), AM (1968), Brown University; AB, LaSalle College (1967); Law Clerk to Chief Judge Wilson Cowen, US Court of Appeals for the Federal Circuit (1975-1976); International Tax Counsel, US Treasury Department (1987-1989); Adjunct Professor, International Tax Law, Georgetown University Law Center (1999-).

TOWNSEND, John M
Hughes Hubbard & Reed LLP, Washington, DC 202 721 4640
townsend@hugheshubbard.com
Recommended in Arbitration
Specialization: Partner; Chair of Arbitration and ADR Group. International disputes, including arbitration, litigation in US federal and state courts, mediation. Also competition law. Represented American Arbitration Association as amicus curiae in United States Supreme Court case involving consumer arbitration. Represented American company in ICC arbitration to enforce technology license and in European Commission proceeding challenging the license as restrictive of competition. Represented Federal Republic of Germany as amicus curiae in appeal from trademark injunction.
Prof. Memberships: Board of Directors and Executive Committee and Chair of Law Committee of American Arbitration Association; Trustee and member of Arbitration and Competition Law Committees of US Council for International

Business; Panel of Distinguished Neutrals of CPR Institute for Dispute Resolution; LCIA North American Users Council; ABA; IBA; UIA; American Law Institute; College of Commercial Arbitrators.
Career: With *Hughes Hubbard & Reed* since 1971, in New York, Paris, and Washington. Admitted to bars of New York 1972 and District of Columbia 1990.
Publications: Author of 'Arbitration Across the Civil Law - Common Law Divide' (with Siegfried Elsing), Arbitration International, February 2002; 'Recent Developments in NAFTA Arbitration', ADR Currents, Sept.-Dec. 2001; 'Nonsignatories and Arbitration', ADR Currents, Sept. 1998; 'The Case for Site Licenses', ECLR, March 1999.
Personal: Born 21st March, 1947. BA Yale University 1968; JD Yale University 1971. Fluent French.

TRITT, Cheryl
Morrison & Foerster LLP, Washington, DC
202 887 1510
ctritt@mofo.com
Recommended in Communications
Specialization: Partner advising on a range of telecommunications issues, especially wireless, satellite, multimedia, and international matters. Counsels clients on the regulatory implications of various transactional matters, including mergers, acquisitions, stock spin-offs, and new business ventures. As former head of the 350 person Common Carrier Bureau, directed all FCC matters involving the interstate and the international regulatory activities of telecommunications carriers, including cellular, satellite, and long distance and local telephone companies. Oversaw several major policy proceedings that encouraged the development of advanced telecommunications networks and greater competition among telecommunications service providers (eg video dial tone and expanded interconnection dockets). Also had primary responsibility for a number of significant international proceedings affecting international accounting rates, market entry policies and foreign ownership issues.
Prof. Memberships: Member, American Bar Association. Member, Federal Communications Bar Association.
Career: Admitted to practice in the District of Columbia and Illinois. Joined *Morrison & Foerster* in 1993, after serving as Chief of the Common Carrier Bureau of the Federal Communications Commission (FCC). Currently serves as co-head of firm's Communications practice.
Personal: BS, cum laude, University of Nebraska; MS, Journalism, Northwestern University; JD, cum laude, Northwestern University School of Law, 1976.

TUCKER, Stefan
Venable LLP, Washington, DC
202 962 4800
Recommended in Real Estate

VALENTINE, Debra
O'Melveny & Myers LLP, Washington, DC
202 383 5300
Recommended in Antitrust

VARDAMAN, John
Williams & Connolly LLP, Washington, DC 202 434 5081
jvardaman@wc.com
Recommended in Litigation
Specialization: With more than 35 years of experience, he has significant experience in complex civil and criminal litigation. He has appeared in state and federal courts nationwide at the trial and appellate levels, and the United States Supreme Court. Over the past decade, he has served as national trial counsel to large corporations faced with mass tort and mass disasters claims. These cases have involved products such as chemicals, medical devices, and pharmaceutical products. He also served as lead counsel in multi-plaintiff litigation arising from airline and rail crashes and represented individuals and corporations in complex commercial litigation.

VARNEY, Christine
Hogan & Hartson LLP, Washington, DC
202 637 6823
cvarney@hhlaw.com
Recommended in Antitrust
Specialization: Partner in the Washington, DC office of *Hogan & Hartson LLP*, member of the firm's Antitrust, Competition and Consumer Protection Practice Group and head of the Internet Law Practice Group. Provides competition policy and regulatory advice as well as full service assistance in the areas of privacy, business planning and corporate governance, intellectual property and general liability issues to companies doing business globally. Representations have included Compaq Computer Corporation, Netscape, Ebay, AOL, DoubleClick, Real Networks, Dow Jones Corporation, Washington Post Interactive and serving as Chief Counsel to the Clinton/Gore Campaign, General Counsel to the 1992 Presidential Inaugural Committee, and General Counsel to the Democratic National Committee from 1989 to 1992.
Prof. Memberships: Chair, Committee on Election Law, American Bar Association (1998-1999); American Bar Association (1986-present); (New York State Bar Association (1986-present); Secretary/Treasurer, Vice-President's Residence Foundation (1998-99) National Lawyers' Council (1985-present).
Career: Served as a Federal Trade Commissioner from 1994 to 1997. At the Federal Trade Commission, was the Administration's leading official on a wide variety of Internet issues. Also pioneered the application of innovation market theory analysis to transactions in both electronic high technology and biotechnology. Led the government's effort to examine privacy issues in the information age, resulting in Congressional and agency hearings, proposed industry standards and increased government enforcement of laws protecting privacy. Prior to becoming a Federal Trade Commissioner, was Assistant to the President of the United States and Secretary to the Cabinet. Was the primary point of contact between the President and the 20 members of his Cabinet. Was responsible for the overall coordination of several major issues and initiatives between the White House and the agencies.
Publications: Author/co-author of many articles, including: 'Internet Privacy: Enforcement Actions'; 'The Death of Privacy?' and 'Innovation Markets in Merger Review Analysis'.
Personal: Has lectured extensively, both in the United States and abroad, on various legal issues. Has also been involved in an ongoing international dialogue on comparative political processes and competition policy with foreign government officials through the Organization for Economic Cooperation and Development (OECD). Received her JD from Georgetown University Law Center in 1986, MPA from Syracuse University, magna cum laude, in 1978, and BS from State University of New York at Albany in 1977. Joined *Hogan & Hartson LLP* in 1991, rejoined in 1997. Current member of the District of Columbia Bar.

VERRILLI, Donald
Jenner & Block, Washington, DC
202 639 6095
dverrilli@jenner.com
Recommended in Litigation
Specialization: Co-chairs appellate and Supreme Court, and telecommunications practices. Has argued US Supreme Court cases including FCC v Next Wave, Verizon v FCC, and MCI v AT&T. Has argued cases in federal appellate and state supreme courts involving constitutional, statutory construction, administrative, copyright and criminal law.
Career: Admitted to New York Bar (1987) and District of Columbia (1989). Clerked for Supreme Court Justice Brennan, 1984-85, and DC Circuit Judge Wright, 1983-84. Served as Special Counsel to the President in the confirmation of Justice Breyer (1994).
Personal: Received a JD with honors from Columbia University (1983); Editor in Chief, 'Columbia Law Review'.

VERVEER, Philip L
Willkie Farr & Gallagher, Washington, DC
202 303 1117
pverveer@willkie.com
Recommended in Communications
Specialization: Senior Partner in Telecommunications Group. A well recognised authority in antitrust and communications law both in private practice and among governmental personnel, including particularly the agencies responsible for antitrust and communications matters. Served as a trial attorney in the Antitrust Division from 1969 to 1977, as a supervisory attorney in the Bureau of Competition of the Federal Trade Commission from 1977 to 1978 and as bureau chief in the Federal Communications Commission from 1978 to 1981. Served in the Antitrust Division of the Department of Justice, and was the first lead counsel in the investigation and prosecution that led to the Bell System divestiture. Provides counseling and administrative agency representation to a variety of communications clients.
Prof. Memberships: Federal Communications Bar Association; American Bar Association and The District of Columbia Bar.
Career: Admitted in 1969. Joined *Willkie Farr & Gallagher* as a partner in 1983. Served in the Antitrust Division of the Department of Justice (1969-1977). Also worked in the Bureau of Competition at the Federal Trade Commission (1977-1978). Chief of the Federal Communications Commission's Cable Television Bureau, the Broadcast Bureau, and the Common Carrier Bureau (1978-1981). Received from President Carter the Distinguished Presidential Rank Award of excellent service, one of the highest awards given to federal government employees. 1996: Served as Chairman of the Federal Advisory Committee on Public Safety Wireless spectrum needs through the year 2001.
Personal: Received a JD in 1969 from the University of Chicago and a BSFS in 1966 from Georgetown University.

VILLA, John K
Williams & Connolly LLP, Washington, DC
202 434 5117
jvilla@wc.com
Recommended in Litigation
Specialization: Described by the January 2002 'American Lawyer' as 'perhaps the premier [legal] malpractice defense lawyer in the nation', he focuses on legal malpractice, corporate, financial services-related, and securities litigation (both civil and criminal). He has been lead counsel in both trial and appellate proceedings involving the defense of claims against law firms, financial institution directors, officers and their financial institutions. In a leading legal publication, he was named as one of the '100 Most Influential Lawyers in America' as the 'first lawyer that other attorneys and law firms turn to when caught up in the S&L and banking scandals.'

VOLLMANN, Alan
Holland & Knight LLP, Washington, DC
202 955 3000
avollman@hklaw.com
Recommended in Real Estate
Specialization: Partner in the Real Estate

DISTRICT OF COLUMBIA

Department. He has substantial experience in representing international development companies, life insurance companies, banks, pension funds and other institutional investors in real estate transactions nationwide. His experience encompasses a wide range of equity and debt transactions, commercial leases, representing landlords and tenants, workouts and foreclosures. He is an adjunct professor of the Berman Real Estate Institute of Johns Hopkins University and is the author of numerous articles on developments in real estate law. He is a graduate of the Catholic University School of Law, Washington, DC, where he was Editor in Chief of the 'Law Review'.

VOLLMER, Andrew
Wilmer, Cutler & Pickering, Washington, DC 202 663 6202
Andrew.Vollmer@wilmer.com
Recommended in Arbitration

Specialization: Partner in firm's securities and litigation sections. Main areas of practice are international arbitration and litigation and securities enforcement matters. International arbitration and litigation experience includes international civil litigation issues and Foreign Sovereign Immunities issues related to various US court proceedings, complex commercial arbitrations, international law issues, and constitutional issues in the foreign affairs area. Has advised clients in connection with internal investigations, resulting litigation, and corporate governance, including advising directors in connection with control and other financial transactions. Has also represented clients in litigation involving the US securities laws, including private cases in US courts, SEC and internal investigations, SEC civil injunctive actions, SEC administrative proceedings, NASD disciplinary proceedings, and international aspects of SEC investigations and enforcement proceedings.
Career: Admitted to District of Columbia Bar (1978). Joined firm in 1978 and became partner in 1986. Spent more than four years in firm's London office and has taught International Civil Litigation in US Courts at Stanford Law School and Georgetown University Law Center.
Personal: Graduate of Miami University (BA 1975) and the University of Virginia (JD 1978).

WADLOW, R Clark
Sidley Austin Brown & Wood, Washington, DC 202 736 8000
Recommended in Communications

WALD, Douglas
Arnold & Porter, Washington, DC
202 942 5000
Douglas_Wald@aporter.com
Recommended in Antitrust

Specialization: Specializes in antitrust and trade regulation, and general litigation. Since joining the firm, his experience has involved a broad range of antitrust matters, including counseling, private litigation (including federal class actions), and representation before governmental agencies. He has advised clients on matters involving marketing, pricing, and distribution restrictions (Sherman Act 1), price discrimination (Robinson-Patman Act), monopolization (Sherman Act 2), and joint ventures and acquisitions (Clayton Act 7). He has also represented clients on appellate matters such as 3M Company v Browner, 17 F. 3d 1453 (D. C. Cir. 1994) (applicability of federal statute of limitations to agency civil penalty proceedings).
Career: Prior to joining *Arnold & Porter* in 1980, he clerked for Judge William H Timbers on the US Court of Appeals for the Second Circuit.
Personal: He graduated in 1979 from Harvard Law School (JD), and was an editor of the 'Harvard Law Review'. He received an AB from Harvard College in 1975.

WARD, Erica A
Skadden, Arps, Slate, Meagher & Flom LLP, Washington, DC 202 371 7050
eward@skadden.com
Recommended in Projects

Specialization: Specializing since 1981 in project finance, with a particular concentration in the energy sector, representing independent power companies, utilities and commercial and investment banks in the development, financing, purchase or sale of industrial and energy facilities. Represented Duquesne Light Company in the $1.7 billion sale of its generating facilities and NRG Energy in its $2 billion construction revolving credit facility.
Career: BA, Stanford University, 1972; JD, University of Michigan Law School, 1975 (Managing Editor, Michigan Law Review); Deputy Director, Domestic Policy Staff, The White House, 1980-81, in charge of energy, environment and interior issues.

WARIN, Roger
Steptoe & Johnson LLP, Washington, DC
202 429 3000
Recommended in Insurance

WATERS, Jennifer
Crowell & Moring LLP, Washington, DC
202 624 2500
Recommended in Energy

WAXMAN, Seth
Wilmer, Cutler & Pickering, Washington, DC 202 663 6800
Seth.Waxman@wilmer.com
Recommended in Litigation

Specialization: Partner in firm's litigation section, focuses on Supreme Court, appellate, and complex civil and criminal trial litigation; corporate advice on complex litigation and public policy challenges. He has argued 33 cases in the Supreme Court and has tried and argued dozens of other high profile, complex civil and criminal cases in federal and state courts across the United States.
Prof. Memberships: Fellow, American College of Trial Lawyers, American Academy of Appellate Lawyers, American Law Institute, American Bar Foundation. Director, 'Legal Affairs' magazine, Supreme Court Institute, Supreme Court Historical Society. Admitted, District of Columbia, United States Supreme Court, all federal courts of appeals.
Career: Former Solicitor General of the United States (1997-2001), he also served in a number of other senior positions in the United States Government. In 18 years of private practice he has garnered numerous awards for trial and appellate litigation. He sits on the law faculty at Georgetown University and previously taught at Harvard University's Kennedy School of Government.
Personal: Harvard College (AB 1973, summa cum laude); Rockefeller Fellow, 1973-74; Yale Law School (JD 1977).

WEINSTEIN, Ken
Latham & Watkins LLP, Washington, DC
202 637 2166
ken.weinstein@lw.com
Recommended in Environment

Specialization: Partner, Litigation and Environment, Land and Resources Departments. Has 25 years experience in chemical regulation and pesticide law; lead trial counsel in many groundbreaking cases. Assists companies in facilitating regulatory approvals from the EPA and successfully defended many products against regulatory challenges. Representative clients include CropLife America, American Chemistry Council, Bayer, BASF, DuPont, FMC, Monsanto, Rohm and Haas, Syngenta, Uniroyal and Valent.
Prof. Memberships: ABA, founder of Committee on Pesticides and Chemical Regulation.
Publications: Co-authored two treatises on pesticide regulation and one on toxic substances regulation.
Personal: JD, Georgetown University, 1973. BS, City University of New York, 1969.

WEISEL, Sheldon
Shaw Pittman, Washington, DC
202 663 8000
Recommended in Real Estate

WELLEN, Robert
Ivins, Phillips & Barker, Washington, DC
202 393 7600
Recommended in Tax

WENNER, Adam
Chadbourne & Parke LLP, Washington, DC 202 974 5600
Recommended in Energy

WEST, Joseph
Arnold & Porter, Washington, DC
202 942 5225
Joseph_West@aporter.com
Recommended in Construction

Specialization: Partner in charge of the Government Contracts Practice. Has concentrated his practice on resolving claims and disputes relating to government and construction contracts. He has represented clients in connection with the identification, evaluation, preparation and litigation of claims by or against owners, buyers, prime and subcontractors and other parties to government and commercial agreements involving primarily the defense, aerospace, and construction industries. Also has substantial experience in general commercial litigation and has developed considerable experience in alternative dispute resolution (ADR) techniques, including arbitration, mediation, and mini-trials, and third-party neutral evaluations. He is the firm's representative to the CPR Institute for Dispute Resolution. He has significant experience before the United States Court of Federal Claims (and its predecessor, the United States Claims Court), the Federal District Courts and Circuit Courts of Appeal, several state courts and various administrative tribunals (including the Contract Appeals Board, the General Accounting Office Board, and Small Business Administration Board).
Prof. Memberships: He is a Fellow of the American College of Construction Lawyers.

WIACEK, Raymond
Jones Day, Washington, DC
202 879 3908
rjwiacek@jonesday.com
Recommended in Tax

Specialization: Coordinator of the firm's tax group. Practice involves the tax and business practice aspects of corporate and international transactions, including structured and cross-border financings, project finance, mergers, acquisitions, restructurings, transfer pricing and international licensing. Representative clients include Bank of America, Bridgestone/Firestone, Dow Corning, Isuzu Motors, JP Morgan, and Pfizer. Testified numerous times on international tax matters and proposed regulations before the House Ways and Means Committee, the Senate Finance Committee, the Senate Foreign Relations Committee, and the Internal Revenue Service and was recently named as one of the world's top tax lawyers in a leading tax publication. Has also served as an adjunct tax professor at Georgetown University Law Center.

WILEY, Richard E
Wiley Rein & Fielding LLP, Washington, DC 202 719 7000
Recommended in Communications

LEADERS — DISTRICT OF COLUMBIA

WILLIAMS, William
Fulbright & Jaworski LLP, Washington, DC 202 662 4673
wwilliams@fulbright.com
Recommended in Energy
Specialization: He was an attorney for the Federal Energy Regulatory Commission from 1977 to 1980. The majority of his practice deals with the representation of interstate pipelines and other clients before the Federal Energy Regulatory Commission and in related appellate matters. He has also represented clients in state regulatory proceedings. In addition to his regulatory practice, he advises clients involved in litigation or commercial transactions with regulated companies.
Prof. Memberships: Virginia Bar, District of Columbia Bar, Federal Energy Bar Association.
Personal: Lives in Falls Church, Virginia; two children, William and Erin; leisure activitites include running, tennis and activities with the children.

WILLNER, Keith
Mayer, Brown, Rowe & Maw, Washington, DC 202 263 3215
kwillner@mayerbrownrowe.com
Recommended in Real Estate
Specialization: Represents institutions in major real estate financing, acquisition, sale and leasing transactions. Counsels major REITs, pension funds, banks, insurance companies, credit companies, and private investors on their real estate needs. Structures and executes acquisitions and dispositions of major commercial property types. Structures investment and ownership vehicles to purchase and operate real estate projects. Assists clients in permanent, construction, mezzanine, securitized, and syndicated loans on all types of commercial real estate. Handles complex portfolio and multistate transactions. Serves as national leasing counsel for leading companies across US and has done major headquarters leases.
Career: Joined *Mayer, Brown, Rowe & Maw* as partner, 1996. Formerly with *Morrison & Foerster; Lane and Edson, P.C.; Bronson, Bronson & McKinnon.* Served on Steering Committee of the Real Estate Section of DC Bar Association and as Chair of Commercial Transactions Committee and Commercial Leasing Committee.
Publications: Articles in numerous publications, including 'Mortgage and Real Estate Executives Report', 'CREI Interactive', 'The Corridor Real Estate Journal', and 'Real Estate Rescues'. Frequent speaker and author on real estate topics.
Personal: Born 10 December 1959. University of Virginia School of Law, JD, 1984; Virginia Tax Review. University of Virginia, BA, magna cum laude, 1981; Phi Beta Kappa.

WOLFF, Paul
Williams & Connolly LLP, Washington, DC 202 434 5079
pwolff@wc.com
Recommended in Litigation
Specialization: With almost 40 years of trial experience, he concentrates in civil and criminal litigation, including white-collar crime; civil and criminal antitrust; commercial litigation; UCC; products liability (both plaintiff- and defense-side); medical malpractice (both plaintiff- and defense-side); ERISA; unfair competition; trademarks and trade secrets; patents; intentional torts; airplane crash litigation; race discrimination; banking matters; officer and director liability and fiduciary duties; energy related matters (both civil and criminal); and other various matters. He has also argued numerous appeals in various US circuit courts and state supreme courts and has participated in dozens of other trials and appellate matters.

WYRON, Richard
Swidler Berlin Shereff Friedman LLP, Washington, DC 202 424 7500
Recommended in Insolvency

YANNUCCI, Thomas
Kirkland & Ellis, Washington, DC 202 879 5056
thomas_yannucci@dc.kirkland.com
Recommended in Litigation, Media & Entertainment
Specialization: Acted as trial and appellate counsel in both individual and class action suits involving claims in the following areas: defamation, antitrust, intellectual property, securities, government enforcement and regulatory matters (DOJ, FDA, EPA, FTC, SEC, ITC, FEC, CIA, NLRB), RICO, insurance coverage, ERISA, international trade and white collar crime. Has handled both jury and bench trials, and has appeared in state and federal courts as well as in arbitrations. He also has served as an arbitrator for complex commercial cases for the American Arbitration Association.
Personal: University of Notre Dame, AB, 1972. University of Notre Dame Law School, JD, 1976.

YDE, Paul
Freshfields Bruckhaus Deringer LLP, Washington, DC 202 777/969 4500
Recommended in Antitrust

ZAHLER, Robert
Shaw Pittman, Washington, DC
202 663 8000
Recommended in Communications

ZWEIFACH, Gerson
Williams & Connolly LLP, Washington, DC 202 434 5534
gzweifach@wc.com
Recommended in Media & Entertainment
Specialization: Listed by his peers as one of 'America's Top Lawyers,' his litigation practice includes antitrust, securities, libel and complex commercial cases, as both plaintiffs' and defense counsel before juries and courts across the US. In the antitrust field, he has successfully defended monopolization, tying and patent antitrust actions. In the securities arena, he represented both plaintiffs and defendants, including defending a 'Big 5' accounting firm in securities class action litigation. In the media field, he has defended movie studios, book publishers, tabloids, and television networks against a wide variety of high profile claims.

FLORIDA

OVERVIEW

CONTENTS: Antitrust p.151; Banking p.152; Construction p.153; Corporate/M&A p.155; Employment: Mainly Plaintiff p.157; Mainly Defendant p.158; Environment p.160; Insolvency p.161; Insurance p.164; Litigation: p.164; Real Estate p.167; Tax p.169; Individuals' Profiles p.171.

FLORIDA'S TOP TEN
1. Holland & Knight
2. Greenberg Traurig
3. Akerman Senterfitt
4. Carlton Fields
4. Steel Hector & Davis
5. Kenny Nachwalter Seymour Arnold Critchlow & Spector
6. Hunton & Williams
6. Shutts & Bowen
7. White & Case

Ranking based on Chambers' research within the state.

All quotes in the text are from interviews with clients and competitors.

OVERVIEW: Three firms are clearly ahead of the pack in Florida: they command the greatest resources and enjoy the highest profiles.

Holland & Knight, a Goliath among law firms in this region, tops *Chambers'* tables. With 11 offices in the state, it achieves rankings in ten sections, amply demonstrating its depth of resources. In particular, the firm boasts the largest tax team in Florida, with Bill Townsend named best in the state for local matters. In construction and real estate, Holland & Knight benefits from its size, experience and high-profile client base, while other areas of strength include banking, litigation and corporate finance. A recent merger with McBride Baker & Coles has doubled the size of its Chicago practice, and this ambitious and expansive outfit is now setting its sights on European growth.

Greenberg Traurig is an old-line firm of impeccable quality. *Chambers'* research reflects this: it heads four of the six sections in which it appears. Real estate is one of its cornerstones, where, according to commentators, excellent transactional experience raises it head and shoulders above its rivals. The dominant corporate practice handles lots of cross-border work, especially in Latin America, such as Telefónica's recent series of Mexican acquisitions. Multi-jurisdictional expertise and transactional prowess characterize many practice areas. In tax, for example, it is second to none for complex corporate issues, while stellar performer Mark Bloom heads an insolvency powerhouse renowned for cross-border work. Its litigation team, too, is celebrated for complex, international disputes, although observers might know it better for Barry Richard's representation of George W Bush before the Florida Supreme Court during the 2000 presidential election.

The third of Florida's dominant trio is **Akerman Senterfitt**. With over 360 lawyers, it is the largest law firm exclusive to Florida and fields the largest corporate and commercial litigation departments in the state. Corporate M&A, where it earns a top band ranking in *Chambers'* tables, is a particular strength. The team is packed with quality attorneys, though it is crackerjack lawyer Stephen Roddenberry who stands out, particularly for his association with important client Huizenga Holdings. The firm's impressive deal list includes advising Wackenhut in its $570 million merger with Group 4 Falck, a transaction where the firm's antitrust practice also came into its own. The firm offers a full range of services, including insolvency, real estate, tax and banking. In the latter, Tom Cardwell has an outstanding reputation, especially for his work on behalf of the Florida Bankers Association.

Carlton Fields boasts a strong network across the state, including large offices in Orlando, Miami and Tampa. Any description of it should perhaps start with construction and real estate, where its huge depth and long list of high-end clients ensure a strong profile. The practice has benefited from the activity in the retail and residential sectors that has accompanied the state's burgeoning reputation as a center for the hospitality industry. The firm offers a range of other services, however, including a sophisticated and successful antitrust team, and expertise in insurance, tax and insolvency.

Steel Hector & Davis is a traditional high-quality firm. It only appears in three of *Chambers'* tables, but ranks near the top in all three. Its tax department, for example, contains some of the finest tax attorneys in the state according to sources, while the firm remains one of the corporate/M&A leaders. An impressive deal list supports its high profile. For example, the firm handled $4 billion in debt and equity offerings during 2001 and boasts major clients like Florida Power & Light. Growing international capacity is focused particularly on Latin America: its network now extends to Argentina, Brazil, Venezuela and the Dominican Republic.

Another small but top-quality firm is **Kenny Nachwalter Seymour Arnold Critchlow & Spector**. This litigation boutique is a favorite of many high-profile clients, especially for antitrust and securities litigation. Its unique and sophisticated antitrust practice has a national name for plaintiff work, particularly representing plaintiffs who opt out of class actions. Attorneys handle the most complex cases, where they distinguish themselves by creativity, knowledge and sheer hard work. Mike Nachwalter and cream of the crop Scott Perwin are two outstanding names.

Hunton & Williams now boasts about 850 lawyers in 16 offices worldwide. Miami is among the newest of these, having opened in 1999. Yet, in that short time it has established itself as a considerable player statewide, with a substantial group of dedicated attorneys. Major practice areas include litigation and antitrust, where the firm has gained expertise in headline cases such as acting for BellSouth in a $2 billion class action. Banking and finance expertise covers securitisation and restructuring as well as regulatory work.

The state's highest profile banking firm, however, is **Shutts & Bowen**, the preeminent banking regulatory firm in Florida. In the regulatory field, Bowman Brown stands out as a national star. He recently represented Royal Bank of Canada in its acquisition of Barclays' Latin American and US banking business, a transaction involving client assets of $2.9 billion. The firm also boasts strong corporate and real estate departments, which clients say offer New York quality without New York costs.

White & Case's finance strength and the Latin American dimension of much of its work makes a Miami office essential. Having opened there in 1987, it is now the buzzing hub of the firm's Latin America and Caribbean practice, with about 60 lawyers. The firm has acted in some of the most interesting investments in the region, such as the $300 million securitization by Brazilian mining company Companhia Vale do Rio Doce. Alongside the international strength, sources acknowledge that the firm is increasingly making its mark in Florida itself.

ANTITRUST

FLORIDA

ANTITRUST

FLORIDA
Leading firms (Antitrust)

1 KENNY NACHWALTER SEYMOUR ARNOLD *Miami*

2 AKERMAN SENTERFITT *Miami, Orlando*
CARLTON FIELDS *Tampa*
HUNTON & WILLIAMS *Miami*

3 HOLLAND & KNIGHT LLP *Miami, Tallahassee*
TRENAM, KEMKER, SCHARF, BARKIN, FRYE *Tampa*
ZUCKERMAN SPAEDER LLP *Miami*

Leading individuals (Antitrust)

1 PERWIN Scott *Kenny Nachwalter Seymour,* Miami
ROUNSAVILLE Keith *Akerman Senterfitt,* Orlando

2 BLECHMAN Bill *Kenny Nachwalter Seymour,* Miami
SILVERMAN Lawrence *Akerman Senterfitt,* Orlando

3 COUTROULIS Chris *Carlton Fields,* Tampa
HOFFMAN Jerome *Holland & Knight LLP,* Tallahassee
LAROSE Edward *Trenam, Kemker, Scharf,* Tampa
LITCHFORD Hal *Litchford & Christopher,* Orlando
NAGIN Stephen *Nagin Gallop Figuerdo,* Coconut Grove

4 RAVIKOFF Ronald *Zuckerman Spaeder LLP,* Miami
SINGER Stuart *Boies, Schiller & Flexner LLP,* Miami

Firms and Individuals are listed alphabetically in each band.

Kenny Nachwalter Seymour Arnold Critchlow & Spector

The Firm: Antitrust has long been a hallmark of this, the *"premier antitrust plaintiffs' firm in Florida."* Peers identified it as a *"unique and sophisticated"* practice; it is nationally renowned for its representation of plaintiffs who opt out of antitrust class actions, largely in Sherman Act conspiracy cases. Clients extolled the group's *"creativity, knowledge and sheer hard work."* The group is *"without peer"* in the state due in part to its *"wealth of superintelligent attorneys and trial experience."* High-profile work includes acting in the generic drug cases against manufacturers on behalf of retailers Walgreen, Eckerd, Kroger and Albertson's.

The Lawyers: Amid this *"formidable"* group, **Scott Perwin** is the *"cream of the crop."* He is a ubiquitous presence in antitrust, with rivals acknowledging that for *"sheer brains and quality of work, there is nobody better."* He recently acted for budget carrier Spirit Airlines in predatory pricing claims in two long-haul markets against Northwest Airlines.

The *"first-rate"* **Bill Blechman** also won widespread praise. He has acted for the plaintiffs in the vitamins antitrust litigation against Takeda Vitamin & Food USA in the US District Court for the District of Columbia.

The Clients: Walgreen; Eckerd; Kroger; Albertson's and Spirit Airlines.

Akerman Senterfitt

see firm details p.760

The Firm: The group's 13 dedicated antitrust attorneys Floridawide are a regular feature in antitrust class action defense and grand jury investigations by the US DOJ. It boasts particular industry expertise in the pharmaceutical, healthcare and telecom sectors, and is active in the interface between consumer actions and antitrust. Recent highlights include acting for private security services provider Wackenhut in its successful merger with Group 4 Falck, a matter that went before the UK Competition Commission. The group was also lead counsel for the workers' compensation insurance Industry in a conspiracy class action.

The Lawyers: The firm's prominent name, and dean of the Florida antitrust bar, is **Keith Rounsaville** (see p.177). *"Academic"* in style, peers extolled his *"exceptional knowledge of antitrust law"* and *"technical excellence."* He is active in the defense of grand jury investigations, and in pharmaceutical and healthcare antitrust claims. *"Young and sharp,"* **Lawrence Silverman** (see p.178) was described to researchers as a *"rising star of the new generation."* Clients pointed to his *"strong economics background"* providing a distinct advantage in his understanding of the commercial aspects of a case. Working in the intersection between antitrust and consumer law, he is currently lead counsel for the defense in an arsenic-treated wood class action.

The Clients: AOL Time Warner, Wackenhut and Metropolitan Casualty Insurance are typical clients of the firm.

Carlton Fields

The Firm: The antitrust practice at this well-established firm is a *"significant force"* in counseling matters and in class action defense. Peers identified a particular strength in class certification defense work, where a *"sophisticated and successful"* practice has won many supporters. The group also advises corporate clients on the antitrust implications of franchising, pricing practices, marketing and other business activities.

The Lawyers: The *"bright and articulate"* **Chris Coutroulis** is adjudged *"prominent in antitrust defense."* He is renowned for his work defending class certifications, where he has acted in the past for clients such as Florida Power, Zeneca and Mobil Oil.

The Clients: Phillips Petroleum Company and CIGNA are examples of the group's clients.

Hunton & Williams

The Firm: Although smaller than its competitors, the group maintains a busy antitrust defense practice, and is frequently seen in high-profile civil and criminal cases across a range of industries. The group acted for BellSouth in a $2 billion antitrust class action brought on behalf of consumers.

The Lawyers: The team includes general litigator Marty Steinberg. He and the firm represented Boeing in antitrust litigation brought by an airline leasing company alleging restraint of trade, and have acted for Honeywell in Robinson-Patman Act litigation.

The Clients: BellSouth, Honeywell and Boeing.

Holland & Knight LLP

see firm details p.820

The Firm: Powered by a strong litigation practice, the antitrust, trade regulation and competition practice group at this *"huge"* full-service firm acts in antitrust litigation defense for a national client base. The group is skilled in RICO, consumer fraud investigations and unfair trade litigation. The team also acts on large-scale M&A, and counsels clients on legal strategies regarding federal and state legislation.

The Lawyers: **Jerome Hoffman** (see p.174) is a former head of the antitrust division in the Florida Attorney General's Office. He is particularly prominent in antitrust law in the healthcare industry.

The Clients: The firm has a national and international client base drawn from a wide range of industries such as pharmaceutical, manufacturing, hi-tech and leisure and media.

Trenam, Kemker, Scharf, Barkin, Frye, O'Neill & Mullis PA

The Firm: The group undertakes civil and criminal antitrust litigation defense in federal and state courts as well as compliance counseling for clients. The active antitrust unit in theFlorida Attorney General's Office provides the firm with a steady stream of defense work in antitrust investigations. The firm recently settled major class action litigation on behalf of the American Optometric Association, regarding allegations of conspiracy in the marketing of disposable contact lenses.

The Lawyers: Antitrust specialist **Ed LaRose** was praised as a *"scholarly"* attorney, active in class action defense work. He is a former chair of the antitrust committee of the Florida Bar Association. Past highlights include successfully defending Océ Printing Systems in a class certification hearing.

The Clients: Océ Printing Systems and the American Optometric Association.

Zuckerman Spaeder LLP

The Firm: This national firm of litigation specialists boasts a respected antitrust practice that focuses on criminal antitrust work and counseling. The team has been involved in high-profile criminal cases, including the Whitewater and Salt Lake City Olympic Committee matters. Major antitrust engagements have included acting for SPX in a case regarding monopolization in the afterparts market. The drafting of compliance programs for clients that are the subject of criminal antitrust investigations is also a key strength. In addition, the team counsels healthcare industry clients that are engaged in joint agreements with antitrust ramifications.

The Lawyers: Ronald Ravikoff is renowned among peers for his criminal antitrust defense work. He is currently representing a client in the solid waste removal industry.

The Clients: SPX; major corporates and individuals.

Other Notable Practitioners

Name partner **Hal Litchford** of Orlando-based Litchford & Christopher is active in the interface of unfair trade practices and antitrust, where peers described him as possessing a *"superb level of knowledge."* **Stephen Nagin** of Nagin Gallop Figuerdo in Coconut Grove undertakes both plaintiffs' and defendants' work in antitrust and IP matters. Interviewees pointed to his *"excellent antitrust credentials."* **Stuart Singer** of Boies, Schiller & Flexner LLP was acclaimed as an *"unbelievably smart"* antitrust litigator. Although the firm is a relative newcomer to the Florida legal landscape, its Miami, Fort Lauderdale and Orlando offices are active in antitrust litigation in Costa Rica, Honduras and Hawaii. Singer acted in antitrust litigation in North Carolina, in which the firm garnered a major victory for client Philip Morris.

BANKING & FINANCE

FLORIDA
Leading firms (Banking & Finance)
1. SHUTTS & BOWEN *Miami, Orlando*
2. HOLLAND & KNIGHT LLP *Miami, Tampa*
3. AKERMAN SENTERFITT *Orlando*
   GUNSTER, YOAKLEY & STEWART, PA *Miami*
   HUNTON & WILLIAMS *Miami*
   WHITE & CASE LLP *Miami*

Leading individuals (Banking & Finance)
1. BROWN Bowman *Shutts & Bowen*, Miami
2. ALVAREZ Victor *White & Case LLP*, Miami
   AVILA Alcides *Holland & Knight LLP*, Miami
   JONES Rod *Shutts & Bowen*, Orlando
   LOUMIET Carlos *Hunton & Williams*, Miami
   STUTTS Charles *Holland & Knight LLP*, Tampa
   VAZQUEZ-BELLO Clemente *Gunster, Yoakley*, Miami
3. CARDWELL Thomas *Akerman Senterfitt*, Orlando
   GREELEY Jack *Smith Mackinnon PA*, Orlando

Firms and individuals are listed alphabetically in each band.

Shutts & Bowen

The Firm: The firm's financial services practice fields 18 banking and finance specialists. Market sources lauded it as *"without a shadow of a doubt the preeminent banking regulatory firm in Florida."* The group represents a host of financial institutions in regulatory and supervisory matters involving the Federal Reserve system and the Florida Department of Banking and Finance. Banks are also represented in M&A and transactional matters, and on loan documentations and credit agreements.

The Lawyers: Bowman Brown (see p.172) is chairman of the financial services industry practice and judged *"a national star"* for his far-reaching regulatory expertise. A powerhouse in chartering and agency work, he represents both domestic and foreign banks, including one of the principal players in Latin America. He acted for Royal Bank of Canada in its acquisition of Barclays' Latin American private banking division. **Rod Jones** (see p.175) is a former director at the Florida Department of Banking and Finance. Rivals referred to him as *"a massive player"* in the bank regulatory arena. He has acted as counsel for the Committee on Commerce of the Florida House of Representatives, during which he advised on revisions to state codes regarding financial institutions.

The Clients: Citibank; JPMorgan Chase; Barclays Bank; ABN AMRO; Dresdner Bank; Merrill Lynch; American Express; Banco Sudameris Brasil and Royal Bank of Canada.

Holland & Knight LLP
see firm details p.820

The Firm: Observers described this Florida-based global firm as *"a supreme outfit that represents a number of prestigious lenders locally, and on a national and international basis."* The group operates out of 11 offices in the state, with about 20 attorneys advising on transactional and regulatory banking matters. Bond-connected credit facilities, creditors' rights, financial institution regulations and bank regulatory matters all feature in the workload.

The Lawyers: Alcides Avila (see p.171) heads the financial services practice group for south Florida, and is described by clients as *"a top professional."* His client base comprises state and national banks, and bank holding companies. He also counsels foreign banks on the establishment of banking operations in the US. Peers perceived **Charles Stutts** (see p.178) as *"an extremely capable lawyer who excels in community banking work."* He is a former general counsel to the Florida Comptroller's Office and the Florida Department of Banking and Finance. Stutts represents domestic banks and savings associations, international banking corporations, and trust companies on regulatory requirements. He acts as primary counsel to the Financial Service Centers of Florida and also represents a number of members in the trade association.

The Clients: Bank of America; Wachovia; Prudential Financial; AmSouth Bank; SouthTrust Bank and CCS Financial Services.

Akerman Senterfitt
see firm details p.760

The Firm: Observers agreed that this sizable firm offers *"great resources and deep quality."* It is endorsed for its representation of local and domestic banks in both transactional and regulatory matters. The group counsels the Florida Bankers Association, and has played an integral role in drafting a host of the state's banking laws. In addition, the team handles loans and commercial credit transactions including asset-based, securitized and syndicated loans.

The Lawyers: The banking community holds chairman and chief executive **Tom Cardwell** (see p.172) in high esteem by virtue of his role as general counsel to the Florida Bankers Association, a trade group of some 293 commercial banks. Cardwell has advised on a state law initiative concerning predatory lending. He also acted in an initiative set up by the IRS concerning interest payments and declarations on the deposit accounts of US nonresidents. Cardwell was dubbed *"a stellar performer"* by his competitors.

The Clients: Florida Bankers Association, Wachovia and Bank of America are clients. The group also acts for many smaller community banks.

Gunster, Yoakley & Stewart, PA

The Firm: The firm's corporate department includes a financial services group that advises on regulatory compliance, banking M&A, securities, broker-dealer issues, litigation and creditors' rights. But it was in the field of bank regulatory advice that attorneys were said to excel. Researchers were informed that *"the firm is great for 'know your customer' regulatory issues."*

The Lawyers: Clemente Vazquez-Bello, a member of the financial institutions practice

group, was described by interviewees as *"one of the premier national experts in the area of money laundering."* He acts for both domestic and foreign banks.
The Clients: The firm's client base includes local, national and international banks.

Hunton & Williams
The Firm: *"Certainly a growing presence in Florida"* is how many eminent practitioners judged this international practice. Clients commended the banking and finance group's experience in securitizations and bank regulatory and compliance issues. The team also advises on restructurings and workouts in connection with the firm's stand-alone bankruptcy group.
The Lawyers: *"Accomplished"* **Carlos Loumiet** joined the firm early in 2001 from Greenberg Traurig, where he headed the international and banking practices. He has advised on a groundbreaking securitization in Ecuador and on the financing for a proposed toll road in the Dominican Republic. He acted on the creation of a web-based process allowing institutional investors to place funds at a number of Federal Deposit Insurance Corporation-insured banks simultaneously. In addition, Loumiet helped the Government of Panama to remove itself from the Financial Action Task Force on Money Laundering's list of noncooperative countries.
The Clients: The World Bank Group; Deutsche Bank; Bank of America; First Union National Bank; Banco Uno; Primerica and SunTrust Banks.

White & Case LLP
The Firm: The Miami office of this international giant advises a range of local, national and international banks; work undertaken includes advising them on the structuring of US operations as well as on business expansion both domestically and overseas. The group fields three partners active in bank lending and regulatory issues who manage *"some substantial and highly relevant issues."*
The Lawyers: **Victor Alvarez** was described as a *"hugely respected attorney,"* particularly for his work on syndicated loans. He represents financial institutions in structured finance transactions, often with a Latin American dimension. Recent transactions include representing Banco BVA in a $100-200 million syndicated loan for a group of Mexican corporates, and advising ING Barings on the close of a $150 million syndicated loan to Panamco, a Panamanian soft drink bottler for Coca-Cola. Also represented BellSouth in its activities in Colombia.
The Clients: Bank of America; BSCH; Banco BVA; ING Barings, Standard Chartered Bank and Union Planters Bank.

Other Notable Practitioners
Jack Greeley of Orlando-based Smith Mackinnon PA is skilled in the formation of new financial institutions such as community banks, ultimately representing many of these entities after their establishment. His peers described him as an attorney who *"understands all the issues,"* including state and federal charters of incorporation matters and business capital requirements.

CONSTRUCTION

FLORIDA
Leading firms (Construction)

1 CARLTON FIELDS *Miami, Orlando, Tampa*
LEIBY TAYLOR STEARNS *Fort Lauderdale*
2 BOOSE CASEY CIKLIN LUBITZ *West Palm Beach*
HOLLAND & KNIGHT LLP *Orlando*
SIEGFRIED, RIVERA, LERNER *Miami*
STEPHEN RAKUSIN PA *Fort Lauderdale*
3 BECKER & POLIAKOFF, PA *Fort Lauderdale*
GRAY, HARRIS & ROBINSON, PA *Orlando*
MOYE, O'BRIEN, O'ROURKE, PICKERT *Orlando*
PECKAR & ABRAMSON, ROSENBERG *Miami*
WELBAUM, GUERNSEY, HINGSTON *Miami*

Firms are listed alphabetically in each band.

Carlton Fields
The Firm: One of the largest firms in Florida, it fields a talented pool of construction lawyers from its Tampa, Orlando and Miami offices. All manner of construction law work is undertaken, in both the contentious and noncontentious arenas. Interviewees pointed to its *"huge depth, broad services and long list of high-end clients."*
The Lawyers: **George Meyer**, the former chair of the construction law committee of The Florida Bar, was described to researchers as *"certainly among the best transactional construction lawyers in Florida."* His background as a construction engineer affords him an *"understanding of the complexities,"* and he has advised on multifaceted public and private development projects, including stadiums and arenas such as the Philadelphia Phillies Ballpark. He also provided contract advice on a 300-unit timeshare development, and counseled on the development of Argonne National Laboratory at The University of Chicago. Chair of the construction law group **Mike Nuechterlein** was described by peers as *"a true gentleman and a first-rate lawyer."* He has been active in litigation arising from a $73 million claim involving a waste water treatment plant in Pinellas County, Florida. He also advised on security improvements valued at $3 billion for the Hillsboro County aviation department, and represented condominium associations in the Panhandle area. **Bruce King** has particular expertise in surety cases, and is respected for his litigious skills. **Charles Cacciabeve** was frequently recommended as an attorney who was *"consistently involved in important projects with notable engineering clients."* He represented subcontractor Addison Steel in a case concerning Orlando International Airport, and a large contractor client in a $42 million bid protest in the federal arena.
The Clients: The firm advises owners, developers, public bodies, large general contractors, designers and engineers. The roster includes: Hunt Construction Group; Orange County, Florida; Kellogg Brown & Root; St. Paul ; The Hartford; AIG; Lucent Technologies and Fairfield Resorts.

Leiby Taylor Stearns Linkhorst & Roberts PA
The Firm: Despite being smaller in size, this Fort Lauderdale construction boutique was respected by competitors for its *"highly specialized expertise."* Its 12 attorneys counsel a mix of general contractors and subcontractors, owners, developers, architects and designers.
The Lawyers: Founder of the firm **Larry Leiby** was heartily endorsed as *"the father of lien law"* and *"the most respected and experienced attorney in the field."* He wrote the Florida Construction Law Manual, and was the founder of The Florida Bar's construction law committee. He represented a client in contractual issues and alleged construction defects and Mursten Construction in a dispute arising from nonpayments relating to a shore club on Miami Beach. Elsewhere, he represented Dooley & Mack Constructors against the Florida Board of Education over disputes concerning payment.
The Clients: Hewitt-Kier Construction, Bostic Steel and Dooley & Mack Constructors.

Boose Casey Ciklin Lubitz Martens McBane & O'Connell
The Firm: The firm is home to *"a clutch of useful attorneys who are well versed in the nuances of construction litigation."* It has attracted an impressive array of general contractors as clients and has also advised school boards.
The Lawyers: **Bruce Alexander** is an expert in construction lien law and construction litigation.

FLORIDA — CONSTRUCTION

FLORIDA
Leading individuals (Construction)

★ **LEIBY Larry** *Leiby Taylor Stearns*, Fort Lauderdale

1
- **ALEXANDER Bruce** *Boose Casey Ciklin*, West Palm Beach
- **MEYER George** *Carlton Fields*, Tampa
- **O'NEAL-COBLE Leslie** *Holland & Knight LLP*, Orlando
- **RAKUSIN Steve** *Stephen Rakusin PA*, Fort Lauderdale
- **SIEGFRIED Steven** *Siegfried, Rivera, Lerner*, Miami
- **WELBAUM Earl** *Welbaum, Guernsey, Hingston*, Miami

2
- **HORNREICH Michael** *Greenberg Traurig LLP*, Orlando
- **KING Bruce** *Carlton Fields*, Miami
- **NUECHTERLEIN Mike** *Carlton Fields*, Tampa
- **REISMAN Steven** *Peckar & Abramson*, Miami
- **WEINTRAUB Lee** *Becker & Poliakoff PA*, Fort Lauderdale
- **WEISS Christopher** *Holland & Knight LLP*, Orlando

3
- **ASHBY Kimberly** *Akerman Senterfitt*, Orlando
- **BROWN Daryl** *Brown Clark Christopher*, Sarasota
- **CACCIABEVE Charles** *Carlton Fields*, Orlando
- **GURLEY David** *Gurley Dramis*, Sarasota
- **KEINER Jeffrey** *Gray, Harris & Robinson PA*, Orlando
- **LESSER Steven** *Becker & Poliakoff PA*, Fort Lauderdale
- **MOYE James** *Moye, O'Brien, O'Rourke, Pickert*, Orlando
- **ROSENBERG Donald** *Peckar & Abramson*, Miami
- **WILSON Michael** *Gray, Harris & Robinson PA*, Orlando

Individuals are listed alphabetically in each band.

Interviewees described him as *"a supremely talented and knowledgeable attorney."* He has advised Suffolk Construction on numerous condominium developments in Broward County, and represented clients such as large local contractors Catalfumo Construction & Development, and The Weitz Company, based in Des Moines, Iowa.
The Clients: The Clark Construction Group, Suffolk Construction and The Weitz Company.

Holland & Knight LLP
see firm details p.820
The Firm: Market commentators recognized that *"Holland & Knight clearly has the depth, experience and client connections."* The Orlando office was particularly commended for its work in the tourism industry; much of the attorneys' workload there relates to hotel developments and hospitality-related matters.
The Lawyers: **Leslie O'Neal-Coble** (see p.176), who was described by competitors as an *"absolute dean of the bar,"* chairs the national construction law team. She is active in drafting and negotiating contracts for owners, contractors and subcontractors, and has extensive trial experience. Her recent caseload includes representing owners in the hospitality field, such as Marriott International, and contractors such as Bovis Lend Lease and Holder Construction as well as acting on public works for the University of Florida. **Chris Weiss** (see p.179) was widely endorsed by peers for his *"sophisticated work for substantial contractors"* such as Turner Construction Company. He is active in construction litigation, with an emphasis on defect disputes, design or delay claims, lien foreclosures and arbitration.
The Clients: Marriott International; Bovis Lend Lease; Holder Construction; Turner Construction Company and University of Florida.

Siegfried, Rivera, Lerner, De La Torre & Sobel PA
The Firm: Approximately 20 attorneys undertake civil trial work, construction litigation and transactional matters. Rivals were impressed by *"the wide array of notable cases that the firm attracts."* The group counts a number of large general contractors among its clients.
The Lawyers: Peers roundly praised **Steve Siegfried** as an *"experienced, highly practical and knowledgeable attorney."* One of the leading construction litigators in the state, he also has a high degree of expertise in lien law.
The Clients: Greenberg Construction; Miller & Solomon General Contractors; Sunhouse Construction and Dacra Construction.

Stephen Rakusin PA
The Firm: This boutique firm in Fort Lauderdale is home to one partner and three associates. Although the firm cannot compete with larger rivals in terms of volume, it does impress observers with its highly sophisticated construction litigation. Peers expressed admiration for both the *"expert knowledge"* of these attorneys and their ability to attract *"high-end clients."*
The Lawyers: Firm founder **Steve Rakusin** was described by interviewees as *"certainly among the elite - a must for any list."* Respected for his writings on lien law, Rakusin is an experienced construction litigator and recently represented a client in a complex contract dispute claim with a surety.
The Clients: The firm acts for owners, developers, contractors and subcontractors.

Becker & Poliakoff PA
The Firm: Rivals perceive the firm to have *"the ability to take on a broad range of construction cases at any one time."* Contractors, subcontractors, sureties and architects are represented, and the firm has developed a profile for public work, particularly in the development of schools. Its expertise in condominium-related construction was also singled out. About a dozen attorneys are dedicated to construction matters.
The Lawyers: Peers described **Lee Weintraub** as *"a fantastic attorney and a credit to the rest of us."* He principally represents owners, contractors, subcontractors and bond sureties. He has advised clients such as The School Board of Broward County and developer Engle Homes, and has worked on a defect case relating to Sunrise Middle School in Fort Lauderdale. **Steve Lesser** is best known for his representation of homeowner Phillipe Moransais in a landmark case before the Florida Supreme Court that effectively made architects, engineers and design professionals accountable for their own negligence. Peers view Lesser as *"an experienced attorney who has been at the head of the pack for many years."* He serves as special construction litigation counsel to The School Board of Broward County.
The Clients: Owners and developers are the predominant clients of this mid-sized Florida full-service outfit. Acts for The School Board of Broward County and Engle Homes.

Gray, Harris & Robinson PA
The Firm: This large full-service firm has six offices in Florida; its Orlando base is frequently cited by competitors as *"a key source of legal representation for construction matters."* Public work programs undertaken in Orange County, Florida have been a steady stream of activity, involving the review of contract documents, bid dispute representation, arbitration and litigation. Attorneys have also worked on the development of sewage treatment plants, pipeline projects, jails and county buildings.
The Lawyers: Rivals described **Michael Wilson** as *"one of the leading lights for construction law in Orlando."* He is experienced in construction litigation, having conducted disputes in state and federal courts throughout Florida. Wilson represents a range of clients including owners, contractors and lenders. On the transactional side, he frequently advises on contract drafting and negotiation. **Jeffrey Keiner** was praised for his defense of architects and engineers. He specializes in professional and environmental claims, land use and real estate litigation.
The Clients: B&M Construction Company, Beers Construction and Hunt Construction Group.

Moye, O'Brien, O'Rourke, Pickert & Martin, LLP
see firm details p.855
The Firm: The Orlando office of this 11-lawyer boutique firm was commended to researchers for its representation of *"significant worldwide clients."* The practice in Florida is ably supported by the firm's Chicago headquarters. Its construction law work encompasses general trial and appellate practice, state and federal arbitrations and dispute resolution board proceedings. The firm also advises on construction-related contracts, bonds, surety law and construction liens.
The Lawyers: *"Right at the top of the tree,"* senior partner **James Moye** (see p.176) was respected by peers for his work with large general contractors. Active across the range of construction law, he also advises on labor relations and employment law as they affect the construction sector.
The Clients: Balfour Beatty Construction and Centex Homes.

CORPORATE/M&A | FLORIDA

Peckar & Abramson, Rosenberg, Reisman & Stein LLP
see firm details p.863

The Firm: This firm was created in 2000 through an amalgamation of the Florida firm Rosenberg, Reisman & Stein with the nationally recognized New Jersey firm of Peckar & Abramson. Nine construction law attorneys work from the Miami office, overseeing building works in south and central Florida as well as construction and development matters in The Bahamas and the Caribbean.

The Lawyers: Observers singled out **Stephen Reisman** (see p.176) as *"the greatest asset of this firm - aggressive in style but always ethical."* Reisman undertakes a substantial volume of work for Turner Construction Company but his client list includes other general contractors, subcontractors and owners. Senior partner **Donald Rosenberg** (see p.177) represents owners, developers and lenders in transactional and litigious matters. Competitors viewed him as *"the senior figure within the firm and a highly dependable attorney."*

The Clients: The client roster is primarily composed of prominent local, national and international contractors and construction managers.

Welbaum, Guernsey, Hingston, Greenleaf & Gregory LLP

The Firm: This Miami firm is most respected for its surety representation, where peers deem it *"second to none."* The team represents contractors, subcontractors, architects, engineers and real estate developers in the construction industry.

The Lawyers: **Earl Welbaum** was recognized as a long-standing leader in his field. One commentator claimed: *"Those who have been trained by Welbaum now read like a who's who of Florida's top construction lawyers."* Welbaum is undoubtedly one of the most experienced lawyers in surety defense, and is also respected for his work in fidelity law, building construction law and insurance and commercial litigation.

The Clients: Beauchamp Construction; Bovis Lend Lease; Clark Contractors; Commercial Union Insurance; Hanover Insurance; Industrial Indemnity Company; JJW Construction; United Pacific Insurance Company and Western Surety Company.

Other Notable Practitioners

"Tenacious" **Kim Ashby** (see p.171) at the Orlando office of Akerman Senterfitt was commended for her expertise in construction litigation and her skills as an appellate lawyer. Rivals were impressed by the demeanor of **Mike Hornreich** at Greenberg Traurig, LLP; they agreed that he is *"intelligent and honorable - he organizes cases so that they get resolved early."* Hornreich continues to represent The Clark Construction Group, Hensel Phelps Construction, Washington Group International and Odebrecht Construction, a Brazilian company. At Brown Clark Christopher & DeMay in Sarasota, **Daryl Brown** was recommended as *"a talented attorney"* who works with contractors, lenders, sureties and insurance companies in all forms of complex litigation and negotiated settlements. Founder member of Gurley Dramis, **David Gurley** was described to researchers as *"a great choice for surety representation."* His expertise spans surety and construction law, insurance coverage and construction disputes.

CORPORATE

FLORIDA
Leading firms (Corporate/M&A)

1. **AKERMAN SENTERFITT** Miami
   GREENBERG TRAURIG LLP Fort Lauderdale, Miami
2. **STEEL HECTOR & DAVIS LLP** Miami
3. **FOLEY & LARDNER** Jacksonville
   HOLLAND & KNIGHT LLP Jacksonville, Tampa
4. **KIRSCHNER & LEGLER** Jacksonville
   SHUTTS & BOWEN Miami
   TRENAM, KEMKER, SCHARF, BARKIN Tampa
   WHITE & CASE LLP Miami

Firms are listed alphabetically in each band.

Akerman Senterfitt
see firm details p.760

The Firm: From a *"relatively low profile"* five years ago, the firm's standing has grown rapidly thanks both to the quality of its attorneys and close ties to a powerful corporate client base. The firm's relationship with Huizenga Holdings is seen as a principal factor in its success. Commentators assess the practice as *"dynamic"* across the state, and particularly in south Florida where it has *"a number of strong lawyers"* driving its corporate and securities operations.

The Lawyers: Observers credit New York-trained **Stephen Roddenberry** (see p.177) - chiefly associated with bringing Huizenga to Akerman Senterfitt - with much of its expanding reputation: *"He joined the firm and it took off."* A *"crackerjack lawyer,"* Roddenberry impresses contemporaries with his ability to maintain control over transactions while being responsive to his clients' needs. He advised Wackenhut in its acquisition by Group 4 Falck for $570 million. Peers agree that **Jonathan Awner** (see p.171) *"has made impressive accomplishments in a short space of time."* A *"well-schooled"* corporate specialist, he was counsel to AutoNation in its spin-off of ANC Rental, a deal that was tax-free to AutoNation stockholders.

The Clients: Boca Resorts; Embraer; Huizenga Holdings; Miami Dolphins; NationsRent; Wackenhut; IVAX; New River Capital Partners; Republic Services and Spherion.

Greenberg Traurig LLP
see firm details p.808

The Firm: Historical roots in Miami plus an enviable client base make the firm a *"national leader"* in the opinion of many commentators. The corporate practice, along with real estate, represents the firm's core strength. Its long-standing corporate securities specialists are said to be *"easy to deal with"* and enjoy a reputation for being *"dominant in the field."* Transactions are frequently cross-border affairs with a pronounced Latin American component. The firm advised Latin American flag carriers TACA Group in several financings and acquisitions, and acted on Telefónica's Mexican acquisitions. Elsewhere, attorneys represented Equity One in its acquisitions of United Investors Realty Trust and the US properties of Canadian-owned Centrefund Realty.

The Lawyers: The highly respected **Daniel Aronson** (see p.171) drew strong acclaim for his work in venture capital, public offerings and M&A. *"Hugely experienced"* **Gary Epstein** (see p.173) is often called on by rivals when conflicts arise. He has undertaken a *"profusion"* of private placements for public clients. These include advising on the acquisition by RailAmerica of the StatesRail companies for $90 million in a cash and common stock purchase.

The Clients: Raymond James & Associates; Equity One; TACA Group; Telefónica; RailAmerica and Ryder System are typical clients of the firm.

Steel Hector & Davis LLP

The Firm: Traditionally one of the *"premier firms in Florida,"* interviewees pointed to its long history in the Miami area, where it is said to have *"all-around capabilities."* The volume of securities transactions remains high; in 2001, its attorneys handled $4 billion in offerings inclusive of debt and equity. On the corporate side, the firm represented Florida's largest private utility in the cross-border purchase and joint ownership of a power plant. Abroad, its attorneys advised a Swedish power and energy company in the development of a venture in the electric utility industry in Latin America.

The Lawyers: **Thomas McGuigan** was warmly recommended as a leading corporate attorney. Rivals acknowledged that he *"excels"* as a resourceful lawyer.

The Clients: American Airlines, AIG American General and FPL Group.

FLORIDA — CORPORATE/M&A

FLORIDA
Leading individuals (Corporate/M&A)

1 MCGUIGAN Thomas *Steel Hector & Davis LLP*, Miami
RODDENBERRY Stephen *Akerman Senterfitt*, Miami

2 AWNER Jonathan *Akerman Senterfitt*, Miami
RASMUSSEN Robert *Glenn Rasmussen Fogarty*, Tampa

3 ARONSON Daniel *Greenberg Traurig*, Fort Lauderdale
DAVIS Gardner *Foley & Lardner*, Jacksonville
EPSTEIN Gary *Greenberg Traurig LLP*, Miami
FELMAN David *Hill, Ward & Henderson PA*, Tampa
LEISNER Richard *Trenam, Kemker, Scharf*, Tampa
SADLER Luther *Foley & Lardner*, Jacksonville
YADLEY Gregory *Shumaker, Loop & Kendrick*, Tampa

4 BROWN Bowman *Shutts & Bowen*, Miami
CANNON Kinder *Holland & Knight LLP*, Jacksonville
DOLINER Nathaniel *Carlton Fields*, Tampa
GRAMMIG Robert *Holland & Knight LLP*, Tampa
JAMIESON Michael *Holland & Knight LLP*, Tampa
KIRSCHNER Kenneth *Kirschner & Legler*, Jacksonville
LEGLER Mitchell *Kirschner & Legler*, Jacksonville
TEBLUM Gary *Trenam, Kemker, Scharf, Barkin*, Tampa

Individuals are listed alphabetically in each band.

Foley & Lardner
The Firm: The firm attracted recommendations for its profile in Jacksonville where it possesses a *"respected and key corporate practice."* Attorneys handled the $1 billion stock sale of a telecom company to an industry buyer, a transaction that illustrates the group's capacity to handle large deals. It was also involved in a $460 million stock and cash acquisition of an air equipment manufacturer.
The Lawyers: **Gardner Davis** is a member of the firm's business law department and its transactional and securities, finance, and business reorganizations practice groups. Davis, who represents public companies, can draw on a *"substantial knowledge of corporate law and the inner workings of M&A transactions."* **Luther Sadler** was described by interviewees as a *"tremendous attorney."* He served as lead counsel to the internet-based mortgage banking firm Mortgage.com in its IPO.
The Clients: Exelon; Gambro Healthcare; Roche Diagnostics and Mortgage.com.

Holland & Knight LLP
see firm details p.820
The Firm: Ten offices make it ubiquitous in Florida and several interviewees agreed that the firm has developed one of the most prominent practices in Tampa. A deep bench of *"talented lawyers"* secures the firm a following. Said one interviewee: *"its strength is in its size."*
The Lawyers: A *"30-year-long successful career"* distinguishes **Kinder Cannon** (see p.172), who possesses *"one of the strongest backgrounds in securities law in north Florida."* Peers described **Robert Grammig**'s (see p.174) assets as *"wise judgment and years of experience."* He advised on several secondary offerings for Raymond James & Associates and Robert W Baird. His corporate transactions include representation on German household products manufacturer Danke's divestiture of major European operations, and Jabil Circuit's acquisition of facilities in Malaysia. The *"first-rate"* **Michael Jamieson** (see p.175) acted on a foreign client's $650 million acquisition of a securities services provider in Florida, and was involved in a $450 million public company acquisition in Texas.
The Clients: Clients consist of a mix of long-standing traditional Tampa businesses and new hi-tech companies. Harris Corporation is a major client. Others include: Jabil Circuit; Raymond James & Associates; Danke; Reptron Electronics; Brown & Brown; Paxson Communications; Pacer International; Rock Creek Capital; Credicorp; Kos Pharmaceuticals; ProxyMed; Kforce; Hughes Supply and Broadwing.

Kirschner & Legler
The Firm: This two-man boutique was founded in 2001. The firm undertakes general corporate work, representing Stein Mart and Winn-Dixie as general counsel and primary counsel respectively.
The Lawyers: The *"consummate"* **Kenneth Kirschner** was formerly senior counsel to the New York firm LeBoeuf, Lamb, Greene & MacRae. **Mitchell Legler** benefits from a *"superlative reputation"* in the securities arena. He has guided several companies through IPOs and also advised Dutch pension funds on investments in US real estate.
The Clients: Stein Mart, Winn-Dixie and insurance companies form part of the client base.

Shutts & Bowen
The Firm: The Miami arm of this *"transactionally minded"* firm is assessed by interviewees as *"clearly visible"* in the corporate finance market. One client appreciated its *"New York quality without New York costs."* In particular, the firm is respected for its regulatory work in banking and Latin American deals. Attorneys advised Royal Bank of Canada during its acquisition of Barclays Bank's Latin American and US private banking business, which had total client assets of $2.9 billion.
The Lawyers: Borrowers respect **Bowman Brown** (see p.172) as a *"trustworthy counsel"* and regard him as the firm's *"top-flight"* attorney. He advised Royal Bank of Canada on several private banking operation acquisitions.
The Clients: Citibank and Royal Bank of Canada are typical of the firm's client roster.

Trenam, Kemker, Scharf, Barkin, Frye, O'Neill & Mullis PA
The Firm: Well known for its bankruptcy practice, market observers believe the firm's corporate and securities profile is growing. The group has pooled tax and corporate specialists into one department, and attracts international investment banks and NYSE-listed companies as clients.
The Lawyers: Leading corporate and securities attorney **Richard Leisner** has *"an impressive record of transactions and clients."* His tax-oriented practice is broadly centered on capital formation and corporate transactions, covering venture-capitalized start-ups and private placements through to IPOs and ongoing SEC reporting. Contemporaries respect **Gary Teblum** as a *"major securities lawyer."* Teblum heads the corporate and business transactions practice group, and leads the firm's business/tax department.
The Clients: HCA and Home Depot are clients.

White & Case LLP
The Firm: *"Certainly making their mark in Florida,"* opine competitors. The team in Miami is respected for its advice to domestic and international investors on Latin American acquisitions. Market opinion felt that the sum of the practice's collective breadth tended to prevail over the profiles of individual members.
The Lawyers: Jorge L Freeland is head of the domestic corporate and securities department in Miami. The firm advised Royal Ahold and Velox Retail Holdings on a joint venture, Disco Ahold International Holdings, which they used to acquire equity interests in supermarket chains in South America. Attorneys also completed a $300 million securitization by Brazilian mining company Companhia Vale do Rio Doce of its US dollar-denominated iron ore export sales.
The Clients: Royal Ahold, Velox Retail Holdings and South American privatization agencies.

Other Notable Practitioners
"As good as they come," **Robert Rasmussen** at Glenn Rasmussen Fogarty & Hooker received robust recommendations as a *"technically proficient"* attorney. He advised on Ceridian's acquisition of ABR Information Services in a $750 million cash transaction. **David Felman** of Hill, Ward & Henderson, PA, was admired by interviewees as *"a strong M&A lawyer."* He is counsel for Tampa-based private equity firm Lovett Miller and has acted for a number of angel investors. Managing partner in the Tampa office of Shumaker, Loop & Kendrick, LLP, **Gregory Yadley** was recommended for his *"quality work"* in public offerings and company sell-offs. **Nathaniel Doliner** is group leader of the corporate, securities and taxation practice group at Carlton Fields. Doliner specializes in transactions involving manufacturing and technology companies.

EMPLOYMENT & LABOR LAW

FLORIDA

EMPLOYMENT & LABOR LAW

MAINLY PLAINTIFF

FLORIDA
Leading firms
(Employment: Mainly Plaintiff)

1
- ROTHSTEIN, ROSENFELDT DOLIN *Fort Lauderdale*
- SUGARMAN & SUSSKIND *Coral Gables*

2
- AMLONG & AMLONG *Fort Lauderdale*
- CHONIN & SHER *Miami*
- EGAN, LEV & SIWICA *Orlando*
- KELLY & McKEE *Tampa*

Leading individuals
(Employment: Mainly Plaintiff)

1
- CHONIN Neil *Chonin & Sher, Miami*
- LINESCH David *The Linesch Firm, Palm Harbor*
- SUGARMAN Robert *Sugarman & Susskind, Coral Gables*
- WEISBERG Robert *Sole Practitioner, Coral Gables*

2
- McKEE Robert *Kelly & McKee, Tampa*
- ROSENFELDT Stuart *Rothstein, Fort Lauderdale*
- ROTHSTEIN Scott *Rothstein, Fort Lauderdale*
- SIWICA Richard *Egan, Lev & Siwica, Orlando*
- THOMAS Archibald *Archibald J. Thomas, III, Jacksonville*

3
- AMLONG Karen *Amlong & Amlong, Fort Lauderdale*
- AMLONG William *Amlong & Amlong, Fort Lauderdale*
- DOLIN Susan *Rothstein, Rosenfeldt, Fort Lauderdale*
- EGAN Joseph *Egan, Lev & Siwica, Orlando*
- KELLY Mark *Kelly & McKee, Tampa*
- SUSSKIND Howard *Sugarman & Susskind, Coral Gables*

Firms and individuals are listed alphabetically in each band.

Rothstein, Rosenfeldt Dolin & Pancier

The Firm: Interviewees endorsed this specialist plaintiffs' practice as *"a superb outfit with a fine reputation."* Eight attorneys focus largely on labor and employment law, while also undertaking civil rights, personal injury and commercial litigation cases.
The Lawyers: **Stuart Rosenfeldt** was named as *"a superb technician who knows the law inside out."* He has been active in class actions and jury trials, and regularly advises on issues including pregnancy and race discrimination, and sexual harassment. *"Effective"* **Scott Rothstein** is an experienced trial lawyer, while **Susan Dolin** was held in high regard by defense attorneys, who found her *"able to captivate the courtroom."* Dolin's caseload includes harassment, discrimination and ADA work.

Sugarman & Susskind

The Firm: A prestigious member of the employment and labor law fraternity. The firm is thought to excel as a *"preeminent"* union and labor law group, advising unions and employees on collective bargaining negotiations and discrimination matters.
The Lawyers: **Bob Sugarman** has represented unions for many years, and has a niche specialty in pension-related issues. Defense attorneys endorsed him as *"the finest union lawyer in the state."* **Howard Susskind** impressed many of *Chambers'* sources as *"a diligent and hard-working attorney."*

Amlong & Amlong

The Firm: Four attorneys at the firm represent plaintiffs in employment matters, which have, of late, included several notable whistle-blower cases. Leading commentators recognized that the firm has *"celebrated some key wins."*
The Lawyers: **William Amlong** is a former investigative and political reporter for The Miami Herald turned employment defense attorney. *"An extremely effective litigator,"* he was involved in a successful whistle-blower case in which he represented two City of Riviera Beach police lieutenants. **Karen Coolman Amlong** was likewise described as a *"tenacious opponent who has enjoyed a great degree of success."* Aside from her prolific employee representation, Coolman Amlong also acts on marital and family law matters.

Chonin & Sher

The Firm: This *"well-respected outfit"* is home to three attorneys who specialize in plaintiffs' representation in the employment and labor spheres. The firm also takes on civil rights, personal injury and commercial litigation cases.
The Lawyers: Firm founder **Neil Chonin** was described to researchers as *"first among equals in the world of labor and employment law."* A skilled trial lawyer, he is respected for his *"professionalism."*

Egan, Lev & Siwica

The Firm: This Orlando practice fields four lawyers who for many years have supplied *"high-quality advice on traditional labor law."* Union representation is the group's key strength, and its caseload has included matters argued before the Florida Supreme Court.
The Lawyers: Defense lawyers view **Richard Siwica** as a *"formidable opponent,"* citing his representation of a host of unions, such as those of the firefighting profession. **Joe Egan** is another traditional labor lawyer who is active in union representation. He was termed by competitors as *"a tough customer but a straight shooter."*
The Clients: Florida Building Trades Council, the Florida AFL-CIO and the National Education Association are clients.

Kelly & McKee

The Firm: Prominent in the Tampa region, this *"excellent team"* consists of two partners, both of whom were perceived to excel in the plaintiffs' field.
The Lawyers: **Robert McKee** was recommended for both his litigation and mediation experience. He advises on a varied mix of discrimination and harassment claims. He recently acted for Palestinian professor Sami Al-Arian, an alleged terrorist, who claimed that bigotry was behind his dismissal from the faculty of the University of South Florida. **Mark Kelly** was singled out for his *"great courtroom abilities."* A seasoned plaintiff attorney, *"he knows the nuances of the law inside out."*

Other Notable Practitioners

Palm Harbor-based **David Linesch** (see p.1754) heads the labor and employment boutique, The Linesch Firm. His workload encompasses both management and employee representation, but it is the latter that has earned him the reputation of being *"one of the preeminent attorneys in the state."* He is well versed in claims regarding equal pay and injuries in the workplace and in harassment, discrimination and ADA matters.

Bob Weisberg is *"never overly aggressive"* in his handling of employment law issues. He recently acted on a complex sexual harassment case before the Florida Fourth District Court of Appeal.

Archibald Thomas is a *"supremely competent and ethical"* attorney. He works out of the three-lawyer firm, the Law Offices of Archibald J. Thomas, III, and is proficient in sex, age and Title VII discrimination, employee rights, wrongful termination and non-compete agreements litigation.

FLORIDA

EMPLOYMENT & LABOR LAW — MAINLY DEFENDANT

FLORIDA
Leading firms
(Employment: Mainly Defendant)

1. **FORD & HARRISON LLP** *Orlando, Tampa*
2. **ZINOBER & MCCREA PA** *Tampa*
3. **COFFMAN, COLEMAN, ANDREWS** *Jacksonville*
   MORGAN, LEWIS & BOCKIUS LLP *Miami*
   MULLER MINTZ *Miami*
   THOMPSON, SIZEMORE & GONZALEZ *Tampa*
4. **ALLEN, NORTON** *Coral Gables, Orlando, Tampa*
   FISHER & PHILLIPS LLP *Fort Lauderdale*
   FOLEY & LARDNER *Jacksonville*
   FOWLER WHITE BOGGS BANKER *Tampa*
5. **AKERMAN SENTERFITT** *Orlando*
   JACKSON LEWIS *Miami, Orlando*

Leading individuals
(Employment: Mainly Defendant)

1. **ALLEY John-Edward** *Ford & Harrison LLP, Tampa*
   CONNOR Terence *Morgan, Lewis & Bockius, Miami*
   GONZALEZ Thomas *Thompson, Sizemore, Tampa*
   ZINOBER Peter *Zinober & McCrea PA, Tampa*
2. **CASEY Michael** *Muller Mintz, Miami*
   COLEMAN Patrick *Coffman, Coleman, Jacksonville*
   DICKINSON John *Constangy, Brooks, Jacksonville*
   FLEMING Joseph *Greenberg Traurig LLP, Miami*
   GARWOOD Thomas *Ford & Harrison LLP, Orlando*
   HAMILTON Russell *Morgan, Lewis & Bockius, Miami*
   HYDE Kevin *Foley & Lardner, Jacksonville*
   ROBINSON John *Fowler White Boggs Banker, Tampa*
3. **ANDREWS William** *Coffman, Coleman, Jacksonville*
   BLUE James *Allen, Norton & Blue PA, Tampa*
   BROWN James *Ford & Harrison LLP, Orlando*
   CAULKINS Charles *Fisher & Phillips, Fort Lauderdale*
   FARMER Guy *Foley & Lardner, Jacksonville*
   GROGAN Michael *Coffman, Coleman, Jacksonville*
   KORNREICH David *Muller Mintz, Miami*
   MCCREA Richard *Zinober & McCrea PA, Tampa*
4. **BRAMNICK James** *Muller Mintz, Miami*
   NORTON Robert *Allen, Norton & Blue PA, Coral Gables*
   NORTON Susan *Allen, Norton & Blue PA, Tampa*

Firms and individuals are listed alphabetically in each band.

Ford & Harrison LLP

The Firm: One of the larger employment and labor boutiques in the US. Four of the firm's ten offices are situated in Florida, and rivals have commented on its *"tremendous growth,"* believing that *"it has rounded up some of the best people in the state."* Its attorneys have been described as *"exemplary - they produce quality work throughout."* The group represents employers on discrimination claims, employee benefits and ERISA issues, and also advises on traditional labor law matters.

The Lawyers: Peers place **John-Edward Alley** *"in a class of his own."* He has represented Publix Super Markets in class actions, counseled Skyline Mobile Homes on union-related issues, and advised a sheet metal manufacturer on union-organizing drives. **Tom Garwood** was endorsed by observers for his *"ethical approach - he gives the employment and labor bar a good name."* Skilled in labor law, he advises Walt Disney World, Sheraton Hotels & Resorts, Westin Hotels & Resorts, Lockheed Martin and the Orlando Utilities Commission among others. *"Hugely respected"* **Jim Brown** represents employers before the NLRB, the State of Florida Public Employees Relations Commission and the Department of Labor. His experience incorporates civil rights litigation, such as race, age, disability and sex discrimination and sexual harassment claims.

The Clients: Walt Disney World; Danka; Publix Super Markets; Sheraton Hotels & Resorts; Westin Hotels & Resorts; Darden Restaurants; Lockheed Martin; Clear Channel Communications; DHL Airways and the Orlando Utilities Commission.

Zinober & McCrea PA

The Firm: This smaller firm fields about 15 attorneys, who specialize in labor and employment. Interviewees singled out the firm's key strength: *"It is fantastic for litigation,"* while its attorneys are trusted as *"very professional - you can deal with them on a handshake."*

The Lawyers: **Pete Zinober** was described by peers as *"a successful and extremely confident trial attorney."* His recent caseload has included counseling restaurant groups such as McDonald's and Applebee's International. He also represented the University of South Florida in a case involving alleged religious discrimination and harassment of two former employees. Clients spoke of name partner **Rich McCrea** as *"a hugely skilled attorney in whom we have the utmost faith."* He has successfully defended two companies, Correctional Services, Inc. and the Agency for Community Treatment Services, in separate whistle-blower cases. He also successfully defended Infinity Broadcasting and Infinity Radio against a claim of gender discrimination and retaliation. McCrea also represented York Bridge Concepts in an arbitration arising from the enforcement of non-compete agreements against former executives.

The Clients: McDonald's; Applebee's International; University of South Florida; Ceridian; Infinity Broadcasting; Tenet Healthcare and US Airways.

Coffman, Coleman, Andrews & Grogan

The Firm: This group has a dominant presence in northern Florida and has been dubbed *"the preeminent firm in Jacksonville."* Attorneys advise on employment litigation and labor law matters in equal measures, with an emphasis on management representation. The group is experienced in a range of employment issues such as race and sex discrimination, national origins, whistle-blower cases, and wage and hour work.

The Lawyers: **Patrick Coleman** is *"a superb lawyer, at the top of his game."* He is frequently involved in complex employment litigation and is a certified mediator. He has acted for a large maritime company and a healthcare organization, and counts Schering-Plough and Blue Cross and Blue Shield of Florida as clients. **Bill Andrews** is a *"highly esteemed"* attorney who has of late represented a large distributor of natural and specialty health food products on wage and hour and OSHA matters. Also involved in collective actions under the FLSA. **Mike Grogan** was praised by peers as *"incredibly hard working in order to achieve his successful results."* Active at state and federal levels, he has advised on the dismissal of a civil rights action against the Broward County Property Appraiser. Grogan also represented Columbia County and the Florida Community College at Jacksonville in collective bargaining matters.

The Clients: Blue Cross and Blue Shield of Florida; Winn-Dixie; Schering-Plough and Unilever.

Morgan, Lewis & Bockius LLP

The Firm: The Miami office of this international firm places a heavy bias on employment and labor law within its remit as a full-service operation. It is skilled in both employment litigation and labor matters and is home to attorneys who are described as *"high quality - bright, analytical and ethical individuals."*

The Lawyers: Researchers were informed that **Terry Connor** was *"well versed in the law."* Much of his work involves clients from the aviation, transport, pharmaceutical and medical industries. Connor acted for Ortho-McNeil Pharmaceutical in a sexual harassment case. **Russell Hamilton** focuses his practice on labor, employment and employee benefits matters for a client base of employers and employers' associations.

The Clients: Principally represents employers and management.

Muller Mintz

The Firm: One of the largest labor and employment boutiques in the state, it has a bias toward employment law, while approximately 20% of the workload lies in labor law matters. Its attorneys have displayed an *"ability to tackle sophisticated*

EMPLOYMENT & LABOR LAW

FLORIDA

public sector cases." Although some commentators pointed to *"an aggressive streak"* in the group's approach to cases, they agreed that its lawyers are *"hard-working and successful."*

The Lawyers: Eminent attorney **Mike Casey** *"is a leading light in the profession."* He primarily works in the employment field and has acted on large class actions, including discrimination charges against companies involved in the hospitality and manufacturing sectors. He is also involved in labor issues related to the motion-picture industry. **David Kornreich** impressed peers as *"an outstanding practitioner"* of labor law, most notably for his representation of public sector bodies including school boards and government entities. Clients singled out **Jim Bramnick** for *"his ability to get the job done with the minimum of fuss."* He is frequently involved in cases covering race or sex discrimination, OSHA, whistle-blower, and wage and hour matters.

Thompson, Sizemore & Gonzalez

The Firm: This 13-lawyer outfit represents employers in high-end discrimination litigation and labor law matters. Peers reported that the firm contains *"some of the most respected and influential attorneys in the state."*

The Lawyers: Defendant attorneys claimed that **Tom Gonzalez** is *"feared by those on the other side because of his brilliance."* He counsels management on union matters, employment litigation, arbitration and mediation. Gonzalez has been active in the defense of civil rights claims, age discrimination, and wage and hour matters. His clients include Verizon, TECO Energy and Outback Steakhouse.

The Clients: University of South Florida; Verizon; TECO Energy and City of Tampa.

Allen, Norton & Blue PA

The Firm: This employment firm has four offices spread across Florida, with particular strength in Coral Gables and Orlando. Peers agreed that its representation of management is conducted by *"a clutch of very fine attorneys."*

The Lawyers: In the Tampa office, **Jim Blue** was described as a *"wise and experienced"* attorney. He has acted as counsel for Boeing and Anheuser-Busch. Coral Gables-based **Bob Norton** concentrates on labor law, with about a third of his time taken up by employment litigation. A *"conscientious attorney,"* he impresses with his trial skills. Norton acted to defeat a union-organizing campaign in the medical field that was rejected by the employees. In the same office, **Susan Norton** has been active in ADA Title III cases.

The Clients: American Express; Starwood Hotels and Resorts Worldwide; Disney and British Airways.

Fisher & Phillips LLP

The Firm: The firm added an Orlando office to its Fort Lauderdale base in Florida in 2001. Adjudged *"a professional outfit with straight-shooting lawyers"* by peers, the firm covers labor, employment, civil rights, employee benefits and business immigration law.

The Lawyers: Observers described **Charles Caulkins** as *"a top-rate attorney - a traditional union player."* Caulkins' practice includes involvement before labor relations boards and proceedings. He has also acted in litigation, appeals, collective bargaining and administrative hearings.

The Clients: The firm's client base includes employers, management and public bodies.

Foley & Lardner

The Firm: This group of 16, with a strong bias toward employment law, operates from five offices across Florida. Peers pointed to the Jacksonville practice as the hub of the group and described it as *"one of the best full-service firms in the field."*

The Lawyers: *"A seasoned attorney,"* **Guy Farmer** has been involved in a series of age discrimination cases, in which he represented the pulp and paper manufacturer Rayonier. He also defended Gulf Terminal, a subsidiary of Toyota, in a class action. **Kevin Hyde**, a senior partner in the Jacksonville office, is regarded as *"a true class act."* He has advised Fortune 100 manufacturing companies on sexual harassment claims, collective wage and hour matters and race discrimination issues.

The Clients: Kmart; Johnson Controls; Rayonier; Visteon; Stein Mart; UPS and Wal-Mart.

Fowler White Boggs Banker

The Firm: This large full-service firm, headquartered in Tampa, fields a group of 12 attorneys that devotes the majority of its time to employment law and discrimination litigation. The team was described to researchers as *"one of the best in the region."*

The Lawyers: Rivals appreciate that **John Robinson** is *"a top guy who runs a steady ship."* A *"hard-working and imposing figure,"* he has been successful in class actions, and has handled some notable race discrimination cases. His clients include Motel 6.

The Clients: Work is undertaken for management.

Akerman Senterfitt

see firm details p.760

The Firm: The workload at this firm includes defense of claims of sexual harassment, ADA and the full range of discrimination. The team also advises on traditional labor matters such as union election campaigns, negotiating collective bargaining agreements and handling unfair labor practice charges, secondary boycotts and strikes.

The Lawyers: Kevin Shaughnessy presides over the firm's employment practice group, which exclusively represents employers.

The Clients: The group represents corporations of all sizes, public bodies and municipalities.

Jackson Lewis

The Firm: This countrywide firm has a network of 20 offices to draw upon for national cases. The group's remit extends from employment and labor matters to include immigration work.

The Lawyers: The firm's Orlando office, managed by Diane Stanton, stood out during the course of our research. Peers contend that it has *"smart lawyers with good judgment."* The Miami office, headed by David Block, was also commended for its consistently high standard of advice.

Other Notable Practitioners

John Dickinson of construction boutique Constangy, Brooks & Smith, LLC heads the firm's five-lawyer Jacksonville office. Sources singled out his employment and labor law experience, judging him *"particularly skilled in the arena of wage and hour compliance."* **Joe Fleming** (see p.173) of Greenberg Traurig LLP is *"incredibly hard working and extremely intelligent."* An active general litigator, he has an impressive track record in employment matters. Fleming has represented several airlines, including the national carriers of several Central American countries. He also acts as general counsel advising on union-related issues.

FLORIDA — ENVIRONMENT

ENVIRONMENT

FLORIDA
Leading firms (Environment)

1. **HOPPING, GREEN & SAMS PA** *Tallahassee*
2. **HOLLAND & KNIGHT LLP** *Orlando, Tallahassee*
   LEWIS, LONGMAN & WALKER PA *West Palm Beach*
3. **GREENBERG TRAURIG LLP** *Miami, West Palm Beach*
   GUNSTER *West Palm Beach, Fort Lauderdale*
   OERTEL, HOFFMAN, FERNANDEZ *Tallahassee*
   WHITE & CASE LLP *Miami*

Leading individuals (Environment)

1. **HALSEY Douglas** *White & Case LLP*, Miami
2. **HOPPING Wade** *Hopping, Green & Sams*, Tallahassee
   SELLERS Lawrence *Holland & Knight LLP*, Tallahassee
3. **COGLIANESE Matthew** *Bilzin Sumberg Dunn*, Miami
   PRESTON William *Sole Practitioner*, Tallahassee
   SMALLWOOD Mary *Ruden, McClosky*, Tallahassee
4. **BARKETT John** *Shook, Hardy & Bacon*, Miami
   COLE Terry *Oertel, Hoffman, Fernandez*, Tallahassee
   CURTIN Lawrence *Holland & Knight LLP*, Tallahassee
   GOLDSTEIN Michael *Akerman Senterfitt*, Miami
   GREEN William *Hopping, Green & Sams*, Tallahassee
   LEWIS Terry *Lewis, Longman & Walker*, West Palm Beach
   LOCKETT Laurel *Carlton Fields*, Tampa
   MALEFATTO Alfred *Greenberg Traurig*, West Palm Beach
   MATTHEWS Frank *Hopping, Green*, Tallahassee
   SCHULMAN Clifford *Greenberg Traurig LLP*, Miami
   SIMS Roger *Holland & Knight LLP*, Orlando

Firms and individuals are listed alphabetically in each band.

Hopping, Green & Sams PA

The Firm: This environmental and regulatory boutique attracted plaudits for its work with Fortune 500 companies. A leading attorney said: *"If I had to move to Tallahassee, it would be the first firm I'd want to join."* Observers noted the firm's participation in lobbying and administrative hearings. Lawyers cultivate a broad statewide practice, and demonstrate *"unparalleled skill"* in air pollution matters. The team has been involved in water work issues on behalf of large consortia in the regulatory community, and in rulemaking for Florida's water program.

The Lawyers: Wade Hopping is an active lobbyist at the state capital, performing *"powerful and effective legislative work."* Formerly a legislative assistant to the governor and a Florida Supreme Court judge, Hopping enjoys widespread recognition for his legislative expertise. The *"talented"* William Green (see p.1748) is an environment litigator able to draw on *"years of unmatched experience."* He helped to establlish rulings on phosphorous standards for the Everglades. Frank Matthews (see p.17499417) *"special role"* in liaising with the local, state and federal agencies also drew admiration.

The Clients: Attorneys advised the Florida Electric Power Coordinating Group and the Florida Manufacturing and Chemical Council on regulatory requirements and compliance issues. Other clients include: DuPont; Florida Power & Light; Florida Water Environment Association Utility Council; Gulf Power; Lloyd's; ExxonMobil and Sugar Cane Growers Cooperative of Florida.

Holland & Knight LLP
see firm details p.820

The Firm: Peers endorsed this Florida heavyweight, particularly citing a *"first-class"* team in Tallahassee. The firm's attorneys are regarded as *"prominent market figures"* steeped in legislative and regulatory matters, who participate in the formulation of state legislation and regulatory policies. They also act in an array of administrative and civil litigation matters involving permitting, enforcement and hazardous waste. The firm obtained a number of state and federal approvals, and advised on initial air construction permits for manufacturing plants. It also secured wetlands permits for phosphate mining companies, and air, water and deep well permits for clients such as Tropicana Products.

The Lawyers: Lawrence Sellers (see p.178) is a leading lobbyist, and a *"tremendous choice"* for key environmental topics of the day. Competitors said they would not hesitate to refer clients to him. Lawrence Curtin (see p.173) heads the environmental law group. He received market commendations for his *"substantial"* involvement in the field. In Orlando, *"old hand"* Roger Sims (see p.178) is considered a *"true leader"* in solid waste landfill matters.

The Clients: Tampa Electric, El Paso and Tropicana Products are clients of the firm.

Lewis, Longman & Walker PA

The Firm: This relatively new three-office environmental practice features a number of former government-salaried lawyers. The West Palm Beach office can lay claim to an *"esteemed"* statewide reputation. Rivals frequently refer work to the firm's attorneys, who they describe as *"professional"* and *"client-minded."* The firm has advised on the regulation of urban and agricultural encroachment on Lake Okeechobee and the Everglades ecosystem. Attorneys have also advised residential, commercial and agribusiness developers on both a national and regional basis in matters related to the CWA and environmental resource permits, rulemaking and comprehensive plan compliance.

The Lawyers: Singled out from the team is the *"impressive"* Terry Lewis. Combining land use and environmental expertise, he represents governmental bodies and private clients in state agency rulemaking proceedings.

The Clients: Southwest Florida Water Management District; Sugar Cane Growers Cooperative of Florida; West Coast Inland Navigation District; St Lucie County; Palm Beach County and Leon County.

Greenberg Traurig LLP
see firm details p.808

The Firm: Commentators regard the firm, one of the oldest and largest in Florida, as a *"recognizable competitor"* in the market. Its depth and experience in transactional real estate work contributes to its *"comprehensive"* planning and permitting environmental practice. Attorneys have sought approvals for a luxury assisted - living facility to be constructed at a former landfill site, and advised on coastal permits for beach restoration and park improvements. Elsewhere, rock mining companies approached the team to secure permitting for industrial plants to process limestone. Wetlands permitting and regulatory approvals for marinas also form a major part of the workload.

The Lawyers: Credited with a *"fine insight"* into the regulatory agencies, Alfred Malefatto (see p.175) specializes in environmental permitting for power plant development projects. He obtained approvals for a repowering project and a stand-alone 700MW power plant. Clifford Schulman (see p.177) has developed *"a real reputation"* in southern Florida for hazardous waste and water quality matters. He is respected as a land use lawyer with environmental expertise.

The Clients: Fisher Island; City of Riviera Beach; Village of Wellington; City of West Palm Beach; Toll Brothers; GL Homes and Angle Homes.

Gunster, Yoakley & Stewart PA

The Firm: Nominated by interviewees for its practices in West Palm Beach and Fort Lauderdale, the environmental group weaves together lawyers with real estate, land use and litigation expertise. The group advises institutional investors, developers, landowners, lenders and local government bodies. In recent representative matters, the team has counseled on due diligence and transactions for stock and asset purchases, and the acquisitions of industrial and commercial properties across the country. Attorneys also represented potentially responsible parties involved in state and federal Superfund sites across the US.

The Lawyers: Rick Burgess, based in the real estate department in the Fort Lauderdale office, is the key contact in the environment team, following the departure of Michael Goldstein to Akerman Senterfitt in January 2003.

The Clients: AutoNation; Flagler Development Company; Florida East Coast Industries; SBA Communications; Sonesta International Hotels; The St Joe Company; Starwood Hotels & Resorts Worldwide; US Sugar; WCI Communities; WR Grace; Wal-Mart and Wyndham Hotels & Resorts.

ENVIRONMENT | FLORIDA

Oertel, Hoffman, Fernandez & Cole PA
The Firm: It is admired as a *"regulatory boutique of quality,"* and rivals say they frequently encounter the firm's lawyers in environmental matters. Several attorneys formerly served on the governing boards of state agencies and held in-house posts at the Florida Department of Environmental Regulation. As a result, the firm continues to exert an influence in rule development issues regarding water and air quality. The regulatory team advises manufacturing and industrial clients on air pollution, industrial and hazardous waste, usage and groundwater issues. Local government bodies also figure prominently on the client roster. Attorneys have advised both Escambia and Hernando Counties on waste and air pollution matters.
The Lawyers: **Terry Cole** received commendation from interviewees as a *"genuine environment specialist with vast experience."* Cole's practice combines substantive contributions to water and air quality rules in Florida with environmental dispute resolution.
The Clients: Florida Fruit & Vegetable Association, Florida Pulp and Paper Association and WR Grace.

White & Case LLP
The Firm: The arrival of Doug Halsey in mid-2000 bolstered the Miami environmental practice of this global giant. Predominantly transaction-driven, the team focuses on analyzing business risk and liability. The regulatory practice works in a distinctly international framework, and liaises closely with land use and litigation departments. It advises clients, including manufacturers, and property owners, developers and operators, in enforcement actions brought by the EPA/Florida Department of Environmental Protection and local government bodies.
The Lawyers: The first point of reference for many sources is **Doug Halsey**. His involvement in both Superfund and cleanup work *"has significantly shaped the view of the field."* Halsey is equally respected as an environmental litigator. Under his lead, the firm represented Waste Management in permitting for dumps and landfills. Banking clients have also turned to the team for assistance with environmental liability. Attorneys further advised clients facing regulatory restriction s in land use activities.
The Clients: Mellon Bank, Clear Channel Outdoor, Orkin and Tarmac America are clients of the firm.

Other Notable Practitioners
Rivals describe **Matthew Coglianese** (see p.173) of Bilzin Sumberg Dunn Baena Price & Axelrod LLP as *"an environment specialist in the pure sense."* A litigation and regulatory expert with Superfund and CERCLA experience, he represents potentially responsible parties, who have included Florida Power & Light, Exxon, Chevron and several Florida municipalities. Tallahassee-based sole practitioner **William Preston** *"works extremely well with the regulatory agencies, who hold him in regard."* Preston is said to *"excel"* in water and hazardous waste issues. **John Barkett** of Shook, Hardy & Bacon enjoys a reputation as a *"groundbreaker"* in the mediation of cleanup disputes at a national level. Capable of *"intelligently mapping out the solutions,"* Barkett *"has created the template for this area."* **Laurel Lockett** at Carlton Fields emerged during *Chambers'* research as one of the most respected regulatory attorneys in Florida, receiving applause for compliance work *"of the highest quality."* **Michael Goldstein** (see p.174) has left Gunster, Yoakley & Stewart, PA for the Miami office of Akerman Senterfitt. During the course of *Chambers'* research, he was deemed *"big in brownfield redevelopment"* and compliance issues by peers. They believed he *"has taken a lead with the state program and its clientele."* Chair of the Florida Brownfields Association, Goldstein was recently appointed by the Florida Pollution Prevention Roundtable to its brownfields committee. Florida EPA **Mary Smallwood** (see p.174), at Ruden, McClasky, Smith, Schuster & Russell PA, is considered an *"A-grade lawyer"* who commands strong market esteem. Smallwood's varied practice has featured Everglades restoration project permitting for wetlands and work for private sector chemical processing industries.

INSOLVENCY/CORPORATE RECOVERY

FLORIDA
Leading firms
(Insolvency/Corporate Recovery)

1. BERGER SINGERMAN *Fort Lauderdale*
   GREENBERG TRAURIG LLP *Fort Lauderdale, Miami*
   STICHTER, RIEDEL, BLAIN & PROSSER *Tampa*
2. KOZYAK TROPIN & THROCKMORTON *Miami*
   SMITH HULSEY & BUSEY *Jacksonville*
3. AKERMAN SENTERFITT *Orlando*
   CARLTON FIELDS *Tampa, West Palm Beach*
   HOLLAND & KNIGHT LLP *Miami, Tampa*
   STEARNS WEAVER MILLER *Miami, Tampa*
4. FERRELL SCHULTZ CARTER *Aventura, Miami*
   GENOVESE JOBLOVE & BATTISTA PA *Miami*
   GLENN RASMUSSEN FOGARTY & HOOKER *Tampa*
   GRONEK & LATHAM *Orlando*
   KLUGER, PERETZ, KAPLAN & BERLIN PA *Miami*

Firms are listed alphabetically in each band.

Berger Singerman
The Firm: This prominent firm has three offices across the state covering a wide variety of disciplines, yet it is in insolvency matters that these attorneys are felt to excel. Consistently spoken of in superlatives, observers stated that *"it has emerged to a significant degree - they seem to be involved in almost every major case."* The firm's 43 attorneys represent a client base that includes creditors, debtors and creditors' committees.
The Lawyers: Interviewees suggested that the co-chief executive of the firm, **Paul Singerman**, was *"a leading light in this field, and arguably the best in the state."* His practice is concentrated on loan workouts, insolvency and related commercial transactions. Among a plethora of notable recent cases is the reorganization of Advanced Promotion Technologies. Singerman has also acted as special litigation counsel to the chief restructuring officer of American Tissue and its 25 affiliated debtors, and advised on the reorganizations of BellSouth Telecommunications, Mars Music and Roadhouse Grill.
The Clients: AT&T; Coca-Cola Enterprises; Florida Department of Transportation; Florida Power & Light; Northern Trust Bank of Florida and The Related Group of Florida.

Greenberg Traurig LLP
see firm details p.808
The Firm: Perceived to be one of the most prestigious Florida firms, Greenberg Traurig is an insolvency powerhouse in this region. Approximately 12 of the 42 attorneys in its reorganization, bankruptcy and restructuring group are Florida-based, and several of them have an emphasis on cross-border matters. Eminent insolvency practitioners acknowledge that *"Greenberg has an incredible depth of quality of attorneys."* These attorneys have recently been involved in, among others, the airline, air cargo carrier, aviation support, hospitality and real estate industries.
The Lawyers: The national cochair of the bankruptcy department **Mark Bloom** (see p.172) was described to researchers as *"an absolutely stellar performer."* He advises both debtors and creditors, and has acted for the international air cargo carrier Fine Air in a Chapter 11. Also advised the retailer Gerald Stevens, a national florist that went into liquidation. Observers labeled **Brian Gart** (see p.173) as *"a proficient lawyer who works on high-end matters."* Primarily representing debtors and creditors' committees, he worked with Bloom on the Fine Air Chapter 11 and advised its

FLORIDA

INSOLVENCY/CORPORATE RECOVERY

FLORIDA
Leading individuals
(Insolvency/Corporate Recovery)

1
- **BLOOM Mark** *Greenberg Traurig LLP,* Miami
- **BUSEY Stephen** *Smith Hulsey & Busey,* Jacksonville
- **KOZYAK John** *Kozyak Tropin & Throckmorton,* Miami
- **RIEDEL Harley** *Stichter, Riedel, Blain & Prosser,* Tampa
- **SINGERMAN Paul** *Berger Singerman,* Fort Lauderdale
- **SORIANO Robert** *Carlton Fields,* Tampa

2
- **BAENA Scott** *Bilzin Sumberg Dunn Baena Price,* Miami
- **CARTER Francis** *Ferrell Schultz Carter,* Miami
- **COHEN Jules** *Akerman Senterfitt,* Orlando
- **GILBERT Leonard** *Holland & Knight LLP,* Tampa
- **GLENN Robert** *Glenn Rasmussen Fogarty,* Tampa

3
- **BERLIN Howard** *Kluger, Peretz, Kaplan & Berlin,* Miami
- **GART Brian** *Greenberg Traurig LLP,* Fort Lauderdale
- **GENOVESE John** *Genovese Joblove & Battista,* Miami
- **OLSON John** *Stearns Weaver Miller Weissler,* Tampa
- **REDMOND Patricia** *Stearns Weaver Miller,* Miami
- **STICHTER Don** *Stichter, Riedel, Blain & Prosser,* Tampa
- **THROCKMORTON Charles** *Kozyak Tropin,* Miami
- **WARREN Jeffrey** *Bush Ross Gardner Warren,* Tampa

4
- **MAY Rodney** *Gronek & Latham,* Orlando
- **SHUKER Scott** *Gronek & Latham,* Orlando
- **WOLFSON Mark** *Foley & Lardner,* Tampa

Individuals are listed alphabetically in each band.

related company Arrow Air. Gart also acted for Tutor Time Learning Centers on its Chapter 11 filing, advised Tasco Worldwide, a manufacturer of optical equipment on its liquidation, and acted for Empire of Carolina and its subsidiaries concerning cross-border issues related to toy manufacturing.
The Clients: Tutor Time Learning Centers; Fine Air; Gerald Stevens; US Diagnostic; UniCapital; Applebee's International; Valeo Electrical Systems and Tasco Worldwide.

Stichter, Riedel, Blain & Prosser
The Firm: Based in Tampa, this outstanding bankruptcy boutique contains 11 partners and two associates, and has a client base that features a bias toward debtors. Chapter 11 filing is a regular component of the workload. Researchers were informed that *"for debtors' work, this is undoubtedly the first port of call."*
The Lawyers: Name partner **Harley Riedel** was lauded by contemporaries, who were impressed with both *"the way he generates business and the way he instills confidence in his clients."* Riedel's *"thorough knowledge of the law"* extends across the insolvency and restructuring fields. He advised on the Chapter 11 of Koger Properties, acted on the court-approved sale of a major telecom cable company, and was involved in the winding up of JumboSports, a sports clothes retailer. **Don Stichter** represents clients on issues involving Chapter 11, bankruptcy litigation, debt restruc-

turings and workouts. Other attorneys referred to him *"as a long-standing dean of the bar."*
The Clients: The Bank of Tampa; First Union National Bank; Koger Properties and JumboSports.

Kozyak Tropin & Throckmorton
The Firm: *"If we had a conflict I would not hesitate to recommend them,"* stated one competitor about this litigation and bankruptcy boutique. About half of the firm's 18 lawyers undertake bankruptcy matters. The majority of clients represented are either creditors or creditors' committees.
The Lawyers: Firm founder **John Kozyak** is an experienced practitioner on all aspects of bankruptcies, workouts and related subjects. Sources singled him out as a *"resourceful, practical and personable"* attorney. **Chuck Throckmorton** is *"easy to deal with and highly effective."* He represents creditors, trustees and high net-worth individuals. Past highlights included working on the Abraham D Gosman bankruptcy case.
The Clients: The Ritz-Carlton Hotel Company and Bank of America are clients of the firm.

Smith Hulsey & Busey
see firm details p.881
The Firm: Peers contend that this full-service firm fields the principal bankruptcy group in the north of the state. Seven of its 37 lawyers are active in the insolvency sphere and they were collectively described as *"sophisticated, if aggressive, litigators."*
The Lawyers: Chair of the firm **Steve Busey** is engaged in both bankruptcy and litigation. His bankruptcy experience includes the representation of debtors, creditors and committees in Chapter 11 reorganizations of public companies. Busey also acts in bankruptcy litigation in courts throughout Florida, in both insolvency and fiduciary disputes.
The Clients: Debtors; creditors' committees; secured and unsecured lenders; commercial landlords and trustees.

Akerman Senterfitt
see firm details p.760
The Firm: This prominent Florida firm has huge resources within its nine offices. Twenty-eight attorneys make up the bankruptcy and creditors' rights practice group, which acts predominantly on the creditors and creditors' committee side. Onlookers viewed the group as *"strong in corporate restructurings,"* and the choice of many leading clients.
The Lawyers: Peers described **Jules Cohen** (see p.173) as *"a terrific top-flight attorney,"* while clients were delighted with *"his skillful maneuvering - he represents our interests extremely well."* His highlights include acting as cocounsel for Crédit Lyonnais, which had a secured claim of $114 million against Gencor Industries, an affiliated group

of manufacturing companies, in its Chapter 11 case. Also represented SunTrust Bank in matters arising from a $35 million loan on inventory and receivables of Golden Gen Growers, a citrus processing company, which filed under Chapter 11.
The Clients: Crédit Lyonnais; SunTrust Bank; Teacher Retirement System of Texas and Ford.

Carlton Fields
The Firm: A serious contender in the market, the firm has 19 attorneys based in the bankruptcy, creditors' rights and insolvency practice group. The work undertaken relates to large reorganizations, Chapter 11s and some Chapter 7 matters. The group principally advises secured creditors, including banks and financial institutions, while occasionally debtors feature in the workload. Practitioners judged this to be *"a strong practice with good depth."*
The Lawyers: Chair of the department **Rob Soriano** was described as a *"calm and methodical attorney - everything you could ask for in a lawyer."* He represented Anchor Glass Container on matters arising from the $500 million restructuring of its balance sheet, having previously filed for special permission to pay off the general unsecured creditors during the course of business. Also acted on the reorganization of a nonprofit hospital system.
The Clients: First Union National Bank; Citibank; Morgan Guarantee and GE Capital.

Holland & Knight LLP
see firm details p.820
The Firm: One of the largest national firms, it has 11 offices in Florida, which are home to about 25 attorneys who concentrate on bankruptcy, creditors' rights, debt restructuring and workouts. Sources enthused about the ability of *"this talented group of attorneys to handle the most sophisticated cases."* A range of clients are represented including secured and unsecured creditors, creditors' committees, Fortune 500 corporations, public and closely held companies and partnerships.
The Lawyers: Former president of the Florida bar, **Lenny Gilbert** (see p.174) is chair of his firm's national practice group for financial institutions and creditors' rights. An *"unbelievably experienced and effective practitioner,"* his highlights include representing Bank of America in the Gerald Stevens case and representing IMC Global in its acquisition of Agrifos, a phosphate mining company, which had filed for Chapter 11.
The Clients: JPMorgan Chase; Bank of America; Wachovia; HSBC and Washington Mutual.

Stearns Weaver Miller Weissler Alhadeff & Sitterson PA
The Firm: This three-office full-service firm was endorsed by peers for its involvement in a *"substantial amount of high-end matters.* "The team acts on Chapter 11 reorganizations, Chapter 7 liquidations, financial restructuring and workouts.

INSOLVENCY/CORPORATE RECOVERY — FLORIDA

Its caseload includes advising creditors' committees as court-appointed examiners, trustees bankruptcy litigation and pre-bankruptcy planning.
The Lawyers: Rivals were impressed by **John Olson**'s *"tough, effective style,"* which combines well with his depth of knowledge: *"he also knows his subject inside out."* Olson represented Lehman Brothers in its debt restructuring of an apartment complex in Orlando. Also acted for Caesars Palace and its interests in a matter involving Planet Hollywood restaurants. **Patricia Redmond** was commended as a *"hugely respected attorney."* She acts for a number of creditors' committees and trustees including involvement in the case of International Air Leases, in which a large recovery was sought following a fraudulent transfer of funds. Redmond also represented St Paul Fire and Marine Insurance Company in the reorganization of one of its debtors.
The Clients: The firm acts for Lehman Brothers and Caesars Palace. Hotels, real estate-related companies and airlines are on the client roster.

Ferrell Schultz Carter Zumpano & Fertel PA
The Firm: This respected firm operates in the US from offices in Miami and Aventura, providing *"high-quality advice on bankruptcy matters."* Five attorneys are dedicated to serving a client base that is split among institutional creditors, debtors and, to a lesser extent, private investors.
The Lawyers: Researchers were told that **Frank Carter** possesses *"an absolutely brilliant mind."* He acted for JPMorgan Chase and Citicorp as trustees in the bankruptcy of the leasing company Commercial Money Center. Carter advised on the out-of-court restructuring activity of the aviation firm Fine Air and represented Bay View Bank in its dealings with a fried-food restaurant chain.
The Clients: JPMorgan Chase and Citicorp are clients of the firm. The group also acts for creditors, debtors, trustees, private investors and creditors' committees.

Genovese Joblove & Battista PA
The Firm: A litigation and bankruptcy boutique, this 20-lawyer firm was endorsed as *"a specialist in insolvency matters."* The firm is frequently involved in cross-border cases, including creditors' litigation, out-of-court workouts and insolvency proceedings.
The Lawyers: **John Genovese** heads the firm's reorganization and insolvency practice. His expertise extends to troubled loan workouts, bankruptcy, insurance insolvencies and expert testimony, although there is an emphasis on complex bankruptcy litigation. Onlookers described him as *"a dean of the bar - smart and aggressive."*
The Clients: Creditors; creditors' committees; debtors and trustees.

Glenn Rasmussen Fogarty & Hooker
The Firm: Founded in 1983, this Tampa firm has grown to 19 attorneys. Despite its smaller size, the firm is skilled in a broad range of practice areas, including a respected banking and insolvency group. Rival attorneys informed researchers that this firm *"conducts top-drawer work for creditors and a variety of banks."*
The Lawyers: **Bob Glenn** represents all manner of clients, such as lenders, lessors, trustees, committees, and debtors in Chapter 11 filings. He is also experienced in mortgage foreclosures and lender liability defense. Peers believe him to be *"hard-working and thorough in his approach."*
The Clients: Lenders, lessors, trustees, committees and debtors use the firm.

Gronek & Latham
The Firm: Formed in around 1996 as a breakaway from the large full-service firm of Foley & Lardner, this outfit now comprises 18 attorneys. Leading insolvency practitioners described it as *"without doubt one of the best firms for debtors' representation in Orlando."* The bankruptcy practice group is made up of four attorneys, whose practice features Chapter 11 filings on behalf of businesses, and creditors' representation.
The Lawyers: Former corporate banking officer **Scott Shuker** was singled out for his expertise in the debtors' market, although his clients also include secured and unsecured creditors. Much of his workload incorporates bankruptcy, creditors' rights, asset purchases, secured lending and general contract-related matters. **Rodney May** is a former special counsel to the SEC, which has provided him with experience in a host of large bankruptcy cases. He is described as a *"knowledgeable, diligent and energetic"* attorney. His practice involves handling business reorganizations, bankruptcy matters and creditors' rights issues.
The Clients: Secured and unsecured creditors, creditors' committees, trustees and government agencies.

Kluger, Peretz, Kaplan & Berlin PA
The Firm: This is *"an efficient organization,"* experienced in bankruptcy and creditors' rights issues. Clients include debtors, trustees and creditors such as financial institutions, trade and government entities and service organizations.
The Lawyers: Founder and managing partner **Howard Berlin** chairs the bankruptcy and creditors' rights department. Sources endorsed him as an *"articulate and informed"* lawyer who undertakes matters for corporate debtors, secured lenders, creditors' committees and individual creditors. He acted on the Gerald Stevens case, advising creditors, and represented creditors in the SunCruz Casinos bankruptcy. Also acted for the trustees of the Piper Aircraft Corporation.
The Clients: Secured and unsecured creditors and debtors and trustees.

Other Notable Practitioners
Scott Baena (see p.172) was brought into the full-service Miami firm Bilzin Sumberg Dunn Baena Price & Axelrod LLP from Stroock & Stroock & Lavan LLP to head the restructuring and bankruptcy department. His cases have included serving as counsel to the Official Committee of Asbestos Property Damage Claimants in the Chapter 11 cases of WR Grace, US Gypsum and National Gypsum. He also served as special bankruptcy litigation counsel in the Chapter 11 of Heilig Meyers and its affiliates, and represented the subordinated bondholders of Southeast Banking Corporation in its Chapter 11 case. **Jeff Warren** of Bush Ross Gardner Warren & Rudy, PA was commended to researchers for his role as lead bankruptcy counsel to the debtor in the Celotex Corporation Chapter 11, one of the largest Chapter 11 cases ever resolved in the US. Sources described him as *"a learned attorney."* **Mark Wolfson** of Foley & Lardner's Tampa office chairs the litigation department and is a member of the business reorganizations practice group. He represents secured creditors, creditors' committees, stockholders, and parties to contracts, such as landlords and franchisers. *"One of the smartest and most influential attorneys around,"* Wolfson has been active in assessing the Uniform Commercial Code and the enactment of its Revised Article 9, for which he drafted many of the Florida non-uniform provisions.

INSURANCE

FLORIDA
Leading firms (Insurance)
1. FOWLER WHITE BOGGS BANKER *Tampa*
2. CARLTON FIELDS *Miami*
3. HOLLAND & KNIGHT LLP *Jacksonville, Miami*
   KATZ, KUTTER, HAIGLER, ALDERMAN *Tallahassee*
   PENNINGTON, MOORE, WILKINSON *Tallahassee*

Firms are listed alphabetically in each band

Fowler White Boggs Banker
The Firm: This Tampa-based firm boasts a broad insurance practice encompassing coverage litigation, regulatory work, personal injury matters and insurance defense. A *"large skilled team,"* which includes Donald Cox, is particularly renowned for insurance litigation, in which field rivals concede that it *"gets great results."* A dedicated casualty department has experience litigating insurance claims related to products liability and healthcare.

Carlton Fields
The Firm: This full-service firm boasts a large and active insurance practice spanning three of its six Florida offices. Some eight partners act in insurance class action defense and regulatory litigation. Substantial insurance areas include property and casualty, life and health, professional liability and marine as well as workers' compensation cases and errors and omissions coverages.

The Tallahassee office is recognized by peers and clients for its regulatory and administrative work. Daniel Brown practices insurance litigation and regulation there. The group also acts for health maintenance organizations before the Florida Department of Insurance, and in insurance coverage litigation.

Holland & Knight LLP
see firm details p.820.
The Firm: This large international firm has grown enormously in recent years, and was endorsed to researchers for an insurance regulatory and coverage practice that *"covers the waterfront."* The team, which includes regulatory lawyer Thomas Jones, advises continuing care providers and life, health, property and casualty insurers on compliance issues, market conduct and M&A matters. Lawyers in Jacksonville and Miami are active in insurance coverage litigation.

Katz, Kutter, Haigler, Alderman, Bryant & Yon PA
The Firm: The firm's insurance regulatory group is among the largest in the state, with 18 practitioners representing insurance company clients before both the Florida Department of Insurance and the state Agency for Health Care Administration. Their experience includes licensing new companies, gaining approval for both traditional and innovative products and rating systems, and handling complex reinsurance arrangements and mergers. Interviewees reported that local political changes have affected the firm's influence with insurance regulators, but noted that it remains the *"premier insurance regulatory firm"* in Florida.
The Lawyers: Firm founders Allan Katz and Ed Kutter are said to be *"in the know"* and were widely proclaimed as the *"preeminent regulatory lawyers in Florida."*

Pennington, Moore, Wilkinson, Bell & Dunbar PA
The Firm: *"Well connected"* with the Florida Department of Insurance, this Tallahassee outfit won high praise from insurance company clients. The six-attorney team, featuring Mark Delegal, was recommended for its expertise in insurance lobbying. However, the group also advises on a variety of insurance regulatory matters, ranging from the formation of insurance companies, corporate insurance work and licensing matters to acquisitions of the books of businesses and agencies. Attorneys additionally act in reinsurance cession and ceding and in insurance litigation. Enjoying good relations with regulators, the group was said to *"really open doors"* for insurance company clients, which include Vanguard Fire & Casualty, Golden Rule Insurance Company and American Pioneer Title Insurance Company.
The Clients: Vanguard Fire & Casualty, Golden Rule Insurance Company and American Pioneer Title Insurance Company.

LITIGATION

FLORIDA
Leading firms
(Litigation: General Commercial)
1. BEDELL, DITTMAR, DEVAULT *Jacksonville*
   HILL, WARD & HENDERSON PA *Tampa*
   KENNY NACHWALTER SEYMOUR ARNOLD *Miami*
   PODHURST, ORSECK, JOSEFSBERG, EATON *Miami*
2. AKERMAN SENTERFITT *Orlando*
   COLSON HICKS EIDSON *Miami*
   GREENBERG TRAURIG LLP *Miami*
   RICHMAN GREER WEIL BRUMBAUGH *Miami*
   SHOOK, HARDY & BACON *Miami*
3. HOLLAND & KNIGHT LLP *Tallahassee*
   HUNTON & WILLIAMS *Miami*
   JONES, FOSTER, JOHNSTON *West Palm Beach*
   KING, BLACKWELL & DOWNS, PA *Orlando*
   KOZYAK TROPIN & THROCKMORTON *Miami*
   STEEL HECTOR & DAVIS LLP *Miami*

Firms are listed alphabetically in each band.

Bedell, Dittmar, DeVault, Pillans & Coxe
The Firm: This prestigious Jacksonville litigation boutique comprises 14 attorneys who display *"quality across the board."* Peers described it as *"clearly one of the outstanding ligitation outfits in the state"* and commended the high standards attained by the group. The attorneys principally represent corporates in a range of disputes, covering antitrust, IP, products liability and professional liability matters. The team also advises on employment and personal injury cases.
The Lawyers: Peers endorsed **John DeVault** for *"his capacity to handle complex cases."* Interviewees agreed that *"his professional style is respected statewide."* He largely works on complex commercial litigation and legal malpractice defense. Recent cases include advising a land development company that was involved in a dispute in Nocatee, a 15,000-acre master-planned community in northeastern Florida.

GENERAL COMMERCIAL

The Clients: Bank of America; AT&T; Kraft; EMC and Florida Rock Industries.

Hill, Ward & Henderson PA
The Firm: A key presence in litigation, the firm was praised by interviewees for its *"superb leadership"* on some very complex cases. Over 30 attorneys comprise the litigation group, practicing before both federal and state courts. The firm was singled out for its expertise in insurance defense matters.
The Lawyers: Firm president and head of the litigation group **Ben Hill** was described as a *"top-flight lawyer"* in both commercial litigation and legal malpractice work. Some interviewees suggested that Hill was *"one of the best commercial litigators in the state."* He acted on a products liability case for DaimlerChrysler.
The Clients: Attorneys Liability Assurance Society; Florida Lawyers Mutual Insurance Company; RJ Reynolds and DaimlerChrysler.

LITIGATION | FLORIDA

FLORIDA
Leading individuals
(Litigation: General Commercial)

[1]
- **DEVAULT John** *Bedell, Dittmar, DeVault,* Jacksonville
- **HILL Benjamin** *Hill, Ward & Henderson PA,* Tampa
- **JOSEFSBERG Robert** *Podhurst, Orseck,* Miami
- **NACHWALTER Michael** *Kenny Nachwalter,* Miami

[2]
- **ASTIGARRAGA José** *Astigarraga Davis,* Miami
- **COLSON Dean** *Colson Hicks Eidson,* Miami
- **PODHURST Aaron** *Podhurst, Orseck, Josefsberg,* Miami
- **STEARNS Eugene** *Stearns Weaver Miller Weissler,* Miami
- **STUBBS Sidney** *Jones, Foster, Johnston,* West Palm Beach

[3]
- **CARDWELL Thomas** *Akerman Senterfitt,* Orlando
- **DAVIDSON Barry** *Hunton & Williams,* Miami
- **DAVIS Alvin** *Steel Hector & Davis LLP,* Miami
- **GREER Alan** *Richman Greer Weil Brumbaugh,* Miami
- **KING David** *King, Blackwell & Downs, PA,* Orlando
- **LILES Rutledge** *Liles, Gavin, Costantino,* Jacksonville
- **MOSS Edward** *Shook, Hardy & Bacon,* Miami
- **RICHARD Barry** *Greenberg Traurig LLP,* Tallahassee
- **RICHMAN Gerald** *Richman Greer Weil,* Miami
- **SEARCY Christian** *Searcy Denney Scarola,* West Palm Beach
- **THOMSON Parker** *Hogan & Hartson LLP,* Miami

[4]
- **EIDSON Mike** *Colson Hicks Eidson,* Miami
- **FEAGIN Robert** *Holland & Knight LLP,* Tallahassee
- **POPE Wallace** *Johnson, Blakely, Pope, Bokor,* Clearwater
- **ROSS David** *Greenberg Traurig LLP,* Miami
- **STEINBERG Marty** *Hunton & Williams,* Miami
- **TROPIN Harley** *Kozyak Tropin & Throckmorton,* Miami
- **WADSWORTH Murray** *Wadsworth, Davis,* Tallahassee
- **WAKSHLAG Stanley** *Akerman Senterfitt,* Miami
- **WALBOLT Sylvia** *Carlton Fields,* St Petersburg

Individuals are listed alphabetically in each band.

Kenny Nachwalter Seymour Arnold Critchlow & Spector

The Firm: This Miami-based litigation boutique has grown steadily in both size and reputation over the past two decades. Home to 20 attorneys, the firm was endorsed by peers as *"respected by the courts and a favorite of many high-profile clients."* Active across a range of litigation and trial proceedings, the firm stands out in particular for its *"sophisticated handling of antitrust and securities litigation."*

The Lawyers: Senior partner **Mike Nachwalter** draws on a *"wealth of experience in complex cases."* He has advised on securities issues for clients such as Florida Power & Light and the president of a Miami bank. Nachwalter also acted for Clear Channel Communications in an antitrust case.

The Clients: Unilever; Eckerd; The Kroger Company and Florida Power & Light.

Podhurst, Orseck, Josefsberg, Eaton, Meadow, Olin & Perwin

The Firm: This 13-lawyer Miami-based litigation group is frequently seen on larger, complex cases. Rivals acknowledged that *"virtually every lawyer has a huge depth of ability."* The team advises on aviation, automotive and products liability claims and medical malpractice disputes. Researchers were also informed that the group had developed an enviable appellate practice.

The Lawyers: **Bob Josefsberg** is respected for his mix of commercial and criminal litigation. Josefsberg's *"seasoned approach"* has impressed many, and he displays a *"broad array of skills on diverse issues."* He was particularly lauded for his *"superb trial performances."* **Aaron Podhurst** is a *"talented attorney"* who conducts much of his litigation in the aviation sector. He is also recommended for his expertise in personal injury and products liability matters.

The Clients: The firm acts for local and national corporates. Litigation clients include Ryder System, Lennar and Florida East Coast Properties.

Akerman Senterfitt
see firm details p.760

The Firm: The firm has one of the largest litigation departments in the state with about 70 attorneys in its nine Florida offices. Interviewees agreed that the firm has *"a good share of top-class litigators"* who undertake all types of commerical litigation, including securities law and antitrust, construction, employment and products liability cases.

The Lawyers: In Orlando, **Tom Cardwell** (see p.172), chairman and chief exective of the firm, is especially respected for his work in banking and general commercial litigation. Cardwell is general counsel for the Florida Bankers Association trade group, and has acted for Lockheed Martin in contract disputes. He also litigated on behalf of the Florida House of Representatives concerning the reapportionment of voting boundaries in the state. **Stanley Wakshlag** (see p.179) advises on antitrust and securities matters as part of his wider general commercial litigation practice. He was commended to researchers as a *"down-to-earth attorney - you can trust him to be reasonable."*

The Clients: Florida Bankers Association; IVAX; Ernst & Young; PwC; Lockheed Martin and AutoNation.

Colson Hicks Eidson

The Firm: This 16-lawyer litigation team earned plaudits from interviewees for the *"uniformly high quality of its lawyers and their ethical modus operandi."* Its activities in high-profile products liability cases have formed the basis for much of the group's litigation profile. However, it is also proficient in general commercial disputes, IP-related litigation, aviation, professional liability, insurance and white-collar crime matters.

The Lawyers: Contemporaries described **Dean Colson** as *"a preeminent trial figure."* Acting for either plaintiffs or defendants, Colson undertakes general commercial litigation and personal injury representation. **Mike Eidson** specializes in products liability, medical and legal malpractice matters, aviation litigation, and admiralty law. He is praised for his *"professional attitude and effective manner."* Both Eidson and Colson also have considerable experience in class action cases.

The Clients: Clients are drawn from local and national corporates.

Greenberg Traurig LLP
see firm details p.808

The Firm: Complex commercial litigation matters, including disputes played out in the international sphere, are the staple diet of this substantial full-service firm. Its six offices throughout the state field about 45 litigation attorneys. Observers commended the firm's *"talented trial lawyers"* who are experienced in jury trials and in arguing cases before state, federal and appellate courts. The firm is active in products liability and securities, IP, employment and construction disputes.

The Lawyers: **Barry Richard** (see p.177) bolstered his profile with his representation of George W Bush in the 2000 presidential election, which included cases heard before the Florida Supreme Court. Peers describe him as *"outstanding on his feet."* Richard has litigated on behalf of the Florida Senate on constitutional issues such as legislative reapportionment and a tax challenge to a reform bill. He has also acted for Anheuser-Busch and Ford in litigation actions. Clients describe **David Ross** (see p.177) as a *"calm, efficient and reassuring attorney."* While rivals pointed to his antitrust skills, Ross also undertakes a wide range of commercial matters. He has acted as trial counsel to Lorillard Tobacco Company in major class actions, and defended the Sugar Cane Growers Cooperative of Florida and Delta Air Lines in separate employment class action cases. Ross also represented Wal-Mart in an antitrust case.

The Clients: Cisco Systems; Wal-Mart; Lorillard Tobacco Company; Anheuser-Busch; Delta Air Lines and Hilton Hotels.

Richman Greer Weil Brumbaugh Mirabito & Christensen

The Firm: Described to researchers as *"an excellent firm for plaintiffs' representation,"* the group is equally prolific in defendant matters. Twenty-two attorneys undertake general trial and appellate cases in both state and federal courts. The firm advises on real estate disputes and trust and probate matters.

The Lawyers: **Alan Greer** *"has a great commercial brain"* and takes a *"thorough approach"* to sophisticated cases. His highlights include representing - together with **Gerry Richman** - Arthur Andersen's non-US operations in professional liability litigation, and acting for the Government of Panama in defense of failed bank BCCI's attempt to recover monies. Although some find Richman's style to be *"more aggressive than Greer's,"* he remains respected as a *"polished and professional attorney."* Richman has a track record in class action cases and is

FLORIDA

LITIGATION

well versed in contractual disputes. He has advised a private client on issues arising from a proposed development on exclusive Fisher Island, the former Vanderbilt estate south of Miami Beach.
The Clients: Arthur Andersen, Government of Panama and Bal Harbor Club.

Shook, Hardy & Bacon
see firm details p.876
The Firm: This Midwest-based firm is prominent in the litigation sector, partly due to its high-profile involvement in tobacco cases. The group fields 73 litigation attorneys in its Miami and Tampa offices, who practice both trial and appellate law. Interviewees pointed to *"a clutch of exemplary major trial lawyers"* who are regularly seen on the defendant's side in complex disputes. Products liability, insurance, IP and antitrust are all areas of activity for the firm.
The Lawyers: Manager of the Miami office, **Ed Moss** is respected as *"the driving force at Shook, Hardy & Bacon and one of the top products liability lawyers in town."* He has represented the DuPont family in a complex national commercial dispute, and advised Boeing in a products liability matter arising from an aircraft disaster. Elsewhere, Moss represented Home Depot in defense of a major class action.
The Clients: Philip Morris; Lorillard Tobacco Company; Eli Lilly; Home Depot and Clear Channel Communications.

Holland & Knight LLP
see firm details p.820
The Firm: Described to researchers as *"a Goliath among law firms in this region,"* the group is respected for its depth of resources and its preponderance of *"top trial guns."* Its 11 offices across the state field litigators experienced at both state and federal level. The group advises local and national clients on general commercial disputes such as antitrust, construction litigation, IP, employment, tax and environmental issues.
The Lawyers: Peers reported that **Bob Feagin** (see p.173) is *"a talented attorney who has served the firm ably for many years."* Despite his role as managing partner of the firm, Feagin continues to litigate substantial cases, focusing on antitrust matters. He has recently served as the senior trial lawyer representing Lykes Bros in a case arising from the valuation of businesses and real property, which resulted in a widely publicized dissenters' rights dispute.
The Clients: Mid-sized and large public and private companies.

Hunton & Williams
The Firm: This large international firm can draw on the support of 16 offices worldwide. Its Miami office, opened in 1999, has quickly gained a reputation among market observers as *"a substantial group of dedicated attorneys."* Approximately half of the office's 47 attorneys conduct litigation. Areas of strength include antitrust and unfair competition issues, securities disputes, class actions and IP and employment litigation.
The Lawyers: Clients value **Barry Davidson** for his *"class action experience and reassuring demeanor."* Peers point to his *"thorough knowledge of the law."* Davidson represented Service Corporation International in a class action arising from alleged misburials at its Menorah Gardens cemetery in West Palm Beach. He also acted on a patent infringement case for Hilton Hotels, which involved its phone system. Commentators described **Marty Steinberg** as a *"highly qualified lawyer with sound judgment."* His caseload has included an antitrust matter for Honeywell, a products liability case for Pfizer and a large business dispute involving a casino.
The Clients: Georgia-Pacific; GE; United Airlines; ExxonMobil; Hilton Hotels; Pfizer and Honeywell.

Jones, Foster, Johnston & Stubbs, PA
see firm details p.825
The Firm: This long-established West Palm Beach firm has a forte in litigation, borne from its background in insurance defense. It has developed into a strong all-around general commercial litigation group, advising on contract disputes and professional liability and eminent domain matters. Attorneys have also established a successful track record defending in construction litigation related to indoor air quality, so-called 'sick building syndrome' cases. Competitors viewed the group as *"a traditional and highly respected team."*
The Lawyers: President of the firm **Sid Stubbs** (see p.178) remains an active force in the litigation field, winning a following for his *"many years of experience."* Professional liability remains one of his strong suits and he is a popular choice for legal malpractice defense. Stubbs has also advised Florida Power & Light on several claims.
The Clients: Abbott Laboratories; Humana; Florida Power & Light; Michelin and HCA.

King, Blackwell & Downs
The Firm: This Orlando boutique won a high degree of commendation from other practitioners as *"a focused team that crops up on many major cases."* Attorneys here were commended as particularly proficient in complex commercial litigation and personal injury matters.
The Lawyers: **David King** was singled out to researchers as *"top of the class in Orlando."* Adept in commercial litigation, eminent domain and personal injury cases, King was endorsed for his *"deft touch - he gets just the right balance between assertiveness and conciliation."*
The Clients: The firm acts for local and national companies.

Kozyak Tropin & Throckmorton
The Firm: Operating from a single office in Miami, this 18-lawyer firm has core strengths in commercial litigation, bankruptcy-related disputes and trademark matters. Interviewees described the firm as *"incredibly strong for creditors' rights and securities disputes,"* while others pointed to the *"wholehearted and earnest service that it provides to plaintiff clients."*
The Lawyers: Firm founder **Harley Tropin** was recommended as a specialist in complex commercial litigation and IP law. A prominent figure in the market due to his lectures on these matters, he was described by peers as *"well respected by the judges in the federal courts."*
The Clients: The firm predominantly acts for plaintiffs, including large employers, newspapers and financial institutions.

Steel Hector & Davis LLP
The Firm: *"A litigation powerhouse,"* the firm was commended to researchers for its work with major clients such as Florida Power & Light. This large full-service firm can draw upon 130 lawyers working from five offices in the state, and from offices in South America and the UK. The team acts in domestic and international disputes, across a range of disciplines including securities law, antitrust, products liability, IP, bankruptcy and insurance coverage claims.
The Lawyers: Peers extolled **Alvin Davis**, chair of the firm, for his *"intelligence and expertise"* and his involvement in complex high-profile cases. He has acted as lead counsel for a host of prominent companies such as American Airlines and Florida Power & Light, and advised Rust-Oleum in a franchising dispute in Latin America.
The Clients: American Airlines; Knight Ridder; Florida Power & Light; Medtronic; AIG and Rust-Oleum.

Other Notable Practitioners
In Miami, **Eugene Stearns** chairs the litigation department at Stearns Weaver Miller Weissler Alhadeff & Sitterson, PA. Described to researchers as *"a litigator right at the top,"* Stearns recently won a $1 billion jury verdict against Exxon on behalf of a class of Exxon dealers. Based in Jacksonville, **Rutledge Liles** is managing partner of the six-lawyer litigation boutique Liles, Gavin, Costantino & Murphy, a plaintiff-focused operation. Interviewees portrayed Liles as a *"robust and seasoned trial lawyer."* He has recently advised on legal malpractice cases and represented a fiber-optics company involved in a dispute with railroad companies. **Christian Searcy** is president of the West Palm Beach litigation boutique Searcy Denney Scarola Barnhart & Shipley, PA and has a mixed commercial and personal injury practice. **Parker Thomson** (see p.178) is a highly rated litigation and appellate attorney who recently

REAL ESTATE — FLORIDA

joined the DC-based full-service firm Hogan & Hartson LLP. Managing partner of the firm's Miami office, Thomson was commended by peers as *"one of the finest appellate attorneys in the state."* He represented the family of the late Dale Earnhardt, the NASCAR driver who died in a crash at the 2001 Daytona 500, in a dispute concerning press rights to photographs. He also represented the State of Florida in a dispute about the prevention of oil drilling in the Gulf of Mexico. **Wally Pope**, a general litigation attorney in the Clearwater office of Johnson, Blakely, Pope, Bokor, Ruppel & Burns, PA, was endorsed by peers as *"a first-class lawyer who deals with sophisticated cases."* **Murray Wadsworth** is a founder member of Wadsworth, Davis & Wadsworth, PA. He specializes in eminent domain, personal injury and medical malpractice claims. At the St Petersburg office of Carlton Fields, **Sylvia Walbolt** is a respected appellate attorney who has a wealth of experience in antitrust litigation. She acted in an appeal that saw the reversal of a jury verdict for a police officer in a First Amendment employment retaliation case. Peers view **José Astigarraga** of Astigarraga Davis as the nation's leading Spanish speaking arbitration practitioner, and as such, he is judged to be a key figure in the Miami market. He represents US and non-domestic corporates worldwide at the ICC, AAA and other international arbitration boards, including ad hoc boards. Astigarraga has recently been involved in arbitrations arising out of power industry disputes.

REAL ESTATE

FLORIDA
Leading firms (Real Estate)

1. **GREENBERG TRAURIG LLP** Miami
2. **BILZIN SUMBERG DUNN BAENA PRICE** Miami
3. **LOWNDES DROSDICK DOSTER KANTOR** Orlando
   STEARNS WEAVER MILLER WEISSLER Miami
4. **AKERMAN SENTERFITT** Orlando
   CARLTON FIELDS Tampa
   HOLLAND & KNIGHT LLP Miami
   LEBOEUF, LAMB, GREENE & MACRAE Jacksonville
   ROGERS, TOWERS, BAILEY, JONES Jacksonville
5. **DEAN, MEAD, EGERTON, BLOODWORTH** Orlando
   FOLEY & LARDNER Tampa
   RUDEN, MCCLOSKY, SMITH, Fort Lauderdale
   SHUTTS & BOWEN Miami

Leading individuals (Real Estate)

1. **BILZIN Brian** Bilzin Sumberg Dunn Baena Price, Miami
   GORSON Matthew Greenberg Traurig LLP, Miami
2. **ALHADEFF Richard** Stearns Weaver Miller, Miami
   PRICE Stanley Bilzin Sumberg Dunn Baena Price, Miami
3. **BOZARTH Stephen** Dean, Mead, Egerton, Orlando
   FITZGERALD Randi Lowndes Drosdick Doster, Orlando
   KANTOR Hal Lowndes Drosdick Doster Kantor, Orlando
   MITCHELL Stephen Squire, Sanders & Dempsey, Tampa
   WALKER William White & Case LLP, Miami
4. **HANSON Karl** LeBoeuf, Lamb, Greene, Jacksonville
   PAPPAS Lynn Pappas Metcalf Jenks, Jacksonville
   RIDLEY Fred Foley & Lardner, Tampa
   SAUL Gary Greenberg Traurig LLP, Miami
   SCHEU William Rogers, Towers, Bailey, Jacksonville
   SEAY James Holland & Knight LLP, Orlando
   SLATER Jim Broad and Cassel, Orlando
   SOLLNER Richard Trenam, Kemker, Scharf, Tampa
   SOMERSTEIN Barry Ruden, McClosky, Fort Lauderdale
   STANFORD Douglas Smith, Gambrell, Jacksonville

Firms and individuals are listed alphabetically in each band.

Greenberg Traurig LLP
see firm details p.808

The Firm: A national firm that is considered by many observers to stand *"head and shoulders"* above its Florida rivals for real estate, it has been geared toward the sector for about 25 years and can claim coverage across the state. The real estate department is noted for its *"excellent crop"* of transactional lawyers, and undertakes substantial residential development work, government contracts and zoning matters.
The Lawyers: Carrying on the work of such icons of the industry as Al Quentel, Bob Traurig and David Kenin is **Matt Gorson** (see p.174), the team's leading light. An extensive and powerful client base that includes The Trump Group, together with a *"take-no-prisoners attitude,"* have earned him a fearsome reputation among his peers. **Gary Saul** (see p.177), who also works out of the Miami office, has been labeled *"one of the leading figures in condominium development in the whole US"* by a fellow professional. His work has included representing developers and lenders in numerous residential, commercial and mixed-use condominium projects in south Florida, as well as an involvement in homeowners' associations and office projects.
The Clients: Clients include The Related Group of Florida, Swire Pacific Holdings and the Swerdlow Group.

Bilzin Sumberg Dunn Baena Price & Axelrod LLP
see firm details p.772

The Firm: Major players in south Florida, the firm was originally part of New York law firm Rubin, Baum, Levin, Constant, Friedman & Bilzin until it became an independent practice in January 1998. It is now home to more than 70 attorneys, and is widely regarded as *"an emerging force"* with some *"highly sophisticated attorneys."* Interviewees were particularly impressed with the firm's real estate development group.
The Lawyers: *"First-class talent"* **Brian Bilzin** (see p.172) appeals to competitors for his ability *"to get the transaction done."* His recent work includes representing LNR Property in its purchase of unrated certificates in a $700 million securitization of commercial mortgage loans by JPMorgan Chase. Highly rated for his land use practice, **Stanley Price** (see p.176) advised Boca Developers in obtaining the necessary approvals for the development of the Peninsula and the Hamptons South, two luxury high-rise condominiums in Aventura.
The Clients: Lennar Partners, LNR Property and Boca Developers feature in the roster.

Lowndes Drosdick Doster Kantor & Reed PA

The Firm: This powerhouse in the central Florida region is regarded as a traditional real estate firm and was commended to researchers as *"comfortably top of the list"* in Orlando. Transactional expertise features heavily at a department that includes a number of major REITs among its client portfolio.
The Lawyers: Taking up the mantle from the legendary John Lowndes, **Hal Kantor** was singled out by peers as *"an outstanding attorney who knows the law inside out."* Opponents endorse **Randi Fitzgerald** as a *"lawyer of substance."* Her recent workload includes advising on the two million sq ft development of the Brevard Crossings regional mall in Cocoa, which incorporates retail space, a hotel and a cinema. She also acted on the 7000-acre Lake Nona Development project, and advised on a project concerning the construction of a road network and bridge over Interstate 5.
The Clients: Clients include: Brevard Crossings; The Ginn Company; Southhampton Properties and Lake Nona Property Holdings.

Stearns Weaver Miller Weissler Alhadeff & Sitterson PA

The Firm: Offices in Miami, Fort Lauderdale and Tampa give the firm excellent statewide coverage. Both peers and clients applauded the group for its tax credit and bond-financed property specialization, while affordable housing is another niche area of expertise. Clients drew the attention of researchers to the efficiency of *"a team of high-quality attorneys."*
The Lawyers: Foremost among the team is **Richard Alhadeff**, who serves on the firm's executive committee. Rivals appreciate the *"ease in dealing with him; he works toward the right end and is always reasonable."* He represented Bank of America in a $186 million loan to finance the construction of a condominium project, and

FLORIDA — REAL ESTATE

advised The Related Group of Florida on the disposal of $60 million worth of apartment communities.
The Clients: JMB Realty is another leading client.

Akerman Senterfitt
see firm details p.760
The Firm: The largest law firm based exclusively in Florida, it covers the full spectrum of real estate advice, encompassing M&A, financing, leasing and development as well as workouts and reconstructions. Managing stockholder Drake Batchelder in Fort Lauderdale and chairman Charles Schuette in Miami preside over a department that, although not packed with star names, was regularly endorsed by rivals for its *"uniformly high standard and strong team ethic."*
The Clients: The firm advised on the $320 million acquisition of the Boca Raton Hotel & Club, and acted for Arena Development Company on the $185 million development of National Car Rental Center. Other clients include the TriLegacy Group and Fletcher Realty & Builder.

Carlton Fields
The Firm: Tampa may be the firm's most noted stronghold, but it also operates from five other offices across Florida. The real estate group has a sound reputation from its involvement in luxury residential condominium developments and large shopping center projects. Clients appreciate the group as *"a reasonably priced option which never disappoints us with the standard of its work."* Ed Lester and Ruth Kinsolving are the team's leading names and the firm's clients include Citibank and First Union.

Holland & Knight LLP
see firm details p.820
The Firm: In spite of the firm's well-publicized recent round of cost cutting, its real estate operation in Florida remains a respected force. Rivals acknowledge that the group's *"size, experience and high-profile client base"* keep it *"in the picture,"* particularly on the transactional side.
The Lawyers: **James Seay** (see p.177) is the outstanding name at the firm's Orlando office. *"A bright and inventive attorney,"* he advises on a full range of transactional and land use projects. Seay's recent caseload has included multimillion dollar transactions for Beazer Homes USA, and apartment and office building projects on behalf of Connterre Corporation.
The Clients: Other clients include Marriott International, Highwoods Properties and Interstate Hotel Corporation.

LeBoeuf, Lamb, Greene & MacRae LLP
see firm details p.838
The Firm: Based in Jacksonville, this national and international heavyweight's real estate reputation is largely founded on its widely recognized financing and M&A expertise.
The Lawyers: Two attorneys particularly are seen to stand out. **Doug Stanford** was praised by clients for his *"timely and technically capable advice."* His recent work has included representing an owner-developer in a $250 million statewide mortgage financing, and advising the purchaser on acquisitions valued at $100 million of grocery stores and gas stations in the southern US. **Karl Hanson** (see p.174) was also endorsed to researchers as a *"proficient attorney who gets good results."*
The Clients: Clients include: Flagler Development Company; Sawgrass Country Club; The St. Joe Company; Washington Mutual and Winn-Dixie.

Rogers, Towers, Bailey, Jones & Gay PA
The Firm: Operating from offices in Jacksonville and St. Augustine, the firm's real estate group represents sellers, purchasers, investors, lenders and contractors in a broad variety of transactional matters. The department is also recognized by peers to possess *"the most extensive land use expertise in Jacksonville;"* beyond the US, the firm has undertaken a joint venture with Lehman, Lee & Xu, one of the largest firms in China, which will give it a presence in seven cities across Asia.
The Lawyers: **Bill Scheu** is regarded by opponents as the firm's marquee name. His workload principally revolves around shopping center and office building acquisitions and sales, and he has advised on about $200 million worth of shopping center transactions for Regency Centers.
The Clients: Other clients include First Union, Wachovia Bank and Gate Petroleum Company.

Dean, Mead, Egerton, Bloodworth, Capouano & Bozarth PA
The Firm: Smaller than some of its principal rivals, the firm has nevertheless established a solid profile in and around Orlando, and appears especially frequently on hotel-related real estate work.
The Lawyers: **Stephen Bozarth** is the senior figure at the Orlando office. Fellow professionals see him as *"an accomplished all-round attorney with an effervescent personality and style."* His practice primarily involves the acquisition of undeveloped real estate, often on behalf of local financial institutions, although he also has expertise in land use and zoning.
The Clients: Clients include A Duda & Sons, SunTrust Bank and First Citrus Bank.

Foley & Lardner
The Firm: Best known for its advice on the contentious aspects of real estate, the Florida branch of this national firm has no discrete real estate department, choosing instead to service its commercial property clientele from its business law department. Transactional matters also figure in the firm's workload.
The Lawyers: The practice is noted for its golf course development work in western Florida, a particular specialty of Tampa-based **Fred Ridley** who appeals to clients for his *"wealth of experience and thorough professionalism."* He recently worked on a 16-acre entertainment project in downtown Tampa, and has represented numerous developers in high-rise condominium and golf course projects.
The Clients: Clients include: Textron; Pacific Life Insurance Company; Meadowbrook Golf Group; WCI Communications and EcoGroup International

Ruden, McClosky, Smith, Schuster & Russell PA
The Firm: Although relatively young, the firm has already carved out an enviable reputation for itself. Clients were quick to praise its expertise in areas of the sector such as development structuring, while the Fort Lauderdale office is said to be *"particularly strong in land use."*
The Lawyers: **Barry Somerstein** has a notably broad practice, and is respected by peers as *"a deal-maker with an easy manner."* Much of his workload involves leasing and leasehold financing, typically on behalf of a landlord clientele.

Shutts & Bowen
The Firm: Now a mid-sized firm by Florida standards, it has expanded to include five offices in the state, one in London and one in Amsterdam. The group is primarily known for its *"prestigious"* land use practice, although it also handles a range of development projects and traditional commercial transactions. Clients expressed *"absolute confidence"* in the group, which is headed from Miami by Judith Burke. The client roster includes landlords, tenants, developers, owners, lenders and borrowers.

Other Notable Practitioners
Stephen Mitchell is a partner at Squire, Sanders & Dempsey LLP in Tampa. Described to researchers as *"a great networker,"* he has been involved in a number of big-ticket hotel projects. Tampa-based **Richard Sollner**, who works for Trenam, Kemker, Scharf, Barkin, Frye, O'Neill & Mullis PA, was commended to researchers as *"creative when the obvious answer is not apparent, and efficient in crossing the finishing line."* **Lynn Pappas** of Pappas Metcalf Jenks & Miller in Jacksonville has been characterized as *"a major player who is extremely driven."* She chairs the Jacksonville Chamber of Commerce, and has a practice that encompasses land use and transactional advice. Her clients include Arvida Realty Sales. **Jim Slater** is a highly regarded transactional real estate lawyer at Broad and Cassel, working out of Orlando. His recent projects include $20-60 million apartment developments with ZOM companies. **Bill Walker** at White & Case LLP was described by peers as *"a tenacious attorney with a strong client following."* He has represented companies such as Arvida and JMB Realty.

TAX

FLORIDA

FLORIDA
Leading firms (Tax)

1
- DEAN, MEAD, EGERTON, BLOODWORTH *Orlando*
- GREENBERG TRAURIG LLP *Miami, Orlando*
- HOLLAND *Lakeland, Miami, Tallahassee, Tampa*
- STEEL HECTOR & DAVIS LLP *Miami*

2
- BAKER & MCKENZIE *Miami*
- PACKMAN, NEUWAHL & ROSENBERG *Coral Gables*
- TESCHER GUTTER CHAVES *Boca Raton, Miami*

3
- AKERMAN SENTERFITT *Miami*
- BARNETT, BOLT, KIRKWOOD & LONG *Tampa*
- TRENAM, KEMKER, SCHARF *St Petersburg, Tampa*
- WHITE & CASE LLP *Miami*

4
- AUGUST & KULUNAS *West Palm Beach*
- CARLTON FIELDS *Tampa*
- JOHNSON, BLAKELY, POPE *Clearwater, Tampa*

Firms are listed alphabetically in each band.

Dean, Mead, Egerton, Bloodworth, Capouano & Bozarth PA

The Firm: Tax is thought to be *"an integral part of the firm's history."* Over a third of the practice's 45 attorneys focus on tax, and the firm has established a reputation for handling substantial matters. Clients consider them the *"first port of call"* for tax questions, describing the practice as *"one of the best in the state."* Departmental subgroups focus on corporate reorganizations, nonprofit and charitable organizations, partnerships, S Corps, LLCs, state and local tax, tax planning and tax controversies.

The Lawyers: In Orlando, practice chair **Charlie Egerton** is a *"likeable and effective tax attorney,"* commended by peers for his deep expertise in real estate and partnership taxation. His recent caseload has included a US Supreme Court certiorari proceeding in relation to an S Corp matter and advice to an NFL team on the tax implications of franchise selling. **Lauren Detzel** was thought to be a *"leading light"* in estate planning. Detzel acts for companies and high net-worth individuals on probate administration and estate taxation.

The Clients: Jacksonville Jaguars; Yesawich, Pepperdine & Brown; Williams Construction Group; A Duda & Sons and Hughes Supply.

Greenberg Traurig LLP
see firm details p.808

The Firm: A large full-service firm, thought to be *"second to none"* for corporate taxation. With 31 tax attorneys distributed across six Florida offices, the firm brings to bear *"enormous depth and resources"* on transactional matters. The practice covers international tax, M&A, tax-exempt organizations, ERISA and employee benefits, estate planning and state and local tax issues. Attorneys were praised as *"bright and forward-thinking."*

The Lawyers: Orlando-based **Joel Maser** (see p.175) was particularly praised for his expertise in partnerships and in state and local tax issues. However, his broad-based practice encompasses all aspects of federal, state and local tax, domestic and international tax planning, and M&A-related matters. Recent clients have included hotels, large public companies and condominium developers. Peers praise him as *"supremely bright and first-rate on state and local tax law."* Although less visible on daily matters, **Norman Lipoff**, who chaired the firm's tax department for 20 years, continues to attract comment for his *"long experience in the field."* The firm mourns the sad loss of its hugely respected head of practice, Shep King.

Holland & Knight LLP
see firm details p.820

The Firm: Despite recent departures, this *"mammoth"* Florida operation possesses the largest tax group in the state. Commended for a *"wide pool of talent,"* the firm is best known for estate planning and state and local matters. Much of this work is handled from the Tallahassee office, with practitioners in Tampa, Orlando, Jacksonville and Fort Lauderdale covering work related to federal or transactional matters.

The Lawyers: Tallahassee attorney **Bill Townsend** (see p.179) was acclaimed *"best in the state"* for state and local matters. This *"extremely experienced individual"* represents clients before the Florida Department of Revenue on issues of sales tax, corporate income tax, gross receipts, intangibles and IP taxation. He has advised a number of national banks, manufacturers and telecom companies on refund claims, disclosure matters and their corporate income tax filing status. **Andrew Weinstein** (see p.179) heads the firm's south Florida practice from the Miami office and has a *"fantastic reputation"* for tax controversy and litigation. He counsels a national banking chain on M&A tax matters and complex tax litigation situations and recently provided tax planning advice to a wealthy Chicago-based individual and a Taiwanese shipping company. In Tampa, *"talented"* **Bernard Barton** (see p.172) undertakes federal, state and local tax matters. He has experience structuring corporate, individual and partnership federal tax packages. Recent highlights include representing a TV broadcaster in an IRS audit and acting for a multinational service provider in transactional and M&A tax issues. **Ed Koren** (see p.175) chairs the national trusts and estates practice group. Operating from the firm's Tampa and Lakeland offices, he advises business owners and executives on partnerships, S Corps and the use of buy-sell and split dollar agreements. Koren also handles tax controversies, both as counsel and expert witness. Miami-based **Bruce Stone** (see p.178) is another highly experienced trusts and estate lawyer. He represents high net-worth domestic clients in connection with the multigenerational transfer of wealth, and has extensive experience in the use of trusts, expatriation and other tax provisions. Stone is also well versed in probate and trusts litigation.

Steel Hector & Davis LLP

The Firm: This *"traditional"* five-office Florida firm is said to contain *"some of the finest tax attorneys in the state."* Matters covered include domestic and international transactions, partnership agreements and personal estates as well as exempt and charitable planning and controversy work. Much of the workload relates to benefits and employee compensation matters. The practice is additionally noteworthy for its international capabilities, with practitioners in Central and South America and Europe providing tax support on international transactions.

The Lawyers: Commended to researchers as *"hot on tax,"* **Sam Ullman** handles all aspects of corporate taxation, including transactional work and controversy matters. Clients mentioned that he was *"the first person you'd think of when a difficult tax issue comes up."* **Sherwin Simmons** is widely renowned as a *"senior statesman"* of the Florida tax bar and was thought to lend *"gravitas"* to the practice. This experienced attorney counsels international business clients, including two very significant family enterprises, on tax concerns. Simmons acted in a large income tax case, and has advised individuals on the ramifications on trusts and estates of divorce.

The Clients: Internet transaction companies, public and private companies and high net-worth individuals comprise the client roster.

Baker & McKenzie
see firm details p.767

The Firm: This huge international firm excels at high-level international tax and transfer pricing matters thanks to a well-developed global network that spans 35 countries. The Miami office is thought to be particularly well placed to use the firm's full resources in the Latin American and Caribbean markets. Interviewees unanimously agreed that the firm was *"the finest in Florida for international taxation."*

The Lawyers: *"Hard-working"* senior partner **Bob Hudson** (see p.174) was consistently referred to as *"the best international tax lawyer around."* His other areas of specialty include general tax planning, private banking, tax controversy and litigation, M&A and transfer pricing.

Packman, Neuwahl & Rosenberg

The Firm: The 15-lawyer tax boutique based in Coral Gables has attorneys who were recognized for their *"high level of specialization and technical*

FLORIDA — TAX

FLORIDA
Leading individuals (Tax)

[1]
- **BOKOR Bruce** *Johnson, Blakely, Pope, Bokor,* Clearwater
- **EGERTON Charles** *Dean, Mead, Egerton,* Orlando
- **GRAGG Lawrence** *White & Case LLP,* Miami
- **HUDSON Robert** *Baker & McKenzie,* Miami
- **KOREN Ed** *Holland & Knight LLP,* Lakeland
- **LEDERMAN Alan** *Broad and Cassel,* Miami
- **PANOFF Robert** *Robert E Panoff PA,* Miami
- **RAATTAMA Henry** *Akerman Senterfitt,* Miami
- **ROSENBERG Michael** *Packman, Neuwahl,* Coral Gables
- **STONE Bruce** *Holland & Knight LLP,* Miami
- **TESCHER Donald** *Tescher Gutter Chaves,* Boca Ratón
- **TOWNSEND William** *Holland & Knight LLP,* Tallahassee
- **ULLMAN Samuel** *Steel Hector & Davis LLP,* Miami

[2]
- **AUGUST Jerald** *August & Kulunas,* West Palm Beach
- **BARTON Bernard** *Holland & Knight LLP,* Tampa
- **COMITER Richard** *Comiter & Singer,* Palm Beach Gardens
- **MASER Joel** *Greenberg Traurig LLP,* Orlando
- **O'NEILL Albert** *Trenam, Kemker, Scharf, Barkin,* Tampa
- **SIMMONS Sherwin** *Steel Hector & Davis LLP,* Miami
- **WARNER Jonathan** *Jonathan H. (Jason) Warner,* Miami
- **WEINSTEIN Andrew** *Holland & Knight LLP,* Miami

[3]
- **BARNETT Leslie** *Barnett, Bolt, Kirkwood & Long,* Tampa
- **BOLT Robert** *Barnett, Bolt, Kirkwood & Long,* Tampa
- **BRONSTEIN Joel** *Bronstein, Carlson,* St Petersburg
- **BURKE David** *Carlton Fields,* Tampa
- **DETZEL Lauren** *Dean, Mead, Egerton,* Orlando
- **DOLINER Nathaniel** *Carlton Fields,* Tampa
- **GUTTER Marvin** *Tescher Gutter Chaves,* Boca Ratón
- **HOROWITZ Mitchell** *Fowler White Boggs Banker,* Tampa
- **JOSEPHER Richard** *Tescher Gutter Chaves,* Boca Ratón
- **PIERCE Robert** *Ausley & McMullen,* Tallahassee
- **WEBER Victoria** *Hopping, Green & Sams,* Tallahassee

Individuals are listed alphabetically in each band.

ability." The firm is best known for international taxation and estate planning, but also handles a small amount of immigration law and transactional real estate work.
The Lawyers: Name partner **Michael Rosenberg** was described by competitors as an *"attorney of the highest caliber."* An experienced international tax and estate planning lawyer, Rosenberg advises high net-worth individuals on US and foreign investments and the tax consequences of immigration to the US.

Tescher Gutter Chaves Josepher Rubin Ruffin & Forman PA
The Firm: The 2002 merger of Tescher Chaves Ruffin & Forman with Gutter Josepher & Rubin created a powerful tax boutique, which operates out of offices in Boca Ratón and Miami. A nine-attorney group of *"exemplary practitioners"* handles all aspects of tax, including corporate, international, state and local taxation and tax planning and controversy work.
The Lawyers: Known locally as *"a dean of individual estate planning,"* **Don Tescher** represents shareholders of public companies in personal planning matters and also undertakes income tax, estate issues and tax planning for individuals. **Marvin Gutter** was praised as a *"proactive, top-class attorney."* Much of his work relates to general business taxation. **Richard Josepher** undertakes a large share of controversy and compliance work. Interviewees particularly remarked on his knowledge of partnership tax, calling him *"a superb and learned individual."*

Akerman Senterfitt
see firm details p.760
The Firm: The largest law firm operating exclusively from Florida, Akerman Senterfitt has nine offices across the state. The Miami office was singled out for its wide-ranging expertise in international, state and local tax and planning matters. However, the firm received most praise for its strong practice in charitable and tax-exempt organizations.
The Lawyers: In Miami, **Hank Raattama** (see p.176) was acknowledged as a leading name in charitable and tax-exempt organizations' work. Praised as a *"diligent and experienced"* attorney, Raattama handles tax-exempt transactions, and compliance and regulatory matters for colleges, universities, healthcare facilities and charities, among others.

Barnett, Bolt, Kirkwood & Long
The Firm: This *"exemplary tax boutique"* comprises 16 attorneys advising on all aspects of corporate and personal taxation. The group is best known for its strength in estate planning and controversy matters, but also advises on a large share of partnership and real estate transactions.
The Lawyers: **Les Barnett** was acknowledged as a *"brilliant practitioner who has been at the top of the game for some time."* He is notable for his work in estate planning, in which he represents several families and limited partnerships. Barnett also handles tax controversy, S Corp and M&A matters. Cofounder **Bob Bolt** was similarly recommended as a *"fine lawyer and a real nice guy."* He recently advised a private corporation with a $100 million property portfolio on a tax-free spin-off under US Code Section 355 and represented Florida personal injury firms participating in the tobacco industry ruling's securitization vehicle, called the Litigation Settlement Monetized Fee Trust, on pass-through certificates.

Trenam, Kemker, Scharf, Barkin, Frye, O'Neill & Mullis PA
The Firm: Tax attorneys work as part of larger teams in three distinct practice groups: business transactions and planning; ERISA and employee benefits; and estates and trusts. The firm has offices in Tampa and St. Petersburg and was thought to possess *"a fine stable of lawyers."*
The Lawyers: The firm's leading tax practitioner is **Al O'Neill**, deemed by peers to be *"something of a genius."* This senior attorney concentrates on ERISA, partnership taxation, corporate tax planning and controversy work.
The Clients: Publix Super Markets; AmeriSteel; Chico's; Discount Auto Parts and numerous dot.com companies.

White & Case LLP
The Firm: Researchers were frequently informed of this firm's *"excellence in international taxation and state and local matters."* An extensive global network of offices yields a substantial amount of sophisticated taxation issues. Its tax attorneys in the Miami office are particularly known for their work on inbound investments on behalf of Latin American clients. In addition to international matters, the firm handles a considerable amount of domestic M&A and general corporate taxation.
The Lawyers: **Larry Gragg** was singled out by peers as *"a don of real estate taxation."* He has significant expertise in REIT work and represents several prominent local real estate developers such as Crocker & Company, Stiles Corporation and Codina Group. His broader practice encompasses state and local tax issues, domestic and international transactions and business counseling.

August & Kulunas
The Firm: This three-lawyer tax boutique is the favorite choice of competitors when referring work in conflicted situations. Described as a *"shining light for federal taxation issues,"* the group also undertakes state and local tax matters, controversy work, employee benefits, estate planning, and probate work. Attorneys were particularly recommended for their knowledge of S Corp regulations.
The Lawyers: *"Hard-working"* **Jerry August** was singled out by peers for his *"experience and keen intellect."* August is well known for his prolific articles on tax issues. His wide-ranging practice covers all aspects of federal, state and local taxation as well as litigation, tax fraud, estate planning and employee benefits.

Carlton Fields
The Firm: This sizable full-service firm has six offices across Florida, which attracts national clients. Best known for its domestic work, the group *"ably covers all the angles."* It provides transactional tax planning and analysis to Fortune 500 companies and nonprofit organizations.
The Lawyers: Practice head **David Burke** rates highly as a *"brilliant"* tax attorney who *"facilitates deal negotiations."* His practice covers international tax planning, M&A, and state and federal tax controversy matters. Burke has advised such clients as The John Nuveen Company, Salomon Smith Barney and the State of Florida on various tax issues. On the tax controversy side, he recently rep-

resented AdTranz, formerly a subsidiary of ABB, on a $10.5 million state and local matter, and worked on a $15 million matter for a sports franchise. **Nat Doliner** chairs the firm's business transaction group and focuses on M&A and corporate tax planning. Recent deals include advising a large commercial business on the tax aspects of a $170 million acquisition, and handling the $350 million sale of a manufacturing company. Widely respected for his *"levelheaded"* advice, Doliner recently counseled on tax issues relating to the formation of a large group of medical diagnostic facilities.
The Clients: Salomon Smith Barney; AdTranz; State of Florida; The John Nuveen Company and Fortune 100 companies.

Johnson, Blakely, Pope, Bokor, Ruppel & Burns PA
The Firm: This full-service Florida outfit has six tax lawyers advising on corporate and real estate transactions, and estate and tax planning. Controversy matters are handled in cooperation with a strong litigation practice. The firm's two offices in Tampa and Clearwater are said to possess a *"good clutch of tax attorneys."*
The Lawyers: A *"complete tax lawyer,"* **Bruce Bokor** is considered one of the *"elite"* of the Florida tax bar. His practice emphasizes tax planning for charitable institutions. He successfully defended three brothers in an IRS challenge by establishing that monies coming into the US from Asia qualified as gifts rather than income.
The Clients: The firm has advised GE Capital and other financial institutions and regularly serves as external tax counsel to Transitions Optical, the global leader in photochromic lens technology and manufacture.

Other Notable Practitioners
In Miami, **Alan Lederman** was singled out at Broad and Cassel as a *"frighteningly intelligent"* tax attorney. Described as a *"walking LexisNexis,"* Lederman is active in establishing trusts for foreign investors. *"Hard-working"* sole practitioner **Robert Panoff** applies an *"incredibly analytical mind"* to tax compliance work. **Jonathan** (**Jason**) **Warner**, another sole practitioner, primarily represents high net-worth individuals on inbound and outbound investments. Peers view him as *"a diligent and well-rounded lawyer."* **Richard Comiter** with the Palm Beach Gardens-based firm Comiter & Singer was particularly praised for his expertise in partnership matters. In St Petersburg, **Joel Bronstein** at Bronstein, Carlson, Gleim & Smith, PA *"uses sound business knowledge to good effect"* in corporate taxation and estate planning. At Tampa-based Fowler White Boggs Banker, **Mitchell Horowitz** handles tax controversy matters in the local and federal courts and was commended by peers for his *"sound legal judgment."* In Tallahassee, **Robert Pierce** of Ausley & McMullen was deemed to be *"one of the finest state and local taxation lawyers in north Florida."* Similarly, **Vicky Weber** at Hopping, Green & Sams PA was reported to *"know tax law inside out."* She represents national and multinational businesses and trade associations on tax planning and controversy matters.

Leaders in Florida

ALEXANDER, Bruce
Boose Casey Ciklin Lubitz Martens McBane & O'Connell, West Palm Beach
561 832 5900
Recommended in Construction

ALHADEFF, Richard
Stearns Weaver Miller Weissler Alhadeff & Sitterson, P.A., Miami 305 789 3200
Recommended in Real Estate

ALLEY, John-Edward
Ford & Harrison LLP, Tampa
813 261 7800
Recommended in Employment

ALVAREZ, Victor
White & Case LLP, Miami 305 371 2700
Recommended in Banking & Finance

AMLONG, William
Amlong & Amlong, Fort Lauderdale
954 462 1983
Recommended in Employment

ANDREWS, William
Coffman, Coleman, Andrews & Grogan, Jacksonville 904 389 5161
Recommended in Employment

ARONSON, Daniel H
Greenberg Traurig LLP, Fort Lauderdale
954 768 8201
aronsond@gtlaw.com
Recommended in Corporate/M&A
Specialization: Public and private securities offerings; venture capital; mergers and acquisitions; leveraged buy-outs; strategic alliances and joint ventures; takeover (and anti-takeover) advice and planning; corporate governance, strategic and crisis planning.
Prof. Memberships: Florida Venture Capital Conference, Co-Chairman. Chairman and Executive Committee Member, Florida Venture Forum. Member, State of Florida, Capital Development Board and Capital Development Advisory Committee. Member, Executive Advisory Board, Council for Entrepreneurship and Innovation. Member, Board of Directors, Cypress Equity Fund Management Corp. Member, Executive Council, The Florida Bar, Business Law Section. Member, American Bar Association, Business Law Section, Committee on Federal Regulation of Securities.
Publications: Author, 'Raising Capital for the Emerging Business: A Primer for Entrepreneurs', Donnelley (4th Edition - 2001). Author, 'Venture Capital Transactions: Current Themes, Key Objectives and Structural Attributes' (19th Annual Federal Securities Institute, Glasser LegalWorks, Feb. 2001). Business Journal, January 26, 2001.

ASHBY, Kimberly
Akerman Senterfitt, Orlando
407 843 7860
kashby@akerman.com
Recommended in Construction
Specialization: Shareholder who focuses her practice in the areas of commercial litigation, construction litigation, eminent domain and appellate law. She is Board Certified in appellate law and has been named as one of the 'Top 5 Women in Construction Litigation in 1998' by the Orlando Business Journal, as well as one of the 'Top 40 under 40' by the Orlando Business Journal.
Prof. Memberships: Chair of the Ad Hoc Subcommittee for Construction Law Certification. She was also appointed to the Florida Bar Appellate Rules Committee and is General Counsel for Central Florida Builders Exchange.

ASTIGARRAGA, José
Astigarraga Davis, Miami
305 372 8282
Recommended in Litigation

AUGUST, Jerald
August & Kulunas, West Palm Beach
561 835 9600
Recommended in Tax

AVILA, Alcides
Holland & Knight LLP, Miami
305 374 8500
aavila@hklaw.com
Recommended in Banking & Finance
Specialization: Partner in the Business Law Department, focusing on the international and domestic banking law and commercial transactions practice areas. A significant portion of his practice involves the representation of state and national banks, bank holding companies, Edge Act corporations, international bank agencies and representative offices. Specific areas of experience include counseling foreign banks, bank holding companies, and foreign investors on establishing banking operations in the United States; licensing, de novo charters, and regulatory compliance matters; complex bank holding company formations; bank acquisitions; and the general representation of banking clients before all state and federal regulatory agencies. He also represents his clients in a variety of transactional matters including domestic and international secured and unsecured lending transactions; letter of credit transactions; mergers and acquisitions; and product expansion.

AWNER, Jonathan L
Akerman Senterfitt, Miami
305 374 5600
jawner@akerman.com
Recommended in Corporate/M&A
Specialization: Chair of the firm's Corporate Practice Group. He has broad experience in public and private securities transactions, mergers and acquisitions, private equity investments, and corporate governance issues. He has served as lead issuer's counsel in underwritten public equity and debt offerings that have raised over $4 billion, including the largest IPO of a Florida-based company in history. He also has represented buyers, sellers, boards of directors and

FLORIDA LEADERS

other stakeholders in over 300 mergers and acquisitions with an aggregate transaction value exceeding $10 billion. His clients include leading public companies, private equity firms and entrepreneurs.

BAENA, Scott
Bilzin Sumberg Dunn Baena Price & Axelrod LLP, Miami 305 350 2403
sbaena@bilzin.com
Recommended in Insolvency
Specialization: Chairs the firm's Restructuring and Bankruptcy Department with personal expertise in creditor's rights, workouts, bankruptcy and commercial loan transactions.
Prof. Memberships: American Law Institute, American Bar Foundation and The Florida Bar.
Career: Admitted to The Florida Bar in 1974 and currently licensed to appear before the Supreme Court of the United States; United States Courts of Appeals for the First, Third and Eleventh Circuits. He has counseled high-visibility clients in many major bankruptcy proceedings, both nationally and in Florida, including, asbestos committees in WR Grace and Celotex; special litigation counsel to Heilig-Meyers; counsel to liquidating trustees of Crown Vantage, Conti Financial and Southern Pacific Funding.
Personal: JD (with honors) 1974, and BBA (Accounting) 1970 from The George Washington University.

BARKETT, John
Shook, Hardy & Bacon LLP, Miami
305 358 5171
Recommended in Environment

BARNETT, Leslie
Barnett, Bolt, Kirkwood & Long, Tampa
813 253 2020
Recommended in Tax

BARTON, Bernard
Holland & Knight LLP, Tampa
813 227 8500
bbarton@hklaw.com
Recommended in Tax
Specialization: Partner in the Business Law Department, practicing in the areas of federal, state and local taxation with an emphasis in tax planning and in administrative and litigated disputes. He structures corporate, individual and partnership federal tax packages as part of business transactions. He handles leveraged lease sale/leaseback transactions and the tax aspects of tax-exempt financing. Some of the substantive areas of his state tax experience include sales and use taxes, corporate income tax, documentary stamp tax, intangible tax, ad valorem tax and various excise taxes. He is a member of the Section of Taxation of the American Bar Association, The Florida Bar, and the Executive Council of The Florida Bar Tax Section, for which he served as chairman of various committees.

BERLIN, Howard
Kluger, Peretz, Kaplan & Berlin P.L., Miami 305 379 9000
hberlin@kpkb.com
Recommended in Insolvency
Specialization: Co-chair of the Bankruptcy & Creditors' Rights Department. Has more than 20 years experience representing corporate debtors, secured lenders, creditors' committees and individual creditors in federal, bankruptcy and state court insolvency proceedings, as well as out of court workouts, debt restructuring negotiations and business reorganization proceedings. Has successfully reorganized a variety of business enterprises.
Prof. Memberships: Member of the American Bar Association, Dade County Bar Association, previously served as chairman of the Florida Bar Business Law Section and Bankruptcy UCC Committee. Completed the American Arbitration Association's 40-hour Circuit Court Mediation Training Program.
Career: Admitted to the Florida Bar (1979), the US District Court, Southern and Middle Districts of Florida (1979), and to the US Court of Appeals, Eleventh Circuit (1981). A founder and managing member of *Kluger, Peretz, Kaplan & Berlin PL* Served as an adjunct faculty member of the Nova University Banking Institute, the Freidt School of Business and Entrepreneurship.
Publications: Co-author of the 1987 revisions to Chapter 727 of the Florida Statutes' Assignments for the Benefit of Creditors and Chapter 247 of the Ohio Transaction Guide's Personal Bankruptcy Planning.
Personal: Earned a JD from the University of Miami School of Law (1979) and a BA from George Washington University in Washington DC (1976). Serves as mayor of the city of Bal Harbour, Florida.

BILZIN, Brian
Bilzin Sumberg Dunn Baena Price & Axelrod LLP, Miami 305 350 2363
bbilzin@bilzin.com
Recommended in Real Estate
Specialization: Partner in the real estate and general business departments. His practice includes all major real estate matters, from sales, purchases, and leases to financing, workouts, and reorganizations. In the area of general business law, he handles mergers and acquisitions, joint ventures, and lending matters, including structured financings.
Prof. Memberships: American Bar Association, The Florida Bar, New York State Bar Association, Association of the Bar of the City of New York and Dade County Bar Association.
Career: Admitted to New York Bar (1971), Florida (1978). He is the firm's founding partner and counsel to several of South Florida's foremost public and private companies. He is a director of LNR Property Corporation (NYSE:LNR).
Personal: JD from Boston University, 1970; AB from University of Michigan, 1967.

BLECHMAN, Bill
Kenny Nachwalter Seymour Arnold Critchlow & Spector, Miami
305 373 1000
Recommended in Antitrust

BLOOM, Mark D
Greenberg Traurig LLP, Miami
305 579 0537
bloomm@gtlaw.com
Recommended in Insolvency
Specialization: Financial restructuring and reorganization and bankruptcy, involving the representation of debtors, trustees, secured and unsecured creditors and official committees and purchasers of troubled companies and their assets
Prof. Memberships: Bankruptcy Bar Association of the Southern District of Florida. American Bar Association, Section of Litigation Leadership. United Way of Miami-Dade County. Fellow, American College of Bankruptcy; Eleventh Circuit Regent.
Publications: Co-author, 'Businesses Should Brace for Change,' Miami Daily Business Review, August 2001. Contributing Author, Norton Bankruptcy Law Treatise. Co-author, 'Saybrook Manufacturing: The Death of Cross Collateralization and the Mootness Doctrine,' Norton Bankruptcy Law Adviser, September 1992.

BLUE, James
Allen, Norton & Blue, P.A., Tampa
813 251 1210
Recommended in Employment

BOKOR, Bruce
Johnson, Blakely, Pope, Bokor, Ruppel & Burns, PA, Clearwater
727 461 1818
Recommended in Tax

BOLT, Robert
Barnett, Bolt, Kirkwood & Long, Tampa 813 253 2020
Recommended in Tax

BOZARTH, Stephen
Dean, Mead, Egerton, Bloodworth, Capouano & Bozarth PA, Orlando
407 841 1200
Recommended in Real Estate

BRAMNICK, James
Muller Mintz, Miami
305 358 5500
Recommended in Employment

BRONSTEIN, Joel
Bronstein, Carlson, Gleim & Smith, PA, St Petersburg 727 898 6688
Recommended in Tax

BROWN, Bowman
Shutts & Bowen, Miami
305 379 9107
BBROWN@SHUTTS-LAW.COM
Recommended in Banking & Finance, Corporate/M&A
Specialization: Chairman of the Executive Committee and the Financial Services Industry Practice Group of *Shutts & Bowen LLP*, a 150 lawyer firm with offices in Florida in Miami, Fort Lauderdale, West Palm Beach, Orlando and Tallahassee.
Prof. Memberships: Member Florida, New York and District of Columbia Bar Associations; serves on the Committee on Banking Law of the Association of the Bar of the City of New York.
Career: Served as Adjunct Professor of Banking Law at the University of Miami School of Law and as Chairman of the Florida Bar Banking Law & Credit Regulation Committee. He also served as General Counsel of the Florida International Bankers Association, Inc., a Trustee of the Pan American Development Foundation, a Washington, DC-based affiliate of the Organization of American States, and is a member of the Florida International Banking and Finance Council established by the Florida Legislature in 1990.
Publications: Editor of 'International Banking Centres' published by Euromoney, London, 1982; and 'Private Banking and the Law', published by LatinFinance in 1992. He serves as a member of the Editorial Advisory Board of Banking and Financial Services Policy Report.
Personal: Received his MBA and JD degrees from Cornell University.

BROWN, Daryl
Brown Clark Christopher & DeMay, PA, Sarasota 941 957 3800
Recommended in Construction

BROWN, James
Ford & Harrison LLP, Orlando
407 418 2300
Recommended in Employment

BURKE, David
Carlton Fields, Tampa
813 223 7000
Recommended in Tax

BUSEY, Stephen
Smith Hulsey & Busey, Jacksonville
904 359 7700
Recommended in Insolvency

CACCIABEVE, Charles
Carlton Fields, Orlando
407 849 0300
Recommended in Construction

CANNON, Kinder
Holland & Knight LLP, Jacksonville
904 353 2000
kcannon@hklaw.com
Recommended in Corporate/M&A
Specialization: Partner in the Business Law Department, focusing on the corporate finance, securities, mergers and

FLORIDA

acquisitions, venture capital and franchising law practice areas. He has represented a broad range of businesses in public and private offerings of equity and debt securities and preparation of disclosure documents required under the securities laws; in business acquisitions and divestitures; and in the development, marketing and expansion of franchise programs. He has extensive experience in venture capital financings, corporate credit facilities, leveraged buy-outs, joint ventures and other capital transactions. Part of his practice has been devoted to providing such corporate finance services to technology start-up and emerging companies. His professional experience has been augmented by several years as a business executive responsible for corporate development and marketing at a manufacturing company serving international markets.

CARDWELL, J Thomas
Akerman Senterfitt, Orlando
407 843 7860
tcardwell@akerman.com
Recommended in Banking & Finance, Litigation

Specialization: Listed in a leading US legal publication in the categories of business litigation and banking law and is a Fellow of the American College of Trial Lawyers. Has extensive experience representing clients in litigation, administrative, and regulatory matters. Served as General Counsel for The Florida Bankers Association since 1982. He is currently Chairman and CEO of the firm.

CARTER, Francis
Ferrell Schultz Carter Zumpano & Fertel PA, Miami 305 371 8585
Recommended in Insolvency

CASEY, Michael
Muller Mintz, Miami
305 358 5500
Recommended in Employment

CAULKINS, Charles
Fisher & Phillips LLP, Fort Lauderdale
954 525 4800
Recommended in Employment

CHONIN, Neil
Chonin & Sher, Miami
305 443 5125
Recommended in Employment

COGLIANESE, Matthew
Bilzin Sumberg Dunn Baena Price & Axelrod LLP, Miami 305 350 2404
mcoglianese@bilzin.com
Recommended in Environment

Specialization: Partner practicing in the area of environmental law, emphasizing CERCLA, RCRA, brownfields redevelopment, the Clean Air Act, the Clean Water Act, and state and local environmental matters.
Prof. Memberships: American Bar Association, Dade County Bar Association,

The Florida Bar, Los Angeles County Bar Association and State Bar of California.
Career: He has substantial experience in environmental litigation before state and federal tribunals and administrative agencies. His practice also includes environmental counseling, permitting and corporate due diligence.
Personal: JD from the University of Miami, 1984; PhD from Texas A&M University, 1981; BS from University of Rhode Island, 1976.

COHEN, Jules
Akerman Senterfitt, Orlando
407 843 7860
jcohen@akeman.com
Recommended in Insolvency

Specialization: Shareholder with extensive experience in bankruptcy and creditors' rights litigation. He was selected as the best bankruptcy attorney in Orlando by the Orlando Business Journal for 2002, and is certified in business bankruptcy law by the American Board of Bankruptcy Certification.
Prof. Memberships: Past Chair of the Business Law Section and Bankruptcy Committee of The Florida Bar, Board Member Emeritus, Southeastern Bankruptcy Law Institute and Fellow of the American College of Bankruptcy. He is a frequent lecturer on Bankruptcy for The Florida Bar, Attorney's Title Insurance Fund, National Business Institute and other organizations.

COLE, Terry
Oertel, Hoffman, Fernandez & Cole PA, Tallahassee 850 521 0700
Recommended in Environment

COLEMAN, Patrick
Coffman, Coleman, Andrews & Grogan, Jacksonville 904 389 5161
Recommended in Employment

COLSON, Dean
Colson Hicks Eidson, Miami
305 476 7400
Recommended in Litigation

COMITER, Richard
Comiter & Singer, Palm Beach Gardens
561 626 4742
Recommended in Tax

CONNOR, Terence
Morgan, Lewis & Bockius LLP, Miami
305 579 0300
Recommended in Employment

COOLMAN AMLONG, Karen
Amlong & Amlong, Fort Lauderdale
954 462 1983
Recommended in Employment

COUTROULIS, Chris
Carlton Fields, Tampa
813 223 7000
Recommended in Antitrust

CURTIN, Lawrence
Holland & Knight LLP, Tallahassee
850 224 7000
larry.curtin@hklaw.com
Recommended in Environment

Specialization: Partner in the Real Estate Department, practicing environmental and administrative law. He has represented and counseled clients on a variety of matters in the environmental area. Since beginning his environmental practice, he has been involved in the implementation of a number of important regulatory statutes, including the Clean Water Act, the Clean Air Act, the Resource Conservation and Recovery Act, and the Comprehensive Environmental Response, Compensation and Liability Act, as well as the development and implementation of Florida's environmental and growth management laws. His practice involves participation in legislative activities, the formulation of rules and regulatory policies, and administrative and civil litigation involving permitting, enforcement, and hazardous waste matters. He has extensive experience in the permitting of major industrial facilities in Florida.

DAVIDSON, Barry
Hunton & Williams, Miami
305 810 2500
Recommended in Litigation

DAVIS, Alvin
Steel Hector & Davis LLP, Miami
305 577 7000
Recommended in Litigation

DAVIS, Gardner
Foley & Lardner, Jacksonville
904 359 2000
Recommended in Corporate/M&A

DETZEL, Lauren
Dean, Mead, Egerton, Bloodworth, Capouano & Bozarth PA, Orlando
407 841 1200
Recommended in Tax

DEVAULT, John
Bedell, Dittmar, DeVault, Pillans & Coxe, Jacksonville 904 353 0211
Recommended in Litigation

DICKINSON, John
Constangy, Brooks & Smith, LLC, Jacksonville 904 356 8900
Recommended in Employment

DOLIN, Susan
Rothstein, Rosenfeldt Dolin & Pancier, Fort Lauderdale 954 522 3456
Recommended in Employment

DOLINER, Nathaniel
Carlton Fields, Tampa
813 223 7000
Recommended in Corporate/M&A, Tax

EGAN, Joseph
Egan, Lev & Siwica, Orlando
407 422 1400
Recommended in Employment

EGERTON, Charles
Dean, Mead, Egerton, Bloodworth, Capouano & Bozarth PA, Orlando
407 841 1200
Recommended in Tax

EIDSON, Mike
Colson Hicks Eidson, Miami
305 476 7400
Recommended in Litigation

EPSTEIN, Gary
Greenberg Traurig LLP, Miami
305 579 0894
epsteing@gtlaw.com
Recommended in Corporate/M&A

Specialization: Public offerings; mergers and acquisitions; corporate planning; financing transactions.
Prof. Memberships: Chairman of the Board, American Israel Chamber of Commerce, Florida. President, Miami Beach Jewish Community Center

FARMER, Guy
Foley & Lardner, Jacksonville
904 359 2000
Recommended in Employment

FEAGIN, III, Robert R
Holland & Knight LLP, Tallahassee
850 224 7000
bob.feagin@hklaw.com
Recommended in Litigation

Specialization: Prior to becoming *Holland & Knight* managing partner in June 2001, he organized and headed the firm's antitrust and trade regulation practice. He was lead counsel for the firm's clients in major antitrust litigation, including the Justice Department's challenge to territorial agreements among electric utilities; a class action suit against a major fast-food franchiser for alleged tying violations; a price-fixing suit involving an alleged national conspiracy among rebar steel manufacturers; an FTC proceeding to block the merger of a major food processor into an international conglomerate; and a monopolization claim against a leading pharmaceutical company by a retail drugstore chain. He also litigated other types of commercial claims and for many years defended numerous phosphate mining companies against multi billion dollar damage claims arising out of Florida activities in alleged state-owned lands.

FELMAN, David
Hill, Ward & Henderson, PA, Tampa
813 221 3900
Recommended in Corporate/M&A

FITZGERALD, Randi
Lowndes Drosdick Doster Kantor & Reed, PA, Orlando 407 843 4600
Recommended in Real Estate

FLORIDA LEADERS

FLEMING, Joseph
Greenberg Traurig LLP, Miami
305 579 0517
flemingj@gtlaw.com
Recommended in Employment

Specialization: Labor and employment; environmental, land use and natural resources; entertainment; arts and sports law; intellectual property; defamation law; media law; constitutional law.
Prof. Memberships: American Law Institute American Bar Association (ALI-ABA). Past Member, Board of Directors, National Center for Preservation Law. Chair, Emerging Issues Committee, American Bar Association's State and Local Government Law Section. Member, America Arbitration Association's Miami Employment Advisory Council and the AAA's Arbitrators Panel Past Chair of the following Florida Bar Sections: the Environmental and Land Use Section; the Entertainment, Arts and Sports Law Section; and the Labor and Employment Law Section.
Publications: Lecturer at numerous seminars, and author of numerous law review articles and published chapters in books on environmental and labor law (Railway Labor Act, Bureau of National Affairs [BNA], International Labor and Employment Law [BNA Supplement]).

GART, Brian
Greenberg Traurig LLP, Fort Lauderdale
954 768 8212
gartb@gtlaw.com
Recommended in Insolvency

Specialization: Chapter 11 business reorganizations; workouts and out of court loan and debt restructurings; acquisition and sale of assets under Section 363 of the Bankruptcy Code Debtor-in-Possession Financing; complex merger, acquisition and divestiture transactions with respect to distressed business entities and/or their assets bankruptcy litigation.
Prof. Memberships: Executive Council of the Business Law Section of The Florida Bar. Chair, Bankruptcy/UCC Committee of the Business Law Section of the Florida Bar. Member, Business Bankruptcy Committee, American Bar Association Section of Business Law (Member of the Committee on Official Creditors' Committees). Member, American Bankruptcy Institute, Business Reorganization Committee. Member, Bankruptcy and Insolvency Section, Commercial Law League.
Publications: Contributing Author, 2001-02 Bankruptcy Law Update, Aspen Publishers. Regular contributor and lecturer on bankruptcy reorganization and debtor/creditor rights for the Business Law Section of The Florida Bar and Nova Southeastern University Shepard Broad Law Center.

GARWOOD, Thomas
Ford & Harrison LLP, Orlando
407 418 2300
Recommended in Employment

GENOVESE, John
Genovese Joblove & Battista P.A., Miami 305 349 2300
Recommended in Insolvency

GILBERT, Leonard
Holland & Knight LLP, Tampa
813 227 8500
lgilbert@hklaw.com
Recommended in Insolvency

Specialization: Partner in the Business Law Department, practicing in the areas of commercial finance, insolvency, and commercial litigation and maintains an active transactional practice. He is chair of the Financial Institutions and Creditors' Rights National Practice Group. His emphasis has been in the representation of financial institutions and other institutional lenders. In his bankruptcy practice, he has represented numerous state, national and international banks, and other financial institutions and public bodies, secured and unsecured creditors' committees and equity and has been involved in restructuring LBO transactions. He has served as president of The Florida Bar and is active in other professional associations. He has written for various publications and has lectured for The Florida Bar, the American Bar Institute, PLI, the International Bar Association and International Insolvency.

GLENN, Robert
Glenn Rasmussen Fogarty & Hooker, Tampa 813 229 3333
Recommended in Insolvency

GOLDSTEIN, Michael
Akerman Senterfitt, Miami
305 374 5600
mgoldstein@akerman.com
Recommended in Environment

Specialization: Shareholder, represents public and private companies, lenders, and individuals in all phases of environmental business transactions and works extensively with real estate development principals and professionals to coordinate regulatory approvals for complex commercial, mixed use, industrial, and marina related projects throughout Florida. His practice has statewide emphasis on the remediation and redevelopment of Brownfield sites including Brownfields related transactional, administrative, legislative, and policy matters for clients in the private and public sectors.
Prof. Memberships: Serves as Chairman of Florida Brownfields Association and the Miami-Dade County Brownfields Oversight Committee. Writes and speaks frequently on environmental restoration and economic revitalization related issues.

GONZALEZ, Thomas
Thompson, Sizemore & Gonzalez, Tampa 813 273 0050
Recommended in Employment

GORSON, Matthew
Greenberg Traurig LLP, Miami
305 579 0777
gorsonm@gtlaw.com
Recommended in Real Estate

Specialization: Real estate, commercial lending and governmental negotiations.
Prof. Memberships: Chairman, Downtown Miami Charter School. Board Member, City of Miami Downtown Development Authority. Board Member, Tulane University President's Council.

GRAGG, Lawrence
White & Case LLP, Miami
305 371 2700
Recommended in Tax

GRAMMIG, Robert
Holland & Knight LLP, Tampa
813 227 8500
rgrammig@hklaw.com
Recommended in Corporate/M&A

Specialization: Partner in the Business Law Department, practicing in the areas of corporate finance, securities law, general corporate law and international business transactions. His practice currently includes a wide range of corporate, securities and commercial law matters, including: public offerings registered under the federal and state securities laws; private placements under the federal and state securities laws; mergers and acquisitions; periodic reporting and compliance matters under the Securities Exchange Act of 1934; corporate governance matters; contests for corporate control; and other commercial law matters. He has devoted a significant part of his practice to international business transactions, representing both United States and foreign entities.

GREELEY, Jack
Smith Mackinnon PA, Orlando
407 843 7300
Recommended in Banking & Finance

GREEN, William
Hopping, Green & Sams PA, Tallahassee
850 222 7500
Recommended in Environment

GREER, Alan
Richman Greer Weil Brumbaugh Mirabito & Christensen, Miami
305 373 4000
Recommended in Litigation

GROGAN, Michael
Coffman, Coleman, Andrews & Grogan, Jacksonville 904 389 5161
Recommended in Employment

GURLEY, David
Gurley Dramis, Sarasota
941 365 4501
Recommended in Construction

GUTTER, Marvin
Tescher Gutter Chaves Josepher Rubin Ruffin & Forman PA, Boca Ratón
561 998 7847
Recommended in Tax

HALSEY, Douglas
White & Case LLP, Miami
305 371 2700
Recommended in Environment

HAMILTON, Russell
Morgan, Lewis & Bockius LLP, Miami 305 579 0300
Recommended in Employment

HANSON, JR, Karl B
LeBoeuf, Lamb, Greene & MacRae, LLP, Jacksonville 904 354 8000
Kbhanson@llgm.com
Recommended in Real Estate

Specialization: He is an experienced commercial real estate attorney concentrating in acquisitions, dispositions, development, financing, leasing and management of real property. He represents clients in all facets of ownership in the real estate area. He has served as counsel to mortgage banking companies in regard to their operations and financing. He is also an experienced real property title insurance attorney, representing several major national title insurance companies in insuring large real estate transactions.
Prof. Memberships: American Bar Association; The Florida Bar; Jacksonville Bar Association.
Career: Joined *LeBoeuf* in 1988.
Personal: University of North Carolina (BA) 1968; University of Florida (JD) 1971.

HILL, Benjamin
Hill, Ward & Henderson, PA, Tampa
813 221 3900
Recommended in Litigation

HOFFMAN, Jerome
Holland & Knight LLP, Tallahassee
850 224 7000
jerome.hoffman@hklaw.com
Recommended in Antitrust

Specialization: Partner in the Litigation Department, representing clients in litigation with special emphasis on antitrust, consumer fraud, RICO, and Medicaid and Medicare fraud and other health care matters. He served as General Counsel for the Agency for Health Care Administration from 1995 to 1997, where he supervised 40 attorneys responsible for prosecuting Medicaid overpayments; regulating hospitals, nursing homes, assisted living facilities and home health agencies; prosecuting disciplinary cases before the Board of Medicine and other health care professional licensing boards and providing general legal services to the Agency. He also served as chief of the Antitrust Section of the Florida Attorney General's Office for eight years, handling cases involving bid rigging, price fixing, monopolization and other restraints of trade, as well as merger reviews.

FLORIDA

HOPPING, Wade
Hopping, Green & Sams PA, Tallahassee
850 222 7500
Recommended in Environment

HORNREICH, Michael
Greenberg Traurig LLP, Orlando
407 420 1000
Recommended in Construction

HOROWITZ, Mitchell
Fowler White Boggs Banker, Tampa
813 228 7411
Recommended in Tax

HUDSON, Robert
Baker & McKenzie, Miami
305 789 8906
bob.hudson@bakernet.com
Recommended in Tax
Specialization: Tax planning and tax controversy work, particularly for international private banks and high-net worth clients, foreign client structuring into US real estate and businesses, preimmigration US tax planning and US mutinational outbound planning.
Prof. Memberships: American Bar Association, New York State Bar, Florida Bar (Tax Sections); International Fiscal Association; International Tax Planning Association; American College of Tax Counsels.
Career: International Partner, *Baker & McKenzie*, Miami (1986 to date); Partner, *Stearns, Weaver, Miller* et al, Miami (1977-1986); Associate, *Wender, Murase & White*, New York (1973-1977); Law Clerk, Hon. Don N Laramore, US Circuit Court of Appeals for Federal Circuit (1972-1973).
Publications: 'Federal Tax Considerations of Foreign Investment in the US Real Estate' BNA Portfolio; published over 50 articles to date on a wide range of international tax topics for TMIJ, Tax Notes International, ALI/ABA, PLI, Business Entities Journal, International Tax Journal, etc.
Personal: Active within the South Florida civic and cultural community, serving as a board member (and Vice-Chrmn.) of the Performing Arts Center Foundation, the Concert Association of Florida, and formerly the Greater Miami Chamber of Commerce, World Trade Center, Rotary Club of Miami and the Japan Society of South Florida.

HYDE, Kevin
Foley & Lardner, Jacksonville
904 359 2000
Recommended in Employment

JAMIESON, Michael
Holland & Knight LLP, Tampa
813 227 8500
mjamieson@hklaw.com
Recommended in Corporate/M&A
Specialization: Partner in and chair of the Business Law Department. His experience includes SEC registered public offerings and exempt offerings of securities; corporate acquisitions, dispositions, redemptions and reorganizations; SEC periodic reporting and compliance matters; financing transactions for regulated industries; Eurodollar financing transactions and other international business transactions; secured lending; equipment leasing; venture capital financing; industrial development revenue bond financing; corporation, partnership, limited liability company and business trust matters; buy sell, voting trust and other shareholder agreements; employee compensation, stock purchase, stock option and benefit plans; corporate governance matters; and employment contracts. He serves or has served on the American Bar Association Committee on Corporate Laws and the Committee on Federal Regulation of Securities and is a member of The American Law Institute.

JONES, Rod
Shutts & Bowen, Orlando
407 835 6909
rjones@shutts-law.com
Recommended in Banking & Finance
Specialization: Partner in *Shutts & Bowen's* Financial Services Industry Practice Group and has been with the firm since 1989. Prior thereto, he was the Director of the Division of Banking of the Florida Department of Banking and Finance, where he had responsibility for licensing and supervising more than 500 state chartered financial institutions.
Prof. Memberships: Florida Bar.
Career: Served for four years as staff counsel and banking analyst for the Committee on Commerce of the Florida House of Representatives. He was involved in drafting major revisions to the Florida Financial Institutions Codes, including legislation authorizing cross-industry mergers, conversions and acquisitions of Florida financial institutions and the Regional Reciprocal Banking Act of 1984. He has been an instructor at the Florida School of Banking; Interstate and Cross-Industry Acquisitions, Mergers and Conversions of and by Florida Financial Institutions, Corporations, Banking and Business Law Section, and New Bank Formations, Banking Law Institute and Executive Enterprises, Inc.
Personal: Graduated with honors from Florida State University and from the Florida School of Banking of the College of Business of the University of Florida.

JOSEFSBERG, Robert
Podhurst, Orseck, Josefsberg, Eaton, Meadow, Olin & Perwin, Miami
305 358 2800
Recommended in Litigation

JOSEPHER, Richard
Tescher Gutter Chaves Josepher Rubin Ruffin & Forman PA, Boca Ratón
561 998 7847
Recommended in Tax

KANTOR, Hal
Lowndes Drosdick Doster Kantor & Reed, PA, Orlando 407 843 4600
Recommended in Real Estate

KEINER, Jeffrey
Gray, Harris & Robinson, PA, Orlando
407 843 8880
Recommended in Construction

KELLY, Mark
Kelly & McKee, Tampa
813 248 6400
Recommended in Employment

KING, Bruce
Carlton Fields, Miami
305 530 0050
Recommended in Construction

KING, David
King, Blackwell & Downs, PA, Orlando
407 422 2472
Recommended in Litigation

KIRSCHNER, Kenneth
Kirschner & Legler, Jacksonville
904 346 3200
Recommended in Corporate/M&A

KOREN, Ed
Holland & Knight LLP, Lakeland
863 682 1161
ed.koren@hklaw.com
Recommended in Tax
Specialization: Partner in the Business Law Department and chair of the Trusts and Estates National Practice Group. He practices in estate planning and probate matters, including the use of life insurance and other vehicles to plan for needed estate liquidity; the use of revocable and irrevocable trusts, family limited partnerships and S corporations to minimize estate taxes; and the use of buy-sell, split dollar and other agreements for business owners and executives. A considerable portion of his practice is related to planning for owners of closely held business interests and the determination of the value of entities. He often handles tax controversies involving succession and income taxes, and is involved in various forms of probate and trust litigation, both as counsel and as an expert witness.

KORNREICH, David
Muller Mintz, Miami 305 358 5500
Recommended in Employment

KOZYAK, John
Kozyak Tropin & Throckmorton, Miami
305 372 1800
Recommended in Insolvency

LAROSE, Edward
Trenam, Kemker, Scharf, Barkin, Frye, O'Neill & Mullis PA, Tampa
813 223 7474
Recommended in Antitrust

LEDERMAN, Alan
Broad and Cassel, Miami
305 373 9435
Recommended in Tax

LEGLER, Mitchell
Kirschner & Legler, Jacksonville
904 346 3200
Recommended in Corporate/M&A

LEIBY, Larry
Leiby Taylor Stearns Linkhorst & Roberts, PA, Fort Lauderdale
954 382 9199
Recommended in Construction

LEISNER, Richard
Trenam, Kemker, Scharf, Barkin, Frye, O'Neill & Mullis PA, Tampa
813 223 7474
Recommended in Corporate/M&A

LESSER, Steven
Becker & Poliakoff, P.A., Fort Lauderdale
954 987 7550
Recommended in Construction

LEWIS, Terry
Lewis, Longman & Walker PA,
West Palm Beach 561 640 0820
Recommended in Environment

LILES, Rutledge
Liles, Gavin, Costantino & Murphy, Jacksonville 904 634 1100
Recommended in Litigation

LINESCH, David
The Linesch Firm, Palm Harbor
727 786 0000
Recommended in Employment

LITCHFORD, Hal
Litchford & Christopher, Orlando
407 841 0325
Recommended in Antitrust

LOCKETT, Laurel
Carlton Fields, Tampa
813 223 7000
Recommended in Environment

LOUMIET, Carlos
Hunton & Williams, Miami
305 810 2500
Recommended in Banking & Finance

MALEFATTO, Alfred J
Greenberg Traurig LLP, West Palm Beach 561 650 7908
malefattoa@gtlaw.com
Recommended in Environment
Specialization: Environmental law; land use and zoning law; administrative and governmental law.
Prof. Memberships: Member, Executive Council, Environmental and Land Use Law Section of The Florida Bar from 1985 to 1993; served as Section Chairman from 1991-92. Gubernatorial Appointee to Board of Treasure Coast Regional Planning Council, 1984-86. Board Member, The Forum Club of the Palm Beaches. Board Member and Vice President, Friends of the Academy of Environmental Science and Technology, Inc. Board Member, Grassy Waters Preserve.

FLORIDA LEADERS

MASER, Joel
Greenberg Traurig LLP, Orlando
407 418 2389
maserj@gtlaw.com
Recommended in Tax
Specialization: Federal, state and local taxation; tax planning; foreign tax planning; mergers and acquisitions.
Prof. Memberships: Active member, Executive Council, The Florida Bar Tax Section and has served as Chairperson of several committees within the Tax Section. Member, Tax Section's Long Range Planning Committee and is serving as the Tax Section's workshop director. Director, Tax Section's State Tax Advisory Division, 1991-95.

MATTHEWS, Frank
Hopping, Green & Sams PA, Tallahassee 850 222 7500
Recommended in Environment

MAY, Rodney
Gronek & Latham, Orlando
407 481 5800
Recommended in Insolvency

MCCREA, Richard
Zinober & McCrea, P.A., Tampa
813 224 9004
Recommended in Employment

MCGUIGAN, Thomas
Steel Hector & Davis LLP, Miami
305 577 7000
Recommended in Corporate/M&A

MCKEE, Robert
Kelly & McKee, Tampa
813 248 6400
Recommended in Employment

MEYER, George
Carlton Fields, Tampa
813 223 7000
Recommended in Construction

MITCHELL, Stephen
Squire, Sanders & Dempsey LLP, Tampa 813 202 1300
Recommended in Real Estate

MOSS, Edward
Shook, Hardy & Bacon LLP, Miami
305 358 5171
Recommended in Litigation

MOYE, James E
Moye, O'Brien, O'Rourke, Pickert & Martin, LLP, Orlando 407 622 5250
jmoye@moohp.com
Recommended in Construction
Specialization: Construction, commercial litigation, management labor relations law, employment relations law. Has extensive experience representing US and international contractors and engineering firms in the USA, the Caribbean basin, Central America and Canada in multi-million dollar claims.
Prof. Memberships: State Bar of Georgia; The Florida Bar; American Bar Association (Member, Sections on Labor and Employment Law, Forum on the Construction Industry); Court of Federal Claims Bar Association.
Career: Admitted to Georgia Bar (1982), Florida (1989); senior partner of *Moye, O'Brien, O'Rourke, Pickert & Martin, LLP* (with affiliate offices in Chicago, Illinois); admitted to US District Court, Middle and Southern Districts of Florida and US District Court, Northern District of Georgia; US Court of Appeals, Fifth, Eleventh and DC Circuits; US Supreme Court.
Personal: Received a BSE (cum laude) from University of Central Florida in 1978 and a JD from University of Florida in 1981; inducted into Eta Kappa Nu (Electrical Engineering National Honor Society), Tau Beta Pi (Engineering National Honor Society) and Omicron Delta Kappa; member of the President's Leadership Council and the University of Florida Law Review from 1980 through 1981.

NACHWALTER, Michael
Kenny Nachwalter Seymour Arnold Critchlow & Spector, Miami
305 373 1000
Recommended in Litigation

NAGIN, Stephen
Nagin Gallop Figuerdo, Coconut Grove
305 854 5353
Recommended in Antitrust

NORTON, Robert
Allen, Norton & Blue, P.A.,
Coral Gables 305 445 7801
Recommended in Employment

NORTON, Susan
Allen, Norton & Blue, P.A.,
Tampa
813 251 1210
Recommended in Employment

NUECHTERLEIN, Mike
Carlton Fields, Tampa
813 223 7000
Recommended in Construction

OLSON, John
Stearns Weaver Miller Weissler Alhadeff & Sitterson, P.A., Tampa 813 223 4800
Recommended in Insolvency

O'NEAL-COBLE, Leslie
Holland & Knight LLP, Orlando
407 425 8500
loneal@hklaw.com
Recommended in Construction
Specialization: Partner in the Litigation Department and chair of the Construction Law National Practice Group. She has extensive trial experience in commercial litigation, especially construction-related cases, including representation of owners, general contractors, subcontractors, architects, engineers and sureties for 24 years. She has handled lien claims, payment and performance bond claims, delay and disruption claims, construction defect claims, professional malpractice claims, 'sick building' claims, mold claims and other construction matters throughout the country. She also has handled virtually all types of fidelity and surety bond claims. Her practice also includes reviewing, drafting and negotiating contracts for construction projects on behalf of owners, contractors and subcontractors. She is the author of Contemplating Litigation and Its Alternatives, a chapter in 'Representing the Contractor' (Wiley, 2001).

O'NEILL, Albert
Trenam, Kemker, Scharf, Barkin, Frye, O'Neill & Mullis PA, Tampa
813 223 7474
Recommended in Tax

PANOFF, Robert
Robert E Panoff PA, Miami
305 670 6547
Recommended in Tax

PAPPAS, Lynn
Pappas Metcalf Jenks and Miller, Jacksonville 904 353 1980
Recommended in Real Estate

PERWIN, Scott
Kenny Nachwalter Seymour Arnold Critchlow & Spector, Miami
305 373 1000
Recommended in Antitrust

PIERCE, Robert
Ausley & McMullen, Tallahassee
850 224 9115
Recommended in Tax

PODHURST, Aaron
Podhurst, Orseck, Josefsberg, Eaton, Meadow, Olin & Perwin, Miami
305 358 2800
Recommended in Litigation

POPE, Wallace
Johnson, Blakely, Pope, Bokor, Ruppel & Burns, PA, Clearwater 727 461 1818
Recommended in Litigation

PRESTON, William
William D Preston, PA, Tallahassee
850 668 4986
Recommended in Environment

PRICE, Stanley
Bilzin Sumberg Dunn Baena Price & Axelrod LLP, Miami 305 350 2374
sprice@bilzin.com
Recommended in Real Estate
Specialization: Chairs the firm's Land Use and Government Law Department. He has worked in the forefront of land use law and is frequently consulted on the subjects of owners' and developers' rights, and complex zoning and permitting issues.
Prof. Memberships: The Florida Bar and New York State Bar.
Career: Has assisted numerous owners and developers in matters involving difficult zoning and planning issues. In addition to representing his clients, he works with government and regulatory agencies, developers, and landowners on land use policy.
Personal: JD from Syracuse University, 1969; BS (with honors) from New York University, 1966.

RAATTAMA, Henry
Akerman Senterfitt, Miami
305 374 5600
hraattama@akerman.com
Recommended in Tax
Specialization: Shareholder who focuses his practice in the areas of charitable and tax-exempt organizations and estate planning. He is listed in a leading US legal publication in Taxation, recipient of the Gerald T Hart Outstanding Tax Attorney for 1998-1999, and has chaired the Tax Section of The Florida Bar and The Florida Bar Tax Certification Committee. He is also the recipient of the James W McLamore Volunteer of the Year Award 1999, and the Outstanding Professional Advisor for 2002. Frequently lectures on tax matters and has taught in the University of Miami Graduate Tax Program.

RAKUSIN, Steve
Stephen Rakusin PA, Fort Lauderdale
954 356 0496
Recommended in Construction

RASMUSSEN, Robert
Glenn Rasmussen Fogarty & Hooker, Tampa 813 229 3333
Recommended in Corporate/M&A

RAVIKOFF, Ronald
Zuckerman Spaeder LLP, Miami
305 358 5000
Recommended in Antitrust

REDMOND, Patricia
Stearns Weaver Miller Weissler Alhadeff & Sitterson, P.A., Miami 305 789 3200
Recommended in Insolvency

REISMAN, Stephen H
Peckar & Abramson, Rosenberg, Reisman & Stein LLP, Miami 305 358 2600
sreisman@pecklaw.com
Recommended in Construction
Specialization: Managing partner of *Peckar & Abramson's* Florida Offices. His primary area of practice is construction law and includes the representation of construction managers, general contractors, subcontractors and owners in the negotiation and preparation of construction documents, and the negotiation, mediation, arbitration and litigation of construction contract claims, construction and design defect claims, insurance claims, and related matters. His construction law practice also includes project administration assistance for the early identification and resolution of potential conflicts and disputes.
Prof. Memberships: He serves on the Construction Advisory Council and Panel of Arbitrators for the American Arbitration Association. He is a member

of the American Bar Association (Construction Industry Forum and Litigation Section), the Academy of Florida Trial Lawyers, the Florida Bar (Litigation and Business Law Sections) and the Construction Association of South Florida.
Career: He is admitted to practice law before the United States Supreme Court, the United States Court of Appeals for the Fifth and Eleventh Circuits, the United States District Court for the Southern and Middle Districts of Florida, the United States Bankruptcy Court for the Southern District of Florida as well as all courts of the State of Florida. He is the managing partner of *Peckar & Abramson's* Florida offices and formerly a partner of *Rosenberg, Reisman & Stein,* which merged with *Peckar & Abramson* in 2000.
Publications: He has authored several articles and conducted seminars on various construction law topics for The Florida Bar, National Business Institute, Construction Specifications Institute, Construction Association of South Florida, 'Southeast Construction,' and Lorman Educational Services.
Personal: He is a graduate of Emory University (1973) and the University of Miami School of Law (1976).

RICHARD, Barry
Greenberg Traurig LLP, Tallahassee
850 425 8503
richardb@gtlaw.com
Recommended in Litigation
Specialization: Complex commercial litigation; state and federal constitutional law; government and election law; appellate practice.
Prof. Memberships: Charter member, American Academy of Appellate Lawyers. Member, Florida Legislature, 1974-78. Former Deputy Attorney General for the State of Florida.
Publications: Author, 'Rule 11 Sanctions: Risks to Non-lead Counsel,' The National Law Journal, September 2001. Author, 'Defending Mega-Suits,' The National Law Journal, April 16, 2001. Chapter author, 'Technology,' Successful Partnering Between Inside and Outside Counsel, West Publishing Company. Chapter author, Federal Practice Guide on Appellate Procedure in the Eleventh Circuit published by Lawyers Cooperative Publishing Company.

RICHMAN, Gerald
Richman Greer Weil Brumbaugh Mirabito & Christensen, Miami
305 373 4000
Recommended in Litigation

RIDLEY, Fred
Foley & Lardner, Tampa 813 229 2300; Pinellas County: 813 442 3296
Recommended in Real Estate

RIEDEL, Harley
Stichter, Riedel, Blain & Prosser, Tampa
813 229 0144
Recommended in Insolvency

ROBINSON, John
Fowler White Boggs Banker, Tampa
813 228 7411
Recommended in Employment

RODDENBERRY, Stephen
Akerman Senterfitt, Miami
305 374 5600
sroddenberry@akerman.com
Recommended in Corporate/M&A
Specialization: Shareholder in the Corporate Practice Group where he focuses his practice in the areas of securities, mergers and acquisitions, private equity and venture capital, international and public finance. He has additional industry experience as counsel in aviation, entertainment and sports and banking and financial institutions. Representative clients include Boca Resorts, Inc., Miami Dolphins, Huizenga Holdings, Inc. and Embraer Aircraft Corporation.
Prof. Memberships: He is a member of the American Bar Association, Sports Lawyers Association and the Florida Bar Foundation.

ROSENBERG, Donald S
Peckar & Abramson, Rosenberg, Reisman & Stein LLP, Miami 305 358 2600
drosenberg@pecklaw.com.
Recommended in Construction
Specialization: Partner in *Peckar & Abramson's* Miami office. His primary areas of practice are in complex real estate, financial transactions, corporate law, probate and banking as well as in matters involving construction, where he represents owners, developers, lenders and general contractors.
Prof. Memberships: He is a member of the Florida Bar, the Dade County Bar Association and the American Bar Association.
Career: He is admitted to practice before the United States Supreme Court, the United States Court of Appeals for the Eleventh Circuit, the United States District Court for the Southern District of Florida as well as all courts of the State of Florida. He is a partner in *Peckar & Abramson's* Miami office and formerly a partner at *Rosenberg, Reisman & Stein* which merged with *Peckar & Abramson* in 2000. Served as a member of the Board of Directors of Cedars Medical Center for 11 years and acted as its chairman for 9 1/2 years. He has also been a longtime advisor to the YWCA and served as a Director of the Zoological Society of Florida. He is currently a member of the Board of Trustees of Barry University, serves as a member of its executive, finance and audit committees and chairs its investment committee. He has been recognized on of America's best lawyers in real estate law by a leading legal publication (1989-2003).
Publications: He has lectured for the Florida Bar and other organizations regarding condominiums and other related topics.

Personal: He is a graduate of the University of Virginia and the University of Miami School of Law (1956).

ROSENBERG, Michael
Packman, Neuwahl & Rosenberg, Coral Gables 305 665 3311
Recommended in Tax

ROSENFELDT, Stuart
Rothstein, Rosenfeldt Dolin & Pancier, Fort Lauderdale 954 522 3456
Recommended in Employment

ROSS, David L
Greenberg Traurig LLP, Miami
305 579 0523
rossd@gtlaw.com
Recommended in Litigation
Specialization: Complex commercial litigation; class-action lawsuits; securities; labor; antitrust and trade regulation; product liability; insurance regulation.
Prof. Memberships: Past Chairman, Business Law Section, The Florida Bar. Past Chairman, Business Litigation Committee, The Florida Bar. Member, American Bar Association's Litigation Section. Member, Board of Trustees, Coconut Grove Playhouse, 1991-1995. Member, Actor's Playhouse Citizen's Board, 1998-1999.
Publications: Co-Author: 'The Florida Antitrust Act of 1980,' The Florida Bar Journal; Author, 'Local Governments and the Antitrust Laws After City of Eau Claire: Is the Fire Finally Out?', Stetson Law Review.

ROTHSTEIN, Scott
Rothstein, Rosenfeldt Dolin & Pancier, Fort Lauderdale 954 522 3456
Recommended in Employment

ROUNSAVILLE, Keith
Akerman Senterfitt, Orlando
407 843 7860
krounsaville@akerman.com
Recommended in Antitrust
Specialization: Shareholder and Chair of the firm's Antitrust and Trade Regulation Practice. Served as lead trial counsel in grand jury investigations and criminal and civil antitrust actions in Florida, Alabama, Georgia, Colorado, Indiana, Texas, Maryland and Virginia. Practice also involves complex litigation in health care, intellectual property and environmental law. Industry experience includes pharmaceuticals, optical lenses, industrial chemicals; building, petroleum, automotive, and citrus products; and thoroughbred horseracing.
Prof. Memberships: Member of the American Law Institute and the American Bar Association's Antitrust, Intellectual Property, Natural Resources & Environmental Law sections.

SADLER JR, Luther
Foley & Lardner, Jacksonville
904 359 2000
Recommended in Corporate/M&A

SAUL, Gary
Greenberg Traurig LLP, Miami
305 579 0846
saulg@gtlaw.com
Recommended in Real Estate
Specialization: Real estate, condominiums and financing.
Prof. Memberships: Member, The Florida Bar's Condominium and Planned Development Committee Former board member of, and lecturer for, the Dade County Chapter of the Community Association Institute.

SCHEU, William
Rogers, Towers, Bailey, Jones & Gay, PA, Jacksonville 904 398 3911
Recommended in Real Estate

SCHULMAN, Clifford
Greenberg Traurig LLP, Miami
305 579 0613
schulmanc@gtlaw.com
Recommended in Environment
Specialization: Environmental regulation and permitting; coastal regulation and permitting; FEMA Regulatory issues; solid waste; resource recovery; utilities; zoning, land use and comprehensive planning.
Prof. Memberships: Member, Executive Council and Chairman of the Environmental and Land Use Law Section of The Florida Bar. Member, Executive Committee, Aventura Marketing Council.
Publications: Co-editor of The Florida Bar Environmental Law Section newsletter in 1979 and 1980 and Editor in Chief of the continuing legal education manual Environmental Regulation and Litigation in Florida (1981 edition). Co-authored the chapter entitled 'Inverse Condemnation' in Volume 2 of that manual.

SEARCY, Christian
Searcy Denney Scarola Barnhart & Shipley, PA, West Palm Beach
561 686 6300
Recommended in Litigation

SEAY, James
Holland & Knight LLP, Orlando
407 425 8500
jseay@hklaw.com
Recommended in Real Estate
Specialization: Partner in the Real Estate Department. Practices in the area of commercial real estate law, with particular emphasis on the representation of developers of commercial, mixed-use and residential projects, and acquisition and disposition of income-producing properties. His broad experience includes multistate financings of real estate projects, tax-deferred exchanges, sale and purchase of agricultural property; acquisitions, financings, and sales of restaurants; and acquisitions, financings, and sales of office and industrial properties, residential subdivisions, apartment complexes and shopping centers. He has served as a member of the Judge Advocate Division of the United

FLORIDA LEADERS

States Marine Corps. He received his BS degree, with merit, from the United States Naval Academy in 1970 and earned his JD from the University of Florida in 1974.

SELLERS, Lawrence
Holland & Knight LLP, Tallahassee
850 224 7000
larry.sellers@hklaw.com
Recommended in Environment

Specialization: Partner in the Real Estate Department, practicing administrative and governmental law, with a concentration in environmental matters. He regularly provides advice on permitting and enforcement matters involving a variety of federal, state, regional and local administrative agencies. He has substantial experience in administrative law, including adjudicatory hearings and rulemaking. For more than 18 years, he also has represented clients before the Florida Legislature, primarily on various environmental, land use and administrative law issues. He also represents clients on growth management matters. He is a past-chair of the Environmental and Land Use Law Section of The Florida Bar. He is also chairman of the Florida Chamber's Infrastructure and Environmental Committee and a member of the Chamber's Board of Governors and Legislative Policy Council.

SHUKER, Scott
Gronek & Latham, Orlando
407 481 5800
Recommended in Insolvency

SIEGFRIED, Steven
Siegfried, Rivera, Lerner, De La Torre & Sobel, PA, Miami 305 442 3334
Recommended in Construction

SILVERMAN, Lawrence
Akerman Senterfitt, Miami
305 374 5600
lsilverman@akerman.com
Recommended in Antitrust

Specialization: Shareholder who is Board Certified in Antitrust and Trade Regulation and is AV Rated by Martindale-Hubbell. He has significant experience in antitrust and trade regulation, commercial litigation and class actions. Also the 2001 Pro Bono Attorney of the Year by the Dade County Bar Association.
Prof. Memberships: Serves on The Florida Bar CLE Committee and The Florida Bar Journal Editorial Board. He is also an Adjunct Professor at Nova Southeastern University, Shepard Broad School of Law.

SIMMONS, Sherwin
Steel Hector & Davis LLP, Miami
305 577 7000
Recommended in Tax

SIMS, Roger
Holland & Knight LLP, Orlando
407 425 8500
rsims@hklaw.com
Recommended in Environment

Specialization: Partner in the Litigation Department, practicing in the areas of water law and environmental and land use law. He is experienced in groundwater, surface water, wetlands, solid waste and hazardous waste issues. He deals with many agencies on a regular basis, including the Department of Environmental Protection, Department of Community Affairs, Southwest Florida and St. Johns Water Management Districts. He has particular experience in the permitting of large projects, including developments of regional impact. He currently serves on the American Bar Association Standing Committee on Environmental Law.

SINGER, Stuart
Boies, Schiller & Flexner LLP, Miami
305 539 8400
Recommended in Antitrust

SINGERMAN, Paul
Berger Singerman, Fort Lauderdale
954 525 9900
Recommended in Insolvency

SIWICA, Richard
Egan, Lev & Siwica, Orlando
407 422 1400
Recommended in Employment

SLATER, Jim
Broad and Cassel, Orlando
407 839 4200
Recommended in Real Estate

SMALLWOOD, Mary
Ruden, McClosky, Smith, Schuster & Russell PA, Tallahassee 850 681 9027
Recommended in Environment

SOLLNER, Richard
Trenam, Kemker, Scharf, Barkin, Frye, O'Neill & Mullis PA, Tampa
813 223 7474
Recommended in Real Estate

SOMERSTEIN, Barry
Ruden, McClosky, Smith, Schuster & Russell, PA, Fort Lauderdale
954 764 6660
Recommended in Real Estate

SORIANO, Robert
Carlton Fields, Tampa 813 223 7000
Recommended in Insolvency

STANFORD, Douglas
Smith, Gambrell & Russell, LLP, Jacksonville 904 598 6100
Recommended in Real Estate

STEARNS, Eugene
Stearns Weaver Miller Weissler Alhadeff & Sitterson, P.A., Miami 305 789 3200
Recommended in Litigation

STEINBERG, Marty
Hunton & Williams, Miami
305 810 2500
Recommended in Litigation

STICHTER, Don
Stichter, Riedel, Blain & Prosser, Tampa 813 229 0144
Recommended in Insolvency

STONE, Bruce
Holland & Knight LLP, Miami
305 374 8500
bstone@hklaw.com
Recommended in Tax

Specialization: Partner in the Business Law Department, practicing in estate planning (both domestic and foreign) and adversarial trust and estate matters. He represents a number of wealthy domestic clients in connection with the multigenerational transfer of wealth, with extensive experience in the use of trusts and other techniques. He is the principal author of Florida legislation authorizing long term 'dynasty' trusts and permitting the restructuring of trusts. He has successfully planned a number of transactions to terminate, modify, or restructure existing irrevocable trusts to respond to needs caused by changes in family circumstances, business reorganizations, and resolution of family disputes. He has significant experience in the conduct of probate and trust litigation, involving such matters as violations of fiduciary duties by personal representatives and trustees, will and trust construction proceedings, and will contests.

STUBBS, Sidney
Jones, Foster, Johnston & Stubbs, PA, West Palm Beach 561 659 3000
sstubbs@jones-foster.com
Recommended in Litigation

Specialization: Commercial litigation with focus on law firm litigation ranging from firm dissolutions to charges of malpractice; corporate merger and acquisition disputes; and eminent domain cases including some of the largest and most complex in Florida history.
Prof. Memberships: Fellow, American College of Trial Lawyers; Life Fellow, American Bar Foundation; and Certified Civil Trial Advocate, National Board of Trial Advocacy. Has served as a member of The Florida Bar Board of Governors and President of The Palm Beach County Bar Association.
Career: Florida Bar, admitted 1966; Special Counsel to The Honorable Bob Graham, Governor, State of Florida 1983; current Shareholder and President of the firm.
Personal: JD University of Florida College of Law with honors (1965), Executive Editor of the 'University of Florida Law Review'; BS, History, Florida State University.

STUTTS, Charles
Holland & Knight LLP, Tampa
813 227 8500
cstutts@hklaw.com
Recommended in Banking & Finance

Specialization: Partner in the Business Law Department, with an emphasis on securities and banking law. As former general counsel to the Florida Comptroller's Office and the Department of Banking and Finance, he helped develop the agency's policies on banking, mortgage lending and securities regulation. He directed the agency's securities enforcement efforts and coordinated prosecutions under Florida's antifraud provisions with its federal counterparts including the US Securities and Exchange Commission and Commodity Futures Trading Commission. He also helped draft revisions to Florida's banking laws in 1988 and 1989, and served on the Comptroller's Task Force on Banking Sunset. He devotes a substantial portion of his practice to federal and state supervision and regulation of banks, trust companies, securities broker-dealers and investment advisers.

SUGARMAN, Robert
Sugarman & Susskind, Coral Gables
305 529 2801
Recommended in Employment

SUSSKIND, Howard
Sugarman & Susskind, Coral Gables
305 529 2801
Recommended in Employment

TEBLUM, Gary
Trenam, Kemker, Scharf, Barkin, Frye, O'Neill & Mullis PA, Tampa
813 223 7474
Recommended in Corporate/M&A

TESCHER, Donald
Tescher Gutter Chaves Josepher Rubin Ruffin & Forman PA, Boca Ratón
561 998 7847
Recommended in Tax

THOMAS, Archibald
Law Offices of Archibald J. Thomas, III, Jacksonville 904 396 2322
Recommended in Employment

THOMSON, Parker
Hogan & Hartson LLP, Miami
305 459 6613
pdthomson@hhlaw.com
Recommended in Litigation

Specialization: Managing partner of the Miami office of *Hogan & Hartson LLP* and a member of the firm's Litigation Group. His practice focuses primarily on complex commercial litigation (including class action and multi-state litigation), corporate law, communications/media law, appellate litigation, environmental law, and constitutional law. He has regularly represented private and public clients, including the state of Florida, in the US Supreme Court, the 11th Circuit Court of Appeals, the Florida Supreme Court, and the various state and federal courts throughout Florida. He has presented oral argument before the US Supreme Court in three cases, before the Florida Supreme Court in dozens of cases, and has been personally involved in over one hundred complex appeals involving issues ranging from the First Amendment, media law, environmental law, jurisdiction, sovereign immunity, and civil rights. He has substantial experience representing both private clients

and the press concerning Florida's public records and sunshine acts, as well as the federal Freedom of Information Act.
Prof. Memberships: He is a member of the Florida, Massachusetts and the District of Columbia Bars, and is admitted to practice before numerous federal, district and appellate courts, including the US Supreme Court, the 11th Circuit Court of Appeals and the Florida Supreme Court.
Career: He joined *Hogan & Hartson* in the fall of 2001. He practiced with a large firm in Massachusetts for two years before moving to Florida and establishing a boutique litigation firm that became recognized as one of the nation's top small law firms.
Personal: He graduated from Princeton University, cum laude, in 1953, and from Harvard Law School, magna cum laude, in 1958. His commitment to public service has earned him numerous awards for significant pro bono contributions, for volunteer legal assistance to the poor and other civic efforts. His community activities include: service as president of the Miami-Dade Performing Arts Center Trust since 1989, president of the Appleseed Center for Law & Justice, Inc. since 1996, chairman of the Dade County Fair Campaign Practices Committee from 1985 to 1991, and chairman of Florida's Advocacy Center for Persons with Disabilities from 1979 through 1997.

THROCKMORTON, Charles
Kozyak Tropin & Throckmorton, Miami
305 372 1800
Recommended in Insolvency

TOWNSEND, William
Holland & Knight LLP, Tallahassee
850 224 7000
bill.townsend@hklaw.com
Recommended in Tax

Specialization: Partner in the Business Law Department, practicing in the areas of state and local taxation and multistate taxation. He has represented clients on legislative tax matters, including the taxation of computer services, corporate income tax issues, and sales tax exemption matters. Additionally, he has extensive experience in handling client matters before the Florida Department of Revenue and the revenue departments of several other states on sales tax, corporate income tax, gross receipts tax, telecommunications tax issues, documentary stamp tax, transfer taxes, intangibles tax, state taxation of intellectual property and electronic commerce taxation (e-commerce). He served as Assistant Attorney General and General Counsel for the Florida Department of Revenue.

TROPIN, Harley
Kozyak Tropin & Throckmorton, Miami 305 372 1800
Recommended in Litigation

ULLMAN, Samuel
Steel Hector & Davis LLP, Miami
305 577 7000
Recommended in Tax

VAZQUEZ-BELLO, Clemente
Gunster, Yoakley & Stewart, P.A., Miami 305 376 6000
Recommended in Banking & Finance

WADSWORTH, Murray
Wadsworth, Davis & Wadsworth, PA, Tallahassee 850 224 9037
Recommended in Litigation

WAKSHLAG, Stanley
Akerman Senterfitt, Miami
305 374 5600
swakshlag@akerman.com
Recommended in Litigation

Specialization: Shareholder who is listed in a leading US legal publication in the category of Business Litigation and is AV Rated by Martindale-Hubbell. He focuses his practice in the areas of securities litigation and regulatory proceedings, commercial litigation, antitrust and trade regulation and class actions. His litigation experience includes the representation of major institutional clients in the area of complex commercial litigation including lender liability, banking, securities, antitrust, ERISA, trademark and copyright infringement, foreclosure, partnership and corporate litigation. His experience has resulted in numerous favorable judicial opinions, many of which have been published.

WALBOLT, Sylvia
Carlton Fields, St Petersburg
727 821 7000
Recommended in Litigation

WALKER, William
White & Case LLP, Miami
305 371 2700
Recommended in Real Estate

WARNER, Jonathan
Law Offices of Jonathan H. (Jason) Warner, PA, Miami 305 670 0007
Recommended in Tax

WARREN, Jeffrey
Bush Ross Gardner Warren & Rudy, PA, Tampa 813 224 9255
Recommended in Insolvency

WEBER, Victoria
Hopping, Green & Sams PA, Tallahassee 850 222 7500
Recommended in Tax

WEINSTEIN, Andrew
Holland & Knight LLP, Miami
305 374 8500
aweinstein@hklaw.com
Recommended in Tax

Specialization: Partner in the Business Law Department, focusing on the tax practice area. His practice involves complex domestic and international tax, trust and estate planning for private clients and high net worth families. He has served as lead counsel in complex international planning for clients with assets substantially in excess of 10 figures. He also has considerable experience in the handling of federal tax disputes at both the administrative and trial levels. He has written and spoken extensively and is the partner in charge of the firm's tax, trust and estates practice in South Florida. He is Board Certified in Tax Law.

WEINTRAUB, Lee
Becker & Poliakoff, P.A., Fort Lauderdale 954 987 7550
Recommended in Construction

WEISBERG, Robert
Robert Weisberg – Sole Practitioner, Coral Gables 305 666 6095
Recommended in Employment

WEISS, Christopher
Holland & Knight LLP, Orlando
407 425 8500
cweiss@hklaw.com
Recommended in Construction

Specialization: Partner in the Litigation Department, practicing in the area of commercial litigation with particular emphasis on construction law, defects in construction, design claims, delay, disruption and acceleration claims, lien foreclosures, and arbitration on behalf of contractors, subcontractors, materialmen, developers and public bodies. He is a frequent lecturer and coordinator of programs and seminars on construction industry issues throughout the state of Florida. He is the author of many articles in the areas of commercial litigation and construction law for bar and trade association publications; and is an active member and panelist of the American Arbitration Association, Associated Builders and Contractors, the Construction Financial Management Association, Associated General Contractors of America and the American Subcontractors Association.

WELBAUM, Earl
Welbaum, Guernsey, Hingston, Greenleaf & Gregory LLP., Miami 305 441 8900
Recommended in Construction

WILSON, Michael
Gray, Harris & Robinson, PA, Orlando 407 843 8880
Recommended in Construction

WOLFSON, Mark
Foley & Lardner, Tampa
813 229 2300;
Pinellas County;
813 442 3296
Recommended in Insolvency

YADLEY, Gregory
Shumaker, Loop & Kendrick, LLP, Tampa 813 229 7600
Recommended in Corporate/M&A

ZINOBER, Peter
Zinober & McCrea, P.A., Tampa
813 224 9004
Recommended in Employment

GEORGIA

OVERVIEW

CONTENTS: Antitrust: p.181; Banking: p.182; Construction: p.183; Corporate/M&A p.186; Employment: Mainly Plaintiff p.188; Mainly Defendant p.189; Energy: p.191; Environment: p.192; Insolvency: p.193; Intellectual Property: p.194; Litigation: p.197; Real Estate p.199; Tax: p.201; Individuals' Profiles p.202.

GEORGIA'S TOP EIGHT
1. Alston & Bird
2. King & Spalding
3. Kilpatrick Stockton
4. Troutman Sanders
5. Sutherland Asbill & Brennan
6. Powell, Goldstein, Frazer & Murphy
7. McKenna Long & Aldridge
8. Rogers & Hardin

Ranking based on Chambers' research within the state.

All quotes in the text are from interviews with clients and competitors.

OVERVIEW: Alston & Bird and **King & Spalding**, Georgia's two heavyweights, emerged as leaders in *Chambers'* research. Many sources, especially those from the traditional corporate sphere, regard King & Spalding as the "strongest all-around business practice" in the state. *Chambers'* research suggests, though, that Alston & Bird has the edge. This ambitious firm has strength in finance, and tops the tables for banking, insolvency and tax, as well as litigation and environment. Its preeminent insolvency practice obtains great results for clients, while Neal Batson, an independent examiner in the Enron case, claims the state's only star ranking in *Chambers'* tables. In tax, the 50-lawyer team is strong across the board, while the firm's banking group is said to be synonymous with megadeals. In other areas, such as energy, the firm's profile rests heavily on its reputation for innovative financing. In the corporate field, the firm is thought to be closing the gap on King & Spalding, and is building strong practices in such areas as IP, healthcare, technology and biotech.

Nonetheless, **King & Spalding** reigns supreme in M&A. A glimpse at its transaction list shows why. The firm has acted in such huge and complex deals as Georgia-Pacific's $1.5 billion sale of four pulp and paper plants and SunTrust Banks' $9 billion acquisition of Crestar Financial. Commentators keep returning to its long-standing links with a blue-ribbon corporate client base. This includes names like Home Depot and Coca-Cola, who it advised in its antitrust action against PepsiCo. The firm boasts probably the strongest antitrust team in the state. It also has a robust DC office and the best-developed national practice of all Georgian firms. It undertakes sophisticated transactional work in most major market sectors, and heads *Chambers'* litigation, real estate, employment and environment tables.

Kilpatrick Stockton perhaps lacks some of the national and international profile of the leading two, but is nonetheless a major force in the region. It has a solid practice in banking and corporate finance, while its insolvency team is one of the state's best. The jewel in its crown, however, is its IP practice. Its profile was boosted recently when it took on a team from boutique Jones & Askew, and it now commands real breadth of IP expertise under trademark star Miles Alexander. The team won a high-profile victory recently in 'The Wind Done Gone' copyright infringement case.

Troutman Sanders is more international in scope than many in Georgia, with offices in places like Hong Kong and London. Its forte is energy, where it gains its sole top band ranking. Here, its position is sustained by a raft of gigantic clients, such as Georgia Power and Southern Company, one of the country's largest electricity generators. The team works closely with a high-quality electricity regulatory group in DC, where its main antitrust strength also resides. Alongside energy, the team acts for a top-flight list of entertainment clients like CNN and Time Warner Entertainment, and enjoys a steady stream of mid-market corporate and finance work.

Another firm known for a major presence in energy is **Sutherland Asbill & Brennan**. It has been at the forefront of energy litigation and has a great reputation for fostering regulatory change. Its profile in tax is even higher. Here, former IRS chief counsel Jerold Cohen stands out among an army of tax lawyers renowned for their toughness. In IP, this is another firm that benefited from the demise of Jones & Askew. Its relatively young department is bolstered by the firm's DC strength. Interviewees claim that this is a go-to firm for anyone requiring detailed legal knowledge, especially in complex, technology-driven fields.

Powell, Goldstein, Frazer & Murphy tops *Chambers'* banking table, where its deep client base includes most of Georgia's community banks. It recently handled the $350 million sale of First South Bank in Florida to BB&T. A quietly efficient insolvency practice also wins plaudits, as does a corporate team that has developed a niche in healthcare.

The June 2002 merger of McKenna & Cuneo with Long Aldridge & Norman created a firm of almost 400 lawyers across the country. Most industry sources consider it too early to say how the merger will bed down. However, many expect the new **McKenna Long & Aldridge** to boost its profile across the region. The corporate team is known for its skillful handling of work with a political element, such as matters involving public utilities. Its "eclectic" client base includes media and biotech companies and telecom interests. The firm recently assisted a company in several telecom-related acquisitions in Europe totaling $2 billion. The firm's environmental team is also known for its good connections, and works well with an impressive group in DC.

Industry sources say that what **Rogers & Hardin** lacks in size, it makes up for in talent. Its twin focuses are corporate and litigation. On the corporate side, adept and exceedingly smart Edward Hardin helps the firm retain a high profile. The firm's reputation for litigation, meanwhile, owes much to CB Rogers, a role model for aspiring litigators, and Richard Sinkfield, the quintessential trial lawyer. It recently assisted an investment bank in connection with litigation surrounding WorldCom. The firm was praised for its development into other niches. One of the most successful is employment, where Hunter Hughes has an unrivaled mastery of his subject.

ANTITRUST

GEORGIA
Leading firms (Antitrust)

1. **BONDURANT, MIXSON & ELMORE LLP** Atlanta
   KING & SPALDING LLP Atlanta
2. **ALSTON & BIRD LLP** Atlanta
3. **ROGERS & HARDIN** Atlanta
4. **VAUGHAN & MURPHY** Atlanta
5. **KILPATRICK STOCKTON LLP** Atlanta
   TROUTMAN SANDERS LLP Atlanta

Leading individuals (Antitrust)

1. **BONDURANT Emmet** Bondurant, Mixson, Atlanta
2. **GRADY Kevin** Alston & Bird LLP, Atlanta
   POWERS Tony Rogers & Hardin, Atlanta
   ROSS Mickey King & Spalding LLP, Atlanta
3. **HARRIS Steve** Alston & Bird LLP, Atlanta
   MURPHY Charles Vaughan & Murphy, Atlanta
   RHODES Tom Smith, Gambrell & Russell LLP, Atlanta
4. **ALLEN Randall** Alston & Bird LLP, Atlanta
   SAUNTRY June Ann Troutman Sanders LLP, Atlanta
   VAUGHAN David Vaughan & Murphy, Atlanta
5. **CASHDAN Jeff** King & Spalding LLP, Atlanta
   MARSHALL John Powell, Goldstein, Frazer, Atlanta
   NEWTON Trammell Jones Day, Atlanta
   ROGERS CB Rogers & Hardin, Atlanta
   RUSS Michael King & Spalding LLP, Atlanta

Firms and individuals are listed alphabetically in each band.

Bondurant, Mixson & Elmore LLP
The Firm: With only about 25 lawyers, this is not among the largest firms, yet competitors acknowledge that it *"has a good deal of antitrust experience and has grown well."* Its forte is litigation, with antitrust litigation held to be *"one of its main practice areas, and definitely its strongest."* The firm has defended companies and individuals in antitrust class actions, multi-district proceedings and federal and state criminal grand jury investigations and trials. Unlike most large firms it takes on both defendants' and plaintiffs' work in antitrust class actions.
The Lawyers: **Emmet Bondurant** is *"the dean of antitrust in this state."* Sources describe him as *"an aggressive trial lawyer first and foremost – he's sharp, stubborn and a real street fighter who gets great results for his clients."* With 40 years of experience in the field and many prominent cases under his belt, there are no gaps in his antitrust expertise. He is acting as lead counsel for Delta Air Lines in a passenger class action antitrust case currently pending in the US District Court in Detroit, MI.
The Clients: The firm boasts clients of the quality of Delta Air Lines; Michelin; Bausch & Lomb; Scientific-Atlanta and Golden Peanut Company.

King & Spalding LLP
see firm details p.829
The Firm: This is *"probably the strongest antitrust firm in the state,"* researchers were told, because *"the quality of the people here is exceptional."* Sources consider it to possess more of a national antitrust practice than the other large general practice firms in the state. The team is boosted by the antitrust capacity of its DC office, and it provides sophisticated, solutions-oriented advice on all aspects of trade regulations and competition law. It also advises clients on potential competitive risks, legitimate arrangements with competitors, entry into new markets and product distribution systems. On the contentious side, the team is respected for its handling of complex antitrust investigations and litigation – over half its business litigation team practices antitrust at times. An excellent trial record prompted peers to single out the group as their first port of call for referrals. The firm's more senior attorneys have fostered strong agency relationships, which has benefited the antitrust group.
The Lawyers: **Mickey Ross** (see p.209) is *"a walking antitrust encyclopedia,"* according to his peers. *"More the brains behind the operation"* than the face fronting it, he spends part of his time on employment law now, but continues to advise on antitrust matters and takes on large cases when required. **Jeff Cashdan** (see p.204) is the youthful chair of the State Bar of Georgia's antitrust section. He undertakes antitrust litigation, M&A and business practice counseling on an increasingly national level. He recently represented defendants, which included Belgian pharmaceutical and chemical company UCB, in several federal and state actions that alleged an international cartel in the sale of vitamins. He has also represented Home Depot in an antitrust action filed against Visa and MasterCard. Cashdan is also cocounsel for Coca-Cola in an ongoing antitrust action brought by PepsiCo, alleging monopolization in the fountain beverage segment. His cocounsel in that matter is **Michael Russ** (see p.210), a general litigator with a strong antitrust focus and substantial experience of acting for corporations in antitrust class actions.
The Clients: Rivals respect the fact that *"the firm has represented huge clients like Coca-Cola for years."* Other important clients include Sprint, UCB and GE.

Alston & Bird LLP
The Firm: This large firm has its national antitrust headquarters in Atlanta, and consequently has the biggest antitrust group on the ground in the state. Forty years ago it was the first firm in the Southeast to form a separate antitrust and trade regulation practice, which now comprises about 20 partners. The team provides antitrust and other competition-related counseling for its top-class corporate client base. It also undertakes complex antitrust disputes, unfair competition and trade regulation litigation, and acts in cases relating to both criminal and government investigations.
The Lawyers: **Kevin Grady** is currently vice chair of the antitrust section of the ABA, and will serve as its chair in 2003-2004. According to competitors, he is *"a true antitrust specialist"* by virtue of the fact that *"he covers the counseling side as well as the litigation work."* He has represented clients in FTC investigations, antitrust criminal grand juries and Hart-Scott-Rodino merger filings. The healthcare industry is a particular area of expertise, though he also advises clients in the heavy equipment and automotive distribution sector and printing, chemical products, steel and insurance fields. Recent merger work has seen him represent Sabre in its $6 billion transaction with EDS, negotiating and successfully attaining DOJ approval after a second request. On the litigation front Grady recently received a favorable decision for the defendant in a $50 million antitrust lawsuit brought by a physician against Newnan Hospital. Chair of the group **Randall Allen** leads its merger counseling efforts, frequently appearing before the DOJ and FTC on behalf of large public corporations. *"A bright attorney,"* he advises on compliance and risk assessment issues related to pricing, distribution and strategic planning. He acted for Mohawk Industries in a nationwide grand jury investigation of alleged price – fixing in the carpet industry. **Steve Harris** focuses on federal and transnational antitrust litigation, advising on the establishment and operation of joint ventures and distribution agreements. He has been active in EC and South American trust work, including two issues related to EC mergers and one non-merger Article 82 case. Harris has represented a US tire company in the defense of antitrust litigation in the Florida courts and represented a multinational oil company in a series of antitrust cases pending in Georgia. Competitors consider him *"intelligent and knowledgeable – ideal for behind-the-scenes advice,"* while clients praise him as *"meticulous and well versed in international competition laws and regulations."*
The Clients: The firm recently mounted a successful defense of Boral Industries in the FTC's investigation and ultimate challenge of its joint venture with a competitor in the building products industry. Other clients include Borden Chemical, Nokia and Imerys, along with a number of telecom companies and banks.

GEORGIA — ANTITRUST

Rogers & Hardin
The Firm: This small, cerebral antitrust team, centered on three partners, is renowned for its quality. According to sources, it is *"an excellent firm"* that *"you can really trust on complex antitrust matters."* The group principally handles litigation and transactional services and has extensive experience of antitrust and franchising law. Its contentious workload includes private litigation, class action defense and representation in governmental investigations. The group also provides antitrust advice under federal and state antitrust legislation.

The Lawyers: Tony Powers conducts litigation defense for clients involved in government claims of price-fixing, and monopolization allegations. Peers agree that he is *"sharp and really knows antitrust law."* He represented Covad Communications Company in a case it brought against BellSouth, alleging the monopolizing of telecom access in a certain area. Powers also represented Baker's Carpet Gallery in a case against Mohawk Industries over a distributorship termination issue. **CB Rogers** is a renowned general litigator with considerable experience in antitrust matters.

The Clients: The firm's client base is drawn from a range of sectors, including transportation, construction, distribution and healthcare, as well as from trade associations. Prominent names include Worldspan, NASCAR and Baker's Carpet Gallery.

Vaughan & Murphy
The Firm: This *"great small firm"* punches well above its weight in the antitrust arena, due in part to its long-standing concentration on the sector. Interviewees express particular admiration for the efficiency with which the team manages its workload, with many attorneys happy to *"send a fair amount of work there."* The firm mixes antitrust with other contentious matters, such as white-collar crime.

The Lawyers: *"Decent and talented"* **Charles Murphy** is held by some sources to be *"the best in the smaller firms at handling the antitrust grand jury work."* He defended E Roy Anderson, a former president of Harbert International Establishment, of Liechtenstein, in a criminal jury trial in Alabama, arising from charges that he had attempted to rig bids and defraud USAID on contracts (value $200 million) for infrastructure projects in Egypt. Researchers were told that Murphy forms *"a really strong team"* with his partner **David Vaughan** (formerly of King & Spalding), who is endorsed as a *"bright and capable"* antitrust specialist with many years' experience.

The Clients: The firm's client base includes Compaq; Hewlett-Packard; Davis Broadcasting; Wheatstone Energy Group and EchoStar.

Kilpatrick Stockton LLP
The Firm: This full-service firm boasts a team of experienced antitrust lawyers. It assists clients in FTC proceedings, and has considerable experience before the DOJ and federal courts throughout the US. It is also active in merger notifications and agency antitrust reviews under the Hart-Scott-Rodino Act. Private unfair competition litigation under the Lanham Act is also undertaken by the team. The work is coordinated through the DC office by the firm's head of antitrust Stanley Gorinson.

The Lawyers: In the Georgia office, Steve Clay and Miles Alexander lead the way in the antitrust work, along with attorneys drawn from the corporate and litigation groups. The team has represented a telecom company in multiple antitrust actions in Georgia and Florida, eight of those cases involving class actions. The diverse practice incorporates litigation services to the healthcare industry, including both merger and unfair competition advice. It has advised on matters under both the Sherman and Cartwright Acts, and acted in claims related to the motion-picture industry. In the pharmaceutical industry, the team has acted on the alleged abuse of patents, trademarks and copyrights. It also defended a national franchiser against vertical price-fixing claims.

The Clients: Telecom companies, healthcare providers and pharmaceutical manufacturers and franchisers.

Troutman Sanders LLP
The Firm: This firm boasts more international scope than many in Georgia thanks to a network of offices in locations such as London and Hong Kong. Its antitrust base is in DC, though it also has an effective Atlanta office handling litigation and transactional antitrust work. The group recently handled a Section 2 monopolies case for a Siemens entity.

The Lawyers: June Ann Sauntry is the Atlanta office's highest profile antitrust expert, though she also spends time in the DC office. She covers the full range of antitrust matters, including civil and criminal litigation, business counseling and antitrust compliance, and some Hart-Scott-Rodino work. Most of her antitrust litigation is on the defendants' side, although she does undertake plaintiffs' matters, and she advises clients on antitrust compliance, government investigations and reviews of M&A transactions. Sauntry recently obtained the closure of a FTC investigation into a large association of physicians, with no charges being filed, and succeeded in obtaining clearance from US and Canadian authorities for the merger of their two largest auto haul-away services.

The Clients: The firm acts for: major motion-picture production and distribution companies; cable-programming companies; chemical and construction companies; medical institutions and medical equipment manufacturers; electric utilities and banks and other financial institutions. Names include: YKK; Southeastern Electric Exchange; AGCO; Chickasha Cotton Oil Company; Bill Harbert International Construction; Komatsu Forklift USA; SQM North America and Southern Company.

Other Notable Practitioners
Tom Rhodes of Smith, Gambrell & Russell LLP is a business litigator, endorsed by interviewees as *"smart and thoroughly experienced in antitrust litigation."* **John Marshall** of Powell, Goldstein, Frazer & Murphy LLP is another general litigator with considerable antitrust experience. Sources say that they have *"never seen him fail to deliver in an antitrust case."* At Jones Day, **Trammell Newton** (see p.208) *"does a great job for his clients."* Much of his caseload lies on the litigation side.

BANKING & FINANCE

Alston & Bird LLP
The Firm: Its name is synonymous with banking megadeals – in the past few years the 52-strong team has advised on nearly 500 acquisitions, totaling more than $50 billion, for financial institutions such as First Union. A niche practice in insurance and a strong DC presence has helped ensure that the firm *"is doing bigger deals with bigger institutions."*

The Lawyers: John Douglas (see p.205), who heads the practice, was described by one client as someone who *"would always strive to go the extra distance."* Within a period of three months he negotiated a global settlement of all claims in connection to a failed thrift with a debt value of $600-700 million. He advised a group of six international banks – including Bank of America and Barclays – in global payments processing procedures. *"A figure of great integrity,"* he has also helped steer the structuring of banks in countries such as Indonesia, Russia and, recently, Afghanistan. **Harvey Hill** was labeled by peers as *"a really brilliant strategist."* He took on Fortis' sale of its financial advising arm to Hartford Financial Services Group in a deal valued at $1.1 billion, with assumed liabilities of $3 billion. Adding muscle to the firm's transactional practice is **Ralph (Chip) MacDonald** (see p.208), who represented Saks Fifth Avenue in the sale of its credit card division to Household International for

BANKING & FINANCE — GEORGIA

GEORGIA
Leading firms (Banking & Finance)

1. ALSTON & BIRD LLP *Atlanta*
   POWELL, GOLDSTEIN, FRAZER & MURPHY *Atlanta*
2. KILPATRICK STOCKTON LLP *Atlanta*
3. KING & SPALDING LLP *Atlanta*
4. SMITH, GAMBRELL & RUSSELL LLP *Atlanta*
   TROUTMAN SANDERS LLP *Atlanta*

Leading individuals (Banking & Finance)

1. CHEATHAM Richard *Kilpatrick Stockton LLP, Atlanta*
   DOUGLAS John *Alston & Bird LLP, Atlanta*
   MOELING Walter *Powell, Goldstein, Frazer, Atlanta*
2. HILL Harvey *Alston & Bird LLP, Atlanta*
   KNUDSON Kathryn *Powell, Goldstein, Frazer, Atlanta*
3. CONRAD Albert *King & Spalding LLP, Atlanta*
   SCHWARTZ Robert *Smith, Gambrell & Russell, Atlanta*
4. DOBBS Edward *Parker, Hudson, Rainer, Atlanta*
   MACDONALD Ralph *Alston & Bird LLP, Atlanta*
   POWELL Thomas *Troutman Sanders LLP, Atlanta*

Firms and individuals are listed alphabetically in each band.

$300 million in cash and $1.5 million in receivables. In an innovative partial sale transaction, he advised Atlanta Capital Management Company in a $130 million deal with Eaton Vance.
The Clients: Wachovia; CheckFree; BNP Paribas; BBVA; UnumProvident; Regions Financial and Union Planters.

Powell, Goldstein, Frazer & Murphy LLP
The Firm: Rivals agree that the group has carved *"a deep client base,"* navigating through banking laws for the majority of the community banks in Georgia.
The Lawyers: Shining star **Walter Moeling** has advised both buyers and sellers on regulatory issues arising from acquisitions; key deals included Royal Bank of Canada's $150 million acquisition of Eagle Bancshares, and the $350 million sale of First South Bank in Florida to BB&T. Considered to have a *"pragmatic business mind,"* he also counseled the underwriter in a $10 million trust-preferred offering for a bank and guided other financial institutions in their privatization strategies. Peers believe that Moeling and his colleague **Kathryn Knudson** *"make a great team."* Knudson's forte is in de novo banks and their holding companies and other affiliates. She also handes corporate governance and regulatory issues for public banks.
The Clients: Habersham Bank; Gwinnett Commercial Group; Synovus Financial and FLAG Financial.

Kilpatrick Stockton LLP
The Firm: The firm is well versed in the general corporate and regulatory side of banking, and represents a broad range of institutions including community banks, independent banking holding companies and the domestic offices of international banks.
The Lawyers: The practice's engine is considered to be **Richard Cheatham** (see p.204), who peers described as *"probably the most brilliant lawyer in his field in this town."* Clients praised his technical creativity. He handled several transactions in which community banks were acquired by international companies, and piloted other financial institutions through the regulatory process.
The Clients: Community banks in the Southeast, credit unions and national financial institutions.

King & Spalding LLP
see firm details p.829
The Firm: Singled out by observers as a *"sophisticated"* transactional practice. The group has represented some of the biggest clients in town, including SunTrust Banks, *"a client that everybody else would give their left arm to have."* Other deals include a $550 million refinancing of pharmaceutical services company Caremark Rx, and a $250 million revolving credit facility in connection with the acquisition of Zacky Farms, a chicken processing facility.
The Lawyers: **Albert Conrad** (see p.205), a leading senior attorney described to researchers as *"someone who handles difficult issues well,"* was responsible for several significant syndicated credit facilities arranged by SunTrust Banks. He guided a $450 million real estate revolving credit facility involving Dollar General and a $500 million senior revolving credit facility for AGL Capital.
The Clients: Bank One; ING Capital; GE Capital; UPS Capital; Coca-Cola Financial; American Express financial services and Bank of Nova Scotia.

Smith, Gambrell & Russell LLP
The Firm: Regarded by peers as a *"low-profile but high-quality operation,"* the team fields a former regional counsel for the Southeast Division of the Office of Thrift Supervision, and a former Federal Reserve Bank of Atlanta chief executive. The bulk of the firm's workload contains transactional and regulatory matters for de novo banks, thrifts and other financial institutions located primarily in the Southeast.
The Lawyers: **Robert Schwartz** (see p.210), who according to clients is *"both fair and firm in negotiations,"* advised Franklin Financial in the $240 million sale of an Ohio bank. He also represented FNB Corporation in several acquisitions, one of which was valued at $450 million.
The Clients: Financial institutions, federal credit unions, bank holding companies and thrift holding companies.

Troutman Sanders LLP
The Firm: This firm has established a reputation in handling M&A and capital formation transactions for community banks and thrifts. Competitors described the practice as having a *"solid grip"* on the handling of deals under $100 million.
The Lawyers: At the helm is **Thomas Powell** (see p.209), who represented Century South Banks in its sale to BB&T and advised PAB Bankshares in its $15 million acquisition of Friendship Community Bank. A *"buttoned-up, thorough and precise"* lawyer, according to one client, Powell is also active in chartering de novo banks, including First Chatham Bank in Savannah and National Bank of Georgia in Athens, Georgia.
The Clients: Cotton States Insurance Group; Presidential Financial; Southeastern Banking; First Community Bancorp and National Bank of Walton County.

Other Notable Practitioners
Edward Dobbs of Parker, Hudson, Rainer & Dobbs LLP has earned distinction in the areas of banking and insolvency. He represents banks and other financial institutions in medium to large syndicated loan facilities, and also advised a group led by Bank of America in a Chapter 11 proceeding involving Fine Air, an air cargo firm.

CONSTRUCTION

Griffin Cochrane & Marshall
The Firm: The firm is firmly established as a leading construction boutique. Commentators regard it as a *"small but effective"* team, well known for representing some of the country's largest contractors in work across the US. It offers a full range of construction services, including *"top-class"* skills in litigation and alternative dispute resolution (ADR), and is also active in advising clients on contract performance and dispute avoidance. Clients and competitors confirm that, due to the core of *"good, strong, younger lawyers,"* the firm's profile has not been damaged by the recent retirement of some highly respected attorneys. The preeminent Buck Griffin has moved into mediation and arbitration but *"still hangs his shingle there,"* and is always on hand for counseling and advice. One interviewee summed up the firm with the comment that *"in terms of being a player in major commercial, industrial and public practices, I would rate them as one of the best."*

GEORGIA

CONSTRUCTION

GEORGIA
Leading firms (Construction)

1
- GRIFFIN COCHRANE & MARSHALL *Atlanta*
- SMITH, CURRIE & HANCOCK LLP *Atlanta*

2
- KILPATRICK STOCKTON LLP *Atlanta*

3
- ALSTON & BIRD LLP *Atlanta*
- HENDRICK PHILLIPS SALZMAN & FLATT *Atlanta*
- KING & SPALDING LLP *Atlanta*
- SUTHERLAND ASBILL & BRENNAN LLP *Atlanta*

4
- SHAPIRO FUSSELL WEDGE SMOTHERMAN *Atlanta*
- SMITH, GAMBRELL & RUSSELL LLP *Atlanta*

5
- WEINBERG, WHEELER, HUDGINS, GUNN *Atlanta*

Leading individuals (Construction)

1
- ABERNATHY Thomas *Smith, Currie & Hancock,* Atlanta
- FLETCHER Jennifer *Griffin Cochrane,* Atlanta
- KELLEHER Thomas *Smith, Currie & Hancock,* Atlanta

2
- GENBERG Ira *Smith, Gambrell & Russell LLP,* Atlanta
- HENDRICK David *Hendrick Phillips Salzman,* Atlanta
- HINCHEY John *King & Spalding LLP,* Atlanta

3
- SMITH Tony *Sutherland Asbill & Brennan LLP,* Atlanta
- SPANGLER John *Alston & Bird LLP,* Atlanta
- SWEENEY Neal *Kilpatrick Stockton LLP,* Atlanta

4
- ASSELIN Thomas *Smith, Gambrell & Russell,* Atlanta
- COLEMAN Aubrey *Smith, Currie & Hancock,* Atlanta
- DIAL David *Weinberg, Wheeler, Hudgins, Gunn,* Atlanta
- SALZMAN Martin *Hendrick Phillips Salzman,* Atlanta
- SHAPIRO Ben *Shapiro Fussell Wedge,* Atlanta

5
- BECK Philip *Smith, Currie & Hancock LLP,* Atlanta
- BUTLER James *Smith, Currie & Hancock LLP,* Atlanta
- CORGAN Brian *Kilpatrick Stockton LLP,* Atlanta
- DORRIS William *Kilpatrick Stockton LLP,* Atlanta
- HUGHS William *Alston & Bird LLP,* Atlanta
- MOLAVI Kamyar *Seyfarth Shaw,* Atlanta
- PHILLIPS Stephen *Hendrick Phillips Salzman,* Atlanta
- STAIR Kent *Carlock Copeland Semler & Stair,* Atlanta

Firms and individuals are listed alphabetically in each band.

The Lawyers: Leading the pack is *"bright, detail-oriented and persistent"* **Jennifer Fletcher** (see p.206), who enjoys an outstanding market reputation. She is one of the youngest members of The American College of Construction Lawyers and national trial lawyer for major construction clients such as Bovis Lend Lease, for whom she *"runs cases all around the country."* Interviewees note that she is possessed of *"the prime litigator's skills, in that she is tenacious and thorough,"* and observed that clients *"keep bringing her into complex disputes."*
The Clients: The group acts for large national and international contractors, including Bovis Lend Lease.

Smith, Currie & Hancock LLP
The Firm: Researchers were told that this is *"the founding firm in town,"* to which *"most construction practices in Atlanta can trace their roots."* Eighteen of the firm's 30 lawyers concentrate on construction law; the emphasis is on construction litigation, although the group also handles a volume of advisory work. A comprehensive knowledge of construction matters assists the team in advising a broad range of clients, including contractors, subcontractors, construction managers, owners, architects, engineers, sureties, insurers, suppliers and developers, both in and out-of-state. Interviewees report that the group has a particularly strong position among contractors, and many sources consider it *"the leading boutique for bench strength, competence and capability."*
The Lawyers: Managing partner **Tom Kelleher** is nationally recognized as a construction litigator, *"hugely experienced"* in arguing disputes involving bidding, differing site conditions, project delays and terminations. He draws upon substantial ADR and mediation skills in handling government contracts work for a large base of contractor clients. Sources praise his *"extremely thoughtful, analytical and practical"* approach, and claim that *"from a strategic standpoint, he is outstanding."* His recent work includes a high-rise condominium project, work for hospitals in Charlestown, Atlanta and St Louis, remediation of a Government nuclear facility and a project involving a private research hospital. **Tom Abernathy** represents owners, general contractors, subcontractors and guarantors on a range of issues, many concerning public contract projects. These include bid protests and performance problems related to changes in work, delays and suspension of work, and the termination of contracts. Competitors consider him *"a real gentleman, who is pleasant and productive to work with."* He recently advised a public US-based steel company in the construction of two steel mills. **Aubrey Coleman** is a *"highly professional"* senior lawyer with a focus on construction litigation. **James Butler** concentrates on the negotiation, arbitration and litigation of construction contracts, with a niche in related environmental issues. Hailed by fellow attorneys as *"a fantastic lawyer,"* he is known as an active seminar speaker on some of the most complex construction matters, and is conversant with the intricacies of design-build projects. **Philip Beck** is *"just great,"* according to clients. He deals with construction disputes and has tried cases before a variety of forums across the US. He is also active in drafting and reviewing design and construction contracts for owners, developers, general contractors, subcontractors and architect/engineers and acts as an arbitrator in construction claims country wide.
The Clients: Turner Construction Company; Caddell Construction Company; Endress +Hauser Systems & Gauging; Golder Associates; Birmingham Steel; Williams Group International; Gebr. Pfeiffer; C Construction Company and Pearce Construction.

Kilpatrick Stockton LLP
The Firm: The team here is said by competitors to be populated by *"good adversarial construction people,"* with *"litigation as its center of gravity."* Dispute prevention and resolution are certainly key to this practice, but, being part of a sizable full-service law firm, it offers a range of services to its clients, including planning, financing, environmental compliance, and contract negotiation and review. The group was formed about five years ago with a team of six construction specialists from Smith Currie & Hancock, and has since developed a group in Atlanta that competitors acknowledge is a *"pretty healthy size."* The team acts principally for a client base of public and private real estate owners, but also represents general contractors, real estate developers and design and engineering firms. Sources admire the group's *"substantial competence and ability to handle complex construction matters."*
The Lawyers: **Neal Sweeney** is best known for litigation in connection with large public works and infrastructure projects. As well as dispute resolution, he does a great deal of consulting work, and competitors say that he is an *"effective"* attorney who *"immediately comes to mind"* for complex construction work. He recently secured a $38.5 million settlement for Odebrecht Construction in a case against a US Army corps of engineers concerning extra costs incurred during the construction of a large dam in southern California. Another case saw him gain a settlement of over $60 million for Siemens Transportation Systems, concerning delays to the 'Tren Urbano' light rail project in Puerto Rico. *"Talented"* **Brian Corgan** covers litigation, ADR and contractual work for a variety of commercial and industrial construction projects. His clients include owners, contractors, design professionals and engineering and materials testing firms. **Bill Dorris** is recognized as being *"experienced and active"* in the public sector, and has advised general contractors working on hospital projects in at least seven states. Competitors note that much of his work takes him outside Georgia, though he retains a strong reputation in the state.
The Clients: Odebrecht Construction; Siemens Transportation Systems; Kitchell and Winter Construction Company.

Alston & Bird LLP
The Firm: This large, general practice firm boasts a *"top-flight construction group,"* according to peers. The 12-attorney team commands a sizable presence in the local market. Typical work includes negotiating and drafting construction and design contracts, project finance, insurance matters and lien avoidance strategies on behalf of owners and contractors. The group is also active in matters relating to both litigation and ADR, including mediation, arbitration and jury and

CONSTRUCTION — GEORGIA

nonjury trials. An even balance of work in litigation and transactional matters is thought to lend greater depth to the group's construction abilities. According to interviewees, the team gives *"great advice to people who are about to get into a construction project, helping to negotiate contracts as well as advising on the prevention and control of disputes,"* and offers a *"supportive approach."*

The Lawyers: John Spangler chairs the firm's construction law group. According to sources, he has *"expanded the department effectively,"* putting together a *"great group of people."* Peers find him *"exceptionally reasonable"* to work opposite in litigious matters. He also advises an impressive list of contractors and owners on complex transactional issues. He has recently advised on a spate of major stadium construction agreements relating to work on Georgia Dome, Turner Field, Philips Arena and the NFL Stadium in Houston. He acts as national lead counsel for major US contractor, Beers Skanska, and regularly handles projects of about $300 million. Senior construction lawyer **Bill Hughs** earns praise from owner clients as *"an active and intelligent member of the construction community."* He divides his time between transactional work and dispute resolution, and is especially noted for his work in the energy sector. He recently acted for a private electric power generation company in litigation involving $30 million in claims arising from delays in the design and construction of a combined cycle electric power plant. He also contributed to the drafting of the A sociated Owners and Developers (AOD) document, which set new guidelines on how users craft standard form construction agreements.

The Clients: Beers Skanska; Barton Malow; Mallory & Evans; Georgia Aquarium; Manhattan Construction Company; GE Power Systems; Mirant; Dynegy; Prudential Insurance Company of America; Liberty Mutual; Lend Lease; Andritz; Industrial Developments International; MEAG-Power and Six Continents Hotels.

Hendrick Phillips Salzman & Flatt PC
see firm details p.817

The Firm: This *"strong boutique"* has been active in the construction market for 25 years. Five full-time partners act exclusively on construction matters for a large base of contractor and subcontractor clients. Contractors, and in particular specialty contractors, appreciate the *"high-quality"* construction practice and the personal service it provides, as do the smaller number of owners and developers for whom the team also acts. The firm is increasingly involved in work on a national level, though it remains very visible within the state. Most of the team's work is contentious, emphasizing construction disputes and litigation avoidance.

The Lawyers: David Hendrick (see p.207) is said to be the rock upon which the firm is founded. *"Highly respected in the construction community,"* market sources dub him a *"smart and experienced"* attorney who *"has built up a fine firm of lawyers."* He has a busy practice in litigation, which includes extensive trial work, and ADR, and he is increasingly spending time on preventative work and business counseling, for example, helping businesses choose the wisest delivery system for their projects. His typical clients are contractors and subcontractors. **Martin Salzman** has a reputation as an outspoken and effective practitioner. One source described him as *"the real deal in construction law."* **Stephen Phillips** is best known for his extremely specialized work with the roofing industry, representing roofing contractors and design professionals. Competitors consider him *"technically very highly qualified."*

The Clients: Sentex Communications; Siemens Energy & Automation; Keene Construction; Arcadis Geraghty & Miller International and John W Rooker & Associates.

King & Spalding LLP
see firm details p.829

The Firm: Like many large full-service firms, King & Spalding concentrates on representing its existing client base of mainly owners, developers and lenders. According to competitors, this stable of *"good clients with construction needs"* is one of its greatest strengths, as is the team's depth of skills, especially in contract negotiation, project delivery system analysis and dispute resolution. Its energy sector expertise is especially noted. The firm's role in the 1996 Olympics is still mentioned by market sources, and many of them date the birth of its real construction strength to that time. These days, the firm has a *"fine construction department"* of about 13 lawyers, and is active on the global stage.

The Lawyers: Head of the firm's contracting practice **John Hinchey** (see p.207) is a *"standout"* practitioner, focusing chiefly on commercial and transactional construction matters. Interviewees consider him a *"smart, thoughtful attorney"* with a profound grasp of construction contracts. Peers often refer to his work on negotiating and drafting the design and construction agreements for the Atlanta Olympic games, and acknowledge that since then he has *"developed the practice well and been able to attract some sophisticated clients."* Having served as chairman of the ABA Forum on the Construction Industry and devoted years to the practice, he is now a valued arbitrator and mediator in numerous cases across the US. He was also on the committee that drafted the influential AOD agree ment. Increasingly involved in dispute resolution, Hinchey is currently serving as lead counsel for an affiliate of Coca-Cola in a dispute with Bechtel, over the design and construction management of a large concentrate manufacturing plant in Ireland. Additionally, he is representing Turner Broadcasting System in all aspects of its $1.2 billion construction program nationwide.

The Clients: The firm represents corporations such as Turner Broadcasting System, UPS and Coca-Cola and a number of major developers, manufacturers and oil, gas and energy companies.

Sutherland Asbill & Brennan LLP
see firm details p.887

The Firm: The firm might be best known for its high-class tax practice, but it can boast experience in all facets of construction law. It has a particularly high profile for litigation and arbitration proceedings, though the group does place emphasis on conflict avoidance and early resolution, using advice and counseling. When litigation is needed, however, a good track record before federal and state courts, government boards of contract appeals, agencies and industry arbitration panels helps achieve favorable results. Market sources acknowledge that the team produces *"extremely high-quality work."*

The Lawyers: The retirement of construction legend Jim Groton has left **Tony Smith** (see p.210) as the firm's outstanding practitioner in this field. Heading up the construction industry disputes group, Smith handles complex, multi-party construction-related disputes and displays particular expertise in large-scale civil and energy projects. Peers proclaim him a *"tremendous and fearless strategic thinker"* with *"extraordinary intellectual ability"* and *"fantastic trial skills."* He has a name in international construction arbitration and is currently involved in a LCIA arbitration in which he is representing an independent power producer and instructing a barrister in connection with various construction, engineering and insurance issues arising from the development and construction of a UK power project.

The Clients: InterGen; The Beck Group; Milwaukee Metropolitan Sewerage District; HOK; Florida State Board of Administration; Rinker Materials and LG&E Energy.

Shapiro Fussell Wedge Smotherman Martin & Price LLP

The Firm: A strong construction boutique with a growing profile, it now has about 25 lawyers, with the majority of its 12 partners devoted to litigation and arbitration. Though dedicated to construction work, the firm provides a full range of corporate services for construction clients, including employment and insurance advice. However, the majority of its work is in construction litigation, negotiation, dispute prevention, mediation and arbitration, and more than half the firm's activity now takes place outside Georgia.

The Lawyers: Ben Shapiro works primarily in litigation and is thought to be *"well connected"*

with trade associations and construction bar groups. He acts for a mix of developers, suppliers, architects and engineers, but has a particular name in the market for representing contractors and subcontractors. Peers say that he has a *"broad-based reputation"* and *"can be relied upon when you need to get the job done."*
The Clients: The firm advises developers, suppliers, contractors, subcontractors, architects and engineers on all aspects of construction law.

Smith, Gambrell & Russell LLP
The Firm: This long-established general practice firm boasts a strong construction and litigation group. It is capable of handling a wide variety of construction projects on an international scale, for a client base that includes owners, developers, construction managers and contractors.
The Lawyers: Ira Genberg heads the construction law and litigation departments. Clients are attracted by his excellent track record in complex construction trials, many of which take place outside Georgia; indeed, most sources confirm that he is better known on the national and international stage than the local one. His national profile is bolstered by his position as general counsel to the AOD group, the country's largest alliance of owners and developers. He gained a great number of plaudits for heading the committee drafting the influential AOD agreement. He has also recently won a ground-breaking victory against the House of Commons in the UK, establishing a new legal precedent throughout the EU. *"Smart and prominent"* **Tom Asselin** has a background in civil engineering and construction management that lends him a *"real edge"* in terms of his depth of technical insight into the relevant issues.
The Clients: Foster Wheeler; Shimizu America; Home Depot; Marriott International; Tyco International; Tracer Industries; Kerzner International; Sierra Aluminum Company; HLK Cladding Systems and BHN.

Weinberg, Wheeler, Hudgins, Gunn & Dial LLC
The Firm: Competitors rate this as a *"good construction group,"* notable for its focus on litigation and dispute resolution, much of which is in connection with government contract s claims and bid protests. Typical dispute work relates to projects such as the renovation of federal courthouses and office buildings and the construction of dams, schools, highways, prison buildings, aircraft hangers and barracks. Although the firm's focus is on trials and arbitrations, the team also undertakes contract negotiation and drafting.
The Lawyers: David Dial wins considerable market plaudits for his *"strategic thinking and leadership."* He undertakes general construction litigation, including trial work and arbitrations, and often tackles the overlap between general construction disputes and insurance defense.
The Clients: The firm acts for a range of contractors, developers, owners, suppliers, architects and engineers.

Other Notable Practitioners
Kent Stair of Carlock Copeland Semler & Stair LLP is respected among peers as a *"highly rated technical lawyer."* His practice encompasses litigation, arbitration and mediation in addition to malpractice and insurance defense work. **Kamyar Molavi** stands out from the small team at Seyfarth Shaw. This *"fine attorney"* wins high marks from competitors for his *"vast experience"* gleaned as a former project manager and estimator for construction companies. His work centers on litigation before federal and state courts and arbitration panels.

CORPORATE/M&A

GEORGIA
Leading firms (Corporate/M&A)
1. KING & SPALDING LLP *Atlanta*
2. ALSTON & BIRD LLP *Atlanta*
3. MCKENNA LONG & ALDRIDGE *Atlanta*
   ROGERS & HARDIN *Atlanta*
   SUTHERLAND ASBILL & BRENNAN LLP *Atlanta*
   TROUTMAN SANDERS LLP *Atlanta*
4. KILPATRICK STOCKTON LLP *Atlanta*
   PARKER, HUDSON, RAINER & DOBBS LLP *Atlanta*
   POWELL, GOLDSTEIN, FRAZER & MURPHY *Atlanta*

Firms are listed alphabetically in each band.

King & Spalding LLP
see firm details p.829
The Firm: With its blue-ribbon corporate clientele and *"some long bloodlines,"* the firm enjoyed overwhelming support from peers as *"the strongest all-around business practice"* in Georgia. *"Just about everybody I've worked with over there has been impressive,"* one rival said. Clients appreciated the specializations covering *"every possible issue that could arise, no matter how small a niche practice area that might be."* The firm represented UPS in its joint venture, estimated at $1 billion, with Ford to deliver cars to dealerships in North America, and acted for Home Depot cofounder Arthur Blank in his $545 million acquisition of the Atlanta Falcons football team.
The Lawyers: Bruce Hawthorne (see p.206), portrayed by competitors as a *"first-rate dealmaker,"* has established a stellar reputation in the telecom industry. He acted as key negotiator for Sprint in many of its most high-profile deals, including a proposed merger with MCI WorldCom. Leading the group's M&A practice is **Michael Egan** (see p.205), who clients seek out for his *"superb analytical skills"* and his ability to *"keep in mind a broader picture of what you're trying to accomplish."* He took UPS through its $180 million purchase of Mail Boxes Etc and piloted Georgia-Pacific's sale of four pulp and paper plants, totaling about $1.5 billion. Respected for being a *"no-boundaries kind of a guy,"* **Bill Baxley** (see p.203) has enhanced his reputation by smoothly steering through several hostile transactions. Rivals consider him to be *"one of the best corporate lawyers around."* Baxley helped SunTrust Banks to acquire Crestar Financial in a $9 billion deal that allowed the financial holding company to expand into Virginia, Maryland and DC. **Russell Richards** (see p.209), whose bread-and-butter workload lies in the midmarket, is known to clients for his *"keen sense of what strategy is appropriate."* His practice combines *"not only technical knowledge but also savvy management."* Richards advised AHL Services in its $180 million sale of an aviation business and Lanier Worldwide in its $1 billion acquisition by copier/printer manufacturer Ricoh. **William Spalding** (see p.210), whose strength lies in venture capital, is clearly *"one of the names"* in the state. He advised Georgia-Pacific on the spin-off and sale of a $4.6 billion timber asset. **John Kelley** (see p.208), noted for having *"a good understanding of the nuances of corporate governance, securities and management,"* has handled several acquisitions for UPS. In addition to his expertise in the technicalities of the law, observers agreed that Kelley is *"effective, without creating hassles or undue posturing."* **Jeffrey Stein** (see p.210) can be *"encyclopedic, almost professorial in his approach to securities law,"* and yet he *"never loses sight of the deal."* Portrayed by one client as an advocate with a *"command of the field,"* Stein represented UPS in a $2.1 billion equity public offering. The *"brain"* behind the firm's Islamic finance and investment practice is **Donald Knight Jr** (see p.208), who was commended for the *"impressive"* results of his representation of Crescent Capital Management. **Alan Prince** (see p.209), whose *"excellent execution skills"* in complex matters

CORPORATE/M&A

GEORGIA

GEORGIA
Leading individuals (Corporate/M&A)

1
- EGAN Michael *King & Spalding LLP*, Atlanta
- HARDIN Edward *Rogers & Hardin*, Atlanta
- HAWTHORNE Bruce *King & Spalding LLP*, Atlanta
- NURKIN Sidney *Alston & Bird LLP*, Atlanta

2
- BAXLEY Bill *King & Spalding LLP*, Atlanta
- JEFFRIES Hill *Alston & Bird LLP*, Atlanta
- LONG Clay *McKenna Long & Aldridge*, Atlanta
- RICHARDS Russell *King & Spalding LLP*, Atlanta

3
- GOLDEN Jonathan *Arnall Golden Gregory LLP*, Atlanta
- KAUFMAN Mark *Sutherland Asbill & Brennan*, Atlanta
- KELLEY John *King & Spalding LLP*, Atlanta
- SMITH James *Troutman Sanders LLP*, Atlanta
- SPALDING William *King & Spalding LLP*, Atlanta
- STEIN Jeffrey *King & Spalding LLP*, Atlanta

4
- CURTIS Vaughan *Alston & Bird LLP*, Atlanta
- FOX Steven *Rogers & Hardin*, Atlanta
- GROUT Robert *Troutman Sanders LLP*, Atlanta
- HUDSON Paul *Parker, Hudson, Rainer*, Atlanta
- HYMAN Thomas *Sutherland Asbill & Brennan*, Atlanta
- KNIGHT Donald *King & Spalding LLP*, Atlanta
- MCNEILL Thomas *Powell, Goldstein, Frazer*, Atlanta
- STOCKTON David *Kilpatrick Stockton LLP*, Atlanta

Up-and-coming individuals
- PRINCE Alan *King & Spalding LLP*, Atlanta

Individuals are listed alphabetically in each band.

---

garnered praise among rivals and clients alike, has advised such institutional clients as Cousins Properties in its corporate matters. Described as someone who *"definitely will have a much bigger role"* in the future, Prince has already established a practice that was said to be *"a good balance between corporate finance and M&A."*

The Clients: Coca-Cola; Budget Group; Turner Broadcasting System; AFC Enterprises; CaremarkRx; Milliken & Company and Jefferson-Pilot.

Alston & Bird LLP
The Firm: Market sources agreed that the firm is *"closing the gap"* with King & Spalding by its recruitment of *"a tremendous amount of talent"* in the past five years. Particular areas of growth include IP, healthcare and technology. Representing clients on *"the front end of a lot of high-profile deals,"* the group steered Wachovia through its purchase of certain assets of E-Risk Services, which enable Wachovia to market specialty insurance products to the private business sector.

The Lawyers: Coordinating the life sciences practice team is **Sidney Nurkin** (see p.209), who rivals noted was one of the most *"distinguished in Atlanta"* for private equity and corporate governance issues. He advised CGW Southeast Partners in a series of transactions ranging from $50-250 million and counseled AMVESCAP on matters concerning several of its mutual funds. *"Bright and capable, with tremendous integrity,"* Nurkin also represented an Atlanta-based software company in the acquisition of several of its competitors. **Hill Jeffries** (see p.207), hailed by observers as a *"get-it-done kind of a lawyer with his eye on the goal,"* advised Banc of America Securities and Salomon Smith Barney in a $500 million shelf takedown and global offering of debt securities by Coca-Cola. *"One of those people who never gets flustered,"* Jeffries also acted for AMVESCAP in a $300 million Rule 144A offering. Peers commended **Vaughan Curtis** (see p.205), a generalist with a healthcare bent, for his *"great judgment."* He counseled board members on corporate governance, change of control and anti-takeover issues, as well as representing underwriters and issuers in public and private offerings.

The Clients: UPS; WebMD; CNN; MAPICS; Indus International and AGL Resources.

McKenna Long & Aldridge
The Firm: Peers respect this practice for its skillful handling of politically oriented matters, pointing particularly to its experience in transactions involving public utilities. The group also counsels an *"eclectic"* range of clients that include telecom, biotech and media companies. For example, the team advised one company in several telecom-related acquisitions in Europe, totaling about $2 billion, and represented a geotechnical engineering business in its $400 million sale to MACTEC.

The Lawyers: Cochairman **Clay Long** was described by competitors as *"one of the best corporate lawyers in town."* He advised clients such as Coca-Cola Enterprises and President Baking Company in purchasing and selling assets. He has also established a stellar reputation in intricate assignments such as acting for the State of Georgia in negotiating water rights with Florida and Alabama.

The Clients: Monsanto; Delta Air Lines; AGL Resources; First Capital Management and Alliance Technology Ventures.

Rogers & Hardin
The Firm: Viewed by commentators as a *"collection of the best talent,"* this boutique firm advises directors and special committees in complex corporate matters. By way of illustration, the group advised brokerage firms such as Salomon Smith Barney and Paine Webber (now UBS Paine Webber) in their roles in the WorldCom matter. However, due to its smaller size, peers commented that the team lacks *"the ability to tap into the resources that much bigger firms have."*

The Lawyers: Founder **Edward Hardin** was endorsed by rivals and clients as *"an adept facilitator"* who is *"exceedingly smart."* He counseled a Scientific-Atlanta special committee in a litigation regarding stockholders' derivatives. He also helped in the restructuring of an integrated steel and wire producer that had $250 million of debt. Distinguished as a *"dogged negotiator,"* **Steven Fox** won accolades for his representation of international sports broadcasting company ISB, including its negotiations of the broadcast agreement for the Athens 2004 Olympics. Clients praised both his *"boundless energy"* and his ability to *"persevere through the most difficult problems."*

The Clients: Arthur Andersen, JDN Realty and Keystone Consolidated Industries.

Sutherland Asbill & Brennan LLP
see firm details p.887

The Firm: A rigorous corporate team with equal reach in DC. The firm benefits from what sources deemed *"an active practice in the tech industry"* and a strong tax group. Attorneys handled two private placements totaling $35 million, acting for the manufacturer of an innovative material that bonds silicon to fabric. The group also advised RTM Restaurant Group in a series of acquisitions valued over $100 million.

The Lawyers: *"Analytical and creative,"* **Mark Kaufman** (see p.207) earned stripes for an innovative deal allowing battery maker Rayovac to acquire all of Varta's consumer subsidiaries outside Germany and to become the majority owner of a new joint venture entity that will conduct all consumer battery operations in Germany. Impressed by his *"flexibility to think outside of the box,"* other clients, such as Netzee, a provider of online banking and billing services, turned to him to handle a series of dispositions. **Thomas Hyman** (see p.207) is acclaimed by clients as *"a technical phenomenon"* who manages to *"show just the proper amount of anger."* His practice is heavily concentrated on M&A. He has advised on the consolidations of Coca-Cola bottling companies, and piloted construction materials producer Rinker Materials through its $540 million acquisition of Kiewit Materials.

The Clients: Six Continents, Overend and Co and Nextec Applications.

Troutman Sanders LLP
The Firm: The group has attracted bellwether clients, such as Southern Company, ensuring its reputation for supplying professional advice to public utilities. Adjudged a *"significant firm with great political ties,"* the group also represented Mirant in several major acquisitions. M&A expertise is just part of its range of experience here, which also include securities offerings, joint ventures and corporate restructurings.

The Lawyers: Practice group leader **James Smith** impressed rivals as an adept analyst who is *"able to pierce through and understand complex issues."* His ability to bring clients together was said to be *"outstanding,"* and he has acted for a venture capital satellite telecom in its raising of

GEORGIA

EMPLOYMENT & LABOR LAW

about $60 million. He also advised Matria Healthcare in a $125 million Rule144A placement and helped Allied Holdings restructure more than $100 million in credit agreements. **Robert Grout** (see p.206), leader of the firm's corporate section, assisted AGCO in its $350 million acquisition of Ag-Chem Equipment. Described by commentators as *"exceptional,"* Grout also steered Securicor in its acquisition of airport security specialist Argenbright Securities.
The Clients: Southern Company; Georgia Power; CNN and CompuCredit.

Kilpatrick Stockton LLP
The Firm: The firm advises clients on public and private offerings, M&A transactions and corporate financing options. This group represented Atlanta-based information serivces company Equifax in its spin-off of Certegy, a payment services business.
The Lawyers: Chair of the corporate group **David Stockton** enjoys *"one of the best reputations at the firm,"* representing numerous businesses in initial and secondary public offerings. He has also advised special committees and management groups, among others, in privatizing transactions.

The Clients: Interland; BellSouth; Krispy Kreme and Allied Capital.

Parker, Hudson, Rainer & Dobbs LLP
The Firm: *"A general corporate boutique with a healthcare bent,"* the firm represents large hospitals and hospital systems in corporate transactions. Attorneys here have helped set up HMOs for hospitals and also advised on the establishment of large affiliations between hospitals and physicians.
The Lawyers: The group's managing partner, **Paul Hudson** stands out as *"one of the best in healthcare."* He has advised such clients as a non-profit health care group in transactions including sales and mergers. He also directed the sales of businesses at values ranging from $5-$55 million.
The Clients: Food distributors, consulting firms, web-based businesses and insurance companies.

Powell, Goldstein, Frazer & Murphy LLP
The Firm: The firm is respected for its broad-reaching corporate practice, which features M&A, joint ventures and securities issues in its workload. The team has also developed niches in areas such as healthcare, where it advises on *"important strategic acquisitions,"* such as representing one hospital in the purchase of another.
The Lawyers: A *"creative advocate who does a good job for his clients,"* **Thomas McNeill** has earned top marks from rivals for his work in the structuring and financing of acquisitions and divestitures. He masterminded a tax-free spin-off involving three NYSE-listed corporations in the restaurant and food service industries. Also helped consolidate a public and private company to form a publicly traded hotel operator.
The Clients: Food cooperatives, retailers, manufacturers of scientific instruments and web service providers.

Other Notable Practitioners
Jonathan Golden of Arnall Golden Gregory LLP has an *"intense"* approach to deals and a *"wealth of contacts,"* sources said. Golden, who can *"cut to the chase and bring out the salient points of the problem quickly,"* was referred to as well versed in stockholders' disputes and other complex transactions. He counseled RoPro US Holdings in its $500 million sale to Deutsche Bank and advised SYSCO in several transactions totaling about $1 billion.

EMPLOYMENT & LABOR LAW — MAINLY PLAINTIFF

GEORGIA
Leading firms
(Employment: Mainly Plaintiff)
1. **BONDURANT, MIXSON & ELMORE LLP** Atlanta
   PARKS, CHESIN, WALBERT & MILLER Atlanta
2. **BUCKLEY & KLEIN, LLP** Atlanta
3. **STANFORD FAGAN & GIOLITO** Atlanta

Leading individuals
(Employment: Mainly Plaintiff)
1. **BUCKLEY** Edward *Buckley & Klein, LLP,* Atlanta
   PARKS Lee *Parks, Chesin, Walbert & Miller,* Atlanta
2. **BONDURANT** Emmet *Bondurant, Mixson* Atlanta
   BRAMLETT Jeffrey *Bondurant, Mixson,* Atlanta
   MILLER Harlan *Parks, Chesin, Walbert,* Atlanta
   NELSON Pat *Sole Practitioner,* Athens
3. **FAGAN** James *Stanford Fagan & Giolito,* Atlanta
   GIOLITO Robert *Stanford Fagan & Giolito,* Atlanta
   KLEIN Daniel *Buckley & Klein, LLP,* Atlanta
   SCHWARTZ Debra *Thompson, Rollins,* Decatur

Firms and individuals are listed alphabetically in each band.

Bondurant, Mixson & Elmore LLP
The Firm: The firm was heavily endorsed to researchers as *"the best plaintiff group out there,"* although it also represents management on occasions, and has a burgeoning litigation practice. Consistently involved in some of the most complex cases in the state, the team's crowning moment came when, acting as cocounsel, it obtained an historic settlement of $192.5 million in a class action race discrimination lawsuit against a Fortune 100 employer. The prevailing economic climate has also dictated that the firm has frequently represented executives and senior managers in the negotiation of severance packages with US and multinational employers.
The Lawyers: A team of *"smart and aggressive"* attorneys is spearheaded by **Emmet Bondurant** (see p.203). Market commentators endorsed him as *"an icon of the plaintiff bar,"* while contemporaries consider him a *"formidable opponent"* in the courtroom. **Jeffrey Bramlett** was also singled out to researchers as an *"aggressive courtroom litigator who really fights his clients' corner."*

Parks, Chesin, Walbert & Miller
The Firm: A team of *"first-rate attorneys"* has built an impressive reputation in the field of employment discrimination. It is often seen as the firm of choice for reverse discrimination race cases, where it has sued a number of public employers. In light of the current economic situation, the group has increasingly acted in a number of age discrimination cases resulting from reductions in workforces.
The Lawyers: **Lee Parks** was described to researchers as a *"smooth operator,"* and was acclaimed by competitors as a trial lawyer who is both *"tenacious and professional."* **Harlan Miller** is another respected name, whose *"straight-talking, bulldog"* approach to a case is said to *"make life difficult"* for defense attorneys.

Buckley & Klein
The Firm: Having recently split off from Greene, Buckley, Jones & McQueen, the firm has quickly established a reputation for professionalism when handling complex cases. Lawyers represent individuals and groups in discrimination cases and have negotiated severance packages for executives. It has had success in a reverse discrimination case brought under Title VII by three white male managers where it won a verdict for $2.9 million. It has also acted for a number of attorneys in a case brought against the EEOC claiming age and race discrimination.
The Lawyers: Both name partners are well known about town and were commended for both their ethics and their commitment to their clients' cause. **Edward Buckley** received market acclaim as a dazzling trial lawyer. His *"impassioned"* courtroom style may ruffle some feathers, but he earns the respect of opposing counsel and the courts. By comparison, **Daniel Klein**'s

EMPLOYMENT & LABOR LAW — GEORGIA

approach is more low key, although he won plaudits from interviewees for his *"reliability and integrity."*

Stanford Fagan & Giolito
The Firm: The firm is best known for its representation of unions but its varied caseload also includes a full spectrum of discrimination cases. Its lawyers are experienced in race, age, sex and disability lawsuits at the trial and appellate level. In the labor arena, the group has acted for unions in arbitrations, mediations and contract negotiations.

The Lawyers: **James Fagan** was widely acknowledged as *"one of the few genuine labor specialists in Georgia,"* while **Robert Giolito** (see p.206), who devotes most of his practice to labor issues, also won plaudits for his employment work.

The Clients: Its client base includes international and local labor organizations in healthcare, manufacturing and construction industries, as well as individual employees.

Other Notable Practitioners
Pat Nelson (see p.208), a sole practitioner based in Athens, won strong market commendation. His *"understated and softly spoken"* manner is considered to be particularly effective in jury trials, where he has scored a number of recent successes.

At Thompson, Rollins, Schwartz & Borowski in Decatur, **Debra Schwartz** was endorsed to researchers as an *"excellent advocate who doesn't overplay her hand."* Focusing primarily on employment discrimination, she also handles traditional labor matters.

EMPLOYMENT & LABOR LAW — MAINLY DEFENDANT

GEORGIA
Leading firms
(Employment: Mainly Defendant)

1
- KILPATRICK STOCKTON LLP *Atlanta*
- KING & SPALDING LLP *Atlanta*
- PAUL, HASTINGS, JANOFSKY & WALKER *Atlanta*

2
- ALSTON & BIRD LLP *Atlanta*

3
- ELARBEE, THOMPSON, SAPP & WILSON *Atlanta*
- FISHER & PHILLIPS LLP *Atlanta*
- FORD & HARRISON LLP *Atlanta*
- OGLETREE, DEAKINS, NASH, SMOAK *Atlanta*
- ROGERS & HARDIN *Atlanta*
- TROUTMAN SANDERS LLP *Atlanta*

4
- CONSTANGY, BROOKS & SMITH LLC *Atlanta*
- JACKSON LEWIS *Atlanta*

Leading individuals
(Employment: Mainly Defendant)

1
- ASHE Lawrence *Paul, Hastings, Janofsky, Atlanta*
- HUGHES Hunter *Rogers & Hardin, Atlanta*
- WYMER John *King & Spalding LLP, Atlanta*

2
- BOICE William *Kilpatrick Stockton LLP, Atlanta*
- BOISSEAU Richard *Kilpatrick Stockton LLP, Atlanta*
- JOHNSTON Mike *King & Spalding LLP, Atlanta*

3
- BUCKLER Robert *Troutman Sanders LLP, Atlanta*
- COIL James *Kilpatrick Stockton LLP, Atlanta*
- DEAKINS Homer *Ogletree, Deakins, Nash, Atlanta*
- JOHNSON Weyman *Paul, Hastings, Janofsky, Atlanta*
- OAKLEY Mary Ann *Holland & Knight LLP, Atlanta*
- WEIRICH Geoffrey *Paul, Hastings, Janofsky, Atlanta*

4
- CLINEBURG William *King & Spalding LLP, Atlanta*
- DENNARD Lane *King & Spalding LLP, Atlanta*
- HUNTER Forrest *Alston & Bird LLP, Atlanta*
- MATCHETT Sam *King & Spalding LLP, Atlanta*
- PERRIN Martha *Ogletree, Deakins, Nash, Atlanta*
- RIDDELL Stephen *Troutman Sanders LLP, Atlanta*
- WILSON Stanford *Elarbee, Thompson, Sapp, Atlanta*

Firms and individuals are listed alphabetically in each band.

Kilpatrick Stockton LLP
The Lawyers: Star name **Richard Boisseau** has a broad practice, including inter alia, collective bargaining negotiations and unfair labor practices. A talented and visible employment group includes **William Boice** (see p.203), a pure litigator by trade, who also devotes a substantial portion of his practice to employment-related issues. He has tried numerous multiple plaintiffs' discrimination cases and is widely recognized by peers as an excellent trial lawyer. Interviewees agreed that the key to his success lay in his creative approach and his *"knack of appealing to both judges and juries."* **James Coil** also won substantial market acclaim for his employment litigation practice.

The Clients: The Pepsi Bottling Group; The Perrier Group of America; Wells Fargo Home Mortgage; BellSouth; Sara Lee and EntreMed.

King & Spalding LLP
see firm details p.829

The Firm: Commentators consistently recommended this *"top-dollar firm"* as one of the market leaders in Georgia, citing both the caliber of its lawyers and their glittering portfolio of clients. Attorneys regularly represent companies in some of the most high-profile class action cases, and clients acknowledged that *"they may not be cheap, but it is money well spent."*

The Lawyers: **John Wymer** (see p.211) is one of the state's most renowned practitioners and widely acknowledged as an excellent litigator. Wymer's strength is said to lie in the simplicity of his manner: *"He isn't overly legalistic and can reduce complicated matters to their essence."* He secured a summary judgment in favor of Gerber Products in a class action age discrimination case in Michigan and also acted as lead counsel in Mathis, et al. v Home Depot where class certification was successfully defeated. **Mike Johnston** (see p.207) has been involved in several high-profile cases including the Coca-Cola/Abdallah nationwide class action alleging race discrimination that was recently settled. Competitors acknowledged him for *"a string of fine, recent results."*

Bill Clineburg (see p.204) is known primarily for employment litigation; he represented Lever Brothers at trial and appellate level in an ADA case that established law favorable to employers. Although lacking the profile of some of his colleagues, **Sam Matchett** (see p.208) is recognized by industry insiders as a *"talented"* employment litigator who frequently defends employers in cases brought under Title VII, ADEA and ADA. Labor law specialist **Lane Dennard** (see p.205) has been involved in several important corporate downsizings and restructurings in recent years.

The Clients: Home Depot; MassMutual; McDonald's; Novartis Consumer Health; SmithKline and Manpower International.

Paul, Hastings, Janofsky & Walker LLP
see firm details p.861

The Firm: The firm's employment group was repeatedly praised to researchers for its outstanding reputation in employment discrimination matters, and has been involved in many of the nation's largest class action cases. Covering a full spectrum of employment matters, it is perceived to be particularly strong in Title VII defense. Such is the group's reputation in this area that, by comparison, its labor law capacity is overshadowed.

The Lawyers: *"The dean of the defense bar,"* **Lawrence Ashe** (see p.202) is acknowledged as an exceptional trial lawyer who *"knows his stuff inside out, is well prepared and looks at cases from all the angles."* Although his 'take-no-prisoners' style does not meet with universal approval, his vast experience and successful track record are beyond dispute. He receives valuable support from class action specialist **Geoffrey Weirich** (see p.211), who notably represented Boeing in a series of putative class actions alleging discrimination on the basis of race, national origin and gender. Weirich also regularly handles matters under Titles I and III of the ADA. Also respected

GEORGIA

EMPLOYMENT & LABOR LAW

by his peers is **Weyman Johnson** (see p.207), an expert in labor law, who also devotes a percentage of his practice to matters arising from OSHA and FLSA.
The Clients: Publix Super Markets; Saturn; New United Motor Manufacturing; Educational Testing Service and Buckeye Technologies.

Alston & Bird LLP
The Firm: The employment team at this large corporate firm was endorsed to researchers for both the quality of its work and its ability to attract a stable of impressive clients. Interviewees also emphasized the team player ethos and uniform excellence of the group. Attorneys cover a plethora of employment and labor-related matters ranging from defense of employment claims through policy advice, including immigration issues, to union avoidance strategies. Clients are also advised on the labor and employment implications of corporate transactions.
The Lawyers: The team has defended First Union National Bank in a class action brought by current and former employees, alleging age discrimination, and has acted for UPS in connection with its affirmative action planning and litigation on a nationwide basis. **Forrest Hunter** is a respected generalist; his unflappable manner and *"client-oriented attitude"* struck a particular chord with the market.
The Clients: UPS; Alcoa; First Union National Bank; Wachovia Bank; SunTrust Bank and Fortis.

Elarbee, Thompson, Sapp & Wilson LLP
The Firm: This well-established boutique has developed expertise in employment law, but is best known for the strength of its traditional labor practice. Its sizable team of about 30 lawyers advises management on a range of issues, including wage and hour compliance and union avoidance. Plaintiffs' lawyers considered this to be a *"straight-shooting and reliable"* group.
The Lawyers: **Stanford Wilson** was applauded by peers for his *"common sense."* He successfully represented Willamette Industries in an age and disability case in which summary judgment was granted in favor of Willamette on all the plaintiffs' claims. In the labor law arena, the firm is awaiting a decision on a case against the NLRB relating to the enforcement and administration of the NLRA.
The Clients: Engelhard; Florida Power; ChoicePoint; Citibank; Lockheed Martin and Goodyear Dunlop Tire Corporation.

Fisher & Phillips LLP
The Firm: Although this versatile team advises on all facets of labor and employment law, it was particularly commended for its traditional labor and Title VII defense work. The Atlanta office, home to the firm's largest group of lawyers, suc-cessfully defended Emory University against claims of race and disability discrimination in the US District Court in Atlanta. It was also successful in having class action allegations dismissed in a sex discrimination lawsuit brought against Target Stores. In the traditional labor arena, the firm has helped both Laurel Heights Hospital, Atlanta and Jefferson-Pilot Broadcasting to defeat union-organizing campaigns.
The Lawyers: The Atlanta office is home to the firm's largest group of lawyers. They were endorsed by opposing counsel as *"versatile and ethical."*
The Clients: The group acts for large multinationals as well as smaller entrepreneurial businesses. It has advised companies from the agricultural, automotive, banking, construction, education, health, insurance and manufacturing industries.

Ford & Harrison LLP
The Firm: Possessing a string of offices throughout the Southeast, this boutique firm was recommended to researchers as an *"excellent option"* for cost-effective advice and work. Although the firm represents clients from all industries, it is particularly associated with its work in the airline sector. The firm's labor practice is seen to be its core strength, though it also has acknowledged capabilities in employment litigation.
The Lawyers: The Atlanta office is headed by Lash Harrison who has amassed over 30 years' experience in the sector. Other attorneys include Thomas Kassin who has expertise in the airline industry.
The Clients: The group represents clients throughout the US including air carriers, manufacturers, hospitals, retailers and restaurant chains.

Ogletree, Deakins, Nash, Smoak & Stewart PC
The Firm: The Atlanta office of this national firm is widely seen as *"one of the top boutiques in the state."* Best known for its union prevention work, its varied practice also extends to employment litigation, employee benefits and immigration. Lawyers frequently advise clients on preventative strategies but were also recognized as talented litigators.
The Lawyers: **Homer Deakins** heads a team of over 20 lawyers and is *"the lifeblood of the firm, handling all the important matters."* He was endorsed to researchers as a pioneer of employment law, having practiced exclusively in this area throughout his career. Renowned for her employment litigation practice, **Martha Perrin** was also strongly recommended as a prominent local attorney.
The Clients: The roster includes multinational companies from the energy, manufacturing, automobile and healthcare industries.

Rogers & Hardin
The Firm: The firm is home to one of the state's outstanding lawyers, Hunter Hughes, and is best known for its litigation work. The group has been involved in cases on behalf of management but has also acted in prominent employment discrimination class actions. It also has expertise in wrongful discharge and employment torts including defamation, intentional infliction of emotional distress and fraud. Lawyers from the Atlanta office also advise on employment policies and practices in connection with work force reductions.
The Lawyers: **Hunter Hughes** is *"a name everyone knows,"* and was recommended as an excellent litigator. He has made his name as the mediator of choice in high-profile cases such as the Coca-Cola class action. Peers respect his *"air of gravitas"* and *"unrivaled mastery of his subject."*
His reputation is generally believed by contemporaries to outweigh that of his firm, which is felt to lack the depth of some of its principal competitors.
The Clients: The group continues to represent a number of blue-chip companies, including major airlines, and also acts for mid-sized public and private companies.

Troutman Sanders LLP
The Firm: Respected full-service firm, which has developed a highly rated, stand-alone labor and employment practice. A large team continues to represent an impressive regional clientele, such as Georgia Power and Georgia-Pacific. The firm has also acted for Lucent Technologies in an age discrimination case where it was able to persuade the court not to allow the case to proceed as a class action and all classwide claims were dismissed.
The Lawyers: The *"forthright"* **Robert Buckler** (see p.467668) has vast experience, and has litigated employment claims under Title VII, FLSA, ADEA and ADA in both state and federal courts. He successfully defended Georgia-Pacific in a race discrimination class action that was eventually voluntarily dismissed by the employees' lawyers. **Stephen Riddell** was commended to researchers as a talented employment litigator who successfully represented Southern Company and several of its subsidiaries in a class action race discrimination lawsuit.
The Clients: UPS; AT&T; Turner Broadcasting System; Mirant; Randstad Temporary Services; AGCO and Allied Holdings.

Constangy, Brooks & Smith LLC
The Firm: This boutique firm has a strong reputation for labor law, and also advises extensively on employment issues. It lays claim to one of the largest OSHA practices in Atlanta and, in addition, advises on business immigration and employee benefits.
The Lawyers: The group gained peer recognition for its ability to attract *"talented and respected*

ENERGY & NATURAL RESOURCES — GEORGIA

lawyers." Some lawyers, including James Smith, are NLRB alumni while others have previously gained experience from in-house positions.

The Clients: The firm acts for a number of high-profile corporations, including Boeing, Johnson & Johnson, Kmart, Marriott International and Sara Lee.

Jackson Lewis

The Firm: The firm's ability to handle a wide range of cases, coupled with the resources of its nationwide network, mean that it is *"certainly a player,"* according to competitors. The Atlanta office is best known for its counseling work, but has also enjoyed recent success on the contentious side.

The Lawyers: This substantial group is led by Stephen Munger. His team has experience in a broad spectrum of employment discrimination cases but is also versed in labor law. The group has handled strikes and collective bargaining agreements and can also provide advice on immigration.

The Clients: Clients include public and private businesses and nonprofit organizations.

Other Notable Practitioners

Mary Ann Oakley (see p.209) of Holland & Knight was consistently recommended to researchers as a consummate employment lawyer who is *"astute and switched-on."* Although she now represents management, experience as a plaintiffs' lawyer is said to have given her *"a sense of perspective and an ability to see both sides of the argument."*

ENERGY & NATURAL RESOURCES

GEORGIA
Leading firms (Energy & Natural Resources)

1. SUTHERLAND ASBILL & BRENNAN LLP *Atlanta*
   TROUTMAN SANDERS LLP *Atlanta*
2. ALSTON & BIRD LLP *Atlanta*
   MCKENNA LONG & ALDRIDGE *Atlanta*
3. KING & SPALDING LLP *Atlanta*

Leading individuals (Energy & Natural Resources)

1. BRADLEY Michael *Sutherland Asbill & Brennan, Atlanta*
   GREENE Kevin *Troutman Sanders LLP, Atlanta*
   KILGORE Cada *Sutherland Asbill & Brennan, Atlanta*
2. DOWDY Craig *McKenna Long & Aldridge, Atlanta*
   FORRY Robert *Troutman Sanders LLP, Atlanta*
3. DEGNAN Peter *Alston & Bird LLP, Atlanta*
   SWENSON Erik *King & Spalding LLP, Atlanta*
   WELLS Della *Alston & Bird LLP, Atlanta*

Firms and individuals are listed alphabetically in each band.

Sutherland Asbill & Brennan LLP
see firm details p.887

The Firm: Sits at the forefront of the field with an *"impressive knowledge of the industry."* The firm was described by competitors as *"a player"* in fostering regulatory changes. Its energy practitioners have litigated landmark cases and assisted in the restructuring of energy-related industries through key transactions they have handled.

The Lawyers: Michael Bradley (see p.203) displays *"an incredible amount of energy and vast experience."* He has cultivated a niche practice representing independent power producers, and has helped to steer the development of several power plants, ranging from $250-400 million, primarily in the Southeast. **Cada Kilgore** (see p.208), described by clients as *"diligent in researching and spotting potential problems,"* has extensive experience in financing power supply matters. For example, Kilgore represented Oglethorpe Power in many of its deals, including a $92 million bond issue. According to peers, he is *"practical and has a good feel for what matters in the field."*

The Clients: JPMorgan Chase, Goldman Sachs and Old Dominion Electric Cooperative.

Troutman Sanders LLP

The Firm: *"One of the busiest"* energy practice groups in Georgia, the 15-strong team defended Mirant in a series of antitrust actions in California alleging manipulation of the state's energy market. The firm is also involved in transactional and regulatory matters, and advises on project developments on behalf of utilities and energy marketers.

The Lawyers: Leading the firm's public utilities department is **Kevin Greene** (see p.206), who is *"well spoken, persistent and good at thinking on his feet,"* according to rivals. He has represented clients before the Georgia Public Service Commission and other agencies. *"One of the most politically astute"* of the state's energy attorneys, Greene has also helped clients to devise strategies to comply with the CAA. Competitors noted the skill of **Robert Forry** in crafting creative regulatory solutions for his clients, including matters relating to the FERC. Forry's *"knowledge of the business"* has enabled him to effectively lobby for changes in Georgia's statutes.

The Clients: Georgia Power, Southern Company and Kansas City Southern.

Alston & Bird LLP

The Firm: Described by peers as a *"significant force,"* the practice is known to clients for its *"innovative"* approach to financing. It has advised the state's municipal gas and electric authorities in such deals as a series of bond transactions for a combustion turbine project.

The Lawyers: Peter Degnan (see p.205), said to be a *"strategist"* in contracting and permitting, is especially proficient in matters relating to power-generating facilities. He has also played a key role in advising the 49-member Municipal Electric Authority of Georgia. **Della Wager Wells** was described by peers as a *"terrific"* transactional lawyer. She concentrates on matters involving taxable and tax-exempt financings for electric and gas facilities, along with other public projects.

The Clients: Mirant; The Southeast Alabama Gas District and Municipal Gas Authority of Mississippi.

McKenna Long & Aldridge

The Firm: Ten lawyers here cover a diverse range of energy law issues. The firm was particularly recommended to *Chambers'* researchers for its work in financing power plants, negotiating permits and litigating such issues as land use.

The Lawyers: Leading the practice is **Craig Dowdy** (see p.205), *"the name on the natural gas side,"* according to competitors. He represented Atlanta Gas Light Company in many of its public policy and legislative proposals relating to industry regulations. He also litigated for Chattanooga Gas Company in a cost of equity dispute.

The Clients: Virginia Natural Gas; AGL Resources; Cleco and Public Service Company of New Mexico.

King & Spalding LLP
see firm details p.829

The Firm: A fledgling practice benefiting from the firm's enormous corporate presence. The group represents underwriters in several projects, such as Baconton Power's gas-fired generating facility. Practitioners also assisted in development issues arising from projects, including a coal-fired generator project costing more than $1 billion.

The Lawyers: Erik Swenson (see p.210), endorsed by clients as an *"outstanding attorney,"* has helped to draft energy legislation, in addition to his transactional work. He has advised a group of 42 electric cooperatives in antitrust and restructuring matters and also counseled Exxon-Mobil in its efforts to develop gas fields in Saudi Arabia.

The Clients: Crédit Lyonnais, UPS and Home Depot.

GEORGIA

ENVIRONMENT

GEORGIA
Leading firms (Environment)

1 ALSTON & BIRD LLP *Atlanta*
 KING & SPALDING LLP *Atlanta*
2 KILPATRICK STOCKTON LLP *Atlanta*
 MCKENNA LONG & ALDRIDGE *Atlanta*
 TROUTMAN SANDERS LLP *Atlanta*
3 HUNTER, MACLEAN, EXLEY & DUNN *Savannah*

Leading individuals (Environment)

1 BARMEYER Patricia *King & Spalding LLP, Atlanta*
 DEHIHNS Lee *Alston & Bird LLP, Atlanta*
 HORDER Richard *Kilpatrick Stockton LLP, Atlanta*
2 JOHNSON John *Troutman Sanders LLP, Atlanta*
 STOKES James *Alston & Bird LLP, Atlanta*
 TISDALE Charles *King & Spalding LLP, Atlanta*
3 ERNST Andrew *Hunter, Maclean, Exley, Savannah*
 KAZMAREK Edward *McKenna Long & Aldridge, Atlanta*
 OAKES Leslie *King & Spalding LLP, Atlanta*
 TOULME Nill *Alston & Bird LLP, Atlanta*
4 GALLO Barbara *McKenna Long & Aldridge, Atlanta*
 HOGFOSS Robert *Hunton & Williams, Atlanta*
 O'DAY Stephen *Smith, Gambrell & Russell, Atlanta*
 POPE David *Carr, Tabb, Pope & Freeman, Atlanta*

Firms and individuals are listed alphabetically in each band.

Alston & Bird LLP
The Firm: A strong team of advocates who *"can handle just about anything you throw at them."* The 20-lawyer group litigated on behalf of corporate powerhouses such as Dow Chemical in some of the country's biggest asbestos claims. Through lobbying efforts, the firm also helped deflect regulations that would have imposed add-on controls to a coal-fired power plant, saving their client millions of dollars.
The Lawyers: **Lee DeHihns** (see p.205), *"the person to go to if you need to negotiate with the EPA,"* earned his laurels defending permits in appeals and other environmental challenges. An *"environmental generalist,"* DeHihns defended Gwinnett County in connection with a controversial permit for a proposed waste water treatment facility. *"Rainmaker"* **James Stokes** represented Atlantic Steel Company in a 140-acre cleanup in preparation for a residential and retail project. He also negotiated a favorable settlement relating to a CWA complaint before the case was officially filed. **Nill Toulme** (see p.211), reputed by peers to be *"effective without being unnecessarily abrasive,"* led a landmark case for Bank of America establishing the scope of fiduciary protection from liability under Superfund. Clients praised Toulme for *"not overworking a case."*
The Clients: UPS, Electrolux Home Products North America and Georgia-Pacific.

King & Spalding LLP
see firm details p.829
The Firm: Clients reported that when *"a lot of horsepower"* is required, this old-line firm delivers. The group is representing the State of Georgia in an ongoing high-profile water dispute involving Florida and Alabama, and acting for the West Georgia Regional Water Authority concerning a permit for a public drinking water reservoir.
The Lawyers: An expert in *"walking the fine line between clients, regulatory agencies and environmental groups,"* **Patricia Barmeyer** (see p.203) defended Georgia in a series of lawsuits related to compliance with the CAA. At stake was a $1.9 billion transportation plan for Atlanta. She also advised a developer in a permit appeal to allow residential construction on marshland. A *"pioneer in Superfund defense,"* **Charles Tisdale** (see p.211) was acknowledged for his rare ability to *"be aggressive without offending anyone."* Tisdale advised businesses involved in several Superfund sites, including a 70-acre landfill in Georgia and a waste treatment and storage facility in North Carolina. He is also an expert in the RCRA, which regulates hazardous waste. **Leslie Oakes** (see p.209), a former engineer at the state Environmental Protection Division, has established a name for himself in the areas of complex air and water pollution. Described by peers as *"competent and combative,"* Oakes handled environmental due diligence aspects of a number of complex transactions involving industrial facilities and properties.
The Clients: GE; Honeywell; Brown & Williamson Tobacco; Bridgestone/Firestone and Inland Paperboard and Packaging.

Kilpatrick Stockton LLP
The Firm: The group earned *"high marks"* from rivals in environmental litigation. With a strong technical team that includes former engineers, the firm can flex its muscles in the areas of land use, permit challenges and due diligence reports. The group defended Atlanta against an EPA challenge determining whether city sewer plants were sufficiently upgraded to protect the Chattahoochee River.
The Lawyers: At the helm of the environmental team is **Richard Horder** (see p.207), known among rivals as a *"bulldog"* in the courtroom. He won a $20 million verdict for Loews Hotels in a case involving PCB contamination and represented a paper mill in a challenge by an environmental group over excessive biological oxygen demand (BOD) in the Altamaha River. Horder also specializes in obtaining permits in areas inhabited by endangered species, such as the habitats of Georgia's red-cockaded woodpecker and the nocturnal beach mice of Florida and Alabama.
The Clients: Sun Chemical, Georgia-Pacific and Aronov Realty.

McKenna Long & Aldridge
The Firm: Recognized by peers as *"politically well connected, particularly at local and state levels,"* the firm recently bolstered its reputation by hiring three heavy-hitting environment lawyers from Kilpatrick Stockton.
The Lawyers: **Barbara Gallo** (see p.206), praised by clients for her *"extreme depth of knowledge,"* defended several electric power plants in litigation relating to air permits. She counseled one client in the redevelopment of a brownfield site and helped another gain a groundwater withdrawal permit to access drinking water. *"A strategic thinker with good interpersonal skills,"* **Edward Kazmarek** (see p.208), one of the three new recruits, is respected by peers for his work in negotiating cleanups on hazardous waste sites. In a case closely watched by the railroad industry, he was able to defeat plans for a large intermodal transfer station in Cobb County.
The Clients: Duke Energy; Williams Energy Partners; Hood Industries and Transco Products.

Troutman Sanders LLP
The Firm: The firm boasts *"gigantic clients"* such as Southern Company – one of America's largest generators of electricity – and was said to be especially skilled in maneuvering through regulatory agencies such as the EPA. The group advised a statewide coalition of industries, including paper, energy and cement manufacturing companies, on various regulatory issues. Another matter involved handling permitting and regulatory issues for a coal-fired electric utility facility.
The Lawyers: **John Johnson** (see p.207), who clients described as *"very knowledgeable and very confident, "* advised a wood products manufacturer in negotiating the terms of cleanup for a groundwater contamination incident. He also helped negotiate for a national mobile home manufacturer savings of nearly $800 million in potential fines from the EPA.
The Clients: Georgia Power, Delta Air Lines and Kerr-McGee.

Hunter, Maclean, Exley & Dunn PC
The Firm: *"A force to be reckoned with"* in wetlands and power project development, the Savannah firm represented a developer in obtaining a precedent-setting permit for a 1750-acre industrial site in Chatham County.
The Lawyers: Leading the land use and environmental practice is **Andrew Ernst** (see p.205), acknowledged by rivals as *"the most experienced and well-known environment attorney on the*

INSOLVENCY/CORPORATE RECOVERY — GEORGIA

coast." Praised primarily for his skill at obtaining permits, Ernst advised Westin Hotels & Resorts in a 560-acre development that included an 18-hole golf course on Hutchinson Island, near Savannah's historic district. He also resolved wetland issues for a client who wanted to develop a business park south of Savannah in Liberty County.

The Clients: Savannah Economic Development Authority, CSX Realty Development and Liberty County Development Authority.

Other Notable Practitioners

Robert Hogfoss of Hunton & Williams is esteemed by peers for his *"low-key and very effective"* approach to environmental law. Known for his *"analytical"* solutions to the CAA and other regulatory problems, Hogfoss has advised some of the country's largest oil pipelines in enforcement actions concerning spills. **Stephen O'Day** of Smith, Gambrell & Russell LLP represents both plaintiffs and defendants in environmental disputes. He advised Alabama landowners in a suit against Chevron and advised a pipeline company concerning allegations of underground gasoline contamination. In a separate suit, he is challenging a permit that would allow treated sewage to be released into Lake Lanier near Atlanta. **David Pope** of Carr, Tabb, Pope & Freeman LLP primarily represents plaintiffs and was said by rivals to have *"battled with the best of them."* He represents environmental organizations, property owners and homeowners in mass environmental and toxic tort lawsuits.

INSOLVENCY/CORPORATE RECOVERY

GEORGIA
Leading firms (Insolvency/Corporate Recovery)

1. ALSTON & BIRD LLP *Atlanta*
2. KILPATRICK STOCKTON LLP *Atlanta*
   MCKENNA LONG & ALDRIDGE *Atlanta*
3. KING & SPALDING LLP *Atlanta*
   TROUTMAN SANDERS LLP *Atlanta*
4. LAMBERTH, CIFELLI, STOKES & STOUT *Atlanta*
   PARKER, HUDSON, RAINER & DOBBS LLP *Atlanta*
   POWELL, GOLDSTEIN, FRAZER & MURPHY *Atlanta*

Leading individuals (Insolvency/Corporate Recovery)

★ BATSON Neal *Alston & Bird LLP, Atlanta*
1. CAMPBELL Charles *McKenna Long, Atlanta*
   DOBBS Edward *Parker, Hudson, Rainer, Atlanta*
   PARDO James *King & Spalding LLP, Atlanta*
2. AUSTIN Jesse *Paul, Hastings, Janofsky, Atlanta*
   CONNOLLY Dennis *Alston & Bird LLP, Atlanta*
   DIEHL Mary *Troutman Sanders LLP, Atlanta*
   LUREY Alfred *Kilpatrick Stockton LLP, Atlanta*
   MEIR Dennis *Kilpatrick Stockton LLP, Atlanta*
3. CIFELLI James *Lamberth, Cifelli, Stokes, Atlanta*
   KAUFMAN Mark *McKenna Long & Aldridge, Atlanta*
   STEIN Grant *Alston & Bird LLP, Atlanta*
4. BORDERS Sarah *King & Spalding LLP, Atlanta*
   COHEN Ezra *Troutman Sanders LLP, Atlanta*
   DORSEY Rufus *Parker, Hudson, Rainer, Atlanta*
   MARSH Gary *McKenna Long & Aldridge, Atlanta*
   WILLIAMSON Robert *Scroggins & Williamson, Atlanta*

Up-and-coming individuals
NAGLE Shannon *Powell, Goldstein, Atlanta*
ROSENBLATT Paul *Kilpatrick Stockton LLP, Atlanta*

Firms and individuals are listed alphabetically in each band.

Alston & Bird LLP

The Firm: Acclaimed by clients for getting *"great results,"* the team combines full-service proficiency in representing corporate debtors with specializations that include handling assets from bankrupt companies. The firm assisted Atlanta Gas Light Company in its acquisition of telecom assets from a bankrupt company.

The Lawyers: Neal Batson is *"obviously in a class by himself,"* and competitors said it was no surprise when Batson was appointed in May 2002 as independent examiner in the Enron case. Prior to then, he had counseled debtors including LaRoche Industries, Glenoit Corporation of Canada and a Tennessee-based automotive parts manufacturer supplying GM. An *"unbeatable"* practitioner with *"a litigation edge,"* Batson has also advised creditors such as Six Continents Hotels in bankruptcies. **Dennis Connolly** is thought to be *"well versed on both the transactional and litigation sides."* Clients pointed to him as a master in *"knowing when to negotiate and when to litigate."* Connolly represented The Krystal Company and Einstein Bros Bagels in bankruptcy proceedings. **Grant Stein** (see p.210), who rivals portray as a *"tenacious attorney,"* piloted such complex matters as the sale of Bill's Dollar Store, with its 400 southeastern US locations, within 60 days. *"Good at navigating through difficult issues,"* according to a client, Stein helped to recover about $100 million in loans to a nursing home development for Pacific Life Insurance Company, and steered Tri-State Outdoor Media Group through its $140 million bankruptcy.

The Clients: Prudential; South Fulton Medical Center; North American Royalties and Cajun Electric Power Cooperative.

Kilpatrick Stockton LLP

The Firm: Known to rivals for its *"depth of experience,"* the firm has advised debtors, such as Midway Airlines, in bankruptcy filings. Its creditors' representations have included BellSouth in proceedings against WorldCom, and KFC in a franchise-related matter in Atlanta. The firm's pool of talent includes Joel Piassick, whose focus on areas such as advising boards of directors in corporate restructurings has helped to earn the firm a reputation for adding a *"heightened level of sophistication to the field."*

The Lawyers: Competitors described **Alfred Lurey** (see p.208), whose practice leans toward complex transactional bankruptcy work, as an *"extraordinarily bright"* lawyer who will *"outwork an opponent."* He represented the restaurant chain Roadhouse Grill in its bankruptcy filings. A tough litigator who *"knows the code cold,"* **Dennis Meir** advised a business that bought debts from credit card companies. He also litigated a case involving a brake components manufacturer in a $20 million bankruptcy. *"You're never going to have an easy day when he's on the other side,"* claimed one competitor. **Paul Rosenblatt** has concentrated on telecom-related bankruptcies. He counseled BellSouth in connection with the WorldCom case.

The Clients: Vista Eyecare, GE Capital and Nextel International.

McKenna Long & Aldridge

The Firm: Rivals say that this 20-strong team is a *"talented practice able to take on any kind of case."* In a recent highlight, the firm represented a credit card processor in connection with the Premier Cruise Line bankruptcy.

The Lawyers: **Charles Campbell** has a reputation for *"unquestioned integrity,"* and received recommendations from both clients and competitors alike for his handling of high-stakes matters. *"There's nobody else I'd rather have on my team,"* one client said. Campbell represented a principal creditor in a reorganization involving a chain of 88 convenience stores in Texas. He also advised one of the last domestic cellophane manufacturers in its sale of assets to a Belgian company. **Mark Kaufman** (see p.208), who competitors cast as *"a straight shooter with a boisterous personality,"* has tackled many of the firm's major debtors' cases, including one involving Big Rivers Electric, a cooperative in Kentucky. *"A brand-name bankruptcy lawyer,"* Kaufman also focuses part of his practice on creditors' rights. **Gary Marsh** was said by competitors to be a *"tenacious advocate"* who is able to *"understandi and follow the intricacies"* of bankruptcy law. He represented Sentinel Trust Company in numerous receiverships and foreclosures involving independent living and nursing homes.

GEORGIA

INSOLVENCY/CORPORATE RECOVERY

The Clients: Atlanta Gas Light Company, GMAC and Flexel.

King & Spalding LLP
see firm details p.829
The Firm: A practice with a traditional bent on creditors' representation, King & Spalding is also turning its attention to representing debtors. It has recently advised The New Power Company in an $80 million restructuring case. The firm also fields corporate specialists, such as Paul Ferdinands, who handle the buying and selling of assets in bankruptcies.
The Lawyers: **James Pardo** (see p.209) was said by one client to give clients *"more bang for the buck"* than any other bankruptcy lawyer in Georgia. He advised clients involved in the PG&E, US Air and Enron bankruptcy proceedings. *"A problem solver,"* he also represented GE Capital in matters relating to a failed textile company and a sporting goods manufacturer. **Sarah Borders** (see p.203), noted by peers for her adroitness and versatility, represented the primary secured lender with respect to the sale of $125 million worth of assets to a Tennessee textile company. She also advised LJM2 in its relationship with Enron.
The Clients: AMEC; Texaco; Home Depot and SunTrust Banks.

Troutman Sanders LLP
The Firm: Market observers described the attorneys here as *"thorough – they keep their eyes on the ball."* The team is respected for its *"tremendous success"* in representing creditors.
The Lawyers: Much of the firm's profile is centered around two leading names. **Mary Grace Diehl** is *"the hub of the action,"* a rival said. She is skilled in the representation of financial institutions in corporate restructurings, and has advised on the Chapter 11 proceedings involving Wolf Camera and Just For Feet. *"Smart, practical and tough,"* she has also defended adversary proceedings in Bankruptcy Court. **Ezra Cohen** (see p.204), a former bankruptcy judge, also commands *"a great deal of respect"* from peers. He represented GE Capital as secured creditor in matters involving Private Jet Enterprises. In one client's judgment, Cohen is *"a gentleman and a scholar."*
The Clients: Bank of America, Schlumberger Resource Management Services and Kimberly-Clark.

Lamberth, Cifelli, Stokes & Stout PA
see firm details p.834
The Firm: *"Perhaps the strongest"* bankruptcy boutique firm in the state, acknowledged peers. The 14-strong team has represented debtors-in-possession for Chapter 11 cases, counseled creditors' committees and acted as trustees in restructurings. The market awaits the effect on the firm of Paul Bonapfel's appointment as a US Bankruptcy Judge in spring 2002.
The Lawyers: **James Cifelli** (see p.204) is a *"diehard litigator,"* who has earned respect from rivals for his *"bulldog"* courtroom demeanor. He has defended clients in connection with numerous bankruptcy-related issues. *"If you have a nasty piece of litigation, he's the one,"* a competitor said.
The Clients: Electronic Medical Distribution; M2Direct; Flooring America; First American Health Care of Georgia and RDM Sports Group.

Parker, Hudson, Rainer & Dobbs LLP
The Firm: Sources agreed that the nine-lawyer group, which is *"well respected in secured lenders work,"* has established a reputation for excellence in its handling of medium-sized cases.
The Lawyers: Peers noted that **Edward Dobbs** was *"exceptionally bright and technically proficient."* Particularly suited for *"cases that involve a substantial amount of negotiation,"* Dobbs was involved in the restructurings of Pillowtex, Kellstrom Industries and a Tennessee sports equipment manufacturer. **Rufus Dorsey** (see p.205), portrayed as *"impressive"* by peers, has more of a litigation edge, though his practice also focuses on representing financial institutions in bankruptcy filings.
The Clients: Bank of America, Fleet Bank and Wachovia.

Powell, Goldstein, Frazer & Murphy LLP
The Firm: Peers deemed the firm to be *"quietly efficient"* and carving a reputation for counseling debtors. Highlights have included advice to Wolf Camera in its $200-300 million restructuring.
The Lawyers: **Shannon Lowry Nagle** is always *"a name to watch,"* according to competitors. *"Aggressive and dynamic,"* Nagle steered a pay phone service provider and a chain of nursing homes through reorganizations. On the creditors' side, she represented a client involved in healthcare facilities in Chapter 11 proceedings.
The Clients: ETS Pay Phones, Hallmark Healthcare and RDM Sports Group.

Other Notable Practitioners
Jesse Austin (see p.202) of Paul, Hastings, Janofsky & Walker LLP is a *"master"* of debtor-in-possession loans. Interviewees spoke of him as a *"sophisticated"* practitioner who has mainly represented financial institutions in their role as lenders to bankrupt companies. Austin focuses on either the agent bank or syndicate member in restructurings involving businesses such as KinderCare Learning Centers for example. Clients endorsed **Robert Williamson** of Scroggins & Williamson as an *"effective and cost-conscious"* attorney. He has cultivated a niche in Chapter 11 debtors' cases, particularly those involving small to medium-sized transactions. *"Smart, with great experience,"* Wiliamson represented a major textile manufacturer in its recent reorganization.

INTELLECTUAL PROPERTY

Kilpatrick Stockton LLP
The Firm: This long-standing practice group remains one of the largest in the firm, if not the country. Based in Atlanta, its network of offices in places like DC and London help to ensure it has *"a terrific presence in IP."* The firm's recent merger with local IP boutique, Jones & Askew, has served to bolster its already strong profile. Competitors acknowledge that this is one of the few places in the state where you can find *"real breadth of IP expertise in a general practice firm."* The group possesses a wealth of contentious and noncontentious knowledge across the range of trademark, copyright and patent law. In particular, it is said to have a depth of copyright experience rarely seen in the region. The group also conducts IP counseling and litigation for service providers, goods manufacturers and suppliers, and acts as outside trademark counsel for a number of Fortune 500 companies. A keen focus on biotech issues is found here, and the team acts for key start-ups in the region.
The Lawyers: According to interviewees, trademark guru, and cochairman of the firm, **Miles Alexander** *"was practicing in IP before IP was cool."* *"He casts a long shadow"* over the market, and remains actively involved in market developments, despite now taking on more management responsibilities and an *"elder statesman"* role. **Tony Askew**'s arrival from Jones & Askew has boosted the team. Described as *"one of the deans of the patent bar,"* many agree that he is *"as good as they come."* Askew is best known for his patent, trademark and copyright litigation practice, though he also undertakes some trademark and patent counseling. **Jim Ewing**'s main focus is on

INTELLECTUAL PROPERTY — GEORGIA

GEORGIA
Leading firms (Intellectual Property)

1
- KILPATRICK STOCKTON LLP *Atlanta*
- NEEDLE & ROSENBERG *Atlanta*

2
- ALSTON & BIRD LLP *Atlanta*
- KING & SPALDING LLP *Atlanta*

3
- FINNEGAN HENDERSON FARABOW *Atlanta*
- SUTHERLAND ASBILL & BRENNAN LLP *Atlanta*
- TROUTMAN SANDERS LLP *Atlanta*

4
- POWELL, GOLDSTEIN, FRAZER *Atlanta*
- SMITH, GAMBRELL & RUSSELL LLP *Atlanta*
- THOMAS KAYDEN HORTSTEMEYER *Atlanta*

Leading individuals (Intellectual Property)

1
- ALEXANDER Miles *Kilpatrick Stockton LLP, Atlanta*
- NEEDLE Bill *Needle & Rosenberg, Atlanta*

2
- ASKEW Anthony *Kilpatrick Stockton LLP, Atlanta*
- BABER Bruce *King & Spalding LLP, Atlanta*
- BLACKSTOCK Jerry *Hunton & Williams, Atlanta*
- FLINN Patrick *Alston & Bird LLP, Atlanta*
- NODINE Larry *Needle & Rosenberg, Atlanta*

3
- BANKOFF Joseph *King & Spalding LLP, Atlanta*
- BECK Joseph *Kilpatrick Stockton LLP, Atlanta*
- EWING Jim *Kilpatrick Stockton LLP, Atlanta*

4
- ELGISON Martin *Alston & Bird LLP, Atlanta*
- HAWKINS Holmes *King & Spalding LLP, Atlanta*
- LUNSFORD Rodgers *Smith, Gambrell, Atlanta*
- ROSENBERG Sumner *Needle & Rosenberg, Atlanta*
- SALYERS Douglas *Troutman Sanders LLP, Atlanta*
- TAYLOR Roger *Finnegan Henderson, Atlanta*
- VANDERBROEK Mark *Troutman Sanders LLP, Atlanta*

5
- BREWSTER William *Kilpatrick Stockton LLP, Atlanta*
- FLEMING JD *Sutherland Asbill & Brennan LLP, Atlanta*
- JOHNSON Jim *Kilpatrick Stockton LLP, Atlanta*
- NORTH John *Sutherland Asbill & Brennan LLP, Atlanta*
- ROSENBLOUM Robert *Greenberg Traurig LLP, Atlanta*
- YOUNG Jeffrey *Alston & Bird LLP, Atlanta*

Firms and individuals are listed alphabetically in each band.

---

covenant issues. **Jim Johnson** (see p.207), respected for his work in the biochemical sphere, often advises on the IP issues relating to financings for start-ups and midlevel biotech companies, such as EntreMed, MetaMorphix, Bioniche Life Sciences and Sensor Medics. He has also directed the prosecution of patent applications for Angiostatin, Endostatin and Panzemä on behalf of Children's Hospital Harvard.

The Clients: The firm's impressive client base includes Van Der Bilt University; Smith & Nephew; BellSouth; Equifax; Delta Air Lines; Continental Airlines; Japan Airlines; Dotcast; BMG Entertainment; Houghton Mifflin Company; The Estate of Martin Luther King Jr; Sony Music Entertainment; Citigroup; Sara Lee; IMAX; Random House; GE; Acuity Brands; adidas; Waffle House; Harley-Davidson; General Mills; REM; DaimlerChrysler and Hewlett-Packard.

Needle & Rosenberg

The Firm: One of the largest dedicated IP boutiques in the Southeast. The group has an enviable reputation across the full range of patent, trademark and copyright litigation, based in part on its excellent track record in the federal and state courts. One commentator observed that *"the fine technical skills"* of its *"wonderful lawyers"* are what make the group so strong in understanding the complexity of IP issues. According to competitors, it is best known for its *"patent prosecution strength,"* winning a healthy share of the referrals market. However, the group stands out for its top-flight abilities in portfolio management and the litigation side of the practice. The group displays expertise in IP issues relating to electrical engineering, mechanical, software, biotech and chemical patent practices, and now serves many of the top 50 US chemical and pharmaceutical companies.

The Lawyers: **Bill Needle** (see p.208), the firm's founder, has practiced patent, trademark, copyright and trade secret law exclusively over his 32-year career. Peers appreciate his mix of practicality and technical skill, and consider him *"a clear leader of the patent lawyers in town."* Although Needle is best known for his patent practice, he is *"equally conversant with trademark and copyright issues."* Recognition of his prowess in this area is reflected in his appointment by US District Court judges to serve as a Special Master in patent infringement cases. **Larry Nodine** heads up the firm's copyright group. A *"true star,"* Nodine's breadth of expertise encompasses a particular aptitude for trademark and copyright work. *"Cerebral attorney"* **Sumner Rosenberg** has a patent practice focusing on computer software and hardware, and also acts in trademark protection. A *"technically skilled"* practitioner, he *"has won a lot of respect in the community,"* and interviewees reported that, although his profile is not as high as those of his two colleagues, many consider *"the quality of his work to be every bit as good."*

The Clients: Typical clients of the firm include University of Florida; Medical University of South Carolina; Shaw Industries Group and Original Appalachian Artworks.

Alston & Bird LLP

The Firm: The acquisition in 1997 of North Carolina IP boutique, Bell Seltzer Park & Gibson, effectively doubled the firm's practice in this area and brought in its previously lacking patent capability. Work is now evenly split between the North Carolina and Georgia offices, and rivals believe that this arrangement has worked well for the firm. *"The North Carolina backup has helped the Atlanta group build a superb patent litigation practice,"* said one. Sources claim that the firm's focus on this area also gives it an edge over the competition: *"Alston's group does IP 24/7 whereas with most other firms it merely forms part of their general practice."* The group covers the full range of patent, trademark and copyright matters, including IP-related antitrust. It enjoys particular strength in the technology sector, ably handling biotech, chemical, electronics and computer patent-related matters, assisting businesses in the protection and enforcement of their trademarks, domain names and copyrights. An IP transactional group, formed following the takeover of Bell Seltzer Park & Gibson, handles promotion and advertising agency agreements, and corporate financings involving IP assets.

The Lawyers: *"Impressive"* **Patrick Flinn** ploughs his energy into patent infringement litigation. He has carved out a reputation for the representation of patent owners and plaintiffs, especially in the resolution of technology-based disputes over patents, trade secrets and copyright matters. He represented Scientific-Atlanta in the enforcement of its patent portfolio, which encompasses technologies including RF cable transmission, Moving Pictures Experts Group (MPEG) encoding and other digital broadcast methods. Flinn also recently defended Diamond Power International, a subsidiary of The Babcock & Wilcox Company, in a patent infringement suit filed by Clyde Bergemann. **Marty Elgison** founded the firm's IP practice, and is currently the coordinator of its different IP groups. He has litigated every kind of IP case there is, but, over the past five years, has focused on counseling and transactional work. Observers credited him as *"experienced and respected"* in issues related to sports, the media and e-commerce. This is further reflected in his advice to trademark owners alleging infringement, including several famous marks in American sports. Recent recruit **Jeff Young** has a growing name as a *"good patent*

---

obtaining patent rights, and sources noted his strengths in IP strategy and portfolio management, and patent litigation. Also experienced in trademarks, trade secrets and copyright matters, peers consider him a *"superb and impressive"* practitioner. The group also boasts *"the reigning expert in copyright,"* **Joseph Beck** (see p.203), whose much admired practice is now taking on an increasingly international slant. He successfully defended Houghton Mifflin Company in the high-profile copyright infringement case brought by the estate of Margaret Mitchell (author of 'Gone with the Wind') against the publication of 'The Wind Done Gone'. **Bill Brewster** (see p.204), the firm's youthful managing partner, enjoys a *"particularly good reputation in the trademark area,"* though his practice also covers copyright and unfair competition and restrictive

GEORGIA

INTELLECTUAL PROPERTY

prosecutor," and is a valuable addition to the firm's mechanical patents group. He is active in protecting and enforcing IP rights in European countries, and analyzing the potential for enforcement of patents inside and outside the client's industry.
The Clients: The firm acts for a wealth of impressive names including: NASCAR; GE Capital; Sabre Holdings and its subsidiary Travelocity; Bertelsmann Group; AER Energy Resources; Six Continents Hotels; EGO North America; Peachtree Software; Sidel; Palmer & Cay; The Estate of Robert T (Bobby) Jones; Unitrin; UPS; Alpine Medical; Akeva LLC; Go Medical Industries; Emory University; Carquest and Beazer Homes USA.

King & Spalding LLP
see firm details p.829
The Firm: According to market sources *"you won't find any better than this outstanding law firm."* The firm has built upon its highly regarded litigation group, and, as competitors acknowledge, *"over the past few years it has been adding some true IP lawyers."* This level of growth has also been seen in New York, where the practice has developed its trademark expertise, ensuring a formidable national profile. The group in Georgia conducts both litigation and transactional work, and its expertise extends across such areas as protecting and enforcing the rights of the firm's software and media clients and research universities. The group has the resources to secure and enforce clients' trademarks and copyrights worldwide, and has defended against patent, trademark and copyright suits across the US.
The Lawyers: *"An excellent litigator,"* **Bruce Baber** (see p.203) heads the IP group, and brings to it his background in general dispute resolution. His work covers the range of copyright and patent litigation, though some competitors consider that his greatest presence is in the trademark sphere. Much of his caseload takes him outside of Georgia, and he has been involved in adversarial patent and trademark proceedings before the International Trade Commission (ITC) in DC, and the US Patent and Trademark Office (USPTO). He recently represented a beverage company in a trademark and trade dress infringement action in a federal court in Alabama. Also acted for an Atlanta real estate developer in an action also in a federal court to enforce its exclusive rights to the federally registered name of a well-known, multi-use real estate development. **Joseph Bankoff** (see p.203) is an experienced trial lawyer, whose *"great courtroom presence"* has impressed many of our interviewees. They acknowledge that *"he knows his way around the block on patent litigation,"* and that he skillfully handles the overlap between antitrust and IP. He is experienced in multi-district patent litigation, relating to software, copyright, trade secrets and distribution channels. Bankoff represented Scientific-Atlanta as lead counsel in a complex case involving 200 other lawyers. **Holmes Hawkins** (see p.206) is a skilled patent litigator with federal court expertise in a range of hi-tech cases. He acted for a leading provider of enterprise software to the financial services industry in an alleged breach of development agreements. Also represented an Atlanta-based software company in a patent infringement action involving web-based strategic e-sourcing solutions.
The Clients: The firm's typical clients include Scientific-Atlanta; UPS; Digimark; Coca-Cola; Carvel; SeeBeyond Technology; Visa USA; FleetBoston Financial; Providian Financial; S1; EMS Technologies; Mercer University and Dornier MedTech.

Finnegan Henderson Farabow Garrett & Dunner LLP
The Firm: This large IP boutique has its primary base in DC, which provides a valuable source of work for the smaller Atlanta team. It is most visible in the field of patents, where competitors acknowledge that it is *"particularly good at getting patent rights and defending them."* Alongside acquiring, licensing and enforcing their clients' patents, the *"excellent lawyers"* here are experienced in trademarks, copyrights and trade secrets work. Sources note that the firm *"has grown fairly steadily,"* winning a respected profile in the state.
The Lawyers: Patent and trademark lawyer **Roger Taylor** has impressed peers as a *"smart, astute"* attorney who *"keeps his feet on the ground."*

Sutherland Asbill & Brennan LLP
see firm details p.887
The Firm: Researchers were told that the IP team here is quite a recent development, but that the firm has now *"gained a fine reputation."* It benefited from the breakup of IP boutique Jones & Askew, taking on a team of their lawyers, and has since recruited more people, including a couple from Alston & Bird. Much of the firm's trademark strength is in its DC office, but the larger IP group in Atlanta enjoys a greater patent and copyright capacity. Together they offer a full range of contentious and noncontentious IP services, particularly those related to complex technical fields including biotechnology, pharmaceuticals, computer law, chemical technology, telecommunications and minerals.
The Lawyers: According to clients, **JD Fleming** (see p.205) is *"the ultimate professional."* He is *"perceptive, balanced and candid in his presentation of the facts"* and *"works well with in-house counsel"* while being *"wonderfully eloquent in court."* An IP litigation specialist, he concentrates on patent protection and infringement litigation, copyright, and interference practice. He acted in the high-profile 'The Wind Done Gone' copyright infringement case, where he was assigned to file an amicus brief. His caseload of late has included hi-tech matters, such as serving as lead counsel to Gemstar in a multi-district patent dispute centered around a consolidated group of patent infringement cases brought by a number of companies, including Scientific-Atlanta, concerning set-top boxes. Defended Mineral Technologies' division Specialty Minerals Inc. (SMI) in a patent infringement case regarding Omya's chemically precipitated calcium carbonate (PCC) production. **John North** (see p.209) heads the firm's IP group, and concentrates on litigation, principally patent infringement and trade secret misappropriation, as well as related antitrust issues. Many of his clients are outside Georgia, but his visibility within the state is increasing with high-profile cases in Atlanta. In one such instance, he served as lead counsel for an international telecom company in a set of patent cases currently pending in Georgia, a matter that also involves antitrust claims against the client.
The Clients: Lanier Worldwide; GE Power Systems; Jordan Outdoor Enterprises; Coca-Cola; Specialty Minerals Inc. (SMI); Gemstar; Ford; Dow Chemical; Minerals Technologies and Burlington Industries.

Troutman Sanders LLP
The Firm: This small IP group is a relative newcomer to the market. It offers a full range of legal services in the IP sphere, with a focus on litigation. Market sources say that they are *"trying hard"* and are *"visible in a number of important cases."*
The Lawyers: **Doug Salyers** is active in patent work, representing defendants in matters such as patent infringement actions. Competitors consider him a *"really impressive"* IP litigator, with the skill and knowledge to get *"great results for his clients."* The firm's highest profile name on the trademark side is litigator **Mark VanderBroek** (see p.211).
The Clients: The group advises national corporates and local businesses, often drawn from the hi-tech community.

Powell, Goldstein, Frazer & Murphy LLP
The Firm: The team here has long-standing experience in the protection of IP rights. It occupies a niche in the technology arena, working with a number of telecom companies and biotech groups, and has considerable expertise in the structure, negotiation and implementation of licenses, IP enforcement and portfolio management. The firm operates a technology and IP litigation group, headed by Bill Ragland (who is president-elect of the Atlanta Bar Association for Spring 2003), and a technology and IP transactions group, led by Scott

INTELLECTUAL PROPERTY — GEORGIA

Killingsworth. The latter group is notably adept at detailed IP counseling and is dedicated to assisting clients in maximizing the value of their IP and technology assets. The group as a whole is felt to have lost some profile recently with the departure of Jerry Blackstock to Hunton & Williams, the impact bearing on IP litigation. One recent successful matter, however, came when the litigation group represented AudioFAX IP in a patent infringement case against Cisco Systems involving AudioFAX's pioneering fax-processing technology. Cisco took a license to AudioFAX's patents, and a consent judgment of patent validity and enforceability was entered by the U.S. District Court. Over 25 licenses have now been obtained for AudioFAX, including other recent cases and license deals with Sprint and 3Com.

The Clients: The firm regularly serves as counsel in anticounterfeiting and trademark enforcement actions for Rolex, Louis Vuitton, Tommy Hilfiger, Burberry Limited and Oakley. The group also advises biotech groups, and telecom and IT companies.

Smith, Gambrell & Russell LLP

The Firm: The firm boasts a small but popular IP team, which sources acknowledge is making an impact on the market with its sophisticated, high-quality advice. Much of its work involves assisting clients with the protection of inventions and the development of patent portfolios. The group also advises on the availability of trademarks, service marks and copyrights. On the contentious side, it has experience of IP and unfair competition disputes in administrative agencies and state and federal courts.

The Lawyers: Rodgers Lunsford has a good name in the market, especially for nonpatent litigation. According to interviewees, he is *"always there in trademark litigation,"* and he conducts a substantial number of broader IP disputes throughout the US. He also supervises litigation abroad and counsels clients in IP registrations and trademark matters.

Thomas Kayden Hortstemeyer & Risley LLP

The Firm: Market sources commend this IP boutique for its experience in the electrical and software sectors. Managing partner Scott Horstemeyer heads the team of *"young, talented lawyers,"* some of whom have degrees in electrical, mechanical or computer engineering, giving the group real depth of understanding of the technical issues. Interviewees note that it engages in *"a volume of patent application work"* and is active in both trademark and license procurement. The team also acts in litigation on behalf of its clients.

The Clients: The firm advises a number of patent agents.

Other Notable Practitioners

Jerry Blackstock has recently joined Hunton & Williams from Powell, Goldstein, Frazer & Murphy LLP. Peers consider him *"one of the great Atlanta IP lawyers"* with a *"pragmatic attitude"* and *"good judgment."* He recently acted as lead trial counsel for the defense in the Riverwood International v RA Jones & Co case, successfully gaining a unanimous jury decision invalidating Riverwood's claim that three of Jones' drinks packaging machines violated their patents. He also acts for, inter alia, Personalized Media Communications, Integrity Media, Siemens Diematic, Earthlink, GlaxoSmithKline and RLI Insurance Company. Sources say that his presence is expected to put Hunton & Williams firmly on the IP map in Georgia. **Robert Rosenbloum** (see p.209) of Greenberg Traurig LLP is considered to be an *"excellent young copyright attorney."* He excels in transactional entertainment-related IP matters, including negotiating licensing and merchandising agreements in the entertainment, software and technology fields. He also provides trademark and unfair competition counseling to a client list that includes Microsoft, Univision Music Group, MuchMusic USA, ARTISTdirect Records, and various recording artists such as Jimmy Buffett and Shaggy.

LITIGATION — GENERAL COMMERCIAL

GEORGIA
Leading firms
(Litigation: General Commercial)

1
- ALSTON & BIRD LLP *Atlanta*
- KING & SPALDING LLP *Atlanta*

2
- BONDURANT, MIXSON & ELMORE LLP *Atlanta*
- KILPATRICK STOCKTON LLP *Atlanta*
- ROGERS & HARDIN *Atlanta*
- SUTHERLAND ASBILL & BRENNAN LLP *Atlanta*

3
- DOFFERMYRE, SHIELDS, CANFIELD *Atlanta*
- POWELL, GOLDSTEIN, FRAZER *Atlanta*
- TROUTMAN SANDERS LLP *Atlanta*

Firms are listed alphabetically in each band.

Alston & Bird LLP

The Firm: Possesses vast resources and operates with a clear focus on client service. Peers agreed that this premier firm has an *"admirable track record"* in complex national and international business disputes. The practice is well equipped for controversies of any type, but was highlighted for its leading position in securities class actions and medical malpractice defense matters.

The Lawyers: *"At the top of the list,"* **Judson Graves** was warmly endorsed by observers as an *"accomplished"* business trial litigator. Graves represents MAG Mutual Insurance Company and Grady Memorial Hospital and has acted for the Earnhardt family in its high-profile dispute over autopsy photographs of Dale Earnhardt. **Oscar Persons** has built a *"powerful reputation"* in securities class action defense on behalf of clients such as Scientific-Atlanta and Claris Corporation.

Peter Bassett is another eminent securities litigator, who has distinguished himself in work related to the Securities Act of 1933 and Securities Exchange Act of 1934. He recently defended a major healthcare corporation against a financial disclosure class action filed in Alabama.

The Clients: UPS; Verizon; Bank of America; HealthSouth; Dow Chemical; Cox Communications; Georgia-Pacific; Genuine Parts Company; Alcoa; Delta Air Lines; Prudential Insurance Company of America; WestPoint Stevens; Providian; Vulcan Materials Company; GlaxoSmithKline and 3M.

King & Spalding LLP

see firm details p.829

The Firm: A litigation powerhouse with an edge in *"sophisticated and challenging"* business disputes. Peers commended its deep bench of trial-savvy litigators who are experienced in matters spanning *"antitrust to securities and most things in-between."* Particular strengths include products liability and personal injury defense, toxic and environmental torts and general contract disputes.

The Lawyers: **Byron Attridge** (see p.202) maintains a broad practice that increasingly emphasizes appellate work, and rivals applauded his *"vigor in tackling complex cases."* His recent appellate matters include a bond contract case on behalf of St. Paul Insurance and a products liability case for Volkswagen. **Michael Russ** (see p.210) is an *"extremely organized and meticulous"* litigator who coordinates many of the firm's substantial cases. After years of representing Coca-Cola in trial and appellate matters, Russ is now recognized for his skill in handling complex antitrust matters. He recently represented a textile manufacturer in an arbitrated insurance dispute. **Chilton Varner** (see p.211) is acknowledged as

GEORGIA

LITIGATION

GEORGIA
Leading individuals
(Litigation: General Commercial)

1
- BONDURANT Emmet *Bondurant, Mixson*, Atlanta
- DALTON John *Troutman Sanders LLP*, Atlanta
- GRAVES Judson *Alston & Bird LLP*, Atlanta
- MARSHALL John *Powell, Goldstein, Frazer*, Atlanta
- ROGERS CB *Rogers & Hardin*, Atlanta
- SINKFIELD Richard *Rogers & Hardin*, Atlanta

2
- ATTRIDGE Byron *King & Spalding LLP*, Atlanta
- CHANDLER John *Sutherland Asbill*, Atlanta
- PERSONS Oscar *Alston & Bird LLP*, Atlanta
- RUSS Michael *King & Spalding LLP*, Atlanta
- VARNER Chilton *King & Spalding LLP*, Atlanta

3
- BASSETT Peter *Alstn & Bird LLP*, Atlanta
- BOICE William *Kilpatrick Stockton LLP*, Atlanta
- BUTLER James *Butler, Wooten, Fryhofer*, Columbus
- CAHOON Susan *Kilpatrick Stockton LLP*, Atlanta
- CLAY Stephens *Kilpatrick Stockton LLP*, Atlanta
- FLEMING John *Sutherland Asbill & Brennan*, Atlanta
- HAYNES Joseph *King & Spalding LLP*, Atlanta
- SHIELDS Robert *Doffermyre, Shields*, Atlanta

Individuals are listed alphabetically in each band.

---

the leader of *"one of the best products liability defense teams in the country."* *"A brilliant lawyer and strategist,"* she impresses with her *"effective courtroom demeanor."* In addition to her role as GlaxoSmithKline's national counsel for the anti-depressant Seroxat/Paxil, Varner recently defended Purdue Pharma in mass tort litigation related to the painkiller OxyContin. Described to researchers as *"thoroughly ethical,"* **Joseph Haynes** (see p.206) is a general business litigator skilled in securities and accounting malpractice matters. Haynes represented Arthur Andersen in the collapse of Golden Bear, and was appointed liaison counsel for the cigarette industry in an alleged price-fixing case arising out of wholesale pricing practices.

The Clients: Schering-Plough; GM; ExxonMobil; GE; 3M; UPS; GlaxoSmithKline; Honeywell; Georgia-Pacific; Hercules; UCAR International; Coca-Cola; Jefferson-Pilot; MassMutual; Chevron-Texaco; Milliken & Company; Brown & Williamson Tobacco and Ernst & Young.

Bondurant, Mixson & Elmore LLP

The Firm: *"Marshaled to take on high-quality work,"* the firm was described to researchers as *"undoubtedly the best-established litigation boutique in Georgia."* Its team of 23 litigators has a reputation for tenacious representation whether in defense or prosecution. Highlights include a landmark jury verdict in the Six Flags business tort litigation, and a $192.5 million settlement in an employment discrimination class action brought against Coca-Cola.

The Lawyers: The firm's *"rainmaker,"* **Emmet Bondurant** (see p.203), was universally endorsed as a *"cerebral"* attorney *"who takes the time to find the silver bullet."* Bondurant's broad practice has a subspecialization in complex antitrust disputes. He defended Michelin North America against a tortious interference claim, and represented Golden Peanut Company at the appellate level in a major breach of contract claim.

The Clients: Avon Products; Bed Bath & Beyond; Brink's Home Security; Conoco; Delta Air Lines; Four M; Lincare; Michelin North America; Primerica Financial Services and the State of Georgia.

Kilpatrick Stockton LLP

The Firm: Commentators agreed that this firm remains active across a diverse spread of commercial litigation, and boasts a number of respected attorneys in its ranks. Recent matters handled by the team include major contract disputes on behalf of BellSouth and a series of commercial arbitrations in respect of heavy industrial equipment and IT outsourcing.

The Lawyers: **William Boice** is a tactical litigator with the capacity to *"identify the winning strategic themes in a case."* Respected for his class action defense work, he has defeated the certification of a class action involving thousands of potential plaintiffs in the Northern District of Georgia. **Susan Cahoon** is thought to be as *"solid as a rock, and highly analytical."* Her practice includes business disputes arising out of breaches of licensing agreements. Cahoon represented the Oklahoma Medical Research Foundation in a large breach of contract and patent infringement dispute related to the sepsis drug Xigris. Interviewees described **Stephens Clay** as a *"savvy lawyer"* who litigates in a *"patrician style."* He is active in IP, antitrust and products liability litigation, as well as in arbitrations and mediations. Clay represented a large Atlanta hospital in a business tort claim brought against a neighboring hospital.

The Clients: BellSouth; Equifax; DuPont; Massachusetts Water Resource Authority; Odebrecht Construction; Cingular Wireless; RJ Reynolds; Krispy Kreme; Sara Lee; Delta Air Lines and Lockheed Martin.

Rogers & Hardin

The Firm: Litigation and corporate matters form the bedrock of this mid-sized firm, but the development of other niche areas has impressed many interviewees. Peers commended the firm's civil trial practice for its *"impressive resumé"* in areas ranging from broker-dealer and insurance litigation to complex antitrust disputes.

The Lawyers: Veteran litigator **CB Rogers** is a *"role model"* for attorneys in this field and is thought to bring *"great analytical depth"* to sophisticated disputes. He defended a major national investment bank in litigation arising out of the WorldCom collapse, and successfully represented a group of finance companies seeking to enjoin several local governments from enforcing ordinances related to predatory and other lending practices. Rogers' success is felt to have been equaled in recent years by his colleague **Richard Sinkfield** (see p.210). *"The quintessential trial lawyer,"* Sinkfield has built his reputation on a *"magnificent courtroom presence"* that opponents concede has left them with *"a lot of scar tissue."* He defended Arthur Andersen against claims made by creditors of its former clients, and a major nursing home provider in connection with patient care cost accounting and alleged unfair trade practices claims.

The Clients: Transit Communications; T2 Medical; Policy Management Systems; Southeast Hotel Properties and Florida Hotel Properties.

Sutherland Asbill & Brennan LLP
see firm details p.887

The Firm: Endorsed for its capabilities in all aspects of traditional business litigation, this *"respected outfit"* has developed specialties in school funding litigation and accountants' and other professional liability.

The Lawyers: **John Chandler** (see p.204) is a *"sharp and courageous"* attorney who has built a *"top-rate"* reputation defending accounting and law firms in *"tough"* malpractice and securities fraud cases. Chandler also represents State Farm, recently defending it in a diminished value class action that settled in 2002. Interviewees also singled out **John Fleming** (see p.206) as a general commercial litigator who brings a *"strong intellectual component"* to his caseload. He is best known for his long-standing representation of Ford, and handles a broad array of matters including franchise and tax litigation. He represented Ford in a class action brought by 160 former truck dealers.

The Clients: Ford; Ford Motor Credit; Gemstar-TV Guide; InterGen; Rinker Materials; KPMG; PwC; Ernst & Young and State Farm. Also advises major law firms in Atlanta and New York.

Doffermyre, Shields, Canfield, Knowles & Devine

The Firm: Interviewees commended this team of *"ethical and effective"* attorneys who *"bring a lot of passion to their work."* Although emphasizing medical malpractice, personal injury and products liability work, the firm also undertakes a fair amount of toxic tort and general business litigation.

The Lawyers: The *"leading light"* of the practice, **Robert Shields** (see p.210), won high praise from opponents as a *"craftsman"* whose *"technical aptitude and non-bombastic"* courtroom manner ensure his high profile. While Shields' practice embraces personal injury, medical malpractice

REAL ESTATE — GEORGIA

and toxic torts litigation, he is widely respected for being *"capable of trying any kind of case."*
The Clients: The firm advises local, national and international corporates.

Powell, Goldstein, Frazer & Murphy LLP

The Firm: Its litigation services cover a range of commercial areas including banking, securities and general business disputes as well as products liability and professional liability matters.
The Lawyers: The firm's reputation for quality litigation derives from the *"phenomenal"* stature of *"big-hitter"* **John Marshall** (see p.208). Interviewees agreed that in addition to his *"excellent judgment"* and conversance with technical areas of the law, Marshall's greatest asset is the credibility he enjoys before both appellate and trial judiciaries. His recent practice has included banking litigation and defense of malpractice suits brought against members of the legal profession.
The Clients: Fortune 500 companies; banks; real estate companies and law firms in Georgia.

Troutman Sanders LLP

The Firm: Renowned for its representation of energy and entertainment clients, this commercial litigation practice was credited with *"strong capabilities"* in complex 'bet-the-company' types of cases.
The Lawyers: Peers described **John Dalton** as *"articulate without being pretentious, aggressive without being offensive and bright without being pedantic."* He was singled out for his strong examination skills and *"tireless"* attention to files. He represented Time Warner Entertainment in its appeal against the jury verdict in the Six Flags Over Georgia litigation, and defended Court TV in a high-profile case brought by the family of a murder victim.
The Clients: CNN; Court TV; Time Warner Entertainment and John Portman.

Other Notable Practitioners

"One of the strongest plaintiff attorneys in the state, if not the country," **James Butler** of Butler, Wooten, Fryhofer, Daughtery & Sullivan LLP was described to researchers as *"a real nemesis of corporate America."* A tenacious advocate, Butler's practice in business torts, products liability and environmental cases has yielded some of the largest awards in Georgian history. Butler acted for a number of investors in the Six Flags litigation.

REAL ESTATE

GEORGIA
Leading firms (Real Estate)

1. **KING & SPALDING LLP** Atlanta
2. **ALSTON & BIRD LLP** Atlanta
3. **KILPATRICK STOCKTON LLP** Atlanta
   SUTHERLAND ASBILL & BRENNAN LLP Atlanta
4. **HOLT NEY ZATCOFF & WASSERMAN LLP** Atlanta
   MCKENNA LONG & ALDRIDGE Atlanta
   POWELL, GOLDSTEIN, FRAZER & MURPHY Atlanta
   TROUTMAN SANDERS LLP Atlanta

Leading individuals (Real Estate)

1. **STEPHENSON Mason** King & Spalding LLP, Atlanta
2. **ADAMS Al** Sutherland Asbill & Brennan LLP, Atlanta
   ARNOLD Scott King & Spalding LLP, Atlanta
   CARSSOW Tim Kilpatrick Stockton LLP, Atlanta
   GRIFFIN John Troutman Sanders LLP, Atlanta
   PAKENHAM Tim Alston & Bird LLP, Atlanta
   PARKS John Powell, Goldstein, Frazer, Atlanta
3. **ADDISON James** Troutman Sanders LLP, Atlanta
   ALDRIDGE John McKenna Long & Aldridge, Atlanta
   FRYER William King & Spalding LLP, Atlanta
   HOLT Robert Holt Ney Zatcoff & Wasserman, Atlanta
   HYATT Wayne Hyatt & Stubblefield PC, Atlanta
   JORDAN James Sutherland Asbill & Brennan, Atlanta
   KAUSS Andrew Kilpatrick Stockton LLP, Atlanta
   NEY James Holt Ney Zatcoff & Wasserman, Atlanta
   RUSCHE Mark Alston & Bird LLP, Atlanta
   THOMPSON William Powell, Goldstein, Atlanta

Firms and individuals are listed alphabetically in each band.

King & Spalding LLP
see firm details p.829
The Firm: A combination of a steady flow of sophisticated transactions and the high profile of its leading practitioners has given this *"outstanding"* firm an edge over its competitors. Commentators identified the firm's particular strengths in equity investment and secured financings on behalf of institutional investors, although *"they do excellent traditional real estate and development work, too."*
The Lawyers: **Mason Stephenson** (see p.210) is a *"heavy hitter"* who brings a *"gentlemanly"* demeanor to his transactional practice, the bulk of which comprises multi-property, multi-jurisdictional transactions for GE Capital Real Estate and sale and leasing work on behalf of Technology Park/Atlanta. Stephenson also advised on the Kimco Realty Opportunity Portfolio, a joint venture between GE Capital Real Estate and Kimco Realty to acquire $1 billion worth of real estate. *"Terrifically talented, hardworking and diligent,"* **Scott Arnold** (see p.202) supports a more traditional, development practice on behalf of clients including Hines and Reynolds Plantation. Arnold's recent practice also involved the formation of REITs on behalf of The Brookvale Group, Kuwait Finance House and William E Simons & Sons Realty. With a practice split between Atlanta and New York, **William Fryer** (see p.206) was commended to researchers as a *"brilliant corporate strategist"* specializing in REITs and capital markets transactions on behalf of clients in the real estate industry. He advised on the formation of the Lend Lease Global Properties investment fund and on the acquisition of 1290 Avenue of the Americas.
The Clients: Hines; Lend Lease Real Estate Investments; The Brookvale Group; William E Simon & Sons Realty; Reynolds Plantation; GE Capital Real Estate; Post Properties; Edens & Avant; ING Clarion; RECAP; Kuwait Finance House and Cornerstone Properties.

Alston & Bird LLP
The Firm: *"Among the pick of the firms if you're looking for depth and experience."* This large Atlanta-based firm has assembled a *"first-rate"* real estate practice with specialties in both institutional investment and the development and ownership of industrial and hotel properties.
The Lawyers: A team of *"fine real estate lawyers"* is headed by **Tim Pakenham** (see p.209), a *"strong"* attorney who has *"distinguished himself nicely"* in his representation of Home Depot and Six Continents Hotels. He is representing Home Depot cofounder Bernard Marcus in the building of a 250,000 sq ft aquarium in Atlanta. Although his practice also covers acquisitions, dispositions and joint venture formation, **Mark Rusche** is recognized as a leading specialist in complex commercial leasing. One client described him as possessing *"the expertise, talent and personality to be able to shift between geographical areas to consummate a transaction."* Rusche is lead real estate attorney for KPMG in its transactions in the southeastern US, and advises Prudential Real Estate Investors in connection with acquisitions and joint ventures relating to senior housing projects.
The Clients: Bank of America; Home Depot; INVESCO; KPMG; Lend Lease Real Estate Investments; Pacific Life Insurance Company; Prudential Real Estate Investors; Six Continents Hotels; UPS and Verizon.

GEORGIA

REAL ESTATE

Kilpatrick Stockton LLP
The Firm: *"A significant participant in the market,"* this firm is distinguished by its hardball negotiating style and technical acumen. Among other matters, the firm recently advised on the Lindbergh City Center project in Atlanta and set up a $225 million investment fund on behalf of Avanti Properties Group.
The Lawyers: *"Hard as nails but enormously capable,"* **Tim Carssow** brings a *"global"* perspective to transactions. His practice involves a mixture of zoning and real estate work with recent highlights including the One Glenlake office building and a multi-use development with a novel ownership structure in Atlanta. **Andrew Kauss** is a detail-oriented attorney known for fiercely representing his clients. His practice encompasses development, real estate investment, capital formation and major commercial office transactions. Recent matters include development of a 3.5 million sq ft office space for BellSouth in the Atlanta metropolitan area and a headquarters lease for Cingular Wireless.
The Clients: Wachovia Bank; Avanti Properties Group; ING; GMAC; BellSouth; Carter & Associates; Cingular Wireless; Pope & Land Enterprises and Retail Planning Corporation.

Sutherland Asbill & Brennan LLP
see firm details p.887
The Firm: *"Highly respected in Atlanta,"* this comprehensive practice shines brightest in the areas of retail, mixed-use, hotel and resort development, and timberland investment and finance. The strength of the firm reflects the reputations of two *"superb"* practitioners who perform *"fine work for some good clients"* including Home Depot and Sembler Retail.
The Lawyers: Al Adams (see p.202) has forged his name representing entrepreneurial clients in *"innovative deals that are off the beaten path."* Clients endorsed him as *"extremely bright, insightful and always available."* Recent projects include the Mall of Georgia and the Piazza at Paces mixed-use development. Lauded for his *"technical proficiency, speed and good judgment,"* **Jim Jordan**'s (see p.207) practice emphasizes development and leasing on behalf of clients in the retail arena. Jordan advises Home Depot in respect of its EXPO design centers and acted for Holder Properties in connection with the Millenium in Midtown office project.
The Clients: Home Depot; Sembler Retail; Ben Carter Properties; Holder Properties; Six Continents Hotels; Florida State Board of Administration; Wachovia Bank; CapMark Services; Martin Marietta Materials; UBS Realty Advisors; Starwood Urban Investments; Cornerstone Realty Advisors; Patillo Construction; Ronus Properties and Westbrook Partners.

Holt Ney Zatcoff & Wasserman LLP
The Firm: *"Development-oriented,"* but serving financier and banking and insurance clients also, this boutique firm is perceived as a *"good old Southern practice"* that *"sticks to its knitting."*
The Lawyers: *"An effective deal-maker,"* **Robert Holt** represents developers and investors in a range of residential and commercial real estate projects. He recently represented a group of Dutch investors providing a mezzanine loan for construction of a Dallas apartment project. **James Ney** is a *"good technician"* whose practice emphasizes zoning, land use and general commercial real estate transactions on behalf of clients in a range of sectors including the telecom industry. He has advised a mid-sized Californian investment trust and other developer clients in their acquisitions and financings in the Atlanta area.
The Clients: Childress Klein Properties; Coca-Cola; Trammell Crow Residential; Equity Office Properties Trust; Gables Residential Trust; Highwoods Properties; Lincoln Property; Ohio Teachers' Retirement Fund and Starwood Capital Group.

McKenna Long & Aldridge
The Firm: Although the firm *"covers the spectrum"* of commercial real estate, its *"strong, good-sized"* practice is most identified with workout and conduit lending work on behalf of banks, insurance companies, pension funds and risk capital investors.
The Lawyers: John Aldridge is a *"clear specialist"* in the financial restructuring of distressed real estate projects. He maintains a broad national and international practice on behalf of investment banks, financial institutions and other investors. Aldridge recently restructured a major loan by a New York investment bank on an industrial warehouse project in Poland and a loan by a US company on a Manhattan office building.
The Clients: Column Financial; GMAC Commercial Mortgage; JPMorgan Mortgage Capital; KSL Recreation; Lehman Brothers Holdings; Lennar Corporation; Midland Loan Services; Morgan Stanley Real Estate Funds; PNC Bank; The Mills Corporation; Wachovia Bank and Prudential Mortgage Capital Company.

Powell, Goldstein, Frazer & Murphy LLP
The Firm: The firm is recognized as *"one of the big firms in town"* with a robust real estate practice embracing niches in affordable housing, public transportation and hospitality.
The Lawyers: *"As good as anybody around,"* **John Parks** won plaudits for his *"terrific"* real estate lending, transactional and M&A work. He acted for ING in a $125 million loan secured by six regional shopping centers. *"Senior statesman"* **William Thompson** now concentrates on healthcare real estate transactions for clients including Northside Hospital.
The Clients: Pulte Homes; ING; Bank of America; Compass Bank; Bank of North Georgia; AIMCO; Metropolitan Atlanta Rapid Transit Authority; Trammell Crow Residential; International Paper and insurance companies.

Troutman Sanders LLP
The Firm: With strengths in large project development, commercial leasing and real estate lending, this diverse practice possesses a number of exceptional attorneys and an enviable stable of clients.
The Lawyers: John Griffin is an *"outstanding technician"* known for representing entrepreneurial clients across the gamut of real estate transactional work. He recently advised Wells Capital on both the Windy Point project and the Dana Corporation facilities, and represented Cousins Properties on transactions including the Avenue Concept shopping center in West Cobb, just outside Atlanta. **Jim Addison** is a *"detail-oriented and thorough"* attorney excelling in finance transactions on behalf of borrowers.
The Clients: Bank of America; Cousins Properties; Chick-fil-A and Wells Capital.

Other Notable Practitioners
A *"true national expert,"* **Wayne Hyatt** of Hyatt & Stubblefield, PC is *"preeminent"* in the specialist area of planned communities including residential, commercial and resort condominiums, large mixed-use developments, golf course communities and destination resorts.

TAX

GEORGIA

TAX

GEORGIA
Leading firms (Tax)

1. **ALSTON & BIRD LLP** Atlanta
   SUTHERLAND ASBILL & BRENNAN LLP Atlanta
2. **KING & SPALDING LLP** Atlanta
3. **CHAMBERLAIN, HRDLICKA, WHITE** Atlanta
4. **KILPATRICK STOCKTON LLP** Atlanta
   POWELL, GOLDSTEIN, FRAZER Atlanta

Leading individuals (Tax)

1. **AUGHTRY** David *Chamberlain, Hrdlicka,* Atlanta
   COALSON John *Alston & Bird LLP,* Atlanta
   COHEN Jerold *Sutherland Asbill & Brennan,* Atlanta
   WOODWARD Robert *King & Spalding,* Atlanta
2. **BLOOM** Herschel *King & Spalding LLP,* Atlanta
   COOK Philip *Alston & Bird LLP,* Atlanta
3. **ALLEN** Pinney *Alston & Bird LLP,* Atlanta
   HASSON James *Sutherland Asbill,* Atlanta
   WASSERMAN Michael *Holt Ney Zatcoff,* Atlanta
   WHITE Benjamin *Alston & Bird LLP,* Atlanta
4. **ABRAMS** Harold *Kilpatrick Stockton LLP,* Atlanta
   BEAUDROT Charles *Morris, Manning,* Atlanta
   BRADLEY William *Sutherland Asbill,* Atlanta
   CLARK Reginald *Sutherland Asbill,* Atlanta
   CRISAFI Frank *Powell, Goldstein, Frazer,* Atlanta
   HARRIS Morton *Hatcher, Stubbs, Land,* Columbus
   THROWER Randolph *Sutherland Asbill,* Atlanta

Firms and individuals are listed alphabetically in each band.

Alston & Bird LLP

The Firm: *"Strong across the board,"* the 50-lawyer team consistently delivered breadth and depth to clients, according to competitors. Its expertise spans transactional matters, international tax planning, legislative and regulatory issues and dispute resolution.

The Lawyers: Distinguished among the firm's *"array of talented people,"* **John Coalson** has established *"national prominence"* in tackling complex state and local tax matters, with a focus on unclaimed properties. He won a case for Delta Air Lines, establishing its right to claim Georgia's state tax exemption for certain manufactured goods and saving his client millions of dollars. **Philip Cook** is described by peers as being *"thorough, efficient and incredibly responsive to clients."* He led a precedent-setting courtroom battle to obtain IRS deductions on sales commissions for Verizon. He also advised several banks on cross-border leverage leases. Cochair of the firm's tax section is **Pinney Allen** (see p.202), said to be a *"crackerjack"* lawyer with a *"darn good"* record of solving complex federal tax structural problems involving M&A. He is skilled in the movement and redeployment of assets in order to achieve corporate goals. **Benjamin White** *"wows people"* by using what clients called his *"fantastic"* analytical skills to devise solutions to problems that other attorneys have dismissed as unsolvable. Clients say that *" he always has your best interests at heart"* in his specialist practice of tax planning for charitable organizations. In addition to Duke University, J Bulow Campbell Foundation and Coca-Cola Foundation, he also advises some of the wealthiest individuals in the region, who have assets worth billions.

The Clients: Bank of America; Bertelsmann; Prudential; UPS; Panasonic USA; Bose; CNN and Home Depot.

Sutherland Asbill & Brennan LLP
see firm details p.887

The Firm: An *"army of tax lawyers renowned for their toughness,"* the group was said by competitors to be the first contact for controversial or complex tax litigation.

The Lawyers: **Jerold Cohen** (see p.204), a former chief counsel to the IRS, won a landmark case for Ingram Industries that resulted in the deduction of the cost of maintaining barge towboats. The decision overturned a previous IRS demand for $2.46 million. **James Hasson** (see p.206) is *"as good as they come"* in tax planning for charitable organizations. He handled a $300 million tax-exempt bond financing transaction for Duke University. A specialist in controversial matters, Hasson has expertise in corporate sponsorship payments, executive compensations and government reimbursements to healthcare providers. A national timber tax specialist, **William Bradley**'s (see p.203) dexterity extends beyond that niche due to what clients described as his combination of *"extremely competent"* negotiation skills and *"a great deal of integrity."* He argued before the US Courts of Appeals in a closely watched case involving methods of claiming depletion on timber properties. **Reginald Clark** (see p.204), whose work attains *"high standards,"* earned commendations from competitors for transactional work such as acquisitions and restructurings. **Randolph Thrower** (see p.210), the *"ambassador"* of the firm, represented the Muscogee County Homeowners and Nonprofit Foundation, which was challenging a 19-year-old property tax assessment freeze.

The Clients: Nortel Networks; Coca-Cola Enterprises; Procter & Gamble; Philip Morris and Forest Capital Partners.

King & Spalding LLP
see firm details p.829

The Firm: Dovetailing with the firm's stunning corporate presence, its tax group was singled out by competitors as one of the best on the transactional side of federal tax law. The firm has expertise in M&A, international tax planning and controversy work.

The Lawyers: Among the throng of former US Treasury and IRS officials in this firm is highflier **Bob Woodward** (see p.211), who was recommended by peers and clients for his *"commanding presence"* and *"breadth of experience."* Woodward specializes in esoteric tax work such as off-balance sheet financing. The primary go-to tax lawyer for blue-chip clients such as Lockheed Martin, Woodward advised the company on tax matters when it acquired Comsat. Peers hailed **Herschel Bloom** (see p.203) as *"a good businessman as well as a talented lawyer."* His diverse practice includes advising corporations, for example UPS, and defending companies against both criminal investigations by the IRS and tax controversies by the State of Georgia. But his pièce de résistance is partnership matters, especially those pertaining to real estate investment trusts.

The Clients: Sprint; UPS; SunTrust Banks; International Paper; Jefferson-Pilot and Post Properties.

Chamberlain, Hrdlicka, White, Williams & Martin

The Firm: More than a third of the practitioners at this boutique firm talk tax. Founded by trial lawyers from the IRS and the US DOJ's tax division, the firm still packs a powerful punch in defending clients in high-profile tax controversies.

The Lawyers: Dominating the practice is **David Aughtry** (see p.202), *"one of the best trial lawyers around,"* who was commended by peers for his *"ability to communicate complex issues in simple ways."* One key courtroom battle involved IRS corporate tax shelter allegations, while other cases have led the way for claiming certain federal income tax deduction entitlements.

The Clients: The firm advises public companies, privately-owned businesses, trusts, estates and tax-exempt organizations.

Kilpatrick Stockton LLP

The Firm: An all-around tax firm with regional presence as well as an international reach. The group was said to pool its expertise in areas such as tax planning, federal tax controversies and international counseling.

The Lawyers: *"A jack-of-all-trades tax lawyer,"* **Harold Abrams** has earned his stripes battling the IRS in controversies that have included valuations, particularly those involving estates and gifts. Abrams has a *"stable of impressive clients"* who seek his advice for planning estates, wills and trusts.

The Clients: Real estate development companies, textile manufacturers, beer/wine distributors and other private companies use the firm.

GEORGIA — LEADERS

Powell, Goldstein, Frazer & Murphy LLP
The Firm: Peers described this group of a dozen practitioners as primarily a transactional tax firm. The team also includes notable tax litigators such as former IRS trial attorney William Kinzer, who has represented a major airline and other public companies in controversy matters.
The Lawyers: *"Incredibly sharp"* is how interviewees described **Frank Crisafi** (see p.205), a merger specialist and international tax planner, who sources say is detail-driven. He has helped financial institutions to structure taxable dispositions of stocks and assets, particularly in Sub S elections, in which the tax liability may be shifted to individual shareholders. Crisafi has also advised start-up companies and foreign subsidiaries of domestic corporations.
The Clients: Technology-based manufacturers, a footwear/apparel manufacturer, an aerospace manufacturer and an appliance company figure in the client roster.

Other Notable Practitioners
Michael Wasserman of Holt Ney Zatcoff & Wasserman LLP has a doctorate in mathematics, and displays a knack for reaching creative solutions by *"thinking from a different angle."* His stable of clients include real estate juggernaut Trammell Crow Company and tax-exempt organizations such as The University Financing Foundation. Competitors described **Charles Beaudrot** of Morris, Manning & Martin LLP as an *"energetic"* generalist who concentrates on partnerships. He represented PowerTel in its acquisition by Deutsche Telekom, and worked on another wireless telecom joint venture. Although competitors believe **Morton Harris** of Columbus-based Hatcher, Stubbs, Land, Hollis & Rothschild LLP is *"not a garden-variety business tax"* practitioner, he is endorsed as an effective tax planner, particularly in matters relating to employee benefits or tax-qualified plans.

Leaders in Georgia

ABERNATHY, Thomas
Smith, Currie & Hancock LLP, Atlanta
404 521 3800
Recommended in Construction

ABRAMS, Harold
Kilpatrick Stockton LLP, Atlanta
404 815 6500
Recommended in Tax

ADAMS, JR, Alfred
Sutherland Asbill & Brennan LLP,
Atlanta 404 853 8014
agadams@sablaw.com
Recommended in Real Estate
Specialisation: Firmwide Chair of the Real Estate Group. Practices primarily in the areas of real estate and creditors' rights, representing foreign and US investors, lenders and developers in connection with virtually every type of real estate project. Has worked extensively in the acquisition and development area and on mortgage and joint venture financing of commercial projects. Has developed considerable experience in real estate workouts, foreclosures and bankruptcy reorganizations. Has spoken frequently at such seminars as the Georgia Real Property Institute and ICSC Law Conference and at other continuing legal education seminars on topics such as retail development and leasing, real estate workouts and creditors' rights, commercial real estate sales and acquisitions, partnerships and joint ventures. Serves on the editorial advisory boards of the 'Journal of Applied Real Property Analysis' and the 'Retail Law Strategist'.
Prof. Memberships: From 1988-89, served as the Chair of the Real Property Section of the State Bar of Georgia, and has also served as the Co-Chair of the State Bar of Georgia's Committee on Legal Opinions in Real Estate Transactions. Fellow in the American College of Mortgage Attorneys and is a member of the Georgia Bar Association. International Council of Shopping Centers and the National Association of Industrial and Office Parks. Member of the Board of Visitors of Duke Law School.
Publications: 'Springing Exclusive - Another Technique to Resolve Exclusive Use Issues', 'Retail Law Strategist', (2002); 'Developing a Shopping Center on a Ground Lease', 'Retail Law Strategist', (2001); 'The Mortgagee's Guide to Single Asset Bankruptcy Reorganizations', 98 'Commercial Law Journal' 351(1993).
Personal: JD with distinction, Duke University School of Law, 1974, Order of the Coif, Administrative Law Editor, Duke Law Journal; AB, Duke University, 1970.

ADDISON, James
Troutman Sanders LLP, Atlanta
404 885 3000
Recommended in Real Estate

ALDRIDGE, John
McKenna Long & Aldridge, Atlanta
404 527 4000
Recommended in Real Estate

ALEXANDER, Miles
Kilpatrick Stockton LLP, Atlanta
404 815 6500
Recommended in Intellectual Property

ALLEN, Pinney
Alston & Bird LLP, Atlanta
404 881 7000
Recommended in Tax

ALLEN, Randall
Alston & Bird LLP, Atlanta
404 881 7000
Recommended in Antitrust

ARNOLD, Scott
King & Spalding LLP, Atlanta
404 572 4908
sarnold@kslaw.com
Recommended in Real Estate
Specialisation: Represents investors (both foreign and domestic) in large commercial properties throughout the US in commercial real estate transactions. Represents real estate investment funds and developers in consolidating within the commercial real estate industry. Assists domestic investors in acquiring and divesting properties.
Prof. Memberships: American College of Real Estate Lawyers; American Bar Association; Atlanta Bar Association; State Bar of Georgia.
Personal: BA, Economics, University of Missouri, Phi Beta Kappa, 1972; JD, magna cum laude, University of Michigan Law School, 1975.

ASHE, Lawrence
Paul, Hastings, Janofsky & Walker LLP, Atlanta 404 815 2201
lawrenceashe@paulhastings.com
Recommended in Employment
Specialisation: Concentrates practice in employment law, litigation and civil rights matters. Founding/Original Chair of the firm's Atlanta office.
Prof. Memberships: Past Chair - EEO Law Committee of the Defense Research Institute; Management Chair - ABA Test & Validation Subcommittee, President (1977-80) and Director of the Atlanta Urban League; Chair - Jury Trial Subcommittee of the ABA Litigation Section; Founding Director - American Employment Law Council. Special Assistant Attorney General for the State of Georgia for employment and civil rights law (1980-97).
Personal: AB degree, High Honors - Princeton University (1962); LLB degree, Honors - Harvard Law School (1967).

ASKEW, Anthony
Kilpatrick Stockton LLP, Atlanta
404 815 6500
Recommended in Intellectual Property

ASSELIN, Thomas
Smith, Gambrell & Russell, LLP, Atlanta
404 815 3500
Recommended in Construction

ATTRIDGE, Byron
King & Spalding LLP, Atlanta
404 572 4787
battridge@kslaw.com
Recommended in Litigation
Specialisation: Commercial litigation, including professional liability, environmental, security transactions, trademark, creditors' rights and product liability. Extensive experience in appellate litigation in federal and state courts.
Prof. Memberships: American Bar Association; American College of Trial Lawyers (Chair, Committee on Complex Litigation); Atlanta Bar Association (former President); Fellow, National Center of State Courts (Board); State Bar of Georgia (former member, Board of Governors and former Chairman, State Board of Bar Examiners).
Personal: AB, Princeton University, 1955; LLB, Emory University School of Law, 1961.

AUGHTRY, David
Chamberlain, Hrdlicka, White, Williams & Martin, Atlanta 404 659 1410
Recommended in Tax

AUSTIN, Jesse
Paul, Hastings, Janofsky & Walker LLP, Atlanta 404 815 2208
jessaustin@paulhastings.com
Recommended in Insolvency
Specialisation: Concentrates practice in bankruptcy law, particularly Chapter 11 reorganization cases and large commercial workouts. A principal focus of his workout and insolvency practice is the representation of institutional senior secured lenders in syndicated credit facilities, with particular experience in debtor-in-possession lending and in the health-

GEORGIA

care, communications, retail and forest products industries. Also closes senior credit facilities and assists other financial services lawyers in structuring senior credit facilities and negotiating subordination provisions of subordinated debt issues.
Personal: BS, Business Administration, Phi Beta Kappa, University of North Carolina (1976). JD, with distinction and MBA from Emory University (1980).

BABER, Bruce
King & Spalding LLP, Atlanta
404 572 4826
bbaber@kslaw.com
Recommended in Intellectual Property
Specialisation: Intellectual property and technology law with focus in patent, trademark, trademark counterfeiting, false advertising and copyright infringement cases before the International Trade Commission and the United States Patent and Trademark Office. Substantial experience in the protection of trademarks, copyrights and other forms of intellectual property, including registration applications prosecution and implementation of worldwide protection strategies.
Prof. Memberships: American Bar Association; Atlanta Bar Association; State Bar of Georgia.
Personal: BA, with distinction, Princeton University, 1976; JD, cum laude, Duke University, Order of the Coif, 1979.

BANKOFF, Joseph
King & Spalding LLP, Atlanta
404 572 4796
jbankoff@kslaw.com
Recommended in Intellectual Property
Specialisation: Technology, communication disputes and contracts relating to software, copyrights, trade secrets, distribution channels and traditional/new media organizations. Experienced trial lawyer in patent, copyright, trade secret, media and technology-related matters.
Prof. Memberships: American Bar Association; American Law Institute; Atlanta Bar Association; Georgia Center for Advanced Telecommunications Technology (Board); Illinois State Bar; National Institute for Trial Advocacy (Board of Trustees); State Bar of Georgia.
Personal: BS, Purdue University, 1967; JD, University of Illinois, Omicron Delta Kappa, Order of the Coif, 1971.

BARMEYER, Patricia
King & Spalding LLP, Atlanta
404 572 3563
pbarmeyer@kslaw.com
Recommended in Environment
Specialisation: Regulatory compliance and environmental litigation in the areas of water, waste, air and environmental tort issues.
Prof. Memberships: American Bar Association (member, Section on Natural Resources, Energy and Environmental Law); American Bar Foundation; Atlanta Bar Association; Fellow, Atlanta Volunteer Lawyers Foundation (past President); State Bar of Georgia.
Personal: BA, Hollins College, 1968; JD, cum laude, Harvard University, 1971.

BASSETT, Peter
Alston & Bird LLP, Atlanta 404 881 7000
Recommended in Litigation

BATSON, Neal
Alston & Bird LLP, Atlanta
404 881 7000
Recommended in Insolvency

BAXLEY, Bill
King & Spalding LLP, Atlanta
404 572 3580
bbaxley@kslaw.com
Recommended in Corporate/M&A
Specialisation: Domestic and international mergers and acquisitions and joint ventures in the consumer products, telecom, banking, insurance, transportation, retail and restaurants industries, involving public company mergers, private company acquisitions and dispositions, joint ventures, strategic investments, going private transactions, special committee representations, tender offers and proxy contests.
Prof. Memberships: American Bar Association; State Bar of Georgia.
Personal: BS, summa cum laude, University of Alabama, 1986; JD, magna cum laude, Harvard University, 1989. Named one of the top 15 young Atlanta lawyers by 'The Fulton County Daily Report' in 2002.

BEAUDROT, Charles
Morris, Manning & Martin, LLP, Atlanta
404 233 7000
Recommended in Tax

BECK, Joseph
Kilpatrick Stockton LLP, Atlanta
404 815 6500
Recommended in Intellectual Property

BECK, Philip
Smith, Currie & Hancock LLP, Atlanta
404 521 3800
Recommended in Construction

BLACKSTOCK, Jerry
Hunton & Williams, Atlanta
404 888 4000
Recommended in Intellectual Property

BLOOM, Herschel
King & Spalding LLP, Atlanta
404 572 4929
hbloom@kslaw.com
Recommended in Tax
Specialisation: Corporate, partnership and real estate tax matters, particularly real estate investment trusts, life insurance companies and state tax issues and controversies.
Prof. Memberships: American Bar Association; American College of Tax Counsel; American Law Institute; State Bar of Georgia (former Chairman, Tax Section).
Personal: AB, magna cum laude, Vanderbilt University, 1965; JD, cum laude, Harvard University Law School, Phi Beta Kappa; Omicron Delta Kappa, 1968. Former Associate Professor of Law at University of Mississippi Law School. Frequent speaker on corporate and partnership tax subjects.

BOICE, William
Kilpatrick Stockton LLP, Atlanta
404 815 6500
Recommended in Employment, Litigation

BOISSEAU, Richard
Kilpatrick Stockton LLP, Atlanta
404 815 6500
Recommended in Employment

BONDURANT, Emmet
Bondurant, Mixson & Elmore, LLP, Atlanta 404 881 4100
Recommended in Antitrust, Employment, Litigation

BORDERS, Sarah
King & Spalding LLP, Atlanta
404 572 3596
sborders@kslaw.com
Recommended in Insolvency
Specialisation: Insolvency law issues, extensive experience representing creditors and debtors in large workouts, restructurings and bankruptcy cases in the retail, textile, real estate and healthcare industries.
Prof. Memberships: American Bar Association; American Bankruptcy Institute; American Law Institute (former President); Atlanta Bar Association; Best Lawyers in America; State Bar of Georgia.
Personal: BS, Louisiana State University, 1984; JD, University of Virginia, 1988. Frequent speaker on restructuring issues.

BRADLEY, Michael
Sutherland Asbill & Brennan LLP, Atlanta 404 853 8145
msbradley@sablaw.com
Recommended in Energy
Specialisation: Has practiced in the field of energy and telecommunications law since 1982, starting his career in government practice as an Assistant Attorney General for the State of Georgia. From 1982 to 1985, while serving in that role, and from 1986 to 1991, under appointment as a Special Assistant Attorney General, represented the Georgia Public Service Commission and its litigation staff at the trial and appellate level in every major electric and telecommunications matter to come before the agency. Such matters included all aspects of the five year process of phasing into rates Georgia Power Company's investment in Plant Vogtle and, in telecommunications, all aspects of beginning the transition under state law to competition in the telecommunications markets in Georgia. Since 1992, practice has focused on private sector clients in the electric and telecommunications arenas. Since 1995, predominant practice has been electric, centering on representation of independent power producers. His independent power practice has covered all aspects of power project development, culminating in financial closing of power projects. Listed (since 1992) in a leading US legal publication as one of the best lawyers in America.
Prof. Memberships: State Bar of Georgia.
Personal: JD, cum laude, University of Georgia School of Law, 1982; MA, with honors, University of Georgia, 1979; BA, magna cum laude, Catawba College, 1976.

BRADLEY, William H
Sutherland Asbill & Brennan LLP, Atlanta 212 389 5020
whbradley@sablaw.com
Recommended in Tax
Specialisation: Particularly experienced in handling complex tax controversies. Has handled such matters at all administrative levels within the Internal Revenue Service and has litigated tax issues in the Tax Court, the United States District Court, the Court of Federal Claims and in the Eleventh and Ninth Circuit Court of Appeals. Has worked extensively in the area of tax treatment of various loss funding programs. Also has extensive experience in the area of timber taxation and finance and has handled timber transactions and controversies for clients in all the major timber growing regions in the country.
Prof. Memberships: Served as Vice-Chair of the Forest Resources Committee of the American Bar Association and as General Counsel of Georgia Cities in Schools. Served as a member of the Board of Visitors of Emory University and the Duke University School of Environment. Member of the Board of Directors of the World Forestry Center and of the Lawyers Committee for Civil Rights under Law. Also a member of the Atlanta Bar Association and a frequent lecturer at tax seminars and other meetings.
Career: After law school, became a law clerk to Judge Edward C McLean on the Southern District of New York before serving for two years as an officer in the US Army. Served as managing partner of Sutherland's Atlanta office from 1991 to 1995. From 1976 through 1986, served as an adjunct professor of law at Emory University, teaching corporate tax to graduate attorneys in the LLM Taxation Program.
Publications: Has published recent articles on tax treatment of various loss funding programs in 'The American Journal of Tax Policy' and 'The Journal of Taxation'.

GEORGIA LEADERS

Personal: JD, cum laude, Harvard Law School, 1968, Editor, 'Harvard Law Review', 1966-68; BA, with high honors, Emory University, 1965.

BRAMLETT, Jeffrey
Bondurant, Mixson & Elmore, LLP, Atlanta 404 881 4100
Recommended in Employment

BREWSTER, William
Kilpatrick Stockton LLP, Atlanta
404 815 6500
Recommended in Intellectual Property

BUCKLER, Robert
Troutman Sanders LLP, Atlanta
404 885 3000
Recommended in Employment

BUCKLEY, Edward
Buckley & Klein LLP, Atlanta
404 781 1100
Recommended in Employment

BUTLER, James
Butler, Wooten, Fryhofer, Daughtery & Sullivan, LLP, Columbus 706 322 1990
Recommended in Litigation

BUTLER, James
Smith, Currie & Hancock LLP, Atlanta
404 521 3800
Recommended in Construction

CAHOON, Susan
Kilpatrick Stockton LLP, Atlanta
404 815 6500
Recommended in Litigation

CAMPBELL, Charles
McKenna Long & Aldridge, Atlanta
404 527 4000
Recommended in Insolvency

CARSSOW, Tim
Kilpatrick Stockton LLP, Atlanta
404 815 6500
Recommended in Real Estate

CASHDAN, Jeff
King & Spalding LLP, Atlanta
404 572 4818
jcashdan@kslaw.com
Recommended in Antitrust

Specialisation: Antitrust, merger and acquisition and complex business litigation counseling, including securities, purported class actions and appellate matters.
Prof. Memberships: American Bar Association (Vice-Chair, Sherman Act Section 2, Antitrust and Litigation Sections); Editorial Board for the 2000 Annual Review of Antitrust Law Developments; 'Antitrust Law Journal' (former Editor); Atlanta Bar Association; Illinois State Bar; State Bar of Georgia (Chair, Antitrust Section).
Personal: BA, cum laude, Claremont McKenna College, 1987; London School of Economics and Political Science; JD, University of Chicago, 1990.

CHANDLER, John
Sutherland Asbill & Brennan LLP, Atlanta 404 853 8029
jachandler@sablaw.com
Recommended in Litigation

Specialisation: Tries business cases. Has represented clients in numerous complex professional liability, securities, insurance and RICO cases. Has represented all of the Big Four accounting firms, several local accounting firms, several law firms, insurance companies, individuals and partnerships.
Prof. Memberships: Served as President of the Atlanta Bar Association, the Atlanta Council of Younger Lawyers, the Atlanta Legal Aid Society, the Atlanta Volunteer Lawyers Foundation, Travelers Aid of Metropolitan Atlanta. Chair of the Fulton County Ethics Board and Chair of the City of Atlanta Board of Ethics. Member of the Board of Governors of the State Bar of Georgia. Member of the International Association of Defense Counsel, Past President of the Bleckley American Inn of Court, a Master of the Lumpkin American Inn of Court, member of the Board of Visitors of the University of Tennessee College of Arts and Sciences, a Fellow of the American Bar Foundation and a Fellow of the American College of Trial Lawyers.
Personal: JD, Vanderbilt University School of Law, 1972, Order of Coif, Managing Editor, 'Vanderbilt Law Review'; BS, University of Tennessee, 1966.

CHEATHAM, Richard
Kilpatrick Stockton LLP, Atlanta
404 815 6500
Recommended in Banking & Finance

CIFELLI, James
Lamberth, Cifelli, Stokes & Stout, PA, Atlanta 404 495 4495
jcifelli@lcsslaw.com
Recommended in Insolvency

Specialisation: Senior partner in bankruptcy litigation. Has represented debtor in reorganization in cases such as Hays Microcomputer Products, Inc., Beau Rivage, Ltd., Colorocs Corporation, Tennessee Chemical Company, Gilbert & Bennett Manufacturing, Inc., Gulf Properties Financial Services, Inc., Micro Mart, Inc., and Vintage Enterprises, Inc. Has represented trustees or liquidating agents in RDM Sports Group, Inc., All American of Ashburn, Inc., Preferred Alliance, Inc., and QOS Networks, Inc. Also has represented substantial creditor interests in significant reorganization and liquidation cases. Handles discharge, dischargeability, and avoidance action adversary litigation for both prosecution and defense in individual and business bankruptcy cases.
Prof. Memberships: State Bar of Georgia; Atlanta Bar Association (board member, Bankruptcy Section).

Career: Admitted to bar, Connecticut, 1976, Georgia, 1977. Joined present firm in 1976, became partner in 1982.
Publications: Numerous course materials for presentation at seminars on bankruptcy, commercial litigation, and collection, for Atlanta Bar Association, PLI, and other private seminar companies.
Personal: Received BA from Duke University, 1973; JD from Vanderbilt University School of Law, 1976.

CLARK, Reginald J
Sutherland Asbill & Brennan LLP, Atlanta 404 853 8032
rjclark@sablaw.com
Recommended in Tax

Specialisation: A tax practitioner with particular experience in corporate taxation and in planning corporate acquisitions, restructurings and other transactions. Practice includes advising a number of cooperative organizations, both tax-exempt and taxable. Also experienced in handling tax controversies and representing clients before the National Office of the Internal Revenue Service in connection with requests for rulings or technical advice.
Prof. Memberships: Former Adjunct Professor of Law in the Emory University School of Law's Graduate Tax Program. Presently Secretary of the Corporate Tax Committee of the American Bar Association's Tax Section, and has spoken at a number of tax seminars and bar programs. Former member of the Editorial Board of the Georgia State Bar Journal, and served on a state bar task force which drafted legislation authorizing the formation of limited liability companies in Georgia. Recently elected to membership in the American Law Institute.
Personal: JD, with distinction, Duke University School of Law, 1978, Notes and Comments Editor, 'Duke Law Journal'; AB, Duke University, 1975 Phi Beta Kappa.

CLAY, Stephens
Kilpatrick Stockton LLP, Atlanta
404 815 6500
Recommended in Litigation

CLINEBURG, William
King & Spalding LLP, Atlanta
404 572 4701
bclineburg@kslaw.com
Recommended in Employment

Specialisation: Employment litigation, representing Fortune 100 automotive, chemical, tobacco, computer, oil, textile and retail companies. Also represents hospitals and colleges in state and federal courts throughout the country.
Prof. Memberships: American Bar Association (member, EEO Subcommittee, Labor and Employment Law Section); Atlanta Bar Association; fellow, College of Labor and Employment Lawyers; State Bar of Georgia.

Publications: Co-author, 'Employment Discrimination,' 35 Mercer Law Review 1169 (1984).
Personal: BA, Brown University, 1965; JD, cum laude, University of Georgia School of Law, 1970.

COALSON, John
Alston & Bird LLP, Atlanta
404 881 7000
Recommended in Tax

COHEN, Ezra
Troutman Sanders LLP, Atlanta
404 885 3000
Recommended in Insolvency

COHEN, Jerold
Sutherland Asbill & Brennan LLP, Atlanta 404 853 8038
njcohen@sablaw.com
Recommended in Tax

Specialisation: Represents a number of US and foreign clients in all aspects of domestic and international tax planning and controversy matters. Has been involved in planning and structuring corporate acquisitions and dispositions. Has successfully litigated a number of federal tax cases and has handled numerous matters before the Internal Revenue Service and the Treasury Department. Has also handled legislative matters for clients, has testified on a number of occasions before the two Congressional tax writing committees and has worked with the Joint Committee on Taxation on tax legislative matters. Has been nominated by his peers for inclusion in several leading US legal publications.
Prof. Memberships: In 1979, was appointed by President Carter to serve as Chief Counsel for the Internal Revenue Service, a position he held until 1981. That same year, presented with the Commissioner's Award for outstanding service to the Internal Revenue Service and the General Counsel of the Treasury's Award for outstanding service to the Treasury Department. A former Chair of the Internal Revenue Service Advisory Council and currently serves as Chair of the American College of Tax Counsel. A past Chair of the Tax Section of the American Bar Association, a member of the Board of Advisors of the Virginia Tax Review, a past member of the Little Brown and Commerce Clearing House Tax Advisory Boards and Vice Chair of the American College of Tax Counsel. Served as a member of the Board of Advisors of the Internal Revenue Service's Continuing Professional Education Program and as a member of the Advisory Group to the Staff of the Senate Finance Committee on its Subchapter C Revision Act and is now a member of the American Law Institute, and its Tax Advisory Board. Served as an advisor to its Subchapter C Project, and a consultant to its Tax Integration Project.

Publications: Has published in 'The Journal of Taxation', 'The Tax Lawyer', Practicing Law Institute publications, 'The Journal of the American Bar Association' publications and the N.Y.U Tax Institutes, and has spoken at numerous tax institutes such as the American Law Institute, Practicing Law Institute, state bar and university tax programs. Appointments include: Internal Revenue Service Advisory Counsel (1999-), Chair, ABA Tax Section (1995-96); Chair Elect, ABA Tax Section (1994-95); Vice Chair and Member of Council, ABA Section of Taxation; Chair, Formation of Tax Policy Committee, ABA Section of Taxation (1982-86); Chair, Taxation Committee, ABA Section of Litigation (1981-83); Chair, Corporate Stockholder Relationships Committee, ABA Section of Taxation (1977-79); Vice Chair, Committee on Taxation, ABA Section of Individual Rights and Human Responsibilities (1976-79); Adjunct Professor of Law, Emory University (1967-76); Vice Chair, American College of Tax Counsel.
Personal: LLB, magna cum laude, Harvard Law School, 1961, Book Review Editor, 'Harvard Law Review'; BBA, Tulane University, 1957, Beta Gamma Sigma.

COIL, James
Kilpatrick Stockton LLP, Atlanta
404 815 6500
Recommended in Employment

COLEMAN, Aubrey
Smith, Currie & Hancock LLP, Atlanta
404 521 3800
Recommended in Construction

CONNOLLY, Dennis
Alston & Bird LLP, Atlanta
404 881 7000
Recommended in Insolvency

CONRAD, Albert H
King & Spalding LLP, Atlanta
404 572 4807
cconrad@kslaw.com
Recommended in Banking & Finance
Specialisation: Representing banks and lending institutions in private debt financings and major financing transactions. Serves as the principal outside lawyer for a number of the firm's corporate and REIT clients.
Prof. Memberships: American Bar Association (Banking Law Section); American College of Commercial Finance Lawyers (former Chair, Uniform Commercial Code Committee); Atlanta Bar Association; State Bar of Georgia (Chair, Corporate and Banking Law Section).
Personal: BS, with highest honors, University of Tennessee, 1972; JD, University of Virginia, Omicron Delta Kappa; Phi Kappa Phi; Order of the Coif, 1975. Frequent speaker on lending-related topics.

COOK, Philip
Alston & Bird LLP, Atlanta
404 881 7000
Recommended in Tax

CORGAN, Brian
Kilpatrick Stockton LLP, Atlanta
404 815 6500
Recommended in Construction

CRISAFI, Frank
Powell, Goldstein, Frazer & Murphy LLP, Atlanta 404 572 6600
Recommended in Tax

CURTIS, Vaughan
Alston & Bird LLP, Atlanta
404 881 7000
Recommended in Corporate/M&A

DALTON, John
Troutman Sanders LLP, Atlanta
404 885 3000
Recommended in Litigation

DEAKINS, Homer
Ogletree, Deakins, Nash, Smoak & Stewart, PC, Atlanta 404 881 1300
Recommended in Employment

DEGNAN, Peter
Alston & Bird LLP, Atlanta
404 881 7000
Recommended in Energy

DEHIHNS, Lee
Alston & Bird LLP, Atlanta
404 881 7000
Recommended in Environment

DENNARD, H Lane
King & Spalding LLP, Atlanta
404 572 5121
ldennard@kslaw.com
Recommended in Employment
Specialisation: Over 28 years labor and employment experience representing unionized and union-free employers, including labor/employment cases in state and federal courts. Labor advice in corporate transactions, including sale of businesses, mergers and acquisitions and outsourcing of products and services.
Prof. Memberships: American Bar Association (Labor and Employment Sections); Atlanta Bar Association; Fellow, College of Labor and Employment Lawyers; South Carolina Bar; State Bar of Georgia.
Personal: AB, Mercer University, 1966; JD, University of Georgia, Phi Delta Phi, 1973. Author of numerous articles on labor and employment law.

DIAL, David
Weinberg, Wheeler, Hudgins, Gunn & Dial, LLC, Atlanta 404 876 2700
Recommended in Construction

DIEHL, Mary Grace
Troutman Sanders LLP, Atlanta
404 885 3000
Recommended in Insolvency

DOBBS, Edward
Parker, Hudson, Rainer & Dobbs LLP, Atlanta 404 523 5300
Recommended in Banking & Finance, Insolvency

DORRIS, William
Kilpatrick Stockton LLP, Atlanta
404 815 6500
Recommended in Construction

DORSEY, Rufus
Parker, Hudson, Rainer & Dobbs LLP, Atlanta 404 523 5300
Recommended in Insolvency

DOUGLAS, John
Alston & Bird LLP, Atlanta
404 881 7000
Recommended in Banking & Finance

DOWDY, Craig
McKenna Long & Aldridge, Atlanta
404 527 4000
Recommended in Energy

EGAN, Michael
King & Spalding LLP, Atlanta
404 572 4753
megan@kslaw.com
Recommended in Corporate/M&A
Specialisation: Mergers and acquisitions, joint ventures and strategic alliances. Substantial experience representing international companies in cross-border transactions. Serves as counsel for the Atlanta Falcons NFL franchise. Served as European Transactions Counsel to The Coca-Cola Company.
Prof. Memberships: American Bar Association; International Bar Association; State Bar of Georgia.
Personal: BA, University of North Carolina, 1978; JD, cum laude, Harvard University, Phi Beta Kappa, 1982; Morehead Scholar, University of North Carolina.

ELGISON, Martin
Alston & Bird LLP, Atlanta
404 881 7000
Recommended in Intellectual Property

ERNST, Andrew
Hunter, Maclean, Exley & Dunn, PC, Savannah 912 236 0261
Recommended in Environment

EWING, Jim
Kilpatrick Stockton LLP, Atlanta
404 815 6500
Recommended in Intellectual Property

FAGAN, James
Stanford Fagan & Giolito, Atlanta
404 897 1000
Recommended in Employment

FLEMING, JD
Sutherland Asbill & Brennan LLP, Atlanta 404 853 8062
jdfleming@sablaw.com
Recommended in Intellectual Property
Specialisation: Practices primarily in the areas of civil and tax litigation and has substantial trial experience in controversies involving science and technology, including product liability, patent infringement, trade secrets, intellectual property, environmental matters, industrial technology, occupational health and safety, and federal taxation. These matters have been before local, state and federal trial courts and agencies in Florida, Georgia, Illinois, Nebraska, New Jersey, New York, Ohio, Oregon, South Carolina, Tennessee, Texas, Virginia and Wisconsin, and before the United States Courts of Appeals for the First, Fourth, Fifth, Sixth, Seventh, Eleventh, DC and Federal Circuits. Has handled challenges to regulations and rule-making proposals of the Environmental Protection Agency, Occupational Safety and Health Administration and Federal Energy Regulatory Commission involving effluent limitations, underground injection, permissible occupational exposure levels and fuel conversions. Has also handled a number of significant enforcement actions dealing with toxic chemical and harmful physical agent exposures and civil actions arising from exposures and registration activities.
Prof. Memberships: Has served on numerous committees of the Section of Science and Technology and the Litigation Section of the American Bar Association (ABA). From 1985 to 1986, he was Chair of the Section of Science and Technology. From 1987 to 1990, he was a member of the National Conference of Lawyers and Scientists and was Chair of the ABA delegation to the Conference from 1988 to 1990. Served on the ABA Standing Committee on Technology and Information Systems from 1997 through 2001. Served in 1990 as Section Delegate to the ABA House of Delegates. In 1994 and 1995, he was a member of the ABA Board of Governors, a member of the Operations Committee of the Board of Governors and Board of Governors Liaison to the Section of Intellectual Property Law, the National Conference of Administrative Law Judges, the Coordinating Group on Bioethics and the Law, and the Coordinating Group on Energy Law. Returned to the House of Delegates in 1994 and served through 1996. In 1995 and 1996, he was Chair of the ABA Special Committee on Citation Issues. In 1996 and 1997, he was a member of the ABA Coordinating Commission on Legal Technology and he is now a member of the ABA Standing Committee on Technology and Information Systems. Has served on the Editorial Board of Jurimetrics, the official publication of the Section of Science and Technology, and on the Editorial Board of the Georgia State Bar Journal. From 1990 to 2001, served as a member of the Georgia Appellate Practice and Educational Resource Center, to

GEORGIA LEADERS

which he was appointed by the Judges of the United States District Court for the Northern District of Georgia. Fellow of the American College of Trial Lawyers, Fellow of the American Bar Foundation, Fellow of the American Inns of Court Foundation, and a Fellow of the American Institute of Chemists. Member of the American Institute of Chemical Engineers and is a Registered Professional Engineer in Georgia and California.
Personal: JD, with distinction, Emory University School of Law, 1967, First Honor Graduate, Editor in Chief, 'Journal of Public Policy Law' (now 'Emory Law Review'); PhD, Georgia Institute of Technology, 1959; BS, with highest honors, Georgia Institute of Technology, 1955.

FLEMING, John H
Sutherland Asbill & Brennan LLP, Atlanta 404 853 8065
jhfleming@sablaw.com
Recommended in Litigation
Specialisation: Firmwide Chair of the Litigation Group. Has been responsible for a wide variety of cases in many different courts, but has had particularly extensive experience in complex business litigation, including franchise litigation, professional liability litigation, intellectual property litigation, major litigation involving insurance companies and banks and tax litigation. Experienced, both as an attorney and an arbitrator, in arbitration and in other alternative dispute resolution mechanisms. Since 1998, has served as Eastern Regional Counsel for dealer and general litigation for an automobile manufacturer and was Southeast Regional Counsel for the five years before that. Has successfully represented a major hotelier in several lawsuits in the southeast. Other accomplishments include trial victories for both owners of intellectual property and alleged infringers, favorable jury verdicts in state and federal court in Georgia and elsewhere, successful defense of RICO class action claims in consumer litigation and an arbitration award for an insurance company in excess of $55,000,000. Handled an appointed death penalty case, from 1980 through 1992, in which he had the death penalty reversed once by the United States Supreme Court and twice by the Georgia Supreme Court, and finally won before a jury (and Court TV) in Madison, Georgia. During 1991 through 1996, served as an adjunct professor in the Pretrial Litigation course at Emory Law School.
Career: Prior to joining the firm, clerked in Dallas with Judge Irving Goldberg of the United States Court of Appeals for the Fifth Circuit.
Personal: JD, magna cum laude, Harvard Law School, 1975,Senior Editor, 'Harvard Law Review'; MA, Florida State University, 1972; BA, Emory University, 1970, Phi Beta Kappa.

FLETCHER, Jennifer
Griffin Cochrane & Marshall, Atlanta 404 523 2000
Recommended in Construction

FLINN, Patrick
Alston & Bird LLP, Atlanta 404 881 7000
Recommended in Intellectual Property

FORRY, Robert
Troutman Sanders LLP, Atlanta 404 885 3000
Recommended in Energy

FOX, Steven
Rogers & Hardin, Atlanta 404 522 4700
Recommended in Corporate/M&A

FRYER, William
King & Spalding LLP, Atlanta 404 572 4911
bfryer@kslaw.com
Recommended in Real Estate
Specialisation: Mergers, acquisitions, funds formation and project developments with emphasis on real estate securitizations.
Prof. Memberships: American Bar Association; Atlanta Bar Association; The Lovett School (Trustee); State Bar of Georgia; University of Virginia School of Law (Alumni Council).
Personal: BA, University of Virginia, 1971; JD, University of Virginia, Phi Beta Kappa, Omicron Delta Kappa, Order of the Coif, 1974.

GALLO, Barbara
McKenna Long & Aldridge, Atlanta 404 527 4000
Recommended in Environment

GENBERG, Ira
Smith, Gambrell & Russell, LLP, Atlanta 404 815 3500
Recommended in Construction

GIOLITO, Robert
Stanford Fagan & Giolito, Atlanta 404 897 1000
Recommended in Employment

GOLDEN, Jonathan
Arnall Golden Gregory LLP, Atlanta 404 873 8500
Recommended in Corporate/M&A

GRADY, Kevin
Alston & Bird LLP, Atlanta 404 881 7000
Recommended in Antitrust

GRAVES, Judson
Alston & Bird LLP, Atlanta 404 881 7000
Recommended in Litigation

GREENE, Kevin
Troutman Sanders LLP, Atlanta 404 885 3000
Recommended in Energy

GRIFFIN, John
Troutman Sanders LLP, Atlanta 404 885 3000
Recommended in Real Estate

GROUT, Robert
Troutman Sanders LLP, Atlanta 404 885 3000
Recommended in Corporate/M&A

HARDIN, Edward
Rogers & Hardin, Atlanta 404 522 4700
Recommended in Corporate/M&A

HARRIS, Morton
Hatcher, Stubbs, Land, Hollis & Rothschild, LLP, Columbus 706 324 0201
Recommended in Tax

HARRIS, Steve
Alston & Bird LLP, Atlanta 404 881 7000
Recommended in Antitrust

HASSON JR, James K
Sutherland Asbill & Brennan LLP, Atlanta 404 853 8083
jkhasson@sablaw.com
Recommended in Tax
Specialisation: Practices in the areas of tax, health care and finance. Regularly represents closely-held businesses, universities, private foundations, hospitals and other religious, charitable and educational organizations. Practice consists both of advising clients and resolving conflicts with the Internal Revenue Service, the Centers for Medicare and Medicaid Services and other federal and state governmental agencies. Much of the advising portion of his practice focuses on the design and negotiation of acquisition or affiliation contracts, financing arrangements, organizational structures and tax planning for business continuity. Has published numerous articles and speaks extensively at various conferences around the country. Served from 1987 through 1990 as a member of the Exempt Organization Advisory Group to the Commissioner of the Internal Revenue Service, and served for almost 20 years as an Adjunct Professor of Law in the graduate tax program at Emory University School of Law.
Prof. Memberships: Member of the American and Atlanta Bar Associations. Currently serves as Division Coordinator of the American Bar Association's Tax Section to the Tax Exempt and Governmental Entities Division of the IRS. Formerly chaired the Exempt Organizations Committee of the Tax Section of the American Bar Association, and remains actively involved in the work of that Committee. Fellow of the American College of Tax Counsel. Member of the Foundation Lawyers Group, the National Association of College and University Attorneys and the American Health Lawyers Association. In addition to his professional activities, chairs the Board of Trustees of Reinhardt College, former Chair of the Board of Directors of The Foxfire Fund and of the Metropolitan Atlanta Crime Commission, and a graduate of Leadership Atlanta.
Personal: JD, Duke University School of Law, 1970, Order of the Coif, Comment and Project Editor, 'Duke Law Journal'; BA, Duke University, 1967.

HAWKINS, Holmes
King & Spalding LLP, Atlanta 404 572 2443
hhawkins@kslaw.com
Recommended in Intellectual Property
Specialisation: Intellectual property law, focusing on patent litigation, including patent infringement lawsuits involving computer systems and software, internet-related technologies, telecommunications and electronics systems, financial service models, consumer products, medical devices, patents, trademarks, copyrights and licensing matters.
Prof. Memberships: American Bar Association; Atlanta Bar Association; American Intellectual Property Law Association; Georgia Institute of Technology, Atlanta (Visiting Professor); State Bar of Georgia (Intellectual Property Section).
Personal: BEE, high honors, Georgia Institute of Technology, 1990; JD, cum laude, University of Georgia, 1993. National Institute of Trial Advocacy, National Trial Skills program, Colorado.

HAWTHORNE, Bruce
King & Spalding LLP, Atlanta 404 572 4903
bhawthorne@kslaw.com
Recommended in Corporate/M&A
Specialisation: Complex mergers and acquisitions transactions, including strategic joint ventures, tender offers and proxy fights, merchant banking and leveraged buyout transactions. Corporate finance, representing issuers, underwriters and institutional investors in public offerings, venture capital transactions, Rule 144A transactions, Eurobond offerings and debt and equity securities private placements.
Prof. Memberships: American Bar Association; BTI Consulting Group, Inc.'s Client Service All Star Team; State Bar of Georgia.
Personal: BBA, with distinction, University of Michigan, 1971; MBA, University of Detroit, 1972; JD, Vanderbilt University, Beta Gamma Sigma, Order of the Coif, 1975.

HAYNES, Joseph B
King & Spalding LLP, Atlanta 404 572 4792
bhaynes@kslaw.com
Recommended in Litigation
Specialisation: Civil and commercial litigation, representing accounting firms in malpractice, securities litigation and professional liability matters, including

antitrust, commercial contract litigation, franchisor franchisee relationships, internal corporate investigations, class action lawsuits, derivative shareholder suits, civil RICO claims, banking litigation, construction contract suits, corporate espionage and competitive intelligence.
Prof. Memberships: American Bar Association; American College of Trial Lawyers; Atlanta Cancer Society; State Bar of Georgia; State Bar of New York; Atlanta Chamber of Commerce (Public Affairs Committee).
Personal: BA, University of the South, 1962; LLB, New York University, Phi Beta Kappa, Omicron Delta Kappa, 1965.

HENDRICK, David
Hendrick Phillips Salzman & Flatt PC, Atlanta
Recommended in Construction

Specialisation: Construction law and construction contract counseling and construction dispute and claim resolution, including negotiation, mediation, arbitration, administrative processes, and judicial litigation. Also, represents local, state, and national construction industry trade associations.
Prof. Memberships: American College of Construction Lawyers, fellow and past President; American Bar Association, Forum on Construction, member and past Division Steering Committee Chair; Atlanta Bar Association, Construction Law Section, member and past Chairman; American Arbitration Association, Large, Complex Case National Arbitrator Panel Member and previously served as member of the AAA Large Case Dispute Resolution Committee; Georgia Bar Association, member; District of Columbia Bar Association, member.
Personal: BS (Chem. Eng), Tufts University, 1968; JD University of Virginia, 1973; Law Clerk to Honorable Albert J Henderson, Judge, United States District Court, ND Ga 1973-75.

HILL, Harvey
Alston & Bird LLP, Atlanta
404 881 7000
Recommended in Banking & Finance

HINCHEY, John
King & Spalding LLP, Atlanta
404 572 4922
jhinchey@kslaw.com
Recommended in Construction

Specialisation: Construction and commercial contracting matters, including large capital companies; consulting firms; private and public schools and universities; state, city and county governments; public authorities; medical institutions; public utilities; private developers and owners; and design professionals.
Prof. Memberships: American Arbitration Association; American Bar Association; American College of Construction Lawyers; Atlanta Bar Association; Chartered Institute of Arbitrators; International Bar Association; London Court of International Arbitration; State Bar of Georgia.
Personal: AB, Emory University, 1964; LLB, Emory University, 1965; M.Litt., Oxford University, 1980; LLM, Harvard University, 1966.

HOGFOSS, Robert
Hunton & Williams, Atlanta
404 888 4000
Recommended in Environment

HOLT, Robert
Holt Ney Zatcoff & Wasserman, LLP, Atlanta 770 956 9600
Recommended in Real Estate

HORDER, Richard
Kilpatrick Stockton LLP, Atlanta
404 815 6500
Recommended in Environment

HUDSON, Paul
Parker, Hudson, Rainer & Dobbs LLP, Atlanta 404 523 5300
Recommended in Corporate/M&A

HUGHES, Hunter
Rogers & Hardin, Atlanta 404 522 4700
Recommended in Employment

HUGHS, William
Alston & Bird LLP, Atlanta
404 881 7000
Recommended in Construction

HUNTER, Forrest
Alston & Bird LLP, Atlanta
404 881 7000
Recommended in Employment

HYATT, Wayne
Hyatt & Stubblefield, PC, Atlanta
404 659 6600
Recommended in Real Estate

HYMAN, JR, Thomas
Sutherland Asbill & Brennan LLP,
Atlanta 404 853 8098
tbhyman@sablaw.com
Recommended in Corporate/M&A

Specialisation: Focuses practice on the corporate and finance areas, with heavy concentration on the purchase and sale of businesses and the representation of purchasers and sellers in taxable and non-taxable transactions throughout the United States. This has particularly involved transactions in nationwide business consolidations. Frequent lecturer on purchases and sales of businesses at state and national bar programs.
Prof. Memberships: Member of the American Bar Association Committee on Negotiated Acquisitions and Co-Chair of that Committee's Subcommittee on Joint Ventures. Member of the Board of Trustees of Randolph-Macon Woman's College and former member of the Board of Directors of the Alliance Theatre Company.
Personal: JD, with honors, University of Florida College of Law, 1969, Phi Kappa Phi, Order of the Coif and Executive Editor, University of Florida Law Review; BA, with honors, Yale University, 1966.

JEFFRIES, Hill
Alston & Bird LLP, Atlanta
404 881 7000
Recommended in Corporate/M&A

JOHNSON, Jim
Kilpatrick Stockton LLP, Atlanta
404 815 6500
Recommended in Intellectual Property

JOHNSON, Weyman
Paul, Hastings, Janofsky & Walker LLP, Atlanta 404 815 2209
weymanjohnson@paulhastings.com
Recommended in Employment

Specialisation: Practices exclusively in labor and employment law and employee benefits litigation, representing management. Practices in both employment litigation and traditional labor relations, as well as in matters under the Fair Labor Standards Act, the Occupational Safety and Health Act, and the Employee Retirement Income Security Act.
Career: Frequent speaker on legal, business, and community affairs, and a contributing editor to various publications, writing on labor and employment law issues.
Personal: AB degree, Mercer University, cum laude, (1973); JD degree, University of Georgia School of Law (1979). Acted as the Decisions Editor of the 'Georgia Law Review'.

JOHNSON, John
Troutman Sanders LLP, Atlanta
404 885 3000
Recommended in Environment

JOHNSTON, Mike
King & Spalding LLP, Atlanta
404 572 3581
mjohnston@kslaw.com
Recommended in Employment

Specialisation: Labor, ERISA and employment law matters, representing clients in pharmaceutical, grocery, food service and distribution, soft drinks, manufacturing, technology, entertainment and healthcare industries.
Prof. Memberships: American Bar Association; Atlanta Bar Association; the Florida Bar; State Bar of Georgia.
Personal: BS, with academic distinction, US Air Force Academy, 1975; LLM, Georgetown University, 1986; JD, with high honors, University of Florida, Order of the Coif, 1980.

JORDAN, James B
Sutherland Asbill & Brennan LLP, Atlanta 404 853 8101
jbjordan@sablaw.com
Recommended in Real Estate

Specialisation: Chair of the firm's Retail Practice Group and a member of the American College of Real Estate Lawyers. Devotes a substantial portion of his time to retail development and leasing matters. Has experience and expertise in representing developers and retailers as to the entire gamut of retail product types ranging from freestanding facilities to neighborhood and power center developments to enclosed regional malls. Represented Ben Carter Properties and Simon Properties in connection with a wide variety of development and leasing matters at the Mall of Georgia, a regional mall and entertainment/lifestyle center consisting of more than 2,000,000 square feet located in suburban Atlanta. Currently represents Home Depot in connection with the rollout of its Expo Design Center stores and on a regional basis in connection with the development and leasing of Home Depot home improvement stores. Also regularly represents landlords and tenants in office and industrial development matters and leasing transactions, with a particular emphasis on the development and leasing of telecommunication facilities. Is a regular contributor to local and national continuing legal education seminars. Recent speaking engagements include presentations at two recent International Council of Shopping Centers National Law Conference programs and chairing a breakfast roundtable at a recent International Council of Shopping Centers University of Shopping Centers.
Prof. Memberships: Member of the International Council of Shopping Centers (member of Law Committee) and past chair of the Real Property Law Section of the State Bar of Georgia, as well as past chair of the legislative and legal opinion committees of this Section. Co-author of the 'Report on Legal Opinions to Third Parties in Georgia Real Estate Secured Transactions' (Real Property Law Section of the State Bar of Georgia, October 15, 1997), which establishes a model opinion for use in Georgia secured loan transactions.
Personal: JD, magna cum laude, University of Michigan, 1980,Order of the Coif, Phi Beta Kappa; BBA, with highest honors, University of Michigan, 1977.

KAUFMAN, Mark
Sutherland Asbill & Brennan LLP, Atlanta 404 853 8107
mdkaufman@sablaw.com
Recommended in Corporate/M&A

Specialisation: Co-chairs the firm's Corporate teams. Practices in the areas of corporate and securities law. Practice focuses on the general representation of corporations, with an emphasis on day to day counseling and problem solving. Has extensive experience in the representation of public corporations, including all aspects of SEC reporting, and in acquisitions and sales of businesses, having worked on more than 50 in the last several years. In addition, has been significant-

GEORGIA LEADERS

ly involved in public and private offerings of securities and has represented underwriters in public offerings of securities. Has extensive experience with fast-growth companies, including their start-up, financing and public offering and sale. In addition, represents companies in a wide variety of businesses, including consumer products, finance, fulfillment, healthcare, hospitality, internet banking, manufacturing, quick service restaurants and textiles, among many others. Experienced in acquiring businesses in Europe and Latin America.
Prof. Memberships: Served for 20 years as Legal Counsel to the Atlanta Bar Association and the Atlanta Bar Foundation.
Personal: JD, with distinction, Duke University School of Law, 1974, Order of the Coif, Note and Comment Editor, 'Duke Law Journal'; BA, Northwestern University, 1971.

KAUFMAN, Mark
McKenna Long & Aldridge, Atlanta
404 527 4000
Recommended in Insolvency

KAUSS, Andrew
Kilpatrick Stockton LLP, Atlanta
404 815 6500
Recommended in Real Estate

KAZMAREK, Edward
McKenna Long & Aldridge, Atlanta
404 527 4000
Recommended in Environment

KELLEHER, Thomas
Smith, Currie & Hancock LLP, Atlanta
404 521 3800
Recommended in Construction

KELLEY, John
King & Spalding LLP, Atlanta
404 572 3401
jkelley@kslaw.com
Recommended in Corporate/M&A
Specialisation: Corporate finance transactions and securities matters in Rule 144 and Regulation S public offerings and private placements in the technology, real estate, healthcare and manufacturing industries. Advises corporations regarding SEC reporting and disclosure requirements, securities transactions and compliance matters. Merger and acquisition transactions, including tender offers, leveraged buy-outs, going private transactions, stock and asset sales and partnership and joint venture transactions.
Prof. Memberships: American Bar Association; Atlanta Bar Association; The Florida Bar; State Bar of Georgia.
Personal: AB, cum laude, Hamilton College, 1982; JD University of Virginia, Phi Beta Kappa, 1985.

KILGORE III, Cada
Sutherland Asbill & Brennan LLP,
Atlanta 404 853 8196
ctkilgore@sablaw.com
Recommended in Energy
Specialisation: Practice includes the representation of lenders, underwriters, utilities and other electric industry participants in financings, mergers and acquisitions, power project and corporate transactions and power supply matters. Experience includes publicly-issued and privately-placed bond financings, a variety of secured and unsecured loan arrangements, leasing transactions, corporate restructurings, mergers and acquisitions and government-guaranteed financings. Practice has included construction and permanent financings for electric power plants, mortgage bond financings for electric generation, transmission and distribution systems, power supply arrangements, retail competition, stranded cost recovery and other aspects of industry restructuring.
Prof. Memberships: Member of the Business Law Section, the Section of Public Utility, Communications and Transportation and the Section of Environment, Energy and Resource Law of the American Bar Association; the Electric Cooperative Bar Association; the G&T Lawyers' Association and the G&T TAC Subcommittee.
Personal: MBA, University of Georgia, 1979; JD, magna cum laude, University of Georgia School of Law, 1979, Order of the Coif, Notes Editor, 'Georgia Law Review'; BBA, magna cum laude, Georgia College, 1975, Phi Kappa Phi.

KLEIN, Daniel
Buckley & Klein LLP, Atlanta
404 781 1100
Recommended in Employment

KNIGHT JR, Donald
King & Spalding LLP, Atlanta
404 572 4764
dknight@kslaw.com
Recommended in Corporate/M&A
Specialisation: Domestic mergers and acquisitions, including advising non-US investors in structuring, negotiating and effecting investments relating to corporate acquisitions, venture capital investments, real estate investments and complex securities portfolios.
Prof. Memberships: American Bar Association; Atlanta Bar Association; State Bar of Georgia; International Bar Association; International Fiscal Association; INTERTAX (Contributing Editor); (Advisory Board) North American Free Trade & Investment Report; Tax Management International Journal (Advisory Board).
Personal: BA, highest honors, Mississippi State University, 1961; MA, Emory University, 1963; LLB, University of Virginia, Order of the Coif, 1967. Frequent speaker and author on international law and taxation matters.

KNUDSON, Kathryn
Powell, Goldstein, Frazer & Murphy LLP,
Atlanta 404 572 6600
Recommended in Banking & Finance

LONG, Clay
McKenna Long & Aldridge, Atlanta
404 527 4000
Recommended in Corporate/M&A

LUNSFORD, Rodgers
Smith, Gambrell & Russell, LLP, Atlanta
404 815 3500
Recommended in Intellectual Property

LUREY, Alfred
Kilpatrick Stockton LLP, Atlanta
404 815 6500
Recommended in Insolvency

MACDONALD, Ralph
Alston & Bird LLP, Atlanta
404 881 7000
Recommended in Banking & Finance

MARSH, Gary
McKenna Long & Aldridge, Atlanta
404 527 4000
Recommended in Insolvency

MARSHALL, John
Powell, Goldstein, Frazer & Murphy LLP,
Atlanta 404 572 6600
Recommended in Antitrust, Litigation

MATCHETT, Sam
King & Spalding LLP, Atlanta
404 572 2414
smatchett@kslaw.com
Recommended in Employment
Specialisation: Employment relationship matters, emphasis in labor and employment litigation in state and federal courts, governmental agencies and arbitration tribunals, including employment discrimination matters. Advice on avoidance of employee-related problems, presenting seminars concerning all aspects of employment law. Litigation involving Civil Rights Acts of 1866 and 1964, Age Discrimination in Employment Act and Americans with Disabilities Act.
Prof. Memberships: Appeals Court of Georgia; Georgia State Bar; Institute of Applied Management and Law (IAML) (faculty member).
Personal: BA, magna cum laude, Morehouse College, 1981; JD, University of Georgia, 1984.

MCNEILL, Thomas
Powell, Goldstein, Frazer & Murphy LLP,
Atlanta 404 572 6600
Recommended in Corporate/M&A

MEIR, Dennis
Kilpatrick Stockton LLP, Atlanta
404 815 6500
Recommended in Insolvency

MILLER, Harlan
Parks, Chesin, Walbert & Miller, Atlanta
404 873 8000
Recommended in Employment

MOELING, Walter
Powell, Goldstein, Frazer & Murphy LLP,
Atlanta 404 572 6600
Recommended in Banking & Finance

MOLAVI, Kamyar
Seyfarth Shaw, Atlanta
404 892 6412
Recommended in Construction

MURPHY, Charles
Vaughan & Murphy, Atlanta
404 577 6550
Recommended in Antitrust

NAGLE, Shannon
Powell, Goldstein, Frazer & Murphy LLP,
Atlanta 404 572 6600
Recommended in Insolvency

NEEDLE, Bill
Needle & Rosenberg, Atlanta
404 688 0700
Recommended in Intellectual Property

NELSON, Pat
Pat Nelson-Sole Practitioner, Athens
706 549 5598
Recommended in Employment

NEWTON, Trammell
Jones Day, Atlanta 404 581 8308
tnewton@jonesday.com
Recommended in Antitrust
Specialisation: Broad experience in all facets of antitrust and trade regulation practice. Has appeared in numerous civil and criminal antitrust matters in both state and federal trial and appellate courts, including the US Supreme Court. Litigation experience includes the defense of a number of class actions, in connection with antitrust and other complex commercial matters. Has also represented clients before state and federal antitrust enforcement agencies in a large number of regulatory matters, with particular emphasis on Clayton Act merger investigations. Additionally, has provided counseling on, and litigated with respect to, a broad range of trade regulation matters, including trade practice rules and state and federal franchise and distributor/dealer termination laws. Regularly counsels companies on structuring business arrangements so as to minimize antitrust risk and has conducted audits, internal investigations, and compliance programs for a variety of clients.
Prof. Memberships: Member of the ABA (Antitrust Law Section), the State Bar of Georgia (Antitrust Section), and the bars of the US District Court for the Northern District of Georgia, the US Court of Appeals for the Eleventh Circuit, and the US Supreme Court.

NEY, James
Holt Ney Zatcoff & Wasserman, LLP,
Atlanta 770 956 9600
Recommended in Real Estate

LEADERS
GEORGIA

NODINE, Larry
Needle & Rosenberg, Atlanta
404 688 0700
Recommended in Intellectual Property

NORTH, John
Sutherland Asbill & Brennan LLP,
Atlanta 404 853 8358
jlnorth@sablaw.com
Recommended in Intellectual Property
Specialisation: Practices primarily in the area of intellectual property. Has substantial experience in controversies involving patent infringement and trade secret misappropriation, and related unfair competition and antitrust controversies. Also has experience handling trademark infringement and trademark opposition. Has tried cases in state and federal court, and has arbitrated and mediated a number of disputes. Has been admitted to practice before all Georgia state courts, the United States District Court for the Northern District of Georgia, and the Eleventh, Federal and Third Federal Circuit Courts of Appeal. Serves as lead patent counsel to one of the nation's major entertainment copmanies in one of the largest sets of patent and antitrust cases pending in the United States.
Prof. Memberships: Member of the Intellectual Property Law, Science and Technology and Litigation Sections of the American Bar Association. Council member of the Science and Technology Section, as well as Vice Chair of the Section's standing Committee on Scientific Evidence, Section Liaison of the American Bar Association's standing Committee of Publishing Oversight, and editor of the Section's 'Scientific Evidence Review'. Past President of the Atlanta Chapter of the Federal Bar Association.
Personal: JD, cum laude, Emory University School of Law, 1987, Notes & Comments Editor, 'Emory Law Journal'; BA, magna cum laude, Duke University, 1984.

NURKIN, Sidney
Alston & Bird LLP, Atlanta
404 881 7000
Recommended in Corporate/M&A

OAKES, Leslie
King & Spalding LLP, Atlanta
404 572 3314
loakes@kslaw.com
Recommended in Environment
Specialisation: Experienced in permitting and enforcement actions, air and water pollution and hazardous waste. Environmental due diligence in a number of complex transactions involving industrial facilities and properties. Over 11 years as environmental engineer with the Environmental Protection Division, Georgia Department of Natural Resources.
Prof. Memberships: American Bar Association; State Bar of Georgia.

Personal: BME, Georgia Institute of Technology, 1974; MS Georgia State University, 1981; JD, Georgia State University, 1986.

OAKLEY, Mary Ann
Holland & Knight LLP, Atlanta
404 817 8500
maoakley@hklaw.com
Recommended in Employment
Specialisation: Partner in the Litigation Department, practicing for more than 28 years in the area of labor and employment law, appeals, and alternative dispute resolution. She has substantial experience in administrative proceedings, trials, and appellate practice in all aspects of labor and employment law. She has advised numerous clients about personnel, human resources, and employment practices, including drafting contracts, policies and procedures. She has experience training employers in a wide variety of employment matters including discrimination, harassment, retaliation and Fair Labor Standards Act issues. She is a trained mediator and arbitrator, has served as a Special Master for the Georgia Commission on Equal Opportunity, was on the editorial review board of 'The Georgia Labor Letter', and has published many articles on employment law matters.

O'DAY, Stephen
Smith, Gambrell & Russell, LLP, Atlanta
404 815 3500
Recommended in Environment

PAKENHAM, Tim
Alston & Bird LLP, Atlanta
404 881 7000
Recommended in Real Estate

PARDO JR, James
King & Spalding LLP, Atlanta
404 572 4794
jpardo@kslaw.com
Recommended in Insolvency
Specialisation: Financial restructuring transactions, focusing on representation of secured and unsecured creditors in both bankruptcy cases and out of court debt restructurings.
Prof. Memberships: American Bankruptcy Institute; Fellow, American College of Bankruptcy; State Bar of Georgia (past Chairman, Bankruptcy Section); 'Collier on Bankruptcy' and 'Collier Bankruptcy Manual' (former contributing Editor); Southeastern Bankruptcy Law Institute (Director).
Personal: BA, with honors, University of Virginia, Phi Beta Kappa, 1979; JD, University of Virginia, Order of the Coif, 1979. Frequent lecturer on bankruptcy and commercial litigation.

PARKS, Lee
Parks, Chesin, Walbert & Miller, Atlanta
404 873 8000
Recommended in Employment

PARKS, John
Powell, Goldstein, Frazer & Murphy LLP, Atlanta 404 572 6600
Recommended in Real Estate

PERRIN, Martha
Ogletree, Deakins, Nash, Smoak & Stewart, PC, Atlanta 404 881 1300
Recommended in Employment

PERSONS, Oscar
Alston & Bird LLP, Atlanta
404 881 7000
Recommended in Litigation

PHILLIPS, Stephen
Hendrick Phillips Salzman & Flatt PC, Atlanta 404 522 1410
smp@hpsf-law.com
Recommended in Construction
Specialisation: Construction law; commercial roofing.
Prof. Memberships: Fellow, American College of Construction Lawyers. Counsel, National Roofing Contractors Assocation; National Roofing Legal Resource Center.
Career: 1976-81 *Stokes & Shapiro*, Atlanta, GA. 1981 - present *Hendrick, Phillips, Salzman & Flatt*.
Publications: 'Construction Technology for Lawyers: Roofing Systems'; 'Liabilities of Parties Engaged in Re-roofing Construction Projects'; 'Roofing Contractor's Guide to Mold'; 'Roofing Warranties'; 'Avoiding Problems With Additional Insureds'; 'Avoiding Problems With Defective Materials'; 'Avoiding OSHA Liability Resulting from Employee Misconduct'; 'Indemnification Agreements'; 'How To Combat Proprietary Specifications'.
Personal: Born: December 9, 1949, Philadelphia, PA; George Washington University, BA 1971; Emory University, JD 1976.

POPE, David
Carr, Tabb, Pope & Freeman, LLP, Atlanta 404 442 9000
Recommended in Environment

POWELL, Thomas
Troutman Sanders LLP, Atlanta
404 885 3000
Recommended in Banking & Finance

POWERS, Tony
Rogers & Hardin, Atlanta 404 522 4700
Recommended in Antitrust

PRINCE, Alan
King & Spalding LLP, Atlanta
404 572 3595
aprince@kslaw.com
Recommended in Corporate/M&A
Specialisation: Corporate finance transactions and securities matters, representing issuers and underwriters in connection with initial and secondary public offerings, 'shelf' offerings, Rule 144A offerings and other private placement transactions. Extensive experience in public offerings of equity securities, including initial public offerings, SEC reporting and disclosure requirements and corporate governance issues. Private merger and acquisition transactions, including mergers, tender offers and stock and asset transactions.
Prof. Memberships: American Bar Association; Atlanta Bar Association; State Bar of Georgia.
Personal: BA, cum laude, Wake Forest University, 1986; JD, cum laude, University of Georgia, 1989.

RHODES, Tom
Smith, Gambrell & Russell, LLP, Atlanta
404 815 3500
Recommended in Antitrust

RICHARDS, Russell
King & Spalding LLP, Atlanta
404 572 4695
rrichards@kslaw.com
Recommended in Corporate/M&A
Specialisation: Representing clients in connection with the acquisition and sale of publicly-held and privately-owned companies and establishing domestic and international joint ventures in the United States and in Canada, Mexico, South America, the United Kingdom and Continental Europe.
Prof. Memberships: American Bar Association; Atlanta Bar Association; BTI Consulting Group, Inc.'s 2002 Client Service All-Star Team; State Bar of Georgia.
Personal: BS, high honors, University of Tennessee, 1971; JD, high honors, Duke University, 1974.

RIDDELL, Stephen
Troutman Sanders LLP, Atlanta
404 885 3000
Recommended in Employment

ROGERS, CB
Rogers & Hardin, Atlanta 404 522 4700
Recommended in Antitrust, Litigation

ROSENBERG, Sumner
Needle & Rosenberg, Atlanta
404 688 0700
Recommended in Intellectual Property

ROSENBLATT, Paul
Kilpatrick Stockton LLP, Atlanta
404 815 6500
Recommended in Insolvency

ROSENBLOUM, Robert
Greenberg Traurig LLP, Atlanta
678 553 2250
rosenbloumb@gtlaw.com
Recommended in Intellectual Property
Specialisation: Entertainment and intellectual property.
Prof. Memberships: Executive Committee (Member-at-Large), Georgia State Bar Entertainment and Sports Law Section. Member, ABA Entertainment and Sports Law Section. Member, Copyright Society of the United States.
Publications: 'Sorting Through the Confusion: Interpreting Standard Recording Agreement Provisions in the Digital Era,'

GEORGIA   LEADERS

'The Entertainment Law Reporter', November 1999. 'A Very Welcome Return: Copyright Reversion and Termination of Copyright Assignments in the Music Industry,' 'ABA Entertainment and Sports Lawyer'.

ROSS, Mickey
King & Spalding LLP, Atlanta
404 572 4876
mross@kslaw.com
Recommended in Antitrust
Specialisation: Over 25 years experience in employment and healthcare litigation, including employment and separation agreements, personnel policies and handbooks, EEO and diversity training, FLSA and FMLA compliance, restrictive covenants, retirement incentives and reductions-in-force. Numerous employment cases under Title VII, the ADA, the ADEA, 'a7 1981, the FMLA, and state law. Involved in ADR, including mediation, arbitration, and summary jury trials.
Prof. Memberships: American Bar Association; Atlanta Bar Association; State Bar of Georgia.
Personal: AB, University of Florida, 1971; JD, magna cum laude, Phi Beta Kappa, Omicron Delta Kappa, Harvard University, 1974.

RUSCHE, Mark
Alston & Bird LLP, Atlanta
404 881 7000
Recommended in Real Estate

RUSS, Michael
King & Spalding LLP, Atlanta
404 572 4774
mruss@kslaw.com
Recommended in Antitrust, Litigation
Specialisation: Corporate and securities litigation, SEC and tax investigations, as well as general commercial disputes. Specializes in representation of corporate clients in securities and antitrust class actions and internal corporate investigations.
Prof. Memberships: American Bar Association; American College of Trial Lawyers; The District of Columbia Bar; State Bar of Georgia.
Personal: AB, Duke University, 1966; JD, Duke University, Order of the Coif, 1969.

SALYERS, Douglas
Troutman Sanders LLP, Atlanta
404 885 3000
Recommended in Intellectual Property

SALZMAN, Martin
Hendrick Phillips Salzman & Flatt PC, Atlanta 404 522 1410
Recommended in Construction

SAUNTRY, June Ann
Troutman Sanders LLP, Atlanta
404 885 3000
Recommended in Antitrust

SCHWARTZ, Debra
Thompson, Rollins, Schwartz & Borowski, Decatur 404 377 7717
Recommended in Employment

SCHWARTZ, Robert
Smith, Gambrell & Russell, LLP, Atlanta
404 815 3500
Recommended in Banking & Finance

SHAPIRO, Ben
Shapiro Fussell Wedge Smotherman Martin & Price, LLP, Atlanta
404 870 2200
Recommended in Construction

SHIELDS, Robert
Doffermyre, Shields, Canfield, Knowles & Devine, Atlanta 404 881 8900
Recommended in Litigation

SINKFIELD, Richard
Rogers & Hardin, Atlanta 404 522 4700
Recommended in Litigation

SMITH, George A (Tony)
Sutherland Asbill & Brennan LLP, Atlanta 404 853 8092
gasmith@sablaw.com
Recommended in Construction
Specialisation: Head of the firm's Construction Industry Disputes Practice Group and the International Arbitration and Dispute Resolution Practice Group. Has substantial experience in the areas of construction contract negotiation, arbitration, and litigation, both domestically and abroad. Practicing law since 1973, has extensive experience as lead trial attorney in large, complex, multi-party, construction-related disputes. Has represented the full spectrum of construction clients, including: EPC contractors, general contractors, owners, architects/engineers, subcontractors, sureties, and insurors. His success as a litigator is reflected in the many multi-million dollar jury verdicts, arbitration awards, or settlements he has obtained on behalf of clients, including: a $24 million settlement for the Milwaukee Metropolitan Sewerage District against a large engineering contractor; a $3.2 million jury verdict against the Florida Department of Transportation; a $29 million jury verdict/judgment against a mechanical subcontractor and its surety on a large hospital project in Wilmington, Delaware; an $8.7 million arbitration award on behalf of a terminated contractor on a large hospital project in Los Angles; a $1.5 million arbitration award against the Cobb County Water and Sewer Authority; and, as co-counsel, a $26 million arbitration award on behalf of the general contractor on the Liberty Place mixed-use project in Philadelphia. Internationally, has served as an advocate or arbitrator for cases in Egypt, the United Kingdom, Malaysia, the Turks and Caicos Islands, the Bahamas, the US Virgin Islands, and others.
Prof. Memberships: Member of the International, American, Georgia and Kentucky Bar Associations. Fellow of the American College of Construction Lawyers and the Center for International Legal Studies, and is a Member of the Chartered Institute of Arbitrators and the London Court of International Arbitration.
Publications: Lectured and written extensively on topics related to the construction industry, publishing over 50 articles and speaking at over 75 programs and seminars during the course of his legal career.
Personal: JD, with high distinction, University of Kentucky, 1973, Delta Theta Phi, Order of the Coif; BA, with distinction, University of Kentucky, 1970.

SMITH, James
Troutman Sanders LLP, Atlanta
404 885 3000
Recommended in Corporate/M&A

SPALDING, William
King & Spalding LLP, Atlanta
404 572 3385
bspalding@kslaw.com
Recommended in Corporate/M&A
Specialisation: Private equity and investment funds, representing strategic funds and in private equity transactions ranging from non-control investments in technology and biotech companies to control investments and sales of established operating companies. Representing publicly-held corporations in corporate governance and SEC compliance and reporting matters.
Prof. Memberships: American Bar Association; Atlanta Bar Association; State Bar of Georgia.
Personal: AB, with honors, Dartmouth College, 1981; JD, summa cum laude, Washington & Lee University, 1984.

SPANGLER, John
Alston & Bird LLP, Atlanta
404 881 7000
Recommended in Construction

STAIR, Kent
Carlock Copeland Semler & Stair, LLP, Atlanta 404 522 8220
Recommended in Construction

STEIN, Grant
Alston & Bird LLP, Atlanta
404 881 7000
Recommended in Insolvency

STEIN, Jeffrey
King & Spalding LLP, Atlanta
404 572 4729
jstein@kslaw.com
Recommended in Corporate/M&A
Specialisation: Corporate finance transactions and securities matters, focusing on public offerings, representing corporate issuers and underwriters in shelf registrations of investment-grade debt securities, medium-term note programs, high-yield securities offerings and initial public offerings of common stock. Advice regarding SEC reporting and disclosure requirements, securities transactions and corporate governance and compliance matters.
Prof. Memberships: American Bar Association (Legal Opinions Committees); New York State Bar Association; New York City, County and State Bar Associations (Tri-Bar Legal Opinion Committee); State Bar of Georgia.
Personal: BA, summa cum laude, Yeshiva University, 1977; JD, Harvard University, 1980.

STEPHENSON, Mason
King & Spalding LLP, Atlanta
404 572 4945
mstephenson@kslaw.com
Recommended in Real Estate
Specialisation: Commercial real estate law, representing banks, credit companies, life insurance companies, pension funds and institutional investors in secured financings and equity investments in income properties, including office buildings, hotels, apartments and industrial properties. Extensive experience in workout, restructure and foreclosure of real estate investments.
Prof. Memberships: American College of Real Estate Lawyers; Atlanta Bar Association (former Chairman, Real Estate Section); State Bar of Georgia (former member, Executive Committee, Real Estate Section).
Personal: AB, cum laude, Phi Beta Kappa, Davidson College, 1968; JD, University of Chicago, 1971. Frequent lecturer on commercial real estate and ethics topics.

STOCKTON, David
Kilpatrick Stockton LLP, Atlanta
404 815 6500
Recommended in Corporate/M&A

STOKES, James
Alston & Bird LLP, Atlanta
404 881 7000
Recommended in Environment

SWEENEY, Neal
Kilpatrick Stockton LLP, Atlanta
404 815 6500
Recommended in Construction

SWENSON, Erik
King & Spalding LLP, Atlanta
404 572 3540
eswenson@kslaw.com
Recommended in Energy
Specialisation: Nationwide representation of energy project participants, including developers, equity investors and lenders and industrial companies in energy matters, including the purchase and sale of electricity and energy regulation matters.

Prof. Memberships: District of Columbia Bar; New York State Bar.
Personal: BA, cum laude, Columbia College; JD, Columbia University School of Law, 1982. Lectures before energy industry leaders on project development and energy regulation. Regular contributor to energy industry publications.

TAYLOR, Roger
Finnegan Henderson Farabow Garrett & Dunner LLP, Atlanta 404 653 6400
Recommended in Intellectual Property

THOMPSON, William
Powell, Goldstein, Frazer & Murphy LLP, Atlanta 404 572 6600
Recommended in Real Estate

THROWER, Randolph
Sutherland Asbill & Brennan LLP, Atlanta 404 853 8149
rwthrower@sablaw.com
Recommended in Tax
Specialisation: Works primarily in the area of Federal taxation, including civil and criminal tax controversies, litigation, estate planning and administration, general corporate and individual tax-related matters. From 1969-71, served as US Commissioner of Internal Revenue. In 1993, received the American Bar Association Medal, the ABA's highest honor, for his extensive public, professional and government service. In 1995, received the Court of Federal Claims Special Service Award, given in recognition of his many contributions to the Court, and received the Tax Section's Distinguished Service Award for 1996.
Career: Served as trustee on the boards of several universities and colleges and served as Chair of the Ethics Committee of the City of Atlanta from 1980 until 1992. Joined *Sutherland* in 1936 and has practiced in both the Washington and Atlanta offices.
Personal: Honorary LLD, Emory University, 1984; JD, first honors, Emory University School of Law, 1936; BPh, Emory University, 1934.

TISDALE JR, Charles
King & Spalding LLP, Atlanta
404 572 4820
ctisdale@kslaw.com
Recommended in Environment
Specialisation: 30 years experience in environmental law, representing clients on air, water, and superfund and hazardous waste issues before state and federal agencies and in litigation.
Prof. Memberships: American Bar Association; Chemical Waste Litigation Reporter (Board); Clean Air Campaign; the Georgia Conservancy; Research Atlanta; State Bar of Georgia (former Chairman, Environmental Law Section).
Personal: BA, cum laude, Vanderbilt University, 1969; JD, with distinction, Emory University, Order of the Coif; Omicron Delta Kappa, 1972.

TOULME, Nill
Alston & Bird LLP, Atlanta
404 881 7000
Recommended in Environment

VANDERBROEK, Mark
Troutman Sanders LLP, Atlanta
404 885 3000
Recommended in Intellectual Property

VARNER, Chilton
King & Spalding LLP, Atlanta
404 572 4789
cvarner@kslaw.com
Recommended in Litigation
Specialisation: 25 years courtroom experience defending corporations in product liability, commercial and civil disputes. Trial and appellate counsel for large automotive, pharmaceutical and medical device manufacturers. Mass tort litigation, class actions and MDL litigation, including attorney-client privilege and Daubert issues.
Prof. Memberships: American Bar Association; American College of Trial Lawyers; Atlanta Bar Association; Emory University (Trustee); Product Liability Advisory Council (member); State Bar of Georgia.
Personal: AB, with distinction, Phi Beta Kappa, Smith College, 1965; JD, with distinction, Emory University, Order of the Coif, 1976. Distinguished Alumni Award, Emory University Law School.

VAUGHAN, David
Vaughan & Murphy, Atlanta
404 577 6550
Recommended in Antitrust

WASSERMAN, Michael
Holt Ney Zatcoff & Wasserman, LLP, Atlanta 770 956 9600
Recommended in Tax

WEIRICH, Geoff
Paul, Hastings, Janofsky & Walker LLP, Atlanta 404 815 2400
geoffweirich@paulhastings.com
Recommended in Employment
Specialisation: Exclusively represents employers in defending employment discrimination claims. Has handled more than two dozen employment class actions and is widely recognized for his extensive experience in such complex cases, as well as in matters arising under either Title I or Title III of the Americans with Disabilities Act.
Publications: Editor in Chief (Third Cumulative Supplement) to the Lindemann & Grossman treatise, 'Employment Discrimination Law'.
Personal: MA, Labor and Industrial Relations and BA, Economics, (Michigan State University). JD, (Duke University School of Law). Served as Executive Editor of the 'Duke Law Journal', and received high honors and Order of the Coif.

WELLS, Della
Alston & Bird LLP, Atlanta
404 881 7000
Recommended in Energy

WHITE, Benjamin
Alston & Bird LLP, Atlanta
404 881 7000
Recommended in Tax

WILLIAMSON, Robert
Scroggins & Williamson, Atlanta
404 893 3880
Recommended in Insolvency

WILSON, Stanford
Elarbee, Thompson, Sapp & Wilson, LLP, Atlanta 404 659 6700
Recommended in Employment

WOODWARD, Robert
King & Spalding LLP, Atlanta
404 572 3353
bwoodward@kslaw.com
Recommended in Tax
Specialisation: Business tax issues, focusing on corporate mergers, acquisitions, restructurings and financings. Experience in tax, business and estate planning issues relating to corporate executives and closely held businesses and owners in tax controversies.
Prof. Memberships: American Bar Association (Chair, Subcommittee on Tax-Free Acquisitions); Atlanta Tax Forum (former President and Trustee); Georgia Federal Tax Conference (Trustee); State Bar of Georgia.
Personal: BA, magna cum laude, Washington & Lee University, 1971; JD, Yale University, 1975.

WYMER, John
King & Spalding LLP, Atlanta
404 572 2413
jwymer@kslaw.com
Recommended in Employment
Specialisation: Representing employers, (private and public) in labor and employment-related disputes, class action litigation, employment discrimination cases, sexual harassment claims, National Labor Relations Board matters, arbitrations, wage/hour disputes and labor negotiations.
Prof. Memberships: Alabama State Bar; Fellow, The College of Labor and Employment Lawyers; Management Labor and Employment Law Roundtable.
Publications: 'Personnel Law Desk Manual' (contributing Editor), State Bar of Georgia.
Personal: BA, University of Alabama, 1971; JD, University of Virginia, 1974. Instructor, the California Labor and the Institute for Applied Management and Law.

YOUNG, Jeffrey
Alston & Bird LLP, Atlanta
404 881 7000
Recommended in Intellectual Property

HAWAII

CORPORATE/M&A

CONTENTS: Corporate/M&A p.212; Employment: Mainly Plaintiff p.213; Mainly Defendant p.214; Litigation: General Commercial p.215; Real Estate p.216; Individuals' Profiles p.218.

HAWAII'S TOP TWO
1. Goodsill Anderson Quinn & Stifel
2. Cades Schutte Fleming & Wright

Ranking based on Chambers' research within the state.

All quotes in the text are from interviews with clients and competitors.

OVERVIEW: With over 70 attorneys, **Goodsill Anderson Quinn & Stifel** is one of the largest law firms in Hawaii. The Honolulu-based firm provides a full range of legal services, but is said to be strongest in corporate and real estate law. A large corporate team boasts expertise in capital markets transactions, while the real estate department has figured prominently in a series of groundbreaking transactions. These include advising on the first horizontal property regime under Hawaiian condominium law and completing documentation for the first mixed-use residential, office and commercial condominium project to be approved in the Kakaako Development District in Honolulu. Key clients include American Savings Bank, Hawaiian Airlines, Dole Foods and Macy's.

Cades Schutte Fleming & Wright is its closest competitor, both in size and strength. Lawyers in the firm's corporate, employment, litigation and real estate groups received commendation throughout the market for their quality of service and breadth of experience. Litigation is a particularly strong suit for the practice; interviewees regularly noted the firm's successful court record as well as its skill at alternative dispute resolution. A highly rated real estate practice handles real estate finance, title work and real estate litigation, while the corporate section is supported by the state's largest tax and land use practices. It also features in the employment rankings for its combined defendant and plaintiff practice. The firm's attorneys act as local counsel to clients such as Citibank, Wal-Mart and Merrill Lynch.

CORPORATE/M&A

HAWAII
Leading firms (Corporate/M&A)
1. GOODSILL ANDERSON QUINN & STIFEL Honolulu
2. CADES SCHUTTE FLEMING & WRIGHT Honolulu
3. CARLSMITH BALL LLP Honolulu
   CASE BIGELOW & LOMBARDI Honolulu
4. GELBER, GELBER, INGERSOLL Honolulu

Leading individuals (Corporate/M&A)
1. **CASE Daniel** Case Bigelow & Lombardi, Honolulu
   KIM Gregory Goodsill Anderson Quinn & Stifel, Honolulu
   REBER David Goodsill Anderson Quinn, Honolulu
2. **CHUN Nelson** Cades Schutte Fleming, Honolulu
   SCHULL Gunner Cades Schutte Fleming, Honolulu
3. **CASE James** Carlsmith Ball LLP, Honolulu
   GELBER Stephen Gelber, Gelber, Ingersoll, Honolulu

Firms and individuals are listed alphabetically in each band.

Goodsill Anderson Quinn & Stifel

The Firm: The oldest and largest general practice firm in Hawaii is home to the state's largest corporate group. It handles a diverse range of work including M&A and securities law, while enjoying the support of a small but capable tax group. The corporate team is set apart by its strong foothold in the capital markets arena. Historically the firm has focused on advising large Hawaiian companies; however, it is increasingly acting for national and international clients. This caseload involves all transactional and regulatory compliance advice and the provision of dispute avoidance counseling. The team also covers municipal funding and bond offerings, and advises on the applicability of Hawaiian franchise laws to various commercial arrangements. Rivals acknowledged: *"If I had a corporate client and there was a conflict, Goodsill is the only firm I would feel comfortable referring to."*

The Lawyers: David Reber is a senior lawyer dedicated to the corporate arena. According to sources, he is a *"smart and experienced"* practitioner who *"knows the technical aspects of the field inside out."* His workload includes M&A, securities offerings and regulation, corporate governance and fiduciary duties. He is also experienced in handling commercial disputes. He has represented Hawaiian Electric Company in a $40 million State of Hawaii Department of Budget and Finance special purpose revenue bond financing. His colleague **Greg Kim** is a *"highly capable corporate lawyer with a niche in technology."* He spearheaded the firm's work with start-ups and hi-tech companies, currently a fast-growing sector in Hawaii, and is often involved in the angel financing stage of development. His workload also features institutional work with Goodsill Anderson's large corporate clients. IP is another string to his bow, and Kim has provided counseling on numerous domestic and international licensing and distribution agreements for computer software and hardware manufacturers.

The Clients: Typical clients include: Hawaiian Electric Industries; Hawaiian Electric Company; American Savings Bank; Hawaiian Airlines; Bank of Hawaii; DTRIC Insurance; Servco Pacific; Dole Foods; Coffee Partners Hawaii; Hawaii Biotech; Hoana Technologies; Hoku Scientific and Assist-Guide.

Cades Schutte Fleming & Wright

The Firm: Some interviewees singled out the corporate practice at this, one of Hawaii's oldest and largest, firms as among the most comprehensive in the state. It offers clients a full range of services and considerable transactional experience. A team of about six dedicated corporate partners is supported by Hawaii's largest tax and land use practices. Clients appreciate the firm's *"professional attitude, expertise and reasonable rates,"* and praised its skill in assisting with business formations and structuring.

The Lawyers: Nelson Chun acts for an impressive selection of Hawaiian companies, and local entrepreneurs. These include the largest dairy producer in the state and one of its largest supermarket chains. Clients value his responsiveness and lateral thinking: *"He's quick at responding to requests and good at finding alternative solutions to problems."* Typically his work includes M&A, business formation and structuring, and general advice on operational and contractual issues. He has advised one of the three hospitals involved in a $100 million combination, resulting in the creation of one of Hawaii's largest healthcare organizations. **Gunner Schull** heads the corporate department. Peers described him as a *"careful, thoughtful and technically adept"* corporate lawyer with many years of experience. A notably *"non-adversarial"* practitioner, he has focused on M&A, and business and franchising law. He has acted in a group of nonpublic corporate redemption and split-up transactions ranging from $10-100 million, and in the formation of limited liability joint ventures for real estate development projects with budgets of up to $200 million.

The Clients: The firm acts for a range of clients, including: Arthur Andersen; Inter Island Petroleum; Aloha Petroleum; Theo Davies Group; Tori Richard; Oceanic Institute; Edward Enterprises; The Queen's Health Systems; Alexander & Baldwin; City Mill Company; AES and Meadow Gold Dairies.

CORPORATE/M&A — HAWAII

Carlsmith Ball LLP
The Firm: A merger with a Los Angeles firm has given the Hawaii-based Carlsmith Ball mainland US strength, while retaining its focus on the Asia-Pacific region. Its forte lies in assisting US and foreign corporations in transactions throughout the Pacific area. M&A, reorganizations, regulatory advice and stockholder relations all feature in the workload here. The group is also active in a range of financing matters, including project finance, bonds, venture capital and federal and state offerings. Competitors agree that the team as a whole possesses considerable depth, and *"definitely has the resources to keep transactions moving."*
The Lawyers: According to observers, **Jim Case** is an *"active business lawyer who gets things done."* Over the past 40 years he has acted as general counsel to Hawaiian businesses in many fields. His workload of late incorporates the tourism, agricultural, real property and utilities sectors. He has acted for Hawaii's oldest company, C Brewer & Company, in its liquidation, which involved tax advice and the sales of all corporate assets, both business entities and lands.
The Clients: The firm represents clients within the construction, finance, telecom and energy sectors. It has a special emphasis on foreign investors. Client names include ML Macadamia Orchards, City Mill and The Admiral Thomas.

Case Bigelow & Lombardi LC
The Firm: Interviewees have a healthy respect for this *"reputable and talented"* medium-sized firm. Its corporate team is visible in a range of work, including the formation and operation of corporations, joint ventures and partnerships, M&A and financings. It also provides commercial advice on issues such as profit-sharing agreements, pensions and other employee benefit plans. Attorneys work closely with colleagues in the real estate group, enabling them to skillfully draft and close real estate transactions that are structured as corporate mergers or stock transfers.
The Lawyers: **Dan Case** (see p.218), the firm's senior director, concentrates on corporate and trust law for major firms active in Hawaii. Market commentators pointed to his *"good practical sense and sound judgment"* and his *"knack of sorting the important issues from the smaller ones."*
The Clients: The firm acts for local corporates and international entities.

Gelber, Gelber, Ingersoll & Klevansky LC
The Firm: This small firm has built up a *"quality reputation"* for its business advice. Although its size prevents it from taking on the volume of the larger corporate matters, peers consider the team to be quite visible in the field, and to offer high-quality assistance on a variety of corporate issues, including transactional M&A and corporate governance advice.
The Lawyers: The standout practitioner here, according to interviewees, is **Steve Gelber** (see p.218). He received plaudits as a *"sharp and knowledgeable"* practitioner in both the local business and tax law arenas. Competitors agree that he is a *"highly impressive"* and constructive lawyer to have on the other side, producing consistently high standards of transactional advice.
The Clients: The firm attracts a variety of regional clients such as Apartment Management & Investment Co., Employees' Retirement System of the State of Hawaii, Waimanu Associates, Paradise Petroleum, Parker School Trust, E Noa, Herbert Lee & Associates and Arlie & Company.

EMPLOYMENT & LABOR LAW — MAINLY PLAINTIFF

HAWAII
Leading firms
(Employment: Mainly Plaintiff)
1. **NING LILLY & JONES** Honolulu

Leading individuals
(Employment: Mainly Plaintiff)
1. **SIMONS David** Sole Practitioner, Honolulu
2. **HIATT Jerry** Sole Practitioner, Honolulu
   ICHINOSE Susan Sole Practitioner, Honolulu
   NING Ke-Ching Ning Lilly & Jones, Honolulu
   TAKAHASHI Herbert Takahashi Masui, Honolulu

Firms and individuals are listed alphabetically in each band.

Ning Lilly & Jones
The Firm: Clearly the state's leading plaintiff firm, Ning Lilly & Jones recently achieved particular acclaim when it took on a case against a large, prestigious Hawaiian law firm on behalf of one of its dismissed employment lawyers. Ning Lilly & Jones advised on a complaint that the firm had lodged with the state's Office of Disciplinary Counsel, which alleged ethical misconduct, and acted on a range of counter-allegations brought by the plaintiff, ultimately securing a jury verdict in its client's favor.
The Lawyers: **Ke-Ching Ning** is a highly regarded commercial litigator with a growing name for undertaking difficult labor and employment matters. Commentators applauded her determined and skillful handling of plaintiff cases.

Other Notable Practitioners
Formerly part of Simons & Viola, **David Simons** is now a sole practitioner with a dedicated plaintiffs' practice. Simons has enjoyed notable successes in the past few years. One interviewee said: *"He is someone I would recommend if a case had to go to trial."* Simons often represents victims in sex discrimination and sexual harassment cases. For example, he secured a $1.8 million award for a woman who lost her job as general manager of a car dealership because the owners thought they could not attract top male sales personnel to work for a woman. Other claims Simons frequently takes on involve age or arrest and court record discrimination, failure to pay wages, commissions or overtime, and breach of employment contracts. Peers describe sole practitioner **Susan Ichinose** as *"a truly talented lawyer."* She is increasingly visible in arbitration and mediation matters. The *"dynamic"* **Jerry Hiatt** is known best for his *"excellent advocacy skills,"* which make it *"exciting to watch him try a case."* He recently successfully concluded a plaintiff's labor case that resulted in a $2.9 million compensation award against Nissan of Hawaii. **Herbert Takahashi** of Takahashi Masui & Vasconcellos is a *"brilliant"* senior employment attorney with vast experience of union work. *"The guy everyone fears,"* admiring defense attorneys reported, adding that *"if you have a pinprick hole in your case, he will make it big enough to drive a truck through."*

HAWAII

EMPLOYMENT & LABOR LAW

EMPLOYMENT & LABOR LAW — MAINLY DEFENDANT

HAWAII
Leading firms
(Employment: Mainly Defendant)

1. **MARR HIPP JONES AND PEPPER** Honolulu
   TORKILDSON, KATZ, FONSECA, JAFFE Honolulu
2. **WATANABE ING KAWASHIMA & KOMEIJI** Honolulu
3. **ALSTON HUNT FLOYD & ING LC** Honolulu
   CADES SCHUTTE FLEMING & WRIGHT Honolulu

Leading individuals
(Employment: Mainly Defendant)

1. **KATZ Robert** Torkildson, Katz, Fonseca, Jaffe, Honolulu
   MARR Barry Marr Hipp Jones and Pepper, Honolulu
2. **HIPP Ken** Marr Hipp Jones and Pepper, Honolulu
   LEONG Ron Watanabe Ing Kawashima, Honolulu
3. **JOSSEM Jared** Dwyer Schraff Meyer Jossem, Honolulu
   KAWASHIMA James Watanabe Ing, Honolulu

Firms and individuals are listed alphabetically in each band.

Marr Hipp Jones and Pepper
The Firm: This boutique of *"labor law experts"* is primarily involved in defense work for an employer client base. Founded in 1995 by key players from Goodsill Anderson Quinn & Stifel and Carlsmith Ball, it now boasts six labor and employment partners. Adept in all areas of labor and employment law, the group remains best known for labor matters undertaken for its client roster of unionized companies. According to peers, the team comprises *"fine attorneys and respected litigators."*

The Lawyers: Barry Marr is at *"the top of the labor relations and employment law tree."* He has broad experience in both traditional labor and employment law, and has represented employers before arbitrators and administrative agencies and in federal and state courts. His cases have involved breach of contract, wrongful discharge, discrimination, defamation, fraud, and sexual harassment. He is valued as a source of counsel in collective bargaining negotiations. **Ken Hipp** is a *"well-respected"* labor lawyer with over 25 years' experience in counseling, arbitration, mediation and administrative agency practice, and litigation in federal and state courts. In addition he has served as lead negotiator, attorney and mediator in collective bargaining processes across numerous industries.

The Clients: Both Hawaiian and mainland-based companies, including hotels, medical centers, insurance and financial institutions, transportation companies and retailers.

Torkildson, Katz, Fonseca, Jaffe, Moore & Hetherington Attorneys At Law, LC
The Firm: A long tradition in the sector gives the group its strong foothold as one of *"the big names in town."* It boasts three offices across Hawaii and, with 15 attorneys dedicated to labor and employment law, one of the largest departments in the state. The firm has developed a breadth of experience, and practitioners are known among peers as a *"successful litigation outfit"* in jury and bench trials, as well as in arbitrations, mediations and other alternative dispute resolution (ADR) work. The firm is distinguished, however, by its prowess in management labor work, and has taken part in numerous administrative hearings, union organization and election campaigns as well as collective bargaining negotiations. The team excels in preventative counseling.

The Lawyers: Industry sources acknowledge that there are some talented younger partners here. However, the outstanding name remains that of **Bob Katz** (see p.218), who is adjudged *"the undisputed dean of employment law."* He is *"hard-working, smart and experienced"* and highly rated as a trial attorney. Katz has served for several years as cochair of the ABA's employment law section on antitrust and labor relations law.

Watanabe Ing Kawashima & Komeiji
The Firm: This firm is *"really muscling into the employment arena."* It enjoys a good reputation for understanding the needs of Hawaiian businesses and counseling employers of all sizes on effective management of workplace issues. The knowledgeable, experienced team advises on wrongful discharge, ADA and sexual harassment actions, and plant closings, union-organizing drives and wage and hour matters. An especial strength of the labor group is preventative labor law.

The Lawyers: Commentators singled out **Ron Leong** (see p.218), *"definitely a big name in town,"* for his labor negotiation and consulting work. He heads the firm's labor and employment and employee benefits group, and has practiced before various state and federal agencies. He is also active in ADR, arbitration and mediation. **Jim Kawashima** (see p.218), principally known as a general litigator, enjoys a wealth of experience in employment disputes. Researchers were told that *"for heavy-duty litigation, some of the state's leading employment practitioners turn to Mr Kawashima."*

The Clients: First Hawaiian Bank; Halekulani; DFS Hawaii; The Ritz-Carlton, Kapalua; Oceanic Time Warner Cable and MidWeek Printing (Honolulu Star-Bulletin).

Alston Hunt Floyd & Ing Attorneys At Law, LC
The Firm: This litigation-oriented group has substantial experience representing employers in wrongful termination, discrimination, and sexual harassment matters as well as benefits disputes. Peers respect its team of skilled litigators, noting that they are capable of *"impressive work"* in this area. The firm also focuses on ADR, dispute avoidance and the early resolution of claims, and advises on personnel policies and handbooks.

The Lawyers: The firm's key employment players are Ellen Carson and Louise Ing, who are representative of a team that possesses a good grounding in employment discrimination and wrongful termination matters.

Cades Schutte Fleming & Wright
The Firm: One of the two largest law firms in Honolulu, it handles a large volume of employment law, focusing on strategic planning and legal compliance. As well as drafting employee contracts and company handbooks, it also advises on personnel policies. The group has experience of union contract negotiations, and defends its employer client base against litigation and union-organizing campaigns. Despite its profile as one of the state's leading corporate firms, it also undertakes some plaintiff work. Overall, commentators judge it to be a *"pretty effective"* player in the sector. In a well-publicized case, the firm successfully argued that parts of the Hawaii Civil Rights Commission Act were unconstitutional on the grounds that employers risked never receiving a jury trial in employment discrimination cases.

The Lawyers: David Banks chairs the firm's employment law and labor relations group.

Other Notable Practitioners
Jared Jossem of Dwyer Schraff Meyer Jossem & Bushnell has enjoyed an excellent reputation in the labor and employment sphere since the early 1980's, and *"is held in high regard."* His practice encompasses litigation and arbitration, and he also undertakes reviews of personnel policies and issues pertaining to labor management law.

LITIGATION

GENERAL COMMERCIAL

HAWAII
Leading firms
(Litigation: General Commercial)

1 MCCORRISTON MILLER MUKAI *Honolulu*
2 CADES SCHUTTE FLEMING & WRIGHT *Honolulu*
GOODSILL ANDERSON QUINN & STIFEL *Honolulu*
3 ALSTON HUNT FLOYD & ING *Honolulu*
WATANABE ING KAWASHIMA & KOMEIJI *Honolulu*
4 CARLSMITH BALL LLP *Honolulu*
CRONIN, FRIED, SEKIYA, KEKINA *Honolulu*
PAUL, JOHNSON, PARK & NILES *Honolulu*

Leading individuals
(Litigation: General Commercial)

1 MCCORRISTON William *McCorriston Miller,* Honolulu
PORTNOY Jeffrey *Cades Schutte Fleming* Honolulu
2 ALSTON Paul *Alston Hunt Floyd & Ing,* Honolulu
DEZZANI David *Goodsill Anderson Quinn,* Honolulu
HEIHRE Michael *Cades Schutte Fleming,* Honolulu
KOBAYASHI Bert *Kobayashi, Sugita,* Honolulu
3 KAWASHIMA James *Watanabe Ing,* Honolulu
KOMEIJI John *Watanabe Ing Kawashima,* Honolulu
PAUL James *Paul, Johnson, Park & Niles,* Honolulu

Firms and individuals are listed alphabetically in each band.

McCorriston Miller Mukai MacKinnon LLP

The Firm: This started as a litigation boutique in 1989, but has since grown to become the fourth largest firm in Honolulu. It now numbers about 25 partners and, according to market feedback, remains *"one of the best litigation firms"* in the state. The local and national courtroom experience of these attorneys, coupled with their alternative dispute resolution (ADR) prowess, ensures that the team is a sound choice for litigation. Knowledge of the Asian markets, representing Japanese and Korean companies, is another of the team's strengths, and it has a foothold in the health and finance sectors. Typical work includes complex corporate and commercial disputes, insurance coverage disputes, and products and professional liability, and environmental, matters. Sources endorse its work in land-related litigation, where the team benefits from a healthy real estate practice. According to competitors the firm's success is based on close attention to the basics: *"It just has a lot of good lawyers and they work hard."*
The Lawyers: **Bill McCorriston** (see p.218), chair of the firm's litigation section, is established as one of the sector's great names. According to commentators, *"he is articulate, tenacious and cool, and he gets good hard work out of his supporting team."* His *"intelligence,"* along with his *"passion and intensity,"* helps him to get results, while in court he is *"one of the most gifted trial lawyers in Hawaii."* Much of his work is complex and multi-jurisdictional, and includes professional malpractice, antitrust and governmental matters, and construction and environmental disputes. He also does a great deal of insurance litigation.
The Clients: The firm advises local and national clients.

Cades Schutte Fleming & Wright

The Firm: The litigation team is one of the largest in the firm, with about 20 lawyers - including 12 partners - dedicated to the field. A *"highly professional group,"* it has won cases before the courts at every level, including the US Supreme Court. Some sources consider that, as a leading corporate player, the firm is particularly skilled in dispute avoidance and obtaining early settlements. It has built up a successful track record, not just in trials, appeals and administrative proceedings, but also in arbitration, mediation and other ADR processes. The group's workload extends to general corporate disputes, antitrust, IP, business torts and class actions. The group's profile in real estate, trust and construction litigation is considered to be particularly strong.
The Lawyers: According to his peers, **Jeff Portnoy** is *"just excellent."* The *"personable"* chair of the firm's litigation department, he is justly famed for his First Amendment and media cases, and is often the first port of call in Hawaii when the representation of newspapers and television companies is needed. The bulk of his work is in general business litigation and ADR, extending to many areas of law, such as insurance, employment, business torts, and securities. Portnoy is often found representing financial institutions. **Michael Heihre** serves as head of the commercial litigation group, and is especially renowned for his work in business disputes relating to real estate, financial, tax and trust matters. He works on both the defendants' and plaintiffs' sides and has experience of complex multi-state and international disputes. Sources confirm that *"the quality of his work is first rate."*
The Clients: The firm's impressive international client base includes: Merrill Lynch; Honeywell; Norwegian Cruise Lines; Campbell Estate; Theo H Davies & Company; Alexander & Baldwin; Nordic Construction and Odell Construction Company.

Goodsill Anderson Quinn & Stifel

The Firm: This is the largest general practice firm in Hawaii, employing over 70 people. It can boast the biggest, and one of the most diverse, litigation practices. Peers confirm that the group *"has good litigation skills and plentiful resources backing it up."* Its seasoned trial lawyers are experienced in a range of high-profile business disputes, including foreclosures, commercial class actions and tort claims. Possessed of a good trial record, the group is nevertheless deemed to be resolution-oriented, and adept at reducing costs through prevention counseling, risk avoidance audits, early-negotiated settlements and the skillful use of ADR. Sources acknowledged that *"across the board the team takes an effective and reasonable approach."* The litigation team also benefits from working with strong public utilities and communications groups.
The Lawyers: According to competitors, the lawyers here are *"not only good technically, but ethical too."* Chief among them, and *"quite a star,"* is **David Dezzani** (see p.218). He has more than 30 years of experience as a trial lawyer and has been chief counsel on over 100 trials. He enjoys a broad practice, which features construction, employment and personal injury litigation, most of which is on the defendants' side, although about a third of his work is for plaintiffs. In the recent TSA v Shimizu Corporation case, involving a dispute over an option agreement regarding the Four Seasons Hotel on Maui, the plaintiff claimed ownership of the hotel and multi-million dollar damages for alleged misrepresentations and fraud during negotiations to dissolve the partnership which owned the hotel. After nearly two years of litigation involving discovery and depositions in Japan, Hawaii and the US mainland, Dezzani and his team were successful in obtaining summary judgement in favor of the defendant, Shimizu, a result that was recently affirmed by the Supreme Court of Hawaii.
The Clients: The team's client roster includes Hyatt, Unum/Provident Companies, Steamship Mutual Underwriting Association, Wyeth, Pfizer, Castle & Cooke, Tokyu and various hotel owners and healthcare providers.

Alston Hunt Floyd & Ing Attorneys At Law, LC

The Firm: This mid-sized firm has a *"great reputation"* for litigation. It handles a steady stream of commercial and professional malpractice cases, on both the plaintiffs' and defendants' sides. The group is also experienced in complex disputes stemming from failed business transactions.
The Lawyers: A key player and one of the firm's founders, **Paul Alston** has a substantial reputation as a commercial trial lawyer. He handles much of the firm's most important litigation and advisory work. Competitors find him *"tenacious and articulate"* in negotiations, while in court he is *"always well prepared - and then some."* His hard work and high level of thoroughness are said to help ensure that the settlements he achieves for his clients are substantial, even if a case does not reach the trial stage. He has represented both foreign and

HAWAII — LITIGATION

domestic lenders in a variety of disputes involving lender liability claims, disputed liens and securities law violations, with values of up to $100 million. He has also been busy of late representing various property owners, including Dole Foods, in environmental disputes involving contaminated soil and groundwater.

The Clients: Notable clients include Hawaiian Electric Industries, Chuo Mitsui Trust & Banking Company, Thermo Electron and ConocoPhillips.

Watanabe Ing Kawashima & Komeiji

The Firm: Commentators admire this mid-sized firm's close ties to the fabric of Hawaiian culture, and recognize, in particular, the distinct edge this gives its attorneys in jury trials. It is also said to have *"extraordinary political influence"* and excellent relations with government agencies. One rival attorney pointed out that this factor makes the firm a *"particularly good choice for anyone wanting to start a new company in Hawaii."* It has tried an enormous volume of commercial cases, ranging from two-party breach of contract claims to complex international litigation, and is also experienced in many varieties of ADR.

The Lawyers: Two leading figures jointly head this *"competent, creative and thorough"* litigation department. One is highly respected trial lawyer **John Komeiji** (see p.218), who has just become the firm's latest name partner after years of service here. He covers virtually every area of commercial litigation, but has recently focused on the telecom field, taking on the representation of Time Warner Cable in its Hawaiian interests. One of his most recent involvements was in a major case alleging a breach of fiduciary relationship and breach of trust. Damages of $63 million were avoided when the matter settled following Komeiji's cross-examination of the plaintiffs' expert witness, a noted Yale Law School professor. According to peers, a major weapon in **James Kawashima**'s armory is his *"credible, low-key, understated presence, which works well with local juries."* Joint leader of the litigation department, Kawashima has a broad scope to his practice, and regularly represents a diverse mix of corporate clients in complex business disputes.

The Clients: Typical clients include Time Warner Cable, Viacom and its television subsidiary CBS, First Hawaiian Bank, Dole Foods, SSSB and Obayashi.

Carlsmith Ball LLP

The Firm: This firm's network of offices in Hawaii, Guam and Saipan helps give it a strongly Asia-Pacific-oriented outlook, while, as the only Hawaiian firm able to boast offices in LA and DC, it also enjoys more national presence than its competitors. Its team of *"knowledgeable performers"* has a track record in a range of business litigation, which spans insurance defense and liability work, IP, banking and contract disputes. The group concentrates on litigation avoidance and early resolution, and has built strong relationships with courts, regulators and arbitrators in a number of jurisdictions.

The Lawyers: The chairman of the litigation and dispute resolution group is Gary Grimmer. He practices business litigation, along with restructuring, regulatory matters and other commercial work.

Cronin, Fried, Sekiya, Kekina & Fairbanks Attorneys At Law

The Firm: This firm has an outstanding reputation for personal injury work on the plaintiffs' side. Commentators say that, in this field, it is *"almost certainly the top firm."* Its profile for general commercial litigation is lower; however, it does handle general cases, again principally for plaintiffs. Commercial law firms, which have seen it on the other side, attest to the skill and dedication of its attorneys.

The Clients: The firm's client base comprises a broad range of plaintiff clients.

Paul, Johnson, Park & Niles, Attorneys At Law, LC

The Firm: This *"boutique litigation firm"* has a presence both in Honolulu and Maui. Interviewees agree that its attorneys boast *"a good depth of experience in complex commercial litigation."* They have earned a reputation for providing highly effective lead counsel in large, complex commercial cases in Hawaii's courts, and in arbitrations and mediations.

The Lawyers: **James Paul** was consistently singled out for praise by fellow lawyers across Hawaii. His reputation is founded on his depth of knowledge and intelligence, as well as *"a lot of presence and experience"* drawn from commercial disputes.

The Clients: The firm's client base consists chiefly of large Japanese banks and financial institutions.

Other Notable Practitioners

Bert Kobayashi is the outstanding litigator at Kobayashi, Sugita & Goda. According to peers, he is a *"kick-ass guy"* who engages in trial and arbitration work. He is *"tough when he has to be"* and displays *"a lot of credibility."* His practice is mainly defense work in the general commercial sphere, and contains a rich vein of construction litigation.

REAL ESTATE

HAWAII — Leading firms (Real Estate)

1. **ASHFORD & WRISTON** Honolulu
   GOODSILL ANDERSON QUINN & STIFEL Honolulu
2. **CADES SCHUTTE FLEMING & WRIGHT** Honolulu
   MCCORRISTON MILLER MUKAI Honolulu
3. **CARLSMITH BALL LLP** Honolulu
4. **MANCINI WELCH & GEIGER LLP** Kahului
   OSHIMA, CHUN, FONG & CHUNG Honolulu

Firms are listed alphabetically in each band.

Ashford & Wriston

The Firm: This mid-sized real estate and real estate litigation boutique fields about five dedicated partners. Although the group has established a profile for trusts specialization, it boasts a diverse practice covering all areas of real property law, in contentious and noncontentious spheres. The workload includes acquisitions and sales of real estate, condominium development and governance, retail and vacation resort development, and financing issues. It is also skilled in matters pertinent to land use, zoning and timeshare. Its trusts and titling expertise is especially sought after in Hawaii, where much of the land is held in trust, and the group is able to deal effectively with land title disputes, including water and native Hawaiian land matters.

The Lawyers: Observers described **Bruce Graham** as *"charming and wonderful to deal with,"* and *"one of the preeminent trusts lawyers in Hawaii."* Graham possesses *"a vast knowledge of Hawaiian title issues,"* and one of his key clients is the biggest title and escrow company in Hawaii. His practice is focused on the transactional side and deals with commercial leasing, land title matters, real estate transactions and trusts administration.

The Clients: As well as representing some of the largest landowners in the state, the firm acts for a range of developers. It has also worked closely with title, escrow and mortgage companies and other financial institutions.

Goodsill Anderson Quinn & Stifel

The Firm: Sources observed that the firm's position as the state's largest general practice has seen it *"involved in many of the major transactions in Hawaii"* in the past. This experience has *"given its lawyers the chance to learn the nuances of real estate."* The real estate group works closely with colleagues in the firm's taxation, bankruptcy, litigation, labor and environmental law departments to deliver creative solutions to its clients. Active in the development of real estate law in Hawaii, the

REAL ESTATE — HAWAII

HAWAII
Leading individuals (Real Estate)

1 GRAHAM Bruce *Ashford & Wriston*, Honolulu
2 CHUN Deborah *Oshima, Chun, Fong*, Honolulu
LEONG Donna *Cades Schutte Fleming*, Honolulu
3 MILLER Clifford *McCorriston Miller Mukai*, Honolulu
PEAR Charles *McCorriston Miller Mukai*, Honolulu
STEVERSON Randall *Goodsill Anderson*, Honolulu
4 GABRIO Gino *Cades Schutte Fleming*, Honolulu
HAZLETT Mark *Cades Schutte Fleming*, Honolulu
MACKINNON Scott *McCorriston Miller*, Honolulu
MANCINI Paul *Mancini Welch & Geiger LLP*, Kahului
STRAND Robert *Carlsmith Ball LLP*, Honolulu
WELCH Thomas *Mancini Welch & Geiger LLP*, Kahului

Individuals are listed alphabetically in each band.

firm established the first horizontal property regime under Hawaiian condominium law. It has also completed documentation for the first commercial condominium office complex in Hawaii and the first mixed-use residential, office and commercial condominium project to be approved in the Kakaako Development District in downtown Honolulu. Typical work includes development, financing, real estate transactions, leasing and land title work. The group also handles real estate litigation.

The Lawyers: **Randy Steverson** concentrates on real estate development and financing in both the residential and commercial spheres. Interviewees expressed admiration for his transactional expertise, and he is generally known as *"a thorough all-rounder."*

The Clients: The firm boasts an enviable client list of leading corporate firms. Typical names include Macy's, Victoria Ward Centers and Castle & Cooke.

Cades Schutte Fleming & Wright

The Firm: This stable and tight-knit group handles mainly commercial real estate, including hotels, offices and retail projects. Real estate is one of the firm's largest departments, comprising more than 24 attorneys, which gives it a *"highly visible real property profile."* The group has expertise in transactional work of all levels of sophistication, and has acted in the development of condominiums, golf courses, shopping centers, office buildings, industrial property projects, time-sharing clubs and telecom sites. The group is adept in the purchase and sale of real property, land use, zoning, leasing and title matters. It works closely with attorneys in the firm's tax and litigation practices, and has a particularly strong reputation for title work, real estate finance and real estate litigation.

The Lawyers: *"Tough but honest"* **Donna Leong** is a real estate all-rounder, with a focus on transactional matters. She acts for Outrigger Hotels & Resorts, one of the largest hotel management groups in Hawaii, and has assisted it in its recently announced marketing alliance with timeshare group Fairfield Resorts. She is also active in hospitality law, development issues, land use and zoning, and real property tax appeals. Peers praise her as a *"thorough technician"* who *"works 25 hours a day, eight days a week."* **Gino Gabrio** heads the commercial real estate practice group. He concentrates on real estate transactions, commercial leasing, water rights, regulatory matters and development financing. He has represented Wal-Mart in the acquisition and development of a combined Wal-Mart/Sam's Club store in Honolulu, for which the site acquisition cost alone was $35 million. He is also representing several clients in the acquisition or sale of 15 commercial shopping center, office building and industrial properties, with a total dollar value in excess of $150 million. **Mark Hazlett** is skilled in the corporate and finance aspects of real estate issues, advising on developments such as hotels, resort condominiums, vacation ownership projects, shopping centers and office buildings. He also assists financial institutions in lending, compliance and regulatory matters. Clients confirm that he is *"a superb wordsmith who puts contracts together with an eye to the future and protecting the company."* Hazlett has represented one of Hawaii's largest Japanese developers in the disposition of its Hawaiian assets, including major Honolulu office buildings, an urban shopping center site, a resort hotel and condominium apartments.

The Clients: The firm represents a mix of purchasers, sellers, developers, owners, lenders and hotel managers. Its clients include: Consolidated Resorts; Aston Hotels and Resorts; Citibank; First Hawaiian Bank; American Savings Bank; Outrigger Hotels & Resorts; Alexander & Baldwin; Wal-Mart; LaSalle Investment Management and Cornerstone Group.

McCorriston Miller Mukai MacKinnon LLP

The Firm: Now the fourth largest firm in Honolulu, it has grown from its roots in litigation to become an *"effective"* presence in the real estate sector. The real estate practice group advises on a range of transactional work: not only acquisitions and disposals, leasing and real estate development, but also construction and development loans, restructurings and workouts, and equity investments. Attorneys have developed various specializations that lend the practice great depth. One such is time-sharing, including product design, acquisition and finance on projects both domestically and worldwide. For years it has represented the owner/developer, assisting with the planning, development and construction, of the 404 Piikoi Street Project, which includes the existing Nauru Tower condominium project, and the 1133 Waimanu Street and the Hawaiki Tower condominiums. The group also acts on behalf of the owner of the lands comprising the Hualalai Resort at Historic Kalehu, which has been developed by others under a master development agreement.

The Lawyers: According to commentators, the firm boasts *"individuals who are great in many different areas of real estate."* **Charlie Pear** is a specialist in timeshare and condominium work who *"knows all the timeshare minutiae."* **Cliff Miller** is a *"capable, experienced"* senior lawyer who peers consider *"definitely first cabin."* His expertise covers real estate development, finance and business organization. *"Highly meticulous"* **Scott MacKinnon** is an authority on lease work. MacKinnon incorporates real estate finance, condominium matters, land use, and commercial loans and workouts into his practice.

The Clients: The firm's clients include landowners, developers, retail and investment banks, property managers, insurance companies, architects, construction contractors and others involved in the real estate industry.

Carlsmith Ball LLP

The Firm: The real property and land use group at this established full-service firm has a long-standing reputation for expertise across a broad spectrum of real estate matters. *"It has emerged in the past 15 years as a major presence in real estate."* The talented team acts for developers and landowners in resort, commercial, residential and industrial projects, with an emphasis on complex transactions. Typical work includes the acquisition, development and sale of both raw land and developed properties, tax-deferred exchanges, commercial leasing and construction contracts. The team is also experienced in planning, zoning and land use matters, water rights and environmental issues.

The Lawyers: **Bob Strand** is a *"careful and meticulous"* attorney with 30 years' experience in complex real estate transactions. He also advises on commercial leasing, water law and public utilities matters, and carries out real estate acquisition work for large developers. Peers consider him *"a skilled document drafter,"* with *"broad real estate knowledge."*

The Clients: The firm enjoys a respected client base of developers and major landowners.

Mancini Welch & Geiger LLP

The Firm: *"This is the firm you will be dealing with if the case is Maui-specific,"* said one commentator, and there is general agreement that, although a smaller team, the firm's high-quality work dominates the real estate scene in Maui. Typical work includes condominium development and zoning; the practitioners here have superior knowledge of the nuances of zoning law specifically applicable to Maui.

HAWAII LEADERS

The Lawyers: Interviewees commended **Tom Welch** as *"the only Hawaiian lawyer outside Honolulu that everyone - in real estate at least - can name."* His practice includes zoning, and municipal and general real estate law. **Paul Mancini** has a similar practice to Welch's, though many commentators consider that Mancini's real strength lies in his land use work on Maui.

The Clients: The firm handles local work for Marriott Hotels, among others.

Oshima, Chun, Fong & Chung

The Firm: This is *"a smaller group, but a worthy competitor,"* according to peers. Attorneys here are known for their efforts in real estate development, leasing, land use and environmental matters, and have represented clients in some large and complex projects. The team handles a range of work including purchase and sale agreements, land acquisition and development projects, condominium, resort and retail property matters, and leasing. It has built healthy political bridges in Hawaii, and was recommended to researchers as particularly effective in government zoning work and obtaining land use permits.

The Lawyers: *"Excellent"* **Deborah Chun** assists borrowers and lenders in asset-based and commercial real estate financing. She also represents developers in the acquisition and development of hotel, shopping center, office, condominium and residential projects. Her extensive experience includes counseling local and mainland lenders on state and federal regulations related to consumer lending. Market commentators agreed that *"everyone is impressed by her."*

The Clients: The firm advises financial institutions and developers on a range of real estate matters.

Leaders in Hawaii

ALSTON, Paul
Alston Hunt Floyd & Ing Attorneys At Law, A Law Corporation, Honolulu
808 524 1800
Recommended in Litigation

CASE, Daniel
Case Bigelow & Lombardi A Law Corporation, Honolulu 808 547 5400
Recommended in Corporate/M&A

CASE, James
Carlsmith Ball LLP, Honolulu
808 523 2500
Recommended in Corporate/M&A

CHUN, Deborah
Oshima, Chun, Fong & Chung, Honolulu
808 528 4200
Recommended in Real Estate

CHUN, Nelson
Cades Schutte Fleming & Wright, Honolulu 808 521 9200
Recommended in Corporate/M&A

DEZZANI, David
Goodsill Anderson Quinn & Stifel, Honolulu 808 547 5600
Recommended in Litigation

GABRIO, Gino
Cades Schutte Fleming & Wright, Honolulu 808 521 9200
Recommended in Real Estate

GELBER, Stephen M
Gelber, Gelber, Ingersoll & Klevansky A Law Corporation, Honolulu
808 524 0155
Recommended in Corporate/M&A

GRAHAM, Bruce
Ashford & Wriston, Honolulu
808 539 0400
Recommended in Real Estate

HAZLETT, Mark
Cades Schutte Fleming & Wright, Honolulu 808 521 9200
Recommended in Real Estate

HEIHRE, Michael
Cades Schutte Fleming & Wright, Honolulu 808 521 9200
Recommended in Litigation

HIATT, Jerry
Mr Jerry Hiatt - Sole Practitioner, Honolulu 808 885 3400
Recommended in Employment

HIPP, Ken
Marr Hipp Jones and Pepper, Honolulu 808 536 4900
Recommended in Employment

ICHINOSE, Susan
Ms Susan Ichinose – Sole Practitioner, Honolulu 808 585 0333
Recommended in Employment

JOSSEM, Jared
Dwyer Schraff Meyer Jossem & Bushnell, Honolulu 808 524 8000
Recommended in Employment

KATZ, Robert
Torkildson, Katz, Fonseca, Jaffe, Moore & Hetherington Attorneys At Law, A Law Corporation, Honolulu 808 523 6000
Recommended in Employment

KAWASHIMA, James
Watanabe Ing Kawashima & Komeiji, Honolulu 808 544 8300
Recommended in Employment, Litigation

KIM, Gregory
Goodsill Anderson Quinn & Stifel, Honolulu 808 547 5600
Recommended in Corporate/M&A

KOBAYASHI, Bert
Kobayashi, Sugita & Goda, Honolulu 808 539 8700
Recommended in Litigation

KOMEIJI, John
Watanabe Ing Kawashima & Komeiji, Honolulu 808 544 8300
Recommended in Litigation

LEONG, Donna
Cades Schutte Fleming & Wright, Honolulu 808 521 9200
Recommended in Real Estate

LEONG, Ron
Watanabe Ing Kawashima & Komeiji, Honolulu 808 544 8300
Recommended in Employment

MACKINNON, D Scott
McCorriston Miller Mukai MacKinnon LLP, Honolulu 808 529 7300
Recommended in Real Estate

MANCINI, Paul
Mancini Welch & Geiger LLP, Kahului
808 871 8351
Recommended in Real Estate

MARR, Barry
Marr Hipp Jones and Pepper, Honolulu 808 536 4900
Recommended in Employment

MCCORRISTON, William
McCorriston Miller Mukai MacKinnon LLP, Honolulu 808 529 7300
Recommended in Litigation

MILLER, Clifford
McCorriston Miller Mukai MacKinnon LLP, Honolulu 808 529 7300
Recommended in Real Estate

NING, Ke-Ching
Ning Lilly & Jones, Honolulu
808 528 1100
Recommended in Employment

PAUL, James
Paul, Johnson, Park & Niles, Attorneys At Law, A Law Corporation, Honolulu
808 524 1212
Recommended in Litigation

PEAR, Charles
McCorriston Miller Mukai MacKinnon LLP, Honolulu 808 529 7300
Recommended in Real Estate

PORTNOY, Jeffrey
Cades Schutte Fleming & Wright, Honolulu 808 521 9200
Recommended in Litigation

REBER, David
Goodsill Anderson Quinn & Stifel, Honolulu 808 547 5600
Recommended in Corporate/M&A

SCHULL, E Gunner
Cades Schutte Fleming & Wright, Honolulu 808 521 9200
Recommended in Corporate/M&A

SIMONS, David
David Simons - Sole Practitioner, Honolulu 808 536 3255
Recommended in Employment

STEVERSON, Randall
Goodsill Anderson Quinn & Stifel, Honolulu 808 547 5600
Recommended in Real Estate

STRAND, Robert
Carlsmith Ball LLP, Honolulu
808 523 2500
Recommended in Real Estate

TAKAHASHI, Herbert
Takahashi Masui & Vasconcellos, Honolulu 808 526 3003
Recommended in Employment

WELCH, Thomas
Mancini Welch & Geiger LLP, Kahului
808 871 8351
Recommended in Real Estate

CORPORATE/M&A

IDAHO

CONTENTS: Corporate/M&A p.219; Employment: Mainly Plaintiff p.219; Mainly Defendant p.220; Litigation p.220; Real Estate p.221; Individuals' Profiles p.222.

IDAHO'S TOP TWO
1. Hawley Troxell Ennis & Hawley
2. Stoel Rives

Ranking based on Chambers' research within the state.

All quotes in the text are from interviews with clients and competitors.

OVERVIEW: The largest firm based in Idaho, **Hawley Troxell Ennis & Hawley** has deep roots in the state and offers a broad-based service from its three offices. Over half the firm's attorneys focus on litigation, and litigator Craig Meadows is seen to be the star of the firm. Described locally as the traditional choice for real estate advice, the firm represents large-scale developers, borrowers and lenders on a variety of projects. Real estate attorney Brian Ballard and his team are widely known for their work on shopping centers and office buildings. A highly regarded corporate practice offers first-rate business expertise and receives particular commendation for its advice on business formation. Clients include Boise Cascade and Washington Group International.

Leading West Coast full-service firm **Stoel Rives** is thought to be expanding its Idaho corporate practice, which comes highly recommended for its corporate, finance and securities advice and work in the energy and telecom sectors. Corporate/M&A attorney Paul Boyd is considered the firm's leading practitioner for commercial matters. The litigation department has also doubled in size in recent years and now handles a full range of cases in state and federal courts. The team is particularly known for business-related litigation, personal injury and products liability claims. The firm has a strong client base in its real estate practice, and can call on substantial resources within its network of Western offices. Its national profile has the group representing clients outside the state on commercial transactions, acquisitions and sales and leasings. Real estate specialist Quentin Knipe is widely praised. American Ecology Corporation and Nu-West Industries are among the firm's clients.

CORPORATE/M&A

IDAHO
Leading Firms (Corporate/M&A)
1. HAWLEY TROXELL ENNIS & HAWLEY LLP *Boise*
   STOEL RIVES LLP *Boise*

Leading individuals (Corporate/M&A)
1. BOYD Paul *Stoel Rives LLP, Boise*
   MILLER Nicholas *Hawley Troxell Ennis, Boise*

Firms and Individuals are listed alphabetically in each band.

Hawley Troxell Ennis & Hawley LLP
The Firm: Noted by peers as the *"largest firm based in Idaho,"* this business-oriented group promotes a broad-based corporate, commercial and financial practice. While the primary focus of the group is to provide business formation support, the group also offers broader general corporate/commercial counsel for everything from contract negotiations and joint ventures to public offerings and acquisitions.

The Lawyers: Said to have *"first-rate business expertise,"* **Nick Miller** chairs the firm's business and finance group. Specializing in corporate finance and transactions, venture capital and municipal bond finance, he also covers the niche area of bonds for hospitals and healthcare bodies. He has recently represented Highway 12 Venture Fund in its investment in Vigilos.

The Clients: Telemetric Corporation, Highway 12 Venture Fund and Boise State University are represented.

Stoel Rives LLP
The Firm: Drawing on the expertise from this large Portland, Oregon-based business law firm's seven other offices, the Boise group offers strong corporate, finance and securities counsel. The group covers all areas of corporate and commercial law, with a focus on the telecom and energy industries.

The Lawyers: Named as the firm's leading light, **Paul Boyd** received high praise from clients who claimed they *"wouldn't use anyone else"* and peers who stated that *"if I were going to set up my own firm, I'd want him with me."* Focusing on M&A transactions, joint ventures and venture capital financing, he recently worked on the $93 million joint venture acquisiton of a natural wood products manufacturing company. Boyd also regularly practices outside the state, including representing a $30 million acquisition of a hazardous waste landfill.

The Clients: ProClarity Corporation, American Ecology Corporation and Woodgrain Millwork are among the firm's clients.

EMPLOYMENT & LABOR LAW

MAINLY PLAINTIFF

IDAHO
Leading Firms (Corporate/M&A)
1. MAUK & BURGOYNE *Boise*

Leading individuals
(Employment: Mainly Plaintiff)
1. BURGOYNE Grant *Mauk & Burgoyne, Boise*
2. MAUK Bill *Mauk & Burgoyne, Boise*

Firms and Individuals are listed alphabetically in each band.

Mauk & Burgoyne
The Firm: Spontaneously recommended by peers, this niche litigation firm specializes in representing public and private sector employees nationwide. Its expertise spans wage claims litigation, discrimination litigation and ERISA matters.

The Lawyers: Grant Burgoyne is applauded by peers as the *"number-one plaintiff attorney in Idaho"* for his representation of federal employees. Described as *"reasonable and energetic"* in his approach, Burgoyne's accomplishments include pioneering the representation of law enforcement officers and firefighters regarding enhanced retirement benefits. **Bill Mauk** was also recommended to researchers as a *"principal attorney in the development of employment law in Idaho."* He is engaged in trial and appellate litigation with an emphasis on employment law.

IDAHO

EMPLOYMENT & LABOR LAW — MAINLY DEFENDANT

IDAHO
Leading Firms
(Employment: Mainly Defendant)

1. **HALL, FARLEY, OBERRECHT & BLANTON** Boise
2. **MOFFATT THOMAS BARRETT ROCK** Boise
   STOEL RIVES LLP Boise

Leading individuals
(Employment: Mainly Defendant)

1. **DALE Candy** Hall, Farley, PA, Boise
2. **BERENTER Steven** Hawley Troxell Ennis, Boise
   CHANDLER Harry Stoel Rives LLP, Boise
   DALE James Moffatt Thomas Barrett Rock, Boise

Firms and individuals are listed alphabetically in each band.

Hall, Farley, Oberrecht & Blanton, PA
The Firm: *"The number-one employment law firm,"* claim interviewees. The group has avoided being marginalized as a regional firm for traditional labor and employment law by staking its claim to major national clients. The group predominantly defends management in judicial and administrative proceedings on complaints of wrongful discharge, discrimination, harassment, civil rights, and wage and hour claims. It also provides counseling and training on related preventative practices.
The Lawyers: The key name here is **Candy Wagahoff Dale**, who is described as an *"aggressive litigator"* with *"a clear understanding of legal strategies."* Her practice encompasses HR issues, policies and procedures, and investigations into employer misconduct issues. She has defended Symms Fruit Ranch in the Ninth Circuit Court of Appeals against a claim that a tractor breached OSHA safety regulations. Her practice has recently expanded to include alternative dispute resolution. Although named as the firm's star, peers acknowledge that she is supported by *"a strong contingent of other labor and employment attorneys and associates."*
The Clients: Major national businesses use the firm.

Moffatt Thomas Barrett Rock & Fields
The Firm: Described by peers as *"a close second"* to Hall, Farley, Oberrecht & Blanton, this Boise-based firm is said to be successfully *"building its employment department."* It provides aggressive representation, advising on a range of labor and employment-related matters from regulatory and other compliance issues to collective bargaining. The group recently secured the dismissal of a lawsuit against a major Idaho manufacturer, brought by the EEOC, which alleged violations of Title VII of the Civil Rights Act. The firm also offers preventative advice to management through training on personnel policies and the development of employment literature.
The Lawyers: *"Analytical"* **James Dale** was recommended as the leading figure within the group for his skill in *"spotting the issues and consulting clients on preventative strategies."* He represents management from the manufacturing, hi-tech and retail sectors, with a practice that spans sex discrimination and wrongful terminations to negotiating with unions and collectively bargained actions. Dale served as counsel for the employer in the significant Mitchell v ZiLOG case, which is regularly cited in opinions discussing the doctrine of at-will employment in Idaho.
The Clients: Albertson's and GM are examples of the firm's client portfoilio.

Stoel Rives LLP
The Firm: Peers describe this *"large and aggressive"* Portland, Oregon-based business law firm as receiving *"recognition from Idaho's major corporations."* The Boise office draws on the resources of the firm's seven other offices in the Northwest. The group provides counseling and litigation services across the full spectrum of labor, employment, employee benefits and workers' compensation law.
The Lawyers: Following stints in both the Boise and Portland offices, the *"well-connected"* **Harry Chandler** has a reputation that secures *"recognition well beyond Idaho."* He represents management in labor law and employment discrimination matters, employment contract matters and tort litigation. Experienced in administrative practices, he also offers mediation and client counseling.
The Clients: Gentle Dental Service and Weyerhaeuser are clients of the group.

Other Notable Practitioners
Steven Berenter of Hawley Troxell Ennis & Hawley LLP was recommended to researchers as an *"exceedingly competent, high-quality litigator."* He is the chairman of the firm's labor and employment practice group, advising clients such as Washington Group International and Futura. He recently acted for St Luke's Regional Medical Center in a wage dispute class action, and was commended for his experience in counseling on preventative measures.

LITIGATION — GENERAL COMMERCIAL

IDAHO
Leading Firms
(Litigation: General Commercial)

1. **HAWLEY TROXELL ENNIS & HAWLEY LLP** Boise
2. **ELAM & BURKE, PA** Boise
   HOLLAND & HART LLP Boise
3. **COSHO, HUMPHREY, GREENER & WELSH** Boise
   MOFFATT THOMAS BARRETT ROCK Boise
   STOEL RIVES LLP Boise

Firms are listed alphabetically in each band.

Hawley Troxell Ennis & Hawley LLP
The Firm: A group of highly respected attorneys is thought to place this *"class law firm"* at the *"top of the heap."* Half of the firm's attorneys devote their time primarily to litigation, advising on everything from IP, antitrust and securities to environmental and employment litigation.
The Lawyers: *"Consummate professional"* **Craig Meadows** is seen as the undisputed star of the firm. Described by peers as *"a master of the profession,"* he is the cohead of the firm's litigation group, focusing on commercial litigation, legal malpractice, insurance law, products liability and aviation. Researchers were also directed toward **Merlyn Clark**, described as the *"dean of Idaho law"* by colleagues. His practice focuses on complex civil litigation, including real property, contract and commercial law, business entities and ERISA.
The Clients: Clients include Boise Cascade, JR Simplot Company, Albertson's and Washington Group International.

Elam & Burke, PA
The Firm: Possessing a large corporate clientele, this traditional firm was routinely commended as *"a tough competitor"* because of the depth offered by its bench of respected attorneys. The firm offers all-around litigation advice, including antitrust, aviation, contract, civil rights, environmental, products liability and tort disputes.
The Lawyers: Several names were recommended

LITIGATION

IDAHO

IDAHO
Leading individuals
(Litigation: General Commercial)

1
- BITHELL Walter *Holland & Hart LLP*, Boise
- GREENER Richard *Cosho, Humphrey, Greene*, Boise
- MEADOWS Craig *Hawley Troxell Ennis*, Boise

2
- BURKE Carl *Elam & Burke, PA*, Boise
- CLARK Merlyn *Hawley Troxell Ennis & Hawle*, Boise
- DINGEL Allyn *Elam & Burke, PA*, Boise
- DRYDEN William *Elam & Burke, PA*, Boise

3
- ANDERSEN Steven *Holland & Hart LLP*, Boise

Individuals are listed alphabetically in each band.

to researchers, including **Carl Burke**, whose father was one of the firm's founding partners. Noted for having a *"fatherly way in court"* himself, his practice covers contract disputes, products liability cases, environmental law and mediation. Clients acclaimed **William Dryden** as *"the first person we call when litigation matters arise."* A *"hard, aggressive litigator,"* his practice ranges from ski resort-related litigation for Bogus Basin Recreational Association to employment discrimination cases for Farmers Insurance. **Allyn Dingel** was also noted as *"one of the most entertaining attorneys you could meet."* Primarily responsible for the firm's lobbying and legislative practice, he also extends his skills to commercial transactions, insurance defense and administrative practice.

The Clients: Clients include: City of Boise; Midwest Insurance; Washington Group International and Thompson Creek Mining Company.

Holland & Hart LLP
see firm details p.8190

The Firm: Market appraisal for this firm is implicitly bound up with the reputation of its leading light **Walter Bithell** (see p.222). Described by peers as *"creative,"* he emphasizes individual and class action plaintiffs' tort litigation, including commercial, personal injury, insurance and securities litigation. He has been representing landowners in a class action against DuPont, seeking damages for crop damage allegedly done by the herbicide Oust. He receives strong support from **Steve Andersen** (see p.222), who has developed an expertise in IP, tort and business litigation, including professional negligence, personal injury and products liability litigation.

The Clients: Clients include the Nez Perce Tribe.

Cosho, Humphrey, Greener & Welsh, PA

The Firm: The firm's workload consists primarily of a civil and appellate practice, covering such areas as environment, insurance, construction and general litigation.

The Lawyers: **Richard Greener**, a *"good strategist who sorts through to the key issues,"* received substantial market endorsement. *"A real player,"* he has a catalog of significant clients, including recently representing Nokia in a business failure lawsuit. In another high-profile case he successfully defended Micron Technology in a $7 million wrongful termination lawsuit, brought by one of the company's former research and development engineers.

The Clients: Clients include Regence BlueShield, JR Simplot Company and Boise Cascade.

Moffatt Thomas Barrett Rock & Fields

The Firm: Half of this *"traditional"* law firm's attorneys work within the litigation practice, focusing on commercial, employment, environmental, personal injury and complex litigation. One of Idaho's oldest law firms, it has three offices in the state with attorneys representing clients in all areas except criminal and family law. The firm recently successfully defended a client that was being sued by the EEOC.

The Clients: Clients include: Micron; Chubb; Zurich American Insurance Company and GM.

Stoel Rives LLP

The Firm: Having doubled in size in recent years, the Boise office of this Western b2b firm handles a full range of cases in state and federal courts and before administrative agencies. The emphasis lies in business-related litigation, personal injury and products liability claims. The team provides regional counsel to a range of national companies, with specialty areas including bankruptcy, construction and design, patents, trademarks, copyrights and utilities.

The Clients: Clients include GlaxoSmithKline and Fred Meyer.

REAL ESTATE

IDAHO
Leading Firms (Real Estate)

1
- GIVENS PURSLEY LLP *Boise*
- HAWLEY TROXELL ENNIS & HAWLEY LLP *Boise*

2
- MEULEMAN & MILLER, LLP *Boise*
- SPINK BUTLER CLAPP *Boise*
- STOEL RIVES LLP *Boise*

Firms are listed alphabetically in each band.

Givens Pursley LLP

The Firm: Competitors acclaimed this mid-sized Boise-based firm as the state's *"number-one real estate transactional firm."* *"Well-connected politically,"* it represents a range of entrepreneurial developers and investors in acquisitions, dispositions, ground leases, limited partnerships and other securities syndications. Land use and entitlement law is a key strength of the group. It also counsels borrowers and lenders in financing transactions involving commercial and residential projects and agricultural properties.

The Lawyers: **Christopher Beeson** is viewed as the practice's driving force. His *"user-friendly approach"* is reinforced by *"the highest ethical standards."* His practice is focused on commercial transactions, including joint ventures and equity syndications for shopping centers, offices and hotel developments.

The Clients: The group acts for national and regional real estate investment companies and developers, title insurance companies, financial institutions and venture capital firms.

Hawley Troxell Ennis & Hawley LLP

The Firm: Acknowledged by peers as a *"quality practice with a long history behind it."* The group was endorsed for representing borrowers and lenders, in acquisition and development financing, securitized commercial mortgage financing, and refinancing and loan modifications. It has a forte in the development of shopping centers, office buildings and lodging facilities. The firm is frequently seen representing large-scale developers in exchanges of real estate and the negotiation and preparation of leases.

The Lawyers: **Brian Ballard** was described to researchers as a *"straightforward"* attorney. He focuses on real property and land use law, and has been active of late in shopping center acquisitions and developments on sites in Utah, California and Texas for his primary client Albertson's. He also specializes in IRS Section 1031 tax-deferred exchanges. Researchers had their attention drawn to *"deal-maker"* **Donald Knickrehm**. Noted for his representation of investors and developers in leasing, investment, zoning and subdivision matters, he has recently been involved in the acquisition of several sites in Idaho for a fast-food chain client.

The Clients: Albertson's, Micron and Washington Group International are represented.

Meuleman & Miller, LLP

The Firm: This small, Boise-based firm built its reputation on real estate and construction law. It has now expanded into a more comprehensive mix of business law and litigation. The group represents construction businesses throughout the

IDAHO

LEADERS

IDAHO
Leading individuals (Real Estate)

1 BEESON Christopher *Givens Pursley LLP,* Boise
2 BALLARD Brian *Hawley Troxell Ennis & Hawley,* Boise
   MILLER Robert *Meuleman & Miller, LLP,* Boise
   SPINK Michael *Spink Butler Clapp,* Boise
3 GOWLAND Kimbal *Meuleman & Miller, LLP,* Boise
   KNICKREHM Donald *Hawley Troxell Ennis,* Boise
   KNIPE Quentin *Stoel Rives LLP,* Boise

Individuals are listed alphabetically in each band.

West, and assists investors, national tenants, developers, real estate brokers, title insurance companies and lending institutions in a range of real estate matters.
The Lawyers: Several individual lawyers were recommended to researchers, an indication of the firm's depth. Among them, **Robert Miller** was singled out by contemporaries as a *"top-rate developer's lawyer."* He and **Kimbal Gowland** advise on transactions involving retail developments for clients such as Albertson's.

The Clients: Albertson's; Contractors Northwest; Micron; Idaho Power Company; Western Construction; Bronco Motors and Hawkins-Smith Developers.

Spink Butler Clapp
The Firm: Described by contemporaries as *"strong competitors,"* this small firm of four attorneys was heavily endorsed for its land use practice. The firm offers a full range of real estate advice, including sales and acquisitions, zoning and related litigation.
The Lawyers: Much of the group's reputation is attributed to **Michael Spink**, who has recently acted for the Neighborhood Housing Services (NHS) and Wal-Mart in separate Idaho Supreme Court land use appeals, relating to a mobile home park and superstore development respectively. Peers described him as *"one of the city's most respected real estate litigators,"* and he has a following of dedicated clients who trust his *"sound judgment."*
The Clients: The firm advises, among others, Wal-Mart, Costco Wholesale, Harris Family Ranch, John L Scott Real Estate, S-Sixteen Ltd Partnership, Commonwealth Title and Neighborhood Housing Services (NHS).

Stoel Rives LLP
The Firm: Vast resources and a string of Western offices have resulted in a widely held profile for this firm. Due to its national presence, much of the group's time is dedicated to the representation of local and national clients outside the state, on commercial transactions, acquisitions, sales and leasings. Rivals commend this *"good team of respected lawyers,"* despite its relatively lower local profile.
The Lawyers: Among its leading lawyers is **Quentin Knipe**, who has been assisting Albertson's in its plans to divest a 741,000 sq ft distribution center near Houston, Texas. He has also represented the retailer in developing a co-anchored shopping center on a 50-acre site outside Seattle.
The Clients: The group acts for, among others, Albertson's, Nu-West Industries and Darigold.

Leaders in Idaho

ANDERSEN, Steven
Holland & Hart LLP, Boise
208 383 3930
sandersen@hollandhart.com
Recommended in Litigation
Specialisation: Partner practicing in tort and commercial litigation including products liability, professional negligence, and personal injury. Has tried cases involving insurance disputes, partnership dissolution claims by and against banks, patent and intellectual property claims, as well as automobile, medical malpractice and product defects.
Prof. Memberships: American Bar Association (Litigation and Business Sections), Idaho State Bar (Continuing Legal Education Committee, Professional Conduct Board).
Career: Admitted to the Idaho Bar (1980), US Court of Appeals, Ninth Circuit (1985).
Personal: Received a JD (with honors) from Brigham Young University in 1981 and a BA (summa cum laude) from Brigham Young University in 1977.

BALLARD, Brian
Hawley Troxell Ennis & Hawley LLP, Boise 208 344 6000
Recommended in Real Estate

BEESON, Christopher
Givens Pursley LLP, Boise
208 388 1200
Recommended in Real Estate

BERENTER, Steven
Hawley Troxell Ennis & Hawley LLP, Boise 208 344 6000
Recommended in Employment

BITHELL, Walter
Holland & Hart LLP, Boise
280 342 5000
wbithell@hollandhart.com
Recommended in Litigation
Specialisation: Partner with practice emphasis on individual and class action plaintiffs' tort litigation, including business and commercial, personal injury, products liability, professional liability, commercial, insurance, securities and general litigation.
Prof. Memberships: Fellow of the American College of Trial Lawyers, American Inns of Court No. 130 (Master of the Bench), American Trial Lawyers Association (Board of Governors), Idaho Trial Lawyers Association, Idaho State Bar, Western Trial Lawyers Association, University of Idaho Foundation (Board of Directors), University of Idaho Alumni Association, The American Society of Writers on Legal Subjects (SCRIBES).
Career: Admitted to Idaho Bar (1968), US Court of Federal Claims (1991), US Court of Appeals, Ninth Circuit (1992), US Supreme Court. Former Idaho Deputy Attorney General, General Counsel for the Idaho State Department of Insurance and General Counsel for the Idaho State Tax Commission.
Personal: Received JD from University of Idaho (1968) and a BS from the University of Idaho (1965).

BOYD, Paul
Stoel Rives LLP, Boise 208 389 9000
Recommended in Corporate/M&A

BURGOYNE, Grant
Mauk & Burgoyne, Boise 208 345 2654
Recommended in Employment

BURKE, Carl
Elam & Burke, PA, Boise 208 343 5454
Recommended in Litigation

CHANDLER, Harry
Stoel Rives LLP, Boise 208 389 9000
Recommended in Employment

CLARK, Merlyn
Hawley Troxell Ennis & Hawley LLP, Boise 208 344 6000
Recommended in Litigation

DALE, James
Moffatt Thomas Barrett Rock & Fields, Boise 208 345 2000
Recommended in Employment

DINGEL, Allyn
Elam & Burke, PA, Boise 208 343 5454
Recommended in Litigation

DRYDEN, William
Elam & Burke, PA, Boise 208 343 5454
Recommended in Litigation

GOWLAND, Kimbal
Meuleman & Miller, LLP, Boise
208 342 6066
Recommended in Real Estate

GREENER, Richard
Cosho, Humphrey, Greener & Welsh, PA, Boise 208 344 7811
Recommended in Litigation

KNICKREHM, Donald
Hawley Troxell Ennis & Hawley LLP, Boise 208 344 6000
Recommended in Real Estate

KNIPE, Quentin
Stoel Rives LLP, Boise 208 389 9000
Recommended in Real Estate

MAUK, Bill
Mauk & Burgoyne, Boise 208 345 2654
Recommended in Employment

MEADOWS, Craig
Hawley Troxell Ennis & Hawley LLP, Boise 208 344 6000
Recommended in Litigation

MILLER, Nicholas
Hawley Troxell Ennis & Hawley LLP, Boise 208 344 6000
Recommended in Corporate/M&A

MILLER, Robert
Meuleman & Miller, LLP, Boise
208 342 6066
Recommended in Real Estate

SPINK, Michael
Spink Butler Clapp, Boise 208 388 1000
Recommended in Real Estate

WAGAHOFF DALE, Candy
Hall, Farley, Oberrecht & Blanton, PA, Boise 208 395 8500
Recommended in Employment

OVERVIEW ILLINOIS

CONTENTS: Antitrust p.224; Banking & Finance p.226; Communications/Technology p.229; Construction p.231; Corporate/M&A p.232; Employment p.235; Energy & Natural Resorces p.238; Environment p.239; Insolvency p.240; Insurance p. 242; Intellectual Property p. 243; Litigation p.245; Media & Entertainment p.247; Real Estate p.249; Tax p.251; Individuals' Profiles p.253.

ILLINOIS'S TOP TEN
1. Mayer, Brown, Rowe & Maw
2. Sidley Austin Brown & Wood
3. Kirkland & Ellis
4. Winston & Strawn
5. Skadden, Arps, Slate, Meagher & Flom
6. Sonnenschein Nath & Rosenthal
7. Schiff Hardin & Waite
8. Jenner & Block
9. McDermott, Will & Emery
10. Latham & Watkins

Ranking based on Chambers' research within the state.

All quotes in the text are from interviews with clients and competitors.

OVERVIEW: Leading the pack is classic Chicago firm, **Mayer, Brown, Rowe & Maw**, which appears most often in the top band position of *Chambers'* rankings. The firm grew up with many of the Midwest's major banking and corporate entities and has emerged as a full-service practice with traditional strength in the areas of M&A, banking, tax and antitrust. The firm's mergers with UK firm Rowe & Maw and the Frankfurt office of Germany's Gaedertz expanded Mayer Brown's profile far beyond its US roots. Within M&A, Bob Helman remains a senior statesman of the corporate bar, while banking and finance specialist Robert Baptista shines at the top of the rankings. The firm stands alone in the state for its strength in communications, with Theodore Livingston well known for his role as lead external counsel to Ameritech. The large corporate team relies on strong support from the real estate, environmental and energy practices, where the firm also received top band ratings.

Sidley Austin Brown & Wood emerged as a close second in Chicago. Like Mayer Brown, Sidley Austin's history is closely bound to that of the city, and a long-standing friendly rivalry exists between the two. The practice is respected both nationally and internationally for its expertise in capital markets transactions. Securitizations are a strong suit for the firm, and Sidley Austin's muscle in this area was augmented both by its merger in 2001 with New York's Brown & Wood and the recruitment of insurance securitization specialists from Katten Muchin Zavis. Strong ties to the financial institutions' community keep the firm in the top tier for banking, with senior attorney Bruce Bernstein at the helm. Managing partner Tom Cole and his premier corporate team are highly esteemed throughout the country for their work on big-ticket M&A. In antitrust, the group, under the leadership of litigator Thomas Ryan, acts for AT&T on competition issues. A top-ranking environmental practice acts for clients GE and BP, among others.

Staffed by tough attorneys, Chicago-headquartered **Kirkland & Ellis** enjoys a reputation as an "institutional bruiser," which puts the firm in a league of its own for high-stakes litigation. The practice's star, David Bernick, was hailed as a class performer with a flair for mass tort cases. The ferocious style of the partnership is thought to permeate even the corporate departments where the firm is equally renowned as a private equity powerhouse. Jack Levin is nationally regarded as a guru in the field, while the corporate practice regularly tops tables for LBOs and debt financings. An outstanding bankruptcy practice, led by Jamie Sprayregen, appeared as debtor's counsel in the restructurings of WR Grace and Conseco. In antitrust, Tefft Smith and his team earn top band recognition for work on such matters as Kraft's cheese price-fixing case. The firm is also considered strong in IP and tax.

Litigation is **Winston & Strawn**'s claim to fame with star attorney Dan Webb topping the charts for his confident style and enormous trial experience. This consistently outstanding lawyer receives plaudits for his ongoing antitrust work for Microsoft. A deep bench of business-minded attorneys was felt to be at ease across a range of fields. The firm is in the top band in media and entertainment where well-connected Stephen Durchslag reigns as an expert in advertising law. A midmarket banking practice is strongly recommended for asset-based finance and commercial lending, while a highly respected corporate team earns praise for work in securities and private equity transactions. A diverse client roster includes Antares Capital, Motorola and Nestlé.

The international monolith, **Skadden, Arps, Slate, Meagher & Flom**, looms large in Chicago for its world-class restructuring practice, which is internationally recognized as one of the most dominant debtors' practices in the US. The practice centers around forceful Jack Butler who has led major restructurings for companies such as US Airways. While New York remains the focus of the firm's leviathan corporate practice, Chicago attorney Charles Mulaney plays a leading role on a number of high-profile M&A and corporate finance transactions. Despite its emphatically East Coast origins, the firm has succeeded in building up a following among indigenous Midwest clients, among them Sears Roebuck, who the group recently represented in its $1.9 billion purchase of Lands' End. The combined strength of the bankruptcy and corporate practices is balanced by the quality service provided by its highly rated banking and finance, tax and litigation teams.

Sonnenschein Nath & Rosenthal makes a strong showing across a range of areas. Praised in Chicago for its local feel, the firm has offices nationally in LA, New York, San Francisco, DC, St. Louis, West Palm Beach, Kansas City and Short Hills, NJ. In the corporate department, Don Lubin is prominent for his corporate governance advice to the boards of public and private companies, and appears frequently as counselor to key client, McDonald's. The firm has strong ties to Chicago hi-tech interests and the downturn in the technology market has contributed to the expertise of the firm's insolvency practice. The real estate group focuses on leasing and finance transactions and is able to contribute considerable experience in related environmental matters. Sonnenschein also makes a respectable showing in media and entertainment as well as antitrust, acting for such clients as Allstate, Midas and Random House.

Schiff Hardin & Waite is the only full-service firm to feature in Illinois' construction rankings, where it tops the tables for its work on behalf of owners, developers, contractors and architects. Here, Paul Lurie and Mark Friedlander, acknowledged to be the premier practitioners in the state, have led the team handling the development of O'Hare International Airport's terminal six construction project. At the top of the insurance rankings is reinsurance expert David Spector, who has represented insurance companies in several major receivership cases. An able corporate department acts for Newell Rubbermaid and NiSource, while regulatory specialist Owen MacBride makes an appearance in both the communications and energy rankings. Since its acquisition of labor boutique Brittain, Sledz, Morris & Slovak about three years ago, Schiff Hardin has commanded a strong profile in employment matters. The firm also receives praise for its handling of environmental claims, with Sheldon Zabel singled out as the dean of the environmental bar.

Jenner & Block places a heavy emphasis on litigation and ranks highly in a number of areas due to its strength in contentious matters. Changes at management level have not affected the firm's presence in the market. Firm chair Jerold Solovy is

www.ChambersandPartners.com All quotes in the text are from interviews with clients and competitors. 223

ILLINOIS — ANTITRUST

considered a household name for headline cases and, together with Tom Sullivan, leads an outstanding litigation practice. Darryl Bradford's communications team enjoys a considerable profile within the industry as longtime counsel to WorldCom. A strong environmental practice includes a number of individuals with valuable government experience. The firm ranks highest in media and entertainment, however, with David Sanders widely esteemed for expertise in libel and privacy issues. The firm is also seen to be increasing its insolvency capacities and the recent recruitment of Robert Osborne from Kirkland & Ellis signals a developing corporate practice.

A native Chicago firm that has grown to international stature, **McDermott, Will & Emery** now possesses offices in New York, DC, Boston, LA, Silicon Valley, Orange County, Miami as well as London, Munich and Düsseldorf. Close ties to Bank of America ensure its place in the banking and finance tables. The group is recognized for strength in asset-based lending, securitization and restructuring transactions. Expertise in finance has helped bolster the firm's corporate practice where the firm acts for a loyal base of Midwestern companies and is developing a noteworthy niche in sports law. McDermott Will secures its highest ranking in tax, with Lowell Yoder widely recommended as a preeminent international tax practitioner in Chicago's largest tax team. The firm also appears in the Chicago commercial litigation rankings, acting for Lockheed Martin, Medtronic and Hitachi among others.

LA-based **Latham & Watkins** boasts a strong Chicago branch, which forms part of its extensive global network of 21 offices across the US, Europe and Asia. Benefiting from a firmwide focus on finance, the Chicago team has earned renown for asset-backed lending, while David Crumbaugh has achieved particular prominence in workout-related financings. A strong corporate practice draws upon a base of both local and national clients, including Bally Total Fitness and Sears Roebuck, and receives substantial support from a highly rated tax department. The Chicago insolvency practice, featuring David Heller, acts primarily on behalf of creditors and has advised in restructuring proceedings for major lenders. Clients include GE Capital and Bank of America.

ANTITRUST

ILLINOIS

Leading firms (Antitrust)

1. KIRKLAND & ELLIS
   MAYER, BROWN, ROWE & MAW
   SIDLEY AUSTIN BROWN & WOOD
2. EIMER STAHL KLEVORN & SOLBERG
   SONNENSCHEIN NATH & ROSENTHAL
3. WINSTON & STRAWN

Leading individuals (Antitrust)

1. ABRAMS Lee *Mayer, Brown, Rowe & Maw*
   RYAN Thomas *Sidley Austin Brown & Wood*
   SMITH Tefft *Kirkland & Ellis*
2. EIMER Nathan *Eimer Stahl Klevorn & Solberg*
   LANGAN Andrew *Kirkland & Ellis*
3. CHEFITZ Joel *Howrey Simon Arnold & White*
   FINKE Robert *Mayer, Brown, Rowe & Maw*
   FREED Michael *Much Shelist Freed Denenberg, Ament*
   FREEMAN Lee *Freeman, Freeman & Salzman*
   MCCAREINS Mark *Winston & Strawn*
   MCLAUGHLIN Mark *Mayer, Brown, Rowe & Maw*
   SILBERMAN Alan *Sonnenschein Nath & Rosenthal*
   SLATER Paul *Sperling & Slater*
   TREECE John *Sidley Austin Brown & Wood*
4. BUSEY Roxane *Gardner Carton & Douglas*
   JOSEPH Robert *Sonnenschein Nath & Rosenthal*
   MARX David *McDermott, Will & Emery*

Up-and-coming individuals

KLEVORN Andrew *Eimer Stahl Klevorn & Solberg*
MUTCHNIK James *Kirkland & Ellis*

Firms and individuals are listed alphabetically in each band.

Kirkland & Ellis
see firm details p.830

The Firm: Tenacity and ferocity are the hallmarks of this superb antitrust practice, best known for its *"trial-readiness"* and sophisticated merger analysis. Interviewees agreed that despite a generational shift and the recent departure to the FTC of Robbie Robertson, it is *"still the starting point"* for antitrust advice in Chicago.

The Lawyers: **Tefft Smith** (see p.273) is *"a true expert in the field,"* who was highly recommended to researchers for antitrust litigation requiring aggressive defense. His split practice between Washington DC and Chicago reflects an increasing emphasis on M&A and joint venture counseling as well as advice in respect of EU and other international antitrust laws. He was lead counsel to Kraft on its defense of a nationwide cheese price-fixing case, and acted for Dean Foods in its recent merger with Suiza Foods. Described by opponents as *"personable and down-to-earth,"* **Andrew Langan** (see p.264) is an antitrust litigator, noted for his adept management of complex disputes. He recently defended Abbott Laboratories in a brand name prescription drugs case, and has represented BP America in a class action relating to the company's trading of Alaska North Slope crude oil. **James Mutchnik** (see p.268) is fast forging a name in the area of criminal antitrust work, where he draws on his prior experience as a prosecutor at the antitrust division of the US Department of Justice.

The Clients: Clients include: Sara Lee; Dean Foods; 3M; International Truck & Engine; Health Care Service Corporation; Tetra Pak; Packaging Corporation of America; Cambridge Protection Industries; Bently Nevada; Dow Agro Science; Illinois Tool Works; Terra Industries; Chiquita Brands International; Bain Capital; Briggs & Stratton; Colgate-Palmolive; IPSCO and Morgan Stanley.

Mayer, Brown, Rowe & Maw
see firm details p.843

The Firm: This firm is reaping the rewards of efforts to grow a robust counseling practice alongside its strength in antitrust litigation, with peers commending its *"excellent transactional experience"* in pre-merger notifications and the antitrust implications of distribution and franchise agreements.

The Lawyers: At the helm of the practice, **Lee Abrams** (see p.253) is held in universally high regard as an *"elder statesman"* of the Chicago antitrust bar, although opponents report that his *"gentlemanly approach"* disguises *"a tough negotiating style where necessary."* He has acted as lead trial lawyer for Ford in the ChoiceParts antitrust litigation, and is defending News Corporation against monopolization claims made in respect of coupon dispensers in retail stores. Having recently diversified his practice beyond litigation defense work, **Robert Finke** (see p.259) is now recognized as a first-rate counselor in the areas of marketing and distribution arrangements. Clients value his pragmatic analysis and his ability to *"cut through the esoteric arguments that often float around."* **Mark McLaughlin** (see p.267) was endorsed to researchers as *"a highly skilled, thoughtful and effective lawyer"* who is sure to have *"done his homework before he turns up."* Both Finke and McLaughlin were instrumental in securing victory in a large boat and marine engine antitrust suit brought against Brunswick Corporation by a group of boatbuilders and their buying cooperative.

ANTITRUST — ILLINOIS

The Clients: Clients include: ANGUS Chemical; Whirlpool Corporation; US Golf Association; Merrill Lynch; BASF; AOL Time Warner and Cargill.

Sidley Austin Brown & Wood
see firm details p.877

The Firm: Having steered AT&T through its complex divestiture, this firm boasts an institutional knowledge of antitrust that competitors concede is *"hard to match."* In addition to its impressive stable of Fortune 100 clients in the telecom, healthcare, consumer product, oil and mining industries, the firm's antitrust practice is noted for a *"keep-your-head-low-and-get-the-job-done"* attitude, and its collegiate approach to problem-solving.

The Lawyers: Thomas Ryan is an accomplished litigator whose *"extraordinary charm"* is said to endear him to *"courts, judges and juries alike."* Much of his current practice is devoted to defending antitrust cases brought against a major oil company in respect of a range of pricing and other practices. Commended to researchers as an *"outstanding"* attorney who demonstrates *"leadership and good judgment,"* **John Treece** has built a national reputation on the back of his defense of GD Searle in a brand name prescription drugs litigation. He represented Citibank in currency conversion fee antitrust litigation, and counseled appliance maker Maytag in its recent acquisition of Amana's major appliance business.

The Clients: Clients include: AT&T; BP Amoco; Citibank; Brunswick Corporation; IMC Global; Kimberly-Clark; US Cellular; Merrill Lynch, Pierce, Fenner & Smith; Microsoft: Pharmacia; ABA; AMA; Borden; IBP; Magna International and Tupperware Corporation.

Eimer Stahl Klevorn & Solberg
see firm details p.792

The Firm: This spin-off from Sidley Austin Brown & Wood is regarded locally as a *"high-quality"* litigation boutique offering substantial experience in complex antitrust matters, and a specialization in price-fixing defense.

The Lawyers: A *"true client magnet,"* **Nathan Eimer** (see p.258) is admired for his creativity in settlement negotiations but is considered *"mature and well-versed enough"* to take cases to trial if necessary. He successfully represented Dow Chemical before the FTC in respect of the company's merger with Union Carbide, and acted for Land O'Lakes in a case alleging price-fixing in relation to milk, cream and butter sold to dairy processors. Boasting an impressive combination of *"brainpower and personality,"* **Andrew Klevorn** (see p.263) is said by peers to display *"good instincts"* in counseling clients through government clearance procedures for proposed mergers and acquisitions. Eimer and Klevorn recently steered CITGO Petroleum through both a large FTC investigation of gasoline price-fixing and a US Senate investigation of gasoline pricing.

The Clients: Clients include: Kimberly-Clark; Conoco; Praxair; Holcim (US); Corn Products International; RR Donnelley & Sons and The Williams Companies.

Sonnenschein Nath & Rosenthal
see firm details p.882

The Firm: Longtime representation of McDonald's has spawned for this firm a subspecialization in the antitrust implications of franchise and distribution agreements, although strategic advice and litigation support are offered across the gamut of competition issues.

The Lawyers: Known to clients for his *"professorial"* stature and conceptual mastery of antitrust laws, **Alan Silberman** (see p.272) combines deep expertise in vertical restraints issues with a broad experience of antitrust compliance cases. He has advised Six Continents Hotels on restraint of trade questions arising from frequency programs, and recently assisted Sara Lee in the restructuring of its distribution relationships, following its acquisition of Earthgrains. Silberman has also been retained by both McDonald's and Prudential Real Estate Affiliates in respect of antitrust issues arising from the controversial Puerto Rico Dealer's Contract Act, commonly known as Law 75. **Robert Joseph** (see p.263) is widely regarded as a *"good technician,"* and has a mixed counseling and litigation practice that appeals to clients for *"assisting us to sort out pricing objectives and compliancy issues."* Both Silberman and Joseph represented online parts exchange company ChoiceParts in its high-profile antitrust suit against GM, DaimlerChrysler and Ford, alleging restricted access to parts information.

The Clients: Clients include: Allstate; Midas; Owens Corning; Red Bull North America; Salton; Owens-Illinois and Pella Corporation.

Winston & Strawn
see firm details p.904

The Firm: Antitrust expertise at this firm pivots on its celebrated litigation talent and its dedicated team of antitrust and trade regulation attorneys. Best known for its lead role in the long-running Microsoft antitrust litigation, the practice is also recommended for its expert handling of sensitive antitrust criminal investigations.

The Lawyers: *"A real player and a real competitor,"* **Mark McCareins** (see p.267) *"brings a litigator's perspective to the area of antitrust."* Clients commend him for the *"overwhelmingly calm influence"* he exerts on the process of taxing antitrust disputes. He successfully represented Abbott Laboratories in a recent arbitration. This involved claims by Baxter Healthcare that Abbott's exclusive license in respect of an inhalant anesthetic (sevoflurane) violated Section 1 of the Sherman Act.

The Clients: Clients include: AE Staley Manufacturing; GE; Hyatt Hotels; Interstate Bakeries; Luxottica Group; The Marmon Group; Premark International; SBC Communications; Smurfit-Stone Container and Verizon.

Other Notable Practitioners

The recruitment of **Joel Chefitz** from Katten Muchin Zavis Rosenman was described to researchers as *"a real coup,"* and marks the arrival in Chicago of Washington DC firm Howrey Simon Arnold & White. Chefitz received acclaim for his antitrust work on behalf of the Chicago Bulls and the Chicago White Sox, and for his role as lead antitrust counsel to TWA in its sale to American Airlines. According to interviewees, **Michael Freed** of Much Shelist Freed Denenberg Ament & Rubenstein, PC is undoubtedly *"among the top people in Chicago"* for plaintiff antitrust work. Specializing in class action work, his *"formidable"* reputation stems from his involvement in major antitrust litigation, including brand name prescription drugs and commercial tissue cases. Accredited by peers with *"good trial instincts"* and *"great probity,"* **Lee Freeman** at Freeman, Freeman & Salzman boasts a unique practice, where prosecution of high-stakes treble damage actions sits beside defense of restraint of trade suits and government investigations. He was defense counsel for Forest Laboratories in a brand name prescription drugs case, and represented Cargill and The Iams Company in a vitamin antitrust case. Sperling & Slater's **Paul Slater** is considered by contemporaries to possess both the *"intellectual horsepower and the substantive knowledge"* to handle complex litigation on behalf of antitrust plaintiffs. Specializing in healthcare antitrust cases, **Roxane Busey** of Gardner Carton & Douglas is highly regarded as a counselor and advocate for hospitals and other healthcare providers, as well as professional and trade associations. McDermott, Will & Emery's **David Marx** (see p.266) is also known as a healthcare specialist with a market reputation for *"hard-driving, single-minded"* pursuit of his clients' interests. He recently defended Banner Health System in an antitrust suit filed by a Colorado surgery center.

ILLINOIS — BANKING & FINANCE

BANKING & FINANCE

ILLINOIS
Leading firms (Banking & Finance)

1. MAYER, BROWN, ROWE & MAW
   SIDLEY AUSTIN BROWN & WOOD
2. LATHAM & WATKINS
   WINSTON & STRAWN
3. GOLDBERG, KOHN, BELL, BLACK, ROSENBLOOM
4. CHAPMAN AND CUTLER
5. KATTEN MUCHIN ZAVIS ROSENMAN
   KIRKLAND & ELLIS
   MCDERMOTT, WILL & EMERY
   SKADDEN, ARPS, SLATE, MEAGHER & FLOM LLP
   VEDDER, PRICE, KAUFMAN & KAMMHOLZ

Leading individuals (Banking & Finance)

1. BAPTISTA Robert *Mayer, Brown, Rowe & Maw*
   BERNSTEIN Bruce *Sidley Austin Brown & Wood*
   CLARK James *Sidley Austin Brown & Wood*
   CRUMBAUGH David *Latham & Watkins*
   MURRAY Gregory *Winston & Strawn*
2. ALBRECHT Thomas *Sidley Austin Brown & Wood*
   FORRESTER Paul *Mayer, Brown, Rowe & Maw*
   KOHN Richard *Goldberg, Kohn, Bell, Black, Rosenbloom*
   ROKOSZ Ronald *Chapman and Cutler*
   SCHWARTZ Donald *Latham & Watkins*
   WILLIAMS Douglas *Sidley Austin Brown & Wood*
3. BOEHRER Charles *Winston & Strawn*
   DOETSCH Douglas *Mayer, Brown, Rowe & Maw*
   DRANOFF David *Goldberg, Kohn, Bell, Black, Rosenbloom*
   JACOBSON Ronald *Winston & Strawn*
   LITWIN Stuart *Mayer, Brown, Rowe & Maw*
   MCMENAMIN Robert *McDermott, Will & Emery*
   STERN Gary *Sidley Austin Brown & Wood*
4. BARROW Peter *Neal Gerber & Eisenberg*
   DORAN James *Latham & Watkins*
   FRANSON Marc *Chapman and Cutler*
   GOLD Michael *Sidley Austin Brown & Wood*
   LATIMER Kenneth *Duane Morris LLP*
   LOOMAN James *Sidley Austin Brown & Wood*
   MASON David *Goldberg, Kohn, Bell, Black, Rosenbloom*
   PICKENS Scott *Schiff Hardin & Waite*
   SHULRUFF Stuart *Katten Muchin Zavis Rosenman*

Firms and individuals are listed alphabetically in each band.

Mayer, Brown, Rowe & Maw
see firm details p.843

The Firm: The practice ranks highly for its *"depth of talent,"* with a number of individuals recognized for *"tremendous knowledge and ability"* in a range of areas. *"Strong across the board,"* the group receives highest praise for its structured finance work; it undertakes a volume of syndicated facility matters for investment banks. Noted strength also exists in relation to asset-backed commercial paper work. The practice has steadily accrued significant expertise in sophisticated and innovative financings, and its reputation for *"exotic"* structures now extends well beyond the Chicago market.

The Lawyers: Still regarded as the *"leader of the practice,"* **Robert Baptista** (see p.254) is a *"great guy and excellent lawyer."* His more traditional practice remains active in secured and unsecured loans, financings and restructurings. Peers endorse him as a *"sharp, practical"* attorney for his skill in documentation and talents as a *"deal-closer."* *"Terrific"* **Paul Forrester** (see p.259) has broad expertise in project finance and complex structured finance and often represents major investment banks on syndicated facilities. With much of his practice based in Latin America, *"first-class"* **Douglas Doetsch** (see p.257) concentrates on securitizations, capital markets activities, restructurings and project work. He recently represented Banco do Brasil on a $300 million securitization and a $450 million securitization of diversified payment rights. Doetsch reportedly commands a *"wealth of knowledge"* in the field and is commended by clients as a *"leading light"* within the banking sector. His representation of Banc of America Securities as arranger on a $250 million securitization of diversified payment rights for Banco Itau has helped to consolidate his position *"at the cutting edge in financial future flows."* The *"talented and creative"* **Stuart Litwin** (see p.265) specializes in the securitization of auto leases, auto loans and equipment leases, and has a reputation as a leading attorney in this area. A *"trusted adviser,"* he recently counseled a large German auto manufacturer on the financing of auto lease and loan portfolios, and has been involved in the development of securitization structures for the fleet leasing industry.

The Clients: Bank One; Capital One; Bank of America; Citigroup; CSFB; Deutsche Bank; Fifth Third Bank; GE Capital; Porsche; Subaru of America; Volkswagen and Volvo Commercial Finance.

Sidley Austin Brown & Wood
see firm details p.877

The Firm: The practice received glowing market commendation as a *"top-notch"* banking team with a long roster of *"consistently high-quality"* practitioners. A 17-partner banking and finance group in Chicago works closely with a sizable New York team on complex financings and enjoys a national profile as regular advisers to major financial institutions such as Bank of America, Bank One, Citibank and GE Capital on syndicated and acquisition financing. The group covers the full range of commercial finance work but is particularly prominent in the securitization field where a highly respected team is often seen at the forefront of market developments. Current market conditions, however, have ensured that restructuring and refinancing matters have driven much of the practice's recent workload.

The Lawyers: Seen as the leader of the practice, *"elder statesman"* **Bruce Bernstein** enjoys a considerable reputation for expertise in secured transactions and restructurings for commercial banks and asset-based lenders. He recently represented Andersen Worldwide, the Swiss cooperative that serves as the central coordinating entity of the Arthur Andersen organization, in connection with the restructuring and settlement of claims against third parties and indebtedness to institutional creditors. Interviewees commend **James Clark** as a *"no-nonsense lawyer"* who *"doesn't get hung up on small points."* This *"classic Midwestern gentleman"* oversees the firm's relationship with Bank One and has been largely occupied with workouts and restructurings. Particularly hailed as a *"wonderful advocate for his clients,"* Clark played a leading role in the workout of CMS Energy. Cohead of the firm's international securitization practice, **Thomas Albrecht** rates highly as a *"spectacular lawyer"* with deep experience in the securitization of assets ranging from trade receivables, CLOs and CBOs to royalty payment streams and whole businesses. His current practice emphasizes the restructuring and redocumentation of existing securitizations and the application of securitization techniques in financing private equity and M&A transactions. **Douglas Williams** was described by peers as a *"talented draftsman"* with an *"extremely thoughtful"* approach to deal work. He has lately been active in restructuring secured and unsecured financings for Bank One and JPMorgan Chase. *"As smart as they come,"* **Gary (Skip) Stern** was recommended for his ability to *"simplify complex information."* A key figure within the team, his practice encompasses securitization, structured finance and bankruptcy work. A *"strong, capable attorney,"* **James Looman** undertakes securitization work for prominent banking clients. He has advised Bank of America in restructuring a credit facility for a large US winemaker and acted for Citigroup in a $1.6 billion accounts receivable securitization facility for a cellular phone company. His work for Bank One includes a $100 million securitization of sub-prime auto loans, and a $500 million securitization of auto loans and leases for a European car manufacturer. *"Eminently practical,"* **Michael Gold** *"knows all the right moves"* in complex financings. This highly regarded practitioner focuses on secured and unsecured syndicated financings, advising clients Bank of America and GE Capital on acquisition finance, restructurings and debtor-in-possession financings.

The Clients: Bank One; Citibank; Bank of America; JPMorgan Chase; GE Capital and La Salle National Bank.

BANKING & FINANCE ILLINOIS

Latham & Watkins
see firm details p.835

The Firm: Widely regarded as a key Chicago practice for asset-backed lending work, this West Coast-based firm has earned renown in the area for having *"as fine a group of lawyers as you will find."* With the firm's excellent workout practice operating at full steam, the team has been engaged in a large amount of 'clean up' work amending credit facilities. They have also been active on a $150 million secured facility for Foothill Capital and a $140 million secured financing for Congress Financial.

The Lawyers: *"First-class"* **David Crumbaugh** (see p.256) is a popular choice with clients who describe him as a *"whirlwind"* for his speed and thoroughness in transactions. This prominent Chicago lawyer combines a *"sharp, learned"* style with *"superb business sense."* Crumbaugh specializes in commercial and corporate finance and has been visible acting on a volume of workout arrangements. Practice head **Donald Schwartz** (see p.272) was commended as a *"straight-shooting"* practitioner with wide experience in the field. He is frequently found acting for Bank of America and Deutsche Bank in transactional and out-of-court insolvency matters. He recently represented the US agent in a multi-bank workout of a Canadian construction company. **James Doran** (see p.257) is a *"hard-working, creative"* attorney who focuses on secured financings and mezzanine investments, particularly leveraged change-of-control transactions and refinancings. Clients report that his *"even keel"* approach to negotiations ensures *"fast, smooth"* transactions.

The Clients: Antares Capital; Bank of America; Bank One; CIT Group; Citibank; Congress Financial; Deutsche Bank; Fleet Capital; Foothill Capital; GE Capital; LaSalle Bank; Royal Bank of Canada and Transamerica Business Capital.

Winston & Strawn
see firm details p.904

The Firm: *"Excellent and deep,"* the firm is not felt to be at the level of market leaders, but nevertheless wins a broad set of representations and is a popular choice among banks for cash flow, leveraged and asset-based financings. The practice has particular emphasis on the acquisition of debt and loan portfolios, and on the representation of portfolio managers in the acquisition of liquid senior debt.

The Lawyers: The *"premier"* attorney at the practice, **Gregory Murray** (see p.268) is *"absolutely top tier."* This *"low-key"* lawyer represents US and foreign banks and other financial institutions in large syndicated secured and unsecured loan transactions. He recently led the $3.5 billion letter of credit issuance facility for Swiss Re. Judged by clients to be *"exceptionally well-versed in law,"* **Charles Boehrer** (see p.254) can deploy an *"extraordinarily balanced"* approach in the meeting room. He continues to focus on cash flow syndicated loans, including restructuring, add-on facilities and amendments. *"A truly smart individual,"* **Ronald Jacobson** (see p.262) *"gets deals done,"* ensuring a *"a bunch of loyal clients."* His wide-ranging practice covers leveraged finance, structured investment and private equity matters.

The Clients: Antares Capital; Bank of America; Bank One; Denali Capital; Deutsche Bank; Friedman, Billings & Ramsey Group; La Salle National Bank; Madison Capital Funding; PPM America; Stein Roe & Farnham; Tricor Pacific Capital; WestLB; William Blair & Company and Wynnchurch Capital

Goldberg, Kohn, Bell, Black, Rosenbloom & Moritz, Ltd

The Firm: *"A unique animal with a tremendous academic pedigree and a history of achievement,"* the group is beloved for its *"quality, depth"* and *"awfully talented lawyers."* With an undisputed reputation for technical excellence, practitioners are routinely found on midmarket work and reportedly can be relied upon to *"get the deal done."* Although still largely perceived as a regional practice, the group has picked up work from New York companies looking for an alternative to Wall Street firms. A growth in mezzanine lender representation has accompanied an increasing volume of restructuring and asset-based work.

The Lawyers: Resoundingly popular among peers, the *"top-tier"* **Richard Kohn** is widely revered as a *"scholarly"* practitioner. Founding partner and head of the firm's commercial finance department, Kohn maintains a high profile within the market, in part due to his position as co-general counsel of the Commercial Finance Association. Although some commentators feel that his various academic and regulatory/legislative roles keep him increasingly out of the deal room, Kohn is warmly recommended as an expert in international lending. **David Dranoff** has a broad commercial finance practice and was deemed *"highly qualified"* in this area. He handles a growing number of syndicated transactions, restructurings and innovative asset-based transactions. Recent engagements include advising the agents in the restructuring of a $200 million multi-bank asset-based facility within the steel industry and a $60 million going private cash flow acquisition financing for a leisure games distributor. A *"thoroughly excellent"* attorney, **David Mason** concentrates primarily on restructuring-related financings. Clients praised his *"impressive knowledge of the A to Z of commercial finance,"* pointing to his experience that ranges from acquisition finance to workouts.

The Clients: Allied Capital; AmSouth Capital; Antares Capital; Bank of America; Bank of Montreal; Bank One; Congress Financial; FB Commercial Finance; Fleet Capital; Foothill Capital; GE Capital; GMAC Business Credit; Harris Trust & Savings Bank; LaSalle Bank; Madison Capital Funding; Merrill Lynch; Transcap Trade Finance; CIT Group and US Bancorp.

Chapman and Cutler

The Firm: This firm remains a *"steady"* player in the market. Well known for its work for clients Bank of Montreal and Harris Trust & Savings Bank, the group includes a handful of *"talented lawyers"* and was commended for its leading municipal bond practice. While not perceived to be the deepest of practices, the firm's corporate finance department is notable for its specialty in representing major US and foreign insurance companies in the private placement market and is judged to have a *"good reputation"* in this area.

The Lawyers: The flagship name at the firm continues to be **Ron Rokosz**, a *"class individual"* who earns *"tremendous respect"* from the Chicago market for some *"sophisticated work."* In addition to advising on cross-border and political risk issues, Rokosz undertakes syndicated lending work and some collateralization and workout matters. He acts frequently for ABN AMRO, who he recently advised on a $500 million credit card asset securitization transaction. He also completed a $175 million secured syndicated loan and letter of credit facility for Harris Trust & Savings Bank and the Bank of Montreal. The *"popular"* **Marc Franson** has built a practice centered around the consumer finance industry. He regularly represents retailers, banks and credit card companies in consumer credit transactions, securitization programs and related litigation.

The Clients: ABN AMRO; Babcock & Brown; Bank of America; Bank of Montreal; Bank of Tokyo-Mitsubishi; Bank of New York; Bank One; Barclays Bank; BNP Paribas; Capstar Partners; Chase Securities; CNA Insurance Companies; CSFB; Fifth Third Bank; First Union; Fleet Capital; GE Capital; Goldman Sachs; ING Bank; Lehman Brothers; MassMutual; Merrill Lynch; Morgan Stanley; Motorola; Nexstar Financial; Salomon Smith Barney; State Farm; Van Kampen Funds; Wells Fargo and William Blair & Company.

Katten Muchin Zavis Rosenman
see firm details p.827

The Firm: The firm is a regular player in small and mid-level financings, and has expanded its coverage through a merger with New York firm Rosenman & Colin. In a slow M&A market, the commercial finance practice has been kept busy advising companies seeking new and restructured credit lines. Recent matters include representing the lead lender in a $110 million senior secured loan to a catalog retailer and acting for the lead lender in $70 million worth of senior secured loans to a national chain of vitamin shops. High-end work includes advising the lead lender in a $1 billion unsecured loan to a national energy company. The practice has picked up new clients following the takeover of Heller Financial, and a noteworthy project finance practice represents major money center banks on projects such as water filtration or nuclear plants.

The Lawyers: Noted for his *"clear-sighted approach,"* name partner **Stuart Shulruff** (see p.272) is said to *"understand clients' objectives."* His practice covers senior and mezzanine financing and equity co-investments. He represented the lead lenders in a $105 million senior loan to a national distributor of home healthcare products and a $110 million secured loan to an international manufacturer of high-volume mail and document processing systems.

The Clients: Antares Capital; FINOVA Capital; First Source Financial; Fleet Capital; GE Capital; LaSalle Bank; Madison Capital Funding and Merrill Lynch Capital Services.

Kirkland & Ellis
see firm details p.830

The Firm: Although rarely found representing major lenders, the firm is still deemed an *"important market presence"* due to its strong sponsor client base. In keeping with the firm's general profile, the group has a heavy emphasis on LBO and private equity transactions, acting for a range of equity investors, pension funds, mezzanine lenders, buyout sponsors and borrowers. In addition to an established practice in aircraft finance, the group is developing a reputation for representing investors in mezzanine securities.

The Lawyers: Partners Christopher Butler and Andrew Kaufman handle secured and unsecured financing transactions from within the firm's corporate transactional department.

McDermott, Will & Emery
see firm details p.846

The Firm: This comprehensive practice acts for both lenders and borrowers in all areas of finance, including asset-based lending, securitizations, and financial product transactions. Bank of America remains a key client for the firm; the group recently advised the bank on a $110 million syndicated secured credit facility with infoUSA, an $85 million credit agreement with DeVry, and a $40 million multi-bank credit agreement with Liquid Container and Midway Games. At present, restructuring work is proving a driving force for the practice. Members recently acted for one of the creditors of Daewoo Group and in a $35 million restructuring for Strategies Equipment Supply Corporation. Recent issuer representation includes acting for Dairy Farmers of America in a $350 million credit facility. Also active within the private placement market, practitioners regularly advise large insurance and pension funds on mezzanine and private equity financings.

The Lawyers: Widely regarded as the practice's key attorney, *"highly responsive"* **Robert McMenamin** (see p.267) *"does a great job for clients."* A recent highlight of his practice was a $240 million credit agreement for Kellwood Company. Elizabeth Majers chairs the firm's global corporate finance group and oversees much of the group's private placement financings.

The Clients: Bank of America; Bell & Howell; Dairy Farmers of America; Hilco Capital and Kellwood Company.

Skadden, Arps, Slate, Meagher & Flom LLP & Affiliates
see firm details p.878

The Firm: Better known for its top-tier insolvency practice, the Chicago branch of the New York goliath regularly advises CSFB, Deutsche Bank and Goldman Sachs in relation to financings and investments in troubled companies. In addition, a high profile in blue-chip M&A ensures a significant role as borrower's counsel on large domestic and international transactions. The group has garnered a reputation for acting on *"big-time securitizations"* for both institutional lenders and corporate borrowers. A small, specialized group of partners possess niche expertise in a variety of areas. Particular strength exists in relation to aircraft finance; the group regularly acts for US Airways in aircraft mortgage and lease transactions, large secured financings and debt restructurings. Individual practitioners concentrate on tax-advantaged financial products and on the representation of sponsors, investors and placement agents in the formation and operation of US and offshore private investment funds.

The Lawyers: Randall Rademaker is the contact partner within the Chicago banking and institutional investing group.

The Clients: The group provides regular counsel to international financial institutions CSFB, Deutsche Bank and Goldman Sachs, and acts at a national level for a large base of multinational corporations on finance matters.

Vedder, Price, Kaufman & Kammholz

The Firm: Highly recommended for leasing work, the firm has a strong midmarket focus and appears on a volume of traditional commercial finance and asset-based transactions. Members advise banking and savings institutions throughout the US on the formation and expansion of bank and thrift holding companies, securities underwritings and placements, and loan and lease documentation. The group's highest profile, however, remains in the area of equipment finance, where the team was identified as having *"one of the best aircraft finance practices in the country."* Expertise in this area extends to structuring and negotiating leveraged leases, operating leases, subleases, conditional sales and securitizations in relation to aircraft acquisitions, sales and leases.

The Lawyers: John McEnroe is the group's contact partner. Attorneys skilled in related areas of tax, ERISA, bankruptcy and securities provide support on a range of transactions.

The Clients: The finance and transactions group advises underwriters, investment banks and assorted lenders and financiers on domestic and international transactions and regularly counsels US Ex-Imbank on aircraft finance matters.

Other Notable Practitioners

Scott Pickens of Schiff Hardin & Waite receives *"high marks from clients"* as a respected midmarket practitioner. His practice emphasizes asset-based lending, including cash flow transactions and mezzanine finance. At Duane Morris LLP, **Kenneth Latimer** is recognized for his work representing financial institutions on M&A, loan workouts, real estate and lease financing. **Peter Barrow** of Neal Gerber & Eisenberg *"understands the drill and is easy to work with."* With a broad commercial finance practice extending from equipment lease transactions to multicurrency financings, Barrow is a popular choice for client referrals.

COMMUNICATIONS/TECHNOLOGY

ILLINOIS
Leading firms (Communications)

1 MAYER, BROWN, ROWE & MAW
2 JENNER & BLOCK
   SIDLEY AUSTIN BROWN & WOOD
3 BAKER & MCKENZIE
4 KIRKLAND & ELLIS
   MEYER CAPEL, PC Champaign
5 O'KEEFE ASHENDEN LYONS & WARD
   SCHIFF HARDIN & WAITE
   SONNENSCHEIN NATH & ROSENTHAL

Leading individuals (Communications)

1 BRADFORD Darryl *Jenner & Block*
CARPENTER David *Sidley Austin Brown & Wood*
LIVINGSTON Theodore *Mayer, Brown, Rowe & Maw*
2 BINNIG Christian *Mayer, Brown, Rowe & Maw*
COVEY Tyson *Mayer, Brown, Rowe & Maw*
FRIEDMAN Dennis *Mayer, Brown, Rowe & Maw*
HAMILL John *Jenner & Block*
KIRCHHOEFER Gregg *Kirkland & Ellis*
MASCHERIN Terri *Jenner & Block*
MUNCY Dennis *Meyer Capel, PC, Champaign*
PETERSON Brad *Mayer, Brown, Rowe & Maw*
3 DOW Robert *Mayer, Brown, Rowe & Maw*
GORDON Mark *Gordon & Glickson*
KELLY Henry *O'Keefe Ashenden Lyons & Ward,*
MENSIK Michael *Baker & McKenzie*
MUENCH John *Mayer, Brown, Rowe & Maw*
SMEDINGHOFF Tom *Baker & McKenzie*
4 BRO Ruth *Baker & McKenzie*
DOCKSEY Ross *Sonnenschein Nath & Rosenthal*
EISNER Rebecca *Mayer, Brown, Rowe & Maw*
MACBRIDE Owen *Schiff Hardin & Waite*
MURPHY Joseph *Meyer Capel, PC, Champaign*
ROONEY John *Sonnenschein Nath & Rosenthal*
ROY Paul *Mayer, Brown, Rowe & Maw*

Firms and individuals are listed alphabetically in each band.

Mayer, Brown, Rowe & Maw

see firm details p.843

The Firm: An unmatched competence across the full range of communications law allows the firm to reign supreme at the top of the Illinois rankings. It provides comprehensive *"first-rate"* advice on telecom, IT and e-commerce issues to a clientele that values the group's *"responsive"* manner. The anchor of the firm's reputation in this area remains its *"broad base of experience and depth"* in telecommunications law. In this field, the group's long-standing advice to Ameritech ensures that it is acknowledged by peers as *"far and away the dominant player."*

The Lawyers: The team handles a huge volume of telecom litigation and regulatory work at both state and federal levels, under the guidance of *"renowned rainmaker"* **Theodore Livingston** (see p.265), leading external counsel to Ameritech. He was endorsed to researchers as a *"powerful advocate,"* and is noted for his fluency in the technicalities of the law. Contemporaries also singled out *"his judgment in assembling such a great group of people,"* transforming what one observer described as the *"Ted Livingston show"* into a full cast affair. Prominent among the group's leading names is **Christian Binnig** (see p.254), a trial and regulatory attorney, who is recognized to combine profound legal knowledge with *"great presence in the hearing room."* Complementing his strength on his feet is *"softly spoken and calm"* **Tyson Covey** (see p.256), who is said to be able to create *"incredible briefs at the drop of a hat."* Livingston, Binnig and Covey successfully represented Ameritech in proceedings brought in several states by competitors seeking the unbundling of Ameritech's digital subscriber line broadband architecture. Leading the firm in telecommunications arbitrations is **Dennis Friedman** (see p.260), whose *"frightening"* level of knowledge prompted the comment that *"he's a compendium of decisions."* In addition to his intellectual rigor, he was endorsed as an *"excellent writer"* who is *"great with witnesses."* **John Muench** (see p.268) is regarded as a *"strategic"* and *"terrifically creative"* telecom litigator. Clients consider him to be *"astute, diplomatic and responsive."* **Robert Dow** (see p.257) assists Muench in complex jurisdictional and constitutional appellate matters, and is highly recommended as a *"superb"* lawyer in this field. Muench and Dow have recently represented Ameritech in numerous cases before the US Courts of Appeal and the US Supreme Court concerning the scope of the federal courts' power to review state commission determinations under the Telecommunications Act of 1996. Elsewhere, the firm has a solid reputation for transactional IT expertise. The firm's young star in the area and *"a name you hear on a consistent basis"* is **Brad Peterson** (see p.269), who is thought to have *"a good sense of where the market is going."* He advised McDonald's on Enterprise Resource Planning system license and integration contracts, as well as appearing on outsourcing deals on behalf of Bank One and technology transactions on behalf of CNA Financial Corporation. **Paul Roy** (see p.271) is respected for his *"outstanding"* drafting skills and *"thorough understanding of technology outsourcing law."* He has performed technology and outsourcing transactions on behalf of Dow Chemical, Pharmacia and Cap Gemini Ernst & Young. The firm's *"front runner"* in e-commerce law is the *"rock solid"* **Rebecca Eisner** (see p.258), a *"good transactional lawyer"* whose reputation for *"thorough"* analysis and *"good business sense"* has earned strong market recognition. She has advised on a number of technology and e-commerce transactions for ONDEO Nalco, WW Grainger and the Chicago Mercantile Exchange.

The Clients: Among the firm's clients can be found: Ameritech; BellSouth; McDonald's; Bank One and Cap Gemini Ernst & Young.

Jenner & Block

see firm details p.822

The Firm: As longtime outside counsel to WorldCom, the firm is a veteran of a number of spectacular battles in the telecom sector, and has earned itself a reputation as a hotbed of lawyers *"raised and nurtured on the nuances of the industry."* Although it advises on all aspects of the industry, the team has forged its name through a long history of success in both regulatory and commercial litigation.

The Lawyers: The star of the practice is **Darryl Bradford** (see p.255), whose blend of technical and analytical expertise, strong oral advocacy skills and general *"worldliness"* is said to locate him within *"the top 1%"* of telecom attorneys nationwide. He has recently appeared for NextWave Communications in spectrum litigation before the US Supreme Court, and has conducted a series of reciprocal compensation disputes on behalf of WorldCom in states including California, New York and Illinois. **Terri Mascherin** (see p.266) is highly regarded by peers as an effective trial court advocate who always makes *"an impressive appearance for her client."* She recently conducted a range of interconnection proceedings on behalf of WorldCom. **John Hamill** (see p.261) was acclaimed to researchers as a *"terrific advocate"* and *"exceptionally hard worker."* He specializes in complex jurisdictional issues arising from the Telecommunications Act of 1996.

The Clients: WorldCom; NextWave Communications; McLeodUSA and Focal Communications.

Sidley Austin Brown & Wood

see firm details p.877

The Firm: The core of this firm's telecom practice may have shifted to Washington DC, but the location in Chicago of the *"phenomenal"* **David Carpenter** ensures that the group's profile in its home state remains high. As AT&T's principal appellate attorney, Carpenter is among the most experienced and respected telecom lawyers in the country. He has been credited as a pioneer of the important bridge between telecommunications and antitrust law, an endeavour punctuated by several high-profile US Supreme Court appearances. Although also celebrated as a strong oral advocate, it is his *"enormous intellectual power,"* *"meticulous"* briefs and litigation strategy that are thought to distinguish him from other practi-

ILLINOIS

COMMUNICATIONS/TECHNOLOGY

tioners in this area. He played a pivotal role in the recent US Supreme Court decision which upheld the FCC's pricing standard for network elements.
The Clients: The firm is well-known for its representation of AT&T.

Baker & McKenzie
see firm details p.767
The Firm: Renowned for its global capacity in this area of law, the firm in Chicago boasts a sophisticated IT practice with a characteristically international aspect.
The Lawyers: At the helm stands **Michael Mensik** (see p.267), a transactional attorney who was praised by one competitor as *"a walking encyclopedia on global IT law."* He is particularly noted for his multi-jurisdictional expertise, and is regarded by clients as *"an excellent strategist."* Recent transactions include a $75 million deal on behalf of Compaq to provide 'thin client' technology to American Express, and advising Borders on the negotiation of an online services outsourcing agreement with Amazon.com. Noted more for his academic wisdom than as an aggressive negotiator, **Tom Smedinghoff** (see p.273) is widely regarded as *"an authority"* on e-commerce, following years of research and advisory experience with various national and international policy bodies. He acts as e-commerce counsel to a range of Fortune 500 companies in the banking, insurance and manufacturing industries. The respected **Ruth Hill Bro** (see p.255) has a strong reputation in the field of privacy law, providing risk management counseling to a number of large multinational companies.
The Clients: Compaq; Apple; divine; Borders Group; CSG Systems International; JDA Software Group; Orbitz; Johnson & Johnson; Baxter Healthcare. The firm also advises government agencies.

Kirkland & Ellis
see firm details p.830
The Firm: This *"tremendously good"* IT practice is thought to profit from the firm's historical strengths in IP and corporate transactional work, and covers a broad range of licensing, outsourcing and system acquisition transactions, in addition to technology-related joint ventures and strategic alliances.
The Lawyers: **Gregg Kirchhoefer** (see p.263) enjoys industrywide respect for the *"deep technical background"* he brings to the sophisticated technology transactions that typify his practice. Described to researchers as a *"tireless negotiator who knows IT inside and out,"* he was recommended by peers as *"a wonderful choice to run a big deal."* He recently negotiated the restructuring of a broad-based outsourcing arrangement, valued at several billion dollars, between a large financial services client and a leading services provider. Other successes include advising a large financial commodities exchange on a strategic alliance leading to the outsourcing of an electronic trading exchange.
The Clients: Accenture; Allegiance Telecom; Allstate; American National Red Cross; Chicago Board of Trade; GM; Hitachi; IBM; Morgan Stanley; PwC; Tribune Company and WW Grainger.

Meyer Capel, PC
The Firm: Notwithstanding its downstate location, this small but *"accomplished"* firm continues to demonstrate solid credentials against larger Chicago competitors. Specializing in regulatory work on behalf of competitive wireless carriers and a number of independent telephone companies, the firm has recently earned acclaim for its role in telephone numbering and reciprocal compensation disputes.
The Lawyers: **Dennis Muncy** was described by peers as a *"real old fox,"* whose sophisticated arguments belie the image of a *"a small-town guy."* He is active in state regulatory issues such as access charge reform and the establishment of a universal service fund. He is assisted by **Joseph Murphy**, who has recently advised Cingular Wireless on area code disputes. Contemporaries acknowledge his ability *"to think through and grasp any number of complex and arcane issues."*
The Clients: Citizens Communications; Illinois Independent Telephone Association; Gallatin River Communications; Geneseo Telephone Company; Shawnee Telephone Company; Associated Network Partners; Cingular Wireless; Ameritech Advanced Data Services of Illinois; FairPoint Communications and SBC Communications.

O'Keefe Ashenden Lyons & Ward
The Firm: Outside counsel for a wide range of competitive local exchange carriers, this firm has a sound reputation as a smaller practice *"trying to gain a foothold"* in the telecom arena. Although dividing its work between regulatory and litigation matters, its reputation is strongest before the Illinois Commerce Commission (ICC), where competitors report that *"we see them doing pretty well."*
The Lawyers: **Henry Kelly** is considered to be a *"thorough"* and *"analytical"* practitioner who advises an impressive carrier clientele. He recently advised on pricing investigations and line loss complaints against Ameritech, contributing to his reputation as *"one of the voices for competition."*
The Clients: WorldCom; AT&T Wireless; Z-Tel Communications; Talk America Radio Networks; Level 3; Illinois Public Telecommunications Association; Delta Phones; Cbeyond Communications and International Payphone.

Schiff Hardin & Waite
The Firm: The firm has recently represented several competitive local exchange carriers in rulings relating to retail service standards and wholesale service standards for telecom carriers.
The Lawyers: The departure of Carrie Hightman to Ameritech is seen as a serious blow to this telecom-focused team, but commentators agree that **Owen MacBride** *"deserves a lot of credit"* for maintaining the firm's presence in Illinois. Drawing on his experience in the energy sector, he is a skilled regulatory attorney, known for his technical dexterity and calm handling of matters before the ICC.
The Clients: McLeodUSA; Allegiance Telecom of Illinois; RCN Telecom Services of Illinois; TDS Metrocom; NuVox Communications of Illinois and Illinois Consolidated Telephone Company.

Sonnenschein Nath & Rosenthal
see firm details p.882
The Firm: Competitors know this telecom practice, built around a small but *"seasoned"* team of former administrative law judges, for the *"strong historical perspective"* that it brings to regulatory work on behalf of its principal client Verizon. The group is felt to be attuned to the inner workings of the ICC, and lawyers here are noted for their *"straight-shooting"* style.
The Lawyers: **John Rooney** (see p.270) is a former ICC chief hearing examiner, who won acclaim for his role in the development of an intrastate universal service fund for smaller local exchange carriers and for his contributions to legislative amendments. The firm also boasts strong credentials in the area of IT outsourcing, where **Ross Docksey** (see p.257) is recognized for his technical mastery and *"business savvy."* He recently advised Aon Consulting and its subsidiary on a large human resources outsourcing agreement with AT&T.
The Clients: Verizon; Citizens Telecommunications Company of Illinois; Accenture; PwC and Aon Consulting.

Other Notable Practitioners
Described to researchers as Chicago's *"original technology lawyer,"* Gordon & Glickson's **Mark Gordon** enjoys kudos nationally for his trailblazing boutique practice in IT law. He advises on a range of strategic IT projects for clients including Hyatt Corporation, Pratt & Whitney, Morgan Stanley and the City of Chicago.

CONSTRUCTION

ILLINOIS
Leading firms (Construction)

1 SCHIFF HARDIN & WAITE
STEIN, RAY & HARRIS

2 BELL, BOYD & LLOYD
CONWAY & MROWIEC

3 BEDRAVA & LYMAN Oak Brook
PIPER RUDNICK

4 MUCH SHELIST FREED DENENBERG AMENT

Leading individuals (Construction)

1 FRIEDLANDER Mark *Schiff Hardin & Waite*
LURIE Paul *Schiff Hardin & Waite*
STEIN Steven *Stein, Ray & Harris*

2 LYMAN Bill *Bedrava & Lyman, Oak Brook*
SKLAR Stanley *Bell, Boyd & Lloyd*

3 CONWAY Tim *Conway & Mrowiec*
DASH James *Much Shelist Freed Denenberg Ament*
KIKOLER Stephen *Much Shelist Freed Denenberg Ament*
LAURIE Ty *Schiff Hardin & Waite*
RAY Stephen *Stein, Ray & Harris*
RUFF Randolph *Ogletree, Deakins, Nash, Smoak*

Firms and individuals are listed alphabetically in each band.

Schiff Hardin & Waite
The Firm: The group's nine dedicated partners represent an impressive range of clients, including property owners, developers, contractors, architects and engineers, and are known to be particularly well versed in construction procurement matters. The team can now boast national recognition, and, according to market observers, is the only full-service firm in Chicago that *"comes even close"* to the caliber of leading boutique Stein Ray & Harris.
The Lawyers: The presence at the firm of a host of *"excellent younger people"* is acknowledged by rivals to safeguard the construction legacy left by a number of Illinois' premier practitioners. Among these is the *"grandfather of construction law,"* **Paul Lurie**, a trailblazing lawyer who commands *"the utmost respect"* from his peers. He has a reputation as *"a champion of mediation"* who has *"seen everything there is to see,"* and is credited with the development of the careers of a number of the state's leading construction attorneys. **Mark Friedlander** is considered to be a shining testament to Lurie's tuition. Described to researchers as *"a visionary attorney,"* he was the recipient of glowing client references as *"a man whose judgment we trust implicitly."* He features prominently on consultative, transactional and contentious work, and is renowned for his pioneering work on design-build agreements. Cochairman of the construction group, **Ty Laurie** was firmly endorsed by both peers and clients. Opponents concede that he *"really knows the industry,"* and appreciate the fact that *"his word is his bond."* He is best known as a strong litigator with sound experience of complex construction disputes in both state and federal courts.
The Clients: The firm represented the City of Chicago in the extensive O'Hare International Airport terminal six construction and expansion project, and advised on most of the transactional work for the Chicago Bears' $632 million renovation of their Soldier Field stadium. Other clients include: Exelon; Jones Lang LaSalle; MCL Companies; NiSource; Sears Roebuck; DeStefano & Partners; Holabird & Root; Perkins & Will; VOA Associates; Interlake Material Handling; Midwesco Industries and Primary Energy.

Stein, Ray & Harris
see firm details p.884
The Firm: A *"well-oiled machine,"* according to market commentators, the most successful construction law boutique in Illinois now has 20 lawyers working out of its sole office in Chicago. Representing design professionals, contractors and owners, the group has tried or arbitrated an impressive range of multimillion dollar disputes. In one of the highest stakes designer liability cases to be tried in Illinois in recent years, the firm prevailed on behalf of Knight Architects Engineers Planners in litigation over two deaths and five injuries arising from the 1993 steel collapse at the new Chicago Post Office. The team's caseload also includes advice on contract negotiations, insurance procurement and analysis, and claim avoidance and licensing. The firm is currently active in assisting the University of Chicago with its huge construction program, refining some of the design and construction contracts it originally drafted, and recently arbitrated a $12 million claim against underwriters at Lloyd's.
The Lawyers: The firm's esteemed rainmaker **Steven Stein** (see p.273) is said to have *"tremendous name recognition."* A prolific lecturer, he is acknowledged by peers to combine *"thorough knowledge of the law"* with *"a wonderful strategic capability to work through a dispute."* He was especially singled out to researchers for his outstanding advocacy. **Stephen Ray** (see p.270) also received consistent market recommendation. His caseload has encompassed general consulting services for contractors and design professionals, and complex litigation. He acted as lead counsel in a $7.5 million breach of contract claim brought by one of the country's largest general contractors against a structural steel subcontractor.
The Clients: The firm is currently active in assisting the University of Chicago with its huge construction program, refining some of the design and construction contracts it originally drafted, and recently arbitrated a $12 million claim against underwriters at Lloyd's. Among its clients can be found: Pepsi Bottling Company; Dominican University; AIMCO; Bovis-Lend Lease; Chicago Bridge & Iron Company; Clark Construction Group; Hunt Corporation; McShane Construction; Gilbane Building Company; Walsh Construction Company; Graycor; Jacobs Engineering Group; Fluor; Black & Veatch and Pizza Hut.

Bell, Boyd & Lloyd
The Firm: Many observers perceive the department to function *"almost as a boutique construction litigation firm within a bigger firm."* A group of about a dozen lawyers advises on a roughly even split of transactional and litigation work, and has seen notable recent growth in healthcare projects. Acting as construction counsel for Loyola University Medical Campus, the firm prepared the contracts for the expansion of hospital facilities. On the contentious side, the group acted for Elmhurst Memorial Hospital on the resolution of a major construction defects dispute.
The Lawyers: One of the *"elder statesmen"* of construction law in Illinois, **Stan Sklar** still gains extensive admiration for his *"extraordinary industry contacts."* He is particularly noted for expertise in alternative dispute resolution, although he has also both prosecuted and defended numerous mechanics lien claims.
The Clients: Elmhurst Memorial Hospital; Loyola University Medical Campus; Draper & Kramer; Kraft and Abbott Laboratories.

Conway & Mrowiec
The Firm: Commended to researchers as *"a class act in Chicago,"* this small boutique developed from a split with Stein, Ray & Harris six years ago. Concentrating exclusively on construction and public contracts, and possessing a strong name for contentious work, the firm has recovered from owners or successfully defended against subcontractors on over 60 different construction projects. Although the group comprises just five lawyers, clients trust the team's ability to *"get the work done promptly,"* while the firm is appreciated by rivals for being *"resolution-oriented and not too battle-ready."*
The Lawyers: **Tim Conway** is regarded as the firm's outstanding name. A *"levelheaded"* attorney, he represents contractors, construction managers and design builders in a range of arbitration and litigation. Contemporaries believe that he *"comes alive"* in court, where his technical mastery and *"smooth style"* make him *"highly effective for jury cases."*
The Clients: The firm acts for, inter alia, contractors, engineering companies, construction managers and design builders.

ILLINOIS — CORPORATE/M&A

Bedrava & Lyman
The Firm: This boutique maintains a reputation both for contentious and non-contentious work in the construction sector, but is predominantly noted for its prowess in litigation, arbitration and mediation.
The Lawyers: Spearheaded by venerable construction expert **Bill Lyman**, currently president of the Society of Illinois Construction Attorneys, the group is well known for its extensive contractor clientele. Lyman himself was commended to researchers for his *"invaluable insight into the industry"* and his *"superb handling of client relationships."* Although he does handle commercial transactions, he is most associated with contentious practice, notably mechanics lien claims.
The Clients: The firm's clients include Testing Service Corporation, Garbe Iron Works and Warren F Thomas Plumbing Company.

Piper Rudnick
see firm details p.867
The Firm: The firm has a healthy track record in a wide range of transactional and dispute resolution matters throughout the construction sector. The firm advised the Sofitel hotel group in Chicago on a large recent construction dispute, achieving a settlement in its client's favor in defense of a multmillion dollar claim.
The Lawyers: Although it lacks the headline individual attorneys of its principal competitors, the department, which includes Dennis Powers, is recognized for its *"national and international scope."*
The Clients: Eddie Bauer; Sofitel Accor Hotels & Resorts; Hiffman Schaffer; Enclos; Boeing; Equity Office Properties Trust; Equity Residential and Power Construction Company.

Much Shelist Freed Denenberg Ament & Rubenstein, PC
The Firm: Best known for its general commercial practice, the firm owes its market profile to the presence of a pair of *"particularly sophisticated"* attorneys. **Jim Dash** and **Stephen Kikoler** are regarded as an *"excellent double act,"* and both were commended by clients for their *"great attention to detail."* Dash focuses on the contentious side, including mechanics lien claims, while Kikoler's practice encompasses both this and transactional matters.
The Clients: Brandenburg Industrial Service Company; DiPaolo Construction Company; EW Corrigan Construction Company; Osman Construction; Robinette Demolition and Tire N' Tracks.

Other Notable Practitioners
Possessed of a *"high level of experience,"* **Randolph Ruff** at Ogletree, Deakins, Nash, Smoak & Stewart, PC was pointed out to researchers for doing *"an excellent job for his clients."* These include companies such as Pepper Construction Company, Capitol Construction Group, Shaw Construction Company and JN Gray Company.

CORPORATE/M&A

ILLINOIS
Leading firms (Corporate/M&A)

1
- KIRKLAND & ELLIS
- MAYER, BROWN, ROWE & MAW
- SIDLEY AUSTIN BROWN & WOOD
- SKADDEN, ARPS, SLATE, MEAGHER & FLOM LLP

2
- WINSTON & STRAWN

3
- KATTEN MUCHIN ZAVIS ROSENMAN
- MCDERMOTT, WILL & EMERY
- SONNENSCHEIN NATH & ROSENTHAL

4
- LATHAM & WATKINS
- SCHIFF HARDIN & WAITE

Firms are listed alphabetically in each band.

Kirkland & Ellis
see firm details p.830
The Firm: *"An all-around solid corporate practice,"* its trump card remains a huge and preeminent private equity group that is national in scope and operation. Peers concede that no other Midwest practice operates in the same league. Although the firm has been hit by the downturn in venture capital work, such is its grip on the market that its caseload remains prolific.
The Lawyers: The firm continues to benefit from the presence of **Jack Levin** (see p.265), described simply as *"the consummate attorney."* An undisputed doyen of the Chicago legal scene, he earns the highest respect for his *"innovative and inquiring mind."* His status as a private equity lawyer is matched by a superlative reputation as a tax attorney. The *"combative"* M&A practice, although slightly overshadowed by its private equity counterpart, contains a number of top-level, experienced attorneys. Its aggressive style may not appeal to all commentators, but no one denies that the team is *"crammed with incredibly smart people."* The corporate caseload is underpinned by the firm's outstanding blue-chip debtor bankruptcy practice, and attorneys have kept active by handling the corporate aspects of insolvency cases. Regarded as one of the *"most accessible"* senior attorneys at the firm, **Carter Emerson** (see p.258) was commended to researchers as a *"first-class individual in the traditional corporate mould."* He concentrates on complex M&A, LBOs and IPOs, recently representing Dean Foods on its $1.5 billion merger with Suiza Foods and advising on the sale of OSCA to BJ Services. The popular **Kevin Evanich** (see p.258) has a general corporate practice, and represents both institutional clients and some privately held companies. He advised on the sale of SecurityLink to ADT for $1 billion, and acted on the disposal of Anchor Food Products to a consortium of HJ Heinz and McCain Foods and that of Bently Nevada to a division of GE, each for over $600 million. **Bill Kirsch** (see p.263) is rated as another of the group's *"key players."* Employing an *"assertive"* style in the meeting room, he has advised on various private equity fund structures, and represented Reiman Publications on its purchase by Reader's Digest. Other highlights include the acquisition of TWA by American Airlines, and representing Madison Dearborn Partners on its acquisition of Jefferson Smurfit, one of the largest LBOs in European history. **Jeffrey Hammes** (see p.261) acts for clients such as Bain Capital, Golden Gate Capital and Hidden Creek Industries. His LBO and restructuring practice has included advising on a $700 million LBO for Golden Gate Capital and on Dade Behring's $1.5 billion debt for equity restructuring.
The Clients: A recent highlight for the firm was advising GTCR Golder Rauner on its $800 million acquisition of TSI Telecommunication Services. Other clients include: Adolph Coors Company; American Medical Laboratories; BioChem Pharma; Dean Foods; Doncasters; Gaylord Container; GM; Great Lakes Chemical Corporation; Lands' End; Madison Dearborn Partners; PayPal; Thomas H Lee Company; TWA; Willis Stein & Partners and William Blair & Company.

Mayer, Brown, Rowe & Maw
see firm details p.843
The Firm: *"The classic Chicago firm,"* it is *"always on the shortlist"* for major companies, and maintains its enviable reputation for *"depth, breadth and sheer hard work."* The firm's deeply entrenched relationships with a powerful clientele and a bench of experienced lawyers ensure its undisputed position as one of the clear market leaders.
The Lawyers: Senior statesman **Bob Helman** (see p.262) is one of the great names of corporate America. This *"first-class, totally professional individual"* remains on hand to dispense the wisdom gained from years of experience building the firm's relationships with clients such as Northern Trust. *"Wonderfully creative"* **Scott Davis** (see p.256) is an M&A attorney who is now generally seen as one of the group's leading assets. He has

CORPORATE/M&A — ILLINOIS

ILLINOIS
Leading individuals (Corporate/M&A)

1
- **COLE Thomas** *Sidley Austin Brown & Wood*
- **HELMAN Robert** *Mayer, Brown, Rowe & Maw*
- **LEVIN Jack** *Kirkland & Ellis*
- **MULANEY Charles** *Skadden, Arps, Slate, Meagher*
- **WANDER Herb** *Katten Muchin Zavis Rosenman*

2
- **DAVIS Scott** *Mayer, Brown, Rowe & Maw*
- **LOWINGER Frederick** *Sidley Austin Brown & Wood*
- **LUBIN Donald** *Sonnenschein Nath & Rosenthal*
- **WALL Robert** *Winston & Strawn*

3
- **EMERSON Carter** *Kirkland & Ellis*
- **EVANICH Kevin** *Kirkland & Ellis*
- **KUNKEL William** *Skadden, Arps, Slate, Meagher & Flom*
- **QASIM Imad** *Sidley Austin Brown & Wood*
- **THOMAS Frederick** *Mayer, Brown, Rowe & Maw*

4
- **AIZENSTEIN Neal** *Sonnenschein Nath & Rosenthal*
- **CHOI Paul** *Sidley Austin Brown & Wood*
- **CULLEN Gary** *Skadden, Arps, Slate, Meagher & Flom LLP*
- **KIRSCH Bill** *Kirkland & Ellis*
- **OSBORNE Robert** *Jenner & Block*
- **TOTH Bruce** *Winston & Strawn*

5
- **FRIEDLI Helen** *McDermott, Will & Emery*
- **GERSTEIN Mark** *Latham & Watkins LLP*
- **GOODMAN Stuart** *Schiff Hardin & Waite*
- **HAHN Arthur** *Katten Muchin Zavis Rosenman*
- **HAMMES Jeffrey** *Kirkland & Ellis*
- **MEADOWS Stanley** *McDermott, Will & Emery*
- **SCHNEIDMAN Ed** *Mayer, Brown, Rowe & Maw*
- **SHEPRO Richard** *Mayer, Brown, Rowe & Maw*

Up-and-coming individuals
- **NAPOLITANO Steven** *Katten Muchin Zavis Rosenman*
- **THEISS Paul** *Mayer, Brown, Rowe & Maw*

Firms and individuals are listed alphabetically in each band.

played a key role in the firm's relationship with Devon Energy, representing the company on the $4.6 billion acquisition of Anderson Exploration, and the $3.5 billion acquisition of Mitchell Energy & Development. **Frederick Thomas** (see p.274) maintains a general corporate practice with a heavy bias toward M&A. Clients commended this *"responsive and knowledgeable"* attorney for his *"sound and unflappable judgment"* and his ability to *"analyze tough situations quickly."* He has recently handled matters for Etex Group and Marley in connection with sales of US subsidiaries, and represented Marconi on the sale of Marconi Data Systems to Danaher for $400 million. Newly ranked **Ed Schneidman** (see p.272) has built his reputation around M&A work in the publicly listed real estate industry. An *"understated guy who works likes a Trojan,"* he is said by peers to have a *"reflective and practical"* style. He advised on Archstone Communities Trust's acquisition of Charles E Smith Residential Realty in a stock-for-stock merger valued at $1.9 billion, and acted for Cabot Industrial Trust on its two-step acquisition by CalWest Industrial Properties for $2.2 billion. **Paul Theiss** (see p.274) continues to be regarded as an up-and-coming member of the department, and acted for iPCS in an $899 million stock-for-stock transaction with AirGate PCS, while **Richard Shepro** (see p.272) retains his share of market approval for his corporate and securities practice.
The Clients: Cabot Industrial Trust, iPCS, Etex Group, Marley, Marconi, Devon Energy and Northern Trust are among the firm's clients.

Sidley Austin Brown & Wood
see firm details p.877
The Firm: Rivals view this as the *"epitome of the old-line firm,"* and such is its standing as a premier corporate practice that *"even the man on the street knows who they are."* The firm enjoys a top-notch reputation among the Chicago business community, and is known by clients both for its expertise in big-ticket M&A and as a group of *"collegial"* attorneys who *"appear to practice law because they enjoy it."*
The Lawyers: In spite of the recognized depth at the firm, the principal name clearly remains that of the firm's managing partner **Tom Cole**. Peers report that despite the extra burden of managerial responsibilities, he is still *"one of the few big deal lawyers outside New York."* He is said to possess a *"fabulous individual brand name,"* and appears on the largest and most complex transactions. The *"talented"* **Frederick Lowinger** is also judged to have a top profile. Peers report that he *"gets to the issues fast, and resolves deals quickly,"* as when he advised on the sale of Howard Publications to Lee Enterprises for $750 million. Clients insisted to researchers that *"extremely effective negotiator"* **Imad Qasim** *"knows the art of a deal."* Among a raft of loyal clients, he represents Concord EFS on corporate work, advising inter alia on a $1.2 billion common stock offering and the acquisition of The Logix Companies and Core Data Resources. He also advised Tellabs on the $355 million acquisition of Ocular Networks. **Paul Choi** is said to have *"the kind of business acumen that wins boardroom confidence."* He has notable experience of defending clients from hostile takeovers, having represented Barrett Resources in its response to Shell Oil's hostile bid, and its subsequent sale to The Williams Companies for $2.8 billion. In addition, he has a healthy track record of advising on the formation and conclusion of joint ventures.
The Clients: Like every one of its competitors, the firm has felt the bite of the recent downswing in large M&A transactions, but it remains busy counseling some of the nation's largest corporations. These include: Aon; Bank One; Brunswick Corporation; DrKW; Exelon; Federal-Mogul; GE; Kimberly-Clark; KPMG Consulting; Merrill Lynch; RR Donnelley & Sons; Morgan Stanley Dean Witter; ServiceMaster; Starwood Hotels & Resorts Worldwide; Tellabs; Telephone & Data Systems and Tribune Company.

Skadden, Arps, Slate, Meagher & Flom LLP & Affiliates
see firm details p.878
The Firm: By far the most successful group from out of town, the firm's corporate department in Chicago has clearly established itself as a significant and freestanding entity. Peers recognize that the team *"gets its share of major indigenous Chicago business."* Despite the trying prevailing economic climate, the firm has remained busy in its key area of blue-chip public M&A, and the corporate team has also frequently been active in conjunction with the office's outstanding restructuring practice.
The Lawyers: A small group of *"tireless"* individuals are universally commended as having *"done a marvellous job"* in the Midwest. The long-term prospects of the firm are emphasized by the relative youth of its headline attorneys, exemplified by **Gary Cullen** (see p.256). He won the approval of peers for his advice to Sears Roebuck on its $1.9 billion purchase of Lands' End, and was described by clients as a *"practical, down-to-earth"* attorney. The team's flagship partner, however, remains **Charles Mulaney** (see p.268). Active in M&A, corporate finance and corporate governance, he is acknowledged to be *"at the peak of his powers."* He was commended to researchers for his *"terrifically energetic"* presence and his portfolio of blue-chip clients, including Ameritech, Hartmax, LaSalle Partners and Sara Lee. **Bill Kunkel** (see p.264) also won plaudits as a *"pragmatic, no-nonsense"* lawyer. His practice combines both M&A and corporate finance, and he represented SUPERVALU on its acquisition of Richfood Holdings, and Dow Chemical on its acquisition of CanStates Holdings.
The Clients: An impressive client base includes: Abbott Laboratories; AFFINA; AMCORE Financial; American Equity Investment Life Holding; AutoNation; Ball Corporation; Bank One; Bank of America; Bank of Montreal; Bear Stearns; BMO Nesbitt Burns; Brera Capital Partners; CCC Information Services; Chicago Mercantile Exchange; CIBC World Markets; Classic Communications; CSFB; Danka Business Systems; DrKW; Ecolab; Entergy-Koch; Goldman Sachs; Ivex Packaging; Kemper Insurance; Lake Capital Management; Legg Mason Wood Walker; Merrill Lynch; Morgan Stanley; National Steel; Newcor; Northern Trust; O'Reilly Automotive; Playboy Enterprises; Prudential Vector Healthcare Group; Safeguard International Fund; Sara Lee; Sears Roebuck; Steelcase; SUPERVALU; Unitrin and US Airways.

Winston & Strawn
see firm details p.904
The Firm: A respected firm that *"does a bit of everything"* and *"gets some good deals,"* it was generally highlighted to researchers for its excellent corporate finance practice, and has seen out the downturn in big-ticket work with smaller M&A

ILLINOIS

CORPORATE/M&A

transactions and financings. The team has advised on various workouts, including representing the senior debt holders on the restructuring of the debt of Huntsman Corporation and Huntsman International, and acting for the senior debt holders on the restructuring of the debt of Orius.

The Lawyers: Still *"the best-liked lawyer in Chicago,"* **Bob Wall** (see p.275) *"shows up everywhere"* and remains a hugely popular choice for investment banks. He represented Merrill Lynch in an international offering of $215 million of equity for CNH Global, and acted for Salomon Smith Barney in a $250 million offering for GATX Financial. Clients highlighted his *"creativity"* and *"business sense,"* and his recent M&A record includes representing Kellogg in connection with the sale of its Bakeline unit to an affiliate of Soros Capital. The respected **Bruce Toth** (see p.275) has a broad corporate practice and has maintained his levels of activity, representing Booth Creek Management Corporation on its $125 million acquisition of Kings Delight, and acting for the owners on the sale of Romano Brothers to Southern Spirits for $155 million.

The Clients: The firm acts for: AirGate PCS; Argosy Gaming Company; Barr Laboratories; Cap Gemini; Citizens Utility; Clear Channel; DrKW; Exelon; Fortune Brands; Iberdrola; Kellogg; Lear Corporation; Luxottica; Merrill Lynch; Morgan Stanley; Motorola; Morning Star; Newell Rubbermaid; Pliant Corporation; Prime Group Realty Trust; Prime Retail; Salomon Smith Barney; Smurfit-Stone Container; Telefónica and Urban Shopping Centers.

Katten Muchin Zavis Rosenman
see firm details p.827

The Firm: Although the collapse of the hi-tech bubble has been less than helpful, the firm's merger with New York firm Rosenman & Colin is generally reckoned to have boosted the corporate practice and extended its reach and volume. The team is particularly recommended for its corporate finance work, and is acknowledged to have *"some excellent people."*

The Lawyers: The firm's profile continues to be principally associated with the distinguished figure of **Herb Wander** (see p.275). Described by some commentators as *"the best lawyer in town,"* he is perceived to be one of the premier securities lawyers in the country. He is also admired for his wealth of experience in investment banking transactions. Peers respect **Arthur Hahn** (see p.261) as an attorney who *"understands the negotiating dynamic."* He has a diverse practice representing banks and brokerage firms, international equity and commodity exchanges, and technology companies. Rising name **Steve Napolitano** (see p.269) has a private equity and emerging company practice, and is involved in a broad range of M&A, LBOs and restructurings. Contemporaries observe that he has *"done a wonderful job building up a healthcare practice,"* and he is known for his private equity work in the regulated healthcare arena, acting as lead counsel on private and public transactions.

McDermott, Will & Emery
see firm details p.846

The Firm: It still does not have the profile of the market leaders in Chicago, but the corporate department is usually conceded to be part of a *"good franchise that is getting better."* A recent niche development has been a practice in the sports industry, including the financing of new arenas and the securitization of naming rights.

The Lawyers: *"One of the elder statesmen"* of the sector, the esteemed **Stan Meadows** (see p.267) has a general M&A practice, and has recently worked on a number of deals in the alcoholic beverage industry around the $100 million mark. He also advised on the sale of a food company for $500 million. The *"user-friendly and knowledgeable"* **Helen Friedli** (see p.260) has a varied practice, and is renowned for her work in the private arena. Popular with clients, she is reported to combine successfully the roles of *"tough negotiator"* and *"calming spirit."* She advised Hewitt Associates on its merger with Bacon & Woodrow.

The Clients: In spite of its international network of offices, the firm's client base remains noticeably strong in the industrial heartland of the Midwest. Clients include: Apple; Apple Oil & Gas; Arjo Wiggins Appleton; BAE SYSTEMS; Barrick Gold; Brightdart; Brokat Technologies; Centerpulse; CSFB; Cross Atlantic Technology Fund and Co-Investment 2000 Fund; Durlacher; Health Net; Hewitt Associates; Honeywell; IDT; Juergen Bartels; J O Hambro Capital Management; Kellwood Company; KPS Special Situations Fund; Kvaerner; LION Bioscience; Maynard Oil; Medal Entertainment & Media; North American Scientific; PRG-Schultz International; ProQuest Company and Schmalbach-Lubeca.

Sonnenschein Nath & Rosenthal
see firm details p.882

The Firm: Picked out by peers for its *"pure quality on public M&A,"* the firm has continued to feature prominently on public and private M&A and venture capital work.

The Lawyers: Showing *"no sign of stepping back,"* **Don Lubin** (see p.265) is said to be *"well known in the Chicago business community."* He was recommended particularly for *"his tact with sensitive matters,"* and he counts the boards of several major corporations among his clientele. **Neal Aizenstein** (see p.253) also stood out to interviewees as an attorney with a sound practice in M&A, public offerings and debt financings.

Latham & Watkins
see firm details p.835

The Firm: Regularly seen by rivals on the other side of transactions, the firm has successfully staked its claim to a share of the Midwest corporate market. Recent highlights for the firm include undertaking two acquisitions for the First Health Group, multiple complex securities transactions for Citadel Investment Group, and representing Reliant Pharmaceuticals on its acquisition by Alkermes for over $900 million.

The Lawyers: Coleader of the firm's M&A group, **Mark Gerstein** (see p.261) focuses on M&A and securities. Clients emphasize his ability to put issues in a *"business context, and then point the way forward."* He represented Merrill Lynch as financial adviser to Ivex Packaging on its sale and related spin-off, and advised Salomon Smith Barney as financial adviser to Paragon Brands for its $750 million sale to Tyco. More locally, he acted for Liberty Publishing Group on its recapitalization and IPO.

The Clients: The firm acts for: Bally Total Fitness; Citadel Investment Group; CSFB; DRL Enterprises; Hanover Compressor Company; IDEX; Integra LifeSciences; Koch Industries; Libbey; Manor Care; Merrill Lynch; Orbitz; The Pritzker Organization; Salomon Smith Barney and Sears Roebuck.

Schiff Hardin & Waite

The Firm: The firm retains its presence in the market through work encompassing IPOs, securities, M&A and corporate counseling. Recent highlights have included the $205 million sale of Cole-Parmer Instrument Company to Fisher Scientific International, the $225 million sale of First National Bancorp to Bank of Montreal, and the merger of Triple S Plastics with Eimo.

The Lawyers: The department's prominent name continues to be **Stuart Goodman**, a highly respected figure among his contemporaries. Head of the firm's corporate and securities practice, he has been the principal outside counsel to Newell Rubbermaid for more than 30 years. The firm advised that client on its $419 million acquisition of the remaining shares of American Tool Companies.

The Clients: The firm acts for a range of loyal, high-profile clients such as Newell Rubbermaid and NiSource. Other clients include: Anixter International; CIB Marine Bancshares; Franklin Electric; Koch Poultry; NorthWestern Corporation; Laidlaw Transit; Modine Manufacturing Company; Northern Trust; Tuthill and Wintrust Financial.

Other Notable Practitioners

Robert Osborne (see p.269) has been recruited from Kirkland & Ellis to Jenner & Block to chair the firm's corporate practice. This *"able practitioner"* received strong peer endorsement for his work for clients Lands' End and Sears Roebuck. Market commentators wait to see how his practice will develop at his new firm.

EMPLOYMENT & LABOR LAW

MAINLY PLAINTIFF

ILLINOIS
Leading firms
(Employment: Mainly Plaintiff)
1. ABRAHAMSON VORACHEK & MIKVA
   MINER, BARNHILL & GALLAND
2. MEITES, MULDER, BURGER & MOLLICA
3. ASHER, GITTLER, GREENFIELD, COHEN & D'ALBA
4. DOWD, BLOCH & BENNETT
   STOWELL & FRIEDMAN

Leading individuals
(Employment: Mainly Plaintiff)
1. GALLAND George *Miner, Barnhill & Galland*
2. ABRAHAMSON Vicki *Abrahamson Vorachek & Mikva*
   GITTLER Marvin *Asher, Gittler, Greenfield, Cohen & D'Alba*
   MEITES Thomas *Meites, Mulder, Burger & Mollica*
   MIKVA Mary *Abrahamson Vorachek & Mikva*
   MOLLICA Paul *Meites, Mulder, Burger & Mollica*
   PLATT Steven *Arnold & Kadjan*
3. BENNETT Barry *Dowd, Bloch & Bennett*
   D'ALBA Joel *Asher, Gittler, Greenfield, Cohen & D'Alba*
   NATHAN KAHAN Penny *Penny Nathan Kahan & Associates*

Firms and individuals are listed alphabetically in each band.

Abrahamson Vorachek & Mikva
The Firm: This *"top-caliber group"* is renowned for its professionalism and for the quality of its work, and was clearly endorsed to researchers as one of the two leading plaintiff firms in Chicago. Regarded by interviewees as *"tough and competitive attorneys"* in the courtroom, the firm nevertheless has a reputation for being prepared to settle claims where possible. The firm recently won a decision on summary judgment in Kielczynski v Village of LaGrange, a sex discrimination case involving a female police officer. It also received a favorable decision from the Chicago Commission on Human Relations regarding the unlawful termination of a worker's contract on the grounds of his race.
The Lawyers: **Mary Mikva** is a former US Supreme Court clerk who garnered praise for her *"ability to keep focused on the important things"* and for her dedication to her clients. Originally a defense lawyer, **Vicki Abrahamson** is now considered one of the top members of the plaintiffs' bar: *"She gets great results and really does her homework."*
The Clients: The firm tends to focus more on the representation of single plaintiffs rather than class groups, and is said to be selective about the cases that it takes on and thorough in its approach.

Miner, Barnhill & Galland
The Firm: *"An obvious leading firm,"* it was principally recommended to researchers for the outstanding and consistent quality of its partners. The team was also praised for its determination and commitment. It is best known for its track record in employment discrimination class action cases. Here it has had success representing large groups of plaintiffs in sexual harassment and race discrimination cases.
The Lawyers: Although the group as a whole won widespread acclaim, it was **George Galland** who received most attention. Our interviewees endorsed him as *"one of the outstanding plaintiffs' lawyers in Chicago."* He commands the respect of the courts and opposing counsel and was described as *"a compelling lawyer with tremendous integrity."*
The Clients: The bulk of the firm's work in this area is undertaken on behalf of large parties of plaintiffs although it also acts for smaller groups and individuals.

Meites, Mulder, Burger & Mollica
The Firm: This small team of lawyers focuses primarily on employment and personal injury, and was enthusiastically described by peers as *"the most promising plaintiffs' firm in the country."* Interviewees pointed to both the *"high quality"* of the firm's cases and a number of prominent individuals. The bulk of the team's workload takes the form of class actions and multi-plaintiff cases, and has included a class action filed against Mitsubishi Motor Manufacturing of America, acting as cocounsel with Benassi & Benassi. The case, alleging racial harassment against some 200 employees, was recently settled. In the ERISA field, the group, together with a second plaintiffs' firm, has won class certification in a case against McDonnell Douglas, which is now proceeding to the remedial phase for 1200 class members.
The Lawyers: **Thomas Meites** is said to take an intellectual approach to a case, and has *"a fantastic mind."* **Paul Mollica** also received endorsement as *"one of the brightest lawyers out there,"* who employs a *"low-key"* style to great effect.
The Clients: The group acts for individuals but is best known for its representation of large groups of plaintiffs.

Asher, Gittler, Greenfield, Cohen & D'Alba
The Firm: As one of the oldest union firms in the state, it continues to attract commendation for a practice that encompasses an array of labor matters. Its 12 lawyers are known for their tough negotiating stance and were characterized by opposing counsel as an ethical group. They typically handle collective bargaining agreements, strike management, arbitrations and litigation.
The Lawyers: The *"iconic"* **Marvin Gittler** spearheads the group, and is one of the most respected union lawyers in the market. Defense attorneys acclaim him as *"a worthy adversary,"* and maintain that *"you can cut a deal with him and his word is gospel."* **Joel D'Alba** was also singled out as a *"tough, straight-shooting"* practitioner, who undertakes substantial individual plaintiffs' work.
The Clients: The firm is best known for work in the labor law arena and was acknowledged for its high-level connections with unions on a nationwide level.

Dowd, Bloch & Bennett
The Firm: The vast majority of the work handled by this small team of lawyers involves labor law, and includes collective bargaining and union negotiations. However, a percentage of its time is also devoted to representing individuals in litigation. Here, the firm has experience in negotiating employment agreements and severance packages as well as handling a range of discrimination claims.
The Lawyers: From among an *"aggressive"* group of lawyers, the *"meticulous"* **Barry Bennett** came to the fore. He was endorsed to researchers as a *"tough opponent and an excellent negotiator."*
The Clients: The team benefits from a mixed client base including unions, individuals and groups of plaintiffs.

Stowell & Friedman
The Firm: This small group is famed among peers for its ability to *"pull off some excellent results"* and is best known for its class action expertise. Its *"client-oriented yet objective"* attorneys have experience in a variety of employment discrimination cases. In particular, the group has won most attention for its involvement as cocounsel to the plaintiffs in well-publicized sex discrimination cases against financial institutions such as Merrill Lynch.
The Lawyers: Name partners **Mary Stowell** and **Linda Friedman** were described as *"bright and honest"* lawyers. They were frequently cited as the first port of call for large and high-profile sexual harassment and sex discrimination cases.
The Clients: The group is best known for its representation of large classes of plaintiffs.

Other Notable Practitioners
Steve Platt of Arnold & Kadjan was recommended to researchers as one of the top plaintiffs' lawyers in Chicago. *"A consummate trial lawyer,"* he is an aggressive litigator, said to be *"familiar with all the developments of the law."* Sole practitioner **Penny Nathan Kahan** won market recognition as *"a practical and articulate"* lawyer who *"knows what the issues are."* She has represented individual plaintiffs in a broad sweep of employment matters, including cases filed under Title VII.

ILLINOIS — EMPLOYMENT & LABOR LAW

EMPLOYMENT & LABOR LAW — MAINLY DEFENDANT

ILLINOIS
Leading firms
(Employment: Mainly Defendant)

1. SEYFARTH SHAW
2. FRANCZEK SULLIVAN
   VEDDER, PRICE, KAUFMAN & KAMMHOLZ
3. LANER, MUCHIN, DOMBROW, BECKER, LEVIN
   LITTLER MENDELSON
   SCHIFF HARDIN & WAITE
   WINSTON & STRAWN
4. MATKOV SALZMAN MADOFF & GUNN
   MAYER, BROWN, ROWE & MAW
   ROSS & HARDIES
5. MECKLER, BULGER & TILSON
   SIDLEY AUSTIN BROWN & WOOD

Leading individuals
(Employment: Mainly Defendant)

1. WARNER Michael *Seyfarth Shaw*
2. FRANCZEK James *Franczek Sullivan*
   HARTSTEIN Barry *Vedder, Price, Kaufman & Kammholz*
   JEPSON Edward *Vedder, Price, Kaufman & Kammholz*
   SULLIVAN William *Franczek Sullivan*
3. LOPATKA Kenneth *Matkov Salzman Madoff & Gunn*
   STILLMAN Nina *Vedder, Price, Kaufman & Kammholz*
   YASTROW Joseph *Laner, Muchin, Dombrow, Becker*
4. BRITTAIN Max *Schiff Hardin & Waite*
   CREMENT Anthony *Franczek Sullivan*
   CRYSTAL Jules *Ross & Hardies*
   GANGEMI Columbus *Winston & Strawn*
   GOLDEN Gerald *Neal Gerber & Eisenberg*
   PARSONS David *Littler Mendelson*
   PISKORSKI Thomas *Seyfarth Shaw*
   POWERS John *Seyfarth Shaw*

Firms and individuals are listed alphabetically in each band.

Seyfarth Shaw

The Firm: In what is undoubtedly the firm's best-known practice area, it was repeatedly endorsed as the outstanding group in the state. A diverse and well-rounded practice comprising over 100 lawyers has accumulated a wealth of experience on behalf of some of America's largest corporations. Commentators were especially vocal in their praise for the group's contentious expertise, pointing out that *"they know when to settle and when to fight on."* It has defended an employer in a 'pattern and practice' sexual harassment case involving approximately 80 claimants. Other key engagements include advising a national chain of 40 restaurant and entertainment facilities following EEOC claims that it discriminates in favor of female servers over males.

The Lawyers: Having specialized in the area of employment discrimination since its genesis, **Michael Warner** has developed a reputation as *"the grand eminence of the defense bar."* An expert in the field of class action discrimination cases, he is renowned as an exceptional trial lawyer who is *"particularly effective in front of a jury."* **John Powers** also won acclaim for his client-friendliness, while **Thomas Piskorski** was singled out for his reputation in ERISA litigation.

The Clients: The firm's clients include: Starwood Hotels and Resorts Worldwide; GM; AT&T; Lucent Technologies; United Airlines and Caterpillar.

Franczek Sullivan

The Firm: Founded in 1994, the firm has quickly carved out an impressive reputation for itself, and is considered by many to be the top boutique in Chicago. Clients appreciate the firm's *"obvious commitment,"* although not every commentator delighted in its *"scorched earth policy"* toward litigation. The group represented the City of Chicago in the negotiations of a contract, initially rejected by the union, with the Fraternal Order of Police, Lodge 7. A ruling was made in favor of the City following arbitration. It has also defended a manufacturing facility against multi-plaintiff age and gender claims.

The Lawyers: Several of the firm's founding members are Seyfarth Shaw and Vedder Price alumni, who consistently attracted market recommendation. **James Franczek** is chief labor counsel to the City of Chicago for police and fire union matters, and was warmly endorsed as *"the best attorney in the city for public sector law."* In contrast, **William Sullivan** maintains a wide-ranging practice for predominantly private sector clients in the manufacturing, retail and distribution industries. An experienced trial lawyer, he appeals to peers as *"a wonderful attorney with great judgment."* Although not possessing quite the profile of the name partners, **Anthony Crement** (see p.256) was nevertheless endorsed to researchers as a talented practitioner with a *"good feel for the law."*

The Clients: The firm has litigated numerous employment discrimination claims on behalf of the Chicago Housing Authority. It has also defended a large retail chain in a disability discrimination case. Its other clients include Roadway Express, Safeway and State Farm.

Vedder, Price, Kaufman & Kammholz

The Firm: From a historical standpoint, the firm is one of the most prominent in the state, and has maintained its reputation as a top management firm. While it has latterly built up its corporate department, the firm remains most noted for its traditional strengths in labor and employment. Here, it is capable of handling the full spectrum of work, although its standing is particularly high for employment litigation.

The Lawyers: A team of *"consistently impressive people"* includes a number of high-profile individuals, including practice head **Barry Hartstein**. Described by opponents as *"one of the main go-to guys in Chicago,"* he is an *"aggressive, yet amiable"* litigator with substantial experience in equal employment and wrongful discharge litigation. **Edward Jepson** was also endorsed as a *"lawyer of substance who gets great results,"* and whose personable style was appreciated both by clients and opposing counsel. **Nina Stillman** was also singled out for her work on prominent OSHA cases. The firm successfully represented RR Donnelly & Sons Company in a seven-year litigation in which over 300 former employees brought claims of age discrimination. The group has also won an ADA class action case on summary judgment for Rockwell International brought by the EEOC.

The Clients: The firm's clients include: Bank One; Chicago Sun Times; Rockwell International; Sotheby's; Novartis; 3Com; Avon Products and Dominick's Finer Foods.

Laner, Muchin, Dombrow, Becker, Levin, Tominberg

The Firm: *"One of the most distinguished labor boutiques"* in Chicago, it won regular plaudits for its client-oriented service. The firm places a heavy emphasis on counseling and long-term preventative strategies, with interviewees noting that *"they keep costs down and resolve things quickly, but are also technically excellent litigators."*

The Lawyers: **Joseph Yastrow** is the outstanding practitioner here, and was enthusiastically described to researchers as a *"top-notch guy and a classy litigator."* He handles a full spectrum of labor and employment matters, including ADA, OSHA and wage and hour issues in federal and state court litigation, and has recently defended the City of Highland Park in a racial profiling dispute.

The Clients: The firm is defending the City of Chicago in a state court class action involving healthcare benefits for retirees. It also acts for Burger King; AmeriKing; Allied Waste; Yellow Cab Company; the Chicago Bulls; the Chicago White Sox and the State of Illinois.

Littler Mendelson

The Firm: The Chicago office of this national firm is relatively small in comparison to some of its competitors, but support from an extensive network of offices means that it can cover every area of employment. A plethora of traditional labor matters is routinely handled by a *"sharp and business-savvy"* team, although the firm's real forte is said to lie in employment discrimination class actions.

The Lawyers: Competitors consider **David Parsons** (see p.269) to be an *"intellectually sophisticated"* employment discrimination attorney. He represents clients in federal and state trial and appellate courts.

EMPLOYMENT & LABOR LAW — ILLINOIS

The Clients: The firm represents clients of varying sizes from Fortune 500 companies to small local concerns.

Schiff Hardin & Waite
The Firm: Commentators enthused about this corporate firm's fast rising employment practice, which is said to be *"blossoming into a serious player,"* thanks largely to the acquisition of labor boutique Brittain, Sledz, Morris & Slovak about three years ago. The group has been heavily involved in restrictive covenant issues such as trade secrets, and has also defended a number of age discrimination claims.

The Lawyers: Max Brittain is a well-known local name, who represents clients in matters arising from Title VII of the Civil Rights Act and in NLRB proceedings.

Winston & Strawn
see firm details p.904

The Firm: Although the firm is perhaps best known for litigation, its labor and employment department has evolved into a *"vibrant and respected"* practice.

The Lawyers: The high-profile chairman of the group, **Columbus Gangemi** (see p.260), is credited with much of the firm's success, and has expertise in both labor and employment matters. Representing private sector companies before the NLRB and the EEOC he was especially commended for his affinity with clients: *"He's responsive and quickly arrives at a solution."*

The Clients: The firm advised American Airlines in a class action involving a group of retired pilots, and won a summary judgment for Country Mutual Insurance in a case alleging age and gender discrimination. Other clients include: Sun Chemical; UBS PaineWebber; American Airlines; Experian; Country Companies and Caterpillar.

Matkov Salzman Madoff & Gunn
The Firm: For many interviewees this was a *"choice boutique"* for traditional labor expertise, although our research indicated that the practice extends far beyond these confines. Employment discrimination and executive compensation cases are part of the firm's repertoire, and the team also handles immigration issues. Its alliances with firms in Canada, Japan, Mexico, Puerto Rico and the Caribbean mean that the group advises a number of foreign clients on matters arising from NAFTA, Canadian and Caribbean labor laws and the Mexican Labor Code.

The Lawyers: A respected team of attorneys includes **Ken Lopatka**, a *"shrewd and professional"* labor and employment generalist. He leads the team that successfully represented Yellow Freight System in an ADA case. The group has also managed to overturn a NLRB decision on behalf of Overnite Transportation Company relating to union representation and wage increases.

The Clients: The firm's representative clients include: Aon; CNH Global; Ford; HJ Heinz; Newell Rubbermaid and Wal-Mart.

Mayer, Brown, Rowe & Maw
see firm details p.843

The Firm: This *"fledgling"* group won plaudits from competitors for the *"raw talent"* of its attorneys, although it generally lacks the profile of some of the firm's more established departments. Focusing primarily on employment litigation, the firm also counsels clients on preventative strategies and developments in the law.

The Lawyers: Jim Gladden has helped to develop the group that recently succeeded in having class status denied in a race discrimination case against Abbott Laboratories.

The Clients: The firm has represented Chevron USA in a landmark ADA case before the US Supreme Court, which centered around whether an employer can exclude an individual from a job because it is hazardous to the employee's health. The firm has also acted for: Sears Roebuck; Wal-Mart; Ameritech; City of Chicago and Leo Burnett/Bcom3.

Ross & Hardies
The Firm: A respected employment practice has been carved out of the firm's solid corporate base. Although the focus is heavily weighted towards employment discrimination, the firm also fields a number of individuals who are experienced labor lawyers. Its workload includes wrongful discharge litigation and defending various claims of employment discrimination. It also has experience in employee benefits and collective bargaining.

The Lawyers: The firm's most noteworthy employment practitioner is **Jules Crystal**. A former NLRB attorney, he has experience in collective bargaining agreements and handling strikes, and was endorsed by clients as *"terrific"* to deal with.

The Clients: The firm represents a wide variety of national and regional clients.

Meckler, Bulger & Tilson
The Firm: A small litigation firm, specializing in insurance work and labor and employment issues, that has quickly established a sound reputation since its foundation in 1994. It undertakes a wide variety of labor and employment matters for many of Illinois' largest employers and is active in the defense of employment discrimination, wrongful discharge and workplace tort claims.

The Lawyers: Joe Tilson and Brian Bulger are two of the firm's most high-profile names. Together with a team of specialized practitioners, they have handled several high-profile FLSA, Title VII and ADA cases.

The Clients: The practice advises many of Chicago's largest employers, including: Archer Daniels Midland Company; Cargill; The University of Chicago; Northwestern University; Wm. Wrigley; Allstate and Starbucks.

Sidley Austin Brown & Wood
see firm details p.877

The Firm: The group was endorsed for the quality of its advice and its ability to defend a full range of employment issues. Interviewees acknowledged that it was a growing force in the market. The firm is well known for its litigation capabilities. However, it also advises on employment issues arising from reorganizations and provides training programs to clients.

The Lawyers: The team, which is led by Brian Gold, was praised for its sound client relationships, and is respected by rivals for its *"ferocious"* litigators. The group has been involved in class action and multi-plaintiff wage and hour and employment discrimination cases for a national utility and an investment bank. It has also successfully negotiated a significant collective bargaining agreement within the utility industry.

The Clients: Some of the firm's most significant clients include: AT&T; Exelon; Norfolk Southern; KPMG; Sara Lee and Takeda Pharmaceuticals North America.

Other Notable Practitioners
A *"no-nonsense guy,"* **Gerald Golden** of Neal Gerber & Eisenberg garnered praise for his ability to *"cut to the chase and resolve things quickly."* Having represented clients before the NLRB as well as federal and state courts, he has extensive experience in matters relating to collective bargaining, employment discrimination, employment contract disputes and non-competition agreements.

ENERGY & NATURAL RESOURCES

ILLINOIS
Leading firms
(Energy & Natural Resources)

1 FOLEY & LARDNER
MAYER, BROWN, ROWE & MAW
2 JONES DAY
SCHIFF HARDIN & WAITE
SIDLEY AUSTIN BROWN & WOOD
3 LUEDERS, ROBERTSON, KONZEN *Granite City*
PIPER RUDNICK

Leading individuals
(Energy & Natural Resources)

1 HANZLIK Paul *Foley & Lardner*
MATTSON Stephen *Mayer, Brown, Rowe & Maw*
RIPPIE Glenn *Foley & Lardner*
2 MACBRIDE Owen *Schiff Hardin & Waite*
3 FLYNN Christopher *Jones Day*
ROBERTSON Eric *Lueders, Robertson, Konzen*
RUXIN Paul *Jones Day*
4 THOMAS Dale *Sidley Austin Brown & Wood*
TOWNSEND Christopher *Piper Rudnick*

Firms and individuals are listed alphabetically in each band.

Foley & Lardner
The Firm: *Chambers*' researchers encountered fervent recommendation for a group that has both *"depth"* and *"expertise,"* and which continues to act for blue-blooded clients, including Commonwealth Edison. It is particularly rated for state regulatory work, although the firm's merger with Hopkins & Sutter more than a year ago is thought to have bolstered its practice across the board.
The Lawyers: **Paul Hanzlik** is coleader of the national practice group and is deemed a *"thoroughly high-quality manager."* Although he has accumulated a wealth of all-around experience, the focus of his practice is on the electric utility industry, including the restructuring of electric operations, cooperative ventures and the operation of transmission systems. **Glenn Rippie** galvanized market opinion, and was valued by peers for his willingness to *"look for creative solutions rather than litigating everything."* He has represented energy clients on restructuring matters before state agencies and the FERC.
The Clients: The firm advises, among others, Commonwealth Edison.

Mayer, Brown, Rowe & Maw
see firm details p.843
The Firm: Combining transactional, litigious and regulatory aspects of energy law, the group stands out to rivals for its *"experience and talent."* In the regulatory sphere, the firm represents utilities and non-utility clients in proceedings that typically include rate cases, license approvals and rule-makings.
The Lawyers: A team of approximately ten attorneys includes **Stephen Mattson** (see p.266), who was warmly described to researchers as a *"skilled attorney with good judgment."* His practice touches on energy, sewerage and water matters, and he is frequently seen representing clients before state regulatory agencies, where he is noted for his *"calm and even demeanor."*
The Clients: Following the introduction of competition, the group has also been involved in the unbundling of natural gas services and has recently represented core client Nicor Gas in its 'Customer Select' proceedings before the Illinois Commerce Commission (ICC).

Jones Day
see firm details p.8422
The Firm: Much of the group's activity is centered on the Illinois market, but it maintains an active practice outside the state, and has experience before the FERC and the SEC. In the regulatory arena, the group advises a number of major utilities, including Ameren, in utility rate proceedings and retail power supply contracts. It also maintains an active transactional practice, encompassing mergers, demergers and restructuring.
The Lawyers: Chairing the group is **Paul Ruxin** (see p.271), regarded by peers as a *"knowledgeable regulatory lawyer"* with over 20 years' experience in the field. Typically acting for gas, pipeline and electric public utilities, he has represented Reliant Energy in its restructuring into Reliant Resources and CenterPoint Energy. **Chris Flynn** (see p.259) operates in state and federal regulatory agencies and courts, where observers see him as an *"easy to deal with guy with a good grasp of the facts."*
The Clients: FirstEnergy; Excel; Dominion Resources; Oklahoma Gas & Electric Company and Exelon.

Schiff Hardin & Waite
The Firm: Although the firm is felt by some commentators to lack the depth of personnel of some of its competitors, it remains a respected force for both state and federal matters. Major facets of its *"diverse"* practice involve representing gas companies in FERC proceedings concerning filings for certificates for new facilities and authority to provide new services. The firm also undertakes a high volume of state regulatory work for electric and gas utilities, and has recently acted for Illinois Power in two rate cases before the ICC to establish delivery services tariffs.
The Lawyers: Despite devoting a proportion of his practice to telecom work, **Owen MacBride** was described to researchers as *"one of the most knowledgeable people"* in the energy field. Clients regard him as *"practical and always well prepared,"* and he represented an electric utility client on its activities related to joining a regional transmission organization.
The Clients: NIPSCO; Dynegy Midwest Generation; NSTAR; Primary Energy; Bay State Gas and New England Gas Company.

Sidley Austin Brown & Wood
see firm details p.877
The Firm: A regular fixture in the Illinois energy market, the firm's transactional experience was identified as a particular area of strength. The group is primarily seen advising clients on contracts and M&A. In the regulatory field, the group's *"detailed knowledge"* of the ICC, originating in part from its involvement in the 1997 restructuring legislation, was widely noted.
The Lawyers: A *"deep"* bench of personnel includes **Dale Thomas**, whose *"command of the subject"* and *"creative approach"* to problems appealed to clients. Acting as counsel to the firm, Sarah Read is another prominent player, who frequently advises utilities on restructuring legislation.
The Clients: The firm continues to act for Commonwealth Edison and has advised it on the sale of its nuclear generating plants to its unregulated affiliate Exelon Genco. It is also active for Central and Southwestern System and advises a number of utilities.

Lueders, Robertson, Konzen & Fitzhenry
The Firm: Situated in Granite City, this small firm has an impressive reputation for representing large industrial clients before the ICC and the FERC. Clients saw the group as a key player in shaping the deregulation process, and acknowledged its *"profound understanding of the sector."* The team, which comprises four lawyers, has represented clients, including Illinois Industrial Energy Consumers, in several delivery service rate cases, and has been involved in contract negotiations with electric utilities.
The Lawyers: Opposing attorneys saw **Eric Robertson** as the key individual here. He has amassed a *"wealth of knowledge,"* and was commended to researchers as a *"composed attorney with great personal integrity."*
The Clients: GM; Ford; DaimlerChrysler; Archer Daniels Midland; AE Staley Manufacturing Company; Granite City Steel Division of the National Steel Corporation; Caterpillar and Abbott Laboratories.

ENVIRONMENT — ILLINOIS

Piper Rudnick
see firm details p.867

The Firm: Following the restructuring legislation of 1997, the firm has become renowned for its work on behalf of new competitive suppliers of electricity and natural gas. Here, it is active at the ICC, and has represented a coalition of alternative retail electricity suppliers in delivery services tariff proceedings.

The Lawyers: A small team includes the *"ultra-knowledgeable"* **Chris Townsend** (see p.275) who was described as being *"excellent at the fundamentals of energy law."* He has been involved in the negotiation of a contract between the City of Chicago and a major new competitive energy provider for the purchase of 60% of the city's electricity needs.

The Clients: The group represents independent power producers, and commercial and industrial customers. Its clients include: AES NewEnergy; Blackhawk Energy Services; The New Power Company; Dominion Retail; AXON Field Solutions; eMeter; Florida Power & Light Group and NRG Energy.

ENVIRONMENT

ILLINOIS
Leading firms (Environment)

1. MAYER, BROWN, ROWE & MAW
   SIDLEY AUSTIN BROWN & WOOD
2. JENNER & BLOCK
   SCHIFF HARDIN & WAITE
3. KARAGANIS, WHITE & MAGEL
   ROSS & HARDIES
   SONNENSCHEIN NATH & ROSENTHAL
4. WINSTON & STRAWN

Leading individuals (Environment)

1. ANGELO Percy *Mayer, Brown, Rowe & Maw*
   ZABEL Sheldon *Schiff Hardin & Waite*
2. EGGERT Russell *Mayer, Brown, Rowe & Maw*
   FORT Jeffrey *Sonnenschein Nath & Rosenthal*
   McMAHON Thomas *Sidley Austin Brown & Wood*
   OLIAN Robert *Sidley Austin Brown & Wood*
3. BERGHOFF John *Mayer, Brown, Rowe & Maw*
   FORCADE Bill *Jenner & Block*
   FRANZETTI Susan *Sonnenschein Nath & Rosenthal*
   HARRINGTON James *Ross & Hardies*
   KARAGANIS Joseph *Karaganis, White & Magel*
4. NIJMAN Jennifer *Winston & Strawn*
   RUSSELL James *Winston & Strawn*

Firms and individuals are listed alphabetically in each band.

Mayer, Brown, Rowe & Maw
see firm details p.843

The Firm: One of the largest environment departments in Illinois, it is acknowledged by all interviewees for its ability to offer expertise across the full spectrum of relevant law. It is particularly noted for its litigation capacity, which has seen it defend a large manufacturer in citizen suits under the RCRA. Researchers discovered, however, substantial market endorsement for the group's transactional prowess, and the team also routinely provides regulatory compliance advice to clients from the oil and chemical industries, involving, inter alia, permit negotiations before state and federal agencies.

The Lawyers: **Percy Angelo** (see p.253) is the group's most prominent individual and has been involved in this area of law since its genesis. Her experience includes Superfund and CAA work. Described by opponents as *"a tough negotiator,"* she successfully represented the permit applicant in a US Supreme Court case concerning the CWA. For litigation matters, the *"smart and thoughtful"* **Russ Eggert** (see p.258) is seen as the firm's top gun. He represented the plaintiffs in an appeal pending in the Court of Appeals in San Francisco that challenges the EPA's regulation of agriculture under the CWA. **John Berghoff** (see p.254) was praised by clients for his *"excellent strategic advice and high-quality service."* His practice is focused on environmental litigation, although he has also counseled clients on issues including the CAA and the Federal Water Pollution Control Act.

The Clients: The firm successfully represented a large corporation that was sued by the EPA for violations of asbestos regulations, following vandalism of its closed-down plant. The complaint was dismissed. Multinational corporations, local governments, public interest groups, small business enterprises and individuals all feature in the firm's client base. Leading clients include: Premcor; Illinois Tool Works; ProLogis Trust; The Williams Companies; Caterpillar; IBP; PPL Global; American Farm Bureau; The Alliance of Automobile Manufacturers and Waste Management.

Sidley Austin Brown & Wood
see firm details p.877

The Firm: The firm was one of the first in Illinois to develop an environmental practice, and has since maintained its position as one of the market leaders. The group is able to draw on expertise from its offices in Los Angeles, Washington DC and New York, but maintains a considerable presence in Chicago with a team comprising 18 lawyers. Strong in environmental regulatory and statutory issues, it also lays claim to an accomplished litigation practice, while its transactional side benefits from the firm's impressive corporate client base. Many of its lawyers have been recruited from government and were felt by clients to be *"strong and experienced across the board."*

The Lawyers: Heading the group is **Rob Olian**, described to researchers as *"an astute courtroom litigator,"* who focuses primarily on compliance and enforcement issues. He is defending American Electric Power against claims alleging violations of the CAA's New Source Review and Prevention of Significant Deterioration rules. **Tom McMahon** is a *"senior statesman"* of the bar, who is perceived to be at the stage of his career where he can *"pick and choose"* his cases. Competitors were struck by his ability to *"understand everything and see all the issues,"* and believe that his success lies in his *"grasp of the technical details on which cases turn."* Over the past year, he has represented NCR and Appleton Papers in a polychlorinated biphenyls (PCB) remediation case concerning the Fox River, Wisconsin.

The Clients: Other clients include GE and BP.

Jenner & Block
see firm details p.822

The Firm: An *"active"* market force, the firm is well known for the strength of its environmental litigation arm, but was also recommended to researchers for environmental insurance advice. Direct competitors also felt that the regulatory arm of the practice had developed well, and commented on the depth of this 11-attorney team, which represents a diverse client base on due diligence, litigation and regulatory matters.

The Lawyers: Formerly at the Illinois Pollution Control Board, **Bill Forcade** (see p.259) is an experienced lawyer who focuses on enforcement issues, government regulatory work and lobbying. Endorsed by clients for his *"problem-solving approach,"* he has niche expertise in air emission and control strategies and water resources cases.

The Clients: Carylon; El Paso Corporation; Exelon; General Dynamics; Pactiv; Peoples Energy; Rockwell International and Tenneco Automative.

Schiff Hardin & Waite

The Firm: A small group of lawyers, in conjunction with a core of litigators with environmental capabilities, provides clients with expertise in all areas of environmental law. Over the past year, much of the group's time has been devoted to the defense of Dynegy Midwest Generation in one of the largest air quality enforcement cases filed by the EPA under the New Source Review Enforcement Initiative.

The Lawyers: **Sheldon Zabel** is the key lawyer here. He has been awarded the palm of *"dean of the*

ILLINOIS — ENVIRONMENT

environmental bar" by clients and peers, who asserted that *"he knows all there is to know about the law in this area."* He advised the Steering Committee at the Rose Chemical Superfund site that was characterized as the largest PCB site in the country, and which involved over 750 potentially responsible parties. After 16 years, on-site cleanup has now been completed and administrative work is expected to be completed this year.
The Clients: Ford; Exolon-ESK; BorgWarner; Newell Rubbermaid and NiSource and its operating companies.

Karaganis, White & Magel
The Firm: This boutique firm, focusing almost exclusively on environmental law, is said by observers to comprise a *"sharp group of people who aren't afraid to take on controversial matters."* The six-strong team provides litigation expertise and compliance counseling to a variety of clients, and is often called on by rival law firms to give environmental advice on corporate transactions.
The Lawyers: The group's leading player is **Joe Karaganis**, singled out to researchers as an *"excellent attorney"* who *"has done it all over the years."* He is best known for advising suburban communities around O'Hare Airport on addressing noise and additional forms of pollution. Here, he established a legal precedent in finding that property owners are owed compensation, and secured soundproofing for locally situated schools.
The Clients: The firm successfully represented a large corporation that was sued by the EPA for violations of asbestos regulations, following vandalism of its closed-down plant. The complaint was dismissed. Multinational corporations, local governments, public interest groups, small business enterprises and individuals all feature in the firm's client base.

Ross & Hardies
The Firm: A small, multidisciplinary team has acknowledged strengths in counseling, permitting, enforcement and related litigation. It continues to act for a variety of clients in the metal, chemical, oil and heavy industries.
The Lawyers: Heading the group's eight lawyers is **Jim Harrington**, a veteran environmental practitioner with over 30 years' experience in this field. He is respected by peers for his technical flair and client-oriented approach. As well as acting on regulatory matters, he has undertaken work for a lead paint company, and advised on the cleanup of a heavily contaminated refinery.
The Clients: Major national industrial companies form a part of the firm's client roster.

Sonnenschein Nath & Rosenthal
see firm details p.882
The Firm: Research revealed that although the environment group does not have the profile of some of its competitors, it acts for an impressive list of clients and is home to a number of respected attorneys. Covering regulatory, litigation and transactional advice, the team represented ports in the State of Washington on the negotiation and implementation of government-regulated cleanup actions for waterfront properties. It also acted on behalf of an Illinois municipality before the Illinois Pollution Control Board, in order to revise aspects of the Illinois Water Pollution Control regulations.
The Lawyers: **Jeff Fort**'s (see p.260) practice is centered on the CAA, although his range also extends to environmental compliance matters and transactional work. Peers found him to be *"an excellent technician, who brings lots of experience to the table."* **Susan Franzetti** (see p.260) was endorsed by interviewees as an *"energetic attorney, who thinks outside the box."* She is best known for CWA work, but also covers air pollution, hazardous waste and toxic substance issues, and Superfund matters.
The Clients: Aon; Daubert Chemical Company; McDonald's; National Mining Association and US Airways.

Winston & Strawn
see firm details p.904
The Firm: Although commentators felt that the recent retirement of prominent partner Jane Piggott was a blow to the group, it still secured market recognition for the regulatory and litigation facets of its practice.
The Lawyers: The group's nine lawyers, who have experience in a variety of environmental fields, provide coverage on enforcement, transactional, compliance and legislative work. Of them, **Jen Nijman** (see p.269) has advised clients on a broad range of issues, including the CAA, the RCRA, underground storage tanks and Superfund issues. Said by competitors to be *"good at asserting herself without making enemies,"* she has represented companies from the coatings industry in a number of CAA proceedings. **Jim Russell** (see p.271) has a versatile practice that encompasses transactions and litigation, including enforcement and cost recovery issues.
The Clients: AMSTED Industries; Eaton; Interstate Brands; PMC; Reliant Energy; Renault; SkyGen Energy and Smurfit-Stone Container.

INSOLVENCY/CORPORATE RECOVERY

ILLINOIS
Leading firms
(Insolvency/Corporate Recovery)

1. KIRKLAND & ELLIS
   SKADDEN, ARPS, SLATE, MEAGHER & FLOM LLP
2. SIDLEY AUSTIN BROWN & WOOD
3. LATHAM & WATKINS
4. MAYER, BROWN, ROWE & MAW
5. GOLDBERG, KOHN, BELL, BLACK, ROSENBLOOM
   JENNER & BLOCK
   KAYE SCHOLER LLP
   PIPER RUDNICK
   SONNENSCHEIN NATH & ROSENTHAL

Firms are listed alphabetically in each band.

Kirkland & Ellis
see firm details p.830
The Firm: Clearly one of the two market leaders, this *"marvelous practice"* continues to rate highly for the breadth of its work. The insolvency group advises a range of national and international clients, appearing for debtors, secured and unsecured creditors, financial institutions, lessors and investors. It has been involved in a string of high-profile bankruptcies in recent years, and has acknowledged expertise in complex corporate restructuring, workout and bankruptcy planning and insolvency litigation. The firm has represented Teligent in its restructuring efforts, and Exide Technologies in its Chapter 11 restructuring.
The Lawyers: Much of the team's continuing eminence is attributed to **Jamie Sprayregen** (see p.273). Peers recognize him as *"an enormously hard worker, who deserves every bit of success he gets."* His practice is split between Chicago and New York, and East Coast opponents applaud his *"excellence at negotiating and managing the process."* He has recently represented Conseco and WR Grace on their restructuring activities, while his creditors' work includes the committee of unsecured creditors in the Chapter 11 proceedings of Williams Communications.
The Clients: Clients include: American Commercial Lines; Chiquita Brands International; Dade Behring; Quality Stores; TWA; United Airlines and United Artists Theatre Company.

Skadden, Arps, Slate, Meagher & Flom LLP & Affiliates
see firm details p.878
The Firm: An outstanding national practice with a *"wealth of talent and depth,"* it has profited from the economic downswing, and is now considered by rivals to have *"gone into overdrive."* The Chicago office is the headquarters of the firm's interna-

INSOLVENCY/CORPORATE RECOVERY — ILLINOIS

ILLINOIS
Leading individuals
(Insolvency/Corporate Recovery)

1
- BUTLER Jack *Skadden, Arps, Slate, Meagher & Flom LLP*
- SPRAYREGEN Jamie *Kirkland & Ellis*

2
- BERNSTEIN Bruce *Sidley Austin Brown & Wood*
- HELLER David *Latham & Watkins*
- MUNITZ Gerald *Goldberg, Kohn, Bell, Black, Rosenbloom*
- NYHAN Lawrence *Sidley Austin Brown & Wood*

3
- ADELMAN Howard *Adelman Gettleman Merens Berish*
- BOTICA Matthew *Winston & Strawn*
- MISSNER David *Piper Rudnick*
- PETERSON Ron *Jenner & Block*
- ROSENBLOOM Lewis *McDermott, Will & Emery*
- SNIDER Lawrence *Mayer, Brown, Rowe & Maw*
- SOLOW Michael *Kaye Scholer LLP*

Individuals are listed alphabetically in each band.

tional restructuring practice, and is consistently to be found handling high-profile megabankruptcy cases. Competitors recognize that the firm possesses *"one of the most dominant debtors' practices"* in the US.
The Lawyers: In spite of the departure of David Kurtz to an investment bank, the team retains the services of one of the country's leading practitioners: the *"talented and forceful"* **Jack Butler** (see p.255). The head of the practice, Butler is said to combine the attributes of both *"scholar and street fighter."*
The Clients: It has acted as special counsel to Enron, e.spire Communications, Owens Corning and The Warnaco Group. Among its debtor-in-possession cases, the group has worked on Comdisco, Exodus Communications, Hayes Lemmerz international, ICG Communications, Outboard Marine, Polaroid, Safety-Kleen Services, Service Merchandise Company and Viatel. The group's restructuring workload has including acting for America West Airlines, CoreComm, Cuddy Foods International, McLeodUSA and Xerox. Other clients include: PhyCor; ntl; Kmart; Globix; HCI; IT Group; ZiLOG; Prandium and National Steel.

Sidley Austin Brown & Wood
see firm details p.877
The Firm: Widely regarded as a first-tier creditors' practice, the firm advises an impressive client base of leading financial institutions. However, market commentators have also noted *"real strength"* in debtor work, where the firm has advised on such cases as Federal-Mogul and Pacific Trail.
The Lawyers: The head of the bankruptcy practice is the *"tenacious"* **Lawrence Nyhan** who was endorsed to researchers as a *"great strategist."* Noted for his vast experience of advising lenders, he represented the unsecured creditors' committee in the Chapter 11 of Columbia Gas Transmission, and the senior debt syndicate in the Chapter 11 of Fairchild Aircraft. A top-class banking lawyer, **Bruce Bernstein** also has a superlative reputation as a *"scholarly"* practitioner of restructuring law. He is most frequently associated with his lender work and has represented Andersen Worldwide.
The Clients: Clients include: GE Capital; Fleet Bank; Bank One; Wells Fargo and Bank of America.

Latham & Watkins
see firm details p.835
The Firm: Traditionally regarded as a creditors' practice, it maintains an enviable client list of major lenders, and appeared for the unsecured creditors' committee in the Comdisco bankruptcy.
The Lawyers: The high reputation of the department is largely thought to be the result of *"team effort,"* although researchers did have their attention drawn to the *"charismatic and magnetic"* **David Heller** (see p.262). He advised Bank of America on debtor-in-possession financings such as Owens Corning, WR Grace and Kaiser Aluminum, and was tipped by clients as *"a gifted workouts' attorney."* He has also acted for one of Kmart's largest unsecured creditors, Mattel and affiliates, during the Kmart Chapter 11 proceedings.
The Clients: The firm has been developing its debtors' practice, recently filing the Senior Living Properties Chapter 11 in Dallas involving more than $400 million in secured and unsecured debt. Other clients include: Bank of America; GE Capital; La Salle National Bank; Congress Financial and Foothill Capital.

Mayer, Brown, Rowe & Maw
see firm details p.843
The Firm: Judged to be a major player for creditors' work, the firm has represented a range of banks in major insolvency cases, most notably the Enron affair.
The Lawyers: The leading figure here is **Lawrence Snider** (see p.273), who recently represented Bank of America in connection with the restructuring of TruServ, and has worked on the reorganization of Lason.
The Clients: The firm has also acted for a number of note holders and bondholder insurance companies. Its clients include: Bank of Montreal; CIBC; Bank of Montreal; Toronto-Dominion Bank and Bank One.

Goldberg, Kohn, Bell, Black, Rosenbloom & Moritz, Ltd
The Firm: An established name in the sector, the group is especially respected for its core practice of asset-based lending work. It has also been retained by a large shareholder of Kmart.
The Lawyers: *"Still the dean,"* **Gerald Munitz** is held in the highest regard by peers for the strength of his intellect. He continues to serve as debtors' counsel on a number of the nation's largest Chapter 11s.
The Clients: Major national and international corporates feature on the firm's client roster.

Jenner & Block
see firm details p.822
The Firm: Having *"enhanced its position"* with the acquisition of several new partners, the practice is thought by interviewees to have *"unquestionably increased its capacity."*
The Lawyers: **Ron Peterson** (see p.270) concentrates on representing debtors, trustees, creditors' committees, landlords and secured lenders in Chapter 11 cases. An experienced insolvency litigator who is regularly seen representing unsecured creditors' committees, he was characterized as *"a reliable gunslinger, who trustees like to hire."*
The Clients: The firm has represented a number of parties on the Kmart bankruptcy, including prescription drug and golf club suppliers. It also advises creditors' committees, trustees, debtors and secured lenders.

Kaye Scholer LLP
The Firm: The Chicago office of a New York firm, it has assembled a *"good core bankruptcy group,"* and has increased its depth this year with the addition as counsel of Daniel Zazove, a senior attorney in midmarket Chicago bankruptcy work. The group has represented the largest holder of senior debt in Birmingham Steel, the bondholders in the Chapter 11 of International Knife and the largest bondholder in the Chapter 11 of American Tissue. The firm's debtors' assignments include Spinnaker Industries, DEC International and Geneva Steel.
The Lawyers: The primary individual remains the *"tough, smart and effective"* **Michael Solow**, who continues to act for Van Kampen Funds in numerous cases, including Teligent, Big V, Vencor, Ventas and Breed. His other creditors' work includes advising GE as debtor-in-possession lender and creditor in Kmart's Chapter 11, and JPMorgan Chase as agent for pre- and post-petition lenders in World Kitchen's Chapter 11.
The Clients: Clients include: LaSalle Bank; Foothill Capital; Citibank; Travelers; Crédit Lyonnais; GE Capital; ORIX, Nuveen Investments; United Stationers; Chikol Equity; Cerberus Partners; Huron Consulting; Andersen Worldwide; Deutsche Bank; BNY Asset Solutions and Geneva Steel.

Piper Rudnick
see firm details p.867
The Firm: *"Certainly a major player in Chicago bankruptcy,"* the firm is felt to benefit from a

ILLINOIS — INSURANCE

"good cadre of younger lawyers." It advised on the bankruptcy of Outboard Marine, and has represented lenders and borrowers in Chapters 11 and 7 matters, loan workouts, debt restructuring, creditors' rights issues, debtor-in-possession financing and non-bankruptcy alternatives.

The Lawyers: *"A lawyer for all seasons,"* **David Missner** (see p.268) is recognized as *"one of the most active debtors' lawyers locally,"* often representing creditors' committees. Clients appreciate the fact that he *"likes to get to the bottom line."*

The Clients: Creditors' committees and lenders instruct the firm.

Sonnenschein Nath & Rosenthal
see firm details p.882

The Firm: Although the firm is perceived to have a lower profile than in previous years, it is acknowledged to retain a forte in committee representation. The group also acts for Chapter 11 debtors, debtors-in-possession, secured creditors, unsecured creditors' and equity committees, and asset acquirers.

The Lawyers: Fruman Jacobson is the partner in charge of the national workout, reorganization and bankruptcy practice.

The Clients: The firm advises leading national corporates.

Other Notable Practitioners

Howard Adelman of Adelman Gettleman Merens Berish & Carter is an *"aggressive bankruptcy lawyer"* who is respected by contemporaries as an *"honest and capable"* local practitioner. *"Capable and amiable"* **Matthew Botica** (see p.255) of Winston & Strawn is a *"good lawyer in a terrific position."* Benefiting from the firm's excellent banking and corporate finance practices, he is felt by peers to have *"looked after the firm's institutional client base superbly,"* and is establishing a growing reputation for creditors' work. The esteemed **Lewis Rosenbloom** (see p.270) of McDermott, Will & Emery is a corporate finance and M&A lawyer who represents acquirers and investor groups in the market for distressed companies. He is also active in corporate governance.

INSURANCE

ILLINOIS
Leading firms (Insurance)

1. LORD, BISSELL & BROOK
2. KIRKLAND & ELLIS
   MAYER, BROWN, ROWE & MAW
   PIPER RUDNICK
   SIDLEY AUSTIN BROWN & WOOD
3. BUTLER RUBIN SALTARELLI & BOYD
   LOVELLS
   SCHIFF HARDIN & WAITE

Leading individuals (Insurance)

1. SCHWAB Stephen *Piper Rudnick*
   SPECTOR David *Schiff Hardin & Waite*
2. FORADAS Michael *Kirkland & Ellis*
   GILFORD Steven *Mayer, Brown, Rowe & Maw*
   GOODMAN Mark *Lord, Bissell & Brook*
   MCCULLOUGH Joe *Lovells*
   STINSON James *Sidley Austin Brown & Wood*
3. BATES Robert *Bates & Carey*
   DIGIOVANNI Nick *Lord, Bissell & Brook*
   GAVIN John *Foley & Lardner*
   GOLDMAN Michael *Sidley Austin Brown & Wood*
   HAARLOW John *Lord, Bissell & Brook*
   HAMM Leisa *Lord, Bissell & Brook*
   MENDELSOHN David *Piper Rudnick*
   RUBIN James *Butler Rubin Saltarelli & Boyd*
   SHUGRUE John *Zevnik Horton,*
   WYLIE Kenneth *Sidley Austin Brown & Wood*

Firms and individuals are listed alphabetically in each band.

Lord, Bissell & Brook

The Firm: A full-service insurance practice, it possesses a national reputation in both coverage litigation and transactional matters. Market commentators agree that *"for breadth of work and talent, they win the award."* Clients insist that the firm's reputation also benefits from the *"integrity and cordiality"* of its attorneys. The *"outstanding"* coverage litigation practice is best known for its representation of the London market, and undertakes a volume of toxic tort and products liability matters. Interviewees acknowledge that the practice *"comes up in almost every case,"* noting the advantage it derives from *"a lot of new blood."*

The Lawyers: A *"great school"* for the sector's lawyers, the firm has produced standout attorneys in the shape of **John Haarlow** and **Leisa Hamm**. Haarlow, head of the insurance coverage department, was commended for his representation of underwriters. He has recently defended Equitas on various jurisdictional and contract matters. Hamm focuses on the London market in environmental pollution, products liability and health hazard matters, particularly relating to the lead paint manufacturing, tobacco and pharmaceutical industries. **Nick DiGiovanni** is skilled in reinsurance litigation and arbitrations. A large noncontentious insurance practice undertakes M&A and regulatory matters for major insurance entities. **Mark Goodman** combines his M&A work with advice to US-based insurance companies on new consumer privacy rules. He recently represented a major US reinsurer on the issuance of a financial guarantee policy to support a $100 million tranche of a $400 million future flow asset securitization. Goodman is part of the *"premier regulatory practice in Chicago."*

The Clients: AEGON USA; GE Financial Assurance; General Re; Hannover Re; Hartford Life Insurance Company; Old Republic Group and Swiss Re Life & Health America.

Kirkland & Ellis
see firm details p.830

The Firm: The insurance group derives an advantage from the firm's *"formidable"* litigation prowess. It represents large policyholders, many drawn from its existing corporate client base, and has a national scope. Although characterized as *"aggressive litigators,"* these attorneys are commended for their work in asbestos coverage litigation for several power companies. The team has also represented a brewing company for business interruption claims.

The Lawyers: *"Extremely intelligent and knowledgeable"* **Michael Foradas** (see p.259) was recommended to researchers as an excellent choice on matters bound for trial. Policyholder clients appreciated this *"strategic thinker"* for his *"aggressive and tenacious"* advocacy. He advised a chemical manufacturer in coverage litigation for all its non-owned Superfund liabilities, and represented a telecom client on its Superfund and toxic tort liabilities throughout the country.

The Clients: Alcon Laboratories; BP; Central Hudson; Dow Chemical; Dow Corning; Hughes Aircraft Company; Motorola; Bayer; NL Industries; US Gypsum; Keystone Consolidated Industries; Milwaukee Brewers Baseball Club; Gaylord Container; Honeywell; Newmont Mining; Raytheon Company and S&C Electric.

Mayer, Brown, Rowe & Maw
see firm details p.843

The Firm: An extensive corporate client base underpins the firm's coverage litigation practice. The group represents policyholders and acts as counsel to life companies. M&A, regulatory matters and the development of master policy forms are all features of the practice. The firm also advises on a variety of reinsurance matters. It was recently appointed by the Illinois Department of Insurance to serve as special assistant attorney general.

The Lawyers: **Steven Gilford**'s (see p.261) practice focuses on complex coverage litigation, reinsurance litigation and advising corporations. He was widely recommended for his ability to bring a case to settlement, proving himself an *"excellent strategist and negotiator."* Clients appreciated his

INSURANCE — ILLINOIS

"understanding of how the insurance industry works," which he used to great effect on complex cases. His client roster includes major chemical manufacturers and clients in the automotive industry.
The Clients: Bank of America; BASF; Böhler-Uddeholm; Burlington Northern Santa Fe; Cargill; Caterpillar; Deutsche Financial; Dow Chemical; EniChem; Illinois Tool Works; Kindred Healthcare; Ispat Inland; Philip Services; Ryerson Tull; Tenneco Automotive and Whirlpool.

Piper Rudnick
see firm details p.867
The Firm: It offers expertise across the insurance industry, advising clients such as insurance companies, intermediaries, trade organizations, legislators and receivers. Competitors regard the team as *"litigators by instinct and training."* The firm has a particular reputation for reinsurance, and has developed a niche in e-commerce matters relevant to the insurance industry.
The Lawyers: **Stephen Schwab** (see p.272) sets the tone for the group as *"a trial attorney with bags of insurance experience."* Peers concede that he *"knows what the marketplace is thinking,"* while clients extol him as *"a real pro who knows how to conduct a trial."* His practice covers insolvency and M&A, as well as litigation and reinsurance. **David Mendelsohn** (see p.267) was also recommended for his insolvency and reinsurance work and enjoys a national reputation in the viatical industry.
The Clients: The firm advises insurance companies, trade organizations and receivers.

Sidley Austin Brown & Wood
see firm details p.877
The Firm: The group has consolidated, following the recruitment of partners from Katten Muchin Zavis who specialize in the securitization of insurance products. A merger with New York firm Brown & Wood has allowed the firm to develop a nationally prominent practice in the sector. Peers and clients agree that the group is *"easy to get along with,"* and commend its reinsurance expertise.

The Lawyers: **Kenneth Wylie** is recognized by peers as one of the most *"senior and experienced"* attorneys in the market. Together with the esteemed **Michael Goldman**, he heads the firm's insurance products practice. They represented AIG in the financing of several specialized asset classes, and acted for Zurich Insurance Group in the financing of investment commitments within its holding company system. **James Stinson** is active in insolvency as well as reinsurance work, and has advised on a number of asbestos and toxic tort claims. Regarded by commentators as an *"outstanding litigator,"* he frequently represents state regulators in insurance insolvency cases.
The Clients: The team enjoys a powerful financial services client base, including JPMorgan Chase, AIG and Zurich.

Butler Rubin Saltarelli & Boyd
The Firm: This respected boutique enjoys a high standing for its reinsurance work. It counsels clients on insurance coverage and undertakes litigation.
The Lawyers: Peers commended **James Rubin** (see p.271) as *"a talented lawyer,"* who focuses on reinsurance litigation, including insolvency matters. His client base spans the US, UK and continental Europe, and he has recently tried a reinsurance accounting case, in addition to two reinsurance coverage matters relating to environmental claims.
The Clients: The firm acts for IGF Insurance Company, International Insurance Co, Sphere Drake Insurance and Zenith Insurance Company.

Lovells
The Firm: The Chicago office of this large, London-based firm focuses on the insurance and reinsurance industry, and advises an international clientele that stretches through the US, Europe and China. Clients report that the team *"manages both themselves and cases well."*
The Lawyers: Observers recommended *"hard-hitting"* **Joe McCullough**. A reinsurance specialist, he is renowned for his contentious expertise and is experienced in private arbitration. Peers agree that he is *"an excellent technical attorney*

who gets things done." He advised extensively on losses incurred by 9/11, and has also advised a number of reinsurers seeking revision of their contracts.
The Clients: Everest Reinsurance Co; Hannover Life Reassurance Company; Riunione Adriatica di Sicurtà; Aioi Insurance Co; European Specialty Reinsurance; Manulife Financial; Reliastar Life Insurance Company; Security Life of Denver Insurance Company; Nationwide Insurance Companies; Equitas and NRMA Insurance.

Schiff Hardin & Waite
The Firm: The firm's insurance practice encompasses reinsurance, class action defense litigation and advice on disputes and torts where insurance may be an asset. A key element of the caseload is its advice on the assembly of insurance packages for corporate projects.
The Lawyers: Much of the firm's profile in this area is associated with **David Spector**, *"one of Chicago's top reinsurance experts."* A litigator who has been practicing *"longer than anyone else,"* he has represented insurance companies in a number of major receivership cases.
The Clients: Allstate; Bank of America; Catholic Mutual Group; Gerber Life Insurance Company; The Lincoln National Life Insurance Company; Munich Reinsurance Company; Penn Mutual Life Insurance Company; The Robert Plan Corporation; State Farm; The Tokio Marine and Fire Insurance Co; Transamerica Occidental Life Insurance Company and Trustmark Insurance Company.

Other Notable Practitioners
Robert Bates of Bates & Carey was commended to researchers for his *"excellent understanding of insurance coverage."* Much of his time is spent litigating environmental, asbestos and mass tort claims. **John Gavin** of Foley & Lardner is respected for his insurance M&A practice, although he has also acted for the Illinois Department of Insurance in insurance regulatory issues. **John Shugrue** of Zevnik Horton gained substantial peer approval for his expertise in policyholder coverage litigation. His practice also covers general liability, first-party and fidelity insurance policies.

INTELLECTUAL PROPERTY

Brinks Hofer Gilson & Lione
The Firm: This comprehensive IP boutique has emerged as the leader among specialist firms in Chicago. Interviewees emphasized the *"historical longevity"* of a firm with long-term links to traditional Midwest manufacturing companies, and noted the sheer size of the practice: *"They are bigger than anyone else and undertake so much more work."* The team handles all aspects of contentious, prosecuting and transactional work in patents, trademarks, trade secrets, copyright, e-commerce and related antitrust matters.
The Lawyers: Researchers discovered a consensus that **Roy Hofer** is *"a leader of the IP bar."* Head of the firm's IP litigation group, this *"confident and capable lawyer"* has experience in patent, trade secret, unfair competition, antitrust and contract litigation. The respected **Gary Ropski** is a litigator who also stood out to contemporaries for his work in patent, trademark, trade secret, copyright and IP litigation, representing clients at state, federal and international level.
The Clients: Major national and international corporates are among the firm's client base.

ILLINOIS — INTELLECTUAL PROPERTY

ILLINOIS
Leading firms (Intellectual Property)

1
- BRINKS HOFER GILSON & LIONE
- KIRKLAND & ELLIS

2
- LEYDIG, VOIT & MAYER, LTD
- MAYER, BROWN, ROWE & MAW
- MCANDREWS, HELD & MALLOY, LTD

3
- MARSHALL, GERSTEIN & BORUN
- PATTISHALL, MCAULIFFE, NEWBURY, HILLIARD
- SIDLEY AUSTIN BROWN & WOOD

Leading individuals (Intellectual Property)

1
- HOFER Roy *Brinks Hofer Gilson & Lione*
- WARNECKE Michael *Mayer, Brown, Rowe & Maw*

2
- AMEND James *Kirkland & Ellis*
- MCANDREWS George *McAndrews, Held & Malloy, Ltd*
- STREFF Bill *Kirkland & Ellis*

3
- GERSTEIN Allen *Marshall, Gerstein & Borun*
- HARTMANN Michael *Leydig, Voit & Mayer*
- HILLIARD David *Pattishall, McAuliffe, Newbury*
- KOZAK John *Leydig, Voit & Mayer, Ltd*
- MALLOY Timothy *McAndrews, Held & Malloy*
- NIRO Raymond *Niro, Scavone, Haller & Niro*
- ROPSKI Gary *Brinks Hofer Gilson & Lione*

Firms and individuals are listed alphabetically in each band.

Kirkland & Ellis
see firm details p.830

The Firm: Undoubtedly the premier IP group among the general practice firms, its historic decision to develop an IP capability is widely thought to have paid dividends, and the department has been a stand-alone operation for the past decade. The firm's depth of contentious expertise was frequently observed by interviewees, with trademark litigation regarded as an area of notable strength.

The Lawyers: The *"tenacious"* **Bill Streff** (see p.274) has a mixed practice, combining patent litigation and global strategic transaction work. Credited by peers as a *"high-level strategic thinker,"* he has particular experience in representing Japanese companies in a range of industries including computer systems, telecommunications, satellites and fuel systems technology. **James Amend** (see p.253) was picked out to researchers as *"a bright, practical attorney, who cuts to the chase."* An IP litigator with a heavy focus on patent and trademark cases, he has tried cases in various industries, including electronics, computers, automotive, chemistry, manufacturing and packaging.

The Clients: As well as servicing the firm's institutional clients, including Motorola, Lucent Technologies, Hughes Electronics and Kraft, the team has focused in recent years on cases in the biotech and IT sectors.

Leydig, Voit & Mayer, Ltd

The Firm: This large, historic boutique covers the entire sphere of transactional and contentious IP work. Its lineage is underscored by client relationships that date back to the 1890's.

The Lawyers: Senior figure **John Kozak**'s practice concentrates mainly on patent litigation and features some counseling work. Described to researchers as *"a nice guy and a good lawyer,"* his appearances are most frequent on cases concerning electrical engineering, chemicals and biotech. **Michael Hartmann** specializes in litigation and IP licensing enforcement, notably in the international arena, and has represented clients around Europe and in Japan. He acts both for plaintiffs and defendants, advised a large software manufacturer on infringement allegations and was recently active in the blood filter industry.

The Clients: The firm's roster includes both leading US and international companies.

Mayer, Brown, Rowe & Maw
see firm details p.843

The Firm: A younger practice, which is said to possess *"strong lawyers,"* it is recommended for transactional work, patent prosecution and litigation.

The Lawyers: Much of the firm's reputation in IP is seen to rest with the head of the practice, **Michael Warnecke** (see p.275). Widely regarded to be among the top echelon of IP attorneys, he has litigated at federal and international levels. His primarily contentious practice has included representing large corporations from the electronics and chemical industries among others.

The Clients: Caterpillar, Siemens, Sony and Mitsubishi use the firm.

McAndrews, Held & Malloy, Ltd
see firm details p.845

The Firm: A respected Chicago boutique, which was noted by competitors for its *"well-schooled, aggressive"* lawyers and a substantial client list. An eclectic practice offers litigation, licensing, prosecution, alternative dispute resolution and counseling services.

The Lawyers: Leading patent lawyer **George McAndrews** has a reputation as a *"forthright"* character, and counsels clients on all aspects of patent and trademark law. However, he is best known for his trial performances, notably in the mechanical, electronics and chemical industries, before federal and state courts. Researchers also had their attention drawn to the *"successful and hard-working"* **Tim Malloy** (see p.266), who specializes in the electronics, software, mechanical and medical device industries. He has argued before the US Supreme Court on behalf of Eli Lilly in a case concerning the scope of patent protection for medical devices.

The Clients: The firm advises mechanical, electronics and chemical companies.

Marshall, Gerstein & Borun

The Firm: A specialist IP firm focusing primarily on the contentious side, it has an excellent reputation for patent prosecution, and has also succeeded in developing a name among its peers for biotech work.

The Lawyers: The esteemed **Allen Gerstein**'s litigation practice covers patents, trademarks, copyright and antitrust matters. He has represented a major drug retailer in the US in trademark litigation, and has been heavily involved in litigation relating to computer games software and computer hardware.

The Clients: The firm advises major biotech companies and drug retailers.

Pattishall, McAuliffe, Newbury, Hilliard & Geraldson

The Firm: This boutique is considered to have a fine reputation for the individual quality of its lawyers, and a widely commended trademark practice that some commentators believe to be *"as good as any in the country."* The team focuses its practice on domestic and international trademark, copyright, IT, e-commerce, advertising, trade secret and unfair trade matters. It scores particularly high marks for contentious expertise, with competitors acknowledging the group as *"worthy opponents."*

The Lawyers: Managing partner **David Hilliard** gained universal endorsement for his trademark and competition practice.

The Clients: Leading national and international companies.

Sidley Austin Brown & Wood
see firm details p.877

The Firm: Nationally, the firm is felt to have benefited from its Dallas merger with a team led by the revered Bryan Medlock. The Chicago practice, while not possessing a comparable profile, remains highly regarded, notably for IT-related advice. The IP practice, which features David Pritikin, concentrates entirely on contentious matters, has a large number of patent lawyers and has undertaken significant recent patent litigation cases, particularly in the pharmaceutical and technology industries.

The Clients: Major national and international companies.

Other Notable Practitioners

Ray Niro of Niro, Scavone, Haller & Niro emerged from our research as the number-one choice in Chicago as plaintiffs' counsel for IP cases. He has earned a widespread reputation as a *"litigator to be feared."*

LITIGATION — ILLINOIS

GENERAL COMMERCIAL

ILLINOIS
Leading firms
(Litigation: General Commercial)

1. KIRKLAND & ELLIS
2. MAYER, BROWN, ROWE & MAW
   WINSTON & STRAWN
3. BARTLIT BECK HERMAN PALENCHAR & SCOTT
4. JENNER & BLOCK
   SIDLEY AUSTIN BROWN & WOOD
5. MCDERMOTT, WILL & EMERY
6. JONES DAY
   SKADDEN, ARPS, SLATE, MEAGHER & FLOM LLP

Leading individuals
(Litigation: General Commercial)

★ WEBB Dan *Winston & Strawn*
1. BERNICK David *Kirkland & Ellis*
2. SOLOVY Jerold *Jenner & Block*
   SULLIVAN Thomas *Jenner & Block*
   ZAROV Herbert *Mayer, Brown, Rowe & Maw*
3. BECK Philip *Bartlit Beck Herman Palenchar*
   CONNELLY Vincent *Mayer, Brown, Rowe & Maw*
   FAHNER Tyrone *Mayer, Brown, Rowe & Maw*
   REIDY Daniel *Jones Day*
   VALUKAS Anton *Jenner & Block*
4. CICERO Frank *Kirkland & Ellis*
   GODFREY Richard *Kirkland & Ellis*
   NICKLIN Emily *Kirkland & Ellis*
   SALPETER Alan *Mayer, Brown, Rowe & Maw*
   TARUN Robert *Winston & Strawn*
5. CONLON William *Sidley Austin Brown & Wood*
   DURKIN Thomas *Mayer, Brown, Rowe & Maw*
   STONE Jeffrey *McDermott, Will & Emery*
6. CARLSON Walter *Sidley Austin Brown & Wood*
   CLIFFORD Robert *Clifford Law Offices*
   DOUGLAS Charles *Sidley Austin Brown & Wood*
   GRIMM Terry *Winston & Strawn*
   HICKEY John *Kirkland & Ellis*
   LERMAN Bradley *Winston & Strawn*
   LINKLATER Joe *Baker & McKenzie*
   MOLO Steven *Winston & Strawn*
   POPE Michael *McDermott, Will & Emery*

Firms and individuals are listed alphabetically in each band.

Kirkland & Ellis
see firm details p.830

The Firm: In a league of its own, research revealed this to be the outstanding group in Chicago, with some commentators proclaiming it to be *"one of the best litigation firms in the country."* The group is consistently involved in some of the largest and most prominent cases throughout the US, is famed for its trial practice and is said to have an instinct for trying cases rather than settling them. Researchers had their attention drawn to the team's aggressive and tough approach, while the quality of its lawyers was noted as *"consistently excellent: you are more likely to get someone suited to you here than elsewhere."*

The Lawyers: David Bernick (see p.254) is seen as the group's outstanding practitioner, and has substantial experience in the area of mass torts. Described by contemporaries as an *"incredibly sophisticated courtroom litigator,"* he excels at jury trials where his strength is said to lie in an *"ability to explain complex science issues to everyday people."* In the field of asbestos litigation, where he is an acknowledged expert, he has represented Ford, GM and DaimlerChrysler. He has also acted as national trial counsel for Brown & Williamson in tobacco litigation, and was recently successful in securing a unanimous jury verdict in favor of his client in a union class action case. **Emily Nicklin** (see p.269) is best known for her accountants' liability practice although she has also represented Morgan Stanley in a sex bias case brought by a former female employee. Clients appreciate her responsiveness and enthuse about her ability as *"a terrific trial lawyer."* **Frank Cicero** (see p.255) is an *"engaging and straightforward"* senior member of the group. His workload includes antitrust and securities fraud cases, and has seen him act for BP Amoco in its contested merger with ARCO. **Rick Godfrey** (see p.261) can *"litigate anything,"* and was warmly recommended by clients for his ability to *"grasp the key issues and see the bigger picture."* One of his most notable engagements has been the successful representation of Lincoln Benefit Life in a breach of loan agreement claim and in defense of a $2 billion counter claim for breach of contract. **John Hickey** (see p.262) is a *"personable guy who gets on well with his adversaries."* He successfully represented GM in a motion brought by DaimlerChrysler for an injunction on GM's new sport utility truck, the HUMMER H2. A ruling in favor of GM was granted and is now being appealed.

The Clients: The firm's clients include: Brown & Williamson Tobacco; GM; Dow Corning; Motorola; BP Amoco; Arthur Andersen; Morgan Stanley Dean Witter; 3M; Ameritech and GE.

Mayer, Brown, Rowe & Maw
see firm details p.843

The Firm: Commentators believe that this corporate giant's litigation department has *"evolved nicely over the past few years,"* to the point that it is now considered to be one of the leading forces in the market. Regarded as more scholarly in its approach than some of its competitors, it was commended for its ability to combine *"intellectual firepower,"* excellent trial advocacy and documentation skills. The depth of the group and its national and international scope mean that it covers a comprehensive range of issues, but its appellate practice is thought to take particularly high rank. Post-9/11, the firm was retained by Westfield WTC, the holder of the 99-year lease for the retail space at the World Trade Center, to pursue its insurance claims. In class action litigation, it has successfully defended Oracle in one of the largest securities fraud claims ever brought.

The Lawyers: A team of 100 lawyers includes **Vince Connelly** (see p.256), endorsed to researchers as an *"understated, gentlemanly and well-prepared"* trial attorney. Famed for his ability to *"take on cases late in the day and turn it around for the client,"* he received high praise as a *"skilled tactician."* He has recently obtained favorable jury verdicts for clients in the healthcare, food and steel manufacturing industries. Although now chairman of the firm, **Ty Fahner** (see p.258) remains accepted as a *"sensational trial lawyer."* He is admired for his *"great judgment,"* and recently acted as lead trial counsel for BASF in a vitamins antitrust case. **Alan Salpeter** (see p.271) is a general commercial litigator who has acted for some of the top accountancy firms in recent years. Said to be *"relentless in the pursuit of his clients' interests,"* he appeals to observers as a *"tough and thorough litigator."* **Tom Durkin** (see p.257) was singled out by opposing counsel for his *"unflappability in the courtroom,"* while **Herb Zarov** (see p.276) gained widespread recognition as *"a fine lawyer who doesn't let his ego get in the way."* He has developed particular expertise in mass torts and consumer and securities class actions and has acted as co-national counsel for Union Carbide and Amchem in asbestos litigation.

The Clients: Wal-Mart; Sears Roebuck; Union Carbide; Dow Chemical; Ameritech; Oracle; Ernst & Young and Arthur Andersen.

Winston & Strawn
see firm details p.904

The Firm: *"A litigation powerhouse,"* the firm has the depth of practice to rival the best in the state, and won plaudits from competitors for its *"zealous"* pursuit of its cases. Clients find the team to be *"easy to work with"* and approved its *"consistent record of good results,"* citing the firm's in-depth knowledge of the courts and the local judiciary.

The Lawyers: Although the group maintains a strong stable of *"intelligent, experienced and confident"* lawyers, it is dominated by the *"towering figure"* of **Dan Webb** (see p.276). He was repeatedly endorsed to researchers as one of the outstanding trial lawyers in the country, with commentators remarking that he has *"proved himself again and again in the biggest cases, and won some that were unwinnable."* Currently involved in the antitrust case for Microsoft, he is admired by peers as a tireless worker who has *"great credibility and a good grasp of the central issues."* Other lawyers of note include **Bob Tarun** (see p.274), who received market recommendation as a *"careful lawyer with exceptional trial skills."* His caseload has included filing a federal RICO complaint on behalf of Titan Tire against United Steelworkers, and the ongoing defense of Philip Morris in a US Department of Justice RICO tobacco lawsuit. A *"candid and credible"* attorney, **Brad Lerman** (see p.264) is able to absorb *"a vast amount of information, and knows how to apply it."* He has been heavily involved in tobacco litigation and work for pharmaceutical companies. Although his practice involves both appeals and criminal matters, **Steve Molo** (see p.268) is best known for his sophisticated business litigation, where clients find that *"he gets results."* He has represented SFX Entertainment in a securities fraud case and has acted for Reader's Digest in a consumer fraud class action. The respected **Terry Grimm** (see p.261) specializes in jury trials, and his wide-ranging practice has embraced corporate, antitrust, patent and white-collar cases.

The Clients: Abbott Laboratories; GE; Compaq; Philip Morris; Premark and Caterpillar.

Bartlit Beck Herman Palenchar & Scott

The Firm: This *"fabulous boutique"* is renowned among peers for great quality and for its *"smart and savvy lawyers."* It broke away from Kirkland & Ellis nearly ten years ago and has become a *"much sought after"* shop. A small group of about 40 lawyers focuses on complex commercial litigation, and won particular approval from clients for its alternative fee arrangements.

The Lawyers: Chambers' researchers encountered strong market recommendation for **Phil Beck**, a *"first-rate"* attorney who came to prominence following his representation of George W Bush in the contested Florida election. More recently, he has acted as special trial counsel for the US Department of Justice in the Microsoft antitrust case. Peers believe him to be at *"the peak of his game,"* and admire him for his *"exceptional"* cross-examination skills. **Fred Bartlit** (see p.478053) was also endorsed as an attorney who *"will walk through walls for his clients."* He successfully represented MediaOne/AT&T Broadband in a contract dispute against US WEST over responsibility for telephone class actions.

The Clients: Reebok; GM; Bayer; Johnson & Johnson; United Technologies and AT&T.

Jenner & Block

see firm details p.822

The Firm: Best known for its litigation focus, the firm has a fine reputation for both commercial and criminal work. Although a management shake-up has caused something of a stir in the local market, clients and peers were adamant that the group was *"back on track."*

The Lawyers: **Anton R Valukas** (see p.275) is a former Chicago US Attorney who was endorsed by competitors as *"a sensational trial lawyer and one of the preeminent litigators in Chicago."* Highly rated for his attention to detail and appeal to juries, he has a practice that focuses on the defense of companies in consumer product litigation, product defect and consumer fraud class actions, food contamination, mass accident and environmental claims. In 2001 he obtained a settlement for Sara Lee in several class action cases and has defended Honeywell in a QuiTam suit, involving the fulfillment of various government contracts. Chairman and senior member of the firm, **Jerold Solovy** (see p.273), is a household name in Chicago. Although his profile is not as high as in previous years, he has nevertheless been involved in a number of prominent cases. These include successfully re-arguing an eminent domain case at the Illinois Supreme Court on behalf of the Southwestern Illinois Development Agency, and representing the Kennedy family in litigation resulting from the sale of the Merchandise Mart building. **Tom Sullivan** was also consistently recommended to researchers, and has acted as cocounsel in a lengthy dispute between two major pharmaceutical companies.

The Clients: The roster includes: GE Capital; Ryerson Tull; Steelcase; GE and Honeywell.

Sidley Austin Brown & Wood

see firm details p.877

The Firm: Although the firm is better known as a corporate powerhouse, market commentators also perceived it as home to an accomplished litigation department with a number of excellent individuals. This substantial group provides broad-based expertise, but was principally acknowledged for its strengths in professional liability and antitrust litigation. Groups of lawyers here are loosely organized into practice groups, thus specializing more narrowly than some of the firm's competitors.

The Lawyers: **Bill Conlon**, who heads the general commercial litigation group, was singled out to researchers as *"a first-rate litigator"* whose low-key courtroom style is said to be *"particularly effective."* The *"incisive"* **Walter Carlson** also received market plaudits as a *"superior practitioner"* and is involved in a variety of general commercial litigation, including SEC investigations and corporate governance. **Chuck Douglas** also attracted praise from peers for his *"affable and thorough approach"* and his strong courtroom presence. His reputation lies principally in the area of antitrust litigation, where he has acted for Microsoft, AT&T and Citibank.

The Clients: Bank One, AT&T, GE and Microsoft are among the firm's clients.

McDermott, Will & Emery

see firm details p.846

The Firm: The litigation group may still lack the profile and stature of some of the market leaders, but it is seen to have made *"tremendous strides"* in recent years. The 'trial department' consists of roughly 80 lawyers who draw on the capabilities of other groups for substantive expertise.

The Lawyers: **Jeff Stone** (see p.274) is the group's leading light, and was enthusiastically recommended as *"an up-and-coming superstar nationally."* A former Chicago US attorney, clients find him to be *"likable and direct, with a good courtroom presence."* Particularly well known for products liability expertise, **Mike Pope** (see p.270) also attracted market plaudits as an attorney who *"fights about the right things, and relates well to judges and juries."*

The Clients: Advanced Micro Devices; Lockheed Martin; Medtronic; Hitachi; Caterpillar and Schmalbach-Lubeca.

Jones Day

see firm details p.823

The Firm: The Chicago group is a respected force in the market, but it is often overshadowed by the national reputation of its sister team in Ohio. Although it has acknowledged expertise in a broad spectrum of matters and represents a rostrum of blue blood clients, commentators felt that the department lacked the depth of some of its leading rivals.

The Lawyers: Much of the firm's visibility is ascribed to **Dan Reidy** (see p.270), a *"fabulously gifted"* attorney who divides his time between civil and criminal matters, and is regarded as a consummate trial lawyer. He successfully obtained a motion for summary judgment on behalf of Abbott Laboratories in a patent infringement action brought by TorPharm. Elsewhere, the firm represented TAP Pharmaceutical Products in the settlement of a major four-year criminal, civil and administrative healthcare investigation.

The Clients: Abbott Laboratories; Sherwin-Williams; Bridgestone/Firestone; Bayer; Aventis and AOL Time Warner.

Skadden, Arps, Slate, Meagher & Flom LLP & Affiliates

see firm details p.878

The Firm: A *"tough"* litigation group covering a range of complex commercial matters including breach of contract, fraud and securities. The group, which comprises about 30 litigators, has national and international scope, and is felt to

MEDIA & ENTERTAINMENT — ILLINOIS

benefit regularly from the strength of the firm's corporate department.
The Lawyers: Cases of particular significance include representing Kmart in various litigation matters arising from its bankruptcy, in which senior partners Charles Smith and Tina Tchen were involved.
The Clients: In class action litigation, the team represented Liberty Mutual, and acted for Hartmarx in successfully rebuffing a tender offer for all its outstanding shares. The firm also advises, among others, Champion Enterprises.

Other Notable Practitioners
Joe Linklater (see p.265) of Baker & McKenzie drew recommendations from peers for his international practice, which encompasses anti-kickback and commercial bribery cases. A *"natural in the courtroom,"* he has been involved in the Sotheby's and Christie's auction houses litigation. In the sphere of plaintiffs' personal injury, *Chambers'* interviewees championed **Bob Clifford**. Peers described him as *"emotional but highly effective."* He advised a prominent violinist, who was involved in a commuter train accident, while his firm, Clifford Law Offices, represents clients in complex damages cases resulting from aviation, transportation and products liability claims.

MEDIA & ENTERTAINMENT

ILLINOIS
Leading firms (Media & Entertainment)

1
- JENNER & BLOCK
- WINSTON & STRAWN

2
- HALL DICKLER KENT GOLDSTEIN & WOOD LLP
- HOLLAND & KNIGHT LLP
- SIDLEY AUSTIN BROWN & WOOD
- SONNENSCHEIN NATH & ROSENTHAL

3
- FREEBORN & PETERS
- ROSS & HARDIES

Leading individuals (Media & Entertainment)

1
- HODES Scott *Ross & Hardies*
- O'REILLY Peter *Hall Dickler Kent Goldstein & Wood LLP*
- SALTIEL David *Bell, Boyd & Lloyd*
- SANDERS David *Jenner & Block*
- STRAND Peter *Holland & Knight LLP*

2
- DURCHSLAG Stephen *Winston & Strawn*
- FELCH Patricia *Sole Practitioner, Evanston*
- FIFER Sam *Sonnenschein Nath & Rosenthal*
- KELLEY Timothy *Sole Practitioner*
- KLENK James *Sonnenschein Nath & Rosenthal*
- LABATE Robert *Holland & Knight LLP*
- MENSCH Linda *Sole Practitioner*
- O'BRIEN Richard *Sidley Austin Brown & Wood*

3
- CONWAY Michael *Foley & Lardner*
- GOLDSTEIN Andrew *Freeborn & Peters*
- ZELEK Eugene *Freeborn & Peters*

Up-and-coming individuals
- HEIDELBERGER Brian *Winston & Strawn*

Firms and individuals are listed alphabetically in each band.

Jenner & Block
see firm details p.822
The Firm: As regular outside counsel to high-profile clients in the publishing and broadcast industries, this *"sound and reliable"* Chicago firm shines brighter than most in the fields of media and First Amendment law. Although based on its particular flair for libel and privacy defense, the firm's strong reputation also derives from its comprehensive knowledge across the spectrum of media law, an expertise that has been successfully leveraged for clients involved in new communications media. The team's strength is complemented by the firm's resources in Washington DC that are called upon for large First Amendment matters.
The Lawyers: The Chicago practice is synonymous with **David Sanders** (see p.271), who has earned a reputation as an *"astute"* and *"efficient"* legal adviser with experience across all areas of traditional media law. He and his team have provided both counseling and litigation for a range of media clients, on matters ranging from media business to advertising promotion and media insurance. Sanders recently defended a television network in a libel action relating to a post-9/11 terrorism news report, and routinely defends news organizations against subpoenas brought under state and federal law.
The Clients: ABC; Crain Communications; Chicago magazine and Golfweek are examples of the firm's clients.

Winston & Strawn
see firm details p.904
The Firm: Despite periodic challenges to its *"unique monopoly,"* the firm maintains its reputation as Chicago's *"first and foremost"* advertising and promotional law firm.
The Lawyers: Heading the practice is legendary **Stephen Durchslag** (see p.257), considered to have *"ruled the roost in the Midwest for a long time"* with *"by far its strongest advertising practice."* Clients value his industry contacts: *"He has the relationships; he knows the people; he can get it done."* Recent matters include the representation of Energizer Holdings in a false advertising and unfair competition suit brought against Duracell and parent company Gillette, arising from references in Duracell advertising to 'heavy-duty' batteries. Durchslag heads a team that includes of counsel Mary Hutchings Reed, regarded as an experienced advertising and special events attorney whose *"fabulous"* results *"instill great confidence."* Widely tipped within the industry as Durchslag's *"heir apparent,"* **Brian Heidelberger** (see p.262) is also recommended for the versatility of his practice, which encompasses IP, marketing, IT and advertising law. He recently advised McDonald's in relation to the $10,000,000 Labor Day Giveaway.
The Clients: NutraSweet; Eveready; Burrell Communicatons Group; Wunderman; Wm. Wrigley; Motorola; Nestlé; DDB Chicago and Rubin Postaer.

Hall Dickler Kent Goldstein & Wood LLP
The Firm: The arrival of this *"stellar"* New York-based firm in Chicago has created a stir in the advertising and entertainment law sectors. Acknowledged by peers to *"understand the law and get to the bottom line,"* the Chicago team advises a growing base of local advertising and marketing clients, as well as songwriters, music publishers, producers and managers. The firm provides both counseling and litigation expertise in a range of industry disputes, in addition to negotiating contracts and licensing and merchandising agreements.
The Lawyers: Much of the team's profile in Chicago is connected to former Winston & Strawn partner **Peter O'Reilly**, undoubtedly the dominant local authority on law relating to sweepstakes and contests. He was commended to researchers as a *"superlative professional,"* with the ability to *"defuse fractious situations."*
The Clients: The team advises advertising and promotion agencies, consumer product companies and various entities in the music business.

Holland & Knight LLP
see firm details p.820
The Firm: Market commentators are awaiting with interest the effect on the department of the firm's recent merger with Florida-based Holland & Knight. The firm's media and entertainment capacity is widely recognized as a *"compact and organized"* offering.
The Lawyers: Commentators particularly drew the attention of researchers to two attorneys.

ILLINOIS — MEDIA & ENTERTAINMENT

Heading the practice is **Robert Labate** (see p.264), a *"highly organized"* practitioner, who is said to be particularly knowledgeable on contract negotiations, and is reputed to have excellent Hollywood connections. His practice is a broad one, spanning not only distribution agreements but also corporate restructuring work. He acted as production counsel on both the award-winning PBS documentary 'Refrigerator Mothers' and the recently completed rock documentary 'MC5 * A True Testimonial'. In spite of the fact that he is still an associate, **Peter Strand** (see p.274) is regarded as *"one of the most experienced"* and one of the best music attorneys in Chicago. His *"calm"* pursuit of *"realistic"* goals has earned him the admiration of opponents. A noted generalist, he advises on both transactional and litigation matters, and has a niche in copyright and trademark enforcement cases. Recent highlights include advising a film production company on a major sponsorship agreement with an entity of the Spanish Government.

The Clients: The firm acts for independent film companies, music production companies, talent agencies, artists and writers.

Sidley Austin Brown & Wood
see firm details p.877

The Firm: Better known for its media practice in Washington DC, the firm nevertheless commands a *"highly respectable"* profile in Chicago with its media and First Amendment law practice. Defamation is a cornerstone of the workload, and the team also has expertise in Freedom of Information Act litigation, recently winning a notable case against a government contractor and government agencies.

The Lawyers: The *"knowledgeable"* **Richard O'Brien**, whose practice embraces both IP and media law, was said by clients to provide *"first-rate legal advice."* He successfully defended Crossroads Fund in a recent defamation case brought by Chicago alderman Eugene Schulter. This related to a grant issued by the fund that was used by a neighbourhood organization to publish criticism of the alderman.

The Clients: The firm acts for publishers, authors, broadcasters and artists. Clients include the Chicago Tribune, CBS and Windows to the World Communications.

Sonnenschein Nath & Rosenthal
see firm details p.882

The Firm: Competitors regard this as a *"good, traditional media law firm"* with *"substantial expertise"* in matters of defamation, privacy, subpoena defense, copyright, Freedom of Information and First Amendment matters. The team advises extensively on pre-broadcast and pre-publication review and libel clearance for a range of clients, notably from the print media.

The Lawyers: The *"efficient and trustworthy"* **Sam Fifer** (see p.259) received consistent endorsement for his wide-ranging IP, media and entertainment practice, and has a strong reputation for advice on First Amendment law. Recent highlights include defending Studios USA in a personal injury action brought by a guest on 'The Jerry Springer Show'. **James Klenk** (see p.263) is said to get *"excellent results for his clients,"* and is a respected litigator, often handling libel, privacy and copyright matters. He has recently defended Home Shopping Network in a number of consumer class action claims.

The Clients: The group acts for a range of media clients including the Chicago Tribune Company and several of the Tribune Company's subsidiaries; Time; Random House; Studios USA and NBC.

Freeborn & Peters

The Firm: Although not possessing a pure media/entertainment department, rivals concede that the firm can lay claim to a number of IP lawyers who display *"particular flair"* for handling marketing-connected entertainment matters.

The Lawyers: **Eugene Zelek** combines IP expertise with advertising, licensing and promotional litigation, and is considered by peers to do a *"hell of a good job on entertainment contracts."* **Andrew Goldstein** is also noted for his work on advertising, promotion and entertainment law. Opponents singled him out for his *"good technical skills and sound judgment."*

The Clients: The firm has advised branding and corporate identity consultants on IP rights and handled routine contract negotiations on behalf of a premier merchandise licensing consultant. The firm has advised the Publicity Club of Chicago. Consultancy firms, marketing companies, and consumer and industrial goods and services marketers all form part of its client roster.

Ross & Hardies

The Firm: The IP practice of this firm wins plaudits for its representation of artists, professional sportspersons and other celebrities on a range of matters including trademarks, copyrights and right of publicity.

The Lawyers: When it comes to the fine arts, there is no doubt among observers that **Scott Hodes** is *"the lawyer in this area."* Hodes has been at the forefront of litigation exploring the concept of the moral rights of artists under the Visual Rights Act of 1990. He advises an array of leading art dealers and distinguished international artists including Christo and Jeanne-Claude.

The Clients: Celebrity artists and athletes, among others, feature on the client list.

Other Notable Practitioners

Dominating the realm of theater law, **David Saltiel** at Bell, Boyd & Lloyd was described to researchers as *"incisive, direct and hard-working."* Clients agree that they *"wouldn't dream of using anyone else."* Sole practitioner **Patricia Felch** is highly respected as an *"aggressive"* and *"thorough"* litigator who *"puts her money where her mouth is"* by representing a range of writers and artists in *"tough to handle"* IP matters. She represented 18 medical illustrators in a major copyright infringement claim against Advanstar Communications. *"Particularly strong in music and film,"* sole practitioner **Timothy Kelley** is said to have *"done it all"* in entertainment law, and is considered to operate with the *"highest possible integrity."* Recent highlights include the negotiation of a major label recording contract and a publishing agreement on behalf of Chicago band SOiL. *"Freethinking"* sole practitioner **Linda Mensch** is another *"first-rate and well-known music lawyer,"* who is said to *"know the industry inside out."* **Michael Conway** at Foley & Lardner was also recognized by commentators as a *"capable"* attorney with *"profound experience of libel law."*

REAL ESTATE — ILLINOIS

ILLINOIS
Leading firms (Real Estate)

1. KATTEN MUCHIN ZAVIS ROSENMAN
   MAYER, BROWN, ROWE & MAW
   PIPER RUDNICK
2. SIDLEY AUSTIN BROWN & WOOD
   SONNENSCHEIN NATH & ROSENTHAL
3. BARACK FERRAZZANO KIRSCHBAUM PERLMAN
4. D'ANCONA & PFLAUM LLC
5. GOLDBERG, KOHN, BELL, BLACK, ROSENBLOOM
   KATZ RANDALL WEINBERG & RICHMOND
   NEAL GERBER & EISENBERG
   WINSTON & STRAWN
6. ALTHEIMER & GRAY
   BELL, BOYD & LLOYD
   KIRKLAND & ELLIS
   SCHWARTZ COOPER GREENBERGER KRAUSS

Leading individuals (Real Estate)

1. EDWARDS Charles *Piper Rudnick*
   GEAREN John *Mayer, Brown, Rowe & Maw*
   MATIS Nina *Katten Muchin Zavis Rosenman*
2. ARONSON Virginia *Sidley Austin Brown & Wood*
   GLICKSTEIN David *Piper Rudnick*
   HOMBURGER Tom *Bell, Boyd & Lloyd*
   MEHLMAN Mark *Sonnenschein Nath & Rosenthal*
   MORAN Patrick *Sonnenschein Nath & Rosenthal*
   RANDALL Benjamin *Katz Randall Weinberg & Richmond*
   RUBIN Joel *D'Ancona & Pflaum LLC*
3. FEINSTEIN Fred *McDermott, Will & Emery*
   KURTZON Mike *Schwartz Cooper Greenberger Krauss*
   MORRISON Portia *Piper Rudnick*
   NAGELBERG Howard *Barack Ferrazzano Kirschbaum*
   NOVAK Theodore *Piper Rudnick*
   SMOLEN Lee *Sidley Austin Brown & Wood*
4. AIELLO Anthony *Sidley Austin Brown & Wood*
   BELL Stephen *Goldberg, Kohn, Bell, Black, Rosenbloom*
   CHICO Gery *Altheimer & Gray*
   FERRAZZANO Dennis *Barack Ferrazzano Kirschbaum*
   JACOBSON Kenneth *Katten Muchin Zavis Rosenman*
   KATZ Alvin *Mayer, Brown, Rowe & Maw*
   KIRSCHBAUM Howard *Barack Ferrazzano Kirschbaum*
   KRUEGER Herbert *Mayer, Brown, Rowe & Maw*
   MILLER Lee *Piper Rudnick*
   MURTAUGH Christopher *Winston & Straw*
   ROSENBLOOM Jim *Goldberg, Kohn, Bell, Black*
   SCHILLER Eric *Sonnenschein Nath & Rosenthal*
   SIMON Mark *Katten Muchin Zavis Rosenman*
   SULLIVAN Marcia *Katten Muchin Zavis Rosenman*
   TOMLINSON Stephen *Kirkland & Ellis*

Up-and-coming individuals
BESSETTE-SMITH Suzanne *Barack Ferrazzano*

Firms and individuals are listed alphabetically in each band.

Katten Muchin Zavis Rosenman
see firm details p.827

The Firm: Real estate is the firm's strongest suit, and it is particularly considered to excel in mortgage financing, leasing and development work. The firm serves a broad client base, which includes REITs and developers.

The Lawyers: Among a large and deep team, **Nina Matis** (see p.266) stands out. Although she divides her time between iStar Financial in New York, where she is general counsel and executive vice president, and her practice at the firm's Chicago office, she was commended to researchers as the *"best for real estate in Chicago."* Opponents esteem her as a *"capable, tough negotiator"* and she is particularly known for her work in retail and hotel development. She has most recently acted on the financing and development of The Palladium Company project in West Palm Beach. The department is no one-attorney show, however. Commentators praised the *"intellectually acute"* **Ken Jacobson** (see p.262) and top lenders' lawyer **Mark Simon** (see p.273), whose practice is thought to have *"taken off"* since his defection from Sonnenschein Nath & Rosenthal last year. **Marcia Sullivan** (see p.274) also gained strong market endorsement for her advice to a variety of lenders.

The Clients: Starwood Capital Partners; Blackacre Capital Group; Chicago Bulls; Chicago White Sox and The Palladium Company.

Mayer, Brown, Rowe & Maw
see firm details p.843

The Firm: Commended by both rivals and clients for its *"sophisticated approach,"* the firm is recognized for its *"uniformly high-quality"* work with institutional clients, pension funds and REITs. A large group with a sound transactional reputation, and particular expertise in real estate securitization and complex financing transactions such as mezzanine lending, mortgage warehousing financings and lease financing deals. Clients appreciated the firm's *"one-stop shop"* diversity and its ability to handle both *"gritty local matters and the more complicated lending issues."*

The Lawyers: **John Gearen** (see p.260) stands out for all commentators as a *"top-notch deal-maker."* Regarded as *"a real institutional client lawyer,"* he was firmly endorsed to researchers for his willingness to *"consider all the alternatives to resolving problems."* He recently acted for Cadim in its attempted acquisition of Prime Group Realty Trust. **Herbert Krueger** (see p.264) won peer approval for his work as head of the firm's pension practice, representing tax-exempt pension fund investors in ERISA matters. Some rivals are not keen on **Alvin Katz**'s (see p.263) *"abrasive"* style, but praise him for his representation of the Washington DC-based venture capital firm, The Carlyle Group.

The Clients: The group advised GM in connection with a series of lease financings across the US, as well as negotiating structured lease financings and leveraged lease take-out financing commitments on behalf of Banc One Capital. These were negotiated for the construction of oil and gas production platforms in the Gulf of Mexico. The firm also acts for the Teachers Insurance & Annuity Association of America, the New York State Common Retirement Fund and Lehman Brothers.

Piper Rudnick
see firm details p.867

The Firm: Despite a series of recent layoffs, the firm maintains its significant market presence for real estate. The sheer size of the largest department in Chicago makes uniform judgment on the quality of its work difficult, but it remains generally rated by rivals as *"the most powerful practice in Chicago in terms of attorney and client numbers,"* and is seen as one of the clear market leaders for development work.

The Lawyers: Headed by land use and condemnation *"guru"* **Ted Novak** (see p.269), the firm is also recognized by peers as *"preeminent in Chicago"* in this area. He recently acted for the developer consortium Mesirow Stein Real Estate in the adaptation of the Fort Sheridan military base for residential purposes. He also advised Boeing on the real estate aspects of its relocation to Chicago. The *"elder statesman"* of real estate law in Chicago, **Chuck Edwards** (see p.258) is *"still a name that shines."* Renowned for his work with entrepreneurial developer clients, he is respected by peers as a lawyer who is *"a pleasure to deal with"* and *"knows how to get a deal done."* He and his team are currently acting as local counsel for Donald Trump in the high-profile redevelopment of the old Sun-Times building in downtown Chicago. **Lee Miller** (see p.267) won plaudits from rivals for his *"extensive network of contacts throughout the industry,"* while **David Glickstein** (see p.261) appeals to clients as a *"tough negotiator who responds quickly."* **Portia Morrison** (see p.268) came to the attention of researchers for her work with Hyatt, and is said to be *"quick to reach agreement on issues that would otherwise be deal-breakers."* She recently represented Pritzker Realty Group on the creation of Pritzker Residential Equities, a luxury apartment ownership and operating company. She also acted for Hyatt Hotels in the acquisition and development of its Hyatt Regency Coconut Point Resort & Spa in Naples, Florida.

ILLINOIS   REAL ESTATE

The Clients: The firm represents some of the largest REITs in the US, including Equity Office Properties Trust and Equity Residential Properties Trust.

Sidley Austin Brown & Wood
see firm details p.877

The Firm: The firm's real estate practice may be largely driven by its corporate client base, but this 34-lawyer team received consistent market approval for the *"terrific quality"* of its work. Although smaller than the three leaders, the group handles the full range of corporate real estate work for its Fortune 500 clients, including acquisitions, dispositions and leasing, financing and development work. The team is especially known for its *"highly sophisticated"* financing and commercial mortgage securities practice.

The Lawyers: The leader of the firm's national real estate practice is finance expert **Virginia Aronson**. She is lauded by peers as a *"class act,"* and is recognized for her work in mortgage-backed securitizations, and her understanding of *"gigantic, complicated financing transactions."* Interviewees appreciated her ability to *"represent clients well without causing strife on a deal."* One major client is the Government of Singapore, for whom she advises on real estate investments in the US and Europe. **Lee Smolen** earned widespread endorsement as a *"hard-working and astute attorney."* Particularly known for his work on structured finance transactions, he often works in tandem with Aronson, forming a team that is admired as *"a tough act to follow."* He acted for Wells Fargo on the structuring of an originating loan for securitization on a shopping center portfolio spanning four states, and has represented the same client on a number of hotel financings. Real estate generalist **Tony Aiello** also gained substantial market approval.

The Clients: Crédit Lyonnais, Citigroup/Citibank and Wells Fargo Bank are examples of the firm's client base.

Sonnenschein Nath & Rosenthal
see firm details p.882

The Firm: Acknowledged by peers to be home to *"heavy-hitting real estate partners,"* the department's reputation is greatest for real estate finance, although it also undertakes an array of corporate real estate work, along with advice to institutional lenders.

The Lawyers: Interviewees do not generally consider the firm to possess quite the associate strength in depth of the three market leaders, but a number of partners here stand comparison with some of the finest in the state. *"Phenomenal"* **Pat Moran** (see p.268) won high marks for his lending and development expertise. Liked by peers for his sense of humor and pleasant manner in negotiations, he is known for his ability to *"get deals done."* The *"practical"* **Mark Mehlman** (see p.267) has a sizable development practice, and is regarded by his contemporaries as a *"transactionally aware attorney."* **Eric Schiller** (see p.271) was also recommended to researchers for his advice to major lending banks. Lending lawyer Mark Simon has departed to Katten Muchin Zavis Rosenman.

The Clients: The firm's clients include: Crédit Lyonnais; Goldman Sachs Mortgage Company; McDonald's; The Rockefeller Group; Bank of America; Citibank/Citicorp and La Salle National Bank.

Barack Ferrazzano Kirschbaum Perlman & Nagelberg

The Firm: The *"giant-slayers"* of the Chicago real estate market, this boutique practice of 22 years' standing has the respect of rivals for its work with REITs, and its real estate financing and secured lending expertise. A *"smart and competent"* group of 25 lawyers is perceived not just as a significant real estate presence in Illinois but also as a real competitor to the major firms.

The Lawyers: Much of the team's excellence in real estate is attributed to founding partners, **Dennis Ferrazzano** and **Howard Nagelberg**, who both have established reputations for advising REITs and quasi-REITs. Fellow founder **Howard Kirschbaum** is said by clients to *"stand his ground in negotiations,"* while development lawyer **Suzanne Bessette-Smith** is widely regarded as an up-and-coming talent.

The Clients: First Industrial Realty Trust, Ventas and Equity Office Properties Trust are among the firm's clients.

D'Ancona & Pflaum LLC

The Firm: Although a smaller practice, the group is *"clearly an important player in real estate in Chicago,"* renowned among rivals for its work with pension fund investors. In the 1970's, the group cut its teeth representing the major suburban developer Hamilton Partners, and the team continues to advise on the construction, leasing and financing of office, retail and industrial developments for this, its principal client.

The Lawyers: Chairman of the firm **Joel Rubin** is said to have carved out a *"wonderful niche"* in representing pension fund investors and advisers. Regarded as *"more a deal-maker than a scholar,"* he received high praise from rivals for his negotiation skills.

The Clients: The firm advised a developer on the acquisition of real estate in Chicago, which included a 677,000 sq ft shopping center, a day-care center and more than 100 acres of vacant land. The firm's client base includes Hamilton Partners.

Goldberg, Kohn, Bell, Black, Rosenbloom & Moritz, Ltd

The Firm: The firm's real estate pedigree has been established since its inception, when three of the original five founding partners were real estate lawyers. Today, the 12-lawyer group focuses particularly on the representation of institutional lenders and entrepreneurial developers. Known also for its bankruptcy practice, the firm has recently undertaken a substantial number of workouts, complementing its real estate lending practice.

The Lawyers: **Jim Rosenbloom** was highly commended by rivals as a *"tough but fair"* negotiator, while fellow founder **Stephen Bell** was also strongly endorsed to researchers. The latter has represented Mesirow Realty Development, the facilitator of sale and leaseback financing transactions, and is well known for his relationship with GE Capital/Heller Financial.

The Clients: Bank of America; Fleet Business Credit Corporation; LaSalle Bank; Bank One; Heller Financial; Baum Realty Group and Obayashi.

Katz Randall Weinberg & Richmond

The Firm: First conceived as a specialist real estate practice, this smaller firm maintains its reputation as an *"excellent"* group doing a *"tremendous"* amount of work, particularly on behalf of developers and lenders.

The Lawyers: *"Feisty but good"* **Ben Randall** is at the center of the practice and polarizes opinion among his peers. Recognized as a *"brilliant, impressive lawyer,"* his *"brash"* style in negotiations does not meet with universal approval. However, rivals commend his acute business sense and his *"pure intellectual gift."*

The Clients: Among others, the firm advises: CenterPoint Properties Trust; ORIX Real Estate Equities; Trident Development and FCL Builders.

Neal Gerber & Eisenberg

The Firm: It is primarily known for transactional work, including acquisitions, dispositions, leasing and property management.

The Lawyers: The group, which includes Phil Kayman, acts as lead counsel for Equity Office Properties Trust, the office REIT of flamboyant Chicago entrepreneur Sam Zell.

The Clients: The real estate department is generally associated with its client the Pritzker family, owners of Hyatt. Here, the firm has advised on the acquisition, development and management of hotel properties across the US as well as in Mexico and the Caribbean.

Winston & Strawn
see firm details p.904

The Firm: A Chicago stalwart whose real estate expertise is supported by its considerable corporate client base, the firm is regarded as a *"sound, if*

REAL ESTATE — ILLINOIS

conservative player" in the local market. Recent high-profile work for the department includes representing Shuwa Investment Corporation in the acquisition, financing and sale of several major high-rise real estate developments in downtown Chicago.

The Lawyers: Key practitioner and chair of the real estate group, **Chris Murtaugh** (see p.268) is well known for his advice to developers and investors. He has caught the eye of rivals as an *"experienced and reliable"* performer, who *"does what he says he's going to do and doesn't sweat the small stuff."*

The Clients: Clients include: Prudential Mortgage Capital Company; Ashley Capital; GE Asset Management; Amtrak and The McShane Companies.

Altheimer & Gray
see firm details p.763

The Firm: Despite the presence of offices in Shanghai and Eastern Europe, it was the firm's local land use and zoning practice that garnered the most recommendations from peers. A group of about 60 lawyers also maintains an active practice in representing office and retail developers alongside luxury hotel owners and managers on acquisitions and developments.

The Lawyers: **Gery Chico** chairs the firm. Regarded by rivals as *"probably the preeminent zoning and land use lawyer in the city,"* he brought his considerable client list and ties to City Hall when he joined the firm from Sidley Austin Brown & Wood in 1996.

The Clients: Kimco Realty, GE Capital and J&B Realty Trust all feature on the client list of this firm.

Bell, Boyd & Lloyd

The Firm: A team of 21 lawyers in this full-service Chicago firm represents lenders on financing transactions, as well as a respectable stable of developer clients. In addition to its heavy financing practice, the group also does construction work and general transactional work for a Fortune 500 corporate client base. The firm's land use and construction practices have developed a niche in the development of nursing and healthcare facilities.

The Lawyers: *"Scholarly"* **Tom Homburger**, described to researchers as a *"lawyers' lawyer,"* impresses rivals with his *"tough"* manner in negotiations. Universally praised for his *"wealth of experience"* and intelligence in *"hairy"* transactional work, he specializes in sale and leasebacks, and complex financing and leasing transactions.

The Clients: Homburger and the firm recently represented the Austrian Government in the high-profile New York high-rise development of the Austrian Cultural Institute. Other clients include Arthur Andersen, Budget Rent a Car and Commonwealth Edison.

Kirkland & Ellis
see firm details p.830

The Firm: Although not historically one of the firm's stronger suits in Chicago, the real estate department has recently built a reputation for its *"sophisticated"* work in the less traditional real estate arenas of equity funds and corporate ventures. A substantial proportion of the workload involves the formation of investment funds, representing institutional investors in joint ventures between institutional investors and public real estate companies, and acting for REITs.

The Lawyers: **Steve Tomlinson** (see p.275) won praise from peers as Chicago's leader in the equity funds arena, having *"picked his market and specialized in it."* He has recently acted for CenterPoint Properties Trust in the formation of a joint venture for the development of a $100 million industrial campus, and acted on behalf of a corporate pension fund on the acquisition of a $200 million downtown Chicago property.

The Clients: The firm acts for Jones Lang LaSalle, Transwestern Investment Company and Walton Street Real Estate Fund among others.

Schwartz Cooper Greenberger Krauss
see firm details p.872

The Firm: A Chicago real estate team of approximately 20 lawyers, it has its principal focus on real estate finance. The group represents major lending banks and pension funds, alongside real estate developers, owners and investors in the financing, acquisition, development and disposition of commercial and residential properties, as well as advising on workouts and restructurings.

The Lawyers: Finance specialist **Mike Kurtzon** (see p.264) garnered strong recommendations from clients for his *"knowledge, responsiveness and value for money."* Opponents appreciated his *"productive"* approach to negotiation. In addition to finance work, he has a particular niche in representing lenders on obtaining loans for residential condominiums.

The Clients: The Habitat Company, Robin Construction Corporation and LaSalle Bank National Association feature in the firm's client roster.

Other Notable Practitioners

Fred Feinstein (see p.258) of McDermott, Will & Emery has a real estate pedigree which is considered to eclipse that of his firm. Capable of handling both transactional and contentious matters, this *"excellent"* practitioner has a particularly enviable reputation for development and zoning advice.

TAX

ILLINOIS
Leading firms (Tax)

1. KIRKLAND & ELLIS
   MAYER, BROWN, ROWE & MAW
2. McDERMOTT, WILL & EMERY
3. SIDLEY AUSTIN BROWN & WOOD
4. SKADDEN, ARPS, SLATE, MEAGHER & FLOM
5. BAKER & MCKENZIE
   LATHAM & WATKINS LLP
6. WINSTON & STRAWN

Firms are listed alphabetically in each band.

Kirkland & Ellis
see firm details p.830

The Firm: This *"dynamic"* tax planning and litigation group enjoys an increasingly international reputation, while in Chicago, competitors are clear that *"we bump into them more than any other local firm."* The symbiotic relationship between the firm's corporate lawyers and the tax team enables the latter to offer particularly effective advice in the private equity, venture capital, M&A and capital markets sectors. The group's legendary ability to *"handle complex matters well"* delights clients: *"I will pay whatever they charge, because you get what you pay for."*

The Lawyers: **Jack Levin** (see p.265) *"may be the best tax lawyer in the world,"* according to his contemporaries. A trailblazing academic, as well as an outstanding tax practitioner, he is credited with writing *"the definitive tax treatise."* Although he also channels much of his time into private equity work, he continues to oversee the progress of his talented tax team. Among them is **Jeff Sheffield** (see p.272), whose *"ability to separate what's important from what isn't"* is held in the highest regard. He handled the tax implications of the high-profile $25 billion DIRECTV spin-off. Reputed to possess a *"photographic memory,"* **George Javaras** (see p.263) remains accepted as one of the market leaders in Chicago. He advised on the tax aspects of the restructuring of the Chicago Board of Trade and acted on the acquisition of Bcom3 Group by Publicis Groupe. Former Government attorney **Don Rocap** (see p.270) still has a particularly notable public sec-

ILLINOIS — TAX

ILLINOIS
Leading individuals (Tax)

1
- **BOWEN Stephen** Latham & Watkins LLP
- **FREEMAN Louis** Skadden, Arps, Slate, Meagher & Flom
- **JAVARAS George** Kirkland & Ellis
- **LEVIN Jack** Kirkland & Ellis
- **SHERCK Timothy** Mayer, Brown, Rowe & Maw
- **WILLIAMSON Joel** Mayer, Brown, Rowe & Maw

2
- **LIPTON Richard** Baker & McKenzie
- **ROCAP Don** Kirkland & Ellis
- **SHEFFIELD Jeffrey** Kirkland & Ellis
- **YODER Lowell** McDermott, Will & Emery
- **ZIMBLER Jay** Sidley Austin Brown & Wood

3
- **LEMEIN Gregg** Baker & McKenzie
- **WELKE William** Kirkland & Ellis

4
- **BANOFF Sheldon** Katten Muchin Zavis Rosenman
- **BORDERS Thomas** McDermott, Will & Emery
- **CRAVEN George** Mayer, Brown, Rowe & Maw
- **FITZGERALD Thomas** Winston & Strawn
- **LEDUC André** Skadden, Arps, Slate, Meagher & Flom LLP
- **LUSCOMBE George** Mayer, Brown, Rowe & Maw
- **LYNCH James** Winston & Strawn
- **WOOTTON Bob** Sidley Austin Brown & Wood

Individuals are listed alphabetically in each band.

...tor tax practice. Peers regard him as a *"creative and analytical"* attorney, who *"stays right on top of the issues."* Respected transactional lawyer **Bill Welke** (see p.276) was also endorsed to researchers for his *"good, practical deal sense."*

The Clients: Vestar Capital Partners; GKN; Bain & Company; Leo Burnett McManus; GM; Sara Lee; United Airlines; USG; CNA Financial; Bcom3 Group; Chicago Board of Trade; Alcoa and Navistar International.

Mayer, Brown, Rowe & Maw
see firm details p.843

The Firm: A large and flourishing tax department is recognized to have outstanding expertise in transactional, tax planning and controversy work. In the latter area, the team is acknowledged to be *"preeminent"* and to possess *"enormous bench strength,"* while the firm's big-hitting corporate team gives the tax group access to clients such as Boeing and Pfizer.

The Lawyers: **Tim Sherck** (see p.272) is one of the leading corporate tax lawyers in Chicago. Described to researchers as *"calm, cautious and insightful,"* he has a top name for restructuring work, in addition to his M&A track record. Among recent successes, he advised Nestlé on the tax aspects of its $2.6 billion acquisition of Chef America. Heading the tax controversy group is **Joel Williamson** (see p.276), regarded by clients as an *"exemplary tax litigator"* who *"operates best under pressure."* He won a landmark victory for his client in the Bankers Trust case against the IRS, in which he made innovative use of an 1803 US Supreme Court case and US constitutional law.

George Luscombe (see p.265) gained widespread recommendation for his corporate-focused tax practice. Clients marveled at his ability to *"quote chapter and verse"* on relevant law. Also endorsed to researchers was **George Craven** (see p.256), whose practice includes tax litigation, corporate tax and tax planning issues.

The Clients: Pfizer; Schering-Plough; Dow Chemical; Ameritrade Holding; CIVC Partners; Bank of Montreal; GATX; University of Notre Dame; Goodrich; Boeing; CNF Transportation; Illinois Tool Works; Riggs Bank; UPS; Nestlé; Tribune Company and Bank of America.

McDermott, Will & Emery
see firm details p.846

The Firm: The largest tax group in Chicago offers a proportionally broad range of services, and is recognized by peers to have *"lots of talent."* Tax planning, international tax, corporate, restructuring and financial products expertise, and tax litigation are all covered here. However, a majority of commentators were adamant that the team's overall profile lags slightly, but clearly, behind the two market leaders.

The Lawyers: **Lowell Yoder** (see p.276) was widely recommended as one of Chicago's preeminent international tax practitioners. This *"astute"* attorney has broad expertise in relation to multi-jurisdictional business structures and the use of special-purpose foreign entities. Respected litigator **Tom Borders** (see p.255) also maintains his sound reputation as a trial attorney. The practice suffered a setback in the recent departure of Richard Lipton to Baker & McKenzie.

The Clients: Citigroup; The May Department Stores Company; Allstate; Caterpillar; Case New Holland; United Technologies; BP Amoco; Georgia-Pacific; Shorenstein; Goldman Sachs; Bank of Montreal; IDT; Baylor Health Care System; IKEA and Eli Lilly.

Sidley Austin Brown & Wood
see firm details p.877

The Firm: This smaller practice may not be perceived to have the depth of the market leaders in Illinois, but the firm's *"tight, effective team"* is still considered to be a substantial local and national player. The firm's recent merger has had a particularly beneficial effect in New York, where the tax team has increased dramatically in size and works closely with the group in Chicago. Its access to a fabulous corporate client base gives the team a particularly substantial profile for M&A and capital markets work.

The Lawyers: Leading name **Jay Zimbler** retains an enviable reputation for federal income tax matters, and has a practice that emphasizes contested matters, Subchapter C issues and the taxation of transactions with a foreign element. He has handled a number of complex appellate cases for a variety of multinational corporations. **Bob Wootton** was endorsed to researchers as *"a well-rounded and thoughtful tax attorney."* His practice includes international and domestic tax planning, as well as controversy work and M&A and finance transactions. He advised on the restructuring of Canadian Pacific into five separate public companies, and acted on the merger between PanCanadian Energy and Alberta Energy Company, which formed EnCana, one of the largest independent energy companies in North America.

The Clients: The firm's client base includes: Tribune Company; Telephone and Data Systems; International Minerals and Chemicals; Fairmont Hotels & Resorts and Canadian Pacific Railway.

Skadden, Arps, Slate, Meagher & Flom LLP
see firm details p.878

The Firm: The Chicago office's tax practice is rooted in M&A and bankruptcy expertise. In these areas, an imposing Fortune 500 clientele insists that the firm has *"some wonderful attorneys."* Major public transactions have provided the group with its staple fare. Leading examples have included advising on The Williams Companies' $2.2 billion acquisition of Barrett Resources, a two-step transaction involving a tender offer followed by a forward merger, America General's acquisition by AIG and AIMCO's acquisition of Casden Properties.

The Lawyers: Nationally known as *"an exceptional tax lawyer,"* **Louis Freeman** (see p.260) has long spearheaded the tax group in Chicago. His *"thoughtful, creative"* approach to complex transactional tax matters has earned him the respect of the whole market. He advised Unitrin on the recapitalization and spin-off of Curtiss-Wright. Formerly associated with his asset-based leasing practice, the *"cerebral"* **André LeDuc** (see p.264) has widened his workload to include substantial cross-border transactional work.

The Clients: AIMCO; Anderson-Tully; Banc One Capital; Chicago Mercantile Exchange; Citicorp; Credit Suisse Asset Management; GE Capital; McLeodUSA; Morgan Stanley; ntl; Occidental Petroleum; Square D Company; Unitrin and The Williams Companies.

Baker & McKenzie
see firm details p.767

The Firm: Having gained two new partners over the past couple of years, the tax team is thought by many commentators to be *"on an upswing."* The firm covers all areas of the sector, but is most notable for its focus on international work, controversy and tax planning. Its network of national and overseas offices enables the firm to keep a high profile for advising on the tax aspects of a range of big-ticket cross-border transactions.

The Lawyers: **Gregg Lemein** (see p.264) is thought to be the key figure of the tax department in Chicago. Noted by contemporaries as a *"sophisticated and versatile attorney,"* he has a practice that combines tax litigation with international tax matters. He appeared on the recent case Square D Company v Commissioner, which involved the issue of the timing of deductions for interest payable to a foreign parent company. The recent recruitment of *"energetic and articulate"* **Richard Lipton** from McDermott ,Will is expected to boost the firm's standing in the field. Lipton is an expert in real estate and partnership issues with considerable experience within the telecom sector.

Latham & Watkins LLP
see firm details p.835

The Firm: Noted M&A, partnership and joint venture expertise continue to give the firm a solid presence in Chicago, and peers acknowledge that *"we frequently run into them."*

The Lawyers: The market still perceives, however, that the department's profile in Chicago relies on the presence of **Stephen Bowen** (see p.255).

Extolled to researchers as *"one hell of a lawyer,"* he operates principally in the arena of federal income taxation. Contemporaries regard him as *"a giant"* who has *"consistently delivered results over the years."*

The Clients: Hyatt Hotels & Resorts; Harrah's Entertainment; HCR Manor Care; First Health; The Pritzker Organization and Choice Hotels International.

Winston & Strawn
see firm details p.904

The Firm: Ranked for the first time this year, this broad-based, 20-strong tax group is especially noted for its tax controversy practice, although transactional work is also a key element of the caseload.

The Lawyers: Central to the group's success is the respected **James Lynch** (see p.265). He has advised extensively on federal tax controversy work, often appearing on disputes with the IRS. He led the appeal before the Second Circuit Court of Appeals in New York of the US Tax Court's decision in the Nicole Rose Corporation v Commissioner case, and advised on the $300 million acquisition of Yorkshire Global Restaurants by Tricon Global Restaurants.

Tax litigator **Tom Fitzgerald** (see p.259) is an experienced and highly rated member of the team. He has successfully represented numerous clients before the IRS, and appeared on cases in both the US Tax Court and the US Court of Appeals. He recently advised Smurfit-Stone Container on its acquisition of St Laurent, a $1.2 billion transaction.

The Clients: Sara Lee; Waste Management; Allied Waste Industries; SPX; Tricon Global Restaurants; SBC Ameritech; Bank of America; Smurfit-Stone Container and Boeing.

Other Notable Practitioners

Acclaimed by peers as *"one of the leading partnership guys in the city,"* **Sheldon Banoff** (see p.254) of Katten Muchin Zavis Rosenman is considered to have *"a marvelous intellect,"* which he also puts to use on tax planning and litigation matters. He advised on Fifield's investment in a $110 million condominium project in Los Angeles, and TrizecHahn's acquisition of Whitehall Realty's controlling interest in a 1.2 million sq ft office/retail mixed-use property in LA. Elsewhere, he acted for Greenfield Partners on its acquisition of real estate properties from South East Apartment Fund.

Leaders in Illinois

ABRAHAMSON, Vicki
Abrahamson Vorachek & Mikva, Chicago 312 263 2698
Recommended in Employment

ABRAMS, Lee N
Mayer, Brown, Rowe & Maw, Chicago
312 701 7083
labrams@mayerbrownrowe.com
Recommended in Antitrust

Specialization: Leading attorney in antitrust and franchising litigation. Has represented numerous Fortune 500 corporations, including General Motors, Ford, Eastman Kodak, Citicorp, Sears, NewsCorp, and PitneyBowes, and also the United States Golf Association. Has frequently litigated intellectual property issues.
Prof. Memberships: Member, Panel of Distinguished Neutrals of the Center for Public Resources; American Bar Association: Chair, Franchising Forum, 1982-85; Section of Antitrust Law: Vice Chair, 1991-92; Financial Officer and Council Member, 1977-81; Section of Business Law: Chair, Antitrust Committee, 1995-1999; Fellow, American College of Trial Lawyers. Admitted to practice in Illinois (1957), US Supreme Court (1961).
Career: Joined *Mayer, Brown, Rowe & Maw* in 1957; became partner 1967.
Publications: Author of numerous articles and speeches on antitrust, trade regulation, litigation, and franchising topics.
Personal: Born 28 February 1935. Earned JD with highest distinction from University of Michigan Law School, 1957; served on Law Review Board of Editors. Holds AB from University of Michigan,1955; elected to Phi Beta Kappa in his junior year. Winner, Elijah Watt Sells Award for achieving the highest grade in the United States on the Uniform CPA Examination.

ADELMAN, Howard
Adelman Gettleman Merens Berish & Carter, Chicago 312 435 1050
Recommended in Insolvency

AIELLO, Anthony
Sidley Austin Brown & Wood, Chicago
312 853 7000
Recommended in Real Estate

AIZENSTEIN, Neal
Sonnenschein Nath & Rosenthal, Chicago 312 876 8000
naizenstein@sonnenschein.com
Recommended in Corporate/M&A

Specialization: Partner in Corporate and Securities Group. Has extensive experience in corporate and securities matters, including public and private financings, acquisitions and dispositions, restructurings, joint ventures and partnerships, securities regulation, venture capital transactions and general corporate and securities counselling. Has represented purchasers, sellers and investors in acquisition and disposition transactions. Represented both issuers and underwriters in public and private financings, including IPOs and Rule 144A offerings of both equity and debt securities. Has extensive experience in representing both borrowers and lenders in a wide range of financing transactions such as asset-based loans and private placements.
Prof. Memberships: American Bar Association, Chicago Bar Association.
Career: Certified Public Accountant, Illinois, 1984. Joined *Sonnenschein* in 1986. Admitted to Illinois Bar 1987.
Personal: Born 4 September, 1963; Northwestern University School of Law, JD, Cum Laude, 1987, Dean's List, editor, 'Journal of Criminal Law and Criminology'; University of Illinois, Champaign, Urbana, BS, Accounting, 1984, member, Bronze Tablet, CPA, recipient of Lowden-Wigmore Prize.

ALBRECHT, Thomas
Sidley Austin Brown & Wood, Chicago
312 853 7000
Recommended in Banking & Finance

AMEND, James M
Kirkland & Ellis, Chicago 312 861 2154
james_amend@chicago.kirkland.com
Recommended in Intellectual Property

Specialization: Has significant litigation and counseling experience in the following technology-related fields: electronics, computers, automotive, chemistry, manufacturing and packaging. He has tried many patent infringement cases to judge and jury and has counseled clients on patent infringement and validity questions and licensing. He also has extensive experience in litigating and counseling in trademark, unfair competition, advertising and copyright fields for major US and foreign companies.
Personal: University of Michigan, BS, 1964; University of Michigan, JD, 1967, Editor 'Law Review', Order of the Coif; London School of Economics, Fulbright Scholar,1967-68. Consulting Professor-Stanford Law School, 1996-97, Patents and Intellectual Property.

ANGELO, Percy L
Mayer, Brown, Rowe & Maw, Chicago
312 701 7330
pangelo@mayerbrown.com
Recommended in Environment

Specialization: Environmental law litigator on air, water, solid waste, hazardous waste, noise, TSCA, and NEPA matters. Advises on CAA, CWA, CERCLA, RCRA, and toxic tort litigation and regulatory matters, as well as state and federal cleanup actions throughout US. Represents clients on private cost recovery actions and insurance coverage actions for

ILLINOIS — LEADERS

waste cleanup costs. Advises on environmental issues in business transactions.
Prof. Memberships: Council member, ABA Section on Public Utility, Communications and Transportation Law and member of ABA Section on Natural Resources, Energy, and Environmental Law. Associate Member, Chemical Industry Council of Illinois.
Career: Joined *Mayer, Brown, Rowe & Maw* in 1973; became partner in 1978. Former Attorney-Advisor and Acting Chief, Enforcement Services, Division of Air Pollution Control, Illinois Environmental Protection Agency, 1971-73.
Publications: Include: 'Pollution Control Board Procedures and the Board's New Rules', Environmental Law in Illinois - 2001 Edition, Illinois Institute for Continuing Legal Education ('IICLE'). 'Federal Environmental Liability Concerns in Business Transactions', Environmental Law for Transactional Attorneys - 2001 Edition, IICLE.
Personal: Born 11 September 1945. Stanford University, JD, 1970; Articles Editor, Stanford Law Review. Smith College, BA, 1967. Listed 'Best Lawyers in America' in several legal publications.

ARONSON, Virginia
Sidley Austin Brown & Wood, Chicago
312 853 7000
Recommended in Real Estate

BANOFF, Sheldon
Katten Muchin Zavis Rosenman, Chicago 312 902 5256
sheldon.banoff@kmzr.com
Recommended in Tax
Specialization: Partner, Chicago. Has concentrated in the area of federal income taxation for over 25 years, with particular concentration in investment, real estate, partnership and limited liability company taxation matters. Practice includes the representation of major real estate developers, syndicators, lenders and investors, including both taxable and tax-exempt investors and professional service (including law and accounting) firms.
Prof. Memberships: A past Chairman of the Chicago Bar Association's Federal Taxation Committee, he now serves on its Executive Council. Actively involved in the American Bar Association Section of Taxation, and is a frequent program speaker on tax planning, partnership, limited liability company, executive compensation, and professional firm organization and management matters. Past Chairman of the Chicago Bar Association's Large Law Firm Committee and counsels firms on tax and non-tax matters.
Career: Nationally and internationally known author and lecturer. Former Lecturer in Law at the University of Chicago Law School. Editor of the 'Journal of Taxations' monthly Shop Talk column since 1985, he has also written over 100 leading articles in the tax area. Co-author of two books: 'Illinois Limited Liability Company - Forms and Practice Manual' (Data Trace Legal Publishing Inc. 2002) and 'Limited Liability Companies and S Corporations' (Illinois Institute of Continuing Legal Education 1999). Has annually been selected by a national poll of lawyers as one of the 'Best Lawyers in America' and is profiled in several top legal publications, including 'Chambers Global' directory. Member of the Chicago Federal Tax Forum and in 1994 was elected as a Fellow of the American College of Tax Counsel (one of 17 members in Illinois and 535 in America). A frequent speaker at tax institutes, bar associations, accountants' societies and industry groups.
Personal: Graduated with high honors from the University of Illinois at Chicago with a Bachelor of Science degree in Accounting and received his law degree in 1974 from the University of Chicago Law School, where he was Associate Editor of the 'Law Review'.

BAPTISTA, Robert C Jr
Mayer, Brown, Rowe & Maw, Chicago
312 701 7101
rbaptista@mayerbrown.com
Recommended in Banking & Finance
Specialization: Negotiates and documents secured and unsecured lending agreements, debt restructurings, and other financing transactions. Advises in corporate matters such as borrowing transactions, sale agreements, and long-term production and licensing arrangements.
Prof. Memberships: Admitted to practice in Illinois, 1982.
Career: Served as Judicial Clerk to The Honorable R Lanier Anderson III, US Court of Appeals for the Eleventh Circuit, 1982-83. Joined *Mayer, Brown Rowe & Maw* in 1983 and became a partner in 1989.
Publications: Author of 'Bank Credit as Value in Article 4 of the Uniform Commercial Code', U. Ill. L. Rev. 395, 1981; 'Prior Party Set-Off as a Defense Under U.C.C. Section 3-306', U. Ill. L. Rev. 869, 1981; 'Peoria Savings & Loan Association v. Jefferson Trust & Savings Bank', 70 Ill. B.J. 191, 1981.
Personal: Born 14 September 1948. Earned JD, summa cum laude, at the University of Illinois in 1982, where was editor-in-chief of the 'Law Review'. Received MA, also summa cum laude, from Northern Illinois University in 1976 and BA from Wheaton College in 1970.

BARROW, Peter
Neal Gerber & Eisenberg, Chicago
312 269 8000
Recommended in Banking & Finance

BATES, Robert
Bates & Carey, Chicago 312 762 3100
Recommended in Insurance

BECK, Philip
Bartlit Beck Herman Palenchar & Scott, Chicago 312 494 4400
Recommended in Litigation

BELL, Stephen
Goldberg, Kohn, Bell, Black, Rosenbloom & Moritz, Ltd, Chicago
312 201 4000
Recommended in Real Estate

BENNETT, Barry
Dowd, Bloch & Bennett, Chicago
312 372 1361
Recommended in Employment

BERGHOFF, John C Jr
Mayer, Brown, Rowe & Maw, Chicago
312 701 7315
jberghoff@mayerbrownrowe.com
Recommended in Environment
Specialization: Environmental Practice Leader. Litigates in complex environmental trials and appeals before federal and state courts. Provides counselling and response to environmental and corporate 'crisis' situations.
Prof. Memberships: Adjunct Professor, Northwestern University School of Law, 1996 to date. Lecturer on litigation and environmental issues.
Career: Joined Mayer, Brown, Rowe & Maw as partner, 1986.
Publications: 'NRC Regulations as a Standard for Legal Actions', Practicing Law Institute, New York, 1982, 1983, 1984, Vol. 212, 272. 'The Transportation and the Storage of Spent Nuclear Fuel', Practicing Law Institute, New York, 1982, Vol. 212. Monographs relating to litigation and environmental issues.
Personal: Earned JD, Northwestern University School of Law, 1966; Wigmore Key. Holds BA, with honors, from Northwestern University. Board of Trustees, Northwestern University, 1988-94. Chairman, Board of Alumni Regents, Northwestern University, 1998 to date. Vice Chairman, Board of Trustees, Ravinia Festival, 1996 to present.

BERNICK, David M
Kirkland & Ellis, Chicago 312 861 2248
david_bernick@chicago.kirkland.com
Recommended in Litigation
Specialization: National trial counsel in mass tort litigation in the areas of pharmaceutical litigation, asbestos litigation, including the development of a Chapter 11 strategy for companies with asbestos liabilities, tobacco cost recovery, holocaust labor, breast implants and radiation exposure in state and federal courts. He has also served as trial counsel in securities fraud, product liability, leveraged-buyout, trade secret misappropriation, breach of contract, RICO, securities and monopoly cases. Currently serves on the Judicial Conference Committee on the Rules of Practice and Procedure.
Personal: University of Chicago, BA, 1974. Yale University, MA, 1975. University of Chicago, JD, 1978.

BERNSTEIN, Bruce
Sidley Austin Brown & Wood, Chicago
312 853 7000
Recommended in Banking & Finance, Insolvency

BESSETTE-SMITH, Suzanne
Barack Ferrazzano Kirschbaum Perlman & Nagelberg, Chicago 312 984 3100
Recommended in Real Estate

BINNIG, Christian F
Mayer, Brown, Rowe & Maw, Chicago
312 701 7079
cbinnig@mayerbrown.com
Recommended in Communications
Specialization: Litigator specializing in telecommunications and regulated industries, particularly gas and electricity. Experienced in antitrust, mergers and acquistions, emergency litigation, appellate work, professional malpractice.
Prof. Memberships: American Bar Association, Litigation Section and Public Utilities, Communications and Transportation Law Section; Illinois, 1986. US District Court for the Northern District of Illinois, 1986. Various other US District Courts and Courts of Appeal.
Career: Joined *Mayer, Brown, Rowe & Maw*, 1986; became partner, 1994. Formerly with *Troutman, Sanders, Lockerman & Ashmore*, Atlanta, 1985-86.
Publications: 'Federal and State Supply Issues Separating LDCs from Complete Open-Access Common Carrier Status' (presented as 'Gas Supply Planning and Management as the LDCs Unbundle', Institute of Gas Technology, 1997).
Personal: Born 10 November 1961. University of Michigan Law School, JD, cum laude, 1985. University of Virginia, BA with high distinction, 1982; Phi Beta Kappa.

BOEHRER, Charles
Winston & Strawn, Chicago
312 558 5600
Recommended in Banking & Finance
Specialization: Partner in the Corporate Department. Main area of work is syndicated leveraged finance working with major money centre banks on international and US based transactions. Recently acted as legal counsel for Deutsche Bank in connection with the US$2.07 billion Senior debt for the Huntsman-ICI joint venture, the Huntsman restructuring, and the $1.4 billion Ball Corporation credit facilities. Acts for a number of corporations on matters ranging from merger and acquisitions to general corporate work.
Career: Joined the firm in 1985 as an associate. Partner in 1993. Chairman of the Finance Institutions-Committee of the Chicago Bar Association, 1990.
Personal: University of Wisconsin, Madison, BBA, 1982; University of

LEADERS   ILLINOIS

Michigan, JD, 1985, Editor, Michigan Law Review, Finalist, Campbell Moot Court Competition

BORDERS, Thomas
McDermott, Will & Emery, Chicago
312 984 7552
tborders@mwe.com
Recommended in Tax

Specialization: Partner in Tax Department, main practice areas include federal tax controversies involving audits, administrative appeals, litigation and criminal investigations. Worked on numerous US and international tax cases involving corporate tax matters, as well as analysis of tax incentive investments, valuation, finance and accounting issues.
Prof. Memberships: Member of Chicago Bar Association; American Bar Association (Federal Taxation and Litigation Committees).
Career: Admitted to the Indiana Bar in 1974, Illinois, 1979. Also qualified for the US District Court for the Northern District of Illinois, the US Tax Court, various Circuits of the US Court of Appeals, and the US Court of Federal Claims. Prior to joining *McDermott* in 1986, worked as a trial attorney for the Office of Chief Counsel with the Internal Revenue Service (1975-85), also held position as Adjunct Professor in the graduate tax program at IIT Chicago-Kent College of Law (1987-93). Member of Advisory Board and author for Journal of Taxation of Corporate Transactions and frequent speaker on tax topics.
Personal: Born April 22, 1948. Received BA in 1970 from St. Louis University, JD from Georgetown University Law Centre in 1974, and MBA from Northwestern University in 1984.

BOTICA, Matthew
Winston & Strawn, Chicago
312 558 8095
mbotica@winston.com
Recommended in Insolvency

Specialization: Partner, Corporate Department, Chicago office. Practice concentration in insolvency, bankruptcy, and business reorganization. Co-Chair of the financial restructuring group at *Winston & Strawn*. More than 25 years' experience representing banks, institutional lenders, creditors' committees, trustees, governmental agencies, and other creditors in the bankruptcy, reorganization, and claims trading areas.
Prof. Memberships: American College of Bankruptcy.
Publications: Author of a chapter on chapter 7 'Business Liquidations' in the Illinois Institute for Continuing Legal Education (IICLE) Bankruptcy Practice Handbook.
Personal: Boston College, 1972, summa cum laude, Phi Beta Kappa. Harvard Law School, 1975.

BOWEN, Stephen S
Latham & Watkins LLP, Chicago
312 876 7652
stephen.bowen@lw.com
Recommended in Tax

Specialization: Tax partner, concentrating on federal income taxation of mergers and acquisitions, joint ventures and other business transactions.
Prof. Memberships: Member, American and Chicago Bar Associations; Fellow, American College of Tax Counsel; Member, University of Chicago Tax Conference Planning Committee.
Career: Managing partner, Chicago office. Former chairman of the firm's global tax department. Member of the firm's Executive Committee 1993-97. Regular participant in the PLI's Annual M&A Tax Program.
Publications: Numerous articles on the federal income tax consequences of business transactions.
Personal: JD, University of Chicago, 1972 (Order of the Coif). BA, Wabash College, 1968 (Phi Beta Kappa).

BRADFORD, Darryl
Jenner & Block, Chicago 312 923 2773
dmbradford@jenner.com
Recommended in Communications

Specialization: Co-chairs telecommunications practice. Partner in the class action litigation and appellate and Supreme Court practices. Member of firm's management committee. Has litigated a variety of telecommunications disputes in the deregulated environment. Has represented carriers including WorldCom in battles at the Federal Communications Commission, state commissions, federal Courts of Appeals, and state and federal courts to shape and implement rules that govern local competition. Represents carriers in interconnection disputes and arbitrations and has successfully challenged FCC orders on reciprocal compensation and inter-carrier compensation.
Career: Admitted to Illinois Bar (1980).
Personal: Received a JD from University of Chicago in 1980.

BRITTAIN, Max
Schiff Hardin & Waite, Chicago
312 258 5500
Recommended in Employment

BRO, Ruth Hill
Baker & McKenzie, Chicago
312 861 7985
bro@bakernet.com
Recommended in Communications

Specialization: Focus: privacy, security, e-workplace, e-business. Bro helps clients develop a privacy strategy, including drafting and implementing website, HR, customer, and e-marketing policies and procedures. She also advises on cross-border data protection compliance issues, provides in-house training, and assists in privacy crisis management.
Prof. Memberships: Member, *Baker & McKenzie* Global Privacy Steering Committee; Chair, ABA E-Privacy Law Committee; Member, IICLE Board of Directors.
Career: Admitted in Illinois (1994).
Publications: Numerous publications on privacy and e-business issues; Co-author, 'Online Law' (Addison-Wesley, 1996); Editor, 'The E-Business Legal Arsenal' (ABA, 2003).
Personal: '40 Illinois Attorneys Under 40 to Watch' (2001); JD University of Chicago.

BUSEY, Roxane
Gardner Carton & Douglas, Chicago
312 644 3000
Recommended in Antitrust

BUTLER JR, John Wm (Jack)
Skadden, Arps, Slate, Meagher & Flom LLP & Affiliates, Chicago 312 407 0730
jbutler@skadden.com
Recommended in Insolvency

Specialization: Co-practice leader, Corporate Restructuring Department. Specializes principally in company representation in high-profile restructuring and reorganization cases, including restructurings of Per-Se Technologies, Inc., Rite Aid Corporation and Xerox Corporation and chapter 11 reorganizations involving Comdisco, Inc., FPA Medical Management, Inc., Kmart Corporation, Service Merchandise Company, Inc., Singer, N.V. and US Airways Group, Inc. Special counsel to 360/networks, inc., Enron Corporation and The Warnaco Group, Inc. Has also acted as lead counsel in transactional work with sellers, purchasers and creditors in hundreds of transactions across the Americas and in Asia, Australia, Europe and the Middle East. Listed in every annual edition of the K&A Register, the peer group listing of the top restructuring attorneys and financial advisors in the United States. Five times named by 'Turnarounds & Workouts' in its annual list of the top dozen restructuring lawyers in America. Named as one of the top ten worldwide restructuring lawyers in 2002 by Global Counsel Magazine. Recipient of first-ever Chairman's Award from the Turnaround Management Association in 2001 for his contributions to and standing in the corporate renewal industry. Fellow, American College of Bankruptcy and International Insolvency Institute.
Personal: JD, University of Michigan Law School, 1980; AB, Princeton University, 1977 (magna cum laude).

CARLSON, Walter
Sidley Austin Brown & Wood, Chicago
312 853 7000
Recommended in Litigation

CARPENTER, David
Sidley Austin Brown & Wood, Chicago
312 853 7000
Recommended in Communications

CHEFITZ, Joel
Howrey Simon Arnold & White, Chicago
312 595 1239
Recommended in Antitrust

CHICO, Gery
Altheimer & Gray, Chicago
312 715 4000
Recommended in Real Estate

CHOI, Paul
Sidley Austin Brown & Wood, Chicago
312 853 7000
Recommended in Corporate/M&A

CICERO, Jr, Frank
Kirkland & Ellis, Chicago 312 861 2216
frank_cicero@chicago.kirkland.com
Recommended in Litigation

Specialization: Extensive experience in a wide variety of litigation matters. Areas of practice include professional malpractice, admiralty and maritime law, antitrust and trade regulation, criminal and civil fraud and securities law, trademark and patent claims, commercial contracts, construction litigation, libel, slander, and First Amendment cases, tax disputes, trade secrets, unfair competition, employment contracts, pollution and toxic substance cases, international arbitrations and litigation, dealer and franchise relationships and terminations, trust, estates and ERISA disputes, divorce and domestic relations law, product liability and warranty claims.
Personal: Amherst College, 1953-54. Wheaton College, AB, 1957. Princeton University, MPA, 1962. University of Chicago, JD, 1965.

CLARK, James
Sidley Austin Brown & Wood, Chicago
312 853 7000
Recommended in Banking & Finance

CLIFFORD, Robert
Clifford Law Offices, Chicago
312 899 9090
Recommended in Litigation

COLE, Thomas
Sidley Austin Brown & Wood, Chicago
312 853 7000
Recommended in Corporate/M&A

CONLON, William
Sidley Austin Brown & Wood, Chicago
312 853 7000
Recommended in Litigation

ILLINOIS
LEADERS

CONNELLY, Vincent J
Mayer, Brown, Rowe & Maw, Chicago
312 701 7912
vconnelly@mayerbrown.com
Recommended in Litigation
Specialization: Specializes in securities, antitrust, government contract and program cases, RICO, commercial and financial fraud, and public corruption litigation. Primary trial responsibility in over 70 federal cases, with more than 60 jury trials. Civil litigation representations have included major corporations, corporate directors, and individuals in federal and state court trials, and corporate internal investigations.
Prof. Memberships: Member, American College of Trial Lawyers; Blue Ribbon Committee appointed by the Illinois Supreme Court to review the Attorney Registration and Disciplinary Commission; President, Chicago Inn of Court. Lecturer at Chicago Association of Commerce and Industry; Chicago Bar Association; Department of Justice Trial Advocacy Institute; FBI Training Academy; State Bar Antitrust Seminar.
Career: Joined *Mayer, Brown, Rowe & Maw*, Chicago, 1987; became partner, 1987. Formerly US Attorney's Office, Northern District of Illinois, 1975-87: Chief, Special Prosecutions Division, 1985-87; Chief, Criminal Division, 1983-85.
Publications: 'A Dozen Stops on the Grand Jury Road', Litigation. 'Undercover Work at the Exchanges', Chicago Tribune. 'Unconventional Strategies in White-Collar Criminal Investigations', Litigation.
Personal: Born June 25, 1950. University of Chicago Law School, JD, 1975. University of Notre Dame, BA, summa cum laude, 1972.

CONWAY, Michael
Foley & Lardner, Chicago 312 755 1900
Recommended in Media & Entertainment

CONWAY, Tim
Conway & Mrowiec, Chicago
312 692 1700
Recommended in Construction

COVEY, Tyson J
Mayer, Brown, Rowe & Maw, Chicago
312 701 8600
jcovey@mayerbrownrowe.com
Recommended in Communications
Specialization: Specializes in regulated industries litigation and appeals on behalf of telecommunications and other utility companies in matters before state and federal regulatory agencies and courts.
Prof. Memberships: Admitted in Illinois, 1991; US District Court for the Northern District of Illinois, 1992; US Court of Appeals for the Seventh Circuit, 1992; US Court of Appeals for the Sixth Circuit, 2000.

Career: Joined *Mayer, Brown, Rowe & Maw*, 1996; became partner 2000. Formerly with *Sidley & Austin*, Chicago, 1993-96. US Court of Appeals for the Seventh Circuit, Staff Attorney, 1991-93.
Personal: Born 1965. University of Illinois College of Law, JD, magna cum laude, 1991; Order of the Coif; Administrative Editor, University of Illinois Law Review. Augustana College, BA, magna cum laude, 1987; Phi Beta Kappa.

CRAVEN, George W
Mayer, Brown, Rowe & Maw, Chicago
312 701 7231
gcraven@mayerbrown.com
Recommended in Tax
Specialization: Leading authority on tax aspects of financial transactions, cross-border tax arbitrage, offshore insurance arrangements, and deductibility of alternative risk transfer payments. Advises on acquisitions and dispositions of businesses, including structured financings as well as tax aspects of new financial products such as 'Section 483 Notes', 'Liquid Yield Option Notes'. International tax planning expertise includes Subpart F issues, transactions designed to accelerate or create foreign source income, and redomestication of US insurance companies to foreign jurisdiction.
Prof. Memberships: Admitted to practice in Illinois, 1976, and US Tax Court, 1976. Member of the American Bar Association, Section of Taxation; Financial Transactions Committee.
Career: Joined *Mayer, Brown, Rowe & Maw*, Chicago, in 1981 and became a Partner in 1983. Prior to that, had worked for *Sidley & Austin*, Chicago (1976-80) and *Ogden, Robertson & Marshall*, Louisville (1980-81).
Publications: Lecturer on 'Inversion, Section 367, Section 953(d) and Other International Tax Law Topics of Interest to US Insurers', Federal Bar Association Insurance Tax Seminar, June 7, 2001, Washington, DC; 'Tax Aspects of Securitization of Insurance Risks' at IBC Conference on Insurance Risk & Securitization, November 11-12, 1999, New York City. Moderator and panel member, 'Hot Products and Innovative Financial Instruments', University of Chicago Federal Tax Conference, November 1, 1994; 'Offshore and Captive Insurance Issues', delivered at Tax Executive Institute Seminar, May 1994; 'Money' and 'Property (Other than Money)': An Exploration of 'Amount Realized' Under Section 1001(b), Taxes, December, 1992, paper originally delivered at the 45th University of Chicago Federal Tax Conference, October, 1992.
Personal: Born 11 March 1951. Earned JD, cum laude, from Harvard Law School in 1976 and BA summa cum laude, from the University of Notre Dame in 1973. Also studied at Sophia University, Tokyo (1970-71). Named one of 'North America's Top Tax Advisers' by International Tax Review, June, 2000; profiled in 'The World's Leading Lawyers 2001-2002' and 2002-2003 by Chambers & Partners, Legal Publishers, London.

CREMENT, Anthony
Franczek Sullivan, Chicago
312 786 6140
ajc@franczek.com
Recommended in Employment
Specialization: Founding partner of *Franczek Sullivan P.C.* Has been engaged exclusively in representing employers in labor and employment matters throughout legal career.
Prof. Memberships: Member of the American and Chicago Bar Associations. Also a frequent faculty member of the Illinois Institute of Continuing Legal Education. Has been elected as a Fellow in the College of Labor and Employment Lawyers. He is also a member of the Association of Trial Lawyers of America. Is also an invited member of the International Society for Labor Law and Social Security, United States Branch and a member of the National Arbitration Panel of Arbitrators and Mediators. Has also been named one of the top labor and employment lawyers in Illinois by a leading peer review directory.
Career: Spends a significant portion of time handling employment litigation and has successfully tried cases to verdict before both judges and juries. These cases have involved claims of discrimination, wrongful discharge and benefit claims. Also represents clients in collective bargaining and arbitration, as well as many other aspects of labor and employment law.
Publications: Co-authored the article 'Reductions in Force: Practical Problems and Legal Pitfalls', which appeared in the publication 'Illinois Reporter'.
Personal: Prior to forming *Franczek Sullivan P.C.*, practiced at *Seyfarth Shaw Fairweather & Geraldson* (1969-94), where became a partner in 1975. Graduated from Harvard Law School in 1969. Received a bachelor of arts degree in history from St Joseph's College where was listed in Who's Who Among Students in American Colleges and Universities before graduating magna cum laude in 1966.

CRUMBAUGH, David G
Latham & Watkins LLP, Chicago
312 876 7660
david.crumbaugh@lw.com
Recommended in Banking & Finance
Specialization: Partner in the Finance and Real Estate Department. Represents banks and commercial finance companies in secured lending transactions, both cash flow and asset based, domestic and cross-border, to borrowers in virtually every industry.
Prof. Memberships: Member of the American Bar Association.
Career: Co-chair of the Chicago office Finance and Real Estate Department. Chairman of the Commercial Finance Association's Education Foundation.
Personal: JD, University of Illinois, 1976 (Order of the Coif, managing editor of the University of Illinois Law Review). BS, Illinois State University, 1973.

CRYSTAL, Jules
Ross & Hardies, Chicago 312 558 1000
Recommended in Employment

CULLEN, Gary P
Skadden, Arps, Slate, Meagher & Flom LLP & Affiliates, Chicago 312 407 0680
gcullen@skadden.com
Recommended in Corporate/M&A
Specialization: Partner, Chicago. Represents Fortune 500, middle market and emerging companies in a wide range of industries, as well as investment banking and other financial institutions, in a variety of M&A and corporate finance transactions. Has worked on behalf of buyers and sellers in auctions involving public companies and their business units, other stock and asset acquisitions and dispositions, negotiated and contested takeovers, proxy contests and joint ventures. Also represents issuers and investment banking institutions in initial and other public offerings, private placements of securities, and high-yield debt transactions. Advises on corporate governance and disclosure issues, shareholder rights plans, stockholders' agreements, executive compensation arrangements and other securities and corporate control issues, and counsels investment banking clients in their role as transaction financial advisors.
Career: JD, Columbia University School of Law, 1985; BA, University of Illinois, 1982.

D'ALBA, Joel
Asher, Gittler, Greenfield, Cohen & D'Alba, Chicago 312 263 1500
Recommended in Employment

DASH, James
Much Shelist Freed Denenberg Ament & Rubenstein, PC, Chicago 312 346 3100
Recommended in Construction

DAVIS, Scott J
Mayer, Brown, Rowe & Maw, Chicago
312 701 7311
sdavis@mayerbrown.com
Recommended in Corporate/M&A
Specialization: Firm Practice Leader of the Corporate and Securities Group. Extensive experience in mergers and acquisitions and the problems that arise when there is a real or perceived conflict of interest between a company's officers or directors and its shareholders. Major deals have included representation of Dow Chemical in its acquisition of Union

Carbide (approximate enterprise value US$11.6 billion as of the date of announcement), Devon Energy in its acquisition of Mitchell Energy and Development (approximate value US$3 billion as of the date of announcement), Devon in its acquisition of Anderson Exploration (approximate value US$3.5 billion) and George Weston in its acquisition of Bestfoods Baking from Unilever (approximate value US$1.75 billion). Also advises in litigation matters involving derivative, takeover, and securities fraud litigation.
Prof. Memberships: Vice President, Chicago Police Board, a body appointed by the Mayor of Chicago with disciplinary and supervisory powers over Chicago police officers and the Department.
Career: Joined *Mayer, Brown, Rowe & Maw* in 1977 and became a partner in 1983.
Publications: Author or Co-Author of 'Liability Under Sections 10, 18 and 20 of the Securities Exchange Act of 1934', printed in Understanding the Securities Laws 2000, PLI Corp. Law & Practice Handbook Series, No. B-1198, 2000; 'Merger and Acquisition Agreements in Competitive Bidding Situations: Rights and Obligations Created by Corporation and Contract Law', 17 Securities Regulation Law Journal 3, 1989.
Personal: Born 8 January 1952. Earned JD, cum laude, from Harvard University in 1976 where was a member of the Board of Editors, Harvard Law Review. Holds a BA, cum laude, from Yale University, 1972.

DIGIOVANNI, Nick
Lord, Bissell & Brook, Chicago
312 443 0700
Recommended in Insurance

DOCKSEY, Ross
Sonnenschein Nath & Rosenthal, Chicago 312 876 8000
jdocksey@sonnenschein.com
Recommended in Communications
Specialization: Partner in the Corporate and Securities Group. His practice focuses heavily on corporate transactions, including mergers and acquisitions, the creation of strategic alliances, technology contracting, and the outsourcing of key business functions including finance and administration, human resources, learning and education, supply chain management, information technology, and information services. He also serves as general counsel or principal outside corporate counsel for a number of closely held corporations.
Prof. Memberships: Frequent speaker at conferences and continuing legal education programs, including programs sponsored by the Practicing Law Institute, the Advanced Computer Law Institute, IT Mergers and Acquisitions, Insight Information Co., the Law Practice Technology Roundtable, and the National Association of Web Managers. He is a member of the Human resources Outsourcing Association and was listed by HO Today as one of five leading outsourcing lawyers in the United States.
Personal: University of Minnesota JD cum laude, 1981, United States Military Academy BS, 1973.

DOETSCH, Douglas A
Mayer, Brown, Rowe & Maw, Chicago
312 701 7973
ddoetsch@mayerbrownrowe.com
Recommended in Banking & Finance
Specialization: Chicago Office Practice Leader in Banking and Finance. Partner in International Corporate and Finance practice. Advises on secured and unsecured lending, including lending for leveraged buyouts, workouts and project financings, particularly in cross-border transactions. Represents clients in cross-border securitisation transactions, particularly future cash flow securitisations, debt restructuring and debt exchange offers, with emphasis on restructuring of emerging market debt. Counsels on asset and stock acquisitions and contract negotiations. Works on joint ventures with emphasis on cross-border ventures in Latin America. Advises on Euro-securities offerings, particularly for issues of emerging market companies, and US equity offerings of foreign issuers.
Prof. Memberships: Admitted to practice in Illinois, 1989 and New York, 1987. Member of the American Bar Association and the Illinois Bar Association; Director, Chicago Council on Foreign Relations; President, Mid-America Chapter of US-Mexico Chamber of Commerce.
Career: Joined *Mayer, Brown, Rowe & Maw* in 1988 and became a partner in 1995. Prior to that, worked for *Cleary, Gottlieb, Steen & Hamilton*, New York (1986-88) and, before that, worked as a Consultant for Data Resources, Inc. (1979-82).
Publications: Frequent author of articles and speaker at conferences on such topics as securitisations by emerging market issuers, debt restructuring, international joint ventures, and issuances of debt securities in the Euro-markets.
Personal: Born 6 November 1957. Earned JD from Columbia University in 1986, where he served as Editor-in-Chief, Columbia Journal of Transnational Law. Rotary Graduate Fellow at Université de Dakar, Dakar, Senegal (1982-83). Holds BA, magna cum laude, from Kalamazoo College (1979), where was elected to Phi Beta Kappa. Fluent in French and Spanish.

DORAN, James
Latham & Watkins LLP, Chicago
312 876 7700
james.doran@lw.com
Recommended in Banking & Finance
Specialization: Partner in the Finance and Real Estate Department. Focuses primarily on representing banks, commercial finance companies and other financial institutions in structuring and underwriting loan originations and out-of-court workouts. He frequently represents lead lenders and agents in structuring and underwriting syndicated loan transactions, including leveraged change-of-control transactions and recapitalizations of both public and privately held companies.
Personal: JD, Stanford Law School, 1981. BA, University of Iowa, 1978.

DOUGLAS, Charles
Sidley Austin Brown & Wood, Chicago
312 853 7000
Recommended in Litigation

DOW, Robert M Jr
Mayer, Brown, Rowe & Maw, Chicago
312 701 8441
rdow@mayerbrown.com
Recommended in Communications
Specialization: General and appellate litigation specializing in telecommunications, constitutional law, civil procedure, antitrust, and tort law.
Prof. Memberships: Admitted in Illinois (1993); Supreme Court of the United States; US Courts of Appeals for the Fourth, Fifth, Sixth, Seventh, Ninth, and Eleventh Circuits, Northern District of Illinois. Seventh Circuit Bar Association; Appellate Lawyers Association of Illinois (Director, 2000-02, Treasurer, 2002-03).
Career: Joined *Mayer, Brown, Rowe & Maw*, Chicago, 1995; became partner, 2002. Law Clerk, Honorable Joel M Flaum, US Court of Appeals for the Seventh Circuit, 1993-94. Teaching Fellow, Harvard College, 1992. Recipient, Derek Bok Center Certificate of Excellence in Undergraduate Teaching, 1992.
Publications: 'Invalidation of Ohio Tort Reform Legislation', 2000 'International Journal of Insurance Law' 85-88 (January 2000) (with John E. Muench); 'Arguing for Changes in the Law', 25(2) Litigation 37 (1999) (with James C. Schroeder); 'Linking Trade Policy to Free Emigration: The Jackson-Vanik Amendment', 4 'Harvard Human Rights Journal' 128-138 (1991).
Personal: Born 6 September 1965. Harvard Law School, JD, cum laude, 1993; University of Oxford, Rhodes Scholar, D. Phil in International Relations, 1997, M. Phil in International Relations, 1990; Yale University, BA (History and Political Science), summa cum laude with distinction in both majors, 1987; Phi Beta Kappa.

DRANOFF, David
Goldberg, Kohn, Bell, Black, Rosenbloom & Moritz, Ltd, Chicago 312 201 4000
Recommended in Banking & Finance

DURCHSLAG, Stephen
Winston & Strawn, Chicago
312 558 5288
sdurchsl@winston.com
Recommended in Media & Entertainment
Specialization: Intellectual property, trademark, copyright, advertising, entertainment, and promotion.
Prof. Memberships: Board of Directors, Off the Street Club; Board of Directors, Chicago Advertising Federation; President, Board of Directors, Anshe Emet Synagogue; Trustee, Nathan Cummings Foundation.
Career: Head, Intellectual Property Department. Joined firm as partner, 1989.
Personal: University of Wisconsin, BS, 1962; Hebrew University Jerusalem, 1962-1963; Harvard Law School, LLB, 1966, Felix Frankfurter Scholarship

DURKIN, Thomas M
Mayer, Brown, Rowe & Maw, Chicago
312 701 7997
tdurkin@mayerbrownrowe.com
Recommended in Litigation
Specialization: Specializes in complex civil litigation (including product liability and patent matters) and white collar criminal defense. Tried approximately 50 federal criminal jury trials.
Prof. Memberships: DePaul Law School, Adjunct Professor, Advanced Criminal Procedure, 1996; 1998. Chicago Bar Association Judicial Evaluation Committee, 1993-95. Merit Selection Panel for US Magistrate, Northern District of Illinois, 1994. Assisted Special Counsel Nicholas Bua, Inslaw Investigation, 1991-92. John Marshall Law School, Adjunct Professor, Trial Advocacy, 1988-91.
Career: Joined *Mayer, Brown, Rowe & Maw* as partner, 1993. Former Assistant US Attorney, Northern District of Illinois, 1980-93. First Assistant to US Attorney, 1990-93. Law Clerk to The Honorable Stanley J Roszkowski, Northern District of Illinois, 1979-80.
Publications: 'Doing the Right Thing' (Foreign Corrupt Practices Act), Infrastructure Finance, September 1996. Speaker at seminars on Foreign Corrupt Practices Act. Lecturer, Department of Justice Trial Advocacy Institute and FBI Training Academy in Quantico, Virginia.
Personal: Born 26 December 1953. DePaul University College of Law, JD with honors, 1978; Illinois Law Issue Editor, Law Review. University of Illinois, BS with honors, 1975. Certified Public Accountant, Illinois, 1975. Excellence in Law Enforcement Award, Chicagoland Chamber of Commerce, 1993. Attorney General's John Marshall Award by US Attorney General Thornburgh, 1991.

ILLINOIS
LEADERS

EDWARDS, Charles
Piper Rudnick, Chicago 312 368 4010
charles.edwards@piperrudnick.com
Recommended in Real Estate
Specialization: Real estate; real estate finance.
Prof. Memberships: Past Chair of the Chicago Bar Association Real Property Law Committee and its Real Property Finance Subcommittee.
Career: He concentrates his practice exclusively in the area of complex commercial real estate transactions, including purchase and sale; mortgage financing; leasing; joint ventures and partnerships; condominium development and conversion; cooperative housing transactions; general development and all other aspects of commercial real estate practice. He is also an adjunct professor and frequently lectures on real estate finance and leasing subjects.
Personal: JD, University of Chicago; BBA, University of Wisconsin.

EGGERT, Russell R
Mayer, Brown, Rowe & Maw, Chicago
312 701 7350
reggert@mayerbrownrowe.com
Recommended in Environment
Specialization: Specializes in trials and appeals of complex regulatory and environmental tort litigation. Experienced in responding to environmental crisis or emergency situations and counseling and strategic management of environmental issues. Tried over 50 environmental cases and argued over 40 appeals in state and federal courts and administrative agencies.
Prof. Memberships: American Bar Association, Sections on Natural Resources Law and Litigation.
Career: Joined *Mayer, Brown, Rowe & Maw*, Chicago, 1987; became partner 1987. Former Chief (1983-87) and Deputy Chief (1974-79), Environmental Division and Legal Counsel to the Attorney General of Illinois, Chicago. O'Conor, Karaganis & Gail Ltd., Chicago, 1979-83. Graduate Research Associate in Environmental Law, University of Illinois College of Law, 1973-74.
Personal: Born 28 July 1948. University of Illinois, JD, 1973; University of Illinois, AB, 1970.

EIMER, Nathan P
Eimer Stahl Klevorn & Solberg, Chicago
312 660 7601
neimer@eimerstahl.com
Recommended in Antitrust
Specialization: Antitrust trial lawyer and counselor. He has handled a large number of grand jury investigations of alleged price fixing, including related criminal proceedings and trial. He has also been involved as trial counsel in numerous civil antitrust cases, particularly class actions related to alleged price fixing. His practice also includes counseling clients regarding the antitrust aspects of mergers and acquisitions, and representation of clients before the Federal Trade Commission, the United States Department of Justice, and in related civil proceedings attempting to enjoin a merger. He has represented a large number of major corporations in antitrust matters, including Union Carbide Corporation, CITGO Petroleum Corporation, Kimberly-Clark Corporation, Borden, Inc., CPC, Inc., International Minerals & Chemicals Corporation, Praxair, Inc., Land O'Lakes Inc., and Corn Products International.
Prof. Memberships: Antitrust and Criminal Sections of the American Bar Association.
Career: He was one of the founding members of his firm in July 2000. Prior to that he was a member of the Executive Committee, General Counsel, head of the Commercial & Regulatory Litigation Group, and a partner of *Sidley & Austin*. From 1984 until 1990 he was the head of that firm's New York litigation practice.
Personal: Born June 26, 1949. Received his JD, cum laude, from Northwestern Universtiy School of Law in 1973, where he was a Notes & Comments Editor for the 'Law Review'. Received a BA, magna cum laude, with Highest Distinction in Economics, from the University of Illinois in 1970.

EISNER, Rebecca
Mayer, Brown, Rowe & Maw, Chicago
312 701 8577
reisner@mayerbrownrowe.com
Recommended in Communications
Specialization: Specializes in information technology and electronic commerce law. Counsels clients in complex technology transactions, including technology and business process outsourcing, strategic alliances, joint ventures, licensing agreements, development agreements, consulting services agreements, software licensing, development, maintenance and support agreements, database issues, and telecommunications agreements. Experienced in counseling clients in e-commerce and internet law issues.
Career: Joined *Mayer, Brown, Rowe & Maw*,1989-92; returned, 1996; partner, 2000. Former Associate Group Counsel and Assistant Vice President, Equifax, Inc., Atlanta, 1993-95. Public Relations and Government Affairs Specialist, The Dow Chemical Company, Midland, Michigan, 1984-86.
Publications: Offshore BPO Conference NYC: 'Privacy Issues in BPO'. 'Avoiding Gotchas in Outsourcing', Illinois Institute of Continuing Legal Education, September 2002. 'Making a Good Match: Strategic Alliances In Technology and E-Commerce', i-Street, May 2002. 'Focus on Legal: Smoothing Over the Privacy Potholes in BPO Outsourcing', 'BPO Outsourcing Journal', March 2002. 'Ignorance Isn't Bliss: What You Need To Know About EU Data Privacy Law', 'CIO Magazine', February 2002. Contributing Co-Author to E-Commerce treatise edited by B Smith, 2000, 2001.
Personal: Born 27 August 1962. University of Michigan Law School, JD cum laude, 1989; Michigan Journal of Law Reform. Ohio State University, BA, cum laude, 1984.

EMERSON, Carter W
Kirkland & Ellis, Chicago 312 861 2052
carter_emerson@chicago.kirkland.com
Recommended in Corporate/M&A
Specialization: Carter Emerson has extensive experience in counseling public and private corporations on a wide variety of subjects including corporate and SEC disclosure matters, securities filings and executive compensation. He also has public offering experience, including twelve initial public offerings ("IPOs") for issuers and three for underwriters and many Rule 144A debt offerings. His other principal aspects of practice are corporate transactions such as mergers and acquisitions (including leveraged buyouts), public offerings, debt placements and loans, and venture capital investments.
Personal: Miami University (Ohio), BS 1969. Northwestern University, JD, 1972.

EVANICH, Kevin R
Kirkland & Ellis, Chicago 312 861 2076
kevin_evanich@chicago.kirkland.com
Recommended in Corporate/M&A
Specialization: Corporate practice concentrating in mergers and acquisitions, leveraged buyouts and private equity fund formations. Responsible for structuring, supervising and closing a wide variety of leveraged acquisitions and venture capital and other financings and numerous buyout, venture capital and mezzanine funds. Represents general partners and other fund sponsors in fund formations and gatekeepers and other major investors in fund investments. Lead counsel in representation of numerous portfolio companies of private equity funds. Member of firm management committee.
Personal: University of Wisconsin - Milwaukee, BA, 1976; Northwestern University School of Law, JD, 1980.

FAHNER, Tyrone C
Mayer, Brown, Rowe & Maw, Chicago
312 701 7062
tfahner@mayerbrownrowe.com
Recommended in Litigation
Specialization: Chairman, *Mayer, Brown, Rowe & Maw*. Senior litigator specializing in civil and criminal antitrust, trade regulation matters, product liability, commodities, securities, and multi-district litigation. Represents various banking institutions, as well as telecom providers and companies in the chemical and vitamin industry. Extensive experience regarding internet access class actions, state and federal tax matters, 'white collar' crime, and criminal fraud. Extensive jury trial experience in cases involving financial crimes, including tax, bankruptcy, securities fraud and consumer fraud. Former Attorney General of Illinois - chief legal and law enforcement officer of the State - prosecuting actions on behalf of the People and defending actions brought against the State, its constitutional officers and employees. Argued cases in the US District Court and the Illinois Supreme Court.
Prof. Memberships: American College of Trial Lawyers. American Judicature Society. Americans for Effective Law Enforcement. Former President, Business Integrity Institute. J William Fulbright Board of Foreign Scholarships, Bureau of Educational and Cultural Affairs, United States Information Agency, 1988-93. Chicago Committee of the Chicago Council on Foreign Relations. Civic Committee - Commercial Club of Chicago.
Career: Joined *Mayer, Brown, Rowe & Maw*, 1979-80; returned 1983 to date; became partner 1983; Co-Chairman, *Mayer, Brown, Rowe & Maw* Management Committee, 1998-2001; Chairman, 2001 to date. Former Attorney General, State of Illinois, July 1980 to January 1983. Director, Illinois Department of Law Enforcement, 1977-79. *Freeman, Rothe, Freeman & Salzman*, Chicago, 1975-77. Assistant United States Attorney, Northern District of Illinois, 1971-75.
Personal: Born 18 November 1942. Wayne State University, JD, 1968. Northwestern University, LLM, 1971; Ford Foundation Criminal Justice Fellowship, 1969-71. University of Michigan, BA, 1965.

FEINSTEIN, Fred I
McDermott, Will & Emery, Chicago
312 984 7665
ffeinstein@mwe.com
Recommended in Real Estate
Specialization: Practice includes general transactional and litigation practice, with particular emphasis in real estate development, annexation, zoning and environmental matters. Practice includes governmental relations; purchases, sales, exchanges, and leases of industrial, commercial, retail and farm properties; construction; financing of real estate acquisitions and developments on behalf of both borrowers and lenders; HUD financing; consumer credit; loan pools, REITS and portfolio lending matters; mortgage foreclosures and mechanics' lien matters; loan participation agreements; right of way easements; condemnation litigation; bankruptcy and chancery litigation; real estate taxation matters; condominiums; legal aspects of real estate financing, syndicating and joint venturing for real estate development and multiparcel acquisition; health care, retirement housing, and related development.

Prof. Memberships: Member of the American College of Real Estate Lawyers, Illinois State Bar Association, Real Property Section, 1977-83 (Vice Chairman, 1980-81; Chairman, 1981-82) and Legislative Committee, 1984 to present; Lambda Alpha, Beta Gamma Sigma, Chicago Mortgage Attorneys Association; International Association of Attorneys in Corporate Real Estate; Associate Member, Illinois Mortgage Bankers Association, American Land Title Association, and the Urban Land Institute.
Career: Admitted to practice in Illinois and before the US Supreme Court.
Personal: Received BSC in 1967 and JD in 1970 from DePaul University.

FELCH, Patricia
Patricia A Felch - Attorney at Law, Evanston 847 475 8085
Recommended in Media & Entertainment

FERRAZZANO, Dennis
Barack Ferrazzano Kirschbaum Perlman & Nagelberg, Chicago 312 984 3100
Recommended in Real Estate

FIFER, Sam
Sonnenschein Nath & Rosenthal, Chicago 312 876 8000
sfifer@sonnenschein.com
Recommended in Media & Entertainment
Specialization: Partner and chair of intellectual property and technology group. Has extensive experience in the fields of intellectual property, entertainment and media law, including litigation and counseling. Has advised a wide variety of clients in trademark selection, registration and protection and has counseled clients in negotiating, developing, drafting and implementing licensing and other contractual agreements and protection programs. Also has advised clients, including developers of computer software, in the protection of rights in technology and has drafted and negotiated agreements for the licensing and transfer of rights in intellectual property and technology, as well as in motion pictures, theatrical and television production and distribution, music, newspaper, magazine and book publishing, syndication and talent agreements, advertising compliance and promotion law. He has worked with clients incorporate transactions involving the transfer of rights in intellectual property and technology, and has advised clients with regard to the creation and maintenance of security interests in such rights. In the area of media law, has advised clients and handled precedent-setting litigation in the areas of defamation, rights of privacy and publicity, access to courts, reporters' rights, subpoena defense and freedom of information.
Publications: Has frequently published in the areas of intellectual property and first amendment law, including 'Defamation on the Internet: Nothing to Fear But New Ideas,' presented to the American Bar Association 1997; 'The Price of International Free Speech: Nations Deal with Defamation on the Internet', DePaul Journal of Arts & Entertainment Law 1997; with co-author Greg Naron, 'Changing Horses in Mid-Stream, The Copyright Office's New Rule Makes Broadcasters Pay For 'Streaming' Their Signals Over The Internet,' 3 Vanderbilt Journal of Entertainment Law and Practice 182 (2001). Is a contributor to 'State Trademark and Unfair Competition Law', published by Clark Boardman Company Ltd. of New York and 'The New Role of Intellectual Property in Commercial Transactions', published by John Wiley & Sons Inc. of New York.
Personal: Adjunct professor of law at Northwestern University school of law, entertainment law. Is a member of the American Bar Association's Forum Committee on Communications Law, the International Trademark Association and the Copyright Society of the United States. DePaul University, JD cum laude, 1974, managing editor - DePaul Law Review, Northwestern University, BS Speech, 1971.

FINKE, Robert F
Mayer, Brown, Rowe & Maw, Chicago 312 701 7110
rfinke@mayerbrown.com
Recommended in Antitrust
Specialization: Specializes in civil, criminal, and antitrust litigation. Represents automotive, chemical, and manufacturing companies in toxic tort, mass disaster, or product liability litigation. Represents financing and financial institutions in general commercial contract and business litigation. Experienced in complex litigation, the proper use of outside counsel and alternative dispute resolution. Counsels on antitrust aspects of acquisitions and mergers, workouts and restructures, distribution, pricing, employee confidentiality, trade secret, and non-competition agreements.
Prof. Memberships: American Bar Association, Vice-Chairman, 1976, Council, 1971-75, Section of Legal Education and Admissions to the Bar; Member, Sections of Business, Antitrust, and Litigation; Committee on Corporate Counsel. Economic Club of Chicago. Lawyers Club of Chicago. University Club of Chicago.
Career: Joined *Mayer, Brown, Rowe & Maw*, 1967; became partner, 1973. Law Clerk to The Honorable Richard B Austin, United States District Court for the Northern District of Illinois, 1966-67.
Publications: 'Using Expert Testimony in Lender Liability Litigation', 'The Practical Lawyer', July 1990.
Personal: Born 11 March 1941. Harvard University, JD, 1966. University of Michigan, AB with distinction and high honors, 1963. Trustee, Rush-Presbyterian-St. Luke's Medical Center. Director, Lyric Opera Guild Board.

FITZGERALD, Thomas
Winston & Strawn, Chicago 312 558 5845
tfitzgerald@winston.com
Recommended in Tax
Specialization: Tax issues regarding acquisitions, divestitures, mergers, and reorganizations; tax controversy matters, including corporate reorganisations, intangible valuation, inventory accounting methods, true lease, foreign tax credit and acquisition-related expense issues.
Career: Joined as associate, 1979. Partner, 1986.
Personal: University of Notre Dame, 1976; Notre Dame Law School, JD, 1979.

FLYNN, Christopher
Jones Day, Chicago 312 269 4156
cflynn@jonesday.com
Recommended in Energy
Specialization: Represents electric and gas utilities before federal and state regulatory agencies in federal and state courts and in a number of commercial transactions and other ventures. Since 1984, has represented energy companies in a wide variety of matters, including mergers, restructurings, transmission unbundling, transmission open access tariff development, wholesale and retail power supply contracts, and commercial dispute resolution, as well as traditional utility rate proceedings. Devotes majority of work time to developing competitive retail markets, including retail access tariffs, stranded cost recovery mechanisms, and independent power projects, as well as wholesale marketing initiatives and international energy projects. Experienced in energy privatization projects and other commercial projects in Mexico and has spoken before the Spanish National Electricity Commission regarding transmission access and other transmission issues.

FORADAS, Michael P
Kirkland & Ellis, Chicago 312 861 2308
michael_foradas@chicago.kirkland.com
Recommended in Insurance
Specialization: Partner in litigation group. Extensive experience in commercial, insurance coverage, business torts, mass tort and product liability, trade secret/intellectual property, securities, and antitrust matters. Particular emphasis in representing policy holders in complex insurance coverage litigation, including general and product liability, directors and officers, and business interruption claims. Clients include Dow Chemical, Motorola, ServiceMaster, Brunswick, and other Fortune 500 companies.
Personal: AB, College of William & Mary, 1978; (Phi Beta Kappa). JD, Northwestern University School of Law, 1981. (Editor-in-Chief, Northwestern Law Review; Order of Coif; cum laude). Member, Board of Editors, Insurance Coverage Law Bulletin.

FORCADE, Bill
Jenner & Block, Chicago 312 923 2964
bforcade@jenner.com
Recommended in Environment
Specialization: Partner in the environmental, energy and natural resources law practice. Focuses on air pollution, regulatory and permit compliance, and administrative and judicial enforcement matters. Has a range of experience in environmental law from the perspective of a scientist, government regulator, attorney, expert witness and environmental law judge.
Career: Admitted to Illinois Bar (1976). General counsel for nationwide environmental public interest group Citizens for a Better Environment, 1976-82. Member of the Illinois Pollution Control Board, 1983-93. Governor Ryan appointed him to the Illinois Environmental Regulatory Review Commission in 2000.
Personal: Received a JD from John Marshall in 1976.

FORRESTER, Paul J
Mayer, Brown, Rowe & Maw, Chicago 312 701 7366
jforrester@mayerbrownrowe.com
Recommended in Banking & Finance
Specialization: Partner in corporate finance practice. Specializes in standard credit products (including credit derivatives, collateralized debt obligations, and structured investment vehicles) and project financings in oil and gas, utilities, shipping, refinery and pipeline industries. Represents clients in mezzanine financings, high-yield debt financings, structured financings, equity and commodity-linked securities transactions, venture capital investments, interest rate, currency, and commodity swap transactions, restructurings, reorganizations, and workouts.
Career: Associate (1980) and partner (since 1987) with *Mayer, Brown, Rowe & Maw,* except for one year (1986) with Bildakit Homes Australia. Served variously in Chicago, New York, and London. Associate with *Allen, Allen & Hemsley*, Sydney, 1977-80.
Publications: 'Alternative Investment Collateralized Fund Obligations: What? Why? Now?' Real Estate Finance, November 2002. 'CDOs: Process Not Product', Euromoney's ABS Yearbook 2002. 'Project Finance CDOs: What? Why? Now?', Independent Power Project Finance Yearbook 2001-02. 'Wanted: A New Financing Model (and Acronym?) for Merchant Power Projects', Power Economist, February 1997. 'Political Risk Plagues Alternative Energy Project', Private Power Executive, November/December 1996.

Personal: Born 6 December 1953. Earned JD from Illinois Institute of Technology, Chicago-Kent College of Law, 1985, and LLB from University of Sydney, 1976. Admitted in Illinois, 1988; New York, 1984; and New South Wales, Australia, 1978.

FORT, Jeffrey
Sonnenschein Nath & Rosenthal, Chicago 312 876 8000
jfort@sonnenschein.com
Recommended in Environment

Specialization: Partner and chair of the environmental group. His practice includes all environmental media and all state and federal environmental agencies. He has successfully litigated before all levels of state and federal courts and negotiated with all varieties of state and federal environmental agencies. Reported decisions in which he was a principal advocate include: Kerr-McGee v Lefton, 14 F.3d 321 (7th Cir. 1994); North Shore Gas Company v EPA, 753 F.Supp. 1413 (ND Ill 1990) aff'd, 930 F.2d 1239 (7th Cir. 1991); United States v. Distler, 741 F. Supp. 643 (WD Ky 1990); United States v Outboard Marine Corporation, 1991 US Dist. Lexis 7313 (ND Ill 1991); Illinois State Chamber of Commerce v US EPA, 775 F.2d 1141 (7th Cir. 1985); United States v Riverside Laboratories, 678 F.Supp. 1352; (ND Ill 1988) (counsel for defendant Riverside Laboratories).
Publications: Former chairman of the Environmental Law Committee of the Chicago Bar Association and of the Lake Michigan States Section of the Air & Waste Management Association. Is a frequent lecturer on environmental topics for various professional groups, including the Corporate Counsel Institute and the Illinois Institute for Continuing Legal Education. Also a frequent author, he has published: 'Can Emissions Trading Work Beyond A National Program? Some Practical Observations on the Available Tools', 18 U.Pa. J.Int'l Economic Law 463 (1997); 'Designing an Effective Environmental Compliance Program' (Clark Boardman Callaghan 1993); 'Water Pollution in Illinois' (IICLE 1993 1996); 'Closure and Corrective Actions of Areas Potentially Contaminated with Hazardous Waste' (Illinois Institute for Continuing Legal Education 1993 1996); 'Trends and Developments in Environmental Law: Ongoing Conduct' (Northwestern University Corporate Counsel Institute 1992), and 'Cost Control of Environmental Remediation Projects' (Executive Enterprises 1991). Adjunct Professor of Law at Northwestern University School of Law (1990-93).
Personal: Clerkship for Justice John M Karns, Jr of the Illinois Appellate Court. Northwestern University School of Law, JD, cum laude, 1975, Monmouth College, BA, Economics, 1972.

FRANCZEK, James
Franczek Sullivan, Chicago
312 986 0300
Recommended in Employment

FRANSON, Marc
Chapman and Cutler, Chicago
312 845 3000
Recommended in Banking & Finance

FRANZETTI, Susan
Sonnenschein Nath & Rosenthal, Chicago 312 876 8027
sfranzetti@sonnenschein.com
Recommended in Environment

Specialization: Partner in *Sonnenschein's* Environmental Group, she concentrates in permitting, compliance, administrative and judicial litigation in air, water, hazardous waste and toxic substance matters before local and state environmental agencies, the US Environmental Protection Agency and state and federal courts. She represents clients in resolving Clean Water Act permitting and compliance issues, hazardous and nonhazardous waste management issues, handling state and federal Superfund matters, coordinating and overseeing environmental due diligence and audit projects, establishing environmental management programs and completing Brownfields and other voluntary site remediation projects under state programs. She is also an experienced litigator in both federal and state enforcement defense work, administrative rule-making proceedings and defending and prosecuting private cost recovery actions for environmental remediation costs and injunctive relief.
Prof. Memberships: Member of the Illinois Bar, US Northern District, Illinois, Seventh Circuit Court of Appeals, and Western District, Michigan, Federal Trial Bar.
Publications: Author of 'Water Pollution' in 'Environmental Law in Illinois' (Ill Inst. for CLE 2001); 'Environmental Risks in Leasing', 'The Docket' (April, 1994); 'Comment on the Seventh Circuit's Environmental Regulation of Business', 'Chicago-Kent Law Review' (1991); and a frequent speaker for legal and professional organizations. She is a former instructor of environmental law at Chicago-Kent College of Law and Loyola University of Chicago School of Law and a vice-chair of the ABA Water Quality Committee.
Personal: Loyola University of Chicago Law School, JD, cum laude, 1979, Northwestern University, BA, 1976. Distinguished Achievement Award for Trial Advocacy.

FREED, Michael
Much Shelist Freed Denenberg Ament & Rubenstein, PC, Chicago 312 346 3100
Recommended in Antitrust

FREEMAN, Lee
Freeman, Freeman & Salzman, Chicago
312 222 5100
Recommended in Antitrust

FREEMAN, Louis
Skadden, Arps, Slate, Meagher & Flom LLP & Affiliates, Chicago 312 407 0650
lfreeman@skadden.com
Recommended in Tax

Specialization: Has extensive experience in all aspects of federal tax planning and dispute work, with particular emphasis on corporate acquisitions and dispositions, spin-offs, consolidated groups, financings, joint ventures and partnerships, workouts and restructurings, real estate, financial products, and foreign inbound and outbound transactions. Active in the ABA Tax Section, where served as chair of Committee on Corporate Tax. Is a fellow in American College of Tax Counsel and a member of Tax Advisory Group of the ALI Federal Income Tax Project-Subchapter C.
Career: LLM (in Taxation), New York University, 1972. JD, Harvard Law School, 1966. BBA, University of Cincinnati, 1963.

FRIEDLANDER, Mark
Schiff Hardin & Waite, Chicago
312 258 5500
Recommended in Construction

FRIEDLI, Helen
McDermott, Will & Emery, Chicago
312 984 7563
hfriedli@mwe.com
Recommended in Corporate/M&A

Specialization: Partner in corporate department and a member of the firm's management committee and compensation committee. Main area of work is mergers and acquisitions, takeovers, strategic alliances, public and private offerings of securities and corporate law. Has represented US based purchasers of services, manufacturing and telecom businesses in Europe and European acquirers of businesses in the US.
Prof. Memberships: Member of the Illinois State Bar; American Bar Association and Chicago Finance Exchange.
Career: Admitted to the Illinois Bar in 1980. Received Industrial Management degree in 1977. In 1980, received JD, and joined *McDermott, Will & Emery.*

FRIEDMAN, Dennis G
Mayer, Brown, Rowe & Maw, Chicago
312 701 7319
dfriedman@mayerbrown.com
Recommended in Communications

Specialization: Commercial litigation.
Prof. Memberships: Admitted in Illinois, 1982.
Career: Joined *Mayer, Brown, Rowe & Maw,* 1982; became a partner, 1988. Law Clerk to The Honorable Gerald Bard Tjoflat, United States Court of Appeals for the Eleventh Circuit, 1981-82.

Personal: Duke University, JD, 1981; graduated first in class. Amherst College, BA, cum laude, 1969.

GALLAND, George
Miner, Barnhill & Galland, Chicago
312 751 1170
Recommended in Employment

GANGEMI, Columbus
Winston & Strawn, Chicago 312 558 5811
cgangemi@winston.com
Recommended in Employment

Specialization: National Head, Labor and Employment Practice. Concentrates in all areas of labor and employment relations counseling and litigation, representing clients before the NLRB, the EEOC, the Department of Labor, the US Supreme Court, the US Congress.
Prof. Memberships: Board of Directors, Illinois State Chamber of Commerce, 1995-present; National Labor Relations Board Practice Committee, American Bar Association, 1976-present; Fellow, College of Labor & Employment Lawyers, 1998-present.
Career: Joined firm as associate, 1973. Partner, 1979. Member, Executive Committee; Member, Compensation Committee.
Publications: 'Labor Disputes Planning Workbook, Labor Policy Association, 1999'; 'The Bargaining Order and Related Remedies Under the NLRA', 'The Labor Law Handbook, IICLE, 1998' (with D Barella); 'The Lockout as an Alternative to Union In-Plant Campaign Tactics', 'NLRB Watch, LPA', January 1999.
Personal: Villanova University, AB, 1969; Temple University, Doctoral Fellow-Philosophy, 1970; Villanova University School of Law, JD, 1973, Case & Comments Editor, Villanova Law Review.

GAVIN, John
Foley & Lardner, Chicago 312 755 1900
Recommended in Insurance

GEAREN, John J
Mayer, Brown, Rowe & Maw, Chicago
312 701 7278
jgearen@mayerbrownrowe.com
Recommended in Real Estate

Specialization: Real estate transactions, representing commercial banks, national insurance companies, and pension funds in negotiating acquisition, construction, and permanent financing for real estate projects and in negotiating workouts. Represents developers of real estate projects in obtaining governmental approvals, financing arrangements, and architectural and construction contracts to develop hotels, offices, residential apartments, and single family residential developments. Represents tenants and landlords in office, commercial, and industrial leases.
Prof. Memberships: American College of Real Estate Lawyers. Chicago Bar Association. Chicago Council of Lawyers.

Career: Joined *Mayer, Brown, Rowe & Maw*, 1971; Partner, 1978. Law Clerk to The Honorable Spotswood W Robinson, US Court of Appeals, Washington, DC 1970-71.
Publications: Frequent speaker and panelist on real estate issues, including panel on lenders' issues at the annual Law Conference of the International Council of Shopping Centers.
Personal: Born 1 September 1943. Yale University, JD, 1970; Managing Editor, 'Yale Law Journal'. Oxford University, MA, 1967; Rhodes Scholar. Notre Dame, BA, summa cum laude, 1965. Peer selection to several legal publications. Chairman of the Board, Director, Institute for the International Education of Students.

GERSTEIN, Allen
Marshall, Gerstein & Borun, Chicago
312 474 6300
Recommended in Intellectual Property

GERSTEIN, Mark D
Latham & Watkins LLP, Chicago
312 876 7666
mark.gerstein@lw.com
Recommended in Corporate/M&A
Specialization: Particular expertise in mergers and acquisitions with additional focus on securities and general corporate representation, including technology concerns. Experienced in all aspects of tender offers - defending and advancing; hostile and friendly - and representing both insurgents and management in proxy contests for control of public companies. Also provides counsel to private equity sponsors, financial advisors and boards of directors in change-in-control and going-private transactions.
Career: Co-chair, Global Mergers and Acquisitions group. Adjunct professor, Northwestern University School of Law.
Personal: JD, University of Chicago, 1984. BA, University of Michigan, 1981.

GILFORD, Steven R
Mayer, Brown, Rowe & Maw, Chicago
312 701 7909
sgilford@mayerbrownrowe.com
Recommended in Insurance
Specialization: Commercial litigation. International insurance and reinsurance. Coverage disputes. Insurance fraud, regulation and insolvencies. RICO, attorneys' fee and class action litigation. Insurance defense and coordination. Restrictive covenant disputes.
Career: Joined *Mayer, Brown, Rowe & Maw* as partner, 1987. Formerly with *Isham, Lincoln & Beale*.
Publications: Author: 'Insurance Coverage Actions: Who, Where, and When to Sue', The Brief, Fall 1996, Vol. 26, No. 1, ABA Tort & Insurance Practice Section. 'Prior Attention to Arbitration Clauses Help Ensure Fairness', Legal Update, The Review Worldwide Reinsurance, March 1995. 'Alternatives to Insurance Liquidation: A US Perspective', 7th International Reinsurance Congress, October 1993. 'The Responsibilities and Liabilities of Accountants and Actuaries to Life Insurers and in Life Insurance Insolvencies', ABA National Institute on Life Insurer Insolvency, June 1993.
Personal: Born 2 December 1952. Duke University, JD, 1978; Order of the Coif; Administrative Law Editor and Member of the Editorial Board, 'Law Journal'. Duke University, MA, 1978. Dartmouth College, AB, summa cum laude, 1974. Member, Board of Education, Evanston Township High School. Director, Metropolitan Family Services.

GITTLER, Marvin
Asher, Gittler, Greenfield, Cohen & D'Alba, Chicago 312 263 1500
Recommended in Employment

GLICKSTEIN, David
Piper Rudnick, Chicago 312 368 7270
david.glickstein@piperrudnick.com
Recommended in Real Estate
Specialization: Real estate; real estate finance.
Career: He has extensive experience in a broad range of real estate transactions including acquisitions and dispositions, financing, development, joint ventures and leasing. He represents owners and developers on local, national and international projects and has significant experience representing lenders and borrowers on complex financing transactions and workouts. He is a member of the American College of Real Estate Lawyers and has been listed for many years in a leading legal publication.
Personal: JD, Northwestern University; BBA, University of Wisconsin.

GODFREY, Richard C
Kirkland & Ellis, Chicago 312 861 2391
richard_godfrey@chicago.kirkland.com
Recommended in Litigation
Specialization: Senior litigation partner and member of the firm's Management Committee. He specializes in complex litigation, including jury and bench trials, arbitration, and appellate work in various fields, including class actions, antitrust, environmental contamination claims, franchise and distribution litigation, and business torts and contract disputes.
Prof. Memberships: Member, Board of Visitors, Boston University School of Law. Member, Board of Trustees, Augustana College. Member, Lawyers' Committee, National Center for State Courts. Member, American, Illinois, Chicago, Fifth and Seventh Circuit Bar Associations. Member, Board of Governors, The Mid-America Club.
Personal: Augustana College, BA, 1976. Boston University School of Law, JD, 1979.

GOLD, Michael
Sidley Austin Brown & Wood, Chicago
312 853 7000
Recommended in Banking & Finance

GOLDEN, Gerald
Neal Gerber & Eisenberg, Chicago
312 269 8000
Recommended in Employment

GOLDMAN, Michael
Sidley Austin Brown & Wood, Chicago
312 853 7000
Recommended in Insurance

GOLDSTEIN, Andrew
Freeborn & Peters, Chicago
312 360 6000
Recommended in Media & Entertainment

GOODMAN, Mark
Lord, Bissell & Brook, Chicago 312 443 0700
Recommended in Insurance

GOODMAN, Stuart
Schiff Hardin & Waite, Chicago
312 258 5500
Recommended in Corporate/M&A

GORDON, Mark
Gordon & Glickson, Chicago
312 321 7660
Recommended in Communications

GRIMM, Terry
Winston & Strawn, Chicago
312 558 5782
tgrimm@winston.com
Recommended in Litigation
Specialization: Commercial, anti-trust, patent, and white collar criminal litigation.
Prof. Memberships: Fellow, American College of Trial Lawyers.
Career: Joined firm as associate, 1968. Partner, 1975. Member, Executive Committee. Member, Litigation Department Policy Team.
Personal: Indiana University, Durham University, England, BA, 1964; Indiana University Law School, JD, 1967, Order of the Coif, Law Review.

HAARLOW, John
Lord, Bissell & Brook, Chicago
312 443 0700
Recommended in Insurance

HAHN, Arthur
Katten Muchin Zavis Rosenman, Chicago
312 902 5241
arthur.hahn@kmzr.com
Recommended in Corporate/M&A
Specialization: Chairman of *Katten Muchin Zavis Rosenman's* Financial Services Group. His practice includes: representation of major international banks and brokerage firms in connection with their cash and derivatives products, including interfacing with exchanges, regulatory compliance, principal trading and sales practices issues, litigation and enforcement matters; representation of international equity and commodity exchanges and clearing houses in connection with their business structuring, trading rules, technology initiatives, cross-border Securities Exchange Commission and Commodities Futures Trading Commission licenses and international insolvency issues; representation of technology companies in connection with business strategies, capital formation and mergers and acquisitions.
Prof. Memberships: Currently serves on the Executive Committee of the Institute for Financial Markets, is Chairman of the Illinois Council on Economic Education, and was the founding Faculty Chairman of the Chicago Kent Illinois Institute of Technology Graduate School of Financial Services Law (serving from 1988 through 1999).
Career: Served on the legislative staff of US Senator Paul H Douglas and clerked on the Federal District Court for the Northern District of Illinois. Member of *KMZ Rosenman's* Executive Committee.
Personal: Attended the London School of Economics and Political Science. Received his JD degree from Northwestern University School of Law.

HAMILL, John
Jenner & Block, Chicago 312 923 2684
jhamill@jenner.com
Recommended in Communications
Specialization: Partner in the telecommunications, appellate and Supreme Court, and antitrust and trade regulation practices. Extensively involved in complex telecommunications litigation and counseling including appellate, local competition, antitrust, regulatory and class action matters, especially representing carriers in local competition litigation since adoption of the Telecommunications Act of 1996. Also has regularly represented clients in a wide range of antitrust and unfair competition matters, including federal and state court antitrust lawsuits.
Prof. Memberships: Illinois Appellate Lawyers Association and the Seventh Circuit Bar Association.
Career: Admitted to Illinois Bar (1993).
Personal: Received a JD (cum laude) from Harvard in 1993.

HAMM, Leisa
Lord, Bissell & Brook, Chicago
312 443 0700
Recommended in Insurance

HAMMES, Jeffrey C
Kirkland & Ellis, Chicago 312 861 2476
jhammes@kirkland.com
Recommended in Corporate/M&A
Specialization: He has concentrated his practice on structuring and negotiating complex business transactions including domestic and international mergers, acquisitions, leveraged buyouts and

ILLINOIS

recapitalizations, going private transactions, spinoffs, formation of private equity funds, venture capital investments, debt and equity financings and restructurings and workouts and executive compensation, handling transactions which range in size from several million dollars to over $1 billion.
Personal: University of Wisconsin, BBA, 1980; Northwestern University School of Law, JD, 1985.

HANZLIK, Paul
Foley & Lardner, Chicago 312 755 1900
Recommended in Energy

HARRINGTON, James
Ross & Hardies, Chicago 312 558 1000
Recommended in Environment

HARTMANN, Michael
Leydig, Voit & Mayer, Ltd, Chicago
312 616 5600
Recommended in Intellectual Property

HARTSTEIN, Barry
Vedder, Price, Kaufman & Kammholz, Chicago 312 609 7500
Recommended in Employment

HEIDELBERGER, Brian
Winston & Strawn, Chicago
312 558 5897
bheidelb@winston.com
Recommended in Media & Entertainment
Specialization: Counsels major corporations, e-commerce companies and their advertising/promotion agencies on advertising, marketing, and promotional issues, taking into account copyright, trademark, right of publicity, false advertising, sweepstakes/contest issues, television network guidelines, as well as the Screen Actors Guild Commercials Contract. Has expertise in high-level talent, music and sponsorship negotiations, as well as electronic commerce, web development, software licensing, and other related technology agreements.
Personal: BS in marketing from Indiana University (1991). JD from Chicago Kent College of Law (1994), where he was a Law Review member and a Kent Legal Scholar.

HELLER, David
Latham & Watkins LLP, Chicago
312 876 7670
david.heller@lw.com
Recommended in Insolvency
Specialization: Represented lenders and debtors in workouts and bankruptcy proceedings for 20 years. Represents Bank One as DIP lender in the United Airlines bankruptcy and led the reorganization and sale of GST Telecommunications, one of the first and largest telecom companies sold in Chapter 11.
Career: In 1997, 'Turnarounds & Workouts' selected him as one of the "Top Ten Bankruptcy Attorneys in the Country" stating that he "saved [lender clients] millions in loan losses in 1997".
Publications: Speaker, Commercial Finance Association, US Bankruptcy Judges' Conference and Turnaround Management Association.
Personal: JD, Georgetown University, 1978. BA, Northwestern University, 1974.

HELMAN, Robert A
Mayer, Brown, Rowe & Maw, Chicago
312 701 7020
rhelman@mayerbrownrowe.com
Recommended in Corporate/M&A
Specialization: Senior partner and former chairman of *Mayer, Brown, Rowe & Maw*. Primary practice areas include corporate, business, financial, securities, public utility, and banking. Widely recognized for expertise in tender offers, mergers and acquisitions, corporate restructurings, and corporate governance issues.
Prof. Memberships: Member of the American Bar Association (Chairman, Section of Public Utility Law) 1983-84; American Law Institute; Chicago Bar Association; and Chicago Council of Lawyers.
Career: Admitted to practice in Illinois, 1956, and Supreme Court of the United States, 1963. Joined *Mayer, Brown, Rowe & Maw*, Chicago, as a partner in 1967. Served as Chairman, *Mayer, Brown, Rowe & Maw* management committee from 1984-98, and now serves as Senior Partner. Prior to *Mayer, Brown, Rowe & Maw*, served with *Isham, Lincoln & Beale*, Chicago, from 1956-66.
Publications: Co-Author of 'Commentaries on the Illinois Constitution of 1970' and various articles in legal and trade publications on corporate and public utility matters.
Personal: Born January 27, 1934. Earned BSL (1954) and LLB (1956) at Northwestern University, where was a member of the Order of the Coif and Associate Editor of 'Northwestern University Law Review'. Serves in a range of directorships and civic organisations, including Northern Trust Corporation, Dreyer's Grand Ice Cream, Inc.; TC PipeLines GP, Inc.; Chicago Stock Exchange, 1993-2000; Zenith Electronics Corporation, 1995-99; The Horsham Corporation, 1990-96; Alberta Natural Gas Company, 1993-96; Southern Pacific Transportation Co., 1987-88; The Brookings Institution, Emeritus Trustee; Chicago Council on Foreign Relations, Trustee; Museum of Contemporary Art, Trustee; Aspen Institute, Trustee, 1986-92; Citizens Committee on the Juvenile Court of Cook County, Chairman, 1968-83; Jewish Federation of Metropolitan Chicago, Director, 1991-92; The Learned Hand Human Relations Award of the American Jewish Committee, Recipient, 1989; Justice John Paul Stevens Award of the Chicago Bar Association, Recipient, 2001; Legal Assistance Foundation of Chicago, President, 1973-75; Northwestern University Law School Visiting Committee, Chairman, 1989-92; United Charities of Chicago, Director, 1967-72; and University of Chicago Hospitals, Trustee, 1982-88.

HICKEY, JR, PC, John T
Kirkland & Ellis, Chicago 312 861 2348
john_hickey@chicago.kirkland.com
Recommended in Litigation
Specialization: Member of firm's executive committee. Lead trial counsel in commercial, intellectual property, environmental, product liability, consumer fraud, securities, shareholder derivative, antitrust, and contract litigation in state and federal courts, arbitrations and administrative proceedings throughout the US. Fellow, American College of Trial Lawyers; Leading Lawyers Network Advisory Board (top 1% of IL lawyers).
Personal: Georgetown University, AB, 1974 magna cum laude, Phi Beta Kappa; University of Chicago, JD, 1977.

HILLIARD, David
Pattishall, McAuliffe, Newbury, Hilliard & Geraldson, Chicago 312 554 8000
Recommended in Intellectual Property

HODES, Scott
Ross & Hardies, Chicago 312 558 1000
Recommended in Media & Entertainment

HOFER, Roy
Brinks Hofer Gilson & Lione, Chicago
312 321 4200
Recommended in Intellectual Property

HOMBURGER, Tom
Bell, Boyd & Lloyd, Chicago
312 372 1121
Recommended in Real Estate

JACOBSON, Kenneth
Katten Muchin Zavis Rosenman, Chicago 312 902 5445
Kenneth.Jacobson@kmzr.com
Recommended in Real Estate
Specialization: Partner, Chicago. Concentrates on commercial real estate finance and investment in real estate and real estate-related companies (including, multi-family, office, retail, hotel, resort and mixed-use facilities) for real estate investment trusts, real estate opportunity funds, commercial banks, insurance companies, finance companies and other lenders, as well as developers and other borrowers. Has been involved in complex financings, including mezzanine financing, multi-asset portfolio financing, permanent and line of credit financing, rated and structured financing and other financing and investment activities in a variety of projects such as shopping centers, hotels, resort facilities, office buildings, build-to-suit distribution facilities and multifamily assets. Represents lenders, loan participants, loan purchasers and sellers, investors and borrowers in unsecured and secured lines of credit, construction and permanent financing, mezzanine financing, portfolio financing, workouts, loan dispositions and acquisitions, distressed property transactions and joint ventures. Regularly represents clients in commercial real estate acquisitions and divestitures.
Prof. Memberships: Member of the American College of Real Estate Lawyers, American Bar Foundation and the Chicago Mortgage Attorneys Association. Past President of the Chicago Mortgage Attorneys Association. Served as Vice Chairman of the Legal Opinions in Real Estate Transactions Committee of the Real Property, Probate and Trust Section of the American Bar Association.
Career: Frequent speaker, panelist and author on a variety of topics, including, portfolio transactions, deeds in lieu of foreclosure, limited liability companies and partnerships, mortgage finance, attorneys' opinions and restrictions and easement agreements.
Publications: Co-author of 'Illinois Limited Liability Company Forms and Practice Manual'.
Personal: Graduated, Phi Beta Kappa, from the University of Illinois in 1976 and received his Juris Doctor degree from Stanford Law School in 1979.

JACOBSON, Ronald H
Winston & Strawn, Chicago
312 558 5832
rjacobson@winston.com
Recommended in Banking & Finance
Specialization: Partner, Corporate Department, Chicago office. Practice concentrated in leveraged finance, structured investment, private equity, and debt portfolio purchase matters. Extensive background in advising prominent financing sources in structuring, negotiating, and documenting significant leveraged transaction financings. Substantial experience in complex mezzanine financing, structured investment product, private equity, and leveraged purchase matters.
Prof. Memberships: Member, American Bar Association, Business Law Section. Member, Commercial Finance Association's Education Foundation Founders Leadership Council. Member, Loan Syndications and Trading Association, Inc. Boy Scouts of America Executive Fund Raising Committee, American Bar Association Business Law Section.
Career: Admitted to Illinois Bar, 1988. Joined *Winston & Strawn*, 1990; Partner, 1997. Annual Presenter, *Winston & Strawn* Corporate Associate Training Program. Member, *Winston & Strawn* Associate Evaluation Committee, Billings and Collections Committee, Corporate Associate Training Program and Corporate Associate Mentoring Program.
Personal: Born July 23rd, 1963. BA, 1985, with honors, University of Illinois at

Urbana-Champaign. Received JD, 1988, with honors, Loyola University Chicago School of Law; Managing Editor of Loyola Law Journal. Received MM, 1990, with honors, JL Kellogg Graduate School of Management, Northwestern University, majors in accounting and finance.

JAVARAS, George B
Kirkland & Ellis, Chicago 312 861 2016
george_javaras@kirkland.com
Recommended in Tax

Specialization: George Javaras is a senior tax partner who represents major multi-national corporations in acquisitions, dispositions, spin-offs, joint ventures, tax planning (including executive compensation) and tax controversies. He has structured a large variety of multi-billion dollar acquisitions and dispositions (both domestic and cross-border, taxable and tax free) and planned substantial bankruptcy restructurings. In addition, he has represented a major commodities exchange on its tax matters. His clients are engaged in financial services, manufacturing, natural resources, metal refining, advertising, insurance, communications, transportation, food and apparel, among other industries.
Personal: Northwestern University, BSBA, 1961. University of Chicago Law School, JD, 1964.

JEPSON, Edward
Vedder, Price, Kaufman & Kammholz, Chicago 312 609 7500
Recommended in Employment

JOSEPH, Robert
Sonnenschein Nath & Rosenthal, Chicago 312 876 8165
rjoseph@sonnenschein.com
Recommended in Antitrust

Specialization: Partner and senior member of Antitrust, Franchising and Distribution Group; Chair of the American Bar Association (ABA) Section of Antitrust Law. With 30 years of experience in antitrust and trade regulation litigation and counseling, handles complex issues covering a wide variety of substantive law and procedural litigation questions. Has represented franchisors and other suppliers in a number of antitrust disputes, including class actions, and has counseled them on the legal implications of their distribution strategies and on such issues as tying, resale price maintenance and price discrimination questions.
Prof. Memberships: Previously served as the ABA Antitrust Section's Chair-Elect and Vice-Chair and as Committee Officer on the Section's Council, and as Chair of its Franchising Committee (1984-87). Chair of Videotapes Committee (1987-90), and Chair of its Publications Committee (1991-94). He also was Vice Chair of the Franchising Committee (1981-84) and of the Publications Committee (1990-91).

Publications: Lecturer at ABA Section of Antitrust Law programs and before the ABA Forum on Franchising, where he is a member of the governing board, and at other programs. He has also written extensively.
Personal: University of Michigan, JB cum laude 1971. Member - Michigan Law Review, Alpha Sigma Nu, National Honor Society, Xavier University, AB magna cum laude 1968. Joined *Sonnenschein* after serving as a staff attorney with the Federal Trade Commission's Bureau of Competition from 1971-76.

KARAGANIS, Joseph
Karaganis, White & Magel, Chicago 312 836 1177
Recommended in Environment

KATZ, Alvin Charles
Mayer, Brown, Rowe & Maw, Chicago 312 701 8285
akatz@mayerbrown.com
Recommended in Real Estate

Specialization: Real estate development, finance, management and leasing. Partnerships and joint ventures. General business law.
Prof. Memberships: Lecturer on real estate development and finance, University of Illinois Law School, IIT-Chicago Kent College of Law, Practicing Law Institute, American Conference Institute, and other continuing legal education programs. American Bar Association. The Economic Club of Chicago. Lambda Alpha International. Pension Real Estate Association. Urban Land Institute. National Association of Real Estate Investment Trusts.
Career: Joined *Mayer, Brown, Rowe & Maw*, Chicago as partner, 1990. Formerly with *Neal Gerber & Eisenberg*, Chicago, 1984-90; *Levy and Erens*, Chicago, 1977-84.
Personal: Born 18 January 1952. Stanford University Law School, JD, 1977. University of Michigan, BA with high distinction and honors in economics, 1974. Member, Glencoe, Illinois, Board of Education. Victory Gardens Theater, Director. Northlight Theatre, Director. University of Michigan Alumni Association. Stanford University Law School Alumni Association. Jewish Community Centers of Chicago, former Director. LaSalle Street Council, former Director. The Randolph Street Gallery, Co-founder and former Director. Community Arts Foundation (Body Politic Theatre), former Director. UJA National Men's Cabinet, former member. Wisdom Bridge Theatre, Former Director.

KELLEY, Timothy
Timothy S Kelley - Sole Practitioner, Chicago 312 641 3560
Recommended in Media & Entertainment

KELLY, Henry
O'Keefe Ashenden Lyons & Ward, Chicago 312 621 0400
Recommended in Communications

KIKOLER, Stephen
Much Shelist Freed Denenberg Ament & Rubenstein, PC, Chicago 312 346 3100
Recommended in Construction

KIRCHHOEFER, Gregg
Kirkland & Ellis, Chicago 312 861 2177
gregg_kirchhoefer@kirkland.com
Recommended in Communications

Specialization: Outsourcing (IT, BPO and ASP); telecommunications (including voice, data, video and network management); internet, e-commerce and EDI; strategic alliance, joint venture, consortium and teaming arrangements; system development, software licensing and other computer-related agreements; biotechnology, biogenetics, pharmaceutical and medical device; technology transfer, R&D and licensing agreements; facilities management; entertainment, publishing and new media; bankruptcy-remote and tax-driven intellectual property holding entity mechanisms; intellectual asset-management programs; protection of technology and product development, manufacturing, franchising and distribution arrangements, across a broad spectrum of businesses, technologies and intellectual property rights.
Personal: Saint Louis University, BSC, 1972. Saint Louis University, cum laude, JD, 1982.

KIRSCH, William S
Kirkland & Ellis, Chicago 312 861 2288
william_kirsch@chicago.kirkland.com
Recommended in Corporate/M&A

Specialization: Complex business transactions, private equity fund formations, domestic and international mergers, going private transactions, debt and equity financings and restructurings. Recent lead representations include 2002 Jefferson Smurfit Group public to private transaction, 2001 American Airlines acquisition of TWA, 2002 sale of Gaylord Container Corporation to Temple Inland, 2002 acquisition by Reader's Digest of Reiman Publishing, Packaging Corporation of America leveraged acquisition by Madison Dearborn Partners, 2001 TransWestern Publishing public to private acquisition of WorldPages, Madison Dearborn Partners $4 billion fund formation, Putnam Investments investment in T.H. Lee Partners.
Personal: Northwestern University, BA, 1978. Stanford Law School, JD, 1981.

KIRSCHBAUM, Howard
Barack Ferrazzano Kirschbaum Perlman & Nagelberg, Chicago 312 984 3100
Recommended in Real Estate

KLENK, James
Sonnenschein Nath & Rosenthal, Chicago 312 876 8000
jklenk@sonnenschein.com
Recommended in Media & Entertainment

Specialization: Partner in Litigation and Business Regulation Group and Intellectual Property and Technology Group. Practices in state and federal courts across the country, has tried patent, copyright and trademark cases before juries, judges and the US Patent and Trademark Office. Litigations have run from straightforward patent and copyright claims to more novel claims revolving around the protection of data transmissions over broadcaster television signals. He has litigated a variety of mechanical and electrical patent disputes for Sharp Corporation, Sony, Salton, Inc., Sara Lee, American Express and Juno Lighting. He has litigated hundreds of damage and valuation claims for small and large companies, tangible and intangible assets. He has a special competence in the litigation of reasonable royalties and lost profits for intellectual property intangibles. In the antitrust and franchising area, he has played a leading role in assisting the Chicago Tribune, the Orlando Sentinel, the Eastman Kodak Co., the G. Heileman Brewing Co., and affiliates of The Prudential in restructuring their systems for the delivery of products and services to the public. He regularly handles libel, privacy and copyright matters for the Chicago Tribune Company and other publishers. He served as Chicago litigation counsel for record companies (Sony Music, and A&M Records) and for recording stars (Michael Jackson and the C&C Music Factory).
Prof. Memberships: Member of the firm's Management Committee.
Personal: University of Wisconsin, JD, 1974, Order of the Coif, Articles Editor-'Wisconsin Law Review', Beloit College, BA 1971, Phi Beta Kappa.

KLEVORN, Andrew
Eimer Stahl Klevorn & Solberg, Chicago 312 660 7676
aklevorn@EimerStahl.com
Recommended in Antitrust

Specialization: Antitrust litigator with broad trial experience. His practice spans a wide variety of issues, including the defense of class actions, grand jury investigations, counseling firms with respect to proposed acquisitions and arbitrations, and representation of clients before the Federal Trade Commission and the United States Department of Justice. He has represented a number of leading firms, including, among others, Kimberly-Clark Corporation, R.R. Donnelley & Sons Company, Holcim (US), Inc. and CITGO Petroleum Corporation.
Prof. Memberships: American Bar Asso-

ILLINOIS

ciation, Litigation and Antitrust Sections; Chicago Bar Association.
Career: Admitted to the Illinois Bar, 1987. Member of the trial bar of the United States District Court for the Northern District of Illinois. Partner at *Sidley & Austin*, 1994-2000.
Publications: He has authored a variety of articles in various newspapers and journals, including the 'Wall Street Journal' and the 'National Law Journal', concerning antitrust and other legal issues.
Personal: Born: March 23, 1961. Received his JD, magna cum laude, from the University of Michigan, 1986. Received his AB, with honors, from the University of Chicago, 1983 (economics).

KOHN, Richard
Goldberg, Kohn, Bell, Black, Rosenbloom & Moritz, Ltd, Chicago 312 201 4000
Recommended in Banking & Finance

KOZAK, John
Leydig, Voit & Mayer, Ltd, Chicago
312 616 5600
Recommended in Intellectual Property

KRUEGER, Herbert W
Mayer, Brown, Rowe & Maw, Chicago
312 701 7194
hkrueger@mayerbrownrowe.com
Recommended in Real Estate
Specialization: Advises on the structuring of real estate, private equity and other investment funds. Represents ERISA and governmental pension plans and other institutional investors with respect to investments in such funds. Advises investment managers with respect to the application of the ERISA fiduciary and prohibited transaction rules and tax treatment of ERISA and governmental pension plans and other institutional investors. Represents executives and corporations on employment issues and executive compensation. Represents corporations, trustees, and service providers in fiduciary, administrative, and compliance matters with the Internal Revenue Service, the Department of Labor, and the Pension Benefit Guaranty Corporation.
Prof. Memberships: Pension Real Estate Association Chairman, Governmental Affairs Committee (1995-97). National Advisory Board, NYU Real Estate Institute Pension Fund Investment in Real Estate Annual Conferences (1992-95).
Career: Joined *Mayer, Brown, Rowe & Maw*, Chicago, 1975; became partner, 1981. University of Miami, School of Law Instructor, 1974-75 (Federal Income Tax and International Law).
Publications: Author/Co-Author: 'Investments by US Pension Plans, A Tax and Regulatory Overview', Proceedings of the Canadian Tax Foundation Corporate Management Tax Conference, 1995. 'The Conversion of Common and Collective Trust Funds to Mutual Funds - ERISA, Tax and Bank Regulatory Issues', Proceedings of California Bankers Association, 26th Annual Bank Counsel Seminar, April 1993. 'Reconciling Performance Fees for Pension Fund Real Estate Managers With ERISA', 20 Real Estate Review 4, 17 Winter 1991.
Personal: Born 20 April 1948. University of Chicago, JD, 1974. University of Wisconsin, BA, 1970. Chicago Children's Museum, Director and former Treasurer. Illinois Study Commission on Public Pension Investment Policies, 1981-82 (Commission appointed by Governor Thompson to review state pension fund investment authority and practice; Final Report published March, 1982); Chairman, Committee on Fiduciary Standards.

KUNKEL, William
Skadden, Arps, Slate, Meagher & Flom LLP & Affiliates, Chicago 312 407 0820
wkunkel@skadden.com
Recommended in Corporate/M&A
Specialization: Partner, Chicago. Represents companies in mergers, stock and asset acquisitions and divestitures, takeovers (negotiated and contested), leveraged buyouts, venture capital transactions, restructurings, joint ventures and other strategic alliances, debt and equity underwritings and private placements (representing companies issuing securities and investment banking firms acting as underwriters or placement agents).
Career: JD, Harvard Law School, 1981 (cum laude; Editor-in-Chief, Harvard Environmental Law Review); BS, Creighton University, 1978.

KURTZON, Michael S
Schwartz, Cooper, Greenberger & Krauss, Chartered, Chicago
312 346 1300
mkurtzon@scgk.com
Recommended in Real Estate
Specialization: Principal at *Schwartz, Cooper, Greenberger & Krauss, Chartered*. Chairman of the firm's Real Estate Department, represents major banks and other financial institutions and borrowers in complex financing transactions on a national basis, developers of residential and mixed-use projects and purchasers and sellers of commercial real estate developments including hotels, shopping centers and office buildings.
Prof. Memberships: Fellow: American College of Real Estate Lawyers. Member: American Bar Association, Chicago Bar Association and Illinois State Bar Association.
Publications: Has published various articles and materials for the Illinois Institute of Continuing Legal Education, Community Associations Institute and Chicago Bar Association.
Personal: Born: 1947. Cornell University AB 1969; University of Chicago Law School JD 1973.

LABATE, Robert
Holland & Knight LLP, Chicago
312 263 3600
robert.labate@hklaw.com
Recommended in Media & Entertainment
Specialization: Partner in the Litigation Department, with a transactional practice that includes the development, financing and distribution of feature and documentary films. He represents entertainment companies, screenwriters, bestselling authors, talent agencies and actors in a broad spectrum of contract, financing, distribution, copyright and right of publicity issues. Among his film clients are Kartemquin Educational Films, the award-winning producer of documentary films such as 'Hoop Dreams', 'Stevie' and 'Refrigerator Mothers'. He frequently speaks and writes on entertainment law issues. His law and entertainment, column has appeared in lquote PerformInkrquote for the past four years and he is co-creator of an annual, five-part seminar series, 'The Business of Independent Film Production', which provides information on legal and business aspects of independent film production.

LANGAN, J Andrew
Kirkland & Ellis, Chicago 312 861 2064
andrew_langan@chicago.kirkland.com
Recommended in Antitrust
Specialization: Experience as litigation and trial counsel in commercial, antitrust, and products liability cases including class actions. He has been principal counsel to major corporate clients in high-stakes class actions alleging violations of the antitrust laws, as well as class actions alleging products liability, mass tort and breach of warranty. Has also been principal counsel in high-profile merger investigations and related litigation. He has tried, as lead counsel, seven jury trials, and has been involved in numerous other contested proceedings and appeals.
Personal: University of Illinois at Urbana-Champaign, AB, 1979; Harvard Law School, JD, 1982.

LATIMER, Kenneth
Duane Morris LLP, Chicago
312 499 6700
Recommended in Banking & Finance

LAURIE, Ty
Schiff Hardin & Waite, Chicago
312 258 5500
Recommended in Construction

LEDUC, André
Skadden, Arps, Slate, Meagher & Flom LLP & Affiliates, Chicago 312 407 0770
aleduc@skadden.com
Recommended in Tax
Specialization: Partner, Chicago. Specializes in tax planning for financially distressed corporations, both inside and outside bankruptcy. Also advises on, and designs, tax-advantaged financial products and represents equity investors and financial intermediaries in the leveraged leasing industry. Clients include Comdisco, Inc., Safety-Kleen Corporation, National Steel Corporation, Grove Worldwide LLC, US Airways Group, Inc. and The Goldman Sachs Group, Inc.
Prof. Memberships: American Law Institute Federal Income Tax Advisory Group, 1987-95; Adjunct Professor of Law, Graduate Tax Program, Chicago-Kent College of Law, 1985-90; 1998-present.
Career: Princeton University, AB, summa cum laude, 1975; Harvard Law School, JD, cum laude, 1978; Advisory Council of the Princeton University Department of History, 1980-present.

LEMEIN, Gregg D
Baker & McKenzie, Chicago
312 861 8013
gregg.d.lemein@bakernet.com
Recommended in Tax
Specialization: US federal income taxation of corporations, with emphasis on international tax issues. Extensive experience in international tax planning, transfer pricing and tax controversies before the IRS and in court.
Prof. Memberships: American Bar Association Tax Section.
Career: Joined *Baker & McKenzie* in 1976 and became a partner in 1983.
Publications: Numerous published articles.
Personal: Born February 2, 1950. Northwestern University Law School, JD, magna cum laude, Order of the Coif (1976); Kellogg Graduate School of Management, Northwestern University, MM, with distinction (1976); and University of Illinois, BS, with high honors (1972).

LERMAN, Bradley
Winston & Strawn, Chicago
312 558 7492
blerman@winston.com
Recommended in Litigation
Specialization: White collar criminal defense, complex commercial litigation, corporate investigations.
Career: Joined firm as partner, 1998. Associate Independent Counsel, Madison Guaranty S&L Investigation, Whitewater Investigation, 1994-96; Assistant US Attorney, Northern District of Illinois, 1986-94.
Personal: Yale University, BA in Economics, summa cum laude, 1978, Phi Beta Kappa; Harvard Law School, JD, cum laude, 1981.

LEVIN, Jack S
Kirkland & Ellis, Chicago 312 861 2004
jack.levin@kirkland.com
Recommended in Corporate/M&A, Tax
Specialization: Practice concentrates on complex business transactions, including mergers, acquisitions, buyouts, private equity/venture capital investing, private

equity fund formations, debt and equity restructurings, and executive compensation, emphasizing on tax, corporate, SEC, and structuring aspects, handling transactions ranging in size from several million dollars to over $1 billion.
Personal: Northwestern University School of Business, BS, 1958; Harvard Law School, LLB, 1961 (ranking 1st in class of 500 and serving as officer of 'Harvard Law Review'). CPA and winner of Illinois gold medal. Teaches at Harvard and University of Chicago Law Schools. Author of five books on M&A and private equity.

LINKLATER, Joe
Baker & McKenzie, Chicago
312 861 2794
wjl@bakernet.com
Recommended in Litigation
Specialization: Practice involves criminal and complex civil litigation.
Prof. Memberships: American College of Trial Lawyers, Fellow; American Board of Criminal Lawyers, Fellow; American Bar Association, White Collar Crime Committee, Criminal Justice Section; Chicago Bar Association (President 2000-01); Illinois, California, Colorado, Seventh Circuit and Federal Bar Associations; National Association of Criminal Defense Lawyers; The Chicago Inn of Court, Master; The Wong Sun Society of San Francisco, International Proctor; World's Leading White Collar Crime Lawyers (Euromoney).
Career: Admitted in Illinois, California, Colorado and various federal District Courts and Court of Appeals.

LIPTON, Richard
Baker & McKenzie, Chicago
312 861 7590
richard.m.lipton@bakernet.com
Recommended in Tax
Specialization: Advises on partnerships, LLCs, other pass-through entities, and real estate transactions for multinational corporations and major owners and investors in real estate.
Prof. Memberships: Member of Chicago Bar Association (Federal Taxation Committee, Chair, 1991-92) and American Bar Association (section of taxation: Chair, 2001-02).
Career: Admitted to Illinois Bar and US Tax Court in 1977, District of Columbia, 1978; and US Court of Federal Claims, 1980.
Publications: Contributor and editor to the 'Journal of Taxation'; 'Journal of Pass-Through Entities'; 'Journal of Real Estate Taxation'. Co-author of two treatises. Author of 100+ articles on partnership and real estate taxation.

LITWIN, Stuart M
Mayer, Brown, Rowe & Maw, Chicago
312 701 7373
slitwin@mayerbrownrowe.com
Recommended in Banking & Finance
Specialization: Leading specialist in the securitisation and financing of auto leases, auto loans, equipment leases, dealer floor plan receivables, catastrophic and residual value risk and the creation of asset-backed securities for money market funds. Represents originators, investment banks, commercial banks, asset-backed commercial paper conduits and investors (including money market and other mutual funds) in public and private US and international asset-backed securities transactions. Experience in the securitisation of virtually all asset types.
Prof. Memberships: Former Chairman of Securities Law Committee and Corporate Control Subcommittee, Chicago Bar Association.
Career: Joined *Mayer, Brown, Rowe & Maw* in 1985 and became partner in 1994.
Publications: Author of 'Equipment and Auto Lease Financing: Securitization, Leveraged Leasing and Titling Trusts' (Aspen Law & Business, 2000); 'Equipment and Auto Lease Securitization', Chapter 30 of Equipment Leasing — Leveraged Leasing, Practising Law Institute, 4th Ed., 2000.
Personal: Born 17 June 1959. JD, cum laude, and MBA from University of Chicago in 1985. Certified Public Accountant, Illinois, 1981 (Winner of Elijah Watt Sells Award on Uniform CPA Examination). BS, summa cum laude and Bronze Tablet, from the University of Illinois in 1981. President of the Chicago Lawyers Committee for Civil Rights Under Law President, 1999-2000.

LIVINGSTON, Theodore A
Mayer, Brown, Rowe & Maw, Chicago
312 701 7180
tlivingston@mayerbrown.com
Recommended in Communications
Specialization: Specializes in telecommunications and commercial litigation. Lead counsel for Ameritech Corp. in regulatory and antitrust litigation under the Telecommunications Act of 1996. Represents BellSouth in antitrust litigation under the 1996 Act. Has tried and argued cases in state and federal courts throughout the US.
Prof. Memberships: American Bar Association: Administrative Law and Regulatory Practice Section; Antitrust Law Section; Business Law Section; Communications Law Forum; Dispute Resolution Section; Litigation Section; Business Torts Committee of Litigation Section; Public Utilities, Communications and Transportation Law Section; US District Court for the Northern District of Illinois, 1973; US Supreme Court; US Court of Appeals for the Seventh Circuit, 1975; Various other US courts of appeals and district courts.
Career: Joined *Mayer, Brown, Rowe & Maw*, 1973; became partner, 1980.

Personal: Born 21 July 1946. University of Kansas, JD, 1973; Order of the Coif; Law Review. McPherson College, BA, summa cum laude, 1969.

LOOMAN, James
Sidley Austin Brown & Wood, Chicago
312 853 7000
Recommended in Banking & Finance

LOPATKA, Kenneth
Matkov Salzman Madoff & Gunn, Chicago 312 332 0777
Recommended in Employment

LOWINGER, Frederick C
Sidley Austin Brown & Wood, Chicago
312 853 7000
Recommended in Corporate/M&A

LUBIN, Donald G
Sonnenschein Nath & Rosenthal, Chicago 312 876 8007
dlubin@sonnenschein.com
Recommended in Corporate/M&A
Specialization: Counsels Boards and management of public and private companies on corporate restructurings, takeover defence, joint ventures, corporate governance and mergers and acquisitions. Lead counsel to Sears in its corporate restructuring. Regularly advises other public companies, including Grainger, GUS, Allstate, McDonald's and Molex. Represented committees of independent directors of AON, Focal, Exide, and Wrigley. Lead counsel in GUS take over of Metromail, Safety-Kleen takeover, merger of 360'b0 Communications and Alltel, the sale of Searle to Monsanto, the sale of Holiday Inn's International to Bass, the acquisition of Merrill Lynch Realty by Prudential; advised Lazard in Kraft/Philip Morris transaction. Serves on McDonald's Board, its Executive Committee, Finance Committee and Nominating and Corporate Governance Committee. Serves on Molex Board.
Prof. Memberships: Lawyer's Club, Commercial Club (Executive Committee), Civic Committee (Steering Committee).
Career: Joined *Sonnenschein* in 1957. Chairman of firm 1991-96.
Personal: University of Pennsylvania, BS, 1954; Harvard Law School, LLB, 1957. Chairman, Chicago Metropolis 2020, Trustee, Rush-Presbyterian-St. Luke's Medical Center; former Director, National Museum of American History; Chairman, Anchor Cross Society; former Chairman, Ravinia Festival Association, Highland Park Hospital; Life Trustee, Chicago Symphony Orchestra; former Director, Smithsonian Institution; former member Board of Overseers, Faculty of Arts & Sciences, University of Pennsylvania.

LURIE, Paul
Schiff Hardin & Waite, Chicago
312 258 5500
Recommended in Construction

LUSCOMBE II, George A
Mayer, Brown, Rowe & Maw, Chicago
312 701 7099
gluscombe@mayerbrownrowe.com
Recommended in Tax
Specialization: Partner in Corporate Taxation practice in Chicago. Structures acquisitions and divestitures, taxable and tax-free, business joint ventures, leveraged buyouts, and leasing transactions. Structures partnership, joint venture, and limited liability company vehicles for real estate, natural resources, and new technologies. Structures investment vehicles and companies in various industries, including real estate acquisitions for pension plan trusts. Represents corporations, partnerships, and limited liability companies in matters related to general corporate, partnership, real estate and natural resources taxation.
Prof. Memberships: Admitted to practice in the District of Columbia, 1972, and Illinois, 1969. Adjunct Professor of Taxation, Illinois Institute of Technology/Chicago-Kent College of Law, 1987-93. Member of American Bar Association, Section of Taxation; former Chairman, Committee on Capital Recovery and Leasing; former Editor, Tax Notes column, American Bar Association Journal; and former Chairman of Illinois State Bar Association, Council of Federal Tax Section.
Career: Served in Office of Chief Counsel, Internal Revenue Service, Legislation and Regulations Division, Washington, DC, from 1969-73. Joined *Mayer, Brown, Rowe & Maw* in 1973 and became partner in 1976.
Publications: Author of presentations for Illinois Institute for Continuing Legal Education, American Bar Association, University of Chicago Tax Institute, Tulane Tax Institute, and Canadian Petroleum Tax Society and Canadian Property Forum.
Personal: Born 22 October 1944. Earned LLM, George Washington University in 1972. Awarded JD and Order of the Coif University of Illinois in 1969, and BS with honors, University of Illinois, in 1966. Certified Public Accountant, Illinois, 1966.

LYMAN, Bill
Bedrava & Lyman, Oak Brook
630 575 0020
Recommended in Construction

LYNCH, James M
Winston & Strawn, Chicago
312 558 5935
jlynch@winston.com
Recommended in Tax
Specialization: Partner, corporate department, Chicago office. Practice focuses on US and international corporate and tax aspects of mergers and acquisitions, corporate taxation and tax controversies.
Prof. Memberships: Member, American

ILLINOIS   LEADERS

Bar Association and Chicago Bar Association, American Institute of Certified Public Accountants, American College of Tax Counsel.
Career: Received an LLM from Georgetown University, JD from John Marshall School, and a Bachelor of Science in Business Administration from Xavier University in Cincinnati, Ohio, and is a Certified Public Accountant. Joined *Winston & Strawn* in 2000.

MACBRIDE, Owen
Schiff Hardin & Waite, Chicago
312 258 5500
Recommended in Communications, Energy

MACHLIN, Barry N
Mayer, Brown, Rowe & Maw, Chicago
312 701 8574
bmachlin@mayerbrownrowe.com
Recommended in Projects
Specialization: Partner and Co-Chair of Global Project Finance practice. Represents international banks and financial institutions and multilateral and bilateral official lending agencies. Transactions include the $226 million San Fernando gas pipeline project (Mexico), the $440 million Baijio power project (Mexico), the $800 million Quezon power project (Philippines), a CDMA telecom upgrade financing in Mexico, the $2.5 billion Paiton I project (Indonesia), and the Khalda and Qarun oil concession developments (Egypt). Also represents banks and financial institutions in syndicated lending and Eurodollar transactions, sovereigns, state-owned enterprises and investors in privatisation and restructuring matters, and parties in cross-border investment and financial transactions. Widely experienced in representing clients in connection with transactions throughout Europe, Asia and the Middle East.
Prof. Memberships: Admitted to practice in Massachusetts (1985); the District of Columbia (1987); Illinois (2000) and New York (2000).
Career: Joined *Mayer, Brown, Rowe & Maw* as a partner in 1997, serving first in Washington, DC, and currently in Chicago. Partner (first associate) with *White & Case*, Washington, DC, and London, from 1985 to 1997.
Publications: Speaking engagements have included 'Building Infrastructure Projects in Developing Markets' at the Practising Law Institute, 'Project Finance' at the International Bar Association, and 'Venture Capital and Private Equity Investments in Emerging Markets' at the Harvard International Development Conference.
Personal: Born 14 July 1959. Earned JD from Harvard Law School in 1985 and BA, summa cum laude, from Brandeis University in 1982, where was elected to Phi Beta Kappa.

MALLOY, Timothy J
McAndrews, Held & Malloy, Ltd, Chicago
312 775 8000
tmalloy@mhmlaw.com
Recommended in Intellectual Property
Specialization: He has litigated cases on behalf of The Laitram Corporation against IBM involving control and processing circuitry for a high-speed LED printer; on behalf of Ford Motor Company involving an electronic control for an intermittent windshield wiper; on behalf of The Goodyear Tire & Rubber Company involving feedback control systems for aircraft antiskid brake control; on behalf of Cardiac Pacemakers, Inc. involving various electronic and mechanical patents for pacemakers and defibrillators; on behalf of General Foods Corporation involving air cushion bulkheads for railway cars; on behalf of Baxter Corporation involving dialysis controls; on behalf of Advanced Cardiovascular Systems, Inc. involving balloon angioplasty; and on behalf of Stryker Corporation involving surgical instruments and arthroscopy. His arbitration victory of $166 million on behalf of Guidant Corporation was confirmed by the Northern District of California on 23 May 2002 (Civil Action No. 99-05393).
Prof. Memberships: American Bar Association, Illinois Bar Association, American Intellectual Property Law Association, Barristers of the Patent Law.
Career: Began trial practice in patent litigation 1969, partner 1974. Formed *McAndrews, Held & Malloy, Ltd.* with six attorneys in 1988. Continued growing the firm to over seventy attorneys currently in practice at MH&M.
Publications: (1) Practicing Law Institute (PLI): 'Organization, Vendor Support, and Cost Control', (Chapter 6, p. 6-1 - May 2002); 'Patents, Copyrights, Trademarks, And Literary Property, Course Handbook Series, No. G-350'; 'The Ongoing Evolution Of The Law of Patent Damages', (Chapter 6, p. 279 - 8 September 1992); 'Patent Damages Revisited: Recent Issues Before The Federal Circuit', (Chapter 27, p. 277 - 1 October 1994); 'Patents, Copyrights, Trademarks, And Literary Property, Course Handbook Series, No. G-397'; 'Rite-Hite: Has The Federal Circuit Expanded The Legal Limits On Damages Awarded In Patent Infringement Actions?', (Chapter 11, p. 515 - 1995); 'Patents, Copyrights, Trademarks, And Literary Property, Course Handbook Series, No. G-424'; 'Infringement And Equivalents-Has There Been A Significant Change?', (Chapter 28, p. 445 - 1996); 'Patents, Copyrights, Trademarks, And Literary Property, Course Handbook Series, No. G-457';(2) The Metropolitan Corporate Counsel: 'An Alternative For Righting The Wrongs Of An Arbitration Panel In IP Disputes', (Vol. 10, No. 6 - June 2002); 'Intellectual Property Disputes And Arbitration', (Vol. 10, No. 9 - September 2002); 'A Modified Jury Trial Schedule: A Win-Win-Win Situation', (Vol. 10, No. 11, p. 29 - November 2002) (3) Intellectual Property Today: 'The Shape Of Things Past And Things To Come', (Vol. 7, No. 1, p. 6 - January 2000).
Personal: Received from the University of Notre Dame a JD in 1969 and a BS in electrical engineering in 1966.

MARX, David
McDermott, Will & Emery, Chicago
312 984 7668
dmarx@mwe.com
Recommended in Antitrust
Specialization: Partner in the Litigation Department. Concentrates practice in civil and criminal antitrust litigation and counseling, and trade regulation matters. Responsible for antitrust practice in Chicago office. Serves corporate and health care industry clients, and individuals who are the subjects or targets of investigations or enforcement proceedings initiated by federal or state antitrust agencies, and in private civil litigation.
Prof. Memberships: Member of the American Bar Association, including its antitrust and litigation sections and a past chair of the Antitrust Committee of the Chicago Bar Association and the former chair of the Antitrust Law Committee of the American Health Lawyers Association.
Career: Admitted to the Illinois and New York bars, the Supreme Court of the United States, the US Court of Appeals for the District of Columbia Circuit, and the 3rd, 7th and 8th Circuit Courts of Appeals. Adjunct professor at Loyola University Chciago School of Law (teaching antitrust in the health care field).

MASCHERIN, Terri
Jenner & Block, Chicago 312 923 2799
tmascherin@jenner.com
Recommended in Communications
Specialization: Partner in the telecommunications, litigation, antitrust and trade regulation, bankruptcy, intellectual property and technology law, and trade secrets practices. Represents clients in trials, appeals and regulatory appeals and has first-chaired jury and bench trials and argued appeals in both state and federal court. Acts as lead counsel for WorldCom in several actions under the Telecommunications Act of 1996, and counsels telecommunications providers in matters involving compliance with FCC detariffing orders.
Prof. Memberships: American Bar Association and Chicago Bar Association (Board of Managers).
Career: Admitted to Illinois Bar (1984).
Personal: Received a JD (cum laude) from Northwestern University in 1984.

MASON, David
Goldberg, Kohn, Bell, Black, Rosenbloom & Moritz, Ltd, Chicago 312 201 4000
Recommended in Banking & Finance

MATIS, Nina
Katten Muchin Zavis Rosenman, Chicago 312 902 5560
Nina.Matis@kmzr.com
Recommended in Real Estate
Specialization: Chair of Real Estate Practice. Concentrates heavily in all areas of commercial real estate development and acquisition (including residential, office, retail, hotel and mixed use developments), financing (including rated and structured financing) and partnership law. Extensive experience in the organization and investment activities of debt and equity funds comprised of pension funds and of domestic and foreign investors and in investment and organizational matters relating to REITS.
Prof. Memberships: Member of the American College of Real Estate Lawyers, Ely Chapter of Lambda Alpha International, Chicago Finance Exchange, Urban Land Institute, REFF, Chicago Real Estate Executive Women, The Chicago Network and The Economic Club of Chicago.
Career: Member of the firm's Executive Committee and the Board of Directors. Served as Adjunct Professor at Northwestern University School of Law teaching Real Estate Transactions. In addition, she is General Counsel and Executive Vice President to iStar Financial Inc. and a member of the Board of Directors of New Plan.
Personal: Graduated from Smith College, Northampton, Massachusetts with a BA (Honors) in Political Science and holds a law degree from New York University School of Law (1972). Listed in leading publications including Sterling's 'Who's Who' .

MATTSON, Stephen J
Mayer, Brown, Rowe & Maw, Chicago
312 701 7082
smattson@mayerbrownrowe.com
Recommended in Energy
Specialization: Advises gas, telecommunications, industry associations, sewer and water utilities, and oil and products pipelines before state regulatory agencies in all proceedings, including ratemaking, certificate, investigations, rulemaking and eminent domain cases. Represents public utilities and others in appeals from orders of state regulatory agencies, cases involving gross receipts taxes, general litigation and eminent domain proceedings. Advises public utilities and others on all regulatory aspects of functioning as, or dealing with, public utilities and related legal matters.
Prof. Memberships: American Bar Association, Section of Public Utility, Communications and Transportation Law, Vice-Chair, Gas.
Career: Joined *Mayer, Brown, Rowe & Maw*, 1970; became partner, 1978. US Army (missile officer), 1965-67.
Publications: Lecturer, seminars spon-

sored by the Institute of Gas Technology, the Center for Regulatory Studies, Gas Mart, the Midwest Regional Business and Economics Utilities Conference, the Illinois State Bar Association and the Chicago Bar Association.
Personal: Born 11 October 1943. University of Illinois College of Law, JD, cum laude, 1970; Order of the Coif; Member and Articles Editor, Law Review. University of Illinois, BA, cum laude, 1965.

MCANDREWS, George
McAndrews, Held & Malloy, Ltd, Chicago
312 775 8000
Recommended in Intellectual Property

MCCAREINS, Mark
Winston & Strawn, Chicago
312 558 5902
rmccareins@winston.com
Recommended in Antitrust

Specialization: Antitrust, trade regulation, intellectual property, and unfair competition litigation.
Prof. Memberships: American Bar Association; American Inns of Court; American Bar Foundation.
Career: Joined firm as associate, 1981. Partner, 1988. Member, Library Committee; Litigation Department Advisory Committee.
Publications: Senior Editor, Handbook on Civil Discovery, American Bar Association, Antitrust Section, 2001; Board of Editors, The Health Care and Antitrust Manual, 1994-2001. Author: Report of the Task Force on Civil Ligitation, American Bar Association, Section on Antitrust Law, September 2001; Evaluating Secular/Non-Secular Hospital Affiliations: Lessons from Poughkeepsie, Antitrust Health Care Chronicle, Vol. 14, No. 3, Fall 2000.
Personal: Northwestern University, BA, with honors, 1978; Washington University, JD, 1981, Editor-in-Chief, Washington University Law Quarterly.

MCCULLOUGH, Joe
Lovells, Chicago 312 832 4400
Recommended in Insurance

MCLAUGHLIN, Mark T
Mayer, Brown, Rowe & Maw, Chicago
312 701 7066
mmclaughlin@mayerbrownrowe.com
Recommended in Antitrust

Specialization: Litigation and counseling on antitrust and other distribution matters. Has litigated substantial antitrust cases involving a variety of industries and issues, including monopolization claims, challenges to acquisitions, and group boycott, exclusive dealing, sham litigation and price discrimination claims, and claims involving practices in foreign commerce. Chicago Office Practice Leader for litigation.
Prof. Memberships: Part-time Faculty, Loyola University of Chicago School of Law (antitrust courses), 1983, 1986,
1988-90. Governing Committee, ABA Forum on Franchising, 1992-95. ABA Section of Antitrust Law, Chair, Membership Committee, 1993-96. American Bar Association, Section of Antitrust Law, Forum on Franchising. Chicago Bar Association. Commercial Arbitration Panel. American Arbitration Association. Illinois, 1978. US District Court for the Northern District of Illinois and Trial Bar, 1978. US Court of Appeals for the Seventh and Eleventh Circuits, 1982. US District Court for the Central District of Illinois, 1992. US District Court for the Eastern District of Wisconsin, 1992.
Career: Joined *Mayer, Brown, Rowe & Maw* in 1978; became partner, 1985.
Personal: Born 20 April 1953. University of Notre Dame, JD, magna cum laude, 1978; Law Review. University of Notre Dame, BA, summa cum laude, 1975. Board of Directors, American Diabetes Association, Northern Illinois Affiliate, Inc., 1985-94; Chairman, 1990-92.

MCMAHON, Thomas
Sidley Austin Brown & Wood, Chicago
312 853 7000
Recommended in Environment

MCMENAMIN, J Robert
McDermott, Will & Emery, Chicago
312 984 3618
rmcmenamin@mwe.com
Recommended in Banking & Finance

Specialization: Partner in the corporate department of *McDermott, Will & Emery's* Chicago office. Has 30 years' experience in banking, finance, commercial and corporate law. Experience includes syndicated loans, project financing, leveraged acquisition financing, capital financing, asset-based lending, subordinated debt and mezzanine financing, ESOP lending, securitisation, credit enhancement, workouts and restructurings, both in the private and public markets.
Prof. Memberships: American Bar Association; The Lawyers Club of Chicago and The Economic Club of Chicago. Vice president and director of The Lawyers Club of Chicago. Past chairman of the Advisory Board of Holy Trinity High School.
Career: Received bachelor's degree from the University of Notre Dame in 1968 and graduated from Notre Dame Law School in 1971. Clerked in the US Court of Appeals for the 7th Circuit during 1971-72. Thereafter, practised law at *Mayer, Brown & Platt* until 1989, when joined *McDermott, Will & Emery*.

MEADOWS, Stanley
McDermott, Will & Emery, Chicago
312 984 7570
smeadows@mwe.com
Recommended in Corporate/M&A

Specialization: Partner in corporate department and a member of the firm's corporate finance group. Focuses practice in public and private offering of securities, mergers and acquisitions, joint ventures and corporate restructuring. Has spent considerable time representing acquirers of financially distressed companies and lenders and debtors in negotiating debt restructuring for pharmaceutical, telecom and other technology companies in joint ventures, and insurance and energy companies in acquisitions, debt financing and public offerings. During the last year, has acted for purchasers of European telecom assets, a new pan-European web hosting business and several European manufacturing businesses, together with the associated financings. Has also represented professional sport franchises, including financing, arena and player issues and legislative matters.
Prof. Memberships: Member of the Illinois State Bar and the Florida State Bar.
Career: Admitted to the Illinois Bar in 1970. Received undergraduate degree from the University of Illinois in 1966 and JD from the University of Chicago Law School in 1970.

MEHLMAN, Mark
Sonnenschein Nath & Rosenthal, Chicago 312 876 8000
mmehlman@sonnenschein.com
Recommended in Real Estate

Specialization: Has a broad based real estate practice that includes real estate financing (including conduit lending), troubled loan workouts, real estate acquisitions and dispositions, and partnership and joint venture relationships. He has lectured frequently on various real estate topics, including real estate acquisitions, multi-property, multi-state loan transactions, troubled loan workouts and lessons learned by lenders as a result of their troubled loan experiences.
Prof. Memberships: He is a member of the Council of the Real Property and Probate Section of the American Bar Association and previously served as an Advisory Group Chairman of a number of financing related subcommittees. He is also a member of the American College of Real Estate Lawyers where he is a member of the Board of Governors and was recently asked to join the Anglo-American Real Property Institute and the National Conference of Lawyers and Certified Public Accountants. He is listed in many leading legal publications, at state, regional, national and global level.
Career: He serves on *Sonnenschein's* Policy and Planning Committee.
Personal: University of Michigan, LLB,
1973; Administrative Editor, 'University of Michigan Journal of Law'; Reform University of Illinois, BA, 1969.

MEITES, Thomas
Meites, Mulder, Burger & Mollica, Chicago 312 263 0272
Recommended in Employment

MENDELSOHN, David
Piper Rudnick, Chicago 312 368 7272
david.mendelsohn@piperrudnick.com
Recommended in Insurance

Specialization: Homeland security; corporate and securities; insurance and reinsurance.
Prof. Memberships: Associate of Fellows and Legal Scholars of the Center for International Legal Studies.
Career: Practices in the areas of general corporate, technology and e-commerce and insurer and reinsurer transactional and regulatory matters. He also counsels clients on compliance and information management matters, such as records management and retention, contracts management, money laundering, data privacy and security, E&O risk management and ethics.
Personal: JD, Chicago-Kent College of Law, Illinois Institute of Technology; Lancaster Gate School of Law; LLB, University College of London.

MENSCH, Linda
Linda S Mensch PC - Sole Practitioner, Chicago 312 922 2910
Recommended in Media & Entertainment

MENSIK, Michael
Baker & McKenzie, Chicago
312 861 8941
michael.s.mensik@bakernet.com
Recommended in Communications

Specialization: Focus: information technology; outsourcing; e-commerce. Advises companies on various aspects of their domestic and foreign operations, including technology transfer, intellectual property protection, antitrust issues, and tax planning. He counsels multinationals on how to structure their outsourcing arrangements, from BPO deals to vendor to vendor strategic alliances. He also helps technology and e-commerce companies go global via the internet or agents/distributors or other corporate vehicles (joint ventures and alliances).
Prof. Memberships: Global Coordinator *Baker & McKenzie* IT Practice; Editor, 'Global e-Law Alert'.
Career: Admitted in Illinois (1980).
Publications: Outsourcing Journal (4 articles, 2002); 'International Software Licensing', 'Software Localization' (Computer Lawyer 1997, 1991).

MIKVA, Mary
Abrahamson Vorachek & Mikva, Chicago 312 263 2698
Recommended in Employment

ILLINOIS LEADERS

MILLER, Lee I
Piper Rudnick, Chicago 312 368 4029
lee.miller@piperrudnick.com
Recommended in Real Estate
Specialization: Real estate.
Prof. Memberships: American College of Real Estate Lawyers.
Career: Co-Chair of the firm and concentrates his practice in commercial real estate and has represented clients in a wide range of commercial real estate transactions, including acquisitions and dispositions, portfolio acquisitions of properties and loans, complex financing, joint venture formation, syndications, construction contract negotiations, lease preparation, restructuring and workout of troubled real estate projects and real estate securitization and fund investment. Has lectured extensively before bar, trade and professional associations on a variety of topics.
Personal: JD, Georgetown University Law Center; BSBA, Georgetown University.

MISSNER, David
Piper Rudnick, Chicago 312 368 2170
david.missner@piperrudnick.com
Recommended in Insolvency
Specialization: Bankruptcy reorganization, commercial transactions and banking law.
Prof. Memberships: American Bar Association; Illinois State Bar Association; Chicago Bar Association.
Career: He is a frequent lecturer on banking and bankruptcy-related topics for the Chicago Bar Association, Illinois Institute for Continuing Legal Education and other professional and trade organizations.
Publications: 'Chapter 11', 'Representing the Debtor and Representing the Creditor with a Secured Claim', both published by Illinois Institute for a Continuing Legal Education.
Personal: BA degree, Miami University, Oxford, Ohio; JD Degree, Northwestern University School of Law. Interests include tennis, hiking and rafting.

MOLLICA, Paul
Meites, Mulder, Burger & Mollica, Chicago 312 263 0272
Recommended in Employment

MOLO, Steven
Winston & Strawn, Chicago
312 558 5978
smolo@winston.com
Recommended in Litigation
Specialization: Represents corporations and individuals in complex business litigation, as well as white-collar criminal matters, throughout the United States. Former prosecutor in Chicago and has tried many civil and criminal cases before juries, judges, administrative tribunals, and arbitral forums. His practice frequently includes the representation of companies in multi-party litigation involving parallel litigation in several courts. He has handled numerous class action claims in state and federal courts and is experienced in dealing with matters adjudicated through the MDL process. The British publication Euromoney named him in its list of 'The World's Leading White Collar Crime Lawyers'; and The Illinois Legal Times profiled him in its article, 'The Next Generation of Killer Litigators.' Crain's Chicago Business named him to its list of '40 Under 40' Chicago business leaders.
Prof. Memberships: Serves as adjunct professor at Northwestern University Law School. Member of the faculty of the National Institute for Trial Advocacy. Writes and lectures frequently on the subjects of trial practice, evidence, and corporate criminal liability. Fellow, American Academy of Appellate Lawyers. Past president, Chicago Inn of Court.
Career: Joined as an associate, 1986. Partner, 1989. Member of the firm's Executive Committee.
Publications: Co-author of the treatise Corporate Internal Investigations.
Personal: BS and JD from the University of Illinois.

MORAN, Patrick G
Sonnenschein Nath & Rosenthal, Chicago 312 876 8132
pmoran@sonnenschein.com
Recommended in Real Estate
Specialization: Partner in the Real Estate Group. He handles a wide variety of commercial real estate and related financing matters, with an emphasis on leasing, development and financing. He has worked extensively with major office landlords and tenants during his career in the development and leasing of more than 10 million square feet of office space. His current financing practice focuses on multistate secured and unsecured revolving credit loans to Reits and other real estate companies, as well as traditional project loans secured by office buildings, apartment projects, shopping centers, golf courses, hotels and mixed use projects.
Prof. Memberships: Member of the American College of Real Estate Lawyers.
Personal: Georgetown University, JD 1976, Harvard College, BA 1972.

MORRISON, Portia
Piper Rudnick, Chicago 312 368 4013
portia.morrison@piperrudnick.com
Recommended in Real Estate
Specialization: Real estate; lodging and timeshare; real estate finance.
Prof. Memberships: American College of Real Estate Lawyers.
Career: She represents investors, developers and lenders in multi-family, office, retail, hotel and industrial development and redevelopment projects; construction of infrastructure and buildings; sales and leasing activities; and construction and permanent financing. She has an extensive practice in real estate investment and finance, representing lenders, investors and borrowers, in structuring financing through traditional mortgage loans, joint venture formations, structured debt placements, mezzanine loans and other financing and investment mechanisms.
Personal: JD, University of Chicago; MA, University of Wisconsin; BA, Agnes Scott College.

MUENCH, John E
Mayer, Brown, Rowe & Maw, Chicago
312 701 7059
jmuench@mayerbrown.com
Recommended in Communications
Specialization: Litigation.
Prof. Memberships: Admitted in Illinois, 1976. US District Court for the Northern District of Illinois, 1976.
Career: Joined *Mayer, Brown, Rowe & Maw*, 1983; became partner, 1985. Assistant Professor of Law, University of Illinois College of Law, Champaign, 1978-83. Law Clerk to The Honorable John Paul Stevens, Associate Justice, Supreme Court of the United States, Washington, DC, 1977-78. Law Clerk to The Honorable Robert A Sprecher, US Court of Appeals for the Seventh Circuit, 1976-77.
Personal: Born 21 July 1948. Northwestern University School of law, JD, magna cum laude, 1976; Order of the Coif. College of the Holy Cross, AB, magna cum laude, 1970.

MULANEY, Charles
Skadden, Arps, Slate, Meagher & Flom LLP & Affiliates, Chicago 312 407 0500
cmulaney@skadden.com
Recommended in Corporate/M&A
Specialization: Partner, Chicago. Concentrates in mergers and acquisitions (both friendly and hostile), corporate financings (public and private), restructurings, and general corporate governance. Has advised clients on a wide range of corporate matters, including joint ventures, divestitures and spinoffs, and has represented issuers and underwriters in public and private securities offerings. Lecturer, Corporate Counsel Institute sponsored by Northwestern University School of Law. Member of the executive committee of the Ray Garrett, Jr. Corporate and Securities Law Institute.
Career: JD, Yale Law School, 1974 (Editor, Yale Law Journal); AB, Georgetown University, 1971 (summa cum laude); Law Clerk, The Honorable Judge Edward Weinfeld, Southern District of NY, 1974-75.

MUNCY, Dennis
Meyer Capel, Champaign
217 352 1800
Recommended in Communications

MUNITZ, Gerald
Goldberg, Kohn, Bell, Black, Rosenbloom & Moritz, Ltd, Chicago 312 201 4000
Recommended in Insolvency

MURPHY, Joseph
Meyer Capel, Champaign
217 352 1800
Recommended in Communications

MURRAY, Gregory
Winston & Strawn, Chicago
312 558 5669
gmurray@winston.com
Recommended in Banking & Finance
Specialization: Partner in the Corporate Department. Concentration in syndicated leveraged finance representing numerous prominent US and foreign lending institutions in a variety of senior and subordinated credit facilities, cross-border facilities and structured finance transactions. Extensive experience in structuring multi-tiered acquisition and tender facilities. In recent years has represented agent bank in financings aggregating in excess of US$40 billion.
Career: Joined *Winston & Strawn* as an associate in 1974. Elected as partner in 1980. Member of firm executive committee.

MURTAUGH, Christopher D
Winston & Strawn, Chicago
312 558 5798
cmurtaugh@winston.com
Recommended in Real Estate
Specialization: Chairman of real estate department. More than 25 years' experience focusing on commercial property acquisition and disposition, real estate development, and lending activities.
Prof. Memberships: Member of the American College of Real Estate Lawyers, Order of the Coif, Chicago, Illinois, Florida, and American Bar Associations. Member of the Urban Land Institute and International Council of Shopping Centers.
Career: Joined as associate, 1974. Partner, 1979. Member of the Compensation Committee, Insurance Committee, and the Billing and Collections Committee
Personal: University of Illinois, 1967. JD, University of Illinois College of Law, 1970.

MUTCHNIK, James
Kirkland & Ellis, Chicago 312 861 2350
james_mutchnik@chicago.kirkland.com
Recommended in Antitrust
Specialization: Represents corporate and individual clients in antitrust, white collar crime, commercial, bankruptcy, and patent litigation in federal and state courts throughout the United States and before a variety of federal and state investigative agencies. In the antitrust area, litigates various matters ranging from alleged price fixing to price discrimination and representing clients in dealing with the antitrust aspects of mergers, acquisitions and joint ventures. Counsels a wide range of small and large companies in diverse industries on pricing, marketing, distribution and dealer termination issues.

Personal: University of Pennsylvania, BS, May 1986. Northwestern University School of Law, JD, May 1989.

NAGELBERG, Howard
Barack Ferrazzano Kirschbaum Perlman & Nagelberg, Chicago 312 984 3100
Recommended in Real Estate

NAPOLITANO, Steven
Katten Muchin Zavis Rosenman, Chicago 312 902 5615
steven.napolitano@kmzr.com
Recommended in Corporate/M&A

Specialization: Partner and Co-Chair of Private Equity and Emerging Growth Companies Practice. National practice focused on representing private equity funds and emerging growth companies in connection with mergers, acquisitions, leveraged buyouts, venture capital financings, industry consolidations and corporate restructurings. Substantial experience with private equity transactions involving both private and public targets, including complex management sponsored 'going private' transactions and PIPE financings. Frequently represents equity funds, emerging-growth companies and senior management teams in connection with complex incentive compensation arrangements. Significant experience with private equity, M&A and venture capital transactions in the health care sector.

Prof. Memberships: American Bar Association, Association for Corporate Growth and The Executives' Club of Chicago, where he serves as a member of the Technology Committee. Serves on the Board of Directors of NovaMed Eyecare, Inc. (Nasdaq: NOVA) and is a member of the Limited Partner Advisory Board of Psilos Group Partners, II, a New York-based venture capital fund specializing in health care and new media investing. Serves on the Boards of Directors of the Malignant Hyperthermia Association of the United States (MHAUS) and United Cerebral Palsy of Chicago.

Career: Member of the *KMZ Rosenman* Board of Directors, Executive and Operating Committee, and Strategic Marketing Committee.

Personal: Received BA degree in Economics from the University of Notre Dame in 1981, where he was elected to the Omicron Epsilon Delta national economics society, and completed graduate work in Monetary Theory at the London School of Economics. He earned his JD degree from the Boston University School of Law in 1985, where he was a G Joseph Tauro Scholar, American Jurisprudence Award recipient and an Editor of the American Journal of Law and Medicine.

NATHAN KAHAN, Penny
Penny Nathan Kahan & Associates, Chicago 312 855 1660
Recommended in Employment

NICKLIN, Emily
Kirkland & Ellis, Chicago 312 861 2387
emily_nicklin@chicago.kirkland.com
Recommended in Litigation

Specialization: Has been lead trial counsel in cases (both individual and class action) in a number of areas including: professional liability for accountants and consultants, securities, contract, tort (including product liability and personal injury), employment discrimination, constitutional law and municipal law. Has been lead trial counsel in both jury and bench trials, as well as arbitrations, in various state and federal venues including Arkansas, California, Idaho, Illinois, Iowa, Michigan, Missouri, Nebraska, Nevada, New York, Pennsylvania, Texas, and Washington, DC.

Personal: University of Chicago, BA, 1975. University of Chicago, JD, 1977.

NIJMAN, Jennifer
Winston & Strawn, Chicago
312 558 5771
jnijman@winston.com
Recommended in Environment

Specialization: Enforcement-related issues, including common law liability and toxic tort, private cost recovery, and all aspects of the Superfund process; represents clients in permitting and siting, compliance issues, and transactions, including energy projects.

Prof. Memberships: President, Chicago Bar Association; American Bar Association, Environmental Litigation Committee; Illinois State Bar Association; Board Member, Public Interest Law Initiative, Center for Conflict Resolution (Certified mediator for the Center of Conflict Resolution); Member, Economic Club of Chicago.

Career: Joined as associate, 1994. Partner, 1995. Member, Diversity Committee; Member, Hiring Committee.

Publications: 'Environmental Law', Illinois Institute of Continuing Legal Education, Starting Points, April 2001; 'Coordination of a Large Environmental Permitting Effort', Natural Resources & Environment, Spring 2001 (winner of 2002 Burton Award for Legal Achievement)

Personal: University of Illinois, BA in Psychology, 1984; University of Chicago Law School, JD, 1987, The Legal Forum.

NIRO, Raymond
Niro, Scavone, Haller & Niro, Chicago
312 236 0733
Recommended in Intellectual Property

NOVAK, Theodore
Piper Rudnick, Chicago 312 368 4037
theodore.novak@piperrudnick.com
Recommended in Real Estate

Specialization: Real estate; governmental affairs, zoning, land use, public incentives and eminent domain.

Prof. Memberships: Member, American College of Real Estate Lawyers (ACREL).

Career: He has been instrumental in the acquisition, public financing, condemnation, rezoning and development of all types of property. He has extensive litigation experience in trial and appellate courts. He is a lecturer at the University of Chicago Law School and is an Adjunct Professor at Northwestern University School of Law, teaching a course on land use, zoning and condemnation.

Personal: JD, Chicago-Kent College of Law, Illinois Institute of Technology; BS, University of Illinois.

NYHAN, Lawrence
Sidley Austin Brown & Wood, Chicago
312 853 7000
Recommended in Insolvency

O'BRIEN, Richard
Sidley Austin Brown & Wood, Chicago
312 853 7000
Recommended in Media & Entertainment

OLIAN, Robert
Sidley Austin Brown & Wood, Chicago
312 853 7000
Recommended in Environment

O'REILLY, Peter
Hall Dickler Kent Goldstein & Wood LLP, Chicago 312 819 4170
Recommended in Media & Entertainment

OSBORNE, Robert Stephen
Jenner & Block, Chicago 312 923 2690
rosborne@jenner.com
Recommended in Corporate/M&A

Specialization: Chairs corporate practice. Has extensive experience in securities transactions, mergers and acquisitions and related transactions, including spin-offs by General Motors of EDS, the defence business of Hughes Aircraft and Delphi Automotive Systems. Acted for several large public companies in cross-border acquisitions, joint ventures and securities offerings. Represented GM in several of the world's largest public offerings of equity securities.

Career: Admitted to Illinois bar (1979). Former *Kirkland & Ellis* partner and management committee member. Joined *Jenner & Block* in 2002. General Counsel of Lands' End, 1986-95.

Personal: Received a JD (magna cum laude) from Harvard Law School in 1979.

PARSONS, David
Littler Mendelson, Chicago
312 372 5520
dparsons@littler.com
Recommended in Employment

Specialization: Shareholder in the employment litigation department. He has tried a significant number of jury cases to favorable verdicts for his clients, including, Whirlpool Corporation, Baxter Healthcare and International Truck and Engine Corporation. He has significant class action experience and works extensively in the unfair competition arena, including, enforcing/defending lawsuits involving alleged breaches of noncompete and confidentiality provisions in employment agreements.

Prof. Memberships: The American Bar Association (Trial Practice Committee, Litigation Section and Labor and Employment Law Section), the Defense Research Institute and the Seventh Circuit Bar Association.

Career: Prior to joining *Littler Mendelson*, he was Chairperson of the Employment Practice Group at *Wildman, Harrold, Allen & Dixon*, and before that, he was founding partner of *Matkov, Griffin, Parsons, Salzman and Madoff*, an employment and labor boutique firm in Chicago. He also was at *Seyfarth, Shaw, Fairweather and Geraldson* (where he began his legal career) for 10 years, the last four years as a partner. He is admitted to practice before the Supreme Court of Illinois; the United States Supreme Court; the United States Courts of Appeal for the Fourth, Fifth, Sixth, Seventh, Eighth, and Eleventh Circuits; the United States District Court for the Northern District of Illinois (including its trial bar); and the United States District Courts for the Central District of Illinois, the District of Columbia, the Northern District of Indiana, the Southern District of Indiana, the District of Arizona, the Eastern District of Wisconsin, and the Western District of Michigan.

Personal: Received a BA degree from Denison University and a JD degree from the University of Illinois.

PETERSON, Brad L
Mayer, Brown, Rowe & Maw, Chicago
312 701 8568
bpeterson@mayerbrownrowe.com
Recommended in Communications

Specialization: Outsourcing. Information technology transactions. Joint ventures and strategic alliances. Corporate and securities transactions. E-commerce.

Prof. Memberships: Admitted in Illinois, 1988.

Career: Joined *Mayer, Brown, Rowe & Maw*, 1995; became partner, 1998. Formerly at *Wildman, Harrold, Allen & Dixon*, Chicago, 1992-95; *Kirkland & Ellis*, Chicago, 1988-92. International Business Machines Corporation, Marketing Representative, Chicago, 1982-85.

Publications: 'The Smart Way to Buy Information Technology: How to Maximize Value and Avoid Costly Pitfalls' (AMACOM Books, New York, 1998, 250 pages). Author of many articles on outsourcing, alliances, and technology transactions.

Personal: Born May 29, 1959. Harvard Law School, JD with honors, 1988; Managing Editor, Harvard Journal of Law and Public Policy. University of Chicago Graduate School of Business, MBA, cum

ILLINOIS LEADERS

laude, 1982; Beta Gamma Sigma. Northwestern University, Computer Studies, 1977-80; Phi Beta Kappa.

PETERSON, Ron
Jenner & Block, Chicago 312 923 2981
rpeterson@jenner.com
Recommended in Insolvency
Specialization: Co-chairs bankruptcy/corporate restructuring practice. Has extensive experience in commercial, insolvency and bankruptcy law, focusing on representing debtors, trustees, creditors' committees, landlords and secured lenders in Chapter 11 cases. Counsel to creditors' committees in Chapter 11 cases of hardware stores Handy Andy Home Centers and Payless Cashways Inc, and attorney for the debtor in Harrah's Jazz Company and Armstrong's Inc bankruptcy cases. Chapter 7 trustee of large accounting firm Lester Witte & Company.
Career: Admitted to Illinois bar (1974). Chapter 7 trustee for the Northern District of Illinois.
Personal: Received a JD from University of Chicago in 1973.

PICKENS, Scott
Schiff Hardin & Waite, Chicago
312 258 5500
Recommended in Banking & Finance

PISKORSKI, Thomas
Seyfarth Shaw, Chicago 312 346 8000
Recommended in Employment

PLATT, Steven
Arnold & Kadjan, Chicago
312 236 0415
Recommended in Employment

POPE, Michael
McDermott, Will & Emery, Chicago
312 984 7780
mpope@mwe.com
Recommended in Litigation
Specialization: Partner in the Trial Department and heads international product liability practice. Product liability practice includes complex class action lawsuits. Currently represents the nation's largest automobile insurer in a major class action challenging the company's policy on replacement auto parts. Has extensive experience handling reinsurance disputes, in the interpretation of excess and umbrella liability insurance policies, and in professional liability and complex business litigation. Active in ADR, both as an advocate and as an arbitrator.
Prof. Memberships: Chairman of the Board of Trustees of the National Judicial College and president of the Illinois Equal Justice Foundation. Past president of the International Association of Defense Counsel, Lawyers for Civil Justice, and the American Board of Professional Liability Attorneys. Fellow, American College of Trial Lawyers, International Society of Barristers and the International Academy of Trial Lawyers (Board of Directors, 2000-03). Member, American Law Institute; member, Chicago Bar Association (Board of Managers, 1987-90), Illinois State Bar Association (Chair, Special Committee on Discovery Reform, 1994-1995), American Bar Association, Defense Research Institute, Seventh Circuit Bar Association (First Vice President 2002-03) and Product Liability Advisory Council.
Personal: Received BS from Loyola University of Chicago and JD from Northwestern University School of Law, cum laude.

POWERS, John
Seyfarth Shaw, Chicago 312 346 8000
Recommended in Employment

QASIM, Imad
Sidley Austin Brown & Wood, Chicago
312 853 7000
Recommended in Corporate/M&A

RANDALL, Benjamin
Katz Randall Weinberg & Richmond, Chicago 312 807 3800
Recommended in Real Estate

RAY, Stephen E
Stein, Ray & Harris, Chicago
312 641 3700
ser@steinrayharris.com
Recommended in Construction
Specialization: Partner in Construction Law Practice that provides consulting services on a nationwide basis, to contractors and design professionals. He specializes in handling complex construction design disputes including construction defect, construction delay, active interference, and mechanics liens claims.
Prof. Memberships: Chicago Bar Association; Builders Association of Greater Chicago; Chicago Building Congress (member, Professional Services Division); Construction Financial Managers Association; Design-Build Institute of America.
Career: Admitted to Illinois Bar (1981). A partner of *Stein, Ray & Harris* since the firm's inception in 1991.
Personal: Received a JD from Cornell University in 1981 and a BA (magna cum laude) from Colgate University in 1978.

REIDY, Daniel
Jones Day, Chicago 312 269 4140
dereidy@jonesday.com
Recommended in Litigation
Specialization: Litigation Group Coordinator. Chair, Corporate Criminal Investigations practice. Commercial litigation work includes patent infringement, False Claims Act, partnership disputes, board of director liability litigation, securities law, theft of trade secrets, environmental insurance coverage and coordination of product liability defense. Criminal work includes antitrust violations, health care fraud, insider trading, defense contracting, bank and mail fraud, questioned overseas payments, violations of US export restrictions and questionable payments to public officials. Extensive lead counsel trial experience. Substantial appellate experience. Numerous high profile cases. Former Prosecutor in the US Attorney's Office specialising in political and judicial corruption. Lead prosecutor in the Greylord judicial corruption project. Numerous public corruption cases, including the conviction of a Chicago alderman.
Prof. Memberships: Fellow of the American College of Trial Lawyers. Member of ABA, The Federal Bar Association, The Chicago Council of Lawyers, The Chicago Bar Association. Trial practice tutor. Speaker at criminal defense and civil litigation seminars.

RIPPIE, Glenn
Foley & Lardner, Chicago 312 755 1900
Recommended in Energy

ROBERTSON, Eric
Lueders, Robertson, Konzen & Fitzhenry, Granite City 618 876 8500
Recommended in Energy

ROCAP, Donald E
Kirkland & Ellis, Chicago 312 861 2266
donald_rocap@chicago.kirkland.com
Recommended in Tax
Specialization: His practice focuses on the tax aspects of complex business transactions, including mergers, acquisitions, leveraged buyouts, formation of private equity funds, and debt and equity restructurings and workouts. Is a lecturer at the University of Chicago Law School and is a Volume co-author of 'Mergers, Acquisitions, and Buyouts,' by Martin Ginsburg and Jack Levin, and a Special Editor of 'Structuring Venture Capital, Private Equity, and Entrepreneurial Transactions,' by Jack Levin.
Personal: Duke University, BA, 1977. University of Virginia School of Law, JD, 1980.

ROKOSZ, Ronald
Chapman and Cutler, Chicago
312 845 3000
Recommended in Banking & Finance

ROONEY, John
Sonnenschein Nath & Rosenthal, Chicago 312 876 8000
jrooney@sonnenschein.com
Recommended in Communications
Specialization: Partner in the Energy and Telecommunications Practices. He works extensively on electric energy, natural gas and telecommunications regulatory and legislative issues. Such matters include counseling on developing tariffs and resolving operational issues related to the implementation of retail open access for industrial and commercial customers, the possible unbundling of other utility services and the development of regulatory rules for the restructured electric energy market. He has been involved in litigation on issues including the development of rates, performance based regulation plans, terms and conditions for the provision of delivery services to customers, the development of rates and rules for the provision of unbundled metering service and issues concerning delivery services tariff uniformity. Recently, he also has been involved with performing due diligence work associated with the acquisition of electric generating facilities. He also has worked extensively on behalf of telecommunications carrier, Verizon North Inc., and Verizon South Inc., on numerous regulatory and legislative issues in Illinois, including litigation involving unbundled network elements, the possible development of an intrastate universal service fund, collocation, and rulemakings on interconnection and costing issues, payphone compensation, area code exhaust, deployment of advanced telecommunications services, and review of various legislative proposals. par par
Career: He formerly served as Chief Administrative Law Judge at the Illinois Commerce Commission.
Personal: The John Marshall Law School, JD 1988; 'Law Review', Loyola University, BBA 1985.

ROPSKI, Gary
Brinks Hofer Gilson & Lione, Chicago
312 321 4200
Recommended in Intellectual Property

ROSENBLOOM, Jim
Goldberg, Kohn, Bell, Black, Rosenbloom & Moritz, Ltd, Chicago
312 201 4000
Recommended in Real Estate

ROSENBLOOM, Lewis S
McDermott, Will & Emery, Chicago
312 984 6943
lrosenbloom@mwe.com
Recommended in Insolvency
Specialization: As debtor's counsel, restructured Gillett Holdings, the Funding Systems companies and Axiohm Technologies. Represented the Unsecured Creditors Committee in the Federated Department Stores cases and the Senior Bondholders Committee in the Continental Airlines chapter 11 cases. Assumed senior restructuring and corporate advisory responsibilities in the landmark public company reorganisation and class litigation settlement involving Mercury Finance, and currently represents the Directors of Armstrong Holdings. Has also been involved in the purchase, sale and financing of many billions of dollars of distressed company assets and securities.
Prof. Memberships: American, Illinois State, and Chicago bar associations, and fellow, American College Bankruptcy. Serves on the Board of Advisors to the

Bankruptcy and Commercial Law Advisor and as managing editor of the Annual Survey of Bankruptcy Law for Lenders.
Career: Received his bachelor's degree from Lake Forest College and was named College Scholar of his graduating classes. Received his law degree, summa cum laude, from DePaul University. Admitted: Illinois bar, various US District Courts (including the Northern District of Illinois trial bar), numerous circuits of the US Court of Appeals, and the US Supreme Court.

ROY, Paul J N
Mayer, Brown, Rowe & Maw, Chicago
312 701 7370
proy@mayerbrownrowe.com
Recommended in Communications

Specialization: Partner in Corporate, Information Technology, Telecommunications and Outsourcing Practices. Represents corporate clients in a broad range of information technology, telecommunications and outsourcing transactions, including the outsourcing of data and voice networks, data centers, personal computers, help desks, applications development and maintenance, call centers, finance and accounting functions, logistics, human resources and other business process functions. Representative transactions also include software and systems development and implementation, systems integration, strategic alliances and joint ventures. Clients include domestic and international corporations of various sizes, and in a variety of industries, including chemicals, telecommunications, software and computer equipment manufacturing, pharmaceutical, life sciences, banking and finance, securities trading, insurance, professional associations, auditing, consulting, consumer products, and distribution.
Prof. Memberships: Admitted to practice in Illinois. Member of the American Bar Association.
Career: Joined *Mayer, Brown, Rowe Maw*, 1985. Formerly with The Associates Commercial Corporation, Chicago, manager - personal computer software development, business systems analyst, 1982-85. Borg Warner Corporation, Automotive Parts Division, warehouse department manager, financial analyst, 1979-82.
Personal: Born 15 April 1955. Loyola University of Chicago, JD, 1985. Northwestern University, MBA, 1982. Colby College, BA, 1978.

RUBIN, James
Butler Rubin Saltarelli & Boyd, Chicago
312 696 4443
jrubin@butlerrubin.com
Recommended in Insurance

Specialization: Trial lawyer, partner and head of reinsurance litigation and arbitration practice group. Represented insurance and reinsurance companies in over 200 complex reinsurance disputes. Firm counsels insurers and reinsurers regarding transactions, reinsurance wordings, and commutations. Experience includes matters in litigation, arbitration and mediation, involving disparate issues such as the proper allocation of losses, fraud, contract interpretation, finite contract disputes, the authority of agents, the conclusiveness of commutations, and claims by and against companies in receivership or operating under schemes of arrangement. Practice also includes insurance coverage litigation and the defense of professional liability claims.
Prof. Memberships: Active in ARIAS US and sits on both its ethics and publications committees.
Career: 1971, admitted to Illinois Bar, US District Court, Northern District of Illinois including Trail Bar and US Court of Appeals, Seventh Circuit; 1983, US District Court, Northern District of California and US Supreme Court. Partner at *Winston & Strawn* prior to founding *Butler Rubin Saltarelli & Boyd* in 1981 with three other *Winston & Strawn* partners.
Publications: Authored ARIAS's Code of Conduct for Arbitrators (with two other industry representatives).
Personal: Received JD from Loyola University (1971; member of Law Review) and AB from the University of Illinois (1967).

RUBIN, Joel
D'Ancona & Pflaum LLC, Chicago
312 602 2000
Recommended in Real Estate

RUFF, Randolph
Ogletree, Deakins, Nash, Smoak & Stewart PC, Chicago 312 558 1220
Recommended in Construction

RUSSELL, James
Winston & Strawn, Chicago
312 558 6084
jrussell@winston.com
Recommended in Environment

Specialization: Environmental law and environmental litigation: administrative, civil, and criminal environmental enforcement litigation and cost recovery litigation before state and federal courts and agencies; rulemakings before state agencies and USEPA; permit appeals, permit negotiations, and regulatory counseling; all environmental aspects of corporate transactions and lender liability.
Career: Joined as partner, 1986.
Personal: Ohio Wesleyan University, 1965; The Ohio State University College of Law, JD, 1969.

RUXIN, Paul
Jones Day, Chicago
312 269 1546
paultruxin@jonesday.com
Recommended in Energy

Specialization: Immediate past Professional Personnel Partner and Chairman, Energy Specialized Industry Practice. Practice concentrates on the representation of natural gas, pipeline, electric and telephone public utilities before state and federal regulatory bodies and in the courts. On behalf of clients is regularly involved in the development, acquisition, and sale of energy resources and independent power and energy-related projects, the structure and restructuring of public utility and other energy businesses, the impact of the antitrust laws on regulated utilities, and the general litigation and commercial problems of the energy and public utility industries.
Prof. Memberships: Member of the ABA (Public Utility Law Section), the Energy Bar Association, the Ohio State Bar Association (Public Utility Law Section), the Cleveland Bar Association, and The Chicago Bar Association. Frequent speaker at utility industry meetings and seminars and is currently listed in the public utilities section of a leading American legal publication.

RYAN, Thomas
Sidley Austin Brown & Wood, Chicago
312 853 7000
Recommended in Antitrust

SALPETER, Alan N
Mayer, Brown, Rowe & Maw, Chicago
312 701 7051
asalpeter@mayerbrownrowe.com
Recommended in Litigation

Specialization: Senior litigator with approximately 70 bench and jury trials and 20 appeals. Commercial litigation cases focusing on alleged malpractice suits against lawyers, accountants and consultants; alleged securities fraud; multiple kinds of class actions; disputes over information technology; contested mergers or acquisitions; business torts; corporate governance and fiduciary duties; consumer class actions.
Career: Joined *Mayer, Brown, Rowe & Maw*, Chicago, 1972; became partner, 1979. Co-head Litigation Department, 1994-2000.
Publications: Co-author of a number of articles and chapters in books on a range of legal issues. Swiss Reinsurance New Markets - Conference for Global Accounting Firms: Risk Management Challenges - Defending Accountants Against Litigation in the US; Numerous Presentations: The Inside Story of Lexecon v. Milberg Weiss; Guest Lecturer, Boalt Hall School of Law (University of California at Berkeley). Lorman Education Services.

Personal: Born 7 October 1947. Villanova University, JD, 1972; Managing Editor, Villanova Law Review. The American University, BS with highest honors, 1969.

SALTIEL, David
Bell, Boyd & Lloyd, Chicago
312 372 1121
Recommended in Media & Entertainment

SANDERS, David P
Jenner & Block, Chicago
312 923 2963
dsanders@jenner.com
Recommended in Media & Entertainment

Specialization: Co-chairs media and First Amendment practice. Provides litigation and counseling services on many types of media and First Amendment law issues to publishers, broadcasters and others in news and entertainment fields. Has successfully defended numerous libel and privacy cases. Has served as regular outside counsel to media clients including ABC Inc, Crain Communications Inc, Chicago Magazine and Golfweek. Also has extensive experience in handling complex business litigation.
Prof. Memberships: American Bar Association, Chicago Council of Lawyers (chairs Federal Judicial Evaluations Committee), Libel Defense Resource Center.
Career: Admitted to Illinois bar (1974).
Personal: Received a JD from Georgetown University in 1974.

SCHILLER, Eric
Sonnenschein Nath & Rosenthal, Chicago 312 876 8000
eschiller@sonnenschein.com
Recommended in Real Estate

Specialization: Partner in the Real Estate and Finance Groups. Has more than 25 years of experience representing major corporate and institutional clients on a nationwide basis in a wide variety of real estate and commercial finance matters. He is particularly active and expert in financing, joint ventures, commercial leases, real estate acquisition and sales matters and workouts. His experience includes extensive work on multi-state, multi-asset real estate and commercial transactions. He has handled matters involving virtually every type of real estate, including office buildings, industrial buildings, shopping centers, hotels and apartment complexes. In the workout area, has been actively involved in representing parties in connection with troubled real estate on a nationwide basis. He is highly experienced in counseling lenders in syndication groups with respect to large loan transactions, both as agent and as co-lender.
Prof. Memberships: Elected to the American College of Real Estate Lawyers and member of the Chicago and American Bar Associations.

Publications: He has lectured and written on subjects including complex multi-bank financing transactions, equity and mezzanine investments and the restructuring of troubled loans for both ACREL and ALI-ABA.
Personal: Northwestern University School of Law, JD, 1971, Editorial Board, Law Review, Indiana University, BA with honors, 1968.

SCHNEIDMAN, Edward J
Mayer, Brown, Rowe & Maw, Chicago
312 701 7348
eschneidman@mayerbrown.com
Recommended in Corporate/M&A
Specialization: Mergers of publicly and privately held corporations, partnerships, limited liability companies and other entities. Stock and asset acquisitions and divestitures. Corporate and partnership liquidations and reorganizations. General corporate governance and compliance. Public and private offerings. Real estate investment trusts and other public and private real estate-related entities. Limited partnerships, mortgage pools and institutional funds, including group trusts, separate accounts, and tax-exempt title-holding corporations. Federal and state securities law compliance.
Prof. Memberships: Illinois, 1980. US District Court for the Northern District of Illinois, 1980.
Career: Joined *Mayer, Brown, Rowe & Maw*, Chicago, 1980; became partner 1987. Corporate Practice Area Administrator since 1996-2002.
Publications: Illinois Continuing Legal Education Seminars, Partnership Law and Aspects of Oil and Gas Law. American Association of Equipment Lessors Lawyer Forum.
Personal: Born 20 September 1955. Duke University School of Law, JD with honors, 1980. University of Pennsylvania, BSE magna cum laude, 1977.

SCHWAB, Stephen
Piper Rudnick, Chicago 312 368 2150
stephen.schwab@piperrudnick.com
Recommended in Insurance
Specialization: International commerce and litigation; litigation; insurance and reinsurance.
Career: He is a commercial litigator who concentrates his practice in the areas of insurance and reinsurance, litigation, arbitration and mediation, transactions and regulation. He has published an extensive list of book chapters, law review articles and pieces for trade publications on insurance and reinsurance-related subjects. He has lectured at numerous presentations on insurance and reinsurance topics to a wide variety of audiences throughout the world.
Personal: JD, Dickinson School of Law; BA, Northwestern University.

SCHWARTZ, Donald
Latham & Watkins LLP, Chicago
312 876 7631
donald.schwartz@lw.com
Recommended in Banking & Finance
Specialization: Co-head of the Banking and Leveraged Finance Group. Principally represents banks, commercial finance companies and other lenders in transactional and out of court insolvency matters, as well as entities borrowing or leasing from financial institutions. Experienced in issues faced by lenders, including acquisitions of loan portfolios and business units and serving as lead counsel on domestic and cross-border financings.
Prof. Memberships: ABA Commercial Finance Services Committee.
Career: Associate General Counsel, Commercial Finance Association 1997-2002. Member, Editorial Advisory Board, Journal of Bankruptcy Law and Practice.
Personal: JD, University of Chicago, 1974 (Order of the Coif). BA, Macalester College, 1971.

SHEFFIELD, Jeffrey T
Kirkland & Ellis, Chicago 312 861 2454
jeffrey_sheffield@chicago.kirkland.com
Recommended in Tax
Specialization: Concentrates his practice in the areas of business planning; mergers, acquisitions and venture capital investing; tax planning for public and closely-held entities; and executive compensation.
Publications: He has authored or co-authored several articles, including 'How VC/PE Funds Can Deliver Special LTCG Tax Benefits to Individual LPs and GPs'.
Personal: University of Chicago, BA, 1976, Phi Beta Kappa; Harvard Law School, JD, 1979. Former Lecturer at Law, University of Chicago Law School (teaching Business Planning). Former Adjunct Professor, IIT-Kent Graduate Tax Program (teaching tax-free reorganizations, corporate income tax, advanced income tax).

SHEPRO, Richard Warren
Mayer, Brown, Rowe & Maw, Chicago
312 701 7007
rshepro@mayerbrown.com
Recommended in Corporate/M&A
Specialization: Chicago Office Practice Leader for Corporate and Securities law. Represents and counsels on acquisitions, restructurings, and securities law; negotiations and planning for acquisitions and sale of publicly traded and private businesses, both in the US and internationally; offshore corporations; international investment; insurance and reinsurance companies; venture capital and private equity fund work; proxy and consent solicitations; public and private offerings; broker-dealer and investment advisor regulation; special complex corporate planning problems; and joint ventures and other arrangements.
Prof. Memberships: Admitted to practice in California, 1981; Illinois, 1979; US District Court for the Northern District of Illinois, 1981; US Court of Appeals for the Ninth Circuit, 1981; US Supreme Court, 1993. Member of the American Law Institute; Chicago Council of Lawyers, Board of Governors, 1986-89; Chairman, Election Law Committee, 1987-93. Fellow of the Chicago Bar Foundation. Board of Directors of LaSalle Club.
Career: Served as Law Clerk to The Honorable Judge James R Browning, Chief Judge, US Court of Appeals for the Ninth Circuit, 1979-81. Joined *Mayer, Brown, Rowe & Maw* in 1981 and became partner in 1986. Lecturer, University of Chicago Law School. Former Visiting Professor, Northwestern University School of Law. Lectured at the London Business School, Ecole des Hautes Etudes Commerciales, and at professional associations. Taught at Harvard University.
Publications: Co-author of 'Bidders & Targets: Mergers and Acquisitions in the US' (Oxford, England and Cambridge, Massachusetts: Basil Blackwell, 1990). Has written many articles on mergers, corporate law issues, and securities law for US and foreign publications, including 'Financial Times', 'Harvard Business Review', and 'Business Lawyer'.
Personal: Born 9 May 1953. Earned JD cum laude from Harvard University in 1979, where served as Supreme Court Note Editor of the Law Review. Holds MSc (1976) from The London School of Economics and AB magna cum laude (1975) from Harvard University. Special Assistant Attorney General of the State of Illinois, 1981-82. Staff Member, US Senate Judiciary Committee, 1978-79. Speaks French and Russian.

SHERCK, Timothy C
Mayer, Brown, Rowe & Maw, Chicago
312 701 7148
tsherck@mayerbrownrowe.com
Recommended in Tax
Specialization: Represents and counsels on all tax aspects of acquisitions and dispositions of business, including consolidated return, carryforward, spinoff and asset basis issues; tax-free reorganisations; corporate joint ventures; tax aspects of business financial restructurings, workouts, and bankruptcy, including debt exchanges and modification, cancellation of indebtedness income, loss carryforwards, and related matters such as tax liens and tax-related aspects of bankruptcy law; acquisitions of financially troubled business; and preparation and handling of requests for private letter rulings before the IRS National Office.
Prof. Memberships: Admitted to practice in Illinois, 1975. Member, American Bar Association Section of Taxation (corporate tax committee); member, American College of Tax Counsel; member, Planning Committee, University of Chicago Law School Federal Tax Conference.
Career: Served as Law Clerk to The Honorable Walter R Mansfield, US Court of Appeals for the Second Circuit, New York, 1974-75. Joined *Mayer, Brown, Rowe & Maw* in 1975 and became partner in 1981.
Publications: Author of 'Treatment of Options in Applying Stock Ownership Tests in the Corporate World', 66 Taxes 935 (1988); 'Restructuring Today's Financially Troubled Corporation', 68 Taxes 881 (1990); 'Applying the Property-Services Distinction in Corporate Transactions: The New Economy Tests the Limits', 68 Taxes 120 (2001) (co-author).
Personal: Born 27 February 1949. Earned JD, cum laude, from Harvard Law School in 1974, where was Comment Editor for the Law Review. Holds a BA cum laude (1971) from Northwestern University.

SHUGRUE, John
Zevnik Horton, Chicago
312 977 2500
Recommended in Insurance

SHULRUFF, Stuart
Katten Muchin Zavis Rosenman, Chicago 312 902 5694
stuart.shulruff@kmzr.com
Recommended in Banking & Finance
Specialization: Partner, Chicago. Concentrates his practice in all aspects of corporate finance (senior financing, mezzanine financing and equity co-investments) for a wide variety of institutional and entrepreneurial finance clients such as Antares Capital Corporation, Dymas Funding Company LLC, Heller Financial, Inc., General Electric Capital Corporation, LaSalle Bank National Association, First Source Financial LLP, FINOVA Capital Corporation, Fleet Capital Corporation, Prairie Capital, Madison Capital Funding LLC, Merrill Lynch Capital, and Midwest Mezzanine Fund.
Prof. Memberships: Illinois Bar Association, Chicago Bar Association.
Personal: Graduated with High Honors from the University of Illinois at Urbana-Champaign in 1981 with a Bachelor of Science degree in Accountancy. Successfully completed the Certified Public Accountant's examination in 1981. Graduated cum laude from Loyola University School of Law in 1984.

SILBERMAN, Alan
Sonnenschein Nath & Rosenthal, Chicago 312 876 8000
asilberman@sonnenschein.com
Recommended in Antitrust
Specialization: Partner and Chair of the Antitrust, Franchising and Distribution Group. More than 30 years' experience in antitrust and franchising litigation, counseling and related transactional represen-

tation, as well as in general commercial litigation. He has represented franchisors in a number of negotiated, litigated and arbitrated disputes with franchisees and third parties and regularly represents franchising clients in domestic and international activities. He regularly counsels McDonald's Corporation on a wide range of franchise law, franchise relationship, marketing and trade regulation matters. He has acted as counsel for insurance companies in various cases involving the legality of provider arrangements and similar claim handling practices designed to obtain competitive prices for insurance companies and their policyholders. He is a frequent speaker on antitrust topics relating to marketing, distribution, franchising, litigation and insurance.
Prof. Memberships: Member of the Bureau of National Affairs' Antitrust and Trade Regulation Advisory Board, Member of the Illinois Franchise Advisory Board, appointed by the Attorney General of Illinois.
Career: Co-Chair of Practising Law Institute's Annual Antitrust Law Institute, served as Chair of the American Bar Association (ABA) Section of Antitrust Law 1993-94. Previously served as member of the Council of the ABA Section of Antitrust Law and as member of its Special Committee on the Role of the Federal Trade Commission, and member of the ABA House of Delegates. Following graduation from law school, he served as Law Clerk to the late Honorable Hubert L Will, United States District Judge (Northern District of Illinois). President of the National Ramah Commission, Inc. of the Jewish Theological Seminary of America.
Personal: Yale University LLB 1964, Northwestern University BA with Distinction 1961.

SIMON, Mark
Katten Muchin Zavis Rosenman, Chicago + 312 902 5301
Mark.Simon@kmzr.com
Recommended in Real Estate
Specialization: Partner, Chicago. Represents banks, insurance companies and pension fund advisors making loans and other real estate investments. Frequently acts as agent's counsel on syndicated REIT credit facilities and construction loans in excess of $100 million. Substantial experience documenting mezzanine loans and joint venture investments. Has handled a considerable number of workouts for both lending institutions and developers, including restructuring the indebtedness of entire real estate companies.
Prof. Memberships: Past chair of the Chicago Bar Association real estate finance subcommittee. Represents not for profit organizations redeveloping urban sites on a pro bono basis.
Publications: Co-author of an article on legal opinions and speaks frequently at seminars on real estate finance.
Personal: Graduated magna cum laude from Carleton College in 1976 and with honors from the University of Michigan Law School in 1979.

SKLAR, Stanley
Bell, Boyd & Lloyd, Chicago
312 372 1121
Recommended in Construction

SLATER, Paul
Sperling & Slater, Chicago
312 641 3200
Recommended in Antitrust

SMEDINGHOFF, Thomas J
Baker & McKenzie, Chicago
312 861 8670
smedinghoff@bakernet.com
Recommended in Communications
Specialization: Focus: e-business; security; digital signatures and PKI; information technology; privacy. Acts as e-business counsel for clients worldwide, and is internationally recognized for leadership in addressing legislative and public policy issues relating to electronic security and digital signatures.
Prof. Memberships: *Baker & McKenzie's* North American e-commerce practice coordinator; Member, US Delegation to United Nations Commission on International Trade Law (UNCITRAL); Chair, ABA E-Commerce Law Division; Chair, Illinois Commission on Electronic Commerce (1996-98).
Career: Admitted in Illinois (1978).
Publications: Editor and primary author, 'Online Law' (Addison-Wesley, 1996); numerous e-transaction, security, and IT articles.
Personal: JD University of Michigan Law School (1978).

SMITH, Tefft W
Kirkland & Ellis, Chicago 312 861 2212
tefft_smith@dc.kirkland.com
Recommended in Antitrust
Specialization: A senior partner with *Kirkland & Ellis*, he leads the firm's 110-person Antitrust and Competition Practice. Has 30 years of civil and criminal antitrust and merger trial experience and has led government criminal, class-action, price fixing and civil antitrust cases for US and international companies. Has managed many sensitive mergers and acquisitions through the clearance process and has expedited numerous multinational transactions, requiring coordination of EU, member-state, and other national filings. Has appeared in many courts, including the United States Supreme Court.
Personal: Brown University, BA, 1968. University of Chicago, JD, 1971.

SMOLEN, Lee
Sidley Austin Brown & Wood, Chicago
312 853 7000
Recommended in Real Estate

SNIDER, Lawrence K
Mayer, Brown, Rowe & Maw, Chicago
312 701 7858
lsnider@mayerbrownrowe.com
Recommended in Insolvency
Specialization: Firm Practice Leader for Bankruptcy and Insolvency. Serves as bankruptcy/insolvency/restructuring counsel to numerous banks, financial institutions and creditor committees, including Tru Serv Corporation lenders; Quaker Coal Company, Inc., lenders; Midcom Communications, Pegasus Gold, and Handy Andy Home Improvement Centers, Inc, creditors' committee. Also served or serves as debtor's counsel or special restructuring counsel to companies such as Lason, Inc., Metal Management, Inc, Paging Net, Inc; DirecTV Latin America; Acted as special counsel to Chrysler Financial Corporation in 1992 on US$6.7 billion refinancing.
Prof. Memberships: National Bankruptcy Conference (Chairman, Mass Torts Committee). American College of Bankruptcy (Director). American Bankruptcy Institute. American Bar Association, Business Bankruptcy Committee. Chicago Bar Association, Bankruptcy and Reorganization Committee, 1991-93. Detroit Bar Association, Chairman, Debtor-Creditor Law Committee, 1980-88. State Bar of Illinois, Commercial, Banking and Bankruptcy Law Section Council, 1992-93. State Bar of Michigan: Chairman, Debtor Creditor Business Law Section, 1980-84; Chairman, Business Law Section, 1985-86.
Career: *Mayer, Brown, Rowe & Maw*, Chicago, as a partner in 1991. Prior to that, served with *Jaffe, Snider, Raitt & Heuer*, Detroit (1968-91) and *Weisswasser, Jaffe and Grant*, Detroit, (1963-68).
Publications: Author or co-author: 'Recent Decision Regarding Creditors' Committees', 21 ABI Journal, March 2002; 'Creditors' Committee Member Inaction: Any Liability?' The Bankruptcy Strategist, July, 1998; 'The Secured Creditor's Right to Receive Current Interest Payments During Chapter 11', 9 Norton Law Adviser, September, 1997; 'Bankruptcy Law' (Bankruptcy Commission Proposal on Creditors' Committees), 'National Law Journal', January 27, 1997.
Personal: Born: 1938. Earned his JD from the University of Michigan Law School (1963) as well as his BA from the University of Michigan (1960). Adjunct Professor of Law, Wayne State University Law School (Bankruptcy/Debtor-Creditor Law), 1973-84. Trustee, Columbia College Chicago, Illinois; Chairman, Museum Advisory Committee, Museum of Contemporary Photography (Chicago); Member, Acquisition Committee, Photography Department, The Art Institute of Chicago.

SOLOVY, Jerold S
Jenner & Block, Chicago 312 923 2671
jsolovy@jenner.com
Recommended in Litigation
Specialization: Firm's Chairman also serves on the firm's policy committee and chairs one of its litigation groups. Has extensive experience in state and federal litigation, both at the trial and appellate levels, and has argued several cases before the United States Supreme Court. Focuses on litigating complex business matters and insurance coverage issues. Has a national reputation in defending class actions in both federal and state courts, and has handled many high-profile intellectual property and securities cases.
Career: Admitted to Illinois Bar and District of Columbia (1955).
Personal: Received an LLB (cum laude) from Harvard in 1955.

SOLOW, Michael
Kaye Scholer LLP, Chicago
312 583 2300
Recommended in Insolvency

SPECTOR, David
Schiff Hardin & Waite, Chicago
312 258 5500
Recommended in Insurance

SPRAYREGEN, James H M
Kirkland & Ellis, Chicago 312 861 2481
james_sprayregen@chicago.kirkland.com
Recommended in Insolvency
Specialization: Experience includes the representation of significant companies as debtors in bankruptcy proceedings or in non-bankruptcy fora and large creditors in bankruptcy and insolvency proceedings. On behalf of his clients, he has handled a wide variety of matters involving such issues as deleveraging, fraudulent conveyances, equitable subordination, substantive consolidation, preferences, and successor liability. In addition, he has extensive experience in representing boards of directors in troubled situations, the acquisition of companies and assets of companies out of bankruptcy proceedings or from insolvent debtors.
Personal: University of Michigan, BA, 1982; University of Illinois College of Law, JD, 1985.

STEIN, Steven GM
Stein, Ray & Harris, Chicago
312 641 3700
sgms@steinrayharris.com
Recommended in Construction
Specialization: Firm partner and leading authority in construction law; specializes in trial and arbitration of complex design and construction matters; works extensively in the drafting and negotiation of design and construction related agreements.
Prof. Memberships: Chicago and American Bar Associations; American College of Real Estate Lawyers; American College of Construction Lawyers (Fellow and

ILLINOIS — LEADERS

Member); Design-Build Institute of America.
Career: Admitted to Wisconsin Bar (1976), Illinois (1978); Supreme Court (1980). Partner since the firm's inception.
Publications: Editor in Chief: 'Construction Law' and 'AIA Legal Citator', 1993.
Personal: Received a JD from University of Chicago (1976; BA from the University of Wisconsin (1973).

STERN, Gary
Sidley Austin Brown & Wood, Chicago
312 853 7000
Recommended in Banking & Finance

STILLMAN, Nina
Vedder, Price, Kaufman & Kammholz, Chicago 312 609 7500
Recommended in Employment

STINSON, James
Sidley Austin Brown & Wood, Chicago
312 853 7000
Recommended in Insurance

STONE, Jeffrey
McDermott, Will & Emery, Chicago
312 984 2064
jstone@mwe.com
Recommended in Litigation
Specialization: Partner in the Trial Department and head of White Collar Criminal Defense Practice Group. Concentrates on white collar criminal defense, complex commercial litigation, internal investigations and RICO. Represents individuals and corporations in criminal prosecutions and complex commercial litigation.
Prof. Memberships: Member, American Bar Association and the Chicago Council of Lawyers. Fellow of the American College of Trial Lawyers. Member of the board of directors, Harvard Law Society of Illinois; national chairman, Stanford Fund, and Vice Chair, Stanford's campaign for Undergraduate Education.
Career: Admitted to practice before the Illinois bar, the US District Court for the Northern District of Illinois (trial bar), the US Court of Appeals for the Seventh Circuit and the Supreme Court of the United States. Prior to joining *McDermott, Will & Emery*, served in the United States Attorney's Office in Chicago, most recently as deputy chief of the Criminal Receiving and Appellate Division. As assistant US attorney, tried federal jury trials in the area of white collar crime, focusing on complex financial crime, fraud, public corruption and tax prosecutions.
Personal: Received BA with honors and distinction from Stanford University and JD cum laude from Harvard Law School.

STRAND, Peter
Holland & Knight LLP, Chicago
312 263 3600
peter.strand@hklaw.com
Recommended in Media & Entertainment
Specialization: Sr Counsel in the Business Law Department, focusing on the entertainment and intellectual property practice areas. He represents artists, managers, songwriters, recording artists, musicians, television and film writers, independent record labels, publishing companies, production companies and writers in litigation and transactional matters. He assists clients in protecting and enforcing copyrights and trademarks and licensing or exploiting their creative works. His services include reviewing clients' intellectual property and creating and implementing a plan to secure and protect intellectual property rights; licensing; trademark clearance, registration and defending applications before the Patent and Trademark Office; litigation before the Trademark Trial and Appeal Board and state and federal litigation of trademark rights; copyright registration and enforcement and defense in state and federal courts.

STREFF, Jr, William A
Kirkland & Ellis, Chicago 312 861 2126
william_streff@kirkland.com
Recommended in Intellectual Property
Specialization: William A. Streff, Jr. has been practicing intellectual property law for almost 30 years, concentrating in intellectual property litigation, including jury trials, and transactions, including international strategic alliances, involving computer hardware, firmware, software and systems; semiconductor processing technology and circuitry, including DRAMs, CCDs and MPUs; optical networks; satellite and cable communications systems; avionics; high definition and satellite television systems; and digitally controlled fuel systems. He is one of the leaders of the Firm's 175-member Intellectual Property Department and is a member of the Firm Management Committee.
Personal: Northwestern University, BSME, 1971. Northwestern University School of Law, JD, 1974.

SULLIVAN, Marcia
Katten Muchin Zavis Rosenman, Chicago 312 902 5535
Marcia.Sullivan@kmzr.com
Recommended in Real Estate
Specialization: Partner, Chicago. Concentrates on commercial real estate finance for commercial banks, insurance companies, finance companies and other lenders. Has been involved in complex financing for a variety of projects across the nation - shopping centers, hotels, office buildings, build-to-suit, apartments and for-sale residential. Has represented lenders and investors in unsecured and secured lines of credit, permanent financing, workouts and foreclosures. Has also represented lenders, investors, servicers, trustees and borrowers in loan securitizations, as well as in portfolio transactions and structured finance. In conjunction with real estate financing, represents lenders in loan participations, co-lender arrangements and interest rate risk protection products. Regularly represents developers and investors in real estate acquisitions and divestitures, development, leasing and financing.
Prof. Memberships: Served as President and member of Chicago Real Estate Executive Women and Chicago Real Estate Education Initiative, co-chaired the 13th National Forum for Women Corporate Counsel.
Career: Speaker at CREW Network 2002 National Convention; member of Editorial Advisory Board of Real Estate Chicago; speaker with Lolita Didrickson at the Hugh O'Brian Youth Foundation Leadership Seminar, served as Adjunct Professor for the Chicago-Kent College of Law, leader of the firm's Women's Forum.
Personal: Graduated, Phi Beta Kappa, from DePauw University in 1972 and received her Juris Doctor degree from the Indiana University School of Law, where she was an associate editor of the 'Indiana Law Review'.

SULLIVAN, Thomas
Jenner & Block, Chicago 312 222 9350
Recommended in Litigation

SULLIVAN, William
Franczek Sullivan, Chicago
312 986 0300
Recommended in Employment

TARUN, Robert
Winston & Strawn, Chicago
312 558 5804
rtarun@winston.com
Recommended in Litigation
Specialization: Business litigation, corporate internal investigations, white collar criminal defense.
Prof. Memberships: Fellow, American College of Trial Lawyers.
Career: Executive Assistant US Attorney (Chicago) 1982-85; Deputy Chief, Criminal Division 1979-82. Lecturer in Law, University of Chicago Law School. Sensitive investigations in 30 countries and civil and criminal matters in over 25 federal (US) districts.
Publications: Co-Author, 'Corporate Internal Investigations' (LJSP 2003); Editorial Board, 'Business Crimes Bulletin'.
Personal: Stanford, AB (1971), DePaul, JD (1974), University of Chicago, MBA (Finance) (1982).

THEISS, Paul W
Mayer, Brown, Rowe & Maw, Chicago
312 701 7359
ptheiss@mayerbrownrowe.com
Recommended in Corporate/M&A
Specialization: Chicago Office Practice Leader for Corporate and Securities Group. Emphasizes mergers and acquisitions, securities offerings, and corporate governance matters. Mergers and acquisitions work has included both public and private transactions, including in the telecommunications, industrial and gaming sectors. Regularly represents both issuers and underwriters in public debt and equity offerings and Rule 144A private placements, with recent emphasis on equity and high-yield debt issuances. Other specialties include private equity, outsourcing transactions and domestic and international joint ventures.
Prof. Memberships: Admitted in Illinois, 1985.
Career: Joined *Mayer, Brown, Rowe & Maw*, Chicago, 1985, and became partner in 1993.
Personal: Born 11 April 1960. Earned JD at University of Chicago, 1985, and BA at Amherst College, 1982.

THOMAS, Dale
Sidley Austin Brown & Wood, Chicago
312 853 7000
Recommended in Energy

THOMAS, Frederick B
Mayer, Brown, Rowe & Maw, Chicago
312 701 7035
fthomas@mayerbrownrowe.com
Recommended in Corporate/M&A
Specialization: Partner in general corporate practice in Chicago. Advises clients on stock acquisitions, asset acquisitions, mergers, joint ventures, financings, tender offers, shareholder disputes, and a variety of other matters involving US, foreign and multinational businesses. Provides advice to boards of directors and management regarding corporate governance and securities matters. Extensive representation of clients in telecommunications and information technology businesses. Represents large US corporations, other US clients of various types and foreign corporations.
Prof. Memberships: Admitted to practice in Illinois, 1974. Member of the American Bar Association, Section of Business Law; Chicago Council of Lawyers; and the Planning Committee for Ray Garrett, Jr. Corporate and Securities Law Institute. Member of the Visiting Committee of the University of Chicago Law School.
Career: Served as Law Clerk to The Honorable John C Godbold, US Court of Appeals for the Fifth Circuit, Montgomery, AL, from 1974-75. Joined *Mayer, Brown, Rowe & Maw*, Chicago, in 1975. Served in London office from 1978-81 and became partner in 1981. Serves on

LEADERS ILLINOIS

Management Committee of *Mayer, Brown, Rowe & Maw.*
Personal: Born 13 August 1949. Earned JD at the University of Chicago in 1974 (awarded the Joseph Henry Beale Prize and served as Comment Editor, University of Chicago Law Review). Holds AB, magna cum laude (1971), from Dartmouth College (elected to Phi Beta Kappa). Serves on the Board of Managers of the YMCA of Metropolitan Chicago. Board of Directors of St. Gregory Episcopal School and the Board of Trustees of LaRabida Children's Hospital. Adjunct Professor of Law (teaching corporations) at the University of Notre Dame, London Law Center, 1980-81.

TOMLINSON, PC, Stephen G
Kirkland & Ellis, Chicago 312 861 2386
stephen_tomlinson@kirkland.com
Recommended in Real Estate
Specialization: As the senior partner in *Kirkland & Ellis'* Real Estate Practice Group, his practice focuses on complex business transactions for real estate investment trusts (REITs), real estate private equity sponsors, institutional investors and real estate operating companies engaged in acquisitions and dispositions, operating company investments and formations, and multi-investor fund formations and investments. He has a broad base of experience in transactions regarding hospitality, office, industrial, retail and multi-family properties and operating companies in both the private and public market contexts.
Personal: University of Michigan, AB, 1981; University of Michigan, JD, 1984.

TOTH, Bruce
Winston & Strawn, Chicago
312 558 5723
btoth@winston.com
Recommended in Corporate/M&A
Specialization: Partner in the Corporate Department concentrating on financing, securities, and mergers and acquisitions. Recent M&A transactions include representation of Keebler Foods in its US$4.2 billion sale to Kellogg Company and its acquisitions of Austin Quality Foods, Inc and Presidents International Inc; representation of Huntsman Packaging in the sale of the company to Chase Capital Partners in a US$1.1 billion recapitalisation transaction; representation of Corporate Brands Foods America in its acquisition by IBP, Inc; representation of Booth Creek in its acquisition of Montreal Canadiens for US$270 million; representation of Booth Creek in its US$250 million recapitalisation of Packerland Packaging; representation of Northland Holdings, Inc. in the sale of 50 percent of its outstanding stock to Adsteam Marine Limited, and representation of Booth Creek in its acquisition with Hicks, Muse, Tate & Furst of Swift Foods Company for $1.4 billion. Editor; BNA Corporate Practice Series - Board of Directors.
Career: Joined *Winston & Strawn* as an associate in 1982. Elected as partner in 1987. Member of firm executive committee. Chairman, corporate department (1994-2001).
Personal: Born February 14, 1953. Received BS, summa cum laude, Georgia Institute of Technology. Received MBA, and JD, Stanford University.

TOWNSEND, Christopher
Piper Rudnick, Chicago 312 236 7516
christopher.townsend@piperrudnick.com
Recommended in Energy
Specialization: Energy; environmental; litigation; homeland security; communications; lodging and timeshare.
Career: He concentrates his practice in all aspects of energy, public utility, communications and environmental law and regulation. He represents commercial and industrial energy users and competitive electric, communication, and natural gas providers in proceedings before administrative agencies and appellate courts. He regularly assists large industrial and commercial consumers in negotiating natural gas, electric, on-site generation and chilled water supply contracts. He has worked closely with developers of independent power plants, counseling them on regulatory and administrative law issues.
Personal: JD, University of Iowa; BA, Augustana College.

TREECE, John
Sidley Austin Brown & Wood, Chicago
312 853 7000
Recommended in Antitrust

VALUKAS, Anton
Jenner & Block, Chicago 312 923 2903
avalukas@jenner.com
Recommended in Litigation
Specialization: Former United States Attorney (1985-89) chairs one of the firm's litigation groups and serves on firm's policy committee. Handles high-profile civil and white-collar criminal litigation concerning government contracts, fraud and compliance issues, plus conflict of interest, ethics violations and internal corporate investigations. Has defended corporations in class action and mass tort actions involving product defect and consumer fraud, food contamination, mass accident, and toxic exposure and environmental claims. Has extensive experience in media, health care and antitrust law.
Career: Admitted to Illinois Bar (1968). Held several Justice Department positions (1970-76).
Personal: Received a JD from Northwestern in 1968.

WALL, Robert
Winston & Strawn, Chicago
312 558 5699
rwall@winston.com
Recommended in Corporate/M&A
Specialization: Senior partner in Corporate Department. Concentration in mergers and acquisitions and corporate finance for public companies. Represented clients in these areas since 1977. Recently, represented Keebler Foods Company in $4.2 million sale to Kellogg Company; represented Salomon Smith Barney in $250 million debt financing of 30-year notes for Maytag Corporation; represented Morgan Stanley in $442 million stock offering of CDW Computer Centers; represented AirGate PCS, Inc., network partner of Sprint, in connection with its $802 million acquisition of iPCS, Inc. Frequent speaker at seminars and member of various securities and merger and acquisition organisations.
Prof. Memberships: Member, Editorial Board, Mergers and Acquisitions and Corporate Control Law Reporter; Member, Executive Committee, Northwestern University's Ray Garrett Securities Institute.
Career: Joined firm as associate, 1977. Partner, 1984. Co-Chairman, Library Committee.
Personal: University of Virginia, 1970; Northwestern University, BA, with distinction, 1973; Santa Clara University, JD, summa cum laude, 1977, Comments Editor, Santa Clara Law Review.

WANDER, Herb
Katten Muchin Zavis Rosenman, Chicago 312 902 5267
hwander@kmzr.com
Recommended in Corporate/M&A
Specialization: Partner, Chicago. Concentrates on all aspects of business law, especially corporate governance, securities law and M&A transactions. Has been the chief legal architect for many major M&A transactions - both negotiated and hostile - including the successful defense of Commercial Intertech Corp and the hostile acquisitions of West Point-Pepperell and Safety-Kleen Corp. He was appointed by the SEC to be one of two securities lawyers to make a presentation at the SEC's April 2001 Regulation FD Roundtable.
Prof. Memberships: Served as Chair of the ABA's 53,000 member Business Law Section and presently serves as Chair of The Ray Garrett Jr. Corporate and Securities Law Institute. Appointed by the President of the American Bar Association to serve on the Commission on Multidisciplinary Practice. He was a Director and President of the Jewish Federation of Metropolitan Chicago and the Jewish United Fund; is a Trustee and Officer of the Michael Reese Health Trust; and is a Director of Telephone & Data Systems Inc. He is serving his second term as a member of the Legal Advisory Committee to the New York Stock Exchange Board of Governors and is a member of its Corporate Governance Subcommittee. In 2002 he was nominated by his peers as one of the world's leading practitioners in the field of corporate governance and is listed in The International Who's Who of Corporate Governance Lawyers.
Publications: Has authored numerous articles and book reviews in the 'Yale Law Journal,' the 'Business Lawyer,' the 'Southwestern Law Journal,' the 'Northwestern University Law Review,' the 'Review of Securities and Commodities Regulation,' 'INSIGHTS,' and the 'New York Law Journal' and served as co-editor of 'Selected Articles on Federal Securities Law.' He was the first Editor of the Business Law Section's magazine, 'Business Law Today', and was the editor of Volume 49 (1993-94) of 'The Business Lawyer'. Frequently speaks at institutes and programs of various business and legal organizations.
Personal: Bachelor's degree from the University of Michigan and a law degree from Yale Law School, where he was on the board of editors of the Yale Law Journal.

WARNECKE, Michael O
Mayer, Brown, Rowe & Maw, Chicago
312 701 8602
mwarnecke@mayerbrownrowe.com
Recommended in Intellectual Property
Specialization: First chair in numerous major patent litigation cases. Experienced in international patent, technology licensing, and other IP matters. Frequent expert witness, arbitrator, and mediator.
Prof. Memberships: Fellow, American College of Trial Lawyers. American Bar Association.
Career: Joined *Mayer, Brown, Rowe & Maw*, Chicago, 1996; became partner 1996. Formerly with *Keck, Mahin & Cate*, Chicago, 1991-96; *Neuman, Williams, Anderson & Olson*, Chicago, 1967-91; US Patent and Trademark Office, US Patent Examiner, Group 350, Washington, DC, 1963-67.
Publications: Frequent lecturer. Selected by the People's Republic of China trade delegation to host two-day seminar for American automotive and after-market companies and the Chinese delegation on the legal aspects of doing business in China. Frequent lecturer and speaker, nationally and internationally, on intellectual property law, including Federal Court of Australia, IP Colloquium II, Melbourne, Australia, March 2001; Presentation to Federal Bench on United States litigation on how to determine issues to litigate and the conducting of Markman hearings on claim construction.
Personal: Born 28 June 1941. George Washington University, JD, 1967. Purdue University, BS, 1963.

ILLINOIS LEADERS

WARNER, Michael
Seyfarth Shaw, Chicago
312 346 8000
Recommended in Employment

WEBB, Dan
Winston & Strawn, Chicago
312 558 5856
dwebb@winston.com
Recommended in Litigation

Specialization: National trial practice in the areas of major commercial, civil, regulatory, and white-collar criminal cases.
Prof. Memberships: Fellow, American College of Trial Lawyers.
Career: Joined *Winston & Strawn* as partner, 1985. Head, Litigation Department; Member, Executive Committee.
Publications: Co-author, Corporate Internal Investigations (Law Journal Seminars Press).
Personal: Western Illinois University, 1967; Loyola University School of Law, JD 1970. Iran-Contra Special Trial Counsel; US Attorney, Northern District of Illinois, 1981-85; Illinois Department of Law Enforcement, 1979-80; Assistant US Attorney, 1970-76.

WELKE, William R
Kirkland & Ellis, Chicago 312 861 2143
william_welke@chicago.kirkland.com
Recommended in Tax

Specialization: Mr. Welke focuses his practice on the tax aspects of complex business transactions and entities, including: mergers, acquisitions, and leveraged buyouts; venture capital and other private equity investments; formation of private equity funds; joint ventures and partnerships; debt and equity restructurings; and executive compensation.
Personal: Massachusetts Institute of Technology, SB, 1980. University of Michigan Law School, JD, 1983.

WILLIAMS, Douglas
Sidley Austin Brown & Wood, Chicago
312 853 7000
Recommended in Banking & Finance

WILLIAMSON, Joel V
Mayer, Brown, Rowe & Maw, Chicago
312 701 7229
jwilliamson@mayerbrownrowe.com
Recommended in Tax

Specialization: Firm Practice Leader for Tax Controversy. Has tried in excess of 50 tax cases. Represented clients in six major international transfer pricing cases (Eli Lilly, G.D. Searle, Nestlé Westreco, Seagate Technology, Inc., National Semiconductor and United Parcel Service). Has also represented clients in cases involving financial products (Saba Partnership); captive insurance (Humana and Gulf Oil); Subpart F issues (The Limited); constructive triangular dividends (Gulf Oil); R&D moratorium (Intel Corporation); entitlement to Brazilian foreign tax credits (The Riggs Bank and Bankers Trust); Iranian losses and foreign tax credits (Continental Bank); tax accounting: sale and leaseback transactions (Comdisco); foreign source income on export sales (Intel Corporation); IRC Section 338 liquidations; trademark valuation, sale of assets for preferred stock and the proper role of IRS trial counsel in the audit examination process and summons enforcement (Nestlé Holdings, Inc) R&D allocation to DISC (Boeing).
Prof. Memberships: Admitted to practice in Illinois, 1986; Kentucky, 1970; US District Court for the Northern District of Illinois; Trial Bar for the Northern District of Illinois; various Circuit Courts of Appeal; US Court of Federal Claims; US Tax Court; US Supreme Court. Member of the American Bar Association.
Career: Special Trial Attorney, Chief Counsel's Office, United States Department of Treasury, Cincinnati, Ohio, 1972-85. Joined *Mayer, Brown, Rowe & Maw* as partner in 1986.
Publications: 'Litigating Transfer Pricing Cases' and 'Tax-Advantaged Transactions', Co-Author, Practicing Law Institute, 2001, 2002; 'Mrs. Gregory's Great-Grandchildren: The Lost Generation', 'Journal of Taxation of Global Transactions' (Summer 2002) (with Thomas C Durham and Stuart E Thiel); 'The Future of Section 482 Audits and Litigation', Co-Author, Practicing Law Institute, 1999, 2000; 'The Real World of Transfer Pricing Today', Taxes, March 1999.
Personal: Born 26 May 1945. Earned JD from University of Kentucky in 1970, where he was a member of the Order of the Coif, Law Review, Moot Court Board, and National Moot Court Team. Holds BA (1967) from Davidson College. Mentioned in a number of leading legal publications. Served as Officer, Criminal Trial Attorney, US Army, at Ft. Bragg, NC, and in the Republic of South Vietnam from 1970-72.

WOOTTON, Bob
Sidley Austin Brown & Wood, Chicago
312 853 7000
Recommended in Tax

WYLIE, Kenneth
Sidley Austin Brown & Wood, Chicago
312 853 7000
Recommended in Insurance

YASTROW, Joseph
Laner, Muchin, Dombrow, Becker, Levin, Tominberg, Chicago 312 467 9800
Recommended in Employment

YODER, Lowell
McDermott, Will & Emery, Chicago
312 984 7523
lyoder@mwe.com
Recommended in Tax

Specialization: Partner in tax department and co-chair of International Tax Practice. Focuses on international tax planning for multinationals. Advises on cross-border acquisitions, mergers, financings and restructurings. Advises on foreign tax credits, expense allocations, sourcing of income, Subpart F and passive foreign investment companies.
Prof. Memberships: Member of the Illinois Bar Association; American Bar Association; American College of Tax Counsel.
Career: Admitted to the Illinois Bar in 1982. Federal Clerkship, 1982-83, Honorable James M. Sprouse, US Circuit Court of Appeals for the Fourth Circuit. Joined McDermott, Will & Emery in 1983. Editor-in-Chief of 'Journal of Taxation of Global Transactions' and board member of 'Journal of International Taxation' and 'Tax Management International Journal'. Frequent speaker for Practising Law Institute, Tax Executives Institute and International Fiscal Association. Adjunct Professor of International Tax Law.
Publications: Author of three treatises on Subpart F (rules that apply to foreign operations of US multinationals); author of numerous articles on international tax topics including classification of foreign entities, affect of foreign losses on the use of foreign tax credits, and the treatment of foreign partnerships.
Personal: Attended University of Illinois College of Law 1979 to 1982 (JD, magna cum laude).

ZABEL, Sheldon
Schiff Hardin & Waite, Chicago
312 258 5500
Recommended in Environment

ZAROV, Herbert
Mayer, Brown, Rowe & Maw, Chicago
312 701 7317
hzarov@mayerbrownrowe.com
Recommended in Litigation

Specialization: Senior litigator and firm practice leader in litigation. Extensive experience in mass torts, federal securities law class actions, and complex commercial litigation. Served as national counsel for The Dow Chemical Company in multi-district breast implant litigation and currently national co-counsel for Union Carbide Corporation in asbestos litigation. Also experienced in securities, appellate, and tax litigation.
Prof. Memberships: Admitted in Illinois, 1979; US Supreme Court, 1996; US District Court for the Northern District of Illinois, 1979; US Court of Appeals for the Third Circuit, 1992; US Court of Appeals for the Sixth Circuit, 1995; US Court of Appeals for the Seventh Circuit, 1981; US Court of Appeals for the Ninth Circuit, 1991; US Tax Court, 1984; US Court of Claims, 1985.
Career: Joined *Mayer, Brown, Rowe & Maw*, 1986; became partner in 1987. Member of management committee. Prior firm: *Friedman & Koven*, Chicago, 1977-86. Taught English and American Studies at Smith College from 1973-76. Also taught at Washington University of St. Louis, University of Missouri, Roosevelt University, Wilson Junior College (now Kennedy-King), pre-1973.
Personal: Born 7 June 1945. Earned JD from University of Chicago, 1979, and MA from University of Chicago, 1968. Earned BA from Columbia University, 1967. Published 'Milton and the Rhetoric of Rebellion' in the 'Milton Quarterly', 1973.

ZELEK, Eugene
Freeborn & Peters, Chicago
312 360 6000
Recommended in Media & Entertainment

ZIMBLER, Jay
Sidley Austin Brown & Wood, Chicago
312 853 7000
Recommended in Tax

CORPORATE/M&A

INDIANA

CONTENTS: Corporate/M&A p.277; Employment: Mainly Plaintiff p.278; Mainly Defendant p.279; Litigation: General Comercial p.280; Real Estate p.281; Individuals' Profiles p.283.

INDIANA'S TOP FOUR
1. Baker & Daniels
2. Ice Miller
3. Barnes & Thornburg
4. Sommer Barnard Ackerson Attorneys

Ranking based on Chambers' research within the state.

All quotes in the text are from interviews with clients and competitors.

OVERVIEW: A major player in the region, **Baker & Daniels** ranks equal first in the state. The firm has been described as a legal Goliath, with 350 lawyers across seven offices. Litigation is a particular strength, although the firm has also gained a reputation for corporate work and boasts one of the largest employment groups in the Midwest. Litigator Chris Scanlon is highly praised, as is Jim Aschleman for his securities and M&A work. Clients include Eli Lilly and Bank One.

Ice Miller, the largest firm in Indianapolis, is traditionally known for its litigation expertise, particularly within the insurance sector. However, the firm is now moving toward a more general corporate and commercial portfolio. Its employment team also has a strong reputation, as does its real estate department. Chic Born is recognized for his traditional labor work, while Richard Thrapp is known statewide for his lending experience. Clients include Emerson Electrical Company and Buckingham Companies.

The largest firm in the state, **Barnes & Thornburg** represents a number of Fortune 500 companies. It has been called a powerhouse in commercial litigation and is also praised for its employment and real estate groups. The firm does a wide variety of corporate work and has been especially active in recent state bank mergers. John Maley is singled out for his litigation skills, Kenneth Yerkes for employment and Dave Warshauer for real estate. Clients include Roche Diagnostics and Tomkins.

Sommer Barnard Ackerson Attorneys has boosted its profile in litigation through a merger with DC-based firm, The Ackerson Group. It is also considered to punch above its weight in the corporate sector, where it has an experienced team. Litigator Linda Pence has attracted several high-profile cases since she joined the firm, while Jim Strain is widely respected for his corporate knowledge. The firm has been involved in the Microsoft litigation, and Vectren and Eli Lilly are among its corporate clients.

CORPORATE/M&A

INDIANA
Leading firms (Corporate/M&A)
1. BAKER & DANIELS *Indianapolis*
   ICE MILLER *Indianapolis*
2. BARNES & THORNBURG *Indianapolis*
3. SOMMER BARNARD ACKERSON *Indianapolis*
4. KRIEG DEVAULT LLP *Indianapolis*
5. HENDERSON DAILY WITHROW *Indianapolis*
   LEAGRE CHANDLER & MILLARD LLP *Indianapolis*

Leading individuals (Corporate/M&A)
1. ASCHLEMAN James *Baker & Daniels*, Indianapolis
   STRAIN Jim *Sommer Barnard Ackerson*, Indianapolis
2. BRIDGE Catherine *Barnes & Thornburg*, Indianapolis
   BROWN Jeff *Baker & Daniels*, Indianapolis
   HUMKE Steven *Ice Miller*, Indianapolis
   SNYDER Jack *Ice Miller*, Indianapolis
   THORNBURGH John *Ice Miller*, Indianapolis
   THRAPP Richard *Ice Miller*, Indianapolis
3. BOEGLIN Daniel *Baker & Daniels*, Indianapolis
   HICKS Robert *Sommer Barnard Ackerson*, Indianapolis
   SWHIER Claudia *Barnes & Thornburg*, Indianapolis
   WILDMAN Bob *Henderson Daily Withrow*, Indianapolis
4. GREISING Robert *Krieg DeVault LLP*, Indianapolis
   MILLARD David *Leagre Chandler & Millard*, Indianapolis

Firms and individuals are listed alphabetically in each band.

Baker & Daniels
The Firm: Employing 350 lawyers worldwide and with five offices in Indiana, this firm is acknowledged by interviewees as a *"preeminent player"* in the region. It has a superb reputation and boasts experience in a variety of corporate/commercial transactions, such as representing issuers in securities offerings, acquisitions and corporate governance. On the private equity side, it represents financial investors and management participants. It also acts for investment advisers, broker-dealers and other financial institutions in connection with the structuring and offering of various investment vehicles, including hedge funds, mutual funds and asset-backed securities.

The Lawyers: **Jim Aschleman** is chairman of the corporate finance group. Peers describe him as *"immensely knowledgeable"* and *"straight-shooting."* He has *"first-rate"* experience of all aspects of securities and M&A work, and is involved in a wide range of financings and IPOs. Leading the firm's private capital and venture capital group is **Jeff Brown** . Sources regard him as an *"incredibly valuable asset"* to the firm. An *"energetic attorney,"* he is adept at *"focusing on the central issues"* in tough deals. *"Amiable"* **Dan Boeglin** chairs the business and finance team. Rivals describe him as *"a sharp guy"* who *"inspires lots of confidence."* His experience, especially in the establishment of joint ventures and strategic partnering arrangements, helps him to stay in *"control of a deal."*

The Clients: Typical clients include Wabash National, Bank One, National City and Ely Lilly.

Ice Miller
The Firm: This is the largest firm in Indianapolis, with a 50-plus corporate/M&A team. Peers consider it a *"strong pacesetter,"* active in a wide range of corporate/commercial work. Its representation of Delco Remy International, a spin-off from GM, has expanded from advising on employee benefits' plans to a role as general corporate counsel.

The Lawyers: **Steve Humke** is founding partner of the strategic advisors group. Peers regard him as a *"sharp and colorful"* attorney who *"serves his clients well."* His focus is on assisting high-growth, owner-managed companies to expand. *"Dynamic"* **Richard Thrapp** is renowned across the state for his lending experience. Peers consider him *"pragmatic, bright and good on detail."* He is also active in the city and state bar associations. Clients value *"guru"* **Jack Thornburgh** for his *"superb grasp of venture capital"* and his *"ability to switch between the big picture and the details."* He is also considered a *"superb counsel to high-growth emerging companies."* Many sources rate him *"one of the best corporate lawyers in the city"* for his mix of skills. He undertakes a great deal of work for entrepreneur

INDIANA
EMPLOYMENT & LABOR LAW

Scott Jones, the inventor of voice mail. Winning praise from the market as a *"consummate gentleman and seasoned veteran,"* **Jack Snyder** boasts *"a widely respected and prominent reputation"* and oversees many major transactions. He represents the Indianapolis Motor Speedway and took the leading role in the negotiation of TV contracts with ABC and ESPN.
The Clients: The firm enjoys a large and growing client base. Important clients include Delco Remy International; The Steak n Shake Company; Biomet Orthopedics; Eli Lilly; German American Bancorp and Crossmann Communities.

Barnes & Thornburg
The Firm: The largest firm in Indiana is a major corporate player. However, market opinion does not consider that it has quite the same prominence in this sector as some of its traditional rivals. The firm is, nonetheless, active in a great variety of corporate work and has been busy assisting clients throughout the consolidation of Indiana's financial sector. It has been involved in a number of thrift/bank mergers.
The Lawyers: *"Bright securities lawyer"* **Cathy Bridge** is one of the firm's stars. She chairs the business, tax and real estate department, and won consistent praise from peers and clients for her *"technically strong and solution-oriented"* advice on securities matters. She has also represented insurers in M&A and regulatory matters. *"High-flying banking expert"* **Claudia Swhier** enjoys a good reputation for her work in corporate securities. Peers rate her as a *"leader in the legal and regulatory arena of the financial institutions industry"* and she is renowned for representing banks and financial institutions.
The Clients: The firm has a large and varied client base, including such names as Tomkins, Eli Lilly, The Children's Museum of Indianapolis and DePuy Orthopaedics.

Sommer Barnard Ackerson
The Firm: The firm concluded a merger in August 2002 with DC litigation experts The Ackerson Group, adding to its litigation strength. On the corporate side, peers commented that it is *"moving in the right direction"* and is able to *"give the larger firms a run for their money."* Though smaller than some of its rivals, with about 20 attorneys in corporate law, the team is widely experienced, especially at the midmarket level, and enjoys expertise in all aspects of M&A and securities work.
The Lawyers: The *"unquestionable leader,"* **Jim Strain** (see p.284) is said by interviewees to be *"incredibly smart"* with *"unusual technical expertise."* Formerly of Barnes & Thornburg, his *"substantial IPO experience"* and all-around corporate knowledge earned him market recommendations as *"one of the top corporate lawyers in the city."* He was lead outside counsel for the City of Indianapolis in the public-private agreement it made with NiSource and the $500 million purchase of the company's Indianapolis water utility assets, a two-year deal that closed in April 2002. He is currently involved in advisory work relating to the Sarbanes-Oxley legislation. **Bob Hicks** (see p.283) has been representing gaming and racetrack interests in acquisitions in Colorado. Market sources consider him a *"first-class, practical transactional lawyer with an entrepreneurial spirit."* He returned to Sommer Barnard in January 2002, after a six-year absence during which he held senior positions at medical claims processor RealMed and its largest shareholder, the CIT Group.
The Clients: The firm's client base includes names like Eli Lilly and Vectren.

Krieg DeVault LLP
The Firm: With three offices in the region, peers describe the firm as *"active and prominent in the representation of banks"* and financial institutions in Indiana. It boasts about 40 lawyers under its corporate and securities umbrella, giving it an edge over its smaller rivals.
The Lawyers: The firm's standout name is **Bob Greising**, a *"leader"* in the corporate arena, with an *"increasingly diversified"* practice. Peers acknowledge his expertise in all areas of general commercial advice, corporate finance and secured lending. He also has a niche in the technology sector and has advised many start-ups on commercial issues, including negotiations concerning venture capital.
The Clients: GE; Bank One, Indiana; Bridgestone/Firestone and First Indiana Bank.

Henderson Daily Withrow & DeVoe
The Firm: This *"small but capable shop"* has about 30 lawyers in its one Indianapolis office. Interviewees considered it a good, solid outfit within the limits imposed by its smaller size.
The Lawyers: **Bob Wildman** leads the corporate practice. Peers describe him as a *"strong and capable lawyer,"* particularly known for his representation of emerging companies.
The Clients: Typical clients of the firm include American United Life Insurance Company, Verizon Wireless and Morgan Stanley.

Leagre Chandler & Millard LLP
The Firm: This mid-sized firm has nearly 30 lawyers at its Indianapolis office. It focuses on helping emerging companies with their expansion plans. In early 2002, the firm represented a shareholder group in its hostile takeover of the publicly traded Californian entertainment company that owns leading comedy brand National Lampoon.
The Lawyers: *"Impressive"* **David Millard** enjoys a strong reputation among peers. He is especially well known for representing smaller private entities and start-ups in general commercial and smaller securities transactions.
The Clients: The firm represents a number of important clients. It is counsel to Obsidian Enterprises, recognized by The Indianapolis Business Journal in 2002 as one of the fastest growing publicly held companies in central Indiana.

EMPLOYMENT & LABOR LAW — MAINLY PLAINTIFF

INDIANA
Leading firms
(Employment: Mainly Plaintiff)

1. **MACEY MACEY & SWANSON** Indianapolis
2. **FILLENWARTH, DENNERLINE** Indianapolis
   HASKIN LAUTER & LARUE Indianapolis
   LOWE GRAY STEELE & DARKO LLP Indianapolis

Firms are listed alphabetically in each band.

Macey Macey & Swanson
The Firm: According to market opinion, this firm is *"head and shoulders above"* the opposition when it comes to representing plaintiffs on complex labor and employment matters. It has a traditional labor background, and is staffed by a group of talented lawyers who are said to *"know the field inside out."*
The Lawyers: The group's star name is **Barry Macey**. Interviewees describe him as a *"bright, capable and experienced guy"* with an excellent reputation on the local circuit. He has been seen around on many of the most interesting union cases.

Fillenwarth, Dennerline, Groth & Towe
The Firm: The employment group represents many of the labor unions in Indianapolis. It has a name for employment discrimination and lobbying work regarding legislation on workers' compensation issues.
The Lawyers: The firm boasts some *"top people,"* including **Frederick (Ricky) Dennerline**. He has a high standing in the state as a benefits lawyer.

Haskin Lauter & LaRue
The Firm: The firm handles a large workload with *"high volumes"* of employment litigation. Many commentators consider it to have a strong and growing reputation, with one even describing it as *"hot on the heels of Macey Macey & Swanson."*
The Lawyers: The *"unshakable"* **Denise LaRue**

EMPLOYMENT & LABOR LAW

INDIANA

INDIANA
Leading individuals
(Employment: Mainly Plaintiff)

1. **MACEY Barry** *Macey Macey & Swanson,* Indianapolis
2. **DENNERLINE Frederick** *Fillenwarth,* Indianapolis
   LAPOINTE Mary Jane *Lowe Gray Steele,* Indianapolis
   LARUE Denise *Haskin Lauter & LaRue,* Indianapolis

Individuals are listed alphabetically in each band.

is an *"outstanding adversary"* according to competitors. She has a background in the Indiana Civil Rights Commission, having been its hearing officer for some time.

Lowe Gray Steele & Darko LLP
The Firm: This mid-sized, 23-lawyer firm includes six labor and employment specialists. Their workloads range from advising the management of private businesses to representing major public sector unions.

The Lawyers: Researchers were told that this firm is expected to become much more of a force in the near future. This anticipation is due to the energy and determination of *"unique"* **Mary Jane Lapointe**, a *"straight-shooting, ethical and diligent discrimination lawyer"* with *"no self-inflated importance."* Competitors are impressed by the good reputation she is building with her plaintiffs' work.

EMPLOYMENT & LABOR LAW   MAINLY DEFENDANT

INDIANA
Leading firms
(Employment: Mainly Defendant)

1. **BAKER & DANIELS** Indianapolis
   ICE MILLER Indianapolis
2. **BARNES & THORNBURG** Indianapolis
   OGLETREE, DEAKINS, NASH, SMOAK Indianapolis
3. **BOSE MCKINNEY & EVANS LLP** Indianapolis

Leading individuals
(Employment: Mainly Defendant)

1. **BORN SR** *Ice Miller,* Indianapolis
   EBERT Kim *Ogletree, Deakins, Nash,* Indianapolis
   MILLER David *Baker & Daniels,* Indianapolis
2. **BOLDT Michael** *Ice Miller,* Indianapolis
   YERKES Kenneth *Barnes & Thornburg,* Indianapolis
3. **EMERSON Dan** *Bose McKinney & Evans,* Indianapolis
   KLAPER Martin *Ice Miller,* Indianapolis
   NEIGHBOURS John *Baker & Daniels,* Indianapolis
   SWIDER David *Bose McKinney & Evans,* Indianapolis
   UTKEN Greg *Baker & Daniels,* Indianapolis

Firms and individuals are listed alphabetically in each band.

Baker & Daniels
The Firm: The firm boasts one of the largest employment groups in the Midwest, with about 30 labor and employment attorneys in Indiana. Five offices in the state give it a strongly entrenched position. Market sources note the firm's strength across the full range of employment and traditional labor work. The group attracted particular praise for its representation of management in union matters, union avoidance and labor contracts.

The Lawyers: **Greg Utken** chairs the practice and has broad experience in labor and employment law. However, he now focuses on traditional labor issues with some employment discrimination work. According to sources, he is still active after almost 30 years in the profession and is *"heavily involved in counseling and strategic planning."* Peers respect his knack of *"getting companies through the land mines."* **John Neighbours** has a good name in the market as a *"solid all-around generalist."* His *"considerable strength"* in the traditional labor arena, especially employment litigation, collective bargaining and union avoidance, is said to have earned him a national reputation. *"Incredibly client-friendly"* **David Miller** was praised by clients and competitors for his energy and ability. He represents many healthcare institutions nationally and, in addition to day-to-day counseling, is particularly focused on traditional labor matters and union avoidance.

The Clients: The team has acted for some important clients, including Conseco, Eli Lilly and Guidant.

Ice Miller
The Firm: According to market commentators, this is a *"top notch"* employment team with some *"high-quality lawyers."* It has recently added half a dozen attorneys from the now-defunct Johnson Smith. This enhances what was already one of the deepest benches in Indianapolis, allowing the firm to draw on almost 30 employment specialists, ten of whom have over 20 years' experience each. The firm covers the range of employment law but gained especially high marks from observers for its traditional labor work.

The Lawyers: **Chic Born** was recognized for his *"array of talents."* In particular, he won praise for a *"solid base in traditional labor"* and *"substantial collective bargaining experience"* nationally as well as in Indiana. His work in the OSHA arena was also well regarded. *"Outstanding"* **Martin Klaper** has a diverse labor and employment practice. He is active in negotiating and arbitrating labor contracts, as well as in advising companies on their internal systems for dealing with employment issues. Almost exclusively a construction labor lawyer, **Michael Boldt** has *"an excellent reputation in a discrete area."* Interviewees describe him as *"solutions-oriented and nonconfrontational"* with a *"high level of credibility with the unions."*

Barnes & Thornburg
The Firm: Indiana's largest firm boasts a complement of more than 50 labor and employment lawyers. Sources agree that this makes it a *"big player,"* and *"something of a one-stop shop"* for employment advice. It handles the full spectrum of labor law, including counseling, employment litigation and traditional labor matters. Currently it is felt to lean slightly toward discrimination and litigation, in accordance with market trends.

The Lawyers: **Kenneth Yerkes** chairs the firm's employment group. Competitors describe him as a *"well-known and knowledgeable"* employment lawyer with a *"good name statewide and nationally."* His practice is evenly split between employment litigation and traditional labor matters. Commentators praised his experience in a range of areas, including collective bargaining and union avoidance planning. He has worked on arbitration agreements with unions on behalf of Finish Line.

The Clients: Roche Diagnostics; Hillenbrand Industries; Anthem; Bristol-Myers Squibb and Ameritech.

Ogletree, Deakins, Nash, Smoak & Stewart, PC
The Firm: Market sources consider this firm to have a growing employment profile in the state. It is felt to be expanding rapidly, and recent recruits from Johnson Smith and Locke Reynolds have helped it to build its reputation as a leading player in the labor law arena. It now boasts about 160 attorneys based in 14 offices, and its single Indianapolis office has grown to include about a dozen labor and employment lawyers. Peers commented that the group has a strong employee benefits and immigration practice.

The Lawyers: **Kim Ebert**, formerly of Locke Reynolds, leads the group. Competitors say he has *"the right balance of personality and intelligence"* to ensure long-term success. The *"cream of the crop,"* Ebert has a well-rounded practice covering traditional labor issues, employment counseling, advisory work, affirmative action planning and litigation.

INDIANA

LITIGATION

Bose McKinney & Evans LLP
The Firm: Market sources question how visible the firm – acknowledged to be a major presence in the state – is in the labor and employment arena. Its size and importance, however, make it a definite player.

The Lawyers: The most widely recognized lawyers are **David Swider** and **Dan Emerson**. Emerson chairs the employment group. He is said by peers to be a *"great lawyer with an effective bull-in-a-china-shop approach."* His practice emphasizes employment litigation and general client counseling. Swider, meanwhile, is noted for his professional and cordial style. He particularly advises on affirmative action plans and employment handbooks, and represents management in labor matters, including litigation and discrimination.

LITIGATION

INDIANA
Leading firms
(Litigation: General Commercial)

1. BAKER & DANIELS *Indianapolis*
   BARNES & THORNBURG *Indianapolis*
2. ICE MILLER *Indianapolis*
3. BINGHAM MCHALE LLP *Indianapolis*
   SOMMER BARNARD ACKERSON *Indianapolis*
4. BOSE MCKINNEY & EVANS LLP *Indianapolis*
   MCTURNAN & TURNER *Indianapolis*
5. KRIEG DEVAULT LLP *Indianapolis*

Leading individuals
(Litigation: General Commercial)

1. MCTURNAN Lee *McTurnan & Turner*, Indianapolis
   PENCE Linda *Sommer Barnard Ackerson*, Indianapolis
   SCANLON Chris *Baker & Daniels*, Indianapolis
   WHISTLER Philip *Ice Miller*, Indianapolis
   YEAGER Jay *Baker & Daniels*, Indianapolis
2. CAMPBELL Dave *Bingham McHale LLP*, Indianapolis
   ELBERGER Ronald *Bose McKinney*, Indianapolis
   FICKLE Stanley *Barnes & Thornburg*, Indianapolis
   MACGILL Robert *Barnes & Thornburg*, Indianapolis
   MALEY John *Barnes & Thornburg*, Indianapolis
   TURNER Wayne *McTurnan & Turner*, Indianapolis
3. DEPREZ Anne *Barnes & Thornburg*, Indianapolis
   HOKANSON Jeffrey *Ice Miller*, Indianapolis
   MITCHELL Marvin *Mitchell Hurst Jacobs*, Indianapolis
   SHOCKLEY Steve *Sommer Barnard*, Indianapolis
   TITTLE Dave *Bingham McHale LLP*, Indianapolis

Firms and Individuals are listed alphabetically in each band.

Baker & Daniels
The Firm: Widely acknowledged as a *"legal Goliath."* It boasts 350 lawyers across seven offices, five of them in Indiana, and continues to earn high marks from clients and competitors for the strength and experience of its commercial litigation practice. Attorneys have experience of all aspects of commercial litigation, including contract, insurance, business tort, business and securities fraud, RICO and trade secrets matters.

The Lawyers: *"First-rate all-rounder"* **Chris Scanlon** enjoys a broad-based workload. Commentators note his *"big background in insurance coverage litigation."* He also has extensive experience of a range of other areas. These include securities litigation, where he has participated in actions under both state and federal securities laws, including securities class actions. Meanwhile *"savvy"* **Jay Yeager** was praised for his *"excellent brief-writing and trial skills."* His cases have included aviation litigation, insurance company acquisition and financing matters, fraud, and public entity disputes.

Barnes & Thornburg
The Firm: This is the largest firm in Indiana and among the biggest in the Midwest. Competitors and clients recognize it as a *"powerhouse"* in the area of commercial litigation. Its *"deep and talented pool"* of more than 340 lawyers is spread across six offices, four of them in Indiana, and includes over 100 litigation lawyers. The firm has an emphasis on products liability, toxic tort and medical defense litigation.

The Lawyers: **John Maley**, the president of the Indianapolis Bar Association, is regarded by peers as an *"extraordinarily sharp guy"* and *"one of the most efficient lawyers in Indiana."* He litigates a wide array of matters, including employment discrimination, noncompetition, trade secrets, products liability and IP cases. *"Appellate whiz"* **Stan Fickle** has a name as *"the appellate lawyer"* in Indiana. He has successfully handled appeals before the Court of Appeals and Indiana Supreme Court, several federal appellate courts and the US Supreme Court. Sources praise him for his *"excellent written work"* and *"extensive experience"* of ERISA matters and utility regulation. He was recently successful on behalf of an Illinois resident against Rush Prudential HMO in a healthcare litigation case. **Anne Deprez** is *"bright and quick on her feet,"* according to interviewees. She was particularly noted for her strength in securities, antitrust and class action work. **Rob MacGill** chairs the litigation group. He was described as *"one of the top guys"* and a *"highly qualified and aggressive lawyer"* with a reputation for developing national defense strategies in products liability litigation.

The Clients: The firm's client list includes names such as Whirlpool, DePuy Orthopaedics, Georgia-Pacific, Dow Chemical and Mitsubishi.

GENERAL COMMERCIAL

Ice Miller
The Firm: Ice Miller's profile is aided by being the largest law firm in Indianapolis, and competitors are quick to recognize it as a major player in the sector. Its name is consistently associated with expertise in insurance defense. However, it is now expanding its focus to cover the full range of litigation counsel, and has been busy in areas such as commercial contract litigation, IP and trade regulation disputes.

The Lawyers: **Phil Whistler** is a *"fine and bright lawyer,"* according to peers, with a *"thorough and logical"* approach. Clients value his advice on complex business and contractual disputes. He is currently representing a university that is tracking down historically significant relics. Sources describe **Jeff Hokanson** as a *"responsive"* lawyer, with a talent for *"keeping things moving."* He was noted for his experience in creditors' rights, bankruptcy and general commercial litigation.

The Clients: The firm acts for some important corporates and institutions, including Emerson Electrical Company and Community Hospital.

Bingham McHale LLP
The Firm: In January 2002 Bingham Summers Welsh & Spilman and McHale Cook & Welch merged to form Bingham McHale. Interviewees dubbed this a *"vital consolidation."* The merged entity is now the fourth largest firm in Indiana, employing about 110 lawyers in three Indiana offices.

The Lawyers: There are *"many competent lawyers"* at this firm, according to peers. In litigation, two names were consistently highlighted. *"Not one to overplay his hand,"* **Dave Campbell** received much acclaim as a *"good courtroom lawyer"* with almost 30 years of experience. Rivals particularly admire his *"terrific knack of simplifying incredibly complex facts."* Campbell, who had early experience in insurance defense, now boasts a diverse practice, ranging from antitrust and securities litigation to general contractual litigation. **Dave Tittle** also has a high standing among peers. He, too, has made the transition to commercial litigation from an insurance defense background, and carries out a lot of products liability work.

LITIGATION

INDIANA

Sommer Barnard Ackerson
The Firm: The firm has boosted its profile in the area through a recent merger with DC-based litigation firm, The Ackerson Group. The expanded practice now consists of 80 lawyers across two Indiana offices.
The Lawyers: The recruitment of **Linda Pence** (see p.284) from Johnson Smith was recognized as an *"important addition"* for the firm. *"A real go-getter"* who has attracted a number of high-profile cases, she is described by sources as an *"experienced, tough, methodical and direct litigator."* She has a strong US Department of Justice background, and concentrates on complex civil and white-collar criminal litigation. Her extensive experience of defending individuals and corporations in white-collar investigations, including government procurement contract fraud and tax fraud, came in for particular praise. In **Steve Shockley** (see p.284), head of the appellate practice, she is said to have a *"solid lieutenant,"* with talent as a deposition-taker and brief writer.
The Clients: High-profile litigation matters include the Microsoft litigation and the White River fish kill litigation.

Bose McKinney & Evans LLP
The Firm: The firm has a solid market reputation in commercial litigation. It can count on almost 100 lawyers in four offices in Indiana and one in Washington DC, many of whom have contentious experience. Interviewees note that it has been involved in some impressive litigation. In one case it successfully represented William Warren and WOWemployers.com in a lawsuit brought by Warren's previous company, Monster.com.
The Lawyers: **Ron Elberger** emerged from *Chambers'* research as a *"savvy, dogged, aggressive and experienced litigator."* He is recognized for his strength in appellate law and public sector litigation, particularly for schools and municipalities. Sources also note his expertise in entertainment law, where he represents TV personality David Letterman.

McTurnan & Turner
The Firm: This 12-person niche firm, based in Indianapolis, concentrates on complex commercial litigation. Market sources consider it a *"player in the sector on the strength of the reputation of its name partners."* It undertakes defense work almost exclusively, and is currently assisting Ameritech, the regional telecom player, in a large class action age discrimination case. It also undertakes a steady stream of professional negligence cases, often representing some of the state's larger law firms.
The Lawyers: **Lee McTurnan** was formerly with Sidley & Austin in Chicago. Peers consider him a *"talented, well-paced litigator with a strong courtroom presence,"* and rate him highly for his *"incredible thoroughness"* and sound strategic advice. **Wayne Turner** earned high marks from interviewees for his *"sharp intellect"* and all-around excellence in commercial litigation – he is *"more a decathlete than an athlete,"* according to one source. He has been involved in cases across a range of sectors, including the firm's major work for Ameritech and litigation in the automotive sector.
The Clients: Alongside its law firm clients, the firm represents top names such as Ameritech and DaimlerChrysler.

Krieg DeVault LLP
The Firm: This medium-sized firm boasts over 80 lawyers in its three Indiana offices. Its Indianapolis office is one of the largest in the city. Commentators acknowledge that it has *"a respected name"* for commercial litigation. However, market opinion is that its profile is highest in the fields of banking and creditors' rights litigation, and that it is less visible in general commercial cases.
The Lawyers: The litigation department is headed by Max Hittle Jr.
The Clients: American Express, Bank One, Indiana and Conseco.

Other Notable Practitioners
Marvin Mitchell of Mitchell Hurst Jacobs & Dick is said by commentators to be *"an accomplished lawyer"* who is *"organized, practical and hard as nails."* He is felt to be the premier general commercial litigator at a firm that focuses on personal injury work for plaintiffs.

REAL ESTATE

INDIANA
Leading firms (Real Estate)

1. BARNES & THORNBURG *Indianapolis*
   ICE MILLER *Indianapolis*
2. BAKER & DANIELS *Indianapolis*
   WALLACK SOMERS & HAAS PC *Indianapolis*
3. BOSE McKINNEY & EVANS LLP *Indianapolis*
   DANN PECAR NEWMAN & KLEIMAN, *Indianapolis*
4. BINGHAM McHALE LLP *Indianapolis*
   SOMMER BARNARD ACKERSON *Indianapolis*
5. KRIEG DEVAULT LLP *Indianapolis*

Firms are listed alphabetically in each band.

Barnes & Thornburg
The Firm: The largest law firm in the state has a *"highly respected"* 30-strong real estate team. It is experienced in the full range of commercial real estate services, including land use, leasing and condemnation. Historically, the firm has represented both lenders and larger corporate developers, and it boasts a client list with a Fortune 500 flavor.
The Lawyers: *"Top-drawer"* **Dave Warshauer** has returned to private practice following a stint as executive vice president of a development company. Market sources describe him as *"one to watch."* He has impressed with his *"wide range of capabilities in both simple and sophisticated transactions,"* and his advice in relation to zoning, land use and general development work. Work has included a major zoning case, securing approval for a limestone quarry. *"Practical"* **Dick Johnson** is recognized for his knowledge and experience in real estate finance. Peers acknowledge that this has given him a national reputation, and many regard him as one of the *"leading lending lawyers in the Midwest."* He has been involved in two of the firm's major construction finance deals: a $52 million deal for Jefferson Pointe Shopping Center in Fort Wayne and a $66 million transaction for Bank One, Indiana. **Stephen Lee** is described as *"unflinching"* and *"appropriately aggressive."* Researchers were told that he is *"one of the most effective real estate lawyers around,"* with particular strength in leasing and land development planning.
The Clients: Important clients include Eli Lilly, Georgia-Pacific, Whirlpool and Bank One, Indiana.

Ice Miller
The Firm: Among the firm's more than 230 lawyers, about 16 attorneys practice real estate law. Competitors and clients were full of praise for the skills of these *"first-rate legal architects."* The firm is traditionally known for representing developers, but has skills across the range of real estate transactions, from construction and acquisition to development and finance. The firm assisted a local development team in obtaining governmental incentives, which allowed it to construct a 600-room Marriott Convention Center Hotel in the heart of Indianapolis. These incentives included a favorable long-term ground lease, a large subsidy toward improvements, and the construction by the local government of skyway connectors linking the hotel with the Indianapolis Convention Center.
The Lawyers: The firm's real estate team is *"superbly led"* by its chair **Zeff Weiss**. Interviewees repeatedly praised him as a *"brilliant tactician and*

INDIANA   REAL ESTATE

INDIANA
Leading individuals (Real Estate)

1
- SOMERS George *Wallack Somers & Haas*, Indianapolis
- WEISS Zeff *Ice Miller*, Indianapolis

2
- BAYT Phillip *Ice Miller*, Indianapolis
- WALLACK Barry *Wallack Somers & Haas*, Indianapolis
- WARSHAUER David *Barnes & Thornburg*, Indianapolis

3
- HAAS Karl *Wallack Somers & Haas PC*, Indianapolis
- JOHNSON Richard *Barnes & Thornburg*, Indianapolis
- LEE Stephen *Barnes & Thornburg*, Indianapolis
- LISHER Mary *Baker & Daniels*, Indianapolis
- NICELY Phil *Bose McKinney & Evans LLP*, Indianapolis
- O'BRYAN Rory *Harrison & Moberly LLP*, Indianapolis
- SCIMIA Joe *Baker & Daniels*, Indianapolis
- SOLADA Mary *Bingham McHale LLP*, Indianapolis

4
- ABRAMS Jeffrey *Dann Pecar Newman*, Indianapolis
- CARLINO James *Bose McKinney & Evans*, Indianapolis
- DINWIDDIE Thomas *Wooden & McLaughlin*, Indianapolis
- LAWSON Jack *Beckman Lawson, LLP*, Fort Wayne
- SCHWARZ James *Dann Pecar Newman*, Indianapolis
- STERNER Dan *Sommer Barnard Ackerson*, Indianapolis

Individuals are listed alphabetically in each band.

---

strategist" with an *"enormous depth of real estate knowledge and a sure grasp of the vital business issues."* He is particularly admired for his skill in land use, zoning and development in the housing market. **Phil Bayt** has taken on the role of managing partner. Competitors rate him as a *"practical, intelligent and experienced"* lawyer with a focus on development work, especially the creation of ownership and development strategies. He has represented Manser Development, the Indianapolis Motor Speedway and various hotel developers, and conducts a great deal of work for Indiana's growing gaming industry.

The Clients: The firm services a top-quality client base, including names like Whiteco Industries and Buckingham Companies.

Baker & Daniels
The Firm: This regional giant is deemed by market sources to be an important local player, with a depth of expertise and some good real estate clients. Its bench is a respectable size, at approximately 18 lawyers. However, the firm has faced the loss, in recent years, of a number of senior attorneys. George Somers and Karl Haas left in 1999 to form their own firm, and Rory O'Bryan has also departed, for boutique firm Harrison & Moberly.

The Lawyers: The team retains a core of outstanding real estate lawyers. **Joe Scimia** was recommended to *Chambers'* researchers as a *"smart and sound negotiator."* He chairs both the firm's real estate and environmental law team and its land use and planning services group. Clients value his broad experience, which includes representing developers, contractors, lenders, land-lords, tenants and property owners in a variety of real estate transactions. Equally valuable is his *"thorough and at times tenacious"* approach. **Mary Lisher** also won plaudits from the market. *"Bright, capable and unquestionably honest,"* she is said by peers to *"catch all the issues."* Her strengths are felt to lie on the real estate development side, especially industrial parks. She was lead attorney for the Union Station hotel/retail development in Indianapolis, including advising on all related financing and leasing matters. She has also served as attorney for the AmeriPlex Project, a mixed-use advanced technology and commerce park.

The Clients: United Airlines.

Wallack Somers & Haas PC
see firm details p.895

The Firm: This seven-person boutique was launched in 1999. It concentrates on serving the commercial real estate and business communities in Indianapolis. Though small, it boasts a wealth of expertise: the three name partners alone have over 60 years' combined experience. Market sources consider the firm to have a focus on developers and investors. However, it represents a diversified clientele, including municipalities in their redevelopment efforts.

The Lawyers: Karl Haas (see p.283) was formerly a star at Baker & Daniels. Clients value his *"highly intelligent and analytical"* approach. He has worked on major urban renewal projects for downtown Indianapolis and boasts a good mix of municipal clients. **Barry Wallack** (see p.285) is an exceptionally skilled attorney, who competitors describe as a *"massive lenders' lawyer."* They acknowledge, however, that the breadth of his experience extends across the entire field, including small business issues and retail development. **George Somers**' (see p.284) practice focused on representing commercial developers. He received warm recommendations for his *"practical"* approach and *"excellent grasp of the commercial issues."*

The Clients: Despite its youth, the firm already boasts a large and growing client base, including such names as Allstate Life Insurance Company, ReliaStar Life Insurance Company, City of Carmel, Indiana, Fifth Third Bank, Browning Investments and Kite Development.

Bose McKinney & Evans LLP
The Firm: According to market sources, this mid-sized Indiana firm is *"historically sound"* in the real estate arena. It can count on almost 100 lawyers in five offices, including a dedicated real estate team of about ten. Like many of its larger rivals, it is geared toward representing commercial real estate developers. However, sources also point to a widely admired niche in planning, land use and zoning.

The Lawyers: *"Zoning guru"* **Phil Nicely** is considered by many to be *"one of the best land use lawyers in the city."* He is enormously experienced and was primarily responsible for advising on all of the real estate issues involved in the formation of Duke Realty, where he is currently counsel to the board of directors. He receives *"impressive support"* from *"knowledgeable"* **Jim Carlino**. Carlino's practice is focused on real estate transactions, although he also has financing experience. He has acted as local counsel in a $450 million sale and leaseback transaction for a power company in southern Indiana. He also helped to arrange a partnership agreement for GE Capital regarding an investment in a coke-producing facility in northern Indiana.

The Clients: Important clients of the group include Duke Realty, First Indiana Bank and Panther Racing.

Dann Pecar Newman & Kleiman, PC
The Firm: This firm has nearly 30 lawyers in its Indianapolis office. It commands respect from peers for the strength of its real estate team. Its good position in the market is said to stretch back to the solid relationship forged by the late Philip Pecar with Simon Property Group. This major Indianapolis-based client is the largest publicly traded REIT in North America. Sources also often refer to the firm's niche expertise in shopping center development.

The Lawyers: *"Technically strong"* **Jim Schwarz** undertakes a large amount of work for Simon Property Group. He acted as developer's counsel in the development and financing of the Mall of America, the largest of its kind. A *"smart and experienced"* lawyer, he carries out a broad range of real estate services, including substantial lending work. The 11-man real estate team also contains *"aggressive business developer and rainmaker"* **Jeff Abrams**, who is highly regarded for his transactional work for small to medium-sized private developers and lenders.

The Clients: The firm's best-known client is Simon Property Group.

Bingham McHale LLP
The Firm: The January 2002 merger that created Bingham McHale brought into being a firm with about 110 lawyers in three Indiana offices. Its enhanced real estate group is attracting much positive feedback from the market, and commands a particularly good reputation for its expertise in zoning issues.

The Lawyers: The chair of the real estate group is **Mary Solada**, a *"shining light"* for the firm who is *"well known and well connected"* in the real estate community. She represents both private sector and governmental clients in a wide range of areas including real estate acquisitions and redevelopments, but peers consider her *"especially highly thought of"* in land use, zoning and planning.

LEADERS — INDIANA

She holds a position as general counsel for the Capital Improvement Board of Marion County, Indiana. Her broad experience includes advising on the development of Conseco Fieldhouse for the NBA's Indiana Pacers, 'Victory Field' and the RCA Dome stadium.
The Clients: Clients of the firm include Gatorade Trust, Shell Oil, Thomson multimedia and Time Warner Cable.

Sommer Barnard Ackerson
The Firm: This *"quality"* 84-lawyer firm pulled off a merger in August 2002 with DC litigation experts, The Ackerson Group. Rivals acknowledge that it is a player in this field; however, it is not felt to have as high a profile in real estate as in some other areas.

The Lawyers: Dan Sterner (see p.284) stands out here as a *"superb lawyer"* with a high market profile. He represents a broad base of clients on matters relating to real estate acquisitions, development, leasing and financing.

Krieg DeVault LLP
The Firm: This firm has a long-established presence in the marketplace, serving the real estate community from three Indiana offices. Competitors praise the firm for its real estate finance expertise, especially for its work on behalf of banks and lenders.
The Lawyers: The real estate and environment group, chaired by Andrew Buroker, includes about 20 lawyers.
The Clients: Bank One, Indiana, Fifth Third Bank, Indiana and GE.

Other Notable Practitioners
"Incredibly smart" **Rory O' Bryan**, formerly of Baker & Daniels, is now *"the shining light"* at boutique firm Harrison & Moberly LLP. He attracts consistent plaudits for his vast real estate experience. **Tom Dinwiddie** is a *"bright"* real estate specialist at Wooden & McLaughlin LLP. Peers often see him putting his *"depth of experience"* to use for commercial developers. **Jack Lawson**, of Fort Wayne firm Beckman Lawson LLP, is considered by many to be one of the *"most respected zoning lawyers in the state."* Peers acknowledge that he is both highly skilled and *"incredibly devoted"* to his clients' interests.

Leaders in Indiana

ABRAMS, Jeffrey
Dann Pecar Newman & Kleiman, PC, Indianapolis 317 632 3232
Recommended in Real Estate

ASCHLEMAN, James
Baker & Daniels, Indianapolis
317 237 0300
Recommended in Corporate/M&A

BAYT, Phillip
Ice Miller, Indianapolis
317 236 2100
Recommended in Real Estate

BOEGLIN, Daniel
Baker & Daniels, Indianapolis
317 237 0300
Recommended in Corporate/M&A

BOLDT, Michael
Ice Miller, Indianapolis
317 236 2100
Recommended in Employment

BORN, S R
Ice Miller, Indianapolis
317 236 2100
Recommended in Employment

BRIDGE, Catherine
Barnes & Thornburg, Indianapolis
317 236 1313
Recommended in Corporate/M&A

BROWN, Jeff
Baker & Daniels, Indianapolis
317 237 0300
Recommended in Corporate/M&A

CAMPBELL, Dave
Bingham McHale LLP, Indianapolis
317 635 8900
Recommended in Litigation

CARLINO, James
Bose McKinney & Evans LLP, Indianapolis 317 684 5000
Recommended in Real Estate

DENNERLINE, Frederick
Fillenwarth, Dennerline, Groth & Towe, Indianapolis 317 353 9363
Recommended in Employment

DEPREZ, Anne
Barnes & Thornburg, Indianapolis
317 236 1313
Recommended in Litigation

DINWIDDIE, Thomas
Wooden & McLaughlin LLP, Indianapolis 317 639 6151
Recommended in Real Estate

EBERT, Kim
Ogletree, Deakins, Nash, Smoak & Stewart, PC, Indianapolis 317 916 1300
Recommended in Employment

ELBERGER, Ronald
Bose McKinney & Evans LLP, Indianapolis 317 684 5000
Recommended in Litigation

EMERSON, Dan
Bose McKinney & Evans LLP, Indianapolis 317 684 5000
Recommended in Employment

FICKLE, Stanley
Barnes & Thornburg, Indianapolis
317 236 1313
Recommended in Litigation

GREISING, Robert
Krieg DeVault LLP, Indianapolis
317 636 4341
Recommended in Corporate/M&A

HAAS, Karl
Wallack Somers & Haas PC, Indianapolis 317 231 9000
kph@wshlaw.com
Recommended in Real Estate
Specialisation: Partner at *Wallack, Somers & Haas*, concentrating in a broad range of real estate projects representing developers, lenders, investors and municipalities. He has provided counsel for these clients regarding purchasing, financing, developing, leasing, refinancing and selling office, retail, industrial, hotel and residential properties. In addition, he has provided counsel for numerous urban renewal projects, including Conseco Fieldhouse, home of the Indiana Pacers.
Career: Indiana State Bar admission 1985; *Baker & Daniels* (Associate 1985; Partner 1992-99).
Personal: Indiana University (BS, highest distinction, 1982); Indiana University School of Law, Indianapolis (JD, graduated first in class 1985).

HICKS, Robert
Sommer Barnard Ackerson Attorneys, PC, Indianapolis 317 713 3500
bhicks@sbalawyers.com
Recommended in Corporate/M&A
Specialisation: Firm Director focusing practice on complex business and commercial transactions, private equity and venture capital transactions, business advisory services, and tax and estate planning matters. Lead Counsel to sellers and buyers in numerous merger and acquisition transactions ranging in transaction sizes from $5 Million to approximately $650 Million and covering multiple industries. Lead Counsel in several private equity and joint venture transaction. Certified Public Accountant; Adjunct Professor, Tax and Business Law, Butler University, 1987-94.
Prof. Memberships: Indianapolis, Indiana State, and American Bar Associations. Indiana Certified Public Accountant Society.
Career: Admitted to Indiana Bar (1987); passed CPA Examination, May 1984. Chairman of the Board and Chief Executive Officer, RealMed Corporation (Indianapolis), 1999-2001; Executive Vice President, Strategic Development, the CIT Group, Inc. (Toronto, Chicago and New Jersey) 1998-2001; *Sommer Barnard Ackerson* Director from 1994 through 1996 and Associate from 1988 through 1994; *Ice Miller Donadio & Ryan* Associate from 1986 through 1988.
Publications: Author of numerous articles in various business and tax magazines and publications.
Personal: Received a BS in Business Administration and Accounting, with High Honors, from Butler University in 1984. Earned a JD from Marshall-Wythe School of Law; College of William & Mary, in 1986. Order of the Coif and William & Mary Law Review, 1985-1986.

HOKANSON, Jeffrey
Ice Miller, Indianapolis
317 236 2100
Recommended in Litigation

HUMKE, Steven
Ice Miller, Indianapolis
317 236 2100
Recommended in Corporate/M&A

JOHNSON, Richard
Barnes & Thornburg, Indianapolis
317 236 1313
Recommended in Real Estate

INDIANA — LEADERS

KLAPER, Martin
Ice Miller, Indianapolis
317 236 2100
Recommended in Employment

LAPOINTE, Mary Jane
Lowe Gray Steele & Darko LLP,
Indianapolis 317 236 8020
Recommended in Employment

LARUE, Denise
Haskin Lauter & LaRue,
Indianapolis 317 955 9500
Recommended in Employment

LAWSON, Jack
Beckman Lawson, LLP, Fort Wayne
219 422 0800
Recommended in Real Estate

LEE, Stephen
Barnes & Thornburg, Indianapolis
317 236 1313
Recommended in Real Estate

LISHER, Mary
Baker & Daniels, Indianapolis
317 237 0300
Recommended in Real Estate

MACEY, Barry
Macey Macey & Swanson, Indianapolis
317 637 2345
Recommended in Employment

MACGILL, Robert
Barnes & Thornburg, Indianapolis
317 236 1313
Recommended in Litigation

MALEY, John
Barnes & Thornburg, Indianapolis
317 236 1313
Recommended in Litigation

MCTURNAN, Lee
McTurnan & Turner, Indianapolis
317 464 8181
Recommended in Litigation

MILLARD, David
Leagre Chandler & Millard LLP,
Indianapolis 317 808 3000
Recommended in Corporate/M&A

MILLER, David
Baker & Daniels, Indianapolis
317 237 0300
Recommended in Employment

MITCHELL, Marvin
Mitchell Hurst Jacobs & Dick,
Indianapolis 317 633 7680
Recommended in Litigation

NEIGHBOURS, John
Baker & Daniels, Indianapolis
317 237 0300
Recommended in Employment

NICELY, Phil
Bose McKinney & Evans LLP,
Indianapolis 317 684 5000
Recommended in Real Estate

O'BRYAN, Rory
Harrison & Moberly LLP, Indianapolis
317 639 4511
Recommended in Real Estate

PENCE, Linda L
Sommer Barnard Ackerson Attorneys,
PC, Indianapolis 317 713 3500
lpence@sbalawyers.com
Recommended in Litigation
Specialisation: Co-chairs the litigation department and heads up the white collar criminal practice at *Sommer Barnard Ackerson*. Concentrates her practice on federal white collar criminal defense and complex civil litigation, including government procurement contract fraud, tax fraud, Medicare/Medicaid fraud, violations of securities laws, antitrust violations, rules and regulation, bribery, bid-rigging, embezzlement, official misconduct, RICO, insurance and bank fraud, customs and currency violations, and other related matters.
Prof. Memberships: National Association of Criminal Defense Lawyers, American Bar Association, Indiana State Bar Association.
Career: Admitted to Indiana Bar (1974) and District of Columbia Bar (1982). Spent nine years with the US Department of Justice as the Chief, Special Projects Branch; Deputy Chief, Government Fraud Section, Criminal Division; and Trial Attorney, Civil Division.
Personal: Received a BA and JD from Indiana University in 1971 and 1974.

SCANLON, Chris
Baker & Daniels, Indianapolis
317 237 0300
Recommended in Litigation

SCHWARZ, James
Dann Pecar Newman & Kleiman, PC,
Indianapolis 317 632 3232
Recommended in Real Estate

SCIMIA, Joe
Baker & Daniels, Indianapolis
317 237 0300
Recommended in Real Estate

SHOCKLEY, Steven C
Sommer Barnard Ackerson Attorneys,
PC, Indianapolis 317 713 3500
sshockley@sbalawyers.com
Recommended in Litigation
Specialisation: Member of the Litigation Department and the head of the Appellate Practice Department. A registered lobbyist in the State of Indiana and is also a member of the firm's Governmental Affairs Practice. Represented Indiana State Bar Association in original actions in Indiana Supreme Court to enjoin unauthorized practice of law. Represented the state circuit in original actions in the Indiana Supreme Court seeking jurisdictional writ.
Prof. Memberships: Indianapolis, Indiana State, Florida and American Bar Associations.
Career: Admitted to Indiana Bar (1984) and Florida Bar (1986). Associate with Florida law firm, Holland and Knight from 1986-88. Law Clerk to Hon. Stanley B Miller, Indiana Court of Appeals (1984-1986). Indiana Law Review, 1983-84.
Publications: Authored 'Crossed Signals: Copyright Liability for Resale Carriers of Television Broadcasts', in the 'Indiana Law Review, 1983'.
Personal: Received a BA and JD from Indiana University in 1978 and 1984.

SNYDER, Jack
Ice Miller, Indianapolis 317 236 2100
Recommended in Corporate/M&A

SOLADA, Mary
Bingham McHale LLP, Indianapolis
317 635 8900
Recommended in Real Estate

SOMERS, George W
Wallack Somers & Haas PC,
Indianapolis 317 231 9000
gws@wshlaw.com
Recommended in Real Estate
Specialisation: Partner at *Wallack, Somers & Haas*, concentrating in all types of real estate development. He has provided counsel to local, regional and national developers regarding the acquisition, construction, leasing, financing and disposition of retail, office and mixed-use developments.
Career: Indiana State Bar admission 1979; *Baker & Daniels* (Associate 1979; Partner 1985-99). James B Duke Scholar, Phi Beta Kappa.
Personal: Graduated St Olaf College (BA, magna cum laude, 1969); Harvard University (MTS, cum laude, 1971); Duke University (MA, 1974); University of Chicago (JD, 1979).

STERNER, Dan G
Sommer Barnard Ackerson Attorneys,
PC, Indianapolis 317.713.3500
dsterner@sbalawyers.com
Recommended in Real Estate
Specialisation: Extensive experience in commercial real estate law, representing developers and financial institutions. International experience in real estate acquisitions, distribution licensing, and manufacturing, concentrating on Europe, Far East, and Australia.
Prof. Memberships: The Indianapolis, Indiana State and International Bar Associations.
Career: Admitted to the Indiana Bar in 1962. Partner in *Sommer Barnard Ackerson, PC* since joining the firm in 1996.
Personal: Received a BA from Northwestern University in 1955 and a JD from Indiana University in 1962. Note Editor Indiana Law Journal from 1961-62.

STRAIN, James A
Sommer Barnard Ackerson Attorneys,
PC, Indianapolis 317 713 3500
strain@sbalawyers.com
Recommended in Corporate/M&A
Specialisation: Managing Partner/Director of the firm and Chairman of Business Law Practice Group. Has represented many clients in mergers and acquisitions matters, both friendly and hostel, including the Consolidated City of Indianapolis, Vectren Corporation, Indiana Energy, Control Devices, Excel, Amoco Corporation, Escient, Inc., Profitt's, Inc. (now Saks Incorporated), CTS Corporation.
Prof. Memberships: The American Bar Association, Seventh Circuit Bar Association (President, 1995-96 term), Indiana State Bar Association.
Career: Admitted to Indiana Bar in 1969. Law Clerk to Judge John S Hastings, United States Court of Appeals for Seventh Circuit, 1970-71 and Law Clerk to then Associate Justice William H Rehnquist, United States Supreme Court, October Term 1972. A partner of *Sommer Barnard Ackerson Attorneys, PC* since joining the firm in 1996. Participated in both national and state panels on issues of corporate governance, state regulation of takeovers and securities laws. Panelist for the 19th Annual Ray Garrett Jr. Corporate and Securities Law Institute. Lecturer in law at the Indiana University School of Law-Indianapolis; Adjunct Professor of Law at the Indiana university School of Law, Bloomington.
Personal: Received a JD (with honors, Order of the Coif) from Indiana University School of Law in 1969 and an AB from Indiana University in 1966. Admitted to Southern District of Indiana, Seventh Circuit, and US Supreme Court. Active in Indianapolis charitable activities principally involving music and theatre.

SWHIER, Claudia
Barnes & Thornburg, Indianapolis
317 236 1313
Recommended in Corporate/M&A

SWIDER, David
Bose McKinney & Evans LLP,
Indianapolis 317 684 5000
Recommended in Employment

THORNBURGH, John
Ice Miller, Indianapolis 317 236 2100
Recommended in Corporate/M&A

THRAPP, Richard
Ice Miller, Indianapolis 317 236 2100
Recommended in Corporate/M&A

TITTLE, Dave
Bingham McHale LLP, Indianapolis
317 635 8900
Recommended in Litigation

TURNER, Wayne
McTurnan & Turner, Indianapolis
317 464 8181
Recommended in Litigation

UTKEN, Greg
Baker & Daniels, Indianapolis
317 237 0300
Recommended in Employment

WALLACK, Barry Z
Wallack Somers & Haas PC,
Indianapolis 317 231 9000
bzw@wshlaw.com
Recommended in Real Estate
Specialisation: Partner at *Wallack, Somers & Haas*, concentrating in leasing, lending, borrowing, development, operation and syndication. He has represented clients in $300 million public debt offerings, sales and purchases of real estate projects of all sizes, development of numerous apartment projects, leasing of office buildings and shopping centers, and lender representation in all types of mortgage loans.
Career: Indiana State Bar admission 1965; *Baker & Daniels* (Associate 1965-69); *Klineman Rose Wolf & Wallack* (Partner 1969-93; Managing Partner 1986-93); *Wallack & Wallack* (Partner 1994-99).
Personal: Graduated University of Wisconsin (BS, 1962; JD, 1965).

WARSHAUER, David
Barnes & Thornburg, Indianapolis
317 236 1313
Recommended in Real Estate

WEISS, Zeff
Ice Miller, Indianapolis
317 236 2100
Recommended in Real Estate

WHISTLER, Philip
Ice Miller, Indianapolis 317 236 2100
Recommended in Litigation

WILDMAN, Bob
Henderson Daily Withrow & DeVoe,
Indianapolis 317 639 4121
Recommended in Corporate/M&A

YEAGER, Jay
Baker & Daniels, Indianapolis
317 237 0300
Recommended in Litigation

YERKES, Kenneth
Barnes & Thornburg, Indianapolis
317 236 1313
Recommended in Employment

IOWA

CORPORATE/M&A

CONTENTS: Corporate/M&A p.286; Employment: Mainly Plaintiff p.288; Mainly Defendant p.288; Litigation: General Commercial p.289; Real Estate p.290; Individuals' Profiles p.292.

IOWA'S TOP TWO
1. Belin Lamson McCormick Zumbach Flynn
2. Nyemaster, Goode, Voigts, West, Hansell & O'Brien

Ranking based on Chambers' research within the state.

All quotes in the text are from interviews with clients and competitors.

OVERVIEW: Des Moines-based **Belin Lamson McCormick Zumbach Flynn** is highly visible representing key state, national and global businesses in local Iowan matters. The firm offers a full range of legal services and ranks highly in corporate/M&A, real estate, employment defense and litigation. The real estate practice is said to include some of the most outstanding property lawyers in the state. Recent high-profile work includes the acquisition and development of a 200-acre entertainment and shopping center complex in West Des Moines, and the demutualization of AmerUS Life. Clients include Mid-America Group and the Meredith Corporation.

With offices in Des Moines and Ames, **Nyemaster, Goode, Voigts, West, Hansell & O'Brien** is Iowa's largest law firm, as well as one of the oldest. The firm is particularly noted for the strength of its employment practice, where attorneys defend management in all aspects of employment and labor law. An esteemed corporate department represents a varied client base that ranges from Fortune 500 companies to small local businesses and individuals. Recent transactional work

includes counseling Equitable of Iowa Companies on its sale to ING Group for $2.2 billion in cash and stock. The firm's client list also includes MidAmerican Energy Holdings Company, the City of Des Moines and GMAC Real Estate.

CORPORATE/M&A

IOWA
Leading firms (Corporate/M&A)
1. **BELIN LAMSON MCCORMICK** Des Moines
2. **NYEMASTER, GOODE, VOIGTS, WEST** Des Moines
3. **DAVIS, BROWN, KOEHN, SHORS** Des Moines
   LANE & WATERMAN Davenport
4. **BRADSHAW, FOWLER, PROCTOR** Des Moines
   SHUTTLEWORTH & INGERSOLL PLC Cedar Rapids
5. **AHLERS & COONEY PC** Des Moines
   BRADLEY & RILEY PC Cedar Rapids
6. **BROWN, WINICK, GRAVES, GROSS** Des Moines
   MOYER & BERGMAN PLC Cedar Rapids

Leading individuals (Corporate/M&A)
1. **HANSELL Edgar** *Nyemaster, Goode, Voigts,* Des Moines
   KRAMBECK James *Belin Lamson,* Des Moines
   ZUMBACH Steven *Belin Lamson,* Des Moines
2. **ADAMS Garth** *Belin Lamson,* Des Moines
   STREIT Gary *Shuttleworth & Ingersoll,* Cedar Rapids
   WATERMAN Dana *Lane & Waterman,* Davenport
3. **CARROLL Frank** *Davis, Brown, Koehn,* Des Moines
   CORTESIO John *Bradshaw, Fowler, Proctor,* Des Moines
   DONOHUE Michael *Moyer & Bergman,* Cedar Rapids
   NEUMANN Gordon *Nyemaster, Goode,* Des Moines
   REASONER Carroll *Shuttleworth,* Cedar Rapids
4. **BROWN Donald** *Davis, Brown, Koehn,* Des Moines
   HINTZE John *Ahlers & Cooney PC,* Des Moines
   JOHNSON Edward *Bradshaw, Fowler,* Des Moines
   RILEY Byron *Bradley & Riley PC,* Cedar Rapids

Firms and individuals are listed alphabetically in each band.

Belin Lamson McCormick Zumbach Flynn PC
The Firm: Market sources placed the firm *"at the forefront"* of Iowa's corporate legal market. The practice serves as counsel to many of Iowa's *"prime businesses"* and acts for national and international corporate clients on local legal matters. The corporate team is said to work well with other groups at the firm and with in-house counsel. It was involved in the demutualization of AmerUS Life. Other matters included acting in the recapitalization of Color Converting Industries and in a recent sale of assets by Southern Culvert and Wheeler Consolidated to Hydro Conduit.

The Lawyers: According to many, **Steven Zumbach** (see p.293) has emerged as *"the leader of Iowa's corporate law community."* Clients reported that he combines *"a great grasp of business issues with a sound legal background."* He is visible acting for high-profile public companies such as Meredith Corporation; however, the bulk of his practice is devoted to private corporations. He recently represented EMCO Enterprises in its sale of stock to Andersen Corporation. **James Krambeck**'s *"prompt and efficient"* advice has helped many family-owned start-ups to become national businesses. He has broad experience of advising insurance companies on the formation of mutual holding companies. Younger partner **Garth Adams** also earned praise from market commentators. He assisted R&R Realty Group in setting up a Delaware limited liability company.

The Clients: The firm's impressive client base includes: National Travelers Life; Mid-America Group; R&R Realty Group; Meredith Corporation; EMCO Enterprises; AmerUS Life and Color Converting Industries.

Nyemaster, Goode, Voigts, West, Hansell & O'Brien PC
The Firm: The largest law firm in Iowa, the firm is also one of the oldest, and maintains a strong foothold in the local market. Clients range from Fortune 500 corporations to individuals and small businesses. Researchers were told that the firm has *"one of the most effective corporate practices around,"* and that its lawyers possess all the necessary skills to ensure that transactions run smoothly. The firm acted as legal counsel to Equitable of Iowa Companies in its sale to ING Group for $2.2 billion in cash and stock.

The Lawyers: Clients rate **Edgar Hansell** as a *"top-notch lawyer with a large corporate practice."* He is involved in the buying and selling of businesses, and was singled out for his work on behalf of insurance companies and medical clinics. **Gordon Neumann** is highly regarded for his skill in a broad spectrum of corporate transactions. He serves as chair of the Des Moines/Polk County consolidation commission.

The Clients: The firm acts for clients Zurich American Insurance Company, MidAmerican Energy Holdings Company and FMC, as well as biotech businesses and construction companies, among others.

Davis, Brown, Koehn, Shors & Roberts PC
The Firm: This well-established team enjoys a diverse corporate practice. It was commended to researchers as an *"excellent"* source of business advice, and represents a widespread industrial client base in all aspects of business formation and operation, M&A, joint ventures and securities regulation. Commentators reported that the firm has been increasingly involved in acquisitions and joint ventures for real estate developers, insurance agencies and agricultural businesses in the state.

The Lawyers: **Frank Carroll** won considerable plaudits from clients, who point especially to his tax and business background. His colleague, **Donald Brown**, was thought by some to be *"as good as it gets"* for corporate advice in the state.

CORPORATE/M&A — IOWA

The department recently represented a service company and an insurance agency in stock acquisitions.

The Clients: The firm serves a range of clients in the fields of agribusiness, banking, broadcasting, construction, healthcare, real estate, telecommunications and manufacturing, alongside state and national trade associations, nonprofit organizations and educational institutions.

Lane & Waterman

The Firm: Established in 1854, the firm is widely respected in western Iowa as Davenport's leading corporate practice. A second office in Rock Island, IL further boosts the firm's position. Clients range from Fortune 500 corporations to local family-run enterprises. The firm has a strong profile in the banking sector, representing, among others, Wells Fargo, US Bank and Quad City Holdings in various commercial projects.

The Lawyers: *"The guy to go to"* here, according to interviewees, is **Dana Waterman**, managing partner and grandson of the firm's founder. He is a well-regarded corporate lawyer with a name in the local market for M&A and corporate divestitures. He recently represented Lee Enterprises in its $694 million acquisition of Howard Publications.

The Clients: The firm is local counsel to Deere & Company, representing it in various acquisitions. Other clients include Lee Enterprises, Sears Manufacturing Company and US Bank.

Bradshaw, Fowler, Proctor & Fairgrave PC

The Firm: Interviewees recommended the firm as one of the most highly regarded corporate practices in Des Moines. The practice fields a large and growing team of over 40 lawyers. Clients praised the team's *"effectiveness"* in the fields of M&A, business litigation and business formation. The group enjoys a strong profile among Iowa's leading businesses, and is especially visible in the insurance, mortgage lending and banking sectors.

The Lawyers: Clients admired **John Cortesio** for his *"extremely fine intellect."* He commands a varied corporate practice encompassing commercial litigation, utilities law, antitrust, unfair competition and trade regulation. **Edward Johnson** was also recommended as *"a good man to turn to for complete corporate advice."* He has over 30 years' experience of handling transactional work, and is noted for his specialization in estate planning.

The Clients: The firm's client base includes Iowa Insurance Guaranty Association, Zurich American Insurance Company and Farmland Mutual Insurance Company.

Shuttleworth & Ingersoll PLC

The Firm: The firm traces its history back to 1853 and is widely acclaimed as one of the leaders in Cedar Rapids. *"Outstanding"* lawyers provide a complete range of legal services to clients state and nationwide. The corporate group represents public and private companies and nonprofit organizations in a range of sectors including banking and insurance. The practice's workload includes business formations, acquisitions and disposals.

The Lawyers: Clients nominated **Gary Streit** as an *"impressive"* corporate lawyer with a particular specialty in corporate tax. He advises private and public companies on M&A, estate planning and tax matters. **Carroll Reasoner** has a *"great deal of experience"* in the industry, according to sources. She is highly regarded for her knowledge of commercial lending and healthcare law.

The Clients: Typical clients include: Gazette Communications; US Bank; Quaker Oats Company; Federated Mutual Insurance Company; Fireman's Fund; PMX Industries and KCRG/Cedar Rapids TV Company.

Ahlers & Cooney PC

The Firm: The firm enjoys a reputation for offering *"first-class"* advice in state regulation and municipal bond offerings. It acts on a large share of Iowa's bond work, serving as bond counsel to most of its counties, public school districts, community colleges, universities and the State of Iowa Board of Regents. The firm also advises on legislative proposals relating to tax-exempt bonds and public sector finance issues. The corporate department complements the firm's finance practice, ensuring clients a *"complete service."* Matters handled range from assisting on transactions to corporate tax advice.

The Lawyers: **John Hintze** chairs the business law department. Market commentators described him as a *"senior figure"* in the field. He is well known for his representation of public businesses, many of them in the real estate sector. Typical work includes establishing new entities, acquiring and disposing of assets, and forming joint ventures. His group recently represented the City of Iowa City in negotiations with Plaza Towers over the sale of property in the central business district urban renewal area.

The Clients: The firm's client base includes the State of Iowa Board of Regents, Iowa Association of School Business Officials and Iowa Public Agency Investment Trust.

Bradley & Riley PC

The Firm: This relatively young outfit has developed rapidly from a personal injury law firm to a fully fledged commercial player with notable litigation strength. It gained high marks from the market for its *"young and dynamic"* corporate practice, which provides statewide services from offices in Cedar Rapids and West Des Moines. Clients reported that it has developed into *"one of the firms that count."*

The Lawyers: Interviewees recommended **Byron Riley** as a *"high-quality"* business lawyer.

The Clients: Alliant Energy; Mount Mercy College; Heartland Hotel; Merit Construction Company and MidAmerica Housing Partnership.

Brown, Winick, Graves, Gross, Baskerville and Schoenebaum PLC

The Firm: Originally specializing in tax law, the firm has now established its reputation as a full-service entity with *"multitalented"* lawyers. It offers legal services on a regional and national level through its offices in Des Moines and Pella, Iowa and DC.

The Lawyers: Although felt to lack an outstanding M&A star, the corporate team was said to include *"a number of good, active business lawyers."* The group is headed by John Hunter.

The Clients: The group acts for a mix of clients in the manufacturing and commercial sectors, along with healthcare providers, doctors, governmental agencies, banks, financial institutions, estates, trusts and partnerships.

Moyer & Bergman PLC

The Firm: Interviewees recognized this full-service firm as having one of the top business and tax practices in Cedar Rapids. Its lawyers handle complex litigation and advise clients on the formation, operation and dissolution of corporations, partnerships and joint ventures.

The Lawyers: In the opinion of clients, **Michael Donohue** is both a *"nice guy and a good corporate lawyer."* He was said to have a great deal of experience, especially in the fields of corporate finance and insolvency.

The Clients: Typical clients include: Bankers Trust; Cedar Graphics, Inc; GE Capital; Omega Communications; State Farm Insurance Companies; US Bank; United States Liability Insurance Group; West Bend Mutual Insurance Company and Westfield Group.

IOWA — EMPLOYMENT & LABOR LAW

EMPLOYMENT & LABOR LAW — MAINLY PLAINTIFF

IOWA
Leading firms
(Employment: Mainly Plaintiff)
1. MOYER & BERGMAN PLC *Cedar Rapids*

Leading individuals
(Employment: Mainly Plaintiff)
1. CONLIN Roxanne *Conlin & Associates*, Des Moines
2. O'BRIEN Dorothy *O'Brien & Greve PC*, Davenport
   VISSER Kevin *Moyer & Bergman PLC*, Cedar Rapids
3. RILEY Tom *Tom Riley Law Firm PLC*, Cedar Rapids
   SMITH MacDonald *Smith & McElwain*, Sioux City

Firms and individuals are listed alphabetically in each band.

Moyer & Bergman, PLC
The Firm: Based in Cedar Rapids, this full-service firm has a market reputation for plaintiffs' representation, and is one of the largest firms in the state. Practice areas include employment and labor law, workers' compensation, litigation and risk management. Attorneys are licensed to practice in state, federal and appellate courts.

The Lawyers: Kevin Visser represents both plaintiffs and defendants, but was particularly commended for his *"spectacular"* reputation in plaintiff-sided employment matters.

The Clients: The firm acts for both plaintiffs and defendants.

Other Notable Practitioners
Des Moines' **Roxanne Conlin** of Conlin & Associates garnered widespread praise in the market for her representation of plaintiffs in discrimination and civil rights suits and malpractice and professional negligence cases. Described as a *"formidable advocate,"* she was hailed as *"one of the top plaintiff attorneys in the country"* by interviewees, who noted her *"high-profile"* case-load. Market commentators speculate that she has probably won *"more million dollar verdicts than anyone in Iowa."* Recent cases have included sex discrimination, sexual harassment, equal pay and retaliation matters. **Dorothy O'Brien** of O'Brien & Greve comes highly recommended for her wrongful termination and civil rights discrimination work. She also enjoys a reputation for specializing in age, gender and race issues. With a practice focusing on employment law, O'Brien is considered a *"dynamite"* plaintiff lawyer. *"Successful and aggressive"* **Tom Riley** of Tom Riley Law Firm PLC was noted for his experience in personal injury and civil rights cases. Thought by some to be *"the best on the union side,"* **MacDonald Smith** of Smith & McElwain maintains a strong standing for labor union representation throughout the state.

EMPLOYMENT & LABOR LAW — MAINLY DEFENDANT

IOWA
Leading firms
(Employment: Mainly Defendant)
1. AHLERS & COONEY PC *Des Moines*
   BELIN LAMSON MCCORMICK *Des Moines*
   DAVIS, BROWN, KOEHN, SHORS *Des Moines*
   DICKINSON, MACKAMAN, TYLER *Des Moines*
   NYEMASTER, GOODE, VOIGTS, WEST *Des Moines*
2. BRADLEY & RILEY PC *Cedar Rapids*
   SHUTTLEWORTH & INGERSOLL PLC *Cedar Rapids*
   SIMMONS PERRINE ALBRIGHT *Cedar Rapids*
   WHITFIELD & EDDY PLC *Des Moines*

Leading individuals
(Employment: Mainly Defendant)
1. HARTY Frank *Nyemaster, Goode, Voigts*, Des Moines
2. ADAMS Helen *Dickinson, Mackaman, Tyler*, Des Moines
   BAIER Kelly *Bradley & Riley PC*, Cedar Rapids
   KENNEDY Elizabeth *Ahlers & Cooney*, Des Moines
   LA SUER Gene *Davis, Brown, Koehn, Shors*, Des Moines
   MUCHMORE Iris *Simmons Perrine*, Cedar Rapids
   SAMUELSON Jaki *Whitfield & Eddy PLC*, Des Moines
   SWANGER James *Belin Lamson*, Des Moines
   ZAIGER Mark *Shuttleworth & Ingersoll*, Cedar Rapids

Firms and individuals are listed alphabetically in each band.

Ahlers & Cooney PC
The Firm: *"Highly regarded for all aspects of corporate law,"* the Des Moines-based firm enjoys a high standing among local Iowan businesses for employment defense work. Attorneys practice in state and federal courts, in both trial and appellate proceedings. The group litigates numerous employment issues for a client list that includes some of the state's largest employers as well as a number of national corporations.

The Lawyers: Chair of the firm's local government and employment law departments, **Elizabeth Gregg Kennedy** was recommended to researchers for wide experience in employment defense.

The Clients: Attorneys advise small and large companies, counties, school districts, community colleges, public sector bodies and cities.

Belin Lamson McCormick Zumbach Flynn PC
The Firm: *Chambers'* researchers were informed that the practice is *"capable of handling a broad range of matters"* and is well known in the market for its representation of substantial corporations. Clients hold the firm's employment attorneys in the *"highest regard."* The group advises employers on unions and governmental regulatory entity work and represents corporate clients in litigation before arbitration panels, civil rights commissions and state and federal courts.

The Lawyers: Clients commend the *"incredibly responsive"* **James Swanger**, for his *"integrity and honesty."* Interviewers were told he conducts himself with the *"utmost professionalism"* and produces *"excellent results."*

The Clients: The firm acts for a number of locally owned businesses as well as foreign and national corporations with Iowan interests.

Davis, Brown, Koehn, Shors & Roberts PC
The Firm: With three offices across the state, the firm represents large and small businesses, international corporations, healthcare organizations and municipalities. Attorneys have experience in all aspects of employment law. Market sources point to the firm's reputation for dealing with private sector clients, crediting it with *"broad corporate capabilities."*

The Lawyers: *"Knowledgeable and competent,"* **Gene La Suer** was commended by clients for employment-related matters, as well as general litigation.

The Clients: Attorneys are visible representing local, national and international businesses on a host of employment matters.

Dickinson, Mackaman, Tyler & Hagen PC
The Firm: Interviewees report that the firm possesses a large team of *"pretty darn smart"* employment lawyers and is known in the market for the size and quality of its labor and employment defense practice. The firm advises clients across a number of industry sectors and was said to contain *"highly educated and experienced people."* Its market profile is enhanced by an additional office in DC.

The Lawyers: *"An outstanding name"* in the field, **Helen Adams** was recommended to researchers for her employment and trial law practice.

The Clients: Trade industry associations; local and national companies; cocounsel to national

LITIGATION — IOWA

firms acting in Iowa; Iowan counsel for out-of-state businesses, and individual clients.

Nyemaster, Goode, Voigts, West, Hansell & O'Brien PC
The Firm: One of the largest and oldest full-service firms in the state, it has offices in Ames and West Des Moines. It receives high marks from interviewees, who cite the group's expertise in management representation in employment defense and labor law matters. Matters handled include OSHA, employment discrimination, wrongful discharge, union negotiations and wage and hour issues. The firm offers both advice and litigation services to clients.
The Lawyers: Clients retain a *"huge amount of respect"* for **Frank Harty**, naming him a *"high-quality employment lawyer."* This *"scholarly"* attorney was particularly noted for his writing and speaking on employment law matters.
The Clients: The firm is visible acting for a spread of Iowan and Midwest clients. These range from large corporates such as Deere & Company to smaller, privately owned businesses and individuals.

Bradley & Riley PC
The Firm: Lauded as an *"excellent all-around business practice,"* this 26-attorney firm has offices in Cedar Rapids and Des Moines. *"Well-rounded"* attorneys offer the full gamut of employment law services.
The Lawyers: *"One of the best employment lawyers around,"* **Kelly Baier** was strongly recommended to our interviewers.
The Clients: The practice advises Iowan public and private companies on a variety of employment matters.

Shuttleworth & Ingersoll PLC
The Firm: Clients acclaimed this large, established Iowan firm for the quality of its employment practice. Attorneys possess broad experience in employment discrimination claims, union issues and other employment matters.
The Lawyers: Interviewees identified **Mark Zaiger** as *"one of the best,"* particularly noting his large volume of cases.
The Clients: AEGON USA; Amana Society; local and national businesses and individuals.

Simmons Perrine Albright & Ellwood PLC
The Firm: Commended as a top firm for labor and employment law, this 30-attorney practice enjoys a strong regional following.
The Lawyers: **Iris Muchmore** was recommended to researchers for both defendants' and plaintiffs' work. Sources feel she is a *"highly skilled employment lawyer."*
The Clients: The firm represents both plaintiffs and defendants.

Whitfield & Eddy PLC
The Firm: Employment is among the firm's core practice areas. The department supplies legal counsel on issues relating to discrimination, wrongful termination, civil rights and employment policy.
The Lawyers: Defense attorney **Jaki Samuelson** earned praise for her *"first-rate trial abilities."*
The Clients: National and international businesses; smaller local companies; insurance companies and agricultural lenders.

LITIGATION — GENERAL COMMERCIAL

IOWA
Leading firms
(Litigation: General Commercial)

1
- AHLERS & COONEY PC *Des Moines*
- BELIN LAMSON MCCORMICK ZUMBACH *Des Moines*
- BRADSHAW, FOWLER, PROCTOR *Des Moines*
- LANE & WATERMAN *Davenport*

2
- NYEMASTER, GOODE, VOIGTS, WEST *Des Moines*
- SHUTTLEWORTH & INGERSOLL PLC *Cedar Rapids*

3
- ELDERKIN & PIRNIE PLC *Cedar Rapids*
- FINLEY, ALT, SMITH, SCHARNBERG *Des Moines*
- WHITFIELD & EDDY PLC *Des Moines*

Firms are listed alphabetically in each band.

Ahlers & Cooney PC
The Firm: *Chambers'* researchers were told that this *"top-drawer"* firm is highly regarded in Iowa for its expertise in complex commercial litigation. Founded in 1887, the Des Moines-based firm is thought to be one of the biggest local competitors, and is recommended by clients as a *"first-class"* practice.
The Lawyers: Litigator **Richard Santi** was commended to our researchers for his defense work: an area in which the market deemed him *"competent and capable."*
The Clients: The firm represents local, national and international corporate clients in litigious matters.

Belin Lamson McCormick Zumbach Flynn PC
The Firm: Clients named the firm as a *"go-to practice"* for any type of litigation. The firm's strength in litigation is complemented by its substantial reputation for its expertise in general corporate work.
The Lawyers: **Roger Stetson** is described as a *"top-flight dispute lawyer"* with a *"superb"* reputation in the field. Noted by market sources as a *"passionate oral advocate,"* **Mark McCormick** has a high profile for appellate work, but is also known to act in commercial litigation. Clients consider him extremely skilled in products liability and tax litigation cases and commend him as a *"skilled and persuasive writer."* **David Charles** was acclaimed as *"among the best"* for his work in trade secrets, commercial litigation, personal injury and employment matters.
The Clients: The firm acts for a number of Iowan corporations and represents national and multinational businesses on state law matters.

Bradshaw, Fowler, Proctor & Fairgrave PC
The Firm: The full-service firm covers a range of practice areas from its Des Moines office, but was particularly singled out to *Chambers'* researchers for its *"excellent"* standing in litigation matters.
The Lawyers: Clients recommend **Michael Figenshaw** as a skilled trial lawyer, describing him as *"without peer"* for his medical negligence expertise. His practice also includes general and civil litigation, personal injury and insurance defence.
The Clients: The firm has acted for the likes of MidAmerican Energy Company and Principal Financial Group.

Lane & Waterman
The Firm: Descended from a partnership formed in 1854, the firm now comprises over 40 attorneys, with two offices, in Davenport and Rock Island. The litigation department was hailed as a *"significant local practice"* with experience across a range of fields.
The Lawyers: **Robert Waterman** was hailed by clients as a talented litigator with noteworthy expertise in commercial litigation and medical malpractice suits. His practice also encompasses products liability and environmental insurance litigation. **Thomas Waterman** enjoys a reputation as an up-and-coming litigator with impressive advocacy skills.
The Clients: The practice has acted for Lee Enterprises and Isle of Capri Casinos and advises a number of major media companies, railroads, manufacturers, financial institutions, utilities and contractors.

IOWA — LITIGATION

IOWA
Leading individuals
(Litigation: General Commercial)

1
- FIGENSHAW Michael *Bradshaw, Fowler*, Des Moines
- FINLEY Thomas *Finley, Alt, Smith*, Des Moines
- ROBY Patrick *Elderkin & Pirnie PLC*, Cedar Rapids
- SANTI Richard *Ahlers & Cooney PC*, Des Moines
- STETSON Roger *Belin Lamson McCormick*, Des Moines
- WATERMAN Robert *Lane & Waterman*, Davenport

2
- CHARLES David *Belin Lamson McCormick* Des Moines
- COLLINS Kevin *Shuttleworth & Ingersoll*, Cedar Rapids
- CRITELLI Nicholas *Law Chambers*, Des Moines
- HOUGHTON Robert *Shuttleworth*, Cedar Rapids
- JAMES Dwight *The James Law Firm PC*, Des Moines
- MCCORMICK Mark *Belin Lamson*, Des Moines
- RICCOLO John *Riccolo & Baker PC*, Cedar Rapids
- SAPP Richard *Nyemaster, Goode, Voigts*, Des Moines
- WATERMAN Thomas *Lane & Waterman*, Davenport

Individuals are listed alphabetically in each band.

Nyemaster, Goode, Voigts, West, Hansell & O'Brien PC
The Firm: Iowa's largest law firm, the practice was identified as a leading player in corporate and commercial litigation with related strength in estate planning and general corporate law. Practitioners undertake a variety of matters from offices in Des Moines and Ames.

The Lawyers: Recommended for his litigation work, **Richard Sapp** is known within the market for experience in products liability cases.

The Clients: The firm's client base ranges from large corporations to small local businesses and individuals.

Shuttleworth & Ingersoll PLC
The Firm: One of the oldest law firms in the state, founded in 1853, Shuttleworth & Ingersoll attorneys were recommended for experience in federal, state and appellate courts. The 40-strong practice also handles alternative dispute resolution (ADR) and undertakes matters both in and out of state.

The Lawyers: An *"outstanding commercial litigator,"* **Kevin Collins** is senior vice president within the firm. His practice covers all aspects of business litigation, including ADR, construction disputes, personal injury and civil litigation, as well as immigration law and OSHA matters. Clients praised **Robert Houghton** for his defense work. Matters handled include products liability cases, drug and medical device litigation, civil litigation, personal injury and medical malpractice claims.

The Clients: The practice acts for a variety of businesses both in and out of state, including banks, insurance companies, public companies and nonprofit organizations.

Elderkin & Pirnie PLC
The Firm: This well-established Iowan firm is known to handle commercial litigation and business law. Market sources endorsed the firm for the broad range of matters covered.

The Lawyers: Clients singled out *"top-tier"* attorney **Patrick Roby** for his litigation experience and *"dominant courtroom presence."* His practice includes civil litigation.

The Clients: Clients include Acme Electric Company, Home Mortgage Corporation and Bruce McGrath Pontiac.

Finley, Alt, Smith, Scharnberg, Craig, Hilmes & Gaffney PC
The Firm: Acclaimed by interviewees as an *"excellent litigation firm,"* researchers were informed of its strong reputation for medical malpractice work. Based in Des Moines, the full-service firm has 14 attorneys with experience in both federal and state courts.

The Lawyers: Esteemed among clients as the *"first port of call for medical negligence questions,"* **Thomas Finley** has a reputation as a *"top-tier"* defense lawyer.

The Clients: The firm has acted for Minnesota Lawyers Mutual as well as many other businesses and individuals throughout the state. It is well known for its large base of hospital and transportation company clients.

Whitfield & Eddy PLC
The Firm: *Chambers'* researchers heard of the firm's *"well-respected"* litigation section and skilled trial attorneys. Practice areas covered include corporate and business matters, commercial transactions and litigation, and insurance defense.

The Clients: The firm's client base includes insurance companies, agricultural interests and other entities.

Other Notable Practitioners
Nicholas Critelli of Law Chambers Nicholas Critelli PC distinguished by his qualification as both a UK barrister and a US attorney, assists members of the bar as local or trial counsel. He is also elected vice president of The Iowa State Bar Association for the 2002-2003 term. Areas of advocacy for the chambers include commercial and business litigation, as well as mediation and arbitration work. Market sources commended *"top-notch"* **Dwight James** of The James Law Firm PC for plaintiffs' representation in personal injury suits, professional malpractice law, and products liability issues. *"Highly qualified"* **John Riccolo** of Riccolo & Baker PC also attracts comment for his plaintiffs' work and experience in personal injury cases.

REAL ESTATE

IOWA
Leading firms (Real Estate)

1
- BELIN LAMSON MCCORMICK *Des Moines*

2
- CONNOLLY, O'MALLEY, LILLIS *Des Moines*
- DAVIS, BROWN, KOEHN, SHORS *Des Moines*
- SIMMONS PERRINE *Cedar Rapids, Iowa City*

3
- DICKINSON, MACKAMAN, TYLER *Des Moines*
- MOYER & BERGMAN PLC *Cedar Rapids*
- NYEMASTER, GOODE, VOIGTS, WEST *Des Moines*

4
- ACKLEY, KOPECKY & KINGERY *Cedar Rapids*
- BRADLEY & RILEY PC *Cedar Rapids*
- BRADSHAW, FOWLER, PROCTOR *Des Moines*
- LANE & WATERMAN *Davenport*
- SHUTTLEWORTH & INGERSOLL PLC *Cedar Rapids*

Firms are listed alphabetically in each band.

Belin Lamson McCormick Zumbach Flynn PC
The Firm: The firm acts as legal counsel to real estate developers, financial institutions, contractors, owners, landlords and tenants throughout central Iowa. It offers a full range of legal services relating to the acquisition, development, financing and management of real estate. The firm is said to attract *"top-class talent"* and produces *"some of the most outstanding lawyers in Iowa."* The practice acts for R&R Realty Group in community development projects. It is also leading local counsel to General Growth Properties, and recently assisted the company in its acquisition and development of the 200-acre Jordan Creek Town Center entertainment and shopping venue in West Des Moines.

The Lawyers: Developer clients identify **William Bartine** as a *"longtime player"* in the field. He has been involved in many of the redevelopment projects in the City of Des Moines, and has often represented real estate developers in property acquisition. He and his partner **Jeremy Sharpe** are regarded as *"key figures"* in the Iowan market. Sharpe acts as counsel for the Mid-America Group and for Knapp Properties in developing real estate projects across the state. He is said by clients to be *"extremely knowledgeable in the real estate area, and has the talent and ability to handle complicated transactions."*

The Clients: AmerUs Life; GuideOne Insurance; Wheeler Consolidated; General Growth Properties; Mid-America Group; Iowa Health System and Knapp Properties.

REAL ESTATE | IOWA

IOWA
Leading individuals (Real Estate)

1
- BARTINE William *Belin Lamson*, Des Moines
- KUBICEK David *Simmons Perrine Albright*, Cedar Rapids
- SHARPE Jeremy *Belin Lamson McCormick*, Des Moines

2
- COLACINO Antonio *Nyemaster, Goode*, Des Moines
- DETTMANN David *Lane & Waterman*, Davenport
- ERICKSON David *Davis, Brown, Koehn*, Des Moines
- HOLCOMB James *Bradshaw, Fowler*, Des Moines
- LILLIS William *Connolly, O'Malley, Lillis*, Des Moines
- NELSON Stephen *Moyer & Bergman PLC*, Cedar Rapids

3
- DOUGLAS Robert *Davis, Brown, Koehn*, Des Moines
- MOORE Dan *Berenstein, Moore, Berenstein*, Sioux City
- SEYFER Greg *Bradley & Riley PC*, Cedar Rapids
- TYLER Paul *Dickinson, Mackaman, Tyler*, Des Moines

4
- ANDEWEG Robert *Brown, Winick, Graves*, Des Moines
- DOWNER Robert *Meardon, Sueppel*, Iowa City
- KINGERY Gregory *Ackley, Kopecky*, Cedar Rapids
- LEFF Philip *Leff, Haupert, Traw & Willman*, Iowa City
- PROWELL William *Shuttleworth*, Cedar Rapids

Individuals are listed alphabetically in each band.

Connolly, O'Malley, Lillis, Hansen & Olson LLP

The Firm: A real estate boutique that specializes in land planning, zoning matters and real estate litigation. Lawyers of the firm *"do unique work"* appearing before governmental bodies, state councils and committees. The firm has been involved in some of the most high-profile cases in downtown Des Moines and surrounding areas. Attorneys represented G&L Clothing in the controversial rezoning and sale of a Des Moines city park to Crescent Chevrolet and to G&L. The firm was also involved in a dispute over the acquisition of a city street by two west-side churches.

The Lawyers: Chambers' researchers were told that **William Lillis** adds weight to the firm's historically strong market reputation. According to clients, his is the *"first name you hear for real estate matters in the city."* Lillis is involved in major Des Moines area rezoning and development issues and is said to *"understand politics, development and land use issues."*

The Clients: The firm recently assisted Meredith Corporation with matters surrounding its new Des Moines office building. Other clients include R&R Realty Group, Ronald W Cheney Revocable Trust and G&L Clothing.

Davis, Brown, Koehn, Shors & Roberts PC

The Firm: A prominent and highly thought of firm, said to handle substantial amounts of real estate work for developers, banks, insurance companies, landowners and individual investors. It is counsel to, among others, the Iowa Manufactured Housing Association and the Des Moines Metropolitan Planning Organization, and maintains a solid reputation for public projects.

The Lawyers: **David Erickson** is mainly involved in developing residential real estate projects. He commands a loyal following among local clients, who refer to him as an *"outstanding attorney with a solid-gold reputation."* His colleague **Robert Douglas** is endorsed for his *"clear thinking, and problem-solving attitude."* Douglas is especially known for his work representing hospital and healthcare entities in real estate matters.

The Clients: Des Moines Metropolitan Planning Organization, Iowa Manufactured Housing Association and Wells Fargo Mortgage.

Simmons Perrine Albright & Ellwood PLC

The Firm: This full-service firm has a long track record as a litigation firm, appearing in arbitrations and mediations before both federal and state courts. However, it has also established a *"fully fledged"* real estate practice. Attorneys in both the Cedar Rapids and Iowa City offices undertake real estate matters for individuals and corporate clients, state and nationwide.

The Lawyers: Chairman of the Title Standards Committee for The Iowa State Bar Association, **David Kubicek** represents buyers and lenders in the acquisition and financing of properties. Clients expressed confidence in his abilities, commenting that *"there is nothing he can't handle."*

The Clients: Kleiman Construction; Wells Fargo; City of Iowa City; Hills Bank & Trust Company; Commercial Federal Bank; The Greater Cedar Rapids Community Foundation; Iowa Comprehensive Petroleum Underground Storage Tank Fund and Mutual Service Insurance Companies.

Dickinson, Mackaman, Tyler & Hagen PC

The Firm: Originally a tax firm, Dickinson Mackaman has, according to market sources, expanded its practice to include *"one of the best real estate practices in Des Moines."* The real estate and commercial group is well known for its focus on representing creditors and lending institutions in real estate finance and development. The firm is involved in the development of all types of real estate property, including condominiums, commercial and industrial. Attorneys are active in gaining approvals before planning, zoning and other governmental boards and in title examinations.

The Lawyers: **Paul Tyler** attracted market plaudits for his extensive real estate practice and emphasis on real estate finance. He is visible acting as local Iowa counsel to banks such as Wells Fargo and Wells Fargo Mortgage.

The Clients: Adventure Lands of America; Associated Builders and Contractors of Iowa; Des Moines Area Association of Realtors; Hills Bank & Trust Company; US Cellular; Urbandale Community School District and Waukee State Bank.

Moyer & Bergman PLC

The Firm: One of Iowa's largest full-service firms, it was said to represent many of the state's major developers. For example, it recently assisted WDG Investment Company in the refinancing of a large apartment building and Bankers Trust in rebuilding a complex. The group also closed a large deal for Cedar Graphics, Inc.

The Lawyers: **Stephen Nelson** is thought to be one of the most frequently retained lawyers in this area. He has a great reputation in the market for handling statewide real estate developments, including some prestigious commercial properties. His expertise also extends to zoning matters. He has recently undertaken major work for Ag Services of America.

The Clients: Bankers Trust; Fauser Oil; First Financial Center; GreatAmerica Leasing Corporation; Omega Communications; SAFECO; State Farm Insurance Companies; US Bank and Westfield Group.

Nyemaster, Goode, Voigts, West, Hansell & O'Brien PC

The Firm: This large, active real estate practice serves state, national and international clients through its Des Moines and Ames offices. Many of its clients are in the public utility, pipeline and insurance industries. The firm assisted the City of Des Moines with the acquisition of land for the expansion of the airport. It has also acted for bidders in connection with the construction of new federal buildings in Des Moines.

The Lawyers: **Antonio Colacino** has nearly 30 years' experience in the field. Clients consider him to be an *"excellent lawyer with a broad-based real estate practice."* He has acted in large real estate purchases and sales, and leasing. He represents a number of municipalities in the Midwest, as well as many of Iowa's landowners, and has been visible in statewide pipeline and natural gas projects, including the Alliance Pipeline Project.

The Clients: City of Des Moines; GMAC Real Estate; pipeline companies; insurance companies; public utilities and real estate developers.

Ackley, Kopecky & Kingery

The Firm: Much of this firm's work is in the areas of real estate, tax preparation, and general corporate and litigation advice. In the real estate arena, lawyers handle most types of general transactional work. They are involved in many smaller and mid-sized projects, including single-family and residential developments.

The Lawyers: **Greg Kingery** is the team's highest profile name, according to interviewees. He is involved in a number of real estate projects in Cedar Rapids.

The Clients: The firm is known to act for both buyers and lenders.

IOWA

REAL ESTATE

Bradley & Riley PC
The Firm: The firm's real estate practice enjoys a steady flow of transactional and financing work. Its strengths in the fields of banking and tax are said to complement its real estate expertise and to be a draw to real property clients.
The Lawyers: Greg Seyfer is the outstanding name in the firm's real estate team. According to clients, he is *"honest, trustworthy and competent: all the things you want in an attorney."* His workload includes representing commercial and residential developers in the acquisition of land, the financing of projects and the leasing of property.
The Clients: Guaranty Bank and Trust Company, United Fire & Casualty Company and McLeodUSA are clients.

Bradshaw, Fowler, Proctor & Fairgrave PC
The Firm: The firm's real estate practice is particularly known for representing lenders in real estate transactions, disputes and related matters. Its experience extends to issues surrounding competing interests in the selling or buying of properties, bankruptcy proceedings, environmental due diligence, and title issues.
The Lawyers: James Holcomb is an *"experienced and seasoned"* real estate attorney. He is regarded by sources as *"outstanding"* on the lending side of real estate transactions. His stable client base includes Wells Fargo and Principal Financial Group, the largest financial group in Des Moines.
The Clients: AmerUs Leasing Company, Earlham Savings Bank and Farmland Mutual Insurance Company are clients.

Lane & Waterman
The Firm: This firm is considered by clients to have *"the best real estate practice in eastern Iowa."* The firm advises on a range of real property matters, including the sale and purchase of multimillion dollar real estate developments.
The Lawyers: David Dettmann is a highly respected senior lawyer who has done *"considerable work in the field."* He was warmly praised for his involvement in commercial and industrial developments in the Quad City area.
The Clients: Davenport Community School District; Russell Construction; Quad City Bank & Trust; Deere & Company; Sears Manufacturing Company; Farm Bureau Mutual Insurance Co and Verizon Wireless.

Shuttleworth & Ingersoll PLC
The Firm: This *"top-notch"* real estate team represents residential and commercial developers and landlords, real estate brokers, property managers and mortgage lenders. It handles counseling, planning, due diligence and drafting in connection with the acquisition and disposition of properties, leasings and development projects.
The Lawyers: Bill Prowell received widespread plaudits as the firm's biggest name in real estate transactions and zoning issues.
The Clients: Gazette Communications; General Growth Management; US Bank; AEGON USA; United Fire & Casualty Company and Universal Underwriters Group.

Other Notable Practitioners
Dan Moore of Berenstein, Moore, Berenstein, Heffernan & Moeller is much praised for his work in Sioux City. He is, according to clients, an *"effective"* choice for residential, commercial, industrial and agricultural developments.
Robert Downer of Meardon, Sueppel & Downer is a well-known real estate lawyer, active in real estate planning matters. Researchers were told that Downer knows the real estate market *"inside out."* He represents commercial and industrial developers and handles complex zoning matters.
Robert Andeweg of Brown, Winick, Graves, Gross, Baskerville and Schoenebaum PLC is *"just great,"* according to clients. He is involved in city development and redevelopment projects and is also commended for his work as local counsel for Allied Insurance.
Philip Leff of Leff, Haupert, Traw & Willman LLP stands out for his real estate work in Iowa City. Interviewees had a high opinion of his knowledge of subdivision matters.

Leaders in Iowa

ADAMS, Garth
Belin Lamson McCormick Zumbach Flynn, PC, Des Moines 515 243 7100
Recommended in Corporate/M&A

ADAMS, Helen
Dickinson, Mackaman, Tyler & Hagen, P.C., Des Moines 515 244 2600
Recommended in Employment

ANDEWEG, Robert
Brown, Winick, Graves, Gross, Baskerville and Schoenebaum PLC, Des Moines 515 242 2400
Recommended in Real Estate

BAIER, Kelly
Bradley & Riley, PC, Cedar Rapids 319 363 0101
Recommended in Employment

BARTINE, William
Belin Lamson McCormick Zumbach Flynn, PC, Des Moines 515 243 7100
Recommended in Real Estate

BROWN, Donald
Davis, Brown, Koehn, Shors & Roberts, PC, Des Moines 515 288 2500
Recommended in Corporate/M&A

CARROLL, Frank
Davis, Brown, Koehn, Shors & Roberts, PC, Des Moines 515 288 2500
Recommended in Corporate/M&A

CHARLES, David
Belin Lamson McCormick Zumbach Flynn, PC, Des Moines 515 243 7100
Recommended in Litigation

COLACINO, Antonio
Nyemaster, Goode, Voigts, West, Hansell & O'Brien, PC, Des Moines 515 283 3100
Recommended in Real Estate

COLLINS, Kevin
Shuttleworth & Ingersoll PLC, Cedar Rapids 319 365 9461
Recommended in Litigation

CONLIN, Roxanne
Conlin & Associates, Des Moines 515 282 3333
Recommended in Employment

CORTESIO, John
Bradshaw, Fowler, Proctor & Fairgrave, PC, Des Moines 515 243 4191
Recommended in Corporate/M&A

CRITELLI JR, Nicholas
Law Chambers Nicholas Critelli PC, Des Moines 515 243 3122
Recommended in Litigation

DETTMANN, David
Lane & Waterman, Davenport 563 324 3246
Recommended in Real Estate

DONOHUE, Michael
Moyer & Bergman, PLC, Cedar Rapids 319 366 7331
Recommended in Corporate/M&A

DOUGLAS, Robert J
Davis, Brown, Koehn, Shors & Roberts, PC, Des Moines 515 288 2500
Recommended in Real Estate

DOWNER, Robert
Meardon, Sueppel & Downer, Iowa City 319 338 9222
Recommended in Real Estate

ERICKSON, David
Davis, Brown, Koehn, Shors & Roberts, PC, Des Moines 515 288 2500
Recommended in Real Estate

FIGENSHAW, Michael
Bradshaw, Fowler, Proctor & Fairgrave, PC, Des Moines 515 243 4191
Recommended in Litigation

FINLEY, Thomas
Finley, Alt, Smith, Scharnberg, Craig, Hilmes & Gaffney PC, Des Moines 515 288 0145
Recommended in Litigation

HANSELL, Edgar
Nyemaster, Goode, Voigts, West, Hansell & O'Brien, PC, Des Moines 515 283 3100
Recommended in Corporate/M&A

HARTY, Frank
Nyemaster, Goode, Voigts, West, Hansell & O'Brien, PC, Des Moines 515 283 3100
Recommended in Employment

HINTZE, John
Ahlers & Cooney, PC, Des Moines 515 243 7611
Recommended in Corporate/M&A

LEADERS

IOWA

HOLCOMB, James
Bradshaw, Fowler, Proctor & Fairgrave, PC, Des Moines 515 243 4191
Recommended in Real Estate

HOUGHTON, Robert
Shuttleworth & Ingersoll PLC, Cedar Rapids 319 365 9461
Recommended in Litigation

JAMES, Dwight
The James Law Firm PC, Des Moines 515 246 8484
Recommended in Litigation

JOHNSON, Edward
Bradshaw, Fowler, Proctor & Fairgrave, PC, Des Moines 515 243 4191
Recommended in Corporate/M&A

KENNEDY, Elizabeth Gregg
Ahlers & Cooney, PC, Des Moines 515 243 7611
Recommended in Employment

KINGERY, Gregory
Ackley, Kopecky & Kingery, Cedar Rapids 319 364 2463
Recommended in Real Estate

KRAMBECK, James
Belin Lamson McCormick Zumbach Flynn, PC, Des Moines 515 243 7100
Recommended in Corporate/M&A

KUBICEK, David
Simmons Perrine Albright & Ellwood P.L.C., Cedar Rapids 319 366 7641
Recommended in Real Estate

LA SUER, Gene
Davis, Brown, Koehn, Shors & Roberts, PC, Des Moines 515 288 2500
Recommended in Employment

LEFF, Philip
Leff, Haupert, Traw & Willman LLP, Iowa City 319 338 7551
Recommended in Real Estate

LILLIS, William
Connolly, O'Malley, Lillis, Hansen & Olson LLP, Des Moines 515 234 81 57
Recommended in Real Estate

MCCORMICK, Mark
Belin Lamson McCormick Zumbach Flynn, PC, Des Moines 515 243 7100
Recommended in Litigation

MOORE, Dan
Berenstein, Moore, Berenstein, Heffernan & Moeller, Sioux City 712 252 0020
Recommended in Real Estate

MUCHMORE, Iris
Simmons Perrine Albright & Ellwood P.L.C., Cedar Rapids 319 366 7641
Recommended in Employment

NELSON, Stephen
Moyer & Bergman, PLC, Cedar Rapids 319 366 7331
Recommended in Real Estate

NEUMANN, Gordon
Nyemaster, Goode, Voigts, West, Hansell & O'Brien, PC, Des Moines 515 283 3100
Recommended in Corporate/M&A

O'BRIEN, Dorothy
O'Brien & Greve PC, Davenport 563 355 6060
Recommended in Employment

PROWELL, William
Shuttleworth & Ingersoll PLC, Cedar Rapids 319 365 9461
Recommended in Real Estate

REASONER, Carroll
Shuttleworth & Ingersoll PLC, Cedar Rapids 319 365 9461
Recommended in Corporate/M&A

RICCOLO, John
Riccolo & Baker PC, Cedar Rapids 319 365 9200
Recommended in Litigation

RILEY, Byron
Bradley & Riley, PC, Cedar Rapids 319 363 0101
Recommended in Corporate/M&A

RILEY, Tom
Tom Riley Law Firm PLC, Cedar Rapids 319 363 4040
Recommended in Employment

ROBY, Patrick
Elderkin & Pirnie PLC, Cedar Rapids 319 362 2137
Recommended in Litigation

SAMUELSON, Jaki
Whitfield & Eddy, PLC, Des Moines 515 288 6041
Recommended in Employment

SANTI, Richard
Ahlers & Cooney, PC, Des Moines 515 243 7611
Recommended in Litigation

SAPP, Richard
Nyemaster, Goode, Voigts, West, Hansell & O'Brien, PC, Des Moines 515 283 3100
Recommended in Litigation

SEYFER, Greg
Bradley & Riley, PC, Cedar Rapids 319 363 0101
Recommended in Real Estate

SHARPE, Jeremy
Belin Lamson McCormick Zumbach Flynn, PC, Des Moines 515 243 7100
Recommended in Real Estate

SMITH, MacDonald
Smith & McElwain, Sioux City 712 255 8094
Recommended in Employment

STETSON, Roger
Belin Lamson McCormick Zumbach Flynn, PC, Des Moines 515 243 7100
Recommended in Litigation

STREIT, Gary J
Shuttleworth & Ingersoll PLC, Cedar Rapids 319 365 9461
Recommended in Corporate/M&A

SWANGER, James R
Belin Lamson McCormick Zumbach Flynn, PC, Des Moines 515 243 7100
Recommended in Employment

TYLER, Paul
Dickinson, Mackaman, Tyler & Hagen, P.C., Des Moines 515 244 2600
Recommended in Real Estate

VISSER, Kevin
Moyer & Bergman, PLC, Cedar Rapids 319 366 7331
Recommended in Employment

WATERMAN, Thomas
Lane & Waterman, Davenport 563 324 3246
Recommended in Litigation

WATERMAN, Dana
Lane & Waterman, Davenport 563 324 3246
Recommended in Corporate/M&A

WATERMAN, Robert
Lane & Waterman, Davenport 563 324 3246
Recommended in Litigation

ZAIGER, Mark
Shuttleworth & Ingersoll PLC, Cedar Rapids 319 365 9461
Recommended in Employment

ZUMBACH, Steven E
Belin Lamson McCormick Zumbach Flynn, PC, Des Moines 515 283 4625
sezumbach@belinlaw.com
Recommended in Corporate/M&A

Specialisation: Partner in the firm of *Belin Lamson McCormick Zumbach Flynn*, a professional corporation. Specializes in corporate transactional practice focusing on mergers, acquisitions and financing transactions for closely held companies. Also a Certified Public Account; PhD in Economics with emphasis on finance. Based on his background in law, economics and accounting, he brings an interdisciplinary approach to the corporate transactional practice.
Career: Has a long record of public service, having served as a member of the State Board of Regents, Chair of the Greater Des Moines Chamber of Commerce Federation, Chair of the Greater Des Moines Committee, Chair of the Greater Des Moines Partnership, President of the Iowa State University Alumni Association, and Deputy National Chair of the Iowa State University Partnership for Prominence Capital Campaign.
Personal: BS 1973, Iowa State University; JD 1975, University of Iowa; PhD in Economics 1980, Iowa State University.

KANSAS

CORPORATE/M&A

CONTENTS: Corporate/M&A p.294; Employment: Mainly Plaintiff p.295; Mainly Defendant p.295; Litigation: General Commercial p.296; Real Estate p.297; Individuals' Profiles p.299

KANSAS'S TOP FIVE
1. Foulston Siefkin
1. Stinson Morrison Hecker
2. Lathrop & Gage
3. Shook, Hardy & Bacon
3. Shughart Thomson & Kilroy

Ranking based on Chambers' research within the state.

All quotes in the text are from interviews with clients and competitors.

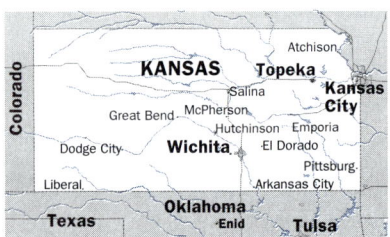

OVERVIEW: **Foulston Siefkin** has a first-class litigation team, famed for its strengths in antitrust and trade regulation as well as in class actions, bankruptcies and creditors' rights. This firm is also recommended for defendant employment work and traditional trade union matters. The corporate department is recognized for its work in M&A, while corporate lawyer William Trenkle is admired for his skill in aircraft financing, corporate governance and securities matters. Top litigator Mikel Stout was singled out for his work in complex litigation and environmental matters. Clients include Boeing and Candlewood Hotels.

Stinson Morrison Hecker matches Foulston Siefkin in *Chambers'* research. The firm has a corporate department with a reputation for excellence in M&A and venture capital transactions. Its real estate department garners respect for transaction and land use work, while its litigation department enjoys a depth of expertise in commercial and consumer class actions. Carl Circo is seen as an excellent deal facilitator in commercial real estate transactions. Clients include Sprint and State Street.

Lathrop & Gage, ranked in second place, has long-established roots in both Kansas and Missouri. Its corporate department attracts company giants such as AT&T and Colgate-Palmolive. The excellence of the firm's litigators on business issues has given the firm a major presence in this specialty. Joseph Hatley in the litigation department is highly respected for his work in telecom matters. The firm's real estate department is highly regarded for working with municipalities and private developers.

Shook, Hardy & Bacon, in third place alongside Shughart Thomson, has carved a sterling reputation for its litigation department, representing tobacco and pharmaceutical companies, among others, in highly complex cases in state and federal courts. Bill Sampson and David Erickson won plaudits for their litigation talents. Its corporate department is also well regarded for its breadth of expertise.

Shughart Thomson & Kilroy's trial lawyers are involved in high-profile business litigation cases on such matters as antitrust and class actions in both the local and national arenas. The corporate department is endorsed for its securities and joint ventures experience. Cochair of the firm's IP and technology practice, Lawrence Swain stood out as a clear leader, and one of the best in his field. Clients include the Major League Baseball Players Association and Commerce Bank.

CORPORATE/M&A

KANSAS
Leading firms (Corporate/M&A)
1. BLACKWELL SANDERS PEPER MARTIN *Overland Park*
   FOULSTON SIEFKIN LLP *Overland Park, Wichita*
   STINSON MORRISON HECKER LLP *Overland Park*
2. LATHROP & GAGE LC *Overland Park*
   POLSINELLI SHALTON & WELTE PC *Overland Park*
   SHOOK, HARDY & BACON LLP *Overland Park*
   SHUGHART THOMSON & KILROY PC *Overland Park*
   SPENCER FANE BRITT & BROWNE LLP *Overland Park*

Leading individuals (Corporate/M&A)
1. ADAMS Stephen *Blackwell Sanders, Overland Park*
   SWAIN Lawrence *Shughart Thomson, Overland Park*
   TRENKLE William *Foulston Siefkin LLP, Overland Park*

Firms and individuals are listed alphabetically in each band.

Blackwell Sanders Peper Martin LLP
The Firm: One of the leading firms in the area, it acts in high-profile M&A, debt financing and public and private securities offerings. Observers praised the group for a *"powerful presence"* and *"intelligent coverage,"* and applauded its involvement in *"exceptional transactional deals."*
The Lawyers: Peers recommend **Stephen Adams** for his negotiating skills and his *"superb work"* for healthcare and real estate clients. He has completed affiliations for major hospitals, and advised on acquisitions for physician practices and real estate companies.
The Clients: Aquila; Blue Valley Recreation Commission; The Denzer Group; MC Real Estate Services; Medical Plaza Partners; The Missouri Foundation for Health and American Italian Pasta Company.

Foulston Siefkin LLP
The Firm: Observers pointed to the firm's corporate group's *"consistently high-quality advice."* More than 60 attorneys practice from the firm's three Kansas offices in Wichita, Overland Park and Topeka, serving clients throughout the state and beyond.
The Lawyers: **William Trenkle**'s practice includes corporate governance, securities matters, franchising, aircraft financing and M&A. He has been recognized by peers for his *"great capability"* and the *"superb job"* he does for his clients.

Stinson Morrison Hecker LLP
The Firm: Commentators agree this firm has one of the *"most established clientele"* of any firm in this sector. It is highly respected for its work in M&A, venture capital and private equity transactions and has displayed facility in asset securitization. In its network of seven offices throughout the Midwest, its Kansas office in Overland Park in particular has allowed the firm to *"broaden its wings,"* according to clients, to provide *"outstanding quality."*
The Lawyers: Based in Kansas City, MO, Lawrence Bigus is the most senior contact for the firm's corporate team.
The Clients: The firm advises clients drawn from the local area, and those with a greater regional reach.

Lathrop & Gage LC
The Firm: Commentators praised the 130-year-old firm's corporate department for its *"wide-ranging"* practice and *"loyal clientele."* This dynamic group is active in M&A, securities offerings, venture capital and mezzanine financings and attracts major national and international clients.
The Lawyers: Harry Wigner is a key member of the corporate practice.
The Clients: AT&T; Bank of America; Bayer; Colgate-Palmolive; Ford; GM; Harry Cooper Supply; Kimco Realty; Burlington Northern & Santa Fe Railway and Royal Oak Enterprises.

Polsinelli Shalton & Welte PC
The Firm: Praised highly by peers for its *"broad reach and expertise,"* the group acts for national corporations as well as small local businesses. It is involved in transactional matters and corporate governance across a range of industries, including manufacturing, transportation, construction, finance, healthcare and insurance.
The Lawyers: Much of the firm's profile in corporate matters lies with Jim Polsinelli in the Kansas City, MO office. In Overland Park, Stanley Woodworth is one of the lead members of the team.

EMPLOYMENT & LABOR LAW

KANSAS

The Clients: Stowers Institute for Medical Research; Intell Management and Investment Company; University of Kansas Hospital Authority and Key Commercial Mortgage.

Shook, Hardy & Bacon LLP
see firm details p.876
The Firm: Commentators agreed that this firm is a *"major force"* in the representation of bidders, target companies, dealer managers and financial advisers in all types of transactions. Its ability to *"handle any possible deal"* has impressed many. Its workload has included takeovers, exchange offers, going-private transactions, and a variety of multistep acquisitions.
The Lawyers: This national and international firm has a base of *"trusted and respected"* attorneys in Overland Park. Bob Grossman is the key contact for the corporate group here.

Shughart Thomson & Kilroy PC
The Firm: Joint ventures, public and private issuers of securities and M&A are just some of the areas in which this corporate group specializes. Peers pointed to the *"high-quality services"* it offers to clients and described attorneys here as pragmatic and deal-focused.
The Lawyers: Lawrence Swain is the partner in charge of the Overland Park office and cochairs the firm's IP and technology practice group. His practice incorporates corporate and business law. His competitors praise him for the great job he does for his clients and the *"smooth approach"* he brings to the deal table.
The Clients: Automobile dealerships; manufacturers; credit and finance companies; electrical construction contractors; food processors, packagers and distributors, and healthcare and oil refining companies.

Spencer Fane Britt & Browne LLP
The Firm: Market watchers agree the *"quality of service is consistent"* at Spencer Fane Britt & Browne. Its corporate group has experience in the acquisition and sale of publicly traded and closely held businesses, tender offers, takeovers and anti-takeover measures. Attorneys are also knowledgeable in public company securities regulation, and alternative commercial transactions such as franchising and joint ventures.
The Lawyers: The firm's business and finance group is chaired by Michael McCann.

EMPLOYMENT & LABOR LAW — MAINLY PLAINTIFF

KANSAS
Leading firms
(Employment: Mainly Plaintiff)
1. **MCCULLOUGH, WAREHEMAN & LABUNKER** Topeka
2. **DEPEW AND GILLEN LLC** Wichita
   RALSTON POPE & DIEHL LLC Topeka

Leading individuals
(Employment: Mainly Plaintiff)
1. **ALEGRIA** David *McCullough, Wareheman,* Topeka
2. **PETERSON** Ken *Morris, Laing, Evans, Brock,* Wichita
   RALSTON Eugene *Ralston Pope & Diehl LLC,* Topeka
   RATHBUN Randy *Depew and Gillen LLC,* Wichita

Firms and individuals are listed alphabetically in each band.

McCullough, Wareheman & Labunker
The Firm: This Topeka-based, six-lawyer team has secured a strong reputation for the *"high quality"* of its plaintiff employment law work.
The Lawyers: Much of the team's standing is attributed to **David Alegria**, deemed by defendant rivals to be *"articulate, tenacious, and bright"* in plaintiff employment law. He primarily focuses on employment issues pertaining to employee retaliatory discharge and workers' compensation.

Depew and Gillen LLC
The Firm: This established eight-attorney firm in Wichita fields a group of three attorneys who handle employment-related issues.
The Lawyers: Randy Rathbun received endorsements from the market for both his plaintiff employment litigation work and his expertise in environmental issues.

Ralston Pope & Diehl LLC
The Firm: A small but growing firm for plaintiff employment work. The firm's general practice also focuses on personal injury and products liability law.
The Lawyers: The backbone of the firm's plaintiff employment department is **Eugene Ralston**, who was praised for his *"excellent labor and employment trial skills."*

Other Notable Practitioners
At Morris, Laing, Evans, Brock & Kennedy, Chartered, **Ken Peterson** has extensive experience in labor litigation, representing both employees and employers. Rivals especially noted his expertise in dealing with plaintiff work.

EMPLOYMENT & LABOR LAW — MAINLY DEFENDANT

KANSAS
Leading firms
(Employment: Mainly Defendant)
1. **FOULSTON SIEFKIN LLP** Wichita
2. **MARTIN & CHURCHILL CHARTERED** Wichita
3. **MARTIN, PRINGLE, OLIVER, WALLACE** Wichita
   MORRIS, LAING, EVANS, BROCK Wichita

Firms are listed alphabetically in each band.

Foulston Siefkin LLP
The Firm: Considered by the market to be the *"best firm"* in Kansas for defendant labor and employment matters. A long-established player in this area of law in the state, it fields a group of 23 attorneys specializing in both litigation and counseling. Commentators were also keen to highlight the practice's skill in handling trade union issues. Attorneys received accolades from clients for their *"thoroughness"* and *"high degree of professionalism"* on employer labor issues.
The Lawyers: *"Outstanding lawyer"* sums up the market consensus for team leader **Doug Stanley**. He has extensive experience in helping employers with union avoidance campaigns, and clients praised his *"grasp of the detail in labor issues"* and *"moderation"* in handling trade union negotiations. Interviewees acknowledged that **Kathleen Babcock** has *"a lot of experience"* and *"deep knowledge,"* won from her long track record defending employers involved in federal discrimination litigation cases. She is admired for her *"precision to detail"* and *"graciousness"* in advocacy.
The Clients: Popular with the aeronautics industry, the firm's client base includes Boeing, Bombardier, Learjet, Air One Transport and the Cessna Aircraft Company. Candlewood Hotels, Pizza Hut and Amazon.com are also leading clients.

KANSAS

EMPLOYMENT & LABOR LAW

KANSAS
Leading individuals
(Employment: Mainly Defendant)

1 RUPE Alan *Husch & Eppenberger LLC*, Wichita
2 BABCOCK Kathleen *Foulston Siefkin LLP*, Wichita
STANLEY Douglas *Foulston Siefkin LLP*, Wichita
3 CHURCHILL Stanley *Martin & Churchill*, Wichita
MANN Terry *Martin, Pringle, Oliver, Wallace*, Wichita
OVERMAN Robert *Morris, Laing, Evans*, Wichita
4 HILL Donald *Martin & Churchill Chartered*, Wichita
WORTH Diane *Morris, Laing, Evans, Brock*, Wichita

Up-and-coming individuals
MCCLELLAN Roger *Martin, Pringle, Oliver*, Wichita

Individuals are listed alphabetically in each band.

Martin & Churchill Chartered

The Firm: According to market observers, this firm is one of the few labor and employment boutiques representing management. Comprising seven lawyers, it has impressed many as a force in traditional labor union issues. Attorneys here advise employers on all aspects of contract negotiations and unfair labor practice charges. The firm also counsels management on employee disciplinary actions.

The Lawyers: The firm's reputation in traditional labor is attributed to partner **Stanley Churchill**, *"one of the top union lawyers in the state."* He has extensive experience on all union-related issues, such as advice on employee disciplinary actions and terminations. The market also applauded **Donald Hill** for his counseling on federal compliance laws and regulations.

The Clients: Brittain Machine; The Coleman Company; GE; Hay and Forage Industries; Hutchinson Hospital Corporation; INTRUST Bank; Koch Industries and Kansans for the Right to Work.

Martin, Pringle, Oliver, Wallace & Bauer LLP

The Firm: This Wichita-based, full-service firm is one of the largest firms in Kansas.

The Lawyers: **Terry Mann** garnered market kudos for her *"competency and intelligence"* as an employment discrimination defense litigator. Peers also singled out **Roger McClellan** as *"a rising star"* in employment litigation.

Morris, Laing, Evans, Brock & Kennedy, Chartered

The Firm: Prevailing market opinion recognizes this firm's sustained effort to develop its labor and employment practice. The four-lawyer group also benefits from the support of its colleagues in commercial litigation. There is a strong emphasis here on employment litigation, centered on OSHA and ERISA-related matters, in which the team has represented employers as well as employees.

The Lawyers: Interviewees singled out **Robert Overman** for his *"experience"* and his *"breadth of knowledge"* of labor and employment law. Overman's practice is said to have achieved *"a fine balance"* among employment litigation, employer counseling and traditional labor issues involving arbitrations and union avoidance. Peers also praised **Diane Worth** for her *"tenacious"* employment litigation style, seen particularly in her representation of both employers and employees in discrimination cases.

The Clients: Bauersfeld Enterprises; Butler County Community College; Midwest Drywall Company; Excel Corporation; Hutchinson Community College and Raytheon Aircraft Company.

Other Notable Practitioners

Set apart from the rest of the labor and employment litigators in Kansas is **Alan Rupe**, of regional firm Husch & Eppenberger LLC. Clients and admiring peers tagged Rupe the *"best and most effective labor and employment trial lawyer in the state."* Rivals acknowledged that he stands out due to his success in both defendants' and plaintiffs' employment trials, but noted that his *"aggressive"* and distinctive courtroom style is an acquired taste. Commercial clients appreciated his *"skilled advocacy"* and *"personal involvement"* in their employment discrimination cases. Over the past two years, he has successfully defended Wal-Mart on employment matters in a succession of cases. Rupe's other clients include Blue Cross and Blue Shield Association, and Sedgwick County.

LITIGATION

KANSAS
Leading firms
(Litigation: General Commercial)

1 FOULSTON SIEFKIN LLP *Overland Park, Wichita*
SHOOK, HARDY & BACON LLP *Overland Park*
SHUGHART THOMSON & KILROY PC *Overland Park*
STINSON MORRISON HECKER LLP *Overland Park*
2 HITE, FANNING & HONEYMAN LLP *Wichita*
LATHROP & GAGE LC *Overland Park*
3 HUSCH & EPPENBERGER LLC *Wichita*
SPENCER FANE BRITT & BROWNE LLP *Overland Park*

Firms are listed alphabetically in each band.

Foulston Siefkin LLP

The Firm: Applauded by observers as one of the *"main players"* in the market, the largest Kansas law firm – more than 60 attorneys in three Kansas offices – fields an *"exceptionally brilliant"* trial team. The group handles commercial litigation, antitrust and trade regulation, business torts, bankruptcies and creditors' rights, class actions and class action defense.

The Lawyers: **Mikel Stout**, whose work was hailed by peers as *"incomparable,"* handles complex litigation cases in specialty areas such as environmental matters. He is also skilled in mediation and dispute resolution. **Charles Efflandt**, group leader of the firm's environmental department, focuses on environmental and toxic tort litigation, regulatory enforcement and compliance issues. Competitors admired his *"strength and knowledge"* and his *"ability to convince"* juries.

The Clients: The firm represents and advises a wide range of clients from large corporations and small and medium-sized businesses to lenders and trusts.

Shook, Hardy & Bacon LLP
see firm details p.876

The Firm: With over 600 attorneys in ten offices worldwide, this international law firm has grown considerably from its Kansas City beginnings. The litigation group focuses on arbitration, business torts, commodities and securities litigation, contract disputes and fraud. Observers within the jurisdiction praise them for handling *"highly complex"* cases and attorneys here are respected as a *"dominant force"* in trials.

GENERAL COMMERCIAL

The Lawyers: Overland Park-based **Bill Sampson**, who concentrates on antitrust and general commercial litigation, has broad experience in federal and state courts, and has been active both nationally and internationally. Observers commented on his *"superior courtroom demeanor"* and the *"superb quality of advice"* that he provides to clients. **David Erickson** has tried numerous environmental, toxic tort, business litigation and professional liability cases. Competitors agreed that he is one of the *"finest"* environmental litigation attorneys in the state.

The Clients: Tobacco and pharmaceutical companies are represented by the firm.

Shughart Thomson & Kilroy PC

The Firm: This firm is one of the Midwest's better-known trial law firms. Attorneys here undertake business litigation in federal and state courts on a local, regional and national basis. The trial practice, which was recommended highly for its *"incredible sophistication,"* incorporates antitrust, banking, class actions, contract cases, fraud, and business disputes in its caseload.

LITIGATION

KANSAS

KANSAS
Leading individuals
(Litigation: General Commercial)

1
- **HITE Richard** *Hite, Fanning & Honeyman LLP,* Wichita
- **SAMPSON Bill** *Shook, Hardy & Bacon LLP,* Overland Park
- **STOUT Mikel** *Foulston Siefkin LLP,* Wichita

2
- **EFFLANDT Charles** *Foulston Siefkin LLP,* Overland Park
- **HINDERKS Mark** *Stinson Morrison Hecker,* Overland Park
- **MUSIL Gregory** *Shughart Thomson & Kilroy* Overland Park
- **REBEIN David** *Rebein Bangerter PA,* Dodge City

3
- **ERICKSON David** *Shook, Hardy & Bacon,* Overland Park
- **HATLEY Joseph** *Lathrop & Gage LC,* Overland Park
- **MACKAY Douglas** *Husch & Eppenberger LLC,* Wichita

Individuals are listed alphabetically in each band.

The Lawyers: Competitors applauded **Gregory Musil** for his *"high standards."* He has been particularly active in commercial litigation, business torts and property taxation matters.
The Clients: Health Midwest; Block Financial Corporation; Sprint; Jack Henry & Associates; Major League Baseball Players Association; Kansas City Power & Light; Associated Wholesale Grocers; Horizon Organic Dairy; Commerce Bank; JE Dunn Construction Company and Dickinson Financial.

Stinson Morrison Hecker LLP
The Firm: With more than 300 attorneys in offices throughout the Midwest as well as Phoenix and DC, this firm has a litigation department that is heavily involved in appellate law, business torts, general commercial litigation, banking, white-collar crime and construction matters. Peers agreed that its healthy client roster is attracted to the *"quality of its tremendous attorneys."*
The Lawyers: **Mark Hinderks**, cochair of the firm's construction litigation practice group, has broad experience in commercial litigation and arbitrations. Hinderks' recent caseload has included business purchase disputes, commercial and consumer class actions, securities litigation, contract disputes and industrial accident claims. Competitors applauded his *"good jury presence"* and his success in securing a *"well-established"* clientele.
The Clients: The firm has advised Sprint in 17 class actions arising from a billing issue.

Hite, Fanning & Honeyman LLP
The Firm: This 20-strong litigation boutique advises on issues such as civil litigation and business disputes, oil and gas litigation and products liability defense. Observers acknowledged that these attorneys have the skill and capacity to handle cases of *"unimaginable complexity."* Attorneys here specialize in medical malpractice, general insurance defense, probate work and general business and commercial disputes.
The Lawyers: Competitors pointed to **Richard Hite**'s *"superb knowledge"* of the law and his *"brilliant way"* with the jury. Active in public and community affairs, he was recommended for his experience in general business litigation and products liability matters.
The Clients: The firm advises petroleum and natural gas suppliers with their activities in southwestern Kansas.

Lathrop & Gage LC
The Firm: Competitors agreed that a *"loyal clientele"* and *"splendid"* attorneys have made this litigation group a major presence in Kansas. Although the group concentrates much of its energies in general commercial and business litigation, it remains a *"renowned force"* for its outstanding telecom work.
The Lawyers: **Joseph Hatley** is active across a range of matters including bankruptcy, telecom, education and environmental litigation and general business disputes. Peers especially endorsed his *"outstanding"* work with telecom companies.
The Clients: GM; The Greater Kansas City Chamber of Commerce; GMAC Commercial Mortgage Corporation; GST Steel; Royal Oak Enterprises; Russell Stover Candies; SSSB; Science City at Union Station; Seaboard; AMLI Residential Properties; AT&T; Baird, Kurtz & Dobson and Bank of America.

Husch & Eppenberger LLC
The Firm: This full-service Midwest law firm is widely respected by peers for its practice in toxic tort and general business litigation. The group is also experienced in environmental and health law, antitrust, construction disputes and class actions.
The Lawyers: **Douglas Mackay** has handled numerous lawsuits for major corporations in federal and state courts. Observers commended his *"wit"* and *"resilience"* when undertaking trial proceedings.
The Clients: The firm represents major retailers and chemical, pharmaceutical, multinational and international corporates.

Spencer Fane Britt & Browne LLP
The Firm: This three-office Kansas/Missouri firm is respected by clients and peers alike for its hard-working attorneys who ensure they give *"good value for money."* Active across a range of sectors, including IP, environmental issues and class actions, the group is also recommended for its expertise in areas such as alternative dispute resolution, mediation and arbitration.
The Lawyers: Nick Badgerow, who heads the litigation group in Kansas, focuses on litigation in business and employment matters, including construction, trade secrets, intellectual property and employment discrimination.
The Clients: The litigation group advises both local and national corporations.

Other Notable Practitioners
Formerly with Foulston Siefkin LLP, **David Rebein** of newly established Rebein Bangerter PA centers his practice around commercial litigation, employment law and insurance defense. He is widely respected by peers for his *"refined"* work and the complexity of his cases.

REAL ESTATE

KANSAS
Leading firms (Real Estate)

1
- **POLSINELLI SHALTON & WELTE PC** Overland Park
- **STINSON MORRISON HECKER LLP** Leawood

2
- **LATHROP & GAGE LC** Overland Park

3
- **HINKLE ELKOURI LAW FIRM LLC** Wichita
- **MORRIS, LAING, EVANS, BROCK,** Wichita
- **TRIPLETT, WOOLF & GARRETSON LLC** Wichita

4
- **ADAMS & JONES CHARTERED** Wichita
- **FLEESON, GOOING, COULSON & KITCH** Wichita

Firms are listed alphabetically in each band.

Polsinelli Shalton & Welte PC
The Firm: With a reputation in the market as *"the regional specialists"* for residential, commercial and land use development, this 11-lawyer team is a popular choice for developers. The firm handles billion dollar development project deals in Johnson County, dominating the Kansas City development market with an overall expertise in planning and zoning.
The Lawyers: Interviewees attribute the firm's reputation to land use expert **John Petersen**, who they describe as *"so politically connected that developers flock to him."* **Stanley Woodworth** was also recommended for his strengths in partnership law and residential real estate development.
The Clients: The group typically acts for a client base of Fortune 500 companies such as Wal-Mart and Sprint, for whom it negotiated the 240-acre land purchase and financing, including a $4 million tax incentive, for the development of its world headquarters. It also acted for the National Association of Stock Auto Car Racing in a $400-500 million deal establishing Kansas City as a venue on the circuit. Other clients include

KANSAS   REAL ESTATE

KANSAS
Leading individuals (Real Estate)

1 CIRCO Carl *Stinson Morrison Hecker LLP*, Leawood
HEAVEN Lewis *Lathrop & Gage*, Overland Park
PETERSEN John *Polsinelli Shalton*, Overland Park

2 STALLINGS John *Hinkle Elkouri Law Firm LLC*, Wichita
WOODWORTH Stanley *Polsinelli Shalton* Overland Park

3 GOODELL Gerald *Goodell, Stratton, Edmonds*, Topeka
HARNDEN Ronald *Triplett, Woolf*, Wichita
SCHRAG Donald *Morris, Laing, Evans, Brock*, Wichita
SHORTLIDGE Neil *Stinson Morrison Hecker*, Overland Park

4 BUCKLEY Mert *Adams & Jones Chartered*, Wichita
STARK Stephen *Fleeson, Gooing, Coulson LLC*, Wichita

Up-and-coming individuals
DOERR Brian *Duggan Shadwick & Doerr*, Overland Park

Individuals are listed alphabetically in each band.

Hanover Development, Home Depot and Trammell Crow.

Stinson Morrison Hecker LLP
The Firm: The firm enjoys a long-established reputation in the region, and is highly rated by the market for all aspects of real estate transaction work and municipal land use. Acknowledged by clients and peers as *"leaders in transactional work,"* the group derives its strength from the firm's sheer size – over 100 attorneys – throughout the Midwest.
The Lawyers: Carl Circo focuses on commercial transactions and was endorsed by peers for being *"easy to work with"* and *"a deal facilitator."* Neil Shortlidge is also recognized as a prominent figure in land use.
The Clients: The team represents a number of municipalities in land use and development cases, including the Cities of Olathe, Roeland Park and Overland Park. The firm's base of commercial and financial institution clients features: Farmland Industries; State Street; US Bank; SSB Realty and Corporate Woods.

Lathrop & Gage LC
The Firm: Observers consider the firm to be *"a leader in the public sector."* The team offers a broad base of experience working with both municipalities and private developers on land use issues. They also have great expertise in negotiating development matters with governmental entities. Interviewees particularly recommended the group for substantial municipal zoning work; the firm advised the City of Overland Park on a $200,000 design change on the intersection of a local highway. The group also negotiated on behalf of Deffenbaugh Industries to obtain a permit for large sanitary landfills.
The Lawyers: Lewis (Pete) Heaven is the group's leading figure. This well-respected attorney received excellent market feedback for being *"smart and unassuming."*
The Clients: Clarkson Construction; Rodrock Development; AT&T; The Atchison, Topeka and the Santa Fe Railway; Bank of America; Bayer; AMLI Residential Properties Trust; Block & Company; Browning-Ferris Industries and Burlington Northern Santa Fe.

Hinkle Elkouri Law Firm LLC
The Firm: This prestigious Wichita-based law firm has a primary focus on commercial, industrial and multi-family real estate.
The Lawyers: The seven-lawyer group has close ties with the Wichita community. *"Results-oriented"* attorney John Stallings spearheads the practice group.
The Clients: City of Wichita; Sedgwick County; Kansas Development Finance Authority; Wichita Public Schools; Wichita Public Building Commission and Raytheon Aircraft.

Morris, Laing, Evans, Brock & Kennedy, Chartered
The Firm: A full-service firm operating out of Wichita and Topeka. This established seven-lawyer team boasts a wide range of expertise in all real estate matters. Much of its client base is derived from the local community.
The Lawyers: *"Coolheaded"* transactions specialist Donald Schrag is thought by peers to be *"very knowledgeable about the law."*
The Clients: The firm acts for oil and gas companies such as ONEOK and for banks, including The Emprise Banks of Kansas, US Bank, Southwest National Bank and Twin Lakes National Bank.

Triplett, Woolf & Garretson LLC
The Firm: Rivals describe the Wichita firm as having a *"burgeoning real estate practice."* The three-lawyer team has a strong emphasis on financial and commercial transactions.
The Lawyers: Ron Harnden has the firm's highest profile. Clients endorse him for his deep legal experience and *"real understanding of the business."*
The Clients: Vantage Point Properties; Dean & Deluca; Plaza Real Estate; Ablah Enterprises and Ritchie Development.

Adams & Jones Chartered
The Firm: This smaller team of *"first-rate attorneys"* was deemed a powerful force within the Wichita real estate market. The practice's workload is 90% made up of commercial real estate deals on behalf of a wide range of local and national clients.
The Lawyers: Mert Buckley received general market commendation for his knowledge of commercial real estate.
The Clients: The firm acted as outside counsel to the City of Wichita in a $40 million public-private venture for development of a Hyatt hotel, conference center and parking garage. Represented the ground owner in the negotiation of a long-term lease to acquire national retail doughnut franchise Krispy Kreme's first site in Wichita. The firm has also advised First American Title Insurance Company and INTRUST Bank on real estate matters.

Fleeson, Gooing, Coulson & Kitch LLC
The Firm: Prevailing market opinion gives this full-service firm an entry onto *Chambers'* real estate rankings. This *"reputable"* group is best known for real estate financing and tax matters.
The Lawyers: The force behind the group, Stephen Stark, elicits praise from commentators for his expertise on real estate financing.
The Clients: GE Energy & Industrial Services and Fugate Enterprises.

Other Notable Practitioners
Gerald Goodell of Goodell, Stratton, Edmonds & Palmer LLP, is a respected Topeka-based real estate attorney with experience in the healthcare industry and condominium development. His clients include The Menninger Foundation, the Topeka Urban Renewal Agency and Kansas Medical Mutual Insurance. Brian Doerr of Duggan Shadwick & Doerr is proclaimed by peers as a *"rising talent"* in commercial real estate and financing. He is visible acting for clients such as The Provo Group and Country Club Bank.

Leaders in Kansas

ADAMS, Stephen
Blackwell Sanders Peper Martin LLP, Overland Park 913 696 7000
Recommended in Corporate/M&A

ALEGRIA, David
McCullough, Wareheman & Labunker, Topeka 785 233 2323
Recommended in Employment

BABCOCK, Kathleen
Foulston Siefkin LLP, Wichita
316 267 6371
Recommended in Employment

BUCKLEY, Mert
Adams & Jones Chartered, Wichita
316 265 8591
Recommended in Real Estate

CHURCHILL, Stanley
Martin & Churchill Chartered, Wichita
316 263 3200
Recommended in Employment

CIRCO, Carl
Stinson Morrison Hecker LLP, Leawood
913 451 5100
Recommended in Real Estate

DOERR, Brian
Duggan Shadwick & Doerr, Overland Park 913 498 3536
Recommended in Real Estate

EFFLANDT, Charles
Foulston Siefkin LLP, Overland Park
913 498 2100
Recommended in Litigation

ERICKSON, David
Shook, Hardy & Bacon LLP, Overland Park 913 451 6060
Recommended in Litigation

GOODELL, Gerald
Goodell, Stratton, Edmonds & Palmer, LLP, Topeka 785 233 0593
Recommended in Real Estate

HARNDEN, Ronald
Triplett, Woolf & Garretson LLC, Wichita
316 630 8100
Recommended in Real Estate

HATLEY, Joseph
Lathrop & Gage LC, Overland Park
913 451 5100
Recommended in Litigation

HEAVEN, Lewis
Lathrop & Gage LC, Overland Park
913 451 5100
Recommended in Real Estate

HILL, Donald
Martin & Churchill Chartered, Wichita
316 263 3200
Recommended in Employment

HINDERKS, Mark
Stinson Morrison Hecker LLP, Overland Park 816 691 2600
Recommended in Litigation

HITE, Richard
Hite, Fanning & Honeyman LLP, Wichita
316 265 7741
Recommended in Litigation

MACKAY, Douglas
Husch & Eppenberger, LLC, Wichita
316 264 3339
Recommended in Litigation

MANN, Terry
Martin, Pringle, Oliver, Wallace & Bauer, L.L.P., Wichita 316 265 9311
Recommended in Employment

MCCLELLAN, Roger
Martin, Pringle, Oliver, Wallace & Bauer, L.L.P., Wichita 316 265 9311
Recommended in Employment

MUSIL, Gregory
Shughart Thomson & Kilroy PC, Overland Park 913 451 3355
Recommended in Litigation

OVERMAN, Robert
Morris, Laing, Evans, Brock & Kennedy, Chartered, Wichita 316 262 2671
Recommended in Employment

PETERSEN, John
Polsinelli Shalton & Welte, A Professional Corporation, Overland Park
913 451 8788
Recommended in Real Estate

PETERSON, Ken
Morris, Laing, Evans, Brock & Kennedy, Chartered, Wichita 316 262 2671
Recommended in Employment

RALSTON, Eugene
Ralston Pope & Diehl LLC, Topeka
785 273 8002
Recommended in Employment

RATHBUN, Randy
Depew and Gillen LLC, Wichita
316 262 4000
Recommended in Employment

REBEIN, David
Rebein Bangerter PA, Dodge City
620 227 8126
Recommended in Litigation

RUPE, Alan
Husch & Eppenberger, LLC, Wichita
316 264 3339
Recommended in Employment

SAMPSON, Bill
Shook, Hardy & Bacon LLP, Overland Park 913 451 6060
Recommended in Litigation

SCHRAG, Donald
Morris, Laing, Evans, Brock & Kennedy, Chartered, Wichita 316 262 2671
Recommended in Real Estate

SHORTLIDGE, Neil
Stinson Morrison Hecker LLP, Overland Park 816 691 2600
Recommended in Real Estate

STALLINGS, John
Hinkle Elkouri Law Firm LLC, Wichita
316 267 2000
Recommended in Real Estate

STANLEY, Douglas
Foulston Siefkin LLP, Wichita
316 267 6371
Recommended in Employment

STARK, Stephen
Fleeson, Gooing, Coulson & Kitch, LLC, Wichita 316 267 7361
Recommended in Real Estate

STOUT, Mikel
Foulston Siefkin LLP, Wichita
316 267 6371
Recommended in Litigation

SWAIN, Lawrence
Shughart Thomson & Kilroy PC, Overland Park 913 451 3355
Recommended in Corporate/M&A

TRENKLE, William
Foulston Siefkin LLP, Overland Park
913 498 2100
Recommended in Corporate/M&A

WOODWORTH, Stanley
Polsinelli Shalton & Welte, A Professional Corporation, Overland Park
913 451 8788
Recommended in Real Estate

WORTH, Diane
Morris, Laing, Evans, Brock & Kennedy, Chartered, Wichita 316 262 2671
Recommended in Employment

KENTUCKY

CORPORATE/M&A

CONTENTS: Corporate/M&A p.300; Employment: Mainly Plaintiff p.301; Mainly Defendant p.302; Litigation: General Commercial p.303; Real Estate p.304; Individuals' Profiles p.305.

KENTUCKY'S TOP FOUR
1. Frost Brown Todd
2. Greenebaum Doll & McDonald
3. Stites & Harbison
3. Wyatt, Tarrant & Combs

Ranking based on Chambers' research within the state.

All quotes in the text are from interviews with clients and competitors.

OVERVIEW: Top-ranking firm Frost Brown Todd is the product of a merger in 2000 between Kentucky's Brown, Todd & Heyburn and Ohio's Frost & Jacobs to form Mid-America's largest regional law firm. Close to 400 lawyers act from offices in Indiana, Tennessee, Ohio and Kentucky. The Kentucky practice is considered to be a leader for corporate matters, where a team led by Ed Glasscock boasts particular strength in IP. The firm also earns praise for its litigation and labor and employment practices, with attorneys Winston Miller and Patton Pelfrey both appearing in Chambers' rankings. Bank of Louisville, UPS and Brown & Williamson Tobacco are representative clients.

As **Greenebaum Doll & McDonald** celebrates its 50th year, it marks a successful period of growth that has seen the firm develop from a small Louisville office to a multi-state practice with offices in Kentucky, Ohio, Tennessee and DC. A respected corporate practice receives praise for its work in tax, securities and M&A. The firm was also recommended for the strength of its employment defense group, where Richard Cleary was singled out as a leader in the field. The firm's real estate and litigation practice groups also performed well in the ranking tables. Clients include LG&E Energy and Papa John's International.

A well-established firm, **Stites & Harbison** is best known for its litigation capacity, which is considered one of the best in the state. Interviewees identified premier litigator and former firm managing partner Charles (Mike) Cronan as among the crème de la crème in this field. Its strength in contentious matters feeds into the firm's highly rated real estate and corporate practices. Peers consider top-ranked real estate attorney Fred Joseph to shine in a cutting-edge practice. The firm has additional offices in Indiana, Tennessee, Georgia and DC. Clients include American Electric Power, JPMorgan and KFC.

Full-service firm **Wyatt, Tarrant & Combs** ranks joint third with Stites & Harbison. Backed by the resources of more than 200 lawyers in Kentucky, Indiana and Tennessee, the firm appears in the top tier for corporate and employment law and was highly rated in both commercial litigation and real estate. Of eight lawyers ranked, four emerged as in the top band in their respective areas. A broad spectrum of clients includes Merrill Lynch, Fruit of the Loom and LG&E Energy.

CORPORATE/M&A

KENTUCKY
Leading firms (Corporate/M&A)
1. **FROST BROWN TODD LLC** Louisville
   GREENEBAUM DOLL & MCDONALD Louisville
   STITES & HARBISON PLLC Louisville
   WYATT, TARRANT & COMBS Bowling Green, Louisville
2. **STOLL, KEENON & PARK LLP** Lexington
3. **OGDEN NEWELL & WELCH** Louisville

Leading individuals (Corporate/M&A)
1. CONNER Stewart *Wyatt, Tarrant & Combs*, Louisville
   GLASSCOCK Ed *Frost Brown Todd LLC*, Louisville
2. BRADLEY Craig *Stites & Harbison PLLC*, Louisville
   LYNDRUP Peggy *Greenebaum Doll*, Louisville
   MACDONALD Alan *Frost Brown Todd LLC*, Louisville
   STRAUS James *Frost Brown Todd LLC*, Louisville
   TANNON Jay *Frost Brown Todd LLC*, Louisville
   YOUNG Cynthia *Wyatt, Tarrant & Combs LLP*, Louisville
3. CATRON Stephen *Wyatt, Tarrant*, Bowling Green
   DOLSON Scott *Frost Brown Todd LLC*, Louisville
   LESTER David *Stoll, Keenon & Park LLP*, Lexington
   NORTHAM Patrick *Greenebaum Doll*, Louisville
   SEIFFERT James *Stites & Harbison PLLC*, Louisville

Firms and individuals are listed alphabetically in each band.

Frost Brown Todd LLC
see firm details p.798

The Firm: The November 2000 merger of Kentucky's Brown, Todd & Heyburn with Ohio's Frost & Jacobs created this *"mammoth"* law firm. The mid-American giant has close to 400 lawyers in seven offices, including two in Kentucky. Its *"tremendously deep and talented bench"* represents a large number of public companies and venture capital firms. The group's increased strength in IP was noted by commentators.

The Lawyers: Clients claimed that the corporate team has thrived under the *"tremendous leadership"* of *"great and well-connected rainmaker"* **Ed Glasscock**. He earned plaudits for his *"unique combination of practical deal-making capabilities, enormous energy and commitment to his clients."* He represented Bank of Louisville MidAmerica Bancorp in its recent $372 million merger with North Carolina-based bank holding company BB&T. Clients also complimented **Alan MacDonald** on his *"practical and highly analytical approach to business needs."* MacDonald is particularly valued as a *"top securities lawyer, with an excellent understanding of Sarbanes-Oxley."* He has worked on a large debt placement for ResCare and has also represented Horizon Natural Resources, the fourth largest coal producer in the US. The firm has created an international practice, led by *"incredibly personable"* **Jay Tannon**. He was praised by peers as an *"excellent attorney, who has worked tirelessly to cultivate a unique niche."* Tannon counsels North American and international businesses on M&A, joint ventures, investments, product distribution and licensing arrangements. He has acted in major projects for UPS, Powerscreen International and Beatrice Foods Canada. The firm was also praised for its strong banking practice, led by **Jim Straus**, a *"leading M&A lawyer in the banking arena."* Straus was valued by clients for his *"logical approach and ability to simplify complicated matters."* **Scott Dolson** also won market praise. A *"technically sophisticated, bright lawyer with a tax-flavored practice,"* Dolson has been seen advising in the acquisition of an insurance company and counseling individuals and corporates on wealth-transfer planning.

The Clients: Bank of Louisville MidAmerica Bancorp; ResCare; Horizon Natural Resources; UPS; Yum! Brands and Brown & Williamson Tobacco.

Greenebaum Doll & McDonald PLLC

The Firm: Interviewees considered this to be *"one of the leading corporate and tax firms in Kentucky."* It earned particularly high marks for its M&A and IP work. It now fields over 170 lawyers from six offices, four of them in Kentucky.

The Lawyers: **Peggy Lyndrup** chairs the corporate and commercial practice group. Peers described her as a *"seasoned deal lawyer"* and an *"excellent technician, very much in the trenches."* Her practice covers M&A, corporate formations, joint ventures, trademark licensing and product distribution. Her *"solid stable of clients"* includes sporting goods manufacturer Hillerich & Bradsby. *"Indefatigable worker"* **Pat Northam** was admired by clients for his *"incredible foresight and knowledge of regulatory issues."* He is said to have an *"extremely sophisticated"* grasp of energy matters.

The Clients: In addition to Hillerich & Bradsby,

CORPORATE/M&A — KENTUCKY

the firm represents LG&E Energy and Papa John's International, among others.

Stites & Harbison PLLC
The Firm: Market sources were quick to praise this *"quality corporate powerhouse."* It has 200 lawyers in eight offices, four of which are located in Kentucky, and enjoys a reputation as a commercial front runner. The firm's expertise in complex M&A and corporate finance was particularly noted.
The Lawyers: Observers admired *"outstanding and instinctive corporate and securities lawyer"* **Craig Bradley**. He was said to be *"solutions-oriented and nonconfrontational,"* with a *"superb ability to prioritize."* He won especial praise for his work with emerging growth companies, as did his colleague **Jim Seiffert**. Clients also praised Seiffert for his *"incredible wisdom"* and *"invaluable knowledge"* of tax, cooperatives and unusual business structures.
The Clients: Steel Technologies; AEGON USA Investment Management; American Electric Power; Fidelity National Bank and Zurich-American Insurance Group.

Wyatt, Tarrant & Combs LLP
The Firm: This *"top-notch giant"* can draw upon *"considerable depth and breadth"* in its seven offices, four located in Kentucky. The well-connected firm boasts over 200 lawyers and is particularly known for its strength in the energy sector, in which it represents LG&E Energy.
The Lawyers: Interviewees singled out **Stewart Conner**, managing partner of the firm, for his outstanding corporate and securities work. He has *"oceans of experience"* in the corporate finance and banking sectors. Commentators also praised *"solid, bright and capable"* **Cynthia Young**. She scooped high marks for her wide experience of securities work and her representation of financial institutions. Her corporate governance and regulatory work also won plaudits. The *"well-connected"* president-elect of the state bar association, **Stephen Catron**, was recommended by peers for his *"goal-oriented nature and devotion to his clients' needs."* Operating out of the Bowling Green office, Catron focuses on corporate, banking and real estate law. He played a key role in the development of the Bowling Green-Warren County Convention Center.
The Clients: LG&E Energy; Liberty Mutual Group; Merrill Lynch and Fruit of the Loom.

Stoll, Keenon & Park LLP
The Firm: Interviewees described this as a *"highly respected old-line firm."* It has four offices in the state, and was noted for its *"overall strength and size"* in Lexington, the state's second legal market place after Louisville. The firm has close links to Kentucky's important horse racing industry and represents Keeneland Association, a thoroughbred race course and sales company, along with a number of stud farms.
The Lawyers: According to sources, *"smooth and conciliatory"* **David Lester** is a *"strong transactional attorney."* He is especially active in business formations and commercial lending matters and is said to be *"both good to work with, and against."*
The Clients: Keeneland Association; Lexington Herald-Leader; Lexmark International; Breeders' Cup and Caterpillar.

Ogden Newell & Welch
The Firm: This *"quality firm"* is perhaps better known for civil and commercial litigation. Sources confirmed, however, that it is also a player in the corporate arena. It has about 40 lawyers in Kentucky who handle a variety of corporate work from debt and equity financing to M&A and divestitures. It represents both lenders and borrowers in connection with real estate and business loans.
The Lawyers: The corporate team includes Thomas Rutledge.
The Clients: Kentucky Medical Insurance Company; United Medical; Zurich and Kentucky Utilities Company.

EMPLOYMENT & LABOR LAW — MAINLY PLAINTIFF

KENTUCKY
Leading firms
(Employment: Mainly Plaintiff)

1. **LAW OFFICES OF THOMAS CLAY** Louisville
2. **PRIDDY, EISENBERG, MILLER & MEADE** Louisville
   SALES, TILLMAN & WALLBAUM Louisville
   SEGAL, STEWART, CUTLER, LINDAY Louisville

Leading individuals
(Employment: Mainly Plaintiff)

1. **CLAY Thomas** *Law Offices of Thomas Clay,* Louisville
2. **COAN Marvin** *Hummel, Coan, Miller & Sage,* Louisville
   CUTLER Irwin *Segal, Stewart, Cutler,* Louisville
   MEADE Don *Priddy, Eisenberg, Miller,* Louisville
   PRIDDY Al *Priddy, Eisenberg, Miller & Meade,* Louisville
   SALES Kenneth *Sales, Tillman & Wallbaum,* Louisville
   SEGAL Herbert *Segal, Stewart, Cutler, Linday,* Louisville
3. **FRIEDMAN David** *Fernandez Friedman,* Louisville
   MORRIS Doug *Oldfather & Morris,* Louisville

Firms and individuals are listed alphabetically in each band.

Law Offices of Thomas Clay
The Firm: This five-lawyer firm is focused on plaintiffs' discrimination cases. It has thrived on the reputation of *"aggressive, shrewd, heavy hitter"* **Tom Clay**. Clay's skills and experience have earned him wide recognition as the *"leader of the pack"* in Kentucky. His reputation as a formidable opponent was strengthened recently by a large, successful verdict against Philip Morris.

Priddy, Eisenberg, Miller & Meade
The Firm: This *"ethical and trustworthy"* firm enjoys a solid profile, thanks in part to the strong reputations of two of its name partners. **Al Priddy** is considered by many to be the *"top labor lawyer in town."* He represents a number of unions. His colleague, **Don Meade**, was described to researchers as *"extremely bright and well organized."* His experience covers both traditional labor and plaintiffs' employment work.

Sales, Tillman & Wallbaum
The Firm: Formerly with Segal Stewart, **Ken Sales** was admired by interviewees for his *"tremendously successful record"* as a plaintiffs' lawyer. He represents unions in disputes with employers.

Segal, Stewart, Cutler, Linday, Janes & Berry
The Firm: This firm is a notable player across the personal injury, labor and employment law sectors. According to market sources, the formidable group benefits from the high standing of veteran **Herb Segal**, still a *"leading labor union lawyer,"* and his *"talented and competitive"* younger colleague **Irwin (Buddy) Cutler**. The firm represents, inter alia, major unions of autoworkers and machinists.

Other Notable Practitioners
The *"thoroughly smart and experienced"* **Marvin Coan**, of Hummel, Coan, Miller & Sage, was praised by interviewees as a *"trial attorney with the highest integrity."* He has earned particular respect in the employment discrimination arena.

Oldfather & Morris is best known as a medical malpractice boutique. However, **Doug Morris** of the firm has branched out into employment litigation, where he is establishing a solid reputation. **David Friedman** of Fernandez Friedman Grossman & Kohn PLLC was recommended to researchers as a talented lawyer, particularly in the constitutional field. He has also acted in the employment discrimination domain, arguing sexual harassment and race, age and gender discrimination cases, and acts as general counsel for the American Civil Liberties Union.

KENTUCKY

EMPLOYMENT & LABOR LAW

EMPLOYMENT & LABOR LAW — MAINLY DEFENDANT

KENTUCKY
Leading firms
(Employment: Mainly Defendant)

1
- GREENEBAUM DOLL & MCDONALD PLLC *Louisville*
- WYATT, TARRANT & COMBS LLP *Louisville*

2
- FROST BROWN TODD LLC *Louisville*
- SMITH & SMITH *Louisville*
- STOLL, KEENON & PARK LLP *Lexington*

3
- DINSMORE & SHOHL LLP *Louisville*

Leading individuals
(Employment: Mainly Defendant)

1
- CLEARY Richard *Greenebaum Doll, Louisville*
- HOPSON Edwin *Wyatt, Tarrant & Combs LLP, Louisville*
- PELFREY Patton *Frost Brown Todd LLC, Louisville*

2
- GRIFFITH Richard *Stoll, Keenon & Park LLP, Louisville*
- SMITH James *Smith & Smith, Louisville*

3
- BECKER Wendy *Greenebaum Doll, Lexington*
- COCKRUM James *Frost Brown Todd LLC, Louisville*
- DAWAHARE Debra *Wyatt, Tarrant & Combs, Lexington*
- ESCHELS Philip *Greenebaum Doll, Louisville*
- FLEISCHAKER Jon *Dinsmore & Shohl LLP, Louisville*
- GREENE Kimberly *Dinsmore & Shohl LLP, Louisville*
- SAVARISE Jeff *Greenebaum Doll & McDonald, Louisville*

Firms and individuals are listed alphabetically in each band.

Greenebaum Doll & McDonald PLLC

The Firm: This firm received praise from market sources for its *"considerable muscle"* and deep bench in the labor and employment arena. Over the past 12 months, the firm has been involved in some key cases, including a major ADA case for Toyota Motor Manufacturing, Kentucky against Williams. The group also acted for Union Underwear Co against Barnhart.

The Lawyers: Chair of the employment group **Richard Cleary** was unanimously commended as a *"leading authority with a national reputation in the labor and employment field."* With his *"incredible expertise"* he is a *"well-known highflier"* at the NLRB. Researchers were told that he also *"runs a tight ship,"* full of experienced attorneys. These include **Jeff Savarise**, whose *"excellent legal analysis"* enables him to *"cut right through to the important issues,"* according to peers. Interviewees also admire *"fast-climbing and forward-looking"* **Philip Eschels**. He is widely experienced in discrimination, harassment and non-compete disputes, and has acted as corporate counsel for Toyota. *"Meticulous and conscientious"* **Wendy Becker** is highly regarded for her advice on employment discrimination, particularly in regard to sexual harassment matters. Based in Lexington, Becker is recognized as a focused practitioner who *"keeps her eye on the ball."*

The Clients: The firm's top-flight client base also includes The Kroger Company and National Linen Service.

Wyatt, Tarrant & Combs LLP

The Firm: This firm has a considerable presence across the state. Its strong labor and employment practice wins the respect of peers and clients alike. The group covers everything from employment litigation to the representation of management in their union dealings, with FMLA, ADA and wage and hour cases continuing to be key areas.

The Lawyers: **Ed Hopson**, who chairs the firm's employment group, has over 30 years of trial experience. His strengths are in employment law, and, particularly, traditional labor issues, winning him unanimous respect from market sources. He was noted for his experience in unfair labor practice hearings before the NLRB, and praised for his responsiveness and ability to evaluate cases quickly. He defended the City of Louisville, Division of Fire, in a wage and hour dispute, which reduced the City's exposure to overtime by $6 million. *"Experienced and competent"* **Debra Dawahare**, based in the firm's Lexington office, was warmly praised by clients for her *"wide experience of discrimination cases"* and her *"innate ability to connect with juries."*

The Clients: GE; Kuhlman Electric; Allstate and Fruit of the Loom.

Frost Brown Todd LLC
see firm details p.798

The Firm: Frost Brown Todd boasts a potent mix of labor and employment attorneys. It enjoys a strong reputation in the market for both traditional and cutting-edge work, and has experience of a range of sectors.

The Lawyers: The *"engaging"* cochair of the labor and employment group, **Patton Pelfrey**, is admired by clients for his *"straightforward approach."* His ability to form *"good relationships with both allies and opponents"* was also noted, as were his long-standing connections with the NLRB. His practice is split between traditional labor matters and corporate-related advice. Sources also admired the *"excellent legal insight and assertiveness"* of **Jim Cockrum**, who represents a wide range of employers in the manufacturing and service industries.

The Clients: UPS; East Kentucky Power Cooperative; Avenir Corp; Louisville Gas & Electric; Kentucky Association of Electric Cooperatives and AK Steel.

Smith & Smith

The Firm: This labor and employment specialist boutique was described to researchers as a *"go-to firm in Kentucky."* For many years it has held a preeminent reputation for labor law in Louisville, and still remains a key player. It is particularly noted for its experience in representing the management of small to mid-sized companies in resisting union-organizing campaigns. Other strengths include OSHA, wage and hour disputes and the full range of employment litigation.

The Lawyers: **Jim Smith** has almost 30 years' experience in the field. He was lauded by peers as an *"excellent labor lawyer,"* with wide experience and an *"easygoing, practical approach."* He has represented Chubb Group and Churchill Downs, among others.

The Clients: The firm acts for a range of private and public companies, many in the insurance sphere. Clients include Churchill Downs, American Commercial, Cardinal Aluminium Company and Chubb Group.

Stoll, Keenon & Park LLP

The Firm: The firm was praised to researchers as a *"strong player,"* especially in the Lexington market. Its labor and employment team focuses on advice and litigation on behalf of employers. ADA, sexual harassment and age discrimination continue to be strong areas for the group. It also handles a volume of race discrimination claims and has represented a Japanese company in a Hispanic discrimination suit.

The Lawyers: The team, which has about ten full-time attorneys in the field, pulled off a coup when it recruited *"bright and knowledgeable"* **Rick Griffith** from Stites & Harbison. He is well known for his strength as a trial lawyer, and is admired by peers for his *"excellent demeanor"* and *"ability to get things done."*

The Clients: The firm represents a large client base, including Lexington Herald-Leader, Alliance Tobacco and Kentucky Medical Services Foundation.

Dinsmore & Shohl LLP

The Firm: This Cincinnati-based firm is still considered relatively new to Kentucky. It now has three offices in the state, however, and market sources confirm that it has a growing presence in the local labor and employment market.

The Lawyers: Former Wyatt, Tarrant & Combs partner **Jon Fleischaker** is known as a preeminent First Amendment lawyer, defending radio and television stations, and newspapers. His practice also includes a large volume of employment litigation. *"Intuitive and practical"* **Kimberly Greene** is another knowledgeable employment lawyer, with a strong litigation profile. She also carries out a large amount of First Amendment work.

The Clients: The firm represents numerous employers, including Fortune 500 companies.

LITIGATION: GENERAL COMMERCIAL — KENTUCKY

KENTUCKY
Leading firms
(Litigation: General Commercial)

1 FROST BROWN TODD LLC *Louisville*
   STITES & HARBISON PLLC *Louisville*
2 GREENEBAUM DOLL & MCDONALD PLLC *Louisville*
   STOLL, KEENON & PARK LLP *Lexington*
   WYATT, TARRANT & COMBS LLP *Louisville*
3 MIDDLETON REUTLINGER PSC *Louisville*
   OGDEN NEWELL & WELCH *Louisville*

Leading individuals
(Litigation: General Commercial)

1 CRONAN Charles *Stites & Harbison, Louisville*
   HAYNES Greg *Wyatt, Tarrant & Combs LLP, Louisville*
2 COLLIER Philip *Stites & Harbison PLLC, Lexington*
   HENLEIN Carl *Frost Brown Todd LLC, Louisville*
   MILLER Winston *Frost Brown Todd LLC, Louisville*
   REED John *Reed Weitkamp Schell & Vice, Louisville*
3 BALLANTINE John *Ogden Newell & Welch, Louisville*
   BEEMAN Arthur *Frost Brown Todd LLC, Louisville*
   CASSIS Charlie *Frost Brown Todd LLC, Louisville*
   HINKLE Samuel *Stoll, Keenon & Park LLP, Louisville*
   HOULIHAN Robert *Stoll, Keenon & Park, Lexington*
   ISON Eric *Greenebaum Doll & McDonald, Louisville*
   MILLIMAN Jim *Middleton Reutlinger PSC, Louisville*
   SNYDER Sheryl *Frost Brown Todd LLC, Louisville*

Firms and individuals are listed alphabetically in each band.

Frost Brown Todd LLC
see firm details p.798

The Firm: This newly merged firm has formidable resources in commercial litigation and now fields over 100 lawyers in the specialty from its Midwest office network. Clients enthused about its strong all-around skills in commercial litigation, particularly insurance, IP, environmental and mineral disputes. The firm served as lead counsel for 30 major products manufacturers in the San Juan Dupont Plaza Hotel Fire litigation, one of the largest cases ever filed, which culminated in a 13-month-long jury trial in Puerto Rico.

The Lawyers: *"Excellent and accomplished"* department chair **Winston Miller** was praised for his understanding of clients' needs and his considerable experience in products liability, employment, toxic tort and general business litigation. **Carl Henlein** is a *"tremendous products liability and mass torts attorney"* with a national reputation. Peers highlighted his skill in determining strategy and coordinating actions. He has played a major part in the lead paint litigation defense for ICI Paints. *"Outstandingly energetic and creative IP lawyer"* **Arthur Beeman** also enjoys a national reputation, while *"skilled and combative"* **Sheryl Snyder** has a high profile for governmental and constitutional matters. In a 30-year career, Snyder has made the appellate oral argument in over 25 reported decisions, including the Oklahoma City bombing civil litigation. He has also been involved in defending a governor in an alleged sex scandal. Peers admired his *"incredible ability to get his mind around the issues."* **Charlie Cassis** has a traditional strength in insurance cases, though he also boasts considerable experience in mass tort and has been active in litigation on behalf of Brown & Williamson Tobacco.

The Clients: In addition to representing Brown & Williamson Tobacco, Anthem, and UPS, the largest employer in the state, the firm carries out work for AK Steel and ICI.

Stites & Harbison PLLC

The Firm: Peers admire this firm for its *"overwhelmingly large"* state presence in commercial litigation. Having *"long been the backbone"* of the 170-year-old giant, its commercial litigation practice is experienced in a wide range of work. Market sources particularly drew our attention to expertise in employment, construction and environmental litigation.

The Lawyers: *"Outstanding, levelheaded and well-prepared litigator"* **Charles (Mike) Cronan** outshone most of his rivals in the state. His *"incredible presence"* and *"vast analytical experience"* of complex business litigation were said to give him the edge. Particular strengths include products liability and professional malpractice defense, particularly for the medical profession. *"Honorable, skillful and feisty"* **Phil Collier** was recommended for his ability to *"understand the financial heart of a transaction."* Said by fellow professionals to be *"reassuringly fair and good to work with or against,"* Collier has worked on cases involving directors and other officers, and auditors. He also undertakes complex contractual disputes.

The Clients: Electrolux; American Electric Power and Regional Airport Authority of Louisville and Jefferson County.

Greenebaum Doll & McDonald PLLC

The Firm: This 50-year-old firm may be better known for its corporate practice, but it also handles the full range of commercial litigation from its four Kentucky offices. It enjoys a particularly strong profile for manufacturing and healthcare litigation. The team acted for Toyota Motor Manufacturing, Kentucky in the high-profile Toyota v Williams case. It has also represented a real estate developer in a complex commercial dispute with a national financial services firm, securing a $27.5 million settlement.

The Lawyers: **Eric Ison**, who chairs the litigation and dispute resolution group, earned sustained market commendations. Sources describe him as a *"talented and reliable go-to trial attorney."*

The Clients: The firm represented Staples in defense of a $13 million breach of contract claim. Other clients include Toyota Motor Manufacturing North America, Papa John's International, LG&E Energy and Merrill Lynch.

Stoll, Keenon & Park LLP

The Firm: This *"premier Kentucky corporate firm"* enjoys a strong litigation profile despite its smaller presence in Louisville. It is well connected in the Lexington market, and was admired by sources for its expertise in many areas of commercial litigation, including complex bankruptcy, IP and employment matters. The group has been particularly busy in fraud and securities litigation, and acts in a large volume of lender liability cases for banks and financial institutions.

The Lawyers: *"Smart and relentless"* **Sam Hinkle** is the partner in charge of the Louisville office and chairs the firm's environmental practice. He was recommended to researchers as a popular and *"practical"* commercial litigator who can be relied upon to pay *"incredible attention to detail."* His practice includes contractual, environmental, bankruptcy and franchise litigation. **Bob Houlihan** was admired for his great track record in libel defense and defamation cases. His impressive stable of media clients includes names like the Lexington Herald-Leader. Industry sources say that he is *"impressive in closing arguments"* and *"never one to leave any stone unturned."*

The Clients: The firm's client base includes Lexmark International, Lexington Herald-Leader and Fifth Third Bancorp.

Wyatt, Tarrant & Combs LLP

The Firm: The firm's litigation team was considered to be among its strongest practice groups. It covers all types of business-related disputes, including non-compete and trade secrets, employment litigation, business torts and environmental matters. The group's high-profile caseload has included representing a former governor facing allegations of improper conduct.

The Lawyers: *"Incredibly skillful trial lawyer"* **Greg Haynes** chairs the litigation department. He earned widespread market plaudits for being *"smart, quick on his feet and composed"* and has built up *"oceans of experience"* over a 30-year career. He has been lead counsel in, interalia, stockholder class actions and complex securities cases.

The Clients: The firm recently represented Thornton Oil in a major commercial dispute. Other important clients include Bank One Kentucky, Ford, Fruit of the Loom, Pfizer and Liberty Mutual Group.

KENTUCKY

REAL ESTATE

Middleton Reutlinger PSC
The Firm: Interviewees noted that this old-line Louisville firm is enjoying a growing reputation, and is *"in the mix with a good stable of clients."* It has a decent reputation in commercial litigation, including contract, IP and class actions.
The Lawyers: Market sources praised *"talented and aggressive"* **Jim Milliman**. He has acted in a range of complex litigation, including representing a number of coal companies in a $2 billion dispute with 500 insurance carriers concerning Black Lung coverage. His experience of trade secret cases includes acting for Brown & Williamson Tobacco in a highly publicized whistle-blower case, in which the company's right to protect its confidential information was successfully upheld.
The Clients: The firm's client base includes Brown & Williamson Tobacco, Chevron USA, Fifth Third Bank, The Kroger Company and National Technical Systems.

Ogden Newell & Welch
The Firm: This 40-strong Louisville firm is considered an important player in the market. Its commercial litigation practice covers a range of matters including professional malpractice defense.
The Lawyers: Commentators said the firm has thrived under the influence of the outstanding **John (Jack) Ballantine**. He currently spends much of his time as a mediator, but also has an extensive civil trial practice, almost exclusively on the defense side. Market sources particularly noted his high profile for defense in medical malpractice cases.
The Clients: The firm's enviable client list includes Zurich and Louisville Gas & Electric.

Other Notable Practitioners
Commentators praised **John Reed** of smallish Louisville firm, Reed Weitkamp Schell & Vice PLLC, as *"one of the most experienced and smartest"* commercial litigators in the state. He is said to be *"a skilled and formidable adversary,"* particularly well qualified in complex antitrust matters.

REAL ESTATE

KENTUCKY
Leading firms (Real Estate)
1. FROST BROWN TODD LLC *Louisville*
2. STITES & HARBISON PLLC *Louisville*
   WYATT, TARRANT & COMBS LLP *Louisville*
3. GREENEBAUM DOLL & MCDONALD PLLC *Louisville*

Leading individuals (Real Estate)
1. JOSEPH Alfred *Stites & Harbison PLLC,* Louisville
   MARTIN Timothy *Frost Brown Todd LLC,* Louisville
   VINCENTI Mike *Wyatt, Tarrant & Combs,* Louisville
2. AHEARN Dale *Frost Brown Todd LLC,* Louisville
   HADEN Bill *Stites & Harbison PLLC,* Louisville
   HINES Barry *Stites & Harbison PLLC,* Louisville
   PRICE Glenn *Greenebaum Doll & McDonald,* Louisville
   SAFFER David *Wyatt, Tarrant & Combs LLP,* Louisville
3. CLARK Jude *Frost Brown Todd LLC,* Louisville
   GATHRIGHT Joe *Gathright & Hardy,* Louisville

Firms and individuals are listed alphabetically in each band.

Frost Brown Todd LLC
see firm details p.798
The Firm: The firm's large group of professionals was universally endorsed as the front runner in Kentucky. Its real estate attorneys offer the full breadth of services, from acquisitions to zoning, to both developers and lenders. The Cincinnati office, in particular, just over the Kentucky state line, carries out a large volume of lending work. The team has historically been active in major commercial and residential development projects, with lifestyle centers featuring as a growth area.
The Lawyers: **Tim Martin** commands a diverse practice with a lending and refinancing focus. The *"intelligent, user-friendly and well-connected"* Martin was praised for his ability to see the most critical issues in a transaction, and to *"furrow unplowed legal ground."* He represents a number of major institutional and local lenders, handling matters such as land use, development and acquisitions. Tough competitor **Dale Ahearn** boasts lengthy experience in the shopping and retail development arena, which earned him widespread plaudits from industry sources. He acts for retailers, developers and lenders in commercial developments, both state and nationwide. Clients noted that **Jude Clark**, former in-house counsel for AEGON USA Realty Advisors, is a *"knowledgeable and competent"* real estate attorney with a *"broad perspective."* He regularly represents lenders in secured credit arrangements involving real estate and other assets.
The Clients: Morgan Stanley; CIBC; GE Capital; NTS Development Company; Hogan Development; US Bank; UPS and Bank One.

Stites & Harbison PLLC
The Firm: This firm has a *"well thought of, responsive and efficient"* real estate team, according to clients. In addition to the conventional real estate services, it covers all aspects of relocation and condemnation law. The firm's roles as counsel to the Regional Airport Authority of Louisville and Jefferson County for the expansion of Louisville's primary airport, and to the Louisville Waterfront Development Corporation for the redevelopment of the city's riverfront, have boosted its profile.
The Lawyers: **Fred Joseph**, one of the deans of real estate law, is felt to be *"among the wisest real estate attorneys"* in the state, with a *"terrific understanding of complex matters."* His broad experience and increasing involvement in unique, cutting-edge real estate projects have earned him a national reputation. He undertakes considerable work for the Housing Authority of Louisville in connection with the redevelopment of dilapidated public housing in the city. Rising star **Barry Hines** represents commercial lenders and undertakes large amounts of conduit lending work. His *"incredible insight and foresight"* help him to remove pitfalls from deals, according to clients. He has acted in many national loan closings for JPMorgan. *"Detailed and timely"* **Bill Haden** chairs the real estate and finance group. His broad experience includes letters of credit, real estate-linked bond deals and the sale of shopping centers.
The Clients: JPMorgan; KFC; Louisville Waterfront Development Corporation and Regional Airport Authority of Louisville and Jefferson County.

Wyatt, Tarrant & Combs LLP
The Firm: This more than 200-lawyer regional powerhouse is recommended by industry sources as a good choice for multiparty real estate transactions. Its considerable strength in lending is held to be a major advantage.
The Lawyers: *"Technically skilled, upfront and professional"* **Mike Vincenti** chairs the firm's real estate and lending group. Sources praised his expertise in real estate leasing, development and loan work, as well as his *"personable"* manner and *"understanding of subtle issues."* He recently acted for high-rise landlords in leasing negotiations, and is representing the developer in a waterfront condominium project. *"Hard-working"* **David Saffer** regularly assists lenders in commercial real estate transactions. Saffer is said to be *"rising quickly upward,"* and peers noted that his previous experience as senior vice president at Ohio Valley National Bank has allowed him to *"walk the walk and talk the talk."*
The Clients: Union Planters, Bank One and Jefferson County Board of Education.

Greenebaum Doll & McDonald PLLC
The Firm: According to interviewees, attorneys here retain their reputation as tough, top-class negotiators. The firm is clearly on the radar in the real estate market, and was particularly flagged as being responsive to top developers' needs. The group also represents lenders, and was considered to be especially strong in zoning.

KENTUCKY

The Lawyers: Peers and clients warmly recommended **Glenn Price**. He enjoys a *"stellar reputation"* as *"one of the best zoning lawyers in the state."* Market sources admired his *"vast understanding of zoning-related, government and building permits"* and his *"ability to zero in on clients' needs."*

The Clients: Bayer Properties, Jewish Hospital and NTS Development Company

Other Notable Practitioners

"Responsive and personable" **Joe Gathright** of Gathright & Hardy is visible on commercial lending transactions, frequently acting for National City Bank of Kentucky. Recommended for his representation of mid-sized clients in smaller transactions, Gathright has also advised Porcelain Metals, Cave Hill Cemetery Company and Duane Realty.

Leaders in Kentucky

AHEARN, Dale
Frost Brown Todd LLC, Louisville
502 589 5400
Recommended in Real Estate

BALLANTINE, John
Ogden Newell & Welch, Louisville
502 582 1601
Recommended in Litigation

BECKER, Wendy
Greenebaum Doll & McDonald PLLC, Lexington 859 231 8500
Recommended in Employment

BEEMAN, Arthur
Frost Brown Todd LLC, Louisville
502 589 5400
Recommended in Litigation

BRADLEY, Craig
Stites & Harbison PLLC, Louisville
502 587 3400
Recommended in Corporate/M&A

CASSIS, Charlie
Frost Brown Todd LLC, Louisville
502 589 5400
Recommended in Litigation

CATRON, Stephen
Wyatt, Tarrant & Combs LLP, Bowling Green 270 842 1050
Recommended in Corporate/M&A

CLARK, Jude
Frost Brown Todd LLC, Louisville
502 589 5400
Recommended in Real Estate

CLAY, Thomas
Law Offices of Thomas Clay, Louisville
502 561 2005
Recommended in Employment

CLEARY, Richard
Greenebaum Doll & McDonald PLLC, Louisville 502 589 4200
Recommended in Employment

COAN, Marvin
Hummel, Coan, Miller & Sage, Louisville
502 585 3545
Recommended in Employment

COCKRUM, James
Frost Brown Todd LLC, Louisville
502 589 5400
Recommended in Employment

COLLIER, Philip
Stites & Harbison PLLC, Lexington
859 226 2300
Recommended in Litigation

CONNER, Stewart
Wyatt, Tarrant & Combs LLP, Louisville
502 589 5235
Recommended in Corporate/M&A

CRONAN, Charles
Stites & Harbison PLLC, Louisville
502 587 3400
Recommended in Litigation

CUTLER, Irwin
Segal, Stewart, Cutler, Linday, Janes & Berry, Louisville 502 568 5600
Recommended in Employment

DAWAHARE, Debra
Wyatt, Tarrant & Combs LLP, Lexington
859 233 2012
Recommended in Employment

DOLSON, Scott
Frost Brown Todd LLC, Louisville
502 589 5400
Recommended in Corporate/M&A

ESCHELS, Philip
Greenebaum Doll & McDonald PLLC, Louisville 502 589 4200
Recommended in Employment

FLEISCHAKER, Jon
Dinsmore & Shohl LLP, Louisville
502 540 2300
Recommended in Employment

FRIEDMAN, David
Fernandez Friedman Grossman & Kohn PLLC, Louisville 502 589 1001
Recommended in Employment

GATHRIGHT, Joe
Gathright & Hardy, Louisville
502 569 2030
Recommended in Real Estate

GLASSCOCK, Ed
Frost Brown Todd LLC, Louisville
502 589 5400
Recommended in Corporate/M&A

GREENE, Kimberly
Dinsmore & Shohl LLP, Louisville
502 540 2300
Recommended in Employment

GRIFFITH, Richard
Stoll, Keenon & Park, LLP, Louisville
502 568 9100
Recommended in Employment

HADEN, Bill
Stites & Harbison PLLC, Louisville
502 587 3400
Recommended in Real Estate

HAYNES, Greg
Wyatt, Tarrant & Combs LLP, Louisville
502 589 5235
Recommended in Litigation

HENLEIN, Carl
Frost Brown Todd LLC, Louisville
502 589 5400
Recommended in Litigation

HINES, Barry
Stites & Harbison PLLC, Louisville
502 587 3400
Recommended in Real Estate

HINKLE, Samuel
Stoll, Keenon & Park, LLP, Louisville
502 568 9100
Recommended in Litigation

HOPSON, Edwin
Wyatt, Tarrant & Combs LLP, Louisville
502 589 5235
Recommended in Employment

HOULIHAN, Robert
Stoll, Keenon & Park, LLP, Lexington
859 231 3000
Recommended in Litigation

ISON, Eric
Greenebaum Doll & McDonald PLLC, Louisville 502 589 4200
Recommended in Litigation

JOSEPH, Alfred
Stites & Harbison PLLC, Louisville
502 587 3400
Recommended in Real Estate

LESTER, David
Stoll, Keenon & Park, LLP, Lexington
859 231 3000
Recommended in Corporate/M&A

LYNDRUP, Peggy
Greenebaum Doll & McDonald PLLC, Louisville 502 589 4200
Recommended in Corporate/M&A

MACDONALD, Alan
Frost Brown Todd LLC, Louisville
502 589 5400
Recommended in Corporate/M&A

MARTIN, Timothy
Frost Brown Todd LLC, Louisville
502 589 5400
Recommended in Real Estate

MEADE, Don
Priddy, Eisenberg, Miller & Meade, Louisville 502 569 2888
Recommended in Employment

MILLER, Winston
Frost Brown Todd LLC, Louisville
502 589 5400
Recommended in Litigation

MILLIMAN, Jim
Middleton Reutlinger, P.S.C., Louisville
502 584 1135
Recommended in Litigation

MORRIS, Doug
Oldfather & Morris, Louisville
502 637 7200
Recommended in Employment

NORTHAM, Patrick
Greenebaum Doll & McDonald PLLC, Louisville 502 589 4200
Recommended in Corporate/M&A

PELFREY, Patton
Frost Brown Todd LLC, Louisville
502 589 5400
Recommended in Employment

KENTUCKY LEADERS

PRICE, Glenn
Greenebaum Doll & McDonald PLLC,
Louisville 502 589 4200
Recommended in Real Estate

PRIDDY, Al
Priddy, Eisenberg, Miller & Meade,
Louisville 502 569 2888
Recommended in Employment

REED, John
Reed Weitkamp Schell & Vice PLLC,
Louisville 502 589 1000
Recommended in Litigation

SAFFER, David
Wyatt, Tarrant & Combs LLP, Louisville
502 589 5235
Recommended in Real Estate

SALES, Kenneth
Sales, Tillman & Wallbaum, Louisville
502 589 5600
Recommended in Employment

SAVARISE, Jeff
Greenebaum Doll & McDonald PLLC,
Louisville 502 589 4200
Recommended in Employment

SEGAL, Herbert
Segal, Stewart, Cutler, Linday, Janes &
Berry, Louisville 502 568 5600
Recommended in Employment

SEIFFERT, James
Stites & Harbison PLLC, Louisville
502 587 3400
Recommended in Corporate/M&A

SMITH, James
Smith & Smith, Louisville 502 587 0761
Recommended in Employment

SNYDER, Sheryl
Frost Brown Todd LLC, Louisville
502 589 5400
Recommended in Litigation

STRAUS, James
Frost Brown Todd LLC, Louisville
502 589 5400
Recommended in Corporate/M&A

TANNON, Jay Middleton
Frost Brown Todd LLC, Louisville
502 589 5400
Recommended in Corporate/M&A

VINCENTI, Mike
Wyatt, Tarrant & Combs LLP, Louisville
502 589 5235
Recommended in Real Estate

YOUNG, Cynthia
Wyatt, Tarrant & Combs LLP, Louisville
502 589 5235
Recommended in Corporate/M&A

BANKING & FINANCE — LOUISIANA

CONTENTS: Banking & Finance p.307; Corporate/M&A p.308; Employment: Mainly Plaintiff p.310; Mainly Defendant p.311; Litigation: General Commercial p.312; Real Estate p.314; Individuals' Profiles p.316.

LOUISIANA'S TOP FOUR
1. Phelps Dunbar
2. Jones Walker Waechter Poitevent Carrère & Denègre
3. Liskow & Lewis
4. Stone Pigman Walther Wittmann

Ranking based on Chambers' research within the state.

All quotes in the text are from interviews with clients and competitors.

OVERVIEW: Now celebrating its 150th anniversary, **Phelps Dunbar** boasts an extensive commercial practice from offices in Louisiana, Texas, Florida and the UK. The firm is historically known for its banking and finance expertise, but also makes a strong showing in the real estate, litigation and corporate rankings. James Stuckey is the best-known personal property finance lawyer in the state, while Philip Claverie is well regarded for his real estate financing advice. Clients include Philip Morris and Hilton Hotels.

Louisiana's largest law firm, **Jones Walker Waechter Poitevent Carrère & Denègre**, is highly rated for its corporate and securities work, with corporate attorney Richard Wolfe praised as one of the best legal minds in the state. A top-tier litigation practice features Harry Hardin, identified by interviewees as a key commercial litigator. The real estate department benefits from the firm's activity at local, regional and national levels. Here, Donald Bradford was identified as a leader in transactional real estate work. The firm has additional offices in Texas, Florida and DC. Clients include Cisco Systems and CSX Transportation.

Full-service firm **Liskow & Lewis**, in third place, is noted for its real estate group, which has a loyal following of local energy clients. The firm is considered to have one of the best litigation departments in the state, where again it has carved out a niche in energy issues. On the corporate side, too, it provides advice to numerous oil and gas companies, while the banking and finance department counsels many corporations prominent in the state's mineral industry. Real estate financing expert Marilyn Maloney is much praised, as is Donald Abaunza in the litigation department. Clients include ChevronTexaco, Shell Oil and Amerada Hess.

Stone Pigman Walther Wittmann ranks fourth in Louisiana. This well-established firm is esteemed for its litigation practice, considered the best in the state. Its strength here feeds into its real estate practice, where the firm has developed long-standing relationships with key clients. The corporate practice, serving mid-sized to large private companies, is also praised. Peers recommend top litigator Phillip Wittmann, who has represented RJ Reynolds in a products liability class action. Clients include Marathon Oil and Dole Food Company.

BANKING & FINANCE

LOUISIANA
Leading firms (Banking & Finance)
1. LISKOW & LEWIS PLC *New Orleans*
   PHELPS DUNBAR LLP *New Orleans*
2. CARVER, DARDEN, KORETZKY *New Orleans*
   MCGLINCHEY STAFFORD *New Orleans*
3. KEAN, MILLER, HAWTHORNE *Baton Rouge*

Leading individuals (Banking & Finance)
1. CLAVERIE Philip *Phelps Dunbar LLP, New Orleans*
   MALONEY Marilyn *Liskow & Lewis PLC, New Orleans*
   WILLENZIK David *McGlinchey Stafford, New Orleans*
2. CROMWELL David *Pettiette, Armand, Shreveport*
   STUCKEY James *Phelps Dunbar LLP, New Orleans*
3. REYMOND Leon *Liskow & Lewis PLC, New Orleans*
   ROUSSEL Randy *Phelps Dunbar LLP, Baton Rouge*
   TESSIER Frank *Carver, Darden, Koretzky, New Orleans*

Firms and individuals are listed alphabetically in each band.

Liskow & Lewis PLC
The Firm: This long-established firm retains close ties to oil and gas corporates and also serves as regional and national adviser to clients prominent in the Louisiana mineral industry. Its banking and finance practice primarily acts as local counsel to national or out-of-state banks and financial institutions. The firm acted as regional counsel to both the Resolution Trust Corporation and the Federal Deposit Insurance Corporation in matters involving the insolvency of banks and the recovery of assets from failed financial institutions.

The Lawyers: Highly experienced commercial lending attorney **Marilyn Maloney** advises Bank One on general banking and finance matters. She also represents Ochsner Clinic Foundation, Louisiana Offshore Oil Port (LOOP) and INEOS Oxide, Europe's leading producer of ethylene glycol, in their acquisitions in the state. **Leon Reymond** is highly regarded for his work in commercial real estate and corporate and project financing transactions. He chiefly represents owners and lenders in handling real estate and oil and gas properties.

The Clients: Bank One; LOOP; INEOS Oxide; Columbian Chemicals; JPMorgan Chase; Kelley Oil & Gas; Amerada Hess; Hibernia National Bank; Devon Energy; Hunt Oil Company and Crompton Corporation.

Phelps Dunbar LLP
see firm details p.864

The Firm: Currently celebrating its 150th anniversary, this New Orleans firm has expanded both nationally and internationally to offices in Texas, Florida and the UK. It is strong in banking and finance and has long been recognized as a *"prominent lenders' practice."* Clients and peers agreed that its extensive practice fields some of the top players in the state. Commercial lending and project finance, public and structured finance, oil and gas financing and government and regulatory counseling all feature in their caseload.

The Lawyers: *"Pragmatic"* **Philip Claverie** (see p.316) was highly praised for his *"experience and efficiency"* in commercial and real estate transactions. He has represented regional and national financial institutions in connection with the funding of several major office buildings and hotels in the New Orleans area. Peers recommend **James Stuckey** (see p.318) as an excellent banking attorney and the *"best-known personal property finance lawyer in the state."* He represents lenders in oil and gas loans and real estate and construction financings. He also advises companies on computer software development agreements, software licensing and marketing contracts. **Randy Roussel** (see p.318) focuses on real estate, banking and commercial transactions. He regularly represents commercial developers Wampold Companies and Whitney National Bank.

The Clients: A diverse client base ranges from local emerging businesses to multinational corporations. Retailers, restaurant chains, petrochemical companies, oil and gas producers, lenders, developers, utilities, banks and individual investors figure in its roster.

LOUISIANA

BANKING & FINANCE

Carver, Darden, Koretzky, Tessier, Finn, Blossman & Areaux LLC

The Firm: Since the firm's inception ten years ago, Carver Darden has distinguished itself as a leading Louisiana banking and finance practice. The group represents local and regional banks, financial institutions and real estate developers.

The Lawyers: Frank Tessier was singled out by competitors as the *"driving force"* behind the firm's banking and finance practice. He served as local counsel to lenders in the construction of the Astor Crowne Plaza, a 500-room downtown hotel near New Orleans' famous French Quarter. Tessier also regularly advises major client Whitney National Bank in its financings and corporate transactions.

The Clients: Whitney National Bank; Hibernia National Bank; Deutsche Bank; Latter & Blum; Marriott International; Nexen Petroleum USA; Nexen Chemicals USA; The Laitram Corporation and Hancock Bank.

McGlinchey Stafford

see firm details p.847

The Firm: The firm is renowned for having an extensive and profound commercial practice group. It mainly represents lending clients in banking and finance transactions, but is also singled out for its consultations with banks and financial institutions in their compliance with federal and state laws and regulations. It has an impressive client list of auto manufacturing companies, representing firms such as Mercedes-Benz Credit Corporation and Toyota Motor Credit Corporation. Another area of note is its national representation of consumer finance services.

The Lawyers: Regulatory expert **David Willenzik** (see p.318) is widely recognized as a specialist in asset-based lending and consumer financial services. He enjoys a national reputation for consumer credit transactions and serves as national and state compliance counsel to large consumer financial services providers.

The Clients: Citibank; Bank of America; Wells Fargo; Hancock Bank; US Trust Company of California; Louisiana Bankers Association; American Honda Motor Company; DaimlerChrysler and Advanta.

Kean, Miller, Hawthorne, D'Armond, McCowan & Jarman LLP

The Firm: This full-service Baton Rouge firm is highly regarded for its emphasis on real estate financings. The practice has strong links to power plant companies and also serves as general counsel to clients such as Lamar Corporation and the Louisiana Chemical Association. Attorneys here have broad experience in loan structuring, lender liability issues, commercial loan documentation, real estate lending and regulatory matters.

The Lawyers: Isaac McPherson Gregorie is the department's contact partner at the Baton Rouge office.

The Clients: Union Planters Bank; Whitney National Bank; Lamar Corporation and Louisiana Chemical Association.

Other Notable Practitioners

Name partner **David Cromwell** of Pettiette, Armand, Dunkelman, Woodley, Byrd & Cromwell in Shreveport, received market commendation as *"the best banking and commercial lawyer in town."* He also handles commercial litigation and acts as lenders' counsel to banks and financial institutions including Bank One, AmSouth Bank and Regents Bank. Peers and clients praised him as an outstanding lawyer who is *"knowledgeable, professional and eloquent in court."*

CORPORATE/M&A

LOUISIANA
Leading firms (Corporate/M&A)

1
- CORRERO FISHMAN HAYGOOD New Orleans
- JONES WALKER WAECHTER New Orleans

2
- PHELPS DUNBAR LLP New Orleans
- STONE PIGMAN WALTHER WITTMANN New Orleans

3
- ADAMS AND REESE LLP New Orleans
- TAYLOR, PORTER, BROOKS Baton Rouge

4
- LISKOW & LEWIS PLC New Orleans
- McGLINCHEY STAFFORD New Orleans

5
- KANTROW, SPAHT, WEAVER Baton Rouge
- KEAN, MILLER, HAWTHORNE Baton Rouge
- SHER GARNER CAHILL RICHTER KLEIN New Orleans

Firms are listed alphabetically in each band.

Correro Fishman Haygood Phelps Walmsley & Casteix LLP

The Firm: This highly regarded corporate boutique established itself as a force in the mid 1990's by *"poaching the best and the brightest"* from leading Louisiana firms. The now 18-strong group of *"high-caliber"* attorneys is recommended for its strength in corporate, banking and securities matters. Members represent both public and private companies across a wide range of industries.

The Lawyers: Competitors rate **Anthony (Andy) Correro** as *"the top securities guy in the state."* His extensive practice encompasses security compliance, corporate governance, M&A transactions, credit finance and general corporate work with a particular emphasis on banking matters. Regarded by peers as *"clearly the best and most senior"* attorney in the field, Correro has trained most of the prominent corporate lawyers in the state. Name partner **Louis Fishman** also has extensive experience in the field and enjoys a fine reputation.

The Clients: The firm recently represented Petroleum Helicopter in a $200 million syndicated note facility and assisted First Bank in closing a $5 million loan. Other clients include: MidSouth Bancorp; IBERIABANK Corporation; TL James & Co; First Bank & Trust; Bank One; Whitney National Bank; The Times-Picayune Publishing Corporation; US Unwired and Asco Group.

Jones Walker Waechter Poitevent Carrère & Denègre LLP

see firm details p.826

The Firm: The largest Louisiana law firm boasts one of the leading corporate and securities practices in the state. About 18 New Orleans lawyers handle diverse transactions for public and private companies. Recognized as a *"major player"* in the field, the firm acts as principal outside counsel to Freeport-McMoRan Copper & Gold, CenturyTel and Stewart Enterprises. The team advised Conrad Industries on the adoption of a stockholders' rights plan and counseled SCP Pool Corporation in its acquisition of Fort Wayne Pools.

The Lawyers: *"Well-connected"* practice head **Richards McMillan** (see p.317) is renowned among peers for his *"business acumen."* His partner **Richard Wolfe** (see p.318) was praised as *"one of the best legal minds in the state."* Wolfe recently served as underwriters' counsel in a secondary offering of 2 million shares of Monarch Casino & Resort for $25 million.

The Clients: The team advised Superior Energy Services in its acquisition of Workstrings and acted for Lamar Advertising on the acquisition of DeLite Outdoor Advertising of Ohio. Other clients include: International Shipholding Corporation; Tidewater; BNCCORP; Conrad Industries; Gulf Island Fabrication; Horizon Offshore; OMNI Energy Services; Stratus Properties; Trico Marine Services; Bayou Steel and McIlhenny Company.

Phelps Dunbar LLP

see firm details p.864

The Firm: This *"old-line"* Gulf South firm is distinguished by its dominant international focus and strong securities practice. A team of *"excellent"* corporate attorneys represent public and

CORPORATE/M&A — LOUISIANA

LOUISIANA
Leading individuals (Corporate/M&A)

1
- CORRERO Anthony *Correro Fishman*, New Orleans
- MCMILLAN Richards *Jones Walker*, New Orleans

2
- CAVERLY Joseph *Stone Pigman Walther*, New Orleans
- FULLMER Mark *Phelps Dunbar LLP*, New Orleans

3
- KANTROW Lee *Kantrow, Spaht, Weaver*, Baton Rouge
- WHITTAKER Scott *Stone Pigman Walther*, New Orleans
- WOLFE Richard *Jones Walker Waechter*, New Orleans

4
- BOULET Virginia *Adams and Reese LLP*, New Orleans
- CAMPBELL John *Taylor, Porter, Brooks*, Baton Rouge
- FISHMAN Louis *Correro Fishman*, New Orleans
- WOGAN John *Liskow & Lewis PLC*, New Orleans

5
- BUTLER Patrick *Phelps Dunbar LLP*, New Orleans
- FANTACI James *McGlinchey Stafford*, New Orleans
- KLEIN Steven *Sher Garner Cahill Richter*, New Orleans
- MILLER Ben *Kean, Miller, Hawthorne*, Baton Rouge

Individuals are listed alphabetically in each band.

---

private companies in connection with stock and asset sales, mergers and other business activities. Large matters are coordinated across offices in Louisiana, Mississippi, Texas, Florida and London, UK.
The Lawyers: The practice's *"principal figure"* is **Mark Fullmer** (see p.317), who competitors recommended for his handling of a volume of transactional matters for an entrepreneurial client base. *"Promising"* younger partner **Patrick Butler** (see p.316) was also recognized for his securities experience.
The Clients: The team represented a New Orleans-based regional bank holding company in its acquisition of other financial institutions in mergers valued at over $270 million. It also counseled a national bank in its acquisition of three insurance agencies in three separate transactions. Other work included acting for a Louisiana-based sugar refining company in its purchase of a refinery and related businesses.

Stone Pigman Walther Wittmann LLC
The Firm: A well-established firm with an excellent reputation among peers for its corporate and banking practice. Comprising *"really bright and highly respected attorneys,"* the team represents mid-sized to large private corporations in real estate financings, lending transactions, bonds counseling, M&A, multi-state financings and general corporate counseling. The firm is local and regional counsel to national and international companies such as Textron and Canadian National/Illinois Central Railroad.
The Lawyers: *"Straightforward"* **Joseph Caverly** chairs the firm's business group and inspires admiration in both clients and peers for his *"knowledge, experience and easygoing style."* *"Hard-nosed"* **Scott Whittaker** leads the corporate and securities team. Clients praise his ability to attract and train *"fantastic and sharp corporate lawyers who are always available."*
The Clients: Bank One; Lehman Brothers; Occidental Chemical; Marathon Oil; ASARCO; Morgan Keegan & Company; Waste Management; America's Best Contacts & Eyeglasses; Kaiser Aluminum & Chemical Corporation; Paramount Pictures and Warner Bros.

Adams and Reese LLP
The Firm: Better known for its litigation capacities, the firm is thought to have recently *"invested substantial effort and resources"* into expanding its corporate department. The group provides advice to public and private firms throughout the Gulf South region, and is often associated with major client UNIFAB International. Practitioners advise companies on day-to-day operations, the structuring of anti-takeover protection and various types of commercial and financial transactions. The firm is increasingly involved in securities regulatory work and corporate governance.
The Lawyers: The firm's corporate and securities department was boosted by the appointment as special counsel in April 2002 of highly respected attorney **Virginia Boulet** (see p.316). Boulet was recommended by interviewees for her *"long experience in the field."*
The Clients: The firm advises a number of clients in the airline, banking and thrift, software, healthcare, communications, manufacturing, oil and gas, education, leisure and pharmaceutical industries.

Taylor, Porter, Brooks & Phillips LLP
The Firm: The oldest and most respected of the Baton Rouge firms, Taylor Porter boasts almost a century of experience in corporate and banking transactions. It has a loyal following of long-standing institutional clients. Attorneys here are highly regarded for their extensive experience in business formations, M&A and reorganizations and for their *"business-oriented"* approach to deal negotiations.
The Lawyers: **John Campbell** received widespread commendation from peers across the state. He is well known for his representation of banks in corporate, commercial and financial transactions.
The Clients: Bank One; Entergy; Louisiana State University; Blue Cross and Blue Shield of Louisiana; American Electric Power; Bechtel; Turner Industries Holding Company; Pennington Oil Company; Coca-Cola Bottling Company United; Dow Chemical; The Parish of East Baton Rouge and Goodyear.

Liskow & Lewis PLC
The Firm: A full-service firm, it is historically known for representing clients in the energy industry. The group provides corporate advice to many of the country's major oil and gas producers. Matters covered include M&A, due diligence, secured lending, contractual issues and environmental compliance. The firm also represents lenders and borrowers statewide in financings and secured transactions.
The Lawyers: **John Wogan** is a sought-after general corporate adviser who represents financial institutions in Baton Rouge and across the state. He is highly regarded in the corporate community by clients who view him as an *"extremely able business attorney."*
The Clients: Amerada Hess; Bank One; BP America; ChevronTexaco; Columbian Chemicals; ExxonMobil; Gaylord Chemical; Hibernia National Bank; Hunt Oil; JP Morgan Chase; Kelley Oil & Gas; Pennzoil-Quaker State Company; Prudential Securities; Shell; Travelers; Todd Shipyards Corporation and Unocal.

McGlinchey Stafford
see firm details p.847
The Firm: This large commercial firm is highly esteemed for its *"shrewd"* advice on corporate governance, M&A and business formations. With six offices in four southeastern states, the firm serves regional, national and international manufacturers, financial institutions, insurance companies and healthcare providers.
The Lawyers: **Jim Fantaci** (see p.317) acts for a number of healthcare institutions on M&A, asset sales and purchases.
The Clients: Bank of America; Chase Manhattan; Monogram Credit Card Bank of Georgia; Whitney National Bank; BMW; Ford; Caterpillar; Kaiser Aluminum; Phillips Petroleum Company; The Lamar Corporation; AIG; ARAMARK; CIGNA Healthcare of Louisiana; United Healthcare and State Farm.

Kantrow, Spaht, Weaver & Blitzer
The Firm: This 70-year-old, established Louisiana boutique benefits from a strong profile in litigation. The group handles transactional matters and corporate and securities work, including the representation of public companies, reorganizations and creditors' rights matters. Attorneys here are also active in commercial counseling.
The Lawyers: Peers regard **Lee Kantrow** as one of the *"top"* corporate lawyers in Baton Rouge, noting his *"varied skills and expertise in the area."* As a longtime player in the field, Kantrow has developed close relationships with many local and regional corporate businesses, representing them in equity and debt financings and M&A transactions.
The Clients: Air Products and Chemicals; Allied Waste Industries; American Excess Underwriters; Archer Daniels Midland; CIGNA Property and Casualty Companies; Citizens Bank; First American

LOUISIANA

EMPLOYMENT & LABOR LAW

Title Insurance Company; General Health System; The Baton Rouge Clinic, AMC; The Shaw Group; United Artists Theatre Circuit and Whitney National Bank.

Kean, Miller, Hawthorne, D'Armond, McCowan & Jarman LLP

The Firm: This full-service firm represents a wide range of local, national and international industries from offices in Baton Rouge, New Orleans, Lake Charles, Covington and Plaquemine. The firm serves as local counsel to a number of national chemical and refinery companies.

The Lawyers: Senior practitioner **Ben Miller** was recommended as *"the patri arch"* of the practice and a leading lawyer in the field. His practice covers general business advice and M&A transactions. He regularly advises Baton Rouge-based Lamar Advertising, a large owner/operator of outdoor advertising structures, on corporate matters.

The Clients: Union Planters Bank; Whitney National Bank; Hancock Bank of Louisiana; Louisiana Chemical Association; Transcontinental Gas Pipeline; Transco Energy Company; Amoco Production Company; Big River Industries; CNG Producing; Duke Energy; Exxon Mobil; Helena Chemical and Louisiana Energy Users Group.

Sher Garner Cahill Richter Klein McAlister & Hilbert LLC

The Firm: This business and litigation boutique has grown steadily in stature since its 1999 inception. Lawyers here, who can draw upon experience gleaned from larger practices, advise on M&A and real estate transactions, joint ventures and related tax matters. A loyal client base has a heavy emphasis on leisure, hotel and real estate organizations. The firm has recently expanded its practice in Latin America and provides corporate counseling to start-ups and small businesses in Argentina, Puerto Rico and the Caribbean.

The Lawyers: Peers describe **Steven Klein** as a *"conscientious, detailed and knowledgeable"* attorney. He is well known for his expertise in corporate tax and limited liability partnerships.

EMPLOYMENT & LABOR LAW

LOUISIANA
Leading firms
(Employment: Mainly Plaintiff)
1. **ROBEIN URANN & LURYE PLC** Metairie
2. **AVANT & FALCON** Baton Rouge

Leading individuals
(Employment: Mainly Plaintiff)
1. **ROBEIN Louis** Robein Urann & Lurye PLC, Metairie
2. **FALCON Floyd** Avant & Falcon, Baton Rouge
   LURYE William Robein Urann & Lurye PLC, Metairie
3. **CRAFT Jill** Craft & Craft PLC, Baton Rouge
   HAYNIE Barbara Kingsmill Riess LLC, New Orleans
   MACMURDO Bruce Law Office of R Bruce, Baton Rouge
   MCGOEY William Evans and Clesi PLC, New Orleans
4. **REINHARDT William** William H Reinhardt, Metairie
   WELLS Randall Randall G Wells, Baton Rouge

Firms and individuals are listed alphabetically in each band.

Robein Urann & Lurye PLC

The Firm: Acknowledged as Louisiana's leading firm for unions, the practice represents private and public sector labor unions in all industries across the state. Defendant lawyers esteem the group as *"worthy opponents,"* commenting: *"We know that we're in for a tough case when they're on the other side."* Attorneys were praised as *"outstanding and well-prepared"* in their court presentations.

The Lawyers: Leading labor lawyer **Louis Robein** is *"deeply experienced"* in both labor union matters and employment discrimination cases. Colleague **William Lurye** is an *"honorable and trustworthy"* lawyer who is seen to handle a large share of plaintiff work in New Orleans.

The Clients: International Association of Fire Fighters; United Food & Commercial Workers International Union; Communication Workers of America; Louisiana Association of Educators; Iron Workers Welfare Fund; Laborers' International Union of North America (and Locals); Seafarers International Union and International Union of Operating Engineers.

Avant & Falcon

The Firm: This small boutique firm is highly regarded in the market for its representation of plaintiffs.

The Lawyers: **Floyd Falcon** is regarded as Baton Rouge's best plaintiffs' attorney. He has a long track record of public sector representations, including work for government employees and the firefighters' and police unions.

The Clients: Louisiana AFL-CIO; Louisiana State Police; Louisiana State Troopers Association; Baton Rouge Union of Police; Baton Rouge Firefighters Association; Louisiana Firefighters Association; American Federation of State County & Municipal Employees and the City of Baton Rouge.

MAINLY PLAINTIFF

Other Notable Practitioners

Jill Craft of Craft & Craft PLC is a notable plaintiffs' attorney in Baton Rouge, who is admired by employers' lawyers for *"having lots of guts."* She was particularly recommended for obtaining numerous successful verdicts in sexual harassment cases. New Orleans lawyer **Barbara Haynie** of Kingsmill Riess LLC was widely endorsed as an accomplished plaintiffs' attorney. A highlight of her practice was her successful representation of the plaintiff in the US Supreme Court age discrimination case Oubre v Entergy Operations. She also represents businesses as policy adviser and in defense litigation. **Bruce Macmurdo** of the Law Office of R Bruce macmurdo LLC in Baton Rouge is an established lawyer, who peers recommended as a *"knowledgeable and diligent"* plaintiffs' attorney. He has been involved in some important discrimination cases, including Greer v Dresser Industries, where he won a $4.4 million verdict for six employees under Louisiana's age discrimination law.

William McGoey of Evans and Clesi PLC is highly respected as *"a tough opponent who knows the law inside out."* Known for his *"sharp mind,"* **William Reinhardt** of William H Reinhardt Jr PLC mainly represents individuals in employment discrimination cases. Sole practitioner **Randall Wells** is a longtime player in the field who was commended as one of the top plaintiff and union attorneys in Baton Rouge.

EMPLOYMENT & LABOR LAW — LOUISIANA

EMPLOYMENT & LABOR LAW — MAINLY DEFENDANT

LOUISIANA
Leading firms
(Employment: Mainly Defendant)

1
- THE KULLMAN FIRM PLC *New Orleans*

2
- JONES WALKER WAECHTER *New Orleans*

3
- FISHER & PHILLIPS LLP *New Orleans*
- KEAN, MILLER, HAWTHORNE *Baton Rouge*

4
- ADAMS AND REESE LLP *New Orleans*
- MCGLINCHEY STAFFORD *New Orleans*
- PHELPS DUNBAR LLP *New Orleans*

5
- BREAZEALE, SACHSE & WILSON LLP *Baton Rouge*
- TAYLOR, PORTER, BROOKS *Baton Rouge*

Leading individuals
(Employment: Mainly Defendant)

1
- MALONE Ernest *The Kullman Firm PLC,* New Orleans
- MCCALLA Robert *Fisher & Phillips LLP,* New Orleans

2
- D'ARMOND William *Kean, Miller,* Baton Rouge
- PREIS Fredrick *McGlinchey Stafford,* New Orleans
- SHAPIRO Howard *Shook, Hardy & Bacon,* New Orleans

3
- ADAMS Mark *Jones Walker Waechter,* New Orleans
- FOSTER Murphy *Breazeale, Sachse,* Baton Rouge
- PHARIS Michael *Taylor, Porter, Brooks,* Baton Rouge
- PYBURN Keith *Fisher & Phillips LLP,* New Orleans

4
- ALESSANDRA Nan *Phelps Dunbar LLP,* New Orleans
- CROCHET Vicki *Taylor, Porter, Brooks,* Baton Rouge
- DUNCAN Brooke *Adams and Reese,* New Orleans
- KIGGANS Thomas *Phelps Dunbar LLP,* Baton Rouge
- LEWIS Sidney *Jones Walker Waechter,* New Orleans
- MITCHELL Michael *Fisher & Phillips LLP,* New Orleans

Firms and individuals are listed alphabetically in each band.

The Kullman Firm PLC
The Firm: This well-established firm has gained national recognition for its representation of employers and management in labor and employment matters. Twenty New Orleans attorneys advise on all areas of discrimination law and are heavily involved in collective bargaining, arbitration hearings and day-to-day counseling. Peers praised the group as a *"strong and effective"* team with an ability to inspire *"tremendous client loyalty."* Practitioners are also experienced in representing industrial and commercial clients before administrative agencies and federal and state courts.
The Lawyers: **Ernest Malone** has an excellent reputation in the market as *"one of the best in the business."* His practice emphasizes counseling and administrative work rather than litigation.
The Clients: ChemFirst; Cintas; Consolidated Freightways; Dow Chemical; Entergy; Fleming Companies; Halliburton; Huhtamaki Van Leer; Ingram Industries; Lear Siegler Services; Northwest Airlines; PepsiAmericas; Sysco; Tenet Healthcare and Whitney National Bank.

Jones Walker Waechter Poitevent Carrère & Denègre LLP
see firm details p.826
The Firm: Offices in Louisiana, Florida, Texas and DC serve the firm's comprehensive labor and employment practice. This noteworthy practice counsels an array of companies both locally and nationwide and was described by peers as *"one of the most prestigious firms in the field."* Clients range from multinational corporations to individual executives, reflecting the firm's strong commercial orientation. Matters covered include employment litigation, traditional labor arbitration and advise to managements on union protection.
The Lawyers: Peers credit practice head **Mark Adams** (see p.316) with building up the firm's profile in labor and employment law. Adams has a successful record in state and federal employment lawsuits and continues to represent employers in contract negotiations, collective bargaining and labor arbitrations. **Sidney Lewis** (see p.317) advises management and human resources personnel throughout the US on traditional labor/management relations and regularly handles EEOC and NLRB charges on behalf of employers.
The Clients: Home Depot; McDermott International; The University of Louisiana; Riverwood International Corporation; CSX Transportation; New Orleans Public Belt Railroad Commission and Allied Waste Industries.

Fisher & Phillips LLP
The Firm: A national law firm with a New Orleans team of 15 labor and employment lawyers. The group specializes in labor, employment, civil rights, employee benefits and business immigration law. Attorneys represent managements in federal and state courts in complex litigation and class action cases involving employment discrimination claims. The team also provides regular counseling to employers on preventative strategies and labor relations.
The Lawyers: The recent recruitment of **Robert McCalla** was thought to *"add weight"* to the firm's already *"solid"* reputation. McCalla attracted comment for his *"long and successful career,"* which includes three years at the NLRB. **Keith Pyburn** is extremely active in employment litigation and has particular expertise in disability and illness discrimination. Managing partner **Michael Mitchell**, who has 20 years of employment law experience, is recognized as a *"leader"* in the market. He focuses on collective bargaining and unfair labor practice proceedings and is nationally sought after both as an adviser and a speaker in the field of preventative training.
The Clients: State of Louisiana; City of New Orleans; Wal-Mart and companies from the marine, glass and paper industries.

Kean, Miller, Hawthorne, D'Armond, McCowan & Jarman LLP
The Firm: This major Louisiana firm offers employment services from five offices across the state. The firm was envied for its strong institutional client base that includes local, national and international clients with particular concentration in the industrial, petrochemical and refining industries. The firm is frequently associated with key client, Turner Industries, who the team has represented for the last 30 years. The employment group has extensive experience representing and counseling management in various aspects of labor relations and employment matters, but receives most recognition for its strength in employment litigation. Practitioners handle discrimination and wrongful employment cases in state and federal courts and before the EEOC.
The Lawyers: A former labor lawyer for the City of Baton Rouge, **William D'Armond** heads the firm's ten-strong employment practice. This *"top dog"* attorney was recommended for his *"excellent"* research and effective defense strategies.
The Clients: Baton Rouge Industrial Contractors Association; Louisiana Chemical Association; Greater Baton Rouge Association of Realtors; Coca-Cola Bottling Company United; Duke Energy; ExxonMobil; Kaiser Aluminum & Chemical Corporation; Lyondell Petrochemical; Occidental Chemical and Anco Industries.

Adams and Reese LLP
The Firm: A regional firm with over 200 attorneys in five key cities in the Gulf South region and in DC. Members represent employers in employment discrimination cases before the EEOC. The firm handles wage and hour, discrimination and union organization cases as well as workers' compensation retaliation claims before state and local courts and human rights commissions. The firm is seen to be strengthening its ERISA practice through the addition of experienced practitioners.
The Lawyers: **Brooke Duncan** enjoys a significant reputation for management counseling. His practice encompasses administrative proceedings before federal, state and local agencies, collective bargaining and arbitrations for unionized employers. He also counsels private and public employers on labor relations, defending discrimination claims, wage and hour issues and OSHA and workplace regulations compliance.
The Clients: A varied clientele includes private and public companies ranging from hospitals and

LOUISIANA

EMPLOYMENT & LABOR LAW

nursing homes to manufacturing interests and multinational corporations.

McGlinchey Stafford
see firm details p.847

The Firm: An expanding 15-attorney practice, highly regarded for its comprehensive labor and employment capabilities. The firm has garnered both a local and national reputation from its representation of banks, hotels and hospitals as well as clients in the chemical, gaming and oil and gas industries. Members advise on union arbitrations, litigation, employment practices and employee benefits compliance and preventing and opposing union organization.

The Lawyers: Rated for his *"striking experience in the field,"* practice head **Fredrick Preis** (see p.318) provides advice and training to employers in day-to-day employment matters. Preis successfully co-argued before the Louisiana Supreme Court in New Orleans Campaign for a Living Wage, et al v The Small Business Coalition to Save Jobs, et al in which he urged that the City of New Orleans' adoption of a local minimum wage be struck down.

The Clients: AIG; American Home Products; ARAMARK; Bank of America; Bank One; Caterpillar; CHRISTUS Health; CIGNA Healthcare; First National Bankers Bank; Ford; Jackson Municipal Airport; Kaiser Aluminum; Maytag Corporation; State of Louisiana and Wal-Mart.

Phelps Dunbar LLP
see firm details p.864

The Firm: The firm possesses a well-known regional practice, serving management clients from offices in New Orleans, Baton Rouge, Jackson and Tampa. The group acts for clients in various industries in both the public and private sectors with respect to labor relations, civil rights and constitutional law and in all aspects of arbitration and litigation. Members also defend state agencies, municipalities and public officials in constitutional and civil rights suits arising from employment relationships. The team successfully handled a disability discrimination case and FMLA claim for Dow Chemical, and achieved a substantial court victory for Williams Gas Pipelines in a race discrimination case.

The Lawyers: New Orleans practice coordinator **Nan Alessandra** (see p.316) has an active employment litigation practice, representing employers in discrimination claims for sex, age, disability, race and religion, sexual harassment cases and EEOC charges. *"All-arounder"* employment and labor attorney **Thomas Kiggans** (see p.317) heads the Baton Rouge practice and earned peer recognition for his *"fair and straight-shooting"* style. Kiggans successfully represented Microsoft in a wage and hour case that went to the Fifth Circuit Court of Appeals.

The Clients: Louisiana Lottery Corporation; Turner Industries; The Shaw Group; Chubb Group; Fairfield Industries; Hilton Hotels; Louisiana Workers' Compensation Corporation; Philip Morris; Sysco; Texas Gas Transmission and Textron.

Breazeale, Sachse & Wilson LLP

The Firm: This preeminent Baton Rouge firm is seen to be expanding its practice in labor and employment. The group acts for employers in matters ranging from litigation prevention to management training. Commentators pointed to the firm's success in employment litigation and its strong trial record for discrimination cases. The majority of the firm's client base is drawn from the construction industry, although banking, retail, transport and manufacturing clients also feature heavily. The firm serves as employment counsel to the Trucking Association in Louisiana.

The Lawyers: **Murphy Foster** is identified as the *"best-known labor and employment attorney in Baton Rouge."* His practice areas are labor and employment, and construction. He serves as general counsel to Associated Builders and Contractors International and Louisiana Motor Transport Association.

The Clients: IBM; Reynolds Metal; Bank One and Morgan Keegan & Company.

Taylor, Porter, Brooks & Phillips LLP

The Firm: A *"traditional"* Baton Rouge practice, it has a loyal following among state and national corporates. Typical work includes assisting management in negotiating collective bargaining agreements, defending against class actions arising out of discrimination claims, representing employers in suits brought by the EEOC and advising on the development of manuals and handbooks. Its strong public company client base is supplemented by governmental agencies, private companies and individuals.

The Lawyers: **Michael Pharis** was said to *"shine"* for his work in traditional labor law and employment litigation. **Vicki Crochet** was widely respected for her excellence in representing management in employment discrimination claims.

The Clients: Alliance Bank of Baton Rouge; Bank One; Blue Cross and Blue Shield Association; BP America Production Company; Bridgestone/Firestone; Louisiana State University; Southern University and A and M College; Louisiana Home Builders Self Insurers Fund and Turner Industries Holding Company.

Other Notable Practitioners

Howard Shapiro of Shook, Hardy & Bacon LLP, is highly esteemed for his work in employee benefits and discrimination litigation and ERISA matters. Competitors commended him as an *"extremely effective"* attorney who adds stature to the firm's recently established New Orleans office.

LITIGATION

GENERAL COMMERCIAL

Jones Walker Waechter Poitevent Carrère & Denègre LLP
see firm details p.826

The Firm: A full-service firm with offices outside the state in addition to ones in New Orleans, Baton Rouge and Lafayette. Its *"army"* of lawyers has expertise in commercial litigation, including specialists on the maritime and healthcare industries. Work is mainly in defense and the firm's clients are typically companies active in a whole host of disputes, including class actions, in areas such as medical malpractice, bankruptcy, products and professional liability, fraud and toxic tort.

The Lawyers: Chair of the appellate practice group **Harry Hardin** (see p.317) was recommended to researchers as a specialist in commercial business litigation. He has a niche in railroad law, and has advised on a matter on behalf of railroad owner CSX Transportation, a class action toxic tort case involving a fire on CSX-owned tracks.

The Clients: The firm's litigators have defended Cisco Systems and Cisco Capital in suits brought by investors arising out of the bankruptcy of a telecom company. Further clients include major record companies, such as Universal Music, MCA and Island Records on copyright defense litigation, and CSX Transportation, J Ray McDermott and American Commercial Barge Line.

Liskow & Lewis PLC

The Firm: *"One of the best firms in the area,"* it mainly acts for defendants in complex litigation cases including class actions and multi-state and multiparty proceedings. While the firm's reputation lies firmly in the energy arena (*"they are at the top for oil and gas"*), the practice also litigates in maritime, healthcare, employment, securities, tax and professional liability matters. In the energy

LITIGATION
LOUISIANA

LOUISIANA
Leading firms
(Litigation: General Commercial)

[1]
- JONES WALKER WAECHTER New Orleans
- LISKOW & LEWIS PLC New Orleans
- STONE PIGMAN WALTHER WITTMANN New Orleans

[2]
- GAINSBURGH, BENJAMIN, DAVID New Orleans
- GORDON, ARATA, MCCOLLAM New Orleans
- KEAN, MILLER, HAWTHORNE Baton Rouge
- PHELPS DUNBAR LLP New Orleans

[3]
- ADAMS AND REESE LLP New Orleans
- FRILOT, PARTRIDGE, KOHNKE New Orleans
- HERMAN, HERMAN, KATZ & COTLAR New Orleans

Leading individuals
(Litigation: General Commercial)

[1]
- HERMAN Russ *Herman, Herman, Katz*, New Orleans
- MARTZELL Jack *Martzell & Bickford APC*, New Orleans
- MEUNIER Gerald *Gainsburgh, Benjamin*, New Orleans
- WITTMANN Phillip *Stone Pigman Walther*, New Orleans

[2]
- ABAUNZA Donald *Liskow & Lewis PLC*, New Orleans
- CHEATWOOD Roy *Phelps Dunbar LLP*, New Orleans
- HARDIN Harry *Jones Walker Waechter*, New Orleans
- JARMAN William *Kean, Miller, Hawthorne*, Baton Rouge
- MCCOLLAM John *Gordon, Arata*, New Orleans

Firms and individuals are listed alphabetically in each band.

---

markets, attorneys have acted on significant royalty litigations involving both royalty owners and state bodies, and in expropriation or condemnation matters.

The Lawyers: **Donald Abaunza** is rated by peers as *"an all-around savvy lawyer"* whose focus is on admiralty and energy. He has defended Caltex in a large maritime collision case in the Philippines, in which over 4000 people died. He also represented Poseidon in a case involving a collision between a moving drilling rig and a pipeline.

The Clients: ChevronTexaco; Shell Oil; ExxonMobil; Caltex; Poseidon; El Paso; Enterprise Products; Hibernia Bank; Ochsner Clinic Foundation; New Orleans Hornets and LOOP.

Stone Pigman Walther Wittmann LLC

The Firm: Named by some clients to be *"the top litigation firm in Louisiana"* and *"a lawyers' law firm,"* even competitors agree that the firm is home to *"some really outstanding litigators."* It undertakes a spectrum of litigation, mainly on the defense side. Class actions and complex disputes, including insurance and bank regulation, products liability, regulation, IP and securities matters are on the agenda here.

The Lawyers: Several lawyers in the group were recommended to researchers, but most frequently cited was **Phillip Wittmann**. Peers remarked upon his tenacity and commitment as well as his *"outstanding skill,"* deeming him *"one of the deans."* He has represented RJ Reynolds in a products liability class action, and also acted for Dole Food Company in a products liability mass action involving the use of a chemical on fruit-bearing plants in Central and South America and the Philippines.

The Clients: The firm has recently represented insurance companies in class actions involving bad faith claims. Clients in this area include Chubb Group and Liberty Mutual. In IPL, the firm has acted in protecting the patent rights of Laitram. Other typical clients include: RJ Reynolds; Dole Food Company; Allstate; Metropolitan Property & Casualty; New Orleans Saints and International Paper.

Gainsburgh, Benjamin, David, Meunier & Warshauer

The Firm: A *"distinguished plaintiff's firm"* that clients recommended heartily to researchers. The firm has a general tort practice with experience in areas including medical malpractice, products liability, admiralty/maritime, criminal law, and railroad and other personal injury litigation.

The Lawyers: **Gerald Meunier**, a specialist in personal injury litigation, class actions, maritime law and products liability litigation, is highly regarded by his courtroom peers and adversaries. He is described as *"articulate, professional and ethical,"* and was commended for his involvement in major class actions.

The Clients: The firm is best-known for its work with plaintiffs across a broad range of litigation.

Gordon, Arata, McCollam, Duplantis & Eagan LLP

The Firm: A mid-sized firm of about 45 lawyers, it has offices in New Orleans, Baton Rouge and Lafayette. Recommended to researchers for its litigation prowess, particularly in the energy-related field, the firm's litigators are also involved in corporate and securities litigation, medical malpractice, products liability, and environmental litigation. The firm typically represents clients as both plaintiffs and defendants.

The Lawyers: **John McCollam**, whose commercial litigation practice has an emphasis on onshore and offshore energy, is considered by peers to be *"close to the top of his game."* Recent highlights include representation of BP America in a major pipeline project in Louisiana, and advice to ChevronTexaco in litigation involving outer continental shelf (OCS) federal leases.

The Clients: In ongoing tobacco litigation, the firm has acted as local counsel for Lorillard Tobacco. Clients include BP America, ChevronTexaco and Intergia Entergy.

Kean, Miller, Hawthorne, D'Armond, McCowan & Jarman LLP

The Firm: Employs over 100 attorneys in the state with its main office in Baton Rouge. The firm has a historic focus on chemical and petrochemical industries, and boasts a variety of high-profile clients, who commented to researchers that they would have no hesitation in recommending the firm. Industry-related litigation is largely on the defense side and includes work in environmental law and asbestos and toxic tort litigation. In addition, the firm has a large business group handling contract disputes and commercial arbitrations, bankruptcy and construction disputes, and insurance and products liability defense.

The Lawyers: Environmental and oil and gas litigation specialist **Bill Jarman** is highly respected in the litigation bar, and acts for longtime client ChevronTexaco in cases involving oil field environmental damage.

The Clients: The firm is general counsel to a host of local industrial companies, and has a practice in acting as local counsel for large, out-of-state clients. ChevronTexaco, BP Amoco and ExxonMobil are clients of the firm.

Phelps Dunbar LLP
see firm details p.864

The Firm: The firm has a network of offices in Louisiana, Mississippi, Texas and Florida, and an office in London, UK, to facilitate its work in the European insurance market. The substantial commercial litigation practice represents defendants in fraud, bankruptcy and First Amendment matters, products liability and contract issues. The firm is involved in traditional litigation, appellate work, class actions and alternative dispute resolutions.

The Lawyers: **Roy Cheatwood** (see p.316), practice group coordinator, was recommended to researchers for his trial expertise in commercial and energy litigation. Attorneys at the firm have been involved in bankruptcy litigation representing Wells Fargo as the creditors' committee, and have represented a consortium of insurers (including State Farm) in a lawsuit arising from a fraudulent inducement to pay medical bills.

The Clients: Clients are drawn from industries such as oil and gas, energy, minerals, railroad, construction, gaming, healthcare and insurance. The firm represented the defendants in WRT Liquidation Trust v LLOG Exploration Company, et al, a fraudulent conveyance action valued at upward of $100 million. In the New Orleans Tank Car Leakage class action (approximately 10,000 members), the firm acted on behalf of GATX. Other clients include Wells Fargo and State Farm.

Adams and Reese LLP

The Firm: Peers commend the firm's work and its *"honest, reliable"* lawyers. The firm has offices in New Orleans & Baton Rouge, and offices out-of-state such as Houston, TX, Jackson, MI and Mobile, AL. The commercial litigation practice group has

LOUISIANA

REAL ESTATE

expertise in areas including labor, antitrust, class actions, construction, environment, gaming and IP.
The Clients: The firm advises clients drawn from the Gulf South region and beyond, across industries such as shipping, oil and gas exploration and banking.

Frilot, Partridge, Kohnke & Clements LC
The Firm: Following a split from Louisiana firm Lemle & Kelleher in 1994, the firm of Frilot Partridge now numbers about 60 lawyers. This is a litigation firm that principally does defense work for corporate clients, with a good proportion made up of class actions. Its *"terrifically talented lawyers"* advise on admiralty and maritime matters, products and professional liability, energy and environmental disputes, insurance coverage and healthcare.
The Lawyers: George Frilot and the group have represented longtime client Murphy Oil USA in class actions. Attorneys have also advised on putative class actions, representing Nintendo of America in claims alleging that children have become epileptic as a result of using its products.
The Clients: Murphy Oil USA; Nintendo of America; Monsanto; Rheem Manufacturing; ExxonMobil; Emerson Electric and Chevron-Texaco.

Herman, Herman, Katz & Cotlar LLP
The Firm: This litigation firm is well regarded for its representation of plaintiffs. Practice areas include business and commercial law, medical and professional negligence, and railroad and tobacco litigation. The firm's recent activities have included action in a race discrimination case against life insurer Unitrin, which has resulted in a $27 million settlement to reimburse about 467,000 policyholders.
The Lawyers: Russ Herman is described by peers as an *"extremely talented guy"* who *"enjoys an outstanding reputation, particularly in tobacco litigation."* He is currently involved in a class action against the tobacco industry. Recent successes also include securing over $1.2 million in a case involving wrongful death of an offshore maritime worker.
The Clients: The firm is particularly known for plaintiff representation in a wide range of matters.

Other Notable Practitioners
Jack Martzell, of New Orleans firm Martzell & Bickford APC, was recommended to researchers as *"a great lawyer with the most talent in the courtroom."* He acts on behalf of plaintiffs and defendants. Martzell's eclectic practice embraces plaintiffs' personal injury cases, medical malpractice work, in which he currently acts on behalf of both defendants and plaintiffs, oil and gas-related litigation, white collar criminal defense work, domestic relations, class actions and representation of professionals before regulatory agencies. Examples of cases include litigation in Louisiana on behalf of the Republic of Sri Lanka and its subsidiary, the Sri Lanka Cement Company, now in mediation at The World Bank.

REAL ESTATE

LOUISIANA
Leading firms (Real Estate)

1
- LISKOW & LEWIS PLC *New Orleans*
- PHELPS DUNBAR LLP *New Orleans*
- SHER GARNER CAHILL RICHTER *New Orleans*
- STEEG AND O'CONNOR LLC *New Orleans*
- STONE PIGMAN WALTHER WITTMANN *New Orleans*

2
- JONES WALKER WAECHTER *New Orleans*
- LEMLE & KELLEHER LLP *New Orleans*
- MCGLINCHEY STAFFORD *New Orleans*

Leading individuals (Real Estate)

1
- CLAVERIE Philip *Phelps Dunbar LLP*, New Orleans
- MALONEY Marilyn *Liskow & Lewis PLC*, New Orleans
- SHER Leopold *Sher Garner Cahill Richter*, New Orleans
- STEEG Robert *Steeg and O'Connor LLC*, New Orleans
- TALLEY Susan *Stone Pigman Walther*, New Orleans

2
- BRADFORD Donald *Jones Walker*, Baton Rouge
- COLVIN Keith *McGlinchey Stafford*, New Orleans
- GOOD Julian *Lemle & Kelleher LLP*, New Orleans
- REYMOND Leon *Liskow & Lewis PLC*, New Orleans
- SCHNEIDER Michael *Stone Pigman*, New Orleans

Firms and individuals are listed alphabetically in each band.

Liskow & Lewis PLC
The Firm: This full-service firm, considered by observers to be *"one of the best in Louisiana"* for real estate, is specially commended for its representation of lenders and developers. Its recognized strength in the local energy industry corresponds with activity in both industrial and metropolitan real estate matters. Attorneys here attract clients from Louisiana and out of state.
The Lawyers: Peers rate Marilyn Maloney as *"one who would be first on my list of referrals."* She has a leaning toward real estate financing, and represents banks and institutional lenders. She acts both as general counsel and as local counsel for out-of-state institutional clients. Leon Reymond is respected for his work in the acquisition, operation and leasing of both commercial real estate and oil and gas properties.
The Clients: The firm acts for major financial institutions, and clients are also drawn from the healthcare and energy industries.

Phelps Dunbar LLP
see firm details p.864
The Firm: Peers recommended the firm for its *"high-quality lawyers"* and its breadth of expertise. The real estate practice is geared toward commercial clients; the firm's strength in corporate matters gives it an advantage in the real estate market. The real estate group is spread across both the New Orleans and Baton Rouge offices; the former focuses mainly on lender clients and the latter on developers. Work includes transactional leasing, acquisition and disposition as well as financing, restructuring, zoning and land use, and title insurance.
The Lawyers: *"Top-notch"* Philip Claverie (see p.316) is known for his specialty in real estate financing, and represents both developers and lenders. He has advised lenders on real estate financing matters in connection with office buildings and hotels in New Orleans and on apartment buildings throughout the Gulf South region.
The Clients: The firm advises commercial and industrial developers, owners, tenants and financial institutions.

Sher Garner Cahill Richter Klein McAlister & Hilbert LLC
The Firm: Competitors acknowledge that this New Orleans firm, founded in 1999 by former McGlinchey Stafford lawyers, has a *"large amount of talent,"* which has led to its *"involvement in the biggest deals."* Servicing a loyal band of clients, the full-service firm has a reputation as one that *"acts aggressively on behalf of its clients."* Attorneys here have a strong profile in real estate matters, including financial and commercial real estate transactions, and real estate-related litigation.
The Lawyers: Interviewees recommended this large group of attorneys for their diverse talents and their *"client focus, business acumen and thorough, affordable work."* Managing member Lee Sher has a wide practice, and clients praised him as *"responsive and easy to work with."*
The Clients: Recent work includes representing Burrus Investment Group in its acquisition of six hotels, and sale of one hotel, in a single $100 million transaction. Clients in the development area include Realm Realty, Boston Market, Greystar

REAL ESTATE

LOUISIANA

and the World Trade Center of New Orleans. Other high-profile clients include food service distributor Ameriserve, and Wal-Mart, a long-time client, which the firm has represented in its entry into the Puerto Rican market.

Steeg and O'Connor LLC
The Firm: Researchers were informed that this nine-attorney firm, a *"quality boutique,"* has a historic claim on New Orleans' real estate market. The real estate practice handles transactions, financing and development, and displays ability also in title insurance, industry-related litigation and commercial and residential closings.
The Lawyers: While interviewees were quick to cite Moise Steeg as *"the dean of the bar, with a world of connections,"* his son, **Robert Steeg**, was particularly singled out by *Chambers'* researchers as *"the future of the firm."* Observers were impressed with the latter's *"timely and efficient manner"* and his high visibility on complex transactions.
The Clients: The group advises banks, insurance companies, real estate developers and owners.

Stone Pigman Walther Wittmann LLC
The Firm: The real estate, finance and construction practice group of this full-service firm is involved in commercial real estate transactions locally, regionally and nationally. Representing owners, the firm offers regulatory and transactional advice on zoning and land use and in leasing, construction, and environmental issues. Researchers heard praise for the firm's ability to build long-standing relationships with its clients. Additionally, the firm's strength in litigation is carried through to its real estate group.
The Lawyers: The *"highly experienced"* **Susan Talley** has expertise in many areas of real estate, including development, financing, leasing, and purchase and sales. Peers commented on her *"extremely active"* practice, while a client said: *"We are confident that she has our best interests at heart; she offers us expert guidance."* Talley represents Simon Property in connection with its ownership of New Orleans Shopping Centre and Dominion Tower, an urban mixed-use project. Work for this client has included acquisition, financing, development and leasing. She also acts as local counsel to Sydran Services, a Burger King franchisee, and for Catalyst Old River Hydro-electric Partnership. **Michael Schneider** also has experience in diverse real estate transactions, and was recommended for his *"careful approach and talent in handling deals."*
The Clients: Recent matters include acting on zoning and building restriction issues for Longue Vue House and Gardens in New Orleans, and on real estate and financing matters on behalf of Barriere Construction.

Jones Walker Waechter Poitevent Carrère & Denègre LLP
see firm details p.826
The Firm: This is the largest law firm in the state, and fields over 200 lawyers firmwide from three Louisiana locations and three out-of-state offices. The practice is therefore active on the local, regional and national stages in the acquisition and financing of commercial and industrial properties such as retail and mixed-use properties. The group also advises on zoning and permitting work, and leasing matters on behalf of both landlords and tenants.
The Lawyers: Donald Bradford (see p.316) in the firm's Baton Rouge office was recommended to *Chambers* as a leader in his field. His work concentrates on development and transactional issues arising from commercial and industrial property and title insurance.
The Clients: Regional and national clients, including developers, investors and lenders make up its client list.

Lemle & Kelleher LLP
The Firm: This full-service firm's real estate practice centers largely on institutional lenders, developers and investors. Its transactional experience encompasses acquisition, construction and complex financing, and the firm acts on projects such as industrial facilities, land and riverboat-based casinos and retail and office facilities. The group has a high degree of experience in handling leasing, land use, environmental and regulatory compliance. Advice on enforcement matters includes foreclosures of mortgages againt income-producing properties in federal and state courts, and bankruptcy work involving real estate.
The Lawyers: Julian Good was roundly commended for his reputation in real estate circles.
The Clients: The firm's clients span an impressive range of industries and it works on projects that include industrial, retail and office facilities. The firm represents The Rouse Company as developers of two shopping centers in the state and also acts for life insurance company Aetna in connection with its major interest in an office building in New Orleans. In addition to acting as local counsel for institutional clients, the firm acts for Hibernia National Bank in matters involving workouts and repossessions.

McGlinchey Stafford
see firm details p.847
The Firm: The firm's presence throughout the southeastern US allows it to handle transactions on a regional basis and to cover multiple states. Competitors described it as *"a well-known player,"* and clients said the firm was *"always our preferred choice."* The real estate group is primarily commercial, with a large capacity for developer, lender, public finance and bond work. Additionally, the firm advises on leasing, and sale and leasebacks, and on financings such as real estate secured loans. The firm also has its own title insurance agency.
The Lawyers: Head of the real estate section, **Keith Colvin** (see p.316) has a focus in commercial real estate, in which he represents developers and lenders. One competitor enthused that it is *"a pleasure to get him on the other side,"* thanks to his knack for getting deals done.
The Clients: Large transactions undertaken by the firm include a $530 million project for Occidental Chemical. In real estate finance, the firm is involved in asset-based lending, representing lenders exclusively; it arranged, for example, a $130 million credit facility for Foothill Capital. The group also acts in both development and financing in the hospitality industry; work locally has included projects connected with the New Orleans Ritz-Carlton, the New Orleans Astor Crown Plaza and the New Orleans Cotton Exchange hotels.

LOUISIANA LEADERS

Leaders in Louisiana

ABAUNZA, Donald
Liskow & Lewis, PLC, New Orleans
504 581 7979
Recommended in Litigation

ADAMS, Mark
Jones Walker Waechter Poitevent Carrère & Denègre, LLP, New Orleans
504 582 8258
madams@joneswalker.com
Recommended in Employment
Specialization: Partner and Section Head of *Jones Walker's* Labor and Employment Law Section. Accomplished advocate who has successfully defended employers for more than 20 years before federal and state courts, administrative agencies, arbitrators, and arbitral tribunals. Experienced in collective bargaining and all types of employment dispute resolution. Skilled in development of effective personnel policies and procedures and supervisor training programs, creative strategies for resolution of labor and employment issues relating to mergers and acquisitions, and practical solutions for the multitudinous day-to-day human resource issues from employee screening and hiring to discipline and termination. "A lawyer's area of practice as stated here is one to which (s)he devotes a substantial portion of his/her professional practice and should not be considered a 'specialization' unless certified by the Louisiana Board of Legal Specialization (or similar body in any other state in which such lawyer is licensed to practice)."
Prof. Memberships: American Bar Association, Labor and Litigation Sections; Louisiana State Bar, admitted since 1981; Mississippi State Bar, admitted since 1981. Also admitted: United States Supreme Court; United States Courts of Appeal for the Second, Fifth, Sixth, Eighth, and Eleventh Circuits; all United States District Courts in Louisiana and Mississippi and numerous others.
Career: Joined *Jones Walker*, 1981; partner since 1986; member of firm's Executive Committee since 2001.
Publications: Editor in Chief, Louisiana Employment Law Letter, since 1992; other publications too numerous to list.
Personal: Native of Mississippi; resident of New Orleans since 1981.

ALESSANDRA, Nan
Phelps Dunbar LLP, New Orleans
504 584 9297
alessann@phelps.com
Recommended in Employment
Specialization: Partner and the practice coordinator of the employment law group in the New Orleans office. She practices in the areas of labor and employment, civil rights, constitutional law, consumer credit litigation, and general business litigation. Her employment litigation practice includes representing employers in discrimination claims for age, sex, disability, race, religion, and sexual harassment, and handling EEOC charges and other administrative complaints through the administrative and judicial process.
Personal: Loyola University, JD, cum laude, 1985; Loyola Law Review. Hunter College in New York; University of New Orleans, BA, 1982.

BOULET, Virginia
Adams and Reese LLP, New Orleans
504 585 0331
bouletv@arlaw.com
Recommended in Corporate/M&A
Specialization: Special counsel specializing in corporate, securities and banking law. Author of numerous Louisiana banking and corporate statutes. Has represented numerous banks, securities firms and corporate firms in Louisiana and Mississippi in mergers and acquisitions, corporate restructurings, corporate takeovers and defenses, raising capital and making investments.
Prof. Memberships: American Bar Association; Louisiana Bar Association; Association of Louisiana Bank Counsel.
Career: Admitted to Louisiana bar in 1983. From 1983 to March 1992, associate and partner with the New Orleans based firm of *Jones, Walker, Waechter, Poitevent, Carrere & Denegre*. From 1992 to March 2002, partner with the New Orleans based firm of *Phelps Dunbar, LLP*. Serves as a director of CenturyTel, Inc., a NYSE corporation headquartered in Monroe, Louisiana.
Personal: Received a JD degree (cum laude, Order of the Coif) from Tulane University Law School in 1983. Received a BA degree from Yale University in 1975.

BRADFORD, Donald E
Jones Walker Waechter Poitevent Carrère & Denègre, LLP, Baton Rouge
225 248 2028
dbradford@joneswalker.com
Recommended in Real Estate
Specialization: All areas of commercial real estate law including acquisition and dispositions, joint ventures, secured lending, landlord and tenant relationships, architectural and construction contracts, and title insurance for office buildings, enclosed malls, lifestyle centers, planned unit developments, mixed use residential and recreational developments, and industrial developments; private and public developments. "A lawyer's area of practice as stated here is one to which (s)he devotes a substantial portion of his/her professional practice and should not be considered a 'specialization' unless certified by the Louisiana Board of Legal Specialization (or similar body in any other state in which such lawyer is licensed to practice)."
Prof. Memberships: American Bar Association, International Council of Shopping Centers.
Career: Admitted to practice in 1966 and has continuously practiced in the area of real estate. Partner, *Jones Walker*. Recommended in real estate by a leading US legal publication since 1987.
Personal: Born 1941; resident of Baton Rouge, Louisiana.

BUTLER, Patrick
Phelps Dunbar LLP, New Orleans
504 584 9298
butlerr@phelps.com
Recommended in Corporate/M&A
Specialization: Partner in the business group in the New Orleans office. He practises primarily in the areas of corporate and securities law and mergers and acquisitions. Has extensive experience in the purchase and sale of businesses (both asset and stock transactions) for large, publicly-traded corporations and for smaller, privately-held firms. He also handles federal and state securities law matters, including the registration of offerings with the Securities and Exchange Commission and state securities regulators.
Personal: Duke University, JD, with honors, 1986. University of Notre Dame, BA, cum laude, 1983.

CAMPBELL, John
Taylor, Porter, Brooks & Phillips, LLP, Baton Rouge 225 387 3221
Recommended in Corporate/M&A

CAVERLY, Joseph
Stone Pigman Walther Wittmann LLC, New Orleans 504 581 3200
Recommended in Corporate/M&A

CHEATWOOD, Roy C
Phelps Dunbar LLP, New Orleans
504 584 9266
cheatwor@phelps.com
Recommended in Litigation
Specialization: Partner and the practice coordinator of the commercial litigation group in the New Orleans office, where he practises in the fields of construction, contract, corporate and securities, oil and gas, energy and minerals, trade secrets, legal malpractice and commercial litigation. He represents local, national, and international concerns in complex commercial matters before trial and appellate courts and regulatory authorities. He also represents clients in various forms of alternative dispute resolution and has been selected to arbitrate disputes for other litigants.
Personal: Tulane University, JD, 1974; Moot Court Board. University of South Florida, BA, 1968.

CLAVERIE, Philip deV.
Phelps Dunbar LLP, New Orleans
504 584 9223
claverip@phelps.com
Recommended in Banking & Finance, Real Estate
Specialization: Partner in the firm's business group in the New Orleans office. His business practice includes banking, commercial, real estate and probate. He represents various financial institutions in dozens of transactions involving financing of real estate construction, mergers and acquisitions and working capital. He also represents several real estate developers in connection with various development projects, from major office buildings to shopping centers.
Personal: Tulane University, JD, 1966; Index Editor, Associate Editor, Tulane Law Review; Order of the Coif; Phi Delta Phi; Omicron Delta Kappa. Princeton University, AB, magna cum laude, 1963.

COLVIN, Keith
McGlinchey Stafford, New Orleans
504 596 2730
kcolvin@mcglinchey.com
Recommended in Real Estate
Specialization: Manager of Real Estate Section of *McGlinchey Stafford* concentrating in commercial real estate and representing developers, owners, and lenders in a wide variety of projects including industrial plants, shopping centers and malls, apartment complexes, hotels, office buildings, residential condominium and townhome developments, and golf course and resort developments. Licensed title insurance agent.
Prof. Memberships: American College of Real Estate Lawyers; American College of Mortgage Attorneys, Board of Regents; International Association of Attorneys and Executives in Corporate Real Estate; Louisiana Land Title Association; Metro-Vision Economic Development Partnership, Executive Committee.
Publications: Author and editor of the initial working draft of the Louisiana Uniform Title Standards as Chairman of the Uniform Title Standards Committee of the Louisiana State Bar Association, 1991-94. The Louisiana Uniform Title Standards were published by the Louisiana State Bar Association in 2000 after a period of promulgation and discussion

CORRERO, Anthony
Correro Fishman Haygood Phelps Walmsley & Casteix LLP, New Orleans
504 586 5252
Recommended in Corporate/M&A

CRAFT, Jill
Craft & Craft, A Professional Law Corporation, Baton Rouge 225 344 6090
Recommended in Employment

CROCHET, Vicki
Taylor, Porter, Brooks & Phillips, LLP,
Baton Rouge 225 387 3221
Recommended in Employment

CROMWELL, David
Pettiette, Armand, Dunkelman, Woodley,
Byrd & Cromwell L.L.P., Shreveport
318 221 1800
Recommended in Banking & Finance

D'ARMOND, William
Kean, Miller, Hawthorne, D'Armond,
McCowan & Jarman, LLP, Baton Rouge
225 387 0999
Recommended in Employment

DUNCAN, Brooke
Adams and Reese LLP, New Orleans
504 581 3234
Recommended in Employment

FALCON, Floyd
Avant & Falcon, Baton Rouge
225 387 4462
Recommended in Employment

FANTACI, James
McGlinchey Stafford, New Orleans
504 596 2791
jfantaci@mcglinchey.com
Recommended in Corporate/M&A
Specialization: Practice includes negotiation and preparation of asset purchase, stock purchase, merger agreements for acquisition of businesses; confidential private placement memoranda; franchise agreements and disclosure documents; formation of corporations, limited liability companies and partnerships; and business restructuring. Advices on liquidations, shareholder (buy-sell) agreements, employment contracts, and other business oriented documents.
Prof. Memberships: American Bar Association; Jefferson Chamber of Commerce; Jefferson Parish Economic Development Commission; New Orleans Regional Chamber of Commerce.
Publications: Louisiana Limited Liability Company Forms and Practice Manual (1996).
Personal: Received JD from University of Virginia (1971) and BA from University of Rochester in (1968).

FISHMAN, Louis
Correro Fishman Haygood Phelps Walmsley & Casteix LLP, New Orleans
504 586 5252
Recommended in Corporate/M&A

FOSTER, Murphy
Breazeale, Sachse & Wilson, L.L.P.,
Baton Rouge 225 387 4000
Recommended in Employment

FULLMER, Mark
Phelps Dunbar LLP, New Orleans
504 584 9324
fullmerm@phelps.com
Recommended in Corporate/M&A
Specialization: Partner in the business group in the New Orleans office. He represents start-up companies as well as companies in the mature stages of their growth cycle. His practice in the area of corporate and securities includes all aspects of public and private company representation, including public offerings, private placements, and mergers and acquisitions. He has also represented both venture capital funds and investors in private equity transactions.
Personal: Louisiana State University, JD, 1976; Order of the Coif; Louisiana Law Review. University of New Orleans, BS in Accounting, 1976.

GOOD, Julian
Lemle & Kelleher, LLP, New Orleans
504 586 1241
Recommended in Real Estate

HARDIN III, Harry S
Jones Walker Waechter Poitevent Carrère & Denègre, LLP, New Orleans
504 582 8170
hhardin@joneswalker.com
Recommended in Litigation
Specialization: Senior partner concentrating in all aspects of commercial business litigation, including contract litigation, antitrust, trademark, copyright, professional responsibility and environmental law; frequently speaks/instructs malpractice avoidance, professionalism, and ethics; chairs Louisiana Supreme Court Judicial Oversight Committee; six years as US Fifth Circuit Representative on ABA Federal Judiciary Committee. "A lawyer's area of practice as stated here is one to which (s)he devotes a substantial portion of his/her professional practice and should not be considered a 'specialization' unless certified by the Louisiana Board of Legal Specialization (or similar body in any other state in which such lawyer is licensed to practice)."
Prof. Memberships: American Bar Association: Section of Litigation, Antitrust, Patent Trademark & Copyright, Tort & Insurance Practice; Louisiana State Delegate; past president Louisiana State Bar.
Career: After 30 years of outstanding performance at the trial bar his leadership in the legal community, and community at large, is widely recognized. 1971 Jones Walker, (1973-77 1st Lt. JAG U.S. Army), partner in 1976; chairs Appellate Practice Group; listed in a leading US legal publication.
Publications: Managed Care and Antitrust: The PPO Experience, ABA Press (contributing author); 'Pitfalls for In-House Counsel', The Brief, ABA Press.
Personal: New Orleans native; Harvard (BA, cum laude); Tulane University (JD)

HAYNIE, Barbara
Kingsmill Riess L.L.C, New Orleans
504 581 3300
Recommended in Employment

HERMAN, Russ
Herman, Herman, Katz & Cotlar LLP,
New Orleans 504 581 4892
Recommended in Litigation

JARMAN, William
Kean, Miller, Hawthorne, D'Armond,
McCowan & Jarman, LLP, Baton Rouge
225 387 0999
Recommended in Litigation

KANTROW, Lee
Kantrow, Spaht, Weaver & Blitzer, Baton
Rouge 225 383 4703
Recommended in Corporate/M&A

KIGGANS, Thomas
Phelps Dunbar LLP, Baton Rouge
225 376 0247
kigganst@phelps.com
Recommended in Employment
Specialization: Partner and the practice coordinator of the employment law group in the Baton Rouge office. He also practices labor and employment law out of the firm's Houston, Texas office. Represents primarily employers in both litigation and counseling in all areas of labor and employment, including discrimination, ERISA, sexual harassment, employee defamation, and other employment-related tort claims, employment contracts, OSHA, union matters, wage and hour, drug testing, and drafting and implementing employment policies.
Personal: Louisiana State University, JD, 1984; Board of Editors, Louisiana Law Review. Louisiana Tech University, BA, magna cum laude, 1981.

KLEIN, Steven
Sher Garner Cahill Richter Klein McAlister & Hilbert, LLC, New Orleans
504 299 2100
Recommended in Corporate/M&A

LEWIS, Sidney
Jones Walker Waechter Poitevent Carrère & Denègre, LLP, New Orleans
504 582 8352
slewis@joneswalker.com
Recommended in Employment
Specialization: Labor and employment law. A partner in the firm's Labor and Employment Law Section, he is an experienced litigator in federal, state and administrative judicial forums. A large part of his practice is devoted to advising and counseling employers with respect to union organizing drives and in the development, maintenance and administration of personnel policies, procedures and employee relations to minimize exposure to litigation and union organizing. In this regard, he regularly conducts supervisor and management training programs. He is a frequent speaker for human resource associations. "A lawyer's area of practice as stated here is one to which (s)he devotes a substantial portion of his/her professional practice and should not be considered a 'specialization' unless certified by the Louisiana Board of Legal Specialization (or similar body in any other state in which such lawyer is licensed to practice)."
Prof. Memberships: American Bar Association Labor and Employment Law Section; Louisiana State Bar Association.
Career: Admitted in Louisiana, 1985; Joined *Jones Walker* as partner in 1999; Tulane School of Law, JD, 1985; University of Alabama, BA, 1982.
Publications: 'Sexual Harassment in Employment Law', BNA Books (Contributing Author); 'Louisiana Employment Law Letter' (Associate Editor); 'Jones Walker's Labor and Employment Tip Sheet' (electronic newsletter) (Co-Editor).
Personal: Native of New Orleans, Louisiana.

LURYE, William
Robein Urann & Lurye A Professional
Law Corporation, Metairie
504 885 9994
Recommended in Employment

MACMURDO, Bruce
Law Office of R Bruce Macmurdo LLC,
Baton Rouge 255 344 1333
Recommended in Employment

MALONE, Ernest
The Kullman Firm A Professional Law
Corporation, New Orleans
504 596 4105
Recommended in Employment

MALONEY, Marilyn
Liskow & Lewis, PLC, New Orleans
504 581 7979
*Recommended in Banking & Finance,
Real Estate*

MARTZELL, Jack
Martzell & Bickford, APC, New Orleans
504 581 9065
Recommended in Litigation

MCCALLA, Robert
Fisher & Phillips LLP, New Orleans
504 522 3303
Recommended in Employment

MCCOLLAM, John
Gordon, Arata, McCollam, Duplantis &
Eagan LLP, New Orleans 504 582 1111
Recommended in Litigation

MCGOEY, William
Evans and Clesi, PLC, New Orleans
504 523 8523
Recommended in Employment

MCMILLAN II, L Richards
Jones Walker Waechter Poitevent Carrère & Denègre, LLP, New Orleans
504 582 8188
rmcmillan@joneswalker.com
Recommended in Corporate/M&A
Specialization: Corporate, securities, corporate finance, mergers and acquisitions, corporate governance. "A lawyer's area of practice as stated here is one to which (s)he devotes a substantial portion of his/her professional practice and

should not be considered a 'specialization' unless certified by the Louisiana Board of Legal Specialization (or similar body in any other state in which such lawyer is licensed to practice)."
Prof. Memberships: He is past chairman of the Corporate Law Section of the Louisiana State Bar Association and a former member of the Committee on Negotiated Acquisitions of the American Bar Association.
Career: He joined *Jones Walker* in 1976 after serving three years in the Navy JAG Corps and became a partner in 1979. He served as head of the firm's corporate and securities practice from 1987 to 2002 and as a member and chairman of the firm's executive committee from 1990 through 2002. He has broad industry experience, with significant representations of clients in banking, chemical manufacturing, computer technology, consumer services, defense contracting, manufacturing, mining, ocean shipping, offshore construction, oil and gas exploration and production, oil and gas services, and retailing. He also has business operational experience, having served as chairman, from 1986 through the current date and as president from 1989 through 1999, of a privately held integrated manufacturing company producing water purification equipment.
Personal: Born New Orleans, Louisiana, 1947; Washington and Lee University (BS, 1969); Tulane University School of Law (JD, 1972); Order of the Coif; US Navy Judge Advocate General's Corps (1972-75); New York University School of Law (LLM in Taxation, 1976).

MEUNIER, Gerald
Gainsburgh, Benjamin, David, Meunier & Warshauer, New Orleans
504 522 2304
Recommended in Litigation

MILLER, Ben
Kean, Miller, Hawthorne, D'Armond, McCowan & Jarman, LLP, Baton Rouge
225 387 0999
Recommended in Corporate/M&A

MITCHELL, Micheal
Fisher & Phillips LLP, New Orleans
504 522 3303
Recommended in Employment

PHARIS, Michael
Taylor, Porter, Brooks & Phillips, LLP, Baton Rouge 225 387 3221
Recommended in Employment

PREIS, Fredrick
McGlinchey Stafford, New Orleans
504 596 2716
epreis@mcglinchey.com
Recommended in Employment
Specialization: Heads national labor/employment law section representing employers. Past chairman Louisiana and New Orleans Bar Association Labor Law Sections.
Prof. Memberships: Charter member National Academy of Hospitality Industry Attorneys; past president Louisiana Hospital Association Society of Hospital Attorneys; board member Louisiana Association of Business and Industry and Jefferson Chamber of Commerce; board of editors 'The Corporate Counselor' national newsletter.
Career: Co-argued 2002 case before Louisiana Supreme Court urging New Orleans attempt to adopt minimum wage be nullified - court overwhelmingly agreed.
Publications: Numerous employment law articles in periodicals including 'Loyola Law Review', 'CityBusiness', and 'The Developing Labor Law'; co-author business law book, 'Executive Compensation', published by Matthew Bender.
Personal: Prior to military service, received degrees from Louisiana State University Business Administration School and Law School.

PYBURN, Keith
Fisher & Phillips LLP, New Orleans
504 522 3303
Recommended in Employment

REINHARDT, William
William H Reinhardt Jr, PLC, Metairie
504 832 9984
Recommended in Employment

REYMOND, Leon
Liskow & Lewis, PLC, New Orleans
504 581 7979
Recommended in Banking & Finance, Real Estate

ROBEIN, Louis
Robein Urann & Lurye A Professional Law Corporation, Metairie
504 885 9994
Recommended in Employment

ROUSSEL, Randy
Phelps Dunbar LLP, Baton Rouge
225 376 0234
rousselr@phelps.com
Recommended in Banking & Finance
Specialization: Partner in the business group in the Baton Rouge office. His general business practice is concentrated in the areas of real estate, banking, and commercial transactions. Has represented Wampold Companies, Waffle House, Whitney National Bank, Gross Builders, Inc., and a variety of multifamily and commercial developers.
Personal: Louisiana State University, JD, 1984; Louisiana Law Review; Order of Coif; Beta Alpha Psi; Louisiana Bar Association Civil Law Award for the highest grade point average in Louisiana Civil Law courses. Louisiana State University, BS, 1977

SCHNEIDER, Michael
Stone Pigman Walther Wittmann LLC, New Orleans 504 581 3200
Recommended in Real Estate

SHAPIRO, Howard
Shook, Hardy & Bacon LLP, New Orleans
504 310 4055
Recommended in Employment

SHER, Leopold
Sher Garner Cahill Richter Klein McAlister & Hilbert, LLC, New Orleans
504 299 2100
Recommended in Real Estate

STEEG, Robert
Steeg and O'Connor LLC, New Orleans
504 582 1199
Recommended in Real Estate

STUCKEY, James
Phelps Dunbar LLP, New Orleans
504 584 9239
stuckeyj@phelps.com
Recommended in Banking & Finance
Specialization: Partner in the business group in the New Orleans Office. He practices in the areas of commercial finance, real estate, banking, and leasing. His lending practice includes representing lenders in oil and gas loans, real estate and construction financings, and secured working capital loans. He advises clients in negotiations of a wide variety of contracts, including computer software development and licensing contracts, and major lease development agreements.
Personal: Tulane University, JD, magna cum laude, 1983; Editor, Tulane Law Review; Order of the Coif. Davidson College, AB, magna cum laude, 1980.

TALLEY, Susan
Stone Pigman Walther Wittmann LLC, New Orleans 504 581 3200
Recommended in Real Estate

TESSIER, Frank
Carver, Darden, Koretzky, Tessier, Finn, Blossman & Areaux L.L.C, New Orleans
504 585 3800
Recommended in Banking & Finance

WELLS, Randall
Randall G. Wells, Baton Rouge
225 928 5157
Recommended in Employment

WHITTAKER, Scott
Stone Pigman Walther Wittmann LLC, New Orleans 504 581 3200
Recommended in Corporate/M&A

WILLENZIK, David S
McGlinchey Stafford, New Orleans
504 596 2708
dwillenzik@mcglinchey.com
Recommended in Banking & Finance
Specialization: Heads firm's business law practice. Nationally known in banking and bank regulatory law; commercial finance law; asset based lending; equipment leasing; consumer financial services law; Louisiana and UCC security device litigation; defense of lender liability claims; consumer credit litigation and class action defense. Financial services clients include regional, money center, and international banks, consumer and commercial finance companies, manufacturers, equipment lessors, insurance companies, securities firms, venture capital companies, and project finance lenders. Practice includes negotiating and documenting commercial and consumer loans secured by all types of UCC collateral, real estate, aircraft, and vessels; project finance; leveraged leases; acquisition and leveraged buy-out financings; letters of credit. Initiator and primary drafter of numerous Louisiana laws that apply to banking, commercial finance and consumer credit transactions.
Prof. Memberships: ABA Business Law Section, Commercial Financial Services, Consumer Financial Services, Banking Law, and UCC Committees; American College of Commercial Finance Lawyers; American College of Consumer Financial Services Attorneys; American Law Institute; Consumer Banker's Association Lawyers Committee.
Publications: West, Louisiana Secured Transactions.

WITTMANN, Phillip
Stone Pigman Walther Wittmann LLC, New Orleans 504 581 3200
Recommended in Litigation

WOGAN, John
Liskow & Lewis, PLC, New Orleans
504 581 7979
Recommended in Corporate/M&A

WOLFE, Richard
Jones Walker Waechter Poitevent Carrère & Denègre, LLP, New Orleans
504 582 8182
rwolfe@joneswalker.com
Recommended in Corporate/M&A
Specialization: Partner concentrating in corporate and securities law, particularly mergers and acquisitions, with over 35 years experience in corporate matters, including representing issuers and underwriters in initial and subsequent public equity offerings and advising public and private companies in matters involving tender offers, proxy contests, venture capital transactions, spinoffs, private offerings of securities, special litigation committees in derivative stockholder suits, foreign joint ventures, and related matters. "A lawyer's area of practice as stated here is one to which (s)he devotes a substantial portion of his/her professional practice and should not be considered a 'specialization' unless certified by the Louisiana Board of Legal Specialization (or similar body in any other state in which such lawyer is licensed to practice)."
Career: Joined Monroe & Lemann, New Orleans, in 1963, partner in 1968, headed Corporate Department 1970-96; joined *Jones, Walker, Waechter, Poitevent, Carrère & Denègre LLP* as partner, 1997.
Personal: Princeton University (AB, magna cum laude, 1959); Harvard University (JD 1962); Tulane University (M Civ L 1965); Phi Beta Kappa.

MAINE

CORPORATE/M&A

CONTENTS: Corporate/M&A p.319; Employment: Mainly Plaintiff p.320; Mainly Defendant p.321; Litigation: General Commercial p.322; Real Estate p.323; Individuals' Profiles p.325.

MAINE'S TOP FOUR
1. Pierce Atwood
2. Verrill & Dana
3. Drummond Woodsum & MacMahon
4. Bernstein, Shur, Sawyer & Nelson

Ranking based on Chambers' research within the state.

All quotes in the text are from interviews with clients and competitors.

OVERVIEW: Pierce Atwood, the largest firm in the state, recently boosted its profile in the market through its merger with New Hampshire firm, Sanders & McDermott. The firm is highly praised for the strength of its litigation group, with William Kayatta identified as a noted individual. A team of 30 litigators commands expertise in areas as diverse as IP, environmental and energy law. Clients appreciated the firm's high-quality and cost-effective service. The corporate team, led by Jim Zimpritch, is particularly known for M&A work. Clients include MBNA and UnumProvident.

Verrill & Dana's strong corporate department handles a range of public offerings, reorganizations, takeover contests and private placements. Partner Greg Fryer is credited with expanding the scope of the firm's noted securities practice. The real estate department, featuring key member Charles Oestreicher, is admired for its high-caliber client base and experience in the field. The firm also received comment for its litigation practice, where the bulk of the work it undertakes is commercial. Clients include Fleet National Bank and MaineHealth.

Portland-based **Drummond Woodsum & MacMahon** has developed a school law niche in handling public sector and education-related work. It also has a long-standing corporate practice, led by Mike High, which is known for financial transactions, particularly venture capital work. A respected employment team specializes in work for state schools and municipalities but also handles discrimination issues for private companies. Clients include Citizens Bank and Goodwin Motor Group.

Bernstein, Shur, Sawyer & Nelson has a forte in real estate, where a 12-attorney team is praised for being capable and assertive. The group advises on all aspects of real estate, including acquisitions, financings and litigation. The firm also has two wholly-owned subsidiaries - a title company and an environmental engineering company - to assist clients. Charles Miller is a widely admired member of the team. Clients include FPL Energy and University of Maine System.

CORPORATE/M&A

MAINE
Leading firms (Corporate/M&A)
1. PIERCE ATWOOD Portland
2. VERRILL & DANA LLP Portland
3. DRUMMOND WOODSUM & MACMAHON Portland
   EATON PEABODY Bangor

Leading individuals (Corporate/M&A)
1. ZIMPRITCH James Pierce Atwood, Portland
2. FRYER Greg Verrill & Dana LLP, Portland
3. CHAMPOUX David Pierce Atwood, Portland
   HIGH Michael Drummond Woodsum & MacMahon
   MCKAY Daniel Eaton Peabody, Bangor

Firms and individuals are listed alphabetically in each band.

Pierce Atwood
see firm details p.865

The Firm: *"The first name on the list,"* asserted many of our interviewees. The firm's 30-strong corporate group was recommended to researchers for large corporate matters requiring *"a lot of troops."* Clients believed the team *"quite clearly has the horsepower"* and can provide a *"one-stop shop"* covering the gamut of corporate issues. M&A has been a steady source of work, and the group has been active in resort developments, biotech and international transactions. Other areas of experience include venture capital, IP, e-commerce and banking work. Recent highlights included the representation of a $300 million bank holding company acquired by a New England holding company. The team also represented a marine biotech company in a venture capital financing with Norwegian investors, and advised on an $850 million acquisition of a nuclear generating facility.

The Lawyers: Department head **Jim Zimpritch** (see p.326) was singled out as a leading attorney for securities, acquisitions and banking law. Zimpritch combines scholarliness with a practical outlook, and brings a broad-ranging expertise to the deal table. His time is divided between M&A and general corporate governance and regulatory issues. **David Champoux** (see p.325) enjoys a broad practice that encompasses securities law, M&A, venture capital financing and SEC reporting and compliance. He has advised on a number of ski resort development deals, and worked in the energy sector.

The Clients: MariCal; Atlantic Salmon of Maine; American Skiing; Fjord Seafood USA; Anthem Blue Cross and Blue Shield of Maine; Acadia Trust; FPL Energy; Dead River Company; The First National Bank of Damariscotta; Engineered Materials of Maine and Sensor Research and Development.

Verrill & Dana LLP
The Firm: Clients expressed high regard for the caliber of this firm's 14 business lawyers, while peers pointed to their broad range of expertise. The firm is respected for its securities practice, which sits alongside its work in bankruptcy, ERISA, tax and IP. Representative matters include the planning and formation of corporations, financial transactions including equity and bond offerings, and SEC compliance work.

The Lawyers: Greg Fryer has been a key figure in the growth of the firm's securities group. He was recommended by both competitors and clients for his handling of M&A and venture capital transactions. Fryer was further singled out by clients for his expertise in venture fund investments and his work in the nonprofit arena.

The Clients: The firm's strength in depth is exemplified by its role as general counsel to an enviable roster of long-standing clients. Among this number are: Maine and out-of-state hi-tech companies; banks and other financial institutions; utilities; manufacturers; nonprofit institutions; and hospitals and other healthcare facilities.

Drummond Woodsum & MacMahon
see firm details p.791

The Firm: Peers endorsed this long-standing corporate practice for its good value legal services covering the full gamut of business needs. The team of 12 has a recognized expertise in lending and financial transactions. Acquisition activity, particularly in the venture capital sector, has been a growth area and the team has also been engaged in bankruptcy matters, with a steady diet of venture capital representations. Recently, the firm represented management in its buyout of CDC Group's interests in Rainforest Aquaculture Products. The group also advised Calpine in the contracting, permitting and financing of a 560MW generating facility in Westbrook, Maine.

The Lawyers: Market commentators credited

MAINE

EMPLOYMENT & LABOR LAW

the chair of the business and commercial services group, **Mike High** (see p.325), with the development of the corporate practice. He is regarded as a *"great candidate"* for his excellent judgment, broad experience and hard-working ethic. High advised Binax on its capital formation and acquisition program and Colby College on bond issuances.

The Clients: Fresh Samantha; Stonewall Kitchen; Citizens Bank; KeyBank; Fleet National Bank and Cherryfield Foods.

Eaton Peabody

The Firm: *"Far and away the most prominent business firm in eastern Maine,"* claimed interviewees. This nine-strong, Bangor-based group has developed a practice to rival the most high-profile Portland firms. It advises on a full range of corporate issues, and is recommended especially for its securities expertise and knowledge of landfill licensing. The firm has an active timberland practice, and is well known for its lobbying activities. The group advised a public company on a hostile takeover defense, and acted for another in a threatened stockholder derivative litigation.

The Lawyers: Group chair **Dan McKay** was described by peers as a *"jack of all trades."* They agreed that his breadth of talent did not come at the expense of quality, pointing to his eye for detail and approachable manner. McKay's own area of expertise is securities law, in line with the firm's reputation. In addition to his broad transactional practice, he also advises on antitrust and issues arising from the healthcare sector.

The Clients: The firm represents medium-sized companies statewide. Its client base is largely governed by the firm's geographic location; for example, it frequently acts for Canadian companies looking to establish US operations. Clients include: hi-tech manufacturers; software developers and publishers; forest product corporates; healthcare companies and banks.

EMPLOYMENT & LABOR LAW — MAINLY PLAINTIFF

MAINE
Leading firms
(Employment: Mainly Plaintiff)

1. **BERMAN & SIMMONS** Portland
   MCTEAGUE, HIGBEE, CASE, COHEN Topsham
   REBEN, BENJAMIN & MARCH Portland

Leading individuals
(Employment: Mainly Plaintiff)

1. **WEBBERT David** *Johnson & Webbert LLP*, Augusta
2. **REBEN Howard** *Reben, Benjamin & March*, Portland
   YOUNG Jeffrey *McTeague, Higbee, Case*, Topsham
3. **GAUSE John** *Berman & Simmons*, Portland
   WEBBER Rebecca *Linnell Choate & Webber*, Auburn

Firms and individuals are listed alphabetically in each band.

Berman & Simmons

The Firm: The practice's reputation is pinned to practitioners' litigation prowess and *"fearless"* courtroom style. With a track record for obtaining big jury verdicts, the group is said to *"get straight to the nitty-gritty."* A diverse workload of workers' compensation, discrimination and labor relations matters is complemented by particular strength in the related areas of personal injury, defamation and civil rights. Commentators tipped this developing practice as a *"major player for the future."*

The Lawyers: Employment specialist **John Gause** takes a *"scholarly"* approach to litigation and possesses notable expertise in disability claims. Opponents cited as a key strength his *"clear understanding of the law,"* commenting: *"He knows just what to say to make you worry."*

McTeague, Higbee, Case, Cohen, Whitney & Toker PA

The Firm: Based in Topsham, the firm is recognized for its strong background in union representation and workers' compensation matters. Eleven attorneys concentrate on labor law, workplace discrimination, workers' compensation and personal injury issues. The group represents both individuals and unions and has experience negotiating and administering collective bargaining agreements. Litigation strengths include discrimination and wrongful termination claims, whistle-blower and retaliation cases, and claims for unpaid wages and benefits. Union clients recommended the practice as *"the only ones we trust."* The firm recently acted in Guy Carrier et al v JPB Enterprises concerning the application of faltering business defense to an employer's obligation to give 60 days' notice of a plant closure.

The Lawyers: Jeffrey Young commanded respect for his representation of employees and unions in discrimination cases, wage and hour and ERISA matters. Recommended for his *"straightforward, intelligent representation of his clients' interests,"* Young was described as a *"whole package"* lawyer offering *"tenacity, astute analysis and impressive trial skills."* He notably acted in Karen Romano v U-Haul, the first sex discrimination case to consider punitive damages following the Kolsted decision.

The Clients: International Association of Machinists, District Lodge 4 and Local 6 - Shipbuilders; Northern New England District Council of Carpenters; International Brotherhood of Electrical Workers; United Association of Plumbers and Pipefitters; International Brotherhood of Firemen and Oilers; and Utility Workers Union.

Reben, Benjamin & March

The Firm: This small Portland firm practices labor and employment law alongside insurance, personal injury, commercial and contract law. With a strong background in litigation, the practice is divided evenly between employee and union representation and personal injury work. Practitioners were said to *"come up with well-thought-out solutions"* to complex employment problems. The firm acts as special counsel to a number of unions and recently represented a university faculty union in a highly publicized case concerning the disciplining of a professor.

The Lawyers: *"Passionate and experienced"* **Howard Reben** splits his practice between plaintiff personal injury work and employment litigation. Recommended for his activities on behalf of unions, Reben is particularly skilled at out-of-court dispute resolution. Clients regard him as a *"safe pair of hands,"* appreciating his willingness to *"dedicate himself to a cause."*

The Clients: The Associated Faculty of the University Union; Maine Education Association; Teamsters' Union; Stagehand Workers' Union and Bath Ironworks Security Guard Union.

Other Notable Practitioners

At Johnson & Webbert LLP in Augusta, **David Webbert** is thought to be *"in a league of his own"* for *"pure courtroom horsepower."* His exclusively plaintiffs' practice also covers criminal defense and general business litigation. Peers placed Webbert in the top tier for his talent for arguing strong cases, observing: *"If there's a hook to hang his case on, he will find it."* Recent successes have included a $450,000 settlement in Moses Sebunya v Cumberland County for free speech retaliation, and a favorable ruling in Peter Kleban v The University of Maine from the Maine Human Rights Commission, which found that asthma is covered

EMPLOYMENT & LABOR LAW — MAINE

under a broader definition of disability in the Maine Human Rights Act than in the ADA. Webbert is currently working on federal and state legislative issues concerning federal income tax and employment settlements and judgments, and the individual liability of supervisors under the Maine Human Rights Act.

Rebecca Webber of Linnell Choate & Webber LLP earned peer recommendation for her *"passion, and excellent people skills."* She undertakes litigation for both plaintiffs and defendants, but is best known for her many successes on behalf of individuals. She negotiated a $80,000 out-of-court settlement for emotional damages in Perkins and Swift v Lewiston Police Department. More recently, Webber upheld a jury verdict awarding $215,000 to the plaintiff in Crowley v LL Bean. Fellow professionals described her as a *"dogged and devoted"* client advocate.

EMPLOYMENT & LABOR LAW — MAINLY DEFENDANT

MAINE
Leading firms
(Employment: Mainly Defendant)

1. **MOON, MOSS, MCGILL & SHAPIRO** Portland
2. **EATON PEABODY** Bangor
   PIERCE ATWOOD Portland
3. **DRUMMOND WOODSUM & MACMAHON** Portland
   RUDMAN & WINCHELL LLC Bangor

Leading individuals
(Employment: Mainly Defendant)

1. **MCGILL Linda** Moon, Moss, McGill & Shapiro, Portland
   MOON Richard Moon, Moss, McGill & Shapiro, Portland
2. **JOHNSTON Thomas** Eaton Peabody, Bangor
   PAYNE Clare Eaton Peabody, Bangor
3. **ERWIN James** Pierce Atwood, Portland
   HEWEY Melissa Drummond Woodsum, Portland
   MCGUIRE Frank Rudman & Winchell LLC, Bangor
   PRINGLE Harry Drummond Woodsum, Portland
   SHAPIRO Jonathan Moon, Moss, McGill, Portland

Firms and individuals are listed alphabetically in each band.

Moon, Moss, McGill & Shapiro
The Firm: Rated by peers as *"the boutique employment firm"* in Maine, the practice comprises ten *"feisty and experienced"* labor and employment specialists. Participation in national forums has established the group as a key presence both in Maine and out of state. The team advises management clients in unionized and non-unionized industries on employment litigation, employee benefits and executive compensation. Practitioners have experience in related areas of civil rights liability, immigration, workplace safety, IP and business planning. The group is characterized by a *"ferocious"* litigation style and a *"high level of integrity."* Clients appreciate the *"personal attention"* and *"quality service"* on offer here.
The Lawyers: The *"dean"* of the practice, **Richard Moon** draws upon 25 years' experience in labor and employment law. His *"dogged"* approach to litigation makes him *"a force to be reckoned with."* He advises employers on NLRA and occupational safety matters, discrimination cases, employment-at-will, benefits, privacy and immigration issues. He frequently represents clients in US Department of Labor audits. Recommended for her expertise in sexual harassment cases, **Linda McGill** represents public and private sector employers on matters including union management negotiations, Title VII, ADA, workplace safety and wage and hour issues. Up-and-coming **Jonathan Shapiro** won peer acclaim for his *"punchy"* litigation style and *"aggressive"* approach. He undertakes both litigation and employment counseling, and has experience in designing and reviewing affirmative action plans.
The Clients: Clients range from sole proprietorships to multi-state corporations, and include banks, hospitals, manufacturers, transport companies and public utilities. The group has provided employment advice to hi-tech companies, service industry corporates, and hospitality and retailing entities.

Eaton Peabody
The Firm: The *"best bet in Bangor,"* the employment relations and benefits practice represents employers in response to union-organizing campaigns and employee actions. The six-lawyer group negotiates labor contracts, drafts employment handbooks and advises on OSHA and workers' compensation matters. Practitioners received particular recognition for both their *"strong business focus"* and impressive representations before the Maine Human Rights Commission. The Bangor base provides the team with a strong perspective on the fishing, forestry and agricultural industries as well as on Canadian affairs.
The Lawyers: Group chair **Thom Johnston** attracted comment for his *"impressive"* handling of discrimination cases, labor contract negotiations and arbitrations, and union organization campaigns. This *"down-to-earth"* individual has a *"wide-ranging knowledge"* of matters such as the federal Worker Adjustment and Retraining Notification Act, drug and alcohol testing, discipline and discharge issues. Peers described **Clare Payne** as *"thorough and creative,"* particularly singling her out for her counseling skills. Her practice includes representation of public, private and nonprofit employers before arbitrators, the Maine Human Rights Commission, the Maine Labor Relations Board and other commissions and courts. Much of her workload involves consultation with clients regarding personnel handbooks and policies, discipline, discharge and wage and hour issues as well as sexual harassment investigations.
The Clients: The firm enjoys the patronage of significant clients. Among them are: New Balance Athletic Shoe; Webber Oil; The Jackson Laboratory; Eastern Maine Medical Center; Charlotte White Center and the County of Aroostook.

Pierce Atwood
see firm details p.865
The Firm: A *"one-stop shop"* that *"handles it all."* Twelve Portland employment attorneys cover the gamut of employment issues for management clients. The group has recently litigated a number of sex and disability discrimination defenses, workers' compensation cases and FMLA, ADA and OSHA claims. The recent recruitment of an ERISA lawyer is expected to boost the firm's practice in the area. Rivals rate the firm as having the size and resources necessary to take on sophisticated cases. *"Expert"* attorneys received high marks for their excellent written submissions and attentive service. The group is said to *"attract good clients and keep them."*
The Lawyers: *"Straight shooter"* **James Erwin** (see p.325), a former Maine Human Rights Commissioner, was recommended by peers for his *"sensitivity"* toward clients and his *"deep legal knowledge."* His litigation-based practice encompasses a volume of sex discrimination and sexual harassment suits. Erwin recently acted in Plumley v Southern Container, which prevailed on brief, and represented WorldCom in the First Circuit Court of Appeals.
The Clients: MBNA, IDEXX Laboratories, Fairchild Semiconductor, Sears Roebuck, International Paper and Dead River Company.

Drummond Woodsum & MacMahon
see firm details p.791
The Firm: This six-attorney employment team benefits from the firm's renowned school law niche in handling public sector and education-related work. Attorneys work in conjunction with non-legal staff in counseling on discrimination law compliance, and wage and hour, FMLA,

MAINE — LITIGATION

OSHA and wrongful discharge issues. The group also advises on litigation and administrative hearings, collective bargaining and conflict management. While the bulk of the group's workload is on behalf of state schools and municipalities, the practice also handles discrimination matters for private companies. Commentators recommended this *"collegial"* group of *"top-notch"* attorneys as having the *"knowledge and versatility"* to address any employment problem.

The Lawyers: Melissa Hewey (see p.325) maintains a litigation practice that focuses on sexual harassment and discrimination, civil rights and whistle-blower claims. A *"bright litigator,"* Hewey is a strong advocate for employers in alternative dispute resolution proceedings and Maine Human Rights Commission hearings. Clients valued her *"sound advice."* Harry Pringle (see p.326) heads the firm's public sector group and commands extensive experience in traditional labor issues. While less visible *"in the trenches,"* Pringle is widely recognized for his counseling expertise and has a loyal following among education clients.

The Clients: Binax; Media Power; Casco Bay Island Transit District; CYRO Industries; Cherryfield Foods; Goodwin Motor Group; Stonewall Kitchen and RICH Tool & Die.

Rudman & Winchell LLC

The Firm: This Bangor-based firm attracted attention for its *"aggressive"* employment trial attorneys who *"know when to hold, and when to fold."* The firm traditionally focuses on the defense side, but also maintains a substantial plaintiffs' practice. Typical work includes advising employers on personnel management and compliance with Maine's mandatory sexual harassment training statute. Praised by clients for givng *"cost-effective"* service, practitioners can be relied on *"not to raise false expectations in their clients."* Members have particular experience in labor relations, collective bargaining, workers' compensation, and wage and hour and business immigration matters.

The Lawyers: *"Bright and thorough"* Frank McGuire heads the firm's employment group. He maintains a generalist employment practice, covering litigation and tribunals, labor relations and employee benefits. McGuire undertakes both defendant and plaintiff work, and wins peer acclaim for his *"extensive knowledge of the field."*

The Clients: Clients vary from smaller Maine entities to national corporations in the healthcare, utilities, manufacturing, service and hospitality industries.

LITIGATION

MAINE
Leading firms
(Litigation: General Commercial)

1. **PIERCE ATWOOD** Portland
2. **BERNSTEIN, SHUR, SAWYER & NELSON** Portland
   HARVEY & FRANK Portland
   NORMAN, HANSON & DETROY LLC Portland
3. **BERMAN & SIMMONS** Portland
   PRETI, FLAHERTY, BELIVEAU, PACHIOS Portland
4. **VERRILL & DANA LLP** Portland

Leading individuals
(Litigation: General Commercial)

1. **KAYATTA William** Pierce Atwood, Portland
2. **DETROY Peter** Norman, Hanson & DeTroy, Portland
   FRANK Robert Harvey & Frank, Portland
   HARVEY Charles Harvey & Frank, Portland
3. **CULLEY Peter** Pierce Atwood, Portland
   PETRUCCELLI Gerald Petruccelli Martin, Portland
   ROBITZEK William Berman & Simmons, Portland
   RUBIN Peter Bernstein, Shur, Sawyer, Portland

Firms and individuals are listed alphabetically in each band.

Pierce Atwood
see firm details p.865

The Firm: This *"top-caliber"* team is thought to be *"second to none"* for *"expertise and resources"* across a range of areas. A 30-strong *"army"* of litigators represents plaintiffs and defendants in matters ranging from personal injury to complex commercial litigation including liability actions, securities litigation, consumer rights, ERISA, class actions and bankruptcies. Clients cite the group's *"cost-effective, high-quality service"* as a major attraction. Growth areas include IP, environment and energy-related litigation. The firm also attracted comment for a strong alternative diputed resolution (ADR) practice.

The Lawyers: *"Outstandingly bright"* William Kayatta (see p.325) was consistently recommended to researchers for *"analytical and strategic abilities unsurpassed by anyone in the state."* Considered the firm's leading litigator, this talented attorney was commended for skill in *"organizing and deploying his troops in complex cases."* Kayatta focuses on complex, high-stakes commercial cases and has an active appellate practice. Deemed an *"excellent tactition and strategist"* by peers, Peter Culley (see p.325) is an experienced trial lawyer *"capable of handling any type of commercial litigation."* Eighty percent of his practice is devoted to civil and white-collar criminal litigation.

The Clients: Recent work includes representation of Maine Yankee in an action against Stone & Webster for breach of a contract to decommission a nuclear power plant, with a $64 million judgment entered for Maine Yankee. The firm acted for Cohesive Technologies in a patent infringement case against Waters Corporation and represented Great Northern Paper on an appeal against an action alleging a breach of contract to permit unlimited access to 671,000 acres of undeveloped forest lands. Other clients include: Gorham Savings Bank; Anthem Insurance Companies; UnumProvident; Hannaford; Maine Medical Center; MBNA; ACT and the State of California.

Bernstein, Shur, Sawyer & Nelson PA

The Firm: The firm's 20-strong litigation practice includes a specialized business litigation group, lauded by interviewees for *"high-quality work."* Experienced attorneys are *"capable of handling large cases"* and command extensive expertise in energy and waste-related litigation, employment litigation and insurance defense. Commentators particularly noted the group's *"robust"* ADR practice, with the majority of litigators given advanced training as mediators and arbitrators.

The Lawyers: Chair of the business litigation practice Peter Rubin is respected by peers and rivals as a *"tenacious opponent."* In addition to a comprehensive commercial litigation practice, Rubin spends a significant amount of his time on products liability and PI work.

The Clients: The firm recently settled a multi-million dollar contract dispute with Central Maine Power and the Maine Public Utilites Commission over power supply rates. Practitioners assisted national counsel from Chicago in a patent infringement case against competitors in Texas and California. Other clients include: Wal-Mart; McKesson General; Shipyard Brewing Company; UnumProvident; Owens-Illinois; IDEXX Laboratories; Halliburton; Travelers Insurance; Groupe Arno (Quebec, Canada) and Benton Falls.

Harvey & Frank

The Firm: Founded seven years ago, this *"hard-working,"* two-attorney litigation boutique was felt to have made a profound impact on the market. The *"excellent and effective duo"* has built up a loyal client base who appreciate the pair's willingness to *"tailor their services to meet our needs."* Rivals told researchers that they often refer work to the firm for specialized expertise and courtroom representation. The bulk of the practice is devoted to commercial litigation; PI and medical malpractice are also covered.

The Lawyers: Rivals heaped praise on Charles

LITIGATION

MAINE

Harvey as a *"smart, aggressive and articulate"* trial attorney. He concentrates on civil trials, appeals and dispute resolution. **Robert Frank** divides his practice between commercial and administrative litigation, and antitrust and trade regulation counseling. In addition to *"outstanding courtroom abilities,"* Frank was recommended as having *"intellectual depth"* in areas outside of the law, and a strong scientific expertise in particular.

The Clients: The firm represented dissenting stockholders of Ocean National Bank resisting a tender offer by Chittenden Corporation of Vermont. It obtained the first federal court order requiring the management of a target to provide stockholder access to proxies. Attorneys successfully defended a national retail chain against an $11 million suit by owners of a smaller chain alleging fraudulence in stock sales. Other notable work includes representation of a contractor in arbitration arising from the construction of a large university building and acting for a paper manufacturer in a contract arbitration concerning the pricing of raw materials. The firm also represents: Georgia-Pacific; Maine Medical Center; Movie Gallery; Medical Mutual Insurance Co. of Maine; Dexter Shoe Company; Maine Technical College System and the State of Maine.

Norman, Hanson & DeTroy LLC
The Firm: This mid-sized firm has over 25 experienced trial attorneys. The firm is preeminent in insurance defense and, over the past five years, has cemented an *"excellent"* reputation in complex commercial litigation, products liability and civil rights. The team also provides a wide variety of ADR services.

The Lawyers: The firm's *"muscle"* on the commercial side is generally attributed to **Peter DeTroy**. Recommended to researchers as *"a utility fielder who can try almost any type of case,"* he stands out for his *"impeccable judgment and common sense."* Interviewees nominated him as the *"most sought-after mediator in the state."*

The Clients: Camden National Bank; MaineHealth; AutoZone; Bath Iron Works and Carlisle Corporation.

Berman & Simmons
The Firm: This 17-attorney litigation boutique came highly recommended to researchers. The *"high-quality firm"* has the second largest litigation group in Maine and was described as *"preeminent for the kind of work they do."* Purely plaintiff, the majority of their work is PI and medical malpractice; however, **William Robitzek**, Jack Simmons and Steven Silin were recommended as excellent commercial litigators. They typically act for *"David against Goliath,"* representing smaller businesses, sole proprietorships and minority stockholders in contract disputes, unfair competition cases, antitrust violations, class actions and litigation in breach of fiduciary duty. Recommended by clients as *"results-oriented"* and *"able to move the case to the bottom line as quickly and effectively as possible,"* virtually all their work is contingent fee-based.

The Clients: The firm has acted as local counsel on numerous class actions, including a $45 million securities fraud case and an $11 million indirect vitamin purchaser litigation. Other clients include Schiavi Homes, Global Protein Products and Fitzpatrick Dairy.

Preti, Flaherty, Beliveau, Pachios & Haley LLC
The Firm: One of Maine's larger firms with over 80 attorneys, Preti Flaherty was recommended to researchers as having a *"solid, capable"* litigation team, with an emphasis in insurance defense work. Members have expertise in most areas of commercial litigation, including contracts, professional liability, media and communications cases and environmental suits.

The Clients: The firm represents a variety of corporate clients, including those in the telecom, publishing, healthcare, manufacturing and energy industries.

Verrill & Dana LLP
The Firm: Perceived to be rebuilding after the departure of three of their foremost litigators, Verrill & Dana's 20-attorney litigation team was nonetheless recommended as *"bringing a lot to the table."* The bulk of the group's workload is commercial. The practice is broad-based; however, researchers were told that current strengths lie in IP and antitrust issues.

The Clients: International Paper; Duke Energy; Jasper Wyman and Son; Bowdoin College and Bar Harbor Banking and Trust Company.

Other Notable Practitioners
Gerald Petruccelli of Petruccelli Martin & Haddow LLP was acclaimed for *"outstanding intellect"* and *"strong analytical skills."* An *"academic"* lawyer with a talent for legal interpretation, Petruccelli was said to *"get to the issues quickly"* and *"obtains good results in novel cases and difficult circumstances."* His litigation practice generally involves one-time client relationships. He and his team have represented Big Five accounting firms, contractors, bonding companies, liability insurers, risk pools, banks, hospitals, real estate developers and pharmaceutical manufacturers.

REAL ESTATE

MAINE
Leading firms (Real Estate)
1. BERNSTEIN, SHUR, SAWYER & NELSON Portland
   JENSEN BAIRD GARDNER & HENRY Portland
2. DRUMMOND WOODSUM & MACMAHON Portland
   PIERCE ATWOOD Portland
   VERRILL & DANA LLP Portland
3. PERKINS, THOMPSON, HINCKLEY Portland

Firms are listed alphabetically in each band.

Bernstein, Shur, Sawyer & Nelson PA
The Firm: Real estate is a significant practice area for the firm, with 12 full-time attorneys acting on real estate acquisitions, financings and litigation. Rivals praise this *"capable, assertive"* team for the *"horsepower they bring to the table,"* while clients noted the group's skill at coordinating multi-state transactions. Practitioners have expertise in all aspects of real estate from project planning and environmental risk assessment to representation of banks and lending institutions. The firm has two wholly-owned subsidiaries, a title company and an environmental engineering company, to assist clients in development needs.

The Lawyers: *"Lawyer's lawyer"* **Nathan Smith** was recommended to researchers as an experienced real estate attorney with an *"easygoing"* demeanor. Interviewees particularly noted his expertise in environmental and land conservation law. Practice chair **Jaimie Schwartz** was singled out as being *"knowledgeable and extremely talented."* He focuses on commercial real estate transactions and commercial leasing.

The Clients: Recent deals include: the acquisition, financing and leasing of the 75,000 sq ft Atlantic National Trust Building in Portland; the acquisition, permitting, construction and financing of the RiverPlace Development – a 136-luxury-apartment building – including the first tax increment financing used for housing in Maine; and a $28 million conservation easement acquisition by the

MAINE — REAL ESTATE

MAINE
Leading individuals (Real Estate)

1 MILLER Charles *Bernstein, Shur, Sawyer*, Portland
WEBBER Walter *Jensen Baird Gardner*, Portland
2 COLE Kenneth *Jensen Baird Gardner*, Portland
SMITH Nathan *Bernstein, Shur, Sawyer PA*, Portland
3 KEELER Dennis *Pierce Atwood*, Portland
LEDDY Bruce *Perkins, Thompson, Hinckley*, Portland
OESTREICHER Charles *Verrill & Dana LLP*, Portland
PATTERSON Robert *Verrill & Dana LLP*, Portland
SCHWARTZ Jaimie *Bernstein, Shur, Sawyer*, Portland

Individuals are listed alphabetically in each band.

New England Forestry Foundation. Other clients include: FPL Energy; Portland Natural Gas Transmission System; First American Title Insurance Company; University of Maine System; Ram Management; Bramlie Development Corporation and RE Management Company.

Jensen Baird Gardner & Henry
The Firm: A mid-sized firm of 23 *"high-caliber"* attorneys with a strong reputation in real estate. Rivals describe the practice as a *"hands-on"* team, distinguished by practitioners' thoroughness, experience and talent for *"closing a deal."* The group represents developers and lenders, commercial landlords and tenants as well as individuals.
The Lawyers: Acclaimed for his *"depth of knowledge and solid strategic ability,"* **Walter Webber** concentrates on commercial development activity. Webber is well known for his *"admirable work ethic"* and specialized knowledge of shopping center development. He was responsible for the permitting and development of the Maine Mall, the largest shopping center in the state. Rivals praise **Kenneth Cole** for his common sense and practicality. This *"extremely careful attorney"* was thought to possess good negotiating skills and a thorough knowledge of real estate law. His practice covers a wide variety of governmental, real estate and title issues. Clients include large residential builders, Kasprzak, Inc and numerous Greater Portland municipalities.
The Clients: The firm worked with Wal-Mart to locate ten stores in Maine and represented Plum Creek Timber Company in the sale of conservation easements to the State of Maine and the sale and development of recreational homes on Maine lakes. Other clients include: Packard Development, SR Weiner & Associates, Banknorth and Camden National.

Drummond Woodsum & MacMahon
see firm details p.791
The Firm: Five attorneys specialize in commercial real estate work as a subsection of the firm's expanding corporate team. Interviewees praised the group's experience, commenting that the quality of work it receives rivals that of the major state players. Attorneys advise owners, developers, lessees and lenders and act as Maine counsel for a number of out-of-state lenders.
The Lawyers: Ronald Ward and Richard Shinay are the contact attorneys for the real estate practice.
The Clients: Legal counsel for the contracting, siting, permitting and construction loan financing of a 560MW, gas-fired electric generating facility in Westbrook, Maine, and represented local Community School District as real estate counsel and bond counsel in the authorization, site acquisition and construction of a $19 million school project. Also acts for Colby College, Stonewall Kitchens, Boyd Properties, Sunrise Properties and Congress Properties.

Pierce Atwood
see firm details p.865
The Firm: Maine's largest law firm, Pierce Atwood possesses a six-lawyer real estate practice with a reputation for *"sophisticated, high-quality work."* The group's focus is commercial; it represents developers and lenders, and advises clients on matters such as timberland development and real estate syndications. Clients recommend this *"unusually thorough"* practice as *"the place to go to when the devil is in the detail."* Rivals considered it an *"aggressive"* practice with strength in real estate litigation.
The Lawyers: *"Smart and thorough"* **Dennis Keeler** (see p.504004) heads the firm's real estate practice group. Rivals and clients priased his *"responsive and results-oriented approach."* He is involved in all aspects of real estate law with an emphasis on development, permitting, leasing and financing.
The Clients: The practice assisted FPL Energy Seabrook in the acquisition of a nuclear power plant in New Hampshire and represented Nestlés Waters of North America in connection with a synthetic lease of approximately 500,000 sq ft in Portsmouth, NH for a warehouse/distribution facility. Other clients include: Dead River Properties, Fairway Villas and Kimco Realty.

Verrill & Dana LLP
The Firm: This *"competent and experienced"* practice continues to hold its own in a competitive market. Rivals envy the firm's *"quality client base"* and *"good depth of lawyers."* The team represents lenders, developers and lessees in commercial, retail and industrial transactions and developments and acts for high-income residential purchasers and sellers. The practice also boasts expertise in title problems, boundary disputes, easements, real estate trusts and zoning matters.
The Lawyers: Well respected for *"long experience in the field,"* **Charles Oestreicher** was recommended to researchers for high-end residential work. His practice focuses on the ownership, purchase and sale of real estate, title matters, easements, zoning and real estate brokerage law.
Clients lauded **Robert Patterson** for his *"expeditious handling of transactions,"* while rivals referred to him as a *"practical and thorough"* attorney. He represents clients in all aspects of commercial real estate law and finance, with an emphasis on commercial financing. In addition to representing numerous lending institutions and developers in Maine, he serves as local counsel to many out-of-state lenders in a wide variety of commercial loan transactions.
The Clients: Banknorth; Fleet National Bank; Camden National Bank; MaineHealth; JB Brown & Sons; JM Huber Corporation; Turnpike Mall and the Maine Governmental Facilities Authority.

Perkins, Thompson, Hinckley & Keddy PA
The Firm: A six-attorney real estate practice continues to uphold the mid-sized firm's traditional strength in this area. The group focuses on three principal areas: representation of businesses and residential developers, representation of large property owners, and secured lender financing of real estate acquisitions and construction.
The Lawyers: **Bruce Leddy** brings to the group more than 30 years' experience of Maine-based real estate transactions. Rivals and clients roundly applauded his *"depth of knowledge"* of the area. The bulk of his practice is dedicated to leasing work and he also works in the forest products area.
The Clients: The firm recently represented Plum Creek Land Company before Maine's Land Use Regulation Commission in obtaining permits to develop 89 camp lots and negotiated a conservation easement on a lake in Maine's unorganized territory. Members acted for the October Corporation in all phases of the acquisition and development of a century-old facility, Pineland in New Gloucester, ME and regularly advise CB Richard Ellis/Boulos Property Management on real estate issues.

Leaders in Maine

CHAMPOUX, David
Pierce Atwood, Portland 207 791 1100
DChampoux@PierceAtwood.com
Recommended in Corporate/M&A
Specialization: Concentrates in corporate, finance, and general transactional representation, including all aspects of corporate, securities, and commercial law, focusing on representing corporations and individuals in a wide variety of transactional settings. Experience includes securities law, special purpose entities such as limited liability companies, M&A, venture capital financing, and SEC reporting and compliance.
Prof. Memberships: New York Bar (1985); Maine Bar (1987). Chair, Maine Bar's Business Law Section (2001).
Career: Partner, (1993-). Listed in a leading legal publication, 2003-2004 edition, for corporate, M&A, and securities.
Personal: University of Virginia School of Law, JD 1984; Harvard College, AB (cum laude)1981.

COLE, Kenneth
Jensen Baird Gardner & Henry, Portland
207 775 7271
Recommended in Real Estate

CULLEY, Peter
Pierce Atwood, Portland 207 791 1288
pculley@pierceatwood.com
Recommended in Litigation
Specialization: Chair, Litigation Department. Extensive experience in representing corporate interests in jury trials in all courts. Represents manufacturers, financial institutions, and professional service firms in a broad range of matters, including business litigation, professional liability and product liability actions.
Prof. Memberships: International Association of Defense Counsel; American Board of Trial Advocates; Fellow, American College of Trial Lawyers.
Career: Served as Chief of Criminal Division of Department of Attorney General, State of Maine; founding partner of a Portland litigation firm before joining *Pierce Atwood*.
Personal: Boston University, JD 1968; University of Maine, AB 1965.

DETROY, Peter
Norman, Hanson & DeTroy, LLC, Portland 207 774 7000
Recommended in Litigation

ERWIN, James
Pierce Atwood, Portland 207 791 1100
jerwin@pierceatwood.com
Recommended in Employment
Specialization: Partner and Chair, Labor and Employment Department. Representation of management in federal, state and administrative proceedings, and counseling, training and related preventative services.
Prof. Memberships: ABA (Employment and Labor Relations Committee, Litigation Section); American Judicature Society (Director 2001-); American Counsel Association (Director 2002-); Maine State Bar Association; Maine Trial Lawyers Association.
Career: Maine Bar (1978); Assistant Attorney General, State of Maine (homicide prosecutions) 1978-83; Commissioner, Maine Human Rights Commission (1985-87); Technology Partner 1993-98; Marketing Partner (2000-).
Publications: 'Model Jury Instructions', 'Employment Litigation', 2d ed. (ABA 2003) (Board of Editors); 'Employment Litigation Handbook' (ABA 1998) (Chapter Author).
Personal: Boston University School of Law, JD 1978; Dartmouth College, AB (cum laude, High Distinction) 1975.

FRANK, Robert
Harvey & Frank, Portland
207 775 1300
Recommended in Litigation

FRYER, Greg
Verrill & Dana, LLP, Portland
207 774 4000
Recommended in Corporate/M&A

GAUSE, John
Berman & Simmons, Portland
207 774 5277
Recommended in Employment

HARVEY, Charles
Harvey & Frank, Portland
207 775 1300
Recommended in Litigation

HEWEY, Melissa
Drummond Woodsum & MacMahon, Portland 207 772 1941
mhewey@dwmlaw.com
Recommended in Employment
Specialization: Focuses her practice on complex civil litigation including school law and employment matters, defense against discrimination, sexual harassment and civil rights claims. She has extensive experience in a variety of forms of alternative dispute resolution, including arbitration and mediation.
Prof. Memberships: She is a member of the American Trial Lawyers Association as well as the Maine State and Cumberland County Bar Associations. She serves on the Local Rules Committee of the United States District Court and is a member of the Gignoux Inn of Courts. She has been selected by her peers to be included in a leading US legal publication.
Career: Joined *Drummond Woodsum and MacMahon* in 1987 and is Chair of the Trial Services Group.
Personal: She is a graduate of Wesleyan University (1980) and a magna cum laude graduate of the University of Maine School Law.

HIGH, Michael E
Drummond Woodsum & MacMahon, Portland 207 772 1941
mhigh@dwmlaw.com
Recommended in Corporate/M&A
Specialization: Has extensive experience in representing businesses, investors, lenders and borrowers throughout New England in a wide range of corporate and commercial matters, including mergers and acquisitions, corporate finance, shareholder matters, private placements, venture capital financing, technology licensing and transfers, and intellectual property.
Prof. Memberships: Listed in a leading US legal publication and is immediate past Chair of the Business Law Section of the Maine State Bar Association. He was co-chair of a Bar Sub-committee that oversaw the adoption of Revised Article 9 in Maine, and a State Task Force Leader on the Corporate Law Revision Committee of the Business Law Section that revised and recommended the adoption of the new Maine Business Corporation Act (effective 1 July 2003).
Career: Practiced at *Choate, Hall & Stewart* in Boston, MA for several years before joining *Drummond Woodsum and MacMahon*. He is Chair of the firm's Business and Commercial Services Group.
Personal: Graduated from Cornell Law School (1983) where he was an articles editor of the 'International Law Journal'.

JOHNSTON, Thomas
Eaton Peabody, Bangor 207 947 0111
Recommended in Employment

KAYATTA JR, William
Pierce Atwood, Portland 207 791 1100
wkayatta@pierceatwood.com
Recommended in Litigation
Specialization: Complex civil litigation; class actions; life and disability.
Prof. Memberships: Fellow, American College of Trial Lawyers; Chair, Maine Professional Ethics Commission (2002); President-elect, Maine Bar Foundation (2003).
Career: Argued UNUM v Ward to USSCT; successfully defended $846 million asset purchase deal in FPL Energy v CMP; recovered $44 million in action arising out of nuclear plant decommissioning in Maine Yankee v Federal Insurance Co.
Personal: Harvard Law School, JD 1979 (magna cum laude) (Harv.L.Rev 1978-79); Amherst College, BA 1976 (magna cum laude); Clerk, Chief Judge Frank M Coffin, US 1st Circuit Court of Appeals (1980).

KEELER, Dennis
Pierce Atwood, Portland 207 791 1331
dkeeler@pierceatwood.com
Recommended in Real Estate
Specialization: Chair, Real Estate Group. Practices primarily in the real estate development area, with emphasis on representing developers and owners of retail centers, office buildings, commercial and industrial projects and large residential/resort developments throughout New England and the mid-Atlantic Coast area.
Prof. Memberships: Colorado Bar (1981); Maine Bar (1984); Secretary and Member, Board of Directors of Maine Real Estate Development Association; Member, International Council of Shopping Centers.
Career: Partner (1990-). Practiced in Denver, Colorado. Selected for inclusion in a leading legal publication, 2003-2004 edition, for real estate law.
Personal: University of Denver, JD 1981; University of Maryland, BA 1975.

LEDDY, Bruce
Perkins, Thompson, Hinckley & Keddy, P.A., Portland 207 774 2635
Recommended in Real Estate

MCGILL, Linda
Moon, Moss, McGill & Shapiro, Portland
207 775 6001
Recommended in Employment

MCGUIRE, Frank
Rudman & Winchell LLC, Bangor
207 947 4501
Recommended in Employment

MCKAY, Daniel
Eaton Peabody, Bangor 207 947 0111
Recommended in Corporate/M&A

MILLER, Charles
Bernstein, Shur, Sawyer & Nelson, PA, Portland 207 774 1200
Recommended in Real Estate

MOON, Richard
Moon, Moss, McGill & Shapiro, Portland
207 775 6001
Recommended in Employment

OESTREICHER, Charles
Verrill & Dana, LLP, Portland
207 774 4000
Recommended in Real Estate

PATTERSON, Robert
Verrill & Dana, LLP, Portland
207 774 4000
Recommended in Real Estate

MAINE LEADERS

PAYNE, Clare
Eaton Peabody, Bangor 207 947 0111
Recommended in Employment

PETRUCCELLI, Gerald
Petruccelli Martin & Haddow LLP,
Portland 207 775 0200
Recommended in Litigation

PRINGLE, Harry
Drummond Woodsum & MacMahon,
Portland 207 772 1941
hpringle@dwmlaw.com
Recommended in Employment
Specialization: Has extensive experience in employment litigation, labor negotiations, National Labor Relations Board and Maine Labor Relations Board proceedings, Title VII litigation, and discrimination cases before the courts, the Equal Employment Opportunity Commissions and the Maine Human Rights Commission.
Prof. Memberships: He has been a member of the Board of Directors of the National School Board Association Council of School Board Attorneys. He has been listed in labor and employment law by a leading US legal publication for over ten years.
Career: He is a past President of the Maine Council of School Board Attorneys. He joined the firm in 1973, is Chair of the Public Sector Group, is a lead instructor for school law courses at two area universities, and is a frequent lecturer on employment law issues.
Publications: Editor of 'Maine School Law' and has authored numerous articles on school and employment law issues including 'Significant Cases in Maine School Law'.
Personal: He graduated from Harvard Law School (cum laude 1973) and from Princeton University (1968 magna cum laude, Phi Beta Kappa).

REBEN, Howard
Reben, Benjamin & March, Portland
207 874 4771
Recommended in Employment

ROBITZEK, William
Berman & Simmons, Portland
207 774 5277
Recommended in Litigation

RUBIN, Peter
Bernstein, Shur, Sawyer & Nelson, PA,
Portland 207 774 1200
Recommended in Litigation

SCHWARTZ, Jaimie
Bernstein, Shur, Sawyer & Nelson, PA,
Portland 207 774 1200
Recommended in Real Estate

SHAPIRO, Jonathan
Moon, Moss, McGill & Shapiro, Portland
207 775 6001
Recommended in Employment

SMITH, Nathan
Bernstein, Shur, Sawyer & Nelson, PA,
Portland 207 774 1200
Recommended in Real Estate

WEBBER, Rebecca
Linnell Choate & Webber LLP, Auburn
207 784 4563
Recommended in Employment

WEBBER, Walter
Jensen Baird Gardner & Henry, Portland
207 775 7271
Recommended in Real Estate

WEBBERT, David
Johnson & Webbert, LLP, Augusta
207 623 5110
Recommended in Employment

YOUNG, Jeffrey
McTeague, Higbee, Case, Cohen, Whitney & Toker, PA, Topsham
207 725 5581
Recommended in Employment

ZIMPRITCH, James B
Pierce Atwood, Portland 207 791 1100
jzimpritch@pierceatwood.com
Recommended in Corporate/M&A
Specialization: Broad corporate experience. Active M&A practice. Extensive experience in corporate and securities, banking, insurance, shareholder disputes, director duties, structuring investments and general commercial law. Involved in nearly every takeover fight in Maine in last 20 years. Represents emerging, middle-market, and large publicly held companies.
Prof. Memberships: American Law Institute; ABA Corporate Laws Committee; Maine: Chair, Corporate Law Revision Committee (2000-); past Chair, Business Law Section; frequent lecturer.
Career: Partner, *Pierce Atwood*, (1978-).
Publications: 'Maine Corporation Law & Practice', the definitive treatise.
Personal: Duke Law School, JD 1973; 'Duke Law Journal', 1972-73; Dartmouth College, AB 1970.

CORPORATE/M&A

MARYLAND

CONTENTS: Corporate/M&A p.327; Employment: Mainly Plaintiff p.328; Mainly Defendant p.329; Litigation: General Commercial p.330; Real Estate p.331; Individuals' Profiles p.351.

MARYLAND'S TOP THREE
1. Piper Rudnick
2. Venable
3. Hogan & Hartson

Ranking based on Chambers' research within the state.

All quotes in the text are from interviews with clients and competitors.

OVERVIEW: The largest firm in the state, **Piper Rudnick** also has the most respected litigation department. Known particularly for its work on products liability cases, the litigation group acts for the firm's wide base of corporate and real estate clients. It has recently been active in the WorldCom and Enron affairs. On the corporate side the practice works extensively with emerging companies. A nationwide reach attracts high-profile clients to both the real estate and employment practices. The firm's cochair, Francis Burch in the litigation department has substantial jury trial experience, while Richard Hafets, who leads the labor and employment practice, was identified by interviewees as a brilliant practitioner. Clients include AEGON USA and Deutsche Bank.

Large, full-service firm **Venable** is commended in the region as a one-stop shop for labor and employment matters, and is also respected for its corporate and real estate work. Within litigation, the firm carving out a niche with a growing plaintiffs' practice that handles claims against professional advice businesses. Employment attorney Ron Taylor is one of the most recognized names in the market. Clients include MBNA and American Red Cross.

Top DC firm **Hogan & Hartson** boasts a respected local office in Maryland with noteworthy strength in corporate and M&A work. A team of 15 lawyers combines corporate work for the law firm's national clients with advice to local Maryland businesses. Corporate attorney Walter Lohr is credited with building up an impressive roster of commercial clients. The litigation department was also praised, with George Beall singled out as a senior figure in the market. Clients include News Corporation and the State of Maryland.

CORPORATE/M&A

MARYLAND
Leading firms (Corporate/M&A)
1. **PIPER RUDNICK LLP** Baltimore
2. **HOGAN & HARTSON LLP** Baltimore
   VENABLE LLP Baltimore
3. **MILES & STOCKBRIDGE PC** Baltimore

Leading individuals (Corporate/M&A)
1. **SMITH Robert** Piper Rudnick LLP, Baltimore
2. **COOK Bryson** Venable LLP, Baltimore
   TILGHMAN Richard Piper Rudnick LLP, Baltimore
3. **HANKS James** Ballard Spahr Andrews, Baltimore
   LOHR Walter Hogan & Hartson LLP, Baltimore
   SILVER Michael Hogan & Hartson LLP, Baltimore
   WASHBURNE Thomas Venable LLP, Baltimore
   WATKINS John Wilmer, Cutler, Baltimore
   WEBB Thompson Miles & Stockbridge, Baltimore

Firms and individuals are listed alphabetically in each band.

Piper Rudnick LLP
see firm details p.867

The Firm: Peers reported that this sizable practice can field a *"contingent of able business attorneys."* It is best known for its work with emerging companies, and has been active in transactions across the $50-500 million deal range. The group has also counseled clients on corporate governance and the Sarbanes-Oxley Act.
The Lawyers: **Robert (Jay) Smith** (see p.335) was singled out to researchers as setting the mould for the all-around corporate practitioner, while some identified his skill in securities offerings as most prominent. Cochair of the practice, he is active in M&A, and IPOs for emerging companies. *"Highly regarded"* among the Maryland corporate bar, **Richard Tilghman** (see p.335) is experienced in the representation of emerging growth companies. Also acts for underwriters in the public or private offering of equity securities.
The Clients: CSFB; Deutsche Bank Alex. Brown; Human Genome Sciences; Legg Mason Wood Walker; The Ryland Group and T Rowe Price Associates.

Hogan & Hartson LLP
see firm details p.818

The Firm: *"Definitely a presence,"* this DC firm has succeeded in developing a respected corporate practice. A team of 15 lawyers combines work for the firm's national client base with advice to Maryland-based companies such as CIENA .
The Lawyers: **Walter Lohr** (see p.333) represents private and public companies across the full range of corporate and securities work, including some contested matters. Peers described him as a lawyer of *"substantial experience,"* and he has a client roster filled with investment banks, manufacturing companies and hi-tech enterprises. Clients emphasized that he is *"prepared and ready for every kind of transaction,"* adding: *"He cannot be thrown a curveball."* **Michael Silver** (see p.334) has a broad corporate and securities practice, advising issuers, underwriters and placement agents, nationwide. His clients have included healthcare and telecom equipment manufacturers, and he recently represented LabCorp in its cross-border acquisition of a provider of laboratory testing services. Clients described him as a *"sharp, knowledgeable, responsive and creative"* attorney.
The Clients: News Corporation; Host Marriott; Havas; Sithe Energies; Orbital Sciences; CIENA; E*TRADE Financial and LabCorp.

Venable LLP
The Firm: Interviewees respect the firm as a serious corporate player with significant capabilities, which tend toward more regional and private company work. It fields a *"bunch of good people,"* who represent corporate clients in a wide range of business transactions, including both domestic and international M&A and joint ventures, and the creation of offshore ventures.
The Lawyers: One of the firm's *"shining stars,"* **Bryson Cook** was highlighted to researchers for his *"creativity."* His experience as a *"first-rate"* tax lawyer has ensured his *"great reputation"* among the local business community. He regularly undertakes M&A work for a large international hotel company, and has represented the sellers of several sports facilities in Maryland. **Thomas (Tuck) Washburne** was also identified as a *"terrifically able"* lawyer. His practice includes venture capital financing and M&A.
The Clients: The firm's client base includes Fortune 100 companies, international and regional entrepreneurs, private companies, venture capitalists and underwriters. The group is also developing a focus on emerging growth industries.

Miles & Stockbridge PC
The Firm: This midmarket corporate practice is endorsed for its *"significant"* presence in the corporate sector. The firm is distinguished by its long-standing relationship with Black & Decker, and continues to benefit from the presence of the firm's chair, Lowell Bowen who, although less visible, continues to be considered by many as a valuable asset.
The Lawyers: Researchers have had their attention drawn to **Thompson Webb**, a *"calm, reflective"*

MARYLAND — EMPLOYMENT & LABOR LAW

attorney. He represents large public companies in financial transactions and general corporate work, across a range of industries.

The Clients: The firm acts for Black & Decker, and a range of local and national corporates.

Other Notable Practitioners
Although **James Hanks** of Ballard Spahr Andrews & Ingersoll LLP is found less often in a transactional context, he remains a *"recognized authority"* on Maryland corporate law. He regularly advises Fortune 500 companies, real estate and investment groups, and is judged to have a *"national reputation"* in this specialty. At the small Baltimore branch of Wilmer, Cutler & Pickering, *"superb"* **John (Jay) Watkins** (see p.335) focuses on securities offerings and M&A for clients such as Sinclair Broadcast Group and Legg Mason.

EMPLOYMENT & LABOR LAW — MAINLY PLAINTIFF

MARYLAND
Leading firms
(Employment: Mainly Plaintiff)

1
- ABATO, RUBENSTEIN AND ABATO PA *Baltimore*
- KAHN, SMITH & COLLINS PA *Baltimore*
- LEBAU & NEUWORTH LLC *Baltimore*

2
- ALBERTINI, SINGLETON, GENDLER *Baltimore*

Leading individuals
(Employment: Mainly Plaintiff)

1
- SINGLETON John *Albertini, Singleton*, Baltimore

2
- CAHILL Kathleen *Kathleen Cahill*, Baltimore
- GODOFF Stephen *Stephen Godoff*, Baltimore
- HEDIAN Victoria *Abato, Rubenstein and Abato*, Baltimore
- LEBAU Steve *Lebau & Neuworth LLC*, Baltimore
- SMITH Joel *Kahn, Smith & Collins PA*, Baltimore

3
- GAGLIARDO Thomas *Sole Practitioner*, Silver Spring
- GOLD Carl *Sole Practitioner*, Baltimore
- ROSENBERG James *Abato, Rubenstein*, Baltimore

Firms and individuals are listed alphabetically in each band.

Abato, Rubenstein and Abato PA
The Firm: The firm's level of knowledge and expertise has ensured that it received frequent nominations as one of the state's prime choices for traditional labor law. It acts for a variety of local unions, including those that represent musicians, carpenters, and food distribution and transit workers. In its full-service workload, the firm is particularly active in contract and collective bargaining negotiations, arbitrations and the management of strikes.
The Lawyers: The pick of the talented team, **Vickie Hedian** has *"a wonderful combination of intellectual abilities, practicality and personality."* She is ably supported by *"straight-shooting"* **Jim Rosenberg**, who was characterized as a *"problem solver who isn't overly adversarial."*

Kahn, Smith & Collins PA
The Firm: The group is best known for a client list that largely comprises public labor unions. Peers were impressed with the firm's dogged pursuit of its clients' interests. It has acted for state employees such as firefighters, while a proportion of the practice is also devoted to the representation of individuals. Cases are brought in response to claims of age, race, sex and disability discrimination.
The Lawyers: **Joel Smith** spearheads the team and was consistently recommended to researchers as *"one of the brightest lawyers"* at the bar. His *"tenacious"* style combines with a *"creative and innovative"* approach to cases.

Lebau & Neuworth LLC
The Firm: The group covers the waterfront of employment law, and its expertise extends to employee benefits and union representation. Management firms reported that it measured up best in employment discrimination cases, where a high-quality service was displayed. It has been involved in negotiations, mediations and litigation with a number of Fortune 500 companies. The group has had particular success in cases involving sexual harassment claims, as well as those involving violations of federal wage and hour laws.
The Lawyers: Name partner **Steve Lebau**'s background in management representation was felt by interviewees to lend him a valuable perspective. He is a *"skilled and practical"* attorney who does a *"tremendous job representing his clients' interests."*
The Clients: The group acts primarily for individuals ranging from senior executives to hourly workers. It also represents a number of nonprofit organizations.

Albertini, Singleton, Gendler & Darby LLP
The Firm: A compact group of lawyers that is heavily involved in union representation before federal and state courts and agencies. It has acted for the AFL-CIO in a NLRB case involving dozens of unfair labor practice allegations against offshore oil platform operators in the Gulf of Louisiana. The firm's focus also extends to discrimination cases, and it has brought several ADA cases against fire departments on behalf of clients.
The Lawyers: Researchers were impressed with the respect that the *"tremendously talented"* **John Singleton** commanded from peers and opposing counsel. *"Straightforward and honest,"* he maintains a low-key approach, and has enjoyed extensive success on behalf of unions and individuals.
The Clients: AFL-CIO; International Organization of Masters, Mates & Pilots; Baltimore Building and Construction Trades Council and International Union of Operating Engineers.

Other Notable Practitioners
Kathleen Cahill of The Law Offices of Kathleen Cahill LLC won renown for her formidable approach to employment discrimination cases, where interviewees saw her as a *"tremendously talented"* practitioner. **Stephen Godoff** of The Law Offices of Stephen Godoff is a well-known union attorney, endorsed by peers as *"a practical and savvy negotiator."* Sole practitioner **Tom Gagliardo** caught the attention of the market for his handling of discrimination cases: *"He has perspective and knows when to settle and when to proceed."* Although sole practitioner **Carl Gold** does not focus exclusively on employment law, he was also recommended in this arena as an excellent jury trial lawyer.

MARYLAND

EMPLOYMENT & LABOR LAW — MAINLY DEFENDANT

MARYLAND
Leading firms
(Employment: Mainly Defendant)

1
- PIPER RUDNICK LLP *Baltimore*

2
- MILES & STOCKBRIDGE PC *Baltimore*
- SHAWE & ROSENTHAL LLP *Baltimore*
- VENABLE LLP *Baltimore*
- WHITEFORD, TAYLOR & PRESTON LLP *Baltimore*

3
- GORDON, FEINBLATT, ROTHMAN *Baltimore*

Leading individuals
(Employment: Mainly Defendant)

1
- HAFETS Richard *Piper Rudnick LLP, Baltimore*
- PONTONE Kathleen *Miles & Stockbridge PC, Baltimore*
- SILVESTRI Stephen *Miles & Stockbridge PC, Baltimore*
- TAYLOR Ronald *Venable LLP, Baltimore*

2
- AYRES Jeffrey *Venable LLP, Towson*
- GARDNER Russell *Piper Rudnick LLP, Baltimore*
- KELLNER Robert *Gordon, Feinblatt, Rothman, Baltimore*
- MCGEE Emmett *Piper Rudnick LLP, Baltimore*
- POKEMPNER Joseph *Whiteford, Taylor, Baltimore*
- WOLF Larry *Whiteford, Taylor & Preston LLP, Baltimore*

3
- MCGUIRE Michael *Shawe & Rosenthal LLP, Baltimore*
- PALTELL Eric *Kollman & Saucier PA, Baltimore*
- SHAWE Stephen *Shawe & Rosenthal LLP, Baltimore*

Firms and individuals are listed alphabetically in each band.

Piper Rudnick LLP
see firm details p.867

The Firm: The size of this firm allows it to maintain a presence in the local market and provide, with the aid of a network of offices, a nationally focused practice. Employment law is the team's key strength, and it advises a broad group of clients, often representing large corporates in complex class actions. For example, it successfully represented a telecom company in a lengthy arbitration involving claims of race, age and sex discrimination, FMLA retaliation and denial of stock options.

The Lawyers: A group of *"fine"* lawyers is able to draw on the support of a respected litigation arm. *"Brilliant attorney"* **Richard Hafets** (see p.333) leads the labor and employment practice. He advises clients on union avoidance and labor management relations. **Russell Gardner** (see p.333) concentrates primarily on employment law; peers regard him as a skilled attorney in discrimination cases. **Emmett McGee** (see p.334) was endorsed by peers for both the quality of his work and his *"thorough"* approach.

The Clients: The group has represented a delivery company in a multi-plaintiff race case alleging discrimination in compensation, terms and conditions of employment and discipline. It has also successfully defended a home-building company in a sex discrimination and sexual harassment case. Clients include: Lockheed Martin; ExxonMobil; UPS; WorldCom; Hershey Foods and New World Pasta Company.

Miles & Stockbridge PC

The Firm: An active force in the local market, the firm's attorneys provide day-to-day advice on both labor and employment matters. Its expertise extends to immigration issues, OSHA and employee benefits. The group's presence was felt most keenly in employment litigation, advising on issues related to the FMLA and the ADA. The firm's labor law capability was acknowledged by competitors, and it is lent weight by the profile of several NLRB alumni.

The Lawyers: From among a sizable group of *"smart and practical"* lawyers, **Kathleen Pontone** was singled out as one who *"is not afraid to litigate, but takes a long-term perspective."* She won a settlement in a major sexual harassment case brought by the EEOC. Other areas of her expertise include employment cases that raise indoor air quality issues. **Stephen Silvestri**'s eclectic practice has seen him involved in employment, labor and employee benefits matters. He impressed competitors as an *"energetic"* lawyer, *"thorough in his knowledge."*

The Clients: The group represents manufacturers, financial institutions, hospitality providers and food distributors. It also acts for clients involved in multi-family and commercial real estate operations. Nonprofit associations, including schools, clubs and charitable organizations, also form part of the client roster.

Shawe & Rosenthal LLP
see firm details p.873

The Firm: A labor and employment boutique, this group of *"fine adversaries"* has established itself as one of the *"most competitive"* in the market. Opposing counsel referred to its attorneys as *"conversant, and expert,"* in employment law, and pointed to their well-honed negotiating skills. The group has experience in class actions across the country, with defense of sexual harassment cases and age discrimination claims prominent in the workload. The group defended Calvert County Public Schools in an age and race discrimination case brought under the ADEA and Title VII. The firm is also experienced in labor law and active in collective bargaining agreements.

The Lawyers: A group of 15 lawyers includes **Stephen Shawe** (see p.334), son of one of the firm's founding partners. He was recommended by observers as a practical lawyer, experienced in a range of labor matters, who *"fights hard, but not to the death."* **Michael McGuire** (see p.334) also caught the attention of interviewees as an *"easy-to-deal-with"* attorney with a varied base of experience.

The Clients: Prominent clients include McDonald's, GEICO Insurance, Mid-Atlantic Isotopes, Amtrak, FedEx and Lafarge.

Venable LLP

The Firm: This firm continues to be regarded as an excellent *"one-stop shop"* for labor and employment questions throughout the mid-Atlantic region. The group acts for clients from a range of industries, including manufacturing and the financial and public service sectors, and has recently been involved in a broad spectrum of discrimination cases including the defense of age, race and disability claims. The team's experience also extends to traditional labor issues including union elections, collective bargaining and union arbitration.

The Lawyers: As one of the most recognized names in the market, **Ron Taylor** was endorsed as an *"experienced and trustworthy"* lawyer who provides high-quality service to his clients. **Jeff Ayres** is a talented litigator, also recommended for his *"detail-oriented"* approach. Together with a mid-sized group of attorneys, they have successfully defended a large financial institution in a US Department of Labor enforcement proceeding.

The Clients: Johns Hopkins; MBNA; Allfirst Bank; Giant Food and American Red Cross.

Whiteford, Taylor & Preston LLP

The Firm: Described by peers as a *"substantial"* practice, this firm provides coverage on labor, employment and ERISA matters. The team is built around a number of seasoned veterans. A group of younger lawyers tends to focus on employment-related issues. The firm has negotiated settlements with the EEOC, advised on union-organizing campaigns, and has been active in developing employment policies and procedures.

The Lawyers: The firm's best-known lawyers emanate from the traditional labor arm of the practice. **Joe Pokempner** is a former NLRB attorney who commands respect as a prominent labor attorney. **Larry Wolf** was highly recommended by union lawyers, who referred to him as *"one of the most intelligent lawyers around."*

The Clients: The firm's clients include auto dealerships, manufacturers, fast-food chains and healthcare organizations.

Gordon, Feinblatt, Rothman, Hoffberger & Hollander LLC

The Firm: Although the firm may not be best known for its employment practice, those familiar

MARYLAND

LITIGATION

with it spoke of an *"experienced and fair"* group who were adept at developing *"good client rapport."* Clients from a broad array of industries are not only represented in employment litigation but also benefit from the firm's traditional labor component, which is on hand to assist with collective bargaining agreements and union elections. Several of the team's individuals are well versed in business immigration matters and in the design and drafting of employee benefits plans. The group also has experience in implementing reductions in workforces, drafting and negotiating employment agreements and defending discrimination charges.

The Lawyers: **Robert Kellner** heads the practice, and was warmly regarded by our interviewees as a *"reasonable and pleasant"* attorney. His advice pertaining to employee benefits received particular endorsement. He has successfully defended Raytheon in a federal lawsuit involving claims under ERISA.

The Clients: The group regularly represents the Mid-Atlantic Permanente Medical Group, the Kennedy Krieger Institute, Hendersen-Webb and the Merchants Terminal Corporation as well as a number of financial institutions located in the state.

Other Notable Practitioners
At Kollman & Saucier PA, **Eric Paltell** was described as a *"knowledgeable and personable"* younger attorney and a valuable addition to this smaller firm. Previously at Piper Rudnick LLP, he has defended employers in a full range of labor and employment disputes.

LITIGATION

GENERAL COMMERCIAL

MARYLAND
Leading firms
(Litigation: General Commercial)
1. **KRAMON & GRAHAM PA** Baltimore
   PIPER RUDNICK LLP Baltimore
2. **HOGAN & HARTSON LLP** Baltimore
   VENABLE LLP Baltimore

Leading individuals
(Litigation: General Commercial)
1. **GRAHAM Andrew** *Kramon & Graham PA*, Baltimore
2. **BEALL George** *Hogan & Hartson LLP*, Baltimore
   BURCH Francis *Piper Rudnick LLP*, Baltimore
   LEWIN John *Venable LLP*, Baltimore
   MATHIAS Robert *Piper Rudnick LLP*, Baltimore
   SHEA James *Venable LLP*, Baltimore
   ULWICK James *Kramon & Graham PA*, Baltimore
3. **IMMELT Stephen** *Hogan & Hartson LLP*, Baltimore
   MURPHY William *Murphy & Shaffer*, Baltimore
   NILSON George *Piper Rudnick LLP*, Baltimore
   STRAIN Paul *Venable LLP*, Baltimore

Firms and individuals are listed alphabetically in each band.

Kramon & Graham PA
The Firm: A litigation boutique, its lead figures are judged to be *"head and shoulders above anyone in the state."* It is a popular choice for referrals, and represents several major law firms in malpractice suits. The group's business dispute expertise incorporates professional negligence, breaches of contract and unfair competition. The team is also experienced in alternative dispute resolution.

The Lawyers: By common consent, name partner **Andrew Graham** is a *"premier trial lawyer."* He is often found defending other law firms, while peers observe that *"he can handle anything and everything."* Graham was recently involved in representing a number of auto dealerships in claims against a large car manufacturer. **James Ulwick** is a *"fabulous lawyer with great judgment,"* who undertakes both plaintiffs' and defendants' work in a wide variety of commercial arenas, most recently antitrust. He is a *"creative"* attorney who *"gives good advice,"* and peers report on his success in jury trials.

The Clients: Business clients include small local companies and national corporations.

Piper Rudnick LLP
see firm details p.867

The Firm: Peers acknowledge that the Baltimore office of this national firm has the *"biggest practice around"* and as such is clearly capable of complex multi-state commercial litigation. Fielding *"first-class"* litigation partners, it has a noted strength in products liability, as part of its broad-based commercial practice. Its lead lawyers are helped by the *"best supporting cast of anyone in the state."* A stand-alone practice, the litigation group also serves the firm's private, public corporation and real estate clients. Recently, it has been active in the WorldCom and Enron affairs, but has also had high-profile roles in diet drug litigation, and in representing two major tobacco companies.

The Lawyers: Peers applaud the firm's cochair **Francis Burch** (see p.332) for his *"significant jury trial experience."* Advising on business, securities and corporate control litigation, he has worked on cases involving products liability, IP and toxic tort, and in patent disputes. He employs a *"polite but energetic and focused"* approach to the courtroom, and has represented major defense contractors in the prosecution of a multimillion dollar claim against the seller of a defense contracting business. His international experience includes representing the world's largest developer of outlet malls in litigation in Puerto Rico. **Robert Mathias** (see p.334) has impressed peers with his skill in *"relating well to juries."* He acts for both plaintiffs and defendants, in IP, complex financial and contract disputes. *"A bright, hard-working litigator,"* Mathias has represented a telecom company in dispute over the cancellation of a $6 billion contract, and acted for a computer equipment manufacturer in a dispute involving over $100 million in claims. *"A terrific lawyer,"* **George Nilson** (see p.334) has a general corporate litigation practice, which has a specialty in products liability. He recently represented two major tobacco manufacturers in benefits fund and state Medicaid reimbursement litigation and a statewide class action.

The Clients: AEGON USA; American Home Products; Deutsche Bank; GM; Harley-Davidson; International Paper; Lockheed Martin; Marriott International; Microsoft; Subaru of America and WorldCom.

Hogan & Hartson LLP
see firm details p.818

The Firm: Commended by interviewees as a *"talented local office,"* the Baltimore branch of this DC firm fields some strong lawyers as part of the firm's national litigation practice. The group is active in products and professional liability, antitrust, complex contractual disputes, and IP and insurance matters.

The Lawyers: **George Beall** (see p.332) is an *"effective, poised trial lawyer of absolute integrity."* A *"real professional"* and a senior figure in the market, he practices at state and federal level, handling regulatory and compliance matters. He currently represents the Baltimore Ravens NFL team. An *"extremely smart lawyer,"* **Stephen Immelt** (see p.333) focuses on healthcare and general civil litigation. He has advised clients in the healthcare sector on a wide variety of disputes including whistle-blower and antitrust litigation.

The Clients: Baltimore Ravens; State of Maryland; Maryland Stadium Authority; Duratek and LabCorp.

Venable LLP
The Firm: A regional firm that has secured its place on national cases. The group undertakes

REAL ESATE

MARYLAND

commercial litigation for corporate clients, including contract and corporate governance work. The firm has a growing plaintiffs' practice exercising claims against professional advice businesses, and has seen a growth in its workload from the shakeout of the internet boom. Stockholder disputes, IP and patents are also areas of concentration.

The Lawyers: John Lewin was described to researchers as a *"tough, effective litigator - professional, and a pleasure to work with."* He focuses on antitrust, securities fraud, trade secrets, and other business tort and contract matters. Observers described **James Shea** as a *"wonderful litigator."* Managing partner of the firm, he focuses on commercial and products liability litigation. Singled out for his technical skills, **Paul Strain** is often found representing pharmaceutical companies and other manufacturers in products liability and surety matters.

The Clients: Manufacturers and clients drawn from the hi-tech community are found on the firm's client roster.

Other Notable Practitioners
William Murphy of Murphy & Shaffer is respected for his work as local counsel. He represents individuals and small businesses in commercial disputes and is judged by interviewees to be a *"smart, capable lawyer."*

REAL ESTATE

MARYLAND
Leading firms (Real Estate)

1 BALLARD SPAHR ANDREWS *Baltimore*
PIPER RUDNICK LLP *Baltimore*
2 GORDON, FEINBLATT, ROTHMAN *Baltimore*
SHULMAN, ROGERS, GANDAL, PORDY *Rockville*
VENABLE LLP *Baltimore*
3 LINOWES AND BLOCHER LLP *Silver Spring*
SAUL EWING LLP *Baltimore*
WHITEFORD, TAYLOR & PRESTON LLP *Baltimore*
WILMER, CUTLER & PICKERING *Baltimore*

Leading individuals (Real Estate)

1 FISHER Morton *Ballard Spahr Andrews*, Baltimore
FISHMAN David *Gordon, Feinblatt, Rothman*, Baltimore
LEVIN Edward *Piper Rudnick LLP*, Baltimore
POLLAK Mark *Wilmer, Cutler & Pickering*, Baltimore
2 FISH Ronald *Ballard Spahr Andrews*, Baltimore
RENO Russell *Venable LLP*, Baltimore
SHULMAN Lawrence *Shulman, Rogers*, Rockville
3 GARFINK Roger *Saul Ewing LLP*, Baltimore
LEVINE Richard *Piper Rudnick LLP*, Baltimore
SHEPHERD Kevin *Venable LLP*, Baltimore
TRUITT Raymond *Ballard Spahr Andrews*, Baltimore
WRIGHT James *Venable LLP*, Baltimore
4 BARBUTI Thomas *Whiteford, Taylor*, Baltimore
CHRISS Timothy *Gordon, Feinblatt, Rothman*, Baltimore
MACHEN John *Piper Rudnick LLP*, Baltimore

Firms and individuals are listed alphabetically in each band.

Ballard Spahr Andrews & Ingersoll LLP
see firm details p.769

The Firm: The Baltimore office of this Philadelphia-based firm was acclaimed as one of the leading practices in Maryland, and was praised for its broad array of services. The team represents a mix of developers and institutional lenders and is frequently involved in complex commercial projects, including several downtown developments in and around Baltimore. The group's scope also extends to leasing, zoning and land use aa well as environmental issues arising from real estate.

The Lawyers: Researchers were impressed with the praise that was consistently bestowed upon a sizable group of *"capable and excellent"* attorneys. **Morton Fisher** was singled out as *"one of the leading real estate lawyers in the US."* He is a former chair of ACREL and continues to maintain a high profile in bar associations. Interviewees also endorsed **Ronald Fish** as a *"businesslike"* and knowledgeable attorney, skilled in real estate development. **Ray Truitt** was recommended as a visible younger lawyer in leasing and restructuring matters.

The Clients: The group regularly represents a supermarket chain, and has acted for a retailer in the acquisition and leasing of sites. It has also been involved in the preparation of a design, build and construction contract for a 450,000 sq ft perishable goods warehouse.

Piper Rudnick LLP
see firm details p.867

The Firm: Interviewees acknowledged that the firm maintains a profile in the local market, but felt that its nationwide scope was one of its main assets. The group acts for a range of lenders, including institutional and commercial banks, but the main emphasis of the practice is on the representation of developers. The group's portfolio includes suburban, city and retail development projects. Attorneys are on hand to advise on land use and zoning issues. The Baltimore group is also able to draw on the strength of colleagues in nearby DC. Highights have included acting for The Ryland Group in the acquisition of properties for residential development in the DC area, and advising Continental Realty in the sale and acquisition of apartment projects and shopping centers in Maryland and Florida.

The Lawyers: **Ed Levin** (see p.333), a seasoned campaigner, is principally known for his lender-oriented practice. Peers pointed to his *"pragmatic and get-the-deal-done"* style as his most valuable attribute. **Richard Levine** (see p.333) is a recent recruit from Miles & Stockbridge. He is a tax specialist, well versed in the structuring of real estate deals. **John Machen** (see p.334) was also recommended as a prominent player in the local market, where he has been involved in the renovation of historic buildings.

The Clients: AEGON USA Realty Advisors; The Ryland Group; Liberty Property Trust; Continental Realty; Constellation Real Estate and LaSalle Investment Management.

Gordon, Feinblatt, Rothman, Hoffberger & Hollander LLC

The Firm: Although smaller than some of its main rivals, the group stood out for the quality of its work on behalf of developers. It has also broadened its client base to include public entities and lenders. A varied workload has seen the group act for a REIT in the acquisition and financing of shopping centers in Maryland, Virginia and Pennsylvania, including lease negotiations. It has also represented a national bank in its acquisition, construction and Government subsidization of a credit-processing facility.

The Lawyers: The department's eight lawyers include **David Fishman**, who was recommended for his academic work and as *"a great guy to work with."* He has amassed a rich experience in the field, including litigation skills and the ability to *"keep the deal going."* **Tim Chriss** has been heavily involved in office development and leasing, and was tipped as the cream of the firm's younger attorneys.

The Clients: Mid-Atlantic Realty Trust; FRP Development; MedStar Health Systems; Bank One; American Port Services; Maryland Bankers Association and City of Baltimore.

Shulman, Rogers, Gandal, Pordy & Ecker PA

The Firm: *"A premier real estate shop"*, this group is frequently seen operating in the DC metropolitan area, where it is involved in commercial and residential developments. In commercial leasing, the group has acted for both tenants and landlords. It also has strengths in land use and zoning.

The Lawyers: A group numbering about 20 lawyers includes the highly experienced **Lawrence Shulman**. A commercial real estate and leasing expert, he is a fellow of ACREL and was described to researchers as a *"bright and truly excellent"* practitioner.

MARYLAND — REAL ESTATE

The Clients: The firm has experience representing banks, insurance companies and developers.

Venable LLP
The Firm: Market commentators agreed that this firm had succeeded in raising its regional profile, and is respected for its work on behalf of national companies. The group is involved in all aspects of real estate financing on behalf of borrowers and lenders. It also advises on the leasing, purchase and sale of commercial properties.

The Lawyers: Although the firm's other Maryland offices include Towson and Rockville, the majority of the real estate practitioners are based in Baltimore. **Russell Reno**, a senior member of the group, enjoys widespread recognition across the region. He divides his time between the representation of developers and lenders, and was described by peers as *"a hugely knowledgeable leader."* The *"talented"* **Kevin Shepherd** is one of the cochairs of the firm's real estate group. His client base includes developers and pension funds, and he impresses with his *"hard-working and detail-oriented"* approach. His colleague, **Jim Wright**, is a *"practical and pragmatic"* lawyer with substantial experience in the hotel industry.

The Clients: The firm's clients include financial institutions, developers, life insurance companies, pension funds and retailers.

Linowes and Blocher LLP
The Firm: Based in Silver Spring, the firm is supported by additional Maryland offices in Annapolis, Columbia and Frederick. Its reputation rests primarily on the high quality of its advice pertaining to land use and zoning laws; interviewees applauded its ability to guide clients successfully through the morass of regulations. It has also broadened its scope to provide coverage on real estate transactions and financing and environmental law.

The Lawyers: Although no single individual came to the fore, the firm undoubtedly lays claim to an experienced team. Name partner Joseph Blocher is active in zoning law, while partner David Cohen advises on real estate transactions.

The Clients: The stable of clients includes landowners, builders, real estate developers and investors, and entrepreneurs.

Saul Ewing LLP
The Firm: The real estate practice at this firm is regarded as heavily transactional in nature, and it has gained expertise from its work on a variety of real estate projects. Its workload typically involves advising on the acquisition, financing and construction of commercial, residential, retail and industrial facilities.

The Lawyers: Although smaller in size, the group fields a number of experienced attorneys. **Roger Garfink** is widely regarded as the group's key individual. With over 30 years in the business, Garfink has amassed a wealth of experience in the sector. He is currently handling financing and leasing matters for borrowers and landlords.

The Clients: The firm represents a number of institutional lenders including insurance companies, pension funds and commercial banks. It also acts for owners and developers, corporations and entrepreneurs.

Whiteford, Taylor & Preston LLP
The Firm: This well-balanced practice, with a strong statewide profile, is involved in real estate finance and development for an even mix of borrower and investor clients. It has recently experienced an upturn in residential sector work, and is also frequently involved in downtown urban redevelopment programs such as shopping mall and hotel matters.

The Lawyers: The focus of **Tom Barbuti**'s practice is commercial leasing, where he has earned a reputation as a *"bright and thorough"* attorney. He is experienced in both construction law and real estate finance. The group also fields a number of individuals who specialize in zoning and land use matters.

The Clients: The firm acts for a broad range of national and regional clients.

Wilmer, Cutler & Pickering
see firm details p.901

The Firm: This developer-based practice was recommended as a group of accomplished practitioners. The DC office supports a Baltimore operation, which has been involved in a number of significant transactions, such as advising Maryland Transit Administration on a public-private partnership for the development of a $300 million town center project. The group has also advised Bank of America on a major redevelopment project in downtown Baltimore, and represented the National Aquarium in Baltimore on expansion plans.

The Lawyers: Mark Pollak (see p.334) is credited with much of the group's profile in this area. He was highly recommended by peers for his urban redevelopment work.

The Clients: Equitable; National Aquarium in Baltimore; Maryland Transit Administration and Bank of America.

Leaders in Maryland

AYRES, Jeffrey
Venable LLP, Towson 410 494 6200
Recommended in Employment

BARBUTI, Thomas
Whiteford, Taylor & Preston LLP, Baltimore 410 347 8700
Recommended in Real Estate

BEALL, George
Hogan & Hartson LLP, Baltimore
410 659 2715
gbeall@hhlaw.com
Recommended in Litigation
Specialization: Partner in the Baltimore office of *Hogan & Hartson L.L.P.* and a member of the firm's Litigation Group. Focuses on civil and criminal litigation in both state and federal courts. Involved in every major contested takeover of a Maryland corporation between 1975 and 1990, representing some of the largest companies in the country. Handles regulatory, compliance and criminal matters involving 'white collar' offenses. Currently represents a Baltimore-based professional sports team.
Prof. Memberships: A fellow of the American College of Trial Lawyers. Serves as chairman of the US District Court for Maryland Magistrate Selection Panel; a member of the Maryland ADR Commission; and Chairman of the Fourth US Circuit Court of Appeals Advisory Committee on Rules and Procedures. A permanent member of the Judicial Conference for the Fourth US Circuit Court of Appeals and of the American Law Institute. Served on the Board of Governors of the Maryland Bar Association and the Executive Committee of the Baltimore City Bar Association, and a member of both.
Career: Served as law clerk for the late Honorable Simon E Sobeloff, then chief judge of the United States Court of Appeals for the Fourth Circuit. Following his clerkship, joined a Baltimore law firm concentrating in civil litigation, where became partner before assuming responsibilities as United States Attorney. Upon leaving the US Department of Justice, continued trial work as a partner with another Baltimore-based firm. (Presidential appointment as United States Attorney for the District of Maryland (1970-75).
Personal: JD from the University of Virginia School of Law, president of the law school student body, member of the National Moot Court Team and elected to a number of honor societies, including Omicron Delta Kappa.

BURCH JR, Francis B
Piper Rudnick LLP, Baltimore
410 580 4040
frank.burch@piperrudnick.com
Recommended in Litigation
Specialization: Litigation; class action; patent litigation; securities litigation.
Prof. Memberships: Fellow of the American College of Trial Lawyers; Member of The American Law Institute.
Career: He is co-chairman of the firm

and has been listed in a leading legal publication for over ten years. He represents public and private companies, as well as individuals, in the defense and prosecution of claims under the federal securities laws, in corporate control related litigation and in a broad spectrum of business litigation, including intellectual property matters.
Personal: JD, University of Maryland; AB, Georgetown University; serves on the Board of Johns Hopkins Medicine.

CAHILL, Kathleen
The Law Offices of Kathleen Cahill, LLC
Baltimore 410 321 6171
Recommended in Employment

CHRISS, Timothy
Gordon, Feinblatt, Rothman, Hoffberger & Hollander, LLC, Baltimore
410 576 4000
Recommended in Real Estate

COOK, Bryson
Venable LLP, Baltimore 410 244 7400
Recommended in Corporate/M&A

FISH, Ronald
Ballard Spahr Andrews & Ingersoll LLP, Baltimore 410 528 5600
Recommended in Real Estate

FISHER, Morton
Ballard Spahr Andrews & Ingersoll LLP, Baltimore 410 528 5600
Recommended in Real Estate

FISHMAN, David
Gordon, Feinblatt, Rothman, Hoffberger & Hollander, LLC, Baltimore
410 576 4000
Recommended in Real Estate

GAGLIARDO, Thomas
Thomas J Gagliardo (Sole Practitioner), Silver Spring 301 589 1900
Recommended in Employment

GARDNER, Russell H
Piper Rudnick LLP, Baltimore
410 580 4154
russell.gardner@piperrudnick.com
Recommended in Employment
Specialization: Labor and employment law; class action litigation.
Career: His practice encompasses all areas of management-side labor and employment discrimination. He regularly advises on union-avoidance matters, including representation before the National Labor Relations Board, employment discrimination and OSHA matters, and defense of employment claims, including ERISA claims, in state and federal courts across the nation. He has experience in drafting and enforcing employment agreements and non-competition agreements. He has written and lectured extensively on a variety of employment topics, particularly for the Americans with Disabilities Act.
Personal: JD, Syracuse University; BA, Alfred University.

GARFINK, Roger
Saul Ewing LLP, Baltimore
410 332 8600
Recommended in Real Estate

GODOFF, Stephen
The Law Offices of Stephen Godoff, Baltimore 410 539 0717
Recommended in Employment

GOLD, Carl
Carl R Gold (Sole Practitioner), Baltimore 410 337 5545
Recommended in Employment

GRAHAM, Andrew
Kramon & Graham, PA, Baltimore
410 752 6030
Recommended in Litigation

HAFETS, Richard J
Piper Rudnick LLP, Baltimore
410 580 4168
richard.hafets@piperrudnick.com
Recommended in Employment
Specialization: Homeland security; labor and employment law; class action litigation.
Career: He practices in all areas of labor and employment law, including union avoidance, traditional labor-management relations, employment litigation, EEO and affirmative action, OSHA, and general personnel. He is primary labor counsel to many Fortune 500 companies, healthcare institutions, charities, and civic organizations, and represents many of the firm's significant clients. Prior to joining *Piper Rudnick*, he worked with the National Labor Relations Board.
Personal: JD, American University; BS, American University.

HANKS, James
Ballard Spahr Andrews & Ingersoll LLP, Baltimore 410 528 5600
Recommended in Corporate/M&A

HEDIAN, Victoria
Abato, Rubenstein and Abato, PA, Baltimore 410 321 0990
Recommended in Employment

IMMELT, Stephen
Hogan & Hartson LLP, Baltimore
410 659 2757
sjimmelt@hhlaw.com
Recommended in Litigation
Specialization: Focuses primarily on white collar criminal litigation and complex litigation in the health and general commercial fields. Devotes a substantial part of his practice to healthcare issues. Has represented academic health centers and medical schools, hospitals, medical device and pharmaceutical companies, clinical laboratories, and other providers of healthcare in connection with a wide variety of governmental investigations, both civil and criminal in nature, involving issues arising under federal and state laws that govern health care providers. With regard to general civil litigation, has handled numerous commercial matters, with cases involving health care, whistleblower claims, education, officers and directors liability, securities fraud, and a variety of business torts.
Prof. Memberships: Permanent member of the Judicial Conference in the United States Court of Appeals for the Fourth Circuit. Association memberships include: American Health Lawyers Association, ABA Health Law Section and the National Association of College and University Attorneys. Member of the District of Columbia and Maryland Bars.
Career: Following law school, served one year as a law clerk to the Honorable Harrison L Winter, Circuit Judge for the United States Court of Appeals for the Fourth Circuit. After commencing private practice in Baltimore, was appointed as an Assistant United States Attorney for the District of Maryland, effective November 1979. During his service in that office, participated in numerous criminal trials dealing with political corruption, fraud, tax evasion, and conspiracy charges. Returned to private practice in the Fall of 1983 and joined *Hogan & Hartson L.L.P.* in August 1989.
Personal: Graduated from Yale College, cum laude, in 1974 and from the University of Maryland in 1977. While in law school, he served as Editor-in-Chief of the 'Maryland Law Review'.

KELLNER, Robert
Gordon, Feinblatt, Rothman, Hoffberger & Hollander, LLC, Baltimore
410 576 4000
Recommended in Employment

LEBAU, Steve
Lebau & Neuworth, LLC, Baltimore
410 296 3030
Recommended in Employment

LEVIN, Edward J
Piper Rudnick LLP, Baltimore
410 580 4700
edward.levin@piperrudnick.com
Recommended in Real Estate
Specialization: Real estate; real estate finance.
Prof. Memberships: Member of the American College of Real Estate Lawyers (ACREL).
Career: He has lectured at and chaired seminars sponsored by the American College of Real Estate Lawyers, the American Bar Association, the Maryland Institute for Continuing Professional Education of Lawyers, Inc, and the Section of Real Property, Planning and Zoning of the Maryland State Bar Association.
Publications: Co-author of Maryland Real Estate Leasing Forms - Practice; author of numerous articles on attorneys' opinions and other real property-related matters.
Personal: JD, University of Virginia; BA, The Johns Hopkins University, with honors.

LEVINE, Richard E
Piper Rudnick LLP, Baltimore
410 580 4400
rich.levine@piperrudnick.com
Recommended in Real Estate
Specialization: Business tax; real estate; corporate and securities.
Prof. Memberships: Fellow of American College of Tax Counsel.
Career: He is nationally recognized in the area of partnership and real estate taxation and represents many of the leading real estate entrepreneurs in the Maryland area. He focuses his practice on sophisticated real estate transactions which frequently involve complex tax issues. He is also listed in alternative legal publications.
Personal: JD, University of Maryland 1975; LLM, Georgetown University Law Center; BS, Mechanical Engineering, Bucknell University.

LEWIN, John
Venable LLP, Baltimore
410 244 7400
Recommended in Litigation

LOHR JR, Walter
Hogan & Hartson LLP, Baltimore
410 659 2764
wglohr@hhlaw.com
Recommended in Corporate/M&A
Specialization: Partner in the Baltimore office of *Hogan & Hartson L.L.P.* and member of the Corporate, Securities and Finance Group. Represents clients in a broad range of transactions, including public and private offerings of securities, mergers and acquisitions, and organization of partnerships and joint ventures. Has been involved in matters where corporate control was contested. In addition to transactional work, provides ongoing representation to corporations, partnerships and other business enterprises. Clients have included both private and publicly-held interests.
Prof. Memberships: Serves on the Board of Directors of a New York Stock Exchange listed, publicly-held corporation, as well as several privately-held corporations. Served on the Advisory Board of a venture capital limited partnership sponsored by a major US life insurance company.
Career: Served for two years as an Assistant Attorney General for the State of Maryland, where he principally represented higher education agencies in litigation and other matters. From 1977 to 1987, was partner in the corporate and securities department of a large law firm based in Baltimore. From 1988 to 1992, was a sole practitioner, representing a small number of clients in connection with business and investment interests.
Personal: Graduated from Princeton University in 1966 and from Yale Law School in 1969. Is a Trustee of the Baltimore Museum of Art and a past trustee and officer of Gilman School.

MARYLAND — LEADERS

MACHEN, John
Piper Rudnick LLP, Baltimore
410 580 4444
jack.machen@piperrudnick.com
Recommended in Real Estate
Specialization: Real estate.
Career: He practices in the areas of commercial real estate financing and real estate development, including property acquisition, disposition, and leasing. He has represented lenders and developers in a variety of commercial enterprises, including shopping centers, office buildings, condominiums, townhouses, and apartments, with respect to acquisition, construction and permanent financing, syndication, leasing, sale, foreclosures, and negotiated workouts.
Personal: JD, University of Maryland; BA, Princeton University.

MATHIAS, Robert
Piper Rudnick LLP, Baltimore
410 580 4209
robert.mathias@piperrudnick.com
Recommended in Litigation
Specialization: Litigation; class action litigation; patent litigation; securities litigation; white collar.
Prof. Memberships: American College of Trial Lawyers, Fellow, Complex Litigation Committee.
Career: His primary areas of practice are business litigation, intellectual property litigation and white collar criminal advice to corporate clients. He has tried cases and argued appeals in the federal and state courts in a number of jurisdictions and has extensive experience with many different types of alternative dispute resolution. He is listed in several leading legal publications.
Personal: JD, Harvard Law School, BA, Yale University.

MCGEE JR, Emmett F
Piper Rudnick LLP, Baltimore
410 580 4211
emmett.mcgee@piperrudnick.com
Recommended in Employment
Specialization: Labor and employment law.
Career: He represents employers in all aspects of employment law and human resource management, including employment discrimination, wage and hour issues and affirmative action planning. His practice includes litigation in state and federal courts throughout the US, as well as before administrative agencies and arbitration panels. He also has extensive experience in areas of employment contracts, trade secrets and restrictive covenants, and related litigation, as well as the litigation of ERISA claims and stock option claims.
Personal: JD, University of Virginia; BA, Johns Hopkins University.

MCGUIRE, J Michael
Shawe & Rosenthal LLP, Baltimore
410 752 1040
mcguire@shawe.com
Recommended in Employment
Specialization: Labor management relations on behalf of management; employment discrimination; human resources advice and counsel; employment agreements; employment tort and contract litigation; employment handbooks, policies, and procedures; wage and hour laws; Occupational Safety and Health Acts; Family and Medical Leave Act; Workers' Adjustment and Retraining Act.
Prof. Memberships: Bar Admissions: Maryland (State and Federal); US Court of Appeals for the 4th, 9th and 11th Circuits. American Bar Association; Maryland State Bar Association; Maryland Association of Defense Trial Counsel.
Personal: University of Maryland School of Law, JD, cum laude, 1978 Recipient, Joseph Bernstein Prize; University of Maryland, BA 1975.

MURPHY, William
Murphy & Shaffer, Baltimore
410 783 7000
Recommended in Litigation

NILSON, George
Piper Rudnick LLP, Baltimore
410 580 4227
george.nilson@piperrudnick.com
Recommended in Litigation
Specialization: Environmental; litigation; class action litigation; state legislation and public policy; white collar.
Career: He has had significant involvement in environmental controversies (hazardous waste, toxic torts, gasoline contamination, landfill litigation, removal of asbestos products from buildings), public and administrative law, election law controversies, tobacco litigation, cable television controversies, consumer controversies (range of regulatory and litigation issues presented by automobile dealers, condominium developers/sellers, time-share ventures and commercial lenders), zoning and litigation relating to real estate development, and complex civil litigation generally.
Personal: LLB, Yale University; BA, Master of Urban Studies, Yale School of Art and Architecture; BA, Yale College.

PALTELL, Eric
Kollman & Saucier PA, Baltimore
410 727 4300
Recommended in Employment

POKEMPNER, Joseph
Whiteford, Taylor & Preston LLP, Baltimore 410 347 8700
Recommended in Employment

POLLAK, Mark
Wilmer, Cutler & Pickering, Baltimore
410 986 2860
Mark.Pollak@wilmer.com
Recommended in Real Estate
Specialization: Partner in firm's business transactions section, with more than 30 years of experience in real estate development and finance and municipal finance matters. Known particularly for involvement in the public financing of complex real estate projects, major sports stadiums, and the creation of public-private partnerships for development of central business districts. Has been involved with development activities in downtown Baltimore, Maryland and works closely with the business community for the betterment of Baltimore City. Recently selected as one of two top real estate lawyers in a poll of lawyers conducted by a US magazine.
Prof. Memberships: American College of Real Estate Lawyers; National Association of Bond Lawyers; American Planning Association.
Career: Admitted to Maryland Bar (1972). Joined firm in 1999.
Personal: Graduate of Brooklyn College (BA, cum laude, 1968) and the University of Pennsylvania (JD 1972; Masters in City Planning 1972). Member, Board of Directors and Executive Committee for the Baltimore Children's Museum Downtown Partnership of Baltimore, Inc.

PONTONE, Kathleen
Miles & Stockbridge PC, Baltimore
410 727 6464
Recommended in Employment

RENO, Russell
Venable LLP, Baltimore 410 244 7400
Recommended in Real Estate

ROSENBERG, James
Abato, Rubenstein and Abato, PA, Baltimore 410 321 0990
Recommended in Employment

SHAWE, Stephen D
Shawe & Rosenthal LLP, Baltimore
410 752 1040
sshawe@shawe.com
Recommended in Employment
Specialization: Labor-management relations on behalf of management; employment discrimination; human resources advice and counsel; employment tort and contract litigation; employment handbooks, policies, and procedures; wage and hour laws; Occupational Safety and Health Acts; Affirmative Action Programs; Family and Medical Leave Act; Workers' Adjustment and Retraining Act; appellate litigation; class actions; and alternative dispute resolution.
Prof. Memberships: Bar Admissions: Maryland (State and Federal); US Court of Appeals for the 4th Circuit; Supreme Court of the United States. American Bar Association; Maryland State Bar Association; Bar Association of Baltimore City.
Personal: Education: Harvard Law School, LLB, 1965; Williams College, BA, cum laude, 1962.

SHEA, James
Venable LLP, Baltimore
410 244 7400
Recommended in Litigation

SHEPHERD, Kevin
Venable LLP, Baltimore
410 244 7400
Recommended in Real Estate

SHULMAN, Lawrence
Shulman, Rogers, Gandal, Pordy & Ecker, PA, Rockville 301 230 5200
Recommended in Real Estate

SILVER, Michael J
Hogan & Hartson LLP, Baltimore
410 659 2741
mjsilver@hhlaw.com
Recommended in Corporate/M&A
Specialization: Practices in the areas of corporate, securities, mergers and acquisitions and general business law. Has represented underwriters and issuers on a large number of public and private securities offerings and has extensive experience in a wide variety of public and private mergers and acquisitions, corporate organization and governance issues, and general securities law advice to public companies. Has acted as outside counsel on securities and mergers and acquisitions matters to a wide variety of companies, including Deutsche Bank, CIENA Corporation, Laboratory Corporation of America Holdings, Wabash National Corporation, Guilford Pharmaceuticals Inc. and Martek Biosciences Corporation.
Prof. Memberships: Maryland Bar since 1980.
Career: Associate at *Piper & Marbury* 1980-87, Partner from 1987 until 1992. Joined *Hogan & Hartson LLP* as a Partner in 1992.
Personal: Was identified as one of fewer than 100 lawyers in North America in a 2002 national survey of General Counsel at Fortune 1000 companies for "delivering truly outstanding and superior client service". Received his AB, magna cum laude, from Harvard University in 1977, and his law degree from the University of Chicago Law School in 1980.

SILVESTRI, Stephen
Miles & Stockbridge PC, Baltimore
410 727 6464
Recommended in Employment

SINGLETON, John
Albertini, Singleton, Gendler & Darby LLP, Baltimore 410 243 9400
Recommended in Employment

SMITH, Joel
Kahn, Smith & Collins, PA, Baltimore
410 244 1010
Recommended in Employment

MARYLAND

SMITH JR, Robert (Jay) W
Piper Rudnick LLP, Baltimore
410 580 4266
jay.smith@piperrudnick.com
Recommended in Corporate/M&A
Specialization: Business and technology; biosciences; corporate and securities; mergers and acquisitions; venture capital and emerging companies.
Career: His practice focuses on public and private offerings of debt and equity securities, mergers and acquisitions, and general representation of public and private companies. A significant portion of his practice includes representation of issuers and underwriters in connection with the sale of securities by existing public companies, as well as the initial public offering of securities by emerging companies in the technology, biotechnology and real estate industries.
Personal: JD, University of Maryland; BS, The Wharton School of Finance, University of Pennsylvania.

STRAIN, Paul
Venable LLP, Baltimore
410 244 7400
Recommended in Litigation

TAYLOR, Ronald
Venable LLP, Baltimore
410 244 7400
Recommended in Employment

TILGHMAN JR, Richard
Piper Rudnick LLP, Baltimore
410 580 4274
richard.tilghman@piperrudnick.com
Recommended in Corporate/M&A
Specialization: Business and technology; biosciences; corporate and securities; mergers and acquisitions; homeland security.
Career: He practices in the area of corporate and securities law, primarily representing growth oriented companies and underwriters in the public or private offering of equity securities. He also has substantial experience in a wide range of private and public offerings of debt and asset-backed securities, including various transactions under Rule 144A and various structured finance transactions. He currently represents a number of growth oriented public and private companies, providing securities, corporate and general business advice.
Personal: JD, University of Maryland; BA, Union University.

TRUITT, Raymond
Ballard Spahr Andrews & Ingersoll LLP, Baltimore 410 528 5600
Recommended in Real Estate

ULWICK, James
Kramon & Graham, PA, Baltimore
410 752 6030
Recommended in Litigation

WASHBURNE, Thomas
Venable LLP, Baltimore 410 244 7400
Recommended in Corporate/M&A

WATKINS, John (Jay) B
Wilmer, Cutler & Pickering, Baltimore
410 986 2820
John.Watkins@wilmer.com
Recommended in Corporate/M&A
Specialization: Partner in firm's business transactions section, whose general corporate and securities practice has a particular emphasis on securities offerings transactions (both public and private), equity and debt investments, mergers and acquisitions, and real estate investment trusts (REITS). Has advised a wide range of clients on complex corporate and securities matters and has handled acquisitions and securities offerings transactions for many public and private companies. Also has represented numerous investment banking firms, as well as merchant banking, private equity, and venture capital funds in connection with securities offering matters, acquisitions of controlling interests, and debt and equity investments.
Prof. Memberships: ABA Business Law Section (Federal Regulation of Securities and Partnerships and Unincorporated Business Organizations Committees).
Career: Admitted to Maryland (1981) and District of Columbia (1998) bars. Partner of the firm since joining in 1996. Has been an instructor in numerous continuing education courses in the area of corporate and securities laws.
Personal: Graduate of The Johns Hopkins University (BA 1977, with honors) and the University of Michigan Law School (JD 1981).

WEBB, Thompson
Miles & Stockbridge PC, Baltimore
410 727 6464
Recommended in Corporate/M&A

WOLF, Larry
Whiteford, Taylor & Preston LLP, Baltimore 410 347 8700
Recommended in Employment

WRIGHT, James
Venable LLP, Baltimore 410 244 7400
Recommended in Real Estate

MASSACHUSETTS

ANTITRUST

CONTENTS: Antitrust p.336; Banking & Finance p.338; Corporate/M&A p.339; Employment: Mainly Plaintiff p.341; Mainly Defendant p.342; Environment p.344; Insolvency p.346; Intellectual Property p.348; Litigation: General Commercial p.348; Private Equity p.350; Real Estate p.351; Tax p.353; Individuals' Profiles p.354.

MASSACHUSETTS' TOP SEVEN
1. Goodwin Procter
1. Hale and Dorr
2. Ropes & Gray
3. Foley Hoag
4. Bingham McCutchen
5. Mintz Levin Cohn Ferris Glovsky and Popeo
6. Testa, Hurwitz & Thibeault

Ranking based on Chambers' research within the state.

All quotes in the text are from interviews with clients and competitors.

OVERVIEW: Two firms share first place in *Chambers'* tables in Massachusetts. **Goodwin Procter** has a stable of excellent attorneys who performed well during our research. The talented group, under the guidance of chairman and managing partner Regina Pisa, is noted for its corporate practice's commercial and financial mastery, while the banking practice is admired for its quality throughout the ranks. The tax group is transactions-oriented and a strong competitor. The firm has in its portfolio a number of impressive matters and clients, including work for Citizens Financial and Boston Private Financial Holdings.

Hale and Dorr joins Goodwin Procter at the top. Its litigation group enjoys a fabulous reputation for its top-quality lawyers and their ability to tackle complex matters. The firm's top-level corporate and commercial work is weighted toward technology clients, and competitors complimented the firm's branding in this area. Leader of the corporate practice Mark Borden and his group offer the whole package in major M&A and financing matters. A large number of skilled insolvency attorneys were recommended, and the firm has an enviable tax capability. Litigator Bill Lee tops the tables as the leading IP specialist in the state.

Ropes & Gray is an established and prominent competitor, with a leading litigation practice. The firm also tops the tables with its large tax group and an imposing corporate group that represents many impressive commercial and financial institutions. The top-tier labor and employment group benefits from the presence of top lawyers in all disciplines. Additionally, the firm's expertise in antitrust, private equity, insolvency and banking comes highly recommended. Among the firm's high-profile clients are Goldman Sachs and Fidelity.

Foley Hoag is a leader for its environmental practice, led by two respected experts, Laurie Burt and Seth Jaffe. The group's work in urban redevelopment and Superfund matters is particularly impressive. A stalwart contender in many of *Chambers'* tables, its litigation leader Michael Keating is worthy of peers' praise, and mention must also be made of the firm's successful groups specializing in corporate matters, IP, labor and employment, antitrust, and banking and finance.

Bingham McCutchen's formation in July 2002 combined the established presence in Boston of Bingham Dana with West Coast firm McCutchen, Doyle, Brown & Enersen. The resulting powerhouse has combined Bingham Dana's reputation for quality corporate and litigation representation with McCutchen Doyle's West Coast presence and capabilities. The firm is a leader in the Boston market for antitrust and banking, with admirable practices in litigation, corporate/M&A, tax and labor and employment. Attorneys here have a number of big-ticket transactions under their belts, along with high-profile clients such as Fleet Bank and the Boston Red Sox.

Researchers found that **Mintz Levin Cohn Ferris Glovsky and Popeo** is particularly admired for both its dynamic environmental practice and its insolvency practice. The firm's litigation group also wins praise for its resolute representation of its clients. Litigator Robert Popeo's name was mentioned to researchers in several practice areas and he remains a key member of the firm. Clients include AOL, Fleet Bank and Compaq.

Testa, Hurwitz & Thibeault's private equity practice soars above competitors' and two top-ranked individuals, Robin Painter and David Tegeler, lead the pack in this area. The firm suffered a blow in December 2002 with the death of founding partner and highly influential Dick Testa. Managing partner William Asher leads a large and highly active corporate practice with a focus on tech-oriented clients. The firm's tax practice is of notable size and weight, and Dean Gordanier was mentioned as one of the cream of the crop.

ANTITRUST

MASSACHUSETTS
Leading firms (Antitrust)

1. BINGHAM MCCUTCHEN LLP *Boston*
   NUTTER, MCCLENNEN & FISH LLP *Boston*
2. HALE AND DORR *Boston*
   ROPES & GRAY *Boston*
3. CHOATE HALL & STEWART *Boston*
   FOLEY HOAG LLP *Boston*
   PALMER & DODGE *Boston*

Firms are listed alphabetically in each band.

Bingham McCutchen LLP

The Firm: The firm boasts one of the largest competition teams in Boston, with 12 dedicated attorneys focusing on antitrust and trade regulation matters. The group offers counseling services and has experience in both civil and criminal litigation. Noteworthy expertise exists in relation to government enforcement issues, compliance programs, pricing and distribution, monopolization, licensing, M&A, alliances and joint ventures and standards setting.

The Lawyers: Interviewees identified **John (Jack) Curtin** as one of Boston's *"leading lights"* in antitrust. An *"accomplished and gifted"* lawyer, Curtin devotes a significant proportion of his general commercial litigation practice to complex antitrust cases. He recently acted in international price-fixing cartel matters in the isostatic graphite and carbon fiber industries. **Daniel Goldberg** enjoys considerable renown for his work in drafting the Massachusetts Antitrust Act. His practice encompasses merger review, product distribution and general antitrust counseling.

The Clients: Attorneys have represented vitamin and feed additive companies in indirect purchaser litigation arising from international price-fixing cartel allegations, and acted for Supermercados Amigos in the antitrust clearance of its acquisition by Wal-Mart. Other clients include GM, Toyota, FLEXcon, BMW of North America, Porche Cars of North America, Massachusetts Society of Certified Public Accountants, Freightliners and Sterling Truck Corporation.

Nutter, McClennen & Fish LLP

The Firm: A ten-lawyer team offers antitrust counsel in connection with M&A and joint venture transactions and provides day-to-day advice on antitrust compliance to the firm's large base of corporate clients. Attorneys possess considerable litigation experience in both the federal and state courts and in trade regulation investigations, and have advised on cases involving monopolization, exclusive dealing, business irregularities and multi-defendant conspiracy.

The Lawyers: Interviewees report that **Neil Motenko** is *"highly sought after for antitrust, both in and outside the state,"* for his *"impressive array of skills."* His practice is largely focused on antitrust issues, of which much is litigation, acting both for

MASSACHUSETTS

Leading individuals (Antitrust)

1
- CURTIN John *Bingham McCutchen LLP,* Boston
- MOTENKO Neil *Nutter, McClennen & Fish LLP,* Boston

2
- ARMISTEAD Cary *Ropes & Gray,* Boston
- BRUNELL Richard *Foley Hoag LLP,* Boston
- BUCHANAN Robert *Choate Hall & Stewart,* Boston
- BURLING James *Hale and Dorr,* Boston
- MILLER Michelle *Hale and Dorr,* Boston
- PATTON William *Ropes & Gray,* Boston

3
- FUGUET Howard *Ropes & Gray,* Boston
- GOLDBERG Daniel *Bingham McCutchen LLP,* Boston
- SCOTT Thane *Palmer & Dodge,* Boston
- WOOD Lisa *Nutter, McClennen & Fish LLP,* Boston

Individuals are listed alphabetically in each band.

plaintiffs and defendants. He is particularly renowned for his work in the healthcare sector and cochairs the firm's healthcare group. In addition to his litigation practice, Motenko provides general antitrust advice on dealing with the DOJ and the FTC. Market sources commend **Lisa Wood** as an *"active lawyer who knows her field inside out."* She cochairs the antitrust group and in this area is mainly involved in litigation, which is in large part civil defense work.

The Clients: Clients are drawn from industry sectors such as manufacturing, distribution, retail, technology, healthcare, chemical and real estate.

Hale and Dorr

The Firm: The 12-strong antitrust practice is one of the largest in the rankings and earns respect from peers for *"breadth of experience."* The group's workload is divided between civil litigation and Government-initiated matters (such as Hart-Scott-Rodino merger matters and investigations). The practice has a heavy focus on technology-related matters, benefiting from the firm's concentration of clients in this sector.

The Lawyers: Cochair of the antitrust group, **James Burling** advises on both government and private matters and enjoys a loyal following among clients within the pharmaceutical, biotech and computer industries. He acts in three cases asserting monopolization claims against Ocean Spray regarding cranberry products. He represented Avid Technology in a monopolization and conspiracy case in the US District Court Central District of California and in the Ninth Circuit Court of Appeals. **Michelle Miller** is vice chair of both the antitrust and trade regulation group and the litigation group. She acts on antitrust class actions, merger investigations and antitrust counterclaims in IP cases and advises clients on the antitrust aspects of distribution and licensing agreements. Representative work includes price-fixing class actions pending in the state court in Massachusetts, and an antitrust counterclaim arising out of a patent infringement suit for ASML (a Netherlands-based company), pending in the US District Court Northern District of California.

The Clients: Other clients include EMC, Analog Devices and Wyeth.

Ropes & Gray
see firm details p.870

The Firm: The Boston antitrust group of this large firm numbers three attorneys, all of whom were recommended to researchers. They offer guidance in a range of transactional and litigious antitrust issues. These include distribution, licensing, government enforcement, mergers and price-fixing and extend to international representation and advice in industries including hi-tech, sport and healthcare.

The Lawyers: Head of the trial and litigation department, **Bill Patton** (see p.358) is highly commended by peers. His general litigation experience includes a significant practice in antitrust and IP issues. Clients recommend **Cary Armistead** (see p.354) for his *"practical, business-oriented manner."* His antitrust practice includes handling government investigations and analysis of proposed or actual mergers and acquisitions. He works both within the US and internationally, and advises on European competition laws. **Howard Fuguet** (see p.356) is considered a strong counselor with particular expertise in the corporate securities arena. His antitrust practice encompasses pricing, distribution and marketing issues, advising on joint ventures and acquisitions, and representing clients in front of the DOJ and FTC.

The Clients: The group advises a large number of private equity firms such as Fenway Partners and Berkshire Partners on antitrust issues. Highlights include representation of Bain Capital as part of a consortium of investors that acquired Burger King for $1.5 billion. The firm also advises retail clients Timberland and Gillette.

Choate Hall & Stewart

The Firm: This Boston firm's antitrust work includes litigation, managing antitrust issues in transactions, and advising on state and federal antitrust law.

The Lawyers: Commercial litigator **Robert Buchanan** is widely respected for his focus on antitrust litigation and counseling. This *"able"* attorney represented a hi-tech company in bringing its merger through a second request investigation by the FTC.

The Clients: Antitrust clients include venture capital and hi-tech companies, healthcare institutions and professional associations.

Foley Hoag LLP

The Firm: The firm's trade regulation practice comprises six Boston attorneys and an additional specialist in the DC office. The group is experienced in antitrust litigation and regularly advises clients on antitrust issues arising out of transactions and federal and state regulations.

The Lawyers: Researchers were told that **Richard Brunell** possesses a *"thorough knowledge"* of antitrust law. His practice emphasizes defense litigation and includes Hart-Scott-Rodino filings and investigations, and other governmental investigations, as well as private litigation, class action defense, price-fixing cases, and unfair and deceptive practices claims. He also provides pre-merger advice and counsels on distribution issues. He has defended several companies against price-fixing allegations in the Massachusetts state court, including multinational vitamin manufacturers and makers of food flavor enhancers, and has acted on behalf of American Honda Motor Co in private antitrust and unfair practices cases. The group is led by Gloria Larson, a former Massachusetts Secretary of Consumer Affairs and Business Regulation.

The Clients: Representative matters include ongoing work for PG&E Corp and its national energy group in a federal case involving several claims including Section 7 of the Clayton Act and price-fixing claims. The firm provides antitrust counseling to trade groups that include the Financial Services Technology Consortium and the Banking Industry Technology Secretariat.

Palmer & Dodge

The Firm: A four-attorney practice offers a full range of antitrust litigation and counseling services. Attorneys are adept at advising on avoidance of antitrust-related risk and government actions as well as the prosecution and defense of complex litigation.

The Lawyers: Group chair **Thane Scott** was said to *"do an excellent job for his clients."* He focuses on trade regulation, and is active in both counseling and litigation at the state and federal court level.

The Clients: A stable base of clients ranges from NYSE-listed corporations to small companies.

MASSACHUSETTS — BANKING & FINANCE

BANKING & FINANCE

MASSACHUSETTS
Leading firms (Banking & Finance)

1. **BINGHAM MCCUTCHEN LLP** Boston
   GOODWIN PROCTER LLP Boston
2. **EDWARDS & ANGELL LLP** Boston
   FOLEY HOAG LLP Boston
3. **ROPES & GRAY** Boston

Leading individuals (Banking & Finance)

1. **CURTIN Neal** Bingham McCutchen LLP, Boston
   MAYER William Goodwin Procter LLP, Boston
2. **BARR Lynne** Goodwin Procter LLP, Boston
   COOGAN Peter Foley Hoag LLP, Boston
   PISA Regina Goodwin Procter LLP, Boston
   SMITH Edwin Bingham McCutchen LLP, Boston
   SMITH Philip Ropes & Gray, Boston
3. **COUKOS Steven** Edwards & Angell LLP, Boston
   EHRLICH Kenneth Nutter, McClennen & Fish, Boston
   LYONS Gregory Goodwin Procter LLP, Boston

Firms and individuals are listed alphabetically in each band.

Bingham McCutchen LLP

The Firm: The 2002 merger between Bingham Dana and McCutchen Doyle has given extra weight to this already highly respected banking group, which now houses 15 full-time partners. The firm has a strong restructuring orientation, with the remaining workload divided between asset-based lending, and mezzanine, acquisition and cashflow financing, often involving multiple jurisdictions. In the restructuring sphere, the group undertakes debtor-in-possession financing and has advised senior bank lenders in workouts and bankruptcies such as those of Republic Technologies and NationsRent.

Peers recommended this *"strong institution"* for its association with large, sophisticated clients, describing the attorneys here as *"good caretakers of a relationship."* Clients point to the firm as *"the main players,"* noting its international reach and depth of experience. A historical relationship with the former Bank of Boston and extensive current dealings with Fleet Bank ensure this group its outstanding profile. Highlights include representing Eastern Bank in its acquisition of Allied American Insurance Agency and advising senior lenders in major bankruptcy matters

The Lawyers: Cochair of the firm's financial institutions, corporate and regulatory group **Neal Curtin** is a *"long-term player"* and *"éminence grise,"* experienced in the most sophisticated transactions. Curtin is active in M&A for banks and bank holding firms, and company conversions and restructurings. His workload has an international element, often undertaking transactions in sub-Saharan Africa, South America and the Caribbean. A key relationship builder at the firm, Curtin is admired for his tough negotiating skills and a personable approach. He has handled Fleet Bank's acquisition of Liberty Financial asset management companies, and handled the reprivatization of Uganda Commercial Bank for The Bank of Uganda. *"Dean of the bar,"* **Edwin Smith** chairs the finance-related area. His practice focuses on debt financings, workouts, bankruptcies and international transactions. He has advised senior lenders on high-profile bankruptcies, including Enron, Covanta Energy, NationsRent and Adelphia, and was part of the drafting committee of the Uniform Commercial Code dealing with secure financings. Described as a *"leading scholar and commentator,"* his wealth of experience includes debtor-in-possession financings and complex syndicated transactions.

The Clients: Fleet Bank; State Street Bank; Eastern Bank; Union Bank of California; Deutsche Bank; Citigroup; JPMorgan Chase; Wachovia; Crédit Agricole and Standard Chartered Bank.

Goodwin Procter LLP
see firm details p.805

The Firm: The substantial banking group at Goodwin Procter won broad acclaim from both peers and clients for its extensive practice and deep bench of experienced attorneys. Its representation of community banks is well known in the market, and the firm has succeeded in securing a profile for its growing activity with larger financial entities. Peers respected the team as a strong referral candidate for regulatory work, and also recommended its M&A, FCC and securities law expertise. Clients stressed the importance of the *"high level of consistency"* among the firm's lawyers, who produce uniformly *"top-notch work"* while remaining responsive to commercial deadlines. Researchers were informed that the firm has successfully developed its banking practice, and that the emergence of a third generation of practitioners is set to retain command of a strong market share. The group's move into the New York market is expected to help it develop a greater national presence. The firm has already established a base in DC, which provides a valuable resource for tracking developments on a federal level. Recently, the Boston-based group worked on major transactions for Citizens Financial, and assisted Phoenix Insurance in the establishment of banks. The team has also aided Boston Private Financial Holdings in its acquisition of a bank in California.

The Lawyers: In this *"stable of excellent lawyers,"* clients identified several *"good lieutenants,"* including **William Mayer**. Respected for his representation of community banks, Mayer advises on bank regulatory matters involving state and federal law, offerings of debt and equity securities, and bank formations and reorganizations. Peers recommended his *"top-flight advice,"* sound judgment and vast experience, and pointed to his strong litigation background. *"A class act,"* **Lynne Barr** won broad acclaim for her expertise in electronic banking and consumer and retail banking matters, involving contract negotiations and issues arising from privacy laws. Her clients include Fidelity Investments, Fleet Bank and GE Consumer Finance, and she is general counsel to both the Massachusetts Bankers Association and the Electronic Funds Transfer Association. **Regina Pisa** remains highly visible in the banking arena despite her duties as managing partner of the firm. Her practice focuses on M&A and securities activities. Respected for her work with Citizens Bank, Pisa was commended as *"a hard-working and effective counselor."* The broad regulatory and transactional banking practice of **Greg Lyons** contains niche work advising financial institutions on how to broaden their activities. Clients reported that *"his energy levels are off the chart,"* and valued his close management of a case.

The Clients: Citizens Financial; Fifth Third Bancorp; Chittenden Corporation and NYCE.

Edwards & Angell LLP

The Firm: Close historical ties as outside counsel to Fleet Bank and its affiliates earn this firm a high profile in the banking and finance arena. Peers acknowledge that this relationship gives the group *"a real advantage,"* allowing its attorneys to develop the depth of experience that sees it *"able to handle anything thrown at them."* A variety of lending and commercial finance issues are undertaken, while the regulatory practice was the subject of frequent plaudits by market commentators. More recently the focus here has been on developing the client base to service the needs of smaller financial institutions.

The Lawyers: Observers pointed to **Steven Coukos**, *"a bright young lawyer,"* who is credited with being the group's driving force, particularly in the development of its relationships with smaller finance houses. The *"energetic and strong"* Coukos has a practice focusing on banking regulation, M&A and corporate and securities law. He has advised FleetBoston in acquisitions and joint ventures, and has a broad clientele that includes regional and community banks.

The Clients: Fleet Bank; Citizens Bank; Keybank; Sovereign Bank; PNC Bank; community banks and thrifts.

Foley Hoag LLP

The Firm: Distinguished by its representation of New England-based community banks and thrift institutions. A group of seven attorneys undertakes a broad spectrum of banking and finance

CORPORATE/M&A — MASSACHUSETTS

matters, including the representation of bidders and targets in acquisition financing, securities issues and regulatory work. The group counsels smaller finance houses and provides securities advice to larger banks. Interviewees recommended the breadth of experience available, and the *"intellectual horsepower"* of its attorneys. Clients appreciate that *"they have the staff to cover almost everything,"* and recommended them especially for their *"general interpretation of banking law for the introduction of new products."*
The Lawyers: *"One of the real class performers in the business,"* **Peter Coogan** provides counsel to various financial institutions on the creation of de novo banks, M&A in the financial arena, and bank reorganizations. Coogan earns the respect of peers with his understanding of UCC and banking regulation matters. They refer to his *"intellectual capacity and knowledge"* and his *"style and carriage,"* while clients appreciate his understanding of technical details and his high level of personal involvement.
The Clients: Banknorth Group; Abington Bancorp; Seacoast Financial Services Corporation; Provident Bank; Benjamin Franklin Savings Bank; Randolph Savings Bank and UniBank for Savings.

Ropes & Gray
see firm details p.870
The Firm: This blue blood firm has capitalized on its outstanding corporate reputation to develop a dedicated banking practice. The group represents both lenders and borrowers in cash flow transactions, capital raisings, mutual fund and FCC work. The group has recently handled a $400 million credit facility to the United States Can Company, and a $465 million facility to Domino's Pizza. Commentators describe attorneys here as *"attaining high professional standards."* They have secured key client relationships, such as the representation of Fleet Bank. Although less visible in a regulatory role, the depth of this *"pedigree"* firm's bench affords it the capabilities to undertake high-quality transactions for the biggest clients.
The Lawyers: Cohead of the private equity group, **Philip Smith** (see p.359) specializes in LBO and private equity financings, syndicated bank loans, and high yield debt. Smith has represented Boston Ventures, Bain Capital, Berkshire Partners and Fenway Partners in lending transactions. A senior figure in the market, he is a *"recognized expert"* among peers.
The Clients: Fleet Bank; ABN AMRO; JPMorgan Chase and Sankaty Advisors.

Other Notable Practitioners
A new recruit to Nutter McClennen & Fish LLP, **Kenneth Ehrlich** serves as corporate and regulatory counsel to banks and savings institutions. His workload is evenly divided between large banks and smaller community institutions. Interviewees endorsed Ehrlich's representation of community banks and credit unions, and remarked that he is *"smart, capable and will work hard to get the job done."* The market anticipates that he will grow the firm's practice. Ehrlich's clients include: Mellon Financial; State Street; Citizens Bank; ChartBank and Navisbank.

CORPORATE/M&A

MASSACHUSETTS
Leading firms (Corporate/M&A)

1. GOODWIN PROCTER LLP Boston
   HALE AND DORR Boston
   ROPES & GRAY Boston
2. BINGHAM MCCUTCHEN LLP Boston
   SKADDEN, ARPS, SLATE, MEAGHER Boston
   TESTA, HURWITZ & THIBEAULT LLP Boston
3. FOLEY HOAG LLP Boston
   MINTZ LEVIN COHN FERRIS GLOVSKY Boston
   PALMER & DODGE Boston
   WEIL, GOTSHAL & MANGES LLP Boston

Firms are listed alphabetically in each band.

Goodwin Procter LLP
see firm details p.805
The Firm: Interviewees were clear that there are *"three primary competitors"* in the Boston corporate market, with this firm a long-standing participant. This large group is respected for its broad coverage and singled out for its financial services practice. The firm counsels clients on financing and fund formation work, M&A, joint ventures and public and private offerings of shares. Clients praised the group's *"body of knowledge and experience"* and described their ease in *"entrusting to them our company's important issues."*
The Lawyers: The firm's REIT practice is particularly admired by peers and **Gilbert Menna** was noted as *"the REIT specialist in town."* He is active in corporate governance and M&A activities, securities and tax work for REIT clients that include AvalonBay Communities, Beacon Capital Partners and Boston Properties. Chairman and managing partner of the firm and chair of the banking practice, **Regina Pisa** has an active M&A practice in the financial services industry. Clients enthuse that she is *"a brilliant strategist who works to the benefit of the client and the transaction."* **Laura Hodges Taylor** gains similar plaudits: *"she offers great business judgment, seeing around corners and anticipating issues."* She has a broad base of experience, with a focus on venture capital, private equity investments and hedge funds. **Stephen Carr** is also rated highly for his practice in M&A, securities and corporate matters.
The Clients: The group acts on behalf of some major clients in the corporate and financial worlds. The firm has acted for Citizens Financial Group on its acquisitions, including those of Medford Bancorp in Massachusetts and Commonwealth Bancorp in Pennsylvania. Further clients include Arthur D Little, Storage USA and Key3Media.

Hale and Dorr
The Firm: Market sources commended the firm's work with technology clients. The corporate team numbers about 120 lawyers and is involved in venture capital financing, public offerings and M&A as well as governmental and regulatory affairs and tax advice. While the firm's expertise in IPOs is widely acknowledged, this activity has been less prominent in the current economic climate. Competitors admired the firm for its *"significant breadth and quality,"* and clients told researchers they had found the group *"strong and aggressive in business."*
The Lawyers: Mark Borden is chair of the corporate department and won praise from his peers for having *"done a great job of building a first-rate team."* *"A competitive force,"* Borden's *"thoughtful approach, great personal skills and outstanding legal knowledge"* have impressed many. His practice is split between advising public companies and start-ups in transactional matters. Peers described **Paul Brountas** as a *"dean of the bar"* and *"a father of the practice."* Chair of the life sciences group, **Steven Singer** *"really stands out"* in his field.
The Clients: The firm acts for a broad range of technology clients, including leaders in the software, biotech, internet infrastructure and telecom sectors. The firm recently acted for Staples in its acquisition of Medical Arts Press, and in a senior note offering through underwriters valued at over $300 million. A major client in the life sciences area is Millennium Pharmaceuticals; the firm advised on its $2 billion acquisition of COR Therapeutics. Other clients include: Raytheon; Analog Devices; Thermo Electron Corporation and PerkinElmer.

Ropes & Gray
see firm details p.870
The Firm: The corporate group is the largest in the firm, and comprises about 250 attorneys in the Boston office alone. Competitors see the firm as *"a traditional and tremendous player in the institutional market."* The full-service corporate group is especially well regarded in areas such as healthcare

MASSACHUSETTS — CORPORATE/M&A

MASSACHUSETTS
Leading individuals (Corporate/M&A)

1
- **ASHER William** *Testa, Hurwitz & Thibeault,* Boston
- **BORDEN Mark** *Hale and Dorr,* Boston
- **HIGGINS Keith** *Ropes & Gray,* Boston

2
- **BROUNTAS Paul** *Hale and Dorr,* Boston
- **MENNA Gilbert** *Goodwin Procter LLP,* Boston
- **SINGER Steven** *Hale and Dorr,* Boston

3
- **CARR Stephen** *Goodwin Procter LLP,* Boston
- **ENGEL David** *Bingham McCutchen LLP,* Boston
- **NUTT Robert** *Ropes & Gray,* Boston
- **PISA Regina** *Goodwin Procter LLP,* Boston
- **TAYLOR Laura** *Goodwin Procter,* Boston

4
- **GOODMAN Louis** *Skadden, Arps, Slate, Meagher,* Boston
- **KELLER Stanley** *Palmer & Dodge,* Boston
- **MALT Brad** *Ropes & Gray,* Boston
- **ROSENBLUM Peter** *Foley Hoag LLP,* Boston
- **WESTRA James** *Weil, Gotshal & Manges LLP,* Boston

Individuals are listed alphabetically in each band.

and life sciences, investment management, private equity, securities and capital markets.

The Lawyers: A number of lawyers from this *"excellent corporate group,"* which is chaired by David Chapin, were recommended to researchers. **Keith Higgins** (see p.357) received much praise from leaders in the field, who endorsed him as a *"knowledgeable and confident attorney who takes charge and has integrity."* He is head of the firm's securities practice and also advises on venture capital and executive compensation issues. **Robert Nutt** (see p.357) is respected as a member of Boston's *"old guard"* whose loyal clients heartily recommended his work to researchers. His is a general corporate and commercial practice, including experience in large syndicated transactions, high yield debt, M&A and private equity. **Bradford Malt** (see p.357) is a founder of the firm's private equity practice and his clients in this area include Bain Capital, Fenway Partners and Merrill Lynch Private Equity Partners . Market sources commended his practice as *"dynamic and creative,"* adding: *"If you want private equity advice, Ropes & Gray is clearly the best place to go."*

The Clients: The firm has represented Berkshire Partners in its $500 million acquisition of The William Carter Company, a manufacturer of children's clothing, and represented XTRA in its $800 million acquisition by Berkshire Hathaway. The group recently advised the investor group in the acquisition (valued at $1.66 billion) of Boston-based publisher Houghton Mifflin from Vivendi Universal. It also acted on behalf of the financing sources in the acquisition of the Boston Red Sox baseball team. Further high-profile clients include Goldman Sachs, Fidelity and Morgan Stanley.

Bingham McCutchen LLP

The Firm: This is a vast international firm formed in July 2002 by the merger of Boston-based Bingham Dana with West Coast firm McCutchen, Doyle, Brown & Enersen. There are now about 150 corporate lawyers in the Boston office, who have expertise in a full range of transactional issues and corporate governance matters. The firm has a strong reputation for work with mutual funds. Clients endorsed Bingham McCutchen for displaying *"consistent high quality,"* and for fielding lawyers who *"strike a balance between legal and business needs."*

The Lawyers: Leaders in the field consider the lawyers here to be *"extraordinarily capable,"* and named many to researchers. Clients asserted that **David Engel**, cochair of the corporate group, produced first-rate work. Engel is a general corporate and securities lawyer and was heavily involved in coordinating the recent merger.

The Clients: The firm acts as counsel to Raytheon, Boston Scientific and Cubist Pharmaceuticals, and has been involved in big-ticket transactions in this area, including the sale of LeukoSite to Millennium Pharmaceuticals, a deal valued at about $1 billion. High-profile M&A transactions in the past year have included the sale of the Boston Red Sox for approximately $700 million. In the sports sector, the firm also represents the New England Patriots football team and soccer side, New England Revolution. Financial clients include Heritage Partners and Gemini Investors.

Skadden, Arps, Slate, Meagher & Flom LLP & Affiliates

see firm details p.878

The Firm: The Boston office of this international firm houses about 50 lawyers, half of whom are corporate specialists. The group is active in corporate and M&A matters. Clients told researchers of the benefits of being represented by *"a fully fledged powerhouse law firm,"* as the group can draw upon the support of its offices across the US and overseas. Competitors commented on the firm's skill in handling sizable deals.

The Lawyers: The group's lawyers were described to researchers as *"typical Skadden Arps high-caliber attorneys."* **Louis Goodman** (see p.356) heads the Boston office and counsels clients on financings, acquisitions and restructurings. He has recently acted in JW Childs Associates' acquisition of Esselte, a cross-border deal reportedly valued at approximately $542 million, and Ascential Software's acquisitions of Vality Technology (value $100 million) and Torrent Systems (value $46 million).

The Clients: Big-ticket transactions include representing Textron in the sale of its automotive trim business, valued at $1.24 billion, and acting for Houghton Mifflin in its acquisition in 2001 by Vivendi Universal for a reported value of $2.2 billion. Further clients of the Boston group include SG Cowen Securities, Genuity and Fidelity.

Testa, Hurwitz & Thibeault LLP

The Firm: Market sources considered this Boston firm to be a *"tremendous competitor in the hi-tech arena."* The business practice group services technology-oriented clients, private equity houses and investment banking firms. Its roster includes startups to Fortune 1000 companies, acting both as general counsel and in specialized transactions. Matters handled by the firm include the formation of new businesses, M&A, public offerings, strategic alliances, spin-offs and compliance issues.

The Lawyers: William Asher, managing partner, wins praise as a *"technically skilled and trusted adviser."* His practice is focused on business and securities law, and incorporates work for technology companies, investors and underwriters. Interviewees mourned the sad loss at the end of 2002 of the firm's legendary corporate partner, Dick Testa.

The Clients: The firm acts for domestic and foreign clients, including investment banks and private equity investors, government agencies, educational institutions, corporations, charitable organizations and individuals.

Foley Hoag LLP

The Firm: The corporate department is largely technology-focused, although its attorneys have experience in a wider industry base. The group has expertise in purchases and sales, MBOs, public offerings and corporate restructurings. A substantial practice representing investment advisers and private investment funds is also at the firm's core.

The Lawyers: The team was described by competitors and clients alike as *"smart players."* Co-managing partner of the firm **Peter Rosenblum** is, according to clients, *"smart and analytical."* His broad range of activities includes handling corporate transactions and counseling companies such as investment advisers and hedge funds.

The Clients: The firm's clients are mainly involved in the technology industries, and also come from the retail, financial, manufacturing and energy sectors. Highlights include the acquisition of substantial forestry industry assets in Latin America on behalf of UBS Timber Investors and a large secondary public offering for CACI, valued at $170 million. The team also advised on the merger of PRI Automation with Brooks Automation. The firm acts for prominent venture funds including Polaris Venture Partners, TVM Technoventures and Argo Capital, and for investment funds and advisers including Acadian Asset Management and Numeric Investors.

EMPLOYMENT & LABOR LAW — MASSACHUSETTS

Mintz Levin Cohn Ferris Glovsky and Popeo PC
The Firm: The firm's business law group offers expertise in corporate and commercial issues including M&A, banking and investment services. Interviewees spoke highly of the firm's skill in representing hi-tech clients.
The Lawyers: Market sources described the firm as having *"a collection of excellent lawyers."* The firm's managing partner Irwin Heller is based in the Boston office and has a commercial practice that includes acting for early stage technology companies.
The Clients: The firm's clients range from small businesses to Fortune 500 companies. Action is undertaken on behalf of investment companies, trade associations, government agencies and nonprofit organizations. International clients include multinationals from Europe, Asia, the Middle East and South America.

Palmer & Dodge
The Firm: Observers consider this Boston firm to be an *"experienced player"* in the Massachusetts' corporate world. The firm has know-how in the technology industry, incorporating work for biomedical, telecom and IT companies, and conducting licensing, IP, venture capital financings and public offerings for its clients.
The Lawyers: **Stanley Keller** is a business and securities lawyer who was often recommended by leaders in the field as *"an influential lawyer."*
The Clients: Clients range from small, private companies to NYSE-listed corporations and international clients.

Weil, Gotshal & Manges LLP
see firm details p.897
The Firm: This well-respected international firm opened an office in Boston on 1 September 2002, mainly populated by local lawyers from Hutchins Wheeler & Dittmar. At the time of press, it housed about 20 attorneys in its Boston office, and planned to increase this number in coming years. The group is focused on private equity matters, with expertise also in venture capital and M&A matters. Market predictions for the group were favorable: *"Undoubtedly they will be competing in the private equity arena."* Clients also spoke positively of the firm, describing the team as *"packed with wonderful attorneys."*
The Lawyers: Observers agreed that the most visible individual in the group is **James Westra** (see p.359), who has broad experience in private equity, M&A and venture capital finance. Competitors testified to his fine reputation, and clients spoke of him as *"one of the very best lawyers we've ever worked with."*
The Clients: Among the firm's private equity clients is Boston-based Thomas H Lee Company, for which the firm recently acted as lead in raising $6.1 billion in one fund. The firm also acts for Berkshire Partners, Summit Partners and Highland Capital Partners.

EMPLOYMENT & LABOR LAW — MAINLY PLAINTIFF

MASSACHUSETTS

Leading firms (Employment: Mainly Plaintiff)

[1] MESSING, RUDAVSKY & WELIKY PC Boston
PYLE ROME LICHTEN & EHRENBERG Boston
SEGAL ROITMAN & COLEMAN Boston
[2] PERKINS SMITH & COHEN LLP Boston
RODGERS, POWERS & SCHWARTZ Boston

Leading individuals (Employment: Mainly Plaintiff)

[1] SHILEPSKY Nancy *Perkins Smith & Cohen,* Boston
[2] LICHTEN Harold *Pyle Rome Lichten,* Boston
MESSING Ellen *Messing, Rudavsky & Weliky,* Boston
RUDAVSKY Dahlia *Messing, Rudavsky,* Boston
SULLIVAN Mary *Segal Roitman & Coleman,* Boston
[3] NEWMAN Jody *Dwyer & Collora,* Boston
POWERS Kevin *Rodgers, Powers & Schwartz,* Boston
RAPAPORT David *Rapaport & Rapaport,* Boston
SCHWARTZ Harvey *Rodgers, Powers,* Boston

Firms and individuals are listed alphabetically in each band.

Messing, Rudavsky & Weliky PC
The Firm: According to peers, this plaintiffs' firm stands out as one where the lawyers *"know how to litigate a case and negotiate a successful outcome."* The firm represents individuals and unions on matters that are primarily related to discrimination, civil rights and contracts.
The Lawyers: Competitors have a *"professional respect"* for this firm's lawyers, who are considered to offer *"passionate commitment"* to their clients. **Ellen Messing** was described to researchers as *"smart and tough,"* with an *"expert plaintiffs' practice."* **Dahlia Rudavsky** won praise from defendant attorneys as a lawyer who *"really knows what she's doing."*
The Clients: The firm's clients range from blue-collar workers to highly paid executives, and include federal employees, clerical workers and academics. The firm acted in a sex discrimination case brought by a female police office against the president and fellows of Harvard University. It also advised a whistle-blower working for a Massachusetts municipality.

Pyle Rome Lichten & Ehrenberg
The Firm: Peers describe the firm as *"impressive, effective and aggressive."* It comprises seven lawyers who focus on labor and employment law, representing both employees and unions.
The Lawyers: **Harold Lichten** comes particularly recommended for his *"dynamic and highly visible"* practice. He divides his time between matters concerning individual employee's' rights and unions.
The Clients: The firm has litigated a number of cases under the ADA, including an action on behalf of a deaf mechanic denied a job working for United Airlines, which resulted in damages for the plaintiff. It was also successful in an action on behalf of an individual with a hearing impairment denied a job as an officer with the Boston Police Department. Unions represented by the firm include the International Brotherhood of Electrical Workers, United Steelworkers, United Food and Commercial Workers, Service Employees International Union, and firefighter and police unions.

Segal Roitman & Coleman
The Firm: Market sources told researchers that th is firm is *"one of the best for union work."*
The Lawyers: A number of lawyers here were recommended to *Chambers*. Of these, **Mary Sullivan**, in particular, wins praise as an *"effective"* attorney who is *"impressive in her thinking and presentation."*

Perkins Smith & Cohen LLP
The Firm: This firm has offices in Boston, Providence and DC. The labor, employment and employee benefits group in Boston comprises about 12 attorneys who advis e on discrimination and wrongful termination proceedings. The firm also advises employers.
The Lawyers: **Nancy Shilepsky** advises both employers and employees, and is widely acknowledged by peers to be *"an excellent attorney"* and *"a force."* Interviewees point to her plaintiffs' work as *"the best in town."* She is chair of the group and cochair of the executive advocacy group. Her practice includes discrimination-related litigation and advice on separation agreements and restrictive covenants.
The Clients: The firm advises employers, executives and employees.

MASSACHUSETTS — EMPLOYMENT & LABOR LAW

Rodgers, Powers & Schwartz
The Firm: This seven-attorney firm specializes in employment law and civil rights litigation, representing plaintiffs in race, age and gender discrimination matters. Peers describe it as *"a preeminent plaintiffs' firm."*

The Lawyers: **Kevin Powers** is a litigator and also spends a proportion of his time on noncompetition work. Sources told researchers that he is considered to be *"one of the top plaintiff lawyers around,"* and that *"his knowledge is as deep as you could ask for."* **Harvey Schwartz** is a civil rights and employment attorney. Peers described him as *"aggressive, strategic and bright."*

The Clients: Recent cases include action for a court clerk suing a state court judge for violation of constitutional rights, and action for a police officer suing a chief of police and mayor for his demotion in a case involving alleged violation of the officer's constitutional right to free speech. The firm has acted on behalf of a plaintiff in a race discrimination case against the Massachusetts Bay Transportation Authority; at trial the plaintiff received a $5.5 million jury award.

Other Notable Practitioners
Jody Newman of Dwyer & Collora has carved a reputation among peers as a *"tough but effective lawyer."* She focuses on plaintiffs' litigation in employment disputes and has experience in alternative dispute resolution. **David Rapaport** of Rapaport & Rapaport is, according to peers' *"a high-quality litigator and a pleasure to work with."* He acts for both employers and employees, focusing on major cases including statutory discrimination and arbitrations. Recent cases include a national origin case, acting on behalf of a plaintiff dismissed by a large mutual fund.

EMPLOYMENT & LABOR LAW — MAINLY DEFENDANT

MASSACHUSETTS
Leading firms
(Employment: Mainly Defendant)

1. **ROPES & GRAY** Boston
2. **BINGHAM McCUTCHEN LLP** Boston
   FOLEY HOAG LLP Boston
   GOODWIN PROCTER LLP Boston
   MORGAN BROWN AND JOY LLP Boston
   SEYFARTH SHAW Boston
3. **HALE AND DORR** Boston
   MINTZ LEVIN COHN FERRIS GLOVSKY Boston
4. **JACKSON LEWIS** Boston
   PALMER & DODGE Boston
   TESTA, HURWITZ & THIBEAULT LLP Boston

Leading individuals
(Employment: Mainly Defendant)

1. **ALFRED Richard** Seyfarth Shaw, Boston
   CASEY David Bingham McCutchen LLP, Boston
   GORDON Robert Ropes & Gray, Boston
2. **DAMON Lisa** Seyfarth Shaw, Boston
   JOY Robert Morgan Brown and Joy LLP, Boston
   LUKEY Joan Hale and Dorr, Boston
   NAGLE James Goodwin Procter LLP, Boston
   TELEGEN Arthur Foley Hoag LLP, Boston
   WARD Richard Ropes & Gray, Boston
3. **BELLO Kenneth** Mintz Levin Cohn Ferris, Boston
   BENOIT Wilfred Goodwin Procter LLP, Boston
   JACOBS Neil Hale and Dorr, Boston
   MALONE Judith Palmer & Dodge, Boston
   PICKETT Andrew Jackson Lewis, Boston

Up-and-coming individuals
   COHEN Bret Pepe & Hazard LLP, Boston

Firms and individuals are listed alphabetically in each band.

Ropes & Gray
see firm details p.870

The Firm: This group of about 15 lawyers handles a broad range of labor and employment matters on the management side. Its litigious experience includes proceedings before government agencies, while on the noncontentious side the group counsels clients on day-to-day policy issues. Additionally, the firm is involved in representing companies, healthcare institutions and schools in union issues. Clients enthused that the group *"works cooperatively and solves issues creatively,"* and that *"the wonderful thing about working with them is the access to top lawyers in all disciplines."*

The Lawyers: There are *"a number of excellent lawyers"* in this group. **Robert Gordon** (see p.356) was recommended by peers as a *"highly skilled attorney with great judgment,"* and clients praised his *"practical assistance"* to their businesses. His practice is oriented toward disputes. Recent successes include the defense of a bank in the Supreme Court in an age discrimination claim. **Richard Ward** (see p.359) wins the respect of his competitors for his *"sophisticated and engaging trial manner."* His specialty is employment litigation, including contract and discrimination claims, wage and hour disputes and labor arbitrations.

The Clients: The firm successfully represented a major Fortune 100 financial institution in the defense of a challenge to its cash balance retirement plan. It also represented Hazen Paper Company in a successful ADEA case heard in the Supreme Court. In the healthcare industry, it advises Partners Health Care, New England Medical Center Hospitals and University of Massachusetts Medical Center. Further clients include Fleet Bank, Harvard University, Gillette and Terra Lycos.

Bingham McCutchen LLP
The Firm: Competitors told researchers that this *"outstanding employment group"* deserved some of the *"highest marks."* The full-service labor and employment group numbers 17 lawyers in Boston; they counsel management clients in day-to-day matters and give transactional advice on employment-related issues. Additionally, the firm is experienced in employment-related litigation.

The Lawyers: Chair of the labor and employment group **David Casey** concentrates his practice in litigation, where sources claim he *"takes no prisoners."* Formerly a plaintiff litigator, he has for several years litigated on the defendants' side, in which he is described as *"professional and respected."*

The Clients: The firm represents employers in industries including manufacturing, technology, education, healthcare and hospitality. Principal clients include Hewlett-Packard, Compass Group, EMC and Harvard University. Casey has recently acted on behalf of Harvard in a case involving claims of gender bias in the university police force.

Foley Hoag LLP
The Firm: Market observers portrayed the group as *"impressive, highly competent and aggressive on behalf of their clients."* With about 25 lawyers, the group is particularly well regarded for its traditional labor work, in which it is said to *"represent a lot of major players."* It has experience before the NLRB, and at arbitrations and collective bargaining proceedings. Dispute work includes a wide range of discrimination claims, and the firm also offers advice on transaction-related employment issues.

The Lawyers: Competitors spoke of their *"utmost respect"* for **Arthur Telegen**'s work. Telegen chairs the firm's labor and employment department, and his practice has a focus on labor relations, advising unionized employers. His successes include a contract negotiation on behalf of an international brewer, involving multiple proceedings in the federal courts and before the NLRB.

The Clients: The firm's recent highlights include an action on behalf of a large US employer in a wage and hour class action, advice to an employer in ongoing federal multi-employer pension

EMPLOYMENT & LABOR LAW

MASSACHUSETTS

plan act litigation. The group has undertaken ERISA litigation for an association of savings banks, and has defended a variety of clients in state and federal court actions arising from discrimination claims.

Goodwin Procter LLP
see firm details p.805

The Firm: The group of about 16 lawyers in Boston covers the gamut of labor and employment matters, both litigious and non-litigious. The firm services a strong corporate group, particularly acting on issues such as non-compete agreements, employee privacy, trade secrets and work force reductions. Clients spoke highly of their experiences with the firm ; one said: *"We went to Goodwin on a thorny and high-profile matter and they dealt with it efficiently and very satisfactorily."*

The Lawyers: James Nagle is chair of the firm's labor and employment department and defends corporations in state and federal courts and before administrative agencies. Commentators consider ed him *"just as good as they get"* and described him as *"creative and strategic in his thinking."* Clients were impressed by what he brings to the table: *"What distinguishes Goodwin Procter is James Nagle - he's experienced, smart and tough."* **Wilfred Benoit** is also recommended for his work in employment litigation and alternative dispute resolution (ADR), as well as for his labor law work in collective bargaining.

The Clients: The group counsels a wide range of local and national clients, including those involved in the technology, retail, healthcare, financial services and manufacturing industries. Key clients include: Cisco Systems; Compaq; Fidelity Investments; New Balance Athletic Shoe; Putnam Investments and Vicor.

Morgan Brown and Joy LLP

The Firm: Regarded by interviewees as *"the leading local boutique for management in town,"* this firm numbers about 25 full-time labor and employment attorneys. The firm advises clients throughout the US and has experience before the courts and agencies of many states.

The Lawyers: Competitors described the group as having *"lots of first-rate lawyers."* **Robert Joy**, in particular, is considered *"an excellent litigator."*

The Clients: The firm attracts clients from the insurance, retail, healthcare, education and finance sectors.

Seyfarth Shaw

The Firm: This national firm is a long-standing player in the labor and employment market. The Boston branch is regarded by competitors as *"quite a powerhouse,"* having recently acquired 20 local lawyers from Schnader Harrison Segal & Lewis. Representation in labor and employment matters extends from traditional labor work to litigation, class actions and policy counseling. Nationaly spread clients spoke of the advantages of having the resources of a countrywide firm to draw on: *"We have facilities all over the country and it's great to use them nationally."*

The Lawyers: Richard Alfred was described to researchers as *"an impressive and aggressive lawyer."* He spends a large portion of his time in defense litigation, including on disability discrimination and complex sexual harassment cases in various industries, such as pharmaceutical, manufacturing and sales. Clients warmly recommended him as *"an out-of-the-box thinker, client-oriented and involved in details."* Managing partner **Lisa Damon** was described by competitors as *"understated, thoughtful and effective in advancing her clients' claims."* Her practice is focused on discrimination and harassment claims.

The Clients: The firm's Boston office acts as defense counsel for s ome prominent clients that include airlines, hotels and restaurants, and retail, hi-tech, healthcare and property management companies. It has acted as counsel to the Massachusetts State Senate, the Massachusetts Board of Bar Overseers and various state and local entities.

Hale and Dorr

The Firm: Market sources refer to Hale and Dorr as an *"outstanding firm."* Particularly warm comments were made about the employment litigators here. The labor and employment group is retained on a wide range of matters, including general counseling, advising on the workforce implications of business restructuring, unfair competition guidance and union-related issues.

The Lawyers: Joan Lukey is reportedly in the *"top echelon"* of defense litigators, and market commentators describe d her as *"experienced, powerful and resourceful."* Among her cases is the defense of an action brought by the EEOC against a technology company and the Massachusetts Attorney General , challenging the severance plan in place at the company. **Neil Jacobs** chairs the department and was commended by interviewees for his experience in collective bargaining and in litigation.

The Clients: The group attracts clients from manufacturing, construction, education, healthcare and the sports sector. A major success for the firm in 2001 was winning an age discrimination class action in the Massachusetts Appeals Court on behalf of Augat. Clients include Fidelity Investments and Analog Devices.

Mintz Levin Cohn Ferris Glovsky and Popeo PC

The Firm: This well-respected labor and employment practice provides a full range of advice for unionized and nonunionized employers. Its lawyers are experienced in matters of policy and procedure, state and federal employment laws, confidentiality, and non-compete agreements. The group also advises on union matters before the NLRB and collective bargaining.

The Lawyers: Sources described **Kenneth Bello** as a *"tenacious lawyer who does a great job."* His practice includes a portion of traditional union work, alongside his discrimination, harassment and wrongful discharge litigation. He also counsels clients on day-to-day employment-related issues.

The Clients: The firm advises national, regional and local clients.

Jackson Lewis

The Firm: This nationwide boutique provides advice on all aspects of workplace law. Its Boston office fields about 20 attorneys and is, according to market sources, *"clearly a competitor."* The firm undertakes litigation, affirmative action, collective bargaining, arbitrations and ADR. It also counsels employers on issues such as pensions and benefits, union avoidance, wage and hour claims and immigration.

The Lawyers: Andrew Pickett is highly rated by peers. He spends a large proportion of his time in defense litigation and counsels clients on matters including ERISA and restrictive covenants.

The Clients: The firm's recent significant court victories include its representation of Browing Ferris Industries and Allied Waste at trial court and appellate levels in cases concerning effective releases and waivers of employment law claims. The firm also successfully represented Massachusetts-American Water Company in a case of wrongful discharge.

Palmer & Dodge

The Firm: This Boston firm has about 12 attorneys in its labor and employment group. The practice is comprehensive and attracts stand-alone clients as well as those in its existing corporate client base. The firm has expertise in litigation and ADR and offers advice on diverse issues, including compliance, workplace safety, workforce reductions and employee benefits.

The Lawyers: Judith Malone was described to researchers as a *"prominent and successful"* attorney in this area. She advises clients on the development of employment policies and litigates in federal and state courts, and before administrative agencies.

The Clients: The group's clients include financial institutions, biotech and hi-tech companies and traditional manufacturers. The firm has an active practice in representing schools and colleges.

Testa, Hurwitz & Thibeault LLP

The Firm: This team of 20 is respected by peers for its breadth of experience. It advises and trains clients on employment policies and regulatory compliance. A number of litigators act on

MASSACHUSETTS   ENVIRONMENT

discrimination and wrongful dismissal claims. The group additionally acts on employment due diligence in transactional work undertaken by the firm.
The Lawyers: Adam Forman is chair of this well-regarded labor and employment group.
The Clients: A large proportion of the group's clients are private equity firms and those in the technology market. Manufacturing industries, educational institutions and nonprofit organizations also feature in the portfolio. Recent cases include representing a public software company that was sued by a mid-level manager complaining of sexual harassment. The group has also recently handled several discrimination-related class actions on behalf of clients sued by the EEOC.

Other Notable Practitioners
Bret Cohen (see p.355) of Pepe & Hazard LLP was recommended by peers as a *"talented and vigorous"* lawyer. Cohen has established an *"impressive"* practice and *"has a way of inspiring trust"* in his clients. He represents employers in discrimination claims, non-compete agreements and labor-related disputes. A recent success was a trial victory regarding a wage and hour claim made by a senior salesperson seeking over $1 million in compensation against his software company client.

ENVIRONMENT

MASSACHUSETTS
Leading firms (Environment)

1
- FOLEY HOAG LLP *Boston*
- GOODWIN PROCTER LLP *Boston*

2
- HALE AND DORR *Boston*
- MCDERMOTT, WILL & EMERY *Boston*
- MINTZ LEVIN COHN FERRIS GLOVSKY *Boston*

3
- MOEHRKE, MACKIE & SHEA PC *Boston*
- NUTTER, MCCLENNEN & FISH LLP *Boston*

4
- ANDERSON & KREIGER *Cambridge*
- BOWDITCH & DEWEY LLP *Worcester*
- GOULSTON & STORRS *Boston*

Leading individuals (Environment)

1
- BURT Laurie *Foley Hoag LLP, Boston*
- CHILD Ralph *Mintz Levin Cohn Ferris Glovsky, Boston*
- COOKE Susan *McDermott, Will & Emery, Boston*
- DAVIS Christopher *Goodwin Procter LLP, Boston*
- JAFFE Seth *Foley Hoag LLP, Boston*

2
- BATES Jeffrey *McDermott, Will & Emery, Boston*
- GALVANI Paul *Ropes & Gray, Boston*
- HEALY Martin *Goodwin Procter LLP, Boston*
- KIRSCH Robert *Hale and Dorr, Boston*
- LEONARD Stephen *Brown Rudnick Berlack, Boston*
- MOEHRKE Anton *Moehrke, Mackie & Shea PC, Boston*
- PORTER Jeffrey *Mintz Levin Cohn Ferris, Boston*

3
- ABELSON Ned *Goulston & Storrs, Boston*
- ANGLEHART Donald *Testa, Hurwitz & Thibeault, Boston*
- RIKLEEN Lauren *Bowditch, Framingham*

4
- GOODHEART Lisa *Piper Rudnick LLP, Boston*
- KREIGER Arthur *Anderson & Kreiger, Cambridge*
- LEON Michael *Nutter, McClennen & Fish LLP, Boston*

Up-and-coming individuals
- KAHN Adam *Foley Hoag LLP, Boston*

Firms and individuals are listed alphabetically in each band.

Foley Hoag LLP
The Firm: The environmental group of about 16 lawyers was roundly endorsed by peers as *"an excellent competitor."* Work includes advising on complex air regulations, especially relating to energy and manufacturing facilities, and counseling on hazardous waste sites, urban development and brownfield sites. Attorneys are experienced in public-private partnerships. They are active in transactional advice, audit, negotiation, risk management programs, administrative proceedings and dispute resolution.
The Lawyers: A large number of the *"extremely strong"* team was recommended to researchers. According to some competitors, *"nobody has more experience"* than **Laurie Burt**, the founder of the group. Her practice focuses on environmental compliance and land use development projects, including urban redevelopment of brownfield sites and cleanups of complex contaminated properties. Competitors admire **Seth Jaffe**'s *"top representation of his clients' interests,"* and make note of his *"extensive general experience."* Now chair of the firm's administrative law department, he maintains his practice as a general environmental lawyer. He has advised on cleanups under state and federal Superfund law, and represented USGen New England in air regulations and energy-related work. Recently appointed chair of the environmental practice group, **Adam Kahn** was recommended as *"smart and bright."* He has a broad practice that incorporates litigation, compliance and transactional work, and spends a lot of time on brownfield and land use matters and energy projects.
The Clients: Burt has led advice to Fortune 500 companies and public authorities, including the cleanup of brownfield sites with a nearby public water supply, and a major dioxin site in Rhode Island, on behalf of a public-private partnership that owns housing for the elderly on the site. The firm has acted for the Cities of Cambridge, Boston, Everett, and Malden, on permitting and cleanup issues, and represents educational institutions including Williams College and Emerson College. Commercial clients include Invensys Systems, and Martha's Vineyard Golf Partners.

Goodwin Procter LLP
see firm details p.805
The Firm: Competitors described this as a group that *"really maintains a critical mass,"* endorsing its *"highly intelligent lawyers."* About 14 lawyers cover a full range of environmental law, including compliance counseling, contaminated land projects, permitting, litigation and insurance. The firm has a long-standing Superfund practice and has represented many Fortune 500 companies as potentially responsible parties in hazardous waste sites in the Northeast.
The Lawyers: Christopher Davis is *"top of the list of recommendations"* for many of his peers. *"Expert"* in contaminated property issues, a large proportion of his time is spent on Superfund work, state cleanup programs and brownfield redevelopment projects. Chair of the environmental group **Martin Healy** is considered by market sources to be *"without parallel on land use issues."* His focus is on the environmental review and permitting of complex project developments. Issues he is concerned with include wetlands, tidelands, waterfront areas, sewer water and endangered species.
The Clients: The firm acts for the Massachusetts Port Authority regarding the redevelopment of Logan Airport. It is also counsel to Cisco Systems in its development of a major corporate campus in Boxborough, MA. The group has advised Entergy in the acquisition and operation of nuclear power plants, and has counseled long-time client Polaroid on the recovery of cleanup costs.

Hale and Dorr
The Firm: Interviewees spoke of *"an outstanding firm with a number of skilled environmental lawyers."* The practice focuses on high-stakes litigation against governmental claims and in defense of claims regarding responsibility for environmental cleanup costs. In addition, the practice works in support of business transactions, and in permitting and compliance advice work. Clients enthused that they would *"of course recommend Hale and Dorr to anyone."*
The Lawyers: Chair of the environmental group is **Robert Kirsch**. A skilled litigator, he also advises on permitting issues, and has extensive experience within the energy industry. Clients include National Grid USA, for whom Kirsch has defended

ENVIRONMENT — MASSACHUSETTS

claims brought by the Government and by private third parties. The market mourns the sad loss of Paul Wallach, a prominent figure in the practice.

The Clients: In addition to players in the energy industry, clients are drawn from a wide range of disciplines, including biotech, hi-tech, pharmaceuticals, manufacturing and property management and development. The group advises solid waste company Casella Waste Systems on compliance and the environmental aspects of transactional work. The firm has acted on enforcement defense on behalf of Millennium Pharmaceuticals. Further clients include Cabot Corporation, Textron Systems, Tyco International, and the Synthetic Organic Chemical Manufacturers Association.

McDermott, Will & Emery
see firm details p.846

The Firm: This international firm has offices in six US states as well as European offices, and as such the Boston group is prominent on national and international matters. Confidence in the firm's ability was high: *"They are super smart - whatever they are doing you can be sure they'll be good at it,"* agreed peers. In terms of representation, the group is full service. Particular areas of strength include regulatory expertise, in particular hazardous waste and chemical regulation.

The Lawyers: Head of the Boston office's environmental group **Susan Cooke** (see p.355) and partner **Jeff Bates** (see p.354) are considered a particularly strong pairing by competitors and clients alike. Cooke is considered a guru in this area and clients value her ability to appreciate *"the interplay between environmental issues and business activity."* Clients described Bates as *"outstanding for complex regulatory and transactional matters."* Much of his work is outside of the US or for non-US clients, and he acts as liaison partner for the firm's London and Munich offices. He has advised on greenhouse gas emissions trading and on aspects of European environmental, M&A, workers' safety and public law.

The Clients: International matters include action for Bayer, which Bates is representing before the Food and Drug Administration. The team also acted on a project for ON Semiconductor involving the cleanup of sites in the Czech Republic and Slovakia.

Mintz Levin Cohn Ferris Glovsky and Popeo PC

The Firm: This firm has about seven lawyers in its environmental law group, which competitors concede is a *"stand-alone group that wins major clients."* Services provided include planning and permitting advice, transaction-related issues and compliance, in addition to litigation and enforcement actions. The firm has loyal clients, who recommended the firm's *"extremely good resources"* and ability to deal with complex issues. In enforcement actions, the firm has experience before federal and state agencies.

The Lawyers: A large proportion of the group was recommended to researchers. A skilled advocate, **Ralph Child** practices in regulatory, permitting and enforcement issues. Peers praise his *"across-the-board environmental expertise."* Clients point to his recent tenure as general counsel to the Massachusetts Department of Environmental Protection as being a *"great advantage in knowing the law and how it works."* He has advised on the permitting of the Maritimes and Northeast Pipeline project, bringing natural gas from Nova Scotia into the US. **Jeffrey Porter** is manager of the firm's environmental section and a specialist in litigation, compliance and permitting issues. Competitors comment on the large amount of *"interesting cases"* Porter has worked on, which include the Constellation Center, a performing arts center planned for a former gas producing plant in Cambridge, MA.

The Clients: The firm acted for GE as the plaintiff in a federal cleanup cost recovery case against the former owner of an industrial plant. Another major client is drugstore chain CVS, for whom the firm has advised on its national expansion plan. Further clients include TA Realty; Jefferson Properties; Lincoln Properties; Sunrise Development; Aggregate Industries and Boston Sand & Gravel.

Moehrke, Mackie & Shea PC

The Firm: Interviewees pointed to this firm as a boutique that has *"such a high level of experience that it can compete with the big firms."* Eight lawyers are dedicated to environmental law, and the team is best known for its particular strengths in solid and hazardous waste. Its expertise in permitting and licensing, cost recovery actions, and the defense of government enforcement cases is also widely respected.

The Lawyers: While the three name partners were roundly commended to researchers, **Tony Moehrke** was singled out as *"the solid waste guy - no one in-state has more experience than he does."* Additionally, he litigates before local boards, state agencies and state and federal courts on issues including hazardous waste and wetlands.

The Clients: Hazardous waste facilities; solid waste landfills; manufacturing and processing facilities; transfer stations; builders and residential property owners.

Nutter, McClennen & Fish LLP

The Firm: This 11-partner team can draw on additional backup in the litigation department. Interviewees spoke of the *"effective service they provide for their clients"* in the business, government and industry sectors. They offer a full range of counseling and representation in matters ranging from regulatory permitting, compliance and enforcement issues to litigation (at federal and state levels).

The Lawyers: Several of the firm's lawyers were recommended to researchers as being *"highly adept."* The chair of the land use group is **Michael Leon**, who acts for commercial and industrial clients in hazardous waste, solid waste and regulatory issues. He also advises on the environmental implications of his clients' corporate affairs.

The Clients: The firm attracts public sector clients such as state and local boards, bodies and commissions. The firm advised the Massachusetts Port Authority in its joint venture to develop a regional transportation facility on a Superfund site. It also advises clients on the operation of industrial facilities, including paper manufacturers and energy companies.

Anderson & Kreiger

The Firm: Located in Cambridge, this three-partner firm specializes in environmental law and is considered *"extremely talented "* by competitors. The firm offers services in mediation and consultation alongside its prowess in litigation. Its expertise in trial and appellate work incorporates diverse matters such as oil and hazardous waste contamination, land use, environmental insurance, siting, and environmental review.

The Lawyers: Peers spoke of their respect for the long-standing practice of **Arthur Kreiger**.

The Clients: The firm represents public and private clients, including towns, businesses, property owners, landowners, developers and citizen groups.

Bowditch & Dewey LLP

The Firm: This Worcester-based firm has 13 attorneys focused on environmental law. Clients commended them as *"extremely capable,"* and commented on the *"value-for-money"* service offered. The practice is full service, with expertise in regulatory compliance, permitting, Superfund defense and cleanup, brownfield redevelopment, litigation and transaction-related due diligence.

The Lawyers: **Lauren Stiller Rikleen** (see p.359) is focused on enforcement work, and has extensive experience in hazardous waste issues and environmental mediation. Clients are passionate about the benefits of hiring her: *"She's like an insurance policy; my advice to other clients with environmental issues is to hire her first of all."*

The Clients: The firm's clients include colleges and universities. Projects undertaken frequently involve public-private partnerships, and the firm serves as environmental counsel for municipalities.

Goulston & Storrs

The Firm: The firm's environmental group of three lawyers has a significant focus on

MASSACHUSETTS

INSOLVENCY

transaction-related matters, and expertise in brownfield work and environmental insurance. The group is also active in costs recovery, in which it acts on behalf of owners whose land has become contaminated. Supported by a strong real estate practice, the group also works with corporate clients on environmental issues associated with sites owned, leased or being developed.

The Lawyers: Competitors view **Ned Abelson** as *"experienced in environmental real estate issues,"* while clients consider his representation to be *"a valuable resource - he understands the laws, rules and regulations, as well as our business issues and interests."*

The Clients: Important projects for the firm include the new Boston Convention Center Project, advising the Boston Redevelopment Authority on permitting, due diligence, cost recovery negotiations and litigation. The firm advised National Development in its acquisition and redevelopment of a portion of the Woburn, MA Industri-Plex Superfund site, now known as MetroNorth Corporate Center. Also represented the New England Patriots football team on the construction of the $325 million Gillette Stadium in Foxborough, MA. Other clients include Fleet Bank, Beacon Capital Partners and New England Development.

Other Notable Practitioners

Litigator **Paul Galvani** (see p.356) of Ropes & Gray devotes much of his time to environment-related litigation. Competitors admire him as *"tough and effective,"* and note that *"if you were a client you would want to make sure you got him."* His highlights include representing the successors to Stauffer Chemical Company in an LA harbor natural resource damage claim, and representing approximately 20 corporations in a response action/natural resource damage case. Clients testify that **Stephen Leonard** of Brown Rudnick Berlack Israels has *"sensitivity to legal issues and the politics, and helped us to craft a solution that met our needs."* His recent work has included an energy project development. Leonard has a background in government and he counts among his clients Massachusetts Bay Transportation Authority (MBTA), Massachusetts Water Resources Authority (MWRA) and the City of Boston. *"Highly capable"* **Don Anglehart** is the head of Testa, Hurwitz & Thibeault LLP's environmental practice group. He has a background at the EPA regional office in Boston and maintains a state and federal focus in defending companies from actions brought by the Government and the agencies. His clients include public companies involved in pharmaceuticals, biotechnology and specialty materials. **Lisa Goodheart** (see p.356), who has moved to Piper Rudnick LLP, has a substantial environmental practice. Competitors told researchers of their *"huge admiration"* for her work. Representative actions include cost recovery litigation, enforcement, permitting and environmental malpractice.

INSOLVENCY/CORPORATE RECOVERY

MASSACHUSETTS
Leading firms
(Insolvency/Corporate Recovery)

1. **GOODWIN PROCTER LLP** Boston
   HALE AND DORR Boston
2. **MINTZ LEVIN COHN FERRIS GLOVSKY** Boston
3. **COHN KHOURY MADOFF & WHITESELL LLP** Boston
   HANIFY & KING Boston
   ROPES & GRAY Boston
4. **FOLEY HOAG LLP** Boston

Leading individuals
(Insolvency/Corporate Recovery)

1. **COHN Daniel** Cohn Khoury Madoff & Whitesell, Boston
   DALEY Paul Hale and Dorr, Boston
   GLOSBAND Daniel Goodwin Procter LLP, Boston
   MIKELS Rick Mintz Levin Cohn Ferris Glovsky, Boston
   POLEBAUM Mark Hale and Dorr, Boston
   SWAIM Hall Hale and Dorr, Boston
2. **MCCARTHY William** Ropes & Gray, Boston
   MURPHY Harold Hanify & King, Boston
   PAPPONE Michael Goodwin Procter LLP, Boston
   SIGEL John Hale and Dorr, Boston
3. **SCHNEIDER Jon** Goodwin Procter LLP, Boston
   SCHWARTZ Andrew Foley Hoag LLP, Boston

Up-and-coming individuals
BLECK Daniel Mintz Levin Cohn Ferris, Boston
ROSNER Douglas Goulston & Storrs, Boston

Firms and individuals are listed alphabetically in each band.

Goodwin Procter LLP
see firm details p.805

The Firm: One of Boston's larger practices, this group of 12 has carved out an impressive reputation for its versatility and depth of experience. The group advises debtors and borrowers on creditor claims and restructurings in, or outside of, bankruptcy proceedings. It also represents investors seeking to acquire assets from insolvent entities, and defends clients involved in fraudulent transfer and preference claims.

While peers acknowledge that the experience of its senior figures *"gives the team its edge,"* they also endorse the *"talent all the way down."* The firm wins acclaim for the sheer number of cases handled at the highest level. Highlights include providing counsel in the Chapter 11 proceedings of Arthur D Little, GC Companies, Value America and Transcon Insurance.

The Lawyers: Chair of the practice, **Daniel Glosband** represents debtors, secured and unsecured creditors in workouts and bankruptcy proceedings. Non-bankruptcy court liquidations, particularly for failed venture capital clients are his area of expertise. Peers also endorsed his international practice, particularly his understanding of international banking systems. He acted as lead counsel to Arthur D Little, Mitsubishi Heavy Industries (shipbuilding division) and GC Companies in their Chapter 11 proceedings. Corporate partner **Michael Pappone** represents principal parties in large corporate reorganizations both in and out of court and handles workouts for smaller entrepreneurial entities. He also advises venture capital clients who have troubled portfolios. Part of the *"next generation"* at Goodwin Procter, he is respected for involvement in larger, complicated matters such as the Value America Chapter 11 proceedings. **Jon Schneider**'s experience lies in creditors' rights, insolvency and related M&A. Peers recommended him as *"first-rate, smart, creative and ethical."* He has acted for the creditors' committee in the Amcare Medical Services and USAfrica Airlines cases, and acted for the debtor in the Silver Bros proceedings, and the bondholders of Baldwin Builders.

The Clients: Alpha-Beta Technology; Thornhill Global Deposit Fund; Transcon Insurance; Converse; Watts Industries; Filene's Basement and Meditrust Corporation/La Quinta.

Hale and Dorr

The Firm: The 15-strong commercial team has deep foundations in the corporate restructuring market; it is perhaps best known for its representation of hi-tech clients, and its strong debtor orientation. Peers respect the technical knowledge of these attorneys and their sound business judgment. The firm has the capacity – an *"array of top-level talent"* – to handle complex cases. Researchers were impressed by the level of recommendation for this *"smart and aggressive"* team's individual attorneys. Recent work by the group includes the filing of Chapter 11 for Arch Wireless and 20 of its subsidiaries and the representation of a bondholder committee in a prepackaged Chapter 11.

The Lawyers: **Paul Daley** has considerable experi-

INSOLVENCY — MASSACHUSETTS

ence in secured lending, UCC matters, insolvency and reorganizations. His work is evenly divided between debtors and creditors, and his representations have included the CMGI and Charles River Ventures proceedings. Daley's wealth of experience extends to international matters. Commercial department chair **Mark Polebaum** is focused on Chapter 11 reorganizations and out-of-court workouts. He received commendation for his leadership skills and the high quality of his work, which includes the Chapter 11 proceedings of Mattress Discounters and Empresa Eléctrica Del Norte Grande. **Hall Swaim** has represented acquirers of assets from companies in Chapter 11 proceedings. Interviewees agreed that his *"great capabilities in the hi-tech arena"* combine well with a *"tenacious and patient"* approach to debtor work. Peers and clients noted **John Sigel**'s broad finance and structuring practice. His recent representations include Arch Wireless in financial restructurings and Metrobility in its Chapter 11 proceedings.
The Clients: The Kendall Company; Autographics; Computervision; Sequoia Systems; Wang Laboratories; Bank East; Choate-Symmes Hospital; Smith Valve Company; Paragon Park Development and Kurzweil Music Systems.

Mintz Levin Cohn Ferris Glovsky and Popeo PC
The Firm: A 16-strong group advises on the full gamut of insolvency and restructuring issues. Its representations in asset-based lending, workouts and bankruptcy transactions are combined with experience in bondholder and trustee issues. Peers respect the firm's substantial number of *"sophisticated practitioners"* and its recent involvement in high-profile cases. Clients praise the group highly for its *"significant capabilities"* and for successfully protecting the value of estates. A firm with considerable depth, it has undergone continual growth in Boston over recent years. Recently the group represented indenture trustees and bondholder groups in the United Airlines bankruptcy.
The Lawyers: Rick Mikels is regarded by peers as *"the ultimate deal-maker."* His diverse practice has a national focus, concentrating on insolvency and restructuring issues. This *"creative, energetic straight shooter"* was commended as *"a brilliant problem solver."* Clients admired his commitment to a case, asserting that he *"goes beyond the call of duty."* He is active in acquisitions arising out of bankruptcy proceedings, and advised on ACT Manufacturing and Malden Mills' Chapter 11 filings. Rising star **Daniel Bleck** has carved a profile in the market through his involvement in high-profile cases arising from workouts, bankruptcy and creditors' rights.
The Clients: Caribbean Petroleum Refining, Filene's Basement and Mergent are representative clients.

Cohn Khoury Madoff & Whitesell LLP
The Firm: Described by peers as a *"fabulous debtorside boutique."* A seven-attorney team has a far-reaching reputation in bankruptcy, debt restructuring, alternative dispute resolution and business litigation. The group's distressed company practice advises on Chapter 11 filings and tries adversary proceedings in the bankruptcy courts. The team is also involved in related acquisition and investment work. Competitors endorsed the group's counseling skills and its effective partnering with other firms. Clients favor the firm for its clear guidance; its *"strong team perspective builds consensus among the parties."* The group has represented Waste Systems International and Wash Depot Holdings in their successful Chapter 11 reorganizations.
The Lawyers: Peers and clients applaud founding partner **Daniel Cohn**'s (see p.355) representation of debtors. Described as *"one of the go-to guys,"* he is *"a strategist with sound ethical judgment."* Clients reported that he is *"a champion - instrumental in our success ."* Peers agreed, noting: *"He misses nothing."* Cohn was involved in the Waste Systems International and Wash Depot Holdings Chapter 11 proceedings, and also represented a stockholder of Wolverine Proctor & Schwartz in an out-of-court debt restructuring.
The Clients: NordicTrack; Diam International; New Hampshire Electric Co-operative; Furniture.com; Wang Laboratories and HealthCo International.

Hanify & King
The Firm: This 34-strong trial firm is known for its capacity to handle a high volume of bankruptcy and financial restructuring work. The practice covers a range of issues, including Chapter 7 and Chapter 11 proceedings, asset acquisitions and creditor representation. The *"effective"* litigation practice has impressed market commentators with its *"high-quality debtor advice."* Peers were keen to emphasize that the firm has all the resources of its larger competitors .
The Lawyers: Group director **Harold Murphy** was endorsed by peers for his debtor work. He specializes in bankruptcy and commercial law, including the representation of debtors, creditors' committees, trustees and secured and unsecured creditors in Chapter 11 reorganizations and Chapter 7 liquidations. His ability to *"pull victory out of the ashes of defeat"* has impressed many, who also appreciate his *"no-nonsense bottom line"* approach.
The Clients: The firm advises regional and local businesses.

Ropes & Gray
see firm details p.870
The Firm: The group of 11 attorneys advises private equity clients in connection with their troubled portfolios, and represents bondholders in bankruptcies and workouts. The firm's *"intellectual"* attorneys are respected for producing *"top-quality"* creditor work and earn plaudits for their bondholder representations. The team advised the acquirers of eToys and US internetworking in Chapter 11 proceedings, and represented the official committee of bondholders in the restructuring of Archibald Candy. Also advised on the restructuring of the $500 million debt of Trump's Castle Associates.
The Lawyers: William McCarthy (see p.357) is head of the firm's creditors' rights department and represents both debtors and creditors in reorganization cases nationwide. *"Technically knowledgeable, bright and aggressive,"* he commands respect for his effective litigation and good business sense. McCarthy has represented funds managed by Bain Capital in the prepackaged Chapter 11 of Dade Behring and the Chapter 11 of Mattress Discounters. He also represented Gillette in relation to the Chapter 11 proceedings of Arthur D Little .
The Clients: Enron; York Funding (Cayman); Colorado's Ocean Journey and House2Home.

Foley Hoag LLP
The Firm: The firm's bankruptcy group has experienced notable growth in recent years, and now boasts nine attorneys. They advise on all aspects of bankruptcies, reorganizations and workouts, with a particular strength in bankruptcy-related litigation. The firm's client base includes debtors and creditors, although its work with creditors' committees has earned particular recognition in the market. Peers acknowledge that the firm contains *"plenty of intellectual assets,"* while clients express confidence in the *"professional manner and forward thinking"* of its attorneys. The team has advised Benchmark Electronics in its $70 million acquisition of the majority of assets of ACT Manufacturing, and acted for the creditors' committee in Malden Mills pending Chapter 11 proceedings.
The Lawyers: Group head **Andrew Schwartz**'s practice specializes in the representation of creditors' committees, and, with his background in litigation, is a familiar sight in complex insolvency disputes. Clients praise Schwartz for his professionalism and communication and management skills; they appreciate that his negotiation skills *"help to move the case forward."* He has represented Disney in the bankruptcy of Toysmart.com and PwC in the bankruptcy of Flagship Healthcare Center.
The Clients: Amex Life Assurance Company; International Data Group; Mitsubishi Electronics America and Spalding Sports Worldwide.

Other Notable Practitioners
At Goulston & Storrs, **Douglas Rosner** has earned the respect of peers with his advice to the

MASSACHUSETTS
INTELLECTUAL PROPERTY

creditors' committee of Arthur D Little. His practice focuses on complex Chapter 11 and Chapter 7 cases, workouts and related litigation, for both creditors and debtors. Sources portrayed him as a *"smart and low-key"* attorney. He has advised the creditors' committees of USM Corporation, and the office landlords in WorldCom. Rosner has also acted as special financing counsel for Malden Mills and is currently representing a creditor group in the cross-border insolvency of United Pan-Europe Communications.

INTELLECTUAL PROPERTY

MASSACHUSETTS
Leading firms (Intellectual Property)
1. HALE AND DORR *Boston*
2. FOLEY HOAG LLP *Boston*
3. CHOATE HALL & STEWART *Boston*
   FISH & RICHARDSON *Boston*
   GOODWIN PROCTER LLP *Boston*

Leading individuals (Intellectual Property)
1. LEE Bill *Hale and Dorr, Boston*
2. FRANK Robert *Choate Hall & Stewart, Boston*
   WARE Donald *Foley Hoag LLP, Boston*
3. HENNESSEY Gilbert *Fish & Richardson, Boston*
   WARE Paul *Goodwin Procter LLP, Boston*

Firms and individuals are listed alphabetically in each band.

Hale and Dorr
The Firm: Its IP prosecution and litigation groups provide a wide range of IP services to a broad client base. The group's litigation prowess was repeatedly recommended to *Chambers'* researchers. Attorneys have defended Dynatech and Whistler against Cincinnati Microwave in a patent infringement dispute over radar detectors.
The Lawyers: IP litigator **Bill Lee** is recognized among his peers as the *"leading star in Boston."* He deals predominantly with patent disputes, but is also known to represent clients in trademark and trade secrets cases. He recently represented Biogen against Berlex Laboratories in a Court of Appeal patent infringement dispute involving a product used to treat multiple sclerosis.
The Clients: GE; Intel; Procter & Gamble; Wyeth; Boston Scientific; Analog Devices and Biogen.

Foley Hoag LLP
The Firm: This full-service firm offers counseling and prosecution services in patent, copyright, trademarks and trade secrets matters as well as general IP litigation. Peers singled out the *"significant depth"* of the team and its strong trial experience.
The Lawyers: *"Top patent litigator"* **Donald Ware** specializes in biomedical patent litigation. He was counsel for Johns Hopkins University and Baxter Healthcare in patent litigation against CellPro involving human stem cell technology.
The Clients: Selfcare; Polaroid; Baxter Healthcare; Abiomed; Hoffmann-La Roche and Robert Reiser & Company.

Choate Hall & Stewart
The Firm: The IP prosecution and litigation groups of this general practice firm are well regarded by competitors for their experience in a wide spectrum of services. Patent litigations include the representation of Teradyne against AMP and Transkaryotic Therapies against Amgen over a European Patent Office patent.
The Lawyers: Peers repeatedly recommended **Robert Frank** for his IP litigation skills. He focuses on patents, copyrights and trade secrets, and was involved in a copyright infringement dispute on behalf of EMC. Also represented Japanese company Eisai in a patent infringement dispute.
The Clients: Harvard University; Dana Farber Cancer Institute; FileNet; Aventis and Cabot Corporation.

Fish & Richardson
The Firm: This *"fine"* boutique provides all-round IP services to its broad client base. Its litigation group fields senior patent prosecutors with a great depth of expertise. The firm's areas of focus include companies in the biotech, optics, telecom, pharmaceuticals and software industries.
The Lawyers: **Gilbert Hennessey** (see p.356) provides patent litigation and prosecution services to his client base, which includes hi-tech entities. Successes include the representation of a Swiss company in a patent infringement dispute involving produce flow meters, and the defense of a Massachusetts-based firm in a patent dispute involving medical equipment used for detecting and diagnosing cancer.

Goodwin Procter LLP
see firm details p.805
The Firm: This firm boasts IP practice groups in the fields of copyrights, patents, trademarks, trade secrets and litigation. The high degree of trial experience among these attorneys was commended to *Chambers'* researchers.
The Lawyers: **Paul Ware** is *"great to work with,"* claim interviewees, and has, as a patent litigator, obtained recognition among peers.
The Clients: Boston Scientific; Citizens Financial; Compaq; GE; NYCE Corporation; Teva Pharmaceuticals USA; Eli Lilly and Amgen.

LITIGATION

MASSACHUSETTS
Leading firms (Litigation: General Commercial)
1. HALE AND DORR *Boston*
   ROPES & GRAY *Boston*
2. BINGHAM MCCUTCHEN LLP *Boston*
   FOLEY HOAG LLP *Boston*
3. GOODWIN PROCTER LLP *Boston*
   MINTZ LEVIN COHN FERRIS GLOVSKY *Boston*
   TODD & WELD *Boston*
4. GOULSTON & STORRS *Boston*

Firms are listed alphabetically in each band.

Hale and Dorr
The Firm: Noted for its *"aggressive"* approach to litigation, this group has a historically strong reputation for representing all facets of commercial and business disputes. It is particularly well known for its expertise in IP and securities litigation. Attorneys here also specialize in the defense of hi-tech corporate disputes, with many practitioners holding relevant advanced scientific degrees. The group represents both plaintiffs and defendants, and acted for Massachusetts General Hospital in a license contract dispute with CenterCare. It also won a $32 million trade secrets case in Delaware.

GENERAL COMMERCIAL

The Lawyers: Interviewees noted that this group has *"several fabulous lawyers."* Among them, **Joan Lukey** was recommended as a *"first-rate trial lawyer."* She has particularly strong expertise in employment litigation, while also covering the range of general commercial and business disputes. These include environmental, contract, trade secrets and IP issues. She represented SAIC in a dispute with the seller of land it had purchased, after discovering the area was polluted.
The Clients: GE; Intel; Procter & Gamble; Wyeth; Boston Scientific; Analog Devices; BIOGEN and SAIC.

LITIGATION — MASSACHUSETTS

MASSACHUSETTS
Leading individuals
(Litigation: General Commercial)

1
- KEATING Michael *Foley Hoag LLP,* Boston
- POPEO Robert *Mintz Levin Cohn Ferris,* Boston
- RENEHAN Richard *Goulston & Storrs,* Boston
- TODD Owen *Todd & Weld,* Boston

2
- KOCIUBES Joseph *Bingham McCutchen LLP,* Boston
- LUKEY Joan *Hale and Dorr,* Boston
- MULDOON Robert *Sherin and Lodgen,* Boston

3
- BARSHAK Edward *Sugarman, Rogers,* Boston
- CURTIN John *Bingham McCutchen LLP,* Boston
- DONOVAN John *Ropes & Gray,* Boston
- GALVANI Paul *Ropes & Gray,* Boston
- MAHONY Gael *Holland & Knight LLP,* Boston
- PIERCE Rudolph *Goulston & Storrs,* Boston

Individuals are listed alphabetically in each band.

Ropes & Gray
see firm details p.870

The Firm: This large Boston-based firm was recommended by sources for its *"skill, ethical conduct and sophistication"* in handling litigation on a national level. Much of the group's work comes from its respected institutional corporate client base, and the full-service practice actively competes on a national level rather than serving on local cases. It covers all types of litigation including bankruptcy, government enforcement, healthcare, employment and IP. It successfully defended Goldman Sachs and Deutsche Bank in claims of an antitrust conspiracy in gold and gold derivatives.

The Lawyers: Possesses a stable of *"outstandingly competent lawyers."* One key member mentioned to researchers was environmental law and litigation specialist **Paul Galvani** (see p.355). He also has an extensive practice in commercial litigation and IP matters, and as an experienced trial lawyer, has defended complex litigation, including securities and legal malpractice cases. He represented Massachusetts Continuing Legal Education in a copyright dispute relating to the publication of a listings guide. **John Donovan** (see p.355) was also noted for his expertise in securities and corporate governance litigation. He was described as a *"smart lawyer"* who instilled *"confidence in his clients."* Donovan works nationally on the gamut of complex business disputes, including investment litigation. He represented Fidelity in a trade secrets case relating to customer loyalty programs.

The Clients: Fidelity; Goldman Sachs; GE; Timberland and Lloyd's syndicates.

Bingham McCutchen LLP

The Firm: Competitors acknowledge that the firm provides *"strong competition with trial prowess."* It is best known for its work in general finance litigation and corporate disputes. Following the merger with McCutchen, Doyle, Brown & Enersen, the group has expanded its antitrust, IP, sports and media litigation practices. It has a weighty portfolio of Japanese clients, and offers a special focus on distribution and franchise-related litigation for the automotive industry. The group represented Japanese manufacturers in price-fixing allegations relating to civil and criminal proceedings.

The Lawyers: Peers endorsed *"an outstanding group of trial lawyers."* **Joseph Kociubes**, the key name mentioned to researchers, was described by peers as *"a top-notch litigator."* His broad commercial practice includes advice to financial institutions and internet consulting companies on disputes relating to patents and technology rights. He has a large practice that has acted in breach of contract disputes relating to M&A. Kociubes has also defended a law firm against a legal malpractice case. **John (Jack) Curtin** is a widely respected general commercial litigator who combines *"outstanding advocacy"* with an in-depth knowledge of the law.

The Clients: Harvard University; Fleet Bank; Bain & Company; Toyota; Major League Soccer; Boston Red Sox and The Boston Globe.

Foley Hoag LLP

The Firm: Colleagues recommended this full-service group for its *"strong expertise in accounting litigation,"* derived from its work with clients of the caliber of PwC. Attorneys also have expertise in IP, environmental, and labor and employment litigation. The group combines its trial prowess with skills in alternative dispute resolution, mediation and arbitration.

The Lawyers: Michael Keating has impressed as *"a good litigator, and a diplomat"* in his handling of general civil and business disputes. Head of the litigation practice group, he is also president of the Boston Bar Association. He represents both defendants and plaintiffs in the hi-tech and manufacturing industries, which includes IP litigation such as trademark, patent, fiduciary and eminent domain disputes. Keating has acted on a patent case relating to the manufacture of a device to inspect cargo for contraband.

The Clients: Lucent Technologies; Boston Communications Group; American Science and Engineering and PwC.

Goodwin Procter LLP
see firm details p.805

The Firm: Attorneys at this sizable full-service firm work nationally on high-stakes disputes. Areas covered include patent and trademark infringement, multi-district mass tort products liability, nonpublic company and partnership disputes, and non-compete disputes. Observers singled out the firm's strong representation of REITs and involvement in public equity disputes. It also provides counseling on litigation avoidance and risk management.

The Lawyers: Shepard Remis is cochair of the IP litigation practice. He has extensive experience in internet and e-commerce litigation, products liability and mass tort litigation. Paul Ware, an IP litigation specialist, is another key member of the firm.

The Clients: Boston Scientific; Citizens Financial; Compaq; GE; NYCE Corporation; Teva Pharmaceuticals USA; Eli Lilly and Amgen.

Mintz Levin Cohn Ferris Glovsky and Popeo PC

The Firm: Sources acknowledge that the firm comprises *"tenacious litigators who are great when you need a tough fight."* Offices across the Northeast and in Los Angeles support the Boston-based litigation group, which is active in corporate and commercial litigation in such areas as biotech, international trade, privacy and employment disputes. The group is well known for its political connections and was commended for its lobbying work. Also offers expertise in alternative dispute resolution.

The Lawyers: The group's leading light is **Robert Popeo**. Described by peers as a *"heavyweight litigator,"* he is said to offer a combination of *"high-level legal skills, sharp elbows in the courtroom and political influence."* He acts for corporate and individual clients in civil and criminal litigation, and has represented GE in its alleged contamination of the Housatonic River.

The Clients: Boston College; Arbella; BIOGEN; AOL; Compaq and Fleet Bank.

Todd & Weld

The Firm: The group is known for representing both plaintiffs and defendants in all areas of business litigation. As a litigation boutique, the firm divides its attorneys into specialist practice groups, such as construction, labor and employment, IP, medical malpractice, probate and real estate, among others. A trial-focused firm, the group is also experienced in pretrial negotiations, arbitrations and mediation.

The Lawyers: Owen Todd is a *"tough all-round trial lawyer."* A former justice of the Massachusetts Superior Court, he now covers civil and criminal litigation, arbitrations and meditation. He defended Cardinal Bernard Law in a civil case of alleged negligent supervision of a priest accused of sexual abuse. He also represented an attorney in a dispute for additional bonus compensation from his former employer.

The Clients: Individuals; partnerships; limited liability entities; public corporations; close corporations and trusts and joint ventures.

Goulston & Storrs

The Firm: This mid-sized firm is predominantly recommended for its *"well-known"* real estate-related litigation practice, which includes financing and contract disputes, and zoning and development permits. However, the group also

MASSACHUSETTS — PRIVATE EQUITY

has substantial experience in general commercial litigation derived from IP, environmental, insurance and employment matters. Attorneys have represented Microsoft in an aspect of its antitrust case, relating to the access of documents about the company's competitors. Also acted for Pebble Beach Golf Club in an IP case concerning the club's trademark.

The Lawyers: Peers commended **Rudolph Pierce** as *"a terrifically capable trial lawyer."* He is a former justice of the Massachusetts Superior Court, and now actively tries cases relating to business contracts, tax, securities and insurance matters. He has defended the Massachusetts Bay Transportation Authority against a lawsuit challenging its method of choosing a supplier for a new fare collection system. He was joined in 2003 by **Richard Renehan** from Hill & Barlow. Renehan is described by interviewees as *"the lawyer's lawyer"* for his specialty in legal malpractice disputes. Active at both the trial and appellant levels, he also represents other professionals, such as school, police and corporate officials. Renehan has represented many major law firms in New England, and a senior member of the Massachusetts bar in disciplinary proceedings for professional misconduct.

The Clients: Malden Mills; Arvin Industries; Pebble Beach Golf Club; Microsoft and Rockwell International.

Other Notable Practitioners

Robert Muldoon of Sherin and Lodgen was recommended to researchers as *"a guru for ethical considerations and legal analysis."* He has extensive experience in the defense of legal malpractice, land use and real estate development disputes. He was part of a team that successfully defended Teva Pharmaceuticals against a patent infringement lawsuit brought by SmithKline Beecham. *"One of the very best,"* according to peers, is **Edward Barshak** of Sugarman, Rogers, Barshak & Cohen PC, who was recommended for his tort and insurance defense experience. He also specializes in the trials of complex disputes and professional liability claims. Another key name mentioned to researchers was **Gael Mahony** (see p.357), formerly of Hill & Barlow PC and now based in the Boston office of Holland & Knight LLP. He was endorsed as *"a long-standing luminary,"* who focuses on complex business litigation. He defended Volvo in a class action that claimed purchasers of automobiles were tricked into overpaying for their vehicles.

PRIVATE EQUITY — FUND FORMATION

MASSACHUSETTS
Leading firms
(Private Equity: Fund Formation)
1. **TESTA, HURWITZ & THIBEAULT LLP** Boston
2. **ROPES & GRAY** Boston
3. **GOODWIN PROCTER LLP** Boston
   HALE AND DORR Boston

Leading individuals
(Private Equity: Fund Formation)
1. **PAINTER Robin** Testa, Hurwitz & Thibeault LLP, Boston
   TEGELER David Testa, Hurwitz & Thibeault LLP, Boston
2. **MALT Brad** Ropes & Gray, Boston
   ROWE Larry Ropes & Gray, Boston
3. **COLLINS Michael** Testa, Hurwitz & Thibeault, Boston
   ROBINS Charles Weil, Gotshal & Manges LLP, Boston
   ROTHERMEL Sarah Hale and Dorr, Boston

Firms and individuals are listed alphabetically in each band.

Testa, Hurwitz & Thibeault LLP

The Firm: Found at the cutting edge of developments in fund formation. The group has been described by market sources as *"the leaders by far in Boston."* The team, which features 15 partners, advises on private equity fund formations and transactional buyouts, both for US and non-US sponsors. Its clients are typically drawn from the larger industry groups and include those derived from the emerging technology and healthcare markets, making the firm a popular choice for established venture capitalists. *"Outstanding lawyers"* enable this firm to dominate the Massachusetts market. Interviewees were also quick to commend a raft of *"junior up-and-coming names."* The group has been busy with buyout club activities and the internal restructuring of funds. It is also active outside the US, with the UK, Ireland, Canada and Israel proving rich sources of work.

The Lawyers: The group has suffered the sad loss of firm founder and legendary private equity adviser, Dick Testa. The firm, however, continues to field a *"deeply talented pool of attorneys."* *"Hugely personable"* **Robin Painter** acts for clients in the US and overseas on capital formations and investment activities. **David Tegeler** was described as *"a leading light"* for his experience in fund structuring, investment and governance issues. **Michael Collins** was recommended to researchers for his work on funds focused on internet and hi-tech developments.

The Clients: The firm has recently acted on fund formations for clients such as: Highland Capital Partners; Adam Street Partners; ACT Venture Capital; Swiss Life Private Equity Partners and Techno Venture Management, a German-US life science fund.

Ropes & Gray

see firm details p.870

The Firm: The *"favorite choice"* of many interviewees, Ropes & Gray is a national force in the tax-efficient structuring of funds. Its attorneys were complimented by peers for their understanding of the transactional side of private equity and *"identifying the needs of their clients."* Enjoying a wide breadth of experience, the group has acted on fund of funds, hedge funds and LBO pools. It has recently advised key client Goldman Sachs on a series of private equity fund arrangements, and acted for Harvard University on its fund structurings.

The Lawyers: *"Technically skilled"* **Brad Malt** (see p.357) was respected for his tax knowledge and *"effective and practical"* solutions to investment structuring. His clients include Bain Capital, Butler Capital and Fenway Partners, and he advises equity and mezzanine groups on LBO and hedge funds. Interviewees deemed **Larry Rowe** (see p.358) to be a *"real presence"* in fund structurings, particularly for his expertise in hedge funds and pension funds. Rowe also acts for some of the largest endowment funds in the country.

The Clients: Alongside a raft of private equity houses and venture capitalists, the firm also advises pension funds, educational endowment funds and private foundations. Typical clients include: Bain Capital Partners; BancBoston Capital; Goldman Sachs; Charlesbank Capital Partners; Merrill Lynch; Golden Gate Capital and Boston Ventures.

Goodwin Procter LLP

see firm details p.805

The Firm: *"A sizable group"* has firmly established a respected name for itself in the private equity and venture capital arena. The private investment funds' attorneys here are considered by observers to be *"the real specialists"* in the creation of funds, such as LBO, real estate and hedge funds. The group is supported by a strong corporate team, which assists in the execution of investments both nationally and overseas. The group operates with a cross-industry approach that ensures breadth of experience. Attorneys were described as *"practical and easy to work with,"* keeping, as they do, *"a clear focus on the end result."*

The Lawyers: David Watson is a key member of the corporate department who acts on the establishment of private equity funds across the US and internationally. He and the team have advised on mezzanine and hedge funds, REITs and forestry funds.

The Clients: Among others, the group advises: Advent International; AEW Capital Management;

Alta Communications; Beacon Capital Partners; Lend Lease Real Estate Investments; MPM Capital and TA Associates.

Hale and Dorr
The Firm: Peers singled out the investment management group here as home to *"intelligent lawyers blessed with sound technical judgment."* The fund formation team is integrated within the corporate practice to provide seamless advice on the creation and structuring of funds and their subsequent transactional lifespan. Currently, more than 200 open and closed funds are represented by the practice. Attorneys have been active in the establishment of venture capital funds that focus on the local hi-tech start-up market, and in the creation of offshore funds to invest in emerging markets such as Eastern Europe and Latin America.
The Lawyers: Sarah Rothermel is well established in the Boston market, and was described to researchers as *"the creative force behind Hale and Dorr."* Much of her work is for regional venture capital funds, with Village Ventures as a key client. She has also been active on restructuring issues and separation agreements for a range of private equity and venture capital funds.
The Clients: Greylock, Matrix Private Equity and Draper Fisher Jurvetson are clients of the firm.

Other Notable Practitioners
Charles Robins (see p.358) has left Hutchins, Wheeler & Dittmar to join the newly established Boston office of Weil, Gotshal & Manges LLP. He brings both a *"wealth of experience"* and strong ties to Thomas H Lee Partners to the firm.

REAL ESTATE

MASSACHUSETTS
Leading firms (Real Estate)
1. GOULSTON & STORRS Boston
2. GOODWIN PROCTER LLP Boston
3. HALE AND DORR Boston
   PIPER RUDNICK LLP Boston
4. MINTZ LEVIN COHN FERRIS GLOVSKY Boston
   NUTTER, MCCLENNEN & FISH LLP Boston
5. BROWN RUDNICK BERLACK ISRAELS Boston

Leading individuals (Real Estate)
1. KRASNOW Jordan Goulston & Storrs, Boston
2. GLAZER Michael Goodwin Procter LLP, Boston
   HAMILTON John Hale and Dorr, Boston
   HAROZ Michael Goulston & Storrs, Boston
   KWASNICK Raymond Goulston & Storrs, Boston
   ROTTENBERG Alan Goulston & Storrs, Boston
   RUDMAN Richard Piper Rudnick LLP, Boston
3. BARKER Christopher Goodwin Procter LLP, Boston
   FISHMAN Robert Nutter, McClennen & Fish, Boston
   HALEY Joseph Goodwin Procter LLP, Boston
   PITTARO Frederick Mintz Levin Cohn Ferris, Boston
   RECK Joel Brown Rudnick Berlack Israels, Boston
   SCHWARTZ Paul Goodwin Procter LLP, Boston
   SHUMAN Melvin Hale and Dorr, Boston
   SIRKIN Joel Hale and Dorr, Boston
   SURKIN Elliot Piper Rudnick LLP, Boston

Firms and individuals are listed alphabetically in each band.

Goulston & Storrs
The Firm: The firm is well known for its historic focus on real estate work, and almost half of its attorneys concentrate on real estate development, acquisition, planning, leasing and finance. Its reputation in the field is such that peers comment: *"You wouldn't come to town without hearing about them."* This full-service group contains specialists in most aspects of real estate law and acts for investors and lenders as well as developers and owners. The team is supported by the firm's strength in related areas of corporate, tax, healthcare, technology and employment law. Clients appreciated the practice's uniformly high standards; one noted: *"I haven't met a lawyer there I don't think is great."*
The Lawyers: A host of lawyers was recommended to researchers. *"Clearly a formidable lawyer,"* Jordan Krasnow was described by competitors as *"the big cheese there."* He was admired for a broad practice that embraces acquisitions and dispositions, financing and development. His work included representation of Beacon Capital Partners in its $270 million acquisition of BP Plaza, a 55-floor office building in LA. Interviewees identified Raymond Kwasnick as a *"dean of the leasing world."* Although the bulk of his practice is given over to leasing matters, Kwasnick is also experienced in general real estate work, including construction, financing and property management. He notably advised Massachusetts General Hospital on the leasing and construction of a 400,000 sq ft research and laboratory facility at Charles River Plaza in Boston. Michael Haroz is considered to be a *"sophisticated and smart lawyer"* who acts both in debt and equity financings and in construction. He recently represented a consortium of lenders making available an unsecured line of credit to a national development company. Haroz also acts for a major Northeastern developer on a potential multi-use (office and retail) development in Montgomery County, MD. Alan Rottenberg is a member of both the firm's corporate and real estate practice groups. Clients told researchers that he *"understands how to close a transaction."* He acts as counsel to institutions such as New England Development, SR Weiner & Associates and Fleet Bank.
The Clients: The firm acted on behalf of AvalonBay Communities on the sale of Longwood Towers, Brookline, MA, and advised Lincoln Property in connection with the acquisition of various sites used for build-to-suit projects. Additional clients include TA Realty, Nationwide Life Insurance Company, Boston Properties and First Essex Bank.

Goodwin Procter LLP
see firm details p.805
The Firm: Interviewees agreed that the firm's 50-strong real estate team is more than a match for other practices in town. The firm is well regarded for its corporate work, and in real estate is thought to excel at the corporate finance aspects of property acquisition and development. Peers acknowledged the firm as an *"important player in finance,"* particularly praising a *"first-class"* REIT practice that features corporate lawyer Gil Menna. The group is also experienced in traditional real estate matters, including development, leasing, acquisitions and dispositions.
The Lawyers: Michael Glazer was singled out for his work on general real estate matters, commercial finance, joint ventures and leasing. His practice emphasizes the representation of institutional investors and lenders in debt and equity transactions, workouts and restructurings. Joseph Haley was often mentioned to researchers as a force in real estate development, financing, permitting, leasing and environmental issues. Group chair Christopher Barker focuses on the institutional and corporate side of the practice, acting on the formation of joint ventures and capital relationships. He recently advised Charlesbank Capital Partners on raising a series of funds with institutional capital, and is also involved in the firm's well-respected REIT practice. Paul Schwartz was recommended for his *"top-quality"* work for institutional investors in real estate-related private market finance, including structuring products to raise funds and handling investment transactions.
The Clients: Clients range from start-ups to multinationals. Among the most recognized are The Prudential Insurance Company of America and Fidelity Investments Real Estate Group. Representative transactions include advising AEW Capital Management on the formation of AEW Partner Funds, a series of real estate opportunity funds. The firm subsequently acted on behalf of AEW Capital Funds in numerous transactions in the US, Canada and Western Europe. The firm

also acted on the formation of Fidelity Real Estate Asset Manager Funds and Fidelity Real Estate Growth Fund, a series of opportunity funds sponsored by Fidelity Investments and managed by Fidelity Management Trust Company. Other matters include representation of Boston Properties in a joint venture to acquire the New York Citicorp Center and in its $1.2 billion acquisition of the Embarcadero Center in San Francisco.

Hale and Dorr
The Firm: A *"major competitor for real estate,"* Hale and Dorr boasts a *"sophisticated group"* of 25 real estate lawyers in Boston. The full-service firm has notable strength in capital management, corporate real estate, and development, particularly of retail projects. In addition, the firm has expertise in institutional debt and equity investment.
The Lawyers: *"Senior statesman"* **John Hamilton** is considered a *"key figure"* in the real estate community. Former managing partner and now chairman of the firm, Hamilton continues to practice in real estate development and leasing. Much of his time is spent counseling Carpenter and Co, who he is representing in a redevelopment project to adapt Boston's Charles Street Jail for use as a hotel. Department chair **Joel Sirkin** handles both transactional and finance matters. Competitors recommended him as a *"high-profile and able lawyer."* **Melvin Shuman**'0s work as a development specialist is well regarded in the state. Representative matters include acting for The Gale Company as developers of a new office tower (of about one million sq ft) in downtown Boston, and on behalf of Boston University in its construction of a 6200-seat ice hockey arena, recreation center and 2300-room student residences.
The Clients: The firm acts for pension funds Fidelity Management Trust Company and AEW Capital Management and for institutional investors, including Equity Office Properties Trust, General Investment & Development with CalPERS and DuPont Pension Funds, and TIAA-CREF. Attorneys also advise developer clients including Cabot, Cabot & Forbes, Campanelli Companies and Spaulding & Slye Colliers and retailers Lowe's, Wal-Mart and Staples. Overseas work includes assisting Taurus Investment Group (composed of German, Austrian and Swiss investors) in acquiring US real estate investments, representing The Gale Company in a joint venture with a large Korean construction company and advising Novartis in the creation of the Novartis Institute for Biomedical Research in Cambridge, MA.

Piper Rudnick LLP
see firm details p.867
The Firm: In January 2003, the former real estate practice group of Hill & Barlow (comprising 24 transactional lawyers and 12 litigators), along with key lawyers from Hill & Barlow's litigation, energy and tax sections, opened a new Piper Rudnick office in Boston. Competitors told researchers that the real estate practice group is *"top quality,"* while clients spoke of its *"significant depth of expertise."* The group offers a full-service commercial representation. The real estate finance practice is weighted toward borrower representation. In development, the firm has particular expertise in large, complex, commercial transactions; its clients are involved in hotels and resorts, multi-family projects and affordable housing as well as office, industrial and apartment projects. The group draws upon the specialties of other practice groups to offer clients representation in complex and multidisciplinary matters.
The Lawyers: **Richard Rudman** (see p.358) specializes in real estate development and finance; his work on projects includes site acquisition, permitting and development planning, leasing, financing and sales. Competitors *"think highly"* of his work, and named him as a lawyer they would *"specifically recommend in cases of conflict."* Interviewees noted that **Elliot Surkin** (see p.359) has *"a good circle of clients."* He focuses on real estate development, finance and tax.
The Clients: The firm represents the owners in the Fan Pier project, a mixed-use office, hotel, residential and retail development in Boston covering over three million sq ft. Other matters include representation of Congress Group Ventures as developers of a 600,000 sq ft office tower under construction in Boston's financial district. The firm also advises pension funds and opportunity funds such as Fidelity Management Trust Company and AEW Capital Management. Additional representative clients are Spaulding & Slye Colliers, Lyme Properties and the Massachusetts Development Finance Agency.

Mintz Levin Cohn Ferris Glovsky and Popeo PC
The Firm: The firm's real estate section in Boston comprises 20 lawyers. It is a full-service development and real estate finance practice, with particular strength in downtown development projects. The firm has its own in-house consulting group, ML Strategies, which offers advice on government and community strategies, environmental issues and media relations. Attorneys possess expertise in multi-family, residential (including affordable housing) and retail developments, as well as in corporate real estate matters. Clients told researchers that the group benefits from the *"broad base and backup of a large full-service firm."*
The Lawyers: Interviewees singled out **Frederick Pittaro** as the firm's leading name in real estate. A development and finance lawyer, Pittaro was recommended by clients as *"the first person to call for a property transaction."*
The Clients: The firm represented Eastern Development on a transaction involving the former Woolworths Building in Boston, and acted for Development Management Corporation on a mixed-use hotel, residential and retail waterfront development in Boston. Financial clients include Ohio State Teachers Retirement Fund and Washington Mutual.

Nutter, McClennen & Fish LLP
The Firm: Thirty real estate practitioners operate from the firm's two Massachusetts offices, handling a diverse array of real estate transactions and financing matters. These include acquisitions and dispositions, land use and permitting, leasing, construction, foreclosures, workouts and restructurings. The group was endorsed by interviewees for its comprehensive experience in the field.
The Lawyers: The *"star of the firm,"* **Robert Fishman** was recommended to researchers as a *"knowledgeable"* attorney with particular expertise in permitting and environmental work. As chair of the land use group, his focus is on land use and environmental permitting, and the development, financing, acquisition and sale of property, as well as leasing, entity formation and conveyancing.
The Clients: The team acts for owners, operators, developers and managers of property. Within real estate finance, the firm represents lenders, brokers and investors. Other clients include educational institutions, hospitals, healthcare providers and nonprofit entities such as governmental authorities and quasi-governmental organizations.

Brown Rudnick Berlack Israels
The Firm: A significant presence in New England, the firm boasts 25 real estate lawyers in its Boston office. With offices also in London, UK and Dublin, Ireland, the firm has international capability. The broad-based practice was commended by competitors for its substantial transactional ability. Attorneys possess noteworthy expertise in areas such as affordable housing, leasing, development, finance, zoning and sitings for telecom buildings and systems.
The Lawyers: Chair of the group **Joel Reck** was described by peers as *"one of the premier transactional lawyers in town."* This *"talented"* attorney has 30 years' experience advising on all aspects of real estate law. His client list includes a number of hi-tech companies, including Sun Microsystems and Teradyne, for whom he acted in the development of a manufacturing, research and office campus.
The Clients: The practice represented the City of Boston and its mayor in connection with the Logan Airport project. International matters include representing PerkinElmer in a large sale-leaseback transaction in Finland. Further clients include Konover, MIT, Sullivan Properties and ABB Energy Capital.

TAX

MASSACHUSETTS

Leading firms (Tax)

1
- GOODWIN PROCTER LLP *Boston*
- HALE AND DORR *Boston*
- ROPES & GRAY *Boston*

2
- BINGHAM MCCUTCHEN LLP *Boston*
- TESTA, HURWITZ & THIBEAULT LLP *Boston*

3
- FOLEY HOAG LLP *Boston*
- SULLIVAN & WORCESTER *Boston*

Leading individuals (Tax)

1
- BLATTNER David *Ropes & Gray, Boston*
- BROWN John *Bingham McCutchen LLP, Boston*
- CUBELL Howard *Goodwin Procter LLP, Boston*
- GORDANIER Dean *Testa, Hurwitz & Thibeault, Boston*

2
- DAVIS Michael *Sullivan & Worcester, Boston*
- RITT Roger *Hale and Dorr, Boston*
- SHAY Stephen *Ropes & Gray, Boston*

3
- DAVENPORT David *Testa, Hurwitz & Thibeault, Boston*
- ELFMAN Eric *Ropes & Gray, Boston*
- SCHNEIDMAN Leonard *Foley Hoag LLP, Boston*

Firms and individuals are listed alphabetically in each band.

Goodwin Procter LLP
see firm details p.805

The Firm: The 15-strong team at Goodwin Procter runs a transactions-oriented practice. Private equity is a specialist area for the group, which also advises on international tax issues and federal and state matters. Market commentators pointed to its reputation for *"covering all bases,"* and the group is particularly renowned for its REITs expertise and capacity to advise on cross-border transactions. According to peers, a combination of wide-ranging knowledge and creative thinking makes this firm a *"major participant."*

The Lawyers: Department chair **Howard Cubell**'s practice is focused on developing tax strategies for domestic and international companies, including advice on the structuring of offshore investment funds. Currently, the majority of Cubell's time is spent representing private equity investors and providing advice on tax controversy cases. His reputation is pinned on his assertive style and creativity: peers described him as *"impressive, a top-notch lawyer,"* while clients applauded his can-do attitude, agreeing that he is *"as good as they get."*

The Clients: Affiliated Managers Group; TA Associates; Advent International; Thomas H. Lee Company; Spectrum Equity Investors and Alta Communications.

Hale and Dorr

The Firm: This full-service firm's tax group of about 20 attorneys covers the gamut of tax issues. In addition to its transactional and controversy expertise, the group has specialist knowledge of the state sales and use tax, and Massachusetts' taxation of out-of-state federal and state banks. Funds-related taxation, debt restructurings, M&A, ERISA and international tax planning are also on the agenda here. The firm is highly recommended for its breadth and experience; according to peers: *"The quality of their work says it all."*

The Lawyers: Despite a three-month sabbatical in 2002, **Roger Ritt** has maintained a major presence in the market with work in M&A, compensation planning, controversies and workouts. The current climate has given Ritt's workload a weighting in bankruptcy, and he has also represented mutual funds in M&A. Peers endorsed his *"professionalism,"* which *"inspires trust."* His highlights include serving as tax counsel in the largest individual bankruptcy case in New England, and acting for creditors' committees in Chapter 11 proceedings.

The Clients: Standish, Ayer & Wood; Student Advantage; Akamai Technologies; Casella Waste Systems; Arch Wireless Holdings; John Hancock Advisers; CMGI and Nortel Networks.

Ropes & Gray
see firm details p.870

The Firm: A commanding presence in the Massachusetts market, some 45 lawyers work on corporate tax, compensation issues, partnerships and international tax planning. A transactions-oriented practice represents institutional investors and funds' sponsors. Tax controversies are also an area of expertise. Market commentators credit the firm's success to its exposure to major clients, agreeing that attorneys have *"honed their skills on sophisticated matters in a culture that encourages creative tax planning."* The sheer size of the department commands respect from peers and clients alike and strength and depth across the board places the firm *"on a different level."* Highlights include advising State Street Bank in securities' issuance, and acting on the consolidations of Putnam Funds and Liberty Funds.

The Lawyers: Senior partner **David Blattner** (see p.354) specializes in federal and corporate tax matters, including advice on structuring M&A transactions and controversies with the IRS. Peers commended his wealth of experience, calling him *"the guru of Ropes & Gray's tax practice,"* while clients praised his transactional prowess. He recently advised Brooks Automation in its tax-free acquisition of PRI Automation. **Stephen Shay**'s (see p.358) varied practice has an international flavor, advising multinational companies, financial institutions and global investors on foreign tax credits, deferral of US taxation and transfer pricing issues. He advised Monitor Clipper Partners on its sale of a French portfolio company and on its acquisition of an interest in a Spanish portfolio company. Interviewees respect him as a *"bright lawyer providing a wonderful service."* **Eric Elfman** (see p.355) has a transactions-focused tax practice, and has worked on a number of tax-free transactions including Millipore's IPO and the spin-off of Mykrolis. Also involved in private equity acquisitions and restructurings, Elfman represented Bain Capital in its acquisition of Houghton Mifflin from Vivendi Universal. Department head Susan Johnston provides advice on mutual fund and investment management matters.

The Clients: Gillette; Cabot Corporation; Timberland; State Street Bank; Harvard University and The J Paul Getty Trust.

Bingham McCutchen LLP

The Firm: The tax department of this major Boston firm offers support on the full range of tax matters. In the transactional arena, the 26-strong group assists the firm's corporate division, while maintaining its strength in federal and state controversy practice. The team has attracted extensive REIT and regulated investment company work, and has advised on leasing and structured finance transactions, tax-exempt bond financings and public utilities and insurers tax law. Clients singled out the high caliber of the attorneys and their professional approach to cases.

The Lawyers: **John Brown** provides tax-planning advice on the structuring of organizations and transactions, often with an international element. Interviewees described him as a *"towering presence"* in the field of tax controversies. Clients likewise acknowledged Brown's track record, commenting that *"his name is on every successful tax case."*

The Clients: Gillette; Reebok; Colgate-Palmolive; Jefferson Smurfit Group; Kimberly-Clark; McDonald's and TransCanada.

Testa, Hurwitz & Thibeault LLP

The Firm: The 23-strong tax team is able to offer specialist expertise in investment funds, corporate restructuring, acquisitions and compensation packages. Market commentators lauded the group for its practice advising technology companies. The firm is also recommended for producing attorneys who *"understand the business needs of their clients."* Its extensive experience in the venture capital fund area has led some sources to deem it *"the cream of the crop in private equity tax matters."* One of the firm's busiest areas of late has been the structuring of international transactions.

MASSACHUSETTS — LEADERS

The Lawyers: *"Head and shoulders above the rest,"* **Dean Gordanier** wins peer recommendation for his funds work. He advises on the tax structuring of domestic and offshore LBOs. Active on an international sphere, he represents US fund managers overseas and foreign entities within the US. He is respected by peers for his *"sharp analytical skills and business focus,"* while his *"encyclopedic"* knowledge makes him *"a real businessman's lawyer."* Gordanier has advised on the overdistributions to fund managers following the bursting of the dot.com bubble. **David Davenport**'s practice incorporates advice to technology companies on cross-border investments and transactions, multi-jurisdictional planning, and litigation at federal and state level.

The Clients: The client roster includes public and private software, biotech and consumer product companies, and electronic, medical device and other manufacturing companies as well as financial institutions and venture capital groups including Atlas Ventures, Concord Ventures (Israel), New Enterprise Associates and North Bridge Venture Partners.

Foley Hoag LLP

The Firm: International tax planning and investment fund structuring is just part of this group's broad range of activities. The team also advises on controversies, REITs, restructurings, and the organization of tax-exempt and governmental entities. The firm recently has been involved in private investment funds and cross-border transactions. Peers noted its ability to *"cover all bases,"* and the sophistication of its tax knowledge. The group has represented the French purchaser of a US software company, and has advised on the migration of European technology companies into the US.

The Lawyers: **Leonard Schneidman**'s tax practice is dominated by international matters arising from cross-border transactions and the tax structuring of hedge and private equity funds. Market commentators are impressed by his *"big-picture outlook,"* noting his *"sound judgment and worldly wisdom."*

The Clients: Abington Bancorp; Acadian Asset Management; Cadre Technologies; International Data Group; International Fashions Apparel Corp; Lasertron; Providence Media Partners; Telco Systems; Transition Systems and Velcro Corporation.

Sullivan & Worcester

The Firm: This tax group of 22 attorneys has recently responded to client demands by adding lateral hires to handle state taxation issues and international tax matters. Peers were keen to stress that, despite the sad loss of senior practitioner Frederic Corneel, a battalion of well-trained troops continues to produce high-quality work. A respected controversy practice is combined with the firm's activities in transactional matters. Specialty areas include tax matters for nonprofit organizations and charities, employee benefits, hedge and LBO funds, and REITs.

The Lawyers: *"A real scholar,"* **Michael Davis** wins broad acclaim from peers for his work on income tax and estate planning matters. He has recently handled the restructuring of an international consulting firm, and the merger and restructuring of two beverage distributors. His *"real concern, deliberation and resourcefulness"* have won him a strong following.

The Clients: It acts for mutual funds and REITs, banks and investment management firms, and corporates in the telecom, consulting, real estate, distribution, hi-tech and construction industries.

Leaders in Massachusetts

ABELSON, Ned
Goulston & Storrs, Boston
617 482 1776
Recommended in Environment

ALFRED, Richard
Seyfarth Shaw, Boston 617 946 4800
Recommended in Employment

ANGLEHART, Donald
Testa, Hurwitz & Thibeault LLP, Boston
617 248 7000
Recommended in Environment

ARMISTEAD III, Ivor Cary
Ropes & Gray, Boston 671 951 7832
iarmistead@ropesgray.com
Recommended in Antitrust
Specialization: Counsels domestic and multinational corporations regarding corporate legal matters and the antitrust laws of the US and the competition laws of European Union and other nations in: joint ventures, mergers, acquisitions, and divestitures; acquisition and licensing of intellectual property rights; distribution of products and services. Assists high-technology and other clients with domestic and international commercial matters including technology transfers, distribution and licensing agreements, and other complex business arrangements.
Career: Massachusetts Bar (1979); District of Columbia Bar (1970). Partner, *Ropes & Gray* (1996).
Personal: JD, cum laude, Columbia Law School (1970). BA, Economics, Michigan State University (1967).

ASHER, William
Testa, Hurwitz & Thibeault LLP, Boston
617 248 7000
Recommended in Corporate/M&A

BARKER, Christopher
Goodwin Procter LLP, Boston
617 570 1000
Recommended in Real Estate

BARR, Lynne
Goodwin Procter LLP, Boston
617 570 1000
Recommended in Banking & Finance

BARSHAK, Edward
Sugarman, Rogers, Barshak & Cohen,
PC, Boston 617 227 3030
Recommended in Litigation

BATES, Jeffrey
McDermott, Will & Emery, Boston
617 535 4068
jbates@mwe.com
Recommended in Environment
Specialization: Practices in the fields of international and environmental law. Has provided counsel to corporations, environmental organizations and governments in connection with international law, environmental litigation, due diligence, product roll-outs, compliance, cleanups, Brownfields development, insurance coverage and products, corporate and governmental policy, and legislation and rulemaking worldwide. Has considerable experience with high profile, complex litigation and controversies. Served as counsel on Doe v. Milosevic (human rights and war crimes violations in Kosovo); New Bedford Harbor, Boston Harbor and Lower Fox River (Wisconsin) litigation and cleanup; Woburn, Massachusetts litigation and cleanup featured in book and film, A Civil Action; appeal of EPA rule implementing WTO Gasoline Standards decision; Caspean Sea delimitation; and anti-corruption matters for Bosnian President, Prime Minister and UN Ambassador.
Prof. Memberships: Admitted to practice before the US Supreme Court, US District Court for the District of Massachusetts, US Court of Appeals for the First Circuit, US Court of Appeals for the District of Columbia and Supreme Judicial Court of Massachusetts.
Personal: Earned BA from Colgate University and JD from University of Virginia Law School.

BELLO, Kenneth
Mintz Levin Cohn Ferris Glovsky and Popeo PC, Boston 617 542 6000
Recommended in Employment

BENOIT, Wilfred
Goodwin Procter LLP, Boston
617 570 1000
Recommended in Employment

BLATTNER, David
Ropes & Gray, Boston 617 951 7281
dblattner@ropesgray.com
Recommended in Tax
Specialization: Senior partner; specializes in federal and corporate tax matters; advises on structuring M&A transactions and controversies with the IRS. Recently worked on buyout and restructuring of cross-border corporate joint venture for privately-owned company and Brooks Automation tax-free acquisition of PRI Automation.
Prof. Memberships: American Bar Association (Tax Section); Boston Tax Forum
Career: Massachusetts Bar (1963). Partner, *Ropes & Gray* (1973).
Personal: JD, magna cum laude, Harvard Law School (1963); undergraduate degree, magna cum laude, Harvard College (1960).

BLECK, Daniel
Mintz Levin Cohn Ferris Glovsky and Popeo PC, Boston 617 542 6000
Recommended in Insolvency

BORDEN, Mark
Hale and Dorr, Boston 617 526 6000
Recommended in Corporate/M&A

BROUNTAS, Paul
Hale and Dorr, Boston 617 526 6000
Recommended in Corporate/M&A

MASSACHUSETTS

BROWN, John
Bingham McCutchen LLP, Boston
617 951 8000
Recommended in Tax

BRUNELL, Richard
Foley Hoag LLP, Boston
617 832 1000
Recommended in Antitrust

BUCHANAN, Robert
Choate Hall & Stewart, Boston
617 248 5000
Recommended in Antitrust

BURLING, James
Hale and Dorr, Boston
617 526 6000
Recommended in Antitrust

BURT, Laurie
Foley Hoag LLP, Boston
617 832 1000
Recommended in Environment

CARR, Stephen
Goodwin Procter LLP, Boston
617 570 1000
Recommended in Corporate/M&A

CASEY, David
Bingham McCutchen LLP, Boston
617 951 8000
Recommended in Employment

CHILD, Ralph
Mintz Levin Cohn Ferris Glovsky and Popeo PC, Boston 617 542 6000
Recommended in Environment

COHEN, Bret A
Pepe & Hazard LLP, Boston
617 695 9090
bcohen@pepehazard.com
Recommended in Employment
Specialization: He is a partner in *Pepe & Hazard LLP's* Labor and Employment Group. His practice includes the representation of domestic and foreign employers in labor matters as well as employment litigation, including claims arising under NLRA, FLSA, Title VII, ADA, ADEA, Mass. Gen. Laws ch. 151B, as well as state common law, breach of contract, wrongful termination and defamation claims. He also has extensive experience litigating executive compensation, non-competition and non-solicitation agreements.
Prof. Memberships: The Labor and Employment Law sections of the American Bar Association, Massachusetts Bar Association, the Boston Bar Association, the Illinois Bar Association and the Missouri Bar Association.
Career: Admitted to the state and federal bars in Illinois (1993), Missouri (1994) and Massachusetts (1997). A partner in *Pepe & Hazard LLP* since joining the firm in 2001. Frequently lectures on practice before the Massachusetts Commission Against Discrimination and Massachusetts civil practice. Past Chair of the New Lawyers Section of the Massachusetts Bar Association (1998-00) and is currently on the MBA Labor and Employment Law Section Council (2001 to present) and a fellow of the Massachusetts Bar Foundation. In August 2000, the Massachusetts Lawyers Weekly selected him as one of the top five up and coming lawyers in the Commonwealth. Member of the Joint Bar Committee (2002 - present), which reviews judicial nominations, and the Boston Bar Association's Committee on Civility (2002 - present).
Publications: 'Ten Commandments to Practising Before the Attorney Assisted Unit of the Massachusetts Commission Against Discrimination,' Massachusetts Bar Association's Section Review (Feb 2003).
Personal: BA from the University of Illinois (1989). JD from St. Louis University (1993) where he was awarded a Certificate in Labor and Employment Law and received the American Jurisprudence Award and the Everett E Hullverson Award.

COHN, Daniel
Cohn Khoury Madoff & Whitesell LLP, Boston 617 951 2505
cohn@ckmw.com
Recommended in Insolvency
Specialization: Founding partner of *Cohn Khoury Madoff & Whitesell LLP*, a law firm specializing in out of court financial restructuring, Chapter 11 reorganization, acquisition of distressed companies. Also extensive experience representing creditors' committees, equity sponsors, suppliers, trustees. Representative matters include: counsel to Waste Systems International, Inc., waste disposal company with liabilities of $150 million, in successful Chapter 11 reorganization (Delaware); counsel to Diam International, Inc., retail display manufacturer with sales of $250 million, in out of court restructure cutting bank debt in half (New York); counsel to successful acquiror of Newcare Health Corp., health-care supplier with revenues of $60 million (Massachusetts); counsel to trustee of Shape Inc., manufacturer of audio/video cassettes, with sales of $100 million, in successful Chapter 11 reorganization (Maine).
Prof. Memberships: American College of Bankruptcy; American Bankruptcy Institute; American Bar Association.
Career: Admitted 1978. Practiced at *Hale and Dorr*, then *Fine & Ambrogne*, before founding *CKMW* in 1990.
Personal: JD (cum laude) Cornell Law School 1978. BA Yale University 1975. Married with four children.

COLLINS, Michael
Testa, Hurwitz & Thibeault LLP, Boston 617 248 7000
Recommended in Private Equity

COOGAN, Peter
Foley Hoag LLP, Boston
617 832 1000
Recommended in Banking & Finance

COOKE, Susan
McDermott, Will & Emery, Boston 617 535 4012
scooke@mwe.com
Recommended in Environment
Specialization: Has worked on environmental and health and safety matters worldwide. Practice includes regulatory analyses and counseling, enforcement actions, permitting activities, Brownfields redevelopment, land use and environmental issues in transactions, and legislative and regulatory proposals. Work has covered site cleanups and liability actions at contaminated sites. Served as coordinating counsel in Superfund negotiations; Brownfields redevelopment projects; EHS audits; due diligence reviews and permitting of industrial, commercial, and large residential properties, including development of environmental opinion format for transactions; chemical regulation and use, including procurement of first waiver under state chemical regulation law to expedite construction of industrial facility and first US exemption from premanufacture notification requirements under federal Toxic Substances Control Act. Clients include major manufacturers and energy, technology, and health sector companies.
Prof. Memberships: Admitted to practice in Massachusetts and before US Patent and Trademark Office. Chaired Hazardous Waste Subcommittee of American Bar Association Business Law Section's Environmental, Energy, and Natural Resources Law Committee.
Publications: General editor and principal author of five volume treatise on hazardous waste and Superfund law.
Personal: BA, Chemistry, Emmanuel College; JD, Boston University; special student, Electrical Engineeering, MIT.

COUKOS, Steven
Edwards & Angell, LLP,
Boston 617 439 4444
Recommended in Banking & Finance

CUBELL, Howard
Goodwin Procter LLP, Boston
617 570 1000
Recommended in Tax

CURTIN, John
Bingham McCutchen LLP, Boston
617 951 8000
Recommended in Antitrust, Litigation

CURTIN, Neal
Bingham McCutchen LLP, Boston
617 951 8000
Recommended in Banking & Finance

DALEY, Paul
Hale and Dorr, Boston 617 526 6000
Recommended in Insolvency

DAMON, Lisa
Seyfarth Shaw, Boston 617 946 4800
Recommended in Employment

DAVENPORT, David
Testa, Hurwitz & Thibeault LLP,
Boston 617 248 7000
Recommended in Tax

DAVIS, Christopher
Goodwin Procter LLP, Boston
617 570 1000
Recommended in Environment

DAVIS, Michael
Sullivan & Worcester, Boston
617 338 2800
Recommended in Tax

DONOVAN, John
Ropes & Gray, Boston 617 951 7566
jdonovan@ropesgray.com
Recommended in Litigation
Specialization: Business litigation, including corporate and securities matters, class actions, disputes in connection with mergers and acquisitions, other complex business transactions. Expertise in corporate and securities litigation as a result of successfully defending high tech corporations, 'old economy' issuers, underwriters and financial services companies in litigation. Appeared and argued such cases in dozens of state and federal jurisdictions, producing successful results at both trial and appellate court levels.
Prof. Memberships: American, Massachusetts, Boston Bar Associations.
Career: Massachusetts Bar (1981). Partner, *Ropes & Gray* (1990).
Personal: JD, summa cum laude, Boston College Law School (1981); undergraduate degree, cum laude, Harvard College (1975).

EHRLICH, Kenneth
Nutter, McClennen & Fish, LLP, Boston
617 439 2000
Recommended in Banking & Finance

ELFMAN, Eric
Ropes & Gray, Boston 617 951 7298
eelfman@ropesgray.com
Recommended in Tax
Specialization: Federal and corporate tax practice focusing on transactions and planning and tax audit and controversy matters; extensive experience in structuring acquisitions, mergers, leveraged buyouts, recapitalizations, preferred stock financings and spin-off transactions, venture capital and private equity deals, technology licensing transactions for biotechnology and life science companies; recent transactions include Millipore Corporation's IPO and spin-off of Mykrolis Corporation; representing Bain Capital in structuring the equity component of the acquisition of Houghton Mifflin from Vivendi and the acquisition of Domino's Pizza, Inc.
Prof. Memberships: Past Chairman, American Bar Association Corporate Tax

MASSACHUSETTS LEADERS

Committee; Policy and Special Projects Subcommittee Member, Boston Bar Association, American Institute of CPAs and Massachusetts Society of CPAs.
Career: Massachusetts Bar (1986); California Bar (1980). Certified Public Accountant (Pennsylvania, 1977). Partner, *Ropes & Gray (1989)*. Previously Attorney-Advisor in US Treasury's Office of Tax Policy, responsible for assisting in formulating tax policy positions in the corporate tax and tax accounting areas.
Publications: Several articles in New York University Institute on Federal Taxation, Taxes, Practicing Law Institute and other national tax publications.
Personal: JD, George Washington University Law School (1980). MS in Accounting, University of Pennsylvania Wharton Graduate School (1976). BS in Economics, University of Pennsylvania Wharton School (1975).

ENGEL, David
Bingham McCutchen LLP, Boston
617 951 8000
Recommended in Corporate/M&A

FISHMAN, Robert
Nutter, McClennen & Fish, LLP, Boston
617 439 2000
Recommended in Real Estate

FRANK, Robert
Choate Hall & Stewart, Boston
617 248 5000
Recommended in Intellectual Property

FUGUET, Howard
Ropes & Gray, Boston 617 951 7000
hfuguet@ropesgray.com
Recommended in Antitrust
Specialization: Corporate and antitrust partner concentrating in corporate representation of public companies, and industry corporate mergers, acquisitions and joint ventures, and concentrating in antitrust matters, including acquisitions and joint ventures; pricing, distribution, and marketing matters; and the representation of clients before the United States Department of Justice and the Federal Trade Commission.
Career: Massachusetts Bar (1962). Partner, *Ropes & Gray* (1971).
Publications: Co-author of Robinson-Patman Act: A Quick Synopsis and other antitrust material for the 1993 Massachusetts Continuing Legal Education Program on 'Antitrust Basics'.
Personal: LLB, Harvard Law School (1962).

GALVANI, Paul
Ropes & Gray, Boston 617 951 7543
pgalvani@ropesgray.com
Recommended in Environment, Litigation
Specialization: Environmental law, commercial litigation, and intellectual property. Experienced trial lawyer who has served as defense counsel in complex commercial and white collar litigation, including in securities, patent, and natural resource damage cases.
Prof. Memberships: Lectured for several years at Harvard Law School; Fellow of the American College of Trial Lawyers; Member of the American Law Institute; Boston Bar Association.
Career: Former law clerk and assistant United States Attorney in the Southern District of New York. New York Bar (1965). Massachusetts Bar (1964). Partner, *Ropes & Gray* (1975).
Publications: 'White Collar Crime Business & Regulatory Defenses', co-author of Chapters: Defending the Criminal Antitrust Action; Government Contract Fraud: Detecting it and Controlling the Damages. 'Natural Resource Lawyers: A Legal, Economic, and Policy Analysis': co-author of Chapter: Scientific and Legal Conundrums in Establishing Injury and Damages: The Natural Resource Damage Assessment Regulations (1995).
Personal: JD, cum laude, Harvard Law School (1964). Undergraduate degree, magna cum laude, Phi Beta Kappa, Williams College (1960).

GLAZER, Michael
Goodwin Procter LLP, Boston
617 570 1000
Recommended in Real Estate

GLOSBAND, Daniel
Goodwin Procter LLP, Boston
617 570 1000
Recommended in Insolvency

GOLDBERG, Daniel
Bingham McCutchen LLP, Boston
617 951 8000
Recommended in Antitrust

GOODHEART, Lisa
Piper Rudnick LLP, Boston
617 406 6023
lisa.goodheart@piperrudnick.com
Recommended in Environment
Specialization: Environmental, Litigation and Real Estate.
Prof. Memberships: Co-Chair of the Boston Bar Association's Environmental Law Section; New England Women in Real Estate.
Career: Trial lawyer concentrating in real estate and business disputes, with experience in environmental cost recovery cases, permitting appeals, and environmental enforcement, insurance and consultant malpractice actions, as well as breach of contract, negligence and fraud cases. She has been named as one of 10 'Lawyers of the Year' in a leading American legal publication.
Personal: JD, University of Pennsylvania Law School, cum laude; BA, Williams College, cum laude, Phi Beta Kappa.

GOODMAN, Louis A
Skadden, Arps, Slate, Meagher & Flom LLP & Affiliates, Boston 617 573 4830
lgoodman@skadden.com
Recommended in Corporate/M&A
Specialization: Head of *Skadden's* Boston office. Advises on a wide range of corporate matters, from financings, acquisitions and restructurings to white collar criminal defense.
Publications: Author, 'Takeover Strategies & Responses: The Battle for Corporate Control'.
Personal: JD, Harvard Law School, 1969; MA Harvard University, 1966; AB Columbia College, 1965.

GORDANIER, Dean
Testa, Hurwitz & Thibeault LLP, Boston
617 248 7000
Recommended in Tax

GORDON, Robert
Ropes & Gray, Boston 617 951 7442
rgordon@ropesgray.com
Recommended in Employment
Specialization: Advising, defending management in employment discrimination, wrongful discharge, employee privacy, defamation, employee benefits, wage and hour, non-competition, and trade secret litigation. Numerous cases to verdict in state and federal courts, dozens of labor and commercial arbitrations. Extensive appellate experience.
Prof. Memberships: American, Massachusetts, Boston bar associations; Steering Committee Member of Labor & Employment Law section- Boston Bar Association.
Career: Connecticut Bar (1995); Rhode Island Bar (1991); Massachusetts Bar (1986). Partner, *Ropes & Gray* (1995).
Publications: Private Settlement as Alternative Adjudication: A Rationale for Negotiation Ethics, 18 U. Mich. J. L. Ref. 503 (1985). New Jersey's Casino Set-Aside Program After Croson, 13 Seton Hall L. J. 155 (1990) (with David O Stewart). Running in the Wrong Direction: Robinson's Off-Track Interpretation of Hicks, (1994 MBA Best of the Sections). Attendance Control Issues under the ADA and FMLA, 12 The Labor Lawyer No. 4 (American Bar Association Summer/Fall 1997) (with Christopher L Ekman). Temporary Employees in the Modern Workplace: Avoiding the Legal Pitfalls, 1999 MCLE Employment Law Conference, pp. 81-147 (Dec. 1999) (with David M Mandel).
Personal: JD, cum laude, University of Michigan Law School (1986); undergraduate degree, Phi Beta Kappa, Wesleyan University (1983).

HALEY, Joseph
Goodwin Procter LLP, Boston
617 570 1000
Recommended in Real Estate

HAMILTON, John
Hale and Dorr, Boston 617 526 6000
Recommended in Real Estate

HAROZ, Michael
Goulston & Storrs, Boston
617 482 1776
Recommended in Real Estate

HEALY, Martin
Goodwin Procter LLP, Boston
617 570 1000
Recommended in Environment

HENNESSEY, Gilbert
Fish & Richardson, Boston
617 521 7838
hennessey@fr.com
Recommended in Intellectual Property
Specialization: Principal in Patents and Litigation Groups in Boston office, specializing in counseling high tech companies in contested matters involving technology IP. Experienced in software and Internet IP matters. He represented Lotus(1-2-3®) in Refac v Lotus defeating one of the first software patents in the US. Also represented Endress + Hauser in Micro Motion v Endress + Hauser, a US patent litigation against a Swiss-based European manufacturer of Coriolis mass flow meters. Other areas of expertise include electronic medical equipment, eg, pacemakers and imaging, patent reissues and re-examinations, domestic and international licensing, IP due diligence for mergers, acquisitions and venture funds, and counseling European companies charged with infringement in the US.
Prof. Memberships: American Intellectual Property Law Association, National Chair of its Giles Rich Moot Court competition in IP law, 1976-78; Boston Patent Law Association; International Bar Association, IP committee.
Career: Admitted to bar of the US Court of Appeals for the Federal Circuit and its predecessor, 1970; District of Columbia bar and courts, 1970; Massachusetts 1979; registered patent attorney, US Patent & Trademark Office since 1970; principal at *Fish & Richardson* since 1987; formerly partner in IP boutique firms, *Kenway & Jenney* (Boston) 1980s, and *Lane, Aitken, Dunner & Ziems*, (DC) 1970s; Office of Naval Research, avionics and antisubmarine warfare, IP advisor 1969-71; arbitrator for the AAA in IP and licensing matters.
Publications: Co-author, 'Patent Practice' (ed. Irving Kayton), Patent Resources Institute, 1976-95 (7 Vols.); co-author, 'Compendium of Packaged Software Licensing Provisions,' (2d ed.), American Intellectual Property Law Association, 1988.
Personal: Earned his bachelor's degree in Physics and Mathematics from Beloit College, where he was elected to the Phi Eta Sigma honor society. He earned his

MASSACHUSETTS

law degree, with honors, from George Washington University. He has sung with various choral groups and has a very active interest in Europe, spending significant time in Paris.

HIGGINS, Keith
Ropes & Gray, Boston 617 951 7386
khiggins@ropesgray.com
Recommended in Corporate/M&A
Specialization: Securities offerings, representing issuers and underwriters, mergers and acquisitions, and venture capital investments. Recognized as one of top IPO lawyers in the country. Securities law aspects of executive compensation arrangements.
Prof. Memberships: American and Boston Bar Associations; Chair, Task Force on Securities Law Opinions; Member, Subcommittee on Executive Compensation, Employee Benefits and Section 16 of Federal Regulation of Securities Committee of Business Law Section of ABA.
Career: Massachusetts Bar (1982). Partner, *Ropes & Gray* (1991).
Personal: JD, summa cum laude, Boston University School of Law (1982). MA, University of Virginia (1975). BA, Florida State University, Phi Beta Kappa (1973).

HODGES TAYLOR, Laura
Goodwin Procter LLP, Boston
617 570 1000
Recommended in Corporate/M&A

JACOBS, Neil
Hale and Dorr, Boston 617 526 6000
Recommended in Employment

JAFFE, Seth
Foley Hoag LLP, Boston 617 832 1000
Recommended in Environment

JOY, Robert
Morgan Brown and Joy LLP, Boston
617 523 6666
Recommended in Employment

KAHN, Adam
Foley Hoag LLP, Boston 617 832 1000
Recommended in Environment

KEATING, Michael
Foley Hoag LLP, Boston 617 832 1000
Recommended in Litigation

KELLER, Stanley
Palmer & Dodge, Boston 617 239 0100
Recommended in Corporate/M&A

KIRSCH, Robert
Hale and Dorr, Boston 617 526 6000
Recommended in Environment

KOCIUBES, Joseph
Bingham McCutchen LLP, Boston
617 951 8000
Recommended in Litigation

KRASNOW, Jordan
Goulston & Storrs, Boston
617 482 1776
Recommended in Real Estate

KREIGER, Arthur
Anderson & Kreiger, Cambridge
617 252 6575
Recommended in Environment

KWASNICK, Raymond
Goulston & Storrs, Boston
617 482 1776
Recommended in Real Estate

LEE, Bill
Hale and Dorr, Boston 617 526 6000
Recommended in Intellectual Property

LEON, Michael
Nutter, McClennen & Fish, LLP, Boston
617 439 2000
Recommended in Environment

LEONARD, Stephen
Brown Rudnick Berlack Israels, Boston
617 856 8200
Recommended in Environment

LICHTEN, Harold
Pyle Rome Lichten & Ehrenberg, Boston
617 367 7200
Recommended in Employment

LUKEY, Joan
Hale and Dorr, Boston 617 526 6000
Recommended in Employment, Litigation

LYONS, Gregory
Goodwin Procter LLP, Boston
617 570 1000
Recommended in Banking & Finance

MAHONY, Gael
Holland & Knight LLP, Boston
617 523 2700
gael.mahony@hklaw.com
Recommended in Litigation
Specialization: Partner in the Litigation Department, specializing in complex business cases. His high profile litigation clients include such companies as Volvo and the Hyatt Hotel chain. In a 'Boston Magazine' survey of Boston lawyers he was named the lawyer of choice for 'betting the company' cases. He has served as a member of the Standing Committee on Rules of Practice and Procedure of the United States Judicial Conference, as chairman of the Advisory Committee of the First Circuit Court of Appeals, as chairman of the Massachusetts Special Commission on Foster Care, and is a member of the Massachusetts Commission on Judicial Conduct. He is a member and former president of the American College of Trial Lawyers.

MALONE, Judith
Palmer & Dodge, Boston 617 239 0100
Recommended in Employment

MALT, Brad
Ropes & Gray, Boston 617 951 7318
Bmalt@RopesGray.com
Recommended in Corporate/M&A, Private Equity
Specialization: Concentrating in corporate finance and mergers and acquisitions, he represents equity and mezzanine partnerships in their fundraising and leveraged buyout activities, as well as pension funds, hedge funds, CBO pools and other clients in alternative investments. Was a founder of *Ropes & Gray's* private equity practice. His clients include leading private equity firms such as Bain Capital, Butler Capital, Fenway Partners, Merrill Lynch Private Equity Partners, Monitor-Clipper Partners, and Saunders, Karp & Megrue. Co-chair of the ALI-ABA Advanced Course of Study on Corporate Mergers & Acquisitions.
Career: Massachusetts Bar (1979). Partner, *Ropes & Gray* (1987). Member of the firm's Policy Committee.
Personal: JD, cum laude, Harvard Law School (1979); undergraduate degree, magna cum laude, Harvard College (1976).

MAYER, William
Goodwin Procter LLP, Boston
617 570 1000
Recommended in Banking & Finance

MCCARTHY, William
Ropes & Gray, Boston 617 951 7466
wmccarthy@ropesgray.com
Recommended in Insolvency
Specialization: Head of *Ropes & Gray's* Creditors' Rights Department. Represents debtors and creditors in reorganization cases. Lectures on debtor/creditor relationship. Debtor's counsel to Genuity, Inc., Bay Financial, J. Bildner & Sons and Monarch Capital; committees relating to York Research, Axiohm Transactions Solutions, Promestar and Grand Union Company; and directors or equity sponsors in Enron Corp., Stone & Webster, Mattress Discounters, Dade Behring and Ampan; Harcourt General, Inc. in GC Comanies and Koger Equity, Inc. in Koger Properties case and distressed investors in Molten Metal, Cumberland Farms, Wang Laboratories, and JPS Textiles.
Prof. Memberships: Massachusetts, Boston, American bar associations. American College of Bankruptcy.
Career: Massachusetts bar (1970); US Marine Corps. 1971-1973; *Ropes & Gray* 1974. Partner 1979.
Personal: JD, Harvard Law School (1970); undergraduate degree, College of the Holy Cross (1967).

MENNA, Gilbert
Goodwin Procter LLP, Boston
617 570 1000
Recommended in Corporate/M&A

MESSING, Ellen
Messing, Rudavsky & Weliky PC, Boston
617 742 0004
Recommended in Employment

MIKELS, Rick
Mintz Levin Cohn Ferris Glovsky and Popeo PC, Boston 617 542 6000
Recommended in Insolvency

MILLER, Michelle
Hale and Dorr, Boston 617 526 6000
Recommended in Antitrust

MOEHRKE, Anton
Moehrke, Mackie & Shea, P.C., Boston
617 266 5700
Recommended in Environment

MOTENKO, Neil
Nutter, McClennen & Fish, LLP, Boston
617 439 2000
Recommended in Antitrust

MULDOON, Robert
Sherin and Lodgen, Boston 617 646 2225
Recommended in Litigation

MURPHY, Harold
Hanify & King, Boston 617 423 0400
Recommended in Insolvency

NAGLE, James
Goodwin Procter LLP, Boston
617 570 1000
Recommended in Employment

NEWMAN, Jody
Dwyer & Collora, Boston 617 371 1006
Recommended in Employment

NUTT, Robert
Ropes & Gray, Boston 617 951 7384
rnutt@ropesgray.com
Recommended in Corporate/M&A
Specialization: Transactions lawyer, experienced at marshalling resources of *Ropes & Gray* in complex capital market transactions. Represents primarily investment advisors, investment banking firms and private equity clients including Putnam Investment Management and Merrill Lynch Investment Managers. Represents committees of public bondholders in large case debt restructurings, including Trump's Castle Associates, DR Holdings (Prime Computer), Premium Standard Farms and Grand Union Company restructurings.
Prof. Memberships: American Bar Association: Secretary, Committee on Corporate Laws; Boston Bar Association: Chair, Corporate Law Committee and Business Law Section; Boston University School of Law: Lecturer, advanced corporation and taxation courses, 1987-1998.
Career: New York bar (1971); Massachusetts bar (1971). Partner, *Ropes & Gray* (1979).
Publications: MCLE/NELI, State Usury Laws and National Banks (May 1981); MCLE/NELI, Ownership and Control of Stock and Closely-Held Corporations (June 1983); MCLE/NELI, Advising the Debtor in a Workout (April 1984); MBA, The New Massachusetts Professional Corporations Act (May 1986); BBA, Exculpation and Indemnification of Directors and Officers (March 1988).
Personal: JD, cum laude, University of Pennsylvania Law School (1970); BA, summa cum laude, Grove City College (1967).

MASSACHUSETTS LEADERS

PAINTER, Robin
Testa, Hurwitz & Thibeault LLP, Boston
617 248 7000
Recommended in Private Equity

PAPPONE, Michael
Goodwin Procter LLP, Boston
617 570 1000
Recommended in Insolvency

PATTON, William
Ropes & Gray, Boston 617 951 7572
wpatton@ropesgray.com
Recommended in Antitrust
Specialization: General litigation matters, including antitrust and intellectual property. Patent cases include State Street Bank v. Signature Financial Group, Inc., 927 F. Supp. 502 (D. MA, 1996), rev'd and remanded, 149 F.3d 1368 (Fed. Cir. 1998), a leading case in area of software and business methods patents, and Genentech, Inc. v. Boehringer Manheim GmbH, 47 F. Supp.2d 91 (D. MA, 1999), involving recombinant DNA technology.
Prof. Memberships: American Bar Association (Antitrust, International, Litigation Sections).
Career: Massachusetts bar (1970); Maine bar (1969). Law clerk to Honorable Frank M Coffin US Court of Appeals for 1st Circuit (1968-69). Assistant to Solicitor General of US (1973-75).
Publications: Monopoly Claims, MCLE, New England Antitrust Conference (1985). Contract Provisions From a Litigation Perspective, MCLE, Eighth Annual New England Computer Law Conference (1986). Obtaining Information Abroad (co-authored), ABA, National Institute on Transnational Litigation: Practical Approaches to Conflict and Accommodations (1984).
Personal: JD, Duke University School of Law (1968); BA, Yale University (1965).

PICKETT, Andrew
Jackson Lewis, Boston 617 367 0025
Recommended in Employment

PIERCE, Rudolph
Goulston & Storrs, Boston
617 482 1776
Recommended in Litigation

PISA, Regina
Goodwin Procter LLP, Boston
617 570 1000
Recommended in Banking & Finance, Corporate/M&A

PITTARO, Frederick
Mintz Levin Cohn Ferris Glovsky and Popeo PC, Boston 617 542 6000
Recommended in Real Estate

POLEBAUM, Mark
Hale and Dorr, Boston 617 526 6000
Recommended in Insolvency

POPEO, Robert
Mintz Levin Cohn Ferris Glovsky and Popeo PC, Boston 617 542 6000
Recommended in Litigation

PORTER, Jeffrey
Mintz Levin Cohn Ferris Glovsky and Popeo PC, Boston 617 542 6000
Recommended in Environment

POWERS, Kevin
Rodgers, Powers & Schwartz, Boston
617 482 7771
Recommended in Employment

RAPAPORT, David
Rapaport & Rapaport, Boston
617 747 7600
Recommended in Employment

RECK, Joel
Brown Rudnick Berlack Israels, Boston
617 856 8200
Recommended in Real Estate

RENEHAN, Richard
Goulston & Storrs, Boston
617 482 1776
Recommended in Litigation

RITT, Roger
Hale and Dorr, Boston 617 526 6000
Recommended in Tax

ROBINS, Charles W
Weil, Gotshal & Manges LLP, Boston
617 772 8302
charles.robins@weil.com
Recommended in Private Equity
Specialization: Partner of *Weil, Gotshal & Manges LLP* and a member of the firm's Private Equity Practice Group concentrating in the areas of business and corporate law and corporate transactions. Represents private investment firms in raising institutional funds for investment in buyouts, recapitalizations and other corporate transactions, as well as structuring, financing and implementing investments. Began career with the office of the Chief Counsel, Internal Revenue Service in Washington, DC, where, among other responsibilities, analyzed the tax structure of redemptive buyouts, the precursor to the modern leveraged buyouts, now having represented a wide spectrum of clients in many aspects of these type transactions. Developed innovative approaches for both private equity investment transactions and the economic allocations as between investors and transaction sponsors. Private equity clients include the Thomas H Lee Partners, LP and Berkshire Partners LLC.
Prof. Memberships: He is a member of the American, Massachusetts and Boston Bar Associations and the tax sections of each.
Career: Spent more than thirty years with the Boston firm of *Hutchins, Wheeler & Dittmar* where he established and built their private equity practice.
Publications: Has written and spoken extensively on issues relating to private investment funds.
Personal: Received his BA, from Bates College, 1961, and LLB from Columbia University School of Law, 1964.

ROSENBLUM, Peter
Foley Hoag LLP, Boston 617 832 1000
Recommended in Corporate/M&A

ROSNER, Douglas
Goulston & Storrs, Boston
617 482 1776
Recommended in Insolvency

ROTHERMEL, Sarah
Hale and Dorr, Boston 617 526 6000
Recommended in Private Equity

ROTTENBERG, Alan
Goulston & Storrs, Boston
617 482 1776
Recommended in Real Estate

ROWE, Larry
Ropes & Gray, Boston 617 951 7407
lrowe@ropesgray.com
Recommended in Private Equity
Specialization: Co-chair of *Ropes & Gray's* Private Equity Group. He specializes in structuring and analyzing private equity and debt investments, investment fund formation and investments, leveraged buyouts, venture capital investments, and international transactions. Extensive experience in organizing funds of funds. Clients include some of the largest endowment funds in the country, funds of funds, investment funds and other institutional investors and advisers.
Prof. Memberships: American, Massachusetts, and Boston bar associations.
Career: Massachusetts bar (1985).
Personal: JD, Harvard Law School (1984). MPP, Harvard University (1984). Undergraduate degree, summa cum laude, Phi Beta Kappa, Dartmouth College (1980).

RUDAVSKY, Dahlia
Messing, Rudavsky & Weliky PC, Boston
617 742 0004
Recommended in Employment

RUDMAN, Richard
Piper Rudnick LLP, Boston
617 406 6027
richard.rudman@piperrudnick.com
Recommended in Real Estate
Specialization: Real Estate.
Prof. Memberships: American College of Real Estate Lawyers.
Career: Focuses his practice on real estate development and finance, property acquisition, leasing, land use and environmental regulation, joint venture arrangements, and construction and design agreements. He has represented the developers of several downtown office towers, and has extensive experience in build to suit developments, hotels, and multi-family apartment projects, including projects with complicated phasing arrangements, environmentally contaminated sites and public/private development agreements. He is listed in a leading American legal directory.
Personal: JD, Harvard University (1982), cum laude; BA, Yale College (1979), summa cum laude.

SCHNEIDER, Jon
Goodwin Procter LLP, Boston
617 570 1000
Recommended in Insolvency

SCHNEIDMAN, Leonard
Foley Hoag LLP, Boston 617 832 1000
Recommended in Tax

SCHWARTZ, Andrew
Foley Hoag LLP, Boston 617 832 1000
Recommended in Insolvency

SCHWARTZ, Harvey
Rodgers, Powers & Schwartz, Boston
617 482 7771
Recommended in Employment

SCHWARTZ, Paul
Goodwin Procter LLP, Boston
617 570 1000
Recommended in Real Estate

SCOTT, Thane
Palmer & Dodge, Boston 617 239 0100
Recommended in Antitrust

SHAY, Stephen
Ropes & Gray, Boston 617 951 7302
sshay@ropesgray.com
Recommended in Tax
Specialization: International tax practice; advises on cross border acquisitions, foreign tax credits, deferral of US taxation, transfer pricing issues, cross border withholding on financial instruments; regularly provides international tax advice to Brooks-PRI Automation, Cabot Corporation, EMC Corporation and The Timberland Company, privately-held FMR Corp. State Street Bank and the mutual fund industry's Investment Company Institute; recently advised private equity fund Monitor Clipper Partners on the sale of a French portfolio company and acquisition of an interest in a Spanish portfolio company and the Baupost Group on multiple European real estate investments.
Prof. Memberships: Member, International Bar Association; Member, International Fiscal Association; Member, American Law Institute (served as Associate Reporter for the ALI's Federal Income Tax Project on Income Tax Treaties); Member of the Tax Section of the American Bar Association (former Chairman of the Committee on Foreign Activities of US Taxpayers); Member, Board of Directors, Outdoor Explorations, Inc.
Career: New York bar (1977). Massachusetts bar (1991).
Personal: JD, Columbia Law School (1976). MBA, Columbia Business School (1976). BA, Wesleyan University (1972).

SHILEPSKY, Nancy
Perkins Smith & Cohen LLP, Boston
617 854 4000
Recommended in Employment

SHUMAN, Melvin
Hale and Dorr, Boston 617 526 6000
Recommended in Real Estate

MASSACHUSETTS

SIGEL, John
Hale and Dorr, Boston 617 526 6000
Recommended in Insolvency

SINGER, Steven
Hale and Dorr, Boston 617 526 6000
Recommended in Corporate/M&A

SIRKIN, Joel
Hale and Dorr, Boston 617 526 6000
Recommended in Real Estate

SMITH, Edwin
Bingham McCutchen LLP, Boston
617 951 8000
Recommended in Banking & Finance

SMITH, Philip
Ropes & Gray, Boston 617 951 7744
psmith@ropesgray.com
Recommended in Banking & Finance
Specialization: Leveraged buyout and private equity transactions including debt and equity components of these matters. Extensive experience in structuring syndicated bank credits, leveraged leases, mezzanine capital transactions, and high-yield debt plus experience with acquisitions and public and private preferred stock financings. Experience includes acquisitions and financings on national and international levels in manufacturing, distribution, leasing, motion picture and entertainment industries.
Prof. Memberships: American Bar Association, various committees; Boston Bar Association, Opinion Committee.
Career: Massachusetts bar (1967). Partner, *Ropes & Gray* (1976).
Personal: JD, Order of the Coif, University of Virginia School of Law (1966). Undergraduate degree, cum laude, Williams College (1963).

STILLER RIKLEEN, Lauren
Bowditch & Dewey LLP, Framingham
508 416 2141
lrikleen@bowditch.com
Recommended in Environment
Specialization: Partner in the Real Estate and Environmental Practice Department. Extensive environmental practice with emphasis on regulatory compliance, representation of parties in governmental enforcement actions, and negotiation and litigation strategies. Significant experience with brownfields and related real estate development projects. Serves as a neutral third party in a broad variety of disputes. Diverse client base includes significant higher education practice. Clients include Harvard University, Dartmouth College, Brown University, Boston University, and Mount Holyoke College.
Prof. Memberships: Trustee at Clark University (1988-Present); Chair of the Environmental League of Massachusetts (2000-Present); also member of the Board of Trustees of the Boston Bar Foundation and the James D St. Clair Court Public Education Project. Past President (1988-99) of the Boston Bar Association. Past Chair (1994-95) of the MetroWest Chamber of Commerce.
Career: Admitted to Massachusetts Bar (1979). Partner at Bowditch & Dewey since 1990. Formerly served as: Assistant Attorney General, Commonwealth of Massachusetts; Assistant Vice President for Negotiations at Clean Sites, Inc.; attorney at New England Region of the United States Environmental Protection Agency; and Assistant Director of the Flaschner Judicial Institute.
Publications: Frequent author and lecturer on environmental issues. In addition, contributes op-ed articles on a variety of topics to the Boston Globe and other publications.
Personal: Received JD from Boston College in 1979 and BA (magna cum laude) from Brandeis University in 1975. Attended Clark University (1971-73). Married to attorney Sander A Rikleen, Partner at *Edwards & Angell LLP*, Boston.

SULLIVAN, Mary
Segal Roitman & Coleman, Boston
617 742 0208
Recommended in Employment

SURKIN, Elliot
Piper Rudnick LLP, Boston
617 406 6030
elliot.surkin@piperrudnick.com
Recommended in Real Estate
Specialization: Real Estate.
Prof. Memberships: American College of Real Estate Lawyers; American Law Institute.
Career: Concentrates his practice on real estate development, finance and taxation. Has acted as general counsel to the developers and owners of many of Boston's significant office, mixed-use and retail projects. He has taught courses in real estate development and finance throughout his career.
Publications: 'When Joint Venturers Can't Agree: The Buy-Sell Revisited,' and 'How Do I Get Out of Here? A discussion of Exit Strategies in Closely-Held Real Estate LLCs'.
Personal: LLB, Harvard Law School, magna cum laude; AB, Princeton University, magna cum laude.

SWAIM, Hall
Hale and Dorr, Boston 617 526 6000
Recommended in Insolvency

TEGELER, David
Testa, Hurwitz & Thibeault LLP, Boston
617 248 7000
Recommended in Private Equity

TELEGEN, Arthur
Foley Hoag LLP, Boston 617 832 1000
Recommended in Employment

TODD, Owen
Todd & Weld, Boston 617 720 2626
Recommended in Litigation

WARD, Richard
Ropes & Gray, Boston 617 951 7444
rward@ropesgray.com
Recommended in Employment
Specialization: Employment litigation, including the trial of employment discrimination cases, contract cases, wage-hour disputes, and labor arbitrations.
Prof. Memberships: Member, Labor and Employment Law Sections, American, Massachusetts, Boston Bar Associations; Member, Association of Trial Lawyers of America; selected as a Fellow to the College of Labor and Employment Lawyers in 2001.
Career: Massachusetts bar (1967). Partner, *Ropes & Gray* (1977).
Personal: LLB, cum laude, Harvard Law School (1967). AB, magna cum laude, Boston College (1964).

WARE, Donald
Foley Hoag LLP, Boston 617 832 1000
Recommended in Intellectual Property

WARE, Paul
Goodwin Procter LLP, Boston
617 570 1000
Recommended in Intellectual Property

WESTRA, James
Weil, Gotshal & Manges LLP, Boston
617 772 8377
james.westra@weil.com
Recommended in Corporate/M&A
Specialization: Has developed a diverse practice as a Corporate and Securities attorney. Has represented several of the leading private equity firms in connection with a number of major investments and acquisitions of both public and private companies, including Snapple Beverage Corp. and HomeSide Lending. Also has broad merger and acquisition, capital markets, venture capital and finance experience, and has often served as counsel to boards of directors with respect to corporate governance matters.
Prof. Memberships: Has been involved in a number of charitable and non-profit activities, and is currently an overseer with the Boston Symphony Orchestra, Chairman of the Board of CAST, Inc., a nonprofit corporation which is a national leader in education innovation, and a member of the board of the Boston Rescue Mission, an organization dedicated to meeting the needs of the homeless. Has also been active in his community of Wenham, Massachusetts, where he currently serves as Chairman of the Board of Appeals.
Career: Before joining *Weil, Gotshal & Manges LLP*, was with the law firm of *Hutchins, Wheeler & Dittmar* since 1977.
Personal: Graduated from Harvard College (AB 1973) and Boston University Law School (JD 1977).

WOOD, Lisa
Nutter, McClennen & Fish, LLP, Boston
617 439 2000
Recommended in Antitrust

MICHIGAN

BANKING & FINANCE

CONTENTS: Banking & Finance p.360; Corporate/M&A p.361; Employment: Mainly Plaintiff p.362; Mainly Defendant p.362; Litigation p.363; Real Estate p.364; Individuals' Profiles p.366.

MICHIGAN'S TOP FIVE
1. Miller, Canfield, Paddock and Stone
2. Dickinson Wright
2. Honigman Miller Schwartz and Cohn
4. Butzel Long
5. Dykema Gossett

Ranking based on Chambers' research within the state.

All quotes in the text are from interviews with clients and competitors..

OVERVIEW: Miller, Canfield, Paddock and Stone ranks first. One of the biggest firms in the state, it covers a wide spectrum of business matters. On the corporate side, it is particularly strong in municipal finance. The firm is highly recommended for its employment practice, and for banking and finance, where it serves as general counsel to major financial institutions. David Joswick is respected for his corporate work. Clients include Comerica and Detroit Edison.

Dickinson Wright, in joint second place, operates from five offices in the state, and represents large corporations and government bodies. It also has a strong international focus. Highly rated litigation and corporate/M&A departments benefit from a strong institutional client base. The firm's employment group is also admired. Lawrence Campbell in the litigation department was nominated as a star lawyer. Clients include Northwest Airlines and Deloitte & Touche.

Honigman Miller Schwartz and **Cohn**, ranked second along with Dickinson Wright, is a national player with a large corporate client list. M&A is a key strength, but the firm also has a top real estate department, with practitioners advising on national retail projects and shopping center developments. A strong litigation practice attracts national and international clients. Cyril Moscow in the corporate department is highly rated, as is real estate group chairman Lawrence McLaughlin. Clients include The Federal Reserve Bank of Chicago and The Taubman Realty Group.

Ranked third, **Butzel Long** is a large, full-service firm boasting one of the biggest employment groups in the state. It is particularly strong on employment litigation. Robert Battista, a prominent name in this department, has become the new chairman of the National Labor Relations Board. The firm is expanding its corporate work and represents a number of privately owned medium-sized companies, particularly within the automotive industry. Justin Klimko is mentioned as an experienced M&A lawyer. Clients include McKechnie and Associated General Contractors of America.

Dykema Gossett has a large employment practice, well-known for its employment-based immigration work. It also has an esteemed corporate department, representing both mid-sized companies and multinationals. Real estate is also considered a strength. Well-respected Joseph Ritok heads the labor and employment group. Clients include Standard Federal Bank and UPS.

BANKING & FINANCE

MICHIGAN
Leading firms (Banking & Finance)
1. BODMAN, LONGLEY & DAHLING LLP *Detroit*
2. MILLER, CANFIELD, PADDOCK & STONE *Detroit*
   WARNER NORCROSS & JUDD LLP *Grand Rapids*

Leading individuals (Banking & Finance)
1. BREAY James *Warner Norcross & Judd,* Grand Rapids
2. JOHNSON Donald *Varnum, Riddering,* Grand Rapids
   JOSWICK David *Miller, Canfield, Paddock,* Detroit
   SHULMAN Larry *Bodman, Longley & Dahling,* Detroit

Firms and individuals are listed alphabetically in each band.

Bodman, Longley & Dahling LLP
see firm details p.773

The Firm: This *"extensive"* practice *"covers all the angles."* Statewide, the group represents many of Michigan's banks and continues to act for multi-state financial services provider, Comerica. Peers respected the firm's regulatory and compliance practice – it acts for more than 80 financial institutions. In addition, the group focuses on commercial loans, industrial revenue and other tax-exempt bond transactions. Loan workouts, bankruptcy proceedings and finance-related litigation are also features of the practice.

The Lawyers: Chairman of the firm's executive committee, **Larry Shulman** (see p.367) was frequently mentioned as an *"efficient"* and *"skillful"* attorney. He represents lenders in syndicated loans, and advises mid-sized companies on both asset-based and unsecured lending. On the transactional front, he has acted on leveraged buyouts and multi-rate, multi-currency facilities. Shulman recently represented a Michigan bank on a transitional $50 million secured credit facility for a Californian hi-tech company.

The Clients: Comerica, Standard Federal Bank, The Huntington National Bank and the Ford family are typical clients of the firm.

Miller, Canfield, Paddock and Stone PLC
The Firm: A *"broad"* banking practice, historically known for representing Comerica. The group serves as general counsel to several leading financial institutions. It advises on the preparation of commercial loan documentation and policy manuals. Renowned for municipal finance. It represents corporate clients in asset-based loans and transactions involving multiple foreign and domestic lenders and borrowers.

The Lawyers: Peers identified **David Joswick** as a specialist in the private placement of debt securities. This *"business-minded"* practitioner has recently advised on restructurings, asset-based financings and subordinated debt financings. He acted on the financing of $1.5 billion medium-term unsecured notes offered by a Detroit-based financial institution.

The Clients: Comerica and Huntington Banks of Michigan are clients

Warner Norcross & Judd LLP
The Firm: This small Grand Rapids group has achieved prominence through its representation of an interstate bank holding company and the Michigan Bankers Association. Peers endorsed the firm's expertise in bankruptcy and loan documentation. Packed with *"lots of talented individuals,"* the group covers issues ranging from commercial lending, consumer credit, negotiable instruments and bank litigation to leveraged leasing, antitrust and regulatory compliance. It is also known for the development of securities brokerage operations, mutual fund programs and arrangements with retailers of variable and fixed annuity products.

The Lawyers: Heading up the group as chairman is its shining star, **James Breay**. Interviewees recommended his regulatory expertise, *"analytical skills"* and *"diplomacy in negotiations."* General counsel for the Michigan Bankers Association, he advises and drafts new regulations for the banking industry. His commercial loan work

CORPORATE/M&A — MICHIGAN

includes documentation for Fifth Third Bank.
The Clients: Michigan Bankers Association and Fifth Third Bank.

Other Notable Practitioners
Donald Johnson of Varnum, Riddering, Schmidt & Howlett LLP was described to researchers as *"a key attorney for independent banks."* He represents the Macatawa Bank on transactional and regulatory matters.

CORPORATE/M&A

MICHIGAN
Leading firms (Corporate/M&A)
1. HONIGMAN MILLER SCHWARTZ & COHN *Detroit*
2. DICKINSON WRIGHT PLLC *Detroit*
   DYKEMA GOSSETT PLLC *Detroit*
   MILLER, CANFIELD, PADDOCK & STONE *Detroit*
3. BUTZEL LONG, PC *Detroit*
4. WARNER NORCROSS & JUDD LLP *Grand Rapids*

Leading individuals (Corporate/M&A)
1. SEMPLE Lloyd *Dykema Gossett PLLC*, Detroit
2. JAFFE Ira *Jaffe, Raitt, Heuer & Weiss, PC*, Detroit
   JOSWICK David *Miller, Canfield, Paddock*, Detroit
   KLIMKO Justin *Butzel Long, PC*, Detroit
   MOSCOW Cyril *Honigman Miller Schwartz*, Detroit
3. KUNZ Donald *Honigman Miller Schwartz*, Detroit
   LARSEN Tracy *Warner Norcross & Judd*, Grand Rapids
   SCHWARTZ Alan *Honigman Miller Schwartz*, Detroit

Firms and individuals are listed alphabetically in each band.

Honigman Miller Schwartz and Cohn
The Firm: Observers claimed this as *"the premier business law firm"* within Michigan. Often aggressive in its approach, the firm *"goes head-to-head with New York firms."* A national player, it works for a large stable of private and publicly held companies. It advises developmental enterprises that are preparing share issues and debt offerings. They have key strengths in M&A, real estate matters, commercial and municipal finance.
The Lawyers: The leader here is **Cyril Moscow**, described by many interviewees as *"a first-class lawyer."* Much of his profile lies with his work drafting state legislation. He is a popular choice for opinions on points of corporate and securities law. Vice president of the firm, **Alan Schwartz** was commended by clients as *"one of the best attorneys available."* He advises on M&A, generational wealth transfers and business dispute resolution. Also recommended was chair of the corporate and securities department **Donald Kunz**. *"Gentlemanly"* in his approach, he counsels public companies in corporate matters, technology and IP law.
The Clients: The firm advises healthcare providers and nonprofit organizations. It represented Exemplar Manufacturing in its expansion into Mexico and Canada. Masco; Mechanical Dynamics; Bank One; Ramco-Gershenson and Crain Communications are typical clients of the firm.

Dickinson Wright PLLC
The Firm: Peers commended the group which has *"ties to the oldest and best-known companies in the area."* Operating from five offices in the state, it represents large corporations and government bodies nationally. A strong international practice has particular focus on the Japanese market. Corporate governance, M&A, securities and private capital are areas of work. Clients spoke of their long relationships with these attorneys, and peers described them as *"a firm that works hard to get things done."*
The Lawyers: Richard Bolton heads the corporate, tax, employee benefits and emerging technology practice. He and the team represent private equity funds in venture capital and mezzanine finance transactions.
The Clients: The group represented LDM Technologies in an exchange offering to the holders of its debt securities. It has also recently conducted six securities offerings on Semco Energy. Other clients include Kmart and Wolohan Lumber Company.

Dykema Gossett PLLC
The Firm: Respected by peers for its midwestern focus. It has a national presence and represents mid-sized corporates and multinationals. It specializes in manufacturing, retail and the financial services sectors. E-commerce, healthcare and biotechnology are also growth areas. Experienced in franchise law, corporate compliance and other regulations. The group was particularly recommended for its government experience.
The Lawyers: Former chairman of the firm, **Lloyd Semple** stands out. He focuses on M&A, divestitures and financings, and is often outside counsel for several Michigan-based automotive businesses. Semple has advised healthcare institutions on securities and bond issues. Described by interviewees as a *"commanding presence."* He represented MascoTech's directors in a $2.2 billion recapitalization agreement with Hartland Industrial Partners.
The Clients: Huntington Investment; UPS; Sears; Bank One; MascoTech; Barton Malow Company and Federal-Mogul.

Miller, Canfield, Paddock and Stone PLC
The Firm: Recommended in the past for its forte in municipal finance. The group now boasts a respected general corporate practice, admired by peers for its international specialty group. Minority business enterprises and governmental incentives are strengths of the group.
The Lawyers: **David Joswick** was recommended to researchers for his *"commercially savvy approach."* His corporate practice focuses on divestitures, especially for manufacturing concerns. He has recently established a joint venture company in the Far East.
The Clients: The group acts for multinational corporations, family-owned businesses, joint ventures and strategic alliances. Like many Michigan-based firms, it has a large automotive client base. For instance, it assisted on several joint ventures between German companies seeking greater opportunities with US entities. Other clients include: Michigan State Housing Authority; Michigan Broadband Authority; Comerica and Tecumseh Products Company.

Butzel Long, PC
see firm details p.777
The Firm: One of the fastest growing firms in Michigan. The business, corporate and taxation practice group has succeeded in matching the firm's historical profile in labor law. Peers envy the firm's *"deep resources."* The corporate group represents midmarket privately owned companies, particularly suppliers to the automotive industry. Internationally, it has a focus on China. M&A, partnerships and joint ventures, and restructuring are key areas for the group. It recently assisted with an $11 million venture capital financing for Arbor Networks, and advised on a $115 million public offering by a REIT.
The Lawyers: **Justin Klimko** (see p.366) impresses interviewees as a *"dedicated, hard worker."* Much of his transactional work occurs outside the state. He is experienced in M&A, corporate governance and securities regulation matters for publicly and privately held companies. He represented an IT company in five acquisition transactions, totaling $40 million.
The Clients: McKechnie; Superior Consultant Company; Takata; William Beaumont Hospital; Valeo and Covansys.

Warner Norcross & Judd LLP
The Firm: This Grand Rapids-based group was endorsed by its larger peers as a leading player in local corporate transactions. Core practice revolves around M&A and reorganizations. Also home to an admired finance team that has ties with the Michigan Bankers Association. Planning, antitrust, franchising and distributorship law are all strengths here. The group has

MICHIGAN — EMPLOYMENT & LABOR LAW

recently worked on several securities offerings – both public and private – and complex recapitalization and exchange offers.
The Lawyers: This group of *"talented"* attorneys is typified by **Tracy Larsen**. Interviewees noted his expertise in corporate and securities law. His work is conducted both in the state and nationally, and features corporate finance, partnerships and joint ventures.
The Clients: Mainly Michigan-based publicly traded corporations and privately held companies.

Other Notable Practitioners
Ira Jaffe of Jaffe, Raitt, Heuer & Weiss, PC was described by peers as possessing *"unimpeachable integrity and energy."* He focuses on limited liability matters, partnerships and restructurings. His approach is often *"aggressive,"* which has attracted entrepreneurs and public companies. Clients include The Crawford Group and Edgemere Enterprises.

EMPLOYMENT & LABOR LAW — MAINLY PLAINTIFF

MICHIGAN
Leading firms
(Employment: Mainly Plaintiff)

1. **PITT DOWTY MCGEHEE & MIRER** Royal Oak
2. **EISENBERG & BOGAS** Bloomfield Hills
   STARK & GORDON Ann Arbor

Leading individuals
(Employment: Mainly Plaintiff)

1. **GORDON Deborah** Stark & Gordon, Ann Arbor
   PITT Michael Pitt Dowty McGehee & Mirer, Royal Oak
2. **BOGAS Kathleen** Eisenberg & Bogas, Bloomfield Hills
3. **GOLDEN Joseph** Sommers, Schwartz, Southfield
   GREEN Philip Green, Green, Adams, Palmer, Ann Arbor

Firms and individuals are listed alphabetically in each band.

Pitt Dowty McGehee & Mirer
The Firm: A favorite among competitors. This small firm specializes in employment litigation and personal injury actions for individuals. Noted for its *"aggressive"* approach. It focuses on financial recovery for both settlement and trial scenarios.
The Lawyers: **Michael Pitt** is reputed to have *"one of the largest plaintiffs' practices."* Described by peers as *"a bulldog."* He has acted on discrimination and wrongful discharge claims in state and federal courts. Pitt represented students in a civil rights class action challenging Michigan's use of a high school test to award college scholarships.
The Clients: Represents individuals in employment, PI and civil rights litigation.

Eisenberg & Bogas
The Firm: A smaller firm active in discrimination, pension issues, breach of conduct and workers' compensation. The group is also involved in pre-suit negotiations for both employees and employers. Peers endorsed its *"client-driven focus."*
The Lawyers: The *"formidable"* **Kathleen Bogas** impressed interviewees. Described as *"fighting hard for her clients on the things that are important."* She focuses on wrongful termination and discrimination disputes. Recently represented an Auburn Hills police officer who claimed she had suffered retaliation following her complaints about the illegal activity of a colleague.
The Clients: Represents individuals and companies in employment, commercial and civil rights litigation.

Stark & Gordon
The Firm: A boutique firm based in Royal Oak. Peers described it as *"one of the best plaintiffs' firms in the state."* It specializes in representing public and private sector employees in wage claims, ERISA and discrimination litigation.
The Lawyers: **Deborah Gordon** is a litigator who acts on wrongful terminations, discrimination and harassment claims. She is respected for being *"efficient and results-focused."*
The Clients: Represents individuals in employment and civil rights litigation.

Other Notable Practitioners
"Smooth" **Philip Green** of Green, Green, Adams, Palmer & Craig was recommended by peers for his experience in employment and civil rights cases. He has represented an Ann Arbor attorney in a race discrimination case. **Joseph Golden** of Sommers, Schwartz, Silver & Schwartz PC has acted in wrongful discharge and discrimination disputes. He is also involved in collective bargaining and arbitrations.

EMPLOYMENT & LABOR LAW — MAINLY DEFENDANT

MICHIGAN
Leading firms
(Employment: Mainly Defendant)

1. **MILLER, CANFIELD, PADDOCK & STONE** Detroit
2. **BUTZEL LONG, PC** Detroit
   DYKEMA GOSSETT PLLC Detroit
   KIENBAUM OPPERWALL HARDY Birmingham
   VERCRUYSSE METZ & MURRAY Bingham Farms
3. **DICKINSON WRIGHT PLLC** Detroit

Firms are listed alphabetically in each band.

Miller, Canfield, Paddock and Stone PLC
The Firm: *"An old, fine Michigan firm,"* agree competitors. Involved in traditional labor law, preventative employment relations and litigation. Attorneys specialize in areas such as workers' compensation, wrongful discharge, strikes and lockouts. The firm has recently defended Detroit Edison in a fair labor standards class action case relating to employees' claims for overtime.
The Lawyers: **Leonard Givens**, the long-standing head of the labor and employment group, is highly regarded. He defended 21st Century Newspapers on an age discrimination case relating to a reduction in the company's workforce. He has advised on the National Labor Relations Act and the Public Employees Relations Act. He recently stood before the Michigan Employment Relations Commission regarding unfair labor practices and recognition of union claims.
The Clients: The group's client base features national corporations and automotive companies. Typical clients are: Detroit Edison; 21st Century Newspapers; Detroit Public Schools; Standex International and Greektown Casino.

Butzel Long, PC
see firm details p.777
The Firm: This *"talented and responsive"* group represents public and private sector employers and multi-employer associations in collective bargaining, unfair labor practice charges, strikes, and wage and hour matters. A sizable presence in employment litigation. The group has acted on class actions relating to sexual harassment and race discrimination. Compliance counseling is also a major component of the practice.
The Lawyers: The administrator of the labor and employment group is John Hancock. He and the team advise on employment and OSHA litigation, arbitrations and collective bargaining

EMPLOYMENT & LABOR LAW

MICHIGAN

MICHIGAN
Leading individuals
(Employment: Mainly Defendant)

1. **KIENBAUM Thomas** *Kienbaum Opperwall*, Birmingham
   VERCRUYSSE Robert *Vercruysse*, Bingham Farms
2. **GIVENS Leonard** *Miller, Canfield, Paddock*, Detroit
   RITOK Joseph *Dykema Gossett PLLC*, Detroit
3. **CONNOLLY Walter** *Foley & Lardner*, Detroit

Individuals are listed alphabetically in each band.

negotiations. Robert Battista has become the chairman of the NLRB.
The Clients: Noted for its strength in representing construction employers' associations and universities. Clients include: Detroit Symphony Orchestra; Associated General Contractors of America; Alpha Stamping Company and Michigan Road Builders Association.

Dykema Gossett PLLC
The Firm: This full-service firm is experienced in labor negotiations, administrative proceedings, union organization and strikes. Peers commend the firm for its expertise in employment-based immigration matters. Head quartered in Detroit, it frequently represents clients throughout the Midwest as well as advising international companies in establishing US affiliates. Active in litigation before federal district and appellate courts.
The Lawyers: Joseph Ritok focuses on traditional labor law, including union relations, arbitrations, workforce restructuring and compliance. Head of the labor and employment group, Ritok is also regional counsel for UPS.

The Clients: Standard Federal Bank, Marshall Field's and UPS.

Kienbaum Opperwall Hardy & Pelton
The Firm: Peers nominate this *"effective"* boutique firm, formed in 1997 by four former partners at Dickinson Wright, for its focus on labor and employment law. For instance, the firm has defended Ford in a class action brought by employees alleging age discrimination. They are specialized in the representation of management on wrongful discharge and discrimination claims and traditional union/management matters.
The Lawyers: Thomas Kienbaum (see p.366) was endorsed by peers as the firm's *"first-rate star."* Much of his work features employment discrimination and wrongful termination, particularly class action suits. He has extensive trial and appellant experience. Kienbaum is defending DaimlerChrysler in an appeal against a $21 million sexual harassment decision.
The Clients: Wal-Mart; Ford; DaimlerChrysler; Avis and Detroit Edison.

Vercruysse Metz & Murray
The Firm: A boutique firm involved in the representation of employers, particularly in the auto-manufacturing and supply industries. The majority of its work consists of litigation arising from sexual harassment claims and ERISA, trade secrets and breaches of fiduciary duty. Experienced in negotiating collective bargaining agreements and unfair labor practice proceedings. The practice has expanded to include a business immigration law group.

The Lawyers: Competitors acknowledge that Robert Vercruysse *"fights for every inch"* in the courtroom. He is president and a founder of the firm. He acts nationally on labor, civil rights and ERISA litigation. He successfully defended an unfair dismissal claim in which the employees claimed termination was a result of their attempts to form a union.
The Clients: Siemens Auto Products; American Axle & Manufacturing; Detroit Newspapers and Northwest Airlines.

Dickinson Wright PLLC
The Firm: The group is admired by peers for its *"savvy style."* Differentiated from its competitors by having dedicated groups. Active in employment litigation, class actions and labor relations. The group also advises on employee benefits and immigration and specializes in preventative counseling.
The Lawyers: Timothy Howlett and the team focus on employee relations. Contract negotiations, discrimination litigation and work force reductions are all part of the workload. The group has recently tried jury cases defending wrongful termination, race, disability and religious discrimination claims.
The Clients: Ameritech; Ford; MGM Grand Detroit Casino and University of Michigan.

Other Notable Practitioners
Peers identified **Walter Connolly** of Foley & Lardner for his litigation experience. He represents large corporations in civil rights class actions. An ex-Miller, Canfield, Paddock and Stone attorney, he acts for clients such as Mitsubishi and Kmart.

LITIGATION

GENERAL COMMERCIAL

MICHIGAN
Leading firms
(Litigation: General Commercial)

1. **BUTZEL LONG, PC** Detroit
   DICKINSON WRIGHT PLLC Detroit
   MILLER, CANFIELD, PADDOCK & STONE Detroit
2. **BARRIS, SOTT, DENN & DRIKER, PLLC** Detroit
   DYKEMA GOSSETT PLLC Detroit
   HONIGMAN MILLER SCHWARTZ & COHN Detroit

Firms are listed alphabetically in each band.

Butzel Long, PC
see firm details p.777
The Firm: *"Backed by deep resources,"* this team of *"quality lawyers"* was recommended for its involvement in a spectrum of disputes arising out of business transactions and operations. The full-service group *"handles good-sized matters,"* ranging from products liability to false advertising claims. Practitioners were particularly praised as being *"conscientious and proactive."*
The Lawyers: Many attribute the group's pre-eminence to **Philip Kessler** (see p.366). President of the firm, he is renowned for his expertise in prosecuting and defending contract disputes, IP, intracorporate and partnership disputes. He also has experience in civil rights defense, having recently represented the University of Michigan in a race discrimination class action relating to admissions decisions. Chairman and chief executive of the firm, **Richard Rassel** (see p.366), was described by peers as *"an excellent general litigator."* Practicing primarily in the area of business litigation, he concentrates on media law, libel and complex business disputes.

The Clients: The firm has represented the University of Michigan, Michigan Press Association and Condé Nast Publications.

Dickinson Wright PLLC
The Firm: Noted for its long roster of major corporate clients, the Detroit-based firm was recommended by competitors for its business and commercial trial experience, including a substantial Japanese practice. Although the practice focuses on litigating administrative and public sector cases, and antitrust and libel suits, the group promotes itself as *"solving problems, not creating them",* by counseling clients on how to prevent such actions.
The Lawyers: Peers described **Lawrence Campbell** as the firm's *"leading light,"* noting his expertise in securities fraud defense, accountant malpractice and contract disputes. *"Highly regard-*

MICHIGAN

LITIGATION

MICHIGAN
Leading individuals
(Litigation: General Commercial)

1. **DRIKER Eugene** Barris, Sott, Denn & Driker, Detroit
2. **CAMPBELL Lawrence** Dickinson Wright PLLC, Detroit
3. **KESSLER Philip** Butzel Long, PC, Detroit
   RASSEL Richard Butzel Long, PC, Detroit
   VON ENDE Carl Miller, Canfield, Paddock, Detroit

Individuals are listed alphabetically in each band.

ed" by clients, he also offers experience in acquisitions, mergers and dissolutions of corporations, as well as labor contract negotiations.
The Clients: Northwest Airlines; Gerber Products; Arbor Drugs; AAA Michigan; Ameritech Mobile Communications and Deloitte & Touche.

Miller, Canfield, Paddock and Stone PLC

The Firm: A *"significant presence"* in the Michigan market, the group is known to represent large corporate clients, public entities and tax-exempt bodies such as hospitals. The litigation department is divided into the specialty areas of business litigation and dispute resolution, products litigation and torts, and state and local tax counseling and litigation. Cases include securing a substantial reduction of a $50 million patent infringement award for a manufacturing client.
The Lawyers: The key name here is the *"poised"* **Carl von Ende**, whose broad experience emphasizes trials and appeals relating to IP, corporate, banking, sales and distribution, and constitutional and real estate matters. He recently won a $16.6 million verdict for Valassis Communications against the Sunflower Group, which was found to have misappropriated trade secrets.
The Clients: Valassis Communications; Mitsubishi; Phillips Petroleum Company; Xerox and the State of Michigan.

Barris, Sott, Denn & Driker, PLLC

The Firm: This boutique firm enjoys a reputation for top-quality work and is described as handling *"unusual and difficult cases."* The practice focuses on business law and litigation. Past cases include defending a public utility against a $500 million lawsuit alleging its inability to complete construction of a nuclear power plant. The group successfully used ADR to allow the partnership to complete the project.
The Lawyers: Market appraisal of the firm is implicitly bound up with the reputation of one of its founding partners and undisputed star, **Eugene Driker** (see p.366). A *"real go-to guy,"* Driker was praised by peers as *"a sophisticated strategist."* Actively involved in general business litigation, contract disputes, antitrust, IP and corporate securities, he is also renowned for his expertise representing other law firms in disputes. His clients include Fortune 500 companies, utilities and government entities, including the City of Detroit, which he recently defended in a dispute related to the process of granting casino gaming licenses.
The Clients: GM; Ford; Dow Chemical; City of Detroit; County of Wayne; State of Michigan; University of Michigan and Wayne State University.

Dykema Gossett PLLC

The Firm: Offering one of the largest litigation groups in the Midwest, this *"traditional"* practice was felt to provide *"sensible, business-oriented"* advice on contentious matters. The firm has recently reorganized itself with an emphasis on corporate counseling and has developed a computer information exchange program to benefit regular clients. The full-service practice covers all areas of law for clients ranging from banks and insurers to retailers, manufacturers and transportation companies. Highlights include the successful defense of a WorldCom subsidiary in a $2 million lawsuit filed by AmeriTex for penalties relating to access charges. Attorneys have also advised Masco Corporation in a trade secrets case against a former employee who left the company to work for a competitor in the home insulation industry.
The Lawyers: The firm possesses a strong stable of attorneys who maintain *"high profiles within the local community."* Daniel Wyllie heads the firm's litigation practice group.
The Clients: WorldCom; Masco; Omega Healthcare Investors; UPS and Sears Roebuck.

Honigman Miller Schwartz and Cohn

The Firm: Deemed a *"worthy competitor"* by peers, this large Michigan-based law firm boasts a national presence. Practitioners are reported to employ an *"aggressive"* approach towards litigation and compete with the country's largest and most prominent law firms for national and international clients, such as Philip Morris and Hewlett-Packard. A steady workload ranges from breach of contract to bankruptcy proceedings. The group recently represented AGIS in suits involving termination of internet services to 'spammers', and represented landowners of property taken for the expansion of Detroit Metropolitan Airport. The firm also boasts a specialist media and entertainment litigation group, assisting publishers and broadcasters in breach of contract cases, invasion of privacy claims and copyright infringement suits.
The Lawyers: Norman Ankers chairs the firm's litigation department.
The Clients: Hewlett-Packard; Intergraph; Philip Morris; Ford; The Detroit Free Press and Wonderware.

REAL ESTATE

MICHIGAN
Leading firms (Real Estate)

1. **HONIGMAN MILLER SCHWARTZ & COHN** Detroit
2. **BUTZEL LONG, PC** Bloomfield Hills, Detroit
   DICKINSON WRIGHT PLLC Bloomfield Hills, Detroit
   MILLER, CANFIELD, PADDOCK & STONE Detroit
3. **DYKEMA GOSSETT PLLC** Detroit
   JAFFE, RAITT, HEUER & WEISS, PC Detroit
   MIRO WEINER & KRAMER, PC Bloomfield Hills

Firms are listed alphabetically in each band.

Honigman Miller Schwartz and Cohn

The Firm: Peers lauded this *"developer-oriented"* group as one of the most prominent real estate practices in the state. This large full-service department strives to offer a *"one-stop shop"* for all areas of real estate law. Attorneys specialize in everything from real estate property tax to government-assisted housing, and particular expertise exists in relation to national retail projects. The team advises on all aspects of the development of shopping centers, retail parks and mixed-use projects from financing through to leasing; it advised the developers of The Mall at Wellington Green in Palm Beach, Florida.
The Lawyers: Lawrence McLaughlin chairs the real estate practice group. Recommended by peers for his work on *"extraordinarily complex deals,"* he focuses on public-private partnerships, construction and structured finance. His client list includes major corporations such as Northwest Airlines, who he represented in the construction of the $1.5 billion Midfield Terminal at Detroit Metropolitan Airport. He also advised GM on the acquisition and redevelopment of phase two of its Renaissance Center headquarters. One interviewee praised him as *"one of the brightest people I have ever worked with."*
The Clients: The Federal Reserve Bank of Chicago; The Taubman Realty Group; Ramco-Gershenson Properties Trust; Slavik Enterprises; Compuware and Scholstak Brothers & Company.

Butzel Long, PC

see firm details p.777
The Firm: Described by peers as a *"strong firm*

REAL ESTATE # MICHIGAN

MICHIGAN
Leading individuals (Real Estate)

1 BROMBERG Steve *Butzel Long, PC,* Bloomfield Hills
MCLAUGHLIN Lawrence *Honigman Miller,* Detroit
2 DAWSON Stephen *Dickinson Wright,* Bloomfield Hills
DUNN William *Clark Hill PLC,* Detroit
3 NIX Robert *Kerr Russell & Weber,* Detroit
TABACK Gary *Sommers, Schwartz, Silver,* Southfield
ZUSSMAN Richard *Jaffe, Raitt, Heuer & Weiss,* Detroit

Individuals are listed alphabetically in each band.

with a significant real estate practice," the group employs a cross-disciplinary approach that allows it to handle complex real estate-related matters. The group has experience in all areas of real estate law from urban redevelopment projects and downtown office facilities to greenfield development of industrial centers and residential properties. The firm is particularly noted for its counsel in the River Place project, the redevelopment of an aging industrial complex into a multi-use residential, office and urban retail shopping center.

The Lawyers: The spotlight falls on **Steve Bromberg** (see p.366) whose *"excellent judgment"* makes him *"stand out from the crowd."* Practicing from the firm's Bloomfield Hills office, he focuses on real property law, land contracts, zoning and finance. Bromberg represents borrowers, lenders, purchasers and sellers in all manner of commercial, retail, apartment and subdivision matters. He was particularly recommended for his involvement with the 26-acre Stroh River Place development.

The Clients: Borrowers and institutional lenders; purchasers and sellers; nonprofit entities and contractors and owners.

Dickinson Wright PLLC

The Firm: Possessing one of the largest real estate practices in the state, this firm offers *"a good standard of attorneys"* with expertise in multi-state financings, national real estate development and leases, land use planning and condemnation. Historically, the group has worked for more corporate clients with real estate requirements than for real estate developers; in recent years, however, the firm has made an effort to attract more owner/developer clients.

The Lawyers: Director of the real estate, banking and environmental practice areas, **Stephen Dawson** is seen as the group's leading light. His practice focuses primarily on real estate finance, mortgage lending, leasing and some real estate development. He regularly advises Daimler-Chrysler Services North America on loan transactions to finance new real estate, including dealerships. At the other end of the scale, Dawson has also represented a small developer of warehouses in West Detroit in its acquisition, development and leasing of properties.

The Clients: Borders Group; Pacific Life Insurance Company; Bank One; Canada Life Assurance Company; Liberty Property Trust and The Related Companies.

Miller, Canfield, Paddock and Stone PLC

The Firm: This full-service Detroit-based firm has a portfolio of large publicly traded corporate clients, providing counsel to developers, lenders, contractors and government entities. Members have advised on the development of GM's new Renaissance Center headquarters and Detroit Metropolitan Airport. The group covers all areas of real estate law from financing to land use, but is especially noted for its affordable housing and construction expertise. Attorneys worked on the $300 million development of Detroit's Comerica Park for Olympia Development, owned by the Ilitch family.

The Lawyers: Peers described attorneys here as *"solid, hard-working and bright."* Stephen Palms is the firm's real estate contact partner.

The Clients: Equitable; Transamerica; Michigan National Bank; McKinley Associates; Michigan State Housing Development Authority and Turner Construction Company.

Dykema Gossett PLLC

The Firm: The practice was felt to be *"in a period of transition"* following some partner and associate departures in recent years. However, this full-service group continues to offer broad representation on real estate matters and emphasizes an interdisciplinary approach. Its capabilities extend to advising on both the planning and business aspects of complex property transactions. Attorneys also counsel on specialty areas such as ADA compliance, casino gaming matters, property management and property tax appeals and exemptions.

The Lawyers: James Adams leads a 22-strong group of *"quality attorneys."*

The Clients: The firm represents lenders, developers, contractors, architects and property managers.

Jaffe, Raitt, Heuer & Weiss, PC

The Firm: Specifically recommended for its representation of entrepreneurs, this smaller firm has distinct strength in commercial transactions. The real estate practice is divided into three subsections (general real estate law, leasing and real estate litigation) and offers specialized counsel in all areas from REIT transactions and property tax disputes to industrial property leases. Described by clients as *"competent, talented and reasonably priced,"* the group received particular praise for its leasing expertise. Work in this area includes negotiating leases on behalf of the owners of the Nebraska Crossing Factory Shops.

The Lawyers: Richard Zussman was commended by peers as an *"able attorney."* A member of the firm's business transactions group, he specializes in commercial real estate including acquisitions, disposals, syndications and development projects. His experience of development work ranges from golf courses to planned development communities.

The Clients: The practice represents a range of developers and tenants, corporate and entrepreneurial clients and has recently handled work for Michigan National Bank.

Miro Weiner & Kramer, PC

The Firm: Historically regarded as a real estate boutique, in recent years the firm has diversified into general corporate and business law. It still maintains, however, a highly regarded real estate presence. Peers describe it as *"a fine firm with fine clients,"* and commend the group's *"high standards of service and quality."* Although smaller than competitors, the practice covers a broad range of real estate issues, from acquisitions and development to leasing and land use.

The Lawyers: Laurence Winoker chairs the real estate department.

The Clients: Comerica; The Taubman Realty Group; Kirco Construction and Malan Realty Investors.

Other Notable Practitioners

Although full-service firm Clark Hill PLC does not have a specific real estate practice group, **William Dunn** was named as a *"star"* within the real estate market. Described as *"a real gentleman,"* this *"standout"* practitioner focuses on real estate lending and leasing for clients such as MetLife. **Robert Nix** of Kerr Russell & Weber *"comes immediately to mind"* for all-around expertise relating to developments, financings and acquisitions. He recently negotiated leases for a new $10 million industrial hi-tech park in Plymouth. **Gary Taback** of Sommers, Schwartz, Silver & Schwartz PC was recommended by peers as an *"excellent attorney"* with expertise in real estate finance. Taback has acted on the development of shopping centers, office buildings and mixed-use projects and recently advised on the acquisition and conversion into condominiums of a 28-story apartment complex in Southfield.

MICHIGAN

Leaders in Michigan

BOGAS, Kathleen
Eisenberg & Bogas, Bloomfield Hills
248 258 6080
Recommended in Employment

BREAY, James
Warner Norcross & Judd LLP,
Grand Rapids 616 752 2000
Recommended in Banking & Finance

BROMBERG, Steve
Butzel Long, Bloomfield Hills
248 258 1616
bromberg@butzel.com
Recommended in Real Estate
Specialization: Represents borrowers and institutional lenders, purchasers and sellers, non-profit entities and contractors and owners in all types of office, commercial, shopping center, apartment and subdivision matters, zoning matters, workouts, reorganizations and foreclosures.
Prof. Memberships: State Bar of Michigan, Detroit, Oakland County and American Bar Associations, American Judicature Society, American College of Real Estate Lawyers, President, American College of Mortgage Attorneys. Past chairman of the Real Property Law Section of the State Bar of Michigan.
Career: Senior Attorney.
Personal: University of Michigan in 1952, with distinction, (Phi Beta Kappa). The University of Michigan Law School (JD, 1954).

CAMPBELL, Lawrence
Dickinson Wright PLLC, Detroit
313 223 3500
Recommended in Litigation

CONNOLLY, Walter
Foley & Lardner, Detroit 313 963 6200
Recommended in Employment

DAWSON, Stephen
Dickinson Wright PLLC, Bloomfield Hills
248 433 7200
Recommended in Real Estate

DRIKER, Eugene
Barris, Sott, Denn & Driker, PLLC,
Detroit 313 596 9303
edriker@bsdd.com
Recommended in Litigation
Specialization: Specialist in commercial litigation, with strong emphasis on antitrust, trade regulation, corporate and professional liability matters. Regularly represents major national and international businesses in complex disputes, both in courts and arbitration. Is often called upon by major area law firms to represent them in their litigation disputes and to mediate or arbitrate cases for their clients.
Prof. Memberships: Fellow, American College of Trial Lawyers; Fellow, International Academy of Trial Lawyers; Life Member, Sixth Circuit Judicial Conference.
Career: Trial lawyer, Antitrust Division, US Department of Justice, Washington DC, 1961-64. Private practice in Detroit, 1964 to present.
Personal: Born 1937. BA, 1959 Wayne State University; JD 1961 Wayne State University; LLM, 1962 The George Washington University; Doctor of Laws (Hon) 2001 Wayne State University.

DUNN, William
Clark Hill PLC, Detroit 313 965 8300
Recommended in Real Estate

GIVENS, Leonard
Miller, Canfield, Paddock and Stone PLC, Detroit 313 963 6420
Recommended in Employment

GOLDEN, Joseph
Sommers, Schwartz, Silver & Schwartz PC, Southfield 248 355 0300
Recommended in Employment

GORDON, Deborah
Stark & Gordon, Ann Arbor
248 542 3784
Recommended in Employment

GREEN, Philip
Green, Green, Adams, Palmer & Craig,
Ann Arbor 734 665 4036
Recommended in Employment

JAFFE, Ira
Jaffe, Raitt, Heuer & Weiss, PC,
Detroit 313 961 8380
Recommended in Corporate/M&A

JOHNSON, Donald
Varnum, Riddering, Schmidt & Howlett LLP, Grand Rapids 616 336 6000
Recommended in Banking & Finance

JOSWICK, David
Miller, Canfield, Paddock and Stone PLC, Detroit 313 963 6420
Recommended in Banking & Finance, Corporate/M&A

KESSLER, Philip J
Butzel Long, Detroit 313 225 7000
kessler@butzel.com
Recommended in Litigation
Specialization: Antitrust litigation, corporate control contests, securities fraud claims, merger and acquisition related litigation, audit malpractice, contract litigation, false advertising claims, intra-corporate and partnership disputes, distributorship litigation, bankruptcy litigation, intellectual property litigation, probate and trust litigation.
Prof. Memberships: Fellow of The American College of Trial Lawyers, a Life member of the United States Court of Appeals, Sixth Circuit Judicial Conference.
Career: President of *Butzel Long*. Extensive experience in federal and state courts.
Personal: School of Law of the University of California at Berkeley (1972) and The University of Michigan (1969, AB, with distinction).

KIENBAUM, Thomas
Kienbaum Opperwall Hardy & Pelton,
Birmingham 248 645 0000
tkienbaum@kohp.com
Recommended in Employment
Specialization: Employment litigation with emphasis on complex or class actions; traditional labor relations.
Prof. Memberships: State Bars of Michigan and Illinois; Fellow, American and State Bar of Michigan Foundations; College of Labor and Employment Lawyers; Advisory Board, National Employment Law Institute.
Career: BA, University of Michigan, 1965; JD, Magna Cum Laude (Order of the Coif) Wayne State University, 1968; Associate, Partner and Chair of Employment Practices Group, *Dickinson Wright Moon Van Dusen & Freeman*, 1968-97; Founding Partner, *Kienbaum Opperwall Hardy & Pelton, PLC*, 1997-present.
Publications: Various, including papers presented on behalf of the National Employment Law Institute, and Institute of Continuing Legal Education.
Personal: Born in Berlin, Germany, 1942; married to Elizabeth Hardy, Founding Partner, *Kienbaum Opperwall Hardy & Pelton, PLC*.

KLIMKO, Justin
Butzel Long, Detroit
313 225 7000
klimkojg@butzel.com
Recommended in Corporate/M&A
Specialization: Securities regulation, corporate financing, mergers and acquisitions.
Prof. Memberships: Past Chair State Bar of Michigan Business Law Section; Co-chair, Corporate Laws Committee; Member of the Legal Opinions Committee, the Negotiated Acquisitions Committee and the Federal Regulation of Securities Committee of the American Bar Association.
Career: Securities regulation matters. Private placements and secured and unsecured financing transactions, venture capital financing, and co-venture transactions. Planning, negotiating and implementing merger and acquisition transactions. Representation of special committees of boards of directors. Advised standing board committees in the performance of their duties.
Personal: Graduate of Ohio University and Duke University Law School.

KUNZ, Donald
Honigman Miller Schwartz and Cohn,
Detroit 313 465 7000
Recommended in Corporate/M&A

LARSEN, Tracy
Warner Norcross & Judd LLP,
Grand Rapids 616 752 2000
Recommended in Corporate/M&A

MCLAUGHLIN, Lawrence
Honigman Miller Schwartz and Cohn,
Detroit 313 465 7000
Recommended in Real Estate

MOSCOW, Cyril
Honigman Miller Schwartz and Cohn,
Detroit 313 465 7000
Recommended in Corporate/M&A

NIX, Robert
Kerr Russell & Weber, Detroit
313 961 0200
Recommended in Real Estate

PITT, Michael
Pitt Dowty McGehee & Mirer, Royal Oak
248 398 9800
Recommended in Employment

RASSEL, Richard E
Butzel Long, Detroit
313 225 7000
rassel@butzel.com
Recommended in Litigation
Specialization: Business litigation, media law, libel and slander law, and complex business disputes.
Prof. Memberships: Chair Multi-Disciplinary Practice Committee, State Bar of Michigan; past Chair of the Media and Law Committee, State Bar of Michigan; Vice-Chair of the Media and Law Committee of the ABA; Chair of the Tort Reform Committee of the Libel Defense Resource Center. Member of American College of Trial Lawyers.
Career: Chairman and Chief Executive Officer of *Butzel Long*.
Personal: BA from University of Notre Dame; JD from University of Michigan.

RITOK, Joseph
Dykema Gossett PLLC, Detroit
313 568 6800
Recommended in Employment

SCHWARTZ, Alan
Honigman Miller Schwartz and Cohn,
Detroit 313 465 7000
Recommended in Corporate/M&A

SEMPLE, Lloyd
Dykema Gossett PLLC, Detroit
313 568 6800
Recommended in Corporate/M&A

SHULMAN, Larry R
Bodman, Longley & Dahling LLP, Detroit
313 259 7777
lshulman@bodmanlongley.com
Recommended in Banking & Finance
Specialization: Concentrates his practice in the representation of lenders in loan originations. His practice also encompasses loan workouts and counseling lenders on lender liability issues. He also represents lenders acting in non-lending capacities such as trustee or escrow agent. He has extensive experience representing lenders providing credit enhancements for commercial paper back-up facilities and municipal bonds. He has handled a wide variety of loan transactions including leveraged buyout and leveraged recapitalization loans, asset-based loans, letter of credit and bankers acceptance facilities and multi-rate, multi-currency loan facilities. He has structured and documented agented and syndicated loan facilities and other commercial transactions.
Prof. Memberships: Real Estate and Corporations sections of the Michigan Bar Association and the Business Law Section of the American Bar Association.

Career: Admitted to Michigan State Bar (1978). Joined *Bodman, Longley & Dahling* in 1978 and became a partner in 1985. Chairman of the firm's Executive Committee since 2000.
Personal: Received a JD (cum laude) from the University of Michigan Law School in 1978 and a BA from the University of Michigan in 1975.

TABACK, Gary
Sommers, Schwartz, Silver & Schwartz PC, Southfield 248 355 0300
Recommended in Real Estate

VERCRUYSSE, Robert
Vercruysse Metz & Murray, Bingham Farms 248 540 8019
Recommended in Employment

VON ENDE, Carl
Miller, Canfield, Paddock and Stone PLC, Detroit 313 963 6420
Recommended in Litigation

ZUSSMAN, Richard
Jaffe, Raitt, Heuer & Weiss, PC, Detroit
313 961 8380
Recommended in Real Estate

MINNESOTA

CORPORATE/M&A

CONTENTS: Corporate/M&A p.368; Employment: Mainly Plaintiff p.370; Mainly Defendant p.371; Litigation: general commercial p.372; Real Estate p.374; Individuals' Profiles p.376.

MINNESOTA'S TOP FIVE
1. Dorsey & Whitney
1. Faegre & Benson
2. Leonard, Street and Deinard
3. Briggs and Morgan
3. Gray, Plant, Mooty, Mooty & Bennett

Ranking based on Chambers' research within the state.

All quotes in the text are from interviews with clients and competitors.

OVERVIEW: International firm **Dorsey & Whitney** originated in Minneapolis and boasts one of the most powerful corporate departments in Minnesota. A full-service group covers areas such as M&A, tender offers and corporate finance. Cochair of the firmwide corporate group Robert Rosenbaum was particularly singled out for praise. The firm was also hailed for its litigation, employment and real estate practices. 3M, Northwest Airlines and American Express Financial Corporation are clients.

The second largest firm in Minnesota, **Faegre & Benson**, shares the top tier, earning high marks across the board for its corporate, real estate, employment and litigation practices. In litigation, top-rated attorneys act in both state and federal courts. Market observers salute the firm for its corporate expertise, especially noting Philip Garon and Kris Sharpe for outstanding work in this area. Clients include Hutchinson Technology, 3M and HMN Financial.

Leonard, Street & Deinard, in second place, is widely respected for its strength in antitrust, franchise and stockholder disputes, fraud and securities litigation. Veteran practitioner Morris Sherman was identified as a "*star*" by competitors for his active practice in M&A and securities transactions. The firm has represented clients New World Power, American Express Tax and Business Services, and Fisher Paper Box Company.

Briggs and Morgan, in equal third place, was praised for its extensive resources and broad coverage of securities regulation, corporate financing and M&A. Senior lawyer Christopher Cleveland was noted as a standout attorney within the corporate department. A litigation practice boasting over 40 partners represents a range of businesses including Fortune 500 pharmaceutical and financial services companies.

Gray, Plant, Mooty, Mooty & Bennett is well known for its diverse litigation practice, said to comprise a number of skillful and accomplished trial attorneys. James Simonson, in particular, was named for his ability to bring his erudition to bear on tough litigation matters. A detail-oriented and experienced real estate department, chaired by John Thiel, also attracted general market commendation. The firm's clients are drawn from sectors such as manufacturing, financial services and technology.

CORPORATE/M&A

MINNESOTA
Leading firms (Corporate/M&A)
1. **DORSEY & WHITNEY LLP** Minneapolis
   FAEGRE & BENSON LLP Minneapolis
   KAPLAN, STRANGIS & KAPLAN Minneapolis
2. **FREDRIKSON & BYRON PA** Minneapolis
   LEONARD, STREET AND DEINARD PA Minneapolis
   LINDQUIST & VENNUM PLLP Minneapolis
3. **BRIGGS AND MORGAN PA** Minneapolis
   GRAY, PLANT, MOOTY, MOOTY Minneapolis
   OPPENHEIMER WOLFF & DONNELLY Minneapolis
4. **HENSON & EFRON** Minneapolis
   LOMMEN, NELSON, COLE Minneapolis
   RIDER, BENNETT, EGAN & ARUNDEL Minneapolis

Firms are listed alphabetically in each band.

Dorsey & Whitney LLP
The Firm: This powerhouse of a firm represents corporate clients, investment banks and management buyout groups, among others, involved in M&A, LBOs, tender offers and corporate financings. The corporate group is valued highly by competitors and clients alike for its "*outstanding management of complex transactions*" and for the experience of its "*top-notch*" corporate attorneys.

The Lawyers: **Robert Rosenbaum** advises public and private corporations in M&A transactions. He received the highest respect from market observers for his "*astonishing erudition*" and "*depth of practice.*" His expertise extends to all aspects of corporate governance, public reporting, public offerings and private placement transactions. **Kenneth Cutler** focuses on emerging growth companies and venture capital financing. Clients appreciated that he is "*devoted to our cause,*" while competitors admired his "*sophisticated*" practice, which includes financing, M&A and SEC-registered public offerings.

Faegre & Benson LLP
The Firm: Home to over 60 attorneys in Minneapolis who are experienced in all aspects of corporate counseling, M&A, securities offerings, structured finance and asset securitizations. Market observers reported on the group's "*superb lawyers*" and their "*extensive skill*" in the representation of buyers, sellers and lenders in spin-offs, LBOs and M&A. Recent transactions included a $2 billion public offering for Wells Fargo and two public offerings for Target Corporation worth $1 billion and $750 million respectively. Also advised on Guidant's $3 billion acquisition of Cook Group.

The Lawyers: **Philip Garon** was commended for his work in private and public financings and hostile takeover defenses for buyers, sellers, equity investors and lenders. Observers and clients within the specialty credited his "*magnificent track record*" to the consistent level of "*proficiency and expertise*" he brings to each transaction. **Kris Sharpe** is head of the corporate finance group and the securities law practice. Market observers hail his "*star status*" within the field and beyond, while his familiarity with newly introduced laws has impressed many. Peers applauded **William Busch** for his "*terrific*" representation of magazines, newspapers and other media organizations. His clients include equity investors, purchasers, sellers and management in the area of M&A.

The Clients: Fastenal; Hutchinson Technology; HMN Financial; Deltak; Wilsons The Leather Experts Management Group; Crescendo Venture Management and Spine-Tech.

Kaplan, Strangis & Kaplan
The Firm: The 15-attorney firm enjoys a "*deep bench of marvellous*" attorneys. They provide a "*first-class*" service across a range of transactional and regulatory issues such as M&A, securities and banking and finance. Clients referred to attorneys "*extensive knowledge,*" claiming: "*We trust them to handle the most complex of deals.*"

The Lawyers: **Ralph Strangis** has been highly recommended by competitors for his work in

CORPORATE/M&A — MINNESOTA

MINNESOTA
Leading individuals (Corporate/M&A)

[1]
- **CUTLER Kenneth** *Dorsey & Whitney LLP,* Minneapolis
- **GARON Philip** *Faegre & Benson LLP,* Minneapolis
- **LAREAU Richard** *Oppenheimer Wolff,* Minneapolis
- **MOORSE Charles** *Lindquist & Vennum,* Minneapolis
- **ROSENBAUM Robert** *Dorsey & Whitney,* Minneapolis
- **SHARPE Kris** *Faegre & Benson LLP,* Minneapolis
- **SHERMAN Morris** *Leonard, Street,* Minneapolis
- **STRANGIS Ralph** *Kaplan, Strangis,* Minneapolis

[2]
- **CLEVELAND Christopher** *Briggs and Morgan,* Minneapolis
- **EFRON Stanley** *Henson & Efron,* Minneapolis
- **KAPLAN Samuel** *Kaplan, Strangis & Kaplan,* Minneapolis
- **LIBBEY Keith** *Fredrikson & Byron PA,* Minneapolis
- **SCALLEN Timothy** *Oppenheimer Wolff,* Minneapolis
- **STAGEBERG Roger** *Lommen, Nelson,* Minneapolis

[3]
- **BUSCH William** *Faegre & Benson LLP,* Minneapolis
- **COSTLEY Kevin** *Lindquist & Vennum PLLP,* Minneapolis
- **GARDIN Lynn** *Fredrikson & Byron PA,* Minneapolis
- **HENNIG Gene** *Rider, Bennett, Egan,* Minneapolis

Individuals are listed alphabetically in each band.

M&A, securities and general corporate law. Clients praised him as *"the number-one guy"* who deals with the *"most highly developed and complex"* transactions. His expertise includes corporate governance, joint ventures and public offerings. **Samuel Kaplan** received approbation for his general corporate practice and his *"outstanding"* contribution to its clients. Peers singled him out for being *"exceptionally bright,"* *"with a "superb expertise"* in all aspects of M&A and securities. Kaplan approaches his workload with *"high ethical standards."*
The Clients: Adams Outdoor Advertising; Allianz Life Insurance Company of North America; Camp Coast to Coast; Minnesota Wine & Spirits Wholesalers; Polaris Industries; TCF Financial Corporation; UnitedHealth Group and US Airways.

Fredrikson & Byron PA
The Firm: Commentators recommended the firm for its diversity of experience and the *"imposing quality"* of its corporate department. Emphasis is placed on stock and asset purchases, mergers and corporate reorganizations, and leveraged and management buyouts. The team is also active in the structuring of joint ventures, the issuance of licenses, spin-offs and the raising of capital. Clients swear by its *"highly knowledgeable"* attorneys.
The Lawyers: **Keith Libbey** represents a variety of major public companies and mid-sized private companies and those seeking venture capital funding. He is widely respected for his extensive experience in advising banks and financial institutions. Sources referred to his *"unbeatable"* involvement in major deals in both national and international markets. **Lynn Gardin** concentrates on corporate, commercial, banking and finance law. Her strength lies in the negotiation and documentation of M&A and restructuring transactions. Clients praised Gardin's knowledge and *"flair"* in structured finance transactions.
The Clients: The firm acts for manufacturers and marketers of a wide range of industrial, commercial, medical and consumer products. Other clients include venture capital investors, and biotech and computer software companies.

Leonard, Street and Deinard PA
The Firm: Market observers and clients alike applauded the firm's *"outstanding"* corporate practice. M&A, securities law, business planning and corporate financings are all on the agenda here. The team also counsels on e-commerce issues and general corporate governance. The group is often active in cross-border transactions.
The Lawyers: **Morris Sherman** is, according to competitors, a *"veteran"* with over 40 years' experience. Hailed by market observers as one of the *"stars"* in the field for his *"amazing"* service to both the community and his clients. Sherman is active in M&A and securities transactions, and the financings of private businesses.
The Clients: American Express Tax and Business Services; Wilkins Automotive; Krenzen Indoor Auto Mall; Grossman Chevrolet; New World Power and Fisher Paper Box Company.

Lindquist & Vennum PLLP
The Firm: The corporate department comprises four key disciplines, which focus on M&A, securities law, business planning and emerging growth companies. Observers spoke about the *"depth and breadth"* of experience found in its *"top-quality"* attorneys. Clients appreciated the no-nonsense approach of these lawyers, who *"get the job done effectively."*
The Lawyers: **Charles Moorse** represents buyers and sellers of private and public companies across a variety of industry groups including manufacturing, technology, retailing, financial services and insurance. Clients commented on his *"respected demeanor,"* which he brings to bear on both transactional and corporate governance issues. **Kevin Costley** specializes in the representation of financial institutions in M&A, capital financing and business expansion strategies. Sources described him as a *"hard-working"* and *"ethical"* attorney. Most of his clients are independent community banks located in the Upper Midwest.
The Clients: Acts for venture capital investors, and manufacturing, hi-tech and computer software companies.

Briggs and Morgan PA
The Firm: Commentators praised the firm's resources and recommended some of its *"remarkable"* attorneys for doing an *"admirable job"* for its clients. The corporate division is active across the range of transactions including M&A, emerging company financings and securities law.
The Lawyers: **Christopher Cleveland**, one of the senior figures of the firm, has a practice that incorporates securities regulation, corporate financing and M&A. Respected by many, Cleveland displays *"terrific knowledge"* and *"first-class skills"* that have won him a following both inside and outside the state.
The Clients: The firm acts for manufacturers, technology companies and a wide range of industrial, commercial and medical corporations.

Gray, Plant, Mooty, Mooty & Bennett PA
The Firm: The corporate group received strong feedback from commentators and clients who were impressed with its *"fine reputation"* and *"enthusiastic and dedicated"* lawyers. The firm advises on a range of M&A and divestitures, and offers support in related areas of the law such as tax, antitrust and employee benefits.
The Lawyers: Franklin Jesse chairs the international practice group and concentrates on business law, M&A, franchising and product distribution.

Oppenheimer Wolff & Donnelly LLP
The Firm: Involved in some major corporate business representations, the practice has advised its clients on securities law, M&A, venture capital and general commercial disputes. Recent representative transactions included advising the Michael family on an £800 million acquisition, acting for Merrill Corporation in a transaction with a value of $360 million and representing VidaMed in a transaction worth $326 million.
The Lawyers: Alongside his corporate transactional practice, **Richard Lareau** has acted as mediator and arbitrator in commercial disputes, securities law and employment matters. He was hailed as a *"connoisseur"* for his *"scholarly"* approach to transactional matters. Clients were impressed by the *"deftness"* of this *"top-notch lawyer."* **Timothy Scallen** chairs the M&A practice group and has over 15 years' experience in handling domestic and international acquisitions for both public and private companies. He comes highly commended by market observers for his *"fine technical talent"* and *"professional"* attitude.
The Clients: The firm acts for: Andersen Windows; Ceridian; Ecolab; Nash Finch Company; Norris Education Innovations and Northern Technologies International. It also represents clients in sectors such as transportation and logistics, medical technology, healthcare and financial services.

Henson & Efron
The Firm: Specializes in the acquisition and divestiture of small corporations and large public companies as well as their divisions and subsidiaries. Attorneys in the corporate practice focus on merger structuring and documentation,

MINNESOTA

EMPLOYMENT & LABOR LAW

acquisition financing and development agreements. Sources in the Minnesota market commented on the *"extraordinary quality"* of individual attorneys who assisted clients with obtaining both equity and debt funding through private placements, IPOs and secondary offerings.

The Lawyers: **Stanley Efron**, the former president of the firm, is valued by many of his competitors for his *"refined"* representation of his clients in transactions arising from business formations, financings and M&A.

The Clients: CSK Auto; Minnesota Freezer Warehouse; Delta International Machinery; NetLink Services; Electronic Enclosures; Schroff; Stannard Soil Anchor Systems and Fiberstar.

Lommen, Nelson, Cole & Stageberg PA

The Firm: Provides a full range of services to large and small businesses. Areas of emphasis include M&A, corporate financing and securities. Although one of the smaller corporate teams in the state, it has been praised for training and employing some of the *"smarter"* and more *"dedicated"* attorneys in the market.

The Lawyers: According to clients and rivals, **Roger Stageberg** is renowned for his *"exceptional knowledge"* and *"way with people."* He is typical of the firm as a whole in the *"high quality of service"* he offers to clients.

The Clients: Pipeline Supply; RJM Construction; Roof Depot; Summit Packaging; United Rentals; The Bergquist Company; Burns International Security Services and Dalsin Industries.

Rider, Bennett, Egan & Arundel LLP

The Firm: A general corporate and business counsel for both large and small companies. Attorneys are praised by clients for their negotiating skills in a variety of business transactions including joint ventures, loan agreements, purchases, franchise opportunities, distribution and technology utilization.

The Lawyers: **Gene Hennig** represents business clients across the US, ranging from emerging growth entities to larger public companies, on a broad spectrum of business activities. Interviewees pointed to his successful combination of technical legal knowledge and clear business sense.

The Clients: Clients vary from emerging entrepreneurs to national conglomerates, including Fortune 500 companies and closely held corporations, school districts and municipalities, non-profit organizations and insurance companies.

EMPLOYMENT & LABOR LAW

MAINLY PLAINTIFF

MINNESOTA
Leading firms
(Employment: Mainly Plaintiff)

[1] MILLER-O'BRIEN, PLLP *Minneapolis*
NICHOLS KASTER & ANDERSON PLLP *Minneapolis*
SPRENGER & LANG PLLC *Minneapolis*
[2] GREGG M CORWIN & ASSOCIATES *Minneapolis*
PEMBERTON, SORLIE, RUFER *Fergus Falls*

Leading individuals
(Employment: Mainly Plaintiff)

[1] KASTER James *Nichols Kaster & Anderson*, Minneapolis
O'BRIEN Maurice *Miller-O'Brien PLLP*, Minneapolis
SCHAEFER Lawrence *Sprenger & Lang*, Minneapolis
[2] CORWIN Gregg *Gregg M Corwin*, Minneapolis
NICHOLS Donald *Nichols Kaster & Anderson*, Minneapolis
PEMBERTON Richard *Pemberton, Sorlie*, Fergus Falls
SPRENGER Paul *Sprenger & Lang PLLC*, Minneapolis

Firms and individuals are listed alphabetically in each band.

Miller-O'Brien PLLP

The Firm: Market observers respect the *"great quality"* of the firm's plaintiff employment representation. Its attorneys litigate claims of age, sex, disability and race discrimination. The firm recently secured a $31 million settlement in a national class action against American Express Financial Advisors, a subsidiary of American Express.

The Lawyers: Name partner **Maurice (Bill) O'Brien** has practiced employment and labor law for about 20 years, concentrating on trial work, arbitrations and mediations. Interviewees agreed that this *"professional"* attorney is *"aggressive when he needs to be,"* and *"always practices at the highest level."*

Nichols Kaster & Anderson PLLP

The Firm: Hailed by sources for its *"tremendous"* trial and appellate experience in state and federal courts. The quality and skill of the firm's plaintiff lawyers is widely recognized. Their broad practice encompasses discrimination and sexual harassment claims, complex class actions and high-profile criminal defense cases.

The Lawyers: **James Kaster** has impressed many in his successful actions, which have led to multimillion dollar verdicts. Observers agreed that he was *"magnificent"* in landmark cases that saw the first verdicts on employee polygraphs in Minnesota. Founder of the firm **Donald Nichols** was successful in Ling Luu v Seagate Technology, a case that resulted in a million dollar jury verdict for the plaintiff whose employment was terminated for reporting sexual harassment in the workplace.

Sprenger & Lang PLLC

The Firm: Founded in 1989, the firm concentrates on complex plaintiffs' litigation, such as the race discrimination class action filed on behalf of 25 current and former African-American employees of agribusiness multinational Cargill.

The Lawyers: Managing partner of the firm **Lawrence Schaefer** specializes in discrimination litigation. His *"first-class"* work has impressed peers who refer to him as *"one of the best attorneys in the state."* **Paul Sprenger** has served as lead counsel in many employment class and multi-plaintiff actions. Observers commended his *"amazing depth"* of knowledge.

Gregg M Corwin & Associates Law Office PC

The Firm: Recommended by market observers as one of the *"finest"* labor and employment law firms in Minnesota. This boutique firm acts on discrimination, wrongful discharge, sexual harassment and civil rights infringement claims

The Lawyers: Interviewees spoke of **Gregg Corwin**'s *"high-quality"* plaintiffs' work. His recent clients have included the Minnesota Association of Professional Employees.

Pemberton, Sorlie, Rufer & Kershner PLLP

The Firm: One of the oldest firms in Minnesota, it was recommended for its *"highly effective"* plaintiffs' representation and the *"great expertise"* of its attorneys. It was also recommended for its strong labor law practice.

The Lawyers: **Richard Pemberton** has over 30 years' experience trying a wide range of jury cases in state and federal courts, including the US Supreme Court. Peers agreed that he also exhibits *"great skill"* in mediation and arbitration.

EMPLOYMENT & LABOR LAW — MINNESOTA

MAINLY DEFENDANT

MINNESOTA
Leading firms
(Employment: Mainly Defendant)

1
- DORSEY & WHITNEY LLP *Minneapolis*
- FAEGRE & BENSON LLP *Minneapolis*

2
- BRIGGS AND MORGAN PA *Minneapolis*
- FELHABER, LARSON, FENLON & VOGT PC *Minneapolis*
- GRAY, PLANT, MOOTY, MOOTY *Minneapolis*
- LEONARD, STREET AND DEINARD PA *Minneapolis*

3
- FLYNN, GASKINS & BENNETT *Minneapolis*
- RIDER, BENNETT, EGAN *Minneapolis*
- ROBINS KAPLAN MILLER & CIRESI *Minneapolis*

Leading individuals
(Employment: Mainly Defendant)

1
- CARRON Reid *Faegre & Benson LLP, Minneapolis*
- D'AQUILA Barbara *Flynn, Gaskins & Bennett, Minneapolis*
- HOBBINS Robert *Dorsey & Whitney LLP, Minneapolis*
- REINHART Robert *Dorsey & Whitney LLP, Minneapolis*
- STUMO Mary *Faegre & Benson LLP, Minneapolis*

2
- DAVIES Scott *Briggs and Morgan PA, Minneapolis*
- SNYDER Stephen *Gray, Plant, Mooty, Mooty, Minneapolis*
- STENMOE Gregory *Briggs and Morgan PA, Minneapolis*
- THOMPSON John *Rider, Bennett, Egan, Minneapolis*
- ZEGLOVITCH Robert *Leonard, Street, Minneapolis*

3
- LANGEVIN Judith *Gray, Plant, Mooty, Mooty, Minneapolis*
- MERLEY Dennis *Felhaber, Larson, Fenlon, Minneapolis*
- ROBINER Susan *Leonard, Street and Deinard, Minneapolis*

Firms and individuals are listed alphabetically in each band.

Dorsey & Whitney LLP
The Firm: This international law firm can draw on the support of 22 offices in the US, Canada, Europe and Asia. Peers described it as a *"powerhouse"* that offers a full service to an enviable client base. *"Brilliant"* attorneys advise on equal employment opportunity compliance and the development of corporate policies. Discrimination litigation and labor relations also feature in its workload.
The Lawyers: Much of the firm's profile in this market lies with its two leading lights: **Robert Reinhart** and **Robert Hobbins**. Reinhart is chair of the labor and employment practice group and is respected as a *"superior litigator,"* "who is equally adept at regulatory compliance and general counselling. Peers applauded Hobbins for his *"extraordinary expertise"* in labor relations and discrimination litigation. They also pointed to his *"fair and ethical"* approach to cases.
The Clients: Cub Foods; Mayo Foundation for Medical Education and Research; National Steel; Northwest Airlines; The Toro Company; Thiele Technologies; US Bancorp and RBC Dain Rauscher.

Faegre & Benson LLP
The Firm: Interviewees endorsed this *"sophisticated practice"* that has over 30 lawyers concentrating exclusively on labor and employment-related issues. Its work has a national and international dimension, and observers referred to the *"tremendous depth and high standards"* of the firm's employment attorneys. Their workload includes race, sex, age and disability discrimination cases and claims of sexual harassment.
The Lawyers: **Mary Stumo** is widely respected by commentators for her *"extraordinary strength"* and *"mental power."* She brings *"the right attitude"* to her work, which includes both litigation and general counseling. **Reid Carron** is the head of the labor and employment practice, and assists employers in their negotiation of union agreements and employee contracts. His competitors recognized him as *"bright and knowledgeable"* and praised his *"vast depth"* of experience.
The Clients: Pennwalt Corporation; Fingerhut Companies; Cowles Media; Land O'Lakes; Metropolitan Waste Control Commission and Abbott Northwestern Hospital.

Briggs and Morgan PA
The Firm: Founded in 1882, this long-standing player counsels on employment law, discrimination litigation, employee benefits and labor law matters. Clients include multinational corporations, nonprofit bodies and educational establishments.
The Lawyers: Peers agreed that **Scott Davies** has secured *"an excellent reputation"* from his employment discrimination practice, which takes him before federal and state courts. *"Highly trusted"* **Gregory Stenmoe** was singled out by market sources for his involvement in a variety of *"innovative"* court cases concerning employers' rights.

Felhaber, Larson, Fenlon & Vogt PC
The Firm: The employment and labor group was endorsed for its activity in national cases, with regard to breaches of contract, employment discrimination claims and whistle-blower matters. Market observers applauded the team's *"great understanding of the law."*
The Lawyers: Interviewees spoke highly of **Dennis Merley**'s *"extensive knowledge"* and *"great demeanor."* He combines litigation work with counseling on risk prevention and employment policies.
The Clients: The firm was respected for its work with healthcare groups. It also acts for Fortune 500 companies, financial institutions and hi-tech companies.

Gray, Plant, Mooty, Mooty & Bennett PA
The Firm: Clients recommended this firm for its *"efficiency"* and *"value for money,"* while competitors praised the talents of its *"outstanding"* lawyers. The labor and employment practice advises clients on the defense of claims and also assists with preventative counseling. Attorneys are also experienced in alternative dispute resolution and other mediation techniques.
The Lawyers: *"Smart"* **Stephen Snyder** is respected by peers and clients alike for his *"terrific"* work as lead counsel in age discrimination class action suits brought against Lennox Industries, Monsanto and Svedala Industries. Market observers spoke of **Judith Langevin**'s *"dynamic attitude"* and the *"wonderful"* job she does for her clients. She defends employers in discrimination and wrongful termination litigation and sexual harassment cases.
The Clients: The firm acts for commercial enterprises and consumer services companies.

Leonard, Street and Deinard PA
The Firm: The areas covered in the labor and employment practice here include discrimination litigation, workplace harassment, whistle-blower litigation, labor law issues and workplace training. Its lawyers were recommended to researchers for their *"good-quality advice and sound judgment."*
The Lawyers: Chair of the group **Robert Zeglovitch** has impressed market observers with his *"great expertise"* and *"dedication to his clients."* **Susan Robiner**'s *"methodical and calm analysis"* of cases has won her a strong following.
The Clients: The firm attracts local and national corporations as well as financial institutions and manufacturers.

Flynn, Gaskins & Bennett
The Firm: Much of the firm's profile lies with its leading light, **Barbara D'Aquila**. Both competitors and clients agree that she is the *"rock"* of the practice, and *"one of the best"* attorneys specializing in employment law in the state. She and the team are respected for their *"extensive practice"* in contract, discrimination and sexual harassment litigation. The group is also active in preventative counseling.
The Clients: The firm acts for financial institutions and major manufacturers.

Rider, Bennett, Egan & Arundel LLP
The Firm: Interviewees recommended this firm for its *"great trial experience,"* which includes whistle-blower claims, sexual harassment cases and ADA and other types of employment discrimination.
The Lawyers: Peers singled out **John Thompson**'s experience in the area of workplace violence,

MINNESOTA — LITIGATION

where he has provided counseling and litigation services to a number of Fortune 500 companies. They commended his *"scholarly and tenacious approach"* to complex cases.
The Clients: The firm acts for businesses in both the public and private sector.

Robins Kaplan Miller & Ciresi
The Firm: This firm was spontaneously recommended to researchers for its work at national level in sexual harassment, employee misconduct and discrimination cases.
The Lawyers: Charles Lentz, who focuses on employment and labor issues with an emphasis on discrimination, harassment and retaliation matters, is a key member of the employment group.
The Clients: Alliant Techsystems; Bearcom Group; Best Buy Company; General Mills; MediaOne Group and The Toro Company.

LITIGATION

MINNESOTA
Leading firms
(Litigation:General Commercial)

1
- ANTHONY OSTLUND & BAER *Minneapolis*
- DORSEY & WHITNEY LLP *Minneapolis*
- FAEGRE & BENSON LLP *Minneapolis*
- ROBINS KAPLAN MILLER & CIRESI *Minneapolis*

2
- BRIGGS AND MORGAN, PA *Minneapolis*
- FREDRIKSON & BYRON, PA *Minneapolis*
- GRAY, PLANT, MOOTY, MOOTY *Minneapolis*
- KELLY & BERENS PA *Minneapolis*
- LINDQUIST & VENNUM PLLP *Minneapolis*
- MASLON EDELMAN BORMAN & BRAND *Minneapolis*
- OPPENHEIMER WOLFF & DONNELLY *Minneapolis*

3
- BASSFORD, LOCKHART, TRUESDELL *Minneapolis*
- LEONARD, STREET AND DEINARD, PA *Minneapolis*
- LOMMEN, NELSON, COLE *Minneapolis*
- WINTHROP & WEINSTINE, PA *Minneapolis*

Leading individuals
(Litigation: General Commercial)

1
- ANTHONY Joseph *Anthony Ostlund & Baer,* Minneapolis
- CIRESI Michael *Robins Kaplan Miller,* Minneapolis
- FRENCH John *Faegre & Benson LLP,* Minneapolis
- KELLY Timothy *Kelly & Berens PA,* Minneapolis
- PENTELOVITCH William *Maslon Edelman,* Minneapolis
- REMELE Lewis *Bassford, Lockhart,* Minneapolis
- SIMONSON James *Gray, Plant, Mooty,* Minneapolis

2
- FRASER Thomas *Fredrikson & Byron PA,* Minneapolis
- GAGNON Craig *Oppenheimer Wolff,* Minneapolis
- KAPLAN Elliot *Robins Kaplan Miller,* Minneapolis
- KEYES Jeffrey *Briggs and Morgan PA,* Minneapolis
- MAGNUSON Roger *Dorsey & Whitney LLP,* Minneapolis
- TINKHAM Thomas *Dorsey & Whitney LLP,* Minneapolis

3
- FIELD Lawrence *Leonard, Street and Deinard,* Minneapolis
- FRUTH Terence *Fruth, Jamison & Elsass,* Minneapolis
- HENNESSEY Robert *Lindquist & Vennum,* Minneapolis
- HUNT Kay *Lommen, Nelson, Cole,* Minneapolis
- LUGER Andrew *Greene Espel PLLP,* Minneapolis
- SYMCHYCH Janice *Dorsey & Whitney,* Minneapolis
- WEINSTINE Robert *Winthrop & Weinstine,* Minneapolis

Firms and individuals are listed alphabetically in each band.

Anthony Ostlund & Baer
The Firm: This boutique firm focuses on complex business litigation, and also displays expertise in the handling of regulatory and enforcement issues. The firm gained high marks from clients for its *"unbeaten success rate"* in resolving the most complex cases and for its *"superb"* attorneys who are equally adept at trial work, mediation and arbitration. Their activities incorporate securities disputes, employment discrimination, fraud, and professional negligence matters.
The Lawyers: One of the firm's founders, **Joseph Anthony** was praised by interviewees for his *"extensive knowledge"* and *"technical skills."* His *"fine performances"* in court have impressed many. He recently secured $16 million in damages following a raiding claim between two members of the investment banking community.
The Clients: The firm attracts national and regional clients from sectors such as banking, healthcare and technology.

Dorsey & Whitney LLP
The Firm: This large international firm has, according to commentators, extensive experience in complex *"high-stakes"* commercial litigation. Among its group of 30 lawyers there can be found a number of *"veteran specialists"* who ensure the high profile of the practice. Securities disputes, antitrust and negligence claims all form part of the group's workload.
The Lawyers: Thomas Tinkham, the chair of the commercial and business litigation group, received praise from commentators for his *"thorough approach to trial preparation."* He has attracted an *"exceptional clientele"* to the firm. **Roger Magnuson** heads the strategic litigation group and has a national reputation for his work in class actions, fraud, antitrust and stockholder disputes. He brings a high level of *"technical sophistication"* to his cases. **Janice Symchych** has an *"extraordinary depth"* of experience in litigation arising from white-collar crime and regulatory enforcement proceedings.
The Clients: University of Minnesota; Mayo Clinic; 3M; Gannett Satellite Information Networks; Northwest Airlines and American Express Financial Corporation.

GENERAL COMMERCIAL

Faegre & Benson LLP
The Firm: Clients acknowledge that the firm has *"made an immense effort"* to satisfy their needs. Its *"terrific individuals"* act in both state and federal courts, including the US Supreme Court on insurance, antitrust, bankruptcy and IP litigation. The firm is national in its reach and much of its work is multi-district in nature. These attorneys can draw upon the specialist knowledge of other practice groups at the firm for environmental, construction and employment litigation.
The Lawyers: President of the Harvard University Law Review, **John French** brings *"charisma"* to what market observers agree are *"crucial, bet-the-company"* cases. As part of his general commercial litigation practice he also advises on antitrust and trade regulations, constitutional law and FTC compliance.
The Clients: 3M; ADC Telecommunications; FSI International; Target Corporation; Hutchinson Technology and Upsher-Smith Pharmaceuticals.

Robins Kaplan Miller & Ciresi
The Firm: Skilled in trial work and alternative dispute resolution, the firm is commended for its *"landmark-setting"* litigation in securities cases. Attorneys advise in both class actions and individual litigation, and have developed a niche in stock holder disputes. Peers and clients alike endorsed the *"great job"* its attorneys do in handling complex litigation matters. The firm acts for plaintiffs and defendants and large corporations and insurance companies can be found on its client list.
The Lawyers: Interviewees believe that **Michael Ciresi** makes an *"outstanding contribution"* to the firm with his work in products liability, IP and regulatory litigation. **Elliot Kaplan** is best known for his *"magnificent advice"* on a range of price-fixing matters, such as cases involving alcoholic beverages and hearing aids.
The Clients: The firm acts for Alliant Techsystems; Cox Communications; Employers Insurance Company of Wausau; Federated Mutual Insurance Company; The Toro Company and Honeywell.

LITIGATION

MINNESOTA

Briggs and Morgan PA
The Firm: The firm's litigation department has over 40 partners and 30 associates, who represent both Fortune 500 companies and smaller entities, including those in the emerging markets. Peers recommended the firm's *"good depth of quality"* and its *"hard-working"* attorneys. The group resolves disputes before tribunals, arbitration panels and administrative agencies throughout the US.
The Lawyers: Commentators pointed to **Jeffrey Keyes**' *"first-rate"* experience in antitrust and franchising law. Clients reported that they *"value his labors hugely"* and trust his *"sound judgment."*
The Clients: The firm acts for Fortune 500 pharmaceutical companies, mortgage bankers and financial services companies.

Fredrikson & Byron PA
The Firm: Drawing on its strong corporate client base, this team of commercial litigators has broad experience covering securities, antitrust, insurance coverage, employment and environmental litigation. The firm is active in price-fixing claims concerning vitamins and milk products.
The Lawyers: Much of the firm's profile lies with the chair of the group, **Thomas Fraser**. Peers recognize his *"immensely focused"* business litigation practice, which includes stock holder and partnership disputes and *"groundbreaking"* class actions.
The Clients: The firm acts for major national and regional corporates.

Gray, Plant, Mooty, Mooty & Bennett PA
The Firm: The group has won credit from clients and peers for its *"exceptionally diverse"* litigation practice, which ranges from small matters for individual clients to complex litigation on behalf of Fortune 500 corporations. Its attorneys are skilled performers in court, *"aggressive when they need to be,"* and have experience in handling arbitrations, mediations and other forms of dispute resolution.
The Lawyers: James Simonson has displayed *"a high level of erudition,"* claim interviewees, in his approach to civil litigation and settlement negotiations.
The Clients: The firm acts for individuals and small and large companies, including manufacturers, financial institutions, and insurance and technology firms.

Kelly & Berens PA
The Firm: The 14-lawyer boutique firm was commended to researchers for its *"effective"* work in real estate, antitrust and employment litigation. The *"clear dedication"* of attorneys here has impressed many market observers.

The Lawyers: Managing partner **Timothy Kelly**'s *"extensive technical skills"* and *"ethical standards"* have set the high standards met by the rest of his group.
The Clients: Regis Corporation; Ceridian; Guidant and TCF Financial Corporation.

Lindquist & Vennum PLLP
The Firm: Interviewees pointed to *"a talented group of lawyers"* spanning two offices in Minnesota and one in Colorado. There are about 50 attorneys who concentrate on litigation matters, including antitrust, fraud, construction, employment and insurance disputes.
The Lawyers: Chair of the group **Robert Hennessey** is a *"seasoned practitioner"* who has developed a strong profile for his work in insurance and antitrust litigation as part of his wider commercial litigation practice.
The Clients: The team advises public and private companies, nonprofit organizations and government agencies.

Maslon Edelman Borman & Brand LLP
The Firm: Picked by some commentators as their choice for *"high-stakes"* litigation. Its attorneys have *"grown up with the culture of high trial standards,"* and are respected for their commitment to clients. The firm's breadth of experience includes contract disputes, products liability, environmental matters and IP.
The Lawyers: William Pentelovitch has displayed an *"unbeatable talent"* in his track record of success in highly complex commercial disputes.

Oppenheimer Wolff & Donnelly LLP
The Firm: A long-standing presence in the Minneapolis market, the team is active in both state and federal courts in cases arising from securities disputes, fraud, breach of contract and insurance coverage claims.
The Lawyers: Interviewees recommended **Craig Gagnon** for his powerful courtroom presence and the dedication he shows to his clients.
The Clients: The firm has attracted clients from the manufacturing, financial services, technology and healthcare industries.

Bassford, Lockhart, Truesdell & Briggs PA
The Firm: Attorneys at the firm have attracted a national client base with their work in business torts, and construction and employment claims. Peers recommended these lawyers for their *"flair"* in the courtroom.
The Lawyers: Lewis Remele (see p.376) was esteemed by interviewees as one of the most *"knowledgeable"* individuals within the specialty.
The Clients: Allina Health System/Medica; American National Can Company; Con-Agra; Minnesota Lawyers Mutual; Illinois Tool Corporation and URS.

Leonard, Street and Deinard PA
The Firm: The department is applauded by commentators for its *"personable"* and *"sensible handling"* of disputes. The group is active in antitrust, franchise and stock holder disputes, fraud and securities litigation.
The Lawyers: Lawrence Field represents a number of Fortune 500 companies in national cases. He was described to researchers as *"good with a jury."*
The Clients: Draws clients from the financial, healthcare, manufacturing and industrial sector.

Lommen, Nelson, Cole & Stageberg PA
The Firm: The business law department, which is chaired by Chris Cuneo, focuses on all aspects of litigation. The firm is active in all areas of business litigation, but is perhaps best-known for its work in PI claims.
The Lawyers: *"Insightful"* **Kay Nord Hunt** is skilled in the handling of PI appeals and professional liability matters.
The Clients: Represents Active Software; PrimeNet Marketing Services; Heat-N-Glo; Heartland Apparel; BHC Marketing; Pipeline Supply; Technology Marketing Group; Minnesota Elevator and US Grain Company.

Winthrop & Weinstine PA
The Firm: Fields around 18 litigation lawyers, who cover all aspects of general commercial and business litigation including banking, antitrust and securities law.
The Lawyers: Robert Weinstine is well known for his *"genial demeanor,"* and has won the *"admiration"* of his peers for his work on complex litigation matters.
The Clients: The firm has advised public and private companies in the manufacturing and financial services arena.

Other Notable Practitioners
Andrew Luger of Greene Espel PLLP was recommended to researchers as respected attorney who combines *"high energy"* with *"technical legal knowledge."* **Terence Fruth** of Fruth, Jamison & Elsass is a senior figure in the market who impresses as *"highly experienced trial attorney,"* who brings his *"sound business acumen"* to every case.

MINNESOTA — REAL ESTATE

REAL ESTATE

MINNESOTA
Leading firms (Real Estate)

1
- DORSEY & WHITNEY LLP *Minneapolis*
- FAEGRE & BENSON LLP *Minneapolis*
- LEONARD, STREET AND DEINARD, PA *Minneapolis*

2
- BRIGGS AND MORGAN, PA *Minneapolis*
- FABYANSKE, WESTRA & HART, PA *Minneapolis*
- FREDRIKSON & BYRON, PA *Minneapolis*
- GRAY, PLANT, MOOTY, MOOTY *Minneapolis*
- OPPENHEIMER WOLFF & DONNELLY *Minneapolis*

3
- FELHABER, LARSON, FENLON & VOGT *Minneapolis*
- LINDQUIST & VENNUM PLLP *Minneapolis*
- RAVICH MEYER KIRKMAN MCGRATH *Minneapolis*
- RIDER, BENNETT, EGAN & ARUNDEL *Minneapolis*
- WINTHROP & WEINSTINE, PA *St Paul*

Leading individuals (Real Estate)

1
- COOK Jay *Dorsey & Whitney LLP, Minneapolis*
- FERRELL Charles *Faegre & Benson LLP, Minneapolis*
- HAMEL Mark *Dorsey & Whitney LLP, Minneapolis*
- KELLEY David *Leonard, Street and Deinard, Minneapolis*
- THIEL John *Gray, Plant, Mooty, Mooty, Minneapolis*
- WESTRA Mark *Fabyanske, Westra & Hart PA, Minneapolis*
- WHEATON John *Faegre & Benson LLP, Minneapolis*

2
- CHRISTY Angela *Faegre & Benson LLP, Minneapolis*
- FINLEY Joseph *Leonard, Street and Deinard PA, Mankato*
- HAYNOR Charles *Briggs and Morgan PA, Minneapolis*
- MASSOPUST Richard *Oppenheimer Wolff, Minneapolis*
- NORWICH Donald *Oppenheimer Wolff Minneapolis*
- ODLAUG Bruce *Lindquist & Vennum PLLP, Minneapolis*
- RAVICH Paul *Ravich Meyer Kirkman McGrath Minneapolis*
- ROM Rebecca *Faegre & Benson LLP, Minneapolis*
- SELLERGREN David *Fredrikson & Byron, Minneapolis*

Firms and individuals are listed alphabetically in each band.

Dorsey & Whitney LLP
The Firm: A team of 30 attorneys provides advice on a full range of real estate matters including development, construction and financing. Competitors agreed that its *"strong history"* and the *"superb quality"* of its attorneys make this group *"one of the best"* within the specialty.
The Lawyers: Jay Cook advises on the development and construction of commercial real estate, and related transactions. Market observers praised his *"magnificent knowledge"* and his *"great expertise"* in the sector. He represented a multinational corporation in the acquisition, construction and development of a 400,000 sq ft headquarters facility in New Jersey. **Mark Hamel**, who has chaired the real estate group since 2002, has advised on developments in the retail, healthcare, office and hotels sector. His peers admire his *"excellent technical knowledge"* and refer to him as a *"top-notch attorney."* Advised a Fortune 500 company with a $180 million synthetic lease financing for various office and manufacturing facilities.
The Clients: Citicorp Leasing; Honeywell International; Odyssey Development Company; TCF Bank and Universal Title Insurance Company.

Faegre & Benson LLP
The Firm: Active in the development, acquisition, financing and management of real estate. The group represents large and small contractors, owners, developers and financial institutions, as well as landlords and tenants in the office, retail and industrial markets. Observers and clients alike value and respect the *"tremendous depth"* of the group, which fields *"hard-working and dedicated"* attorneys.
The Lawyers: John Wheaton has long-standing experience in real estate leasing, litigation and financing matters, which often contain a multi-state element. Sources referred to his *"first-class negotiating skills."* Represents Norwest Bank, TCF Bank, Prudential and other institutional lenders in several construction and mortgage financings. Interviewees applauded **Charles Ferrell**'s *"excellent judgment"* and praisd his work on complex and significant cases. He represented Niketown (Seattle) and negotiated the leases with Nike, Planet Hollywood and Cineplex Odeon for the Niketown project in downtown Seattle. **Angela Christy** came highly recommended by market observers, particularly for her work in the areas of affordable housing and low income housing tax credits. Peers agreed her work shows a *"creativity"* that *"shines through"* in every case she undertakes. **Rebecca Rom** was singled out for her *"great strength"* in land use matters. She advises on affordable housing, real estate development and financing, and real estate transfers.
The Clients: University of Arizona Science and Technology Park; Niketown; major lending institutions; restaurants and shopping centers.

Leonard, Street and Deinard PA
The Firm: Heavily involved in the full range of real estate transactions and related litigation. Competitors acknowledged the *"high skill levels"* of the practice's attorneys, who advise on mortgage lending and real estate developments in affordable housing, on hotel projects, and on the formation of real estate partnerships. Attorneys here have secured a following with their broad coverage and *"analytical resources."*
The Lawyers: *"Smart and thoughtful"* **David Kelley** received a chorus of praise from competitors and clients alike. His representation of banks in particular was acclaimed; his clients include national and state banks, insurance companies, investment banks and municipal agencies. Peers praised **Joseph Finley**, who advises on real estate developments, zoning and land use, for his *"great experience."*
The Clients: US Bancorp Asset Management; Hubbard Broadcasting; Lundgren Bros Construction; Heritage Renovations; The Ackerberg Group; Milestone Hotel Investments and BNC National Bank of Minnesota.

Briggs and Morgan PA
The Firm: Over 20 lawyers represent clients in commercial real estate transactions of all sizes, both throughout the Midwest and nationally. Areas of practice include land acquisitions and sales, real estate tax, leasing and financing. Market observers agreed on the responsive service offered, and expressed their admiration for the *"proficiency"* shown by the firm's attorneys.
The Lawyers: **Charles Haynor** is chair of the commercial department and head of the real estate section. Commentators endorsed his sophisticated work on financing transactions, including term loans and revolving credit facilities.
The Clients: Financial institutions, holding companies and officers and directors involved in bank examination issues.

Fabyanske, Westra & Hart PA
The Firm: Observers commended this boutique, which they referred to as *"small but extraordinary,"* for its client-focused approach. Attorneys here possess the breadth of experience that is associated with those in larger law firms. Their real estate clients include lenders and borrowers, landlords and tenants and developers and contractors.
The Lawyers: **Mark Westra** has been active in development, zoning and land use, and financing options. Westra's *"creativity and intelligence"* was the subject of approbation, and his *"tremendous knowledge"* was widely pointed out to researchers.
The Clients: Cargill Financial Services; Apex Asset Management; Intergroup Realty Trust; Trammell Crow and Eagle Ridge Partners.

Fredrikson & Byron PA
The Firm: Engaged in development, leasing and finance-related matters in industrial, office, retail, entertainment and residential projects. Clients value the group's attorneys for their *"clear understanding of business issues"* and their *"responsive service."* The team advises on business planning, property tax management, zoning and land use proceedings.
The Lawyers: **David Sellergren**'s expertise lies in land use and development, an area in which he is deemed *"a leading light."* Also known for his work in environmental law.
The Clients: Minneapolis West Business Park; Golden Hills Business Park; Hudson Road

Technology Center; Piper Jaffray Tower; Norman Pointe; Grain Belt Brew House; Fortune 500 companies and start-ups.

Gray, Plant, Mooty, Mooty & Bennett PA
The Firm: Market observers praised the group for its *"detailed and methodical handling"* of real estate issues relating to land use, zoning, foreclosures and environmental matters. Attorneys here advise on commercial, industrial, office and retail projects, and have experience of residential developments.
The Lawyers: Chair of the real estate department **John Thiel** possesses an *"incredible knack"* for complex transactions concerning governmental participation and financing. He has also been active in real estate workouts, tax increment financing and debt restructuring.
The Clients: Lenders; developers; governmental entities; tenants and owners.

Oppenheimer Wolff & Donnelly LLP
The Firm: Best known among *Chambers'* interviewees for its work with lenders in real estate financing and workouts. The firm is also active in land use and development issues, construction, management and leasing. Peers respected its *"highly adept"* lawyers and the level of experience they bring to multi-family residential transactions, hospitals and nursing facilities.
The Lawyers: Many observers were impressed with **Donald Norwich**'s *"outstanding technical capabilities"* in the areas of institutional lending, mortgage banking and corporate development issues. **Richard Massopust** combines his work in mortgage financing with development counseling and litigation. Peers endorsed his *"extremely effective"* representation of key lenders in the market.
The Clients: Accenture; ADC; American Express; United Airlines; GE Transportation Systems; Primax Electronics and Syngenta International.

Felhaber, Larson, Fenlon & Vogt PC
The Firm: An active player in the local and regional real estate market. The firm has a broad practice that includes transactional matters, leasing and financing, and zoning issues in both the residential and commercial sphere.
The Lawyers: Timothy Hassett is chair of the real estate department.
The Clients: Fortune 500 companies; construction industry companies; real estate developers; hospitals; banks; hi-tech companies; manufacturers and distribution companies, and advertising firms.

Lindquist & Vennum PLLP
The Firm: The *"high quality and depth"* of the firm's real estate group was praised during the course of *Chambers'* research. Lawyers here advise on real estate transfers, including the negotiation and documentation of acquisitions, construction, leasing and development, and land use.
The Lawyers: Observers singled out **Bruce Odlaug** for his *"expert"* knowledge and *"positive demeanor."* He represents both financial institutions and developers and owners on zoning and land use issues as well as on landlord and tenant matters.
The Clients: Representative clients include owners, managers, investors and developers of commercial and industrial properties in the Twin Cities Metro Area, and in Minnesota. Other clients include nonprofit organizations, oil and gas companies and professional services, restaurants and telecom groups.

Ravich Meyer Kirkman McGrath & Naun PC
The Firm: A boutique firm of about six dedicated attorneys advises developers, investors and managers on all aspects of real estate matters. Peers recognized and praised the *"high standards"* attained by attorneys here who have *"a real understanding of the market."*
The Lawyers: Competitors agreed that **Paul Ravich** shows *"admirable judgment"* in his advice to small and medium-sized businesses and their owners, as well as to developers, investors and managers.
The Clients: Developers; investors and managers.

Rider, Bennett, Egan & Arundel LLP
The Firm: The real estate department received approval from peers and clients alike. It specializes in real estate finance, commercial leasing, residential property development, and related litigation and dispute resolution.
The Lawyers: James Watson, chair of the commercial lending and real estate practice group, is a key contact.
The Clients: Clients include owners, investors and developers of commercial and industrial properties.

Winthrop & Weinstine PA
The Firm: According to market observers, the firm offers a *"decent depth"* and some *"outstanding"* individuals in its real estate department. Areas of focus include zoning and other governmental approvals, leases, land use and eminent domain issues.
The Lawyers: A key member of the real estate group is Todd Urness.
The Clients: Local and national firms, of all sizes, including real estate developers, equity investors, homeowners' associations, nonprofit entities and institutions.

MINNESOTA LEADERS

Leaders in Minnesota

ANTHONY, Joseph
Anthony Ostlund & Baer, Minneapolis
612 349 6969
Recommended in Litigation

BUSCH, William
Faegre & Benson LLP, Minneapolis
612 766 7000
Recommended in Corporate/M&A

CARRON, Reid
Faegre & Benson LLP, Minneapolis
612 766 7000
Recommended in Employment

CHRISTY, Angela
Faegre & Benson LLP, Minneapolis
612 766 7000
Recommended in Real Estate

CIRESI, Michael
Robins Kaplan Miller & Ciresi,
Minneapolis 612 349 8500
Recommended in Litigation

CLEVELAND, Christopher
Briggs and Morgan, Professional
Association, Minneapolis
612 334 8400
Recommended in Corporate/M&A

COOK, Jay
Dorsey & Whitney LLP, Minneapolis
612 340 2600
Recommended in Real Estate

CORWIN, Gregg
Gregg M Corwin & Associates Law Office,
PC, Minneapolis 952 544 7774
Recommended in Employment

COSTLEY, Kevin
Lindquist & Vennum PLLP, Minneapolis
612 371 3211
Recommended in Corporate/M&A

CUTLER, Kenneth
Dorsey & Whitney LLP, Minneapolis
612 340 2600
Recommended in Corporate/M&A

D'AQUILA, Barbara
Flynn, Gaskins & Bennett, Minneapolis
612 333 9500
Recommended in Employment

DAVIES, Scott
Briggs and Morgan, Professional
Association, Minneapolis
612 334 8400
Recommended in Employment

EFRON, Stanley
Henson & Efron, Minneapolis
612 339 2500
Recommended in Corporate/M&A

FERRELL, Charles
Faegre & Benson LLP, Minneapolis
612 766 7000
Recommended in Real Estate

FIELD, Lawrence
Leonard, Street and Deinard Professional Association, Minneapolis
612 335 1500
Recommended in Litigation

FINLEY, Joseph
Leonard, Street and Deinard,
Professional Association, Mankato
507 345 1179
Recommended in Real Estate

FRASER, Thomas
Fredrikson & Byron, PA, Minneapolis
612 347 7000
Recommended in Litigation

FRENCH, John
Faegre & Benson LLP, Minneapolis
612 766 7000
Recommended in Litigation

FRUTH, Terence
Fruth, Jamison & Elsass, Minneapolis
612 344 9700
Recommended in Litigation

GAGNON, Craig
Oppenheimer Wolff & Donnelly LLP,
Minneapolis 612 607 7000
Recommended in Litigation

GARDIN, Lynn
Fredrikson & Byron, PA, Minneapolis
612 347 7000
Recommended in Corporate/M&A

GARON, Philip
Faegre & Benson LLP, Minneapolis
612 766 7000
Recommended in Corporate/M&A

HAMEL, Mark
Dorsey & Whitney LLP, Minneapolis
612 340 2600
Recommended in Real Estate

HAYNOR, Charles
Briggs and Morgan, Professional
Association, Minneapolis
612 334 8400
Recommended in Real Estate

HENNESSEY, Robert
Lindquist & Vennum PLLP, Minneapolis
612 371 3211
Recommended in Litigation

HENNIG, Gene
Rider, Bennett, Egan & Arundel, LLP,
Minneapolis 612 340 7951
Recommended in Corporate/M&A

HOBBINS, Robert
Dorsey & Whitney LLP, Minneapolis
612 340 2600
Recommended in Employment

HUNT, Kay Nord
Lommen, Nelson, Cole & Stageberg, P.A.,
Minneapolis 612 339 8131
Recommended in Litigation

KAPLAN, Elliot
Robins Kaplan Miller & Ciresi,
Minneapolis 612 349 8500
Recommended in Litigation

KAPLAN, Samuel
Kaplan, Strangis & Kaplan,
Minneapolis 612 375 1138
Recommended in Corporate/M&A

KASTER, James
Nichols Kaster & Anderson PLLP,
Minneapolis 612 338 1919
Recommended in Employment

KELLEY, David
Leonard, Street and Deinard
Professional Association, Minneapolis
612 335 1500
Recommended in Real Estate

KELLY, Timothy
Kelly & Berens P.A., Minneapolis
612 349 6171
Recommended in Litigation

KEYES, Jeffrey
Briggs and Morgan, Professional
Association, Minneapolis
612 334 8400
Recommended in Litigation

LANGEVIN, Judith
Gray, Plant, Mooty, Mooty & Bennett, PA,
Minneapolis 612 343 2800
Recommended in Employment

LAREAU, Richard
Oppenheimer Wolff & Donnelly LLP,
Minneapolis 612 607 7000
Recommended in Corporate/M&A

LIBBEY, Keith
Fredrikson & Byron, PA, Minneapolis
612 347 7000
Recommended in Corporate/M&A

LUGER, Andrew
Greene Espel PLLP, Minneapolis
612 373 0830
Recommended in Litigation

MAGNUSON, Roger
Dorsey & Whitney LLP, Minneapolis
612 340 2600
Recommended in Litigation

MASSOPUST, Richard
Oppenheimer Wolff & Donnelly LLP,
Minneapolis 612 607 7000
Recommended in Real Estate

MERLEY, Dennis
Felhaber, Larson, Fenlon & Vogt, PC,
Minneapolis 612 339 6321
Recommended in Employment

MOORSE, Charles
Lindquist & Vennum PLLP, Minneapolis
612 371 3211
Recommended in Corporate/M&A

NICHOLS, Donald
Nichols Kaster & Anderson PLLP,
Minneapolis 612 338 1919
Recommended in Employment

NORWICH, Donald
Oppenheimer Wolff & Donnelly LLP,
Minneapolis 612 607 7000
Recommended in Real Estate

O'BRIEN, Maurice
Miller-O'Brien, PLLP, Minneapolis
612 333 5831
Recommended in Employment

ODLAUG, Bruce
Lindquist & Vennum PLLP, Minneapolis
612 371 3211
Recommended in Real Estate

PEMBERTON, Richard
Pemberton, Sorlie, Rufer & Kershner,
PLLP, Fergus Falls 218 736 5493
Recommended in Employment

PENTELOVITCH, William
Maslon Edelman Borman & Brand, LLP,
Minneapolis 612 672 8200
Recommended in Litigation

RAVICH, Paul
Ravich Meyer Kirkman McGrath & Naun
PC, Minneapolis 612 332 8511
Recommended in Real Estate

REINHART, Robert
Dorsey & Whitney LLP, Minneapolis
612 340 2600
Recommended in Employment

REMELE JR, Lewis A
Bassford, Lockhart, Truesdell & Briggs,
P.A., Minneapolis 612 333 3000
lewr@bassford.com
Recommended in Litigation
Specialization: Civil trial practice involving personal injury, insurance coverage, commercial litigation including contract disputes, securities, fiduciary and shareholder disputes, class actions. Clients include Minnesota Lawyers Mutual Insurance Company; Illinois Tool Corporation; Medica Health Plan; URS; American National Can; and Con Agra.
Prof. Memberships: Minnesota State Bar Association (past president); fellow of the American College of Trial Lawyers, American Board of Trial Advocates and American Bar Foundation; Hennepin County Bar Association (past president).
Career: Admitted to Minnesota state and federal courts, Eighth Circuit Court of Appeals and United States Supreme Court. Shareholder with *Bassford, Lockhart, Truesdell & Briggs, PA* since 1989; chief executive officer since 2001. Listed in leading American publications. Best lawyer in Minnesota by Minnesota Law & Politics, 2001-2003.

MINNESOTA

Personal: JD, Creighton University (cum laude); BA, Harvard University (magna cum laude).

ROBINER, Susan
Leonard, Street and Deinard Professional Association, Minneapolis 612 335 1500
Recommended in Employment

ROM, Rebecca
Faegre & Benson LLP, Minneapolis 612 766 7000
Recommended in Real Estate

ROSENBAUM, Robert
Dorsey & Whitney LLP, Minneapolis 612 340 2600
Recommended in Corporate/M&A

SCALLEN, Timothy
Oppenheimer Wolff & Donnelly LLP, Minneapolis 612 607 7000
Recommended in Corporate/M&A

SCHAEFER, Lawrence
Sprenger & Lang, PLLC, Minneapolis 612 871 8910
Recommended in Employment

SELLERGREN, David
Fredrikson & Byron, PA, Minneapolis 612 347 7000
Recommended in Real Estate

SHARPE, Kris
Faegre & Benson LLP, Minneapolis 612 766 7000
Recommended in Corporate/M&A

SHERMAN, Morris
Leonard, Street and Deinard Professional Association, Minneapolis 612 335 1500
Recommended in Corporate/M&A

SIMONSON, James
Gray, Plant, Mooty, Mooty & Bennett, PA, Minneapolis 612 343 2800
Recommended in Litigation

SNYDER, Stephen
Gray, Plant, Mooty, Mooty & Bennett, PA, Minneapolis 612 343 2800
Recommended in Employment

SPRENGER, Paul
Sprenger & Lang, PLLC, Minneapolis 612 871 8910
Recommended in Employment

STAGEBERG, Roger
Lommen, Nelson, Cole & Stageberg, P.A., Minneapolis 612 339 8131
Recommended in Corporate/M&A

STENMOE, Gregory
Briggs and Morgan, Professional Association, Minneapolis 612 334 8400
Recommended in Employment

STRANGIS, Ralph
Kaplan, Strangis & Kaplan, Minneapolis 612 375 1138
Recommended in Corporate/M&A

STUMO, Mary
Faegre & Benson LLP, Minneapolis 612 766 7000
Recommended in Employment

SYMCHYCH, Janice
Dorsey & Whitney LLP, Minneapolis 612 340 2600
Recommended in Litigation

THIEL, John
Gray, Plant, Mooty, Mooty & Bennett, PA, Minneapolis 612 343 2800
Recommended in Real Estate

THOMPSON, John
Rider, Bennett, Egan & Arundel, LLP, Minneapolis 612 340 7951
Recommended in Employment

TINKHAM, Thomas
Dorsey & Whitney LLP, Minneapolis 612 340 2600
Recommended in Litigation

WEINSTINE, Robert
Winthrop & Weinstine, A Professional Association, Minneapolis 612 347 0700
Recommended in Litigation

WESTRA, Mark
Fabyanske, Westra & Hart PA, Minneapolis 612 338 0115
Recommended in Real Estate

WHEATON, John
Faegre & Benson LLP, Minneapolis 612 766 7000
Recommended in Real Estate

ZEGLOVITCH, Robert
Leonard, Street and Deinard Professional Association, Minneapolis 612 335 1500
Recommended in Employment

MISSISSIPPI

CORPORATE/M&A

CONTENTS: Corporate/M&A p.378; Employment: Mainly Plaintiff p.379; Mainly Defendant p.380; Litigation: General Commercial p.381; Real Estate p.382; Individuals' Profiles p.383.

MISSISSIPPI'S TOP THREE
1. Butler, Snow, O'Mara, Stevens & Cannada
2. Phelps Dunbar
3. Watkins & Eager

Ranking based on Chambers' research within the state.

All quotes in the text are from interviews with clients and competitors.

OVERVIEW: Mississippi's largest law firm, **Butler, Snow, O'Mara, Stevens & Cannada**, came first in the state for overall excellence, with seven lawyers ranked across three practice areas. In corporate and real estate, it was a family affair with business chair Barry Cannada and his son, financial services chair Don Cannada, both emerging in pole positions. Highlight matters for the firm include advising on a land acquisition for a $600 million power plant.

Old-line New Orleans firm **Phelps Dunbar**, in second place, commands extensive resources across its network of regional offices. The firm garnered widespread accolades for its strength in employment law where both Tommy Siler and Gary Friedman earned top-tier rankings. A first-rate litigation practice features Reuben Anderson, the first African-American Supreme Court Justice in Mississippi. Clients include GE and GM.

Jackson firm **Watkins & Eager** was recognized for its excellent, long-standing reputation in litigation. Within the employment arena, Kenny Milam was voted a top attorney for employment discrimination defense. The firm acts for a wide and varied client list that includes McDonald's and RJ Reynolds.

CORPORATE/M&A

MISSISSIPPI
Leading firms (Corporate/M&A)
1. BUTLER, SNOW, O'MARA, STEVENS *Jackson*
   WATKINS LUDLAM WINTER & STENNIS *Jackson*
2. BRUNINI, GRANTHAM, GROWER & HEWES *Jackson*
   PHELPS DUNBAR LLP *Jackson*
   WATKINS & EAGER PLLC *Jackson*
3. BAKER, DONELSON, BEARMAN *Jackson*
   MCGLINCHEY STAFFORD PLLC *Jackson*
   WISE CARTER CHILD & CARAWAY *Jackson*

Leading individuals (Corporate/M&A)
1. CANNADA Barry *Butler, Snow, O'Mara, Stevens, Jackson*
   DRINKWATER Robert *Brunini, Grantham, Jackson*
2. CHATHAM Henry *Wise Carter Child & Caraway, Jackson*
   HISE Daniel *Butler, Snow, O'Mara, Stevens, Jackson*
   HODGE Clifton *Phelps Dunbar LLP, Jackson*
   PAINTER William *Baker, Donelson, Bearman, Jackson*
   SHEPHERD Thomas *Watkins Ludlam Winter, Jackson*
   WEEMS Walter *Brunini, Grantham, Grower, Jackson*
3. FAIR George *Watkins & Eager PLLC, Jackson*
   GRISHMAN David *Watkins Ludlam Winter, Jackson*
   HAFTER Jerome *Phelps Dunbar LLP, Jackson*
   MENDENHALL William *McGlinchey Stafford, Jackson*

Firms and individuals are listed alphabetically in each band.

Butler, Snow, O'Mara, Stevens & Cannada PLLC

The Firm: Recommended for its *"strong business law practice,"* this large Mississippi firm is a clear front runner in the corporate law arena. Said to possess *"deep resources,"* the firm also boasts sophisticated practices in healthcare, real estate, IP and complex litigation.

The Lawyers: Interviewees hailed the chair of the business practice, **Barry Cannada**, as *"the very best for corporate work,"* citing his accounting background and big-ticket experience as particular assets. His general transactional M&A practice includes antitrust and securities work. Cannada recently acted for a healthcare company on acquisition work and represented a grocery store chain in multimillion dollar sales and acquisition transactions. *"Well-respected"* **Dan Hise** was recommended for his strength in securities law and a particular focus on securities regulation. This *"trustworthy"* attorney also covers healthcare law, gaming law and a variety of corporate transactions.

The Clients: The practice frequently represents banks and other financial institutions as well as corporate clients in the healthcare and manufacturing sectors.

Watkins Ludlam Winter & Stennis PA

The Firm: This 70-attorney firm boasts a niche in business transactions and was commended by peers for its *"broad corporate client base."* The *"first-rate"* corporate practice is sole Mississippi counsel to Nissan in legal matters relating to the construction of the company's billion dollar plant in the state. The corporate department is additionally supported by the strength of the firm's large tax practice.

The Lawyers: Well known for his expertise in corporate and gaming matters, **Thomas Shepherd** represents corporations and insurance companies in areas of law such as healthcare, securities, corporate and administrative/gaming. He represented Don Barden in its $140 million acquisition of Fitzgeralds Hotel and Casino, and acted for Boyd Gaming in the $7.5 million acquisition of a property from Isle of Capri Casinos. Peers recommend **David Grishman** for his focus on representing entrepreneurs. His practice encompasses corporation law, tax, trusts and estates, and franchise work. Clients praise him as a reliable attorney who will *"get the job done."*

The Clients: Nissan; Park Place Entertainment; AmSouth Bank and American Express.

Brunini, Grantham, Grower & Hewes PLLC

The Firm: Best known in the market as a traditional heavyweight in litigation, the firm also receives widespread praise for its strong business practice.

The Lawyers: Chairman of the firm's commercial department, **Robert Drinkwater** was consistently commended by peers and clients for his general commercial practice. Market sources praised him as a *"tremendously smart"* attorney who *"knows his stuff,"* noting particularly his representation of major financial institutions. His generalist practice covers real estate, banking, lending, securities, corporate finance, M&A and commercial transactions. Interviewees also identified *"highly esteemed"* **Walter Weems** as a strong business lawyer with experience in commercial transactions, lending, real estate, M&A, and general corporate and contract matters.

The Clients: Albertson's; Cooper Industries; Genesis Power; Waverly Group; Shell Oil; North American Coal and Enterprise Rent-A-Car.

Phelps Dunbar LLP
see firm details p.864

The Firm: Benefiting from the firm's network of regional offices, Phelps Dunbar's Jackson branch received high marks for its corporate expertise. Commentators spoke of a *"top-notch"* corporate department that receives strong support from partners in the New Orleans office.

The Lawyers: **Clifton Hodge** (see p.383) is widely respected as a *"bright and able"* corporate law expert. His practice spans both commercial litigation and business disputes. Hodge has extensive experience advising on business disputes and corporate and securities matters, including securities fraud, financial institution issues, directors' and officers' liability and breaches of contract. Recent matters include representation of Isle of

CORPORATE/M&A

Capri Casinos in a contract dispute and handling corporate work for Blue Cross and Blue Shield of Mississippi. *"Brilliant"* **Jerome Hafter** (see p.383) was said by peers to *"eat, sleep and drink business law."* Interviewees recommended him as an expert on the UCC. His practice incorporates business and corporate law, acquisitions, bankruptcy, taxation, casinos and gaming, IP licensing and commercial litigation.
The Clients: Blue Cross and Blue Shield of Mississippi; Isle of Capri Casinos; Southern Farm Bureau Life Insurance Company and Whitney National Bank.

Watkins & Eager PLLC
The Firm: The 58-lawyer firm, covering a wide range of practice areas, traditionally has a strong reputation in litigation. Within corporate law, market sources noted the group for its *"depth of expertise."*
The Lawyers: Said to *"know business law through and through,"* **George Fair** was singled out by peers and clients for his involvement in big cases. He divides his practice between litigation and corporate transactions and possesses noteworthy experience in banking, utility regulations, lending and general business. Client recommended him as a lawyer who *"instills confidence."*
The Clients: Trustmark National Bank; International Paper; Blossman Gas; Freide Goldman Halter; Dollar General; Pruet Oil Company and Willmut Gas Company.

Baker, Donelson, Bearman & Caldwell
The Firm: Able to draw on over 250 attorneys in multiple offices throughout the Southeast, this firm boasts *"deep resources"* and earns its ranking for the quality of its corporate advice.
The Lawyers: Peers admire *"sharp"* attorney **William Painter** for his legal knowledge of many sectors, noting particularly his work in the healthcare arena. His general business law practice is complemented by a background in tax and securities. He heads the corporate group and maintains a broad practice that encompasses healthcare matters, M&A, tax and corporate transactions. Painter recently represented a public company in a $75 million acquisition.
The Clients: Baptist Memorial Health Care; River Oaks Health System; Singing River Hospital System; University of Mississippi and public companies.

McGlinchey Stafford PLLC
see firm details p.76257
The Firm: One of the largest law firms in the Southeast, the firm possesses six offices in four states and maintains a diverse commercial and defense practice.
The Lawyers: The practice's profile was felt to rely heavily on the *"excellent reputation"* of **William Mendenhall** (see p.383), a corporate attorney with *"great technical knowledge."* Visible on a volume of smaller transactions, Mendenhall was endorsed for his generalist practice that embraces corporate advice, business transactions and commercial real estate matters. He regularly represents local clients in business acquisitions, commercial lending transactions and insurance regulatory matters.
The Clients: Clients include national and international manufacturers, suppliers, service companies, banks, financial services providers, insurance companies, healthcare providers and other individual and business interests.

Wise Carter Child & Caraway, PA
The Firm: A 44-lawyer firm based in Jackson. Interviewees recommended the practice for its unique strength in public utilities and nuclear power matters.
The Lawyers: *"Well-rounded"* **Henry Chatham** received peer praise as a general business attorney who *"really knows his stuff."*
The Clients: Jackson Coca-Cola Bottling Company; Blue Cross and Blue Shield of Mississippi; Mississippi Hospital Association and Entergy Mississippi.

EMPLOYMENT & LABOR LAW — MAINLY PLAINTIFF

MISSISSIPPI
Leading firms
(Employment: Mainly Plaintiff)
1. **WAIDE & ASSOCIATES** Tupelo
2. **HORN & PAYNE** Jackson
   MAXEY WANN Jackson
   ROGER K DOOLITTLE & RICHARD REHFELT Jackson

Leading individuals
(Employment: Mainly Plaintiff)
1. **WAIDE James** Waide & Associates, Tupelo
2. **DOOLITTLE Roger** Roger K Doolittle & Richard, Jackson
   FYKE Marcie Baria Fyke Hawkins & Stracener, Jackson
   HORN Dennis Horn & Payne, Jackson
3. **WANN Mark** Maxey Wann, Jackson

Firms and individuals are listed alphabetically in each band.

Waide & Associates
The Firm: The firm's reputation lies with its *"star lawyer,"* **Jim Waide**. Market sources endorsed his trial prowess: he is *"quick on his feet"* and *"a great performer in the courtroom"* with a *"terrific track record."*

Horn & Payne
The Firm: Interviewees endorsed the employment practice of *"trustworthy, intelligent and aggressive"* **Dennis Horn**. Defendant attorneys agreed that he is *"attentive to files"* and a strong litigator in discrimination, and wage and hour cases. He works alongside his wife at Horn & Payne.

Maxey Wann
The Firm: Sources respected the firm's involvement in employment and labor law issues. **Mark Wann** is an experienced employment attorney who combines this field with his work in general commercial and nursing homes litigation. The firm has represented unions in labor negotiations and has expanded its defense and commercial work, including representation of casinos.

Roger K Doolittle & Richard Rehfelt
The Firm: Much of the firm's profile lies with *"seasoned veteran"* **Roger Doolittle**. Observers endorsed his *"litigation prowess"* and deep experience on behalf of unions, which includes arbitrations, hearings and appearances before the NLRB. Doolittle was also praised for his workers' compensation work.

Other Notable Practitioners
Formerly with Maxey Wann, the *"immensely talented"* **Marcie Fyke** moved to Baria Fyke Hawkins & Stracener in September 2002. The firm undertakes civil litigation, including medical malpractice, nursing home litigation and PI, and she brings to it a respected employment practice. Peers recommended her as *"well-prepared and a hard fighter."* Fyke is experienced in discrimination suits, and sexual harassment and whistleblower cases.

MISSISSIPPI

EMPLOYMENT & LABOR LAW

MAINLY DEFENDANT

MISSISSIPPI
Leading firms
(Employment: Mainly Defendant)

1
- PHELPS DUNBAR LLP *Jackson*
- THE KULLMAN FIRM PC *Jackson*
- WATKINS & EAGER PLLC *Jackson*

2
- BALCH & BINGHAM *Jackson*
- BUTLER, SNOW, O'MARA, STEVENS *Jackson*

(Employment: Mainly Defendant)

1
- FRIEDMAN Gary *Phelps Dunbar LLP*, Jackson
- MILAM Kenneth *Watkins & Eager PLLC*, Jackson
- SILER Thomas *Phelps Dunbar LLP*, Jackson
- SMITH Taylor *The Kullman Firm PC*, Columbus

2
- FARRELL Michael *The Kullman Firm PC*, Jackson

3
- CRUTCHER Pepper *Balch & Bingham*, Jackson
- MOELLER Armin *Balch & Bingham*, Jackson

Firms and individuals are listed alphabetically in each band.

Phelps Dunbar LLP
see firm details p.864

The Firm: Its three Mississippi offices give the firm a highly visible presence with a strong line of about 15 labor and employment attorneys. The firm runs the full gamut of employment law, and also undertakes a significant amount of police liability and civil rights disputes. Sexual harassment, and sex and race discrimination remain key facets of the firm's practice, while its labor activity involves collective bargaining and contract negotiations.

The Lawyers: Commentators endorsed **Tommy Siler** (see p.384) as *"excellent, professional and personable."* He has carved a fine reputation in employment discrimination, particularly for his trial courtroom experience, which has recently included an ADA and a race discrimination claim. Regional practice coordinator of the group, his *"focused attention to files"* has secured him a following in the market. Clients described **Gary Friedman** (see p.383) as *"conscientious and dependable."* He is respected for his representation of municipalities, particularly the Mississippi Municipal Liability Plan, a pool insuring municipalities against civil rights lawsuits. Friedman *"leaves no stone unturned"* in his cases and is experienced in federal litigation, wrongful termination and sexual harassment.

The Clients: Mississippi Municipal Workers' Compensation Group; Mississippi Municipal Liability Plan; Philip Morris and GM.

The Kullman Firm PC

The Firm: This New Orleans-based labor and employment group can draw on the support of five offices in the Southeast. Interviewees spoke of it as *"one of the originals"* in this area, with an excellent reputation across employment discrimination litigation, labor law issues and preventative counseling.

The Lawyers: Its attorneys are *"skilled in negotiations and arbitrations."* The *"tenacious"* **Taylor Smith** was recommended by commentators for his *"incredible knowledge of labor law."* Clients claimed Smith's *"impeccable credentials"* were especially visible in employment discrimination, union organization and avoidance, and contract negotiation. *"Dedicated"* **Mike Farrell** heads up the Jackson office. Peers lauded him for his extensive employment litigation work, especially in the areas of sexual harassment, wage and hour cases and FMLA.

The Clients: Weyerhaeuser; Sanderson Plumbing Products; North Mississippi Medical Center and Action Lane.

Watkins & Eager PLLC

The Firm: One of the oldest firms in the region, it is widely recognized for its prowess in litigation. A team of about six employment attorneys concentrates on employment litigation defense and some ERISA litigation.

The Lawyers: Rival firms credited the well-respected **Kenny Milam** with an extensive knowledge of the law and a strong presence in the courtroom. He has a wide experience of ADA, age and sexual harassment cases. Milam also has experience in the labor arena, handling many union elections and contract negotiations.

The Clients: The Kroger Company; Lazy Boy Chair Company; Mississippi Baptist Medical Center and Nissan North America.

Balch & Bingham
see firm details p.768

The Firm: The commercial litigation practice of this firm was strengthened by its 2001 merger with Eaton & Cottrell. Two of its six offices are in Mississippi, and the firm can boast 15 lawyers in the labor and employment practice group. Retaliation lawsuits, and race discrimination and sexual harassment cases remain core areas of practice, while the group also advises on arbitration enforcement agreements.

The Lawyers: **Armin Moeller** (see p.384) was endorsed by market sources for his wisdom in labor relation matters, representing employers in maintaining nonunion status, collective bargaining negotiations and arbitration proceedings. He has received a defense jury verdict on race and sex discrimination claims in favor of the Mississippi Department of Education. He also defeated unionization efforts among vessel owners' tugboat crews. Former chair of the labor and employment section of the Mississippi Bar, **Pepper Crutcher**'s (see p.383) practice includes union representation campaign advice before the NLRB. He also undertakes OSHA cases and wage and overtime payment disputes.

The Clients: Circuit City Stores, AmSouth Bank and Delta Air Lines.

Butler, Snow, O'Mara, Stevens & Cannada PLLC

The Firm: The eight-attorney labor and employment group of this firm was recommended by observers as a *"highly capable team."* It handles the range of employment issues, with experience in sexual harassment, gender and race discrimination litigation.

The Lawyers: The labor and employment group is under the stewardship of Paula Ardelean.

The Clients: Clients include Fortune 500 companies and local businesses spanning the shipbuilding, retail, healthcare and manufacturing sectors.

LITIGATION

MISSISSIPPI

LITIGATION

GENERAL COMMERCIAL

MISSISSIPPI
Leading firms
(Litigation: General Commercial)

1 PHELPS DUNBAR LLP *Jackson*
   WATKINS & EAGER PLLC *Jackson*
2 BAKER, DONELSON, BEARMAN *Jackson*
   BRUNINI, GRANTHAM, GROWER *Jackson*
   BUTLER, SNOW, O'MARA *Jackson, Gulfport*
3 BRADLEY ARANT ROSE & WHITE LLP *Jackson*
   FORMAN PERRY WATKINS KRUTZ *Jackson*

Leading individuals
(Litigation: General Commercial)

1 DRINKWATER Wayne *Bradley Arant Rose, Jackson*
   PERRY Alan *Forman Perry Watkins Krutz, Jackson*
2 ANDERSON Reuben *Phelps Dunbar LLP, Jackson*
   BASS Ross *Phelps Dunbar LLP, Jackson*
   GOODMAN William *Watkins & Eager, Jackson*
   REED William *Baker, Donelson, Bearman, Jackson*
   SHAPLEY Christopher *Brunini, Grantham, Jackson*
   ULMER Michael *Watkins & Eager PLLC, Jackson*
3 GALLOWAY Robert *Butler, Snow, O'Mara, Gulfport*
   HENEGAN John *Butler, Snow, O'Mara, Stevens, Jackson*
   JONES Walker *Baker, Donelson, Bearman, Jackson*
   KAUFMAN David *Brunini, Grantham, Grower, Jackson*
   WELCH Scott *Butler, Snow, O'Mara, Stevens, Jackson*

Firms and individuals are listed alphabetically in each band.

Phelps Dunbar LLP
see firm details p.864

The Firm: From its origins in New Orleans, Phelps Dunbar's reach has extended to eight offices with three in Mississippi. Interviewees highlighted the firm's litigation prowess, describing its attorneys as *"the principal competitors involved in the most complex cases."* The team acted in the welding rod litigation for Lincoln Electric, where welders had alleged claims of Parkinson's disease, brought on by fume inhalation.

The Lawyers: **Reuben Anderson** (see p.383) has a career spanning three decades, which includes his role as the first African-American Supreme Court Justice in Mississippi. Peers agree that he is a *"fantastic court advocate"* having grown up in civil rights litigation. His practice, which includes regulatory, governmental and gaming matters, is combined with his duties on the board of directors of Minact and Trustmark National Bank. **Ross (Rick) Bass** (see p.383) is the managing partner of the Jackson office and practice coordinator. Sources endorsed him as a *"worthy adversary - incredibly efficient at managing the details."* His practice includes complex commercial and products liability litigation, and he has defended a UK public company against thousands of Mississippi asbestos claims.

The Clients: Lincoln Electric; GE; BancorpSouth Bank and GM.

Watkins & Eager PLLC
The Firm: This well-established Jackson firm enjoys *"a long history in litigation,"* claimed peers. The group fields about 60 lawyers, who were recommended to researchers for their expertise in products liability and insurance defense.

The Lawyers: **Mike Ulmer** has extensive trial expertise in mass tort and products liability litigation. Interviewees pointed to the *"long hours he puts in for his clients,"* among which are RJ Reynolds and DIRECTV. His *"terrific"* reputation is borne in part from his involvement in the tobacco and satellite litigation. He has represented the manufacturers in the welding rod litigation and acted for Sherwin-Williams Company in the lead paint litigation. Peers labeled *"the smooth-mannered"* **Bill Goodman** as *"unquestionably formidable."* He was praised for his *"great judgment and moderating influence."* His commercial litigation experience comprises advice to banks and companies in contract disputes and fraud.

The Clients: RJ Reynolds; McDonald's; Bridgestone/Firestone and Pfizer.

Baker, Donelson, Bearman & Caldwell
The Firm: The firm operates from a single office of about 40 attorneys in Mississippi. The litigation group has expanded over the years and interviewees describe it as *"a key player"* with a strong track record in healthcare litigation and products liability.

The Lawyers: Sources acknowledge that **Bill Reed** is a *"smart and devoted lawyer,"* while clients enthused *"he would certainly make our dream team."* He gained considerable experience in the asbestos litigation and undertakes a significant amount of medical malpractice and toxic torts. Managing partner **Walker (Bill) Jones** was lauded by observers for his *"ability to make the issues relevant to a local jury."* His *"hands-on approach"* has secured him a following in the market.

The Clients: The firm has acted for Philip Morris in the renowned tobacco litigation, Lloyd's, Terra Industries and Quorum Health Group,

Brunini, Grantham, Grower & Hewes PLLC
The Firm: The firm was strengthened by its merger with Alston & Jones, a general civil litigation firm, in December 2002. It fields more than 60 lawyers in its Jackson office, who were described by clients as *"proactive and effective."* The group has handled mass tort and pharmaceutical litigation and toxic tort matters such as asbestos, silica and the welding rod litigation. Antitrust and stockholder suits remain core areas for the firm. The firm serves as litigation counsel for WorldCom, representing former chief executive Bernie Evers in class action and ERISA lawsuits. The firm also acts for Choctaw Maid Farms in contract disputes.

The Lawyers: Clients valued **Chris Shapley** as an *"aggressive lawyer, quick on his feet."* He enjoys a statewide reputation secured by his experience in products liability, medical device and insurance coverage litigation. Shapley also acts on personal injury, pharmaceutical and toxic tort litigation. **David Kaufman** has extensive experience in handling complex commercial and mass tort cases. He has a *"respected and growing reputation"* in the market and acts for key client WorldCom.

The Clients: The firm's extensive and diverse client list includes WorldCom, for whom they handle all litigation work in Mississippi, Ingalls Shipbuilding, Blue Cross and Blue Shield of Mississippi, Mississippi Chemical and Choctaw Maid Farms.

Butler, Snow, O'Mara, Stevens & Cannada PLLC
The Firm: Two of the firm's three offices are based in Mississippi. The firm's large commercial litigation team was respected by peers for its *"bench of talented attorneys."* The practice incorporates mass tort, pharmaceutical, medical device and banking litigation.

The Lawyers: Interviewees believe that **Bob Galloway** of the Gulfport office epitomized the *"conscientious, smart and tirelessly studious"* litigator. His practice focuses on products liability, maritime litigation and professional liability defense. He also represents casinos on the Mississippi coast in gaming litigation. Peers acknowledged that the *"organized"* **John Henegan** has *"a good view of the bigger picture."* His practice centers on media-related issues, especially defamation defense. **Scott Welch** was recommended to researchers for his ability to communicate clearly to jurors. He is experienced in products liability involving industrial products in the workplace and personal injury matters. He also represents trucking companies and insurers in transportation litigation.

The Clients: The firm represents a wide variety of clients drawn from the gaming, manufacturing and transportation industries.

Bradley Arant Rose & White LLP
The Firm: This well-established Alabama firm has recently opened its Jackson office, which can draw on the resources of over 180 lawyers across five offices. The litigation team in the Mississippi office focuses on high-stakes business and employment litigation. The firm has represented Pfizer in pharmaceutical litigation and is heavily involved in the current silica litigation.

MISSISSIPPI — REAL ESTATE

The Lawyers: Wayne Drinkwater was described by clients as *"one of the most persuasive and well-organized litigators in the state."* They also agreed that he is *"knowledgeable about all the relevant cases and issues"* and is *"an excellent brief writer."* He is active in products liability and constitutional matters, and is currently involved in the silica litigation.

The Clients: Pfizer, Georgia-Pacific and other Fortune 500 companies, manufacturers, insurance companies and financial institutions.

Forman Perry Watkins Krutz & Tardy PLLC

The Firm: The 17-year-old firm was considered by peers to be *"a key player"* in products liability and commercial litigation. Much of its profile in the latter rests with *"the brainpower"* of **Alan Perry**. Interviewees pointed to his accounting background and described him as *"brilliant with the economics and financial implications of an issue."* He is heavily involved in commercial and banking litigation, while the firm is also prominent in asbestos litigation.

The Clients: Mississippi Valley Gas Company; GE; Georgia-Pacific and BancorpSouth.

REAL ESTATE

MISSISSIPPI
Leading firms (Real Estate)
1. **BUTLER, SNOW, O'MARA, STEVENS** Jackson
   WATKINS LUDLAM WINTER & STENNIS PA Jackson
2. **BRUNINI, GRANTHAM, GROWER** Jackson
3. **TAYLOR, COVINGTON & SMITH PA** Jackson

Leading individuals (Real Estate)
1. **CANNADA Don** *Butler, Snow, O'Mara, Stevens*, Jackson
   CLEMENT Rodney *Brunini, Grantham*, Jackson
   TOHILL Jim *Watkins Ludlam Winter & Stennis*, Jackson
2. **DAVIS Mark** *Watkins Ludlam Winter & Stennis*, Jackson
   SMITH William *Taylor, Covington & Smith*, Jackson
3. **CORSO Ann** *Butler, Snow, O'Mara, Stevens*, Jackson
   GUNN Paul *Taylor, Covington & Smith PA*, Jackson

Firms and individuals are listed alphabetically in each band.

Butler, Snow, O'Mara, Stevens & Cannada PLLC

The Firm: The largest Mississippi-based law firm boasts a sizable real estate practice, considered tops for its *"overall depth and expertise."* Peers admire the group's client roster, which features a string of headline names.

The Lawyers: Front runner **Don Cannada** was widely commended for his involvement in *"big projects."* Described as *"diligent and trustworthy,"* Cannada has an excellent reputation, derived from his long-standing experience in the specialty. As chairman of the financial services group, his transactional practice centers on real estate and finance matters. He recently represented the owner/developer of a more than 2000-acre planned community that will include lakes and golf courses. Cannada was also involved in land acquisition for a $600 million power plant, and represented an owner/developer in a 1050 sq ft regional shopping center deal. Market sources endorsed **Ann Corso** for her *"well-rounded"* real estate practice and *"sound lawyering."* Her experience includes commercial real estate and business acquisitions, and financing transactions.

The Clients: The practice represents regional and local developers, and lenders.

Watkins Ludlam Winter & Stennis PA

The Firm: This *"large, established firm"* received universal praise for its *"first-rate"* real estate group. Practitioners regularly advise on construction and permanent loan financings, foreclosures, secured transactions, and commercial leasing and development.

The Lawyers: Senior attorney **Jim Tohill** was named by interviewees as a *"top guy"* in the real estate arena. Praised for his thorough knowledge of real estate law, Tohill was also commended for his tendency to *"focus on the important issues."* His practice is primarily focused on commercial real estate development and lending with a specialty in public-private joint venture development. Highlight matters include construction financing for the Nissan plant, an $800 million project using public and private lenders. He also continues to advise on transactions in relation to the 50,000-acre Ross Barnett Reservoir project. **Mark Davis** was also highly recommended for his large development real estate work. His practice encompasses corporate, commercial, contract and real estate law.

The Clients: Jim Wilson & Asssociates; Maurice H Joseph; Mattiace Properties and Underwood Commercial Real Estate.

Brunini, Grantham, Grower & Hewes PLLC

The Firm: A strong general real estate practice, with a niche in representing electric power generating plants in their real estate, environmental and land use needs.

The Lawyers: Said by peers to be *"aggressive, yet easy to work with,"* **Rod Clement** received endorsement for his *"dedication"* to real estate matters. His practice focuses on commercial real estate and secured transactions. He frequently advises developers of shopping centers and office developments, borrowers, lenders and title insurers in secured financings and has extensive experience in leasing retail and commercial properties and telecom sites. Recent projects include financings for the construction of power plants and the development of offshore mineral interests, and acquisitions of multiple properties in Mississippi and other states by retail franchisees. Senior attorney Richard Dortch remains a *"considerable resource"* for the practice.

The Clients: The group serves as general counsel to several national companies acting in Mississippi. Other clients include Mattiace Properties and Trustmark National Bank.

Taylor, Covington & Smith PA

The Firm: A five-lawyer real estate boutique, recommended by interviewees for its representation of local developers.

The Lawyers: Praised as *"good with clients,"* *"versatile"* **William Smith III** attracted comment for a broad-based commercial real estate practice, which covers both the corporate and real estate aspects of shopping center and retail outlet acquisitions and developments. Smith is particularly recommended for his niche in environmental law pertaining to convenience store chains. Peers see him to be following in the steps of his father, William Smith Jr, a renowned real estate specialist, who remains on hand at the firm for strategic advice. **Paul Gunn** also received high marks for his general commercial real estate practice. Commentators especially noted his expertise in multi-family housing matters. Recent transactions include advising on a number of multimillion dollar transactions involving multi-family developments, involvement in commercial retail and office finance and development, and counseling on REIT finance and timberland investment.

The Clients: The firm's commercial real property clients include developers of office buildings, retail shopping complexes and convenience stores together with timberland and investment property companies. Attorneys represent numerous developers of multi-family properties, condominiums and single-family properties. Real estate finance clients include local, regional and national lenders, financial institutions, mortgage companies, insurance companies and REITs.

Leaders in Mississippi

ANDERSON, Reuben
Phelps Dunbar LLP, Jackson
601 360 9339
andersor@phelps.com
Recommended in Litigation
Specialization: The first African-American Supreme Court Justice in Mississippi, and a partner in the general litigation group in the Jackson office. He practices in the areas of commercial litigation, regulatory and governmental matters and gaming. In addition to his work at the firm, he has cultivated a professional resume spanning three decades of legal service. Key positions have included the Jamie L Whitten Chair of Law and Government at the University of Mississippi, Fall of 1995 and Mississippi Supreme Court Justice, 1985-90.
Personal: University of Mississippi, JD, 1967. Tougaloo College, BA, 1964.

BASS JR, Ross
Phelps Dunbar LLP, Jackson
601 360 9332
bassr@phelps.com
Recommended in Litigation
Specialization: Managing partner of the firm's Jackson office and regional practice coordinator of the commercial litigation practice group. He practices in the area of complex commercial and product liability litigation and has substantial experience in the representation of financial institutions and litigation and settlement of class actions. Admitted in Mississippi and Georgia in 1973 and the US Supreme Court in 1977.
Personal: University of Mississippi, JD, with honors, 1973; Editor-in-Chief, Mississippi Law Journal. Vanderbilt University; Belhaven College, BA, 1970.

CANNADA, Barry
Butler, Snow, O'Mara, Stevens & Cannada, PLLC, Jackson 601 948 5711
Recommended in Corporate/M&A

CANNADA, Don
Butler, Snow, O'Mara, Stevens & Cannada, PLLC, Jackson 601 948 5711
Recommended in Real Estate

CHATHAM, Henry
Wise Carter Child & Caraway, Professional Association, Jackson
601 968 5500
Recommended in Corporate/M&A

CLEMENT, Rodney
Brunini, Grantham, Grower & Hewes, PLLC, Jackson 601 948 3101
Recommended in Real Estate

CORSO, Ann
Butler, Snow, O'Mara, Stevens & Cannada, PLLC, Jackson
601 948 5711
Recommended in Real Estate

CRUTCHER JR, Pepper
Balch & Bingham, Jackson
601 965 8137
pcrutcher@balch.com
Recommended in Employment
Specialization: For more than twenty years, has advised and represented employers in defense of their lawful discretion to hire, direct, and discharge their employees. Continuing litigation in state and federal courts, predominantly in Mississippi and Louisiana, and administrative litigation and investigations conducted by the National Labor Relations Board, which polices relations between employers and labor unions. Much of practice before the NLRB consists of union representation campaign advice, an increasingly unusual hybrid of law and politics. Practice includes the drafting and enforcement of confidential non-union employment dispute arbitration agreements, traditional arbitration of union contract grievances, and negotiation of traditional labor agreements. Also frequently presents continuing education programs for clients and industry groups and has testified before subcommittees of the Mississippi Legislature on related topics.
Prof. Memberships: Mississippi Bar, Section of Labor and Employment Law; Louisiana Bar Association, Section of Labor and Employment Law; Federalist Society of Mississippi, Chairman; Federalist Society for Law and Public Policy Studies, Labor and Employment Practice Group, Executive Committee; Fifth Circuit Bar Association.
Career: Admitted to Louisiana Bar (1982) and to Mississippi Bar, (1986). Partner at *Balch & Bingham LLP* since joining in 2002; *Phelps Dunbar LLP* (Jackson, Mississippi, 1989-2002); *Miller, Milam & Moeller* (Jackson, Mississippi, 1985-89); *Kullman, Inman, Bee, Downing & Banta* (New Orleans, Louisiana, 1983-85); *Kullman, Lang, Inman & Bee* (New Orleans, Louisiana, 1982-83).
Personal: Received JD from University of Virginia in 1982 and received BA (magna cum laude) from University of Mississippi in 1979.

DAVIS, Mark
Watkins Ludlam Winter & Stennis PA, Jackson 601 949 4900
Recommended in Real Estate

DOOLITTLE, Roger
Roger K Doolittle & Richard Rehfelt, Jackson 601 957 9777
Recommended in Employment

DRINKWATER, Robert
Brunini, Grantham, Grower & Hewes, PLLC, Jackson 601 948 3101
Recommended in Corporate/M&A

DRINKWATER, Wayne
Bradley Arant Rose & White LLP, Jackson 601 948 8000
Recommended in Litigation

FAIR, George
Watkins & Eager PLLC, Jackson
601 948 6470
Recommended in Corporate/M&A

FARRELL, Michael
The Kullman Firm A Professional Law Corporation, Jackson 601 355 1994
Recommended in Employment

FRIEDMAN, Gary
Phelps Dunbar LLP, Jackson
601 360 9355
friedmag@phelps.com
Recommended in Employment
Specialization: Partner in the labor and employment group in the Jackson office. He is general counsel to the Mississippi Municipal Liability Plan, the Mississippi Municipal Workers' Compensation Group, and the Mississippi Drug Testing Consortium. Has assisted public and private employers throughout the state in matters involving labor and employment problems.
Personal: University of Mississippi, JD, with distinction, 1982; Articles Editor, Mississippi Law Journal; Phi Delta Phi. Georgia Institute of Technology, BS in Industrial Engineering, 1971.

FYKE, Marcie
Baria Fyke Hawkins & Stracener, Jackson 601 969 9692
Recommended in Employment

GALLOWAY, Robert
Butler, Snow, O'Mara, Stevens & Cannada, PLLC, Gulfport
228 864 1170
Recommended in Litigation

GOODMAN, William
Watkins & Eager PLLC, Jackson
601 948 6470
Recommended in Litigation

GRISHMAN, David
Watkins Ludlam Winter & Stennis PA, Jackson 601 949 4900
Recommended in Corporate/M&A

GUNN, Paul
Taylor, Covington & Smith PA, Jackson
601 969 7817
Recommended in Real Estate

HAFTER, Jerome
Phelps Dunbar LLP, Jackson
601 360 9347
hafterj@phelps.com
Recommended in Corporate/M&A
Specialization: Partner in the business group in the Jackson office. He practices in the areas of business and corporate law, agricultural law, biotechnology, acquisition transactions, bankruptcy, taxation, casinos and gaming law, intellectual property licensing, commercial litigation and employment advice and litigation. Served as a law clerk to the Honorable Charles Clark, United States Court of Appeals, Fifth Circuit in 1972-73. He is admitted to practice in Mississippi.
Personal: Oxford University, MA, 1974. Yale University, JD, 1972; Associate Editor, Yale Law Journal. Oxford University, BA, first class honours, 1969. Rice University, BA, summa cum laude, 1967.

HENEGAN, John
Butler, Snow, O'Mara, Stevens & Cannada, PLLC, Jackson
601 948 5711
Recommended in Litigation

HISE, Daniel
Butler, Snow, O'Mara, Stevens & Cannada, PLLC, Jackson
601 948 5711
Recommended in Corporate/M&A

HODGE JR, Clifton
Phelps Dunbar LLP, Jackson
601 360 9331
hodgec@phelps.com
Recommended in Corporate/M&A
Specialization: Partner in the general litigation group in the Jackson office. He practices in the areas of commercial litigation and business transactions. His litigation practice involves many types of business disputes and corporate and securities matters, including securities fraud, financial institution issues, and director and officer liability. Frequently advises corporate boards of directors concerning duties and responsibilities of board members, corporate procedure, and board decisions concerning threatened litigation.
Personal: Harvard University, LLM (concentration on corporate law), 1970. University of Mississippi, JD, 1967; Assistant Editor, Mississippi Law Journal. University of Mississippi, BBA in Accounting, 1964.

HORN, Dennis
Horn & Payne, Jackson
601 373 0170
Recommended in Employment

JONES, Walker
Baker, Donelson, Bearman & Caldwell, Jackson 601 351 2400
Recommended in Litigation

KAUFMAN, David
Brunini, Grantham, Grower & Hewes, PLLC, Jackson 601 948 3101
Recommended in Litigation

MISSISSIPPI
CORPORATE/M&A

MENDENHALL, William
McGlinchey Stafford, PLLC, Jackson
601 960 8400
bmendenhall@mcglinchey.com
Recommended in Corporate/M&A
Specialization: Partner in the business and tax section concentrating in corporate practice, business transactions and commercial real estate.
Prof. Memberships: The American Bar Association, the Hinds County Bar Association, and the Mississippi Bar.
Career: Admitted to the Mississippi Bar in 1984. In 1993, appointed by Secretary of State Dick Molpus to the Secretary of State's Business Law Advisory Group, which he continues to serve in this capacity.
Personal: Received a JD (cum laude) in 1984, and a BA (magna cum laude) in 1980 from the University of Mississippi. Named Woodward White's Best Lawyers in America.

MILAM, Kenneth
Watkins & Eager PLLC, Jackson
601 948 6470
Recommended in Employment

MOELLER Jr, Armin J
Balch & Bingham, Jackson
601 965 8156
amoeller@balch.com
Recommended in Employment
Specialization: Practice concentrates on labor relations and the defense of adverse employment decisions; litigation; drafting and negotiating contracts, including information technology project agreements; and litigatin claims against information technology companies. Represents employers in maintaining non-union status; collective bargaining negotiations and arbitration; race, sex, religion, age, disability, sexual/workplace harassment discrimination and retaliation claims; handling EEOC, NLRB, OSHA and other administrative claims through judicial process; drafting employment, severance, noncompetition and confidentiality contracts; and affirmative action and OFCCP compliance. Also conducts client training programs.
Prof. Memberships: Best Lawyers in America since 1989; Mississippi Defense Lawyers Association, President, 1988-89; Mississippi Bar, Labor and Employment Law Section Chairman, 1987-88; Multi-State Seminar, Program Chairman since 1984; American Bar Association Developing Labor Law Committee, Chapter Editor since 1978; College of Labor and Employment Law.
Career: Admitted to Louisiana Bar (1972) and to Mississippi Bar (1975); Partner at *Balch & Bingham LLP* since joining in 2002; *Phelps Dunbar LLP* (1989-2002); *Miller, Milam & Moeller* (1982-89); *Fuselier, Ott, McKee & Moeller* (1975-82); National Labor Relations Board (1972-75).

PAINTER, William
Baker, Donelson, Bearman & Caldwell, Jackson 601 351 2400
Recommended in Corporate/M&A

PERRY, Alan
Forman Perry Watkins Krutz & Tardy, PLLC, Jackson 601 960 8600
Recommended in Litigation

REED, William
Baker, Donelson, Bearman & Caldwell, Jackson 601 351 2400
Recommended in Litigation

SHAPLEY, Christopher
Brunini, Grantham, Grower & Hewes, PLLC, Jackson 601 948 3101
Recommended in Litigation

SHEPHERD, Thomas
Watkins Ludlam Winter & Stennis PA, Jackson 601 949 4900
Recommended in Corporate/M&A

SILER JR, Thomas
Phelps Dunbar LLP, Jackson
601 360 9357
silert@phelps.com
Recommended in Employment
Specialization: Partner and the regional practice coordinator of the firm's labor and employment practice group. He serves as a member of the firm's policy and planning committee. Since 1983, his practice has been concentrated in the representation of management in labor and employment law matters, and in the defense of civil rights issues.
Personal: University of Mississippi, JD, with distinction, 1983; Assistant Editor, Mississippi Law Journal; Recipient, Phi Delta Phi Award and the Bowling Labor Law Award. Millsaps College, BBA, 1979.

SMITH, Taylor
The Kullman Firm A Professional Law Corporation, Columbus
662 244 8824
Recommended in Employment

SMITH, William
Taylor, Covington & Smith PA, Jackson 601 969 7817
Recommended in Real Estate

TOHILL, Jim
Watkins Ludlam Winter & Stennis PA, Jackson 601 949 4900
Recommended in Real Estate

ULMER, Michael
Watkins & Eager PLLC, Jackson
601 948 6470
Recommended in Litigation

WAIDE, James
Waide & Associates, Tupelo
662 842 7324
Recommended in Employment

WANN, Mark
Maxey Wann, Jackson
601 355 8855
Recommended in Employment

WEEMS, Walter
Brunini, Grantham, Grower & Hewes, PLLC, Jackson 601 948 3101
Recommended in Corporate/M&A

WELCH, Scott
Butler, Snow, O'Mara, Stevens & Cannada, PLLC, Jackson
601 948 5711
Recommended in Litigation

MISSOURI

CORPORATE/M&A

CONTENTS: Corporate/M&A p.385; Employment: Mainly Plaintiff p.387; Mainly Defendant p.387; Litigation: General Commercial p.388; Real Estate p.391; Individuals' Profiles p.392.

MISSOURI'S TOP SIX
1. Blackwell Sanders Peper Martin
2. Stinson Morrison Hecker
3. Bryan Cave
4. Shook, Hardy & Bacon
5. Polsinelli Shalton & Welte
5. Thompson Coburn

Ranking based on Chambers' research within the state.

All quotes in the text are from interviews with clients and competitors..

OVERVIEW: Top-ranking **Blackwell Sanders Peper Martin** boasts a stellar litigation department with a reputation for handling all manner of business, commercial and employment discrimination cases. The corporate practice is the largest in the state and is involved in numerous high-profile M&A transactions. Here, corporate lawyer Ralph Wrobley is considered the firm's standout practitioner. The firm is also an established player in real estate, where it is visible acting on several high-value development projects. In employment law, the team is respected for its advice to employers on labor union contract negotiations. Clients include Home Depot and Hallmark Cards.

Recently merged **Stinson Morrison Hecker** takes second place. The firm's litigators enjoy a high standing among clients on both sides of the Missouri/Kansas state line. Litigator David Everson was particularly singled out for his expertise in antitrust litigation. Under the leadership of John Granda, the corporate finance department covers a broad range of transactions and asset securitizations. Strength in real estate is centered on financing and development work for municipalities. Clients include Boyd Gaming and Wyandotte County.

Bryan Cave receives plaudits for its high-caliber international and national legal expertise. Possessing one of the strongest corporate departments in the state, the firm undertakes substantial work for multinational and domestic corporates. The firm's commercial litigation practice has won great success in federal and state courts, with star litigator Irvin Belzer described as outstanding in a courtroom. The firm also elicited praise for its work counseling businesses on labor and employment regulatory matters. Clients include Anheuser-Busch and Ralston Purina.

The largest firm in the state, **Shook, Hardy & Bacon** enjoys a strong client following in Missouri as well as in neighboring Kansas. Within employment, the firm is lauded for both its class action work and its effective advice to employers on federal compliancy issues. Bill Martucci is highly esteemed as an employment litigator. The firm's litigation practice includes a number of seasoned professionals well known for their representation of the tobacco industry. The corporate department is also highly recommended for LBO work. Clients include Coca-Cola, Unilever and Philip Morris.

In equal fifth place, **Polsinelli Shalton & Welte** was recognized as a politically well-connected firm in the Missouri/Kansas area. Its excellent corporate law department represented Lockton in a $190 million transaction. Name partner Jim Polsinelli was identified as a key figure for his top-notch corporate practice. The real estate practice, featuring ranked practitioner Lonnie Shalton, garners praise for its work on behalf of developers in structuring property deals. The firm also appears in **Chambers**' litigation rankings. Clients include Intell Management and Investment Company and Stowers Institute for Medical Research.

With long-established ties to the St. Louis area, **Thompson Coburn** has a strong general business litigation practice. The corporate department has broad experience working with publicly traded companies on the NYSE. Michael Lause, chairman of the firm's public finance department, was particularly commended for his work in the area. A quality labor and employment practice counsels companies on employment policies and collective bargaining issues. Clients include American Red Cross and Johnson & Johnson.

CORPORATE/M&A

MISSOURI
Leading firms (Corporate/M&A)

1
- **BLACKWELL SANDERS PEPER** Kansas City
- **BRYAN CAVE LLP** Kansas City, St Louis
- **SONNENSCHEIN NATH & ROSENTHAL** Kansas City
- **STINSON MORRISON HECKER LLP** Kansas City

2
- **LATHROP & GAGE LC** Kansas City
- **POLSINELLI SHALTON & WELTE PC** Kansas City
- **THOMPSON COBURN** St Louis

3
- **ARMSTRONG TEASDALE** Kansas City, St Louis
- **LEWIS, RICE & FINGERSH** St Louis
- **SHOOK, HARDY & BACON LLP** Kansas City
- **SHUGHART THOMSON & KILROY PC** Kansas City

4
- **HUSCH & EPPENBERGER LLC** Kansas City
- **SPENCER FANE BRITT & BROWNE LLP** Kansas City

Firms are listed alphabetically in each band.

Blackwell Sanders Peper Martin LLP
The Firm: The corporate law practice, headed by Jim Ash, is the largest in the state with a 43-strong team in Kansas City and 14 lawyers in St. Louis. Active in high-profile M&A, debt financing and public and private securities offering, the group was considered by market commentators to provide "*broad coverage*" to "*the best client base,*" and were involved in the "*most complex transactions*" on their behalf.

The Lawyers: Ralph Wrobley is respected for his broad experience in representing privately held businesses and in M&A. According to observers, he enjoys a "*fine reputation*" as a "*bright and talented attorney with star qualities.*" **Jim Ash**, has undertaken high-value acquisitions in the telecom industry. Competitors respect his "*drive and integrity*" and compliment his "*strong personality.*" **Gary Gilson** impresses with his "*good business sense.*" His accomplishments include the structuring, negotiation and documentation of public and private, domestic and international stock purchases and M&A.

The Clients: Recently the firm advised Aquila on its $1.5 billion acquisition of independent power producer Cogentrix Energy, including the disposal of non-core assets in conjunction with the client's strategic repositioning. The group has also advised the Missouri Foundation for Health, a nonprofit corporation, on a merger valued at $733 million. Additional clients include: American Italian Pasta Company; Atchison Casting; Applebee's International; Home Depot and St. Luke's Health System.

Bryan Cave LLP
The Firm: This "*powerhouse*" of an international firm is respected in the Missouri market for "*consistantly high-quality service.*" Its securities practice incorporates an active transactional presence in the public and private issuance of debt and equity. Also involved in M&A and giving corporate governance advice to public corporations. In a recent highlight, the group acted as cocounsel to HCA, the largest owner of hospitals in the country, in its attempt to purchase Health Midwest, a 13-hospital system in Kansas City. Bryan Cave merged with New York-based Robinson Silverman Pearce Aronsohn & Berman in July 2002, a move that bolstered the firm's transactional reach.

The Lawyers: Recognized constantly as the front runner, **Thomas Van Dyke** gained high marks from competitors for his "*leadership and take-charge attitude.*" His practice centers on securities, M&A and general corporate governance. **James Nouss** specializes in M&A and corporate finance for a "*respected and enviable clientele.*" Peers commend **Donald Lents** for his work on "*complex*

MISSOURI — CORPORATE/M&A

MISSOURI
Leading individuals (Corporate/M&A)

1
- **FISHER Robert** *Sonnenschein Nath*, Kansas City
- **GRANDA John** *Stinson Morrison Hecker*, Kansas City
- **NIXON Richard** *Stinson Morrison Hecker*, Kansas City
- **POLSINELLI James** *Polsinelli Shalton*, Kansas City
- **VAN DYKE Thomas** *Bryan Cave LLP*, Kansas City
- **WROBLEY Ralph** *Blackwell Sanders*, Kansas City

2
- **ASH James** *Blackwell Sanders Peper*, Kansas City
- **GILSON Gary** *Blackwell Sanders Peper*, Kansas City
- **HEETER James** *Sonnenschein Nath*, Kansas City
- **LAUSE Michael** *Thompson Coburn*, St Louis
- **MONROE Bob** *Stinson Morrison Hecker*, Kansas City
- **NOUSS James** *Bryan Cave LLP*, St Louis
- **PRUELLAGE John** *Lewis, Rice & Fingersh*, St Louis

3
- **ESSIG Leonard** *Lewis, Rice & Fingersh*, St Louis
- **FITZGERALD Robert** *Shughart Thomson*, Kansas City
- **HUNTER Rob** *Stinson Morrison Hecker*, Kansas City
- **LENTS Donald** *Bryan Cave LLP*, St Louis
- **MEDVED Joseph** *Lathrop & Gage LC*, Kansas City
- **STAHL Thomas** *Armstrong Teasdale*, Kansas City
- **STEPLETON Jim** *Husch & Eppenberger LLC*, St Louis

Individuals are listed alphabetically in each band.

---

multinational and domestic" mergers, anti-takeover planning, and other corporate governance issues.
The Clients: The group represented Anheuser-Busch in its $1 billion investment in Mexico's Grupo Modelo and its $300 million investment in Chile's CCU. It also advised Ralston Purina in its sale to Nestlé, and acted as special tax counsel in the Niagara Mohawk Holdings' sale to National Grid Group.

Sonnenschein Nath & Rosenthal
see firm details p.882
The Firm: This national firm has established offices in both Kansas City and St. Louis. Peers recommend the corporate group's *"superb attorneys"* who provide *"exceptionally high-quality services."* The corporate practice advises on public offerings, M&A, spin-offs and refinancing. The group is also admired for its ability to attract a wide-ranging clientele, engaged in the manufacturing, telecom, financial services, biotech, IT and healthcare sectors.
The Lawyers: **Robert Fisher** (see p.392) specializes in transactional matters with a particular focus on M&A. He is acclaimed by peers as *"a highly experienced leader"* whose *"deals are run like a well-oiled machine."* *"Smart and practical"* **James Heeter** (see p.392) has substantial experience in complex corporate M&A, entrepreneurial start-up ventures and debt financing.
The Clients: The group advises Jordan Industries, a diversified private holding company with over $2 billion combined revenues. Other clients include: Monsanto; American Safety Razor; H&R Block; Farmland Industries; Waddell & Reed; Black & Veatch; Isle of Capri Casinos; Weary & Associates; Kansas City Southern and Westlake Ace Hardware.

Stinson Morrison Hecker LLP
The Firm: Formed in May 2002 from the combination of two large Kansas City-based law firms, Stinson, Mag & Fizzell and Morrison & Hecker. Interviewees acknowledged that the merger has resulted in *"a broad base of excellent lawyers"* who act for a *"fine institutional clientele."* The corporate group is particularly respected for its M&A work, venture capital and private equity transactions, and asset securitizations.
The Lawyers: **John Granda** chairs the firm's corporate finance division. He is highly regarded for his *"exceptional understanding"* of financings, M&A, securities law and corporate governance. Peers describe **Richard Nixon**, one of the firm's front runners in several major transactions, as a *"most efficient and technically able"* lawyer for disposals, acquisitions, debt and equity financing and joint ventures. Chairman of the financial services division, **Bob Monroe** is *"the banking expert,"* advising on bank holding company mergers and financing issues. Monroe is also *"a superb player"* in the general corporate and commercial arena. **Rob Hunter**, chair of the firm's general business division, represents venture capital investors and entrepreneurs in corporate governance, finance and transactional matters.
The Clients: The firm advises major local, national and international corporates.

Lathrop & Gage LC
The Firm: Kansas City is the firm's largest office, which has nearly doubled in size in the past four years through lateral hires and mergers. Observers agree the firm's corporate department is a *"powerful force,"* attracting *"loyal clients."*
The Lawyers: Endorsed by peers for his *"ethical approach,"* **Joseph Medved** specializes in M&A, securities law and corporate finance.
The Clients: The firm continues to represent its first ever client, the Burlington Northern & Santa Fe Railway. Other clients include: American Royal Association; AT&T; Bank of America; Bayer; Colgate-Palmolive; Ford; GM; Harry Cooper Supply; Kimco Realty and Royal Oak Enterprises.

Polsinelli Shalton & Welte PC
The Firm: The group recently represented Lockton in its sale, at a reported purchase price of $190 million, of an affiliated entity, a transaction that was recognized by observers as *"a standout piece of work."* The corporate group advises on a range of transactional and corporate governance issues; peers deem it *"a force to be reckoned with."*
The Lawyers: *"Leader of the pack"* **Jim Polsinelli** is widely credited with developing the firm into one of the area's largest full-service law firms. His practice focuses on corporate law, with an emphasis on M&A and business succession planning.
The Clients: Stowers Institute for Medical Research; University of Kansas Hospital Authority; Key Commercial Mortgage and Intell Management and Investment Company.

Thompson Coburn
The Firm: Over 250 lawyers work at the firm's main office in the heart of St. Louis. The practice offers *"diversity and depth,"* and provides a full range of corporate legal services to businesses of all sizes, including publicly owned companies listed on the NYSE.
The Lawyers: **Michael Lause** chairs the firm's public finance department, and is active in public finance and corporate and governmental law. Peers applaud his *"high-quality work."*
The Clients: Angelica; Barry-Wehmiller Companies; DaimlerChrysler Services North America; Enterprise Rent-A-Car; Kawasaki Motors; Lorillard Tobacco; Peabody Energy; Unigroup; Union Pacific Railroad and US Bancorp.

Armstrong Teasdale Schlafly & Davis
The Firm: This firm, home to 230 lawyers, gained high marks for its work in the Missouri corporate market; its St. Louis office was especially singled out. Clients include large public and small private corporations, entrepreneurs and individuals. Attorneys are experienced in all aspects of corporate law, and advise on transactional matters such as M&A and corporate governance.
The Lawyers: Interviewees singled out **Thomas Stahl** as a *"bright and talented attorney with tremendous people skills."*
The Clients: The firm acts for retailer bebe stores.

Lewis, Rice & Fingersh
The Firm: Its corporate practice covers disciplines such as securities, corporate finance, M&A, banking and bankruptcies. Sources commend the firm for its *"progressive thinking,"* and appreciate the breadth of a practice that serves the needs of public and private businesses of all sizes and industries, including healthcare and e-commerce.
The Lawyers: Competitors commended the chairman of the corporate practice, **John Pruellage**, for his *"great demeanor"* and advice on complex matters. His expertise covers securities and general corporate law. **Leonard Essig** specializes in advice to financial institutions and corporates on securities law and M&A. He is respected for his thorough work, and peers acknowledge the *"superb job he does for clients."*
The Clients: The group represented St. Louis-based RightCHOICE Managed Care in its $1.3 billion sale to WellPoint Health Networks, one of the nation's largest publicly traded healthcare companies.

EMPLOYMENT & LABOR LAW — MISSOURI

Shook, Hardy & Bacon LLP
see firm details p.876
The Firm: This 575-attorney firm is the largest in the state. The corporate group in Missouri has been involved in all aspects of LBOs, and the acquisitions and financing of public and private companies of all sizes. Observers agree that the recent recruitment of Craig Evans, formerly a partner at Stinson, Mag & Fizzell (now merged to form Stinson Morrison Hecker), who joined the Kansas City office, will be of *"great value"* to the firm. Evans, a securities and M&A attorney, has represented prominent public and private companies.

Shughart Thomson & Kilroy PC
The Firm: Endorsed by peers for its *"dynamic"* corporate practice. Attorneys have attracted clients involved in equity and debt issuance, joint ventures and M&A.

The Lawyers: Peers recognize **Bob Fitzgerald**, who also serves as the firm's treasurer, for his *"strong business sense"* and reputation for technical knowledge.
The Clients: Recent M&A transactions have included activity in the automobile dealership sector. The firm has also advised on transactions involving furniture manufacturers, computer software and credit and finance companies, electrical construction contractors, food processors, packagers and distributors, and healthcare and oil refining entities.

Husch & Eppenberger LLC
The Firm: Clients agree that, with its 285 attorneys, the firm provides *"cost-effective and efficient representation"* on a range of corporate matters. The firm engages in general corporate governance, financings, M&A, real estate syndications and securities representation of public corporations.
The Lawyers: **James Stepleton**, whose practice includes M&A, venture capital and securities law, was praised by his peers for his *"comprehensive knowledge of corporate law."*
The Clients: The group advises national and international clients as well as local industries.

Spencer Fane Britt & Browne LLP
The Firm: The firm's corporate services include the acquisition and sale of publicly traded and closely held businesses, tender offers, M&A and anti-takeover measures. The corporate group acts for a range of national and local clients ranging from start-ups to large publicly traded companies. Active industry sectors include manufacturing, retail, technology and public utilities.

EMPLOYMENT & LABOR LAW — MAINLY PLAINTIFF

MISSOURI
Leading firms
(Employment: Mainly Plaintiff)
1. THE MEYERS LAW FIRM LC *Kansas City*
   THE POPHAM LAW FIRM PC *Kansas City*
2. DKE LAW OFFICE *Kansas City*

Leading individuals
(Employment: Mainly Plaintiff)
1. EGAN Dennis *The Popham Law Firm PC*, Kansas City
   MEYERS Martin *The Meyers Law Firm LC*, Kansas City
2. KETCHMARK Michael *DKE Law Office*, Kansas City

Firms and individuals are listed alphabetically in each band.

The Meyers Law Firm LC
The Firm: This firm has a strong market reputation for plaintiffs' employment discrimination work. A four-member team specializes in all aspects of age, sex, race and disability discrimination as well as sexual harassment claims.
The Lawyers: The firm's backbone in employment discrimination litigation is **Martin Meyers**. He has won the respect of the market with his *"aggressive trial techniques."* Peers also recognized his ability to *"communicate effectively to a courtroom jury."*

The Popham Law Firm PC
The Firm: The five-lawyer firm has achieved a statewide reputation, according to interviewees, through its *"skilled employment plaintiffs' litigation practice."* The group remains focused on representing employees in discrimination cases, predominantly involving wrongful discharge.
The Lawyers: Considered by rivals to be *"a premier trial attorney in Missouri,"* **Dennis Egan** has a reputation in the market for handling complex litigation and high-profile employment discrimination cases.

DKE Law Office
The Firm: Interviewees agree that the firm has the capabilities to handle *"high-quality"* employment litigation cases.
The Lawyers: Much of their reputation is owed to **Michael Ketchmark**, who is acknowledged by defendant lawyers to be a *"highly intelligent trial lawyer."*

EMPLOYMENT & LABOR LAW — MAINLY DEFENDANT

MISSOURI
Leading firms
(Employment: Mainly Defendant)
1. BLACKWELL SANDERS PEPER *Kansas City*
2. BRYAN CAVE LLP *St Louis*
   SHOOK, HARDY & BACON LLP *Kansas City*
   SPENCER FANE BRITT & BROWNE LLP *Kansas City*
3. ARMSTRONG TEASDALE SCHLAFLY *Kansas City*
   BIOFF, FINUCANE, COFFEY, HOLLAND *Kansas City*
   CONSTANGY, BROOKS & SMITH LLC *Kansas City*
   THOMPSON COBURN *St Louis*

Firms are listed alphabetically in each band.

Blackwell Sanders Peper Martin LLP
The Firm: This 30-lawyer team was endorsed by clients as *"exceptionally knowledgeable,"* and characterized for their *"high degree of professionalism"* in the courtroom. The firm's strong track record in winning trial cases has impressed many commentators, who refer to its *"years of experience and reputation"* in the region. The team offers a broad range of experience working with employers in discrimination litigation, as well as on traditional labor matters involving contract negotiations.
The Lawyers: Undoubtedly a high-profile name on the team is **John Phillips**. Sources described him as an *"intelligent and capable"* attorney. He also elicits praise from clients for his *"successful management skills"* in deploying a legal team, and his ability to achieve results for employers in an *"amicable way."*
The Clients: Chubb Group; Hallmark Cards; Dairy Farmers of America; AccoustiSeal; Saint Luke's Health System; Sunshine Biscuits/Keebler Company and Harcros Chemicals.

Bryan Cave LLP
The Firm: Interviewees pointed to the firm's superb network of offices across the US and overseas, which is believed to give it an enviable spread of resources dedicated to advice on labor and employment matters. The 35-member department was commended for its *"breadth of knowledge"* and a *"diverse client base."* One area of particular strength is the team's handling of *"complex"* union negotiations on behalf of clients.
The Lawyers: Peers admire **Jerry Hunter** for his *"strong"* labor policy skills and *"vast"* regulatory experience. They endorsed him as *"a leading labor union specialist"* in the state.

MISSOURI

EMPLOYMENT & LABOR LAW

MISSOURI
Leading individuals
(Employment: Mainly Defendant)

[1] MARTUCCI William *Shook, Hardy & Bacon,* Kansas City
[2] PHILLIPS John *Blackwell Sanders Peper,* Kansas City
[3] FINUCANE Brian *Bioff, Finucane, Coffey,* Kansas City
   HUNTER Jerry *Bryan Cave LLP,* St Louis
   WHITACRE Jack *Spencer Fane Britt,* Kansas City
[4] DONNELLY Paul *Stinson Morrison Hecker,* Kansas City
   JANOWITZ Robert *Constancy, Brooks,* Kansas City
   ROWE Jack *Lathrop & Gage LC,* Kansas City
   VERING John *Armstrong Teasdale Schlafly,* Kansas City
   YATES Jack *Husch & Eppenberger LLC,* Kansas City

Individuals are listed alphabetically in each band.

The Clients: Walgreen Co; Waste Management; Abb; Ganett Company Newspapers and GM.

Shook, Hardy & Bacon LLP
see firm details p.876
The Firm: This full-service firm is best known for its extensive litigation experience in employment matters. The 26-lawyer team has a growing reputation in the region, developing a broad-based employment practice that assists corporate clients in class actions, ERISA and discrimination claims. The group also counsels employers on non-litigation policy issues such as FMLA, ADA and other federal compliance acts.
The Lawyers: **Bill Martucci** garners the admiration and respect of peers and clients for his *"tenacious"* litigation skills and *"breadth of knowledge"* on employment policy issues. His ability to *"effectively"* communicate an employer's point of view to a jury has impressed many interviewees, who also point to his success in establishing a client base that contains a number of Fortune 500 names.
The Clients: Coca-Cola; Unilever; Miller Brewing; Kraft; Data Systems International; Bristol-Myers Squibb and Saks Fifth Avenue.

Spencer Fane Britt & Browne LLP
The Firm: The firm is considered by market commentators to be *"the best traditional labor firm"* in Missouri. The 19-member team received endorsement from Kansas City peers for its expertise in representing employers involved in charges of unfair labor practice before the NLRB. The group also provides *"quality counseling"* to clients on federal compliance issues.
The Lawyers: **Jack Whitacre** was endorsed for his *"knowledge, experience and ability to get the job done."* Competitors respected him for his *"loyal"* client base and solutions-oriented approach to traditional labor issues.
The Clients: Procter & Gamble; Honeywell; La Petite Academy; UMB Bank and Commerce Bank.

Armstrong Teasdale Schlafly & Davis
The Firm: A long-established player in Missouri, the firm remains well-regarded for employment and labor law matters. Commentators highlighted the practice's aptitude in advising employers on preventative employment law measures and compliance with federal regulations. The 20-member practice group also represents employers in disputes before federal and state courts, and before arbitration panels.
The Lawyers: Team leader **John Vering** is respected for his employment litigation prowess. Interviewees endorsed his *"professionalism"* and *"logical approach to problems."*
The Clients: General Mills; IBM; North Kansas City Hospital; Aurora Foods; McDonald's; Ameren; Columbia Public Schools; Sprint and Curry Investment Company.

Bioff, Finucane, Coffey, Holland & Hosler LLP
The Firm: Considered by the market to be a *"smaller firm with an excellent reputation in traditional labor law."* This 13-member firm specializes in labor and employment matters and was commended to researchers for its *"great litigation expertise."*
The Lawyers: Sources appreciated **Brian Finucane** as an *"extremely hard-working lawyer"* who has *"a lot of experience."* His skill in handling appellate court cases was singled out.
The Clients: GE Capital; Farmers; UMB Bank and ADT Security Services.

Constancy, Brooks & Smith LLC
The Firm: A small but growing force in labor and employment, especially for counseling employers on government laws and changing regulations. The firm operates across a *"high-quality"* network of offices in the southern and Midwestern states, specializing in all aspects of management labor and employment litigation and counseling.
The Lawyers: Office head **Robert Janowitz** was praised for his expertise in handling traditional labor areas, such as union avoidance and NLRB issues on behalf of employers.
The Clients: McDonald's; National Express Corporation; St. John's Health System; IPC International and Greater Kansas City Community Foundation.

Thompson Coburn
The Firm: Our researchers were drawn to this firm, following positive recommendations from other labor and employment lawyers in the state. The 28-lawyer team was applauded by peers for its *"excellence"* in providing *"top-level"* employment policy counseling and collective bargaining *"know-how"* to clients.
The Lawyers: The Missouri office is based in St. Louis and the lead partner for labor and employment law is Richard Jaudes.
The Clients: Deutsche Financial Services; American Red Cross; Johnson & Johnson; United Van Lines and Union Pacific Railroad.

Other Notable Practitioners
Jack Yates of Husch & Eppenberger LLC is considered by Missouri peers to be an *"experienced employment litigator."* His *"sound reputation"* extends to counseling management clients on labor and employment regulatory issues. At Stinson Morrison Hecker LLP, **Paul Donnelly** was recommended by clients for his *"depth of knowledge"* and *"forceful"* ERISA litigation skills. **Jack Rowe** of Lathrop & Gage LC advises management on traditional labor matters. Commentators singled him out as a *"focused attorney."*

LITIGATION

Berkowitz, Stanton, Brandt, Williams & Shaw LLP
The Firm: Founded in 1997, this 30-attorney boutique is recognized by peers for its *"tremendous depth and expertise"* in complex commercial litigation. The firm has represented clients at state and federal level and in appellate court proceedings.
The Lawyers: **David Oliver** undertakes complex commercial disputes and can boast a wide-ranging experience that includes class actions in state and federal courts. Peers point to his *"smooth approach"* and *"long-standing trial experience."* He is respected for his work as lead trial counsel in a sequence of key environmental cases, in which a class action was defeated.
The Clients: BASF; BMW of North America; Ford; George K Baum & Company; KPMG; Kansas City Life Insurance Company; ONEOK; Land Rover North America; Mazda Motor; UBS PaineWebber; Pullman Power; Prudential Securities; SAFECO; Stifel, Nicolaus & Company; Sunset Financial Services; The Budd Company; Wal-Mart and Westar Energy.

GENERAL COMMERCIAL

Blackwell Sanders Peper Martin LLP
The Firm: Handles every type of business and commercial litigation with its *"power team"* of over 100 *"top-notch"* litigation lawyers. Peers also applauded its *"high standards"* achieved in *"extraordinary litigation and arbitration"* throughout both state and federal courts. The group represents a variety of clients in areas such as securities

LITIGATION — MISSOURI

MISSOURI
Leading firms
(Litigation: General Commercial)

1
- BERKOWITZ STANTON BRANDT *Kansas City*
- BLACKWELL SANDERS PEPER MARTIN *Kansas City*
- BRYAN CAVE LLP *Kansas City, St Louis*
- ROUSE HENDRICKS GERMAN MAY PC *Kansas City*
- SHOOK, HARDY & BACON LLP *Kansas City*
- SHUGHART THOMSON & KILROY PC *Kansas City*
- STINSON MORRISON HECKER LLP *Kansas City*

2
- ARMSTRONG TEASDALE *Kansas City, St Louis*
- KOHN, SHANDS, ELBERT, GIANOULAKIS *St Louis*
- SPENCER FANE BRITT & BROWNE LLP *Kansas City*
- THOMPSON COBURN *St Louis*

3
- GALLOP, JOHNSON & NEUMAN LC *St Louis*
- HUSCH & EPPENBERGER LLC *Kansas City*
- LATHROP & GAGE LC *Kansas City*
- LEWIS, RICE & FINGERSH *St Louis*
- POLSINELLI SHALTON & WELTE PC *Kansas City*
- SONNENSCHEIN NATH & ROSENTHAL *Kansas City*

Leading individuals
(Litigation: General Commercial)

★ **WARD Larry** *Shughart Thomson & Kilroy, Kansas City*

1
- **BELZER Irvin** *Bryan Cave LLP, Kansas City*
- **EVERSON David** *Stinson Morrison, Kansas City*
- **GERMAN Charles** *Rouse Hendricks German, Kansas City*
- **GRIFFIN James** *Blackwell Sanders Peper, Kansas City*
- **KOHN Alan** *Kohn, Shands, Elbert, Gianoulakis, St Louis*
- **OLIVER David** *Berkowitz Stanton Brandt, Kansas City*
- **VOIGTS Gene** *Shook, Hardy & Bacon LLP, Kansas City*

2
- **GOZA Kirk** *Shook, Hardy & Bacon LLP, Kansas City*
- **HURSH Lynn** *Armstrong Teasdale Schlafly, Kansas City*
- **MASSEY Ray** *Thompson Coburn, St Louis*
- **WALSH Thomas** *Bryan Cave LLP, St Louis*

3
- **HUNT Jeffrey** *Gallop, Johnson & Neuman LC, St Louis*
- **KOKORUDA Thomas** *Shughart Thomson, Kansas City*
- **PRICE Jim** *Spencer Fane Britt & Browne, Kansas City*
- **SHORT Barry** *Lewis, Rice & Fingersh, St Louis*
- **TRIPP David** *Stinson Morrison Hecker LLP, Kansas City*
- **VIRTEL James** *Armstrong Teasdale Schlafly, St Louis*
- **WOLF Jerome** *Sonnenschein Nath, Kansas City*

Firms and individuals are listed alphabetically in each band.

Bryan Cave LLP

The Firm: Recommended highly by observers for its *"high-caliber"* attorneys and the *"tremendous job"* they do for their clients. The firm represents clients in federal and state courts including all types of commercial disputes as well as administrative and regulatory proceedings. In recent highlights, the firm is advising major UK insurance carriers on delayed start-up policies relating to a power plant in Missouri, and has successfully defended a financial institution in a consumer class action asserting that protection insurance was excessive in price and scope.

The Lawyers: **Irvin Belzer** has won a following with his *"intelligent approach"* and his *"fabulous charisma."* Coleader of the commercial litigation client service group, he is active in complex commercial disputes, receiving particular plaudits for his *"thorough and outstanding"* representation of lenders, and involvement in real estate litigation. **Thomas Walsh**, currently the leader of the appellate client service group, has tried numerous lawsuits in state and federal courts. Respected by peers for his *"effective litigation,"* he covers a range of subjects including civil commercial transactions, constitutional issues, trademarks and antitrust.

The Clients: The group has advised GMAC Commercial Mortgage and GMAC Commercial Credit on litigation involving defaulted loans and restructurings. Also represented a variety of banks such as Union Bank, Commerce Bank and Bank of America, and has acted for Viron Corporation.

Rouse Hendricks German May PC

The Firm: Hailed by peers for its *"superb and effective"* 12-lawyer team, this litigation boutique represents a large number of closely held businesses, major law and accounting firms and regional banks. Many of its peers acknowledged that it *"excels constantly"* in its representation of businesses and individuals and their involvement in criminal investigations and internal corporate investigations.

The Lawyers: **Charles German**, one of the market's favorites, was commended as an *"astonishingly smooth"* trial lawyer. He focuses on corporate litigation, capital markets, securities and white-collar criminal defense. His consistent *"trial victories"* are widely respected and applauded.

The Clients: Employers Reinsurance Corporation; Fru-Con Construction; Goodyear; Health Midwest; Interstate Bakeries; Kansas City Power & Light; Southwestern Bell Yellow Pages; Sprint and Station Casinos.

Shook, Hardy & Bacon LLP

see firm details p.876

The Firm: Market observers respect the *"depth and amazing strength"* and the *"stamina"* displayed by the group when dealing with *"highly complex"* trials. Its *"extremely experienced"* attorneys are perhaps best known for their representation of the tobacco industry, and undertake a range of commercial litigation such as securities disputes, and antitrust, environmental and employment-related matters.

The Lawyers: **Gene Voigts** has handled a range of civil and criminal cases in state and federal courts. Observers acknowledged that his *"outstanding grasp of technical issues"* is beneficial when arguing cases at all levels of the state and federal appellate systems. **Kirk Goza** concentrates on business and complex litigation, toxic tort and products liability cases. He has over 20 years of experience in trying *"momentous"* lawsuits, and his peers agree he has done a *"terrific job"* representing Fortune 500 companies in class actions.

The Clients: The firm is best known for its work with Philip Morris.

Shughart Thomson & Kilroy PC

The Firm: Competitors agree that the *"forceful"* litigation department, with its extensive knowledge and *"energetic"* attorneys, is *"one of the main players"* within the jurisdiction. In a recent highlight the firm successfully acted for Block Financial in a breach of contract dispute brought against AOL, arising from the sale of CompuServe to WorldCom with a simultaneous transfer to AOL.

The Lawyers: **Lawrence Ward** has spent 35 years trying cases and arguing appeals in both state and federal courts around the country. Peers and clients refer to him as a *"real gentleman,"* praising his *"star qualities."* An *"unbeatable"* litigator, he is experienced in antitrust, class actions, fraud, securities, professional negligence, IP and environmental law. **Thomas Kokoruda** is chair of the litigation and healthcare litigation department. His trial practice focuses on hospital liability, physician malpractice and medical staff privilege litigation. His peers agree he is *"good with the jury"* and respect his *"strong personality."*

The Clients: Health Midwest; Block Financial; Sprint; Jack Henry & Associates; Major League Baseball Players Association; Kansas City Power & Light; Associated Wholesale Grocers; Horizon Organic Dairy; Commerce Bank; JE Dunn Construction and Dickinson Financial.

Stinson Morrison Hecker LLP

The Firm: Distinguished by market observers for training and attracting some of the *"most outstanding"* attorneys in the region. The firm is respected for *"superb quality"* and its capacity to act on complex disputes, which include antitrust, appellate law, banking, commercial and consumer lending, business torts and construction-related matters.

The Lawyers: **David Everson**'s *"fantastic attitude"* and *"superior"* work in antitrust and commercial litigation has won him a following, particularly for his experience in technology litigation and white-collar crime. **David Tripp** has been involved in environmental matters concerning

disputes, IP, insurance, antitrust and real estate-related litigation.

The Lawyers: **James Griffin** has handled complex civil litigation through mediation, arbitration and at trial proceedings. Market observers commented on his *"bright, professional and persistent manner"* and applauded his *"effective courtroom demeanor."*

The Clients: Clients include: American Italian Pasta Company; Atchison Casting; Applebee's International; Harcos Chemicals; Home Depot and Saint Luke's Health System.

MISSOURI LITIGATION

toxic substances, air and water pollution and chemical regulation under a variety of federal, state and local laws. He is widely known by his competitors for his *"expertise and broad knowledge"* in environmental litigation, which has been applied to issues in both administrative and judicial tribunals.
The Clients: Clients include large national and international companies in industries such as manufacturing, banking and environment.

Armstrong Teasdale Schlafly & Davis
The Firm: A team of 70 attorneys in the litigation department make it one of the firm's largest practice groups. Observers commented on the firm's *"strong"* attorneys and the *"continuously great service"* they provide with litigation matters being actively and aggressively pursued nationwide. Areas of experience include commercial contract disputes, IP, environmental and toxic torts, products liability and antitrust litigation.
The Lawyers: **Lynn Hursh**'s practice includes business litigation, and contract and toxic torts such as chemical explosions, large fires and petroleum leaks. He has been recommended highly by peers for his *"astonishing trial performances."* **James Virtel** frequently acts in commercial utility and environmental litigation. Market observers pointed to his good *"jury tactics"* and his *"approachable demeanor."*
The Clients: The firm advises ICI.

Kohn, Shands, Elbert, Gianoulakis & Giljum LLP
The Firm: Generally known by peers for its *"strong trial"* department, the firm specializes in general trial, appellate, business and commercial litigation.
The Lawyers: **Alan Kohn**'s *"tremendous trial expertise"* has seen him act in business and civil litigation, legal malpractice claims, securities litigation, class actions and appellate law.
The Clients: The firm attracts both local and national clients.

Spencer Fane Britt & Browne LLP
The Firm: Market observers comment on the *"complexity of cases"* attracted by the firm, which require *"immense"* trial experience. Alternative dispute resolution, including arbitration and mediation, is offered both nationally and locally. Environmental litigation, products liability, class actions and toxic torts are just some of the specialist areas covered by the firm.
The Lawyers: **Jim Price**, the chair of the firm's environmental department, advises on regulation and compliance issues and insurance coverage litigation.
The Clients: Spencer Fane serves clients throughout the region, nationally and internationally, including names such as Bebe Stores.

Thompson Coburn
The Firm: Covers general business, antitrust, estate and trust, banking and finance and securities litigation. Its peers recommend the firm's breadth of experience in state and federal courts all over the country, in national and international tribunals, and arbitration panels worldwide. Attorneys were also endorsed for their *"in-depth knowledge"* of a variety of industries.
The Lawyers: Trial attorney **Raymond Massey** advises clients in the heavy industrial machinery sector including railroads and construction project companies. Peers spoke of his *"exceptional skill"* in representing towing companies and various water-related construction companies in all aspects of litigation: according to market observers he has *"significant trial experience"* in maritime and tort law-related issues.
The Clients: Clients include large national and international companies and small businesses in almost every industrial and service sector.

Gallop, Johnson & Neuman LC
The Firm: This firm offers a variety of litigation advice including in contractual disputes, lender liability, antitrust, insurance coverage, and security broker-dealer disputes. The firm is applauded for its *"respectable"* client representation in disputes arising from investor and securities fraud, white-collar crime and secured transactions.
The Lawyers: **Jeffrey Hunt** combines his work in complex commercial litigation and general civil litigation with medical malpractice claims. His 18-year-old practice, which has encompassed the representation of major companies in fraud litigation, and contract and licensing disputes in federal and state courts, has won him the respect of his peers.
The Clients: Represents large and small companies, private organizations and individuals.

Husch & Eppenberger LLC
The Firm: Recommended by competitors for its *"methodical"* trial work and its *"talented attorneys."* The group's activities incorporate a range of complex litigation issues handled by lawyers with substantial jury and trial experience in state and federal courts and arbitration forums nationwide. Areas of experience include general business litigation, antitrust, toxic torts and class actions.
The Lawyers: Robert Best is the key contact for the firm's litigation group
The Clients: Clients include individuals, local, regional and national businesses, financial institutions, and charitable and governmental organizations.

Lathrop & Gage LC
The Firm: Interviewees agree that the firm, which covers a range of litigation matters, offers *"good-quality, cost-effective"* advice. Experience on offer includes general commercial litigation and antitrust. Its attorneys have been praised by observers for being *"consistently hard-working in their effort"* to represent clients effectively.
The Lawyers: Richard Bien is the manager of the litigation department.
The Clients: Allied Waste; GM; Sprint and Bank of America.

Lewis, Rice & Fingersh
The Firm: Recommended by competitors for its *"capable and deft"* attorneys especially prominent in the St. Louis market. Attorneys are skilled in antitrust, environmental, admiralty, products liability, e-commerce, securities and white-collar crime issues.
The Lawyers: **Barry Short** was singled out for his *"dexterous"* litigation skills, which are on display in business litigation, environmental and toxic torts and white-collar crime.
The Clients: Clients include banking organizations, manufacturers, wholesalers and retailers, publishers and broadcasters, maritime firms, real estate brokers and developers, insurance companies, healthcare providers and professional firms.

Polsinelli Shalton & Welte PC
The Firm: Recommended by the market for its *"diverse"* practice. The group acts on disputes arising from industries such as construction, manufacturing, telecommunications, automotive, pharmaceutical and finance.
The Lawyers: Cathy Dean, the chair of the general and commercial litigation practice, is a key contact within the firm.
The Clients: Acts across a range of industries attracting clients on a local, regional and national level.

Sonnenschein Nath & Rosenthal
see firm details p.882
The Firm: Competitors recommended the firm's *"highly skilled"* attorneys, who handle cases in federal and state courts throughout the country. The group draws on the resources in its nine offices throughout the US to provide coordinated advice on antitrust, securities disputes, insurance coverage, IP, products liability and white-collar crime.
The Lawyers: **Jerome Wolf** (see p.393), who heads the Kansas City litigation group, was commended by peers for his *"all-embracing"* experience in environmental, antitrust and construction litigation.
The Clients: Bank of America; Citicorp; Crédit Lyonnais; Enterprise Rent-A-Car Company; GE; Kansas City Southern Industries; 3M; Nissan; Sony Computer Entertainment America; Sun Microsystems and The University of Chicago.

REAL ESTATE

MISSOURI

Leading firms (Real Estate)

1 LEWIS, RICE & FINGERSH *Kansas City*

2 BLACKWELL SANDERS PEPER MARTIN *Kansas City*
POLSINELLI SHALTON & WELTE PC *Kansas City*
STINSON MORRISON HECKER LLP *Kansas City*
WHITE GOSS BOWERS MARCH *Kansas City*

3 LATHROP & GAGE LC *Kansas City*

4 KING HERSHEY PC *Kansas City*

Leading individuals (Real Estate)

1 CARR William *Lewis, Rice & Fingersh,* Kansas City
O'FLAHERTY Michael *Stinson Morrison,* Kansas City

2 FENLEY David *Blackwell Sanders Peper,* Kansas City
FRANTZE David *Stinson Morrison Hecker,* Kansas City
MILLER Charles *Lewis, Rice & Fingersh,* Kansas City
SHALTON Lonnie *Polsinelli Shalton,* Kansas City
WHITE Michael *White Goss Bowers March,* Kansas City

3 BOWERS James *White Goss Bowers March,* Kansas City
DIGIOVANNI Pete *Lewis, Rice & Fingersh,* Kansas City
MARCH Aaron *White Goss Bowers March,* Kansas City

4 DAGENAIS Don *Lathrop & Gage LC,* Kansas City
FREILICH Robert *Freilich, Leitner & Carlisle,* Kansas City
KING Richard *King Hershey PC,* Kansas City

Firms and individuals are listed alphabetically in each band.

Lewis, Rice & Fingersh

The Firm: Clients refer to this as *"one of the best real estate firms,"* while peers respect it as *"consistently honest"* in its negotiations. The 17-lawyer team here handles all aspects of commercial real estate. Acts for developers and investors in transactions involving the acquisition, financing and leasing of office buildings, entertainment complexes and shopping centers.

The Lawyers: A high-profile name on the team is undoubtedly **Bill Carr**, who earns admiration from attorneys on both sides of the Missouri/Kansas state line. Interviewees laud him especially for his *"breadth of experience"* and *"leasing expertise."* Reinforcing the high standing of the team is **Charles Miller**. Clients endorse Miller's *"honesty"* and *"integrity,"* which is combined with a deep understanding of the technicalities of the law. **Pete DiGiovanni** received accolades from clients as a *"problem solver"* and a *"great legal draftsman."*

The Clients: The group currently represents Farmland Industries and has advised it on a new company headquarters. Also represents: American Multi-Cinema; MD Management; Sprint Spectrum; Helzberg Diamonds and Bank of America.

Blackwell Sanders Peper Martin LLP

The Firm: An established real estate player in Kansas City, the firm remains highly rated among market commentators. The group has worked on development projects totaling $802 million in 2001. Commentators referred approvingly to the firm's *"excellent relationships"* with developers. The workload of this 32-member team also embraces the full range of acquisitions, sales and leasing work.

The Lawyers: The group's leading figure is **David Fenley**. Peers acknowledged him to be a *"mover and shaker"* in Kansas City on development projects and transactions. Clients appreciated his *"no-nonsense approach"* and noted that he *"gets the job done."*

The Clients: Represented Aquila in its corporate relocation, securing state and local tax incentives totaling $15 million and negotiating 200,000 sq ft of space in downtown Kansas City. The group also represented AG Edwards & Sons in its acquisition and development of a $165 million St. Louis headquarters. Other clients include Harrah's Entertainment and Highwoods Properties.

Polsinelli Shalton & Welte PC

The Firm: The real estate lawyers at this firm have a reputation in the market for being *"politically connected"* and *"strong in zoning matters."* The 22-lawyer group also benefits from the support of finance department colleagues in the structuring of commercial real estate transactions.

The Lawyers: Much of the team's reputation is owed to founding partner **Lonnie Shalton**, who is widely acclaimed by market observers to be a *"strong real estate specialist."* He has extensive experience in negotiating property acquisitions.

The Clients: The group has represented Intell Management and Investment Company in 3 acquisitions: the Planet Hollywood Hotel in New York's Times Square; the 1.5 million sq ft Insurance Exchange Building in Chicago; and the 250,000 sq ft MCI building in St. Louis. Other clients include Sprint and Block & Company.

Stinson Morrison Hecker LLP

The Firm: Rivals point to a *"balanced"* practice group, which fields attorneys who combine *"a depth of knowledge"* with a *"tenacity to get the job done."* These lawyers also display *"expertise in transactions"* and exemplify *"great intelligence in negotiations."* The group is popular with both municipalities and developers.

The Lawyers: **Michael O'Flaherty**, chair of the real estate group, is a *"well-established"* figure in the real estate market. Interviewees consider him to be *"efficient"* in transactions and *"a pleasure to work with."* Commentators also endorsed **David Frantze**, who has the ability to handle seamlessly any type of real estate matter. Clients appreciated that he is *"always looking for solutions."*

The Clients: Represented Wyandotte County in redeveloping a shopping center. Other Missouri municipalities represented include Lee's Summit and Springfield. DeBruce Graine and Boyd Gaming also use the firm.

White Goss Bowers March Schulte & Weisenfels PC

The Firm: This young but growing team was recommended to researchers as a powerful force in real estate, especially for its city approval work. Clients endorsed the seven-lawyer team as being the *"best in Kansas City"* for zoning and development, while rivals also pointed to its *"superb expertise"* in planning and economic incentives.

The Lawyers: According to clients and competitors, *"big gun"* **Mike White** has an *"excellent reputation"* in zoning and government entitlement matters. **Aaron March** also elicits praise for his rezoning and neighborhood development skills. Rounding out this top-notch team is **James Bowers**, who brings extensive land use experience.

The Clients: ABN AMRO; Knight Ridder; Toys 'R' Us; Harley Davidson; Gateway 2000 and John Q Hammons.

Lathrop & Gage LC

The Firm: Commentators highlighted this 45-member practice group's aptitude for *"sophisticated"* real estate transactions, and its success in securing a diverse client base.

The Lawyers: **Don Dagenais** received positive feedback from the market for his skill in commercial real estate sales and purchases.

The Clients: The Greater Kansas City Chamber of Commerce; Colgate-Palmolive; The Children's Mercy Hospital; GM; Kansas City Area Transportation Authority and Kansas City Life Insurance Company.

King Hershey PC

The Firm: Market observers respect this smaller firm, describing it as *"devoted to the understanding of land use law."* The firm is also experienced in real property matters, municipal finance and development issues.

The Lawyers: **Richard King** is considered by peers to be a *"talented attorney."* King is often found advising on high-profile developments in Kansas City, and is respected for his representation of Missouri municipalities.

The Clients: Quality Hill Redevelopment, Home Builders Association of Greater Kansas City and City of Fulton, Missouri.

Other Notable Practitioners

Robert Freilich of Freilich, Leitner & Carlisle is a well-respected attorney with a national reputation in land use and city subdivisions. His expertise extends to growth management for municipalities. Among his clients are the City of Liberty and Livingston County, Missouri, Highwoods Properties and Hunt Midwest Real Estate Development.

MISSOURI — LEADERS

Leaders in Missouri

ASH, James
Blackwell Sanders Peper Martin LLP,
Kansas City 816 983 8000
Recommended in Corporate/M&A

BELZER, Irvin
Bryan Cave LLP, Kansas City
816 374 3200
Recommended in Litigation

BOWERS, James
White Goss Bowers March Schulte & Weisenfels, A Professional Corporation, Kansas City 816 753 9200
Recommended in Real Estate

CARR, William
Lewis, Rice & Fingersh, Kansas City
816 421 2500
Recommended in Real Estate

DAGENAIS, Don
Lathrop & Gage LC, Kansas City
816 292 2000
Recommended in Real Estate

DIGIOVANNI, Pete
Lewis, Rice & Fingersh, Kansas City
816 421 2500
Recommended in Real Estate

DONNELLY, Paul
Stinson Morrison Hecker LLP, Kansas City 816 691 2600
Recommended in Employment

EGAN, Dennis
The Popham Law Firm PC, Kansas City
816 221 2288
Recommended in Employment

ESSIG, Leonard
Lewis, Rice & Fingersh, St Louis
314 444 7600
Recommended in Corporate/M&A

EVERSON, David
Stinson Morrison Hecker LLP, Kansas City 816 691 2600
Recommended in Litigation

FENLEY, David
Blackwell Sanders Peper Martin LLP, Kansas City 816 983 8000
Recommended in Real Estate

FINUCANE, Brian
Bioff, Finucane, Coffey, Holland & Hosler LLP, Kansas City 816 842 8770
Recommended in Employment

FISHER, Robert
Sonnenschein Nath & Rosenthal,
Kansas City 816 460 2400
gfisher@sonnenschein.com
Recommended in Corporate/M&A
Specialization: Practices corporate law, specializing in transactional matters, principally in mergers and acquisitions. He has represented his largest client, Jordan Industries, Inc., since its founding in 1982. Jordan Industries, Inc. ('JII') is a diversified private holding company with combined pro forma 2001 revenues of more than $2 billion. Since its founding, JII has successfully acquired more than 100 middle market companies, both domestic and foreign. Has served as corporate counsel for approximately 25-30 acquisitions or dispositions each year of companies operating in such areas as telecommunication products, electric motors, temporary staffing, specialty printing and information management agriculture and financial services. Domestic companies, which he represents on transactional matters, include Monsanto Company, American Safety Razor Company, H&R Block, Inc., Farmland Industries, Waddell & Reed, Inc., Black & Veatch, Isle of Capri, Inc., Weary & Associates, and numerous private equity firms. Has served as counsel on numerous foreign transactions in Canada, Mexico, Spain, Italy, India, China, Japan and Brazil.
Prof. Memberships: American Bar Association; Kansas City Metropolitan Bar Association; Missouri Bar Association; Director - Jordan Industries Inc.
Career: Georgetown University Law School, LLM, Taxation, 1966. Georgetown University Law School, JD, 1964. University of Notre Dame, BA, 1961.

FITZGERALD, Robert
Shughart Thomson & Kilroy PC,
Kansas City 816 421 3355
Recommended in Corporate/M&A

FRANTZE, David
Stinson Morrison Hecker LLP,
Kansas City 816 691 2600
Recommended in Real Estate

FREILICH, Robert
Freilich, Leitner & Carlisle, Kansas City
816 561 4414
Recommended in Real Estate

GERMAN, Charles
Rouse Hendricks German May PC,
Kansas City 816 471 7700
Recommended in Litigation

GILSON, Gary
Blackwell Sanders Peper Martin LLP,
Kansas City 816 983 8000
Recommended in Corporate/M&A

GOZA, Kirk
Shook, Hardy & Bacon LLP, Kansas City
816 474 6550
Recommended in Litigation

GRANDA, John
Stinson Morrison Hecker LLP, Kansas City 816 691 2600
Recommended in Corporate/M&A

GRIFFIN, James
Blackwell Sanders Peper Martin LLP,
Kansas City 816 983 8000
Recommended in Litigation

HEETER, James
Sonnenschein Nath & Rosenthal,
Kansas City 816 460 2452
j1h@sonnenschein.com
Recommended in Corporate/M&A
Specialization: Has nearly 30 years of corporate and healthcare legal experience. In his corporate practice, he has represented a diverse range of companies and business entities, including some of Kansas City's best-known and fastest-growing businesses. He has substantial experience in complex corporate transactions such as mergers and acquisitions and debt financings, as well as entrepreneurial start-up ventures. He serves as general counsel to a number of companies and in that role works directly and closely with the companies' senior management, boards of directors and shareholders. In his healthcare practice, hehas served as general counsel for a major Kansas City hospital and as special counsel to other Midwest hospitals. He has handled a wide variety of complex healthcare transactions and represents some of the area's largest physician groups. He has also represented state and local governments in the 'privatization' of healthcare facilities and services such as community mental health centers and ambulance services.
Prof. Memberships: Active in a host of local and state civic and political affairs. From 1983 through 1987, he served as a member of the City Council of Kansas City, Missouri and presently serves as a member of the Civic Council of Greater Kansas City. Member of the American Bar Association, The Missouri Bar, the Kansas City Metropolitan Bar Association, the American Academy of Healthcare Attorneys, the National Health Lawyers Association, the Missouri Society of Hospital Attorneys and the Kansas City Society of Hospital Attorneys.
Career: Harvard Law School, JD cum laude 1973. University of Missouri-Columbia, AB with honors 1970

HUNT, Jeffrey
Gallop, Johnson & Neuman, L.C.,
St Louis 314 615 6217
Recommended in Litigation

HUNTER, Jerry
Bryan Cave LLP, St Louis 314 259 2000
Recommended in Employment

HUNTER, Rob
Stinson Morrison Hecker LLP, Kansas City 816 691 2600
Recommended in Corporate/M&A

HURSH, Lynn
Armstrong Teasdale Schlafly & Davis,
Kansas City 816 221 3420
Recommended in Litigation

JANOWITZ, Robert
Constancy, Brooks & Smith, LLC,
Kansas City 816 472 6400
Recommended in Employment

KETCHMARK, Michael
DKE Law Office, Kansas City
816 842 1515
Recommended in Employment

KING, Richard
King Hershey, A Professional Corporation, Kansas City 816 842 3636
Recommended in Real Estate

KOHN, Alan
Kohn, Shands, Elbert, Gianoulakis & Giljum,LLP, St Louis 314 241 3963
Recommended in Litigation

KOKORUDA, Thomas
Shughart Thomson & Kilroy PC, Kansas City 816 421 3355
Recommended in Litigation

LAUSE, Michael
Thompson Coburn, St Louis
314 552 6000
Recommended in Corporate/M&A

LENTS, Donald
Bryan Cave LLP, St Louis 314 259 2000
Recommended in Corporate/M&A

MARCH, Aaron
White Goss Bowers March Schulte & Weisenfels, A Professional Corporation, Kansas City 816 753 9200
Recommended in Real Estate

MARTUCCI, William
Shook, Hardy & Bacon LLP, Kansas City
816 474 6550
Recommended in Employment

MASSEY, Ray
Thompson Coburn, St Louis
314 552 6000
Recommended in Litigation

MEDVED, Joseph
Lathrop & Gage LC, Kansas City
816 292 2000
Recommended in Corporate/M&A

MEYERS, Martin
The Meyers Law Firm LC, Kansas City
816 444 8500
Recommended in Employment

MILLER, Charles
Lewis, Rice & Fingersh, Kansas City
816 421 2500
Recommended in Real Estate

MONROE, Bob
Stinson Morrison Hecker LLP, Kansas City 816 691 2600
Recommended in Corporate/M&A

NIXON, Richard
Stinson Morrison Hecker LLP, Kansas City 816 691 2600
Recommended in Corporate/M&A

MISSOURI

NOUSS, James
Bryan Cave LLP, St Louis
314 259 2000
Recommended in Corporate/M&A

O'FLAHERTY, Michael
Stinson Morrison Hecker LLP, Kansas City 816 691 2600
Recommended in Real Estate

OLIVER, David
Berkowitz Stanton Brandt Williams & Shaw LLP, Kansas City 816 561 7007
Recommended in Litigation

PHILLIPS, John
Blackwell Sanders Peper Martin LLP, Kansas City 816 983 8000
Recommended in Employment

POLSINELLI, James
Polsinelli Shalton & Welte, A Professional Corporation, Kansas City 816 753 1000
Recommended in Corporate/M&A

PRICE, Jim
Spencer Fane Britt & Browne LLP, Kansas City 816 474 8100
Recommended in Litigation

PRUELLAGE, John
Lewis, Rice & Fingersh, St Louis
314 444 7600
Recommended in Corporate/M&A

ROWE, Jack
Lathrop & Gage LC, Kansas City
816 292 2000
Recommended in Employment

SHALTON, Lonnie
Polsinelli Shalton & Welte, A Professional Corporation, Kansas City 816 753 1000
Recommended in Real Estate

SHORT, Barry
Lewis, Rice & Fingersh, St Louis
314 444 7600
Recommended in Litigation

STAHL, Thomas
Armstrong Teasdale Schlafly & Davis, Kansas City 816 221 3420
Recommended in Corporate/M&A

STEPLETON, Jim
Husch & Eppenberger, LLC, St Louis
314 421 4800
Recommended in Corporate/M&A

TRIPP, David
Stinson Morrison Hecker LLP, Kansas City 816 691 2600
Recommended in Litigation

VAN DYKE, Thomas
Bryan Cave LLP, Kansas City 816 374 3200
Recommended in Corporate/M&A

VERING, John
Armstrong Teasdale Schlafly & Davis, Kansas City 816 221 3420
Recommended in Employment

VIRTEL, James
Armstrong Teasdale Schlafly & Davis, St Louis 314 621 5070
Recommended in Litigation

VOIGTS, Gene
Shook, Hardy & Bacon LLP, Kansas City 816 474 6550
Recommended in Litigation

WALSH, Thomas
Bryan Cave LLP, St Louis
314 259 2000
Recommended in Litigation

WARD, Larry
Shughart Thomson & Kilroy PC, Kansas City 816 421 3355
Recommended in Litigation

WHITACRE, Jack
Spencer Fane Britt & Browne LLP, Kansas City 816 474 8100
Recommended in Employment

WHITE, Michael
White Goss Bowers March Schulte & Weisenfels, A Professional Corporation, Kansas City 816 753 9200
Recommended in Real Estate

WOLF, Jerome
Sonnenschein Nath & Rosenthal, Kansas City
816 460 2400
jwolf@sonnenschein.com
Recommended in Litigation

Specialization: Concentrates in complex civil and commercial litigation, with extensive experience in environmental, antitrust, intellectual property, franchise litigation, construction litigation and alternative dispute resolution. Before joining *Sonnenschein Nath & Rosenthal* as the founding Managing Partner of the Kansas City office in 1994, he practiced law with *Spencer Fane Britt & Browne* from 1966-94, and held positions with *Spencer Fane* as one of its Managing Partners, 1978-85, Chairman of Litigation Group, 1984-94, and Litigation Chair, 1994. He was an officer in the US Army Judge Advocate General's Corps from 1963-66, defending general courts martial and representing the US government with respect to government contracts. He is Chairman of *Sonnenschein's* firmwide marketing committee and heads the Kansas City litigation group. He has served as the founding Managing Partner of the Kansas City office and as a member of the firm's Management Committee.

Prof. Memberships: Kansas City Bar Association - Past President; Kansas City Bar Foundation - Founding President; American Law Institute; Center for Public Resources National Commission to Study Arbitration Procedures, Chairman; Civil Justice Reform Act of 1990 Advisory Group (1991-present), US District Court, Western District of Missouri (See August 1994 ABA Journal, p. 28); American Arbitration Association Western Missouri and Kansas Complex Case ADR Neutral Panel; Best Lawyers in America.

Career: Harvard Law School, JD 1962. Yale University, BA magna cum laude 1959, Phi Beta Kappa.

Publications: 'Environmental Audits and Their Uses in Liability Defense and Allocation, Corporate Decision Making, and Environmental Compliance' - Presented at Urban Land Institute Environmental Panel, New Orleans, Louisiana, April 28, 1989. 'The Corporate Analyst,' Volume 2, Number 1, November 1989: Business Laws, Inc. 'Environmental Law: Identifying, Limiting and Avoiding Liability' - Presented at the Northwestern University School of Law 28th Annual Corporate Counsel Institute in Chicago and San Francisco, fall of 1989. 'Trial: Closing Argument - For Defendant' - Missouri Products Liability Handbook, Chapter 34(b), Continuing Legal Education, University of Missouri-Kansas City School of Law (Copyright 1995). 'The Early Assessment Program: A Unique Opportunity to Avoid Cost and Delay' - Journal of The Missouri Bar, March-April 1995. 'Sharing the Financial Costs of a Dispute: Final Cost Allocation Strategies' - Center For Public Resources Practice Guide on Multiparty Cooperation, Part 3, Key Issues In Cooperative Defense, Chapter 8. Lecturer - Northwestern University Corporation Counsel Institute, 1989. Lecturer - Numerous seminars for the Missouri Bar and Kansas City Metropolitan Bar Association on trial practice and alternative dispute resolution. Lecturer - Numerous seminars on environmental law and alternative dispute resolution nationally, including for Risk Management Technologies, Inc., Superfund Information Network, at the American Bar Association Environmental Conference in Keystone, Colorado, and the Environmental Enforcement Committee of the Litigation Section meeting in Steamboat Springs, Colorado.

WROBLEY, Ralph
Blackwell Sanders Peper Martin LLP, Kansas City
816 983 8000
Recommended in Corporate/M&A

YATES, Jack
Husch & Eppenberger, LLC, Kansas City 816 421 4800
Recommended in Employment

MONTANA

CORPORATE/M&A

CONTENTS: Corporate/M&A p.394; Employment: Mainly Plaintiff p.395; Mainly Defendant p.395; Litigation: General Commercial p.396; Real Estate p.398; Individuals' Profiles p.398.

MONTANA'S TOP TWO
1. Crowley, Haughey, Hanson, Toole & Dietrich
2. Garlington, Lohn & Robinson

Ranking based on Chambers' research within the state.

All quotes in the text are from interviews with clients and competitors.

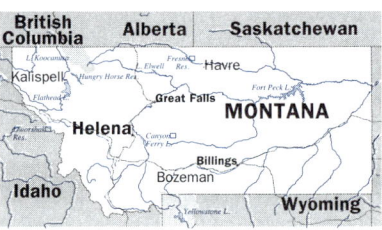

OVERVIEW: The largest firm in Montana and ranked first, **Crowley, Haughey, Hanson, Toole & Dietrich** was said to possess a deep bench of responsive and intelligent attorneys. The corporate practice acts for a broad range of national and international clients, and is highly visible on key M&A transactions. Attorneys also recently advised on the $65 million refinancing of a national healthcare provider. In real estate, its more than 30 attorneys were felt to be capable of handling real estate transactions involving any degree of complexity. A strong litigation practice covers a variety of cases, while the labor and employment team was recognized for its expertise in discrimination litigation, general counseling and risk assessment. First Interstate Bank of Commerce and John Deere are clients.

Garlington, Lohn & Robinson, in second place, is a full-service firm, respected for its breadth of coverage and the quality of its attorneys. It fields a highly rated litigation practice from its Missoula office. Sources also spoke of the great depth of its employment practice, which has a strong track record in age, sex and race discrimination actions, and wrongful dismissal cases. Clients include Burlington Northern & Sante Fe Railway and the Anaconda Company.

CORPORATE/M&A

MONTANA
Leading firms (Corporate/M&A)

1. **CROWLEY, HAUGHEY, HANSON, TOOLE** Billings
   DORSEY & WHITNEY LLP Great Falls
2. **CHRISTIAN, SAMSON, JONES & CHISHOLM** Missoula
   GARLINGTON, LOHN & ROBINSON PLLP Missoula
   HOLLAND & HART LLP Billings

Leading individuals (Corporate/M&A)

1. **CHISHOLM David** Christian, Samson, Jones, Missoula
   ELLINGSON Mae Dorsey & Whitney, Missoula
   LAMDIN William Crowley, Haughey, Hanson, Billings
   MANNING John Dorsey & Whitney LLP, Great Falls
2. **BROWN Stephen** Garlington, Lohn & Robinson, Missoula
   HINGLE Charles Holland & Hart LLP, Billings
   PETERSEN Laurence Holland & Hart LLP, Billings

Firms and individuals are listed alphabetically in each band.

Crowley, Haughey, Hanson, Toole & Dietrich PLLP

The Firm: A strong regional presence is enjoyed by this, the largest firm in Montana. Its corporate practice has a deep bench of *"responsive and intelligent"* attorneys who are highly visible on key M&A transactions. The firm acts for a broad spread of both national and international corporate clients. Attorneys recently advised on the $65 million refinancing of a national healthcare provider.

The Lawyers: William Lamdin, a key figure in the firm's corporate practice, handles corporate financing and mergers. Competitors singled out Lamdin as an *"experienced attorney who understands the details;"* his refinancing expertise was particularly esteemed. Clients also responded positively, commenting that Lamdin *"carries a lot of respect to the deal table."*

The Clients: Represents a wide range of clients, including national and international corporations, local business people, farmers and ranchers.

Dorsey & Whitney LLP

The Firm: This national firm has offices in Missoula and Great Falls and has impressed market observers with its *"excellent full-service offering."* While the closure of a large office in Billings and the consequent staff loss has reduced the firm's capacity within the state, its highly specialist corporate team has retained the respect of clients. The firm is considered a sound choice for complex technical transactions and related tax issues.

The Lawyers: Sources endorsed **Mae Nan Ellingson**'s expertise both in corporate matters and bond issues. Peers regard her as a *"first choice for complicated bond work,"* while clients describe her as *"an effective attorney."* Corporate securities specialist **John (Jack) Manning** is *"a terrific securities and M&A lawyer,"* and *"certainly one of the best in Montana."* Clients pointed to his *"great commercial understanding,"* and were impressed by his portfolio of *"big-ticket securities work."*

The Clients: The firm acts for public and private companies, including seven NASDAQ and one NYSE-listed companies.

Christian, Samson, Jones & Chisholm PLLC

The Firm: This nine-attorney Missoula firm has a general civil practice and undertakes a variety of corporate and M&A work for business interests in the state.

The Lawyers: A recent recruit from Holland & Hart, **David Chisholm** is respected for his work with banks, both on corporate transactions and finance-related matters. Clients cited him as *"an eminent practitioner in this field,"* while peers were full of admiration for his *"excellence in bank acquisition work."*

The Clients: Missoula Federal Credit Union; John Deere Credit; Norwest Corporation; Stewart Title Guaranty Company; Hensler Farms; Cook Ranches; McCrumb Construction; Northwest Media and Rocky Rail Services.

Garlington, Lohn & Robinson PLLP

The Firm: Clients value this firm's *"broader-based approach,"* and competitors respect its *"first-class operation,"* which fields *"good lawyers in virtually every area."*

The Lawyers: Stephen Brown has a strong track record in environmental matters as they relate to business transactions. Peers applauded Brown as one of the state's leading corporate lawyers for his *"analysis of issues"* and *"incredible drafting skills."* He is *"levelheaded in the biggest transactions"* and *"easy to work with on either side of the table."*

The Clients: Missoula Light and Water, The Milwaukee Railroad and the Anaconda Company.

Holland & Hart LLP

see firm details p.819

The Firm: The firm indicated its commitment to the Montana market through its merger at the end of 2002 with the well-established Petersen, Jones, Hingle & Sterup. Attorneys from this firm have joined the Billings office, bolstering the firm's corporate practice. Sources anticipate that this move to consolidate its Montana presence will be rewarded in coming years, particularly with its work in M&A, joint ventures and corporate financings.

The Lawyers: Chuck Hingle's (see p.398) high level of experience in corporate transactions, and particularly in the state's banking sector, has won him a following. Interviewees described him as *"an efficient and knowledgeable attorney."* Business generalist **Laurence Petersen** (see p.399) has an excellent reputation for his *"broad expertise,"* which also includes specialist tax knowledge. Clients agree that he is *"much respected in the state."*

The Clients: The firm acts as legal counsel to individuals and companies of all sizes, from emerging businesses to large public corporations, located throughout the US and internationally.

MONTANA

EMPLOYMENT & LABOR LAW — MAINLY PLAINTIFF

MONTANA
Leading firms
(Employment: Mainly Plaintiff)

[1]
- **EDWARDS FRICKLE HALVERSON** Billings
- **GOETZ, GALLICK, BALDWIN & DOLAN** Bozeman
- **HOYT & BLEWETT** Great Falls

Leading individuals
(Employment: Mainly Plaintiff)

[1]
- **BLEWETT Alexander** Hoyt & Blewett, Great Falls
- **EDWARDS Clifford** Edwards Frickle Halverson, Billings
- **GOETZ James** Goetz, Gallick, Baldwin & Dolan, Bozeman

Firms and individuals are listed alphabetically in each band.

Edwards Frickle Halverson & Anner-Hughes
The Firm: This plaintiffs' firm in Billings won the respect of the market for its work advising on a variety of different actions, including wrongful discharge and gender-based discrimination.
The Lawyers: A **Clifford Edwards**' *"first-rate advocacy skills"* impressed many market observers. A *"persuasive, forceful character,"* Edwards also possesses *"a depth of technical knowledge."*

Goetz, Gallick, Baldwin & Dolan PC
The Firm: This five-lawyer Bozeman litigation boutique provides general trial and appellate-level advocacy. Sources respect the group's *"understanding of how to manage plaintiffs' cases"* and its expertise in labor and employment law.
The Lawyers: Competitors praised **James Goetz** as *"just about the best litigator around."* He is particularly known for his representation of plaintiffs in constitutional cases involving First Amendment rights. Clients described him as *"a great legal scholar"* and referred to the *"excellent value-added advice"* he provides.

Hoyt & Blewett
The Firm: This litigation boutique in Great Falls has produced an *"excellent employment practice,"* adjudged *"first-rate"* by competitors. Clients particularly pointed to its skill in discrimination litigation and labor law matters.
The Lawyers: Respected litigator **Alexander Blewett** is well known in the state for his plaintiffs' practice. This *"tenacious and competitive"* attorney has impressed defendant lawyers who endorse his commitment, saying he is *"passionate about his clients."*

EMPLOYMENT & LABOR LAW — MAINLY DEFENDANT

MONTANA
Leading firms
(Employment: Mainly Defendant)

[1]
- **GARLINGTON, LOHN & ROBINSON PLLP** Missoula
- **HOLLAND & HART LLP** Billings

[2]
- **CROWLEY, HAUGHEY, HANSON, TOOLE** Billings
- **GOUGH, SHANAHAN, JOHNSON** Helena
- **HUGHES, KELLNER, SULLIVAN & ALKE** Helena
- **UGRIN, ALEXANDER, ZADICK & HIGGINS** Great Falls
- **WORDEN, THANE & HAINES PC** Missoula

Leading individuals
(Employment: Mainly Defendant)

[1]
- **BENDER Jeanne** Holland & Hart LLP, Billings
- **FETSCHER Candace** Garlington, Lohn, Missoula
- **SULLIVAN John** Hughes, Kellner, Sullivan, Helena
- **ZADICK Gary** Ugrin, Alexander, Zadick, Great Falls

[2]
- **HATTERSLEY Thomas** Gough, Shanahan, Helena
- **LEHMAN Steven** Crowley, Haughey, Hanson, Billings
- **THANE Jeremy** Worden, Thane & Haines PC, Missoula

Firms and individuals are listed alphabetically in each band.

Garlington, Lohn & Robinson PLLP
The Firm: Sources spoke of the *"great depth to this employment practice."* The seven-strong employment group has a strong track record in employment-related controversy work such as age, sex and race discrimination actions, and wrongful dismissals.
The Lawyers: **Candace Fetscher** is regarded by peers as a *"thorough litigator"* and one who stays *"up to date on developments in employment law and regulations."* She is widely consulted on both litigation and risk management. Her *"ethical"* approach combined with her *"skillful advocacy"* makes her a popular choice with clients.
The Clients: The firm acts for: Amtrak; Bank of America; Bristol-Myers Squibb; Burlington Northern & Santa Fe Railway; First National Bank of Montana; Missoula County and WR Grace.

Holland & Hart LLP
see firm details p.819
The Firm: This respected national practice is regarded as a *"strong presence"* for employment-related counseling and discrimination litigation. Clients value the *"sound judgment"* of its attorneys and their wide-ranging experience.
The Lawyers: Jeanne Bender (see p.398) is held in high regard by *Chambers'* interviewees as *"a no-nonsense problem solver."* Clients appreciate that she is *"accessible, anticipates the stumbling blocks and puts you at ease."*
The Clients: The firm acts for a variety of private individual and corporate clients across Montana, and as local counsel for national businesses.

Crowley, Haughey, Hanson, Toole & Dietrich PLLP
The Firm: This firm has carved itself a reputation as a *"strong litigation outfit,"* with specialist knowledge of labor and employment matters. Its attorneys have the *"range of skills to handle all types of cases."* Interviewees agreed that its advice on discrimination litigation, general counseling and risk assessment attains *"consistently high standards."*
The Lawyers: Clients laud **Steven Lehman** as a *"great trial lawyer"* who offers *"support on a wide range of areas."* His particular specialties lie in the areas of discrimination law and union organization.
The Clients: First Interstate Bank of Commerce; Noranda Minerals; Montana Power Company; Northwest Farm Credit Services; Mid-Rivers Telephone Cooperative; Kennecott Corporation and Deaconess Medical Center, Billings.

Gough, Shanahan, Johnson & Waterman
The Firm: Well respected in Helena and surrounding area for its employment defense work. The group has experience in litigation arising out of discrimination claims and wrongful dismissal. The wide variety of clients attracted to the firm provides testimony to its profile across a number of industries.
The Lawyers: Thomas Hattersley's *"thoroughness in trial preparation and analytical approach"* have impressed many market observers.
The Clients: American Farm Bureau Federation; Great American Federal Savings & Loan Association; Carroll College; Kaiser Cement Corporation; Hanson Natural Resources Company and Montana Mining Association.

Hughes, Kellner, Sullivan & Alke
The Firm: This small Helena firm was endorsed for its involvement in *"litigation that has a powerful employment element."* The firm has been particularly active in counseling clients in the insurance and medical provision sectors.
The Lawyers: Clients commended **John Sullivan** as *"an effective and experienced lawyer in both mediation and litigation."*

MONTANA

LITIGATION

The Clients: Morrison Maierle; Dick Anderson Construction; Prudential Property and Casualty and Utah Medical Insurance Association.

Ugrin, Alexander, Zadick & Higgins PC
The Firm: Based in Great Falls, this litigation practice boasts *"top-quality people"* with notable successes in employment cases. Attorneys are known to be undaunted by challenges; interviewees reported that they *"take on cases that other firms would be hesitant to handle"* and have an excellent case record in discrimination and unfair dismissal claims.
The Lawyers: **Gary Zadick** was warmly recommended as an able employment litigator with *"remarkable jury appeal."* Although best known for his employment litigation work, Zadick has a growing arbitration practice and is well liked by clients for his *"down-to-earth and constructive"* approach.
The Clients: ARCO; Attorneys Liability Protection Society; Coltec Industries; Sinclair Oil; The Medical Protective Company; Montana Municipal Insurance Authority; Smith's Food & Drug Centers; Truck Insurance Exchange and United Building Centers.

Worden, Thane & Haines PC
The Firm: One of the larger Missoula firms active in the employment sector. Its labor and employment practice focuses on commercial advice and risk management counseling to public and private institutions and insurance companies.
The Lawyers: Clients respect name partner **Jeremy Thane** as *"a tough negotiator"* who advises management on compliance risk assessment and litigation.
The Clients: Sammons Trucking; First Interstate Bank; First National Bank of Montana; Triple W Equipment and The WGM Group (Engineering).

LITIGATION

GENERAL COMMERCIAL

MONTANA
Leading firms
(Litigation: General Commercial)

1
- CROWLEY, HAUGHEY, HANSON, TOOLE Billings
- GARLINGTON, LOHN & ROBINSON PLLP Missoula

2
- DORSEY & WHITNEY LLP Missoula
- HOYT & BLEWETT Great Falls
- POORE, ROTH & ROBINSON PC Butte

3
- BOONE, KARLBERG PC Missoula
- BROWN LAW FIRM PC Billings
- CHRISTENSEN, MOORE, COCKRELL Kalispell
- GOETZ, GALLICK, BALDWIN & DOLAN Bozeman
- GOUGH, SHANAHAN, JOHNSON Helena

Leading individuals
(Litigation: General Commercial)

1
- CHRISTENSEN Dana Christensen, Moore, Kalispell
- GOETZ James Goetz, Gallick, Baldwin & Dolan, Bozeman
- ROBINSON Donald Poore, Roth & Robinson PC, Butte
- STRONG Keith Dorsey & Whitney LLP, Great Falls

2
- BLEWETT Alexander Hoyt & Blewett, Great Falls
- COX Randy Boone, Karlberg PC, Missoula
- DALY Lawrence Garlington, Lohn & Robinson, Missoula
- EDWARDS Clifford Edwards Frickle, Billings
- HINGLE Charles Holland & Hart LLP, Billings
- SHANAHAN Ward Gough, Shanahan, Johnson, Helena

Firms and individuals are listed alphabetically in each band.

Crowley, Haughey, Hanson, Toole & Dietrich PLLP
The Firm: The largest firm in the state. Its litigation group is widely respected among interviewees as *"an efficient and effective operation,"* while clients appreciate that it *"offers a full service, with experience of a range of industries."* The litigation practice spans the full gamut of cases, including bad faith litigation, insurance defense, environmental issues and workers' compensation matters.
The Lawyers: The group has displayed great strength in depth, with *"high-quality attorneys"* providing *"the range of skills a client needs."* Although no single individual stood out during *Chambers'* research, the group, which includes Steve Lehman and Bill Mattix, was endorsed by peers for setting high standards for the rest of the market.
The Clients: The firm acts for: First Interstate Bank of Commerce; John Deere; Farmers; Transamerica Insurance; Montana State Compensation Insurance Fund and Equitable. The firm recently acted successfully for the Burlington Northern & Santa Fe Railway against a $250 million judgment in Crow Tribal Court concerning the ownership of a large tract of land.

Garlington, Lohn & Robinson PLLP
The Firm: A *"broad-based firm"* of *"extremely talented lawyers,"* according to competitors. Its well-respected litigation department is particularly active in insurance coverage and defense against negligence claims, including medical malpractice, products liability and employment-related litigation.
The Lawyers: Peers described **Larry Daly** as a *"powerful advocate,"* while clients portrayed him as *"a top trial lawyer who really knows his stuff."* His expertise lies in medical malpractice, products liability and professional negligence defense, and he also undertakes a substantial amount of insurance coverage defense.
The Clients: The firm acts for manufacturers, healthcare providers, retailers and financial institutions.

Dorsey & Whitney LLP
The Firm: A sizable national firm with two branch offices in Montana. Although the firm lost capacity with the recent closure of its full-service Billings branch, it retains the healthy respect of competitors and clients. Peers portrayed its experience in commercial litigation as *"excellent,"* while clients pointed to the group as a *"reasonable, cost-effective service."* The litigation practice includes trial and appellate-level matters arising from securities disputes, insurance coverage, malpractice, products liability, and cases in the banking and finance, natural resources and environmental sectors.
The Lawyers: **Keith Strong** is active in professional malpractice cases, securities disputes and products liability defense. Peers and clients appreciate this *"knowledgeable, hard-working litigator"* for his track record in big-ticket, complex litigation. He has secured favorable verdicts for clients in the federal district courts and Montana Supreme Court.
The Clients: The firm acts for a number of public and private companies.

Hoyt & Blewett
The Firm: A litigation boutique, adjudged a *"first-class operation"* by competitors. Clients agreed that the firm, although a smaller group, is *"as good as any in the state."* The team has impressed with its work in securing a $7 million verdict for its client BNSF in a 2002 case against Dorn.
The Lawyers: **Alexander Blewett** has a strong profile among our interviewees as *"an extremely competitive attorney who is passionate about his clients."* He specializes in plaintiffs' litigation and has been dubbed *"a genteel bulldog"* by appreciative clients.
The Clients: Champion Enterprises; Sturm,Ruger & Comapny; Unocal; Zurich; Hertz; State Farm; John Hancock Life Insurance Company; University of Great Falls and City of Great Falls.

Poore, Roth & Robinson PC
The Firm: This mid-sized firm, with offices across the state, has derived an advantage through the success of what competitors have dubbed its *"great team approach."* Attorneys approach their cases by *"focusing on research and legal analysis,"* and combining this with strong courtroom skills. The firm's main sources of litigation cases are insurance defense, environmental and natural resources law, business disputes, personal injury and workers' compensation matters.
The Lawyers: **Donald Robinson** is one of the state's most eminent practitioners. He received

LITIGATION

MONTANA

strong commendations from clients as a respected litigator who *"does an excellent job of deflecting negative energy, particularly in the courtroom."* His practice encompasses a wide range of litigation including employment and labor relations disputes, commercial litigation, and contract and torts disputes.
The Clients: Allstate; Blue Cross and Blue Shield of Montana; First Citizens Bank; Northern Montana Hospital; Hartford Accident and Indemnity Company and Lexington Insurance Company.

Boone, Karlberg PC
The Firm: A mid-sized firm based in Missoula, it is respected by observers as *"actively engaged in state and federal court civil litigation."* The practice covers statewide matters, with an emphasis on insurance coverage, products liability and personal injury matters. Competitors acknowledged that the firm *"gets good results in trials,"* due to the success of its *"tenacious lawyers."* The group fields *"good brief writers and clear thinkers."*
The Lawyers: A number of lawyers at the firm were singled out by interviewees. Among them, **Randy Cox** received praise from a number of peers as a strong and *"tenacious advocate,"* who *"consistently gets good results in trials."* He was also praised for his excellent *"writing and analytical"* abilities.
The Clients: US Fidelity & Guaranty Company, Industrial Indemnity Company and Farmers Alliance Mutual Insurance Company.

Brown Law Firm PC
The Firm: This 16-strong group of *"highly competent trial lawyers"* has impressed peers with its *"good record of defense work."* The firm has been described as *"number one in Billings"* for litigation. Its *"hard-working"* attorneys advise on civil and criminal trial matters, and enjoy an active appellate practice. Mediation and arbitration are also areas of expertise.
The Lawyers: Rockwood Brown is a key member of the litigation team.
The Clients: The firm acts for financial institutions, manufacturers, retailers and distribution companies.

Christensen, Moore, Cockrell, Cummings & Axelberg PC
The Firm: This small firm, based in Kalispell, represents clients in all aspects of civil trial and appellate litigation, including environmental and natural resources regulatory disputes. Competitors endorsed its attorneys' *"hard-working and ethical"* approach to litigation. Clients reported that the firm has a *"clear perspective on how to manage a case,"* and that attorneys *"really gear up for litigation."*
The Lawyers: Peers rate **Dana Christensen** as a *"first-rate lawyer"* with a *"prime"* insurance defense and medical malpractice caseload, while clients pointed to his *"excellent trial skills."*
The Clients: Allstate; Attorneys Liability Protection Society; ASARCO; CNA Insurance Companies; Montana Municipal Insurance Authority and National Farmers Union.

Goetz, Gallick, Baldwin & Dolan PC
The Firm: The five-lawyer Bozeman-based litigation boutique provides general trial and appellate-level support in commercial and business litigation, personal injury cases, and products liability, employment and First Amendment litigation.
The Lawyers: **James Goetz** was commended by rivals as *"one of the best litigators in the state,"* and he was picked as the *"number-one choice for any piece of significant litigation"* by clients. His long-standing practice features a mixture of trial and appellate work including constitutional, environmental and plaintiffs' personal injury cases.
The Clients: The firm's client base consists mostly of local and regional businesses, and private individuals.

Gough, Shanahan, Johnson & Waterman
The Firm: A mid-sized firm with a *"first-class"* group of litigators. Their credentials include general civil and trial experience and specialist knowledge of construction, insurance defense and natural resources disputes.
The Lawyers: While researchers came across several names in the course of interviews, the most prominent litigator at the firm was **Ward Shanahan**. Sources commended him as an *"efficient and professional"* defense attorney.
The Clients: American Farm Bureau Federation and Western Energy Company are clients.

Other Notable Practitioners
A Clifford Edwards of Edwards Frickle Halverson & Anner-Hughes received plaudits from market observers as *"one of Montana's most successful litigators."* Clients valued him as *"a person you can trust,"* and endorsed his skill across a range of litigation cases. In January 2003, Petersen, Jones, Hingle & Sterup PLLC combined with Holland & Hart LLP. **Charles Hingle** (see p.398), a key attorney at the latter firm, received a number of positive recommendations for his success as a *"highly effective litigator"* with *"exceptional technical ability."*

REAL ESTATE

MONTANA
Leading firms (Real Estate)
1. **CROWLEY, HAUGHEY, HANSON, TOOLE** Billings
   GARLINGTON, LOHN & ROBINSON PLLP Missoula
2. **HEARD & HOWARD** Columbus
   MOULTON, BELLINGHAM, LONGO Billings
   ROBERT M KNIGHT Missoula
   WORDEN, THANE & HAINES PC Missoula

Leading individuals (Real Estate)
1. **DOCKERY** Michael *Crowley, Haughey, Hanson,* Billings
   HEARD Richard *Heard & Howard,* Columbus
   KNIGHT Robert *Robert M. Knight,* Missoula
   WAGNER William *Garlington, Lohn & Robinson,* Missoula
2. **HAINES** Harry *Worden, Thane & Haines PC,* Missoula
   JONES John *Moulton, Bellingham, Longo,* Billings

Firms and individuals are listed alphabetically in each band.

Crowley, Haughey, Hanson, Toole & Dietrich PLLP
The Firm: Interviewees agreed that this large regional firm has the capacity to *"handle most real estate transactions."* The more than 30 attorneys in the firm's commercial group were respected for their *"sound management of large-scale projects,"* involving complex financing, development and land use issues.
The Lawyers: **Michael Dockery** is widely respected as a *"top real estate lawyer who knows the law extremely well."* Clients said that they *"would choose him for large deals,"* and were consistently impressed with the standard and quality of work that he produced. Dockery's expertise includes the subdivision and development of real property, and he is well versed in the environmental considerations related to real estate transactions.
The Clients: The firm acts for First Interstate Bank of Commerce. Insurance clients include: Farmers; The Home Insurance Companies; Transamerica Insurance Company; Montana State Compensation Insurance Fund and Equitable.

Garlington, Lohn & Robinson PLLP
The Firm: This real estate group fields" *attorneys who are extremely able, and interested in finding solutions to problems."* Both peers and clients acknowledge that when the firm is on one side of the deal table, *"matters will be resolved."*
The Lawyers: Commercial lawyer **William Wagner** has won a following among peers with his *"driven attitude"* and *"confident demeanor that assists the smooth running of transactions."*
The Clients: The Milwaukee Railroad and the Anaconda Company are clients.

MONTANA — LEADERS

Heard & Howard
The Firm: A small Columbus firm that undertakes a variety of commercial matters. It has carved a strong reputation for its work in real estate development and financing.
The Lawyers: Competitors endorsed **Richard Heard** as a *"first-class negotiator"* who has a *"depth of knowledge."* Clients viewed him as being *"responsive and committed to our needs."*
The Clients: The firm acts for small local clients and larger national developers.

Moulton, Bellingham, Longo & Mather PC
The Firm: A mid-sized firm in Billings that is active in a range of real estate work, from residential property to large real estate transactions. Also experienced in land development and condominium projects, and subdivisions of real property.
The Lawyers: Commercial generalist **John Jones** is recommended for his experience in real estate-related transactions. Sources commented on his *"intellectual approach,"* while clients valued his prompt advice and availability for consultation on a range of issues.
The Clients: St Vincent Healthcare; Lee Enterprises; Kampgrounds of America. Also advises automobile manufacturers, utilities and financial institutions.

Robert M. Knight
The Firm: A Missoula real estate boutique that focuses on commercial developments, ranch properties and related real property issues.
The Lawyers: Peers commended **Robert Knight** for his *"outstanding level of experience"* and *"excellent depth of knowledge."* Clients admired his *"analytical abilities"* and pointed to his talent for presenting ideas and drafting documentation.
The Clients: The firm acts for a variety of private and public companies, and individuals with large real property portfolios.

Worden, Thane & Haines PC
The Firm: The real estate practice of this mid-sized firm represents clients in both commercial and residential matters, including ranches and farms.
The Lawyers: **Harry Haines** undertakes all forms of real estate work. He is respected by competitors for his breadth of experience, particularly on residential property matters.
The Clients: Employers Association of Western Montana; Western Security Bank; Sammons Trucking; First Interstate Bank; Missoula County Public Schools and Missoula County Airport Authority.

Leaders in Montana

BENDER, Jeanne Matthews
Holland & Hart LLP, Billings
406 252 2166
jbender@hollandhart.com
Recommended in Employment
Specialization: Partner practicing in commercial and natural resources litigation, and employment counseling and litigation. Has represented commercial and nonprofit entities in a variety of claims including breach of contract, wrongful discharge, discrimination, wage and hour claims and labor issues. Has appeared before the Montana Human Rights Commission and the State Department of Labor and Industry. Regularly makes presentations on sexual harassment, wrongful discharge, discrimination, fair labor standards and related topics.
Prof. Memberships: American Bar Association Foundation, Montana Bar Association, American Bar Association, ABA sections on Litigation and Labor and Employment Law and Torts and Insurance Law, Past President, Montana Association of Female Executives, Montana Defense Trial Lawyers Association.
Career: Admitted the Montana (1985) and Colorado (1987) Bars, the United States District Court and the Ninth Circuit Court of Appeals. Editor of the Montana Employment Law Letter.
Personal: Received a JD (1985) and a BA (1965) from the University of Montana.

BLEWETT, Alexander
Hoyt & Blewett, Great Falls
406 761 1960
Recommended in Employment, Litigation

BROWN, Stephen Ross
Garlington, Lohn & Robinson, PLLP, Missoula 406 523 2500
Recommended in Corporate/M&A

CHISHOLM, David
Christian, Samson, Jones & Chisholm, PLLC, Missoula 406 721 7772
Recommended in Corporate/M&A

CHRISTENSEN, Dana
Christensen, Moore, Cockrell, Cummings & Axelberg PC, Kalispell
406 751 6000
Recommended in Litigation

COX, Randy
Boone, Karlberg PC, Missoula
406 543 6646
Recommended in Litigation

DALY, Lawrence
Garlington, Lohn & Robinson, PLLP, Missoula 406 523 2500
Recommended in Litigation

DOCKERY, Michael
Crowley, Haughey, Hanson, Toole & Dietrich, PLLP, Billings 406 252 3441
Recommended in Real Estate

EDWARDS, Clifford
Edwards Frickle Halverson & Anner-Hughes, Billings 406 256 8155
Recommended in Employment, Litigation

ELLINGSON, Mae Nan
Dorsey & Whitney LLP, Missoula
406 721 6025
Recommended in Corporate/M&A

FETSCHER, Candace
Garlington, Lohn & Robinson, PLLP, Missoula 406 523 2500
Recommended in Employment

GOETZ, James
Goetz, Gallick, Baldwin & Dolan PC, Bozeman 406 587 0618
Recommended in Employment, Litigation

HAINES, Harry
Worden, Thane & Haines, PC, Missoula 406 721 3400
Recommended in Real Estate

HATTERSLEY, Thomas
Gough, Shanahan, Johnson & Waterman, Helena 406 442 8560
Recommended in Employment

HEARD, Richard
Heard & Howard, Columbus
406 322 4429
Recommended in Real Estate

HINGLE, Charles
Holland & Hart LLP, Billings
406 252 2166
chingle@hollandhart.com
Recommended in Corporate/M&A, Litigation
Specialization: A partner whose practice focuses on business bankruptcy and creditor's rights, but he has extensive experience in banking, real estate and commercial litigation. He has been certified as a business bankruptcy specialist by the American Board of Certification since 1993.
Prof. Memberships: Louisiana State Bar Association, Montana State Bar Association, Wyoming State Bar Association, American Bankruptcy Institute, Roster of Neutrals, American Arbitration Association.
Career: Admitted to the Louisiana (1976), Montana (1980), and Wyoming (1996) State Bars.
Personal: Received a JD from Louisiana State University (1976) and a BA from Tulane University (1972).

JONES, John
Moulton, Bellingham, Longo & Mather, PC, Billings 406 248 7731
Recommended in Real Estate

KNIGHT, Robert
Robert M. Knight, Missoula
406 721 5440
Recommended in Real Estate

LAMDIN, William
Crowley, Haughey, Hanson, Toole & Dietrich, PLLP, Billings 406 252 3441
Recommended in Corporate/M&A

LEHMAN, Steven
Crowley, Haughey, Hanson, Toole & Dietrich, PLLP, Billings 406 252 3441
Recommended in Employment

MANNING, John
Dorsey & Whitney LLP, Great Falls
406 727 3632
Recommended in Corporate/M&A

PETERSEN, Laurence
Holland & Hart LLP, Billings
406 252 2166
lpetersen@hollandhart.com
Recommended in Corporate/M&A
Specialization: Partner whose practice focuses on tax, estate planning, real estate, and natural resources. He has extensive experience with probates; formation of LLC's, partnerships and corporations; coal leasing, acquisitions, and entity formations; purchase and sale of oil and gas and entity formation; and health care.
Prof. Memberships: Montana Bar Association, Yellowstone County Bar Association, ACTEC.
Career: Admitted to the Montana Bar (1967).
Personal: Received a JD from the University of Montana (1967) and a BS in Economics from the University of Pennsylvania (1964). Received LLM from New York University (Taxation, 1970).

ROBINSON, Donald
Poore, Roth & Robinson, P.C., Butte
406 497 1200
Recommended in Litigation

SHANAHAN, Ward
Gough, Shanahan, Johnson & Waterman, Helena 406 442 8560
Recommended in Litigation

STRONG, Keith
Dorsey & Whitney LLP, Great Falls
406 727 3632
Recommended in Litigation

SULLIVAN, John
Hughes, Kellner, Sullivan & Alke, Helena
406 442 3690
Recommended in Employment

THANE, Jeremy
Worden, Thane & Haines, PC, Missoula
406 721 3400
Recommended in Employment

WAGNER, William
Garlington, Lohn & Robinson, PLLP, Missoula 406 523 2500
Recommended in Real Estate

ZADICK, Gary
Ugrin, Alexander, Zadick & Higgins, PC, Great Falls 406 771 0007
Recommended in Employment

NEBRASKA

CORPORATE/M&A

CONTENTS: Corporate/M&A p.400; Employment: Mainly Plaintiff p.401; Mainly Defendant p.401; Litigation: General Commercial p.402; Real Estate p.404; Individuals' Profiles p.405.

NEBRASKA'S TOP THREE
1. Baird, Holm, McEachen, Pedersen, Hamann & Strasheim
2. McGrath, North, Mullin & Kratz
3. Fraser Stryker Law Firm

Ranking based on Chambers' research within the state.

All quotes in the text are from interviews with clients and competitors..

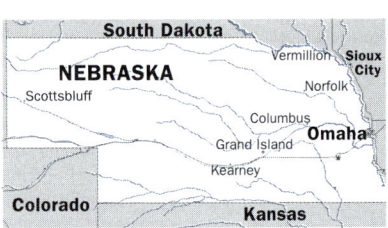

OVERVIEW: Baird, Holm, McEachen, Pedersen, Hamann & Strasheim emerged as Nebraska's preeminent firm in *Chambers'* research. Strong litigation and corporate groups top the charts for breadth and depth. Competitors admire the firm's solid, historic presence, and high visibility across the board. In addition to a full portfolio of impressive litigation and corporate representations, a growing employment practice has recently stepped into the limelight following work on the much-publicized wrongful termination case of Gasper v Wal-Mart. Clients include Airlite Plastics, Tenaska and IBP.

In second place, **McGrath, North, Mullin & Kratz** is widely recognized for the strong, assertive style of its attorneys and commands respect for its formidable list of Fortune 100 clients. The depth of the litigation and employment law benches warrants particular mention. However, the firm also secures top band rankings in the corporate and real estate tables. Clients include ConAgra Foods, First Data Corporation and Adesta Communications.

Fraser Stryker Law Firm, ranked third, was said to have a leading edge over competitors in corporate and employment law. Notable representations include advising on a $210 million convention center and arena in Omaha, and handling a race-based class action for an electric public utility company. The firm's litigators were praised for their deep level of resources and advocacy experience, while the five-attorney real estate practice was recommended for broad expertise in the field. Clients include Level 3 Communications, Mutual of Omaha Insurance Company and State Farm.

CORPORATE/M&A

NEBRASKA
Leading firms (Corporate/M&A)
1. BAIRD, HOLM, MCEACHEN, PEDERSEN *Omaha*
   BLACKWELL SANDERS PEPER MARTIN *Omaha*
   FRASER STRYKER LAW FIRM *Omaha*
   MCGRATH, NORTH, MULLIN & KRATZ PC *Omaha*
2. ABRAHAMS KASLOW & CASSMAN LLP *Omaha*
   CLINE, WILLIAMS, WRIGHT, JOHNSON *Lincoln*
   ERICKSON & SEDERSTROM PC *Omaha*

Leading individuals (Corporate/M&A)
1. FREEMAN Robert *Fraser Stryker Law Firm, Omaha*
   HEFFLINGER David *McGrath, North, Mullin, Omaha*
   KASLOW Howard *Abrahams Kaslow, Omaha*
   KATELMAN John *Blackwell Sanders Peper, Omaha*
2. BURT Donald *Cline, Williams, Wright, Johnson, Lincoln*
   RICHARDSON Todd *Blackwell Sanders Peper Omaha*
   SEDERSTROM Charles *Erickson & Sederstrom, Omaha*
   STRASHEIM Jerrold *Baird, Holm, McEachen, Omaha*
   ZEILINGER John *Baird, Holm, McEachen, Omaha*

Firms and individuals are listed alphabetically in each band.

Baird, Holm, McEachen, Pedersen, Hamann & Strasheim LLP
The Firm: Thirty-three attorneys at this well-established firm advise on a range of general commercial matters, including M&A, joint venture agreements, securities law, franchise matters and antitrust law. The group undertakes extensive bank holding company regulatory work and advises governmental entities on bond issuance. Sources describe the firm as *"preeminent for sheer quality,"* and agree that its attorneys *"measure up with their professional approach and high ethics."*

The Lawyers: **John Zeilinger**'s practice is divided evenly among banking, securities and M&A, and it is for bank regulatory matters and financing that he is best known. A former bankruptcy judge, **Jerrold Strasheim** combines his transactional work with commercial litigation. Peers commend his work in corporate restructuring and his *"smooth handling"* of a deal.

The Clients: Bank holding, telecom and technology companies and healthcare entities.

Blackwell Sanders Peper Martin LLP
The Firm: The relatively recently founded office of this Kansas City firm has the resources behind it to provide clients with a full repertoire of corporate and commercial services. The group's activities include handling financing, equipment leasing, outsourcing, franchising relationships and technology licensing matters. Peers commend the team's *"sophisticated advice,"* which has attracted key local and regional clients. Clients are *"totally thrilled"* with the firm for its *"talented"* corporate attorneys, who have displayed a breadth of expertise.

The Lawyers: In addition to his real estate practice, **John Katelman** advises on M&A and securities law, and represents institutional lenders in financing options. Rivals place him *"at the top"* of the commercial market. Rising star **Todd Richardson** has impressed with his work in mergers, asset and stock purchase transactions, corporation formations and securities placements.

The Clients: Gallup; Allianz Life Insurance Company; Centris Federal Credit Union; First National Bank of Omaha; Omaha Steaks and Power Genetics Company.

Fraser Stryker Law Firm
The Firm: The firm has 23 attorneys with corporate experience, covering the full gamut of issues. It has expertise in bank lending and the negotiation of venture capital for new businesses. Peers are impressed by its attorneys' creative and aggressive approach to the deal table, while clients praised their handling of acquisitions and securities law issues, saying *"they have the size and experience to deal with complex transactions."*

The Lawyers: **Robert Freeman**'s practice incorporates general commercial issues, and real estate and estate planning matters. Much of his time has been devoted to his work on a new $210 million convention center and arena in Omaha. Freeman was recommended by peers for his *"strong work ethic"* and *"brilliant strategic advice."*

The Clients: Level 3 Communications; Peter Kiewit Sons'; Kiewit Construction Company; Omaha Childrens Hospital; real estate developers and construction companies.

McGrath, North, Mullin & Kratz PC
The Firm: The firm's representation of ConAgra Foods across the board has helped to develop this widely respected corporate practice. The team advises on M&A, tax issues, estate planning, securities and antitrust matters. Attorneys are also skilled in insurance issues, bankruptcy and IP. The large group is a high-profile player in the commercial market, successfully attracting *"some of the best clients and deals around."*

The Lawyers: **David Hefflinger**'s practice incorporates securities, tax and business law. His experience in tax planning has ensured that his profile as *"one of the state's top lawyers"* is an *"excellent resource"* for the corporate team.

The Clients: ConAgra Foods.

EMPLOYMENT & LABOR LAW — NEBRASKA

Abrahams Kaslow & Cassman LLP
The Firm: Fifteen of this small firm's attorneys cover the corporate waterfront with a business transactions practice that incorporates commercial litigation. The group handles M&A, restructuring and company formations. It also represents lenders in secured loan transactions. The group has expertise in the independent power production arena and represents purchasers and providers of technology services. Interviewees described it as a *"strong, old-line firm,"* and its lawyers are of *"the highest caliber."*
The Lawyers: *"An outstanding lawyer,"* **Howard Kaslow** concentrates on corporate law, and estate planning for high net-worth individuals. Peers reported that he is an influential attorney for tax and corporate matters. Clients praised him as *"smart and diligent, with impeccable credentials."*
The Clients: Data Transmission Network; Tenaska; CSG Systems International; American National Bank; Grace/Mayer Insurance Agency; Heartland Promotions; First National Bank of Omaha; Huse Publishing Company; Kwik Shop and Cox Communications.

Cline, Williams, Wright, Johnson & Oldfather LLP
The Firm: This Lincoln-based firm has a small Omaha office that advises on M&A, securities, insurance and finance law. The group is particularly commended by competitors for its commercial litigation prowess and its work in the municipal bond field, and in the public and private placing of securities.
The Lawyers: **Donald Burt**'s *"outstanding reputation"* is built on his work in corporate, finance and business law. A *"hard-working lawyer,"* he is *"a great manager of a deal."*
The Clients: Clients include healthcare providers, banks and financial services, insurance companies and retailers

Erickson & Sederstrom PC
The Firm: The nine corporate attorneys at this firm advise on company formations, corporate governance and the range of corporate transactional activities. Acquisitions and sales, private and public funding, franchise arrangements, and securities are on the agenda here. Peers endorsed the firm as a professional *"trusted"* organization.
The Lawyers: **Charles Sederstrom** attracts market recommendation for his corporate, banking and healthcare practices. Peers portray him as a *"wonderful rainmaker"* for a team that *"meets high standards."*
The Clients: National and international clients including banks, insurance companies, healthcare services, food producers, retailers and utilities.

EMPLOYMENT & LABOR LAW — MAINLY PLAINTIFF

NEBRASKA
Leading firms
(Employment: Mainly Plaintiff)
1. BROOM, JOHNSON, CLARKSON & LANPHIER Omaha
   BYAM & HOARTY Omaha
   DOWD & DOWD Omaha

Leading individuals
(Employment: Mainly Plaintiff)
1. BROOM Bob *Broom, Johnson, Clarkson* Omaha
   DOWD Tom *Dowd & Dowd,* Omaha
   HOARTY Tom *Byam & Hoarty,* Omaha

Firms and individuals are listed alphabetically in each band.

Broom, Johnson, Clarkson & Lanphier
The Firm: The firm advises plaintiffs in discrimination cases at state and federal levels, and counsels on civil rights matters and immigration issues. Market observers identify the firm as one that practices to a consistently high standard. The firm also occasionally counsels the management of nonprofit organizations.
The Lawyers: Here **Bob Broom** is a key attorney for employment issues, including discrimination and ERISA cases. Broom is respected by peers for his work in civil rights actions, and has earned a reputation as *"a hard-working, ethical and highly skilled advocate."*

Byam & Hoarty
The Firm: This small firm runs a general civil trial and appellate practice that includes employment issues in its repertoire. Competitors endorse the firm's plaintiff employment practice for the strong advocacy skills of its attorneys.
The Lawyers: Interviewees described **Tom Hoarty** as *"a gentleman,"* with an effective courtroom demeanor. Highly knowledgeable Hoarty has long-standing experience defending management.

Dowd & Dowd
The Firm: This is a specialist firm with a consistently high workload. The team of Tom Dowd and his two sons represent individuals in workers' compensation, personal injury, malpractice and discrimination cases. They also represent unions in labor relations issues. In a recent highlight, the firm won a favorable jury verdict in a disability discrimination case in the Eighth Circuit Court of Appeals. **Thomas Dowd** wins high acclaim for his representation of unions. Defendant attorneys described him as a *"real bulldog"* and an *"excellent advocate"* in court. His sons, Michael and Timothy, are also respected for their continuation of his *"polished"* practice.

EMPLOYMENT & LABOR LAW — MAINLY DEFENDANT

Fraser Stryker Law Firm
The Firm: Three full-time labor and employment attorneys here represent public and private employers on labor issues such as arbitrations, union organizations and collective bargaining agreements. Disability cases under the ADA have increased in number, adding to the group's steady diet of wrongful discharge and discrimination litigation work. The group is also devoted to preventative work, and advises clients on training and policy development. Peers recommend these attorneys for their depth of knowledge, while clients point to their experience both in Nebraska and out of state. In a recent highlight, the group advised on a race-based class action for an electric public utility company.
The Lawyers: **Robert Rossiter** advises on both litigation and preventative work, and has recently been involved in a number of ADA-related cases. For clients, Rossiter is *"far and away the first choice"* for employment litigation, while peers note that he is a familiar presence *"in the trenches."* **George Rozmarin** is an *"expert"* in traditional labor relations. He is also active in preventative counseling, and impresses with his *"sound advice."*
The Clients: The firm advises both private and public businesses.

McGrath, North, Mullin & Kratz PC
The Firm: The six-strong employment group covers the waterfront of employment discrimination litigation and labor relations, though

NEBRASKA

EMPLOYMENT & LABOR LAW

NEBRASKA
Leading firms
(Employment: Mainly Defendant)

1. **FRASER STRYKER LAW FIRM** Omaha
   MCGRATH, NORTH, MULLIN & KRATZ PC Omaha
2. **BAIRD, HOLM, MCEACHEN, PEDERSEN** Omaha
3. **BLACKWELL SANDERS PEPER MARTIN** Omaha
   HARDING SCHULTZ & DOWNS Lincoln

Leading individuals
(Employment: Mainly Defendant)

1. **BARRETT Patrick** McGrath, North, Mullin, Omaha
   ROSSITER Robert Fraser Stryker Law Firm, Omaha
   ROZMARIN George Fraser Stryker Law Firm, Omaha
2. **HARDING William** Harding Schultz & Downs, Lincoln
   MILLER Roger McGrath, North, Mullin & Kratz, Omaha
3. **BOGUE Stevenson** McGrath, North, Mullin, Omaha
   HEDICAN Chris Baird, Holm, McEachen, Omaha
   MCGRATH Brian Blackwell Sanders Peper, Omaha

Firms and individuals are listed alphabetically in each band.

recent activity has been concentrated on wage and hour cases, and OSHA and immigration claims. Competitors adjudge it their *"first choice,"* impressed by its long-standing presence and deep resources. It has an enviable client roster of Fortune 100 companies, and has developed a niche with its employee benefits practice. Peers respect the high-caliber lawyers here, agreeing that *"it would be hard to go beyond them for quality advice."*
The Lawyers: In a close group, **Patrick Barrett**'s representation of management in labor and employment matters stands out. Peers described him as *"confident, cordial, and cooperative,"* noting that he *"doesn't play games, and is honest with the law."* **Roger Miller** spends a portion of his employment practice involved in counseling and strategic matters. His practice has recently involved an ADA discrimination class action, and a suit filed by a legal competitor over trade secret allegations. Peers also endorsed his union-related representations. **Stevenson Bogue**'s practice incorporates OSHA and immigration work, where he is carving a reputation. Interviewees admire him for *"not getting hung up on details,*" and for *"dealing with the issues at hand."*
The Clients: include Eaton Corporation; McDonald's; ShopK. Stores; Pamida; Roberts Dairy and Life Care Centers of America.

Baird, Holm, McEachen, Pedersen, Hamann & Strasheim LLP
The Firm: A team of 14 attorneys advise on litigation and labor relations, compliance issues and employee benefits. The firm impresses with its wide representation of public and private employers, particularly in the healthcare and communications sectors. Client loyalty is secured through its *"highly visible and very supportive"* attorneys. Recent successes include the highly publicized wrongful termination case of Gasper v Wal-Mart, and the wrongful termination and disability discrimination case of Orr v Wal-Mart.
The Lawyers: **Chris Hedican**'s litigation prowess is displayed in his work on wrongful termination and discrimination cases, which include claims arising from non-compete and employee fiduciary matters. Clients enthused about his aggressive trial style, describing him as an *"outstanding advocate."*
The Clients: Gordmans; FBG Services Corp oration; PharMerica and Analysts International.

Blackwell Sanders Peper Martin LLP
The Firm: In this recently established office, the two attorneys developing the employment practice have impressed clients as *"business thinkers."* The team represents management in traditional labor law, employment-related litigation and human resources counseling. It also advises on immigration matters and corporate compliance. Litigation activities have focused on race, age and disability discrimination claims. Recent successes include obtaining summary judgments in the ERISA case of Bohbot v Eaton Corporation, and in the race and sex discrimination Rodriuez v JC Penney Company case.
The Lawyers: **Brian McGrath** is well versed in wage and hour issues, litigation and regulatory compliance. Clients value his skill in *"getting issues off the table"* and in *"damage limitation."* They also appreciate his comprehensive explanations and describe him as *"sensitive to a company's nuances."*
The Clients: Anheuser-Busch; Applebee's International; Boeing; Manpower; Prudential Insurance Company of America; Tenet Healthcare and Roberts Dairy.

Harding Schultz & Downs
The Firm: Despite the firm's smaller size, this Lincoln-based group has a substantial labor and employment practice, covering litigation, compliance and OSHA. Its traditional labor work has included advice on strikes and picketing, boycotts and labor relation negotiations, including arbitration. Clients also recommend the group, especially for NLRB matters, in which *"they are the ones you want to use."*
The Lawyers: **William Harding**'s practice incorporates collective bargaining and labor relations alongside employment litigation. Interviewees praised his expertise in public sector representations, public bargaining and NLRB work. He was described as having *"a strategic mind, backed by solid resources."*
The Clients: The firm attracts clients from the retail, utilities, communications, healthcare and manufacturing sectors.

LITIGATION

Baird, Holm, McEachen, Pedersen, Hamann & Strasheim LLP
The Firm: This Omaha-based general commercial litigation practice handles a broad spectrum of cases, including technology and IP disputes, bankruptcies, and antitrust and securities litigation. A long-established presence, it is respected among peers for its *"breadth of experience"* and *"academic"* attorneys. The team has represented a nuclear generator company in issues arising from the review of its license application. It has also successfully acted for First Data Corporation in a tax dispute with the Nebraska Department of Revenue.
The Lawyers: Amid his broad general commercial litigation practice, **Tom Johnson** has impressed market observers with his advice to third party payers on issues relating to patient care costs. He has also advised the producers in Entergy Industries' bad faith litigation stemming from efforts to license a nuclear waste disposal facility. Peers acknowledge that he *"stays one step ahead"* of his opponents.
The Clients: Airlite Plastics; Oriental Trading Company; IBP; Tenaska; Champion Home Builders Company; Woodmen of the World Life Insurance and Nebraska Methodist Health Systems.

Fraser Stryker Law Firm
The Firm: The 15 litigators handle a full portfo-

GENERAL COMMERCIAL

lio of commercial issues, including securities, malpractice cases and the defense of RICO claims. The group advises healthcare professionals, accountants and engineers in negligence cases, and acts on products liability and insurance defense. Peers endorsed the group's deep level of resources and advocacy experience. They also acknowledged that the firm's substantial client roster ensures its involvement in high-profile, complex representations.
The Lawyers: **Joseph Meusey**'s caseload includes complex commercial matters, professional liability and personal injury work. He is described by interviewees as *"a top-notch litiga-*

LITIGATION — NEBRASKA

NEBRASKA
Leading firms
(Litigation: General Commercial)

1. BAIRD, HOLM, MCEACHEN, PEDERSEN *Omaha*
   FRASER STRYKER LAW FIRM *Omaha*
   MCGRATH, NORTH, MULLIN & KRATZ PC *Omaha*
2. CLINE, WILLIAMS, WRIGHT, JOHNSON *Lincoln*
3. BLACKWELL SANDERS PEPER MARTIN *Omaha*
   ERICKSON & SEDERSTROM PC *Omaha*
   LAMSON, DUGAN & MURRAY LLP *Omaha*

Leading individuals
(Litigation: General Commercial)

1. JOHNSON Thomas *Baird, Holm, McEachen, Omaha*
   LAMSON William *Lamson, Dugan & Murray, Omaha*
2. CULHANE Thomas *Erickson & Sederstrom PC, Omaha*
   KNOWLES Leo *McGrath, North, Mullin & Kratz, Omaha*
   MEUSEY Joseph *Fraser Stryker Law Firm, Omaha*
   PETERSON Alan *Cline, Williams, Wright, Lincoln*
3. DAHLK Thomas *Blackwell Sanders Peper Martin, Omaha*
   FITZGERALD James *McGrath, North, Mullin, Omaha*
   PASSARELLI John *McGrath, North, Mullin, Omaha*

Firms and individuals are listed alphabetically in each band.

---

tor" and *"an old hand in jury trials."* His *"personable demeanor"* and extensive trial preparation have won him a following in the market.

The Clients: Level 3 Communications; Mutual of Omaha Insurance Company; State Farm; Omaha Public Power District and Peter Kiewit Sons'.

McGrath, North, Mullin & Kratz PC
The Firm: The 35 litigators here advise on IP, construction, products liability and insurance coverage litigation as part of their commercial litigation practice. The team is frequently involved in out-of-state matters, and competitors say it is a *"key candidate"* for tough cases. Attorneys have a *"strong, aggressive approach"* to litigation and *"a real courtroom presence,"* according to sources. Clients praise the firm's *"specialist technical knowledge."*

The Lawyers: Leo Knowles has secured a national reputation for his *"impressive courtroom performance and jury appeal."* He is active across a range of commercial disputes, particularly in products liability matters. John Passarelli's practice focuses on marketing and distribution disputes. He has also handled patent and trademark litigation for high-profile national clients who valued his *"preparation, advocacy skills and strong personality."* James Fitzgerald has a broad general practice that makes him *"a key contender"* in the litigation market.

The Clients: ConAgra Foods; First Data Corporation; Ag Processing; Peter Kiewit Sons'; Werner Construction; Mutual of Omaha Insurance Company and Adesta Communications.

Cline, Williams, Wright, Johnson & Oldfather LLP
The Firm: Peers consider this Lincoln-based firm to have a *"well-rounded"* broad litigation practice, which is defense-oriented, but maintains a healthy plaintiffs' practice. The group's specialist areas include medical malpractice, environmental litigation, contract and tort disputes and professional negligence. The group is increasingly turning its attention to the growing areas of employment litigation and creditor work for financial institutions.

The Lawyers: A significant proportion of Alan Peterson's commercial litigation practice has been devoted to his successful representation of the four neighboring states in a dispute with the State of Nebraska over a proposed license for a low-level nuclear waste site. He has also been developing a niche specialty in defending the freedom of the press, involving advice on privacy and libel issues. Peers describe Peterson as a *"formidable opponent"* who is highly *"attuned to ethical issues."*

The Clients: University of Nebraska; University of Nebraska Foundation; Nebraska Broadcasters Association; Nebraska Press Association; GM and State Farm.

Blackwell Sanders Peper Martin LLP
The Firm: The firm's 10 Omaha-based commercial litigators run an increasingly busy practice. Cited as the *"hottest practice area in the firm,"* the group has attracted complex commercial cases including products liability and creditor work. It also undertakes a substantial amount of securities litigation. Clients endorsed the group's current strengths, saying they were *"totally thrilled"* with its expertise, and also anticipated future growth, asserting that it is *"the one to watch."*

The Lawyers: Clients enthused about Tom Dahlk's *"impressive courtroom demeanor and substantial successes."* Peers credit him with developing the practice. He concentrates entirely on complex business litigations, and RICO and securities matters, often involving multiple districts or appellate arguments.

The Clients: Waddell & Reed Financial; U Save Foods; Purina Mills; Ag Processing; Consolidated Nutrition; Matrix Bancorp and The Gallup Organization.

Erickson & Sederstrom PC
The Firm: The 8-strong litigation team is experienced in personal injury, construction and products liability claims in addition to its general commercial litigation for both defendants and plaintiffs. Additionally, the firm is widely believed by peers to have strong, beneficial political connections. Peers commend the group's administrative skills and its expertise in the healthcare industry.

The Lawyers: Skilled in insurance defense, Tom Culhane has recently also been active in construction and contract disputes. Interviewees recommend him for his *"extremely high-quality"* advocacy skills.

The Clients: Construction companies, hospitals and medical facilities and insurance carriers.

Lamson, Dugan & Murray LLP
The Firm: A group of 15 litigators represents commercial clients in fraud and UCC actions, bankruptcies and securities litigation. Employment litigation and regulatory matters are also key strengths of the firm. Sources described attorneys here as *"ethical, careful and very talented litigators,"* singling out their *"high-quality work"* in insurance defense and medical malpractice cases.

The Lawyers: Department chair William Lamson's commercial litigation practice incorporates environmental issues, insurance and professional negligence cases. He recently acted in a contract dispute regarding the sale of electricity from a nuclear power plant. Lamson impresses competitors with his legal knowledge and his superb courtroom presence, which combine to place him *"head and shoulders above the rest."*

The Clients: Nebraska Public Power District; Union Pacific Railroad; Dow Chemical; GM; Georgia-Pacific; Nissan North America; Tenet Healthcare and AlliedSignal.

NEBRASKA — REAL ESTATE

REAL ESTATE

NEBRASKA
Leading firms (Real Estate)

1
- FULLENKAMP, DOYLE & JOBEUN *Omaha*
- MCGRATH, NORTH, MULLIN & KRATZ PC *Omaha*

2
- BAIRD, HOLM, MCEACHEN, PEDERSEN *Omaha*
- BLACKWELL SANDERS PEPER MARTIN *Omaha*
- FRASER STRYKER LAW FIRM *Omaha*
- GAINES PANSING & HOGAN *Omaha*

3
- CROKER, HUCK, KASHER, DEWITT *Omaha*

Leading individuals (Real Estate)

1
- FULLENKAMP John *Fullenkamp, Doyle,* Omaha
- HAMANN Lee *McGrath, North, Mullin & Kratz,* Omaha
- KATELMAN John *Blackwell Sanders Peper,* Omaha
- RIEKE Robert *Fraser Stryker Law Firm,* Omaha

2
- BACKMAN John *Gaines Pansing & Hogan,* Omaha
- DYE Scott *Baird, Holm, McEachen, Pedersen,* Omaha
- HOGAN Dennis *Gaines Pansing & Hogan,* Omaha
- HUCK Robert *Croker, Huck, Kasher, DeWitt,* Omaha
- SLUSKY Jerry *Gross & Welch PC,* Omaha

Up-and-coming individuals
- BUSER James *Gaines Pansing & Hogan,* Omaha

Firms and individuals are listed alphabetically in each band.

Fullenkamp, Doyle & Jobeun
The Firm: This Omaha-based firm fields four attorneys, who specialize in land use and zoning issues, environmental matters and real estate development. The team's work for sanitary and improvement districts is widely respected. Competitors endorse this *"first-class group"* for its efficiency and knowledge in the development field, which combine to place it *"right at the top of the market."* Recent representations include advising Pentagon Federal Credit Union in the purchase of an office building in Omaha, and acting for Muscatine Plaza in the sale of a shopping center and subsequent purchases of the Empire Park Shopping Center and the Harvey Oaks Shopping Center in Omaha.
The Lawyers: **John Fullenkamp**'s broad base of experience makes him *"first choice"* for zoning and development matters. Rivals agree that he *"has the edge,"* with his client roster of key real estate businesses.
The Clients: Regional developers, telecom companies and local power district entities.

McGrath, North, Mullin & Kratz PC
The Firm: One of the larger players in the Nebraska legal market, five of its attorneys practice real estate law. The firm's work for major client ConAgra Foods is credited as the source of much of its profile in real estate matters, and the group remains most visible on the transactional side. Interviewees recommended the firm's deep resources and the quality of its advice.

The Lawyers: Managing director **Lee Hamann** divides his time among business law, leasing issues and real estate matters. His role as key counsel to ConAgra has given him a national presence. Peers endorsed his technical knowledge and agreed that he *"knows how to run a smooth transaction."*
The Clients: ConAgra Foods; Omaha Airport Authority; Physicians Mutual Insurance Company and Valmont Industries

Baird, Holm, McEachen, Pedersen, Hamann & Strasheim LLP
The Firm: The firm's five real estate lawyers act on a range of real estate-related areas, incorporating financing, building management and leasing, construction contracts, environmental compliance, purchase and sale transactions, Section 1031 exchanges, and zoning and land use. The group specializes in healthcare facility construction. Market sources pointed to the firm's *"real expertise"* in financing issues, such as tax structurings and REITs.
The Lawyers: **Scott Dye**'s practice concentrates on real estate and construction issues, and he has extensive experience in purchase, sale and lending transactions, Section 1031 exchanges, tax increment financing, zoning and land use planning, public bidding and contracting. He was described as the firm's *"leading force"* in real estate transactions.
The Clients: Omaha Public Schools; Airlite Plastics; First Data Resources; Nebraska Methodist Health System and Great Western Bank.

Blackwell Sanders Peper Martin LLP
The Firm: Commands the attention of the market for its representation of major real estate clients in substantial transactions. The firm covers the gamut, and is widely respected for its advice on sophisticated financing options such as synthetic leasing. It is also involved in development projects and sales and purchases. The team advised The Gallup Organization in its acquisition and development of the $45 million Gallup University in Omaha. It has also represented the developer of a new 48,000 sq ft medical office building, and acted for Omaha's largest federal credit union in the acquisition of several sites and building contracts for new buildings.
The Lawyers: **John Katelman** specializes in downtown redevelopment projects, assisting businesses to work in partnership with local government. His recent highlights have included work on the ConAgra Campus, First National Bank of Omaha and Omaha World-Herald projects. Sources described Katelman as a *"formidable competitor"* in the transactional market, while clients viewed him as *"definitely an expert"* in the development of contracts.

The Clients: Advised Avaya in the sale of land for a major retail development in southwest Omaha. The firm also acts for Wells Fargo; First National Bank of Omaha; Centris Federal Credit Union; Grubb & Ellis/Pacific Realty; The Gallup Organization and First Data Resources.

Fraser Stryker Law Firm
The Firm: The firm's five full-time real estate practitioners advise on a broad array of issues, including property development, contractor agreements and environmental matters. Historically, the firm has undertaken extensive leasing and right of way work, and it has built up a following among regional developers. Competitors and clients recommend the group for its lending, purchases and sales activities. The group advised Pentagon Federal Credit Union on the purchase of an office building in Omaha and acted for Tetrad Corporation on the purchase of an office building.
The Lawyers: Clients described **Robert Rieke** as *"one of the best real estate attorneys in town."* Much of his reputation derives from his transactional activities, including acquisitions and lending.
The Clients: The firm advises regional developers and telecom companies.

Gaines Pansing & Hogan
The Firm: The three-lawyer team is heavily involved in development and zoning real estate issues in the Omaha area. The group also counsels on mortgage financing, and has impressed observers with its work on sanitary and improvement district matters. These *"highly competent"* lawyers are also recommended for their responsive advice and *"dedication to their clients."*
The Lawyers: **Dennis Hogan**'s real estate practice focuses on zoning and development issues, and municipal and construction law. His work on sanitary improvement districts has ensured his profile as the *"leading light"* of the group. **John Backman**'s practice incorporates real estate, construction, lender financing, creditors' rights and commercial matters. Peers reflect that they would *"refer anything to him,"* and, like Hogan, Backman is respected for his work in development and sanitary and improvement district matters. Interviewees also identified rising talent **James Buser**, particularly endorsing his work in lending matters and zoning changes.
The Clients: Real estate developers; sanitary and improvement districts; lenders, including banks and life insurance companies, and business entities.

Croker, Huck, Kasher, DeWitt, Anderson & Gonderinger PC
The Firm: The six real estate attorneys at this firm focus their activities on the Omaha area, rep-

NEBRASKA

resenting developers and banks. The group has expertise in governmental issues and represents some 35 sanitary and improvement districts. Market observers recommend the firm's expertise in development work, and endorse its capacity to handle all areas of a real estate transaction.

The Lawyers: **Robert Huck** enjoys long-standing expertise in sanitary and improvement district matters. Development and rezoning occupy the majority of his time. Huck also advises clients in matters before assessors and the Nebraska State Board of Equalization.

The Clients: Sanitary and improvement districts; banks; real estate developers and homeowners' associations.

Other Notable Practitioners

At Gross & Welch PC, **Jerry Slusky** won market commendation for his specialist expertise in zoning, municipal law, and financing matters, including tax appeals and tax-deferred transactions. He has advised on an 80-acre mixed-use project in Lincoln, NE, which includes a public school, residential homes and 30,000 sq ft of retail space.

Leaders in Nebraska

BACKMAN, John
Gaines Pansing & Hogan, Omaha
402 397 5500
Recommended in Real Estate

BARRETT, Patrick
McGrath, North, Mullin & Kratz, PC, Omaha 402 341 3070
Recommended in Employment

BOGUE, Stevenson
McGrath, North, Mullin & Kratz, PC, Omaha 402 341 3070
Recommended in Employment

BROOM, Bob
Broom, Johnson, Clarkson & Lanphier, Omaha 402 346 8323
Recommended in Employment

BURT, Donald
Cline, Williams, Wright, Johnson & Oldfather LLP, Lincoln 402 474 6900
Recommended in Corporate/M&A

BUSER, James
Gaines Pansing & Hogan, Omaha
402 397 5500
Recommended in Real Estate

CULHANE, Thomas
Erickson & Sederstrom, PC, Omaha
402 397 2200
Recommended in Litigation

DAHLK, Thomas
Blackwell Sanders Peper Martin LLP, Omaha 402 964 5000
Recommended in Litigation

DOWD, Tom
Dowd & Dowd, Omaha 402 341 1020
Recommended in Employment

DYE, Scott
Baird, Holm, McEachen, Pedersen, Hamann & Strasheim LLP, Omaha
402 344 0500
Recommended in Real Estate

FITZGERALD, James
McGrath, North, Mullin & Kratz, PC, Omaha 402 341 3070
Recommended in Litigation

FREEMAN, Robert
Fraser Stryker Law Firm, Omaha
402 341 6000
Recommended in Corporate/M&A

FULLENKAMP, John
Fullenkamp, Doyle & Jobeun, Omaha
402 334 0700
Recommended in Real Estate

HAMANN, Lee
McGrath, North, Mullin & Kratz, PC, Omaha 402 341 3070
Recommended in Real Estate

HARDING, William
Harding Schultz & Downs, Lincoln
402 434 3000
Recommended in Employment

HEDICAN, Chris
Baird, Holm, McEachen, Pedersen, Hamann & Strasheim LLP, Omaha
402 344 0500
Recommended in Employment

HEFFLINGER, David
McGrath, North, Mullin & Kratz, PC, Omaha 402 341 3070
Recommended in Corporate/M&A

HOARTY, Tom
Byam & Hoarty, Omaha 402 397 0303
Recommended in Employment

HOGAN, Dennis
Gaines Pansing & Hogan, Omaha
402 397 5500
Recommended in Real Estate

HUCK, Robert
Croker, Huck, Kasher, DeWitt, Anderson & Gonderinger, PC, Omaha
402 391 6777
Recommended in Real Estate

JOHNSON, Thomas
Baird, Holm, McEachen, Pedersen, Hamann & Strasheim LLP, Omaha
402 344 0500
Recommended in Litigation

KASLOW, Howard
Abrahams Kaslow & Cassman LLP, Omaha 402 392 1250
Recommended in Corporate/M&A

KATELMAN, John
Blackwell Sanders Peper Martin LLP, Omaha 402 964 5000
Recommended in Corporate/M&A, Real Estate

KNOWLES, Leo
McGrath, North, Mullin & Kratz, PC, Omaha 402 341 3070
Recommended in Litigation

LAMSON, William
Lamson, Dugan & Murray, LLP, Omaha
402 397 7300
Recommended in Litigation

MCGRATH, Brian
Blackwell Sanders Peper Martin LLP, Omaha 402 964 5000
Recommended in Employment

MEUSEY, Joseph
Fraser Stryker Law Firm, Omaha
402 341 6000
Recommended in Litigation

MILLER, Roger
McGrath, North, Mullin & Kratz, PC, Omaha 402 341 3070
Recommended in Employment

PASSARELLI, John
McGrath, North, Mullin & Kratz, PC, Omaha 402 341 3070
Recommended in Litigation

PETERSON, Alan
Cline, Williams, Wright, Johnson & Oldfather LLP, Omaha 402 397 1700
Recommended in Litigation

RICHARDSON, Todd
Blackwell Sanders Peper Martin LLP, Omaha 402 964 5000
Recommended in Corporate/M&A

RIEKE, Robert
Fraser Stryker Law Firm, Omaha
402 341 6000
Recommended in Real Estate

ROSSITER, Robert
Fraser Stryker Law Firm, Omaha
402 341 6000
Recommended in Employment

ROZMARIN, George
Fraser Stryker Law Firm, Omaha
402 341 6000
Recommended in Employment

SEDERSTROM, Charles
Erickson & Sederstrom, PC, Omaha
402 397 2200
Recommended in Corporate/M&A

SLUSKY, Jerry
Gross & Welch, P.C., Omaha
402 392 1500
Recommended in Real Estate

STRASHEIM, Jerrold
Baird, Holm, McEachen, Pedersen, Hamann & Strasheim LLP, Omaha
402 344 0500
Recommended in Corporate/M&A

ZEILINGER, John
Baird, Holm, McEachen, Pedersen, Hamann & Strasheim LLP, Omaha
402 344 0500
Recommended in Corporate/M&A

NEVADA

CORPORATE/M&A

CONTENTS: Corporate/M&A p.406; Employment: Mainly Plaintiff p.407; Mainly Defendant p.408; Litigation p.419; Real Estate p.xxx; Individuals' Profiles p.xxx.

NEVADA'S TOP FIVE
1. Lionel Sawyer & Collins
2. Jones Vargas
3. Hale Lane Peek Dennison and Howard
3. Kummer Kaempfer Bonner & Renshaw
4. Schreck Brignone

Ranking based on Chambers' research within the state.

All quotes in the text are from interviews with clients and competitors.

OVERVIEW: Ranked first in the state, **Lionel Sawyer & Collins** is strong across a number of areas, including corporate work, real estate and litigation. In the largest firm in Nevada, a respected corporate practice works closely with the firm's real estate financing experts, attracting quality transactional work from high-profile clients. The firm also boasts the largest private law practice in Nevada. Jeffrey Zucker was named one of the best corporate lawyers in the state and managing partner Paul Hejmanowski ranks in *Chambers'* tables as a leading commercial litigator. Clients include Bank of America and HCA.

Peers acknowledged **Jones Vargas**, in second place, as a giant on the corporate scene. The firm is known for its skill in handling complex transactions, and enjoys particular renown for its advice to bond issuers and underwriters. Here corporate lawyer Douglas Crosby is considered top in his field. Within litigation, a highly rated team, featuring Kirk Lenhard, acts regularly for public and private companies on commercial disputes. The firm also attracts comment for the strength of its real estate practice. Clients include Kodak and Hilton Hotels.

Full-service firm **Hale Lane Peek Dennison** and Howard is particularly strong in real estate; its Reno office has attracted some of the state's best lawyers in this field. The firm also has a successful track record in corporate work and general commercial litigation. Karen Dennison is noted for her transactional work in real estate and David Garcia earns praise as a respected member of the corporate team. Clients include Bank of America and Marnell Corrao Associates.

Kummer Kaempfer Bonner & Renshaw ranks joint third. The firm has doubled in size in less than ten years, adding particular strength to its litigation practice. The practice specializes in general commercial disputes, with Thomas Kummer noted as an outstanding senior trial lawyer. Clients include Olympic Group and Monarch Casino & Resort.

Although smaller than many competitors, **Schreck Brignone** punches above its weight, and advises on corporate and commercial transactions, particularly for clients in the hospitality and gaming industries. The firm's forte is in real estate where it is known for its work with local and out-of-state hotel-casino clients. Terry Jones was identified as a key lawyer within the real estate team. He recently represented Sierra Health Services on one of the largest sale and leaseback transactions in Nevada history. Other firm clients include MGM Mirage and Mandalay Resort Group.

CORPORATE/M&A

NEVADA
Leading firms (Corporate/M&A)

1. JONES VARGAS *Las Vegas*
   LIONEL SAWYER & COLLINS *Las Vegas*
2. HALE LANE PEEK DENNISON AND HOWARD *Reno*
   KUMMER KAEMPFER BONNER, *Las Vegas*
   SCHRECK BRIGNONE *Las Vegas*
   WOODBURN AND WEDGE *Reno*
3. MARSHALL HILL CASSAS & DE LIPKAU *Reno*

Leading individuals (Corporate/M&A)

1. FOWLER John *Marshall Hill Cassas & De Lipkau, Reno*
   ZUCKER Jeffrey *Lionel Sawyer & Collins, Las Vegas*
2. BONNER Michael *Kummer Kaempfer, Las Vegas*
   CROSBY Douglas *Jones Vargas, Las Vegas*
   GARCIA David *Hale Lane Peek Dennison, Reno*
   GOLDSTEIN Mark *Lionel Sawyer & Collins, Las Vegas*
   SCHULHOFER Ellen *Schreck Brignone, Las Vegas*
   SCHUMACHER Kirk *Woodburn and Wedge, Reno*
   WOLOSON Kenneth *Haney, Woloson, Las Vegas*
3. BUCKLEY Michael *Jones Vargas, Las Vegas*
   KIM Robert *Kummer Kaempfer Bonner, Las Vegas*

Firms and individuals are listed alphabetically in each band.

Jones Vargas

The Firm: Interviewees spoke of a *"well-respected and sophisticated"* practice that serves the Nevada corporate and commercial community. Its size ensures prominence in the marketplace and a reputation for *"great depth."* The firm houses *"reputable and talented individual lawyers in the field,"* skilled in complex transactions, including M&A, joint ventures, securities issues and partnership structures. The team advises both bond issuers and underwriters. Litigation is also a strength of the firm.

The Lawyers: *"Top-notch"* **Douglas Crosby** enjoys a broad spectrum of clients, mainly in the hospitality and gaming industries. Observers described him as *"the main man to go to"* for corporate formation, governance and financial representation. **Michael Buckley** works alongside Crosby, and is recommended for his work in real estate finance and corporate and general business transactions.

The Clients: The firm serves as Nevada counsel for Pharmacia, International Game Technology and the Mandalay Resort Group. Other clients include: Kodak; Sears Roebuck; Harrah's Entertainment; American Gaming Association and Peppermill Hotel Casino.

Lionel Sawyer & Collins

The Firm: Clients commended this *"incredibly strong"* corporate group, which benefits from close working ties with the firm's real estate financing practice. It is active in disposals, acquisitions and the financing of businesses in Nevada. The group is supported by attorneys experienced in IP and state and federal tax matters.

The Lawyers: Senior lawyer **Jeffrey Zucker** is regarded as *"one of the best corporate lawyers in the state."* He represents privately and publicly held companies in M&A, joint ventures and real estate projects. He also counsels on business conflict resolution. Described as the *"top dog"* in the field, **Mark Goldstein**'s practice encompasses corporate finance and real estate transactions. He recently represented Deutsche Bank as Nevada counsel in connection with the proposed $350 million second mortgage notes due in 2010 of Wynn Las Vegas, LLC. He was also selected by international firm Freshfields Bruckhaus Deringer as Nevada counsel for Barclays Bank in a derivatives financing for a large Nevada financial institution.

The Clients: The firm advises major banks such as BankWest of Nevada; Bank of America; Citibank (Nevada) and First Republic Bank.

CORPORATE/M&A

NEVADA

Other clients include GE Capital Assurance, Reliant Energy, Park Place Entertainment and Mikohn Gaming.

Hale Lane Peek Dennison and Howard
see firm details p.810

The Firm: The corporate group is blessed with a broad background and extensive experience on complex M&A transactions and securities issues. According to market commentators, the firm provides *"fierce competition"* in the corporate field, and has gained a reputation among clients of being *"one of the firms that count."*

The Lawyers: Peers agreed that **David Garcia** (see p.413) *"would definitely be at the top of my list."* His *"depth of knowledge"* has impressed, particularly in relation to start-ups' venture capital financings, publicly traded corporations' M&A transactions, and public and private securities offerings.

The Clients: The group advises lenders, publicly traded companies and developers. Marnell Corrao Associates and Bank of America are examples of the firm's clients.

Kummer Kaempfer Bonner & Renshaw
see firm details p.833

The Firm: Respected for its *"integrity and expertise,"* the firm's corporate group is best known for its experience in handling securities issues, IPOs and venture capital financings, divestitures and reorganizations. It also counsels on ongoing compliance matters for federal and state securities. The firm is known for its work for Rio Hotel & Casino in its $1 billion merger with Harrah's Entertainment and was the lead securities counsel to Herbst Gaming when it recently completed a $170 million senior secured debt offering.

The Lawyers: **Michael Bonner** (see p.412) was endorsed as a *"premier"* securities attorney by peers who rate his *"timely delivery and depth of technical knowledge."* Clients view him as *"more qualified than anyone, with an integrity that is unquestionable."* He is general and securities counsel to Monarch Casino & Resort and Marnell Corrao Associates, and has represented Paul-Son Gaming in its acquisition of French company Bourgogne et Grasset. Another *"super corporate guy"* is **Robert Kim** (see p.413). A *"pleasure to work with – especially as he is so talented,"* Kim was part of the team that represented eRoomSystem Technologies in its IPO.

The Clients: The firm is viewed as a *"key adviser"* to publicly held companies such as Monarch Casino & Resort. It has advised private companies, and investors in start-up financings. Other clients include: Marnell Corrao Associates; Paul-Son Gaming; eRoomSystem Technologies and Herbst Gaming.

Schreck Brignone
The Firm: Respected in the gaming industry, the firm is perceived as *"influential"* in its advice on corporate and commercial transactions for the hotel, gaming and casino industries in Las Vegas. It serves as local corporate counsel for public and private gaming and nongaming corporations, including Park Place Entertainment and Phillips Petroleum Company.

The Lawyers: Responsible for the firm's corporate department, **Ellen Schulhofer** is *"incredibly active in the area."* She acts as local counsel in equity and debt offerings for state and out-of-state firms. She recently advised Wynn Resorts on its IPO and the financing of a new hotel-casino, 'Le Rêve'. Schulhofer also represented Aristocrat in its acquisition of Casino Data Systems.

The Clients: The firm acted as Smart & Final's special Nevada counsel in its $87.1 million, five-year synthetic lease financing. Other clients include: Station Casinos; Park Place Entertainment; Phillips Petroleum Company; The Riviera Hotel and Casino; Wynn Resorts and Aristocrat.

Woodburn and Wedge
The Firm: This comprehensive law firm has developed an *"exceptionally strong"* corporate practice, which has ensured it a loyal clientele among mining, utility and real estate companies. M&A, licensing, business organization and tax issues all form part of the firm's portfolio.

The Lawyers: **Kirk Schumacher** is respected as a *"top-dollar"* securities and corporate lawyer who *"stays on top of Nevada corporate law."* He counsels on corporate governance, corporate financing and equity securities matters. Interviewees agree that he is a responsive attorney who *"always has his clients' needs at heart."* He acts as Nevada corporate counsel to Tenet Healthcare, Glamis Gold and Fortune 100 companies.

The Clients: L-3 Communications; Household International; Glamis Gold; Tenet Healthcare; Bank of America and Sierra Pacific Resources.

Marshall Hill Cassas & De Lipkau
The Firm: Much of the reputation of this *"high-quality"* corporate group is tied to the success of **John Fowler**. He is endorsed by peers as *"a driving force and a spokesperson for the corporate community"* in Reno. Fowler is the author of a study of Nevada corporate law and is viewed as one of the *"most experienced corporate attorneys"* in the state. He acts for public corporations and limited liability companies in M&A, financings and reorganizations.

The Clients: Cargill; Wells Fargo; Independence Mining Company and Southern Nevada Water Authority.

Other Notable Practitioners
Kenneth Woloson of Haney, Woloson & Mullins is recommended as *"an outstanding, articulate and bright"* corporate lawyer, who benefits from a strong tax and business transactional background. Woloson has been involved as general and local counsel to a number of gaming and nongaming clients in connection with acquisitions, sales, leasing and financing transactions.

EMPLOYMENT & LABOR LAW

MAINLY PLAINTIFF

NEVADA
Leading individuals
(Employment: Mainly Plaintiff)

1. **ENGLAND** Kathleen *Brenske & Christensen*, Las Vegas
   MARKS Daniel *Sole Practitioner*, Las Vegas
   SEGERBLOM Richard *Sole Practitioner*, Las Vegas
2. **CHAPIN** Patrick *Sole Practitioner*, Henderson
   ELLSWORTH Carolyn *Ellsworth Law Firm*, Las Vegas
   LYONS Keith *Keith M Lyons*, Las Vegas

Individuals are listed alphabetically in each band.

Notable Practitioners
Kathleen England (see p.497865) of Brenske & Christensen has become a *"pioneer"* in employment discrimination and civil rights matters, having worked on an *"incredible selection of employment cases."* Sole practitioner **Daniel Marks** (see p.497868) has set many landmark cases in this field in Nevada; he won the largest wrongful termination judgment in Nevada against the Las Vegas Hilton. *"Superb"* sole practitioner **Richard Segerblom** (see p.497867) has won significant lawsuits in the employment discrimination area. He is, claim peers, *"helping people more than any of us could ever dream of."* Sole practitioner **Patrick Chapin** (see p.497743) is widely known for his skill in representing clients in employment discrimination and disability cases. In February 2003, the two-partner law firm of Lyons & Ellsworth dissolved. Its key players continue to advise on discrimination claims against employers from their newly formed firms. The former deputy district attorney and in-house

NEVADA

EMPLOYMENT & LABOR LAW

counsel for Mirage Resorts, **Carolyn Ellsworth** (see p.497739), is described as a *"first-rate"* lawyer. She specializes in wage and hour cases and now practices as Ellsworth Law Firm PC. **Keith Lyons** (see p.497870) has formed Keith M Lyons. Interviewees endorsed him as one of the state's leading plaintiff attorneys. He has impressed many with his *"creative and thoughtful"* approach to equal rights issues

EMPLOYMENT & LABOR LAW — MAINLY DEFENDANT

NEVADA
Leading firms (Employment: Mainly Defendant)

1. KAMER ZUCKER & ABBOTT *Las Vegas*
   SMITH & KOTCHKA LTD *Las Vegas*
2. LIONEL SAWYER & COLLINS *Las Vegas*
   PIPER RUDNICK LLP *Las Vegas*
3. SCHRECK BRIGNONE *Las Vegas*

Leading individuals (Employment: Mainly Defendant)

1. BRIGNONE Andrew *Schreck Brignone, Las Vegas*
   KAMER Gregory *Kamer Zucker & Abbott, Las Vegas*
   MOSS Gary *Piper Rudnick LLP, Las Vegas*
   RICCIARDI Mark *Ricciardi Law Group, Las Vegas*
2. COLE Howard *Lionel Sawyer & Collins, Las Vegas*
   FERENBACH Cam *Lionel Sawyer & Collins, Las Vegas*
   KOTCHKA Malani *Smith & Kotchka Ltd, Las Vegas*
   SMITH Gregory *Smith & Kotchka Ltd, Las Vegas*
   ZUCKER Carol *Kamer Zucker & Abbott, Las Vegas*
3. EFROYMSON Kevin *Sole Practitioner, Las Vegas*
   MORGAN Ann *Jones Vargas, Reno*
   PAUSTIAN Kathleen *Sullivan, Hill, Lewin, Las Vegas*

Firms and individuals are listed alphabetically in each band.

Kamer Zucker & Abbott
The Firm: This traditional labor and employment law firm has grown to become one of the most prominent in the state. Attorneys are commended as experts in the representation of employers, including *"high-profile"* clients as varied as Clark County School District and the New York-New York Hotel & Casino.
The Lawyers: A *"brilliant trial attorney"* **Gregory Kamer** is former counsel to the NLRB in Washington DC and founder of the firm. He recently represented MGM Mirage's Golden Nugget and 35 other downtown hotels and casinos in talks, described as the most difficult collective bargaining negotiations since 1984, with the Culinary Workers Union. **Carol Zucker** is skilled in employment litigation and also represents clients before federal and state regulatory agencies. She successfully defended the nation's sixth largest public school district in a sexual harassment retaliation case (Clark County School District v Breeden).
The Clients: The firm acts for: Las Vegas Metropolitan Police Department; Clark County School District; New York-New York Hotel & Casino; Golden Nugget; MGM Mirage and Nevada Federal Credit Union.

Smith & Kotchka Ltd
The Firm: Adjudged a *"hugely successful"* labor and employment law firm, peers reported that *"if they are on the other side, then you know you're in for a big battle."* The majority of the firm's clients are in the hotel and casino industry but it also represents public employers and national and regional companies. The group has extensive experience in handling wrongful termination cases, union contract disputes, industrial insurance compensation claims, and employee benefits and labor/management relations.
The Lawyers: Gregory Smith is former in-house counsel for the Nevada Resort Association, and is experienced in the representation of management in employment litigation, counseling and strategic advice. **Malani Kotchka** was commended as *"thorough and accurate"* in her approach to labor and wage and hour matters.
The Clients: Boyd Gaming; Stardust Hotel & Casino; Eldorado Casino; City of Las Vegas; Las Vegas Valley Water Districts; Associated Builders & Contractors; Silver State Materials; Marnell Corrao Associates; McDonald's and GES Exposition Services.

Lionel Sawyer & Collins
The Firm: The largest law firm in Nevada, it houses a *"first-rate"* employment litigation practice, with strength in the representation of clients in termination and harassment lawsuits. The firm also advises management in the design of employment policies, unionization campaigns and collective bargaining negotiations. The firm won summary judgment twice in the notable case, Folkerson v Circus Circus.
The Lawyers: Cam Ferenbach is a *"high-quality trial attorney,"* respected for his work on federal claims. *"Knowledgeable"* **Howard Cole** has represented management in lawsuits claiming wrongful termination, sexual harassment and discrimination.
The Clients: The Venetian Casino Resort; International Game Technology; Mandalay Resort Group; Colorado Belle Hotel & Casino; Konami Gaming and The Four Queens Casino Hotel.

Piper Rudnick LLP
see firm details p.867
The Firm: The Las Vegas-based office is best known for its work in the hotel and gaming industries; union issues and collective bargaining are areas of expertise. Peers agree that attorneys here have deep resources enabling them to provide integrated corporate and labor advice, both nationally and internationally. The firm recently represented employers involved in jurisdictional disputes over the assignment of work to employees represented by different labor unions at two major constructions projects in Las Vegas.
The Lawyers: Gary Moss (see p.414) is a senior attorney who clients admire for his *"persuasive advocacy."* Peers regard him as *"tough, but a pleasure to work with or against."* Moss acts on union issues and employment discrimination-related litigation. He recently represented Golden Gate Hotel & Casino in negotiations with the Culinary Workers Uinon over healthcare plans, successfully ending a nine-day strike in downtown Las Vegas.
The Clients: Mandalay Resort Group; New York-New York Hotel & Casino; Golden Gate Hotel & Casino; Nevada Labor Commission; MGM Mirage; Stations Casinos and Stratosphere Gaming.

Schreck Brignone
The Firm: Peers agreed that the firm *"has established its place"* in the labor and employment law field. Its long-standing representation of the gaming and hospitality industries has ensured its prominence, but the firm has a much wider reach, advising statewide and national business and government entities.
The Lawyers: Interviewees recommended **Andrew Brignone** as an *"assertive lawyer who maintains the human touch."* He has been active for the past 25 years in employment and employee benefits law and is *"one of the most frequently named lawyers"* for such matters.
The Clients: The firm's clients are drawn from the gaming and hospitality industries, construction, healthcare services and state and national businesses.

Other Notable Practitioners
Mark Ricciardi of Ricciardi Law Group, a partner in Fisher & Phillips LLP, is a *"dedicated and hard-*

LITIGATION

NEVADA

working lawyer." His practice encompasses large and small businesses, and features litigation and counseling. Sole Practitioner **Kevin Efroymson** was applauded by peers as the long-standing "*dean of labor law.*" **Ann Morgan** of Jones Vargas' Reno office is a strong generalist who "*knows how to handle a case in court and is familiar with every aspect of labor law.*" **Kathleen Paustian** of Sullivan, Hill, Lewin, Rez & Engel was described as a "*top player*" in the state for her work on behalf of local and national business clients.

LITIGATION

GENERAL COMMERCIAL

NEVADA
Leading firms
(Litigation: General Commercial)

1 JONES VARGAS *Las Vegas*
   LIONEL SAWYER & COLLINS *Las Vegas*
2 KUMMER KAEMPFER BONNER *Las Vegas*
3 CAMPBELL & WILLIAMS *Las Vegas*
   HALE LANE PEEK DENNISON *Las Vegas, Reno*
   HARRISON, KEMP & JONES *Las Vegas*
   MCDONALD CARANO WILSON MCCUNE *Reno*
4 MORRIS PICKERING & SANNER *Las Vegas*
5 LAXALT & NOMURA *Reno*
   ROBISON, BELAUSTEGUI, SHARP & LOW *Reno*

Leading individuals
(Litigation: General Commercial)

1 CAMPBELL Donald *Campbell & Williams*, Las Vegas
   KENNEDY Dennis *Lionel Sawyer & Collins*, Las Vegas
   LENHARD Kirk *Jones Vargas*, Las Vegas
2 JONES Randall *Harrison, Kemp*, Las Vegas
   KUMMER Thomas *Kummer Kaempfer*, Las Vegas
   MORRIS Steve *Morris Pickering & Sanner*, Las Vegas
   PEEK Stephen *Hale Lane Peek Dennison*, Las Vegas
3 HEJMANOWSKI Paul *Lionel Sawyer*, Las Vegas
   KEMP Will *Harrison, Kemp & Jones*, Las Vegas
   LAXALT Bruce *Laxalt & Nomura*, Reno
   ROBISON Kent *Robison, Belaustegui*, Reno
   WILSON Thomas *McDonald Carano Wilson*, Reno

Firms and individuals are listed alphabetically in each band.

Jones Vargas
The Firm: Established as one of the most prominent law firms statewide, a large proportion of the practice is devoted to commercial and civil litigation. According to peers it sits "*at the top of the list for litigation,*" representing local, national and international clients in multi-state or multi-district litigation and appellate work before the Nevada Supreme Court.
The Lawyers: "*A strong adversarial litigator,*" **Kirk Lenhard** is recognized as "*among the top litigators in Las Vegas.*" The firm is defending McCarran International Airport in a case concerning three high-stakes lawsuits challenging the airport's authority to limit the height of nearby buildings.

The Clients: Hilton Hotels; Lehman Brothers; MGM Mirage; National American Insurance Company and New York-New York Hotel & Casino.

Lionel Sawyer & Collins
The Firm: "*A highly respected firm,*" it has the largest private law practice in Nevada, with substantial resources devoted to commercial litigation. In civil matters the firm advises on contract disputes, foreclosures, lender liability, gaming and IP matters. The firm won the respect of its peers and clients by acting as lead counsel in "*the most prominent cases.*" One such matter involved a class action case against major casinos in the US.
The Lawyers: "*Heavy hitter*" **Paul Hejmanowski** combines his work in complex commercial disputes with his duties as managing partner of the firm. **Dennis Kennedy** is one of the market's "*main trial lawyers.*" His practice encompasses healthcare cases and drug lawsuits, often involving class actions. He represents a range of healthcare providers, and is involved in defending RJ Reynolds in claims brought against the tobacco industry.
The Clients: HCA and Sunrise Hospital and Medical Center are represented.

Kummer Kaempfer Bonner & Renshaw
see firm details p.833
The Firm: Doubling its size in less than a decade has ensured that the firm is "*a well-established force*" for Nevada litigation matters. The firm focuses on general commercial disputes and all aspects of civil and appellate litigation. The team also has experience in construction disputes and securities claims.
The Lawyers: Founding member of the firm **Thomas Kummer** (see p.414) is an "*outstanding senior trial lawyer,*" who engages in commercial disputes, professional malpractice and aviation litigation.
The Clients: Olympic Group; Rio Hotel & Casino; AIG Aviation; State Farm and Republic Services.

Campbell & Williams
The Firm: Peers and clients alike acknowledge that this "*small firm has a considerable impact*" in the market. Its "*first-rate litigators*" are engaged mainly in catastrophic injury cases, commercial litigation and corporate criminal defenses.
The Lawyers: The founder of the firm, **Donald Campbell**, is "*an extraordinary talent,*" who has attracted commendation as "*one of the most respected plaintiffs' attorneys in Las Vegas.*" He has successfully handled high-profile lawsuits in both civil and white-collar criminal matters and has a "*persuasive and compelling*" approach to litigation. In a recent case, Campbell settled a civil case in favor of the client against GM, Exxon and Husky Energy.
The Clients: The firm acts for, among others, The Wall Street Journal, The Trump Organization, Las Vegas Review-Journal and Coast Resorts.

Hale Lane Peek Dennison and Howard
see firm details p.810
The Firm: This firm is renowned for its primarily commercial practice, with an emphasis on real estate transactions. It has also established a "*well-respected*" full-service litigation practice, representing clients from an industrywide spectrum, including financial institutions, hotels and casinos, business organizations and e-commerce companies.
The Lawyers: Observers acknowledged that litigator **Stephen Peek** (see p.414) has "*quite a reputation state and nationwide.*" A former deputy district attorney, he is "*an aggressive and direct lawyer – clients love to have him on their side.*" He represented The Venetian Casino Resort in a claim against the construction manager Lehrer McGovern Bovis for deficient and incomplete work in the $150 million expansion of the 3000-room hotel and casino, shopping mall and convention facility.
The Clients: Bank of America; The Venetian Casino Resort; iGo; contractors; developers; manufacturers; retailers and title companies.

Harrison, Kemp & Jones, LLP
see firm details p.813
The Firm: Established recently, this specialist litigation outfit is an offshoot of Jones, Jones, Close & Brown. The group has "*excelled and advanced*" in its development as a leading civil law practice. Its workload includes complex commercial litigation and corporate counseling.
The Lawyers: Peers described **Randall Jones** (see p.413) as "*a talented lawyer,*" who devotes his

NEVADA — LITIGATION

practice to complex commercial cases. *"Definitely a player in the litigation scene,"* **Will Kemp** (see p.413) is involved in national and multi-district litigation.
The Clients: The firm has defended Las Vegas City Council against large construction lawsuits, and won a landmark decision in a $28 million class action lawsuit against health benefits company Humana, filed over a decade ago on behalf of 84,000 Nevada patients and employers. The firm also acts for MGM Grand Hotel & Casino, Continental Casualty Company, MacDonald Properties and City of Las Vegas.

McDonald Carano Wilson McCune Bergin Frankovich & Hicks LLP
The Firm: Producing some of *"the top litigators"* in Reno, this statewide firm is experienced in business, employment, real estate, construction, environmental and insurance litigation. The litigation group has successfully represented Reno City Council and several business and casino owners in the fight against the petition for the downtown Reno train trench.
The Lawyers: A respected trial lawyer, **Thomas (Spike) Wilson** represents state and national clients in complex commercial litigation, arbitration and mediation. As a former state senator, he is respected for his knowledge of governmental affairs and regulations, and appears before state and governmental agencies.
The Clients: AT&T Communications of Nevada; The Associated General Contractors of America; Eldorado Hotel Casino; Reliance Insurance Company and Reno City Council.

Morris Pickering & Sanner
The Firm: Commended by peers as a *"dominant litigation firm,"* it handles complex, sensitive litigation for hospitals, pharmaceutical companies, automobile manufacturers and other public and private entities, on a local, state and national basis.
The Lawyers: Described by some as one of the *"best trial attorneys in Las Vegas,"* **Steve Morris** has *"extraordinary legal and personal skills."* He enjoys a national reputation in tort litigation, and, together with his partners, successfully defended American Pacific in a securities fraud class action.
The Clients: The group acts for American Pacific, Sierra Pacific Power Company and Southwest Gas.

Laxalt & Nomura
The Firm: Interviewees endorsed the group as *"one of the top firms for litigation in northern Nevada."* It is respected for its *"aggressive"* approach to the statewide representation of businesses, employers, manufacturers and insurers.
The Lawyers: *"Top-drawer"* litigator **Bruce Laxalt** (see p.414) is a former chief deputy district attorney of Reno. An established trial attorney, he is commended for his involvement in *"high-profile cases,"* arising from personal injury, employment and general commercial matters.
The Clients: The firm successfully defended Atlantis Hotel Casino in a federal court age discrimination employment suit. It has also acted for Caterpillar in a $2 million products liability suit. Other clients of the firm include: Wells Fargo; International Game Technology; Johnson & Johnson and Yellow Freight System.

Robison, Belaustegui, Sharp & Low
The Firm: This small general practice firm has *"an established and well-deserved reputation"* for representing clients in state and nationwide commercial and civil litigation cases.
The Lawyers: **Kent Robison** was described by peers as a *"dynamic trial attorney"* and one of the most active in the state. He specializes in business tort and commercial litigation, and has won admiration for his experience in personal injury and legal and medical malpractice matters.
The Clients: American Airlines; Alliance Insurance Companies; Corrao Construction Co; Wells Fargo and American General Realty Advisors.

REAL ESTATE

NEVADA
Leading firms (Real Estate)

1
- GOOLD PATTERSON DEVORE ALES *Las Vegas*
- HALE LANE PEEK DENNISON AND HOWARD *Reno*
- JONES VARGAS *Las Vegas*
- LIONEL SAWYER & COLLINS *Las Vegas*

2
- KUMMER KAEMPFER BONNER *Las Vegas*
- SCHRECK BRIGNONE *Las Vegas*

3
- ALLISON, MACKENZIE, RUSSELL, *Carson City*
- DEANER, DEANER, SCANN, MALAN, *Las Vegas*

4
- GORDON & SILVER, LTD *Las Vegas*
- MCDONALD CARANO WILSON MCCUNE, *Reno*
- SANTORO, DRIGGS, WALCH, *Las Vegas*

Firms are listed alphabetically in each band.

Goold Patterson DeVore Ales & Roadhouse
The Firm: A *"big player"* in the real estate market, the firm is judged by peers and clients alike to be a *"stable and prominent"* force. Its primary focus is commercial and real estate transactions, representing developers and other businesses in southern Nevada. The firm acted as local counsel to a national car dealer as borrower in a $325 million financing transaction. Development highlights of late include advising the builders of Lake Las Vegas Resort's MonteLago Village – a 1370-acre, $500 million resort and commercial village complex.
The Lawyers: Interviewees pointed to two leading figures: **Barry Goold** was commended as *"an exceptional lawyer,"* while colleague **Jeffrey Patterson** enjoys a strong following for his work in the bankruptcy field.
The Clients: Arnold Palmer Enterprises; Bank of America; DR Horton; Desert Oak Development; John Laing Homes; Koll Real Estate; Plaster Development and William Lyon Homes.

Hale Lane Peek Dennison and Howard
see firm details p.810
The Firm: This statewide law firm has a full-service approach, although observers perceive that the real drive to the practice lies with its real estate division, based in the Reno office. Real property law is at *"the heart of the firm,"* and it has attracted some of the *"top players"* in the field.
The Lawyers: *"Bright"* real estate lawyer **Karen Dennison** (see p.413) is *"heavily involved"* in the transactional market, particularly in timeshare and residential developments. **Stephen Novacek** (see p.414) provides *"advice that counts"* in the areas of secured and unsecured loans and the development of commercial projects.
The Clients: The firm represents new and expanding businesses in the Las Vegas Metropolitan Area. Real estate developers, lenders and sellers use the firm.

Jones Vargas
The Firm: One of the most prominent firms in Nevada, it is at the forefront of developments in one of the most rapidly growing states in the US. Possessed of *"super guys in the field,"* the real estate team is *"frequently on the scene"* representing master developers in establishing homeowners' associations. This work also involves the sale of properties to merchant builders and related financing matters.
The firm represents a client who is master planning a 1900-acre community in North Las Vegas, including the development of commercial sites and selling residential sites to merchant builders. It has also been involved in assisting a developer to acquire easements for a proposed monorail in Las Vegas.

REAL ESTATE / NEVADA

NEVADA
Leading individuals (Real Estate)

1
- BUCKLEY Michael *Jones Vargas*, Las Vegas
- DENNISON Karen *Hale Lane Peek Dennison*, Reno
- GOOLD Barry *Goold Patterson DeVore Ales*, Las Vegas
- ZUCKER Jeffrey *Lionel Sawyer & Collins*, Las Vegas

2
- DEANER Charles *Deaner, Deaner, Scann*, Las Vegas
- JONES Terry *Schreck Brignone*, Las Vegas
- SHARP DeArmond *Robison, Belaustegui*, Reno

3
- BARKSDALE David *Kummer Kaempfer*, Las Vegas
- BERGIN Leo *McDonald Carano Wilson*, Reno
- BUTT Layne *Lionel Sawyer & Collins*, Las Vegas
- CURTIS Patricia *Snell & Wilmer LLP*, Las Vegas
- MACE James *Gordon & Silver, Ltd*, Las Vegas
- PATTERSON Jeffrey *Goold Patterson*, Las Vegas
- WHITTEMORE David *Lionel Sawyer*, Las Vegas

4
- DRIGGS Jay *Santoro, Driggs*, Las Vegas
- FIORENTINO Mark *Kummer Kaempfer*, Las Vegas
- FRANKOVICH John *McDonald Carano*, Reno
- NOVACEK Stephen *Hale Lane Peek Dennison*, Reno
- PETERSON Karen *Allison, MacKenzie, Ltd*, Carson City
- RICE Stephen *Jones Vargas*, Las Vegas
- YOKEN Stephen *Gordon & Silver, Ltd*, Las Vegas

Individuals are listed alphabetically in each band.

The Lawyers: *"Top player"* **Michael Buckley** is the leader of the firm's real estate and commercial practice. He represents both developers and lenders in master-planned community projects. **Stephen Rice** has acted as general counsel to The LandWell Company in the largest brownfield redevelopment project of its type in the country. He also advised Shadow Creek Ranch Development Company on a 3000-acre master-planned community in Texas.

The Clients: North Valley Enterprises; The LandWell Company; Shadow Creek Ranch Development Company; City of Las Vegas; Howard Hughes Corporation; Nevada Development Authority and Wells Fargo.

Lionel Sawyer & Collins

The Firm: This *"top-notch"* firm houses a well-respected real estate practice that represents major local and national owners and developers. Alongside its experience in financing and purchasing matters, the group is skilled in land use planning and zoning law.

The Lawyers: At the top of the tree is the *"remarkable"* **Geoffrey Zucker**. *"A hugely respected force,"* he is involved in large commercial real estate transactions, mainly for hotels and casinos. *"Prominent"* **David Whittemore** represents real property developers in the acquisition, financing and development of housing and commercial projects. Another key team member is **Layne Butt**, who represents banks and life insurance companies in real estate financings, and advises on complex development work.

The Clients: MGM Mirage; Regent Hotel & Casino; The Venetian Casino Resort; Lady Luck Casino Hotel Las Vegas; Home Depot; Hilton Grand Vacations Company and CVS/pharmacy.

Kummer Kaempfer Bonner & Renshaw
see firm details p.833

The Firm: The firm is *"well connected"* to the Las Vegas business community and is applauded for its *"high-quality"* advice on commercial, residential and industrial projects. Peers pointed to its strength in land use, planning and government regulations. The firm has become one of the leading law firms in southern Nevada for planning and zoning matters.

The Lawyers: Head of the real estate practice **David Barksdale** (see p.412) brings his experience as a former in-house lawyer for a real estate development group to the team. Interviewees commented on his *"sharp mind – his advice is always spot on."* Barksdale represents owners and developers in the acquisition and financing of shopping centers, office buildings and residential projects. **Mark Fiorentino** (see p.413) is a government affairs lawyer who has carved a name for himself as the firm's land use and zoning specialist. He lobbies before the Nevada legislature and briefs state and local government agencies on zoning and licensing matters.

The Clients: Triple Five Development; Laurich Properties; Citibank; Merrill Lynch; Marnell Corrao Associates and Monarch Casino & Resort.

Schreck Brignone

The Firm: This respected real estate practice is *"prominent"* for its work within the Nevada gaming industry. The firm represents state and out-of-state hotel-casino clients in real property transactions, and advises on the financing of complex issues. It advised American Nevada and Del Webb in their acquisition and development of a master-planned community in North Las Vegas.

The Lawyers: One of the *"primary"* figures in the market, **Terry Jones** was endorsed for his business acumen. He has served as Nevada counsel to Goldman Sachs in the $1.2 billion financing of The Venetian Casino Resort project. Most recently, Jones represented Sierra Health Services on one of the largest sale and leaseback transactions in Nevada history.

The Clients: MGM Mirage, Mandalay Resort Group and Park Place Entertainment are key clients. Other clients include: Station Casinos; Horseshoe Club Hotel & Casino; Silver Legacy Resort Casino; Goldman Sachs; Sierra Health Services and Stephen Wynn.

Allison, MacKenzie, Russell, Pavlakis, Wright & Fagan, Ltd

The Firm: Home to the *"best real estate lawyers in northern Nevada."* The firm serves private and public entities, alongside non-profit clients across the state and nationwide.

The firm represented Lincoln County and its private partner, Vidler Water Company, in an application to pump 7000 acre-feet of water from the Tule Desert Groundwater Basin to supply a proposed $650 million power plant in southern Lincoln County.

The Lawyers: **Karen Peterson** has a statewide profile as a *"specialist"* on water rights-related real estate matters. One interviewee judged her to be *"one of the most prominent lawyers in this area."*

The Clients: The firm serves as general counsel to Carson City School District, Nevada State Board of Accountancy and Vidler Water Company, among others. Other clients include: Capital City Entertainment; Carson-Tahoe Hospital; Nevada Land & Resource; Northern Nevada Industrial Gas Users; Associates Commercial Corporation and Lincoln County.

Deaner, Deaner, Scann, Malan & Larsen

The Firm: A smaller but *"extremely creative"* real estate firm, it focuses on transactional real estate matters, litigation and development financing for Nevada, national and international clients.

The Lawyers: Founder of the firm **Charles Deaner** is regarded by peers as the *"dean of Nevada real estate law,"* and has been practicing in this area *"longer than most."*

The Clients: Continental American Management; Deere Credit Services; Investment Equity Builders; John Laing Homes; Land Title of Nevada; Nevada Federal Credit Union and the City of North Las Vegas.

Gordon & Silver, Ltd

The Firm: Interviewees commended this firm as one of the oldest and most *"reputable"* practices in the state. The group recently handled the $31 million sale of the Oasis in Mesquite, Nevada to the Las Vegas mogul, Randy Black Sr.

The Lawyers: The chairman of the corporate and real estate department, **Stephen Yoken** is *"meticulous"* in his representation of major banks and financial institutions, developers and landowners. His main clients are the Bank of America and Wells Fargo.

Clients described themselves as *"extremely satisfied"* with **James Mace**. He is respected for his *"thorough handling"* of acquisitions, disposals and financings within the real estate market.

The Clients: The firm's client roster spans large national financial institutions, local real estate developers and individuals, and includes: Bank of America; Nevada State Bank; Nevada Title Company; Hard Rock Hotel & Casino; Turnberry Pavilion Partners; Delta Air Lines and Turner Associates.

NEVADA

REAL ESTATE

McDonald Carano Wilson McCune Bergin Frankovich & Hicks LLP

The Firm: Athough the firm is perhaps better known for its work in gaming law, it is well regarded for its *"broad-based"* real estate department in Reno. The firm has strong ties to Nevada's gaming and construction industries and advises on the sale and acquisition of developed and undeveloped real property, and financing and land use, including zoning matters.

The Lawyers: Interviewees endorsed **Leo Bergin** as *"one of the most well-known real estate attorneys in Nevada."* Managing partner of the firm, he represents several large developers in Nevada in all aspects of land sale and acquisition, and financings through securitizations. Bergin also represents home builders, local banks, farm credit organizations, title companies and the Nevada Department of Transportation. Peers claim that *"if there is a big real estate transaction, he is most likely to be involved."* **John Frankovich** is a key figure in the Reno market. He advises on entitlement processes, obtaining approvals for projects from state and federal agencies and represents most of the downtown Reno casinos and shopping centers.

The Clients: Associated General Contractors of America; AT&T Communications of Nevada; Bank One; Eldorado Hotel & Casino and Reno-Sparks Association of Realtors.

Santoro, Driggs, Walch, Kearney, Johnson & Thompson

The Firm: Competitors agree that this firm *"punches above its weight."* Although smaller in size, it can lay claim to *"good real estate lawyers that are on the scene frequently."* The firm is active in the areas of planned development, homeowners' associations, land use and real property.

The Lawyers: The *"front man"* of the real estate practice, **Jay Douglas Driggs**, is regarded by peers and clients alike as *"a deal-maker with excellent negotiating skills."* He advises on the purchasing and sale of real estate, for both lenders and borrowers. He has handled foreclosures and long-term leases for, among others, First American Equities.

The Clients: The firm represents American Nevada and other Nevada developers and property managers in real estate acquisitions financings. Other clients include: First American Equities; American Pacific; Bank of America; Capital Pacific Homes; Textron Financial and Union Pacific Railroad.

Other Notable Practitioners

DeArmond Sharp of Robison, Belaustegui, Sharp & Low is an attorney in *"the top league;"* he represents both investment trusts and businesses in real estate lending transactions. **Patricia Curtis** of Snell & Wilmer is commended as *"a long-time player with a respected name in the industry."* She heads the firm's newest office in Las Vegas, and represents large developers in real estate financings, including asset secured and unsecured loans. Textron and power plants are also clients.

Leaders in Nevada

BARKSDALE, David A
Kummer Kaempfer Bonner & Renshaw,
Las Vegas 702 792 7000
dbarksdale@kkbr.com
Recommended in Real Estate
Specialization: Partner and head of the firm's real estate transactional practice. Has substantial experience with acquiring, developing and financing commercial shopping centers, office buildings and multi-family residential projects; acquiring and managing industrial/office projects; acquiring and developing hotel-casinos; negotiating and documenting construction contracts; handling foreclosures and workouts; financing the acquisition of hotel-casinos; negotiating and closing financing throughout all stages of the development process; and negotiating and documenting leases for retail, office and industrial properties. Represents The Rouse Company, The Berkley Group, World Market Center, Toll Brothers, Citibank and Marnell Corrao Associates.
Prof. Memberships: Member of the American Bar Association, the State Bar of Nevada and the State Bar of California. Member of the Executive Committee of the Business Law Section of the State Bar of Nevada. Adjunct professor with the University of Nevada, Las Vegas lecturing in real estate and construction law.
Career: Admitted California Bar (1989), Nevada Bar (1993). General Counsel of Triple Five National Development Corporation (1997-1999). Partner with *Kummer Kaempfer Bonner & Renshaw* (2000-present).
Personal: Las Vegas native. JD from Hastings College of the Law, University of California, in 1988; BA and BS, both magna cum laude, from Oral Roberts University in 1985.

BERGIN, Leo
McDonald Carano Wilson McCune
Bergin Frankovich & Hicks LLP, Reno
775 788 2000
Recommended in Real Estate

BONNER, Michael J
Kummer Kaempfer Bonner & Renshaw,
Las Vegas 702 792 7000
mbonner@kkbr.com
Recommended in Corporate/M&A
Specialization: Managing Partner. Practice concentration in business transactions, securities and gaming law. Has acted as counsel on IPOs, follow-on offerings, private placements, M&A and restructuring transactions. Has counseled publicly held companies on federal securities law disclosure and corporate governance matters, including Rio Hotel & Casino, Inc., Paul-Son Gaming Corporation and Monarch Casino & Resort, Inc. Has counseled acquirors and acquirees in M&A, roll-ups and other acquisition-related transactions. Has represented hotel-casino resort operators, including ITT Corporation in 1997 control contest, Atlantis Casino Resort (Reno), Rio Suite Hotel Casino, Aladdin Hotel & Casino, and Maxim Hotel & Casino as well as manufacturers, suppliers, lenders and officers and directors in transactional and licensing approvals before the Nevada Gaming regulatory agencies.
Prof. Memberships: Former chairman, corporations sub-committee, Business Law Committee, State Bar of Nevada; former vice chairman, Southern Nevada Disciplinary Board, State Bar of Nevada; trustee, Nevada Development Authority; member, International Association of Gaming Attorneys and Young President's Organization.
Career: Admitted to Nevada Bar (1981). Founding stockholder of *Kummer Kaempfer Bonner & Renshaw* (1994) and stockholder of predecessor firm.
Personal: Las Vegas native; JD, University of California, Los Angeles (1981); BS (High Distinction), University of Nevada, Las Vegas (1978).

BRIGNONE, Andrew
Schreck Brignone, Las Vegas
702 382 2101
Recommended in Employment

BUCKLEY, Michael
Jones Vargas, Las Vegas 702 734 2220
Recommended in Corporate/M&A, Real Estate

BUTT, Layne
Lionel Sawyer & Collins, Las Vegas
702 383 8888
Recommended in Real Estate

CAMPBELL, Donald
Campbell & Williams, Las Vegas
702 382 5222
Recommended in Litigation

CHAPIN, Patrick
Patrick N. Chapin, Henderson
702 433 8780
Recommended in Employment

COLE, Howard
Lionel Sawyer & Collins, Las Vegas
702 383 8888
Recommended in Employment

LEADERS
NEVADA

CROSBY, Douglas
Jones Vargas, Las Vegas 702 734 2220
Recommended in Corporate/M&A

CURTIS, Patricia
Snell & Wilmer LLP, Las Vegas
702 784 5200
Recommended in Real Estate

DEANER, Charles
Deaner, Deaner, Scann, Malan & Larsen, Las Vegas 702 382 6911
Recommended in Real Estate

DENNISON, Karen D
Hale Lane Peek Dennison and Howard, Reno 775 327 3000
Recommended in Real Estate
Specialization: All aspects of real estate law, including real estate acquisition, development, leasing, sale and financing, with a focus on master planned communities and resort developments, including time share.
Prof. Memberships: American College of Real Estate Lawyers, the American College of Mortgage Attorneys, the American Resort Development Association State Legislative Committee, State Bar of Nevada and State Bar of California.
Career: Shareholder for 28 years in the law firm of *Hale Lane Peek Dennison and Howard*.
Publications: 'Advanced Principles of Title Insurance'; 'Foreclosure and Repossession'.
Personal: JD degree from the University of San Francisco Law School in 1971.

DRIGGS, Jay Douglas
Santoro, Driggs, Walch, Kearney, Johnson & Thompson, Las Vegas
702 791 0308
Recommended in Real Estate

EFROYMSON, Kevin
Kevin C. Efroymson, Las Vegas Null
Recommended in Employment

ELLSWORTH, Carolyn
Ellsworth Law Firm, Las Vegas
702 366 0533
Recommended in Employment

ENGLAND, Kathleen
Brenske & Christensen, Las Vegas
702 385 3300
Recommended in Employment

FERENBACH, Cam
Lionel Sawyer & Collins, Las Vegas
702 383 8888
Recommended in Employment

FIORENTINO, Mark H
Kummer Kaempfer Bonner & Renshaw, Las Vegas 702 792 7000
mfiorentino@kkbr.com
Recommended in Real Estate
Specialization: Partner and head of land use and government affairs practice. Practices extensively before the Nevada State Legislature and local government authorities on zoning, licensing and general business matters. Substantial experience with zoning matters, state and local gaming license and tax matters. Drafts ordinances, legislation, and regulations on a variety of zoning, gaming and general business issues. Represents Boyd Gaming Corporation, Herbst Gaming, Chelsea Property Group, Pulte Homes, Astoria Homes, and Lamar Advertising. Registered lobbyist with the Nevada State Legislature, Clark County and Cities of Las Vegas and Henderson.
Prof. Memberships: Member, American Bar Association, Clark County Bar Association, International Association of Gaming Attorneys, and Nevada Gaming Attorneys. Served as Circuit Governor, Law Student Division, American Bar Association, Former member, Clark County Comprehensive Planning Steering Committee. Served on Clark County Committee rewriting the County's Zoning Code and the City of Las Vegas Master Plan Committee.
Career: Admitted to Nevada Bar (1992); partner, *Kummer Kaempfer Bonner & Renshaw* (1999); former associate, Lionel, Sawyer & Collins (1992-1995).
Publications: Member, Drake University Law Review. Published article on federal preemption of tobacco litigation. Contributing author to International Casino Law (1993) and Nevada Gaming Law (1995).
Personal: JS, Drake University (1992); BS, Arizona State University (1986).

FOWLER, John
Marshall Hill Cassas & De Lipkau, Reno
775 323 1601
Recommended in Corporate/M&A

FRANKOVICH, John
McDonald Carano Wilson McCune Bergin Frankovich & Hicks LLP, Reno
775 788 2000
Recommended in Real Estate

GARCIA, David A
Hale Lane Peek Dennison and Howard, Reno 775 327 3000
dgarcia@halelane.com
Recommended in Corporate/M&A
Specialization: Stockholder, Business Ventures Group, practicing primarily corporate and securities law. Extensive experience in mergers and acquisitions, venture capital, and public and private securities offerings. Additional experience with corporate partnering transactions and technology development, distribution and licensing arrangements.
Prof. Memberships: Member of Business Law Sections of State Bars of California and Nevada (Executive Committee) and the American Bar Association.
Career: Began career with *Wilson Sonsini Goodrich & Rosati* in Silicon Valley. Left in 1993 to help start Venture Law Group, where he practiced until joining Hale Lane in 1997.
Personal: JD, cum laude, Harvard Law School. AB Stanford University.

GOLDSTEIN, Mark
Lionel Sawyer & Collins, Las Vegas
702 383 8888
Recommended in Corporate/M&A

GOOLD, Barry
Goold Patterson DeVore Ales & Roadhouse, Las Vegas 702 436 2600
Recommended in Real Estate

HEJMANOWSKI, Paul
Lionel Sawyer & Collins, Las Vegas
702 383 8888
Recommended in Litigation

JONES, J Randall
Harrison, Kemp & Jones LLP, Las Vegas
702 385 6000
r.jones@hkj-law.com
Recommended in Litigation
Specialization: Practice embraces all aspects of civil litigation including residential construction defect cases, numerous class actions, a wide range of commercial litigation, administrative law problems such as land use and zoning challenges, bad faith denials of insurance coverage matters, medical malpractice cases, catastrophic injury and wrongful death actions.
Prof. Memberships: American Bar Association, Association of Trial Lawyers of America, Nevada Trial Lawyers Association, Nevada Bar Association, Clark County Bar Association, American Arbitration Association (Civil Arbitrator & Mediator), Nevada Law Foundation, Nevada Legal Services, and Nevada Medical/Legal Screening Panel (panel member).
Career: Named Trial Lawyer of the Year in 1998 by the Nevada Trial Lawyers Association and a member of the American College of Trial Lawyers in 2002, he received his BA from the University of Nevada (1978), his JD from California Western School of Law (1981), where he now serves as a Trustee, and was admitted to the Nevada Bar in 1981.

JONES, Terry
Schreck Brignone, Las Vegas
702 382 2101
Recommended in Real Estate

KAMER, Gregory
Kamer Zucker & Abbott, Las Vegas
702 259 8640
Recommended in Employment

KEMP, Will
Harrison, Kemp & Jones LLP, Las Vegas
702 385 6000
w.kemp@hkj-law.com
Recommended in Litigation
Specialization: Focusing primarily on complex and multi-district product liability litigation, has served on the Plaintiffs' Committees, and acted as trial counsel, for such cases as the: MGM Multi-District Fire Litigation (87 deaths and thousands of injuries in 1980 fire), San Juan Dupont Plaza Multi-District Fire Litigation (97 deaths and thousands of injuries in 1986 fire), Peachtree 25th Fire Litigation (5 deaths in 1991 fire), Breast Implants Products Liability Litigation, Castaño Tobacco Litigation, the Orthopedic Bone Screw Products Liability Litigation (defective spinal implants), Fen/Phen Diet Drug Litigation, Baycol Cholesterol Drug Litigation, and Meridia Drug Litigation.
Prof. Memberships: American Bar Association, Association of Trial Lawyers of America, Nevada Trial Lawyers Association, Nevada Bar Association, Clark County Bar Association.
Career: Received BA from Loyola University in Los Angeles, California (1975); JD (1978) from Northwestern University; admitted to the Nevada Bar (1978).
Publications: Primarily related to tort litigation including "Recent and Future MDL/Mass Tort Issues in Nevada," Communiqué, April, 2002; 'Modern Trends in Fire Litigation,' 16th International Conference on Fire Safety, (1991); 'American Law: The Victim's Only Hope,' The Brief (1985); and 'Settling With a Joint Tortfeasor in Vicarious Liability Cases,' NTLA Advocate (1984).

KENNEDY, Dennis
Lionel Sawyer & Collins, Las Vegas
702 383 8888
Recommended in Litigation

KIM, Robert C
Kummer Kaempfer Bonner & Renshaw, Las Vegas 702 792 7000
rkim@kkbr.com
Recommended in Corporate/M&A
Specialization: Senior associate. Practice concentration on general corporate, transactional, securities and gaming law. Member of legal teams representing: ITT Corporation (1997 takeover defense); Rio Hotel & Casino, Inc. (1998 $1.0 billion acquisition by Harrah's Entertainment, Inc.); Carefree Holdings Limited Partnership (1999 $60 million roll-up transaction); eRoomSystem Technologies, Inc. (2000 IPO); and, USA Capital First Trust Deed Fund, LLC (2002 $120 million equity offering). Represents public corporations in complying with the requirements of the 1934 Securities Exchange Act and companies in private placements of debt and equity securities.
Prof. Memberships: Member, State Bar of Nevada, State Bar of California, American Bar Association and the National Registry of Who's Who; Vice Chairman and Treasurer, Executive Committee, Business Law Section, State Bar of Nevada (committee responsible for proposing and preparing amendments to Nevada's business entity statutes). President and Co-Founder, Asian Bar Association of Las Vegas.
Career: Admitted to Nevada Bar (1996) and California Bar (1998).
Publications: Authored articles for Nevada Business Journal and American Bankruptcy Institute Journal. Speaker at seminars on business entity selection, limited-liability companies and venture capital.

NEVADA

Personal: JD and MBA, University of Southern California (1996); BA, Government, Cornell University (1992). Born in New York, New York. Proficient in Korean.

KOTCHKA, Malani
Smith & Kotchka Ltd, Las Vegas
702 382 1707
Recommended in Employment

KUMMER, Thomas F
Kummer Kaempfer Bonner & Renshaw, Las Vegas 702 792 7000
tkummer@kkbr.com
Recommended in Litigation
Specialization: Senior litigation partner. Practice concentration encompasses business/commercial, professional malpractice, solid waste/resource recovery and aviation litigation. Has represented ITT Corporation (1997 hostile takeover), Exxon Mobil, Republic Services, Aerospatiale, Pan American World Airways, America West Airlines, Inamed Corporation, Mandalay Resort Group, and Las Vegas Metropolitan Police Department. Has appeared in US and Nevada District Court, the 9th Circuit Court of Appeals, and the Nevada Supreme Court.
Prof. Memberships: State Bar of Nevada; American Bar Association; Clark County Bar Association; American Trial Lawyers Association; Defense Research Institute; served for 8 years on the Ethics and Professional Responsibility Committee of the State Bar of Nevada, and chaired that Committee for three years; appointed by the Nevada Supreme Court to act as a Supreme Court Settlement Conference Judge.
Career: St. Louis University, BSC (1965) and JD (1968). Admitted to Missouri Bar (1968-inactive) and Nevada Bar (1971). Founding partner, *Kummer Kaempfer Bonner & Renshaw* (1994); former partner, predecessor firm (1982-*Vargas & Bartlett*).
Personal: Active member of Las Vegas community, participates in several community and church organizations. Currently serves as board member and legal counsel to HELP of Southern Nevada and participates as a Big Brother in the Big Brother and Big Sisters program in Southern Nevada.

LAXALT, Bruce
Laxalt & Nomura, Reno 775 322 1170
blaxalt@laxalt-nomura.com
Recommended in Litigation
Specialization: Defense civil litigation, primarily in product liability, commercial, emloyment/civil rights, and professional liability, for such clients as Caterpillar Inc., General Motors, Navistar International, Tamrock Oy (now Sandvik), numerous Nevada hotel/casinos and law firms. Over sixty cases tried to jury verdict with over 93% success rate. Multiple high exposure cases resolved pre-trial through confidential settlement.
Prof. Memberships: State Bar of Nevada; American Board of Trial Advocates.
Career: Nevada State Bar, 1976; US District Court (Nevada), 1980; US Court of Appeals (9th Circuit), 1982. 1976-77: staff attorney, US Department of Justice (Washington, DC); 1977-78: law clerk, Nevada Supreme Court Justice Gordon Thompson; 1978-82: deputy, Assistant Chief, and Chief Criminal Deputy, Washoe County District Attorney's Office (Reno, Nevada); 1982-86: partner, *Beckley, Singleton, DeLanoy & Jamison*, Chtd. (Reno and Las Vegas); 1986-present: partner, *Laxalt & Nomura, Ltd.* (Reno and Las Vegas).
Personal: BA (Philosophy), Stanford University, 1973; JD, Stanford Law School, 1976.

LENHARD, Kirk
Jones Vargas, Las Vegas 702 734 2220
Recommended in Litigation

LYONS, Keith
Keith M Lyons, Las Vegas
702 432 8655
Recommended in Employment

MACE, James
Gordon & Silver, Ltd, Las Vegas
702 796 5555
Recommended in Real Estate

MARKS, Daniel
Daniel Marks, Las Vegas 702 386 9600
Recommended in Employment

MORGAN, Ann
Jones Vargas, Reno 775 786 5000
Recommended in Employment

MORRIS, Steve
Morris Pickering & Sanner, Las Vegas
702 474 9400
Recommended in Litigation

MOSS, Gary
Piper Rudnick LLP, Las Vegas
702 737 3433 gcmoss@verner.com
Recommended in Employment
Specialization: Labor and employment law.
Career: His labor and employment law practice includes federal and state court employment discrimination and wrongful discharge litigation, collective bargaining negotiations, arbitrations, union organizing campaigns, cases before federal and state administrative agencies, wage and hour matters, and labor and employment law issues relating to sales, mergers, acquisitions, shutdown and bankruptcies. He has extensive experience in advising clients regarding strikes and other forms of labor disputes, union organizing attempts, corporate campaigns, and arbitration of disputes arising under collective bargaining agreements.
Personal: JD, University of Iowa; BA, University of Illinois.

NOVACEK, Stephen V
Hale Lane Peek Dennison and Howard, Reno 775 327 3000
Recommended in Real Estate
Specialization: All aspects of real estate law with a focus on real estate finance, including residential and commercial construction and permanent loan transactions. He also has extensive experience in commercial asset-based lending transactions.
Prof. Memberships: Member: Nevada, Washoe County, Clark County, and American Bar Associations.
Career: He joined *Hale Lane* in 1974 and has been a shareholder since 1980.
Personal: BS (Finance) from the University of Nevada and JD from Willamette University College of Law.

PATTERSON, Jeffrey
Goold Patterson DeVore Ales & Roadhouse, Las Vegas 702 436 2600
Recommended in Real Estate

PAUSTIAN, Kathleen
Sullivan, Hill, Lewin, Rez & Engel, Las Vegas 702 382 6440
Recommended in Employment

PEEK, J Stephen
Hale Lane Peek Dennison and Howard, Las Vegas 702 222 2500
speek@halelane.com
Recommended in Litigation
Specialization: In over 30 years of trial court experience in commercial litigation, he has represented a wide range of clients before state courts and federal courts including the Ninth Circuit Court of Appeals. As a prominent trial lawyer, he is focused on every step of the litigation process, always aiming to obtain the best result for clients. Under his leadership, the firm's litigation group in Las Vegas has grown to represent a wide variety of local, regional, and national companies engaged in complex commercial transactions.
Prof. Memberships: Member: Nevada, Clark County, Washoe County and American Bar Associations, Nevada Trial Lawyers Association and the American Trial Lawyers Association.
Career: Deputy District Attorney, Washoe County District Attorney's Office. He joined *Hale Lane* in 1973, becoming a shareholder in 1975.
Personal: He received his BA from the University of Nevada and his JD from Georgetown University Law School where he was a member and editor of the 'Georgetown University Law Review'.

PETERSON, Karen
Allison, MacKenzie, Russell, Pavlakis, Wright & Fagan, Ltd, Carson City
775 687 0202
Recommended in Real Estate

RICCIARDI, Mark
Ricciardi Law Group, Las Vegas
702 252 3131
Recommended in Employment

RICE, Stephen
Jones Vargas, Las Vegas 702 734 2220
Recommended in Real Estate

ROBISON, Kent
Robison, Belaustegui, Sharp & Low, Reno 775 329 3151
Recommended in Litigation

SCHULHOFER, Ellen
Schreck Brignone, Las Vegas
702 382 2101
Recommended in Corporate/M&A

SCHUMACHER, Kirk
Woodburn and Wedge, Reno
775 688 3000
Recommended in Corporate/M&A

SEGERBLOM, Richard
Richard S. Segerblom, Las Vegas
702 388 9600
Recommended in Employment

SHARP, DeArmond
Robison, Belaustegui, Sharp & Low, Reno 775 329 3151
Recommended in Real Estate

SMITH, Gregory
Smith & Kotchka Ltd, Las Vegas
702 382 1707
Recommended in Employment

WHITTEMORE, David
Lionel Sawyer & Collins, Las Vegas
702 383 8888
Recommended in Real Estate

WILSON, Thomas
McDonald Carano Wilson McCune Bergin Frankovich & Hicks LLP, Reno
775 788 2000
Recommended in Litigation

WOLOSON, Kenneth
Haney, Woloson & Mullins, Las Vegas
702 474 7557
Recommended in Corporate/M&A

YOKEN, Stephen
Gordon & Silver, Ltd, Las Vegas
702 796 5555
Recommended in Real Estate

ZUCKER, Carol
Kamer Zucker & Abbott, Las Vegas
702 259 8640
Recommended in Employment

ZUCKER, Jeffrey
Lionel Sawyer & Collins, Las Vegas
702 383 8888
Recommended in Corporate/M&A, Real Estate

NEW HAMPSHIRE

CORPORATE/M&A

CONTENTS: Corporate/M&A p.415; Employment: Mainly Plaintiff p.417; Mainly Defendant p.417; Litigation: General Commercial p.418; Real Estate p.420; Individuals' Profiles p.421.

NEW HAMPSHIRE'S TOP THREE
1. McLane, Graf, Raulerson & Middleton
2. Sheehan Phinney Bass & Green
3. Devine Millimet & Branch

Ranking based on Chambers' research within the state.

All quotes in the text are from interviews with clients and competitors.

OVERVIEW: The largest New Hampshire firm, **McLane, Graf, Raulerson & Middleton** operates from four offices across the state and takes top billing. The firm's litigators received widespread endorsement for their outstanding trial capabilities. The labor and employment department boasts significant prowess and undertakes a volume of consulting and advisory work for employers. In commercial law, the firm serves corporate clients in a broad range of matters and possesses noteworthy experience in revolving loans, public and private equity offerings, and venture capital transactions. The real estate group acts on financings and transactional matters, and benefits from an extensive support base when advising on large-scale projects. Clients include BayCorp Holdings and Microsoft.

Traditionally strong in the corporate arena, **Sheehan Phinney Bass & Green** maintains its profile, providing services in M&A, commercial lending and public finance, and securities and venture capital. Clients of the labor and employment group here appreciate these attorneys' dedication and their ability to resolve employment disputes quickly, particularly noting the firm's established system of information exchange. In litigation, the firm commands a strong reputation, especially in relation to healthcare, technology and IP disputes. The real estate department is diverse in its practice and undertakes a variety of matters ranging from covenants and restrictions to 0zoning board work and appeals. This New Hampshire firm recently opened a Boston office. Raytheon, UPS and University of New Hampshire are clients.

Recommended for its resources and wide-ranging experience, **Devine Millimet & Branch**'s corporate group represents public and private companies in M&A, banking and finance, governmental affairs, IP and telecom matters. The employment group is well regarded for its excellent risk management counseling and training services. Considered preeminent for insurance defense, the litigation group is seen to be expanding steadily into the commercial sector, undertaking increasing amounts of contractual disputes and securities cases. In real estate, the firm focuses heavily on commercial work, acting for financial institutions and developers. Hi-tech companies and educational establishments feature in its client roster.

CORPORATE/M&A

NEW HAMPSHIRE
Leading firms (Corporate/M&A)

1. MCLANE, GRAF, RAULERSON Manchester
   SHEEHAN PHINNEY BASS & GREEN Manchester
2. COOK, LITTLE, ROSENBLATT & MANSON Manchester
   DEVINE MILLIMET & BRANCH PA Manchester
3. NIXON PEABODY LLP Manchester
   ORR & RENO PA Concord
4. HINCKLEY, ALLEN & SNYDER LLP Concord

Leading individuals (Corporate/M&A)

1. REISCHE Alan Sheehan Phinney Bass, Manchester
   SAMUELS Richard McLane, Graf, Raulerson, Manchester
2. COHEN Steven Devine Millimet & Branch, Manchester
   COOK James Cook, Little, Rosenblatt, Manchester
   LITTLE Curtis Cook, Little, Rosenblatt, Manchester
3. CASTALDO Neil Hinckley, Allen & Snyder, Concord
   HOOD James Nixon Peabody LLP, Manchester
4. BURGER Peter Orr & Reno PA, Concord
   BURKE Steven McLane, Graf, Raulerson, Manchester

Firms and individuals are listed alphabetically in each band.

McLane, Graf, Raulerson & Middleton PA
see firm details p.849

The Firm: This well-established New Hampshire firm provides legal services to corporate clients on a broad range of matters, including business formation, contracts, M&A, corporate finance and administrative law. Attorneys here have experience in complex business affairs such as revolving loans, public and private equity offerings, and venture capital transactions, and are quite at home in international M&A. Sources underlined the firm's *"excellent"* reputation for tax and estate planning, and for banking expertise.

The Lawyers: *"Intelligent, disciplined and organized"* **Richard Samuels** (see p.423) is highly respected by rivals and clients alike for his experience, knowledge and attention to detail. He chairs the firm's corporate department, and focuses on larger clients. His practice has a particular emphasis on securities law and M&A. **Steven Burke** (see p.421) chairs the tax department and is a CPA. Industry sources hold him in high regard, and he is widely seen as Samuels' heir apparent. He concentrates on business and corporate tax at both state and federal levels as well as estate planning, ERISA matters and employee benefits.

The Clients: The firm recently represented BayCorp Holdings in connection with its interest in the Seabrook Nuclear Power Plant, representing 17% of an $800 million transaction. It also acted for Telecommunications Systems of New Hampshire in its 2002 sale to Telephone & Data Systems (TDS). Other clients include: Quinn Bros Corporation; KeySpan Energy Delivery; NEXIQ Technologies; KeyBank; City of Claremont NH and Microsoft.

Sheehan Phinney Bass & Green PC
see firm details p.875

The Firm: This regional firm is traditionally strong in the corporate arena. Retaining a high profile, it fields about 30 attorneys in its business practice. The group provides services in the areas of business formation and planning, M&A, contracts, commercial lending and public finance, securities and venture capital, and IP and technology. The firm boasts niche expertise in serving hospitals and other nonprofit institutions in financing and compliance work. Over the past 18 months it has advised on more than a billion dollars of tax-exempt financings in New Hampshire and Massachusetts.

The Lawyers: Peers were unanimous in naming **Alan Reische** (see p.423) the *"dean of the corporate bar,"* agreeing that *"there is no one in his league."* He received an unusual volume of plaudits, and was described as *"one of the few genuinely brilliant lawyers in the state,"* bringing *"innovative approaches to complicated corporate problems."* His practice is primarily focused on corporate planning, generational and succession planning, secured lending and M&A.

The Clients: The group recently represented Oxford Health Care Plans in its acquisition of

NEW HAMPSHIRE

CORPORATE/M&A

MedSpan, for approximately $19 million in cash. It also assisted Mary Hitchcock Memorial Hospital and Dartmouth-Hitchcock Clinic in refinancing outstanding debt and acquiring funds for major new construction projects. Other representative clients include: Vox Radio Group; University of New Hampshire; Dartmouth College; State of New Hampshire Turnpike System; Covenant Health System; Coral Energy Resources and Sigma Data.

Cook, Little, Rosenblatt & Manson PLLC
The Firm: *"Business lawyers for entrepreneurs"* is how this eight-lawyer corporate boutique is described. It focuses on business law, with five partners concentrating on transactional work. According to the market, these are *"outstanding lawyers, who have done a tremendous amount of financing work"* for the firm's mainly entrepreneurial, technology-based clients. Its expertise covers everything required by fledgling companies, including business formation, securities matters, licensing, IP rights, equity and debt financings, corporate governance and stock option plans.
The Lawyers: According to industry sources, **Curtis Little** is an *"uncommonly experienced and practical business lawyer"* with a knack of going straight to the crux of matters. His practice straddles the corporate and banking spheres, and he represents a range of local businesses and financial institutions in connection with major financings, securities matters, real estate purchases, leases and the formation of new companies. **James Cook** concentrates on the entrepreneurial technology-based sector, where he is said by peers to be *"prominent and experienced."* His practice includes advising companies on debt and equity financing arrangements, joint ventures and strategic alliances, licensing agreements and M&A.
The Clients: The firm's dynamic hi-tech work includes representing a biotech firm in a $7 million second-round venture capital financing, and acting for a bank as lead arranger in syndicated loans totaling $32.5 million to a coffee manufacturer. Representative clients include: Granite Systems; Biznews24; Pragmatech Software; EnviroSense; Fleet Bank and Banknorth.

Devine Millimet & Branch PA
The Firm: This firm was warmly recommended to researchers for its resources and wide-ranging experience. The 40 attorneys in its corporate group represent public and private companies, and provide them with a range of services covering M&A, banking and finance, business and tax planning, telecommunications, governmental affairs and IP matters.
The Lawyers: According to sources, **Steven Cohen** is *"a bright guy with major strengths in tax and finance."* A former CPA, his practice encompasses M&A, business planning, federal and state taxation, technology and IP law.
The Clients: Clients include hotels, manufacturers, distributors and software companies.

Nixon Peabody LLP
see firm details p.858
The Firm: The New Hampshire office of this large, multi-practice law firm was established in 1992. Interviewees said: *"Its status as part of a large network is a unique selling point - its work has a national and even international flavor."* This ability to draw on the firm's enormous resources gives the office in Manchester a huge advantage, according to commentators, and it is further bolstered by the fact that many of its attorneys have a background in the state's larger indigenous firms. The corporate group provides a full range of services to its business clients, but was particularly praised for its expertise in bankruptcies and workouts.
The Lawyers: **James Hood**, formerly with McLane, Graf, Raulerson & Middleton, was recommended to researchers as a *"top-class, smart and personable"* attorney. His practice covers corporate governance, restructuring, M&A, debt and equity financing, company and joint venture formation, and distribution arrangements. He also has experience in bank regulatory issues and the law relating to public utilities.
The Clients: Clients are a blend of New Hampshire-based companies and national or international ones requiring representation in the state.

Orr & Reno PA
The Firm: Peers praised the 14 corporate attorneys at this traditional New Hampshire firm as *"without exception, competent and careful lawyers."* The group advises clients on a full range of business affairs including M&A and divestitures, tax-exempt and conventional financing and leasing, regulatory compliance, environmental issues and IP. Market sources consider the firm to have a particular niche in the healthcare sector, in which the firm boasts a specialist group of eight.
The Lawyers: **Peter Burger** was particularly recommended to researchers for his skills in tax and financing. However, his broad practice also includes M&A, e-commerce and technology, IP and immigration law. Fluent in German, he represents many US subsidiaries of German, Swiss or Austrian-owned companies, including Lindt & Sprüngli (USA), which he assists with all major contracts, including a recent review of lines of credit in excess of $45.5 million.
The Clients: The firm recently assisted PAK 2000 with a multimillion dollar asset financing. Other clients include: Concord Litho Group; Linchris Hotel; Audley Construction; ActivMedia Robotics; Atlantic Bridge Network and Innoserv Gmbh.

Hinckley, Allen & Snyder LLP
The Firm: This corporate-focused regional firm boasts offices in Boston and Providence as well as in New Hampshire, where its Concord branch currently has about seven lawyers but is in a period of expansion. Attorneys focus on higher end work in the areas of M&A, recapitalizations, IPOs and contractual affiliations between corporates. In complex matters, the group can draw on the specialized services offered by its other offices. Rivals and clients alike say the firm has *"strength and expertise in healthcare issues."*
The Lawyers: **Neil Castaldo** is *"a bright, very thorough guy,"* who some sources consider *"one of the top lawyers in the state."* He is best known for his niche focus on healthcare issues. He has wide experience, however, in general corporate affairs, including providing strategic advice on corporate direction, litigation management and M&A.
The Clients: Recent work for the firm includes representing Fleet Bank in connection with a $70 million term loan to Florida Office Associates, and assisting American National Power as part of a $1.4 billion nationwide financing of various power plants. Other clients include: Hasbro; CVS; Modern Continental Construction; Textron and the Dartmouth-Hitchcock Medical Center.

NEW HAMPSHIRE

EMPLOYMENT & LABOR LAW

MAINLY PLAINTIFF

NEW HAMPSHIRE
Leading firms
(Employment: Mainly Plaintiff)

1. BACKUS MEYER SOLOMON ROOD *Manchester*
   STEIN VOLINSKY & CALLAGHAN PA *Concord*
2. COOK & MOLAN *Concord*

Leading individuals
(Employment: Mainly Plaintiff)

1. VOLINSKY Andru *Stein Volinsky & Callaghan, Concord*
2. MACLELLAN Eleanor *Sulloway & Hollis, Concord*
   MEYER Jon *Backus Meyer Solomon Rood, Manchester*
3. MOLAN Richard *Cook & Molan, Concord*

Firms and individuals are listed alphabetically in each band.

Backus Meyer Solomon Rood & Branch LLP

The Firm: This small firm has offices in Manchester and Concord. The *"sound"* general trial practice is well known for its representation of plaintiffs in a variety of claims concerning discrimination, wrongful discharge and constitutional rights in the workplace.
The Lawyers: Star constitutional lawyer **Jon Meyer** was highly commended by peers as a *"talented trial advocate"* for his employment work and specialty in First Amendment matters. Interviewees reported that this *"cerebral"* lawyer possesses *"top-notch briefing and writing skills."* His excellent track record in cases before the US and New Hampshire Supreme Courts makes him a popular choice among clients.
The Clients: The practice provides legal advice to plaintiffs and defendants in the insurance, retail and education sectors.

Stein Volinsky & Callaghan PA

The Firm: This small Concord firm represents employees in wrongful termination, harassment and discrimination disputes and in severance and employment contract negotiations. Peers reported that the firm was extremely well known for its employment practice, which places an emphasis on trial work and risk management.
The Lawyers: A *"plaintiffs' favorite,"* **Andru Volinsky** is renowned for his *"effective advocacy"* in a number of high-profile cases. This *"skilled trial attorney"* earned praise as a *"persuasive, all-around"* practitioner.
The Clients: Clients include employees in the technology and communications industries, as well as a number of education and public sector bodies.

Cook & Molan

The Firm: This labor boutique is widely respected for its representation of unions and union members on a wide variety of employment and labor matters.
The Lawyers: Top labor lawyer **Dick Molan** is regarded as *"a player in the big leagues."* Recommended as *"the most highly regarded union lawyer in the state,"* Molan boasts a substantial practice in the area. His workload includes counseling, negotiations, and labor and employment advocacy work.
The Clients: The practice acts for a diverse portfolio of union clients, including The Professional Firefighters of New Hampshire, United Steelworkers and Concord Police Patrolmen's Association.

Other Notable Practitioners

Within the defendant employment practice at Concord firm, Sulloway & Hollis PLLC, **Eleanor MacLellan** stands out for her *"fantastic"* work on behalf of plaintiff employees. She maintains a mixed plaintiffs' and defendants' practice and was highly recommended as a *"tenacious and well-prepared"* trial advocate.

EMPLOYMENT & LABOR LAW

MAINLY DEFENDANT

NEW HAMPSHIRE
Leading firms
(Employment: Mainly Defendant)

1. DEVINE MILLIMET & BRANCH PA *Manchester*
   FLYGARE SCHWARZ & CLOSSON PLLC *Exeter*
   GALLAGHER, CALLAHAN AND GARTRELL *Concord*
2. MCLANE, GRAF, RAULERSON *Manchester*
   SHEEHAN PHINNEY BASS & GREEN *Manchester*
   SULLOWAY & HOLLIS PLLC *Concord*

Leading individuals
(Employment: Mainly Defendant)

1. BROTH Mark *Devine Millimet & Branch , Manchester*
   FLYGARE Thomas *Flygare Schwarz & Closson, Exeter*
   JOHNSTONE Andrea *Gallagher, Callahan Concord*
   REIDY James *Sheehan Phinney Bass, Manchester*
2. JOHNSON Linda *McLane, Graf, Raulerson, Manchester*
   KAPLAN Edward *Sulloway & Hollis PLLC, Concord*
   WOLOWITZ David *McLane, Graf, Raulerson, Portsmouth*

Firms and individuals are listed alphabetically in each band.

Devine Millimet & Branch PA

The Firm: This is a five-attorney labor and employment practice that focuses on providing preventative employment advice to management clients. Clients commend the firm's *"excellent"* risk management counseling and training services relating to sexual harassment, discipline and discharge, and compensation systems. Other matters handled include collective bargaining and union relations matters, executive compensation arrangements and ERISA litigation.
The Lawyers: Litigator **Mark Broth** was recommended as a talented trial lawyer who *"puts a lot of time into a case."* This *"tenacious"* attorney is known for his *"tough"* stance in the courtroom. His practice centers on the representation of employers in union and other traditional labor disputes and negotiations.
The Clients: The firm represents employer clients in a range of sectors, including those in the manufacturing, education, service, healthcare and hi-tech industries. Practitioners also advise local government bodies on employment matters.

Flygare Schwarz & Closson PLLC

The Firm: This small employment boutique in Exeter concentrates on defense work against claims of age and disability discrimination, wrongful discharge, sexual harassment and breach of contract. The firm enjoys an excellent reputation among peers for its skilled trial attorneys and strong following among municipal clients.
The Lawyers: Market sources commend **Tom Flygare** as a *"top practitioner"* who *"knows his stuff"* both in and out of the courtroom. Clients call him an *"able advocate and careful counselor,"* noting his extensive knowledge of law and procedure.
The Clients: The firm acts for: Rivier College; Notre Dame College; Freudenberg-NOK; Spaulding Composites; Citizens Bank; Kinderworks; City of Portsmouth; City of Keene; New Hampshire College; Saint Anselm College; Holderness School; Derryfield School and Pinkerton Academy.

Gallagher, Callahan and Gartrell PA

The Firm: This *"brisk and busy"* department, based in Concord, provides a host of labor and employment practices. Interviewees particularly

NEW HAMPSHIRE — EMPLOYMENT & LABOR LAW

commented on the group's specialty in mediation, praising members' abilities to *"take complex laws and make them practical for the client."* The team is involved in a number of discrimination and wage claims. Additionally, the firm's powerful banking arm provides a substantial amount of employment-related work.

The Lawyers: *"Bright"* **Andrea Johnstone** was identified as a leading light at the employment bar. Interviewees admired her work in risk management matters, commending her as an *"efficient and effective"* counselor to administrative bodies. Even rivals expressed willingness to refer important clients to her, thanks to her *"deep understanding of the law."*

The Clients: The group is known to act for a number of local banking clients as well as municipalities and an array of corporate clients in the education, media, electricity and oil and gas sectors.

McLane, Graf, Raulerson & Middleton PA
see firm details p.849

The Firm: The largest New Hampshire firm was noted for its *"strong trial capability"* in defending against employment claims. Attorneys also provide counseling services to mid-sized public and private companies.

The Lawyers: *"Excellent"* **David Wolowitz** (see p.423) is visible handling a volume of discrimination cases. He is well known for his large client portfolio of private educational institutions whom he advises on every aspect of their legal requirements. Peers recommend **Linda Johnson** (see p.422) for her skill in mediation and *"level-headed"* advice to employers. Although better known for her risk management work, Johnson is said to be *"an aggressive advocate for her client when necessary."*

The Clients: Clients range from small businesses to the New Hampshire branches of large multi-national corporations. These include numerous banks and technology companies, manufacturers and distributors, hospitals and educational institutions.

Sheehan Phinney Bass & Green PC
see firm details p.875

The Firm: A sizable New England firm, well regarded for its labor and employment practice. Members are said to be *"highly involved in the community"* and possess strength in preventative employment counseling. Contentious claims are handled by trial attorneys in the firm's general litigation practice. Peers particularly commend the firm's *"excellent information-sharing systems."*

The Lawyers: **Jim Reidy** (see page 422) is considered a *"key figure"* in the market for his lobbying efforts in connection with employment legislation reform. This highly respected practitioner focuses on the representation of management (public and private employers) through counseling, training and advice on avoiding employment disputes or claims.

The Clients: The team acts for public and private companies of all sizes. The firm has an emphasis on healthcare and hi-tech clients, but also undertakes work for a number of colleges, pipeline companies and financial institutions.

Sulloway & Hollis PLLC

The Firm: This large Concord-based firm is recognized for its employment advice to several local companies and healthcare institutions. Attorneys were commended as *"able and accessible."*

The Lawyers: Commentators singled out **Edward Kaplan** as a *"persuasive"* advocate who *"gives his best for clients"* in the courtroom. Clients report *"he is always well prepared"* and *"puts a lot of thought into identifying the issues that will arise in trial."* His practice concentrates on discrimination and labor matters before state and federal administrative agencies and state and federal courts.

The Clients: The firm acts for a large concentration of insurance companies, but also advises manufacturing, healthcare and education clients on a range of employment matters.

LITIGATION — GENERAL COMMERCIAL

NEW HAMPSHIRE
Leading firms
(Litigation: General Commercial)

1. **MCLANE, GRAF, RAULERSON** Manchester
2. **ORR & RENO PA** Concord
   SHEEHAN PHINNEY BASS & GREEN Manchester
3. **DEVINE MILLIMET & BRANCH PA** Manchester
   GALLAGHER, CALLAHAN AND GARTRELL Concord
   SULLOWAY & HOLLIS PLLC Concord
   WADLEIGH, STARR & PETERS PLLC Manchester
   WIGGIN & NOURIE Manchester

Firms are listed alphabetically in each band.

McLane, Graf, Raulerson & Middleton PA
see firm details p.849

The Firm: A 30-strong troop of litigators comprises *"an outstanding group, with several high-profile members,"* according to interviewees. The team received unequivocal endorsement for its trial capabilities. Plaintiff and defendant representation is provided in state and federal courts in such matters as securities law, trade secrets, non-compete agreements, contractual disputes, employment law, personal injury and complex commercial issues. Observers highlight attorneys' *"huge amount of expertise,"* particularly in the computer software and products liability spheres, both of which have been very productive for the firm in recent years. The IP group also commands respect among peers, and has both trademark and patent expertise.

The Lawyers: **Jack Middleton** (see p.422) is a major rainmaker for the firm and, with over 40 years' trial experience, he is *"one of the more senior and respected members of the New Hampshire bar."* He has tried a wide variety of commercial matters for both plaintiffs and defendants, recently focusing on products liability and patent infringement litigation. According to interviewees, **Bruce Felmly** (see p.422) is *"a superb trial lawyer: bright, hard-working and dynamic in the courtroom."* He has made a name for himself in high-profile products liability cases on both the plaintiff and defendant sides. Felmly also handles personal injury and complicated medical malpractice work. His current caseload includes representing Hyundai on a products liability case in the First Circuit Court of Appeals. Sources identified **Wilbur Glahn** (see p.422) as *"an experienced lawyer who commands respect in the commercial arena."* Focusing on complex business issues, he has tried cases relating to corporate governance, stockholder disputes, breaches of fiduciary duty and IP. Glahn also has extensive experience in constitutional litigation.

The Clients: The firm represented Carpet One against Mercator Software in a case alleging negligence, breach of contract, and intentional misrepresentation relating to a faulty software design and purchase contract. It has also acted for Microsoft against PC Connection in a computer software trademark and copyright infringement case, concerning alleged software piracy. Other clients include: BAUER Nike Hockey USA; Abbott Laboratories; Chicago Title Insurance Company; KeySpan Energy Delivery; Verizon; KeyBank National Association; BAE Systems and HSBC.

Orr & Reno PA

The Firm: Clients and competitors applaud this 15-member team for their *"high-quality commercial litigation work."* The group's size and *"effective, creative approach"* gives it *"a strong New Hampshire presence."* The firm represents both plaintiffs and defendants across the full range of civil matters, from traditional corporate issues, to IP, bankruptcy, immigration, products liability and securities litigation. Market sources recom-

LITIGATION — NEW HAMPSHIRE

NEW HAMPSHIRE
Leading individuals
(Litigation: General Commercial)

1
- **FELMLY Bruce** *McLane, Graf, Raulerson,* Manchester
- **GLAHN Wilbur** *McLane, Graf, Raulerson,* Manchester
- **HILLIARD Russell** *Upton and Hatfield LLP,* Concord
- **MIDDLETON Jack** *McLane, Graf, Raulerson,* Manchester
- **WHEAT James** *Wadleigh, Starr & Peters,* Manchester

2
- **DANENBARGER Wright** *Wiggin & Nourie,* Manchester
- **HARVELL Michael** *Sheehan Phinney Bass,* Manchester
- **MOORE George** *Devine Millimet & Branch,* Manchester
- **SNOW Ronald** *Orr & Reno PA,* Concord

3
- **COUSER Richard** *Orr & Reno PA,* Concord
- **VAN OOT Martha** *Orr & Reno PA,* Concord

Individuals are listed alphabetically in each band.

---

mended the team in particular for its handling of healthcare and corporate governance issues.

The Lawyers: Ronald Snow is the senior trial lawyer in the firm. He concentrates on complex civil litigation and medical malpractice cases, but also has extensive courtroom experience in products liability defense. A *"creative, hard-working and tactically astute litigator,"* Snow commands enormous respect from the market. He recently acted as lead counsel defending Dartmouth-Hitchcock Medical Center et al against the City of Lebanon, which was attempting to enforce a real property tax. The case was settled in New Hampshire Superior Court in such a way as to preserve the tax-exempt status of the medical center. *"Bright, well-prepared and thorough"* **Richard Couser** is experienced in the gamut of commercial cases, including environmental, products liability, tax abatement and IP matters. He is also busy in his role as a trained arbitrator and mediator. He recently acted as plaintiff counsel for PMC Corporation against Houston Wire & Cable Company in claims of breach of contract and misrepresentation. **Martha Van Oot** was recommended to researchers as a *"good tactician and an outstanding lawyer."* She practices in complex commercial litigation, bankruptcies and workouts, legal and other professional malpractice defense, and employment matters. She is also frequently retained as a private mediator.

The Clients: Amerisure Companies; Bank of New York; Dartmouth-Hitchcock Medical Center; Fleet Bank; Manufacturers' and Merchants' Mutual Insurance Company; New York Times and Sears Roebuck.

Sheehan Phinney Bass & Green PC
see firm details p.875

The Firm: The business litigation group, numbering 16 attorneys, continues to enjoy a strong reputation in the field, despite the retirement of several senior partners. The team is renowned for representing many New Hampshire businesses, especially in the healthcare and technology industries. The spectrum of its work ranges from multiparty business cases and M&A litigation, to antitrust and unfair trade practices disputes, and employment and labor relations. The firm's strong IP practice gives it a good profile for trademark-related work. It has served as leading counsel for a class action of 15,000 taxpayers seeking refunds of interest and dividends tax.

The Lawyers: Market sources acclaim **Michael Harvell** (see page 422) for his dynamic courtroom appearances and quick financial mind. He has frequently litigated stockholder and partnership disputes and employment matters as well as issues involving lender liability and other commercial disputes. He is also experienced in environmental and IP matters.

The Clients: The firm successfully defended Loon Mountain Recreation against a challenge to an $18 million merger transaction. Other clients include Dartmouth College; Aprisma Management Technologies; BioSan Labs; Citizens Bank; Coral Energy Resources; Exeter Clinic; Ford; Taxtron; New London Hospital; Skillsoft and UPS.

Devine Millimet & Branch PA
The Firm: Historically known for insurance defense, this firm, according to market sources, still handles *"an enormous amount of insurance work, and is the preeminent firm in the state for this."* Rivals comment that it is deploying the trial skills learned in this field and is *"branching out into the commercial sector."* A group of about 20 provides a broad range of civil legal advice on contractual disputes, corporate securities and employment work as well as on more traditional insurance defense issues such as products liability, medical and legal malpractice, and personal injury defense.

The Lawyers: George Moore was recommended to researchers as a *"good, flexible trial lawyer."* Moore has developed a sound reputation in the commercial field; clients unanimously praised his dedication and perseverance. His practice focuses on corporate disputes between stockholders, contract and corporate governance issues and professional malpractice.

The Clients: The firm recently acted in the $6 million settlement of a trade secret claim against a Chinese corporation, and in the $3 million settlement of a breach of contract claim involving the sale of electric power.

Gallagher, Callahan and Gartrell PA
The Firm: Although this is a full-service firm, it has a particularly strong focus on governmental and regulatory issues, and owes much of its market profile to regulatory and legislative work. Its expertise covers commercial contracts, consumer protection, unfair competition, stockholder rights, business dissolutions, real estate titles and insurance coverage.

The Lawyers: The four partners in the litigation section won praise from market sources for being *"excellent in the courtroom."* The team includes David Garfunkel.

The Clients: Clients include insurance companies, hospitals, small businesses, utilities, manufacturers and hi-tech companies.

Sulloway & Hollis PLLC
The Firm: Four of the partners in the litigation group of this mid-sized firm specialize in commercial work. They represent plaintiffs and defendants in a range of business disputes, including antitrust, securities and copyright issues. Commentators particularly highlighted the team's skills and experience in the areas of medical malpractice and personal injury. Irvin Gordon is a contact partner for the group.

The Clients: Clients are drawn from a number of sectors, including insurance, manufacturing, healthcare, utilities and technology.

Wadleigh, Starr & Peters PLLC
The Firm: This mid-sized New Hampshire firm enjoys a strong reputation for insurance defense. The civil litigation group, about 15 in number, practice in virtually every area of the field. Attorneys here have extensive experience in complex construction litigation and healthcare disputes. Market sources particularly endorsed its expertise in professional malpractice defense.

The Lawyers: Commentators described **James Wheat** as *"an experienced, versatile trial lawyer,"* and resoundingly applauded his *"stamina, courage and tremendous workload."* He represents both plaintiffs and defendants in a variety of commercial disputes, and has considerable expertise in construction litigation and legal malpractice defense.

The Clients: Clients include educational institutions, financial institutions, healthcare providers, insurance companies, manufacturers and retailers.

Wiggin & Nourie
The Firm: This firm has a long history of acting in litigation relating to insurance coverage and defense. It fields a team of experienced trial lawyers who provide both defense and plaintiff representation in such matters as breach of contract, trade secrets, employment and antitrust litigation. The firm has developed a particular niche in the area of class action work on behalf of automobile dealers.

The Lawyers: Wright Danenbarger has over 30 years' experience in trying commercial cases and was resoundingly praised by peers as a *"formidable adversary."* His practice covers litigation in general commercial, IP, construction and personal injury cases.

NEW HAMPSHIRE — REAL ESTATE

The Clients: Clients include auto franchises, medical groups, real estate developers, construction companies, manufacturers, energy corporations, financial institutions, insurance companies, governmental agencies and individuals.

Other Notable Practitioners
Russell Hilliard of Upton & Hatfield LLP won sustained praise from peers for his *"excellent trial skills, professionalism, credibility and work ethic."* He handles a wide range of commercial litigation, and was highly recommended for his skills as a mediator.

REAL ESTATE

NEW HAMPSHIRE
Leading firms (Real Estate)

1 GALLAGHER, CALLAHAN AND GARTRELL *Concord*
MCLANE, GRAF, RAULERSON *Manchester*
SHEEHAN PHINNEY BASS + GREEN *Manchester*
SULLOWAY & HOLLIS PLLC *Concord*

2 DAVIS & BOGHIGIAN PC *Nashua*
DEVINE MILLIMET & BRANCH PA *Manchester*
WADLEIGH, STARR & PETERS PLLC *Manchester*

3 NUNGESSER & HILL *Meredith*
UPTON AND HATFIELD LLP *Concord*
WINER & BENNETT LLP *Nashua*

Leading individuals (Real Estate)

1 DAVIS Jefferson *Davis & Boghigian PC, Nashua*
ROTCH Peter *McLane, Graf, Raulerson, Manchester*

2 GARTRELL Donald *Gallagher, Callahan, Concord*
HILL Douglas *Nungesser & Hill, Meredith*
IMSE Peter *Sulloway & Hollis PLLC, Concord*
MANCHESTER Susan *Sheehan Phinney Bass, Manchester*
TUCKER William *Wadleigh, Starr & Peters, Manchester*

3 UPTON Robert *Upton and Hatfield LLP, Concord*

Firms and individuals are listed alphabetically in each band.

Gallagher, Callahan and Gartrell PA
The Firm: The five-attorney real estate practice of this large, Concord-based firm has strong links to the firm's banking practice. The group handles real estate sales and acquisitions and undertakes title matters for insurance clients. The firm also offers expertise in real estate tax issues, such as assessments and abatements and state and federal tax matters. Competitors regard the group as a *"high-quality"* team with extensive capacity in real estate development and condominium law. The firm also attracts comment for its lobbying efforts, with a number of practitioners involved in promoting legislative reform within the state legislature.
The Lawyers: Interviewees recommend **Don Gartrell** as one of New Hampshire's leading real estate lawyers, particularly noting his skill in drafting documentation. He counsels several municipalities in the state on zoning matters, drawing upon extensive experience in the crossover between property and municipal law. Peers and clients praise him as a *"very able negotiator."*
The Clients: BAE SYSTEMS; Bank of New Hampshire; Citizens Bank New Hampshire; Concord Monitor; Dartmouth College; GM; JPMorgan Chase; Manchester Sand, Gravel and Cement Company; MBNA America Bank; Nike; PG&E Co; Providian National Bank; Savings Bank of Walpole; Southern New Hampshire Bank & Trust Company; St Anselm College and Subaru of America.

McLane, Graf, Raulerson & Middleton PA
see firm details p.849
The Firm: Attorneys in the firm's four New Hampshire offices handle real estate finance and acquisition in conjunction with a highly respected commercial lending practice. Typical work includes construction finance, leasing, zoning and land use matters. The real estate practice is closely supported by specialists in related areas of bankruptcy, litigation and environmental law. Clients complimented the group's strength in transactional work, citing the firm's *"extensive support base for large-scale projects."*
The Lawyers: *"Refined"* **Peter Rotch** (see p.423) elicits praise for his considerable transactional ability and *"commercial outlook."* Interviewees described him as a *"strong advocate for his clients,"* noting his recent involvement in a number of difficult real estate and restructuring matters.
The Clients: BayCorp Holdings; Chicago Title Insurance Company; Community Bank & Trust Company; Citizens Bank New Hampshire; City of Portsmouth; GE Capital Asset Funding; GE Capital Small Business Finance; Heidelberg Web Systems; Hyundai ; Manchester Water Works; Microsoft; Monadnock Paper Mills; Nashua Motor Express; Pfeiffer Vacuum Technology; Sheraton Hotel - Portsmouth; Souhegan Nursing Association; Summit Packaging Systems and Synagro Technologies.

Sheehan Phinney Bass & Green PC
see firm details p.875
The Firm: The real estate department of this large New England firm was acknowledged for a diverse practice, which encompasses advice on covenants, conditions, zoning board applications and appeals, and compliance with New Hampshire land sales and condominium registration requirements. The firm also acts as agent to several title insurance companies.
The Lawyers: Known particularly for her condominium practice, **Susan Manchester** (see page 422) is highly regarded in the market for *"excellent"* work in property finance. This *"practical"* attorney enjoys a reputation for *"solving problems."* Clients especially value her ability to *"see the big picture"* in large and complex transactions.
The Clients: Anthem Insurance; AscendantOne; BioSan Labs; Boston & Maine Corporation; Brookstone; City of Manchester; Coca-Cola Bottling of Northern New England; Concord Monitor; Dartmouth College; Exeter Hospital; First USA; Ford Motor Credit Company; Gillette; Hampshire Paper Corporation; Honeywell; Maritimes & Northeast Pipeline LLC; New Hampshire Insurance Department; Raytheon; Sigma Data; St. Joseph's Hospital; Tyco International and UPS.

Sulloway & Hollis PLLC
The Firm: The largest firm in New Hampshire's state capital, *"strong in real estate"* and well respected for its work for private and public corporations, hospitals, developers, lenders and public entities, in connection with commercial financing and bond issues in a wide variety of real estate projects. The practice attracts particular comment for its representation of banks and commercial lenders. Matters covered range from tax-exempt financings and leasing negotiations to zoning challenges and title insurance claims.
The Lawyers: Identified as an *"old hand"* in the field, **Peter Imse** received general commendation as a *"sophisticated"* real estate practitioner with noteworthy expertise in condominium matters. His practice covers zoning and land use planning, title insurance, commercial finance and tax-exempt municipal finance. Clients praise his *"team-oriented approach"* and *"depth of experience."*
The Clients: American Honda Finance Corporation; Public Service Company of New Hampshire.; Fleet Bank; AMICA Mutual Insurance Company; American Insurance Association; Chicago Title Insurance Company; Merrill Lynch Credit Corporation; CIGNA; Travelers Group; Citizens Bank New Hampshire and Liberty Mutual.

REAL ESTATE — NEW HAMPSHIRE

Davis & Boghigian PC
The Firm: This two-partner Nashua firm specializes in commercial real estate matters. The team boasts long-standing ties to a number of eminent lender and developer clients in the state and earns kudos in the market for its *"careful and steady"* approach to transactional work.
The Lawyers: Jefferson Davis received widespread recommendation as a *"practical and solutions-driven"* lawyer, highly visible in his work on behalf of lenders in real estate financing. He was named as *"our first choice for real estate matters"* by clients who commend his skill in complex and sophisticated transactions.
The Clients: Andover Bank; Bank of New Hampshire; Centrix Bank & Trust; First Essex Bank; Fleet Bank - New Hampshire; KeyBank National Association; Lawyers Title Insurance Corporation and Southern New Hampshire Bank & Trust Company.

Devine Millimet & Branch PA
The Firm: With three offices in New Hampshire, the large New England firm is thought to command *"extensive resources."* The real estate practice focuses heavily on commercial work, acting for financial institutions and developers. The firm advised on the development of the Center of New Hampshire in Manchester, a construction project funded by several different sources of finance. Part of this project involved the first commercial development of *"air rights"* in the state.
The Lawyers: Although no single individual stood out during *Chambers'* research, the group, which includes Karen McGinley and Susan Duprey, was endorsed by peers for setting high standards within the market.
The Clients: The firm acts for service, manufacturing, hi-tech and research businesses, individual entrepreneurs, colleges and universities, public companies, hospitals, professional corporations and governmental bodies throughout New England.

Wadleigh, Starr & Peters PLLC
The Firm: Market sources recognized this Manchester-based practice for its *"diverse and excellent"* real estate offerings. Practitioners undertake work for financial institutions, development firms, local businesses and contractors. Particular expertise exists in the overlap between land use planning and municipal law.
The Lawyers: William Tucker earned praise as a *"bright and experienced"* real estate attorney with an extensive background in representing developers in shopping center projects. Peers noted his skill in title work and zoning procedures, describing him as *"one of the best deal makers in the state."* Clients appreciate his *"tactical brilliance and sense of humor."*
The Clients: American Contractors Insurance Group; BancBoston Mortgage Corporation; Bank of New Hampshire; Fitchburg Mutual Insurance Company; Ford; Honeywell; KeyBank National Association; Kollsman; Nations Title Insurance Company; New England Development Company; Risk Enterprise Management; Scandia Plastics and Toyota Motor Credit Corporation.

Nungesser & Hill
The Firm: This Meredith-based real estate boutique handles a variety of work in the commercial real property sphere.
The Lawyers: Name partner **Douglas Hill** was highly recommended as *"an extremely thorough and knowledgeable"* real estate attorney. Interviewees report: *"He knows how to get to the heart of a question and find a solution."* Clients consider him a *"pleasure to deal with."*
The Clients: The firm acts for smaller local companies, individuals and mid-sized institutions statewide on a full range of real estate transactions.

Upton and Hatfield LLP
The Firm: A mid-sized firm with offices in Concord and Hillsborough. The firm's diverse real estate practice covers financing, sales and leasing transactions, as well as real estate development. Attorneys advise on the purchase and sale of almost every type of real estate, from condominiums to subdivisions. Competitors commented on the firm's impressive portfolio of work undertaken for the state's municipalities.
The Lawyers: Robert Upton was named as an *"extremely experienced"* real estate practitioner with a *"great depth of knowledge."* Noted for his *"remarkable rapport with clients,"* Upton was said to act for a *"select"* client base, to which he provides *"exceptional service."*
The Clients: The firm represents a variety of clients as borrowers and lenders, contractors and developers, buyers and sellers, and tenants and landlords.

Winer & Bennett LLP
The Firm: This small Nashua firm is well known locally for its real estate capacity. Rivals praised the group's *"consistently high-quality"* work.
The Lawyers: The firm has a strong real estate practice and is well established in the locality for its expertise. While no individual emerged as a market leader, the group, which includes J Bradford Westgate and Peter Bennett, was highly regarded by peers for its property practice.
The Clients: Banknorth; Bank of New Hampshire; Granite Bank; Brookstone; Semikron International; Banknorth Leasing; ExxonMobil; Cadec; First Colebrook Bank; Resonetics; Clearview Software International; Pennichuck Water Works; Nashua YMCA; Apex Telecommunications; Spaceflight Systems and Design Mentor.

Leaders in New Hampshire

BROTH, Mark
Devine Millimet & Branch PA, Manchester 603 669 1000
Recommended in Employment

BURGER, Peter
Orr & Reno, PA, Concord 603 224 2381
Recommended in Corporate/M&A

BURKE, Steven
McLane, Graf, Raulerson & Middleton PA, Manchester 603 628 1454
steve.burke@mclane.com
Recommended in Corporate/M&A
Specialization: Concentrates on M&As and business ventures, including tax implications of transactions, ESOPs, pension plans, ERISA, executive compensation and corporate governance arrangements. Also advises on tax and estate planning for business owners, IRS and state tax matters. He is also a Certified Public Accountant.
Prof. Memberships: New Hampshire & Massachusetts Bars, New Hampshire Society of CPAs, American Institute of Certified Public Accountants.
Career: Shareholder, Director, and Tax Department Chair; Current President, Board of Directors and Executive Committee-NH Society of CPAs; Past President-Tax Section NH Bar; Past President and Treasurer-NH Employee Benefits Council; Adjunct Professor-Franklin Pierce Law School. Listed in leading US legal publication.
Personal: BA, Bates College, 1981; MBA, University of Lowell, 1984; JD Franklin Pierce Law School, 1987; LLM in Taxation, Boston University School of Law, 1990.

NEW HAMPSHIRE — LEADERS

CASTALDO, Neil
Hinckley, Allen & Snyder LLP, Concord 603 225 4334
Recommended in Corporate/M&A

COHEN, Steven
Devine Millimet & Branch PA, Manchester 603 669 1000
Recommended in Corporate/M&A

COOK, James
Cook, Little, Rosenblatt & Manson PLLC, Manchester 603 621 7100
Recommended in Corporate/M&A

COUSER, Richard
Orr & Reno, PA, Concord 603 224 2381
Recommended in Litigation

DANENBARGER, Wright
Wiggin & Nourie, Manchester 603 669 2211
Recommended in Litigation

DAVIS, Jefferson
Davis & Boghigian, PC, Nashua 603 595 0210
Recommended in Real Estate

FELMLY, Bruce
McLane, Graf, Raulerson & Middleton PA, Manchester 603 628 1448
bruce.felmly@mclane.com
Recommended in Litigation
Specialization: Co-chair, *McLane's* Litigation Department. Concentrates in complex commercial defense and plaintiff trial practice, including products liability, antitrust, insurance recovery, employment, and contract claims. Recent representation of clients has included Microsoft Corporation, Abbott Labs, Hyundai Motor Company, Bayer Corporation, Carpet One, Dartmouth College, and KeySpan.
Prof. Memberships: Fellow of the American College of Trial Lawyers, American and New Hampshire Trial Lawyer's Associations, and a Fellow of the American and New Hampshire Bar Foundations.
Career: Shareholder and Director since 1979; In 2002, he received the New Hampshire Bar Association's Distinctive Service to the Legal Profession Award. President of the New Hampshire Bar Association (1995-96).
Personal: JD, Cornell Law School, 1972.

FLYGARE, Thomas
Flygare Schwarz & Closson PLLC, Exeter 603 778 7300
Recommended in Employment

GARTRELL, Donald
Gallagher, Callahan and Gartrell, PA, Concord 800 528 1181
Recommended in Real Estate

GLAHN, Wilbur
McLane, Graf, Raulerson & Middleton PA, Manchester 603 628 1469
bill.glahn@mclane.com
Recommended in Litigation
Specialization: Business and commercial litigation, including issues of corporate governance and control, breaches of fiduciary duty and dissenters' rights, contract disputes, securities law, and taxation. Constitutional litigation.
Prof. Memberships: New Hampshire and American Bar Associations, New Hampshire Trial Lawyers Association.
Career: Admitted to practice in the state and federal courts in New Hampshire (1976) and Massachusetts (1972); First Circuit Court of Appeals (1976); Supreme Court of the United States (1978). Former Assistant Attorney General and head of the Civil Division of the Office of the Attorney General (New Hampshire).
Personal: Trinity College, BA with honors 1969 (Phi Beta Kappa); University of Chicago Law School, JD 1972.

HARVELL, Michael
Sheehan Phinney Bass + Green PC, Manchester 603 627 8133
mharvell@sheehan.com
Recommended in Litigation
Specialization: A member and director of the firm, he practices in the areas of coprporate law and corporate litigation. He has frequently litigated shareholder and partnership disputes, employment matters, intellectual property disputes, commercial disputes and fiduciary disputes.
Prof. Memberships: New Hampshire Bar Association; Bar of the United States Supreme Court.
Personal: BA from Yale University in 1968 and JD (cum laude) from Boston University in 1975. Former Chair and Trustee, Strawbery Banke Museum; Vice Chair and Director, NH Preservation Alliance; Former President and Director, Child & Family Services of NH; Former Trustee, NH Society for the Protection of NH Forests; Former Director, Greater Piscataqua Community Foundation.

HILL, Douglas
Nungesser & Hill, Meredith 603 279 8182
Recommended in Real Estate

HILLIARD, Russell
Upton and Hatfield, L.L.P., Concord 603 224 7791
Recommended in Litigation

HOOD, James
Nixon Peabody LLP, Manchester 603 628 4000
Recommended in Corporate/M&A

IMSE, Peter
Sulloway & Hollis, PLLC, Concord 603 224 2341
Recommended in Real Estate

JOHNSON, Linda
McLane, Graf, Raulerson & Middleton PA, Manchester 603 628 1267
linda.johnson@mclane.com
Recommended in Employment
Specialization: Co-Chair, *McLane's* Employment Practice. Concentrates on corporate risk management and defendant litigation. Formulates employment and personnel policies and handbooks, advises on employee discipline, termination, discrimination claims, wage and hour compliance, and other personnel matters. Conducts harassment and other workplace trainings. Defends companies in State and Federal Courts and before Administrative Agencies.
Prof. Memberships: Past President, Manchester Area Human Resources Association; active member, National Society for Human Resource Management, and Employment Law Sections of the New Hampshire and American Bar Associations; member, Human Resource Committee of the New Hampshire Business and Industry Association.
Career: Shareholder and Director. Awards: 2002 Marilla Ricker Award from New Hampshire Women's Bar Association, and the 2002 New Hampshire Civil Liberties Union award for pro bono work on a civil rights matter.
Personal: JD, Boston University, 1984.

JOHNSTONE, Andrea
Gallagher, Callahan and Gartrell, PA, Concord 800 528 1181
Recommended in Employment

KAPLAN, Edward
Sulloway & Hollis, PLLC, Concord 603 224 2341
Recommended in Employment

LITTLE, Curtis
Cook, Little, Rosenblatt & Manson PLLC, Manchester 603 621 7100
Recommended in Corporate/M&A

MACLELLAN, Eleanor Holmes
Sulloway & Hollis, PLLC, Concord 603 224 2341
Recommended in Employment

MANCHESTER, Susan
Sheehan Phinney Bass + Green PC, Manchester 603 627 8245
smanchester@sheehan.com
Recommended in Real Estate
Specialization: Member and director of the firm and is the head of the Real Estate and Lending Practice Group. Her practice is in the areas of zoning and land use, commercial leasing, conveyancing, condominium, construction and commercial lending.
Prof. Memberships: New Hampshire Bar Association. American Bar Association.
Personal: BA, magna cum laude, Brown University 1977. JD, Boston University 1980. Heritage United Way, Board Chair.

MEYER, Jon
Backus Meyer Solomon Rood & Branch LLP, Manchester 603 668 7272
Recommended in Employment

MIDDLETON, Jack
McLane, Graf, Raulerson & Middleton PA, Manchester 603 628 1446
jack.middleton@mclane.com
Recommended in Litigation
Specialization: Concentrates on arbitration and mediation, utilizing 45 years experience as a trial lawyer and 24 years as a New Hampshire District Court Judge. In addition, he has a strong trial practice in commercial litigation.
Prof. Memberships: Former Secretary, member, Board of Governors, American Bar Association (ABA); member, ABA House of Delegates; Fellow, American College of Trial Lawyers; former president, New Hampshire and New England Bar Associations, the National Conference of Bar Foundations and National Conference of Bar Presidents; former chairman, New Hampshire Bar Foundation.
Career: Shareholder and Director since 1962. New Hampshire District Court Judge (1964-87). Listed in several leading US legal publications.
Personal: JD, Boston University, 1956.

MOLAN, Richard
Cook & Molan, Concord 603 225 3323
Recommended in Employment

MOORE, George
Devine Millimet & Branch PA, Manchester 603 669 1000
Recommended in Litigation

REIDY, James
Sheehan Phinney Bass + Green PC, Manchester 603 627 8217
jreidy@sheehan.com
Recommended in Employment
Specialization: Employment law. Advises and represents public and private employers in matters of counseling, training, and ways to effectively avoid and/or defend against employment disputes or claims.
Prof. Memberships: Chairman, New Hampshire High Tech Council's Human Resources Exchange; Board, Manchester Area Human Resources Association.
Career: Chair, Employment Law and Employee Benefits Practice; founder/moderator of NHLABORNET Internet discussion group for human resource professionals; recipient of 2001 New Hampshire Business and Industry Award for work on behalf of employers.
Publications: Many. Please see www.sheehan.com
Personal: BA Assumption College 1980. MPA Northeastern University 1981. JD (cum laude) New England School of Law 1989.

NEW HAMPSHIRE

REISCHE, Alan
Sheehan Phinney Bass + Green PC, Manchester 603 627 8225
areische@sheehan.com
Recommended in Corporate/M&A
Specialization: Corporate finance, business acquisitions and mergers and business succession planning.
Prof. Memberships: Director, New Hampshire International Trade Association; member, Continuing Legal Education and Professionalism Committees, New Hampshire Bar Association; member, Governor's Advisory Committee on Capital Formation; Vice-Chairman, New Hampshire Workforce Opportunity Council; Director, Court Appointed Special Advocates of New Hampshire; member, Venture for Growth committee of the New Hampshire Community Loan Fund.
Career: Associate and member, *Sheehan Phinney Bass + Green*, Prof Assn., Manchester, New Hampshire, 1965-2003. Admitted to the New Hampshire Bar; United States District Court, District of New Hampshire; Tax Court of the United States.
Personal: Married to Joan B Lazarus, 1965; children, James F Reische, Ann Arbor MI (b 1966); Margaret Ann Reische, Seattle WA (b 1969).

ROTCH, Peter
McLane, Graf, Raulerson & Middleton PA, Manchester 603 628 1305
peter.rotch@mclane.com
Recommended in Real Estate
Specialization: Chair of *McLane's* Real Estate Department. His practice is focused on commercial property development and financing. He works with investors and corporate clients who wish to develop and finance real estate. He is an agent for all of the major title insurance companies. Recent projects include obtaining property and easements for a major gas powered electric generating facility.
Prof. Memberships: Fellow of the American College of Real Estate Lawyers; member, New Hampshire and American Bar Associations.
Career: Admitted in New Hampshire - 1966; Shareholder and Partner, 1974. Listed in leading US legal publication.
Personal: Dartmouth College (1963-AB), University of Chicago Law School (1966-JD).

SAMUELS, Richard
McLane, Graf, Raulerson & Middleton PA, Manchester 603 628 1470
richard.samuels@mclane.com
Recommended in Corporate/M&A
Specialization: Chair of *McLane's* Corporate Department. Concentrates practice in corporate and commercial transactions, securities law, banking, and utilities regulatory matters. Advises on merger and acquisition transactions and securities matters, including public and private offerings of equity securities, entity formation, governance, and commercial matters. An author of New Hampshire's Business Corporation Act and Limited Liability Company Act.
Prof. Memberships: Co-chair for Fiscal Policy of the Fiscal Policy and Economic Development Committee of the Business & Industry Association of New Hampshire. New Hampshire liaison to the American Bar Associations Business Law Section's Committee on State Regulation of Securities.
Personal: BA, Union College, 1974; MA, Duke University, 1976; JD, Cornell University, 1980. Listed in leading US legal publication.

SNOW, Ronald
Orr & Reno, PA, Concord 603 224 2381
Recommended in Litigation

TUCKER, William
Wadleigh, Starr & Peters PLLC, Manchester 603 669 4140
Recommended in Real Estate

UPTON, Robert
Upton and Hatfield, L.L.P., Concord 603 224 7791
Recommended in Real Estate

VAN OOT, Martha
Orr & Reno, PA, Concord 603 224 2381
Recommended in Litigation

VOLINSKY, Andru
Stein Volinsky & Callaghan PA, Concord 603 228 1109
Recommended in Employment

WHEAT, James
Wadleigh, Starr & Peters PLLC, Manchester 603 669 4140
Recommended in Litigation

WOLOWITZ, David
McLane, Graf, Raulerson & Middleton PA, Portsmouth 603 436 2818
david.wolowitz@mclane.com
Recommended in Employment
Specialization: Concentrates in risk management and litigation on behalf of corporations relating to all aspects of employment law, with a particular focus on mental health issues in the workplace. Recent representation of clients includes BAE Systems, Inc., Nike, Inc., Universal Instruments Corp. as well as healthcare and educational organizations, including St. Paul's School.
Prof. Memberships: Admitted to practice before the state and federal courts in New Hampshire and Massachusetts. Member of the New Hampshire and American Bar Associations.
Career: Shareholder and Director since 1991; Guest faculty Harvard Law School, Trial Advocacy Workshop (1984-present).
Personal: 1968, AB, Washington University; 1971, MA, Harvard University; 1975, JD, University of Michigan.

NEW JERSEY

CORPORATE/M&A

CONTENTS: Corporate/M&A p.424; Employment: Mainly Plaintiff p.426; Mainly Defendant p.426; Litigation p.428; Real Estate p.429; Individuals' Profiles p.430.

NEW JERSEY'S TOP SIX
1. Lowenstein Sandler
2. Drinker Biddle & Shanley
3. Greenbaum, Rowe, Smith, Ravin, Davis & Himmel
3. McCarter & English
3. Sills Cummis Radin Tischman Epstein & Gross
4. Pitney, Hardin, Kipp & Szuch

Ranking based on Chambers' research within the state.

All quotes in the text are from interviews with clients and competitors.

OVERVIEW: **Lowenstein Sandler** emerged in Chambers' research as New Jersey's premier firm. A full-service firm, its forte is corporate law, in which the firm earns a top-band ranking. Securities and M&A attorney Peter Ehrenberg attracted particular praise for his expertise in the field. A highly respected litigation department also won recognition for its clutch of fine attorneys. Clients include AT&T and Ernst & Young.

Drinker Biddle & Shanley, in second place, resulted from the merger in 1999 of Philadelphia-based Drinker Biddle & Reath with local firm Shanley & Fisher. This New Jersey practice has swiftly garnered a reputation for excellence. The litigation group was acknowledged as a major player in the state with Tom Campion singled out for both his experience and ability. Interviewees also noted the strength, particularly in leasing matters, of the firm's real estate practice. Clients include Chubb and Morgan Guarantee Trust.

Sharing third place, smaller firm **Greenbaum, Rowe, Smith, Ravin, Davis & Himmel** was credited with having some top-class individuals spread across its practice areas. The real estate group was distinguished for its strength in land use and zoning with Peter Buchsbaum noted for his work in these areas. Commentators also lauded the firm's corporate and litigation practices for their high standards of service and quality. Clients include Merrill Lynch and Russell-Stanley.

One of the largest and oldest firms in the state, **McCarter & English** attracts many high-end clients thanks to its depth of resources. Top ranked for litigation, the firm is considered second to none for products liability matters, while the corporate group has been greatly strengthened by the arrival of attorneys from Krugman & Kailes. Clients include Wachovia Bank and The Prudential Insurance Company of America.

Sills Cummis Radin Tischman Epstein & Gross featured prominently in the New Jersey lists with venture capitalist and M&A specialist Victor Boyajian top ranked in corporate law. Jeffrey Newman leads an experienced team in the real estate department, who are considered to produce outstanding work. Clients include JPMorgan Chase and Dun & Bradstreet.

Ranked fourth, well-established New Jersey firm **Pitney, Hardin, Kipp & Szuch** boasts a prestigious history in the state. Real estate attorney Glenn Geiger was named as a superb transactional lawyer, while Joseph Lunin was commended for his expertise in corporate law. Clients include AT&T Wireless and The Gale Company.

CORPORATE/M&A

NEW JERSEY
Leading firms (Corporate/M&A)

1. **LOWENSTEIN SANDLER PC** *Roseland*
2. **MCCARTER & ENGLISH** *Cherry Hill, Newark*
   SILLS CUMMIS RADIN TISCHMAN *Newark*
3. **DRINKER BIDDLE & SHANLEY LLP** *Florham Park*
   HALE AND DORR *Princeton*
   MORGAN, LEWIS & BOCKIUS LLP *Princeton*
   PITNEY, HARDIN, KIPP & SZUCH LLP *Morristown*
4. **GREENBAUM, ROWE, SMITH,** *Roseland, Woodbridge*

Firms are listed alphabetically in each band.

Lowenstein Sandler PC
see firm details p.841

The Firm: Widely recognized by interviewees as *"one of the most sophisticated corporate practices"* in the state. Out of about 200 lawyers in the firm, nearly a quarter are in the corporate group. The team serves clients at all phases of their development, from capital raising through to stock issuance and M&A. Restructuring is also a core area of practice. Clients valued the *"resources of the firm and the breadth of skills of its attorneys."*

The Lawyers: Chair of the corporate department, **Peter Ehrenberg** (see p.431) focuses on securities law and M&A. Researchers heard high praise from clients who found him *"incredibly smart, creative and responsive."* **Alan Wovsaniker** (see p.432) was recommended for his work in M&A, securities, banking and business planning. He also has experience with PIPE transactions; his recent work in this area has included financings for LifeCell, a public biotech. **John MacKay** (see p.431) has a reputation as *"one of the deans of New Jersey corporate law,"* and advises on stockholder disputes, reorganizations and corporate governance issues.

The Clients: The firm's clients include national and regional public and private companies. The group, led by Ehrenberg, recently acted for Vestcom in its sale for approximately $70 million. The team also represented long-standing client Bergen Brunswig in its $7.5 billion joint venture with AmeriSource Health to form Amerisource-Bergen.

McCarter & English
The Firm: The respected litigation practice at this firm is complemented by what interviewees called *"a strong presence in corporate law."* The firm has recently been bolstered by the addition of 11 attorneys from Krugman & Kailes, which has increased the Newark office's corporate team to about 30. They are supported by colleagues in the firm's other New Jersey office in Cherry Hill, and by bases in five other states. Attorneys here are active on M&A, securities, tax, venture capital and business formation matters.

The Lawyers: A number of lawyers were recommended to researchers. Of these, **Michael Guariglia** was widely respected for his tax expertise. He counsels clients on tax, estate planning and other corporate issues, and has experience before state and federal administrative bodies and courts. **Ken Thompson** was recommended to researchers for his skills as *"a deal-doer."*

The Clients: The firm acts on behalf of major names in such industries as insurance, finance and healthcare. Clients include: Provident Bank; The Prudential Insurance Company of America; Wachovia Bank and Fleet Bank.

CORPORATE/M&A

NEW JERSEY

NEW JERSEY
Leading individuals (Corporate/M&A)

1 BOYAJIAN Victor *Sills Cummis Radin Tischman*, Newark
EHRENBERG Peter *Lowenstein Sandler PC*, Roseland
SORIN David *Hale and Dorr*, Princeton

2 GUARIGLIA Michael *McCarter & English*, Newark
LUNIN Joseph *Pitney, Hardin, Kipp & Szuch LLP*, Morristown
MACKAY John *Lowenstein Sandler PC*, Roseland
THOMPSON Ken *McCarter & English*, Newark
WOVSANIKER Alan *Lowenstein Sandler PC*, Roseland

3 AIELLO John *Giordano Halleran & Ciesla PC*, Middletown
COHEN Steven *Morgan, Lewis & Bockius LLP*, Princeton
DAVIS Alan *Greenbaum, Rowe, Smith*, Woodbridge
FELTON Raymond *Greenbaum, Rowe*, Woodbridge

Individuals are listed alphabetically in each band.

Sills Cummis Radin Tischman Epstein & Gross PC

The Firm: This New Jersey-based firm has extended its reach nationally by establishing offices in New York and, more recently, in California. It has more than 40 attorneys in the New Jersey corporate group, which peers consider to be *"a principal player in the corporate arena."* The group advises on securities and regulatory compliance issues, and has experience with transactions such as complex M&A, divestitures, joint ventures and LBOs.

The Lawyers: Several of the firm's lawyers were described to researchers as *"stellar performers."* **Victor Boyajian** is chair of the capital markets group and corporate technology practice, and is respected for his work in venture capital financing, M&A and spinoffs. The group can also draw on the experience of managing partner Steve Gross.

The Clients: Local, national and international clients range from emerging companies to Fortune 500 businesses. The firm recently acted for Tacit Networks in raising $7.3 million in equity funding. Another recent representation was advising Italian medical technology firm Snia in its $116 million acquisition of CarboMedics, a US mechanical heart valves manufacturer.

Drinker Biddle & Shanley LLP

The Firm: Market observers considered this firm to be a *"homegrown leader"* following its merger with national firm Drinker Biddle & Reath in 1999. The corporate lawyers in New Jersey number about 20, with further support from attorneys with banking and finance expertise. The full-service practice advises on M&A, capital markets, corporate governance and private equity.

The Lawyers: Stewart Lavey is associate head of the corporate and securities group.

The Clients: The group's clients range from NYSE-listed and international companies to locally based midmarket businesses. The firm has a long-standing relationship with The BISYS Group, advising on its acquisitions, and has represented Selective Insurance Group, Kestrel Technologies and Chubb. The team acted for long-term client Degussa in its joint venture with Engineered Carbons.

Hale and Dorr

The Firm: The firm's Princeton office is driven by its corporate and transactional groups, which comprise about 30 lawyers. Amid its broad corporate practice, the firm specializes in representing technology and emerging hi-tech companies in a range of corporate governance, securities, venture capital and M&A issues.

The Lawyers: The group's lawyers were described to researchers as *"smart and client oriented."* Its leading light is **David Sorin**, who competitors dubbed *"one of the best lawyers in the state."* He is active in venture capital and M&A matters, and has wide experience in stock issuance.

The Clients: The team has acted for the former owners of Sensors Unlimited in its acquisition from Finisar. The firm advised New Jersey Technology Council Venture Fund on its financing of KidBiz and acted for Edison Venture Fund on the financing of Maptuit. Clients of the group include Intelligroup, GoAmerica and CollaGenex Pharmaceuticals.

Morgan, Lewis & Bockius LLP

The Firm: This international firm established its Princeton office about a decade ago. Its corporate group of about ten attorneys serves clients in the Massachusetts technology sector, and the pharmaceutical and life sciences industries. Its activities include securities, M&A, venture capital financings and strategic alliances.

The Lawyers: Market sources recommend **Steven Cohen** for his work in venture capital and emerging growth companies matters. He also provides advice on general corporate governance.

The Clients: The firm acted on a $15 million venture capital financing for a pharmaceutical company, and a $12 million financing for biotech company Transave. The group has also worked on several large life science firm's strategic alliances, including representing Aventis in its collaboration with Genta. Further clients include Pharmacia, Princeton Lightwave, PharmaSeq and Paytrust.

Pitney, Hardin, Kipp & Szuch LLP

The Firm: Market sources consider this firm to have *"a track record in corporate transactions."* Its New Jersey offices in Morristown and Red Bank field transactional attorneys who advise on corporate and securities matters such as M&A, tax issues and financing.

The Lawyers: Interviewees acknowledge that **Joseph Lunin**, who represents businesses, partnerships and nonprofit corporations, has *"sound judgment and a wealth of experience."*

The Clients: The firm acts for public and private companies in the technology, financial services, banking, retail, healthcare, pharmaceuticals, manufacturing and service industries, among others.

Greenbaum, Rowe, Smith, Ravin, Davis & Himmel LLP

The Firm: This 12-attorney group operates from two offices in the state, in Woodbridge and Roseland. Interviewees respect the *"quality of their service"* and their breadth of practice. Attorneys are experienced in company formation, financing issues, franchising, M&A and general corporate governance.

The Lawyers: Chair of the corporate department **Alan Davis** advises on financings, business planning and corporate transactions. Clients value his *"outstanding guidance on complex matters."* He represented Hatco in Germany, in the formation of a joint venture and in IP issues. Interviewees also recommend **Raymond Felton** for his extensive experience in corporate and securities law.

The Clients: Recent highlights for the firm included the acquisition and disposition of dry dock facilities in New York and the sale of a money management group to a NYSE-listed financial services business. The firm also advises on the corporate activities of automobile dealerships. Clients include: Sorrento Networks; Russell-Stanley; Entrada Networks and Englert.

Other Notable Practitioners

John Aiello is chair of the corporate and securities department at Giordano Halleran & Ciesla PC. Peers *"think the world"* of his deep knowledge of M&A, securities and financing.

NEW JERSEY

EMPLOYMENT & LABOR LAW

EMPLOYMENT & LABOR LAW — MAINLY PLAINTIFF

NEW JERSEY
Leading firms (Employment: Mainly Plaintiff)

1. SMITH MULLIN *Montclair*
2. JENNINGS SIGMOND *Cherry Hill*
3. GREEN LUCAS SAVITS & MAROSE *West Orange*
   OXFELD COHEN *Newark*
   REITMAN PARSONNET PC *Newark*

Leading individuals (Employment: Mainly Plaintiff)

★ MULLIN Neil *Smith Mullin*, Montclair
  SMITH Nancy *Smith Mullin*, Montclair
1. LUCAS Walter *Green Lucas Savits & Marose*, West Orange
   MCMORAN Bruce *McMoran & O'Connor*, Tinton Falls
2. COHEN Arnold *Oxfeld Cohen*, Newark
   CRANGLE Mary *Jennings Sigmond*, Cherry Hill
   SIMONOFF Howard *Jennings Sigmond*, Cherry Hill
   STRAUSS Jesse *Reitman Parsonnet PC*, Newark
3. OXFELD Sanford *Oxfeld Cohen*, Newark
   WONG Linda *Wong Fleming*, Princeton

Firms and individuals are listed alphabetically in each band.

Smith Mullin
The Firm: This three-lawyer firm was lauded by both defendant attorneys and management clients: *"The ability of these attorneys is outstanding - they are often awarded multimillion dollar judgments."*
The Lawyers: Neil Mullin takes on employment litigation and civil rights cases for plaintiffs. Peers agree that his work is *"exemplary - he is one of the finest plaintiffs' lawyers in the state."* **Nancy Smith** was described as *"dynamic, committed and passionate."* She has recently represented a female Essex County sheriff's officer in an appellate hearing relating to claims of sex discrimination and sexual harassment.

Jennings Sigmond
The Firm: Interviewees agreed that this firm *"excels in union representation."*
The Lawyers: Mary Crangle's extensive practice places her *"right at the top of the game."* **Howard Simonoff** was roundly admired for his union representation. *"He has earned a great reputation following many years of experience,"* according to sources.

Green Lucas Savits & Marose
The Firm: Based in West Orange, this practice was recommended for its handling of *"a large volume of high-profile work."* Five lawyers here work on a range of discrimination matters.
The Lawyers: Competitors endorsed **Walter Lucas** as *"a confident plaintiffs' lawyer who has had some significant victories."* He focuses on employment discrimination, sexual harassment, wrongful discharge and civil rights cases.

Oxfeld Cohen
The Firm: This small outfit in Newark won the admiration of defense attorneys for having a *"clutch of great lawyers."*
The Lawyers: Arnold Cohen is *"well versed in traditional labor law,"* while **Sanford (Sandy) Oxfeld** was described by peers as *"a talented, committed lawyer."* He recently represented a plaintiff in the New Jersey Appellate Court who was seeking additional salary for services he had performed while holding the position of Assistant Counsel in Essex County.

Reitman Parsonnet PC
The Firm: Market observers thought that this Newark firm was *"extremely strong on the union side."*
The Lawyers: Jesse Strauss is the chair of the employment and labor section of the New Jersey State Bar Association. Competitors said Strauss was *"a very talented lawyer whom we all respect."*

Other Notable Practitioners
Bruce McMoran works out of the three-lawyer office of McMoran & O'Connor in Tinton Falls. He represents employees and unions in employment litigation and traditional labor law. Interviewees endorsed him as *"a supreme courtroom lawyer - practical and reasonable."* **Linda Wong** is a name partner of the nine-lawyer Princeton-based practice Wong Fleming PC. She was said to have had *"some notable victories in recent times,"* and was described as being *"very effective."*

EMPLOYMENT & LABOR LAW — MAINLY DEFENDANT

NEW JERSEY
Leading firms (Employment: Mainly Defendant)

1. CARPENTER, BENNETT & MORRISSEY *Newark*
   STANTON HUGHES DIANA CERRA *Morristown*
2. COLLIER, JACOB & MILLS *Somerset*
   GROTTA, GLASSMAN & HOFFMAN *Roseland*
   LUM DANZIS DRASCO & POSITAN *Roseland*
3. BALLARD SPAHR ANDREWS *Voorhees*
   GENOVA, BURNS & VERNOIA *Livingston*
   PITNEY, HARDIN, KIPP & SZUCH LLP *Morristown*

Firms are listed alphabetically in each band.

Carpenter, Bennett & Morrissey
The Firm: The firm has strong leanings toward labor and employment law with approximately 40% of its 80 or so lawyers engaged in this area. Competitors were impressed with its *"good depth,"* while clients appreciated its *"frequency in getting fine results."* The majority of the work is employment law and discrimination matters, with about 20% devoted to labor law including union negotiations and OSHA issues.
The Lawyers: Head of the labor and employment group **Frank Dee** was widely recommended to researchers as *"a supremely gifted lawyer."* Much of his work is employment litigation and ERISA-related. He represented Johnson & Johnson on a discrimination and retaliation matter, and has acted for a large US brokerage company in a case alleging widespread discrimination.
The Clients: AT&T; Lucent Technologies; Rutgers, The State University of New Jersey; Merrill Lynch; Schering-Plough and Avaya.

Stanton Hughes Diana Cerra Mariani & Margello
The Firm: This employment and labor boutique, founded in 1995 by a group of Shanley & Fisher attorneys, has grown from four lawyers to 12. Market sources agree that the firm comprises *"smart and dedicated attorneys,"* and that *"all of the names on the letterhead are first class."* Work here primarily covers all aspects of employment litigation as well as the counseling and training of clients; a smaller amount of labor work is also taken on.
The Lawyers: Interviewees commended **Pat Stanton** as a *"top-drawer lawyer - he understands the details."* He has recently appeared for CBS before the NLRB on union issues, and has counseled a major retailer regarding the employment law implications of acquiring a large number of other stores. Elsewhere, he has been acting for a food wholesaler on three collective bargaining matters. **Richard Mariani** was singled out for his *"great integrity."* He recently represented a township in New Jersey, which was being sued together with its police department over reverse race discrimination and reverse racial harassment.

EMPLOYMENT & LABOR LAW

NEW JERSEY

NEW JERSEY
Leading individuals
(Employment: Mainly Defendant)

[1]
- CARMAGNOLA Domenick *Lum Danzis Drasco*, Roseland
- DEE Frank *Carpenter, Bennett & Morrissey*, Newark
- POSITAN Wayne *Lum Danzis Drasco & Positan*, Roseland
- STANTON Patrick *Stanton Hughes Diana*, Morristown
- SUFLAS Steve *Ballard Spahr Andrews*, Voorhees

[2]
- ALITO Rosemary *McCarter & English*, Newark
- GENOVA Angelo *Genova, Burns & Vernoia*, Livingston
- JACOB Cynthia *Collier, Jacob & Mills*, Somerset
- RIDLEY John *Drinker Biddle & Shanley LLP*, Florham Park

[3]
- EISENBERG Theodore *Grotta, Glassman*, Roseland
- KEYSER Denise *Ballard Spahr Andrews*, Voorhees
- MARIANI Richard *Stanton Hughes Diana*, Morristown

Individuals are listed alphabetically in each band.

Mariani has also represented a public utility in an age discrimination case, and an international engineering company in a disability discrimination case.

The Clients: Gap; CNA Financial; CBS; FirstEnergy; Penske; Pfizer and United States Golf Association.

Collier, Jacob & Mills

The Firm: This labor and employment boutique boasts some 18 attorneys, and is described by observers as *"one of the preeminent practices in the state."* Its employment litigation caseload includes age, sex, race and disability discrimination, as well as whistle-blower, ERISA and wrongful termination claims.

The Lawyers: Firm director **Cynthia Jacob** concentrates her practice on employment litigation. Interviewees described her as *"a seasoned trial lawyer, much in demand for high-profile gender cases."* Jacob also frequently acts in wrongful terminations, benefit disputes as well as race, sex and age discrimination and other civil rights litigation.

The Clients: Local, regional and national corporations.

Grotta, Glassman & Hoffman

The Firm: *"An absolute powerhouse for labor law,"* claimed a host of interviewees in reference to this large boutique firm. Founded in 1966, the firm now also has offices in California and New York, and fields about 54 lawyers across the three states. Observers noted that attorneys take *"a tough stance"* in their cases, which include both employment and labor law matters.

The Lawyers: The firm's managing principal, Theodore (Ted) Eisenberg, was recommended to researchers for carrying on the fine work of name principals Jerold Glassman and Harold Hoffman, and *"serving his clients extremely well."* He advises on all aspects of labor law, including labor relations and compliance issues, wage and hour matters and equal opportunity guidelines.

The Clients: The firm advises national as well as local clients.

Lum Danzis Drasco & Positan

The Firm: This group has recently secured a notable ruling from the New Jersey Supreme Court relating to the sexual harassment case of Gaines v Bellino, and is perceived by peers to have *"a superb reputation."* Interviewees also spoke of the *"top-class individuals"* in the firm's 12-strong employment and labor group.

The Lawyers: Head of the department **Wayne Positan** was endorsed as *"a tough attorney, and supremely confident."* He recently represented Pepsi Bottling Group in a wage and hour case before the New Jersey Supreme Court. He has also acted for the University of Medicine and Dentistry of New Jersey in discrimination and whistle-blower cases. Younger attorney **Domenick Carmagnola** was recommended to researchers as *"a shining star, destined for the top."* He handled the Gaines v Bellino case before the New Jersey Supreme Court, which dealt with employer's responsibilities in sexual harassment cases.

The Clients: State of New Jersey and Marotta Scientific Controls are clients.

Ballard Spahr Andrews & Ingersoll LLP
see firm details p.769

The Firm: This Philadelphia-based firm opened its 40-lawyer office in New Jersey three years ago. The employment and labor group comprises seven attorneys who joined from Archer & Greiner in 2002. Although newly established, interviewees believe that *"they have several top-quality lawyers who will guide them through."*

The Lawyers: Steven Suflas was widely respected as *"a highly ethical lawyer"* in labor and employment matters. He has advised a large international chemical manufacturer before the NLRB on an unfair labor practice issue, and he has negotiated an initial labor agreement for a large hotel chain. **Denise Keyser** has represented the Gannett Company in workplace harassment litigation. She has also handled labor cases for Dupont and the confectionery company Barry Callebaut.

Genova, Burns & Vernoia

The Firm: Market sources acknowledged that the firm is *"extremely proficient"* in employment matters, particularly in relation to the public sector. This boutique of about 25 lawyers represents management in all forms of employment litigation and labor law issues. It also provides counseling to clients in areas such as policy implementation and workplace training.

The Lawyers: Founding partner **Angelo Genova** was regarded as an *"extremely bright and well-connected attorney."* His recent labor caseload has included work on collective bargains for two of the largest agencies in the state: the New Jersey Sports and Exposition Authority and the New Jersey Transit rail system. He has also been appearing before the New Jersey Supreme Court on wage issues in the construction industry.

The Clients: Atlantic Mutual, EDS and ADP are clients.

Pitney, Hardin, Kipp & Szuch LLP

The Firm: The employment group continues the firm's tradition as a preeminent New Jersey practice. About 25 of the firm's 150 attorneys focus on this area, and interviewees informed researchers that both traditional labor law issues and employment litigation were conducted to a high degree of rigor.

The Lawyers: The group is headed by Patrick McCarthy, and while no individual was singled out for specific praise, the entire department was applauded for its uniform excellence.

Other Notable Practitioners

John Ridley joined the large national practice Drinker Biddle & Reath LLP in 2002, and cochairs the firm's labor and employment law group out of the New Jersey office. He was deemed *"highly experienced"* in the representation of employers in class and collective actions in race and age discrimination litigation. Former Carpenter Bennett & Morrissey attorney **Rosemary Alito** is a widely respected figure in the Newark office of the large full-service regional firm, McCarter & English LLP. Interviewees referred to her *"huge reputation as an academic."* She represented former New Jersey Governor Christine Whitman in a wrongful termination suit brought by a superintendent of state police. She also handled an appeal case on behalf of WWOR-TV against a former anchorwoman who alleged sex, religious and disability discrimination.

NEW JERSEY

LITIGATION

LITIGATION

NEW JERSEY
Leading firms
(Litigation: General Commercial)

1
- **DRINKER BIDDLE & SHANLEY LLP** Florham Park
- **GIBBONS, DEL DEO, DOLAN, GRIFFINGER** Newark
- **MCCARTER & ENGLISH** Newark

2
- **GREENBAUM, ROWE, SMITH, RAVIN,** Woodbridge
- **LOWENSTEIN SANDLER PC** Roseland

3
- **GREENBERG DAUBER EPSTEIN** Newark
- **PITNEY, HARDIN, KIPP & SZUCH LLP** Morristown
- **RIKER, DANZIG, SCHERER, HYLAND** Morristown
- **SILLS CUMMIS RADIN TISCHMAN EPSTEIN** Newark
- **WALDER, HAYDEN & BROGEN PA** Roseland

Leading individuals
(Litigation: General Commercial)

1
- **BERRY Andrew** McCarter & English, Newark
- **CAMPION Thomas** Drinker Biddle & Shanley Florham Park
- **GIBBONS John** Gibbons, Del Deo, Dolan, Newark
- **GRIFFINGER Mike** Gibbons, Del Deo, Dolan, Newark
- **LUSTBERG Lawrence** Gibbons, Del Deo, Dolan, Newark
- **ROWE Paul** Greenbaum, Rowe, Smith, Ravin, Woodbridge

2
- **GOLDSTEIN Bruce** Saiber Schlesinger Satz, Newark
- **HARRIS David** Lowenstein Sandler PC, Roseland
- **HAYDEN Joe** Walder, Hayden & Brogen PA, Roseland
- **KROVATIN Gerald** Krovatin & Associates LLC, Newark
- **ORLOFF Larry** Orloff, Lowenbach, Stifelman, Roseland
- **WALDER Justin** Walder, Hayden & Brogen, Roseland

3
- **GREENBERG Melvin** Greenberg Dauber Epstein, Newark
- **HIMMEL Michael** Greenbaum, Rowe, Smith, Woodbridge
- **KRAUS Alan** Latham & Watkins LLP, Newark
- **REILLY Gregory** Lowenstein Sandler PC, Roseland
- **ROLNICK Lawrence** Lowenstein Sandler PC, Roseland

Firms and individuals are listed alphabetically in each band.

Drinker Biddle & Shanley LLP

The Firm: The firm's two New Jersey offices comprise 70 litigators with experience in securities and stockholders' litigation, insurance disputes, products liability and antitrust suits. Competitors note the group's success in attracting high-end work. Practitioners are recommended for their *"efficient"* handling of cases and *"high-quality documents."* The firm also offers alternative dispute resolution (ADR) services for its large client base of domestic and international corporations.

The Lawyers: **Tom Campion** earned plaudits from peers for his *"vast experience and huge ability."* He coheads the firm's professional liability claims practice group and undertakes a wide range of commercial litigation cases. He recently represented Johnson & Johnson in a large products liability suit.

The Clients: The firm advises large and mid-sized public corporations, including a number of Fortune 500 companies.

Gibbons, Del Deo, Dolan, Griffinger & Vecchione

The Firm: A well-developed commercial litigation practice that covers a range of areas including antitrust, employment, securities, products liability, IP and environmental suits. Researchers were told that the firm possesses a *"clutch of fine litigators"* with broad experience in the field. Members also handle ADR proceedings, acting as arbitrator or mediator in business conflicts.

The Lawyers: Hailed as a *"dean of the bar,"* **Mike Griffinger** earned praise for long-standing litigation experience. He focuses primarily on securities cases, commercial disputes and antitrust matters. He recently acted for Hoffman-La Roche in a class action suit and represented Fresenius in fraudulent conveyance litigation. Former Chief Judge of the Third Circuit Court of Appeals, **John Gibbons** is widely respected by peers, who describe him as a *"client magnet."* He heads the firm's ADR group and undertakes a volume of appellate work in both state and federal courts. He acted as liaison defense counsel on litigation arising out of Nazi era slave labor claims and represented two New Jersey hospitals in antitrust matters. Interviewees also commended **Larry Lustberg** as a *"star"* practitioner with a particular niche in criminal and white-collar crime litigation. He chairs the firm's white-collar criminal defense department and has experience in general commercial litigation, and public interest and constitutional law.

The Clients: Aventis; Hilton Hotels; McDonald's; Pfizer; Mitsubishi and Toyota.

McCarter & English

The Firm: One of the oldest and largest of the New Jersey firms, McCarter & English boasts a sizable litigation practice with numerous specialized subgroups. The team particularly excels in toxic tort and mass products liability matters and has been involved in major pharmaceutical, medical, chemical and environmental litigation. Market sources acknowledged the firm as a *"major player"* in the field. Other matters handled include employment claims, fraud cases, insurance defense and securities litigation.

The Lawyers: Chair of the firm's executive committee, **Drew Berry** was lauded as a *"first-rate attorney"* with *"real depth of expertise."* His broad-based practice encompasses complex commercial litigation, mass tort work and products liability cases.

The Clients: Clients range from individuals to Fortune 500 companies. A diverse client base includes a substantial concentration of pharmaceutical, medical and manufacturing interests.

GENERAL COMMERCIAL

Greenbaum, Rowe, Smith, Ravin, Davis & Himmel LLP

The Firm: Approximately half of the firm's 95 attorneys act on commercial litigation matters, including products liability, IP, antitrust, professional liability and white-collar crime. Competitors were impressed by the quality of the team's attorneys, commenting: *"They have several individuals in the top echelon of the profession."*

The Lawyers: Recommended for expertise in antitrust and banking litigation, **Michael Himmel** was named as a *"superb trial attorney."* He heads the white-collar crime and criminal defense practice group. Notable work includes filing a securities class action on behalf of the State of New Jersey pension fund against EDS. He also counseled the US Attorney's Office and the IRS in suits against a number of public corporations and high net-worth individuals. Chair of the litigation department **Paul Rowe** was identified as a *"marvelously talented commercial litigator."* His caseload includes patent litigation, breach of contract claims, construction disputes and stock fraud cases.

The Clients: The firm has advised Fortune 500 companies and financial institutions First Union and Merrill Lynch.

Lowenstein Sandler PC
see firm details p.841

The Firm: A 90-strong litigation practice that covers a diverse range of matters, including products liability, business torts, partnership disputes, copyright claims and antitrust. Commentators acknowledged its concentration of *"fine, able attorneys."*

The Lawyers: Current chair of the litigation group **Dave Harris** (see p.431) elicited praise for his *"ability to get results."* His recent caseload has included several stockholder disputes. He also handles IP litigation, environmental insurance coverage and breach of contract claims.

Researchers were told that general commercial litigator **Larry Rolnick** (see p.432) is *"wise beyond his years."* He has lately acted for the large investment management company, WR Huff Asset Management, in a claim against Deloitte & Touche and represented European media company, KirchMedia, in litigation against Paramount Pictures and Viacom. **Greg Reilly** (see p.432) commands respect as a *"man of intellect and integrity."* He recently represented pharmaceutical company, Merck, in several class actions and derivatives cases and frequently advises Rutgers, The State University of New Jersey on issues such as IP and construction litigation.

The Clients: AT&T; RCM Technologies; Ernst & Young; TNT and CBS.

REAL ESTATE   # NEW JERSEY

Greenberg Dauber Epstein & Tucker
The Firm: The highly regarded practice covers the full gamut of business litigation, including products liability cases, franchise disputes, RICO and antitrust matters, environmental claims and stockholder disputes. The team contains a number of accomplished litigators with government experience. Practitioners have particular expertise in appellate work and have appeared before the New Jersey Supreme Court and the US Court of Claims.
The Lawyers: Mel Greenberg was distinguished as a *"highly rated attorney who can handle a wide range of cases."* He represents corporate clients in business litigation at the state and federal courts and has experience arguing cases before the New Jersey Supreme Court and the New Jersey Appellate Division.
The Clients: The firm represents corporations, entrepreneurs, financial institutions and municipalities.

Pitney, Hardin, Kipp & Szuch LLP
The Firm: This *"comprehensive"* 50-lawyer litigation practice is subdivided into 11 separate practice groups, undertaking work in areas such as products liability, professional liability and general commercial litigation. Clients recommend the group's across-the-board expertise and *"attentive service."* Dennis Kearney oversees the firm's litigation department.

The Clients: Clients range from small local corporations to Fortune 500 companies.

Riker, Danzig, Scherer, Hyland & Perretti LLP
The Firm: This large full-service firm in Morristown is said to be *"on the shortlist of many companies in the area"* for litigation matters. Headed by Gerald Liloia, the 39-strong litigation group covers general commercial litigation, products liability, PI, IP and securities litigation.
The Clients: AT&T, Chubb Group and Schering-Plough.

Sills Cummis Radin Tischman Epstein & Gross PC
The Firm: Interviewees recommended the firm as an *"impressive New Jersey practice with a history of fine litigators."* An *"able"* team, headed by Barry Epstein, undertakes a volume of commercial and business litigation for high-profile clients.
The Clients: Clients include large regional and national companies, many within the pharmaceutical, manufacturing, banking and insurance sectors.

Walder, Hayden & Brogen PA
The Firm: Market sources particularly praised this smaller practice for its strength in white-collar crime work. Nevertheless, this 19-attorney team is equipped to handle a full complement of civil and commercial cases, including environmental torts, professional ethics matters, chancery proceedings and stockholder disputes.
The Lawyers: Interviewees recognized Joe Hayden as a *"top-notch"* litigator with a specialty in criminal defense and white-collar crime. *"Versatile"* Justin Walder was also noted for a broad-based practice that spans complex commercial litigation and white-collar crime.
The Clients: The practice represents both companies and individuals in a range of litigious matters.

Other Notable Practitioners
Alan Kraus (see p.431) at Latham & Watkins LLP was named as a *"fine all-purpose litigator"* by interviewees. His practice emphasizes complex commercial litigation, products liability, professional liability, toxic torts and IP litigation. Senior partner Bruce Goldstein of Saiber Schlesinger Satz & Goldstein LLC in Newark is widely respected as an *"upstanding and honorable attorney"* with experience in white-collar crime, antitrust, and professional liability and business litigation. Peers endorsed Gerry Krovatin of Krovatin & Associates LLC as a *"brilliant lawyer,"* known to represent some *"notable clients."* His reputation lies largely in his *"sterling"* work in criminal defense and white-collar crime cases. Larry Orloff at Roseland firm Orloff, Lowenbach, Stifelman & Siegel is noted as a *"talented securities specialist"* with broad expertise in professional liability matters.

REAL ESTATE

NEW JERSEY
Leading firms (Real Estate)

1
- GREENBAUM, ROWE, SMITH, RAVIN, Woodbridge
- RIKER, DANZIG, SCHERER, HYLAND Morristown

2
- DOLLINGER & DOLLINGER Paramus
- DRINKER BIDDLE & SHANLEY LLP Florham Park
- SILLS CUMMIS RADIN TISCHMAN EPSTEIN Newark

3
- COLE, SCHOTZ, MEISEL, FORMAN Hackensack
- LOWENSTEIN SANDLER PC Roseland
- PITNEY, HARDIN, KIPP & SZUCH LLP Morristown

Leading individuals (Real Estate)

1
- DOLLINGER Martin Dollinger & Dollinger, Paramus
- HULL Gerald Drinker Biddle & Shanley, Florham Park

2
- MORRISON Victoria Riker, Danzig, Scherer, Morristown
- NEWMAN Jeffrey Sills Cummis Radin Tischman, Newark

3
- BUCHSBAUM Peter Greenbaum, Rowe, Smith, Woodbridge
- KAHN Richard Cole, Schotz, Meisel, Forman &, Hackensack
- SCHACHTER Robert Greenbaum, Rowe, Woodbridge

4
- GEIGER Glenn Pitney, Hardin, Kipp & Szuch, Morristown
- STEINBERG Joseph Lowenstein Sandler PC, Roseland

Firms and individuals are listed alphabetically in each band.

Greenbaum, Rowe, Smith, Ravin, Davis & Himmel LLP
The Firm: This large full-service firm operates from offices in Woodbridge and Roseland. Market observers recognized the group's proficiency in real estate matters. It fields *"extremely talented real estate attorneys."* Approximately 20 of its lawyers are active in development financing and zoning issues.
The Lawyers: Peter Buchsbaum heads the firm's land use group and peers describe him as *"one of the go-to guys."* His recent caseload has involved rezoning and regulatory approvals for private development. He represented the New Jersey Farm Bureau in its challenge to the Township of East Amwell's 10-acre downzoning ordinance. He has also represented the City of Long Branch in the formulation of redevelopment plans. Robert Schachter chairs the firm's real estate department and was dubbed by competitors as *"the complete lawyer."* His recent caseload has included a joint venture among three developers active in downtown Englewood, NJ. He also advised the owner of four office buildings in the Edision/Woodbridge Metropark area on leasing issues.

The Clients: New Jersey Builders Association; Toll Brothers; Pulte Homes; K Hovnanian; City of Long Branch and New Jersey Farm Bureau.

Riker, Danzig, Scherer, Hyland & Perretti LLP
The Firm: This full-service 150-lawyer outfit operates out of Trenton and has its headquarters in Morristown. Competitors commend the group of five attorneys as *"a highly visible presence"* in the market, which can draw upon the firm's extensive resources.
The Lawyers: Interviewees singled out Vicky Morrison for *"her ability to pinpoint the important issues of a case, and to get the job done."* Her practice comprises transactional, development and financing issues. She is also well versed in related tax and bankruptcy matters. The team can also draw on the support of well-respected Peter Berkley.
The Clients: Fortune 500 companies, banks and financial institutions, and owners and tenants.

NEW JERSEY

REAL ESTATE

Dollinger & Dollinger
The Firm: The firm is home to a nine-attorney group that interviewees were quick to recommend for *"great knowledge and understanding of the market."* Real estate work undertaken includes acquisitions and dispositions, leasings and financings. Zoning, planning and land use also form part of the firm's workload.
The Lawyers: Martin Dollinger was consistently endorsed by peers for his *"comprehensive knowledge of the law and reasonable approach."* His recent caseload has included office lease transactions for KPMG nationwide. He also represented a landlord of Gotham Industrial Park who leased premises to Unisys. Elsewhere, he has worked on a zoning project for the homebuilder K Hovnanian Companies.
The Clients: KPMG; Snapple Beverage; K Hovnanian Companies and Mac Company.

Drinker Biddle & Shanley LLP
The Firm: The firm has two offices in this state, in Florham Park and Princeton, which contain about 150 attorneys. Competitors commended the group as *"excellent in real estate, particularly for leasing matters."*
The Lawyers: Cohead of the firm's real estate practice group, **Gerald Hull** was described by interviewees as *"a class act,"* prominent in real estate financing. He has represented clients in the acquisition of the Newark Legal and Communications Center, and advised on the sale of the assets of Bellemead Development and on the $80 million sale of a Park Avenue corporate complex.
The Clients: Morgan Guarantee Trust; Chubb; Matrix Realty Group and The Gale Company.

Sills Cummis Radin Tischman Epstein & Gross PC
The Firm: This large full-service firm has added offices in New York and San Francisco to its bases in Newark and Atlantic City. Some 20 lawyers cover a broad range of real estate matters such as retail and office leasing, shopping center and resort development, finance, litigation, zoning and land use. Clients recommended the team to researchers, with one stating: *"They have a proven track record and do some outstanding work for us."*
The Lawyers: Chair of the firm's real estate department, **Jeffrey Newman** has a broad practice that encompasses transaction, litigation and finance-related matters. He has litigated for Bloomingdale's and for Target Stores, the latter of which he also represents in leasings.
The Clients: Federated Department Stores; Target Stores; Novartis; JPMorgan Chase; Citicorp; Toys 'R' Us; International Flavors and Fragrances and Dun & Bradstreet.

Cole, Schotz, Meisel, Forman & Leonard PA
The Firm: Currently in its 75th year, the Hackensack-based firm has some 13 partners and four associates focused on real estate matters and can draw on the support of an office in New York. Interviewees described its attorneys as *"exemplary"* in their work on acquisitions and sales, leasing, development, financing and land use.
The Lawyers: Market sources commended **Richard Kahn** as *"one of the state's smartest and sharpest lawyers."* He is experienced in shopping center development and supermarket leasing.
The Clients: Landlords; tenants; lending institutions; developers and property owners and investors.

Lowenstein Sandler PC
see firm details p.841
The Firm: This is one of the largest firms in New Jersey with almost 200 attorneys. Competitors suggested the firm's overall reputation ensures it a place on *"a large amount of high-end work."* The real estate department operates from the firm's two offices in the state, in Roseland and Somerville. Attorneys are active in leasing, and acquisitions of industrial and residential real estate, and advise owners and property managers in all phases of real estate property transactions.
The Lawyers: Cochair of the real estate group firmwide, **Joseph Steinberg** (see p.432) combines his *"great expertise"* in asset-based and mortgage lending transactions with leasing, and land use and zoning issues. His recent caseload has included an application for a fast-food operation in Fair Lawn, NJ, and the development of a 306-unit housing venture in Englewood, NJ.
The Clients: Fortune 500 companies, lessors and lessees, and owners and developers.

Pitney, Hardin, Kipp & Szuch LLP
The Firm: Researchers were informed that this firm *"has a great group of real estate lawyers."* About 150 attorneys work out of Morristown, giving the firm a massive presence in the state, while around 15 attorneys concentrate on real estate matters. Active across the range of transactional and financing issues, the firm was singled out for its strength in land use, zoning and development.
The Lawyers: Peers respected **Glenn Geiger** for his work in transactional and land use matters. He has been working on two high-profile land use cases: he has represented St. Mary's Abbey in a zoning matter in the Washington Valley Historic District, and advised Canfield Building Associates in its proposed development of an 800-townhouse project in the Mine Hill Township, Morris County.
The Clients: AT&T Wireless; K Hovnanian Companies; The Gale Company and Matzel & Mumford.

Leaders in New Jersey

AIELLO, John
Giordano Halleran & Ciesla PC, Middletown 732 714 3900
Recommended in Corporate/M&A

ALITO, Rosemary
McCarter & English, Newark 973 622 4444
Recommended in Employment

BERRY, Andrew
McCarter & English, Newark 973 622 4444
Recommended in Litigation

BOYAJIAN, Victor
Sills Cummis Radin Tischman Epstein & Gross, A Professional Corporation, Newark 973 643 7000
Recommended in Corporate/M&A

BUCHSBAUM, Peter
Greenbaum, Rowe, Smith, Ravin, Davis & Himmel LLP, Woodbridge 732 549 5600
Recommended in Real Estate

CAMPION, Thomas
Drinker Biddle & Shanley LLP, Florham Park 973 360 1100
Recommended in Litigation

CARMAGNOLA, Domenick
Lum Danzis Drasco & Positan, Roseland 973 403 9000
Recommended in Employment

COHEN, Arnold
Oxfeld Cohen, Newark 973 642 0161
Recommended in Employment

COHEN, Steven
Morgan, Lewis & Bockius LLP, Princeton 609 919 6600
Recommended in Corporate/M&A

CRANGLE, Mary
Jennings Sigmond, Cherry Hill 856 667 6950
Recommended in Employment

DAVIS, Alan
Greenbaum, Rowe, Smith, Ravin, Davis & Himmel LLP, Woodbridge 732 549 5600
Recommended in Corporate/M&A

DEE, Frank
Carpenter, Bennett & Morrissey, Newark 973 622 7711
Recommended in Employment

DOLLINGER, Martin
Dollinger & Dollinger, Paramus 201 599 8400
Recommended in Real Estate

NEW JERSEY

EHRENBERG, Peter H
Lowenstein Sandler PC, Roseland
973 597 2350
pehrenberg@lowenstein.com
Recommended in Corporate/M&A
Specialization: Chair of the Corporate Department and M&A and Corporate Finance Practice, has extensive experience in securities, mergers and acquisitions, and business law. He represents issuers and investment firms in the private and public offering of debt and equity securities, and participates in complex merger and acquisition transactions, recapitalizations, employment benefit matters, secured and unsecured borrowings, and securities offerings.
Prof. Memberships: New Jersey State Bar Association (Director, Corporate and Business Law Section and Chair, Securities Law Committee); American Bar Association.
Career: Corporate, M&A, and Securities Law; 'All-Star Lawyer Deal Makers' by NJBIZ; New Jersey Bar and Federal Courts (1973).
Publications: 'Corporate Governance ebook:' provides Sarbanes-Oxley regulations including Regulation FD, Reporting Obligations, Corporate Governance Proposals and Compliance Recommendations;' 'Structuring the Transaction When the Tax Advisors Leave the Room,' New Jersey Lawyer; 'Why Private Companies Should Not Ignore the Sarbanes-Oxley Act,' Wall Street Lawyer; 'The Unintended Victim: Ramifications Of The Sarbanes-Oxley Act For Private Companies,' Metropolitan Corporate Counsel; 'Peter H. Ehrenberg: An Experienced Securities Lawyer Sheds Light On The New Corporate Governance Reform Statute,' Metropolitan Corporate Counsel.
Personal: JD, Yale University (1973) and Editor of the Yale Law Journal; BA, Trinity College (Phi Beta Kappa)(1969).

EISENBERG, Theodore
Grotta, Glassman & Hoffman, Roseland
973 992 4800
Recommended in Employment

FELTON, W Raymond
Greenbaum, Rowe, Smith, Ravin, Davis & Himmel LLP, Woodbridg
732 549 5600
Recommended in Corporate/M&A

GEIGER, Glenn
Pitney, Hardin, Kipp & Szuch LLP, Morristown 973 966 6300 New York City: 212 687 6000
Recommended in Real Estate

GENOVA, Angelo
Genova, Burns & Vernoia, Livingston
973 533 0777
Recommended in Employment

GIBBONS, John
Gibbons, Del Deo, Dolan, Griffinger & Vecchione, Newark 973 596 4500
Recommended in Litigation

GOLDSTEIN, Bruce
Saiber Schlesinger Satz & Goldstein, LLC, Newark 973 622 3333
Recommended in Litigation

GREENBERG, Melvin
Greenberg Dauber Epstein & Tucker, Newark 973 643 3700
Recommended in Litigation

GRIFFINGER, Mike
Gibbons, Del Deo, Dolan, Griffinger & Vecchione, Newark 973 596 4500
Recommended in Litigation

GUARIGLIA, Michael
McCarter & English, Newark
973 622 4444
Recommended in Corporate/M&A

HARRIS, David L
Lowenstein Sandler PC, Roseland
973 597 2378
dharris@lowenstein.com
Recommended in Litigation
Specialization: Chair-elect of the Litigation Department. Has more than 23 years of trial and appellate experience in business litigation emphasizing trade secret, trademark, labor and employment insurance coverage, as well as civil rights litigation.
Prof. Memberships: ACLU; Trial Lawyers of NJ; NJ Commission on Racism and Racial and Religious Violence (Commissioner, 1990-1994); ABA (Intellectual Property Committee); NJ State, Garden State, National and Essex County Bar Associations.
Career: Business Litigation; Top Ten Litigators in NJ, National Law Journal; NJ Supreme Court (1979), US District Court, District of NJ (1979), Pennsylvania Supreme Court (1979), US Court of Appeals, Third Circuit (1982), US District Court, Eastern District of NY (1987), US Court of Appeals, Fourth Circuit (1987), US Court of Appeals, Sixth Circuit (1993) and US District Court, Southern District of NY (2001).
Publications: 'Preparing Experts with Kumho in Mind,' The Practical Litigator; 'The Absolute Pollution Exclusion: Subterfuge, Confusion and Fair Resolution,' ABA Monograph; 'Meet Legal Needs of Poor Through Organization, Not Mandatory Pro Bono,' NJ Law Journal; 'Protecting Trade Secrets: Steps to Take When Information is Firmly Lodged in Employees' Heads,' NJ Lawyer.
Personal: JD, Rutgers University Law School (1979); MEd(1972) and BA (1970), Pennsylvania State University.

HAYDEN, Joe
Walder, Hayden & Brogen P.A., Roseland
973 992 5300
Recommended in Litigation

HIMMEL, Michael
Greenbaum, Rowe, Smith, Ravin, Davis & Himmel LLP, Woodbridge
732 549 5600
Recommended in Litigation

HULL, Gerald
Drinker Biddle & Shanley LLP, Florham Park 973 360 1100
Recommended in Real Estate

JACOB, Cynthia
Collier, Jacob & Mills, Somerset
732 560 7100
Recommended in Employment

KAHN, Richard
Cole, Schotz, Meisel, Forman & Leonard, P.A., Hackensack
201 489 3000
Recommended in Real Estate

KEYSER, Denise
Ballard Spahr Andrews & Ingersoll LLP, Voorhees 856 761 3400
Recommended in Employment

KRAUS, Alan E
Latham & Watkins LLP, Newark
973 639 7293
alan.kraus@lw.com
Recommended in Litigation
Specialization: Partner, Litigation Department. Extensive trial experience in complex litigation, including product liability, toxic tort and commercial litigation. Has represented RJ Reynolds Tobacco Company, The Prudential Insurance Company, IBM, Campbell Soup Company and PriceWaterhouse Coopers. Also has experience in securities fraud, patent litigation, professional malpractice, employment, consumer fraud and class action matters.
Prof. Memberships: American College of Trial Lawyers.
Publications: Co-author of New Jersey Practice: Appellate Practice and Procedure.
Personal: JD, University of North Carolina School of Law, with high honors, 1978. BA, Wesleyan University, with high honors, 1975.

KROVATIN, Gerald
Krovatin & Associates LLC, Newark
973 424 9777
Recommended in Litigation

LUCAS, Walter
Green Lucas Savits & Marose, West Orange 973 736 4949
Recommended in Employment

LUNIN, Joseph
Pitney, Hardin, Kipp & Szuch LLP, Morristown 973 966 6300 New York City: 212 687 6000
Recommended in Corporate/M&A

LUSTBERG, Lawrence
Gibbons, Del Deo, Dolan, Griffinger & Vecchione, Newark 973 596 4500
Recommended in Litigation

MACKAY 2ND, John R
Lowenstein Sandler PC, Roseland
973 597 2416
jmackay@lowenstein.com
Recommended in Corporate/M&A
Specialization: Has more than 30 years of experience in business law and handles corporate and business planning and counseling matters, including mergers, acquisitions and sales of business corporations; organization and operation of business corporations and banking associations; resolution of shareholder disputes; and structuring of shareholder relationships. He is the author of the definitive guide to New Jersey Corporate Law, New Jersey Business Corporations: Law and Practice (2nd ed. 1996).
Prof. Memberships: New Jersey Corporation Law Revision Commission. Chair (1978-1987) and Secretary (1969-74); ABA Committee on Corporate Laws; President of Rutgers University School of Law Alumni Association (1980-81); Trustee for United Way of Essex and West Hudson (1979-86); American, New Jersey State and Essex County Bar Associations; former Adjunct Faculty at Rutgers University School of Law and Seton Hall University School of Law.
Career: Corporate, M&A, and Securities Law category; New Jersey Bar (1965).
Publications: 'Court Adopts Modified Business Judgment Rule,' New Jersey Law Journal.
Personal: LLB (with honors), Rutgers University School of Law (1965) and Editor in Chief of the Rutgers Law Review; AB, Bowdoin College (1956).

MARIANI, Richard
Stanton Hughes Diana Cerra Mariani & Margello, Morristown 973 656 1600
Recommended in Employment

MCMORAN, Bruce
McMoran & O'Connor, Tinton Falls
732 758 8181
Recommended in Employment

MORRISON, Victoria
Riker, Danzig, Scherer, Hyland & Perretti LLP, Morristown 973 538 0800
Recommended in Real Estate

MULLIN, Neil
Smith Mullin, Montclair 973 783 7607
Recommended in Employment

NEWMAN, Jeffrey
Sills Cummis Radin Tischman Epstein & Gross, A Professional Corporation, Newark 973 643 7000
Recommended in Real Estate

ORLOFF, Larry
Orloff, Lowenbach, Stifelman & Siegel, Roseland 973 622 6200
Recommended in Litigation

OXFELD, Sanford
Oxfeld Cohen, Newark 973 642 0161
Recommended in Employment

POSITAN, Wayne
Lum Danzis Drasco & Positan, Roseland
973 403 9000
Recommended in Employment

NEW JERSEY

REILLY, Gregory B
Lowenstein Sandler PC, Roseland
973 597 2460
greilly@lowenstein.com
Recommended in Litigation
Specialization: Chair of the firm's Litigation Department. Has more than 25 years of litigation experience representing United States and foreign companies and their principals, with an emphasis in federal and state court injunction and damage actions in the areas of business torts, employment law and corporate governance. He has represented clients at jury trials, bench trials, administrative proceedings and appeals. He has advised both public and private corporations concerning compliance with state and federal governmental legislation and regulations regarding employment relationships. Coordinates the firm's representation of Rutgers, the State University of New Jersey, and has represented Rutgers, as a state entity, in connection with numerous cases pertaining to constitutional issues.
Prof. Memberships: National Association of College and University Attorneys; American, New Jersey State and Essex County Bar Associations.
Career: New Jersey and Federal Courts (1973), the US Court of Appeals, Third Circuit and US Tax Court (1975).
Publications: A Practical Guide to New Jersey Employment Law: The Employer's Resource, 'Managing the Workforce: Private Employees' Right to Organize and the New Jersey Anti-Injunction Act.'
Personal: JD, Rutgers University School of Law (1973); BA Princeton University (1967).

RIDLEY, John
Drinker Biddle & Shanley LLP, Florham Park 973 360 1100
Recommended in Employment

ROLNICK, Lawrence M
Lowenstein Sandler PC, Roseland
973 597 2468
lrolnick@lowenstein.com
Recommended in Litigation
Specialization: Chair of the Securities Litigation Practice. Has extensive experience in complex commercial litigation, with emphasis in securities and class action litigation. He has represented public companies in class action litigation, institutional investors in securities litigation and directors and officers in defense of alleged breach of fiduciary duty claims. He has successfully argued before the New Jersey Supreme Court on questions of first impression on securities law issues and defended clients in actions brought by the SEC, NASD and NYSE.
Prof. Memberships: New Jersey State Bar Association's Securities Litigation and Regulatory Enforcement Committee (Co-founder and Chair); New Jersey State and American Bar Associations; Trustee of the Federal Bar Association, District of New Jersey.
Career: New York Bar (1985), the US District Court, Southern and Eastern Districts of New York (1991) the New Jersey Bar and the US District Court, District of New Jersey (1992), the US Court of Appeals, First and Second Circuit (1999).
Publications: 'Complex Litigation: Defending Consumer Fraud Class Actions,' New Jersey Law Journal.
Personal: JD, Rutgers University School of Law (cum laude, 1984) and Officer of Rutgers Law Review; BA, Rutgers University (with high honors, 1981) and Henry Rutgers Scholar.

ROWE, Paul
Greenbaum, Rowe, Smith, Ravin, Davis & Himmel LLP, Woodbridge
732 549 5600
Recommended in Litigation

SCHACHTER, Robert
Greenbaum, Rowe, Smith, Ravin, Davis & Himmel LLP, Woodbridge
732 549 5600
Recommended in Real Estate

SIMONOFF, Howard
Jennings Sigmond, Cherry Hill
856 667 6950
Recommended in Employment

SMITH, Nancy
Smith Mullin, Montclair 973 783 7607
Recommended in Employment

SORIN, David
Hale and Dorr, Princeton 609 750 7600
Recommended in Corporate/M&A

STANTON, Patrick
Stanton Hughes Diana Cerra Mariani & Margello, Morristown 973 656 1600
Recommended in Employment

STEINBERG, Joseph LeVow
Lowenstein Sandler PC, Roseland
973 597 2518
jsteinberg@lowenstein.com
Recommended in Real Estate
Specialization: Co-Chair of the firm's Real Estate Practice. Has more than 40 years of experience in financial and real estate transactions. He represents financial institutions in term, revolving, asset-based and mortgage lending transactions, as well as in 'workouts' within and outside formal insolvency proceedings. His real estate practice includes assisting clients in leasing, acquisitions, sale and mortgage transactions, as well as with related environmental problems. He regularly appears before governmental agencies, particularly municipal planning and zoning boards.
Prof. Memberships: Harvard Alumni Association, Regional Director (1996-99); Harvard Club of New Jersey, President (1980-81); President of the New Jersey Association on Correction (1972-74); New Jersey Department of Institutions and Agencies (Ad Hoc Committee on Children's Services); Trustee of Pitzer College in Claremont, CA (1986-89); New Jersey State, American and Essex County Bar Associations.
Career: New Jersey Bar (1960) and the US Supreme Court (1996).
Personal: LLB, Harvard University School of Law (cum laude)(1959); BA, Harvard University (magna cum laude and Phi Beta Kappa)(1956).

STRAUSS, Jesse
Reitman Parsonnet PC, Newark
973 642 0885
Recommended in Employment

SUFLAS, Steve
Ballard Spahr Andrews & Ingersoll LLP, Voorhees 856 761 3400
Recommended in Employment

THOMPSON, Ken
McCarter & English, Newark
973 622 4444
Recommended in Corporate/M&A

WALDER, Justin
Walder, Hayden & Brogen P.A., Roseland
973 992 5300
Recommended in Litigation

WONG, Linda
Wong Fleming, Princeton 609 951 9520
Recommended in Employment

WOVSANIKER, Alan
Lowenstein Sandler PC, Roseland
973 597 2564
awovsaniker@lowenstein.com
Recommended in Corporate/M&A
Specialization: Co-Chair of the Closely Held Business Services Practice, has 25 years of experience in mergers and acquisitions, business planning, securities regulation and corporate finance. He successfully consolidated seven private companies into Vestcom International, consummating the initial public offering. He also successfully consolidated 11 private companies into Consolidated Delivery & Logistics and consummated the initial public offering.
Prof. Memberships: District V-C Ethics Committee, Supreme Court (1994-98) and Chair (1997-98); Trustee of the Essex County Bar Association(1996-99), Chair of the Essex County Bar Association's Corporate Law Committee (1999-present) and Chair of the Essex County Bar Association's Banking Law Committee (1994-97); New Jersey State and American Bar Associations; former Adjunct Faculty of Rutgers University Law School and Seton Hall University Law.
Career: New Jersey Bar in 1977.
Publications: 'Ten Ways to Succeed and Prosper When Selling Your Business', Commerce Magazine; 'Equity Compensation: Cash-Poor Employers Have Options', The National Law Journal; 'Update on the Sarbanes-Oxley Act: SEC Adopts Final Rules Relating to Corporate Codes of Ethics, Audit Committee Financial Experts and New Form 8-K Disclosure.'
Personal: JD, Harvard University (magna cum laude, 1977); AB, Brown University (magna cum laude and Phi Beta Kappa, 1974).

NEW MEXICO — CORPORATE/M&A

CONTENTS: Corporate/M&A p.433; Employment: Mainly Plaintiff p.434; Mainly Defendant p.434; Litigation: General Commercial p.435; Real Estate p.437; Individuals' Profiles p.438.

MEXICO'S TOP THREE
1. Rodey, Dickason, Sloan, Akin & Robb
2. Modrall, Sperling, Roehl, Harris & Sisk
3. Keleher & McLeod

Ranking based on Chambers' research within the state.

All quotes in the text are from interviews with clients and competitors.

OVERVIEW: Ranked first, the 60-lawyer firm **Rodey, Dickason, Sloan, Akin & Robb** is among New Mexico's largest full-service practices. Interviewees praised the firm's strength across the board, particularly noting its prowess in litigation, where the group regularly appears in both state and federal courts. Bruce Hall is considered to be the linchpin of the group and is respected for his effective, engaging style. In corporate, the firm also acts for research organizations in the state, such as Los Alamos National Laboratories, which bud hi-tech spin-offs. It represents the University of New Mexico as well as national corporate clients such as AT&T and GM.

Modrall, Sperling, Roehl, Harris & Sisk, in second place, operates from four New Mexico offices in Albuquerque, Santa Fe, Las Cruces and Roswell, offering a full range of legal services. The firm was felt to shine especially in the areas of corporate law and commercial litigation. Bonnie Paisley was singled out for her prowess in securities work. The corporate practice group has a high profile in M&A and strategic planning matters. Clients include BP Amoco, Bank of America and Burlington Resources.

Albuquerque-based **Keleher & McLeod** earns widespread praise for its sensitivity to local needs and issues. The large full-service firm offers noteworthy expertise in public utility and regulatory work and is seen to be steadily expanding its base of private sector clients. Key clients include the largest utility in the state, PNM (Public Service Company of New Mexico), Wells Fargo and RJ Reynolds.

CORPORATE/M&A

NEW MEXICO
Leading firms (Corporate/M&A)
1. **MODRALL, SPERLING, ROEHL** Albuquerque
   SUTIN, THAYER & BROWNE Albuquerque
2. **KELEHER & MCLEOD PA** Albuquerque
   RODEY, DICKASON, SLOAN, AKIN Albuquerque

Leading individuals (Corporate/M&A)
1. **BUCHHOLTZ David** Sutin, Thayer, Albuquerque
   MOORE Charles Keleher & McLeod PA, Albuquerque
2. **BARLOW Richard** Barlow & Wilcox PA, Albuquerque
   PAISLEY Bonnie Modrall, Sperling, Roehl, Albuquerque
3. **BENDICKSEN Perry** Sutin, Thayer & Browne, Santa Fe
   BETZER Stan Betzer Roybal & Eisenberg, Albuquerque
   BROWNE Graham Sutin, Thayer & Browne, Albuquerque
   PARKER James Modrall, Sperling, Roehl, Albuquerque
4. **BROWN Duane** Modrall, Sperling, Roehl, Albuquerque
   HEYMAN Robert Sutin, Thayer & Browne, Albuquerque
   MCDONALD Randall Foster Johnson, Albuquerque
   SCHULER Alison Schuler, Messersmith, Albuquerque

Firms and individuals are listed alphabetically in each band.

Modrall, Sperling, Roehl, Harris & Sisk PA

The Firm: Market sources credit the firm with having *"unrivaled breadth in corporate law,"* and point out that it has built up a *"sophisticated client base."* The firm's strong tax and finance capability reinforces its corporate backbone. Attorneys here are prominent in big-ticket transactions, both locally and regionally, and are noted for being *"politically well connected."* They advise on all aspects of forming and managing businesses, providing contacts for local venture capital providers or angel investors and acting for established businesses on bonds, securities and stockholder agreements. They are *"one of the few groups in New Mexico truly able to handle M&A matters,"* according to clients. Attorneys are also heavily involved in strategic planning matters for large clients, both inside and outside of the state.

The Lawyers: Bonnie Paisley's prowess in the securities arena impressed many interviewees. She advises New Mexico's hi-tech companies, whose businesses include software and hardware development and telecom infrastructure, on start-up issues and the tax benefits of public financings. Jim Parker, *"the kind of guy that everyone knows well,"* advises clients primarily on tax matters and employee benefits-related work. An all-arounder, he was endorsed as *"a long-standing figure in the corporate market."* Duane Brown is widely considered to be *"possibly the best bond lawyer in the state."* Chair of the firm's public finance group, Brown is also counsel to New Mexico Finance Authority, which issues pooled and stand-alone bond issues, and acts for the New Mexico Hospital Equipment Loan Council.

The Clients: Manufacturers particularly are attracted to the firm's strength in natural resources issues. The firm also advises technology start-ups and established businesses, and healthcare companies.

Sutin, Thayer & Browne

The Firm: Corporate and commercial work is an area in which these lawyers shine. Peers pointed to the firm's *"significant presence,"* advising on M&A and in complex corporate work. Fourteen out of a total of about 20 partners are business/corporate lawyers, advising public and private firms and venture capitalists on planning and operations, structured and commercial financings and M&A. Attorneys here also act on securities issues, due diligence and employee benefit-related issues.

The Lawyers: Commentators cite David Buchholtz as *"a true bond specialist"* whose work centers on advice to issuers and underwriters of public finance. A *"reliable and efficient attorney,"* he advises on a wide variety of securities-related work. Perry Bendicksen in the Santa Fe office focuses primarily on venture capital, municipal finance and M&A. He advises out-of-state lenders on compliance with state consumer finance laws and has represented several major companies that have located facilities in New Mexico, assisting them with industrial revenue bonds and other incentives. Graham Browne is *"a key figure"* in business and tax planning and restructuring. He represented a privately owned local engineering firm in its $75 million acquisition by a large national company. *"Incredibly bright"* Robert Heyman represents major local banks as well as out-of-state financial institutions on regulatory and transactional matters. He also leads the firm's work in bond counseling for the State of New Mexico and other agencies.

Keleher & McLeod PA

The Firm: The firm's strong background in the public utilities sector has afforded its attorneys opportunities to handle substantial corporate matters. Attorneys act as primary outside counsel to the Public Service Company of New Mexico (PNM), one of the largest utilities in the

NEW MEXICO

EMPLOYMENT & LABOR LAW

region, and are credited with producing *"quality work."* The firm is also continuing to expand its corporate client base, acting on contract negotiations, financings and antitrust, tax and employment issues. Interviewees singled out lawyers here for their success in *"taking on complex cases and regulatory matters."*

The Lawyers: The firm's *"business guru,"* **Charles Moore**, has extensive experience in asset sales and purchases, corporate financings and, particularly, in securities matters. He recently handled an attempted multibillion dollar utility companies merger. Sources described him as a *"top-notch attorney,"* and spoke of his *"integrity, and hard-working approach."*

The Clients: Access Anytime Bancorp; TPL; GE Capital; Bankers Trust; Acorn Ventures; New Mexico State Investment Council and Laguna Industries.

Rodey, Dickason, Sloan, Akin & Robb PA

The Firm: Commentators noted that this firm, one of the largest in New Mexico with more than 60 attorneys on staff, has the capacity to handle major M&A projects. It can draw upon the diverse expertise and experience of colleagues in such areas as litigation and tax. The corporate team has a growing reputation for its work in the securities and bonds arena, owing to national laboratories in the state budding a number of hi-tech spin-offs requiring finance.

The Lawyers: John Salazar chairs the firm's business department.

The Clients: Bank of the West; Wells Fargo; Las Vegas Telecom; Diamond Tail Estates; GE; Mississippi Potash; Peabody Energy; Sun Healthcare Group; University of New Mexico and AT&T.

Other Notable Practitioners

Market observers agree that **Richard Barlow** of Barlow & Wilcox PA *"continually produces superior work"* in corporate matters. Best known for his tax expertise, Barlow also advises on employee benefits and trusts, and attracts clients from outside New Mexico as well as local firms. **Stan Betzer** of Betzer Roybal & Eisenberg PC chiefly takes on securities matters, M&A and stockholder disputes. As general counsel to Santa Fe Natural Tobacco Company, much of his time was spent advising on its $350 million acquisition by RJ Reynolds in 2002. **Randy McDonald** of Foster Johnson McDonald Lucero Koinis LLP is a corporate lawyer with an IP specialty focused toward technology matters. Interviewees pointed to his *"impressive ability"* across a practice that is increasingly broad in scope. *"Sharp"* **Alison Schuler** of Schuler, Messersmith, Daly & Lansdowne stands out for her *"effective handling"* of corporate and commercial matters.

EMPLOYMENT & LABOR LAW — MAINLY PLAINTIFF

NEW MEXICO
Leading firms
(Employment: Mainly Plaintiff)
1. TINKLER & BENNETT Santa Fe

Leading individuals
(Employment: Mainly Plaintiff)
1. KEY Chris Sole Practitioner, Albuquerque

Firms and individuals are listed alphabetically in each band.

Tinkler & Bennett

The Firm: Market observers acknowledge that this small Santa Fe-based boutique has *"won some pretty prominent cases,"* which ensure its reputation as *"a top plaintiffs' firm."* Attorneys take on sexual harassment cases, personal injury and professional malpractice cases. Mediation work is also entered into by both partners.

The Lawyers: Stephen Tinkler and Merit Bennett are the firm's partners.

Other Notable Practitioners

Chris Key operates as a sole practitioner focused on plaintiffs' work. Interviewees singled him out as an employment litigator who *"thinks through his cases and simplifies them in a way that your average jury can understand."* Possessed of a celebrated presence in the courtroom, he *"is not afraid of a battle."*

EMPLOYMENT & LABOR LAW — MAINLY DEFENDANT

NEW MEXICO
Leading firms
(Employment: Mainly Defendant)
1. GILKEY & STEPHENSON PA Albuquerque
2. NOEDING & MOODY PC Albuquerque
   RODEY, DICKASON, SLOAN, AKIN Albuquerque

Firms are listed alphabetically in each band.

Gilkey & Stephenson PA

The Firm: This boutique specializes in the representation of employers in the defense of employment-related litigation. The firm also advises on labor relations, and engages in counseling clients on personnel policies and procedures. Additionally attorneys engage in a lot of work with credit unions and financial institutions. Peers agree that the firm enjoys a *"great reputation,"* which is boosted by its success rate in both federal and state courts.

The Lawyers: Duane Gilkey's practice sees him involved in litigation and arbitration about 75% of the time, dealing with discrimination, wrongful discharge and a range of other issues. Peers respect his *"enormous experience,"* affording *"excellent judgment."* Widely considered to be Gilkey's protégé, **Barbara Stephenson** is a skilled employment litigator who also defends administrative claims and counsels clients on personnel issues.

The Clients: The firm's client base consists of large employers in the region.

Noeding & Moody PC

The Firm: Despite being just five years old, this specialist labor and employment boutique is devoted to serving employers throughout the Southwest. The two name partners broke away from Hinkle Hensley Shanor & Martin and carved a reputation for their prowess in litigation. The firm also has a growing labor relations practice, and combines this with office consultation, emphasizing preventative measures.

The Lawyers: Sources respect **Nicholas Noeding** as *"a gifted and insightful employment lawyer,"* who has taken on a wealth of work in the healthcare, construction and public utilities sectors. He is active in wrongful discharge litigation, civil rights and employment discrimination defense and collective bargaining.

The Clients: Ethicon, National Electrical Con-

LITIGATION

NEW MEXICO

NEW MEXICO
Leading individuals
(Employment: Mainly Defendant)

1 GILKEY Duane *Gilkey & Stephenson*, Albuquerque
2 EASTHAM John *Krehbiel Bannerman*, Albuquerque
   STEPHENSON Barbara *Gilkey & Stephenson*, Albuquerque
3 NOEDING Nicholas *Noeding & Moody*, Albuquerque
   TINNIN Robert *Hinkle Hensley Shanor*, Albuquerque

Individuals are listed alphabetically in each band.

tractors Association (New Mexico Chapter); Presbyterian Medical Services; St Vincent Hospital; New Mexico Board of Bar Commissioners; Integrated Electrical Services and Protection Technologies Los Alamos.

Rodey, Dickason, Sloan, Akin & Robb PA
The Firm: The firm provides a full-service employment law practice representing local, regional and national employers. Trial strength is a key factor in the practice and the attorneys here are experienced at both state and federal court level, and before various equal opportunities and workers' rights agencies. Much of its dispute work revolves around Title VII litigation. Attorneys are also skilled in alternative dispute resolution and preventative counseling, advising on employment terminations, early retirement plans and personnel policies.
The Lawyers: Scott Gordon is the leader of the firm's employment law practice group.
The Clients: Los Alamos National Laboratory; Honeywell; Presbyterian Healthcare Services; Sandia National Laboratories and Northrop Grumman.

Other Notable Practitioners
John (Jack) **Eastham** of Krehbiel Bannerman & Williams PA is active in discrimination, unlawful termination suits and compensation issues. He has helped draft legislation at state level. He also provides employment litigation and in-depth advice as well as preventative counseling. His clients include Lovelace Health Plan, SBS Technologies, Lockheed Martin and Honeywell. **Bob Tinnin** of Hinkle Hensley Shanor & Martin LLP is praised by peers for his *"deep well of knowledge on labor law issues."* His clients include Sprint, Sandia National Laboratories, Johnson Controls and various state hospitals. He has advised several large companies in responding to union-organizing drives in the healthcare and broadcast industries, involving bargaining units of up to 350 employees.

LITIGATION

GENERAL COMMERCIAL

NEW MEXICO
Leading firms
(Litigation: General Commercial)

1 MODRALL, SPERLING, ROEHL Albuquerque
   RODEY, DICKASON, SLOAN, AKIN Albuquerque
2 KELEHER & MCLEOD PA Albuquerque
   MILLER, STRATVERT & TORGERSON Albuquerque
3 BROWNING & PEIFER Albuquerque
   EAVES BARDACKE BAUGH KIERST Albuquerque
   HINKLE HENSLEY SHANOR & MARTIN Roswell
   MADISON HARBOUR MROZ Albuquerque
4 FREEDMAN BOYD DANIELS Albuquerque

Leading individuals
(Litigation: General Commercial)

1 HALL Bruce *Rodey, Dickason, Sloan*, Albuquerque
   HARRIGAN Kenneth *Modrall, Sperling, Roehl*, Albuquerque
2 CARPENTER Bill *Carpenter & Chávez Ltd*, Albuquerque
   MCGINN Randi *McGinn & Carpenter PA*, Albuquerque
3 BARDACKE Paul *Eaves Bardacke Baugh*, Albuquerque
   GALLEGOS Jean *Gallegos Law Firm PC*, Santa Fe
   MADISON William *Madison Harbour Mroz*, Albuquerque
   MILLER Ranne *Miller, Stratvert & Torgerson*, Albuquerque
   PEIFER Charles *Browning & Peifer*, Albuquerque
   THROCKMORTON Rex *Rodey, Dickason*, Albuquerque
4 BROWNING James *Browning & Peifer*, Albuquerque
   DURKOVICH Stephen *Durkovich Salazar*, Albuquerque
   GOLDBERG Joseph *Freedman Boyd Daniels*, Albuquerque
   SNEAD William *Sole Practitioner*, Albuquerque
   TORGERSON Alan *Miller, Stratvert*, Albuquerque
   WOLF Wayne *Wolf Taylor & McCaleb*, Albuquerque
   WORD Terry *Word & Bodargus*, Albuquerque

Firms and individuals are listed alphabetically in each band.

Modrall, Sperling, Roehl, Harris & Sisk PA
The Firm: Peers enthused that this is *"a terrific law firm,"* which has steadily built a formidable reputation in commercial litigation. A substantial workload is taken from natural resources and Indian law matters as well as products liability defense. The firm takes a broad-based approach to general litigation cases, and *"effectively"* conducts appellate cases in state, tribal and federal courts.
The Lawyers: Sources consider **Ken Harrigan** to be *"one of the top guns"* on New Mexico's legal scene. He takes on a diverse range of highly complex litigation matters, encompassing products liability defense, insurance and some personal injury work. His *"fantastic skill, longevity and tenacity"* have impressed many, who also note he brings *"eloquence and thoroughness,"* to court. He represented a foreign company in a complex and protracted breach of contract litigation involving claims in excess of $350 million.
The Clients: Burlington Resources; BP Amoco; Albuquerque Public Schools; Western Commerce Bank; Bank of America and SAFECO Insurance Company.

Rodey, Dickason, Sloan, Akin & Robb PA
The Firm: This firm is seen to be vying with Modrall Sperling for top billing in New Mexico; commentators said: *"They are both excellent firms, packed with talented lawyers."* Clients praised Rodey Dickason attorneys for being *"extremely thorough and equipped with good local knowledge,"* adding that they are *"thoroughly prepared, confident and very good value, too."* Competitors noted the firm's strong track record arguing before both federal and state courts on contract disputes, antitrust and IP-related matters.
The Lawyers: Linchpin of the firm's litigation group, **Bruce Hall** is regarded by peers as *"a lawyer's lawyer, ethical and honorable - he looks out for the best solution for his clients."* He combines a general business disputes caseload with employment litigation and stands out for an *"engaging approach that makes him extremely effective, and respected by both judge and jury."* He successfully defended a dispute between the family owners of the 20,000-acre Salman Ranch in northeast New Mexico over contractual issues. Managing director **Rex Throckmorton** demonstrates *"excellent judgment"* in all his commercial litigation dealings. Peers spoke of his *"poise"* and *"calm, but direct manner,"* while a client said that when taking on a case from another firm, *"he changed the mood and the momentum, and subsequently gained a good result for us."* He acted for The Williams Companies in a recent case brought by BP Amoco concerning the interpretation of a price provision in their contract.
The Clients: AT&T; Bank of America; Bank of the West; Diamond Tail Estates; Ford; GE; GM; Honeywell; Los Alamos National Laboratories; Microsoft and University of New Mexico.

Keleher & McLeod PA
The Firm: This is very much a firm of local lawyers, with a strong sense of community. Historically it is best known for its work with public utilities, affording it expertise in regulatory work that peers consider second to none. It continues to represent PNM, the largest utility in New Mexico, and also acts for a wide range of corporate and state clients
The Lawyers: Headed by the firm's president,

NEW MEXICO

LITIGATION

Charles Pharris, the litigation group is said to *"really cover the waterfront."*
The Clients: Public Service Company of New Mexico (PNM); Presbyterian Healthcare Services; New Mexico Lottery; Wells Fargo; RJ Reynolds and State of New Mexico - Risk Management Division.

Miller, Stratvert & Torgerson PA
The Firm: Observers respect this firm for its pre-eminent appellate practice and point to its *"specialist"* skills in medical malpractice and insurance defense. Attorneys here are applying their collective litigation skills to a broader commercial stage, and commentators said they had a *"huge amount of respect for these lawyers."*
The Lawyers: Founder and director **Ranne Miller** is said to be *"one of the finest lawyers you will see in a courtroom."* His expertise extends to medical malpractice, products liability, professional liability and complex commercial litigation. **Alan Torgerson** is *"trusted by plaintiffs and defendants,"* according to his peers. An *"aggressive advocate,"* Torgerson is equally at home dealing with commercial litigation and liability cases or medical malpractice and wrongful death matters.
The Clients: The group acts for a strong list of clients that includes Zurich Financial Services Group, Medical Protective Insurance Companies and Lovelace Hospital.

Browning & Peifer
The Firm: Sources called this *"a small, but excellent firm"* whose litigators *"work harder than anyone else."* It is engaged, somewhat unusually, in almost equal amounts of plaintiffs' and defendants' work. In testimony to the quality of the its work, peers cited this group as a popular choice for referrals.
The Lawyers: **Chuck Peifer** shines as an accomplished commercial litigator, who is skilled in securities and general civil matters. Interviewees reported: *"He gives a commitment to a case that the larger firms can not."* Peifer recently acted for the plaintiffs in Howard v Everex Systems, a securities class action fraud that he won on appeal. He is also active in a statewide class action for Wal-Mart. Clients valued **Jim Browning** as *"probably the hardest working lawyer in the state,"* while peers considered him *"exceptionally smart and thorough"* in his approach to a case. He has advised on class actions against life insurance providers, and represented the State of New Mexico in a number of cases where oil companies alleged that they had overpaid state taxes.
The Clients: Wal-Mart; AOL; Qwest; Mellon Bank and Lloyd's.

Eaves Bardacke Baugh Kierst & Kiernan PA
The Firm: This firm undertakes an even balance of plaintiffs' and defendants' matters. Interviewees felt its strength lies in its business litigation and professional liability practices, and noted that *"the firm has done a great deal of highly successful class action work."*
The Lawyers: **Paul Bardacke**'s work in complex commercial litigation is coupled with mediation matters, giving him a first-rate understanding of how to resolve business disputes. Observers appreciate that he is *"particularly good with juries."*
The Clients: A wide variety of defendant and plaintiff clients are represented by this firm.

Hinkle Hensley Shanor & Martin LLP
The Firm: The only ranked firm that has offices outside the state. Although it has three offices in Texas, Hinkle Hensley specializes in oil and gas work from its Roswell, New Mexico base, and is competitive with local firms in both size and manpower. Lawyers here are said to *"display expertise in complex commercial litigation."* Areas of activity include antitrust, securities law and banking matters. The firm won a $1.5 million judgment for DKD Electric Company against a major pipe manufacturer for the supply of defective material.
The Lawyers: Marshall Martin, the firm's managing partner, heads litigation efforts at the firm.
The Clients: First State Bank; SouthWestern Public Service Company; Phillips Petroleum Company; ARCO and DKD Electric Company.

Madison Harbour Mroz & Brennan PA
The Firm: This dynamic commercial litigation team was highly recommended; peers claimed: *"The quality per person here is higher than at any other firm in the state."* The firm mainly acts on insurance coverage disputes and contract disputes.
The Lawyers: **Bill Madison** is a skilled litigator, and is extensively involved in insurance defense.
The Clients: Insurance companies and other large commercial entities are clients.

Freedman Boyd Daniels Hollander Goldberg & Cline PA
The Firm: While this modestly sized practice does a fair amount of criminal litigation work, it is the commercial litigation and appellate practice that has produced its well-deserved reputation. Peers laud the *"smart, creative and experienced trial lawyers"* in the team.
The Lawyers: **Joe Goldberg** (see page 438) has a substantial reputation as an expert in voter redistricting. Clients also described him as *"a very fine antitrust lawyer."* He acted as lead counsel for a number of companies, including mining firms and building contractors, in a case concerning price-fixing among commercial explosives manufacturers, which was settled for more than $75 million.
The Clients: The Peters Corporation; NuCity Publications; BHP Copper; Amherst Technologies and Flexitallic Corporation.

Other Notable Practitioners
Respected plaintiffs' attorney **Bill Carpenter** of Carpenter & Chávez Ltd represents clients in a broad range of matters, including products liability, insurance bad faith, toxic tort and general commercial litigation. Peers said he was *"highly effective in court."* **Randi McGinn** of McGinn & Carpenter PA was dubbed *"one of the best trial lawyers in the state."* Active at both state and federal levels, she was recommended as a *"dynamo in the courtroom, extremely persuasive and charming."* **Wayne Wolf** of Wolf Taylor & McCaleb was identified as *"a superb trial lawyer."* He is active in complex litigation, insurance defense and products liability cases. **Jean Gallegos** of Gallegos Law Firm PC in Santa Fe has earned a *"reputation as one of the finest plaintiffs' lawyers in New Mexico."* He is engaged largely in oil and gas and natural resources-related litigation. Interviewees cited sole practitioner **William Snead** in Albuquerque as an attorney who was *"able to see all sides of the case."* At Durkovich Salazar & Sullivan, **Stephen Durkovich** continues to shine as an *"honorable and effective"* medical malpractice specialist, who is equally adept in commercial cases. Gifted litigator **Terry Word** of Word & Bogardus most frequently represents plaintiffs in medical malpractice, personal injury and wrongful death cases, and has also been involved in business disputes.

REAL ESTATE

NEW MEXICO
Leading firms (Real Estate)
1. MYERS OLIVER & PRICE *Albuquerque*
2. HURLEY TOEVS STYLES HAMBLIN *Albuquerque*
   MODRALL, SPERLING, ROEHL *Albuquerque*
   RODEY, DICKASON, SLOAN, AKIN *Albuquerque*
3. KELEHER & MCLEOD PA *Albuquerque*

Leading individuals (Real Estate)
1. PRICE Charles *Myers Oliver & Price,* Albuquerque
2. HURLEY Patrick *Hurley Toevs Styles,* Albuquerque
   MYERS John *Myers Oliver & Price,* Albuquerque
   SALAZAR John *Rodey, Dickason, Sloan,* Albuquerque
   STYLES Mark *Hurley Toevs Styles Hamblin,* Albuquerque
3. EK Dale *Modrall, Sperling, Roehl, Harris,* Albuquerque
   GOLDBERG Catherine *Rodey, Dickason,* Albuquerque
   KELEHER William *Keleher & McLeod PA,* Albuquerque

Firms and individuals are listed alphabetically in each band.

Myers Oliver & Price
The Firm: Interviewees commended this firm of *"truly outstanding lawyers"* for its expertise in commercial real estate, including land use and zoning, finance and transactional work. The attorneys here are *"pragmatic and reasonable,"* drawing on *"a tremendous well of knowledge."*
The Lawyers: **Charles Price**'s *"complete knowledge of real estate,"* has brought him a lot of respect. He was commended for his *"careful handling of deals and strong technical skills."* **John Myers**' work is primarily centered on zoning, land use and eminent domain matters. Peers consider him to be *"a real deal-maker"* with his deep knowledge of the law and political connections.
The Clients: The firm advises real estate developers and investment companies.

Hurley Toevs Styles Hamblin & Panter PA
The Firm: This boutique's real estate work chiefly involves structuring, negotiating and implementing all types of commercial and real estate transactions. The group represents clients in development and construction projects and was recommended to researchers for its skill in handling real estate financings.
The Lawyers: **Patrick Hurley**'s work in real estate development, leasing and financing transactions has earned him a reputation as a specialist in his field. Peers reported: *"He's smart and tough - an excellent lawyer."* **Mark Styles** was dubbed *" an outstanding transaction lawyer."* His clients include large owners and developers, who recommend his attention to detail, particularly his *"thoroughness in reviewing the factual information relating to the transaction."*
The Clients: Owners, developers, and banks and other financial institutions make up the team's varied client base.

Modrall, Sperling, Roehl, Harris & Sisk PA
The Firm: Rivaling the Rodey Dickason firm in size and scope, Modrall Sperling's real estate team has the capacity to advise on the full range of real estate issues. Attorneys here are best known for their representation of buyers and sellers of commercial and residential properties and ranches. Peers acknowledge that these skilled practitioners have become particularly *"well known over the years, having represented a number of large ranching interests"* and undertaken the associated land use issues, border disputes and tribal concerns involved.
The Lawyers: **Dale Ek** has been a pivotal member of the team for about 30 years. Commended as an *"experienced and knowledgeable"* attorney, he is particularly effective in dealing with ranch and agricultural concerns.
The Clients: Among the team's clients are Bank of America, Wells Fargo, Bank of Albuquerque and Duke Energy.

Rodey, Dickason, Sloan, Akin & Robb PA
The Firm: This full-service heavyweight was endorsed for its *"high-quality service."* Attorneys are adept at dealing with every stage of a real estate development including related litigation matters. They advise on acquisitions and sales, development and construction, financing and land use matters.
The Lawyers: Head of the land use group **John Salazar** combines his litigation work in eminent domain matters with extensive transactional activity. Clients agree: *"He is the best there is for land use issues."* Strong in condemnation work, he is credited with a *"deep understanding of real estate matters"* and strong negotiation skills. He has advised on the renovation and redevelopment of Albuquerque's Winrock Shopping Mall for The Prudential Insurance Company of America. **Catherine Goldberg** is head of the real estate banking group and counsels lenders and borrowers on real estate financing. Peers considered her to be *"thorough and sharp – a highly ethical attorney."* She recently concluded the $20 million purchase agreement for a large office building, also assisting in the related land use and zoning issues.
The Clients: American Stores Properties; AT&T Wireless; Diamond Tail Estates; High Desert Investment; Roberson Construction Company and Santa Teresa Real Estate Development.

Keleher & McLeod PA
The Firm: This senior group of lawyers primarily engages in real estate transactions and financing, development and property management for commercial projects, timeshare ventures and condominiums. The team is advantageously backed by lawyers with strong construction knowledge and by a number of litigators with respected trial capabilities.
The Lawyers: Sources call **Bill Keleher** *"a deal doer."* *"He is innovative in trying to find a way through the minefield, discovering alternatives that work for both sides."* Real property title matters and negotiations and documentation for commercial property transactions are his main focus.
The Clients: The real estate group's clients include a number of landowners and development groups.

NEW MEXICO   LEADERS

Leaders in New Mexico

BARDACKE, Paul
Eaves Bardacke Baugh Kierst & Kiernan PA, Albuquerque 505 888 4300
Recommended in Litigation

BARLOW, Richard
Barlow & Wilcox PA, Albuquerque 505 248 1300
Recommended in Corporate/M&A

BENDICKSEN, Perry
Sutin, Thayer & Browne, A Professional Corporation, Santa Fe 505 988 5521
Recommended in Corporate/M&A

BETZER, Stan
Betzer Roybal & Eisenberg PC, Albuquerque 505 797 0105
Recommended in Corporate/M&A

BROWN, Duane
Modrall, Sperling, Roehl, Harris & Sisk, PA, Albuquerque 505 848 1800
Recommended in Corporate/M&A

BROWNE, Graham
Sutin, Thayer & Browne, Albuquerque 505 883 2500
Recommended in Corporate/M&A

BROWNING, James
Browning & Peifer, Albuquerque 505 247 4800
Recommended in Litigation

BUCHHOLTZ, David
Sutin, Thayer & Browne, Albuquerque 505 883 2500
Recommended in Corporate/M&A

CARPENTER, Bill
Carpenter & Chavez Ltd, Albuquerque 505 243 1336
Recommended in Litigation

DURKOVICH, Stephen
Durkovich Salazar & Sullivan, Albuquerque 505 247 2367
Recommended in Litigation

EASTHAM, John
Krehbiel Bannerman & Williams PA, Albuquerque 505 837 1900
Recommended in Employment

EK, Dale
Modrall, Sperling, Roehl, Harris & Sisk, PA, Albuquerque 505 848 1800
Recommended in Real Estate

GALLEGOS, Jean
Gallegos Law Firm PC, Santa Fe 505 983 6686
Recommended in Litigation

GILKEY, Duane
Gilkey & Stephenson PA, Albuquerque 505 242 4466
Recommended in Employment

GOLDBERG, Catherine
Rodey, Dickason, Sloan, Akin & Robb, PA, Albuquerque 505 765 5900
Recommended in Real Estate

GOLDBERG, Joseph
Freedman Boyd Daniels Hollander Goldberg & Cline PA, Albuquerque 505 842 9960
jg@fbdlaw.com
Recommended in Litigation
Specialization: Complex commercial litigation; antitrust.
Prof. Memberships: American Law Institute; American Bar Association; American Trial Lawyers Association.

HALL, Bruce
Rodey, Dickason, Sloan, Akin & Robb, PA, Albuquerque 505 765 5900
Recommended in Litigation

HARRIGAN, Kenneth
Modrall, Sperling, Roehl, Harris & Sisk, PA, Albuquerque 505 848 1800
Recommended in Litigation

HEYMAN, Robert
Sutin, Thayer & Browne, Albuquerque 505 883 2500
Recommended in Corporate/M&A

HURLEY, Patrick
Hurley Toevs Styles Hamblin & Panter PA, Albuquerque 505 888 1188
Recommended in Real Estate

KELEHER, William
Keleher & McLeod, PA, Albuquerque 505 346 4646
Recommended in Real Estate

KEY, Chris
The Law Office of Chris Key, Albuquerque 505 242 9097
Recommended in Employment

MADISON, William
Madison Harbour Mroz & Brennan PA, Albuquerque 505 242 2177
Recommended in Litigation

MCDONALD, Randall
Foster Johnson McDonald Lucero Koinis LLP, Albuquerque 505 243 3000
Recommended in Corporate/M&A

MCGINN, Randi
McGinn & Carpenter PA, Albuquerque 505 843 6161
Recommended in Litigation

MILLER, Ranne
Miller, Stratvert & Torgerson, PA, Albuquerque 505 842 1950
Recommended in Litigation

MOORE, Charles L
Keleher & McLeod, PA, Albuquerque 505 346 4646
Recommended in Corporate/M&A

MYERS, John
Myers Oliver & Price, Albuquerque 505 247 9080
Recommended in Real Estate

NOEDING, Nicholas
Noeding & Moody PC, Albuquerque 505 878 0515
Recommended in Employment

PAISLEY, Bonnie
Modrall, Sperling, Roehl, Harris & Sisk, PA, Albuquerque 505 848 1800
Recommended in Corporate/M&A

PARKER, James
Modrall, Sperling, Roehl, Harris & Sisk, PA, Albuquerque 505 848 1800
Recommended in Corporate/M&A

PEIFER, Charles
Browning & Peifer, Albuquerque 505 247 4800
Recommended in Litigation

PRICE, Charles
Myers Oliver & Price, Albuquerque 505 247 9080
Recommended in Real Estate

SALAZAR, John
Rodey, Dickason, Sloan, Akin & Robb, PA, Albuquerque 505 765 5900
Recommended in Real Estate

SCHULER, Alison
Schuler, Messersmith, Daly & Lansdowne, Albuquerque 505 872 0800
Recommended in Corporate/M&A

SNEAD, William
The Law Office of William E. Snead, Albuquerque 505 842 8177
Recommended in Litigation

STEPHENSON, Barbara
Gilkey & Stephenson PA, Albuquerque 505 242 4466
Recommended in Employment

STYLES, Mark
Hurley Toevs Styles Hamblin & Panter PA, Albuquerque 505 888 1188
Recommended in Real Estate

THROCKMORTON, Rex
Rodey, Dickason, Sloan, Akin & Robb, PA, Albuquerque 505 765 5900
Recommended in Litigation

TINNIN, Robert
Hinkle Hensley Shanor & Martin LLP, Albuquerque 505 768 1500
Recommended in Employment

TORGERSON, Alan
Miller, Stratvert & Torgerson, PA, Albuquerque 505 842 1950
Recommended in Litigation

WOLF, Wayne
Wolf Taylor & McCaleb, Albuquerque 505 888 6600
Recommended in Litigation

WORD, Terry
Word & Bodargus, Albuquerque 505 842 1905
Recommended in Litigation

OVERVIEW

NEW YORK

CONTENTS: Antitrust p.440; Arbitration p.443; Banking p.445; Capital Markets: Debt & Equity p.448; Capital Markets: Derivatives p.451; Capital Markets: Securitization p.453; Communications p.456; Construction p.458; Corporate/M&A p.459; Employment: Mainly Plaintiff p.466; Mainly Defendant p.466; Energy p.468; Environment p.468; Insolvency p.470; Insurance p.476; Intellectual Property p.478; Litigation: General Commercial p.480; Media p.485; Private Equity: Buyouts & Investments p.487; Private Equity: Fund Formation p.488; Projects p.490; Real Estate p.492; Shipping p.496; Tax p.498

NEW YORK'S TOP TEN

1. Skadden, Arps, Slate, Meagher & Flom
2. Simpson Thacher & Bartlett
3. Davis Polk & Wardwell
4. Sullivan & Cromwell
5. Cravath, Swaine & Moore
6. Weil, Gotshal & Manges
7. Shearman & Sterling
8. Wachtell, Lipton, Rosen & Katz
9. Debevoise & Plimpton
10. Cleary Gottlieb Steen & Hamilton

Ranking based on Chambers' research within the state.

All quotes in the text are from interviews with clients and competitors.

OVERVIEW: In a year when deal volume dropped 10.6% and value fell 40% from 2001, **Skadden, Arps, Slate, Meagher & Flom** – among the most corporate-focused of the New York elite firms – might have been expected to fare badly. However, it triumphantly topped the 2002 US M&A tables, and also emerged a clear winner in *Chambers'* rankings. M&A lies at the core of Skadden Arps' practice. A juggernaut in the corporate marketplace, sources say it helped to invent the game and has gone on reinventing it ever since. Deemed the grandfather of M&A, Jo Flom remains on hand for advice and mentoring, while the team includes a list of such top names as Roger Aaron, Peter Atkins, Blaine Fogg, Morris Kramer and leading powerbroker Ken Bialkin. Together, they have concluded deals on the scale of Pfizer's $60 billion acquisition of Pharmacia, representing Goldman Sachs, and American General in relation to Prudential's unsuccessful acquisition bid and subsequent sale to AIG for $23 billion. Many of the firm's other key teams, such as its enormous litigation group, and the tax department coheaded by superstar Matt Rosen, have a strong transactional focus. Another point of strength is Skadden Arp's securitization practice, which tops our tables thanks to its quality and deep resources as well as the matchless reputation of Thomas Kunz.

Simpson Thacher & Bartlett boasts the second largest practice in New York after Skadden Arps, and also follows it in *Chambers'* rankings. However, this blue-blooded operation tops five of our tables, three more than its larger rival. The firm's approach is smoothly pragmatic: it gets maximum results with minimum posturing, according to clients. Simpson Thacher's most notable strength, perhaps, is private equity. The firm has a long-standing commitment to this sector under chairman Dick Beattie and the team, which includes standout practitioner Charles Cogut. This has secured the firm a blockbuster LBO practice and clients of the caliber of Kohlberg Kravis Roberts & Company and The Blackstone Group. This leveraged finance profile is important to its banking practice, as is its close relationship with JPMorgan Chase, for whom it recently acted on $18 billion of syndicated loans to GE Capital. Sources agree that this is a go-to firm for financing work, with some observers describing it as the main driver in this market. It is, indeed, a major driver in many markets, ranging from corporate through tax to insurance, where it is handling coverage issues for Swiss Re as lead insurer of the World Trade Center. Commercial litigation is also an outstanding area: peers say the firm can litigate any matter under the sun. It also heads our antitrust tables, in which its practice has been boosted by the recent recruitment of Kevin Arquit from Clifford Chance.

Davis Polk & Wardwell, ranked third, is another distinguished outfit with a strong relationship to Wall Street financial institutions, particularly JPMorgan Chase (which it is representing in connection with Enron's Chapter 11 proceedings), Morgan Stanley, CSFB and Citibank. It is known in the market for its consistent high quality and practical, user-friendly approach, and boasts outstanding attorneys such as Brad Smith, dubbed by peers the dean of the finance bar. The firm can claim a transactional record as good as any, acting, for example, in the $72 billion acquisition of AT&T Broadband by Comcast. Davis Polk enjoys a high profile in debt and equity capital markets. With about 70 capital markets lawyers across the world, the group handles work like Lucent Technologies' recent $1.75 billion offering. Tax is another area of strength, and Avishai Shachar's close-knit team offers top-class advice on domestic and international matters. Internationally, the firm boasts a particularly good reputation for Latin American work. And, with a 'best friends' network including Slaughter and May, Hengeler Mueller and Uría & Menéndez in the UK, Germany and Spain respectively, Davis Polk is a natural choice for high-end cross-border transactions.

Clients commend **Sullivan & Cromwell** for the excellence exhibited by its top-drawer lawyers. Nowhere is this more evident than in capital markets, where it tops two of *Chambers'* tables. Sources particularly admire the way the firm has established an international network, appreciating its consistent quality across Europe and Asia. In Latin America too, Sullivan & Cromwell enjoys a stream of headline deals, including recent SEC-registered bond offerings by Brazil and Mexico, each totaling over $3 billion. The firm handles an impressive range of domestic and international work, where its envied relationship with Goldman Sachs often sees it representing the financial adviser. It is in finance sector M&A, however, that its reputation is highest. This is largely due to the standing of incredibly hard-working firm chairman Rodge Cohen, who appears on many of the sector's biggest deals, such as First Union's 2001 merger with Wachovia. This reputation for banking M&A somewhat overshadows the firm's traditional banking profile, although it does command a top-tier name for banking regulatory expertise. Another area of unusual strength is tax, in which the team won particular plaudits for its advice on multi-jurisdictional transactional matters.

Cravath, Swaine & Moore is known as one of the most focused and profitable firms in New York. Our research bears this out. It appears in only eight *Chambers'* tables; nonetheless, it tops five of these, including the core areas of debt and equity capital markets, banking and tax. The firm makes no secret of its concentration on complex, high-end work, and wins warm praise from blue-chip clients who rely on it to tackle the toughest cases. The firm's focus is emphatically domestic. However, this does not prevent it from handling top-class, cross-border deals, including Alcon Laboratories' $2.2 billion IPO, in which it represented parent company Nestlé. Cravath Swaine's corporate department is widely acknowledged for producing talented generalists. Perhaps its best-known star is Allen Finkelson, principal corporate partner for IBM. Its litigation expertise has helped it acquire a reputation for pushing through difficult or contested deals. The firm's antitrust team, which represented AOL Time Warner in a case against Microsoft, was particularly singled out for praise.

Any discussion of **Weil, Gotshal & Manges** must begin with insolvency. Interviewees universally recognize it as the number-one firm in this area; it scooped the lead roles in the Chapter 11s of both Enron and WorldCom, the largest bankruptcy filings in US history. The team also claims Global Crossing and Bethlehem Steel as clients. Equally strong in both debtors' and creditors' representation, it counsels a host of top financial institutions. Martin Bienenstock and Marcia Goldstein were warmly commended for the panache with which they've taken up leadership of the bankruptcy practice following Harvey Miller's departure. Although insolvency accounts for the firm's only top band ranking in *Chambers'* tables,

NEW YORK — ANTITRUST

it makes a solid showing across the board. Private equity is an area of traditional strength, thanks to the firm's key relationship with Hicks, Muse, Tate & Furst. This LBO activity, coupled with the flow of troubled company M&A linked to restructuring, has gained the firm a reputation as an improving practice within M&A. An impressive roster of telecom and media clients accounts for many of its highest profile deals, such as NBC's $1.98 billion acquisition of Telemundo Communications. The firm's international ambitions are also attracting interest. It has now built an impressive European network, augmenting it recently with additional offices in Germany.

Shearman & Sterling is another firm with a major international presence. Its rapid expansion throughout Europe, Asia and the Middle East has seen it build a convincing global network. Indeed, rivals hold the firm up as the very model for US law firms wanting to establish a European presence. The firm has buoyant core practices in corporate/M&A and capital markets. A stream of cross-border and domestic transactions has included such choice work as Anglo American's $17.6 billion acquisition of De Beers. Work for the underwriter on China Telecom's $1.43 billion global offering and dual listing can be attributed to both the firm's strong Asian profile and its long-standing experience in the telecom sector. With its international reach, project finance is another area of strength for the firm.

Wachtell, Lipton, Rosen & Katz remains universally acknowledged as the M&A market leader. It focuses on the biggest, most complicated transactions, advising AT&T, for example, on AT&T Broadband's $72 billion merger with Comcast. This was handled by Richard Katcher, a widely admired market figure. The firm's star, though, is Martin Lipton, who commentators regard as a legend in his lifetime. Wachtell Lipton's profile does not depend upon a handful of great names, however; researchers were told that there are no bad lawyers at the firm. Clients also say that attorneys here can handle anything that is thrown at them, although they are held to be especially good on securities litigation and white-collar defense. The firm's relatively small size and focus on headline M&A give it a boutique atmosphere, as does its unusual business model, involving roughly even numbers of partners and associates. Since the 1980's, the firm has been involved in many of the most bitter hostile takeovers, where Lipton's invention of the 'poison pill' defense became famous. This helped the firm to develop prowess in complex litigation, a prowess it retains.

Debevoise & Plimpton has an especially high profile for private equity, in which it enjoys an enviable relationship with Clayton, Dubilier & Rice. This is highest in fund formation, where sources say that its talented attorneys and a hugely active, sophisticated client roster have made the firm a market leader. It also serves an impressive body of insurance clients, earning top-flight accolades in insurance M&A. Headline work includes AXA Financial's $11.5 billion sale of its controlling stake in Donaldson, Lufkin & Jenrette to Credit Suisse, and a number of high-profile demutualizations. Debevoise & Plimpton is also identified as having the leading international arbitration team in New York.

Cleary Gottlieb Steen & Hamilton is the closest rival to Shearman & Sterling for the depth and quality of its global network. It regularly represents foreign multinationals investing in the US, and many US clients rate it the premier choice for international M&A. In capital markets, Cleary Gottlieb's international strength lifts it into the upper echelons. The firm's first-class tax practice, too, is identified with the cutting-edge structures associated with international M&A, a field in which Les Samuels is considered a guru. Indeed, the profile of its cross-border work can threaten to eclipse that of its domestic practice, though it retains a strong reputation for M&A in the financial services, technology and travel industries. Clients appreciate both the firm's excellent response time and the authority and confidence of its attorneys.

ANTITRUST

NEW YORK
Leading firms (Antitrust)

1
- CRAVATH, SWAINE & MOORE
- SIMPSON THACHER & BARTLETT

2
- SKADDEN, ARPS, SLATE, MEAGHER & FLOM LLP
- WEIL, GOTSHAL & MANGES LLP

3
- BOIES, SCHILLER & FLEXNER LLP
- DAVIS POLK & WARDWELL
- SHEARMAN & STERLING
- SULLIVAN & CROMWELL LLP
- WACHTELL, LIPTON, ROSEN & KATZ

4
- CLIFFORD CHANCE US LLP
- DEBEVOISE & PLIMPTON
- FRIED, FRANK, HARRIS, SHRIVER & JACOBSON

Firms are listed alphabetically in each band.

Cravath, Swaine & Moore

The Firm: Distinguished for its litigation expertise, this group has snagged some of *"the most complex transactions and high-profile clients"* in recent months, sources report. For example, it led AOL Time Warner in an antitrust suit against Microsoft, which alleged that the personal computer operating systems provider had illegally attempted to force AOL's Netscape from the market. The firm also boasts an array of *"strong and well-rounded"* individuals, partly due to its tradition of rotating associates through various practices and discouraging strict specialization.

The Lawyers: Interviewees singled out **Bob Joffe** as a *"most effective communicator;"* he is consistently sought after for his *"polite but precise"* methods. Popular among media clients, Joffe advised AOL Time Warner in a deal involving AT&T and Comcast to unwind Time Warner Entertainment (TWE), and also counseled Warner Bros. concerning online music matters. Leading the firm's litigation department is **Evan Chesler**, who rivals described as *"spectacular."* In addition to his work as lead partner in the Netscape case, Chesler defended Bristol-Myers Squibb against allegations that the pharmaceutical company misused patents to block the generic production of popular anti-anxiety drug Buspirone. *"Accomplished"* **Ron Rolfe** continues to advise British American Tobacco against price-fixing claims in federal and state putative class actions. He also acted for Brown & Williamson Tobacco in an antitrust suit against Philip Morris alleging anticompetitive marketing practices.

The Clients: IBM; Alcoa; Royal Dutch/Shell Group of Companies and Lazard Frères.

Simpson Thacher & Bartlett

The Firm: Already possessing a *"deep well of antitrust experience,"* the group has coolly established its dominance in the field through its recent recruitment of superstar Kevin Arquit from Clifford Chance. The antitrust group benefits from synergies with the corporate department, but elicits praise from rivals for its *"proactive"* efforts to attract large antitrust cases. The firm is known for its list of investment banking and blue-chip corporate clients, especially in the media and entertainment arena.

The Lawyers: One of *"the best transactional guys around,"* **Kevin Arquit** was said to give *"a gigantic boost"* to both the firm's business portfolio and its credibility among government agencies. A former director of the FTC's bureau of competition, he has obtained antitrust clearance for clients in the airline, pharmaceutical, optics and computer hardware industries, among others. **Charles Koob**, cochair of the firm's litigation department, acted for Virgin Atlantic Airways in a private action against British Airways concerning incentive agreements. *"Highly regarded in the courtroom,"* Koob successfully defended Appleton Papers in a criminal price-fixing trial. *"Absolutely at the very top of the heap"* is **Kenneth Logan**. He successfully defended Viacom and Paramount

ANTITRUST — NEW YORK

NEW YORK
Leading individuals (Antitrust)

1
- **ARQUIT Kevin** *Simpson Thacher & Bartlett*
- **HAWK Barry** *Skadden, Arps, Slate, Meagher*
- **JOFFE Bob** *Cravath, Swaine & Moore*

2
- **BOIES David** *Boies, Schiller & Flexner LLP*
- **COLLINS Wayne Dale** *Shearman & Sterling*
- **HARTY Ronan** *Davis Polk & Wardwell*
- **KOOB Charles** *Simpson Thacher & Bartlett*
- **LOGAN Kenneth** *Simpson Thacher & Bartlett*
- **STANDISH Peter** *Weil, Gotshal & Manges LLP*

3
- **AXINN Stephen** *Axinn Veltrop & Harkrider LLP*
- **BYOWITZ Michael** *Wachtell, Lipton, Rosen*
- **GOLDEN Arthur** *Davis Polk & Wardwell*
- **GOLDFEIN Shepard** *Skadden, Arps, Slate*
- **GOTTS Ilene** *Wachtell, Lipton, Rosen & Katz*
- **JAFFE Helene** *Weil, Gotshal & Manges LLP*
- **VICTOR Paul** *Weil, Gotshal & Manges LLP*
- **WARDEN John** *Sullivan & Cromwell LLP*

4
- **BARTEL Paul** *Davis Polk & Wardwell*
- **BLUMKIN Linda** *Fried, Frank, Harris*
- **BOAST Molly** *Debevoise & Plimpton*
- **CHESLER Evan** *Cravath, Swaine & Moore*
- **EVANS Martin Frederic** *Debevoise & Plimpton*
- **PEARLSTEIN Debra** *Weil, Gotshal & Manges*
- **PRINCE Kenneth** *Shearman & Sterling*
- **ROLFE Ron** *Cravath, Swaine & Moore*
- **STOLL Neal** *Skadden, Arps, Slate, Meagher*

5
- **ARONSON Clifford** *Skadden, Arps, Slate*
- **BURKE Arthur** *Davis Polk & Wardwell*
- **FASTOW Jay** *Weil, Gotshal & Manges LLP*
- **JOHNSTON Elaine** *White & Case LLP*
- **MEIKLEJOHN Stuart** *Sullivan & Cromwell LLP*
- **QUINN Yvonne** *Sullivan & Cromwell LLP*
- **TRINGALI Joseph** *Simpson Thacher*
- **WEINER Michael** *Skadden, Arps, Slate*

Individuals are listed alphabetically in each band.

Skadden, Arps, Slate, Meagher & Flom LLP & Affiliates
see firm details p.878

The Firm: Endorsed by the market for its *"sheer strength, particularly on the merger side,"* the team was said to be *"everywhere."* The firm advised Christie's in connection with civil price-fixing allegations, and defended the American Stock Exchange against US DOJ allegations that it conspired with other exchanges to prevent the listing of equity options on more than one exchange. In addition, the firm's prominent Brussels practice bolsters its antitrust cachet and international standing.

The Lawyers: Lauded by rivals as *"a brilliant EU and international antitrust specialist,"* **Barry Hawk** (see p.518) advised Cendant on its $1.8 billion acquisition of Galileo International, a provider of computerized reservation systems to the travel industry. He also represented Covisint, a b2b internet marketplace created by Ford, DaimlerChrysler, GM, Renault, Nissan and Peugeot Citroën. Interviewees noted that the firm's antitrust group leader, **Shepard Goldfein** (see p.515), was a *"tenacious fighter"* in the courtroom. Although particularly noted for his litigation skills in high-profile battles involving the National Football League, Goldfein covers a variety of issues in his practice, including treble damages class action price-fixing cases. In addition to handling the Christie's case, he defended three financial services companies against price-fixing allegations. **Neal Stoll** (see p.538), credited with *"excellent judgment and effective advocacy skills,"* counsels clients on a range of antitrust issues including monopolization, distribution practices and the Robinson-Patman Act. He argued on behalf of the US Tobacco Company in a case alleging the tobacco giant had engaged in anticompetitive behavior against Conwood Company. **Michael Weiner** (see p.542), whose focus is on antitrust investigations and litigation, represented Hexel in a price-fixing class action suit involving carbon fiber. He also handled matters for Christie's and Cendant, and advised Renault in connection with its stake in Covisint. **Clifford Aronson** (see p.504), rated by peers as *"an excellent deal lawyer,"* acted for such companies as The Coastal Corporation in its $16 billion merger with El Paso Energy.

The Clients: Textron; Honeywell; CEMEX; CIBC Oppenheimer and SG Cowen Securities.

Weil, Gotshal & Manges LLP
see firm details p.897

The Firm: One of the largest practices in the country, with about 50 practitioners in New York alone, the group has *"experience that runs the whole gamut,"* sources said. Though the firm has an especially tight grip on midmarket matters, it has also been linked to such prominent deals as EchoStar's $26 billion acquisition of GM's satellite television unit, DIRECTV.

The Lawyers: **Peter Standish** (see p.537), who was recommended for his *"tremendous experience and judgment,"* led the team acting for GM in the EchoStar deal. He also steered Wal-Mart through its acquisition of Supermercados Amigo, the largest supermarket chain in Puerto Rico. *"A classy lawyer,"* **Helene Jaffe** (see p.519) garnered praise for her *"tough, take-no-prisoners"* approach. She helped secure a summary judgment for American Airlines in a predatory-pricing case filed by the US DOJ. A generalist with an extensive international reach, **Paul Victor** (see p.540) has advised companies from Japan, Germany, China, France and Singapore. On the criminal front, he has handled international cartel matters involving such products as lysine, nucleotides, carbon fiber and vitamins. A *"hard worker"* who concentrates mostly on M&A counseling and general antitrust litigation, **Debra Pearlstein** (see p.529) advised Vivendi Universal on its sale of Boston publisher Houghton Mifflin. She also counseled PentaSafe Security Technologies in a $251 million sale to NetIQ, a San Jose network management software company. **Jay Fastow** (see p.512), commended by peers for his antitrust litigation expertise, represented MasterCard in an unfair pricing case involving currency conversion. He also appealed a federal antitrust lawsuit for the NYSE that involved the listing of security options.

The Clients: CBS; L'Oréal; Matsushita Electric Industrial Company; Toray Industries; Kyowa Hakko and Mitsubishi Heavy Industries.

Boies, Schiller & Flexner LLP

The Firm: A national litigation boutique is built around star attorney David Boies. The firm represents both plaintiffs and defendants in complex commercial litigation and international arbitration; it maintains an *"exceptional"* reputation based on its record of securing large sums in antitrust class action suits. One high-profile case resulted in a $512 million settlement against Christie's and Sotheby's auction houses. The firm also handled an anticompetitive claim concerning the drug Hytrin, manufactured by Abbott Laboratories. Antitrust expert Don Flexner in DC was said to complement the team.

The Lawyers: Described by peers as a *"celebrity lawyer,"* **David Boies** has an envied client roster that includes the likes of Calvin Klein and Tyco International. His specialty is high-stakes litigation and, thanks to the boutique nature of his firm, Boies is able to take on the more controversial matters that larger firms might shy away from due to conflicts of interest. This *"clear and persuasive advocate"* advised Spanish Broadcasting System (SBS), the US' largest Hispanic-owned radio operator, in a lawsuit alleging that Clear Channel Communications and Hispanic Broadcasting Corporation (HBC) interfered in recent negotiations that could have led to a SBS-HBC merger.

The Clients: EchoStar, Adelphia Communications and Florida Power & Light are clients.

---

against conspiracy and price discrimination allegations in Texas and California, and advised Universal Music Group concerning press*play*, a joint venture with Sony that offers online music subscription services. Clients esteem Logan as a *"brilliant tactician"* with the ability to balance economic and litigious considerations. *"Energetic and smart,"* **Joseph Tringali** has litigated civil antitrust actions for such financial powerhouses as Lehman Brothers and JPMorgan Chase.

The Clients: Wyeth; Vivendi Universal; Viacom; Virgin Atlantic Airways; CR Bard; The Blackstone Group and Kohlberg Kravis Roberts & Company (KKR).

NEW YORK

ANTITRUST

Davis Polk & Wardwell
The Firm: This *"well-rounded"* group receives a steady flow of work from the firm's extensive corporate base, and earns plaudits for its antitrust defense on major transactions. Rivals particularly commended the team's successes in fending off challenges from private groups and government authorities as well as in representing companies in cross-border reviews. The group defended AstraZeneca against anticompetitive allegations involving products such as the cancer drug Tamoxifen. It also represented Comcast in its $72 billion merger with AT&T Broadband.

The Lawyers: With a *"good head on his shoulders"* and *"a lot of credibility with the agencies,"* **Ronan Harty** was praised by peers for his transactional prowess. In addition to handling the Comcast/AT&T merger, Harty advised advertising company Bcom3 in its $3.5 billion sale to Publicis. Leader of the firm's competition and antitrust team, **Arthur Golden**, is esteemed as a *"top strategist."* He led the practice's representation of AstraZeneca and is currently acting for Hoffman-La Roche in ongoing proceedings alleging worldwide vitamin price-fixing. **Paul Bartel** rates highly for his work in international antitrust matters. Recent work includes representation of Royal Caribbean Cruises in its unsuccessful proposed merger with P&O Princess Cruises, and the defense of Time Distribution Services, a joint venture between Time and The New York Times, against allegations brought by French publisher Hachette. **Arthur Burke** focuses on antitrust advisory work and is said to offer clients a *"good perspective on legal developments."* Recent matters include counseling EMTEC in a cartel case, and defending subsidiaries of Emerson Electric against charges of monopolization.

The Clients: Bertelsmann; Roche Holding; Syngenta; Texas Instruments; International Paper; JPMorgan Chase and Morgan Stanley.

Shearman & Sterling
The Firm: Commended for fielding a collection of *"strong personalities,"* the team was endorsed for both its *"tremendous"* expertise in global antitrust and its domestic transactional experience. Three full-time antitrust partners in New York focus on M&A defense. They piloted Quest Diagnostics in its proposed merger with Unilab and Aventis through the sale of its agricultural chemical division. A large multinational client base and strong groups in Germany, the UK and Belgium also guarantee the practice's international profile.

The Lawyers: **Dale Collins** (see p.509), described by one client as *"a brilliant economist and great lawyer,"* handled a prominent Canadian antitrust review for Viacom, and provided antitrust advice to Movielink, a joint venture among five motion picture studios to provide an online movie rental service. Practice head **Kenneth Prince** earned a reputation for being *"meticulous"* through his work with such clients as Novartis, BASF and Cadbury Schweppes/Dr Pepper. He was said to be particularly effective when *"a client needs a lot of hand-holding."*

The Clients: Corus; The BOC Group; Lafarge and Pathmark Stores.

Sullivan & Cromwell LLP
see firm details p.886

The Firm: An *"exceptional"* antitrust group, nestled within the firm's litigation department. The practice was particularly endorsed for its mastery of *"large, difficult issues that require fighting on several fronts."* While continuing to represent Microsoft in various antitrust-related lawsuits, the team also acted for clients with interests in the cable television, pharmaceutical and airline industries.

The Lawyers: *"Smart and articulate"* **John Warden** (see p.541) was commended by peers for his ability to *"see the big picture."* He continues to lead a team of attorneys in defending Microsoft against a number of anticompetitive allegations involving its product development and distribution practices. The software giant battled against nine non-settling states and the District of Columbia, which sought to impose more stringent controls than those included in the US DOJ settlement. There are also scores of separate private class actions relating to Microsoft's Windows operating system. As partner in charge of coordinating the firm's antitrust practice, **Yvonne Quinn** (see p.531) was recommended for her *"bright and aggressive"* approach. Rivals described her as *"a deep thinker"* with *"practical know-how."* She defended Cablevision Systems against anticompetitive allegations relating to the broadcast of local sports. **D Stuart Meiklejohn** (see p.525), perceived by peers as *"a smart lawyer with impeccable judgment,"* concentrates on merger reviews and other antitrust proceedings. He represented a chemical and pharmaceutical group in its acquisition of another chemical business to form one of the world's largest producers of certain compounds.

The Clients: British Airways; Philips; Goldman Sachs and Network Solutions.

Wachtell, Lipton, Rosen & Katz
see firm details p.892

The Firm: Particularly noted for its analytical dexterity in merger reviews, the group *"gets its hands on a lot of high-profile transactions"* due to the firm's prominent corporate profile. Clients praise the team for its *"aggressive, tough and smart"* lawyers who *"you can count on, no matter what the problem."* The firm represented AT&T in its $72 billion sale of AT&T Broadband to Comcast; the deal combined the largest and third largest cable TV players at the time.

The Lawyers: Leading the antitrust practice is **Michael Byowitz** (see p.508), a *"lawyer's lawyer,"* who is also said to possess business savvy. This *"practical academic"* represented Goodrich in its $1.5 billion acquisition of TRW's Aeronautical Systems unit, and advised Raytheon in a defense industry joint venture with Thales. Interviewees described **Ilene Gotts** (see p.516) as *"the go-to lawyer for mergers at Wachtell,"* adding *"...and they do a lot of mergers!"* An *"extremely hands-on"* antitrust specialist, she oversaw *"landscape-changing deals"* such as representing General Mills in its acquisition of Pillsbury. She also navigated Phillips Petroleum through its $10 billion merger with Tosco and a separate $35 billion merger with Conoco.

The Clients: HotJobs.com; Cardinal Health; Newmont Mining; Valero and VoiceStream.

Clifford Chance US LLP
see firm details p.783

The Firm: Commentators perceived the recent defection of Kevin Arquit to Simpson Thacher & Bartlett as *"clearly a blow"* in the short term, and anticipated challenges for the firm in rebuilding its New York practice. However, a strong DC team, including star attorney Steve Newborn, should *"help fill the gap"* left by Arquit. The firm's strong transactional practice complements its antitrust capacities. Practitioners were particularly praised for their ability to *"take a complex problem and figure out how to clear it through the government."* The team acted for MasterCard in an antitrust lawsuit brought by retailers, and also successfully represented Quaker Oats before the FTC, EC and other global authorities in connection with its merger with PepsiCo.

The Clients: Mylan Laboratories; Merck; Siemens; Shell Oil and the Major League Baseball Players Association.

Debevoise & Plimpton
see firm details p.788

The Firm: Although antitrust reviews and counseling remain the practice's bread and butter, the firm is thought to be making its mark in antitrust litigation. The recent arrival of Molly Boast, former director of the FTC's bureau of competition, *"adds agency credibility"* to the practice, and promises to boost the firm's profile in the area. The group represented Swedish Match in a case against US Tobacco involving distribution practices and a potential exclusionary sale.

The Lawyers: Presiding partner **M Frederic (Ric) Evans** (see p.512) was said to tackle anticompetitive issues with a litigator's *"ability to see a few steps ahead."* He has been involved in a series of private lawsuits involving distribution and monopolization in the technology industry. **Molly Boast** (see p.506), *"a forceful litigator with good merger-analysis skills,"* advised American Express in a lawsuit involving British Airways. She also represented

ARBITRATION — NEW YORK

MidAmerican Energy Holdings, a unit of Warren Buffett's Berkshire Hathaway, in its acquisition of a natural gas pipeline from Dynegy.
The Clients: Pernod Ricard, Allied Worldwide and Waste Management are additional clients.

Fried, Frank, Harris, Shriver & Jacobson
see firm details p.796
The Firm: Boasting strong transactional capabilities, the team was said to focus on matters relating to the pharmaceutical, defense, energy, media and technology industries. The group often collaborates with the firm's IP and technology practices; for example, in its work as lead counsel to Datek in its merger with Ameritrade. Although the bulk of the group's workload continues to be merger review matters, the team also represented The Scotts Company in a lawsuit alleging that the global leader in lawn and garden products had conspired with Monsanto to monopolize the US consumer herbicide market.
The Lawyers: Praised by peers as an *"effective"* advocate, **Linda Blumkin** (see p.506) acted for El Paso in its $24 billion merger with The Coastal Corporation. She also frequently represents corporations in private antitrust litigation, and has participated in international arbitrations involving competition issues.
The Clients: Microsoft; Northrop Grumman; BellSouth; Charter Communications; Invensys and MGM.

Other Notable Practitioners
"An excellent stand-up litigator," **Stephen Axinn** of Axinn, Veltrop & Harkrider LLP garnered praise for his representation of SunGard in a case in which the financial services data provider outbid Hewlett-Packard for Comdisco. **M Elaine Johnston** of White & Case LLP, who helped gained antitrust clearance for a merger between Metso and Svedala Industri, is particularly experienced in cross-border issues. She also advised Deutsche Bank in its acquisition of Zurich Scudder Investments, and UPM-Kymmene in its purchase of MACtac, a global pressure-sensitive materials business.

ARBITRATION — INTERNATIONAL

NEW YORK
Leading firms
(Arbitration (International))

1
- DEBEVOISE & PLIMPTON

2
- SIMPSON THACHER & BARTLETT
- SKADDEN, ARPS, SLATE, MEAGHER & FLOM LLP
- SULLIVAN & CROMWELL LLP
- WHITE & CASE LLP

3
- FRESHFIELDS BRUCKHAUS DERINGER LLP

4
- BAKER & MCKENZIE
- CLEARY GOTTLIEB STEEN & HAMILTON
- SHEARMAN & STERLING
- THELEN REID & PRIEST LLP

Leading individuals
(Arbitration (International))

1
- AKSEN Gerald *Thelen Reid & Priest LLP*
- CARTER James *Sullivan & Cromwell LLP*
- DONOVAN Donald *Debevoise & Plimpton*
- RIVKIN David *Debevoise & Plimpton*

2
- FREYER Dana *Skadden, Arps, Slate, Meagher*
- FRIEDLAND Paul *White & Case LLP*
- GARFINKEL Barry *Skadden, Arps, Slate*
- KERR John *Simpson Thacher & Bartlett*
- REED Lucy *Freshfields Bruckhaus Deringer*
- SMIT Robert *Simpson Thacher & Bartlett*

3
- GOLDSTEIN Marc *Proskauer Rose LLP*
- LINDSEY David *Clifford Chance US LLP*
- NEUHAUS Joseph *Sullivan & Cromwell LLP*
- NEWMAN Lawrence *Baker & McKenzie*
- ROVINE Arthur *Baker & McKenzie*
- SCHNABL Marco *Skadden, Arps, Slate*
- WEISBURG Henry *Shearman & Sterling*

Firms and individuals are listed alphabetically in each band.

Debevoise & Plimpton
see firm details p.788
The Firm: Undoubtedly the leading arbitration team in New York, it was commended to researchers as a *"meaningful and frighteningly competent"* group. Attorneys are currently acting on a multibillion dollar AAA arbitration between a US and European company that are in dispute over an investment venture in Latin America. The team also represented a US oil company in ICC arbitrations arising from disputes in Latin America and Africa.
The Lawyers: *"Trusted, respected and full of integrity,"* **Donald Donovan** (see p.511) is involved in multiple arbitration matters both as a practitioner and an arbitrator. His track record includes an ICSID arbitration of a construction project in Venezuela. Peers praise the *"terrific"* **David Rivkin** (see p.532) as a key lawyer in the field. He handles international arbitration throughout the world for the ICC, AAA and the IACAC. His resumé includes acting for GE in a long-running dispute with a German engineering company, and he has also been involved in an arbitration concerning the Salt Lake City Winter Olympics.
The Clients: The firm advises on various types of arbitrations in the fields of power, energy, construction, engineering, joint venture and insurance and reinsurance disputes, and frequently appears on cases involving sovereign states.

Simpson Thacher & Bartlett
The Firm: The international arbitration group has experience at all the major arbitration boards, including the ICC, AAA, LCIA, ICSID and UNCITRAL, for clients from a vast range of industries. The group scored one of its greatest coups when it represented Accenture in obtaining its final separation from Arthur Andersen and Andersen Worldwide through a complex ICC arbitration.
The Lawyers: Interviewees regard **John Kerr** as a *"substantial and respected"* figure who focuses his practice on ICC, AAA, UNCITRAL and various ad hoc arbitrations of IP, foreign investment expropriation and insurance disputes. He has appeared on an IP dispute at the AAA relating to a medical product, an IP dispute at the ICC between two international pharmaceutical firms and an ad hoc arbitration in the UK on an insurance claim. As an arbitrator, he is involved in an IP dispute at the ICC involving heavy equipment licensing. **Robert Smit** is regarded as *"a name on the rise,"* and principally serves as counsel in AAA, ICC and ad hoc arbitrations. However, one of his major cases saw him represent a large US company in an ICSID arbitration regarding expropriation in India. Ad hoc arbitrations have included disputes in the utilities and construction industries.

Skadden, Arps, Slate, Meagher & Flom LLP & Affiliates
see firm details p.878
The Firm: The firm's international arbitration group represents domestic and foreign clients in arbitrations before international bodies as varied as the ICC, ICSID, the Arbitration Institute at the Stockholm Chamber of Commerce (SCC) and UNCITRAL. The team also advises on the drafting and enforcement of international arbitration awards.
The Lawyers: The head of the firm's arbitration practice is **Dana Freyer** (see p.513), who handles domestic and international arbitrations under UNCITRAL, ICC, AAA, the Arbitration Institute at the SCC and other bodies' rules, in addition to drafting dispute resolution contract clauses. Recommended to researchers for her *"versatility and profound knowledge of the law,"* she is representing a large telecom company in a $1.5 billion claim at the ICC in Geneva. **Barry Garfinkel** (see p.514), hailed as the *"grandfather of international arbitration,"* has vast experience in the international profession. In addition to serving as arbitrator for ICC

NEW YORK

ARBITRATION

and ad hoc arbitral tribunals, he is advising on an international AAA arbitration concerning the drug industry, and an arbitration at The Hague in connection with biotech business issues. **Marco Schnabl** (see p.535) has a sound reputation for representing companies and sovereign states on a range of international disputes. He recently represented a client against the Government of Argentinia in ICSID proceedings.
The Clients: Clients are drawn from the construction, manufacturing, metals, mining, oil and gas, power and energy and financial services industries.

Sullivan & Cromwell LLP
see firm details p.886
The Firm: Focusing on international commercial arbitrations, the group is acknowledged for its *"excellent bench of scholarly attorneys."* Its range of services includes drafting arbitration clauses for joint ventures and other commercial agreements, and developing strategies to resolve complex international disputes.
The Lawyers: James Carter (see p.508) is renowned for his work as counsel on ICSID joint venture disputes, and also appears for clients from the technology, pharmaceutical and natural resources industries, among others. A figure of international stature, he is regarded by contemporaries as a *"leading light and a wonderful talent."* **Joseph Neuhaus** (see p.527) is viewed by competitors as a *"solid and detail-oriented"* practitioner. The coordinator of the firm's arbitration group, he has a practice that emphasizes Latin American matters. He was recently involved in an ICC arbitration between European and Latin American parties, which arose from a contract dispute in the retail industry.
The Clients: The firm represents such industries as technology, pharmaceutical and natural resources.

White & Case LLP
The Firm: Although its international arbitration group does not enjoy quite the same status as its matchless DC counterpart, the New York office has a recognized presence for arbitration and an expanding team.
The Lawyers: Commended to researchers as *"a leader in New York,"* **Paul Friedland** is the team's principal drawing card, and focuses his practice on ICC and ICSID disputes. Peers recognize his *"practical approach"* to cases; his recent caseload has included two ICC cases in connection with the power and construction industries.

Freshfields Bruckhaus Deringer LLP
The Firm: The arbitration group has been increasingly active in representing investors and conducting arbitrations in the emerging markets of central and Eastern Europe, Asia, Africa and Latin America. The team works closely with its acclaimed offices in Paris and London.
The Lawyers: Head of the department **Lucy Reed** serves as counsel and arbitrator on a high volume of cases, and is admired by contemporaries as *"a super-energetic"* attorney. Focusing on ICSID arbitrations, she represented CMS Energy in an ICSID case, and sits on the Eritrea-Ethiopia Claims Commission dealing with the peace agreement between those countries.

Baker & McKenzie
see firm details p.767
The Firm: A regular participant in disputes under all international arbitration rules, the group has seen an increase in cases from Latin America, often in relation to joint ventures.
The Lawyers: *"Well known in the arbitration club,"* **Arthur Rovine** (see p.533) counsels clients extensively on ICC disputes. He advised on a multimillion dollar ICC arbitration relating to high-speed railways in Taiwan. **Lawrence Newman** (see p.527) also has a respected name, both as counsel and as an arbitrator. He appeared on an ICC arbitration for an American-based investor involved in a Polish telecom project.

Cleary Gottlieb Steen & Hamilton
see firm details p.782
The Firm: A *"strong team of lawyers"* represents a variety of foreign sovereign states, domestic and international corporates and individuals. The group also advises on the drafting of contracts and arbitration clauses. It represented a Fortune 500 company on its $50 million employee benefits-related claim before the AAA, acted for the Government of Russia before the Arbitration Institute of the SCC on a sovereign debt dispute, and is defending the Bank for International Settlements in arbitration proceedings at The Hague.

Shearman & Sterling
The Firm: This firm's arbitration group boasts experience at all major arbitration institutions. Although the New York team remains overshadowed by the firm's extraordinary arbitration group in Paris, it is, nonetheless, a respected presence. The group represented a UK hotel management company in an ICSID arbitration against Egypt in a dispute arising from the lease, refurbishment and subsequent expropriation of two leading hotels in Egypt.
The Lawyers: Henry Weisburg specializes in cross-border finance, investment and insurance disputes and represents parties in AAA, ICSID and LCIA arbitrations.

Thelen Reid & Priest LLP
see firm details p.888
The Firm: The firm's presence in this area owes everything to legendary counsel and arbitrator **Gerald Aksen** (see p.503). A *"brilliant strategist,"* according to contemporaries, he has now participated in over 200 arbitrations in 18 countries. His range has been vast, handling disputes in, among others, the technology, environmental, construction, shipbuilding and licensing and trade sectors.

Other Notable Practitioners
Marc Goldstein of Proskauer Rose LLP has a respected name in New York, and counsels American and European clients from the hi-tech, pharmaceutical, communications, merchandising, finance and entertainment industries. He represented a US technology company at the ICC regarding distribution rights in the Middle East, and was involved in a distribution dispute at the ICC in relation to European-made luxury goods. **David Lindsey** of Clifford Chance US is noted for his work on reinsurance, joint venture and other contractual disputes at tribunals, including the ICC, UNCITRAL and ICSID. Focusing in particular on Latin America, he is currently involved in an ICSID arbitration against the Government of Argentina on behalf of a US energy company. He has also represented a US power company on a dispute arising from its investments in Brazil.

BANKING & FINANCE

Cravath, Swaine & Moore
The Firm: Strong ties to JPMorgan Chase – through a long-standing association from the days of Chemical Bank – continue to ensure a presence in the top flight for this skilled banking group. In addition, the firm attracts clients of the caliber of Citigroup, CSFB and SSSB. Peers acknowledge that its success in securing a *"long list of prestigious clients"* is due to its *"extremely talented attorneys."* Clients value their *"responsive approach,"* claiming: *"We trust them to tackle the toughest cases."* Well versed in large, complex financings, the group regularly attracts multi-currency loan syndications and acquisition financings of the highest order.
The Lawyers: Competitors pointed to **Rob Kiessling** as a key figure in the firm's acquisition finance and restructuring practice. Clients agreed that Kiessling, a *"tough negotiator,"* combines *"technical prowess"* with an *"ability to get the job done."* He has represented JPMorgan Chase in a $4 billion financing for Hewlett-Packard and a

BANKING & FINANCE — NEW YORK

NEW YORK
Leading firms (Banking & Finance)

1
- CRAVATH, SWAINE & MOORE
- DAVIS POLK & WARDWELL
- SIMPSON THACHER & BARTLETT

2
- SHEARMAN & STERLING
- SULLIVAN & CROMWELL LLP

3
- MILBANK, TWEED, HADLEY & MCCLOY
- SKADDEN, ARPS, SLATE, MEAGHER & FLOM LLP
- WHITE & CASE LLP

4
- WEIL, GOTSHAL & MANGES LLP

5
- CLEARY GOTTLIEB STEEN & HAMILTON
- MAYER, BROWN, ROWE & MAW

Leading individuals (Banking & Finance)

1
- COHEN Rodgin *Sullivan & Cromwell LLP*
- COOPER Jim *Cravath, Swaine & Moore*
- HIRSCHBERG William *Shearman & Sterling*
- HUCK Francis *Simpson Thacher & Bartlett*
- KIESSLING Rob *Cravath, Swaine & Moore*
- PARKER Allen *Cravath, Swaine & Moore*
- SMITH Bradley *Davis Polk & Wardwell*

2
- DOUGLAS James *Skadden, Arps, Slate*
- HYLTON Hartwell *Simpson Thacher & Bartlett*
- LEVIN Peter *Davis Polk & Wardwell*
- LINDAUER Erik *Sullivan & Cromwell LLP*
- ROSSMAN Vladimir *Shearman & Sterling*
- TORTORIELLO Robert *Cleary Gottlieb Steen*
- VARDELL James *Cravath, Swaine & Moore*
- WEBSTER Robert *Pillsbury Winthrop LLP*

3
- BERG Eric *White & Case LLP*
- DOKOS Daniel *Weil, Gotshal & Manges LLP*
- GEARY Sean *White & Case LLP*
- GOLDMAN Mike *Cravath, Swaine & Moore*
- HALLIDAY Joseph *Skadden, Arps, Slate*
- KNIGHT James *Simpson Thacher & Bartlett*
- NECKLES Peter *Skadden, Arps, Slate*
- PULEO Frank *Milbank, Tweed, Hadley*
- WIEMAN Lawrence *Davis Polk & Wardwell*
- WOJCIECHOWSKI Mark *Mayer, Brown*

4
- BURESH James *Simpson Thacher & Bartlett*
- FLORACK James *Davis Polk & Wardwell*
- GUYNN Randall *Davis Polk & Wardwell*
- HANRAHAN Marc *Skadden, Arps, Slate*
- MATTEI Andrew *Mayer, Brown, Rowe & Maw*
- MILLARD John *Shearman & Sterling*
- SIMMS Marsha *Weil, Gotshal & Manges LLP*
- WALKER John *Simpson Thacher & Bartlett*
- WEISS Gregory *Simpson Thacher & Bartlett*
- WIGHT Richard *Milbank, Tweed, Hadley*

Firms and individuals are listed alphabetically in each band.

$700 million financing for the Indonesian company Freeport-McMoRan Copper & Gold. **Allen Parker** was described by peers as *"one of the best analytical problem solvers"* and *"fun to work with."* Parker specializes in syndicated loan transactions largely in connection with acquisition financings and leveraged recapitalizations. He frequently represents JPMorgan Chase as financial sponsor on LBO fund work.

"Smart and confident" **Jim Cooper** *"has certainly achieved greater prominence over recent years,"* asserted interviewees. Clients reported that they are *"comfortable with his style."* Much of his activities concern large secured financings, such as those for Reader's Digest and Ryman Publications. He has also acted on credit facilities for Sotheby's auctioneers and closed a transaction for King Pharmaceuticals. **James Vardell** was described as *"an attorney who has got the whole package and is willing to listen to the needs of his clients."* His recent highlights include representing JPMorgan as lead bank in the complex $2.9 billion refinancing facility for Crown Cork & Seal, which had components on both sides of the Atlantic. He also closed a large financing for JC Penney, and advised on a $6.5 billion secured facility for Lucent Technologies. **Mike Goldman**, the youngest partner of the group, was likewise spoken of in glowing terms. According to one peer, *"he is creative, responsive and protects his clients fiercely."*

The Clients: Among the firm's roster of clients are JPMorgan Chase, Goldman Sachs, SSSB, Citigroup, CSFB and Bank of America.

Davis Polk & Wardwell

The Firm: Best known for its enduring relationship with JPMorgan, the group continues to advise a host of other leading finance houses. Home to *"thorough professionals,"* peers commend their *"integrity and practical, user-friendly approach."* The group's skill in investment grade work was singled out to researchers, and it has a strong track record in bank regulatory matters.

The Lawyers: Few earned as many plaudits as *"the hugely admired and respected"* **Brad Smith**. His practice encompasses structured finance and leveraged acquisition financing. *"Dean of the finance bar,"* Smith was involved in the $72 billion acquisition of AT&T Broadband by Comcast, and acted for JPMorgan Chase, Citibank and Bank of America on the refinancing of bank facilities for distressed companies. *"Blessed with intelligence,"* **Peter Levin** has been involved in the $4 billion cross-border restructuring for Nortel Networks, and acted for Bank of America in a $4 billion debt restructuring for Qwest. Interviewees commended **Larry Wieman** as *"one of the smartest lawyers I have ever met."* Respected for his work with both lenders and borrowers, he advises on the credit risks involved in cross-border securities and derivatives transactions. A *"thorough and thoughtful lawyer,"* **Jim Florack** is well versed in the use of structured financings and high yield debt offerings, representing institutions such as JPMorgan Chase, CSFB and Morgan Stanley. His cross-border activities often have a Latin American angle. **Randall Guynn**, the cohead of the firm's financial institutions group, is a senior bank regulatory attorney. Possessed of *"a long history in this sphere,"* he brings an *"innovative mind"* to a range of regulatory matters, cross-border collateral transactions, securities settlements and payment systems.

The Clients: JPMorgan Chase, Morgan Stanley, CSFB, Citibank and Bank of America are examples of the firm's client base.

Simpson Thacher & Bartlett

The Firm: Endorsed by peers as *"one of the broadest practices,"* the firm handles *"work of superior quality,"* which has resulted in its profile as *"the main driver in this market."* Well resourced with dedicated banking attorneys, the group has impressed clients who *"trust their smart, practical"* lawyers. Clients also noted the depth of quality in the team, recommending its well-trained associates who possess a clear understanding of complex financing arrangements and an innovative approach to the development of new products. The group maintains its close relationship with JPMorgan Chase, ensuring a healthy flow of syndicated loans and investment grade financings. A firmwide reputation for prowess in the private equity markets has also furnished the banking group with a strong profile for leveraged financings. High yield debt and the restructuring of debt in relation to bankruptcy are also key strengths of the team.

The Lawyers: **Frank Huck** is a specialist in syndicated commercial lending and a seasoned lawyer, who has been a member of the firm for some 30 years. He is *"a supremely talented attorney and a force in the banking market,"* claimed one rival; Huck has *"all the qualities you look for to ensure smooth negotiations."* He recently represented JPMorgan Chase in $18 billion of syndicated loans to GE Capital, and advised on a large syndicated loan to AOL Time Warner. He also advised on Comcast's acquisition of AT&T Broadband, and acted on the financing of $4 billion of bank facilities as part of the Lucent Technologies restructuring. **Hartwell Hylton** was applauded for his *"fine attention to detail."* Much of his work involves representing clients, such as Lehman Brothers, JPMorgan Chase and UBS Warburg, in complex multi-currency financings and restructurings. **James Knight**, expert in leveraged financings, principally represents JPMorgan and The Blackstone Group. *"A class act,"* Knight is thought to *"protect his clients' interests well."* **James Buresh** is *"a favorite for detailed documentation,"* syndicated lending and high yield financing, while *"practical"* **Gregory Weiss** was respected for his work in syndicated financings. *"Thoughtful and intelligent"* **John Walker** is the firm's preeminent bank regulatory attorney. His recent highlights include acting as global counsel for the mergers and corporate splits on 1 April 2002 involving The Fuji Bank, The Industrial Bank of Japan and The Dai-Ichi Kangyo Bank. He advised JPMorgan Chase on a $20 billion discount window credit facility at the Federal

NEW YORK

BANKING & FINANCE

Reserve Bank of New York, and has counseled the Central Bank of Afghanistan (pro bono) on commercial banking and central banking laws.
The Clients: JPMorgan Chase; CIBC; Barclays; Lehman Brothers; Bear Stearns; Toronto-Dominion Bank; Bank of America; UBS Warburg; Société Générale; Mizuho Corporate Bank; Shinsei Bank and Greenwich Capital Markets.

Shearman & Sterling
The Firm: *"Strong on both sides of the coin,"* the firm's prowess in regulatory and finance matters continues to impress interviewees. Consistently endorsed as *"one of the best for investment grade finance,"* the group is popular for *"high-end complex"* matters. Its long-standing ties to Citigroup provide an enviable flow of senior debt financings, and the group is respected for the resources committed to the development of its overseas offices. London, Paris, Frankfurt and Düsseldorf are home to established finance teams, supporting complex cross-border transactions and debt restructuring programs.
The Lawyers: **William Hirschberg** (see p.518) is cohead of the firm's banking practice. Interviewees described him as an authority on acquisition and leveraged financings, workouts and structured products: *"A deeply experienced attorney – he has seen it all."* Among recent highlights, he represented Bank of America as debt coordinator in the restructuring of the $1.2 billion bank debt of US industries. He also advised Citibank, JPMorgan Chase, CSFB and Goldman Sachs as joint lead arrangers and book runners in a $4 billion credit facility for AT&T.
Vladimir Rossman (see p.533) was commended for his efforts, which *"go above and beyond the call of duty"* for *"clients who are ferociously loyal to him."* An expert in cross-border matters, he is accomplished in CBOs, CLOs and other structured financings, LBOs and restructurings. **John Millard** (see p.525) was praised for *"his expertise in the Latin American sphere."* He represents borrowers, financial institutions and issuers in South America, and is proficient in privatizations, project financings and SEC-registered Rule 144A/Regulation S debt and equity offerings.
The Clients: The firm advises, among others, Citigroup, Bank of America, SSSB and JPMorgan Chase.

Sullivan & Cromwell LLP
see firm details p.886
The Firm: *"By far and away the leaders for bank regulatory matters."* The group fields partners who have *"substantial experience"* in advice to both US and international financial institutions on compliance issues and participation before federal and state authorities. The firm's prowess in financial institutions M&A continues to enjoy a higher profile than its syndicated loans work.
The Lawyers: **H Rodgin (Rodge) Cohen** (see p.509) is a key figure in the bank regulatory market: *"He has no equals."* Clients described him as *"flexible, thoughtful and willing to listen."* Cohen advises a host of financial institutions, including the 11 member banks of the New York Clearing House, to whom he clarified new statutes relating to terrorism and money laundering in the wake of 9/11. Peers recommended **Erik Lindauer** (see p.523) for his *"fine syndicated loan work."* He is also experienced in bankruptcy and restructuring and the provisions under the Uniform Commercial Code (UCC). His *"stylish and sensible"* advice is often seen in the hi-tech and media spheres.
The Clients: New York Clearing House; UBS Warburg; Sanpaolo IMI; DrKW; National Australia Bank; Bank of Tokyo-Mitsubishi; Royal Bank of Canada; Barclays; HBOS; The Bank of New York; Mellon Financial and AmSouth Bank.

Milbank, Tweed, Hadley & McCloy
The Firm: A force in the banking and project finance sphere, the group has *"some extremely talented attorneys"* and *"a clear focus on this area."* The global finance team is particularly respected for its work in the Latin American bond market.
The Lawyers: **Frank Puleo** is a *"talented attorney,"* who consistently *"sees the big picture."* His broad-based practice encompasses both financing and bank regulatory matters. He has advised on structured financings, CBOs and CDOs by JPMorgan Chase and Citigroup, and has acted on transactional work for CIBC. Puleo acted on a $2.5 billion bank debt for an ailing telecom company and arranged bank facilities for an energy company.
Richard Wight was endorsed by clients as *"a supremely able and technically knowledgeable lawyer."* Skilled in cross-border transactions, he has organized a $1.25 billion credit facility for in-orbit satellites company, PanAmSat, and advised on a $1.4 billion bank credit facility for cable TV provider Mediacom Broadband, and a $1.8 billion facility for Motorola. In the bankruptcy sphere, Wight has advised administrative agents on a $2.25 billion bank credit facility for Global Crossing, and an $800 million bank credit facility for FrontierVision Operating Partners.
The Clients: JPMorgan Chase, Citigroup, Deutsche Bank, CIBC and CSFB are typical of the firm's client base.

Skadden, Arps, Slate, Meagher & Flom LLP & Affiliates
see firm details p.878
The Firm: Although some commentators pointed to the firm's lack of traditional ties to the major finance houses, it remains *"a notable presence in the New York banking and finance arena – with both depth of talent and some real big hitters."* By virtue of its preeminence in M&A work, the group derives an abundance of acquisition finance cases and has carved itself a name for leveraged loan facility work.
The Lawyers: Department cohead **Jim Douglas** (see p.511) was commended as *"a massive player"* in the market, and one who brings a *"practical and down-to-earth"* approach to the table. He has advised on a $400 million restructuring for America West Airlines – the first such deal to be guaranteed by the Air Transportation Stabilization Board, post 9/11. He advised on the $10.6 billion restructuring of ntl.
Cohead **Joe Halliday** (see p.517) recently represented lenders to Sunbeam on a $1.7 billion financing agreement in pre-bankruptcy, as well as exit financing. He has also been involved in restructurings for clients of the caliber of Xerox and Kmart. **Peter Neckles** (see p.527) has a mixed borrower and lender practice. *"Affable and technically first rate"* he has acted on the refinancing of a bank debt for Wyndham International ($2.2 billion) and advised on a $250 million debtor-in-possession (DIP) financing for the web hosting company Exodus, obtained from GE. *"Extremely proficient attorney"* **Marc Hanrahan** (see p.517) has a strong track record in acquisition financings for clients such as Goldman Sachs, CSFB and Barclays Bank.
The Clients: Deutsche Bank/Bankers Trust; Goldman Sachs; CSFB; ABN AMRO; BNP Paribas and Barclays.

White & Case LLP
The Firm: The operation enjoys a global reach and has secured ties with Deutsche Bank, courtesy of its long association with Bankers Trust. Home to *"a clutch of intelligent attorneys,"* interviewees spoke of the firm's *"deep resources"* in staffing complex transactions. The group has a powerful presence in Europe and the Far East, ensuring its prominence on cross-border matters.
The Lawyers: Head of the global banking practice is **Eric Berg**. Interviewees described him as *"a bright and experienced attorney, who always has his eye on the ball."* Others point to Berg's ability to focus on the key elements of a case. He frequently represents lead agents and underwriters in leveraged finance transactions and has been involved in high yield debt securities transactions, workouts and recapitalizations.
Another senior statesman, **Sean Geary**, was one of the pioneers of the use of leveraged acquisitions of public companies through syndicated bank loans. *"A flamboyant, gregarious and first-rate practitioner,"* his recent work has included representing JPMorgan Chase in a $1.5 billion restructuring for Wyndham Hotels, and representing Goldman Sachs in a large financing package for The Carlyle Group, in its acquisition of a

BANKING & FINANCE — NEW YORK

specialty fiber production company. He also represented Deutsche Bank in an $800 million financing for United Defense in relation to its Crusader system.
The Clients: Deutsche Bank/Bankers Trust; Morgan Stanley; JPMorgan Chase; Goldman Sachs and Bank of America.

Weil, Gotshal & Manges LLP
see firm details p.897
The Firm: As New York's leading bankruptcy firm, much of the banking group's profile is derived from its work in restructuring and debt refinancing for distressed companies. Competitors acknowledged that the group had gained further prominence in recent times *"gleaning a great deal of work from major banks,"* such as its strengthening relationship with Citibank. Aside from its prowess in restructuring, the group is proficient in credit transactions, acquisition financings and highly leveraged syndicated lending, working on both investment grade and non-investment grade matters.
The Lawyers: Daniel Dokos (see p.511), who heads the firm's banking group, was described by peers as *"a top performer."* He undertakes a steady flow of work for SSSB, and recently worked on a complex $1.3 billion cross-border issue, where SC Johnson Commercial Markets acquired a subsidiary of Unilever. Peers described **Marsha Simms** (see p.536) as *"a talented and hard-working individual."* Largely active for borrowers, she has recently represented Sotheby's, The FINOVA Group and Estée Lauder.
The Clients: The firm acts for SSSB, Citigroup and Goldman Sachs.

Cleary Gottlieb Steen & Hamilton
see firm details p.782
The Firm: Researchers were informed that the group's profile lies with its *"handful of exemplary bank regulatory lawyers."* The group has a healthy track record in advising clients on issues such as the implications of, among others, the Gramm-Leach-Bliley Act and its affect on the merchant banking sector.
The Lawyers: Bob Tortoriello (see p.540) has *"an adventurous mind – he's willing to push the boundaries."* His practice focuses on capital markets financings, regulatory and compliance issues, securities, financial institution M&A and restructurings. He has recently counseled on issues surrounding the Sarbanes-Oxley Act, the Bank Holding Company Act, the Glass-Steagall Act and the International Banking Act. He also advises on domestic and foreign bank expansion into all types of nonbank services and related transactions.
The Clients: The group acts for CSFB, Bank of America, Commerzbank, Crédit Lyonnais and Crédit Agricole Indosuez.

Mayer, Brown, Rowe & Maw
see firm details p.843
The Firm: The 12-partner banking and finance group that operates from the New York office is acknowledged to have continued its strong growth of recent years. Used by many of the largest Canadian banks, the firm undertakes an impressive array of work, including syndicated financings, acquisition financings and securitizations. Regulatory expertise also features in the group's portfolio.
The Lawyers: Mark Wojciechowski (see p.542) was the subject of praise from both clients and peers, who were impressed by his *"hard-working attitude."* He undertakes major transactional financings for Bank of America. He also represents borrowers, recently acting for Arthur Andersen in a global syndicated loan facility. Peers identified **Andrew Mattei** (see p.524) as *"one destined for the top."* His practice encompasses highly leveraged financings – including syndicated lending and acquisition financings – and restructurings and workouts. He represented a German bank in facilities provided to a US company in order to acquire a German defense company, and has assisted Canadian corporates on their acquisitions in the US.
The Clients: Bank of America; JPMorgan Chase; CSFB; Wachovia Bank; Toronto-Dominion Bank; The Bank of Nova Scotia and Dresdner Bank.

Other Notable Practitioners
Robert Webster (see p.541), of Pillsbury Winthrop LLP's New York office, is regarded as one of the leading bank regulatory attorneys. The *"scholarly"* Webster advises financial institutions, foreign central banks and governments. He recently counseled The Bank of New York on its M&A activities. Webster also continued to counsel on the ramifications of the USA PATRIOT Act, the Sarbanes-Oxley Act and the Gramm-Leach-Bliley Act and on the regulations of the Office of Foreign Assets Control. His typical clients include Société Générale, DenNorske Bank, Banco Internacional of Mexico, CSFB, and Deutsche Bank.

CAPITAL MARKETS — DEBT & EQUITY

NEW YORK
Leading firms
(Capital Markets: Debt & Equity)

1
- CRAVATH, SWAINE & MOORE
- DAVIS POLK & WARDWELL
- SULLIVAN & CROMWELL LLP

2
- CLEARY GOTTLIEB STEEN & HAMILTON
- SHEARMAN & STERLING
- SIMPSON THACHER & BARTLETT
- SKADDEN, ARPS, SLATE, MEAGHER & FLOM LLP

3
- CAHILL GORDON & REINDEL
- LATHAM & WATKINS LLP

4
- SIDLEY AUSTIN BROWN & WOOD
- WEIL, GOTSHAL & MANGES LLP

Firms are listed alphabetically in each band

Cravath, Swaine & Moore
The Firm: *"At the top end of the spectrum,"* this *"uniformly impressive"* team of *"superb"* lawyers was said to excel in complex transactions. Observers noted that the group is strong right across the range of equity, debt and high yield work, and maintains close relationships with key underwriting institutions, including CSFB, Salomon Smith Barney and JPMorgan Chase. Although not perceived to have the international reach of some rivals, the New York practice is supported by additional capital markets practitioners in both the London and Hong Kong offices. The group's cross-border capacity is demonstrated by its representation of parent company Nestlé in Alcon Laboratories' $2.2 billion IPO. Cravath Swaine has preserved its *"stellar reputation"* despite a difficult market, largely thanks to its *"high concentration of remarkable attorneys"* and the *"client confidence"* they inspire.
The Lawyers: *"A leader in the field,"* **John White** is thought to *"merit highest commendation."* This *"thoughtful and client-friendly"* attorney advises on offerings, high yield and investment grade debt, and exercises *"impeccable judgment"* in securities law matters. He recently acted for Banc of America Securities, Merrill Lynch and Salomon Smith Barney as financial advisers to Goodrich's $200 million stock offering. *"One of the best in the business,"* **Kris Heinzelman** represents investment banks in IPOs and debt work, and is judged a *"great lawyer"* by peers and clients. **Marc Rosenberg** was on sabbatical this year but market commentators expect him to renew his profile after his return in 2003.

NEW YORK
CAPITAL MARKETS

NEW YORK
Leading individuals
(Capital Markets: Debt & Equity)

1
- QUINN Linda *Shearman & Sterling*
- WHITE John *Cravath, Swaine & Moore*
- WILLIAMS William *Sullivan & Cromwell*

2
- DAVENPORT Kirk *Latham & Watkins LLP*
- HEINZELMAN Kris *Cravath, Swaine & Moore*
- MALLOW Matthew *Skadden, Arps, Slate*
- MORISON Francis *Davis Polk & Wardwell*
- SANDLER Richard *Davis Polk & Wardwell*
- SMALL Jeffrey *Davis Polk & Wardwell*

3
- FORD Paul *Simpson Thacher & Bartlett*
- HARMS David *Sullivan & Cromwell LLP*
- HARTNETT William *Cahill Gordon & Reindel*
- PISANO Vincent *Kirkland & Ellis*
- SLONAKER Norman *Sidley Austin Brown*
- SPERLING Allan *Cleary Gottlieb Steen*
- TEHAN John *Simpson Thacher & Bartlett*

4
- BESHAR Sarah *Davis Polk & Wardwell*
- BOSTELMAN John *Sullivan & Cromwell LLP*
- CLARK James *Cahill Gordon & Reindel*
- CONRAD Winthrop *Davis Polk & Wardwell*
- EVANS Robert *Shearman & Sterling*
- GOLDSCHMIDT David *Skadden, Arps, Slate*
- KORFF Phyllis *Skadden, Arps, Slate, Meagher*
- KROUSE George *Simpson Thacher*
- REITER Glenn *Simpson Thacher & Bartlett*
- ROSENBERG Marc *Cravath, Swaine & Moore*
- SILVERMAN Leslie *Cleary Gottlieb Steen*
- SOUSSLOFF Andrew *Sullivan & Cromwell*
- WEERASINGHE Rohan *Shearman & Sterling*

Individuals are listed alphabetically in each band.

The Clients: CSFB; Salomon Smith Barney; Merrill Lynch; Banc of America Securities and JPMorgan Chase.

Davis Polk & Wardwell
The Firm: The firm possesses a *"long history"* of involvement in capital markets and is relied upon by the likes of Morgan Stanley, JPMorgan Chase and CSFB for its *"experienced and knowledgeable attorneys."* With 70 capital markets lawyers distributed among offices in London, Paris, Frankfurt, Tokyo and Hong Kong, the firm demonstrates a clear international commitment. The 13-partner New York team comprises a *"wealth of talented and responsive people."* Recent activity includes offerings in the insurance industry, capital-raising transactions for financial institutions, and a number of restructurings and spin-offs in conjunction with the firm's highly rated Latin American practice. The strength of the debt and equity practice is complemented by the sophistication of the firm's tax and equity derivatives teams.

The Lawyers: Richard Sandler attracts praise as an *"all-round impressive capital markets lawyer."* This *"independent thinker"* is said to take a *"creative"* approach to transactions. Interviewees report that he is *"willing to take risks and is always on the mark in his judgments."* Sandler coheads the global capital markets group with **Jeffrey Small**, who was described as a *"star"* with a *"real reputation among practitioners."* Clients observed: *"The more complicated the transaction, the better he is."* Known for his long-standing relationship advising Morgan Stanley, Small recently represented the underwriters in the $305 million public offering by Bermuda-based Bunge. He also represented the bankers in Lucent Technologies' $1.75 billion offering. Senior attorney **Francis Morison** is considered to be a *"stalwart of the capital markets industry"* and remains active on major transactions. He has lately worked on investment grade debt deals, drawing upon long-standing relationships with issuer clients among the Fortune 500. Morison recently advised JP Morgan Securities as underwriters to a $500 million SEC-registered offering of high yield notes by SPX. **Sarah Beshar** is a *"talented"* younger capital markets lawyer, who has experience of representing underwriters and issuers in public equity and debt work. She has seen activity in spin-offs and restructurings, secondary equity offerings and has advised on new legislation. Clients singled out **Winthrop Conrad** for his *"breadth of knowledge on US securities law,"* and combined experience of M&A and securities offerings of all types. *"Good at managing thorny issues,"* Conrad has recently tended toward underwriter representation. He advised Morgan Stanley on Premcor's $460 million IPO, Aon's $900 million equity and equity linked financing, and a $225 million common stock offering for The St Joe Company. Other matters include representing CSFB in Flowserve's $270 million common stock offering, and acting for Banc of America Securities in a $75 million common stock offering for Nu Skin Enterprises.

The Clients: Morgan Stanley; CSFB; JPMorgan Chase; Banc of America Securities and Deutsche Bank.

Sullivan & Cromwell LLP
see firm details p.886

The Firm: The firm owes its *"long-standing leadership position"* to a team of *"top-drawer"* attorneys with a knack for delivering *"on-the-money advice."* Recognized as a serious international contender, the firm is said to be *"building a global base"* with noteworthy capital markets capabilities in both Paris and Frankfurt. In Latin America, the firm was recently involved in the first exchange offers by Colombia and Peru. It also acted in SEC-registered global bond offerings by Brazil and Mexico totaling $3.5 billion and $3.25 billion respectively. As principal securities counsel to Goldman Sachs, the group advises the investment bank on capital-raising matters and serves as underwriter's counsel on offerings and debt work. The firm's strength in issuer representation was demonstrated in 2001 by its work on the $3 billion demutualization of Prudential Financial. In 2002, the firm represented BP as the guarantor on $2.3 billion of SEC-registered notes offerings, and acted for Cingular Wireless in a $2 billion issuance of long-term debt securities. Practitioners also advised long-term client Tenaris in a worldwide stock-for-stock exchange offer valued at approximately $2.4 billion. Competitors concede: *"They have a whole group of uniformly terrific people."*

The Lawyers: A *"dean of the bar,"* **Bill Williams** (see p.542) elicited admiration for his regular involvement in the firm's headline matters. *"At the top of the profession,"* Williams is active in industry and regulatory developments and commands wide experience of international securities offerings. He recently acted for Banco Bilbao Vizcaya Argentaria as global coordinator of Spain's largest natural gas supplier Enagás' €917 million IPO. Peers recognize him as *"one of the leading intellects"* in capital markets. **David Harms** (see p.517) is *"a strong lawyer who knows his stuff."* He coordinates the firm's broker-dealer regulation practice, and also focuses on IPOs and giving advice to financial institutions in capital market transactions. A *"terrific guy and excellent lawyer,"* **Andrew Soussloff** (see p.537) undertakes M&A work in addition to his capital markets focus. He represented Goldman Sachs as underwriters in the $127 million offering by Asbury Automotive Group. On the issuer side, he advised Panama's largest electricity generating group in a $170 million global offering. **John Bostelman** (see p.507) was tipped as an *"extremely thoughtful, hardworking attorney,"* who possesses *"excellent judgment."* He handles public and private securities offerings, broker-dealer regulation, investment management, commodities and derivatives matters.

The Clients: Goldman Sachs; Merrill Lynch; JP Morgan Chase Securities; Morgan Stanley and Inco.

Cleary Gottlieb Steen & Hamilton
see firm details p.782

The Firm: *"Highly respected in international finance,"* the firm's worldwide network of offices is felt to lift it to a place among the major players in debt and equity work. Peers identify real strength in Latin America, Europe and Asia. While some interviewees feel that the firm's domestic presence lags behind its international profile, the practice earns universal acclaim for the *"pure quality"* of its attorneys. The group possesses historical ties to Salomon Smith Barney and is perceived to be popular with issuers overseas, particularly in Europe. In Latin America the firm is highly visible representing sovereign entities in securities transactions. Peers continued to cite the move by Alan Beller to the SEC as a loss, but confirmed the firm is *"one of the best in the business."*

The Lawyers: Among the practice's many *"sound and practical attorneys,"* **Les Silverman** (see p.536) is seen to be *"picking up the slack"* as a result of Beller's departure. *"An experienced and accomplished securities lawyer,"* he focuses on US securities law, often representing Latin American companies in their US offerings. Although traditionally focused on issuer work, Silverman has become increasingly involved in underwriter representation. He led the firm's representation of Companhia de Concessoes Rodoviarias, as issuer, in its $126 million IPO in Brazil and US Rule 144A placement. He also represented the underwriters, co-led by Morgan Stanley and UBS, in the IPO of the Chicago Mercantile Exchange, the first flotation by a financial exchange in the US. *"Outstanding"* **Allan Sperling** (see p.537) maintains a broad capital markets practice, focusing primarily on domestic issues and overseeing much of the group's work for Salomon Smith Barney. He acted as underwriters' counsel for Salomon on the IPO by Travelers in March 2002, the largest ever IPO in the US insurance sector, and was also involved in a follow-on offering by St. Paul.

The Clients: Salomon Smith Barney; Goldman Sachs; Morgan Stanley; CSFB; Merrill Lynch; Deutsche Bank; Deutsche Telekom; Instinet; Interpublic; Kookmin Bank; Nortel Networks; Petrobras; Sony; TELMEX; American Express; BP; McDonald's; United Technologies and Vodafone.

Shearman & Sterling
The Firm: The firm has followed an aggressive policy of international expansion in recent years and is now acknowledged as a major global player for complex capital markets work. Interviewees deemed it *"one of the deepest firms in the world in terms of securities capability,"* and remarked on the group's ability to coordinate large projects among strong practices in the US, Europe and Asia. A dry period for US capital markets has seen the firm looking at new products and ancillary issues as well as exploring opportunities originating from its international offices. The firm is noted for a preeminent record in Asian capital markets work.

The Lawyers: A prominent figure in the industry, the *"savvy and knowledgeable"* **Linda Quinn** (see p.531) is a former director of the corporation finance division of the SEC. She advises investment banking and corporate clients on capital markets, derivatives and securities matters. Although she is seen more in an advisory role than in transactional matters, her close connections to the SEC and other regulators are thought to raise the profile of the firm. *"A real deal-maker's lawyer,"* **Rohan Weerasinghe** (see p.541) is *"one of the best."* His diverse corporate finance practice encompasses IPOs, cross-border offerings and high yield debt issuances. He represented Merrill Lynch and CSFB in IDEX's follow-on common stock offering of $180 million. Also acting for the underwriters, Weerasinghe worked on American Seafoods' $175 million offering of senior subordinated notes, Duane Reade's $330 million senior convertible note offering, and an offering of $617 million of pass-through certificates by American Airlines to finance the acquisition of aircraft. High yield debt work included acting for Pathmark Stores on $200 million of senior subordinated notes. **Robert Evans** is a *"strong young partner,"* who is identified by peers as a future leader in the firm. Evans is most visible representing investment banks, particularly Merrill Lynch, and has substantial expertise in public offerings and convertible securities. He recently represented the underwriters of China Telecom's $1.43 billion global offering and dual listing on the New York and Hong Kong Stock Exchanges.

The Clients: Merrill Lynch; CSFB; Bank of China; Salomon Smith Barney and Deutsche Bank Securities.

Simpson Thacher & Bartlett
The Firm: Sources indicate that the firm has succeeded in dovetailing its capital markets practice with its considerable corporate/M&A representation. The practice is still driven by investment bank clients, but attorneys are developing their representation of corporate and financial institution issuers. Clients consider the group their *"first choice"* for emerging capital markets work. The firm twice achieved headline status in the past year, representing Accenture in its $1.8 billion IPO and Travelers in its $3.8 billion IPO. Other issuer work included advising on $300 million of notes for Northwest Airlines, and acting for JPMorgan Chase Capital X on its $1 billion offering. The firm's largest investment bank client is Lehman Brothers, who it represents as issuer of its own securities, and as underwriter and placement agent for offerings in domestic and international capital markets. On the underwriters side, the firm advised on German bank group KfW's bond issuances, which had an aggregate value of $10 billion, multiple stock issuances by BlackRock, and MBNA America Bank's $15 billion global bank note program.

The Lawyers: *"Practical"* **John Tehan** is well known for his long-standing expertise in high yield matters, but has recently been shifting his focus to IPO work, following his heavy involvement with the firm's representation of Accenture. He has also undertaken some follow-on offerings, and corporate reorganization work. **Paul Ford** continues to focus on international capital markets and Rule 144A offerings, with a growing emphasis on Asian transactions. He acted as special counsel to Bank of China and also represented Korea Telecom in a joint venture with Morgan Stanley. Head of the corporate department, **George Krouse** focuses on corporate and securities law. He represented Peabody Energy in its $257 million stock offering. Underwriter work includes Six Flags' $480 million senior note issuance, and a note issuance by Wal-Mart totaling $1.5 billion. **Glenn Reiter** acts on domestic US securities offerings, but has a focus on cross-border offerings and M&A. He undertakes both equity and debt offerings and structured finance, frequently in Latin America and Canada. Clients characterize him as a *"grounded"* attorney who *"always knows the right answer and conveys it constructively."*

The Clients: Key underwriter clients include: Salomon Smith Barney; CSFB; JPMorgan Chase; Kreditanstalt für Wiederaufbau (KfW); Merrill Lynch and Banc of America Securities. The firm has also undertaken issuer work for Accenture, Northwest Airlines, American Electric Power and Duke Energy.

Skadden, Arps, Slate, Meagher & Flom LLP & Affiliates
see firm details p.878

The Firm: While the firm's debt and equity capabilities are often overshadowed by its immense corporate/M&A profile, Skadden Arps' enormous size and international reach has the capital markets group acting on headline securities deals. The practice is less dependent on specific underwriter relationships than many of its rivals, but does regularly act for Merrill Lynch and Goldman Sachs, representing the latter on a $1.2 billion equity offering for Fox Entertainment Group. The firm notably acted in the Citigroup spin-off of Travelers Property Casualty involving a $5.1 billion IPO and the subsequent distribution to Citigroup stockholders of approximately $11.6 billion of Travelers' common stock. Attorneys also represented The Gap in a $1.4 billion convertible note offering, and worked for IBM on an equity issue in 75 countries as part of its acquisition of PwC Consulting.

The Lawyers: Peers revere the *"terrific judgment"* of **Matthew Mallow** (see p.524). Head of the firm's finance department, Mallow oversees the firm's practice, providing advice on major transactions. He has experience advising major investment banks and corporations such as American Express and Cartier. Mallow recently represented NASDAQ in connection with its transformation from a wholly-owned subsidiary of the NASD to

NEW YORK

CAPITAL MARKETS

an investor-owned stock market, a matter involving private placements of equity and debt, bank credit agreements and other activities. **David Goldschmidt** (see p.515) advises investment banks and issuers across a range of industries. On the underwriter side, he acted for CSFB in a $715 million offering of equity units and in a $775 million offering of common stock for Nortel Networks. Acting increasingly for corporate issuers, Goldschmidt recently represented Fisher Scientific in a $150 million note offering and a $200 million common stock offering, and advised Nabors Industries on a $500 million offering of two classes of senior notes. **Phyllis Korff** (see p.521) counsels corporate clients on new legislation and advises on securities refinancings. She acted for Huntsman on public debt issues and worked on several IPOs in the financial services area.

The Clients: Merrill Lynch; Goldman Sachs; CSFB; Lehman Brothers; Morgan Stanley; NASDAQ; Citigroup; Travelers; CEMEX; Xerox and Huntsman.

Cahill Gordon & Reindel

The Firm: Principally seen in the domestic high yield debt market, the firm's reputation is pinned to an excellent profile and market share in this area. A popular firm with peers and clients alike, the practice rates highly for its *"deep bench of qualified people"* who have the *"brains and confidence to be pragmatic and flexible."* Cahill Gordon is highly visible as outside counsel to Goldman Sachs, but also acts for most of the major investment banks. It represented CSFB and Merrill Lynch in a $275 million offering of convertible subordinated notes for Barnes & Noble, and advised CSFB and Goldman Sachs on a $210 million offering of common stock by Dal-Tile International. Other matters included the representation of Vail Resorts on a $160 million offering of senior subordinated notes underwritten by Deutsche Bank.

The Lawyers: Regularly active for Deutsche Bank, **Bill Hartnett** is *"one of the deans of the business."* Clients believe he *"cannot be beaten"* for his knowledge of high yield matters, referring to him as the *"captain"* of the practice. Among his team, the *"exceptionally smart"* **James Clark** stands out for his experience in both high-profile debt and equity issues and corporate M&A.

Described by clients as a *"solution-based lawyer,"* he is a *"popular personality"* in the meeting room where his legal knowledge and market experience allow him to *"quietly second guess his opponents."* He represented CSFB and UBS Warburg in a $350 million offering of senior notes for MailWell, Merrill Lynch in a $165 million offering of second lien notes for WestPoint Stevens, and SSSB in a €150 million offering for Antenna TV.

The Clients: Banc of America Securities; CIBC World Markets; CSFB; Deutsche Bank Securities; Goldman Sachs; JPMorgan Chase; Lehman Brothers; Merrill Lynch; SSSB and UBS Warburg.

Latham & Watkins LLP
see firm details p.835

The Firm: Together with Cahill Gordon, the firm is considered a market leader for high yield debt work and maintains an excellent reputation in that area. Clients reported that the quality of the New York practice has discernibly improved in recent years, and expressed their confidence in its *"legally sharp and commercially savvy attorneys."* The firm represented Lehman Brothers on L-3 Communications' $702 million offering of common stock. Work for Goldman Sachs included JohnsonDiversey's $300 million offering, and National Waterworks' $200 million offering. The firm also represented UBS Warburg in a $400 million offering by Ventas Capital, and CSFB in AmerisourceBergin's $300 million offering.

The Lawyers: Kirk Davenport (see p.510) rates highly as a *"true businessman's lawyer"* who *"negotiates to get a deal done."* He is well known for his representation of investment banks, particularly Lehman Brothers, Goldman Sachs and CSFB. Clients report that he is *"one of a few lawyers who could cross the table and do our job as an investment banker."* Others assert: *"He is excellent with our clients and likes to make things happen."*

The Clients: CSFB; Goldman Sachs; Lehman Brothers; UBS Warburg and Dresser.

Sidley Austin Brown & Wood
see firm details p.877

The Firm: The practice is felt to excel within its niche as a lower margin group, and a close relationship with Merrill Lynch ensures the firm's place on the map. Like other firms, it has experienced a drop-off in high yield and IPO work recently, but has seen some activity in principal protective debt-linked products and in advisory work connected with to the Sarbanes-Oxley Act.

The Lawyers: *"Veteran"* practitioner **Norman Slonaker** focuses on global offerings, investment grade debt securities, medium term note programs and Rule 144A offerings. Researchers were told of both his *"encyclopedic knowledge of US securities law"* and ability to find *"creative solutions to problems."* In this vein, he has been exploring new product classes, working for DEPFA Bank on a $2 billion German Pfandbriefe (mortgage bond) to be sold in the US under Rule 144A restrictions.

The Clients: The group counsels Merrill Lynch, Morgan Stanley, Fannie Mae and other financial institutions, corporate and sovereign issuers and underwriters.

Weil, Gotshal & Manges LLP
see firm details p.897

The Firm: While lacking the market profile of its major rivals, the firm has represented a basket of investment banks on basic debt and equity work. The practice, which features Jeremy Dickens, advised Lehman Brothers on $200 million of senior notes for Hanger Orthopedic Group, and on the $483 million IPO of Peabody Energy Group. Issuer representation includes $877 million of liquid yield option notes for Franklin Resources, and $480 million of senior notes for Six Flags. IPO work includes the $374 million offering of LIN TV.

The Clients: Lehman Brothers; Salomon Smith Barney; CSFB and Merrill Lynch.

Other Notable Practitioners

Recently recruited from Skadden Arps, **Vince Pisano** (see p.530) at Kirkland & Ellis has a general corporate finance practice, with an emphasis on investment grade debt matters and securities restructuring. He has closed a convertible debt deal for Gabelli Group, and worked on an equity issue for IBM in 75 countries as part of its acquisition of PwC Consulting. In the REIT industry, Pisano has completed debt and equity financings for Anthracite Capital and Archstone-Smith. Investment grade debt work includes issuances for UST and Norfolk Southern. The market awaits his success in developing Kirkland & Ellis' practice, and hence its profile in the field.

CAPITAL MARKETS — NEW YORK

CAPITAL MARKETS

NEW YORK
Leading firms
(Capital Markets: Derivatives)

1
- CLEARY GOTTLIEB STEEN & HAMILTON
- SULLIVAN & CROMWELL LLP

2
- CADWALADER, WICKERSHAM & TAFT
- DAVIS POLK & WARDWELL

3
- ALLEN & OVERY

4
- SHEARMAN & STERLING
- SKADDEN, ARPS, SLATE, MEAGHER & FLOM LLP

5
- MAYER, BROWN, ROWE & MAW
- STROOCK & STROOCK & LAVAN LLP

Leading individuals
(Capital Markets: Derivatives)

1
- CUNNINGHAM Dan *Allen & Overy*
- RAISLER Kenneth *Sullivan & Cromwell LLP*
- ROSEN Edward *Cleary Gottlieb Steen*

2
- BRANDOW John *Davis Polk & Wardwell*
- GILBERG David *Sullivan & Cromwell LLP*
- GROSSHANDLER Seth *Cleary Gottlieb Steen*
- MITCHELL David *Cadwalader, Wickersham*
- OSBORN John *Skadden, Arps, Slate, Meagher*
- WEST Holland *Shearman & Sterling*

3
- BUDOFSKY Daniel *Davis Polk & Wardwell*
- COLLINS Joseph *Mayer, Brown, Rowe & Maw*
- HEFTLER Thomas *Stroock & Stroock*

4
- GOLDSTEIN Marvin *Stroock & Stroock*
- KLEIN Linda *Dewey Ballantine LLP*
- REEDER Robert *Sullivan & Cromwell LLP*
- STROMFELD Lary *Cadwalader, Wickersham*

Firms and individuals are listed alphabetically in each band.

Cleary Gottlieb Steen & Hamilton
see firm details p.782
The Firm: This *"premier Wall Street practice"* *"tops most people's lists"* for complex derivatives work. Clients value the group's *"expertise in a variety of legal specialties"* and *"active participation in legislative processes."* Excellent relationships with regulators and investment banks are said to give the firm a *"comprehensive view of the market."* Interviewees report that the firm is *"in high demand"* and tends to focus on high-end matters. The firm recently acted in the creation of EnergyClear, an energy derivatives clearing facility.
The Lawyers: *"One of the leading practitioners on Wall Street,"* **Ed Rosen** (see p.532) has played a *"critical"* role in recent legislative reviews. This *"smart and knowledgeable"* attorney boasts a *"broad range of expertise"* and was named by clients as *"great for black letter law issues."* He concentrates chiefly on documentation and financial market regulation, and has acted as counsel to several industry associations. Frequently tipped as *"New York's leading derivatives bankruptcy lawyer,"* **Seth Grosshandler** (see p.516) is widely felt to be without peer in this arena. Primarily involved in private transactions, Grosshandler works with a number of major derivatives dealers in analyzing credit risks and structuring transactions. He led the firm's representation of The Bond Market Association in developing the Cross-Product Master Agreement Version 2.1, and worked with the firm's bankruptcy and litigation team in claims against Enron.
The Clients: The group has experience advising sovereign issuers, foreign banks, end-users and credit rating agencies on derivatives matters.

Sullivan & Cromwell LLP
see firm details p.886
The Firm: Active on transactions, product development, regulatory advice, compliance and litigation, this *"fine firm"* occupies a *"visible and prominent"* place in the market. The six-partner practice advises clients on derivative structures, including regulatory and bankruptcy issues, and remains highly active in equity-indexed and equity derivatives products. In the past year, the firm has advised an increasing number of energy companies on compliance and review efforts, relating to post-Enron legislative initiatives. Practitioners also offer regulatory expertise concerning hedge funds and the structuring of new business ventures. The team serves as regular adviser to the Intercontinental Exchange, who it represented in its 2001 acquisition of the International Petroleum Exchange of London.
The Lawyers: Widely recommended for his regulatory commodities work, **Kenneth Raisler** (see p.531) spearheads the firm's activities in energy and energy derivatives. Raisler, considered *"one of the top names"* in this area, chairs the firm's commodities, futures and derivatives group. He is extremely well thought of by clients who praise his skill at *"coming up with creative solutions."* *"Astute"* **David Gilberg** (see p.514) has a general focus on the derivatives and trading markets, which encompasses regulatory advice, new products and new ventures. He has lately been active in the energy markets, advising on documentation and regulatory compliance. *"Technically adroit,"* Gilberg is also well known for his work on electronic trading and the development of new exchanges. *"An encyclopedia of knowledge,"* **Robert Reeder** (see p.531) earns kudos from clients as an *"extremely responsive"* lawyer with wide-ranging expertise. A *"cautious"* adviser, Reeder has experience establishing triple A-rated derivative products for companies, and advising commercial and investment banks on derivative instruments.
The Clients: OneChicago, UBS Warburg and InterContinental Exchange are clients.

DERIVATIVES

Cadwalader, Wickersham & Taft
see firm details p.778
The Firm: *"Certainly a significant practice,"* the firm has a broad coverage in transactional and regulatory work, with notable expertise in the development of new products. An envied client base includes major broker-dealers, commercial investment banks and end-users, including corporations, sovereign issuers and money managers. The firm's headline matter in the past year was its work as special counsel to the debtors for trading issues in the Enron bankruptcy proceedings.
The Lawyers: *"A fine attorney who knows his stuff,"* **David Mitchell** (see p.526) is said to be *"wonderful"* for commodities and futures issues. Focused on advising clients on trading, structuring transactions, and legal and regulatory issues pertaining to risk management, Mitchell has lately been occupied with matters pertaining to the Enron proceedings. **Lary Stromfeld**'s (see p.538) practice centers around the development, negotiation and documentation of a wide variety of financial products. He also assists clients in the creation of a full range of structured derivative products that rely upon embedded derivatives.

Davis Polk & Wardwell
The Firm: This practice holds a preeminent position for its advice on equity derivatives, and boasts a dedicated group that focuses on the creation of off-balance sheet products for major investment banks. The equity derivatives group includes over 35 securities and tax lawyers advising on equity-related transactions. The team maintains particularly close ties to Morgan Stanley and Goldman Sachs, and has lately been active in the creation of a number of derivatives linked to the retail and energy markets. Clients report that members of the firm are able to *"not just define legal risk, but think about things as we think about them."* Attorneys here are further distinguished by possessing a *"firm grasp of the underlying economic issues."* The firm is highly recommended for its work on hedge fund and mutual-linked products, and is seen to be expanding into asset classes outside the equity arena.
The Lawyers: **John Brandow** heads the equity derivatives group, and *"has his finger on the pulse of the industry."* Clients report: *"He can jump into our shoes and tell us what we need to do."* An equity derivatives specialist, Brandow advises major investment banks on new products and the convergence of capital markets and over-the-counter (OTC) work.
He recently advised the underwriters on convertible securities offerings for Lucent Technologies, AIG, and Chubb, and advised AT&T on the monetization of its holdings of Cablevision tracking

stock. *"One of the best derivatives lawyers out there,"* **Dan Budofksy** undertakes OTC work as well as some distributed transactions involving institutional markets. He continues to work on a variety of hedging transactions, including restructurings.
The Clients: Morgan Stanley; JPMorgan Chase; Bank of America and CSFB.

Allen & Overy
The Firm: This *"top-quality"* firm is perceived to be *"making a push"* in the market and fielding some *"significant players."* It is best known for its coveted role as chief US, European and Asian counsel to ISDA (International Swaps and Derivatives Association). The firm also advised the Norwegian Futures & Options Clearing House and the International Maritime Derivatives Exchange on US, UK and Swiss regulatory matters in connection with the establishment of an electronic trading facility for cash-settled futures contracts for the transportation of maritime freight.
The Lawyers: An attorney who *"knows the industry's whole history,"* **Dan Cunningham** is the long-standing counsel to ISDA, and is hailed as a specialist in OTC work. He and his team advise Phibro and Citicorp with respect to set-off and collateralization issues under derivatives documentation.
The Clients: International Swaps and Derivatives Association (ISDA) is the firm's key client.

Shearman & Sterling
The Firm: The firm looms large on the international scene, thanks to its well-developed global network. In New York, a smaller team of derivatives specialists collaborates with the firm's structured products attorneys as part of an integrated practice. Rivals praise the group's efforts to expand the practice. Building from a solid base in commodities work, the team has *"made strides"* in developing its equity derivatives capacities, and is involved increasingly in the development of hybrid and synthetic products. Practitioners cover a range of asset classes, including currency, equity and weather derivatives, and boast considerable regulatory expertise. Clients report that the group's focus on documentation *"helps keep the wheels of commerce turning."*
The Lawyers: A *"popular figure"* with end-users, **M Holland West** reflects the firm's *"multidisciplinary"* approach, and specializes in derivatives, structured products and securitizations. West coheads the firm's securitization and derivatives group and is well known for his commodities exchange focus.
The Clients: Citicorp; Salomon Smith Barney; Deutsche Bank; The Bank of Nova Scotia; Merrill Lynch; The TCW Group; JPMorgan Chase and Morgan Stanley.

Skadden, Arps, Slate, Meagher & Flom LLP & Affiliates
see firm details p.878
The Firm: The practice's strength and focus, reflecting the nature of the firm, is perceived to be in transactional rather than regulatory work. Attorneys integrate derivatives into a wide range of transactions, and handle an increasing amount of work involving securities with embedded derivatives features. Practitioners advise a large corporate client base on derivatives-related risk and are noted for a particular strength in income derivatives. The group has seen growth in real estate and insurance-related derivatives and benefits from a thorough knowledge of international tax regimes in advising on cross-border work.
The Lawyers: *"Talented and hard-working,"* **John Osborn** (see p.528) is a *"major figure in the industry."* Head of the firm's derivative financial products practice, Osborn is said to employ a *"generalist"* approach, and possesses a *"refined insight into the market."* He has acted on a wide spectrum of transactions for banks, dealers and end-users, but tends to concentrate on work for institutional end-users, particularly in relation to securities offerings with derivatives features. He recently acted for the underwriter and interest rate swap provider in a major domestic offering of asset-backed securities. Other matters include advising the issuer and currency swap provider in a combined offshore and domestic private offering of repackaged complex mortgage-backed securities.
The Clients: Citibank; Deutsche Bank; Goldman Sachs and Merrill Lynch.

Mayer, Brown, Rowe & Maw
see firm details p.843
The Firm: The firm fields a ten-partner derivatives team from offices in Chicago, DC, New York and London. Its Chicago origins mean the firm is active in the Chicago and Midwest exchanges, and the group has attracted particular mention for its strength in commodities work. Described as *"good people, without exception,"* attorneys here were said to possess a depth of knowledge not only in futures and regulation issues, but also in the full range of transactional, operational and regulatory matters, including arbitration and litigation. The team includes a number of individuals with experience in the Commodity Futures Trading Commission (CFTC), US Treasury or SEC, who can advise on compliance with currency control, banking, securities insurance and partnership regulation. The 2002 linkup with UK firm Rowe & Maw has given Mayer Brown wider access to the London corporate market and European bond issuers.
The Lawyers: Identified by peers as the practice's *"mover and shaker,"* **Joseph Collins** (see p.509) heads the firm's derivatives group from its Chicago office. In addition to substantial expertise in swaps and futures, Collins is increasingly involved in the development of managed products, hedge funds and alternative investments. and counsels corporate clients on new legislation.
The Clients: The firm represented Ameritrade Holding in its merger agreement with Datek Online Holdings.

Stroock & Stroock & Lavan LLP
The Firm: The *"go-to practice for physical commodities,"* the group is commonly cited for its work for Goldman Sachs in this area. *"High-quality"* name practitioners won recognition among interviewees. The team handles both litigation and documentation issues, and has lately acted on a number of credit derivative structures. The firm is heavily involved in the energy markets, advising project developers, electric and gas utilities, oil companies and financial institutions in the use of complex derivatives for hedging and other strategic purposes.
The Lawyers: Managing partner **Thomas Heftler** focuses on commodities and derivatives transactions relating to energy, metals and currencies. He regularly acts for Goldman Sachs and its commodity merchant affiliates in trading, finance, new product development and joint ventures. **Marvin Goldstein** concentrates on commodities and derivatives, counseling clients as dealers and participants in those markets. In addition to work in energy trading, Goldstein handles more traditional commodities, including metals, coffee, sugar and cocoa.
The Clients: AIG; Bear Stearns; CSFB; Goldman Sachs; Hess Energy Trading; JPMorgan Chase and UBS Warburg.

Other Notable Practitioners
An *"expert in documentation,"* **Linda Klein** (see p.521) leads the derivatives group of Dewey Ballantine LLP, and has long experience in OTC derivatives. She regularly advises dealers and end-users on interest rate, currency, commodity price, credit, equity and weather derivatives, and their use in CDO, securitization and project finance structures. She has recently counseled REITs and investment managers on the application of synthetic CDOs and other derivatives.

CAPITAL MARKETS

NEW YORK

CAPITAL MARKETS

SECURITIZATION

NEW YORK
Leading firms
(Capital Markets: Securitization)

1
ORRICK, HERRINGTON & SUTCLIFFE
SIDLEY AUSTIN BROWN & WOOD
SKADDEN, ARPS, SLATE, MEAGHER & FLOM LLP

2
CADWALADER, WICKERSHAM & TAFT
MAYER, BROWN, ROWE & MAW

3
CLEARY GOTTLIEB STEEN & HAMILTON
CRAVATH, SWAINE & MOORE
SIMPSON THACHER & BARTLETT

4
MCKEE NELSON LLP

5
WEIL, GOTSHAL & MANGES LLP

6
DEWEY BALLANTINE LLP
FRIED, FRANK, HARRIS, SHRIVER & JACOBSON
THACHER PROFFITT & WOOD

Leading individuals
(Capital Markets: Securitization)

1
COWAN Cameron *Orrick, Herrington*
DE SEAR Edward *Orrick, Herrington*
KRAVITT Jason *Mayer, Brown, Rowe & Maw*
KUNZ Thomas *Skadden, Arps, Slate*
MARTIN Renwick *Sidley Austin Brown*

2
AUERBACH Reed *McKee Nelson LLP*
CURTIS Susan *Skadden, Arps, Slate, Meagher*
ISAACSON Laurence *Fried, Frank, Harris*
SCHETMAN Richard *Cadwalader*
SHAW Gregory *Cravath, Swaine & Moore*
WIPPERMAN Robert *McKee Nelson LLP*

3
CITRON Diane *Mayer, Brown, Rowe & Maw*
DIANGELO Christopher *Dewey Ballantine*
EISENBERG David *Simpson Thacher*
KADLICK Richard *Skadden, Arps, Slate*
KAPLAN Cathy *Sidley Austin Brown & Wood*
NOCCO Frank *Weil, Gotshal & Manges LLP*
PALMA Laura *Simpson Thacher & Bartlett*

4
ARNHOLZ John *McKee Nelson LLP*
GLASS Adam *Sidley Austin Brown & Wood*
GLICK Anna *Cadwalader, Wickersham & Taft*
KUDENHOLDT Stephen *Thacher Proffitt*

Up-and-coming individuals
HOROWITZ Richard *Thacher Proffitt & Wood*
STRINGFELLOW James *Skadden, Arps, Slate*

Firms and individuals are listed alphabetically in each band.

Orrick, Herrington & Sutcliffe
see firm details p.859

The Firm: This *"top-notch"* team was lauded by interviewees for its significant commitment to the area. The firm is noteworthy for the sheer size of its securitization practice group; clients reported that *"Orricks has a large staff suitable for running multiple deals,"* and added that *"there is never a resource problem."* The group excels at volume securitization work but a *"deep bench"* of able practitioners permits the leading lights to concentrate on high-end work. Ten New York partners work closely with large groups of structured finance specialists in the DC, LA, San Francisco, London and Tokyo offices on the securitization of novel asset classes. A recent merger with the Paris branch of Watson Farley & Williams will further expand the practice's international reach. In addition to a substantial workload of traditional asset-backed and CDO securitizations, the firm is active in the securitization of credit card receivables due to strong relationships with major credit card issuers. Researchers were told that the firm has *"a lot of intellectual capital"* and distinguishes itself in complex work.

The Lawyers: Described by clients as *"the real thing,"* chair of the structured finance group **Ed De Sear** (see p.510) combines *"a great bedside manner"* with a *"phenomenal"* showing on innovative structures. He has attracted particular praise from rivals for successfully expanding the practice beyond credit card work. His own practice emphasizes asset-backed securities, including the securitization of legal fees for plaintiff lawyers in tobacco litigation settlements.

"A great deal-maker," De Sear's background as an investment banker is said to give him a *"businesslike approach"* to securitizations. Recent matters include two issuances of credit card loss-indexed certificates jointly developed by Goldman Sachs and Bank of America, which provided protection to Bank of America against credit card losses on a leveraged basis.

"Extraordinarily strong" DC-based **Cam Cowan** (see p.134) was hailed by clients and peers as an *"exceptional lawyer"* with a *"ubiquitous"* market presence. He has taken on industry roles in response to a troubled market, but remains predominantly active in credit card work, drawing upon close relationships with MBNA America Bank and Capital One.

The Clients: JPMorgan Chase and Wachovia Securities are also clients.

Sidley Austin Brown & Wood
see firm details p.877

The Firm: This *"superlative"* practice, created by the 2001 merger of Sidley & Austin with Brown & Wood, combines strength in volume and cutting-edge work. A *"huge"* department is perceived to be *"taking over"* the market in commodity work (*"They are in everything"*), while retaining its reputation for quality. *"Strong commitment"* to the field is shown by the 170-lawyer global securitization group, practicing from offices in New York, LA, Chicago, San Francisco and Seattle as well as London, Hong Kong, Tokyo and Singapore. Highlights include the representation of DZ Bank and The Bank of Nova Scotia in the first synthetic CDO to be listed on the Frankfurt Stock Exchange. The firm also represented KBC Bank in two managed synthetic CDOs, and Wachovia Bank in a static pool arbitrage synthetic CDO. The firm advised Deutsche Bank in its first US credit-linked note arbitrage synthetic CDO, and UBS Warburg in a hybrid CDO.

The Lawyers: *"A talented lawyer and great guy to boot,"* **Renwick Martin** is also described as a *"total class act."* He undertakes a variety of transactions, mostly asset-backed, and has been heavily occupied with CDOs. In addition to his work for major underwriters, Martin's *"unassailable character"* is said to *"do a lot for the industry."* A *"veteran of the field,"* **Cathy Kaplan** maintains an eclectic practice that includes growing amounts of synthetic risk transfer structures and corporate bond repackaging. Cohead of the New York securitization practice, she specializes in cross-border transactions. She represented Deutsche Bank in its Blue Spice CP transactions, and was involved in a recent Samsung securitization. **Adam Glass** focuses largely on synthetic products and credit derivatives, while continuing to do some franchise loan securitization and SEC-registered corporate bond repackaging. His practice includes credit derivatives work for US, UK and Hong Kong entities. He recently represented Bank of America Securities as underwriter in the $560 million static pool synthetic CLO securitization by Northwest Farm Credit.

The Clients: Banc One; Commerzbank; Deutsche Bank; Fannie Mae; Lehman Brothers; Merrill Lynch; Swiss Re; Wells Fargo and Zurich Re.

Skadden, Arps, Slate, Meagher & Flom LLP & Affiliates
see firm details p.878

The Firm: This firm's sizable securitization practice – *"at the top of the market"* – is known for both its *"quality and deep resources."* A major market presence (*"They do a ton"*), the firm has *"a lot of good people,"* and attorneys here are characterized as *"seasoned"* and *"solution-oriented."* Researchers were particularly impressed with the level of commendation for the firm's individual attorneys, while commentators noted their depth in credit cards, auto loans and revolving master trusts work. The group continues to figure prominently as adviser to larger issuers in traditional securitizations involving credit card and trade receivables, mortgages and auto loans. It has also seen an increase in transactions using securitization in bankruptcy or restructuring situations and the restructuring of existing CDOs.

The Lawyers: Credited with *"building a mighty practice"* at the firm, **Thomas Kunz** (see p.522) is

NEW YORK

CAPITAL MARKETS

a *"giant in the industry."* Although increasingly absorbed by managerial responsibilities, Kunz is judged *"matchless"* for his *"broad expertise, knowledge, and ingenuity with new asset classes."* He represents underwriters, issuers, depositories and credit enhancers in asset-backed securities transactions and credit-enhanced securities issuances. Researchers were told the *"excellent"* **Susan Curtis** (see p.509) *"works hard for her client"* and often *"takes the lead"* on complex transactions. Possessing long experience of the CBO market as counsel for underwriters and collateral managers, Curtis recently handled a number of CDO transactions involving mortgage-backed and asset-backed securities.

Richard Kadlick (see p.519) focuses on CDOs and CBOs, and has noteworthy expertise in instruments backed by both family and commercial mortgage loans. He also undertakes 'principal finance' work involving asset acquisition for the purposes of portfolio securitization. *"Well-respected"* **James Stringfellow** (see p.538) has a general securitization practice, with a background in traditional asset-backed work. His current practice emphasizes newer products, including synthetic CDOs, and credit default swap type transactions for such clients as Deutsche Bank.

The Clients: UBS Securities; Bank One; Chase Manhattan; Ford Motor Credit; Morgan Stanley; Goldman Sachs; CSFB; Fleet Bank; Salomon Smith Barney; JP Morgan Securities; John Hancock and New York Life.

Cadwalader, Wickersham & Taft
see firm details p.778

The Firm: Most often recommended for its leading commercial mortgage practice, the firm is also visible on some *"significant"* credit card securitizations. Clients describe a *"deep"* team with the *"scope to take on multiple transactions"* and the *"brainpower to handle innovative projects."* The firm has been involved in municipal, asset-backed fund of fund and project finance CBOs, as well as CBO restructurings for Lehman Brothers, Salomon Smith Barney, CSFB and Morgan Stanley. The group has seen a high volume of activity in residential and commercial mortgage-backed securitizations as counsel to Federal Home Loan Mortgage Corporation (Freddie Mac) and the Student Loan Marketing Association (Sallie Mae).

The Lawyers: Clients depend upon **Richard Schetman** (see p.534) for his *"clear and honest explanations of legal risk."* He represents underwriters, credit enhancers, issuers, institutional investors and trustees, and has extensive experience in structuring commercial paper vehicles and vehicles for repackaging corporate, asset-backed and non-US securities. Schetman recently advised Lehman Brothers in structuring a synthetic CBO program, and undertook over 40 repackagings in 2002 involving credit products, stripping and principal-protected and auction rate structures. He also counseled UBS on tobacco legal fee settlement transactions. A *"past master"* of the field, **Anna Glick** (see p.515) has worked in multi-class securitization since its inception, representing issuers, underwriters and institutional investors. Glick has particular experience in the securitization of commercial mortgage loans. Clients report: *"She knows the market inside and out and can walk you through any deal."*

The Clients: CSFB; Deutsche Bank; Lehman Brothers; Morgan Stanley and Salomon Smith Barney.

Mayer, Brown, Rowe & Maw
see firm details p.843

The Firm: The locus of the firm's securitization practice is seen to be shifting from Chicago to New York as a result of Jason Kravitt's 2001 move to the New York office. However, the two groups act as an integrated practice, and receive additional support from offices in Charlotte, Houston, London, Frankfurt and Paris. Recommended as a *"major player"* in the field, the firm received particular praise for its expertise in commercial paper conduit work. The team also has extensive experience in the securitization of trade receivables through the use of MTNs.

The Lawyers: A *"figurehead"* for the industry, **Jason Kravitt** (see p.522) was widely recognized as an *"intellectual leader"* in the securitization bar. Active in securitization sector initiatives, Kravitt earns praise for *"pulling together the industry"* in response to regulatory issues. In 2002, Kravitt was elected secretary of the American Securitization Forum, a newly formed trade association. *"Extremely well versed in the history of securitization as well as in the technical aspects of structured deals,"* he is also said to be *"clearly well ahead"* with respect to multi-seller conduits. Despite Kravitt's increased involvement in regulatory and management issues, clients report that they would *"hire him in a heartbeat."* Cohead of the firm's securitization practice, **Diane Citron** (see p.509) was described by peers as *"a diamond"* for her *"dedication"* and expertise in commercial mortgage-backed securities (CMBS) matters. She is well known for her work on Australian mortgage-backed deals and occasional industry involvement. Clients praise her *"commercial savvy"* and *"credibility with the SEC."* Citron recently worked on a cross-border warehouse financing using commercial mortgage loans originated by a major financial company, and also acted for Australian bank Members Equity on its first SEC issuance of mortgage-backed securities.

The Clients: Citigroup; Deutsche Bank; Bank of America; Morgan Stanley; Merrill Lynch; GMAC; GMAC Commercial Mortgage; Commonwealth Bank of Australia; Westpac; St George Bank; GE Capital Services; Crédit Lyonnais and CSFB.

Cleary Gottlieb Steen & Hamilton
see firm details p.782

The Firm: Although a significant presence in the New York market, the firm earns greatest recognition for the strength of its cross-border practice, which draws upon an extensive network of global offices. Staffed across the New York and DC offices, the group has experience of a range of asset classes. The team undertakes commercial and residential mortgage work for Goldman Sachs, and serves as principal underwriter's counsel on public offerings of mortgage-backed securities and debt by Freddie Mac and Sallie Mae. The firm, which features Andrea Podolsky, was repeatedly recommended for its CDO work and advises most of the major investment banks. Practitioners also possess expertise in relation to convertible and synthetic assets as well as European high yield assets. In this regard, it recently worked on a CDO transaction involving the securitization of a $1 billion loan and lease operations in multiple jurisdictions, and synthetic transfers of assets. Overseas, the firm is active in the securitization of telephone, oil, power and credit card receivables, and receives particular attention for its Latin American and European market activities.

The Clients: CSFB; Deutsche Bank; GE Capital; Goldman Sachs; Merrill Lynch; Morgan Stanley and Salomon Smith Barney.

Cravath, Swaine & Moore

The Firm: This specialized team comprising two securitization partners and a tax partner enjoys special status as a *"niche player"* in the market. Although not felt to possess the depth of its major competitors, the practice earns high marks for the *"high quality"* and *"intellectual acumen"* of its attorneys. Credit card securitization, particularly on behalf of key client Citigroup, forms the bedrock of the practice. The team also regularly acts for the firm's major corporate clients as buyers or sellers of securitized trade receivables.

The Lawyers: The firm's profile hinges on the *"excellent"* **Greg Shaw**, head of the asset-backed securities group. This *"user-friendly"* attorney *"thinks through all the issues"* and was particularly noted by peers for his experience in esoteric securitizations. Shaw recently represented Hertz in the creation of a special purpose vehicle to finance its rental car fleet, and acted for Providian Bank in the sale of some sub-prime assets

The Clients: Citigroup, Providian Bank and Hertz are clients.

Simpson Thacher & Bartlett

The Firm: Forming part of the firm's focus on M&A, the firm's *"select"* securitization practice is geared towards one-off, high-end matters rather than volume activity. Much of the firm's securitization work takes place in the context of other financings and structured deals. The three-partner team frequently advises Chase as issuer in their credit card program.

The Lawyers: Recommended for her ability to *"get to the heart of things,"* **Laura Palma** handles securitization transactions as part of a general corporate finance practice. Her focus on rental car financing kept her busy in a difficult year for the rental car industry. Palma represented Lehman Brothers as structuring agent in the establishment of a rental car fleet financing program for Hertz. She also acted for a group of banks led by JPMorgan Chase in connection with the restructuring of the Avis rental car fleet financing program. Other work includes representing JP Morgan Securities as structuring agent in a $3 billion single-seller commercial paper program established by DaimlerChrysler Services North America. Head of the asset-backed practice, the *"excellent"* **David Eisenberg** is well known for his work for Chase on credit card and auto loan securitizations. He has also lately been involved in private credit card work and a film financing for a major film production company.

The Clients: JPMorgan Chase; JP Morgan Securities; Lehman Brothers; The Blackstone Group; Northwest Airlines; American Electric Power; DreamWorks SKG and Dillard's.

McKee Nelson LLP

The Firm: The arrival in mid-2002 of a respected securitization team from Stroock & Stroock & Lavan has dramatically increased this firm's depth and profile in the area. While many market commentators reserved judgment on the new practice, clients were enthusiastic: *"They have some of the best talent in New York focusing on structured products."* Although yet to truly distinguish itself in high-end products, the group has a *"great grasp of the market"* and *"growing firepower."* The firm represented Sallie Mae in its first securitization backed only by consolidation loans, valued at $2 billion.

The Lawyers: The firm now boasts 32 securitization specialists, distributed between the New York and DC offices. Tipped as *"the next big star,"* **Reed Auerbach** (see p.504) focuses on asset-backed securities and esoteric asset classes, often working as designated underwriter's counsel for such clients as Deutsche Bank. He has a notable practice representing underwriters on auto loan and auto lease transactions, student loans, and equipment contracts. Auerbach has also been involved in the securitization of tobacco agreements, royalty streams and golf courses. He recently acted for Sallie Mae as issuers' counsel in a private student loan transaction. **Robert Wipperman** (see p.542) focuses on residential mortgage work, both prime and sub-prime. He has worked on numerous net interest margin securities deals and represented Banc of America Securities and Goldman Sachs as underwriters of a $4.1 billion home equity securitization. Noted for his *"keen business understanding,"* Wipperman *"always gives sound advice"* and is said to be *"unsurpassed in his ability to work with the SEC."* DC-based **John Arnholz** is a *"great lawyer and excellent manager."* He represents issuers and underwriters, focusing on cross-border and global offerings. He has experience advising on residential mortgage and home equity loans, debt obligations, auto, franchise and high loan-to-value (LTV) loans.

The Clients: Deutsche Bank Securities; Lehman Brothers; CSFB; Greenwich Capital Markets and Goldman Sachs.

Weil, Gotshal & Manges LLP
see firm details p.897

The Firm: A firm with a *"strong presence,"* it is said to be *"moving up"* in the marketplace. The group has grown rapidly in recent years and now numbers 40 lawyers; peers particularly congratulated the firm for making *"canny"* strategic lateral hires. The group's workload encompasses a varied range of asset classes and an even balance of issuer and underwriter representation. The firm represented Financial Security Assurance as credit enhancer in a $1.8 billion automobile retail installment securitization. Work for the main institutional banks includes the securitization of a portfolio of non-investment grade bank loans for JPMorgan Chase and Goldman Sachs. Acting for Lehman Brothers as arranger and committed lender, the firm worked on the establishment of a securitized warehouse facility for Household Finance.

The Lawyers: Singled out for his skill at managing deals and resources, **Frank Nocco** (see p.528) inspires *"tremendous client loyalty"* through his *"hard-working ethic."* With notable strength in rental car securitization, he has represented ANC Rental for several years, including counseling in its Chapter 11 proceedings. He recently acted for Lehman Brothers in connection with the establishment of a synthetic structured commercial paper conduit for Abbey National Treasury Services. He also represented the structuring agent in connection with the establishment of Fenway Funding, a $5 billion multi-seller, asset-backed extendible commercial paper conduit.

The Clients: ANC Rental; BMW; CSFB; Financial Security Assurance; GE Capital; Goldman Sachs; JPMorgan Chase; Lehman Brothers; MBIA; Merrill Lynch and Morgan Stanley.

Dewey Ballantine LLP
see firm details p.790

The Firm: A *"traditional"* practice, thought to be *"among the best"* for home equity loan securitization. Five New York partners receive referral work from practices in DC, LA, Menlo Park, London, Hong Kong and Warsaw. The firm has a strong following among auto loan clients and received praise for its handling of sub-prime assets. Practitioners also have expertise in credit card receivables, commercial paper and commercial trade finance payment items as well as foreign currency transactions.

The Lawyers: **Chris DiAngelo** (see p.510) maintains a domestic focus on credit card programs for Household International, mortgage work for UBS Warburg and Morgan Stanley, and auto payment securitizations. Clients characterize him as a *"manager of projects,"* with a *"sixth sense for where the market is at"* and a *"deep understanding of legal implications."*

The Clients: Ford; Honda; Household International; Morgan Stanley and UBS Warburg.

Fried, Frank, Harris, Shriver & Jacobson
see firm details p.796

The Firm: This small New York practice, comprising three partners and 15 associates, receives support from practitioners in DC and London on complex structured products. The group was lauded for its work on credit-linked offerings for Morgan Stanley, Barclays and Bear Stearns, and for its related strength in credit derivatives. The firm recently advised Goldman Sachs in a 'CRISP' transaction, a synthetic securitization of consumer credit card assets.

The Lawyers: Considered a leading market figure in CDO work, **Laurence Isaacson** (see p.519) rates as a *"remarkable"* attorney with an *"innovative"* approach to transactions. He continues to act for commercial and investment banks and insurance companies on a variety of CDOs, including some emerging markets work. He recently represented Goldman Sachs in a synthetic CDO that combined techniques from the synthetic, cash flow and unfunded (super senior) markets, and represented Deutsche Bank in an emerging market CDO that also mixed cash flow and synthetic structures. Isaacson additionally represented JPMorgan, as initial purchaser, in a $550 CFO managed by Man-Glenwood.

The Clients: Goldman Sachs; Deutsche Bank; Morgan Stanley; JPMorgan and UBS Warburg.

Thacher Proffitt & Wood

The Firm: This 50-attorney practice focuses predominantly on residential and commercial mortgage securitizations and is recognized for its *"groundbreaking work"* in the field. Sources report the group has become a *"significant presence in the sub-prime market"* and has broad expertise in asset securitizations involving auto loan, student loan, credit card and healthcare exports and municipal receivables. Attorneys here also advise on regulatory issues and the use of swaps and derivatives in securitization structures.

The Lawyers: Chairman of the structured finance practice group, **Stephen Kudenholdt**

earns peer recommendation for his focus on residential mortgage loan securitization and resecuritization transactions involving various classes of mortgage-backed securities. Kudenholdt recently worked on a number of offshore resecuritization transactions. *"Market-savvy"* **Richard Horowitz** is said to demonstrate *"excellent judgment"* in his *"shrewd analysis of legal risk."* Horowitz concentrates on residential, multi-family and commercial loan securitizations and has established a *"loyal following among issuer clients."*

COMMUNICATIONS

NEW YORK
Leading firms (Communications)
1. MILBANK, TWEED, HADLEY & MCCLOY
2. SHAW PITTMAN LLP
3. KAYE SCHOLER LLP
   MORRISON & FOERSTER LLP
   SKADDEN, ARPS, SLATE, MEAGHER & FLOM LLP
   WEIL, GOTSHAL & MANGES LLP
4. BROWN RAYSMAN MILLSTEIN FELDER
   HALE AND DORR
   WILLKIE FARR & GALLAGHER

Leading individuals (Communications)
1. HALVEY John *Milbank, Tweed, Hadley*
2. HUDANISH David *Mayer, Brown, Rowe*
3. DELANEY John *Morrison & Foerster LLP*
   EPSTEIN Michael *Weil, Gotshal & Manges*
   KRAUS Bruce *Willkie Farr & Gallagher*
   LEVI Stuart *Skadden, Arps, Slate, Meagher*
   NESGOS Peter *Milbank, Tweed, Hadley*
   STERN Akiba *Shaw Pittman LLP*
   TANENBAUM William *Kaye Scholer LLP*

Firms and individuals are listed alphabetically in each band.

Milbank, Tweed, Hadley & McCloy
The Firm: The firm's communications and space practice group is admired for its industry expertise in relation to IT, space and satellites, telecommunications, and corporate finance transactions. Researchers heard that the firm has a long-standing reputation in outsourcing deals. Recent work in this area includes representing AT&T on both an HR outsourcing deal with Aon and a $2.6 billion outsourcing deal with Accenture regarding customer care and sales. On the IT/business processing side, the firm advises the NYSE and Deloitte Consulting on outsourcing and system integration work. The New York practice is seen to be expanding following recent recruitment, and interviewees particularly commended the firm's efforts to enlarge its international coverage.
The Lawyers: Within the New York market, **John Halvey** is *"clearly the name in outsourcing; most of the players in that area have worked with him at some stage."* Halvey's 1999 departure to serve as executive vice president of Safeguard Scientifics was seen to be a setback for the firm, and his recent return to practice has given the group a timely boost. *"Tough but fair,"* **Peter Nesgos** was described by one client as *"one of the world's most preeminent space lawyers."* He represents financial institutions, space manufacturers and satellite operators, principally in financial transactions. A recent highlight was his representation of the underwriters (Morgan Stanley, Merrill Lynch and Lehman Brothers) in the Intelsat bond offering and proposed IPO.
The Clients: AT&T; NYSE; Deloitte Consulting; Morgan Stanley; Merrill Lynch; Lehman Brothers; CSFB; Goldman Sachs and Fleet.

Shaw Pittman LLP
The Firm: Established in 1994, the New York office's technology practice focuses on strategic transactions for large institutions, including agreements involving software and software systems, enterprise resource systems, integration and maintenance. The DC office's *"top-notch"* reputation for outsourcing is echoed by the New York practice, with competitors applauding the firm's work in this area. Attorneys represent a number of high-profile financial institutions such as HSBC, whom the practice advised on its formation of a strategic relationship with Yahoo! and an agreement to provide global online payment services through Yahoo!'s PayDirect service. The group advises multinational media conglomerate Vivendi on acquisitions and disposals and maintains a long-standing relationship with insurance and investment company The Hartford.
The Lawyers: Akiba Stern was described as *"the one to go to"* for IT and corporate transactions. Clients noted his facility for *"closing enormous deals."* His deal resumé includes advising Aventis on a multinational full-scope outsourcing transaction and negotiating HSBC's global strategic technology alliance with Yahoo!
The Clients: HSBC; Vivendi; The Hartford; Aventis; Independence Savings Bank and MetLife.

Kaye Scholer LLP
The Firm: The firm's technology and e-commerce practice group is a full-service, coordinated team that has expertise in areas including industry-related transactions, IP, e-commerce, the internet, IT, outsourcing, computer law, privacy and litigation.
The Lawyers: The firm's attorneys have substantial IP and technology industry experience. This applies particularly to practice chair, **Bill Tanenbaum**, who commands the respect of peers for his ability and success, and of clients for his efficiency and responsiveness.
The Clients: Recent work includes acting for Merrill Lynch in acquiring technology, and for the Guardian Life Insurance Company in outsourcing, IT licensing and transactions, and computer dispute resolution. The firm also represented Cendant in outsourcing, IT licensing and transactions, and in international privacy compliance programs. Additional IT clients of the firm include AOL Time Warner, JPMorgan Chase, Rockefeller Group Telecommunications, ACNielsen, Galileo International and the United States Tennis Association.

Morrison & Foerster LLP
see firm details p.854
The Firm: The New York practice is one of the largest in the firm's international network. A 15-strong technology transaction group advises on IP and technology issues including privacy policies, trademarks, copyrights, patents, licensing, joint ventures and outsourcing. Expertise in the technology industry ranges from hi-tech (including IT, e-commerce and telecommunications) through life sciences to broadcast and new media (including TV and multimedia).
The Lawyers: Described by peers as *"the cornerstone of the practice,"* **John Delaney** (see p.510) is admired for both his industry knowledge and his extensive legal skills. A technology licensing lawyer, his focus is on joint ventures and licensing agreements. He has experience in internet-related issues and in general outsourcing work.
The Clients: The group provides outsourcing advice to clients in the defense and aerospace, financial services, insurance, medical and healthcare, real estate, technology and telecom sectors. Clients of the technology transaction group are local, national, international and multinational businesses. These include entertainment, multimedia, software, telecom, online trading, investment and credit card companies, and websites and banks.

COMMUNICATIONS

NEW YORK

Skadden, Arps, Slate, Meagher & Flom LLP & Affiliates
see firm details p.878

The Firm: Hailed as "*a firm that really understands the technology underlying and transforming the industry,*" Skadden Arps is respected among industry specialists for its "*holistic approach*" to technology and communications. Praise for the firm's strong corporate base is unanimous, and interviewees identified several leaders in M&A and venture capital who were felt to have "*given Skadden a leg up through their experience.*" Telecom corporation ntl remains a major client for the firm and attorneys have lately been advising on the company's financial restructuring and pre-arranged bankruptcy.

The Lawyers: The IT and e-commerce group is led by **Stuart Levi** (see p.523), a specialist in strategic alliances who also focuses on outsourcing and portal agreements. Recent work in this area has included acting on a major strategic alliance for Citigroup with Microsoft, allowing for the provision of online alerts to Citigroup's users through Microsoft's .NET services.

The Clients: Financial institutions and hi-tech companies.

Weil, Gotshal & Manges LLP
see firm details p.897

The Firm: The firm's reputation in the communications and technology industries plays on its noted strengths in corporate/M&A and restructuring matters, as well as bringing to the fore Weil Gotshal's technology-specific capability. "*They have expertise in IP, antitrust and licensing and a presence in new media activities,*" one industry insider told researchers. The firm's preeminence in bankruptcy and restructuring advice serves it well in the current industry climate; the firm is currently handling major telecom restructurings for WorldCom and Global Crossing and represented the committee of unsecured creditors of Iridium in its bankruptcy proceedings. Competitors also remarked upon the strength of the group's technology M&A practice. Recent deals include acting as US counsel to Pirelli on its acquisition, through a consortium, of Olivetti, the controlling company of Telecom Italia. The firm also represented Pirelli in a research and development transaction with the Massachusetts Institute of Technology.

The Lawyers: **Michael Epstein** (see p.512) commands "*obvious stature*" in IP circles. His expertise in this and e-commerce is an asset to the practice, as is his work advising on transactional matters.

The Clients: WorldCom; Global Crossing; Pirelli; Hughes and Vivendi.

Brown Raysman Millstein Felder & Steiner LLP

The Firm: The firm has grown from an IT-focused practice to a general corporate firm through the January 2002 addition of core commercial practices from the New York firm of Baer Marks & Upham and is now widely admired as a "*diversified technology boutique with very good transactional lawyers.*" A dedicated IT group provides counsel in areas such as development, procurement, licensing, distribution and transfer of software, hardware, and telecom products and services. The outsourcing group's activities include IT operations, business process outsourcing, and facilities and real property operations. The firm is a longtime player in e-commerce matters and advises clients, ranging from start-ups to large public and private institutions, on development and hosting agreements, joint ventures, and portal and content transactions.

The Lawyers: In New York, managing partner Richard Raysman focuses on computer law, outsourcing and IP.

The Clients: Clients range from internet start-ups through investment banks, entertainment and media companies, and financial services and insurance firms to software and technology infrastructure vendors.

Hale and Dorr

The Firm: Recommended in particular for its IT and IP expertise, this tech-focused firm advises telecom, software, electronics and life sciences clients on matters such as transactions, licensing agreements, joint ventures, outsourcing and strategic alliances. The New York internet and e-commerce group draws on experience in corporate and business law as well as in IP, litigation, licensing and strategic alliance issues, government affairs and tax matters. Additionally, the office has lawyers with expertise in telecom and wireless-related industries.

The Clients: Clients include software providers and commercial entities joining the e-commerce market. In telecom matters, the firm acts on behalf of network providers, designers and manufacturers of products used in communications, computer and industrial markets, and wireless operating companies.

Willkie Farr & Gallagher
see firm details p.900

The Firm: A dedicated telecom and media group possesses expertise in an array of corporate and commercial transactions, working closely with the firm's litigation department on industry-led litigation. In recent years, the firm has attracted market comment for its work in prominent telecom restructurings. Most notably, practitioners have been advising 360networks concerning ongoing restructuring work and developing a restructuring plan, and acting on corporate finance, M&A and litigation for long-term client Loral Space & Communications.

The Lawyers: "*Smooth dealer*" **Bruce Kraus** (see p.522) has lately been visible advising XO Communications on a debt restructuring in response to a takeover battle between US financier Carl Icahn and Forstmann Little & Co and Mexican telecom carrier Téléfonos de México.

The Clients: Clients are drawn from industries such as IT, software, TV (including cable operators and cable programmers) and finance providers investing in technology-related enterprises. These include: XO Communications; 360networks; Globalstar; Loral Space & Communications and UBS Warburg.

Other Notable Practitioners

David Hudanish (see p.519), formerly with the now defunct Brobeck, Phleger & Harrison LLP, has joined Mayer, Brown, Rowe & Maw following the Brobeck Phleger dissolution. Interviewees recommended his expertise, which is "*heavily focused on tech solutions.*" Hudanish concentrates on sophisticated IT and business process outsourcing transactions and was lauded by clients for his "*quick understanding of complex needs.*" Recent work includes representing DuPont in negotiating a worldwide enterprise resource planning system with Accenture (customizing the software) and CSC (hosting).

NEW YORK — CONSTRUCTION

CONSTRUCTION

NEW YORK
Leading firms (Construction)

1
- PECKAR & ABRAMSON, PC
- POSTNER & RUBIN
- THELEN REID & PRIEST LLP

2
- ROSS & COHEN LLP
- ZETLIN & DE CHIARA

3
- GOETZ FITZPATRICK MOST & BRUCKMAN LLP

4
- BERMAN, PALEY, GOLDSTEIN & KANNRY
- LEPATNER & ASSOCIATES LLP
- MAZUR, CARP & RUBIN PC
- SACKS MONTGOMERY

Leading individuals (Construction)

1
- GROVE Barry *Thelen Reid & Priest LLP*
- PECKAR Robert *Peckar & Abramson PC*

2
- POSTNER William *Postner & Rubin*
- RUBIN Robert *Postner & Rubin*

3
- ROSS Allen *Ross & Cohen LLP*
- ZETLIN Michael *Zetlin & De Chiara*

4
- GOETZ Peter *Goetz Fitzpatrick Most*
- LEPATNER Barry *LePatner & Associates*
- MACPHERSON Robert *Postner & Rubin*
- MAZUR Sayward *Mazur, Carp & Rubin PC*

Firms and individuals are listed alphabetically in each band.

Peckar & Abramson PC
see firm details p.863

The Firm: The New York branch of this New Jersey-headquartered firm is thought to be *"on every contractor's shortlist of top firms."* The firm is wholly dedicated to the construction industry and represents general contractors and construction managers on litigation, alternative dispute resolution (ADR), contract documentation, environmental concerns, labor relations and OSHA compliance. The team has been active on some of the largest matters in the region and, as a founding member of the International Construction Law Alliance, receives frequent referrals to represent international clients involved in US development projects. Practitioners have experience advising on stadium, airport and other large commercial projects. The firm has additional offices in San Francisco, Miami, Fort Lauderdale and Los Angeles.

The Lawyers: Founding partner **Robert Peckar** (see p.529) was said to be *"without question, a major figure in New York construction."* Although based in New Jersey, he spends much of his time practicing from the New York office and attracts widespread praise for his success in building up a *"formidable outfit."* Peckar counsels construction and insurance companies on a global basis, often intervening in a troubleshooting capacity on complex cases. This *"insightful"* practitioner is particularly active in national and international arbitration and ADR proceedings and is experienced in litigating multiparty disputes. Recent work includes acting as contract counsel on the development of the AOL Time Warner Center at Columbus Circle and representing contractors in the resolution of a dispute relating to the construction of a court building.

The Clients: The team counsels major contractors, owners, design professionals, and other construction industry participants on construction disputes and contractual matters.

Postner & Rubin

The Firm: Generally acknowledged as a *"key name in the industry,"* this eight-lawyer construction boutique operates from offices in NYC and Holmdel, New Jersey. Practitioners advise at all stages of the construction process, undertaking a range of transactional and contentious matters. Projects typically involve marine and highway construction, energy plants and housing, healthcare and industrial facilities. The team represents owners, contractors, suppliers and construction managers in the US and abroad. They have most notably advised in relation to the Times Square Subway renovation project and the John F Kennedy International Airport $150 million cogeneration project. The firm also maintains a leading profile in ADR and has counseled a private developer of the $100 million Hudson River hydroelectric project on dispute avoidance and management.

The Lawyers: The firm's founding partners attract a wealth of market comment. Identified as a *"renowned figure in the field,"* **Bill Postner** is considered particularly well versed in construction contracts, including their negotiation, drafting and implementation. His partner, **Bob Rubin** focuses principally on contentious work. Rubin was noted for his *"supreme mediation skills"* by clients and peers who appreciated the *"huge amount of service he's dedicated to the industry."* The two partners have been involved in some high-profile matters: the development of the AOL Time Warner headquarters in New York; and representation of the contractors of the Brooklyn Navy Yard cogeneration plant on related litigation. *"Talented"* **Robert Macpherson** was cited for his expertise in mediation and arbitration proceedings. He has also been involved in an asbestos abatement dispute concerning a 375,000 sq ft facility.

The Clients: Clients include Fortune 500 companies, public utilities, public agencies and private companies.

Thelen Reid & Priest LLP
see firm details p.888

The Firm: Thelen Reid & Priest stands alone as the only full-service New York firm to cover construction law in significant depth. An *"enormous"* bicoastal national practice benefits from an historic reputation for large infrastructure projects that dates back to the 1930's. Practitioners have noteworthy experience in negotiating government contracts and are able to assist clients on bidding and procurement issues. The current practice acts for a large number of contractors and is closely associated with key client, Bechtel. The firm advises on related insurance, litigation, tax and employment matters and maintains a web site, constructionweblinks.com, dedicated to construction law issues.

The Lawyers: The dominant figure in the New York office is **Barry Grove** (see p.516). His advice on contentious matters is said to be *"second to none."* Clients remarked on his *"mature"* approach to mediation, arbitration and litigation proceedings, commenting that *"he is tough but not confrontational; he helps settle disputes."* He advises Bechtel Power and Raytheon on construction disputes, and has recently acted on cases concerning power and pipeline projects.

The Clients: Bechtel, Bovis Lend Lease, URS and other contractors are clients.

Ross & Cohen LLP
see firm details p.871

The Firm: This New York boutique was recommended as a *"highly competent outfit,"* offering *"great depth and quality."* Seventeen lawyers handle a mix of construction and real estate issues, advising on transactional and litigious matters. A loyal client base of contractors, construction managers, sureties and designers are *"extremely happy with the service they provide; we wouldn't use anyone else."*

The Lawyers: Founding partner **Allen Ross** (see p.533) is widely admired for his long experience in the field. Well liked within the industry, Ross has an active practice mediating in disputes with claims and counter claims ranging from $1-10 million. Ross has been sitting as chairman of a dispute review board on an ongoing $500 million contract dispute and has also counseled on a construction default involving a $20 million performance bond.

The Clients: The Related Companies; Forest Electric Company; Forest City Ratner Companies; The American-Scandinavian Foundation and Albert Einstein College of Medicine of Yeshiva University.

Zetlin & De Chiara

The Firm: Hailed as a *"brilliant young firm,"* Zetlin & De Chiara specializes in the representation of architects, designers and engineers, which together comprise nearly three-quarters of the firm's client

CONSTRUCTION — NEW YORK

base. The team is also known to undertake matters on behalf of owners, developers, contractors and government agencies. Members advise on design and construction litigation, contract negotiations and related employment, insurance, and health and safety issues. The 20-lawyer practice acts primarily from the firm's Manhattan office, with regional branches in Long Island and New Jersey.
The Lawyers: *"Bright and energetic,"* name partner **Michael Zetlin** was felt to be the *"top attorney for design professionals."* Zetlin serves as general counsel to both the American Institute of Architects and the American Society of Civil Engineers. His recent litigation experience includes advising on a $40 million cogeneration facility dispute and acting as counsel on a $600 million claim relating to Caissons disease (Decompression Sickness) on a tunneling project.
The Clients: Large national and international engineering firms, architects, large corporates and contractors.

Goetz Fitzpatrick Most & Bruckman LLP
The Firm: This well-resourced boutique contains *"plenty of good people who know what they're doing."* Eleven partners practice exclusively within the construction industry, advising on risk management, insurance analysis, arbitration, mediation and litigation arising from contract disputes, defect claims and catastrophic failures. Practitioners have also developed expertise in relation to trade regulation, employment, environment, finance and copyright matters pertaining to project development.
The Lawyers: Founding partner **Peter Goetz** is well known for his lectures and articles on construction law and arbitration. This *"meticulous lawyer"* received warm recommendation from peers who frequently refer work to him in conflict situations.
The Clients: The firm acts for Fortune 500 companies, engineers, owners, developers, sureties and construction managers.

Berman, Paley, Goldstein & Kannry
The Firm: The firm attracts most praise for its high-quality civil and public construction work. Practitioners are said to be *"very experienced at local civil works,"* and have advised on numerous bridge, tunnel, highway, power plant and sewage treatment plant projects. The practice's primary emphasis is on construction law; however, the group has also built up a substantial niche in environmental matters.
The Lawyers: Jack Kannry is managing partner of the ten-member firm.
The Clients: The firm's client base includes contractors, construction managers, architects, private owners and governmental entities. Among them are: Slattery Skanska; Granite Halmar Construction Company; Lawler, Matusky & Skelly Engineers; Kiska Construction; Tully Construction and Interworks Systems.

LePatner & Associates LLP
see firm details p.839
The Firm: This smaller, six-lawyer practice was said to be *"very good for transactional matters."* The team includes two in-house design consultants who advise on contract negotiation, drafting and disputes. The firm handles all aspects of construction law, with notable expertise in architects' and engineers' liability in cases of errors or omissions in design.
The Lawyers: Name partner **Barry LePatner** (see p.523) was described as a *"deeply experienced"* attorney with an *"innovative"* approach to commercial transactions, contract law and liability issues. He also elicits praise for his writing and seminars.
The Clients: A diverse client base consists of corporate owners, architects, engineers and designers.

Mazur, Carp & Rubin PC
The Firm: Acknowledged as a *"top firm with a fine reputation,"* this smaller boutique was founded with an emphasis on construction litigation and ADR; it was felt to possess a *"collection of very fine lawyers."* Of the firm's nine attorneys, six provide general business counseling and litigation services to construction interests, while the remainder focus on probate, trust and estate matters.
The Lawyers: Sayward Mazur forms part of the *"old guard"* of New York construction lawyers. He has written extensively on mediation and construction contract disputes and was recommended by peers as an accomplished litigator.
The Clients: Large national companies; contractors; owners; designers and sureties.

Sacks Montgomery
The Firm: Nine attorneys divide their time between the firm's New York headquarters and a smaller Connecticut office. Construction and surety law are the firm's primary focus areas. Clients describe the group as a *"highly ethical"* team that *"has been in the field for 30 years and know what they're doing."* The group received particular mention for expertise on government contracts.
The Lawyers: Founding partners Harry Sachs and David Montgomery practice from the firm's main New York office.
The Clients: Sureties; construction managers; insurers; municipalities; developers and engineers.

CORPORATE/M&A

NEW YORK
Leading firms (Corporate/M&A)
1. WACHTELL, LIPTON, ROSEN & KATZ
2. SKADDEN, ARPS, SLATE, MEAGHER & FLOM
3. CRAVATH, SWAINE & MOORE
   DAVIS POLK & WARDWELL
   SIMPSON THACHER & BARTLETT
   SULLIVAN & CROMWELL LLP
4. SHEARMAN & STERLING
5. CLEARY GOTTLIEB STEEN & HAMILTON
   FRIED, FRANK, HARRIS, SHRIVER & JACOBSON
6. CADWALADER, WICKERSHAM & TAFT
   DEBEVOISE & PLIMPTON
   WEIL, GOTSHAL & MANGES LLP
   WILLKIE FARR & GALLAGHER

Firms are listed alphabetically in each band.

Wachtell, Lipton, Rosen & Katz
see firm details p.892
The Firm: In a *"league of their own"* for public M&A, this *"small and select"* 60-lawyer team regularly attracts headline deals. Said to have *"positioned themselves as a market elite,"* the firm focuses only on the most complicated mergers, divestitures, financings and spin-offs, and is famed for a *"unique business model"* based on a roughly even partner-to-associate ratio. Both its *"well-defined focus"* on big-ticket M&A and its relatively small size contribute to a *"boutique-y feel"* and has helped it achieve a *"name brand recognition"* that is unmatched in the marketplace. The group established its dominance in the 1980's as a leading counsel for targets of hostile takeovers, and has continued to attract megadeals on the back of its stellar reputation. Noteworthy tax and litigation practices further the transactional needs of major blue-chip clients. Even with no overseas offices, the firm still appears on many of the highest profile cross-border deals. Most recently, the group has acted for French advertising group Publicis in its $3 billion acquisition of Bcom3 Group, and joint venture with Tokyo-based Dentsu. Domestically, the firm has managed to remain busy in a slow transactional market. Most attribute the firm's success to its *"consistently outstanding"* attorneys. Practitioners are deemed to be *"to a person, excellent;" "there are no bad lawyers at Wachtell."* In addition to a host of reputable *"M&A veterans,"* the firm was praised for a concentration of younger partners, said to be *"firing all pistons."* Although the firm is acknowledged to be *"staggeringly expensive,"* clients believe that attorneys here are *"worth every penny,"* commenting that *"they give new meaning to client service."*
The Lawyers: The history of New York M&A is

NEW YORK

CORPORATE/M&A

NEW YORK
Leading individuals (Corporate/M&A)

★ LIPTON Martin *Wachtell, Lipton, Rosen*

[1]
- AARON Roger *Skadden, Arps, Slate, Meagher*
- BEATTIE Richard *Simpson Thacher & Bartlett*
- COHEN Rodgin *Sullivan & Cromwell LLP*
- FLOM Joseph *Skadden, Arps, Slate, Meagher*
- HERSCH Dennis *Davis Polk & Wardwell*
- KRAMER Morris *Skadden, Arps, Slate*
- STEPHENSON Alan *Cravath, Swaine & Moore*

[2]
- BASON George *Davis Polk & Wardwell*
- BLOCK Dennis *Cadwalader, Wickersham*
- LEWKOW Victor *Cleary Gottlieb Steen*

[3]
- BROWN Meredith *Debevoise & Plimpton*
- FINLEY John *Simpson Thacher & Bartlett*
- FRAIDIN Stephen *Fried, Frank, Harris, Shriver*
- HELENIAK David *Shearman & Sterling*
- SCHELL Michael *Skadden, Arps, Slate*

[4]
- AQUILA Francis *Sullivan & Cromwell LLP*
- EMMERICH Adam *Wachtell, Lipton, Rosen*
- KATZ David *Wachtell, Lipton, Rosen & Katz*
- LEDERMAN Lawrence *Milbank, Tweed*
- MADDEN John *Shearman & Sterling*
- NUSBAUM Jack *Willkie Farr & Gallagher*
- RUEGGER Philip *Simpson Thacher & Bartlett*

[5]
- DOUGLAS Peter *Davis Polk & Wardwell*
- HALL Richard *Cravath, Swaine & Moore*
- KERR Diane *Davis Polk & Wardwell*
- MILLS Phillip *Davis Polk & Wardwell*
- NUSSBAUM Andrew *Wachtell, Lipton*
- SAEED Faiza *Cravath, Swaine & Moore*
- WHITE Fred *Skadden, Arps, Slate*

- ATKINS Peter *Skadden, Arps, Slate, Meagher*
- COGUT Charles *Simpson Thacher & Bartlett*
- FINKELSON Allen *Cravath, Swaine & Moore*
- HERLIHY Edward *Wachtell, Lipton, Rosen*
- KATCHER Richard *Wachtell, Lipton, Rosen*
- STAPLETON Benjamin *Sullivan & Cromwell*

- BIALKIN Kenneth *Skadden, Arps, Slate*
- FLEISCHER Arthur *Fried, Frank, Harris*
- SPATT Robert *Simpson Thacher & Bartlett*

- BROWNSTEIN Andrew *Wachtell, Lipton*
- FOGG Blaine *Skadden, Arps, Slate, Meagher*
- GELSTON Philip *Cravath, Swaine & Moore*
- MORPHY James *Sullivan & Cromwell LLP*
- WASSERMAN Craig *Wachtell, Lipton, Rosen*

- CONDON Creighton *Shearman & Sterling*
- KADEN Lewis *Davis Polk & Wardwell*
- KLING Lou *Skadden, Arps, Slate, Meagher*
- LYONS Peter *Shearman & Sterling*
- NEFF Daniel *Wachtell, Lipton, Rosen & Katz*
- PIERCE Morton *Dewey Ballantine LLP*
- VLAHAKIS Patricia *Wachtell, Lipton, Rosen*

- GITTES Franklin *Skadden, Arps, Slate*
- KENNEDY Thomas *Skadden, Arps, Slate*
- MEYERSON Lee *Simpson Thacher & Bartlett*
- NATHAN Charles *Latham & Watkins LLP*
- RINALDI Joseph *Davis Polk & Wardwell*
- SCHUMER Robert *Paul, Weiss, Rifkind*

Up-and-coming individuals
- COCHRAN Eric *Skadden, Arps, Slate*
- O'BRIEN Clare *Shearman & Sterling*
- SHIM Paul *Cleary Gottlieb Steen & Hamilton*
- TOWNSEND Robert *Cravath, Swaine & Moore*

Individuals are listed alphabetically in each band.

Andrew Brownstein (see p.507) was recognized as a *"highly accomplished"* practitioner with a *"down-to-earth"* approach to M&A and corporate governance matters. Interviewees described him as a *"thoughtful negotiator"* who *"always does the best for his clients."*

Adam Emmerich (see p.512) maintains a varied practice, acting in a range of mergers, joint ventures and financings both in the US and abroad. He is said to *"inspire confidence"* by his ability to *"cut through the nonsense."* He recently represented Security Capital in its $5.1billion acquisition by GE Capital, and acts for Wal-Mart in an assortment of international matters. Clients observe that Emmerich, although *"assertive"* in negotiations, *"knows when to step aside,"* but is *"not a man who suffers fools gladly."* **David Katz** (see p.520) was said to be an *"energetic young star"* with a reputation as *"one of the hardest working lawyers you could meet."* His *"far-sighted"* approach makes him *"ideal for a tough situation where you need to plan 15 steps ahead."* He has recently been active in a number of transactions in the mining and energy sectors with colleague **Daniel Neff** (see p.527), who was recommended as a *"strong advocate for his clients."* A *"sharp"* lawyer, Neff was reported to *"always have time for questions,"* and *"doesn't just tell you what you want to hear."* Katz and Neff jointly advised Anadarko Petroleum on its $265 million acquisition of Howell Corporation.

Often associated with media clients, **Pat Vlahakis** (see p.541) was felt to be a *"world-class"* attorney, and *"not afraid to make enemies"* in difficult negotiations. Her *"deft handling of technical issues"* inspires *"tremendous client loyalty."* *"Able"* younger lawyer **Andrew Nussbaum** (see p.528) was noted for her wide experience in the entertainment industry. He has had a busy year representing Philip Morris in a $5.6 billion agreement to merge Miller Brewing into South African Breweries.

The Clients: AT&T; AIG; USA Networks; Publicis; General Mills; Security Capital; Wal-Mart; Kellogg; The McGraw-Hill Companies; Miller Brewing Company and Raytheon.

Skadden, Arps, Slate, Meagher & Flom LLP & Affiliates
see firm details p.878

The Firm: The *"juggernaut"* of the corporate M&A market, the firm regularly tops league tables for transactional volume. From its inception, the firm has historically played a prominent role in the biggest US and international transactions. As one interviewee commented: *"They helped invent the game, and have gone on reinventing it ever since."* Skadden Arps remains *"highly focused"* on top-level M&A, and is able to *"throw the whole weight of their resources behind a transaction,"* which, for a global M&A practice of

---

inextricably linked with that of founding partner **Martin Lipton** (see p.524), now widely acclaimed as a *"legend in his lifetime"* for his role in the invention and development of the 'poison pill' defense. A prominent figure in the *"pantheon of the gods,"* Lipton is beloved of corporate board members who continue to view him as a primary contact for *"strategic and troubleshooting"* advice. Senior partner **Richard Katcher** (see p.520) *"proves you can be a nice person and still succeed."* As lead counsel to AT&T in AT&T Broadband's $72 billion merger with Comcast, Katcher was thought to be *"one of the few busy M&A lawyers in America at the moment."* He was highly recommended to researchers as a *"flexible"* attorney, able to *"take a broad or detailed view, depending on what is needed."*

Additionally, the firm attracts particular praise for the strength of its banking M&A practice, led by the *"phenomenal"* **Ed Herlihy** (see p.518). An *"astute"* practitioner, Herlihy has played a leading role in many of the major banking combinations of recent years, and remains a *"dynamic force"* in the financial services sector. Commended for having done a *"tremendous job"* of forging relationships with major investment banks, he numbers Wachovia and FirstStar (now US Bancorp) among his clients. Herlihy's *"right-hand man"* is younger partner **Craig Wasserman** (see p.541), a *"savvy operator"* who *"knows what he's talking about."* The two are said to *"do a nice Mutt & Jeff routine"* and work closely on a large share of financial institution transactions. Most recently the pair acted for State Street in its $1.5 billion acquisition of part of Deutsche Bank's global securities service businesses, and for Golden State Bancorp in its $5.8 billion acquisition by Citigroup.

CORPORATE/M&A

NEW YORK

270 lawyers, is no small feat. The firm is a recognized player both domestically, and internationally, where an extensive network of 12 global offices helps maintain a steady flow of cross-border megadeals. In the US, Skadden Arps has substantial corporate practices in major commercial centers, including LA, Chicago and DC. The firm is seen as *"an obvious choice for principal representation,"* and a busy bankruptcy practice has the corporate department working on divestitures and acquisitions arising out of restructuring arrangements. In keeping with the firm's *"hard-driving"* image, Skadden Arps' partners can be *"aggressive in pursuit of their clients' interests."* The enormous size of the practice allows attorneys to specialize in specific areas, and researchers were told that personalities tend to dominate. Although the firm was not perceived to be as uniform in quality as smaller competitors, interviewees agreed that *"the top lawyers at Skadden Arps are the best anywhere."*

The Lawyers: The 30-partner NY M&A group contains a large number of *"market-leading lawyers."* **Jo Flom** (see p.513), the acknowledged *"grandfather of M&A"* remains a potent figurehead and *"mentor"* for the practice. Deemed to have *"near-mythic status"* in the marketplace for his historic role in the development of both the firm and the practice area, Flom continues to be available to offer *"strategic advice"* on transactions, but now focuses largely on business development. At the helm of the practice is a group of core practitioners who *"grew up under Flom's tutelage."* Chief among these is **Roger Aaron** (see p.503), the senior partner in charge of all of Skadden Arps' corporate practice areas. Observers say there's *"no baloney"* about this *"wise and thoughtful"* attorney. A *"tried and true"* practitioner, Aaron has long-standing experience representing major US and foreign companies in a variety of mergers, joint ventures, and negotiated and contested takeovers. His *"low-key"* manner is thought to have a *"calming influence"* on heated negotiations. Aaron has lately been acting for financial advisers Goldman Sachs in connection with Pfizer's $60 billion acquisition of Pharmacia. Aaron's partner, **Peter Atkins** (see p.504), is said to have a *"tremendous aptitude for the game,"* and receives the ultimate praise from rivals who say that *"he's one of the few lawyers I'd call on to represent me."* Atkins' *"impressive resumé of deals"* includes headline transactions within the telecom, airline, healthcare, defense and financial services sectors. Atkins is currently leading the firm's representation of major defense contractor TRW in connection with Northrop Grumman's $5.9 billion unsolicited takeover bid, and represented IBM in its $3.5 billion acquisition of PwC Consulting. A *"personality-and-a-half,"* **Morris Kramer** (see p.522) is soundly commended for his expertise in hostile transactions. Noted for his *"intellectual brilliance,"* Kramer reportedly *"relishes a good scrap"* and enters into negotiations with *"surprising gusto."* He represented American General in connection with Prudential's unsuccessful $22 billion acquisition bid. Another of *"Flom's colonels,"* **Blaine (Fin) Fogg** (see p.513) is considered an *"éminence grise"* at the M&A bar. He *"knows everything there is to know about corporate transactions,"* and received especial praise for his leadership abilities and willingness to *"teach and support younger partners."* The practice's major *"powerbroker"* is **Ken Bialkin** (see p.505), who is credited with having single-handedly *"sewn up the firm's relationship with Citibank."* Bialkin's ability to *"bring in the clients"* is legendary. He has a huge following among clients in the financial services, banking and insurance industries, who appreciate his *"clear-sighted"* advice. Bialkin's practice spans all aspects of corporate, regulatory and securities matters. He represented Citigroup in its $5.8 acquisition of Golden State Bancorp. **Michael Schell** (see p.534) brings to the table a *"wealth of experience"* in unsolicited and contested bids. Highly regarded by retail and manufacturing clients, Schell maintains close ties to valued client DaimlerChrysler, who he has represented in a range of international transactions. Interviewees report that Schell's *"legal skills are beyond question"* and clients particularly admire his *"straight-up advice"* on strategic issues: *"He'll tell you right away if you're making a mistake."* Described as a *"steady and reliable"* counselor, Schell *"can play the tough guy when he needs to."* He has recently been acting for Alcoa in connection with its acquisition and joint venture discussions with Australia's Western Mining Corporation and Norway's Elkem. Acting in both LBOs and public company acquisitions, **Lou Kling** (see p.521) was recommended as a corporate generalist. Although acknowledged to be *"not everyone's cup of tea,"* Kling is a jealously guarded name among clients who consider him an *"absolute jewel."* *"Well connected"* to companies in the technology, defense and pharmaceutical industries, Kling recently acted for Unilab in its $860 acquisition by Quest Diagnostics. Widely respected for his *"keen intellect,"* he *"has an eye on getting the best deal for clients"* and is a frequent favorite of firms hoping to *"intimidate the other side."* *"Efficient and business-minded"* practitioner **Franklin Gittes** (see p.514) was praised for *"honing in on the important issues - he gets down to the nitty-gritty right away."* He heads the firm's M&A practice, together with younger partner **Tom Kennedy** (see p.521), who was described as *"the most unpretentious lawyer you could ever hope to meet."* This *"down-to-earth"* practitioner, who is principal corporate counsel to broadband company ntl, specializes in mergers and corporate finance in the internet, telecom and IT industries. In a quiet transactional market, he has lately been active on a number of debt restructuring matters for technology clients. Most notably, he has been advising ntl on its pending 'pre-negotiated' Chapter 11 bankruptcy. Cohead of the financial M&A practice, **Fred White** (see p.542) remains a *"key figure"* in banking M&A, and also handles associated public offerings and regulatory matters for financial service firms. **Eric Cochran** (see p.509) enters the tables as an up-and-coming name, after receiving general commendation in the market. Cochran has been assisting Atkins in representing TRW.

The Clients: Citigroup;TRW; American General; Unilab; News Corporation; DaimlerChrysler; Warner-Lambert; Compaq and Temple-Inland.

Cravath, Swaine & Moore

The Firm: Another *"obvious choice for principal representation,"* this group has a noteworthy record in both initiating and defending against hostile bids, but also appears frequently for targets, acquirers and financial advisers on a range of other complex transactions. *"Classically New York,"* the firm is felt to focus primarily on US-based work. Smaller corporate practices in the UK and Hong Kong support the New York headquarter office on cross-border transactions. Held up by some as the model of *"a complete firm,"* the practice benefits from both international *"prestige"* and close relationships with influential corporate and financial clients. Its antitrust and commercial litigation practices are highly rated and complement the team's transactional strength, enhancing the group's *"ability to push through a difficult or contested deal."* The firm was commended for its *"emphasis on training"* and received recognition for producing *"high-caliber"* younger partners with a *"comprehensive view"* of all aspects of corporate law. Cravath Swaine's lawyers are known to be *"corporate generalists."* The corporate department divides itself into small partner-associate clusters that focus on specific client relationships.The result is a *"collegial atmosphere"* with a reputation for *"pure quality"* at all levels of practice. Practitioners bring a *"terrific blend of intellectual ability and pragmatism"* to transactions and are characterized by a *"deliberative approach"* to decision-making.

The Lawyers: **Allen Finkelson** is widely respected for his long experience in M&A transactions and general corporate counseling. *"Bright and amusing,"* Finkelson was noted for the *"panache"* with which he approaches deal-making. With a background in both law and finance, Finkelson is valued by peers for his *"wide-ranging perspective;"* they commented that *"he's seen it all before."* He serves as principal corporate partner for IBM, who he recently represented in its negotiation of a strategic alliance with Hitachi. **Alan Stephenson** was similarly recommended for his *"deep experience and insight."* An *"enterprising public company*

NEW YORK

CORPORATE/M&A

man," Stephenson has been visible on a number of high-level transactions, most notably acting for Nestlé in its $10.3 billion acquisition of Ralston Purina. A winning combination of an *"easy-going manner"* and *"keen intellectual analysis"* render Stephenson a *"highly effective negotiator."* *"Unflappable"* **Philip Gelston** is a *"no-nonsense"* attorney who *"doesn't make mistakes."* He has acquired a reputation for cross-border work and recently acted for BAE SYSTEMS in its $146 million disposition of its Gaithersburg operations to Integrated Defense Technologies. Younger partner **Richard Hall** was reported to be particularly *"good at sifting out material quickly and presenting alternative solutions."* Clients have confidence in his *"excellent judgment,"* and especially commend his thoroughness – *"You never have to re-read his papers."* Another member of the *"next generation"* of Cravath Swaine lawyers, **Faiza Saeed**, was mentioned as someone who is *"rising quickly through the ranks."* She is commonly associated with the firm's major media clients, most notably Vivendi Universal who she represented in both its acquisition of USA Networks' entertainment assets and its $1.5 billion strategic alliance with EchoStar. Interviewees agreed that she has a *"promising future"* ahead of her. Rated as an up-and-coming practitioner with particular expertise in telecom transactions, **Robert Townsend** is a *"strong personality"* who has a *"remarkable rapport with clients."*

The Clients: Bristol-Myers Squibb; Nestlé; Johnson & Johnson; Vivendi Universal; AOL Time Warner; IBM; BAE SYSTEMS and United Airlines

Davis Polk & Wardwell
The Firm: This *"distinguished"* corporate group is heir both to valuable institutional relationships with the likes of Morgan Stanley and a *"legacy of excellence"* in its attorneys. Twenty dedicated M&A partners are supported by highly rated securities and tax practices in offering *"full-service coverage with boutique quality."* The firm provides US corporate and capital markets advice from offices in Europe and Asia, and benefits from a complementary 'best friends' relationship with major firms Hengeler Mueller (Germany), Uría & Menéndes (Spain) and Slaughter and May (UK), in advising on a range of cross-border matters. The group received particular praise for the strength of its Latin American practice, which is largely run out of the New York office. Commentators believe that Davis Polk's global lockstep compensation system promotes a *"cooperative team spirit"* throughout the firm. Particular strength exists in relation to technology and communications matters, in which practitioners are regarded as *"ahead of the curve."*

The Lawyers: The practice's *"top gun"* is **Dennis Hersch**, a highly respected M&A specialist who *"cut his teeth in the hostile takeovers of the 1980's."* A *"class act,"* Hersch is said to *"play his hand extremely well in the boardroom."* He was noted both for his skill in managing a large team and for a *"human"* approach that lets him *"read people, find creative solutions, and persuade others to accept them."* In a quiet transactional market, he has attracted enormous attention through his representation of Comcast in its proposed $72 billion acquisition of AT&T Broadband. He coheads the M&A group with **George (Gar) Bason**, who divides his time between M&A and merchant banking transactions. Praised for his *"mental acuity,"* Bason has an *"impressive ability to digest complex documents."* A *"genuine advocate for his clients,"* he reportedly has a *"unique talent for finding the sweet spot in a deal."* Clients additionally appreciate his *"easy-going"* manner and knack for *"hilarious"* impersonations - *"there's no better person to alleviate pressure and make everyone comfortable."* He recently advised CSG Systems International on its $300 million acquisition of the billing and customer care assets of Lucent Technologies. **Lewis Kaden** brings a background in employment law to his broad-based corporate and litigation practice. The 'éminence gris" of the practice, Kaden is *"smart, and reassuring in the boardroom."* He has developed a busy practice advising on corporate governance matters, and continues to draw recommendations for his experience in insurance sector mergers. A *"keen analyst."* **Peter Douglas** remains for many the *"first port of call for difficult questions."* His practice emphasizes unusual structures connected with multinational acquisitions, recapitalizations and spin-offs. Offering *"instrumental strategic advice,"* Douglas is valued for his *"deep experience, and contacts at the investment banks - he knows who to call and can even tell you their phone numbers off the top of his head."* **Diane Kerr** is a *"dominant figure for Latin American M&A."* A member of the firm's Latin American and Spain practice group, she most notably acted for Citibank in its 2001 acquisition of Mexico's Grupo Financiero Banamex-Accival (Bannacci) bank. A *"real professional,"* **Phillip Mills** is a *"no-nonsense"* attorney, qualified at both the Australian and New York bar. He has experience in takeover defense strategies and public and private transactions, and counsels on corporate governance and fiduciary duties, particularly in the biotech industry. In the past year, Mills has advised ImClone Systems in both a strategic relationship with Bristol-Myers Squibb and its defense against a hostile bid by Carl Icahn. He is also serving as lead counsel to steel company The LTV Corporation in connection with asset dispositions arising from its bankruptcy. *"Polished"* practitioner **Joseph Rinaldi** has established a high profile for major cross-border deals. Operating from both the New York and Paris offices, Rinaldi led the firm's representation of Bcom3 Group in its $3 billion acquisition by French advertising group Publicis. Peers spoke of him as a *"legal sophisticate."*

The Clients: Comcast; ImClone Systems; Citigroup; Bcom3 Group; JPMorgan Chase; C-MAC Industries; LVMH; ABN AMRO; Deutsche Telekom; Reed Elsevier; Ford and NetIQ.

Simpson Thacher & Bartlett
The Firm: The strength of this *"outstanding M&A franchise"* is cemented by close relationships with *"key movers and shakers in all segments of the market."* The firm's *"blockbuster LBO practice"* and long-standing ties to leading buyout sponsors KKR and The Blackstone Group produce a volume of both private and public portfolio deal work that keeps the group *"active at all levels."* Thirty New York partners maintain a broad-based corporate practice, appearing in negotiated transactions, mergers, joint ventures, proxy contests and spinoff transactions. In addition to representing US and multinational businesses as targets and acquirers, the group regularly appears as counsel to financial advisors on significant transactions and has considerable experience advising boards of directors' special committees. This is a group that *"knows how to get things done."* Clients report that they can count on Simpson Thacher partners to *"hit the ground running,"* and achieve *"maximum results with the minimum amount of posturing."*

The Lawyers: The firm's overall success is closely linked to the tremendous reputation of firm chairman **Richard Beattie**. A *"rainmaker par excellence,"* Beattie is credited with cultivating valuable ties to flagship clients KKR and JPMorgan Chase. Although experienced in a range of public and private transactional work, his chief role is seen to be that of a general counselor. Many of America's leading corporate directors look on him as their own *"consigliere,"* able to advise on everything from corporate governance and investigations to litigation and crisis management. Head of the firm's M&A group, **Charles Cogut** is said to *"always have the big picture in mind."* Like many Simpson Thacher partners, Cogut covers both private equity transactions and public company M&A and ranks highly in both sections of *Chambers'* research. He oversees the firm's representation of many KKR portfolio companies and regularly represents Wyeth (formerly American Home Products), Northwest Airlines and Silver Lake Partners. A *"wise"* perspective and *"nerves of steel"* serve him well in difficult negotiations. Cogut recently advised American Home Products as shareholders in connection with Amgen's acquisition of Immunex. Visible both in boardrooms and on the lecture circuit, **Rob Spatt** has to his credit a large volume of high-end transactions. Described as a *"formidable intellect"* with an *"encyclopedic knowledge"* of corporate law, Spatt has extensive experience representing

CORPORATE/M&A — NEW YORK

financial advisers in M&A. Most notably he has been acting for financial advisers to Comcast in its bid for AT&T's broadband business. He recently advised HJ Heinz in the structuring of a reverse Morris Trust transaction, in which a spun-off entity merged with Del Monte Foods. *"Tireless in transactions,"* partner **John Finley** was noted for his *"amazing head for detail."* In addition to frequent representation of Goldman Sachs, JPMorgan Chase and Lehman Brothers as financial advisers, Finley has recently handled the acquisition of Williams Pipe Line Company by Williams Energy Partners and advised the Edgar M Bronfman family in its minority investment in A&G Group. **Philip (Pete) Ruegger** has a leading profile for LBOs and public transactions in the telecom and healthcare sectors. Interviewees recommend him as a *"bright and practical"* attorney who is *"on his toes"* in deal negotiations. Ruegger's regular clients include Blackstone, Accenture, Travelers, and CR Bard. Best known for his work in financial institutions' M&A, **Lee Meyerson** has acted in such high-profile deals as the merger of Wachovia and First Union and Chase Manhattan's acquisition of JPMorgan. He continues to advise an array of banks and financial service clients on M&A and capital markets transactions.

The Clients: Kohlberg Kravis Roberts & Company; The Blackstone Group; Wyeth; L-3 Communications; Willamette Industies; Accenture; HJ Heinz; Premcor; Global Crossing; Ingersoll-Rand and American Electric Power.

Sullivan & Cromwell LLP
see firm details p.886

The Firm: One of the earliest firms to focus on international expansion, Sullivan & Cromwell now boasts a highly developed global network that attracts the highest profile cross-border deals. Multinational blue-chip clients appreciate the firm's strength and *"consistent quality"* across Europe and Asia, commenting that *"they can go anywhere we need to."* With the assistance of the international partnership, a *"top-caliber"* group of 50 NY M&A lawyers constitutes an *"overwhelming brute force"* in the marketplace. Practitioners are known to be both hard-working and thorough in their due diligence: *"You can count on them to cross every t and dot every i."* The group represents US and foreign acquirers, targets and stockholders in a variety of corporate transactions, but earns highest acclaim for its preeminent financial institutions practice. A coveted long-standing relationship with Goldman Sachs sees the group acting on a large volume of domestic and international deals. Even more notably, the firm has a *"gold-plated"* reputation for financial institutions' M&A, having acted as counsel in most major bank mergers of recent years.

The Lawyers: Most observers attribute the firm's dominance in banking M&A to the colossal reputation of firm chairman **H Rodgin (Rodge) Cohen** (see p.509). Renowned for having a *"work ethic your wife would shoot you for,"* the hard-working Cohen was said to *"put in more hours than any associate."* His high visibility as both firm administrator and active practitioner has prompted peers to speculate that *"there must be two of him."* Recommended for both his regulatory and transactional expertise, Cohen has worked on the first US public offering by a foreign bank, advised on legislative reform efforts and played a key role as counselor in a recent spate of consolidation in the banking sector. Notable transactional work includes counseling First Union in its 2001 merger with Wachovia, and advising Mexico's Grupo Financiero Banamex-Accival (Banacci) in its acquisition by Citigroup. Envied for his *"photographic memory,"* Cohen *"has everything you need to know at his fingertips."* Long experience in the field has endowed him with the *"ability to figure out what all the regulators are thinking."* He and the senior partner of the M&A group, the *"patrician"* **Ben Stapleton** (see p.537), are considered the practice's *"senior statesmen."* An influential figure in the M&A market, Stapleton was noted for his *"impeccable judgment"* and *"straight-shooting"* manner. Clients testify: *"He will tell you the parts you need to worry about."* Stapleton commands formidable experience in big-ticket international deals, with particular expertise in the telecom and energy sectors. Managing partner of the M&A group, the *"engaging"* **James Morphy** (see p.526), rates highly for his experience defending against hostile bids. He is visible acting for Goldman Sachs as both financial adviser and principal, and is said to *"know the issues financial advisers deal with inside and out."* Interviewees describe him as a *"man of his word,"* who is *"unafraid to take risks in order to get the best deal for his client."* Morphy is currently advising the Milton Hershey Schools Trust board in its bid to sell its 77% voting stock in Hershey Foods. *"Outstanding"* **Frank Aquila** (see p.504) has had an active year representing Diageo both in its $1.5 billion sale of Burger King to a consortium led by Texas Pacific and in its $800 million disposal of the Malibu brand to Allied Domecq. He also continues to represent EchoStar in ongoing work in connection with its combination with Hughes Electronics. Recently returned from London, Neil Anderson has attracted attention for his representation of Pharmacia in connection with its acquisition by Pfizer.

The Clients: EchoStar; Pharmacia; Diageo; Goldman Sachs; The Bank of New York; AIG; Wachovia; Spieker Properties; US Bancorp; AXA Financial and Philips.

Shearman & Sterling

The Firm: Publicity surrounding the firm's 2001 associates' layoff appears to have had little effect on its standing as a *"major global presence."* The firm has made an enormous push toward international expansion and has built a successful network of offices throughout Europe, Asia and the Middle East, incorporating both US and local law practitioners. Rivals are particularly envious of the firm's highly developed practices in London, Paris and four German cities, and look upon the firm as an *"example of how to crack Europe."* Success in a volume of high-profile cross-border deals is matched by a steady flow of US domestic work. The firm receives particular kudos for having *"done a great job of mining investment banking relationships to come up with corporate relationships."* In New York, a corporate group of 11 partners and 50 associates works closely with practitioners in DC and San Francisco/Menlo Park on public and private acquisitions, joint ventures and spinoffs. In addition to strong relationships with major financial institutions such as CSFB, Deutsche Bank and Morgan Stanley, the firm has a highly developed media and telecom practice, acting for the likes of Viacom and Ericsson. Shearman & Sterling partners were commended for their *"awareness of international issues,"* and were described as a *"forthright"* group who *"know there's more than one way to skin a cat."*

The Lawyers: Despite the heavy management duties requisite in leading an international firm, senior partner **David Heleniak** remains visible on transactions. A man who *"makes things happen,"* Heleniak oversees the firm's relationships with investment banks Morgan Stanley, Goldman Sachs and Merrill Lynch as well as corporate groups Novartis, Pechiney and The Thomson Corporation. He recently advised Anglo American in its $17.6 billion acquisition of De Beers. Cohead of the M&A group, **Peter Lyons** enters the tables following his return to New York from Silicon Valley where he attracted considerable attention by his efforts to build up the firm's technology and telecom practice. *"Brilliant and irascible,"* Lyons has a lot of deal credits to his name, particularly in the chemical, healthcare and biotech industries. He recently advised Expedia in connection with its $1.5 billion acquisition by USA Networks. Interviewees praise him as an *"unpretentious"* attorney who *"doesn't stand on ceremony."* *"Corporate generalist"* **John Madden** rates highly for his extensive cross-border experience and *"strategic instincts."* Especially active in the telecom sector, Madden has appeared in numerous M&A and joint venture transactions and, more recently, in a concentration of restructuring matters. Clients rely on him to *"make sure it all gets done."* Recent work includes acting for the financial advisers to GM in its disposition of Hughes Electronics to EchoStar. Considered the

NEW YORK

CORPORATE/M&A

"first port of call for M&A" in the media and entertainment industries, **Creighton Condon** (see p.509) regularly advises Viacom on significant corporate matters, and recently acted for New England Sports Ventures in buying the Boston Red Sox. A *"talented negotiator,"* Condon is admired for his ability to *"take control of a situation."* Commentators reported that *"he makes sure you can get your point across, and win it."* Younger partner **Clare O'Brien** (see p.528) was ranked as an up-and-coming attorney following general market recommendation. Dual-qualified in Ireland and the US, O'Brien was praised for her *"clear understanding of European law aspects"* and *"good feel for the essentials."* She recently acted for Quest Diagnostics in its $860 million acquisition of Unilab.
The Clients: Viacom; Georgia-Pacific; CSFB; Ericsson; British Telecommunications; Citigroup; Pechiney; Merrill Lynch; Goldman Sachs; Thomson; Novartis; Danone and Quest Diagnostics.

Cleary Gottlieb Steen & Hamilton
see firm details p.782
The Firm: Heavily focused on international work, the firm is a *"powerful global player,"* rivaling Shearman & Sterling in the depth of its international network. Strong local law practices in Germany, France, UK, Belgium, Italy, Hong Kong and Japan bring in a wealth of cross-border transactions, and the firm regularly appears as counsel to foreign companies making investments in the US. Even corporate clients that look elsewhere for domestic US deals acknowledge that Cleary Gottlieb's is their *"number one choice for international M&A."* The preeminence of its transatlantic practice tends to overshadow the group's US-based work; however, the firm was particularly distinguished for its expertise in M&A deals in the financial services, technology and travel industries. Outstanding capital markets and tax practices bolster the firm's reputation of being *"all things to all men,"* and boasting global reach and *"deep and comprehensive resources."* Eight New York corporate partners are said to possess *"vast experience in highly complex deals"* and received particular praise for their *"understanding of legal risk and how to work with non-US clients."* Clients appreciate the group's service-oriented outlook, *"excellent response time"* and ability to *"communicate with clarity."* Cleary Gottlieb's attorneys were said to exude *"authority and confidence."* The firm represented private equity firms Texas Pacific Group, Bain Capital Partners and Goldman Sachs Capital Partners in their $2.26 billion winning bid to acquire Burger King from Diageo.
The Lawyers: The *"superb"* **Victor Lewkow** (see p.523) is New York's *"key M&A guy."* Well-liked by clients who can rely on him to *"take sensible positions,"* he maintains close relationships with Nortel Networks, HSBC and Prudential. Commended for his *"impressive technical skill,"* Lewkow is a lawyer who *"doesn't sweat the small stuff."* He has lately been acting as US counsel to South African Breweries in its $5.6 billion acquisition of Miller Brewing from Philip Morris. *"Able"* younger partner **Paul Shim** (see p.535) was commended for his *"client-oriented"* approach. Interviewees remarked: *"He'll return your call within an hour, no matter where he is."* Visible acting for technology, private equity and financial institution clients, Shim has lately handled a number of transactions for semiconductor producers such as South Korea's Hynix Semiconductor. Shim also acted for Nortel Networks in its $108 million disposal of certain assets of its optical components business to Bookham Technology.
The Clients: Nortel Networks; HSBC; Prudential; South African Breweries; Texas Pacific Group and Nortek.

Fried, Frank, Harris, Shriver & Jacobson
see firm details p.796
The Firm: This *"well-established"* practice enjoys a long-standing reputation for *"excellence"* on corporate matters, including US and international M&A, dispositions, joint ventures, takeovers and proxy fights. The 41-partner NY corporate department comprises *"talented people with great reputations,"* and embraces a number of *"old hands"* in the market. Its public M&A work overlaps greatly with a busy private equity practice, where the firm continues to serve as principal outside counsel to major buyout firm Forstmann Little. The firm has also sustained valuable relationships with investment banks Goldman Sachs, Merrill Lynch and Lazard Fréres, and appears frequently as counsel to the financial advisers on large transactions. The group handles Europe-based transactions in conjunction with its London practice, which has grown in profile since Sandy Krieger's 2001 move to head up the office. The firm has additional corporate partners in DC, LA and Paris and receives a volume of US-Canadian cross-border deals due to its formal alliance with Toronto-based McCarthy Tétrault.
The Lawyers: Seen by fellow practitioners to occupy *"a tier above the stars,"* senior partner **Art Fleischer** (see p.513) is *"a steady hands-type lawyer"* who *"has seen it all before."* This *"sage"* attorney is renowned for his *"superb deal judgment"* and tendency to *"get involved in everything."* Regarded as an *"influential figure"* for his role in the development of standard M&A procedure, Fleischer continues to lead the firm's M&A practice and recently counseled Goldman Sachs as financial adviser to Anthem's $4 billion merger with Trigon Healthcare. Another *"high achiever,"* **Stephen Fraidin** (see p.513) attracts comment both for his *"dry wit"* and *"exceptional legal ability."* Fraidin undertakes much of the group's work for Forstmann Little and has become increasingly involved in corporate governance matters. In public M&A, this *"top-notch professional"* regularly counsels blue-chip clients such as Procter & Gamble and Adelphia on transactional matters and corporate governance. Recent work includes his representation of MGM in connection with NBC's purchase of its 20% stake in the Bravo cable channel, and acting for CommScope in a joint venture with Furukawa Electric to acquire Lucent Technologies' fiber-optic cable division.
The Clients: Goldman Sachs; Invensys; Forstmann Little & Company; Procter & Gamble; Lazard Fréres; Sara Lee; Merrill Lynch; Datek Online Holdings and The Rouse Company.

Cadwalader, Wickersham & Taft
see firm details p.778
The Firm: Despite a comparatively lower profile in the M&A market than its competitors, the firm scored a major coup by landing one of the very few megadeals of recent months: Pfizer's acquisition of Pharmacia. The firm has only relatively recently established itself as a go-to M&A practice following its 1998 recruitment of Dennis Block; commentators agreed that Cadwalader Wickersham owes its success in the field to the efforts and profile of this *"controversial figure."*
The Lawyers: Described as a *"law unto himself,"* **Dennis Block** (see p.506) is a *"tough negotiator"* with a wide-ranging practice incorporating transactional work, litigation and general corporate counseling. He heads both the firm's corporate/M&A and litigation departments and ranks highly in Chambers for his work in each field. A *"flamboyant personality,"* he tends to elicit strong reactions; interviewees commented that *"you either love him or hate him."* Even rivals acknowledged, however, that *"he works like a demon, and clients adore him."* He was commended for giving his clients *"top priority and attention"* and has forged close relationships with the likes of Bear Stearns, Quaker Oats, GE and GM. As Pfizer's traditional outside counsel, he and his team represented the company in its $60 billion bid for Pharmacia.
The Clients: Pfizer; The Quaker Oats Company; Bear Stearns; Schroders; GM; GE and Toys 'R' Us.

Debevoise & Plimpton
see firm details p.788
The Firm: Although better known for its preeminent private equity buyout and fund formation practices, the firm maintains a busy *"traditional"* public M&A practice. Attorneys typically handle a mix of work in public and private deals, which interviewees believe contributes to the group's *"balanced, well-rounded approach."* A core NY group is supported by six satellite offices comprising US and local law practitioners, of which Paris is generally considered the strongest. The *"market leader in insurance M&A,"* the firm has a heavy concentration of

insurance clients. In 2000, Debevoise & Plimpton acted for AXA Financial on the $11.5 billion sale of its controlling interest in Donaldson, Lufkin & Jenrette to Credit Suisse, and, more recently, acted for insurance company Anthem in its proposed acquisition of Blue Cross & Blue Shield of Kansas. The group also appears frequently as counsel to financial advisers and has been representing Goldman Sachs as financial adviser to Comcast in its $72 billion acquisition of AT&T Broadband. Members of this *"classic New York"* practice are said to be a *"hard-working bunch"* who exude *"old world affability."*

The Lawyers: The 26-partner corporate group is cochaired by **Meredith Brown** (see p.507), a practitioner of considerable *"stature"* who peers view as *"a dean of the M&A bar."* A *"gentleman's gentleman,"* Brown has long experience dealing with boards of directors in a range of corporate and securities matters. Described as both *"reasonable and fair-minded"* he is known to take a *"cerebral approach."* He has been leading the firm's representation of Cogentrix Energy in its $415 million acquisition by Aquila. The group continues to work for Pernod Ricard in its joint venture with Diageo in connection with the sale of Seagram's mixers business to Coca-Cola, and acted for Westfield America Trust in a $5.3 billion acquisition of Rodamco North America.

The Clients: AXA Financial; Pernod Ricard; Hasbro; Chrysler; Goldman Sachs; Westfield America Trust; Greater Media; Provident Mutual Life Insurance Company; Domtar; Deutsche Banc Alex. Brown and Clayton, Dubilier & Rice.

Weil, Gotshal & Manges LLP
see firm details p.897

The Firm: This *"highly responsive"* group of 20 New York partners and 43 associates is felt to be *"improving its position"* within the M&A market. The firm continues to grow both nationally and internationally and in the past year has opened corporate practices in Frankfurt, Singapore and Boston, bringing its total number of offices across the US, Europe and Asia to 14. This *"knowledgeable"* group was praised for its *"cohesiveness,"* and ability to coordinate *"seamless service"* across multiple jurisdictions. Rivals particularly admired the firm's *"balanced corporate strategy."* Traditionally, the firm has been recognized for its strength in private equity, and its ties with marquee client Hicks, Muse, Tate & Furst still generate a volume of LBO activity and public portfolio deals. In addition, an unrivaled bankruptcy practice sees the group acting on a substantial number of troubled company M&A work. The group has a large base of telecom and media clients and recently acted for NBC in a $1.98 billion acquisition of Telemundo Communications that involved attorneys in the New York, Dallas and Frankfurt offices. The group continues to represent Hughes Electronics and the board of directors of GM in a proposed $34.74 billion merger with EchoStar, and acted for General Dynamics in connection with its unsuccessful offer to acquire TRW.

The Lawyers: Although the substantial group generally received *"high marks"* from clients and peers as a *"knowledgeable"* team well suited to large and complicated deals, no single individual emerged from *Chambers'* research. Tom Roberts chairs the New York corporate department while Fred Green and Howard Chatzinoff cohead the M&A practice. All three practitioners handle a mix of M&A and private equity deals.

The Clients: Hughes Electronics; General Dynamics; GE; GE Capital; NBC; Enron; American Airlines and Hicks, Muse, Tate & Furst.

Willkie Farr & Gallagher
see firm details p.900

The Firm: Although the firm is better known for its strength in private equity practice, it gets involved in a number of large M&A transactions and private equity portfolio deals thanks to a long-standing relationship with flagship client Warburg Pincus. In the past year, the corporate practice has benefited considerably from the firm's high profile for major bankruptcy work. This ties in particularly well with Willkie Farr's additional focus on hi-tech and telecom matters, making the practice a *"key player"* for troubled company M&A within the distressed technology markets. The firm has also witnessed increased activity in real estate M&A, most recently acting for Developers Diversified Realty in a $811 million acquisition of JDN Realty. Interviewees also remarked upon the complementary strength of the firm's corporate practices in Paris and London, praising the group for its ability to *"put together all the pieces"* on large international transactions. The firm has opened additional offices in Germany, Italy and Belgium, further augmenting its cross-border capacities.

The Lawyers: Heading the 21-partner corporate practice is **Jack Nusbaum** (see p.528), a *"top-flight generalist,"* who is well known as Willkie Farr's relationship partner for buyout fund Warburg Pincus. Although increasingly involved in management issues due to his chairman's duties, Nusbaum maintains his transactional practice, and acts on larger M&A and LBO deals. Sources commend him as a *"truly impressive"* attorney with considerable *"stature"* in the market.

The Clients: Warburg Pincus; Zurich Financial Services; XO Communications; TELMEX; Comp USA and Simon Property Group.

Other Notable Practitioners

Lawrence Lederman chairs the Milbank, Tweed, Hadley & McCloy international corporate practice. A *"zealous advocate for his clients,"* Lederman was recommended by peers for his long experience in the field and *"gutsy"* approach to negotiations.

At Dewey Ballantine LLP, *"pragmatic"* **Mort Pierce** (see p.530) is well known as the leading attorney for financial advisers on M&A transactions. Peers report that he *"pops up all the time"* in deals: *"His name is on everything."* Pierce retains particularly strong ties to CSFB and, thanks to his tremendous deal activity, enjoys a *"wide perspective on the market."* Clients praise his *"terrific business judgment"* and *"constructive"* corporate advice. Despite his preeminent reputation for financial advisory work, Pierce also handles transactions on behalf of targets and acquirers, and most notably acted as corporate counsel to Sony Corporation of America in its joint $453 million acquisition with Royal Philips Electronics and others of InterTrust Technologies.

The recruitment of **Chuck Nathan** (see p.526) from Fried, Frank, Harris, Shriver & Jacobson to Latham & Watkins LLP is expected to *"shake up"* the latter's New York corporate practice. This *"thoughtful"* practitioner has *"seen deals from every angle,"* thanks to his experience both as a lawyer and as an investment banker. He is currently global cochair of the firm's M&A practice and, since his arrival, has acted as adviser to Hughes Electronics in connection with its spin-off and $25.8 billion acquisition by EchoStar.

"Straight-shooting" **Robert Schumer** (see p.535) at Paul, Weiss, Rifkind, Wharton & Garrison LLP received high marks for the *"superb caliber of his work."* Clients called him a *"calming force in a nerve-wracking situation,"* and praised his ability to be *"forceful without being obnoxious."* This *"unflappable"* attorney coheads the firm's M&A group and attracted attention for his work as counsel to AOL Time Warner as joint venture partner to AT&T Broadband in the $9 billion restructuring of its stake in Time Warner Entertainment Company.

NEW YORK

EMPLOYMENT & LABOR LAW

EMPLOYMENT & LABOR LAW — MAINLY PLAINTIFF

NEW YORK
Leading firms
(Employment: Mainly Plaintiff)
1. OUTTEN & GOLDEN LLP
   VLADECK, WALDMAN, ELIAS & ENGELHARD PC
2. GOODMAN & ZUCHLEWSKI LLP
3. COHEN WEISS & SIMON

Leading individuals
(Employment: Mainly Plaintiff)
1. OUTTEN Wayne *Outten & Golden LLP*
   VLADECK Judith *Vladeck, Waldman, Elias*
2. GOODMAN Janice *Goodman & Zuchlewski*
   LIDDLE Jeffrey *Liddle & Robinson LLP*
   ZUCHLEWSKI Pearl *Goodman & Zuchlewski*
3. RASKIN Debra *Vladeck, Waldman, Elias*
   VLADECK Anne *Vladeck, Waldman, Elias*

Firms and individuals are listed alphabetically in each band.

Outten & Golden LLP
The Firm: A boutique firm that has been praised as the best plaintiffs' firm in New York. It represents employees, executives and partners in all areas of employment law both on the litigation and the transactional sides. Famous for its class action work, it currently serves as cocounsel on a number of high-profile class action cases involving discrimination and wage and hour issues against MetLife, Wal-Mart, A&P and Donna Karan.
The Lawyers: *"Conscientious and practical"* **Wayne Outten** deals with any employee law matters and has been especially recommended for his gender, race and sex discrimination work.
The Clients: Clients include employees, partners and executives from various industries.

Vladeck, Waldman, Elias & Engelhard PC
The Firm: This boutique firm represents employees, both on an individual and a classwide basis, in all fields of employment law, including discrimination, breach of contract, defamation and employment negotiations. Interviewees commended the firm for its long-established market profile, which ensures it *"a wealth of experience"* and a *"presence on landmark cases."*
The Lawyers: **Judith Vladeck** was described as a *"genuine pioneer and grande dame of the plaintiffs' bar."* She deals with all aspects of employment law, and is willing to *"rattle the cage"* at all times. One management attorney commented on her success in class action discrimination work. **Anne Vladeck** is respected as an *"attorney who has seen it all"* and has developed strong mediation skills. **Debra Raskin** has likewise been acknowledged by a number of interviewees as a skilled trial lawyer.
The Clients: The firm attracts clients from various industries.

Goodman & Zuchlewski LLP
The Firm: This boutique firm offers the entire spectrum of employment law services with an emphasis on discrimination issues. It has recently dealt with a number of high-profile discrimination and wage and hour claims against The New York Times and the American Stock Transfer & Trust Company.
The Lawyers: *"Formidable opponent"* **Janice Goodman** is highly recognized for her discrimination work and considered to be a determined lawyer who cannot be intimidated. More laid-back **Pearl Zuchlewski** has been recommended for providing very creative work. Her practice is partly focused on the securities industry and she is known for her knowledge on arbitration issues.
The Clients: Clients are drawn from all industries including the financial services and advertising industries.

Cohen Weiss & Simon
The Firm: This highly respected firm represents both individuals and unions but has in particular been noted as a *"top firm"* for union work. It provides litigation and transactional services in all employee matters especially for the airline industry. A significant amount of its work is devoted to collective bargaining agreements. A leading figure is Stephen Moldof.
The Clients: Clients include: Air Line Pilots Association; Association of Professional Flight Attendants; National Association of Letter Carriers; American Federation of Television & Radio Artists (AFTRA); Directors Guild of America and American Guild of Musical Artists.

Other Notable Practitioners
Some observers found **Jeffrey Liddle** of Liddle & Robinson LLP to be an *"aggressive advocate;"* however, all agree that he *"gets results for his clients and that's what counts."* He specializes in advice to the securities industry.

EMPLOYMENT & LABOR LAW — MAINLY DEFENDANT

NEW YORK
Leading firms
(Employment: Mainly Defendant)
1. PROSKAUER ROSE LLP
2. MORGAN, LEWIS & BOCKIUS LLP
3. EPSTEIN BECKER & GREEN PC
   KAYE SCHOLER LLP
   SULLIVAN & CROMWELL LLP
4. BENETAR BERNSTEIN SCHAIR & STEIN
   JACKSON LEWIS
   O'MELVENY & MYERS LLP
   ORRICK, HERRINGTON & SUTCLIFFE

Firms are listed alphabetically in each band.

Proskauer Rose LLP
The Firm: Several commentators consider the firm's labor and employment practice to be *"in a league of its own,"* and certainly, it is home to a number of the sector's best-known figures.
The Lawyers: Cochair of the group **Allen Fagin** received universal plaudits as a *"sharp and details-oriented lawyer."* He represents clients in all types of employment litigation, breach of contract, defamation and wrongful discharge, in addition to providing preventative counseling. **Bettina (Betsy) Plevan** has been at the forefront of the industry for many years, and was commended to researchers as a *"wonderful litigator who cares deeply about the profession."* A significant part of her practice focuses on employee discrimination issues and she has recently handled claims against Citibank, CBS, Donna Karan International and Spin Magazine. **Paul Salvatore** focuses on employment law and litigation as well as union/management relations and collective bargaining. Admired for his ability to *"add a human element to his work,"* he successfully defended the NYSE against a discrimination and sexual harassment claim.
The Clients: Clients include: MetLife; AT&T; Deloitte & Touche; ING Barings; Philip Morris; Citigroup; Lazard Fréres; Willis Group; Bristol-Myers Squibb; Polo Ralph Lauren and The New York Times Company.

Morgan, Lewis & Bockius LLP
The Firm: The firm features a large and respected labor and employment group with a massive presence both in Philadelphia and New York, and is notable both for its expertise in class action and defense work, and for its *"bare-knuckle"* approach to such cases. The overall standard of technical competence is said by clients to be *"well above average."*
The Lawyers: **Andrew Schaffran** is viewed by other lawyers as *"a good speaker who provides*

EMPLOYMENT & LABOR LAW

NEW YORK

NEW YORK
Leading individuals
(Employment: Mainly Defendant)

1
FAGIN Allen *Proskauer Rose LLP*
PLEVAN Bettina *Proskauer Rose LLP*
ROGERS, Theodore *Sullivan & Cromwell*
WAKS Jay *Kaye Scholer LLP*

2
CURLEY Michael *Morgan, Lewis & Bockius*
GREEN Ronald *Epstein Becker & Green PC*
SALVATORE Paul *Proskauer Rose LLP*

3
BERNSTEIN Michael *Benetar Bernstein Schair*
DELIKAT Michael *Orrick, Herrington*

4
SCHAFFRAN Andrew *Morgan, Lewis*

Individuals are listed alphabetically in each band.

---

impressive case results." He is known for representing securities firms and other financial services organizations in all aspects of employment law and has recently represented Merrill Lynch in a discrimination class action. Another recent case involved issues relating to the proper scope of judicial review of arbitration awards. The firm scored a coup with the recruitment of **Michael Curley** from O'Melveny & Myers, thereby gaining a noted transportation and entertainment specialist, who is said by clients to *"understand industry issues perfectly."*

The Clients: Clients include: Comcast; Paramount Pictures and Kidder, Peabody & Company.

Epstein Becker & Green PC

The Firm: Its New York office serves as headquarters for the firm's labor and employment practice, which is among the largest in the world. The group is particularly famous for its litigation and class action defense work, and was singled out to researchers for its aggressive approach. It recently defended foreign multinationals against class actions by US citizens, who were claiming unlawful hiring preferences for foreign nationals. Other work includes counseling and client education with respect to post-9/11 trauma claims.

The Lawyers: Clients strongly endorsed **Ronald Green** as a *"pragmatic business thinker."* He recently defended a global pharmaceutical company in a reverse discrimination case, and won a victory for a well-known designer in a sexual harassment claim. Additionally, he is a veteran of negotiating collective bargaining agreements, notably for a large Japanese telecom company.

The Clients: Clients include major domestic and international corporates.

Kaye Scholer LLP

The Firm: Recommended to *Chambers'* researchers as a firm with a *"really positive atmosphere,"* its labor and employment practice group has recently handled a number of substantial class actions involving age and sex discrimination, plant closures and wage and hour issues.

The Lawyers: Peers attribute much of the group's prestige to **Jay Waks**, the cochair of the employment department. He is renowned for his discrimination and alternative dispute resolution work and for his skill in negotiating executive compensation packages. Leading market figures characterize him as an attorney who *"knows the law, chapter and verse."*

Sullivan & Cromwell LLP

see firm details p.886

The Firm: The group's highest profile comes through its work on behalf of the financial and insurance services industries, for whom it provides a full range of services, including advice in connection with large-scale layoffs, litigation of disputes and negotiation of agreements.

The Lawyers: The star of the show is managing partner of the labor and employment group, **Theodore Rogers** (see p.532), revered by clients for his *"practical advice, sensible approach and passion for his work."* He represented Microsoft in a landmark contractor litigation settlement, and advised MSNBC on its successful defense against the American Federation of Television & Radio Artists (AFTRA).

The Clients: Clients include Barclays Capital, Goldman Sachs and The Grand Union Company.

Benetar Bernstein Schair & Stein

The Firm: A boutique labor and employment law firm with *"top-class contacts,"* its workload encompasses the gamut of labor and employment issues, including discrimination and wrongful termination litigation, collective bargaining, strikes, arbitration, NLRB proceedings and preventative measures.

The Lawyers: Leading light **Michael Bernstein** appeals to his peers as a *"creative lawyer who is respectful of his opponents,"* while clients waxed lyrical about his ability to *"listen to us and find the right options."*

The Clients: Clients include major domestic and international corporates.

Jackson Lewis

The Firm: A large, *"effective"* employment boutique, which is said by commentators to be *"one of the most aggressive on the block"* for countering union organization. Possessing 20 regional offices, the firm has established a sound reputation for advice on termination of contract issues, and also deals extensively with ERISA matters, data protection and immigration issues for foreign employees.

The Lawyers: William Krupman is the name most often singled out at the firm.

The Clients: Clients include major US and foreign corporates.

O'Melveny & Myers LLP

The Firm: Clients view the firm's labor and employment group as one that *"exudes competence."* It advises on all aspects of labor and employment relations, including preventative counseling, alternative dispute resolution, class actions, employment discrimination and wage and hour issues. However, the group recently suffered the loss of the respected Michael Curley to local rival Morgan, Lewis & Bockius, and with him, his niche expertise in employment matters affecting the transportation and entertainment industries.

The firm represented major recording companies in ongoing collective bargaining negotiations with AFTRA. It also secured a victory for NBC against AFTRA in NLRB proceedings.

The Clients: Clients include: Columbia Pictures; California Institute of Technology; Ford; Sony and US Airways.

Orrick, Herrington & Sutcliffe

see firm details p.859

The Firm: This Californian firm's labor and employment group, while arguably not as prominent as in its home state, was still recommended to researchers as *"a big New York player."* The group represents employers in all facets of labor and employment law, with emphasis on discrimination and wrongful termination litigation, advice on affirmative action compliance, workplace health and safety, wage and hour issues and work force reductions and reorganizations.

The Lawyers: **Michael Delikat** (see p.510) gained widespread endorsement for his *"great intellectual curiosity."* An active trial lawyer, he also counsels clients on various workplace issues and corporate transactions. He represented Carrols in a class action for sexual harassment brought by the EEOC. The firm successfully advised JPMorgan Chase on obtaining an injunction to prevent an employee from using customer information.

The Clients: Citigroup; Morgan Stanley; UBS Warburg; Merrill Lynch and PrimeMedia.

NEW YORK

ENERGY & NATURAL RESOURCES

NEW YORK
Leading firms (Energy & Natural Resources)
1. LEBOEUF, LAMB, GREENE & MACRAE LLP
2. SKADDEN, ARPS, SLATE, MEAGHER & FLOM LLP
   THELEN REID & PRIEST LLP
3. SIMPSON THACHER & BARTLETT

Leading individuals (Energy & Natural Resources)
1. BAKER William *Thelen Reid & Priest LLP*
2. LAMB William *LeBoeuf, Lamb, Greene*
3. ADLER Sheldon *Skadden, Arps, Slate*
   COTTER James *Simpson Thacher & Bartlett*
   DAVIS Steven *LeBoeuf, Lamb, Greene*

Firms and individuals are listed alphabetically in each band.

LeBoeuf, Lamb, Greene & MacRae LLP
see firm details p.838
The Firm: A *"wealth of experience"* in the industry, coupled with a significant transactional capability brought the firm to the fore. Historically a force in regulation, the group's standing is particularly high for its command of PUHCA (Public Utility Holding Company Act of 1935) matters. In addition, it is now frequently seen acting on big-ticket M&A deals on behalf of oil and gas producers, natural gas pipelines, energy exchanges and publicly owned utilities.
The Lawyers: Leading the energy practice, **Steve Davis** (see p.510) won praise from peers for his *"calming influence"* in transactions involving domestic and foreign companies. Renowned for his strong corporate background, **Bill Lamb** (see p.522) has established himself as an important player in utility M&A. Together, these two individuals led the team that advised on Pepco's acquisition of Conectiv and represented MidAmerican Energy Holdings in its acquisition of Kern River Gas Transmission Company.
The Clients: MidAmerican Energy Holdings; E.ON; National Grid Group; Pepco and Western Resources.

Skadden, Arps, Slate, Meagher & Flom LLP & Affiliates
see firm details p.878
The Firm: In keeping with the firm's reputation for a stellar corporate department, the group garnered most praise for its transactional experience. Although the team is ably supported by an acclaimed regulatory arm in DC, the New York group handles a range of transactions including utility M&A and the divestiture of generating assets. Highlights have included representing New England Electric System and its subsidiaries in the sale of generation assets to USGen Acquisition Corporation and acting for Orange and Rockland Utilities in its merger with Consolidated Edison.
The Lawyers: Within the four-partner team, **Sheldon Adler** (see p.503) was singled out as an experienced corporate lawyer, well versed in utilities M&A. He advised Centrica on its $150 million acquisition of CPL Retail Energy and WTU Retail Energy from American Electric Power.
The Clients: New England Electric System; Orange and Rockland Utilities; Sithe; Centrica and AES.

Thelen Reid & Priest LLP
see firm details p.888
The Firm: This long-standing energy group is renowned for the *"extensive"* reach of its practice that incorporates regulatory, transactional and financing aspects of energy law. Peers felt that the securities side of the practice was particularly notable; however, the group is also frequently seen representing clients, especially utilities, in regulatory proceedings. Although experienced in the natural gas sector, the practice's profile is highest in the electricity markets where its workload has been dominated by the demands of deregulation.
The Lawyers: Bridging the corporate and regulatory aspects of energy law, **Bill Baker** (see p.505) was acclaimed by competitors as *"the world expert on the 35 Act [PUHCA]."* His *"superb"* reputation attracts a steady stream of work to the practice, particularly in relation to acquisitions of US utilities by foreign companies.
The Clients: Allete; Calpine; DQE; Entergy; FirstEnergy; FPL Group; PPL Corporation and TXU and various subsidiaries.

Simpson Thacher & Bartlett
The Firm: Interviewees acknowledged the firm as a *"flourishing force"* in the market, particularly praising the strength of its transactional arm. The team consists principally of lawyers from the M&A and capital markets groups focusing on the energy industry transactions. However, there is also a regulatory component to the practice.
The Lawyers: An experienced M&A lawyer, **Jim Cotter** was recommended by peers as a *"practical and no-nonsense"* attorney. His team has represented American Water Works in its acquisition by RWE and acted for American Electric Power on the sale of its Texas retail business to Centrica. The group has also completed a $750 million equity-linked securities financing for Duke Energy.
The Clients: American Water Works; American Electric Power; Conectiv; Duke Energy and KeySpan.

ENVIRONMENT

NEW YORK
Leading firms (Environment)
1. CRAVATH, SWAINE & MOORE
   DAVIS POLK & WARDWELL
   SIVE PAGET & RIESEL PC
2. ARNOLD & PORTER
   NIXON PEABODY LLP *Albany*
   SIDLEY AUSTIN BROWN & WOOD
   SIMPSON THACHER & BARTLETT
3. CARTER LEDYARD & MILBURN LLP
   DEWEY BALLANTINE LLP
4. SULLIVAN & CROMWELL LLP
   WHITEMAN, OSTERMAN & HANNA *Albany*
   YOUNG, SOMMER, WARD, RITZENBERG *Albany*

Firms are listed alphabetically in each band.

Cravath, Swaine & Moore
The Firm: A *"strong core of lawyers"* focuses its efforts on providing support to the firm's famed transactional practice. The group was praised for providing clients with *"real-world advice;"* its repertoire includes the environmental issues arising from M&A transactions, securities offerings and secured finance. It is also on call to advise on toxic tort litigation and other contentious environmental issues, and additionally counsels clients on regulatory law.
Some of the group's key engagements have included representing Bristol-Myers Squibb on its acquisition of DuPont's pharmaceutical business, and acting for Nestlé on its purchase of Purina's pet food business. It also acted for IBM on the sale of its hardware business to Hitachi, and for Conoco on its merger with Phillips Petroleum.
The Lawyers: **Jeff Smith** was identified as the group's star individual. A *"smart, humorous and creative"* attorney, he was praised by commentators for his regulatory experience.
The Clients: RWE-DEA; Nestlé; Shell; Conoco; Bristol-Myers Squibb and IBM.

Davis Polk & Wardwell
The Firm: This specialized practice focuses almost exclusively on the environmental aspects of transactions, and *"adds real value"* to the firm's powerful corporate group. The bulk of the workload involves assessing environmental liability in M&A and credit transactions, bankruptcy

ENVIRONMENT

NEW YORK

NEW YORK
Leading individuals (Environment)

1
- GERRARD Michael *Arnold & Porter*

2
- ADAMS Katherine *Sidley Austin Brown*
- FLESHER Gail *Davis Polk & Wardwell*
- SMITH Jeffrey *Cravath, Swaine & Moore*
- STEVER Donald *Dewey Ballantine LLP*

3
- KAFIN Robert *Proskauer Rose LLP*
- PAGET David *Sive Paget & Riesel PC*
- RIESEL Daniel *Sive Paget & Riesel PC*

4
- KASS Stephen *Carter Ledyard & Milburn*
- ROSENBERG Mark *Sullivan & Cromwell LLP*
- SACRIPANTI Peter *McDermott, Will & Emery*
- SOMMER Dean *Young, Sommer, Ward, Albany*

Individuals are listed alphabetically in each band.

proceedings, real estate matters and securities offerings. Here, the group's eight lawyers advise a range of clients from the paper, chemical, petroleum and real estate industries.

The Lawyers: Clients described **Gail Flesher** as an *"exceptional"* attorney who *"doesn't get bogged down in the details."* She led a team that advised on the environmental aspects of the $496.8 million IPO of common stock in Premcor, and the $72 billion merger between Comcast and AT&T Broadband.

The Clients: AES; AstraZeneca; Morgan Stanley; Roche and Highlands Gas.

Sive Paget & Riesel PC

The Firm: This boutique is well known for its long-term involvement in the environmental regulatory arena and was noted by interviewees for its broad-based practice. It continues to maintain its position as one of the few purely environmental firms in New York City, and was recommended for the quality of its counseling and its litigation capabilities. In particular, commentators underlined the group's local knowledge and *"ability to provide a cost-efficient service."* An eclectic client base comprises community and environmental groups, as well as Fortune 500 companies.

The Lawyers: **David Paget** was thought to be *"strong in a variety of environmental areas,"* but is best known for his work on environmental impact statements. Formerly chief of the environmental protection unit at the US Attorney's office in NY, **Dan Riesel** maintains his reputation as a *"leading litigator."* An assorted workload has included success in several multiparty toxic tort cases. The group also defended a Fortune 500 corporation against multimillion dollar claims for the cleanup of hazardous waste.

The Clients: Duracell; Kraft Foods; Cooper Industries; Goodyear; CIGNA and the Commonwealth of Puerto Rico.

Arnold & Porter
see firm details p.765

The Firm: The group provides advice on the full spectrum of environmental work, encompassing transactional, contentious and regulatory aspects of the law. Its key areas of strength were pinpointed as Superfund, RCRA and land issues, where it has represented BP/ARCO on the formulation of a land use plan for the redevelopment of a contaminated site near the Hudson River.

The firm represented KeySpan Energy on licensing work and associated litigation in connection with four new electric power plants, appeared in a trial relating to coastal erosion and acted in the defense of several contaminated property cases.

The Lawyers: The firm's chief draw card is undoubtedly the ubiquitous **Mike Gerrard** (see p.514), who was repeatedly championed by clients and competitors as *"a classic environmental lawyer."* An active member of bar associations and a prolific writer, Gerrard is said to have a *"broad awareness of everything that is going on in the environmental field."*

The Clients: BP/ARCO; GE; KeySpan Energy; Wyeth and Pfizer.

Nixon Peabody LLP

The Firm: Possessing a string of offices across the state, including bases in Albany and Rochester, the group is best known for its legislative and regulatory work. Commentators felt that this *"a strong group"* of knowledgeable practitioners was better suited to day-to-day environmental issues rather than 'bet-the-company' cases.

Attorneys here are supported by a non-legal, in-house environmental team that advises on scientific issues. The team's areas of specialization include enforcement defense, in which it negotiates settlements with state and federal agencies on behalf of potentially responsible parties. Other mainstays of the practice are advise on site permitting and environmental management systems.

The Lawyers: John Greenthal and Scott Turner are members of this respected team. Attorneys acted as counsel to Athens Generating Company in the siting, licensing and development of the Athens Generating Project, and served as waste water counsel to three communities in enforcement actions brought by the EPA.

The Clients: Georgia-Pacific; KeySpan Energy; Mobil; SPX; Tampa Electric Company and Xerox.

Sidley Austin Brown & Wood
see firm details p.877

The Firm: Nationally, the firm has a strong regulatory background in environmental work, and is widely recognized for its stellar Chicago and DC offices. However, a *"young and diverse"* group in New York has in no way been overshadowed, and has forged its own reputation, largely through excellence in contentious matters. It routinely manages toxic tort cases, and has recently represented a number of energy companies, including BP and CITGO Petroleum on various matters in the State of New York. In the regulatory field, the group counsels on major statutes, such as RCRA, CWA and CAA. The firm acted for American Electric Power in litigation involving the New Source Review provisions of the CAA.

The Lawyers: **Kate Adams** (see p.503) is the most high profile of the group's ten attorneys, and is credited by opponents as a *"good negotiator with great insight."* She led a team that represented GE in litigation and other matters relating to the Hudson River.

The Clients: GE; American Electric Power; Reckson Associates Realty; BP; Consolidated Edison; Forest City Ratner Companies; Lucent Technologies and Sun Chemical.

Simpson Thacher & Bartlett

The Firm: Much of the group's practice is devoted to advising on the environmental aspects of a wide range of transactions. The firm counsels clients on LBOs, syndicated loans, M&A and sale and leaseback transactions. However, competitors were especially vocal in their praise for the quality of the group's advice on insurance matters.

The Lawyers: Adeeb Fadil is one of three attorneys who work in conjunction with the litigation department on enforcement and permit proceedings, and cleanup cases under Superfund law.

The Clients: The group advised American Water Works on the environmental aspects of its sale of five regional subsidiaries to Aquarion Company. A number of blue-chip multinational corporations are also clients.

Carter Ledyard & Milburn LLP
see firm details p.780

The Firm: Since the firm recruited several lawyers from an environmental boutique in 1994, Carter Ledyard has established a reputation for fielding a *"thoroughly capable group."* Now numbering a bout 12 attorneys, the group has advised clients on corporate compliance and environmental audits, environmental litigation and the permitting and regulation of projects and facilities. The firm represented United Water New Rochelle on its construction of a pump station.

The Lawyers: **Stephen Kass** (see p.520) is one of three directors who lead the practice and a recognized face at the environmental bar. His wide-ranging practice has seen him assist the New York Power Authority on its overall strategy, environmental review and air quality permitting. In particular, he advised in relation to the peak demand for power in the city in the summer of 2001.

The Clients: New York Power Authority; Archer Daniels Midland; Nabisco; The Trump Organization and First National Bank of Chicago.

NEW YORK

INSOLVENCY/CORPORATE RECOVERY

Dewey Ballantine LLP
see firm details p.790

The Firm: Environmental litigation is at the heart of this team's practice, although it also engages in environmental due diligence on both domestic and international transactions. Highlights have included advice to a European chemical company on the sale and remediation of a manufacturing facility in the US. It has also assisted in the negotiation of remedial settlements, and provided regulatory advice to a US corporate following the discovery of PCBs and other contaminants under its facility.

The Lawyers: Easily the most recognizable individual of the group, **Don Stever** (see p.538) has over 30 years' experience and was described to researchers as *"a qualified and serious environmental lawyer."* His practical experience includes advice to clients on air, water, waste and Superfund matters.

The Clients: The firm acts for mining, aircraft engineering, oil and pharmaceutical companies as well as investment and commercial banks.

Sullivan & Cromwell LLP
see firm details p.886

The Firm: Although clients conceded that they were initially drawn to the firm by the strength of its corporate department, they were adamant that the support provided by the environmental group gave *"added worth to the service we received."* The group focuses on M&A transactions, advising buyers and sellers on actual and potential environmental problems, and also counsels on insurance and reinsurance matters.

A proportion of the practice is devoted to litigation, where typical cases include toxic tort, Superfund and indemnity matters.

The Lawyers: Mark Rosenberg (see p.533) heads the group and is an active member of various bar associations. Described by rivals as a *"tough and pragmatic"* lawyer, he and his team assisted Amgen on its acquisition of Immunex, and also acted for Powergen in E.ON's purchase of the company.

The Clients: WMC; Amgen; Cogentrix Energy; Powergen; Unilab; American Water Works and NRG Energy.

Whiteman, Osterman & Hanna

The Firm: Primarily focusing on environmental permitting and enforcement, this small group from Albany was universally acclaimed as a *"well-established and high-quality"* offering. Although little of the firm's environmental work extends beyond the state boundary, peers saw this as a distinct advantage, maintaining that *"they really understand the local issues."*

The team advises on all environmental aspects of major developments such as shopping centers, and also represents clients in a host of contentious cases including Superfund and private cost recovery suits. One such matter is the group's representation of Honeywell in relation to the Onondaga Lake Superfund site in Syracuse. The firm also represented GM in connection with a mixed residential and commercial brownfield redevelopment at a former manufacturing site on the Hudson River.

The Lawyers: Phil Gitlen cochairs the firm's environmental practice group.

The Clients: GM; Honeywell; DaimlerChrysler; International Paper; Occidental Chemical; The Terminix International Company and Phelps Dodge.

Young, Sommer, Ward, Ritzenberg, Wooley, Baker & Moore LLC

The Firm: *"A major player upstate,"* this Albany-based boutique was described to researchers as an active and value-for-money concern. Taking on a broad range of cases, the ten-strong group is best known for regulatory counseling. The areas in which it has particular experience include hazardous and solid waste, air, water, wetlands issues and historic preservation.

The Lawyers: Renowned for his litigation skills, **Dean Sommer** has a respected track record in defending clients in enforcement cases.

The Clients: A varied client portfolio includes Fortune 500 companies, smaller businesses, developers and municipalities.

Other Notable Practitioners

Bob Kafin leads a group of four environmental attorneys at Proskauer Rose LLP. Involved in the sector for over 30 years, he is respected for his ability to assess environmental liability and compliance in a variety of transactions. At McDermott, Will & Emery, **Peter Sacripanti** (see p.534) elicited praise from interviewees as an *"aggressive litigator."* He recently negotiated a large hazardous waste settlement for a multinational corporation.

INSOLVENCY/CORPORATE RECOVERY

Weil, Gotshal & Manges LLP
see firm details p.897

The Firm: Still *"at the top of the tree for overall presence and talent,"* the practice retains its historic position as *"the number-one firm on everyone's list for big cases."* Weil Gotshal was one of the first full-service firms to focus on bankruptcy work and is now reaping the rewards. The group is among the largest in the city, with a NY restructuring practice of about 70 lawyers, who are supported by additional attorneys in Dallas, Houston and Miami. The team is distinguished by its equal strength in both creditors' and debtors' representation. Traditionally, the firm has maintained *"spectacular client relationships"* with restructuring groups at CSFB and Citibank while at the same time managing to establish itself as the city's premier debtors' practice. Known for work on *"phenomenally high-profile cases,"* the practice has, in the past year alone, appeared as debtors' counsel in some of the largest corporate restructurings in US history: WorldCom; Enron; and Global Crossing. Expertise ranges across numerous sectors, including the healthcare, motion picture, airline and banking industries. Rivals envy the group's *"deep bench of major talent,"* remarking that *"the practice is strong all the way down."* The bankruptcy group benefits from the firm's expertise in related areas of tax, corporate and trade regulation, and works closely with members of the environmental practice on toxic tort-related insolvencies.

The Lawyers: Historically, the bankruptcy practice has been associated with Harvey Miller – a *"colossus"* – and the firm owes much of its preeminence in the field to his efforts in building up the practice. Despite Miller's recent departure to an investment banking boutique, the strength of the team is seen to be unaffected. Interviewees report that Miller's legacy has been to leave the practice *"in good hands."* His immediate successors, **Martin Bienenstock** (see p.505) and **Marcia Goldstein** (see p.515), have assumed coleadership of the practice. Bienenstock, described as *"one of the most qualified lawyers in America,"* is acting as lead attorney for energy trader Enron in its Chapter 11 proceedings involving $62 billion in assets. Known to be both *"adaptable and clear-sighted,"* Bienenstock was praised for his ability to be *"aggressive in his tactics and techniques without raising his voice."* The *"fabulously able"* Goldstein is described as an *"accomplished and talented"* attorney who has acquired an impressive resumé acting for both creditors and debtors in large restructuring and insolvency matters. She is leading the firm's representation of WorldCom, the largest bankruptcy filing in US corporate history at $107 billion. Also recommended was *"creative"* attorney **Stephen Karotkin** (see p.520), said to be *"deeply experienced"* in connection with asbestos and toxic tort-related restructurings. He continues as debtors' counsel to Armstrong World Industries in its ongoing Chapter 11, and is currently acting for the lenders in the Integrated Health Services bankruptcy.

INSOLVENCY/CORPORATE RECOVERY — NEW YORK

NEW YORK
Leading firms
(Insolvency/Corporate Recovery)

1
- WEIL, GOTSHAL & MANGES LLP

2
- WILLKIE FARR & GALLAGHER

3
- DAVIS POLK & WARDWELL
- MILBANK, TWEED, HADLEY & McCLOY
- SHEARMAN & STERLING
- SKADDEN ARPS SLATE MEAGHER & FLOM LLP
- WACHTELL, LIPTON, ROSEN & KATZ

4
- AKIN GUMP STRAUSS HAUER & FELD LLP
- DEBEVOISE & PLIMPTON
- FRIED, FRANK, HARRIS, SHRIVER & JACOBSON
- JONES DAY
- LATHAM & WATKINS LLP
- PAUL, WEISS, RIFKIND, WHARTON & GARRISON

5
- CADWALADER, WICKERSHAM & TAFT
- KASOWITZ BENSON TORRES & FRIEDMAN
- KRAMER LEVIN NAFTALIS & FRANKEL LLP
- MORGAN, LEWIS & BOCKIUS LLP
- STROOCK & STROOCK & LAVAN LLP

6
- BINGHAM McCUTCHEN LLP
- BROWN RUDNICK BERLACK ISRAELS
- CLEARY GOTTLIEB STEEN & HAMILTON
- OTTERBOURG, STEINDLER, HOUSTON & ROSEN
- SIMPSON THACHER & BARTLETT

Firms are listed alphabetically in each band.

The Clients: Enron; WorldCom; Global Crossing; Bethlehem Steel; Sunbeam Products; CSFB; Citibank; BNP Paribas and Deutsche Bank.

Willkie Farr & Gallagher
see firm details p.900
The Firm: *"New York's premier debtors' shop,"* this 26-lawyer group represents large companies in all aspects of Chapter 11 bankruptcies, workouts and out-of-court restructurings. Successful corporate teams in London and Paris provide support on cross-border transactions and insolvency matters involving non-US legal structures. Practitioners work closely with individuals in the firm's tax, ERISA and real estate practices to provide *"all-round advice."* Clients appreciate the *"depth of resources"* available to them, commenting that *"they have every expertise we need in-house."* The group receives frequent referrals from fellow practitioners who commend the team as a *"top-notch quality"* outfit that *"knows how to run a big case."* The firm has strong links with technology clients and is now frequently called on to handle the bankruptcy proceedings of many of the companies it helped to launch. Most notably, the group is currently acting on major telecom bankruptcies for Adelphia Communications, XO Communications and 360networks. While primarily a company-side practice, the group does undertake occasional work for secured and non-secured creditors and shareholder committees.

The Lawyers: Much of the practice is felt to revolve around department head **Myron Trepper** (see p.540), who is described as *"a born bankruptcy lawyer."* Clients praise his *"sophisticated judgment"* and *"low-key manner,"* while peers refer to him as an *"eye in the storm"* because of his ability to remain calm in difficult negotiations. Well respected in the market for his *"broad experience"* in insolvency-related transactions, Trepper leads the group's representation of cable television company Adelphia Communications in a Chapter 11 filing involving assets of $24 billion. He has been assisted in this by **Marc Abrams** (see p.503), a *"sharp and efficient debtors' lawyer"* who is applauded for his ability to *"focus on the things that matter."* Younger partner **Matthew Feldman** (see p.512) enters the ranks as an up-and-coming practitioner following general market recommendation of him as a *"constructive and results-oriented"* attorney who *"keeps his eye on the prize."*
The Clients: Adelphia Communications; Big V Supermarkets; 360networks and XO Communications.

Davis Polk & Wardwell
The Firm: With long-standing institutional ties to JPMorgan Chase and Citibank, the group is known principally for its creditors' work, which remains the focus of the practice. This *"classy operation"* consists of eight partners and 22 associates acting for creditors, debtors-in-possession (DIP), lenders, agent banks and financial advisers in a range of corporate restructuring and insolvency matters. This *"busy"* team is characterized by the *"consistently high quality"* and *"creative thinking"* of its members.
Although the focus is on creditors' representation, the group does undertake restructuring work on behalf of debtors and recently represented Bertelsmann in connection with Napster's bankruptcy proceedings. While out-of-court work is the primary emphasis of the practice, individual practitioners are adept in large-scale bankruptcy litigations. The group is particularly distinguished by the depth of its expertise in litigation and bankruptcy proceedings arising from asbestos and environmental tort claims. It continues to act as counsel to the official committee of unsecured creditors of Owens Corning in its Chapter 11. The firm also has noted expertise relating to the restructuring of derivatives and structured products in the context of large corporate collapses, and much of the team's daily work involves advising financial institutions on the credit risks associated with derivatives, securities transactions and other international financings. In addition, the practice has recently developed an online data system to assist clients in case analysis and multi-jurisdictional structures.
The Lawyers: *"Top-notch"* attorney **Don Bernstein** was praised as *"one of the smartest lawyers around."* Considered to have *"gained the respect of the banks,"* Bernstein is frequently seen acting for lenders, but also rates highly for his *"broad range of experience"* in debtor representation and legislative initiatives. Bernstein is well liked throughout the market for his *"pleasant demeanor;"* peers report that *"he can pick your pockets and you'll smile afterward."* Recently he has recently been acting as counsel to JPMorgan Chase as a member of the creditors' committee and DIP lender in Enron's Chapter 11, as agent for a syndicate of lenders in connection with the Bethlehem Steel bankruptcy, and again as lender's counsel in the Polaroid Chapter 11. Senior attorney **Stephen Case** is known as a *"great scholar of bankruptcy law"* with a *"talent for applying the law to complex cases."* As the principal lawyer to the official committee of unsecured creditors for Owens Corning, he is seen to be a *"material player in resolving asbestos cases,"* and is roundly praised as a *"deliberative"* lawyer with a flair for *"innovative solutions."*
The Clients: JPMorgan Chase; Morgan Stanley; Goldman Sachs; Bertelsmann; LTV; Goodman International; Lomas Financial and Safeguard Business Systems.

Milbank, Tweed, Hadley & McCloy
The Firm: The firm's financial restructuring practice has enjoyed a *"banner year,"* appearing as counsel in some of the highest profile bankruptcies going. This *"diverse practice"* acts both for debtors and creditors, as well as lender syndicates and equity security holders in Chapter 11s and international and domestic corporate restructurings. However, its most recent successes have been in creditors' representation. In the past year, the firm has acted as counsel to the official committee of unsecured creditors to Enron, and represented agent banks in the bankruptcies of both Global Crossing and Adelphia Communications. The restructuring practice is organized at a national level with a NY team of six partners and 24 associates acting closely with a substantial LA-based group. Practitioners were commended for finding solutions with *"maximum efficiency and minimum bluster."* Notable work on behalf of debtors includes acting for Belgium corporate Lernout & Hauspie Speech Products and its units L&H Holdings USA and Dictaphone in Chapter 11 proceedings, and representing Fruit of the Loom in its bankruptcy filing involving assets of $2.2 billion. Particular strength exists in relation to options, exchange offers and prepackaged restructuring plans. Milbank Tweed's representation of the official committee of unsecured creditors in PG&E's $21 billion Chapter11 filing is being led out of the firm's West Coast offices in LA and Palo Alto.
The Lawyers: The NY practice is synonymous with *"polished attorney"* **Luc Despins**, and many attribute the group's recent *"resurgence"* to Despins' efforts to rebuild the practice. As cochair

NEW YORK
INSOLVENCY/CORPORATE RECOVERY

NEW YORK
Leading individuals
(Insolvency/Corporate Recovery)

[1]
- BERNSTEIN Donald *Davis Polk & Wardwell*
- BIENENSTOCK Martin *Weil, Gotshal & Manges LLP*
- DESPINS Luc *Milbank, Tweed, Hadley & McCloy*
- GOLDEN Daniel *Akin, Gump, Strauss, Hauer & Feld*
- NOVIKOFF Harold *Wachtell, Lipton, Rosen & Katz*
- TREPPER Myron *Willkie Farr & Gallagher*

[2]
- ABRAMS Marc *Willkie Farr & Gallagher*
- BAKER Jan *Skadden, Arps, Slate, Meagher*
- BALL Corinne *Jones Day*
- BARTNER Douglas *Shearman & Sterling*
- CASE Stephen *Davis Polk & Wardwell*
- FEINTUCH Richard *Wachtell, Lipton, Rosen & Katz*
- GOLDSTEIN Marcia *Weil, Gotshal & Manges LLP*
- KORNBERG Alan *Paul, Weiss, Rifkind, Wharton*
- SCHELER Brad *Fried, Frank, Harris, Shriver & Jacobson*
- TODER Richard *Morgan, Lewis & Bockius LLP*

[3]
- FRIEDMAN David *Kasowitz Benson Torres & Friedman*
- GROSS Steven *Debevoise & Plimpton*
- HANDELSMAN Lawrence *Stroock & Stroock & Lavan*
- PANTALEO Peter *Simpson Thacher & Bartlett*
- ROSENBERG Robert *Latham & Watkins LLP*
- ZIRINSKY Bruce *Cadwalader, Wickersham & Taft*

[4]
- BOROWITZ Peter *Debevoise & Plimpton*
- ECKSTEIN Kenneth *Kramer Levin Naftalis & Frankel*
- HYMAN Alan *Proskauer Rose LLP*
- KAROTKIN Stephen *Weil, Gotshal & Manges LLP*
- WEISFELNER Edward *Brown Rudnick Berlack Israels*

[5]
- HAZAN Scott *Otterbourg, Steindler, Houston & Rosen*
- MILMOE Gregory *Skadden, Arps, Slate, Meagher*
- SCHONHOLTZ Margot *Clifford Chance US LLP*
- SHIMSHAK Stephen *Paul, Weiss, Rifkind, Wharton*

Up-and-coming individuals
- FELDMAN Matthew *Willkie Farr & Gallagher*
- HARRIS Adam *O'Melveny & Myers LLP*
- MASON Richard *Wachtell, Lipton, Rosen & Katz*

Individuals are listed alphabetically in each band.

of the national practice group, he has acquired *"an enormous amount of deal know-how."* Rivals consider his appointment as lead attorney for the official committee of unsecured creditors of Enron in its $63 billion Chapter 11 a *"tremendous feather in his cap."*
The Clients: JPMorgan Chase; Citigroup; Fruit of the Loom; AM Cosmetics; Lernout & Hauspie Speech Products; Safety Components International and HomePlace Stores.

Shearman & Sterling
see firm details p.874
The Firm: The practice rates highest for its strength in cross-border restructurings and has appeared as counsel on many large international bankruptcies, acting for US and foreign banks, debtors, investors, bondholders and acquirers. Traditionally, the firm's long-standing ties to major financial institutions have fostered a heavily creditor-oriented practice. In recent years, however, the group has managed to establish itself as a market presence for debtors' representation, and the team now handles equal amounts of debtor, bank and bondholder work. These *"highly skilled lawyers"* are warmly commended for their *"calm, professional approach to complicated issues"* and willingness to do a *"lot of client hand-holding."* Members have lately been involved in a number of large telecom restructurings, most notably as debtors' counsel to Global TeleSystems in a combined US Chapter 11 and Dutch bankruptcy proceeding. Niche expertise exists in relation to the use of Section 304 ancillary proceedings in large US non-insolvency cases, garnered through the firm's involvement in the BCCI, Peregrine Investment Holdings and KELM/Walbrook insolvencies.
The Lawyers: Practice head **Doug Bartner** (see p.505) earns kudos for his *"constructive can-do attitude."* Clients value his connections with leading lending institutions, commenting: *"He knows all the key players and can get all the creditors on board before filing."* This *"unflappable"* practitioner has recently been visible acting for the lenders in the $2 billion DIP financing for WorldCom. On the debtor side, Bartner represented Pathmark Stores in its prepackaged Chapter 11, and led the firm's representation of both Versatel Telecom and Global TeleSystems in prenegotiated Chapter 11s. The recent addition to the firm of a former southern district of New York bankruptcy judge is expected to boost the practice.
The Clients: Citibank; Versatel Telecom; Winstar Communications; Grapes Communications; Mpower Communications; Global TeleSystems; Pathmark Stores; Crown Vantage and Merrill Lynch.

Skadden, Arps, Slate, Meagher & Flom LLP & Affiliates
see firm details p.878
The Firm: At a national level, the firm competes with the likes of Weil Gotshal on the basis of size and strength. Interviewees frequently remark on the group's *"overall strength, expertise and manpower,"* noting that *"they have a lot of attorneys at their disposal."* The firm's profile for corporate restructuring is slightly higher in Chicago, where, despite the loss of David Kurtz, the group regularly features at the top of bankruptcy rankings. However, the 35-lawyer NY team is not far behind, and the two offices are said to *"operate seamlessly"* on major matters. The practice's worldwide coverage is further supplemented by strong teams in Delaware and LA. It is weighted toward debtors' representation, but undertakes substantial work for creditors, acquirers and investors in Chapter 11 cases. Expertise ranges from prepackaged and prearranged bankruptcies to DIP financings and bankruptcy-related litigation. A *"powerhouse"* corporate department assists on related acquisitions and dispositions, and advises clients on implementing changes to their capital structures. A *"strong coterie of attorneys"* has *"all the tools"* necessary to tackle large cases, and benefits from in-house expertise in environmental, litigation and employment issues. Skadden Arps' attorneys were described as *"aggressive"* and *"results-oriented;"* clients reported that *"they can handle anything we give them."*
The Lawyers: The principal name at the NY practice is **D J (Jan) Baker** (see p.504), a *"no-nonsense"* attorney with the *"right temperament to handle any situation."* His largely debtors' practice encompasses out-of-court restructurings and Chapter 11s for a loyal base of manufacturing, retail, oil and gas, and financial institution clients. His *"intelligence and personal integrity"* wins him *"enormous credibility with judges."* Baker has been leading the firm's representation of Owens Corning in its asbestos-related Chapter 11, and is engaged in ongoing work in connection with the Sterling Chemicals and Safety-Kleen bankruptcies. Clients particularly commend his leadership abilities: *"He's terrific at organizing a team, and delegates work on an efficient basis."* Cohead of the firm's corporate restructuring group, **Greg Milmoe** (see p.525) is described as a *"fabulous switch-hitter"* with wide-ranging experience. A securities lawyer by training, Milmoe handles a mix of bankruptcy and public and private M&A practice but has gravitated increasingly toward restructuring work. This *"unflappable"* attorney is said to contribute both noteworthy expertise in prepackaged bankruptcies and a *"good philosophic outlook."* He recently acted for Polaroid in obtaining approval from the US Bankruptcy Court for the District of Delaware for the sale of a 65% stake in the company to One Equity Partners.
The Clients: Owens Corning; Safety-Kleen; ntl; Sterling Chemicals; Vlasic Foods International; CSFB; Deutsche Bank and Goldman Sachs.

Wachtell, Lipton, Rosen & Katz
see firm details p.892
The Firm: This firm has built a *"superb"* creditors' practice on the back of strong relationships with financial institutions and insurance companies, and acts almost exclusively in this domain. While interviewees continue to cite Chaim Fortgang's 2001 departure as a loss for the practice, researchers were assured that *"there has been no diminution of talent"* in the *"happy, cohesive"* group. Clients and competitors alike recommend this *"absolutely excellent"* practice for its *"high-caliber"* attorneys and *"deep experience"* in the field. The 15-attorney group is perhaps strongest in the overlap between creditors' rights work and troubled company M&A, where the team benefits from the support and *"unmatched"* reputation of the firm's corporate/M&A practice. The firm recently

INSOLVENCY/CORPORATE RECOVERY — NEW YORK

represented CSFB in the Kmart bankruptcy, and the banks in World Kitchen proceedings.

The Lawyers: Chair of the creditors' rights practice, **Harold Novikoff** (see p.528) was mentioned as *"one of the best in the business"* for debt restructurings and insolvency-related transactions. Peers said this *"world-class talent"* possesses *"star quality."* He is recognized for his sophisticated work on behalf of major investment banks, including the development of bankruptcy-remote vehicles, troubled LBO, loan structuring and lender liability matters. *"Detail-oriented"* **Richard Feintuch** (see p.512) covers *"bankruptcy, and more."* Clients appreciate his *"straightforward"* approach to negotiations and *"broad deal perspective."* He typically represents creditors in large Chapter 11s and out-of-court restructurings, and is also heavily involved in both healthy and distressed M&A transactions. Feintuch has recently been representing the creditors in the Fruit of the Loom bankruptcy. Younger partner **Richard Mason** (see p.524) was identified as part of the *"next generation"* of insolvency attorneys. This *"energetic"* individual was ranked as an up-and-coming practitioner following general market recommendation.

The Clients: JPMorgan Chase, CSFB and Bank of America are clients.

Akin Gump Strauss Hauer & Feld LLP
see firm details p.761

The Firm: A nationwide bankruptcy practice with branches in DC, LA and Texas. In NY, seven partners appear in *"prominent cases,"* typically representing either bondholder or creditors' committees. Members have advised in connection with many recent high-profile technology bankruptcies, such as those of XO Communications and Adelphia Communications. The team is felt to have *"great contacts"* with distressed investors and hedge fund managers. Peers commended the practice for a tendency to *"nurture younger attorneys,"* while bondholder clients praised the *"fast, first-rate service"* they habitually receive.

The Lawyers: The *"face of the practice"* is department head **Daniel Golden** (see p.515). Commentators describe him as being *"at the epicenter of the bondholder community."* Golden has acted as lead counsel to the creditors' and bondholders' committees in a long list of large public restructurings and Chapter 11 proceedings. He is currently representing the official committee of unsecured creditors in the WorldCom bankruptcy. Known to be a strong advocate for his clients, Golden was commended for his ability to *"cut through the minutiae"* and understand business decisions. Clients reported that he is in a *"unique position to get things done."*

The Clients: The practice acts predominantly for bondholders' and creditors' committees. In addition to work on the WorldCom bankruptcy, the firm was chosen to advise the official committee of unsecured creditors in FLAG Telecom Holdings, and represented the official bondholders committee in steel company LTV's Chapter 11. Other notable work includes acting for the official committee of unsecured creditors in both the Exide Technologies and the XO Communications restructurings.

Debevoise & Plimpton
see firm details p.788

The Firm: Restructuring is an important link in the firm's full-service corporate practice. Four corporate partners and two litigators specialize in out-of-court restructurings and bankruptcy cases, drawing support from partners in the tax, corporate and litigation departments. Practitioners have deep expertise in prepackaged Chapter 11 situations and maintain a reputation for *"consensus-building."* The practice is largely creditor-oriented, and was felt to do a *"good job representing bondholders, and balancing that with the firm's institutional clientele"* of banks and private equity funds. The group often represents investors in, and acquirers of, distressed companies and has recently been developing a profile for international insolvency work.

The Lawyers: Steven Gross (see p.516) heads the firm's bankruptcy and workouts practice. Particularly recommended for bondholder representation, he acts for a range of debtors, creditors and investors in a volume of prepackaged and prearranged bankruptcies. This *"effective operator"* has a reputation for remaining *"smooth and calm"* in the boardroom. He represents the official creditors committee in the AMF Bowling Worldwide Chapter 11 proceeding, and is advising Leiner Health Products in prepackaged Chapter 11 preparations. His partner, **Peter Borowitz** (see p.507), has been hailed as an *"intellectual genius."* Acting exclusively on the creditor side, Borowitz is said to find *"creative solutions"* to complex problems. Although known as an *"academic"* at the bar, clients value him as a *"tenacious"* negotiator who is prepared to *"take tough, hard decisions."*

The Clients: The firm represents the bondholders committee on the Delaware and Netherlands bankruptcy proceedings of Global TeleSystems. On the debtor side, the group has acted for both Wheeling-Pittsburgh Steel and Reliance Group Holdings in their respective Chapter 11 filings.

Fried, Frank, Harris, Shriver & Jacobson
see firm details p.796

The Firm: Six partners and 25 associates maintain a mixed practice, acting equally for corporate debtors and bondholders as well as a range of creditors, trustees, investors and acquirers. The practice is transaction-oriented and acts frequently on *"innovative"* capital markets-driven restructurings. On the creditor side, the firm acts regularly for Goldman Sachs in bankruptcy arrangements. Although the emphasis in the practice is on out-of-court restructurings and recapitalizations, the team includes specialist bankruptcy litigators handling formal Chapter 11 proceedings. The team is reported to be *"aggressive in representing client's interests."*

The Lawyers: The practice is widely associated with the *"forceful personality"* of department chair **Brad Scheler** (see p.534), who receives praise for *"building up a fine practice."* Scheler can be relied upon to *"tell it like it is,"* and clients report that he is able to *"get on the phone and work out the strategic points of a deal in ten minutes – he saves us cash and heartache."* He continues to counsel Loews Cineplex on post-Chapter 11 matters and is currently advising the unofficial committee of bondholders in both the Telewest and Conseco restructurings.

The Clients: The firm advised the official creditors committee in ntl's Chapter 11, and acted for the official committee of unsecured creditors in Sunterra's Chapter 11. The firm has also acted for ANC Rental and Rand McNally on restructuring matters. In addition, the group represents institutional investors Forstmann Little & Company, Goldman Sachs, AEA Investors and Franklin Resources in connection with investments in distressed companies.

Jones Day
see firm details p.823

The Firm: The 2001 recruitment of key partners from Weil Gotshal has dramatically boosted the NY profile of this Cleveland-based firm. While the firm is still felt to be stronger in the Midwest, the NY group is quickly establishing a reputation for complicated debtor work. Four partners and eight associates work closely with specialists in Cleveland, Chicago, DC and Atlanta on large bankruptcies and corporate reorganizations. The team was praised as a *"high-quality outfit"* backed by *"enormous national resources."* Practitioners have extensive experience in international restructurings and troubled company M&A.

The Lawyers: Felt to be a *"real presence"* in the market, **Corinne Ball** (see p.505) has apparently *"landed on her feet"* at Jones Day. As a headline lateral hire, her move helped bring the firm into the spotlight for restructuring matters. This *"quirky"* practitioner is reported to have a talent for *"getting things done."* She has long-standing experience advising on major international bankruptcies, frequently acting on behalf of creditors and bondholder groups. She is currently lead counsel to IBM in its effort to acquire the worldwide assets of Comdisco. Peers describe her as a *"dynamo"* at the negotiating table.

The Clients: The firm is representing Burlington Industries in its Chapter 11 filing, and acts for Globalstar in its $3.4 billion bankruptcy. Other work includes representing Napster in their

NEW YORK

INSOLVENCY/CORPORATE RECOVERY

Delaware Chapter 11, and acting as Chapter 11 counsel to broadband provider Williams Communications Group. Much of the firm's work is staffed across multiple offices.

Latham & Watkins LLP
see firm details p.835
The Firm: This expanding practice consists of four partners, one of counsel member and ten associates. The practice is broad-based, acting for debtors, bondholders, bank groups and investment banks. With strong restructuring groups in both Chicago and LA, the firm also receives praise for geographic coverage that extends to Europe and Asia. The group has developed particular expertise in telecom workouts and Chapter 11 cases, appearing as debtors' counsel in the bankruptcies of Orbcom, Birch Telecom and ITC DeltaCom. Practitioners are able to call upon colleagues in related areas of tax, litigation, real estate and environment when advising on out-of-court restructurings, corporate governance and the disposition of distressed assets. Clients appreciate the *"integrated advice"* provided by the firm.
The Lawyers: Robert Rosenberg (see p.533) *"goes beyond the call of duty"* for his clients. Described as a *"master orchestrator,"* this *"business-minded"* practitioner is visible representing investment banks in refinancings and restructurings. He is currently advising the independent committee of the board of Allegiance Telecom, and is acting as counsel to the cochair of the Enron creditors committee and to the major trade creditors of WorldCom.
The Clients: The group frequently acts for CSFB, Lehman Brothers, UBS Warburg, Deutsche Bank and Crédit Lyonnais in out-of-court restructurings. It is representing CSFB as financial adviser in the ntl Chapter 11. Corporate clients include GE and Wells Fargo.

Paul, Weiss, Rifkind, Wharton & Garrison LLP
see firm details p.862
The Firm: This *"collegial"* five-partner group rates highly for its *"knowledgeable and dedicated"* members. Although somewhat more visible as counsel to creditors committees, the practice *"covers the waterfront,"* acting for a range of debtors, official and unofficial creditors, equity security holders and purchasers of distressed companies' assets. Partners were said to be *"highly accessible"* and to display *"first-rate analytical skills."* The group emphasizes a multidisciplinary approach and works closely with practitioners in the tax, corporate, litigation and real estate departments when advising on complex Chapter 11 cases or out-of-court restructuring matters. The recent departure of a partner to the bench has not been seen to materially affect the group's strength in the area.
The Lawyers: Chair of the bankruptcy department **Alan Kornberg** (see p.521) *"doesn't yield to the yellers and screamers."* This *"diligent"* practitioner *"gets right to the issue,"* and is admired for his ability to *"anticipate the company's interests."* Clients appreciate his *"constructive"* advice, describing him as an *"excellent quarterback"* who ably *"coordinates strategy and keeps everything moving."* Kornberg has recently been advising the Californian Public Utilities Commission in connection with the PG&E bankruptcy. Partner **Stephen Shimshak** (see p.536) is acclaimed as a *"fine analyst"* with an *"eye for the right deal."*
The Clients: The group represented the official creditors committee of Armstrong World Industries in an asbestos-related Chapter 11, and acted for the unofficial bondholders committee in the restructuring of United Pan-Europe Communications. The firm has also acted as special counsel to the creditors committee of ICG Communications, and represented the unofficial committee of noteholders of Intermedia Communications, a subsidiary of WorldCom. Other clients include: Derby Cycle; Hutchison Whampoa; Viacom; Oaktree Capital and California Public Utilities Commission.

Cadwalader, Wickersham & Taft
see firm details p.778
The Firm: The restructuring group has undergone several changes in recent years with a number of recruitments and defections at both partner and associate level. The current NY practice consists of five partners, 17 associates and five special counsel. These attorneys focus on advising commercial and investment banks, mutual funds and investment management firms as creditors on large financial restructuring matters and Chapter 11 insolvencies. On the debtors side, industry expertise ranges across the commodities, energy, gaming, media, aerospace and insurance sectors. Drawing upon an additional three-partner group in London, the group acts on complex international restructurings and advises foreign entities on Section 304 ancillary proceedings.
The Lawyers: One of the *"war horses"* of the business, **Bruce Zirinksy** (see p.543) attracts considerable market attention for his *"bright"* manner and *"tactical"* methods. Chair of the financial restructuring practice, Zirinsky is often seen as bondholders counsel on complex matters. Peers admire his *"hard-working ethic."*
The Clients: The practice represents the bondholder committee in the Telewest Communications Chapter 11 proceedings, and acts for the official committee of unsecured creditors in the ntl bankruptcy. Attorneys frequently represent financial institutions Merrill Lynch, CSFB and Lehman Brothers as creditors to workout and bankruptcy arrangements.

Kasowitz Benson Torres & Friedman
The Firm: Bankruptcy and creditors' rights are core areas for the firm. In NY, the firm maintains its *"boutique"* reputation as *"one of the biggest names in the distressed debtor community."* Three partners, eight associates and one special counsel concentrate primarily on bondholder litigation, in which they are thought to be *"highly successful and strategic."* Practitioners are said to *"have a natural flair for disrupting plans and turning cases to their own direction."*
The Lawyers: Department head **David Friedman** has made a name for himself as a leading lawyer for bondholders in litigated cases. This *"smart and aggressive"* attorney is well known for his *"creativity."* Peers report that he *"works hard to find solutions."*
The Clients: The firm typically represents DIP, commercial lenders, equity security holders trustees, and hedge funds. Recent notable work includes acting for the bondholders of Adelphia in the company's bankruptcy, and representing the holders of $3 billion of bonds issued by MCI in connection with the WorldCom Chapter 11 proceedings.

Kramer Levin Naftalis & Frankel LLP
see firm details p.832
The Firm: This 25-strong practice acts predominantly on behalf of creditors committees, bank groups and bondholders, and has appeared on some of the largest industrial bankruptcies of recent years. Practitioners here are felt to be *"highly focused"* and commended for producing *"quality work."* A five-lawyer subgroup specializes in distressed debt trading; the firm is developing a *"steady"* practice representing purchasers of troubled securities. In addition, the group occasionally acts in court-ordered investigations in connection with reorganizations and bankruptcy proceedings.
The Lawyers: Kenneth Eckstein (see p.511) chairs the firm's creditors' rights and bankruptcy department, and elicits praise for having *"put together a good practice."* This *"effective"* practitioner is highly recommended for his bondholder and creditor committee representation. He continues to advise the 47-member bank group that holds $1.6 billion in unsecured debt in Owens Corning in connection with the company's asbestos-related bankruptcy.
The Clients: The practice acts as counsel to the official committee of unsecured creditors in the $1.4 billion Adelphia Business Solutions bankruptcy, and for the official unsecured creditors committee of Bethlehem Steel. Attorneys represent the senior secured noteholders in connection with Sterling Chemicals' Chapter 11, and acted for the official committee of equity security holders of WR Grace in bankruptcy filings.

INSOLVENCY/CORPORATE RECOVERY

NEW YORK

Morgan, Lewis & Bockius LLP
The Firm: Widely associated with major client JPMorgan Chase, the firm has a preeminent reputation for DIP financings. This relationship has seen the group acting on large-scale bankruptcies of the likes of LTV and Caldor. In addition to a volume of bank representation, the practice has developed a niche acting for REITs, owners, developers and property investors in the disposal and acquisition of the real estate assets of distressed companies. The national bankruptcy practice is composed of 45 lawyers, concentrated largely in the NY and Philadelphia offices.

The Lawyers: Acknowledged as *"one of the deans of the bankruptcy bar,"* **Richard Toder** leads the firm's bankruptcy and financial restructuring practice. He is perceived to have a *"highly specialized"* practice representing institutional creditors and creditors committees. He has acted for JPMorgan Chase as agent for syndicates in the Iridium and LTV bankruptcies. This *"outgoing"* attorney displays *"tremendous ability and personal integrity."* He was observed to have a *"great rapport with judges,"* and even rivals noted he was *"a pleasure to deal with."*

The Clients: The practice represents a number of institutional lenders, namely Wachovia and Bank of New York. The firm has represented JPMorgan Chase as DIP lenders in the Kmart, Armstrong and Burlington Industries bankruptcies. Other work includes representing Mellon Bank as agent to lending groups owed $1.5 billion in connection with Genesis Health Care's Chapter 11, and acting for CSFB as agent for a syndicate in the Enron bankruptcy.

Stroock & Stroock & Lavan LLP
The Firm: The firm's historical reputation for restructuring work has been invigorated by the recent addition of ten attorneys from Dewey Ballantine, bringing the total count up to nine partners and 21 associates. Noteworthy industry expertise exists in the steel, retail, airline, real estate and communications sectors. Practitioners are said to *"appear consistently"* as counsel to lenders, bondholders and trade creditors on a volume of small and mid-sized bankruptcies. The group is felt to maintain *"high standards of quality,"* offering counseling on risk management, derivatives and structured finance. Well known for its energy trading practice, the firm currently represents a number of purchasers of assets of Enron.

The Lawyers: *"Calm, cool and collected"* **Lawrence Handelsman** was thought to be a *"savvy"* practitioner with long experience in the field. He cochairs the firm's insolvency department, and has acted as counsel to creditors committees in the Chapter 11 filings for LTV, Wheeling-Pittsburgh Steel and AEI Resources.

The Clients: A stable of financial institution clients include ABN AMRO, CSFB, Lehman Brothers and JPMorgan Chase. On the debtor side, the practice has represented AMF Bowling Worldwide and Coleco Industries in Chapter 11 cases.

Bingham McCutchen LLP
The Firm: The product of a 2002 merger between Bingham Dana and McCutchen, Doyle, Brown & Enersen, this firm now boasts a 100-lawyer restructuring practice split between the NY and Hartford offices. Practitioners focus on creditors' work, representing a range of banks, insurance companies, mutual funds and distressed debt investors on out-of-court restructurings, Chapter 11s and troubled company M&A. Although active in the US, the group is most visible internationally, where attorneys advise on major cross-border restructurings. In addition to its main New York/Connecticut axis, the firm maintains small restructuring practices in Boston, San Francisco, London and Singapore.

The Lawyers: Commentators trace the firm's prestige in cross-border bankruptcy to the now retired Richard Gitlin and his original Hartford-based firm Hebb & Gitlin, which was absorbed by Bingham Dana in 1999. Interviewees have called him *"the foremost authority on international insolvency."* The recruitment of former federal bankruptcy judge Tina Brozman is also felt to further boost the practice.

The Clients: The firm represented the public debtholders in the out-of-court restructuring of AT&T Canada, and acted as counsel to the creditors committee in the $14 billion Asia Pulp & Paper debt restructuring. Other work includes representing Raytheon in connection with the Washington Group International bankruptcy, and acting for the DIP lender in Republic Technologies International. GE Capital, Fleet Bank, MetLife, Deutsche Bank and John Hancock Life Insurance are also active clients of the firm.

Brown Rudnick Berlack Israels
The Firm: The niche New York Berlack Israels & Liberman practice merged in 2002 with the larger Boston-based Brown Rudnick firm. However, this is not seen to have affected the group's status as *"one of New York's most notorious bondholder practices."* This small practice is equally feared and admired for taking *"an aggressive stance"* on behalf of distressed investors. Commentators reached the consensus that *"clients come first"* with this niche practice.

The Lawyers: A *"contentious"* figure in the bankruptcy bar, **Ed Weisfelner** is the face of the practice. Known to be a *"passionate advocate for clients,"* Weisfelner is said to employ *"attack dog"* strategies in bondholder litigation. Clients commended both his *"accessibility"* and his *"ability to think outside of the box."*

The Clients: The firm has associations with financier Carl Icahn, and played a significant role in the Global Crossing bankruptcy. Work is typically on behalf of bondholders and investors in troubled companies.

Cleary Gottlieb Steen & Hamilton
see firm details p.782

The Firm: Although insolvency is not felt to be an area of concentration for the firm, a small practice here comprises *"some terrifically talented people"* with broad experience in the field. The group handles both debtors' and creditors' work and receives substantial amounts of international bankruptcy matters off the back of the firm's highly regarded cross-border corporate practice. Most notably, the firm acted for Chile power company Edelnor in a prepackaged Chapter 11. Practitioners possess niche expertise in sovereign debt restructuring and work closely with members of the capital markets group in advising major Wall Street banks on derivatives exposure. Clients rely on this *"responsive"* group for their *"top-notch advice"* on distressed M&A, exit strategies, workouts, restructuring matters and bankruptcy litigation. Major matters include representation of Bridge Information Systems in its liquidation and sale of assets to Reuters, and acting for Abbey National Bank in LTV's second bankruptcy. In M&A, the firm represented Cable & Wireless in its acquisition of Exodus Communications out of Chapter 11.

The Lawyers: James Bromley and Thomas Moloney are the contact partners for the firm's restructuring group.

The Clients: Abbey National Bank; Bridge Information Systems; Covanta Energy; Edelnor; Morgan Stanley; Lehman Brothers; Fleet Bank; Goldman Sachs; Oaktree and Nortel Networks.

Otterbourg, Steindler, Houston & Rosen
The Firm: This *"old-line"* middle market practice is renowned for its representation of trade creditors in retail Chapter 11 cases. Highly respected within this niche area, the firm has been retained to act on such high-profile matters as the Kmart and Fruit of the Loom bankruptcies. Attorneys frequently appear in bankruptcy court on large cases throughout the country and are said to enjoy a *"great book of business."*

The Lawyers: *"Experienced"* attorney **Scott Hazen** attracts praise for his *"smooth"* negotiating style and work on *"high-profile cases."* Hazen recently acted for the official committee of unsecured creditors in the US Airways Chapter 11.

The Clients: The firm typically represents creditor committees in workouts and Chapter 11 proceedings and is particularly well known for its work on behalf of trade creditors.

Simpson Thacher & Bartlett
The Firm: While the restructuring practice is still perceived largely as a service department for the firm's highly rated M&A and LBO practice, the

NEW YORK

INSURANCE

group was significantly enhanced by the recruitment of Peter Pantaleo from O'Melveny & Myers. The ten-partner team typically represents lenders and maintains strong ties with JPMorgan Chase. Practitioners are said to possess *"broad experience of sophisticated transactions"* and offer *"consistently solid"* service and advice.

The Lawyers: The 2001 lateral hire of *"superb lawyer"* **Peter Pantaleo** was felt to *"shore up"* the Simpson Thacher restructuring practice. Since his arrival Pantaleo has reportedly *"taken up the gauntlet,"* bringing the firm increasingly into the spotlight for agent bank and senior lender representation. Peers hold him in high esteem him as a *"talented"* attorney who *"doesn't give anything away"* in negotiations.

The Clients: The firm has represented bank groups in the Chapter 11 reorganizations of Kmart, Sunbeam and Adelphia Communications. Attorneys regularly act for lenders JPMorgan Chase and Wachovia Securities in out-of-court workouts and Chapter 11s. The practice is also advising a large capacity purchaser in the 360networks insolvency proceedings.

Other Notable Practitioners

Alan Hyman at Proskauer Rose LLP received praise for his work as debtors' counsel. His *"affable and easygoing"* manner is reputed to *"charm and impress judges."* Clients have described him as a *"bridge-builder"* who is nonetheless prepared to *"stamp his feet and draw a line in the sand"* when necessary. Hyman recently represented the Museum Company in bankruptcy proceedings.

Margot Schonholtz heads the practice at Clifford Chance US LLP and is often seen acting for large syndicated creditors. Rated as a *"smart, tough negotiator,"* Schonholtz is said to display *"keen business sense."* She represented Bank of America as agent to the senior secured lender in the Williams Communication Chapter 11.

"No-nonsense" attorney **Adam Harris** is now heading the restructuring practice at O'Melveny & Myers LLP. This younger partner was rated by peers as an up-and-coming practitioner.

INSURANCE

NEW YORK
Leading firms (Insurance)

1. LEBOEUF, LAMB, GREENE & MACRAE LLP
2. DEBEVOISE & PLIMPTON
3. DEWEY BALLANTINE LLP
4. ANDERSON KILL & OLICK
   SIMPSON THACHER & BARTLETT
   SKADDEN, ARPS, SLATE, MEAGHER & FLOM LLP
   SULLIVAN & CROMWELL LLP
5. CADWALADER, WICKERSHAM & TAFT
   STROOCK & STROOCK & LAVAN LLP
6. CLIFFORD CHANCE US LLP
   EDWARDS & ANGELL
   FRIED, FRANK, HARRIS, SHRIVER & JACOBSON
   MENDES & MOUNT LLP
   WILSON, ELSER, MOSKOWITZ, EDELMAN

Firms are listed alphabetically in each band.

LeBoeuf, Lamb, Greene & MacRae LLP
see firm details p.838

The Firm: *"The big dog"* of the insurance industry, the firm's historical reputation for regulatory work is complemented by its acknowledged expertise in insurance litigation and industry-specific transactions. The group's *"dominance"* is often attributed by market commentators to its strong bench of insurance specialists, who cover most angles of the industry.

The Lawyers: Alex Dye (see p.511), described to researchers as *"the strongest corporate insurance lawyer at the practice,"* has a particularly high profile. He recently represented Nationwide Financial Services in its acquisition of Provident Mutual Life Insurance for $1.56 billion.

Among a slew of highly rated names, a further three attorneys stood out. **Don Henderson**'s (see p.518) renowned regulatory background earned him widespread endorsement from his peers, while **John Nonna** (see p.528) comes recommended as *"a fine mainstream choice"* for reinsurance work. **Cynthia Shoss** (see p.536) gained high marks for her skill in complex demutualizations. She earned plaudits for her work on the demutualization of Prudential, and is reported by clients to be *"a pleasure to work with."*

The Clients: The firm maintains its historical relationship with Lloyd's and continues to represent Lloyds' US interests. Recent work also includes acting for AEGON in its $10.8 billion acquisition of Transamerica, and representing Goldman Sachs and other underwriters in The Principal Financial Group's $2.1 billion IPO following demutualization. Other clients include: Nationwide Financial Services; Prudential; Safety Insurance Group; Sun Life Financial Services of Canada; Morgan Stanley; Allstate and CSFB.

Debevoise & Plimpton
see firm details p.788

The Firm: Strong in both regulatory and financial matters, the firm is best known for its work in the life insurance industry and demutualizations. Elsewhere, the group represented Prudential in its acquisition of Gibraltar Life Insurance, a deal involving the acquisition of the reorganized Kyoei Life Insurance and an investment of $1.2 billion.

The Lawyers: The firm's reported preeminence in demutualizations and the life insurance industry are specifically credited to the presence of **Wolcott Dunham** (see p.511): *"The father of the practice."* *"Erudite and scholarly,"* he is thought by a number of commentators to be *"on a higher plane."* Rival practitioners admire him for his *"even-keeled"* manner and ability to get issues out on the table, and one enthused: *"I would go to him if I had a bet-your-life deal."*

Tom Kelly (see p.520) has also worked on prominent demutualizations and public offerings, including the Principal Life Insurance demutualization and IPO, a deal worth $7 billion. He was named by one competitor as *"the most impressive young lawyer I see opposite me."*

The Clients: The firm acted on the demutualization of Provident Mutual Life Insurance, in which Provident was acquired by Nationwide Financial Services for approximately $1.6 billion. It also advised Phoenix on its $1.8 billion demutualization.

Dewey Ballantine LLP
see firm details p.790

The Firm: The practice's focus is on transactional matters; M&A and capital markets financings form the basis of the workload, and the firm also offers coverage in securitization, insurance bankruptcy and reinsurance. The group's M&A transactions have included representing Irish Life & Permanent on the sale of several US properties. It has also advised underwriters in offerings for both PMA Capital and Philadelphia Consolidated.

The Lawyers: Jeff Liebmann (see p.523) and **Bill Rosenblatt** (see p.533) stand out as the group's two leaders. The former was commended to researchers as a *"hard-working and smart"* attorney, specializing in M&A and the life insurance industry. Rosenblatt, an experienced securities lawyer, garnered praise from clients for his *"concentration on the real issues."*

The Clients: The firm took public MONY in the demutualization of what was Mutual of New York, and represented Cathay Financial Holdings on its issue of $700 million worth of convertible bonds. Irish Life & Permanent and Radian Reinsurance are also clients.

INSURANCE — NEW YORK

NEW YORK
Leading individuals (Insurance)

★ **DUNHAM** Wolcott *Debevoise & Plimpton*

[1] **ANDERSON** Eugene *Anderson Kill & Olick*
   DYE Alexander *LeBoeuf, Lamb, Greene & MacRae LLP*
   LIEBMANN Jeff *Dewey Ballantine LLP*
   OSTRAGER Barry *Simpson Thacher & Bartlett*
   ROSENBLATT William *Dewey Ballantine LLP*
   VYSKOCIL Mary Kay *Simpson Thacher & Bartlett*

[2] **GABAY** Donald *Stroock & Stroock & Lavan LLP*
   SULLIVAN Robert *Skadden, Arps, Slate, Meagher*

[3] **HENDERSON**, Donald *LeBoeuf, Lamb, Greene*
   KELLY Thomas *Debevoise & Plimpton*
   NONNA John *LeBoeuf, Lamb, Greene & MacRae LLP*
   ROWEN Andrew *Sullivan & Cromwell LLP*
   SHOSS Cynthia *LeBoeuf, Lamb, Greene & MacRae LLP*
   TORCHIANA William *Sullivan & Cromwell LLP*

[4] **CHAFFETZ** Peter *Clifford Chance US LLP*
   PEARSON Nick *Edwards & Angell*
   SCHOENBERG Clifford *Cadwalader, Wickersham*
   SCHWARTZ Steven *Clifford Chance US LLP*

Individuals are listed alphabetically in each band.

Anderson Kill & Olick

The Firm: The firm of choice for insurance policyholders, its insurance practice group exclusively represents policyholders in disputes with insurance companies. Here, its reputation for diligently fighting the corner of its clients, in and out of court, is unrivalled.

The Lawyers: Name partner **Eugene Anderson** is well known to market insiders as a *"real leader who has advanced the cause of policyholders."* In his field of expertise, his *"passion"* and status as a *"trailblazer"* is almost legendary. Peers particularly cited advances made by him in environmental matters, and he is known also for his work in asbestos and toxic tort cases. Anderson is supported by a substantial group of lawyers, who gained client endorsement for their *"creativity and good strategy."*

The Clients: The firm successfully represented Weyerhaeuser in the Washington Supreme Court in a policy dispute with its insurer, Commercial Union. It also acted for Fuller-Austin Insulation in its court dispute with its insurers concerning asbestos-related claims. It has also advised on several claims made following the World Trade Center (WTC) disaster. Other clients include: Textron; United Capital; ABC Bus Company; ATOFINA Chemicals; Quest Diagnostics and ICI Risk & Insurance Services.

Simpson Thacher & Bartlett

The Firm: Acknowledged to be the insurance company's favored insurance law firm, it is especially valued for its insurance and reinsurance litigation expertise.

The team has advised Swiss Re on insurance and reinsurance coverage issues following the 9/11 attacks, including representing it as the lead insurer to the property insurance program for the WTC. This has involved litigation with the WTC leaseholder, Larry Silverstein, in which he has contended that the WTC suffered two occurrences of attack, which should effectively double any insurance recovery. Reinsurance work for the group has included action for Travelers and American General. The firm has also been involved in asbestos-related work on behalf of Travelers, St. Paul and CNA.

The Lawyers: Two leading partners particularly stand out in this area. **Barry Ostrager** has *"a towering reputation"* as an all-around litigator, but his profile is highest in the insurance sector, where he is known as a *"formidable opponent."* He has been retained by ACE USA for an appeal in a surety bond case.

Mary Kay Vyskocil, extolled to researchers as an *"effective and high-caliber courtroom performer,"* is, like Ostrager, involved in commercial as well as insurance litigation. She has advised on matters in which insureds sought coverage for expenses arising from Y2K data processing upgrades, including action for Industrial Risk Insurers.

The Clients: Swiss Re; Industrial Risk Insurers; ACE USA; Travelers; American General; St. Paul; CNA and AIG.

Skadden, Arps, Slate, Meagher & Flom LLP & Affiliates
see firm details p.878

The Firm: *"A powerhouse firm with a growing insurance practice group,"* according to competitors. It is best known in insurance circles for its M&A prowess. The department also extends to corporate and coverage litigation and regulatory advice.

The Lawyers: By common consent, the key to the practice is **Bob Sullivan** (see p.539), whose practice incorporates claims litigation, insurance and reinsurance transactions, and regulatory matters.

The Clients: The firm represented Citigroup on its acquisition of Golden State Bancorp for a reported $5.8 billion, and acted for Sul América Companhia Nacional de Seguros in its sale of a 49% stake to ING Groep. Other matters include advising American General on its sale to AIG, a deal valued at $23 billion, and its advice to Travelers in connection with its 2002 IPO. The firm also advises Sul América Companhia Nacional de Seguros, Swiss Re and Liberty Mutual.

Sullivan & Cromwell LLP
see firm details p.886

The Firm: Another major player in transactional insurance work, the firm has a caseload that encompasses insurance financings, M&A, and mutual and offshore company advice. It provides transactional support to an impressive roster of clients, notably representing St. Paul on a number of large deals. The group recently advised Anthem on its acquisition of Trigon Healthcare, acted for Royal Bank of Canada on its acquisition of Business Men's Assurance Company of America, and represented SCOR in its disposition of certain interests. Elsewhere, it acted for Daido Life on its demutualization and IPO, represented AIG and other founders on the establishment of Allied World Assurance and advised SCOR on the establishment of Irish Reinsurance Partners.

The Lawyers: **Andrew Rowen** (see p.533), *"a senior and respected corporate man,"* coordinates the insurance practice group, while *"excellent professional"* **William Torchiana** (see p.540) earned universal acclaim for his work in financings and M&A.

The Clients: St. Paul; Anthem; Royal Bank of Canada; SCOR; Daido Life; AIG; Everest Re; Prudential; Chubb and Hartford Life.

Cadwalader, Wickersham & Taft
see firm details p.778

The Firm: Competitors commented on the strength of the whole group, which is especially recommended for its work in reinsurance, but also has sound transactional experience. Securities, demutualizations and M&A are all catered for and the firm fields a robust litigation department.

The firm has been involved in litigation concerning the Unicover matter, recently scoring a success in the New York Appellate Division. It also advised on two high-profile catastrophe bonds, one for Swiss Re and another for Munich Re, the latter of which was valued at $300 million.

The Lawyers: **Cliff Schoenberg** (see p.535), a reinsurance litigation and arbitration specialist, was recommended to researchers by both opponents and clients as a *"clear and responsive"* attorney.

The Clients: Berkshire Hathaway; Legion Insurance; General Re; Munich Re; National American Insurance; Ambac; ACE and PartnerRe.

Stroock & Stroock & Lavan LLP

The Firm: The firm maintains a respected status for its insurance regulatory expertise. The department is home to five former New York Insurance Department regulators.

The Lawyers: **Donald Gabay**, endorsed to researchers as an *"exceedingly competent guy with a user-friendly manner about him,"* has a practice that emphasizes regulatory compliance. However, he has also been involved in corporate transactions, demutualizations, securitizations and litigation.

The Clients: A varied clientele includes major insurance companies and smaller, local groups, property/casualty insurers and life and health companies.

NEW YORK — INSURANCE

Clifford Chance US LLP
see firm details p.783
The Firm: The firm was recommended by commentators as a *"solid"* choice for a range of insurance matters, including corporate, financial, regulatory, insolvency and litigation advice.
The Lawyers: **Peter Chaffetz** is experienced in insurance and reinsurance litigation and insurance insolvency matters. He has recently taken a significant role in the Unicover dispute, in which he has represented Sun Life Assurance Company of Canada. He has also been involved in matters arising from both the WTC attacks and the Enron insolvency. His colleague **Steven Schwartz** is also highly regarded as an experienced reinsurance lawyer.
The Clients: The firm advised the New York State Insurance Department on both Nationwide Financial Service's acquisition of Provident Mutual Life Insurance and the demutualizations of Phoenix Home Life Mutual Insurance and Principal Mutual Holding. It also acted for Prudential on its acquisition of a controlling interest in Apolo Operadora de Sociedades de Inversión, a Mexican private mutual fund company. Sun Life Assurance and John Hancock are also clients of the firm.

Edwards & Angell
The Firm: **Nick Pearson** is thought to be the leading asset of a firm that is widely acknowledged to be *"making an aggressive push"* in the insurance market. He represents both domestic and international clients on the formation, acquisition and sale of insurance and reinsurance companies. He is also well versed in reinsurance arbitrations. The team also advises on regulatory issues, insurance defense litigation and securitizations.
The Clients: The firm advises property and casualty insurers, life and health insurers, investment banks, brokers and trade associations.

Fried, Frank, Harris, Shriver & Jacobson
see firm details p.796
The Firm: Competitors acknowledged the firm's historical strength in insurance litigation and financing matters. They spoke of a firm that is *"making a real push"* to broaden its insurance portfolio. Led by Richard Brown, the expanded insurance practice group covers dispute resolution, corporate transactions and tax advice. Reinsurance, regulatory advice and insurer insolvency are also catered for by the group.
The Clients: The firm acted for Goldman Sachs as the lead underwriter for the IPO of Platinum Underwriters Holdings, and advised Goldman Sachs and GS Capital Partners 2000 and their affiliates on the formation of Allied World Insurance Holding and Allied World Assurance. Other work has included litigation and arbitration proceedings on behalf of Fortress Re, involving insurer insolvencies and disputes in the insurance aviation market. Other clients of the firm include: Generali Group; Gulf Insurance; Liberty Mutual and AIG.

Mendes & Mount LLP
The Firm: The practice encompasses a wide range of insurance and reinsurance law, with experience in areas such as risk management counseling, professional liability and related transactions. Its dispute resolution capability includes arbitration and litigation, and extends to cases such as personal injury, property damage, products liability and coverage disputes. Peers particularly commended the firm to *Chambers'* researchers for its insurance claims work.
The Lawyers: The large group of insurance specialists at the New York office is led by Thomas Quinn.
The Clients: The group acts for domestic and international insurers and reinsurers.

Wilson, Elser, Moskowitz, Edelman & Dicker LLP
The Firm: The origins of the firm's reputation in the industry lie in insurance claims work. Its New York offices continue to focus on insurance defense litigation on behalf of insurance companies and insureds involved in coverage disputes. The firm represented Royal Insurance in disputes such as the shootings at Columbine High School, CO, and has advised on a number of professional liability issues. These have included acting for a large New York client on medical malpractice matters and consequent disciplinary procedures.
The Lawyers: Leaders in the New York office include Arnold Kideckel, an expert on insurance regulatory matters, workers' compensation and employee liability, along with Perry Kreidman, whose specialties include reinsurance. At the Albany office, Jerry Hoffman's focus in the healthcare industry extends to insurance matters, and regional managing partner Kenneth Shapiro's many concerns include the insurance industry.
The Clients: Royal Insurance, Yasuda, AIG, Travelers and Chubb are examples of the firm's client base.

INTELLECTUAL PROPERTY

NEW YORK
Leading firms (Intellectual Property)
1. FISH & NEAVE
2. CLIFFORD CHANCE US LLP
   FITZPATRICK, CELLA, HARPER & SCINTO
   KENYON & KENYON
3. KIRKLAND & ELLIS
4. MORGAN & FINNEGAN
   PENNIE & EDMONDS LLP
5. BAKER BOTTS LLP
   FISH & RICHARDSON
   JONES DAY
   WEIL, GOTSHAL & MANGES LLP

Firms are listed alphabetically in each band.

Fish & Neave
The Firm: *"Head and shoulders above everyone else"* is the view commentators hold about this boutique firm, unanimously recommended as the state's premier IP law firm. Covering the entire spectrum of IP law, its services include transactions and counseling on patents, trademarks, copyright and trade secrets, including licensing and asset management. The firm's litigation reputation rests in the hands of its *"strong and outstanding"* prosecution team, which successfully represented ZymoGenetics in a case concerning methods of making fibrinogen in the milk of transgenic animals.
The Lawyers: **Herbert Schwartz** continues to be rated by his peers as *"the doyen of the NY bar."* Acclaimed for his profound knowledge of the law, he has a practice that focuses on patents, but extends to all areas of the sector. He successfully appeared for Purdue Pharma in a major patent litigation case against Boehringer Ingelheim. A *"great name,"* **Albert Fey** remains *"a major talent"* for patent litigation. He recently represented Microsoft in a declaratory judgment action for non-infringement and invalidity of patents in the data communications industry. **Jesse Jenner**, *"a brilliant courtroom performer"* specializes in patent, trade secrets and trademark litigation. Among his recent successes was a landmark class action case against Lemelson Medical, Education & Research Foundation, which ruled that there is a prosecution laches defense in cases involving submarine patents.
Biotech specialist **James Haley** is recognized as a *"sharp and careful"* attorney. His time is split between counseling and strategy work, and litigation for clients in the biotech and pharmaceutical industries. He advised Amgen on its high-profile dispute with Aventis/TKT over erythropoietin (EPO) patents. Researchers also noted substantial

INTELLECTUAL PROPERTY — NEW YORK

NEW YORK
Leading individuals (Intellectual Property)

1
- BAECHTOLD Robert *Fitzpatrick, Cella, Harper & Scinto*
- SCHWARTZ Herbert *Fish & Neave*

2
- FEY Albert *Fish & Neave*
- JENNER Jesse *Fish & Neave*
- KIDD John *Clifford Chance US LLP*

3
- FILARDI Edward *Skadden, Arps, Slate, Meagher*
- KATSH Salem *Shearman & Sterling*
- NEUNER Robert *Baker Botts LLP*
- SWEENEY John *Morgan & Finnegan*

4
- BEN-AMI Leora *Clifford Chance US LLP*
- CREEL Thomas *Goodwin Procter LLP*
- DELUCIA Richard *Kenyon & Kenyon*

5
- DESMARAIS John *Kirkland & Ellis*
- GLAZER Steven *Weil, Gotshal & Manges LLP*
- HALEY James *Fish & Neave*
- KOENIGSBERG Fred *White & Case LLP*
- LEE Steven *Kenyon & Kenyon*
- MORGAN Robert *Fish & Neave*
- SOBEL Gerald *Kaye Scholer LLP*

Individuals are listed alphabetically in each band.

endorsement for *"conscientious and intuitive"* litigator **Bob Morgan**. A patent specialist, he has appeared on cases connected with semiconductors, computers and medical and telecom devices. He advised VIA & Centaur on a suit against Intel involving microprocessors, and appeared for Linear Technology against Texas Instruments in a case involving integrated circuits.

The Clients: Amgen; Linear Technology; Purdue Pharma; Microsoft; ZymoGenetics; VIA & Centaur; AT&T; Lucent Technologies; Ford; Biogen and Polaroid.

Clifford Chance US LLP
see firm details p.783

The Firm: Clients commented favorably about this growing IP practice group, which has a particularly strong name for contentious work. The group also provides advice on all relevant IP matters, including licensing, transactional work, prosecution and filing services.

The Lawyers: Global head of the firm's IP group **John Kidd** is regarded by peers and clients as an *"experienced and hard-hitting"* litigator. Although his practice also embraces trademark work, he is best known for his patent expertise, and has a clientele drawn from hi-tech, biotechnology and mechanical devices industries. He acted for Genentech in a dispute over DNA patents, and has appeared on a number of patent cases for Honda. Interviewees praised **Leora Ben-Ami** (see p.505) as an *"aggressive but effective"* litigator who has particular knowledge of the biotechnology industry.

The Clients: Honda; Genentech; DuPont and Pfizer.

Fitzpatrick, Cella, Harper & Scinto
see firm details p.795

The Firm: This boutique firm boasts specialist practice groups in trademark licensing and transactions, copyrights, patent prosecution, pharmaceuticals, electronic and computer technologies, biotech, litigation and e-commerce. Most notable is its pharmaceutical group, which has been repeatedly recommended as *"the obvious leader"* by peers and clients alike. Here, the firm represents AstraZeneca in its suit against producers of generic versions of the drug Prilosec.

The Lawyers: Head of the pharmaceuticals group **Bob Baechtold** (see p.504) is thought by peers to have *"a great track record"* for advising on litigation strategy in the patent sector. Baechtold is viewed by industry leaders as a *"true partner in our business."* He successfully represented Merck in a recent patent dispute, and advised Bristol-Myers Squibb against Rhone Poulenc Rohrer on the basis that it had committed inequitable conduct in acquiring a patent.

The Clients: AstraZeneca; Bristol-Myers Squibb; Novartis; Pharmacia; Merck; Bausch & Lomb and Pfizer.

Kenyon & Kenyon

The Firm: *"A top IP firm with senior people"* provides clients with a range of advice on patents, copyright, trademark, trade secrets and litigation. Its litigation practice has been particularly praised by competitors.

The Lawyers: Head of the firm's chemical/biotechnical practice group, **Richard DeLucia** conducts IP litigation and counsels clients on alternative dispute resolution and litigation avoidance. Noted by peers for his huge workload, he represented Enzon in a patent dispute involving hepatitis drugs, and Amgen against a number of high-profile companies in a dispute involving a patent for an ultrasound agent. *"Clear thinker"* **Steven Lee** focuses on chemical and biochemical litigation, and in particular on biotechnology, pharmaceuticals and polymers. He successfully defended Teva Pharmaceuticals USA in a patent suit brought by GlaxoSmithKline, which invalidated three of its patents on the basis of the doctrines of anticipation and inequitable conduct.

The Clients: Sony; Enzon; Amgen and Teva Pharmaceuticals USA.

Kirkland & Ellis
see firm details p.830

The Firm: The NY office of this successful national IP practice has a sound reputation for litigation, transaction, counseling and various administrative services involving all areas of IP law. Noted for attracting a substantial amount of work, the firm's litigators were recently involved in a high-profile patent infringement suit, successfully defending several cellular telephone companies against MLMC.

The Lawyers: Contemporaries concede that **John Desmarais** (see p.510) *"does an excellent job for the firm"* on patents, trademark and trade secrets litigation. His patent litigation caseload spans all industries, and includes representing Infineon Technologies in its landmark defense against Rambus, which resulted in a ruling that provided new guidance on the existence and scope of patent disclosure obligations. The firm also advised on a trademark infringement suit on behalf of Hermes International against a number of retail companies.

The Clients: Lucent Technologies; Hermes International; Infineon Technologies and Schering-Plough.

Morgan & Finnegan
see firm details p.853

The Firm: Regarded by peers as *"a fine all-round boutique,"* it boasts practice groups for patents, trademarks, copyright, unfair competition, e-commerce and financial systems. The group acted for Thinking Machines in defense of a suit against IBM.

The Lawyers: Researchers were told that **John Sweeney** (see p.539) *"has real presence"* in this field. He is involved in patent, trade secret and trademark litigation. Sweeney represented Bombardier in its patent suit against Yamaha over personal watercrafts, and advised software provider The SCO Group in a patent infringement case involving cell phones.

The Clients: Clients include Bombardier, The SCO Group and Procter & Gamble.

Pennie & Edmonds LLP

The Firm: Despite some personnel losses over the past two years, this boutique firm is still viewed as *"a strong competitor"* by rivals. Noted both for patent and trademark expertise, the firm has practice groups in the areas of biotech and pharmaceuticals, electrical engineering and computer sciences, mechanical engineering, and chemistry. It also offers litigation, procurement and consulting services to clients from all industries.

The Lawyers: Laura Coruzzi chairs the firm's biotech and pharmaceutical group.

The Clients: The biotech and pharmaceutical group is currently representing long-term client Hoffmann-La Roche in a patent dispute against Promega and MJ Research. It is also acting for Boehringer Ingelheim Vetmedica against Schering and Schering-Plough in a patent suit concerning swine vaccines and involving issues surrounding the doctrine of equivalents.

Baker Botts LLP

The Firm: The firm's IP practice groups provide comprehensive services relating to IP transactions and litigation. The litigation group attracted par-

NEW YORK

INTELLECTUAL PROPERTY

ticular praise from market commentators for its handling of a wide range of disputes, including patent, copyright, trademark, unfair competition and trade secret cases.

The Lawyers: Also renowned for his general commercial practice, **Bob Neuner** heads the group, and is regarded as *"one of the best in the business."* He focuses on patent cases, although his expertise also extends to copyright and trademark. Highlights include acting for Infineon Technologies in a patent infringement dispute, and advising Vanguard Products in a dispute concerning a patent for gasketing materials.

The Clients: Vanguard Products; Siemens; Novartis; Alcatel and Cisco Systems.

Fish & Richardson

The Firm: The firm's NY office was noted to researchers for *"really churning out the work,"* and received particularly warm client endorsement for its trademark group, which represented Circle Line-Statue of Liberty & Ellis Island Ferry in a trademark dispute. Also notable is the firm's patent group, which offers the full range of prosecution, litigation and counseling services in a wide spectrum of industries. Representative cases include advising Nokia on design litigation disputes, and acting for Atmel and LSI Logic in litigation claims brought by Philips involving semiconductors.

The Lawyers: David Francescani is the contact partner for the firm's IP practice.

The Clients: 3M; Intel; Eastman Chemical; Alcatel USA; Honda; Mars; Nokia; Calvin Klein; NHL Enterprises; Sanyo; Atmel and LSI Logic.

Jones Day
see firm details p.823

The Firm: The IP practice group focuses on patents, copyright, trademark litigation, advice and counseling. As usual, the firm won substantial plaudits for its contentious expertise, and is said by some clients to be home to *"some brilliant people."* The group represented Bayer on a patent dispute involving glucose meters, appeared for Midco International in a patent dispute relating to medical equipment for brain surgery, and advised Consumers Packaging in a dispute relating to breach of trade secret agreements.

The Lawyers: Theresa Gillis cochairs the firm's technology issues practice.

The Clients: Aventis; Consumers Packaging; Midco International; Bayer; Nokia; BellSouth; PepsiCo and Procter & Gamble.

Weil, Gotshal & Manges LLP
see firm details p.897

The Firm: This respected group is involved in patent, copyright and trademark litigation as well as negotiating and documenting transactions and counseling. It offers ongoing patent advice to Merrill Lynch in respect to its financial products, acts on transactional and litigation matters for the telecom arm of Pirelli, and represents the Weizmann Institute of Science in Israel on various IP matters.

The Lawyers: *"Superbly competent"* **Steve Glazer** (see p.514) litigates all types of patent disputes and also provides advice on licensing and other transactional services. He successfully represented Disney's ABC in a lawsuit brought by ACTV, and acted for Hyper-TV in a dispute over interactive TV patents. In addition, he appeared for ExxonMobil, obtaining a positive ruling for the company with respect to the validity of two of its petrochemical patents.

The Clients: Disney; Hewlett-Packard; AOL Time Warner; ExxonMobil; Merrill Lynch; Reuters; Pfizer; GlaxoSmithKline; News Corporation and Pirelli.

Other Notable Practitioners

Recommended for his intellectual ability, patent litigator **Gerald Sobel** of Kaye Scholer LLP *"knows the minds of judges."* He handles patent litigation for clients in all industries, and is involved in trademark, trade secrets and licensing cases. Peers praise *"fantastic trial lawyer"* **Edward Filardi** (see p.513) of Skadden, Arps, Slate, Meagher & Flom LLP & Affiliates for his *"talent and style."* Specializing in jury trial cases, Filardi primarily deals with patent disputes; he successfully represented Nanomotion in a dispute with a Russian entity involving a patent for piezo-ceramic motors. **Thomas Creel** (see p.509) of Goodwin Procter LLP focuses on patent and trade secrets litigation. He has handled all types of patent cases, but increasingly deals with generic pharmaceutical work. An example of this was his work for Teva Pharmaceuticals USA in its patent infringement defense against a number of high-profile pharmaceutical companies. **Salem Katsh** (see p.520) of Shearman & Sterling heads the firm's IP group. He focuses on patent, trade secrets, trademark, unfair competition and antitrust litigation. He advised Jiangsu Sopo on a trade secrets litigation launched by BP Chemicals. **Fred Koenigsberg** of White & Case LLP is particularly known for his copyright work, and provides transactional, litigation and counseling services in this field. Koenigsberg is general counsel to the American Society of Composers, Authors and Publishers (ASCAP), and represents clients in copyright issues relating to music, motion pictures, literature and the fine arts.

LITIGATION

Paul, Weiss, Rifkind, Wharton & Garrison LLP
see firm details p.862

The Firm: Rivals were loud in their praise for the firm's long litigation tradition, its *"incredible capacity for generating impressive papers,"* and its *"creative approach"* to finding solutions to complex litigation matters. Litigators here have a reputation among their clients as *"terrifically smart guys who know their subject."* The team has extensive experience in handling high-stakes litigation work in capital markets, involving securities, futures and derivatives disputes, and has acted on behalf of bidders, targets and financial advisers in takeover litigation. The firm has represented Citigroup in all matters relating to the Enron bankruptcy. Other key elements of the caseload include insurance and reinsurance litigation, and the firm's track record includes representing Amtrak in a $200 million lawsuit.

The Lawyers: Martin London (see p.524) earned top recommendations from rivals as *"one of the toughest and most vigorous trial lawyers out there."* Noted for defending Morgan Stanley in false accusation claims, he has also represented plaintiffs in commercial libel cases, defended numerous securities litigations for the largest investment banks, and litigated commercial cases involving breach of contract, products liability and insurance.

Dan Beller (see p.505) was also recommended to *Chambers'* researchers as a class action *"guru"* with

GENERAL COMMERCIAL

substantial experience of complex civil matters, including securities and internal corporate investigations. He has a background in criminal defense work, and has appeared on cases including securities fraud, insider trading, RICO and securities manipulation for major clients such as Goldman Sachs and Morgan Stanley. *"Cerebral"* performer **Leslie Fagen** (see p.512) has an established market reputation for products liability, insurance and securities litigation. His track record includes representing one of the largest medical device manufacturers in products liability defense work. He has also defended companies in cases throughout the US concerning alleged defective components in nuclear power plants. Chair of securities **Richard Rosen** (see p.533) has

LITIGATION

NEW YORK

NEW YORK
Leading firms
(Litigation: General Commercial)

1
- PAUL, WEISS, RIFKIND, WHARTON & GARRISON
- SIMPSON THACHER & BARTLETT
- WACHTELL, LIPTON, ROSEN & KATZ

2
- CRAVATH, SWAINE & MOORE
- DAVIS POLK & WARDWELL
- SKADDEN, ARPS, SLATE, MEAGHER & FLOM LLP
- SULLIVAN & CROMWELL LLP

3
- BOIES, SCHILLER & FLEXNER LLP
- CADWALADER, WICKERSHAM & TAFT
- WEIL, GOTSHAL & MANGES LLP

4
- CAHILL GORDON & REINDEL
- CLIFFORD CHANCE US LLP
- KIRKLAND & ELLIS
- KRAMER LEVIN NAFTALIS & FRANKEL LLP
- WILLKIE FARR & GALLAGHER

5
- BAKER BOTTS LLP
- CLEARY GOTTLIEB STEEN & HAMILTON
- CURTIS, MALLET-PREVOST, COLT & MOSLE LLP
- DEBEVOISE & PLIMPTON
- MILBERG WEISS BERSHAD HYNES & LERACH
- SHEARMAN & STERLING

Leading individuals
(Litigation: General Commercial)

1
- BOIES David *Boies, Schiller & Flexner LLP*
- FISKE Robert *Davis Polk & Wardwell*
- REARDON Roy *Simpson Thacher & Bartlett*
- WACHTELL Herbert *Wachtell, Lipton, Rosen & Katz*

2
- DIBLASI Gandolfo *Sullivan & Cromwell LLP*
- LERNER Jonathan *Skadden, Arps, Slate, Meagher*
- LONDON Martin *Paul, Weiss, Rifkind, Wharton*
- NUSSBAUM Bernard *Wachtell, Lipton, Rosen & Katz*
- OSTRAGER Barry *Simpson Thacher & Bartlett*
- VIZCARRONDO Paul *Wachtell, Lipton, Rosen*

3
- CHEPIGA Michael *Simpson Thacher & Bartlett*
- JOSEPH Gregory *Gregory P. Joseph Law Offices LLC*
- KOLB Daniel *Davis Polk & Wardwell*
- MIRVIS Theodore *Wachtell, Lipton, Rosen & Katz*
- NAFTALIS Gary *Kramer Levin Naftalis & Frankel LLP*

4
- BIRNBAUM Sheila *Skadden, Arps, Slate, Meagher*
- BLOCK Dennis *Cadwalader, Wickersham & Taft*
- CASTEL Kevin *Cahill Gordon & Reindel*
- KOOB Charles *Simpson Thacher & Bartlett*
- ROSEN Richard *Paul, Weiss, Rifkind, Wharton*

5
- ALLERHAND Joseph *Weil, Gotshal & Manges LLP*
- BELLER Daniel *Paul, Weiss, Rifkind, Wharton*
- BENEDICT James *Clifford Chance US LLP*
- BRANDES Lawrence *Cadwalader, Wickersham & Taft*
- CHESLER Evan *Cravath, Swaine & Moore*
- DAVIS Fred *Shearman & Sterling*
- FAGEN Leslie *Paul, Weiss, Rifkind, Wharton*
- KAVALER Thomas *Cahill Gordon & Reindel*
- KIERNAN John *Debevoise & Plimpton*
- NEUNER Robert *Baker Botts LLP*
- SAUNDERS Paul *Cravath, Swaine & Moore*

Firms and individuals are listed alphabetically in each band.

---

a wealth of experience in securities, derivatives, commodity futures and banking. In complex business disputes, he has represented underwriting syndicates in securities fraud class actions, and appeared on a number of cases involving open and closed-end funds. Described to researchers as *"incredibly smart, if a touch abrupt,"* he was the defense counsel in two of the most significant commodity futures manipulation class actions of recent decades – the silver and copper markets cases. He recently represented Citigroup, as well as several mutual funds involved in technology and telecom losses.

The Clients: Alberta Energy; Johnson & Johnson; Burgess Services; Citigroup; General Atlantic Partners; Amtrak; Revlon and Sphere Drake Insurance.

Simpson Thacher & Bartlett
The Firm: A litigation group comprising 160 lawyers that encompasses every type of complex commercial case, including insurance and reinsurance, products liability, securities and M&A, and features notable experience of Supreme Court appeals. This *"sophisticated"* team typically represents US and multinational corporations, and earned consistent praise from competitors for its *"remarkable breadth and ability to litigate any matter under the sun."* Expert in takeover litigation, the firm is well known for representing both bidders and targets in LBOs and hostile tender offers. Significant cases have included the American Home Products/Warner-Lambert/Pfizer transaction. The team has also represented JPMorgan Chase and Chase Securities in securities and antitrust class action lawsuits against IPO issuers and underwriters. Other matters include defending clients charged with claims under RICO and the Foreign Corrupt Practices Act and acting for the former directors of HFS in derivative disputes arising from the merger between HFS and CUC International (to form Cendant).

The Lawyers: Senior litigator **Roy Reardon** is nationally acclaimed as a *"terrific and confident lawyer with an amazingly diverse practice."* Revered as a superb trial lawyer who employs a *"calm and balanced"* style of advocacy, he is particularly well known for his work on behalf of GM. He was also commended to researchers for his schooling of the firm's junior litigators, a number of whom have represented Fortune 500 companies in investigations by the SEC and the NYSE. **Mike Chepiga** is respected by clients and competitors for his expertise in securities litigation and for representing investment banks in class and derivative actions. Described to researchers as *"a skilled constructor of convincing arguments,"* he is a leading figure in the securities group, which defended WorldCom in connection with securities actions filed in federal courts in New York and Mississippi. He has represented several major investment banks in IPO-related litigation, and has been involved in recent high-profile M&A disputes. The experienced **Charles Koob** received solid endorsement as a capable and experienced litigator, notably for antitrust matters, while for insurance and reinsurance litigation, the name of **Barry Ostrager** stands out. He was recommended to researchers for his *"tactically astute"* approach to solving complex problems, and represented Andersen Consulting against a highly publicized $14 billion claim by Arthur Andersen. Envied for his loyal client base, Ostrager's run of high-profile cases has continued with his representation of Swiss Re in the insurance dispute over the World Trade Center disaster.

The Clients: JPMorgan Chase; Lehman Brothers; Kohlberg Kravis Roberts & Company; The Blackstone Group; Goldman Sachs; Morgan Stanley; CSFB; Ralph Lauren; Swiss Re and Duke Energy.

Wachtell, Lipton, Rosen & Katz
see firm details p.892

The Firm: *"Superb at everything they do,"* the firm's litigators are universally acknowledged by competitors to be *"savvy, smart and driven."* Although the group is slightly smaller than its principal rivals and tends to have a narrower focus on securities and white-collar defense work, clients insist that it has the capacity to take on *"anything you throw at them."* Since the 1980's, when the firm was a regular player on a number of the country's most acrimonious hostile takeover disputes, it has enjoyed an outstanding reputation for its prowess in the most technically complex matters. Recent examples include representing the leasehold owner of the destroyed World Trade Center, and acting for Philip Morris in successful federal appeals involving third-party medical expenses.

The Lawyers: **Herbert Wachtell** (see p.541) commands universal respect. An *"in-your-face hard-nosed litigator,"* he is rated by competitors as *"a formidable opponent"* in any class action or civil litigation case. He is also regarded as the driving force behind the firm's involvement in most of the landmark corporate governance litigation in Delaware, including the Revlon, Macmillan, Time Warner and Paramount cases.

Top trial lawyer **Paul Vizcarrondo** (see p.540) is also highly regarded as a *"thorough and serious attorney,"* and appeared for AT&T in a dispute with Cablevision concerning the former's attempt to restructure its relationship with Excite@Home. **Bernie Nussbaum** (see p.528) appeals to opponents as a *"a lawyer's lawyer,"* and is valued for his *"rock solid"* counseling work in securities cases. Completing a powerful lineup. **Ted Mirvis** is widely held to possess *"excellent judgment,"* and is known for his appellate court work.

The Clients: Goldman Sachs; Philip Morris; Revlon; Time Warner and AT&T.

NEW YORK

LITIGATION

Cravath, Swaine & Moore
The Firm: The *"formidable record of success"* of the firm's litigation department and its *"enormous scope for handling any type of dispute"* ensure that it takes high rank in New York, in spite of the comparative absence of any real individual stars. Commentators were unanimous about the team's *"great evenness of quality,"* with one client asserting that *"there are no weak links at Cravath Swaine."* The practice covers a diverse range of matters in all sectors of the economy and handles cases at trial and appellate level in federal and state courts as well as in domestic and international arbitration. The group successfully defended CBS in an action seeking to enjoin the merger between Viacom and CBS and represented IBM in an action alleging breach of a patent cross-license agreement. In the field of libel and privacy law, the team is well known for representing national media companies and newspapers. Recently the group defended Newsweek in an action brought by Julie Hiatt Steele alleging breach of confidentiality.

The Lawyers: Evan Chesler is highly regarded as an excellent litigator who has very strong advocacy skills. His style is described as *"crystal clear and effective."* **Paul Saunders** was also endorsed to researchers for his emphasis on international arbitration, IP, securities and antitrust disputes.

The Clients: ABACUS Distribution System; Air-Net Systems; Berlex Laboratories; Bristol-Myers Squibb; British American Tobacco; CBS; DuPont; GE Capital; Hertz; IBM and King World.

Davis Polk & Wardwell
The Firm: The firm's prominence in the field is linked to the individual profiles of the team's *"celebrity litigators"* and their ability to attract headline cases. The practice has notable strength in accountancy-related litigation, in which the team has represented all the major accountancy firms. The firm has advised PwC and Ernst & Young in professional liability matters, and appeared for Salomon Smith Barney in connection with various civil matters relating to limited partnership sales. Elsewhere, the department has represented Hoffman-La Roche in a variety of antitrust issues, and appeared for Alfred Taubman, former chairman of Sotheby's, in recent, much-publicized, civil and criminal cases.

The Lawyers: The firm is thought to owe much of the credit for its eminent position in litigation to the presence of star performer **Bob Fiske**, internationally regarded as *"a craftsman who does without the courtroom histrionics."* Peers especially envied his ability to try a case while simultaneously grasping the PR impact of any litigation matter, and clients pointed to his *"tremendous ability to relate to both judges and juries."* Fiske's huge profile from his time as prosecutor on the Whitewater affair has been consolidated by securities litigation cases on behalf of GE and Bankers Trust, and the successful defense of one of the largest actions ever brought – a $4 billion suit arising from the Three Mile Island disaster.

In accounting litigation, **Dan Kolb** was acclaimed to researchers as an *"undoubted expert,"* and has an impressive portfolio of experience as a trial lawyer in federal, state and appellate courts throughout the US.

The Clients: JP Morgan Securities; Deutsche Bank; JPMorgan Chase; Prudential Securities and Sotheby's.

Skadden, Arps, Slate, Meagher & Flom LLP & Affiliates
see firm details p.878

The Firm: Known for its sheer size and *"huge appetite for work,"* the firm has developed an outstanding reputation for corporate-related litigation. Recent highlights for the department include being appointed special counsel for Enron in conjunction with its reorganization proceedings. The team also defended McKesson HBOC in a major securities class action in the Northern District of California and acted for Robotic Vision Systems in a contested jury trial against General Scanning.

The Lawyers: *"Amazingly thorough"* **Jonathan Lerner** (see p.523) was endorsed to researchers as a *"top-quality"* securities litigator, appealing to clients as an attorney who is *"on top of his briefs and ethically beyond reproach."* He represented Cendant in the $2.8 billion settlement of the largest securities class action approved by the US District Court for the District of New Jersey, and led the team that defended DaimlerChrysler in both individual and class action securities litigation in the US District Court for the District of Delaware. **Sheila Birnbaum** (see p.506) earned market approval as *"a sound negotiator,"* and was particularly recommended for her expertise in complex products liability cases.

The Clients: Afilias; Charles Schwab; Chris-Craft Industries; Citigroup; CSFB; Dresdner Bank; Honeywell; Lockheed Martin; McKesson HBOC; NBA and North Fork Bancorporation.

Sullivan & Cromwell LLP
see firm details p.886

The Firm: Clients raved about the firm's all-around litigation ability, citing the group's *"methodical and thorough"* approach to cases. Although some find the departmental style to be *"a little remote and prescriptive,"* the majority of commentators appreciate the team's breadth of expertise in areas such as antitrust, IP, products liability and securities. The group's recent caseload has included defending the directors of BP in a stockholder derivative action, and representing KPMG in securities actions arising from allegations against Lernaut and Hauspie. The team also represented Bankers Trust in proceedings before the SEC and Commodity Futures Trading Commission.

The Lawyers: Gandolfo DiBlasi (see p.510) is nationally renowned as a securites litigator who *"has clear judgment and is attuned to the business needs of his clients."* Focusing on securities, banking and commodities matters, he has represented clients in a number of class actions in federal courts. He also has a wealth of experience of defending clients in major investigations into alleged insider trading.

The Clients: Goldman Sachs; France Télécom; First Union; Microsoft; Kodak; The Bank of New York; Bankers Trust and BP.

Boies, Schiller & Flexner LLP
The Firm: Interviewees report that the firm owes its renown to the fame of its name partner and star litigator, David Boies. The firm covers the spectrum of commercial disputes, and served as counsel for the lead plaintiffs in a class action case against Sotheby's and Christie's in which the court approved a $512 million settlement. Another recent highlight involved the team's work as co-lead counsel in a price-fixing case against the major manufacturers of bulk vitamins, in which the court approved a $1.1 billion settlement.

The Lawyers: The name of the firm is inextricably linked with that of its brightest star, *"flame thrower extraordinaire"* **David Boies**. Typically found on cases with the highest profile, he was special trial counsel for the DOJ in its antitrust suit against Microsoft, and lead counsel for former Vice President Al Gore in connection with litigation relating to the Presidential election vote count in Florida. Competitors acknowledge that Boies possesses *"tremendous recall and the ability to distill information and get to the heart of things,"* although commentators also point out that success has its price: *"All clients want his personal attention, and he can't be in two places at once."*

The Clients: CBS; CSFB; Ernst & Young and Philip Morris.

Cadwalader, Wickersham & Taft
see firm details p.778

The Firm: A large team of about 100 litigators has its principal reputation in securities and corporate litigation, IP, and insurance and reinsurance. Clients confirm that the group is *"both consistent and competent."*

The Lawyers: Larry Brandes (see p.507) is highly acclaimed as an insurance expert, and also has a burgeoning arbitration practice. He has acted as arbitrator or counsel in more than 200 reinsurance disputes. Corporate man **Dennis Block** (see p.506) is also known as an aggressive litigator. *"Dynamic, pushy and determined,"* his track record includes representing Merrill Lynch in a high-profile securities case in connection with trading on NASDAQ, which resulted in a $1 billion settlement with plaintiffs' firm Milberg Weiss Bershad Hynes & Lerach.

The Clients: General Reinsurance; CIGNA; Commercial Union; ACE; Excel; Zurich; Merrill Lynch; Bear Stearns and Pfizer.

Weil, Gotshal & Manges LLP

see firm details p.897

The Firm: In spite of its experience in a wide range of commercial matters ranging from banking to sports litigation, the firm is inevitably associated with its expertise in bankruptcy litigation. Competitors regard the litigation group as an *"up-and-coming bunch with an excellent cadre of young partners."* In this department, attorneys generally belong to one of four main practice groups: antitrust and trade regulatory litigation; IP and business securities litigation, including work related to derivatives; takeover and internal corporate investigations; and white-collar crime. The firm defended Arthur Andersen in lawsuits brought by hundreds of investors, and represented Sotheby's in connection with stockholders' class action suits arising from price-fixing allegations.

Chambers' researchers also found that the firm has an established reputation for 'busted deal' litigation, recently acting as counsel to GE following its abortive merger with Honeywell. Elsewhere, the group acted for Disney in connection with litigation concerning the TV program 'Who Wants To Be A Millionaire?' and has defended ExxonMobil against the Saudi Arabian Government in courts in New Jersey and Delaware.

The Lawyers: **Joseph Allerhand** (see p.503) is said to be *"on the verge of breaking into the big league,"* and is well regarded within the business and securities community. He has defended Bear Stearns and Merrill Lynch from claims by stockholders, while a number of his colleagues have recently undertaken trial work in accounting and malpractice cases.

The Clients: GE; Merrill Lynch; Pirelli; Sotheby's; McGraw-Hill; BNP Paribas; Arthur Andersen and AK Steel.

Cahill Gordon & Reindel

The Firm: Although the firm's litigation practice has no formal subgroups or specialized departments, it still manages to advise on a huge range of disputes, including securities, corporate governance, insurance and products liability matters. Among a number of high-profile recent cases, the group defended Prudential Securities in multi-district litigation proceedings, in which plaintiffs sought a recovery of $24 billion, following the sale of limited partnerships. The team has represented Time Warner Entertainment in a nationwide class action. In antitrust litigation, the team represented major market makers in connection with DOJ, SEC and NASD investigations into alleged price-fixing in the NASDAQ securities market. Litigators at the firm also represented Sony in an industrywide investigation by the FTC into pricing of compact discs. More esoteric work has involved representing the estate of the daughter of the late Sir Arthur Conan Doyle in litigation over the US copyrights to her father's works, including the Sherlock Holmes stories.

The Lawyers: **Kevin Castel** is a popular attorney, recommended by clients as a litigator who *"leaves no stone unturned."* Noted for a *"larger-than-life"* personality, **Thomas Kavaler** was also recommended to researchers for his expertise in litigation.

The Clients: Prudential Securities; Time Warner Entertainment and Sony.

Clifford Chance US LLP

see firm details p.783

The Firm: This 200-lawyer litigation department is one of the largest in New York, and gains particular kudos for its antitrust and class action expertise. The internal structure of the department comprises loose practice groups divided into antitrust, IP and securities/class action teams. In addition, even though the firm has suffered the loss of criminal defense star Mark Pomerantz to Paul, Weiss, Rifkind, Wharton & Garrison, the department continues to have a strong team of litigators in white-collar regulatory work. Securities disputes range from multiple class action litigation to minor customer complaints.

The Lawyers: **James Benedict** (see p.505) is highly regarded for his securities work, and was endorsed to researchers as a *"thoroughly reliable team player."* He and his team defended Merrill Lynch in an IPO class action, involving more than a thousand complaints and over 300 companies.

The Clients: Litigation clients include Bear Stearns and Merrill Lynch.

Kirkland & Ellis

see firm details p.830

The Firm: Top of the field in Chicago, the firm also has a highly rated litigation department in New York, which gains market plaudits for its *"trial-ready"* philosophy and *"hands-on"* litigators. The workload encompasses commercial and contract disputes, securities and stockholder mass torts, and the team has an excellent track record in winning high-profile products liability cases involving complex scientific and technical issues. IP litigation on behalf of global pharmaceutical and telecom companies is another niche area of expertise, and the firm recently defended HermËs in a trademark infringement case.

The Clients: Infineon Technologies; Siemens and Hermés.

Kramer Levin Naftalis & Frankel LLP

see firm details p.832

The Firm: The team has a strong portfolio of investment bank clients, for whom the firm appears on matters such as federal criminal and SEC investigations of US Treasury auction bidding practices. The group has also acted on derivatives litigation and a variety of complex general commercial disputes spanning numerous industries. Recently, the team succesfully defended Liz Claiborne in stockholder class actions alleging that the company had issued misleading projections, and defended Daiwa Securities America in stockholder actions arising from the underwriting of an unsuccessful Chinese telecom company.

The Lawyers: Specialising in high-profile commercial cases and white-collar criminal defense work, the group is considered to owe much of its reputation to star litigator **Gary Naftalis** (see p.526), who chairs the department. Regarded by opponents as a *"great name,"* he has been representing the chairman of Global Crossing and the former vice chairman and head of Enron's International Division in Government inquiries into corporate accounting irregularities.

The Clients: Salomon Brothers; Daiwa Securities America and Liz Claiborne.

Willkie Farr & Gallagher

see firm details p.900

The Firm: The group has experience of handling the full spectrum of litigation, ranging from routine disputes to complex multi-district class actions. It comprises 64 lawyers, including 28 partners, who work on general commercial and securities litigation, and white-collar criminal and regulatory investigations. Joseph Baio and Mike Young are among the best-known names here.

Notable successes for the department include obtaining a dismissal of claims against Donald Trump brought by the bondholders of the Taj Mahal casino in Atlantic City. The team has also represented Major League Baseball and the National League in numerous matters including the League's disciplinary action against Cincinnati Reds owner, Marge Schott. It also served as counsel to the audit committee of the board of directors at Cendant in connection with an internal investigation into accounting irregularities.

The Clients: Donald Trump and Major League Baseball.

Baker Botts LLP

The Firm: The firm is well known for its civil securities litigation practice, and has defended both corporations and directors in high-stakes securities fraud class action lawsuits. Defending claims arising from employee participation in stock ownership plans is also a major area of expertise, while the group has also regularly appeared on environmental and antitrust cases. The team has prosecuted an international arbitration before ICSID against the Government of

NEW YORK

LITIGATION

Mexico. Team members have also represented a major US company that is claiming damages following the expropriation of some of its investments. Elsewhere, the firm is serving as lead counsel to the Republic of Venezuela in complex civil disputes that deal with issues of state, federal and international law.
The Lawyers: Bob Neuner was frequently cited to researchers as *"a decent and reliable attorney."* His practice emphasizes pretrial and trial aspects of patent, copyright, trademark and trade dress cases.
The Clients: Enron; EPS; Global Marine; CIT and PGS.

Cleary Gottlieb Steen & Hamilton
see firm details p.782
The Firm: Rivals acknowledge the firm's litigation practice as a *"diverse and wide-ranging"* affair. The group represented The Museum of Modern Art against the efforts of state and federal prosecutors to seize two famous paintings on loan to the museum. A solid track record also includes defending Mexico's second largest bank in a federal criminal prosecution for money laundering. Products liability is an area of core expertise, and the team has been involved in cases involving allegedly defective timber products, defective ball bearings in helicopters, toxic torts and mass tort claims. The firm recently defended a Japanese company in one of the largest ever mass tort litigations, involving over 2000 suits filed in the US, Europe and Japan. The group has advised most of the major investment banks in securities and derivatives litigation, has been retained on Rule 10b-5 and other securities actions, has represented clients in SEC investigations, and has served as counsel to the Government of Russia in a complex Stockholm Chamber of Commerce arbitration relating to its foreign debts.
The Clients: Crystallex; Berkeley International; Governments of Nicaragua and Slovenia; Goldman Sachs; Salomon Smith Barney; HSBC; UBS Warburg and Fleet Bank.

Curtis, Mallet-Prevost, Colt & Mosle LLP
The Firm: Although the firm is primarily known for its white-collar crime expertise, under the aegis of the legendary Peter Fleming, the litigation department is by no means limited to this type of work. A respected civil litigation capacity encompasses securities and commodities cases, as well as products liability work. The firm appeared before courts in Delaware and Pennsylvania in defense of a claim against a stockholder in a multinational manufacturing enterprise. Products liability cases have included acting for a large Midwestern electric utility in connection with claims arising from alleged failure to complete nuclear power facilities.
Overseas, the team represented French local governments and private parties in the ongoing Amoco Cadiz oil spill case, involving the grounding of the 'Amoco Cadiz' off the coast of France in 1978.
The Clients: The practice represents major US and international corporates.

Debevoise & Plimpton
see firm details p.788
The Firm: Renowned for its international arbitration prowess, the firm can also lay claim to a large litigation team, which includes eight former Assistant US Attorneys and has a particularly sound reputation for antitrust/merger analysis litigation. The group, where Molly Boast has a recognized name, has handled complex cases in both federal and state courts, and represented Citibank in connection with its role as trustee for Lloyds' trust fund. Its practice was further bolstered by the recent arrival of Mary Jo White, formerly US Attorney for the Southern District of New York.
In products liability, where six partners specialize, the firm has represented Owens Corning in asbestos litigation and American Airlines in connection with the 9/11 terrorist attack. Other cases have seen the group advise American Home Products in diet drug litigation, and represent Procter & Gamble in toxic shock syndrome litigation.
The Lawyers: Cochair of the firm's litigation department, **John Kiernan** (see p.521) handles a volume of 'busted deal' and First Amendment litigation. He recently tried and won a $0.5 billion international arbitration against the Czech Republic under a bilateral investment treaty.
The Clients: Procter & Gamble, Owens Corning and American Home Products.

Milberg Weiss Bershad Hynes & Lerach LLP
The Firm: The nation's largest litigation practice has tentacles extending from California to New York, and focuses on representing aggrieved consumers and investors in class actions throughout the US. Areas of expertise include state and federal securities, consumer fraud, corporate governance, tobacco and whistle-blower litigation. The firm is highly regarded by the courts, which have appointed the group on numerous occasions to lead roles in complex multi-district and consolidated litigations.
In tobacco litigation the group is nationally acclaimed for waging a war on *"big tobacco"* and was responsible for filing the 'Joe Camel' case. In tobacco cases, the group has represented the State of Arkansas, the general public in California and the cities of San Francisco, Los Angeles, and Birmingham, AL, and 14 counties in California. The firm also represented employees in the Union Pension and Welfare Fund cases, which were filed in 40 states.
The Clients: The firm represents employees, overarching groups and state and federal authorities.

Shearman & Sterling
see firm details p.874
The Firm: A general litigation group, it is best known for its work related to M&A, securities and class action litigation. Typical work includes representing Turkcell, a telecom company, which was sued in the Southern District of New York in a class action concerning allegations of omissions in its IPO-related prospectus.
Litigators at the firm also have extensive experience of antitrust work, and benefit from a constant stream of work from a deep pool of major corporate clients. The team advised CSFB in an action against several major investment banks, alleging failure to disclose conflicts of interest by securities analysts. Elsewhere, the firm has established something of a niche in the fine art world, representing The Metropolitan Museum of Art, the Getty Museum and art dealer Richard Green in London in title pursuits and authenticity disputes related to cultural property.
The Lawyers: **Fred Davis** (see p.510) was recommended to researchers for experience in international arbitration and general complex litigation.
The Clients: Ford; Nortel Networks; Firecom; CSFB and The Metropolitan Museum of Art.

Other Notable Practitioners
A renowned general commercial litigator, **Greg Joseph** of Gregory P. Joseph Law Offices LLC left Fried, Frank, Harris, Shriver & Jacobson to establish his own practice and focus on trial work. Rivals enthuse about his expertise in evidence and procedure, noting his *"excellent judgment and ability to solve a problem before it comes to trial."* He represents several major American retail corporations and served as the principal RICO counsel for all the American retailers in a RICO class action brought against the retailers by 50,000 garment workers.

MEDIA & ENTERTAINMENT

NEW YORK

MEDIA & ENTERTAINMENT

NEW YORK
Leading firms (Media & Entertainment)

1
- CAHILL GORDON & REINDEL
- DAVIS WRIGHT TREMAINE LLP

2
- CLIFFORD CHANCE US LLP
- GIBSON, DUNN & CRUTCHER LLP

3
- HOGAN & HARTSON LLP
- PAUL, WEISS, RIFKIND, WHARTON & GARRISON
- PROSKAUER ROSE LLP

4
- COUDERT BROTHERS
- DEBEVOISE & PLIMPTON
- O'MELVENY & MYERS LLP
- WEIL, GOTSHAL & MANGES LLP

Leading individuals (Media & Entertainment)

1
- ABRAMS Floyd *Cahill Gordon & Reindel,*
- KOVNER Victor *Davis Wright Tremaine LLP,*

2
- SCHULZ David *Clifford Chance US LLP,*
- WEISS Jack *Gibson, Dunn & Crutcher LLP,*

3
- HANDMAN Laura *Davis Wright Tremaine LLP,*
- METCALF Slade *Hogan & Hartson LLP,*
- RINGEL Dean *Cahill Gordon & Reindel,*

4
- CENDALI Dale *O'Melveny & Myers LLP,*
- KELLER Bruce *Debevoise & Plimpton,*
- SIMS Charles *Proskauer Rose LLP,*

5
- GOERING Kevin *Coudert Brothers,*
- RICH Bruce *Weil, Gotshal & Manges LLP,*
- SUGARMAN Robert *Weil, Gotshal & Manges LLP,*

Firms and individuals are listed alphabetically in each band.

Cahill Gordon & Reindel

The Firm: The team has a long-standing relationship with Time magazine, and appeared for it in a Supreme Court appeal brought by the Church of Scientology, following the defeat of its action against a 1991 cover story. Other successful cases have included a Sixth Circuit Court of Appeals victory for Time, thereby overturning a libel judgment against the magazine following a suit by the boxer, Randall 'Tex' Cobb.

The Lawyers: Even competitors concede that *"there is no one better than* **Floyd Abrams** *and his colleagues."* The reputation of the First Amendment practice rests firmly on Abrams' preeminence in his field. *"Obviously the biggest name,"* he collects accolades for his success in prominent cases, and was described to researchers as *"an amazing appellate lawyer with an extraordinary Supreme Court record."* The next generation is headed by **Dean Ringel**, who is reported to be an *"extremely thoughtful"* attorney.

The Clients: The New York Times, Time and CNN.

Davis Wright Tremaine LLP

see firm details p.787

The Firm: The New York media practice is seen by competitors as one of the office's strengths, and it is universally acclaimed as *"for years, a leading choice in this field."* First Amendment issues, defamation, privacy and copyright are niche areas of expertise.

The Lawyers: **Victor Kovner** (see p.521), who has been with the firm since it merged with his boutique in 1998, was commended to researchers as *"the first person I'd go to in the media sector. He has a good instinct for the bigger picture as well as superb nuts and bolts lawyering skills."* His recent cases include representing the directors and officers of the Martha Graham Center of Contemporary Dance in trademark and copyright litigation brought by the heir of Martha Graham. He also appeared on behalf of Penthouse magazine in a claim brought against it by Judith Soltesz-Benetton, after the magazine published photographs of her and claimed in error that they were of tennis player Anna Kournikova.

Laura Handman (see p.517) splits her practice between New York and DC, and is admired by peers and clients for her work in the areas of First Amendment, libel, privacy and copyright. She has advised the BBC on litigation in New York, and also serves as US media counsel to The Economist. Her recent caseload includes appearing on the Ninth Circuit Court of Appeals for Little, Brown and Company and author George Stephanopoulos in defense of a libel claim against the publishers brought by Gennifer Flowers.

The Clients: The firm's client roster includes: Wenner Media; Village Voice Media; New York Daily News; Martha Graham Center of Contemporary Dance; Penthouse; BBC; The Economist; AOL Time Warner; Viacom; The New York Times; Random House; CNN; Reed Elsevier and Pearson Education.

Clifford Chance US LLP

see firm details p.783

The Firm: Rogers & Wells' historical strength in litigation remains intact following its merger with Clifford Chance. The media practice is employed by high-profile clients in defending defamation and libel claims and protecting copyright and other IP. The retirement of Dick Winfield recently, who was highly regarded in this area, was generally seen as a setback to the team's profile, but the group has remained a strong and sizable force.

The Lawyers: *"In the forefront of the industry"* is **Dave Schulz** (see p.535), described to researchers as *"one of the more thoughtful lawyers in this area of law."* He is a full-time media litigator and heads the firm's US media litigation group, which concentrates on press issues, notably representing news organizations and reporters. He has advised on Gutnick v Dow Jones, a case involving the publication of documents posted on the internet.

The Clients: The firm has been involved in protecting the media's rights on news-gathering issues, representing Univision in a case asserting invasion of privacy, involving novel claims of constitutional violations by Univision reporters. Elsewhere, a recent success saw the group appearing for the Sing Tao Newspaper Group, and defeating a request for an injunction brought by the Fulan Gong religious sect against articles claimed to be defamatory of their religious views. More recently, the team defended The Associated Press from a suit brought by the Global Relief Foundation, an Islamic charitable organization based in the US, which claimed to be libeled by press accounts suggesting that it was under investigation for supporting terrorist organizations. Other clients include: CNN; Reuters; The New York Times; Time and Hubert Burda Media.

Gibson, Dunn & Crutcher LLP

The Firm: *"Extremely strong on media issues,"* in the opinion of market commentators, the firm is experienced in counseling, litigation, prepublication and pre-broadcast review, as well as contractual negotiations.

The Lawyers: **Jack Weiss**, cohead of the media law practice group, is principal outside counsel to Dow Jones and, according to one interviewee: *"His understanding of the law as it relates to journalists is unparalleled."* He remains heavily involved in a class action on behalf of Dow Jones, which relates to the publication in electronic format of the work of freelance authors, and represented the same client in the international internet case Gutnick v Dow Jones.

The Clients: The firm is defending ABC in libel claims brought by Nina Broyles, who was alleged to be running an agency to import pregnant Russian women for the purpose of arranging adoptions for money. Other matters have included the recent settlement on behalf of Jeppesen Sanderson, a publisher of aircraft navigation charts, in a case brought by the families of victims of an air crash in Dubrovnik, Croatia. The firm also represents Dow Jones and Deloitte & Touche.

Hogan & Hartson LLP

see firm details p.818

The Firm: Following the merger in March 2001 between Hogan & Hartson and New York firm Squadron Ellenoff Plesent & Sheinfeld, the former's New York offices have been augmented to about 125 lawyers. Most notably, it has inherited Squadron Ellenoff's major media client - Rupert Murdoch's media empire, News Corporation - for which the firm handles corporate, tax and litigation matters. Strengths have also been noted in IP, trademark and patent work.

The Lawyers: The leading figure here is **Slade Metcalf** (see p.525), described by competitors as *"the primary lawyer in New York for Rupert Mur-*

www.ChambersandPartners.com · All quotes in the text are from interviews with clients and competitors. · 485

NEW YORK

MEDIA & ENTERTAINMENT

doch," and who is admired for his wide-ranging practice. He defended the New York Post in a libel case brought by a former Miss Universe, in which the Post was successful in maintaining the confidentiality of a source.
The Clients: News Corporation, Dearborn Publishing, New York Post, HarperCollins and Hollywood Reporter form part of the firm's client list.

Paul, Weiss, Rifkind, Wharton & Garrison LLP
see firm details p.862
The Firm: Although its attorneys are not thought to have high individual profiles, as a group, the firm was strongly recommended to researchers for its long-standing entertainment focus. Peers acknowledge the team as: *"A worthy group of adversaries who have had some significant media victories."* The firm has experience across a range of matters, including litigation, rights acquisition, copyright and trademark issues, financing, talent and production agreements, distribution, licensing and strategic partnership.
The Clients: Its client base is drawn from diverse sectors of the industry, including live stage, motion pictures, television, music, the internet, publishing and entertainment attractions.

Proskauer Rose LLP
The Firm: The firm has a sizable entertainment practice in New York, and was widely endorsed by interviewees as *"a bunch of good people."* The team provides a full service to the media and entertainment industry and is thought to be particularly strong for cutting-edge copyright work. The firm served as counsel for the record labels in the widely publicized Recording Industry Association of America (RIAA)'s copyright infringement litigation against Napster, the internet music company that allowed users to download MP3 music files from the internet without payment.
The Lawyers: *"Smart media lawyer"* **Charles Sims** concentrates on copyright, First Amendment issues and defamation law for a range of industries including music and publishing. He acted for LexisNexis in class actions brought by freelance authors against the publishers of the Nexis electronic database.
The Clients: The firm's diverse client base includes record companies, motion-picture studios and publishers, such as LexisNexis, as well as the RIAA.

Coudert Brothers
The Firm: This full-service group handling First Amendment, copyright and trademark, broadcast and news-gathering, and IP issues, among others, for media and entertainment industry clients. Other important elements of the caseload are prepublication review and counseling, corporate work, contractual advice and litigation.
The Lawyers: Head of the litigation department and a specialist in media and publishing, **Kevin Goering** is popular with clients, who commend him as: *"A strong advocate for his clients' position,"* and appreciate his *"personable, energetic and enthusiastic style."*
The Clients: The firm appeared in Beck v Grove/Atlantic (representing Grove/Atlantic), a case in California alleging false attribution of authorship, following publication of the book Doom Fox by Iceberg Slim (aka Robert Beck). In the libel case of Miracle v The New Yorker Magazine, in which the firm advised the latter party, it succeeded in obtaining a motion for summary judgment on behalf of its client. The firm has also acted for Condé Nast Publications; Perseus Books Group; Capital Cities/ABC; Scholastic; Nielsen Media Research and Reed Elsevier.

Debevoise & Plimpton
see firm details p.788
The Firm: The firm offers a full-service corporate media and technology group along with a combined IP and media litigation practice. The corporate group benefits from the firm's strengths in private equity and M&A; recent actions include representing longtime client Charles F Dolan in his unsuccessful efforts to acquire the Boston Red Sox baseball team and the New York Jets football team. Clients enthuse about the speediness and effectiveness of the advice they receive: *"They hold business objectives to be valuable; each question is answered quickly with an eye toward cost control."*
The Lawyers: **Bruce Keller** (see p.520), a specialist in IP litigation, is considered a *"bright and significant"* lawyer, and something of an expert in new media matters. His cadre of high-profile clients includes the NFL, Time and Sony. He successfully represented Sony Pictures in getting dismissed a lawsuit brought by billboard and building owners over the digital depiction of Times Square in the recently released Spiderman movie. Researchers were impressed by the commitment of his clients: *"There is not one tactic that escapes him - he is always one step ahead of the competition."* A recent success for the firm was representing Novartis Consumer Health in a false advertising claim, which was upheld on the Third Circuit Court of Appeals against Johnson & Johnson-Merck Pharmaceuticals.
The Clients: The firm's client base extends across a wide range of the industry, including sports leagues, broadcast companies, the press, and commercial entities involved in advertising. Specific client names include: Charles F Dolan and Cablevision Systems; NFL; Time; Sony; Novartis Consumer Health; The New York Times; American Lawyer; CNN; The Washington Post and Yahoo!

O'Melveny & Myers LLP
The Firm: The firm's strength in the motion-picture and television industry in Los Angeles often overwhelmed interviewees' comments to researchers. However, the New York office is also a center for production, financing, joint venture and litigation work in the media and entertainment sector.
The Lawyers: *"Superb litigator"* **Dale Cendali** is a specialist in IP and media law, who *"thinks quickly on her feet and vigorously defends her clients."* Recent victories include a case involving copyright infringement of the memoirs of General Eisenhower, in which she achieved a $3.4 million judgment, and a trial involving the IP rights of the dancer Martha Graham, in which Cendali represented the Martha Graham Center of Contemporary Dance. She also acted on the protection of the image of Harry Potter on behalf of Warner Bros, and those of The X-Files and Titanic on behalf of 20th Century Fox.
The Clients: The firm acts for, among others, the Martha Graham Center of Contemporary Dance; 20th Century Fox; Warner Bros and E & J Gallo Winery.

Weil, Gotshal & Manges LLP
see firm details p.897
The Firm: The firm does not have a specially designated media practice group, but does have a number of IP, First Amendment, litigation and trade practitioners who specialize in media law.
The Lawyers: The two most frequently recommended to researchers were IP specialists **Bruce Rich** (see p.531) and **Bob Sugarman** (see p.538). The former concentrates on litigation and pre-litigation, and is involved in matters relating to music licensing, First Amendment and copyright for clients in industries including print, broadcast, cable television and new media. Clients praised his *"specialized expertise."* His recent cases include a major test lawsuit for the publishing industry, involving the publication of backlist titles in e-book format, in which he has been retained by Random House.
Sugarman's ability in the courtroom was particularly endorsed to researchers, who heard that he has *"an effective approach and a persuasive trial persona."* He has recently put it to use on behalf of the National Geographic Society, in a case in which authors and photographers have sued for copyright infringement following publication of their work on CD-ROM.
The Clients: Random House; National Geographic Society; Rev Billy Graham; DVD Copy Control Association; Copyright Clearance Center; ABC; CBS and Viacom.

PRIVATE EQUITY — NEW YORK

PRIVATE EQUITY

BUYOUTS & INVESTMENTS

NEW YORK
Leading firms
(Private Equity: Buyouts & Investment)

1. SIMPSON THACHER & BARTLETT
2. DAVIS POLK & WARDWELL
   DEBEVOISE & PLIMPTON
3. KIRKLAND & ELLIS
4. LATHAM & WATKINS LLP
   WEIL, GOTSHAL & MANGES LLP
5. FRIED, FRANK, HARRIS, SHRIVER & JACOBSON

Leading individuals
(Private Equity: Buyouts & Investment)

1. BASON George *Davis Polk & Wardwell*
   BEATTIE Richard *Simpson Thacher & Bartlett*
   COGUT Charles *Simpson Thacher & Bartlett*
2. BLASSBERG Franci *Debevoise & Plimpton*
   FRAIDIN Stephen *Fried, Frank, Harris, Shriver*
   RUEGGER Philip *Simpson Thacher & Bartlett*
3. BICK John *Davis Polk & Wardwell*
   ETTINGER John *Davis Polk & Wardwell*
   NUSBAUM Jack *Willkie Farr & Gallagher*
   RADKE Kirk *Kirkland & Ellis*
4. BOHM Richard *Debevoise & Plimpton*
   GRAEV Lawrence *King & Spalding LLP*
   HOPKINSON Ronald *Latham & Watkins LLP*
   KARABELL David *Carter Ledyard & Milburn LLP*
   ROBERTS Thomas *Weil, Gotshal & Manges LLP*

Firms and individuals are listed alphabetically in each band.

Simpson Thacher & Bartlett
The Firm: *"A stable and potent force,"* agreed market sources. The firm has impressed as one of private equity's most long-standing participants. A deep bench of *"seasoned intellectual heavyweights"* has secured key clients such as KKR, Blackstone and The Carlyle Group. These sit alongside an array of investment banks, such as JPMorgan Chase, which provide high levels of work in the acquisition financings of private equity transactions. The transactional team benefits from a pre-eminent fund formation practice, and has an international reputation for its *"cradle-to-grave"* service.

The Lawyers: **Dick Beattie** is chairman of the firm. He provides *"an unparalleled wealth of experience"* to the firm's major LBO clients who add that, although his managerial duties take him away from the transactional frontline, Beattie remains *"a valuable adviser on complex transactions."* **Charles (Casey) Cogut** is the head of the M&A practice group and has strong ties to KKR and Silver Lake Partners. Interviewees appreciated his *"great understanding"* of the LBO market and his *"confident management of those difficult deals."* Much of **Philip (Pete) Ruegger**'s profile in the private equity market derives from his experience representing The Blackstone Group, advising on its cross-border transactions.

The Clients: The firm represented a consortium of sponsors led by Thomas H Lee Partners and Bain Capital Partners in the LBO of publisher Houghton Mifflin from Vivendi Universal for $1.7 billion. Other clients include: Kohlberg Kravis Roberts & Company (KKR); The Blackstone Group; The Cypress Group; Silver Lake Partners; Vestar Capital Partners; Evercore Capital Partners and Blum Capital Partners.

Davis Polk & Wardwell
The Firm: The breadth of clients attracted to this firm's *"highly respected"* private equity practice is indicative of its coverage among key sector-focused funds. Although best known for its work with merchant banking clients such as the Morgan Stanley portfolio, which includes LBOs and real estate funds, the firm also advises sponsors such as Greenhill Capital Partners and Soros Fund Managment. Supported by its fund structuring specialists, the group enjoys the capacity to advise on the transactional lifespan of a fund. Much of its recent activities have involved recapitalization and workouts for funds affected by the slow LBO market. In a recent highlight, the firm has advised Princes Gate Investors III on its acquisition of the Unique Pub Company and Voyager Pub Group from Nomura International.

The Lawyers: **George Bason** combines his private equity practice with public company M&A and is the relationship partner for DLJ Merchant Banking Partners. Observers credit him with a *"highly commercial approach to the deal"* that ensures the smooth running of a transaction. **John Bick** has been active recently for portfolio clients in the oil and gas and telecom sectors. He is best known for his work with Morgan Stanley Dean Witter Capital Partners, and has advised the group on its investments in a for-profit hospital system and in home and car insurance companies. Managing partner **John Ettinger** can count Greenhill Capital Partners and Pinnacle Holdings among his private equity-related clients. Interviewees valued his *"big picture"* view of the market and dubbed him *"a major rainmaker."*

The Clients: Morgan Stanley Dean Witter Capital Partners, Greenhill Capital Partners and Pinnacle Holdings are clients.

Debevoise & Plimpton
see firm details p.788

The Firm: The firm is able to field 150 lawyers specializing in private equity matters from its eight worldwide offices. A high-profile relationship with marquee client Clayton, Dubilier & Rice ensures the group's visibility not only in the structuring of funds but also in related M&A and in the final close. The group has witnessed a growth in 'club deals', in which it assists groups of private equity houses acting together on key deals. The team advised Providence Equity Partners as part of a consortium for the proposed $8.5 billion acquisition of directory company Qwest-Dex. It also advised on an investment made to an insurance company by Trident II, a fund managed by MMC Capital, the private equity arm of Marsh & McLennan.

The Lawyers: Interviewees singled out **Franci Blassberg** (see p.506) as one of the market's most experienced participants: *"She grew up with private equity and has seen it all."* She is a key contact for Clayton, Dubilier & Rice, advising on its US and international investments, and also acts for Merrill Lynch in its private equity investments. Much of Blassberg's work is M&A-related or concerned with refinancing and recapitalization. She advised on the sale of Aliant Exchange, one of the largest food service providers in the US, to Royal Ahold. Another member of this *"talented team"* is **Richard Bohm** (see p.506), who devotes a portion of his time to public company M&A. On the private equity front, he has advised Kelso & Company on its investment in, and exit from, companies such as Ellis Communications and Charter Communications. Peers described Bohm as *"a sound deal-maker,"* a description which is perceived to be applicable to the team as a whole.

The Clients: Clayton, Dubilier & Rice; The Exxel Group; HarbourVest Partners; Kelso & Company; Providence Equity Partners; Ripplewood Holdings and Schroder Venture Partners.

Kirkland & Ellis
see firm details p.830

The Firm: Sources respect this New York group's *"great depth of transactional talent,"* citing it as a team that has *"grown up with the high standards set by the Chicago office."* Its attorneys have the advantage of *"an excellent all-round knowledge"* in both the structuring of funds, leveraged acquisitions, financing options and stock issuance. Its broad sector coverge incorporates healthcare, e-commerce, biotech, real estate, construction and telecom matters.

The Lawyers: **Kirk Radke** (see p.531) was described to researchers as *"a practical and aggressive transactional force."* Radke is also respected for his advice on the structuring of funds.

The Clients: Vestar Capital; CVC Capital Partners; Bain Capital Partners; Merrill Lynch; Citigroup; Morgan Stanley Capital Partners; Whitney Group; AEA Investors; Cornerstone Partners and Catterton Partners.

NEW YORK

PRIVATE EQUITY

Latham & Watkins LLP
see firm details p.835

The Firm: Competitors agreed that *"this firm has the transactional know-how"* and *"sets high standards"* in the market. Respected for its venture capital work in the technology and life sciences fields, its reputation is enhanced by a powerful West Coast presence. The team represents institutional fund sponsors and investment banks on venture capital, LBO and 'club' fund matters. This truly international firm is also respected for its work on cross-border European investments, and has been active in the restructuring and refinancing of funds.

The Lawyers: The standout partner in the New York group is **R Ronald Hopkinson** (see p.519). Peers appreciate his *"clear business focus,"* while clients applaud him as *"dedicated and hard-working."* He has attracted clients of the caliber of The Carlyle Group and BC Partners.

The Clients: The Carlyle Group; Chase Capital Partners; Bear Stearns and BC Partners.

Weil, Gotshal & Manges LLP
see firm details p.897

The Firm: *"One of the main competitors,"* acknowledged rivals, thanks in part to its strong relationship with Hicks, Muse, Tate & Furst. The firm has recently bolstered its practice group by opening an office in Boston, led by private equity attorneys recruited from Hutchins, Wheeler & Dittmar. This coup has provided the firm with access to major LBO funds such as Thomas H Lee Partners. The team in New York can also draw upon the support of a sizable presence in Dallas, and works in conjunction with offices across Europe and Asia on complex cross-border matters.

The Lawyers: Tom Roberts (see p.532) has spent much of his 20 years in the field advising key client Hicks, Muse, Tate & Furst. Commentators said he was *"attuned to the needs of a big transaction."* Roberts advised GE Capital on its $5.3 billion acquisition via a tender offer of Heller Financial.

The Clients: Hicks, Muse, Tate & Furst; Oak Hill Partners; GE Capital; Capital Z Partners and CSFB.

Fried, Frank, Harris, Shriver & Jacobson
see firm details p.796

The Firm: *"Highly respected and knowledgeable lawyers"* make up the private equity offering at this firm. Peers also pointed to these attorneys' *"diligent and hard-working"* approach to complex investment and financing options for private equity sponsors and investment banking interests. The firm advised GE Capital in the acquisition of a 50% stake in Bank One's Monogram Credit Services (valued at $531 million), and acted for GS Capital Partners 2000 in its acquisition of Berry Plastics for $837.5 million.

The Lawyers: Interviewees claim that **Stephen Fraidin**'s (see p.513) *"huge reputation was earned by being on the top rung for so many years."* His practice combines M&A for companies such as Procter & Gamble with private equity representation, which lately has included the restructuring of LBO funds.

The Clients: Forstmann, Little & Company; AEA Investors; GE Capital; Goldman Sachs; Lehman Brothers; Shamrock Holdings and Thomas Weisel Partners' private equity investment funds.

Other Notable Practitioners

"Hugely respected" **Jack Nusbaum** (see p.528) of Willkie Farr & Gallagher combines buyout work with large-scale M&A. He has recently been active in the telecom sector, and was involved in a buyout involving an automobile manufacturer in Italy. **Lawrence Graev** (see p.516) of King & Spalding LLP was described to researchers as the *"key player there,"* and clear driver for the practice group. Graev is active in leveraged acquisitions, venture capital and growth financings. **David Karabell** (see p.520) has left O'Sullivan LLP to join Carter Ledyard & Milburn LLP. Market sources await the success that this *"classic rainmaker"* is expected to have in building up the profile of this midmarket private equity group.

PRIVATE EQUITY

NEW YORK
Leading firms
(Private Equity: Fund Formation)

1
- DEBEVOISE & PLIMPTON
- SIMPSON THACHER & BARTLETT

2
- DAVIS POLK & WARDWELL
- REBOUL, MACMURRAY, HEWITT, MAYNARD
- WEIL, GOTSHAL & MANGES LLP

3
- AKIN GUMP STRAUSS HAUER & FELD LLP
- KIRKLAND & ELLIS
- SCHULTE ROTH & ZABEL LLP

Firms are listed alphabetically in each band.

Debevoise & Plimpton
see firm details p.788

The Firm: A *"keen focus"* and *"talented, knowledgeable"* attorneys have ensured this firm a place at the forefront of the fund formation market. The group's ability to attract *"hugely active, sophisticated clients"* has meant that it continues to advise on complex and innovative matters, despite the slower economic conditions. Seven partners and a host of associates concentrate on fund formation, and work closely with the firm's offices in Europe and the Far East on cross-border private equity funds. Mezzanine, distressed debt, real estate and hedge funds all feature in the group's workload.

The Lawyers: Clients commend **Woody Campbell** (see p.508) as *"attentive, hard-working and on top of everything: he makes a difference to our business."* Campbell heads the investment management practice group. He is widely respected for both his tax expertise and his work on international funds for investment clients drawn from Asia, Latin America and Europe. **Michael Harrell** (see p.518) brings *"a practical approach to negotiations,"* claim observers. A *"creative thinker,"* he impresses many with his skill in *"spotting the real business issues straight way."* **Rebecca Silberstein** (see p.536) continues to draw commendation as a younger attorney who is *"moving the field forward."* She is best known for her work with the Merrill Lynch portfolio.

The Clients: The group advises a mix of institutional and independent fund sponsors. Clients include: AIG Capital Partners; HarbourVest Partners; Kelso & Company; MMC Capital; Merrill Lynch; Solera Capital; Ripplewood Partners and Zephyr Management.

FUND FORMATION

Simpson Thacher & Bartlett

The Firm: Possesses a *"well-resourced, highly-developed practice"* to which many peers aspire. The firm is home to top-flight groups on both the transactional and fund structuring sides, making it a *"natural port of call"* for clients who require a breadth of experience. Historically known for its work with LBO firm KKR, the group has demonstrated its commitment to the sector through the diversification of its client base, which now ranges from larger LBO funds and midmarket entities to international investors and sector specialists. It acts on the formation of LBO and venture capital funds, fund of funds and multi-class and master/feeder structures. The group has also advised on the restructuring of agreements and on the merger of investment funds.

The Lawyers: Competitors agree that **Tom Bell** is *"just smarter than everyone else."* A *"highly professional adviser,"* he brings to the deal table extensive experience in LBO real estate and venture capital funds. Clients include highly active funds such as The Cypress Group, The Carlyle Group and Evercore Partners. He is also skilled in the documentation of offshore and cross-border

PRIVATE EQUITY

NEW YORK

NEW YORK
Leading individuals
(Private Equity: Fund Formation)

1
- BELL Thomas *Simpson Thacher & Bartlett*
- CAMPBELL Woodrow *Debevoise & Plimpton*
- HARRELL Michael *Debevoise & Plimpton*
- KAWATA Yukako *Davis Polk & Wardwell*
- WOLITZER Michael *Simpson Thacher & Bartlett*

2
- HEWITT William *Reboul, MacMurray, Hewitt*
- TABAK Jeffrey *Weil, Gotshal & Manges LLP*
- VINE Stephen *Akin Gump Strauss Hauer & Feld LLP*
- WOLF Barry *Weil, Gotshal & Manges LLP*

3
- BERGTRAUM Howard *O'Melveny & Myers LLP*
- BRESLOW Stephanie *Schulte Roth & Zabel LLP*
- MACMURRAY John *Reboul, MacMurray, Hewitt*
- RADKE Kirk *Kirkland & Ellis*

4
- BOWIE Scott *Latham & Watkins LLP*
- MCCORMACK William *Reboul, MacMurray, Hewitt*
- SCHWED Robert *Reboul, MacMurray, Hewitt, Maynard*

Up-and-coming individuals
- SILBERSTEIN Rebecca *Debevoise & Plimpton,*

Individuals are listed alphabetically in each band.

funds. **Michael Wolitzer** is a *"bright lawyer, immensely knowledgeable on the technicalities."* He and Campbell were commended as *"facilitators: their pragmatic style makes deals happen."* Much of Wolitzer's practice is international in scope.
The Clients: Kohlberg Kravis Roberts & Company (KKR); The Cypress Group; The Carlyle Group; Evercore Partners; CSFB; The Blackstone Group; Silver Lake Partners and Heartland Industrial Partners.

Davis Polk & Wardwell
The Firm: Although smaller in size than its direct rivals, this practice continues to be held in high esteem for its *"high standards and creativity."* The firm has investment management attorneys in its three offices across the US, who are supported by European and Asian offices on cross-border fund activities. The group has advised on some of the largest private equity funds, including the $5.4 billion DLJ Merchant Banking Partners III. It also advises on hedge funds and venture capital funds focused on emerging growth companies.
The Lawyers: The firm's *"flagship fund formation partner"* is **Yukako Kawata**. An *"impeccably accurate attorney,"* she is respected for her work with merchant banking funds such as CSFB and JPMorgan Chase. Kawata has also been active on hedge funds, advising managers on the creation of investment advisory platforms, and has counseled European clients entering the US on issues arising from the regulation of derivatives and structured products.
The Clients: The group's clients include US and offshore financial services clients as well as private equity houses and hedge fund managers. Among them are: CSFB; Morgan Stanley Dean Witter; JPMorgan Chase; FundPoint Partners; Chilton Investments; Hellman & Friedman and Citadel.

Reboul, MacMurray, Hewitt, Maynard & Kristol
The Firm: *"Long-established"* in the fund formation market, this mid-sized firm has impressed competitors and clients alike with the level of resources it has committed to the sector. The group assists a host of international funds sponsored out of Europe, South Africa and Asia, and is respected for its assistance to LBO funds worldwide. The group advises on venture capital, mezzanine, distressed equity and fund of funds work, and on term arrangements for limited partnerships. It has also been involved in the restructuring of funds. The group remains closely associated with its *"trophy client,"* Welsh, Carson, Anderson & Stowe.
The Lawyers: The firm fields a raft of well-known and respected names. **William Hewitt** was commended as a *"technical, capable"* attorney who wins fans with his *"immense experience and knowledge of the law."* **John MacMurray** is a founding member of the firm, and an *"eminently trustworthy"* adviser. Primarily active in the international market, **William McCormick** advises offshore and domestic private equity investment funds on tax planning, documentation and transactional issues. He recently acted on the formation of the Suala Capital Fund, a $300 million fund focused on Spain, and the Procuritas Capital Investors III, a $250 million fund aimed at the Scandanavian market. Although **Bob Schwed** is less active on the fund formation side, he remains a valuable source of knowledge at the firm, and has been involved in fund restructuring and refinancing.
The Clients: Clients include StarVest Partners, Riverside Holdings and Accolade Partners.

Weil, Gotshal & Manges LLP
see firm details p.897
The Firm: Attorneys across the US and in London and Frankfurt coordinate advice on the structuring of cross-border funds. This cross-border capability has coincided with European activity by the firm's key client, Hicks, Muse, Tate & Furst. The firm's representation of DLJ and Lehman Brothers also typifies its growth. It scored a coup in the 2002 recruitment of former Hutchins, Wheeler & Dittmar private equity lawyers, including Charles Robins, to its newly established Boston office. The team recently acted for Lindsay Goldberg & Bessemer on the $2 billion closing of a new LBO fund.
The Lawyers: Rivals identified **Barry Wolf**'s (see p.543) strong tax background as an important factor in the group's success in attracting new clients. A *"pragmatic and approachable"* attorney, he coheads the group with **Jeff Tabak** (see p.539). Interviewees recommended Tabak for his expertise in hedge fund structuring and limited partnerships.
The Clients: Hicks, Muse, Tate & Furst; Thomas H Lee Partners; Capital Z Partners; Oak Hill Partners; Odyssey Partners; Olympus Real Estate; CSFB; Ulysses Partners; GE Capital; New Century Holdings and Wingate Partners.

Akin Gump Strauss Hauer & Feld LLP
see firm details p.761
The Firm: Respected for its involvement in *"complex arrangements,"* the group remains best known for its activities in hedge funds, in which it has *"really made its mark,"* according to peers. The investment management group also counsels offshore, private equity and real estate funds as well as fund of funds, and has the international capacity to assist on cross-border arrangements and transactions.
The Lawyers: **Stephen Vine** (see p.540) was recommended as *"a top-flight attorney,"* who has done much to drive the New York funds group forward. His work has included advice to funds focused on emerging markets, real estate opportunities and individual countries.
The Clients: The firm advises financial institutions, private equity houses and hedge fund managers.

Kirkland & Ellis
see firm details p.830
The Firm: The fund formation activities of this group are bolstered by the buyout expertise of its transactional attorneys. Although the team in New York has yet to match the Chicago office's dominance of its market, it remains a respected operation that focuses on the creation of domestic and international private equity funds. Attorneys in the firm's London and DC offices ensure an integrated service in available for international clients.
The Lawyers: **Kirk Radke** (see p.531) is better known for his transactional experience, but remains respected for his work in the creation of buyout funds. He and the team recently closed a $3 billion newly created fund for Citigroup Venture Capital.
The Clients: Vestar Capital Partners; CVC Capital Partners; Bain Capital Partners; Merrill Lynch; Citigroup; Morgan Stanley Capital Partners; Whitney Group; AEA Investors; Cornerstone Partners and Catterton Partners.

Schulte Roth & Zabel LLP
The Firm: The firm remains best known for being *"the hedge funds' specialists,"* but observers acknowledge that it has a growing presence in private equity fund formation. It has advised on the formation of domestic and offshore private

NEW YORK

PROJECTS

investment funds such as Cerberus Institutional Funds, and assisted institutional groups launching new funds - Lazard Asset Management's Worldwide Opportunities Fund being one example. In the private equity arena, the group has advised on the formation of Athena Real Estate Partners and Brookside Pecks Capital Partner. Institutional clients have sought out the group's counsel on the organization of hybrid registered fund products, including registered hedge funds.
The Lawyers: *"Smart"* **Stephanie Breslow** attracts plaudits for her skill in *"getting to the bottom of a deal."* Singled out to researchers as the practice's leading light, she was commended for her knowledge of the tax and regulatory issues arising from hedge funds, private equity funds and limited partnerships.
The Clients: Financial institutions, hedge fund managers and private equity houses.

Other Notable Practitioners
Howard Bergtraum of O'Melveney & Myers LLP was described to researchers as *"an attorney who has seen it all."* He is active in the formation of cross-border funds and their subsequent lifespan for clients such as JPMorgan Chase, Deutsche Bank, Société Générale and Toronto-Dominion Bank. Bergtraum has also been involved in agreement amendments and in the restructuring of funds. **Scott Bowie** (see p.507) of Latham & Watkins LLP is respected for his work with Kohlberg Kravis Roberts & Company (KKR), The Carlyle Group and Bear Stearns. He recently closed the KKR Millenium Fund, and has advised fund managers on restructuring issues and the liquidation of assets.

PROJECTS

NEW YORK
Leading firms (Projects)

1. LATHAM & WATKINS LLP
2. MILBANK, TWEED, HADLEY & MCCLOY
   SKADDEN, ARPS, SLATE, MEAGHER & FLOM LLP
   WHITE & CASE LLP
3. CHADBOURNE & PARKE LLP
   SULLIVAN & CROMWELL LLP
4. DEWEY BALLANTINE LLP
   FRESHFIELDS BRUCKHAUS DERINGER LLP
   SHEARMAN & STERLING
   SIMPSON THACHER & BARTLETT
5. DAVIS POLK & WARDWELL
6. ORRICK, HERRINGTON & SUTCLIFFE

Firms are listed alphabetically in each band.

Latham & Watkins LLP
see firm details p.835
The Firm: Peers commended the firm as an *"awesome force;"* many believed the projects group was *"in a league of its own."* Despite the depressed market, the group has enjoyed an active year advising in sophisticated domestic and international transactions. Its traditional strength lies in power projects, although interviewees noted that the group had diversified into oil and gas, telecom and infrastructure projects.
A *"young and aggressive"* team of lawyers acts for national and international developers but its work on behalf of lenders continues to elicit the most praise. Clients repeatedly spoke of a businesslike group that was *"easy to work with and pragmatic."* Deal highlights include acting for CSFB in a $2 billion revolving credit facility extended to a subsidiary of NRG Energy to enable the construction and acquisition of power plants throughout the US.
The Lawyers: The sizable group lays claim to *"three of the best guys in the field."* The *"extraordinarily capable"* **Dave Gordon** (see p.515) was respected for his ability to *"keep the lines of communication open."* **Bill Voge** (see p.541) was endorsed as a projects lawyer with *"all-around expertise."* He is experienced in international transactions and represents sponsors, banks and underwriters in Latin America and the Middle East. Despite being based on the West Coast, **Andy Singer** (see p.72) has a practice in New York that has earned him a reputation as *"hands down, the dominant bank lawyer in power deals."* He represented Citibank and Société Générale in the $2.8 billion debt financing of TECO Energy's and Panda Energy International's El Dorado and Gila River power facilities, in Arkansas and Arizona respectively.
The recruitment from Freshfields Bruckhaus Deringer in 2002 of *"technically astute"* **Jonathan Rod** (see p.532) has helped to bolster the group's experience in structured financing and bond issues. **Michèle Penzer** (see p.529) was endorsed by clients as *"a terrific younger lawyer."*
The Clients: CSFB; Citibank; Société Générale; JPMorgan Chase; Deutsche Bank; Goldman Sachs; ABN AMRO; BNP Paribas; InterGen; RAS Laffan LNG Company (Rasgas) and AES.

Milbank, Tweed, Hadley & McCloy
The Firm: This *"powerful"* group was adjudged by peers to be a *"hugely successful group"* with a long-standing history in the sector. The practice is supported by a string of respected overseas offices, and is also active on the domestic front. The New York-based group brings a *"sophisticated and intellectual"* approach to complex multi-jurisdictional projects. This *"pool of talented attorneys"* forms one of the premier lender firms. *"Adept at anything,"* it consequently acts for sponsors, government agencies and multilateral institutions in power, oil and gas, natural resources and infrastructure projects. Acting as sponsor's counsel, the firm represented Termobahia in a $243 million project financing in Brazil.
The Lawyers: **Jonathan Green** was identified by interviewees as a *"top-flight player,"* especially in Latin American projects. **Eric Silverman** manages the group. He was acknowledged to be a *"clever"* attorney and talented rainmaker. **Richard Brach** was commended for his *"gravitas and quality advice;"* he is respected for his mining expertise. **Douglas Harris** is a project finance *"guru"* who is experienced in structured and leveraged leasing.
The Clients: Citibank; Bank of America; CSFB; TECO Energy; Société Générale; Japan Bank for International Cooperation and KfW.

Skadden, Arps, Slate, Meagher & Flom LLP & Affiliates
see firm details p.878
The Firm: Clients claim that this *"top-notch"* operation is one of the most seasoned in the market, and is *"always on the shortlist."* Much of the firm's activity has been in the domestic sphere but it also commands respect for its activities on the international stage, supported by well-established overseas offices. The overall market impression was of a *"business-minded and practical"* group that is *"good at guiding clients through the deals."* Highlights for the team include representing BNP Paribas as agent in the $1 billion Rio Pollmeros petrochemical project in Brazil. It also advised DZ Bank in the $497 million development of an 885MW generating plant in Fluvanna, Virginia.
The Lawyers: The leading light of the practice is **Hal Moore** (see p.526). Opposing counsel found him *"insightful and results-oriented,"* and he is a popular choice for complex projects. He represented Edison Mission Energy on the restructuring and refinancing of a $1.8 billion lease financing at Homer City, Pennsylvania and also acted for CSFB in the $1 billion bank financing of the Kern River gas pipeline project in Nevada and Utah.
The Clients: Edison Mission Energy; NRG Energy; Barclays Capital; Citibank; CSFB; Lehman Brothers and Goldman Sachs.

PROJECTS

NEW YORK

NEW YORK
Leading individuals (Projects)

1
- GORDON David *Latham & Watkins LLP*
- MOORE Harold *Skadden, Arps, Slate, Meagher*
- SCAVONE Arthur *White & Case LLP*
- SHUTRAN Richard *Dewey Ballantine LLP*
- SINGER Andrew *Latham & Watkins LLP*
- VOGE William *Latham & Watkins LLP*

2
- GREEN Jonathan *Milbank, Tweed, Hadley & McCloy*
- RICH Frederic *Sullivan & Cromwell LLP*
- WACHSBERGER Chaim *Chadbourne & Parke LLP*

3
- ALEXANDER Troy *White & Case LLP*
- BAECHER John *Chadbourne & Parke LLP*
- BRACH Richard *Milbank, Tweed, Hadley & McCloy*
- BURKE Ted *Freshfields Bruckhaus Deringer LLP*
- HARRIS Douglas *Milbank, Tweed, Hadley & McCloy*
- JACOBSON Martin *Simpson Thacher & Bartlett*
- SILVERMAN Eric *Milbank, Tweed, Hadley & McCloy*
- WARNER Waide *Davis Polk & Wardwell*

4
- GALVIS Sergio *Sullivan & Cromwell LLP*
- GOODWILLIE Eugene *White & Case LLP*
- ROD Jonathan *Latham & Watkins LLP*
- URDA KASSIS Cynthia *Shearman & Sterling*

5
- HADLEY Joseph *Davis Polk & Wardwell*
- MANN Christopher *Sullivan & Cromwell LLP*
- MEYERS Michael *Orrick, Herrington & Sutcliffe*
- MILLARD John *Shearman & Sterling*
- OLIVIER Jeanne *Shearman & Sterling*
- PENZER Michèle *Latham & Watkins LLP*

Individuals are listed alphabetically in each band.

White & Case LLP

The Firm: An extensive overseas network of offices has ensured the firm's profile for international project finance. Peers commended its success in attracting a broad client base: lenders, sponsors, export credit agencies and multilateral agencies provide a steady stream of complex work. Much of the firm's activity has been in the oil and gas area although it has also secured work in the faltering power sector. Key engagements here include representing various lenders in the Termobahia power project in Brazil and acting for the Japan Bank for International Cooperation (JBIC) in the financing of the Altamira II power project in Mexico.

The Lawyers: Peers described **Art Scavone** as a *"superb"* lawyer who *"sees diverse points of view and is a real pleasure to work with."* He represents both lenders and agencies, and has acted for US Ex-Im Bank in the financing of the Shin satellite project in Thailand. **Troy Alexander**'s lender-based practice has led to his involvement in power and telecom projects in Latin America. He won praise for his skill in managing large groups of lenders with divergent interests. **Gene Goodwillie** is a senior member of the group. He continues to elicit praise for his *"vast knowledge"* of the field and his impressive client roster.

The Clients: 2International Finance Corporation (IFC); US Ex-Im Bank; Inter-American Development Bank; JBIC; Deutsche Bank; Bank of America; GE Capital; Saudi Aramco; Mirant; Conoco; TECO Energy and Panda Energy International.

Chadbourne & Parke LLP
see firm details p.781

The Firm: This firm, which has *"substantial size and depth,"* is active in both domestic and international markets and is most closely affiliated with the power industry. The group is an active participant in the Latin American market and has a broader reach than its principal reputation for power projects suggests. On the domestic front, the practice opened a Houston office in August 2002 and also received support from its respected DC office.

The Lawyers: Chaim Wachsberger (see p.541) is a veteran of the sector and remains recognized as the firm's star attorney. Peers and clients applaud his *"smooth, commercial"* style, and his client-focused attitude. **John Baecher** (see p.504) was also recommended for his representation of sponsors. He has acted for AES on the AES Andres LNG project in the Dominican Republic.

The Clients: Key clients include AES; El Paso; Duke Energy; IFC; Overseas Private-Investment Corporation (OPIC); EBRD and CSFB.

Sullivan & Cromwell LLP
see firm details p.886

The Firm: This *"stellar"* practice was perceived to be an increasingly important player and was commended for the quality of its attorneys. It was deemed a powerful force in Latin American markets, and is active on a broader international stage and on the domestic front. Much of its expertise lies in the extractive industry, such as oil and gas, where it is best known for its representation of sponsors. One of the group's highlights includes achieving financial closure on the Oleoducto de Crudos Pesados (OCP) Ecuador pipeline project in Ecuador.

The Lawyers: Fred Rich (see p.531) won plaudits from clients who described him as an *"absolute gem."* They saw his analytical style as invaluable in explaining complex matters: *"He comes up with the solution at just the right time."* *"Expert"* **Sergio Galvis** (see p.514) coordinates the Latin American practice, while peers continue to acknowledge **Chris Mann** (see p.524) as a *"practical and savvy"* lawyer.

The Clients: The group has represented the upstream and downstream sponsor consortia on the Camisea gas project in Peru. It also acted for the project company and sponsor consortium on the $2.9 billion Baku-Tblisi-Ceyhan (BTC) pipeline project. Other clients include: Anglo American; BP; Conoco; ExxonMobil and Total-FinaElf.

Dewey Ballantine LLP
see firm details p.790

The Firm: Although a smaller group than its direct competitors, the firm was endorsed by observers for its *"healthy deal flow"* from North and South America. Support provided by a respected energy regulatory group has meant that the firm is most visible on energy-related projects. It remains active in infrastructure projects, and was involved in the financing of a toll road in Chile.

The Lawyers: Much of the firm's profile lies with **Rich Shutran** (see p.536) who peers say is an icon of the industry: *"He is world-class – I'd love to hire him."* Shutran was described as a practical negotiator, adept at representing both sponsors and lenders. He led the team that acted for the lending group on the La Rosita power project in Mexico.

The Clients: The group acts for developers, lenders, investors and underwriters. PG&E, Citibank, BNP Paribas, XL Capital and Dresdner Bank are typical clients.

Freshfields Bruckhaus Deringer LLP

The Firm: The global network was seen as one of this firm's principal strengths and commentators applauded the team's depth and market presence: *"It is a substantial international player."* Jonathan Rod's departure to Latham & Watkins is not thought to have affected the firm's profile. The development of strong relationships with lenders, sponsors and multilateral agencies is seen as key to its success. The group acted on the financing of the $5 billion Baku-Tblisi-Ceyhan pipeline from Azerbaijan to Turkey on behalf of US Ex-Im Bank, Japan Bank for International Cooperation and other multilaterals.

The Lawyers: Ted Burke was described as a *"fantastic"* lawyer, with a loyal client following. He has close relationships with institutional lenders. Burke led the team that represented Tractebel in the financing of five gas-fired power plants in the US. The group also acted for WestLB and other lenders in the $237 million Atlas methanol project in Trinidad and Tobago.

The Clients: Typical clients include OPIC; US Ex-Im Bank; Deutsche Bank; Tractebel; IFC; ArcLight Capital Partners; WestLB and JPMorgan.

Shearman & Sterling
see firm details p.874

The Firm: Strongly international in focus, the group was applauded by peers for its cross-border reach, which includes expertise in Latin America. It acts for an even balance of lenders and sponsors, with oil and gas transactions and restructurings dominating its caseload of late. Interviewees acknowledged the firm to be a *"tech-*

NEW YORK — PROJECTS

nically sound" operation, home to a number of respected individuals.
The Lawyers: Cynthia Urda Kassis (see p.540) is a *"highly intelligent"* attorney who has represented the lender group - including long-standing client Citibank - in the $290 million project financing of the Altimara II power project in Mexico. Her colleague **Jeanne Olivier** (see p.528) was noted for work in the telecom sector. **John Millard** (see p.525) was endorsed for his oil and gas expertise, particularly in the Latin America market.
The Clients: The group acted for WestLB in the construction of the Oleoducto de Crudos Pesados (OCP) Ecuador pipeline. Also represented AES Oasis in the development and financing of one of the first independent power producers in Qatar. Citibank, Barclays Capital and JBIC are typical clients.

Simpson Thacher & Bartlett

The Firm: Described to researchers as a *"thoroughly capable"* concern that is particularly visible in the domestic market. The group is buoyed by the firm's strong banking practice and attorneys advise on a range of transactions involving in capital markets offerings, and lease and structured finance techniques. Its projects portfolio includes the financing of power plants, pipelines, satellite and telecom systems and various infrastructure facilities.
The Lawyers: **Martin Jacobson** continues to be identified by interviewees as the group's top gun. *"He doesn't work at being famous - he just gets the deals done."* Highlights for Jacobson and the group have included representing the lenders in the securitized lease project financing of a 792MW merchant power plant in California. The practice also acted for the lenders on the construction and term project financing of two Cogentrix Energy tolling agreement power plants in Louisiana and Oklahoma.
The Clients: Citibank; Société Générale; Crédit Lyonnais; JPMorgan Chase; CSFB; GE; GE Capital; Lehman Brothers and Bank of America.

Davis Polk & Wardwell

The Firm: There was broad consensus that, while the group was unable to match the deal volume of some competitors, it clearly provided *"high-quality advice."* Many of its forays into the projects arena have been in Latin America. It is particularly active in oil and gas where it has assisted on exploration and development. Other areas of expertise are nonrecourse and limited recourse financings, leasings and capital markets financings.
The Lawyers: **Waide Warner** was identified as the lynchpin of practice. He is *"an effective communicator of complex ideas."* **Joe Hadley** was enclosed for his expertise in structured and high yield finance.
The Clients: The firm acts for international sponsors and agency lenders including OPIC. It has represented the borrowers in a telecom project in Bolivia, and in a cell phone transaction in the Caribbean. Other activities include the restructuring of telecom, power, petrochemical and oil and gas projects in several Latin American countries.

Orrick, Herrington & Sutcliffe
see firm details p.859

The Firm: Attorneys are drawn from the global energy, communications and infrastructure group, which includes supporting offices in the UK and the Far East. They advise on the structuring of complex financings in both the domestic and international fields. The group has consistently displayed a level of experience in the transactional sphere that is matched by regulatory expertise. The team is also active in asset divestitures and M&A and has developed a niche strength in renewable energy projects. In particular it has assisted clients in both the US and Europe on wind technology facilities.
The Lawyers: **Mike Meyers** (see p.525) heads the group that acted for Tomen as sponsor in a $100 million power project in Guam. Other key engagements have included representing a consortium of gas and electric companies as sponsors in the Bolivia-to-Brazil gas pipeline project.
The Clients: Typical clients are investor-owned utilities, municipal utilities and lenders. Tomen Power; Aquila; PPL Global; Constellation Energy Group; Lucent Technologies and PG&E use the firm.

REAL ESTATE

NEW YORK
Leading firms (Real Estate)

1 FRIED, FRANK, HARRIS, SHRIVER & JACOBSON
  PAUL, HASTINGS, JANOFSKY & WALKER LLP
  SKADDEN, ARPS, SLATE, MEAGHER & FLOM LLP

2 SHEARMAN & STERLING
  SULLIVAN & CROMWELL LLP
  WEIL, GOTSHAL & MANGES LLP
  WILLKIE FARR & GALLAGHER

3 PAUL, WEISS, RIFKIND, WHARTON & GARRISON
  PROSKAUER ROSE LLP
  STROOCK & STROOCK & LAVAN LLP

4 CADWALADER, WICKERSHAM & TAFT
  CLEARY GOTTLIEB STEEN & HAMILTON
  DEBEVOISE & PLIMPTON
  KRAMER LEVIN NAFTALIS & FRANKEL LLP
  LATHAM & WATKINS LLP

5 BRYAN CAVE ROBINSON SILVERMAN
  KATTEN MUCHIN ZAVIS ROSENMAN
  SIMPSON THACHER & BARTLETT
  WACHTELL, LIPTON, ROSEN & KATZ

Firms are listed alphabetically in each band.

Fried, Frank, Harris, Shriver & Jacobson
see firm details p.796

The Firm: An enormously prestigious name in NY real estate circles, this firm is acknowledged for its *"broad group of excellent lawyers."* Its status remains highest for its unrivaled corporate leasing work, although the department is also known to cooperate profitably with the firm's tax and insolvency teams.
The Lawyers: Chair of the real estate department **Jonathan Mechanic** (see p.525) is thought to be *"far and away the most notable lawyer in New York for leasing work."* Known in the market as a man who *"does not suffer fools gladly,"* his recent work has included representing Equitable in connection with the $400 million disposal of its interest in 1515 Broadway. He also advised on the financing of 199 Water Street for Jack Resnick & Sons. Another senior practitioner, **Josh Mermelstein** (see p.525), is seen by contemporaries as more low-key, but still *"an absolutely top performer."* He has represented Brookfield in post-9/11 issues, and has acted for Reckson Associates, a REIT, which recently completed a long-term project relating to 919 Third Avenue. The firm scored a coup in its recent recruitment of **Steve Lefkowitz** (see p.523) from Pillsbury Winthrop. Widely acknowledged as an outstanding land use attorney, Lefkowitz has advised on the AOL Time Warner development, and worked with the NYSE on a new facility on Wall Street at Broadway. He has also acted on land use matters for Whitehall Funds, Forest City Enterprises and Morgan Stanley.
The Clients: The group has a particularly significant client in Jack Resnick & Sons, a landlord company that owns about five million sq ft of commercial space in the city. Other clients include UBS PaineWebber; CSFB; Tishman Speyer Properties; Millennium & Copthorne Hotels and Lazard Frères Real Estate Investors.

Paul, Hastings, Janofsky & Walker LLP
see firm details p.861

The Firm: Having absorbed leading real estate boutique Battle Fowler in recent years, the firm's capabilities in this sector are widely recognized to be among the nation's finest. Peers applauded *"an enormous group that comes up on deal after*

REAL ESTATE

NEW YORK

NEW YORK
Leading individuals (Real Estate)

1
- **BOXER** Leonard *Stroock & Stroock & Lavan LLP*
- **EDELMAN** Marty *Paul, Hastings, Janofsky & Walker*
- **LINDENBAUM** Samuel *Kramer Levin Naftalis*
- **MECHANIC** Jonathan *Fried, Frank, Harris, Shriver*
- **NEEDELL** Benjamin *Skadden, Arps, Slate, Meagher*
- **SHENKER** Joseph *Sullivan & Cromwell LLP*

2
- **LEFKOWITZ** Stephen *Fried, Frank, Harris, Shriver*
- **LIPSON** Lawrence *Proskauer Rose LLP*
- **PINOVER** Eugene *Willkie Farr & Gallagher*
- **POMERANTZ** Alan *Weil, Gotshal & Manges LLP*
- **SELVER** Paul *Paul, Hastings, Janofsky & Walker LLP*
- **SIMKIN** Steven *Paul, Weiss, Rifkind, Wharton*

3
- **ADLER** Arthur *Sullivan & Cromwell LLP*
- **CHADAKOFF** Richard *Latham & Watkins LLP*
- **FORELLE** John *Simpson Thacher & Bartlett*
- **HACKETT** Kevin *Shearman & Sterling*
- **HOROWITZ** Steven *Cleary Gottlieb Steen & Hamilton*
- **LASCHER** Alan *Weil, Gotshal & Manges LLP*
- **MERMELSTEIN** Joshua *Fried, Frank, Harris, Shriver*
- **SMITH** Chris *Shearman & Sterling*
- **STEIN** Joshua *Latham & Watkins LLP*
- **URIS** Harvey *Skadden, Arps, Slate, Meagher & Flom*

4
- **ALDEN** Steven *Debevoise & Plimpton*
- **FELTENSTEIN** Martha *Skadden, Arps, Slate, Meagher*
- **FORTE** Joseph *Dechert*
- **IVANHOE** Robert *Greenberg Traurig LLP*
- **NEVELOFF** Jay *Kramer Levin Naftalis & Frankel LLP*
- **PANOVKA** Robin *Wachtell, Lipton, Rosen & Katz*
- **ROSEN** Philip *Weil, Gotshal & Manges LLP*
- **WEINBERGER** Michael *Cleary Gottlieb Steen*
- **WHITE** Christopher *Cadwalader, Wickersham & Taft*

Individuals are listed alphabetically in each band.

The Clients: Clients include GE, AOL Time Warner and Bear Stearns.

Skadden, Arps, Slate, Meagher & Flom LLP & Affiliates
see firm details p.878

The Firm: A massive real estate department is noted for possessing vast resources and consequent ability to field teams able to handle the full spectrum of relevant law. Transactional work naturally constitutes the major proportion of the caseload, and the team advises a vast array of blue-chip clients.

The Lawyers: Ben Needell (see p.527) is regarded as the dean of the practice group, and was unanimously endorsed by contemporaries as *"one of the great names."* This legendary rainmaker was also singled out to researchers for his hard-nosed, *"rather confrontational"* style, an assertiveness which was generally agreed to typify the department. His hugely varied practice encompasses purchase and sale transactions, financings, securitized real estate loans, development, partnership law, REITs, syndications, leases and pension fund investments. **Harvey Uris** (see p.540) is another *"feisty but supremely gifted attorney."* He has niche expertise in capital markets-related real estate transactions, and over the past year, has represented Deutsche Banc Alex Brown on a range of matters. His name is frequently mentioned in the same breath as the respected **Martha Feltenstein** (see p.513), whose strongest suit is said to lie in real estate development, in which she has represented IBM on a number of occasions.

The Clients: The team also acts for Larry Silverstein, The Port Authority of New York and New Jersey, Queens West Development and The Carlyle.

Shearman & Sterling
see firm details p.874

The Firm: A prominent player in the real estate finance market, this *"sophisticated"* group regularly appears on big-ticket transactions for a powerful client portfolio of major financial institutions. Development, leasing, workouts and restructuring are other major elements of the team's caseload.

The Lawyers: Contemporaries regularly acclaim **Kevin Hackett** (see p.517) as *"an extremely smart attorney."* He has advised on some major real estate fund work, including the formation of a $2 billion fund for CSFB aimed at European and US real estate projects. **Chris Smith** (see p.536), the head of the property group, was described to researchers as a *"reasonable and practical"* opponent, and was recognized for his financing and equity investment expertise. Smith's practice embraces both national and international matters, and has involved residential property, offices, shopping centers and hotels. He acted for the Kuwait Investment Company on the restructuring and subsequent partial disposal of its $11 billion US property portfolio.

The Clients: A recent surge in European investment in the NY property market has given the firm particularly substantial instructions from its German banking clientele. Clients include: Goldman Sachs; Morgan Stanley; Citibank; Deutsche Bank Securities; HypoVereinsbank; Alcazar Trust; Barrow Street Capital; Tishman Speyer; CSFB; Viacom; Pyramid Development Company; Trizec Properties; Hyatt Regency Hotels and Sheraton Hotels & Resorts.

Sullivan & Cromwell LLP
see firm details p.886

The Firm: Best known for its association with the large investment bank Goldman Sachs (particularly their Whitehall Funds), the real estate group here is also thought to benefit from the presence of the firm's first-rate tax department. Clients praised the team for the *"streak of excellence running through its lawyers."* It primarily excels on the financing side of real estate law, advising on securitizations, IPOs and REIT work; for example, the firm represented Spieker Properties on the largest ever REIT M&A transaction, valued at $7.2 billion.

The Lawyers: The star turn is **Joe Shenker** (see p.535), a *"big-picture guy"* who market commentators say has *"one of the best brains in New York."* Clients appreciate his *"amazing ability to process and understand information."* He represented Vornado Realty Trust on its $1.6 billion acquisition of Charles E Smith Commercial Realty, and advised Whitehall Funds on its $1.85 billion sale of the Rockefeller Center. **Arthur Adler** (see p.503) has an excellent reputation for his expertise in leaseback work. Contemporaries regard him as *"a tough opponent, but one who is prepared to listen to rational arguments."*

The Clients: Goldman Sachs, Whitehall Funds, Jacobs Realty Investors, Prologis Trust, UBS, Hyatt Regency Hotels, Philips and Allegheny Power form part of the firm's extensive client roster.

Weil, Gotshal & Manges LLP
see firm details p.897

The Firm: The home of the world's finest insolvency group, the firm was also credited by rivals with possessing *"the best practice for real estate restructuring and refinancing"* in New York. The team is regularly seen on some of the largest deals in New York, and is widely regarded as one of the most forceful units in the city. No one doubts its success: *"They certainly get results."* Land use and development are other acknowledged areas of sector expertise.

The Lawyers: Senior partner **Alan Pomerantz** (see p.530) represents some enormous clients. He advised Brookfield on a three million sq ft

deal," notably on property development matters. The firm was also singled out to researchers for the diversity of its practice, which covers the spectrum of relevant work from litigation to financing.

The Lawyers: Observers viewed **Marty Edelman** (see p.511) as one of the premier names in this field; clients were loud in their praise of an attorney who they consider to be *"in a class of his own."* He recently advised on a $600 million land purchase in Manhattan, one of the largest assemblages of property in New York, and has also been active in the hospitality sector in Japan and Mexico. For land use matters, **Paul Selver** (see p.535) is seen as one of the foremost practitioners in the city. He advised on the redevelopment of nine acres of East River frontage in Manhattan, where a joint venture between Fisher Brothers Realty and Sheldon H Solow acquired a number of properties from utility company Con Edison. Commentators regard him as a *"permanently busy attorney"* with *"great instincts."*

NEW YORK — REAL ESTATE

development project on the West Side of Manhattan, and has frequently acted for Silverstein Properties and Goldman Sachs. He was commended to researchers as *"a fearsome negotiator and exceptional attorney."* **Alan Lascher** (see p.522) *"has been at the top of the tree for years,"* and was recently involved in large-scale leasings, notably on behalf of major companies seeking new premises in the wake of the destruction of the World Trade Center. He also represented Empire Blue Cross Blue Shield in a $1 billion tenancy matter, advised on a 250,000 sq ft leasing in the Rockefeller Center, and acted for Lehman Brothers on its acquisition of 745 Seventh Avenue from Morgan Stanley. **Phil Rosen** (see p.532) is a respected real estate generalist, whose practice covers development, securitizations, REITs, lending, and lease work. His recent caseload has included acting for Brookfield in the $800 million securitized financing of 245 Park Avenue, and representing the Lower Manhattan Development Corporation in the redevelopment of the World Trade Center site post-9/11.

The Clients: Blackstone Realty; Boston Properties; Empire Blue Cross Blue Shield; Schottenstein Stores and Value City Department Stores.

Willkie Farr & Gallagher
see firm details p.900

The Firm: This firm brings its corporate and telecom strengths to bear on a *"solid"* real estate department that handles substantial property M&A, financing and REIT work. Clients, which include major investment banks, enthused about *"a cooperative group that gets everyone involved on a deal."*

The Lawyers: **Gene Pinover** (see p.530) has by far the highest profile in the department, and is widely known as *"an attentive and skilled guy with no overbearing ego."* Over the past year, Pinover's workload has included a host of major deals such as his representation of a large REIT, New Plan Excel Realty Trust, on disposals and acquisitions worth $1 billion. He also acted for CBL & Associates Properties on numerous property acquisitions, and represented Simon Property Group on its purchase of 13 regional malls from Rodamco North America.

The Clients: The firm advised Paramount Group on the acquisition of the one million sq ft 180 Maiden Lane property, and 745 Fifth Avenue. The firm has also acted for Paramount Group, Merrill Lynch and New Plan Excel Realty Trust.

Paul, Weiss, Rifkind, Wharton & Garrison LLP
see firm details p.862

The Firm: Contemporaries regard this as an *"active, diverse and accomplished"* real estate group. Although the firm covers all areas of relevant law, it is particularly well known for handling high-end transactional work.

The Lawyers: The head of the real estate department, **Steve Simkin** (see p.536), came in for specific praise. Peers regard him as a *"smart and tough"* all-around lawyer, and clients appreciated his *"understanding of how to get deals done."* He advised principal client GMAC on matters such as the $1.3 billion construction financing of the Columbus Center, a $250 million financing of State Street's Boston headquarters and a $335 million securitized loan to Lucent Technologies. His work has also included advising on the $725 million acquisition of the Citigroup Center as well as appearing on a variety of real estate litigation.

The Clients: The firm also acts for Starwood Hotels & Resorts Worldwide and the Cayre Family.

Proskauer Rose LLP

The Firm: One of the most prominent firms in New York for leasing work, it advises a powerful roster of landlord and owner clients. It enjoys a particularly noteworthy relationship with Vornado Realty Trust, a company that owns, leases and develops office, retail and industrial properties.

The Lawyers: The leader of the firm's real estate department, **Larry Lipson**, is a veteran of numerous big-ticket leasings, financings and real estate M&A transactions. Described to researchers as *"a great worker for his client's cause,"* he acted for DLJ Real Estate Funds (now part of CSFB) on the purchase of hotels and the refinancing of an apartment building.

The Clients: The firm acts for property firms such as Alexanders.

Stroock & Stroock & Lavan LLP

The Firm: Commentators regard this as a *"nicely balanced"* real estate group, which covers a wide range of transactional and contentious matters in the sector. However, the 45-attorney team has its highest profile for development work, and is considered to know the local market as well as any of its rivals.

The Lawyers: The firm's real estate head, **Leonard Boxer**, was characterized by peers as *"one of the luminaries, without a doubt."* Clients described him as: *"a great deal-maker with a balanced perspective and absolute integrity, who just gets the job done."* He has been acting in a senior advisory capacity to Larry Silverstein, the owner of the World Trade Center, and remains heavily involved elsewhere in development work and arbitration.

The Clients: Donald Trump; JPMorgan Chase; Bear Stearns and The Lefrak Organization.

Cadwalader, Wickersham & Taft
see firm details p.778

The Firm: The real estate group remains in the public eye as one of the preeminent forces for lending work in general, and public securitized financing in particular.

The Lawyers: The leader of the firm's real estate group is the respected **Chris White** (see p.542), who was retained by Conseco in a $1 billion real estate dispute with Donald Trump. He also represented HypoVereinsbank in the second largest construction financing in New York, and GMAC in connection with financing for the World Trade Center.

The Clients: The firm's client base includes banks and corporations such as Morgan Stanley, Lehman Brothers, Conseco, GMAC and HypoVereinsbank.

Cleary Gottlieb Steen & Hamilton
see firm details p.782

The Firm: Rivals say this comparatively young real estate team boasts *"some of the finest up-and-coming talent in the game."* Commentators frequently drew researchers' attention to the group's expertise in high-end transactions, notably commercial mortgage-backed securitizations, and a clientele that includes some of the world's major investment banks.

The Lawyers: **Steve Horowitz** (see p.519) is well versed in a variety of real estate finance matters including joint ventures, restructurings and securitized lending, and was labeled *"an ideal guy for complex situations."* He has acted for Kindred Healthcare on lease financing deals totaling $700 million, and advised Deutsche Bank on equity, mortgage and mezzanine financings. Impressed interviewees regard **Michael Weinberger** (see p.541) as *"a major star in years to come."* He is often involved in deals for Goldman Sachs, and advised on the enormous single mortgage asset loan to Tishman Speyer in connection with the Rockefeller Center.

The Clients: Goldman Sachs; Morgan Stanley; Whitehall Funds; Deutsche Bank; Kindred Healthcare; Texas Pacific Group; Bank of America; JP Morgan Investment Management and TrizecHahn.

Debevoise & Plimpton
see firm details p.788

The Firm: Acting from within the firm's corporate department, the real estate group was most commonly recommended to researchers for its shopping center and mall work, which is acknowledged by peers to be *"of exceptionally good quality."*

The Lawyers: Leading light **Steven Alden** (see p.503) is said to *"run a tight ship."* This *"learned and experienced attorney"* is renowned among contemporaries for his *"consistently sound judgment."* Alden recently represented an insurance company on the $260 million financing of a joint venture office purchase in Boston, and on a $350 million financing package for a shopping center acquisition in Texas.

The Clients: The firm advises Westfield, one of

REAL ESTATE — NEW YORK

the biggest shopping center developers in the US; it acted on the $5.3 billion deal in which Westfield and two other parties acquired Rodamco North America's assets in the US. The firm has also acted for Talcott Investors and Unilever.

Kramer Levin Naftalis & Frankel LLP
see firm details p.832

The Firm: Although relatively small, the firm's real estate department is distinguished by the presence of some outstanding individual attorneys, notably on the development side. The practice has also established a niche in condominium work.

The Lawyers: The team is thought to have been clearly strengthened by the recruitment of a land use group from the former Rosenman & Colin. Chief among them is **Samuel Lindenbaum** (see p.524), esteemed by some as the *"finest land use practitioner in the state."* He has advised on expansions to the Museum of Modern Art and the Morgan Library in the city, and represented major developers such as Lennar Corporation and Jack Resnick & Sons. Lindenbaum has also undertaken substantial nonprofit work. **Jay Neveloff** (see p.527) has an excellent reputation for his developer practice; he advised The Related Companies in the condominium documentation used by the eight owners and lenders. Neveloff has continued his long-standing relationship with Donald Trump, including handling recent work on the Trump World Tower. He was also active in a $1 billion refinancing deal, which was canceled post-9/11, for the General Motors Building in Manhattan.

The Clients: Tishman Speyer; Sheldon Solow; Vornado Realty Trust; Rockrose Development; CSFB and Deloitte & Touche.

Latham & Watkins LLP
see firm details p.835

The Firm: The firm's real estate capacity is perceived to be largely driven by its finance department, but the property group is acknowledged to contain *"some highly effective individuals,"* who have a particular expertise in secured lending.

The Lawyers: Richard Chadakoff (see p.508), head of the firm's national real estate practice group, has a solid name for lending work and securitized financings. He acted for GE on multiple leases over the past year, including a $200 million joint venture loan portfolio involving 12 shopping centers. He also represented a well-known real estate advisory fund in the acquisition of 11 shopping centers. **Joshua Stein** (see p.538) was widely commended as *"an extremely intelligent and academically rigorous performer."* Over the past 12 months, he has regularly acted on secured lending for office projects. His work includes advising on the $100 million refinancing of the Washington Harbor complex in DC, and the refinancing of the Daily News Building in NY and the First Union Financial Center in Miami.

The Clients: Bayerische Landesbank; Bear Stearns; CSFB; Deutsche Bank; Lehman Brothers and Morgan Stanley.

Bryan Cave Robinson Silverman

The Firm: Robinson Silverman Pearce Aronsohn & Berman received a boost to its profile through its 2002 merger with St. Louis, MO giant Bryan Cave; the NY office of the firm is now known as Bryan Cave Robinson Silverman. Although this *"classy little local firm"* has not been as frequently visible as the market leaders on very large deals, observers await developments. The practice is viewed as a *"true jack of all trades."* Attorneys here handle the full spectrum of work from sales, acquisitions, leasing, construction, development and real estate finance to cooperatives, condominiums, housing and REIT work.

The Lawyers: Steven Bloom presides over this *"talented group."*

The Clients: Clients include owners, operators, developers and managers.

Katten Muchin Zavis Rosenman
see firm details p.827

The Firm: Providing a diverse range of services, the firm's real estate department advises owners, residential and commercial developers, investors and syndicators, construction and permanent lenders, investment funds and partnerships. Attorneys' workload here includes development work, such as site acquisition, land use and construction as well as structured and securitization financing, and mezzanine-secured debt financing.

The Lawyers: Clients asserted that the team, despite some recent departures, retains its reputation for *"high, all-round quality."*

The Clients: Owners; residential and commercial developers; investment funds and partnerships.

Simpson Thacher & Bartlett

The Firm: Ranked for the first time this year, the firm's real estate department has acquired its standing from its financing expertise. Structured debt, securitized financings and leasing are areas of specific ability, while the firm also advises extensively on joint ventures, equity investments and real estate M&A.

The Lawyers: John Forelle was endorsed to researchers as *"a prudent and hands-on attorney."* His practice concentrates on real estate finance, including securitizations and REIT work.

The Clients: Blackstone Real Estate Partners; Lazard Frères Real Estate Investors; The Carlyle Group; JE Robert Real Estate Funds; Westbrook Real Estate Partners; Bankers Trust; HypoVereinsbank; Mitsui Trust; Westdeutsche ImmobilienBank; Lehman Brothers and Equitable.

Wachtell, Lipton, Rosen & Katz
see firm details p.892

The Firm: This firm was described as *"supreme at what they do, but rather narrow in its remit."* Almost all the firm's real estate work revolves around M&A and REITs, areas in which it was consistently and highly praised.

The Lawyers: Robin Panovka (see p.529) was labeled by peers as *"a great attorney with some high-profile clients."* Highlights include representing Silverstein Properties in conjunction with 7 World Trade Center, acting for Security Capital in its acquisition of Storage USA and advising Lend Lease Real Estate Investments in its acquisition of AMRESCO.

The Clients: The firm also acts for Tishman Speyer.

Other Notable Practitioners

Robert Ivanhoe (see p.519), who chairs the national real estate practice group for Florida firm Greenberg Traurig LLP, is renowned as a *"natural deal-maker."* He represented SL Green Realty on a $480 million joint venture in early 2002 to acquire the Viacom headquarters at 1515 Broadway, which was, at the time, one of the largest real estate transactions in the city post-9/11. He also worked on the acquisition of the Seagram Building at 375 Park Avenue for a major investor, and on the sale of 1370 Avenue of the Americas for Westbrook Partners and Stellar Management. **Joe Forte** (see p.513), who left Thacher Proffitt & Wood in the summer of 2002 to join Dechert, is one of the pioneers of the commercial mortgage-backed securitization sector. Researchers were told that Forte is *"a fine attorney with a huge array of contacts."*

NEW YORK

SHIPPING

NEW YORK
Leading firms (Shipping)

1. HEALY & BAILLIE LLP
2. HILL RIVKINS & HAYDEN LLP
   HOLLAND & KNIGHT LLP
   SEWARD & KISSEL
3. FREEHILL HOGAN & MAHAR LLP
   NOURSE & BOWLES LLP
   WATSON, FARLEY & WILLIAMS
4. BURKE & PARSONS
   CARTER LEDYARD & MILBURN LLP
   GILMARTIN, POSTER & SHAFTO
5. CICHANOWICZ, CALLAN, KEANE, VENGROW
   CLARK, ATCHESON & REISERT
   DEORCHIS & PARTNERS LLP
   NICOLETTI HORNIG CAMPISE SWEENEY & PAIGE

Leading individuals (Shipping: Finance)

1. HENGEN Nancy *Holland & Knight LLP*
   OSBORNE John *Watson, Farley & Williams*
   POSTER Robert *Gilmartin, Poster & Shafto*
   RUTKOWSKI Larry *Seward & Kissel*
2. CHANG Leo *Watson, Farley & Williams*
   TENEV Jovi *Holland & Knight LLP*
   WHALEN Thomas *Carter Ledyard & Milburn LLP*
   WOLFE Gary *Seward & Kissel*

Leading individuals (Shipping: Litigation)

★ KIMBALL John *Healy & Baillie LLP*
1. BURKE Ray *Burke & Parsons*
   HAYDEN Raymond *Hill Rivkins & Hayden LLP*
2. HONAN William *Holland & Knight LLP*
   HOOPER Chester *Holland & Knight LLP*
   NOURSE David *Nourse & Bowles LLP*
3. BURRELL Lizabeth *Levy Phillips & Konigsberg LLP*
   COHEN Michael *Nicoletti Hornig Campise*
   PARÉ Jay *Nourse & Bowles LLP*
4. CLARK Peter *Clark, Atcheson & Reisert*
   DEORCHIS Vincent *DeOrchis & Partners LLP*
   GUTOWSKI Peter *Freehill Hogan & Mahar LLP*
   KENNEDY Donald *Carter Ledyard & Milburn LLP*
   LAMBERT LeRoy *Healy & Baillie LLP*
   STARER Brian *Holland & Knight LLP*
5. GINOS Geoffrey *Nicoletti Hornig Campise Sweeney*
   GREENBAUM Jack *Healy & Baillie LLP*
   HEARD Keith *Burke & Parsons*
   INGRAM John *Healy & Baillie LLP*
   KEANE Paul *Cichanowicz, Callan, Keane, Vengrow*

Firms and individuals are listed alphabetically in each band.

Healy & Baillie LLP
see firm details p.815

The Firm: A weak market has not dented the profile of this classic admiralty firm, which is now regarded as the best in town. With the exception of ship finance, its strength in depth is such that teams of the highest quality are available in all areas of maritime law. A reduction in casualty work has been offset by a rise in shipping-related bankruptcies, and the firm continues to excel in core charter party litigation on behalf of owners and protection & indemnity (P&I) clubs.

The Lawyers: Under the leadership of **John Kimball** (see p.521), the practice has *"gone from strength to strength."* He is universally respected by peers, and greatly in demand from clients looking for *"succinct, savvy advice,"* notably in charter party disputes, about which he has written a leading text. **LeRoy Lambert** (see p.522) was widely praised by owners for his expertise in both time and voyage charters, while **Jack Greenbaum** (see p.516) was described to researchers as a technical lawyer who *"battles hard to win."* He represented the managers of Navigator Gas vessels in an arbitration with the owners. He also obtained a summary judgment in favor of Ocean Rig, the owner of two drilling rigs, against Safra National Bank of New York on a $15 million letter of credit. **John Ingram** (see p.519) is rated as *"one of the best cargo defense attorneys in New York - the last of a dying breed,"* and has developed particular expertise in the pollution field.

The Clients: Premier Product Tankers; Ocean Rig; P&I clubs; shipowners; banks; charterers and insurance companies.

Hill Rivkins & Hayden LLP

The Firm: The 9/11 terrorist attacks forced the firm to find new downtown premises, but the shipping practice bounced back in late 2001 with the acquisition of a four-lawyer team from the now defunct Kirlin, Campbell & Keating. The firm continues to be active in the maritime, insurance and energy sectors for a clientele of insurers, reinsurers, underwriters and commodity traders. A Spanish-speaking partner heads up a vigorous Latin American practice, which is involved in a number of disputes in Chile and Argentina. The firm's Houston office, and in particular its ties to the Mexican market, is also thought to add an important dimension to the unit.

The Lawyers: **Ray Hayden**, who became president of The Maritime Law Association of the United States in May 2002, remains the team's dominant individual. A tough approach to litigation is the hallmark of a man regarded by many as *"the most capable cargo lawyer in New York."* He takes on policy defense work for large insurers, as well as major casualty work. The rest of the team drew a share of market endorsement, especially those lawyers with expertise in ship finance and bankruptcy. One highlight has been the firm's involvement in the case of the 'P36' drilling rig, which sank off the coast of Brazil in 2001 incurring a $500 million loss.

The Clients: Key client American Bureau Of Shipping has been added to this cargo plaintiff firm's lengthy portfolio. Its other clients include Lloyd's, CNA, St. Paul, ACE and AIG.

Holland & Knight LLP
see firm details p.820

The Firm: The firm's maritime unit may have lost some of its former profile in New York, but it still received market plaudits for its mix of expertise. Admiralty litigation, ship contracts and ship finance advice are offered alongside services such as bankruptcy, tax and environmental law.

The Lawyers: **Bill Honan** (see p.518), who runs the New York office, was recommended to researchers for charter party and freight, demurrage and defense (FD&D) work, principally in arbitration. The respected **Chet Hooper** (see p.518) handles cases on behalf of international logistics operators, cargo interests and shipowners and their P&I clubs. In 2002, he handled a complex case for a leading distribution company concerning the tracking of goods around the world. **Brian Starer** (see p.537), now back from management duties, is increasingly taking on casualty litigation matters. He represented The Swedish Club in litigation over an abandoned cargo ship, the 'M/V Anemone'. Salvage experts and former mariners add practical experience to the firm's wet department, which pioneered the use of electronic bills of lading, and recently completed the documentation for a large, new, luxury cruise ship. For the ship finance team, bankruptcies and workouts now complement the usual diet of synthetic lease transactions – usually for equipment values of greater than $100 million – and traditional bank lending work. **Nancy Hengen** (see p.518) is noted for her *"thorough, technical approach"* to asset finance transactions, while **Jovi Tenev** (see p.539) is also frequently seen acting for major financial institutions. Hengen's team represented a borrower in a US Title XI ship financing bond transaction, and has been active in the start-up of a fast ferry operation. Attorneys also worked on domestic prepackaged shipping bankruptcies in 2002 on behalf of bondholders, and were involved in lending work for vessels registered in Liberia, the Marshall Islands and Vanuatu.

The Clients: Banks; financial institutions; shipowners and energy and oil companies.

SHIPPING — NEW YORK

Seward & Kissel
The Firm: A favorite with large shipowners and their lending banks, this esteemed ship finance practice garnered widespread praise. Litigation is said to be a growing feature of the team, but it scores most highly in transactions. The finance team offers expertise in stock exchange listings for shipping lines, in offshore shipping investment funds and in bankruptcy (both for companies and creditors). It has a resident shipping tax specialist.
The Lawyers: **Larry Rutkowski** is seen by contemporaries as the *"classic ship financier,"* and is said to have a *"great following in the banking community."* He led on the Fleet/Nordea/Den norske Bank/Bank of Scotland $200 million syndicated revolving credit facility for SEACOR SMIT, and the JPMorgan Chase/Den norske Bank/Nordea/Hamburgische Landesbank $350 million credit facility for Overseas Shipholding Group. **Gary Wolfe**'s (see page 543) practice tends more toward capital markets and securities deals than pure asset financing. He is noted for high visibility in public offerings, in which field he advises leading shipowning issuers; examples include the Dampskibsselskabet TORM NASDAQ listing and the Stelmar Shipping secondary offering. Elsewhere, the firm's litigators advised Silja Line on the Commodore Cruises bankruptcy and Exmar in the Enron LNG bankruptcy.
The Clients: Nordea; Den norske Bank; DVB Nedship Bank; Fortis Capital; The Bank of New York; Deutsche Schiffsbank; Stelmar Shipping; General Maritime Corporation; American Marine Advisors; Northern Navigation; Pacific Coast Shipping; Dampskibsselskabet TORM and Exmar.

Freehill Hogan & Mahar LLP
The Firm: Commentators noted that this increasingly prolific team has *"moved successfully into the full-service admiralty firm mould."* Clients and peers are united in their praise for a practice that has *"bucked the market trend by increasing its staff and taking on more work,"* and is consequently considered to be an *"obvious destination for the vast majority of cases."* Although the West of England P&I Club remains a key client, the practice has shed its historical 'one-client firm' tag and now acts for a number of clubs, owners, charterers and banks. One of the largest practices in New York, it has teams working on personal injury-related matters (such as deaths at sea), property-related work (explosions and casualties) and transactions (ship contract agreements).
The Lawyers: George Freehill remains an influential rainmaker and a sounding board for the firm's clients. However, it is **Peter Gutowski** who now gains the most market endorsement. A *"robust litigator,"* he is active in casualty matters, contract work and arbitration, and has won high praise for his *"effectiveness in bringing cases to a quick conclusion."* The team was involved in a high-profile casualty case involving the tanker 'Virgo', which collided with Maine-based fishing vessel 'Starbound' off the coast of New England.
The Clients: Phoenix; West of England P&I Club; SKULD; American P&I Club; Gard Services; Maersk and Stolt - Nielsen.

Nourse & Bowles LLP
The Firm: This respected admiralty litigation firm is renowned for its high-quality case - handling skills and thorough commitment to disputes. Interviewees say it has built a *"credible brand,"* with market consensus suggesting that what the firm lacks in size, it makes up for in technical proficiency. The team undertakes the full spectrum of traditional litigation, including collisions, sea damage and container losses. As well as advising oil companies and commodity traders, the firm has an extensive P&I club client portfolio.
The Lawyers: **David Nourse** received widespread endorsement for his charter party litigation and arbitration skills, while **Jay Paré**'s drafting ability also drew consistent market approval.

Watson, Farley & Williams
see firm details p.896
The Firm: Still a premier choice for ship finance work despite the loss of Craig Stearns to Orrick, Herrington & Sutcliffe, the firm represents shipowners and banks in finance and leasing transactions, and has niche expertise in securitizations. The firm advised Fortis on a $175 million syndicated financing of five container ships to be built in China and chartered to China Shipping Group. Although dominated by its transactional practice, the firm houses a number of contentious partners who handle ship litigation and arbitration. Specific attention is paid to the cruise line sector, oil pollution and bankruptcies. A team acted for Stena Line on the restructuring of StenTex following the merger of Texaco and Chevron. The firm also advised the chartering subsidiary of Phillips Petroleum Company on the sale and charterback with Teekay Shipping of five tankers in Korea.
The Lawyers: Leasing expert **John Osborne**, the team's heaviest hitter, is seen as *"the key to its success,"* and has built up a formidable client roster. **Leo Chang**'s advice to banks, shipowners and financial institutions is a success with in-house counsel, who regard him as *"someone who manages his time efficiently."*
The Clients: Van Ommeren Clipper; Citibank; DVB Nedship Bank; Royal Bank of Scotland; Société Générale; Teekay Shipping; Royal Caribbean Cruises; Fortis and Stena Line.

Burke & Parsons
The Firm: Sluggish market conditions and an accompanying reduction in casualty work have not helped this maritime boutique, but it continues to enjoy healthy market approval for its *"extremely loyal client base."* The seven-lawyer team represents major shipowners on their admiralty claims, taking in FD&D, charter party matters, oil spills and pollution. It also counsels on cargo defense and ship finance for Japanese trading companies. The firm advised on a naval pollution case arising from an incident that occurred off the coast of Portland, ME.
The Lawyers: Charter party litigator **Ray Burke** is one of the market's leading lights, and was described by major clients as an *"exceptionally reliable and user-friendly attorney."* He receives valuable support from **Keith Heard**, who is said to *"know case law inside out."*
The Clients: Hyundai, OSG and Teekay Shipping.

Carter Ledyard & Milburn LLP
see firm details p.780
The Firm: The firm's shipping practice can call on support from the tax, insolvency and environmental departments. Ship finance is the team's forte, although there has been a rise in litigation and restructuring cases. Transocean Sedco Forex was the team's client in arbitration and litigation in New York arising from the bareboat charter of 'Peregrine X'. The firm also acted for the United States Trust Company of New York in lender liability litigation over the collapse of Adriatic Tankers, and advised SeaStreak America (a subsidiary of Sea Containers) in the development of its New York passenger ferry program. Restructuring activity has included advising the mortgagee of the five Navigator Gas carrier vessels on a $304 million debt issue, and acting for the mortgagee and secured note holders in the foreclosure on President Casinos' riverboat casino vessels.
The Lawyers: **Tom Whalen**'s (see p.542) experience and knowledge of ship financing techniques draws approval from clients and opposing solicitors. *"He's not a shouter,"* say shipowners, but he *"quietly gets on with it."* He has built up substantial knowledge of the German market through his work for financial institutions such as KfW and Commerzbank. Litigation expertise is provided by **Donald Kennedy** (see p.521), who takes on the bulk of the group's P&I and FD&D work, and is said to *"know the lie of the land."*
The Clients: Nordisk Skibsrederforening; Polish Steamship Company; United States Trust Company of New York; The Bank of New York; The East Asiatic Company; Norwegian Hull Club; Frachtcontor Junge & Co; Stephenson Harwood; Sea Containers; SeaStreak America; Nichimen America; Kreditanstalt für Wiederaufbau (KfW) and Commerzbank.

NEW YORK

SHIPPING

Gilmartin, Poster & Shafto
The Firm: This partner-heavy corporate and securities shipping boutique is said to be a favored destination for referrals from other firms. Ship finance and bankruptcy are key elements of the eight-lawyer unit's workload, and the group often acts as cocounsel alongside larger firms. Highlights have included representing financial institutions in a triple net lease financing of maritime equipment and advising an Asian-based client on a LNG joint venture. The team also advised a committee of noteholders in connection with a vessel-secured high yield issue and acted for the borrower in the financing of articulated tug/barge combinations.
The Lawyers: The death of former bankruptcy judge Howard Buschman was a loss to its restructuring capability, but the firm is still felt to contain some fine individuals. Foremost among them is *"finance guru"* **Robert Poster**, who acts for banks and shipowners, and is renowned for his expertise in leasing, vessel documentation and the shipping regulatory framework. Other partners act for carriers on LNG projects and synthetic leases, and advise banks on financing for oil field vessels, tugs and barges. Lawyers are also able to advise on the interaction between ship finance and tax, and occasionally appear on major litigation cases.
The Clients: US banks and leasing companies; naval architects; New York law firms; a major Japanese LNG carrier; a domestic marine operating company; a South American liner carrier and a Japanese maritime organization.

Cichanowicz, Callan, Keane, Vengrow & Textor LLP
The Firm: Known for its strong P&I club and shipowning connections, the firm's expertise stretches across the admiralty spectrum and includes marine cargo and ship contract advice.
The Lawyers: Senior lawyer **Paul Keane**, rated by peers for his *"hard-working and robust"* approach to litigation, is often consulted by major clubs for his knowledge of cargo and bills of lading. Other partners are noted for their expertise in tankers and marine insurance.
The Clients: Astra Oil; CMA CGM; Contship Containerlines; Duke Energy; Enjet; Evergreen Marine; Hanjin Shipping Co.; Hapag-Lloyd; Koch Petroleum Group; NYK LINE; Senator Lines; Sprague Energy; Texas Petrochemical and YANG MING LINE.

Clark, Atcheson & Reisert
The Firm: A *"technically skilled"* wet unit, which attracts market endorsement for its tradition of recruiting seamen, engineers, naval architects and graduates of the US Merchant Marine Academy. The firm is widely regarded as a natural choice for complex cases involving the mechanical aspects of ships, such as engine faults and equipment malfunctions. It has handled a number of cases involving large fruit shipments, and frequently represents non-vessel operating common carriers. Elsewhere, the firm has acknowledged expertise in ship finance and insurance.
The Lawyers: Cargo expert and licensed chief engineer **Peter Clark** is one of the firm's three partners, and frequently serves as both advocate and arbitrator.

DeOrchis & Partners LLP
The Firm: **Vince DeOrchis** is the partner in charge of this respectable admiralty litigation firm, which is recognized for its visibility on behalf of P&I clubs, shipping lines and underwriters. Cargo defense forms the main thrust of the practice's activity, but the team also advises on hull claims, personal injury, collision, pollution and charter party disputes.

Nicoletti Hornig Campise Sweeney & Paige
The Firm: This marine and insurance firm received a major boost with the arrival in 2002 of a senior team from the former shipping practice at Burlingham Underwood.
The Lawyers: Leading academic **Michael Marks Cohen**, now of counsel, has a *"first-rate legal brain,"* and is said to *"like trying out new theories."* Clients, however, backed his *"practical usability."* Cohen has a charter party practice and specializes in on-the-spot advice to clients as disputes emerge. **Geoff Ginos** was recommended by clients for his versatile approach and charter party skills. He advises on casualty and cruise-related work and construction defect cases. Admiralty litigator Terry Stoltz was the other key lateral hire.
The Clients: The group's key client is ConocoPhillips. It also has established relationships with chemical trader Vinmar International and tanker company OMI.

Other Notable Practitioners
Liz Burrell left Burlingham Underwood LLP in 2002 to join Levy Phillips & Konigsberg LLP. She is a prominent figure at The Maritime Law Association of the United States and an active contract drafter. *Chambers'* researchers heard widespread praise for her reliability and *"impeccable writing ability."*

TAX

NEW YORK
Leading firms (Tax)

1. CLEARY GOTTLIEB STEEN & HAMILTON
   CRAVATH, SWAINE & MOORE
   DAVIS POLK & WARDWELL
   SULLIVAN & CROMWELL LLP
2. SKADDEN, ARPS, SLATE, MEAGHER & FLOM LLP
   WACHTELL, LIPTON, ROSEN & KATZ
3. SIMPSON THACHER & BARTLETT
4. DEBEVOISE & PLIMPTON
   SHEARMAN & STERLING
   WEIL, GOTSHAL & MANGES LLP
5. FRIED, FRANK, HARRIS, SHRIVER & JACOBSON
   PAUL, WEISS, RIFKIND, WHARTON & GARRISON
   ROBERTS & HOLLAND LLP

Firms are listed alphabetically in each band

Cleary Gottlieb Steen & Hamilton
see firm details p.782
The Firm: Most prominent in the financial products arena, this firm is a market leader for high-end and innovative tax work. The team is thought to have *"tied their chariot to the financial institutions practice,"* and appears advising investment banks such as Goldman Sachs and Morgan Stanley on a variety of cutting-edge structures and transactions. In addition, a well-developed global network has the group acting as US tax counsel on a large proportion of cross-border M&A transactions. Thirty New York tax practitioners work closely with colleagues in London, Paris, Frankfurt, Brussels, Rome and Milan as part of an integrated worldwide tax practice. Commentators routinely point to the group's *"extraordinary amount of tax talent"* and consistent standard of quality at all levels of the practice. One rival noted that *"any firm would be glad to have any one of their lawyers."*
The Lawyers: Senior practitioner **Les Samuels** (see p.534) was recommended as a *"guru"* for international tax-based transactions. A former US Treasury official, he is thought to be *"plugged into"* market and legislative developments. He advises both corporate and financial clients on M&A and foreign direct investment in the US. Samuels recently advised South African Breweries in connection with its $3.6 billion acquisition of Miller Brewing. In financial products, the firm owes its high profile to the *"dynamic duo"* of **Ed Kleinbard** (see p.521) and **Jim Peaslee** (see p.529), both of whom are at the *"top of the form"*

TAX
NEW YORK

NEW YORK
Leading individuals (Tax)

1
- CANELLOS Peter *Wachtell, Lipton, Rosen & Katz*
- ROSEN Matthew *Skadden, Arps, Slate, Meagher*
- SCHLER Michael *Cravath, Swaine & Moore*
- STEINBERG Lewis *Cravath, Swaine & Moore*
- TODRYS Steven *Simpson Thacher & Bartlett*
- TRIER Dana *Davis Polk & Wardwell*

2
- BLESSING Peter *Shearman & Sterling*
- HEITNER Kenneth *Weil, Gotshal & Manges LLP*
- SCHWARTZ Jodi *Wachtell, Lipton, Rosen & Katz*
- SHACHAR Avishai *Davis Polk & Wardwell*
- SOLOMON Andrew *Sullivan & Cromwell LLP*
- TAYLOR Willard *Sullivan & Cromwell LLP*
- YOUNGWOOD Alfred *Paul, Weiss, Rifkind, Wharton*

3
- COHEN Ben *Cahill Gordon & Reindel*
- GOLDRING Stuart *Weil, Gotshal & Manges LLP*
- GORDON Steve *Cravath, Swaine & Moore*
- INDOE William *Sullivan & Cromwell LLP*
- REINHOLD Richard *Willkie Farr & Gallagher*
- SAMUELS Leslie *Cleary Gottlieb Steen & Hamilton*
- SCHARFSTEIN Joel *Fried, Frank, Harris, Shriver*
- STAFFARONI Robert *Debevoise & Plimpton*

4
- AMDUR Martin *Weil, Gotshal & Manges LLP*
- ANDERSEN Richard *Arnold & Porter*
- BRANNAN William *Cravath, Swaine & Moore*
- CHINN Adam *Wachtell, Lipton, Rosen & Katz*
- EINHORN David *Wachtell, Lipton, Rosen & Katz*
- FRIEDMAN Gary *Debevoise & Plimpton*
- GARDNER Stephen *Kronish Lieb Weiner & Hellman*
- HAIMS Bruce *Debevoise & Plimpton*
- LEE Carolyn *Roberts & Holland LLP*
- PHILLIPS Barnet *Skadden, Arps, Slate, Meagher*
- POLLACK Martin *Weil, Gotshal & Manges LLP*
- REICH Yaron *Cleary Gottlieb Steen & Hamilton*
- ROSEN Burt *Debevoise & Plimpton*
- SICULAR David *Paul, Weiss, Rifkind, Wharton*

Up-and-coming individuals
- THURSTON Sally *Skadden, Arps, Slate, Meagher*
- WOLLMAN Diana *Sullivan & Cromwell LLP*

Leading individuals
(Tax: Financial Products)

1
- DIMON Samuel *Davis Polk & Wardwell*
- HARITON David *Sullivan & Cromwell LLP*
- KLEINBARD Edward *Cleary Gottlieb Steen & Hamilton*
- PEASLEE James *Cleary Gottlieb Steen & Hamilton*

2
- BROWN Dickson *Simpson Thacher & Bartlett*
- KAYLE Bruce *Milbank, Tweed, Hadley & McCloy*
- MILLER David *Cadwalader, Wickersham & Taft*
- MORGAN Charles *Skadden, Arps, Slate, Meagher*
- NIJENHUIS Erika *Cleary Gottlieb Steen & Hamilton*
- SCARBOROUGH Robert *Freshfields Bruckhaus*

Up-and-coming individuals
- SIT Po *Davis Polk & Wardwell*

Individuals are listed alphabetically in each band.

---

for capital markets and structured products tax work. A *"consummate tax lawyer,"* Kleinbard engages in tax planning for major US investment banks and has been handling international work for the Securities Industry Association. He is best known for his work developing innovative financial products, but also undertakes a share of transactional M&A matters. Peaslee is similarly considered *"hot"* on derivatives and financial products matters, and is said to have *"built up a tremendous reputation in the area."* Interviewees recommend this *"enormously talented"* practitioner for his expertise in relation to REMICs and other mortgage-backed securities structures and foreign tax credits. **Erika Nijenhuis** (see p.527) also focuses on financial products work. Noted for her *"keen intellect,"* this younger partner is reported to be *"making her mark"* as an expert in derivatives and structured products. Well-respected **Yaron Reich** (see p.531) maintains a mixed practice, encompassing M&A, partnerships, tax litigation and the taxation of financial institutions. He advises the Institute of International Bankers on US tax matters.

The Clients: Goldman Sachs; Morgan Stanley; Citigroup; Securities Industry Association; CSFB; South African Breweries; Texas Pacific Group; McDonald's and Deutsche Telekom.

Cravath, Swaine & Moore

The Firm: Acknowledged as one of the *"premier tax departments in NY,"* the five-partner practice rates highly for the *"depth and quality of its individuals."* Much of the team's work involves providing tax support on high-profile M&A and spin-off transactions. A *"rigorous training model"* here is thought to produce strong corporate generalists who are acknowledged as *"terrific across the board."* In addition to a high level of transactional work, the firm offers advice on securities and financial products, and general counseling. The firm has had notable success within the telecom and technology industries and advises such blue-chip clients as Vivendi Universal, Lucent Technologies and IBM on transactional matters.

The Lawyers: A remarkable team of quality practitioners keeps Cravath Swaine firmly at the top of the rankings. *"Superb"* partner **Lewis Steinberg** was praised as both *"smart and well-spoken."* Peers described him as a *"Renaissance attorney,"* and admired his *"range and versatility."* Steinberg's practice is weighted towards cross-border M&A, but also encompasses financial products and securities offerings. He regularly advises Vivendi Universal on tax issues, most recently in relation to its $10.3 billion acquisition of USA Networks. **Michael Schler** maintains a similarly diverse practice, covering structured finance, M&A, and securitization transactions. Prominent in the specialty due to his numerous articles on tax and corporate finance, this *"intellectually gifted"* practitioner can be relied upon to *"consider a question from every angle."* A *"frank and principled"* adviser, he is reported to display *"the courage of his convictions."* Schler acted for Newport News Shipbuilding in its $2.6 billion acquisition by Northrop Grumman. **Steve Gordon** undertakes general corporate counseling, with particular expertise in restructuring arrangements. Clients admire his *"low-key"* style, commenting that *"he does it right, without the histrionics."* Gordon frequently handles tax matters for Bristol-Myers Squibb. Well known partnerships expert **William Brannan** specializes in real estate and joint venture transactions. He has lately been advising PwC Consulting on its acquisition by IBM.

The Clients: Vivendi Universal; Johnson & Johnson; IBM; Unilever; Nestlé; Lucent Technologies; BAE SYSTEMS and Bristol-Myers Squibb.

Davis Polk & Wardwell

The Firm: This *"distinguished"* 11-partner practice boasts a *"huge amount of talent"* in the tax arena. The team *"covers the waterfront,"* advising on large international mergers, dispositions and restructurings. The group has a growing profile in structured finance and investment fund work, and is thought to benefit from *"established connections with financial intermediaries."* A small tax controversy practice also represents clients on contested tax matters. Practitioners were commended for *"working well together as a team,"* and interviewees observed that *"they all know what their colleagues are doing."* A strong group of well-respected senior attorneys is supported by a number of *"promising young attorneys"* coming through the ranks.

The Lawyers: *"Extraordinarily talented"* **Dana Trier** was acclaimed *"one of the best general tax lawyers in New York."* His broad-based practice spans both cross-border M&A and financial products; peers insist that he is *"good at whatever he turns his hand to."* In financial products, he serves as lead counsel to CSFB in connection with convertibles and equity derivatives. Trier recently acted as tax counsel to PwC Consulting in connection with its over $3 billion sale to IBM. Department head **Avishai Shachar** focuses largely on M&A, IPOs and spin-offs. Popular with clients for his *"savvy business sense,"* Shachar *"knows how to make a deal work."* He acted as lead tax counsel to Comcast in its acquisition of AT&T Broadband. **Sam Dimon** advises institutional clients Deutsche Bank, Morgan Stanley and JPMorgan Chase on equity derivatives and equity-related financial products. *"Clever and level-headed,"* he is reported to exercise *"impeccable judgment."* His current position as chairman of the NY State Bar Association Tax Section is considered a *"tribute to his intellect and skills."* Young

NEW YORK   TAX

partner **Po Sit** was additionally recommended as an *"up-and-coming talent"* in derivatives and financial products.
The Clients: JPMorgan Chase; Morgan Stanley; Deutsche Bank; Comcast and Banc of America Securities.

Sullivan & Cromwell LLP
see firm details p.886
The Firm: This *"well-resourced"* practice is thought to be one of the most diverse; its workload encompasses transactional M&A, financial instruments, partnerships and real estate finance, tax planning and controversy work. Its profile is greatest in international matters, where the group enjoys a global reputation for handling multi-jurisdictional M&A and joint venture transactions. It also advises foreign corporates on the tax aspects of their US securities offerings. In New York, ten partners receive support on cross-border matters from a smaller Paris practice that offers both US and French tax expertise. Practitioners have experience structuring tax-advantaged financial instruments and have been involved in the development of income preferred securities (MIPS and QUIPS), automatic common exchange securities (ACES) and privately placed indexed securities and derivatives.
The Lawyers: Managing partner of the tax group **Andrew Solomon** (see p.536) was praised by competitors for *"looking after his clients' interests."* He maintains a broad-based practice, with particular expertise in cross-border M&A and finance in the insurance, oil and gas and technology industries. He acted for AIG in its acquisitions of SunAmerica and Chiyoda Mutual Life, and for Dexia in its acquisitions of Financial Security Assurance and the PwC business, Global Structured Finance. **David Hariton** (see p.517) is a *"confident and creative lawyer"* who is noted for his *"high sense of ethics."* He is a *"definite force"* in the financial products market, in which he is active in the development of debt-equity hybrids and equity-indexed swaps. Although Hariton is most prominent for his involvement in novel financial instruments, his practice also extends into M&A and domestic and foreign partnerships. *"Dean of the tax practice"* **Willard Taylor** (see p.539) divides his time between the firm's Paris and New York offices. Highly recommended for international tax matters, Taylor represented BP in connection with its US expansion and acquisitions of ARCO and Amoco. *"Smart as a whip,"* **Bill Indoe** (see p.519) concentrates on M&A transactions, representing investment banks and principals on various acquisitions, divestitures, and spin-off arrangements. This *"gentlemanly"* practitioner also handles Title 1 ERISA issues for investment fund clients such as Whitehall Funds. Clients describe him as a *"consummate technician,"* who is able to *"get the tax perfect, without interfering in the deal."* Highlights of his practice include advising Pharmacia in connection with its acquisition by Pfizer, and acting for eBay in its acquisition of PayPal. Commended as *"sharp, motivated and interested,"* **Diana Wollman** (see p.543) was identified as an up-and-coming tax practitioner.
The Clients: AIG; Goldman Sachs; Diageo; UBS Warburg; Barclays Bank; Philips; Microsoft; Bank of New York; Allianz and Vornado Realty Trust.

Skadden, Arps, Slate, Meagher & Flom LLP & Affiliates
see firm details p.878
The Firm: The New York team is the largest in the firm's national practice, with 13 partners and 30 associates advising on a variety of transactional matters. They work closely with partners in DC, Chicago and LA in coordinating tax advice on large mergers, spin-offs and restructurings. The firm's global reputation as a corporate *"powerhouse"* attracts high-quality international deals, and attorneys frequently advise both US and multinational clients in cross-border M&A and hybrid financings, international joint ventures and US and Euromarket securities offerings. Recent highlights include advising Lockheed Martin on federal tax issues relating to the restructuring and privatization of its global satellite company Intelsat, and representing Shionogi & Co in a pharmaceutical joint venture with GlaxoSmithKline. A *"deep bench"* of talent was said to include a large number of skilled younger attorneys. Rivals describe the team as a *"bunch of all-round solid performers."*
The Lawyers: *"Superstar"* **Matt Rosen** (see p.533) is said to have *"done or supervised more M&A deals than anyone alive."* Cohead of the firm's tax group, this *"thoughtful"* practitioner maintains a broad generalist practice covering domestic and cross-border M&A, REIT and partnership transactions and financial instruments. He receives particular praise for his skill at managing a team and for his *"low-key"* approach to negotiations.
Barnet Phillips (see p.530) is highly regarded as a REIT and partnerships expert. Rated by clients as *"bright and responsive,"* Phillips advises fund managers BlackRock, Gabelli Asset Management and Allen & Company, and other clients such as MacAndrews & Forbes and Northstar on tax planning and acquisitions. He recently represented Genuity on the sale of its assets to Level 3 Communications. Former IRS official **Charles Morgan** (see p.526) is well known for his *"deep experience"* in financial products. He has a strong client following in the hedge fund community where he has been involved in the development of creative swap arrangements and hybrid instruments. Morgan regularly advises Bear Stearns, Merrill Lynch and Deutsche Morgan Grenfell on the tax consequences of complex financial products. **Sally Thurston** (see p.539) was nominated by peers and clients as a *"gifted"* up-and-coming practitioner with a focus on international transactions. She recently advised TRW in connection with its $5.9 billion acquisition by Northrop Grumman.
The Clients: Bear Stearns; Citibank; Deutsche Morgan Grenfell; BlackRock; Merrill Lynch; Morgan Stanley; Lockheed Martin; MacAndrews & Forbes and Plum Creek.

Wachtell, Lipton, Rosen & Katz
see firm details p.892
The Firm: This *"superb"* practice has a *"niche focus"* on high-profile M&A transactions. Although narrower in scope than many of its competitors, the group retains a *"stellar reputation"* in the field as *"New York's best M&A tax practice."* The six-partner practice supports a thriving corporate client roster on big-ticket acquisitions, joint ventures, spin-offs and financings. Particular expertise exists in workouts and restructuring transactions. Practitioners here are thought to be the *"brightest and best in the business"* with *"impressive deal experience"* to their credit. The firm advised USA Networks on its $10.3 billion acquisition by Vivendi Universal.
The Lawyers: *"Dean of the practice,"* **Peter Canellos** (see p.508) enjoys a reputation as *"one of the giants"* of the tax bar. He is considered a specialist in domestic and international corporate acquisitions, and writes extensively on the subject. His partner **Jodi Schwartz** (see p.535) was described as *"one of the hardest working tax lawyers alive."* This *"energetic"* practitioner was commended as particularly *"good under pressure."* She focuses on transactional matters, and is thought to be taking an increasingly leading role within the practice. Clients appreciate her *"practical commercial sense."* Schwartz recently acted for AT&T Broadband in its acquisition by Comcast. The REIT specialist **David Einhorn** (see p.512) rates highly for his *"creative"* advice on complicated structures. He represented Dreyer's Grand Ice Cream in its $2.5 billion merger with Nestlé. *"Quirky"* **Adam Chinn** (see p.509) advises on executive compensation and ERISA matters and was recommended as the *"young turk"* of the practice.
The Clients: The firm advises blue-chip domestic and international corporates, including AT&T Broadband, USA Networks, Trigon Healthcare, Dreyer's Grand Ice Cream and Publicis, among others.

Simpson Thacher & Bartlett
The Firm: This *"balanced"* six-partner team handles a varied workload of public company and private equity transactions. With experience representing a large institutional base of buyout funds such as KKR, The Blackstone Group and The Cypress Group, the practice here is consid-

ered a market leader for tax matters relating to fund formation, LBOs and venture capital deals. However, the practice also undertakes a share of public company M&A and is best known for its niche strength in financial institution mergers. The firm also represents equity investors in leasing and project finance transactions, and coordinates cross-border matters with practitioners in the London and Hong Kong offices.

The Lawyers: Head of the tax department, **Steve Todrys** was identified as the *"intellectual leader of the practice."* Acknowledged as *"one of the standouts of the profession,"* Todrys is well known for his role as lead counsel to investment fund KKR, who he advised on its acquisition of the Bell Canada directories and pending acquisition of Legrand from Schneider. His practice is a mixture of cross-border and domestic M&A with private equity transactions. He recently advised on the spin-off of CarMax by Circuit City and on the spin-off of several businesses of HJ Heinz and their susequent merger with Del Monte. Clients value both his *"sharp, analytical mind"* and *"wonderful common sense,"* and particularly commended his ability to *"distill and present complex material."* *"Astute"* financial products specialist **Dickson Brown** *"knows his way around derivatives."* He advises investment banks Lehman Brothers and JPMorgan Chase on the creation of financial instruments, and also undertakes a share of regulatory and accounting matters.

The Clients: Kohlberg Kravis Roberts & Company (KKR); JPMorgan Chase; The Blackstone Group; The Cypress Group; Silver Lake Partners; AOL Time Warner; The Carlyle Group; Accenture and Lehman Brothers Merchant Banking.

Debevoise & Plimpton
see firm details p.788

The Firm: A *"classy outfit,"* it focuses on taxable and tax-free acquisitions, dispositions and restructurings. The practice is best known for its work on behalf of investment funds Oaktree Capital, AIG Private Equity Portfolio and Providence Equity Partners as sponsors to investment partnerships, mortgage-backed securities and hedge funds. Practitioners advise on the tax aspects of private equity portfolio deals as well as on large public company M&A. The firm has also developed specialized expertise in relation to tax-advantaged cross-border leasing transactions and lease portfolio transfers. It is seen to be expanding its international capabilities and now comprises 50 tax lawyers worldwide. In addition, the group handles a large insurance practice, advising on demutualizations and on other transactions within the insurance industry. Recent highlights include Sithe Energies' $2.5 billion sale of domestic and international assets, and Swiss International Air Line's lease of 50 aircraft, valued in excess of $1 billion.

The Lawyers: Department head **Bruce Haims** (see p.517) is a *"careful, confident"* lawyer with a wide-ranging practice that incorporates general tax advice, M&A, partnership arrangements, investment funds and executive compensation. He is best known, however, for his work advising high net-worth individuals and company owners in the sports and entertainment fields on both personal and corporate tax planning. He recently acted for a private company on the restructuring of $1.5 billion of assets and conversion into an S Corp. The *"effective"* **Robert Staffaroni** (see p.537) concentrates on corporate finance and international transactions. This *"thoughtful"* attorney regularly advises American Airlines on public and private financings, and counsels Zurich Capital Markets on hedge funds and derivatives. **Gary Friedman** (see p.514) is thought to be a *"dynamic"* young partner with particular strength in international M&A. Clients feel that he *"takes their interests to heart,"* underlining Friedman's *"accessibility"* and *"dedication."* He acted for Domtar on its $1.7 billion acquisition of four paper mills and has lately been advising eircom in tax issues arising from its purchase by Valentia Telecommunications, a consortium led by Providence Equity Partners. *"Talented"* **Burt Rosen** (see p.532) was recommended for his expertise in equipment and structured finance. He regularly advises DaimlerChrysler and Misys on leasing, acquisitions and cross-border finance and acted for Swiss International Air Lines (formerly Crossair) on its acquisition of the Swissair lease portfolio.

The Clients: American Airlines; Prudential Insurance; L'Oreal; Zurich Capital Markets; DaimlerChrysler; eircom; Mitsui; Rolls-Royce; GE Capital; Misys; Swiss International Air Lines; Clayton, Dubilier & Rice; AIG Private Equity Portfolio and Oxygen Media.

Shearman & Sterling
see firm details p.874

The Firm: The practice is seen to be in a state of *"flux"* following some recent partner departures. However, the firm remains highly rated for its international tax expertise. An integrated global practice group includes tax practitioners in the US, France, Germany and the UK who act on a volume of cross-border M&A and finance transactions. Commentators consistently praise the practice's *"broad coverage,"* observing that *"they have the know-how to complete a deal anywhere in the world."* The group was also thought to be strong on financial instruments and real estate securitization matters. A dedicated leasing sub-group focuses on international leasing transactions, and the firm has also developed a practice offering tax counseling to technology start-ups.

The Lawyers: Widely hailed as a *"leading light in international taxation,"* **Peter Blessing** (see p.506) divides his time between the firm's New York and Munich offices. Active in cross-border finance and restructuring matters, Blessing was thought to have a *"comprehensive"* knowledge of international treaties and tax arbitrage regulations.

The Clients: British Telecom; Corning; Citigroup; GKN; Novartis; CSFB; TrizecHahn; Conoco; Merrill Lynch and Thyssen Industrie.

Weil, Gotshal & Manges LLP
see firm details p.897

The Firm: While not perceived to be as visible as competitors on large M&A deals, the firm has a thriving tax practice based on its unrivaled reputation for major bankruptcy matters. This *"able young group"* provides tax support for a volume of complex restructurings, workouts and troubled company M&A transactions. While the bulk of this work is on the corporate side, the practice also has ties to a number of banks, investment funds and insurance companies, and counsels creditors on tax planning and transactional matters. The team is additionally recommended for its strength in tax controversy work; attorneys represent clients in IRS and US Treasury audits and in litigation at federal, state and appellate courts.

The Lawyers: *"Understated"* attorney **Kenneth Heitner** (see p.518) was praised for his *"excellent business judgment."* Considered a *"standout talent,"* Heitner advises on a range of merger, joint venture and restructuring transactions. Described as both *"user-friendly"* and an *"effective communicator,"* he is popular with peers and clients alike. One interviewee asserted: *"If you just had him, you'd have a strong department."* He coheads the practice with **Martin Pollack** (see p.530) who was recommended for his expertise in partnerships, joint ventures and limited liability companies. The *"terrific"* **Stuart Goldring** (see p.515) is highly regarded as a specialist in bankruptcy-related tax matters. He has experience advising debtors, creditors and potential investors in distressed companies. **Martin Amdur** (see p.503) maintains a broad-based practice that includes venture capital partnerships and REITs, reorganizations, spin-off transactions and IRS tax audit representations.

The Clients: The firm advises blue-chip domestic and international corporates. Practitioners provided tax advice to Hughes Electronics in connection with its $23 billion acquisition by EchoStar, and counseled Invensys in the $880 million disposal of its subsidiary Rexnord to The Carlyle Group.

Fried, Frank, Harris, Shriver & Jacobson
see firm details p.796

The Firm: A nine-partner practice, split between the New York and DC offices, covers all areas of corporate tax including domestic and interna-

NEW YORK

TAX

tional M&A, restructurings and capital markets transactions. The firm was particularly recommended for its expertise in real estate transactions and advises both US and foreign clients on the tax aspects of REITs and partnership agreements. Practitioners have lately been advising a group of Thailand-based investors on the acquisition and financing of NY's Plaza Atheneé Hotel. Strong ties to buyout funds such as Forstmann Little & Company provide a steady flow of private equity representations. Individual practitioners focus on capital markets and structured finance transactions, displaying particular expertise in the CDO and CBO areas.

The Lawyers: Joel Scharfstein (see p.534) is the practice's key figure. This *"personable"* attorney focuses largely on M&A and partnership matters. Scharfstein is said to possess an *"instinctive business sense,"* and was praised for his ability to *"get a deal wrapped up in 15 minutes."* Highlights of his practice include representing Procter & Gamble in its notable $1 billion peanut-butter-and-jam deal involving the spin-off of Jif/Crisco and its merger with JM Smucker, and acting for Northrop Grumman in its acquisition of Newport News Shipbuilding. Scharfstein also handles private equity, hedge fund and exchange fund work for Goldman Sachs. In DC, part-time consultant professor Martin Ginsburg continues to attract comment as a *"tax sage"* and valuable resource to the firm.

The Clients: Goldman Sachs; Procter & Gamble; Invensys; Forstmann Little & Company; The Dial Corporation; Morgan Stanley; Dow Jones & Company and Kimco Realty.

Paul, Weiss, Rifkind, Wharton & Garrison LLP

see firm details p.862

The Firm: The firm has a historical reputation for *"across the board"* strength in tax matters. Six partners and 14 associates cover the gamut of corporate tax, acting in a range of public and private M&A, REITs, reorganizations and bankruptcy-related transactions. Members also undertake a substantial amount of tax litigation in tax and district courts. The group is said to be *"stocked with good people,"* and interviewees see the appointment of a tax partner as chairman as an indication of the firm's commitment to the area.

The Lawyers: Firm chairman **Alfred Youngwood** (see p.543) commands considerable stature at the bar for his *"incisive analysis"* of issues and long experience in the field. He concentrates on acquisitions, reorganizations and financings for foreign and US corporates. He recently represented AOL Time Warner in its restructuring of Time Warner Entertainment. Also prominent is partner **David Sicular** (see p.536), who was noted for his expertise in insolvency restructurings and cross-border finance. Sicular acted for PCA International on its debt refinancing and Rule 144A offerSee firm index on page 957ing of $165 million of senior notes. He also advised on the tax aspects of Alberta Energy's acquisition by PanCanadian Energy.

The Clients: AOL Time Warner; Fomex; EMI; Carnival; British Telecom and PCA International.

Roberts & Holland LLP

The Firm: Proclaimed the *"leaders in state and real estate tax,"* this *"well-run"* tax boutique received kudos for *"sticking to their knitting."* The 40-attorney firm handles nothing but tax, with half the practice devoted to state and local tax, and half to federal tax. Matters covered include employee benefits, estate and personal planning and tax controversy. In corporate tax, the firm is seen to be less active than competitors on transactional matters and is thought to compete directly with accounting firms in general tax counseling. The firm's reputation is greatest for state and local tax matters and real estate taxation. However, strength also exists in international tax in which individuals advise on intercompany transactions and foreign business activities in the US.

The Lawyers: **Carolyn Lee** is well known for her focus on state and local taxation matters and the taxation of real property transactions. Fellow attorneys describe her as an *"extremely talented"* practitioner with *"tremendous ability."*

The Clients: The firm acts for major US corporates, foreign institutions and high net-worth individuals and families.

Other Notable Practitioners

Ben Cohen at Cahill Gordon & Reindel is well known as an *"intellectual"* tax attorney with expertise in foreign partnerships. He is frequently seen acting for GE Capital. *"Knowledgeable"* **Richard Reinhold** (see p.531) at Willkie Farr & Gallagher handles both M&A and financial products work. A *"direct and efficient"* attorney, Reinhold was recommended as someone who *"anticipates problems"* and *"cuts quickly to the bottom line."* Chair of the Milbank, Tweed, Hadley & McCloy tax practice, **Bruce Kayle** is well known at the bar for his expertise in credit derivatives, REMICs and CDOs. Peers report that this *"thoughtful"* practitioner always *"comes up with the right answers."* **Stephen Gardner** at Kronish Lieb Weiner & Hellman LLP was said to be *"as good a litigator as there is in the Western world."* He is visible representing Fortune 500 clients in the oil, financial services, banking and entertainment industries on tax controversy matters. *"Talented"* **Richard Andersen** (see p.504) remains the sole NY tax partner at Arnold & Porter. He is recognized as an expert in international tax and regulatory matters and advises sovereign states and foreign investors on tax aspects of US capital market transactions. Financial products and structured finance specialist **David Miller** (see p.525) is credited with *"single-handedly building up the practice"* at Cadwalader, Wickersham & Taft. He works frequently with CSFB, Citibank and Banc of America Securities. Clients value his *"detailed and comprehensive"* documentation. At Freshfields Bruckhaus Deringer, **Robert Scarborough** also earns praise for his work in international structured finance and financial instruments. The former chair of the state bar association tax section, Scarborough is rated highly for his *"solid judgment on hard issues."*

Leaders in New York

AARON, Roger S
Skadden, Arps, Slate, Meagher & Flom LLP & Affiliates, New York
212 735 3300
raaron@skadden.com
Recommended in Corporate/M&A
Specialization: Senior partner in charge of all corporate practice areas, including mergers and acquisitions, finance, banking and institutional investing, tax, employee benefits, investment companies, and restructuring and bankruptcy organisation. Is a frequent lecturer at various seminars and symposiums on M&A, corporate and securities law matters.
Personal: AB, Dartmouth College, 1964 (magna cum laude). MBA, Amos Tuck School of Business Administration, Dartmouth College, 1965 (with High Distinction), LLB, JD, Yale Law School, 1968.

ABRAMS, Floyd
Cahill Gordon & Reindel, New York
212 701 3900
Recommended in Media & Entertainment

ABRAMS, Marc
Willkie Farr & Gallagher, New York
212 728 8200
mabrams@willkie.com
Recommended in Insolvency
Specialization: Partner in the Business Reorganisation and Restructuring Department. Has been instrumental, on behalf of debtors, in several complex chapter 11 cases and non-judicial restructurings including Adelphia Communications Corp; Alliance Entertainment Corp; Allis-Chalmers Corp; AMF Bowling Worldwide Inc; APS Holdings Inc; Brooks Fashion Stores Inc; Community Newspapers Inc; Days Inns of America, Inc; Hechinger Company; Integrated Resources Inc; Orion Pictures, Inc; Petrie Retail Inc; Phoenix Steel Corp; Prime Hospitality Corp; LTV Corporation; The Multicare Companies; Woodward & Lothrop Incorporated and US Internetworking, Inc. Has also been actively involved (on the committee side) in the AM International Inc, Strawberries Inc, Lone Star, Inc and RCM Global Long Term Capital Appreciation Fund chapter 11 cases. Has extensive experience representing individual creditors, landlords, general partners and other parties in interest. International experience includes issues or matters involving the insolvency laws of Argentina, Australia, Bermuda, Canada, France, Germany, Mexico, Russia, Spain, Switzerland, The Netherlands and the UK among other nations.
Prof. Memberships: The Association of the Bar of the City of New York (Committee on Bankruptcy and Corporation Reorganisation), the International Bar Association, the Turnaround Management Association and the American College of Bankruptcy.
Career: Admitted to Delaware Bar (1978), Pennsylvania (1981) and New York (1985). A partner of *Willkie Farr & Gallagher* since joining the firm in 1990. A certified mediator of the US Bankruptcy Court for the Southern District of New York.
Personal: Received a JD (cum laude) from Widener University in 1978 and a BA (cum laude) from Villanova University in 1975.

ADAMS, Katherine
Sidley Austin Brown & Wood, New York
212 839 5300
Recommended in Environment

ADLER, Arthur S
Sullivan & Cromwell LLP, New York
212 558 4000
adlera@sullcrom.com
Recommended in Real Estate
Specialization: Partner in the firm's Commercial Real Estate Group. Expertise includes mortgage, mezzanine debt and preferred equity financings; securitisations and other rated public and private investment vehicles; sale-leasebacks and lease-backed financings; joint ventures and partnerships for development and investment projects; acquisitions and dispositions of improved and unimproved properties; construction contracting; insurance; and commercial office leasing. Clients include Goldman, Sachs & Co. and its affiliated Whitehall Street Real Estate Funds; Barclays Bank; Prudential Financial Group; Philips Electronics; Vornado Realty Trust; and The New York Giants.
Prof. Memberships: American Bar Association; New York State Bar Association; and Association of the Bar of the City of New York.
Career: Joined *Sullivan & Cromwell* in 1983; Partner since 1990.
Personal: Born 1958. Columbia University (AB, 1979); Columbia Law School (JD, 1982).

ADLER, Sheldon S
Skadden, Arps, Slate, Meagher & Flom LLP & Affiliates, New York
212 735 2135
sadler@skadden.com
Recommended in Energy
Specialization: Partner, New York. Primarily responsible for development of the firm's utility merger and acquisition practice, a subgroup of the Corporate Department that handles utility acquisition transactions. Represents a wide variety of clients in merger and other acquisition transactions. Involved in many recent public utility merger transactions. Has also been involved in many recent generation assets divestiture transactions. Clients include Sierra Pacific Resources, New England Electric Systems, Centrica plc., CMS Energy Corporation, and Orange & Rockland Utilities.
Personal: JD, Yale Law School, 1979 (Editor, 'Yale Law Journal'); BA, City College of New York, 1976.

AKSEN, Gerald
Thelen Reid & Priest LLP, New York
212 603 2000
Recommended in Arbitration

ALDEN, Steven M
Debevoise & Plimpton, New York
212 909 6481
smalden@debevoise.com
Recommended in Real Estate
Specialization: Partner and head of *Debevoise & Plimpton*'s Real Estate Department (1982-present). His practice concentrates in all aspects of real estate, including purchases and sales, development and leasing, and lending and borrowing. He advises clients on purchase and sale issues, financing issues, including the design and structure of mortgage loans, participating and contingent interest mortgages, sale leasebacks, leasehold mortgages, mezzanine financings, restructuring and refinancing existing loans, and workouts, bankruptcies and foreclosures.
Prof. Memberships: American College of Real Estate Lawyers; American College of Mortgage Attorneys; Association of the Bar of the City of New York's Committee on Real Property Law; American Land Title Association; New York Land Title Association; American Bar Association; New York State Bar Association; Chairman of the Board of Symphony Space.
Career: Joined *Debevoise & Plimpton* in 1971 and became a partner in 1979.
Publications: Author of numerous articles on real estate and real estate financing and is a frequent contributor to real estate publications and legal periodicals.
Personal: University of California at Los Angeles, AB, magna cum laude, 1967, Phi Beta Kappa; University of California at Berkeley, Boalt Hall School of Law, JD, 1970.

ALEXANDER, Troy
White & Case LLP, New York
212 819 8200
Recommended in Projects

ALLERHAND, Joseph
Weil, Gotshal & Manges LLP, New York
212 310 8725
joseph.allerhand@weil.com
Recommended in Litigation
Specialization: Serves as the co-head of the firm's Business and Securities Litigation Department and has been with the firm for over 20 years. Recognized expert in securities, class action and derivative litigation, corporate control contests, and mass actions. An experienced trial lawyer who has tried high profile cases in state and federal courts, and before arbitration panels for many clients of the firm including, Bear Stearns, Hicks Muse, International Paper, TWA/Carl Icahn, GAF, GE Capital and Entravision. Practice includes extensive litigation at the trial and appellate levels of a broad spectrum of complex business, securities, and corporate actions, including actions for securities fraud, breach of fiduciary duties, proxy contests and tender offers for corporate control, and violations of federal and state regulations governing securities and banking. Frequently counsels boards of directors and special committees in connection with corporate transactions. Also provides representation in proceedings before the United States Securities and Exchange Commission.
Publications: Articles include, 'Altris Dispels Notion of Automatic Liability for Botched Audits', Securities Reform Act Litigation Reporter, September 2002, 'EBankerUSA.com Takes Bespeaks Caution Doctrine to Bank', 'New York Law Journal', October 2, 2002, 'Courts Make Waves in PSLRA's Safe Harbor', 'New York Law Journal', June 14, 2001 and 'Court of Chancery Orders Tyson-IBP Merger', 'Business & Securities Litigator', August 2001.
Personal: BA, Columbia University (1975); JD, Georgetown University Law Center (1978).

AMDUR, Martin
Weil, Gotshal & Manges LLP, New York
212 310 8224
martin.amdur@weil.com
Recommended in Tax
Specialization: New York-based partner in the firm's Tax Department. Broad-based practice, ranging from the formation of private venture capital partnerships and the structuring of their investments, including taxable acquisitions and dispositions, to tax-free spin-offs and other reorganisations involving both domestic and multinational corporations. Advises on domestic and international financings, including derivatives, sophisticated real estate investments, secured finance transactions involving receivables and other intangibles, and executive compensation. Regularly represents taxpayers before the Internal Revenue Service.
Prof. Memberships: Fellow of the American College of Tax Counsel.
Personal: AB, Cornel University (1964); LLB, Yale University Law School (1967); LLM, New York University School of Law (1968).

NEW YORK

LEADERS

ANDERSEN, Richard E
Arnold & Porter, New York
212 715 1000
Richard_Andersen@aporter.com
Recommended in Tax

Specialization: Practices international tax law, both for foreign enterprises and individuals investing and doing business in the United States and for US companies' and investors' overseas activities. He has extensive experience in cross-border mergers, acquisitions and joint ventures; multinational securities offerings; the establishment of overseas branches or subsidiaries by US multinationals; foreign investment in the United States; cross-border licensing; the organization and operation of global investment funds; the design of international financial products; cross-border financing and leasing transactions; foreign tax credit planning; international transfer pricing issues; and the impact of tax treaties on US and foreign individuals and companies.
Prof. Memberships: He is a member of numerous professional associations, including the USA Branch Council of the International Fiscal Association.
Career: He has written or co-authored numerous articles on international tax matters, books on tax treaties and the foreign tax credit, and a portfolio on the US withholding tax on foreign persons. He is a frequent speaker in the United States and overseas on international topics and teaches international taxation at New York University Law School.

ANDERSON, Eugene
Anderson Kill & Olick, New York
212 278 1000
Recommended in Insurance

AQUILA, Francis J
Sullivan & Cromwell LLP, New York
212 558 4000
aquilaf@sullcrom.com
Recommended in Corporate/M&A

Specialization: M&A and corporate matters. Advises US and non-US companies on structuring, negotiating and documenting acquisitions, divestitures, mergers, tender offers and joint ventures. Extensive experience involving divisions and subsidiaries, defense from hostile bids, mergers of equals and cross-border acquisitions. Representation of Diageo in its sale of Burger King Corporation, EchoStar in its proposed combination with Hughes Electronics, British Airways in its proposed alliance with American Airlines, Medtronic in its acquisition of MiniMed and Medical Research Group, Earthgrains in its acquisition by Sara Lee, Newbridge Networks in its acquisition by Alcatel, Pillsbury in its acquisition by General Mills, SITA s.c. in the sale of the SITA Foundation's interest in Equant to France Telecom, and Diageo and Guinness UDV in their acquisition of the Seagram wines and spirits business.
Prof. Memberships: American Bar Association; Association of the Bar of the City of New York; New York State Bar Association.
Career: Joined *Sullivan & Cromwell* in 1983; Partner since 1992.
Personal: Born 1957. Columbia University (AB, 1979); Brooklyn Law School (JD, 1983). Serves on the National Advisory Board of the NALP Foundation for Education & Research, the Board of Advisors of the Salvation Army of Greater New York and the Executive Committee of St. Peter's University Hospital and Health System, where he is also Vice Chairman of the Board of Trustees.

ARONSON, Clifford H
Skadden, Arps, Slate, Meagher & Flom LLP & Affiliates, New York
212 735 2644
caronson@skadden.com
Recommended in Antitrust

Specialization: Represents clients in antitrust matters relating to mergers and acquisitions. Has experience advising clients on other types of antitrust matters and representing them before federal and state antitrust agencies as well as grand juries.
Career: Instructor, Wharton School, University of Pennsylvania; regular speaker on mergers and acquisitions, Wharton's Executive Education Program; vice-chair, Clayton Act Committee of the Antitrust Section of the American Bar Association.
Publications: Co-editor, 'Mergers and Acquisitions - Understanding the Antitrust Laws,' American Bar Association.
Personal: JD, Georgetown University Law Center, 1980; BS, Wharton School, University of Pennsylvania, 1977 (cum laude).

ARQUIT, Kevin
Simpson Thacher & Bartlett, New York
212 455 2000
Recommended in Antitrust

ATKINS, Peter Allan
Skadden, Arps, Slate, Meagher & Flom LLP & Affiliates, New York
212 735 3700
patkins@skadden.com
Recommended in Corporate/M&A

Specialization: Involved since 1968 in *Skadden*'s M&A, corporate, securities, restructuring and financial practices. Represents acquirors, targets and investment banks in mergers, acquisitions, takeovers, leveraged buyouts and joint ventures. Involved in all phases of transactions, including planning, structuring, negotiation and implementation. Counsels clients on other corporate, securities and business related matters, including corporate governance, director's duties and responsibilities, disclosure issues and investigations. Transactional involvement in airline, defense and aerospace, energy, financial institutions, forest products, health care, information technology, insurance, media and telecommunications, retail and utilities industries.
Personal: AB, Brooklyn College, 1965; LLB, Harvard University, 1968.

AUERBACH, Reed
McKee Nelson LLP, New York
917 777 4400
rauerbach@mckeenelson.com
Recommended in Capital Markets

Specialization: Represents underwriters and issuers in connection with public and private offerings of asset-backed and mortgage-backed securities and related interim warehouse financings, whole loan purchases, repurchase agreements and residual financings. Has broad-based experience with a wide variety of assets, including prime and non-prime auto loans, auto leases, equipment leases, royalty streams and other intellectual property rights, student loans, dealer floor plan receivables, telecommunication receivables, litigation settlement fees, Australian mortgage loans, manufactured housing contracts, recreational vehicle loans, boat loans, home equity loans, credit card receivables, and insurance premium finance agreements.
Career: Prior to joining *McKee Nelson*, was a partner at the New York office of *Strook & Strook & Lavan*. At *McKee Nelson*, is managing partner of the firm's New York office. Received a JD from Columbia University School of Law in 1985, where he served as Editor of the 'Journal of Transnational Law' and was a Harlan Fiske Stone Scholar.

AXINN, Stephen
Axinn Veltrop & Harkrider LLP, New York
212 728 2200
Recommended in Antitrust

BAECHER, John
Chadbourne & Parke LLP, New York
212 408 5100
jbaecher@chadbourne.com
Recommended in Projects

Specialization: Senior project finance partner concentrating on project finance and related general corporate and commercial law. Represents developers, lenders and investors in the development and financing of privately-financed independent power projects, transmission and distribution systems, ports and other associated facilities. Assists several of the largest global independent power companies in the expansion of their US holdings and in their international development and acquisition activities in Latin America and the United Kingdom. Advises developers and lenders in evaluating and responding to RFPs issued by governments and investor-owned utilities relating to the acquisition or development of projects.
Prof. Memberships: New York State Bar Association; United States District Court, Southern District of New York.

BAECHTOLD, Robert
Fitzpatrick, Cella, Harper & Scinto, New York 212 218 2100
rbaechtold@fchs.com
Recommended in Intellectual Property

Specialization: Lead counsel in litigation for major corporate clients, including Bristol-Myers Squibb, Warner-Lambert, Merck, Yamanouchi, GD Searle, Novartis, AstraZeneca, Bausch & Lomb, Pharmacia, SmithKline Beecham, Pfizer, Sanofi-Synthelabo, GSK, Hoffman La Roche, American Cyanamid, Takeda, SC Johnson & Son, Hoechst Celanese, Hoechst-Roussel, American-Maize Products, EI du Pont, and Union Carbide. Cases in 2002 include successfully asserting AstraZeneca patents against validity challenges to its $5 billion per year Prilosec's product and successfully defending a multi-billion dollar infringement claim and receiving an award of over $32 million in attorneys fees for client Bristol-Myers Squibb. Selected as one of the ten best patent lawyers in the world, in 'Euromoney's' "Best of the Best" survey in 2000 and 2002.
Prof. Memberships: President-elect, Federal Circuit Bar Association; Founding Fellow, American Intellectual Property Law Association; member of the Bars of New York, New Jersey and Pennsylvania and of several Federal District Courts and Courts of Appeal. Previously served as: Member, Advisory Committee of the Court of Appeals for the Federal Circuit; Board of Directors, American Intellectual Property Law Association and New York Intellectual Property Law Association; President, New Jersey Patent Law Association.
Career: Research Chemist, American Cyanamid Co. (1958-62); Patent Agent, M&T Chemicals (1962-65); *Ward, McElhannon, Brooks and Fitzpatrick*, joined 1965, partner 1969; *Fitzpatrick, Cella, Harper & Scinto*, founding partner, 1971.
Personal: Rutgers University (BS Chemistry); Seton Hall University School of Law (JD magna cum laude). Married with three children, five grandchildren. Enjoys music, golf, tennis, sailing and travel.

BAKER, D J (Jan)
Skadden, Arps, Slate, Meagher & Flom LLP & Affiliates, New York
212 735 2150
jbaker@skadden.com
Recommended in Insolvency

Specialization: Partner, New York. Has represented numerous public companies in restructurings. Advises officers and directors on duties and governance. Has had primary responsibility in numerous Chapter 11 cases and out-of-court restructurings. Some major matters in which he has played a leading role include: American Pad & Paper (Debtor); CIRCLE K (Debtor); FirstCity Bank Corporation (Acquiror); FoxMeyer Drug Company (Debtor); Gen-Tek (Debtor);

LEADERS NEW YORK

Global Marine (Debtor); Iridium (Committee); KCS Energy (Committee); M Corp. (Debtor); MicroAge (Debtor); Owens Corning (Debtor); Safety-Kleen (Debtor); and Sterling Chemicals (Debtor). **Personal:** JD, University of Houston Law School (editor in chief, 'Houston Law Review'); AB, Harvard University (cum laude).

BAKER JR, William T
Thelen Reid & Priest LLP, New York
212 603 2000
wbaker@thelenreid.com
Recommended in Energy

Specialization: Senior partner, chair of the firm's Utility Services Practice Group and co-chair of the firm's Energy, Utility and Infrastructure Practice. He advises public utility company clients, both electric and gas, and specializes in corporate matters with an emphasis on financing and corporate restructuring and on regulatory matters, primarily under the Public Utility Holding Company Act of 1935 (PUHCA). He was an active participant in the debate and analysis leading to reform of the PUHCA as part of the Energy Policy Act of 1992 and the Telecommunications Act of 1996, as well as in the review and study of the Act by the Securities and Exchange Commission in 1994-95.
Prof. Memberships: Chairman Emeritus of the Edison Electric Institute Legal Committee and Chairman of the Public Utility Holding Company Act of 1935 Counsel Group. Member of the Association of the Bar of the City of New York, and the American Bar Association (Member, Section on Business Law and Chair of the subcommittee on the Public Utility Holding Company Act of 1935; Member, Section on Public Utility, Transportation and Communications Law).
Personal: University of Virginia (JD, 1968); Yale University (BA, cum laude, 1965). Born in New York City, New York.

BALL, Corinne
Jones Day, New York 212 326 7844
cball@jonesday.com
Recommended in Insolvency

Specialization: Has more than 23 years experience in business finance and restructuring, with a focus on out-of-court and international restructurings, M&A involving distressed companies, and working out troubled portfolio companies. Is currently lead counsel for IBM in its effort to acquire the worldwide assets of Comdisco. Has led large and complex restructurings, including the Olympia & York Companies, Drexel Burnham Lambert, and Sammi Atlas. Has been the lead attorney for the Bondholder Committee in the Iridium Chapter 11 case, the largest US bidder for Daewoo Motor, one of the largest potential bidders for Hyundai Securities; the second lender in GST Telecommunications, Viatel Inc, RSL, and American MetroCom, as well as the lead lawyer for the largest aircraft lessor to VARIG in its restructuring; and counsel to the agent bank to Telergy, Inc, Ceteco, the Pittsburgh Penguins, the Phoenix Coyotes, the Detroit Redwings, and the Baltimore Ravens. Worked with insolvency and restructuring investments in troubled companies and finance for major lenders and investors such as IBM; General Electric Capital Corporation; General Motors; Citibank; Lazard Freres; Pirelli; Rothschild, Inc; WL Ross & Co; and SG Gowan Sports, among others. Also works extensively on corporate governance in restructuring, focusing on the accountability and other fiduciary duties of officers and directors in financially distressed situations.
Prof. Memberships: Member of the American Bar Association, currently serving as the chair of the task force on European Insolvency and chair of the New York chapter of the ABA Women Rainmakers. Member of the American College of Bankruptcy, the Association of the Bar of the City of New York, and the Corporate and Securities Law Advisory Committee of the Practising Law Institute.
Career: Admitted, New York, 1979. Joined the firm in 2001.
Publications: Contributing author to the treatise 'Reorganising Failing Businesses', recently published by the American Bar Association, focusing on cross-border insolvency. Articles and materials on insolvency and corporate governance have been published by the American Bar Association, the American Bankruptcy Institute, INSOL, the Practising Law Institute, the National Conference of Bankruptcy Judges, 'The Business Lawyer', the 'Journal of Securities/Commodities Regulation', and the 'Distress Investors Conference', among others.
Personal: Williams College (Phi Beta Kappa; BA magna cum laude, 1975); The George Washington University (JD with honours, 1978).

BARTEL, Paul
Davis Polk & Wardwell, New York
212 450 4000
Recommended in Antitrust

BARTNER, Douglas
Shearman & Sterling, New York
212 848 4000
Recommended in Insolvency

BASON, George
Davis Polk & Wardwell, New York
212 450 4000
Recommended in Corporate/M&A, Private Equity

BEATTIE, Richard
Simpson Thacher & Bartlett,
New York 212 455 2000
Recommended in Corporate/M&A, Private Equity

BELL, Thomas
Simpson Thacher & Bartlett, New York
212 455 2000
Recommended in Private Equity

BELLER, Daniel
Paul, Weiss, Rifkind, Wharton & Garrison LLP, New York 212 373 3312
dbeller@paulweiss.com
Recommended in Litigation

Specialization: A leading trial lawyer and litigator, has worked extensively in complex civil and criminal matters, including antitrust, securities, real estate and commercial litigations; internal corporate investigations and compliance; and white collar criminal defense. Has handled nearly every type of trial and litigation, including insider trading, RICO, contract, tort, mortgage foreclosure and real estate, intellectual property and bankruptcy and constitutional law. Also, represents corporate and individual clients in criminal and government enforcement investigations and has successfully handled cases involving money laundering, corruption, bribery, the Foreign Corrupt Practices Act, government procurement fraud and tax evasion.

BEN-AMI, Leora
Clifford Chance US LLP, New York
212 878 3140
leora.benami@cliffordchance.com
Recommended in Intellectual Property

Specialization: Serves as Chair of the region's Intellectual Property Group and is a member of the region's management group. Her practice covers all areas of technology, including biotechnology, pharmaceutical and chemistry, medical devices, mechanical devices and electronics. The verdict she won in Glaxo v Genentech was cited by the 'National Law Journal' as 'defense verdict of the year'; and she is also listed as 'highly recommended' in intellectual property by a leading legal publication.

BENEDICT, James
Clifford Chance US LLP, New York
212 878 8274
james.benedict@cliffordchance.com
Recommended in Litigation

Specialization: Serves as global head of the firm's Litigation and Dispute Resolution Practice and is a member of the region's Management group. He recently served as Managing Partner of the Americas region. He specializes in complex commercial litigation, with emphasis on multiparty class and derivative suits in state and federal courts across the nation. He has handled trial and appellate civil litigation, involving securities and antitrust issues, for some of the largest corporations in America, including Coca-Cola, MasterCard, Merrill Lynch and Prudential Financial. Has published over three dozen articles and is active in professional and charitable organizations.

BERG, Eric
White & Case LLP, New York
212 819 8200
Recommended in Banking & Finance

BERGTRAUM, Howard
O'Melveny & Myers LLP, New York
212 408 2400
Recommended in Private Equity

BERNSTEIN, Donald
Davis Polk & Wardwell, New York
212 450 4000
Recommended in Insolvency

BERNSTEIN, Michael
Benetar Bernstein Schair & Stein,
New York 212 697 4433
Recommended in Employment

BESHAR, Sarah
Davis Polk & Wardwell, New York
212 450 4000
Recommended in Capital Markets

BIALKIN, Kenneth J
Skadden, Arps, Slate, Meagher & Flom LLP & Affiliates, New York
212 735 2130
kbialkin@skadden.com
Recommended in Corporate/M&A

Specialization: Extensive experience in representing insurance companies, broker-dealers, investment banks and other financial institutions. Has represented US and non-US companies in connection with US public and private offerings, and government and regulatory investigations by agencies as the SEC and the Department of Justice.
Prof. Memberships: Legal Advisory Committee (or subcommittees thereof) of the Board of Directors of the New York Stock Exchange, Inc. (1981-present); Chair, Ad Hoc Committee on Insider Trading Legislation, Section on Business Law, American Bar Association (1987-present).
Personal: AB University of Michigan, 1950; Certificate of Attendance, London School of Economics, 1952; JD Harvard Law School, 1953.

BICK, John
Davis Polk & Wardwell, New York
212 450 4000
Recommended in Private Equity

BIENENSTOCK, Martin
Weil, Gotshal & Manges LLP, New York
212 310 8530
martin.bienenstock@weil.com
Recommended in Insolvency

Specialization: Partner in the Business Finance Restructuring Department of *Weil, Gotshal & Manges LLP*. Has practised with the firm for 24 years. Practice consists of representing creditors, debtors and investors in restructuring troubled companies in and out of chapter 11, counseling boards of directors for companies facing material problems and counseling firms that create or trade

derivatives. Led the firm's representation of numerous statutory creditors' committees in such cases as Caldor Corporation; Discovery Zone; Lomas Mortgage USA, Inc; New Valley Corporation; Ames Department Stores, Inc; National Gypsum Corporation and IFRB Corporation. In out-of-court restructurings, is frequently involved in the firm's representation of Chase Manhattan Bank; Citicorp; Bank of Montreal; Barclays Bank PLC and Banque Paribus. On the debtor's side, was actively involved in the firm's representation of G-I Holdings, Inc; KCS Energy Inc; Pergament; Bradlees; Texaco Inc; and Global Marine Inc.
Prof. Memberships: American College of Bankruptcy Lawyers; American College of Commercial Finance Lawyers.
Publications: Wrote a 1,000 page treatise on chapter 11, entitled 'Bankruptcy Reorganization', published by Practicing Law Institute. Frequently speaks at programmes arranged by the American Bar Association, the Southwest Legal Foundation, the New York State Bar Association, the Practising Law Institute and other institutions.
Personal: JD, University of Michigan (1977); BS, University of Pennsylvania, Wharton School (1974).

BIRNBAUM, Sheila L
Skadden, Arps, Slate, Meagher & Flom LLP & Affiliates, New York
212 735 2450
sbirnbau@skadden.com
Recommended in Litigation
Specialization: Head of *Skadden's* Products Liability Department. Practices primarily in the areas of products liability, toxic torts and insurance coverage litigation. Represents corporations in complex mass tort and insurance litigation.
Career: Associate Dean of the Graduate Division (1982-84), Professor of Law (1978-84) and Adjunct Professor of Law (1984-present), New York University School of Law; Professor of Law, Fordham University School of Law (1972-78).
Publications: Co-author, 'Practitioner's Guide to Litigating Insurance Coverage Actions'.
Personal: LLB, New York University School of Law, 1965; MA, Hunter College, 1962; BA, Hunter College, 1960 (cum laude; Phi Beta Kappa).

BLASSBERG, Franci J
Debevoise & Plimpton, New York
212 909 6531
fjblassberg@debevoise.com
Recommended in Private Equity
Specialization: Partner at *Debevoise & Plimpton* and co-head of *Debevoise & Plimpton's* Private Equity Group. Practice concentrates in the areas of private equity and mergers and acquisitions. She represents private equity clients in their acquisition and related activities and has extensive experience counselling private and public companies in domestic and international acquisitions and divestitures, securities offerings and other transactions. Recent representations include: Clayton, Dubilier & Rice in its US and cross-border transactions; USA Group in its sale to SLM Holding Corp (Sallie Mae); North Castle Partners in its acquisitions and investment activities and Merrill Lynch in a variety of its private equity activities. She is a frequent speaker at seminars and has co-chaired for many years the annual Advance ALI-ABA Course of Study on Corporate Mergers and Acquisitions sponsored by the American Law Institute - American Bar Association Committee on Continuing Professional Education.
Career: Joined *Debevoise & Plimpton* in 1977 and became partner in 1985.
Publications: Originated and acts as Editor in Chief of 'The Debevoise & Plimpton Private Equity Report' and is a frequent contributor to legal and other periodicals.
Personal: Cornell University, BA, with Distinction, 1975; Cornell Law School, JD, magna cum laude, 1977.

BLESSING, Peter
Shearman & Sterling, New York
212 848 4000
Recommended in Tax

BLOCK, Dennis
Cadwalader, Wickersham & Taft, New York 212 504 5555
dennis.block@cwt.com
Recommended in Corporate/M&A, Litigation
Specialization: Head of *Cadwalader's* Corporate Department, he concentrates on mergers and acquisitions and other corporate transactions, corporate governance, and securities law. Has handled numerous M&A transactions, both hostile and friendly, on behalf of acquirers and targets, joint ventures, self-tender offers, spin-offs, and other corporate restructurings. Has participated in many highly visible transactions including Pfizer Inc.'s acquisition of Pharmacia, Vivendi Universal's acquisition of Houghton Mifflin Co, Pepsi-Cola's acquisition of Quaker Oats, Pfizer Inc.'s acquisition of Warner-Lambert, and US West's merger with Qwest, among many others. Has represented numerous Board Committees involved in corporate transactions, and public companies, investment and commercial banks, and entrepreneurs in connection with major issues of public interest and debate, including the Business Roundtable regarding corporate governance issues, Texaco regarding discrimination matters, Cendant directors, and Merrill Lynch (negotiator on the US$1 billion settlement of Orange County and Nasdaq).
Career: Graduate of Brooklyn Law School, where he now serves as an Adjunct Professor teaching Advanced Corporate Law. Was Branch Chief of Enforcement at the New York Regional Office of the Securities and Exchange Commission.
Publications: Participated in drafting 'The Corporate Directors Guidebook' and portions of the Revised Model Business Corporation Act. A frequent author and lecturer whose many publications include 'The Business Judgment Rule: Fiduciary Duties of Corporate Directors' (co-author), 'The Corporate Counsellor's Deskbook' (co-editor), and a monthly column in the New York Law Journal. Member of the editorial boards of several legal publications.

BLUMKIN, Linda R
Fried, Frank, Harris, Shriver & Jacobson, New York 212 859 8085
Linda.Blumkin@FriedFrank.com
Recommended in Antitrust
Specialization: Antitrust partner. Focuses practice in antitrust litigation and counseling, with special emphasis on M&A (including the premerger notification requirements of the Hart-Scott Rodino Act) compliance and litigation matters. Regularly represents clients before the FTC and in dealings with the Antitrust Division of the Department of Justice and litigates in federal court. Representative clients include El Paso Corporation, the Scotts Company and Hunter Douglas Inc.
Prof. Memberships: Former Chair, American Bar Association's Clayton Act Committee, Antitrust Section; member of the ABA's Sections on Antitrust Law and Litigation; member of the Association of the Bar of the City of New York, where formerly a member of the Committee on Trade Regulation, the Committee on Women in the Profession and the Committee on Science and Law; member of the Executive Committee of the New York State Bar Association's Antitrust Law Section.
Career: Qualified in 1968 in New York. Joined firm in 1967 and rejoined as a partner in 1979. Assistant Director for General Litigation, Bureau of Competition, Federal Trade Commission (1977-79); Associate at *Breed, Abbott & Morgan* (1973-77); and assistant professor at Boston University's School of Management (1972-73); assistant professor at Boston University's School of Law (1971).
Publications: Co-edited 'Corporate Sentencing Guidelines: Compliance and Mitigation' (Law Journal Seminars Press).
Personal: Born 1944. Achieved LLB, cum laude, in 1967, LLM in 1973 from Harvard Law School. Received AB, cum laude, in 1964 from Barnard College, where was elected to Phi Beta Kappa.

BOAST, Molly S
Debevoise & Plimpton, New York
212 909 1069
msboast@debevoise.com
Recommended in Antitrust
Specialization: Partner at *Debevoise & Plimpton*, practice concentrates on antitrust and other complex litigation, merger analysis, antitrust counselling. Served in the Bureau of Competition of the Federal Trade Commission, as Senior Deputy Director and as Director. Principal responsibility for successful litigation challenges to BP/ARCO and Heinz/Beech-Nut mergers. Oversaw litigation challenges to patent settlement agreements between branded and generic pharmaceutical manufacturers. Current representations include plaintiffs and defendants in antitrust and other major litigations, a party in a joint Department of Justice/EU price fixing investigation and merger parties.
Prof. Memberships: Federal Bar Council; ABA Section of Antitrust Law, American Law Institute.
Career: *LeBoeuf, Lamb, Greene & MacRae*, LLP 1979-99 (partner 1988-99); Federal Trade Commission (1999-2001); joined *Debevoise & Plimpton* as partner in 2001.
Publications: The George Washington Law Review, 'Federal Trade Commission Remedies: Shattering the Myths', Vol. 69, number 5/6, October/December 2001. Speeches: 'Protecting Privilege Under US Law', IBA 6th Annual Competition Conference, Florence, Italy, 9/2002; 'Antitrust Limits To Patent Settlements and Licenses', ABA Antitrust Section Fall Forum, Washington, DC, 11/2002.
Personal: College of William and Mary, BA with honours 1970; Columbia School of Journalism, MS 1971; Columbia University School of Law, JD 1979.

BOHM, Richard D
Debevoise & Plimpton, New York
212 909 6226
rdbohm@debevoise.com
Recommended in Private Equity
Specialization: Partner and co-chair of *Debevoise & Plimpton's* Private Equity Practice Group and Media and Technology Practice Group. His clients include financial sponsors such as Kelso & Company and Schroder Venture Partners, and their respective investment funds and portfolio companies, and media companies for whom he advises with respect to acquisitions, divestitures, joint ventures, public offerings, private offerings, bank financings, licensing and other corporate matters. Recent representations include representing Kelso in the sale of Charter Communications to Paul Allen and representing Goldman, Sachs & Co in taking Charter public; and representing the purchaser in taking private the Cleveland Indians major league baseball team.
Prof. Memberships: Association of the

LEADERS NEW YORK

Bar of the City of New York; American Bar Association.
Career: Joined *Debevoise & Plimpton* in 1978 and became a partner in 1986.
Personal: Stanford University, BA with Honors, 1975; Harvard Law School, JD, cum laude, 1978.

BOIES, David
Boies, Schiller & Flexner LLP, New York
914 749 8200
Recommended in Antitrust, Litigation

BOROWITZ, Peter L
Debevoise & Plimpton, New York
212 909 6525
plborowitz@debevoise.com
Recommended in Insolvency
Specialization: Partner at *Debevoise & Plimpton*. His practice concentrates on creditors' rights in bankruptcy and debt restructuring.
Prof. Memberships: American Bar Association.
Career: Joined *Debevoise & Plimpton* in 1978 and became a partner in 1986.
Publications: 'Waiving Subrogation Rights and Conjuring Up Demons in Response to 'Deprizio', 45 'Business Lawyer' 2151 (1990); 'A New Twist on Twist Cap: Invalidating a Preferential Letter of Credit in In re Air Conditioning', 103 'Banking Law Journal' 368 (1986) and 'Real Property Foreclosure as a Fraudulent Conveyance: Proposals for Solving the Durrett Problem', 38 'Business Lawyer' 1605 (1983).
Personal: Harvard College, AB, summa cum laude, 1974; Harvard Law School, JD, magna cum laude, 1978. 'Harvard Law Review'. Sears Prize.

BOSTELMAN, John T
Sullivan & Cromwell LLP, New York
212 558 4000
bostelmanj@sullcrom.com
Recommended in Capital Markets
Specialization: Coordinates *S&C*'s global securities practice. Areas of focus include public and private securities offerings, investment management, commodities and derivatives and broker-dealer regulation. Broad securities experience includes SEC-registered public offerings, unregistered Rule 144A offerings and Regulation S offerings for issuers in variety of businesses, including those in banking, computers, electronics, entertainment, investment companies, natural gas, publishing, radio broadcasting, retailing, telecommunications, securities brokerage and steel.
Prof. Memberships: American Bar Association (Vice Chair of the Securities Registration Subcommittee of the Federal Regulation of Securities Committee); Association of the Bar of the City of New York; New York State Bar Association.
Career: Joined *Sullivan & Cromwell* in 1979; partner since 1986.
Personal: Born 1953. Yale University (BA, 1975); Columbia Law School (JD, 1979).

BOWIE, Scott
Latham & Watkins LLP, New York
212 906 1285
scott.bowie@lw.com
Recommended in Private Equity
Specialization: Partner in the New York office. Represents a broad array of management buyout, venture capital, debt and other investment fund sponsors, whose funds range from US$100 million to US$6 billion of committed capital. Representative clients include Kohlberg Kravis Roberts & Co., The Carlyle Group and Bear Stearns.
Prof. Memberships: New York and California Bar Associations.
Career: Joined *Latham & Watkins* in 1988 and became partner in 1996.
Personal: JD, University of California, Los Angeles, 1988. Undergraduate studies were at The London School of Economics and at Occidental College, where he received an AB, cum laude with Highest Honors, in 1984.

BOXER, Leonard
Stroock & Stroock & Lavan LLP,
New York 212 806 5400
Recommended in Real Estate

BRACH, Richard
Milbank, Tweed, Hadley & McCloy,
New York 212 530 5000
Recommended in Projects

BRANDES, Lawrence
Cadwalader, Wickersham & Taft,
New York 212 504 6946
larry.brandes@cwt.com
Recommended in Litigation
Specialization: An experienced reinsurance litigator who has acted as counsel, arbitrator or umpire in more than 500 reinsurance arbitrations and litigations, a number of which have established industry precedents. A frequent lecturer on reinsurance arbitration and litigation, he has addressed the Independent Reinsurance Underwriters, the Society of CPCU, the American Bar Association, the British Commercial Bar Association, Executive Enterprises, Inc., and numerous Mealey's conferences. Co-Chair of Mealey's 2003 Insurance Insolvency and Reinsurance Roundtable.
Prof. Memberships: New York State Bar Association; American Bar Association - Tort and Insurance Practice Section; Association of the Bar of the City of New York (served as a member of the Insurance Law Committee and Chairman of the Reinsurance Subcommittee); and British Commercial Bar Association (Honorary Overseas Member).
Career: Former Executive Vice President of APP-CAP Reinsurance Company, Ltd., Hamilton, Bermuda; former Chairman of the Board of Directors of National Consulting Services, Inc., a professional reinsurance auditing company.
Personal: BA, with distinction, University of Virginia (1971); JD, New York University School of Law (1974)(member of the Law Review).

BRANDOW, John
Davis Polk & Wardwell, New York
212 450 4000
Recommended in Capital Markets

BRANNAN, William
Cravath, Swaine & Moore, New York
212 474 1000
Recommended in Tax

BRESLOW, Stephanie
Schulte Roth & Zabel LLP, New York
212 756 2000
Recommended in Private Equity

BROWN, Dickson
Simpson Thacher & Bartlett, New York
212 455 2000
Recommended in Tax

BROWN, Meredith
Debevoise & Plimpton, New York
212 909 6528
mmbrown@debevoise.com
Recommended in Corporate/M&A
Specialization: Partner; co-chair of *Debevoise & Plimpton*'s Corporate Department (1991-2002) and Mergers and Acquisitions Group (1985-present). Works primarily on mergers and acquisitions and securities matters. Recent representations include Zurich Scudder Investments in its sale to Deutsche Bank, Goldman Sachs as financial advisor to AT&T in selling its broadband business to Comcast, and Chrysler in its merger with Daimler.
Career: Judicial Clerk, US Court of Appeals, Second Circuit (1965-66). Joined *Debevoise & Plimpton* in 1966 and became a partner in 1973.
Publications: Co-author 'Takeovers: A Strategic Guide to Mergers & Acquisitions' (Aspen Law & Business, 2001); Editor, 'International Mergers & Acquisitions' (Kluwer 1988); Co-editor, 'Mechanics of Global Offerings' (Kluwer 1995).
Personal: Harvard College, AB, summa cum laude, 1961; Harvard Law School, JD, magna cum laude, 1965.

BROWNSTEIN, Andrew R
Wachtell, Lipton, Rosen & Katz,
New York 212 403 1233
arbrownstein@wlrk.com
Recommended in Corporate/M&A
Specialization: Specializes in mergers and acquisitions, takeovers, leveraged buyouts, corporate governance and securities law matters. Has been a leading participant in numerous precedent setting transactions, including: the takeover defenses of Household International, Inc., Phillips Petroleum Company, Inc., Revlon and Universal Foods; the complex restructurings of WR Grace & Co.'s medical services and packaging divisions in successive Morris Trust transactions with Fresenius AG and Sealed Air Corporation; and Household International's acquisition of Beneficial Corporation. More recently, advised Phillips Petroleum Company, in its merger with Conoco, Inc., its acquisitions of Tosco Corporation and ARCO Chemical Company's Alaskan assets and its joint ventures with Chevron and Duke Energy Corporation, counselled the Special Committee of the Board of Directors of The Hertz Corporation in connection with a going private proposal from Ford Motor Company, and represented Amoco Corporation in its merger with British Petroleum Corporation and Reynolds in its merger with Alcoa Inc. Also active in the technology area; represented Proxicom, Inc. in its merger with Dimension Data plc, Packard BioScience Company in its merger with PerkinElmer Inc. and HotJobs.com, Ltd. in its merger with TMP Worldwide Inc. Also represents several leading private equity investors, including Apollo Advisors LP and Warburg, Pincus & Co Inc.
Prof. Memberships: Has been an adjunct professor of securities law at Rutgers University Law School; was past chairman of the Ray Garrett Jr Corporate and Securities Law Institute at Northwestern University School of Law; is on the executive planning committee of that Institute; and is co-chairman of the Annual M&A Lawyers Institute held in New York City.
Career: Partner at *Wachtell, Lipton, Rosen & Katz* since 1985, member of the management committee of the firm. Clerked for the Honorable Leonard Garth of the US Court of Appeals for the Third Circuit.
Publications: Frequent author and lecturer on legal subjects.
Personal: Graduated from the University of Pennsylvania in 1975 (BA, English, BS, Economics), from the Wharton School of the University of Pennsylvania in 1976 (MBA) and from Harvard Law School in 1979 (JD), where he was Articles Editor of the 'Harvard Law Review'.

BUDOFSKY, Daniel
Davis Polk & Wardwell, New York
212 450 4000
Recommended in Capital Markets

BURESH, James
Simpson Thacher & Bartlett,
New York 212 455 2000
Recommended in Banking & Finance

BURKE, Arthur
Davis Polk & Wardwell, New York
212 450 4000
Recommended in Antitrust

BURKE, Ray
Burke & Parsons, New York
212 354 3800
Recommended in Shipping

NEW YORK — LEADERS

BURKE, Ted
Freshfields Bruckhaus Deringer LLP, New York 212 277 4000
Recommended in Projects

BURRELL, Lizabeth
Levy Phillips & Konigsberg LLP, New York 212 605 6200
Recommended in Shipping

BYOWITZ, Michael H
Wachtell, Lipton, Rosen & Katz, New York 212 403 1268
mhbyowitz@wlrk.com
Recommended in Antitrust

Specialization: Heads the Antitrust Department, focusing on antitrust law and policy, and principally advising multinational corporations on major domestic and international mergers, acquisitions, joint ventures and corporate takeovers. Represents many clients before the Department of Justice, the Federal Trade Commission, and State Attorneys General in the United States and consults on investigations by foreign antitrust authorities in the European Union, Canada, Mexico, South America, Australia and elsewhere.
Prof. Memberships: A leader of the American Bar Association's Section of International Law & Practice; Chair of the Section's General Division and former Chair of its Business Regulation Division, its Public International Law Division and its International Antitrust Law Committee; and served as Chair of the Antitrust and Trade Regulation Committee of the Association of the Bar of the City of New York.
Career: Partner at *Wachtell, Lipton, Rosen & Katz*. Served as Senior Trial Attorney and Trial Attorney with the Department of Justice's Antitrust Division from 1979-83.
Publications: Writes articles on antitrust issues and is a contributor to legal publications, including two ABA books, 'The International Lawyer's Deskbook' and 'The Merger Review Process'. Frequent speaker on International Antitrust Law and Compliance in the United States and abroad.
Personal: Graduated from Columbia University in 1973 (AB) and from New York University School of Law in 1976 (JD), where he was awarded the Order of the Coif and served as an editor of the 'Law Review'.

CAMPBELL JR, Woodrow W
Debevoise & Plimpton, New York 212 909 6779
wwcampbell@debevoise.com
Recommended in Private Equity

Specialization: Partner and head of *Debevoise & Plimpton*'s Investment Management Practice Group (1990-present). His practice concentrates on organising private equity, venture capital, hedge and other similar private investment pools and has a significant international component with clients active in Europe, Latin America and Asia. Frequent speaker at conferences, serving, for example, as the Chair of PLI 2002 Private Equity Forum. He is a member of the Association of the Bar of the City of New York (Securities Regulation Committee, 1992-95), the International Bar Association, Section on Business Law (founder and Chair of Committee 11 Private Investment Companies, 1995-97) and the American Bar Association (Subcommittee on Investment Companies and Investment Advisors, 1995-2000). He is a member of the Board of Visitors of the Columbia Law School. In 2001 he completed a term on the Board of Directors of the 'Columbia Law Review'.
Prof. Memberships: Association of the Bar of the City of New York; International Bar Association; American Bar Association.
Career: Served in US Marine Corps, to rank of Captain (1967-70). Judicial Clerk, US Court of Appeals, Second Circuit (1973-74). Joined *Debevoise & Plimpton* in 1974 and became a partner in 1982.
Personal: Yale College, BA, 1966; Columbia Law School, JD, 1973.

CANELLOS, Peter C
Wachtell, Lipton, Rosen & Katz, New York 212 403 1241
pcanellos@wlrk.com
Recommended in Tax

Specialization: Specializes in the tax aspects of the corporate acquisitions, dispositions and financings that constitute *Wachtell, Lipton, Rosen & Katz*'s major practice areas, whose large and complex transactions frequently involve multinational tax considerations.
Prof. Memberships: Served as Chairman of the New York State Bar Association Tax Section.
Career: Partner at *Wachtell, Lipton, Rosen & Katz*. Clerked for the Honorable Judge Charles D Breitel of the New York Court of Appeals and was a Fulbright Scholar at the University of Amsterdam in the Netherlands.
Publications: Frequent writer and lecturer on tax matters. Published articles include: 'Contingency and the Debt/Equity Continuum' (with Deborah Paul, in the 'Journal of Financial Products', 2002); 'A Tax Practitioner's Perspective on Substance, Form and Business Purpose in Structuring Business Transactions and in Tax Shelters' (in 'SMU Law Review', 2001); 'Reasonable Expectations and the Taxation of Contingencies' (in 'Tax Lawyer', 1997); 'Dividend Access Shares' (49th IFA Congress, Cannes, 1995); and 'Corporate Inversions and Similar Transactions' (in the 54th NYU Annual Institute on Federal Taxation, 1995).
Personal: Graduated summa cum laude from Columbia University (BA), where he was elected to Phi Beta Kappa, and magna cum laude from Columbia Law School in 1967 (LLB), where he was editor in chief of 'Columbia Law Review'.

CARY, George
Cleary Gottlieb Steen & Hamilton, Washington, DC 202 974 1500
gcary@cgsh.com
Recommended in Antitrust

Specialization: Antitrust counseling and litigation, focusing on mergers and acquisitions. Representative clients and transactions: Dow Chemical (Union Carbide), Time Warner (AOL and EMI), SmithKline Beecham (GlaxoWelcome), Cable & Wireless (MCI Internet), Northern Telecom (Bay Networks), Conoco (Phillips Petroleum).
Prof. Memberships: California and DC Bars. ABA Antitrust Section, (past Chair, Government Antitrust Litigation Committee).
Career: Joined firm as a partner, 1998. Deputy Director, Bureau of Competition, Federal Trade Commission (1995-98) (responsible for merger enforcement), Partner, Irell & Manella (1984-95). JD, Boalt Hall School of Law, UC Berkeley (1976), BA, (Economics) UC Santa Cruz (1973). Trial Attorney, FTC Bureau of Competition (1976-84).

CARTER, James H
Sullivan & Cromwell LLP, New York 212 558 4000
carterj@sullcrom.com
Recommended in Arbitration

Specialization: Partner in Litigation Department and Coordinator of *Sullivan & Cromwell*'s Arbitration Practice. Principal area of practice is international arbitration, as counsel and arbitrator, in ICC, LCIA, AAA, CPR, ICSID, ad hoc proceedings and other fora. Typical cases are international joint venture, investment and intellectual property licensing disputes.
Prof. Memberships: AAA Executive Committee Chair and Chair of International Arbitrator Training Development Group; AAA and CPR Arbitration Rules Revisions committees; LCIA Court member; Court of Arbitration for Sport member; former Member, NAFTA Advisory Committee on Private Commercial Disputes; member, WIPO Arbitration Consultative Commission; Swiss Arbitration Association; International Arbitration Institute; former Chair, American Bar Association Section of International Law and Practice; former Chair, New York State Bar Association International Dispute Resolution Committee; former Chair, Association of the Bar of the City of New York Council on International Affairs; former VP, American Society of International Law.
Career: Joined *Sullivan & Cromwell* in 1970. Became partner in 1977.
Publications: 25 arbitration articles.
Personal: Born 1943. Graduate of Yale College and Yale Law School; Fulbright Scholar at Cambridge University.

CASE, Stephen
Davis Polk & Wardwell, New York 212 450 4000
Recommended in Insolvency

CASTEL, Kevin
Cahill Gordon & Reindel, New York 212 701 3900
Recommended in Litigation

CENDALI, Dale
O'Melveny & Myers LLP, New York 212 326 2000
Recommended in Media & Entertainment

CHADAKOFF, Richard
Latham & Watkins LLP, New York 212 906 1210
richard.chadakoff@lw.com
Recommended in Real Estate

Specialization: Head of firm's 75-member Global Real Estate Department. Experience in the business and legal aspects of commercial real estate development, investment, financing, leasing and related transactions. Representation of foreign and domestic developers, owners, lenders, borrowers, tenants, landlords and venturers, both institutional and noninstitutional. Primary real estate financing counsel for General Electric Capital Corporation for past 20 years and its lead counsel for corporate leasing and real estate projects.
Personal: JD, Georgetown University Law Center, 1972. MBA, Harvard University, 1974.

CHAFFETZ, Peter
Clifford Chance US LLP, New York 212 878 4910
peter.chaffetz@cliffordchance.com
Recommended in Insurance

Specialization: Serves as the US practice group leader for reinsurance litigation and arbitration, and he was recently elected to serve on the firm's partnership council. He has played a prominent role in some of the most significant reinsurance issues in recent years including major coverage disputes against London reinsurers, disputes arising from managing general agencies and the fallout from the collapse of the Unicover Occupational Accident Pool. Regularly speaks and publishes in the field.

CHANG, Leo
Watson, Farley & Williams, New York 212 922 2200
Recommended in Shipping

CHEPIGA, Michael
Simpson Thacher & Bartlett, New York 212 455 2000
Recommended in Litigation

LEADERS NEW YORK

CHESLER, Evan
Cravath, Swaine & Moore, New York
212 474 1000
Recommended in Antitrust, Litigation

CHINN, Adam D
Wachtell, Lipton, Rosen & Katz,
New York 212 403 1213
Recommended in Tax
Specialization: Specializes in both merger and acquisition tax practice and its transaction, related executive compensation practice, with a particular emphasis on transactions involving financial services institutions.
Career: Partner at *Wachtell, Lipton, Rosen & Katz*.
Publications: Has written and spoken frequently on tax and executive compensation issues. Is the author of the chapter on 'Change of Control Arrangements in Executive Compensation' ('Law Journal' Seminars-Press 1996) and 'Bank Mergers: Change of Control Employment Arrangements and Employee Benefit Aspects of Merger Agreements', 15 'Bank and Corporate Governance Law Reporter' at 8 (September 1995).
Personal: Graduated from Oxford University, England in 1982 (BA), from the College of Law, England in 1983 (CPE) and cum laude from New York University in 1987 (JD) where he was Order of the Coif and Editor, 'New York University Law Review' and author: Note 'Attacking Tax Shelters 183 Leaves the Farm and Goes to the Movies', 61, 'New York University Law Review', 89, 1986.

CITRON, Diane
Mayer, Brown, Rowe & Maw, New York
212 506 2520
dcitron@mayerbrownrowe.com
Recommended in Capital Markets
Specialization: Partner and Co-Head of the firm's Securitization Practice. Represents investment banks and financial institutions in structuring and developing foreign and domestic residential and commercial mortgage-backed programs and conduits for the issuance of MBS and CMBS in the United States and global markets. Represents underwriters and issuers in public and private offerings of asset-backed securities. Experienced in interest rate, currency, and total return swaps as used in connection with various structured financings. Represents financial institutions, corporations, and development companies in issuance of corporate debt, limited partnerships, initial public offerings, thrift mergers and acquisitions, and acquisitions of commercial and residential real estate portfolios as well as portfolios of other financial assets. Previous government experience.
Prof. Memberships: Admitted to practise in California, 1985, and District of Columbia, 1978. Adjunct Professor, John Marshall Law School, Real Estate LLM Program, 'Real Estate Securitization'

1995-99. Chair, Subcommittee on Education, American Securitization Forum.
Career: Joined *Mayer, Brown, Rowe & Maw* as a partner (1992); *Skadden, Arps, Slate, Meagher & Flom* (1987-92); *Brown & Wood* (1985-87); *Orrick, Herrington & Sutcliffe* (1984-85); and *Wasserman, Orlow, Ginsberg & Rubin* (1977-80). Staff Attorney, SEC, Division of Enforcement (1980-83) and Senior Counsel, Federal Home Loan Mortgage Corporation (1983-84).
Publications: Author, 'The Legal Aspects of Lease Securitization', 'Banking and Financial Services Reporter', Vol. 9, No. 16, September 29, 1993. Lectures widely on securitization at industry-related conferences.
Personal: Born 9 October 1953. JD, Case Western Reserve University School of Law, 1978; BA, Franklin and Marshall College, 1975. Fluent in Spanish.

CLARK, Jim
Cahill Gordon & Reindel, New York
212 701 3900
Recommended in Capital Markets

CLARK, Peter
Clark, Atcheson & Reisert, New York
212 297 0257
Recommended in Shipping

COCHRAN, Eric L
Skadden, Arps, Slate, Meagher & Flom LLP & Affiliates, New York
212 735 2596
ecochran@skadden.com
Recommended in Corporate/M&A
Specialization: Partner, New York. Concentrates in mergers and acquisitions, securities law and general corporate law.
Career: Regularly on the faculty of Practising Law Institute seminars, speaking on corporate and securities topics.
Personal: JD, New York University School of Law, 1986; MS, New York University, 1984; and BA, Williams College, 1982.

COGUT, Charles
Simpson Thacher & Bartlett, New York
212 455 2000
Recommended in Corporate/M&A, Private Equity

COHEN, Ben
Cahill Gordon & Reindel, New York
212 701 3900
Recommended in Tax

COHEN, H Rodgin
Sullivan & Cromwell LLP, New York
212 558 4000
cohenhr@sullcrom.com
Recommended in Banking & Finance, Corporate/M&A
Specialization: Regulatory, acquisitions and securities laws matters for domestic and foreign banking and financial institutions. Advises on regulatory matters with the four banking regulatory agencies and other governmental agencies; represents many of the largest US and non-US banking institutions, and the New York

Clearing House. Matters include bank product and geographic powers, restrictions on bank operations, insurance of bank deposits, the Community Reinvestment Act, and Bank Secrecy Act and money laundering. Engaged in most of the major US bank acquisitions, including First Union-Wachovia, Wells Fargo-Norwest, US Bancorp-Firstar and numerous others. In cross-border transactions, engaged in Allianz-Dresdner, UBS-PaineWebber, Société Générale-Paribas, Mitsubishi-Bank of Tokyo and numerous others. Worked on the first US public offering by a foreign bank and on numerous US offerings by US and foreign banks. Participated in the resolution of most major US bank failures.
Prof. Memberships: ABA; ABCNY; NYSBA; West Virginia Bar Association; Westchester County Bar Association.
Career: Joined *S&C* 1970. Partner since 1977; Vice Chairman in 1999; Chairman since 2000.
Publications: Frequent speaker on banking law matters; author of numerous articles on commercial banking issues.
Personal: Born 1944. Harvard College (AB, magna cum laude, 1965); Harvard Law School (LLB, 1968). Member, Board of Advisors, Banking Law Review; Member, National Board of Contributors of the American Lawyer Newspaper Group; Trustee, New York Presbyterian Hospital and Hackley School.

COHEN, Michael Marks
Nicoletti Hornig Campise Sweeney & Paige, New York 212 220 3830
Recommended in Shipping

COLLINS, Joseph P
Mayer, Brown, Rowe & Maw, New York
212 506 2657
jcollins@mayerbrownrowe.com
Recommended in Capital Markets
Specialization: Practice Leader, Futures, Securities, and Derivatives Law Practice. Represents brokerage firms, investment management clients, trading and investment advisors, hedge fund operators, investment companies, banks, and pension plans. Practice encompasses securities, futures, forwards, swaps, options, and hybrid securities. Lead attorney in Refco Group's acquisitions of Lind-Waldock, LFG, and Main Street Trading Company and Ameritrade's acquisition of Datek. Active in investment funds and structured derivative transactions.
Prof. Memberships: Member, ABA, Chair, Committee on Regulation of Futures and Derivatives Instruments; Association of the Bar of the City of New York, Futures Regulation Committee; past Chair, Futures Law Committee of the Chicago Bar Association; Faculty, IIT-Kent College of Law's Financial Services Law Graduate Program.
Career: Joined *Mayer, Brown, Rowe & Maw* as partner in 1994 following 19

years with *Schiff Hardin & Waite*.
Publications: Participant at ABA Committee on Regulation of Futures and Derivatives Instruments Conferences, SIA and FIA Law and Compliance Conferences, Kent Financial Services Law Conferences, and various other panels and workshops regarding derivative instruments and securities.
Personal: Born 9 April 1950. JD, New York University School of Law, 1975; Root-Tilden Scholar. AB (magna cum laude), College of the Holy Cross, 1972. Circuit Secretary, NYU School of Law Root-Tilden Scholarship Program.

COLLINS, Wayne Dale
Shearman & Sterling, New York
212 848 4000
Recommended in Antitrust

CONDON, Creighton
Shearman & Sterling, New York
212 848 4000
Recommended in Corporate/M&A

CONRAD, Winthrop
Davis Polk & Wardwell, New York
212 450 4000
Recommended in Capital Markets

COOPER, Jim
Cravath, Swaine & Moore, New York
212 474 1000
Recommended in Banking & Finance

COTTER, James
Simpson Thacher & Bartlett, New York
212 455 2000
Recommended in Energy

COWAN, Cameron
Orrick Herrington Sutcliffe, New York
See Washington DC
Recommended in Capital Markets

CREEL, Thomas
Goodwin Procter LLP, New York
212 813 8800
Recommended in Intellectual Property

CUNNINGHAM, Dan
Allen & Overy, New York 212 610 6300
daniel.cunningham@allenovery.com
Recommended in Capital Markets
Specialization: Acquisitions, mergers and disposals, securities, and derivatives.
Career: JD Harvard Law School 1975. Admitted to the New York Bar 1980. Partner, *Allen & Overy*, 2001.

CURLEY, Michael
Morgan, Lewis & Bockius LLP, New York
212 309 6000
Recommended in Employment

CURTIS, Susan M
Skadden, Arps, Slate, Meagher & Flom LLP & Affiliates, New York
212 735 2119
scurtis@skadden.com
Recommended in Capital Markets
Specialization: Partner, New York. Represents underwriters, placement agents, issuers and banks in asset-backed securi-

NEW YORK — LEADERS

ties transactions and other financings. Has acted as counsel in public offerings and private placement and Regulation S transactions involving the issuance of asset-backed notes, asset-backed certificates, preferred stock, commercial paper and medium-term notes. Active as counsel for underwriters and collateral managers in the collateralised bond obligation market from its inception. Has acted as deal counsel in both cash-flow CBOs and market value CBOs; and in transactions involving the repackaging of bonds, asset-backed securities, swaps and other derivative instruments.
Personal: JD, Vanderbilt University, 1981; BA, University of Tennessee, 1977 (summa cum laude; Phi Beta Kappa).

DAVENPORT, Kirk A
Latham & Watkins LLP, New York
212 906 1284
kirk.davenport@lw.com
Recommended in Capital Markets
Specialization: Chairman of the firm's Corporate Finance Practice Group. Extensive experience in corporate finance, general securities and corporate matters. Represents underwriters, placement agents, initial purchasers and issuers in public and private high yield and convertible debt and equity offerings. Also represents broker-dealers in other engagements, including dealer manager and consent solicitation agent engagements, and represents mezzanine lenders in acquisition financings. Clients include domestic and foreign investment banks, NYSE-listed companies, foreign corporations, leveraged buyout funds and mezzanine investment funds.
Personal: JD, University of Michigan, 1984, magna cum laude, Order of the Coif. BA, Brown University, 1981.

DAVIS, Fred
Shearman & Sterling, New York
212 848 4000
Recommended in Litigation

DAVIS, Steven H
LeBoeuf, Lamb, Greene & MacRae, LLP, New York 212 424 8000
sdavis@llgm.com
Recommended in Energy
Specialization: His practice focuses primarily on companies active in the energy industry, including integrated electric and gas companies and independent power producers. He advises US and non-US clients in connection with mergers and acquisitions. He works in bankruptcy proceedings involving energy companies and provides restructuring advice for independent power producers.
Prof. Memberships: Director of United American Energy Corporation; President of the Board of Trustees of the Tuxedo Park School.
Career: Joined *LeBoeuf* in 1977; Co-Chair of the firm since 1999.

Personal: He attended Yale University (BA) 1970; Yale University (JD) 1977.

DE ORCHIS, Vincent M
DeOrchis & Partners, LLP, New York
212 344 4700
Recommended in Shipping

DE SEAR, Edward
Orrick, Herrington & Sutcliffe, New York
212 506 5060
eddesear@orrick.com
Recommended in Capital Markets
Specialization: Specialises in asset-backed securities, both in the US and abroad. Particular expertise in the areas of securitisation of credit card receivables, auto loans, leases, trade receivables, mutual fund fees, bank loans, tobacco company payments, and catastrophe risk coverage assets. Represents issuers, underwriters, credit enhancers, placement agents, and trustees.
Career: Partner and head of *Orrick's* Structured Finance Group. *Milbank, Tweed, Hadley & McCloy*, partner, 1993. Salomon Brothers, investment banker in pioneering asset-backed group, 1982-88. *Brown, Wood, Ivey, Mitchell & Pett*, partner and associate, 1973-82.
Personal: University of Virginia School of Law, JD, 1973. Columbia University, AB.

DELANEY, John
Morrison & Foerster LLP, New York
212 468 8040
jdelaney@mofo.com
Recommended in Communications
Specialization: Partner concentrating on high technology and intellectual property matters. Advises clients ranging from Fortune 500 companies to early-stage start-ups on technology licensing and liability issues including outsourcing, privacy, reseller agreements, joint ventures, online promotions, digital contracts, auctions, domain names, trademark registration, unfair competition and trade secrets. Counsels clients on intellectual property issues in connection with corporate finance transactions and mergers and acquisitions. Clients include well-known internet companies, such as iVillage and Multex, and more traditional companies as Hertz and A&E Television Networks. Has also represented clients in a range of patent, trademark and other intellectual property disputes, including recent domain name victory on behalf of hockey legend Mario Lemieux.
Prof. Memberships: Co-Chair, PLI Annual Conference ('The Outsourcing Revolution'); Board Member, Volunteer Lawyers for the Arts; Board Member, iMentor.
Career: Admitted to practice in California and New York. Currently serves as Co-Chair, Technology Group for the firm's New York office. Listed by a leading American legal publication as one of the 'lawyers for the new economy.' Included

by a leading New York business publication in its 'Technology 100,' a list of individuals 'likely to shape the direction and growth of New York's economy for years to come.'
Personal: BA, University of Notre Dame, 1986; JD, Columbia Law School, 1989.

DELIKAT, Michael
Orrick, Herrington & Sutcliffe, New York
212 506 5230
mdelikat@orrick.com
Recommended in Employment
Specialization: Counsels a broad range of major corporations in all facets of labor and employment law, with a concentration in the financial services and publishing industries. Has an active trial and appellate practice and handles a number of high-visibility class action and impact cases, including major trade secret protection cases. Counsels clients on employment law issues relating to all corporate transactions. Speaker at prestigious programs on labor and employment law and frequently quoted and interviewed by major publications.
Career: Chair of *Orrick's* Employment Law Department. Harvard Law School, JD, 1977. Cornell University, BS, 1974.

DELUCIA, Richard
Kenyon & Kenyon, New York
212 908 6217
rdelucia@kenyon.com
Recommended in Intellectual Property
Specialization: Is a partner of *Kenyon & Kenyon* and chair of the firm's Life Sciences Practice Group and a member of the firm's Litigation Practice Group. He has over 20 years of patent litigation experience. He has been chief trial counsel in over 100 cases, and has prevailed on behalf of his clients in many well-known jury and non-patent trials. The National Law Journal cited his jury verdict over Mitsubishi Heavy Industries in a patent trial involving printing press technology, where sucess was valued at approximately 900 million dollars, as one of that year's largest jury verdicts. Also counsels clients on issues relating to licensing and the validity, enforcability and infringement of patents, trademarks and copyrights. Among notable clients which he has represented are BASF Corp, RJR Nabisco, Sony Corporation of America, Amersham, Bio-Technology General, and Maxwell House Coffee.
Prof. Memberships: Is the 2002-03 President of the New York Intellectual Property Law Association and has served as the Chairman of the Litigation Committee of the New Jersey Intellectual Property Law Association.
Publications: He is a frequent lecturer and author of many articles pertaining to intellectual property law and litigation.

DESMARAIS, John M
Kirkland & Ellis, New York
212 446 4739
john_desmarais@ny.kirkland.com
Recommended in Intellectual Property
Specialization: Served for three years as an Assistant US Attorney in the Southern District of New York, where he tried criminal jury trials, before joining *Kirkland & Ellis* in 1997. He specializes in intellectual property litigation and is a member of the bars of New York and Washington, DC, the US Supreme Court, the Federal Circuit Court of Appeals, and various other federal district courts and courts of appeal. He is also registered to practice before the United States Patent and Trademark Office.
Personal: Manhattan College, BChE, 1985; New York University School of Law, JD, 1988.

DESPINS, Luc
Milbank, Tweed, Hadley & McCloy, New York 212 530 5000
Recommended in Insolvency

DIANGELO, Christopher
Dewey Ballantine LLP, New York
212 259 6718
cdiangelo@deweyballantine.com
Recommended in Capital Markets
Specialization: Focuses his practice on financial services/structured finance. With more 20 years' experience in the financial services industry, he and the other members of the group represent a wide variety of clients in the industry, including issuers, lenders, underwriters, and bond insurers on a variety of programs and projects, including asset-backed debt, municipal debt, straight corporate debt and equity, warehouse lines, regulatory matters and acquisitions.
Career: Joined *Dewey Ballantine* in 1984, and has been a partner since 1992. Prior to *Dewey Ballantine*, on staff at the New York State Housing Finance Agency.
Personal: Columbia University Law School, JD, 1984; City University of New York, Economics, MA, 1987; Williams College, Economics and Religion, BA, 1979.

DIBLASI, Gandolfo V
Sullivan & Cromwell LLP, New York
212 558 4000
diblasig@sullcrom.com
Recommended in Litigation
Specialization: Litigation partner whose practice focuses on securities, banking and commodities matters. Represents clients in securities and commodities class actions in federal courts throughout the nation, most recently as liaison counsel for the underwriters in the ongoing IPO allocation class actions, as well as counsel for Oxford Health Plans, Inc., UnumProvident Corporation, the directors and officers of Iridium and the directors and officers of Sensormatic Electron-

ics Corporation. Also active in civil and criminal investigations of the financial services industry, most recently the civil inquiries involving research analysts and initial public offerings, certain Arthur Andersen partners, the government securities market, the municipal securities market, Orange County, and the Denver Airport bond issues, as well as criminal cases alleging insider trading and market manipulation. Has handled investigations by self-regulatory organizations, such as the New York Stock Exchange, and NASD.
Prof. Memberships: American Bar Association; Association of the Bar of the City of New York; New York State Bar Association; Federal Bar Council.
Career: Joined *Sullivan & Cromwell* in 1978. Partner since 1985.
Publications: Contributing author of the treatise Business Crime.
Personal: Born in 1953. Yale University (BA, 1975). Yale Law School (JD, 1978).

DIMON, Samuel
Davis Polk & Wardwell, New York
212 450 4000
Recommended in Tax

DOKOS, Daniel S
Weil, Gotshal & Manges LLP, New York
212 310 8576
daniel.dokos@weil.com
Recommended in Banking & Finance
Specialization: Partner in the firm's New York office. An experienced banking law advisor, with particular expertise in secured lending and acquisition finance. Has represented both financial institutions and corporate borrowers in connection with leveraged acquisition and recapitalisation transactions, syndicated lending, asset-based lending and cross-border financings, as well as representing lenders in connection with loan restructurings, debtor-in-possession financings, workouts and exit financings.
Career: Joined the firm in 1998 from the New York office of *Sidley & Austin*.
Personal: AB, Dartmouth College (1979); JD, University of Virginia (1982).

DONOVAN, Donald Francis
Debevoise & Plimpton, New York
212 909 6233
dfdonovan@debevoise.com
Recommended in Arbitration
Specialization: Partner at *Debevoise & Plimpton*. Has argued international law, arbitration law, commercial law, and other issues before the United States Supreme Court, the United States Courts of Appeals for the Second, Fourth, Ninth, and District of Columbia Circuits, and other federal and state courts throughout the country; has argued before the International Court of Justice on behalf of Mexico, Germany, and Paraguay, as well as before the International Criminal Tribunal for the Former Yugoslavia and the Tribunal Established by the 1930 Hague Agreement; has conducted arbitrations in venues throughout the world under a wide variety of rules, including those of ICSID, the ICC, and the AAA; regularly sits as arbitrator in international cases.
Prof. Memberships: Vice President, International Council for Commercial Arbitration; Chair, Advisory Board of Directors, Institute for Transnational Arbitration; Chair, US National Committee, ICC; Executive Council, American Society of International Law.
Career: Legal Assistant, Howard M Holtzmann, Iran-US Claims Tribunal (1985-86). Judicial Clerk, Associate Justice Harry A Blackmun, US Supreme Court (1984-85). Joined *Debevoise & Plimpton* in 1987 and became a partner in 1991.
Publications: Include: The Scope and Enforceability of Provisional Measures in International Commercial Arbitration: A Survey of Jurisdictions, the Work of UNCITRAL, and Proposals for Moving Forward, ICCA Congress Series No. 11 (forthcoming 2003); 'United States Report', 'International Handbook on Commercial Arbitration' (ICCA, rev'd ed 1999); Power of Arbitrators to Issue Procedural Orders, 10 'ICC International Court of Arbitration Bulletin' 57 (Spring 1999).
Personal: University of Virginia, BA, 1977; Stanford Law School, JD, 1981. Competent in Spanish.

DOUGLAS, James M
Skadden, Arps, Slate, Meagher & Flom LLP & Affiliates, New York
212 735 2868
jdouglas@skadden.com
Recommended in Banking & Finance
Specialization: Partner, New York. Co-head, *Skadden*'s Banking and Institutional Investing Group. Represents numerous financial institutions, investors and corporate clients in all areas of private financings. Concentrates in the areas of acquisition financings, bridge financings and restructurings. Listed in several leading US legal publications.
Personal: JD, Fordham University, 1981 (cum laude; Member, Fordham Law Review); BA, State University of New York at Binghamton, 1978.

DOUGLAS, Peter
Davis Polk & Wardwell, New York
212 450 4000
Recommended in Corporate/M&A

DUNHAM JR, Wolcott B
Debevoise & Plimpton, New York
212 909 6595
wbdunham@debevoise.com
Recommended in Insurance
Specialization: Partner at *Debevoise & Plimpton*; co-chair of firm's Insurance Industry Group. Has handled numerous insurance company M&A deals and public offerings, capital raising by insurance companies and their affiliates, demutualizations, workouts and insolvencies, reinsurance and regulatory matters. Advised boards of directors and was lead outside counsel to The Equitable, John Hancock, Metropolitan Life, Phoenix Home Life and Principal Mutual Holding Company in their demutualizations, Provident Mutual Life in its sponsored demutualization, and Pacific Mutual and Ohio National in their mutual holding company reorganizations; advising American Council of Life Insurers on the streamlining of state regulation and on optional federal chartering. Has advised boards and managements in hostile takeover situations.
Prof. Memberships: Former Chair, Committee on Insurance Law of The Association of the Bar of the City of New York; former Chair, Committee on Insurance Law of the American Bar Association Section on Administrative Law; Association of Life Insurance Counsel; Fellow of the American College of Investment Counsel.
Career: Joined *Debevoise* in 1969; became a partner in 1977.
Publications: Has spoken and written on many insurance-related topics; Chair, annual Practising Law Institute program on Insurance Industry Mergers & Acquisitions; Editor and Co-author, four-volume treatise, New York Insurance Law.
Personal: AB, magna cum laude, Harvard College, 1965; LLB, cum laude, Harvard Law School, 1968.

DYE, Alexander M
LeBoeuf, Lamb, Greene & MacRae, LLP, New York 212 424 8642
adye@llgm.com
Recommended in Insurance
Specialization: Specializes in corporate transactions involving the insurance industry. He has advised strategic and financial buyers in some of the largest and most novel mergers and acquisitions transactions in the insurance industry. He has worked on restructurings, demutualizations and conversions of life and property-casualty insurers as well as Blue Cross/BlueShield entities. He also represents US and offshore issuers and underwriters in offerings of equity, debt and hybrid securities by insurers and insurance holding companies.
Career: Joined *LeBoeuf* in 1981.
Personal: Brown University (BA magna cum laude) 1978; University of Michigan (JD) 1981.

ECKSTEIN, Kenneth
Kramer Levin Naftalis & Frankel LLP, New York 212 715 9229
keckstein@kramerlevin.com
Recommended in Insolvency
Specialization: Is partner and chairman of *Kramer Levin Naftalis & Frankel LLP* Creditors' Rights and Bankruptcy Department. He has practiced in the area of corporate reorganization and bankruptcy since 1979.
Prof. Memberships: A frequent lecturer and author in the areas of bankruptcy and corporate reorganization. He is a member of the Section on Corporation, Banking and Business Law of the American Bar Association. He is also a former member of the Committee on Bankruptcy and Corporate Reorganization of the Association of the Bar of the City of New York.
Career: Chairs a department of seven partners and 18 associates and has played a prominent role in many of the largest and most complex chapter 11 reorganization cases and out of court workouts over the past 24 years. His recent representations include Official Creditor Committees for Dow Corning Corporation, Big V, SGL Carbon Corp., Cityscape Financial, Olympia & York, Integrated Resources, SLM International, Financial News Network and Buddy L and bank groups for Owens Corning, Mediq/PRN, Glenoit, Feuer Leather and several recent out of court restructuring transactions. He has also represented the debtors in the bankruptcy of The Wiz, Inc. and has represented bondholders, acquirors and other major creditors in Enron, Warnaco, NTL, Leap Wireless, Amerco, Big City Radio, Jitney Jungle, LTV, New Valley, Herman's Sporting Goods, Tucson Electric and Farley Industries. He has led his firm's representation of the Examiner in Bruno's Inc. and the Independent Restructuring Advisor in Coram Healthcare. He has also represented the Trustee in Island Mortgage and in Sharp International. He regularly represents a wide range of lending and other financial institutions and distressed investors in chapter 11 cases, workouts and out of court restructurings. These institutions include JP Morgan Chase, CSFB, BNP-Paribas, Goldman Sachs, Alliance Capital, Fleet Bank, Barclays, Elliott Associates, Angelo Gordon and others.
Personal: Received a JD degree from New York University in 1979 and a BA degree cum laude from the University of Pennsylvania in 1976.

EDELMAN, Marty
Paul, Hastings, Janofsky & Walker LLP, New York 212 856 7100
martyedelman@paulhastings.com
Recommended in Real Estate
Specialization: Concentrates his practice on large, complex real estate and corporate transactions. He has been involved in all stages of legal development of pioneering financial structures, including participating mortgages, institutional joint ventures in real estate, and joint ventures between US financial sources and European real estate companies. He has also done extensive work in Europe, Canada, Mexico and recently in Japan.
Prof. Memberships: Board of Directors - Cendant Incorporated, Acadia Realty Trust and Capital Trust. Advisory Board -

Columbia University's Law School and Business School. Advisor - Soros Real Estate Partners, Millennium Partners and The Related Companies.

EINHORN, David M
Wachtell, Lipton, Rosen & Katz,
New York 212 403 1213
dmeinhorn@wlrk.com
Recommended in Tax

Specialization: Specializes in the tax aspects of the joint ventures, corporate reorganizations, acquisitions, dispositions, financings, and restructurings that constitute *Wachtell, Lipton, Rosen & Katz's* primary practice, which transactions frequently involve multinational businesses and raise complex multinational tax issues.
Prof. Memberships: Tax Sections of the New York State Bar Association; Association of the Bar of the City of New York.
Career: Partner at *Wachtell, Lipton, Rosen & Katz* since 1982. Often lectures on tax matters at professional seminars.
Personal: Graduated from Fordham Law School in 1976 (JD) and from New York University Law School in 1979 (LLM).

EISENBERG, David
Simpson Thacher & Bartlett, New York
212 455 2000
Recommended in Capital Markets

EMMERICH, Adam O
Wachtell, Lipton, Rosen & Katz,
New York 212 403 1234
aoemmerich@wlrk.com
Recommended in Corporate/M&A

Specialization: Mergers and acquisitions and securities law matters. Practice includes a broad and varied representation of public and private corporations and other entities in a variety of industries throughout the United States and abroad, in connection with mergers and acquisitions, divestitures, spin-offs, joint ventures, and financing transactions. Also has extensive experience in takeover defense and corporate governance issues.
Prof. Memberships: Association of the Bar of the City of New York; New York State and American Bar Association; New York County Lawyers Association; Securities Law Committee of the American Society of Corporate Secretaries; and the Corporate Academic Bridge Group of the NYU Center for Law and Business. Member, board of directors of the American Friends of the Israel Museum and of the Ramaz School, president of the American Friends of the Israel Antiquities Authority. Previously served on the Visiting Committee of the University of Chicago Law School and currently a co-chair of its capital campaign, and as chair of the Young Lawyers Division of the UJA-Federation in New York. Member of the board of directors of the Lawyers Alliance for New York.
Career: Joined *Wachtell, Lipton, Rosen & Katz* in 1986 and named a partner in 1991. BA, Swarthmore College and JD with honors, University of Chicago. Topics and Comments Editor of the University of Chicago Law Review; Order of the Coif; Olin Fellow in law and economics. Law clerk to Hon. Abner J Mikva, United States Court of Appeals for the District of Columbia Circuit. A frequent speaker at bar and professional conferences on topics relating to mergers and acquisitions.
Personal: Born 15 December 1960. Married with three children.

EPSTEIN, Michael
Weil, Gotshal & Manges LLP, New York
212-310-8432
michael.epstein@weil.com
Recommended in Communications

Specialization: Partner in the New York office. A nationally recognized expert in intellectual property and information technology. Has extensive experience litigating and counselling corporations worldwide, and has negotiated and resolved some of the largest and most complex intellectual property disputes. Practice involves substantial transactional work, including significant e-commerce, structuring and negotiating technology and intellectual property acquisitions, technology transfer and licensing arrangements, and joint ventures and other targeted alliances. Chair of the firm's 100 lawyer Technology and Proprietary Rights Group, and co-chair of the firm's 140 lawyer Trade Practice and Regulatory Law Department.
Prof. Memberships: American Bar Association, section of Intellectual Property Law; Licensing Executive Society.
Career: *Weil, Gotshal, & Manges, LLP* 1979 to present; Co-chair, Trade Practices and Regulatory Law Department; Chair, Technology and Proprietary Rights Practice Group. Member of the Firm Management Committee.
Publications: Author of the treaties 'Epstein on Intellectual Property and Modern Intellectual Property'. Co-author of 'On-Line Internet Law', 'International Intellectual Property', and co-editor of 'Drafting License Agreements', 'The Corporate Counsellor's Deskbook', 'The Departing Employee', 'Doing Business in Eastern Europe', 'Biotechnology Law', 'The Trademark Law Revision Act', 'Joint Ventures and Other Cooperative Business Arrangements' and 'Trade Secrets, Restrictive Covenants, and Other Safeguards'. Author of numerous articles on intellectual property law, computer law, unfair competition, trade law, licensing, and non-compete agreements. Founder and co-editor of 'The Journal of Proprietary Rights' and a member of the Editorial Boards of the 'Computer Lawyer', 'Intellectual Property Strategist', and 'Cyberspace Lawyer'.
Personal: BA, Lehigh University (1975); JD, New York University School of Law.

ETTINGER, John
Davis Polk & Wardwell, New York
212 450 4000
Recommended in Private Equity

EVANS, Martin Frederic
Debevoise & Plimpton, New York
212 909 6293
mfevans@debevoise.com
Recommended in Antitrust

Specialization: Presiding partner at *Debevoise & Plimpton* since July 1998. His practice concentrates in antitrust matters and complex civil litigation. Has advised on numerous merger investigations before the Federal Trade Commission, the Department of Justice and EU and other competition authorities. He has led defences of government and private enforcement actions involving, among other industries, insurance, mining and pharmaceuticals.
Prof. Memberships: American Bar Association; Association of the Bar of the City of New York.
Career: Joined *Debevoise & Plimpton* in 1972 and became a partner in 1981.
Personal: University of Virginia, BA, with Honors, 1969; Yale Law School, JD, 1972.

EVANS, Robert
Shearman & Sterling, New York
212 848 4000
Recommended in Capital Markets

FAGEN, Leslie
Paul, Weiss, Rifkind, Wharton & Garrison LLP, New York 212 373 3231
lfagen@paulweiss.com
Recommended in Litigation

Specialization: Joined *Paul, Weiss, Rifkind, Wharton & Garrison LLP* in 1976 and became a partner in its Litigation Department in 1982. He is co-chair of the department and has served as a member of the firm's Management Committee. His litigation practice has been concentrated in the fields of product liability, intellectual property, insurance, antitrust, environmental and securities law. Over the last 26 years, he has litigated on behalf of plaintiffs and defendants at the trial and appellate level in federal and state courts in multiple jurisdictions and has had extensive experience in alternative dispute resolution proceedings.

FAGIN, Allen
Proskauer Rose LLP, New York
212 969 3000
Recommended in Employment

FASTOW, Jay N
Weil, Gotshal & Manges LLP,
New York 212 310 8644
jay.fastow@weil.com
Recommended in Antitrust

Specialization: Antitrust/financial services litigator and advisor with a wide-ranging competition and financial services litigation practice, acting for corporations and financial institutions in trial-level and appellate courts from New York to Guam. Has acted as a Liaison Counsel for defendants in both Nasdaq Market-Makers Antitrust Litigation and Stock Exchange Options Trading Antitrust Litigation, as well as in Mastercard International Inc. Internet Gambling Litigation.
Publications: 'Where the Money Is: Litigation Under Section One of the Sherman Act in the Financial Services and Securities Industries', 115 'The Banking Law Journal', 774-786 (1998).
Personal: BA, magna cum laude, Brandeis University (1974); JD, Yale University Law School (1977).

FEINTUCH, Richard D
Wachtell, Lipton, Rosen & Katz,
New York 212 403 1248
rdfeintuch@wlrk.com
Recommended in Insolvency

Specialization: Representation of both debtors and creditor groups in large Chapter 11 cases, as well as out of court restructurings. In addition, regularly represents corporate clients in merger and acquisition and other corporation transactions, specializing in the negotiation of complex credit arrangements.
Career: Partner at *Wachtell, Lipton, Rosen & Katz* since 1984.
Personal: Graduated magna cum laude from the Wharton School of the University of Pennsylvania in 1974 (BS, economics) and from New York University School of Law in 1977 (JD). While at New York University, he was the Executive Editor of 'New York University Law Review'.

FELDMAN, Matthew
Willkie Farr & Gallagher, New York
212 728 8651
mfeldman@willkie.com
Recommended in Insolvency

Specialization: Partner in the Business Reorganization and Restructuring Department. Clients include debtors, creditors, lenders, landlords, governmental agencies, and bank committees. Has been significantly involved in numerous complex chapter 11 cases and non-judicial restructurings, including his recent representation of XO Communications, Inc., Global Crossing, Ltd., Big V Supermarkets, Inc. and Golden Books Entertainment. Represented several debtors in cross-border insolvency cases and foreign restructurings including Petroleum Geo-Services ASA, Millicom Cellular SA, ish GmbH & Co. KG and Kabel Baden-Wurttemberg GmbH & Co. KG, two of the largest German cable television companies, Livent Inc., Teleglobe, Inc., Converse Corporation, Alliance Entertainment Corp. and AIOC Corporation. Regularly represents investors seeking to acquire assets or businesses from companies operating in chapter 11.
Prof. Memberships: Connecticut Bar

Association, the American Bar Association, and the American Bankruptcy Institute.
Career: Admitted to the Bars of New York, Connecticut, and Massachusetts as well as the Southern and Northern Districts of New York and the District of Massachusetts.
Personal: Received a JD from New York University School of Law in 1988 and a BA (magna cum laude) from Tufts University in 1985.

FELTENSTEIN, Martha
Skadden, Arps, Slate, Meagher & Flom LLP & Affiliates, New York
212 735 2272
mfeltens@skadden.com
Recommended in Real Estate
Specialization: Partner, New York. Active in all aspects of *Skadden*'s real estate practice, including real estate development, acquisitions, leasing, joint ventures, financing, public and private offerings of real estate securities, and commercial mortgage securitization. Also represents US and non-US clients in their acquisition and development of hotels, shopping centers, office buildings and residential properties in the United States and abroad.
Personal: JD, Columbia University, 1981; M Phil., School of Oriental and African Studies, University of London, 1977; BA, Princeton University, 1975.

FEY, Albert
Fish & Neave, New York 212 596 9000
Recommended in Intellectual Property

FILARDI, Edward V
Skadden, Arps, Slate, Meagher & Flom LLP & Affiliates, New York
212 735 3060
efilardi@skadden.com
Recommended in Intellectual Property
Specialization: Partner, New York. Has extensive experience in patent, trade secret, unfair competition and antitrust-related matters, specifically regarding litigation and dispute resolution. Registered US patent attorney with extensive jury trial and appellate experience; has litigated patent and trademark cases for both plaintiffs and defendants. Has served as lead trial counsel in matters involving various technologies including medical devices, chemicals, pharmaceuticals, computers, telecommunications, and mechanics in federal and state courts as well as before the International Trade Commission. Also has significant experience in international litigation related to pharmaceutical, chemical and fabricated materials industries, and has served as advisory lead counsel in coordinating litigation in France, Germany, the Netherlands, the UK, Japan, Denmark and Sweden. Has been an arbitrator and a court-appointed neutral evaluator in intellectual property rights infringement matters.
Personal: JD, New York Law School,

1968 (Articles Editor, Law Review); BS, Iona College, 1965.

FINKELSON, Allen
Cravath, Swaine & Moore, New York
212 474 1000
Recommended in Corporate/M&A

FINLEY, John
Simpson Thacher & Bartlett, New York
212 455 2000
Recommended in Corporate/M&A

FISKE, Robert
Davis Polk & Wardwell, New York
212 450 4000
Recommended in Litigation

FLEISCHER JR, Arthur
Fried, Frank, Harris, Shriver & Jacobson, New York 212 859 8120
Arthur.Fleischer@FriedFrank.com
Recommended in Corporate/M&A
Specialization: Senior partner. Has led the firm's M&A practice for more than 30 years. Represents corporate clients as acquirers and targets and many of the leading investment banks. Practice encompasses negotiated and contested transactions. Advises special committees formed to review buyout proposal and corporate restructurings.
Prof. Memberships: Member of the American Bar Association, Section of Corporation, Banking and Business Law, Committee on Federal Registration of Securities; American Law Institute; Advisory Committee of the Securities Regulation Institute of the University of California; Association of the Bar of the City of New York.
Career: Qualified in 1959. Associated with *Fried Frank* in 1957 and became a partner in 1958.
Personal: Born 1933. Achieved LLB in 1958 and BA 1953 from Yale University.

FLESHER, Gail
Davis Polk & Wardwell, New York
212 450 4000
Recommended in Environment

FLOM, Joseph H
Skadden, Arps, Slate, Meagher & Flom LLP & Affiliates, New York
212 735 3100
jflom@skadden.com
Recommended in Corporate/M&A
Specialization: Partner, New York. Leading attorney in M&A area. Credited with pioneering many of the strategies used by bidders, targets and investment bankers. Practice includes all forms of corporate transactions.
Career: Director, UrbanAmerica, LLC (1998-Present); Advisory Board, RRE Investors, LLC (1999-present); Director, Wm. Wrigley Jr. Company (1977-94); Warnaco Group, Inc. (1997-2000); Trustee, Petrie Stores Liquidating Trust (1996-present).
Personal: LLB, Harvard Law School, 1948 (cum laude; Editor, 'Harvard Law Review'); College of the City of NY; LHD, Honorary Doctorate in Humane Letters, Queens College, 1984; LLD, Honorary Doctorate of Law, Fordham University, 1990; Chairman, Woodrow Wilson International Center for Scholars (1994-98).

FLORACK, James
Davis Polk & Wardwell, New York
212 450 4000
Recommended in Banking & Finance

FOGG, Blaine V (Fin)
Skadden, Arps, Slate, Meagher & Flom LLP & Affiliates, New York
212 735 3900
bfogg@skadden.com
Recommended in Corporate/M&A
Specialization: Senior partner, New York. Concentrates on mergers, acquisitions, restructurings and other corporate and business transactions. Advises on a wide variety of matters, including negotiated mergers, acquisitions and leveraged buyouts; unsolicited tender offers; proxy contests; corporate restructurings and reorganizations; and public and private securities offerings.
Prof. Memberships: American Bar Association; New York State Bar Association; Association of the Bar of the City of New York.
Personal: Born March 29, 1940. Attended Williams College (AB, 1962) and Harvard Law School (JD, 1965). Married, with three children and one grandchild. Interests include golf, art and travel.

FORD, Paul
Simpson Thacher & Bartlett, New York
212 455 2000
Recommended in Capital Markets

FORELLE, John
Simpson Thacher & Bartlett, New York
212 455 2000
Recommended in Real Estate

FORTE, Joseph
Dechert, New York 212 698 3500
Recommended in Real Estate

FRAIDIN, Stephen
Fried, Frank, Harris, Shriver & Jacobson, New York 212 859 8140
Stephen.Fraidin@FriedFrank.com
Recommended in Corporate/M&A, Private Equity
Specialization: Senior member of *Fried Frank*'s Corporate Department. Practice includes the general representation of major companies and investment groups, as well as acquisitions and proxy contests. Has advised Forstmann Little & Co. in the creation of its leveraged buyout funds and in a series of negotiated acquisitions, dispositions and restructurings involving over $40 billion; Procter & Gamble Co. in a number of multibillion-dollar acquisitions, including its $4.95 billion acquisition of Bristol Myers Squibb Company's Clairol business and the combination of its Jif/Crisco business with JM Smucker Company in a Morris Trust transaction for $1 billion on a pretax basis; Datek Online Holdings Corp. in the acquisition of its 20% interest in Bravo, a subsidiary of Cablevision Systems Corporation, by National Broadcasting Company, Inc.
Prof. Memberships: Association of the Bar of the City of New York; American Bar Association; Yale Law School Association.
Career: Qualified in 1965. Joined *Fried Frank* in 1964, becoming a partner in 1971. Visiting Lecturer, Yale Law School; Member of the board of directors, Children's Scholarship Fund.
Personal: Born 1939. Received LLB from Yale University in 1964 and BA from Tufts University in 1961.

FREYER, Dana H
Skadden, Arps, Slate, Meagher & Flom LLP & Affiliates, New York
212 735 2506
dfreyer@skadden.com
Recommended in Arbitration
Specialization: Partner, New York. International and US Commercial Litigation and Arbitration; Alternative Dispute Resolution; Corporate Compliance Program Design; and Legal Risk Management. Handles all types of US and international commercial litigation and arbitration, including international arbitrations under the UNCITRAL, ICC, AAA, other arbitration rules, mediations and other ADR proceedings. Works in structuring dispute resolution alternatives to litigation, drafting dispute resolution contract clauses, and developing conflict management and dispute handling systems. Advises clients on the development and implementation of ethics and compliance programs, including management structures and control systems, to prevent and detect violations of law; the management of claims, litigation and other legal risks; and the organisation of their law departments. Has worked on the design and implementation of compliance programs, including training programs and monitoring and auditing systems.
Prof. Memberships: Admitted in New York and Illinois; Arbitrator, American Arbitration Association; President, Westchester Legal Services, Inc. (1985-87), Director (1978-present); Member, Committee on Arbitration and Alternative Dispute Resolution (1987-90); Advisory and Special Committees on Alternative Dispute Resolution, Bar Association of the City of New York (1992-95); American Arbitration Association Corporate Counsel Committee and Law Committee, International Section; International Bar Association. Advisory Board, Bureau of National Affairs' Alternative Dispute Resolution Report (1987-90); AAA Dispute Resolution Journal (1996-present); World Arbitration and Mediation Report (1990-present).

NEW YORK — LEADERS

Personal: JD, Columbia University, 1971; BA, Connecticut College, 1965.

FRIEDLAND, Paul
White & Case LLP, New York
212 819 8200
Recommended in Arbitration

FRIEDMAN, David
Kasowitz Benson Torres & Friedman, New York 212 506 1700
Recommended in Insolvency

FRIEDMAN, Gary M
Debevoise & Plimpton, New York
212 909 6261
gmfriedman@debevoise.com
Recommended in Tax

Specialization: Partner at *Debevoise & Plimpton*. His practice concentrates in the area of federal income taxation with particular emphasis on mergers and acquisitions and international taxation. Recent representations include the consortium in the acquisition of Eircom (US tax matters).
Prof. Memberships: Executive Committee, Tax Section of the New York State Bar Association; co-chair, Committee on US Activities of Foreign Taxpayers; New York State Bar Association; American Bar Association; Tax Foundation.
Career: Judicial Clerk, US Court of Appeals, Seventh Circuit (1983-84). Joined *Debevoise & Plimpton* in 1984 and became a partner in 1991.
Publications: Regular contributor, 'New York Tax Club'.
Personal: Princeton University, AB, 1979; University of Chicago Law School, JD, 1983; New York University, LLM in Taxation, 1990.

GABAY, Donald
Stroock & Stroock & Lavan LLP, New York 212 806 5400
Recommended in Insurance

GALVIS, Sergio J
Sullivan & Cromwell LLP, New York
212 558 4000
galviss@sullcrom.com
Recommended in Projects

Specialization: Coordinates *S&C's* Latin America practice. Has broad and diverse experience in project financings, M&A, securities offerings, restructurings and privatisations. For more than 18 years has advised Latin American businesses and governments, foreign investors, and international investment banks and companies, in some of the most significant transactions in Latin America. Represents borrowers, sponsors and lenders in project financings, including the ongoing Camisea gas project (Peru), the OCP pipeline project (Ecuador), the Petrozuata heavy oil project (Venezuela), and the Tesoro, Pelambres, Collahuasi, El Abra, Zaldivar, Cerro Colorado and Escondida mining projects (Chile). Represents bidders, acquirors and sellers in M&A transactions, including: Tenaris in acquiring the outstanding stock of Siderca (Argentina), Tamsa (Mexico) and Dalmine (Italy); Koch Industries in the acquisition from Mexico's Saba Group of Saba's 50% stake in KoSa; CSU (Costa Rica) in its supermarkets joint venture with Paiz Ahold in Central America, and; Telefonica in its acquisition of Hicks, Muse's Argentine investment in CEI. Acts for borrowers and lenders in restructurings throughout the region, including Amazonia/Sidor (Venezuela) and Siderca (Argentina). Has advised governments and other parties on sovereign debt restructuring mechanisms.
Prof. Memberships: American Bar Association; Association of the Bar of the City of New York (former Member of the Committee on Inter-American Affairs and the Committee on Securities Regulation); International Bar Association.
Career: Judicial Clerk to the Honorable Lawrence W. Pierce, US Court of Appeals (2nd Circuit) 1983-84. Joined *S&C* in 1984; partner since 1991.
Publications: Has spoken at numerous conferences, seminars and law schools on a variety of legal topics, and has written articles for 'The Miami Herald', 'Project Finance International' and 'Latin Lawyer', among other publications. In spring 2003, will publish review in International Finance entitled 'Sovereign Debt Restructurings - The Market Knows Best'. Previously co-authored 'On Third World', 25 Harv. Int'l L.J. 83 (1984), cited in 'The IMF Survey' (June 24, 2002) as a 'path-breaking article' on mechanisms for resolving debt crises.
Personal: Born 1958 in Cali, Colombia. College of William and Mary (1980); Harvard Law School (1983). General Counsel and a Director of the Council of the Americas. Member, Council on Foreign Relations.

GARDNER, Stephen
Kronish Lieb Weiner & Hellman LLP, New York 212 479 6000
Recommended in Tax

GARFINKEL, Barry
Skadden, Arps, Slate, Meagher & Flom LLP & Affiliates, New York
212 735 2500
bgarfink@skadden.com
Recommended in Arbitration

Specialization: Of Counsel, New York. Heads *Skadden's* international litigation and arbitration practice. Has been in charge of many of the firm's more significant trials and appeals. Has served as lead counsel in major international arbitrations. Has acted as an arbitrator in ICC, UNCITRAL, and AAA arbitrations. Has advised major US and foreign companies on transnational arbitration matters.
Prof. Memberships: Chairman and Trustee, Practising Law Institute; Advisory Committee, Institute for Transnational Arbitration; International Arbitration Committee, American Arbitration Association; American Arbitration Association (Complex Cases), London Court of International Arbitration and ICC; Fellow, American College of Trial Lawyers.
Personal: LLB, Yale University, 1955 (Managing Editor, 'Yale Law Journal').

GEARY, Sean
White & Case LLP, New York
212 819 8200
Recommended in Banking & Finance

GELSTON, Philip
Cravath, Swaine & Moore, New York
212 474 1000
Recommended in Corporate/M&A

GERRARD, Michael
Arnold & Porter, New York
212 715 1000
Michael_Gerrard@aporter.com
Recommended in Environment

Specialization: Heads the firm's New York Environmental Practice.
Prof. Memberships: He has chaired the Executive Committee of the Association of the Bar of the City of New York, and the Environmental Law Section of the New York State Bar Association, and is now the vice chair of the American Bar Association's Section of Environment, Energy, and Resources.
Career: He has practiced environmental law in New York since 1978. He has been an adjunct professor at Columbia Law School and the Yale School of Forestry and Environmental Studies.
Publications: He has written or edited five books, two of which were named Best Law Book of the Year by the Association of American Publishers: the nine-volume 'Environmental Law Practice Guide' (Matthew Bender 1992) and the three-volume 'Brownfields Law and Practice: The Cleanup and Redevelopment of Contaminated Land' (Matthew Bender 1998).

GILBERG, David J
Sullivan & Cromwell LLP, New York
212 558 4000
gilbergd@sullcrom.com
Recommended in Capital Markets

Specialization: Practice involves a broad range of derivatives and related matters, including the development of electronic exchanges and trading facilities for the trading of securities, derivatives and financial instruments, the structuring of indexed products, over-the-counter derivatives and other financial instruments, and the development and implementation of structured transactions, private funds and other managed trading vehicles. Also advises commercial banks, investment banks, trading companies, trading advisers and other types of clients on legal and regulatory issues related to the trading of securities, derivatives and other financial products.
Prof. Memberships: American Bar Association; Association of the Bar of the City of New York (Member, Committee on Futures Regulation).
Career: Served as an Adjunct Professor of Law at Georgetown University Law Center, teaching a course on the regulation of derivative products. Joined *Sullivan & Cromwell* in 1992. Served as Special Counsel, 1994-95. Became a Partner of the firm in 1996.
Publications: Author of several articles on derivatives and speaker at numerous derivatives industry conferences.
Personal: Born 1956. Graduated from the University of Pennsylvania (BA, MA, 1978) and Harvard Law School (JD, 1981). Admitted to the Bar in New York and Washington, DC.

GINOS, Geoff
Nicoletti Hornig Campise Sweeney & Paige, New York 212 220 3830
Recommended in Shipping

GITTES, Franklin M
Skadden, Arps, Slate, Meagher & Flom LLP & Affiliates, New York
212 735 3760
fgittes@skadden.com
Recommended in Corporate/M&A

Specialization: Partner, New York. Recent representations include: Johns Manville in its US$3 billion acquisition by Berkshire Hathaway Inc.; MacMillan Bloedel Limited in its US$2.45 billion acquisition by Weyerhauser Company; and HSB Group, Inc. in its US$1.2 billion acquisition by American International Group, Inc.
Prof. Memberships: American Bar Association; New York State Bar Association; Association of the Bar of the City of New York.
Career: Admitted to the bar in 1973 in District of Columbia and in 1975 in New York. Law Clerk, Hon. John Briggs, Jr., US Court of Appeals for the Third Circuit (1973-74). Joined *Skadden, Arps* in 1978; became a partner in 1981.
Personal: Born in Newark, NJ, 1947. Lehigh University (BSChE, 1969); Georgetown University (JD, 1973).

GLASS, Adam
Sidley Austin Brown & Wood, New York
212 839 5300
Recommended in Capital Markets

GLAZER, Steven D
Weil, Gotshal & Manges LLP, New York
212 310 8806
steven.glazer@weil.com
Recommended in Intellectual Property

Specialization: Leads the Patent Litigation and Counseling Practice Group located in the firm's New York office. He is a broadly experienced practitioner in patent litigation and related counseling issues, particularly in matters requiring expertise in high technology. He has represented clients in complex litigation involving such diverse technical fields as

digital electronics, computer networking, encryption, wastewater treatment, genetic engineering, sweetener chemistry, semiconductors, petrochemicals, and computer software. Clients include ExxonMobil, ST Microelectronics, Pirelli, UnitedHealth Group, Walt Disney, ABC, VF Corp., News Corp., Thomason Multimedia, GlaxoSmithKline, Avaya and General Electric. He is also a registered patent attorney.
Prof. Memberships: American Intellectual Property Law Association, New York Intellectual Property Law Association, New York and New Jersey State Bar Associations, American Bar Association and the Institute of Electrical and Electronics Engineers.
Publications: Frequent author and lecturer on intellectual property and related litigation topics. A Co-editor of 'Intellectual Property & Technology Law Journal' and member of the Editorial Board of 'Patent World'.

GLICK, Anna
Cadwalader, Wickersham & Taft, New York 212 504 6309
anna.glick@cwt.com
Recommended in Capital Markets
Specialization: Capital markets partner whose work includes multi-class securitization, structured mortgage finance, securitization of commercial mortgage loans, federal securities laws issues particular to these securitizations, and related securities compliance matters. Also works in CBOs (particularly those backed by asset and mortgage securities) and securitization of residential mortgage loans and other products. Represents issuers, underwriters and institutional investors active in the primary and secondary capital markets. Structures partnerships, trusts and joint ventures, establishes warehouse financing programs and master repurchase facilities. Works closely with the Real Estate Department to advise on rating agency and securitization issues (origination of large and conduit-size mortgage loans pending securitization). Concentrates on federal securities law, registration of public securities, financings, and other business arrangements for closely-held corporations.
Career: JD in 1982 from New York University School of Law (member of the 'Law Review' and Order of the Coif).

GOERING, Kevin
Coudert Brothers, New York
212 626 4400
Recommended in Media & Entertainment

GOETZ, Peter
Goetz Fitzpatrick Most & Bruckman LLP, New York 212 695 8100
Recommended in Construction

GOLDEN, Arthur
Davis Polk & Wardwell, New York

212 450 4000
Recommended in Antitrust

GOLDEN, Daniel
Akin Gump Strauss Hauer & Feld, LLP, New York 212 872 1000
Recommended in Insolvency

GOLDFEIN, Shepard
Skadden, Arps, Slate, Meagher & Flom LLP & Affiliates, New York
212 735 3610
sgoldfei@skadden.com
Recommended in Antitrust
Specialization: Practice Leader, Antitrust Group. Handles a variety of cases from antitrust litigation to white collar criminal investigations and mass disaster litigation. Also advises on antitrust issues (general compliance programs to antitrust patent licensing issues), and has worked on securities class action litigations and several antitrust takeover cases.
Prof. Memberships: Chairman, Sports Law Committee, Association of the Bar of the City of NY (1999-present).
Publications: Co-author, monthly trade regulation column, 'New York Law Journal' (1983-present).
Personal: JD, Rutgers University, 1975 (Editor, Rutgers Law Review); MA, Political Science, University of Chicago, 1977; AB, Rutgers University, 1970 (Phi Beta Kappa).

GOLDMAN, Mike
Cravath, Swaine & Moore, New York
212 474 1000
Recommended in Banking & Finance

GOLDRING, Stuart
Weil, Gotshal & Manges LLP, New York
212 310 8312
stuart.goldring@weil.com
Recommended in Tax
Specialization: Bankruptcy and restructurings, mergers and acquisitions, consolidated returns. Major cases include: Armstrong World Industries bankruptcy; Pacific Gas and Electric Company bankruptcy; Macy's bankruptcy; Eastern Airlines bankruptcy; American Airlines acquisition of TWA; Reuters, Inc. acquisition of Bridge Trading.
Prof. Memberships: Member, Executive Committee of the Tax Section of the New York State Bar Association (Co-Chair, Committee on Bankruptcy and Taxes); member, Association of the Bar of the City of New York (member of former Tax Council); member, Tax Section of the American Bar Association.
Career: Partner (1992-present), Associate (1983-91), *Weil, Gotshal & Manges LLP*; frequent speaker at tax institutes; member of the Corporate Tax and Business Planning Advisory Board for Tax Management; admitted to the Bar, NY (1984).
Publications: Treatise: 'Tax Planning for Troubled Corporations: Bankruptcy and Nonbankruptcy Restructurings' (Panel

Publications, Aspen Publishing; rev. 2001) (with Gordon D Henderson) (formerly titled 'Failing and Failed Businesses'). Has published numerous articles on tax issues relating to financially troubled companies.
Personal: New York University School of Law (LLM in Taxation, 1983); graduate editor of the 'Tax Law Review'; University of Michigan Law School (JD, magna cum laude, 1982); Order of the Coif; University of Michigan School of Business Administration (BBA, with high distinction, 1979).

GOLDSCHMIDT, David J
Skadden, Arps, Slate, Meagher & Flom LLP & Affiliates, New York
212 735 3574
dgoldsch@skadden.com
Recommended in Capital Markets
Specialization: Partner, New York. Represents investment banks and US and international issuers in a variety of financing matters, including public offerings and private placement of debt and equity securities, and international securities offerings. Focuses primarily on offerings technology and Internet-related companies, as well as REITs. Also focuses on representing investment banks and issuers in private and public offerings of debt and equity securities of Israeli companies.
Personal: JD, New York University School of Law, 1987 (Member, Review of Law and Social Change); BA, New York University, 1984 (magna cum laude).

GOLDSTEIN, Marc
Proskauer Rose LLP, New York
212 969 3495
mgoldstein@proskauer.com
Recommended in Arbitration
Specialization: Counsel in numerous cases involving arbitration under UNCITRAL, ICC, WIPO, IACAC, AAA, Singapore Centre, and Danish Institute rules, including arbitration-related litigation before US courts.
Prof. Memberships: Member, Swiss Arb. Assoc. (ASA), Intl. Arb.Institute (IAI), Institute for Transnational Arbitration, AAA-IADR Advisory Committee, London Intl. Arb. Club; former chair, ABA-SILP International Arb. Committee; Fellow, Chartered Inst. of Arbitrators.
Career: JD 1980 University of Virginia, BA 1976 University of Pennsylvania.
Publications: Author of numerous publications on international dispute resolution.

GOLDSTEIN, Marcia
Weil, Gotshal & Manges LLP, New York
212 310 8000
marcia.goldstein@weil.com
Recommended in Insolvency
Specialization: Partner in the Business Finance and Restructuring Department of *Weil, Gotshal & Manges LLP* for more than 25 years. Has represented bank groups, secured and unsecured creditors,

debtors statutory creditors' committees, trustee, and other parties in major debt restructurings and chapter 11 cases, including Regal Cinemas, Inc; Washington Group International, Inc; AMF Bowling Worldwide, Inc; United Companies Financial Corp; CRIMI MAE, Inc; Babcock & Wilcox, Inc; Purina Mills, Inc; SGL Carbon Corp; Marvel Entertainment, Inc; Paragon Trade Brands, Inc; Donald J Trump and affiliates; Allied Department, Stores, Inc; Anacomp, Inc; Metalurg, Inc; Elder-Beerman Stores, Inc; Southland, Inc; Gitano, Inc; American Healthcare; Piecegoods Shops, Inc; Silas Creek Retain, Inc; CISC, Inc; Telesphere, Inc; Telemundo, Inc; Storage Technology, Inc; Nucorp Energy, Inc; Lionel Corp; Tomlinson, Inc; Food Fair, Inc; White Motor Corp; and WT Grant Co.
Career: Certified mediator in the Southern District of New York and has served as a mediator in a number of chapter 11 cases. Also served as a chapter 11 trustee. Is on the Advisory Board of Colliers Bankruptcy, 15th Ed, has been a visiting lecturer in bankruptcy at Yale Law School, is a member of the National Bankruptcy Conference, and chairs the Committee on Legislation, and is a member of the American College of Bankruptcy. Member of the Association of the Bar of the City of New York, served as the Chair of the Committee on Bankruptcy and Corporate Reorganization. Member of the American Bar Association, served on the Chapter 11 Committee and related sub-committees in the Section of Corporation, Banking and Business Law.
Publications: Frequently lectures and publishes material for continuing legal education programmes.
Personal: JD, Cornell Law School (1975); AB, Cornell University (1973).

GOLDSTEIN, Marvin
Stroock & Stroock & Lavan LLP,
New York 212 806 5400
Recommended in Capital Markets

GOODMAN, Janice
Goodman & Zuchlewski LLP, New York
212 869 1940
Recommended in Employment

GOODWILLIE, Eugene
White & Case LLP, New York
212 819 8200
Recommended in Projects

GORDON, David A
Latham & Watkins LLP, New York
212 906 1251
david.gordon@lw.com
Recommended in Projects
Specialization: Represents primarily banks, financial institutions and sponsors in connection with all phases of the development, financing and restructuring of energy, telecommunications and other infrastructure and industrial projects. Experienced in the development,

financing and restructuring of private power projects, including portfolio financings and domestic and multijurisdictional telecommunications projects, including submarine cable, 'last mile' and telecom hotel projects. Transactional experience includes the structuring of projects and related financing, due diligence and coordination and negotiation of project and financing agreements.
Career: Managing Partner, *Latham & Watkins*' New York office.
Personal: JD, Syracuse University College of Law, 1986.

GORDON, Steve
Cravath, Swaine & Moore, New York
212 474 1000
Recommended in Tax

GORRELL, JR, J Warren
Hogan & Hartson LLP, New York
212 918 5500
jwgorrell@hhlaw.com
Recommended in Corporate/M&A
Specialization: The chairman of *Hogan & Hartson LLP* and a co-director of the firm's Corporate, Securities and Finance Practice Group. His practice, which is primarily transactional, covers several different areas and has involved many different industries. He represents publicly and privately held companies and their controlling shareholders in all aspects of their businesses, including mergers and acquisitions, equity and quasi-equity securities offerings and private placements, senior and subordinated debt financings, tender offers and exchange offers, restructurings and recapitalizations, joint ventures, and general business matters. He also represents a number of major national and regional investment banking firms in connection with domestic and international offerings of both debt and equity securities, including initial public offerings, primary and secondary offerings (including 144A placements), and corporate restructurings and reorganizations. In the last several years, a significant part of his practice has been focused on the real estate industry and related businesses. He has been the partner principally responsible for the major publicly and privately offered real estate investment trust (REIT) offerings and mergers and acquisitions in which numerous public company and investment banking clients have been involved.
Career: He joined *Hogan & Hartson LLP* as an associate in 1979 and became a partner in 1986. He was one of 12 corporate lawyers in the United States recognized as a Dealmaker of the Year for 1998 by a leading legal publication.
Personal: He received his undergraduate degree in economics in 1976 from Princeton University, where he graduated magna cum laude. He received his law degree in 1979 from the University of Virginia School of Law. He is a member of the New York and the District of Columbia Bars.

GOTTS, Ilene Knable
Wachtell, Lipton, Rosen & Katz, New York 212 403 1247
ikgotts@wlrk.com
Recommended in Antitrust
Specialization: Specializes in antitrust matters, particularly relating to mergers and acquisitions. Recent international transactions in which she has served as antitrust counsel include: Diageo plc/General Mills, Inc., Deutsche Telekom AG/VoiceStream Wireless Corporation, Comcast/AT&T Corp./Time Warner Entertainment, The British Petroleum Company plc./Amoco Corp., Phillips Petroleum Company/Tosco Corporation, Fort James Corp./Georgia-Pacific Corp., and Morton International Inc./Rohm & Haas Co.
Prof. Memberships: Has long been an active participant in the Antitrust Section of the American Bar Association; currently serves on the council and is the Chair of the Task Force on the Merger Review Process; and previously served as the Chair of the Section's Clayton Act Committee.
Career: Partner at *Wachtell, Lipton, Rosen & Katz*. Previously worked as a staff attorney in the Bureau of Competition of the Federal Trade Commission in conduct and merger investigations, and in the FTC Bureau of Consumer Protection. In 1995, served as the President of the Washington Council of Lawyers. Chair of the Antitrust and Trade Regulation Section of the Federal Bar Association from 1995-97. Currently a member of the American Law Institute, and the New York State Bar Association's Antitrust Section Executive Committees.
Publications: Frequent guest speaker; published over 85 articles on antitrust related topics; editor of the second edition of the, 'ABA Merger Review Process Handbook'; a member of the advisory board of the Antitrust & Trade Regulation Report; and the editorial board of 'The Antitrust Counselor' and 'The Practical Lawyer' publications.
Personal: Graduated magna cum laude from the University of Maryland (BA), where she was elected to membership in Phi Beta Kappa; and cum laude from Georgetown University Law Center in 1984 (JD).

GRAEV, Lawrence
King & Spalding LLP, New York
212 556 2167
lgraev@kslaw.com
Recommended in Private Equity
Specialization: Private equity investment funds, including fund formation, structuring, negotiation and execution of leveraged acquisitions and venture capital and growth financings and divestitures, public offerings and recapitalizations. Represents investment and merchant banking organizations in their various corporate finance transactions and numerous high technology, e-commerce, telecommunications, healthcare and industrial and service businesses in their day to day operations, merger and acquisition, corporate finance transactions and strategic relationships.
Prof. Memberships: American Bar Association; New York State Bar Association.
Personal: BS, Cornell University, 1966; JD, The George Washington University, 1969.

GREEN, Jonathan
Milbank, Tweed, Hadley & McCloy, New York 212 530 5000
Recommended in Projects

GREEN, Ronald
Epstein Becker & Green PC, New York
212 351 4500
Recommended in Employment

GREENBAUM, Jack
Healy & Baillie LLP, New York
212 943 3980
Recommended in Shipping

GROSS, Steven R
Debevoise & Plimpton, New York
212 909 6586
srgross@debevoise.com
Recommended in Insolvency
Specialization: Partner and head of *Debevoise & Plimpton*'s Bankruptcy and Workouts Group (1985-present). His practice concentrates on bankruptcy and corporate restructuring and includes representation of debtors, creditors and investors. Recent debtor representations include: Reliance Group Holdings, Inc and Leiner Health Products Inc. Recent creditor representations include: AMF Bowling Worldwide, Inc and Global TeleSystems, Inc (Europe BV). Recently completed transactions include: Zenith Electronics Corporation; Phonetel Technologies, Inc; Aurora Foods, Inc and DecisionOne Corporation. Recently represented proposed investors in the Chapter 11 cases of Vlasic Foods International; Crown Vantage and USA Floral Products.
Prof. Memberships: American Bar Association; Association of the Bar of the City of New York; City Bar Committee on Bankruptcy and Corporate Reorganisation.
Career: Joined *Debevoise & Plimpton* in 1973 and became a partner in 1981.
Publications: Co-author of 'Collier Business Workout Guide' (Matthew Bender, 2002).
Personal: Columbia University, BA, 1968 and MA, 1969; Cambridge University, LLB, 1971; Yale Law School, JD, 1973.

GROSSHANDLER, Seth
Cleary Gottlieb Steen & Hamilton, New York 212 225 2000
sgrosshandler@cgsh.com
Recommended in Capital Markets
Specialization: Creditors' rights, derivative products, securities transactions, financial institutions and structured finance, with particular emphasis on risks to counterparties and investors in the event of insolvency.
Prof. Memberships: Member of the Bar in New York.
Career: Joined the firm in 1983; became partner in 1992. JD, Law Review Editorial Board, cum laude, Order of the Coif, Northwestern University School of Law (1983), BA, Phi Beta Kappa, Reed College (1979).
Publications: He lectures and is widely published on various aspects of creditors' rights and derivative products and securities transactions.

GROVE, Barry
Thelen Reid & Priest LLP, New York
212 603 6540
barrygrove@thelenreid.com
Recommended in Construction
Specialization: Trial lawyer with substantial litigation, mediation, dispute review board and arbitration experience in all phases of construction claims on major projects such as dams, tunnels, pipelines, powerhouses, wastewater treatment plants, waste to energy projects, cement plants, highways, bridges, mass transit, telecommunications and municipal, industrial and highrise buildings. He also has extensive experience in insurance disputes, including builder's risk claims; contract formation and contract administration and project structuring advice to owners and contractors.
Prof. Memberships: His is a member of the California, New York and District of Columbia Bars. He is admitted to practice before the US Supreme Court; US District Court, Northern District of California; US District Court, Southern District of California; US District Court, Southern District of New York; Ninth Circuit Court of Appeals and US Court of Claims. He retains pro haec vice admissions: Mississippi, Nevada, Alaska, Michigan, Utah, Wyoming and New Jersey. He is also a member of the American Bar Association, Litigation Section and Construction Law Committee and is a Charter Member of the American College of Construction Lawyers where he served as Secretary, 1992; Treasurer, 2000-01 and President Elect, 2002. He has served on Center for Public Resources, Construction Panel, the AAA Arbitration Panel and is a member of the London Court of International Arbitration.
Career: His speaking engagements include the ABA Annual Meeting, 1981, 1987 and 1989; Fall Meeting, 1983 and Forum Committee on the Construction Industry, 1985. He has lectured at the Practicing Law Institute construction law courses 1980 through 1990, 1993 and 1998 and was an Instructor at the NITA Federal Practice Programs, 1980, 1981,

1982 and 1984 and at the Hastings College of Trial Advocacy, 1982, 1983 and 1984. He has spoken at the ENR Construction Seminar, 1983 through 1987; and ENR's Building Successfully Without Disputes, 1992. He has presented at the B Warren Hart Memorial Lecture Series on Construction Law, 1983 and the Construction Law Superconference, 1985-98 and 2001. He spoke at the Forbes Conference on Project Financing and Construction in the 1990's, 1992; Forbes Conference on Rebuilding America, 1993 and 1994; and the Forbes Conference on Worldwide Infrastructure Partnerships, 1998. He spoke on Resolving Disputes in International Construction Contracts through ADR Techniques, Geneva, 1992; on Identifying, Minimizing and Quantifying Construction Risks, London, 1996 and on Arbitration in an ADR World, Hong Kong, 1996. Served as Chairman, World Conference on Construction Risk, Paris, Singapore, 1994-96 and Consultant to the Government of the Special Administrative Region of Hong Kong, 1998.
Publications: Publications include: Contributing author, 'Construction Litigation: Representing the Owner', Wiley, 1983. Contributing author, 'Construction Litigation: Representing the Contractor', Wiley, 1985. Contributing author, 'Construction Law Treatise', Matthew Bender, 1987. Contributing author, 'Construction Failures', Wiley, 1989. Contributing author, 'Construction Subcontracting', Wiley, 1990. Contributing author, 'Proving and Pricing Construction Claims', Wiley, 1990. Contributing author, 'Construction Subcontracting', Wiley, 1991. Contributing author, 'Construction Litigation: Representing the Contractor', 2nd Ed., Wiley, 1992. Contributing author, 'Lien and Bond Laws', Wiley, 1992. Contributing author, 'Design-Build Construction Workbook', Wiley, 1992. Contributing author, 'Construction Law', Wiley, 1992.
Personal: He received his JD in 1966 from the University of Virginia Law School and his BA in French in 1963 from the Washington and Lee University.

GUTOWSKI, Peter
Freehill Hogan & Mahar LLP, New York
212 425 1900
Recommended in Shipping

GUYNN, Randall
Davis Polk & Wardwell, New York
212 450 4000
Recommended in Banking & Finance

HACKETT, Kevin
Shearman & Sterling, New York
212 848 4000
Recommended in Real Estate

HADLEY, Joseph
Davis Polk & Wardwell, New York
212 450 4000
Recommended in Projects

HAIMS, Bruce D
Debevoise & Plimpton, New York
212 909 6441
bdhaims@debevoise.com
Recommended in Tax
Specialization: Partner and Head of *Debevoise & Plimpton*'s Tax Department (1995-present). His practice concentrates in general tax advice, mergers and acquisitions, partnerships, investment funds and executive compensation. He provides personal and business tax advice to individuals and companies involved in media, communications and entertainment. Represents high net worth individuals in the integration of business and personal income tax and estate tax planning in business transactions as well as in tax controversies.
Prof. Memberships: Association of the Bar of the City of New York; New York State Bar Association; International Fiscal Association.
Career: US Army Captain (1965-67). Joined *Debevoise & Plimpton* in 1967 and became a partner in 1973.
Publications: 'Assignment of Income - Has Ferguson Hastened the Ripening Process?' (87 Tax Notes 807, May 8, 2000); 'The Estate Planner As Transactional Lawyer' (55 NYU Institute on Federal Taxation, 1997); 'A Practitioner's Guide to the Preparation for and Conduct of a Tax Audit' (53 NYU Institute on Federal Taxation, Chapter 24, 1995).
Personal: University of Pennsylvania, BS, 1962; Harvard Law School, LLB, magna cum laude, 1965; New York University, LLM in Taxation, 1972.

HALEY, James
Fish & Neave, New York
212 596 9000
Recommended in Intellectual Property

HALL, Richard
Cravath, Swaine & Moore, New York
212 474 1000
Recommended in Corporate/M&A

HALLIDAY, Joseph W
Skadden, Arps, Slate, Meagher & Flom LLP & Affiliates, New York
212 735 3260
jhallida@skadden.com
Recommended in Banking & Finance
Specialization: Founder and Co-head, *Skadden*'s Banking and Institutional Investing Group, represents commercial banks, investment banks, insurance companies and borrowers from the same. Practice involves banking and restructurings.
Prof. Memberships: Member, Banking Law Committee, NY State Bar Association; Member, TriBar Legal Opinion Committee.
Personal: LLB, Fordham University, 1963 (cum laude; Editor in Chief, 'Fordham Law Review'); AB, Fordham University, 1960 (egregia cum laude).

HALVEY, John
Milbank, Tweed, Hadley & McCloy, New York 212 530 5000
Recommended in Communications

HANDELSMAN, Lawrence
Stroock & Stroock & Lavan LLP, New York 212 806 5400
Recommended in Insolvency

HANDMAN, Laura
Davis Wright Tremaine LLP, New York
202 508 6624
laurahandman@dwt.com
Recommended in Media & Entertainment
Specialization: Partner, media law, litigation, intellectual property. Experience defending newspapers/electronic publishers in libel actions and other First Amendment matters. Clients include The New York Times, BBC, Discovery Communications, Amazon.com.
Prof. Memberships: Past chair, Communications/Media Law Committee of Association of the Bar, New York City. Founder/past chair, Media Law Committee, DC Bar. Past president, Defense Counsel section, Libel Defense Resource Center.
Career: Frequent lecturer/author on media/intellectual property law.
Publications: 'Internet and Intellectual Property,' Inter American Press Association, October 2001. 'Congress, the Networks and Exit Polls,' Communications Lawyer, Winter 2001.
Personal: JD, (magna cum laude), Boston University, 1977. BA, (cum laude), Yale, 1973.

HANRAHAN, Marc
Skadden, Arps, Slate, Meagher & Flom LLP & Affiliates, New York
212 735 2274
mhanraha@skadden.com
Recommended in Banking & Finance
Specialization: Partner, New York. Concentrates on corporate law matters with a particular focus on representing banks and other financial institutions. Has extensive experience representing lenders in acquisition financings, including leveraged buyouts, tender offers and other going private transactions.
Personal: JD, University of Texas, 1980 (cum laude, Order of the Coif); BA, University of California at Santa Barbara, 1977 (summa cum laude).

HARITON, David P
Sullivan & Cromwell LLP, New York
212 558 4000
haritond@sullcrom.com
Recommended in Tax
Specialization: Practice focuses on US federal income tax matters, including taxation of financial instruments, transactions and products; cross-border investment; and international operations. Represents the securities industry association on federal income tax matters.
Prof. Memberships: New York State Bar Association (current Secretary and Chair-elect for 2005, Tax Section).
Career: Joined *Sullivan & Cromwell* in 1985. Partner since 1994.
Publications: Has written extensively on federal income tax treatment of contingent debt instruments, debt-equity hybrids, foreign currency obligations, foreign currency swaps, equity-indexed swaps, recapitalizations, interest expense allocation, and outbound distributions and liquidations. Lectures for Practicing Law Institute, New York University Institute on Federal Income Taxation, University of Chicago Law School and other groups.
Personal: Born 1957 in New York, New York. Graduate of Stanford University (BA, 1981) and Stanford Law School (JD, 1985; member, Order of the Coif).

HARMS, David B
Sullivan & Cromwell LLP, New York
212 558 4000
harmsd@sullcrom.com
Recommended in Capital Markets
Specialization: Focuses on a wide variety of general securities and corporate law matters, including SEC-registered offerings, private placements, international corporate finance, high-yield debt financing, internet offerings and trading practices and negotiated merger and acquisition transactions. Also serves as co-coordinator of *Sullivan & Cromwell*'s securities finance practice and coordinator of the firm's broker-dealer regulation practice.
Prof. Memberships: Association of the Bar of the City of New York.
Career: Judicial Clerk to the Honorable Edward Weinfeld, US District Court (S.D.N.Y.) 1984-85. Joined *Sullivan & Cromwell* in 1985. Became a partner of the firm in 1992.
Publications: 'E-Offerings and the 1933 Act: Applying the Old Rules in a New Arena' in 'The Internet Age: What Securities Lawyers Need to Know to Survive', Practising Law Institute (2000); 'Integration Under the 1933 Act: The SEC Provides New Safe Harbors' in 'The Review of Securities & Commodities Regulation' (2001); and 'Behind the Numbers: A Review of Six Accounting Problem Areas in the News' in 'What Every Lawyer Needs to Know About Accounting Now - or Else!', Practising Law Institute (2002).
Personal: Born 1954. Attended the State University of New York at Purchase (BA, 1978) and New York University Law School (JD, 1984; Editor in Chief, NYU Law Review).

HARPER, Conrad
Simpson Thacher & Bartlett, New York
212 455 2000
Recommended in Arbitration

NEW YORK — LEADERS

HARRELL, Michael P
Debevoise & Plimpton, New York
212 909 6349
mpharrel@debevoise.com
Recommended in Private Equity
Specialization: Partner at *Debevoise & Plimpton*. His practice concentrates on advising sponsors of, and investors in, private investment funds, including leveraged buyout, venture capital, international private equity, merchant banking and telecommunications funds. He writes and speaks frequently on private equity funds and co-teaches a course on private equity funds at Columbia Law School in New York City.
Prof. Memberships: Chair, New York Private Investment Funds Forum (2002); Member, Executive Committee of Specialised Investment Funds Committee of the International Bar Association; Member, American Bar Association and Association of the Bar of the City of New York; Member, Advisory Board, New York Chapter of the Private Equity CFOs Association.
Career: Joined *Debevoise & Plimpton* in 1986 and became a partner in 1996. He was based in the firm's London office from 1991-93.
Publications: Co-author, 'Private Equity Funds' (2002); Advisory Board, 'Private Equity Partnership Terms and Conditions' (Asset Alternatives, 2000 and 2003); Co-author, Internet Incubators: How to Invest in the New Economy Without Becoming an Investment Company,' 'The Business Lawyer' (American Bar Association, 2000).
Personal: Dartmouth College, AB, cum laude, 1982; University of California at Los Angeles, JD, 1985.

HARRIS, Adam
O'Melveny & Myers LLP, New York
212 408 2400
Recommended in Insolvency

HARRIS, Douglas
Milbank, Tweed, Hadley & McCloy,
New York 212 530 5000
Recommended in Projects

HARTNETT, Bill
Cahill Gordon & Reindel, New York
212 701 3900
Recommended in Capital Markets

HARTY, Ronan
Davis Polk & Wardwell, New York
212 450 4000
Recommended in Antitrust

HAWK, Barry E
Skadden, Arps, Slate, Meagher & Flom LLP & Affiliates, New York
212 735 3892
bhawk@skadden.com
Recommended in Antitrust
Specialization: Partner, New York & Brussels. Advises clients primarily in the areas of European Union and national antitrust laws and merger controls, European Union regulatory law, US antitrust law and merger control laws throughout the world. Has advised on EU and European Law in connection with M&A, joint ventures, privatisations, distribution and licensing, enforcement actions and litigation, public procurement, project financing, state aids or government subsidies, and various regulatory matters.
Prof. Memberships: Co-Chair, Associates Committee, Antitrust Section, American Bar Association (1994-present).
Personal: LLB, University of Virginia School of Law, 1965; AB, Fordham College, 1962.

HAYDEN, Raymond
Hill Rivkins & Hayden LLP, New York
212 669 0600
Recommended in Shipping

HAZAN, Scott
Otterbourg, Steindler, Houston & Rosen, New York 212 661 9100
Recommended in Insolvency

HEARD, Keith
Burke & Parsons, New York
212 354 3800
Recommended in Shipping

HEFTLER, Thomas
Stroock & Stroock & Lavan LLP, New York 212 806 5400
Recommended in Capital Markets

HEINZELMAN, Kris
Cravath, Swaine & Moore, New York
212 474 1000
Recommended in Capital Markets

HEITNER, Kenneth H
Weil, Gotshal & Manges LLP, New York
212 310 8288
kenneth.heitner@weil.com
Recommended in Tax
Specialization: Tax partner in the New York office of *Weil, Gotshal & Manges* and co-head of the firm's Tax Group. Has been a partner with the firm since 1981. Skills as a corporate tax advisor are widely recognized and regularly acts on the full range of tax issues affecting corporations transacting their business in the United States and abroad as well as on numerous tax-efficient structures for cross-border transactions.
Prof. Memberships: Executive Committee, New York State Bar Association, Tax Section; Member, American Bar Association; Member, Bar Association of the City of New York; Member, Tax Club.
Personal: BA, Rutgers University (1969); JD, New York University School of Law (1973); LLM (1977).

HELENIAK, David
Shearman & Sterling, New York
212 848 4000
Recommended in Corporate/M&A

HENDERSON, JR, Donald B
LeBoeuf, Lamb, Greene & MacRae, LLP, New York 212 424 8694
dhenders@llgm.com
Recommended in Insurance
Specialization: A corporate lawyer with extensive experience in insurance mergers and acquisitions, public and private financing and related insurance regulatory matters. His experience includes purchases and sales of businesses, including both stock and asset transactions, and purchases and sales of specific blocks of business. A frequent public speaker, has also has written on insurance and corporate issues for numerous publications, including 'Best's Review', 'Business Insurance', 'The National Underwriter', 'International Insurance Law Review', 'Reactions and Reinsurance'.
Personal: University of Alabama (BS) 1971; University of Alabama Law Center (JD) 1974; New York University (LLM) 1976.

HENGEN, Nancy
Holland & Knight LLP, New York
212 513 3200
nhengen@hklaw.com
Recommended in Shipping
Specialization: Partner in Business Law Department. She represents clients in secured and unsecured financing transactions in connection with commercial vessels and other 'big ticket' equipment financing, including leveraged and single-investor leases, synthetic leases, loan agreements and related security documentation, ship mortgages, Title XI financing, and other US governmental financing programs and vessel construction contracts. She has represented US and foreign banks, financial institutions and other investors, as well as borrowers and lessees in loan and leasing transactions involving equipment and facilities. Her practice includes mergers and acquisitions in the shipping industry and corporate transactions. She is also experienced in the formation and governance of corporations established under Liberian, Vanuatu and Marshall Islands laws and has dealt extensively with those jurisdictions and other 'flags of convenience.'

HERLIHY, Edward D
Wachtell, Lipton, Rosen & Katz,
New York 212 403 1207
edherlihy@wlrk.com
Recommended in Corporate/M&A
Specialization: Specializes in the largest and most complex bank and financial institution mergers and acquisitions and recapitalizations throughout the United States and is often called upon to represent companies involved in takeover battles and proxy contests, including investment banking firms in connection with a wide variety of financial institution matters.
Career: Partner at *Wachtell, Lipton, Rosen & Katz*.
Publications: Writes and lectures regularly on issues involving banking and financial matters.

HERSCH, Dennis
Davis Polk & Wardwell, New York
212 450 4000
Recommended in Corporate/M&A

HEWITT, William
Reboul, MacMurray, Hewitt, Maynard & Kristol, New York 212 841 5700
Recommended in Private Equity

HIRSCHBERG, William
Shearman & Sterling, New York
212 848 4000
Recommended in Banking & Finance

HONAN III, William J
Holland & Knight LLP, New York
212 513 3200
whonan@hklaw.com
Recommended in Shipping
Specialization: Partner in the Litigation Department. He has extensive experience in arbitration, mediation and maritime law, especially as to maritime contracts. He is vice-chairman of the Documentary Committee of Intertanko, an entity that represents most of the privately owned tanker owners in the world. He is also a member of the Arbitration Committee of the ABA Section of Dispute Resolutions, is a member of the Committee on Arbitration and ADR of the International Bar Association and is a member of the Committee on Maritime Arbitration of the Maritime Law Association of the United States. He has written articles featured in 'Lloyd's of London Press' and 'Seatrade' and speaks often on a variety of subjects concerning arbitration and maritime law.

HOOPER, Chester
Holland & Knight LLP, New York
212 513 3200
chooper@hklaw.com
Recommended in Shipping
Specialization: Partner in the Litigation Department. His practice involves the defense of vessel interests against claims for cargo damage, multimodal carriage of cargo and drafting bills of lading. He has tried numerous cargo cases on behalf of vessel interests. He was president of The Maritime Law Association of the United States from May 1994 until May 1996 and is a Titulary member of the Comitè Maritime International. He has published numerous articles on admiralty cargo issues and has lectured extensively on the subject of the carriage of goods. He was navigator of the USS TRUCKEE (AO-147) while on active duty in the US Navy and also sailed as a third mate in the United States Merchant Marine.

HOPKINSON, R Ronald
Latham & Watkins LLP, New York
212 906 1840
ron.hopkinson@lw.com
Recommended in Private Equity

Specialization: Corporate partner, New York office. Primarily focuses on mergers and acquisitions and corporate restructurings. Represents merchant banking organizations and leveraged buyout groups, including The Carlyle Group, Welsh Carson and BC Partners. Served as lead counsel to The Carlyle Group and Welsh Carson on their US$7.05 billion buyout of QwestDex. Other acquisition and restructuring clients include Hubbell Incorporated, Mark IV Industries, Vought Aircraft, Park Place Entertainment, First Washington Realty Trust and General Cigar Holdings.
Prof. Memberships: Admitted to practice in New York and District of Columbia.
Personal: JD, Harvard University, 1988, cum laude. BA, Harvard University, 1984, magna cum laude, Phi Beta Kappa.

HOROWITZ, Richard
Thacher Proffitt & Wood, New York
212 789 1200
Recommended in Capital Markets

HOROWITZ, Steven
Cleary Gottlieb Steen & Hamilton, New York 212 225 2000
shorowitz@cgsh.com
Recommended in Real Estate

Specialization: Real estate finance, joint ventures, capital markets and mortgage finance. Clients include Deutsche Bank, Salomon Brothers and Goldman Sachs.
Prof. Memberships: Member of the Board of Governors of the American College of Real Estate Lawyers and of the Board of Directors of the Legal Aid Society.
Career: Joined firm in 1987, became partner in 1989. Previously a partner at *Hill & Barlow*. JD degree, cum laude, Harvard Law School (1978). MPP degree, cum laude, Kennedy School of Government at Harvard (1978).
Publications: Frequent lecturer and author for continuing legal education seminars.
Personal: Resides in New York and is married with three children.

HUCK, L Francis
Simpson Thacher & Bartlett, New York
212 455 2000
Recommended in Banking & Finance

HUDANISH, David
Mayer, Brown, Rowe & Maw, New York
212 506 2500
Recommended in Communications

HYLTON, Hartwell
Simpson Thacher & Bartlett, New York
212 455 2000
Recommended in Banking & Finance

HYMAN, Alan
Proskauer Rose LLP, New York
212 969 3000
Recommended in Insolvency

INDOE, William F
Sullivan & Cromwell LLP, New York
212 558 4000
indoew@sullcrom.com
Recommended in Tax

Specialization: Focuses on the tax structuring of complex financial transactions, with particular experience in M&A, divestitures and spin-offs. Has represented investment banks as well as principals in hundreds of complex transactions, including: tax-free mergers; cross-border acquisitions; conversions of 'C corps' into real estate investment trusts; sales of privately owned businesses; divestitures accomplished through joint ventures; and transactions involving asset managers. Renders tax advice in securities offerings; participates in the preparation and negotiation of employment and severance arrangements, stock option and other incentive compensation plans, and resolution of employee benefit issues both in the ordinary course and in change of control situations.
Prof. Memberships: American Bar Association; Association of the Bar of the City of New York; New York State Bar Association.
Career: Joined *Sullivan & Cromwell* in 1968. Elected a Partner of the firm in 1976.
Personal: Born 1942. Attended Lehigh University (BA, 1964) and the University of Virginia Law School (LLB, 1968). Director, Rho Capital Partners, Inc; Director, The Haven Capital Management Trust.

INGRAM, John
Healy & Baillie LLP, New York
212 943 3980
Recommended in Shipping

ISAACSON, Laurence B
Fried, Frank, Harris, Shriver & Jacobson, New York 212 859 8554
Laurence.Isaacson@FriedFrank.com
Recommended in Capital Markets

Specialization: Corporate partner. Concentrates practice in structured finance, particularly in complex securitisations, and the development, offering and sale of structured products. Clients include commercial and investment banks, insurance companies and other institutional investors and participants in the structured finance market. Has assisted Bear, Stearns & Co., Deutsche Bank AG, Goldman, Sachs & Co., the International Finance Corporation, JP Morgan Chase & Co., Morgan Stanley & Co., SG Cowen Securities Corporation and UBS AG in the structuring and offering of collateralized debt obligations, credit linked transactions and other structured products.
Prof. Memberships: Association of the Bar of the City of New York; American Bar Association.
Career: Qualified in 1987. Joined *Fried, Frank* in 1997 as a partner. Previously he was a partner in the New York office of *Orrick, Herrington & Sutcliffe LLP*. He began his career at *Milbank, Tweed, Hadley & McCloy*.
Personal: Born 1963. Received JD from Duke University in 1987 and BA from Cornell University in 1984.

IVANHOE, Robert
Greenberg Traurig LLP, New York
212 801 9200
Recommended in Real Estate

JACOBSON, Martin
Simpson Thacher & Bartlett, New York
212 455 2000
Recommended in Projects

JAFFE, Helene D
Weil, Gotshal & Manges LLP, New York
212 310 8572
helene.jaffe@weil.com
Recommended in Antitrust

Specialization: Co-chair of the Trade Practices and Regulatory Department and practices in the principal areas of transactional, counseling and litigation aspects of advertising, marketing and antitrust issues (particularly regarding mergers, acquisitions, and Hart-Scott-Rodino matters). She has been involved in numerous Lanham Act advertising, trademark, and trade dress cases (injunctions as well as judge/jury trials) involving a broad spectrum of consumer products and services, such as over-the-counter drugs, cosmetics, and foods, as well as challenges for these products, among others, at the networks, industry self-regulatory boards, and various international, federal and state regulatory agencies. She appears regularly before both the international, federal, and state antitrust enforcement agencies and the federal judiciary representing clients who are either buying or selling companies here or abroad as well as clients whose pricing, promotional, or marketing practices are under investigation. Among the mergers/joint ventures handled: General Motors' sale of Hughes and DirecTV to Echostar; American Airlines' purchase of TWA; Haliburton's purchase of Dresser Industries; CBS' purchase of Outdoor Systems, Inc.; GAF's joint venture with Johns Manville; and CBS' sale of its Power Generation business to Siemens. In addition, she has been lead trial counsel in some of the largest antitrust cases for American Airlines, including the Department of Justice's predation case against America in which summary judgement was just granted, US Airways' antitrust conspiracy challenge to the American/British Airways alliance and American's lawsuit against United Airlines' acquisition of Air Wisconsin. Finally, she has done extensive work in the healthcare area, in particular, for some of the leading pharmaceutical companies.
Prof. Memberships: Member of the Trade Regulation Committee of the Association of the Bar of the City of New York.
Personal: Adjunct Associate Professor at New York University School of Law, teaching a graduate course in Federal Trade Commission Law. She has served as the Chair of the Consumer Protection Committee, Vice-chair of the Clayton Act Committee and on the Council of the ABA's Antitrust Section, Chair of the Committee on Trade Regulation of the New York County Lawyer's Association. She lectures and writes extensively on antitrust, merger advertising, and marketing issues. She is a 1976 graduate of Columbia Law School where she was a Harlan Fiske Stone Scholar.

JENNER, Jesse
Fish & Neave, New York
212 596 9000
Recommended in Intellectual Property

JOFFE, Bob
Cravath, Swaine & Moore, New York
212 474 1000
Recommended in Antitrust

JOHNSTON, Elaine
White & Case LLP, New York
212 819 8200
Recommended in Antitrust

JOSEPH, Gregory
Gregory P. Joseph Law Offices LLC, New York 212 407 1200
Recommended in Litigation

KADEN, Lewis
Davis Polk & Wardwell, New York
212 450 4000
Recommended in Corporate/M&A

KADLICK, Richard F
Skadden, Arps, Slate, Meagher & Flom LLP & Affiliates, New York
212 735 2716
rkadlick@skadden.com
Recommended in Capital Markets

Specialization: Partner, New York. Represents principally underwriters, financial institutions, banks and borrowers in mortgage-backed and asset-backed securities transactions; credit enhancers in credit-enhanced securities issuances. Has acted as counsel in a variety of public offerings, private placements and transactions in which structured securities instruments have been backed by single-family and commercial mortgage loans, credit card receivables, under-performing and non-performing assets, home equity loan receivables, auto loan receivables, boat loan receivables, federal agency securities, auto and equipment leases and various other assets.
Personal: JD, Georgetown University, 1982; BA, Hamilton College, 1979 (summa cum laude; Phi Beta Kappa).

NEW YORK — LEADERS

KAFIN, Robert
Proskauer Rose LLP, New York
212 969 3000
Recommended in Environment

KAPLAN, Cathy
Sidley Austin Brown & Wood, New York
212 839 5300
Recommended in Capital Markets

KARABELL, David
Carter Ledyard & Milburn LLP, New York
212 732 3200
Recommended in Private Equity

KAROTKIN, Stephen
Weil, Gotshal & Manges LLP, New York
212 310 8000
stephen.karotkin@weil.com
Recommended in Insolvency
Specialization: Since joining the firm in 1976, has concentrated in the area of business reorganisations, debt restructurings, debtor and creditors' rights and financing transactions. Was involved in the representation of Texaco Inc, Revere Copper and Brass Incorporated and The Western Company of North America in their cases under chapter 11 of the Bankruptcy Code. Was counsel for the Bank lending group in the restructure of the Indebtedness of Tosco Corporation, a major independent oil refiner, and also was involved in the international restructuring of Massey Ferguson, Inc; represented the United Illuminating Company in its bid for Public Service Company of New Hampshire (Seabrook Nuclear Power Plant) and Alco Standard Corporation in its acquisition of Saxon Industries, Inc in its asbestos-related chapter 11 case. Also represented Fine Host Corporation, a contract food service management company, in its chapter 11 case and was involved in the restructuring of two major corporations located in Argentina. Currently, representing the lenders in the Integrated Health Services, Inc chapter 11 case, and is representing Armstrong World Industries in its pending chapter 11 case. Has been involved in numerous financing transactions, including representing the financial institutions in their pre and post-petition loans to Harvard Industries, Inc. Has been involved in many other debtor in possession financing transactions including current representation of the debtor in possession lenders in the Winstar Communications chapter 11 case. Has represented both lenders and borrowers in connection with several restructuring transactions.
Prof. Memberships: Member of the American Bar Association and its Section of Business Law and the New York State Bar Association. Was vice-chairman of the Litigation Subcommittee of the Business Bankruptcy Committee of the American Bar Association.
Career: Has lectured on numerous occasions, including various lectures at the National Conference of Bankruptcy Judges and recently at the Goldman Sachs Distressed Debt Conference.
Personal: JD, New York University School of Law (1976); BS, Union College (1973).

KASS, Stephen
Carter Ledyard & Milburn LLP, New York
212 732 3200
Recommended in Environment

KATCHER, Richard D
Wachtell, Lipton, Rosen & Katz,
New York 212 403 1222
rdkatcher@wlrk.com
Recommended in Corporate/M&A
Specialization: Specializes in mergers and acquisitions and corporate and securities law and governance. Has participated in numerous mergers and acquisitions and related matters, representing both acquirers and targets as well as investment bankers. Transactions include Monsanto's merger with Pharmacia, Warner Lambert's merger with Pfizer, AT&T Corp's acquisitions of MediaOne Group and Tele-Communications, Inc, the break-up of AT&T Corp, including the AT&T Broadband/Comcast transaction, Lilly Industries, Inc's sale to The Valspar Corporation, Hussmann International, Inc's sale to Ingersoll-Rand Company, American Stores' sale to Albertson's, Browning Ferris' sale to Allied Waste Industries, AT&T Corp's acquisition of McCaw Cellular, AT&T's disposition of Lucent Technologies and NCR Corp, and Monsanto's disposition of Solutia Inc. Cross-border transactions include the sale of Pet Incorporated to Grand Metropolitan and the sale of a greater than majority interest in Genentech Inc to Hoffman-LaRoche. Also represented clients in joint ventures and recapitalizations and has counseled boards and non-management directors on governance issues and investigations and on other crisis situations.
Prof. Memberships: Member of the Board of Trustees of New York University; former Chairman of the Special Committee on Mergers, Acquisitions and Corporate Control Contests of the Association of the Bar of the City of New York; member of the Securities Regulation Committee of the New York State Bar Association and the Association of the Bar of the City of New York.
Career: Partner at *Wachtell, Lipton, Rosen & Katz* since 1971; chairman of *Wachtell Lipton's* management committee.
Publications: Frequent lecturer on continuing legal education programs.
Personal: Graduated from Lafayette College in 1963 (BA) and from New York University School of Law in 1966 (LLB). A member of the 'New York University Law Review', a member of the Order of the Coif and a John Norton Pomeroy Scholar.

KATSH, Salem
Shearman & Sterling, New York
212 848 4000
Recommended in Intellectual Property

KATZ, David A
Wachtell, Lipton, Rosen & Katz,
New York 212 403 1309
dakatz@wlrk.com
Recommended in Corporate/M&A
Specialization: Specializes in the areas of mergers and acquisitions, complex securities transactions and corporate governance matters, and has been involved in many major international and domestic corporate transactions.
Prof. Memberships: Member of the American Bar Association (Section on Business Law); on the Editorial Board of the Committee on Corporate Practice; member of the Committee on Negotiated Acquisitions Task Force on Public Company Acquisitions; member of the Federal Securities Laws Committee, the New York State Bar Association (Section on Business Law); and the Association of the Bar of the City of New York (admitted to New York Bar).
Career: Partner at *Wachtell, Lipton, Rosen & Katz* since 1996. Adjunct Professor at New York University School of Law, Senior Professional Fellow at New York University Center for Law and Business and Adjunct Professor at the Owens Graduate School of Management at Vanderbilt University.
Publications: Has written extensively.
Personal: Graduated from Brandeis University and from New York University School of Law.

KAVALER, Thomas
Cahill Gordon & Reindel, New York
212 701 3900
Recommended in Litigation

KAWATA, Yukako
Davis Polk & Wardwell, New York
212 450 4000
Recommended in Private Equity

KAYLE, Bruce
Milbank, Tweed, Hadley & McCloy,
New York 212 530 5000
Recommended in Tax

KEANE, Paul
Cichanowicz, Callan, Keane, Vengrow & Textor LLP, New York 212 344 7042
Recommended in Shipping

KELLER, Bruce P
Debevoise & Plimpton, New York
212 909 6118
bpkeller@debevoise.com
Recommended in Media & Entertainment
Specialization: Supervises *Debevoise & Plimpton's* Intellectual Property Litigation Practice. Has litigated numerous widely-publicized cases, including those involving the Howard Stern radio show, the hit motion picture Spiderman, NFL television broadcasts, websites operated by The Washington Post, USA Today and other news organizations and numerous television commercials. Recent reported cases include Novartis v J&J Merck, 290 F.3d 578 (3rd Cir. 2002); Pharmacia v Alcon, 201 F. Supp 2d 335 (D.N.J. 2002); CNN v. Go SMS, 56 U.S.P.Q. 2d 1959 (S.D.N.Y. 2000); Infinity Broadcasting v. Kirkwood, 150 F 3d 104 (2d Cir. 1998).
Prof. Memberships: Advisor, American Law Institute's Restatement of the Law: Unfair Competition; Advisory Board of BNA's Patent, Trademark Copyright Journal, the Advertising Compliance Service, The Entertainment Law Reporter. Former Counsel to the International Trademark Association (INTA).
Career: Joined *Debevoise & Plimpton* in 1982; became partner in 1988.
Publications: 'Copyright Law: A Practitioner's Guide' (PLI 2001); 'The Game's the Same: Why Gambling in Cyberspace Violates Federal Law', 108 Yale L.J. 1569 (1999); 'Condemned To Repeat The Past: The Reemergence of Misappropriation And Other Common Law Theories of Protection For Intellectual Property', 11 Harv. J.L. & Tech. 131 (1996).
Personal: Cornell University, BS 1976; Boston University, JD 1979.

KELLY, Thomas
Debevoise & Plimpton, New York
212 909 6907
tmkelly@debevoise.com
Recommended in Insurance
Specialization: Partner at *Debevoise & Plimpton* and co-chair of firm's Insurance Industry Group and a member of the Banking Group. Practice focuses on mergers and acquisitions of insurance companies, demutualizations, public offerings and other capital raising by insurers, and insurance and bank regulatory matters. In April 2002, a leading American legal publication named him one of the Top 10 Dealmakers of the Year in the US. Recent representations include Provident Mutual Life Insurance Company in its demutualization and merger with Nationwide Financial Services and Principal Financial Group and The Phoenix Companies in their demutualization and IPOs.
Prof. Memberships: Association of the Bar of the City of New York.
Career: Joined *Debevoise & Plimpton* in 1984 and became partner in 1993. Law Clerk to Honorable Eugene H Nickerson, EDNY from 1983-84.
Publications: 'The Financial Holding Company Opportunity: Issues for Insurance Organizations' (forthcoming in the 'Review of Banking and Financial Services').
Personal: Columbia University, AB cum laude, 1979; Harvard Law School, JD cum laude, 1983. Serves on the Board of Symphony Space and the Investment Committee of the Social Science Research Council.

LEADERS

NEW YORK

KENNEDY, Donald
Carter Ledyard & Milburn LLP, New York
212 732 3200
Recommended in Shipping

KENNEDY, Thomas H
Skadden, Arps, Slate, Meagher & Flom LLP & Affiliates, New York
212 735 2526
tkennedy@skadden.com
Recommended in Corporate/M&A
Specialization: Partner, New York. Mergers, acquisitions, corporate finance, and other transactions with an emphasis on the telecommunications and information technology industries. Coordinator of the firm's corporate technology practice. Prior technology transactions include Ascend Communications, AOL, Compaq, NTL Inc., US Airways, Tradeweb, and Viewpointe Archive, among others. Experience in many hostile transactions, leveraged buyouts and governance matters representing (among many) Foot Locker, Hasbro, and Singer.
Prof. Memberships: Association of the Bar of the City of New York.
Personal: JD, Georgetown University Law Centre, 1981; BA, University of Virginia, 1978.

KERR, Diane
Davis Polk & Wardwell, New York
212 450 4000
Recommended in Corporate/M&A

KERR, John
Simpson Thacher & Bartlett, New York
212 455 2000
Recommended in Arbitration

KIDD, John
Clifford Chance US LLP, New York
212 878 3136
john.kidd@cliffordchance.com
Recommended in Intellectual Property
Specialization: Serves as global head of the firm's Intellectual Property Group and was formerly managing partner of the group. His practice focuses on representing plaintiffs or defendants in intellectual property trials and jury trials. He is a former patent examiner, and is a frequent speaker and author on intellectual property litigation, trial strategy and alternate dispute resolution. He was listed as 'highly recommended' for IP in the United States by a leading legal publication.

KIERNAN, John S
Debevoise & Plimpton, New York
212 909 6692
jskiernan@debevoise.com
Recommended in Litigation
Specialization: Practice focuses on broad range of commercial and quasi-commercial domestic and international litigation and arbitration, including international treaty claims, securities actions, derivative and class actions, intellectual property disputes, consumer fraud actions, libel and other First Amendment litigations,

accountants liability suits and mass tort actions. Co-Chair of firm's Litigation Department; Chair of its Ethics Committee.
Prof. Memberships: Association of the Bar of the City of New York (Chair, Nominating Committee, 2002-present; Chair, Committee on Pro Bono and Legal Services, 1997-2000); Litigation Section of the American Bar Association (Co-Chair, Discovery and Pretrial Practice Committee, 2002-present; Co-Chair, Committee on State Justice Initiatives, 1998-2000; Member, State Justice Initiatives Task Force, 1995-97; Co-Chair, 1997-98; Member, Task Force on Settlement Ethics, 2000-present); New York State Bar Association; Federal Bar Council (Co-Chair, Mentoring Committee, 1993-present; Public Service Committee, 2000-present).
Career: Joined *Debevoise* in 1981, became partner in 1988. Law Clerk to Hon Walter R Mansfield of the Second Circuit. Director of Legal Services for New York City (Vice-Chair, 1994-2003, Chair, 2003-present); Director of Justice Resource Center (Chair, 1995-present); Lawyers Committee for Civil Rights Under Law (Executive Committee, 1997-present, Regional Co-Chair, 2000-present); Volunteers of Legal Service (President, 2000-present); former Trustee (1993-99) and Mayor (1999-2001), Pelham Manor, New York.
Publications: Lecturer at annual ALI-ABA Seminars on Acountants Liability, 1989-2000. Written numerous articles on substantive issues in litigation; co-editor, three volume Litigation Manual (3rd ed, 1999).
Personal: Harvard, BA, 1976 magna cum laude in English; Harvard Law School, JD, 1980 magna cum laude. Editor, 'Harvard Law Review', 1978-80.

KIESSLING, Rob
Cravath, Swaine & Moore, New York
212 474 1000
Recommended in Banking & Finance

KIMBALL, John
Healy & Baillie LLP, New York
212 943 3980
Recommended in Shipping

KLEIN, Linda B
Dewey Ballantine LLP, New York
212 259 6721
lklein@deweyballantine.com
Recommended in Capital Markets
Specialization: She leads the firm's Derivatives Group and is also a member of practice groups involved with capital markets transactions generally, the emerging markets, in particular, lending of various sorts, including debtor-in-possession financing, private placements and commercial bank credit agreements, and secondary-market transactions.
Prof. Memberships: Bar of the State of New York since 1980.

Career: With *Dewey Ballantine LLP* since 1996.
Personal: Columbia University School of Law, JD, 1979; Columbia University, PhD, Latin American Literature 1971, with distinction.

KLEINBARD, Edward
Cleary Gottlieb Steen & Hamilton, New York 212 225 2000
ekleinbard@cgsh.com
Recommended in Tax
Specialization: Federal income tax matters, including taxation of new financial products, financial institutions and international mergers and acquisitions.
Prof. Memberships: Member of the American College of Tax Counsel, American Association of Financial Engineers, International Fiscal Association.
Career: Joined the firm in 1977 and became partner in 1984. JD, Yale Law School (1976); MA and BA, Brown University (1973).
Publications: 'Contingent Interest Convertible Bonds and the Economic Accrual Regime' (co-author) in 'Tax Notes'. 'Disclosing Book - Tax Differences' (co-author) in 'Tax Notes'. 'The US Taxation of Equity Derivative Instruments,' in the 'Handbook of Equity Derivatives'. 'Corporate Tax Shelters and Corporate Tax Management' in 'The Tax Executive'.

KLING, Lou R
Skadden, Arps, Slate, Meagher & Flom LLP & Affiliates, New York
212 735 2770
lkling@skadden.com
Recommended in Corporate/M&A
Specialization: Partner, New York. Has extensive experience in mergers and acquisitions of public and private companies, subsidiaries and divisions, including negotiated and contested acquisitions, leveraged buyouts and recapitalizations. Has also represented borrowers, issuers, underwriters and lenders in a broad spectrum of financing transactions.
Publications: Co-author of a leading treatise on acquisitions, 'Negotiated Acquisitions of Companies, Subsidiaries and Divisions'.
Personal: JD, New York University, 1977 (Order of the Coif; New York University Law Review); MA, Mathematics, University of Illinois, 1974; BA, New York University, 1973 (magna cum laude; Phi Beta Kappa).

KNIGHT, James
Simpson Thacher & Bartlett,
New York 212 455 2000
Recommended in Banking & Finance

KOENIGSBERG, Fred
White & Case LLP, New York
212 819 8200
Recommended in Intellectual Property

KOLB, Daniel
Davis Polk & Wardwell, New York
212 450 4000
Recommended in Litigation

KOOB, Charles
Simpson Thacher & Bartlett, New York
212 455 2000
Recommended in Antitrust, Litigation

KORFF, Phyllis G
Skadden, Arps, Slate, Meagher & Flom LLP & Affiliates, New York
212 735 2694
pkorff@skadden.com
Recommended in Capital Markets
Specialization: Partner, New York. Represents US and international issuers and investment banks in a variety of financing matters. Has worked on equity and debt financings, both investment grade and high-yield, in the US and international markets. Has worked on numerous initial public offerings and other offerings registered with the Securities and Exchange Commission, as well as offerings exempt from SEC registration pursuant to Rule 144A and Regulation S. Has extensive experience in representing Israeli companies.
Personal: JD, NY University School of Law, 1981 (Notes Editor, NY University Law Review); EdM., Boston University, 1967; BA, Brooklyn College, 1964.

KORNBERG, Alan
Paul, Weiss, Rifkind, Wharton & Garrison LLP, New York 212 373 3209
akornberg@paulweiss.com
Recommended in Insolvency
Specialization: Chair of the Bankruptcy Department. Handles out-of-court restructurings and workouts, chapter 11 cases (including transnational insolvency matters), bankruptcy-related acquisitions, advising on the structuring of financial transactions and bankruptcy-related litigation. Clients include noteholder committees, debtors, lenders and other creditors, equity holders, court-appointed fiduciaries and investors that focus on distressed situations. Serves as regular insolvency counsel to several financial institutions and insurance companies, and represents official and unofficial creditors and equity security holder committees in restructuring matters and in chapter 11 cases. Represents California Public Utilities Commission in the Pacific Gas & Electric Company chapter 11 case.

KOVNER, Victor
Davis Wright Tremaine LLP, New York
212 489 8230
victorkovner@dwt.com
Recommended in Media & Entertainment
Specialization: Partner, communications, intellectual property and commercial litigation. Represents public and private companies and insurers, as well as national broadcast/print media in all aspects of communications law, includ-

ing defamation, privacy, copyright, press access, reporter's privilege and related First Amendment issues. Clients include McGraw-Hill (Standard & Poors and Platts), Cantor Fitzgerald, Disney (Buena Vista Books), Random House, St. Martin's Press, HarperCollins, Ziff Davis Media, Wenner Media, Village Voice Media, US News & World Report, and Employers Reinsurance.
Prof. Memberships: Legal Affairs Committee, Magazine Publishers of America. Lawyer's Committee, Association of American Publishers. Co-founder, Libel Defense Resource Center.
Career: Admitted New York Bar in 1962. *Hays, Sklar & Herzberg* (1963-66), *Lankenau, Kovner* (1966-98), except for leave to serve as Corporation Counsel of the City of New York (1990-91). *Lankenau Kovner* merged with *DWT* in 1998.
Publications: Annual author and lecturer on recent developments in the law of invasion of privacy and newsgathering, Practising Law Institute's Communications Law Seminar (1979-2002).
Personal: JD, Columbia, 1961. BA, Yale, 1958. Member, New York State Commission on Judicial Conduct (1976-89 and Chair in 1989). Member, New York State Commission on Public Access (2002-present).

KRAMER, Morris J
Skadden, Arps, Slate, Meagher & Flom LLP & Affiliates, New York
212 735 2700
mkramer@skadden.com
Recommended in Corporate/M&A
Specialization: Partner, New York. Practice includes both friendly and hostile transactions and has involved many of the largest and most publicised deals of the last 20 years. Counsels bidders, targets and their financial advisors in non-negotiated acquisition situations, as well as having extensive experience in strategic and negotiation issues involving public and private company mergers, acquisitions and dispositions. Also advises shareholders, boards of directors and managements in leveraged and management buyouts, proxy fights and other corporate control transactions. Extensive international experience, having represented parties from around the globe in transactions into and from North America, as well as cross-border intra-European deals.
Personal: LLB, Harvard University, 1966; AB, Dartmouth College, 1963.

KRAUS, Bruce R
Willkie Farr & Gallagher, New York
212 728 8237
bkraus@willkie.com
Recommended in Communications
Specialization: Corporate finance, mergers and acquisitions, restructurings, and general corporate advice for telecommunications clients. Industry experience includes undersea cable, competitive local exchange carriers (CLECs), long distance and internet backbone networks, fixed and mobile wireless networks (LMDS, PCS, SMR), paging, geosynchronous telecommunications satellites and low earth orbit satellite constellations. Transaction types include public equity offerings, private equity in public companies, high yield debt and preferred stock offerings, secured bank financing, mergers and tender offers, private acquisitions, privatisations, judicial and out-of-court restructurings, international project finance and strategic joint ventures.
Career: Partner, *Willkie Farr & Gallagher*; Law clerk to Chief Judge, US Court of Appeals. Selected conferences and articles: 1995: Practising Law Institute (PLI): 'Doing Deals: Acquisitions'. 1996: New York University: 'The World Wide Web and the Academic Medical Enterprise'. 25 August 1997: National Law Journal, 'Pyrrhic Victory in Spectrum Auction'. 1997: Satellite Financing and Strategic Alliances (Conference Chairman). 1998: Space Finance, 'Structuring Global Satellite Systems'. 1997, 1998 & 1999: PLI Conferences: 'Telecommunications Deals' (Co-Chairman, 2000 session and 2001 sessions). ALI-ABA 'The Communications Marketplace' (2000).
Personal: Yale Law School, JD 1979 (Editor, 'Yale Law Journal'); Harvard College, AB 1975 (magna cum laude, economics); Phillips Academy.

KRAVITT, Jason H P
Mayer, Brown, Rowe & Maw, New York
212 262 2622
jkravitt@mayerbrownrowe.com
Recommended in Capital Markets
Specialization: Founder of the firm's securitisation practice and senior partner in that practice. Variety of finance and regulatory related practices. Represents industry groups with regard to securitisation regulatory initiatives, including the Bank for International Settlements' risk-based capital consultative papers, the FFIEC's risk-based capital projects, FASB's Standards on Securitization and Consolidation, SEC initiatives.
Prof. Memberships: Adjunct Professor of Law at Northwestern University Law School, an Adjunct Professor of Finance at the Kellogg Graduate School of Management of Northwestern University, and a Fellow in the American College of Commercial Finance Lawyers. One of three founding members, secretary, and chair of Legal, Regulatory, Accounting and Tax Committee, American Securitization Forum and Executive Committee Member, European Securization Forum.
Career: Joined *Mayer, Brown, Rowe & Maw*, 1973; became partner, 1979. Co-Chairman of the firm in 1998-2001.
Publications: Editor of, and contributing author to, 'Securitization of Financial Assets', Aspen Law & Business, 1996 (2nd Ed).
Personal: Born 19 January 1948. Phi Beta Kappa graduate of The Johns Hopkins University (member of the Advisory Board to the Dean of School of Arts & Sciences). JD, cum laude, Harvard Law School, 1972; diploma in comparative law, Cambridge University, 1973. Chairman, The Cameron Kravitt Foundation.

KROUSE, George
Simpson Thacher & Bartlett, New York
212 455 2000
Recommended in Capital Markets

KUDENHOLDT, Stephen
Thacher Proffitt & Wood, New York
212 789 1200
Recommended in Capital Markets

KUNZ, C Thomas
Skadden, Arps, Slate, Meagher & Flom LLP & Affiliates, New York
212 735 3240
ckunz@skadden.com
Recommended in Capital Markets
Specialization: Partner, New York. Represents underwriters, issuers and credit enhancers in asset-backed securities transactions. Counsel in public offerings and private placement transactions involving the issuance of pass-through certificates, asset-backed notes and bonds, commercial paper notes and participation certificates. Worked on transactions in which structured finance techniques were utilised to enable non-traditional financings to access the capital markets. Has also worked on a number of transactions in which special purpose companies are established to issue securities to purchase trade receivables or other assets from, or to make loans to, numerous companies.
Personal: JD, Cornell University, 1975 (magna cum laude; Order of the Coif; Phi Kappa Phi; Editor, 'Cornell Law Review'); BA, Colgate University, 1972 (magna cum laude; Phi Beta Kappa).

LAMB, William S
LeBoeuf, Lamb, Greene & MacRae, LLP, New York 212 424 8000
blamb@llgm.com
Recommended in Energy
Specialization: Advises energy companies on a wide variety of structural and corporate matters. A significant portion of his practice involves advice relating to PUHCA. He has participated in a wide variety of corporate transactions, representing bidders and targets in both negotiated and unsolicited mergers and acquisitions and underwriters and issuers in financings and corporate governance matters.
Prof. Memberships: Committee on Business Law, American Bar Association; American Institute of Certified Public Accountants
Career: Joined *LeBoeuf* in 1983, becoming a partner in 1991.
Personal: Educated at New York University (BS magna cum laude) 1978; NYU Law School (JD) 1983.

LAMBERT, LeRoy
Healy & Baillie LLP, New York
212 943 3980
Recommended in Shipping

LASCHER, Alan
Weil, Gotshal & Manges LLP, New York
212 310 8000
alan.lascher@weil.com
Recommended in Real Estate
Specialization: Has a national real estate acquisition and finance practice, advising institutional investors and lenders, real estate developers, investment bankers and retailers in a variety of transactional areas, including portfolio acquisitions and financings. Is a nationally recognised figure in the area of portfolio acquisitions and financings, having closed the first 'auction sale' of a portfolio of assets by the RTC, the first third-party financing of a portfolio of assets, and the first 'blind pool' arrangement for the acquisition of portfolios of assets. Worked with the title insurance industry to develop a product that would be applicable to portfolio transactions, both acquisitions and financings thereof. Has worked for lenders and borrowers in connection with loan and workout transactions. This has included construction and permanent real estate loans, participating loans, sale/leasebacks, corporate financings such as LBO acquisition facilities, revolver and term loans, syndicated real estate financings and debt restructurings involving single asset commercial real estate loans as well as real estate, retail and services businesses. Took an innovative approach to structuring a financing of General Motors Building in New York City. Specialises in development/tax orientated transactions, these include institutional joint venture and construction projects involving retail, office, warehouse and industrial facilities; including a tax-orientated joint venture transaction involving 53 State Street in Boston, a building that, but for the innovative structure, would not have been built. Handles leasing transactions, including department store, specialty retail store and multi floor office space leases.
Career: Has lectured on RTC acquisitions and financings, real estate workouts, shopping centre acquisition, financing and leasing, real estate related tax matters, and general real estate matters. Has spoken before various trade group conferences, including those of The American College of Real Estate Lawyers, The Banking Law Institute, the Management Exchange, Infocast and the Construction Management Association of America. Is a member of numerous trade and/or educational groups, such as the

Law Committee of the Real Estate Board of New York, The American College of Real Estate Lawyers and the International Council of Shopping Centers. Recently been appointed to the Advisory Board of Chicago Title Insurance Company.
Personal: LLB, Brooklyn Laws (1967); BS, Union College (1963).

LEDDY, Mark
Cleary Gottlieb Steen & Hamilton, Washington, DC 202 974 1570
mleddy@cgsh.com
Recommended in Antitrust
Specialization: US and European antitrust law, including civil and criminal litigation, analysis of competitive issues in mergers and acquisitions, and appearances before antitrust regulatory agencies and courts.
Prof. Memberships: Bars in Massachusetts and the District of Columbia. Admitted to practice before US Supreme Court and US Courts of Appeal.
Career: Joined the firm as a partner in 1986. Worked for US Department of Justice (1972-86); named Deputy Assistant Attorney General (1984). Adjunct Professor at Georgetown Law School (1996). JD Boston College Law School (1971), BA Boston College (1968).

LEDERMAN, Lawrence
Milbank, Tweed, Hadley & McCloy, New York 212 530 5000
Recommended in Corporate/M&A

LEE, Carolyn
Roberts & Holland LLP, New York
212 903 8700
Recommended in Tax

LEE, Steven J
Kenyon & Kenyon, New York
212 908 6305
slee@kenyon.com
Recommended in Intellectual Property
Specialization: His practice has centered around chemical and biochemical litigation, especially biotechnology, pharmaceuticals and polymers. Recent litiagtions have concerned generic versions of Nabumetone, Zantac, Seldane, Hytrin, and other drugs including oral contraceptives, antihypertensives, antibiotics, monoclonal antibodies for septic shock and against stem cells, machines for the synthesis of DNA, transdermal drug delivery systems, coatings for aluminium cans, paints for automobiles and striped toothpaste. Also prosecutes patent applications in these areas, counsels inventors and patent owners on the scope and validity of their intellectual properties and gives guidance to clients introducing new products and services as to any potential for infringement of the valid patent rights of others. Typical clients include pharmaceutical companies, both generic and brand-name, manufacturers of basic chemicals and plastics, universities and university professors.

Career: Has been practicing chemistry for eleven years when, in 1984 he exchanged a position of Associate Professor of Chemistry at Fordham University for a position as associate attorney at *Cahill Gordon & Reindel* in New York City, specializing in commercial litigation. In 1986 he joined *Kenyon & Kenyon* where he now co-chairs the Chemical/Life Sciences practice Group.
Publications: He is a frequent lecturer and author of many articles pertaining to intellectual property law and litigation. He has presented numerous speeches on patent-related aspects of the Wax-Hatch Act, speeches to the bar on drug litigationion, and teaches an anuual course in patent prosecution in the chemical/pharmaceutical area for the Practicing Law Institute. He recently published the article, 'Third party without remedy' in Orange book case in the November 11, 2002 edition of 'The National Law Journal'.

LEFKOWITZ, Stephen
Fried, Frank, Harris, Shriver & Jacobson, New York 212 859 8780
Stephen.Lefkowitz@FriedFrank.com
Recommended in Real Estate
Specialization: Real estate. Primary practice is real estate development, with emphasis on financing arrangements, planning, land use and zoning and large-scale, complex projects involving public/private development arrangements. Has represented AOL Time Warner, New York Mercantile Exchange, MetroTech Center, 42nd Street Development Project, Battery Park City, New York Stock Exchange.
Prof. Memberships: Secretary, member of board of directors and member of executive committee of Alliance for Downtown New York.
Career: Qualified in New York in 1962. Joined *Fried Frank* in 2003. Formerly, senior partner at *Pillsbury Winthrop LLP*. Counsel to New York State Senate Committee on Housing and Urban Development (1976). General counsel to New York State Urban Development Corporation (1971-75). Associate professor at Columbia University School of Law (1976-82).
Personal: Born 1937. Achieved LLB, magna cum laude, in 1962 from Harvard Law School, where he was member of Law Review. Received BA from Yale College, summa cum laude, in 1959; elected to Phi Beta Kappa.

LEPATNER, Barry
LePatner & Associates LLP, New York
212 935 4400
Recommended in Construction

LERNER, Jonathan J
Skadden, Arps, Slate, Meagher & Flom LLP & Affiliates, New York
212 735 2550

jlerner@skadden.com
Recommended in Litigation
Specialization: Partner, New York. Federal court litigator, emphasizing securities, corporate and commercial litigation, control contests, legal ethics and commercial arbitration. Significant current cases include defending DaimlerChrysler, AG and McKesson Inc. in securities litigations and representation of CTF Hotels against Marriott International.
Prof. Memberships: Federal Bar Council (Trustee 1995-98) (Chairman of Board 1998-2000); Chair, ABCNY Committee on Professional and Judicial Ethics (1999-2002).
Career: Departmental Disciplinary Committee, Appellate Division, First Judicial Department; Hearing Panel Chairman (1984-90; 1992-98); Adjunct Professor, Brooklyn Law School (2001-present); Lecturer, Columbia University School of Law (1989-92).
Personal: JD, St. John's University, 1973 (Magna Cum Laude); BA, Harpur College, 1970.

LEVI, Stuart D
Skadden, Arps, Slate, Meagher & Flom LLP & Affiliates, New York
212 735 2750
slevi@skadden.com
Recommended in Communications
Specialization: Partner and head of *Skadden*'s Information Technology and E-Commerce practice. Represents a broad spectrum of clients, ranging from early stage start-ups to global corporations seeking to use information technologies and the internet to enhance current business models and create new opportunities. Counsels on a variety of issues, including strategic alliances such as 'click and mortar' deals, portal deals and joint marketing relationships; Web site policies; IP matters; privacy issues; and M&A.
Career: Co-chair, Practising Law Institute's annual 'Internet Law Institute.'
Personal: JD, Harvard Law School, 1986 (cum laude); BA, Computer Science, Columbia University, Columbia College, 1983 (magna cum laude).

LEVIN, Peter
Davis Polk & Wardwell, New York
212 450 4000
Recommended in Banking & Finance

LEWKOW, Victor
Cleary Gottlieb Steen & Hamilton, New York 212 225 2000
vlewkow@cgsh.com
Recommended in Corporate/M&A
Specialization: Domestic and international mergers and acquisitions. Clients include South African Breweries (in its acquisition of Miller Brewing to form SABMiller), Synopsys Inc. (in its acquisition of Avant!), HSBC (in its acquisition of Republic National Bank), Nortel Networks (in various acquisitions), and

Deutsche Bank (in its acquisition of Bankers Trust).
Prof. Memberships: Association of the Bar of the City of New York.
Career: JD, magna cum laude, Comment Editor of the Law Review, University of Pennsylvania Law School (1973). Member, Editorial Advisory Board of 'The M&A Lawyer.' Adjunct Professor at New York University Law School (teaching Mergers and Acquisitions).

LIDDLE, Jeffrey
Liddle & Robinson, LLP, New York
212 687 8500
Recommended in Employment

LIEBMANN, Jeff S
Dewey Ballantine LLP, New York
212 259 6230
jliebmann@deweyballantine.com
Recommended in Insurance
Specialization: He has 20 years of experience in the corporate and insurance areas and has spoken at various industry seminars including those sponsored by Infoline, Bowrings and the American Bar Association. He is an Associate Member of the Society of Actuaries.
As counsel for the State of Indiana, he was primary architect for the insurance restructurings of the Baldwin-United life insurance subsidiaries. He has served as counsel for Nationwide Mutual Insurance Company in its deaffiliation from Employers of Wausau, as counsel to New England Mutual Life Insurance Company in its merger with Metropolitan Life Insurance Company, as counsel to Metropolitan Life Insurance Company in its acquisition of GenAmerica Corporation, and as counsel to MONY Group in its closed block securitization.
Prof. Memberships: New York State Bar Association; American Bar Association; Society of Actuaries.
Personal: Harvard University, JD, 1978, cum laude; Princeton University, AB, Mathematics, 1971, cum laude.

LINDAUER, Erik D
Sullivan & Cromwell LLP, New York
212 558 4000
lindauere@sullcrom.com
Recommended in Banking & Finance
Specialization: Transactional banking, secured lending, commercial law (Uniform Commercial Code), corporate reorganisations and bankruptcy. Advises domestic and foreign borrowers under lending agreements in the United States and abroad, US and non-US banking organisations, the New York Clearing House Association and CLS Bank. Experience includes a broad range of complex secured and unsecured financings, including project, cable television and energy financings. Recent engagements include representation of Prudential Financial, Inc.'s negotiation of bank lines in connection with the demutualization

NEW YORK

of The Prudential Insurance Company of America; representation of Allegheny Energy in connection with the renegotiation and securing of its unsecured bank lines; and AIG Financial Products in connection with various structured investments.
Prof. Memberships: American Bar Association; Association of the Bar of the City of New York (Member, Banking Law Committee); New York State Bar Association.
Career: Joined *Sullivan & Cromwell* in 1981; Partner since 1989.
Personal: Born 1956. State University of New York at Albany (BA, 1978); State University of New York Law School at Buffalo (JD, 1981). Legal advisor to the Government Securities Working Group of the Russia-American Bankers Forum (Moscow, 1992); instructor on legal matters at the Forum Academy for Advanced Studies in Banking and Finance (Moscow, 1993).

LINDENBAUM, Samuel H
Kramer Levin Naftalis & Frankel LLP, New York 212 715 7840
slindenbaum@kramerlevin.com
Recommended in Real Estate

Specialization: Is of counsel to *Kramer Levin Naftalis & Frankel LLP* and a member of the Land Use Department. For more than 30 years, his extensive experience in land use and zoning has been utilized in handling special permits, zoning changes, variances, landmark proceedings, air rights transfers, tax abatements and economic development incentives for many of the city's most prominent commercial and residential developments and for the expansion programs of many of the city's leading non-profit institutions.
Prof. Memberships: He is Chairman of the Executive Committee of the Board of Directors of the American Friends of the Israel Museum, a member of the Board of Overseers of the Albert Einstein College of Medicine, Chair of the Executive Committee of the Jewish Association for Services for the Aged, a member of the Board of Trustees of the Real Estate Institute of Baruch College, and a member of the Board of the Real Estate Committee of UJA-Federation. He is Vice President and a member of the Executive Committee of the Board of Governors of the Real Estate Board of New York, and a member of the Advisory Board of the Peggy Guggenheim Collection in Venice. He is a founder, Director and Vice President of the Association for a Better New York, and a former member of the New York State Council on the Arts (1976-86 and 1994-99).
Career: Represents non-profit organizations, major corporations, financial institutions and commercial and residential developers such as Carnegie Hall, Columbia University, the Guggenheim Museum, the Archdiocese of New York, Yeshiva University, Weill Cornell Medical College, Bear Stearns, Tishman Speyer Properties, Vornado Realty Trust, Glenwood Management, Millennium Partners, and the Resnick, Silverstein and Solow Organizations. Current projects for which he acts as counsel include the expansions of the Museum of Modern Art and the Pierpont Morgan Library, a new tower atop the Hearst headquarters building on Eighth Avenue, redevelopment of the former Alexander's site on Lexington Avenue and East 59th Street by Vornado, redevelopment of the Con Edison properties at First Avenue and East 40th Street, and Sheldon Solow's new residential towers on York Avenue and 60th Street. Recent approvals include renovations of Rockefeller Center and the Chrysler Building, and the new Penn Center Special Signage District. Other major approvals in recent years include Trump's Riverside South development and New York Hospital's expansion over the FDR Drive.
Personal: Earned a BA degree cum laude from Harvard College in 1956 and a JD degree from Harvard Law School in 1959. After graduating from law school, he was awarded a Fulbright Fellowship.

LINDSEY, David
Clifford Chance US LLP, New York
212 878 8019
david.lindsey@cliffordchance.com
Recommended in Arbitration

Specialization: Concentrates on international commercial arbitration, international litigation and reinsurance, with a focus on international commercial contracts and power/energy projects. He has represented numerous corporate clients in arbitration matters under the rules of the ICC, the LCIA, the AAA, the SMA and UNCITRAL. He also advises on large, complex commercial litigation matters and represents major reinsurers in various types of disputes. Is a frequent lecturer and is co-editor and author of International Arbitration in Latin America.

LIPSON, Lawrence
Proskauer Rose LLP, New York
212 969 3000
Recommended in Real Estate

LIPTON, Martin
Wachtell, Lipton, Rosen & Katz, New York 212 403 1200
mlipton@wlrk.com
Recommended in Corporate/M&A

Specialization: Specializes in corporate law, corporate governance and mergers and acquisitions.

LOGAN, Kenneth
Simpson Thacher & Bartlett, New York
212 455 2000
Recommended in Antitrust

LONDON, Martin
Paul, Weiss, Rifkind, Wharton & Garrison LLP, New York 212 373 3000
Recommended in Litigation

LYONS, Peter
Shearman & Sterling, New York
212 848 4000
Recommended in Corporate/M&A

MACMURRAY, John
Reboul, MacMurray, Hewitt, Maynard & Kristol, New York 212 841 5700
Recommended in Private Equity

MACPHERSON, Robert
Postner & Rubin, New York
212 269 2510
Recommended in Construction

MADDEN, John
Shearman & Sterling, New York
212 848 4000
Recommended in Corporate/M&A

MALLOW, Matthew J
Skadden, Arps, Slate, Meagher & Flom LLP & Affiliates, New York
212 735 3930
mmallow@skadden.com
Recommended in Capital Markets

Specialization: Partner, New York. Head of *Skadden*'s Finance department. Represents investment banks, issuers and corporations in a variety of financing matters, including initial public offerings and insurance company offerings.
Prof. Memberships: Board of Trustees, Brown University (1990-96, 1997-present).
Career: Guest lecturer on the securities law framework of private placements in a course entitled 'Enterpreneurial Management,' at Harvard Business School.
Personal: LLM, New York University, 1968; LLB, New York University, 1967; AB, Brown University, 1964.

MANN, Christopher L
Sullivan & Cromwell LLP, New York
212 558 4000
mannc@sullcrom.com
Recommended in Projects

Specialization: Project finance, joint venture, M&A, general corporate and securities matters. Has represented sponsors of a potential LNG project in Venezuela; the project entity in the Camisea gas project (Peru); TotalFinaElf, PDVSA and Statoil in the Sincor extra heavy oil project (Venezuela); Ampol Exploration Limited in the Kutubu oil project (Papua New Guinea); WMC in the Zarmitan gold project (Uzbekistan); and sponsors in merchant power projects in Argentina, Brazil and Zimbabwe. Represents Anglo American plc on a variety of matters, as well as Republic of South Africa in its international bond offerings.
Prof. Memberships: Association of the Bar of the City of New York (Former Chair, Project Finance Committee); American Bar Association.
Career: Judicial Clerk to the Honorable Ralph K Winter, US Court of Appeals for the 2nd Circuit, 1989-90. Joined *S&C* in 1990; Partner since 1998.
Personal: Born 1963. Harvard College (AB, 1985); Cambridge University (M Phil, 1987); Harvard Law School (JD, 1989).

MARTIN, Renwick
Sidley Austin Brown & Wood, New York
212 839 5300
Recommended in Capital Markets

MASON, Richard G
Wachtell, Lipton, Rosen & Katz,
New York 212 403 1252
rgmason@wlrk.com
Recommended in Insolvency

Specialization: Specializes in *Wachtell, Lipton, Rosen & Katz*'s insolvency practice, representing bank and bondholder groups and creditors' committees in many large Chapter 11 cases and out-of-court restructurings, including the Pacific Gas & Electric Company, Rand McNally & Company, Allegheny Energy Supply, Inc. and subsidiaries of LTV Corp. matters, and borrowers in leveraged buyouts, mergers and other complex financing transactions.
Prof. Memberships: Active member of the Association of the Bar of the City of New York (recently serving on its Committee on Bankruptcy & Corporate Reorganization), the New York State Bar and the American Bar Association.
Career: Partner at *Wachtell, Lipton, Rosen & Katz* since 1994. Recently named one of the 'Outstanding Young Bankruptcy Lawyers of the Year' by the 'Turnarounds & Workouts'. Has given numerous seminars on bankruptcy subjects for the Practicing Law Institute and other prominent organizations.
Publications: Co-author of 'Collier's Bankruptcy Practice Guide'.
Personal: Graduated magna cum laude from Virginia Commonwealth University in 1983 (BS, Economics) where he was inducted into the Phi Kappa Phi honor fraternity; and cum laude from New York University in 1987 (JD) where became a member of the Order of the Coif and was on the staff of the 'Annual Survey of American Law'.

MATTEI, Andrew
Mayer, Brown, Rowe & Maw, New York
212 506 2572
amattei@mayerbrownrowe.com
Recommended in Banking & Finance

Specialization: Corporate finance. Represents both domestic and foreign banks, other financial institutions. Areas of expertise: highly leveraged, syndicated lending transactions, with emphasis on acquisition financing (including tender offer financings) and corporate recapitalizations. Focuses on senior, secured financings and subordinated financings (including bridge financings). Many cross-border transactions - for example, representing the Agents (Scotia Capital, Credit Suisse First Boston and Canadian Imperial Bank of Commerce) in 2001

Cdn. $1.7 billion acquisition of Bell Acti-Media (Canada) by KKR. Routinely represents lenders in workouts and restructurings of troubled credits.
Prof. Memberships: Admitted in New York, 1988.
Career: Joined *Mayer, Brown, Rowe & Maw*, New York, 1987; became partner, 1996.
Publications: Contributing author: 'How to Buy a U.S. Business: A Guide to Negotiated and Hostile Acquisitions'. Chapter 5: 'Senior and Subordinated Acquisition Financing'. 'Advising Illinois Financial Institutions', Chapter 11, Multi-Bank Credit Facilities, 1997 and 2001. Co-author: 'Proposed Rule 144A and Related Concerns', 'Journal of International Banking Law', 1989. 'Reproposed Rule 144A and Related Concerns', Butterworth's 'Journal of International Banking and Financial Law', 1989.
Personal: Born 15 November 1957. JD, Fordham University School of Law, 1987; 'Fordham Urban Law Journal'. BS, with honors, State University of New York, Cortland, 1979.

MAZUR, Sayward
Mazur Carp Rubin, New York
212 686 7700
Recommended in Construction

MCCORMACK, William
Reboul, MacMurray, Hewitt, Maynard & Kristol, New York 212 841 5700
Recommended in Private Equity

MECHANIC, Jonathan
Fried, Frank, Harris, Shriver & Jacobson, New York 212 859 8222
Jonathan.Mechanic@FriedFrank.com
Recommended in Real Estate
Specialization: Chairman of the real estate department. Practice includes acquisitions, dispositions, financings, joint ventures and commercial leasing. Representations have included Conde Nast Publications Inc., Jack Resnick & Sons, UBS PaineWebber, Tishman Speyer Properties.
Prof. Memberships: Association of the Bar of the City of New York; New York State Bar Association; American Bar Association; New York University Real Estate Institute; and Chicago Title Insurance Company advisory boards.
Career: Qualified in New York in 1978. Joined firm in 1987 as partner. General counsel and managing director of HRO International (1983-87).
Personal: Born 1952. JD in 1977 from New York University and BA, magna cum laude, from Brandeis University in 1974.

MEIKLEJOHN, D Stuart
Sullivan & Cromwell LLP, New York
212 558 4000
meiklejohns@sullcrom.com
Recommended in Antitrust
Specialization: Advises clients in dealing with the Antitrust Division of the US Department of Justice, the FTC and the European Commission in merger transactions that might be thought to raise antitrust issues, as well as matters involving potential criminal and civil liability. Also represents clients in the defense of such claims. Clients have included Algroup, Alumax, AMAX, Amersham, BASF, BBA, Carnation, Compagnie Generale d'Investissements et Participations, DeLaRue, Eisai, Global Industrial Technologies, Hoechst, Imasco, Internorth, Mallinckrodt, Microsoft, Solvay, TI Group and Upjohn. Advises clients in a full range of commercial litigation matters, judicial proceedings, investigations by federal and state authorities, arbitrations, and other forms of dispute resolution.
Prof. Memberships: American Bar Association; New York State Bar Association; Association of the Bar of the City of New York.
Career: Joined *Sullivan & Cromwell* in 1975. Partner since 1983.
Personal: Born 1950 in Chicago, Illinois. Graduate of Harvard College (AB, 1971) and Harvard Law School (JD, 1975). Co-Chairman, Lawyer's Committee for Civil Rights Under Law; Director and Treasurer, The Legal Aid Society; Chairman, Union Settlement Association.

MERMELSTEIN, Joshua
Fried, Frank, Harris, Shriver & Jacobson, New York 212 859 8000
Joshua.Mermelstein@FriedFrank.com
Recommended in Real Estate
Specialization: Real estate partner. Practice includes representation of financial institutions, owners, developers, opportunity funds and offshore investors. Clients include Millenium & Copthorne Hotels plc; Brookfield Financial Properties, Inc; Reckson Associates Realty Corp.; Lazard Freres & Co's Real Estate Funds; and Credit Suisse First Boston Corporation.
Prof. Memberships: New York State Bar Association; Association of the Bar of the City of New York; member of Board of Directors of United Help, Inc.
Career: Qualified in 1981. Joined *Fried Frank* in 1980, becoming partner in 1986.
Personal: Born 1955. Received JD in 1980 from Columbia University Law School, where he was Harlan Fiske Stone Scholar, and AB from Columbia in 1977.

METCALF, Slade
Hogan & Hartson LLP, New York
212 918 3637
srmetcalf@hhlaw.com
Recommended in Media & Entertainment
Specialization: He is a partner in the New York office of *Hogan & Hartson* LLP and a member of the firm's Litigation and Intellectual Property Groups. He handles litigation and general consultation for a variety of media entities. He focuses his practice on issues involving libel, invasion of privacy, copyright, and trademark law and regularly represents newspapers, magazines, book publishers, television and radio stations, motion picture studios, photographic agencies, literary agents, and authors.
Prof. Memberships: He is a member of American Bar Association and is currently a part of the Forum Committee on Communications Law. With the New York State Bar Association, he currently serves as a member of the Committee on Media Law, the Entertainment, Arts and Sports Law Section, and the Committee on Cyberspace Law. Within the Association of the Bar of the City of New York, he presently serves on the Committee on Entertainment Law, and has previously served on the Committee on Art Law, the Committee on Copyright and Literary Property, and the Committee on Communications Law. He is a former chairman of the Legal Affairs Committee of the Magazine Publishers of America, Inc., and has participated in numerous bar association committees regarding media, communications, art, copyright and literary property. He was also a trustee of the Copyright Society of the USA and has lectured extensively on media law at forums including conferences of the Practicing Law Institute, the Magazine Publishers of America and the American Society of Magazine Editors.
Career: He is admitted to practice before the US Supreme Court and has litigated on behalf of clients in a number of federal district and appellate courts. In addition to the US Supreme Court, he is admitted to practice before the US Court of Appeals for the Second, Third, Fifth, Ninth, and Eleventh Circuits and the US District Court for the Southern and Eastern Districts of New York. For the past several years, he has been listed in a leading legal publication.
Publications: An active speaker and writer on media law topics, he is the author of a legal treatise entitled 'Rights and Liabilities of Publishers, Broadcasters and Reporters', which is updated annually and has been a leading media law resource book since 1981.
Personal: He received his AB in 1968 from Princeton University and his JD in 1973 from New York University School of Law. He is a member of the New York State Bar.

MEYERS, Michael
Orrick, Herrington & Sutcliffe, New York 212 506 5270
mmeyers@orrick.com
Recommended in Projects
Specialization: Expert in infrastructure project development and finance, focusing on developers, lenders, and equity investors in power, telecommunications, industrial, and other infrastructure projects in the US and internationally. Recent projects: representation of participants in US and international electric industry workouts; a multinational corporation in restructuring power generation business worldwide, including sale of US fossil-fired generation portfolio and establishment of worldwide wind energy company; and developers of several wind power projects in the US.
Career: Florida State University, BS, summa cum laude, 1976. Stanford Law School, JD, 1979. *Graham & James*, associate and partner, 1979-93. *Orrick, Herrington & Sutcliffe*, partner, 1993-present.

MEYERSON, Lee
Simpson Thacher & Bartlett, New York
212 455 2000
Recommended in Corporate/M&A

MILLARD, John
Shearman & Sterling, New York
212 848 4000
Recommended in Banking & Finance, Projects

MILLER, David
Cadwalader, Wickersham & Taft, New York 212 504 6318
david.miller@cwt.com
Recommended in Tax
Specialization: Tax partner whose practice includes matters relating to the taxation of financial instruments and derivatives, cross-border lending transactions and other financings, international and domestic mergers and acquisitions, multinational corporate groups and partnerships, bankruptcy and workouts, high net worth individuals and families, and public charities and private foundations. Speaks regularly at conferences and universities. Author of numerous articles for legal publications.
Prof. Memberships: New York State Bar Association, Tax Section (Co-chair, Committee on Tax Policy); American Bar Association; Tax Forum.
Personal: BA, University of Pennsylvania (summa cum laude, 1986); JD, Columbia Law School (1989; Notes and Comments Editor, Columbia Law Review); LLM, New York University School of Law (1994); clerk to the Honorable Mary M Schroeder of the Ninth Circuit Court of Appeals (1989-90). Awarded 2001 Burton Award for Legal Achievement (recognizing exceptional legal writing).

MILLS, Phillip
Davis Polk & Wardwell, New York
212 450 4000
Recommended in Corporate/M&A

MILMOE, J Gregory
Skadden, Arps, Slate, Meagher & Flom LLP & Affiliates, New York
212 735 3770
jmilmoe@skadden.com
Recommended in Insolvency
Specialization: Co-lead, firm's Corporate Restructuring Group. Experience includes in court and out of court

NEW YORK

restructurings, hostile and negotiated mergers and acquisitions, leveraged buyouts, and corporate financings (including IPOs). Draws on experience from various legal disciplines to develop pragmatic, sometimes novel, solutions to complex problems. Recent bankruptcy representations include Genuity Inc., Exodus Communications, ICG Communications and Viatel, Inc.; recent out of court restructurings include Aurora Foods and the creditors of Abraxas Petroleum. Was active on behalf of underwriters in public offerings for REITS and related M&A transactions in the 1990s.
Personal: JD, Fordham University, 1975 (Articles Editor, 'Fordham Law Review'); AB, Cornell University, 1970.

MIRVIS, Theodore N
Wachtell, Lipton, Rosen & Katz, New York 212 403 1204
TNMirvis@wlrk.com
Recommended in Litigation

Specialization: Specializes in litigation involving corporate governance and complex securities matters, directors' fiduciary duties in mergers and acquisitions.
Prof. Memberships: American Law Institute and Planning Committee, Tulane Corporate Law Institute.
Career: Partner at *Wachtell, Lipton, Rosen & Katz* since 1982; Law Clerk, Honorable Henry J Friendly, United States Court of Appeals for the Second Circuit, 1976 term.
Publications: Author of numerous articles on corporate governance; and co-author, *Wachtell & Mirvis*, New York Practice under the CPLR.
Personal: Graduated summa cum laude from Yeshiva College in 1973 (BA) and magna cum laude from Harvard Law School in 1976 (JD). While at Harvard Law School, he was Editor of 'Harvard Law Review', vol 88, and Case Editor of 'Harvard Law Review', vol 89.

MITCHELL, David S
Cadwalader, Wickersham & Taft, New York 212 504 6285
david.mitchell@cwt.com
Recommended in Capital Markets

Specialization: Capital Markets partner concentrating on derivatives transactions, including regulatory, transactional and litigation advice relating to the commodities, securities, and banking businesses. Practice includes matters relating to all aspects of the listed and over the counter derivatives markets. Advises a diverse group of clients on trading activities, including documentation, transactional, regulatory and compliance, and insolvency matters, and the development of new products and electronic trading platforms. Clients include commercial and investment banks, dealers, trading companies, insurance companies, investment managers, corporate and institutional end users of derivative products, and industry trade associations.
Prof. Memberships: American Bar Association; Association of the Bar of the City of New York; New York State Bar Association.
Personal: BA, City College (1976) (summa cum laude, Phi Beta Kappa); JD, New York Law School (1979) (magna cum laude); LLM, New York University School of Law (1980); admitted 1980, New York. Member of the firm since 1990.

MOORE, Harold F
Skadden, Arps, Slate, Meagher & Flom LLP & Affiliates, New York
212 735 3252
hmoore@skadden.com
Recommended in Projects

Specialization: Partner, New York. General corporate and bank finance lawyer with a concentration in project finance. Has been the lead lawyer in over 110 domestic and international project financings, representing underwriters, banks and issuers in some of the most complex projects financed in recent years.
Personal: JD, Notre Dame, 1980 (summa cum laude; Articles Editor, Notre Dame Law Review; Thomas J White Scholarship; Peters Scholarship; Farabaugh Prize for High Scholarship in Law); PhD, Fordham University, 1971; MA, Fordham University, 1970; BS, Fordham University, 1968.

MORGAN, Charles
Skadden, Arps, Slate, Meagher & Flom LLP & Affiliates, New York
212 735 2470
cmorgan@skadden.com
Recommended in Tax

Specialization: Partner, New York. Practice emphasizes financial product development and international tax matters. Advises clients in connection with the design, operation and/or tax consequences associated with complex financial products as well as the tax consequences associated with international transactions and legal structures.
Prof. Memberships: Certified Public Accountant; Executive Committee Member, NY State Bar Association Tax Section (1986-Present).
Career: Price Waterhouse, concentrating in international tax; Associate Chief Counsel, Internal Revenue Service (1984-1986); Special Assistant to the Commissioner of the Internal Revenue Service (1982-1984).
Personal: LLM, NY University, 1981; JD, Pepperdine University, 1977; BS, Wharton School, University of Pennsylvania, 1972.

MORGAN, Robert
Fish & Neave, New York
212 596 9000
Recommended in Intellectual Property

MORISON, Francis
Davis Polk & Wardwell, New York
212 450 4000
Recommended in Capital Markets

MORPHY, James C
Sullivan & Cromwell LLP, New York
212 558 4000
morphyj@sullcrom.com
Recommended in Corporate/M&A

Specialization: M&A advice for a wide variety of friendly and hostile acquisitions, representing buyers, sellers and financial advisors. Recent transactions include: advising Hershey Foods Corporation in efforts to explore sale of company; Hewlett-Packard/Compaq merger; split-up and sale of Carter Wallace; Reader's Digest recapitalization; special committee of NCH in buyout by controlling shareholder; Goldman Sachs acquisition of Spear, Leeds & Kellogg; UBS merger with PaineWebber; Alliance Capital acquisition of Sanford Bernstein; and Union Camp merger with International Paper.
Prof. Memberships: American Bar Association; Association of the Bar of the City of New York.
Career: Joined *S&C* in 1979. Partner since 1986. Managing Partner, M&A Group.
Publications: Contributing author to three-volume treatise, New York and Delaware Business Entities: Choice, Formation, Operation, Financing and Acquisitions (West Publishing) and second treatise, Transactional Lawyer's Deskbook (West Publishing).
Personal: Born 1954. Harvard College (BA, Phi Beta Kappa, 1976); Harvard Law School (JD, 1979). Board of Trustees, Greenwich Academy; Board of Governors, Wianno Club.

NAFTALIS, Gary P
Kramer Levin Naftalis & Frankel LLP, New York 212 715 9253
gnaftalis@kramerlevin.com
Recommended in Litigation

Specialization: One of the nation's leading trial lawyers, co-chair of *Kramer Levin Naftalis and Frankel LLP* and head of the firm's litigation practice. For more than 25 years, he has represented individuals and corporations in all phases of complex civil, criminal, and regulatory matters including those involving allegations of insider trading, market manipulation, accounting irregularities and other financial fraud.
Prof. Memberships: He is a fellow of the American College of Trial Lawyers and a member of the White Collar Crime Committee and council member of the Criminal Justice Section of the American Bar Association. He is also a member of the Federal Bar Council, the New York State Bar Association, The Association of the Bar of the City of New York and the International Bar Association.
Career: During his 25+ year career, he has successfully represented numerous securities industry clients, including Salomon Brothers in the federal criminal and SEC investigations of US Treasury auction bidding practices, and Kidder, Peabody in connection with the Wall Street insider trading scandal. He is actively involved in representing significant figures in the government's current inquiries concerning corporate accounting irregularities. For example, he represents the Chairman of Global Crossing; the Chief Financial Officers of Cendant and Oxford Health Systems; the General Counsel of Rite Aid; and the former Vice Chairman and head of Enron's International Division. He also represents senior officials from major investment banks and accounting firms in current financial fraud probes. Previously, he successfully defended the general counsel and chief financial officer of the Southland Corporation against proxy fraud charges and the former head of the New York City Transit Authority on conflict of interest charges. He also successfully represented a prominent Saudi Arabian banker against state criminal charges and in proceedings before the Federal Reserve Board relating to the disposition of his interest in the Bank of Credit and Commerce International, as well as complex civil litigation brought against him by the liquidators of BCCI seeking $10 billion in damages. All US civil, criminal and regulatory charges were ultimately dismissed. He formerly served as an Assistant US Attorney in the Southern District of New York (1968-74), holding the title of Deputy Chief of the Criminal Division. He also served as special counsel to the US Senate Subcommittee investigating abuses in the nursing home industry (1975). He was a lecturer in law at Columbia Law School from 1976-88 and was a member of the faculty of Harvard Law School in 1979. In 1993, he was selected by the American Bar Association to be lead defense counsel for Ethel Rosenberg in its Trial of the Century program: United States v Julius and Ethel Rosenberg. Ethel Rosenberg was found not guilty by the jury.
Personal: Received his AB degree from Rutgers University in 1963, his MA from Brown University in 1965, and his LLB from Columbia Law School in 1967.

NATHAN, Charles
Latham & Watkins LLP, New York
212 906 1730
charles.nathan@lw.com
Recommended in Corporate/M&A

Specialization: Co-Chair, Global Mergers and Acquisitions Group. Represents companies and financial advisors in high-profile US and global M&A transactions, including Amgen's $16 billion acquisition of Immunex.
Prof. Memberships: Co-Chair, Annual Institute on Securities Regulation in Europe. Chair, Securities Regulation Committee, Association of the Bar of the City of New York. Chair, Subcommittee

LEADERS

NEW YORK

on Business Combinations and Proxy Statements, ABA Committee of Federal Regulation of Securities.
Career: Managing Director, head of Financial Institutions M&A at Smith Barney, 1993-95; Managing Director, co-head of domestic M&A at Salomon Brothers, 1987-92.
Publications: Regular columnist for 'The Daily Deal'.
Personal: JD, Yale Law School, 1965. BA, John Hopkins University, 1962.

NECKLES, Peter J
Skadden, Arps, Slate, Meagher & Flom LLP & Affiliates, New York
212 735 2466
pneckles@skadden.com
Recommended in Banking & Finance
Specialization: Partner, New York. Represents corporate borrowers and institutional lenders in bank loan transactions, with an emphasis on corporate restructurings, workouts, debtor-in-possession loans, bankruptcy reorganizations, acquisition financings and other highly leveraged financings.
Personal: JD, Fordham University School of Law, (cum laude; Editor, Fordham Law Review); BS, Rensselaer Polytechnic Institute.

NEEDELL, Benjamin F
Skadden, Arps, Slate, Meagher & Flom LLP & Affiliates, New York
212 735 2600
bneedell@skadden.com
Recommended in Real Estate
Specialization: Partner and head of *Skadden's* Real Estate Department. Practice emphasizes purchase and sale transactions, financings, securitized real estate loans, real estate development, partnership law, real estate investment trusts, syndications, major headquarters leases, hotel operation, development and financing, and matters relating to pension fund investments in real estate.
Prof. Memberships: Member, Board of Directors, Rock and Roll Hall of Fame (1986-present); Wenner Media, Inc. (1978-present); Stratton Mountain School (1980-Present), Chairman (1988-93).
Personal: LLB, St John's University, 1966 (Editorial Board, St John Law Review); BA, Rutgers University, 1963.

NEFF, Daniel A
Wachtell, Lipton, Rosen & Katz,
New York 212 403 1218
daneff@wlrk.com
Recommended in Corporate/M&A
Specialization: Specializes in mergers and acquisitions. During 25 years of practice has been extensively involved in negotiations as well as hostile acquisitions, and has represented bidders and targets, public and private companies, leveraged acquirers and special committees of directors. Has represented companies in divestitures, cross-border transactions and proxy contests and has coun-

selled managements and boards of directors concerning acquisition matters and other significant issues. Recently represented VoiceStream Wireless Corporation in its merger with Deutsche Telekom AG; Kellogg Company in its acquisition of Keebler Foods Company; Litton Industries, Inc in its merger with Northrop Grumman Corporation; Orion Power Holdings, Inc in its sale to Reliant Resources, Inc; Unocal Corporation in its acquisition of Pure Resources, Inc; Mirage Resorts, Incorporated in its merger with MGM Grand, Inc; Anadarko Petroleum Corporation in its acquisitions of Union Pacific Resources Group Inc and Howell Corporation; Vivendi, SA in its acquisitions of United States Filter Corporation and Cendant Software Corporation; and Transamerica Corporation in its merger with Aegon NV and its acquisition of Whirlpool Financial Corporation. In the last several years, represented Western Atlas Inc in its merger with Baker Hughes Incorporated; Newmont Mining Corporation in its initially unsolicited acquisition of Santa Fe Pacific Gold Corporation; and Vons Companies in its merger with Safeway Inc, and has represented special board committees of Wausau Insurance, Hayes Wheels International and Enron Oil & Gas Company.
Prof. Memberships: Member of the Law Review at Columbia University School of Law.
Career: Partner at *Wachtell, Lipton, Rosen & Katz* since 1984.
Personal: Graduated magna cum laude from Brown University and from the Columbia University School of Law.

NESGOS, Peter
Milbank, Tweed, Hadley & McCloy,
New York 212 530 5000
Recommended in Communications

NEUHAUS, Joseph E
Sullivan & Cromwell LLP, New York
212 558 4000
neuhausj@sullcrom.com
Recommended in Arbitration
Specialization: Practice focuses on international commercial litigation in arbitral and court settings. Recent work includes antitrust, patent, and other intellectual property disputes.
Prof. Memberships: Program Chair, Institute for Transnational Arbitration; Member, New York State Bar Association Committee on Professional Ethics; American Society of International Law; Association of the Bar of the City of New York.
Career: Judicial clerkships for Justice Lewis F Powell, Jr. of US Supreme Court and for the Iran-United States Claims Tribunal. Joined *Sullivan & Cromwell* in 1987. Partner since 1992.
Publications: Co-author of A Guide to the UNCITRAL Model Law on International Commercial Arbitration: Legislative History and Commentary (Kluwer,

1989); author of 'Settlement and Release' in Commercial Contracts: Strategies for Drafting and Negotiating (Moskin ed.) (Aspen 2001).
Personal: Born in Glen Ridge, New Jersey. Graduate of Dartmouth College (BA, 1979) and Columbia University School of Law (JD, 1982). Reading knowledge of Spanish.

NEUNER, Robert
Baker Botts LLP, New York
212 705 5000
Recommended in Intellectual Property, Litigation

NEVELOFF, Jay
Kramer Levin Naftalis & Frankel LLP,
New York 212 715 9290
jneveloff@kramerlevin.com
Recommended in Real Estate
Specialization: Is a partner at *Kramer Levin Naftalis & Frankel LLP* where he concentrates on real estate and other commercial transactions. He represents numerous nationally recognized real estate developers and owners, as well as major international lending and financial institutions, in commercial lending transactions, loan restructurings and workouts.
Prof. Memberships: Served for several years as the Vice-Chair of the American Bar Association Committee on Partnerships, Joint Ventures and Other Investment Vehicles. He is an active member of both The American College of Real Estate Lawyers and American Law Institute, and is a member of the Practicing Law Institute Real Estate Advisory Committee. He also served as the Vice-Chair of the International Health Network Society and has throughout his career represented owners, developers and lenders in connection with senior citizen assisted living facilities.
Career: Has represented developers of numerous mixed-use, commercial, retail and residential projects including Trump Tower (a joint venture between Donald Trump and Equitable Life), The Galleria (developed by Morgan Guaranty Trust Company), 500 Park Avenue (developed by Equitable Life) and Trump International Hotel and Tower, the former Gulf + Western Building (a joint venture of General Electric Investment Trust, Donald Trump and The Galbreath Organization); numerous regional and local shopping centers as well as other commercial projects throughout the country. He also represents a number of real estate funds in their acquisition of properties including those managed by Credit Suisse First Boston. He regularly represents numerous lending and other financial institutions in restructuring loans and other business relationships as well as in the development of new and innovative financing products. These institutions include BNP-Paribas. Additionally, he regularly assists clients actively involved in numerous hotel transactions including

the acquisition of numerous hotels, the development of hotels (most recently a Westin Hotel on behalf of its owner, CSX Transportation) in Savannah, Georgia as well as Trump International Hotel, and loan restructurings relating to numerous hotels including The Plaza Hotel in New York.
Personal: Received a JD degree from New York University in 1974 and a BA degree from Brooklyn College in 1971.

NEWMAN, Lawrence W
Baker & McKenzie, New York
212 891 5000
lawrence.w.newman@bakernet.com
Recommended in Arbitration
Specialization: Partner in Litigation Department of New York office. Areas of work are litigation in the United States of transnational commercial disputes and international commercial arbitration, to a great extent in matters involving foreign languages (French, Spanish, Portuguese) and law. Lead attorney for BellSouth International in an arbitration (1994-99) that resulted in an award of $19.5 million against a French telecommunications company on the basis of fraudulent concealment of information in the sale of shares in a cellular telephone company. Was also lead attorney in arbitration between US and Mexican companies in which client obtained an award based on breach of contract and fraud.
Prof. Memberships: Member of various bar organizations including the American Law Institute; former Chairman of the United States Iranian Claimants Committee (USICC), the national organisation of US businesses with claims arising out of the Iranian revolution.
Career: Member of the bar since 1961. Attorney, US Securities & Exchange Commission's Special Study of Securities Markets, 1961-63; Assistant US Attorney, Southern District of New York, 1964-69. Associate and Partner, *Baker & McKenzie* New York office 1969 to present.
Publications: Co-author of 'Litigating International Disputes' (West Group 1996) 'The Practice of International Litigation' (Juris Publishing, 2d. Ed. 1999); general editor of a series of books on international litigation, including 'Enforcement of Foreign Judgments' and 'Attachment of Assets'. Since 1982 the author of column in the New York Law Journal 'International Litigation'.
Personal: Born July 1935. Harvard College 1957; Harvard Law School 1960. Leisure interests include writing, publishing, travel and golf.

NIJENHUIS, Erika
Cleary Gottlieb Steen & Hamilton,
New York 212 225 2000
enijenhuis@cgsh.com
Recommended in Tax
Specialization: US income tax, especially financial products and international tax planning. Clients include Citigroup,

NEW YORK

Goldman Sachs, Lehman, Merrill Lynch, Morgan Stanley.
Prof. Memberships: NYSBA Tax Section Executive Committee; co-chair of financial products subcommittee.
Career: Joined the firm in 1990, became partner in 1997. LLM in Taxation, NYU (1996), JD, University of Pennsylvania (1987).
Publications: Articles on tax shelter disclosure and listing rules, contingent interest convertible bonds, securities futures, off-shore itrading in securities,i global dealing operations, mandatory convertible debt instruments, and swaps and other derivative financial instruments.

NOCCO, Frank
Weil, Gotshal & Manges LLP, New York
212 310 8918
frank.nocco@weil.com
Recommended in Capital Markets
Specialization: Partner in the New York office of *Weil, Gotshal & Manges*. Co-head of the Structured Finance/Derivatives Group and works closely with counterparts in London and in other offices worldwide. Specialises in representing issuers, underwriters, credit enhancers and trustees in corporate and structured securities offerings, both in the US and abroad. Has participated in the securitisation of auto loans, commercial loans, student loans, franchisee loans, mortgage loans, and equipment loans, credit card receivables (both MasterCard/Visa and private label), trade receivables, equipment and vehicle leases, high-yield and other non-conventional assets, such as royalty receivables, oil and gas production payments, synthetic securities and various other derivative products, insurance premium finance contracts and intellectual property. Experienced in structuring single-seller and multi-seller commercial paper vehicles, owner trusts, master trusts, grantor trusts, REMIC's and off-shore and domestic special purpose corporation vehicles that can issue a variety of debt and equity securities, including collateralised loan obligations and collateralised bond obligations. Also has experience with other kinds of securities work such as initial public offerings and subordinated debt offerings. Named as a leading practitioner in several legal publications. Has spoken at various industry conferences and most recently spoke at the 2001 ABA Annual meeting on the topic of 'Cross-Border Securitisations'.
Personal: Law degree from Columbia University School of Law in 1988; undergraduate degree, magna cum laude, from Columbia College, Columbia University in 1985, and elected to Phi Beta Kappa.

NONNA, John M
LeBoeuf, Lamb, Greene & MacRae, LLP, New York 212 424 8311
Jnonna@llgm.com
Recommended in Insurance
Specialization: He practices in the areas of commercial litigation and arbitration including insurance and reinsurance disputes. He has lectured at numerous conferences on trial practice, arbitration and mediation, insurance and reinsurance coverage, and related topics. He is co-editor of the New York State Bar Association treatise, Insurance Law Practice. Has served as Mayor of the Village of Pleasantville, New York. He was a member of the 1972 and 1980 United States Olympic Teams. He was named a Paul Harris Fellow by Rotary International.
Career: Joined *LeBoeuf* in 1999.

NOURSE, David
Nourse & Bowles LLP, New York
212 952 6200
Recommended in Shipping

NOVIKOFF, Harold S
Wachtell, Lipton, Rosen & Katz, New York 212 403 1249
hsnovikoff@wlrk.com
Recommended in Insolvency
Specialization: Specializes in creditors' rights, bankruptcy, debt restructurings, and derivative and financial markets transactions. During the past year, has represented major creditors of 360 networks, Swissair Group, World Kitchen, National Century Financial Enterprises, Budget Rent-a-Car and Navigator Gas.
Prof. Memberships: Member of the Law Review of Columbia University Law School; former chair of the Committee on Bankruptcy and Corporate Reorganization of the Association of the Bar of the City of New York; and is a member of the National Bankruptcy Conference and the American College of Bankruptcy.
Career: Partner at *Wachtell, Lipton, Rosen & Katz* since 1981.
Publications: Contributing author to 'Collier on Bankruptcy'.
Personal: Graduated with distinction from Cornell University in 1972 (BS) and from Columbia University Law School in 1975 (JD).

NUSBAUM, Jack H
Willkie Farr & Gallagher, New York
212 728 8060
jnusbaum@willkie.com
Recommended in Corporate/M&A, Private Equity
Specialization: Chairman of the firm and leads its mergers and acquisitions practice group. In addition to mergers and acquisitions, main focus includes Internal Investigations, Corporate Governance and fiduciary duties. Extensive experience has involved many of the most notable US and cross-border transactions of the past two decades including the completed multibillion dollar merger between Veritas Software, Seagate Technology and Silver Lake Partners; the merger of Nasdaq with the American Stock Exchange; the leveraged buyout of RJR Nabisco; the acquisition of McCaw Cellular Communications by AT&T; the acquisition of Magma Copper by Broken Hill Proprietary Limited; various going private transactions and various restructurings. Headed the team responsible for the 1998 Cendant Report, the internal investigation of Cendant Corporation on behalf of its Audit Committee.
Prof. Memberships: American Bar Association.
Career: Admitted in 1965, has spent entire career with *Willkie Farr & Gallagher*, becoming a partner in 1971, co-chairman of the firm in 1988 and sole chairman in 1995. Director of publicly held corporations including WR Berkley Corporation, Prime Hospitality Corp, Strategic Distribution Inc, Neuberger Berman Inc, and the Topps Company Inc; Trustee Prep for Prep and the Joseph Collins Foundation; Board of Visitors of Columbia University Law School; Member of the Legal Advisory Committee to the Board of Directors of the New York Stock Exchange.
Personal: Graduate of the Wharton School of the University of Pennsylvania and of Columbia Law School.

NUSSBAUM, Andrew J
Wachtell, Lipton, Rosen & Katz, New York 212 403 1269
ajnussbaum@wlrk.com
Recommended in Corporate/M&A
Specialization: Specializes in mergers and acquisitions, international corporate transactions, corporate governance and securities matters.
Prof. Memberships: Member of the American Bar Association and the New York State Bar Association.
Career: Partner at *Wachtell, Lipton, Rosen & Katz*. Rhodes Scholar; Law Clerk, Honorable Antonin Scalia US Supreme Court; Law Clerk, Honorable Ruth Bader Ginsburg, US Court of Appeals, District of Columbia Circuit. Editor in Chief, 'The University of Chicago Law Review'.
Publications: Has written various professional publications on Mergers and Acquisitions Law and Delaware Corporate Law.
Personal: Graduated with high honors from University of Chicago Law School, from Oxford University (MA) and summa cum laude from Amherst College; fluent in Russian and Spanish.

NUSSBAUM, Bernard W
Wachtell, Lipton, Rosen & Katz, New York 212 403 1266
bwnussbaum@wlrk.com
Recommended in Litigation
Specialization: Specializes in corporate and securities litigation.
Prof. Memberships: Admitted to practice in the United States District Courts for the Southern and Eastern Districts of New York, the United States Court of Appeals for the Second Circuit, and the United States Supreme Court; and member of the Association of the Bar of the City of New York (Vice President from 1984 to 1985), the New York State Bar Association, the American Bar Association, and the Federal Bar Council (President from 1990 to 1992).
Career: Partner at *Wachtell, Lipton, Rosen & Katz* since 1968. Has served in both the public and private sectors throughout career, working as an Assistant Attorney in the United States Attorney's Office for the Southern District of New York after graduating from law school, as Senior Associate Counsel to the United States House of Representatives Judiciary Committee's impeachment inquiry in 1974 regarding President Richard Nixon and as Counsel to the President during the Clinton Administration in 1993 and 1994. Has been a lecturer at Columbia University Law School.

O'BRIEN, Clare
Shearman & Sterling, New York
212 848 4000
Recommended in Corporate/M&A

OLIVIER, Jeanne
Shearman & Sterling, New York
212 848 4000
Recommended in Projects

OSBORN, John W
Skadden, Arps, Slate, Meagher & Flom LLP & Affiliates, New York
212 735 3270
josborn@skadden.com
Recommended in Capital Markets
Specialization: Partner, New York. Head of Derivative Financial Products practice with major focus on development of new securities products. Represents commercial and investment banks and other dealers in derivative products as well as major corporations and other end-users of the products; and has analyzed, developed, negotiated and documented the full range of transaction types, including hybrid and structured notes, swaps and various types of forwards and options. Transactions, including structured products and joint ventures, have involved a broad spectrum of reference instruments and indices, including credit-related attributes, interest rates and currencies, equity, debt and asset-backed securities and commodities. Represented issuers, underwriters, placement agents and swap counterparties in a wide range of offerings of securities with derivatives features.
Prof. Memberships: Primary and documentation contact to the International Swaps and Derivatives Association; American and New York State Bar Associations; Bar Association of the City of New York (former member of Securities Regulation and Futures Regulation Committees).
Career: Chairman and speaker at the Practising Law Institute and other confer-

LEADERS
NEW YORK

ences on derivatives and related matters; Branch Chief, Trading Practices, Division of Market Regulation, US Securities and ExchangeCommission (1978-79); Staff Attorney, Office of Market Structure and Trading Practices (1975-78).
Personal: JD, University of Pennsylvania School of Law, 1975; BA, Michigan State University, 1972 (Phi Beta Kappa).

OSBORNE, John
Watson, Farley & Williams, New York
212 922 2200
Recommended in Shipping

OSTRAGER, Barry
Simpson Thacher & Bartlett, New York
212 455 2000
Recommended in Insurance, Litigation

OUTTEN, Wayne
Outten & Golden LLP, New York
212 245 1000
Recommended in Employment

PAGET, David
Sive Paget & Riesel PC, New York
212 421 2150
Recommended in Environment

PALMA, Laura
Simpson Thacher & Bartlett, New York
212 455 2000
Recommended in Capital Markets

PANOVKA, Robin
Wachtell, Lipton, Rosen & Katz,
New York 212 403 1352
rpanovka@wlrk.com
Recommended in Real Estate
Specialization: Specializes in strategic real estate transactions, including mergers and acquisitions of REITs and other real estate companies and related businesses, the formation and investment activity of real estate opportunity funds, and joint ventures, acquisitions, dispositions, financing and development of individual properties and large portfolios, both in the United States and in cross-border transactions. Examples of current representations include representation of the Silverstein Properties group in connection with the redevelopment of the World Trade Center; representation of Taubman Centers, Inc. in connection with Simon Property Group's unsolicited offer; and representation of Apollo Real Estate Advisors in connection with the structuring of various investment vehicles.
Prof. Memberships: Co-Chair, Advisory Board, The REIT Center for the Study of Public Real Estate Operating Companies, New York University; member of the Board of Visitors, Duke University School of Law, 2001; member, Advisory Board: New York University Real Estate Institute; member of the State Bar of Georgia, New York State and American Bar Associations.
Career: Partner at *Wachtell, Lipton, Rosen & Katz.*
Publications: Author, 'Criticism of REITs goes too far - Selling Out or Merging Isn't Always Best for Shareholders', 'Real Estate Issues', Winter 2000/01; 'Taking REITs Private', 'Real Estate Issues', Summer 2000; and 'Public Real Estate Companies Advantages Will Overpower the REIT Bear Market', 'Real Estate Issues', Winter 1999. Co-author, 'REIT M&A Transactions - Peculiarities and Complications', 'The Business Lawyer', February 2000; 'REITs and Rights Plans', 'Property', Winter 2000; 'The 'UP' Factor in UPREIT Change of Control Transactions', 'The REIT Report', Spring 1998; 'REIT Takeovers — Novel Issues Raised by Excess Share Provisions and UPREIT Structures', 'The M&A Lawyer', October 1997; 'Will REIT Takeovers Take Off?', 'CPN's Real Estate Financial Review', Summer 1997; 'REIT Mergers and Acquisitions and Takeover Preparedness: Poison Pills and Excess Shares', 'The REIT Report', Autumn 1995; and 'REIT Mergers and Acquisitions: Structuring Transactions, Protecting Deals and Responding to Unsolicited Offers', 'The REIT Report', Spring 1996; Senior Editor, 'Alaska Law Review' 1984-86; member, Duke Moot Court Board, 1984-86.
Personal: Graduated cum laude from Cornell University (bachelor's degree) and with honors from Duke University (JD).

PANTALEO, Peter
Simpson Thacher & Bartlett, New York
212 455 2000
Recommended in Insolvency

PARÉ, Jay
Nourse & Bowles LLP, New York
212 952 6200
Recommended in Shipping

PARKER, Allen
Cravath, Swaine & Moore, New York
212 474 1000
Recommended in Banking & Finance

PEARLSTEIN, Debra J
Weil, Gotshal & Manges LLP, New York
212 310 8686
debra.pearlstein@weil.com
Recommended in Antitrust
Specialization: Partner in the Trade Practices and Regulatory Law Department, concentrating on antitrust counseling (including merger and acquisition analysis) and litigation. She litigated American Airline's successful defense of a predation lawsuit brought by the Department of Justice and was on the American Airlines trial team in Northwest Airlines v American Airlines (defeating allegations of predatory pricing under section 2 of the Sherman Act); she tried a merger involving the acquisition of oral tobacco products against the Federal Trade Commission; was a senior member of the team that successfully represented Matsushita Electric Industrial Co., Ltd. and Victor Company of Japan, Ltd. in the Go-Video litigation (defeating allegations of conspiracy under section 1 of the Sherman Act) and has represented Matsushita in various antitrust counseling and litigation matters; defended Kyowa Hakko in various federal and state actions alleging price fixing of lysine, and was involved in the Mylan litigation brought by the Federal Trade Commission, various state attorneys general, and multiple private class action plaintiffs alleging violations of federal and state antitrust laws. She has handled transactions requiring department of Justice and Federal Trade Commission approval in various service and manufacturing industries, and coordinated international merger reviews.
Prof. Memberships: American Bar Association's Antitrust Section, Antitrust Section Council.
Personal: Williams College, Princeton University's Woodrow Wilson School for Public and International Affairs and the New York University School of Law.

PEARSON, Nick
Edwards & Angell, New York
212 308 4411
Recommended in Insurance

PEASLEE, James
Cleary Gottlieb Steen & Hamilton,
New York 212 225 2000
jpeaslee@cgsh.com
Recommended in Tax
Specialization: US tax matters, with an emphasis on financial products and structured finance.
Prof. Memberships: Member of the Executive Committee of the New York State Bar Association Tax Section and Chair of the Tax Section from 1991-92.
Career: Joined the firm in 1976 and became partner in 1984. LLM degree, NYU (1979), JD degree, cum laude, Harvard Law School (1976), MA, BA Economics, magna cum laude, Yale University (1973).
Publications: Co-author of Federal Income Taxation of Securitization Transactions (3rd edition) and author of many articles on tax subjects.

PECKAR, Robert S
Peckar & Abramson, PC, New York
212 382 0909
rpeckar@pecklaw.com
Recommended in Construction
Specialization: Is a recognized leader among the construction bar. While he has obtained very substantial recoveries in litigation and arbitration, he has gained recognition for formulating creative, multimillion dollar settlements in the litigation of complex multiparty construction disputes and the implementation of alternative dispute resolution mechanisms to achieve expeditious solutions to complicated construction disputes. Is one of the nation's leading advocates for the appropriate use of Alternative Dispute Resolution (ADR) procedures and serves as an arbitrator in complex international arbitrations.
Prof. Memberships: Is a member of the New Jersey State Bar Association (Chairman, Public Contract Law Section, 1979-81; Chairman, Effective Dispute Resolution Committee, 1990-91; member, New Jersey Supreme Court Committee on Dispute Resolution, 1991-95) as well as a member of the American Bar Association (New Jersey State Chairman, Section on Public Contract Law, Litigation Section, 1979-83; Region II Chairman 1984-88).
Career: Is admitted to practice before the United States Supreme Court, the United States Court of Appeals for the Third, Fourth, Fifth, and Sixth Circuits, the United States Court of Federal Claims, the United States District Court for the Eastern and Southern Districts of New York and the District of New Jersey, as well as the courts of the State of New York and the State of New Jersey. Serves as General Counsel to the Building Contractors Association of New Jersey, the Building Trades Employers Association and the National Construction Financial Management Association (CFMA). He also serves as General Counsel Emeritus to the New York Building Congress, where he has been general counsel for over 15 years. Is a fellow of the American College of Construction Lawyers.
Publications: Throughout his career in construction law, has participated as a guest lecturer to local and national construction industry groups as well as in continuing legal education programs and has otherwise devoted substantial time and effort in service to the construction industry. An author of many articles on construction law topics, he is also a contributing author in several construction law textbooks and the author of 'New Jersey Practice: Construction Law.' National publications such as ENR, cite him frequently.
Personal: Is a graduate of Rutgers University in New Jersey and Columbia University Law School in New York.

PENZER, Michèle
Latham & Watkins LLP, New York
212 906 1245
michele.penzer@lw.com
Recommended in Projects
Specialization: Partner in the New York office. Primary practice is project development and financings, acting for sponsors and banks in the US and internationally. Represented Deutsche Bank, CIBC and Goldman Sachs in the financings of several fiber optic telecommunications systems and collocation facilities. Represented Ras Laffan Liquefied Natural Gas Company in the development and financing of a $3.4 billion liquefied natural gas project in Qatar. Represented various banks and sponsors in the financings of power projects.
Personal: JD, Yale University, 1993. AB, Harvard University, 1990.

NEW YORK — LEADERS

PHILLIPS, IV, Barnet
Skadden, Arps, Slate, Meagher & Flom LLP & Affiliates, New York
212 735 2220
bphillip@skadden.com
Recommended in Tax
Specialization: Partner, tax. Specializes in tax aspects of corporate mergers, acquisitions, divestitures, leveraged buyouts, restructuring and recapitalisations and the structuring of business organisations and investment vehicles, including REITs, regulated investment companies, investment partnerships and exchange funds.
Prof. Memberships: American Bar Association, Tax Section. National Association of Real Estate Investment Trusts.
Career: New York State Bar admission, 1974.
Publications: Co-Author, 'Structuring Corporate Acquisitions-Tax Aspects', Tax Management Inc., (1999).
Personal: BA, Yale University 1970; JD, Fordham Law School 1973; LLM (Tax), New York University 1977.

PIERCE, Morton A
Dewey Ballantine LLP, New York
212 259 6640
mpierce@deweyballantine.com
Recommended in Corporate/M&A
Specialization: He is a vice-chairman of the firm, global chairman of the firm's Corporate Department and has been chairman of the firm's Mergers and Acquisitions Group since 1991. The group consists of more than 60 lawyers based in New York, Washington, Los Angeles and Eastern Europe. He has participated in numerous merger and acquisition matters and related financings. He has represented acquirors, targets, investment bankers and investors in numerous acquisitions, including the Fortis acquisition of American Bankers, the Starwood acquisition of ITT, The Walt Disney Company acquisition of Capital Cities/ABC, the Wells Fargo acquisition of First Interstate Bank and the HCA acquisition of Healthtrust. He also has extensive experience in cross-border merger and acquisition transactions. These include the Guinness/GrandMet merger, the Luxottica Group S.p.A. acquisition of The United States Shoe Corporation, the Eridania Béghin-Say S.A. acquisition of American Maize-Products Company and the Cable & Wireless acquisition of NYNEX CableComms.
Prof. Memberships: American Bar Association: Task Force on Review of the Federal Securities Laws (1991-2000); Advisory Committee to Federal Regulation of Securities Committee (1991-2000); Chairman, Subcommittee on International Securities Matters (1985-91). International Bar Association: Committee on Securities Transactions. Association of the Bar of the City of New York: Chairman, Subcommittee on Securities and Exchange Commission Enforcement Matters (1990-91); Member, Securities Law Committee (1988-91).
Career: Partner, *Dewey Ballantine* since 1986. Chairman, Corporate Department; Chairman, Mergers and Acquisitions Group; member of Executive and Management Committees.
Personal: 1974-75, Oxford University; University of Pennsylvania Law School, JD, 1974; Yale University, BA, Political Science, 1970.

PINOVER, Eugene
Willkie Farr & Gallagher, New York
212 728 8254
epinover@willkie.com
Recommended in Real Estate
Specialization: Partner and chair of the Real Estate Department of *Willkie Farr & Gallagher* in New York. Specialises in representing domestic and foreign real estate clients in acquisitions, sales, restructuring and sophisticated financings and development projects throughout the United States. Practice includes representing public real investment trusts, underwriters and investors in public equity offerings and debt securitisations. Regularly handles acquisition and financing of portfolios and mergers and acquisitions of real estate operating companies.
Prof. Memberships: The Association of Foreign Investors in Real Estate, the Association of the Bar of the City of New York, the American Bar Association, the International Council of Shopping Centers, the New York Advisory Board of Chicago Title Insurance Company; member of the American College of Real Estate Lawyers.
Career: Admitted in 1974, has been with *Willkie Farr & Gallagher* since 1992. A member of the Executive Committee of the Real Estate Advisory Counsel to the Board of Trustees, Dartmouth College.
Personal: Received a JD (cum laude) from New York University School of Law in 1973 and a BA (cum laude) from Dartmouth College in 1969.

PISANO, Vincent J
Kirkland & Ellis, New York
212 446 4980
vpisano@kirkland.com
Recommended in Capital Markets
Specialization: Extensive experience with public and private debt and equity issues, representing major US and foreign corporations, leveraged buyout groups, and US investment banks. He frequently represents major corporate issuers or has been designated by them as underwriters' counsel in a variety of financing situations. For example, for the last 17 years, he has represented the underwriters in capital market transactions for The News Corporation Limited. Has also represented the underwriters in a number of significant initial public offerings, including those of Fox Entertainment and Infinity Broadcasting.
Personal: Vassar College, BA, 1975; St. John's University, JD, 1978.

PLEVAN, Bettina
Proskauer Rose LLP, New York
212 969 3000
Recommended in Employment

POLLACK, Martin
Weil, Gotshal & Manges LLP, New York
212 310 8461
martin.pollack@weil.com
Recommended in Tax
Specialization: Co-head, Tax Department. Federal income tax aspects of partnerships and joint ventures; federal income tax aspects of the restructuring of troubled companies.
Prof. Memberships: New York State Bar Association, Tax Section; New York City Bar Association.
Career: Former Adjunct Associate Professor of Tax Law at New York University School of Law; Member of the Advisory Board of Equipment Leasing Newsletter; Advisory Board of Tax Management.
Publications: Co-author of 'Partnership Buy/Sell Agreements' (Little Brown 1995).
Personal: John Hopkins University (BA, MA); University of Pennsylvania Law School (JD); New York University School of Law (LLM).

POMERANTZ, Alan J
Weil, Gotshal & Manges LLP, New York
212 310 8402
alan.pomerantz@weil.com
Recommended in Real Estate
Specialization: Senior partner of the firm. Has been involved with and supervised some of the largest and most complex developments, acquisitions, public and private financings, leases and restructurings.
Career: Lectures extensively on real estate capital markets, project development, financing, leasing and restructuring in the United States, Europe, the Far East and Latin America, including at the Columbia University Graduate School of Business, New York University School of Law, the University of Amsterdam, the Bar Association of the City of New York, The New York State Bar Association, the Canadian Institute, The Real Estate Syndicators and Securities Institute, The Management Exchange, The Institute for International Research, The Urban Land Institute, The International Council of Shopping Centers, The Metropolitan Corporate Council, the Real Estate Capital Conference, The International Development Research Council (IDRC), and Prentice Hall Law & Business legal education programmes. Has served as the programme chairman for Real Estate Financing for the Practicing Law Institute, and is a member of the Executive Committee and Advisory Board of the Real Estate Institute of New York University, also chairs the Capital Markets Conference. Member of the National Realty Committee and serves on its Commercial Capital Consortium, and Capital Policy Advisory Committees. Counsel to the Real Estate Lenders Association, and on the advisory board of Ticor Title Insurance Co. Vice-chair of the Documents Task Force of the Capital Consortium, an initiative of the National Realty Committee, National Association of Realtors and Mortgage Bankers Association of America that produced a standard set of ratable commercial and multifamily mortgage documents for use in the secondary market, and developed the Capital Markets Initiatives, a set of Guidelines to reduce costs and ease the securitisation process.
Publications: Editor and contributor to 'The Office Building and Office Market', a treatise on the US office building market published jointly by The Appraisal Institute, The American Society of Real Estate Counselors and The Society of Office Industrial Realtors. Served on the editorial board of the London based Journal of 'Property Finance', published by Henry Stewart Publications, and 'The Money Encyclopedia' published by Harper and Row. Editor of the Matthew Bender Publications 'Real Estate Transactions and Real Estate Financing'. Published numerous articles on development, capital markets, financing and restructuring which have appeared in 'The Bankers Magazine', 'Journal of Property Finance', 'Banking Law Journal', 'Real Estate Finance Journal', 'New York Law Journal', 'The Metropolitan Corporate Counsel', 'Shopping Center's Today' and 'The American Banker'.
Personal: JD, New York University School of Law (1968); Diploma, 1969, University of Amsterdam; BA, City College of the City University of New York (1965).

POSTER, Robert
Gilmartin, Poster & Shafto, New York
212 425 3220
Recommended in Shipping

POSTNER, William
Postner & Rubin, New York
212 269 2510
Recommended in Construction

PRINCE, Kenneth
Shearman & Sterling, New York
212 848 4000
Recommended in Antitrust

PULEO, Frank
Milbank, Tweed, Hadley & McCloy, New York 212 530 5000
Recommended in Banking & Finance

LEADERS

NEW YORK

QUINN, Linda
Shearman & Sterling, New York
212 848 4000
Recommended in Capital Markets

QUINN, Yvonne S
Sullivan & Cromwell LLP, New York
212 558 4000
quinn@sullcrom.com
Recommended in Antitrust
Specialization: Coordinates the firm's antitrust practice. Handles a variety of antitrust, commercial and intellectual property litigations for clients in a wide range of industries. Regularly counsels entities in connection with proposed acquisitions, and has provided antitrust counsel in connection with Cablevision Systems' sale of its Bravo programming service to NBC, The St. Paul Companies' disposition of its ongoing reinsurance operations to Platinum Underwriters Holdings, the split-up and sale of Carter-Wallace, Inc., the acquisition of International Petroleum Exchange by IntercontinentalExchange, and the acquisition of Spear, Leeds & Kellogg by Goldman, Sachs & Co.
Prof. Memberships: American Bar Association; Association of the Bar of the City of New York (former Chair of the Antitrust and Trade Regulation Committee); Federal Bar Council; New York State Bar Association.
Career: Joined *Sullivan & Cromwell* in 1980. Partner since 1984.
Publications: Author of 'Practical Aspects of Defending Bank Mergers Before the Federal Reserve Board and the Department of Justice' in 'Antitrust Law Journal' (Summer 1993).
Personal: Born in 1951. University of Illinois (BA, 1973); University of Michigan Law School (JD, 1976); University of Michigan (MA, 1977). Practising Law Institute (Co-Chair or Faculty member, 1998 to date, Annual Antitrust Law Institute). Director, Harlem School of the Arts.

RADKE, Kirk A
Kirkland & Ellis, New York
212 446 4940
kirk_radke@ny.kirkland.com
Recommended in Private Equity
Specialization: Primarily involved in structuring, negotiating and documenting legal aspects of complex business transactions, including leveraged buy-outs, mergers and acquisitions involving private and public companies, corporate divestitures, recapitalizations, private placements and management compensation arrangements. Extensive experience in the formation of leveraged buyout funds.
Personal: Stanford University, BA, 1980, Phi Beta Kappa awarded 1979. University of Virginia, JD/MBA, 1984, Editorial Board, 'Virginia Law Review'; Order of the Coif; William Michael Shermet Award (MBA).

RAISLER, Kenneth M
Sullivan & Cromwell LLP, New York
212 558 4000
raislerk@sullcrom.com
Recommended in Capital Markets
Specialization: Heads the Commodities, Futures and Derivatives Group of *Sullivan & Cromwell*, which is responsible for a full range of regulatory, transactional and litigation advice in the commodities, securities and banking areas to brokerage, investment banking, banking and commercial clients.
Prof. Memberships: American Bar Association (Corporation, Banking & Business Law Section); Association of the Bar of the City of New York (Chairman, Committee on Futures Regulation, 1988-91).
Career: Judicial Clerk to the Honorable Lee P. Gagliardi, US District Court (Southern District of New York). Assistant United States Attorney for the District of Columbia, 1977-82, Criminal and Civil Divisions. Joined the Commodity Futures Trading Commission as Deputy General Counsel; General Counsel from 1983 to 1987.
Personal: Born 1951. Graduated from Yale University (BS, 1973) and New York University School of Law (JD, 1976). Admitted to the Bar in New York and Washington, DC Member, the Working Group of The Group of Thirty Derivatives Project, 1992-93; Member, Board of Directors, Futures Industry Association; Member, Commodity Futures Trading Commission's Technology Advisory Committee; Member, Government Relations Committee, Managed Funds Association.

RASKIN, Debra
Vladeck, Waldman, Elias & Engelhard, P.C., New York 212 403 7300
Recommended in Employment

REARDON, Roy
Simpson Thacher & Bartlett, New York
212 455 2000
Recommended in Litigation

REED, Lucy
Freshfields Bruckhaus Deringer LLP, New York 212 277 4000
Recommended in Arbitration

REEDER, Robert W
Sullivan & Cromwell LLP, New York
212 558 4000
reederr@sullcrom.com
Recommended in Capital Markets
Specialization: Wide array of corporate and securities advice to public companies, such as American International Group, Inc., The Goldman Sachs Group, Inc. and Prudential Financial, Inc. Advises commercial and investment banks, including Goldman, Sachs & Co., Deutsche Bank Securities, Morgan Stanley, UBS and J.P. Morgan, on derivative instruments and 'restricted' and 'control' securities. Has acted in many significant IPOs, including that of The Goldman Sachs Group, Inc. and the first ever initial public offering to consumers by The Boston Beer Company. Has advised on numerous unique and complex securities offerings, including the first SEC-registered convertible MIPs offering. Regular underwriters' counsel in offerings by Corning Incorporated, Delta Air Lines, Inc. and Forest City Enterprises, Inc.. Established AAA-rated structured derivative products companies, including Goldman Sachs Mitsui Marine Derivative Products and GS Financial Products US (the only SEC-registered derivatives product company).
Prof. Memberships: American Bar Association; Association of the Bar of the City of New York; New York State Bar Association.
Career: Judicial Clerk to the Honorable Anthony J Celebrezze, US Court of Appeals (6th Circuit),1984-86. Joined *S&C* in 1986. Partner since 1993.
Personal: Born 1960. Youngstown State University (BS, 1981); Ohio State University Law School (JD, 1984). Director, Teak Fellowship.

REICH, Yaron Z
Cleary Gottlieb Steen & Hamilton, New York 212 225 2000
yreich@cgsh.com
Recommended in Tax
Specialization: Taxation and related matters, including tax aspects of corporate acquisitions, restructurings, insolvencies and financing techniques. Extensive experience in international transactions.
Prof. Memberships: Bar in New York. Admitted to practice before US District Court for the Southern District of New York, US Claims Court and Tax Court.
Career: Joined firm in 1979; became partner in 1986. LLM in Taxation, New York University School of Law (1984); JD, Special Issue Editor of 'Columbia Law Review', Columbia University School of Law (1978), BA, summa cum laude, Columbia College (1975).
Publications: He has published several significant articles on international tax issues.

REINHOLD, Richard L
Willkie Farr & Gallagher, New York
212 728 8292
rreinhold@willkie.com
Recommended in Tax
Specialization: US taxation, domestic and international, relative to mergers and acquisitions, joint ventures, new financial products, corporate restructurings and financial transactions.
Prof. Memberships: New York State Bar Association, Tax Section, Executive Committee (Chair of the Executive Committee, 1996-97); Fellow, American College of Tax Counsel; American Bar Association (Corporate Tax Committee); New York University Tax LLM Advisory Group; Tax Forum; Tax Club.
Publications: 'What is Tax Treaty Abuse? (Is Treaty Shopping an Outdated Concept?)' 53 Tax Lawyer, 663 (2000); 'Section 353(e): How we got here and where we are', 82 Tax Notes, 1485 (1999).

REITER, Glenn
Simpson Thacher & Bartlett, New York
212 455 2000
Recommended in Capital Markets

RICH, Bruce
Weil, Gotshal & Manges LLP, New York
212 310 8170
bruce.rich@weil.com
Recommended in Media & Entertainment
Specialization: Nationally recognized expert in intellectual property law, concentrating on the problems of communications industry clients, including book, magazine and newspaper publishers, broadcasters, cable television entities, and trade associations of these entities. Concentration includes the First Amendment, music licensing, copyright, trademark and antitrust. Heads the nation's pre-eminent practice group representing broadcast and cable television, background music, new media, and other entities in their music license relationships with the music performing rights organizations, the American Society of Composers, Authors and Publishers (ASCAP), Broadcast Music, Inc. (BMI), and SESA, as well as with recording industry insofar as digital delivery of copyrighted materials is concerned. Representative clients of the firm in this area include the ABC and CBS Television Networks, and Lifetime Television. Also actively provides advice to form media clients such as Reuters, HarperCollins and the New York Post in intellectual property matters, including the defense of libel lawsuits, and has represented the Association of American Publishers in its Supreme Court amicus curiae and other First Amendment activities.
Prof. Memberships: A member of the Board of Directors of Expeditionary Learning Outward Bound and of Penn Law School's Board of Overseers.
Personal: University of Pennsylvania (JD, cum laude, 1973); Dartmouth College (AB, magna cum laude, 1970).

RICH, Frederic C
Sullivan & Cromwell LLP, New York
212 558 4000
richf@sullcrom.com
Recommended in Projects
Specialization: Head of Global Project Finance; Co-Head Corporate Practice. Specialization in natural resource and energy projects, political risk management and capital markets. Oil and Gas work includes: financing for AIOC Caspian Sea 'Mega-Project', Baku-to-Ceyhan Pipeline, VLNG and Jose Terminal BOOT projects in Venezuela, Deer

Park Refinery in Texas, and Kutubu Petroleum and Pipeline Project in Papua New Guinea. Mining experience includes Bulyanhulu Project in Tanzania, Batu Hijau Project in Indonesia, Alumbrera Project in Argentina, Kumtor Project in Kyrgyz Republic, Lihir Project in Papua New Guinea and Escondida Project in Chile. Representative clients include BHP-Billiton, BP, ExxonMobil, Goldman Sachs, Rio Tinto, Shell, Sumitomo.
Prof. Memberships: American Bar Association (former Chair, Committee on Privatization); American Society of International Law; International Bar Association.
Career: Joined S&C in 1981. Partner since 1989.
Personal: Born 1956. Princeton University (AB, 1977); King's College, Cambridge (Keasby Fellow, 1978); University of Virginia Law School (JD, 1981). Former term member, Council on Foreign Relations. Chairman, Scenic Hudson Land Trust. Director, The Hudson River Foundation, Scenic Hudson, Inc., the Hudson Highlands Land Trust, Friends of the Palisades Interstate Park Commission, Inc. and Boscobel Restoration Inc.

RIESEL, Daniel
Sive Paget & Riesel PC, New York
212 421 2150
Recommended in Environment

RINGEL, Dean
Cahill Gordon & Reindel, New York
212 701 3900
Recommended in Media & Entertainment

RIVKIN, David W
Debevoise & Plimpton, New York
212 909 6671
dwrivkin@debevoise.com
Recommended in Arbitration
Specialization: Partner at *Debevoise & Plimpton*. His practice concentrates in international arbitration and international litigation. Subjects of disputes have included long-term energy concessions, joint venture agreements, insurance coverage, construction contracts, distribution agreements and intellectual property.
Prof. Memberships: Board of Directors and various committees of the American Arbitration Association; Secretary-Treasurer of the Section of Business Law of the International Bar Association, and immediate past Chair of its Committee on Arbitration and ADR; LCIA Court; ICC Commission on International Arbitration; Director of Divisions, Litigation Section of the American Bar Association. Advisor to the American Law Institute project on Transnational Rules of Civil Procedure; Fellow, Chartered Institute of Arbitrators; former member, NAFTA Advisory Committee on Private Commercial Disputes; US Secretary of State's Advisory Committee on Private International Law.
Career: Judicial Clerk, US Court of Appeals, Seventh Circuit (1980-81). Joined *Debevoise & Plimpton* in 1982 and became a partner in 1988.
Publications: Author of numerous texts on international arbitration and litigation.
Personal: Yale University, BA, 1977; Yale Law School, JD, 1980.

ROBERTS, Thomas A
Weil, Gotshal & Manges LLP, New York
212 310 8479
thomas.roberts@weil.com
Recommended in Private Equity
Specialization: Chairman of the Corporate Department and a member of the 13-member Management Committee of *Weil, Gotshal & Manges*. His practice involves domestic and cross border mergers, acquisitions, divestitures and contested take overs, and private equity. He advises boards of directors on general and strategic matters and is one of the leaders of the firm's team advising clients in crisis management situations. Named in a leading legal publication, 2001. Clients consist of major foreign and domestic, public and private companies, several of the leading private equity funds in the nation, and a number of leading investment banks. His clients include General Electric Company, Vivendi, CSFB Merchant Bank, AMR Corporation, Lehman Brothers, Hicks, Muse, Tate & Furst, TH Lee Company, EDS, Conseco, Inc., Enron, United Health and Capital Z Partners. Recent significant transactions include: matters for General Electric, Hicks, Muse, Tate & Furst, Capital Z and BSFB Merchant Bank. Recent representations include Vivendi in the pending proposed dispositions of Vivendi Universal Publishing and Vivendi Games; CSFB in its proposed acquisition of Nycomed; General Electric in its $5 billion acquisition of Heller Financial and as special Counsel in its terminated $46 billion acquisition of Honeywell; Enron in its terminated $12 billion merger with Dynegy; AMR in its $3 billion acquisition of TWA; and restructurings for Enron, PennCorp Financial Group and Conseco, Inc.
Personal: BA and JD from Georgetown University where he served on the 'Georgetown Law Journal'. His leisure interests include skiing, golf, literature and the theater. A former rodeo cowboy, he was until recently a breeder and exhibitor of American Quarter horses.

ROD, Jonathan
Latham & Watkins LLP, New York
212 906 1363
jonathan.rod@lw.com
Recommended in Projects
Specialization: Corporate finance and project partner in the New York office. Handles a wide variety of securities and finance matters with a principal focus on the oil and gas, energy and telecommunications sectors. Has extensive experience in securities work, including innovative project bond financings in US capital markets. Represented investors and bank groups on export receivable financings and production payment financings. Clients include Citigroup, Credit Suisse First Boston, JPMorgan Chase, West LB and other financial institutions.
Personal: JD, Boston University, 1985. BS (Economics), Wharton School of University of Pennsylvania, 1982.

ROGERS, JR, Theodore O
Sullivan & Cromwell LLP, New York
212 558 4000
rogerst@sullcrom.com
Recommended in Employment
Specialization: Coordinator of the firm's Labor and Employment Law Group. Represents employers with respect to all manner of labor and employment issues. Acted as lead counsel in one of the two consolidated cases in which New York State's highest court upheld the arbitrability of employment discrimination claims. Also focuses on estates litigation, where he has litigated a broad range of issues, including will contests, trust accountings and issues of fiduciary responsibility.
Prof. Memberships: New York State Bar Association (Member, Executive Committee, Labor and Employment Law Section); Association of the Bar of the City of New York; District of Columbia Bar Association. Fellow, College of Labor and Employment Lawyers; Advisory Board member, Center for Labor and Employment Law, New York University School of Law.
Career: Joined *Sullivan & Cromwell* in 1979. Partner since 1987.
Publications: Co-author of West Group's 'Employment Litigation in New York' (1996) and 'Employment Law Deskbook for Human Resources Professionals' (2001). Lecturer on employment law topics, including the Practising Law Institute's annual Employment Law Institutes and the New York State Bar Association's Employment Law Litigation Institutes.
Personal: Born in 1953. AB, Harvard University, 1976 (magna cum laude); JD, Harvard Law School, 1979 (cum laude).

ROLFE, Ron
Cravath, Swaine & Moore, New York
212 474 1000
Recommended in Antitrust

ROSEN, Burt
Debevoise & Plimpton, New York
212 909 6781
brosen@debevoise.com
Recommended in Tax
Specialization: Partner at *Debevoise & Plimpton*. He represents a wide variety of clients in all aspects of tax practice, including equipment financing, international financings and securitisations and mergers and acquisitions.
Prof. Memberships: New York State Bar Association.
Career: Joined *Debevoise & Plimpton* in 1979 and became a partner in 1988.
Publications: Contributing author, 'International Mergers and Acquisitions' (Kluwer 1999).
Personal: State University of New York at Buffalo, BA, BS, 1976; University of Michigan Law School, JD, 1979; New York University, LLM in Taxation, 1985.

ROSEN, Edward J
Cleary Gottlieb Steen & Hamilton, New York 212 225 2000
erosen@cgsh.com
Recommended in Capital Markets
Specialization: Structuring and regulatory analysis of complex securities and derivatives transactions and US securities and commodities law regulation. Counsel to Securities Industry Association, International Swaps and Derivatives Association and Futures Industry Association.
Prof. Memberships: Member ISDA Regulatory Advisory Committee, FIA Board of Directors and CFTC Technology Advisory Committee. Chair, Practicing Law Institute Annual Conference on Swaps and Derivatives.
Career: JD, Columbia University School of Law (1982) (Stone Scholar); BA, MA (Hon.), Oxford University (1975).
Publications: Co-author 'US Regulation of the International Securities and Derivatives Markets'.

ROSEN, J Philip
Weil, Gotshal & Manges LLP, New York
212 310 8000
philip.rosen@weil.com
Recommended in Real Estate
Specialization: Heads the firm's Property Transactions and Finance Group. One of the power brokers of international real estate, he is a leading authority in a broad spectrum of property, including opportunity fund representation, finance (asset-backed, secured and unsecured), development, securitization, real estate investment trusts, portfolio acquisitions, loan restructuring and leasing. He also heads the firm's renowned Hospitality and Gaming Practices. He is also one of the country's leading experts on doing business in Israel and the Middle East, and co-heads the firm's Middle East Practice Group. Client representation includes: CSFB, Brookfield Properties, UBS Securities Starwood Capital, Equtable, Brascan, Lehman Brothers, JP Morgan/Chase, Nomura, Comverser Technology, Fortress Investments, Loews/CAN and Yesuiva University.
Prof. Memberships: Vice Chairman of the Board of Directors of Yeshiva College of Yeshiva University in New York and a Wexner Heritage Foundation Scholar. He is a member of the Conference of Presi-

dents of Major Jewish American Organizations. He is also a member of the International Council of Shopping Centers, the Real Estate Board of New York, the National Association of Real Estate Investment Trusts, and the Urban Land Institute. He is also Vice-Chairman of the Republican Jewish Coalition.
Publications: Written numerous articles and books on opportunity representation, real estate mergers and acquisition, real estate investment trusts, finance, loan restructurings, workouts and turnarounds, leasing, development and securitization. He has also chaired and spoken at seminars on 'Doing Business in Israel and the Middle East', both in the US and Israel. A recognized expert, he has been quoted on many of these topics in newspapers and magazines, including 'The Wall Street Journal', 'The New York Times', 'American Banker', 'Crain's New York Business', 'The American Lawyer', 'Pensions & Investment Age', 'Global Magazine' (Israel), 'Ha' aretz' (Israel) and 'Global Finance' (England).
Personal: JD, Georgetown University Law Center (1981); BA, Yeshiva University (1978).

ROSEN, Matthew A
Skadden, Arps, Slate, Meagher & Flom LLP & Affiliates, New York
212 735 2230
mrosen@skadden.com
Recommended in Tax

Specialization: Co-head, *Skadden*'s Tax Department. Represents clients in every aspect of tax work, with particular emphasis on acquisitions, divestitures and restructurings, both domestic and cross-border. Also handles matters involving partnerships of every type, joint ventures and executive compensation. In addition, practice includes the development of financial instruments and financial products. Clients include many significant public and private companies, investment banks and investment funds.
Prof. Memberships: Co-Chair, Subcommittee on Net Operating Losses, New York State Bar Association (1985-87). Co-Chair, Subcommittee on Bankruptcy, New York State Bar Association (1988-89). Executive Committee Member, Tax Section, New York State Bar Association (1985-89; 2003).
Personal: LLM, New York University, 1979 (Memorial Award for Distinction); JD, Boston University, 1976 (cum laude); BA, Swarthmore College, 1973.

ROSEN, Richard
Paul, Weiss, Rifkind, Wharton & Garrison LLP, New York 212 373 3305
rrosen@paulweiss.com
Recommended in Litigation

Specialization: Litigation partner who chairs firm's Securities Litigation Practice Group, and has significant experience in securities, derivatives, mergers and acquisitions and other complex business disputes. Has represented public companies, underwriting syndicates, open and closed-end investment funds and limited partnerships in securities fraud class actions. Has authored numerous articles on corporate and securities law issues and is a frequent speaker at bar association and securities industry conferences. Representative clients include: Morgan Stanley, Citigroup and Carnival Corporation.

ROSENBERG, Marc
Cravath, Swaine & Moore, New York
212 474 1000
Recommended in Capital Markets

ROSENBERG, Mark
Sullivan & Cromwell LLP, New York
212 558 4000
rosenbergm@sullcrom.com
Recommended in Environment

Specialization: Coordinator of the firm's Environmental Law and Insurance groups. Has extensive litigation and transactional experience in insurance, reinsurance, asbestos, environmental and toxic tort matters, including alter ego, successor liability, fraudulent conveyance, insolvency and bankruptcy issues that often arise in connection therewith. Also has extensive experience in spearheading recoveries of foreign sovereign debt. Has acted as international lead counsel in debt recovery and political risk insurance litigation, and as national counsel in domestic asbestos, environmental and other toxic tort matters.
Prof. Memberships: American Bar Association (former Chair of [i]the Reinsurance Subcommittee, Insurance Coverage Litigation Committee; [ii] of the Directors and Officers Liability Subcommittee, Insurance Coverage Litigation Committee; [iii] of the Toxic and Hazardous Substances and Environmental Law Committee, and; [iv] of the Subcommittee on Revisions to the Comprehensive General Liability Policy. Also has served as the Tort and Insurance Practice Section's Liaison to the ABA Standing Committee on Environmental Law, and as a member of the Tort and Insurance Practice Section's Task Force on Superfund Reauthorization). New York State Bar Association (Chair, Environmental Committee of the International Section).
Career: Joined *Sullivan & Cromwell* in 1980. Partner since 1993.
Publications: Author of several articles on environmental and related insurance and derivative liability issues.
Personal: Born in 1954. BA, Michigan State University, 1977 (magna cum laude); JD, George Washington Law School, 1980 (magna cum laude).

ROSENBERG, Robert
Latham & Watkins LLP, New York
212 906 1370
robert.rosenberg@lw.com
Recommended in Insolvency

Specialization: Global head of Insolvency Practice Group. Member of the Bankruptcy Rules Committee of the US District Court for the District of Delaware. Counsel to Edison International in the refinancing of its $1.2 billion debt, to Wells Fargo Bank as indenture trustee in Enron Corp. and to AOL Time Warner and EDS Corp. in WorldCom. Has also done workouts for Deutsche Bank, Credit Lyonnais, Metropolitan Life, Northwestern Mutual Life and Lehman Brothers.
Career: Former law professor at New York University.
Publications: Numerous.
Personal: JD, Harvard University, 1970. BA, Columbia University, 1967.

ROSENBLATT, William W
Dewey Ballantine LLP, New York
212 259 6500
wrosenblatt@deweyballantine.com
Recommended in Insurance

Specialization: He has had approximately 32 years of experience in corporate finance and securities law, with particular emphasis on the insurance industry. His practice includes representation of parties (including principals, investment bankers and lenders) in all aspects of capital markets, mergers and acquisitions, and private equity transactions as well as product development, contract and regulatory matters. He also focuses on the financial guaranty industry, including corporate finance, transactional, regulatory and product development matters.
Prof. Memberships: Director, National Benefit Life Insurance Company (2000 - present); Director, Sun Alliance (USA) (1996-98); Member, Millburn Township Board of Education (1991-95); Director, Acordia, Inc. (1991-97).
Publications: Chapters in 'New York Insurance Law', 2nd Edition, authored by Wolcott B Dunham Jr (Matthew Bender, 1999).
Personal: Columbia University School of Law, JD, 1971, cum laude; Yale University, BA, American Studies, 1967, honors.

ROSS, Allen
Ross & Cohen, LLP, New York
212 370 1200
aross@rosscohen.com
Recommended in Construction

Specialization: Partner in the Construction Department. He has represented diverse clients involved in the construction process, including owners (public and private), general contractors, subcontractors, sureties and design professionals. He has extensive experience negotiating construction contracts and disputes. He is active as a trial lawyer, arbitrator, mediator and the Chair of a dispute review board for a major public project.
Prof. Memberships: Association of the Bar of the City of New York (Public Contracts Law Section); New York State Bar Association (Construction Law Section); American Bar Association (Forum Committee on Construction, Litigation Section, Alternative Dispute Resolution Committee); International Bar Association; Construction Financial Management Association.
Career: Admitted to New York Bar, 1964. An associate and then partner in *M Carl Levine, Morgulas & Foreman* from 1964-78. A founding partner in *Ross & Cohen, LLP*, in 1978.
Personal: Received an LLB from New York University in 1964 and a BA from Cornell University in 1961.

ROSSMAN, Vladimir
Shearman & Sterling, New York
212 848 4000
Recommended in Banking & Finance

ROVINE, Arthur
Baker & McKenzie, New York
212 891 3550
arthur.w.rovine@bakernet.com
Recommended in Arbitration

Specialization: International commercial arbitration involving complex contracts under US and foreign law. Represents many major corporate clients and has handled cases for and against governments. Previously served in the Office of the Legal Advisor in the Department of State as Assistant Legal Adviser for Treaty Affairs and then as the first US Agent to the Iran-US Claims Tribunal.
Prof. Memberships: Past President, American Society of International Law (2000-02); former Chair, American Bar Association International Law Section (1985-86), Section Delegate to ABA House of Delegates (1986-87); Member: Council on Foreign Relations, the American Arbitration Association (Panel of Arbitrators), the Association of the Bar of the City of New York, the Center for Public Resources (Panel on the Settlement of Transnational Business Disputes), and US Council for International Business (Arbitration Committee).
Career: Taught international law and organization at Cornell and later at Georgetown while in the Department of State. Visiting Lecturer in Law at Yale in 1998, teaching international arbitration.
Publications: Has written widely on international law and international arbitration, and has given many addresses on these topics. Served for ten years as a member of the Board of Editors of the 'American Journal of International Law'.

ROWEN, Andrew S
Sullivan & Cromwell LLP, New York
212 558 4000
rowena@sullcrom.com
Recommended in Insurance

Specialization: Coordinator of *S&C*'s Insurance Group. Focuses on acquisition,

NEW YORK — LEADERS

finance and corporate matters involving insurance companies. Practice includes: acquisitions/divestitures and other change of control transactions, including insurance regulatory approvals; securities offerings and advice as to SEC disclosure issues and inquiries; demutualizations and the establishment of offshore companies; the securitization of insurance risks; and various insurance regulatory matters.
Prof. Memberships: American Bar Association; New York State Bar Association.
Career: Joined *Sullivan & Cromwell* in 1979. Partner since 1987.
Publications: Speaker at various industry conferences.
Personal: Born in 1954. Harvard Law School, (JD, 1979); University of California, Berkeley (AB, 1976).

RUBIN, Robert
Postner & Rubin, New York
212 269 2510
Recommended in Construction

RUEGGER, Philip
Simpson Thacher & Bartlett, New York
212 455 2000
Recommended in Corporate/M&A, Private Equity

RUTKOWSKI, Larry
Seward & Kissel, New York
212 574 1200
Recommended in Shipping

SACRIPANTI, Peter
McDermott, Will & Emery, New York
212 547 5583
psacripanti@mwe.com
Recommended in Environment
Specialization: Partner in charge of *McDermott, Will & Emery*'s New York office. Trial lawyer who focuses practice on complex litigation matters, including toxic torts actions, general commercial disputes, securities actions and class action litigation. His clients include: ExxonMobil, Bristol-Myers Squibb, Honeywell, Citigroup and its Board of Directors, American Home Products, Atofina and Northville Industries.
Prof. Memberships: Member of the bars of the District of Columbia and the states of New York and New Jersey.
Career: Former federal prosecutor, recruited to the Department of Justice under the prestigious Attorney General's Honor Program. Recipient of the prestigious Ellis Island Medal of Honor.
Personal: Received his bachelor's degree from Fordham University, summa cum laude, and law degree from Pace University School of Law, where he was a Ranking Scholar.

SAEED, Faiza
Cravath, Swaine & Moore, New York
212 474 1000
Recommended in Corporate/M&A

SALVATORE, Paul
Proskauer Rose LLP, New York
212 969 3000
Recommended in Employment

SAMUELS, Leslie B
Cleary Gottlieb Steen & Hamilton,
New York 212 225 2050
lsamuels@cgsh.com
Recommended in Tax
Specialization: International taxation and domestic taxation, including tax-related mergers and acquisitions, joint ventures, foreign direct investment in the US, financial products and capital markets activities.
Prof. Memberships: Member of the Association of the Bar of the City of New York and the NYSBA.
Career: Joined the firm in 1968 and became partner in 1975. Served as Assistant Secretary for Tax Policy of the US Treasury Department (1993-96). Vice-Chair, Committee of Fiscal Affairs, OECD (1994-96). LLB, magna cum laude, Harvard Law School (1966), BS Economics, Wharton School of Finance and Commerce, University of Pennsylvania (1963). Fulbright scholar at the London School of Economics and Political Science (1967-68). Certified public accountant.

SANDLER, Richard
Davis Polk & Wardwell, New York
212 450 4000
Recommended in Capital Markets

SAUNDERS, Paul
Cravath, Swaine & Moore, New York
212 474 1000
Recommended in Litigation

SCARBOROUGH, Robert
Freshfields Bruckhaus Deringer LLP,
New York 212 277 4000
Recommended in Tax

SCAVONE, Arthur
White & Case LLP, New York
212 819 8200
Recommended in Projects

SCHAFFRAN, Andrew
Morgan, Lewis & Bockius LLP, New York
212 309 6000
Recommended in Employment

SCHARFSTEIN, Joel
Fried, Frank, Harris, Shriver & Jacobson,
New York 212 859 8172
Joel.Scharfstein@FriedFrank.com
Recommended in Tax
Specialization: Tax partner. Practice focuses on corporate acquisitions and divestitures, partnership transactions, investment partnerships and restructurings.
Prof. Memberships: Member of the Executive Committee of the Tax Section of the New York State Bar Association (1992-2002) and co-chair of its committees on partnerships (1992-94), bankruptcy (1994-96), consolidated returns (1996-98) and basis and cost recovery (1999-2001).
Career: Qualified in New York in 1978. Joined firm in 1977 and became partner in 1984.
Personal: Born 1947. Received JD from the University of Michigan Law School in 1977, AB from Columbia College in 1969 and AM from Harvard University in 1972.

SCHELER, Brad Eric
Fried, Frank, Harris, Shriver & Jacobson,
New York 212 859 8019
Brad.Scheler@FriedFrank.com
Recommended in Insolvency
Specialization: Chairman of the Bankruptcy and Restructuring Department. Practice includes both in and out-of-court restructurings and the rehabilitation of financially distressed businesses. Represents companies experiencing complex financial difficulties, creditors' committees, bondholders' committees, major secured and unsecured creditors, trustees, debtor-in-possession lenders, investment partnerships that buy and sell distressed securities and businesses, and third parties seeking to invest in and/or acquire the assets and businesses of financially troubled companies. Also acts as outside general counsel and strategic adviser to financially strong corporate and institutional clients in connection with financings, mergers and acquisitions, joint ventures and securities transactions.
Prof. Memberships: Fellow of the American College of Bankruptcy; American Bar Association and its Business Bankruptcy Committee, Business Law Section; New York State Bar Association; Association of the Bar of the City of New York; Delaware Bankruptcy Rule and Practice Committee.
Career: Qualified in New York in 1978. Joined *Fried, Frank, Harris, Shriver and Jacobson* in 1981, became partner in 1984, became Chairman of the Bankruptcy and Restructuring Department in 1986. Began career as an associate at *Weil, Gotshal & Manges* (1977-81).
Publications: Contributing author, 'Collier on Bankruptcy'. Co-authors regular column for the 'Uniform Commercial Code Law Journal'; speaker at professional seminars on bankruptcy and restructuring issues; delivered the Benjamin Weintraub Distinguished lecture on bankruptcy law at Hofstra University School of Law, 1994.
Personal: JD in 1977 from Hofstra University School of Law; BA, with high honors, from Lehigh University in 1974.

SCHELL, J Michael
Skadden, Arps, Slate, Meagher & Flom LLP & Affiliates, New York
212 735 3150
mschell@skadden.com
Recommended in Corporate/M&A
Specialization: Partner, New York. Concentrates in mergers and acquisitions, corporate investments and general corporate counseling. Has extensive experience in domestic and cross-border transactions - negotiated and contested. In the past two years counseled Alcoa in a number of initiatives, including acquisition of Fairchild aerospace fastener business, and discussions with Australian mining giant WMC Ltd. In 2000, advised Dexter Corporation's Board in a defense named 'US M&A Deal of the Year' by 'Euromoney'. Has advised Alcoa in its multibillion dollar acquisitions of Reynolds, Alumax and Cordant. Led representation of Daimler-Benz AG in its historic 1998 merger with Chrysler - named 'Investment Dealer's Digest's Deal of the Year.
Prof. Memberships: Member, Board of Trustees, Boston University; Member, Board of Trustees, American Institute for Contemporary German Studies (Johns Hopkins University); Member, Board of Visitors, Boston University Law School; Member, Board of Directors, National Down Syndrome Society; Senior Professional Fellow, Center for Law and Business, New York University.
Personal: JD, Boston University School of Law, 1976; AB, Columbia University, 1969.

SCHETMAN, Richard
Cadwalader, Wickersham & Taft,
New York 212 504 6906
richard.schetman@cwt.com
Recommended in Capital Markets
Specialization: Capital markets partner who concentrates in structured finance, derivative products, other types of financing, and the federal securities laws. Represents underwriters, credit enhancers, issuers, institutional investors, sponsors, and swap counterparties in a wide range of matters, including the securitization of cash flows from such assets as credit card receivables, auto loans, trade receivables, wholesale auto dealer notes, leases, tobacco settlements, and airplane contracts. Extensive experience in structuring commercial paper vehicles and CDOs, synthetic CDOs and vehicles for repackaging corporate, asset-backed and non-US securities. Speaker at various conferences on CDOs, repackagings and other securitization issues.
Prof. Memberships: The Association of the Bar of the City of New York and the American Bar Association.
Career: BA, Brown University (1980); JD, The University of Pennsylvania School of Law (cum laude, 1983) (member of Moot Court Board); joined *Cadwalader* in 1985, became a partner in 1993.

SCHLER, Michael
Cravath, Swaine & Moore, New York
212 474 1000
Recommended in Tax

LEADERS

NEW YORK

SCHNABL, Marco E
Skadden, Arps, Slate, Meagher & Flom LLP & Affiliates, New York
212 735 2312
mschnabl@skadden.com
Recommended in Arbitration

Specialization: Partner, New York. Handles a wide range of international and domestic litigations and arbitrations. Has represented clients in litigations stemming from US and international M&A and changes in corporate control. Also worked on securities class actions both for US and foreign clients, contested proceedings before administrative agencies, SEC investigations, and contract disputes and other commercial litigations. Represented underwriters and Latin American issuers in debt and equity offerings in the industrial, telecommunications, banking and energy sectors.
Personal: JD, Columbia University School of Law, 1981; MPhil, Economics, Columbia University Graduate School of Arts and Sciences, 1977; MS, Management, Sloan School of Management, Massachusetts Institute of Technology, 1973; Lic., Economics, University of Buenos Aires, 1971.

SCHOENBERG, Clifford H
Cadwalader, Wickersham & Taft, New York 212 504 6992
cliff.schoenberg@cwt.com
Recommended in Insurance

Specialization: Litigation partner who has handled scores of multimillion dollar reinsurance arbitrations and litigations, and a wide variety of disputes between insurance companies and their agents. Has litigated direct insurance coverage actions, been retained as an arbitrator and expert in reinsurance arbitrations, and represented insurance companies in regulatory matters before the New York State Insurance Department. Also has acted as coordinating and supervising counsel for federal and state class action lawsuits against insurers, including a large number of actions in the State of Alabama involving significant punitive damage claims. In addition to his extensive litigation and regulatory experience, he has served as lead counsel on insurance company mergers, acquisitions and divestitures. He has written numerous articles and lectured extensively on reinsurance topics. He also serves on the board of directors of Zurich Kemper Life Insurance Company of New York and was formerly Assistant General Counsel of The Home Insurance Company.
Personal: BA, Dickinson College (summa cum laude, 1972); JD, Boston University School of Law (magna cum laude, 1975).

SCHONHOLTZ, Margot
Clifford Chance US LLP, New York
212 878 4990
margot.schonholtz@cliffordchance.com
Recommended in Insolvency

Specialization: Serves as regional head of the Financial Restructuring and Insolvency Group and was recently elected to the firm's partnership council. She represents leading institutional creditors, agents to syndicated lending groups, large lender groups, official and unofficial creditors' committees and commercial lenders in out of court debt restructurings, loan workouts, asset sale transactions and bankruptcy matters. Handles all aspects of bankruptcy and creditors' rights litigation and structures, negotiates and documents complex restructuring transactions. She has particular knowledge of the retail, cable and broadcasting, wireless communications, energy, manufacturing, mining, financial services and healthcare industries.

SCHULZ, David
Clifford Chance US LLP, New York
212 878 8266
david.schulz@cliffordchance.com
Recommended in Media & Entertainment

Specialization: Experienced in media defense and complex litigation, his practice is concentrated on libel, privacy, First Amendment, intellectual property and telecommunications litigation. He has argued precedent-setting cases to New York's highest court - defining the right of press access to judicial proceedings - and in federal appellate courts. His clients include the nation's leading news wire service, national television networks, cable operators, newspapers and national news magazines. Has taught constitutional law for two decades and is the author of numerous articles on press rights. He is often quoted as an expert on First Amendment law in the press.

SCHUMER, Robert B
Paul, Weiss, Rifkind, Wharton & Garrison LLP, New York 212 373 3097
rschumer@paulweiss.com
Recommended in Corporate/M&A

Specialization: Co-head of the M&A group. Concentrates in mergers and acquisitions and joint venture transactions. Has represented numerous major corporations in significant merger and acquisition transactions, many of which involve multibillion-dollar acquisitions or dispositions. Involved in both negotiated transactions and contested takeovers. Also represents special committees of boards of directors and a number of leading investment banking firms in the mergers and acquisitions context. Has also been involved in numerous international and domestic multibillion dollar joint venture arrangements.

SCHWARTZ, Herbert
Fish & Neave, New York
212 596 9000
Recommended in Intellectual Property

SCHWARTZ, Jodi J
Wachtell, Lipton, Rosen & Katz,
New York 212 403 1212
jjschwartz@wlrk.com
Recommended in Tax

Specialization: Specializes in United States federal income taxation with emphasis on mergers, acquisitions and spin-offs.
Prof. Memberships: Member of the New York State Bar Association Tax Section Executive Committee.
Career: Partner at *Wachtell, Lipton, Rosen & Katz* since 1991.
Personal: Graduated magna cum laude from the University of Pennsylvania in 1981 (BS, economics), from the University of Pennsylvania (Wharton School) in 1984 (MBA), magna cum laude from the University of Pennsylvania Law School in 1984 (JD), and from New York University Law School in 1987 (LLM, taxation).

SCHWARTZ, Steven
Clifford Chance US LLP, New York
212 878 4920
steven.schwartz@cliffordchance.com
Recommended in Insurance

Specialization: Specializing in insurance and reinsurance litigation and arbitration, he has represented prominent insurance and reinsurance companies in disputes worth hundreds of millions of dollars, involving property/casualty and life/health reinsurance, insurance insolvency and alternative risk transfer. His experience includes representation of a US ceding company in a series of arbitrations regarding asbestos and other losses, representation of both cedents and reinsurers in disputes relating to pools and managing general agents, as well as recent arbitrations relating to workers' compensation carve-out and personal accident reinsurance. He frequently writes and lectures on reinsurance issues.

SCHWED, Robert
Reboul, MacMurray, Hewitt, Maynard & Kristol, New York 212 841 5700
Recommended in Private Equity

SELVER, Paul
Paul, Hastings, Janofsky & Walker LLP, New York 212 318 6869
paulselver@paulhastings.com
Recommended in Real Estate

Specialization: Practice encompasses all aspects of land use and development law, with a special emphasis on environmental, zoning and historic preservation. He has extensive experience counseling clients in the public and environmental review of complex and large scale projects. Over the past 15 years, he has successfully coordinated the public approval and environmental review process for more than 8,000,000 square feet of office space, more than 7,500 apartments, hundreds of thousands of square feet of retail and entertainment space, hundreds of hotel rooms, and new institutional buildings.
Personal: Harvard College, magna cum laude, (1969); Harvard University Law School (1972).

SHACHAR, Avishai
Davis Polk & Wardwell, New York
212 450 4000
Recommended in Tax

SHAW, Gregory
Cravath, Swaine & Moore, New York
212 474 1000
Recommended in Capital Markets

SHENKER, Joseph C
Sullivan & Cromwell LLP, New York
212 558 4000
shenkerj@sullcrom.com
Recommended in Real Estate

Specialization: Coordinator of the firm's global commercial real estate practice. Broad experience in general representation of major real estate operating companies, securities offerings, negotiated mergers and acquisitions, joint ventures and private equity investment. Regularly represents issuers and underwriters in REIT debt and equity offerings. M&A and joint venture representations include: the investors in the Rockefeller Center Properties merger and subsequent sale; the acquirors in the joint venture acquisition of Westin Hotels Companies, and later Westin in its sale by merger to Starwood Lodging Trust; the international consortium of investors in the acquisition of Canary Wharf PLC, and in Canary Wharf's subsequent IPO; Vornado Realty Trust in all its acquisition activity, including the acquisitions of Mendik Company, Americold, URS, Merchandise Mart and Charles E. Smith Commercial Properties; General Growth in the acquisition of Homart; and the Whitehall Funds in their numerous acquisitions and dispositions worldwide, including both the purchase and sale of Cadillac Fairview (Canada), both the purchase and sale of Hillman Properties, and the acquisitions of Westminster Health Care Holdings PLC (UK) and UNUM (Italy).
Career: Joined *Sullivan & Cromwell* in 1980. Became a partner of the firm in 1986 and member of the firm's Management Committee in 1996.
Personal: Born 1956. Attended CUNY (BS, 1977) and Columbia University (JD, 1980).

SHIM, Paul
Cleary Gottlieb Steen & Hamilton,
New York 212 225 2000
pshim@cgsh.com
Recommended in Corporate/M&A

Specialization: Mergers, acquisitions and leveraged buyouts. Clients include Texas Pacific Group, HSBC, Salomon Smith Barney, American Express, Bank of Montreal, Suntory Limited, Standard Microsystems Corporation.
Career: Joined the firm in 1987, became

partner in 1996. JD degree, cum laude, NYU (1987). BS, MS (Chem. E), MIT (1984).
Publications: 'IBP v. Tyson Foods - Acquiror Must Consummate Merger When Court Finds No 'Material Adverse Effect'' by V Lewkow and P Shim, 'The M&A Lawyer', June 2001. 'Law Puts Parties in a Bind When Announcing Merger' by V. Lewkow and P. Shim, 'The National Law Journal', February 10, 1997.
Personal: Resides in New Jersey with his wife and two children.

SHIMSHAK, Stephen
Paul, Weiss, Rifkind, Wharton & Garrison LLP, New York 212 373 3133
sshimshak@paulweiss.com
Recommended in Insolvency
Specialization: Experience includes restructurings and workouts and a wide range of chapter 11 cases, involving debtors, secured creditors (including banks and other lenders), trustees, asset purchasers and investors. After practicing for two years with *Foley & Lardner* in Wisconsin, he joined *Anderson Russell Kill & Olick* in New York City. From 1984 to 1990, he was an associate in the Bankruptcy Department of *Milbank, Tweed, Hadley & McCloy*. He was a partner with *Milbank* from 1990-91.

SHOSS, Cynthia R
LeBoeuf, Lamb, Greene & MacRae, LLP, New York 212 424 8129
cshoss@llgm.com
Recommended in Insurance
Specialization: She is an experienced insurance regulatory attorney, concentrating especially in demutualizations, restructurings, mergers and acquisitions of insurance companies in the US and other countries. She advises clients in both the private and public sectors on such matters, including with respect to strategy and policy and the enactment of legislation and regulations. Previously, she provided tax counsel to US and multinational clients in connection with transactions, international audits and tax litigation.
Career: Joined *LeBoeuf* in 1982; Managing Partner, London Office 1987-89.
Personal: Newcomb College (BA, cum laude) 1971; Tulane University (JD) 1974; New York University (LLM) 1980, in Taxation.

SHUTRAN, Richard
Dewey Ballantine LLP, New York 212 259 8000
Recommended in Projects

SICULAR, David
Paul, Weiss, Rifkind, Wharton & Garrison LLP, New York 212 373 3082
dsicular@paulweiss.com
Recommended in Tax
Specialization: Tax partner with broad practice in the full range of corporate, partnership and international transactions, including public and private mergers and acquisitions (both domestic and cross-border), financings, bankruptcy and insolvency restructurings, financial products and general tax planning. Clients include public and private companies in the United States and abroad, private equity and other investment funds, private investors and individual entrepreneurs. Member of Executive Committee, New York State Bar Association Tax Section and Tax Forum.

SILBERSTEIN, Rebecca F
Debevoise & Plimpton, New York 212 909 6438
rfsilberstein@debevoise.com
Recommended in Private Equity
Specialization: Partner at *Debevoise & Plimpton*. Her practice focuses on advising financial institutions, investment banks and boutique firms as sponsors of and investors in leveraged buyout, venture capital, private equity, mezzanine merchant banking and other private investment funds. Clients include: Merrill Lynch, MMC Capital, AIG, Kelso & Company, Solera Capital and Fairview Capital Partners.
Career: Joined *Debevoise & Plimpton* in 1993 and became a partner in 2001.
Personal: Yeshiva University, 1990, BA, magna cum laude, in Psychology; Benjamin N. Cardozo School of Law, 1993, JD, summa cum laude, Supervising Editor of the 'Law Review'.

SILVERMAN, Eric
Milbank, Tweed, Hadley & McCloy, New York 212 530 5000
Recommended in Projects

SILVERMAN, Leslie N
Cleary Gottlieb Steen & Hamilton, New York 212 225 2000
lsilverman@cgsh.com
Recommended in Capital Markets
Specialization: Domestic and international finance, particularly cross-border financings and global public offerings and derivatives.
Prof. Memberships: Bar in New York. Admitted to practice before US Court of Appeals (Second Circuit) and US District Court (Southern District of New York).
Career: Joined firm in 1974; became partner in 1982. JD, Law Journal Editor, Yale Law School (1973); BS, summa cum laude, Wharton School of the University of Pennsylvania (1969).
Publications: Co-author of 'US Regulation of the International Securities and Derivatives Markets' (Sixth Edition, 2001).

SIMKIN, Steven
Paul, Weiss, Rifkind, Wharton & Garrison LLP, New York 212 373 3073
ssimkin@paulweiss.com
Recommended in Real Estate
Specialization: Chair of Real Estate Department, maintains an active practice in major financings, acquisitions and development projects, representing both lenders and developers. Experience includes involvement in multi-state mortgage financings. Focus also includes real estate-related litigations and disputes, as well as complex joint ventures and partnership agreements. Shopping centre experience is extensive, having been involved in the purchase, sale or financing of several hundred regional malls. Has represented many major tenants in New York City and elsewhere and has broad experience in the area of commercial office leasing. Major transactions include, World Trade Center, Citicorp Centre and AOL Time Warner Center.

SIMMS, Marsha E
Weil, Gotshal & Manges LLP, New York 212 310 8116
marsha.simms@weil.com
Recommended in Banking & Finance
Specialization: Partner in *Weil, Gotshal & Manges*' Corporate Department. Practices in the areas of debt financing and restructuring. Has extensive experience negotiating financing and restructuring documentation, and has participated in transactions in numerous industries, including retail, telecommunications, energy and manufacturing. Also has represented major lenders providing debtor-in-possession financing and exit financing to newly reorganized companies.
Prof. Memberships: American Bar Association, she is a member of the Council of the Business Law Section, is a member of the Editorial Board of 'Business Law Today', and was the former Chair of the Secured Transactions Subcommittee, UCC Committee of the Business Law Section. She is a member of the Africa Law Initiative Council, a member of the African Commercial Law Subcommittee of the International Law and Practice Section and former Chair of the Coordinating Group on Energy Law. She is a member of the Banking Law Committee and the Committee on Minorities in the Profession of the New York State Bar Association. She is the Treasurer of the American College of Commercial Finance Lawyers and a member of The American Law Institute. She is also a member of the Board of Directors of the American Arbitration Association, a member of the Board of Trustees of the Lawyers' Committee for Civil Rights Under Law and a member of the Board of Trustees of Educational Broadcasting Corporation (Channel 13). Former trustee of the Stanford Alumni Association and was a member of the Stanford Law School Campaign Steering Committee. She serves as the vice-chair of minority recruitment and retention of the firm's Hiring Committee and is a member of the firm's Diversity, Pro Bono and Professional Development Committees.

Career: Has lectured in legal areas related to asset based lending and debt financing for the Practising Law Institute and ALI/ABA, in Africa for American Bar Association technical legal assistance projects as well as in areas related to women and minorities' participation in corporate law practice.
Publications: Co-author of a book on corporate restructurings and bankruptcies published by Euromoney Publications.
Personal: Stanford Law School (JD, 1977); Barnard College (AB, 1974).

SIMS, Charles
Proskauer Rose LLP, New York 212 969 3000
Recommended in Media & Entertainment

SINGER, Andrew
Latham Watkins, California
Recommended in Projects
See California

SIT, Po
Davis Polk & Wardwell, New York 212 450 4000
Recommended in Tax

SLONAKER, Norman
Sidley Austin Brown & Wood, New York 212 839 5300
Recommended in Capital Markets

SMALL, Jeffrey
Davis Polk & Wardwell, New York 212 450 4000
Recommended in Capital Markets

SMIT, Robert
Simpson Thacher & Bartlett, New York 212 455 2000
Recommended in Arbitration

SMITH, Bradley
Davis Polk & Wardwell, New York 212 450 4000
Recommended in Banking & Finance

SMITH, Chris
Shearman & Sterling, New York 212 848 4000
Recommended in Real Estate

SMITH, Jeffrey
Cravath, Swaine & Moore, New York 212 474 1000
Recommended in Environment

SOBEL, Gerald
Kaye Scholer LLP, New York 212 836 8000
Recommended in Intellectual Property

SOLOMON, Andrew P
Sullivan & Cromwell LLP, New York 212 558 4000
solomona@sullcrom.com
Recommended in Tax
Specialization: Managing Partner of the *S&C* Tax Group. Broad-based practice, involving both tax planning and dispute resolution. Regularly advises on structur-

LEADERS

NEW YORK

ing acquisitions, divestitures (including spin-offs) and joint ventures, including cross-border transactions, and on the taxation of complex financial products. Extensive experience in advising financial institutions (including insurance companies), high-technology businesses and natural resource companies. Broad domestic and international M&A experience, recently advising Koninklijke Philips Electronics in its US acquisitions and joint ventures, and First Union/Wachovia Corporation in its transformation into a diversified financial services company that is now the fifth largest bank holding company and fifth largest full-service retail broker dealer (based on client assets) in the United States. Vast experience with organizing and/or taking public offshore insurers, reinsurers and securitization vehicles, including the organization and IPO of International Property Catastrophe Insurance and Global Capital Reinsurance. Regularly represents American International Group, including in its investment in 20th Century, its acquisition of SunAmerica and in various other investments, acquisitions and dispositions.
Prof. Memberships: American Bar Association; New York State Bar Association (Executive Committee Member, Tax Section).
Career: Joined S&C in 1984. Partner since 1992.
Publications: Writes and speaks frequently on taxation of financial products and institutions and international taxation. Contributing author of 'Taxation of Financial Products,' a Clark Boardman treatise. Board of advisors, 'Journal of Taxation of Financial Institutions'.
Personal: Born 1953. Brown University (AB, magna cum laude, 1975); Harvard Law School (JD, magna cum laude, 1984; Editor, Harvard Law Review).

SOMMER, Dean
Young, Sommer, Ward, Ritzenberg, Wooley, Baker & Moore LLC, Albany
518 438 9907
Recommended in Environment

SOUSSLOFF, Andrew D
Sullivan & Cromwell LLP, New York
212 558 4000
soussloffa@sullcrom.com
Recommended in Capital Markets
Specialization: Capital markets transactions, including initial public offerings, recapitalizations, spin-offs and carve-outs, privatisations and other securities offerings for clients from the US, Mexico, South America, Canada and Europe. Has represented major industrial companies, financial institutions and sovereign governments in capital-raising activities in US and international markets. Major role in the return to the international capital markets by Latin American sovereign issuers, including Brady bond exchange offers. Extensive international M&A and joint venture experience. Significant 2002 transactions included the representations of: Pharmacia in the $3.5 billion spin-off of its remaining interest in Monsanto Company; Goldman Sachs and other underwriters in the IPO and subsequent high yield financing for Asbury Automotive; and J.P. Morgan and Salomon Smith Barney in the $1.4 billion exchange offer and underwritten offering of Global Bonds by the Republic of Peru.
Prof. Memberships: Co-Chairman, Securities Law Committee of the International Bar Association.
Career: Joined *Sullivan & Cromwell* in 1981. Partner since 1986. Co-Managing Partner of General Practice Group, which includes the firm's securities, corporate, M&A, financial institutions, project finance and real estate practice areas.
Personal: Graduate of the University of Pennsylvania (BA, MA, 1975) and University of Pennsylvania Law School (JD, 1979).

SPATT, Robert
Simpson Thacher & Bartlett, New York
212 455 2000
Recommended in Corporate/M&A

SPECTOR, Phillip
Paul, Weiss, Rifkind, Wharton & Garrison, Washington, DC
202 223 7300
pspector@paulweiss.com
Recommended in Communications
Specialization: Managing Partner of Washington, DC office and chair of the firm's Communications and Technology Practice Group. Focus is on telecommunications, with particular emphasis on international communications matters. Served as law clerk to Justice Thurgood Marshall of the US Supreme Court, then joined the White House staff as Associate Assistant to the President. Has been involved in key developments in US and international communications policy and is active in contractual negotiations, financings, international transactions and trade, and advocacy before the Congress, the courts and federal agencies, including the FCC. Speaks regularly and writes often on communications, media, and internet issues.

SPERLING, Allan G
Cleary Gottlieb Steen & Hamilton, New York 212 225 2000
asperling@cgsh.com
Recommended in Capital Markets
Specialization: Securities, financial, and corporate matters. Extensive experience representing underwriters, issuers and investors in public and private debt and equity financings, advising financial institutions on securities law and counseling businesses on corporate legal matters.
Prof. Memberships: Bar in New York. Admitted to practice before US Court of Appeals (Second Circuit), US District Court (Southern and Eastern Districts of New York), Member of New York State Bar Association.
Career: Joined firm in 1968; became partner in 1976. LLB, Law Journal Editor, Order of the Coif, Yale Law School (1967), AB, cum laude, Phi Beta Kappa, Columbia University (1964).

STAFFARONI, Robert J
Debevoise & Plimpton, New York
212 909 6365
rjstaffaroni@debevoise.com
Recommended in Tax
Specialization: Partner at *Debevoise & Plimpton*. His practice concentrates on international transactions, corporate finance and leasing, and financial products.
Prof. Memberships: New York State Bar Association; Tax Forum.
Career: Judicial Clerk, US Court of Appeals, Third Circuit (1976-77). Joined *Debevoise & Plimpton* in 1980 and became a partner in 1985.
Publications: 'Size Matters: Section 367(a) and Acquisitions of US Corporations by Foreign Corporations', 'Tax Lawyer' (Spring 1999) and a number of other articles on international taxation.
Personal: Yale University, BA, 1973; University of Pennsylvania Law School, JD, 1976.

STANDISH, Peter D
Weil, Gotshal & Manges LLP, New York
212 310 8650
peter.standish@weil.com
Recommended in Antitrust
Specialization: A senior partner in *Weil, Gotshal & Manges LLP*'s Trade Practices and Regulatory Law Department. His practice covers all areas of antitrust and trade regulation, including joint ventures, licensing, pricing and distribution and marketing issues and focusing heavily on merger and acquisition work. He enjoys an international reputation as an antitrust lawyer and has successfully obtained clearance for scores of strongly contested acquisitions at the Department of Justice and the Federal Trade Commission, as well as in EU merger and competition proceedings and in state attorney general and private actions. Has provided counsel to boards of directors, management and operating officers in areas ranging from corporate governance to procurement, sales, marketing, acquisitions, joint research and development and licensing matters. Also has broad experience in telecommunications and cable competition issues, as well as a wide variety of consumer industrial financial services and defence sectors. Has also represented a wide range of corporations and executives in defending against federal criminal antitrust grand jury investigations. Has been involved in a number of the major antitrust-sensitive merger investigations over the last several years, including Hughes-Boeing, GM-Fiat, AK Steel-Armco, CMS-Duke (Pan Energy), NYNEX / Bell Atlantic, Hughes / Raytheon, L'Oreal / Maybelline and J.C. Penny - Eckerd. Served as the resident partner in charge of the firm's London office from 1990-92, where his practice included advising European clients on US competition law and US and European clients on European Community law. He works closely with the international offices of the firm and a broad spectrum of foreign legal counsel, particularly in European capitals. He also continues to advise on EU and member-state competition matters.
Personal: New York University School of Law (LLB, 1967); University of Rochester (BA, 1964).

STAPLETON, Benjamin F
Sullivan & Cromwell LLP, New York
212 558 4000
stapletonb@sullcrom.com
Recommended in Corporate/M&A
Specialization: Member of M&A Group since 1978 and Senior Partner of group. Has participated in hundreds of transactions during that period and represented bidders, targets and financial advisors in both friendly and contested situations. Represented BP Amoco p.l.c. in its acquisition of Atlantic Richfield Company (ARCO), Glaxo-Wellcome in its merger with SmithKline Beecham and Vodafone AirTouch in its acquisition of equity interests in Japan Telecom from AT&T and BT. Other recent work includes representation of Vodafone in its acquisitions of AirTouch and Mannesmann, The British Petroleum Company plc in its acquisition of Amoco Corporation and SBC Communications Inc. in its acquisitions of Pacific Telesis Group, SNET and Ameritech.
Prof. Memberships: American Bar Association; Association of the Bar of the City of New York; New York State Bar Association.
Career: Joined *Sullivan & Cromwell* in 1969; partner since 1977.
Personal: Born 1943. Harvard College (AB, 1965); Yale Law School (JD, 1969). Director, The Asphalt Green, Inc., New York, New York; Trustee, Amon Carter Museum of Western Art, Ft. Worth, Texas.

STARER, Brian
Holland & Knight LLP, New York
212 513 3200
bstare@hklaw.com
Recommended in Shipping
Specialization: Partner in the Litigation Department. For 25 years his admiralty practice has focused primarily on marine casualties including groundings, sinkings, fires, collisions and environmental pollution. He continues to act as an advisor to shipowners, several international Protection and Indemnity Clubs and hull underwriters on a worldwide basis. He has investigated and advised on all

aspects of maritime and environmental casualties, including property damage, cargo loss, personal injury and death claims, and natural resource and other environmental damage. He has served as casualty counsel on more than 100 ship disasters worldwide and has had articles about the prevention and resolution of maritime disasters appear in publications such as 'Oil & Gas Journal' and 'The Wall Street Journal'.

STEIN, Joshua
Latham & Watkins LLP, New York
212 906 1342
joshua.stein@lw.com
Recommended in Real Estate
Specialization: Partner, Finance and Real Estate Department. Negotiates real estate financing, leases, purchases, sales, restructurings and other transactions for all commercial property types, including hotels, mixed use and portfolios.
Prof. Memberships: American College of Real Estate Lawyers. New York State Bar Association, Secretary, Real Property Law Section, State Bar of California.
Publications: Frequent lecturer and writer on commercial real estate transactions and legal issues. Author, 'New York Commercial Mortgage Transactions' and 'A Practical Guide to Real Estate Practice'.
Personal: JD, Columbia University, 1981, Managing Editor, 'Columbia Law Review'. AB, University of California, Berkeley, 1977.

STEINBERG, Lewis
Cravath, Swaine & Moore, New York
212 474 1000
Recommended in Tax

STEPHENSON, Alan
Cravath, Swaine & Moore, New York
212 474 1000
Recommended in Corporate/M&A

STERN, Akiba
Shaw Pittman LLP, New York
212 603 6861
akiba.stern@shawpittman.com
Recommended in Communications
Specialization: He is part of *Shaw Pittman* Global Sourcing, the world's leading professional services organization for structuring and implementing outsourcing transactions, strategic alliances, and other complex long term sourcing and services arrangements. Consistent with *Shaw Pittman*'s integrated legal/consulting services approach, he helps his clients architect, negotiate and implement commercial strategies, alliance structures, pricing models, governance arrangements, change management, contract administration, and vendor compliance.
Prof. Memberships: He is admitted to practice in New York and Connecticut.
Career: He has advised clients for more than 20 years in all aspects of business law both as in-house counsel and at law firms. He concentrates his practice on information technology and business process outsourcing; information technology and related business transactions; internet-related matters; electronic commerce; technology transfer; licensing; intellectual property; and joint ventures. In recent years he has completed a significant desktop outsourcing transaction for a major insurance company, a large multinational full-scope outsourcing transaction for a leading pharmaceutical company, a global strategic technology alliance between a multinational bank and one of the leading internet portals, and a license agreement permitting the application of one of the world's best known trademarks to consumer electronics. He regularly represents several institutional end-user clients in their acquisitions of computer-based products and services, and related disputes. He has also represented a variety of computer and internet product and services vendors.
Publications: He has lectured widely and has published a number of articles regarding outsourcing, computer and internet law, and intellectual property.
Personal: Received his BA in 1976 from Yeshiva University, his JD in 1979 and an MBA in 1980 from Boston University.

STEVER, Donald W
Dewey Ballantine LLP, New York
212 259 6520
dstever@deweyballantine.com
Recommended in Environment
Specialization: He is an environmental lawyer with more than 30 years of civil and criminal environmental litigation and counseling experience. His practice includes air, water, waste, CERCLA, noise, impact assessment, natural resource damages, environmental torts and constitutional environmental litigation, primarily for industrial clients. His clients include such companies as Wyeth Corporation, Minerals Technologies Inc., Irving Oil Corporation, EDO Corporation, General Electric Company, Novartis, Inc. and ChevronTexaco.
Prof. Memberships: Environmental Law Institute: Executive Committee, Chairman (1995-96; 1999-2003); Board of Directors (1989-97; 1998-present). Village of Sleepy Hollow, NY: Village Trustee (1997 - present). Friends of the Rockefeller State Park Preserve Inc.: Board of Directors (1998 - present). The Hudson Valley Writers' Center Inc.: Board of Directors (1989 - present).
Publications: Law of Chemical Regulation and Hazardous Waste, multi-volume treatise (West Group, 1986); Seabrook and the Nuclear Regulatory Commission, treatise (University Press of New England, 1980).
Personal: University of Pennsylvania, JD, 1968; Lehigh University, BA, Government, 1965, cum laude.

STOLL, Neal R
Skadden, Arps, Slate, Meagher & Flom LLP & Affiliates, New York
212 735 3660
nstoll@skadden.com
Recommended in Antitrust
Specialization: Partner, New York. Represents clients in connection with investigations conducted by the staff of the Department of Justice, Antitrust Division; Part 2 investigations conducted by the staffs of the Federal Trade Commission's Bureau of Competition and Bureau of Consumer Protection; and Part 3 administrative proceedings and appeals; and Federal trial and appellate experience in cases involving distribution practices, the Robinson-Patman Act and acquisitions. Counsels clients on antitrust issues stemming from mergers and acquisitions. Advises corporate clients on other antitrust and consumer protection matters, including compliance programs and advice regarding the implementation of proposed business plans; as well as consumer product companies in connection with the implementation of marketing and promotional business plans. Lectured for the Practising Law Institute and the NY State and City Bar Associations, and has co-authored a treatise and several articles on antitrust and trade regulation matters.
Personal: JD, Fordham University, 1973 (Member, 'Fordham Law Review'); BA, Pennsylvania State University, 1970.

STRINGFELLOW, James S
Skadden, Arps, Slate, Meagher & Flom LLP & Affiliates, New York
212 735 3405
jstringf@skadden.com
Recommended in Capital Markets
Specialization: Partner, New York. Represents issuers, underwriters, placement agents, lenders, agents, managers, investors and other participants in a variety of public and private structured finance transactions. Experience includes credit card, auto loan and other receivable securitizations; collateralized debt obligation issuances (including cash flow, market value and synthetic type transactions); commercial and residential mortgage loan securitizations; asset-backed commercial paper transactions; and resecuritizations and repackagings of various securities and other assets in combination with credit enhancements and derivative products.
Personal: JD, New York University School of Law, 1987; AB, Columbia College, 1983.

STROMFELD, Lary
Cadwalader, Wickersham & Taft, New York 212 504 6291
lary.stromfeld@cwt.com
Recommended in Capital Markets
Specialization: Capital markets partner with particular expertise in OTC fixed income products, credit derivatives, and municipal finance. Represents numerous commercial banks, bond insurers, derivative product companies, broker-dealers, hedge funds, and other financial institutions. Develops, negotiates and documents financial products, including credit derivatives, total return swaps, currency swaps, and fixed income swaps. Assists clients in the creation of structured derivative products that combine securitization techniques and derivative products. Extensively involved in developing and utilizing financial products in the primary and secondary municipal markets, including tender option programs, swaps, repurchase agreements, and other investment products.
Prof. Memberships: Credit Derivatives and General Documentation Committees of the International Swaps and Derivatives Association, Inc.; National Association of Bond Lawyers.
Personal: BA, Brandeis University, magna cum laude, 1977; JD, University of Pennsylvania Law School, 1981.

SUGARMAN, Robert
Weil, Gotshal & Manges LLP, New York
212 310 8184
robert.sugarman@weil.com
Recommended in Media & Entertainment
Specialization: A nationally recognized specialist in the litigation of intellectual property and First Amendment matters. Has litigated significant cases in the libel, privacy, copyright, trademark, trade dress, unfair competition and false advertising areas, and has served as lead counsel in a major patent infringement litigation. Currently representing the licensor of the technology used to the encrypt copyrighted motion pictures on DVD in a trade secret case and the National Geographic Society in copyright litigations arsing out of the publications on a CD-ROM set of all issues of 'National Geographic Magazine'. He has represented a number of recording artists, record companies and music publishers including Julio Iglesias, Michael Bolton, Sony Music, Arista Record, BMG, PolyGram and Warner Chappell in music copyright litigation. He has also represented CBS in First Amendment and copyright litigation, The Daily News in libel litigation, and American Eagle Outfitters, Franklin Resources, Random House and Paco Rabanne in trademarn and trade dress litigation. In non-litigation matters, he represents a number of companies and individuals including Paco Rabanne and Carolina Herrera in intellectual property matters; and Rev Billy Graham and the Trinity Church in publishing matters.
Prof. Memberships: Fellow of the American College of Trial Lawyers, founded and chaired the annual Practising Law Institute Seminar of Litigating Copyright, Trademark and Unfair Competition

Cases from 1982-94 and chaired the Communications and Media Law Committee of the Association of the Bar of the City of New York between 1990 and 1992.
Publications: Co-author of the New York chapter of the annual 'Fifty State Survey', published by the Libel Defense Resource Center. He authored the chapter on intellectual property in 'Masters of Trial Practice', published by Wiley Law Publishers, and has written numerous articles on various subjects dealing with litigation of intellectual property matters.
Personal: Yale University Law School (LLB, 1963); Yale University (BA, 1960).

SULLIVAN, Robert J
Skadden, Arps, Slate, Meagher & Flom LLP & Affiliates, New York
212 735 2930
rsulliva@skadden.com
Recommended in Insurance

Specialization: Has more than 20 years of experience representing insurance and reinsurance companies, and extensive experience with corporate transactions, insurance regulatory matters, reinsurance and complex coverage and major claims litigation.
Career: Managing Director and General Counsel (1992-93), Senior Vice President and General Counsel (1987- 93), Senior Vice President - Government Affairs (1985-87), Vice President - Government Affairs (1977-85), Crum and Forster, Inc.; Assistant Counsel, Swiss Re Holding (North America) Inc. (1976-77); Assistant Counsel, American Insurance Association (1974-76).
Personal: JD, New York Law School, 1974 (Research Editor, 'New York Law Review'); BA, Fordham University, 1971.

SWEENEY, John
Morgan & Finnegan, New York
212 415 8525
JFSweeney@morganfinnegan.com
Recommended in Intellectual Property

Specialization: Trials and appeals, alternative dispute resolution, interference practice, patent, licensing, antitrust, trademark and trade dress in the consumer product, medical device, pharmaceutical and computer technology industries.
Prof. Memberships: The American Bar Association, New York County Lawyers Association, Association of the Bar of the City of New York, American Intellectual Property Law Association and The New York Intellectual Property Law Association, President of The New York Intellectual Property Law Association in 2000.
Career: He has been involved in patent, trade secret and trademark litigation since 1973. His litigation experience includes patent, antitrust, trademark and trade dress bench and jury trials and appeals. He has acted as lead trial counsel for The Procter & Gamble Company, Boehringer Ingelheim Corporation, Bombardier, Inc. ISCO (Illinois Superconductor Corporation), C.R. Bard, Inc., Dot Hill Systems Corporation, Finisar Corporation, Tile Council of America and Arthur D. Little, Inc. in numerous cases. He acted as co-counsel for Digital Equipment Corporation in the Digital/Intel litigation involving microprocessor technology. He has had extensive jury trial practice and has argued many times in the United States Court of Appeals for the Federal Circuit. Before entering legal practice, he worked as a mathematician and computer analyst for the US Army Strategy and Tactics Analysis Group. His work involved mathematical modeling, including war games.
Publications: He is author of: Chapter 10, Injunctions in 'Patent Litigation', edited by Laurence H. Pretty, published 2001 by The Practising Law Institute. John F Sweeney, 'What Is the Zurko Case And What Does It Mean?,' American Conference Institute Seminar on 'Tactical Considerations And Strategies For Success In Litigating Patent Disputes,' March 9-10, 2000, Washington, DC. John F Sweeney, Trying A Patent Case To a Jury And the Federal Circuit At the Same Time, 'The IP Litigator', 2000. John F Sweeney and James F Bush, 'The Doctrines of Equivalents And Prosecution History Estoppel: What Has Warner-Jenkinson Changed?,' The Practising Law Institute, 1999. John F Sweeney and Charles H Sanders, 'The On-Sale Bar To Patentability: Understanding The Doctrine's Past, Present, And Future', The Practising Law Institute, 1998. John F Sweeney and Brenda Pomerance, Significant Developments In Patent Litigation In 1995, 'The IP Litigator', March 28, 1996. John F Sweeney and Elaine J Kaman, 'Inequitable Conduct Developments,' The Practising Law Institute, 1995. John F Sweeney, Midge M Hyman, Scott D Greenberg and Margaret A Bitler, 'Using U.S. Courts And International Treaties To Protect Against Infringement Abroad And At Home,' The Practising Law Institute, 1994. John F Sweeney and Kim D Connolly, 'The Rocky Road To Harmonization: Complications Raised by The Impending United States Transition To A First-To-File Patent System,' 1993. John F Sweeney, Scott D Greenberg and Margaret A Bitler, Heading Them Off At The Pass – Can Counterfeit Goods Of Foreign Origin Be Stopped At The Counterfeiter's Border? 'The Trademark Reporter', 1993. John F Sweeney and Alexandra T Manbeck, Antitrust Law: The Year In Review, '1993 NYIPLA Intellectual Property Annual', 1993.

TABAK, Jeffrey E
Weil, Gotshal & Manges LLP, New York
212 310 8343
jeffrey.tabak@weil.com
Recommended in Private Equity

Specialization: Has a wide-ranging corporate and securities law practice with particular emphasis on private investment entities such as hedge and private equity funds. He is co-head of the firm's Private Equity and Investment Management Practice Group. Has written and spoken on a variety of topics relating to private investment funds. Was actively involved with the firm's representation of Odyssey Partners, LP, a New York-based investment partnership, for more than 10 years in a variety of matters. Represents a variety of sponsors in forming private investment funds as well as institutions investing in such funds. He has also represented other financial services businesses such as Oppenheimer Group, including in the public offerings in 1987 and 1991 of its money management affiliate, Oppenheimer Capital, and its sale of its business in 1997; Oppenheimer Funds, including in its 2001 acquisition of Tremont Advisers; Franklin Resources, including in its 1992 acquisition of Templeton, Galbraith & Hansberger, its 1996 acquisition of Heine Securities Bank, including in its 1995 acquisition of John Govett & Co. Also concentrates and advises clients on the formation and representation of basic business structures, particularly limited and general partnerships and limited liability companies.
Prof. Memberships: American Bar Association; ABA Federal Securities Subcommittee on Private Investment Entities; New York State Bar Association.
Career: Joined firm in 1982. Trustee, Museum of Jewish Heritage. Trustee, HIPPY U.S.A.
Personal: BA, Duke University, 1979; JD, Duke University, 1982. Member, Phi Beta Kappa.

TANENBAUM, William
Kaye Scholer LLP, New York
212 836 8000
Recommended in Communications

TAYLOR, Willard B
Sullivan & Cromwell LLP, New York
212 558 4000
TaylorW@sullcrom.com
Recommended in Tax

Specialization: Specializes in United States tax matters, both federal and state, including advice with respect to the taxation of foreign operations of US corporations, US operations of foreign corporations, mergers and acquisitions and international transactions of all kinds. Has represented domestic and foreign corporations before the Internal Revenue Service and in tax litigation and has worked with the Treasury Department and Congressional staffs on tax legislation.
Prof. Memberships: American Bar Association; American Law Institute (Member, Tax Advisory Group, Federal Income Tax Project); American Society of International Law; Association of the Bar of the City of New York; International Bar Association; International Fiscal Association (Member, US Council); New York State Bar Association (former Chairman, Tax Section).
Career: Joined *Sullivan & Cromwell* in 1965. Partner since 1973.
Publications: Member, Adjunct Faculty of New York University Law School; Member, Tax Advisory Committee, Practicing Law Institute; former Chairman of the Advisory Board, New York University Institute on Federal Taxation. Has lectured and written extensively on US tax matters.
Personal: Born in 1940. Yale Law School (LLB, 1965); Yale University (BA, 1962).

TEHAN, John
Simpson Thacher & Bartlett, New York
212 455 2000
Recommended in Capital Markets

TENEV, Jovi
Holland & Knight LLP, New York
212 513 3200
jtenev@hklaw.com
Recommended in Shipping

Specialization: Partner in the Business Law Department. He has extensive experience representing financial institutions, investment banks, foreign and domestic companies, and airlines in a wide variety of transactions. He practices in all areas of corporate finance, including finance projects in the US and international aerospace, shipping, offshore drilling and rail industries, utilizing complex syndicated loan, leveraged and single-investor leasing structures, and capital markets. He has been involved in domestic and foreign mergers and acquisitions, portfolio purchases, workouts, bankruptcies, restructurings, enforcement and foreclosures, and in US regulatory proceedings. He also served as a trial attorney for the United States Department of Justice, Criminal Division, where he received the Attorney General's Special Commendation for Outstanding Service.

THURSTON, Sally A
Skadden, Arps, Slate, Meagher & Flom LLP & Affiliates, New York
212 735 4140
sthursto@skadden.com
Recommended in Tax

Specialization: Partner, New York. Advises US and international clients on a wide range of tax matters, including tax aspects of mergers and acquisitions, joint ventures, restructurings, divestitures and spin-offs. Advises multinational clients regarding the US tax aspects of cross-border merger and acquisition transactions and tax minimization structures. The former includes utilization of dual-listed company and exchangeable share structures. In US, regularly advises clients on taxable and tax-free acquisitions and divestitures and has significant experience in the partnership taxation area.
Personal: JD, Harvard Law School, 1986 (cum laude); BS, Chemical Engineering, Cornell University, 1983 (with distinction).

NEW YORK   LEADERS

TODER, Richard
Morgan, Lewis & Bockius LLP, New York
212 309 6000
Recommended in Insolvency

TODRYS, Steven
Simpson Thacher & Bartlett, New York
212 455 2000
Recommended in Tax

TORCHIANA, William D
Sullivan & Cromwell LLP, New York
212 558 4000
torchianaw@sullcrom.com
Recommended in Insurance
Specialization: Specializes in finance, acquisition, corporate and regulatory assignments involving insurance and reinsurance companies. Practice has included privatizations, US listings and US and global securities offerings by major non-US insurers and multiline financial institutions in Europe, Asia and Latin America; IPO, demutualization and mutual company financing transactions for US insurers; acquisition, divestiture and other US and cross-border change-in-control transactions, and related regulatory approvals; advice on corporate governance and SEC disclosure matters; Blue Cross/Blue Shield conversion and merger transactions; insurance risk securitization and derivatives; and general insurance regulatory matters.
Prof. Memberships: American Bar Association; Association of the Bar of the City of New York; International Bar Association. Member of New York and Paris bars.
Career: Joined *Sullivan & Cromwell* in 1986; resident in Paris office 1988-92. Partner since 1995.
Personal: Born in 1958. University of Pennsylvania Law School (JD, 1986); Stanford University (AB, 1981).

TORTORIELLO, Robert
Cleary Gottlieb Steen & Hamilton, New York 212 225 2000
rtortoriello@cgsh.com
Recommended in Banking & Finance
Specialization: Bank capital markets and regulatory, securities and compliance matters, financial institution mergers, acquisitions, joint ventures and restructurings, derivative products, and securities offerings. Regulatory counseling concerning the Gramm-Leach-Bliley Act, the Bank Holding Company Act, the Glass-Steagall Act and the International Banking Act.
Career: Joined the firm in 1974, became partner in 1982. JD, magna cum laude, Harvard Law School (1974), BA, summa cum laude, from St. Peters College, New Jersey (1971).
Publications: 'Guide to Bank Underwriting, Dealing and Brokerage Activities' (Glasser LegalWorks, 6th edition, 2002). 'Financial Modernization in the United States: the Gramm-Leach-Bliley Act' ('Journal of International Financial Markets', 2000).

TOWNSEND, Robert
Cravath, Swaine & Moore, New York
212 474 1000
Recommended in Corporate/M&A

TREPPER, Myron
Willkie Farr & Gallagher, New York
212 728 8276
mtrepper@willkie.com
Recommended in Insolvency
Specialization: Firm co-chairman and partner and chair of the Business Reorganisation and Restructuring Department. Has extensive experience in all areas of debtor and creditor representation, as well as in the transactional aspects of corporate reorganisations and insolvency related matters. Has practised continuously in this area for more than 30 years and has been counsel to Petrie Retail; Heilig Meyers Company; Livent, Inc; Paragon Trade Brands, Inc; Alliance Entertainment Corp; Harvard Industries, Inc; Woodward & Lothrop Holdings, Inc; The Grand Union Company; Integrated Resources, Inc; E-II Holdings, Inc; Prime Motor Inns; Orion Pictures and Maxwell Communications, among others. Currently representing Adelphia Communications, Inc.
Prof. Memberships: Association of the Bar of the City of New York and the American Bankruptcy Institute.
Career: Admitted in 1969, has been with *Willkie Farr & Gallagher* since 1989. Is a fellow of the American College of Bankruptcy and lectures on bankruptcy related matters for seminars and panels sponsored by the ALI-ABA, the American Bankruptcy Institute, New York University School of Law, University of Pennsylvania Institute for Law and Economics, and other professional organisations.
Personal: Received a JD from Brooklyn Law School in 1968 and a BA from Hunter College in 1965.

TRIER, Dana
Davis Polk & Wardwell, New York
212 450 4000
Recommended in Tax

TRINGALI, Joseph
Simpson Thacher & Bartlett, New York
212 455 2000
Recommended in Antitrust

URDA KASSIS, Cynthia
Shearman & Sterling, New York
212 848 4000
Recommended in Projects

URIS, Harvey R
Skadden, Arps, Slate, Meagher & Flom LLP & Affiliates, New York
212 735 2212
huris@skadden.com
Recommended in Real Estate
Specialization: Specializes in capital markets-related real estate transactions; commercial mortgage-backed loan origination and securitization transactions, private equity funds and private placements. On behalf of numerous investment banking clients over the past year has originated over $5 billion fixed and floating rate secured whole loans and handled the related pooled mortgage loan securitizations, credit enhanced notes, offerings, non-performing loan acquisition financings, and sale-leaseback transactions in the US, Europe and Asia.
Prof. Memberships: Bar Association City of New York.
Personal: Boston University, JD, cum laude 1979, BA, cum laude, 1976. Skiing; running; tennis. Married, three children.

VARDELL, James
Cravath, Swaine & Moore, New York
212 474 1000
Recommended in Banking & Finance

VICTOR, A Paul
Weil, Gotshal & Manges LLP, New York
212 310 8110
paul.victor@weil.com
Recommended in Antitrust
Specialization: An internationally known expert in antitrust and international trade law. After spending almost three years with the Justice Department's Antitrust Division in Washington, DC, he has spent the past 37 years representing foreign and domestic clients in some of the biggest antitrust and international trade cases ever brought. On the antitrust side, he has recently been heavily involved in criminal and related civil international cartel matters, representing major corporations with respect to such products as lysine, nucleotides, carbon fiber, vitamins, and graphite electrodes, as well as with respect to auction house bidding practices. These matters were generated by US criminal proceedings and also involve related federal and state class actions as well as proceedings in other jurisdictions, such as the EU and Canada. He was also deeply involved on behalf of Matsushita Electric in the famous Matsushita case, decided favorably for his client by the Supreme Court, as well as in the Go-Video v Matsushita antitrust litigation, which was successfully tried to a verdict. On the international trade law side, he has represented various Japanese, French, German, Chinese, Singaporean, Korean and American corporations in antidumping and countervailing duty subsidy cases involving such products as steel, televisions, cellular mobile telephones, paging devices, color picture tubes, compressors, semiconductors, electrolytic manganese dioxide, polyester film, and coated groundwood paper. He has also represented clients before the International Trade Commission in five-year "sunset" reviews.
Prof. Memberships: Currently on the ABA Antitrust Section's International Advisory Board and has, in the past, been Vice-Chair of the Section, twice a member of the Section's Council, a member of the Section's Special Committee on International Antitrust, and twice Chair of its International Antitrust Committee. He is also an Adjunct Professor of Law at Fordham University Law School, Chairman of the Board of Trustees of The Massachusetts School of Law at Andover, a member of the Advisory Board of the Center for American and International Law, an active member of the Commission on Competition Law and of the International Chamber of Commerce (ICC), and former Secretary of the Japan Society in New York.
Career: Has written and lectured widely on various antitrust and international trade law subjects.
Personal: University of Michigan Law School (JD, with honors, 1963); University of Michigan (BBA, 1960).

VINE, Stephen
Akin, Gump, Strauss, Hauer & Feld, LLP, New York 212 872 1000
Recommended in Private Equity

VIZCARRONDO, JR, Paul
Wachtell, Lipton, Rosen & Katz, New York 212 403 1208
pvizcarrondo@wlrk.com
Recommended in Litigation
Specialization: Specializes in corporate and securities litigation and regulatory and white collar criminal matters.
Prof. Memberships: Served on several committees of the Association of the Bar of the City of New York, including the Criminal Law Committee and the Federal Courts Committee, has been a Master of the Federal Bar Council's Inn of Court and is a member of the Columbia Law School Board of Visitors.
Career: Partner at *Wachtell, Lipton, Rosen & Katz* since 1981. Has tried significant cases in courts throughout the United States. Worked as Law Clerk to the Honorable Edward Weinfeld, United States District Judge for the Southern District of New York (1973-74) and as an Assistant United States Attorney in the Southern District of New York (1974-78). Awarded the Department of Justice's Special Achievement Award for his work in the Securities and Commodities Fraud Unit of the United States Attorney's Office. Has taught Trial Practice as an Adjunct Assistant Professor of Law at New York University School of Law and as a faculty member at the National Institute for Trial Advocacy; has lectured on United States federal securities laws for the Practicing Law Institute; and has lectured on litigation issues as a member of numerous continuing legal education panels.
Publications: Wrote the chapter on 'RICO' in Obermaier & Morvillo's 'White Collar Crime; Business and Regulatory Offenses'.
Personal: Graduated from Cornell University in 1970 (BS) and from Columbia University School of Law in 1973 (JD),

where he was a Harlan Fiske Stone Scholar and Articles and Book Reviews Editor of 'Columbia Law Review'.

VLADECK, Anne
Vladeck, Waldman, Elias & Engelhard, P.C., New York 212 403 7300
Recommended in Employment

VLADECK, Judith
Vladeck, Waldman, Elias & Engelhard, P.C., New York 212 403 7300
Recommended in Employment

VLAHAKIS, Patricia A
Wachtell, Lipton, Rosen & Katz, New York 212 403 1206
pavlahakis@wlrk.com
Recommended in Corporate/M&A

Specialization: Specializes in corporate and securities law, concentrating on transactional matters, mergers and acquisitions, hostile takeovers, cross-border transactions and private equity investments, as well as corporate governance. Represented Hellman & Friedman and Warburg Pincus in their investment in Arch Capital, Computer Associates in its proxy fight with Ranger Governance, Fort James in its merger with Georgia-Pacific, Young & Rubicam in its merger with WPP Group, Polygram in its acquisition by Seagrams and Motorola in a number of acquisitions and investments.
Prof. Memberships: Member of the American Bar Association; served for five years as co-chair of the Practicing Law Institute's Annual Institute on Securities Regulation; is a member of the Advisory Board for the Annual Securities Regulation Institute; is a member of the Board of Directors of Phoenix House Foundation, Inc, a not for profit organization for the treatment and prevention of drug addiction.
Career: Partner at *Wachtell, Lipton, Rosen & Katz*.
Publications: Lectured extensively and published numerous articles in the areas of mergers and acquisitions and securities law.
Personal: Graduated summa cum laude from Bryn Mawr College in 1978 (BA) and from Columbia University School of Law in 1981 (JD).

VOGE, William
Latham & Watkins LLP, New York
212 906 1352
bill.voge@lw.com
Recommended in Projects

Specialization: Partner in the New York office. Extensive experience in project development and project financings. Acts for project sponsors, banks, underwriters and other parties on electricity, oil and gas and communication projects in the US and abroad. Activities include structuring complex project financings involving multiple groups and types of lenders.
Prof. Memberships: New York and American Bar Associations.
Publications: Written about political risks, environmental concerns, export credit agencies, disclosure issues, common financing conditions in international projects, and the use of capital markets to finance international projects.
Personal: JD, University of California, Berkeley, 1983. MBA, University of California, Berkeley, 1983.

VYSKOCIL, Mary
Simpson Thacher & Bartlett, New York
212 455 2000
Recommended in Insurance

WACHSBERGER, Chaim
Chadbourne & Parke LLP, New York
212 408 5100
cwachsberger@chadbourne.com
Recommended in Projects

Specialization: Heads *Chadbourne*'s project finance practice. International projects include representing developers of and lenders to power projects, natural gas pipelines and other infrastructure projects. Representation involves complex financing structures, multilateral or export credit agency involvement, and political risk insurance products. Domestic work includes acquisitions, portfolio financings, and project financing and development of greenfield projects. Works with developers on the provision of equity, senior and subordinated debt and negotiation of construction contracts, fuel supply agreements, steam sales and other project-related agreements.
Prof. Memberships: New York State Bar Association; American Bar Association (Section on Corporation, Banking and Business Law).

WACHTELL, Herbert M
Wachtell, Lipton, Rosen & Katz, New York 212 403 1216
hmwachtell@wlrk.com
Recommended in Litigation

Specialization: Specializes in major, complex case litigation.
Prof. Memberships: Member, American Bar Association, Association of the Bar of the City of New York, New York County Lawyers.
Career: Partner at *Wachtell, Lipton, Rosen & Katz* and predecessor, 1958 to date; Assistant US Attorney, Southern District of New York, 1955-57.
Publications: Author: 'New York Practice under the CPLR', First Edition, 1963, Second Edition, 1966, Third Edition, 1970, Fourth Edition, 1973, Fifth Edition, 1976, Sixth Edition, 1986; Practicing Law Institute.
Personal: Graduated from New York University in 1952 (BS), from New York University in 1954 (LLB) where he was Decisions Editor, 'New York University Law Review', Order of the Coif and Root-Tilden Scholar, and from Harvard University in 1955 (LLM).

WAKS, Jay
Kaye Scholer LLP, New York
212 836 8000
Recommended in Employment

WALKER, John
Simpson Thacher & Bartlett, New York
212 455 2000
Recommended in Banking & Finance

WARDEN, John L
Sullivan & Cromwell LLP, New York
212 558 4000
wardenj@sullcrom.com
Recommended in Antitrust

Specialization: General commercial litigation practice covering antitrust, banking, contract, corporate governance and securities areas. Has represented Amax, Bank of New York, British Airways, British Petroleum, Eastman Kodak, First Boston, Goldman Sachs, Gulf Oil, Kennecott, TW Services and Union Carbide in major litigation. Major cases include Berkey Photo v Eastman Kodak, the Union Carbide/GAF takeover litigation and the Bank of New York/Irving Trust takeover litigation. Represented Amax in US v Amax, et al., a criminal antitrust case, and clients in antitrust grand jury investigations. Extensive appellate experience, including constitutional cases and the successful appeal in US v D'Amato; has acted for The New York Clearing House as amicus curiae in numerous cases in courts of appeals and the Supreme Court. Represented Goldman Sachs in antitrust litigation and investigations regarding NASDAQ, and British Airways in the antitrust case brought by Virgin Atlantic. Presently acting for Microsoft in the government antitrust case.
Prof. Memberships: American College of Trial Lawyers; American Law Institute.
Career: Joined *S&C* in 1965. Partner since 1973.
Personal: Born 1941. Harvard College (AB, 1962); University of Virginia Law School (LLB, 1965; Editor in Chief, 'Virginia Law Review'). Honorary Trustee and former President, University of Virginia Law School Foundation; Trustee, American Ballet Theatre.

WARNER, Waide
Davis Polk & Wardwell, New York
212 450 4000
Recommended in Projects

WASSERMAN, Craig M
Wachtell, Lipton, Rosen & Katz, New York 212 403 1232
cmwasserman@wlrk.com
Recommended in Corporate/M&A

Specialization: Specializes in mergers and acquisitions, banking and securities law matters.
Prof. Memberships: Member of the New York State Bar and various bar associations.
Career: Partner at *Wachtell, Lipton, Rosen & Katz*. Law Clerk to Chief Judge Wilfred Feinberg, United States Court of Appeals, Second Circuit.
Publications: Frequent speaker and author on corporate, banking, mergers and acquisitions and securities law topics.
Personal: Graduated summa cum laude from Yale University in 1982 (BA/MA, economics) and from Yale Law School in 1986 (JD) where Phi Beta Kappa and Editor, 'Yale Law Journal', Editor and Senior Articles Editor, 1985-86, 'Yale Journal in Regulation'.

WEBSTER, Robert
Pillsbury Winthrop LLP, New York
212 858 1303
rwebster@pillsburywinthrop.com
Recommended in Banking & Finance

Specialization: He represents financial institutions with particular emphasis on the effect of governmental regulation on both the ordinary conduct of their business and their acquisition and new product development activities. He also advises clients on such diverse governmental actions as capital adequacy directives, restrictions on geographic and functional expansion, anti money laundering initiatives and sanctions in response to international crises, and represents clients subject to supervisory examinations and compliance proceedings. His assignments have included: representation of a US bank resisting a hostile takeover by another US bank, US banks and financial holding companies with respect to the acquisition or disposition of interests in banking and non-banking companies in the US and abroad, European and Asian financial institutions with respect to acquisitions, loans and investments in the US, the US branches and subsidiaries of banks headquartered in Europe, Asia and Latin America with respect to regulatory and compliance matters and Central Banks with respect to matters unique to those institutions.
Career: Admitted to practice: State of New York.
Personal: LLB, Harvard Law School, 1962 (cum laude); AB, Colgate University, 1959 (magna cum laude; Phi Beta Kappa).

WEERASINGHE, Rohan
Shearman & Sterling, New York
212 848 4000
Recommended in Capital Markets

WEINBERGER, Michael
Cleary Gottlieb Steen & Hamilton, New York 212 225 2000
mweinberger@cgsh.com
Recommended in Real Estate

Specialization: Real estate law and commercial mortgage securitizations. Recent transactions include the first fully-rated commercial mortgage securitization in Japan, the origination and securitization of the $1.2 billion financing of Rockefeller Center, and the origination and securitization of a $1.44 billion mortgage

loan to TrizecHahn Office Properties.
Career: Joined firm in 1992, became partner in 2000. JD degree, magna cum laude, Harvard Law School (1991). Law clerk to the Honorable Leonard Garth, U.S. Court of Appeals for the Third Circuit.
Publications: Various articles, including in The Bankruptcy Strategist and Norton Bankruptcy Law Advisor.
Personal: Resides in Brooklyn, New York with his wife and four children.

WEINER, Michael L
Skadden, Arps, Slate, Meagher & Flom LLP & Affiliates, New York
212 735 2632
mweiner@skadden.com
Recommended in Antitrust

Specialization: Partner, New York. Represents clients in antitrust matters arising from merger and acquisition transactions as well as class action and other complex litigations. Has represented a number of major corporations in connection with antitrust investigations of merger, acquisition and joint venture transactions, both consensual and contested. Also represents a number of major corporations with regard to civil and/or criminal antitrust litigation matters. Frequent author and lecturer on variety of antitrust topics.
Personal: JD, Georgetown University Law Center, 1980 (magna cum laude; Editor, 'Georgetown Law Journal'); BA, University of Pennsylvania, 1976 (cum laude).

WEISBURG, Henry
Shearman & Sterling, New York
212 848 4000
Recommended in Arbitration

WEISFELNER, Edward
Brown Rudnick Berlack Israels, New York 212 704 0100
Recommended in Insolvency

WEISS, Gregory
Simpson Thacher & Bartlett, New York
212 455 2000
Recommended in Banking & Finance

WEISS, Jack
Gibson, Dunn & Crutcher LLP, New York
212 351 4000
Recommended in Media & Entertainment

WEST, M Holland
Shearman & Sterling, New York
212 848 4000
Recommended in Capital Markets

WHALEN, Thomas
Carter Ledyard & Milburn LLP, New York 212 732 3200
Recommended in Shipping

WHITE, John
Cravath, Swaine & Moore, New York
212 474 1000
Recommended in Capital Markets

WHITE, W Christopher
Cadwalader, Wickersham & Taft, New York 212 504 6633
christopher.white@cwt.com
Recommended in Real Estate

Specialization: Partner and Chairman of *Cadwalader*'s Real Estate Department. Specializes in commercial real estate with emphasis on debt and equity financing. Represents many of the largest US and foreign institutional investors in the full spectrum of their real estate investment activity. Spearheads *Cadwalader*'s representation of investment banks and institutional lenders in public and private securitizations and other secondary market transactions. Structured acquisition and financing for commercial properties in Europe and Latin America. Represented institutional investors in joint ventures and other investment vehicles for the acquisition and development of hotels, office buildings, shopping centers and internet datacenters. Experienced with hotel and property management agreements and leasing agreements. Structured acquisitions of interests in companies owning and operating hotels, shopping centers, entertainment complexes and office buildings. Experienced in the workout of troubled assets, including restructurings, foreclosures and bankruptcies. Devised procedures for foreclosure by power of sale in New York.
Personal: Graduated from the University of Michigan Law School. Became a partner at *Cadwalader* in 1987.

WHITE III, Fred B
Skadden, Arps, Slate, Meagher & Flom LLP & Affiliates, New York
212 735 2144
fwhite@skadden.com
Recommended in Corporate/M&A

Specialization: Partner, New York. Co-Head, *Skadden*'s financial institutions M&A practice. Represents bank holding companies, commercial banks, acquirers, investors, savings and loan associations, savings banks, consumer finance companies, mortgage banking companies and related services entities. Advises numerous investment banking firms concerning regulatory issues, mergers and acquisitions and public offerings. Represents various institutions before federal banking agencies and consults with major corporations concerning investments in financial institutions and new products in the financial services industry.
Prof. Memberships: Admitted in New York, Delaware, DC, Massachusetts and New Jersey.
Personal: JD, The George Washington University National Law Center, 1972 (with Honours); BA, Wheaton College, 1969.

WIEMAN, Lawrence
Davis Polk & Wardwell, New York
212 450 4000
Recommended in Banking & Finance

WIGHT, Richard
Milbank, Tweed, Hadley & McCloy, New York 212 530 5000
Recommended in Banking & Finance

WILLIAMS JR, William J
Sullivan & Cromwell LLP, New York
212 558 4000
williamsw@sullcrom.com
Recommended in Capital Markets

Specialization: Widely recognized as one of the preeminent securities lawyers in the United States. Played a major role in the development of SEC Regulation S, Rule 144A, Rule 15a-6 (activities of non-US broker-dealers in the US) and Regulation M (trading rules). Enjoys a close working relationship with the most senior staff members of the SEC. Was a member of NASD's Legal Advisory Board and NYSE's Legal Advisory Committee. Chairs the Task Force on Review of Federal Securities Laws of the ABA's Federal Regulation of Securities Committee and is leading a project to modernize federal regulation of public offerings and private placements.
Prof. Memberships: American Bar Association; American Law Institute; American Society of International Law; Association of the Bar of the City of New York; New York State Bar Association.
Career: Joined *S&C* in 1962; partner since 1969.
Personal: Born 1937. College of Holy Cross (AB, 1958); New York University Law School (LLB, 1961; Editor in Chief, 'New York University Law Review'). Trustee, New York University Law School Foundation; Trustee, Sofia American Schools, Inc.; Member, Advisory Committee of Past Presidents, United States Golf Association.

WIPPERMAN, Robert
McKee Nelson LLP, New York
917 777 4600
rwipperman@mckeenelson.com
Recommended in Capital Markets

Specialization: Since 1986 has concentrated exclusively in structured finance transactions. Regularly represents originators, servicers, issuers, purchasers, and underwriters in public offerings and private placements of mortgaged-backed and asset-backed securities, as well as originators in both on-balance-sheet and off-balance-sheet warehouse arrangements. Established and maintained securitization programs for several issuers.
Career: Prior to joining *McKee Nelson*, was a partner in the New York Office of *Stroock & Stroock & Lavan*. At *McKee Nelson*, heads the firm's structured finance group. Received a JD from Boston College Law School in 1979.

WOJCIECHOWSKI, Mark S
Mayer, Brown, Rowe & Maw, New York
212 506 2525
mwojciechowski@mayerbrown.com
Recommended in Banking & Finance

Specialization: Firm Practice Leader in Finance. Corporate, corporate finance, and private equity. Has extensive experience not only in banking and finance but also mergers and acquisitions, joint ventures (domestic and international), and private equity investment.
Prof. Memberships: Admitted to practice in New York (1982). Member of International Law Advisory Committee of the Practising Law Institute; American Bar Association, Section on Corporation, Banking, and Business Law; the New York State Bar Association, Section of International Law and Practice; and the Association of the Bar of the City of New York. Appointments: Chairman, Corporation Law Committee, Association of the Bar of the City of New York.
Career: Joined *Mayer, Brown, Rowe & Maw*, 1986; became partner, 1988. Member, *Mayer, Brown, Rowe & Maw* Executive Committee (Policy and Planning Committee).
Publications: Co-Author, 'How to Buy a US Business: A Guide to Negotiated and Hostile Acquisitions' (1999).
Personal: Born 4 May 1954. JD (cum laude), Indiana University (Bloomington), 1981; AB, Columbia College, 1976.

WOLF, Barry M
Weil, Gotshal & Manges LLP, New York 212 310 8209
barry.wolf@weil.com
Recommended in Private Equity

Specialization: Is a member of the 13-member Management Committee and Co-Head of the Private Equity and Investment Management Practice Group of *Weil, Gotshal & Manges LLP*. He regularly represents a number of private investment funds and their sponsors in their organization and operation. He has extensive experience representing institutional investors in investing in private equity funds, providing both commercial advice as well as tax advice. His background as a tax partner provides him with a unique combination of skills in advising sponsors and investors in connection with fund formation.
Prof. Memberships: A member of the Private Equity Fund Forum, the American Bar Association Tax Section and New York State Bar Association Tax Section.
Personal: BA from the State University of New York at Albany, summa cum laude; received his JD from the University of Michigan Law School, cum laude, and an LLM (tax) from the New York University School of Law.

NEW YORK

WOLFE, Gary
Seward & Kissel, New York
212 574 1223
wolfe@sewkis.com
Recommended in Shipping
Specialization: Securities, capital markets, corporate finance, shipping and environmental, cross-boarder transactions and maritime lease finance
Prof. Memberships: Association of the Bar of the City of New York (Admiralty Committee); New York County Lawyers Association (former Chairman, Maritime Law Committee); US Business Council for Slovenia (former President).
Career: Partner, *Seward & Kissel LLP*, since 1992; associate then partner, *Hill, Betts & Nash*, 1980-91; associate, *Cahill Gordon & Reindel*, 1977-80; Fulbright Dissertation Fellowship, Ljubljana, Slovenia, Belgrade, Yugoslavia (1975-76).
Personal: Yale Law School (JD 1975); Cornell University (Six-Year PhD Program, AB 1971); AIESEC Exchange, Maribor, Slovenia, Zagreb, Croatia (1971).

WOLITZER, Michael
Simpson Thacher & Bartlett, New York
212 455 2000
Recommended in Private Equity

WOLLMAN, Diana L
Sullivan & Cromwell LLP, New York
212 558 4000
wollmand@sullcrom.com
Recommended in Tax
Specialization: Specializes in United States federal tax matters, including a broad spectrum of planning and transactional matters for domestic and foreign corporations, partnerships and investment companies. Has represented clients in tax litigation, as a lobbyist and before the Internal Revenue Service in controversies and requests for private rulings.
Prof. Memberships: New York State Bar Association (Co-Chair, Committee on Reorganizations, Tax Section).
Career: Joined *Sullivan & Cromwell* in 1993. Partner since 2000.
Publications: Speaker at meetings of the Tax Section, New York State Bar Association; Tax Section, American Bar Association; the University of Southern California Annual Major Tax Planning Institute; and the New York University Tax Planning Institute. Has published numerous articles on a variety of topics.
Personal: Born in 1964. University of California Los Angeles Law School (JD, 1991); Harvard University (AB, 1986).

YOUNGWOOD, Alfred D
Paul, Weiss, Rifkind, Wharton & Garrison LLP, New York 212 373 3080
ayoungwood@paulweiss.com
Recommended in Tax
Specialization: Chair of the firm and of Management Committee. Tax partner who concentrates on acquisitions, reorganisations and financings involving both American and foreign business organisations through use of corporate and partnership structures. Has substantial experience in equipment leasing and tax controversy work. Represented clients in: creation of major joint ventures in media and cable television for significant multimedia company; the spin-off of cable television business of one of the world's largest entertainment companies, as well as the sale of its publishing entity; and the multi-billion dollar acquisition of the equipment leasing business of a large corporation by a financial institution.

ZETLIN, Michael
Zetlin & De Chiara, New York
212 682 6800
Recommended in Construction

ZIRINSKY, Bruce
Cadwalader, Wickersham & Taft, New York 212 504 6404
bruce.zirinsky@cwt.com
Recommended in Insolvency
Specialization: Partner and Chairman of the firm's Financial Restructuring Department. For almost 30 years, has counseled debtors, secured and unsecured lenders, creditor committees, public bondholders, shareholders, and investors involved in many of the largest and most complex US and international reorganizations and restructurings, financial transactions, mergers and acquisitions, and litigations across a multitude of industries including telecommunications, energy, airline, health care, manufacturing, retail, food services, financial services, real estate, rail car, shipping, forest products, petroleum, computer, media, casino gaming, and hospitality. Has represented clients in many high-profile reorganization cases, including Adelphia, Arch Wireless, Cadillac Fairview, Chase REIT, Continental Airlines, Dictaphone Corporation, Dow Corning, Eurotunnel, Flag Telecom, Florida Coast Paper, FNN, Glencore Nickel, Harrah's Jazz, Huntsman Corp., Olympia & York, Owens Corning, Pathmark Stores, Resorts International, RSL Communications, Tucson Electric, US Air, USG, and Winstar Communications.
Career: Graduated from the New York University School of Law in 1972. Became a partner and Chair of Financial Restructuring Department at *Cadwalader* in 1998.

ZUCHLEWSKI, Pearl
Goodman & Zuchlewski LLP, New York
212 869 1940
Recommended in Employment

NORTH CAROLINA — BANKING & FINANCE

CONTENTS: Banking & Finance p.544; Corporate/M&A p.545; Employment: Mainly Plaintiff p.547; Mainly Defendant p.547; Litigation: General Commercial p.548; Real Estate p.550; Individuals' Profiles p.552.

NORTH CAROLINA'S TOP THREE
1. Womble Carlyle Sandridge & Rice
2. Kennedy Covington Lobdell & Hickman
2. Robinson, Bradshaw & Hinson

Ranking based on Chambers' research within the state.

All quotes in the text are from interviews with clients and competitors.

OVERVIEW: The 450-lawyer **Womble Carlyle Sandridge & Rice**, operating out of nine offices along the East Coast, is one of the largest firms in the region and tops **Chambers'** tables. The firm, which originated in Winston-Salem, provides legal services in a number of practice areas, and is noted for its determined efforts to expand its national profile and market share. An ambitious recruitment drive has produced a balanced team that was particularly endorsed for strength in litigation and real estate, with William Raper and Alfred Adams singled out respectively. The litigation group is the state's largest, with about 220 attorneys. Key clients include Wachovia Bank, RJ Reynolds and BB&T.

Full-service firm **Kennedy Covington Lobdell & Hickman**, in joint second place, comprises 170 attorneys distributed among four locations around the Carolinas. Peers pinpointed the real estate and corporate groups of this powerhouse firm as market leaders. In the former, the more than 40-strong team rates highly for its great depth, and exhibits particular skill in corporate leasing, zoning and multi-family developments. Allen Prichard acts for both lenders and developers and was praised for his deal management ability. The firm's corporate department is commended for being business-oriented in its approach; it boasts especial expertise in securities and venture capital transactions. Key clients include Bank of America, Duke Energy, Summit Properties and North Carolina State University.

Robinson, Bradshaw & Hinson offers a full range of legal services from its two Carolina offices. Interviewees particularly endorse the firm for its high corporate profile, where Russell Robinson is a leading light. A well-regarded litigation team includes some of the state's leading litigators and is recognized for its excellence, particularly in the banking and power sectors. Market sources also placed the firm among the strongest in the Southeast for its cornerstone banking and finance practice; its work in highly leveraged transactions, mezzanine financing and private equity was highlighted. Key clients include Wachovia, Duke Energy and National Gypsum.

BANKING & FINANCE

NORTH CAROLINA
Leading firms (Banking & Finance)
1. MOORE & VAN ALLEN PLLC *Charlotte*
2. HELMS MULLISS & WICKER PLLC *Charlotte*
   KENNEDY COVINGTON LOBDELL *Charlotte*
   ROBINSON, BRADSHAW & HINSON PA *Charlotte*
   WOMBLE CARLYLE SANDRIDGE *Winston-Salem*
3. CADWALADER, WICKERSHAM & TAFT *Charlotte*
   CARRUTHERS & ROTH, PA *Greensboro*

Leading individuals (Banking & Finance)
1. GREENE Kenneth *Carruthers & Roth, Greensboro*
   HOVIS James *Moore & Van Allen PLLC, Raleigh*
2. BUCK Peter *Robinson, Bradshaw & Hinson, Charlotte*
   FLINT Henry *Kennedy Covington Lobdell, Charlotte*
   HAZLETT Richard *Helms Mulliss & Wicker, Charlotte*
   KUPEC Christopher *Moore & Van Allen PLLC, Raleigh*
   LASSITER Donnell *Kennedy Covington Lobdell, Charlotte*
   MOSER Kenneth *Womble Carlyle, Winston-Salem*
3. CAMPBELL Boyd *Helms Mulliss & Wicker, Charlotte*
   DUNN Thomas *Moore & Van Allen PLLC, Raleigh*
   LEON Christopher *Womble Carlyle, Winston-Salem*
   MCKEITHEN Malloy *Helms Mulliss & Wicker, Charlotte*
   PRYOR Robert *Helms Mulliss & Wicker, Charlotte*

Firms and individuals are listed alphabetically in each band.

Moore & Van Allen PLLC

The Firm: Interviewees believe that the firm has *"a larger banking practice group with more specialists than any other firm in the state."* It represents lenders in all type of financings, including bond issuance, multiple lending transactions and other secured and unsecured transactions. Clients say these attorneys *"stand out for the quality of their advice,"* and described them as *"helpful and professional."* The firm also has a notable bankruptcy practice, representing financial institutions in bankruptcy and reorganization proceedings.

The Lawyers: **James Hovis** is the managing partner of the Charlotte office and the *"senior figure"* in the state for finance and capital markets matters. Sources agree he *"identifies with business needs, is pragmatic and develops strong relations with clients."* **Christopher Kupec** is the head of the private equity group. Banking clients describe him as *"an experienced and responsive individual – he adds value."* **J Thomas Dunn** was mentioned as one of the top attorneys in his field. He practices in capital markets, commercial lending and insolvency, and draws from his experience as the former deputy general counsel and senior vice president for First Union.

The Clients: Banks and financial institutions, including BB&T, Wachovia Bank and Bank of America.

Helms Mulliss & Wicker PLLC

The Firm: A key player in Charlotte, the firm secures a volume of work from its close relationship with Bank of America, the practice's largest client. The group advises on large syndicated loans worldwide for investment banks, and represents state and nationally based clients in loan workouts, restructurings and general bankruptcy work. It also represents numerous counties in the state with their tax-exempt and public finance issues.

The Lawyers: **Richard Hazlett** handles complicated structured financings, including bond issues, as well as syndicated loan transactions. Peers and clients praise his extensive knowledge in the area, and describe him as *"easy to work with, helpful, and gives excellent advice."* **Malloy McKeithen** was recommended for his work in sophisticated financial transactions and tax-exempt financings. **Boyd Campbell** is a corporate finance attorney experienced in the securities and regulatory arena. Clients reported that **Robert Pryor** provides an *"invaluable service"* with his expertise in bankruptcy issues.

The Clients: Bank of America; BB&T; Kitty Hawk Capital and First Charter Bank.

Kennedy Covington Lobdell & Hickman LLP

The Firm: *"A dominant firm in the field,"* say interviewees. Its *"prominent attorneys"* have carved a reputation in commercial lending and private equity financing. It received the highest marks from banking clients for its skill in undertaking complex financial transactions. The team advises on investments in the technology and telecom sector, as well as the oil and gas, manufacturing, healthcare and entertainment industries. It represents a number of lending institutions as agents in secured and unsecured syndicated loan transactions.

The Lawyers: *"A trusted attorney,"* **Henry Flint** co-manages the firm. Peers report that he has a high profile in both debt and equity financings. Sources credit **Donnell Lassiter** with *"an important practice"* in debt financing, including single

CORPORATE/M&A — NORTH CAROLINA

bank and multi-bank syndicated credit transactions.
The Clients: The firm handles all of Wachovia's syndicated credit transactions. Other clients include: LaSalle Bank; First National Bank & Trust; Wells Fargo; Key Bank & Trust and Carousel Capital.

Robinson, Bradshaw & Hinson PA
The Firm: The banking and finance practice is a cornerstone of the firm. The team is experienced in all phases of a financial transaction, particularly loan workouts, restructurings and reorganizations. Sources respect the firm's *"depth and professionalism"* and the quality of its work in highly leveraged transactions, private equity and mezzanine financings.
The Lawyers: Well-connected **Peter Buck** was recommended to researchers as *"an attorney who can do anything in the field."* Clients say that he is their *"first-choice attorney"* for complex, multi-jurisdictional financings.
The Clients: The firm represents both borrowers and lenders. Its largest client is Wachovia Bank, and it advises Piedmont Venture Partners in venture capital financings and acts for borrowers such as National Gypsum.

Womble Carlyle Sandridge & Rice PLLC
see firm details p.906
The Firm: One of the state's most respected full-service firms. Its team is experienced in capital markets transactions, syndicated loans, public underwritings and commercial mortgage loan financings. The team was recommended to researchers for its knowledge of securities law. Clients appreciate that its atttorneys *"bring good business sense to the table,"* while peers value their *"technical legal skills."*
The Lawyers: **Kenneth Moser** has impressed interviewees with his *"commercial attitude."* Clients credit him with *"technical ability; he brings realistic business sense to deals and valuable knowledge to transactions."* **Christopher Leon** is skilled in corporate and real estate financings such as syndicated, and mezzanine loans, securitizations and public/private debt offerings.
The Clients: Piedmont Federal Savings & Loan Association; Bank of America; Wachovia Bank; Royal Bank of Canada and MetLife.

Cadwalader, Wickersham & Taft
see firm details p.778
The Firm: *"A high-quality firm,"* reported market observers, which has over 200 years of experience in the banking and finance arena. The Charlotte office is part of an international network with offices in New York, DC and London, UK. Its attorneys are active in the global banking transactions, asset-based lending, letter of credit and capital markets transactions.
The Lawyers: James Carroll is the managing partner of the Charlotte office, with a practice that includes real estate finance and securitizations.
The Clients: Regional, national and international financial institutions; holding companies; thrifts; funds and insurance companies.

Carruthers & Roth, PA
The Firm: This mid-sized firm fields 25 attorneys who are engaged in secured transactions, asset-based lending, real estate financings and restructuring s . Clients spoke of *"an excellent law firm that provides us with exceptional banking and finance advice."*
The Lawyers: Peers and clients endorsed **Kenneth Greene**'s *"depth of expertise"* in asset-based and secured lending transactions. He has also advised on secured senior credit facilities for companies in a wide spectrum of industries.
The Clients: Fleet Capital ; GE; CIT Group; Wells Fargo; North Carolina Farm Bureau Insurance, Royal & SunAlliance and SAFECO Select Markets.

CORPORATE/M&A

NORTH CAROLINA
Leading firms (Corporate/M&A)

1 KENNEDY COVINGTON LOBDELL *Charlotte*
ROBINSON, BRADSHAW & HINSON PA *Charlotte*

2 HELMS MULLISS & WICKER PLLC *Charlotte*
KILPATRICK STOCKTON LLP *Charlotte*
MOORE & VAN ALLEN PLLC *Charlotte*
SMITH, ANDERSON, BLOUNT, DORSETT *Raleigh*
WOMBLE CARLYLE *Charlotte, Winston-Salem*

3 BROOKS, PIERCE, MCLENDON *Greensboro*
SCHELL BRAY AYCOCK ABEL *Greensboro*

Firms are listed alphabetically in each band.

Kennedy Covington Lobdell & Hickman LLP
The Firm: An *"impressive full-service firm,"* its corporate practice was often recommended as a leader in the state, and clients described its approach as *"both legal and business-minded."* About 25 lawyers are active in corporate M&A and securities issues for the firm. A discrete venture capital group complements the core corporate practice, and debt finance is a particular strength. Recent areas of expansion include fund formation.
The Lawyers: Researchers were left in no doubt that **Northfleet Pruden** is a dominant figure in the field. The time Pruden spends practicing has been limited by his duties as president of the North Carolina Bar Association, and while he cochairs the firm's securities group, his own practice is weighted in favor of M&A. He represented Celebration Associates in its acquisition of a company in Virginia owning land surrounding The Homestead resort. Pruden also acted for the Coca-Cola Bottling Company on a recent public debt offering. **Henry Flint** heads the firm's private equity group and was recommended as *"a talented attorney."*
The Clients: Highlights for the firm include the sale of its client Aurora Communications, owner of a group of radio stations, to Cumulus Media, the second largest owner and operator of radio stations in the US. Other major clients include: Duke Energy; Bank of America; Wachovia; Conso International Corporation; GECC; North Carolina State University and The St. Paul Fire & Marine Insurance Company.

Robinson, Bradshaw & Hinson PA
The Firm: Peers agree that the firm *"produces work of the highest quality"* and that it is a clear leader, *"in terms of both reputation and going after business in the state."* The full range of corporate and commercial advice is on offer here, including M&A, joint venture structurings and financings.
The Lawyers: Sources described **Russell Robinson** as the *"doyen of corporate lawyers and the leading light in the state."* He *"literally wrote the book"* on corporate law for North Carolina. Robinson represented First Union in its $14.5 billion stock-for-stock merger with Wachovia. There was some consensus that **Peter Buck** is the *"heir apparent"* at the firm. He represented Duke Energy in the sale of an energy service business.
The Clients: Highlights for the firm include acting for United Dominion Industries in a $1.9 billion stock merger with SPX. It also acted for Duke Energy in the cash sale of a retail water system to two South Carolina governmental units. The team represented underwriters in a Rule 144A placement of $350 million in senior subordinated notes by Nucor. Further clients include: Wachovia; EnPro Industries; Goodrich; Martin Marietta Materials; National Gypsum and The Cato Corporation.

NORTH CAROLINA   CORPORATE/M&A

NORTH CAROLINA
Leading individuals (Corporate/M&A)

1
- **BUCK Peter** *Robinson, Bradshaw & Hinson,* Charlotte
- **PRUDEN Northfleet** *Kennedy Covington,* Charlotte
- **ROBINSON Russell** *Robinson, Bradshaw,* Charlotte

2
- **BALDWIN Garza** *Womble Carlyle Sandridge,* Charlotte
- **DAGENHART Larry** *Helms Mulliss & Wicker,* Charlotte
- **DAVIS William** *Womble Carlyle,* Winston-Salem
- **FLINT Henry** *Kennedy Covington Lobdell,* Charlotte
- **HOPE Stephen** *Moore & Van Allen PLLC,* Charlotte
- **JERNIGAN John** *Smith, Anderson, Blount,* Raleigh
- **WINSLOW Edward** *Brooks, Pierce,* Greensboro
- **WREN Elizabeth** *Kilpatrick Stockton LLP,* Charlotte

Individuals are listed alphabetically in each band.

Helms Mulliss & Wicker PLLC

The Firm: The firm is deemed by market sources to have retained its reputation as a *"true specialist corporate M&A practice"* following its de-merger from Smith Helms Mulliss & Moore in March 2002. Interviewees also respected the firm as one of the strongest in the state, active from its offices in Charlotte and Raleigh.

The Lawyers: **Larry Dagenhart** was commended as an *"outstanding senior securities and corporate lawyer."* He is relied upon in the referral of major matters and can draw on the support of key attorneys such as Boyd Campbell.

The Clients: The firm recently acted with international firm Freshfields Bruckhaus Deringer for Compass in its £382 million acquisition of Morrison Management Specialists. Other clients include: GE; Bank of America; Unifi; BB&T; Eli Lilly and GM.

Kilpatrick Stockton LLP

The Firm: Interviewees respected the firm for its corporate/commercial work throughout the Carolinas. Clients appreciate a *"well-coordinated full-service practice,"* which they feel benefits from a strong presence throughout the eastern seaboard region. The core practice in Charlotte consists of corporate counseling, venture capital and joint venture work, mostly at a midmarket level. The Raleigh and Winston-Salem offices possess between them considerable healthcare expertise, while Charlotte and Raleigh have niche software practices. Overall, the firm is particularly well geared for deals with a heavy IP aspect, as it has one of the largest IP practices in the US.

The Lawyers: Clients commended **Elizabeth Wren** for being *"excellent, timely and responsive."* She acted out of the Charlotte office for YOUcentric in its acquisition by JD Edwards. Wren also represented RJ Reynolds in a $750 million debt transaction.

The Clients: Other highlights for the firm include acting for Goodrich in its acquisition of a division of Dana in Europe.

Moore & Van Allen PLLC

The Firm: Market observers considered the firm to be *"interchangeable with the best in the state."* Although the firm is best known for its banking prowess, its large M&A group is respected for advising on matters drawn from a wide range of industries. It has offices in Charlotte, Raleigh and Durham, NC and a further base in Charleston, SC, the latter of which is noted for its niche healthcare sector work.

The Lawyers: **Steve Hope** is considered the firm's leading light and is chairman of the corporate group. He advised Rexam Beauty and Closures on its acquisition of the fragrance pumps business of Crown Cork & Seal Company. Hope also assisted Rexam in the sale of its Image Products business to SUN Capital Partners.

The Clients: Highlights for the firm include acting for Nucor on its purchase of the assets of Birmingham Steel. The team also advised Clariant on the sale of its hydrosulfite business in North America to Chemtrade Logistics, and acted for Genesys Telecommunications Laboratories, a US subsidiary of Alcatel, in its acquisition of IBM's CallPath business. Other major corporate clients include Cogentrix Energy, MedCath, Watsco and Red Hat.

Smith, Anderson, Blount, Dorsett, Mitchell & Jernigan LLP
see firm details p.880

The Firm: This Raleigh firm was described by peers as *"a major presence in corporate law."* The team has an outstanding reputation for M&A of public companies, especially those headquartered in and around Raleigh, which includes several global operations. The group also benefits from excellent relations with many of the corporations in the Research Triangle region. As such, it advises boards and special committees and assists in venture capital financings. Its broad-based industry representation has an emphasis on life sciences, IT, services, healthcare and communications.

The Lawyers: Senior partner **John Jernigan** is considered by interviewees to be the firm's outstanding corporate lawyer. He can draw on the support of head of corporate, Gerald Roach.

The Clients: The firm attracts pharmaceuticals, banks and manufacturers to its client roster.

Womble Carlyle Sandridge & Rice PLLC
see firm details p.906

The Firm: The largest full-service firm in North Carolina, it is best known for its huge litigation outfit, while peers admitted *"no statewide table of corporate M&A firms would be complete without it."* Clients praised it as *"an outstandingly well-organized team with seemingly limitless resources in every practice area."* The Winston-Salem base is at the heart of the corporate M&A practice, while its securities work is conducted out of Charlotte. Continued expansion has most recently seen the opening of a small Greensboro office.

The Lawyers: Clients described **Garza Baldwin** as a *"fine lawyer with sound judgment."* **William Davis** is highly rated for his *"specialist expertise in coordinating nationwide deals."* Both lawyers have acted in the recent round of banking M&A, such as that of BB&T's $3.38 billion acquisition of First Virginia Banks. Davis also represented three domestic flooring companies recently purchased by Home Depot.

The Clients: The group advises corporations in the financial services, telecom, IT, healthcare and manufacturing sectors.

Brooks, Pierce, McLendon, Humphrey & Leonard LLP

The Firm: Interviewees endorsed the firm for its *"good resources and breadth of talent."* It is known for the high caliber of its general corporate/commercial work, with the Greensboro office particularly rated for its work in the financial services sector. The firm's Raleigh office is respected for its telecom and media expertise.

The Lawyers: **Edward Winslow** is considered a top M&A and corporate securities lawyer and is particularly well known in finance circles. He was involved in defending Wachovia against the challenge brought by SunTrust Banks to its merger with First Union. The North Carolina Bankers Association is another of Winslow's clients.

The Clients: Major domestic and international corporations.

Schell Bray Aycock Abel & Livingston PLLC

The Firm: This small Greensboro-based boutique came highly recommended by some of the state's top corporate/commercial lawyers. At the core of its corporate practice is securities law, antitrust, taxation and bankruptcy expertise. Specialist areas include joint ventures, LBOs, cash and tax-free mergers and recapitalizations.

The Lawyers: Senior practitioner Michael Abel is a key member of the group.

The Clients: The team advises a number of private and public companies on operating in both domestic and international markets. A concentration of technology and textile sector clients helps to define the practice.

EMPLOYMENT & LABOR LAW — NORTH CAROLINA

EMPLOYMENT & LABOR LAW — MAINLY PLAINTIFF

NORTH CAROLINA
Leading firms (Employment: Mainly Plaintiff)

1. FERGUSON STEIN CHAMBERS WALLAAS *Charlotte*
   PATTERSON HARKAVY & LAWRENCE *Raleigh*
2. ELLIOT PISHKO MORGAN *Winston-Salem*
   LESESNE & CONNETTE *Charlotte*
   SMITH JAMES ROWLETT & COHEN *Greensboro*

Leading individuals (Employment: Mainly Plaintiff)

1. ELLIOT Robert *Elliot Pishko Morgan,* Winston-Salem
   HARKAVY Jonathan *Patterson Harkavy,* Raleigh
   JAMES David *Smith James Rowlett,* Greensboro
   LESESNE Louis *Lesesne & Connette,* Charlotte
2. CONNETTE Edward *Lesesne & Connette,* Charlotte
   GRESHAM John *Ferguson Stein Chambers,* Charlotte
   MORGAN Griffin *Elliot Pishko Morgan,* Winston-Salem
   OKUN Michael *Patterson Harkavy,* Raleigh
   PISHKO David *Elliot Pishko Morgan,* Winston-Salem
   SUMTER Geraldine *Ferguson Stein Chambers,* Charlotte
3. FISHER Stewart *Glenn, Mills & Fisher PA,* Durham
   LAWRENCE Melinda *Patterson Harkavy,* Raleigh
   PAYNE Travis *Edelstein & Payne,* Raleigh
   SMITH Norman *Smith James Rowlett,* Greensboro

Firms and individuals are listed alphabetically in each band.

Ferguson Stein Chambers Wallaas Adkins Gresham & Sumter

The Firm: Interviewees endorsed this firm as one of the most long-standing plaintiffs' practices in the state. The 14 attorneys here have secured an international as well as national reputation in civil rights and employment litigation, with particular emphasis on employment discrimination matters.

The Lawyers: Market sources described **John Gresham** and **Geraldine Sumter** as *"stars at the firm, and top-flight lawyers."* Gresham is a *"polished and experienced attorney,"* active in employment discrimination cases, while Sumter is deemed *"honorable, smart and a great advocate for her clients."*

Patterson Harkavy & Lawrence

The Firm: A nationally recognized boutique with offices in Raleigh and Greensboro. The team is best known for its representation of unions and individuals in labor and employment matters. It also has an extensive practice in workers' compensation, civil rights and personal injury. Clients recommend the firm *"because they have the interests of workers at heart,"* while peers spoke of attorneys' *"great depth of knowledge."* In the employment discrimination area, the firm has secured the single largest sexual harassment verdict in state history. It also represents local, national and international unions in arbitrations and collective bargaining, and before the NLRB.

The Lawyers: Jonathan Harkavy has a strong background in employment litigation, and now devotes a considerable portion of his time to mediation. **Melinda Lawrence** gains plaudits from the market for her expertise in the broad spectrum of labor and employment law. **Michael Okun** serves as the general counsel for the North Carolina AFL-CIO. Clients agreed that he is *"definitely a major player."*

The Clients: AFL-CIO; United Steelworkers; American Federation of Teachers (AFT); American Postal Workers Union (APWU); International Association of Machinists and Aerospace Workers (IAM); Transport Workers Union of America (TWU) and the United Food and Commercial Workers International Union (UFCW).

Elliot Pishko Morgan

The Firm: A *"top-of-the-line"* labor and employment boutique firm, agree interviewees. Six dedicated attorneys here *"know how to put up a hard fight."* They represent clients in employment litigation, social security disability matters, workers' compensation and personal injury matters in state and federal courts.

The Lawyers: Robert Elliot, **David Pishko** and **Griffin Morgan** form a highly respected team of senior lawyers. Defendant attorneys dubbed them *"the best-known plaintiffs' attorneys in Winston-Salem,"* to whom they would *"certainly refer work."*

Lesesne & Connette

The Firm: *"A top-drawer boutique firm,"* according to defendant employment lawyers. The firm has three attorneys and one associate who litigate in employment matters, ERISA claims, civil rights issues and class actions.

The Lawyers: *"First-rate"* plaintiffs' attorneys **Lou Lesesne** and his partner **Edward Connette** were recommended to researchers as *"excellent, creative lawyers who work well together."*

The Clients: Individuals, unions, public employees and an increasing number of medical practices are clients.

Smith James Rowlett & Cohen

The Firm: Four attorneys in this renowned boutique are involved in a variety of civil and criminal litigation matters, including labor and employment and civil rights issues.

The Lawyers: David James is respected for his representation of unions. Peers agree that he is *"a good professional as well as a real gentleman."* Senior attorney **Norman Smith**'s *"long, distinguished career"* has impressed many interviewees.

Other Notable Practitioners

In Durham, market sources were impressed by the litigation skills of **Stewart Fisher** of Glenn, Mills & Fisher PA, while in Raleigh, **M Travis Payne** of Edelstein & Payne was singled out for his *"comprehensive knowledge."*

EMPLOYMENT & LABOR LAW — MAINLY DEFENDANT

Brooks, Pierce, McLendon, Humphrey & Leonard LLP

The Firm: This well-respected corporate law firm has over 100 years' experience representing North Carolina's business elite. The firm houses 65 lawyers in two offices in the state, who are further supported by colleagues in DC. Peers recommend it as *"a top-drawer firm with bright employment lawyers."* It attracts clients from the healthcare, and textile and furniture manufacturing industries as well as banks and restaurants. Attorneys here handle a wide spectrum of employment matters, including ADA and FMLA-related cases. A specialty of note is its familiarity with employment issues, such as employee retirement and benefit plans, retention incentive plans and plant closing procedures, which are impacted by M&A.

The Lawyers: Peers say that **William Cary** and **Daniel McGinn** form an *"absolutely first-rate team."* Cary has extensive experience litigating FLSA-related matters, while McGinn is recognized for his work before the NLRB. Interviewees claim that they represent clients *"in a way that gets problems solved for both parties."*

The Clients: AT&T; Battleground Restaurants; Citicorp; Guilford County Public Schools; LaSalle Bank; Lorillard Tobacco; Moses Cone Health System; Time Warner Cable and Wachovia Bank.

NORTH CAROLINA — EMPLOYMENT & LABOR LAW

NORTH CAROLINA
Leading firms
(Employment: Mainly Defendant)

1 BROOKS, PIERCE, MCLENDON Greensboro
CONSTANGY, BROOKS & SMITH Winston-Salem
2 MAUPIN TAYLOR & ELLIS PA Raleigh
OGLETREE, DEAKINS, NASH, SMOAK Raleigh
3 VAN HOY REUTLINGER ADAMS & DUNN Charlotte
WOMBLE CARLYLE Charlotte, Winston-Salem

Leading individuals
(Employment: Mainly Defendant)

1 CARY William *Brooks, Pierce, McLendon,* Greensboro
DOYLE John *Constangy, Brooks,* Winston-Salem
LOFTIS Randolph *Constangy,* Winston-Salem
MCGINN Daniel *Brooks, Pierce, McLendon,* Greensboro
VAN HOY Philip *Van Hoy Reutlinger Adams,* Charlotte
2 BRADSHAW Penni *Kilpatrick Stockton,* Winston-Salem
FARR Thomas *Maupin Taylor & Ellis PA,* Raleigh
3 BELL Albert *Ward and Smith PA,* New Bern
ERWIN Martin *Smith Moore LLP,* Greensboro
RAINEY Richard *Womble Carlyle Sandridge,* Charlotte
WARD Frank *Maupin Taylor & Ellis PA,* Raleigh

Firms and individuals are listed alphabetically in each band.

Constangy, Brooks & Smith LLC
The Firm: Dubbed by market sources as *"clearly a top labor and employment practice."* The foundation of this practice is work assisting employers with union-related issues such as preventive strategies. The firm has over 50 years' experience, and can draw upon ten offices in eight states. It has a national reputation for representing employers in discrimination claims, wrongful discharge, and wage and hour cases.
The Lawyers: **John Doyle** specializes in employment litigation defense and is the founding chairman of the state bar association's labor and employment law section. Peers admire him as *"a trusted attorney with high ethical standards."* Clients report that he *"provides consistently excellent results."* **W Randolph Loftis** heads the Winston-Salem office and was esteemed as *"among the very best labor and employment litigators in the state."*
The Clients: The team has represented Eaton for over 20 years. Other clients include: Chubb; Duke Energy; GE; Hertz; High Point Regional Hospital; RJ Reynolds; Randolph Hospital and Sara Lee.

Maupin Taylor & Ellis PA
The Firm: This respected and long-established firm has a strong labor and employment practice, which was set up in 1972. According to market observers, the dedicated attorneys here *"do a great job in representing employers."* Employment litigation is their key area of activity, but an emphasis is also placed on general preventive counseling and personnel policies.
The Lawyers: Practice group coordinator **Thomas Farr** (see p.552) is a respected litigator who peers endorse as *"professional and knowledgeable."* **Frank Ward** is a senior attorney in the area of employment discrimination law.
The Clients: The team represents public and private corporations, trade associations, charitable foundations, Fortune 500 companies and emerging technology companies before federal and state courts. Clients include: Kerr Drug; SpectraSite; DaimlerChrysler; Waste Industries USA; BlueCross BlueShield of North Carolina; Alcoa and City of Raleigh.

Ogletree, Deakins, Nash, Smoak & Stewart PC
The Firm: One of the largest labor and employment practices in the country with 14 offices nationwide. Interviewees especially commended its expertise in traditional labor law matters such as union-organizing drives. Attorneys here are experienced in both federal and state courts, and also counsel clients on preventative strategies. Related areas include business immigration, employee benefits and OSHA matters.
The Lawyers: John Burgin is the managing partner of the Raleigh office.
The Clients: Roadway Package Systems; Burlington Industries; Kodak, The Hartford; Public Service Company of North Carolina and Rockwell International.

Van Hoy Reutlinger Adams & Dunn
The Firm: This widely respected labor and employment boutique fields four lawyers who represent public and private employers in the healthcare, manufacturing, and service industries, among others. The team is active in employment litigation, wrongful discharge claims, wage and hour and OSHA matters.
The Lawyers: **Phil Van Hoy** litigates discrimination and wrongful discharge cases in state and federal courts. Interviewees said that he is *"a hugely talented lawyer."*
The Clients: Cape Fear Valley Medical Center; City of Charlotte; Corporate Health International; Duke Energy; The Employers' Association; Pfeiffer University and The Sanger Clinic.

Womble Carlyle Sandridge & Rice PLLC
see firm details p.906
The Firm: This full-service firm receives consistent recommendations for its high-quality advice. The firm operates from offices in four states and DC, ensuring that its labor and employment practice is nationwide in scope. Core areas include employment discrimination litigation and advising clients in union contract negotiations, wage and hour disputes, and OSHA compliance reviews. The group attracts clients from the manufacturing, technology, banking and healthcare sectors as well as government agencies.
The Lawyers: Observers agree that **Richard Rainey** is a highly respected litigator who is *"a familiar sight on complex cases."* He recently advised on Alderman v Inmar Enterprises, an age discrimination case where summary judgment was obtained.
The Clients: Piedmont Federal; Venture First Associates; Associated Aviation Underwriters; Bank of America; Cisco Systems; City of Charlotte; North Carolina Association of County Commissioners; Novartis and Travelers.

Other Notable Practitioners
Penni Bradshaw of Kilpatrick Stockton LLP has extensive experience in employment matters, with a notable expertise in immigration law. She is general employment and labor counsel for, among others, Sara Lee and Krispy Kreme. At Ward and Smith PA, **Albert Bell** has over 30 years' experience litigating employment discrimination suits and civil rights cases in federal and state courts. Clients on the opposing side of the table regard him as *"a tough opponent, but also an honest guy."* Litigator **Martin Erwin** of Smith Moore LLP was recommended to researchers as a *"big hitter"* in employment-related discrimination cases, including ERISA matters.

LITIGATION — GENERAL COMMERCIAL

Robinson, Bradshaw & Hinson PA
The Firm: Although the firm does not match the size of its direct competitors, interviewees agreed that its *"depth of experience"* was unsurpassed, ensuring it a high prominence in the marketplace. The department is home to several of the state's leading litigators and is complemented by a sterling corporate practice. Much of the workload is derived from the power sector or disputes arising from the banking market. The team has defended class actions arising from environmental disputes and has defended banks against claims brought by customers.
The Lawyers: Peers attested to **Ward McKeithen**'s ability to *"battle in court and overwhelm the*

LITIGATION

NORTH CAROLINA

NORTH CAROLINA
Leading firms
(Litigation: General Commercial)

1
- ROBINSON, BRADSHAW & HINSON PA *Charlotte*
- WOMBLE CARLYLE *Charlotte, Winston-Salem*

2
- BROOKS, PIERCE, MCLENDON *Greensboro*
- HELMS MULLISS & WICKER PLLC *Charlotte*
- KENNEDY COVINGTON LOBDELL *Charlotte*
- MOORE & VAN ALLEN PLLC *Charlotte*
- SMITH MOORE LLP *Greensboro, Raleigh*

3
- KILPATRICK STOCKTON LLP *Winston-Salem*
- PARKER, POE, ADAMS & BERNSTEIN LLP *Raleigh*
- SMITH, ANDERSON, BLOUNT, DORSETT *Raleigh*

Leading individuals
(Litigation: General Commercial)

1
- COVINGTON Peter *Helms Mulliss & Wicker,* Charlotte
- COWAN Donald *Smith Moore LLP,* Raleigh
- DAVIS William *Bell, Davis & Pitt PA,* Winston-Salem
- MCKEITHEN Ward *Robinson, Bradshaw,* Charlotte
- RAPER William *Womble Carlyle Sandridge,* Charlotte
- WESTER John *Robinson, Bradshaw & Hinson,* Charlotte
- WILLIAMS Jim *Brooks, Pierce, McLendon,* Greensboro

2
- MERRITT Mark *Robinson, Bradshaw & Hinson,* Charlotte
- SITTON Larry *Smith Moore LLP,* Greensboro
- VAUGHAN Keith *Womble Carlyle,* Winston-Salem

3
- BARBER Timothy *Womble Carlyle Sandridge,* Charlotte
- COONEY James *Womble Carlyle Sandridge,* Charlotte
- COVINGTON George *Kennedy Covington,* Charlotte
- DAVIS Jeffrey *Moore & Van Allen PLLC,* Charlotte
- MCLOUGHLIN JR James *Moore & Van Allen,* Charlotte
- SPEARMAN Robert *Parker, Poe, Adams,* Raleigh
- TAYLOR Daniel *Kilpatrick Stockton,* Winston-Salem

Individuals are listed alphabetically in each band.

its litigators are stationed in North Carolina (about 220 litigators in total) making it by far the largest operation in the state. Tobacco and tax-related litigation have recently provided the firm with high-value cases.

The Lawyers: Peers said **William Raper** was *"more often than not involved in anything complex or high profile."* In addition to a wide-ranging commercial litigation practice, he also provides professional negligence defense. **Keith Vaughan** combines his fee-earning time with duties as managing partner of the firm. He is a respected business litigator and received high praise during *Chambers'* research. Sources believed that head of litigation **Timothy Barber** was *"always destined to become the lead litigator"* at the firm. His practice is perceived as having an emphasis on securities and technology matters. Interviewees report that there is *"no better trial lawyer"* than **James Cooney**. He sustains a practice that brings together business litigation, medical malpractice and criminal defense, as well as appellate representation. Grady Barnhill, though no longer trying cases, remains a valuable source of advice to the group.

The Clients: RJ Reynolds, and regional, national and international corporations are clients.

Brooks, Pierce, McLendon, Humphrey & Leonard LLP

The Firm: Sources agreed that this firm fields *"some of the best litigators in the state and one of the best teams in Greensboro."* In addition to its focus on litigation in the banking and financial services sectors, other areas of activity include IP, contract and complex business disputes.

The Lawyers: Interviewees agreed that **Jim Williams** is a *"formidable opponent."* He defended Wachovia against SunTrust Banks' challenge to its merger with First Union. Williams was most recently involved in a high-profile tobacco antitrust suit.

The Clients: Financial institutions, accounting and consultancy firms, and tobacco companies.

Helms Mulliss & Wicker PLLC

The Firm: Competitors acknowledged that it *"was always a delight to have its litigators on the other side."* The firm's attorneys are *"highly skilled and knowledgeable"* and *"take a reasonable stance"* in their cases. Banking and insurance litigation are strongholds for the firm. Other areas of expertise include media litigation and related First Amendment issues.

The Lawyers: Interviewees respected **Peter Covington**'s *"business acumen,"* at the same time reporting that he is an *"aggressive litigator when necessary."* He acts for banks on securities matters as well as on stockholder disputes. As managing partner of the firm, he spends about one third of his time as a practicing litigator. Though no longer trying cases, Osborne Ayscue is one of the best-known litigators in the state and is a former American College of Trial Lawyers president.

The Clients: Bank of America; Wachovia Securities; Royal & SunAlliance; Unifi and the Charlotte-Mecklenburg School System.

Kennedy Covington Lobdell & Hickman LLP

The Firm: The firm is commended by peers for having *"paid serious attention to its litigation operation."* Although traditionally better known for its premier league corporate outfit, the firm has recently structured its litigation department along industry sector lines. Real estate and securities litigation are noted as particular strengths. Arbitration is also a strong suit, and the firm, led by department head Kiran Mehta, has represented a multinational company in an international arbitration relating to an undersea fiber-optic cable installation.

The Lawyers: **George Covington** practices out of the Charlotte office and is viewed as one of the key players in the market. He represented the initial purchaser of two offerings of asset-backed securities in a lawsuit brought by 14 institutional investors alleging a violation of federal securities laws and common law fraud. Covington also represented a multinational law firm in a suit alleging fraud and malpractice in connection with a failed hi-tech start-up company.

The Clients: AAC Real Estate Services; Bank of America; Coca-Cola Bottling Company; Corning Cable Systems; Duke Energy and subsidiaries including Crescent Resources; Fluor; Framatome ANP DE&S and Summit Properties.

Moore & Van Allen PLLC

The Firm: Clients in the banking and finance sector consistently said the practice *"gave excellent concise and practical advice."* For some it was *"the only firm we would consider using outside New York."* While banking and finance remains widely recognized as the firm's key strength, it has also built up a traditional business litigation practice, and is active in the telecom and heavy industry sectors, among others. The team consists of about 60 litigators and has *"significant operations"* in both Charlotte and Raleigh, not to mention its Durham and Charleston contingents.

The Lawyers: According to clients, the *"astute and aggressive"* **James McLoughlin** *"knows the technicalities of the court and can apply them in a business-minded way."* He recently acted for a publicly listed telecom company in civil and regulatory litigation. McLoughlin also arbitrated a matter between the US subsidiaries of British and French corporations, relating to a dispute over a corporate acquisition. Other recent highlights include acting for a specialized medical service company in arbitration over the pricing of com-

---

opposition." He was consistently described as a *"top-flight litigator,"* often acting on the side of either prosecution or defense in major antitrust and class action securities suits. **John Wester** received a high volume of commendation and is said to *"thrive in the courtroom."* **Mark Merrit** was also well received by peers as *"an extremely smart litigator."* He possesses niche expertise in arbitrations in the construction and securities sectors. He represented First Union when Sun-Trust Banks contested its $14.5 billion stock-for-stock merger with Wachovia.

The Clients: Duke Energy; First Union; Wachovia and McDevitt Street Bovis.

Womble Carlyle Sandridge & Rice PLLC

see firm details p.906

The Firm: There was a clear consensus among interviewees that the firm was top *"for overall depth and quality,"* while clients admitted *"it would always be on the shortlist."* The majority of

NORTH CAROLINA — LITIGATION

plex medical procedures. **Jeffrey Davis** was also recommended to researchers as an *"outstanding trial lawyer in any setting."* His practice includes securities, construction and energy sector litigation.
The Clients: Banks and financial institutions, telecom and healthcare sector corporations and heavy industry manufacturers.

Smith Moore LLP
The Firm: The high-quality advice that interviewees attributed to its lead litigators, combined with the volume of commendation for the team as a whole, makes this a major player in the market. In addition to its core general commercial practice, the firm also covers complex insurance coverage litigation and IP matters. Observers also singled out products liability as one of its main strengths.
The Lawyers: **Donald Cowan** is a *"highly regarded trial lawyer"* who is esteemed for his breadth of knowledge. He is especially well regarded for his representations in antitrust cases. Cowan recently acted for Philip Morris in the DeLoach Suit, a class action by tobacco growers alleging antitrust violations. Peers have *"great respect for"* **Larry Sitton**. Together with Cowan, he acted for Gulf Insurance in a dispute with First Union National Bank (now Wachovia) over the residual value insurance for a leased automobile portfolio. Sitton also acted for the defense in Veronica D Romig et al v Jefferson-Pilot Life Insurance on a pending class action by life insurance policyholders concerning market conduct.
The Clients: Atlantic Coast Conference; Bank of America; Eli Lilly; GE; Miller Brewing Company; Monsanto; Solutia; Stockhausen and Procter & Gamble.

Kilpatrick Stockton LLP
The Firm: Clients described the team as being *"rigorously professional"* in its conduct of complex cases. The practice incorporates securities fraud, products liability, insurance and zoning litigation. It benefits from supporting expertise found in its construction, environmental, government contracts, healthcare and IP departments.
The Lawyers: Winston-Salem-based **Daniel Taylor** is best known for recently representing RJ Reynolds in an antitrust challenge to Philip Morris' retail merchandizing program. Other highlights include involvement in an employment class action, and in business litigation in the waste sector.
The Clients: Public companies; brokers; dealers and manufacturers.

Parker, Poe, Adams & Bernstein LLP
The Firm: Interviewees commended the firm for its general contract and business litigation practice. Attorneys also display niche expertise in antitrust, including trade secrets and IP matters.
The Lawyers: Raleigh-based **Robert Spearman** is considered to be the firm's highest-profile litigator. He heads the antitrust and business tort practice group, and has expertise in areas of public law, including government procurement.
The Clients: A majority of clients are based in the Southeast but the team has recently advised on matters concerning clients as far afield as California. Clients include service industry corporations, pharmaceutical and software companies, and industrial manufacturers.

Smith, Anderson, Blount, Dorsett, Mitchell & Jernigan LLP
see firm details p.880
The Firm: A well-reputed team advises on banking, securities, insurance and real estate litigation. It has recently tackled increasingly complex cases for its growing base of life sciences clients.
The Lawyers: **Carl Patterson** heads the practice and is heavily involved in high-value securities litigation.
The Clients: The firm has successfully acted for Quintiles Transnational in the federal courts, winning injunctive relief relating to the use of de-identified healthcare data by WebMD. It has also acted for individual inventors of cutting-edge technology in a dispute over unpaid royalties that resulted in a multimillion dollar settlement in favor of the inventors.

Other Notable Practitioners
William Davis of Bell, Davis & Pitt PA in Winston-Salem received a high level of commendation for his niche securities litigation practice. Other strands to his practice include general business, banking, and officers' and directors' litigation. He represented Wachovia and its directors during its contested merger with First Union. Davis also represented medical service provider PhyAmerica Physician Services in litigation relating to the restructuring of its debt with healthcare finance firm National Century Financial Enterprises. BB&T is another key client.

REAL ESTATE

NORTH CAROLINA
Leading firms (Real Estate)

1
- KENNEDY COVINGTON LOBDELL *Charlotte*
- WOMBLE CARLYLE *Raleigh, Winston-Salem*

2
- MANNING FULTON & SKINNER *Raleigh*
- MOORE & VAN ALLEN PLLC *Charlotte*
- ROBINSON, BRADSHAW & HINSON PA *Charlotte*

3
- HELMS MULLISS & WICKER PLLC *Charlotte*
- KILPATRICK STOCKTON LLP *Charlotte*
- PARKER, POE, ADAMS & BERNSTEIN *Charlotte*
- POYNER & SPRUILL LLP *Raleigh*
- SMITH MOORE LLP *Greensboro*
- SMITH, ANDERSON, BLOUNT, DORSETT *Raleigh*

Firms are listed alphabetically in each band.

Kennedy Covington Lobdell & Hickman LLP
The Firm: Researchers were left in no doubt as to the great depth of this real estate practice, which totals over 40 lawyers. Interviewees described it as *"having a strong and long-standing presence in the market."* Its expertise in areas as diverse as corporate leasing, multi-family developments and zoning all came in for high praise. In addition to the firm's powerful Charlotte base, it draws support from a small real estate team in Rock Hill, SC, ensuring seamless coverage for clients across the Carolinas.
The Lawyers: Major real estate clients agreed that *"lawyers throughout the firm are approachable, down-to-earth and fair."* Many interviewees favored **Allen Prichard** for his *"sheer deal management ability"* on behalf of both developers and lenders. The *"talented"* **Maynard Tipps** also received favorable reviews from peers and clients alike. He acts primarily for developers and investors, particularly in the lending field. In work typical of the firm's practice, Tipps recently advised the developer/owner on the development, financing and leasing of Brier Creek Commons Shopping Center in Raleigh, a planned buildout in excess of 700,000 sq ft. He also advised on the development of a mixed-use project covering an entire city block in Charlotte's central business district known as Fifth & Poplar. **Charles DuBose**, who is co-managing partner of the firm, and **Glen Hardymon** act mostly on the side of developers. Both were praised as *"outstanding senior real estate lawyers."* Hardymon chairs the real estate development practice group and recently represented the City of Charlotte in its negotiations with the NBA that led to the award of a new NBA franchise to Charlotte.

REAL ESTATE — NORTH CAROLINA

NORTH CAROLINA
Leading individuals (Real Estate)

[1]
- **ADAMS Alfred** *Womble Carlyle,* Winston-Salem
- **OLIVER JR Samuel** *Manning Fulton,* Raleigh
- **PRICHARD Allen** *Kennedy Covington Lobdell,* Charlotte
- **TORSTRICK Brent** *Robinson, Bradshaw,* Charlotte

[2]
- **BRINKLEY Robert** *Helms Mulliss & Wicker,* Charlotte
- **FULTON Charles** *Manning Fulton & Skinner,* Raleigh
- **MELVIN Charles** *Smith Moore LLP,* Greensboro
- **TIPPS Maynard** *Kennedy Covington Lobdell,* Charlotte

[3]
- **DONADIO Donald** *Womble Carlyle Sandridge,* Raleigh
- **DORTON David** *Maupin Taylor & Ellis PA,* Raleigh
- **DUBOSE Charles** *Kennedy Covington Lobdell,* Charlotte
- **HARDYMON Glen** *Kennedy Covington,* Charlotte
- **MASON C Steven** *Smith, Anderson, Blount,* Raleigh
- **OATES J Christopher** *Moore & Van Allen,* Charlotte

Individuals are listed alphabetically in each band.

The Clients: Konover Property Trust; Spectrum Properties; Summit Properties, and Oakwood Homes Corporation.

Womble Carlyle Sandridge & Rice PLLC
see firm details p.906

The Firm: Clients believe that the 450-lawyer firm benefits from its network of nine offices along the East Coast, including in DC. Both the real estate development and lending practices - the latter of which fields *"as much experience as anyone"* – are held in equally high regard. There is an emphasis on the practice's overlap with technology law and the strategic property requirements associated with the sector.

The Lawyers: Winston-Salem-based **Alfred Adams** received the highest volume of commendation at the firm. One client considered him to be *"the best real estate lawyer in the Southeast."* Adams acts for the likes of Lowe's Home Centers, Thomasville Furniture Industries and Lennar. Property finance lawyer **Donald Donadio** was also commended as a *"tough negotiator."* He practices in Raleigh along with William Matthews, a real estate finance lawyer.

The Clients: Major developers in the retail, office, leisure and residential sectors and major lenders.

Manning Fulton & Skinner

The Firm: *"A small firm that does a high percentage of real estate work, it possesses some of the state's leading practitioners."* This was the typical comment on the practice, which is weighted in favor of development in the office sector. The team also advises on the development of shopping centers and acts for a retail sector client nationally. Advice to lenders focused on the real estate market also contributes to the workload.

The Lawyers: **Samuel Oliver** was adjudged *"extremely hard-working and responsive."* He maintains a wide-ranging practice that includes complex property financing work. Peers acknowledge senior practitioner **Charles Fulton**'s role as an essential element in the firm's armory. He recently acted for GE Capital on the acquisition of several 'flex' buildings (properties designed to accommodate both office and industrial functions), one of which was worth $46 million.

The Clients: The firm acts for the likes of Fonville-Morisey Realty, Craig Davis Properties, Highwoods Properties, Carolantic Realty and Tri Properties.

Moore & Van Allen PLLC

The Firm: Best known among market observers for its long-standing real estate lending prowess. The practice also enjoys a traditional development component and was praised for its *"strength in depth."*

The Lawyers: **Chris Oates** heads the practice out of the firm's Charlotte office and is endorsed for *"having the highest level of involvement."* In addition to advising on acquisitions, disposals, development and financing matters, he is also experienced in zoning issues and variances. Smaller teams of real estate lawyers in Raleigh, Durham and Charleston complete the firm's network.

The Clients: Major financial institutions; local and regional developers; institutional investors; insurance companies, and other regional and national corporations.

Robinson, Bradshaw & Hinson PA

The Firm: Renowned among interviewees for *"its superb real estate client base,"* the firm once again performed well in *Chambers'* market research. The team is experienced in all aspects of predevelopment and development matters. It also acts for banks and insurance companies on real estate lending.

The Lawyers: **Brent Torstrick** is considered the firm's top development lawyer. He is particularly experienced in matters relating to retail and residential sector developments.

The Clients: Charlotte-Mecklenburg Hospital Authority, Crescent Resources and Pizzagalli Properties/Pizzagalli Construction Company.

Helms Mulliss & Wicker PLLC

The Firm: The real estate practice received recommendations from market observers for its activities in the industrial and office sectors, and in relation to shopping centers and commercial condominium developments. Attorneys are skilled in developments and acquisitions, entity formation and tax structuring, and zoning. The team also advises on commercial leasing across the US and overseas. Construction law, both non-contentious and litigious, is a further area of experience.

The Lawyers: Charlotte-based **Robert Brinkley** was endorsed by peers as *"technically knowledgeable – he represents his clients' best interests."*

The Clients: Lenders, owners, developers and investors.

Kilpatrick Stockton LLP

The Firm: Observers praised the practice for its *"experienced lawyers and their thorough understanding of real estate and all its complex issues."* The firm's real estate practice consists of over 30 lawyers, about half of which are based in North Carolina. It is concentrated in Raleigh and Charlotte, but also has a small contingent in Winston-Salem. Typically acting on behalf of developers, it has recently been heavily involved in the retail sector. A portion of lending advice also contributes to the workload.

The Lawyers: Gary Joyner and the team recently represented the developer of Triangle Town Center, a 1.3 million sq ft enclosed mall, and assisted the developer in the redevelopment of North Hills Mall and Plaza. The firm also acted on a mixed-use development, known as Mayfair in Wilmington, which included a community center, residential attached and detached dwellings, as well as office and retail space.

The Clients: Major local and regional developers.

Parker, Poe, Adams & Bernstein LLP

The Firm: Sources recommended this *"top-flight real estate practice,"* which is active in development, financing and zoning matters. The firm has a commanding presence in both its Charlotte headquarters and Raleigh branch office. The firm advised on the 1.1 million sq ft Three Wachovia Center in Center City Charlotte, incorporating major office, residential, retail and parking uses. It has also acted on numerous Center City and South End condominiums. A niche expertise in the rail sector has seen the team advising on purchase and sale agreements for NCDOT and Univar USA.

The Lawyers: Chairman for the firm Samuel Woodward is a major figure in the real estate practice.

The Clients: The team advised North Carolina State University on the master-planning and development of the Centennial Campus in Raleigh, a 2000-acre, mixed-use project. Other clients include: Childress Klein Properties; Crescent Resources; Crosland; Charter Properties; Raley-Miller Properties and The Rosen Group.

Poyner & Spruill LLP

The Firm: The team was recommended by clients, who had found it to be *"responsive and dependable over the years."* The team acts for developers on retail buildings and shopping centers, warehouses and offices, as well as large residential properties. Its developers' practice includes advice on equity investment and financing matters. In addition it advises major lenders such as Wachovia, BB&T and, in the case of the Rocky Mount office, Centura Banks (now RBC

NORTH CAROLINA   REAL ESTATE

Centura Banks), on real estate lending issues. Other areas include advising owners on leasing.
The Lawyers: Joseph Dempster and Thomas Eatman are key members of the team.
The Clients: North Carolina Housing Finance Agency; GE Mortgage Insurance Company and Roses Stores.

Smith Moore LLP
The Firm: Clients described these real estate attorneys as *"detail-oriented and thorough in their understanding of our business."* There was consensus among both peers and clients that it is the premier Greensboro real estate outfit with a depth of experience in development, financing and zoning issues.
The Lawyers: Senior real estate practitioner

Charles Melvin was praised as being *"politically wired and well respected in the community."*
The Clients: As well as real estate developers, it represents both domestic and inward investors. Clients include R Twinings and Company, Bonset America Corporation, Liberty Property Trust and Jefferson Pilot Financial.

Smith, Anderson, Blount, Dorsett, Mitchell & Jernigan LLP
see firm details p.65946
The Firm: The practice is highly regarded for its *"top-quality real estate lawyers."* Attorneys are respected for their high-profile representation of lenders, though the practice is well versed in development work.
The Lawyers: Former Moore & Van Allen attor-

ney **Steven Mason** is considered *"one of the best real estate lawyers in town"* by interviewees. As well as banks and financial institutions, he acts for, among others, office and retail developers and investors.
The Clients: Wachovia Bank; Carolina Power & Light; The Pantry; Quintiles Transnational and York Properties.

Other Notable Practitioners
David Dorton of Maupin Taylor & Ellis PA is considered a *"first-class real estate lawyer."* He primarily represents owners and developers as well as some lenders on a range of matters throughout the eastern US, including on issues relating to the Research Triangle.

Leaders in North Carolina

ADAMS, Alfred
Womble Carlyle Sandridge & Rice PLLC, Winston-Salem 336 721 3600
Recommended in Real Estate

BALDWIN, Garza
Womble Carlyle Sandridge & Rice PLLC, Charlotte 704 331 4900
Recommended in Corporate/M&A

BARBER, Timothy
Womble Carlyle Sandridge & Rice PLLC, Charlotte 704 331 4900
Recommended in Litigation

BELL, Albert
Ward and Smith, P.A., New Bern
252 672 5400
Recommended in Employment

BRADSHAW, Penni
Kilpatrick Stockton LLP, Winston-Salem 336 607 7300
Recommended in Employment

BRINKLEY, Robert
Helms Mulliss & Wicker PLLC, Charlotte 704 343 2000
Recommended in Real Estate

BUCK, Peter
Robinson, Bradshaw & Hinson, P.A., Charlotte 704 377 2536
Recommended in Banking & Finance, Corporate/M&A

CAMPBELL, Boyd
Helms Mulliss & Wicker PLLC, Charlotte 704 343 2000
Recommended in Banking & Finance

CARY, William
Brooks, Pierce, McLendon, Humphrey & Leonard, L.L.P., Greensboro
336 373 8850
Recommended in Employment

CONNETTE, Edward
Lesesne & Connette, Charlotte
704 372 5700
Recommended in Employment

COONEY, James
Womble Carlyle Sandridge & Rice PLLC, Charlotte 704 331 4900
Recommended in Litigation

COVINGTON, George C
Kennedy Covington Lobdell & Hickman, L.L.P., Charlotte 704 331 7400
Recommended in Litigation

COVINGTON, Peter
Helms Mulliss & Wicker PLLC, Charlotte 704 343 2000
Recommended in Litigation

COWAN, Donald
Smith Moore, LLP, Raleigh
919 755 8700
Recommended in Litigation

DAGENHART, Larry
Helms Mulliss & Wicker PLLC, Charlotte 704 343 2000
Recommended in Corporate/M&A

DAVIS, Jeffrey
Moore & Van Allen, PLLC, Charlotte
704 331 1000
Recommended in Litigation

DAVIS, William
Bell Davis & Pitt, Winston-Salem
336 722 3700
Recommended in Litigation

DAVIS, William Allison
Womble Carlyle Sandridge & Rice PLLC, Winston-Salem 336 721 3600
Recommended in Corporate/M&A

DONADIO, Donald
Womble Carlyle Sandridge & Rice PLLC, Raleigh 919 755 2100
Recommended in Real Estate

DORTON, David
Maupin Taylor & Ellis, P.A., Raleigh
919 981 4000
Recommended in Real Estate

DOYLE, John
Constangy, Brooks & Smith, LLC, Winston-Salem 336 721 1001
Recommended in Employment

DUBOSE, Buddy
Kennedy Covington Lobdell & Hickman, L.L.P., Charlotte 704 331 7400
Recommended in Real Estate

DUNN, Thomas
Moore & Van Allen, PLLC, Raleigh
919 821 6200
Recommended in Banking & Finance

ELLIOT, Robert
Elliot Pishko Morgan, Winston-Salem
336 724 2828
Recommended in Employment

ERWIN, Martin
Smith Moore, LLP, Greensboro
336 378 5200
Recommended in Employment

FARR, Thomas
Maupin Taylor & Ellis, P.A., Raleigh
919 981 4013
tfarr@maupintaylor.com
Recommended in Employment
Specialization: Practice includes employment discrimination and civil rights litigation; voting rights and constitutional law; labor and employment law; occupational safety and health law. Chair of firm's Labor and Employment Practice Group (which consists of 14 attorneys).
Prof. Memberships: Former Member, Board of Directors, Capital Area Soccer League (CASL), a Raleigh-based youth soccer league with nearly 12,000 registered players. 1995-2001; Former Mem-

ber, Board of Directors of Junior Achievement of Eastern North Carolina, Inc; Former Member of the North Carolina National Federation of Independent Business Guardian Advisory Council; Member of the State Bars of Georgia (1979), Virginia (1980), and North Carolina (1983). The American Bar Association - Member of Litigation and Employment Law Sections; The North Carolina Bar Association - Member of Litigation and Employment Law Sections; The Philadelphia Society - Member; The Federalist Society - Member.
Career: The law firm of *Maupin Taylor & Ellis*, PA, Shareholder, January 1987 to present. Associate, November 1983 to December of 1986. Legal Counsel, North Carolina Republican Party, July 1999 to November of 2001. Chair of Magistrate Judge Merit Selection Committee for United States District Court for the Eastern District of North Carolina, May-June 1999. Permanent Member of Fourth Circuit Judicial Conference as of June 1999. United States Federal Service Impasses Panel, Washington, DC; Member, September 15, 1983 to January 1990. The Panel consists of seven Presidential appointees and is responsible for resolving federal sector collective bargaining impasses. North Carolina State Board of Elections, Raleigh, North Carolina; Member, August 1986 through October 1987. Wake County Board of Elections, Raleigh, North Carolina; Member, June 1985 to August 1986. Law Clerk for the Honorable Frank W Bullock, Jr, United States District Judge for the Middle District of North Carolina; January 1983 to November 1983. United States Office of Personnel Management, Washington, DC. Attorney advisor/special assistant to the General Counsel, August 1982 to

NORTH CAROLINA

LEADERS

December 1982. United States Senate Committee on Labor and Human Resources; Washington, DC; Labor Committee Counsel to Senator John P East, RNC; February 1981 to July 1982. National Right to Work Legal Defense Foundation, Springfield, Virginia; Staff Attorney; August 1979 to January 1981. Areas of practice: Represented employees in litigation involving issues related to freedom of speech, freedom of association, and other First Amendment rights. Court admissions: United States Supreme Court; Supreme Courts of North Carolina, Georgia, and Virginia; United States District Courts for the Eastern, Middle, and Western Districts of North Carolina; United States Courts of Appeal for the Fourth and Sixth Circuits.
Publications: 'Legal Focus: Employment' (regular column in 'Triangle Business Journal' from January 1998 to 2000); 'Employment Law Notebook' (regular column in the 'Campbell Law Observer' from June 1990 until November 1998). 'Unfair and Deceptive Legislation: The Case for Finding North Carolina General Statutes 75-1.1 Unconstitutionally Vague as Applied to an Alleged Breach of a Commercial Contract', Campbell L Rev 421 (1986).
Personal: Georgetown University Law Center, Washington, DC; LLM, Labor Law, 1983; Emory University School of Law; Atlanta, Georgia; JD, 1979; Hillsdale College, Hillsdale, Michigan; BLS 1976; co-salutatorian, summa cum laude.

FISHER, Stewart
Glenn Mills & Fisher, Durham
919 683 2135
Recommended in Employment

FLINT, Henry
Kennedy Covington Lobdell & Hickman, L.L.P., Charlotte 704 331 7400
Recommended in Banking & Finance, Corporate/M&A

FULTON, Charles
Manning Fulton & Skinner, Raleigh
919 787 8880
Recommended in Real Estate

GREENE, Kenneth
Carruthers & Roth, Greensboro
336 273 8651
Recommended in Banking & Finance

GRESHAM, John
Ferguson Stein Chambers Wallaas Adkins Gresham & Sumter, Charlotte
704 375 8461
Recommended in Employment

HARDYMON, Glen
Kennedy Covington Lobdell & Hickman, L.L.P., Charlotte 704 331 7400
Recommended in Real Estate

HARKAVY, Jonathan
Patterson Harkavy & Lawrence, Raleigh
919 755 1812
Recommended in Employment

HAZLETT, Richard
Helms Mulliss & Wicker PLLC, Charlotte
704 343 2000
Recommended in Banking & Finance

HOPE, Stephen
Moore & Van Allen, PLLC, Raleigh
919 821 6200
Recommended in Corporate/M&A

HOVIS, James
Moore & Van Allen, PLLC, Raleigh
919 821 6200
Recommended in Banking & Finance

JAMES, David
Smith James Rowlett & Cohen, Greensboro 336 274 2992
Recommended in Employment

JERNIGAN, John
Smith, Anderson, Blount, Dorsett, Mitchell & Jernigan, L.L.P., Raleigh
919 821 1220
Recommended in Corporate/M&A

KUPEC, Christopher
Moore & Van Allen, PLLC, Raleigh
919 821 6200
Recommended in Banking & Finance

LASSITER, Donnell
Kennedy Covington Lobdell & Hickman, L.L.P., Charlotte 704 331 7400
Recommended in Banking & Finance

LAWRENCE, Melinda
Patterson Harkavy & Lawrence, Raleigh
919 755 1812
Recommended in Employment

LEON, Christopher
Womble Carlyle Sandridge & Rice PLLC, Winston-Salem 336 721 3600
Recommended in Banking & Finance

LESESNE, Louis
Lesesne & Connette, Charlotte
704 372 5700
Recommended in Employment

LOFTIS, Randolph
Constangy, Brooks & Smith, LLC, Winston-Salem 336 721 1001
Recommended in Employment

MASON, Steven
Smith, Anderson, Blount, Dorsett, Mitchell & Jernigan, L.L.P., Raleigh
919 821 1220
Recommended in Real Estate

MCGINN, Daniel
Brooks, Pierce, McLendon, Humphrey & Leonard, L.L.P., Greensboro
336 373 8850
Recommended in Employment

MCKEITHEN, Malloy
Helms Mulliss & Wicker PLLC, Charlotte
704 343 2000
Recommended in Banking & Finance

MCKEITHEN, Ward
Robinson, Bradshaw & Hinson, P.A., Charlotte 704 377 2536
Recommended in Litigation

MCLOUGHLIN, James
Moore & Van Allen, PLLC, Charlotte
704 331 1000
Recommended in Litigation

MELVIN, Charles
Smith Moore, LLP, Greensboro
336 378 5200
Recommended in Real Estate

MERRITT, Mark
Robinson, Bradshaw & Hinson, P.A., Charlotte 704 377 2536
Recommended in Litigation

MORGAN, Griffin
Elliot Pishko Morgan, Winston-Salem
336 724 2828
Recommended in Employment

MOSER, Kenneth
Womble Carlyle Sandridge & Rice PLLC, Winston-Salem 336 721 3600
Recommended in Banking & Finance

OATES, Christopher
Moore & Van Allen, PLLC, Charlotte
704 331 1000
Recommended in Real Estate

OKUN, Michael
Patterson Harkavy & Lawrence, Raleigh
919 755 1812
Recommended in Employment

OLIVER, Samuel
Manning Fulton & Skinner, Raleigh
919 787 8880
Recommended in Real Estate

PAYNE, Travis
Edelstein & Payne, Raleigh
919 828 1456
Recommended in Employment

PISHKO, David
Elliot Pishko Morgan, Winston-Salem
336 724 2828
Recommended in Employment

PRICHARD, Allen
Kennedy Covington Lobdell & Hickman, L.L.P., Charlotte 704 331 7400
Recommended in Real Estate

PRUDEN, Northfleet
Kennedy Covington Lobdell & Hickman, L.L.P., Charlotte 704 331 7400
Recommended in Corporate/M&A

PRYOR, Robert
Helms Mulliss & Wicker PLLC, Charlotte
704 343 2000
Recommended in Banking & Finance

RAINEY, Richard
Womble Carlyle Sandridge & Rice PLLC, Charlotte 704 331 4900
Recommended in Employment

RAPER, William
Womble Carlyle Sandridge & Rice PLLC, Charlotte 704 331 4900
Recommended in Litigation

ROBINSON, Russell
Robinson, Bradshaw & Hinson, P.A., Charlotte 704 377 2536
Recommended in Corporate/M&A

SITTON, Larry
Smith Moore, LLP, Greensboro
336 378 5200
Recommended in Litigation

SMITH, Norman
Smith James Rowlett & Cohen, Greensboro 336 274 2992
Recommended in Employment

SPEARMAN, Robert
Parker, Poe, Adams & Bernstein LLP, Raleigh 919 828 0564
Recommended in Litigation

SUMTER, Geraldine
Ferguson Stein Chambers Wallaas Adkins Gresham & Sumter, Charlotte
704 375 8461
Recommended in Employment

TAYLOR, Daniel
Kilpatrick Stockton LLP, Winston-Salem
336 607 7300
Recommended in Litigation

TIPPS, Maynard
Kennedy Covington Lobdell & Hickman, L.L.P., Charlotte 704 331 7400
Recommended in Real Estate

TORSTRICK, Brent
Robinson, Bradshaw & Hinson, P.A., Charlotte 704 377 2536
Recommended in Real Estate

VAN HOY, Philip
Van Hoy Reutlinger Adams & Dunn, Charlotte 704 375 6022
Recommended in Employment

VAUGHAN, Keith
Womble Carlyle Sandridge & Rice PLLC, Winston-Salem 336 721 3600
Recommended in Litigation

WARD, Frank
Maupin Taylor & Ellis, P.A., Raleigh
919 981 4000
Recommended in Employment

WESTER, John
Robinson, Bradshaw & Hinson, P.A., Charlotte 704 377 2536
Recommended in Litigation

WILLIAMS, Jim
Brooks, Pierce, McLendon, Humphrey & Leonard, L.L.P., Greensboro
336 373 8850
Recommended in Litigation

WINSLOW, Edward
Brooks, Pierce, McLendon, Humphrey & Leonard, L.L.P., Greensboro
336 373 8850
Recommended in Corporate/M&A

WREN, Elizabeth
Kilpatrick Stockton LLP, Charlotte
704 338 5000
Recommended in Corporate/M&A

NORTH DAKOTA

CORPORATE/M&A

CONTENTS: Corporate/M&A p.554; Employment: Mainly Plaintiff p.555; Mainly Defendant p.555; Litigation: General Commercial p.555; Real Estate p.556; Individuals' Profiles p.557.

NORTH DAKOTA'S TOP THREE
1. Vogel, Weir, Hunke & McCormick
2. Serkland Law Firm
3. Pearson Christensen

Ranking based on Chambers' research within the state.

All quotes in the text are from interviews with clients and competitors.

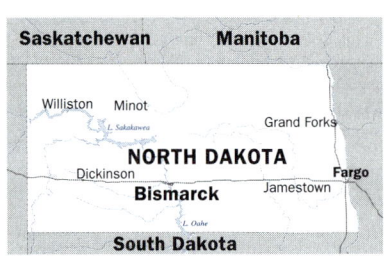

OVERVIEW: Top-ranking **Vogel, Weir, Hunke & McCormick** is one of the larger firms in the state, and boasts a long-standing reputation for fielding the best corporate department in North Dakota. Corporate lawyer Jon Brakke is highly valued for his work in banking and agricultural lending, acting for clients such as FCC National Bank and the Farm Credit Bank of St Paul. The firm is also endorsed for its strength in real estate work and litigation. Ingersoll-Rand, MeritCare Medical Group and Auto-Owners Insurance are clients.

Serkland Law Firm, in second place, enjoys a statewide reputation for excellence in litigation and corporate work. The firm's client base comes from the healthcare, insurance and finance sectors. Commercial litigator Ronald McLean is singled out for personal injury defense and his representation of corporate clients. Clients include Liberty Mutual, State Bank of Fargo and Cenex Harvest States.

Pearson Christensen has key strengths in litigation and corporate work. The firm's business practice acts for numerous insurance companies, while the litigation department has a high standing among municipal authorities. Commentators describe corporate lawyer Douglas Christensen as a tenacious negotiator, while trial lawyer Ronald Fischer is well regarded for his courtroom style. American Universal Insurance, CAN Insurance Companies and the City of Grand Forks figure in the firm's client roster.

CORPORATE/M&A

NORTH DAKOTA
Leading firms (Corporate/M&A)
1. **SERKLAND LAW FIRM PC** *Fargo*
   VOGEL, WEIR, HUNKE & MCCORMICK LTD *Fargo*
2. **CONMY FESTE LTD** *Fargo*
   PEARSON CHRISTENSEN LLP *Grand Forks*
   ZIMNEY, FOSTER, JOHNSON, DITTUS *Grand Forks*

Leading individuals (Corporate/M&A)
1. **BRAKKE Jon** *Vogel, Weir, Hunke & McCormick, Fargo*
   FOSTER John *Zimney, Foster, Johnson, Grand Forks*
   OLSON Richard *Olson Burns Lee PC, Minot*
2. **CHRISTENSEN Douglas** *Pearson Christensen, Grand Forks*
   MINCH Roger *Serkland Law Firm PC, Fargo*
   SINCLAIR Brad *Serkland Law Firm PC, Fargo*
   THOMAS Michael *Conmy Feste Ltd, Fargo*
3. **BOTTRELL Lowell** *Anderson & Bottrell, Fargo*
   JOHNSON Steven *Vogel, Weir, Hunke, Fargo*
   SCHLOSSMAN William *Vogel, Weir, Hunke, Fargo*
   SMITH Sean *Tschider & Smith, Bismarck*

Firms and individuals are listed alphabetically in each band.

Serkland Law Firm PC
The Firm: A well-established firm in Fargo and one of the oldest in North Dakota, it has a reputation in the market for *"excellence"* in loan workouts and bankruptcies. Attorneys here received enthusiastic commendation from the market for their ability to *"get the job done."* The ten-lawyer team focuses on banking, corporate law and creditors' rights.
The Lawyers: Clients endorse **Roger Minch** for his *"thoroughness, timeliness and knowledge"* in bankruptcy and loan collections. Sources also referred to **Brad Sinclair**'s expertise on creditor issues.
The Clients: Town & Country Credit Union; Bremer Bank; State Bank of Fargo and Union State Bank Fargo.

Vogel, Weir, Hunke & McCormick Ltd
The Firm: One of the larger firms in the state, it is home to a business and commercial transactions practice that is widely considered to provide a *"top-quality"* service to clients. About nine attorneys concentrate on all aspects of commercial transactions and securities, bankruptcy and banking law.
The Lawyers: **Jon Brakke** stands at the head of the pack, acknowledged by the market as *"one of the best banking and corporate lawyers in the state."* Interviewees admire both his *"intelligence"* and his *"tough"* banking and bankruptcy representation and litigation skills. He also received accolades for his expertise in the farm credit services arena. **Steve Johnson** chairs the firm's business practice and has an *"excellent statewide reputation"* in corporate law and debtor collections work. **William Schlossman** also elicited praise for his family business law expertise and for his handling of company restructurings.
The Clients: National Sun Industries; Farm Credit Bank of St Paul; FCC National Bank; West Acres Development; ND Automobile Club; Cass County Electric Cooperative and Amity Technology.

Conmy Feste Ltd
The Firm: The seven-lawyer team here has a strong reputation in corporate transactional work. The group's strengths derive from the firm's business practice focused on banking and creditor bankruptcy.
The Lawyers: Interviewees considered **Michael Thomas** to be *"a first-rate creditor bankruptcy attorney."* He has a broad range of experience, including advising banks on loans and drafting loan agreement collaterals.
The Clients: Community First Bank, Wells Fargo and Bremer Bank are clients.

Pearson Christensen LLP
The Firm: This full-service law firm in Grand Forks offers a wide range of expertise in complex commercial and financial transactions. Its client base includes a host of insurance companies, retailers and manufacturers.
The Lawyers: **Douglas Christensen** is the firm's long-standing corporate lawyer. Peers recognize him as an *"tenacious negotiator"* in defending his client's commercial and financial interests. His practice places great emphasis on the insurance industry.
The Clients: American Universal Insurance; Austin Mutual Insurance; Auto-Owners Insurance; Certified Claims Corporation; CNA Insurance Companies; Continental Western Insurance; Dakota Fire Insurance Company and EMC Insurance Companies.

Zimney, Foster, Johnson, Dittus & Flaten, Chartered
The Firm: This nine-member law firm has achieved *"statewide respect"* for its corporate/commercial and banking work. Commentators highlighted the practice's aptitude in creditors' rights, banking regulations and loan agreements. The team also handles commercial paper and secured transactions.
The Lawyers: **John Foster** garners the admiration of peers and clients alike for his general banking and secured transaction work. He was dubbed the *"leading credit union specialist in the state."* Foster is also experienced in loan documentation and business foreclosures.
The Clients: Bremer Bank, Alerus Financial and US Bancorp are clients.

NORTH DAKOTA

EMPLOYMENT & LABOR LAW

Other Notable Practitioners

Lowell Bottrell of Anderson & Bottrell is commended for his work in commercial collections. He represents numerous banks and large machinery companies, and is involved in plant patent licensing in the agriculture sector. **Sean Smith** from Tschider & Smith is a respected Bismarck corporate and tax attorney, with healthcare and business litigation experience. At Olson Burns Lee PC in Minot, **Richard Olson** is recognized by peers as *"one of the leading commercial transactions and bankruptcy lawyers in the region."*

EMPLOYMENT & LABOR LAW — MAINLY PLAINTIFF

NORTH DAKOTA
Leading firms
(Employment: Mainly Plaintiff)
1. NILLES, HANSEN & DAVIES LTD *Fargo*

Leading individuals
(Employment: Mainly Plaintiff)
1. MONSON Patricia *Nilles, Hansen & Davies Ltd, Fargo*

Firms and individuals are listed alphabetically in each band.

Nilles, Hansen & Davies Ltd

The Firm: The six-lawyer employment law practice here handles both employer and employee court trials. The group's standing is boosted by the support of the firm's litigation department, which is considered to be *"one of the largest in the state."*

The Lawyers: The market recommends **Patricia Monson**, cochair of the firm's employment law group, for her employment litigation skills, predominantly representing the employee.

EMPLOYMENT & LABOR LAW — MAINLY DEFENDANT

NORTH DAKOTA
Leading firms
(Employment: Mainly Defendant)
1. DORSEY & WHITNEY LLP *Fargo*
2. ZUGER KIRMIS & SMITH *Bismarck*

Leading individuals
(Employment: Mainly Defendant)
1. HERMAN Sarah *Dorsey & Whitney LLP, Fargo*
2. WARD Patrick *Zuger Kirmis & Smith, Bismarck*

Firms and individuals are listed alphabetically in each band.

Dorsey & Whitney LLP

The Firm: This long-established firm with a national reputation has recently opened a 15-attorney office in Fargo. The three-member labor and employment group here is applauded by interviewees for its *"high-quality work."*

The Lawyers: The center of gravity in this group is managing partner **Sarah Herman**. She is considered to be the *"preeminent"* specialist in collective bargaining and arbitration defense in the state. Clients appreciate her *"empathy, ability to listen and problem-solving skills,"* and peers refer to her *"breadth of knowledge"* of traditional labor law and related employment matters.

The Clients: Blue Cross Blue Shield of North Dakota, Montana Dakota Utilities Resource Group and The JM Smucker Company are clients.

Zuger Kirmis & Smith

The Firm: Rivals acknowledge that this firm's strong employment profile is due to its *"dedicated"* group of attorneys. The employment practice sits under the umbrella of the firm's 13-member litigation group, and has an emphasis on labor and employment litigation, representing the employer.

The Lawyers: **Patrick Ward** has a long track record in handling insurance defense, but market sources also noted his *"burgeoning"* labor and employment litigation work.

The Clients: Great Western Insurance, Grinnell Mutual Reinsurance and Great West Casualty Company feature as clients.

LITIGATION — GENERAL COMMERCIAL

NORTH DAKOTA
Leading firms
(Litigation: General Commercial)
1. NILLES, HANSEN & DAVIES LTD *Fargo*
   SERKLAND LAW FIRM PC *Fargo*
   ZUGER KIRMIS & SMITH *Bismarck*
2. GUNHUS, GRINNELL, KLINGER, SWENSON *Fargo*
   PEARSON CHRISTENSEN LLP *Grand Forks*
   VOGEL, WEIR, HUNKE & McCORMICK LTD *Fargo*

Firms are listed alphabetically in each band.

Nilles, Hansen & Davies Ltd

The Firm: The market acknowledges that this firm produces *"first-class litigators."* The high-caliber 16-lawyer team has largely contributed to the firm's *"top-notch"* reputation in the state. It is a leading force for railroad law, products liability and insurance defense work, representing corporate interests. Clients are also attracted to the related practice strengths that this full-service firm – one of the largest in the state – can provide.

The Lawyers: Leading insurance defense attorney **Duane Ilvedson** is deemed by peers to be an *"excellent trial lawyer"* and *"knowledgeable of the law."* **Richard Henderson** garnered praise for his *"attention to detail"* and *"clear understanding of the issues at stake"* in a court case. **Stephen Plambeck** is also included in the *Chambers'* tables following enthusiastic recommendations for his *"high skills"* *"* as a railroad and products liability litigator.

The Clients: Burlington Northern & Sante Fe Railway; Canadian Pacific Railway; Travelers; DaimlerChrysler and Altru Health System.

Serkland Law Firm PC

The Firm: According to clients and competitors, the firm's lawyers have earned themselves a reputation for both *"high-quality advice"* and for providing *"a broad range of experience"* in litigious matters. This ten-lawyer Fargo firm has a diverse client base, typically acting for finance, healthcare and insurance companies across the state.

The Lawyers: Much of the firm's commercial litigation profile centers on **Ronald McLean**, who receives accolades for his *"common sense and intelligence"* and *"tenacity"* in a courtroom. In addition to personal injury defense work, McLean represents corporate clients such as limited partnerships and stockholders.

NORTH DAKOTA   LITIGATION

NORTH DAKOTA
Leading individuals
(Litigation: General Commercial)

1
- **CARLSON Bruce** *McNair, Larson & Carlson Ltd*, Fargo
- **HILL James** *Zuger Kirmis & Smith*, Bismarck
- **MARING David** *Maring Williams Law Office PC*, Fargo
- **MCLEAN Ronald** *Serkland Law Firm PC*, Fargo

2
- **FISCHER Ronald** *Pearson Christensen*, Grand Forks
- **ILVEDSON Duane** *Nilles, Hansen & Davies Ltd*, Fargo
- **KIRMIS Lyle** *Zuger Kirmis & Smith*, Bismarck
- **KLINGER Edward** *Gunhus, Grinnell, Klinger*, Fargo
- **THIEM Rebecca** *Zuger Kirmis & Smith*, Bismarck

3
- **CAMPBELL Craig** *Gunhus, Grinnell, Klinger*, Fargo
- **DURICK Patrick** *Pearce & Durick*, Bismarck
- **HENDERSON Richard** *Nilles, Hansen & Davies*, Fargo
- **MILLER Charles** *Fleck, Mather & Strutz*, Bismarck
- **PLAMBECK Stephen** *Nilles, Hansen & Davies*, Fargo
- **WEIR Patrick** *Vogel, Weir, Hunke & McCormick*, Fargo

Individuals are listed alphabetically in each band.

The Clients: Liberty Mutual; Cenex Harvest States and Ingersoll-Rand are leading clients.

Zuger Kirmis & Smith

The Firm: Market commentators highlight this Bismarck firm's *"strong aptitude"* for litigation, noting that it boasts an *"excellent statewide reputation"* in commercial litigation matters. The litigation practice mainly handles corporate, insurance and products liability work, and its 13 lawyers benefit from the support of a full-service firm.

The Lawyers: A high-profile name in the firm is **James Hill**, who interviewees commended for his *"intelligence, eloquence and passionate advocacy for clients."* Hill has experience in both railroad and professional liability law. **Rebecca Thiem** also won sustained plaudits for her *"outstanding"* litigation work. Rivals recognize her *"thoroughness"* and *"integrity"* in a courtroom. Managing partner **Lyle Kirmis** also boosts the standing of the firm with his long-established reputation in commercial litigation.

The Clients: Great West Casualty; Attorneys Liability Protection Society; Burlington Northern & Sante Fe Railway; Westfield Group; St. Paul; Mor-Gran-Sou Electric Cooperative; Dan's Supermarket and Prime Cities Broadcasting.

Gunhus, Grinnell, Klinger, Swenson & Guy Ltd

The Firm: A seasoned litigation player in Fargo, this firm has earned itself a reputation as a leader in the market. The 12-attorney firm represents a wide variety of clients in retail, healthcare and regional construction matters, and in multiparty and mass tort litigation including products liability, insurance coverage and employment disputes.

The Lawyers: Interviewees singled out **Ed Klinger** for his commercial and business litigation expertise and *"aggressive"* negotiation skills. **Craig Campbell** has also carved out a market niche in commercial litigation and construction law.

The Clients: Blue Cross Blue Shield of North Dakota; Simmons Lumber; Farmers Insurance Group; Butler Machinery Company and Concordia College.

Pearson Christensen LLP

The Firm: Winning a following across North Dakota, this Grand Forks firm impresses with its *"burgeoning"* litigation practice. The firm is respected as a *"sound option"* for insurance defense work, tax litigation and complex commercial litigation.

The Lawyers: Rivals point to **Ronald Fischer** as a leading light. His *"breadth of knowledge"* and *"ability to relate to jurors"* are contributing factors to the firm's growing reputation in litigation. He also advises many municipalities and specializes in political district subdivisions work.

The Clients: The Cities of Grand Forks and Devils Lake are clients.

Vogel, Weir, Hunke & McCormick Ltd

The Firm: This long-established full-service firm is one of the bigger firms in the state, and is recognized as having a *"proven track record"* in litigation. Clients endorse its attorneys for their *"experience"* and *"knowledge"* in handling a range of disputes.

The Lawyers: Interviewees identified well-respected **Pat Weir** as a *"top-flight"* attorney in medical malpractice defense work. He represents numerous insurance companies and medical institutions.

The Clients: MeritCare Medical Group; CNA Insurance Companies; Dakota Clinic and Auto-Owners Insurance.

Other Notable Practitioners

Heralded by peers as *"one of the most effective business litigators in the state,"* **Bruce Carlson** of McNair, Larson & Carlson Ltd in Fargo divides his practice between insurance defense and stockholder disputes with a special emphasis on agricultural issues. His clients include financial institutions and insurance companies such as Farmland Mutual Insurance. Clients confer *"high praise"* on **David Maring** of Fargo-based Maring Williams Law Office PC for his *"sharp mind"* and his *"ability to communicate clearly in front of a jury."* He is active in commercial litigation and personal injury work, for both plaintiffs and defendants. Maring's clients include First National Bank of Lincolnwood and Catholic Mutual Group, and he also represents lawyers through the Attorneys Liability Protection Society in professional liability cases. In Bismarck, **Pat Durick** of Pearce & Durick is admired by peers for the *"top-notch"* quality of his litigation work. He handles products liability, corporate and insurance defense for such clients as Emerson Electric, utilities, banks and insurance companies (Travelers and Zurich North America). *"A mover and a shaker"* on the Bismarck litigation scene is **Charles Miller** of Fleck, Mather & Strutz Ltd. He has earned the respect of market commentators for his insurance defense, construction and water drainage work on behalf of defendants. Miller works with clients as diverse as the North Dakota Insurance Reserve Fund and the Basin Electric Power Cooperative.

REAL ESTATE

NORTH DAKOTA
Leading firms (Real Estate)

1
- **NILLES, HANSEN & DAVIES LTD** Fargo

2
- **CONMY FESTE LTD** Fargo
- **OHNSTAD TWICHELL PC** Fargo
- **VOGEL, WEIR, HUNKE & MCCORMICK LTD** Fargo

Firms are listed alphabetically in each band.

Nilles, Hansen & Davies Ltd

The Firm: This five-lawyer real estate group handles all types of real estate transactions, including residential and commercial contracts and leases. The team's forte is in title insurance issuance for both residential and commercial projects, an activity that is heavily focused on the Fargo-Moorhead-West Fargo metropolitan area.

The Lawyers: Market commentators denoted group leader **Robert Stroup** as the *"preeminent"* real estate title insurance specialist in the state. He has extensive experience working on commercial transactions on behalf of financial institutions and developers.

The Clients: Bank of America; US Bancorp; Wells Fargo and Olaf Anderson & Son Construction.

Conmy Feste Ltd

The Firm: An eight-attorney firm with a strong emphasis on banking and commercial transactions is home to a *"thriving"* real estate practice. Attorneys here handle general business

REAL ESTATE

NORTH DAKOTA

NORTH DAKOTA
Leading individuals (Real Estate)

1 HUBBARD Paul *Conmy Feste Ltd*, Fargo
STROUP Robert *Nilles, Hansen & Davies Ltd*, Fargo
2 JOHNSON Philip *Wold Johnson PC*, Fargo
SHAFT Grant *Shaft, Reis & Shaft Ltd*, Grand Forks
3 BUEIDE Daniel *Vogel, Weir, Hunke & McCormick*, Fargo
RINDY Dean *Ohnstad Twichell PC*, Fargo

Individuals are listed alphabetically in each band.

foreclosures, commercial real estate transactions and title insurance.
The Lawyers: The mainstay of the real estate group is **Paul Hubbard**, *"one of the most respected real estate lawyers in the state."* Rivals recognize his *"intelligence"* in commercial development transactions.
The Clients: Bremer Bank, Western State Bank and Wells Fargo Mortgages are clients.

Ohnstad Twichell PC
The Firm: Sources considered this 17-attorney firm, based in West Fargo, to be a growing regional presence, with a *"breadth of experience"* in transactions that range from leasing and zoning to foreclosures, and the purchase and sale of real property.
The Lawyers: Peers applaud **Dean Rindy** for his specialty in residential refinancing and construction law. His practice expertise reflects the growing West Fargo property construction market.
The Clients: Gate City Savings Bank and Alerus Finance are clients.

Vogel, Weir, Hunke & McCormick Ltd
The Firm: A long-established commercial player in the state, the firm fields an eight-strong real estate team that benefits from the support of a *"vigorous"* business and banking practice. Attorneys here are highly rated for their land use and development expertise by Fargo commercial and residential developers.
The Lawyers: **Daniel Bueide** wins praise for his *"professionalism"* and *"attention to detail"* in commercial real estate transactions. He specializes in zoning work for investors on land use projects.
The Clients: West Acres Development; Microsoft; Matrix Properties; Ingersoll-Rand and Forum Communications Company.

Other Notable Practitioners
Philip Johnson of Wold Johnson PC is a respected Fargo-Moorhead real estate attorney who works with lenders and developers on commercial management partnerships. His client base comprises some of the leading financial institutions in the state.
In Grand Forks, **Grant Shaft** of Shaft, Reis & Shaft Ltd received strong commendation for his skills on the development side of real estate He works with large tract developers on areas involving commercial retail, strip malls and leasehold interests. He also advises local developers on residential, multi-family projects.

Leaders in North Dakota

BOTTRELL, Lowell
Anderson & Bottrell, Fargo 701 235 3300
Recommended in Corporate/M&A

BRAKKE, Jon
Vogel, Weir, Hunke & McCormick, Ltd., Fargo 701 237 6983
Recommended in Corporate/M&A

BUEIDE, Daniel
Vogel, Weir, Hunke & McCormick, Ltd., Fargo 701 237 6983
Recommended in Real Estate

CAMPBELL, Craig
Gunhus, Grinnell, Klinger, Swenson & Guy, Ltd., Fargo 701 235 2506
Recommended in Litigation

CARLSON, Bruce
McNair, Larson & Carlson Ltd, Fargo 701 293 9190
Recommended in Litigation

CHRISTENSEN, Douglas
Pearson Christensen LLP, Grand Forks 701 775 0521
Recommended in Corporate/M&A

DURICK, Patrick
Pearce & Durick, Bismarck 701 223 2890
Recommended in Litigation

FISCHER, Ronald
Pearson Christensen LLP, Grand Forks 701 775 0521
Recommended in Litigation

FOSTER, John
Zimney, Foster, Johnson, Dittus & Flaten, Chartered, Grand Forks 701 772 8111
Recommended in Corporate/M&A

HENDERSON, Richard
Nilles, Hansen & Davies, Ltd., Fargo 701 237 5544
Recommended in Litigation

HERMAN, Sarah Andrews
Dorsey & Whitney LLP, Fargo 701 235 6000
Recommended in Employment

HILL, James
Zuger Kirmis & Smith, Bismarck 701 223 2711
Recommended in Litigation

HUBBARD, Paul
Conmy Feste Ltd, Fargo 701 293 9911
Recommended in Real Estate

ILVEDSON, Duane
Nilles, Hansen & Davies, Ltd., Fargo 701 237 5544
Recommended in Litigation

JOHNSON, Philip
Wold Johnson PC, Fargo 701 235 5515
Recommended in Real Estate

JOHNSON, Steven
Vogel, Weir, Hunke & McCormick, Ltd., Fargo 701 237 6983
Recommended in Corporate/M&A

KIRMIS, Lyle
Zuger Kirmis & Smith, Bismarck 701 223 2711
Recommended in Litigation

KLINGER, Edward
Gunhus, Grinnell, Klinger, Swenson & Guy, Ltd., Fargo 701 235 2506
Recommended in Litigation

MARING, David
Maring Williams Law Office PC, Fargo 701 241 4141
Recommended in Litigation

MCLEAN, Ronald
Serkland Law Firm, PC, Fargo 701 232 8957
Recommended in Litigation

MILLER, Charles
Fleck, Mather & Strutz, Ltd., Bismarck 701 223 6585
Recommended in Litigation

MINCH, Roger
Serkland Law Firm, PC, Fargo 701 232 8957
Recommended in Corporate/M&A

MONSON, Patricia
Nilles, Hansen & Davies, Ltd., Fargo 701 237 5544
Recommended in Employment

OLSON, Richard
Olson Burns Lee PC, Minot 701 839 1740
Recommended in Corporate/M&A

PLAMBECK, Stephen
Nilles, Hansen & Davies, Ltd., Fargo 701 237 5544
Recommended in Litigation

RINDY, Dean
Ohnstad Twichell PC, Fargo 701 282 3249
Recommended in Real Estate

SCHLOSSMAN, William
Vogel, Weir, Hunke & McCormick, Ltd., Fargo 701 237 6983
Recommended in Corporate/M&A

SHAFT, Grant
Shaft, Reis & Shaft Ltd, Grand Forks 701 772 8156
Recommended in Real Estate

SINCLAIR, Brad
Serkland Law Firm, PC, Fargo 701 232 8957
Recommended in Corporate/M&A

SMITH, Sean
Tschider & Smith, Bismarck 701 258 4000
Recommended in Corporate/M&A

STROUP, Robert
Nilles, Hansen & Davies, Ltd., Fargo 701 237 5544
Recommended in Real Estate

THIEM, Rebecca
Zuger Kirmis & Smith, Bismarck 701 223 2711
Recommended in Litigation

THOMAS, Michael
Conmy Feste Ltd, Fargo 701 293 9911
Recommended in Corporate/M&A

WARD, Patrick
Zuger Kirmis & Smith, Bismarck 701 223 2711
Recommended in Employment

WEIR, H Patrick
Vogel, Weir, Hunke & McCormick, Ltd., Fargo 701 237 6983
Recommended in Litigation

OHIO

OVERVIEW

CONTENTS: Banking & Finance p.558; Construction p.560; Corporate M&A p.562; Employment: Mainly Plaintiff p.564; Mainly Defendant p.654; Environment p.566; Intellectual Property p.568; Litigation: General Commercial p.569; Real Estate p.571; Individuals' Profiles p.573.

OHIO'S TOP FIVE
1. Jones Day
1. Squire, Sanders & Dempsey
2. Thompson Hine
3. Vorys, Sater, Seymour and Pease
4. Baker & Hostetler

Ranking based on Chambers' research within the state.

All quotes in the text are from interviews with clients and competitors.

OVERVIEW: A colossal firm boasting over 1600 lawyers worldwide, **Jones Day** commands an impressive global network of 25 offices. Given the concentration of headline attorneys within its original Cleveland office, it is perhaps unsurprising that the firm emerged in *Chambers'* research as the premier name in the state. It is in litigation that the firm bestrides the market with greatest effect. An enormous litigation group specializes in complex multi-jurisdictional commercial work, most notably in big-ticket products liability disputes. Few firms in the US can compete in staffing major cases with such a stellar array of uniformly impressive trial attorneys. The charismatic John Strauch, who coordinates the firm's national litigation practice, was singled out for his extensive experience in all manner of complex litigation. Bob Weber, the attorney of choice for key client RJ Reynolds, chairs the group's products liability practice. His prowess has lead some to identify him as the firm's brightest star. The firm's litigation proficiency is also in evidence in contentious IP work. Commentators perceived attorneys here to have noteworthy strength in complex technological patent cases. Kenneth Adamo, identified as the cornerstone of the group, maintains a national profile for high-end IP litigation. In noncontentious work, the firm also boasts top-tier practices in the core areas of banking and corporate/M&A. In the former, the highly respected Rachel Rawson coordinates the commercial lending practice in Cleveland. The young and dynamic corporate practice in Cleveland coordinates with colleagues elsewhere in the network to advise large multinationals and Fortune 500 companies on the full range of corporate matters. Considered to excel in high-end M&A, the firm boasts a fine technical lawyer in David Porter and a leading rainmaker in Lyle Ganske.

In joint first place, Cleveland-based **Squire, Sanders & Dempsey** is also a major international law firm with over 750 attorneys spread across 26 offices around the globe. While the firm enjoys a preeminent national profile for its leading bond counsel practice in public financings, its work across the board reflects the firm's roots in the industrial heartlands of Ohio and the Midwest. Under the leadership of the persuasive Tom Kilbane, attorneys from its litigation practice regularly appear in complex financial, industrial and environmental disputes around the country. In particular, Van Carson is said to be a favorite among steel companies involved in environmental disputes. In corporate/M&A, the firm is felt to have a firm grip on the local market through its three offices in Ohio, but is also known for its international work, particularly in Eastern Europe. Mary Ann Jorgenson leads the international business group and has a high profile in the industry. The firm also showed up advising clients in the insolvencies of both Enron and WorldCom. Elsewhere, Samuel Pearlman ensures the firm's significant profile in real estate.

Thompson Hine, with four offices in Ohio, ranks next. Known for its strong Midwestern focus, much of the firm's strengths derive from well-established ties to the local business community. The firm's trump card is undoubtedly its first-rate construction practice, which was identified by interviewees as a clear leader in the field. Jeff Applebaum is singled out as the premier construction lawyer in the state. The firm also has significant depth in its top-ranked real estate practice, where attorneys such as the technically excellent Linda Striefsky stand out. Environmental law is another major area of focus. Here the highly qualified Cleveland team benefits from the focus and vision of Michael Hardy, felt to be among the best environmental litigators in the state. A solid corporate team includes James Carlson, a leading Ohio expert in takeover defense, while the litigation practice features David Hooker, the firm's managing partner and a respected figure among the state's legal fraternity.

Traditional Midwestern firm **Vorys, Sater, Seymour and Pease** maintains a full-service practice that encompasses both commercial and private client work. It is generally acknowledged in the market as the leading law firm in Columbus. One of the firm's glittering names is real estate specialist Stephen Buchenroth, described by clients as bright, knowledgeable and experienced. The firm has a comprehensive practice in real estate transactions and financing, and attorneys here are lauded for their ability to handle anything that comes their way. Vorys Sater is also a regional heavyweight in environmental litigation; Richard Fahey and Scott Doran are standout names here. In banking, detail-oriented Melvin Bedree was appreciated for his commercial instincts. Given the sizable competition, the firm also has an impressive profile in commercial litigation, particularly toxic tort actions, and is often found acting for local insurance clients. David Cupps and his colleague Thomas Ridgley are highlighted names.

Baker & Hostetler's solid performance across a broad range of areas lifts it to a place among the leading firms in Ohio. Labor and employment is the strongest suit for the firm, and the firm secures its sole top-band ranking in this area. From its Cleveland base, attorneys Greg Mersol and Elliot Azoff regularly appear in class action cases across Ohio.

BANKING & FINANCE

Jones Day
see firm details p.823

The Firm: Occupying a *"unique position"* within the market, a top-ranking Ohio banking and finance practice benefits from the firm's extensive national and global resources. The firm is the largest headquartered in the state and maintains integrated practice groups across its 25 worldwide offices.

A *"multidisciplinary"* finance practice encompasses lending and structured finance, capital markets and public offerings, private equity and venture capital matters and works closely with the firm's strong bankruptcy department on refinancing and workout matters. Practitioners enjoy a national reputation for *"considerable expertise"* and *"high standards of quality."* The firm recently represented National City in the refinancing of OM Group and acted for JPMorgan in completing a new credit facility with Hawk Corporation.

The Lawyers: Rachel Rawson (see p.578) coordinates the commercial lending practice in the Cleveland office. Described by peers and clients as a *"young, dynamic"* attorney, Rawson *"knows the market well and gets quickly to the essentials."*

The Clients: National City Corporation; KeyCorp; JPMorgan; US Bank; Bank One; Primus Capital Group; Morgenthaler Venture Partners; Blue Chip Venture Company; Kirtland Capital Partners; Blue Point Capital Partners; Brittany Corporation and Lamson & Session.

BANKING & FINANCE — OHIO

OHIO
Leading firms (Banking & Finance)

1 JONES DAY *Cleveland*
SQUIRE, SANDERS & DEMPSEY LLP *Cleveland*
2 FROST BROWN TODD LLC *Cincinnati*
TAFT, STETTINIUS & HOLLISTER LLP *Cincinnati*
VORYS, SATER, SEYMOUR *Columbus*
3 CALFEE, HALTER & GRISWOLD LLP *Cleveland*
PORTER WRIGHT MORRIS & ARTHUR *Columbus*
THOMPSON HINE LLP *Cleveland*
4 BAKER & HOSTETLER LLP *Cleveland*
STATMAN, HARRIS, SIEGEL & EYRICH *Cincinnati*

Leading individuals (Banking & Finance)

1 BEDREE Melvin *Vorys, Sater, Seymour, Cincinnati*
RUSH Jeffery *Frost Brown Todd LLC, Cincinnati*
SCHLOEMER Jeffrey *Taft, Stettinius, Cincinnati*
2 GRADY Timothy *Porter Wright Morris, Columbus*
GUINN Guy *Calfee, Halter & Griswold LLP, Cleveland*
LERNER Stephen *Squire, Sanders, Cleveland*
MILLS Osborne *Squire, Sanders & Dempsey, Cleveland*
RAWSON Rachel *Jones Day, Cleveland*
3 MIRALDI Leslee *Thompson Hine LLP, Cleveland*
STATMAN Alan *Statman, Harris, Siegel, Cincinnati*

Firms and individuals are listed alphabetically in each band.

Squire, Sanders & Dempsey LLP

The Firm: A *"clear leader"* in the field, the firm has established strong connections within the local banking and finance community. Clients praise the group's *"long-standing commitment"* to the practice area. *"Highly qualified"* practitioners advise on both transactional and regulatory matters. The firm has developed particular expertise in relation to public finance, and is highly regarded for its advice on bonds and other capital-raising activities.

The Lawyers: Cincinnati-based **Stephen Lerner** enjoys a high profile among banking clients for his expertise in workouts and bankruptcy-related finance. *"Veteran attorney"* **Osborne Mills** possesses a broad-based practice, covering commercial and real estate lending, loan workouts and debtor/creditor issues.

The Clients: Town & Country Bank; Bank One; US Bank; JPMorgan Chase and Chevy Chase Bank.

Frost Brown Todd LLC

see firm details p.798

The Firm: The 2000 merger between Frost & Jacobs and Brown, Todd & Heyburn was felt to significantly enlarge the firm's capabilities in the area. The firm regularly represents regional and state banks, thrift holding companies, insurance companies and other financial institutions on banking and finance transactions and complex business litigation. The team recently acted for US Bank in Kentucky in closing a $14 million taxable bond transaction for a shopping center development and completed a $35 million sale and lease transaction for a major Cincinnati hospital.

The Lawyers: Distinguished by his *"remarkable rapport with clients,"* Cincinnati banking and finance attorney **Jeffrey Rush** (see p.578) was recommended for his *"responsive"* attitude and *"ability to explain difficult issues in lay terms."* Rush advised US Bank on a $37 million construction loan to a large regional developer in Minneapolis and acted for the borrower in a $1.2 billion credit facility for a major telecom company.

The Clients: PNC Bank; US Bank; KeyBank; Provident Bank; Western Southern Life Insurance Company; AIG Insurance Group; Central Bank & Trust Company and Liberty Mutual Insurance Group.

Taft, Stettinius & Hollister LLP

The Firm: This well-known Cincinnati firm earns plaudits for its work on public finance and lending transactions. The group advises extensively on bond matters, including state and federal tax aspects of bond financing. Attorneys advise both borrowers and lenders in a range of financial transactions, including commercial and asset-based loans, project finance, real estate lending and letters of credit issues.

The Lawyers: Said to have a *"good head on his shoulders,"* **Jeffrey Schloemer** regularly advises financial institutions and borrowers on cash flow and asset-based financings and equipment leases. Clients praised him as a *"thorough and effective"* attorney who *"understands how bankers think."*

The Clients: US Bank; Federal Home Loan Bank of Cincinnati; First National Bank; Fifth Third Bank; The Prudential Insurance Company of America; Chiquita Brands International and Cincinnati Stock Exchange.

Vorys, Sater, Seymour and Pease LLP

The Firm: An *"old-established Ohio presence,"* the firm boasts a varied client base of major financial institutions and Fortune 500 companies as well as individual investors from across the US. Rivals consider the group to be *"tough competition"* on transactional banking and finance matters. A large share of the group's workload derives from an active bankruptcy department. For example, the team served as cocounsel to Citibank in the Federated Department Stores bankruptcy. Attorneys handle a range of securities transactions and act as bond counsel to a number of public clients, including the Ohio Water Development Authority and the Children's Hospital of Columbus.

The Lawyers: Interviewees recommended *"detail-oriented"* **Melvin Bedree** for expertise in structured finance, asset-based lending and refinancing matters. Banking clients particularly appreciate his *"commercial instincts."*

The Clients: National City Bank; Fifth Third Bank; Provident Bank; US Bank; Bank One; Western Southern Life Insurance Company; Ohio League of Financial Institutions and The Ohio State University.

Calfee, Halter & Griswold LLP

The Firm: This *"excellent"* practice enjoys a strong following in northern Ohio, where it is visible representing a number of emerging and mid-market clients. Attorneys advise investment banks and capital funds on asset securitizations and large refinancings and restructurings in connection with corporate bankruptcies. Researchers were told of the firm's particular reputation in public offerings and public finance matters. Notable work in this domain includes advising on financing the expansion of the Cleveland Hopkins International Airport.

The Lawyers: Considered a *"senior attorney in the field,"* **Guy Guinn** specializes in commercial finance, with wide-ranging expertise in capital formation, lending and workouts.

The Clients: Bank of America; Bank One; US Bank National Association; KeyCorp and LaSalle Bank.

Porter Wright Morris & Arthur

The Firm: This Ohio-headquartered firm benefits from long-standing ties to several Midwestern and national banking clients. The practice has developed an outstanding reputation in leveraged, asset-based and structured finance. Matters covered range from regulatory compliance and transactional advice to loan documentation. Practitioners in the four Ohio offices draw upon the additional resources of the firm's Florida and DC branches.

The Lawyers: **Timothy Grady** enjoys a preeminent reputation in the state for the development of sophisticated loan documentation, mezzanine finance and multi-state commercial financings.

The Clients: The firm is well known in the market as longtime counsel to Huntington Bancshares. Other Ohio-based and national clients include: Fifth Third Bank; National City Bank; KeyCorp; Bank One and Bank of America.

Thompson Hine LLP

see firm details p.890

The Firm: One of the larger firms in the state, Thompson Hine is active in representing banks, borrowers and issuers in complex commercial finance transactions, workouts, and public finance and bank regulatory issues. Interviewees remarked on the practice's *"quality attorneys"* and related strength in banking litigation.

The Lawyers: Deemed a *"top name in the area,"*

OHIO | CONSTRUCTION

Leslee Miraldi (see p.577) represents private and public institutions in a variety of commercial lending matters.
The Clients: KeyCorp; Bank One; Charter One Bank; First Merit; Flowserve; Morgan Stanley; Nationwide Insurance; Sherwin-Williams; Chiquita Brands International; Eaton; Medical Mutual of Ohio; Ohio Bankers Association and Whirlpool.

Baker & Hostetler LLP
The Firm: This *"large and prominent"* practice is well thought of for its banking and finance capabilities, particularly within the field of bankruptcy-related refinancings. Attorneys handle large lender transactions and debt and equity financings. Ohio-based practitioners coordinate substantial matters with lawyers in the firm's Texas, Colorado, New York, California and DC offices.
The Lawyers: Chair of the business practice, Steven Kestner, is the firm's contact partner for finance matters.
The Clients: The group counsels a number of banks, creditors and committees in large bankruptcies and acts for public and private companies, and private equity and venture capital firms on a host of financing matters.

Statman, Harris, Siegel & Eyrich LLC
The Firm: This smaller Cincinnati firm handles its fair share of banking and finance work, and was noted as particularly strong on insolvency matters. In addition to its focus on corporate restructuring and creditors' and debtors' rights, the group also undertakes complex commercial transactions and asset-based financings.
The Lawyers: Name partner **Alan Statman** elicits warm praise from interviewees for his expertise in bankruptcy-related finance. Clients rely on him to *"see us through difficult situations."*
The Clients: Bank One; Fifth Third Bank and K&L Investment Corp.

CONSTRUCTION

OHIO
Leading firms (Construction)
1. **THOMPSON HINE LLP** Cleveland, Columbus
2. **BRICKER & ECKLER LLP** Columbus
   FRANTZ WARD LLP Cleveland
   KEGLER, BROWN, HILL & RITTER Columbus
   SCHOTTENSTEIN, ZOX & DUNN Columbus
   SQUIRE, SANDERS & DEMPSEY LLP Columbus
3. **BENESCH, FRIEDLANDER, COPLAN** Cleveland
   BUCKINGHAM DOOLITTLE Columbus
   ULMER & BERNE LLP Columbus
4. **FROST BROWN TODD LLC** Cincinnati
   HAHN LOESER & PARKS LLP Cleveland

Leading individuals (Construction)
1. **APPELBAUM Jeffrey** Thompson Hine LLP, Columbus
2. **CURRIE Michael** Thompson Hine LLP, Columbus
   GREGORY Donald Kegler, Brown, Hill, Columbus
   HOLMAN Michael Bricker & Eckler LLP, Columbus
   MILLER Barry Benesch, Friedlander, Coplan, Cleveland
   NATALE Andrew Frantz Ward LLP, Cleveland
   REMINGTON Royce Hahn Loeser & Parks, Cleveland
   TARULLO Michael Schottenstein, Zox, Columbus
   WELIN Peter Thompson Hine LLP, Columbus
3. **LEACH Donald** Buckingham Doolittle, Columbus
   PETRO John McNamara & McNamara, Columbus
   ROSATI Jack Bricker & Eckler LLP, Columbus
   ROSENBERG Thomas Ulmer & Berne LLP, Columbus
4. **FRIEDMAN Steven** Squire, Sanders, Columbus
   GURNEY Scott Frost Brown Todd LLC, Cincinnati
   LIGGETT Luther Bricker & Eckler LLP, Columbus

Firms and individuals are listed alphabetically in each band.

Thompson Hine LLP
see firm details p.890
The Firm: Interviewees describe this group as *"clear leaders"* in the construction field. A *"strong, deep team"* boasts *"extremely experienced attorneys,"* and the practice offers a *"cradle-to-grave"* service that includes project consultancy work. The team is involved in *"sophisticated work for sophisticated clients."* The client base has grown from its original focus on local contractors to include architects, construction managers and owners from all over the country. A strong litigation service acts for mainly Ohio-based clients. The team is increasingly known for its work for public and state entities; it is particularly fîted for its work on athletics projects such as the proposed $500 million stadium in St Louis, MO.
The Lawyers: **Jeffrey Appelbaum** (see p.573) was identified as *"the premier construction lawyer in Ohio;"* peers claim he stands *"head and shoulders above everybody else."* He is *"smart, knowledgeable and creative,"* and has a reputation for *"fantastic transactional work"* for owners on complex stadium deals. **Michael Currie** (see p.572) is a respected litigator who has considerable *"panache"* and an *"assertive style."* The *"experienced and effective"* **Peter Welin** (see p.578) has an *"excellent technical background"* that includes a degree in civil engineering. The team has acted on a number of major stadium projects, including as project counsel for both Jacobs Field and Gund Arena in Cleveland and the new St. Louis Cardinals' ballpark.
The Clients: Clients include: Golden State Warriors Arena; Ohio School Facilities Commission; Gilbane Building Company and HOK Sport+Venue+Event.

Bricker & Eckler LLP
The Firm: This diverse group of lawyers includes *"some real stars,"* who have expertise in many different fields and *"intimate industry knowledge."* A largely owners client base is dominated by institutions and laced with selected subcontractors. The firm's profile in construction is considerably boosted by the team's work on Ohio's massive schools rebuilding program. It also represents construction industry professionals before state and federal courts, and administrative agencies.
The Lawyers: A key player on the team is the *"smart and assured"* **Michael Holman**. **Luther Liggett** was endorsed as a *"knowledgeable and established attorney;"* he has a niche in lobbying for the industry. **Jack Rosati** is admired as a *"detailed and powerful litigator"* who brings a *"broad skills base"* to the deal table. The team was chosen as construction counsel for the $600 million Dayton City School District project.
The Clients: Turner Construction Company; Karlsberger Architects; Jefferson County Commissioners; City of Cambridge; American Council of Engineering Companies of Ohio; Columbus Metropolitan Library; Julian Speer Company; Medina City School District and Complete General Construction Company.

Frantz Ward LLP
The Firm: This team's reputation is principally due to the work of its *"fine litigators."* The firm boasts a number of former Thompson Hine partners and is said to be *"doing very well."* It offers advice on a wide range of construction matters, acting for contractors, manufacturers, lenders, owners and design professionals. Claims management and avoidance is a particular specialty of the group.
The Lawyers: The profile of *"knowledgeable"* **Andrew Natale** has soared since his departure from Thompson Hine. He is the key figure in the team, highly respected for his litigation expertise and work in claims.
The Clients: RP Carbone Companies; Hensel Phelps Construction; Tyco International; McNally Tunneling; Ebenisterie Beaubois; The Hartford; Havens Steel and Industrial First.

Kegler, Brown, Hill & Ritter
The Firm: The team represents all segments of the industry, but has a preponderance of subcontractors as clients. It is also respected for its work

for institutional owners. Attorneys here are known for their *"fierce representation"* and *"competitive bid work."*
The Lawyers: The team's strong tie to the American Subcontractors Association (ASA) owes much to the *"straightforward and assertive"* **Donald Gregory**. He is acknowledged as *"a fine, hard-working lawyer"* of considerable experience. Gregory led the team that successfully acted for the ASA in a case in Florida, which resolved the relationship between indemnity and the duty to defend.
The Clients: Clients are drawn largely from among national trade associations, and include the ASA. the National Ground Water Association and the Ceiling & Interior Systems Construction Association.

Schottenstein, Zox & Dunn
The Firm: Many interviewees single out this *"real contractors' firm,"* which is noted for its *"superb, dedicated specialists"* in the Columbus office. The practice is closely identified with its work for The Associated General Contractors (AGC) of America. The workload covers both transactional and litigious matters, and lawyers here bring their extensive industry experience to bear on each case.
The Lawyers: The firm's leading light is the *"eloquent and highly specialist"* **Michael Tarullo**, recognized by commentators as *"one of the best in Columbus."* Tarullo's training as a professional engineer makes him sought after by contractor and subcontractor clients.

Squire, Sanders & Dempsey LLP
The Firm: This international practice is renowned for producing skilled construction litigators as well as attorneys who can advise at every stage on a wide range of projects. Peers comment on the *"fantastic construction service"* attorneys here provide, and note that their reputation has been enhanced by their handling of *"a ton of public bond work."* The practice also undertakes work for owners, and has a caseload that involves claims, litigation and dispute resolution.
The Lawyers: **Steven Friedman** is a *"remarkably bright"* lawyer who is experienced in construction-related disputes, particularly in the representation of public owners. Friedman also has litigation experience in antitrust, contract, employment, trade secrets, municipal and constitutional law.

The Clients: Clients are drawn from many industries and include owners, venture capitalists, operators, contractors, subcontractors, management consultants, architects and government bodies at every level.

Benesch, Friedlander, Coplan & Aronoff LLP
The Firm: This firm is well known for its representation of owners in the process of selecting, and negotiating agreements with, design professionals. A *"diverse"* team undertakes a range of work, including the procurement and negotiation of construction contracts. It has a niche in advising both public bodies and private individuals on competitive bidding disputes.
The Lawyers: **Barry Miller** impresses market commentators with his *"exemplary capability and knowledge."* He is thought to be the driving force behind the practice.
The Clients: Clients include owners, design professionals, contractors and insurers.

Buckingham Doolittle & Burroughs
The Firm: This *"excellent construction group in Columbus"* was singled out by interviewees for offering a quality service *"pretty much across the board."* Lawyers here have a variety of technical backgrounds and advise owners, contractors, developers, subcontractors, engineers, architects and bankers on both public and private construction projects.
The Lawyers: *"Active and assured"* **Donald Leach** heads the team. He is *"famed in the industry"* for his work in major public and private construction projects, and for his high-profile lecturing.
The Clients: Clients include school districts, government agencies, Fortune 500 companies, construction managers, general contractors, subcontractors, suppliers, architects, engineers, financial institutions and real estate developers.

Ulmer & Berne LLP
The Firm: When it comes to insurance defense, commentators agree that this *"smaller, classy practice"* offers high-quality advice. This is a full-service firm in all areas of civil law; in construction it acts primarily on the defense side for architects and engineers. The team also acts for contractors, and occasionally for owners. The focus here is on public and commercial projects, and the team offers a *"decent"* litigation capacity.

The Lawyers: **Thomas Rosenberg** *"knows the industry"* and *"brings a deep pool of experience to the table."* The team is involved in litigation connected with several Wal-Mart operations in central Ohio, and in litigation related to the City of Parma Justice Center.
The Clients: Design Professionals Insurance Company; NBBJ; Correll Construction; General Temperature Control; Landmark Development; Parenteau Builders and The Altman Company.

Frost Brown Todd LLC
see firm details p.798
The Firm: This is a large and respected firm offering *"reliable service"* across a range of disciplines. In construction matters, it was endorsed for servicing industry clients throughout the Midwest and Southeast.
The Lawyers: The big name here is the *"busy and effective"* **Scott Gurney** (see p.575), who is valued for both his construction experience and his litigation skills. The team successfully represented a large contractor against a project owner's $5 million claim for delay and cost overruns in a two week-long arbitration hearing.
The Clients: Construction managers; suppliers; general contractors; surety bond companies; design-build contractors; project owners and developers; specialty and trade contractors and design professionals.

Hahn Loeser & Parks LLP
The Firm: This *"smart group"* is best known among interviewees for its representation of owners and specialty contractors. The team advises private and public clients on projects involving extensive restoration as well as residential developments and construction and new commercial and industrial structures,
The Lawyers: **Royce Remington** heads the group and is widely admired as *"a talented construction guy."*
The Clients: Owners; developers; contractors; material suppliers; design professionals and sureties.

Other Notable Practitioners
John Petro at McNamara and McNamara has a niche practice in sureties and fidelity claims. Peers recommend him as *"one of the top surety lawyers in the state."* He is visible acting for clients such as Aetna Casualty & Surety Co and Home Indemnity Co.

OHIO — CORPORATE/M&A

CORPORATE/M&A

OHIO
Leading firms (Corporate/M&A)

1
- JONES DAY *Cleveland*
- SQUIRE, SANDERS & DEMPSEY LLP *Cleveland*

2
- BAKER & HOSTETLER LLP *Cleveland*
- THOMPSON HINE LLP *Cleveland*
- VORYS, SATER, SEYMOUR AND PEASE *Columbus*

3
- CALFEE, HALTER & GRISWOLD LLP *Cleveland*
- KEATING, MUETHING & KLEKAMP PLL *Cincinnati*
- TAFT, STETTINIUS & HOLLISTER LLP *Cincinnati*

4
- DINSMORE & SHOHL LLP *Cincinnati*
- FROST BROWN TODD LLC *Cincinnati*
- PORTER WRIGHT MORRIS & ARTHUR *Columbus*

Leading individuals (Corporate/M&A)

1
- GANSKE Lyle *Jones Day*, Cleveland
- JORGENSON Mary Ann *Squire, Sanders*, Cleveland
- PORTER David *Jones Day*, Cleveland

2
- CARLSON James *Thompson Hine LLP*, Cleveland
- KAISER Gordon *Squire, Sanders & Dempsey*, Cleveland
- KREIDER Gary *Keating, Muething & Klekamp*, Cincinnati

3
- HOBERG Tim *Taft, Stettinius & Hollister LLP*, Cincinnati
- ROE Clifford *Dinsmore & Shohl LLP*, Cincinnati
- VINCENT George *Dinsmore & Shohl LLP*, Cincinnati

Firms and individuals are listed alphabetically in each band.

Jones Day
see firm details p.823

The Firm: Jones Day's original headquarters at the Cleveland office forms the base of the firm's *"excellent"* international corporate practice. The size and scale of the corporate group ensures its status as *"the first name you think of"* for big-ticket M&A. The firm maintains integrated practice groups across its 25 global offices and has a greater focus on national and international work than many of its Ohio competitors. The broad-based practice advises private individuals and small companies, but is best known for its representation of large multinationals and Fortune 500 companies. Interviewees particularly noted the *"youth and dynamism"* of the Ohio corporate team. During 2002, partners acted in tandem with Jones Day attorneys across the US on LTV's $110 million sale of the company's Tubular Division assets to Maverick Tube Corporation and on the $325 million sale of integrated steel assets to WL Ross & Co. The Ohio team acted for Goodrich in the $142.9 million spin-off of the Engineered Industrial Products division as EnPro Industries, and advised Abbott Laboratories' $75 million sale of the Selsun Blue shampoo business.

The Lawyers: *"A fine technical lawyer,"* **David Porter** (see p.577) focuses on corporate securities and takeover defense. He has particular experience in the aerospace, industrial, real estate, retail and telecom industries, and is well known for his successful defense of Ohio's anti-takeover legislation. He recently represented JM Smucker Company in the $671.1 million acquisition of the Jif peanut butter and Crisco cooking oil businesses from Procter & Gamble. Head of the firm's US M&A practice, **Lyle Ganske** (see p.575) maintains a general corporate, transactional and securities practice and is regarded by interviewees as a leading rainmaker at the firm.

The Clients: Aquila; Abbott Laboratories; FirstEnergy; International Steel Group; Teleglobe; Williams Communications Group; CenterAmerica Property Trust; RJ Reynolds and Bayer.

Squire, Sanders & Dempsey LLP
The Firm: This major full-service firm has deep roots in Cleveland and supplements its volume of local Ohio and Midwest-based work with complex cross-border matters generated by the firm's network of national and international offices. Traditionally, the firm's trump card has been an outstanding national profile in public finance. However, the firm is fully equipped to act on the gamut of corporate finance, M&A, private equity and securities matters. A highly respected insolvency practice has been acting as cocounsel for WorldCom in its Chapter 11 proceedings and as cocounsel to the creditors' committee in the Enron bankruptcy. The group is said to be particularly adept at tax-advantaged financings around the country and handles increasing amounts of work in connection with regulated industries, life sciences and energy. The Columbus and Cincinnati offices tend toward local and midmarket work. Further afield, the firm's expertise in Eastern European corporate work is among the best in the country, and is a *"real strength,"* say interviewees.

The Lawyers: A *"key figure"* within the market, **Mary Ann Jorgenson** was singled out as the firm's most prominent corporate attorney. Head of the firm's international business practice, she advises large public and private companies on M&A and corporate control issues, and counsels corporate officers on legislative changes. She has particular experience in the medical technology, chemical and amusement industries and has been increasingly involved in advisory work for steel industry clients. Jorgenson recently represented Ferro in the purchase of $500 million of assets from Degussa. **Gordon Kaiser** also stands out for his domestic and international M&A and corporate finance experience. He enjoys a loyal client following within the electric utility industry.

The Clients: Ferro; Eaton; Lubrizol and Goodrich.

Baker & Hostetler LLP
The Firm: Headquartered in Cleveland, the firm has grown to be a national presence, with offices in Columbus, Cincinnati and across the US. A varied practice encompasses public M&A, securities and capital raising. The majority of the firm's workload, however, is private, and the team has particular experience in advising clients in the auto parts, healthcare, hospitality and energy industries. Strategic M&A for private equity groups is a particular focus. The group recently counseled a leading Midwest private equity firm in its acquisition of a subsidiary of a Fortune 500 company, and advised Cardinal Health in its recent acquisition of the stock of Magellan Laboratories.

The Lawyers: Steven Kestner chairs the firm's business practice group.

The Clients: Developers Diversified Realty; Lesco; Boykin Management Company; Boykin Hotel Properties; Associated Estates Realty; Morgenthaler Management; The EW Scripps Company and Cardinal Health.

Thompson Hine LLP
see firm details p.890

The Firm: The Cleveland-based firm remains a major force in Ohio for corporate/M&A work with four offices in the state. A broad-based practice represents large manufacturers and mid-sized companies across a range of industries. The firm regularly appears in Ohio takeover defense contests, and is principal outside counsel to a major Ohio bank. Much of the firm's recent work has involved the corporate aspects of restructuring.

The Lawyers: **James Carlson** (see p.573) is widely acknowledged as the firm's leading corporate attorney. Hailed by interviewees as *"a real Midwestern lawyer,"* Carlson focuses on M&A and anti-takeover work. He achieved prominence recently as the lead Ohio lawyer representing TRW against a hostile takeover attempt by Northrop Grumman. He rounds out his practice with counseling on general acquisition strategies. Carlson recently handled a bid by Lubrizol for the worldwide filtration and separations business of USFilter, and the reclassification of the stock of a major public company.

The Clients: Eaton; Goodyear; Jo-Ann Stores; KeyCorp; Lubrizol; Milacron; Noranda; Nordson; Oglebay Norton Company; Omnicare; Polyone and STERIS.

Vorys, Sater, Seymour and Pease LLP
The Firm: Widely viewed as the *"top firm in Columbus,"* Vorys Sater is characterized as a *"fine traditional firm,"* offering full-service capabilities to public companies and private individuals. It boasts deep roots in the central Ohio area and is said to retain a strong regional identity.

CORPORATE/M&A — OHIO

Well-developed practices in Columbus, Cincinnati and Cleveland receive support from practitioners in the DC and Alexandria, VA offices. In addition to a varied portfolio of local companies, the corporate team advises an impressive list of large public companies. Recent work includes advising Dominion Homes on a $44 million issuance, and Wendy's International on a $225 million notes offering. The firm has a specialty in bank and savings and loan M&A and advised Independent Community Bancorp in its $22 million merger into First Citizens Banc Corp. The firm also has a growing venture capital practice and acts as general counsel to several local and regional funds.
The Lawyers: George Jenkins is the contact partner for the Columbus corporate practice.
The Clients: Honda NA; The Kroger Company; Wendy's International; The Scotts Company; Worthington Industries; Big Lots; Athenian Venture Partners; Adena Ventures and River Cities Capital Funds.

Calfee, Halter & Griswold LLP
The Firm: The firm has a *"strong stable of mid-sized clients,"* and is felt to achieve a high profile in the market despite its smaller size. The Cleveland headquarters works closely with a second office in Columbus in coordinating advice on sales and purchases, management buyouts, proxy contests and recapitalizations. Peers identified particular strength in work for start-ups and small companies attempting to grow through acquisition. The firm enjoys a leading reputation for securities work and is well known for its representation of a major regional investment bank. Interviewees commend the practice as a *"good group of business savvy lawyers."*
The Lawyers: Cleveland-based John Mino is the contact partner for corporate/M&A matters.
The Clients: The firm acts for mid-sized public and private companies and Midwestern financial institutions.

Keating, Muething & Klekamp PLL
The Firm: Interviewees associate the Cincinnati practice with its large following of local entrepreneurs and closely held corporations. The firm is said to have developed a strong corporate practice off the back of its long-standing work for American Financial Group. Attorneys typically represent sellers and purchasers in a range of sectors and advise clients in capital-raising activities.
The Lawyers: Premier Cincinnati corporate lawyer, **Gary Kreider**, is judged as *"superbly talented."* Head of the corporate practice, Kreider's reputation extends across the state.
The Clients: AK Steel Holding; American Financial Group; Belcan; Chiquita Brands International; Cintas; Fifth Third Bancorp; Great American Financial Resources; Milacron; Provident Financial Group; Rumpke Consolidated Companies and United Dairy Farmers.

Taft, Stettinius & Hollister LLP
The Firm: A long-established Cincinnati general practice firm with offices across the state, the firm retains long-standing ties to important local clients. The corporate team advises a volume of private small to medium-sized companies, but also has experience of representing NYSE companies, borrowers, creditors and private investment funds. A core team of ten M&A attorneys receives high marks for its work on behalf of entrepreneurial companies and venture capital interests. The firm represents a number of car manufacturers, and, in Columbus, has a heavy focus on the healthcare industry.
The Lawyers: A *"competent, experienced and trustworthy"* attorney, **Tim Hoberg** heads the securities practice group and is responsible for the firm's public company representation. His general corporate practice emphasizes corporate and securities matters and advising special committees of directors. Recent work includes representing Chiquita Brands International in its $45 million sale of interests in the Castellini group.
The Clients: AK Steel ; Avon Products; BASF; The Cincinnati Gas & Electric Company; Cinergy; Cordant Technologies; Ford; G&J Pepsi Cola Bottlers; Morton International; Nissan Motor Acceptance; PSI Energy; SHV North America Corporation and Sandusky International.

Dinsmore & Shohl LLP
The Firm: This Cincinnati-based general practice firm has offices in Columbus and Dayton as well as branches in four other states. In Ohio, the 60-attorney corporate practice represents a variety of listed companies, but stands out for its long experience of handling transactions for Procter & Gamble, such as its purchase of Sunny Delight. However, private company matters remain the lion's share of the group's work. Attorneys recently acted on the reacquisition of a business from Chiquita, and are advising on ongoing transactions for Shire Pharmaceuticals and Standard Register. The group has also seen an increase in transactional work arising from bankruptcy proceedings.
The Lawyers: Managing partner **Clifford Roe** has long experience acting for Procter & Gamble around the country in securities and corporate finance transactions. Chair of the firm's corporate practice, **George Vincent**, was also endorsed to researchers. His practice includes general business and corporate law, especially counseling, M&A and securities matters.
The Clients: Procter & Gamble, Shire Pharmaceuticals and Standard Register.

Frost Brown Todd LLC
see firm details p.798
The Firm: The product of a 2000 merger between Ohio's Frost & Jacobs and Kentucky's Brown, Todd & Heyburn, this large regional firm is well known in Cincinnati for its long association with a local phone company. The corporate practice advises on the full range of M&A, divestitures, joint ventures and strategic transactions, and has experience of small, local asset acquisitions for cash and larger cross-border business acquisitions.
The Lawyers: Theodore Grosser cochairs the firm's M&A practice group.
The Clients: AIG Insurance; Chiquita Brands International; LexisNexis; Brown & Williamson Tobacco; LensCrafters; Waste Management of North America; New Horizon Resources and Anthem Health Plans.

Porter Wright Morris & Arthur
The Firm: This firm, which was founded in 1846, has four offices in Ohio: Columbus, Dayton, Cleveland and Cincinnati. Porter Wright enjoys a high standing in the central Ohio market, where it maintains close relationships with local banks. Practitioners offer *"commercial"* advice on M&A, securities, business formation and venture capital matters to a range of public and private firms.
The Lawyers: Thomas Coady heads the firm's public finance group from the Columbus office.
The Clients: The firm acts for small to mid-sized local businesses and banks, with heavy emphasis on representation of entrepreneurs and private companies.

OHIO — EMPLOYMENT & LABOR LAW

EMPLOYMENT & LABOR LAW — MAINLY PLAINTIFF

OHIO
Leading firms
(Employment: Mainly Plaintiff)
1. SCHWARZWALD & MCNAIR *Cleveland*
2. FAULKNER, MUSKOVITZ & PHILLIPS LLP *Cleveland*
   TOBIAS KRAUS & TORCHIA *Cincinnati*

Leading individuals
(Employment: Mainly Plaintiff)
1. FREKING Randolph *Freking & Betz,* Cincinnati
   GITTES Frederick *Gittes & Schulte,* Columbus
   MCNAIR Eben *Schwarzwald & McNair,* Cleveland
   TOBIAS Paul *Tobias Kraus & Torchia,* Cincinnati
2. KNECHT Denise *Denise J Knecht,* Cleveland
   SCHWARTZ Niki *Gold, Schwartz & Co LPA,* Cleveland
3. MUSKOVITZ Susannah *Faulkner, Muskovitz,* Cleveland
   TORCHIA David *Tobias Kraus & Torchia,* Cincinnati

Firms and individuals are listed alphabetically in each band.

Schwarzwald & McNair
The Firm: Market sources unanimously acknowledged this firm as *"preeminent"* in Ohio for union representation. The practice acts for over 30 labor unions across the state and nationally, and is recommended as the *"best team of union attorneys in the state."*
The Lawyers: Peers and clients alike commend **Eben McNair** for being *"honest, able and a pleasure to work with."* Hailed as a *"leading light"* in labor law, McNair is well known for his representation of many of the state's major unions.
The Clients: The firm is local counsel for international and national unions. United Steelworkers is the firm's key client, although the team also regularly represents United Food & Commercial Workers Union, and serves as general counsel for the Office and Professional Employees International Union.

Faulkner, Muskovitz & Phillips LLP
The Firm: This small but *"dynamic"* union law firm is, according to defendant attorneys, *"the firm we encounter most frequently on the other side of union negotiations."*
The Lawyers: Employment defendant attorneys assert that **Susannah Muskovitz** is *"one of the most difficult opponents in town."* She is highly visible acting for unions and their members on employment and labor law matters.
The Clients: The Teamsters union is a leading client.

Tobias Kraus & Torchia
The Firm: This five-lawyer employment boutique focuses on representing individual plaintiffs in employment claims, but also occasionally handles matters for union clients. The team has a broad expertise in matters ranging from wrongful termination, discrimination, retaliation, family medical leave and sexual harassment claims to negotiations of severance agreements and employment contracts and employee benefits issues.
The Lawyers: A *"prominent figure"* in the field, senior attorney **Paul Tobias** specializes in wrongful termination and discrimination litigation. He is highly regarded, both for his 45 years' experience in employment law, and for his roles as founder of The National Employment Lawyers Association (NELA) and cofounder of Workplace Fairness. Peers were also impressed by **David Torchia**'s track record of successful jury verdicts in the federal and state courts.
The Clients: The firm represents individual employees and unions.

Other Notable Practitioners
Commentators describe **Randolph Freking** of Freking & Betz as *"one of the most impressive, vigorous and active"* plaintiffs' attorneys in Cincinnati. He is particularly admired for his *"terrific trial skills,"* which have won him numerous successful jury verdicts on behalf of employees. In Columbus, **Frederick Gittes** of Gittes & Schulte is *"a real standout"* attorney. This top plaintiffs' attorney represents individual employees, and has a remarkable record in achieving favorable settlements in substantial cases. Described as a *"formidable opponent,"* **Denise Knecht** of Denise J Knecht & Associates Co is a *"hard-driving"* trial attorney. Knecht is recognized for her success in obtaining a number of significant verdicts in the field. Also identified as a *"brilliant trial advocate,"* **Niki Schwartz** of Gold, Schwartz & Co LPA focuses primarily on employment litigation. Schwartz enjoys an outstanding market reputation *"among the best in Cleveland"* for plaintiffs' representation in employment and civil rights claims.

EMPLOYMENT & LABOR LAW — MAINLY DEFENDANT

OHIO
Leading firms
(Employment: Mainly Defendant)
1. BAKER & HOSTETLER LLP *Cleveland*
   DUVIN, CAHN & HUTTON *Cleveland*
2. FRANTZ WARD LLP *Cleveland*
3. JONES DAY *Cleveland*
   MILLISOR CO LPA *Cleveland*
   SQUIRE, SANDERS & DEMPSEY LLP *Cleveland*
4. DINSMORE & SHOHL LLP *Cincinnati*
   FROST BROWN TODD LLC *Cincinnati*
   TAFT, STETTINIUS & HOLLISTER LLP *Cincinnati*
   ULMER & BERNE LLP *Cleveland*

Firms are listed alphabetically in each band.

Baker & Hostetler LLP
The Firm: A large full-service firm with a long track record of representing management in labor and employment matters. Peers acknowledge it to be *"the best employment practice of the larger firms,"* noting its broad client base and *"significant team of excellent attorneys."* The group here excels in statewide class action suits and defends corporate clients against all types of discrimination claims. The team is also known for its labor law capacities and advises employers in connection with wage and hour cases, employee benefits litigation and workers' compensation issues.
The Lawyers: Greg Mersol enjoys an outstanding reputation in the labor and employment community for his success in employment litigation. His practice focuses on the resolution of complex employment disputes through both litigation and alternative procedures. Interviewees consider **Eliott Azoff** to be the firm's *"leading player"* for labor relations matters. He negotiates collective bargaining agreements on behalf of several contractor associations and such newspaper clients as the Scripps-Howard chain and the New York Post. Azoff also serves as both general and labor counsel to a large metropolitan park district. Successful trial lawyer **John Lewis** devotes much of his practice to counseling and alternative dispute resolution. He is well known for winning numerous significant verdicts in state and federal employment discrimination cases.
The Clients: The firm acts as counsel to the East Cleveland School Board. Other clients come from the insurance, retail, real estate, manufacturing, telecom, securities, hotel and education sectors.

Duvin, Cahn & Hutton
The Firm: This growing practice, said to comprise a number of *"brilliant"* labor and employment lawyers, has firmly established itself as Cleveland's *"biggest and best-known law firm in the field."* The

EMPLOYMENT & LABOR LAW — OHIO

OHIO
Leading individuals
(Employment: Mainly Defendant)

[1]
- BARNARD Thomas *Ulmer & Berne LLP*, Cleveland
- DUVIN Robert *Duvin, Cahn & Hutton*, Cleveland

[2]
- FRANTZ Michael *Frantz Ward LLP*, Cleveland
- MERSOL Greg *Baker & Hostetler LLP*, Cleveland
- MILLISOR Kenneth *Millisor Co LPA*, Cleveland
- RYDZEL James *Jones Day*, Cleveland

[3]
- AZOFF Elliot *Baker & Hostetler LLP*, Cleveland
- HAWKINS Michael *Dinsmore & Shohl LLP*, Cincinnati
- LEUKART Barbara *Jones Day*, Cleveland
- MILLSTON David *Squire, Sanders*, Cleveland
- SIEGEL Bradd *Porter Wright Morris & Arthur*, Columbus
- SPRING Gary *Roetzel & Andress PA*, Akron

[4]
- ADAMS Deborah *Frost Brown Todd LLC*, Cincinnati
- KING Roger *Jones Day*, Columbus
- LEWIS John *Baker & Hostetler LLP*, Cleveland
- LIPS Alan *Taft, Stettinius & Hollister LLP*, Cincinnati
- PACE Stanley *Spieht Bell McCurdy & Newell*, Cleveland
- SHEERAN Timothy *Squire, Sanders*, Cleveland
- YUND George *Frost Brown Todd LLC*, Cincinnati

Individuals are listed alphabetically in each band.

firm boasts a national and regional practice and represents public and private employers in all areas of labor relations, including collective bargaining, contract arbitration, union resistance counseling and employment-related litigation.
The Lawyers: Interviewees credit firm founder **Robert Duvin** with building the firm's successful labor and employment practice. Deemed a *"senior statesman"* in the traditional labor law bar, Duvin is esteemed as *"one of the most respected labor lawyers in Ohio."*
The Clients: The firm represents many of northeastern Ohio's supermarkets and has a strong national following among real estate clients such as Simon Property Group. Other clients include: City of Celvel; Wal-Mart; EDS; Ford; Cole National Corporation; Cleveland Browns; Cleveland Indians; Continental Airlines; Lamson & Sessions and Cleveland Marriott.

Frantz Ward LLP
The Firm: This 40-attorney firm, formed only three years ago, has had remarkable success in developing its labor and employment practice into one of the largest in northeastern Ohio. Attorneys here are said to be *"competitive and adept employment litigators"* who have broad experience in labor and employment law matters. Employment discrimination cases remain the bread and butter of the practice; the firm, however, covers the full spectrum of traditional management/union matters, including arbitration proceedings, collective bargaining negotiations and the representation of its employer clients before the NLRB.
The Lawyers: Founding partner **Michael Frantz** was singled out as the firm's most notable practitioner. He focuses primarily on traditional labor law, including contract negotiations, and counsels on union avoidance and administrative issues.
The Clients: The firm represents a diverse group of private and public sector management clients, including Fortune 500 firms and local corporates. It also attracts a substantial share of healthcare industry and non-profit clients.

Jones Day
see firm details p.822
The Firm: The employment lawyers within this 1600-lawyer national firm possess an outstanding reputation in the field for the defense of management clients in employment discrimination and wrongful discharge class actions. The firm also maintains a traditional labor relations practice advising on strikes and collective bargaining. The nationwide team successfully defended Wal-Mart in an action brought by 174,000 current and former Wal-Mart employees alleging violation of Ohio wage and hour laws in Petty v Wal-Mart. The firm also represented Verizon Wireless in multiple proceedings relating to the company's application and interpretation of various labor contracts.
The Lawyers: The *"figurehead"* of the firm's statewide labor and employment practice, **James Rydzel** (see p.578) enjoys an excellent reputation for his *"tremendous trial abilities."* Although he focuses on employment litigation and labor arbitrations, Rydzel is also highly thought of for his work on ERISA and employee benefits issues. He represents Bridgestone/Firestone as a labor counsel in arbitrations, master contract negotiations, and union relations. **Barbara Leukart** (see p.576) counsels clients in a wide spectrum of labor and employment matters, and is commended for her *"bright and assertive attitude"* in discrimination litigation cases. Her practice also includes working with in-house counsel to supervise and manage employment litigation dockets. **Roger King** (see p.576) is well known for his expertise in healthcare-related employment issues. He frequently represents management clients in connection with ADA and FMLA-related matters.
The Clients: Brush Wellman; Penton Media; DTR Industries; Wal-Mart; Kaiser Aluminium and Fortune 500 companies.

Millisor Co LPA
The Firm: A *"talented"* 30-strong labor and employment team serves an extensive and impressive client base from offices in Cleveland, Columbus and Canton. It is deemed a *"progressive"* practice with a specialty in traditional labor law and workers' compensation. Employing a preventative approach on employment-related matters, attorneys counsel clients on union-organizing issues, the employment aspects of acquisitions, the reduction of labor costs and the implementation of affirmative action and employee benefits' plans.
The Lawyers: Clients and peers identified **Kenneth Millisor** as a successful labor and employment lawyer with long experience in the field. He is particularly recommended for his work on labor negotiations.
The Clients: The firm has a long history of advising rubber industry clients, representing Goodyear, Goodrich, General Tires and Uniroil. Other clients include: Brush Wellman; Case Foods; Greater Cleveland Automobile Dealers Association; Kmart; PolyOne and The May Department Stores Company.

Squire, Sanders & Dempsey LLP
The Firm: This prominent global full-service firm, with offices in Cleveland, Columbus and Cincinnati, has an established reputation in the labor and employment field. Attorneys here represent both public and private employers; interviewees particularly noted the team's strength in public sector representation, citing its involvement in employment issues on behalf of school districts and state government agencies. The firm places a strong emphasis on litigation avoidance and offers extensive employment counseling, alternative dispute resolution and arbitration services. Members regularly advise on collective bargaining, health and safety issues and workers' compensation as well as on compliance with state and federal legislation.
The Lawyers: Practice head **David Millston** is widely regarded as a *"talented and experienced"* practitioner. His practice encompasses general employment counseling, employment litigation and arbitration, union avoidance and collective bargaining. **Timothy Sheeran** is recognized as a specialist in education employment law.
The Clients: A broad-based roster of industrial clients features representatives from the aviation, aerospace, steel, transportation, manufacturing, construction and energy sectors.

Dinsmore & Shohl LLP
The Firm: This Cincinnati firm has a long history of involvement in labor and employment law matters and represents corporate clients on a state and national basis. Practitioners counsel US clients on compliance with international labor and employment regulation, and act similarly for foreign companies with respect to their US operations. Areas of representation include employment discrimination, wrongful discharge, labor relations, OSHA, affirmative action plans, wage and hour laws and in-house training.
The Lawyers: **Michael Hawkins** is a *"visible and highly regarded"* labor and employment attorney with over 30 years' experience in the field. He has built a reputation in representing private companies

OHIO — EMPLOYMENT & LABOR LAW

on a state, national and international basis, regularly advising them on discrimination and civil rights claims, collective bargaining negotiations and alternative dispute resolution, mediation and appellate work.
The Clients: Procter & Gamble; GE; GM; Dow Chemical; Rockwell International and United Dairy Farmers.

Frost Brown Todd LLC
see firm details p.798
The Firm: The firm's labor and employment practice handles a wide spectrum of matters including collective bargaining, union avoidance, employment discrimination, workers' compensation, litigation, alternative dispute resolution, immigration and counseling. The labor and employment team represents management clients of all sizes in both the private and public sector. The firm recently secured a $4.3 million federal court judgment for AK Steel against United Steelworkers, after a jury ruled the union acted to slow production through sabotage and the refusal of overtime.
The Lawyers: Deemed a *"big name"* in the market, **Deborah Adams** (see p.573) enjoys a reputation as a *"first-class"* labor and employment attorney with *"terrific trial skills."* **George Yund** (see p.579) was also highly thought of as a *"big hitter with great expertise in the field."*
The Clients: Convergys; Lightyear Communications; Brown & Williamson Tobacco; The Western-Southern Enterprise; Catholic Healthcare Partners; AK Steel and UPS.

Taft, Stettinius & Hollister LLP
The Firm: This old and *"well-connected"* Ohio firm boasts a *"high-powered"* labor and employment practice with a *"national scope."* It serves a varied clientele ranging from banking, manufacturing, transportation and real estate interests to television and radio, healthcare and energy companies. Interviewees note the firm's close ties to long-standing clients AK Steel, The Ohio Casualty Insurance Company and UPS. Attorneys here represent corporate clients in employment cases before federal and state trial and appellate courts, and routinely advise on the employment aspects of M&A transactions.
The Lawyers: Alan Lips was distinguished as a *"significant figure"* in the field, with wide-ranging experience of labor and employment matters. He has argued employment cases before the US Supreme Court and most of the state courts of appeal.
The Clients: Eagle Picher Industries; BMG Music Service; GM; Avon Products; BASF; Chiquita Brands International; The Cincinnati Gas & Electric Company; G&J Pepsi Cola Bottlers; Provident Bank and Federal Home Loan Bank of Cincinnati.

Ulmer & Berne LLP
The Firm: This mid-sized full-service firm serves public and private corporate clients from offices in Cleveland, Cincinnati and Columbus in Ohio, and in Chicago. Employment is a core practice area, with one-quarter of the firm's 125 attorneys able to advise on discrimination claims, workplace regulation, collective bargaining and contract matters. The practice includes a number of specialists who focus on areas such as OSHA compliance, employee benefits and non-competition agreements.
The Lawyers: The firm's labor and employment practice is centered on chairman **Thomas Barnard**, who is named as a *"highly successful attorney"* in the field. The *"top-flight"* practitioner is active in both labor and employment matters, and earns praise for his *"deep and wide knowledge of the law."*
The Clients: Cleveland State University; TRW; CNF; Oglebay Norton; AT&T Wireless and FOX News.

Other Notable Practitioners
In Columbus, **Bradd Siegel** of Porter Wright Morris & Arthur is highly regarded for his work in employment litigation. He recently won a jury trial on behalf of the former safety director for the City of Columbus in a defamation case, and defended SBC Ameritech against age discrimination claims. Hailed as *"the best employment lawyer in Akron,"* **Gary Spring** of Roetzel & Andress PA was praised for his *"incredible client-handling skills."* Spring advises clients such as Babcock & Wilcox, The Akron Beacon Journal and Pentair on a broad spectrum of labor and employment matters. At Spieht Bell McCurdy & Newell Co LPA, **Stanley Pace** was singled out by peers as a *"well-known name in the industry."* Recommended for his expertise in union management issues, Pace has negotiated numerous labor contracts with major unions, and has been involved in a number of union certification and de-certification elections.

ENVIRONMENT

OHIO
Leading firms (Environment)

1
- PORTER WRIGHT MORRIS & ARTHUR Columbus
- SQUIRE, SANDERS & DEMPSEY LLP Cleveland
- THOMPSON HINE LLP Cleveland
- VORYS, SATER, SEYMOUR AND PEASE Columbus

2
- BAKER & HOSTETLER LLP Columbus
- ROETZEL & ANDRESS PA Akron

3
- BRICKER & ECKLER LLP Columbus
- DINSMORE & SHOHL LLP Cincinnati
- MCMAHON, DEGULIS, HOFFMAN Cleveland
- SHUMAKER, LOOP & KENDRICK LLP Toledo
- TAFT, STETTINIUS & HOLLISTER LLP Cincinnati

Firms are listed alphabetically in each band.

Porter Wright Morris & Arthur
The Firm: This group has a reputation for air and water pollution matters and boasts a *"broad-based team."* It achieves particular cachet for its representation of legislative and trade associations, and for its lobbying work. These *"highly professional lawyers"* have developed strong working relationships with the state EPA, and handle issues of compliance arising from federal and state hazardous waste and water pollution laws. The team is well known in the energy sector and frequently acts for utilities to secure generation and transmission permits. Columbus-based, the firm's reach does, however, spread further afield.
The Lawyers: Most fêted of the lawyers here is *"fabulous litigator"* **Christopher Schraff**. Peers describe him as *"a pleasure to work with, forbearing and widely gifted."* They note that Schraff *"understands the fundamentals and can translate that into a good result for his client."* **Robert Brubaker** is *"tightly focused on outstanding air pollution work,"* and is highly regarded for his work with utilities clients.

Squire, Sanders & Dempsey LLP
The Firm: Interviewees reported that the team has *"been at this game in a major way for years"* and conducts *"interesting work of a consistently fine standard."* Its broad client base leans toward heavy industry; many observers described it as *"the steel companies' choice."* The team has adapted well to industrial upheavals in the state and expanded internationally. Lawyers here display a *"great breadth and depth of experience"* and are *"thorough and well-researched"* in all matters. The team acts for municipal and local government authorities. A *"fine all-round"* practice advises on air and water pollution, Superfund, state action cases, contractual indemnities and remediation sites. Clients endorse the group for its ability to handle *"serious issues."*
The Lawyers: The *"well-connected"* **Van Carson** is a favorite with steel companies and has *"a deft touch with agencies."* He has a high profile for air,

ENVIRONMENT — OHIO

OHIO
Leading individuals (Environment)

1
- **HARDY Michael** *Thompson Hine LLP,* Cleveland

2
- **BRUBAKER Robert** *Porter Wright Morris,* Columbus
- **CARSON Van** *Squire, Sanders & Dempsey,* Cleveland
- **LONARDO Joseph** *Vorys, Sater, Seymour,* Columbus
- **NASH David** *Thompson Hine LLP,* Cleveland
- **SCHRAFF Christopher** *Porter Wright Morris,* Columbus
- **TOSI Louis** *Shumaker, Loop & Kendrick LLP,* Toledo

3
- **CYPHERT Michael** *Thompson Hine LLP,* Cleveland
- **DORAN Scott** *Vorys, Sater, Seymour,* Columbus
- **FAHEY Richard** *Vorys, Sater, Seymour,* Columbus
- **JANKE Ron** *Jones Day,* Columbus
- **MCMAHON Michael** *McMahon, DeGulis,* Cleveland
- **MENTEL Michael** *Roetzel & Andress PA,* Akron

Individuals are listed alphabetically in each band.

steel and waste water proceedings. Clients value both his *"strength in adversarial situations"* and his *"ability to defuse and analyze situations."* Carson led the team representing the Association of Metropolitan Sewerage Agencies (AMSA) and the American Iron and Steel Institute (AISI) in a successful challenge to a discharge mixing zone ban.
The Clients: An industry-heavy client list includes: WCI Steel; Phelps Dodge; City of Sandusky; Northeast Ohio Regional Sewer District; White Consolidated Industries; US Steel; Mead-Westvaco; Republic Engineered Products; Ferro and LTV.

Thompson Hine LLP
see firm details p.890
The Firm: Competitors are happy to refer complex matters to this *"highly qualified and professional"* team, especially in matters of hazardous waste litigation. Clients from the electrical utility, automotive, aerospace, and heavy manufacturing industries are *"confident of first-class service."* The group boasts a particularly strong set of lawyers in Cleveland who exhibit *"impressive practical judgment and vision."* Attorneys here specialize in defense against both criminal and civil environmental regulation enforcement proceedings, and advise on federal and state regulatory requirements.
The Lawyers: Michael Hardy (see p.574) is esteemed for his *"leadership qualities;"* he was described as *"perhaps the best litigator in this area."* The *"effective"* David Nash (see p.577) has an *"impressive grasp of the details of a case"* and is *"well known on the block"* for complex cases. Peers admire his *"scholarly"* approach. Michael Cyphert (see p.574) *"knows his cases inside out"* and is frequently seen on large Superfund matters. He *"identifies possible areas of resolution and speaks persuasively to get consensus."*
The Clients: The team defended the City of Akron in a suit involving water entitlements on the Cuyahoga River. A *"great client list"* includes: FirstEnergy; Buckeye Power; Fraser Papers; International Paper; The Stanley Works; Martin Marietta Materials; Eaton and SC Johnson.

Vorys, Sater, Seymour and Pease LLP
The Firm: A regional heavyweight active in *"smart litigation."* The high-flying team here is made up of *"cooperative"* attorneys who act for manufacturing clients, trade groups and real estate developers. The team is experienced in alternative dispute resolution and arbitrations.
The Lawyers: Peers agree that **Joseph Lonardo** remains *"a major player here,"* although he is spending a portion of his time in the firm's DC office. *"Always a fantastic litigator,"* he acted for a group of potentially responsible parties negotiating the remediation of Ashtabula Harbor and the government's claims for natural resource damages under CERCLA. **Richard Fahey** is experienced on the governmental side; he was commended as *"an outstanding lawyer who has seen it all."* **Scott Doran** has earned his spurs with *"pretty hot litigation skills"* and impresses peers with his *"thorough knowledge."* The team represented the Ohio Home Builders Association in negotiations for a new State of Ohio wetlands permitting program.
The Clients: Allied Waste Industries; Dana; GE; Honda of America Mfg; Occidental Chemical; Greif Bros; Worthington Industries; The Scotts Company; Siemens and Borden.

Baker & Hostetler LLP
The Firm: This long-established practice is best known for its wetlands and water pollution expertise, and experience in brownfield and hazardous waste matters. It has a strong track record in litigation and produces attorneys who are credited with *"great background knowledge."* Peers find them *"professional, direct and effective"* in their approach to litigious and transactional matters. The team handles regulatory problems for clients drawn from the petroleum, chemical and manufacturing industries.
The Lawyers: Daniel Gunsett leads the practice group nationally, orchestrating lawyers in ten offices around the country.

Roetzel & Andress PA
The Firm: Peers report that this team is *"shaping up as one of the best"* and *"growing in all the right directions."* It exhibits *"great depth,"* bolstered by lawyers who have a background in government. Good relations with the relevant agencies help ensure a steady flow of work in environmental enforcement defense, permitting for plant expansions and infrastructure projects, brownfield redevelopment and landfill work.
The Lawyers: Michael Mentel is endorsed for his extensive legislative and regulatory experience. He has both *"status and credibility,"* and offers *"a really useful perspective."* The team acts for Marathon Ashland Petroleum on the permitting of a 149-mile petroleum pipeline from Kenova WV to Columbus. Permits have been obtained and the team is now defending three lawsuits that seek to stop the project.
The Clients: Marathon Ashland Petroleum; City of Akron; Lowe's; PPG Industries; Eaton; Pentair; GenCorp; FirstEnergy; The White Rubber Corporation and Seaman Corporation.

Bricker & Eckler LLP
The Firm: Commentators describe this team as *"an effective, low-key"* group. Its lawyers handle the permitting of environmentally sensitive facilities, and are adjudged *"astute at legislative matters."*
The Lawyers: Charles (Chuck) Waterman chairs the firm's environmental law practice group.

Dinsmore & Shohl LLP
The Firm: Respected nationally for its experience in hazardous waste and Superfund work. The team also represents clients in federal and state administrative, civil and criminal environmental litigation matters.
The Lawyers: Peers esteemed lawyers here as *"capable and knowledgeable"* practitioners who are *"robust"* in litigation. Vincent Stamp chairs the firm's environmental practice group.

McMahon, DeGulis, Hoffman & Lombardi LLP
The Firm: Part of the Environmental Law Network (ELN), a trade association that links environmental attorneys from firms in 14 states. The *"innovative"* team here has real breadth, and has won respect for its expertise in cleanup matters.
The Lawyers: Peers extol **Michael McMahon** as *"a fine technician"* who *"understands the regulatory programs, and knows the people at the agencies."* The team advised on the environmental issues for Medina-based coatings and sealants company RPM in its restructuring program known as the Project Pyramid.
The Clients: BP; ChevronTexaco; Yellow Springs Instruments; Imperial Home Decor; Sherwin-Williams; Masco; Weston Companies; GE and TravelCenters of America.

Shumaker, Loop & Kendrick LLP
The Firm: Peers respect the team's *"good depth"* and its ability to attract clients drawn from a range of utilities, industrial companies and small local corporates. Air, water, hazardous waste, toxic substances and Superfund matters are on the agenda here.
The Lawyers: The group's success is due, in the view of many, to the *"flamboyant"* **Louis Tosi**. He *"rules that corner of the state"* and *"performs to a very high level."* He specializes in hazardous waste

and Superfund work, and is admired as *"an aggressive advocate."*

Taft, Stettinius & Hollister LLP
The Firm: Known widely as *"the premier firm in Cincinnati,"* Taft Stettinius fields a well-established environmental practice that has deep roots in litigation and *"great capability,"* according to interviewees. Lawyers are active in defense of enforcement proceedings, pre-acquisition advice and state and federal law compliance. It also undertakes work for defendants in criminal proceedings and some plaintiffs' matters.
The Lawyers: The key individual at the practice is Tom Terp, who advises on Superfund work and organizes PRP (potentially responsible parties) hearings. The team obtained favorable judgments for Helena Chemical Company in a dispute with Chevron, and for Environmental Enterprises Inc on all civil claims brought by the State of Ohio for alleged violations of states hazardous waste regulations.
The Clients: Helena Chemical Company; Sherwin-Williams; Terminix and Environmental Enterprises Inc.

Other Notable Practitioners
Commentators were fulsome in their endorsement of **Ron Janke** (see p.576) of Jones Day, describing him as a *"first-class environmental transactional lawyer."*

INTELLECTUAL PROPERTY

OHIO
Leading firms (Intellectual Property)
[1] FAY, SHARPE, FAGAN, MINNICH & MCKEE Cleveland
JONES DAY Cleveland
WOOD, HERRON & EVANS LLP Cincinnati
[2] CALFEE, HALTER & GRISWOLD LLP Cleveland
FROST BROWN TODD LLC Cincinnati
KILLWORTH, GOTTMAN, HAGAN Dayton
TAROLLI, SUNDHEIM, COVELL Cleveland
[3] ARTER & HADDEN LLP Cleveland
BAKER & HOSTETLER LLP Cleveland
DINSMORE & SHOHL LLP Cincinnati
THOMPSON HINE LLP Cleveland

Leading individuals (Intellectual Property)
[1] ADAMO Kenneth Jones Day, Cleveland
KILLWORTH Richard Killworth, Gottman, Dayton
LYON Charles Calfee, Halter & Griswold LLP, Cleveland
TAROLLI Thomas Tarolli, Sundheim, Covell, Cleveland
[2] BRINKMAN David Wood, Herron & Evans, Cincinnati
DAUCHOT Luke Thompson Hine LLP, Cleveland
FAGAN Christopher Fay, Sharpe, Fagan, Cleveland

Firms and individuals are listed alphabetically in each band.

Fay, Sharpe, Fagan, Minnich & McKee LLP
The Firm: This *"well-thought-of"* IP boutique operates out of Cleveland where it is admired by competitors as a *"sharp and distinguished"* outfit. The bulk of the team's work concerns patent prosecutions, trademarks, copyrights, and licensing agreements. The group is also highly regarded for its litigation of patent infringement, trade secrets and unfair competition suits. A varied client base includes a number of Fortune 500 companies with a heavy concentration of clients from the mechanical and electrical engineering and computer industries.
The Lawyers: The best-known name here is **Christopher Fagan**, an *"established"* figure in the market. His practice emphasizes litigation and IP counseling on patent, trademark and copyright law.
The Clients: A varied client base includes a number of Fortune 500 companies with a heavy concentration of clients from the mechanical and electrical engineering and computer industries.

Jones Day
see firm details p.823
The Firm: This large Cleveland-based *"big-dollar outfit"* handles substantial cases for blue-chip clients. The practice operates across the US, focusing primarily on work for national clients. The IP team has successfully built up a freestanding practice, but nevertheless benefits from the firm's large base of corporate clients and acts for the likes of Cincinnati's industrial giant Procter & Gamble, for example. Commentators believe the team to be *"in a league of its own"* for IP litigation, where attorneys excel at patent cases involving complex technological issues. The team has also played a pivotal role in the defense of key client Texas Instrument's interests, and is currently engaged in a multi-jurisdictional enforcement proceeding against Hyundai.
The Lawyers: Litigator **Kenneth Adamo** (see p.573) is considered the *"cornerstone"* of the Jones Day IP practice. Interviewees report that this *"incredibly hard-working"* attorney is *"always involved in the most important suits."* Peers are astonished that *"he manages to be everywhere,"* adding that he is *"very good indeed, and something of a celebrity."*
The Clients: Abbott Laboreatories; Texas Instruments; Procter & Gamble; Bridgestone/Firestone; GE and Lucent Technologies.

Wood, Herron & Evans LLP
The Firm: This *"impressive patent boutique"* has *"been in the IP game for ever."* It is a stalwart of the Cincinnati scene and famed for its work on technology matters. A *"large and experienced team"* here includes a number of trained scientists and engineers, all reported to be *"enthusiastic, and dedicated to the field."* The firm is seen to be picking up clients from the booming biotech sector, and is able to coordinate its six offices in Ohio and neighboring Kentucky to counsel national clients. The group is currently acting in major biotech infringement litigation.
The Lawyers: Said by interviewees to *"have what it takes,"* **David Brinkman** is the practice's key figure. His expertise encompasses the IP aspects of electronic, mechanical and electrical technologies.
The Clients: IBM; Sony; Goodyear; The Kroger Company; Clopay; Totes; American Eagle Outfitters and Ashland Oil.

Calfee, Halter & Griswold LLP
The Firm: Seen to be a *"real comer"* in the market, this team has made a name for itself in IP litigation and is considered an *"excellent first choice for Cleveland companies."* The carefully *"cherry-picked"* team is perceived to be *"making strides;"* peers report *"seeing them around everywhere."* Among them, the lawyers can draw on knowledge from a number of science and engineering disciplines. The group handles patent and trademark searches, prepares and prosecutes US and international patent, trademark and copyright applications, and works to maintain issued patents and registered trademarks.
The Lawyers: A *"familiar face"* in the field, **Charles Lyon** *"knows his law inside and out."* He handles a volume of litigation work and is particularly recommended for large cases. He has participated in Markman hearings, bench and jury trials, and argued IP cases before multiple state courts of appeal.

Frost Brown Todd LLC
see firm details p.798
The Firm: This firm is a *"notable player"* in the field, with a reputation in trademark litigation and protection. A varied client base is weighted heavily to the manufacturing and technology sectors. Matters covered range from antitrust and trade dress infringement defense to counseling on patent and copyright agreements. The firm's impressive national practice and involvement in *"high-stakes litigation"* is complemented by a capacity to register trademarks and protect patent interests in foreign countries. A team, led by Arthur Beeman, obtained a $28.5 million jury verdict in Gaus v Conair, a patent infringement

INTELLECTUAL PROPERTY — OHIO

case involving electric hair dryers.
The Lawyers: Steven Goldstein chairs the firm's IP department.
The Clients: AK Steel; University of Cincinnati; Cincinnati Children's Hospital; Chiquita Brands International; Battelle Memorial Institute; The Andrew Jergens Company; Convergys; National Association of Professional Baseball Leagues (NAPBL); Meridian Bioscience and Senco.

Killworth, Gottman, Hagan & Schaeff LLP
The Firm: This niche trademark and patent boutique is recognized as a *"major force"* in the Ohio marketplace, and is particularly admired for the strength of its Dayton patents prosecution practice. Lawyers here boast extensive academic and technical backgrounds and have close ties to local law schools. The practice enjoys a sterling reputation in litigation, which is complemented by the quality of its counsel on trademark searches, registration and maintenance.
The Lawyers: Name partner **Richard Killworth** was hailed as a *"first-class litigator"* with a niche in expert witness work.

Tarolli, Sundheim, Covell, Tummino & Szabo LLP
The Firm: The firm earned widespread plaudits as a *"great patent prosecution shop,"* and handles a volume of patent infringement cases and trademark disputes for its clients. The Cleveland-based practice also handles patent and trademark work in the technology sector. Peers commend the *"consistent quality"* of the group's attorneys, who are all registered to practice before the US Patent and Trademark Office.
The Lawyers: Founding partner **Thomas Tarolli** elicited widespread admiration as a *"leading light"* in the field. This *"fantastic"* attorney handles trademark matters and has a specialty in patent issues particular to mechanical technologies.
The Clients: Clients include national and international firms ranging from Fortune 100 corporates to small businesses and individuals.

Arter & Hadden LLP
The Firm: This *"old-line"* litigation firm was felt to have achieved considerable success in expanding the scope of its IP practice. Commentators particularly commend the group's expertise in transactional matters. The practice has a strong technology bent and commands substantial internet-related experience.
The Lawyers: In Cleveland, Alan Ross heads a team of *"highly qualified individuals."*

Baker & Hostetler LLP
The Firm: This is a *"multi-city high-powered"* outfit known for its *"potent teams in DC and Texas."* Clients are drawn from a range of industries in the manufacturing, sport, biotech and entertainment sectors. A strong technology offering includes considerable internet expertise. The team has handled enforcement actions across the globe. It recently represented the ESPN web site in Fantasy Sports Properties v Sportsline.com et al, a patent infringement action heard in the Federal Circuit.
The Lawyers: Bruce Baumgartner heads the Cleveland IP team.
The Clients: The EW Scripps Company; Electrolux Home Products; Progressive Casualty Insurance; OfficeMax; Outback Steakhouse of Florida; Cardinal Health; Major League Baseball Properties; Royal Appliance Mfg Company and University Hospitals of Cleveland.

Dinsmore & Shohl LLP
The Firm: Peers are impressed by this practice's *"commitment to attracting good lawyers."* Commentators applaud the *"consistency"* of this Cincinnati-based practice across the gamut of IP issues, including international trade matters. Attorneys here act for a number of household names, among them, corporate giant Procter & Gamble.
The Lawyers: Lynda Roesch in Cincinnati is the key contact partner for the team.

Thompson Hine LLP
see firm details p.890
The Firm: Possessing a sizable IP team spread throughout Ohio, this firm earns high marks from interviewees for its *"breadth of coverage."* Its highly regarded practice in complex litigation is run out of the Cleveland office and the firm also fields a respected trademark procurement practice from Dayton. A *"strong and commercially focused"* team serves an impressive list of rust-belt clients from such industries as paper, manufacturing and automobiles.
The Lawyers: Commentators singled out **Luke Dauchot** (see p.574) as a *"very fine patent litigator."* His practice combines IP law and complex commercial litigation.

LITIGATION — GENERAL COMMERCIAL

OHIO
Leading firms
(Litigation: General Commercial)

1. **JONES DAY** Cleveland
2. **SQUIRE, SANDERS & DEMPSEY LLP** Cleveland
3. **BAKER & HOSTETLER LLP** Cleveland
   THOMPSON HINE LLP Cleveland
   VORYS, SATER, SEYMOUR AND PEASE Cleveland
4. **ZEIGER & CARPENTER LLP** Columbus

Firms are listed alphabetically in each band.

Jones Day
see firm details p.823
The Firm: The state serves as headquarters for a vast and preeminent national litigation practice. Said by interviewees to possess a *"uniformly impressive"* team in its Cleveland and Columbus offices, the firm fields a remarkable array of top commercial litigators. Peers applaud a group of *"fantastic trial lawyers,"* with *"the kind of hands-on experience"* not always found even at NY firms. Blue-chip clients consider the Cleveland practice's key practitioners to be among *"the finest courtroom performers in the US."* The team is especially respected for its presence on the largest and most complex suits, in which its abilities have frequently been described to researchers as *"in a different league."* *"One of the firms for tobacco litigation,"* it has acted on behalf of the entire US tobacco industry, and has a notable relationship with RJ Reynolds.
The Lawyers: *"A uniquely qualified lawyer,"* according to competitors, **Patrick McCartan** (see p.576) fills the senior statesman role in the litigation group, and has a distinguished client portfolio, which includes Firestone, GM, Gillette, IBM, Pfizer and The Williams Companies. He is renowned for both his appellate work and his advice to corporate boards, although his duties as managing partner mean that he is now less frequently found in the courtroom.

John Strauch (see p.579), coordinator of Jones Day's national litigation practice, is known in the market as *"a charismatic showman"* who is *"great at winning a jury round."* He was a key figure in the firm's defense of RJ Reynolds, defended TRW in a major claims action and acted for Wal-Mart in a class action with more than 700,000 potential class members.

A favorite attorney of tobacco industry clients, **Bob Weber** (see p.579) was commended to researchers as *"our first port of call."* Weber chairs the firm's products liability practice, and clients report that this *"smart, tough"* attorney quickly establishes himself as *"the leading person in any courtroom."* His practice concentrates on multi-jurisdictional litigation, and although his position as the attorney of choice for RJ Reynolds has earned him the title of *"the cigarette king,"* Weber's work on behalf of a leading regional sporting client has also cemented his reputation as a respected and *"courageous"* practitioner.

OHIO — LITIGATION

OHIO
Leading individuals
(Litigation: General Commercial)

1
- **KILBANE Thomas** *Squire, Sanders,* Cleveland
- **MCCARTAN Patrick** *Jones Day,* Cleveland
- **MESSERMAN Gerald** *Messerman,* Cleveland
- **NEWMAN John** *Jones Day,* Cleveland
- **STRAUCH John** *Jones Day,* Cleveland
- **WEBER Robert** *Jones Day,* Cleveland

2
- **HILL Thomas** *Kegler, Brown, Hill & Ritter,* Columbus
- **HOOKER David** *Thompson Hine LLP,* Cleveland
- **SUTTON Jeffrey** *Jones Day,* Columbus
- **WERDER Richard** *Jones Day,* Cleveland
- **YOUNG David** *Squire, Sanders & Dempsey,* Columbus
- **ZEIGER John** *Zeiger & Carpenter LLP,* Columbus

3
- **COGAN Kevin** *Jones Day,* Columbus
- **CRIST Paul** *Jones Day,* Cleveland
- **CUPPS David** *Vorys, Sater, Seymour,* Columbus
- **FARUKI Charles** *Faruki Gilliam & Ireland PLL,* Dayton
- **GALL John** *Squire, Sanders & Dempsey,* Columbus
- **GREER David** *Bieser, Greer, & Landis LLP,* Dayton
- **GROSSMAN Theodore** *Jones Day,* Cleveland
- **HUFFMAN Fordham** *Jones Day,* Columbus
- **KARP Marvin** *Ulmer & Berne LLP,* Cleveland
- **MCDONALD John** *Schottenstein, Zox,* Columbus
- **RIDGLEY Thomas** *Vorys, Sater, Seymour,* Columbus
- **SOLOMON Randall** *Baker & Hostetler LLP,* Cleveland

4
- **MCLAUGHLIN Patrick** *McLaughlin,* Cleveland
- **SAXBE Charles** *Chester, Willcox,* Columbus
- **SCHWARTZ Niki** *Gold, Schwartz & Co LPA,* Cleveland
- **TRAFFORD Robert** *Porter Wright Morris,* Columbus
- **WILKINSON William** *Thompson Hine LLP,* Columbus

Up-and-coming individuals
- **MACE Damond** *Squire, Sanders & Dempsey,* Cleveland

Individuals are listed alphabetically in each band.

Paul Crist's (see p.574) focus on products liability cases has also seen him closely involved in the firm's work for RJ Reynolds. In addition, he gained substantial market endorsement for his securities litigation expertise. **Theodore Grossman** (see p.575) is another attorney who has argued motions on behalf of the entire US tobacco industry. His experience in the DOJ, serving as lead counsel in cases brought by or against a number of federal departments, has provided him with considerable regulatory litigation experience. His recent resumé includes acting for GE Capital in litigation concerning ownership of millions of credit card accounts, and for Northwestern Mutual in an alleged fraud case.

Jack Newman (see p.577) is one of the firm's top commercial practitioners, described by opponents as a *"consummate counter-puncher."* His acclaimed ability to pull together strong teams of associates was exemplified by his work in coordinating the firm's defense, as lead outside counsel, to Cooper Tire & Rubber. A varied practice covers stockholder disputes, corporate governance and banking litigation, and features a particular niche in securities litigation and class actions.

Widely admired by peers as a *"unique Supreme Court practitioner,"* **Jeff Sutton** (see p.579) is a national figure whose star is in the ascendant. About half of his practice is appellate-based, and he cemented his reputation with a staggering four wins in the US Supreme Court in the October 2000 term. These included representing the State of Alabama in a matter relating to the ADA, and Cortez Byrd Chips in relation to the Federal Arbitration Act.

General commercial litigator **Richard Werder** (see p.579) has been particularly active recently in bankruptcy and products liability cases. His *"sheer brainpower"* led clients to enthuse that *"he is so smart, he makes a complex subject seem easy."* He appeared successfully for Lincoln Electric, gaining a defense verdict in a $800 million claim. **Kevin Cogan** (see p.574) is a trial lawyer with a varied practice that has encompassed more esoteric matters, such as a water rights case challenging the City of Akron's use and management of the Cuyahoga River. His broad caseload includes insurance coverage, stockholder representation, labor matters and corporate control contests.

Head of the firm's Columbus office, **Fordham Huffman** (see p.575) has a general litigation practice with special emphasis on products liability, bankruptcy and insurance. Researchers heard sustained market endorsement for this *"pragmatic"* attorney who combines *"analytical ability with a practical approach."* Best known for representing creditors in insurance insolvency proceedings, Huffman recently acted on the $2.5 billion bankruptcy of a funeral business.

Squire, Sanders & Dempsey LLP

The Firm: Originally founded in Cleveland, this historically deep practice now extends far beyond Ohio. The team covers a broad sweep of commercial litigation, particularly environmental cases, heavy industry and complex financial matters, and has wide experience representing government entities. A substantial network of international offices and an array of attorneys who are *"superb advocates in open court"* ensure that the litigation department continues to take high rank both regionally and nationally.

The Lawyers: Described to researchers as *"a persuasive orator,"* **Tom Kilbane** is particularly admired by peers. Clients commented that he has the *"terrific experience and gray hair that command respect in court,"* and noted his ability to *"supervise large cases while mastering the details."* His varied practice embraces antitrust, securities and commercial contracts, as well as some alternative dispute resolution. His client roster includes Bridgestone and BP, and he appeared on an $800 million action in defense of Headwaters. **David Young** is a senior attorney who continues to gain high marks as *"a terrific trial lawyer."* His *"tremendous courtroom presence"* has been deployed on behalf of government officials and in a number of ERISA matters. He represented a national motel chain in relation to commercial speech rights, and has advised several trucking companies on employment claims.

Rivals respect **John Gall** as *"an excellent draftsman"* whose *"astute courtroom manner"* appeals to judges. Although he has a broad range of litigation experience, a significant proportion of his practice now involves IP litigation. His general commercial litigation experience has included defending accounting firms in malpractice suits, representing banks in financial matters and acting in corporate control contests.

Damond Mace was identified to researchers as *"a rising star"* at the firm. His practice takes in construction, contract work and royalty disputes, and was highlighted by his successful representation of DuPont in an environmental trespass claim.

Baker & Hostetler LLP

The Firm: This long-established Cleveland firm also has offices in Cincinnati, Columbus and throughout the US. Peers pointed to the high quality of advice produced by a firm that is *"somewhere between regional and national."* It has a specialty in toxic tort cases, and also undertakes substantial amounts of work in antitrust, banking, bankruptcy and professional negligence litigation.

The Lawyers: **Randall Solomon** was singled out for his expertise in the asbestos field. Clients described him as an *"experienced litigator with heavy trial experience"* and *"extraordinarily responsive."* He has an extensive practice defending the manufacturers of toxic substances, including asbestos, breast implants, and vinyl chloride in litigation that takes place at a regional and national level. General commercial matters, trade secrets and construction litigation also rounds out his practice.

The Clients: The firm acts for regional and national industrial manufacturers; chemical companies; pharmaceutical manufacturers and insurance companies.

Thompson Hine LLP

see firm details p.890

The Firm: Possessing comprehensive statewide coverage, this firm covers the spectrum of commercial litigation, and has developed a particularly strong reputation for construction litigation.

The Lawyers: Managing partner **David Hooker** (see p.575) remains a widely respected figure among Ohio's legal fraternity, although he now splits his time between fee-earning and managerial responsibilities. He forged his reputation in securities, corporate control and contract and construction disputes, and also boasts a track record in accountancy malpractice suits. In a

LITIGATION | OHIO

strong supporting cast, *"formidable adversary"* **Bill Wilkinson** (see p.579) stands out: he is generally regarded as the firm's best litigator in Columbus. His practice focuses on commercial litigation, including tender offers, fraud, breaches of contract and franchise, securities, IP, construction, dealer/distributor and RICO litigation. Domestic and international arbitrations and state and federal administrative hearings and investigations also figure prominently in his caseload.

Vorys, Sater, Seymour and Pease
The Firm: A leading presence in Columbus, this old-line Ohio firm is acknowledged by competitors to have some *"seasoned litigators"* among its leading players. The firm represents a number of local insurance clients, and has historically had a strong and active toxic tort practice.
The Lawyers: Endorsed to researchers as *"an exceptionally bright and experienced litigator,"* **David Cupps** is generally found handling the firm's most complex matters. His practice has recently included securities litigation, professional malpractice suits, pharmaceutical products liability and ERISA cases and matters arising from the duties of trustees. A consistent choice for *"pre-trial paper strategies,"* he is highly regarded by contemporaries who cautioned that *"it would be a mistake to underestimate his jury abilities."*

Thomas Ridgley has extensive experience in insurance defense and corporate control matters. His class action work includes securities, truth in lending, wage and hour, and consumer protection regulations. In addition, he represented Waste Management in a class action relating to a hazardous waste facility, and acted for a state contractor in a class action concerning a nuclear facility.

Zeiger & Carpenter LLP
The Firm: A boutique litigation firm that specializes in particularly complex civil matters, it was founded by several former Jones Day attorneys in the 1980's, and has been building up a respected profile ever since. Among a strong client list are heavyweight names such as Bank One and GM.
The Lawyers: *"One of the finest litigators in Ohio,"* **John Zeiger** is said by clients to be an *"outstanding practitioner and business consultant."* Frequently selected by leading law firms to represent them in malpractice suits, Zeiger earned strong commendation as a *"brilliant strategist"* whose preparation and research is *"flawless."* Elsewhere, his focus on media work has seen him represent AOL, and he has acted for The Columbus Dispatch and its affiliates for well over a decade.
The Clients: Among a strong client list are heavyweight names such as Bank One and GM.

Other Notable Practitioners
The revered **Gerald Messerman** of Messerman & Messerman Co LPA was described by a number of sources as *"the best trial lawyer in Cleveland."* An *"extraordinary"* attorney who has built a reputation as *"certainly the best criminal lawyer in town,"* he also undertakes complex civil matters. **Patrick McLaughlin**, of the small litigation boutique McLaughlin & McCaffrey LLP, is a popular choice for client referrals from major Ohio law firms. A former US attorney for northern Ohio, he has a complex civil practice that has recently included legal malpractice matters, a number of civil RICO cases and several products liability cases for a major tobacco company. Described as *"one of the deans of the commercial trial bar in Ohio,"* **Marvin Karp** of Ulmer & Berne LLP is a senior figure in the state. Karp undertakes corporate and business litigation, including contracts, fraud, corporate governance and some property insurance work. He recently represented the Ohio Attorney General in relation to the proposed sale of Blue Cross, and acted for a German merchant bank in a suit to recover fees.
In Columbus, **Tom Hill** of Kegler, Brown, Hill & Ritter has a practice that emphasizes complex commercial litigation. Respected by opponents as a *"tenacious litigator,"* he recently represented a mining company in a mining rights dispute, and advised the plaintiff on a products liability matter concerning powdered milk.
John McDonald of Schottenstein, Zox & Dunn is said to be *"a natural in a courtroom,"* and is renowned for his general commercial practice. **Charles Saxbe** of Chester, Willcox & Saxbe LLP focuses on commercial contract issues, employment, election law and matters involving the State of Ohio, in addition to his recent involvement in tobacco litigation.
Contemporaries describe **Buzz Trafford**, managing partner of Porter Wright Morris & Arthur, as a *"wonderful commercial litigator."* His practice encompasses corporate control, securities fraud, and professional malpractice, including the recent defense of one of Ohio's largest law firms. **Niki Schwartz** of Gold, Schwartz & Co LPA is another respected generalist who commentators say *"towers above his firm."*
In Dayton, two attorneys were singled out as superior commercial litigators. A trial lawyer with a highly varied commercial practice, **David Greer** of Bieser, Greer, & Landis LLP was described by clients as *"one of the top litigators in Ohio."* His profile is matched by **Charles Faruki**, managing partner of Faruki Gilliam & Ireland PLL, whose practice concentrates on business litigation, IP and products liability cases. He has experience in state and federal courts and before Ohio public agencies the SEC.

REAL ESTATE

OHIO
Leading firms (Real Estate)

1
- THOMPSON HINE LLP *Cleveland*
- VORYS, SATER, SEYMOUR AND PEASE *Columbus*

2
- JONES DAY *Cleveland*
- SQUIRE, SANDERS & DEMPSEY LLP *Cleveland*

3
- BAKER & HOSTETLER LLP *Cleveland*
- BENESCH, FRIEDLANDER, COPLAN *Cleveland*
- BRICKER & ECKLER LLP *Columbus*
- KAHN KLEINMAN *Cleveland*
- PORTER WRIGHT MORRIS & ARTHUR *Columbus*
- SCHOTTENSTEIN, ZOX & DUNN *Columbus*

Firms are listed alphabetically in each band.

Thompson Hine LLP
see firm details p.890
The Firm: Recognized as *"a premier firm in the region,"* Thompson Hine boasts a *"broad group with real depth"* in its core area of developer representation. The practice is subdivided along industry lines and covers the corporate, finance and capital markets aspects of real estate projects and transactions. Cleveland is the center of the practice, although experienced real estate attorneys also work out of the firm's other Ohio branches in Columbus, Cincinnati and Dayton. Competitors envy the firm's *"large stable of quality clients,"* while clients particularly applaud the group's skill at *"sophisticated financings."* Notable work includes representation of a multinational chemical company in a $1 billion joint venture transaction involving multiple properties in the US and Canada.
The Lawyers: Clients recommend **Linda Striefsky** (see p.579) as a *"technically excellent"* practitioner with expertise in real estate financing. She is highly visible in the market representing REITs and lending clients in shopping center acquisitions and financings of multi-state development projects.
The Clients: KeyCorp; KeyBank; Bank One; Charter One Bank; Nationwide Insurance; PolyOne Corporation; Mead/Westvaco; Eaton; Oglebay Norton Company; Forest City Enterprises and Duke Realty.

OHIO — REAL ESTATE

OHIO
Leading individuals (Real Estate)

1. **BUCHENROTH Stephen** *Vorys, Sater,* Columbus
2. **BAKER David** *Bricker & Eckler LLP,* Columbus
- **CONRAD David** *Bricker & Eckler LLP,* Columbus
- **PARIS Zachary** *Jones Day,* Cleveland
- **PEARLMAN Samuel** *Squire, Sanders,* Cleveland
- **REPPERT Richard** *Jones Day,* Cleveland
- **ROSNER Richard** *Kahn Kleinman,* Cleveland
- **STRIEFSKY Linda** *Thompson Hine LLP,* Cleveland

Individuals are listed alphabetically in each band.

Vorys, Sater, Seymour and Pease LLP
The Firm: Peers acknowledge this as *"an outstanding all-round practice."* The team's *"truly excellent lawyers"* are always *"on top of things"* and *"can handle anything that comes their way."* This *"comprehensive"* practice advises on all aspects of development from financing and construction to sale and leasing transactions. It also has noteworthy expertise in multiparty transactions, particularly in relation to public facilities. A blue-chip client base draws on the team's *"statewide quality."* The firm represented Capitol South Community Urban Redevelopment Commission in connection with the Capitol South multi-use development project, and recently handled the foreclosure of a large manufacturing plant in northern Ohio.
The Lawyers: Market sources single out **Stephen Buchenroth** at the Columbus office as a *"terrific, full-package"* attorney. This *"bright, knowledgeable and experienced"* lawyer offers extensive expertise in real estate, zoning, franchising and foreclosures.
The Clients: BancOhio National Bank, Bank One, The Prudential Insurance Company of America, New England Mutual Life Insurance Company, Home Savings of America, Fireman's Fund Mortgage Corporation, Citizens Federal Savings & Loan Association, Ackmor Properties; Abbott Laboratories and The Greater Columbus Convention Center.

Jones Day
see firm details p.823
The Firm: The practice boasts some *"top-flight lawyers"* and is famous for its *"high-class corporate real estate practice."* The team acts primarily for Fortune 500 companies, banks, real estate funds and investors on a range of financing, acquisition and development transactions. It also undertakes work on behalf of regional and national developers. The Cleveland practice acts as a unit with attorneys throughout the Jones Day national network, but attracts a large share of lending work in its own right through key relationships with local Midwest financial institutions. Attorneys in Cleveland have served as lead counsel to Continental Airlines since 1996 in a series of lease/bond financing transactions involving new terminal facilities constructed by Continental at its three hub airports at Cleveland, Newark and Houston.
The Lawyers: **Zachary Paris** (see p.577) is acknowledged as an *"outstanding lawyer with great experience and prestigious clients."* He is particularly involved in the hospitality industry, and has expertise in hotel acquisition and financing as well as the development of shopping centers and industrial parks.
Hailed as an *"absolutely rock-solid attorney,"* **Richard Reppert** (see p.578) is said to provide *"unbeatable quality"* when advising on site acquisitions, development finance and office and industrial leases.
The Clients: Forest City Enterprises; Ray Fogg Building Methods; Interstate Hotels Corporation; FFC Hospitality; KeyBank; Roadway Express; Continental Airlines; The Alderwoods Group and PNC.

Squire, Sanders & Dempsey LLP
The Firm: Renowned as *"one of the best bond practices in the country,"* the firm is a major player in the structuring of debt and equity financings for real estate acquisition and development. Researchers were told of the firm's *"streamlined practice"* and its *"high-caliber"* attorneys who have a *"definite focus on the financial side."* Clients are mainly lenders, equity investors and public entities although the team also occasionally acts for contractors and developers. The practice center is in Columbus, but a smaller group is based in Cleveland.
The Lawyers: Clients remark that **Samuel Pearlman** *"brings a lot to the table,"* including a *"great tax background"* and a *"broad view"* of real estate, corporate and securities matters.
The Clients: A diverse portfolio of clients includes banks, investment funds and insurance companies, municipalities, major developers, hotel managers, shopping centers and apartment complexes and a variety of retail, commercial and industrial tenants.

Baker & Hostetler LLP
The Firm: Commentators report that this group has *"come on strongly"* and is now *"taking work from the competition."* The team has acknowledged breadth and a good number of lawyers noted for their experience and *"entrepreneurial"* approach. The practice developed its REIT capabilities early on and still enjoys an *"excellent name"* in that field. Members typically represent developers and owners on land and business acquisitions and perform leasing work for retail clients.
The Lawyers: Peers noted *"able attorney"* Lawrence Lindberg for his work in property taxation and exemption, and environmental aspects of real estate development.
The Clients: The practice acts for a large concentration of REIT clients but undertakes work for banks and large and small local businesses on real estate financings and property transactions. Attorneys also have experience advising developers of resort hotels, office complexes, condominiums, industrial parks and manufacturing facilities.

Benesch, Friedlander, Coplan & Aronoff LLP
The Firm: A smaller team with a glittering history in this sector also has a *"good niche in sophisticated tax work."* The real estate and environmental teams operate as a combined practice group, and are highly recommended for real estate transactions with complex environmental components. The team fields a *"strong core of able lawyers,"* mostly acting for smaller developers, lenders and owners.
The Lawyers: Howard Steindler chairs the real estate practice group.
The Clients: Clients range from landlords, tenants and owners to developers, lenders and borrowers.

Bricker & Eckler LLP
The Firm: This Columbus-based group commands the respect of peers for its *"excellent advice to lenders"* and *"seriously impressive work."* Nearly half the workload involves mortgage financings. The team also handles development, leasing and acquisitions and sales.
The Lawyers: Widely recognized as *"seasoned lenders' counsel,"* **David Conrad** rates highly for his *"smart, aggressive style."* Clients value **David Baker** for the breadth of his experience and described him as *"reassuringly steady and solid."*
The Clients: Developers; investors; institutional lenders; mortgage bankers; public agencies; investment trusts; wireless communication companies; construction companies; and commercial and industrial landlords and tenants.

Kahn Kleinman
The Firm: This *"innovative, classy boutique"* is said to have *"invested heavily in its relationships with clients."* The firm's focus has grown to include areas such as corporation law, tax, securities and employment; however the firm still retains its traditional reputation for having a forte in the real estate field. Researchers were told that the Cleveland practice comprises *"excellent and active attorneys"* with a *"steady workload"* of real estate finance and development matters.
The Lawyers: **Richard Rosner** is universally admired as *"the attorney for condominium law."* Cochair of the firm's real estate and environmental practice, Rosner represents developers and builders in buying, financing, developing and leasing residential, commercial and industrial properties.

The Clients: Chase Shopping Centers, First Interstate Development and Pulte Homes of Ohio are clients.

Porter Wright Morris & Arthur
The Firm: Based in Columbus, this broad-based real estate practice commands recognized expertise in representing lenders on development projects. The group's transactional workload is mainly generated from a client roster of banks and insurance companies. Practitioners also advise on single family and multi-family residential developments. The team recently closed a $31.5 million commercial mortgage-backed securities loan on behalf of Nationwide Life Insurance for residential apartments in Cincinnati.
The Lawyers: John Rohyans manages the firm's real estate department.
The Clients: Nationwide Life Insurance; Dominion Homes; Huntington National Bank; MTB Corporation; The Great-West Life Assurance Company; Bank One and State Farm.

Schottenstein, Zox & Dunn
The Firm: The Columbus firm remains faithful to its real estate origins and is renowned for work in development and construction. The team acts on both residential and commercial transactions and possesses a noteworthy niche in retail matters, where it represents owners and franchisees both locally and nationally. Peers particularly complimented the team's expertise in leasing matters.
The Lawyers: Randall Arndt chairs the firm's real estate practice.
The Clients: Schottenstein Stores; Limited Brands; Nationwide Realty Investors; DSW Shoe Warehouse; Big Lots; K-B Toys; HoneyBaked Ham; Huntington National Bank and The Provident Bank.

Leaders in Ohio

ADAMO, Kenneth R
Jones Day, Cleveland 216 579 0212
kradamo@jonesday.com
Recommended in Intellectual Property
Specialization: Practices in the area of intellectual property law, including patent, trademark, copyright, unfair competition, trade secrets, bankruptcy, employment contract, and related antitrust matters. He has had extensive trial experience in jury and non-jury matters before the state and federal courts and before the International Trade Commission as well as ex parte and inter partes experience in the US Patent and Trademark Office and with non-US patent and trademark authorities.
Prof. Memberships: He is a member of the ABA (Antitrust, Litigation, and Intellectual Property Law Sections), the American Intellectual Property Law Association, LES, the Cleveland Intellectual Property Law Association, the Intellectual Property Law Association of Chicago, and the Dallas/Fort Worth Patent Association. He has written and lectured extensively on intellectual property law, for both US and non-US publications and organizations, including topics such as motion practice, International Trade Commission proceedings, reexamination, fraud/inequitable conduct in procuring patents, civil RICO in intellectual property matters, attorney disqualification, artificial intelligence and business methods protection, reissue, means plus function claims, combined-reference obviousness, cyberart, the best mode requirement, the doctrine of equivalents/prosecution history estoppel, exhaustion, Internet jurisdiction, software patents, patent marking, traditional litigation and effects of non-US adjudications, and trademark infringement. He has also written and lectured on a wide variety of trial and litigation issues, skills, and training.
Career: Registered to practice before the United States Patent and Trademark Office, Reg. No. 27,299 (1974); admitted 1975 Illinois; 1976 New York; 1984 Ohio; 1988 Texas.
Personal: Rensselaer Polytechnic Institute (BSChE 1972); The Albany Law School of Union University (JD 1975); John Marshall Law School (LLM 1989).

ADAMS, Deborah
Frost Brown Todd LLC, Cincinnati
513 651 6800
Recommended in Employment

APPELBAUM, Jeffrey
Thompson Hine LLP, Columbus
614 469 3200
jeff.Appelbaum@ThompsonHine.com
Recommended in Construction
Specialization: Serves varying roles of trial/transactional attorney, project counsel, project management consultant, mediator, partnering facilitator. Services public/private owners, design professionals, construction managers, contractors on US Canadian projects, served as lead trial lawyer for cases involving millions of dollars of disputed claims, as project counsel for projects involving billions of dollars of construction. Has facilitated 150+ partnering sessions.
Prof. Memberships: American, Cleaveland, Ohio State Bar Associations, Ohio.
Publications: Numerous.
Personal: Received his JD (cum laude) from Cornell Law School; his BA (with distinction) from Cornell University.

AZOFF, Elliot
Baker & Hostetler LLP, Cleveland
216 621 0200
Recommended in Employment

BAKER, David
Bricker & Eckler LLP, Columbus
614 227 2300
Recommended in Real Estate

BARNARD, Thomas
Ulmer & Berne LLP, Cleveland
216 621 8400
Recommended in Employment

BEDREE, Melvin
Vorys, Sater, Seymour and Pease, Cincinnati 513 723 4023
mabedree@vssp.com
Recommended in Banking & Finance
Specialization: Partner who practices in the area of commerical finance, including asset based financing. He has represented many national and regional asset based and structured finance lenders. His practice includes multi-borrower, multijurisdiction, transactions, acquisition financing, asset sales out of bankruptcy, multi-lender deals and capital expenditure financing. His practice also includes negotiating subordinated debt arrangements with institutional providers of mezzanine capital.
Prof. Memberships: Ohio State and American Bar Associations.
Career: Admitted to Ohio Bar, 1984; and US District Court, Southern District of Ohio, 1984.
Personal: University of Cincinnati, JD, 1984; Depauw University, BA, magna cum laude, 1981.

BRINKMAN, David
Wood, Herron & Evans, LLP, Cincinnati
513 241 2324
Recommended in Intellectual Property

BRUBAKER, Robert
Porter Wright Morris & Arthur, Columbus
614 227 2112
Recommended in Environment

BUCHENROTH, Stephen
Vorys, Sater, Seymour and Pease LLP, Columbus 614 464 6366
srbuchenroth@vssp.com
Recommended in Real Estate
Specialization: Real Estate Law; Franchising. Partner in charge of Real Estate Group.
Prof. Memberships: Columbus (Member, Board of Governors, 1986-94; President, 1992-93), Ohio State (Member: Council of Delegates, 1986-88, 1991-; Real Property Section, Board of Governors, 1990; Vice Chair, 1992) and American (Member: Sections on: Antitrust Law; Business Law, Chairman, Franchising Subcommittee of Small Business Committee, 1991-92; Real Property, Probate and Trust Law; Forum Committee on Franchising) Bar Associations; American College of Real Estate Lawyers; Ohio Supreme Court Commission on Continuing Legal Education.
Career: Admitted to Ohio Bar (1974).
Personal: University of Chicago, JD,1974; Wittenberg University, AB, cum laude, 1970.

CARLSON, James
Thompson Hine LLP, Cleveland
216 566 5556
Jim.Carlson@ThompsonHine.com
Recommended in Corporate/M&A
Specialization: Focuses on takeover defense, including shareholder rights plans and preparedness programs; acquisitions and dispositions, including public company mergers; corporate governance; leveraged recaps and buyouts; representation of special board committees; joint ventures, including E-commerce alliances, and SEC filings and compliance.
Prof. Memberships: American Bar Association; Ohio Bar Association, including Tender Offer Subcommittee of Corporation Law Committed.
Publications: Has spoken and published outlines on takeover defense, public company mergers, joint ventures and corporate governance.
Personal: Received JD from Harvard Law School (1975) and a BA from Oberlin College, magna cum laude, Phi Beta Kappa (1969).

OHIO — LEADERS

CARSON, Van
Squire, Sanders & Dempsey L.L.P,
Cleveland 216 479 8500
Recommended in Environment

COGAN, Kevin J
Jones Day, Columbus 614 469 3825
jcogan@jonesday.com
Recommended in Litigation
Specialization: Has extensive trial and jury trial experience in complex litigation, from corporate control contests and securities fraud, to class actions, insurance coverage disputes and water rights. Co-trial counsel in Danaher Corporation v Acme Cleveland and United Dominion Industries v Commercial Intertech, Inc where Jones Day successfully defended the targets of attempted hostile takeovers. In the United Dominion litigation the trial judge upheld the constitutionality of Ohio's Control Share Acquisition Act despite having earlier ruled that the act was unconstitutional. Successfully defended MPW Industrial Services Group in a securities class action filed in Ohio State Court. Co-trial counsel representing Cooper Industries in its insurance coverage dispute with Employer's Insurance of Wausau and other insurance carriers. Successfully defended Buckeye Egg Farm, LP, in a class action relating to Buckeye Egg's use of beneficial insects to control nuisance insects. Defended Buckeye Egg in a state enforcement action in which the state of Ohio sought, unsuccessfully, to place Buckeye Egg in receivership and to seize its assets. Co-trial counsel in the case of Atlantic Richfield Company, et al v Alcan Aluminium Holdings Ltd, an action tried in the US District Court for the Southern District of New York. Successfully defended a central Ohio radiology provider, and its chief executive officer, in a jury trial against claims of fraud and breach of fiduciary duty. Lead trial counsel in an action challenging the city of Akron's use and management of the Cuyahoga River. Lead litigation counsel for Nations Rent in its chapter 11 reorganization.
Career: Admitted 1978 Ohio; 1979 Florida. Joined firm 1986.
Personal: DePauw University (Phi Beta Kappa; BA with high distinction 1975); Case Western Reserve University (Chairman, Moot Court Board; Order of the Coif; JD 1978).

CONRAD, David
Bricker & Eckler LLP, Columbus
614 227 2300
Recommended in Real Estate

CRIST, Paul
Jones Day, Cleveland 216 586 7139
pgcrist@jonesday.com
Recommended in Litigation
Specialization: Fellow of the American College of Trial Lawyers. He has represented clients in complex product liability matters in state and federal trial and appellate courts throughout the US. Paul served as lead trial counsel in Connor v. R.J. Reynolds Tobacco Co. (Duval County, Fla.), a nationally-publicized tobacco liability case that was tried to jury verdict in May 1997, and in Kueper v. R.J. Reynolds Tobacco Co., et al. (St. Clair County, Ill.), a nationally-publicized, two and a half month long tobacco liability case that was tried to a jury and bench verdict in favor of all defendants in January 1993. Has participated in multijurisdictional product liability proceedings pending in the US for other clients in a variety of industries and served as lead or co-counsel in numerous military jury and bench criminal trials. In addition, he has been involved in numerous other litigation matters, including takeovers, securities, general business, real estate, and class actions.
Prof. Memberships: He is a member of the Ohio State Bar Association, the Cleveland Bar Association, and the State Bar of California. He is admitted to practice before the United States District Court for the Northern District of Ohio, the US Court of Appeals for the Sixth Circuit, and the US Court of Military Appeals; and he has been admitted pro hac vice in courts throughout the nation. He has lectured at seminars on trial tactics, evidence, expert witnesses, cross-examination, deposition techniques, federal court mediation, and punitive damages and in programs sponsored by Jones Day and in programs co-sponsored by the National Institute for Trial Advocacy.
Career: Joined firm 1974. Rejoined in 1978.
Personal: University of Nebraska (BA in Chemistry 1971); New York University (Research Editor, Law Review; Order of the Coif; JD cum laude 1974.

CUPPS, David
Vorys, Sater, Seymour and Pease LLP,
Columbus 614 464 6318
dscupps@vssp.com
Recommended in Litigation
Specialization: Partner in the litigation group. Practices in the areas of complex and multi-district litigation; antitrust, intellectual property, securities litigation, and professional malpractice litigation.
Prof. Memberships: American Bar Association, Columbus Bar Association, District of Columbia Bar Association, Ohio State Bar Association.
Career: Admitted to New York Bar (1966), Ohio Bar (1972), District of Columbia Bar (1979).
Personal: Harvard College, AB, 1958. The Ohio State University, JD, summa cum laude, 1965. Order of the Coif. Mershon Fellowship, 1964-65. Editor, Ohio State Law Journal, 1964-65; Fellow, American College of Trial Lawyers and Regent, 1997-2001.

CURRIE, Michael
Thompson Hine LLP, Columbus
614 469 3200
Mike.Currie@ThompsonHine.com
Recommended in Construction
Specialization: Focuses his practice on public and private construction law, real estate law, and commercial and construction litigation. Has represented architects, engineers, public and private owners, contractors, subcontractors, suppliers and sureties in bidding, construction and post-acceptance construction disputes.
Prof. Memberships: American, Columbus, Ohio State Bar Associations, Ohio Contractors Association, Associated General Contractors, Central Ohio Builders Exchange.
Publications: Numerous.
Personal: Received his JD (cum laude) from The Ohio State University College of Law and his BS (cum laude) from The Ohio State University.

CYPHERT, Michael
Thompson Hine LLP, Cleveland
216 566 5500
Mike.Cyphert@ThompsonHine.com
Recommended in Environment
Specialization: Handles environmental counseling, crimes, compliance analysis, energy issues, strategic planning in acquisitions, divestitures, evaluating environmental due diligence investigations, toxic tort litigation, governmental regulatory issues. Lead outside litigation counsel to numerous companies and is coordinating/lead counsel in Superfund litigation to some metal recycling companies.
Prof. Memberships: American, Federal, Ohio State Bar Associations, Defense Research Institute.
Career: Admitted - Supreme Court (Ohio), US District Courts (Norther/Southern Ohio), Sixth Circuit Court of Appeals, Supreme Court (US).
Personal: Received his JD (Order of the Coif), BA from Case Western Reserve University.

DAUCHOT, Luke
Thompson Hine LLP, Cleveland
216 566 5863
Luke.Dauchot@ThompsonHine.com
Recommended in Intellectual Property
Specialization: Focuses on intellectual property and complex litigation commercial litigation. Serves as Business Litigation Group Leader.
Prof. Memberships: American Bar, Master Bencher, Anthony J Celebrezze Inn of Court, Cleaveland Intellectual Property Law Association.
Career: Admitted to practice in Ohio and Illinois state courts, as well as numerous federal district and circuit courts. Associate Member of the Brussels, Belguim Bar.
Personal: Speaks Dutch and French. Received a JD from Case Western Reserve University School of Law and a BA magna cum laude from Case Western Reserve University.

DORAN, Scott
Vorys, Sater, Seymour and Pease LLP,
Columbus 614 464 8248
smdoran@vssp.com
Recommended in Environment
Specialization: Partner and chairman of the Environmental Law Group. He has worked extensively on Superfund, RCRA, toxic tort, and a variety of environmental issues raised by industrial, commercial, and residential real estate developments. An authority on wetland law and regulation, he regularly appears before the Army Corps of Engineers, US EPA, and the Ohio EPA on permit issues and appeals. He participated in the formation of the Ohio Wetlands Foundation, one of the nation's first private wetland mitigation banking programs.
Prof. Memberships: Columbus (Chairman, Environmental Law Committee, 1992-94) and Ohio State Bar Associations.
Career: Admitted to Ohio (1986), US District Court, Southern District of Ohio (1986).
Personal: University of Cincinnati, JD, 1986. Miami University, BA, 1979; Miami University, MS, 1983.

DUVIN, Robert
Duvin, Cahn & Hutton, Cleveland
216 696 7600
Recommended in Employment

FAGAN, Christopher
Fay, Sharpe, Fagan, Minnich & McKee, LLP, Cleveland 216 861 5582
Recommended in Intellectual Property

FAHEY, Richard
Vorys, Sater, Seymour and Pease LLP,
Columbus 614 464 5601
rpfahey@vssp.com
Recommended in Environment
Specialization: Partner, environmental group.
Prof. Memberships: Columbus, Ohio State and American (Vice Chair, Water Quality Committee, Section on Natural Resources, Energy and Environmental Law, 1993-1995) Bar Associations; New Mexico State Bar.
Career: Admitted New Mexico and US District Court, District of New Mexico (1971); US Court of Appeals, Tenth Circuit (1972); Ohio and US District Court, Northern and Southern Districts of Ohio (1973); US Supreme Court (1975).
Publications: Author: 'Groundwater Law in Ohio Past and Future,' 14 Capital University Law Review 43-80, 1984; 'Underground Storage Tanks: The New Federal Regulatory Program,' ABA Natural Resources Monograph Series, 1989, 2nd edition, 1995; Chapter 2, 'Underground Storage Tank Program,' Ohio Environmental Law, Banks-Baldwin, 1992.
Personal: Northwestern University, JD, 1971. San Francisco State University, BA,

OHIO

1966. Professor environmental law, Capital University Law School, 1976-86; Ohio State University Law School, 1986-87; Chairman, Ohio Oil and Gas Regulatory Review Commission, 1986-87.

FARUKI, Charles
Faruki Gilliam & Ireland PLL, Dayton
937 227 3700
Recommended in Litigation

FRANTZ, Michael
Frantz Ward LLP, Cleveland
216 515 1660
Recommended in Employment

FREKING, Randolph
Freking & Betz, Cincinnati
513 721 1975
Recommended in Employment

FRIEDMAN, Steven
Squire, Sanders & Dempsey LLP,
Columbus 614 365 2700
Recommended in Construction

GALL, John
Squire, Sanders & Dempsey LLP,
Columbus 614 365 2700
Recommended in Litigation

GANSKE, Lyle
Jones Day, Cleveland 216 586 7264
lgganske@jonesday.com
Recommended in Corporate/M&A
Specialization: Chairs the firm's M&A/Corporate section and heads the firm's Domestic Mergers & Acquisitions practice. He practices in the general corporate, transactional, and securities law areas, with significant experience in takeover work, takeover preparedness, mergers and acquisitions, corporate governance matters, and general corporate counseling. He has significant expertise in public company transactions and transactions involving regulated industries, including the telecommunications industry and the energy industry.
Prof. Memberships: He is a member of the ABA (Business Law Section) and the Ohio State Bar Association (Corporation Law Committee).
Career: Joined firm 1984. Law Clerk to Judge Craig Wright, Ohio Supreme Court (1985 term).
Publications: He is a frequent speaker on mergers and acquisitions, takeover preparedness, and corporate governance issues and has co-authored many articles, including 'Not Only Does One-Size-Not-Fit-All, But The Same-Size-Does-Not-Always-Fit-One: The Evolving Face Of Corporate Governance At Texas Instruments' ('The Metropolitan Corporate Counsel', March 1998); 'Corporate Governance Out of Focus: The Debate Over Classified Boards' ('The Business Lawyer', May 1999); 'Breaking Up is Hard to Do: Avoiding the Solvency-Related Pitfalls in Spinoff Transactions' ('The Business Lawyer', February 1999); and 'Corporate Bylaws: The Building Blocks of a Corporation &8212; and a Bulwark of Defense' ('Director's Monthly', January 2002).
Personal: Bowling Green State University (BSBA summa cum laude 1981); The Ohio State University (Note and Comment Editor, Law Journal; Order of the Coif; JD with honors 1984).

GITTES, Frederick
Spater Gittes & Schulte, Columbus
614 222 4735
Recommended in Employment

GRADY, Timothy
Porter Wright Morris & Arthur, Columbus
614 227 2112
Recommended in Banking & Finance

GREER, David
Bieser, Greer, & Landis LLP, Dayton
937 223 3277
Recommended in Litigation

GREGORY, Donald
Kegler, Brown, Hill & Ritter, Columbus
614 462 5400
Recommended in Construction

GROSSMAN, Theodore
Jones Day, Cleveland 216 586 7268
tgrossman@jonesday.com
Recommended in Litigation
Specialization: Has tried complex product liability and other significant cases in every section of the country and has argued appeals in a majority of the federal circuits and various state appellate courts. Overall, he has been lead counsel in hundreds of cases, dozens of which have resulted in published opinions. In addition to supervising the defense of hundreds of cases and trying some of the most complex among them, he serves R.J. Reynolds and its co-defendants as the principal cross-examiner of recurrent witnesses, whose testimony is often taken on videotape for use in a wide array of trials. He has been active in class actions and other aggregated litigation since 1983, when he successfully represented the Department of Defense in Brown v. Orr, a putative class action that challenged Air Force career advancement procedures as racially discriminatory. In recent years, he has continued to defend class actions and has also served as lead counsel in a variety of other matters. He has broad experience in regulatory litigation both from his work in private practice and from his work at the Department of Justice. He has served as lead counsel in cases brought by or against almost every federal department and a variety of federal independent agencies.
Prof. Memberships: He has been profiled in several leading US legal directories. He has lectured on cross-examination, deposition techniques and product liability law in NITA presentations and seminars throughout the country and given guest lectures on international trade litigation at the Georgetown University Law Center. He has appeared as counsel on behalf of the Lawyers' Committee for Civil Rights in an action to desegregate the Office of the Attorney General of Mississippi. He was recently inducted into the American College of Trial Lawyers. He has served as a member of the board and as treasurer of the Cleveland Center for Contemporary Art.

GUINN, Guy
Calfee, Halter & Griswold LLP, Cleveland
216 622 8200
Recommended in Banking & Finance

GURNEY, Scott
Frost Brown Todd LLC, Cincinnati
513 651 6800
Recommended in Construction

HARDY, Michael
Thompson Hine LLP, Cleveland
216 566 5500
Mike.Hardy@ThompsonHine.com
Recommended in Environment
Specialization: Leader of the Environmental practice group, focusing his practice on environmental counseling and litigation; environmental compliance analysis and planning in business transactions; and toxic tort litigation.
Prof. Memberships: American, Ohio State, Cleaveland Bar Associations; Defense Research Institute; United States Law Firm Group; Director, Nature Center of Shaker Lakes Canterbury Golf Club, Inc and National Club Association.
Career: Leadership role in Environmental Committees of national, state and local bar associations.
Publications: Numerous.
Personal: Received a JD (cum laude) from the University of Michigan, an AB (magna cum laude) from John Carroll University.

HAWKINS, Michael
Dinsmore & Shohl LLP, Cincinnati
513 977 8200
Recommended in Employment

HILL, Thomas
Kegler, Brown, Hill & Ritter, Columbus
614 462 5403
thill@keglerbrown.com
Recommended in Litigation
Specialization: Is a trial lawyer with over thirty years experience in complex business litigation.
Prof. Memberships: Fellow of the American College of Trial Lawyers; American Bar Association; Columbus Bar Association; Ohio State Bar Association.
Career: Representative cases include: successful defense of a Fortune 100 company in a $500-million dollar fraud claim tried to a jury in federal court in Texas; representation of a publicly-traded company in litigation in federal court in Ohio arising out of a hostile takeover attempt that produced a $20-million dollar settlement for the client; representation of the American Cancer Society in litigation arising out of a $7-million dollar embezzlement of Cancer Society funds; lead trial counsel in Donatos Pizza's successful prosecution of trademark infringement claim involving Donatos 'Edge to Edge' trademark; successful defense of a local university in wrongful discharge litigation brought by discharged faculty members; successful defense of a publicly traded company in federal court litigation alleging defectively manufactured products; defense of a Catholic Diocese in litigation alleging sexual abuse; successful defense of a national pension fund in claims over rights to participate in the fund. Profiled in leading American publications.
Publications: Federal Civil Procedure and Evidence During Trial - 6th Circuit - a two-volume treatise on trial practice in the federal courts in the Sixth Circuit.
Personal: Juris Doctorate, Cornell University Law School, Ithaca, New York, 1970; Bachelor of Arts, Political Science, Grinnell College, Grinnell, Iowa, 1967.

HOBERG, Tim
Taft, Stettinius & Hollister LLP,
Cincinnati 513 381 2838
Recommended in Corporate/M&A

HOLMAN, Michael
Bricker & Eckler LLP, Columbus
614 227 2300
Recommended in Construction

HOOKER, David J
Thompson Hine LLP, Cleveland
216 566 5500
David.Hooker@ThompsonHine.com
Recommended in Litigation
Specialization: Managing director of *Thompson Hine*. Specializes in the trial of complex business disputes with experience in securities litigation, cases about corporate and partnership control, breach of contract actions, tax controversies and construction disputes. Has defended public accountants and consultants in malpractice claims.
Prof. Memberships: Fellow, American College of Trial Lawyers, member American, Cleaveland and Ohio Bar Associations.
Publications: With Jeff Appelbaum: 'Architect Engineer Liability Under Ohio Law' (Cambridge Institute 1989).
Personal: Received his JD from Stanford Law School (member, 'Stanford Law Review') and his BS (with highest honors, Phi Beta Kappa) from Denison University.

HUFFMAN, Fordham
Jones Day, Columbus 614 469 3934
fehuffman@jonesday.com
Recommended in Litigation
Specialization: Partner in Charge of the Columbus office. Practises in the area of general litigation and has extensive experience in insurance regulation and practice, product liability, and bankruptcy litigation. Has served as counsel to the

liquidator of Ambassador Insurance Company in receivership matters and in litigation against the company's former management and auditors. Has represented a variety of clients as creditors in insurance insolvency proceedings, including Allstate, Acordia, and National City Bank, and has advised the Ohio Department of Insurance regarding potential regulatory responses to insurer financial instability. Served as lead litigation counsel to the court-appointed trustee for Cardinal Industries, Inc, whose $2 billion chapter 11 case involved complex, first impression issues of bankruptcy and partnership law affecting tens of thousands of investors and secured lenders. Also regularly represents firm clients in commercial and employment litigation and has coordinated nationwide product liability defense for two firm clients in the building industry.
Prof. Memberships: State Bar of Georgia; Ohio State Bar Association; the Columbus Bar Association.
Career: Admitted 1980 Georgia; 1984 Ohio. Joined firm 1984. Law Clerk to Judge Max Rosenn, US Court of Appeals, Third Circuit (1980 term).
Personal: The Ohio State University (BA 1977; Editor in Chief, Law Journal; JD 1980).

JANKE, Ron
Jones Day, Columbus 216 586 7279
rrjanke@jonesday.com
Recommended in Environment
Specialization: Has experience with the application of environmental laws to many industrial and commercial sectors, including chemical manufacturing, ore and coal mining, ferrous and nonferrous metal manufacturing, coatings, publishing, food processing, banking, transportation, and waste management. Experienced in the major state and federal regulatory programs relating to control of air emissions, wastewater discharges, solid and hazardous wastes, and hazardous materials storage and handling. Has represented clients at more than 100 National Priority List sites and at other sites remediated under federal or state laws; has advised buyers, sellers, and lenders in assessing environmental liabilities in the sale of business operations and real estate, including numerous multi-state or multinational transactions, has advised companies on structure and conduct of compliance audits of existing operations. Has represented clients in state and federal environmental enforcement actions, and in private citizen suits seeking to enforce environmental laws; advised clients in state, federal, and private actions seeking the remediation of or recovery of costs for waste disposal sites and contaminated industrial and commercial properties. Has represented companies in appeals of permits or challenges to the adoption of state or federal regulations.
Prof. Memberships: Served on advisory committees of the US EPA and the Ohio EPA. ABA (Business Law Section, past chairman of the Environmental Controls Committee; Section of Environment, Energy, and Resources); Ohio State Bar Association (Environmental Law Committee); Cleveland Bar Association (Environmental Law Committee); Environmental Law Institute; Ohio Chamber of Commerce (Energy and Environment Committee); Binational Public Forum of the Lake Erie Lakewide Management Plan.
Career: Admitted 1974 Ohio. Joined firm 1974. Lectures extensively on environmental compliance and litigation.
Personal: Wittenberg University (BA cum laude, English 1969); Duke University (Editorial Board, Law Journal; Order of the Coif; JD with distinction 1974).

JORGENSON, Mary Ann
Squire, Sanders & Dempsey L.L.P,
Cleveland 216 479 8500
Recommended in Corporate/M&A

KAISER, Gordon
Squire, Sanders & Dempsey L.L.P,
Cleveland 216 479 8500
Recommended in Corporate/M&A

KARP, Marvin
Ulmer & Berne LLP, Cleveland
216 621 8400
Recommended in Litigation

KILBANE, Thomas
Squire, Sanders & Dempsey L.L.P,
Cleveland 216 479 8500
Recommended in Litigation

KILLWORTH, Richard
Killworth, Gottman, Hagan & Schaeff LLP, Dayton 937 223 0724
Recommended in Intellectual Property

KING, G Roger
Jones Day, Columbus 614 469 3874
gking@jonesday.com
Recommended in Employment
Specialization: Specialises in employment relations matters, with concentration in representing management in matters arising under the National Labor Relations Act, state and federal equal employment statutes, the Americans with Disabilities Act, and the Family and Medical Leave Act. Also represents employers in collective bargaining negotiations, grievance and arbitration matters, and involvement in litigation in state and federal trial and appellate courts regarding labor-related matters. Substantial experience in the areas of covenants not to compete, tortious interference with business issues, substance abuse testing issues, Office of Federal Contract Compliance matters, issues under the Fair Labor Standards Act, wrongful discharge claims, and the development and review of employee policies and procedures.
Prof. Memberships: The College of Labor and Employment Lawyers (Fellow); American, District of Columbia, Ohio State, and Columbus Bar Associations and the labor relations section of each association; Ohio Chamber of Commerce Labor Advisory Committee; the Society of Human Resource Management (SHRM); Member NLRB Region 9 Advisory Committee; American Society for Healthcare Human Resources Administration; Health Care Roundtable; Ohio Society of Hospital Attorneys; Industrial Research Relations Association; American Health Lawyers Association (has served as a board member); Catholic Health Association Legal Affairs Committee; National Employment Relations Committee of SHRM.
Career: Admitted 1971 Ohio; 1973 District of Columbia. Labor Relations Counsel to US Senator Robert Taft Jr (1971-73); Professional Staff Counsel, US Senate Committee on Labor (1973-75). Joined firm 1990. Has testified before committees of the US Congress and administrative agencies. Has been listed in a number of leading American and global legal directories. Has been an active speaker and author for groups throughout the US on labor and employment relations matters.
Publications: An editor of The Developing Labor Law and a contributing editor to HR Advisor.
Personal: Miami University (BS 1968); Cornell University (JD 1971).

KNECHT, Denise
Denise J Knecht & Associates Co,
Cleveland 216 621 4882
Recommended in Employment

KREIDER, Gary
Keating, Muething & Klekamp, P.L.L.,
Cincinnati 513 579 6400
Recommended in Corporate/M&A

LEACH, Donald
Buckingham Doolittle & Burroughs,
Columbus 614 221 8448
Recommended in Construction

LERNER, Stephen
Squire, Sanders & Dempsey L.L.P,
Cleveland 216 479 8500
Recommended in Banking & Finance

LEUKART, Barbara
Jones Day, Cleveland 216 586 7190
bjleukart@jonesday.com
Recommended in Employment
Specialization: Has represented management in all areas of labor and employment relations. She has defended numerous Title VII, age discrimination, and Americans with Disabilities Act cases at the administrative, trial, and appellate levels. Her experience includes the litigation of wrongful discharge, employment contract, and intentional tort cases. On behalf of employers, she has handled cases brought under the Equal Pay Act, Section 301 of the Taft-Hartley Act, the National Labor Relations Act, the Fair Labor Standards Act, the Family and Medical Leave Act, and the Employee Retirement Income Security Act. She has counseled companies on a wide range of employment issues, including advice on union representation campaigns, contract negotiations, the creation and implementation of employment policies, the conduct of discrimination investigations, and corporate management reviews conducted by the OFCCP. In addition, she has extensive experience in supervising and managing large employment litigation dockets in conjunction with in-house counsel and in-house human resources staff.
Prof. Memberships: Pursuant to an appointment by the United States Court of Appeals for the Sixth Circuit, she is currently serving on that court's Advisory Committee on Rules. She has been a member of the Civil Justice Reform Act Task Force for the United States District Court for the Northern District of Ohio and serves as a mediator for the court. She is a member of the Celebrezze Inn of Court, the ABA (Labor and Employment Law Section), and the Ohio State Bar Association. Has been admitted to practice before the US Courts of Appeals for the Sixth, Fifth, and Third Circuits. She has lectured at seminars on various employment law topics.
Career: Joined firm in 1977.
Personal: Barnard College (BA 1971); Case Western Reserve University (Associate Editor, Law Review; Order of the Coif; JD 1975).

LEWIS, John
Baker & Hostetler LLP, Cleveland
216 621 0200
Recommended in Employment

LIGGETT, Luther
Bricker & Eckler LLP, Columbus
614 227 2300
Recommended in Construction

LIPS, Alan
Taft, Stettinius & Hollister LLP,
Cincinnati 513 381 2838
Recommended in Employment

LYON, Charles
Calfee, Halter & Griswold LLP,
Cleveland 216 622 8200
Recommended in Intellectual Property

MACE, Damond
Squire, Sanders & Dempsey L.L.P,
Cleveland 216 479 8500
Recommended in Litigation

MCCARTAN, Patrick F
Jones Day, Cleveland 216 586 7272
pmccartan@jonesday.com
Recommended in Litigation
Specialization: Senior partner with extensive complex case experience on a national basis in areas such as antitrust, taxation, takeovers, officer and director liability, and various kinds of securities

and shareholder litigation. Active in corporate governance matters and in the product liability and consumer class action areas, having defended mass tort litigation throughout the US and having assisted many manufacturers in fashioning programs to cope with emerging developments in product liability law throughout the world. During his term as head of the *Jones Day* Litigation Group (1976-92), the group saw tremendous growth in size. Numbering more than 800 members throughout the firm, the group today has responsibility for a docket averaging close to 4,000 matters pending in state and federal courts in more than 25 jurisdictions throughout the US and before international arbitral tribunals in Geneva, London, Stockholm, and The Hague. As Managing Partner he extended the Firm's geographic reach to Beijing, Houston, Madrid, Menlo Park, Milan, Mumbai, Munich, New Delhi, Shanghai, Singapore, and Sydney and enhanced delivery of the firm's services through Specialized Industry Practice groups.
Prof. Memberships: Fellow of the American College of Trial Lawyers and the International Academy of Trial Lawyers; and an Honorary Overseas Member of the English Commercial Bar Association.
Career: He was Managing Partner of *Jones Day* from 1993-2002 and coordinator of the Firm's Litigation Group from 1976-92. In 2003 he became Senior Partner concentrating on appellate litigation and corporate governance matters.
Personal: University of Notre Dame (AB magna cum laude 1956; Editor in Chief, Law Review; JD 1959)

MCDONALD, John
Schottenstein, Zox & Dunn, Columbus
614 462 2700
Recommended in Litigation

MCLAUGHLIN, Patrick
McLaughlin & McCaffrey, LLP, Cleveland
216 623 0900
Recommended in Litigation

MCMAHON, Michael
McMahon, DeGulis, Hoffman & Lombardi LLP, Cleveland 216 621 1312
Recommended in Environment

MCNAIR, Eben
Schwarzwald & Mcnair, Cleveland
216 566 1600
Recommended in Employment

MENTEL, Michael
Roetzel & Andress, PC, Akron
330 376 2700
Recommended in Environment

MERSOL, Greg
Baker & Hostetler LLP, Cleveland
216 621 0200
Recommended in Employment

MESSERMAN, Gerald
Messerman & Messerman Co, LPA,
Cleveland 216 574 9990
Recommended in Litigation

MILLER, Barry
Benesch, Friedlander, Coplan & Aronoff LLP, Cleveland 216 363 4500
Recommended in Construction

MILLISOR, Kenneth
Millisor & Nobil, Cleveland
440 838 8000
Recommended in Employment

MILLS, Osborne
Squire, Sanders & Dempsey L.L.P,
Cleveland 216 479 8500
Recommended in Banking & Finance

MILLSTON, David
Squire, Sanders & Dempsey L.L.P,
Cleveland 216 479 8500
Recommended in Employment

MIRALDI, Leslee
Thompson Hine LLP, Cleveland
216 566 5500
Leslee.Miraldi@ThompsonHine.com
Recommended in Banking & Finance
Specialization: Partner in the Commercial Finance Group. Focuses on commercial lending, representing financial institutions and public and private companies in senior and subordinated debt facilities. Works with syndicated, multi-bank, foreign and domestic credit facilities, asset based/structured finance facilities, acquisition financing, letter of credit facilities, foreign currency transactions, secured transactions and real estate financing. Representation also includes credit facility restructurings and workouts.
Prof. Memberships: Cleavaland, Lorain County, and Ohio State Bar Associations.
Career: Admitted to Ohio Bar in 1978. Admitted to US Supreme Court; US Court of Appeals, 6th Circuit; and US District Court, Northern District of Ohio.
Personal: Received JD from Ohio State University (1978), MA (summa cum laude) and BA (summa cum laude, Phi Beta Kappa, Alpha Kappa Delta) from Ohio University.

MUSKOVITZ, Susannah
Faulkner, Muskovitz & Phillips, LLP,
Cleveland 216 781 3600
Recommended in Employment

NASH, David
Thompson Hine LLP, Cleveland
216 566 5500
Dave.Nash@ThompsonHine.com
Recommended in Environment
Specialization: Partner, focusing on environmental issues relating to business and real estate transactions, regulatory matters and legislative matters, environmental litigation, and environmental enforcement actions, including civil and criminal defense matters.
Prof. Memberships: Cleaveland (Chair, Environmental Law Section 1997-98) and Ohio State Bar Associations (Chair, Environmental Law Committee, 2000-2001).
Career: Fellow, Ohio Sate Bar Foundation.
Publications: Numerous.
Personal: Received his JD (with honors) from Duke University School of Law, his BA (magna cum laude, Phi Beta Kappa) from Wake Forest University.

NATALE, Andrew
Frantz Ward LLP, Cleveland
216 515 1660
Recommended in Construction

NEWMAN, JR, John (Jack)
Jones Day, Cleveland 216 586 7207
jmnewman@jonesday.com
Recommended in Litigation
Specialization: He is the Cleveland Office coordinator for *Jones Day's* Litigation Group. He has been involved in a wide variety of general business matters, including shareholder actions, bank brokerage lawsuits, takeover contests, lender liability, employee benefits, bankruptcy, tax, consumer and accounting-related litigation, and other commercial controversies.
Prof. Memberships: He is a Fellow of the American College of Trial Lawyers and is a member of the ABA (Litigation Section), the Los Angeles County Bar Association, and the Cleveland Bar Association (Judicial Selection Committee, 1988-1990). He has also served on the board of editors of the Federal Litigation Guide Reporter and was a member of the adviser group for The American Law Institute Project on Complex Litigation (1988-92). He is admitted to practice before the United States Tax and Supreme Courts and various federal district courts and courts of appeals.
Career: Admitted 1970 Illinois; 1972 California; 1976 Ohio. Law Clerk to Judge Irving Hill, United States District Court, Central District of California (1969 term); Assistant United States Attorney, Central District of California (1970-75).
Personal: Georgetown University (BA magna cum laude 1966); Harvard University (Editor, Law Review; JD magna cum laude 1969).

PACE, Stanley Dan
Spieht Bell McCurdy & Newell Co, LPA,
Cleveland 216 696 4700
Recommended on Employment

PARIS, Zachary
Jones Day, Cleveland 216 586 7275
ztparis@jonesday.com
Recommended in Real Estate
Specialization: Practices real estate development, corporate real estate services, and hospitality industry law. He has experience representing developers in most aspects of commercial and industrial development, including the acquisition of undeveloped land and the installation of improvements for office and industrial parks and shopping centers, the construction and leasing of buildings, the negotiation of reciprocal easement agreements for shopping centers, and providing financing through conventional loans, tax-exempt bonds, and equity syndications. The developer clients he frequently represents include Forest City Enterprises, Inc.; Ray Fogg Building Methods, Inc.; and Robert L. Stark Enterprises, Inc. His corporate real estate services work focuses on meeting the real estate needs of corporations and other institutions whose core business is outside the real estate industry. He has been involved in corporate headquarters development projects, ground leases for large industrial properties, and leases and financings for airport expansion projects. Corporate clients for whom he has provided legal services include General Motors Corporation; Gliatech, Inc.; and Continental Airlines, Inc. He also serves as a co-leader of the Firm's hospitality practice. Over the past ten years, he has been involved in most major aspects of the hotel industry, including the acquisition, sale, and/or financing of individual hotels and hotel portfolios; the master leasing of hotel portfolios from REITs; the negotiation and implementation of multilender credit facilities for hotel operators; and the negotiation of management agreements and franchise agreements. One of his principal hotel clients has been Interstate Hotels Corporation, headquartered in Pittsburgh, which *Jones Day* represented in its initial public offering in 1996 and its merger with Patriot American Hospitality, Inc. in 1998 and in its subsequent spin-off and merger with Merister Hospitality in 2002.
Career: Joined firm 1984. Admitted 1973 Ohio. Yale University (BA 1970; JD 1973). Law Clerk to Judge William K Thomas, United States District Court, Northern District of Ohio (1973 and 1974 terms).

PEARLMAN, Samuel
Squire, Sanders & Dempsey L.L.P,
Cleveland 216 479 8500
Recommended in Real Estate

PETRO, John
McNamara & McNamara, Columbus
614 228 6131
Recommended in Construction

PORTER, David
Jones Day, Cleveland 216 586 7215
dporter@jonesday.com
Recommended in Corporate/M&A
Specialization: Practices principally security and corporate finance law. He also has extensive experience in corporate restructurings and corporate governance matters, including takeover defense. His regular corporate clients include aerospace, industrial, real estate, retail, and telecommunications companies, as well as numerous other public companies that call on him for securities disclosure advice. His takeover defense work has included the successful defense of Ohio's antitakeover legislation.

OHIO LEADERS

Prof. Memberships: Member of the ABA (Business Law Section), the Ohio State Bar Association (Corporation Law Section), and the Cleveland Bar Association (Securities Law Section). He has chaired and been a member of subcommittees of the Ohio State Bar Association that have drafted revisions to Ohio's corporate statutes.
Career: Joined firm 1981.
Publications: Has authored numerous articles on securities and takeover planning topics and is a frequent speaker in seminars on such topics. His recent publications include: 'MD&A in Troubled Times' (April 2001); 'Corporate Web Sites and the Securities Laws' (January 2001); 'SEC Ready to Crack Down on Accounting Games' (September 1999); 'Legislation Allows Proxy Votes Via E-Channels' (June 1999); 'The SEC's Plain English Rules: The Rules and Early Comments' (February 1999); 'The Big Event' (December 1998); 'SEC Interpretive Release on Year 2000 Disclosures by Public Companies: Focus on the MD&A' (August 1998); 'The SEC's W.R. Grace Order: The Responsibility of Directors and Officers for Corporate Disclosures' (January 1998); 'Ohio Strengthens, Simplifies Control Share Acquisition Act (October 1997); 'Talks with Analysts Impact Wall Street's Perceptions (April 1997); and 'Decision Gives New Life to Anti-Arbitrageur Provision of Ohio's Control Share Acquisition Act' (April 1997).
Personal: University of California, Davis (BS 1975); Case Western Reserve University (Associate Editor, Law Review; Order of the Coif; JD 1981).

RAWSON, Rachel
Jones Day, Cleveland 216 586 7276
rlrawson@jonesday.com
Recommended in Banking & Finance
Specialization: Coordinates the commercial lending practice in the Cleveland Office. In her practice in the lending/structured finance area, she represents borrowers, institutional lenders, and investors in secured and unsecured lending transactions and other financing transactions and private placements. She has experience in a variety of complex syndicated and single-lender financing transactions, senior and subordinated debt placements, acquisition facilities, multicurrency facilities, workouts and debt restructurings, as well as extensive experience with general asset-based commercial transactions and other working capital facilities. She also has experience with leveraged lease financings, asset securitizations, and venture capital financings.
Prof. Memberships: She is a member of the ABA (Business Law Section) and a member of the Banking and Business Law Section of the Cleveland Bar Association.
Career: Admitted 1991 New York; 1995 Ohio.
Personal: Kenyon College (Phi Beta Kappa; BA magna cum laude 1987);

Columbia University (Research and Writing Editor, Journal of Law and Social Problems; Harlan Fiske Stone Scholar; JD 1990).

REMINGTON, Royce
Hahn Loeser & Parks LLP, Cleveland
216 621 0150
Recommended in Construction

REPPERT, Richard L
Jones Day, Cleveland 216 586 7235
rreppert@jonesday.com
Recommended in Real Estate
Specialization: His practice includes a broad range of commercial real estate transactional matters, including site acquisitions for new developments, purchases and sales of unimproved and improved real property, office and industrial leases, ground leases, and financings for both borrowers and lenders secured by real estate. He specializes in representing life insurance companies, banks, and other institutional lenders, including conduit lenders, in connection with real estate mortgage loans. He is a member of the Firm's Opinions Committee and the Firm's Technology Committee.
Prof. Memberships: He is a member of the ABA (Real Property, Probate and Trust Law Section), the Cleveland Bar Association (chairman of the Real Estate Law Section, 1998-1999), the Ohio State Bar Association, and the American College of Real Estate Lawyers. He is a former contributing editor to Banking and Lending Institution Forms published by A.S. Pratt & Sons, has lectured throughout the country on various issues of real estate law, and is listed in the real estate law section in a leading US publication.
Career: Joined firm 1988. Admitted 1974 Ohio; 1993 Pennsylvania.
Personal: Lehigh University (BA cum laude 1970); Villanova University (Managing Editor, Law Review; Order of the Coif; JD 1974).

RIDGLEY, Thomas
Vorys, Sater, Seymour and Pease LLP, Columbus 614 464 6229
tbridgley@vssp.com
Recommended in Litigation
Specialization: Litigator with experience in all areas of civil litigation including commercial, business, takeover, securities, labor, insurance, environmental, and products liability litigation.
Prof. Memberships: Member of the Columbus, Cincinnati, Ohio State, and American Bar Associations.
Career: Admitted to practice in Ohio (1968), in the United States District Courts for the Northern and Southern Districts of Ohio, the United States Courts of Appeals, Third, Sixth and Tenth Circuits and the US Supreme Court.
Personal: University of Michigan, JD, with distinction, 1965; Princeton University, AB, magna cum laude, 1962. Fellow, American College of Trial Lawyers. Listed in a leading publication in America in the

Business Litigation section for Commercial and Toxic Tort Litigation and in the Personal Injury section for Product Liability Litigation.

ROE, Clifford
Dinsmore & Shohl LLP, Cincinnati
513 977 8200
Recommended in Corporate/M&A

ROSATI, Jack
Bricker & Eckler LLP, Columbus
614 227 2300
Recommended in Construction

ROSENBERG, Thomas
Ulmer & Berne LLP, Columbus Null
Recommended in Construction

ROSNER, Richard
Kahn Kleinman, Cleveland
216 696 3311
Recommended in Real Estate

RUSH, Jeffrey
Frost Brown Todd LLC, Cincinnati
513 651 6800
Recommended in Banking & Finance

RYDZEL, James
Jones Day, Cleveland 216 586 7227
jarydzel@jonesday.com
Recommended in Employment
Specialization: His practice includes counseling in the areas of labor and employment matters, with special focus on employment-related litigation. This includes labor arbitrations and all types of National Labor Relations Board (NLRB) proceedings. His litigation experience includes a large number of ERISA cases, particularly involving retiree medical benefits and severance pay, both individually and on a class basis. His counseling activities have involved all phases of labor relations, including articulation of negotiation goals and strategies, strike preparation, temporary and permanent replacement of strikers, and picket line and Boys Market injunctions. His clients have included both traditional manufacturing operations and white-collar, service-related industries.
Prof. Memberships: He is a member of the ABA (Labor and Employment Law Section and Litigation Section) and the Ohio State Bar Association. He is also a member of the bar of several federal circuits and districts. He was an adjunct professor of law at Case Western Reserve University, where he taught advanced courses in employment litigation, and has lectured extensively on employment matters.
Career: Joined firm 1972. Admitted 1972 Ohio; 1975 Florida.
Personal: Saint Louis University (Phi Beta Kappa; BA magna cum laude 1968); Duke University (Editorial Board, Law Journal; JD with highest honors 1972).

SAXBE, Charles Rockwell
Chester, Willcox & Saxbe LLP, Columbus
614 221 4000
Recommended in Litigation

SCHLOEMER, Jeffrey
Taft, Stettinius & Hollister LLP, Cincinnati 513 381 2838
Recommended in Banking & Finance

SCHRAFF, Christopher
Porter Wright Morris & Arthur, Columbus
614 227 2112
Recommended in Environment

SCHWARTZ, Niki
Gold Schwartz & Company, Cleveland
216 696 6122
Recommended in Employment, Litigation

SHEERAN, Timothy
Squire, Sanders & Dempsey L.L.P., Cleveland 216 479 8500
Recommended in Employment

SIEGEL, Bradd
Porter Wright Morris & Arthur, Columbus
614 227 2112
Recommended in Employment

SOLOMON, Randall
Baker & Hostetler LLP, Cleveland
216 621 0200
Recommended in Litigation

SPRING, Gary
Roetzel & Andress, A Legal Professional Association, Akron 330 376 2700
gspring@ralaw.com
Recommended in Employment
Specialization: Partner with the law firm of *Roetzel & Andress* and concentrates his practice in the areas of employment law and labor law. He is an Adjunct Professor of Law at the University of Akron School of Law teaching Labor Law, Employment Law and Collective Bargaining and Arbitration courses. He has received the Quine award from the Law School as its outstanding Adjunct Professor. He was a regular contributor and on the Editorial Review Board of the Ohio Labor Letter. He is a frequent presenter at various legal and human resource programs.
Prof. Memberships: Member of the Akron, Ohio and American Bar Associations. He is admitted to practice in Ohio, the Northern and Southern Federal Districts of Ohio, the Sixth Circuit Court of Appeals and the United States Supreme Court. He is certified as a specialist in Labor and Employment Law by the Ohio State Bar Association. He is also on the State Bar Association's Committee that administers testing and sets the standards for certification as a specialist in Labor and Employment Law.
Personal: Received his law degree with honors from Ohio State University. While attending law school, he was a member of the Ohio State Law Journal. Following law school he was a law clerk to Justice Paul W Brown of the Ohio Supreme Court.

LEADERS OHIO

STRAUCH, John
Jones Day, Cleveland 216 586 7240
jlstrauch@jonesday.com
Recommended in Litigation
Specialization: He is the coordinator of the firm's 800-plus lawyer Litigation Group, and has extensive experience in complex litigation. He has been involved in matters concerning product liability, corporate takeovers, class actions, federal securities, government regulation, commercial litigation, and antitrust before a variety of state and federal courts.
Prof. Memberships: Is a member of the ABA (Litigation and Antitrust Law Sections), the Ohio State Bar Association, the Cleveland Bar Association (past president), and the Federal Bar Association. He is a Fellow of the American College of Trial Lawyers and a Life Member of the United States Sixth Circuit Judicial Conference and the Ohio Eighth District Judicial Conference. He has lectured at seminars on subjects that include the trial of securities actions, techniques of cross-examination, motion practice, and judicial selection procedures. In connection with various litigation matters, he has been widely quoted in the print media and has appeared on The Today Show, Nightline, David Brinkley, Frontline, Crossfire, Fred Friendly's PBS Managing our Miracles, and ABC, CBS, NBC, and CNN news.
Career: Joined firm 1964. Admitted 1963 New York, 1964 Ohio. Law Clerk to Judge Sterry R. Waterman, United States Court of Appeals, Second Circuit (1963 term).
Publications: Co-author of 'Multidistrict Litigation', Business and Commercial Litigation in Federal Courts (West Group 1998); author of 'The Key to Success in Litigation: Empathy,' in Inside the Minds: Leading Litigators (Aspatore 2002).
Personal: University of Pittsburgh (Phi Beta Kappa; BA in Economics summa cum laude 1960); New York University (Editor-in-Chief, Law Review; Order of the Coif; Root-Tilden Scholar; JD magna cum laude 1963).

STRIEFSKY, Linda
Thompson Hine LLP, Cleveland
216 566 5500
Linda.Striefsky@ThompsonHine.com
Recommended in Real Estate
Specialization: Partner focusing on real estate financing, including real estate investment trusts and multi-state financing transactions; acquisitions and sales; corporate facilities management, including out-sourcing contracts; leasing, easement and related agreements; real estate taxes, including tax complaints, exemptions and abatement.
Prof. Memberships: American, Cleaveland and Ohio State Bar Associations. American College of Real Estate Lawyers; Urban Land Institute.
Publications: Numerous.

Personal: Received her JD from Georgetown University Law Center and her BA from Marywood College (summa cum laude).

SUTTON, Jeffrey
Jones Day, Columbus 614 469 3855
jssutton@jonesday.com
Recommended in Litigation
Specialization: Specializes in commercial, constitutional, and appellate litigation. Has argued 12 cases in the US Supreme Court, including Hohn v US in which the Court invited his participation. Has argued more then 30 cases in other federal and state appellate courts. Has also handled countless cases in the state and federal trial courts.
Career: Admitted 1990 Ohio. Law Clerk to Judge Thomas J Meskill, US Court of Appeals, Second Circuit (1990-91) and Law Clerk to Justice Lewis F Powell Jr (Ret.) and Justice Antonin Scalia, US Supreme Court (1991 Term). With Jones Day from 1992 to 1995; rejoined the firm in 1998. Has taught classes on federal and state constitutional law at The Ohio State University College of Law since 1994. In 1997, he was appointed to the Ohio Supreme Court's Committee on Alternative Dispute Resolution and in that year also received the Outstanding Recent Alumnus Award from The Ohio State University College of Law. While serving as the state solicitor of Ohio, he received the National Association of Attorneys General's Best Brief Award in 1996, 1997, 1998, and 1999.
Personal: Williams College (BA with honors 1983); The Ohio State University (Issue Planning Editor, Law Journal; Order of the Coif; JD summa cum laude 1990).

TAROLLI, Thomas
Tarolli, Sundheim, Covell, Tummino & Szabo LLP, Cleveland 216 621 2234
Recommended in Intellectual Property

TARULLO, Michael
Schottenstein, Zox & Dunn, Columbus
614 462 2700
Recommended in Construction

TOBIAS, Paul
Tobias Kraus & Torchia, Cincinnati
513 241 8137
Recommended in Employment

TORCHIA, David
Tobias Kraus & Torchia, Cincinnati
513 241 8137
Recommended in Employment

TOSI, Louis
Shumaker, Loop & Kendrick LLP, Toledo 419 241 9000
Recommended in Environment

TRAFFORD, Robert
Porter Wright Morris & Arthur, Columbus
614 227 2112
Recommended in Litigation

VINCENT, George
Dinsmore & Shohl LLP, Cincinnati
513 977 8200
Recommended in Corporate/M&A

WEBER, Robert
Jones Day, Cleveland 216 586 7252
rcweber@jonesday.com
Recommended in Litigation
Specialization: Has practiced law at Jones Day for more than 26 years and currently chairs the firm's Product Liability Practice. He has tried cases throughout the United States and is a Fellow of the American College of Trial Lawyers and the International Academy of Trial Lawyers. He also has extensive experience in consumer class actions, corporate derivative litigation, federal and state enforcement actions, and a wide variety of commercial litigation.
Prof. Memberships: Member of The American Law Institute, and Product Liability Advisory Council. Life Member of the Judicial Conference for the Eighth District of Ohio. Served as president of the Cleveland Bar Association and was also honored as a Fellow of the Ohio State Bar Foundation in 1998.
Career: Joined the firm 1976. Admitted Ohio, 1976.
Personal: Yale University (BA cum laude 1972); Duke University (Editorial Board, Law Journal; Order of the Coif; JD 1976).

WELIN, Peter
Thompson Hine LLP, Columbus
614 469 3269
Peter.Welin@ThompsonHine.com
Recommended in Construction
Specialization: Partner focusing his practice on public and private construction contract law, construction contracts, and government procurement law.
Prof. Memberships: American, Columbus and Ohio State Bar Associations, Associated General Contractors of Ohio, Builders Exchange of Central Ohio.
Career: Before entering the legal field, he gained six years of engineering experience with Turner Construction Company.
Publications: Co-Author, 'Ohio Public Contract Law and Construction Claims' (1994).
Personal: Received his JD from The Ohio State University College of Law and his BS from Iowa State University (Civil Engineering).

WERDER, Richard
Jones Day, Cleveland 216 586 7260
riwerder@jonesday.com
Recommended in Litigation
Specialization: Has extensive experience in all kinds of complex litigation including cases involving product liability, consumer class actions, shareholder class and derivative litigation, corporate control contests, information technology contracts, bankruptcy, and general business and commercial litigation. He has served as lead trial counsel in a number of significant trials, including a class action in Illinois in which plaintiffs sought more than $50 million and a consumer protection and product liability action in California in which plaintiffs sought more than $800 million. He has also been heavily involved in various types of bankruptcy court litigation; in alternative dispute resolution procedures arising out of business acquisitions; in takeover defense matters; and in a large number of shareholder class action and derivative lawsuits. He serves as co-chairman of the firm's Technology Issues Practice. He has published in the areas of corporate governance and director and officer liability and in other areas.
Prof. Memberships: Member of the Product Liability Advisory Council, the ABA (Litigation and Business Law Sections), and the Ohio State and Cleveland Bar Associations.
Career: Joined the firm 1984. Admitted Ohio, 1984. Law Clerk to Judge Harry T Edwards, US Court of Appeals, District of Columbia Circuit (1982 term); Law Clerk to Justice Byron R White, United States Supreme Court (1983 Term).
Personal: Canisius College (BA magna cum laude 1979); University of Michigan (Recipient, Henry M. Bates and Class of 1908 Scholarships; Editor in Chief, Law Review; Order of the Coif; JD magna cum laude 1982).

WILKINSON, William
Thompson Hine LLP, Columbus
614 469 3200
william.wilkinson@thompsonhine.com
Recommended in Litigation
Specialization: Partner and former partner-in-charge in the firm's Business Litigation practice group. Focuses his practice on commercial litigation, including tender offer, fraud, breach of contract, franchise, securities, intellectual property, construction, dealer/distribution and RICO litigation; domestic and international arbitration; and state and federal administrative hearings and investigations.
Prof. Memberships: American, Columbus, Ohio State Bar Associations.
Personal: Received his JD and his BA (cum laude) from The University of Akron.

YOUNG, David
Squire, Sanders & Dempsey LLP, Columbus 614 365 2700
Recommended in Litigation

YUND, George
Frost Brown Todd LLC, Cincinnati
513 651 6800
Recommended in Employment

ZEIGER, John
Zeiger & Carpenter LLP, Columbus
614 365 4100
Recommended in Litigation

OKLAHOMA

CORPORATE/M&A

CONTENTS: Corporate/M&A p.580; Employment: Mainly Plaintiff p.581; Mainly Defendant p.582; Litigation: General Commercial p.583; Real Estate p.584; Individuals' Profiles p.585.

OKLAHOMA'S TOP TWO
1. Crowe & Dunlevy
2. McAfee & Taft

Ranking based on Chambers' research within the state.

All quotes in the text are from interviews with clients and competitors.

OVERVIEW: Oklahoma's top-ranked firm, **Crowe & Dunlevy**, is also the largest. This well-established firm has expanded in the past 15 years from its Oklahoma City base to offices in Tulsa and Norman. Peers believe the firm to be unmatched in its breadth of expertise and strength across the state. Crowe & Dunlevy topped every *Chambers'* table, and had more individuals ranked than any of its competitors. In litigation, antitrust and bankruptcy cases were seen as the specialties of star attorney Kent Meyers, who was praised for his solid analytical skills. Consolidation in the oil and gas sector, the principal driving force behind the Oklahoma economy, has produced a substantial flow of work for the firm; litigator Gary Davis was singled out for his particular expertise in this area. Clients of the firm include ExxonMobil, Chevron USA, ConocoPhillips and BancFirst.

Ranked second, **McAfee & Taft** also secured a top-band place in corporate/M&A tables. Founded as a tax firm, and historically strong in the areas of corporate securities, finance and acquisitions, McAfee & Taft still dominates the financial section of the market. Clients describe the practice, in which Theodore Elam and Gary Fuller are leading names, as a sophisticated outfit with a polished, entrepreneurial style. Litigation and employment are also strong suits for the firm. Clients include Devon Energy, Fleming Companies, Dobson Communications and Halliburton.

CORPORATE/M&A

OKLAHOMA
Leading firms (Corporate/M&A)
1. **CROWE & DUNLEVY** Oklahoma City
   MCAFEE & TAFT PC Oklahoma City
2. **CONNER & WINTERS PC** Tulsa
   HARTZOG CONGER CASON Oklahoma City
   MCKINNEY & STRINGER PC Oklahoma City
3. **COMMERCIAL LAW GROUP** Oklahoma City

Leading individuals (Corporate/M&A)
1. **STEWART Michael** Crowe & Dunlevy, Oklahoma City
2. **ELAM Theodore** McAfee & Taft PC, Oklahoma City
   FULLER Gary McAfee & Taft PC, Oklahoma City
   SELF Shannon Commercial Law Group, Oklahoma City
3. **DERRICK Gary** Derrick & Briggs LLP, Oklahoma City
   MOORE Lynnwood Conner & Winters PC, Tulsa
   STRINGER Martin McKinney & Stringer, Oklahoma City

Firms and individuals are listed alphabetically in each band.

Crowe & Dunlevy
The Firm: This *"superb team of top-notch lawyers"* stands out from the majority of its competitors in both reputation and size. Clients felt its experience in more complex matters to be unmatched. The 30 attorneys here have expertise in the full range of commercial matters, including M&A, establishing partnerships and limited liability organizations and taxation. The group was particularly strongly recommended for its public securities work.
The Lawyers: Commentators consider **Michael Stewart** to be *"without doubt the lead securities lawyer at the firm."* Clients highlight his particular expertise in matters relating to the oil and gas, and healthcare industries. His practice focuses on public company representation in financing, securities law and M&A.
The Clients: The firm recently represented Louis Dreyfus Natural Gas in its sale to Dominion Resources for cash, stock and debt assumption totaling $2.3 billion. It also acted for Canaan Energy in its sale to Chesapeake Energy for cash and debt assumption of $118 million. Other clients include: Pre-Paid Legal Services; Southwestern Bell Telephone Company; Bank One Oklahoma; Bank of Oklahoma; BancFirst; GMX Resources; Harold's Stores and Norman Regional Hospital.

McAfee & Taft PC
see firm details p.844
The Firm: Founded as a tax firm, it has historically been strong in the areas of corporate securities, finance and acquisitions. Interviewees commented that the firm boasts *"an extremely sophisticated corporate practice – beyond what some people would expect in Oklahoma."* The 35 lawyers cover a full range of corporate work, routinely handling public and private equity and debt offerings, as well as venture capital investments and strategic alliances. A strong IP group further boosts its profile.
The Lawyers: **Theodore Elam** (see p.585) divides his time between public and private securities issues and M&A. *"A consummate lawyer,"* according to sources, *"he instills confidence in his clients that their deals will be done properly and economically."* His experience includes handling corporate finance matters in the energy, retail, insurance and real estate sectors. He was recently lead counsel on private and public debt and equity offerings totaling $1 billion for Dobson Communications and American Cellular Corporation. *"Analytical and intellectual"* **Gary Fuller**'s *"outstanding ability to find creative solutions"* elicited praise from peers. The bulk of his work lies in corporate planning, debt structuring and M&A.
The Clients: The firm represented Mustang Fuel Corporation in a $92.5 million acquisition of natural gas processing facilities. Other clients include: Devon Energy; Kerr-McGee; Fleming Companies; Dobson Communications and Western Bank.

Conner & Winters PC
The Firm: This established Oklahoma firm boasts a strong team of general corporate attorneys working with both public and private companies. According to sources: *"The firm as a whole does sophisticated work,"* particularly in the Tulsa office, *"where the top talent lies."* The 19 attorneys in the corporate and securities group offers a broad range of services to business clients, including M&A, corporate governance, joint ventures and liquidations. As well as leading corporates, the firm has long experience representing broker-dealers and other industry professionals. It recently handled the sales of two public companies for an aggregate consideration in excess of $100 million.
The Lawyers: **Lynnwood Moore** has handled general corporate advice, securities regulation and M&A for over 30 years. Interviewees praised his *"judgment and deal skills; there is no substitute for experience like his."* Recently he has focused on mergers, asset purchases and sales, and public securities reporting.
The Clients: Recent work includes the disposal of a client's crude oil refineries and related assets for a total consideration of $450 million. Clients include: The Williams Companies; WilTel Communications; Vintage Petroleum; Willbros Group; Dover Resources; Parker Drilling Company; Jameson Inn; Black Hills Corporation; Omni Air International and Global Power Equipment.

CORPORATE/M&A

OKLAHOMA

Hartzog Conger Cason & Neville PC
The Firm: Market sources admire this *"boutique with high-quality lawyers."* Its strong business group has expertise in M&A, capital formation activities, bankruptcies and workouts, and general corporate and securities law advice. Competitors particularly recommended the firm for its *"strong tax background and expertise."* Len Cason is a member of the team.
The Clients: The firm's clientele includes a number of public and privatel businesses, wealthy individuals, trusts and estates, and charitable organizations. Sources particularly noted its private client work.

McKinney & Stringer PC
The Firm: This 12-strong corporate team has a growing profile in the securities area. It is counsel in both public and private offerings, and commands a solid reputation for M&A and related financing, corporate governance, regulation and financial and business planning. The firm was particularly recommended to researchers for its experience representing financial institutions, while competitors also highlighted the firm's strong environmental practice.
The Lawyers: Martin Stringer was admired by interviewees for his knowledge of financing. His practice includes negotiating and structuring business combinations, and counseling corporate and financial institutions on state and federal regulatory and legislative matters.
The Clients: Stage Stores; TEPPCO Crude Oil; Advanced Academics; The Oklahoma Heart Hospital; Chesapeake Energy and First Fidelity Bank.

Commercial Law Group
The Firm: This young corporate boutique has first-class lawyers and a good name for business advice. Its four *"practical and hard-working"* attorneys handle a range of corporate finance and M&A, venture capital investments and bankruptcy matters. Sources note the team's *"businesslike approach"* and commitment to *"getting the best lawyer for the job."*
The Lawyers: Shannon Self is a former certified public accountant with a strong background in tax. Peers rated him *"an A+ lawyer"* with a *"good deal of intuition and experience in sophisticated transactions."* He enjoys a broad practice, but is especially recognized for his expertise in venture capital transactions.
The Clients: The firm has been active in M&A in the energy sector, including transactions for Chesapeake Energy and Canaan Energy. Other clients include Chisholm Private Capital Partners; Infinity Resources; Lazy E Ranch and several local venture capital funds.

Other Notable Practitioners
Gary Derrick of Derrick & Briggs LLP was recommended to researchers as *"outstanding, diligent, hard-working and bright."* A corporate and securities specialist, his work includes public and private securities offerings, M&A, venture capital investments and general contractual work. Recent deals include a spin-off and merger for a public company, and an equity offering for an agricultural cooperative, both of which were valued in excess of $1 million. Clients are drawn from a range of sectors including oil and gas, technology, hospitality, agriculture, manufacturing, insurance, medicine and accounting.

EMPLOYMENT & LABOR LAW

MAINLY PLAINTIFF

OKLAHOMA
Leading firms
(Employment: Mainly Plaintiff)
1. **EDDY & JONES** Oklahoma City
2. **BRIDGER-RILEY & ASSOCIATES PC** Tulsa
   HAMMONS & ASSOCIATES Oklahoma City
   LEONARD & ASSOCIATES PC Oklahoma City

Leading individuals
(Employment: Mainly Plaintiff)
1. **BLEDSOE Gregory** *Gregory Bledsoe*, Tulsa
   EDDY Rand *Eddy & Jones*, Oklahoma City
2. **BRIDGER-RILEY Kay** *Bridger-Riley & Associates*, Tulsa
   HAMMONS Mark *Hammons & Associates*, Oklahoma City
   LEONARD Jana *Leonard & Associates*, Oklahoma City
   NOVICK Steven *Sole Practitioner*, Tulsa

Firms and individuals are listed alphabetically in each band.

Eddy & Jones
The Firm: This team won sustained plaudits from both sides of the table. It specializes in plaintiff representation in a wide variety of employment matters, including discrimination, wrongful discharge and contract work. **Rand Eddy** has made a name for himself as an *"excellent trial lawyer"* who is *"diligent, knowledgeable and appropriately aggressive."* Interviewees admired his determination, commenting that *"he works his cases very hard, and knows how to value them."*

Bridger-Riley & Associates PC
The Firm: This two-person litigation boutique often pits itself against the biggest names in the field, and holds an *"excellent reputation"* for *"beating Goliath."* The firm provides plaintiff representation in employment discrimination and ERISA litigation. **Kay Bridger-Riley** is widely renowned for *"some fantastic trial successes,"* and rivals admiringly referred to her as *"formidable in the courtroom."* Her practice is devoted to civil rights and employment litigation.

Hammons & Associates
The Firm: This firm takes on a wide variety of employment issues, from race and sex discrimination to ERISA work. The team is recommended for its *"staying power,"* and researchers were told that it has gained *"a lot of good results in the courts of appeal."* **Mark Hammons** was applauded for his *"work ethic and good knowledge of issues."*

Leonard & Associates PC
The Firm: This boutique of six was founded in 2001 to represent individuals in employment disputes, and advise them on general issues. It acts for plaintiffs in a spectrum of cases including race, age, gender, and disability discrimination, sexual harassment, retaliation, free speech, whistle-blowing and constitutional concerns. The team's attorneys were praised by sources as *"excellent representatives for their clients."* **Jana Leonard** was particularly recommended to researchers as an *"excellent lawyer who is devoted to her cases."* Her practice focuses predominantly on employment litigation.

Other Notable Practitioners
Gregory Bledsoe of Gregory Bledsoe & Associates in Tulsa is considered by many sources to be *"the leading plaintiffs' lawyer in the state."* He represents clients in a range of matters including sexual harassment, age and race discrimination, equal pay and civil rights cases, and also does some defense work for small businesses. Peers highlighted his negotiation skills, commenting that *"if you were looking to explore settlement possibilities, you would come here."* Recent work includes a successful appeal in the Tenth Circuit on behalf of an employee suing Apollo Metal Specialities for disability discrimination. Also in Tulsa, sole practitioner **Steven Novick** commands respect for his experience and knowledge in the labor field. His practice focuses on employment discrimination and wrongful discharge litigation, and he also acts in civil rights cases. He recently obtained a settlement worth about $250,000 for a police officer who was refused membership of a police pension scheme because of a hearing impairment.

OKLAHOMA — EMPLOYMENT & LABOR LAW

MAINLY DEFENDANT

OKLAHOMA
Leading firms
(Employment: Mainly Defendant)

1 CROWE & DUNLEVY Oklahoma City
2 DOERNER, SAUNDERS, DANIEL Oklahoma City
HALL, ESTILL, HARDWICK, GABLE, GOLDEN Tulsa
MCAFEE & TAFT PC Oklahoma City
3 CONNER & WINTERS PC Oklahoma City
MCKINNEY & STRINGER PC Oklahoma City
STRECKER & ASSOCIATES Tulsa

Leading individuals
(Employment: Mainly Defendant)

1 COURT Leonard Crowe & Dunlevy, Oklahoma City
CREMIN Pat Hall, Estill, Hardwick, Gable, Golden, Tulsa
2 MATTSON Lynn Doerner, Saunders, Daniel, Tulsa
3 BARRETT Gayle Crowe & Dunlevy, Oklahoma City
PLUMB Charles Doerner, Saunders, Daniel, Tulsa
STRECKER David Strecker & Associates, Tulsa
VAN DYKE Peter McAfee & Taft PC, Oklahoma City
4 NEAL Kathy Eldridge Cooper Steichen & Leach, Tulsa
PETRIKIN Ronald Conner & Winters PC, Tulsa
PRIEST Jim McKinney & Stringer PC, Oklahoma City

Firms and individuals are listed alphabetically in each band.

Crowe & Dunlevy
The Firm: This *"stellar group"* is the *"acknowledged market leader in the representation of management,"* according to interviewees. It is a full-service firm capable of *"seamlessly handling a wide variety of issues."* The 13 labor and employment attorneys in the group are housed within the litigation department. They received unequivocal endorsement from the market for their trial abilities. The team's workload includes, inter alia, collective bargaining, union avoidance, discrimination and wrongful discharge, administrative practice, workers' compensation and employee benefits.
The Lawyers: **Leonard Court** chairs the group. His practice is focused on employment discrimination, traditional labor, and wage and hour law. Sources consider him a *"smart, knowledgeable and adept litigator."* He won sustained plaudits from peers for his *"excellent general labor practice,"* while clients praised his *"personable manner and dedication."* **Gayle Barrett** is considered *"knowledgeable and good with her clients."* She spends much of her time litigating the full range of employment – rather than traditional labor – issues. The remainder is spent with clients, developing policies to avoid litigation and resolving human resources problems.
The Clients: Goodyear; Hitachi Computer Products (America); St Anthony's Hospital; Mercy Health Center; Bank One; Continental Airlines; Sheffield Steel; Armstrong World Industries; Bama Foods and Dollar Rent A Car Systems.

Doerner, Saunders, Daniel & Anderson LLP
The Firm: This *"highly respected team"* of 15 covers the full range of management representation, including employment discrimination, wrongful discharge, collective bargaining and grievance arbitration. It is widely recognized in the market for its *"strong position within traditional labor negotiations."* The group also provides planning advice on a range of employment-related personnel matters. Several attorneys have experience in the area of ERISA and employee benefits, involving tax, labor and healthcare issues.
The Lawyers: **Lynn Mattson** represents private and public sector clients in all areas of labor and employment law. Market sources noted his *"outstanding knowledge of traditional labor law"* and *"excellent litigation skills."* His extensive trial experience includes claims under the Davis-Bacon and related acts, and other employment statutes. Preventative advice is now a specialty. According to observers, **Charles Plumb** is *"knowledgeable and thoughtful, with a good trial manner."* He litigates a wide range of labor and employment issues. A large part of his time is also spent counseling employers on compliance with federal and state laws and providing preventative advice.
The Clients: The firm successfully defended several discrimination cases on behalf of St John Medical Center, and CITGO Petroleum. Clients include: AEP/Public Service Company of Oklahoma; Community Care HMO; Key Temporary Personnel; Prudential Securities; Salomon Smith Barney Holdings; Citigroup and PepsiCo.

Hall, Estill, Hardwick, Gable, Golden & Nelson PC
The Firm: Sources consider this to be *"a mature labor and employment practice with a strong client base."* The expanding labor and employment group provides services to corporate clients across a range of areas including discrimination, ERISA and litigation involving trade secrets. The team is a strong advocate of preventative maintenance, and offers counseling services and advice on operational employment matters. It successfully represented an association of employers in a class action filed by the EEOC against a union, achieving a summary judgment for the association.
The Lawyers: Competitors and clients alike unanimously dub **Patrick Cremin** one of the *"preeminent labor and employment guys in the state."* Cremin, a fine litigator with great instincts and a huge amount of experience, concentrates on wrongful discharge and sexual harassment.
The Clients: The firm recently defended WilTel Communications in a government-sponsored litigation alleging religious discrimination against an evangelical Christian. Other clients include: The Williams Companies; Wal-Mart; WorldCom; Bank of Oklahoma; State of Oklahoma and Chubb Group.

McAfee & Taft PC
see firm details p.844
The Firm: This large, Oklahoma City-based firm recently bolstered its profile by absorbing a smaller labor boutique run by Peter Van Dyke. It now enjoys a dominant presence in the market, with sources acknowledging it to have an *"excellent group doing good quality work."* The team of 12 provides management representation across the gamut of labor, employment and employee benefits law. Members are skilled at negotiating, and have litigation experience in state and federal courts, and before government agencies. The team aims at collaboration with clients to avoid litigation through preventative practices.
The Lawyers: *"Zealous and intelligent"* **Peter Van Dyke** (see p.586) spends the bulk of his time on litigation-related issues, which include both labor and employment arbitrations. The balance is spent drafting and reviewing employment policies, handbooks and manuals and consulting with and training employers. He was particularly recommended to researchers for his specialized knowledge of the law relating to labor unions. Recent work has included the defense of a non-competition claim against SYSCO Corporation and named individual employees, a discharge arbitration for Sara Lee, and an arbitration for Halliburton concerning the alleged wrongful termination of an employee's contract.
The Clients: Alongside Halliburton, Sara Lee and SYSCO Corporation, the firm represents a number of other clients, including Fleming Companies, Seagate Technology and Dolese Brothers.

Conner & Winters PC
The Firm: This *"solid, old-line firm"* is developing its presence in the labor and employment arena. Its 13 specialist attorneys represent public and private employers in all aspects of employment work, including wage and hour issues, discrimination and workers' compensation. The group advises clients on ways to minimize potential employment problems. Attorneys also provide representation in employment-related regulatory and administrative matters before a range of bodies, including the EEOC, OSHA, the US Department of Labor and the US DOJ.
The Lawyers: **Ronald Petrikin** divides his time between traditional labor law and employment

LITIGATION

OKLAHOMA

litigation. He was particularly recommended to researchers for his labor-related work, and boasts substantial experience of union-organizing campaigns and the negotiation and arbitration of collective bargaining agreements. Other typical work includes the defense of discrimination and wrongful discharge claims.

The Clients: The firm does a lot of business in the transportation industry. It recently assisted an airline client in fending off a nationwide attempt to unionize its flight attendants. It also helped a client to achieve savings through outsourcing its transportation requirement from unionized drivers to a fleet of owner-operators. Other clients include Omni Air International, Thrifty Car Rental and Link America.

McKinney & Stringer PC

The Firm: The nine attorneys in the firm's employment and workers' compensation group handle a wide range of counseling and litigation, including discrimination, wrongful discharge, and workers' compensation defense. They also provide representation in OSHA matters, and wage and benefits disputes. The majority of the work is corporate defense, but plaintiff work is also undertaken.

The Lawyers: Jim Priest is recognized by peers as an experienced and gifted trial lawyer, and *"an excellent speaker – extraordinary in the courtroom."* He represents both plaintiffs and defendants in labor arbitrations, discrimination cases and wrongful discharge allegations of all kinds. He also provides human resources counseling and training. He recently defended Allstate against allegations of race discrimination.

The Clients: WH Braum; Carlisle FoodService Products; Southern Nazarene University; Mercy Health Center; Tinker Federal Credit Union; The Charles Machine Works; The Nobel Foundation and Express Personnel Services.

Strecker & Associates

The Firm: This labor and employment boutique of three has forged a strong reputation, especially for representing the management of small and medium-sized companies in all aspects of labor and employment law.

The Lawyers: David Strecker is held in high esteem by competitors and clients alike. He was described as *"extremely knowledgeable and experienced, with strong intellectual qualities."* His experience stretches over 20 years in the field, and covers the full range of labor and employment matters.

The Clients: Associated Wholesale Grocers; ASARCO; C&C Harley-Davidson; CogenAmerica Pryor; Cordell Memorial Hospital; Git-n-Go; Plymouth Pharmaceuticals; Taylor Crane & Rigging and Washington Group International.

Other Notable Practitioners

"An exceptional litigator with a high level of legal knowledge and acumen," **Kathy Neal** has recently returned to Oklahoma from Alberta to join the newly founded Eldridge, Cooper, Steichen & Leach PLLC. Her outstanding reputation from previous employment work in the state precedes her. She provides management defense in a wide variety of claims, including wrongful dismissal and public policy torts. Her litigation experience spans Canadian courts, where she was licensed as a barrister and solicitor, as well as US ones.

LITIGATION

GENERAL COMMERCIAL

OKLAHOMA
Leading firms
(Litigation: General Commercial)

1. **CROWE & DUNLEVY** Oklahoma City
2. **MCAFEE & TAFT PC** Oklahoma City
3. **FELLERS, SNIDER, BLANKENSHIP** Oklahoma City
   GABLE & GOTWALS PC Oklahoma City, Tulsa
   MCKINNEY & STRINGER P Oklahoma City
4. **HARTZOG CONGER CASON** Oklahoma City
   KIRK & CHANEY Oklahoma City

Leading individuals
(Litigation: General Commercial)

1. **BAILEY Burck** Fellers, Snider, Blankenship, Oklahoma City
   CORBYN George George S Corbyn Jr, Oklahoma City
   RYAN Patrick Ryan & Whaley, Oklahoma City
2. **HERMES John** McAfee & Taft PC, Oklahoma City
   KIRK James Kirk & Chaney, Oklahoma City
   MCKINNEY Kenneth McKinney & Stringer, Oklahoma City
   MEYERS Kent Crowe & Dunlevy, Oklahoma City
3. **DAVIS Gary** Crowe & Dunlevy, Oklahoma City
   NEVILLE Jack Hartzog Conger Cason, Oklahoma City
   ROBISON Reid McAfee & Taft PC, Oklahoma City
   STURDIVANT James Gable & Gotwals PC, Tulsa

Firms and individuals are listed alphabetically in each band.

Crowe & Dunlevy

The Firm: This firm boasts a stable of *"experienced, highly qualified, hard-working and intelligent litigators."* Clients and competitors alike recognize it as occupying the *"top spot"* in the state. *"A diversified firm with experience in a number of fields,"* its wealth of resources and experience of large, complex cases push it ahead of the pack. The firm's litigation department constitutes approximately half of its total legal staff of 115, and is expert in most aspects of commercial litigation, including antitrust, securities cases, energy, tort, insurance, and products liability defense. The team is conspicuously active in the market and won praise from clients for its *"spotless reputation"* and *"credibility before the jury."*

The Lawyers: Kent Meyers was praised to researchers for his solid analytical skills and profound experience, especially for antitrust and bankruptcy cases. Sources say he is *"quick on his feet"* with an *"excellent manner in court."* **Gary Davis** commands a strong reputation for oil and gas-related litigation. Peers consider his experience and knowledge in this field to be unmatched. Recent work includes defending Chevron USA in the Oklahoma Supreme Court against a class action. He also acted for Conoco in a dispute with the construction company JH Kelly.

The Clients: The team represented ExxonMobil in a class action. Other clients include: ConocoPhillips; Chevron USA; Anadarko Petroleum; Lone Star Steakhouse & Saloon and National Western Life Insurance Company.

McAfee & Taft PC
see firm details p.844

The Firm: This 30-strong team of *"excellent, tough and aggressive"* trial lawyers underscores the depth and breadth of resources that the firm brings to the table. It was praised in particular for its banking and securities work. Researchers were also told of noteworthy expertise in antitrust, oil and gas litigation, IP, products liability, and environmental, labor and employment matters. The group successfully defended Fleming Companies against an appeal by the City of Philadelphia alleging securities fraud due to the omission of information from required SEC filings and statutory company reports.

The Lawyers: John Hermes has experience in a broad range of commercial litigation, from class action products liability to oil and gas and title cases. He was praised to researchers as *"a seasoned litigator"* and a *"thorough, learned lawyer,"* notable for his *"outstanding preparation and presentation"* in court. *"Polished, articulate and intelligent"* **Reid Robison** (has experience in a wide range of commercial litigation, including multi-district and other complex litigation in courts throughout the US.

The Clients: The firm represented Stauth et al and Fleming Companies in an appeal against the

OKLAHOMA

LITIGATION

National Union Fire Insurance Company of Pittsburgh concerning the recoverability of legal fees and expenses incurred by Fleming during action to establish the degree of coverage under executive liability policies. Other clients include: MidFirst Bank; Devon Energy; University of Oklahoma and Oklahoma Publishing Company.

Fellers, Snider, Blankenship, Bailey & Tippens PC
The Firm: This well-respected group of about 20 *"high-quality"* litigators, includes several who market sources consider *"top-flight."* The firm represents both plaintiffs and defendants and has experience in all facets of complex commercial and business litigation, including personal injury and property damage cases.
The Lawyers: **Burck Bailey** is universally acknowledged to be *"a master,"* and one of the field's preeminent practitioners. Interviewees unanimously praised his *"fantastic courtroom ability, control of the situation and knack of getting to the essence of the matter."* He primarily practices in the field of complex business litigation, both civil and criminal, handling a substantial amount of plaintiffs' work.
The Clients: Aetna; American Express; DaimlerChrysler; GE Capital, Hertz; Phillips Petroleum Company; UPS and Wal-Mart.

Gable & Gotwals PC
The Firm: The bias of this Tulsa-based firm is toward business litigation, and about half of its 60 attorneys practice in this area. It represents both plaintiffs and defendants, and covers a broad range of commercial issues. Particular areas of expertise include commercial loans, oil and gas contracts and telecom matters.
The Lawyers: *"Brilliant trial lawyer"* **James Sturdivant** has over 40 years' experience in general business and contract disputes of all kinds. He was recommended to researchers for his expertise in antitrust and First Amendment suits, especially for media clients. He is working on a complaint and intervention case with about $11 million at risk on behalf of an investment bank.
The Clients: Clients range from individuals to Fortune 500 companies, a good number in the oil and gas and communications spheres. Examples include Bank of America, ChevronTexaco, El Paso, The Williams Companies and Capital Resource Partners.

McKinney & Stringer P
The Firm: Business litigation remains the cornerstone of this mid-sized firm's practice. Its litigation team includes about 35 attorneys who were recommended to researchers as *"excellent trial lawyers with good, sophisticated experience."* Its commercial work includes IP, corporate and securities, antitrust and personal injury. The firm has been lead counsel for a city and utility trust authority in a case regarding the pollution of a municipal water supply by the poultry industry.
The Lawyers: **Kenneth McKinney**, a cofounder of the firm, is held by sources to be *"an outstanding and highly credible orator."* Peers highlight his skill in cross-examination and jury argument. He concentrates on general civil litigation, and has extensive experience in environmental work, antitrust cases and class actions involving customer disputes.
The Clients: The firm acted as lead trial counsel for the Hardage Steering Committee in the only Superfund case tried by the DOJ to impose site remediation. Other high-profile clients include AT&T, City of Tulsa, Energetix and Sisters of Mercy Health System.

Hartzog Conger Cason & Neville PC
The Firm: A small firm of 25 lawyers, whose strength traditionally lies in transactional work, Hartzog Conger have over the past few years begun to develop a solid reputation in business litigation. The firm does a considerable amount of securities litigation defense for national accounting firms; other strengths lie in products liability, white-collar criminal defense and oil and gas.
The Lawyers: *"Tough and hard-working"* **Jack (Drew) Neville** cut his teeth in white-collar criminal cases all over the US. With a developing practice in securities defense, he is recognized by many as one of the *"finest commercial litigators in the state."*
The Clients: KPMG; Deloitte & Touche; PwC; Koch Industries; General Dynamics and CMI Corporation.

Kirk & Chaney
The Firm: This boutique firm specializes in business and family law. Market opinion proclaimed it: *"quite small but with excellent lawyers, and fine litigators in particular."* Five partners specialize in trial work and cover a broad range of commercial issues. Interviewees highlight the firm's particular expertise in oil and gas matters.
The Lawyers: **James Kirk** was recommended by interviewees as an *"outstanding trial lawyer."* The majority of his work is commercial, and he has experience in matters ranging from oil and gas to personal injury and securities litigation.
The Clients: Clients here are typically small to medium-sized businesses. Samson Resources Company, Ricks Exploration and Avalon Correctional Services are clients.

Other Notable Practitioners
George Corbyn of George S Corbyn Jr PLLC, was highly recommended to researchers as an *"aggressive and tenacious litigator, conscientious and notoriously well-prepared."* He covers all areas of commercial litigation, employment defense and professional malpractice. He recently won actual and punitive damages for Marlin Oil in an oil and gas abuse of process case, and has also represented Chubb Group, Coregis Group, Executive Risk Indemnity and Midland Claims Administrators. The prosecutor in the Oklahoma Bombing case, **Patrick Ryan** of Ryan & Whaley, has now devoted his practice to commercial work. Interviewees consider him *"a simply outstanding trial lawyer,"* and attest in particular to his abilities in larger, complex cases.

REAL ESTATE

OKLAHOMA
Leading firms (Real Estate)

1
- CROWE & DUNLEVY *Oklahoma City*
- MCAFEE & TAFT PC *Oklahoma City*

2
- MOCK, SCHWABE, WALDO, ELDER *Oklahoma City*
- PHILLIPS MCFALL MCCAFFREY *Oklahoma City*
- SPRADLING, ALPERN & GUM LLP *Oklahoma City*

Firms are listed alphabetically in each band.

Crowe & Dunlevy
The Firm: The historical bias of this real estate group has been toward representing financiers and lenders. The ten members of the team have, however, forged a strong reputation for *"excellent quality work and depth across the board."* Despite the recent retirement of the head of the department, market sources consider the firm *"head and shoulders above other firms in the state."* Regional, national and international clients are represented in a range of issues including acquisitions, sales, leasing and financing as well as related matters such as zoning, governmental jurisdictional issues, economic analysis and the environmental aspects of developments. The team works with the assistance of attorneys practicing in cross-disciplinary areas, to provide broad-based advice for clients.
The Lawyers: **Michael Laird** was recommended to researchers for his *"knowledge and experience."* He spends much of his time representing acquirers and development-side clients and also

REAL ESTATE — OKLAHOMA

OKLAHOMA
Leading individuals (Real Estate)

1
- HASTIE John *Phillips McFall McCaffrey*, Oklahoma City

2
- ELDER James *Mock, Schwabe, Waldo*, Oklahoma City
- HILL Frank *McAfee & Taft PC*, Oklahoma City
- SPRADLING Scott *Spradling, Alpern*, Oklahoma City

3
- HARTMANN James *Crowe & Dunlevy*, Oklahoma City
- LAIRD Michael *Crowe & Dunlevy*, Oklahoma City
- RIGGS Richard *McAfee & Taft PC*, Oklahoma City

Individuals are listed alphabetically in each band.

does a lot of construction work. *"Understated but superb"* **James Hartmann** has a background in commercial leasing and asset-based finance. Much of his work involves traditional real estate issues, including easements, titles and mortgages.
The Clients: The firm was Oklahoma counsel for The Williams Companies on the $175 million mortgage refinancing of Williams Communications' Tulsa headquarters. It also represented Pre-Paid Legal Services in its $25 million corporate headquarters construction project in Ada. Other clients include Snoddy Properties, BancFirst, Corning, Kimco Realty, Norman Regional Hospital Authority and Homeland Stores.

McAfee & Taft PC
see firm details p.844
The Firm: *"A firm that truly represents the entrepreneurial spirit."* This 11-attorney real estate group is most active in the representation of developers, investors, entrepreneurs and owners. The *"seasoned, high-caliber"* team received unequivocal endorsement, in particular for its *"strong tax abilities."* Many of its lawyers have a background in tax, financing or accounting, lending the group specific expertise. The firm has been involved in complex commercial real estate transactions, including leveraged leases, mortgage pass-throughs, shared-appreciation mortgages, tax-free exchanges, multiparty tax-deferred exchanges, tax-exempt financing and other government-enhanced projects.
The Lawyers: **Richard Riggs** is described by market sources as *"pragmatic, practical and a joy to work with."* He was particularly recommended for his extensive experience of representing commercial landlords and tenants. The emphasis of his practice is on real estate purchases and sales, leasing and financing transactions, and secured transactions on personal property. **Frank Hill** is viewed as the team's fulcrum. *"A stellar intellect with sophisticated knowledge and a wonderful demeanor,"* Hill has an expertise that is underpinned by a tax law degree. He is particularly admired for his creative approach to problems. His caseload includes planning transactions, and real estate acquisitions and dispositions.
The Clients: Recent work for the team includes representing OPUBCO Development in the sale of several real estate properties, including Gaillardia Golf & Country Club and WKY radio station, and representing Big Lots Stores in connection with the development of its Durant distribution center. Other clients include: Bank of Oklahoma; MidFirst Bank; Fleming Companies; Devon Energy; Michelin; Price Edwards & Company and the University of Oklahoma Foundation.

Mock, Schwabe, Waldo, Elder, Reeves & Bryant
The Firm: Prevailing market opinion considers this *"small, ethical firm"* to be *"top class."* Three attorneys specialize in commercial real estate work, and have extensive experience of development projects, acquisitions, dispositions, exchanges, conveyances and leases at the local, national and state level. The strength of the firm is considered to lie in financing; it has represented financing institutions in real estate transactions in 26 other states, including work as lead counsel in multi-state transactions.
The Lawyers: **James Elder** was heralded by peers as *"outstandingly experienced, with a fine attention to detail."* He concentrates on financing, sales, development and leasing, and also handles banking law related to those activities.
The Clients: BancFirst; Bank One; Cabot Petroleum; Lincoln National Life Insurance; Local Oklahoma Bank and Pan-American Life Insurance Company.

Phillips McFall McCaffrey McVay & Murrah PC
The Firm: The *"top-notch"* real estate group of this mid-sized Oklahoma firm numbers eight in total. The group handles a wide variety of real estate matters, including litigation, for a client base that includes lenders, developers and managers as well as many title and abstract companies. The firm also represents clients in judicial and administrative proceedings, involving matters such as the impact of state and federal environmental regulations on real estate transactions.
The Lawyers: **John Hastie** is the star and rainmaker of the firm. According to sources, he is *"hands down the best negotiator in the state, with more experience than any other lawyer in town"* and *"excellent and extremely knowledgeable."* His real estate experience goes back more than 30 years. He focuses on representing lenders in real estate financing and also handles reworkings and bankruptcies.

Spradling, Alpern & Gum LLP
The Firm: This smallish firm has historically specialized in real estate. The two attorneys focusing on this area are considered *"well-respected, competent and experienced"* by peers and clients alike. The firm represents both lenders and developers in a broad range of real estate matters, and was recommended for foreclosures in particular.
The Lawyers: **Scott Spradling** won praise for his *"practical, results-oriented advice."* Clients praised his *"dedication and integrity."* Aside from general transactional real estate work, he spends a considerable amount of time on associated legal matters.
The Clients: Anheuser-Busch; Catellus Development; Urban Retail Properties, Ackerman McQueen and Peak Medical.

Leaders in Oklahoma

BAILEY, Burck
Fellers, Snider, Blankenship, Bailey & Tippens, PC, Oklahoma City
405 232 0621
Recommended in Litigation

BARRETT, Gayle
Crowe & Dunlevy, Oklahoma City
405 235 7700
Recommended in Employment

BLEDSOE, Gregory
Gregory Bledsoe & Associates, Tulsa
918 599 8123
Recommended in Employment

BRIDGER-RILEY, Kay
Bridger-Riley & Associates, PC, Tulsa
918 494 6699
Recommended in Employment

CORBYN, George
George S. Cobyn Jr, PLLC, Oklahoma City
405 239 7055
Recommended in Litigation

COURT, Leonard
Crowe & Dunlevy, Oklahoma City
405 235 7700
Recommended in Employment

CREMIN, Pat
Hall, Estill, Hardwick, Gable, Golden & Nelson, PC, Tulsa 918 594 0400
Recommended in Employment

DAVIS, Gary
Crowe & Dunlevy, Oklahoma City
405 235 7700
Recommended in Litigation

DERRICK, Gary
Derrick & Briggs LLP, Oklahoma City
405 235 1900
Recommended in Corporate/M&A

EDDY, Rand
Eddy & Jones, Oklahoma City
405 239 2524
Recommended in Employment

ELAM, Theodore M.
McAfee & Taft, PC, Oklahoma City
405 552 2221
ted.elam@mcafeetaft.com
Recommended in Corporate/M&A
Specialization: Member of the Corporate and Securities Practice Group. Concentrates in corporate and securities matters, corporate finance and mergers and

OKLAHOMA

acquisitions.
Prof. Memberships: Member of the Oklahoma County, Oklahoma and American Bar Associations. Formerly a member of the Young President's Organization.
Career: He has been lead counsel in numerous public and private offerings of securities and mergers and acquistions, tender offers, and in other forms of financing, for businesses involved in telecommunications, technology, energy, mortgage banking, asset-based financing, retailing, insurance and real estate. He has been an Adjunct Professor of Business Planning, Securities Regulation and Corporate Finance at the University of Oklahoma College of Law, and is a frequent lecturer.
Personal: He received a BBA-Finance in 1957 and an LLB in 1959 from the University of Oklahoma. He was a member of the Order of the Coif, Omicron Kelta Kappa and was Note Editor of the Oklahoma Law Review. He is named in leading US publications as a leading lawyer.

ELDER, James
Mock, Schwabe, Waldo, Elder, Reeves & Bryant, Oklahoma City 405 235 1110
Recommended in Real Estate

FULLER, Gary
McAfee & Taft, PC, Oklahoma City
405 235 9621
Recommended in Corporate/M&A

HAMMONS, Mark
Hammons & Associates, Oklahoma City
405 235 6100
Recommended in Employment

HARTMANN, James
Crowe & Dunlevy, Oklahoma City
405 235 7700
Recommended in Real Estate

HASTIE, John
Phillips McFall McCaffrey McVay & Murrah, P.C., Oklahoma City
405 235 4100
Recommended in Real Estate

HERMES, John
McAfee & Taft, PC, Oklahoma City
405 235 9621
Recommended in Litigation

HILL, Frank
McAfee & Taft, PC, Oklahoma City
405 235 9621
Recommended in Real Estate

KIRK, James
Kirk & Chaney, Oklahoma City
405 235 1333
Recommended in Litigation

LAIRD, Michael
Crowe & Dunlevy, Oklahoma City
405 235 7700
Recommended in Real Estate

LEONARD, Jana
Leonard & Associates PC, Oklahoma City 405 239 3800
Recommended in Employment

MATTSON, Lynn
Doerner, Saunders, Daniel & Anderson, LLP, Tulsa 918 582 1211
Recommended in Employment

MCKINNEY, Kenneth
McKinney & Stringer, PC, Oklahoma City
405 239 6444
Recommended in Litigation

MEYERS, Kent
Crowe & Dunlevy, Oklahoma City
405 235 7700
Recommended in Litigation

MOORE, Lynnwood
Conner & Winters, PC, Tulsa
918 586 5711
Recommended in Corporate/M&A

NEAL, Kathy
Eldridge Cooper Steichen & Leach PLLC, Tulsa 918 388 5555
Recommended in Employment

NEVILLE, Jack
Hartzog Conger Cason & Neville, PC, Oklahoma City 405 235 7000
Recommended in Litigation

NOVICK, Steven
Steven Novick - sole practitioner, Tulsa
918 582 4441
Recommended in Employment

PETRIKIN, Ronald
Conner & Winters, A Professional Corporation, Tulsa 918 586 5711
Recommended in Employment

PLUMB, Charles
Doerner, Saunders, Daniel & Anderson, LLP, Tulsa 918 582 1211
Recommended in Employment

PRIEST, Jim
McKinney & Stringer, A Professional Corporation, Oklahoma City
405 239 6444
Recommended in Employment

RIGGS, Richard
McAfee & Taft, PC, Oklahoma City
405 235 9621
Recommended in Real Estate

ROBISON, Reid
McAfee & Taft, PC, Oklahoma City
405 235 9621
Recommended in Litigation

RYAN, Patrick
Ryan & Whaley, Oklahoma City
405 239 6040
Recommended in Litigation

SELF, Shannon
Commercial Law Group, Oklahoma City
405 232 3001
Recommended in Corporate/M&A

SPRADLING, Scott
Spradling, Alpern & Gum, L.L.P., Oklahoma City 405 272 0211
Recommended in Real Estate

STEWART, Michael
Crowe & Dunlevy, Oklahoma City
405 235 7700
Recommended in Corporate/M&A

STRECKER, David
Strecker & Associates, Tulsa
918 582 1716
Recommended in Employment

STRINGER, Martin
McKinney & Stringer, A Professional Corporation, Oklahoma City
405 239 6444
Recommended in Corporate/M&A

STURDIVANT, James
Gable & Gotwals, A Professional Corporation, Tulsa 918 595 4800
Recommended in Litigation

VAN DYKE, Peter
McAfee & Taft, PC, Oklahoma City
405 552 2211
peter.vandyke@mcafeetaft.com
Recommended in Employment
Specialization: Has limited his practice to representing management in all phases of labor and employment related matters, to include: federal and state court litigation; labor and employment arbitrations; union avoidance issues; labor negotiations; federal and state administrative agency practice (NLRB, EEOC, MSHA etc.); supervisory and employee training; and regular consultation on labor and employment issues.
Prof. Memberships: Oklahoma Bar Association and American Bar Association (Labor and Employment Sections).
Career: Shareholder and director of *McAfee & Taft*. Admitted to the New York Bar in 1968; the Oklahoma Bar in 1973; the United States Supreme Court, federal courts of appeal for the Tenth and Fifth Circuits, and federal district courts in Oklahoma and Texas. Has completed the arbitrator course sponsored by the Federal Mediation and Conciliation Service, and a mediation course recognized by the United States District Court for the Western District of Oklahoma, and the Oklahoma district court.
Personal: BS from the University of Rhode Island in 1964; JD (with honors) from Albany Law School of Union University in 1968; LLM in Labor Laws from The George Washington University in 1973.

OREGON
CORPORATE/M&A

CONTENTS: Corporate/M&A p.1; Employment: Mainly Plaintiff p.2; Mainly Defendant p.3; Litigation: General Commercial p.4 Real Estate p.5; Individuals' Profiles p.6.

OREGON'S TOP THREE
1. Stoel Rives
2. Perkins Coie
3. Miller Nash

Ranking based on Chambers' research within the state.

All quotes in the text are from interviews with clients and competitors.

OVERVIEW: Stoel Rives, ranked first, is considered preeminent for both corporate and litigation work. On the corporate side, the firm's national reach attracts top-class clients; it advises the pick of Oregon's blue-chip corporates and, in the first half of 2002 alone, completed 15 transactions valued at between $1 million and $35 million. Henry Hewitt was acknowledged as the firm's star performer for corporate matters. As well, a premier litigation practice handles a wide range of commercial cases. Here, Barnes Ellis, who specializes in securities and major corporate contract disputes, was deemed one of the best case analysts in the Northwest. Widely respected employment and real estate groups also benefit from the firm's impressive client roster, which includes Tektronix and PacifiCorp.

Headquartered in Seattle, **Perkins Coie** takes second place in Oregon, and earns praise for its stylish, incisive handling of corporate transactions. The intelligent and thorough Roy Tucker is a leading light in corporate matters here, taking on M&A and venture capital work requiring a strategic flair. The real estate development practice benefits from the firm's strong regional presence, and has enhanced its reputation recently following the recruitment of a high-profile land use team from Stoel Rives. Richard Cantlin was identified as a rising star in the real estate department. Clients include Louisiana-Pacific and West Hills Development.

Miller Nash, ranked third, is a well-established firm with a strong regional presence. It has an admired commercial litigation practice, and is also a solid player in the corporate and employment arenas. Miller Nash was one of the top firms in the state in the booming 1990's and still retains many major corporate clients. Litigator William Crow is cited for his outstanding trial skills, while Louis Livingston is seen to be making his mark in the employment group. Clients include GlaxoSmithKline and 3M.

CORPORATE/M&A

OREGON
Leading firms (Corporate/M&A)
1. STOEL RIVES LLP
2. PERKINS COIE LLP
3. TONKON TORP LLP
4. ATER WYNNE LLP
   DAVIS WRIGHT TREMAINE LLP
   MILLER NASH LLP

Leading individuals (Corporate/M&A)
1. HEWITT Henry *Stoel Rives LLP*
   TUCKER Roy *Perkins Coie LLP*
2. BOOTH Brian *Tonkon Torp LLP*
3. BAUMAN Todd *Stoel Rives LLP*
   MOORMAN Robert *Stoel Rives LLP*
   NOTO Margaret *Stoel Rives LLP*
   SIMPSON Patrick *Perkins Coie LLP*
   STEPHENS Kenneth *Tonkon Torp LLP*
4. BACA David *Davis Wright Tremaine LLP*
   CAMPBELL William *Ater Wynne LLP*
   MCDONNELL Brendan *Tonkon Torp LLP*

Firms and Individuals are listed alphabetically in each band.

Stoel Rives LLP
The Firm: This firm's *"unparalleled market penetration"* left interviewees in *"no doubt that this is the preeminent corporate practice in Oregon."* Industry knowledge and expertise at every stage of the transactional cycle have ensured the firm a following. The team has completed 15 transactions, valued between $1 million and $35 million, during the first half of 2002.
The Lawyers: The firm houses a number of leading lights. **Henry Hewitt** is a *"terrific business-getter,"* who routinely advises boards and management at Tektronix, PacifiCorp and Electro Scientific Industries on corporate and disclosure issues. He provides the team with a *"great point of reference,"* drawing from his depth of experience. *"Starting to step into a leading role,"* **Todd Bauman** specializes in corporate and securities work on behalf of emerging growth companies. He recently represented Bioject Medical Technologies in a $5.8 million private equity financing, and advised on the restructuring of preferred stock and warrants held by Elan. **Margaret Hill Noto** is a *"capable and well-respected"* attorney who represents *"high-profile local public companies"* in corporate, securities and M&A work. **Robert Moorman** (*"technically wonderful"*) was recommended for his skill in advising on public and private financings. He recently acted for Oregon Steel Mills in its $305 million sale of first mortgage notes to institutional buyers.
The Clients: Clients of the firm include Columbia Management Company/Columbia Funds; Hollywood Entertainment; KinderCare Learning Centers; PacifiCorp; Precision Castparts; StanCorp Financial Group; Tektronix; Columbia Sportswear; Oregon Steel Mills; Pope & Talbot; Electro Scientific Industries; FEI Company; RadiSys; Schnitzer Steel Industries; Bioject Medical Technologies; Microfield Graphics; Paulson Capital and TRM.

Perkins Coie LLP
The Firm: The firm is commonly identified as handling sophisticated transactions. Some interviewees reported that it has an aggressive negotiating style, and brings a *"big city attitude"* to its corporate practice. One competitor noted: *"They really understand the dynamics of public markets and high-growth company finance."* It has impressed with its knowledge of the IPO market.
The Lawyers: *"Intelligent, combative and thorough,"* **Roy Tucker** is *"as good as they get"* for transactions requiring a strategic flair. His practice encompasses M&A advice on behalf of middle-market industrial companies and venture capital work on behalf of emerging growth companies. His recent highlights include two Rule 144A debt financings on behalf of Vancouver-based Teekay Shipping, and a proposed IPO on behalf of Sparkling Spring Water Holdings. **Patrick Simpson** is a senior adviser to publicly held companies *"who certainly knows what he's doing."* *"Respected by the bar"* for his work in corporate finance and M&A work, Simpson provided Oregon corporate law advice to Weyerhaeuser during its takeover of Willamette Industries.
The Clients: The firm's clients include Louisiana-Pacific; Corillian; Datalex; Templex Technology; Teekay Shipping; Sparkling Spring Water Holdings; Merix; CenterSpan Communications; Acres Gaming; Warn Industries; Endeavour Capital and Integra Telecom.

Tonkon Torp LLP
The Firm: This regionally focused firm has secured a following through the emphasis it places on *"excellence, diligence and the depth of legal knowledge."* Staffed by *"homegrown talent,"* it has developed a reputation for *"senior partner attention"* on files. Clients commend both the firm's strong negotiation skills and its user-friendly approach.
The Lawyers: *"Senior statesman"* **Brian Booth** has earned a *"sterling"* reputation for his corporate

OREGON

CORPORATE/M&A

advice to *"the top end of the business community."* Best known for his long-standing relationship with Nike, his practice encompasses M&A, public and private financings and corporate governance. His recent work includes acquisitions for Nike and representation of special board members for Trendwest Resorts and Cascade Corporation. **Kenneth Stephens** was described to researchers as a *"bright lawyer"* with *"strong corporate credentials."* He specializes in corporate and M&A and *"excels"* in broker-dealer registration and SEC compliance issues. He represented New York investors during Weyerhaeuser's takeover of Willamette Industries, and acts as general counsel for M Financial Group. **Brendan McDonnell** has developed an emerging markets practice assisting clients in the technology industry. He acted for SAS Institute in its acquisition of software provider ABC Technologies.
The Clients: Clients of the firm include Nike; Columbia Distributing; Stimson Lumber; M Financial Group; Medical Management International; Key Technology; The Greenbrier Companies; Will Vinton Studios; Centennial Bancorp; Bank of the Northwest and Symbol Technologies.

Ater Wynne LLP
The Firm: The practice is best known for its representation of high-growth private companies and entrepreneurs. During our research it won plaudits for its work on behalf of start-up technology companies.

The Lawyers: Interviewees agree that **William Campbell** has *"a technical mind that allows him to get into hi-tech company strategies and product development concepts."* He acts for clients in the internet, software and hardware, telecom and biotech industries.
The Clients: The firm's client roster features Advanced Silicon Materials; FLIR Systems; Golden Valley Electric Association; Mobilian; Network Elements; Northwest Pipe Company; Oregon Freeze Dry; Pixelworks; Planar Systems and TriQuint Semiconductor.

Davis Wright Tremaine LLP
see firm details p.787
The Firm: The firm is focused on middle-market corporate and M&A work for public and private companies. It enjoys a broad client base, drawn from the financial services, agriculture, technology, telecom and health industries. Recent highlight transactions at the firm include advice on first-round investments and options on behalf of ICO-Teledesic Global, and the sale of DAT Services Division on behalf of Jubitz. The firm has also advised on the merger of ABC Technologies with SAS Institute, and represented both ICO Global and Starbucks on matters arising from strategic partnerships.
The Lawyers: **David Baca** (see p.593) was singled out to researchers for his *"high levels of client service and object-oriented approach"* to transactions. He recently represented the acquirer in a successful tender offer for the Mount Bachelor ski resort.
The Clients: Clients include ICO Global; Advanced Power Technology; Sierra Wireless; Starbucks; Jubitz; Powdr Corporation; Independent Financial Network; ABC Technologies; Chrome Data; National Retail Partners; XO Communications and VRB Bancorp.

Miller Nash LLP
see firm details p.851
The Firm: This well-established firm was commended to researchers as a *"corporate player"* with *"excellent technical abilities and a constantly improving level of service."* It boasts experience in securities, banking regulation and tax law. The firm recently handled a recapitalization on behalf of Gardenburger, and advised the trustee in disposals for New York City-based financial services company ContiFinancial.
The Lawyers: A team led by J Franklin Cable received praise for its representation of Willamette Industries during its long-drawn-out and contested takeover by Weyerhaeuser.
The Clients: Clients of the firm include US Bancorp; Louisiana-Pacific; Rentrak; Southwest Washington Medical Center; Gardenburger; Potlatch; Hyundai Motor America; RB Pamplin; Cingular Wireless; GlaxoSmithKline; WinCo Foods and Merrill Lynch.

EMPLOYMENT & LABOR LAW

MAINLY PLAINTIFF

OREGON
Leading firms
(Employment: Mainly Plaintiff)
1. BUSSE & HUNT
2. CRISPIN & ASSOCIATES

Leading individuals
(Employment: Mainly Plaintiff)
1. BRISCHETTO Stephen *Stephen Brischetto*
   BUSSE Richard *Busse & Hunt*
2. HUNT Scott *Busse & Hunt*
   SNYDER Judy *Hoevet, Snyder & Boise PC*
3. CRISPIN Craig *Crispin & Associates*
   EGGUM Susan *Susan K Eggum, PC*

Firms and individuals are listed alphabetically in each band.

Busse & Hunt
The Firm: Interviewees recommended this *"talented practice"* as one of Portland's oldest and most respected plaintiffs' firms. It has expertise across the range of employment law and litigation matters.
The Lawyers: Having cut his teeth in employment defense, **Richard Busse** was described to researchers as *"a force in the plaintiffs' arena"* with *"a good instinct for winning arguments."* He is best known for his representation of victims of sexual harassment, while his broad practice encompasses discrimination, wrongful discharge and employment fraud. He successfully represented the plaintiff in a recent wrongful discharge case against Oregon Health & Science University. *"Upfront, honest and ethical,"* **Scott Hunt** is a *"refreshing"* addition to the Portland plaintiffs' employment bar. Recognized as an expert in the disabilities area, he won a suit brought under the ADA.

Crispin & Associates
The Firm: The group specializes in the representation of executive-level employees in litigation, contract negotiation and termination counseling. Peers agree that the firm has the capacity to handle a *"large volume of cases."* They also applauded its vigorous advocacy on behalf of employment plaintiffs.
The Lawyers: Opponents report that **Craig Crispin** *"really knows how to evaluate a case."* Recent highlights of his practice include a series of wage and hour/retaliation cases brought against a Portland lawyer. He has also advised in a case brought against a major healthcare group by a lactation consultant alleging interference in economic relations.

Other Notable Practitioners
Sole practitioner **Stephen Brischetto** was described to researchers as a *"premier"* trial and appellate attorney. He has represented plaintiffs in wrongful discharge, statutory discrimination and other employment disputes. According to interviewees, his practice is *"strong on the intellectual and analytical side."* He represented the plaintiff in an employment and breach of contract case brought against Net Value Holdings, and represented a whistle-blower in an action brought against the North Clackamas School District. **Judy Snyder** at Hoevet, Snyder & Boise PC has won acclaim for her plaintiffs' employment practice. She draws on her skills as a former prosecutor, and is described by peers as *"very involved; she is intelligent and good to deal with."* **Susan Eggum** is a sole practitioner, whose *"small shop"* provides *"robust"* representation for victims of employment discrimination and wrongful discharge.

EMPLOYMENT & LABOR LAW — OREGON

MAINLY DEFENDANT

OREGON
Leading firms
(Employment: Mainly Defendant)

1. BARRAN LIEBMAN
2. STOEL RIVES LLP
3. BULLARD SMITH JERNSTEDT WILSON
   MILLER NASH LLP

Leading individuals
(Employment: Mainly Defendant)

1. BARRAN Paula *Barran Liebman*
   LIEBMAN Richard *Barran Liebman*
2. BUCHANAN Paul *Stoel Rives LLP*
   LIVINGSTON Louis *Miller Nash LLP*
   REEVES Edward *Stoel Rives LLP*
   VANCLEAVE Richard *Barran Liebman*
3. AMBURGEY Larry *Amburgey & Rubin PC*
   JERNSTEDT Kenneth *Bullard Smith*
   KITCHEL Chris *Stoel Rives LLP*
4. BERNICK Carol *Davis Wright Tremaine LLP*
   KEITH Calvin *Perkins Coie LLP*
   MARTIN Chrys *Bullivant Houser Bailey PC*
   RODE Helle *Bullard Smith Jernstedt Wilson*

Up-and-coming individuals
   LEINWAND Robert *Stoel Rives LLP*

Firms and Individuals are listed alphabetically in each band.

Barran Liebman
The Firm: Peers agree that this *"outstanding"* boutique provides *"the complete litigation and counseling"* package to management clients across a range of industries. Built around a core of *"seasoned veterans,"* the firm is noted for its *"strong intellectual base"* and commitment to client service.
The Lawyers: **Paula Barran**'s *"awesome"* reputation is built on decades of success defending employers in discrimination and other employment-related lawsuits. While opponents expressed reservations about Barran's *"take no prisoners"* style, clients endorsed her *"superior"* in-house training sessions to which *"senior executives respond very well."* Labor specialist **Richard Liebman** won plaudits as a *"great negotiator,"* whose representation of management is effective without being *"unduly flashy or aggressive."* The recent recruitment from Davis Wright Tremaine of the *"knowledgeable and capable"* **Richard VanCleave** is expected to further fortify the firm's labor relations expertise.
The Clients: Its client base features local and regional corporations.

Stoel Rives LLP
The Firm: Benefiting from its enviable institutional client base, this well-staffed labor and employment practice *"is by far the most visible among the larger firms."* It has a broad practice, offering counseling, labor/management relations and discrimination defense advice and expertise in employee benefits and litigation matters.
The Lawyers: At the helm of the practice, **Paul Buchanan** is a counselor and litigator, who peers report is *"almost deceptively nonaggressive."* He provides routine employment advice to clients, such as Wells Fargo and PacifiCorp. He recently defended a Portland law firm in a multi-plaintiff discrimination, retaliation and wage and hour lawsuit. **Edward Reeves** was described to researchers as *"absolutely the best counselor in Portland."* He advises employers on the full spectrum of employment and labor issues. Clients value his *"deep integrity"* and pragmatic approach to sophisticated work force reorganization, downsizing and post-M&A rightsizing. **Chris Kitchel** enjoys a strong reputation as a *"skilled"* litigator. She successfully defended Gentle Dental against a breach of contract action brought by a former employee who was terminated for failure to comply with company policy. The recruitment of **Robert Leinwand** from San Francisco's Littler Mendelson is expected to bolster the firm's traditional labor practice. A labor counselor with experience in union/management relations and collective bargaining, Leinwand is tipped to become *"a real player."*
The Clients: Wells Fargo; PacifiCorp; Precision Castparts; Kaiser Foundation Health Plans; Tektronix; McDonald's; Columbia Sportswear Company; Oregon Steel Mills; Xerox; Sony Disc Manufacturing; Hynix Semiconductor Manufacturing America; Lattice Semiconductor; City of Lake Oswego; Bechtel; Lewis & Clark College and Verizon Northwest.

Bullard Smith Jernstedt Wilson
The Firm: Despite concerns of a generational shift, this firm retains its title as Portland's *"traditional labor firm."*
The Lawyers: **Kenneth Jernstedt** was singled out to researchers as an *"effective negotiator"* with *"formidable political skills."* Specializing in union contracts and negotiations, he recently negotiated a novel agricultural workers' agreement on behalf of a large Northwestern food processing cooperative. **Helle Rode** has a *"low-key, intelligent and reasonable"* approach. She has built a varied practice that spans employment litigation, advisory work and mediation on behalf of both public and private sector clients. Clients she has defended in recent litigation include Nike, Standard Insurance, Douglas County and ShopKo Stores.
The Clients: Clients of the firm include: American Steel; Chubb; Fred Meyer; Hoffman Construction Company; Legacy Health System; NORPAC Foods; Portland General Electric; Union Pacific Railroad and TriMet. It also advises public entities such as fire departments and health districts.

Miller Nash LLP
see firm details p.851
The Firm: Although the retirement of Donna Cameron has affected the firm's profile in the market, research confirmed that this is a *"good, solid department,"* which continues to grow. The firm has a broad experience of public healthcare and private sector labor and employment matters.
The Lawyers: *"A high-quality lawyer,"* **Louis Livingston** (see p.594) won plaudits from competitors, who acknowledged his *"clear edge"* in negotiations. Much of his recent practice has focused on collective bargaining with organized nursing groups.
The Clients: Providence Health System; Meier & Frank; Weyerhaeuser; Samaritan Health System; Portland School District and CNF Transportation.

Other Notable Practitioners
Rivals from larger firms agree that Amburgey & Rubin PC's **Larry Amburgey** is *"a real competitor and a force to be reckoned with."* He enjoys a mixed practice spanning a range of employment and labor matters, and is experienced in the training of management and arbitrations. He recently handled a number of matters involving illegal workers in the automotive industry. **Carol Bernick** (see p.593) at Davis Wright Tremaine LLP focuses on employment discrimination and wrongful discharge defen s e. She successfully represented a large financial institution in a multimillion dollar wage and hour class action. Perkins Coie LLP's **Calvin Keith** is respected as a *"capable and practical"* litigator. Among other matters, he has defended Starbucks in a discrimination case filed by a transsexual employee. Building on her leadership in disability law, **Chrys Martin** of Bullivant Houser Bailey PC provides representation and counseling to a range of companies, including Kinder Care and Hollywood Entertainment.

OREGON — LITIGATION

LITIGATION — GENERAL COMMERCIAL

OREGON
Leading firms
(Litigation: General Commercial)

1. STOEL RIVES LLP
2. MILLER NASH LLP
   PERKINS COIE LLP
3. MARKOWITZ, HERBOLD, GLADE
4. BULLIVANT HOUSER BAILEY PC
   DAVIS WRIGHT TREMAINE LLP
   STOLL STOLL BERNE LOKTING
5. ATER WYNNE LLP
   SCHWABE, WILLIAMSON & WYATT, PC

Leading individuals
(Litigation: General Commercial)

1. ELLIS Barnes *Stoel Rives LLP*
   MARKOWITZ David *Markowitz, Herbold*
2. CROW William *Miller Nash LLP*
   FORTINO Paul *Perkins Coie LLP*
   HOUSER Douglas *Bullivant Houser Bailey PC*
   STOLL Robert *Stoll Stoll Berne Lokting*
   TONGUE Thomas *Dunn Carney Allen Higgins*
3. ENGLISH Stephen *Bullivant Houser*
   NEUPERT John *Miller Nash LLP*
   O'LEARY Daniel *Davis Wright Tremaine LLP*
   RICHTER Peter *Miller Nash LLP*
   SIMON Michael *Perkins Coie LLP*
4. BERNE Gary *Stoll Stoll Berne Lokting*
   CHADSEY Phillip *Stoel Rives LLP*
   CROWE Austin *Perkins Coie LLP*
   DULCICH Thomas *Schwabe, Williamson*
   GIDLEY James *Perkins Coie LLP*
   GLADE Peter *Markowitz, Herbold, Glade*
   MOWE Gregory *Stoel Rives LLP*
   NEWELL Robert *Davis Wright Tremaine*
   SKERRITT Daniel *Ater Wynne LLP*
   WALTERS Stephen *Stoel Rives LLP*

Firms and individuals are listed alphabetically in each band.

Stoel Rives LLP
The Firm: The firm spans the gamut of business-related litigation and defense of personal injury and product liability claims. It was described to researchers as a *"premier"* litigation practice, which complements the firm's respected transactional expertise.
The Lawyers: **Barnes Ellis** combines *"raw intelligence"* and a *"client-friendly demeanor."* He was endorsed by peers as *"one of the best case analysts in the Northwest."* Specializing in securities and major corporate contract disputes, Ellis recently defended Farmers in overtime pay litigation. He also advised a special committee of the Teledesic Board during a shareholder dispute. **Phillip Chadsey** has won *"national attention"* for his products liability defense work and his advice to companies in the natural resources sector. He has recently advised clients in the timber industry on takings clause claims. *"Professional and down-to-earth,"* **Gregory Mowe** was recommended as an expert in eminent domain and other real estate disputes. He advised North Interstate MAX Project in the contested acquisitions of properties for a new railroad line. **Stephen Walters** was described as *"smart, capable and reasonable."* Within his broad litigation practice, he was endorsed for his expertise in energy-related litigation. He recently represented a Native American tribe in both a securities lawsuit and a breach of contract case involving a $20 million gaming contract. He also defended a government contractor against claims arising out of an alleged industrial accident at the Umatilla Chemical Weapons Depot.
The Clients: Among the firm's clients are Farmers; FLIR Systems; Assisted Living Concepts; Tektronix; H Naito; PacifiCorp; TriMet; NW Natural; BC Metal Fabrication; Butler Ford; Fred Meyer; GlaxoSmithKline; Johnson & Johnson; Janssen Pharmaceutica; Medical Discoveries; 3M and New Holland North America.

Miller Nash LLP
see firm details p.851
The Firm: With a strong regional presence, the firm boasts a broad commercial litigation practice servicing clients in the agricultural, banking, forest products, pharmaceutical and hi-tech industries.
The Lawyers: **William Crow** (see p.593) is *"a gentleman and a scholar"* and one who *"has never lost his golden touch."* He was recommended by interviewees as a solutions-oriented attorney with outstanding trial skills. Much of his recent practice has involved defending pharmaceutical companies in mass tort product litigation. He has acted for GlaxoSmithKline in the vaccine and Baycol matters, and represented the City of Portland in a large environmental waste dumping case. **John Neupert** (see p.594) is an *"excellent strategist"* who peers credit with business acumen. He was involved in the litigation arising out of Weyerhaeuser's takeover of Willamette Industries, and regularly represents parties in large breach of contract disputes. **Peter Richter** (see p.594) is a *"powerhouse trial lawyer"* noted for his ability to run complex cases. He represented a number of union pension funds and trustees in an alleged fraud case.
The Clients: The firm's clients include Abbott Laboratories; GlaxoSmithKline; 3M; Monsanto Chemical; City of Portland; Johnson & Johnson; US National Bank; Weyerhaeuser and timber companies.

Perkins Coie LLP
The Firm: The Portland office of the firm has secured a profile independent of its Seattle headquarters through a combination of broad industry experience and a wealth of *"top-flight"* commercial litigators. Interviewees commented on the *"shrewd"* trial skills of these litigators, and their success in securing high-profile instructions.
The Lawyers: The *"star"* of the practice is **Paul Fortino**, *"a cutting-edge"* attorney who *"undertakes some of the best institutional defense work in town."* He has impressed interviewees with his products liability litigation. His recent highlights include representing 14 of the outside directors of Enron in proceedings in Oregon, and successfully defending Mitsubishi against antitrust and other claims arising out of the Three Gorges Dam project in China. *"Cerebral"* and *"hard-working,"* **Michael Simon** is respected for advocacy on behalf of high-profile corporate and public interest clients. He acted for Weyerhaeuser in litigation arising out of its takeover of Willamette Industries, and successfully represented the Democratic Party in congressional redistricting litigation. Commentators agreed that both **Austin Crowe** and **James Gidley** have applied their well-honed personal injury defense skills to general commercial disputes. Crowe is defending both Brown & Williamson Tobacco in a medical monitoring class action and Corning NetOptics in a major products liability case involving European satellites. Gidley was described to researchers as an *"outstanding"* attorney who *"takes command of a courtroom."* He has recently acted in asbestos and heavy machinery products liability and building materials litigation.
The Clients: The Kroger Company; Mitsubishi; Semitool; Boeing; Genie Industries; Novartis; Hewlett-Packard; Brown & Williamson Tobacco; Union Pacific Railroad; Boise Cascade; UPS; Deere & Company; Altec; ACL; Union Carbide; Dana Corporation; Louisiana-Pacific; Makita and Abbott Laboratories.

Markowitz, Herbold, Glade & Mehlhaf PC
The Firm: Interviewees were consistent in their opinion that this *"exceptional"* firm is Oregon's leading litigation boutique. It has 18 attorneys devoted to resolving sophisticated business disputes. It attracts a range of clients, including financial institutions, utility companies, and media and technology companies.
The Lawyers: *"Always at the top of the list,"* **David Markowitz** brings an *"imaginative approach"* to his cases, displaying *"courtroom*

flair." He represented Andre Agassi in an arbitrated dispute over an endorsement agreement with Nike, and acted for the House of Blues in a royalties dispute with The Blues Brothers. He also represented Portland General Electric in a dispute with union employees over retirement benefits lost as a result of the Enron collapse. **Peter Glade** was endorsed as an *"unassuming but highly skilled"* attorney specializing in contract disputes and accounting and legal malpractice suits. He defended a large regional law firm against professional malpractice claims arising out of the collapse of Capital Consultants.
The Clients: Portland General Electric; Hollywood Entertainment; Sony Pictures Entertainment; Agassi Enterprises; First National Bank of Omaha; US Bank; House of Blues Brands; PeaceHealth; Unified Western Grocers; State of Oregon Department of Justice; Powdr Corporation and Endeavour Capital.

Bullivant Houser Bailey PC
The Firm: An increasingly diversified practice in recent years has seen this firm *"move outside the box"* of insurance defense into the general commercial litigation arena. Interviewees endorsed the firm's breadth of client base.
The Lawyers: **Douglas Houser** commands a *"superb"* reputation as *"Oregon's preeminent attorney on property insurance,"* and is acclaimed as a national expert on arson. He also defended the manufacturer of Wild Turkey bourbon against claims that manufacturers and distillers of spirits had failed to warn customers of the dangers of consuming alcohol. Following **Stephen English**'s *"outstanding"* performance in the Capital Consultants case, peers report that he has *"truly emerged as a broad-based commercial litigator."* English was lead plaintiff's counsel in the litigation arising from the fraud that led to the collapse of Capital Consultants.
The Clients: Among the firm's insurance client base are Travelers, State Farm and St. Paul. Other clients include: Dr Martens; Caterpillar; Rockwell Collins; Louisiana-Pacific; Severn Trent Systems and The Burlington Northern and Santa Fe Railway Company.

Davis Wright Tremaine LLP
see firm details p.787
The Firm: The Portland office of this Seattle-based firm is better known for its transactional expertise; however, it was endorsed to researchers as a *"good shop"* for business litigation. It is recommended for its expertise in business torts, antitrust, intellectual property and partnership disputes, and securities fraud.
The Lawyers: According to interviewees, *"there is no better lawyer for environmental matters"* than **Daniel O'Leary** (see p.594), an environmental and natural resources attorney specializing in Superfund and other large recovery claims. His recent cases include defending the Port of Portland against a citizen suit filed under the Clean Water Act arising from the filling of an island on the Columbia River. **Robert Newell**'s (see p.594) practice emphasizes securities and trade secrets litigation. A *"sharp lawyer with good jury skills,"* he has acted for Kaiser Foundation Health Plan in arbitrations and contract disputes, and represented Oregon Health & Science University in a recent patent dispute with a large East Coast pharmaceutical company.
The Clients: Energy companies, Bank of America, Oregon Health & Science University and the Eastern Oregon Public Land Coalition.

Stoll Stoll Berne Lokting & Shlachter
The Firm: This firm was endorsed as the preeminent plaintiffs' securities fraud practice. Commentators acknowledged that *"many national cases emanate from their office."*
The Lawyers: *"A good jury lawyer with strong strategic vision,"* **Robert Stoll** specializes in plaintiffs' securities and antitrust matters. He has acted as lead plaintiff counsel in derivative cases against Arthur Andersen and others, arising out of the Enron collapse. He also acted for Oregon Public Employees' Retirement Fund in a securities fraud case. **Gary Berne** was commended to researchers as *"articulate, hard-working and committed."* He recently represented a plaintiff class of investors in a high-profile action against Assisted Living Concepts.
The Clients: Among the firm's clients are: Oregon Public Employees' Retirement Fund; Oregon Health & Science University; Paulson Investment; Waddell & Reed; ScanlanKemperBard Companies; Safeway and Hollywood Entertainment.

Ater Wynne LLP
The Firm: Peers described the practice as *"a delight to have on the other side,"* commending its solutions-oriented approach and team ethos. The firm represents all sizes of company, and is noted for its representation of emerging growth companies in securities disputes.
The Lawyers: Mark Turner chairs the firm's litigation department.
The Clients: Its clients include a mix of emerging hi-tech companies, financial institutions and well-established corporates. Among them are: Advanced Silicon Materials; Alliance Capital; Bank of America; Bank of New York; Consolidated Metco; FLIR Systems; Fog Cutter Capital Group; Golden Valley Electric Association; KPMG; Metro One Communications; Northwest Pipe Company; Oregon Health & Science University; Phillips Petroleum and The Schnitzer Group.

Schwabe, Williamson & Wyatt, PC
The Firm: Although the firm is clearly identified with insurance defense, it has emerged as a favorite for advice on commercial disputes and products liability litigation. It has been active on behalf of clients in the pharmaceutical, banking and finance industries.
The Lawyers: *"Still in his ascendancy,"* **Thomas Dulcich** was singled out to researchers as a *"thorough and competent"* attorney whose conduct through a dispute is both *"sharp and personable."* Dulcich specializes in securities, employment, products liability and general business disputes. He recently obtained summary judgment for Maxim Integrated Products in a stock options case.
The Clients: Colonial Pacific Leasing; Kenco Equipment Lease; KeyBank National Association; Nordstrom; Wyeth; Bayer; McKesson; Morgan Stanley; Maxim Integrated Products; Roman Catholic Archdiocese of Portland; Pro-Fac Cooperative and Agrilink Foods.

Other Notable Practitioners
Thomas Tongue (see p.594) at Dunn Carney Allen Higgins & Tongue LLP was praised by peers for his work in complex insurance, professional malpractice and condemnation matters. He was described as *"personable, bright and extraordinarily professional."* He represented a regional law firm in the Capital Consultants case, and has acted for a former Enron director in proceedings brought in Oregon arising out of Enron's collapse.

Identified by peers as a *"skilled opponent,"* **Daniel Skerritt** recently joined Tonkon Torp LLP from Ater Wynne. Focusing on contract, corporate governance and securities disputes, Skerritt is considered equally adept at handling matters on behalf of plaintiffs and defendants. His recent cases include advising the president of ProDX in a dispute over control of the company, and defending Fog Cutter Capital Group in the Capital Consultants case.

OREGON — REAL ESTATE

REAL ESTATE

OREGON
Leading firms (Real Estate)
1. BALL JANIK LLP
2. STOEL RIVES LLP
3. PERKINS COIE LLP
   SCHWABE, WILLIAMSON & WYATT, PC
4. PRESTON GATES & ELLIS LLP
5. DUNN CARNEY ALLEN HIGGINS

Leading individuals (Real Estate)
1. JANIK Stephen *Ball Janik LLP*
2. BALL Robert *Ball Janik LLP*
   CANTLIN Richard *Perkins Coie LLP*
   PAGE Thomas *Stoel Rives LLP*
   RADLER Barbara *Ball Janik LLP*
   SAMUELS Stanley *Preston Gates & Ellis LLP*
3. BENNETT David *Landye Bennett*
   FEUERSTEIN Howard *Stoel Rives LLP*
   MILLER Bradley *Ball Janik LLP*
4. BATEMAN Randall *Preston Gates & Ellis LLP*
   GRANT Eugene *Schwabe, Williamson*
   GUINASSO John *Schwabe, Williamson*
   HAUCK Terry *Schwabe, Williamson*
   MATTHEWS Christopher *Perkins Coie LLP*
   VOBORIL Joseph *Tonkon Torp LLP*

Firms and individuals are listed alphabetically in each band.

Ball Janik LLP
The Firm: Representing the *"lion's share"* of Portland developers and other institutional real estate clients, this *"outstanding"* firm has a reputation for excellence that *"leaves everyone else a distant second."* Peers acknowledge that its reputation pivots on a *"highly developed"* expertise in real estate and land use.
The Lawyers: *" A real hotshot,"* **Stephen Janik** commended for his hybrid real estate and land use practice that interviewees acknowledged is *"hard to compete against."* Described as a deal-maker with *"integrity"* and political acumen, he is recommended as an *"excellent choice for a big deal before the city."* During 2002, Janik represented Oregon Health & Science University in a $600 million expansion project. Complementing Janik, **Robert Ball** is an *"outstanding, top-flight real estate attorney"* with *"exceptional"* technical skills. He led a team that represented Hoyt Street Properties in condominium and apartment projects in the Pearl District of Portland. He also acted for H. Williams Advisors with respect to urban developments in Portland's North Macadam District. *"Consistently gracious and an absolute straight shooter,"* **Barbara Radler**'s expertise in commercial leasing is well known. In addition to serving the firm's long-standing clients, she is general counsel to the commercial Association of Realtors. **Bradley Miller** was also recommended as an *"unflappable and reasonable"* attorney with broad experience in real estate transactions.
The Clients: Crown Pacific Partners; H. Williams Advisors; Hoyt Street Properties; Schnitzer Investment; Commercial Association of Realtors; City of Portland; State of Oregon; Oregon Health & Science University; Costa Pacific Homes; Legacy Health System; Trammel Crow Company; Centex Real Estate; Equity Office Properties Trust; Goldman Sachs Mortgage Company; The May Department Stores Company; Intel; Marsh & McLennan Companies; Opus Northwest and The Prudential Insurance Company of America.

Stoel Rives LLP
The Firm: With *"floor after floor of lawyers"* and the pick of Oregon's blue-chip clients, the firm remains a favorite of many of its peers. It was praised for its expertise in handling large institutional transactions. Interviewees noted the loss to Perkins Coie of a number of land use attorneys, but agreed that the firm's reputation as *"leading counsel"* to real estate users had emerged unscathed.
The Lawyers: **Thomas Page** is recognized as *"one of the real experts"* in complicated leasing deals. A real estate transactional attorney with a *"broad and visible"* practice, he recently represented the City of Portland over a large industrial lease with Aventis. He has also negotiated a series of downtown renewal projects in Lake Oswego on behalf of Graymore Development. **Howard Feuerstein** is a specialist in common interest properties, and was commended for his meticulous drafting. *" thorough is his middle name."* He represented Mark-Taylor in the Hilton Mark-Taylor condominium project, and advised Trendwest Resorts on its condominium residential resort at Seaside.
The Clients: Fred Meyer; Graymore Development; Austin Industries; Stewart Title; Pacific Realty; Freightliner; Trendwest Resorts and Eagle Crest Resort.

Perkins Coie LLP
The Firm: Peers report that this firm's real estate development practice has *"really come on,"* benefiting from a strong regional profile and the addition of a *"star-studded"* land use team from Stoel Rives.
The Lawyers: **Richard Cantlin** was commended to researchers for an ability to *"look at the tapestry and know which two threads to pull."* A consummate deal-maker, he has an eye for the *"big picture."* Cantlin recently advised West Hills Development on a mixed-use development in Wilsonville. *"A rising star in the real estate area,"* **Christopher Matthews** was described to researchers as providing *" a blend of creative thought and technical expertise."* His practice encompasses a broad range of real estate matters, including lease negotiations on behalf of hi-tech tenants and affordable housing projects.
The Clients: Specht Development; PacTrust; West Hills Development; Pacific Western Homes; Safeway; Albertson's; Lowe's Companies; Transwestern Investment Company; Hay Group; Providence Medical Group; Wells Fargo; Ross Island Sand & Gravel Company and Qwest.

Schwabe, Williamson & Wyatt, PC
The Firm: It is recognized by peers as a *"broad and sophisticated"* practice, which advises developers and investors on the gamut of real estate transactions. In keeping with its background in insurance defense, the firm provides real estate investment advice to a number of large insurance companies.
The Lawyers: Interviewees agreed that **Eugene Grant** is a *"technically accomplished"* attorney who *"knows the law backward and upside down."* His recent highlights include the sale of Portland's ADP Plaza, and leasing matters in connection with the 1201 Lloyd Boulevard office building development. *"Engaging"* Practitioner **John Guinasso** *" works like lightning."* His practice focuses on commercial leasing and advice to real estate investors on '1031 exchange' transactions. He has advised on leasing matters for a number of loft projects inlcuding The Gregory and The Edge Lofts (REI store location). **Terry Hauck** is respected for his *"creativity and ability to get the transaction done."* He is recognized as a leader in the acquisition and development of bare land. He recently negotiated leases for two large office spaces in downtown Portland.
The Clients: Louis Dreyfus Property Group; Insignia; St. Paul; UBS Brinson Realty Investors; Simpson Housing; Good Samaritan Hospital Corvallis; Wells Fargo; PS Business Parks; Panattoni Development and Trammell Crow Company.

Preston Gates & Ellis LLP
The Firm: Best known for its work in real estate financing, this *"highly qualified"* group of attorneys combines its expertise in finance, leasing and tax with its knowledge of land use and development matters. The firm acts for vendors, purchasers and developers.
The Lawyers: **Stanley Samuels** won plaudits for his development work on behalf of clients, which included Oregon Pacific Investment and Development Company and Newland Northwest. He was described to researchers as *"friendly, reasonable in negotiations and knowledgeable on the substantive law."* **Randall Bateman** was commended as *"smart and practical"* with a practice focused on low income housing tax credits, shopping center developments, build-to-suit leases and tax-deferred exchanges.
The Clients: The firm advises real estate investment trusts and real estate developers. Clients

include Oregon Corporation for Affordable Housing and Oregon Pacific Investment and Development Company.

Dunn Carney Allen Higgins & Tongue LLP
The Firm: Representation of local developer Gerding/Edlen has enhanced the profile of this Portland firm, with interviewees confirming that *"it is getting stronger and stronger"* in sophisticated development work. The team advises clients on projects including apartments, shopping centers and recreational facilities. It is also involved in multi-family and commercial properties development matters.
The Lawyers: Jonathan Bennett is the real estate practice group leader.
The Clients: Eagle's View Management Company; Eastern Western; Evergreen Associates; Forest Heights Apartments; Gerding/Edlen Development Company; Pan Pacific Retail Properties; Powell Development Co.; Randall Realty; The RREEF Funds and Westwood Commercial Properties.

Other Notable Practitioners
"Technically proficient" **David Bennett** at Landye Bennett Blumstein LLP is considered a *"clear expert"* in the area of condominium and homeowner association work. In addition to his numerous multimillion dollar property deals, he recently advised on a 301-unit apartment complex at McCormick Pier on Portland's waterfront. Tonkon Torp LLP's **Joseph Voboril** was singled out to researchers as a *"consensus builder,"* who is able *"to get the deal done."* He represents a broad range of property owners and developers, and has recently advised the vendor in a $32 million transaction at McCormick Pier Apartments.

Leaders in Oregon

AMBURGEY, Larry
Amburgey & Rubin PC, Portland
503 221 0309
Recommended in Employment

BACA, David C
Davis Wright Tremaine LLP, Portland
503 778 5306
davebaca@dwt.com
Recommended in Corporate/M&A
Specialization: Partner/Co-Chair, Corporate Finance Department. Experience includes acting as lead counsel in public and private securities placements, mergers/acquisitions, general counsel to small and medium-sized businesses; works with underwriters and placement agents in public and private securities placements; acting counsel to 34 Act reporting companies and their boards of directors.
Prof. Memberships: Oregon State Bar (prior chair, Securities Regulation Section).
Career: Admitted to Oregon Bar, 1982. Became partner in DWT predecessor, 1987.
Publications: Speaker at Northwest Securities Institute, and on corporate governance matters.
Personal: JD, (magna cum laude) Harvard School of Law, 1981; BA, (summa cum laude) Linfield College, 1978.

BALL, Robert
Ball Janik LLP, Portland 503 228 2525
Recommended in Real Estate

BARRAN, Paula
Barran Liebman, Portland
503 228 0500
Recommended in Employment

BATEMAN, Randall
Preston Gates & Ellis LLP, Portland
503 228 3200
Recommended in Real Estate

BAUMAN, Todd
Stoel Rives LLP, Portland 503 224 3380
Recommended in Corporate/M&A

BENNETT, David
Landye Bennett Blumstein LLP, Portland
503 224 4100
Recommended in Real Estate

BERNE, Gary
Stoll Stoll Berne Lokting & Shlachter, Portland 503 227 1600
Recommended in Litigation

BERNICK, Carol
Davis Wright Tremaine LLP, Portland
503 778 5233
carolbernick@dwt.com
Recommended in Employment
Specialization: Partner, employment/labor law. Defends employers in discrimination, wrongful discharge, wage/hour claims; trains employers in preventative employment practices, ADA compliance, leave policies, sexual harassment.
Prof. Memberships: Oregon Bar Association. Washington State Bar Association. Bar Counsel, Disciplinary Board, Oregon State Bar Board Member, NW EEO/Affirmative Action Association.
Career: 'Who's Who of Women in Portland Business', Business Journal, 2002. Trial Lawyer of the Year Nomination, Trial Lawyers for Public Justice (representing plaintiffs targeted by national hate group), 1999.
Publications: Editor in chief, 'Oregon Labor Letter', (1994-2001). Principal Editor/Co-Author, 'Oregon Employment Law Deskbook'.
Personal: JD, University of Virginia, 1989. BA, (magna cum laude), Roanoke College, 1985.

BOOTH, Brian
Tonkon Torp LLP, Portland
503 221 1440
Recommended in Corporate/M&A

BRISCHETTO, Stephen
Stephen Brischetto - Sole Practitioner, Portland 503 223 5814
Recommended in Employment

BUCHANAN, Paul
Stoel Rives LLP, Portland 503 224 3380
Recommended in Employment

BUSSE, Richard
Busse & Hunt, Portland 503 248 0504
Recommended in Employment

CAMPBELL, William
Ater Wynne LLP, Portland
503 226 1191
Recommended in Corporate/M&A

CANTLIN, Richard
Perkins Coie LLP, Portland
503 727 2000
Recommended in Real Estate

CHADSEY, Phillip
Stoel Rives LLP, Portland 503 224 3380
Recommended in Litigation

CRISPIN, Craig
Crispin & Associates, Portland
503 293 5770
Recommended in Employment

CROW, William
Miller Nash LLP, Portland
503 205 2354
crow@millernash.com
Recommended in Litigation
Specialization: Trial experience includes antitrust litigation, commercial disputes, securities claims, products liability litigation, and insurance coverage issues. Representative clients: Monsanto Company, Alcoa Corporation, Johnson & Johnson, 3M Company, and Glaxo SmithKline.
Prof. Memberships: American College of Trial Lawyers, International Association of Defense Counsel, American Bar Foundation, and American Arbitration Association Blue Ribbon Arbitration Panel for complex civil litigation.
Career: Named one of Oregon's 10 best litigators by the 'National Law Journal', listed in a leading international review for product liability defense lawyers, and listed in a leading US legal review for the past 10 years. Past president of Oregon State Bar.

CROWE, Austin
Perkins Coie LLP, Portland
503 727 2000
Recommended in Litigation

DULCICH, Thomas
Schwabe, Williamson & Wyatt, PC, Portland 503 222 9811
Recommended in Litigation

EGGUM, Susan
Susan K Eggum, PC, Portland
503 228 9607
Recommended in Employment

ELLIS, Barnes
Stoel Rives LLP, Portland 503 224 3380
Recommended in Litigation

ENGLISH, Stephen
Bullivant Houser Bailey PC, Portland
503 228 6351
Recommended in Litigation

FEUERSTEIN, Howard
Stoel Rives LLP, Portland 503 224 3380
Recommended in Real Estate

FORTINO, Paul
Perkins Coie LLP, Portland
503 727 2000
Recommended in Litigation

GIDLEY, James
Perkins Coie LLP, Portland
503 727 2000
Recommended in Litigation

GLADE, Peter
Markowitz, Herbold, Glade & Mehlhaf PC, Portland 503 295 3085
Recommended in Litigation

GRANT, Eugene
Schwabe, Williamson & Wyatt, PC, Portland 503 222 9981
Recommended in Real Estate

GUINASSO, John
Schwabe, Williamson & Wyatt, PC, Portland 503 222 9981
Recommended in Real Estate

HAUCK, Terry
Schwabe, Williamson & Wyatt, PC, Portland 503 222 9981
Recommended in Real Estate

HEWITT, Henry
Stoel Rives LLP, Portland 503 224 3380
Recommended in Corporate/M&A

HILL NOTO, Margaret
Stoel Rives LLP, Portland 503 224 3380
Recommended in Corporate/M&A

OREGON LEADERS

HOUSER, Douglas
Bullivant Houser Bailey PC, Portland
503 228 6351
Recommended in Litigation

HUNT, Scott
Busse & Hunt, Portland 503 248 0504
Recommended in Employment

JANIK, Stephen
Ball Janik LLP, Portland 503 228 2525
Recommended in Real Estate

JERNSTEDT, Kenneth
Bullard Smith Jernstedt Wilson, Portland
503 248 1134
Recommended in Employment

KEITH, Calvin
Perkins Coie LLP, Portland
503 727 2000
Recommended in Employment

KITCHEL, Chris
Stoel Rives LLP, Portland 503 224 3380
Recommended in Employment

LEINWAND, Robert
Stoel Rives LLP, Portland 503 224 3380
Recommended in Employment

LIEBMAN, Richard
Barran Liebman, Portland
503 228 0500
Recommended in Employment

LIVINGSTON, Louis
Miller Nash LLP, Portland
503 205 2309
livingston@millernash.com
Recommended in Employment
Specialization: Areas of practice include NLRB cases, collective bargaining, arbitration, wage-and-hour matters, and employment discrimination matters. Has written articles and lectured on strikes, NLRB matters, and wage-and-hour issues nationwide and for the American Law Institute/American Bar Association.
Prof. Memberships: Oregon and New York bars.
Career: Partner since 1971; formerly a National Labor Relations Board attorney. Is an elected Fellow of The College of Labor & Employment Lawyers and is listed in a leading US legal publication.
Personal: Received his law degree at Harvard Law School and his bachelor's, magna cum laude, at Yale University

MARKOWITZ, David
Markowitz, Herbold, Glade & Mehlhaf PC, Portland 503 295 3085
Recommended in Litigation

MARTIN, Chrys
Bullivant Houser Bailey PC, Portland
503 228 6351
Recommended in Employment

MATTHEWS, Christopher
Perkins Coie LLP, Portland
503 727 2000
Recommended in Real Estate

MCDONNELL, Brendan
Tonkon Torp LLP, Portland
503 221 1440
Recommended in Corporate/M&A

MILLER, Bradley
Ball Janik LLP, Portland 503 228 2525
Recommended in Real Estate

MOORMAN, Robert
Stoel Rives LLP, Portland 503 224 3380
Recommended in Corporate/M&A

MOWE, Gregory
Stoel Rives LLP, Portland 503 224 3380
Recommended in Litigation

NEUPERT, John
Miller Nash LLP, Portland
503 205 2461
neupert@millernash.com
Recommended in Litigation
Specialization: Practice involves complex commercial litigation, including banking, trade regulation, business torts, intellectual property, and international litigation issues. Also represents clients in environmental litigation matters.
Prof. Memberships: Oregon State Bar, the American Bar, and the Multnomah County Bar Associations. He is admitted to Oregon's federal and state court bars and has practiced in federal courts throughout the West.
Career: Partner; joined the firm in 1978.
Personal: Received his law degree from the University of Oregon and was awarded Order of the Coif; earned his undergraduate degree in political science at the University of Oregon.

NEWELL, Robert D
Davis Wright Tremaine LLP, Portland
503 778 5234
bobnewell@dwt.com
Recommended in Litigation
Specialization: Partner, litigation. Experience includes complex commercial litigation, securities, unfair competition, trade secrets, Uniform Commercial Code and contract litigation.
Prof. Memberships: Oregon Bar Association. California Bar Association. President, Multnomah Bar Association.
Career: Admitted to the Oregon Bar, 1979. Joined as partner via merger, 1990. Serves as Circuit Court pro tem judge.
Publications: Contributing author, 'Federal Civil Litigation in Oregon' (Oregon State Bar). Editor in Chief, 'Civil Pleading and Practice' series (Oregon State Bar). Editorial Board, OSB Litigation Journal. Author/speaker on Oregon legislation, litigating UCC cases, and other litigation topics for lawyers/industry groups.
Personal: JD, University of Oregon, 1976. AB, with honors, Harvard, 1969.

O'LEARY, Daniel
Davis Wright Tremaine LLP, Portland
503 778 5203
danoleary@dwt.com
Recommended in Litigation

Specialization: Partner, litigation department. Civil litigator in state/federal courts since 1963; currently focused on environmental and natural resources issues under state and federal law.
Prof. Memberships: Fellow, American College of Trial Lawyers; American Board of Trial Advocates, Past President; Oregon Trial Lawyers Association, Past President.
Career: Admitted Oregon Bar (1963). Joined DWT as partner, 1994. Multnomah County Bar Association Professionalism Award, 2001. American Board of Trial Advocates, Distinguished Trial Lawyer of Year, 1997.
Publications: Author, 'Dispute Resolution in Transboundary Pollution Cases', Masters Thesis, 1993.
Personal: LLM, Lewis & Clark College, 1993. JD, Lewis & Clark College, 1963. BA, Gonzaga University, 1959.

PAGE, Thomas
Stoel Rives LLP, Portland 503 224 3380
Recommended in Real Estate

RADLER, Barbara
Ball Janik LLP, Portland 503 228 2525
Recommended in Real Estate

REEVES, Edward
Stoel Rives LLP, Portland 503 224 3380
Recommended in Employment

RICHTER, Peter
Miller Nash LLP, Portland
503 205 2366
richter@millernash.com
Recommended in Litigation
Specialization: Has tried more than 200 jury trials involving numerous legal issues.
Prof. Memberships: Member of the American Bar Association, American Board of Trial Advocates, American Inns of Court; Fellow of the American Bar Foundation; admitted to practice in the United States Supreme Court and all Oregon and federal courts.
Career: Partner since 1978 and a co-founder of the Oregon State Bar Trial Advocacy College. Named one of Oregon's 10 best litigators by the 'National Law Journal'. Listed in several leading US legal and non legal publications recognizing him for his accomplishments as a litigator and trial lawyer.

RODE, Helle
Bullard Smith Jernstedt Wilson, Portland
503 248 1134
Recommended in Employment

SAMUELS, Stanley
Preston Gates & Ellis LLP, Portland
503 228 3200
Recommended in Real Estate

SIMON, Michael
Perkins Coie LLP, Portland
503 727 2000
Recommended in Litigation

SIMPSON, Patrick
Tonkon Torp LLP, Portland
503 221 1440
Recommended in Corporate/M&A

SKERRITT, Daniel
Tonkon Torp LLP, Portland
503 221 1440
Recommended in Litigation

SNYDER, Judy
Hoevet, Snyder & Boise PC, Portland
503 228 0497
Recommended in Employment

STEPHENS, Kenneth
Tonkon Torp LLP, Portland
503 221 1440
Recommended in Corporate/M&A

STOLL, Robert
Stoll Stoll Berne Lokting & Shlachter, Portland 503 227 1600
Recommended in Litigation

TONGUE, Thomas
Dunn Carney Allen Higgins & Tongue LLP, Portland 503 224 6440
tht@dunn-carney.com
Recommended in Litigation
Specialization: A partner at *Dunn Carney* since 1973. He specializes in litigation and appeals, arbitration, mediation and healthcare law.
Prof. Memberships: Fellow in the American College of Trial Lawyers; Oregon Association of Defense Counsel; American Judicature Society, member 30+ years; Oregon State Bar, chair of multiple committees and elected delegate; Defense Research Institute member; International Association of Insurance Counsel.
Career: Admitted to Oregon, 1968; US District Court District of Oregon, 1970; US Court of Appeals 9th Circuit, 1971; US Supreme Court, 1971.
Publications: Awards: The Multnomah County Bar Association Professionalism Award; The Oregon State Bar Litigation Section - Owen M Panner Professionalism Award in 2002.
Personal: Received JD from University of Wisconsin in 1968 and a BA from University of Oregon in 1965.

TUCKER, Roy
Perkins Coie LLP, Portland
503 727 2000
Recommended in Corporate/M&A

VANCLEAVE, Richard
Barran Liebman, Portland
503 228 0500
Recommended in Employment

VOBORIL, Joseph
Tonkon Torp LLP, Portland
503 221 1440
Recommended in Real Estate

WALTERS, Stephen
Stoel Rives LLP, Portland 503 224 3380
Recommended in Litigation

OVERVIEW

PENNSYLVANIA

CONTENTS: Antitrust p.595; Banking & Finance p.597; Corporate/M&A p.599; Employment: Mainly Plaintiff p.601; Mainly Defendant p.602; Environment p.604; Insolvency p.606; Intellectual Property p.608; Litigation: General Commercial p.610; Real Estate p.613; Individuals' Profiles p.615.

PENNSYLVANIA'S TOP SIX
1. Morgan, Lewis & Bockius
2. Reed Smith
3. Dechert
4. Ballard Spahr Andrews & Ingersoll
5. Blank Rome
6. Drinker Biddle & Reath

Ranking based on Chambers' research within the state.

All quotes in the text are from interviews with clients and competitors.

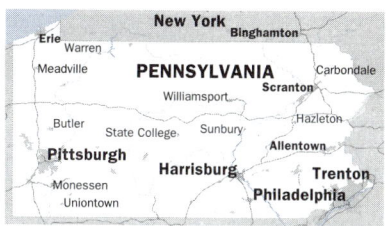

OVERVIEW: At the top of the list are three Pennsylvania classics: **Morgan, Lewis & Bockius; Reed Smith and Dechert.** All were established in the 1870's, proving that in the second oldest state in the union, history still counts for a lot.

Although Reed Smith led in overall strength in the international market, **Morgan, Lewis & Bockius** edged ahead in domestic brand-name awareness; it was cast by clients as the Rolls-Royce of corporate law in the state. The largest firm in Pennsylvania, Morgan, Lewis & Bockius has about 1300 attorneys in its ranks and was felt to be strong across the board. Market sources perceive that its center of gravity has shifted toward New York and DC, where it receives market recognition for its strength in employment, environment, energy, insolvency and antitrust. However, the Philadelphia base has reaped the benefits of the firm's aggressive growth. The corporate department is firmly anchored in traditional M&A, but has broadened its scope to include a large share of technology transactions, nurturing such start-ups as CDNow and Verticalnet. Cochair of the firm's global technology practice is Stephen Goodman, a high-powered attorney who won a top ranking for his expertise in emerging growth markets. The team also topped *Chambers'* list in employment statewide, thanks in part to close relations with bodies such as the NLRB, EEOC and US Department of Labor.

With 16 offices in the US and two in the UK, **Reed Smith** rates highly for its international coverage and is ranked second. The engine of the firm's business development is its employment practice, which was top-ranking statewide. The Pittsburgh-based team forged a formidable reputation at the negotiations table, and its pièce de résistance is a track record of negotiating advantageous contract agreements without strikes. Reed Smith also emerged as a leader in insolvency; it recently expanded its capacities in this area with the recruitment of several partners from Duane Morris.

With the addition of a Frankfurt office in 2002, **Dechert**'s international reach stretches farther afield than any other Pennsylvania firm. Statewide industry sources place Dechert at the top of the heap in litigation. Here, respected attorneys such as Robert Heim keep the practice in the spotlight by defending Philip Morris against individual and class actions in the eastern US. The firm earned top-band ranking in antitrust, with Joseph Tate singled out for his involvement in high-profile cases. He defended FMC and Dead Sea Bromine Group against anticompetitive allegations concerning chemical products. With support from its international network, the firm has cultivated an enviable client roster that includes names such as Siemens, DuPont and Pfizer.

In fourth place is **Ballard Spahr Andrews & Ingersoll**. Renowned for its vigorous cultivation of political ties, the firm boasts several former Philadelphia city solicitors in its attorney roster. Ballard Spahr's growing reputation was boosted recently by the addition of 13 labor lawyers from Montgomery, McCracken, Walker & Rhoads; their public sector expertise is seen to complement the firm's respectable private sector practice. Litigation is the firm's centerpiece. Interviewees particularly praise top-ranking commercial litigator Alan Davis as a wonderfully persuasive advocate and brilliant scholar. In environmental litigation, David Mandelbaum's impressive practice includes major Superfund matters. Real estate is another strong suit for the firm; esteemed strategist Mike Sklaroff chairs the department.

Blank Rome, ranked fifth, leads the pack for banking transactions. The firm focuses on large-scale financings, acting, for example, on behalf of American Business Financial Services in the issuance of more than $1 billion of pass-through certificates. Harvey Forman was particularly recommended for his knowledge of asset-based financing. The firm also earned top-band rankings in real estate and insolvency, with star practitioner Raymond Shapiro acting for a creditors' panel in the reorganization of a prominent US manufacturer.

Drinker Biddle & Reath won endorsement for its concentration of knowledgeable, detail-oriented attorneys. Senior statesman William Clark is said to know Pennsylvania corporate law inside and out. The firm boosted its profile in IP by its merger with boutique firm Seidel, Gonda, Lavorgna & Monaco in 2001; it now combines patent procurement with trademark and copyright work. Arthur Seidel enjoys statewide prominence and was recognized by peers as the driver of the IP practice.

ANTITRUST

PENNSYLVANIA
Leading firms (Antitrust)

1. **DECHERT** *Philadelphia*
2. **MORGAN, LEWIS & BOCKIUS LLP** *Philadelphia*
   PEPPER HAMILTON LLP *Philadelphia*
3. **FINE KAPLAN & BLACK** *Philadelphia*
   MONTGOMERY, MCCRACKEN, WALKER *Philadelphia*
   REED SMITH LLP *Pittsburgh*
4. **BERGER & MONTAGUE** *Philadelphia*
   DRINKER BIDDLE & REATH LLP *Philadelphia*
   DUANE MORRIS LLP *Philadelphia*
   KOHN SWIFT & GRAF *Philadelphia*
   SCHNADER HARRISON SEGAL *Philadelphia*

Firms are listed alphabetically in each band.

Dechert
see firm details p.789

The Firm: *"Clearly first in antitrust,"* acknowledged interviewees, who also pointed to the firm's *"superior depth."* The group fields eight partners in Philadelphia and can draw on members of its offices in DC, New York, London and Brussels. This combined support provides it with the widest range of experience in the state. The team handled such cases as a patent antitrust claim against pharmaceutical companies and a class action against a chemical company concerning a stabilizing agent.

The Lawyers: Sources reckon that **Joseph Tate** is *"the one who gets almost every high-profile case"* in Philadelphia. He focuses on the defense of blue-chip clients and others in class actions, and has defended FMC and Dead Sea Bromine Group against anticompetitive allegations involving chemical products. His practice also involves handling government investigations for such heavyweights as GlaxoSmithKline. Predominantly an antitrust litigator, **George Gordon** was endorsed by peers for his *"substantively strong trial preparation"* and his courtroom prowess. Acting for American Airlines, he successfully argued a case involving alleged conspiracy to fix and reduce commissions for travel agents abroad. He was also involved in class actions involving two pharmaceutical products: an antidepressant and an antiarthritic drug. Observers consider **Stephen Stack** to be *"excellent"* in regulatory

PENNSYLVANIA   ANTITRUST

PENNSYLVANIA
Leading individuals (Antitrust)

1 TATE Joseph *Dechert*, Philadelphia
2 EDWARDS Mark *Morgan, Lewis*, Philadelphia
GORDON George *Dechert*, Philadelphia
KOHN Joseph *Kohn Swift & Graf*, Philadelphia
LIEBENBERG Roberta *Fine Kaplan & Black*, Philadelphia
MATHER Barbara *Pepper Hamilton LLP*, Philadelphia
3 ARMSTRONG Stephen *Montgomery*, Philadelphia
ASHER Steven *Fox Rothschild O'Brien*, Philadelphia
BOOKER Daniel *Reed Smith LLP*, Pittsburgh
BROWN Stephen *Dechert*, Philadelphia
MONTAGUE Laddie *Berger & Montague*, Philadelphia
NEWELL Francis *Montgomery, McCracken*, Philadelphia
SHIEKMAN Laurence *Pepper Hamilton*, Philadelphia
STACK Stephen *Dechert*, Philadelphia
SWIRSKY Sherry *Schnader Harrison Segal*, Philadelphia

Up-and-coming individuals
MACK Wayne *Duane Morris LLP*, Philadelphia
SAINT-ANTOINE Paul *Drinker Biddle*, Philadelphia

Individuals are listed alphabetically in each band.

matters. He helped complete a $5 billion acquisition in the chemical industry within 80 days, and represented a supermarket chain in its purchase of another chain. Chair of the antitrust group, Stack is also experienced in IP-related issues such as patent strategies and licensing. **Stephen Brown** won peer support for his *"skill in handling the intricacies of a complex case."* He has advised on anticompetitive class actions involving such products as automotive refinishing paint.
The Clients: DuPont; Pfizer; Philip Morris; Gerber and Darling International.

Morgan, Lewis & Bockius LLP
The Firm: Renowned for its international capabilities – the firm has offices in London, Frankfurt, Brussels and Tokyo – peers pointed to the support of the DC office as providing a key advantage. The team has five partners focusing on competition law matters statewide, handling complex defenses in private and criminal antitrust litigation. Equipped with what rivals described as *"reach and presence,"* the team represented Degussa-Hüls in a vitamin price-fixing case. On behalf of Pharmacia, the team handled a separate case involving the pricing of prescription drugs.
The Lawyers: Interviewees praised **Mark Edward**'s *"considerable talent"* in regulatory and antitrust litigation. He represented Armstrong Holdings in a monopolization suit concerning hardwood floorings and acted for Westwood One in suing StarGuide Digital Networks for alleged monopolization.
The Clients: Dow Chemical; Sandvik Hard Materials; Law School Admission Council; Dr Pepper; Millipore and Advance Transformer.

Pepper Hamilton LLP
The Firm: The group is esteemed by competitors as establishing a *"nationally important scope"* to its practice. The group includes 12 partners in Pennsylvania and three in DC. It combines a general practice covering such areas as Hart-Scott-Rodino filings and merger counseling with widely respected courtroom battles such as defending Sunoco in an antitrust case alleging conspiracy to benchmark employee pay.
The Lawyers: Barbara Mather, known to sources for her *"high-end antitrust practice,"* counseled Smurfit Container in fighting allegations that it helped to orchestrate an industry wide price increase for linerboards. Mather emerged as one of the most sought-after litigators in the state due to her *"intelligence,"* and her *"good relations with judges."* She has advised several clients in seeking DOJ clearance for key acquisitions. **Laurence Shiekman** chair of the firm's commercial litigation group, earned an *"outstanding reputation"* among competitors for his antitrust expertise. He defended glass manufacturer Pilkington in a price-fixing allegation and advised a national pizza chain concerning monopolization charges by its franchisees.
The Clients: BASF; Bowater; Lesaffre et Cie and Burger King.

Fine Kaplan & Black
The Firm: A *"preeminent"* boutique litigation practice with a flair for antitrust class actions. This firm of a dozen attorneys has represented plaintiffs in some of the nation's most publicized lawsuits. For example, the group has acted as a member of the plaintiffs' executive committee in the vitamin antitrust litigation, which alleges international price-fixing. The team also advised plaintiffs in antitrust matters against the providers of microcrystalline cellulose, a product often used in foods.
The Lawyers: Interviewees considered **Roberta Liebenberg** (see p.617) as *"having risen to the top ranks of the antitrust bar."* She acted on behalf of plaintiffs in bringing anticompetitive charges against manufacturers of corrugated containers.
The Clients: Individuals; retailers; purchasers; suppliers and insurance companies.

Montgomery, McCracken, Walker & Rhoads LLP
The Firm: Peers credited the firm with raising its profile over the past several years. The practice comprises eight partners in Philadelphia, who have *"worked very hard to obtain good results for clients."* The team has secured a reputation for defending multi-district and class actions, advising companies such as one of the largest graphite electrodes producers in battling international price-fixing and other anticompetitive claims.
The Lawyers: As chair of the antitrust practice, **Stephen Armstrong** earned plaudits for his *"careful and thoughtful"* approach to competition law. He defended Air Products & Chemicals against international price-fixing claims. Armstrong also represented Microsoft in statewide antitrust charges and has counseled various clients in issues such as pricing, distribution and evaluations of potential litigation. **Francis Newell**, cochair of the antitrust group, was recognized by interviewees for his *"tremendous experience"* in fending off anticompetitive claims. In one case, he succeeded in obtaining dismissal for a client, Simpson Tacoma Kraft, in the linerboard antitrust case prior to class certification.
The Clients: Delta Air Lines; Amerisource Bergen; UCAR and Menzies Aviation Group.

Reed Smith LLP
The Firm: Marked as *"the premier antitrust defense firm in western Pennsylvania,"* the seven-partner team has seen a steady flow of work arising from an impressive corporate practice. One of the oldest firms in Pittsburgh, the group has also established a UK presence, with four antitrust practitioners stationed in London.
The Lawyers: Daniel Booker, who splits his time between Pittsburgh and DC, received accolades from rivals for his work defending a major aircraft manufacturer against antitrust charges. Commended by peers as *"accomplished"* and *"among the top in Pennsylvania,"* Booker also counseled US Steel in various antitrust issues.
The Clients: Citadel Communications; Matthews International; Highmark and PG Publishing.

Berger & Montague
The Firm: A plaintiffs' boutique, the group was endorsed for its work in complex securities, antitrust and mass torts. Considered by competitors as a *"leading light on the plaintiffs' side,"* the group represented a group of direct purchasers of Cardizem CD, a drug used to control high blood pressure or chest pains – the case resulted in a $110 million settlement. In a separate class action on behalf of purchasers of brand-name prescription drugs, the group obtained a $717 million settlement.
The Lawyers: Interviewees held **H Laddie Montague**, chairman of the antitrust department, in the *"highest regard."* Also described as *"fair minded,"* he successfully convinced the US Seventh Circuit Court of Appeals to reverse a summary judgment involving a lawsuit, which targeted suppliers of high fructose corn syrup, such as Archer Daniels Midland, Staley, Cargill, and others on behalf of purchasers.
The Clients: Schools, employees, retirees, investors and businesses.

Drinker Biddle & Reath LLP
The Firm: Its antitrust expertise is distributed between DC and Philadelphia and the firm main-

ANTITRUST — PENNSYLVANIA

tains what rivals perceive to be an *"active and energetic"* practice. Distinguished in the technology and pharmaceutical areas, the team provided antitrust counseling to Hewlett-Packard in its joint venture with Intel to develop next-generation microprocessors.
The Lawyers: Competitors respect the *"impressive depth of knowledge"* possessed by **Paul Saint-Antoine**, cohead of the antitrust practice. He defended Georgia-Pacific in a lawsuit involving linerboards and advised Cinram International in an antitrust patent dispute involving DVD technology.
The Clients: JFC Technologies and BF Goodrich.

Duane Morris LLP
The Firm: This talented team stretches from San Francisco, Miami and DC to London, UK. It has recently faced the departure of top litigator Michael Baylson, to the federal bench. The group continues to advise on big-ticket cases such as its advice to Swiss and English companies in the antitrust monopolization case against Microsoft. The firm also acts on behalf of plaintiffs, and has argued against FMC and others in a dispute involving microcrystalline cellulose.
The Lawyers: Leader of the antitrust group, **Wayne Mack** won peer endorsements as a *"young and terrific attorney."* He successfully defended a Pennsylvania hospital in an antitrust allegation brought by a surgeon and advised GNC in an antitrust class action involving more than 1500 franchisees.
The Clients: GTE, Lancaster General Hospital and Easton Hospital.

Kohn Swift & Graf
The Firm: Linked to one of the first anticompetitive class actions filed in the US, the firm has *"a lot of antitrust capabilities,"* according to peers. The group has cultivated a *"prominent"* reputation based on complex multi-district suits, with a bent toward representing plaintiffs. It was appointed co-lead counsel for the purchasers of automotive refinishing paint, in a price-fixing case against PPG Industries, DuPont, Sherwin-Williams, BASF and others. The case involves more than 60 class action complaints.
The Lawyers: Firm director **Joseph Kohn** was endorsed by competitors for his *"resourceful and conscientious"* style. He helped obtain a $143 million settlement in a price-fixing case against five top US distributors and three large retailers of compact discs.
The Clients: Employees; retailers; businesses and suppliers.

Schnader Harrison Segal & Lewis LLP
The Firm: Credited by sources with a history of *"real litigation power,"* the firm has represented both plaintiffs and defendants in prominent antitrust disputes. Acting as lead counsel for plaintiffs including the drugstore chain Rite Aid, the team argued a case involving allegations that pharmaceutical companies conspired to keep generic equivalents off the market.
The Lawyers: Rivals acknowledged that **Sherry Swirsky** is an *"accomplished"* lawyer who *"really knows antitrust."* She represented Air France in fighting charges that it conspired to lower commissions for travel agents. She also defended manufacturers of linerboards in a class action alleging price-fixing.
The Clients: International Air Transport Association, UPS and Waste Management.

Other Notable Practitioners
Steven Asher of Fox Rothschild O'Brien & Frankel LLP garnered peer approval for his *"tough, aggressive"* approach, which often results in multimillion dollar settlements. He obtained a $90 million settlement for a class of manufacturers who purchased Sorbates, which is primarily used as a preservative in foods. Asher also secured settlements of $50 million for clients in a suit involving price-fixing in the carpet industry, and $60 million for plaintiffs in an antitrust case against glass manufacturers.

BANKING & FINANCE

PENNSYLVANIA
Leading firms (Banking & Finance)
1. BLANK ROME LLP *Philadelphia*
2. DUANE MORRIS LLP *Philadelphia*
3. BALLARD SPAHR ANDREWS *Philadelphia*
   DRINKER BIDDLE & REATH LLP *Philadelphia*
   MORGAN, LEWIS & BOCKIUS LLP *Philadelphia*
4. KLETT ROONEY LIEBER & SCHORLING *Pittsburgh*
   REED SMITH LLP *Pittsburgh*
   WOLF, BLOCK, SCHORR AND SOLIS *Philadelphia*

Firms are listed alphabetically in each band.

Blank Rome LLP
The Firm: The group of about 15 attorneys is supported by eight other branches nationwide and was considered by competitors to be *"one of the most impressive"* financial service practices in Pennsylvania. The team focuses on large-scale financings, and represented American Business Financial Services in the issuance of more than $1 billion of pass-through certificates, and another $350 million of subordinated debt securities.
The Lawyers: **Harvey Forman** was recommended for his finance and bankruptcy law expertise, with asset-based financing being a mainstay of his practice. Competitors admire his *"studious"* approach and agree that *"bankers really respect him."* Chairman of the leasing and asset securitization group, **Lawrence Flick** blends corporate law adroitness with a deft hand in finance-related transactions. Praised as *"a leading finance lawyer"* in Pennsylvania, he supervised several deals for American Business Financial Services and represented a European multinational company in its acquisition of a portfolio of asset-based loans from a US company. **Joan Stern**, a public finance specialist, won peer endorsements for her *"technically skilled and organized"* style. Rivals complimented her ability to balance the political demands of government-related entities with expertise of the law. She has handled a variety of transactions for the City of Philadelphia and its school district, and focuses on such areas as transportation, utilities, healthcare and housing.
The Clients: Bank of America; CIT Group; Fleet Capital; PNC Bank; Hewlett-Packard and Genesis Health Care System.

Duane Morris LLP
The Firm: Benefiting from an enviable client roster that includes institutional creditors such as Wachovia, the firm earned high marks in structuring difficult transactions, including cross-border deals. Sources described the team as having *"grown nationally in scope,"* with offices in New York, Chicago and San Francisco and it can draw on its London, UK base for international matters. The group also tackles a wide range of business expansion and restructuring issues, alongside its strong public finance practice. The firm represented Bay View Capital and Bay View Bank in a transaction that involved a $3 billion purchase and assumption agreement with US Bank, and a $1 billion mortgage loan purchase by Washington Mutual bank.
The Lawyers: **John Horstmann**, who is also included in *Chambers'* insolvency section for Pennsylvania, has a practice that centers on representing financial institutions, especially in bankruptcy proceedings. His practice also includes commercial loans and matters relating to electronic transfers. **Margery Reed**, viewed by competitors as *"a terrific advocate for clients,"* also has an eye on

PENNSYLVANIA
BANKING & FINANCE

PENNSYLVANIA
Leading individuals (Banking & Finance)

[1]
- **FORMAN Harvey** *Blank Rome LLP,* Philadelphia
- **SHUTER Bruce** *Drinker Biddle & Reath,* Philadelphia

[2]
- **FLICK Lawrence** *Blank Rome LLP,* Philadelphia
- **FRIDY Carl** *Ballard Spahr Andrews,* Philadelphia
- **STERN Joan** *Blank Rome LLP,* Philadelphia

[3]
- **BERGER Lawrence** *Morgan, Lewis,* Philadelphia
- **HERYFORD Craig** *Klett Rooney Lieber,* Pittsburgh
- **HORSTMANN John** *Duane Morris LLP,* Philadelphia
- **LESSER Bruce** *Wolf, Block, Schorr and Solis,* Philadelphia
- **LONDON Alan** *Reed Smith LLP,* Pittsburgh
- **REED Margery** *Duane Morris LLP,* Philadelphia

Individuals are listed alphabetically in each band.

insolvency law while handling a variety of banking and finance matters. Rivals said her forte is in shaping transactions, including syndicated loans and asset-based financings.

The Clients: PNC Bank; Mellon Bank; Citizens Bank; Sovereign Bank; Deutsche Bank and Fleet Bank.

Ballard Spahr Andrews & Ingersoll LLP
see firm details p.769

The Firm: The team possesses a widely recognized talent straddling banking law and litigation, and was described as *"a whole package."* Competitors perceived the team as being especially effective in representing large lending institutions in secured and unsecured commercial loans. The group also specializes in such matters as real estate, healthcare and university finance.

The Lawyers: *"Extremley bright"* **Carl Fridy**, who is partner in charge of the transactional finance group, garnered interviewees' recommendations for his *"thorough knowledge of the law."* Fridy's practice focuses on secured and unsecured commercial lending, and has branched out into such areas as tax-exempt bond financing.

The Clients: Lenders; borrowers; financial institutions and governmental entities.

Drinker Biddle & Reath LLP

The Firm: Deemed a *"terrific"* group by sources, the team primarily represented banks and other financial institutions in a variety of mid-sized secured and unsecured loans. The firm has negotiated, structured and documented multimillion dollar loans, including credit facilities to refinance existing borrowings and to provide working capital. The team handled a $35 million credit facility as part of a complicated international transaction involving 207 banks.

The Lawyers: Sources acclaimed **Bruce Shuter** as *"a sound practitioner who's always effective,"* noting his work on *"sophisticated finance transactions."* He represented clients in syndicated multibank credits and has designed transactions relating to foreign trade finance and loans in industries such as broadcasting and healthcare. He also enjoys a reputation as a *"well-known and able bankruptcy attorney,"* representing lenders in restructuring troubled loans.

The Clients: Financial institutions, manufacturers and media companies.

Morgan, Lewis & Bockius LLP

The Firm: The team was perceived by interviewees as benefiting from its busy corporate department, representing blue-chip companies and others in securing loans. Sources cite its *"center of gravity"* as leaning toward New York and DC, while clients appreciate that the firm is *"well established nationally"* and able to take on complex, multilevel transactions. The team acted for FMC in a $750 million credit facility for debt retirement and working capital.

The Lawyers: Peers described **Lawrence Berger** as a *"substantial"* and *"effective"* practitioner. He has represented private companies and others in sophisticated corporate loans, such as a multimillion dollar securitization of assets. He also advised Rohm and Haas in a term loan agreement worth about $500 million. Competitors also value him as *"a specialist in Uniform Commercial Code."*

The Clients: JPMorgan Chase, Wachovia and Susquehanna Bancshares.

Klett Rooney Lieber & Schorling

The Firm: The Pittsburgh full-service firm has secured a strong regional reputation among rivals for its finance practice. The team handles an array of transactions including representing syndicated bank groups in multimillion dollar loans. The team represents lenders and borrowers, and has structured loans that involve equity features such as warrants, mezzanine financing, and preferred or common stocks.

The Lawyers: Craig Heryford cochair of the firm's finance and technology practice groups, was described by market sources as *"an extremely knowledgeable competitor."* Heryford also was said to *"understand the key business issues involved in this type of transaction."* Although his practice emphasizes finance transactions relating to emerging businesses and venture capital, he is also involved in general corporate work such as M&A.

The Clients: Fortune 500 companies, municipalities and healthcare institutions.

Reed Smith LLP

The Firm: The Pittsburgh-based firm represents an array of clients in such transactions as bank-related M&A, lending and security. It draws recommendations for its extensive international network stretching across the Atlantic to London, UK. Attorneys are also experienced in handling regulatory matters before such Government agencies as the Federal Reserve System, Office of the Comptroller of the Currency and Federal Deposit Insurance Corporation.

The Lawyers: Market sources viewed **Alan London** as *"an excellent consensus builder."* He advises lenders and borrowers in such matters as syndicated facilities, project and acquisition financing, securitization and debt restructuring.

The Clients: National banks; thrifts; mortgage bankers and brokers.

Wolf, Block, Schorr and Solis-Cohen LLP
see firm details p.905

The Firm: Benefiting from a *"good stable of regional clients,"* the firm has a powerful pull on the midmarket, sources said. In addition to traditional commercial lending, the team also represents clients in matters involving asset securitization, debtor-in-possession transactions and tax-free financing.

The Lawyers: Bruce Lesser (see p.617), co-chair of the financial services group, was acclaimed by competitors as *"one of the key names on the banking side."* They commended his *"effective negotiation skills"* and respect his expertise in the structuring and documentation of transactions including asset-based loans. Lesser's practice also includes loan workouts and other bankruptcy-related issues.

The Clients: Wachovia; LaSalle Business Credit; Citizens Bank and PNC Bank.

CORPORATE/M&A

PENNSYLVANIA

CORPORATE/M&A

PENNSYLVANIA
Leading firms (Corporate/M&A)

1
- DECHERT *Philadelphia*
- MORGAN, LEWIS & BOCKIUS LLP *Philadelphia*

2
- BALLARD SPAHR ANDREWS *Philadelphia*
- DRINKER BIDDLE & REATH LLP *Philadelphia*
- PEPPER HAMILTON LLP *Philadelphia*

3
- BUCHANAN INGERSOLL *Pittsburgh*
- REED SMITH LLP *Pittsburgh*

4
- DUANE MORRIS LLP *Philadelphia*
- KIRKPATRICK & LOCKHART LLP *Pittsburgh*

5
- BLANK ROME LLP *Philadelphia*
- COHEN & GRIGSBY PC *Pittsburgh*
- WOLF, BLOCK, SCHORR *Philadelphia*

Leading individuals (Corporate/M&A)

1
- ABELSON Barry *Pepper Hamilton LLP,* Philadelphia
- CLARK William *Drinker Biddle & Reath,* Philadelphia
- GOODMAN Stephen *Morgan, Lewis,* Philadelphia
- WINOKUR Barton *Dechert,* Philadelphia

2
- GARRITY Vincent *Duane Morris LLP,* Philadelphia
- KLEIN Justin *Ballard Spahr Andrews,* Philadelphia
- THOMPSON Thomas *Buchanan Ingersoll,* Pittsburgh

3
- COHEN Charles *Cohen & Grigsby PC,* Pittsburgh
- DENINNO David *Reed Smith LLP,* Pittsburgh
- MCLEAN Michael *Kirkpatrick & Lockhart,* Pittsburgh
- MYERS Marlee *Morgan, Lewis & Bockius,* Pittsburgh
- NEWLIN William *Buchanan Ingersoll,* Pittsburgh

4
- BLUME Fred *Blank Rome LLP,* Philadelphia
- BRAEMER Richard *Ballard Spahr Andrews,* Philadelphia
- HARMELIN Stephen *Dilworth Paxson,* Philadelphia
- HARPER Robert *Klett Rooney Lieber,* Pittsburgh
- KESSLER Mark *Wolf, Block, Schorr,* Philadelphia
- LIPMAN Frederick *Blank Rome LLP,* Philadelphia
- SINGER Alan *Morgan, Lewis & Bockius,* Philadelphia
- SNYDER Henry *Kirkpatrick & Lockhart,* Pittsburgh

Firms and individuals are listed alphabetically in each band.

Dechert
see firm details p.789

The Firm: The firm's *"sophisticated"* corporate profile is among the most diverse in Pennsylvania, advising clients in such areas as cross-border deals, going private transactions and special committee assignments. The team can draw on the support afforded by eight branches in the US and its five offices in Europe. Rivals perceive it as *"a mover and shaker"* especially in M&A relating to investment funds or other financial services, advising clients such as Zurich Scudder Investments and Mellon Bank. The team also led Rohm and Haas in its sale of an agricultural chemicals business to Dow Chemical and advised OraPharma in its sale to Johnson & Johnson.

The Lawyers: Barton Winokur, chair of the firm and *"a major figure"* according to sources, specializes in representing private equity firms. He owes his *"marvelous"* reputation to complex corporate transactions such as a $1.1 billion deal in which an investor group acquired National Golf Properties, the Californian investment trust.
The Clients: Siemens; Pfizer; Baxter International; Citicorp Venture Capital and Starwood Capital Group.

Morgan, Lewis & Bockius LLP
The Firm: *"Strong across the board"* acknowledge interviewees. The largest law firm in the state employs more than 100 corporate lawyers handling deals that range from a few million to tens of billions of dollars. The group also specializes in advising public and private companies on structuring takeover defense mechanisms. The firm was said to be *"the Rolls-Royce of corporate law."* An *"aggressive"* approach to building an emerging growth practice has been viewed by sources as successful.

The Lawyers: Peers endorsed the *"high-power"* **Stephen Goodman** for his *"pre-eminent"* reputation in venture capital transactions. Cochair of the firm's global technology practice, he piloted Universal Display through a $25 million secondary offering, and advised Zany Brainy in its sale to The Right Start for more than $100 million. He was also credited with nurturing such start-ups as CDNow and Verticalnet. **Marlee Myers** is managing partner of the Pittsburgh branch. She is a *"personable"* clients-getter at the firm, who has earned a reputation among competitors as *"an extremely hard worker cut from the New York mold."* She acted for Sandvik in its $175 million acquisition of Valenite. **Alan Singer** employs what rivals call *"an extraordinary mind"* to his practice in securities law, including public and nonpublic offerings. A former SEC official, he also directs companies in regulatory matters.
The Clients: Merrill Lynch; JPMorgan Chase; FreeMarkets and AirClic.

Ballard Spahr Andrews & Ingersoll LLP
see firm details p.769

The Firm: The firm's peers designate it as *"one of the most well-placed firms politically"* in the state. Although the departure of chairman David Cohen to Comcast in 2002 was seen as a setback, the firm has maintained its *"shine,"* particularly in the area of general corporate and securities transactions. Ballard Spahr enjoys broad coverage with seven offices in the mid-Atlantic corridor and western US. The team has progressively established an *"impressive"* list of clients including DuPont. In 2002, it represented DuPont Canada in its purchase of Liqui-Box for $333 million.

The Lawyers: Justin Klein, leader of the securities group, was endorsed by interviewees as *"a great business adviser."* He counseled a group of underwriters led by CSFB in an $80 million offering by Urban Outfitters. He also acted for PMA Capital in a $75 million offering of convertible senior debentures. A point man in M&A for the firm, **Richard Braemer** earned a reputation among peers as *"a first-class, highly skilled practitioner"* who excelled at *"structuring the course of a deal."* He advised a private equity fund in a combined acquisition and merger with another existing portfolio company. He also advised a group of independent directors of Getty Petroleum Marketing, helping to steer the company's sale to LUKOIL, one of Russia's largest oil companies.
The Clients: PNC Financial; GlaxoSmithKline; Sunoco; Metrologic Instruments; Toll Brothers and University of Pennsylvania.

Drinker Biddle & Reath LLP
The Firm: A group of knowledgeable attorneys who *"really dig into the details,"* the practice has solidified its reputation among peers through its advice on complex transactions. In addition to its general corporate transactions, the team also handles structured auctions and other divestitures, and corporate governance. The Philadelphia office is supported by groups in New York, DC and on the West Coast, encompassing some of the nation's most prominent economic zones.

The Lawyers: William Clark, depicted by rivals as *"a senior statesman in Pennsylvania corporate law,"* represented AmerisourceBergen in its $82 million acquisition of Bridge Medical. He also acted as local counsel for Comcast's merger with AT&T. Clients agree that Clark not only *"knows Pennsylvania law inside and out,"* he also renders *"extremely practical advice."*
The Clients: Aetna; Hewlett-Packard; Cott; Delphi Corporation; Comcast and Penske Truck Leasing.

Pepper Hamilton LLP
The Firm: Competitors treat the firm with *"a healthy respect,"* believing that it excels in regional M&A and venture capital financings. The team works closely with attorneys in the firm's ten other offices, three of which are in Pennsylvania, counseling clients in LBOs, recapitalizations and hostile takeovers. In one case, the group defended an electrical components and connectors manufacturer against a hostile tender offer, and the company subsequently merged with a friendly party.

The Lawyers: Chair of the executive committee, **Barry Abelson** concentrates on securities, venture capital and M&A transactions. He has earned a reputation among colleagues as *"a first-class securities lawyer,"* especially for his representation of emerging companies and private equity funds. In addition, he regularly advises boards of

PENNSYLVANIA

CORPORATE/M&A

directors and executives in corporate governance matters.

The Clients: Banks; medical products manufacturers; apparel retailers; software developers and automotive suppliers.

Buchanan Ingersoll

The Firm: Armed with a roster of *"younger, aggressive clients,"* the group was said by peers to have pushed ahead into the new media market. The Pittsburgh-based firm comprises about 55 lawyers in Pennsylvania, in addition to having 11 other offices across the US. The group advised Kennametal in its €188 million acquisition of Widia Group from Milacron, a deal that solidified Kennametal as one of the largest metal cutting tool companies in the world.

The Lawyers: Rivals cast **Thomas Thompson** as a *"well-rounded generalist who is outstanding in dealing with M&A transactions."* He also handles corporate restructurings and some mediation work. He guided three private companies in raising venture capital averaging about $25 million each and a US chemical operation in its $180 million sale to an English joint venture. **William Newlin** was distinguished as a rainmaker who *"has been successful in building a practice outside of Pittsburgh."* He acted for Dick's Sporting Goods in an IPO worth about $60 million.

The Clients: Pitt-Des Moines (PDM); Black Box; Parker/Hunter; NOVA Chemical and Equitable Resources.

Reed Smith LLP

The Firm: Rivals labeled the firm as *"one of the most prestigious practices in Pittsburgh."* It has offices in 13 cities worldwide including London, UK. Mergers with Oakland-based Crosby, Heafey, Roach & May and New York's Parker Duryee Rosoff & Haft have boosted the Pittsburgh-based firm's business capabilities, especially in the corporate and technology sectors. The team represented a prominent publishing company in acquiring several regional publications, and acted for Rocky Mountain Holdings in its sale to Air Methods.

The Lawyers: **David DeNinno** won kudos for his handling of complex commercial transactions, and was said by sources to be *"extremely effective in structuring deals."* His clients include the Pittsburgh Pirates, representing the baseball team in the development of a new stadium. He has also served as principal outside counsel for a number of businesses, including technology-based companies.

The Clients: JG Wentworth and Journal Register.

Duane Morris LLP

The Firm: The *"robust"* firm has nearly doubled in size over the past three years, with 18 branches throughout the US and an office in London, UK. Although it routinely handles general corporate transactions, the team earns respect among peers for its work relating to financial institutions, technology-based businesses and telecom companies. It represented California's Bay View Bank in asset sales that included a $3.5 billion transaction to a Minneapolis bank, and a separate deal valued at about a billion dollars to Washington Mutual.

The Lawyers: **Vincent Garrity**, who garnered praise from interviewees as *"an excellent generalist,"* enjoys a steady flow of M&A deals. He has advised on the sale of a $125 million environmental consulting business and a $500 million purchase of assets. In addition to his advice on corporate governance, he was also recommended for matters relating to takeovers involving Pennsylvania-chartered companies.

The Clients: BMW of North America; JPMorgan Chase; GMAC Commercial Mortgage and PNC Bank.

Kirkpatrick & Lockhart LLP

The Firm: The team has facilitated a full range of transactions including M&A, joint ventures and spin-offs. Its highlights include a series of acquisitions for Westco International, one of the largest electrical products manufacturers. The group has about 50 practitioners in Pittsburgh and Harrisburg, and a dynamic support system throughout offices in eight other US cities. Sources agree that it has *"the credibility and the numbers to handle large sophisticated matters."*

The Lawyers: **Michael McLean**, said by competitors to be *"deeply knowledgeable,"* advised an investment management company in several acquisitions valued between $500,000 and $3 billion each. A *"cordial and thoughtful attorney,"* he represented Eaton in a spin-off IPO and led a voluntary restructuring for Weirton Steel. **W Henry Snyder** is respected by peers for his *"good combination of tax and corporate"* experience. He has established a loyal following among private and smaller companies and has represented several physician practice groups in their acquisitions.

The Clients: United Technologies World Wrestling Entertainment and Education Management Company.

Blank Rome LLP

The Firm: Statewide, the firm employs about 20 general corporate lawyers who were perceived by peers to be *"plugged"* into the community. The group is supported by eight other offices, primarily in the Northeast, and has established a strong reputation in nurturing entrepreneurial companies. The group advised Genesis Health Ventures in public and private finance transactions ranging from $10-200 million in addition to overseeing a $1.4 billion acquisition. Acting on behalf of Nationwide Financial Services, the firm helped navigate the $1.5 billion acquisition of Provident Mutual Life Insurance.

The Lawyers: Managing partner **Fred Blume** won support from rivals for his *"good judgment and practical business sense."* He enjoys a *"substantial"* client roster that includes SunGard and AC Moore. Respected **Frederick Lipman** has represented American Business Financial Services in a $325 million high yield public offering. He also acts for companies such as Hanover Foods in commercial litigation.

The Clients: ARAMARK; Finlay Enterprises; IKON Office Solutions and General Cable.

Cohen & Grigsby PC

The Firm: The group frequently handles deals ranging from $10-50 million. Clients include domestic and foreign companies that require advice in many areas such as tax, accounting and employment law along with general securities matters. The firm advised Instrumentation Engineering in its sale to Singapore-based Flextronics, and Sybron Chemicals in its sale to Novozymes. In addition, one partner specializes in representing German entities, among them Bayer. Peers praised the group's *"excellent capabilities."*

The Lawyers: Chairman of the firm, **Charles Cohen** counsels corporations, financial institutions, venture capitalists and entrepreneurs in reorganizations, capital formations and SEC regulations. Peers respect him as the strategic thinker behind many of the firm's prominent transactions.

The Clients: Giant Eagle; PNC Financial; University of Pittsburgh Medical Center and Ardex.

Wolf, Block, Schorr and Solis-Cohen LLP

see firm details p.905

The Firm: Peers credited the firm with a *"strong tradition"* of securities expertise, and perceived it as having high visibility in the middle market. In addition to a stable of blue-chip clients, the group has advised family-owned businesses and other entrepreneurs through various stages of development prior to taking them public. One of the main attractions at the firm, according to sources, is its IP/IT group, which dedicates more than 20 practitioners to transactional and litigation matters.

The Lawyers: **Mark Kessler** (see p.616), praised by rivals as *"first class,"* centers his practice on M&A, public and private financings. According to competitors, Kessler *"combines excellent common sense with a first-rate technical understanding of the law."*

The Clients: Comcast; Toll Brothers; Legg Mason Wood Walker and Franklin Mutual Series Fund.

EMPLOYMENT & LABOR LAW — PENNSYLVANIA

Other Notable Practitioners

Competitors acclaimed **Stephen Harmelin** of Dilworth Paxson LLP as a *"first-rate lawyer with great business judgment,"* who has assisted a variety of companies through *"complicated situations."* **Robert Harper** of Klett Rooney Lieber & Schorling is respected for his work, especially in matters relating to the healthcare industry. He counseled Universal Health Services in its acquisitions of psychiatric hospitals valued at more than $100 million.

EMPLOYMENT & LABOR LAW — MAINLY PLAINTIFF

PENNSYLVANIA
Leading firms (Employment: Mainly Plaintiff)

1. ROTHMAN GORDON PC *Pittsburgh*
   WILLIG, WILLIAMS & DAVIDSON *Philadelphia*
2. JUBELIRER, PASS & INTRIERI *Pittsburgh*
   MARKOWITZ & RICHMAN *Philadelphia*
   SPEAR, WILDERMAN, BORISH, END *Philadelphia*

Leading individuals (Employment: Mainly Plaintiff)

1. BALLARD Alice *Law Office of Alice Ballard*, Philadelphia
   CONSOLE Stephen *Console Law Offices*, Philadelphia
   EPSTEIN Alan *Spector Gadon & Rosen*, Philadelphia
   KUSHNER Louis *Rothman Gordon PC*, Pittsburgh
   MITCHELL Caroline *Caroline Mitchell*, Pittsburgh
   WILLIG Deborah *Willig, Williams*, Philadelphia
2. JENNINGS Tom *Jennings Sigmond*, Philadelphia
   MURTAGH John *Murtagh & Cahill*, Wexford
   PASS Joseph *Jubelirer, Pass & Intrieri*, Pittsburgh
   PIERCE Patricia *Willig, Williams*, Philadelphia
3. BORISH Warren *Spear, Wilderman, Borish*, Philadelphia
   CARROLL James *Rothman Gordon PC*, Pittsburgh
   CORDES Samuel *Ogg, Cordes, Murphy*, Pittsburgh
   GOODMAN Harold *Raynes, McCarty, Binder*, Philadelphia
   JORDAN Stephen *Rothman Gordon PC*, Pittsburgh
   SPEAR Samuel *Spear, Wilderman, Borish*, Philadelphia
   WILLIAMS Alaine *Willig, Williams*, Philadelphia

Firms and individuals are listed alphabetically in each band.

Rothman Gordon PC
The Firm: The firm maintains a long-standing reputation for excellence in the field. A large team covers a range of labor and employment law from collective bargaining agreements to individual employment negotiations. Attorneys represent clients before a range of tribunals including the NLRB, EEOC and the US Department of Labor, as well as before the state and federal courts.

The Lawyers: The group boasts a number of outstanding labor and employment lawyers. The highest profile belongs to **Louis Kushner**, who *"really stands out for labor advice."* Another strong lawyer on the union side is **Stephen Jordan**, while **Jim Carroll** won praise for his dedicated work on behalf of individuals.

Willig, Williams & Davidson
The Firm: Many market sources consider this *"the premier firm on the union side"* in Pennsylvania. Peers say that its lawyers are *"effective and zealous in representing clients, but they're not zealots – they're pleasant people you can deal with."* The firm represents about 150 unions throughout the East coast, as well as union trust funds and individuals. It also handles the range of employment advice and litigation.

The Lawyers: *"Smart"* **Deborah Willig** commands a strong market profile. She has acted as legal counselor and chief negotiator for a number of labor organizations, and also represents employee benefit funds. **Patricia Pierce** also enjoys an enviable reputation. She was recommended to researchers as an *"extremely professional and tenacious"* trial lawyer. *"Really excellent"* **Alaine Williams** was likewise warmly recommended by interviewees.

Jubelirer, Pass & Intrieri
The Firm: This firm was recommended to researchers for its strong traditional labor advice. Defense attorneys refer to **Joseph Pass** as a *"formidable opponent"* on labor matters. He is attorney to the Allegheny County Labor Council.

Markowitz & Richman
The Firm: This Philadelphia-based firm enjoys a depth of resources on the labor and employment side. Although no individual lawyer stands out, a number of attorneys were mentioned, with commentators praising the general level of competence on offer. Work covers the range of labor and employment advice for individuals and labor organizations.

Spear, Wilderman, Borish, Endy, Spear & Runckel
The Firm: *"There are a lot of good lawyers at this firm,"* according to sources. Particularly singled out for plaudits were **Warren Borish** and **Sam Spear**. The firm has the resources to handle everything from complex collective bargaining agreements to individual employment disputes.

Other Notable Practitioners
Alice Ballard, eponymous head of the Law Office of Alice W. Ballard, enjoys a *"sterling reputation"* and figures among the state's clear leaders. She principally advises employees on issues such as discrimination claims, whistle-blowing and pension rights. Sources note: *"She really knows what she is talking about and has reached the stage in her career when she can afford to concentrate on the good cases."* **Alan Epstein** of Spector Gadon & Rosen PC is known as a *"big verdicts guy"* for his handling of a number of high-profile cases. Peers particularly commended Epstein's *"good courtroom presence."*

"Fantastic" **Stephen Console** stands out at Console Law Offices. He and his team are said to excel in *"managing class actions,"* in which the firm is known for its *"high success rate."* Also at the top of the profession is *"dogged, detailed and outstandingly intelligent"* **Caroline Mitchell** of the Law Offices of Caroline Mitchell. According to some commentators, she is *"probably the best plaintiff-side employment attorney in Pittsburgh."* At Wexford-based Murtagh & Cahill, **Jack Murtagh** is an *"outstanding, intelligent"* lawyer, with a name for both employment and labor work. *"Smart"* **Sam Cordes** of Ogg, Cordes, Murphy & Ignelzi was highly rated for employment litigation: *"Juries love him."* At Jennings Sigmond, **Tom Jennings** is the *"star attraction."* *"Tough, fierce and hard-working,"* he is acknowledged by peers for his *"excellent union work."* **Harold Goodman** at Raynes, McCarty, Binder, Ross & Mundy, also enjoys a good reputation: he has *"been around forever and keeps a high profile."*

PENNSYLVANIA

EMPLOYMENT & LABOR LAW

MAINLY DEFENDANT

PENNSYLVANIA
Leading firms
(Employment: Mainly Defendant)

1
- MORGAN, LEWIS & BOCKIUS LLP *Pittsburgh*
- REED SMITH LLP *Pittsburgh*

2
- BALLARD SPAHR ANDREWS *Philadelphia*
- COHEN & GRIGSBY PC *Pittsburgh*

3
- KLETT ROONEY LIEBER & SCHORLING *Pittsburgh*

4
- BLANK ROME LLP *Philadelphia*
- DECHERT *Philadelphia*
- KIRKPATRICK & LOCKHART LLP *Pittsburgh*
- LITTLER MENDELSON PC *Pittsburgh*
- PEPPER HAMILTON LLP *Philadelphia*

5
- BUCHANAN INGERSOLL *Pittsburgh*
- JACKSON LEWIS *Pittsburgh*

Leading individuals
(Employment: Mainly Defendant)

1
- BEVAN William *Reed Smith LLP, Pittsburgh*
- FRITTON Karl *Reed Smith LLP, Philadelphia*
- LADOV Donald *Cohen & Grigsby PC, Pittsburgh*
- WALL Steven *Morgan, Lewis & Bockius, Philadelphia*

2
- DICHTER Mark *Morgan, Lewis & Bockius, Philadelphia*
- FELIX Thomas *Ballard Spahr Andrews, Philadelphia*
- MUNSCH Martha *Reed Smith, Pittsburgh*

3
- BROWN James *Cohen & Grigsby PC, Pittsburgh*
- CONNORS Eugene *Reed Smith LLP, Pittsburgh*
- DAVIS Doreen *Morgan, Lewis & Bockius, Philadelphia*
- GIOTTO Thomas *Klett Rooney Lieber, Pittsburgh*
- LILLIE Charisse *Ballard Spahr Andrews, Philadelphia*
- LYNCHESKI John *Cohen & Grigsby PC, Pittsburgh*
- OLSON Stephen *Kirkpatrick & Lockhart, Pittsburgh*
- ZONN Sidney *Littler Mendelson PC, Pittsburgh*

4
- BERKOWITZ Alan *Dechert, Philadelphia*
- HORNAK Mark *Buchanan Ingersoll, Pittsburgh*
- JARIN Kenneth *Ballard Spahr Andrews, Philadelphia*
- OUTWATER Lynn *Jackson Lewis, Pittsburgh*
- STOVER Hayes *Kirkpatrick & Lockhart LLP, Pittsburgh*

Up-and-coming individuals
- FOLEY Mark *Klett Rooney Lieber, Philadelphia*

Firms and individuals are listed alphabetically in each band.

Morgan, Lewis & Bockius LLP

The Firm: This national firm boasts a *"terrific reputation"* across the country. Interviewees admire its *"smart people, good training and truly national practice."* It now boasts 180 labor and employment lawyers, more than 45 of them in Pennsylvania. Philadelphia is a particular stronghold; Pittsburgh is said by peers to be less prominent, *"but only because of size, not quality."* The team handles the full range of employment and labor matters, including litigation and regulatory advice. It enjoys close relations with governmental agencies and has worked well with bodies such as the NLRB, US Department of Labor and EEOC. On the labor side, the firm has a strong practice in such key organized industries as transportation, construction, the postal services and major league baseball.

The Lawyers: At the heart of the firm's success are its *"experienced, smart and aggressive lawyers."* Among the best known of these is *"versatile and sharp"* **Steven Wall**. He is involved in a lot of employment counseling, a fast-growing area for the firm according to commentators, and also handles litigation. **Mark Dichter** has a big name in the field. He was recommended to researchers as a *"strong labor and employment generalist,"* who covers a range of employment counseling and disputes work, including employee benefits litigation. He has represented the State of Oregon in a high-profile class action. **Doreen Davis** who joined the firm in May 2001 from Montgomery, McCracken, Walker & Rhoads, enjoys a solid reputation in the field of traditional labor law. She has represented employers in negotiations and arbitrations, appearing before the NLRB, and also has litigation experience.

The Clients: The firm acts for a number of household name clients, some of them exclusively in the labor and employment sphere. These include leading businesses in the entertainment, sports, airlines and financial services sectors. Examples include Merrill Lynch, Honeywell and GE.

Reed Smith LLP

The Firm: According to market sources, labor and employment has *"been the engine of Reed Smith's business development for years."* Its experience in the sector goes back a long time, and it remains arguably the state's *"leading candidate"* for traditional labor matters. Pittsburgh is the center of the employment practice, although the group also has a smaller presence in Philadelphia. Drawing upon a network of offices across the US, the firm offers a full range of advice on matters such as collective bargaining, OSHA, union elections, wage and hour negotiations, right to know and affirmative action. On the employment side, the team is expert in litigation and counseling, and handles a large volume of race and gender discrimination cases. The group boasts a good track record of negotiating advantageous contracts without strikes. It recently negotiated 12 different labor agreements for one of the country's largest waste management companies, covering a number of northeastern states, a process that it settled without any work stoppages.

The Lawyers: Peers recognize a *"number of seasoned practitioners"* here. These include **Bill Bevan** a *"key player on the labor side"* with especially strong experience of the NLRB. He has a particular following in the manufacturing, banking and construction industries. Another *"skilled litigator and negotiator,"* and *"one of the top labor lawyers in the state,"* is **Karl Fritton**. He has experience of negotiating complex labor agreements in a variety of areas. **Gene Connors** is also expert in labor matters. However, his practice also includes a large employment component and Connors frequently counsels major companies on strategic planning and dispute avoidance. Notable successes include helping a brewery client convince the Teamsters Union to brew beer after employees affiliated with a striking union had stopped work. The firm also boasts, in **Martha Munsch**, a *"leader on the employment side,"* who was recommended to researchers as an inspiring litigator.

The Clients: The firm acts for a number of large, multi-state companies across a range of business sectors. These include manufacturing and heavy industry, waste collection and disposal, power generation and transmission, healthcare and railroads, as well as service industries including law, accountancy and education.

Ballard Spahr Andrews & Ingersoll LLP
see firm details p.769

The Firm: Commentators describe this as a firm on the up with a *"growing reputation."* In January 2002 it recruited 13 people from the labor department of Montgomery, McCracken, Walker & Rhoads, adding a heavy-hitting public sector practice to its already respectable private sector practice. Interviewees agree that this move has *"increased its profile a lot"* leaving the firm *"considerably stronger"* and able to challenge the leadership of Morgan Lewis in Philadelphia. The firm now has over 400 lawyers in six US offices, including 40 labor and employment specialists in Pennsylvania. It covers the full range of labor law, including collective bargaining and arbitrations, and boasts particular experience of working at the NLRB. The group also handles a large volume of employment counseling and litigation at both federal and state levels. It assisted Philadelphia's mass transit system, SEPTA, in negotiating new contracts affecting over 5200 unionized workers.

The Lawyers: The highest profile recruit from Montgomery McCracken was veteran labor lawyer **Tom Felix**. He was described to researchers as *"a great deal-maker with a good take on how unions work."* In over 35 years of traditional labor experience he has built up a unique understanding of government labor relations. Another impressive catch for the firm is **Ken Jarin**, praised by interviewees for expertise in public sector work. On the employment side, **Charisse Lillie** is described by peers as a *"fantastic lawyer"* who *"gets a lot of good work and always brings something to the table."*

EMPLOYMENT & LABOR LAW

PENNSYLVANIA

The Clients: The firm represents clients in a variety of sectors including financial services, energy, real estate development, education, healthcare and government. Examples include the City of Philadelphia, SEPTA, the School District of Philadelphia, the Puratos Group and the University of Pennsylvania.

Cohen & Grigsby PC
The Firm: According to market sources, this well-established firm is *"first rate in Pittsburgh."* Only its lower national profile, by comparison with the leading firms, keeps it out of the top tier in the state. The group, which now boasts about 13 labor and employment specialists, enjoys experience of all aspects of labor and employment law with labor law being a particular strength. The firm handles all aspects of union negotiations and counsels executives on strategic decision-making. It also has a number of partners with experience of employment litigation, arbitration and alternative dispute resolution.
The Lawyers: The firm's impressive lawyers are the key to its success. Chief amongst them is **Donald Ladov** (see p.617). He ranks among the most highly rated attorneys in the state, singled out by competitors for his *"superb counseling skills."* He has appeared before a number of regulatory agencies, including the EEOC, NLRB, OSHA and the US Department of Labor. In employment litigation, the firm benefits from the presence of **Jim Brown** (see p.615), a *"major player in employment cases."* **John Lyncheski** remains highly recommended, especially for his substantial practice in the healthcare industry.
The Clients: The firm has a strong niche in the healthcare sector, acting for a number of hospitals and nursing homes. Its experience, however, extends to most of the state's main industries.

Klett Rooney Lieber & Schorling
The Firm: This sizable regional player has strength across the state. Having taken labor and employment lawyers from Pepper Hamilton, it has developed into one of the largest employment and labor groups in Pennsylvania. Based in Pittsburgh, it is set apart by the strength of its traditional labor practice, though it also covers the range of employment law. Alongside the core areas, it has attorneys specializing in employee benefits and OSHA work.
The Lawyers: *"Leading individual"* **Tom Giotto** was described to researchers as a good generalist employment and labor lawyer. Peers particularly envied his *"good relationship with the business community."* **Mark Foley** is said to be an *"impressive and effective"* attorney. He handles both labor and employment law and has a particular specialty in trade secrets law. Within the market, however, Foley is best known for his traditional labor law practice, where he represents a number of local municipalities.

The Clients: The firm represents large employers from sectors like the steel industry, chemicals, healthcare, higher education, hospitality, telecommunications and transport. It acts for both the City of Pittsburgh and the City of Philadelphia.

Blank Rome LLP
The Firm: Market sources recommend this department for its solid advice on all aspects of employment and labor law. It has a sizable team in Pennsylvania handling most aspects of the field. On the traditional labor side, typical work includes union elections and union organization issues, and the team has argued many matters before the NLRB and Pennsylvania Labor Relations board. Meanwhile, on the employment side, the firm argues, among other things, all forms of harassment claims, as well as wage and hour disputes before the US Department of Labor. A specialist team handles ERISA and benefits issues. The firm's management advisory work includes training sessions, such as training the city's Fire Department in harassment avoidance.
The Lawyers: The team is chaired by Michael Hanlon, and includes Margaret McCausland.
The Clients: The firm advises employers from the public and private sectors and has experience of a number of industries.

Dechert
see firm details p.789
The Firm: The firm has a good reputation in the employment sector and receives a steady stream of top-end work from its impressive client roster. Employment litigation is a substantial area of focus, in which the group typically defends against high-profile discrimination claims. The firm also offers a counseling service, assisting companies with advice on compliance procedures. Traditional labor forms a lower proportion of the group's workload; however, it does handle union grievances and bargaining.
The Lawyers: Alan Berkowitz, cochair of the firm's labor and employment group, regularly undertakes employment litigation in the federal and state courts, and handles unfair labor practice proceedings before the NLRB.
The Clients: The firm's clients include household name corporates drawn from a range of sectors.

Kirkpatrick & Lockhart LLP
The Firm: Though this is one of the largest firms in the state, its labor and employment team is not among the most visible. Nonetheless, with about 17 lawyers in Pittsburgh focused on the area, it fields a sizable team, backed by the substantial resources of the firm. The group covers the full range of employment advice and litigation, including discrimination claims and wage and hour negotiations. Within traditional labor, the team is experienced in union work, and possesses a niche in transportation labor matters.
The Lawyers: Steve Olson, the firm's national coordinator for labor and employment, has a good name in the market. He is supported by **Hayes Stover**, who, sources say, is *"well regarded on the traditional labor side."*
The Clients: The firm acts for management across a range of sectors.

Littler Mendelson PC
The Firm: This *"first-tier national firm"* only opened in Pennsylvania in 2001. It established a profile quickly by taking a well-respected team from Buchanan Ingersoll. As yet, it remains a relatively small office, but rivals note the firm's *"growing presence"* across the East Coast and expect its rapid rise to continue. Attorneys with comprehensive experience of employment and labor work are supported by the vast resources of Littler Mendelson's national network.
The Lawyers: Managing shareholder of the Pittsburgh office is **Sid Zonn**, described by market sources as a *"wonderful person"* with a profound knowledge of the law. He has experience of investigating and litigating all types of employment discrimination claims.
The Clients: The firm's clients come from a broad range of sectors, including transport, manufacturing and higher education. They include approximately 60% of the Fortune 500. The office services ex-clients of Buchanan Ingersoll as well as Littler Mendelson's national clients.

Pepper Hamilton LLP
The Firm: The firm may have lost labor lawyers to Klett Rooney, but it remains a *"substantial practice,"* according to the market. Its broad-based team handles a large volume of employment advice and litigation, and includes a robust traditional labor element. The team works closely with a sizable employee benefits group, and is well known for executive compensation issues in the benefits arena. The firm also has niche expertise in regulatory matters specific to the building industry.
The Lawyers: The labor and employment group includes Anthony Haller.
The Clients: The firm represents companies ranging from start-ups to large corporate entities. Although its private sector client base is larger, it also acts for municipalities, hospitals and universities.

Buchanan Ingersoll
The Firm: Despite losing a team to Littler Mendelson, the firm retains a solid labor and employment presence in the state. It operates from offices in Philadelphia, Harrisburg and, especially, Pittsburgh. Typical work includes

PENNSYLVANIA — ENVIRONMENT

developing employment policies and handling litigation, and, on the labor side, collective bargaining and labor arbitrations.

The Lawyers: **Mark Hornak** is *"clearly the pick of the litter"* here, according to peers. He advises employers on litigation and employment practices, and has negotiated collective bargaining agreements for public and private bodies. His clients include media companies, school districts and municipalities.

The Clients: The firm has a wide variety of clients across sectors such as banking, healthcare, hi-tech, hospitality, transport, retail and manufacturing. These include the Sports & Exhibition Authority of Pittsburgh and Allegheny County.

Jackson Lewis

The Firm: This *"strong labor and employment boutique"* operates from 20 major locations across the US, including Pittsburgh. Its lawyers have an excellent track record of counseling employers in litigation avoidance. However, interviewees report they can be *"street fighters"* when the need arises. It covers all aspects of employment and labor law and can draw upon the extensive resources of the network.

The Lawyers: The managing partner of the Pittsburgh office, **Lynn Outwater** was described to researchers as a *"leading individual with a national reputation for advice and counseling."*

The Clients: The firm acts for an impressive roster of national clients.

ENVIRONMENT

PENNSYLVANIA
Leading firms (Environment)

1
- BABST, CALLAND, CLEMENTS Pittsburgh
- MANKO, GOLD, KATCHER & FOX Bala Clynwyd

2
- KIRKPATRICK & LOCKHART Harrisburg, Pittsburgh

3
- DRINKER BIDDLE & REATH Berwyn, Philadelphia

4
- BALLARD SPAHR ANDREWS Philadelphia
- REED SMITH LLP Pittsburgh

5
- DECHERT Philadelphia
- WOLF, BLOCK, SCHORR Philadelphia

6
- FOX ROTHSCHILD O'BRIEN Doylestown, Philadelphia
- JONES DAY Pittsburgh
- KLETT ROONEY LIEBER & SCHORLING Pittsburgh
- MONTGOMERY, MCCRACKEN, WALKER Philadelphia
- MORGAN, LEWIS & BOCKIUS LLP Harrisburg
- SAUL EWING LLP Philadelphia
- SCHNADER HARRISON SEGAL Philadelphia

Leading individuals (Environment)

1
- BABST Chester *Babst, Calland, Clements*, Pittsburgh
- BARNETT Bonnie *Drinker Biddle & Reath*, Philadelphia
- CALLAND Dean *Babst, Calland, Clements*, Pittsburgh
- MANDELBAUM David *Ballard Spahr*, Philadelphia
- MANKO Joe *Manko, Gold, Katcher & Fox*, Bala Cynwyd
- WESTON Timothy *Kirkpatrick & Lockhart*, Harrisburg

2
- BROOMAN David *Drinker Biddle & Reath LLP*, Berwyn
- GOLD Marc *Manko, Gold, Katcher & Fox*, Bala Cynwyd
- NAUGLE Louis *Reed Smith LLP*, Pittsburgh
- RICHMAN Hershel *Dechert*, Philadelphia
- WARREN Kenneth *Wolf, Block, Schorr*, Philadelphia

3
- BOLSTEIN Joel *Fox Rothschild O'Brien*, Doylestown
- COLLINGS Robert *Schnader Harrison Segal*, Philadelphia
- UBINGER John *Jones Day*, Pittsburgh
- WEIN Howard *Klett Rooney Lieber*, Pittsburgh
- WOELFLING Maxine *Morgan, Lewis*, Harrisburg

4
- BERGÈRE Timothy *Montgomery*, Philadelphia
- BOSSERT Terry *Stevens & Lee PC*, Reading
- EVERETT Carl *Saul Ewing LLP*, Philadelphia

Up-and-coming individuals
- CASSIDY Bart *Manko, Gold, Katcher & Fox*, Bala Cynwyd

Firms and individuals are listed alphabetically in each band.

Babst, Calland, Clements and Zomnir PC

The Firm: This is the largest environmental practice in Pennsylvania. It dominates the market in the west of the state and attracts clients from throughout the US. Founded in 1986 as a boutique, the firm has since branched out to other fields, but environment remains the signature practice. The team draws on a range of technical backgrounds and industrial experience. On the regulatory and transactional side, it boasts noted expertise in site remediation, environmental counseling and audits. The litigation group is also well versed in environmental and related construction issues.

The Lawyers: Interviewees were enthusiastic about the *"distinguished group of lawyers"* here. The standout names among them are **Chester Babst** and **Dean Calland**. Babst was singled out for his stellar expertise on air quality issues. Sources say he *"protects his clients' interests impeccably."* Calland is a hazardous waste specialist and is known in the market for his great contacts and transactional know-how. Both were praised as *"intellectually powerful, with lots of experience in complex areas."*

The Clients: Clients of the firm range from major steel and national chemical companies to municipalities within the tristate area. The firm is active in representing utilities, particularly in the power sector.

Manko, Gold, Katcher & Fox LLP

The Firm: Strong recommendations from all sectors of the market put this Bala Cynwyd boutique in the top rank. Its long-standing experience guarantees the firm a lot of referrals from around the state and beyond. Particularly strong in transactional and regulatory work, the group's in-depth knowledge of state and federal legislation, and its highly pragmatic approach, won praise from peers. The attorneys have a mix of technical and environmental agency backgrounds, and are supplemented by an in-house team of technical staff including two qualified engineers. Recent work of note has included land use issues relating to wetlands and steep slopes, and advice on indoor air pollution matters and bioterrorism.

The Lawyers: *"In effect the dean of the environmental bar in Pennsylvania,"* **Joe Manko** was one of the first lawyers in the state to specialize in the field and remains highly rated. According to sources, *"his greatest strength is negotiating on transactional matters."* Superfund and remediation expert **Marc Gold** was also strongly recommended. His practice covers all areas of counseling and and regulation in connection with hazardous waste, and air and water pollution. Despite his relative youth, **Bart Cassidy** is already gaining a reputation as *"one of the best air lawyers in the state."*

The Clients: Clients range from Fortune 500 companies, which the firm represents on a national level, to small local enterprises.

Kirkpatrick & Lockhart LLP

The Firm: Large teams working out of Pittsburgh and Harrisburg give this firm *"a good statewide practice"* in environment. Sources regard the Harrisburg team as more prominent in transactional work, while the Pittsburgh office boasts a wealth of manufacturing clients. The firm undertakes all aspects of regulatory and transactional work, project development and permitting, environmental litigation and natural resources management. The group's expertise extends as far as toxic torts and arranging insurance coverage for environmental liabilities (for some, this is *"the firm of choice"* in this regard). Growth areas over the past 12 months have included advising on the redevelopment of brownfield sites and permitting issues for new power projects. The firm recently advised a specialist steel manufacturer on negotiating the transfer of emission reduction credits, allowing it to increase production.

The Lawyers: Harrisburg-based **Tim Weston** was warmly recommended by market sources. *"A leader in the field,"* he is *"especially well thought of for water resources issues."* His experience includes working as water resources counsel to the largest bottled water company in the US.

The Clients: The firm maintains a broad client

base, including steel and manufacturing industrial companies, energy clients (coal, oil and gas), mining companies and pharmaceutical corporations. It is representing a major aluminum company in an enforcement action brought by the EPA under Section 309 of the CWA.

Drinker Biddle & Reath LLP
The Firm: This *"extensive practice with knowledgeable attorneys"* enjoys a large market presence, especially in the east of the state. It enjoys a formidable name for litigation and boasts expertise ranging from substantial Superfund cases to toxic tort defense work. Its profound involvement in Superfund work is especially well known, and the team has recently assisted clients in two major Superfund cases, involving allocation, insolvency and successor liability issues. The large department, numbering over 25 lawyers, also includes a team of regulatory and transactional specialists. Clients range from major chemical, pharmaceutical and manufacturing companies to environmental consultancies and real estate developers. The firm is especially envied for its substantial body of solid waste industry clients.
The Lawyers: **Bonnie Barnett** is greatly admired by the market. A *"dynamic"* litigator, she is said to be *"great at running groups."* Her focus is on Superfund litigation, but she also advises clients on issues such as regulatory compliance. **David Brooman** is considered *"someone to reckon with."* Commentators admire his *"eclectic"* practice, but consider him especially proficient in the solid waste area.
The Clients: The firm's high-profile client base includes: GlaxoSmithKline; Merck & Co; Georgia Pacific; Millennium Chemicals; Celanese; Hoeganese Corp and United States Pipe & Foundry Company.

Ballard Spahr Andrews & Ingersoll LLP
see firm details p.769
The Firm: This highly rated Philadelphia outfit operates an integrated practice across the eastern region in connection with its Voorhees, NJ office. The firm handles a range of work and was warmly recommended for its litigation skills. It can also draw on the experience of two partners who specialize in criminal investigation and coastal zone matters. Air, water and hazardous waste issues and permit approvals are growing areas of work. The group recently scored a high-profile coup assisting The Phillies in their relocation to a new 43,000-seater ballpark.
The Lawyers: *"Bright and impressive"* litigator **David Mandelbaum** heads the environmental group and works between the firm's Philadelphia and Baltimore MDL offices. He advises clients on environmental matters related to transactions, and is visible in major litigation, including Superfund matters, contamination cases and breach of contract. Competitors praise his *"brilliant and thoughtful"* contribution to the field.
The Clients: The team handles environmental matters for substantial industrial, waste management, real estate and municipal clients.

Reed Smith LLP
The Firm: This Pittsburgh giant has historically been a force in the field, and retains a strong reputation for environmental work. The Pennsylvania team is now positioned as a hub of the firm's national environment practice, which has meant that a large proportion of its work is sourced from outside the state. Advice on the environmental aspects of large corporate and real estate transactions has been an increasing source of work. In addition, the team handles regulatory counseling, matters relating to brownfield sites, and administrative and civil litigation. The firm assisted a client faced with $30 million of cleanup costs at a Superfund site by proving before the Third Circuit Court of Appeals that other parties should share the costs. It also represented a Fortune 500 company in connection with an investigation by the Office of the New Jersey Attorney General, successfully obtaining the return of all documents without charge.
The Lawyers: *"Able and experienced"* **Louis Naugle** heads the practice. Market sources consider him a *"skilled and tenacious litigator"* with a strong track record. He is well known for advising on brownfield redevelopment work, and also has a strong profile for compliance advice and permitting. On the litigation side, he has represented clients in civil enforcement and criminal investigations.
The Clients: Representative environmental clients of the firm include: Wyeth Laboratories; Carmeuse North America; West Chemical Products; East Penn Manufacturing Company; Hercules Incorporated and Graymont Western US.

Dechert
see firm details p.789
The Firm: According to market sources, this highly respected practice is most visible on transaction-related matters. The group's specialist lawyers handle environmental support on deals for blue-chip clients across the US. As well as evaluating the environmental liabilities of M&A and restructurings, typical work includes regulatory and compliance advice and obtaining permits. The firm also boasts broad environmental litigation expertise.
The Lawyers: **Hershel Richman** is a highly respected figure in the market. A *"wonderful lawyer,"* according to market sources, his *"ability to see the big picture"* ensures he maintains a *"substantial network of clients."* His experience includes successfully defending SmithKline, Georgia-Pacific and a company affiliated to BFI in environmental litigation and obtaining permits for the expansion of shopping centers and landfills.
The Clients: The firm services a mix of clients, including local government, real estate developers, land owners, lenders, universities, trade associations, hospitals and major companies.

Wolf, Block, Schorr and Solis-Cohen LLP
see firm details p.905
The Firm: This *"sophisticated and diverse"* Philadelphia practice is seen by many in the market to be increasing its presence in the sector. Traditionally strong on real estate-related work, several recent hires have expanded the team's range of expertise. It now includes advice on regulatory and transactional matters, site remediation and a range of environmental litigation.
The Lawyers: *"Definitely a leading litigator,"* **Kenneth Warren** (see p.619) was formerly with Manko, Gold, Katcher & Fox, and has 20 years' experience in the field. He serves as general counsel to the Delaware River Basin Commission, a federal interstate agency involved in the management of water resources. His experience includes acting as principal trial counsel for GE, and liaison counsel for third parties in the major Superfund case United States v Atlas Minerals and Chemicals.
The Clients: The firm represents a mix of real estate developers and industrial corporations.

Fox Rothschild O'Brien & Frankel LLP
The Firm: This small but well-regarded team is said by interviewees to excel in regulatory and transactional advice. Typical work includes air pollution and hazardous waste matters. The team is especially known for advising on environmental issues associated with real estate developments.
The Lawyers: **Joel Bolstein** is the team's standout environment practitioner. Peers rate him a *"top practitioner for environmental work."* He focuses on brownfield redevelopment work, often assisting developers on obtaining permits, environmental assessments and remediation. As a former deputy secretary at the Pennsylvania Department of Environmental Protection, his grasp of the political environment is much admired.
The Clients: The firm's client base includes developers, lenders and public entities.

Jones Day
see firm details p.823
The Firm: This impressive Pittsburgh practice provides environmental compliance and transactional support for its corporate clients. In contentious matters it can draw on the firm's substantial litigation resources. In this it handles a volume of Superfund work and environmental insurance claims, and has a growing environmental criminal practice. It is involved in restructuring the business of one of its clients, including dispos-

PENNSYLVANIA

ENVIRONMENT

ing of a number of contaminated industrial properties. This includes performing environmental investigations, and often obtaining regulatory approval for cleanup plans. The team has also been involved in defending a client in a federal prosecution for alleged environmental crimes.

The Lawyers: Team coordinator **John Ubinger** (see p.619) is a well-respected environmental practitioner with almost 30 years' experience. He was warmly praised by peers, one of whom described him as *"among the best lawyers in the state."*

The Clients: The firm boasts an impressive list of leading clients. These include: Bridgestone/Firestone; Cargill; Eastman Chemical Company; PCS Phosphate Company; Roadway Express; Sherwin Williams Company; The Arctic Group and The Weir Group.

Klett Rooney Lieber & Schorling

The Firm: This solid generalist practice is *"well regarded, especially in the west of the state."* Its experience covers air and water quality matters, land use and regeneration, solid and hazardous waste and mining issues. Recent work on the regulatory side has included preparing and negotiating Reasonably Available Control Technology (RACT) submittals and agreements, and advice on Pennsylvania's Air Pollution Control Act. On the transactional side, the firm has advised on permitting and environmental issues for industrial properties.

The Lawyers: *"Sharp"* **Howard Wein** heads the environmental team. A former assistant counsel to the Pennsylvania DER, he is respected for his litigation and administrative expertise. He was involved in the development of the recently passed Pennsylvania Land Recycling and Remediation Standards Act.

The Clients: The firm acts for a range of clients including waste management firms, manufacturers and property developers.

Montgomery, McCracken, Walker & Rhoads LLP

The Firm: An environmental group of about nine lawyers assists clients in environmental litigation, regulatory and transactional work, including Superfund laws, permits and reporting, brownfield development and hazardous waste. The firm's expertise in the environmental aspects of real estate transactions was especially recommended.

The Lawyers: Commentators consider environmental practice chair **Tim Bergère** the standout practitioner here. He is especially well regarded for his regulatory work and has advised a major fiberboard manufacturer on environmental regulations.

The Clients: The firm's clients include: Thyssen USA; IKON Office Solutions; Celotex Corp; Simpson Paper Company; Tyco International; Brenntag Mid-South; Henkel Corporation and the Delaware River Port Authority.

Morgan, Lewis & Bockius LLP

The Firm: The firm has a long tradition in the field and a high standing for legal and industry expertise, and government access. Its DC office, in particular, is renowned for the strength of its environmental expertise. The Pennsylvania offices are not so visible, though, and some interviewees regard the firm as *"focused more nationally than locally."* However, sources do see it acting locally, especially on the environmental aspects of transactions.

The Lawyers: Harrisburg-based of counsel **Maxine Woelfling** is known in the market as a *"strong, able"* lawyer with experience in environmental litigation and counseling related to transactions.

The Clients: The firm services an impressive base of major domestic and international clients from a range of industries.

Saul Ewing LLP

The Firm: Although it handles a volume of advice related to transactions, it is for environmental litigation that this firm is best known. Superfund work is seen as a particular area of strength, and the firm also offers a range of regulatory advice. However, some commentators consider the team less visible now than in the past.

The Lawyers: **Carl Everett** won market plaudits, especially for his Superfund work. His practice includes CERCLA matters, and he is involved in CERCLA remediation projects at the Blosenski site in West Caln, PA, and the Galaxy/Spectron site in Elkton, Maryland.

The Clients: Clients range from Fortune 500 companies to individuals, and include players in the energy, chemicals, financial services, manufacturing, real estate, food and waste disposal industries.

Schnader Harrison Segal & Lewis LLP

The Firm: The firm offers a respectable practice of about 15 lawyers based in four offices across the state. The majority of these attorneys focus on litigation, but the group also handles a volume of regulatory and transactional work. Areas of expertise include Superfund matters, air and water emissions, resource development and waste management.

The Lawyers: **Robert Collings** chairs the litigation department, and has substantial experience in issues relating to solid and hazardous waste, and air and water pollution. Competitors also note his expertise in regulatory and transactional advice related to the field. He is currently coordinating environmental tort claims at a national level for a major international manufacturer.

The Clients: Clients are drawn from a variety of sectors, including manufacturing, real estate, financial services and transport.

Other Notable Practitioners

Reading-based **Terry Bossert** of Stevens & Lee PC, is a former chief counsel of the Pennsylvania DEP. Peers consider him a *"strong, solid attorney"* with a *"broad knowledge of state environmental work."*

INSOLVENCY/CORPORATE RECOVERY

Blank Rome LLP

The Firm: *"Essentially one of the best in the region,"* the firm won praise from interviewees as an interdisciplinary group racking up sizable reorganizations, workouts and other bankruptcy-related actions. The team has counseled both debtors and creditors on issues such as debt restructuring, debtor-in-possession financing and inter-creditor relationships.

The Lawyers: **Raymond Shapiro** distinguished as *"one of the deans of the national bankruptcy bar,"* represented the creditors' panel in the reorganization of a prominent US manufacturer. A *"bright and balanced"* person, he was said to get results by *"working through cases methodically and carefully."* **Thomas Biron** earned kudos from both clients and peers for his transactional expertise and litigation skills. He advises clients on debt and equity restructurings, de-leveraging, fraudulent conveyances, and creditors' rights. He represented creditors' committees in major Chapter 11 cases including TWA.

The Clients: Institutional lenders; lender groups; creditors; creditors committees; debtors; plan of reorganization proponents and asset purchasers.

Duane Morris LLP

The Firm: A touchstone in Pennsylvania's insolvency bar, the firm won praise among peers as boasting *"one of the best institutional client bases"* statewide. Although the departure of such talent as Claudia Springer to Reed Smith has been seen as a setback, the firm has corrected this with

INSOLVENCY/CORPORATE RECOVERY — PENNSYLVANIA

PENNSYLVANIA
Leading firms
(Insolvency/Corporate Recovery)

1
- BLANK ROME LLP *Philadelphia*
- DUANE MORRIS LLP *Philadelphia*
- REED SMITH LLP *Pittsburgh*

2
- HANGLEY ARONCHICK SEGAL *Philadelphia*
- KLETT ROONEY LIEBER & SCHORLING *Pittsburgh*
- MORGAN, LEWIS & BOCKIUS LLP *Philadelphia*

3
- ADELMAN LAVINE GOLD & LEVIN *Philadelphia*
- COZEN O'CONNOR *Philadelphia*
- DILWORTH PAXSON LLP *Philadelphia*
- PEPPER HAMILTON LLP *Philadelphia*
- STEVENS & LEE PC *Philadelphia*
- WOLF, BLOCK, SCHORR *Philadelphia*

Leading individuals
(Insolvency/Corporate Recovery)

1
- DWORETZKY Joseph *Hangley Aronchick*, Philadelphia
- SHAPIRO Raymond *Blank Rome LLP*, Philadelphia
- SINGER Paul *Reed Smith LLP*, Pittsburgh
- SYKES David *Duane Morris LLP*, Philadelphia

2
- BLOOM Michael *Morgan, Lewis & Bockius*, Philadelphia
- COLTON Neal *Cozen O'Connor*, Philadelphia
- HORSTMANN John *Duane Morris LLP*, Philadelphia
- SCHORLING William *Klett Rooney Lieber*, Pittsburgh
- SPRINGER Claudia *Reed Smith LLP*, Philadelphia

3
- BIRON Thomas *Blank Rome LLP*, Philadelphia
- CASS George *Buchanan Ingersoll*, Pittsburgh
- KLEBAN Barry *Adelman Lavine Gold & Levin*, Philadelphia
- LAPOWSKY Robert *Stevens & Lee PC*, Philadelphia
- MCMICHAEL Lawrence *Dilworth Paxson*, Philadelphia
- REED Michael *Pepper Hamilton LLP*, Philadelphia
- TEMIN Michael *Wolf, Block, Schorr*, Philadelphia

Firms and individuals are listed alphabetically in each band.

---

recent additions to the group. It continues its involvement in such prominent matters as the Enron, WorldCom and Adelphia Communications bankruptcies.

The Lawyers: Chairman of the firm, **David Sykes** is considered one of the most *"preeminent"* practitioners in Pennsylvania. He advised a Pennsylvanian healthcare provider in a workout and represented creditors in the reorganization of a Pennsylvanian steel company. **John Horstmann** portrayed by clients as *"a fine advocate,"* concentrates on representing creditors, especially banks. He represented a European bank in collecting secured loans and in related litigation concerning a luxury resort hotel and time-share development in the US Virgin Islands.

The Clients: Wachovia; CIGNA; First National Bank of Boston and Fidelity Bank

Reed Smith LLP
The Firm: Pitched as *"a push in the right direction,"* the firm's expansion in the bankruptcy market was deemed by market observers as *"highly successful."* The group has poached several former Duane Morris partners, including Claudia Springer, and added a team of nine bankruptcy lawyers to its New York office. This is in addition to its branches in Wilmington, DE, and London, UK, which combine to provide support on national and international matters. The group received particularly high marks in matters relating to the financial services, healthcare, telecom, technology, manufacturing and retail sectors.

The Lawyers: **Paul Singer** received widespread endorsements as a *"mature, savvy and sophisticated"* lawyer able to *"take on any case, no matter how complex."* He represents both debtors and creditors in bankruptcy and workout matters, including litigation. His forte is advising industrial manufacturers, including steel, railroad and paper companies. As a result, he also gained substantial experience in working with labor unions and government agencies, including Pension Benefit Guaranty. **Claudia Springer** who joined Reed Smith's Philadelphia office in 2002, was viewed by interviewees as a strong transactional lawyer *"with a good following."* Although a generalist, she has successfully developed a niche practice in representing creditors of troubled healthcare institutions.

The Clients: Secured creditors; creditor' committees; asset purchasers; venture funds and financial institutions.

Hangley Aronchick Segal & Pudlin
The Firm: Distinguished for its ability to punch above its weight, the group of six lawyers won peer endorsements particularly in the area of negotiations in multi-party situations. The team also proved adroit in such areas as out-of-court liquidations and restructurings, as well as Chapter 7 and Chapter 11 transactions, advising both creditors and debtors. The healthcare industry is an area of expertise and the team has reorganized a nonprofit group with a 178-bed hospital and a life care community comprising residential units and a nursing home.

The Lawyers: A former city solicitor in Philadelphia, **Joseph Dworetzky** won accolades from Chambers' sources for his *"charismatic ability to work well with groups."* He was also said to display an *"impressive knack for cutting to the heart of the issue"* at the negotiating table, devising strategies in various plans of reorganizations for debtors.

The Clients: Quad Systems, Aetna US Healthcare and IKON Office Solutions.

Klett Rooney Lieber & Schorling
The Firm: The Pittsburgh-based firm was billed by observers as *"a good group of problem solvers,"* able to build consensus under delicate circumstances. The group represented a primary secured lender involved in a bankrupt film lab and storage facility that contained such gems as the original master print of 'Raging Bull'. Acting on behalf of financial institutions, the firm was also involved in the reorganizations of such giants as Adelphia Digital Cable, US Airways and Kmart.

The Lawyers: Sources acknowledge that **William Schorling** is *"up there with the best of them."* He has represented an insurance holding company in its Chapter 11 reorganization. On the creditors' side, he advised lenders in working out troubled domestic and foreign loans, and has litigated on behalf of a group of physicians involved in a bankruptcy-related dispute with a healthcare network.

The Clients: Lenders; creditors; debtors; indenture trustees and committees.

Morgan, Lewis & Bockius LLP
The Firm: Dovetailing well with the firm's respected corporate practice, the bankruptcy group was viewed by peers as a team of *"sophisticated lawyers who win a volume of work outside of Pennsylvania as well."* The firm is focused on the creditors' side, and represents such clients as secured and unsecured financial institutions, funds and lessors. It argued on behalf of a creditors' committee in the Valley Media bankruptcy proceedings, helping to establish the rights of an independent label to liquidate assets.

The Lawyers: **Michael Bloom** regarded by peers as *"smart and aggressive,"* has counseled five major distributors of prepackaged music in major out-of-court restructurings of music retailers and wholesalers. He also represented Air Products and Chemicals in an agreement to provide a debtor-in-possession loan to the bankrupt Agrifos Fertilizer.

The Clients: Morgan Stanley; Video Update; Camelot Music and National Record Mart.

Adelman Lavine Gold & Levin
The Firm: This bankruptcy boutique comprises about 15 attorneys. The firm leans heavily on debtors' representation, such as troubled telecom companies. Although viewed by peers as a contender in the middle market, the group has also acted as local counsel to larger corporations. For example, the team advised a manufacturer of asbestos material in bankruptcy proceedings.

The Lawyers: Interviewees respect **Barry Kleban** as a *"thoughtful and deliberate negotiator."* He acted as lead counsel to several healthcare debtors in bankruptcy proceedings and has directed out-of-court workouts for clients in the metal, plastic and industrial machinery manufacturing sectors.

The Clients: Creditors' committees, nursing homes and continuing care retirement communities.

PENNSYLVANIA

INSOLVENCY/CORPORATE RECOVERY

Cozen O'Connor
The Firm: Interviewees noted that the firm is being largely driven by its star, Neal Colton. The practice has represented debtors and creditors, with emphasis on such areas as real estate insolvencies. In addition to a slew of Chapter 11 proceedings, the team counseled clients in reorganization foreclosures, liquidations and out-of-court transactions.
The Lawyers: Neal Colton is co-chair of the bankruptcy, insolvency and restructuring department. Sources endorsed his *"first-rate mind"* and ability to tackle *"thorny issues that require careful analysis."* A *"master at obtaining assets for unsecured creditors,"* he has represented a number of committees in corporate reorganizations. Colton has also developed a niche practice in representing purchasers of assets from troubled companies.
The Clients: Corporate debtors; landlords; equipment lessors and investors.

Dilworth Paxson LLP
The Firm: Although grounded in litigation, the firm can draw on members with corporate and tax backgrounds to round out the expertise of this *"highly respected team."* The firm acted as national counsel to Dow Chemical in the bankruptcies of United Airlines and US Airways. The team is also known for its work on the debtors' side, and has been involved in non-bankruptcy workouts and restructurings. Examples include a $250 million debt for a real estate developer, a $50 million debt for a healthcare company and a $30 million debt for a truck leasing business.
The Lawyers: Lawrence McMichael, cochair of the litigation department, represented the Holt family in the bankruptcy of Murphy Marine Services, and advised the Rigas family on its stake in the Adelphia Communications reorganization. Rivals admired his ability to gain *"loyalty"* from clients and his *"thoughtful and precise analytical capabilities."*
The Clients: PNC Bank; GE; Merrill Lynch Asset Management and Wilmington Trust.

Pepper Hamilton LLP
The Firm: *"Seen in sophisticated cases,"* Pepper Hamilton was viewed by peers as making its mark on the state's bankruptcy bar through its litigation prowess. The firm represented United States Mineral Products, a defendant in the asbestos litigation, that subsequently filed for bankruptcy. The team is debtors' counsel to VecTour, a tour bus company in a liquidation estimated at $100 million.
The Lawyers: Advice to creditors' committees is a key strength of Michael Reed who won respect among competitors for his *"knowledgeable and effective"* advocacy. He also advises clients in the specialty area of toxic torts and environmental claims relating to bankruptcy law.
The Clients: Debtors; commercial lending institutions; equity holders; trustees; trade associations and governmental agencies.

Stevens & Lee PC
The Firm: Immersed in bankruptcy, the Reading-based firm was respected by interviewees for its *"efficiency,"* especially in dealing with proceedings for debtors in the areas of healthcare, manufacturing and distribution. The group can draw on support from its New Jersey and Delaware branches, and handles an array of transactions on behalf of creditors, including IBM Credit.
The Lawyers: Peers endorsed Robert Lapowsky for his *"tenacious"* advocacy. Respected for his work with debtors, he has also represented creditors and purchasers of assets. For example, he guided Tut Systems through its acquisition of assets from Reflex Communication and ViaGate Technology, and counseled Kay Construction in proceedings involving a troubled care facility in New Orleans.
The Clients: Wachovia; Sovereign Bank; Wilmington Trust; Xerox Financial Services; Anesthesia Solutions; EAL Aviation and Motels of America.

Wolf, Block, Schorr and Solis-Cohen LLP
see firm details p.905
The Firm: About ten dedicated practitioners are housed in Pennsylvania and they can pull on the support from other offices in New York, Delaware and New Jersey. The firm figures prominently among peers for its *"sophisticated work."* It represents both creditors and debtors, emphasizing the litigation side, and also handles such transactional matters as debtor-in-possession financings, debt purchasing and acquisitions of insolvency assets.
The Lawyers: Michael Temin (see p.618), whose practice is predominantly in litigation, was engaged in cases concerning such issues as asset sales. Competitors described him as *"brilliant and ethical,"* adding that he is suited for matters that require *"intellectual depth."*
The Clients: Secured and unsecured creditors; trustees; title insurers; landlords and company executives.

Other Notable Practitioners
George Cass of Buchanan Ingersoll has developed a reputation among peers as a bankruptcy litigator, particularly in the area of appellate law relating to troubled companies. Cast as *"an intellectual giant,"* he has argued issues such as preference and fraudulent conveyance actions, bankruptcy claims and reorganization disputes.

INTELLECTUAL PROPERTY

PENNSYLVANIA
Leading firms (Intellectual Property)

1. WOODCOCK WASHBURN *Philadelphia*
2. AKIN GUMP STRAUSS HAUER *Philadelphia*
   CAESAR, RIVISE, BERNSTEIN, COHEN *Philadelphia*
   DRINKER BIDDLE & REATH *Berwyn, Philadelphia*
   REED SMITH LLP *Philadelphia, Pittsburgh*
   WEBB ZIESENHEIM LOGSDON ORKIN *Pittsburgh*
3. BUCHANAN INGERSOLL *Philadelphia, Pittsburgh*
   DUANE MORRIS LLP *Philadelphia*
   KIRKPATRICK & LOCKHART LLP *Pittsburgh*
   RATNER & PRESTIA *Valley Forge*

Firms are listed alphabetically in each band.

Woodcock Washburn
The Firm: This large Philadelphia boutique remains *"easily the top firm in terms of critical mass"* despite some recent defections. Its combination of experience, resources and impressive clients ensures the practice a genuinely national reputation. As an example, the firm's satellite office in Seattle handles IP work for Microsoft. Many interviewees regard the firm as *"primarily a patent shop,"* and it certainly boasts considerable experience in patent work across all scientific disciplines. Peers were especially quick to praise its expertise in biotech, medical devices and electronics. The group enjoys an unsurpassed profile for patent litigation and has won some notable victories. These include successfully defending nutritional supplement manufacturer Rexall Sundown in a patent infringement action. It is also active in the IP aspects of transactional work, as well as trademarks, copyright and trade secrets.
The Lawyers: Many interviewees considered John Donohue the firm's most prominent lawyer. He heads the trademark and copyright practice, though he is equally well known in the patent field. Peers describe him as *"a top-class all-round IP lawyer."* Dale Heist was also warmly recommended, especially for his work in connection with electrical engineering, while younger attorney Stephen Rocci is seen as a name to watch at the firm.
The Clients: The firm's clients range from start-ups to universities and large technological, pharmaceutical and manufacturing corporations. Examples include: Microsoft; BellSouth; Johnson

INTELLECTUAL PROPERTY — PENNSYLVANIA

PENNSYLVANIA
Leading individuals (Intellectual Property)

1
- MURRAY William *Duane Morris LLP*, Philadelphia
- PANITCH Ronald *Akin Gump Strauss*, Philadelphia
- POKOTILOW Manny *Caesar, Rivise*, Philadelphia
- PRESTIA Paul *Ratner & Prestia*, Valley Forge
- SEIDEL Arthur *Drinker Biddle & Reath*, Philadelphia

2
- BECK Paul *Paul A Beck & Associates*, Pittsburgh
- BERNSTEIN Alan *Caesar, Rivise, Bernstein*, Philadelphia
- BYRNE Richard *Webb Ziesenheim Logsdon*, Pittsburgh
- COHEN Stanley *Caesar, Rivise, Bernstein*, Philadelphia
- COLEN Frederick *Reed Smith LLP*, Pittsburgh
- DONOHUE John *Woodcock Washburn*, Philadelphia
- JACOBS-MEADWAY Roberta *Ballard Spahr*, Philadelphia
- TABACHNICK Gene *Reed Smith LLP*, Pittsburgh
- YEAGER Robert *Kirkpatrick & Lockhart LLP*, Pittsburgh

3
- ALSTADT Lynn *Buchanan Ingersoll*, Pittsburgh
- DICKOS George *Kirkpatrick & Lockhart*, Pittsburgh
- HEIDELBERGER Louis *Reed Smith LLP*, Philadelphia
- HEIST Dale *Woodcock Washburn*, Philadelphia
- MCNICHOL William *Reed Smith LLP*, Philadelphia
- NADEL Alan *Akin Gump Strauss Hauer*, Philadelphia
- WETTACH Thomas *Cohen & Grigsby PC*, Pittsburgh

4
- GUNDERSEN Glenn *Dechert*, Philadelphia
- KYPER James *Kirkpatrick & Lockhart LLP*, Pittsburgh
- MARSHALL John *Drinker Biddle & Reath LLP*, Berwyn
- MONACO Daniel *Drinker Biddle & Reath*, Philadelphia

Up-and-coming individuals
- LINDEFJELD Robert *Jones Day*, Pittsburgh
- ROCCI Stephen *Woodcock Washburn*, Philadelphia

Individuals are listed alphabetically in each band.

& Johnson; UNISYS; ABB; Mobil, University of Pennsylvania and University of Pittsburgh.

Akin Gump Strauss Hauer & Feld LLP
see firm details p.761

The Firm: This prominent IP outfit consists largely of lawyers from the Panitch Schwarze Jacobs & Nadel IP boutique, joined the firm in 1999. As a result of the merger, the Philadelphia office is now one of the hubs of Akin Gump's national IP practice. It boasts broad trademark and patent litigation expertise, while its transactional practice covers all aspects of IP, including the preparation and prosecution of applications before the US Patent and Trademark Office.

The Lawyers: Ronald Panitch has long been a mainstay of the IP bar in Philadelphia. Sources rate him as a *"leader and mentor to many of the IP lawyers around today."* His practice focuses on licensing and counseling, and he wins recommendations for both his patent and trademark work. Patent expert **Alan Nadel** is also highly rated. Previously a biochemist, interviewees were particularly impressed with his knowledge of the chemical and biotech fields.

The Clients: The firm represents domestic and international clients, including Fortune 500 companies, entertainment and pharmaceuticals multinationals, universities, government bodies and individual artists.

Caesar, Rivise, Bernstein, Cohen & Pokotilow Ltd

The Firm: This *"thriving boutique"* boasts a history of excellence in IP that goes back to its foundation in 1926. It covers the range of IP advice, alongside IT and computer law, but also counsels its hi-tech clients on issues such as licensing, employment, royalties and M&A. The team is equally adept at litigation. Sources note that, although it lacks the resources of its larger rivals, the caliber and reputation of its top individuals keep it among the leaders.

The Lawyers: Manny Pokotilow is the best-known practitioner here. Interviewees described him as a top-class litigator who *"does not obfuscate the issues."* Also highly respected is trademark and copyright guru **Stanley Cohen** whose practice covers all aspects of licensing, litigation and advisory work. Also well respected is **Alan Bernstein** who won particular admiration for his expertise in patent law in the chemical, biotech and pharmaceutical fields.

The Clients: The firm's client base ranges from foreign multinationals and Fortune 500 corporations to small companies and individuals.

Drinker Biddle & Reath LLP

The Firm: This large, established firm has enjoyed a greatly enhanced profile in the field following its 2001 merger with IP boutique Seidel, Gonda, Lavorgna & Monaco. It now combines a large patent procurement operation with a noted trademark and copyright practice. Areas of strength on the patent side include biotech, software and mechanical and chemical engineering. The team is active in all areas of IP litigation and counseling, and has related expertise in e-commerce, web marketing and domain names, and brand issues in connection with advertising. It maintains an alliance with Glasgow-based Murgitroyd & Company for clients who require IP protection in the EU.

The Lawyers: Of counsel **Arthur Seidel**, *"a true intellect,"* is seen by market sources as *"the godfather of IP in Philadelphia."* According to some, he remains *"the driver of the practice."* Based in the Berwyn office, **John Marshall** wins praise as an *"outstanding"* litigator. His practice covers litigation in the patent, trademark and copyright fields, including work before domestic and foreign agencies. **Daniel Monaco** is best known for his patent expertise, particularly in the biotech sphere.

The Clients: The firm represents a mix of Fortune 500 companies, multinationals and smaller clients.

Reed Smith LLP

The Firm: The firm is highly rated for its *"breadth of practice."* It boasts a large IP presence in both its Philadelphia and Pittsburgh offices. The group handles the full range of IP work, including trademarks, copyright, unfair competition and trade secrets. It also maintains a computer science practice linked to Carnegie Mellon University.

The Lawyers: In Pittsburgh, **Fred Colen** and **Gene Tabachnick** are major figures. Colen is particularly involved in software protection and technology transfer for new products and research. He was co-lead counsel in Twentieth Century Fox Film Corp v iCraveTV, an important case concerning copyright on the internet. Tabachnick, meanwhile, acted for Litton in Litton Systems v Honeywell. In Philadelphia, **Louis Heidelberger** is known for his work on technology issues, while **Bill McNichol** is busy in drug, biotech and medical devices disputes. His experience includes representing IP interests for the Universities of Washington and Virginia.

The Clients: The team handles all aspects of IP protection for the firm's state, national and international corporate clients, including major corporations in the pharmaceutical, telecom and electronics sectors. It also acts for research universities.

Webb Ziesenheim Logsdon Orkin & Hanson PC

The Firm: According to interviewees, this long-established Pittsburgh boutique enjoys *"a sizable practice"* and some *"fine people."* Its 28 attorneys cover a range of work, including patent, trademark and copyright matters, trade secrets and competition. It is traditionally strong in metallurgical, mechanical engineering and chemical engineering patent work for the steel industries. Several sources noted that they handled a volume of high-quality work, some of it on referral.

The Lawyers: Commentators repeatedly stressed the overall strength of the team here. However, *"bright and accomplished"* **Richard Byrne** won particular plaudits.

The Clients: The firm acts for a mix of corporates across a range of industries including chemical and mechanical engineering.

Buchanan Ingersoll

The Firm: This practice is *"making some headway"* in the area, according to sources. It operates out of offices in Pittsburgh and Philadelphia. The Pittsburgh team focuses largely on mechanical and electrical patent work, while the firm's Philadelphia lawyers do a lot of work for the chemical industry. Both offices handle a large number of internet and computer patents applications and the full range of trademarks, copyright and trade secret matters.

PENNSYLVANIA

INTELLECTUAL PROPERTY

The Lawyers: Lynn Alstadt was particularly strongly recommended for his expertise in patent prosecution and litigation work. This includes obtaining and litigating patents for such diverse products as computers, business methods and toys. He also has broad experience in all aspects of trademarks and copyright.

The Clients: The team's clients are drawn from a range of sectors including the medical products, metal alloys, railroad, window coverings, consumer products and furniture industries.

Duane Morris LLP

The Firm: This Philadelphia firm is said by sources in the market to be consciously raising its profile for IP work. The patent team undertakes a range of counseling and prosecution work. It can draw upon specialist technical expertise in a raft of scientific fields, and has handled patent, trademark and copyright matters relating to among other things, hardware and software, the internet, television and medical electronics. Its IP litigation experience encompasses several landmark cases.

The Lawyers: The acquisition of **William Murray** who rivals acknowledge as *"a leader at the bar,"* has been seen by many in the market as a *"big bonus"* for the firm.

The Clients: The firm's client base includes universities, computer and software companies, pharmaceutical companies and biotech companies.

Kirkpatrick & Lockhart LLP

The Firm: This large IP practice boasts substantial regional and national clients. It is well versed in patent prosecution and litigation work, and enjoys particular expertise in telecommunications, chip manufacture, software, business methods and biotechnology. Recent work includes representing investors in the purchase of businesses whose IP is a premium asset, in industries such as electrical power products, security systems and medical devices. It also advises universities on their licensing programs. Trademarks, copyright, internet and e-commerce law, trade secrets and IP insurance coverage are also handled.

The Lawyers: George Dickos coordinates the firm's IP practice. He is best known in the market for patent prosecution, but also acts in a variety of work across the discipline with a notable hi-tech slant. *"Senior statesman"* **Robert Yeager** is a much-admired litigator with a particular name for patent infringement, while **Jim Kyper** is also active in patent and trademark litigation.

The Clients: The firm's client list includes Carnegie Mellon University, BellSouth Intellectual Property Management and World Wrestling Entertainment.

Ratner & Prestia

The Firm: According to sources this is *"the largest and most successful of the suburban boutique firms."* Most visible in the patent arena, the firm has extensive experience in the preparation, prosecution and licensing of patents in the pharmaceutical, chemical, material science, software and biotech fields. It is also proficient in litigation, copyright and trademark work. It now boasts over 30 attorneys, patent agents and scientific advisers.

The Lawyers: Patent expert **Paul Prestia** is a *"fine lawyer"* according to peers. His experience goes back to 1963 and covers all aspects of the field.

The Clients: The firm has built an enviable following of large domestic and foreign clients. Examples include Matsushita Electronic Industries, Panasonic Technologies, Boston Scientific, UNISYS, GlaxoSmithKline and ITT.

Other Notable Practitioners

Paul Beck of Paul A Beck & Associates is *"an acknowledged leader"* in Pittsburgh. Commentators rate him an excellent patent lawyer and *"one of the nicest people you will ever meet."* He is said to have *"a good reputation among the judges."* Philadelphia-based **Glenn Gundersen** cochairs Dechert's IP group and concentrates on trademarks, copyright, licensing, the internet and advertising. Sources say he has *"good clients in the trademarks sphere"* but that the team lacks profile for patent work.

Roberta Jacobs-Meadway is considered by many to be *"the best in town for trademarks and copyright litigation."* At present, her reputation is felt to eclipse that of her firm, Ballard Spahr Andrews & Ingersoll LLP. However, peers acknowledge that the group is increasingly becoming a force in the region. At Jones Day, **Robert Lindefjeld** (see p.617) is *"talented and active,"* and covers the range of IP work.

Tom Wettach at Cohen & Grigsby PC is also considered, a *"smart lawyer who is good at serving clients' interests."*

LITIGATION

GENERAL COMMERCIAL

Dechert
see firm details p.789

The Firm: Interviewees placed the firm *"head and shoulders above all others in Pennsylvania in terms of international reach and sophistication."* Its *"excellent trial lawyers"* are considered formidable opponents especially in defending mass torts and products liability suits. A team of about a dozen partners in Philadelphia has been linked to some of the nation's most publicized litigation battles, such as acting for Philip Morris over individual cases and class action disputes in the eastern US. The group also has a substantial antitrust practice, and defended GlaxoSmithKline against allegations that it conspired to keep generic drugs out of the market.

The Lawyers: Robert Heim was said to *"command respect in the courtroom."* Possessing what rivals described as *"a sterling reputation"* among judges and juries alike, he *"shone in the tobacco litigation."* Heim, chairman of the litigation department, also advised a major airline involved in a lawsuit alleging conspiracy to reduce travel agent commissions. **Joseph Tate** whose *"aggressive"* style resulted in a successful practice focused on antitrust litigation, defended Israel-based Dead Sea Bromine Group in a criminal price-fixing case. Described as the *"leader of the pack,"* Tate has also counseled clients such as DuPont in several class actions.

The Clients: FMC, Pfizer and Allegiance Healthcare.

Ballard Spahr Andrews & Ingersoll LLP
see firm details p.769

The Firm: The firm's largest practice group – including about 50 partners in Philadelphia – *"knows how to push all the right buttons,"* said competitors. The team roster includes former Philadelphia city solicitor Charisse Lillie as chair of the litigation department, and as such, was viewed as one of the most politically connected statewide. In addition, its diverse practice group includes a lawyer trained in medical device and pharmaceutical products liability, a renowned construction arbitrator and mediator, and a specialist in the use of computer technology in the courtroom.

The Lawyers: Alan Davis whose practice centers on securities-related litigation, won acclaim as *"a wonderfully persuasive advocate, a thorough analyst and a brilliant scholar."* He represented a principal defendant in the Rite Aid securities litigation, a stockholder dispute concerning company disclosures. Special counsel **Donald Goldberg** won unanimous approval as *"the premier white-collar criminal defense lawyer in Pennsylvania."* Also described by peers as *"a hotshot in the courtroom,"* he often defends company executives and

LITIGATION **PENNSYLVANIA**

PENNSYLVANIA
Leading firms
(Litigation: General Commercial)

1 DECHERT Philadelphia
2 BALLARD SPAHR ANDREWS Philadelphia
   MORGAN, LEWIS & BOCKIUS LLP Philadelphia
   REED SMITH LLP Pittsburgh
3 CONRAD O'BRIEN GELLMAN & ROHN Philadelphia
   HANGLEY ARONCHICK SEGAL Philadelphia
   PEPPER HAMILTON LLP Philadelphia
4 AKIN GUMP STRAUSS HAUER Philadelphia
   BLANK ROME LLP Philadelphia
   BUCHANAN INGERSOLL Pittsburgh
   KIRKPATRICK & LOCKHART LLP Pittsburgh
   MONTGOMERY, MCCRACKEN, WALKER Philadelphia
   SCHNADER HARRISON SEGAL Philadelphia
   THORP REED & ARMSTRONG Pittsburgh

Leading individuals
(Litigation: General Commercial)

1 DAVIS Alan *Ballard Spahr Andrews*, Philadelphia
   HANGLEY William *Hangley Aronchick*, Philadelphia
   HEIM Robert *Dechert*, Philadelphia
   MATHER Barbara *Pepper Hamilton LLP*, Philadelphia
   O'BRIEN William *Conrad O'Brien Gellman*, Philadelphia
2 HARKINS John *Harkins Cunningham*, Philadelphia
   MANNINO Edward *Akin Gump Strauss*, Philadelphia
   MCCLENAHAN David *Kirkpatrick & Lockhart*, Pittsburgh
   MCGOUGH Thomas *Reed Smith LLP*, Pittsburgh
   SONNENFELD Marc *Morgan, Lewis*, Philadelphia
   SPRAGUE Richard *Sprague & Sprague*, Philadelphia
   TATE Joseph *Dechert*, Philadelphia
   WYCOFF William *Thorp Reed & Armstrong*, Pittsburgh
3 BLACK Allen *Fine Kaplan & Black*, Philadelphia
   GELLMAN Nancy *Conrad O'Brien Gellman*, Philadelphia
   GOLDBERG Donald *Ballard Spahr Andrews*, Philadelphia
   KLETT Edwin *Klett Rooney Lieber*, Philadelphia
   LAUPHEIMER Ann *Blank Rome*, Philadelphia
   MARION David *Montgomery, McCracken*, Philadelphia
   REICH Abraham *Fox Rothschild O'Brien*, Philadelphia
   RESTIVO James *Reed Smith LLP*, Pittsburgh
   SCHER Howard *Buchanan Ingersoll*, Pittsburgh
   SUPLEE Dennis *Schnader Harrison Segal*, Philadelphia

Firms and individuals are listed alphabetically in each band.

companies in government enforcement and criminal matters.
The Clients: AT&T; Northrop Grumman; DuPont; PNC Bank and Medtronic.

Morgan, Lewis & Bockius LLP
The Firm: The largest firm in Pennsylvania, it has concentrated a portion of its litigation prowess in New York and DC, and appeared all the better for it, according to rivals. The group was said to enjoy one of the most *"vigorous"* practices. Litigators in other cities including Los Angeles, Miami and London, UK, have enhanced Philadelphia's practice, providing clients with one of the most geographically diverse talent pools. Statewide, the team demonstrated a deft hand in areas such as securities, stockholder disputes and employment litigation. Attorneys specialize in what was described as *"big, nasty corporate fights,"* which involved large-scale contract disputes among other issues. The firm won a $29.6 million verdict for Butler Manufacturing Company, a Kansas City producer of pre-engineered building systems, in a case involving Louisiana-Pacific's Inner-Seal Siding product.
The Lawyers: *"Smart and detail-oriented"* **Marc Sonnenfeld** was perceived by rivals and clients as *"able to put together convincing, persuasive arguments."* He acted for a private pharmaceutical company in a case arising out of a short-form merger to eliminate minority stockholders. On behalf of CDNOW, he successfully defended the company against allegations that it failed to disclose crucial information to stock purchasers.
The Clients: Rohm and Haas, Phillips, US Gypsum and PWC.

Reed Smith LLP
The Firm: Competitors delineated the firm as among the top of the heap, with *"global coverage focusing on the ultimate victory as opposed to winning skirmishes."* The team advised American Home Products (now Wyeth) in various drug-related litigation and Mellon Bank in a lawsuit alleging breach of a non-compete agreement. The firm's reach was said to be *"outstanding"* with more than 60 partners in Pittsburgh, Philadelphia and Harrisburg and branch offices in such cities as New York, Los Angeles and London, UK.
The Lawyers: As leader of the litigation department, **Thomas McGough** established a practice grounded in issues involving white-collar crime, media law and appellate litigation. Branded as *"one of the smartest lawyers around,"* he represented AdvancePCS in an antitrust lawsuit in Minnesota and had defended the Scranton Times Tribune in a defamation case. **James Restivo** noted by peers as an attorney *"with a broad vision,"* represented Pittsburgh Corning in asbestos-related litigation.
The Clients: WR Grace, USX, Pittsburgh Post-Gazette and Highmark Blue Cross Blue Shield.

Conrad O'Brien Gellman & Rohn, PC
The Firm: A litigation boutique of about a dozen partners. The firm is consistently sought after for its stable of lawyers, who are judged by peers as among *"the most talented in the city."* The team defeated the certification of a class action involving insurance sales practices, and secured dismissal for AEGON USA in a case involving the sale of variable annuity products.
The Lawyers: **William O'Brien** has a courtroom appeal that peers believe makes him one of the best jury trial lawyers in the state. He has *"Irish charm by the tons"* and the ability to *"speak the language of the jury."* He has handled a long list of high-profile products liability issues including lead paint, tobacco and asbestos. He also counseled clients in defending legal malpractice, class actions and employment discrimination. **Nancy Gellman** was perceived as a productive generalist whose *"tough"* style complements the firm. Her practice involves such issues as insurance coverage, employment wrongful discharge and antitrust. She counseled a global specialty materials company in an insurance case concerning whether an insurer may void a policy purchased under fraudulent circumstances.
The Clients: Fortune 500 companies; entrepreneurs; municipalities and hospitals.

Hangley Aronchick Segal & Pudlin
The Firm: The litigation department was viewed as the foundation of this firm, and sources credited it with *"recruiting the best people."* About 25 attorneys act on behalf of plaintiffs and defendants in a variety of matters, including products liability, toxic torts and other general commercial litigation. The firm has been involved in such well-publicized cases as the Enron bankruptcy, representing issuers of the letters of credit. Acting for the City of Philadelphia, the group had defended civil rights violation claims by protestors at the 2000 Republican National Convention.
The Lawyers: **William Hangley** chair and chief executive of the firm, has counseled a host of clients in disputes involving IP, antitrust, First Amendment and professional malpractice issues. He has advised a mortgage banker in a bankruptcy case involving alleged fraud and successfully obtained a preliminary injunction to prevent the termination of franchising rights for one of his clients. Hailed by peers as a *"stellar litigator"* he has developed a niche in legal malpractice.
The Clients: Universities, banks and private companies.

Pepper Hamilton LLP
The Firm: Depicted by interviewees as a *"superb group"* of general litigators, the team earned high marks for its work in antitrust, stockholder disputes, white-collar crimes and class actions, particularly those that pertain to products liability. Acting for a prominent telecom company, the team obtained summary judgment in a stockholder class action alleging disclosure and accounting improprieties. The firm's seasoned veterans have also established a successful record in appellate litigation.
The Lawyers: Although a generalist, **Barbara Mather** chair of the firm's litigation and dispute resolution department, gained kudos for her expertise in antitrust matters. Displaying what

www.ChambersandPartners.com   All quotes in the text are from interviews with clients and competitors.   611

PENNSYLVANIA

LITIGATION

competitors called *"a steel trap mind,"* she has proved to be *"a good strategist and wise counsel."* Mather represented LaPage in a lawsuit against 3M alleging anticompetitive pricing and predatory conduct in the adhesive tape market. In a separate case, she successfully defended Vlasic Foods International in an alleged securities act violation.
The Clients: ViroPharma and Burger King.

Akin Gump Strauss Hauer & Feld LLP
see firm details p.761
The Firm: Since the firm combined its practice with a prominent IP practice in 1999, it has continued to enjoy recognition in that field. For example, the crew represented Illinois Tool Work in a patent infringement suit and Buena Vista Home Entertainment in a copyright battle against internet service Video Pipeline.
The Lawyers: Peers described the firm as having established its place *"on the map"* of Pennsylvania, though largely built around its litigation department leader, **Ed Mannino** . He is a generalist whose name has been linked to high-profile court cases, and who represented Pennsylvania in challenges to the privatization of the state's schools by citizens groups, the NAACP and others. Called *"a street fighter,"* his *"tough"* style was particularly suited for *"highly complex products liability class actions,"* sources said. Clients reported that Mannino's *"work was exemplary, his performance remarkable and his results often amazing."* He also defeated class action certifications on behalf of such companies as Independence Blue Cross and Allstate.
The Clients: Disney; Wet Seal; Purdue Pharma and Keystone Insurance.

Blank Rome LLP
The Firm: The firm's fulcrum is its litigation department, a sizable group devoted to handling such issues as insurance disputes, municipal liability, real estate controversies and contract-related matters. The team represents company executives, underwriters, brokers and accountants, and also has notable experience in securities-related matters and class action torts.
The Lawyers: **Ann Laupheimer** who gathered peer endorsements for her work in insurance litigation, coordinated the liquidation of Reliance Insurance Company. Rivals noted that the *"smart trial lawyer"* is a first stop for insurance matters, but has also been known to represent blue-chip companies in general commercial lawsuits.
The Clients: ATOFINA Chemicals, Aetna and Pennsylvania Insurance Department.

Buchanan Ingersoll
The Firm: Peers perceived the reputation of this firm to be *"on the upswing"* and the firm has recently acquired a nine-member group in Philadelphia concentrating on IP litigation. Alongside a host of cases concerning the pharmaceutical, hi-tech and chemicals industry, the team also gained distinction for winning jury trials. In a prominent victory for Harman Development, the team obtained a $34.6 million verdict in a battle against Massey Energy involving the cancellation of a long-term coal contract.
The Lawyers: **Howard Scher** whose *"prominence is in ascendancy,"* defended AmerisourceBergen in a national antitrust case involving brand-name prescription drugs. A generalist with an antitrust bent, rivals also credited Scher with being *"a talented courtroom performer."*
The Clients: Kennametal; UPMC Health System; Pitt-Des Moines; Knoll Inc. and ANSYS.

Kirkpatrick & Lockhart LLP
The Firm: Although a general litigation practice, it is in the area of insurance coverage that the firm has cultivated a *"national reputation,"* claimed peers. Its *"outstanding"* litigation department involves about half of the firm's attorneys and the group was also viewed as having had an impact in matters relating to IP and patents. The firm acted for a major supplier of semiconductor equipment in a patent infringement action, and, on behalf of World Wrestling Entertainment (WWE), the team won the right for WWE to enter into a strategic alliance with Viacom.
The Lawyers: If the issue involves *"business judgment as well as acumen of the law,"* then peers recommended **David McClenahan**. Competitors viewed him as *"an exceptionally smart lawyer"* who gets excellent results for his clients. He represented Seven Springs Farm in a precedent-setting decision concerning the right of the board of directors to remove the president and chief executive of the company.
The Clients: National Tax Funding, Marconi and Kidder, Peabody & Company.

Montgomery, McCracken, Walker & Rhoads LLP
The Firm: About 40 partners in Pennsylvania are centered on such areas as products liability, toxic torts and IP. The firm garnered endorsements from market observers for its *"efficiency in utilization of legal resources."* The team defended Delta Air Lines against price-fixing allegations involving commissions to foreign travel agencies, and represented an engineering firm in the collapse of a pier on the Delaware River.
The Lawyers: Armed with what competitors claimed to be a *"legendary reputation,"* **David Marion** has built a reputation as *"a player"* in the fields of antitrust, First Amendment and IP. He advised Sherwin-Williams in a national antitrust case alleging price-fixing of auto refinishing paint and acted for Microsoft in numerous spin-off litigation cases arising from its highly publicized antitrust battle with the DOJ.
The Clients: Oracle; Simpson Tacoma Kraft Company; Hoechst Celanese and The Patriot-News of Harrisburg.

Schnader Harrison Segal & Lewis LLP
The Firm: A pillar in Philadelphia's litigation bar, this traditionally strong group earned the respect of interviewees for its representation of a range of clients. In commercial-related matters, the team succeeded in reducing a $337 million verdict to $40.5 million for a mortgage brokerage company. The firm's scope also includes a strong appellate practice, as well as such niches as maritime law.
The Lawyers: Sources agreed that **Dennis Suplee** has a *"gentle way of being forceful."* He successfully defended ConAgra in a products liability case concerning the company's turkey meat product. He also advised a top chemicals manufacturer in a CERCLA contribution matter. Competitors agreed: *"I would seek him out in any kind of commercial case."*
The Clients: Rohm and Haas, Villanova University and Hilton Group.

Thorp Reed & Armstrong
The Firm: The Pittsburgh-based general practice firm was said to include a dazzling litigation group, largely due to the capabilities of its star litigator, William Wycoff. The group built a successful record of courtroom victories in such areas as antitrust, contract disputes, securities law and other commercial matters.
The Lawyers: **William Wycoff** was hailed by peers as *"an aggressive, respected and ethical lawyer who has gotten great results for clients."* He represented ten national bank directors in a derivatives action lawsuit. He also advised Royal Numico in a breach-of-contract allegation.
The Clients: Mellon Financial Services; PPG Industries; MetLife; National Steel and Grubb & Ellis.

Other Notable Practitioners
John Harkins of Harkins Cunningham earned laurels for his handling of *"a very long list of big cases"* for blue-chip companies including Sunoco, CIGNA and 3M. Renowned for his expertise in such areas as antitrust and securities law, he represented Ikon Office Solutions in an investor class action. **Richard Sprague** of Sprague & Sprague was said to be *"one of the most feared litigators."* He exerts *"a great deal of influence, particularly among the appellate bench,"* and composed his *"enormous"* persona with such cases as a high-profile defamation against The Philadelphia Inquirer newspaper. **Allen Black** (see p.615) of Fine Kaplan & Black won respect from interviewees as an *"extraordinarily competent and bright"* plaintiff attorney with a niche practice in the area of antitrust. **Edwin Klett** of Klett Rooney Lieber & Schorling was said to be a *"mover and shaker,"* successfully representing

REAL ESTATE   # PENNSYLVANIA

UPMC Health System in a challenge to the company's merger with Children's Hospital of Pittsburgh. He also advised the Pennsylvania Insurance Department in an accountant liability case against Arthur Andersen. Acclaimed by colleagues as *"an excellent counselor and advocate,"* **Abraham Reich** has counseled AAMCO Transmissions among other clients regarding franchise-related matters. His expertise also includes representing law firms, including two New York law firms involved in the $3.75 billion Fen-Phen diet drug class action settlement.

REAL ESTATE

PENNSYLVANIA
Leading firms (Real Estate)

1 BALLARD SPAHR ANDREWS *Philadelphia*
BLANK ROME LLP *Philadelphia*
WOLF, BLOCK, SCHORR *Philadelphia*
2 DECHERT *Philadelphia*
DRINKER BIDDLE & REATH LLP *Philadelphia*
MORGAN, LEWIS & BOCKIUS LLP *Philadelphia*
3 SAUL EWING LLP *Philadelphia*
4 SCHNADER HARRISON SEGAL *Philadelphia*

Leading individuals (Real Estate)

1 FALA Herman *Wolf, Block, Schorr*, Philadelphia
OMINSKY Harris *Blank Rome LLP*, Philadelphia
SKLAROFF Mike *Ballard Spahr Andrews*, Philadelphia
2 AICHELE Stephen *Saul Ewing LLP*, Philadelphia
MILLER Henry *Wolf, Block, Schorr*, Philadelphia
3 EBBY Stuart *Hangley Aronchick Segal*, Philadelphia
LANE Robert *Morgan, Lewis & Bockius*, Philadelphia
LORD Craig *Blank Rome LLP*, Philadelphia
4 GOLDBERG Richard *Ballard Spahr Andrews*, Philadelphia
JONES Richard *Dechert*, Philadelphia
PRIMAVERA Carl *Klehr Harrison Harvey*, Philadelphia
RACKOW Julian *Blank Rome LLP*, Philadelphia
ROTWITT Jeffrey *Obermayer, Rebmann*, Philadelphia
STERN Eric *Morgan, Lewis & Bockius*, Philadelphia
5 AXELROTH Lynn *Ballard Spahr Andrews*, Philadelphia
FISCHER John *Drinker Biddle & Reath LLP*, Berwyn
KUTLER Marilyn *Schnader Harrison Segal*, Philadelphia

Firms and individuals are listed alphabetically in each band.

Ballard Spahr Andrews & Ingersoll LLP
see firm details p.769
The Firm: Split into a number of dedicated practice groups, the real estate department also enlists the services of lawyers from the firm's environmental, finance, tax, construction and litigation practices. Clients endorsed the group as *"a cost-effective one-stop shop,"* pointing to its *"premier land use practice,"* and its *"political connections."* (Pennsylvania governor-elect and former mayor of Philadelphia Ed Rendell was a partner here.) Attorneys are recognized for their experience as lenders' counsel in a wide range of financing transactions, and have attracted a following among key developers, ensuring the firm's presence on *"high-impact public-private joint ventures."* The firm is also active in leasing and the management of REITs, and fields a dedicated resorts and hotels group and a long-standing eminent domain/condemnation group.

The Lawyers: Mike Sklaroff chairs the firm's real estate department, and was recommended to researchers as *"among the most dominant real estate lawyers in the region."* He is the firm's rainmaker and *"a strategist who is constantly thinking about the dynamics, money and politics involved in his projects."* His work on development issues and land use is coupled with a strong litigation practice. He has handled three tax appeals for Exelon Generating Company for nuclear generating facilities in Pennsylvania, and has negotiated the long-term lease of the new home of the Philadelphia Orchestra at the Kimmel Center. Managing partner of the Philadelphia office **Lynn Axelroth** heads the construction group and respected for her advice on real estate financings. A *"creative and cooperative attorney,"* she is counsel for The Phillies baseball team, and has advised on the development and construction of its new stadium complex. **Richard Goldberg** heads the real estate development group and has a reputation as *"a real academic figure, up there with national real estate heavyweights."* His broad development practice includes a niche in retail-related projects such as shopping centers, and he advises REITs with multi-state property portfolios. He also represents one of the largest owners of multi-family properties in the City of Philadelphia.

The Clients: The group represents a wide range of clients such as: The Rubinstein Company; The Praedium Group; University of Pennsylvania; Realen Properties; Loews Corporation and SEPTA.

Blank Rome LLP
The Firm: Described by market observers as *"one of the strongest practices in the state, politically well-connected and with excellent attorneys."* The firm's traditional roots in developer work have expanded to include real estate acquisition and financing matters. Peers respect the high-quality attorneys who *"have the X factor that goes toward the smooth execution of a contract."* They are experienced in the complex leasing transactions for commercial office building owners, synthetic structures and other off-balance sheet financings.

The Lawyers: Harris Ominsky is a senior attorney widely praised as a *"true real estate guru."* Interviewees endorsed the *"intellectual underpinning"* he provides the group, a reputation that extends both regionally and nationally. He has represented a residential developer on the acquisition of a residential development business from a REIT, involving 15 communities spread across four states. Benefiting from his experience as a judge, **Craig Lord** concentrates his practice in the areas of real estate development, financing and litigation, and alternative dispute resolution. **Julian Rackow** represents major national and regional developers and lenders on projects, such as shopping centers, luxury hotels and mixed-use facilities. *"He can do anything, but retail work is his greatest strength,"* claimed sources.

The Clients: PREIT-Rubin; Sunoco; Philadelphia Housing Authority; English Village Apartments; Chelbourne Plaza Condominium and Omnicare.

Wolf, Block, Schorr and Solis-Cohen LLP
see firm details p.905
The Firm: Commended to researchers as *"the giant of real estate business,"* the group's efforts are spearheaded by its widely respected Philadelphia office. The real estate practice group, which consists of over 40 attorneys, is national in scope and encompasses the full range of real estate-related transactions. It works in conjunction with the real estate structured finance group, which advises on the origination and securitization of complex commercial mortgage loans. The backing of solid securities, tax and environmental law capabilities in the firm ensure a full service is offered to its clients.

The Lawyers: Herman Fala (see p.616) is chairman of the firm's real estate department and the REIT practice. Interviewees spoke of a *"straightforward and deal-oriented"* attorney, whose broad practice includes corporate transactional matters, financings and development of commercial properties such as office space and hotels. He has recently advised long-term client Liberty Property Trust on its $400 million development of a new office tower in Philadelphia, and acted for a publicly traded REIT in the creation of a joint venture to oversee ownership of a $130 million portfolio of office/warehouse properties. **Henry Miller** (see

PENNSYLVANIA   REAL ESTATE

p.617) has practiced real estate law for over 30 years, representing developers of shopping centers and major high-rise office buildings. Sources respect him as *"a legend in the retail leasing area"* and *"a highly intelligent and personable attorney."*
The Clients: Traditionally the firm's focus was largely on developers, but this has subsequently broadened to include such clients as: Liberty Property Trust; Hilton Hotels; AMC Delancey Group; Citizens Bank; Keystone Property Trust; Deutsche Bank; Wachovia and Lend Lease.

Dechert
see firm details p.789
The Firm: This sizable real estate department is best known for its financial and corporate expertise in advising financial institutions and owner/developer clients. Attorneys are respected for their understanding of tax-efficient investment structures as well as development, planning and construction issues. Interviewees particularly praised the group's *"flawlessly constructed,"* complex financings.
The Lawyers: Rick Jones heads the finance and real estate group in the Philadelphia office and chairs the department internationally. His focus lies in mortgage and capital markets-related transactions, an area in which the firm famously excels. Peers described him as *"extremely intelligent."*
The Clients: The real estate department advises development projects such as shopping centers, offices and business parks and leisure and residential sites. Key clients include Siemens and Sheetz, Crown Cork Seal Company.

Drinker Biddle & Reath LLP
The Firm: Credited by sources as having *"a fantastic group of real estate lawyers,"* this firm concentrates its real estate practice on development issues, financings and leasings. Its attorneys are commended for their familiarity with *"big-ticket deals"* and commentators agree that *"there is no doubt that they could handle any transaction."*
The Lawyers: Interviewees reported that **John Fischer** has *"shown impressive ability"* in his representation of developers in permitting, leasing and development issues. He represents the second largest Philadelphia area office building developer and has assisted this client in the development of five major office parks. He also advises both local and out-of-state lenders in complex, multi-state financing structures.
The Clients: Regional and national owners, developers and lenders.

Morgan, Lewis & Bockius LLP
The Firm: The practice has a strong transactional focus, which interviewees felt ensured *"a large measure of sophisticated corporate client counseling"* in the management of real estate portfolios. Zoning and land use is also an important element of the practice, particularly for the Philadelphia office. Real estate attorneys at this international firm can draw on the support of members of the construction, creditors' rights, environmental and tax practices. Litigation and complex financing are key strengths of the team, which is credited by peers as being home to *"a lot of excellent real estate lawyers."*
The Lawyers: Robert Lane is co-manager of the firm's real estate group, which has nearly tripled in size under his leadership. Recommended to researchers as a *"resourceful"* practitioner, he has advised on the development of facilities for businesses in the media, retail and petroleum industries. He has advised a Fortune 500 company on its world headquarters development, valued at around $250 million, and acted on the buildout of a national wireless telecom system. **Eric Stern** is recommended for his substantial retail real estate expertise. He recently represented REITs involved in build-to-suit lease transactions and on a joint venture with a German investor involving a $22 million office property in New Jersey.
The Clients: Pharmaceutical and chemical companies make up much of the firm's client base, which also includes: Fannie Mae; BP Amoco; McDonald's; Verizon; Forest City Enterprises; American Financial Realty Trust and Brandywine Realty Trust.

Saul Ewing LLP
The Firm: The team has secured its place on high-profile real estate projects throughout the mid-Atlantic region and beyond. Attorneys are experienced in the development and construction of new projects and in the acquisition of existing facilities. They played a major role in the acquisition, zoning approvals and permitting related to transfer stations and landfill sites for one of the nation's largest environmental management companies. Peers pointed to the firm's *"long history with banking clients"* as well as REITs, pension funds and insurance companies, which provide high levels of real estate financing work.
The Lawyers: Managing partner **Steve Aichele** is the former chair of the firm's real estate department, which grew from 17 to 40 attorneys under his leadership. Interviewees respect his efforts as *"one of the premier suburban land use and zoning attorneys,"* singling out his *"sound judgment"* on political issues.
The Clients: The Rouse Company; LMC Properties; The Phoenix Group and various school districts and boroughs.

Schnader Harrison Segal & Lewis LLP
The Firm: The real estate practice group serves a wide range of entrepreneurial, institutional and public sector clients. About 30 full-time real estate lawyers are spread among five separate practice teams covering commercial leasing and shopping center development, construction law, public/private development, creditors' rights and lending. A number of these attorneys litigate in their discrete subspecialties, while an interdisciplinary real estate financing team advises institutional lenders in all aspects of loan transactions. Interviewees spoke of a firm that has *"increased the size of its real estate group substantially."*
The Lawyers: Marilyn Kutler has a background in the public sector and concentrates her practice on government contracts work. Her practice includes real estate sales and project financing, and she has worked extensively with federal, state and local government grant and loan programs. Commentators described her as *"an artist who can really put a deal together."* She was lead counsel to the Philadelphia Authority for Industrial Development, negotiating with the Phillies and The Philadelphia Eagles on new baseball and football stadiums being developed in the city at a cost of over $1 billion.
The Clients: University of Pennsylvania; Brandywine Realty Trust; Philadelphia Authority for Industrial Development; Community Education Partners and Conrail.

Other Notable Practitioners
Stuart Ebby of mid-sized full-service firm Hangley Aronchick Segal & Pudlin is noted to be a *"talented individual – excellent in real estate financing."* Interviewees acknowledged that *"he nurtures good client relationships,"* typically representing large American and Canadian insurance companies. He recently represented the owner of a retail/apartment building in a $21 million commercial mortgage-backed securities loan and advised an insurance company on the refinancing of $80 million in debt secured by an office portfolio. **Jeffrey Rotwitt** of Obermayer, Rebmann, Maxwell & Hippel LLP has *"a powerful presence in real estate."* He is respected for his work with several large, national institutions. A *"real specialist,"* **Carl Primavera**, of Klehr Harrison Harvey Branzberg & Ellers LLP's real estate and finance department, was recommended to researchers for his land use knowledge. He has represented IKEA in the rezoning of land owned by the CSX railroad in Philadelphia, paving the way for a 600,000 sq ft retail center.

PENNSYLVANIA

Leaders in Pennsylvania

ABELSON, Barry
Pepper Hamilton LLP, Philadelphia
215 981 4000
Recommended in Corporate/M&A

AICHELE, Stephen
Saul Ewing LLP, Philadelphia
215 972 7777
Recommended in Real Estate

ALSTADT, Lynn
Buchanan Ingersoll, Pittsburgh
412 562 8800
Recommended in Intellectual Property

ARMSTRONG, Stephen
Montgomery, McCracken, Walker & Rhoads, LLP, Philadelphia
215 772 1500
Recommended in Antitrust

ASHER, Steven
Fox Rothschild O'Brien & Frankel LLP, Philadelphia 215 299 2000
Recommended in Antitrust

AXELROTH, Lynn
Ballard Spahr Andrews & Ingersoll LLP, Philadelphia 215 665 8500
Recommended in Real Estate

BABST, Chester
Babst, Calland, Clements and Zomnir, A Professional Corporation, Pittsburgh
412 394 5400
Recommended in Environment

BALLARD, Alice
Law Office of Alice W. Ballard, Philadelphia 215 893 9708
Recommended in Employment

BARNETT, Bonnie
Drinker Biddle & Reath LLP, Philadelphia 215 988 2700
Recommended in Environment

BECK, Paul
Paul A. Beck & Associates, Pittsburgh
412 343 9700
Recommended in Intellectual Property

BERGER, Lawrence
Morgan, Lewis & Bockius LLP, Philadelphia 215 963 5000
Recommended in Banking & Finance

BERGÈRE, Timothy
Montgomery, McCracken, Walker & Rhoads, LLP, Philadelphia
215 772 1500
Recommended in Environment

BERKOWITZ, Alan
Dechert, Philadelphia 215 994 4000
Recommended in Employment

BERNSTEIN, Alan
Caesar, Rivise, Bernstein, Cohen & Pokotilow Ltd, Philadelphia
215 567 2010
Recommended in Intellectual Property

BEVAN, William
Reed Smith LLP, Pittsburgh
412 288 3131
Recommended in Employment

BIRON, Thomas
Blank Rome Comisky & McCauley LLP, Philadelphia 215 569 5500
Recommended in Insolvency

BLACK, Allen
Fine Kaplan & Black, Philadelphia
215 567 6565
ablack@finekaplan.com
Recommended in Litigation
Specialization: Commercial litigation; complex litigation; class actions; antitrust.
Prof. Memberships: The American Law Institute - Elected Member, Member of Council, Member of Executive Committee. American College of Trial Lawyers (Fellow).
Career: Founding Partner, *Fine Kaplan & Black*, 1975 to present. Previously Judge Advocate General's Corps, United States Navy; Trial Attorney, United States Department of Justice Civil Rights Division; and Law Clerk to Hon. John Minor Wisdom, United States Court of Appeals for the Fifth Circuit, New Orleans. He has taught at the law schools of the University of North Dakota, Rutgers University, Temple University, and the University of Pennsylvania.
Publications: 'Judge Wisdom, the Great Teacher and Careful Writer', 109 Yale LJ 1267 (2000); 'John Minor Wisdom: A Tribute and Memoir by One of His Law Clerks', 69 Miss. L.J. 43 (1999).
Personal: 'Allen Black is quite simply one of the best and most thoughtful lawyers in the country, a highly successful litigator and important contributor to numerous law reform efforts.' Burbank, Litigation in a Free Society: The Roles of Litigation, 80 Washington Univ. L.Q. 705, 719 (2002). Chairman, Bucks County Airport Authority.

BLOOM, Michael
Morgan, Lewis & Bockius LLP, Philadelphia 215 963 5000
Recommended in Insolvency

BLUME, Fred
Blank Rome Comisky & McCauley LLP, Philadelphia 215 569 5500
Recommended in Corporate/M&A

BOLSTEIN, Joel
Fox Rothschild O'Brien & Frankel LLP, Doylestown 267 880 2655
Recommended in Environment

BOOKER, Daniel
Reed Smith LLP, Pittsburgh
412 288 3131
Recommended in Antitrust

BORISH, Warren
Spear, Wilderman, Borish, Endy, Spear & Runckel, Philadelphia 215 732 0101
Recommended in Employment

BOSSERT, Terry
Stevens & Lee A Professional Corporation, Reading 610 478 2000
Recommended in Environment

BRAEMER, Richard
Ballard Spahr Andrews & Ingersoll LLP, Philadelphia 215 665 8500
Recommended in Corporate/M&A

BROOMAN, David
Drinker Biddle & Reath LLP, Berwyn
610 993 2210
Recommended in Environment

BROWN, James
Cohen & Grigsby, PC, Pittsburgh
412 297 4907
jbrown@cohenlaw.com
Recommended in Employment
Specialization: Is a labor and employment attorney who concentrates his practice on representing public and private employers in employment litigation. He has counseled and defended public universities, authorities and commissions, corporations, financial institutions, health care institutions, the construction industry, hotels and retail and manufacturing establishments in all aspects of employment litigation. Is a prolific speaker and author often quoted in professional journals, newspapers and magazine articles both regionally and nationally. Heads the firm's Labor and Employment and Employment Litigation Groups.
Career: BA, University of Louisville, 1967. JD, Duquesne University, 1971. Admitted to practice in Pennsylvania, 1971.

BROWN, Stephen
Dechert, Philadelphia 215 994 4000
Recommended in Antitrust

BYRNE, Richard
Webb Ziesenheim Logsdon Orkin & Hanson, PC, Pittsburgh 412 471 8815
Recommended in Intellectual Property

CALLAND, Dean
Babst, Calland, Clements and Zomnir, PC, Pittsburgh 412 394 5400
Recommended in Environment

CARROLL, James
Rothman Gordon P.C, Pittsburgh
412 338 1100
Recommended in Employment

CASS, George
Buchanan Ingersoll, Pittsburgh
412 562 8800
Recommended in Insolvency

CASSIDY, Bart
Manko, Gold, Katcher & Fox LLP, Bala Clynwyd 484 430 5700
Recommended in Environment

CLARK, William
Drinker Biddle & Reath LLP, Philadelphia 215 988 2700
Recommended in Corporate/M&A

COHEN, Charles
Cohen & Grigsby, PC, Pittsburgh
800 394 4904
Recommended in Corporate/M&A

COHEN, Stanley
Caesar, Rivise, Bernstein, Cohen & Pokotilow Ltd, Philadelphia
215 567 2010
Recommended in Intellectual Property

COLEN, Frederick
Reed Smith LLP, Pittsburgh
412 288 3131
Recommended in Intellectual Property

COLLINGS, Robert
Schnader Harrison Segal & Lewis LLP, Philadelphia 215 751 2000
Recommended in Environment

COLTON, Neal
Cozen O'Connor, Philadelphia
215 665 2000
Recommended in Insolvency

CONNORS, Eugene
Reed Smith LLP, Pittsburgh
412 288 3131
Recommended in Employment

CONSOLE, Stephen
Console Law Offices, Philadelphia
215 545 7676
Recommended in Employment

CORDES, Samuel
Ogg, Cordes, Murphy & Ignelzi, Pittsburgh 412 471 8500
Recommended in Employment

DAVIS, Alan
Ballard Spahr Andrews & Ingersoll LLP, Philadelphia 215 665 8500
Recommended in Litigation

DAVIS, Doreen
Morgan, Lewis & Bockius LLP, Philadelphia 215 963 5000
Recommended in Employment

DENINNO, David
Reed Smith LLP, Pittsburgh
412 288 3131
Recommended in Corporate/M&A

DICHTER, Mark
Morgan, Lewis & Bockius LLP, Philadelphia 215 963 5000
Recommended in Employment

DICKOS, George
Kirkpatrick & Lockhart LLP, Pittsburgh
412 355 6500
Recommended in Intellectual Property

DONOHUE, John
Woodcock Washburn, Philadelphia
215 568 3100
Recommended in Intellectual Property

PENNSYLVANIA
LEADERS

DWORETZKY, Joseph
Hangley, Aronchick, Segal & Pudlin,
Philadelphia 215 568 6200
Recommended in Insolvency

EBBY, Stuart
Hangley, Aronchick, Segal & Pudlin,
Philadelphia 215 568 6200
Recommended in Real Estate

EDWARDS, Mark
Morgan, Lewis & Bockius LLP,
Philadelphia 215 963 5000
Recommended in Antitrust

EPSTEIN, Alan
Spector Gadon & Rosen, PC,
Philadelphia 215 241 8888
Recommended in Employment

EVERETT, Carl
Saul Ewing LLP, Philadelphia
215 972 7777
Recommended in Environment

FALA, Herman
Wolf, Block, Schorr and Solis-Cohen LLP,
Philadelphia 215 977 2000
hfala@wolfblock.com
Recommended in Real Estate
Specialization: Chairman, Real Estate Department, REIT Practice Group, and Hospitality and Gaming Group. Has represented banks, pension funds, publicly traded companies, insurance companies, REITs, and real estate developers in many local and national transactions, including complex acquisitions, mergers, financings, joint venture arrangements, leases, project finance transactions, syndications, public and private debt and equity placements, and transactions involving the development and management of hotels, office buildings and other projects. Has extensive experience in the management, financing, acquisition, development and franchising of hotels.
Prof. Memberships: Member, American College of Real Estate Lawyers, and is listed in a leading US publication as a leading lawyer. Served as Chairman of the Real Property Section of the Philadelphia Bar Association (1998) and on numerous other committees of the Philadelphia Bar Association, including the Professional Responsibility Committee and the Executive Committee of the Real Property Section.
Career: Admitted to the Pennsylvania Bar (1974). Member, Board of Directors of The Wilma Theater Company (Board Chairman from 1995-97). Member, Board of Directors of the Lawyers Club of Philadelphia and the Board of Directors of Central Philadelphia Development Corporation.
Publications: Served as Editor-in-Chief of The Philadelphia Lawyer, and has written numerous articles for that publication. Served as Editor of the Real Property Newsletter, published by the Philadelphia Bar Association.

Personal: Received his BS, summa cum laude, in Physics from the University of Notre Dame in 1971 and JD, cum laude, from Harvard Law School in 1974.

FELIX, H Thomas
Ballard Spahr Andrews & Ingersoll LLP,
Philadelphia 215 665 8500
Recommended in Employment

FISCHER, John
Drinker Biddle & Reath LLP, Berwyn
610 993 2210
Recommended in Real Estate

FLICK II, Lawrence
Blank Rome Comisky & McCauley LLP,
Philadelphia 215 569 5500
Recommended in Banking & Finance

FOLEY, Mark
Klett Rooney Lieber & Schorling,
Philadelphia 215 567 7500
Recommended in Employment

FORMAN, Harvey
Blank Rome Comisky & McCauley LLP,
Philadelphia 215 569 5500
Recommended in Banking & Finance

FRIDY, Carl
Ballard Spahr Andrews & Ingersoll LLP,
Philadelphia 215 665 8500
Recommended in Banking & Finance

FRITTON, Karl
Reed Smith LLP, Philadelphia
215 851 8100
Recommended in Employment

GARRITY, Vincent
Duane Morris LLP, Philadelphia
215 979 1000
Recommended in Corporate/M&A

GELLMAN, Nancy
Conrad O'Brien Gellman & Rohn, PC,
Philadelphia 215 864 9600
Recommended in Litigation

GIOTTO, Thomas
Klett Rooney Lieber & Schorling,
Pittsburgh 412 392 2000
Recommended in Employment

GOLD, Marc
Manko, Gold, Katcher & Fox LLP,
Bala Clynwyd 484 430 5700
Recommended in Environment

GOLDBERG, Donald
Ballard Spahr Andrews & Ingersoll LLP,
Philadelphia 215 665 8500
Recommended in Litigation

GOLDBERG, Richard
Ballard Spahr Andrews & Ingersoll LLP,
Philadelphia 215 665 8500
Recommended in Real Estate

GOODMAN, Harold
Raynes, McCarty, Binder, Ross & Mundy,
Philadelphia 215 568 6190
Recommended in Employment

GOODMAN, Stephen
Morgan, Lewis & Bockius LLP,
Philadelphia 215 963 5000
Recommended in Corporate/M&A

GORDON, George
Dechert, Philadelphia 215 994 4000
Recommended in Antitrust

GUNDERSEN, Glenn
Dechert, Philadelphia 215 994 4000
Recommended in Intellectual Property

HANGLEY, William
Hangley, Aronchick, Segal & Pudlin,
Philadelphia 215 568 6200
Recommended in Litigation

HARKINS, John
Harkins Cunningham, Philadelphia
215 851 6701
Recommended in Litigation

HARMELIN, Stephen
Dilworth Paxson LLP, Philadelphia
215 575 7000
Recommended in Corporate/M&A

HARPER, Robert
Klett Rooney Lieber & Schorling,
Pittsburgh 412 392 2000
Recommended in Corporate/M&A

HARTLE MUNSCH, Martha
Reed Smith LLP, Pittsburgh
412 288 3131
Recommended in Employment

HEIDELBERGER, Louis
Reed Smith LLP, Philadelphia
215 851 8100
Recommended in Intellectual Property

HEIM, Robert
Dechert, Philadelphia 215 994 4000
Recommended in Litigation

HEIST, Dale
Woodcock Washburn, Philadelphia
215 568 3100
Recommended in Intellectual Property

HERYFORD, Craig
Klett Rooney Lieber & Schorling,
Pittsburgh 412 392 2000
Recommended in Banking & Finance

HORNAK, Mark
Buchanan Ingersoll, Pittsburgh
412 562 8800
Recommended in Employment

HORSTMANN, John
Duane Morris LLP, Philadelphia
215 979 1000
Recommended in Banking & Finance, Insolvency

JACOBS-MEADWAY, Roberta
Ballard Spahr Andrews & Ingersoll LLP,
Philadelphia 215 665 8500
Recommended in Intellectual Property

JARIN, Kenneth
Ballard Spahr Andrews & Ingersoll LLP,
Philadelphia 215 665 8500
Recommended in Employment

JENNINGS, Tom
Jennings Sigmond, Philadelphia
215 351 0624
Recommended in Employment

JONES, Richard
Dechert, Philadelphia 215 994 4000
Recommended in Real Estate

JORDAN, Stephen
Rothman Gordon P.C, Pittsburgh
412 338 1100
Recommended in Employment

KESSLER, Mark
Wolf, Block, Schorr and Solis-Cohen LLP,
Philadelphia 215 977 2576
mkessler@wolfblock.com
Recommended in Corporate/M&A
Specialization: Partner in the Corporate/Securities Practice Group and a noted corporate and securities lawyer whose areas of practice include corporate and securities counseling, with emphasis on mergers, acquisitions and public and private financing, including leveraged financing transactions. Clients include: Comcast Corp., Toll Brothers, Inc., Legg Mason Wood Walker, Inc., Franklin Mutual Series Fund Inc., AHP Settlement Trust.
Prof. Memberships: Member, American Law Institute, Philadelphia and American Bar Associations. Serves on American Bar Association's Committee on Regulation of Securities, and served as chairman of the Philadelphia Bar Association's Section of Corporation, Banking and Business Law and the Committee on Securities Regulation. Named by the National Law Journal as a leading figure in the national securities bar.
Career: Admitted to Pennsylvania Bar (1961). Director and former national President of Big Brothers/Big Sisters of America. Member, Board of Directors of Arcadia University. Served as a member of: Board of Trustees of the Albert Einstein Medical Center, the Federation of Jewish Agencies of Greater Philadelphia, and St. Peter's School. Served as President of Jewish Family Service of Philadelphia.
Personal: Received BA from Brown University (1957) and JD from University of Pennsylvania (1960). Clerked for a Pennsylvania Supreme Court Justice and served as Assistant to a Commissioner of the United States Securities and Exchange Commission.

KLEBAN, Barry
Adelman Lavine Gold & Levin,
Philadelphia 215 568 7515
Recommended in Insolvency

KLEIN, Justin
Ballard Spahr Andrews & Ingersoll LLP,
Philadelphia 215 665 8500
Recommended in Corporate/M&A

KLETT, Edwin
Klett Rooney Lieber & Schorling,
Philadelphia 215 567 7500
Recommended in Litigation

LEADERS
PENNSYLVANIA

KOHN, Joseph
Kohn Swift & Graf, Philadelphia
215 238 1700
Recommended in Antitrust

KUSHNER, Louis
Rothman Gordon P.C, Pittsburgh
412 338 1100
Recommended in Employment

KUTLER, Marilyn
Schnader Harrison Segal & Lewis LLP, Philadelphia 215 751 2000
Recommended in Real Estate

KYPER, James
Kirkpatrick & Lockhart LLP, Pittsburgh
412 355 6500
Recommended in Intellectual Property

LADOV, Donald
Cohen & Grigsby, PC, Pittsburgh
412 297 4905
dladov@cohenlaw.com
Recommended in Employment
Specialization: Is a labor lawyer exclusively representing management in all areas of labor/employment law both in the private and public sectors. He has regularly practiced before the National Labor Relations Board, the Equal Employment Opportunity Commission, the Occupational Safety and Health Administration, the US Department of Labor, the Office of Federal Contract Compliance and many other regulatory agencies. Is also a prolific speaker on a wide variety of topics involving human resources and labor and employment law.
Career: BA, Labor Studies, Pennsylvania State University, 1970. JD, University of Pittsburgh School of Law, 1973. Admitted to practice in Pennsylvania, 1973.

LANE, Robert
Morgan, Lewis & Bockius LLP, Philadelphia 215 963 5000
Recommended in Real Estate

LAPOWSKY, Robert
Stevens & Lee A Professional Corporation, Philadelphia
215 575 0100
Recommended in Insolvency

LAUPHEIMER, Ann Blair
Blank Rome Comisky & McCauley LLP, Philadelphia 215 569 5500
Recommended in Litigation

LESSER, Bruce
Wolf, Block, Schorr and Solis-Cohen LLP, Philadelphia 215 977 2000
blesser@wolfblock.com
Recommended in Banking & Finance
Specialization: Co-Chairman of the Financial Services Department and member of the firm's Corporate/Securities Practice Group. Concentrates his practice in the representation of lenders and borrowers in the structuring and documentation of senior, subordinate, debtor in possession and mezzanine financing transactions and in related cred-

itor's rights matters. Additional concentration in bankruptcy and business law.
Prof. Memberships: Member, Pennsylvania Bar Association, Section on Corporation, Banking and Business Law, and the American and Philadelphia Bar Associations.
Career: Admitted to the Pennsylvania Bar (1973). Graduated Villanova School of Law (1973). Member of Law review and Order of the Coif.
Personal: Received his BA from Pennsylvania State University (1969) and his JD from Villanova University (1973).

LIEBENBERG, Roberta
Fine Kaplan & Black, Philadelphia
215 567 6565
rliebenberg@finekaplan.com
Recommended in Antitrust
Prof. Memberships: The American Law Institute; American Bar Association - Litigation Section, Former Co-Chair Class Actions and Derivatives Suits Committee; House of Delegates; Special Advisor Commission on Women in the Profession; Pennsylvania Bar Association - Board of Governors; House of Delegates, Philadelphia Bar Association, Former Chair, Anit-trust Committee.
Career: 2000-present, partner, *Fine, Kaplan & Black*, RPC; 1992-00, Founding partner, *Mager Liebenberg & White* (first female-owned litigation firm in Philadelphia); 1984-92, partner, *Wolf, Block, Schorr and Solis-Cohen*; 1978-92. Associate, *Wolf, Block, Schorr and Solis-Cohen*; law clerk, United States Court of Appeals for the Fourth Circuit.
Publications: 'Anti-trust, Where Are We in 2002?'; Pennsylvania Bar Institute; Speaker, 6th Annual National Class Action Institute, 'New Strategic and Ethical Challenges for Class Counsel', May, 2001 ABA Section of Litigation, 'The Court's Application of Daubert to Proposed Expert Testimony in Anti-trust Cases'.
Personal: Married to Dr Robert Liebenberg; three children - Julie, Katie and David.

LILLIE, Charisse
Ballard Spahr Andrews & Ingersoll LLP, Philadelphia 215 665 8500
Recommended in Employment

LINDEFJELD, Robert
Jones Day, Pittsburgh 412 394 7952
rlindefjeld@jonesday.com
Recommended in Intellectual Property
Specialization: Practises patent, copyright, trademark, trade secrets, and unfair competition law and has been involved in litigation, transactional, opinion, counseling, or appellate work in each of these areas. Has extensive experience in infringement and trade secret litigation in state and federal courts, including the US International Trade Commission under Section 337 of the Tariff Act of

1930, and general business and commercial litigation and appeals. Has also drafted confidentiality, technology transfer, and license agreements involving a wide variety of intellectual property interests, including computer software, mechanical, and the chemical arts. Responsible for preparing and prosecuting patent and trademark applications before the US Patent and Trademark Office.
Prof. Memberships: National council of the American Bar Association's Section of Intellectual Property Law; chaired the section's Continuing Legal Education and the Patent Contracts Other Than Government Committees and the special committee that organized a number of ABA seminars around the US entitled 'Practical Tips On Patent Litigation'; American Intellectual Property Law Association, where he serves as a member of the Professional Programs Committee, past chair of the Pennsylvania Bar Association's Section of Intellectual Property Law; Pennsylvania Bar Institute Intellectual Property Advisory Committee and the Pittsburgh Intellectual Property Law Association, where he serves as secretary/treasurer and has chaired the Professional Programs, Public Relations, and Writing Award Committees; Pennsylvania Bar Association House of Delegates, representing Allegheny County along with other Zone 12 delegates.
Career: Admitted 1994 Pennsylvania; 1994 District of Columbia; registered 1995 to practise before the US Patent and Trademark Office. Law Clerk to Judge Joseph F Weis Jr, US Court of Appeals, Third Circuit (1993-1995). Joined firm 1995.
Publications: Has written and lectured on all aspects of intellectual property law.
Personal: Norwich University, Military College of Vermont (BS in Biology 1986); Widener University (Editor in Chief, Law Review; JD 1993). Fluent in German.

LIPMAN, Frederick
Blank Rome Comisky & McCauley LLP, Philadelphia 215 569 5500
Recommended in Corporate/M&A

LONDON, Alan
Reed Smith LLP, Pittsburgh
412 288 3131
Recommended in Banking & Finance

LORD, Craig
Blank Rome Comisky & McCauley LLP, Philadelphia 215 569 5500
Recommended in Real Estate

LYNCHESKI, John
Cohen & Grigsby, PC, Pittsburgh
800 394 4904
Recommended in Employment

MACK, Wayne
Duane Morris LLP, Philadelphia
215 979 1000
Recommended in Antitrust

MANDELBAUM, David
Ballard Spahr Andrews & Ingersoll LLP, Philadelphia 215 665 8500
Recommended in Environment

MANKO, Joe
Manko, Gold, Katcher & Fox LLP, Bala Clynwyd 484 430 5700
Recommended in Environment

MANNINO, Edward
Akin Gump Strauss Hauer & Feld LLP, Philadelphia 215 965 1200
Recommended in Litigation

MARION, David
Montgomery, McCracken, Walker & Rhoads, LLP, Philadelphia
215 772 1500
Recommended in Litigation

MARSHALL, John
Drinker Biddle & Reath LLP, Berwyn
610 993 2210
Recommended in Intellectual Property

MATHER, Barbara
Pepper Hamilton LLP, Philadelphia
215 981 4000
Recommended in Antitrust, Litigation

MCCLENAHAN, David
Kirkpatrick & Lockhart LLP, Pittsburgh
412 355 6500
Recommended in Litigation

MCGOUGH, Thomas
Reed Smith LLP, Pittsburgh
412 288 3131
Recommended in Litigation

MCLEAN, Michael
Kirkpatrick & Lockhart LLP, Pittsburgh
412 355 6500
Recommended in Corporate/M&A

MCMICHAEL, Lawrence
Dilworth Paxson LLP, Philadelphia
215 575 7000
Recommended in Insolvency

MCNICHOL, William
Reed Smith LLP, Philadelphia
215 851 8100
Recommended in Intellectual Property

MILLER, Henry
Wolf, Block, Schorr and Solis-Cohen LLP, Philadelphia 215 977 2000
hmiller@wolfblock.com
Recommended in Real Estate
Specialization: Partner in the Real Estate Practice Group with more than 30 years experience in real estate. Areas of expertise include representing developers of shopping centers and major high-rise office buildings. Has had extensive experience in representing real estate brokers, REIT's and developers of industrial buildings and industrial parks.
Prof. Memberships: Admitted to the Pennsylvania Bar (1965). Member, American, Pennsylvania and Philadelphia Bar Associations. Served as been Chairman of the Committee on Real Estate

PENNSYLVANIA

LEADERS

Law of the Philadelphia Bar Association. Member, American College of Real Estate Lawyers.
Career: Joined the firm in 1964 and became a partner in 1971. Served as a member of the firm's Executive Committee. Listed in leading US and Global publications as a leading lawyer.
Personal: Received his AB, with Honors, from Lafayette College (1959) and his LLB, cum laude, from the University of Pennsylvania (1963). Law clerk to the Honorable Edwin D Steel, US District Court of Delaware (1963-1965). Has been a member of the board and solicitor of the Association for Jewish Children of Philadelphia; former President and is a board member of the Jewish Family and Children's Agency of Philadelphia; a board member of the Philadelphia Commercial Development Corporation; and former President and is a member of the Advisory Board of Big Brothers/Big Sisters Association of Philadelphia. He also has been a member of the Board of Directors of Philadelphia Child Guidance Clinic.

MITCHELL, Caroline
Law Offices of Caroline Mitchell, Pittsburgh 412 232 3131
Recommended in Employment

MONACO, Daniel
Drinker Biddle & Reath LLP, Philadelphia 215 988 2700
Recommended in Intellectual Property

MONTAGUE, Laddie
Berger & Montague, Philadelphia 215 875 3000
Recommended in Antitrust

MURRAY, William
Duane Morris LLP, Philadelphia 215 979 1000
Recommended in Intellectual Property

MURTAGH, John
Murtagh & Cahill, Wexford 412 935 7555
Recommended in Employment

MYERS, Marlee
Morgan, Lewis & Bockius LLP, Pittsburgh 412 560 3300
Recommended in Corporate/M&A

NADEL, Alan
Akin Gump Strauss Hauer & Feld LLP, Philadelphia 215 965 1200
Recommended in Intellectual Property

NAUGLE, Louis
Reed Smith LLP, Pittsburgh 412 288 3131
Recommended in Environment

NEWELL, Francis
Montgomery, McCracken, Walker & Rhoads, LLP, Philadelphia 215 772 1500
Recommended in Antitrust

NEWLIN, William
Buchanan Ingersoll, Pittsburgh 412 562 8800
Recommended in Corporate/M&A

O'BRIEN, William
Conrad O'Brien Gellman & Rohn, PC, Philadelphia 215 864 9600
Recommended in Litigation

OLSON, Stephen
Kirkpatrick & Lockhart LLP, Pittsburgh 412 355 6500
Recommended in Employment

OMINSKY, Harris
Blank Rome Comisky & McCauley LLP, Philadelphia 215 569 5500
Recommended in Real Estate

OUTWATER, Lynn
Jackson Lewis, Pittsburgh 412 232 0404
Recommended in Employment

PANITCH, Ronald
Akin Gump Strauss Hauer & Feld LLP, Philadelphia 215 965 1200
Recommended in Intellectual Property

PASS, Joseph
Jubelirer, Pass & Intrieri, Pittsburgh
No Number
Recommended in Employment

PIERCE, Patricia
Willig, Williams & Davidson, Philadelphia 215 656 3600
Recommended in Employment

POKOTILOW, Manny
Caesar, Rivise, Bernstein, Cohen & Pokotilow Ltd, Philadelphia 215 567 2010
Recommended in Intellectual Property

PRESTIA, Paul
Ratner & Prestia, Valley Forge 610 993 4204
Recommended in Intellectual Property

PRIMAVERA, Carl
Klehr Harrison Harvey Branzberg & Ellers LLP, Philadelphia 215 568 6060
Recommended in Real Estate

RACKOW, Julian
Blank Rome Comisky & McCauley LLP, Philadelphia 215 569 5500
Recommended in Real Estate

REED, Margery
Duane Morris LLP, Philadelphia 215 979 1000
Recommended in Banking & Finance

REED, Michael
Pepper Hamilton LLP, Philadelphia 215 981 4000
Recommended in Insolvency

REICH, Abraham
Fox Rothschild O'Brien & Frankel LLP, Philadelphia 215 299 2000
Recommended in Litigation

RESTIVO, James
Reed Smith LLP, Pittsburgh 412 288 3131
Recommended in Litigation

RICHMAN, Hershel
Dechert, Philadelphia 215 994 4000
Recommended in Environment

ROCCI, Stephen
Woodcock Washburn, Philadelphia 215 568 3100
Recommended in Intellectual Property

ROTWITT, Jeffrey
Obermayer, Rebmann, Maxwell & Hippel LLP, Philadelphia 215 665 3000
Recommended in Real Estate

SAINT-ANTOINE, Paul
Drinker Biddle & Reath LLP, Philadelphia 215 988 2700
Recommended in Antitrust

SCHER, Howard
Buchanan Ingersoll, Pittsburgh 412 562 8800
Recommended in Litigation

SCHORLING, William
Klett Rooney Lieber & Schorling, Pittsburgh 412 392 2000
Recommended in Insolvency

SEIDEL, Arthur
Drinker Biddle & Reath LLP, Philadelphia 215 988 2700
Recommended in Intellectual Property

SHAPIRO, Raymond
Blank Rome Comisky & McCauley LLP, Philadelphia 215 569 5500
Recommended in Insolvency

SHIEKMAN, Laurence
Pepper Hamilton LLP, Philadelphia 215 981 4000
Recommended in Antitrust

SHUTER, Bruce
Drinker Biddle & Reath LLP, Philadelphia 215 988 2700
Recommended in Banking & Finance

SINGER, Alan
Morgan, Lewis & Bockius LLP, Philadelphia 215 963 5000
Recommended in Corporate/M&A

SINGER, Paul
Reed Smith LLP, Pittsburgh 412 288 3131
Recommended in Insolvency

SKLAROFF, Mike
Ballard Spahr Andrews & Ingersoll LLP, Philadelphia 215 665 8500
Recommended in Real Estate

SNYDER, W Henry
Kirkpatrick & Lockhart LLP, Pittsburgh 412 355 6500
Recommended in Corporate/M&A

SONNENFELD, Marc
Morgan, Lewis & Bockius LLP, Philadelphia 215 963 5000
Recommended in Litigation

SPEAR, Samuel
Spear, Wilderman, Borish, Endy, Spear & Runckel, Philadelphia 215 732 0101
Recommended in Employment

SPRAGUE, Richard
Sprague & Sprague, Philadelphia 215 561 7681
Recommended in Litigation

SPRINGER, Claudia
Reed Smith LLP, Philadelphia 215 851 8100
Recommended in Insolvency

STACK, Stephen
Dechert, Philadelphia 215 994 4000
Recommended in Antitrust

STERN, Eric
Morgan, Lewis & Bockius LLP, Philadelphia 215 963 5000
Recommended in Real Estate

STERN, Joan
Blank Rome Comisky & McCauley LLP, Philadelphia 215 569 5500
Recommended in Banking & Finance

STOVER, Hayes
Kirkpatrick & Lockhart LLP, Pittsburgh 412 355 6500
Recommended in Employment

SUPLEE, Dennis
Schnader Harrison Segal & Lewis LLP, Philadelphia 215 751 2000
Recommended in Litigation

SWIRSKY, Sherry
Schnader Harrison Segal & Lewis LLP, Philadelphia 215 751 2000
Recommended in Antitrust

SYKES, David
Duane Morris LLP, Philadelphia 215 979 1000
Recommended in Insolvency

TABACHNICK, Gene
Reed Smith LLP, Pittsburgh 412 288 3131
Recommended in Intellectual Property

TATE, Joseph
Dechert, Philadelphia 215 994 4000
Recommended in Antitrust, Litigation

TEMIN, Michael
Wolf, Block, Schorr and Solis-Cohen LLP, Philadelphia 215 977 2000
mtemin@wolfblock.com
Recommended in Insolvency
Specialization: Partner, Business Litigation and Financial Services Practice Groups. Deals extensively with problems and opportunities created by business insolvencies, representing debtors, creditors, committees and others participating in the restructuring of insolvent businesses.
Prof. Memberships: Served as an Adjunct Professor at the University of Pennsylvania Law School (ten+ years). Was Chairman of the Eastern District of Pennsylvania Bankruptcy Conference;

Chair of the Rules Subcommittee and Vice-Chair of the Chapter 11 Subcommittee of the Business Bankruptcy Committee of the Business Law Section of the American Bar Association; and Chairman, Bankruptcy Committee of the Section of Corporation, Banking and Business Law of Pennsylvania and Philadelphia Bar Association. Was Chairman of the Section of Corporation, Banking and Business Law of the Philadelphia Bar Association, member of the Board of Governors of the Philadelphia Bar Association. Member, House of Delegates of Pennsylvania Bar Association. Served as Chairman of the Professional Guidance Committee of the Philadelphia Bar Association. He is a Regent of the American College of Bankruptcy and is listed in a leading American publication.
Career: Admitted to the Pennsylvania and Delaware Bars.
Personal: Received his BA, magna cum laude, from Yale University (1954) and his LLB, cum laude, from the University of Pennsylvania (1957).

THOMPSON, Thomas
Buchanan Ingersoll, Pittsburgh
412 562 8800
Recommended in Corporate/M&A

UBINGER JR, John
Jones Day, Pittsburgh 412 394 7908
jwubinger@jonesday.com
Recommended in Environment
Specialization: Co-ordinates the Environmental, Health & Safety practice in Pittsburgh. Since 1974, has had extensive experience in environmental law matters, including the application of environmental laws and regulations to routine business operations; the evaluation of environmental considerations in the purchase, sale, or financing of business assets and real property; the assessment and remediation of contaminated property; alternative dispute resolution strategies; and the litigation of environmental issues against regulatory agencies and private parties. Also counsels clients on strategies for the management or, in some cases, disposition of long-term environmental obligations through environmental risk transfer or 'exit strategy' transactions.
Career: Admitted 1973 Pennsylvania. Joined firm 1990.
Publications: Teaches a course on environmental dispute resolution in the environmental science and management master's degree program at Duquesne University. Has authored articles and frequently participates as a speaker on environmental law and environmental dispute resolution topics. His published work since 2000 includes: Uberinger, Jr. J. W. 'Alternative Dispute Resolution' Proceedings Of The Environmental Law Forum, March 2000, Vol. I (Pennsylvania Bar Institute, 2000); 'Dispute Resolution Strategies for Environmental Professionals: A Framework for Successful Outcomes' Course Book For Air & Waste Management Association Preconvention Course, (Air & Waste Management Association, 2000); Ubinger, Jr. J. W. 'Public Participation: Frim Solicitation of Public Comment Toward Solicitation of Public Involvement' Proceedings Of The Air & Waste Management Association Annual Convention And Exhibition, June 23-27, 2002, (Air & Waste Management Association, 2002).
Personal: Ohio University (BBA cum laude 1970); University of Notre Dame (JD 1973).

WALL, Steven
Morgan, Lewis & Bockius LLP,
Philadelphia 215 963 5000
Recommended in Employment

WARREN, Kenneth
Wolf, Block, Schorr and Solis-Cohen LLP,
Philadelphia 215 977 2000
kwarren@wolfblock.com
Recommended in Environment
Specialization: Partner and chair of the firm's Environmental Practice Group. Principal trial and appellate counsel for General Electric Company and liaison counsel for the Third-Party Plaintiffs in United States v Atlas Minerals & Chemicals, Inc., et al., a leading Superfund allocation case. Has handled numerous enforcement actions, citizen suits, environmental criminal prosecutions, insurance recovery cases, appeals of agency decisions, toxic tort actions, and other environmental cases in courts and tribunals throughout the United States. Has also represented numerous clients in a variety of environmental regulatory and transactional matters including site remediations, permitting, environmental aspects of real estate transactions, environmental management systems, and development of water quality standards and total maximum daily loads. Serves as outside general counsel to the Delaware River Basin Commission, a federal-interstate compact agency managing the water resources of the Delaware River Basin. Serves as an industry stakeholder representative on the National Environmental Justice Advisory Council, a formal federal advisory commitee of the United States Environmental Protection Agency.
Prof. Memberships: Serves as the Chair-Elect of the American Bar Association's Section of Environment, Energy, and Resources. Has previously served on the Section's Council and as a Section committee chair.
Career: Admitted to the Pennsylvania Bar (1980). Joined *Wolf, Block, Schorr and Solis-Cohen* in 1980 and became a partner in 1987.
Publications: Writes a regular column for The Legal Intelligencer on environmental law and is the author of numerous articles on environmental litigation published in journals such as BNA's Toxic Law Reporter, BNA's Environment Reporter and The Environmental Corporate Counsel Report. Author of a chapter in The Law of Environmental Justice.
Personal: Received his BA, magna cum laude, with honors in history, from Brown University (1975) and his JD, magna cum laude, from the University of Pennsylvania (1979). Served as an associate editor of the University of Pennsylvania Law Review. Served as a law clerk to the Honorable Joseph L McGlynn, Jr in the United States District Court for the Eastern District of Pennsylvania (1979-1980).

WEIN, Howard
Klett Rooney Lieber & Schorling,
Pittsburgh 412 392 2000
Recommended in Environment

WESTON, Timothy
Kirkpatrick & Lockhart LLP, Harrisburg
717 231 4500
Recommended in Environment

WETTACH, Thomas
Cohen & Grigsby, PC, Pittsburgh
800 394 4904
Recommended in Intellectual Property

WILLIAMS, Alaine
Willig, Williams & Davidson,
Philadelphia 215 656 3600
Recommended in Employment

WILLIG, Deborah
Willig, Williams & Davidson,
Philadelphia 215 656 3600
Recommended in Employment

WINOKUR, Barton
Dechert, Philadelphia 215 994 4000
Recommended in Corporate/M&A

WOELFLING, Maxine
Morgan, Lewis & Bockius LLP,
Harrisburg 717 237 4000
Recommended in Environment

WYCOFF, William
Thorp Reed & Armstrong, Pittsburgh
412 394 7711
Recommended in Litigation

YEAGER, Robert
Kirkpatrick & Lockhart LLP, Pittsburgh
412 355 6500
Recommended in Intellectual Property

ZONN, Sidney
Littler Mendelson PC, Pittsburgh
412 201 7600
Recommended in Employment

RHODE ISLAND   CORPORATE/M&A

CONTENTS: Corporate/M&A p.620; Employment: Mainly Plaintiff p.620; Mainly Defendant p.621; Litigation: General Commercial p.621; Real Estate p.622; Individuals' Profiles p.623.

RHODE ISLAND'S TOP TWO
1 Edwards & Angell
1 Hinckley, Allen & Snyder

Ranking based on Chambers' research within the state.

All quotes in the text are from interviews with clients and competitors.

OVERVIEW: Full-service firm **Edwards & Angell** houses approximately 300 attorneys across several offices along the US eastern seaboard. Commentators admired the firm's prowess in litigation and corporate law, noting niche strength in industrial and manufacturing trade secrets cases. The firm also rates highly for expertise in banking transactions. A highly respected corporate group acts for an impressive roster of national and international companies such as CVS, G-Tech and Textron.

Hinckley, Allen & Snyder, in joint first place, provides a comprehensive range of legal services from offices in Providence and Boston, MA. Market sources pointed to the firm's considerable profile in litigation matters. In keeping with the group's recognized niche in media law, Hinckley Allen recently handled precedent-setting litigation for a commercial television station. The firm also has an esteemed real estate practice with a strong reputation for environmental work, and a focus on development issues and real estate financing. A diverse client base includes a number of manufacturers, utilities, financial institutions and other regional, national and multinational entities.

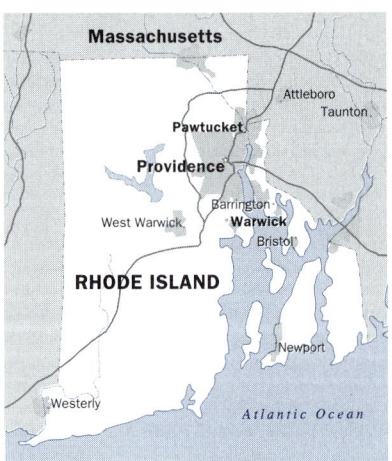

CORPORATE/M&A

RHODE ISLAND
Leading firms (Corporate/M&A)
1 EDWARDS & ANGELL, LLP *Providence*
2 HINCKLEY, ALLEN & SNYDER LLP *Providence*

Leading individuals (Corporate/M&A)
1 CARLOTTI Stephen *Hinckley, Allen & Snyder, Providence*
GRAHAM Christopher *Edwards & Angell, Providence*
2 DUFFELL David *Edwards & Angell LLP, Providence*
JOHNSON Duncan *Edwards & Angell LLP, Providence*
SKEFFINGTON James *Edwards & Angell, Providence*

Firms and individuals are listed alphabetically in each band.

Edwards & Angell, LLP
The Firm: The most highly rated corporate firm in the state. Praised by competitors as *"unavoidable: it is the largest firm and employs experts across the whole spectrum of work."* The team is active on foreign and domestic acquisitions, venture capital funds, company formations and disposals. It also benefits from the support of a highly regarded banking group. In the past year, the team has advised on general M&A and regulatory, securities and tax-related matters. The firm's multi-state setup gives it a large following, and is perhaps one reason why it is described as *"the number-one Rhode Island legal services provider."*

The Lawyers: The team is known for its *"quite excellent attorneys,"* and is thought to provide *"damn good training to its young lawyers."* Prominent among the attorneys is *"corporate star"* **Christopher Graham**. Well known among peers for his venture capital work, he recently advised an international specialty materials conglomerate in the acquisition and sale of business units. Observers also singled out **James Skeffington** as *"a top-flight lawyer carrying out international and regional work."* He is particularly well known for his drafting of legislation. The *"superb"* **Duncan Johnson** impresses with his knowledge of banking law, while **David Duffell**, who has represented a number of outside investors, is described by clients as *"one of the best lawyers you could ever hope to work with."*

The Clients: CVS; G-Tech; Textron and large international and regional corporates.

Hinckley, Allen & Snyder LLP
The Firm: Clients commend the corporate and commercial team for being *"in touch with the ebb and flow of the business world."* The group boasts a strong following, with experience in M&A, sales, recapitalizations and equity/debt securities offerings. The group also advises on venture capital financings, public offerings and regulatory matters involving stockholders and partnerships. The team's recent highlights include a number of high-profile restructurings in Rhode Island, including one for a company with assets valued at over $70 million.

The Lawyers: **Stephen Carlotti** is recognized among peers as *"the firm's luminary."* Clients appreciate his *"high level of experience – he understands the law on a practical level."* He is involved in transactions across the US, in industries ranging from jewelry companies to hi-tech matters. He also has a particular niche in insurance work.

The Clients: The firm's client base is drawn mainly from within New England, but does feature some large national and international names.

EMPLOYMENT & LABOR LAW   MAINLY PLAINTIFF

RHODE ISLAND
Leading firms
(Employment: Mainly Plaintiff)
1 RONEY & LABINGER *Providence*
SAVAGE & SAVAGE *Warwick*

Firms are listed alphabetically in each band.

Roney & Labinger
The Firm: This firm was endorsed by defendant attorneys as a major force in discrimination cases. It has handled a number of sensitive matters involving sex and obesity discrimination. The firm also has a particularly strong history of acting in disputes in the educational arena.

The Lawyers: Interviewees described **Lynette Labinger** as an *"absolutely excellent litigator –* *always a challenge to have on the other side."* She has been involved in a long-running case related to the Title IX mandate and the issue of peer harassment in educational institutions.

Savage & Savage
The Firm: This Warwick-based practice is regarded as one of *"the most highly competent in New England."* It handles a wide range of

EMPLOYMENT & LABOR LAW — RHODE ISLAND

RHODE ISLAND
Leading individuals
(Employment: Mainly Plaintiff)

1. ANDREWS Patricia *Sole Practitioner*, Providence
   GURSKY Marc *Sole Practitioner*, Providence
   LABINGER Lynette *Roney & Labinger*, Providence
   SAVAGE Robert *Savage & Savage*, Warwick

Individuals are listed alphabetically in each band.

employment work, including all types of discrimination claims, sexual harassment, fair employment practices and wrongful dismissal charges.
The Lawyers: Defendant attorneys respect **Robert Savage** as *"a hard-working lawyer, dedicated to his clients."* They singled out his prowess in discrimination litigation.

Other Notable Practitioners
Sole practitioner **Patricia Andrews** was described by market sources as an *"effective, smart and conscientious"* attorney. **Marc Gursky**, also a sole practitioner, is *"a talented litigator,"* best known for his experience in discrimination and workers' compensation matters.

EMPLOYMENT & LABOR LAW — MAINLY DEFENDANT

RHODE ISLAND
Leading firms
(Employment: Mainly Defendant)

1. ADLER POLLOCK & SHEEHAN PC *Providence*
   HOLLAND & KNIGHT LLP *Providence*
   PARTRIDGE SNOW & HAHN LLP *Providence*

Leading individuals
(Employment: Mainly Defendant)

1. BROOKS Robert *Adler Pollock & Sheehan*, Providence
   GAMBOLI Michael *Partridge Snow & Hahn*, Providence
   MCNAMARA Neal *Holland & Knight LLP*, Providence

Firms and individuals are listed alphabetically in each band.

Adler Pollock & Sheehan PC
The Firm: Competitors acknowledge the firm has *"a well-rounded team that offers experience in every quarter."* It represents private and public sector employers, both unionized and non-unionized. Attorneys have acted in federal and state litigation, administrative proceedings and arbitrations arising from discrimination cases and wrongful dismissal. As well as being skilled in labor issues, the firm has advised on collective bargaining and unfair labor practice charges. Commentators say that it has the capacity and knowledge to *"mount a firm defense against most claims."*
The Lawyers: **Robert Brooks** was described to researchers as *"the front runner in the field – he has a superb understanding of all labor issues."* Interviewees particularly commended his work on employment discrimination issues.
The Clients: The firm attracts large national corporates as well as locally based companies.

Holland & Knight LLP
see firm details p.820
The Firm: Peers endorsed the firm's *"top dollar"* employment advice. It counsels management on discrimination and equal opportunity matters, dealing with any contentious issues that arise and advising on personnel policies. Advice on collective bargaining agreements and union-related disputes also forms part of the agenda. Attorneys here have impressed with their *"deep understanding of the law"* and are experienced in handling cases such as wrongful dismissal allegations and whistle-blower matters.
The Lawyers: Highly respected **Neal McNamara** (see p.623) balances his employment advisory work with a strong litigation practice, which features race, gender and age discrimination claims.
The Clients: The Providence office of this large national firm advises both major national and international clients as well as Rhode Island-based entities.

Partridge Snow & Hahn LLP
The Firm: The *"excellent quality of advice"* offered by this firm's attorneys impressed interviewees. Lawyers here have significant experience in the use of mediation and arbitration to resolve disputes. The firm has also handled litigation in front of federal and state courts and various employment commissions. Although peers regard the firm's work on contentious issues as its forte, they also respect its capacity to handle general advisory and personnel policy formation work. The team also assists clients in aspects of non-compete agreements, employee benefits and healthcare and tax matters.
The Lawyers: **Mike Gamboli** cochairs this respected team. A skilled litigator, he is frequently seen handling high-profile discrimination matters.
The Clients: The firm attracts some of the state's largest employers.

LITIGATION — GENERAL COMMERCIAL

RHODE ISLAND
Leading firms
(Litigation: General Commercial)

1. EDWARDS & ANGELL LLP *Providence*
   HINCKLEY, ALLEN & SNYDER LLP *Providence*
2. ADLER POLLOCK & SHEEHAN PC *Providence*
   BLISH & CAVANAGH LLP *Providence*
3. DUFFY & SWEENEY LTD *Providence*
   PARTRIDGE SNOW & HAHN LLP *Providence*

Firms are listed alphabetically in each band.

Edwards & Angell LLP
The Firm: Interviewees regard this firm as *"a litigation powerhouse."* It handles commercial and contract disputes in such sectors as banking, media, environment, pharmaceutical and insurance. A leading force in healthcare cases, the firm also has a niche in trade secrets litigation, which involves various industries and manufacturing processes.
The Lawyers: This *"full-blooded team"* boasts a number of well-regarded names. Chief among them is **Mark Freel**, *"an excellent lawyer who runs the whole gamut of litigation."* He has been active in the past year for Transamerica in a class action concerning the constitutional nature of mortgage escrow procedures. Peers agree that **Mark Pogue** is *"busy on federal court cases."* He litigates in disputes drawn from a wide range of disciplines including commercial, employment and IP matters.
The Clients: Large Rhode Island-based companies and national entities are clients.

Hinckley, Allen & Snyder LLP
The Firm: The firm is respected by competitors and out-of-state practitioners for its ability to maintain a *"consistent level of excellence."* The team's expertise includes contracts, copyright and patent infringement, products liability and environmental issues. The firm has a particular niche in media cases, and has recently been involved in precedent-setting litigation for a commercial television station.
The Lawyers: Market commentators commend **Robert Corrente** for his *"good mind and expert touch – he has all the key requisites of an excellent commercial litigator."* He has acted in a commercial dispute between two companies in the jewelry trade, securing an $11.5 million award, which

RHODE ISLAND — LITIGATION

RHODE ISLAND
Leading individuals
(Litigation: General Commercial)

1
- **CAVANAGH Joseph** *Blish & Cavanagh,* Providence
- **CORRENTE Robert** *Hinckley, Allen & Snyder,* Providence
- **FREEL Mark** *Edwards & Angell LLP,* Providence
- **TARANTINO John** *Adler Pollock & Sheehan,* Providence

2
- **DUFFY Robert** *Duffy & Sweeney Ltd,* Providence
- **POGUE Mark** *Edwards & Angell LLP,* Providence
- **SNOW Stephen** *Partridge Snow & Hahn,* Providence

Individuals are listed alphabetically in each band.

was one of the largest payouts in the state in recent years. He is engaged in work throughout the US, particularly in New Jersey, Pennsylvania and Illinois.

The Clients: The group advises banks, manufacturing companies, utilities, venture capital groups and developers. Clients are based in Rhode Island and nationally.

Adler Pollock & Sheehan PC

The Firm: Regarded in the market as *"one of the major players in litigation."* The firm is active across a broad canvas of commercial litigation such as antitrust, trade regulations, securities, tort claims and construction law matters. It also has a strong employment litigation practice and is experienced in the insurance sector. Recent high-profile cases have been conducted in the healthcare sector.

The Lawyers: Commentators believe that *"nobody has had as good a year as* **John Tarantino.***"* In the past twelve months he has successfully defended the Rhode Island Secretary of State on a constitutional challenge by the Ethics Commission on his right to hold office. He successfully defended a city mayor's chief of staff, who was charged with federal bribery. Tarantino has also played a role in the high-profile lead paint case, in which the State of Rhode Island moved to declare lead paint a public nuisance; Tarantino was successful in representing former lead paint manufacturers.

The Clients: International manufacturers; chemical companies; railroads; IP companies; healthcare providers and real estate developers.

Blish & Cavanagh LLP

The Firm: This litigation boutique is regarded as *"one of the finest practices in Providence."* It is skilled in business litigation, antitrust, securities, environmental, real estate and insurance law. The team also has a well-developed media practice, and has represented newspapers, television stations and other media organizations on a range of First Amendment issues. The group's attorneys have undertaken extensive appellate work before the Rhode Island Supreme Court and the First Circuit Court of Appeals.

The Lawyers: Joseph Cavanagh is recommended by commentators as *"the finest trial lawyer in the state."* He is experienced in many areas, ranging from antitrust to medical malpractice, and was regarded as *"a truly safe pair of hands."*

The Clients: Commercial companies; media organizations; real estate developers and local and state government entities.

Duffy & Sweeney Ltd

The Firm: The activities of an international clientele have ensured the corporate group here its prominence in the state. Peers pointed to the firm's capacity to *"handle high-level commercial work;"* it is active in IP, securities, antitrust, stockholder, insurance, bankruptcy and general commercial work. The team recently acted for the former owner of a hi-tech company in litigation over a post-sale earn out. It also favorably resolved a stockholder dispute involving company valuation issues. Although a smaller practice than some competitors, it handles work in well over a dozen states.

The Lawyers: The *"intelligent, energetic and competitive"* **Robert Duffy** is the key name for the firm. He has recently tried and obtained injunctions in a variety of stockholder, unfair trade practices, trade secrets and unfair competition cases.

The Clients: The group handles work for large private and public companies.

Partridge Snow & Hahn LLP

The Firm: Peers recommend this litigation practice as *"a handy opponent."* Its focus lies in business litigation, and it has advised and litigated in construction matters, antitrust, unfair trade practices, banking and securities cases. The group is highly experienced in arbitration and alternative dispute resolution.

The Lawyers: Stephen Snow was described by commentators as *"one of the state's most experienced litigators."* He has been active in a number of high-profile civil cases, including a precedent-setting antitrust case involving two of Rhode Island's largest health insurance providers.

The Clients: Public and private businesses; financial institutions; colleges; universities; hospitals; insurance companies and government agencies.

REAL ESTATE

RHODE ISLAND
Leading firms (Real Estate)

1
- **HINCKLEY, ALLEN & SNYDER LLP** *Providence*

2
- **ADLER POLLOCK & SHEEHAN PC** *Providence*
- **EDWARDS & ANGELL LLP** *Providence*
- **HOLLAND & KNIGHT LLP** *Providence*

Leading individuals (Real Estate)

1
- **RUBIN David** *Hinckley, Allen & Snyder LLP,* Providence

2
- **BATTY Jerome** *Hinckley, Allen & Snyder,* Providence
- **MARCELLO Matthew** *Hinckley, Allen,* Providence
- **TRACY David** *Holland & Knight LLP,* Providence

Firms and individuals are listed alphabetically in each band.

Hinckley, Allen & Snyder LLP

The Firm: Competitors describe this firm as *"the lions of real estate law"* in Rhode Island. The practice has a strong focus on both development issues and real estate financing. On the transactional side, the team is active in the structuring of joint ventures, sale and leaseback transactions and governmental grant applications. It enjoys a respected profile for environmental work, and has advised at federal and state levels in air, water, hazardous waste and other land use issues.

The Lawyers: Researchers were impressed with the level of commendation for the team's individual members. Among them, **David Rubin** is described as *"a truly sharp lawyer,"* particularly experienced in real estate financing. The *"superb"* **Jerome Batty** has a strong following among New England developers while peers singled out **Matthew Marcello** for his *"sound judgment."*

The Clients: The firm advises major national, regional and local developers, banks and insurance companies.

Adler Pollock & Sheehan PC

The Firm: Peers identified the group as *"one of the major players for real estate work."* It is visible working for developers of projects such as residential property, industrial parks and shopping facilities. It has been active, of late, in the Capital Center Project in Providence, valued at $3 billion and involving five million sqft of real estate. The team has also advised a medical company on its purchase of numerous properties around Rhode Island, a transaction which incorporated zoning approval, construction, permit review and financing matters.

REAL ESTATE — RHODE ISLAND

The Lawyers: Joseph DiStefano handles major commercial property transactions for the firm.
The Clients: The group's client base comprises national and regional developers.

Edwards & Angell LLP
The Firm: The team earns praise from market observers for the *"all-round talent and commitment"* of its attorneys. It represents developers with interests as far afield as Florida and California, handling shopping center developments in the $30-100 million bracket. The group has also represented a major lender in connection with an apartment construction, and shopping center acquisition financing, worth in excess of $20 million. The group also has expertise in zoning and land use, having assisted in the drafting of a historic zoning ordinance.
The Lawyers: Charles Rogers is an experienced member of the real estate team.
The Clients: The firm represents developers, contractors and banks in New England and around the US.

Holland & Knight LLP
see firm details p.820
The Firm: Judged by market observers to enjoy a *"truly national reputation"* in development work, the firm is viewed as *"fast becoming a major competitor."* It is respected for its work in retail development, and has assisted clients with numerous shopping center projects over the past year, both in New England and beyond. Attorneys here also advise on the creation and the subsequent offerings made by REITs.
The Lawyers: David Tracy (see p.623) was described to researchers as *"one of the sharpest and most diligent lawyers around."* He has been active in retail and office development work.
The Clients: Large developers, often involved in retail projects are clients.

Leaders in Rhode Island

ANDREWS, Patricia
Patricia E Andrews - Sole Practitioner, Providence 401 421 0966
Recommended in Employment

BATTY, Jerome
Hinckley, Allen & Snyder LLP, Providence
401 274 2000
Recommended in Real Estate

BROOKS, Robert
Adler Pollock & Sheehan P.C.,
Providence 401 274 7200
Recommended in Employment

CARLOTTI, Stephen
Hinckley, Allen & Snyder LLP, Providence
401 274 2000
Recommended in Corporate/M&A

CAVANAGH, Joseph
Blish & Cavanagh, LLP, Providence
401 831 8900
Recommended in Litigation

CORRENTE, Robert
Hinckley, Allen & Snyder LLP, Providence
401 274 2000
Recommended in Litigation

DUFFELL, David
Edwards & Angell, LLP, Providence
401 274 9200
Recommended in Corporate/M&A

DUFFY, Robert
Duffy & Sweeney, Ltd, Providence
401 455 0700
Recommended in Litigation

FREEL, Mark
Edwards & Angell, LLP, Providence
401 274 9200
Recommended in Litigation

GAMBOLI, Michael
Partridge Snow & Hahn LLP, Providence
401 861 8200
Recommended in Employment

GRAHAM, Christopher
Edwards & Angell, LLP, Providence
401 274 9200
Recommended in Corporate/M&A

GURSKY, Marc
Marc Gursky - Sole Practitioner,
Providence 401 454 7400
Recommended in Employment

JOHNSON, Duncan
Edwards & Angell, LLP, Providence
401 274 9200
Recommended in Corporate/M&A

LABINGER, Lynette
Roney & Labinger, Providence
401 421 9794
Recommended in Employment

MARCELLO, Matthew
Hinckley, Allen & Snyder LLP, Providence
401 274 2000
Recommended in Real Estate

MCNAMARA, Neal
Holland & Knight LLP, Providence
401 751 8500
nmcnamara@hklaw.com
Recommended in Employment
Specialization: Partner in the Litigation Department, focusing on employment law, general commercial litigation, and land use. His employment law practice focuses on both litigation and counseling. He has successfully handled matters involving all major employment related statutes, including Title VII, the ADA, FMLA, ADEA and ERISA, as well as state law employment issues, including non-compete agreements. A major portion of his practice is devoted to counseling clients on a wide range of employee issues in order to prevent matters from reaching litigation. He has developed employment handbooks and policies, conducted internal investigations and also regularly conducts seminars on employment law topics. He has appeared before many Zoning Boards, Planning Boards and Town Councils in Rhode Island regarding land use issues.

POGUE, Mark
Edwards & Angell, LLP, Providence
401 274 9200
Recommended in Litigation

RUBIN, David
Hinckley, Allen & Snyder LLP, Providence
401 274 2000
Recommended in Real Estate

SAVAGE, Robert
Savage & Savage, Warwick
401 732 9500
Recommended in Employment

SKEFFINGTON, James
Edwards & Angell, LLP, Providence
401 274 9200
Recommended in Corporate/M&A

SNOW, Stephen
Partridge Snow & Hahn LLP, Providence
401 861 8200
Recommended in Litigation

TARANTINO, John
Adler Pollock & Sheehan P.C.,
Providence 401 274 7200
Recommended in Litigation

TRACY, David
Holland & Knight LLP, Providence
401 751 8500
dtracy@hklaw.com
Recommended in Real Estate
Specialization: Partner in the Real Estate Department, concentrating his practice in the area of real estate law. His practice involves all areas and aspects of commercial real estate, with particular emphasis on malls, shopping centers, office and mixed use developments, commercial real estate, commercial leasing, condominiums, construction contracts, construction and permanent financing as well as debt restructuring. He represents numerous developers in the acquisition, development and sale of various types of commercial real estate including office buildings, shopping centers and other retail projects as well as lenders in the financing of such projects. He has also represented institutional investors in various Rhode Island and national real estate transactions. He has particular experience in commercial lease transactions and in title insurance issues.

SOUTH CAROLINA

CORPORATE/M&A

CONTENTS: Corporate/M&A p.624; Employment: Mainly Plaintiff p.625; Mainly Defendant p.625; Litigation: General Commercial p.626; Real Estate p.627; Individuals' Profiles p.628.

SOUTH CAROLINA'S TOP FOUR
1. Nexsen Pruet Jacobs & Pollard
1. Haynsworth Sinkler Boyd
2. McNair Law Firm
3. Nelson Mullins Riley & Scarborough

Ranking based on Chambers' research within the state.

All quotes in the text are from interviews with clients and competitors.

OVERVIEW: Nexsen Pruet Jacobs & Pollard has over 120 attorneys practicing from six offices across the Carolinas. The firm offers a full range of legal services and is highly regarded by market commentators in a number of fields. Corporate, litigation and real estate are all areas in which the firm is considered to shine, and Edward Menzie and Wilburn Brewer are the firm's star names. The business group was particularly distinguished for its effective banking section. Key clients of the practice include major financial institutions, insurance companies and manufacturers.

Created in 2001 by a merger between a Columbia and a Greenville firm, **Haynsworth Sinkler Boyd**, in joint first place, now boasts 125 attorneys in four offices across the state. Peers particularly commended the firm for its excellent corporate, litigation and real estate groups, observing noteworthy skill in securities, bonds and other public finance matters. In litigation, the firm was seen to have niche strength in accounting cases. The firm acts for clients across a range of industry sectors and regularly undertakes work for key client Sonoco.

Ranked second, the Columbia-based **McNair Law Firm** boasts widely admired corporate and real estate groups. The latter earns particular praise for its concentration of up-and-coming practitioners. Attorneys operate from nine offices throughout the Carolinas, advising local and national clients such as SCANA Corporation.

The largest firm in South Carolina, **Nelson Mullins Riley & Scarborough** secured a top-band ranking in litigation, in which the firm commands a high profile for major products liability cases. Technology is another focus area for the firm. Deriving support from additional offices in Georgia and North Carolina, the firm offers comprehensive legal advice to local, regional and national companies in all sectors.

CORPORATE/M&A

SOUTH CAROLINA
Leading firms (Corporate/M&A)
1. HAYNSWORTH SINKLER BOYD PA *Columbia*
   MCNAIR LAW FIRM PA *Columbia*
   NEXSEN PRUET JACOBS & POLLARD *Columbia*
2. NELSON MULLINS RILEY *Columbia*
   WYCHE, BURGESS, FREEMAN & PARHAM *Greenville*

Leading individuals (Corporate/M&A)
1. CURRIE John *McNair Law Firm PA, Columbia*
   KING George *Haynsworth Sinkler Boyd PA, Charleston*
   MENZIE Edward *Nexsen Pruet Jacobs, Columbia*
2. BLAKE Joseph *Haynsworth Sinkler Boyd PA, Greenville*
   BOYD William *Haynsworth Sinkler Boyd, Columbia*
   HALL Cary *Wyche, Burgess, Freeman, Greenville*
   KNIGHT Marcus *Nexsen Pruet Jacobs, Columbia*
   MUSSER William *McNair Law Firm PA, Columbia*
   SHOEMAKER James *Wyche, Burgess, Greenville*
   WARREN John *Warren & Sinkler, LLP, Charleston*

Firms and individuals are listed alphabetically in each band.

Haynsworth Sinkler Boyd PA
The Firm: This firm was formed in January 2001 following the merger of Columbia-based Sinkler & Boyd with Haynsworth, Marion, McKay & Guérard from Greenville. Interviewees emphasized the Columbia contingent as being primarily responsible for the corporate group's high profile. Its practice is equally split between transactional and litigious advice, while strength also lies in corporate, securities and public finance matters, including bond issuance.

The Lawyers: **George King** was consistently mentioned when interviewees were asked to give their recommendations. He is seen as being particularly active in the banking sector. **Joseph Blake**, who also holds a management position at the firm, was commended as a *"leading light"* and is often seen acting in healthcare sector M&A. **William Boyd** was singled out to researchers as a key M&A lawyer. In addition to his corporate activity, he has recently been involved in substantial real estate deals.

The Clients: The firm is well known for acting for the likes of Hartsville-based manufacturing company Sonoco. It has also attracted leading clients in the leading telecom, chemical, pharmaceutical, defense, energy and insurance sectors.

McNair Law Firm PA
The Firm: One of the first significant corporate commercial practices established in the state, the firm is named after its founder, a former governor of South Carolina. Peers and clients largely believe that the firm has stood the test of time and developed a broad corporate/commercial practice. It typically advises financial institutions on the sale of assets and the raising of equity capital, and is also heavily involved in municipal finance work. Advice on medium-term note programs and credit lines also contributes to the workload. One of the largest firms in the state, it is based in Columbia and has six other offices in the state and two in North Carolina.

The Lawyers: **John Currie** is credited with having built a *"substantial practice"* at the firm. Peers rate him as *"one of the best lawyers in the state, with the most deal experience."* **William Musser** was commended for his bonds expertise and his heavy involvement in municipal finance.

The Clients: SCANA Corporation, financial institutions and public companies are clients.

Nexsen Pruet Jacobs & Pollard LLC
The Firm: Clients describe the firm as possessing the *"best business group all round."* M&A has accounted for approximately half its workload in recent years, with securities and general corporate governance issues completing the picture. Its strength in the banking sector is widely affirmed by market sources. The Columbia-based team cooperates with lawyers in the firm's Charleston, Greenville, Hilton Head Island and Myrtle Beach offices as necessary. Its client following is so broadly spread that the firm also has an office in Charlotte, North Carolina.

The Lawyers: **Edward Menzie** divides his time between heading the firm's real estate operation and working in corporate M&A. **Marcus Knight** heads a corporate M&A team of five other lawyers in Columbia. Clients praised his *"excellent negotiation skills,"* and his experience acting as local counsel in nationwide deals.

The Clients: Private companies in the distribution, manufacturing, technology, financial, telecom and construction sectors, and restaurant chains are clients.

Nelson Mullins Riley & Scarborough LLP
see firm details p.857

The Firm: There was a strong consensus that the heart of this firm's corporate commercial practice lies in Atlanta. However, with offices in Columbia, Charleston and Greenville in South Carolina, interviewees widely acknowledged the firm's local impact. Its corporate workload

SOUTH CAROLINA

EMPLOYMENT & LABOR LAW

includes venture capital financings, M&A and stock issuance in the telecom and technology sectors, and for healthcare providers and financial institutions.

The Lawyers: Securities attorney Gus Dixon is a key contact in the firm's corporate group.

The Clients: The firm focuses on the technology sector and also acts for several public companies based in the state. Other clients include: Fortune 500 companies and international corporations; regional underwriters; investment banks; financial institutions; healthcare organizations and automotive and textile manufacturers.

Wyche, Burgess, Freeman & Parham PA

The Firm: Peers described the firm as home to a host of *"inspired Ivy League lawyers of the highest caliber."* Interviewees cited corporate finance as being its traditional forte. The firm advises on M&A, joint ventures, securities issues and corporate governance as well as on the related areas of tax and employment matters. The firm was thought to dominate the Greenville market.

The Lawyers: James Shoemaker was highlighted by peers as the outstanding senior figure in the team, and described him as a *"fabulous lawyer."* They also rated **Cary Hall** as a *"great technician."* He divides his time equally between tax matters, in which he is a certified specialist, and corporate M&A. Hall recently advised The South Financial Group in acquiring banks based in South Carolina and Florida and a South Carolina insurance company.

The Clients: Cisco Systems; AVX; Bowater; Delta Woodside Industries; GM; Marzoli International; Michelin North America; Milliken & Company; Pfizer and Chubb Group.

Other Notable Practitioners

John Warren of Warren & Sinkler, LLP was described to researchers as *"an absolutely excellent lawyer, up there with the best in the state."* His practice is equally divided between local and national entities, and he has experience acting on transactions throughout the US and Canada. Banking, insurance, oil and gas and aerospace sector corporations feature among his clientele.

EMPLOYMENT & LABOR LAW — MAINLY PLAINTIFF

SOUTH CAROLINA
Leading firms
(Employment: Mainly Plaintiff)
1. THE LOUTHIAN LAW FIRM PA *Columbia*

Leading individuals
(Employment: Mainly Plaintiff)
1. BURNETTE Malissa *Burnette & Leclair PA,* Columbia
   CROMER Lewis *Cromer & Mabry,* Columbia
   LOUTHIAN JR Herbert *The Louthian Law Firm,* Columbia
   LOUTHIAN SR Herbert *The Louthian Law Firm,* Columbia

Firms and individuals are listed alphabetically in each band.

The Louthian Law Firm PA

The Firm: The firm has an excellent profile based on the high regard in which its two partners are held. **Herbert Louthian Sr** was described as *"a great trial lawyer"* by peers in the sector. **Herbert Louthian Jr** is also considered a prominent labor and employment practitioner, especially with regard to workers' compensation.

Other Notable Practitioners

Malissa Burnette of Burnette & Leclair PA in Columbia received commendations as an *"outstanding litigator."* She is noted for her niche expertise in academic employment. **Lewis Cromer** of Cromer & Mabry is well known for his involvement in high-profile employment cases, predominantly against state agencies as well as large corporations. Typically he represents public employees in whistle-blower and protected class discrimination matters. He also does a portion of defense work on behalf of the County of Richland, EduTek Education Solutions and WLTX-TV.

EMPLOYMENT & LABOR LAW — MAINLY DEFENDANT

SOUTH CAROLINA
Leading firms
(Employment: Mainly Defendant)
1. HAYNSWORTH BALDWIN JOHNSON *Greenville*
   OGLETREE, DEAKINS, NASH, SMOAK *Greenville*
2. ELLZEY & BROOKS LLC *Columbia*
3. GIGNILLIAT, SAVITZ & BETTIS LLP *Columbia*
   NELSON MULLINS RILEY *Columbia*
   NEXSEN PRUET JACOBS & POLLARD *Columbia*

Leading individuals
(Employment: Mainly Defendant)
1. PEARSON Jonathan *Ellzey & Brooks LLC,* Columbia
   SPETH Charles *Haynsworth Baldwin,* Columbia

Firms and individuals are listed alphabetically in each band.

Haynsworth Baldwin Johnson & Greaves LLC

The Firm: Market observers cite this firm as one of the top labor and employment practices in the state. The highest praise was reserved for its expertise in labor law, in which the firm advises on NLRA matters, union issues and negotiations, and unfair labor practices. Associated expertise in immigration, civil rights, health and safety, and workers' compensation was also noted. Its stronghold is considered to be the Greenville base, which is supported by a network of offices in North Carolina, Georgia and Florida.

The Lawyers: Head of the Columbia office, **Charles Speth** is considered the firm's *"foremost litigator."* Interviewees also respect his *"depth of knowledge."*

The Clients: The team acts for clients in all industry sectors, including healthcare, retail and manufacturing, both local and national in scope. It is also experienced in acting for foreign-owned companies in international matters.

Ogletree, Deakins, Nash, Smoak & Stewart PC

The Firm: There was a consensus among clients that this firm is among the highest quality labor and employment firms in the state as well as one of the largest. It was deemed to benefit from a 14-office countrywide network for advice on national issues, while the Greenville office remains its stronghold in South Carolina. Employee benefits matters, immigration and health and safety law specialists support the core practice of discrimination litigation and general employment counseling.

The Lawyers: Market observers commended the 30-year labor law expertise of founder partner Lewis Smoak, while Hamilton Stewart and the team advise on preventative matters as well as employment and labor litigation.

SOUTH CAROLINA — LITIGATION

The Clients: FedEx Ground Package System; GE; Michelin North America; SCANA Corporation and Duke Energy.

Ellzey & Brooks LLC
The Firm: A relatively recent addition to the field, formed in 1997 by attorneys from Ogletree, Deakins, Nash, Smoak & Stewart and Constangy, Brooks & Smith. The firm is largely driven by its labor and employment practice, and has quickly carved out a reputation for the high quality of its work. It is engaged in advocacy before the NLRB, acts in discrimination litigation and offers advice on compliance issues. Small offices in Raleigh and Charlotte, NC and Atlanta, GA complement its Columbia base.
The Lawyers: Jonathan Pearson enjoys an outstanding reputation among peers, who respect his *"high integrity and sound judgment."*
The Clients: Dana; Federal-Mogul and Weyerhaeuser.

Gignilliat, Savitz & Bettis LLP
The Firm: This practice is devoted to labor and employment issues and represents medium to small-sized companies, many of which are in the public sector. It is weighted toward employment law and covers discrimination, breaches of contract, defamation and Section 1983 litigation relating to First Amendment rights.
The Lawyers: Both Vance Bettis and Stephen Savitz are key members of this well-respected and experienced team. The recent death of Julian Gignilliat is considered to have deprived the state of one of its leading labor and employment practitioners.
The Clients: While several large corporations feature in the client base, the general emphasis is on public sector companies.

Nelson Mullins Riley & Scarborough LLP
see firm details p.857
The Firm: Observers endorsed this well-respected employment practice, which sits as a key part of a full-service firm. Current matters include a case that began as a class action and has since become 100 individual race discrimination suits. The practice is also acting on a significant minimum wage appeal. Environmental, tax, ERISA and OSHA expertise also contribute to the core practice.
The Lawyers: Sue Erwin Harper leads the Columbia labor and employment practice. Discrimination and compliance issues form a substantial portion of her workload.
The Clients: The firm represents clients in a broad range of industries including transportation, healthcare, telecom, automotive and other manufacturing, retail, and securities broking. They include companies with operations throughout the Southeast as well as multinationals that have operations in the state.

Nexsen Pruet Jacobs & Pollard LLC
The Firm: Of the state's full-service firms, Nexsen Pruet possesses one of the larger labor and employment groups. The Columbia office focuses on employment law, which is also practiced at the firm's five other offices. In addition the firm has labor lawyers stationed in Greenville and Charleston. The practice incorporates all areas of employment law including litigation, employee handbooks, compliance issues, non-compete covenants and human resources matters.
The Lawyers: A team of 25 lawyers includes six certified specialists in labor and employment law. Victoria Eslinger, who is fluent in several European languages, is experienced in advising European corporations that have operations in the US. The team also advises several Japanese companies on employment matters. The Greenville office was bolstered in 2002 by the recruitment of former Ogletree Deakins partners, Ingrid Blackwelder Erwin and Grantland Burns.
The Clients: Domestic and international corporations.

LITIGATION — GENERAL COMMERCIAL

SOUTH CAROLINA
Leading firms
(Litigation: General Commercial)

1. **HAYNSWORTH SINKLER BOYD** Columbia, Charleston
   NELSON MULLINS RILEY Columbia
   NEXSEN PRUET JACOBS & POLLARD Columbia
2. **WYCHE, BURGESS, FREEMAN** Greenville
3. **BUIST, MOORE, SMYTHE & MCGEE PA** Charleston
   LEATHERWOOD WALKER TODD & MANN Greenville
   MCNAIR LAW FIRM PA Columbia
   YOUNG, CLEMENT, RIVERS & TISDALE Charleston

Leading individuals
(Litigation: General Commercial)

1. **BREWER Wilburn** Nexsen Pruet Jacobs, Columbia
   MORRISON Stephen Nelson Mullins Riley, Columbia
2. **DUKES David** Nelson Mullins Riley, Columbia
   LINTON John Haynsworth Sinkler Boyd, Charleston
   PARHAM James Wyche, Burgess, Freeman, Greenville
   TATE Simmons Haynsworth Sinkler Boyd, Columbia
   TISDALE Thomas Young, Clement, Rivers, Charleston
   YOUNG Rutledge Young, Clement, Rivers, Charleston
3. **CLEVELAND William** Buist, Moore, Smythe, Charleston
   LIGHTSEY Wallace Wyche, Burgess, Freeman, Greenville
   SOWELL Thornwell Sowell Gray Stepp, Columbia

Firms and individuals are listed alphabetically in each band.

Haynsworth Sinkler Boyd PA
The Firm: Interviewees said the caliber of its litigators meant that the firm's general commercial litigation practice would fit naturally among the upper echelons of the market. The team undertakes stockholder litigation, including class actions. It represents banks and financial institutions in lender liability litigation. Other areas of practice include antitrust and unfair trade practices, IP, real estate, business contract disputes and insurance. Complex products liability and asbestos cases that are national in scope also contribute to the workload.
The Lawyers: Columbia-based Simmons Tate is among the most senior litigators in the state. Peers continue to say that they would not hesitate to refer work to him. Charleston-based John Linton was commended to researchers for *"possessing great judgment."*
The Clients: The firm acts for clients such as Duke Energy and Ernst & Young. Commercial litigation in the accounting sector is a niche specialty.

Nelson Mullins Riley & Scarborough LLP
The Firm: Its position in the top three firms for commercial litigation was never in doubt; peers consistently referred to the firm as *"major competition."* Its outstanding products liability profile goes a long way toward establishing its top tier status. Complex multi-action litigation defense is also a central part of the practice.
The Lawyers: Interviewees agree that Stephen Morrison (see p.629) benefits from his in-house general counsel experience and is well connected with larger corporations. He was described by one peer as having *"always been a star - and he still is."* In addition to general commercial litigation, Morrison tackles technology, products liability and securities matters. David Dukes (see p.628), also managing partner at the firm, was commended as *"an extremely hard-working litigator."* His specialties include pharmaceutical and medical device claims and technology litigation. The number of other individual litigators mentioned to researchers indicated the team's considerable depth.
The Clients: Its client base is national, regional and local in scope, and features banks, regional and local brokerage firms, pharmaceutical

LITIGATION

SOUTH CAROLINA

and technology companies and automobile and aircraft manufacturers.

Nexsen Pruet Jacobs & Pollard LLC
The Firm: Interviewees considered the firm to offer *"the best possible all-around representation to clients."* A large team in Columbia wields *"considerable firepower"* from *"trial-savvy"* attorneys. Areas of practice include antitrust matters, construction, healthcare and insurance disputes, and products liability cases. The team is also experienced in mediation and arbitration proceedings.
The Lawyers: Peers praised **Wilburn Brewer** as *"really the best litigator in the state – strong across the board and analytically sound."* He heads the team, and has a specialist antitrust expertise that is echoed in the practice as a whole. Brewer is also well known for his niche legal malpractice claims.
The Clients: Financial institutions; lenders; insurance companies; manufacturers; service companies and electric cooperatives. A considerable number of the firm's clients are nationwide. It recently acted for timber owners throughout the South in an antitrust class action against International Paper.

Wyche, Burgess, Freeman & Parham PA
The Firm: Interviewees consistently referred to this team as a dominant force in commercial litigation in Greenville.
The Lawyers: Market sources pointed to **James Pareham** as a senior figure at the firm, who brings *"experience and a strong courtroom persona"* to his cases. Well-respected **Wallace Lightsey** was suggested to researchers as leading light of the future.
The Clients: The firm acts for corporations in the communication, technology, healthcare, insurance, manufacturing, venture capital and finance sectors.

Buist, Moore, Smythe & McGee PA
The Firm: Peers widely endorsed this group as an *"excellent litigation firm in Charleston."* The team covers such areas as construction, bankruptcy, healthcare and environmental matters. Unfair competition disputes and insurance coverage claims also form part of the workload.
The Lawyers: Interviewees praised **William Cleveland** (see p.628) as a *"smart individual and a talented litigator."* Cleveland heads the team, which includes eight commercial litigators. His specialist areas are securities and IP litigation, and his practice also includes some noncontentious matters.
The Clients: The team advises clients of the caliber of DuPont, and has attracted a following among pharmaceuticals and banks.

Leatherwood Walker Todd & Mann PC
The Firm: A highly respected team of 12 commercial litigators is in the Greenville office. Typical activity includes acting for business entities on contract disputes and providing administrative advice regarding regulatory, debt and antitrust matters.
The Lawyers: Harvey Sanders is a key member of the team and experienced in trade secrets cases.
The Clients: It acts for numerous clients outside the state though most are based in South Carolina itself. They include supermarket chains and insurance companies.

McNair Law Firm PA
The Firm: The firm is felt to possess an *"excellent litigation department"* that is well supported by an extensive network of offices throughout the state. Healthcare sector litigation accounts for a considerable portion of the workload. Much of this is connected with reimbursement disputes on behalf of healthcare providers. The firm also conducts general commercial litigation, including breaches of contract and products liability. Its key industry sectors include real estate, banking, construction and securities.
The Lawyers: The team, consisting of over 30 litigators across six offices, includes Celeste Jones in Columbia.
The Clients: It represents medical product manufacturers and healthcare providers (including hospitals) on a wide range of commercial disputes. These include regulatory work relating to Medicare and other third-party providers, licensing issues and quality of care matters. General commercial litigation clients include transport companies, manufacturers and developers.

Young, Clement, Rivers & Tisdale LLP
The Firm: This firm is said to possess *"exceptional litigators capable of doing the most sophisticated work."* Commercial litigation accounts for half its practice. The operation is based in Charleston, and supported by a Columbia office, with five commercial litigators in each.
The Lawyers: **Rutledge Young** is considered to be *"the true leader at the firm,"* according to market sources. **Thomas Tisdale**, chair of the commercial litigation team, was described as an *"excellent courtroom performer."* In addition to general commercial litigation, he covers niche areas such as IP and products liability litigation, and acts for a number of broadcasting industry clients.
The Clients: BellSouth; The Manitowoc Company; technology, telecom, broadcast media and manufacturing sector corporates. The firm also acts for several national and international corporations.

Other Notable Practitioners
Clients recommended **Thornwell Sowell** of Sowell Gray Stepp & Laffitte LLC in Columbia as an *"outstanding litigator who is retained for the largest cases,"* and singled out his expertise in insurance litigation.

REAL ESTATE

SOUTH CAROLINA
Leading firms (Real Estate)

1 BUIST, MOORE, SMYTHE & MCGEE PA *Charleston*
MCNAIR LAW FIRM PA *Columbia, Charleston*
NEXSEN PRUET JACOBS & POLLARD *Columbia*
2 HAYNSWORTH SINKLER BOYD PA *Columbia*
LEATHERWOOD WALKER TODD *Greenville*

Firms are listed alphabetically in each band.

Buist, Moore, Smythe & McGee PA
The Firm: Peers regularly said that this was the best real estate practice in Charleston. It acts for developers, banks, institutional developers and owners. The practice covers the timber, shopping center, industrial, office and retail sectors on all development, financing and land use issues.
The Lawyers: The *"excellent"* **Foster Gaillard** (see p.629) heads a five-partner commercial real estate department, and acts for one of the largest hotel owner-developers in the state. Gaillard represented the lenders on a high-value loan to a local developer for the refinancing of a 3000-acre planned unit project in Charleston.
The Clients: The firm has recently represented the owner-developer in the refinancing of a high-value loan for a regional shopping center. The team also assisted owner-developers of several large apartment complexes in acquisition, development and permanent financing issues. Condominium projects and industrial facilities acquisitions also contribute to the workload.

SOUTH CAROLINA — REAL ESTATE

SOUTH CAROLINA
Leading individuals (Real Estate)

[1]
- **BOONE Sidney** *McNair Law Firm PA*, Charleston
- **ESTRIDGE Larry** *Womble Carlyle Sandridge*, Greenville
- **MENZIE Edward** *Nexsen Pruet Jacobs*, Columbia

[2]
- **BOYD William** *Haynsworth Sinkler Boyd*, Columbia
- **GAILLARD Foster** *Buist, Moore, Smythe*, Charleston
- **QUATTLEBAUM Marvin** *Leatherwood Walker*, Greenville
- **WARREN John** *Warren & Sinkler, LLP*, Charleston

Individuals are listed alphabetically in each band.

McNair Law Firm PA

The Firm: The team was praised in particular for its *"outstanding young and aspiring lawyers."* About 20 lawyers focus on real estate matters throughout the firm's extensive statewide network. The group is also able to cater for associated issues including tax, zoning, and the structuring of partnerships and joint ventures. Its Georgetown office has recently been involved in coastal development projects.

The Lawyers: Interviewees commended **Sidney Boone** for *"taking charge and getting the deal done."* He heads a small team out of the firm's Charleston office that acts for developers on all aspects of their businesses.

The Clients: Park West Subdivision and Vendue/Prioleau Associates are clients.

Nexsen Pruet Jacobs & Pollard LLC

The Firm: This practice was recommended to researchers for its *"great statewide depth."* Attorneys cover all aspects of real estate investment and development, including areas such as governmental incentives and conservation easements. The real estate team is supported by corporate, securities, healthcare, environmental, tax and bankruptcy departments.

The Lawyers: There were few interviewees who did not spontaneously mention *"high-quality operator"* **Edward Menzie** as a leading real estate lawyer in the state. Based in Columbia, Menzie acts for several major real estate developers.

Haynsworth Sinkler Boyd PA

The Firm: The practice is evenly split between real estate finance and advising developers and large industrial clients on acquisitions. It is active throughout the US, and therefore experienced in interstate land sales regulation as well as matters arising in Canada. Other areas of expertise include resort development and condominium organization and conversion. The real estate team is well supported in associated areas such as litigation and environment.

The Lawyers: The practice of senior lawyer **William Boyd** is weighted in favor of corporate M&A also his involvement in high-end real estate deals has caught the attention of interviewees.

The Clients: Large manufacturers and financial institutions.

Leatherwood Walker Todd & Mann PC

The Firm: The practice was endorsed for its *"fine lawyers"* who are experienced in both development and financing issues. From its Greenville stronghold, the firm is active throughout the Southeast, counseling developers, lenders, sellers, purchasers and financial institutions.

The Lawyers: Of the core nine-lawyer real estate team, **Marvin Quattlebaum** received the highest volume of commendation. He represents purchasers, sellers and developers as well as local and national lenders.

The Clients: Highwoods Properties and Hughes Development Corporation are clients.

Other Notable Practitioners

Senior real estate lawyer **Larry Estridge** of Womble Carlyle Sandridge & Rice PLLC was mentioned as *"having a strong presence"* in the sector. A former Wyche Burgess lawyer, he focuses on both transactional and litigious real estate matters, land use and regulation issues and governmental incentives. He recently acted for an out-of-state developer on zoning and governmental incentives for a 400-acre multi-use technology and research park focusing on the motor sports industry. Another major real estate client for Estridge is Greenville-Spartanburg International Airport. **John Warren** of Warren & Sinkler, LLP is widely recognized for his prowess in both real estate and corporate M&A matters. Peers in the real estate market agreed that he was *"experienced and possessed excellent judgment."*

Leaders in South Carolina

BLAKE, Joesph
Haynsworth Sinkler Boyd PA, Greenville
864 240 3200
Recommended in Corporate/M&A

BOONE, Sidney
McNair Law Firm PA, Columbia
803 799 9800
Recommended in Real Estate

BOYD, William
Haynsworth Sinkler Boyd PA, Columbia
803 765 1818
Recommended in Corporate/M&A, Real Estate

BREWER, Wilburn
Nexsen Pruet Jacobs & Pollard, LLC, Columbia 803 771 8900
Recommended in Litigation

BURNETTE, Malissa
Burnette & Leclair P.A, Columbia
803 251 0202
Recommended in Employment

CLEVELAND, William
Buist, Moore, Smythe & McGee, P.A.,
Charleston 843 722 3400
wcleveland@bmsmlaw.com
Recommended in Litigation
Specialization: Head of the firm's business and commercial litigation group. Handles a broad range of business disputes including those involving intellectual property, securities, lender liability and corporate control issues.
Prof. Memberships: Has just completed his service as President of the International Association of Defense Counsel (IADC), an invitation-only association of approximatley 2200 lawyers who represent corporations and insurers. In 1999, served as Director of the Defense Counsel Trial Academy, a week long school for young lawyers conducted every summer at the University of Colorado in Boulder. Is currently a member of the American Board of Trial Advocates, the Board of Directors of the Defense Research Institute and the Board of Directors of Lawyers for Civil Justice.
Career: Admitted to the bar of California in 1975 and South Carolina in 1979. After finishing law school, practiced with the firm of *Bronson, Bronson & McKinnon* in San Francisco before moving back to his home state of South Carolina.
Publications: Has a special interest in the use of technology in the courtroom and is a frequent speaker on the topic at continuing legal education seminars.
Personal: Received a JD from the Univeristy of Virginia in 1975 and a BA from Yale University in 1972.

CROMER, Lewis
Cromer & Mabry, Columbia
803 799 9530
Recommended in Employment

CURRIE, John
McNair Law Firm PA, Columbia
803 799 9800
Recommended in Corporate/M&A

DUKES, David
Nelson Mullins Riley & Scarborough,
LLP, Columbia 803 799 2000
DED@nmrs.com
Recommended in Litigation
Specialization: Firm managing partner, is resident in Columbia, South Carolina, where he practises in the areas of pharmaceutical and medical device litigation, business litigation, and technology law and litigation, with a concentration on complex litigation.
Prof. Memberships: Served as national coordinating counsel for a leading pharmaceutical company, and he served as national trial counsel for a Fortune 500 developer of computer software throughout the 1990s. Is admitted to practice before the Supreme Court of the United States, the US Court of Appeals for the Fourth and Tenth Circuits, and the US District Court for the District of South Carolina. Is a member of the American Bar Association and a fellow of the Amer-

SOUTH CAROLINA

ican Bar Foundation. He is second vice president of the Defense Research Institute. He is a permanent member of the US Fourth Circuit Judicial Conference and a member of the International Association of Defense Counsel.
Personal: In 1984 received a Juris Doctor, cum laude, from the University of South Carolina School of Law where he was named to The Order of the Coif. Earned a Bachelor of Science in Financial Management from Clemson University in 1981.

ESTRIDGE, Larry
Womble Carlyle Sandridge & Rice PLLC, Greenville 864 255 5400
Recommended in Real Estate

GAILLARD, Foster
Buist, Moore, Smythe & McGee, P.A., Charleston 843 720 4610
fgaillard@bmsmlaw.com
Recommended in Real Estate
Specialization: Head of the Commercial Real Estate Department of his firm, where he routinely handles complex commercial real estate transactions, banking law and business law matters. Has extensive experience in representing corporate and individual clients in all aspects of real estate law, including contract negotiations, zoning and land use issues, financing, regulatory matters and closing the transaction. Clients include owners and developers of shopping centers, office buildings, industrial facilities, apartment complexes, hotels, retail and mixed use developments, and planned unit developments. His practice also includes the representation of various banks and other institutional lenders in all aspects of real estate lending.
Prof. Memberships: South Carolina and American Bar Associations, Immediate Past Chair of Real Estate Practices Section, South Carolina Bar, Member of ABA Books/Media Committee, American College of Real Estate Lawyers.

Career: Admitted to South Carolina Bar (1973). A Principal in *Buist Moore Smythe & McGee*, PA since joining firm in 1986. Listed in a leading US legal directory.
Publications: Contributing Author, Foreclosure and Related Remedies: A State by State Digest (ABA 1995).
Personal: Received BA from Washington & Lee University in 1970 and JD from the University of South Carolina in 1973.

HALL, Cary
Wyche, Burgess, Freeman & Parham, PA, Greenville 864 242 8200
Recommended in Corporate/M&A

KING, George
Haynsworth Sinkler Boyd PA, Columbia 803 765 1818
Recommended in Corporate/M&A

KNIGHT, Marcus
Nexsen Pruet Jacobs & Pollard, LLC, Columbia 803 771 8900
Recommended in Corporate/M&A

LIGHTSEY, Wallace
Wyche, Burgess, Freeman & Parham, PA, Greenville 864 242 8200
Recommended in Litigation

LINTON, Johnny
Haynsworth Sinkler Boyd PA, Charleston 843 722 3366
Recommended in Litigation

LOUTHIAN, Herbert
The Louthian Law Firm PA, Columbia 803 454 1200
Recommended in Employment

LOUTHIAN, Herbert
The Louthian Law Firm PA, Columbia 803 454 1200
Recommended in Employment

MENZIE, Edward
Nexsen Pruet Jacobs & Pollard, LLC, Columbia 803 771 8900
Recommended in Corporate/M&A, Real Estate

MORRISON, Stephen
Nelson Mullins Riley & Scarborough, LLP, Columbia 803 799 2000
SGM@nmrs.com
Recommended in Litigation
Specialization: Partner and chairman of the firm's Litigation I Group, practises in the areas of technology litigation, business litigation, product liability, and securities litigation. He has tried more than 200 cases to jury verdict and has argued more than 60 appeals before state and federal courts including the US Supreme Court. He has been lead trial counsel in more than 20 states and four foreign countries. His business experience includes seven year's service as executive vice president and general counsel to a NYSE traded technology company. He has served on numerous US and international corporate boards and is regularly named to US and international 'Best Lawyer' lists.
Prof. Memberships: Is past president of the Defense Research Institute, Lawyers for Civil Justice and past chairman of the SC Bar House of Delegates. A frequent speaker and teacher, he has served on seminar facilities around the world. He is an adjunct professor of law at the University of South Carolina.
Personal: Recieved a JD from the University of South Carolina School of Law in 1975 and a BBA from the University of Michigan in 1971. In 1997, he completed the Advanced Management Program at Harvard Graduate School of Business.

MUSSER, William
McNair Law Firm PA, Columbia 803 799 9800
Recommended in Corporate/M&A

PARHAM, James
Wyche, Burgess, Freeman & Parham, PA, Greenville 864 242 8200
Recommended in Litigation

PEARSON, Jonathan
Ellzey & Brooks LLC, Columbia 803 255 0000
Recommended in Employment

QUATTLEBAUM, Marvin
Leatherwood Walker Todd & Mann, P.C., Greenville 864 242 6440
Recommended in Real Estate

SHOEMAKER, James
Wyche, Burgess, Freeman & Parham, PA, Greenville 864 242 8200
Recommended in Corporate/M&A

SOWELL, Thornwell
Sowell Gray Stepp & Laffitte LLC, Columbia 803 929 1400
Recommended in Litigation

SPETH, Charles
Haynsworth Baldwin Johnson & Greaves LLC, Columbia 803 799 5858
Recommended in Employment

TATE, Simmons
Haynsworth Sinkler Boyd PA, Columbia 803 765 1818
Recommended in Litigation

TISDALE, Thomas
Young, Clement, Rivers & Tisdale, LLP, Charleston 843 577 4000
Recommended in Litigation

WARREN, John
Warren & Sinkler, LLP, Charleston 843 577 0660
Recommended in Corporate/M&A, Real Estate

YOUNG, Rutledge
Young, Clement, Rivers & Tisdale, LLP, Charleston 843 577 4000
Recommended in Litigation

SOUTH DAKOTA

CORPORATE/M&A

CONTENTS: Corporate/M&A p.630; Employment: Mainly Plaintiff p.631; Mainly Defendant p.631; Litigation: General Commercial p.631; Real Estate p.632; Individuals' Profiles p.633.

SOUTH DAKOTA'S TOP THREE
1. Davenport, Evans, Hurwitz & Smith
2. Woods, Fuller, Shultz & Smith
3. Gunderson, Palmer, Goodsell & Nelson

Ranking based on Chambers' research within the state.

All quotes in the text are from interviews with clients and competitors.

OVERVIEW: Topping the table, **Davenport, Evans, Hurwitz & Smith** is South Dakota's largest and most established full-service firm. It excels in litigation, corporate, real estate and employment law, and has built its reputation on key relationships with prominent financial services clients such as Citibank (South Dakota). Corporate department head David Knudson was deemed a leading banking and healthcare specialist, while Robert Hayes was particularly recommended for both corporate work and real estate matters. Interviewees also identified Susan Brunick Simons as the state's leading labor attorney. The firm's list of active clients includes the Dakota, Minnesota & Eastern Railroad Corporation and Travelers.

In second place, **Woods, Fuller, Shultz & Smith** is a large firm with a long-standing reputation for excellence. The firm elicited praise for its corporate expertise as well as for its complex commercial and employment litigation prowess. An extensive client roster includes many of the state's leading insurance companies. Star litigator Gary Thimsen was heralded for his work in insurance defense and employment discrimination cases. State Farm, Wellmark Blue Cross and Blue Shield and Wal-Mart are regular clients of the firm.

Gunderson, Palmer, Goodsell & Nelson, ranked third, is a fast-growing firm with a top-drawer standing in the state. The firm rates highly for corporate and real estate work, but also received widespread recommendation for outstanding litigation capability. Crisman Palmer is a key member of the firm, and is credited with contributing to the firm's first-class reputation in both insurance defense and lender liability litigation. Clients include Wells Fargo Bank South Dakota and the Coca-Cola Bottling Company of the Black Hills.

CORPORATE/M&A

SOUTH DAKOTA
Leading firms (Corporate/M&A)
1. DAVENPORT, EVANS, HURWITZ *Sioux Falls*
   WOODS, FULLER, SHULTZ & SMITH *Sioux Falls*
2. GUNDERSON, PALMER, GOODSELL *Rapid City*

Leading individuals (Corporate/M&A)
1. GOLDAMMER Vance *Murphy, Goldammer,* Sioux Falls
   HAYES Robert *Davenport, Evans, Hurwitz,* Sioux Falls
   KNUDSON David *Davenport, Evans, Hurwitz,* Sioux Falls
2. CUTLER Richard *Cutler & Donahoe LLP,* Sioux Falls
   DAMGAARD Roger *Woods, Fuller, Shultz,* Sioux Falls
   WIEDERRICH James *Woods, Fuller, Shultz,* Sioux Falls
3. GOETZINGER Patrick *Gunderson, Palmer,* Rapid City
   GROSSENBURG Bradley *Woods, Fuller,* Sioux Falls

Firms and individuals are listed alphabetically in each band.

Davenport, Evans, Hurwitz & Smith LLP
The Firm: Researchers were told that this large full-service Sioux Falls firm has deep roots in the area and continues to grow in strength. An *"excellent"* 14-lawyer business transactions group was recognized for its *"breadth of experience."* The team benefits from the prominence of its financial services clientele and earns particular praise for its expertise in banking and securities matters. Interviewees recommended the group as *"first rate for credit issues,"* and further noted an additional focus on healthcare transactions.

The Lawyers: Interviewees identified practice head **David Knudson** as a *"leading banking transactions attorney,"* widely admired for his corporate acumen and *"practical"* approach. The bulk of his practice is devoted to healthcare, banking and tax incentives. His clients include some of the state's leading financial institutions. *"Premier creditors' rights"* specialist **Robert Hayes** adds to the team's prestige. He has extensive experience in all areas of commercial transactions, including real estate financing, and also appears in *Chambers'* real estate rankings. He advises the Sioux Falls School District on contract and federal regulation matters.

The Clients: Citibank (South Dakota); Sioux Valley Hospitals and Health Systems; First Premier Bank; First National Bank in Sioux Falls; Sioux Falls School District; CorTrust Bank and the Dakota, Minnesota & Eastern Railroad Corporation.

Woods, Fuller, Shultz & Smith PC
The Firm: Rivals and clients deem the firm *"one of the best and most respected practices in South Dakota,"* frequently commenting on Woods Fuller's size and long-standing reputation in Sioux Falls. The 12-strong corporate team received high marks from clients for its attorneys' *"keen legal intelligence"* and *"sharp"* negotiation style. Peers respect the team's *"integrity"* and *"thoroughness"* in facilitating transactions. The group acts for a number of high-profile finance, insurance and agricultural clients, focusing on corporate and banking law and some bankruptcy matters.

The Lawyers: Said to have carved out a niche for himself in commercial finance, **Roger Damgaard** wins plaudits for his *"bright and articulate"* style. His practice emphasizes bankruptcy and lending matters for an envied roster of banking and insurance clients. **James Wiederrich** garnered market accolades for his *"tight grasp"* of general corporate law and commercial loan contracts. He also acts for local soybean processing plants such as South Dakota Soybean Processors on corporate and agricultural issues. Peers acknowledge **Bradley Grossenburg** as an able corporate and tax law adviser. He has a strong following among smaller South Dakota businesses.

The Clients: US Bancorp; Travelers; Home Federal Bank; MetLife; State Farm; John Morrell & Company and South Dakota Soybean Processors.

Gunderson, Palmer, Goodsell & Nelson LLP
The Firm: A rising force in Rapid City, the firm was recognized for its *"quality attorneys."* The business transactions group particularly is seen to be rapidly expanding its profile in the region, and provides general corporate advice on all aspects of business transactions.

The Lawyers: Patrick Goetzinger is said to be cementing a *"solid"* reputation in M&A. He also received positive feedback for his real estate expertise and appears in the *Chambers'* rankings for this area.

The Clients: Wells Fargo Bank South Dakota, Scotchman Industries and the Coca-Cola Bottling Company of the Black Hills.

Other Notable Practitioners
Considered one of the state's most eminent practitioners for corporate and banking matters, **Vance Goldammer** at newly established Murphy, Goldammer & Prendergast is widely admired for his *"first-class"* practice in creditors' rights. His recent move from Boyce Pashby is not thought to affect his stature as a *"leading light"* in the market. Said to have a *"real aptitude"* for problem solving, Goldammer has experience in corporate acquisitions and acts for a number of leading insurance, credit card and financial institutions.

Richard Cutler of Cutler & Donahoe LLP is highly regarded for his *"excellent"* abilities in structuring and financing commercial transactions. He ranks in both the corporate and real estate tables.

EMPLOYMENT & LABOR LAW — SOUTH DAKOTA

EMPLOYMENT & LABOR LAW — MAINLY PLAINTIFF

SOUTH DAKOTA
Leading firms
(Employment: Mainly Plaintiff)
1. FINCH BETTMANN MAKS & HOGUE PC *Rapid City*

Leading individuals
(Employment: Mainly Plaintiff)
1. FINCH Dennis *Finch Bettmann Maks*, Rapid City
2. GROVES William *Sole Practitioner*, Rapid City
   HAGG Rexford *Whiting Hagg & Hagg LLP*, Rapid City
   SIMPSON Michael *Julius & Simpson LLP*, Rapid City

Firms and individuals are listed alphabetically in each band.

Finch Bettmann Maks & Hogue PC
The Firm: Researchers were impressed by the weight of market commendation for this firm. The well-respected practice was cited for having *"extensive experience"* in handling employment plaintiffs' issues. Particular strength exists in workers' compensation litigation.
The Lawyers: The firm's reputation in employment plaintiff's work rests largely on partner **Dennis Finch**, recognized by interviewees as being *"one of the most effective plaintiff attorneys in South Dakota".*

Other Notable Practitioners
William Groves, a sole practitioner in Rapid City, is well respected for his workers compensation litigation skills on behalf of employees. At Julius & Simpson LLP, **Michael Simpson** elicits praise from rivals for his *"congeniality and fairness"* in plaintiff employment law. **Rexford Hagg** at Whiting Hagg & Hagg LLP has also carved out a niche in employee workers' compensation litigation.

EMPLOYMENT & LABOR LAW — MAINLY DEFENDANT

SOUTH DAKOTA
Leading firms
(Employment: Mainly Defendant)
1. DAVENPORT, EVANS, HURWITZ *Sioux Falls*
   WOODS, FULLER, SHULTZ & SMITH *Sioux Falls*
2. BOYCE, PASHBY & WELK *Sioux Falls*

Leading individuals
(Employment: Mainly Defendant)
1. SIMONS Susan *Davenport, Evans*, Sioux Falls
2. HARALDSON Comet *Woods, Fuller, Shultz*, Sioux Falls
   MCKNIGHT Michael *Boyce, Pashby*, Sioux Falls
   SHULTZ Jeff *Woods, Fuller, Shultz & Smith*, Sioux Falls

Firms and individuals are listed alphabetically in each band.

Davenport, Evans, Hurwitz & Smith LLP
The Firm: This 8-lawyer employment and labor practice is a popular choice for banks, customer service companies and small to medium-sized corporations. The team derives particular strength from its highly rated litigation department, which handles numerous ADA and age discrimination cases. Market sources also identified significant expertise in workers' compensation issues.
The Lawyers: **Susan Brunick Simons** is the firm's standout practitioner in labor and employment. She earns plaudits from peers for her *"breadth of experience"* in counseling employers on traditional labor issues such as contracts and agreements and representing them before federal administrative agencies.
The Clients: First Premier Bank; Travelers; Western National Insurance and Sioux Valley Hospitals and Health System.

Woods, Fuller, Shultz & Smith PC
The Firm: A *"rock-solid client base"* and underlying strength in litigation place this firm in an enviable position to advise on a volume of labor and employment matters, say interviewees. Researchers were told of the group's *"long-established"* reputation in the field of workers' compensation. The strong group of employment generalists here also enjoy statewide renown for their defense of insurers and institutional corporate clients on employment cases.
The Lawyers: Group leader **Comet Haraldson** received enthusiastic recommendations from peers who admire his *"proven track record"* and *"high-quality work"* in handling workers' compensation issues for employers. **Jeff Shultz** also earned kudos for his *"strong grasp"* of the employment issues that affect both insurers and self-insured employers.
The Clients: 3M, Wal-Mart and Hy-Vee.

Boyce, Pashby & Welk
The Firm: The caliber of lawyers found in this Sioux Falls firm is considered *"top notch."* The firm is well regarded by fellow attorneys, earning high marks for its expertise in workers compensation.
The Lawyers: **Michael McKnight** received excellent market reviews for both his workers compensation expertise and his defense of employers in the insurance industry.
The Clients: Chubb Insurance, The Avera McKennan Hospital and University Health Center, and Midwest Medical Insurance.

LITIGATION — GENERAL COMMERCIAL

Davenport, Evans, Hurwitz & Smith LLP
The Firm: Interviewees proclaim this Sioux Falls firm to be *"outstanding"* for litigation matters. The 15-attorney litigation team benefits from the resources of a large full-service firm. This *"highly professional"* group has extensive experience handling complex commercial litigation matters, including antitrust and securities fraud. Medical and personal injury defense, in particular, are key strengths. Clients also endorse the *"broad support"* and *"knowledgeable advice"* they receive from the team.

The Lawyers: **Michael Luce** pulled away from the rest of the pack as South Dakota's most preeminent litigator. Market sources noted his wide experience and *"courtroom flair."* His practice focuses on representing businesses in personal injury and products liability cases. Department head **Ed Evans** was deemed *"top-notch"* by commentators for his medical malpractice defense litigation. He received excellent feedback from rivals for his *"tenacious"* style. Described as *"meticulous and intense"* in his courtroom preparation, **Michael Schaffer** earned respect for his specialty in products liability litigation.

The Clients: American International Group; American Society of Composers, Authors and Publishers (ASCAP); Auto-Owners Insurance; Citibank (South Dakota); Continental Western; CorTrust Bank; Daktronics and the Dakota, Minnesota & Eastern Railroad Corporation.

Woods, Fuller, Shultz & Smith PC
The Firm: Eliciting praise from both clients and competitors, this 14-attorney litigation team was heralded as *"one of the best and brightest in the area."* Drawing support from the firm's size and

SOUTH DAKOTA — LITIGATION

SOUTH DAKOTA
Leading firms
(Litigation: General Commercial)

1
- DAVENPORT, EVANS, HURWITZ *Sioux Falls*
- WOODS, FULLER, SHULTZ & SMITH *Sioux Falls*

2
- BOYCE, PASHBY & WELK *Sioux Falls*
- CADWELL SANFORD DEIBERT *Sioux Falls*
- GUNDERSON, PALMER, GOODSELL *Rapid City*

3
- BANGS, MCCULLEN, BUTLER, FOYE *Rapid City*
- COSTELLO PORTER HILL HEISTERKAMP *Rapid City*
- MAY, ADAM, GERDES & THOMPSON LLP *Pierre*

Leading individuals
(Litigation: General Commercial)

1
- LUCE Michael *Davenport, Evans, Hurwitz, Sioux Falls*
- PALMER Crisman *Gunderson, Palmer, Rapid City*
- SANFORD Steven *Cadwell Sanford Deibert, Sioux Falls*
- THIMSEN Gary *Woods, Fuller, Shultz, Sioux Falls*

2
- ANDERSON Robert *May, Adam, Gerdes, Pierre*
- EVANS Ed *Davenport, Evans, Hurwitz, Sioux Falls*
- SCHAFFER Michael *Davenport, Evans, Sioux Falls*
- WELK Thomas *Boyce, Pashby & Welk, Sioux Falls*

3
- CARPENTER Edward *Costello Porter Hill, Rapid City*
- GOODSELL Verne *Gunderson, Palmer, Rapid City*
- HICKEY Michael *Bangs, McCullen, Butler, Rapid City*
- PASHBY Gary *Boyce, Pashby & Welk, Sioux Falls*
- WILBUR Brent *May, Adam, Gerdes & Thompson, Pierre*

Firms and individuals are listed alphabetically in each band.

long-established reputation, litigators here act for an enviable client roster of premier companies. The group acts for small businesses as well as large corporations, advising them on a range of matters such as business tort and construction litigation.
The Lawyers: Gary Thimsen garners praise from interviewees for his *"sharp legal mind."* Described as a *"superb generalist,"* Thimsen handles governmental liability and insurance defense as well as employment discrimination cases.
The Clients: Wal-Mart; Wellmark Blue Cross and Blue Shield; Goodyear; Acuity Insurance; Northwest Airlines; State Farm; US Bancorp; United Airlines and Westfield Companies.

Boyce, Pashby & Welk
The Firm: Despite the loss of three partners to form Murphy, Goldammer & Prendergast, this seven-member litigation practice retains its popularity among interviewees who laud the team for producing *"quality"* work.
The Lawyers: Market sources single out Thomas Welk for his *"highly esteemed"* litigation talents. His *"vast experience"* in stockholder litigation is valued by a clientele of major healthcare corporates such as Avera Health. Gary Pashby enjoys a loyal client following among numerous design and engineering companies. His practice focuses on construction and creditors' litigation.
The Clients: Avera Health; Commercial State Bank, Wagner; Citizens State Bank, Arlington; Banner & Associates; Schmucker, Paul, Nohr & Associates and Zaran Sayre & Associates.

Cadwell Sanford Deibert & Garry LLP
The Firm: Named by clients as a *"sound option"* for complex litigation matters, the firm was endorsed for its *"talented"* litigators. The firm is known to represent many leading finance and insurance institutions in the state.
The Lawyers: Commentators attribute much of the firm's profile in litigation to Steven Sanford, identified as one of the field's most eminent practitioners. Widely admired for his *"tough"* style and courtroom success, he concentrates on commercial, banking and products liability litigation.
The Clients: State Farm; US Bancorp; First National Bank in Sioux Falls and First Premier Bank.

Gunderson, Palmer, Goodsell & Nelson LLP
The Firm: Interviewees named this Rapid City firm as *"one of the fastest growing in South Dakota."* A ten-attorney litigation team enjoys an *"impressive"* reputation for trial success. Attorneys were particularly noted for their expertise in insurance defense.
The Lawyers: Crisman Palmer is the practice's highest profile name in litigation. Acclaimed for his *"legal intellect,"* Palmer focuses on insurance defense, products liability and lender liability claims. Verne Goodsell received enthusiastic recommendations from the market for his *"excellent capabilities"* in litigation. He handles both medical malpractice and products liability cases.
The Clients: Wells Fargo Bank South Dakota, Travelers and Homestake Mining Company.

Bangs, McCullen, Butler, Foye & Simmons LLP
The Firm: Said to have *"a strong presence"* in Rapid City, this expanding firm wins fans across the state for its substantial litigation capabilities. The 15-lawyer litigation team has a strong emphasis on insurance defense work.
The Lawyers: Michael Hickey earned plaudits from peers for his insurance defense work and expertise in water and mineral law. He represents many insurance companies as well as water companies such as Rapid Valley Water Company.
The Clients: Travelers South Dakota, Great American Insurance Group and Wells Fargo Bank.

Costello Porter Hill Heisterkamp Bushnell & Carpenter LLP
The Firm: This Rapid City firm was said by competitors to have a *"burgeoning litigation practice."* The group offers a wide range of expertise in all aspects of commercial litigation.
The Lawyers: Ed Carpenter received positive feedback for his generalist litigation practice. Construction litigation and government contracts are the focal points of his practice.
The Clients: The Ford Motor Company, the National Farmers' Union and Clinical Laboratory of the Black Hills.

May, Adam, Gerdes & Thompson LLP
The Firm: Based in Pierre, this firm is praised by interviewees as *"top notch"* in government regulatory matters. The firm acts for a wide variety of clients, ranging from household name corporations such as Philip Morris and RJ Reynolds to local ranchers.
The Lawyers: Named as an *"excellent trial lawyer,"* Robert Anderson focuses primarily on the representation of insurance companies in litigation. Brent Wilbur was also recognized as a prominent figure in commercial law and lender liability.
The Clients: South Dakota Cable Telecommunications Association; Northern Border Pipeline Company; Farm Credit Services; Bank of Hoven; Philip Morris and RJ Reynolds.

REAL ESTATE

SOUTH DAKOTA
Leading firms (Real Estate)

1
- BANGS, MCCULLEN, BUTLER, FOYE *Rapid City*
- DAVENPORT, EVANS, HURWITZ *Sioux Falls*

2
- BOYCE, PASHBY & WELK *Sioux Falls*
- CUTLER & DONAHOE LLP *Sioux Falls*
- GUNDERSON, PALMER, GOODSELL *Rapid City*

Firms are listed alphabetically in each band.

Bangs, McCullen, Butler, Foye & Simmons LLP
The Firm: Considered a leading real estate player in Rapid City, this firm is highly rated among interviewees for its depth and breadth of expertise. Thanks in part to its location, the firm receives a steady flow of real estate work relating to the state's growing tourism industry. This four-member business practice group handles all aspects of commercial real estate transactions and conservation easements. The group was identified as a *"leading force"* in agriculture-related real estate transactions, and also received praise for its *"excellence"* in business and real estate sales and acquisitions. A loyal client base includes banks, local businesses, hospitals and other public bodies.
The Lawyers: Prevailing market opinion heralds Thomas Foye as an *"outstanding"* real estate

REAL ESTATE — SOUTH DAKOTA

SOUTH DAKOTA
Leading individuals (Real Estate)

1
- CUTLER Richard *Cutler & Donahoe LLP*, Sioux Falls
- DONOHUE Daniel *Davenport, Evans*, Sioux Falls

2
- FOYE Thomas *Bangs, McCullen, Butler, Foye*, Rapid City
- GOETZINGER Patrick *Gunderson, Palmer*, Rapid City
- GREENFIELD Russell *Boyce, Pashby*, Sioux Falls
- HAYES Robert *Davenport, Evans, Hurwitz*, Sioux Falls
- RITER Charles *Bangs, McCullen, Butler, Foye*, Rapid City

Individuals are listed alphabetically in each band.

---

tion of strip malls, residential properties and office buildings. It also attracts comment for its special emphasis on tax credit work.

The Lawyers: Interviewees endorse *"talented"* **Dan Donohue** as *"one of the best in the state"* for complex real estate transactions. **Robert Hayes** appears in both *Chambers'* real estate and corporate rankings, following enthusiastic recommendation from the market.

The Clients: Citibank (South Dakota), Sioux Falls School District, and Sioux Valley Hospitals and Health System.

Boyce, Pashby & Welk

The Firm: This *"top notch"* firm retains its reputation in the market as a *"first-rate"* real estate practice comprising a number of *"tremendous"* attorneys who are esteemed for their *"thorough knowledge of the law."* The group advises on commercial real estate transactions and finance. Clients said they valued the team's *"professionalism,"* noting its *"unique and genuine concern for our company's interests."*

The Lawyers: Clients and competitors recommend **Russell Greenfield** for his *"clear and concise explanations"* of complicated real estate law. His practice is heavily focused on real estate finance and corporate transactions involving bond issues and tax-exempt structures. He also advises on the acquisition and development of commercial and residential properties.

The Clients: Sioux Falls Development Project, Citibank (South Dakota) and First American Bank & Trust Sioux Falls.

Cutler & Donahoe LLP

The Firm: A full-service, ten-member firm with a growing presence in Sioux Falls. Rivals point to a *"burgeoning real estate and transactional team."*

The Lawyers: The firm owes much of its reputation to the individual renown of managing partner **Richard Cutler**, described by interviewees as *"one of the best real estate attorneys in South Dakota."* He counsels on all manner of real estate transactions, including sales, acquisitions and the refinancing of commercial properties. He is visible in the market representing many of the state's top developers. Cutler also figures in the corporate rankings for his skill as a business adviser.

The Clients: Dakota, Minnesota & Eastern Railroad Corporation; Viereck Commercial Real Estate and AH Meyer & Sons.

Gunderson, Palmer, Goodsell & Nelson LLP

The Firm: This *"fast-growing"* Rapid City practice was recommended to researchers as a popular choice for referrals.

The Lawyers: Interviewees singled out **Patrick Goetzinger** for his broad-based practice and expertise in real estate finance.

The Clients: Wells Fargo Bank South Dakota; Scotchman Industries and the Coca-Cola Bottling Company of the Black Hills.

---

attorney with a *"breadth of knowledge in transactions and tax planning."* **Charles Riter** also earned plaudits from peers for his *"top-quality"* commercial real estate development and transactional work.

The Clients: Wells Fargo Bank South Dakota; The Rapid City Journal and Crazy Horse Memorial Foundation.

Davenport, Evans, Hurwitz & Smith LLP

The Firm: Based in Sioux Falls, this well-established seven-member real estate team received high marks for being a *"terrific"* group of *"detail-oriented"* advisers. The real estate practice benefits greatly from the extensive resources of this large full-service firm, and receives strong support from the corporate transactions team on complex commercial real estate matters. This *"business-oriented"* team represents developers and investors in the planning, zoning, development and acquisi-

---

Leaders in South Dakota

ANDERSON, Robert
May, Adam, Gerdes & Thompson, L.L.P., Pierre 605 224 8803
Recommended in Litigation

CARPENTER, Edward
Costello Porter Hill Heisterkamp Bushnell & Carpenter LLP, Rapid City 605 343 2410
Recommended in Litigation

CUTLER, Richard
Cutler & Donahoe LLP, Sioux Falls 605 335 4950
Recommended in Corporate/M&A, Real Estate

DAMGAARD, Roger
Woods, Fuller, Shultz & Smith PC, Sioux Falls 605 336 3890
Recommended in Corporate/M&A

DONOHUE, Daniel
Davenport, Evans, Hurwitz & Smith LLP, Sioux Falls 605 336 2880
Recommended in Real Estate

EVANS, Ed
Davenport, Evans, Hurwitz & Smith LLP, Sioux Falls 605 336 2880
Recommended in Litigation

FINCH, Dennis
Finch Bettmann Maks & Hogue P.C. Rapid City 605 348 6547
Recommended in Employment

FOYE, Thomas
Bangs, McCullen, Butler, Foye & Simmons, LLP, Rapid City 605 343 1040
Recommended in Real Estate

GOETZINGER, Patrick
Gunderson, Palmer, Goodsell & Nelson LLP, Rapid City 605 342 1078
Recommended in Corporate/M&A, Real Estate

GOLDAMMER, Vance
Murphy, Goldammer & Prendergast, Sioux Falls 605 331 2975
Recommended in Corporate/M&A

GOODSELL, Verne
Gunderson, Palmer, Goodsell & Nelson LLP, Rapid City 605 342 1078
Recommended in Litigation

GREENFIELD, Russell
Boyce, Pashby & Welk, Sioux Falls 605 336 2424
Recommended in Real Estate

GROSSENBURG, Bradley
Woods, Fuller, Shultz & Smith PC, Sioux Falls 605 336 3890
Recommended in Corporate/M&A

GROVES, William
William Jason Groves - Sole Practitioner, Rapid City 605 341 4747
Recommended in Employment

HAGG, Rexford
Whiting Hagg & Hagg, Rapid City 605 348 1125
Recommended in Employment

HARALDSON, Comet
Woods, Fuller, Shultz & Smith PC, Sioux Falls 605 336 3890
Recommended in Employment

HAYES, Robert
Davenport, Evans, Hurwitz & Smith LLP, Sioux Falls 605 336 2880
Recommended in Corporate/M&A, Real Estate

HICKEY, Michael
Bangs, McCullen, Butler, Foye & Simmons, LLP, Rapid City 605 343 1040
Recommended in Litigation

KNUDSON, David
Davenport, Evans, Hurwitz & Smith LLP, Sioux Falls 605 336 2880
Recommended in Corporate/M&A

LUCE, Michael
Davenport, Evans, Hurwitz & Smith LLP, Sioux Falls 605 336 2880
Recommended in Litigation

MCKNIGHT, Michael
Boyce, Pashby & Welk, Sioux Falls 605 336 2424
Recommended in Employment

SOUTH DAKOTA

PALMER, Crisman
Gunderson, Palmer, Goodsell & Nelson LLP, Rapid City 605 342 1078
Recommended in Litigation

PASHBY, Gary
Boyce, Pashby & Welk, Sioux Falls
605 336 2424
Recommended in Litigation

RITER, Charles
Bangs, McCullen, Butler, Foye & Simmons, LLP, Rapid City
605 343 1040
Recommended in Real Estate

SANFORD, Steven
Cadwell Sanford Deibert & Garry LLP, Sioux Falls 605 336 0828
Recommended in Litigation

SCHAFFER, Michael
Davenport, Evans, Hurwitz & Smith LLP, Sioux Falls 605 336 2880
Recommended in Litigation

SHULTZ, Jeff
Woods, Fuller, Shultz & Smith PC, Sioux Falls 605 336 3890
Recommended in Employment

SIMONS, Susan Brunick
Davenport, Evans, Hurwitz & Smith LLP, Sioux Falls 605 336 2880
Recommended in Employment

SIMPSON, Michael
Julius & Simpson LLP, Rapid City
605 716 1000
Recommended in Employment

THIMSEN, Gary
Woods, Fuller, Shultz & Smith PC, Sioux Falls 605 336 3890
Recommended in Litigation

WELK, Thomas
Boyce, Pashby & Welk, Sioux Falls
605 336 2424
Recommended in Litigation

WIEDERRICH, James
Woods, Fuller, Shultz & Smith PC, Sioux Falls 605 336 3890
Recommended in Corporate/M&A

WILBUR, Brent
May, Adam, Gerdes & Thompson, L.L.P., Pierre 605 224 8803
Recommended in Litigation

CORPORATE/M&A

TENNESSEE

CONTENTS: Corporate/M&A p.635; Employment: Mainly Plaintiff p.636; Mainly Defendant p.637; Litigation: General Commercial p.638; Real Estate p.639; Individuals' Profiles p.641.

TENNESSEE'S TOP THREE
1. Bass, Berry & Sims
2. Boult, Cummings, Conners & Berry
3. Waller Lansden Dortch & Davis

Ranking based on Chambers' research within the state.

All quotes in the text are from interviews with clients and competitors.

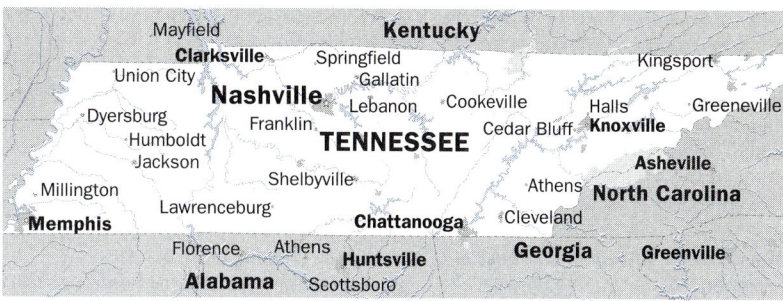

OVERVIEW: Top-ranking Bass Berry & Sims houses over 155 lawyers in its four Tennessee offices. Peers recognize the firm as a strong regional corporate player, particularly in relation to securities transactions. Here, the practice is driven by outstanding market leaders Jim Cheek and Leigh Walton. Head of the labor and employment section, Bill Ozier also earned a top-band ranking for his employment expertise. Clients include HCA and Gaylord Entertainment.

Full-service firm Boult, Cummings, Conners & Berry takes second place in *Chambers'* tables. It was voted the best in the state for real estate, with Tom Trent identified as the practice's standout attorney. He and his team regularly represent Lincoln National in connection with development-related acquisition and credit enhancement transactions. The firm also secured a top-tier ranking in commercial litigation, and is especially well known for its healthcare industry work on behalf of entities such as Saint Thomas Hospital. Other leading clients include Bank of America and GE Capital.

In third place is Waller, Lansden, Dortch & Davis. Covering the A-Z of commercial law, this firm maintains an office in LA in addition to its two Tennessee locations. It takes top ranking in the corporate and employment fields, with Chase Cole and Bob Boston each placing first respectively. Researchers were also told that the firm has noteworthy strength in healthcare issues; it undertakes a large share of work in this area for names such as Province Healthcare Company and HealthSouth.

CORPORATE/M&A

TENNESSEE
Leading firms (Corporate/M&A)
1. **BASS, BERRY & SIMS PLC** Nashville
   WALLER LANSDEN DORTCH & DAVIS Nashville
2. **HARWELL HOWARD HYNE GABBERT** Nashville
3. **BAKER, DONELSON, BEARMAN** Memphis, Nashville
   BOULT, CUMMINGS, CONNERS Nashville
   SHERRARD & ROE PLC Nashville

Leading individuals (Corporate/M&A)
1. **CHEEK James** Bass, Berry & Sims PLC, Nashville
   COLE Chase Waller Lansden Dortch & Davis, Nashville
   WALTON Leigh Bass, Berry & Sims PLC, Nashville
2. **BISHOP George** Waller Lansden Dortch, Nashville
   HILL Reginald Waller Lansden Dortch, Nashville
   MANNER Mark Harwell Howard Hyne, Nashville
3. **BRAUN Stephen** Greenebaum Doll, Nashville
   COWART Richard Baker, Donelson, Bearman, Nashville
   HARDCASTLE Jay Boult, Cummings, Conners, Nashville
   HOLT Berry Boult, Cummings, Conners, Nashville
   HYNE Ernest Harwell Howard Hyne Gabbert, Nashville
   MITCHELL Marlee Waller Lansden Dortch, Nashville
   VOIGT John Sherrard & Roe PLC, Nashville

Firms and individuals are listed alphabetically in each band.

Bass, Berry & Sims PLC
The Firm: With four offices in Tennessee and over 150 lawyers, this *"outstanding"* full-service firm is said to be *"hard to beat"* for quality corporate advice. The firm is widely respected by clients and peers for its strength in securities and banking law. The combined corporate, M&A and securities practice boasts a deep bench of talented attorneys.

The Lawyers: *"Academic"* practice chair **Jim Cheek** emerged as one of the top securities lawyers in the state. Commended as an *"excellent advocate for his clients,"* Cheek represents public and private companies and investment banking firms in capital-raising and M&A transactions. He acts for the independent directors of a number of Merrill Lynch mutual funds. *"Personable"* **Leigh Walton** was named as a *"first-rate"* corporate, securities and healthcare lawyer. She represented Children's Comprehensive Services on its $70 million merger into Kids Holdings and acted for HCA in joint ventures with Quorum Health Group.

The Clients: AmSouth Bank; Bank of America; Gaylord Entertainment and HCA.

Waller Lansden Dortch & Davis
The Firm: Researchers were told that this *"massive corporate heavyweight"* has an edge over competitors in the healthcare sector, where it handles a volume of corporate matters for hospitals, healthcare companies and managed care facilities. Securities is also an area of strength for the practice. The firm is known for its historical role as counsel to HCA and served as lead securities counsel to LifePoint Hospitals in its public offering of 3.6 million shares of common stock. Within Tennessee, the group acts from offices in Nashville and Columbia.

The Lawyers: Peers and clients recommended the *"superbly qualified, experienced and dedicated"* **Chase Cole**. *"Well versed in his clients' business,"* Cole offers *"expert knowledge of securities law and transaction structures."* He counsels a loyal client base on corporate governance, Sarbanes-Oxley compliance and IPO matters. Rivals nominated **George Bishop** as *"one of the best healthcare acquisition attorneys in the region."* Recommended for healthcare acquisition and sales, Bishop is visible in the market representing proprietary health and rural hospital companies. Manager of the business transactions group, **Reggie Hill** was described as an *"excellent deal lawyer"* with vast experience in the areas of M&A, securities, venture capital financing and health law.

He has handled transactional work for HealthSouth, the nation's largest healthcare services provider, and for Symbian. Fellow professionals also praised **Marlee Mitchell** for her dexterity in *"bringing her clients through crisis situations."*

TENNESSEE

CORPORATE/M&A

Chair of the firm's securities group, Mitchell is a *"go-to"* practitioner for securities transactions. Interviewees particularly noted her extensive expertise in broker-dealer legislation.
The Clients: HCA; HealthSouth; Bancorp South; Caterpillar Financial; The Bank of New York; Lifepoint Hospitals; Province Healthcare Company and Verizon Wireless.

Harwell Howard Hyne Gabbert & Manner PC
The Firm: This 30-lawyer Nashville practice earns general acclaim for its strength in corporate transactions, venture capital and bankruptcy work. Clients range from publishing companies to dairies, although the firm remains best known for its substantial focus on healthcare sector work. The firm is representing IT companies engaged in the creation of wireless hospitals.
The Lawyers: Managing partner **Mark Manner** was named as a *"technically superb"* practitioner with *"all-around expertise"* in corporate transactions. His broad-based practice encompasses securities law, M&A, healthcare law, biotechnology, IT and venture capital investments. Clients praise him as a *"proactive"* attorney who contributes impressive intelligence and experience to deal negotiations. *"Always well-prepared,"* **Ernie Hyne** is a *"talented deal lawyer"* with particular expertise in hospital acquisitions. Also active on behalf of venture capital funds and start-up companies, Hyne attains his highest profile in the market for his work for healthcare companies in the hospital, rehabilitation and long-term care industries.
The Clients: National HealthCare Corporation;

Central Parking Corporation and Psychiatric Solutions.

Baker, Donelson, Bearman & Caldwell
The Firm: This large Southeastern firm draws upon over 250 attorneys, distributed among offices in Tennessee, Mississippi, Georgia and DC. Peers commend the firm's large team of experienced attorneys, particularly noting its strength in healthcare transactions.
The Lawyers: Chair of the health law department **Dick Cowart** was singled out by interviewees for his considerable experience in healthcare transactions. His practice is said to have a strong focus on physician relationships and contract matters.
The Clients: American Airlines; Burger King Corporation; Bridgestone/Firestone and The Pillsbury Company.

Boult, Cummings, Conners & Berry PLC
The Firm: Best known as a formidable player in real estate and commercial litigation, the Nashville firm also attracted praise for its advice on general corporate law and knowledge of business matters pertinent to healthcare clients. The firm acted as counsel to a healthcare company in a $100 million private equity financing and acquisition of over 20 ambulatory surgery centers.
The Lawyers: *"Hard-working"* **Jay Hardcastle** is recognized for his healthcare regulatory work and representation of hospitals, surgery centers and physicians in the purchase and sale of healthcare facilities. Head of the firm's health care team, **Berry Holt** earns respect as a *"very fine attorney"*

with long experience representing healthcare providers on a range of business issues. Both Hardcastle and Holt were counsel to Saint Thomas Hospital in its acquisition of Baptist Hospital and three other affiliated Baptist hospitals.
The Clients: Saint Thomas Hospital, Community Health Systems and GM.

Sherrard & Roe PLC
The Firm: Focused on commercial transactions, including M&A, financings and healthcare transactions, the firm is said to offer a broad range of corporate expertise. An expanding practice represents financial institutions, national and multinational companies and local entrepreneurial businesses.
The Lawyers: **John Voight** enjoys a strong following among Tennessee doctors, healthcare providers, hospitals and physicians, who he advises on corporate, litigation and insurance coverage matters. His transactional experience includes advising on the purchase and sale of several hospitals.
The Clients: Gaylord Entertainment Company; State Volunteer Mutual Insurance Company; Nissan North America; AmSouth Bank and Bank of America.

Other Notable Practitioners
"Workaholic" **Stephen Braun** of Greenebaum Doll and McDonald PLLC retains a high profile in the healthcare industry thanks to his experience as former general counsel to Columbia/HCA Healthcare. Commentators admire his *"tremendous ability to cut through complex legalese."*

EMPLOYMENT & LABOR LAW

MAINLY PLAINTIFF

TENNESSEE
Leading firms
(Employment: Mainly Plaintiff)

1. BARRETT, JOHNSTON & PARSLEY Nashville
   BRANSTETTER, KILGORE, STRANCH Nashville
2. DODSON, PARKER, DINKINS & BEHM Nashville
3. BURKHALTER & ASSOCIATES Knoxville
   DONATI & ASSOCIATES Memphis
   STEWART ESTES & DONNELL Nashville

Firms are listed alphabetically in each band.

Barrett, Johnston & Parsley
The Firm: The five-attorney Nashville firm earned accolades from defendant lawyers for its representation of individuals and unions in a wide variety of matters including employment discrimination, wrongful discharge and professional malpractice.
The Lawyers: Widely respected **George Barrett** was flagged up as a *"tenacious and talented"* heavy hitter in the labor arena.

Branstetter, Kilgore, Stranch & Jennings
The Firm: Based in Nashville, this nine-lawyer practice offers a range of legal services in labor and employment law, personal injury and workers' compensation.
The Lawyers: Name partners **Jim Stranch** and **Jan Jennings** were both mentioned as *"intelligent, top-flight"* labor lawyers with a loyal following among union clients. The two have acted for the Teamsters, Tennessee Valley Trades & Labor Council and Nashville Building & Construction Trades Council.

Dodson, Parker, Dinkins & Behm
The Firm: Interviewees rate the nine-attorney Nashville firm for its strength in plaintiffs' employment discrimination work. Clients include Creative Entertainment, Quaker Oats and Sony Music Publishing.
The Lawyers: Plaintiff attorney **Margaret Behm** earns respect with her *"welcoming and confidence-inspiring demeanor."* She is visible representing individuals in a number of wage and hour disputes and discrimination cases.

Burkhalter & Associates
The Firm: This smaller Knoxville team handles plaintiffs' employment litigation and personal injury matters.
The Lawyers: Noted for his *"outstanding work"* on behalf of plaintiffs, **David Burkhalter** is a popular choice for employment referrals.

EMPLOYMENT & LABOR LAW — TENNESSEE

TENNESSEE
Leading individuals
(Employment: Mainly Plaintiff)

1
- BARRETT George *Barrett, Johnston*, Nashville
- BEHM Margaret *Dodson, Parker, Dinkins*, Nashville
- JENNINGS Jan *Branstetter, Kilgore, Stranch*, Nashville
- STRANCH James *Branstetter, Kilgore*, Nashville

2
- BURKHALTER David *Burkhalter*, Knoxville
- BURNETTE Harry *Burnette, Dobson*, Chattanooga
- DONATI Donald *Donati & Associates*, Memphis
- ESTES Reid *Stewart Estes & Donnell*, Nashville

Individuals are listed alphabetically in each band.

Donati & Associates
The Firm: Opponents described the *"excellent, ethical and honest"* **Don Donati** as *"the premier guy in Memphis"* for plaintiffs' work. He represents individual employees on a range of discrimination and wrongful dismissal matters.

Stewart Estes & Donnell
The Firm: This 13-lawyer Nashville practice advises a diverse portfolio of clients on labor and employment law, products liability and IP matters. Clients of the firm include Alliance Insurance Companies, FedEx, Lincoln National Group and Lloyd's.

The Lawyers: **Reid Estes** was named by defendant lawyers as the *"lead class action guy."* Interviewees noted his large caseload of wage and hour disputes.

Other Notable Practitioners
Harry Burnette of the four-man firm Burnette, Dobson & Hardeman was identified as the *"top guy in Chattanooga,"* seen to be *"making a name for himself"* in plaintiffs' work for employees. Clients include Omega Pattern Works, Southern Technologies and Metro Homes.

EMPLOYMENT & LABOR LAW — MAINLY DEFENDANT

TENNESSEE
Leading firms
(Employment: Mainly Defendant)

1
- BASS, BERRY & SIMS PLC *Nashville*
- KIESEWETTER WISE KAPLAN *Memphis*
- KING & BALLOW *Nashville*
- MILLER & MARTIN LLP *Chattanooga, Nashville*
- WALLER LANSDEN DORTCH & DAVIS *Nashville*

2
- BOULT, CUMMINGS, CONNERS *Nashville*
- FORD & HARRISON LLP *Memphis*

Leading individuals
(Employment: Mainly Defendant)

1
- BOSTON Robert *Waller Lansden*, Nashville
- OZIER William *Bass, Berry & Sims PLC*, Nashville
- WAYLAND Eddie *King & Ballow*, Nashville

2
- GARRETT Tim *Bass, Berry & Sims PLC*, Nashville
- KAPLAN Jonathan *Kiesewetter Wise Kaplan*, Memphis
- PHILLIPS John *Miller & Martin LLP*, Chattanooga
- PRATHER Paul *Kiesewetter Wise Kaplan*, Memphis

3
- GERSON Herb *Ford & Harrison LLP*, Memphis
- LONERGAN Matthew *Boult, Cummings*, Nashville
- STEVENS Eric *Miller & Martin LLP*, Nashville
- VANCE Kim *King & Ballow*, Nashville

Firms and individuals are listed alphabetically in each band.

Bass, Berry & Sims PLC
The Firm: A respected labor and employment practice benefits from the firm's remarkable corporate base. The firm successfully represented a Japanese-owned auto parts supplier in preventing union organization and acted for a national tire manufacturer on a number of employment-related lawsuits including disability discrimination, sexual harassment and retaliatory discharge.

The Lawyers: Head of the labor and employment group **Bill Ozier** was recognized for his *"enormous wisdom and broad experience"* in the field. Elected in 2002 to the American College of Labor and Employment Lawyers, Ozier successfully defended a private university in federal court against a claim of retaliatory discharge under Title IX of the Education Amendment Act. He has also advised employers in connection with over 100 union-organizing campaigns. His representation of employers before the NLRB was declared *"second to none."*

His partner **Tim Garrett** also received widespread acclaim as a *"top-flight"* employment attorney known for his knack of *"finding the right angle on a case."* Described to researchers as a *"switch hitter,"* Garrett is adept at both labor and employment issues. His experience in traditional labor law includes union avoidance, contract negotiations and grievance and arbitration procedures. Highlights of his practice include representation of a textile manufacturer in the first FMLA lawsuit filed in Tennessee.

The Clients: Aladdin Industries; Dell; HCA and Paxton Media Group.

Kiesewetter Wise Kaplan Schwimmer & Prather PLC
The Firm: This 20-lawyer Memphis boutique focuses exclusively on management representation in traditional labor, employment and human resources matters and was recognized by peers as a *"major player statewide."* Founded upon the practices of Paul Prather and Jonathan Kaplan, the firm has been successful in expanding its market share in the state and is now able to *"cover the soup to nuts of labor and employment law"* including immigration, discrimination, OSHA and union avoidance.

The Lawyers: **Paul Prather** received widespread plaudits for his *"immense knowledge, experience and amiable demeanor."* He represents management clients in federal and state court employment litigation and in administrative proceedings before the NLRB, the EEOC, and the US Department of Labor. His employment practice covers the full range of discrimination, training and risk avoidance.

The *"dedicated and team-oriented"* **Jonathan Kaplan** was singled out for his expertise in discrimination claims and general employment counseling.

The Clients: The firm acts for a diverse mix of regional and national companies within the manufacturing, healthcare, telecom, hospitality, transportation and chemical industries. Notable names include Johnson Controls, Baptist Memorial Hospital and AT&T.

King & Ballow
The Firm: One of Tennessee's oldest labor and employment practices, the firm boasts a national employment practice of 15 attorneys split between offices in Nashville and San Diego. Well known for its historical ties to regional newspaper and radio clients, the firm has expanded its client base to include companies in the computer, insurance and service industries. Traditional labor strengths include union avoidance and contract negotiations. Within employment, the firm offers expert advice on discrimination, wage and hour and wrongful termination claims.

The Lawyers: In Nashville, litigator **Eddie Wayland** is a *"marquee player"* known for his *"dogged determination"* in employment discrimination suits, sexual harassment cases and union contract negotiations. The remainder of his workload is split between general commercial litigation and media-related defamation cases. Wayland is said to be successful at neutralizing unions and serves as regular counsel to a Florida television station. Particularly *"adroit at anticipating jury reactions,"* Wayland was described by clients as *"one of the smartest courtroom attorneys around."*

Head of the employment discrimination section, **Kim Vance** handles significant amounts of pre-litigation preparation, offering clients counsel on

TENNESSEE
EMPLOYMENT & LABOR LAW

the full range of employment issues and undertaking on-site training. An *"able courtroom performer,"* Vance was also recommended as an expert speaker and writer with a thorough knowledge of ADA and sexual harassment issues.
The Clients: Post News Week, O' Charleys and American Color Graphics.

Miller & Martin LLP
The Firm: A 30-strong labor and employment team has long-standing experience representing management in union relations and labor issues. More recently the firm has developed the practice to emphasize employment discrimination cases. Practitioners advise corporate clients on wage and hour, unfair dismissal and race, sex and disability discrimination charges.
The Lawyers: Plaintiff lawyers acknowledged **John Philips** as both a significant *"rainmaker"* for the firm and as *"one of the most talented defendant lawyers in the state."* Visible as a frequent speaker on employment topics, Philips is heavily involved in corporate training and widely commended for his *"deep substantive knowledge"* of the area. Nashville-based **Eric Stevens** divides his practice between employment counseling and litigation, in which he is particularly recommended for sexual harassment and race discrimination claims. Labor matters include the negotiation of a contract with a telecom union and representation of transport companies in their dealings with the Teamsters.
The Clients: The firm acts as general counsel for Coca-Cola Enterprises, the world's largest soft drink bottler, across the US.

Waller Lansden Dortch & Davis
The Firm: Operating from two offices in Tennessee, the 16-attorney labor and employment group profits from the extensive resources of this large full-service firm. Attorneys provide employment support to an excellent corporate practice, advising institutional clients on matters ranging from sexual harassment to ADA and race discrimination issues. The firm recently acted on a multi-plaintiff race discrimination suit in Chattanooga.
The Lawyers: Manager of the dispute resolution and regulatory group, **Bob Boston** was hailed as an *"excellent"* employment lawyer who combines a *"personable approach"* with a *"great depth of analysis."* Opponents admire him as a *"talented long-term strategist."*
The Clients: UPS, Bridgestone/Firestone and Logan's Roadhouse.

Boult, Cummings, Conners & Berry PLC
The Firm: This *"top-class"* Nashville firm maintains a 14-strong human resources team, which acts closely with a highly respected healthcare practice to serve the diverse employment needs of hospitals and healthcare companies. The group covers the full range of employment discrimination defense and traditional labor work on behalf of management clients. Wrongful termination, breaches of contract and non-compete agreements remain among the busiest areas for the firm.
The Lawyers: **Matt Lonergan**'s *"relaxed, easy style"* serves him well in labor negotiations. Commended for his *"thorough knowledge"* of employment law, Lonergan splits his practice between arbitration work for unionized plants and employment discrimination cases on behalf of local companies and healthcare facilities.
The Clients: Doane Pet Care Company, Saint Thomas Hospital and EJ Footwear.

Ford & Harrison LLP
The Firm: Headquartered in Atlanta, the firm has captured a sizable market share of labor and employment work in Tennessee. Although equipped to handle both labor and employment law issues, the Memphis practice is weighted toward the latter. ADA, sexual harassment, wrongful termination and retaliatory discharge were considered top areas for the firm.
The Lawyers: *"Well-qualified"* **Herb Gerson** enjoys an outstanding market reputation as a *"versatile"* practitioner, adept at both employment litigation and traditional labor issues. Interviewees particularly noted his experience in union avoidance and collective bargaining. Gerson regularly acts for Union Planters Bank and Northwest Airlines.
The Clients: The Athlete's Foot Group; Nestlé USA; FedEx; Union Planters Bank; Darden Restaurants (Red Lobster & The Olive Garden).

LITIGATION

Boult, Cummings, Conners & Berry PLC
The Firm: Renowned for its core practice in litigation, the firm is said to house *"one of the largest and most highly respected"* litigation groups in the state. Twenty-five full-time attorneys focus entirely on commercial litigation, covering such matters as securities, class actions, IP, franchise and commercial finance in addition to personal injury suits. Clients appreciate the *"responsive"* service on offer here.
The Lawyers: **Bill Norton** maintains a busy practice focusing on insolvency and creditors' rights, in which he is visible representing both trade creditors and landlords. Peers view him as one of the best bankruptcy litigators in the state. Managing director **Bob Patterson** was commended as a *"top-drawer trial lawyer for high-stakes litigation."* He acted as counsel to a closely held real estate company in a $97 million capital infusion. Known as a *"meticulous and scientific"* adviser, Patterson has been increasingly involved in risk management and corporate strategy matters. Interviewees praise his *"intricate knowledge of corporate governance issues."*
The Clients: ShoLodge; Bank of America; Foothill Finance; GE Capital; Gibson Guitar and ABECO.

Walker, Bryant, Tipps & Malone
see firm details p.894
The Firm: Formed in 2000 by former Bass, Berry & Sims attorneys, this Nashville-based practice was recognized by peers as *"the best commercial litigation boutique in town."* Twelve attorneys cover most forms of commercial litigation, acting primarily as defense counsel; the team is particularly recommended for its expertise in medical malpractice defense.
The Lawyers: *"Superbly talented"* **Bob Walker** was described to researchers as the firm's *"mover and shaker,"* admired for his *"straightforward"* style and effectiveness with judges and juries. His litigation practice encompasses products liability class actions, stockholder disputes and lender liability litigation. He recently represented two healthcare companies in a class action suit.
The Clients: HCA; BellSouth; Morgan Stanley Dean Witter; Baptist Hospital Healing Institute and KPMG.

GENERAL COMMERCIAL

Bass, Berry & Sims PLC
The Firm: Viewed as one of the state's biggest 'silk stocking' practices, Bass Berry's premier corporate practice receives strong support from a 40-strong litigation team. The group handles all aspects of business litigation for the firm's institutional corporate client base.
The Lawyers: *"Smart and articulate"* **Lee Barfield** earns respect as a *"top-caliber healthcare litigation specialist."* He is actively involved in the defense of hospitals, doctors and nurses in medical malpractice cases. He acts regularly for Vanderbilt University on contentious matters. Interviewees note his skill in managing complex cases and ability to *"relate well to witnesses."*
Chair of the litigation practice group **Wally Dietz** focuses on complex business and commercial

LITIGATION

TENNESSEE

TENNESSEE
Leading firms
(Litigation: General Commercial)

1 BOULT, CUMMINGS, CONNERS Nashville
WALKER, BRYANT, TIPPS & MALONE Nashville
2 BASS, BERRY & SIMS PLC Nashville
BOWEN RILEY WARNOCK Nashville
WALLER LANSDEN DORTCH & DAVIS Nashville
3 BAKER, DONELSON, BEARMAN Nashville
HARWELL HOWARD HYNE GABBERT Nashville
SHERRARD & ROE PLC Nashville

Leading individuals
(Litigation: General Commercial)

1 RILEY Steven *Bowen Riley Warnock*, Nashville
WALKER Robert *Walker, Bryant, Tipps*, Nashville
2 BARFIELD Lee *Bass, Berry & Sims PLC*, Nashville
CAMPBELL Webb *Sherrard & Roe PLC*, Nashville
GABBERT Craig *Harwell Howard Hyne*, Nashville
NORTON Bill *Boult, Cummings, Conners*, Nashville
3 DAVIS Ames *Waller Lansden Dortch & Davis*, Nashville
DIETZ Wallace *Bass, Berry & Sims PLC*, Nashville
PATTERSON Robert *Boult, Cummings*, Nashville

Firms and individuals are listed alphabetically in each band.

been representing the directors of Columbia/HCA in stockholder litigation.
The Lawyers: Described to researchers as an *"aggressive and effective trial lawyer,"* **Steven Riley** *"knows the rules of evidence and procedure intimately."* His general commercial litigation practice emphasizes securities and healthcare suits.
The Clients: AOL Time Warner; Sony Music Entertainment; Vanderbilt University; BMG Entertainment and Thomas Nelson.

Waller Lansden Dortch & Davis
The Firm: Best known for its highly rated healthcare practice, the firm boasts a *"fine litigation department of some depth."* The team handles a volume of medical malpractice suits and managed care contracting litigation, and provides able support to the corporate and securities practice on general business disputes.
The Lawyers: Chairman **Ames Davis** was singled out as an *"accomplished"* commercial litigator with notable experience of securities litigation in state and federal courts. His practice also covers antitrust, healthcare regulation and class actions.
The Clients: UPS, Bridgestone/Firestone and Logan's Roadhouse.

Baker, Donelson, Bearman & Caldwell
The Firm: Tennessee's largest firm, it was recognized as having increased its concentration of quality attorneys. A large litigation team possesses wide-ranging experience of contract disputes, stockholder litigation, insurance defense and business torts. The firm defended a regional shopping center developer in a breach of contract and fiduciary duties action brought by limited partners seeking $10 million in compensatory damages. The firm also ranks in Mississippi for the depth of its litigation practice there.
The Clients: The firm acts for local, regional, national and international clients across numerous industries on complex business litigation.

Harwell Howard Hyne Gabbert & Manner PC
The Firm: Highly recommended for its excellence in commercial restructuring work, bankruptcy and healthcare litigation, this smaller practice earns its place on the echelon of leading Tennessee practices. Clients praise this expanding group of *"talented"* practitioners as *"consistent, professional and extremely prompt."* The firm represents the creditors' committee in connection with Regal Cinemas' restructuring proceedings.
The Lawyers: Distinguished for his skill in negotiation, *"principled"* **Craig Gabbert** splits his practice between bankruptcy and commercial litigation. With considerable experience of workouts, commercial disputes and non-compete agreement litigation, Gabbert is valued for his *"measured advice"* and *"ability to strategically navigate through bankruptcy proceedings."*
The Clients: Nu-Kote Holdings; National HealthCare Corporation; Quorum Health Group and Central Parking Corporation.

Sherrard & Roe PLC
The Firm: Already an established player for corporate matters, the firm is felt to be building up its market share in commercial litigation. Clients praise the group's *"commitment,"* commenting: *"They have a solid understanding of the nature and requirements of our business."*
The Lawyers: A *"decisive and impressive"* trial lawyer, **Webb Campbell** received consistent commendation for his focus on breach of contract, business torts, insurance coverage and commercial disputes. Campbell was involved in the high-profile 2001 dispute between Gaylord Entertainment and Gilmore Entertainment Group.
The Clients: State Volunteer Mutual Insurance; Vanderbilt University; SunTrust Bank; Nissan Motor Manufacturing Corporation USA and Gaylord Entertainment.

litigation, including business torts, trade secrets, internal investigations, banking and commercial law. Dietz served as lead defense counsel to a national bank in a large consumer class action case in federal court.
The Clients: AmSouth Bank; BP America; First Tennessee Bank; HCA; O'Charley's and Vanderbilt University.

Bowen Riley Warnock & Jacobson PLC
The Firm: This 15-lawyer commercial litigation boutique is said to have particularly strong practices in music, entertainment and IP law. Interviewees also noted the firm's expertise in securities and healthcare litigation. The group has

REAL ESTATE

Boult, Cummings, Conners & Berry PLC
The Firm: This Nashville firm boasts one of the largest real estate groups in the state and enjoys an excellent reputation for its representation of local developers and lenders. Attorneys are said to possess particular expertise in relation to zoning, tax structures and bond finance matters. The firm has been involved in the sale of over 200 convenience stores in the region and has handled the sale of 60 travel centers. Practice highlights include advising Lincoln National on acquisition and credit enhancement transactions in connection with development projects across the US.
The Lawyers: Praised as both *"responsive and responsible,"* former managing partner **Tom Trent** earns high marks for his *"creative"* approach to transactions. The practice's *"premier name,"* Trent possesses significant national experience of complex real estate transactions, including acquisitions, workouts, equity participations and bond and tax-driven transactions. **Ann Cargile**

received widespread commendation in the commercial leasing area acting for both landlords and tenants. A member of ACREL, Cargile regularly represents local and national lenders and developers in the acquisition, financing and sale of real estate projects, including condominiums, office buildings, parks and retail centers.
Providing *"effective client service"* is the *"highly respected"* and *"laid-back"* **Bob Wood**, who acts nationally for State Farm Life Insurance. Wood's practice focuses on the representation of

TENNESSEE
REAL ESTATE

TENNESSEE
Leading firms (Real Estate)

1
- BOULT, CUMMINGS, CONNERS *Nashville*

2
- BAKER, DONELSON, BEARMAN *Memphis, Nashville*
- SHERRARD & ROE PLC *Nashville*
- WALLER LANSDEN DORTCH & DAVIS *Nashville*

3
- ARMSTRONG ALLEN PLLC *Memphis*
- BASS, BERRY & SIMS PLC *Nashville*
- BURCH, PORTER & JOHNSON *Memphis*

4
- GLANKLER BROWN PLLC *Memphis*
- STOKES BARTHOLOMEW EVANS *Memphis, Nashville*

Leading individuals (Real Estate)

1
- BROWN Kim *Sherard & Roe*, Nashville
- LIDDON Rob *Baker, Donelson, Bearman*, Memphis
- TRENT Tom *Boult, Cummings, Conners*, Nashville

2
- CATES Thomas *Burch, Porter & Johnson*, Memphis
- DOWSLEY Felix *Bass, Berry & Sims PLC*, Nashville
- HARKAVY Ronald *Armstrong Allen PLLC*, Memphis
- HARRIS Matthew *Waller Lansden Dortch*, Nashville
- HUMPHREYS Hunter *Glankler Brown PLLC*, Memphis
- WEATHERSBY Woods *Stokes Bartholomew*, Memphis

3
- BERRY Dewees *Bass, Berry & Sims PLC*, Nashville
- CARGILE Ann *Boult, Cummings, Conners*, Nashville
- EARTHMAN Douglas *Armstrong Allen PLLC*, Memphis
- HAYNES John *Boult, Cummings, Conners*, Nashville
- KIRKHAM Steven *Waller Lansden Dortch*, Nashville
- WOOD Robert *Boult, Cummings, Conners*, Nashville

Up-and-coming individuals
- RUTTER David *Boult, Cummings, Conners*, Nashville

Firms and individuals are listed alphabetically in each band.

institutional lenders, real estate developers and investors in real estate finance, acquisition and development transactions. Wood also advises a number of title insurance companies, and is involved in commercial lease negotiations, representing both landlords and tenants. **Jack Haynes** was lauded for his *"extensive lending experience"* and is considered a specialist in the acquisition and disposal of investment properties for US and German clients. **David Rutter** was named as an up-and-coming practitioner in the field.
The Clients: Lincoln National; State Farm Life; American Realty and Willis North America.

Baker, Donelson, Bearman & Caldwell
The Firm: The firm's real estate practice is heavily geared toward commercial lending and real estate finance. The group acts for individuals, partnerships, limited liability companies, REITs and private and public corporations in real estate acquisition, development, construction, commercial leasing, land use, management and disposition.
The Lawyers: Interviewees placed Memphis-based **Rob Liddon** *"at the top of the tree,"* praising him as a *"deeply knowledgeable"* attorney with a diverse client base and emphasis on lending work.
The Clients: The firm's clients include financial institutions, major commercial lenders, real estate developers, individual property owners, and public and private companies.

Sherrard & Roe PLC
The Firm: This mid-sized Nashville firm earned plaudits for its *"able and responsive"* real estate practitioners. Attorneys offer counsel on real estate transactions in conjunction with general business advice. Issues covered range from property sales and acquisitions and commercial lending matters to environmental and tax aspects of real estate transactions.
The Lawyers: **Kim Brown** stands out as a *"sharp, even-handed"* attorney with a *"top-notch"* reputation in property-based commercial lending. His practice centers on public and private finance and real estate finance and development.
The Clients: HD Realty, INPHACT and State Volunteer Mutual Insurance Company.

Waller Lansden Dortch & Davis
The Firm: This full-service giant enjoys a solid market reputation for its comprehensive real estate capabilities. A 15-attorney practice group is best known for its representation of large end users and developers in real estate finance transactions. An envied roster of clients includes developers, shopping center owner-operators, hospital management companies, REITs and pension funds groups.
The Lawyers: Partners **Matt Harris** and **Steve Kirkham** both received considerable peer praise. Chair of the real estate working group, Harris was commended for his *"dedication and precision"* and significant experience of acquisitions and disposals within the telecom industry. Frequently called on for his *"informed"* advice on structuring transactions, Kirkham represents entrepreneurial developer clients and multi-family housing clients. Clients report that he possesses the *"ability to find solutions and complete transactions efficiently."*
The Clients: Verizon Wireless; Logan's Roadhouse; HCA and O' Charley's.

Armstrong Allen PLLC
The Firm: The firm's 2000 merger with Harkavy Shainberg Kosten Kaplan & Dunstan is felt to have *"put the firm on the map"* for real estate matters. Building upon its solid base in litigation and commercial law, the firm is steadily enhancing its profile in the field. In addition to developers of shopping malls, hotels and industrial warehouses, the firm also acts for owner clients. Attorneys are currently acting for healthcare providers in the disposal of a hospital.
The Lawyers: Said to stand head and shoulders above his Memphis rivals, **Ron Harkavy** was identified as a critical addition to the firm. Interviewees noted his extensive expertise in the field, particularly with respect to land use and zoning matters.
Doug Earthman maintains a broad-based transactional practice, encompassing commercial real estate, municipal finance and secured financings. He recently advised on a condominium conversion and acted as borrowers' counsel to a Memphis public company in connection with a $25 million synthetic lease line of credit for development projects.
The Clients: Belz Enterprises; Taco Bell; The Regional Medical Center (Memphis) and Memphis Area Association of Realtors.

Bass, Berry & Sims PLC
The Firm: Although better known for its stellar corporate practice, the firm attracts praise for its ability to coordinate complex real estate aspects of commercial transactions.
The Lawyers: *"Scholarly"* **Dewees Berry** counsels clients on matters ranging from zoning, planning, and boundary issues to land use law and lease disputes. His practice covers purchases and sales, financings, leasing and real estate litigation arising from construction suits, mechanic's lien and contract disputes. **Felix Dowsley** received general acclaim for his expertise in commercial lending and real estate finance. Notable work includes representing the owners of a regional chain of restaurants on a $100 million revolving credit facility.
The Clients: Amsouth Bank; Gaylord Entertainment; HCA; The Kroger Company and Vanderbilt University.

Burch, Porter & Johnson
The Firm: The five-attorney real estate group within this old-line Memphis practice benefits from Burch Porter's overall reputation as a *"premier"* firm in the area. Attorneys work closely with the firm's highly rated litigation practice in handling a range of contentious real estate matters.
The Lawyers: *"Excellent"* **Tom Cates** earned distinction as a *"capable and personable"* attorney with long experience of commercial lending and real estate transactions.
The Clients: The firm acts for a number of major national corporations and serves as general counsel to public and private companies, charitable organizations and educational institutions.

Glankler Brown PLLC
The Firm: The Memphis firm boosted its profile in the state through its recruitment of 13 lawyers from Waring Cox, who bring with them a broad range of experience in litigation, securities and transactional matters. Real estate is among the firm's key practice areas.

The Lawyers: *"Hard working"* **Hunter Humphreys** focuses on real estate and secured lending.
The Clients: The firm advises owners, developers, lenders and institutional investors on real estate acquisition and finance.

Stokes Bartholomew Evans & Petree PA
The Firm: A 2000 merger with Evans & Petree created a full-service law firm operating from three offices across the state. A combined 15-lawyer commercial real estate and banking group handles all aspects of real estate financing, acquisition and development. The firm counseled on the construction of the passenger terminal at the Nashville International Airport and represented developers in the construction of the Tom Fazio and Jack Nicklaus golf courses.
The Lawyers: *"Impressive"* vice chair **Woods Weathersby** was particularly recommended for pure land development and zoning issues. He has represented banks and developers in complex commercial loans and large commercial real estate transactions involving multiple parties nationwide.
The Clients: The firm has a strong following among developer clients, acting for names such as Boyle Investment Company.

Leaders in Tennessee

BARFIELD, Lee
Bass, Berry & Sims PLC, Nashville
615 742 6200
Recommended in Litigation

BARRETT, George
Barrett, Johnston & Parsley, Nashville
615 244 2202
Recommended in Employment

BEHM, Margaret
Dodson, Parker, Dinkins & Behm, Nashville 615 254 2291
Recommended in Employment

BERRY, Dewees
Bass, Berry & Sims PLC, Nashville
615 742 6200
Recommended in Real Estate

BISHOP, George
Waller Lansden Dortch & Davis, Nashville 615 244 6380
Recommended in Corporate/M&A

BOSTON, Robert
Waller Lansden Dortch & Davis, Nashville 615 244 6380
Recommended in Employment

BRAUN, Stephen
Greenebaum Doll & McDonald PLLC, Nashville 615 760 7100
Recommended in Corporate/M&A

BROWN, Kim
Sherard & Roe, Nashville 615 742 4521
Recommended in Real Estate

BURKHALTER, David
Burkhalter & Associates, Knoxville
423 524 4974
Recommended in Employment

BURNETTE, Harry
Burnette, Dobson & Hardeman, Chattanooga 423 266 2121
Recommended in Employment

CAMPBELL, Webb
Sherrard & Roe, PLC, Nashville
615 742 4200
Recommended in Litigation

CARGILE, Ann
Boult, Cummings, Conners & Berry, PLC, Nashville 615 244 2582
Recommended in Real Estate

CATES, Thomas
Burch, Porter & Johnson, Memphis
731 524 5000
Recommended in Real Estate

CHEEK, James
Bass, Berry & Sims PLC, Nashville
615 742 6200
Recommended in Corporate/M&A

COLE, Chase
Waller Lansden Dortch & Davis, Nashville 615 244 6380
Recommended in Corporate/M&A

COWART, Richard
Baker, Donelson, Bearman & Caldwell, Nashville 615 726 5600
Recommended in Corporate/M&A

DAVIS, Ames
Waller Lansden Dortch & Davis, Nashville 615 244 6380
Recommended in Litigation

DIETZ, Wallace
Bass, Berry & Sims PLC, Nashville
615 742 6200
Recommended in Litigation

DONATI, Donald
Donati & Associates, Memphis
901 465 9511
Recommended in Employment

DOWSLEY, Felix
Bass, Berry & Sims PLC, Nashville
615 742 6200
Recommended in Real Estate

EARTHMAN, Douglas
Armstrong Allen, PLLC, Memphis
901 523 8211
Recommended in Real Estate

ESTES, Reid
Stewart Estes & Donnell, Nashville
615 244 6538
Recommended in Employment

GABBERT, Craig
Harwell Howard Hyne Gabbert & Manner, P.C., Nashville 615 256 0500
Recommended in Litigation

GARRETT, Tim
Bass, Berry & Sims PLC, Nashville
615 742 6200
Recommended in Employment

GERSON, Herb
Ford & Harrison LLP, Memphis
901 291 1500
Recommended in Employment

HARDCASTLE, Jay
Boult, Cummings, Conners & Berry, PLC, Nashville 615 244 2582
Recommended in Corporate/M&A

HARKAVY, Ronald
Armstrong Allen, PLLC, Memphis
901 523 8211
Recommended in Real Estate

HARRIS, Matthew
Waller Lansden Dortch & Davis, Nashville 615 244 6380
Recommended in Real Estate

HAYNES, John
Boult, Cummings, Conners & Berry, PLC, Nashville 615 244 2582
Recommended in Real Estate

HILL, Reginald
Waller Lansden Dortch & Davis, Nashville 615 244 6380
Recommended in Corporate/M&A

HOLT, Berry
Boult, Cummings, Conners & Berry, PLC, Nashville 615 244 2582
Recommended in Corporate/M&A

HUMPHREYS, Hunter
Glankler Brown, PLLC, Memphis
901 525 1322
Recommended in Real Estate

HYNE, Ernest
Harwell Howard Hyne Gabbert & Manner, P.C., Nashville 615 256 0500
Recommended in Corporate/M&A

JENNINGS, Jan
Branstetter, Kilgore, Stranch & Jennings, Nashville 615 254 8801
Recommended in Employment

KAPLAN, Jonathan
Kiesewetter Wise, Memphis
901 795 6695
Recommended in Employment

KIRKHAM, Steven
Waller Lansden Dortch & Davis, Nashville 615 244 6380
Recommended in Real Estate

LIDDON, Rob
Baker, Donelson, Bearman & Caldwell, Memphis 901 526 2000
Recommended in Real Estate

LONERGAN, Matthew
Boult, Cummings, Conners & Berry, PLC, Nashville 615 244 2582
Recommended in Employment

MANNER, Mark
Harwell Howard Hyne Gabbert & Manner, P.C., Nashville 615 256 0500
Recommended in Corporate/M&A

MITCHELL, Marlee
Waller Lansden Dortch & Davis, Nashville 615 244 6380
Recommended in Corporate/M&A

NORTON, Bill
Boult, Cummings, Conners & Berry, PLC, Nashville 615 244 2582
Recommended in Litigation

OZIER, William
Bass, Berry & Sims PLC, Nashville
615 742 6200
Recommended in Employment

PATTERSON, Robert
Boult, Cummings, Conners & Berry, PLC, Nashville 615 244 2582
Recommended in Litigation

PHILLIPS, John
Miller & Martin LLP, Chattanooga
423 756 6600
Recommended in Employment

TENNESSEE LEADERS

PRATHER, Paul
Kiesewetter Wise, Memphis
901 795 6695
Recommended in Employment

RILEY, Steven
Bowen Riley Warnock & Jacobson,
Nashville 615 320 3700
Recommended in Litigation

RUTTER, David
Boult, Cummings, Conners & Berry, PLC,
Nashville 615 244 2582
Recommended in Real Estate

STEVENS, Eric
Miller & Martin LLP, Nashville
615 244 9270
Recommended in Employment

STRANCH, James
Branstetter, Kilgore, Stranch & Jennings,
Nashville 615 254 8801
Recommended in Employment

TRENT, Tom
Boult, Cummings, Conners & Berry, PLC,
Nashville 615 244 2582
Recommended in Real Estate

VANCE, Kim
King & Ballow, Nashville 615 259 3456
Recommended in Employment

VOIGT, John
Sherrard & Roe, PLC, Nashville
615 742 4200
Recommended in Corporate/M&A

WALKER, Robert
Walker, Bryant, Tipps & Malone,
Nashville 615 313 6000
Recommended in Litigation

WALTON, Leigh
Bass, Berry & Sims PLC, Nashville
615 742 6200
Recommended in Corporate/M&A

WAYLAND, Eddie
King & Ballow, Nashville 615 259 3456
Recommended in Employment

WEATHERSBY, Woods
Stokes Bartholomew Evans & Petree,
P.A., Memphis 901 525 6781
Recommended in Real Estate

WOOD, Robert
Boult, Cummings, Conners & Berry, PLC,
Nashville 615 244 2582
Recommended in Real Estate

OVERVIEW — TEXAS

CONTENTS: Antitrust p.644; Banking & Finance p.645; Communications/Technology p.646; Construction p.647; Corporate/M&A p.649; Employment p.651; Energy & Natural Resources p.653; Environment p.655; Insolvency p.657; Insurance p.658; Intellectual Property p.660; Litigation p.662; Projects p.664; Real Estate p.665; Tax p.667; Individuals' Profiles p.668.

TEXAS' TOP SEVEN
1. Vinson & Elkins
2. Baker Botts
3. Fulbright & Jaworski
4. Haynes & Boone
5. Andrews & Kurth
6. Bracewell & Patterson
7. Akin, Gump, Strauss, Hauer & Feld

Ranking based on Chambers' research within the state.

All quotes in the text are from interviews with clients and competitors.

OVERVIEW: Law firms in Texas are still coming to terms with the fallout from Enron's collapse: for some it has been a boon, bringing lucrative restructuring work; for others, it has represented a significant loss of business.

Enron accounted for some 7% of **Vinson & Elkin's** workload. Yet no one expects the top-ranking firm in the state to suffer lasting damage. The firm easily retains its position in the market as the transactional leaders for oil and gas, and electricity. As energy transactions are the engine of the Texan corporate sector, this gives Vinson & Elkins an almost unassailable position. It regularly appears on the largest M&A, advising Duke Energy, for example, on its $8.5 billion acquisition of Westcoast Energy. Under accomplished attorney Bruce Bilger, the firm has also pursued international projects work, and has built an impressive Latin American practice. But there is more to Vinson & Elkins than energy. It offers a full service, topping *Chambers'* tables in a range of areas, from antitrust to tax. Its superb litigation group, in particular, with charismatic star Harry Reasoner, has developed a name not just for energy matters, but also for complex commercial litigation, IP and antitrust.

In sector after sector, interviewees praised **Baker Botts** as a top-class firm with a presence in all the biggest cases. It is now the clearest challenger to Vinson & Elkins' supremacy. Like its main rival, energy is at the core of its practice. With its growing international reach – it recently opened a Riyadh office, bolstering its burgeoning Middle Eastern profile – the firm enjoys a stream of large, cross-border deals. It has been particularly active in Latin America and in the Caspian Sea region. In David Asmus, the firm boasts the undisputed leader for upstream transactions. Much of the firm's corporate work is energy-related, but its reputation for stand-alone corporate securities advice is outstanding. These two elements - energy and securities - drive a finance practice known for prowess in complex, credit-enhanced transactions. Baker Botts is also renowned for the strength of its communications and IP teams. It is now the clear front runner in this sector, handling deals like Liberty Media's $3.4 billion acquisition of UnitedGlobalCom.

In third place, **Fulbright & Jaworski** is famous for the quality of its communications and IP practice. Clients report that its entrepreneurial team has a uniquely responsive culture, and is as comfortable representing start-ups as it is established players like Compaq, Motorola and AT&T. The firm has particular strength in biotech patent litigation, and, in Lou Pirkey, it boasts a lawyer considered by many to be among the leading trademark attorneys in the country. The firm has strong, active transactional teams and has appeared in top deals, such as Veritas DGC's $3.6 billion merger with Petroleum Geo-Services. However, it is better known for its litigation strength, and many of its departments, such as the well-respected tax team, are more visible on contentious than on noncontentious work.

Haynes & Boone, ranked fourth, operates from seven offices in the state, but has its highest profile in Dallas. This has perhaps limited its visibility in the crucial energy sector, but has not kept it from producing quality work. The firm has a niche in aviation and automobile transactions, acting for American Airlines, for example, in its acquisition of TWA. Communications is another field where the firm enjoys a strong profile. It is known for serving venture capital companies investing in start-ups, but has also built a client base that includes Nokia, Texas Instruments and IBM. The firm's highest profile, however, is in insolvency, in which it is the market leader. Headed by stars Robin Phelan and Bob Albergotti, the team naturally has a share in the Enron work, but is also representing debtors and creditors in a number of other high-profile Chapter 11s.

In fifth place, **Andrews & Kurth** appears in only seven of our Texan tables, but attains strong rankings in many of the core areas. Recent behavior suggests that that firm is focusing on growth. Two mergers with boutique firms in 2001 have substantially bolstered its capacity in communications and insolvency, while some relatively recent recruits from Skadden Arps, notably Mark Thurber, have improved its standing in the important fields of energy and projects. The firm's profile is overwhelmingly transactional. Its corporate group is recognized as one of the top three in the state, with a strong focus on the energy sector. It assists clients such as Duke Energy and NRG Energy, and recently represented InterGen on its $750 million sale to Kinder Morgan Energy Partners. In finance, the firm has close ties to JPMorgan Chase, and a particularly strong name for securitization.

Bracewell & Patterson is another focused firm with a forte in transactional energy work. It stands out most, however, for its strength in financing. The finance group regularly advises a top-flight list of banks on loans to energy and pipeline companies, including a recent $1 billion unsecured credit facility for Dynegy. In Mark Evans and William Hayes, it boasts two of the stars of this field. The homegrown team also regularly acts on high-profile power projects, again frequently for lenders. Clients appreciate its professional approach and ability to turn a deal around quickly. The firm is far from being a finance boutique, however; it provides transactional, regulatory and litigation advice to top-class clients in a variety of sectors.

Akin, Gump, Strauss, Hauer & Feld recently scored a coup by picking up an 18-lawyer litigation team from Brobeck Phleger & Harrison's disintegrating Austin office. The firm has a name for regulatory advice in spheres including energy and insurance. Following internal restructuring, the firm's project development and finance practice is now led out of DC. However, the Houston office still plays a major role in advising energy companies. It is particularly renowned for its links with the former Soviet Union, and regularly assists major player LUKOIL. The Texan offices also handle a large proportion of the firm's national insolvency workload. The practice has developed a niche in bondholder work in large Chapter 11s.

ANTITRUST

TEXAS
Leading firms (Antitrust)

1
SUSMAN GODFREY LLP *Houston*
VINSON & ELKINS LLP *Houston*

2
BAKER BOTTS LLP *Houston*
FULBRIGHT & JAWORSKI LLP *Houston*

3
CARRINGTON, COLEMAN, SLOMAN *Dallas*
HAYNES AND BOONE LLP *Dallas*
THOMPSON & KNIGHT LLP *Dallas*

Leading individuals (Antitrust)

1
MCNEIL Barry *Haynes and Boone LLP, Dallas*
REASONER Harry *Vinson & Elkins LLP, Houston*

2
CARRELL Richard *Fulbright & Jaworski LLP, Houston*
GODFREY Lee *Susman Godfrey LLP, Houston*
OLIVER Rufus *Baker Botts LLP, Dallas*
SUSMAN Stephen *Susman Godfrey LLP, Houston*

3
BAKER Tyler *Carrington, Coleman, Sloman, Dallas*
BEANE Jerry *Strasburger & Price LLP, Dallas*
HUFFMAN Gregory *Thompson & Knight LLP, Dallas*
KRUSE Layne *Fulbright & Jaworski LLP, Houston*
OXFORD Terrell *Susman Godfrey LLP, Dallas*
VAN FLEET Allan *Vinson & Elkins LLP, Houston*

Firms and individuals are listed alphabetically in each band.

Susman Godfrey LLP

The Firm: Revered as *"formidable litigation opponents,"* the most prominent plaintiffs' firm in Texas has cemented its reputation as a *"first-class"* antitrust trial outfit. On behalf of its plaintiff clientele, the firm has been successful in a wide range of price-fixing and predatory pricing cases in industries as diverse as food, steel, airlines and explosives.

The Lawyers: Among a posse of gifted attorneys, **Lee Godfrey** shines. A *"smooth and effective"* courtroom advocate, his *"flair and approachability"* is said by peers to provide a perfect foil for the more *"aggressive"* style of **Stephen Susman**. The latter is regarded in some quarters as *"one of the most intelligent attorneys in Texas."* **Terrell Oxford** in Dallas also received consistent market endorsement as a leading exponent of antitrust litigation.

The Clients: Northwest Airlines, Bell Atlantic and Medtronic figure in the firm's client roster.

Vinson & Elkins LLP

see firm details p.891

The Firm: This *"smart, diligent group"* of about 30 attorneys won praise from rivals for both its litigation and counselling compliance work. Offices in Austin, Dallas and Houston also provide support for the firm's regulatory practice in Washington DC. Notably, the group defended Blockbuster in litigation brought by independent video retailers, alleging pricing conspiracy under the Robinson-Patman Act.

The Lawyers: *"Head and shoulders above the rest,"* **Harry Reasoner** (see p.679) is revered as an antitrust *"guru."* Although now heavily involved in firm management, he maintains his reputation among his peers as an outstanding trial lawyer with *"wonderful judgment."* He represented Sun Microsystems in urging the US Department of Justice to commence antitrust proceedings against Microsoft. *"Top-flight counselor"* **Allan Van Fleet** (see p.681) was singled out to researchers for being *"excellent at holding the client's hand."* A former president of the Texas-Mexico Bar Association, he acts for clients in merger reviews before both the FTC and The Federal Commission on Competition of Mexico, and recently acted for Jindal United Steel in its competition dispute with US Steel.

The Clients: The firms acts for Dell, Halliburton, Sony and Tyco, among others.

Baker Botts LLP

The Firm: An *"experienced and talented"* group of about 12 attorneys is active in a range of antitrust litigation and counseling, including merger control, tying arrangements and antitrust and IP work for its largely energy-focused clientele.

The Lawyers: Described by peers as a *"knowledgeable and well-prepared"* attorney with an *"authoritative"* courtroom manner, the *"well-schooled"* **Rufus Oliver** stands out here. In addition to antitrust litigation, he also offers extensive counseling expertise, and successfully defended American Airlines against competitors' claims of predatory pricing.

The Clients: The firm also acted for Schlumberger in the US Department of Justice review of its sale of its natural gas assets to Hanover Compressor Company. Other clients include Global Marine and American Airlines.

Fulbright & Jaworski LLP

see firm details p.799

The Firm: Chiefly known for its antitrust litigation, this *"deep"* group of 15 attorneys regularly features on high-profile cases, notably acting for Union Pacific in a pipeline dispute with Energy Transportation System. While the firm's DC office handles merger control and regulatory work, offices in Houston, Dallas and Austin are active in counseling and litigation, particularly for energy and technology clients.

The Lawyers: *"First-class analytical abilities"* and *"sound judgment"* are said to give **Richard Carrell** (see p.670) a strong profile in the state. Peers and clients alike appreciated his affable personality and *"wonderful case management skills,"* most recently put to use in the defence of Sony Pictures Entertainment, the owner of Columbia TriStar Motion Picture Group, in the high-profile Robinson-Patman Act suit against Blockbuster and others. He has also acted for oil company Weatherford in predatory pricing litigation. *"Very much up to speed,"* **Layne Kruse** (see p.675) gained high marks from interviewees for his trial expertise. He defended Neighbors Industries in an offshore drilling industry case brought by a class of employees alleging conspiracy to fix wages and benefits.

The Clients: The firm's clients include Neighbors Industries and Sony Picture Entertainment.

Carrington, Coleman, Sloman & Blumenthal, LLP

The Firm: A long-standing force in the Texan litigation market, the firm's antitrust group was highlighted to researchers for its *"outstanding"* trial work. A roster of heavyweight clients enables them to be a frequent presence in big-ticket matters in Texas, acting in treble damages defense cases, Robinson-Patman Act defense matters and criminal antitrust work.

The Lawyers: The *"cerebral"* Rhodes scholar **Tyler Baker** won special praise from peers and clients for his *"sound judgment."* Clients especially appreciated his *"reliability,"* describing him as *"one of the best antitrust counselors out there."* He is recognized for his work with mainstay client Coca-Cola, and is currently acting on a major case brought by small bottlers regarding distribution practices.

The Clients: The group is also defending Navajo Refining in antitrust litigation brought by a consortium of companies including Exxon and The Williams Companies. The firm also advises Kodak.

Haynes and Boone LLP

see firm details p.814

The Firm: The firm has a recognized forte in criminal grand jury defense, but its 25 antitrust lawyers also undertake contentious work in the areas of monopolization, predatory pricing and class action defense, as well as merger and compliance work.

The Lawyers: The firm's eminence in antitrust law is largely attributed to the presence of *"first-class trial lawyer"* and criminal expert **Barry McNeil** (see p.676). Formerly with the antitrust division of the US Department of Justice, he has won national acclaim as a *"nimble and personable"* trial lawyer with *"impeccable timing."* He defended health industry client Hillenbrand Industries in a Section 2 monopolization case brought by Kinetic Concepts. He also provides antitrust counseling to clients on vertical distribution arrangements.

The Clients: Its clients include ExxonMobil, Hillenbrand Industries, Halliburton Energy Services and Waste Management.

BANKING & FINANCE — TEXAS

Thompson & Knight LLP
see firm details p.889

The Firm: The firm's 10-lawyer antitrust group was endorsed to researchers as *"a respected presence throughout the state."* Noted by rivals for a *"significant merger practice,"* the firm is active in both counseling and litigation, as well as in grand jury investigations, recently acting in a high-profile offshore drilling industry class action case.

The Lawyers: The *"unshakable"* **Greg Huffman** (see p.674) won peer endorsement for both his antitrust counseling and trial work. Possessing a *"wonderful trial temperament,"* rivals observed that he *"strikes the right note with juries."* He is currently active in monopolization cases in the tortilla industry, and also gives antitrust advice to the healthcare industry.

The Clients: The firm's client roster features major corporates.

Other Notable Practitioners
At Strasburger & Price LLP in Dallas, **Jerry Beane** has a fine reputation as an antitrust litigator. He recently obtained a favorable verdict for the defense in a price-fixing case involving more than 52,000 plaintiff class members.

BANKING & FINANCE

TEXAS
Leading firms (Banking & Finance)
1. VINSON & ELKINS LLP Houston
2. BRACEWELL & PATTERSON LLP Houston
3. BAKER BOTTS LLP Houston
   MAYER, BROWN, ROWE & MAW Houston
4. ANDREWS & KURTH LLP Dallas

Leading individuals (Banking & Finance)
1. EVANS Mark *Bracewell & Patterson LLP*, Houston
   GOYNE Roderick *Baker Botts LLP*, Houston
   HAYES William *Bracewell & Patterson LLP*, Houston
2. BARBOUR Larry *Vinson & Elkins LLP*, Houston
   KEYES David *Vinson & Elkins LLP*, Houston
   NIEBRUEGGE Michael *Mayer, Brown, Rowe*, Houston
3. BARBOUR David *Andrews & Kurth LLP*, Dallas
   BURNS David *Dewey Ballantine LLP*, Houston
   WEST Glenn *Weil, Gotshal & Manges LLP*, Dallas
   YOUNG William *Vinson & Elkins LLP*, Dallas
4. GILLESPIE Thomas *Jones Day*, Dallas
   MILES Robin *Bracewell & Patterson LLP*, Houston

Firms and individuals are listed alphabetically in each band.

Vinson & Elkins LLP
see firm details p.891

The Firm: Long-established energy expertise and a significant concentration of finance lawyers in Texas make Vinson & Elkins a *"major player"* in the local market. Four main areas of specialization make up the finance practice: syndicated bank lending; project finance; structured finance; and workouts. Rivals especially acknowledge the firm's *"technical mastery"* in debt finance.

Attorneys here primarily represent lenders to energy concerns, typically arranging revolving credit facilities for exploration and production companies. The firm orchestrated a $600 million credit facility for Anadarko Petroleum, as well as leveraged leasing for its transportation assets. It also represented underwriters in a $749 million public bond offering to securitize Reliant Energy's stranded costs. Beyond the energy industry, the firm oversaw the monetizations of healthcare receivables and software license fees for a major computer corporation.

The Lawyers: Researchers found universal approval for **Larry Barbour** (see p.669), a *"talented and persistent banking specialist"* with a particular forte in energy lending. Rated by peers as the *"Albert Einstein"* of the firm, the *"consummate professional"* **David Keyes** (see p.675) combines a noted capacity for the practical application of law with *"the ability to make tough decisions."* In Dallas, the *"triple A"* **William Young** (see p.683) also commands the respect of market commentators as an energy finance lawyer.

The Clients: El Paso; Dynegy; Duke Energy; Wachovia; Anadarko Petroleum; Citibank; Reliant Energy; Merrill Lynch; Shell; CSFB; Valero; JPMorgan Chase; Halliburton and Hicks, Muse, Tate & Furst.

Bracewell & Patterson LLP
see firm details p.774

The Firm: The finance group practices from within the real estate, energy and finance section. Attorneys from the group regularly represent banks on secured and unsecured lending for energy utilities and pipeline companies, as highlighted by the firm's advice on the $1 billion unsecured credit facility for Dynegy. Prior to the bankruptcy of Enron, the firm also represented Citibank and JPMorgan Chase on syndicated loans to Enron's Northern Natural Gas and Transwestern Pipeline companies. Other major transactions have included advising a bank in connection with a $350 million special purpose vehicle to issue top grade commercial paper, and supervising the issue of trust-preferred securities for Prosperity Bank. One leading lender applauded the firm's banking team for getting assignments off the ground *"with speed,"* while another drew attention to its *"first-class"* attorneys who cover *"every conceivable detail."*

The Lawyers: Prominent among the firm's attorneys is **Mark Evans** (see p.672), a syndicated bank finance expert in the oil industry who brings an *"easeful, constructive style"* to the table, which is much appreciated by his opposite numbers. A *"meticulous"* attorney with vast experience in the sector, **William Hayes** (see p.674) operates as a pure banking specialist with extensive knowledge of the energy industry. Meanwhile, **Robin Miles** (see p.677) was endorsed by peers as *"a skilled attorney who we like to see on the other side of a deal."*

The Clients: Citibank; JPMorgan Chase; Barclays; Crédit Lyonnais; Bank One; Société Générale; Crédit Agricole; People's National Bank; Prosperity Bank; Southwestern Bank of Texas; Dynegy and Reliant Energy.

Baker Botts LLP

The Firm: The firm's finance practice is buoyed by the acknowledged excellence of its securities offering. The firm specializes in acquisition financings, margin credit facilities, credit-enhanced transactions, synthetic leases and other types of off-balance sheet financings. Attorneys represented Affiliated Computer Services in the $800 million acquisition of Lockheed Martin's IMS unit, which was financed by a bridge loan led by Bear Stearns. The firm also advised on the securitization of Conoco's accounts receivable and the monetizations of pipelines and future flows, including the contract revenue for EDS' data processing outsourcing agreements.

The Lawyers: Much of the group's profile is linked with the *"prudent and scholarly"* **Roderick Goyne**, who came highly recommended as a *"sophisticated lenders' lawyer"* with wide-ranging experience of securities transactions. He represented three insurance companies on the sale and leaseback of the TXU office headquarters in Dallas, advised Pride International on a convertible debenture offering, and acted on Dell's financing of a plant expansion through a synthetic leasing structure.

The Clients: EDS; Centrex; Dynegy; Affiliated Computer Services; TrinTel Communications; Dell; Pride International and Conoco.

Mayer, Brown, Rowe & Maw
see firm details p.843

The Firm: With recognized strengths in structured finance, securities and advisory work, this *"outstanding"* international firm covers the full range of domestic and international financing matters. The group also weaves together expertise in project finance, reserve-based deals and inventory financings. Attorneys have handled a number of reserve-based financings for energy companies active in the exploration, acquisition, development and reworking of oil wells. In structured finance, meanwhile, the firm has undertaken the lease financing of pipelines as well as oil and gas wells for commercial and investment banks, insurance companies, asset-based lenders and mezzanine investors.

The Lawyers: Practicing exclusively in the energy arena is the firm's leading individual, **Michael Niebruegge** (see p.677). Acknowledged for his technical experience and *"pragmatism"* in getting deals closed, his forte is seen to lie in complex syndicated transactions. These include advising on a $1 billion Citibank financing for Williams Energy Partners, and acting for Deutsche Bank on a range of oil and gas acquisition financings.
The Clients: Bank of America; CIBC; JPMorgan Chase; Deutsche Bank; Bank One; OppenheimerFunds; Citibank and Bank of Montreal.

Andrews & Kurth LLP
see firm details p.764
The Firm: The firm's Dallas office offers a respected asset securitization practice that covers a range of commercial mortgage loans and leases, while structured finance is handled by one of the largest groups of attorneys in the southwestern US. Underwriting public and private offerings of equity and debt securities represents another specialty of the firm. Recent securitizations for the firm include a $545 million residential mortgage loan issued by First Horizon Group, a $963 million commercial mortgage loan supplied by GE Capital, and a $55 million automobile loan negotiated by Consumer Portfolio Services.
The Lawyers: Backed by a team that he leads *"superbly,"* **David Barbour** (see p.669) maintains a broad structured finance practice, which is thought to make him a *"national and international player"* in the field.
The Clients: The firm has developed close institutional ties with JPMorgan Chase. Other clients include First Horizon Group and Onyx Acceptance Financial.

Other Notable Practitioners
Three other practitioners are thought to stand out in this area. In the Houston office of Dewey Ballantine LLP, **David Burns** (see p.670) is regarded as a *"scholarly and studious attorney"* who can handle *"just about any financing deal you care to throw at him."* In Dallas, **Glenn West** (see p.682) of Weil, Gotshal & Manges LLP has a superb name as an acquisition finance specialist, while **Thomas Gillespie**'s (see p.673) reputation in the city also eclipses that of his firm, Jones Day. Gillespie is highly rated by commentators for his *"attention to detail"* on complex financings.

COMMUNICATIONS/TECHNOLOGY

TEXAS
Leading firms (Communications)
1. **BAKER BOTTS LLP** Austin, Dallas, Houston
2. **FULBRIGHT & JAWORSKI LLP** Houston
3. **HAYNES AND BOONE LLP** Houston
   VINSON & ELKINS LLP Dallas
4. **ANDREWS & KURTH LLP** Houston
   BRACEWELL & PATTERSON LLP Dallas, Houston
   JENKENS & GILCHRIST Austin, Dallas
   LOCKE LIDDELL & SAPP LLP Houston
   THOMPSON & KNIGHT LLP Dallas

Leading individuals (Communications)
1. **GRAY Robert** Fulbright & Jaworski LLP, Houston
   SZALKOWSKI Charles Baker Botts LLP, Houston
2. **JEWELL Robert** Andrews & Kurth LLP, Houston
   POWELL Charles Haynes and Boone LLP, Houston
3. **HAMMOND Herbert** Thompson & Knight LLP, Dallas
   HARVEY Dean Vinson & Elkins LLP, Dallas
   MILLS Jerry Baker Botts LLP, Dallas
   PODVIN John Bracewell & Patterson LLP, Dallas
   VOGEL Peter Gardere Wynne Sewell LLP, Dallas

Firms and individuals are listed alphabetically in each band.

Baker Botts LLP
The Firm: Described by peers as *"formidable competitors,"* the firm is highly regarded for its commitment to this area of practice. It is a member of the Texas Nanotechnology Initiative and recently took a shareholder position at STARTech Early Ventures. Communications expertise is offered in tandem with the firm's highly rated IP group, which is acknowledged by clients to deliver *"outstanding"* quality in both litigation and transactional work.
The Lawyers: Jerry Mills is head of the firm's IP group, and a founder of The Dallas Angels, a local investor group that finances emerging technology companies. His resumé includes developing licensing programs for voice mail patents, and extensive licensing and transactional work for Microelectronic Computer Technology. Researchers were consistently informed that **Charles Szalkowski**, head of the technology and emerging growth companies group, was one of the market leaders in Texas. An *"affable, accurate and pragmatic technician,"* he was widely recognized for his venture capital expertise on behalf of private technology companies. He advised on the funding of Questia Media, which raised in excess of $100 million.
The Clients: Telecom and e-commerce matters regularly feature in the firm's workload, and it has secured a raft of high-profile cases, such as representing Liberty Media on its $3.4 billion acquisition of UnitedGlobalCom. Other clients include: Alcatel; Fujitsu; Cisco Systems; Texas Instruments; Questia Media; NuView; Wellogix and Apache Telecom.

Fulbright & Jaworski LLP
see firm details p.799
The Firm: The firm is thought to have one of the most entrepreneurial communications practices in the state. Clients were forthright in their praise for the group's *"uniquely responsive"* culture; it regularly acts for both start-ups and well-established companies. Recent expansion into the area of nanotechnology has established the group as a player in the cellular and telecom sectors. The firm's sizable IP group also dedicates much of its time toward the needs of its technology and emerging business clients, and has developed particular expertise in communications litigation, following the acquisition of practitioners from Arnold White & Durkee in 2000.
The Lawyers: Bob Gray (see p.673) coheads the technology and emerging companies group, and was described to researchers as an *"indispensable"* attorney for any transaction. Commentators were impressed by his combination of *"wisdom, business acumen and enterprise."*
The Clients: Digital Consulting & Software Services; PerformanceRetail; RedMeteor; Compaq; AT&T and Motorola.

Haynes and Boone LLP
see firm details p.814
The Firm: The firm focuses its communications work on venture capital and emerging growth issues, and has notable expertise in technology issues relating to the energy industry. The growth of an office in Richardson's Telecom Corridor - an area about ten miles north of downtown Dallas - has also enabled the firm to penetrate one of the most significant concentrations of hi-tech business in the US.
The Lawyers: Charles (Chuck) Powell (see p.679), head of the firm's technology group, has been lead counsel on a number of large transactions, such as the $60 million merger of an energy service e-commerce company with an online well service and product procurement company. His peers attest to

COMMUNICATIONS/TECHNOLOGY — TEXAS

both his geniality and his ability to inspire *"complete confidence"* in clients and colleagues.

The Clients: The group advises on an impressive spread of work, acting for Trilogy on a going private transaction with pcOrder.com, and advising Nokia on structuring an OEM agreement with a software solutions provider. The firm also advises, among others, Nortel Networks, Texas Instruments, Motorola, IBM and Data General.

Vinson & Elkins LLP
see firm details p.891

The Firm: Endorsed to researchers as *"one of the more traditional firms"* in the Texas communications market, it is best known for transactional e-commerce, telecom and IT work, and has access to an unparalleled corporate clientele. Observers agree that this is one of the few operations to have emerged unscathed from the recent shake-up in the communications industry.

The Lawyers: Cochair of the internet/e-commerce practice group is *"first-rate IT lawyer"* **Dean Harvey** (see p.674). His achievements include assisting an e-commerce consulting company in establishing the largest state governmental portal in the US, and advising a major US airline on its IT-related transactions.

The Clients: The firm advised US Unwired on the $500 million acquisition of IWO Holdings, and represented Leo One USA on its funding efforts to create 'Big LEO'. Other clients include: KPMG; Sun Microsystems; MH2Technologies and Texas Lottery.

Andrews & Kurth LLP
see firm details p.764

The Firm: Advising both start-ups and fully integrated companies, the firm's technology practice group manages all aspects of its clients' e-commerce, IT and telecom requirements. The firm's acquisition of hi-tech boutique Cavazos, Morin, Langenkamp & Ferraro in 2001 is thought to have elevated the practice group's profile in Texas. A significant proportion of the group's recent workload has been e-commerce-related, and the firm is particularly well versed in handling issues that arise from regulatory bodies such as the Public Utility Commission of Texas.

The Lawyers: Peers have praised this predominantly transactional practice for the *"steadiness"* of its attorneys; this reputation has been boosted by **Robert Jewell**'s (see p.674) status in corporate and securities law. He is recognized for his ability to do a *"tremendous job"* for his hi-tech clients on securities, M&A and financing projects.

The Clients: The firm's client base includes: Cisco Systems; Veridian; DataCert; PROIV; Tonic Software and Yahoo!

Bracewell & Patterson LLP
see firm details p.774

The Firm: Although the firm's forte in this sector is recognized to lie on the financing side, its IT, telecom and e-commerce practice group deals with both regulatory and transactional matters at home and abroad.

The Lawyers: **John Podvin** (see p.678), commended to researchers as a *"client-friendly and professional"* attorney, has niche expertise in dealing with privacy and security issues pertaining to the e-banking sector. He has represented a range of financial institutions in their e-commerce work, and obtained an interpretive letter from the Office of the Comptroller of the Currency (OCC) enabling a significant expansion of banks' e-commerce powers.

The Clients: The firm acts for Fortune 100 companies and acts for a broad spectrum of industry sectors, including local and long-distance carriers, wireless, cable and TV companies and financial institutions.

Jenkens & Gilchrist

The Firm: The firm's strength within the field of communications is clearly considered by many to lie in its IP-related capability. The firm has a strong reputation for its e-commerce and telecom expertise, and acts for a range of early stage companies and multinational corporations. A highlight has been the group's advice to Micrografx from inception to its recent merger with Corel.

The Lawyers: A sizable IP and technology group is the third largest practice at the firm. It is thought to possess a number of hard-hitting litigators, under the aegis of an interdisciplinary team, headed by Jerry Welch, John Holzgraefe and Bill Parrish.

The Clients: Ericsson; Compaq; Dallas Semiconductor; Momentum; CompuCom and Belo Interactive.

Locke Liddell & Sapp LLP

The Firm: With growing technology and transactions, and media and telecommunications groups, the firm is thought by some commentators to be *"poised"* to become one of the major players in the Texan communications market. The firm has a particularly comprehensive telecom practice, and regularly acts for some of the most significant companies within the industry. Clients salute the team's *"excellent legal quality"* on issues ranging from venture capital to big-ticket litigation.

The Clients: Past transactions include representing Internet America on its IPO, and acting for AT&T on its successful contentious case against Qwest. The firm also acts for Genesis Park, Compaq, Lucent, GTE and Dynegy Global Communications.

Thompson & Knight LLP
see firm details p.889

The Firm: The firm's technology practice group has a strong transactional slant that caters for most aspects of its clients' e-commerce, telecom and IT needs. Many of the group's attorneys possess prior industry experience, which has allowed the interdisciplinary team to attract a diverse client base.

The Lawyers: One of the firm's leading lights is **Herb Hammond** (see p.673), whose *"technically sound"* reputation has helped to establish the group as *"a force to be reckoned with."*

The Clients: The firm advises emerging growth companies alongside its traditional client base of Fortune 500 companies.

Other Notable Practitioners

Peter Vogel (see p.682) of Gardere Wynne Sewell LLP is a highly respected, Dallas-based attorney, who dedicates his practice exclusively to IT and computer law. His track record includes representing a public utility in a lawsuit to recover $1.5 million in software development costs, following the failure of a project.

CONSTRUCTION

Canterbury, Stuber, Elder, Gooch & Surratt, PC
see firm details p.779

The Firm: In Texas, the firm is widely considered to be *"preeminent"* in construction law. Formed 21 years ago, this 13-lawyer boutique is particularly rated for its contentious expertise, having represented a number of major national contractors and subcontractors in headlinemaking cases.

The Lawyers: Among a team of *"top-classs scholars,"* **Joe Canterbury** (see p.670) was commended as the *"dean of Texan construction lawyers."* A 30-year veteran of the sector, he is a prolific writer and was generally endorsed for his *"practical and solution-oriented"* advice. His colleague **Kyle Gooch** (see p.673) also earned consistent approval for his *"wealth of relevant experience"* and his ability to *"settle cases using sound judgment."*

The Clients: Contractors and subcontractors form part of the firm's client base.

Coats Rose Yale Ryman Lee

The Firm: This Houston firm is regarded as one of those at the forefront of the construction industry in Texas. It offers a broad range of services, advising on real estate, municipal, civil and construction litigation and arbitration.

TEXAS — CONSTRUCTION

TEXAS
Leading firms (Construction)

1 CANTERBURY, STUBER, ELDER, GOOCH *Dallas*
2 COATS ROSE YALE RYMAN LEE *Houston*
   ROLLER & ALLENSWORTH *Austin*
3 FORD WHITE & NASSEN *Dallas*
   JONES DAY *Dallas*
4 COKINOS, BOSIEN AND YOUNG *Houston*
   GOINS, UNDERKOFLER, CRAWFORD *Dallas*
   JENKENS & GILCHRIST *Houston*
   PORTER & HEDGES, LLP *Houston*
5 FISK & FIELDER *Dallas*
   GRIFFITH & NIXON, PC *Dallas*

Leading individuals (Construction)

1 CANTERBURY Joe *Canterbury, Stuber*, Dallas
2 ALLENSWORTH William *Roller & Allensworth*, Austin
   COATS William *Coats Rose Yale Ryman Lee*, Houston
3 COKINOS Greg *Cokinos, Bosien and Young*, Houston
   FORD Jeffrey *Ford White & Nassen*, Dallas
   MEYERS Robert *Jones, Day, Reavis & Pogue*, Dallas
   PEDEN David *Porter & Hedges, LLP*, Houston
   UNDERKOFLER Paul *Goins, Underkofler*, Dallas
   YUNGBLUT Stephen *Jenkens & Gilchrist*, Dallas
4 FISK Hollye *Fisk & Fielder*, Dallas
   FLAKE Richard *Cokinos, Bosien and Young*, Houston
   GOOCH Kyle *Canterbury, Stuber, Elder*, Dallas
   MERWIN Bruce *Haynes and Boone LLP*, Houston

Firms and individuals are listed alphabetically in each band.

The Lawyers: The *"versatile, savvy and well-prepared"* **Bill Coats** has *"been doing construction all his life,"* and is one of the most experienced practitioners in the state. Specializing in representing contractors, he has a national reputation in the industry. He also represented the owners of a $250 million chemical plant near Houston in their dispute with Fluor Enterprises, an engineering and construction company.
The Clients: Since the group was established, it has acted as counsel for The Houston Chapter of the Associated General Contractors of America, the nation's largest and oldest construction trade association. It advises owners and general contractors as well as the City of Houston on its public works projects.

Roller & Allensworth
The Firm: Despite its comparatively small size, this Austin boutique has a reputation that transcends the boundaries of its home state. The group's six attorneys were commended for the *"sageness"* of their counsel on a range of construction-related litigation and arbitrations.
The Lawyers: Leading light **Bill Allensworth** was described as a *"wise and meticulous guy,"* and is renowned for his experience in both litigation and mediation. In addition to his practice, he is an adjunct professor at the University of Texas School of Law.
The Clients: A substantial client portfolio includes a number of notable engineers.

Ford White & Nassen
The Firm: Another nationally recognized construction boutique, it is one of the most significant groups in Texas. Both transactional and contentious work is catered for, although the firm is best known for its litigation prowess.
The Lawyers: The group's leading name is thought to be **Jeffrey Ford**, commended to researchers as a *"personable straight shooter who is easy to work with."* He heads a *"positive and aggressive"* group of all-around construction experts.
The Clients: The firm represents owners, general contractors, subcontractors and major suppliers in both public and private sectors. Clients include: The Beck Group; MDI General Contractors; Spring Valley Construction; University Surety of America and Post Properties.

Jones Day
see firm details p.823
The Firm: The Dallas office of this national giant contains as many as 50 attorneys who can advise on construction transactions and litigation.
The Lawyers: In spite of the firm's formidable resources, the team's principal asset is **Bob Meyers** (see p.677), who is also president of The American College of Construction Lawyers (ACCL), a professional association. Applauded for the versatility of his practice, Meyers advises on construction design and international projects and appears on a variety of contentious cases. Commentators waxed lyrical about his *"understanding of the whole construction process"* and his *"real-world pragmatism."*
The Clients: The firm's clientele includes institutional owners and developers, architects, contractors and suppliers. LCOR and The Robins & Morton Group are leading clients.

Cokinos, Bosien and Young
The Firm: Regarded by rivals as a *"young, go-getting"* Houston firm, it is gaining increased market attention, notably for its construction litigation work on behalf of contractors.
The Lawyers: Among a team of a dozen lawyers, **Rick Flake** and **Greg Cokinos** are thought to stand out. The former was endorsed for the *"professionalism, thoughtfulness and empathy"* of his arbitration and mediation practice. Cokinos, meanwhile, has a burgeoning name as a construction litigator with a *"high-powered clientele."*
The Clients: Owners represent a substantial portion of the firm's client portfolio and surety work figures prominently.

Goins, Underkofler, Crawford & Langdon
see firm details p.804
The Firm: A substantial proportion of this 17-attorney firm's focus is devoted to business litigation in state and federal courts, as well as arbitration and mediation proceedings. The group is also active in construction finance and contract negotiations.
The Lawyers: **Paul Underkofler** (see p.681) represents numerous contractors and subcontractors. He is respected for his *"intellectual integrity"* and is considered to be *"one of the top mediators in the field in Texas."*
The Clients: Construction clients include developers, owners, contractors, construction managers, subcontractors, design professionals and suppliers,

Jenkens & Gilchrist
The Firm: Thought to have taken a *"conscious decision to handle more construction work,"* the firm is now a respected force for arbitration and litigation in the sector.
The Lawyers: The group comprises 20 attorneys, with **Stephen Yungblut** considered to stand out. *"Very sound ethically,"* he was commended to researchers for his *"solid appreciation of the industry and the law."* He recently handled two different international construction arbitrations simultaneously, one in Venezuela and one in India.
The Clients: Dresser-Rand is a leading client.

Porter & Hedges, LLP
The Firm: Possessing more than 80 lawyers, the firm's reputation for construction has been considerably enhanced by its integration with the construction practice of Greenberg Peden in 2001.
The Lawyers: With the merger, the firm acquired the services of **David Peden**, who was praised for his *"massive expertise"* in both the litigation and arbitration of construction, insurance, surety and commercial issues. He represents general contractors, subcontractors, design professionals and owners and has done substantial work for the Houston Contractors Association.
The Clients: The firm advised a subcontractor on the recovery of a delay claim from the US Army Corps of Engineers. It has also appeared for contractors and subcontractors in prosecuting payment, extra work, wrongful termination and delay claims against municipalities, counties, school districts and municipal utility districts. Jerdon Enterprises is a leading client.

Fisk & Fielder
The Firm: Respected five-lawyer firm in Dallas, whose construction expertise centers on the defense

of architects and engineers in professional negligence disputes. The firm has appeared in a litigation involving cracks in the foundation at an elementary school, and advised on a personal injury and property damage action arising from the faulty design and construction of a single-family residence.

The Lawyers: A former architect himself, **Hollye Fisk** is known in Texas as the *"premier architects' lawyer."* Peers saluted his *"steel trap mind,"* and he is considered to be the first port of call for both local and national matters.

The Clients: The firm's clients include Hibbitt, Karlsson & Sorensen (HKS), engineers and architects.

Griffith & Nixon, PC
see firm details p.809

The Firm: This Dallas-based firm provides a full range of services in the areas of construction law, construction litigation and arbitration, business litigation, and insurance defense. Considered by peers to be *"thoroughly professional,"* the 12-attorney group was especially noted for its substantial workload on behalf of subcontractors.

The Lawyers: Scott Griffith leads the construction group at this firm.

Other Notable Practitioners

Bruce Merwin (see p.677), a recent arrival at the Houston office of Haynes and Boone LLP, has a particularly fine reputation for the financing aspects of construction law.

CORPORATE/M&A

TEXAS
Leading firms (Corporate/M&A)

1 BAKER BOTTS LLP *Houston*
 VINSON & ELKINS LLP *Houston, Dallas*
2 ANDREWS & KURTH LLP *Houston*
3 FULBRIGHT & JAWORSKI LLP *Houston*
 WEIL, GOTSHAL & MANGES LLP *Dallas*
4 BRACEWELL & PATTERSON LLP *Houston*
 HAYNES AND BOONE LLP *Dallas*
 HUGHES & LUCE LLP *Dallas*

Leading individuals (Corporate/M&A)

1 JEWELL Robert *Andrews & Kurth LLP, Houston*
 MASSAD Stephen *Baker Botts LLP, Houston*
 O'LEARY Michael *Andrews & Kurth LLP, Houston*
 SWANSON Joel *Baker Botts LLP, Houston*
 WORTLEY Michael *Vinson & Elkins LLP, Dallas*
2 BOONE Michael *Haynes and Boone LLP, Dallas*
 CONLON Michael *Fulbright & Jaworski LLP, Houston*
 KELLY Mark *Vinson & Elkins LLP, Houston*
 KIRKLAND David *Baker Botts LLP, Houston*
3 DAVIDSON Joshua *Baker Botts LLP, Houston*
 DILG Joe *Vinson & Elkins LLP, Houston*
 MCCORMACK William *Hughes & Luce LLP, Dallas*
 STILL Charles *Fulbright & Jaworski LLP, Houston*
 WEST Glenn *Weil, Gotshal & Manges LLP, Dallas*
 WULFE Scott *Vinson & Elkins LLP, Houston*
4 BOGDANOW Alan *Vinson & Elkins LLP, Dallas*
 COHEN Scott *Weil, Gotshal & Manges LLP, Dallas*
 HARRINGTON Michael *Vinson & Elkins LLP, Houston*
 MARSTON Edgar *Bracewell & Patterson LLP, Houston*
 SCHOENBRUN Larry *Gardere Wynne Sewell, Dallas*
 SZALKOWSKI Charles *Baker Botts LLP, Houston*

Firms and individuals are listed alphabetically in each band.

Baker Botts LLP

The Firm: Commentators agree that the firm has consolidated its position in a highly competitive market, and now ranks among the finest corporate teams in Texas. Long-established in Houston, the firm is regarded by some commentators as *"the senior corporate organization"* outside New York. Attorneys in the Houston office advise clients on a range of corporate securities and financial transactions, mostly, but not exclusively, associated with the energy sector. The firm is also considered to run a *"high-quality"* corporate business practice in Dallas.

The Lawyers: Stephen Massad is regarded in some quarters as *"one of the best corporate lawyers in the US,"* and represented Petroleum Geo-Services on its merger with Veritas DGC. This amalgamation created the second largest geophysical services company in the country. A *"hands-on approach"* and wealth of experience is considered to give **Joel Swanson** *"an edge"* on public M&A transactions and leveraged buyouts. He led the team that advised on CSFB's $230 million common stock offering for Pioneer Natural Resources.

Described to researchers as a *"bulldog,"* **David Kirkland**'s assertive style does not obscure his *"smart and meticulous"* nature. He headed the Houston team on Global Marine's $3 billion stock-for-stock merger of equals with Santa Fe International. A newcomer to this year's tables is **Joshua Davidson**, a *"smart, analytical and affable"* practitioner who specializes in IPOs for the energy industry. He has advised on issues for PennVirginia Resource Partners ($136 million) and Shamrock Logistics ($110 million). Practicing from the firm's Houston and Austin offices, the *"quadruple-smart"* **Charles Szalkowski** is said by clients to *"know everything there is to know."* He specializes in venture financings in the biotech and medical technology sectors.

The Clients: Reliant Resources; Transocean; GlobalSantaFe; Valero; Cabot Oil & Gas; Schlumberger; Shell Oil; EDS; Affiliated Computer Services; Equistar Chemicals; Lennox International; Cadbury Schweppes; Merrill Lynch; Goldman Sachs; Conoco; Lyondell; Pride International; Petroleum Geo-Services; Kerr-McGee; NuView; Questia Media and MicroMed Technology.

Vinson & Elkins LLP
see firm details p.891

The Firm: A barrage of adverse publicity relating to the Enron affair has made this an awkward year for the firm. However, observers insist that this *"extraordinary"* group remains preeminent for transactional energy matters, the sector that has lately powered corporate law in the state. Recent M&A deals in this area have included the sale of Triton Energy to Amerada Hess in a $2.9 billion cash tender offer, and advice to Mitchell Energy & Development on its acquisition by Devon Energy for $3.5 billion.

The Lawyers: Michael Wortley (see p.683) is regarded by many experienced observers as the firm's leading player in this sphere, and one of the finest in Texas. Commended to researchers as a *"marvelous technician,"* he advises on private investment fund and portfolio acquisitions, LBOs and public M&A. His track record includes major transactions in the media, food, REIT, technology and healthcare businesses. He piloted through the $1.7 billion acquisition of Dal-Tile International by Mohawk Industries and the $2.9 billion sale of International Home Foods to ConAgra. Competitors agree that **Mark Kelly** (see p.675) *"covers a lot of territory."* His practice centers on advising issuers in IPOs, secondary offerings and high yield debt deals, as well as M&A transactions between public and private companies.

Managing partner of the corporate securities department, **Joe Dilg** (see p.671) is seen by clients as a *"smart"* attorney and a skillful negotiator who *"gets to the bottom line."* New to Chambers' rankings, **Scott Wulfe** (see p.683) received high praise for his *"effective and innovative"* M&A work. *"I'd hire him tomorrow,"* said one leading rival. Dallas-based **Alan Bogdanow** (see p.669) continues to be regarded by clients as a *"fine, versatile corporate lawyer."* Interviewees recognized **Michael Harrington**'s (see p.674) *"solid all-round experience and good judgment."* A leading figure on Devon Energy's acquisition of Mitchell Energy & Development, he also specializes in Rule 144A registered and high yield financings.

The Clients: Devon Energy; Sempra Energy; AES; El Paso; NRG Energy; Unocal; The Williams Companies; Hunt Oil; Pioneer Natural Resources; ConAgra; Dynegy; Shell; Duke Ener-

TEXAS

CORPORATE/M&A

gy; Continental Airlines; Southwest Airlines; Continental Express; Mohawk Industries; Amerada Hess; Halliburton; Hicks, Muse, Tate & Furst; Merrill Lynch; Goldman Sachs; Deutsche Bank; Crédit Lyonnais; CSFB and BNP Paribas.

Andrews & Kurth LLP
see firm details p.764

The Firm: Overall market opinion ranks the firm's corporate and securities practice among the top three most active groups in Texas. As elsewhere in the state, a strong component of the team's workload is energy-related, with highlights including advising Duke Energy on its acquisition of Enron's energy interests, and representing InterGen on its $750 million acquisition by Kinder Morgan Energy Partners.

The Lawyers: Interviewees were unanimous that the group's greatest assets are its two outstanding and well-connected practitioners, **Robert Jewell** (see p.674) and **Michael O'Leary** (see p.677). The *"terrific"* Jewell was endorsed to researchers as a *"hugely talented"* corporate lawyer; he served as counsel to Williams Energy Partners for an IPO worth $320 million. In concert with O'Leary, he also represented Weatherford International on its acquisition of half a dozen overseas companies to expand its oil field equipment and contract drilling services. O'Leary himself was acclaimed by clients as a *"first-tier"* lawyer with strong technical abilities and a *"can-do attitude."* His recent caseload has included advising BJ Services on its $420 million acquisition of OSCA.

The Clients: NRG Energy; Anadarko Petroleum; Williams Energy Partners; Northern Border Partners; American Electric Power; Duke Energy; Weatherford International; BJ Services; Lehman Brothers; Salomon Smith Barney; Banc of America Securities; JPMorgan and CSFB.

Fulbright & Jaworski LLP
see firm details p.799

The Firm: Widely recognized as litigation specialists, the firm is also acknowledged to operate a *"substantial"* corporate practice from its office in Houston. Strong on M&A transactions, the corporate group focuses on oil services companies, chemical processing and hydrocarbons businesses. The team handled Tesoro Petroleum's $1.1 billion acquisition of the Golden Eagle refinery from Valero, acted for Baker Hughes on its WesternGeco joint venture with Schlumberger, and featured on the $3.6 billion merger between Veritas DGC and Norway's Petroleum Geo-Services.

The Lawyers: Other work has included the firm's involvement in the merger between UTI Energy and Patterson Energy. A key player here was the *"outstanding"* **Michael Conlon** (see p.671), who is said by competitors to *"represent the best qualities of the firm."* Leading the transactional team was senior partner **Charles Still** (see p.680), recommended to researchers for his *"uncommon"* technical and negotiating abilities.

The Clients: Veritas DGC; Patterson-UTI Energy; Tesoro Petroleum; Baker Hughes; Shell; Duke Energy; EOG Resources; Weatherford International and Stewart & Stevenson.

Weil, Gotshal & Manges LLP
see firm details p.897

The Firm: Internationally acknowledged for its insolvency, debt and capital market financings, this New York firm continues to make successful inroads into the Texas market. The firm represented Enron on the sale of trading concerns arising from its bankruptcy, notably UBS Warburg's $1.5 billion acquisition of Enron's natural gas and power trading business and the $350 million sale of its Wind Corporation to GE. The firm's Dallas office also advises on major corporate transactions in conjunction with lawyers from New York and Western Europe in industries such as automobiles, technology and broadcasting.

The Lawyers: **Glenn West** (see p.682) and **Scott Cohen** (see p.671) are regarded as the team's leading practitioners in Dallas and drew notable plaudits for their private equity work.

The Clients: A significant amount of business issues from the firm's involvement with leveraged buyout specialist Hicks, Muse, Tate & Furst. Other leading clients include: AMR; Texas Instruments; NextMedia Group; LIN TV; GM; NBC and GE.

Bracewell & Patterson LLP
see firm details p.774

The Firm: This *"sophisticated"* indigenous corporate group is perceived to be particularly strong in Houston, where it provides a distinctly energy-focused M&A and securities offering. The firm has advised on a variety of complex M&A transactions, often involving pipelines, power plants, terminals and infrastructure facilities across the US.

The Lawyers: **Edgar Marston** (see p.676), the *"grand old man"* of corporate law in Houston, continues to be admired by peers for his perennial *"zest."* He represented George Mitchell as shareholder counsel on a deal worth $3 billion, and was also involved in an institutional securities purchase on behalf of Kinder Morgan.

The Clients: Babcock Group; Kinder Morgan; Encompass Services; The Sterling Group; Notre Capital Ventures; Benchmark Electronics; Reliant Energy; Crédit Lyonnais; Société Générale and Citibank.

Haynes and Boone LLP
see firm details p.814

The Firm: Research confirms that Haynes and Boone's strengths lie in Dallas where the firm is said to have a *"forceful"* local practice. Attorneys here have assisted on a variety of strategic acquisitions, notably in the aviation and automobile industries. The firm represented American Airlines on its acquisition of TWA, and also advised Gulf Canada in its sale to Conoco.

The Lawyers: Peers and clients alike consider the firm's cofounder, **Michael Boone** (see p.669), to be a *"powerbroker"* on the Dallas legal and business scenes. Said to have an *"uncompromising"* approach, Boone is widely accepted to be the premier M&A practitioner in the city.

The Clients: AMR; RadioShack; Kirby Corporation; Trinity Industries; El Paso; Bank of America and Gulf Canada.

Hughes & Luce LLP

The Firm: The firm enjoys a substantial profile on the domestic corporate scene, with technology and heavy industry proving to be particularly fruitful sources of work. The corporate and securities group represented Wal-Mart in a $15 billion financing that included public offerings, Rule 144A transactions and private placements. It also advised on EDS' $2.2 billion service contract to manage Sabre's IT infrastructure.

The Lawyers: Top name here is considered to be **William McCormack**, a member of the team that guided Suiza Foods' $10 billion acquisition of Dean Foods to completion. Peers regard him as an attorney with whom *"we can do business."*

The Clients: EDS; Ericsson; Dean Foods; Southwestern Bell Telephone Company; CNA Insurance Companies; Blockbuster; Wal-Mart; Dell; DuPont; AMR and Perot Systems.

Other Notable Practitioners

Larry Schoenbrun (see p.680) of Gardere Wynne Sewell LLP's Dallas office comes *"highly recommended"* as a corporate and securities practitioner. He serves on the special committee of the Arthur Andersen board of directors and attends to affiliate transactions and conflict situations.

EMPLOYMENT & LABOR LAW

TEXAS — MAINLY PLAINTIFF

Leading firms
(Employment: Mainly Plaintiff)

1
- GREGG M ROSENBERG & ASSOCIATES *Houston*
- MANDELL & WRIGHT *Houston*

2
- AHMAD, ZAVITSANOS & ANAIPAKOS, PC *Houston*
- BUTLER & HARRIS *Houston*
- GILLESPIE, ROZEN & WATSKY, PC *Dallas*
- GLICKMAN & HUGHES LLP *Houston*

Leading individuals
(Employment: Mainly Plaintiff)

1
- ROSENBERG Gregg *Gregg M Rosenberg, Houston*
- TUCKER Eliot *Mandell & Wright, Houston*

2
- AHMAD Joseph *Ahmad, Zavitsanos, Houston*
- GILLESPIE Hal *Gillespie, Rozen & Watsky, PC, Dallas*
- GLICKMAN Julius *Glickman & Hughes LLP, Houston*
- HARRIS Margaret *Butler & Harris, Houston*

Firms and individuals are listed alphabetically in each band.

Gregg M Rosenberg & Associates

The Firm: Identified as one of the few dedicated plaintiff employment specialists in Texas, **Gregg Rosenberg** was hailed to researchers as *"a veteran of big cases."* Both unions and opposing lawyers acknowledge him as a *"bright and aggressive"* attorney who has raised his profile by advising on key discrimination and sexual harassment cases. Interviewees insist that *"no one can match his years of experience and courtroom skills."*

Mandell & Wright

The Firm: Senior partner **Eliot Tucker** is one of the state's most prolific employment lawyers. Said by most contemporaries to be *"in a class of his own,"* his practice merges employment, labor and personal injury advice. Although he is seen representing both employees and employers, his reputation is greatest for appearing on behalf of individuals and labor unions in Title VII cases and tort and contract actions. Rivals concede that *"in court, he's a born winner."*

Ahmad, Zavitsanos & Anaipakos, PC
see firm details p.759

The Firm: Researchers had their attention drawn to leading trial lawyer **Joseph Ahmad**. Younger than his nearest competitors, this *"highly capable litigator"* is widely respected in Texas. He is most associated with disability discrimination and breach of contract cases, although executive compensation and employee benefits are also areas of particular expertise. He gained for his clients the first same-sex sexual harassment federal court judgment in Texas.

Butler & Harris

The Firm: Another well-respected employment boutique, it has earned a reputation for acting in *"huge numbers of plaintiff cases."* Although also advising small companies, this two-partner practice is said to be *"brilliant for individual clients."* **Margaret Harris** received substantial market endorsement, notably for her strong track record in sexual harassment cases and wrongful discharge issues.

Gillespie, Rozen & Watsky, PC
see firm details p.803

The Firm: Acting for unions and individual clients, **Hal Gillespie** (see p.672) is a respected figure in the local market. He is the senior partner at an eight-lawyer boutique, which advises primarily on arbitration, mediation, civil trials and appeals involving discharge, discrimination and sexual harassment. Market commentators agree that Gillespie is a *"capable, aggressive and prolific litigator."*

Glickman & Hughes LLP

The Firm: This six-lawyer Houston firm focuses primarily on business litigation, and represents both plaintiffs and defendants in breach of contract, wrongful termination and discrimination cases. *"Classic old-school attorney"* **Julius Glickman** was praised to researchers as *"a fabulous litigator."* During his 30 years in practice, he has obtained some of the most significant verdicts in Texas for wrongful termination, defamation and breach of contract matters. Client: Omnibus International.

EMPLOYMENT & LABOR LAW

TEXAS — MAINLY DEFENDANT

Leading firms
(Employment: Mainly Defendant)

1
- BAKER BOTTS LLP *Houston*
- FULBRIGHT & JAWORSKI LLP *Austin, Houston*
- VINSON & ELKINS LLP *Austin, Dallas, Houston*

2
- BRACEWELL & PATTERSON LLP *Houston*
- LITTLER MENDELSON PC *Dallas, Houston*

3
- AKIN GUMP STRAUSS HAUER *Dallas, San Antonio*
- HAYNES AND BOONE LLP *Dallas, San Antonio*
- JENKENS & GILCHRIST *Dallas, Houston*

Firms are listed alphabetically in each band.

Baker Botts LLP

The Firm: Researchers were impressed by the depth of market recommendation for the firm's employment law expertise. The group is fed by strong corporate and litigation practices, and was acknowledged by all interviewees as *"one of the most experienced in the Texan market."* Opponents perceive the team to be *"stronger in Houston than in Dallas,"* but *"definitely in the premier league in both."* About 20 lawyers advise on the spectrum of employment and labor law, including discrimination claims, wrongful discharge, union-organizing campaigns, labor contract negotiations and unfair labor practices. The energy and telecom industries are particularly fruitful sources of work.

The Lawyers: Both clients and competitors were quick to acknowledge **Richard Brann**'s *"outstanding technical skills."* Even after 30 years of practice, this *"consummate litigator"* is seen to be active in race, age and sex discrimination class actions, as well as wrongful discharge cases. The team represented Exxon Chemical Company (now ExxonMobil Chemical Company) in seven race discrimination cases, and advised CTX Mortgage on a suit filed by nine present and former employees alleging a pattern and practice of discrimination against African-American and Hispanic employees. Other matters include advising Reliant Energy Power Generation against consolidated unfair labor practice charges.

The Clients: CTX Mortgage; ExxonMobil Chemical Company; Reliant Energy; Tejas Gas Corporation; United Way of the Texas Gulf Coast; Post-Newsweek Stations; Greater Houston Emergency Physicians; Hispanic Broadcasting; i2 Technologies US and Jiffy Lube International.

Fulbright & Jaworski LLP
see firm details p.799

The Firm: This is an established team with a *"significant presence in the employment and labor arena,"* which is acknowledged to benefit from its colossal litigation capacity. With four offices in Texas, the group is a leading choice for a wide range of employment work, including employment litigation, civil rights charges, and wage and hour, ERISA and employment benefits matters. It is also noted for its ability to handle traditional labor law and trade secrets work. A long tradition of advising in the healthcare and manufacturing sectors is backed up by a substantial client roster of energy, retail, airline and chemical companies.

The Lawyers: Two individuals' names were singled out to researchers. **John Harper** (see p.673)

TEXAS
EMPLOYMENT & LABOR LAW

TEXAS
Leading individuals
(Employment: Mainly Defendant)

1
- BRANN Richard *Baker Botts LLP*, Houston
- JORDAN Carl *Vinson & Elkins LLP*, Houston

2
- GREIG Brian *Fulbright & Jaworski LLP*, Austin
- HARPER John *Fulbright & Jaworski LLP*, Houston
- MELO Thomas *Bracewell & Patterson LLP*, Houston
- SHEEDER Robert *Jenkens & Gilchrist*, Dallas

3
- HEADLEY Linda *Littler Mendelson PC*, Dallas
- JANSONIUS John *Akin Gump Strauss Hauer*, Dallas
- LONDA Jeffrey *Ogletree, Deakins, Nash*, Houston
- MASLANKA Michael *Godwin Gruber*, Dallas
- SHANK Mark *Hughes & Luce LLP*, Dallas

Individuals are listed alphabetically in each band.

has a superb reputation for labor law expertise (*"He's definitely near the top of the tree"*). Based in Austin, **Brian Greig** (see p.673) was praised for his *"successful handling of major cases,"* and is especially known for his courtroom appearances on restrictive covenant and trade secrets matters.
The Clients: The firm acts for Motorola, and is a popular choice for Fortune 500 companies.

Vinson & Elkins LLP
see firm details p.891
The Firm: The group is an acknowledged master of all areas of employment law, and has a notable client base from the manufacturing, oil and gas and technology industries. The Austin, Dallas and Houston offices are home to an employment team of 30 full-time lawyers, who have long experience of advising on Title VII cases, civil rights litigation and counseling. Clients enthused to researchers about a team that *"always inspires confidence."*
The Lawyers: No observer is in any doubt about the status of **Carl Jordan** (see p.675), recommended as *"one of the leading exponents of employment law in Texas."* Peers admire his ability to deal with *"the most complex cases with the greatest of ease."* His practice encompasses trial cases, discrimination lawsuits and traditional labor law, and he has recently represented clients in connection with numerous class action discrimination lawsuits, involving issues of disparate treatment and disparate impact. He and his team also acted for a national insurance company in an age discrimination and fraud lawsuit brought by several former officers displaced as a result of a nationwide reorganization, obtaining summary judgment on behalf of the employer.
The Clients: The firm acts for Garner Environmental Services. Fortune 500 companies also feature on its client roster.

Bracewell & Patterson LLP
see firm details p.774
The Firm: An active and visible presence in Texas, the firm is respected for employment discrimination, wrongful discharge and wage and hour matters, and has a notably powerful educational institution clientele. The hi-tech, energy and financial industries are other important areas for the group's traditional labour law and counseling work.
The Lawyers: Clearly the outstanding lawyer here is **Thomas Melo** (see p.677), singled out to researchers as *"a smart practitioner who has built up a great client roster."* Contemporaries emphasized his expertise in employment law as it affects educational establishments.
The Clients: American General; San Antonio Spurs; Levi Strauss; Southwest Airlines and Apple.

Littler Mendelson PC
The Firm: A substantial nationwide group is acknowledged by rivals for its *"effective marketing strategy"* and *"ultrasmart attorneys."* Eighteen partners in Houston and Dallas advise on all aspects of employment and labor law, and have a recognized niche in employment litigation.
The Lawyers: **Linda Headley** has built a formidable local name over the past 20 years, defends clients on sexual harassment and trade secrets cases, and represents employers on collective bargaining.
The Clients: Clients are drawn from areas as diverse as real estate, chemicals, manufacturing and energy.

Akin Gump Strauss Hauer & Feld LLP
see firm details p.761
The Firm: Observers thought the firm has *"an increasingly formidable"* employment group in its Dallas and San Antonio offices, which handles all aspects of relevant law across a range of industries, including transportation, hospitality, retail, hi-tech and energy. However, it is most recognized by competitors for its niche expertise in labor law.
The Lawyers: The team's *"shining light"* is considered to be **John Jansonius**, who was recommended to researchers as *"a good choice for complex cases."* His practice combines discrimination litigation work, traditional labor law and arbitration.
The Clients: Fortune 500 companies form part of the firm's clientele.

Haynes and Boone LLP
see firm details p.814
The Firm: Much of the employment team's work revolves around its prime multinational client base, and is supported by strong state coverage, notably in Dallas and San Antonio. The department has a balanced caseload, mixing civil rights cases and counseling with a strong litigation capacity. It also undertakes a variety of traditional labor work and employee benefits matters.
The Lawyers: During the past year, the group, which is led by Jonathan Wilson, advised on a number of discrimination lawsuits, labor unions' cases and workers' compensation matters.
The Clients: AMR; Bank of America; CROSSMARK; Hitachi; CellStar; Aviall and Siemens.

Jenkens & Gilchrist
The Firm: Smaller in size than its competitors, this Dallas-based boutique was warmly recommended to researchers for its *"philosophy of quality over quantity."*
The Lawyers: The team's profile is thought to owe much to the leadership of **Robert Sheeder**, *"one of the first lawyers to come to mind for high-level referrals."* Combining employment-related litigation, arbitration and labor union work in his practice, he is noted as a constant presence on some of the largest cases in the state.
The Clients: The firm is well known for its representation of Fortune 500 companies.

Other Notable Practitioners
A new arrival at Godwin Gruber from Andrews & Kurth LLP, the *"highly experienced"* **Michael Maslanka** earned plaudits from competitors for his employment litigation appearances. Described to researchers as a *"prolific writer and smart practitioner,"* **Mark Shank** is seen by rivals as *"a heavyweight employment lawyer"* at Hughes & Luce LLP, his home since 2001. He was frequently noted for representing hi-tech, telecom and media companies. A senior figure at Ogletree, Deakins, Nash, Smoak & Stewart PC, **Jeffrey Londa** enjoys recognition as *"an extremely professional and hard-working lawyer."* *"Brilliant in front of a jury,"* he specializes in complex employment litigation, collective bargaining and arbitrations.

ENERGY & NATURAL RESOURCES

TEXAS
Leading firms
(Energy & Natural Resources)

1. **VINSON & ELKINS LLP** Houston
2. **BAKER BOTTS LLP** Houston
3. **FULBRIGHT & JAWORSKI LLP** Houston
   KING & SPALDING LLP Houston
4. **AKIN GUMP STRAUSS HAUER & FELD** Houston
   ANDREWS & KURTH LLP Houston
   BRACEWELL & PATTERSON LLP Houston
5. **SKADDEN, ARPS** Houston
6. **LOCKE LIDDELL & SAPP LLP** Dallas

Leading individuals
(Energy & Natural Resources)

1. **ASMUS David** Baker Botts LLP, Houston
   BILGER Bruce Vinson & Elkins LLP, Houston
   COGAN John King & Spalding LLP, Houston
2. **CULOTTA Ken** King & Spalding LLP, Houston
   DILG Joe Vinson & Elkins LLP, Houston
   GOOLSBY George Baker Botts LLP, Houston
   UNGER Timothy Andrews & Kurth LLP, Houston
3. **ALE John** Skadden, Arps, Slate, Meagher, Houston
   BISHOP Doak King & Spalding LLP, Houston
   BOWMAN John Fulbright & Jaworski LLP, Houston
   GREMILLION Todd Akin Gump Strauss, Houston
   KELLEY Jay Vinson & Elkins LLP, Houston
   KUTZSCHBACH George Fulbright & Jaworski, Houston
   TAYLOR Lyndon Skadden, Arps, Slate, Houston
4. **BACKUS Marcia** Vinson & Elkins LLP, Houston
   BLAND Doug Vinson & Elkins LLP, Houston
   DAVIS Platt Vinson & Elkins LLP, Houston
   GUNTER Clifford Bracewell & Patterson LLP, Houston
   MOORE Charles LeBoeuf, Lamb, Greene, Houston
   PATTON David Locke Liddell & Sapp LLP, Houston
   RAFTE Alan Bracewell & Patterson LLP, Houston
   THURBER Mark Andrews & Kurth LLP, Houston

Firms and individuals are listed alphabetically in each band.

Vinson & Elkins LLP
see firm details p.891

The Firm: With almost half of the firm's 860 lawyers across the world focusing on energy practice, Vinson & Elkins maintains its dominant national and international position as one of the world's great energy firms in spite of a tough year. The demise of Enron, one of the group's largest clients, and the attendant unfavorable publicity, have not managed to make a serious dent in the firm's reputation as *"easily the transactional leaders"* for both oil and gas, and electricity matters. The team maintains a continuous involvement in the development and financing of electric power plants, pipelines, and other energy and petrochemical projects around the world and has recently also increased its project development practice in Asia. Regulatory advice and a steady diet of litigation complete its workload.

The Lawyers: **Bruce Bilger** (see p.669), endorsed to researchers as *"accomplished and tough – just a great lawyer,"* is regarded as the group's premier transactional figure. He has been the moving spirit behind the firm's expansion of its portfolio of project developments in Latin America. **Joe Dilg** (see p.671), although recently occupied with managerial responsibilities, retains his reputation as an *"effective leader"* for both domestic and international energy transactions, while **Jay Kelley** (see p.675) enjoys high status as one of the key figures in Texas for finance and project development work. **Marcia Backus** (see p.669) is thought by peers to be a name on the rise. An M&A and joint venture specialist, she also handles big-ticket project financings for both the oil and power sectors. Clients regard her as an *"attentive and smart"* attorney. Now head of the firm's project finance group, **Doug Bland** (see p.669) gained the enthusiastic recommendation of clients who value his *"unequaled commercial awareness."* **Platt Davis** (see p.671) is a highly regarded arbitrator who has represented the natural gas and electric power industries in a range of international disputes.

The Clients: Among a raft of significant transactions, the group represented Duke Energy on its $8.5 billion acquisition of Westcoast Energy, and acted for Reliance Petroleum in the $5.5 billion development of the world's largest greenfield refinery and petrochemical complex in Jamnagar, India. The firm's clients include: Merrill Lynch; Shell Oil; Mitchell Energy & Development; Halliburton; JPMorgan Chase; Fortum; Forest Oil; Occidental Petroleum; Reliance Petroleum and CMS Energy.

Baker Botts LLP

The Firm: A consistent presence on cross-border oil and gas transactions, the firm is recognized by competitors as *"a worthy adversary;"* it remains the principal challenger to Vinson & Elkins' supremacy in this area. A large group represents domestic and international clients on a broad range of oil, gas and electricity matters, with a focus on LNG projects worldwide.
International upstream and midstream matters feature prominently in the caseload, including extensive advice on financial and transportation projects in the Caspian Sea region. In 2001, the firm also opened an office in Riyadh, as a result of its activity in the Middle East. Domestically, the firm has been heavily involved in the deregulation of the electricity industry, and is assisting power distribution companies on filing for bankruptcy after the collapse of the market in California.

The Lawyers: Some commentators believe **David Asmus** to be *"the best energy lawyer in Texas."* Regarded as the market leader on the technical aspects of upstream transactions, he devotes his practice entirely to oil and gas transactions, including joint ventures, M&A work and energy-based financings. He is also heavily involved in international projects work, developing gas fields, building pipelines and advising on offshore projects.
"The preeminent pipeline lawyer in the world," was one rival's assessment of **George Goolsby**, who heads the firm's worldwide energy practice. Renowned for his *"transactional acumen,"* he advised a consortium led by BP on the transportation to and marketing in Georgia and Turkey of natural gas produced in the Caspian Sea region. He also continues to represent the consortium in developing a one million barrel per day crude oil pipeline, running from the Caspian to the Mediterranean Seas.

The Clients: In the field of natural resources, the firm represented Azerbaijan International Operating Company on the formation and structuring of the operating company for the Azeri Project, and in the negotiation of 'early oil' export project routes through Russia and Georgia. Elsewhere, an enviable contentious portfolio has been highlighted by the firm's successful advice to BP Amoco, Amerada Hess and Enterprise Oil in a dispute with Rowan Drilling over the termination of a contract. The firm also acts for Reliant Energy, ExxonMobil, ChevronTexaco, BP, Dynegy, Marathon Oil and Baker Hughes.

Fulbright & Jaworski LLP
see firm details p.799

The Firm: The firm's excellent overall reputation for contentious expertise is often attributed by interviewees to the efforts of its energy practice, where the firm is particularly commended for its track record in international arbitration. However, the energy group advises on the full gamut of regulatory and transactional matters, both at home and on the international stage.

The Lawyers: *"Forthright and commercial"* **George Kutzschbach** (see p.676) has a fine name as a transactional lawyer, often working on deals related to oil and gas exploration. He represented TEPPCO Partners in the $444 million acquisition from Burlington Resources of a 360-mile natural gas pipeline system, and acted for subsidiaries of El Paso on the $294 million lease of a refinery in Corpus Christi, Texas, to affiliates of Valero. *"Outstanding litigator"* **John Bowman** (see p.670) was commended to researchers for his appearances on behalf of oil and gas producers and users in a variety of disputes, including royalty owner matters, joint operating agreement cases, drilling contract disputes and gas contract litigation. He successfully represented a Houston-based independent oil and gas company against claims arising from the purchase of oil and gas properties in Texas and Louisiana.

The Clients: The firm acted for Calpine in connection with a new senior secured $1.6 billion loan facility and an amended $400 million credit facility, and represented Enbridge in its acquisition of Midcoast Energy Resources. It also advises Enterprise Oil, Forest Oil, EOG Resources, El Paso, TEPPCO Partners, Enbridge, TotalFinaElf, Sempra Energy Trading and Plains All American Pipeline.

King & Spalding LLP
see firm details p.829

The Firm: By more than doubling the size of its energy group in the past two years, the firm has become one of the fastest growing in the state, and is now considered by rivals to offer a serious threat to the native Texan practices. Researchers were directed to a team with *"a lot of depth and thoroughly skilled practitioners,"* which provides clients with all-around expertise in oil and gas transactions, LNG and other international project developments, and litigation.

The Lawyers: The outstanding name here is **John Cogan** (see p.671), ExxonMobil's preferred outside counsel, who was universally acclaimed to researchers as *"a top-notch lawyer who can cover anything."* He has advised on corporate and financial transactions and LNG projects throughout the world, notably in Saudi Arabia, and has also been heavily involved in government regulatory matters. Contemporaries rate **Ken Culotta** (see p.671) as an *"honest, straightforward and personable lawyer"* who specializes in international power generation projects. He continues to advise on Haddington Venture's compressed air energy storage project near Norton, Ohio. The *"attentive"* **Doak Bishop** (see p.669) has established a strong profile for expertise in international energy disputes, and has served as counsel and arbitrator for major oil and energy companies in multimillion dollar cases at the International Centre for Settlement of Investment Disputes. He acted for Mobil Argentina and is currently representing Azurix in ICSID arbitrations against Argentina, and is also involved in a large AAA International Rules arbitration for Texaco China.

The Clients: ChevronTexaco; ExxonMobil; Zurich Corporation; Mobil Argentina; El Paso; Williams International; Sempra Energy International and BP Amoco.

Akin Gump Strauss Hauer & Feld, LLP
see firm details p.761

The Firm: Well known in the regulatory field for appearing before federal and state agencies, the firm has recently restructured its energy group. The project development and finance practice is now led out of Washington DC, although the Houston office plays a prominent role in advising energy companies on a range of commercial issues such as major oil and gas development projects. However, it is the firm's international oil and gas expertise, notably in the former Soviet Union, which is reckoned to be its unique selling point. The firm works closely with several Russian and CIS states' key energy companies on a number of high-value transactions.

The Lawyers: Interviewees warmly recommended the *"successful and charismatic"* **Todd Gremillion** for his broad-based oil and gas practice. A veteran of numerous domestic and international transactions, he has acted extensively for Russia's largest oil company, LUKOIL, and has represented a former Soviet republic and its national oil company on oil and gas exploration and production agreements.

The Clients: VimpelCom, LUKOIL, Dynegy, El Paso and Vanco Energy are clients.

Andrews & Kurth LLP
see firm details p.764

The Firm: The firm's *"top-class"* energy practice is renowned for its international capability, and is involved in all types of oil and gas matters, including pipeline projects and power developments at home and abroad. It also represents several major interstate natural gas pipelines, and oil and electricity companies on federal energy regulatory matters.

The Lawyers: The *"extremely accomplished"* **Timothy Unger** (see p.681) has an excellent reputation for representing clients in power projects and gas industry financings. **Mark Thurber** (see p.681), commended to researchers as a *"powerful and ethical lawyer with high standards,"* is involved in energy and infrastructure transactions and energy projects in South America and east Africa.

The Clients: The firm represented Brazos Valley Energy, NRG Energy and STEAG Power on the financing of a 600MW merchant power project, and acted for Williams Energy Marketing & Trading on a $115 million turbine financing and agency agreement project. Other clients include: Anadarko Petroleum; Southern Natural Gas Company; BJ Services and Brazos Valley Energy.

Bracewell & Patterson LLP
see firm details p.774

The Firm: Working closely with its offices in London and Kazakhstan, the energy practice has a solid track record of advising on energy transactions domestically and abroad. The team is noted by peers for its expertise on the regulatory framework of the US energy market, and appeared on recent FERC proceedings in connection with the pricing of power in California.

The Lawyers: **Alan Rafte**'s (see p.679) practice encompasses project finance, M&A transactions and project development. Described to researchers as a *"great negotiator, always looking for reasonable solutions,"* he has represented Shell and Coral Energy Resources on many of their project developments. *"Top-flight"* trial lawyer **Clifford Gunter** (see p.673) has tried international project finance issues for multinational corporations such as Bechtel, Kinder Morgan and KPMG Peat Marwick. The firm represented Kinder Morgan Power on the partnership arrangements with The Williams Companies for the ownership and development of up to six power generation facilities, and advised an affiliate of Calpine on the formation of a limited partnership with Cleco to develop a 1000MW power generation facility in Louisiana.

The Clients: A respected litigation capability has been highlighted by work on a number of power disputes for entities such as El Paso, Calpine, Cinergy and Kinder Morgan. The firm also acts for Reliant Resources, Coral Power, Coral Energy Rersources, Tampa Electric and TransAlta.

Skadden, Arps, Slate, Meagher & Flom LLP & Affiliates
see firm details p.878

The Firm: The Houston office is one of the firm's focal points for energy-related project developments and corporate transactions. The emphasis here lies on the development and financing of electric power projects, where the group typically acts for large developers and international financial institutions. It also benefits from the experience of former FERC personnel to provide a respected regulatory arm to its energy practice.

The Lawyers: **John Ale** (see p.668) is considered by contemporaries to be a *"practical and client-friendly"* attorney, and has a particularly impressive transactional resumé. He recently represented Enron's Azurix on its sale of Wessex Water for £544.6 million. Head of the Houston office is the *"personable"* **Lyndon Taylor** (see p.681), who devotes most of his practice to domestic and international project finance, with a focus on LNG-related projects. He advised El Paso on the negotiation of a 23-year sale and purchase agreement, following which El Paso will purchase LNG from Statoil and its partners in the Sn[Small O oblique]hvit LNG Project in the north of Norway.

The Clients: The firm has represented AES on the $3 billion acquisition of IPALCO Enterprises and the $1.7 billion acquisition of CA Electricidad de Caracas. Dynegy, Cinergy, Entergy and Azurix all feature on the client list.

Locke Liddell & Sapp LLP

The Firm: This *"dynamic"* energy practice is now regarded as a significant player in Texas. It advises its three principal clients – Dynegy, El Paso and Calpine – on a variety of international projects in Latin America and the Far East.

ENVIRONMENT — TEXAS

The team represented Dynegy on its acquisition of 1700MW of generating capacity in upstate New York from Central Hudson Gas & Electric, and served as legal counsel for FPL Energy to build a 75MW wind farm in west Texas, the largest renewable energy project ever constructed in that state. In Latin America, the firm advised Tractebel on the $1 billion acquisition of a controlling interest in Gerasul, a large Brazilian power generation company.

The Lawyers: **David Patton** (see p.678) was endorsed to researchers as an attorney who *"knows both the substantive legal issues and the business concerns involved in a deal."*

The Clients: Dynegy; El Paso; Calpine; Ocean Energy; BP Amoco; TEPPCO Partners; Entergy-Koch Trading; Shell; Atmos Energy and NRG Energy.

Other Notable Practitioners

Charles Moore (see p.677) works from the Houston office of LeBoeuf, Lamb, Greene & MacRae LLP, and has an enviable reputation among peers as a regulatory energy attorney *"of the highest quality."*

ENVIRONMENT

TEXAS
Leading firms (Environment)

1. BAKER BOTTS LLP *Austin*
   VINSON & ELKINS LLP *Austin, Houston*
2. FULBRIGHT & JAWORSKI LLP *Austin, Houston*
3. AKIN, GUMP, STRAUSS, HAUER *Austin, Dallas*
   BRACEWELL & PATTERSON LLP *Houston*
   HAYNES AND BOONE LLP *Austin*
4. THOMPSON & KNIGHT LLP *Dallas*
5. BEIRNE, MAYNARD & PARSONS, LLP *Houston*
   BROWN MCCARROLL, LLP *Austin*

Leading individuals (Environment)

1. CIVINS Jeff *Haynes and Boone LLP, Austin*
   GIBLIN Pamela *Baker Botts LLP, Austin*
2. AMANDES Christopher *Vinson & Elkins LLP, Houston*
   BRADDOCK Patricia *Fulbright & Jaworski, Austin*
   CAGLE Molly *Vinson & Elkins LLP, Austin*
   HESTER Tracy *Bracewell & Patterson LLP, Houston*
3. DINKINS Carol *Vinson & Elkins LLP, Houston*
   DUTTON Diana *Akin Gump Strauss Hauer, Dallas*
   GOLEMON Kinnan *Brown McCarroll, LLP, Austin*
   HARRIS James *Thompson & Knight LLP, Dallas*
   O'BRIEN Eva *Fulbright & Jaworski, Houston*
   SEALS Paul *Akin Gump Strauss Hauer & Feld, Austin*
   SMITH James *Beirne, Maynard & Parsons, Houston*
   STEWART Robert *Baker Botts LLP, Austin*

Firms and individuals are listed alphabetically in each band.

Baker Botts LLP

The Firm: *"A top firm with a presence in all the big cases,"* according to competitors. The department's main strength is thought to lie in a *"stable set of lawyers"* who have general expertise in environmental regulatory matters and a niche in air quality regulatory cases. A renowned international practice puts special emphasis on Mexico, Central and South America and the firm has established a Latin America environmental client group (CIELO).

The Lawyers: The group draws on attorneys with extensive experience of federal and state regulatory agencies, and is headed by *"the face of the firm,"* **Pamela Giblin**. Clients were loud in their praise of an attorney who *"makes a point of being well-informed about laws and potential changes in them."* peers perceive here to be *"on excellent terms with the agencies."* Respected regulatory and litigation attorney **Robert Stewart** is an acknowledged expert in the areas of air emissions, waste water quality and CERCLA issues, and has a broad industrial client portfolio.

The Clients: The firm has appeared on a multistate Title V CAA case, which gained environmental permitting for more than 50 automobile manufacturing plants across the country. They also played a prominent role in revisions to the Clean Air Plan for the Houston-Galveston area. In addition to regulatory work, the team has represented clients in judicial enforcement actions, citizen suits and toxic tort actions in both state and federal courts. Recent successes have included the defense of a major CAA enforcement action against a petroleum refinery, and the prosecution of a multimillion dollar cost recovery claim against the US Government. Exxon, Shell and Dow Chemical are leading clients.

Vinson & Elkins LLP
see firm details p.891

The Firm: Market commentators waxed lyrical about the department's *"historical excellence in both regulatory and contentious work,"* and the firm's environment practice is universally assessed to be one of the two market leaders in Texas. Not only does the firm have one of the largest and most comprehensive national practices, but it also handles a global workload that encompasses South America and eastern Europe.

The Lawyers: Rivals concede that the firm has attracted the *"crème de la crème"* of environment attorneys. **Chris Amandes** (see p.668) was endorsed to researchers as a *"classy and witty advocate, with a good sense of perspective."* His environmental practice includes regulatory work, compliance and counseling on air, water and solid waste issues, where he is said to be *"a skilled interpreter of the regulations."* He successfully represented the plaintiff in a CERCLA cost recovery claim, which resulted in an eight-figure settlement, and defended a foundry and a refinery in two separate state enforcement actions. **Molly Cagle** (see p.670) is a respected generalist who counsels and litigates on behalf of the Texas Chemical Council and clients from the petroleum industry. Known by opponents for her *"tenacity and creativity,"* she negotiated a settlement with the Texas Water Commission in a case involving the largest fine ever sought by that regulatory agency.

The cohead of the practice is **Carol Dinkins** (see p.672), a former US Department of Justice attorney, who maintains offices in both Houston and Washington DC. Researchers had their attention drawn to her *"great negotiating skills,"* which she deploys on behalf of chemical and energy companies as well as municipal and governmental bodies.

The Clients: The group has represented a major petrochemical company in numerous suits alleging property damage and personal injury. It also resolved an enforcement action involving six plants in four states and three EPA regions. The firm acts for power utilities and transportation, energy, aerospace and pesticide manufacturing companies.

Fulbright & Jaworski LLP
see firm details p.799

The Firm: A group of *"experienced and successful"* lawyers is regularly seen in enforcement proceedings, contested permit hearings, and environmental litigation, where the firm's reputation stands comparison with the best in Texas. The team has advised clients on environmental property damage claims stemming from soil and groundwater contamination, and recently successfully represented 70 defendants in one of the largest waste site cases in Texas.

The Lawyers: Many of the team's finest results are credited to former government agency worker **Patricia Finn Braddock** (see p.672), who maintains long-standing relationships with state and federal agencies such as the EPA, Texas Natural Resources Conservation Commmission (TNRCC) and the Texas Resource Commission (TRC). Clients and fellow practitioners alike endorse her as *"a tough, regulatory lawyer who is always accessible to our needs."* She has advised

TEXAS — ENVIRONMENT

industrial and utility clients on enforcement actions for alleged violations of regulations governing air, water and hazardous waste, and defended Crown Central Petroleum against alleged violations of environmental regulations. **Eva Fromm O'Brien** (see p.672) appeals to clients as an *"experienced and effective attorney,"* whose mixed practice includes Superfund recovery actions, pollution issues, enforcement proceedings and transactional work.

The Clients: Crown Central Petroleum, TEPPCO Partners, Duke Energy and The Mason & Hanger Group are clients.

Akin Gump Strauss Hauer & Feld LLP
see firm details p.761

The Firm: The firm gave a boost to its environmental practice in 2000 when it joined forces with boutique firm Cutler & Stanfield. Since then, its respected energy, land use and environment group has developed into a department that represents both public and private sector clients throughout the US. The group has been involved in some of the most high-profile and complex development projects in the country, and has assisted clients in obtaining virtually every kind of environmental permit required under federal and state law.

The Lawyers: Diana Dutton received consistent plaudits as *"an excellent general environment lawyer,"* and heads the department. She represents clients in front of state and federal environmental authorities and has appeared on a number of Superfund actions. A 20-year veteran of the environmental regulatory scene, **Paul Seals** has developed a reputation in the field that goes beyond Texas, and advises a heavyweight institutional clientele.

The Clients: The firm advised on the defense of one of the first multimedia enforcement actions brought by the federal government against one of the largest hazardous waste treatment operators, and has represented numerous industries in connection with alleged violations of the CWA. Petroleum refineries, plastic manufacturers, individual property owners, real estate developers and major oil companies feature in its client portfolio.

Bracewell & Patterson LLP
see firm details p.774

The Firm: Although smaller than some of its principal rivals, the firm is acknowledged to possess some *"excellent environment attorneys,"* with specific experience in preventative regulatory counseling, clean water issues, environmental permits and CAA implementation and compliance.

The Lawyers: Tracy Hester (see p.674) was described to researchers as someone who *"knows how to win a battle,"* and received strong peer recommendation for his *"effective approach to solving problems."* He has organized and managed the environmental due diligence efforts for multiple transactions involving the purchase and sale of power generation facilities throughout the US. Other work has involved the assessment of federal and multi-state waste management requirements and recycling options for a national project to collect and recycle electronic scrap and computer equipment.

The Clients: The firm advises, among others: Goodyear; ChevronTexaco; American Petroleum Institute; Texas Chemical Council and First Wave Marine.

Haynes and Boone LLP
see firm details p.814

The Firm: *"A significant player in the environmental field,"* it counsels large corporations in dealing with the environmental, health and safety aspects of their transactions. The firm has also advised American Premium Underwriters in a recent toxic tort litigation, and acted for a number of companies, including Aviall and Elcor, in another toxic tort litigation involving waste management facilities.

The Lawyers: A sound group of attorneys are said to *"go the extra mile"* for their clients, but all commentators agreed that the group's profile rests largely on the shoulders of the *"simply outstanding"* **Jeff Civins** (see p.670). Regarded by some as *"the best all-round environment lawyer in Texas,"* he represented the State of Texas before federal district courts in an action brought by the US Department of Justice against Koch Industries for violations under the CWA. The case resulted in the largest fine ever levied in Texas against a single company under an environmental statute.

The Clients: El Paso; American Premium Underwriters; Aviall; Cook-Joyce; ENSR; Marathon Oil; Pennzoil Products Company and Safety-Kleen.

Thompson & Knight LLP
see firm details p.889

The Firm: Described by peers as *"one of the finest firms in Dallas,"* it has been active in environmental matters for more than 30 years. The practice has grown from its focus on air pollution litigation to addressing broad-ranging issues such as air and water quality, solid and hazardous waste, energy recovery, toxic substances, hazardous materials and risk assessment. Clients reported on the group's *"high-quality standards – it delivers an outstanding product."* It houses *"top lawyers who provide accurate assistance in a creative and timely manner."* The firm acted for Sparton Technology in a case regarding solvent contamination of groundwater in Albuquerque, New Mexico.

The Lawyers: James Harris (see p.674) *"knows the regulatory regimes well."* Benefiting from an engineering background, he is described by interviewees as *"a rare breed"* who both litigates and practices before state and federal regulatory bodies. Harris has *"the ability to look at the big picture and stay one step ahead of his adversaries."* He successfully defended Fina Oil & Chemical Company in a ten-year groundwater contamination battle in west Texas against the TNRCC.

The Clients: ATOFINA; Ashland Specialty Chemical Company; Centex; Lennox International and Sparton Technology.

Beirne, Maynard & Parsons, LLP
see firm details p.770

The Firm: Highly rated for its civil trial and appellate work, the firm's attorneys are involved in lawsuits ranging from personal injury to toxic torts and class actions on a local, statewide and federal basis.

The Lawyers: Dedicated environment attorney **James Smith** was consistently applauded to researchers as a *"diligent lawyer"* with a niche in regulatory enforcement. Appearing on both civil and criminal matters, he secured a 'not guilty' verdict for a chemical manufacturing company in an alleged environmental criminal case. He also advised a waste disposal company on its successful appeal, on constitutional grounds, against an environmental criminal conviction. Other work includes acting for a major chemical company on a huge CERCLA matter in Texas, and representing a New York-based international manufacturing company before the TNRCC on a groundwater enforcement matter.

The Clients: AIG; ABB; Bayer; Fireman's Fund; Lloyd's; Phillips Petroleum Company; Pakhoed; Rohm & Haas and United Technologies.

Brown McCarroll, LLP

The Firm: This Austin-based firm represents a number of clients in the oil, petrochemical and electrical industries, and is seen by opponents to be both *"ethical and politically well plugged-in."* The firm is most frequently encountered by competitors in legislative work at state and federal level.

The Lawyers: The firm's leading lobbyist is the widely admired **Kinnan Golemon** who *"has been around in this business longer than anyone else in the state"* and *"has his fingers in a lot of different pies,"* according to market commentators. He has represented the Association of Electric Utilities of Texas as well as Exxon and Koch Industries, and obtained the first regulatory flexibility order from the TNRCC for use with the EPA's comparable fuels rule.

The Clients: The firm has assisted clients in lobbying efforts associated with the state's performance review of various Texas environmental agencies. It also negotiated the ground-breaking voluntary air emission reduction agreement between Continental Airlines and the TNRCC (with EPA approval), in lieu of mandatory regulation. Other clients include Cargill, Celanese, Exxon, Shell and Texas Industries.

INSOLVENCY/CORPORATE RECOVERY

TEXAS

TEXAS
Leading firms
(Insolvency/Corporate Recovery)

1. **HAYNES AND BOONE LLP** Dallas, Houston
2. **AKIN GUMP STRAUSS HAUER** Dallas, Houston
   WEIL, GOTSHAL & MANGES LLP Dallas
3. **ANDREWS & KURTH LLP** Houston
   FULBRIGHT & JAWORSKI LLP San Antonio
   VINSON & ELKINS LLP Dallas
   WINSTEAD SECHREST & MINICK Dallas
4. **BAKER BOTTS LLP** Dallas
   COX & SMITH INCORPORATED San Antonio
   GARDERE WYNNE SEWELL LLP Dallas
   THOMPSON & KNIGHT LLP Dallas

Leading individuals
(Insolvency/Corporate Recovery)

1. **ALBERGOTTI Robert** Haynes and Boone LLP, Dallas
   PHELAN Robin Haynes and Boone LLP, Dallas
2. **PEREZ Alfredo** Weil, Gotshal & Manges LLP, Dallas
   STEWART Dan Vinson & Elkins LLP, Dallas
3. **BECKHAM Charles** Haynes and Boone LLP, Houston
   SHEINFELD Myron Akin Gump Strauss, Houston
   WILLIAMSON Deborah Cox & Smith, San Antonio
4. **GIBBS Charles** Akin Gump Strauss Hauer, Dallas
   KAIM Henry Akin Gump Strauss Hauer, Houston
   MCCONNELL Mike Winstead Sechrest & Minick, Dallas
   RAY Hugh Andrews & Kurth LLP, Houston
   SOSLAND Martin Weil, Gotshal & Manges LLP, Dallas
   STROUBE Rey Akin Gump Strauss Hauer, Houston
   STRUBECK Lou Fulbright & Jaworski LLP, San Antonio
   SUTHERLAND Mike Winstead Sechrest, Dallas

Firms and individuals are listed alphabetically in each band.

Haynes and Boone LLP
see firm details p.814

The Firm: Universally accepted as the market leaders in Texas, the firm is home to a number of the most accomplished bankruptcy attorneys in the state. A practice of enormous breadth has simultaneously represented debtors and creditors in Chapter 11 cases, and is also know for its skill in conducting international workouts and business reorganizations.

The Lawyers: The business reorganization and bankruptcy group is led by the *"brilliant"* and *"colorful"* **Robin Phelan** (see p.678), who peers say is *"creative, sophisticated and good on his feet."* **Bob Albergotti** (see p.668) is a *"tenacious and industrious"* attorney who has extensive experience in all aspects of insolvency, bankruptcy and creditors' rights cases. He advised Kitty Hawk as a debtor in Chapter 11 proceedings. Described to researchers as a *"capable and trustworthy negotiator,"* **Charlie Beckham** (see p.669) represented a member of the creditors' committee for the Chapter 11 proceedings of Enron, and has advised a range of creditors, debtors and secured lenders on numerous bankruptcies.

The Clients: Among a host of major transactions, the firm acted for the secured and unsecured creditors in the Chapter 11s for American Homestar and National Airlines. The firm acts for Kitty Hawk; Enron; Amresco; Tri-Union Development; Total Home Care and El Paso Electric.

Akin Gump Strauss Hauer & Feld, LLP
see firm details p.761

The Firm: This *"hard-hitting"* firm recently increased its insolvency capability by recruiting practitioners from Sheinfeld, Maley & Kay. The financial restructuring group in Dallas and Houston is widely acknowledged to undertake a sizable proportion of the firm's national bankruptcy workload. Minimal representation of institutional lenders has enabled the firm to conduct the business of both creditors and debtors, and it has developed particular expertise in representing members of the bondholder community in large Chapter 11s.

The Lawyers: A deep bench of respected lawyers includes **Rey Stroube**, the leader of the financial restructuring group, who has been lead counsel for debtors in a number of major national cases. Commended for his considerable experience in corporate reorganizations, **Myron (Mickey) Sheinfeld** is regarded as the *"grand old man"* of the Texas insolvency bar. **Chuck Gibbs** is thought to be a solid attorney with a sound track record as lead bankruptcy counsel, while the experienced **Henry Kaim** was endorsed to researchers for his expertise in complex Chapter 11s.

The Clients: The firm advised the bondholders in the LTV Steel and Fruit of the Loom cases, and among a raft of similar matters, appeared for the debtors in the Chapter 11 of an international chemical company headquartered in Houston. National Steel and Cable & Wireless are also clients.

Weil, Gotshal & Manges LLP
see firm details p.897

The Firm: The firm has an international reputation for one of the finest insolvency practices in the world, a status that has been reinforced by its position as debtors' counsel to Enron. New York may be the center of the firm's operations, but in Texas, a broad-based department maintains the firm's outstanding traditions and acts for clients across all industries. However, the group has a particularly close association with the aviation industry, where, as elsewhere, large public cases remain the staple of the group.

The Lawyers: *"Personable"* **Martin Sosland** (see p.680) is known to his peers for his enviable clientele of financial institutions, including The Harbor Financial Group and FirstPlus Financial Group. **Alfredo Perez** (see p.678) was endorsed to researchers as a *"smart, pragmatic and tough"* attorney, and has notable expertise in Chapter 11 debtors' representation. His track record has featured bankruptcies such as Cajun Electric Power Cooperative, Kitty Hawk and TransTexas Gas.

The Clients: The firm's client base includes: Enron; Global Crossing; PennCorp Financial Group; Southwestern Life Holdings; Carmike Cinemas; Covad Communications Group; Ameritech and American Airlines.

Andrews & Kurth LLP
see firm details p.764

The Firm: The merger with Mayor, Day, Caldwell & Keeton in 2001 is acknowledged by competitors to have substantially bolstered the firm's capacity in this sector, notably on the contentious side. The group traditionally acts for large debtors and creditors in complex workouts and Chapter 11s, and has represented the debtors in the case of Paracelsus Healthcare and the creditors in the case of Duke Energy. An in-house style of *"raw aggression"* was frequently noted by interviewees.

The Lawyers: **Hugh Ray** (see p.679) was involved in the reorganization of Friede Goldman Halter, and is regarded as a skilled adviser to institutional creditors. The head of the firm's national bankruptcy practice, he is viewed by contemporaries as *"an impressive and experienced"* bankruptcy attorney.

The Clients: Wells Fargo; Duke Energy; Paracelsus Healthcare; Flagstar; First City Bancorporation of Texas; American Rice; Costilla Energy and Friede Goldman Halter.

Fulbright & Jaworski LLP
see firm details p.799

The Firm: The firm's bankruptcy, reorganization, and creditors' rights department was frequently recommended to researchers for its work on big-ticket transactions. The sizable department deals with restructuring, refinancing and insolvency litigation matters for a range of blue-chip clients, often with an involvement in the oil, gas and clinical manufacturing industries. Particular expertise exists in business reorganizations, and the department regularly appears for creditors' committees and trustees.

The Lawyers: **Lou Strubeck** (see p.680) advised on the Chapter 11 for Coho Energy, and is thought by rivals to be the *"best at the practice"* for his creativity and experience in representing creditors.

The Clients: The firm represents many large companies, including Fortune 500 entities.

TEXAS

INSOLVENCY/CORPORATE RECOVERY

Vinson & Elkins LLP
see firm details p.891

The Firm: Historically, the firm's respected bankruptcy lawyers have tended to undertake more creditors' than debtors' work. However, its caseload has also featured advice to substantial debtor corporations, such as Tracor Holdings and El Paso Electric. The group has developed a niche in mass tort Chapter 11s, and represented American General and its affiliates in the case of a consumer-lending subsidiary, which had suffered a $167 million judgment against it.

The Lawyers: **Dan Stewart** (see p.680), cohead of the insolvency and reorganization group, was characterized by some commentators as *"one of the brightest bankruptcy lawyers in the US,"* and is felt to dominate his department. He acted as special counsel to ContiFinancial during its bankruptcy proceedings, and is renowned for his experience in representing financial institutions.

The Clients: The firm advises American General; Tracor Holdings; El Paso Electric and Winstar Communications.

Winstead Sechrest & Minick
see firm details p.902

The Firm: Focusing on large, syndicated senior lender groups and the restructuring of troubled credits in sizable Chapter 11 cases, the firm has one of the largest bankruptcy departments in Texas. Such critical mass also enables the team to take on high-premium debtor cases.

The Lawyers: **Mike McConnell** (see p.676) (a former bankruptcy judge) and **Mike Sutherland** (see p.681) both advised on the WebLink Wireless case, and are regarded by peers as an *"effective double act."*

The Clients: The firm represented senior lenders in the cases of Pillowtex, Metals USA and ProMed-Co, and has advised debtor clients of the stature of Logix Communications and Pinnacle Towers.

Baker Botts LLP

The Firm: Complex debtors' representations, bankruptcy acquisitions and trial experience feature as some of the firm's particular strengths within the sector. The team represents a large institutional client base, and has dealt with the creditors in a number of sizable Chapter 11 cases such as Amresco, Enron and Sterling Chemicals Holdings.

The Lawyers: Experienced in most industries. The group is led by Jack Kinzie.

The Clients: Amresco; Enron; Sterling Chemicals Holdings; NAB Asset Corporation; Imperial Sugar Company and Texas International Company.

Cox & Smith Incorporated

The Firm: Based in San Antonio, the firm has established a reputation for reliability, greatly assisted by the presence of its *"talented"* head of bankruptcy, **Deborah Williamson** (see p.682). A former vice president of the American Bankruptcy Institute, she leads a team that handles all aspects of insolvency work, and is known to excel in the areas of bankruptcy acquisitions, debtors' representations and trustee work.

The Clients: The firm advises AgriBioTech and Vision Technologies Systems (a subsidiary of Singapore Technologies Engineering).

Gardere Wynne Sewell LLP
see firm details p.801

The Firm: The firm has conducted insolvency work for a broad range of clients, including leading players from the financial lending, energy and transportation industries. Its particular forte is felt to lie in corporate restructuring work, both prior to and during bankruptcy proceedings.

The Lawyers: Deirdre Ruckman's creditors' rights and bankruptcy group recently oversaw the restructuring within nine months of a two billion dollar debt for TransTexas Gas, a feat that has helped to boost the firm's reputation both locally and nationally.

The Clients: Jobs.com, TransTexas Gas and WCI Group are clients.

Thompson & Knight LLP
see firm details p.889

The Firm: The firm furthered its bankruptcy and energy expertise through the recruitment of eight attorneys from Morris & Campbell in 2001. Historically, the firm has had a slight creditors' bias, and has represented several former Enron trading partners during their bids for financial recovery.

The Lawyers: Judith Ross is head of the practice. Her group has handled the insolvency cases of a number of high-profile corporations from the energy and finance sectors.

The Clients: The firm acts for The Harbor Financial Group and Forcenergy.

INSURANCE

TEXAS
Leading firms (Insurance)

1	THOMPSON, COE, COUSINS Austin, Dallas, Houston
2	AKIN GUMP STRAUSS HAUER & FELD Austin
	FULBRIGHT & JAWORSKI Austin, Dallas, Houston
3	COOPER & SCULLY, PC Dallas
	HAYNES AND BOONE LLP Dallas
	MARTIN, DISIERE, JEFFERSON Houston
	VINSON & ELKINS LLP Austin, Houston
4	STRASBURGER & PRICE LLP Dallas
	YORK, KELLER & FIELD Austin

Firms are listed alphabetically in each band.

Thompson, Coe, Cousins & Irons, LLP

The Firm: A specialist insurance group, nationally recognized for its expertise in both noncontentious counseling and litigation. It features prominently on major insurance cases in Texas, defending insureds in first and third-party litigation, and acting for carriers in coverage disputes and class action matters.

The firm represented International Insurance Company and United States Fire Insurance Company in a coverage dispute arising from claims,encompassing 25 sites, for environmental damages and bodily injuries against RSR Corporation. It also acted in an asbestos coverage case involving products or premises exposure.

The Lawyers: Leader of the insurance group **Richard Geiger** has won peer admiration as a lobbyist and a regulatory expert. Together with colleague **Jay Thompson**, he represents insurance industry associations and insurance companies before state and federal regulatory agencies. Thompson, who was characterized to researchers as a *"highly respected all-around insurance lawyer,"* has been a key figure in the development of the Texas Insurance Code, in amendments such as the House Bill 2, including issues relating to the benchmark rate system. He was also involved in successfully settling a class action lawsuit against Progressive County Mutual Insurance Company in the Texas Supreme Court dealing with a statute defining unfair discrimination.

"A first-rate trial attorney," **Roger Higgins** has successfully defended a statewide class action seeking to establish coverage for 'diminished value' under the Texas automobile policy. Another recent highlight was the prosecution of a class action on behalf of 134 insurance companies against the State of Texas, which obtained the refund of $105.4 million in premium taxes paid under protest. Although some find **Brian Martin** *"aggressive,"* his *"honest and forthright"* approach has won him many fans. He has been involved in significant insurance coverage disputes and defense matters, and has been appointed as national coverage counsel for United States Fire Insurance Company, regarding exterior insulation finish system cases.

The Clients: Association of Fire and Casualty Companies in Texas (AFACT); Progressive County Mutual Insurance Company; All American Life Insurance Company; Zurich; Employers General

INSURANCE | TEXAS

TEXAS
Leading individuals (Insurance)

1
- **BOND Thomas** *Akin Gump Strauss Hauer,* Austin
- **BROWN Reagan** *Fulbright & Jaworski LLP,* Houston
- **COOPER Brent** *Cooper & Scully, PC,* Dallas
- **MARTIN Christopher** *Martin, Disiere, Jefferson,* Houston
- **MARTIN Ernest** *Haynes and Boone LLP,* Dallas

2
- **GEIGER Richard** *Thompson, Coe, Cousins,* Dallas
- **HUDDLESTON Michael** *Shannon, Gracey, Ratliff,* Dallas
- **MARTIN Brian** *Thompson, Coe, Cousins,* Houston
- **YORK Larry** *York, Keller & Field,* Austin

3
- **CONWAY Susan** *Vinson & Elkins LLP,* Austin
- **HIGGINS Roger** *Thompson, Coe, Cousins,* Dallas
- **KELLER Mary** *York, Keller & Field,* Austin
- **LAWLESS Mark** *Nickens, Lawless & Flack LLP,* Austin
- **MOODY James** *Strasburger & Price,* Dallas
- **THOMPSON Jay** *Thompson, Coe, Cousins,* Austin

4
- **BROWN David** *Vinson & Elkins LLP,* Houston
- **BURNER Burnie** *Long, Burner, Parks & DeLargy,* Austin
- **DAVIS Will** *Heath, Davis & McCalla,* Austin
- **KREBS Arno** *Fulbright & Jaworski LLP,* Houston
- **POWERS Werner** *Haynes and Boone LLP,* Dallas

Individuals are listed alphabetically in each band.

Akin Gump Strauss Hauer & Feld LLP

see firm details p.761

The Firm: Regarded as *"a worthy competitor,"* the firm's insurance practice was extolled to researchers as a *"real powerhouse"* on regulatory matters. The group has extensive experience of the creation and operation of insurance companies under Texas and other state laws. The group is also skilled in reinsurance treaties, merger agreements and the private sale of equity interests.

The Lawyers: The insurance practice group is built around the talents of **Tom Bond**, a former commissioner of insurance for the State of Texas. He is endorsed by peers as *"the lobbyist who matters."* His practice has a national dimension, and he represents a clientele that includes reinsurers, trade associations and e-commerce insurance ventures. A recent highlight saw Bond acting for AIG on Texan regulatory and litigation matters related to its acquisition of American General.

The Clients: The firm has represented Highlands Insurance Group, AMERIGROUP, Liberty Mutual and St. Paul on regulatory, legislative and corporate matters. Other clients include: AIG; National Associations of Insurance Commissioners; Citigroup Travelers and Sierra Health Services.

Fulbright & Jaworski LLP

see firm details p.799

The Firm: Operating with a broad remit, the firm has a substantial track record in representing insurance companies and corporate clients in state and federal cases. The Houston office heads the insurance-related litigation practice, while Austin leads on regulatory issues. Competitors concede: *"We see them on all the big class action cases."* Transactional matters are also catered for, and the group advises on the formation of insurance holding companies and big-ticket M&A.

The Lawyers: *"Leading light"* **Reagan Brown** (see p.670) represents insurance companies and policyholders in litigation and class action cases before state and federal courts. Peers described him as *"a marvelous all-around litigator."* **Arno Krebs** (see p.675) is respected for his advice on insurance coverage cases, and has recently taken on an increased mediation and consultation workload.

The Clients: The group acted for Progressive Northern Insurance Co. in a commercial insurance dispute involving more than $70 million. Obtained a take-nothing jury verdict in favor of the client following a month-long trial. It also acted for Azrock Industries in a lawsuit brought by an insurer on asbestos personal injury cases, successfully obtaining a reversal of the trial court's judgment. The firm also acts for Progressive County Mutual Insurance Company, as well as agents, brokers, underwriters and trade associations.

Cooper & Scully, PC

see firm details p.784

The Firm: Both peers and clients endorsed this firm as *"a top-class insurance practice,"* which represents both insurers and insureds in coverage disputes. The team is focused on advising reinsurers before regulatory authorities and providing coverage opinions regarding claims presented to insurers.

The Lawyers: Clients reported that, for **Brent Cooper** (see p.671), *"work is his life."* He has acted for insurance companies on a number of substantial cases, notably appearing for the plaintiff, St. Paul Guardian, against an attempted declaratory judgment action by Centrum GS. Here, the case was affirmed in part, reversed in part, and remanded.

The Clients: The firm defended Columbia Medical Center of Arlington Subsidiary in an alleged medical malpractice case that was settled in the Court of Appeals in favor of the firm's client. The group also acts for St. Paul Guardian and March Madness Athletic Association.

Haynes and Boone LLP

see firm details p.814

The Firm: Commentators agree the group is one that *"dominates the policyholder market."* It enjoys a *"strong niche"* in sophisticated insurance coverage, and provides substantial counseling and litigation, representing major corporations before state and federal courts.

The Lawyers: *"Outstanding"* **Ernest Martin** (see p.676) concentrates on insurance coverage litigation and bad faith claims. In 1998, he cofounded the statewide insurance law section of The State Bar of Texas. Peers and clients acknowledge that he is a *"superb class action litigator, who produces great results."*
Werner Powers (see p.679) was described to researchers as *"one of the most charismatic lawyers you'll meet."* He represents clients on multimillion dollar coverage litigation cases, and advised Exxon in obtaining coverage for environmental damages arising from the 'Exxon Valdez' oil spill.

The Clients: The firm acted for Advocat on a multimillion dollar case to force insurers to pay, settle or appeal liability exposure in a nursing home litigation. Other clients include: Exxon-Mobil; Telesis; Triton Energy; Panda Energy; American Contractors Insurance Group; Elcor and Texas Health Resources.

Martin, Disiere, Jefferson & Wisdom LLP

see firm details p.842

The Firm: This insurance boutique firm has fast gained an enviable reputation in the industry. It specializes in the defense of first-party insurance lawsuits. The firm draws on the experience of respected trial lawyers to defend major insurance companies on a variety of class action lawsuits and multiparty coverage disputes.

The Lawyers: Peers were particularly impressed with leading light **Chris Martin** (see p.676): *"a knowledgeable and expert insurance trial lawyer."* He represented American States Insurance in the first Texas case to interpret 'sudden and accidental' pollution exclusion, and has been active in other environmental coverage issues.

The Clients: The firm has acted on a long-pending case for State Farm Fire, successfully arguing for the reversal of a $2 million punitive damage award against its client. In another notable case, the group acted as co-lead counsel in a mass tort action brought by 18,000 plaintiffs in an explosion, fire and toxic pollutant case. The firm also acts for American States Insurance.

Vinson & Elkins LLP

see firm details p.891

The Firm: An insurance group that is said by competitors to *"really know its stuff."* It represents policyholders in claims under first-party and liability policies and is active in bad faith insurance disputes. The firm also has expertise in state regulation of the healthcare and medical care sectors.

The Lawyers: The regulatory practice is headed by the esteemed **Susan Conway** (see p.671), who represents healthcare and medical care entities. She serves as counsel to one of the world's largest property and casualty insurers. Characterized to researchers as a *"bright all-rounder,"* Conway regularly participates in annual industrywide rate-setting proceedings for insurance

TEXAS

INSURANCE

firms. The *"cerebral"* **David Brown** (see p.670) leads the insurance coverage group, and has a strong client portfolio of energy companies. He successfully achieved an eight-figure recovery for an energy client in a business interruption loss case. He also represented two Texas Medical Center institutions in property insurance claims arising from losses sustained during Tropical Storm Allison.
The Clients: The firm acted for underwriters at Lloyd's, ILU Companies and Scandinavian underwriters in claims exceeding $1 billion by Exxon for cleanup costs, liability payments, and alleged bad faith, stemming from the 'Exxon Valdez' oil spill. Energy companies, medical institutions, domestic life and casualty insurers and international underwriters use the firm.

Strasburger & Price LLP
The Firm: Offices in several major cities in Texas and a base in Mexico City have ensured the firm has a comprehensive regional coverage and an excellent reputation for insurance work. The firm has appeared for some of the nation's largest primary and excess insurers and reinsurers.
The Lawyers: According to interviewees, **James Hamilton Moody** is one of the *"most significant players in Dallas."* A respected trial attorney, he specializes in insurance business litigation and bad faith claims on behalf of clients that include The Hartford and Allianz Insurance Company.
The Clients: The firm obtained a unanimous take-nothing arbitration award on behalf of the reinsurer of an insolvent Texas insurer, regarding reinsurance for four catastrophic injury claims. It also gained a holding for United States Fire Insurance Company from the Texas Supreme Court that an insurer cannot be liable for bad faith simply because it misinterprets a rule or regulation where the insurer's interpretation is arguable and not legally groundless. Other clients of the firm include: Allianz Insurance Company; Zurich; Universal Underwriters Group and Everest Reinsurance Company.

York, Keller & Field
The Firm: This boutique firm has established itself in Texas as a player of *"the highest quality."* The firm represents insurers in statewide class actions and individual lawsuits, especially in the employee benefits area. It also advises on investigations brought by the Texas Department of Insurance and the Texas Attorney General against various insurance policies. These include allegations of misrepresentation in the sale of homeowners' policies and allegations of mishandling water claims under the Texas homeowner's policy.
The Lawyers: **Larry York** is widely regarded among peers as an *"excellent senior litigator with a first-rate portfolio of insurance work."* He receives valuable support from former general counsel for the Texas Department of Insurance **Mary Keller**. She is regarded in some quarters as *"the best insurance regulator in town,"* and is hailed for her *"access to key institutional contacts."*
The Clients: The firm defended State Farm in a statewide class action, alleging breach of contract under Texas personal auto policy. It also appeared for CIGNA HealthCare of Texas in a statewide class action, arguing breach of contract through CHC Texas' alleged systematic failure to pay contract amounts.

Other Notable Practitioners
Burnie Burner of Long, Burner, Parks & DeLargy is regarded by peers as a *"well-connected leader in the field."* He is best known for representing county mutual insurers in Texas. **Will Davis** of Heath, Davis & McCalla has a strong reputation for representing major insurance companies. At Shannon, Gracey, Ratliff & Miller LLP, **Michael Huddleston** was commended to researchers as *"a cutting-edge lawyer"* who has an excellent name for coverage cases, while **Mark Lawless** of Nickens, Lawless & Flack LLP is respected for his work on behalf of policyholders.

INTELLECTUAL PROPERTY

TEXAS
Leading firms (Intellectual Property)

1
- BAKER BOTTS LLP *Dallas, Houston*
- FULBRIGHT & JAWORSKI LLP *Austin, Houston*

2
- HOWREY SIMON ARNOLD & WHITE *Houston*
- VINSON & ELKINS LLP *Houston*

3
- CONLEY, ROSE & TAYON *Houston*
- SIDLEY AUSTIN BROWN & WOOD *Dallas*
- THOMPSON & KNIGHT LLP *Dallas*

4
- BRACEWELL & PATTERSON LLP *Austin, Houston*
- HAYNES AND BOONE LLP *Dallas*
- JENKENS & GILCHRIST *Dallas*
- JONES DAY *Dallas*
- MCKOOL SMITH *Dallas*
- SLUSSER & FROST LLP *Houston*

Firms are listed alphabetically in each band.

Baker Botts LLP
The Firm: A *"formidable group,"* the team was endorsed to researchers for its expertise in patent prosecution and litigation, particularly in the electronics industry. A *"well-balanced"* team also undertakes client counseling, licensing and litigation in trademark, trade secrets and copyright matters for a broad clientele.
The Lawyers: Practice group head **Jerry Mills** enjoys a reputation for *"outstanding technical competence"* among peers in the patent sphere. Having prosecuted and litigated several well-known telecom patents, including the automated attendant PBX system portfolio and the patent for voice mail, he is now extensively involved in patent portfolio licensing. Here, he acted for Microelectronics and Computer Technology Corporation (MCC) on the licensing of its semiconductor patent portfolio. Leading litigator **Scott Partridge** was also singled out to researchers for the *"versatility"* of his practice. He has acted on nationwide patent and trade secrets matters for Dell, DSC Communications and Alcatel, and advised the Cantor Fitzgerald subsidiary eSpeed on patent litigation against the Chicago Board of Trade and the Chicago Mercantile Exchange.
The Clients: Alcatel; eSpeed; Dell; Texas Instruments and MCC.

Fulbright & Jaworski LLP
see firm details p.799
The Firm: The practice encompasses the full range of IP services, and has particular expertise in biotech patent prosecution and litigation, alongside trademark litigation and counseling. Respected by peers as a *"professional and meticulous"* outfit, the group is seen to have benefited hugely from the acquisition of the Austin office of the former Arnold, White & Durkee.
The Lawyers: *"One of the preeminent trademark attorneys in the country,"* **Lou Pirkey** (see p.678) heads the firm's powerful Austin office. Described by rivals as *"Texan in his approach - he's not a 'Rambo' litigator,"* he represented 3M in color trademark litigation, and also acted for Exxon-Mobil in its high-profile 'cartoon tiger' dispute with Kellogg. Biotech specialist **David Parker** (see p.678) also won peer endorsement for his patent prosecution practice. He successfully acted for Nobel Laureate inventors in their dispute with Barbacid and Bristol-Myers Squibb over patents leading to the indentification of new anticancer compounds. He also advised Invitrogen in a patent dispute with BD Biosciences Clontech.
The Clients: 3M; Exxon; University of Texas; Invitrogen; Compaq; AT&T; For Eyes Optical and Burger King.

INTELLECTUAL PROPERTY — TEXAS

TEXAS
Leading individuals (Intellectual Property)

1
- LAFUZE William *Vinson & Elkins LLP*, Houston
- MEDLOCK Bryan *Sidley Austin Brown & Wood*, Dallas
- PIRKEY Louis *Fulbright & Jaworski LLP*, Austin

2
- MILLS Jerry *Baker Botts LLP*, Dallas
- RICHARD Molly *Thompson & Knight LLP*, Dallas

3
- PARTRIDGE Scott *Baker Botts LLP*, Houston
- PETERSON Pete *Cox & Smith Incorporated*, San Antonio
- SLUSSER William *Slusser & Frost LLP*, Houston
- TURNER Robert *Jones Day*, Dallas

4
- CAWLEY Douglas *McKool Smith*, Dallas
- DILLON Andrew *Bracewell & Patterson LLP*, Austin
- MCCOMBS David *Haynes and Boone LLP*, Dallas
- NORRIS John *Howrey Simon Arnold & White*, Houston
- PARKER David *Fulbright & Jaworski LLP*, Austin
- RAMAN William *Thompson & Knight LLP*, Austin
- SELINGER Jerry *Jenkens & Gilchrist*, Dallas
- TEMPLIN Donald *Haynes and Boone LLP*, Dallas

Individuals are listed alphabetically in each band.

Howrey Simon Arnold & White

The Firm: Despite some high-profile defections and retirements, the *"IP giant"* that has *"been around forever"* retains a powerful presence in Texas. The firm has an outstanding national reputation for patent litigation work, and it is acknowledged to *"cover the waterfront"* of transactional and contentious IP work. This includes patent, trademark, trade secrets and copyright expertise.

The Lawyers: Commentators singled out the *"understated, but excellent"* patent litigator **John Norris** for particular praise. An expert on the chemical and petrochemical industries, he represented Solutia in litigation relating to nylon carpet dyes, as well as acting for Honeywell in litigation to protect patents for heat-activated adhesives.

The Clients: The firm is active in a range of industries spanning herbicides, carpet chemicals, telecommunications, semiconductor processors and golf clubs. Clients include: Callaway Golf; Monsanto; Solutia; DuPont and De Beers.

Vinson & Elkins LLP

see firm details p.891

The Firm: A large group, comprising more than 50 attorneys, was commended for high-quality service to its corporate and stand-alone IP client base. The team's reputation lies principally in patent infringement litigation, although it also undertakes patent prosecution and licensing, and copyright and trademark advice and licensing.

The Lawyers: *"Excellent technician"* **Bill LaFuze** (see p.676) was consistently nominated to researchers as *"top of the heap"* in Texas, and is widely recognized for his patent litigation work in computer-related technology. Rivals appreciate his *"cordial and effective"* approach to negotiations. He acted for Coca-Cola bottlers in a patent infringement case concerning the design of the base of plastic soft drink bottles, and defended Motorola in a high-profile case involving alleged infringement of a patent relating to printed circuit boards.

The Clients: The firm advises a respected corporate client base and attracts stand-alone clients. The firm represents Motorola and Coca-Cola.

Conley, Rose & Tayon

The Firm: One of the few remaining IP boutiques in Texas, it is renowned among rivals for having made patent prosecution a *"successful art form."* A group of about 50 lawyers undertakes patent prosecution, advice work and litigation for a mainly electricity and oil and gas clientele, and also has expertise in the nexus between IP and antitrust law, particularly in the pharmaceutical industry.

The Lawyers: The team, which includes litigator Jeff Tayon, acted for Compaq in transferring its IP portfolio to a subsidiary, and advised Louisiana Wholesale Drug Company in a antitrust class action against Bristol-Myers Squibb.

The Clients: Compaq; Louisiana Wholesale Drug Company; Halliburton and Smith International.

Sidley Austin Brown & Wood

see firm details p.877

The Firm: In Texas, the firm's name for IP is inextricably linked with that of its *"bona fide star,"* patent litigator **Bryan Medlock**. He is revered for his *"sheer persuasiveness"* in court, with peers citing his *"Southern flair"* and *"somewhat folksy"* style of advocacy as keys to his courtroom success.

The Clients: Medlock has acted as a special master, arbitrator and expert witness in patent litigation and often represents the patent interests of long-term client Kimberly-Clark.

Thompson & Knight LLP

see firm details p.889

The Firm: In addition to its high-profile trademark application, litigation and advice practice, the group also performs patent prosecution and litigation, and handles substantial copyright and trade secrets cases.

The Lawyers: The group celebrated a recent coup with the recruitment of trademark *"superstar"* **Molly Richard** (see p.679) from Strasburger & Price. Applauded by contemporaries as *"one of the principal trademark practitioners in the state,"* she advised on the worldwide acquisition of Swiss watch brand Zodiac by Fossil, as well as acting for Hewlett-Packard in internet domain name disputes. Austin-based trademark litigator **Bill Raman** (see p.679) also won peer endorsement, and rivals contend that, together, the pair has made the firm a *"force to be reckoned with."*

The Clients: Fossil and NBA team, the Dallas Mavericks.

Bracewell & Patterson LLP

see firm details p.774

The Firm: The firm's IP group was bolstered with the 2001 recruitment of 22 lawyers from the former boutique Felsman, Bradley, Gunter & Dillon. Where previously the firm was felt to be *"nowhere on the radar,"* peers now regard it as a *"definite force"* in Texas. The bulk of the practice is devoted to patent preparation and prosecution, and the group has niche expertise in the computer software industry.

The Lawyers: **Andy Dillon** (see p.671) was strongly endorsed to researchers by peers and clients for his *"wealth of industry experience."* In addition to representing IBM across the US, he also acts as a patent expert in hi-tech litigation.

The Clients: The firm recently acted for Kent State University in a patent infringement matter relating to liquid crystal displays. It also acts for technology clients IBM and Ericsson.

Haynes and Boone LLP

see firm details p.814

The Firm: This *"strong bunch"* of 50 lawyers practices primarily in patent and trademark prosecution and the full range of IP litigation. The group enjoys a strong reputation among peers for its integration of IP and corporate finance. Twenty-eight registered patent attorneys undertake patent prosecution for both start-up and Fortune 500 companies, as well as asserting patents for business development through licensing and litigation.

The Lawyers: **David McCombs** (see p.676) won consistent market praise for his ability to combine technical mastery of patent litigation with *"business savvy."* He acted as counsel to the US Department of Justice in a dispute between Summit Technology and VISX, concerning the dissolution of patent pooling arrangements for patents on LASIK eye surgery. Commentators also pointed to *"skilled and experienced"* trial lawyer **Don Templin** (see p.681). He undertakes patent, trademark and copyright litigation for both plaintiffs and defendants, and notably achieved a treble damages award for willful patent infringement.

The Clients: The telecom, medical and semiconductor industries are particularly fruitful sources of work. The firm acts for Acutex; Hilite Industries; Nortel Networks; 3M and Hitachi.

Jenkens & Gilchrist

The Firm: A group of about 60 lawyers undertakes the full array of transactional and contentious IP services, including patent and trademark prosecution and litigation, as well as trade secrets and copyright matters. The team also undertakes traditional copyright work, recently acting for the Estate of Buddy Holly.

The Lawyers: Peers view **Jerry Selinger** as the group's *"main player"* and an effective trial lawyer for patent, trademark and trade secrets cases. He

TEXAS | LITIGATION

represented Poly-America in patent infringement litigation relating to patents over a plastic lining for use in landfills. He also pursued litigation in California, Wisconsin and Texas regarding the enforcement of a patent on behalf of DTM Corporation.
The Clients: In addition, the firm advised Ericssonin a dispute withInterDigital Communications over cellular systemspatents. Pfaff, Cardinal Health, Applied Materials and Poly-Americaare clients of the firm.

Jones Day
see firm details p.823
The Firm: A group of 16 lawyers in the firm's Dallas office is primarily known for patent litigation expertise. In addition, the team performs transactional work for a Fortune 500 client base.
The Lawyers: Contemporaries singled out *"superior tactician"* **Robert Turner** (see p.681) for approval. Clients appreciated his *"firm grasp of technical issues,"* and highlighted his *"softly spoken but effective"* courtroom manner. Although the bulk of his practice is devoted to patent litigation, he also acts on trade secrets, trademark and copyright matters, and has a focus on the electronics, telecom and semiconductor industries. He recently obtained a favorable settlement for Spirent in a patent infringement dispute in Hawaii, and has regularly appeared on patent infringement litigation for major client Texas Instruments.
The Clients: The firm recently acted for 35 of the Fortune 500 in a single suit filed by an individual patent owner. Texas Instruments and The MathWorks are clients of the firm.

McKool Smith
The Firm: An emerging force in Texas, this Dallas-based team has added to its ranks in the past year with the recruitment of partners from Hughes & Luce. Rivals concede that the 17-strong group is *"making a serious play"* for the technology market. A number of electrical engineering patent attorneys devote their practices to patent litigation for a technology client base.
The Lawyers: The versatile **Doug Cawley** came in for sustained market plaudits. In addition to patent and trademark issues, his practice also involves the trial of IP antitrust and e-commerce cases.
The Clients: The firm acted for Medtronic in a patent dispute with Johnson & Johnson, as well as successfully representing theatrical lighting manufacturer Vari-Lite in a dispute with Danish rival Martin. Its technology client base includes Ericsson, Excel Telecommunications, EDS and CenturyTel.

Slusser & Frost LLP
see firm details p.879
The Firm: Now in its fourth year, this litigation boutique won praise for its IP litigation practice. The six-lawyer team is renowned for its work on *"high-end strategic issues,"* and has been involved in high-stakes IP litigation since the firm's inception, recently defending Shell against a billion dollar patent infringement claim by Union Carbide.
The Lawyers: Founding partner **Bill Slusser** (see p.680) is an *"outstanding IP litigator"* who is said by opponents to have *"transcended the general litigation tag."* Possessing particular expertise in the chemical industry, he recently achieved a $101 million verdict for BJ Services against Halliburton in a patent dispute relating to oil and gas technology.
The Clients: Shell, Philips and Exxon are clients of the firm.

Other Notable Practitioners
By common consent, the leading IP attorney in San Antonio is **Pete Peterson** of Cox & Smith Incorporated. Described to researchers as a *"knowledgeable specialist,"* he handles a range of patent, trademark and copyright issues at home and abroad.

LITIGATION | GENERAL COMMERCIAL

TEXAS
Leading firms
Litigation: General Commercial)

1. **GIBBS & BRUNS, LLP** Houston
   SUSMAN GODFREY LLP Houston
   VINSON & ELKINS LLP Houston
2. **BAKER BOTTS LLP** Houston
   BECK, REDDEN & SECREST Houston
3. **FULBRIGHT & JAWORSKI LLP** Houston
4. **CARRINGTON, COLEMAN, SLOMAN,** Dallas
   MCDADE FOGLER MAINES LLP Houston
5. **HAYNES AND BOONE LLP** Houston
   MAYER, BROWN, ROWE & MAW Houston

Firms are listed alphabetically in each band.

Gibbs & Bruns, LLP
see firm details p.802
The Firm: This Houston-based boutique continues to be recognized statewide, with both rivals and clients eulogizing its team of *"superb and experienced litigators."* In under 20 years, the firm has grown to 24 attorneys, focusing entirely on commercial litigation, and including expertise in areas as diverse as contract law, securities, trade secrets, IP, antitrust and professional malpractice.
The Lawyers: The team is said to be *"thriving"* under the leadership of **Robin Gibbs**, who was singled out to researchers as *"one of the best trial lawyers in the US."* A 30-year veteran of the bar, he has represented both plaintiffs and defendants on a large range of commercial disputes. Clients highlighted his *"passionate devotion"* to his work, while rivals acknowledged both his *"superb closing arguments"* and his *"ability to relate complex facts to judges and juries."*
Phil Bruns gained widespread endorsement for his *"excellent judgment and sound experience."* He is renowned for his appellate practice and expertise in construction disputes, and was described by commentators as a *"deep thinker"* who *"complements Gibbs perfectly."*
The Clients: The firm acts for Morgan Stanley and Pennzoil.

Susman Godfrey LLP
The Firm: Considered to be *"one of the preeminent litigation groups"* in Texas, this boutique places its emphasis on securities, fraud, breach of contract and patent litigation matters, and undertakes a substantial amount of contingency work.
The Lawyers: Steve Susman spearheads a powerful team, and is regarded by contemporaries as a *"real legal gladiator and a larger-than-life figure."* He has a national profile, and was involved in the Alcatel securities litigation of January 2002, in which the firm secured a $75 million settlement for Alcatel shareholders. Top trial lawyer **Lee Godfrey** has handled complex litigation cases on behalf of both plaintiffs and defendants, including acting for royalty owners in the Lease Oil antitrust litigation, which settled for $194 million. He also advised on a shareholder class action against Shell Oil, which recovered $130 million. Researchers were pointed to his *"knack for getting at the facts,"* and his ability to *"connect with jurors in their own language."*
The *"smart and creative"* **Randy Wilson**, one of the four founding partners, continues to work extensively for Unocal. He also helped to obtain a $21.5 million jury verdict for TeraForce Technology against Cadence Design Systems.
The Clients: The firm advised Enron on its federal securities and shareholder derivatives suits, prior to Enron filing for bankruptcy.

Vinson & Elkins LLP
see firm details p.891
The Firm: *"The biggest and one of the best"* litigation groups in Texas, it not only punches its weight on energy disputes, but is also recognized for its track record in corporate securities, IP and mass torts.
The Lawyers: In Houston, the *"charismatic and charming"* **Harry Reasoner** (see p.679) is regarded as a leading player both locally and on a national level. An *"amazingly talented and thorough trial lawyer"* in all areas of complex commercial litiga-

LITIGATION
TEXAS

TEXAS
Leading individuals
(Litigation: General Commercial)

1
- BECK David *Beck, Redden & Secrest,* Houston
- GIBBS Robin *Gibbs & Bruns, LLP,* Houston
- REASONER Harry *Vinson & Elkins LLP,* Houston
- SUSMAN Stephen *Susman Godfrey LLP,* Houston

2
- BRISTOW Daryl *Baker Botts LLP,* Houston

3
- BRUNS Phil *Gibbs & Bruns, LLP,* Houston
- COLEMAN James *Carrington, Coleman,* Dallas
- GODFREY Lee *Susman Godfrey LLP,* Houston
- TERRELL Irvin *Baker Botts LLP,* Houston

4
- BROWN Reagan *Fulbright & Jaworski LLP,* Houston
- FOGLER Murray *McDade Fogler Maines LLP,* Houston
- KNULL William *Mayer, Brown, Rowe & Maw,* Houston
- MCKOOL Mike *McKool Smith,* Dallas
- MCNIEL Ferguson *Vinson & Elkins LLP,* Houston
- REDDEN Joe *Beck, Redden & Secrest,* Houston
- WILSON Randall *Susman Godfrey LLP,* Houston
- YEATES Marie *Vinson & Elkins LLP,* Houston

Individuals are listed alphabetically in each band.

tion, his success is attributed by clients to his skills as an *"excellent strategist."* **Ferguson McNiel** (see p.677) is also highly rated by contemporaries as a trial lawyer, and has a varied practice that encompasses professional malpractice, toxic tort, products liability and construction claims. He is representing a leading chemical company against nationwide claims for property damage resulting from alleged defects in polybutylene plumbing systems. **Marie Yeates** (see p.683) has a growing reputation for her appellate practice. Commended to researchers as *"an absolutely top-notch attorney,"* she has been involved in appeals arising from general commercial disputes, contract cases and business torts.

Baker Botts LLP
The Firm: Historically rated as one of the best litigation practices in Texas, the firm still gains especially high marks for expertise in its core areas of energy and hi-tech disputes.
The Lawyers: The *"phenomenally bright"* **Daryl Bristow**, endorsed to researchers as a *"great cross-examiner,"* is valued by clients for his *"incredible attention to detail."* He served as lead counsel for the Seminole and Martin Counties, Florida absentee ballot cases in the aftermath of the 2000 presidential election, and represented Dynegy on bankruptcy court adversary proceedings, in which Enron claimed wrongful termination of a merger agreement. **Irvin Terrell** is widely held to be a *"vastly experienced"* trial lawyer with *"a feel for the big cases."* He was trial counsel to President Bush and Vice President Cheney in the election contest, and is renowned for his expertise in disputes arising from a variety of business and election contests.

The Clients: The Houston office was involved in a successful breach of contract suit for ExxonMobil in an natural gas supply production case against Southern California Gas Company. Other clients include Dr Pepper/Seven Up, Allstate and EDS.

Beck, Redden & Secrest
The Firm: A successful spin-off from Fulbright & Jaworski ten years ago, the firm is now rapidly approaching 30 attorneys at its Houston headquarters. The firm's workload covers a wide range of complex commercial litigation, including antitrust, securities, professional malpractice and energy cases.
The Lawyers: The ten-year-old boutique is considered to be prospering under the guidance of the *"outstandingly effective"* **David Beck**. One of the most widely endorsed attorneys in Texas, he is a general commercial litigator who *"knows his material inside out,"* and is widely tipped by clients as *"a marvelous courtroom lawyer."* **Joe Redden** is thought to be *"an excellent foil for Beck,"* and was praised by opponents as *"a good guy to work with."*
The Clients: The firm is currently defending a major oil company in a lawsuit brought by the State of Texas for unpaid royalties on oil and gas production over the past 60 years. It is also defending a class action brought against a major computer company. Clients include Goldman Sachs, Deutsche Bank and ExxonMobil.

Fulbright & Jaworski LLP
see firm details p.799
The Firm: The firm draws on a massive litigation team in Houston, and in spite of a somewhat staid image, the group gained market plaudits for its national and international standing. Energy litigation, class action cases and patent disputes are sources of much work. The team also has expertise in trade secrets and ERISA litigation.
The Lawyers: There was widespread peer commendation for **Reagan Brown** (see p.670), a specialist in insurance and products liability disputes, who was praised to researchers as *"a persuasive advocate"* with a *"great win/loss record."*
The Clients: The firm obtained a favorable judgment in the high-profile Houston pipeline case against the Port of Houston Authority.

Carrington, Coleman, Sloman & Blumenthal, LLP
The Firm: A fixture on the legal landscape of Dallas, the firm now numbers about 90 attorneys, and is widely recognized for its competence in complex business litigation, notably insolvency disputes. Other elements of the caseload include antitrust, securities and IP matters.
The Lawyers: The *"tireless"* **Jim Coleman**, with more than 50 years of experience as a civil trial lawyer, has a reputation among peers as the *"dean of Dallas."* This *"old-school professional"* was

described to researchers as *"a leader who inspires rather than simply commands."* He has represented a number of companies and individuals in claims brought by the Federal Savings and Loan Insurance Corporation, Federal Deposit Insurance Corporation and Resolution Trust Corporation.
The Clients: The firm advises leading corporates and financial institutions.

McDade Fogler Maines LLP
The Firm: Despite only possessing a five-man presence in Houston, the firm receives general recognition as a *"sound organization."* The team principally deals with general commercial litigation, personal injury and white-collar defense.
The Lawyers: The firm is best known for its star litigator, **Murray Fogler**. A *"bright and understated attorney,"* he is said by peers to bring a *"down-to-earth and thoughtful approach"* to his work.
The Clients: Duke Energy; El Paso; Transocean Sedco Forex and Service Corporation International.

Haynes and Boone LLP
see firm details p.814
The Firm: The litigation group, which features Kenneth Broughton, now accounts for more than half the firm's total strength, and covers the full spectrum of commercial disputes. Niche strengths include bankruptcy and reorganization and IP, although the firm's caseload also encompasses consumer class actions, professional liability claims and insurance coverage. Rivals acknowledged the firm as *"a growing force."*
The Clients: The firm advises major corporates and financial institutions.

Mayer, Brown, Rowe & Maw
see firm details p.843
The Firm: The firm's Houston office holds about 40 lawyers, of which nearly a third specialize in litigation. Described to researchers as a *"decent and reputable team,"* it is especially recognized for its ability in energy disputes, and also has substantial experience of construction cases.
The Lawyers: Much of the credit for the firm's profile is ascribed to **Bill Knull**'s (see p.675) *"sound judgment"* and *"first-rate communication skills."*
The Clients: Bank of America, Ernst & Young and GE Power Systems.

Other Notable Practitioners
Mike McKool is the Dallas-based star of the litigation practice at McKool Smith PC. Strongly commended by his peers, he has represented a number of outside directors in litigation filed against former directors of Dallas-based bank holding companies.

TEXAS — PROJECTS

PROJECTS

TEXAS
Leading firms (Projects)
1. VINSON & ELKINS LLP *Houston*
2. ANDREWS & KURTH LLP *Houston*
   BAKER BOTTS LLP *Houston*
3. KING & SPALDING LLP *Houston*
   SKADDEN, ARPS, SLATE, MEAGHER *Houston*
4. BRACEWELL & PATTERSON LLP *Houston*

Leading individuals (Projects)
1. ASMUS David *Baker Botts LLP*, Houston
   BILGER Bruce *Vinson & Elkins LLP*, Houston
   COGAN John *King & Spalding LLP*, Houston
   TAYLOR Lyndon *Skadden, Arps, Slate*, Houston
   UNGER Timothy *Andrews & Kurth LLP*, Houston
2. ALE John *Skadden, Arps, Slate, Meagher*, Houston
   BLAND Doug *Vinson & Elkins LLP*, Houston
   EVANS Mark *Bracewell & Patterson LLP*, Houston
   KELLEY Jay *Vinson & Elkins LLP*, Houston
   KREBS Stephen *Baker Botts LLP*, Houston
   PINKERTON Glenn *Vinson & Elkins LLP*, Houston
   THURBER Mark *Andrews & Kurth LLP*, Houston

Up-and-coming individuals
MAUEL John *Baker & McKenzie*, Houston
THOMPSON Dahl *Andrews & Kurth LLP*, Houston

Firms and individuals are listed alphabetically in each band.

Vinson & Elkins LLP
see firm details p.891

The Firm: The firm has consistently pursued project finance work at home and abroad, and its large and energetic finance practice ensures that it remains *"a cut above the rest"* in Texas. The fallout from Enron notwithstanding, the team's global reach and international experience are thought by commentators to ensure a constant stream of big-ticket work for the firm. At home, the firm represented East Coast Power on the financing of three cogeneration plants in New Jersey. Overseas, attorneys acted as lead counsel for the $800 million Cuiaba Integrated Project in Brazil and the $250 million Centra Gas Pipeline Project in British Columbia and advised on the natural gas pipeline venture between Indonesia and Singapore.

The Lawyers: Recognized for his expertise in power ventures, the *"eminently sophisticated"* **Bruce Bilger** (see p.669) brings a *"smart, level head"* to the intricacies of complex negotiations. He heads a talented team, in which **Doug Bland** (see p.669) is felt to have emerged as *"a real star."* The latter advised the Government of Curaçao on the project financing of an electric power, steam, water and compressed air plant for the Isla Refinery. Interviewees also endorsed **Jay Kelley** (see p.675) as a *"strong player"* on the international scene, where he has advised on projects as far afield as Venezuela, Indonesia, Argentina and the UK. The *"skilled"* **Glenn Pinkerton** (see p.678) was also commended to researchers as a *"rising name"* at the firm. He represented the project company in the development, construction and financing of the first fully integrated merchant gas and power project in Latin America.

The Clients: Duke Energy; Unocal; Shell; JPMorgan Chase; British Gas; BP Amoco; AES; Kinder Morgan; El Paso; Dynegy; Sempra Energy; NRG; ABN AMRO; BNP Paribas; Deutsche Bank; Government of Curaçao; East Coast Power; Mirant and Petrobras.

Andrews & Kurth LLP
see firm details p.764

The Firm: A relatively young team is thought to achieve high visibility in the sector through the *"tremendous skill set"* of its attorneys. The firm's activity is divided equally between domestic and international projects. Its highest profile is in power projects, although gas infrastructure, pipelines and water projects also constitute important elements of the workload.

The Lawyers: A fixture on major domestic and international cogeneration projects, **Timothy Unger** (see p.681) received unanimous endorsement as *"one of the best"* in the market. *"We would love to have him,"* admitted one rival. He is backed by two relatively recent recruits from Skadden Arps: **Mark Thurber** (see p.681), who combines expertise in oil, gas and power projects with *"immense efficiency"* in coordinating suites of transaction documents; and *"up-and-coming star"* **Dahl Thompson** (see p.681), who drew widespread admiration for his *"great commercial sense."*

The Clients: The firm represented Marathon, lead developer for the LNG supply, regasification and power plant project in Baja, Mexico, and also advised on the construction of petrochemical facilities in Trinidad and Rotterdam. On the domestic front, the firm has served as counsel to the developers in connection with the financing of power plants in Oklahoma. Clients of the firm include: NRG; WilliamsEnergy Partners; Duke Energy; KCS Energy and Brazos Valley Energy.

Baker Botts LLP

The Firm: The firm's strength in this area is generally held to be built on the foundations of its top-class corporate securities practice. A proactive structured finance practice has advised on several synthetic leases, worth a total of $2.5 billion, for Reliant Resources to finance four greenfield power facilities. The firm also advised on the joint venture between Conoco and Transocean to finance a drill ship. Overseas, the firm advised on Coral Energy's negotiation of long-term contracts to buy power from InterGen's La Rosita Power Project in Mexicali, Mexico. Attorneys were also counsel for the Baku-Tbilisi-Ceyhan oil pipeline, and advised the Shah Deniz consortium on a natural gas pipeline supplying Azerbaijan, Georgia and Turkey.

The Lawyers: An acknowledged master of upstream and midstream projects, **David Asmus** *"leads by example."* A contributor to the Association of International Petroleum Negotiators (AIPN), he was said by contemporaries to be *"at the forefront"* of drafting and joint operating agreements for oil and LNG ventures. *"Tenacious but diplomatic,"* **Steve Krebs** was fêted for his experience of petrochemical projects, notably in the former Soviet Union. He was singled out to researchers as *"a great negotiator of the elephant hurdles that crop up in global transactions."*

The Clients: Pride International; Global MarineSystems; ExxonMobil; BP Amoco; Reliant Resources; Coral Energy; AES; Occidental Petroleum and EOG Resources.

King & Spalding LLP
see firm details p.829

The Firm: Despite being comparatively new to the state (the Houston office opened in 1995), the firm is conceded by competitors to have built an active international projects practice. Recent financings include a new greenfield LNG facility for the Tangguh Project in Indonesia and major LNG facilities in Angola. The firm is also active in upstream oil and gas fields development for the southern republics of the former Soviet Union, and has undertaken financings for petrochemical plants in Brazil and Mexico, and an $800 million financing for four LNG tankers.

The Lawyers: The outstanding individual at the firm is *"superstar"* **John Cogan** (see p.671), described by one peer as *"the LNG transportation practitioner in town."* His practice has spanned 25 years, and he was extolled to researchers for his *"creative, persuasive and diligent"* style. Advising on some of the world's most high-profile projects, Cogan was lead counsel for two of the three largest core natural gas ventures sponsored by the Government of Saudi Arabia and ten foreign oil companies. In total, these two ventures were estimated to be worth $15 billion. He has also advised on the financing of petrochemical plants in Latin America, and on natural gas infrastructure projects in the Caribbean and the Middle East.

The Clients: ExxonMobil; BP Amoco; ChevronTexaco; El Paso; Ocean Energy and Burlington Resources.

REAL ESTATE | TEXAS

Skadden, Arps, Slate, Meagher & Flom LLP & Affiliates

see firm details p.878

The Firm: Project and infrastructure financings orchestrated from the Houston offices are regarded as one of the strong points of this *"excellent"* firm. Acknowledged to possess *"some of the best lawyers in the business,"* the firm combines a global reach with niche expertise in energy-related non-recourse financings, acquisitions and divestitures. The firm advised NRG in its purchase of four coal-powered plants from FirstEnergy in a deal worth $1.6 billion, and advised on InterGen's development and financing of a power generation plant in Oklahoma. Other areas of focus include LNG work, in which sphere the group advised on British Gas' long-term contracts in Trinidad.

The Lawyers: Lyndon Taylor (see p.681) was described to researchers as *"one of the finest lawyers in Texas."* A specialist in the LNG sector, he has extensive experience of projects in South America, the Far East and Norway. **John Ale** (see p.668) also gained sustained market endorsement. Formerly general counsel at Azurix, he has niche expertise in water infrastructure projects. Peers regard him as an *"outstanding technician."*

The Clients: British Gas; Rolls Royce; Phillips Petroleum Company; WilliamEnergy Partners; NRG; El Paso; Huntsman and InterGen.

Bracewell & Patterson LLP

see firm details p.774

The Firm: Local project and infrastructure financings, frequently on behalf of the lenders, represent a substantial share of the firm's involvement in the energy market. Clients emphasized the *"professional"* approach of partners and the team's ability to *"turn a deal around quickly."* The firm represented InterGen North America in the development and non-recourse senior debt financing of the Texas power generation facility, the Cottonwood Project. It also advised on the Magnolia Project, another power generation project, in Mississippi. The team also assisted Kinder Morgan Power Company on the partnership arrangements for the ownership and development of six power generating facilities.

The Lawyers: Mark Evans (see p.672) is lauded for his *"transactional creativity and flair."* As well as his experience of power projects, he was commended for his knowledge of finance and credit documentation.

The Clients: InterGen; Kinder MorganPower Company; Reliant Energy Power Generation; El Paso Merchant EnergyNorth America; Entergy and Mosbacher Power Company.

Other Notable Practitioners

In Baker & McKenzie's Houston office, **John Mauel** (see p.676)'s reputation for project work is considered to eclipse that of his firm. A power project specialist, he has advised utilities, energy trading companies and lenders on a range of high-profile matters throughout the US and in Brazil, Pakistan, Southeast Asia and the former Soviet Union.

REAL ESTATE

TEXAS
Leading firms (Real Estate)

1
- HAYNES AND BOONE LLP *Dallas*
- JENKENS & GILCHRIST *Dallas*
- VINSON & ELKINS LLP *Houston*
- WINSTEAD SECHREST & MINICK *Dallas, Houston*

2
- ANDREWS & KURTH LLP *Houston*
- BAKER BOTTS LLP *Houston*
- MAYER, BROWN, ROWE & MAW *Houston*

3
- FULBRIGHT & JAWORSKI LLP *Houston*
- JACKSON WALKER LLP *Houston*
- THOMPSON & KNIGHT LLP *Houston*

4
- BRACEWELL & PATTERSON LLP *Dallas*
- GARDERE WYNNE SEWELL LLP *Dallas*
- LOCKE LIDDELL & SAPP LLP *Houston*

Leading individuals (Real Estate)

1
- WALLENSTEIN Jim *Jenkens & Gilchrist, Dallas*

2
- DOW Melvin *Winstead Sechrest & Minick, Houston*
- KATZ Marvin *Mayer, Brown, Rowe & Maw, Houston*
- WEINER Sandford *Vinson & Elkins LLP, Houston*
- WILSON Robert *Haynes and Boone LLP, Dallas*

3
- FIELDS Jack *Andrews & Kurth LLP, Houston*

4
- BOULDEN Michael *Vinson & Elkins LLP, Dallas*
- DOW Andy *Winstead Sechrest & Minick, Dallas*
- DUNLAY Jon *Baker Botts LLP, Houston*
- DUNLOP Fred *Baker Botts LLP, Houston*
- ERWIN Greg *Winstead Sechrest & Minick, Houston*
- NEWSOME Kent *Fulbright & Jaworski LLP, Houston*
- NONDORF Kurt *Jackson Walker LLP, Dallas*
- ROBERTS Harry *Thompson & Knight LLP, Dallas*

Firms and individuals are listed alphabetically in each band.

Haynes and Boone LLP

see firm details p.814

The Firm: The practice is spread across seven offices in Texas, and was thought to possess *"outstanding"* strength in Dallas. Peers and clients consistently recognized the group as *"one of the leading real estate practices in the state."* The real estate department is served by about 30 attorneys, who earned market praise for their *"business-minded outlook."* A comprehensive workload includes advice on real estate finance, development, leasing, sales and acquisitions.

The Lawyers: *"Talented and personable"* **Robert Wilson** (see p.682) enjoys a statewide reputationfor his work on behalf of institutional lenders. Contemporaries acknowledge him as *"an excellent negotiator"* who *"breaks through roadblocks."* He acted for a pension fund in the acquisition of 15 national warehouses, and represents numerousREITs.Wilsonis a member of the American College of Real Estate Lawyers (ACREL).

The Clients: The firm acts for Crédit Lyonnais, Ericsson and Jones Lang LaSalle.

Jenkens & Gilchrist

The Firm: Working from four offices in Texas, the firm was admiringly endorsed to researchers for having *"got real big, real fast."* The real estate team's strength is considered to lie principally in the Dallas office, but nearly 30 attorneys across the state offer a broad range of real estate advice. M&A and financing work is widely recognized as fields of niche expertise for this *"highly talented team."*

The Lawyers: Although commentators emphasized the consistent quality of the group, the *"outstanding"* **Jim Wallenstein** dominates the headlines. A member of ACREL, he was commended to researchers as an *"incredibly cerebral guru of the real estate bar."* Contemporaries agree that his 30 years of experience in commercial real estate law make him *"the one to call"* for the interpretation of new statutes. His workload includes M&A, financing and restructuring, leasing, development, partnership and joint ventures.

The Clients: The firm provides a broad range of real estate and commercial transaction-related services to financial institutions, commercial developers, government agencies and individual investors.

Vinson & Elkins LLP

see firm details p.891

The Firm: The firm undertakes a variety of real estate and construction projects, including offices, shopping malls and industrial facilities as well as infrastructure projects, power plants and pipeline works. In addition to traditional real estate transactions and litigation, the firm is noted by peers for the *"strong nature of its government work,"* earning it the reputation of *"the state's premier regulatory lawyers."*

The Lawyers: Most highly rated is the *"extremely bright"* **Sandy Weiner** (see p.682), president-elect of the ACREL. His principal areas of practice include commercial mortgage finance and synthetic leasing, in which he has represented a number of energy companies in recent multimillion dollar financings. **Mike Boulden** (see p.670) was endorsed to researchers as a *"gifted negotiator,"* and was especially highly commended for his lending work.

TEXAS

REAL ESTATE

The Clients: The broad client base includes energy companies, financial institutions and commercial developers. Clients include GE Capital and Archon Group.

Winstead Sechrest & Minick
see firm details p.902
The Firm: Commentators agree that the firm has *"dramatically enhanced"* its reputation in real estate since expanding in Houston 12 years ago. The firm's *"young and aggressive"* team won consistent praise for its *"extremely broad practice,"* and is acknowledged to have become an *"incredibly efficient regional player."* The July 2001 merger with Houston-based boutique Dow, Cogburn & Friedman was widely regarded as *"a plum acquisition,"* notably for development and finance work. A month later, the firm joined forces with Dallas-based Donohoe, Jameson & Carroll, and can now boast more than 60 attorneys in five offices throughout the state who specialize in real estate and finance advice. Real estate leasing is another area in which the firm is thought to have specific expertise. It also represents developers and owners in the acquisition, development, financing and sale of shopping centers, office buildings, apartment blocks and warehouses.
The Lawyers: Rivals believe that *"outstanding real estate attorney"* **Melvin Dow** (see p.672) has been *"a real catch"* for the firm. *"An excellent analyst and negotiator,"* he advised Weingarten Realty Investors on the acquisition of five shopping malls in California for $277 million. In Houston, he acted for Century Development on the construction of a 37-story office block, known as '1000 Main'. He receives support from **Greg Erwin** (see p.672), an *"intelligent, experienced attorney"* and member of ACREL, and **Andy Dow** (see p.672), cochair of the firm's leasing and development practice, who was singled out to lawyers as an attorney with *"a good blend of commercial and legal knowledge."*
The Clients: The firm advised on the development of a stadium for a new NFL franchise in Texas and acted for the San Antonio Spurs on the development of a new arena. It has been involved in the development of major sports facilities in Florida and Tennessee. Other clients include Century Development and Weingarten Realty Investors.

Andrews & Kurth LLP
see firm details p.764
The Firm: The firm's real estate practice covers the state, with more than 40 lawyers practicing in the Houston and Dallas offices alone. Renowned among peers for its "high caliber on the lending side," the group also handles M&A, land use, leasing, joint ventures and restructuring matters. Development work has included projects for offices, hotels, retail complexes, public buildings and the energy industry.
The Lawyers: Rivals acknowledge that **Jack Fields** (see p.672) *"swims with the big fish."* His broad-based practice is most noted for its commercial emphasis, and he represents both mortgage loan servicers and real estate developers on a range of office, retail and industrial projects.
The Clients: The firm is regional counsel for Wal-Mart. Its other clients include: Fortune 500 companies; developers; institutional lenders; mortgage loan servicers; life insurance companies and pension funds.

Baker Botts LLP
The Firm: The real estate group of this renowned commercial firm gained high marks from observers for its work on behalf of an institutional clientele.
The Lawyers: **John Dunlay** focuses his practice on commercial real estate transactions, and was especially recommended to researchers for his leasing advice. He has represented both landlords and tenants on office leases, advised investors and purchasers on a range of acquisitions, and acted for developers on the financing and leasing of shopping center projects in Dallas.
"Excellent all-rounder" **Fred Dunlop** gained market recognition for his *"sound judgment and technical skill."* His client roster includes developers, institutional lenders and investors. He was involved in the development and operation of the Houston and Dallas Galleria projects, malls covered by glass atriums that incorporated stores and restaurants with office and hotel space.
The Clients: Hines Interests is a major client.

Mayer, Brown, Rowe & Maw
see firm details p.843
The Firm: The most significant real estate department not indigenous to Texas now comprises 50 attorneys in Houston who undertake substantial financing, REIT, development and acquisition work. Clients were impressed by the *"accurate and dependable"* team who are *"both commercial and responsive."*
The Lawyers: The firm's reputation is built around *"one of the premier real estate attorneys in Houston,"* **Marvin Katz** (see p.675). The chair of the City of Houston Planning Commission, Katz was highly acclaimed to researchers as a *"wonderful negotiator"* with a *"sharp understanding of the economics of transactions."* He has advised Bank of Montreal extensively on mortgage lending. The group has also been involved in the development of shopping malls and skyscrapers throughout Texas.
The Clients: The group advises Bank of America, Wells Fargo and Mirant.

Fulbright & Jaworski LLP
see firm details p.799
The Firm: Real estate development and commercial retail leasing form the bedrock of this *"solid and experienced"* Houston team. The firm advised a healthcare company on the acquisition and development of a new hospital in Laredo.
The Lawyers: The group is considered to have *"thrived"* under the aegis of **Kent Newsome** (see p.677). He appeals to contemporaries as a *"vibrant personality who is fast making a name for himself."* Clients appreciate his ability to *"close out transactions efficiently."*
The Clients: The firm has represented buyers, sellers and developers in the acquisition, sale and development of office buildings, retail centers, apartment complexes, hotels and hospitals. Weatherford is a client of the group.

Jackson Walker LLP
The Firm: The firm has a long-established presence in the state, with 325 attorneys in seven regional offices. About 40 attorneys practice real estate law, and the firm is acknowledged to have benefited from the absorption in 2001 of San Antonio boutique Gresham, Davis, Gregory, Worthy and Moore, which enjoyed a fine reputation for real estate transactions. The firm often acts for financial institutions, but its reputation remains highest for real estate M&A, leasing and development.
The Lawyers: **Kurt Nondorf** was noted to researchers as *"an obvious guy to turn to."* He was singled out for his leasing experience, representing landlords and tenants in negotiations for office leases of more than 100,000 sq ft. He also acts as real estate counsel to the Texas Medical Center.
The Clients: The firm represents one of the largest office building REITs in Texas, and has performed substantial local real estate work for foreign investors. Bank of America is a client.

Thompson & Knight LLP
see firm details p.889
The Firm: Especially well known in the Dallas market, the firm was described as a *"solid and reputable"* operation, and is often seen on financings in the real estate sector, notably on the lending side. Other elements of the caseload include shopping center site acquisitions and a range of leasing work.
The Lawyers: **Harry Roberts** (see p.679) has an enviable reputation among peers and clients as *"a savvy and experienced"* attorney.
The Clients: The firm has helped major insurance companies to find permanent financing for real estate projects in the state, and represented a large bank in the synthetic leasing of a $500 million corporate headquarters for a Fortune 500 company.

Bracewell & Patterson LLP
see firm details p.774
The Firm: Energy-related real estate finance and construction are widely seen as the firm's strengths in this sector. However, the group, headed by Allan Wisk, also handles substantial traditional real estate work, advising on the

acquisition and development of shopping malls, golf courses, multi-use urban developments and theaters. Peers regard the team as a *"large and respectable"* player in the local market.

Gardere Wynne Sewell LLP
see firm details p.801

The Firm: Characterized as *"not large, but decent,"* the firm advises on a variety of statewide traditional real estate work. The group, led by Kevin Kelley, advises a clientele that includes entrepreneurs, investors and financial institutions, on the development of retail, leisure and mixed-use projects. Other aspects of the workload have included portfolio acquisitions, disposals and financings.

The Clients: Dallas Area Rapid Transit (DART); Rosewood Property Company; JPMorgan Chase and Bank of America.

Locke Liddell & Sapp LLP

The Firm: The real estate department is respected for its presence on the financing side of transactions, and is acknowledged by peers to be *"making some waves"* in this area. Commercial and residential leasing advice rounds out a practice with "undoubted breadth."

The Lawyers: Jeff Love is the managing partner of the Houston office.

The Clients: A wide range of developers, landlords, tenants and lenders use the firm.

TAX

TEXAS
Leading firms (Tax)
1. VINSON & ELKINS LLP *Dallas, Houston*
2. BAKER BOTTS LLP *Dallas*
   FULBRIGHT & JAWORSKI LLP *Houston*
3. LOCKE LIDDELL & SAPP LLP *Dallas*
   THOMPSON & KNIGHT LLP *Dallas*
4. HUGHES & LUCE LLP *Dallas*

Leading individuals (Tax)
1. KALTEYER Ronald *Locke Liddell & Sapp LLP*, Dallas
2. OSTERBERG Edward *Vinson & Elkins LLP*, Houston
3. ALLISON Christopher *Locke Liddell & Sapp*, Dallas
   ASOFSKY Paul *Weil, Gotshal & Manges LLP*, Houston
   HARDIE Thornton *Thompson & Knight LLP*, Dallas
   HELFAND Thomas *Winstead Sechrest & Minick*, Dallas
   SALCH Steven *Fulbright & Jaworski LLP*, Houston
4. HENKEL Kathryn *Hughes & Luce LLP*, Dallas
   MICCICHE Daniel *Akin Gump Strauss Hauer*, Dallas

Up-and-coming individuals
   WHEAT David *Thompson & Knight LLP*, Dallas

Firms and individuals are listed alphabetically in each band.

Vinson & Elkins LLP
see firm details p.891

The Firm: The department is known for its *"first-rate"* spread of subgroups, which focus on a comprehensive range of tax advice, from international and transactional matters to estate planning issues. It represents both multinational corporations and public entities, and has gained particular recognition for the corporate work that it undertakes for the energy industry. In recent times, the group has also witnessed increased leveraged leasing activity, while its 'Texas Tax' department reflects its expertise in state and local tax issues.

The Lawyers: Peers unanimously agreed that **Ed Osterberg** (see p.678), head of the international and transactional practice group, is *"one of the sharpest tax attorneys in Texas."* His practice includes cross-border joint ventures, M&A, advice on the foreign operations of US multinationals and partnership taxation work. He served as lead US tax lawyer on the $4 billion acquisition of a Canadian energy company, which used exchangeable shares, and has advised on various Eurobond offerings aggregating over $2 billion.

The Clients: The firm advised Goldman Sachs on federal income tax matters in connection with the sale of more than $1 billion of securities issued by Kinder Morgan Management, and acted for National Pipe and Tube on appeal in an ad valorem tax case involving the exhaustion of administrative remedies. Other clients of the firm include: The Williams Companies; ARCO; Penn Virginia; TEPPCO Partners; Boyd Gaming and Duke Energy.

Baker Botts LLP

The Firm: Although the tax group does not possess the high-profile individuals of some of its principal rivals, it is acknowledged by peers as a *"broad, deep and capable"* department. It is divided into distinct but fully integrated subgroups with expertise in business, estate, transactional, controversy and employment-related tax matters.

Led by Stanley Beyer, the group has a significant international reach that has enabled it to represent a number of large oil exploration and production companies. It recently advised on the tax implications of a proposed pipeline project connecting Azerbaijan's Caspian Sea oil reserves to international markets around the Mediterranean Sea. This general reputation for strength in the energy sector has been further bolstered by its niche advisory role to a number of publicly traded partnerships in the industry.

The Clients: Recent work undertaken by the department includes advising Reliant Resources on its $2.9 billion merger with Orion Power Holdings, and representing Cabot Oil & Gas on its merger with Cody Company. The firm's client base also includes: Pride International; Houston Endowment; Rice University; Conoco and Syntroleum.

Fulbright & Jaworski LLP
see firm details p.799

The Firm: Perhaps best known for the strength of its tax controversy and litigation team, the firm in fact provides a complete range of tax services for a diverse clientele. Its comparatively small, but highly active, transactional practice regularly advises on tax matters concerning the energy industry, notably the planning and structuring of M&A transactions. Recent courtroom successes include a favorable verdict in the US Federal Claims Court for the tax refund case brought by the Succession of Betty Felix Helis, who had alleged the overpayment of the estate's tax liability. The firm also successfully represented Prudential Overall Supply in its protracted dispute with the IRS over a challenge made to the company's accounting methodology.

The Lawyers: The group's leading practitioner is generally held to be **Steven Salch** (see p.680), who is said to have *"a finger in many pies."* This versatile attorney's practice encompasses international, state and local tax, and tax controversy, matters.

The Clients: Prudential Overall Supply and Laborers' International Union of North America are represented by the firm.

Locke Liddell & Sapp LLP

The Firm: The firm's tax department boasts one of the largest REIT groups in the US, and it has acquired a solid reputation for the taxation work undertaken by its business tax, employee benefits, and estate planning and probate subgroups. Commentators particularly endorsed the firm's expertise in structuring original business entities in order to reduce state and local tax burdens for its clients. International tax is another growing element of the team's workload.

The Lawyers: **Chris Allison** (see p.668) earned widespread approval as a *"knowledgeable"* attorney, and has extensive experience of corporate and partnership tax matters, as well as appearing on various tax controversy cases. He provides valuable support to **Ron Kalteyer** (see p.675), head of the firm's business tax section, whom

many commentators recognized as the leading tax name in the state. Described to researchers as *"a sharp, technically excellent lawyer, who will do whatever it takes to get the job done,"* his practice embraces corporate, REIT and workout matters.
The Clients: INVESCO Institutional; Service Corporation International; Crescent Real Estate Equities; JPMorgan Chase Bank; Dell; JC Penney Company.

Thompson & Knight LLP
see firm details p.889
The Firm: Described to researchers as *"an innovative and creative tax practice,"* it has historically been known for the volume of work that it has undertaken on behalf of oil and gas companies. The firm gained high market praise for its ability to deal with large tax controversy cases, and is thought to have a particular forte in exempt organization matters and charitable gift planning advice. A substantial estate planning department has also contributed to the department's growing reputation.
The Lawyers: Contemporaries recommended **Thornton Hardie** (see p.673) as an *"outstandingly creative"* tax attorney, and paid particular tribute to his aptitude for tax and business planning advice. He advised a large independent oil and gas company on the acquisition of $300 million worth of oil and gas properties, and acted for a real estate developer on the tax aspects of a $5 million development partnership. **David Wheat** (see p.668) was also identified as an *"especially promising"* corporate tax lawyer. He was special tax counsel on a $1.5 billion stock purchase, and also advised on a recent multibillion dollar merger.
The Clients: The firm advises multinationals, public entities, oil and gas corporations and high net-worth individuals.

Hughes & Luce LLP
The Firm: The strength of the firm's taxation reputation has often been attributed to the influence of senior partner Vester Hughes Jr and his expertise in federal taxation matters. The group's track record for corporate and private client taxation matters continues to earn it a local name as a *"vigorous and impressive"* tax player. The group deals with a broad range of business matters, and frequently advises on partnership tax issues for real estate transactions. Other strengths include oil and gas partnership work, Texas franchise taxation and tax planning for private individuals and closely held family companies.
The Lawyers: Kathy Henkel was recommended to researchers for her estate planning expertise.
The Clients: Communities Foundation of Texas; Merit Energy Company; Waddell & Reed and Estate of Jennette McLendon.

Other Notable Practitioners
In Dallas, **Dan Micciche** of Akin, Gump, Strauss, Hauer & Feld LLP has been acknowledged by peers for the strength of his federal and state taxation work on behalf of corporations, partnerships, limited liability companies and individuals. **Thomas Helfand** (see p.674) of Winstead Sechrest & Minick was characterized to researchers as a *"talented and personable"* attorney with a generalist's tax practice. In Houston, Weil, Gotshal & Manges LLP's **Paul Asofsky** (see p.668) is regarded as an attorney who *"plows his own furrow."* Contemporaries view him as one of the premier tax insolvency lawyers in Texas, and he regularly advises distressed companies on bankruptcy and corporate restructuring.

Leaders in Texas

AHMAD, Joseph
Ahmad, Zavitsanos & Anaipakos, PC, Houston 713 655 1101
Recommended in Employment

ALBERGOTTI, Robert
Haynes and Boone, LLP, Dallas
214 651 5613
robert.albergotti@haynesboone.com
Recommended in Insolvency
Specialization: Represents EOTT Energy Partners, LP in its prenegotiated Chapter 11 proceedings; EOTT is a $10 Billion annual sales operator of crude oil pipelines serving 18 states. Served as principal legal adviser to the California State Assembly in connection with efforts to resolve the California "electricity crisis";. Represented Kitty Hawk, Inc. as Debtor in Possession in its Chapter 11 Proceedings. Kitty Hawk is a non-integrated FAA Certificated airline serving all major US markets with air freight services.

ALE, John
Skadden, Arps, Slate, Meagher & Flom LLP & Affiliates, Houston 713 655 5263
jale@skadden.com
Recommended in Energy, Projects
Specialization: Partner, Houston. Concentrates in US and international energy, infrastructure, finance, and corporate matters. Represents clients in the development, financing and acquisition of energy and water infrastructure projects; privatizations; and acquisitions and divestitures.
Prof. Memberships: Director, Texas Business Law Foundation 1992-97; State Bar of Texas, Business Law Section (Chairman, Partnership Law Committee, 1993-95; Section Council, 1995-97).
Career: Previously Executive Director & General Counsel of Azurix Corp.; Law Clerk, Chief Justice Warren E Burger, US Supreme Court; Law Clerk, Judge Edward Allen Tamm; US Court of Appeals - DC Circuit; JD, University of Virginia, 1979 (Virginia Law Review); BA, University of Virginia, 1976.
Publications: Author, 'Partnership Law for Securities Practitioners' (The West Group).

ALLENSWORTH, William
Roller & Allensworth, Austin
512 708 1250
Recommended in Construction

ALLISON, Christopher
Locke Liddell & Sapp LLP, Dallas
214 740 8692
callison@lockeliddell.com
Recommended in Tax
Specialization: Partner practicing in tax law. Section Coordinator of the firm's Taxation, Trust and Estates Section. Over 20 years of experience in representing clients in the following areas: (i) corporate taxation including corporate formations, liquidations, distributions, reorganizations and recapitalizations, corporation taxation, partnership taxation and taxation of limited liability companies; (ii) tax issues related to investments by tax exempt entities; and (iii) handling federal and state tax controversies at the audit, administrative and court levels.
Prof. Memberships: Member, American Bar Association, Section of Taxation; Member, State Bar of Texas, Section of Taxation; Member, Dallas Bar Association.
Career: Admitted to South Carolina Bar (1977); admitted to the Texas Bar (1981). A partner in *Locke Liddell & Sapp LLP* since 1983; Board Certified in Area of Taxation by the Texas Board of Legal Specialization.
Personal: Received a LLM degree in Taxation, from New York University in 1981; Juris Doctor degree from the University of South Carolina in 1977; Bachelor of Arts degree, cum laude, from Davidson College in 1974.

AMANDES, Christopher
Vinson & Elkins LLP, Houston
713 758 1146
camandes@velaw.com
Recommended in Environment
Specialization: Principal area of practice is environmental law, with emphasis on compliance counseling, enforcement defense, transactional environmental issues, and cost-recovery litigation. Listed in an Leadin US publication in environmental law, since 1995.
Prof. Memberships: Co-Chair: City of Houston's Brownfield Redevelopment Committee, 1996-2000. Air and Waste Management Association.
Career: Admitted to practice: Texas, 1985. Joined *Vinson & Elkins*, 1986; admitted to partnership, 1994. Registered Professional Engineer, Texas, 1983-present.
Personal: Rice University, BA, 1976; Masters of Environmental Engineering, 1978; University of California at Los Angeles, JD, 1985.

ASMUS, David
Baker Botts LLP, Houston
713 229 1234
Recommended in Energy, Projects

ASOFSKY, Paul
Weil, Gotshal & Manges LLP, Houston
713 546 5118
paul.asofsky@weil.com
Recommended in Tax
Specialization: Head of the tax group in *Weil Gotshal*'s Houston office, a position he has held since 1990. Prior to that, he practiced in New York City for 24 years. His practice spans the full range of business tax matters, with emphasis on private equity fund formation and deal execution, structuring business and investment vehicles, capital markets, and debt restructuring and bankruptcy.

Prof. Memberships: Has long been a member of the Section of Taxation of the American Bar Association, where he currently serves as Chair of the Subcommittee on Private Equity Funds of the Committee on Partnerships. He previously chaired two special task forces created by the Section to comment on the tax aspects of bankruptcy legislation. He has been a Conferee of the National Bankruptcy Conference since 1984 and has chaired its Committee on Tax Matters since 1986. He is a Fellow of the American College of Tax Counsel. He has also served as Chair of the Houston Tax Roundtable and the Tax Club in New York City. He is a member of the bars of the states of Texas and New York and is admitted to practice before the United States Courts of Appeals for the Second and Fifth circuits, the United States District Courts for the Southern and Eastern Districts of New York and the Northern and Southern Districts of Texas and the United States Tax Court.
Publications: Has made many appearances as a speaker at the leading tax institutes in the United States and his articles have been published in leading tax periodicals.
Personal: Holds a Bachelor of Arts degree, magna cum laude, from Columbia College, granted in 1962, where he was elected to Phi Beta Kappa. Also holds a Bachelor of Laws degree from the Harvard Law School, cum laude, which was granted in 1965.

BACKUS, Marcia
Vinson & Elkins LLP, Houston
713 758 1101
mbackus@velaw.com
Recommended in Energy

Specialization: Domestic and international acquisition, divestiture and project finance and project development transactions, corporate law, power-related transactions and other energy-related transactions. Is a member of the firm's Management Committee, the Energy Practice Group, and Chair of the Partner Admissions Committee.
Prof. Memberships: Fellow: Houston Bar Association; Keeton Fellow, The University of Texas.
Career: Came to the firm in 1983 and was admitted to the partnership in 1991.
Personal: Attended Georgetown University and graduated from The University of Texas, BA in 1976 and JD in 1983 (Order of the Coif).

BAKER, Tyler
Carrington, Coleman, Sloman & Blumenthal, LLP, Dallas 214 855 3000
Recommended in Antitrust

BARBOUR, David
Andrews & Kurth LLP, Dallas
214 659 4444
dbarbour@akllp.com
Recommended in Banking & Finance

Specialization: Practice includes expertise in various commercial transactions on a national and international basis, including: (i) the representation of issuers and underwriters in public and private offerings of equity and debt securities, with an emphasis in structured debt issuances of mortgage-backed and asset-backed securities; (ii) the negotiation and structuring of various corporate and real estate financings; (iii) the negotiation and structuring of asset and stock acquisitions; and (iv) general corporate, mortgage banking, real estate and securities transactions.
Prof. Memberships: American and Dallas Bar Associations; Member, ABA Section of Business Law, Committee on Developments in Business Financing, Subcommittee on Securitization of Assets.
Career: Admitted to the State Bar of Texas 1974. A partner with *Andrews & Kurth LLP* since 1994.
Publications: Speaker; NYSE and NASDAQ Corporate Governance and Listing Standards Reform, 10th Annual SMU Corporate Counsel Symposium sponsored by the SMU Law Review Association, November 1, 2002, Dallas, Texas.
Personal: Received JD (with honors) from University of Texas School of Law in 1974. Was a member of Chancellors and received Order of the Coif. Received BBA (with highest honors) from University of Texas at Austin in 1971. Was a member of Phi Kappa Phi, Beta Gamma Sigma and Sigma Iota Epsilon.

BARBOUR, Larry
Vinson & Elkins LLP, Houston
713 758 2126
lbarbour@velaw.com
Recommended in Banking & Finance

Specialization: Business transactions, finance, including project and structured finance, and mergers and acquisitions. Has extensive experience in complex syndicated bank transactions, representing either the lenders or the borrower. Worked on all aspects of energy finance and is co-head of the firm's Business & International Section.
Career: Came to the firm in 1977 and was admitted to the partnership in October 1985.
Personal: Graduated from Princeton University, AB in Economics in 1972, New York University, MBA in Finance in 1974, and The University of Texas, JD with high honors, 1977. (Chancellors; Order of the Coif).

BEANE, Jerry
Strasburger & Price LLP, Dallas
214 651 4300
Recommended in Antitrust

BECK, David
Beck, Redden & Secrest, Houston
713 951 3700
Recommended in Litigation

BECKHAM JR, Charles
Haynes and Boone LLP, Houston
713 547 2243
charles.beckham@haynesboone.com
Recommended in Insolvency

Specialization: Has more than twenty years experience helping a broad spectrum of clients with bankruptcy and insolvency problems. He has assisted in a variety of transactions including: representing the co-chair of the Creditors Committee in Chapter 11 of Enron Corp.; represented Agent for Bank Group in Chapter 11 of Tri-Union Development Corporation. Recovered full amount of claim in approximate amount of $123 million for Bank Group; Represented the Receiver for World Manufacturing Ltd. and Manufacturera del Bravo, Ltd., two British Virgin Island corporations. Assisted the Receiver in the recovery of assets in the United States, Mexico, the British Virgin Islands, the Cayman Islands and Switzerland.

BILGER, Bruce
Vinson & Elkins LLP, Houston
713 758 2614
bbilger@velaw.com
Recommended in Energy, Projects

Specialization: Chair of the firm's Energy Practice Group and co-head of the firm's Business & International Section. Practice consists primarily of domestic and international business transactions, including mergers and acquisitions, international infrastructure development projects, project finance, and other corporate transactions, particularly in the energy industry.
Prof. Memberships: Member and Former Trustee: American College of Investment Counsel.
Career: Lecturer and Author: programs and articles on partnership law, corporate law, merger and acquisitions, project finance, and international law topics.
Personal: Graduated from Dartmouth College, BA in 1973, and the University of Virginia, MBA and JD in 1977.

BISHOP, Doak
King & Spalding LLP, Houston
713 751 3205
dbishop@kslaw.com
Recommended in Energy

Specialization: 26 years experience in international arbitration and litigation of oil and gas, energy, construction, and environmental disputes. Lead counsel in 12 foreign investment disputes in ICSID, ISS and UNCITRAL arbitrations. Board Certified in Civil Trial Law.
Prof. Memberships: Vice Chairman, Institute of Transnational Arbitration; Member, US delegation to the NAFTA Advisory Committee on Private Commercial Disputes; Fellow and Chartered Arbitrator, Chartered institute of Arbitrators; Co-Chair, American Bar Association's International Litigation Committee; Co-author, Foreign Investment Disputes; Editor, Advocacy in International Arbitration.
Personal: BA degree, high honors, Southern Methodist University, 1973, JD degree, honors, University of Texas, 1976.

BLAND, Doug
Vinson & Elkins LLP, Houston
713 758 2948
dbland@velaw.com
Recommended in Energy, Projects

Specialization: Partner in Business and International Section. Has a domestic and international business transactions practice focusing on the development, acquisition, divestiture, and financing of energy-related projects. Co-head of Project Finance and Development Practice Group and member of Electric Power Practice Group.
Prof. Memberships: Houston Bar Association.
Career: Admitted to Texas Bar in 1984. Joined *Vinson & Elkins* in 1984; admitted to the partnership in January 1992.
Personal: Graduated from the University of Virginia, BA with high honors in 1981 (Phi Beta Kappa), and the University of Michigan, JD cum laude, in 1984 (Order of the Coif).

BOGDANOW, Alan
Vinson & Elkins LLP, Dallas
214 220 7857
abogdanow@velaw.com
Recommended in Corporate/M&A

Specialization: Primary areas of practice are mergers and acquisitions, public and private financings, and corporate control and governance matters. Represented acquirers, sellers, special committees, and investment bankers in a broad range of merger and acquisition transactions.
Career: Admitted to New York Bar in 1972 and Texas Bar in 1977. Came to the firm as a partner in 2001.
Personal: Graduated cum laude from Brown University, AB in 1968 and Columbia Law School, JD in 1971, served as editor of the 'Columbia Law Review.'

BOND, Thomas
Akin Gump Strauss Hauer & Feld LLP, Austin 512 499 6200
Recommended in Insurance

BOONE, Michael
Haynes and Boone, LLP, Dallas
214 651 5552
mike.boone@haynesboone.com
Recommended in Corporate/M&A

Specialization: A member of the Executive Committee of *Haynes and Boone* and one of the co-founders of the firm. He has extensive experience in mergers and acquisitions, corporate finance and securities transactions. Frequent speaker and writer in his specialty areas.

TEXAS LEADERS

BOULDEN, Michael
Vinson & Elkins LLP, Dallas
214 220 7840
mboulden@velaw.com
Recommended in Real Estate
Specialization: Experience includes construction and permanent lending on commercial real estate; joint ventures and equity participations involving the formation of partnerships and limited liability companies; participating mortgages and real estate and partnership workouts; representing institutional lenders and equity investors; and real estate outsourcing and foreign investment by private equity.
Prof. Memberships: American Bar Association; State Bar of Texas; Dallas Bar Association; Dallas Real Estate Counsel.
Career: Admitted to Texas Bar, 1977. Came to the firm as a partner, 1994.
Personal: Graduated from Rice University, BA in 1973, and Southern Methodist University, JD in 1977.

BOWMAN, John
Fulbright & Jaworski LLP, Houston
512 651 3732
jbowman@fulbright.com
Recommended in Energy
Specialization: Energy and petrochemicals, arbitration and litigation.
Prof. Memberships: Fellow of the College of Commercial Arbitrators and of The Chartered Institute of Arbitrators; member of Association of International Petroleum Negotiators; International Arbitration Club, London; International Arbitration Institute, Paris; Advisory Board of the Institute for Transnational Arbitration; Panel of International Centre for Dispute Resolution; CPR Institute Oil and Gas Panel; LCIA; IBA Committee D; and Houston International Arbitration Club.
Career: He is engaged in an arbitration and litigation practice representing primarily energy and petrochemicals companies. His practice focuses on arbitration, domestic and international, of commercial disputes, including disputes involving state-owned oil companies and Host Governments. He regularly advises regarding dispute resolution agreements, acts as an advocate in arbitrations and judicial proceedings and sits as an arbitrator.
Personal: Married to Katie-Pat Bowman. He received a BA in 1974 and a JD in 1980 from the University of Kansas, where he was editor-in-chief of the 'Kansas Law Review'. He was admitted to practice law in Kansas in 1980 and in Texas in 1983.

BRANN, Richard
Baker Botts LLP, Houston
713 229 1234
Recommended in Employment

BRISTOW, Daryl
Baker Botts LLP, Houston
713 229 1234
Recommended in Litigation

BROWN, David H
Vinson & Elkins LLP, Houston
713 758 2098
dbrown@velaw.com
Recommended in Insurance
Specialization: Principal area of practice is the representation of policyholders in insurance coverage disputes. Has represented a variety of business enterprises, including energy and transportation companies, and health care providers, in insurance litigation and arbitration matters under both first party and liability policies. Represents the Port of Houston Authority in litigation matters.
Prof. Memberships: Member: Houston Bar Association; Texas Association of Defense Counsel; Texas Bar Foundation; and Maritime Law Association.
Career: Admitted to practice: Texas, 1976. Joined *Vinson & Elkins*, 1977; admitted to partnership, 1984.
Personal: Northwestern University, BS, 1972; The University of Texas School of Law, JD with honors, 1975.

BROWN, Reagan
Fulbright & Jaworski LLP, Houston
713 651 5469
rbrown@fulbright.com
Recommended in Insurance, Litigation
Specialization: Trial and appellate litigation, insurance, legal malpractice, and products liability.
Prof. Memberships: Member of the American Board of Trial Advocates. Admitted to practice before the United States Supreme Court, the United States Court of Appeals for the Fifth Circuit.
Career: Admitted to the Texas Bar (1981). A partner of *Fulbright & Jaworski LLP* since 1990. Has tried over 75 cases and arbitration proceedings with over 50 jury cases to verdict.
Personal: Received a BS and BA, summa cum laude, (1978) from Southern Methodist University and a JD, with honors, in 1981 from the University of Texas.

BRUNS, Phil
Gibbs & Bruns, LLP, Houston
713 650 8805
Recommended in Litigation

BURNER, Burnie
Long, Burner, Parks & DeLargy, Austin
512 474 1587
Recommended in Insurance

BURNS, David
Dewey Ballantine LLP, Houston
713 445 1540
dburns@dbllp.com
Recommended in Banking & Finance
Specialization: Finance, banking, reorganization, energy and real estate. His practice has involved the representation of various groups of creditors, borrowers, lessors, lessees and vendors in the financing and the organization or reorganization of companies in numerous industries including oil and gas, electric power projects, information technology, hotels, real estate, contracting and banking. His clients have included Pennzoil Company in the Texaco Chapter 11, Reliant Energy in various reorganizations of power companies, and Fleming Companies in the Kmart Chapter 11. He has also frequently represented JPMorgan Chase Bank, Bank of America and other financial institutions.
Prof. Memberships: Houston Bar Association, American Bar Association, American College of Investment Counsel, American Bankruptcy Institute, and Texas Association of Bank Counsel.
Career: Admitted to practice in 1971, Texas, and to practice in United States District Courts in the Southern District of Alabama and the Southern District of Texas. Private practice since 1971. Partner, *Dewey Ballantine LLP*.
Personal: Born November 26, 1945. AB, University of Oklahoma, 1968 (summa cum laude). JD, Harvard Law School, 1971.

CAGLE, Molly
Vinson & Elkins LLP, Austin
512 542 8552
mcagle@velaw.com
Recommended in Environment
Specialization: Administrative and environmental law.
Career: Admitted to Texas Bar in 1981. Joined *Vinson & Elkins* in 1981 and was admitted to the partnership in January 1989.
Personal: Attended the University of Southwestern Louisiana and graduated from Texas Tech, BS magna cum laude in 1978, and The University of Texas, JD with honors in 1981.

CANTERBURY, JR, Joe
Canterbury, Stuber, Elder, Gooch & Surratt, PC, Dallas 972 239 7493
jcanterbury@canterburylaw.com
Recommended in Construction
Specialization: Construction and labor and employment law; domestic and international arbitration and mediation of construction disputes.
Prof. Memberships: Member, Dallas, Texas and American Bar Associations; Fellow and Former Member of the Board of Governors, American College of Construction Lawyers; Founding Member and Past Chairman, Construction Law Sections of Dallas and Texas Bar Associations; Past Chairman, Labor and Employment Lawyers Council, Associated General Constractors of America; Member, American Arbitration Association National Construction Dispute Resolution Committee; Board Member and Arbitrator, American Arbitration Association; Member, Board of Directors, Dallas Chapter, Associated General Contractors of America (1997-98).
Career: Construction work, United States Navy, followed by college and law school. Active practice of law since 1967, with emphasis on construction law. Founding member and majority shareholder of *Canterbury, Stuber, Elder, Gooch and Surratt*.
Publications: 'Construction Law Handbook', contributing author, Aspen Law & Business (1999-2002); 'Texas Construction Law Manual', Shepards McGraw-Hill (1st Edition 1981, 2nd Edition 1993) Annual Supplements (West); 'Construction Business Handbook', contributing author, McGraw-Hill (1st and 2nd Editions, 1978 and 1984); 'Wiley Construction Law Update', contributing author (1994-2000). Author of numerous articles, speeches and papers on construction law delivered to legal community and industry groups.
Personal: BA, University of Dallas, 1963; JD, Southern Methodist University School of Law, 1966 (Phi Delta Phi); United States Navy 1956-59. Married to the former Patricia Ferguson since 1963, they maintain homes in Dallas, Texas and County Tipperary, Ireland. They have four grown children and five grandchildren. His hobbies include grandchildren, fly fishing and travel.

CARRELL, Richard
Fulbright & Jaworski LLP, Houston
713 651 5447
rcarrell@fulbright.com
Recommended in Antitrust
Specialization: Antitrust, business litigation, securities litigation, contracts, and oil & gas litigation.
Prof. Memberships: The Houston and the American Bar Associations and the State Bar of Texas. Trustee of Baylor College of Medicine and the Kelsey Foundation for Research.
Career: Admitted Texas Bar (1970). A partner of *Fulbright & Jaworski LLP* which he joined in 1970. Served as a member of the firm's Executive and Policy Committees.
Personal: Received a BA from Washington & Lee University in 1965 and a JD from the University of Virginia in 1970.

CAWLEY, Douglas
McKool Smith, Dallas 214 978 4000
Recommended in Intellectual Property

CIVINS, Jeff
Haynes and Boone LLP, Austin
512 867 8477
jeff.civins@haynesboone.com
Recommended in Environment
Specialization: Heads the firm's Environmental Practice Group and has practiced all aspects of environmental law since 1975. He advises clients on regulatory requirements, he assists them in the evaluation and negotiation of corporate transactions, and he represents them in environmental and toxic tort litigation. As an adjunct professor at the University of Texas School of Law, he taught a seminar on Environmental Law Concerns to Business in 1987, and has taught a seminar on Environmental Litigation each

Spring since 1992. He is co-editor of the West Group's 2-volume treatise on Texas Environmental Law and was their consultant on their compilation of 'Texas Environmental Laws'. He has been listed in a leading US legal review since 1989.

COATS, William
Coats Rose Yale Ryman Lee, Houston
713 651 0111
Recommended in Construction

COGAN, JR, John
King & Spalding LLP, Houston
713 276 7371
jcogan@kslaw.com
Recommended in Energy, Projects
Specialization: Chairman, *King & Spalding*'s Global Projects Practice, focusing on international energy, financial and commercial transactions, particularly involving projects for the international exploration, extraction, processing, transportation and sale of hydrocarbons. Named one of the top five international lawyers in Texas.
Prof. Memberships: Corresponding editor of International Legal Materials. Member -Association of International Petroleum Negotiators. Frequent lecturer on international energy matters.
Personal: BA, University of Texas 1965; JD 1968. Attended Universidad Autónoma de Guanajuato, México, Escuela de Derecho in 1968, Universidad Nacional Autónoma de México, Instituto de Derecho Comparativo in 1967, Bucknell University in 1961-62. Work/study program Université de Nantes, France in 1964.

COHEN, R Scott
Weil, Gotshal & Manges LLP, Dallas
214 746 7738
scott.cohen@weil.com
Recommended in Corporate/M&A
Specialization: Dallas-based partner has practiced in the area of corporate and securities law for over 20 years. His practice concentrates on domestic and international mergers and acquisitions, restructurings and public and private offerings of debt and equity securities.
Prof. Memberships: Texas State Bar. Is a member and former chairman of the Corporations Law Committee of the Business Law Section of the Texas Bar. Also serves as a director of the Texas Business Law Foundation.
Personal: JD, Southern Methodist University School, 1979; BBA with honors, University of Texas at Arlington, 1976.

COKINOS, Greg
Cokinos, Bosien and Young, Houston
713 535 5500
Recommended in Construction

COLEMAN, James
Carrington, Coleman, Sloman & Blumenthal, LLP, Dallas 214 855 3000
Recommended in Litigation

CONLON, Michael
Fulbright & Jaworski LLP, Houston
713 651 5427
mconlon@fulbright.com
Recommended in Corporate/M&A
Specialization: Corporation, banking and business.
Prof. Memberships: State Bar of Texas, the District of Columbia Bar and the Houston and American Bar Associations.
Career: He is a partner in *Fulbright & Jaworski* LLP's Houston office. His general corporate practice primarily involves the representation of publicly held corporations in matters involving securities offerings and routine reporting, disclosure issues, secured and unsecured borrowing, mergers, acquisitions and dispositions. He has represented special committees of boards of directors in connection with takeover offers and corporate restructurings.
Personal: He received a BA from Catholic University of America in 1968 and a JD from Duke University in 1971.

CONWAY, Susan
Vinson & Elkins LLP, Austin
512 542 8442
sconway@velaw.com
Recommended in Insurance
Specialization: Texas administrative and regulatory law and litigation; insurance, managed care, and healthcare regulation.
Career: Admitted to Texas Bar in 1982. A partner with *Vinson & Elkins*, which she joined in 1982.
Personal: Graduated from Rice University, BA in 1971, and The University of Texas at Austin, MA in 1979 and JD in 1982.

COOPER, R Brent
Cooper & Scully, PC, Dallas
214 712 9501
brent.cooper@cooperscully.com
Recommended in Insurance
Specialization: Specializes in medical malpractice; premises liability; nursing home liability; appellate practice; insurance law; personal injury; product liability; and torts law. Frequent lecturer, having spoken on insurance litigation, coverage, and bad faith at seminars for the State Bar of Texas, University of Houston Law Center, South Texas College of Law, University of Texas School of Law and Lorman Business Systems.
Prof. Memberships: Admitted to the Dallas Bar Association (1977) and the American Bar Association (Member, Tort and Insurance Law Sections) (1977); State Bar of Texas (1977); Fifth Circuit Bar Association; Texas Association of Defense Counsel; and Defense Research Institute.
Career: Formerly a partner in the firm of *Cowles & Thompson* (1977-93); named partner in the firm of *Cooper & Scully*, PC since starting the firm in 1993. Admitted to practice before the United States Supreme Court, Fifth Circuit Court of Appeals, Eleventh Circuit Court of Appeals, DC Circuit Court of Appeals, Northern District of Texas, Eastern District of Texas, Southern District of Texas, Western District of Texas, Texas Supreme Court, and all Texas State Courts.
Publications: Author of 'Lessor Liability in Aircraft Rental', 42 'Journal of Air Law and Commerce' 447 (1977); 1988 Survey of Insurance Law; 42 'Southwestern Law Journal' 389 (1988); 1989 Survey of Insurance Law; 43 'Southwestern Law Journal' 343 (1989); 1990 Survey of Insurance Law; 44 'Southwestern Law Journal' 329 (1990); 1991 Survey of Insurance Law; 45 'Southwestern Law Journal' 461 (1991); and Cooper, Hensley & Marshall's Texas Rules of Civil Procedure Annotated, 2002 Edition, West Group.
Personal: Received undergraduate degree from Texas A&M University (BBA, summa cum laude, 1974); law degree from Southern Methodist University (JD, cum laude, 1977; Order of the Coif). Certified by the Texas Board of Legal Specialization in Personal Injury Trial Law.

CULOTTA, Ken
King & Spalding LLP, Houston
713 276 7374
kculotta@kslaw.com
Recommended in Energy
Specialization: Advises US and non-US clients in domestic and international oil, gas, LNG, power and natural resources transactions, including mergers and acquisitions, joint ventures, project development and finance, energy management services and other direct and indirect investment transactions. Experienced with industry documentation, including concession, production sharing, joint operating, power purchase, tolling, fuel supply, O&M, construction, gas and electricity transportation and distribution, marketing and other agreements. Languages: German; Spanish.
Prof. Memberships: Member, Association of International Petroleum Negotiators; AIPN Subcommittee Chair (Model Gas Sales Agreement Committee).
Personal: BA University of Texas 1979; JD 1985; Albert Ludwigs-Universität, Freiburg, Germany (DAAD Fellow 1980-81).

DAVIDSON, Joshua
Baker Botts LLP, Houston
713 229 1234
Recommended in Corporate/M&A

DAVIS, Platt
Vinson & Elkins LLP, Houston
713 758 2294
pdavis@velaw.com
Recommended in Energy
Specialization: Principal areas of practice are international arbitration, energy transactions and regulation, and construction law. Listed in 'Chambers Global, The World's Leading Lawyers 2002-2003'.
Prof. Memberships: Advisory Board: Institute for Transnational Arbitration. Member: The Chartered Institute of Arbitrators; International Bar Association; London Court of International Arbitration; Federal Energy Bar Association; and American Bar Association.
Career: Admitted to practice: Texas, 1969; District of Columbia, 1973. Joined *Vinson & Elkins*, 1970; admitted to partnership, 1976.
Personal: The University of Texas, BA, 1966; The University of Texas School of Law, JD, 1970; George Washington University Law School, LLM, 1974.

DAVIS, Will
Heath, Davis & McCalla, Austin
512 478 5671
Recommended in Insurance

DILG, Joe
Vinson & Elkins LLP, Houston
713 758 2062
jdilg@velaw.com
Recommended in Corporate/M&A, Energy
Specialization: Practice focuses on domestic and international business transactions, including acquisitions, divestitures, joint ventures, and financings. Well-versed in all aspects of the domestic and international energy business.
Career: Currently serves as Managing Partner of *Vinson & Elkins*. Director: Society for the Performing Arts; the Business Committee for the Arts, Inc.; and the Greater Houston Partnership. Trustee: The University of Texas Law School Foundation.
Personal: Graduated from Southern Methodist University, BA in economics in 1973, and The University of Texas School of Law, JD with high honors in 1976.

DILLON, Andrew J
Bracewell & Patterson LLP, Austin
512 542 2121
adillon@bracepatt.com
Recommended in Intellectual Property
Specialization: Focuses on patent, trademark and general intellectual property matters primarily in the areas of electronics and software. Co-chairs the firm's Intellectual Property Law Section and is a frequent author and lecturer on the subject of patent law. Recognized by the State Bar of Texas for 'outstanding contributions to the practice of patent law.' Named by a leading state publication as 'go-to lawyer for cutting-edge companies in Texas.'
Career: Admitted: State Bar of Texas. Court Admissions: US Court of Appeals for the Federal Circuit, US Patent and Trademark Office.
Personal: JD, The John Marshall Law School, 1979; BSEE, Purdue University, 1972.

TEXAS LEADERS

DINKINS, Carol
Vinson & Elkins LLP, Houston
713 758 2528
cdinkins@velaw.com
Recommended in Environment
Specialization: Chairs *Vinson & Elkins'* administrative and environmental law practice. Practice includes client counseling on business transactions and permit matters; civil litigation, mediation, and criminal defense.
Prof. Memberships: Chair: Standing Committee on Federal Judiciary, ABA.
Career: Admitted to practice: Texas, 1971. Joined *Vinson & Elkins*, 1973; admitted to partnership, 1980. Served as: Assistant Attorney General in charge of the Environment and Natural Resources Division of the Department of Justice, 1981-83; Deputy Attorney General of the United States, 1984-85.
Personal: The University of Texas, BS, 1968; University of Houston, JD, 1971.

DOW, Melvin
Winstead Sechrest & Minick, Houston
713 650 2724
mdow@winstead.com
Recommended in Real Estate
Specialization: Shareholder in Real Estate Section. Has extensive experience representing clients across various real estate transactions: shopping centers, office buildings, subdivison development.
Prof. Memberships: American Bar Association, Houston Bar Association, and American College of Real Estate Lawyers.
Career: Admitted to State Bar of Texas. Board Certified, Commercial Real Estate Law, Texas Board of Legal Specialization. Listed in Best Lawyers in America.
Personal: Received a JD (magna cum laude) from Harvard Law School in 1951, Editor, 'Harvard Law Review', and a BA (cum laude, Phi Beta Kappa) from Rice University in 1948.

DOW, T Andrew
Winstead Sechrest & Minick, Dallas
214 745 5387
adow@winstead.com
Recommended in Real Estate
Specialization: Shareholder in Real Estate Section and co-chair of leasing and development practice. Extensive experience representing clients in matters involving development, leasing, property management, acquisitions and dispositions, entity and transaction structure, finance, and corporate facilities management.
Prof. Memberships: American and Dallas Bar Associations, International Council of Shopping Centers.
Career: Admitted to State Bar of Texas.
Personal: Received a JD from Southern Methodist University in 1991, where he was the Managing Editor of the 'SMU Law Review'. Recognized as one of the best lawyers in Dallas under 40 in 'D' Magazine, May 2002. Adjunct Professor of Business Law, Dallas Baptist University.

DUNLAY, Jon
Baker Botts LLP, Houston
713 229 1234
Recommended in Real Estate

DUNLOP, Fred
Baker Botts LLP, Houston
713 229 1234
Recommended in Real Estate

DUTTON, Diana
Akin Gump Strauss Hauer & Feld LLP, Dallas 214 969 2800
Recommended in Environment

ERWIN, Greg
Winstead Sechrest & Minick, Houston
713 650 2781
gerwin@winstead.com
Recommended in Real Estate
Specialization: Shareholder in Real Estate Section. Represents developers and owners in the acquisition, development, leasing, financing, and sale of all forms of commerical properties. Experienced in structuring, negotiation and documentation of commercial real estate transactions.
Prof. Memberships: American Bar Association, Houston Bar Association, American College of Real Estate Lawyers.
Career: Admitted State Bar of Texas. Board Certified, Commercial Real Estate Law and Residential Real Estate Law, Texas Board of Legal Specialization.
Personal: Received JD (cum laude) from University of Texas at Austin in 1974 and BA (cum laude) from Southern Methodist University in 1970.

EVANS, Mark
Bracewell & Patterson LLP, Houston
713 221 1300
mevans@bracepatt.com
Recommended in Banking & Finance, Projects
Specialization: Represents commercial banks and other lenders in complex financing transactions such as the representation of the agent in syndicated loans, revolving credit and term loans, leveraged transactions, structured transactions, subordinated and mezzanine investments, credit enhancement for paper and bond transactions, letters of credit and paper facilities, production payment and other oil and gas related credits, project finance, bankruptcy and restructurings. Clients include French, Dutch, Scottish, Japanese and US-based banks who have lended funds to Japanese, Mexican, Canadian, Venezuelan and French companies.
Personal: JD, The University of Texas School of Law, 1977; BBA, The University of Texas at Austin, 1974.

FIELDS, Jack
Andrews & Kurth LLP, Houston
713 220 4348
jfields@akllp.com
Recommended in Real Estate
Specialization: Represents clients in all aspects of a real estate practice, including representing sellers, purchasers, lessors and lessees of commercial real estate of all types; representing mortgage servicers; representing real estate developers in connection with office, multi-family, retail and industrial projects; representing sellers and purchasers of chemical plant facilities; representing land owners in connection with agricultural tax planning matters; and representing real estate lenders, including several major insurance companies, banks and pension funds. Member of firm's legal opinion committee.
Prof. Memberships: Council Member of the Real Estate, Probate and Trust Law Section of the State Bar of Texas, 1988-92, Chairman, Title Insurance Subcommittee, 1990-92; Houston Bar Association; Houston Real Estate Lawyers Council. Representative clients: Wal-Mart/Sam's; Anadarko Petroleum; L.J. Melody Company.
Career: Admitted to the State Bar of Texas in 1978. Joined *Andrews & Kurth* in 1978 as an associate and became partner in 1986.
Publications: Co-authored a law review article on Texas usury laws entitled 'A Topic of Interest: An Analysis of the Status of the Usury Laws of Texas'.
Personal: Received JD (cum laude) from University of Texas School of in 1978. Member of the Order of the Coif. Received BBA (summa cum laude) from University of Houston in 1975. Speaker at State Bar of Texas Advanced Real Estate Law Course.

FINN BRADDOCK, Patricia
Fulbright & Jaworski LLP, Austin
512 536 4547
pbraddock@fulbright.com
Recommended in Environment
Specialization: Toxic tort; Environmental law.
Prof. Memberships: Member of the American Bar Association, the Texas Bar Association and the Travis County Bar Association. Member of the Environmental Advisory Board of the Texas Hospital Association.
Career: Admitted to Texas Bar (1974). A partner in *Fulbright & Jaworski* LLP's Austin office since 1992. Prior to joining the firm, she worked for Texas' environmental regulatory agencies for almost 15 years.
Personal: Received a BA (1971) from the American University and a JD (1974) from St. Mary's University of San Antonio.

FISK, Hollye
Fisk & Fielder, Dallas 214 638 3744
Recommended in Construction

FLAKE, Richard
Cokinos, Bosien and Young, Houston
713 535 5500
Recommended in Construction

FOGLER, Murray
McDade Fogler Maines LLP, Houston
713 654 4300
Recommended in Litigation

FORD, Jeffrey
Ford White & Nassen, Dallas
214 523 5100
Recommended in Construction

FROMM O'BRIEN, Eva
Fulbright & Jaworski LLP, Houston
713 651 5321
efrommobrien@fulbright.com
Recommended in Environment
Specialization: Environmental law, enforcement controversies, environmental crimes, environmental litigation, mergers and acquisitions, permits, and property damage litigation.
Prof. Memberships: Included in leading US publications. Past secretary, vice-chair and chair of the Houston Bar Association's Environmental Law Section. Former chair of the American Bar Association's Real Estate and Probate Section's RCRA and Underground Storage Tank Committee.
Career: Admitted to Texas Bar (1985). Partner at *Fulbright & Jaworski LLP* joining the firm in 1986.
Personal: Received a BS in Chemical Engineering in 1978 from Syracuse University and a JD in 1985 from the University of Houston.

GEIGER, Richard
Thompson, Coe, Cousins & Irons, LLP, Dallas 214 871 8200
Recommended in Insurance

GIBBS, Charles
Akin Gump Strauss Hauer & Feld LLP, Dallas 214 969 2800
Recommended in Insolvency

GIBBS, Robin
Gibbs & Bruns, LLP, Houston
713 650 8805
Recommended in Litigation

GIBLIN, Pamela
Baker Botts LLP, Austin 512 322 2500
Recommended in Environment

GILLESPIE, Hal
Gillespie, Rozen & Watsky, PC, Dallas
214 720 2009
hkg@grwlawfirm.com
Recommended in Employment
Specialization: Union side labor law and plaintiff's side employment law.
Prof. Memberships: National Employment Lawyers Association; AFL-CIO Lawyers Coordinating Committee; College of Labor and Employment Lawyers; American Board of Trial Advocates.
Career: Admitted to State Bar of Texas (1972); United States Supreme Court (1977). A shareholder in the law firm of *Gillespie, Rozen & Watsky, PC* since 1990.
Personal: Received a JD (with Honors) in 1972 and a BA (with Honors) in 1969. Both degrees from the University of Texas at Austin.

GILLESPIE, Thomas
Jones Day, Dallas 214 969 5076
tgillespie@jonesday.com
Recommended in Banking & Finance
Specialization: Lending and structured finance; corporate and commercial law. Represents financial institutions and corporations in complex domestic and cross-border financings, including syndicated credit facilities; project, lease and acquisition financings; debt restructurings and loan workouts; debtor-in-possession credit facilities; letters of credit; derivatives and hedging transactions; recapitalizations; and the private placement of securities. Considerable experience in healthcare, energy, venture capital, transportation and vendor equipment financings.
Prof. Memberships: Member of the New York and Texas bars. Member of American and Dallas Bar Associations. Former member of Texas Business Law Foundation, Texas Association of Bank Counsel and State of Texas Commercial Code Committee. Past Texas Delegate to the Japan-Texas Conference, Tokyo, Japan.
Career: After obtaining an MBA degree from Harvard Business School and prior to attending law school, worked for two years in corporate and aircraft finance for McDonnell Douglas Finance Corporation. After graduating from Cornell Law School, has been in the private practice of law in New York, London and Dallas.
Publications: Co-editor and contributing author of &8216; 'The Commercial Finance Guide'. Contributing author of 'NAFTA and Beyond; A New Framework for Doing Business in the Americas.' Served for 12 years as co-director and speaker on banking and finance for the Institute on Commercial Lending. Organized and delivered programs on loan and collateral documentation as part of in-house credit training for various banks and financial institutions. Past speaker on various commercial finance programs in Texas, Arkansas, New York and London, England.
Personal: Graduate of: California State University, Sacramento (BS cum laude 1966); Harvard University (MBA 1968); Cornell University (JD 1973); Columbia University, Parker School of Foreign and Comparative Law (Foreign and Comparative Law Program, 1975).

GLICKMAN, Julius
Glickman & Hughes LLP, Houston
713 658 1122
Recommended in Employment

GODFREY, Lee
Susman Godfrey LLP, Houston
713 651 9366
Recommended in Antitrust, Litigation

GOLEMON, Kinnan
Brown McCarroll, LLP, Austin
512 472 5456
Recommended in Environment

GOOCH, Kyle
Canterbury, Stuber, Elder, Gooch & Surratt, PC, Dallas 972 239 7493
kgooch@canterburylaw.com
Recommended in Construction
Specialization: Construction litigation and arbitration; construction insurance (builder's risk, commercial general liability, errors and omissions).
Prof. Memberships: Admitted to the Texas and Dallas Bar Associations; Construction Law Section of the Texas Bar (Secretary) (past Treasurer; past Council Member); and American Arbitration Association (arbitrator).
Career: Following graduation from Baylor Law School, he commenced law practice in Dallas, Texas and has practiced consistently in the field of construction and insurance. He has been a member and shareholder of *Canterbury, Stuber, Elder, Gooch & Surratt* since 1981.
Publications: 'Builder's Risk'; 'The Forgotten Insurance, 1999' and other articles on construction and insurance issues.
Personal: Born Greenville, Texas, November 14, 1952; Bachelor of Science - Texas A & M University; JD Baylor University. Married to the former Suzy Davis, they have three children. His hobbies include music, fishing, hunting and following Texas A & M football.

GOOLSBY, George
Baker Botts LLP, Houston
713 229 1234
Recommended in Energy

GOYNE, Roderick
Baker Botts LLP, Houston
713 229 1234
Recommended in Banking & Finance

GRAY, Robert
Fulbright & Jaworski LLP, Houston
713 651 5566
rgray@fulbright.com
Recommended in Communications
Specialization: Corporate & securities laws representation, private placements, venture capital financing, mergers & acquisitions, and public offerings.
Prof. Memberships: Member of the District of Columbia, Houston and American Bar Associations and the State Bars of California and Texas.
Career: Admitted to California Bar (1977), Texas Bar (1978) and District of Columbia Bar (1979). A partner at Fulbright & Jaworski LLP since 1985.
Personal: Received a BBA (1972) and an MBA (1974) from the University of Michigan, a JD,(1977) from the University of San Diego and an LLM (1978) from New York University.

GREIG, Brian
Fulbright & Jaworski LLP, Austin
512 536 4510
bgreig@fulbright.com
Recommended in Employment
Specialization: Labor and employment law, trade secrets, federal practice, commercial litigation, construction litigation, energy.
Prof. Memberships: Member of the Travis County, Federal and American Bar Associations; and the State Bar of Texas. Included in leading US and Global publications.
Career: Partner since 1983, practices in *Fulbright & Jaworski LLP*'s Austin office, where he heads the office's labor and employment practice.
Personal: Received his BA in Economics from Washington & Lee University (1972) and a JD from The University of Texas School of Law (1975).

GREMILLION, Todd
Akin Gump Strauss Hauer & Feld, LLP, Houston 713 220 5800
Recommended in Energy

GUNTER, Clifford
Bracewell & Patterson LLP, Houston
713 221 1213
cgunter@bracepatt.com
Recommended in Energy
Specialization: Maintains an extensive commercial litigation background with a client roster listing some of the nation's largest energy companies. Jury trial experience includes cases involving fraud, theft of trade secrets, breach of contract, construction litigation, antitrust litigation, securities fraud litigation, arbitrations of transnational gas sales contracts and take-or-pay and pricing disputes. Has tried several cases to verdict involving international corporate project finance issues. Has recently argued cases before the Texas Supreme Court and the US Court of Appeals for the Fifth Circuit.
Personal: LLB, The University of Texas School of Law, 1967; BA, The University of Texas at Austin, 1965.

HAMILTON MOODY, James
Strasburger & Price LLP, Dallas
214 651 4300
Recommended in Insurance

HAMMOND, Herbert
Thompson & Knight LLP, Dallas
214 969 1607
herbert.hammond@tklaw.com
Recommended in Communications
Specialization: Patent, trademark, copyright, trade secrets, computer and entertainment law, emphasizing litigation, licensing, and alternate dispute resolution. Recommended in intellectual property law by a leading legal publication 2003-04.
Prof. Memberships: State Bar of Texas. Licensed to Practice before the US Patent and Trademark Office. American Intellectual Property Law Association. Chair, Dallas Bar Association Intellectual Property Section, 1998. Chair, Computer Section, State Bar of Texas, 1994-95; Secretary 1993-94; Treasurer 1992-93; Newsletter Editor 1990-91. Co-chair, State Bar of Texas Committee for the Computerization of the Legal Profession, 1989-90. American Arbitration Association Panel of Arbitrators and Mediators. National Technology Panel of Arbitrators for the American Arbitration Association. Texas General Counsel Forum. Guest Lecturer, SMU Business School. Listed in leading US publication (Intellectual Property Law).
Career: Associated with *Thompson & Knight* since 1994. JD, New York University School of Law, 1976. BS, Physics and Mathematics, magna cum laude, University of New Mexico, 1973; Phi Beta Kappa.
Publications: Publishes and speaks frequently on intellectual property topics.

HARDIE, Thornton
Thompson & Knight LLP, Dallas
214 969 1504
thornton.hardie@tklaw.com
Recommended in Tax
Specialization: Taxation of business transactions; oil and gas taxation and energy finance; tax and business planning for individuals, partnerships, and corporations. Recommended in tax law in the 2001-02 and 2003-04 editions of a leading legal publication.
Prof. Memberships: State Bar of Texas, Taxation Section, various committees. American Bar Association, Taxation Section, various committees. Dallas Bar Association, Taxation Section, various committees, 1987 Chairman. Speaker and panelist, various bar and continuing legal education programs. Chairman, Southwestern Legal Foundation annual institute on oil and gas taxation (1992-94). Fellow, Texas Bar Foundation.
Career: Associated with *Thompson & Knight* since 1976. JD, with honors, The University of Texas School of Law, 1975. BS, Commerce, with high honors, Washington and Lee University, 1973.

HARPER, John
Fulbright & Jaworski LLP, Houston
713 651 5442
ajharper@fulbright.com
Recommended in Employment
Specialization: Labor and employment law.
Prof. Memberships: Member of the State Bar of Texas, the Houston Bar Association and the American Bar Association. Fellow in the College of Labor and Employment Lawyers and is included in a leading US publication.
Career: Admitted to the Texas Bar (1967). Admitted before the United States Court of Appeals for the First, Second, Fifth, Sixth, Eighth, Ninth, Tenth and Eleventh Circuits. Admitted to practice before the United States Supreme Court. Admitted to the US District Courts for the Eastern, Northern, Southern and Western Districts of Texas, and District of Nebraska. Partner since 1975 and currently heads the Firm's Labor and

Employment Law Department.
Personal: Received a BA (1964) from North Texas State University and an LLB, cum laude, (1967) from Southern Methodist University.

HARRINGTON, Michael
Vinson & Elkins LLP, Houston
713 758 2148
charrington@velaw.com
Recommended in Corporate/M&A
Specialization: Corporate financing law, mergers and acquisitions law, and securities offerings law.
Career: State Bar of Texas, Houston Bar Association, and Texas Business Law Foundation.
Personal: Graduated from Yale College, BA in 1969, Cambridge University, Dip. Dev Econ in 1970, and Harvard University, JD in 1973.

HARRIS, James
Thompson & Knight LLP, Dallas
214 969 1102
james.harris@tklaw.com
Recommended in Environment
Specialization: Resolving disputes between private parties and governments in the courtroom and before administrative agencies. Special emphasis on litigation involving environmental matters, land use and zoning, and property tax matters. Experience before a wide range of administrative agencies at the local, state, and federal level.
Prof. Memberships: Admitted to the Texas bar, the United States Supreme Court, five United States Courts of Appeals, and four United States District Courts. Member of the following sections of the American Bar Association: Administrative Law and Reglatory Practice; Urban, State, and Local Government Law; and Natural Resources, Energy, and Environmental Law. Member of the following sections of the State Bar of Texas: Administrative and Public Law, Appellate; and Advocacy; and Environmental and Natural Resources Law. Included in several legal publications.
Career: Has been with *Thompson & Knight* since graduating from law school in 1978.
Publications: In addition to numerous publications on environmental regulation, policy, and related topics, was the lead attorney in the following significant cases: In re Bell Petroleum Services, Inc., 3 F.3d 889 (5th Cir. 1993); Goodner Brothers Aircraft, Inc. v US, 966 F.2d 380 (8th Cir. 1993); Methodist Hospitals of Dallas v Texas Industrial Accident Board, 798 S.W.2d 651 (Tex. App. - Austin 1990, writ dism'd w.o.j.); US v Core Laboratories, Inc., 759 F.2d 480 (5th Cir. 1985); Skelton v Camp, 234 F.2d 292 (5th Cir. 2000); Bland Independant School District v Blue, 34 S.W.3d 542 (Tex. 2000); Comdesco, Inc. v Tarrant County Appraisal Dist., 927 S.W.2d 325 (Tex. App. - Ft. Worth 1996, writ ref'd).
Personal: Graduated from Southern Methodist University in 1975 with a Bachelor of Applied Science in Environmental Systems with High Honors, and The University of Texas School of Law in 1978 with Honors.

HARRIS, Margaret
Butler & Harris, Houston 713 526 5677
Recommended in Employment

HARVEY, Dean
Vinson & Elkins LLP, Dallas
214 220 7815
dharvey@velaw.com
Recommended in Communications
Specialization: Practice focuses on technology related commercial deals in the Internet/e-Commerce area. Counsels clients on Internet related legal issues and assists clients in protecting their intellectual property assets and content and in acquiring and developing technology.
Prof. Memberships: Americal Intellectual Property Law Association; Licensing Executives Society.
Career: Admitted to Texas Bar in 1997. Came to the firm in 1997. Admitted to the partnership in January 2001.
Publications: Regulating Privacy on the Internet: Some Measures Intended to Help May Actually Hurt, 'Texas Lawyer,' 16 April 2001.
Personal: Graduated from West Virginia University, BS summa cum laude,1986 and The University of Texas, JD, 1997.

HAYES, William
Bracewell & Patterson LLP, Houston
713 221 1333
whayes@bracepatt.com
Recommended in Banking & Finance
Specialization: Structuring, drafting and negotiating a wide variety of financing transactions, including secured and unsecured loans, acquisition financings, work-outs of troubled credits, private placements of notes, subordinated debt transactions, sales of accounts receivable, letters of credit and interest rate, currency and commodity derivatives.
Career: Has practiced finance law for more than 25 years, and during the past 20 years has represented the lead banks on numerous syndicated bank credit facilities. Clients include Citibank, NA and JPMorgan Chase Bank.
Personal: JD, Harvard Law School, 1974; BSEE, University of Arkansas, 1970; Tau Beta Pi; Eta Kappa Nu.

HEADLEY, Linda
Littler Mendelson PC, Dallas
214 880 8100
Recommended in Employment

HELFAND, Thomas
Winstead Sechrest & Minick, Dallas
214 745 5342
thelfand@winstead.com
Recommended in Tax
Specialization: Shareholder and Tax Practice Chair. Executive Committee Member. Experienced tax practitioner who represents clients in matters involving corporate organizations, reorganizations, mergers, acquisitions, bankruptcy reorganizations, restructurings, eCommerce, international, partnership formations, transactions and roll-ups, REITs, real estate planning, and state tax planning.
Prof. Memberships: American Bar Association - Tax Section; State Bar of Texas - Tax Section; Dallas Bar Association.
Career: Admitted to State Bar of Texas. Board Certified, Taxation, Texas Board of Legal Specialization.
Personal: Received JD from Southern Methodist University (cum laude, Order of Coif) in 1977 and a BBA from University of Texas at Austin in 1974.

HENKEL, Kathryn
Hughes & Luce LLP, Dallas
214 939 5500
Recommended in Tax

HESTER, Tracy
Bracewell & Patterson LLP, Houston
713 221 1407
thester@bracepatt.com
Recommended in Environment
Specialization: Regulatory counseling with an emphasis on enforcement defense, permitting, cost recovery litigation and environmental aspects of corporate transactions. Represents clients from diverse industrial sectors, including petrochemicals, petroleum and natural gas pipelines, refineries, utilities, local governments, hazardous waste disposal operations and financial institutions.
Career: Past chair of Houston Bar Association Environmental Section. Current Greater Houston Partnership Environmental Advisory Committee member. Current vice-chair, American Bar Association SEER Environmental Crimes and Enforcement Committee. Adjunct Professor, University of Houston Law Center.
Personal: JD, Stone Scholar, Columbia University, 1986; BA, (Plan II Honors Program), The University of Texas at Austin, 1983.

HIGGINS, Roger
Thompson, Coe, Cousins & Irons, LLP, Dallas 214 871 8200
Recommended in Insurance

HUDDLESTON, Michael
Shannon, Gracey, Ratliff & Miller LLP, Dallas 214 245 3090
Recommended in Insurance

HUFFMAN, Gregory
Thompson & Knight LLP, Dallas
214 969 1144
gregory.huffman@tklaw.com
Recommended in Antitrust
Specialization: Commercial litigation, including antitrust and trade regulation litigation and counseling, non-competition covenant litigation and counseling, securities/fraud litigation, complex/multidistrict litigation, white-collar criminal investigations, and mediation and arbitration. Recently recommended in business litigation and antitrust law by a leading US legal publication.
Prof. Memberships: State Bar of Texas. Admitted to practice before the United States District Courts for the Northern, Southern, Eastern, and Western Districts of Texas, United States Courts of Appeals for the Fifth and Tenth Circuits, United States Temporary Emergency Court of Appeals, and United States Supreme Court. State Bar of Texas: chairman, Antitrust and Business Litigation Section (1991-92); chairman, Lawyer Referral Service Committee (1980-81); Certificate of Merit (2001); Presidential Citation (2000); delegate to ABA House of Delegates (July 2000) Member, Dallas Bar Association; secretary/treasurer (1981); founding director and director, Antitrust Section (1981, 1989 to present); founding director, Business Litigation Section (1988); committee chairman (1979, 1980-81, 1986-87, 1999-2001); member, Task Force on Professionalism (1987). Chairman, State Unauthorized Practice of Law Committee, 1981-84. Supreme Court Advisory Commission on Professionalism, 88. Texas Board of Legal Specialization, 1974-77. Fellow, Texas Bar Foundation. Fellow, Dallas Bar Foundation. President, Harvard Law School Association of Texas, 1987-88. Frequent speaker (details available on request).
Career: Assocated with *Thompson & Knight* since 1973. JD, Harvard Law School, 1973. BA, History, with great distinction, Stanford University, 1969; Phi Beta Kappa; Honors; Stanford-in-France. London School of Economics, 1971-72.
Publications: Numerous publications on the practice of law and on antitrust-related topics.

JANSONIUS, John
Akin Gump Strauss Hauer & Feld LLP, Dallas 214 969 2800
Recommended in Employment

JEWELL, Robert V
Andrews & Kurth LLP, Houston
713 220 4200
bjewell@akllp.com
Recommended in Communications, Corporate/M&A
Specialization: Practices in all areas of corporate and securities law, including representation of issuers and underwriters in public and private offerings of equity and debt securities in a variety of industries, the negotiation and structuring of various corporate and partnership debt financings and mergers and acquisitions, both domestic and foreign. Has particular experience relating to real estate investment trusts, the forest prod-

ucts industry, royalty trusts and debt financings.
Prof. Memberships: Served as a member of the Corporation Law Committee of the Corporation, Banking and Business Law Section of the State Bar of Texas since 1986 where was primarily responsible for the rewriting of the Texas Real Estate Investment Trust Act in 1989 and 1995. Also a member of the Texas Business Law Foundation.
Career: Partner of the Business Section. Has been with Andrews & Kurth since 1978 and has been a partner since 1986.
Personal: Graduated from the University of Texas (BBA, Finance, 1975) and received law degree from Southern Methodist University School of Law (JD, 1978). Was Editor of the 'Southwestern Law Journal' from 1977-78.

JORDAN, Carl
Vinson & Elkins LLP, Houston
713 758 2258
cjordan@velaw.com
Recommended in Employment
Specialization: Practice focuses on representing management in labor, ERISA, and employment-related trial work and counseling. Certified in labor and employment law by the Texas Board of Legal Specialization.
Prof. Memberships: Member: Labor and Employment Section and Section's Committee on Equal Employment Opportunity Law, American Bar Association. General Counsel: Texas Employment Law Council. Fellow: American College of Labor and Employment Lawyers.
Career: Admitted to practice: Texas, 1974. Joined *Vinson & Elkins*, 1974; admitted to partnership, 1981.
Personal: Baylor University, BA, 1971; Harvard Law School, JD, 1974.

KAIM, Henry
Akin Gump Strauss Hauer & Feld, LLP, Houston 713 220 5800
Recommended in Insolvency

KALTEYER, Ronald
Locke Liddell & Sapp LLP, Dallas
214 740 8771
rkalteyer@lockeliddell.com
Recommended in Tax
Specialization: Partner heading the firm's Business Tax Section. Practice focuses on partnership tax planning and corporate tax planning, with a specialty in the taxation of REITs and the taxation of workouts and bankruptcies.
Prof. Memberships: American Bar Association Section of Taxation (Partnership Committee: Co-Chairman of Subcommittee on UPREIT Partnerships; former Chairman of Subcommittee on Workouts). American Bar Association Real Property, Probate and Trust Section (Vice-Chairman of the Real Estate Investment Trust Committee).
Career: Admitted to Texas Bar (1979). Law clerk to Judge Homer Thornberry of the United States Court of Appeals for the Fifth Circuit (1980). A partner of *Locke Liddell & Sapp* since joining the firm in 1994.
Publications: Co-author of the treatise entitled 'Federal Tax Aspects of Cancellation of Indebtedness and Foreclosures'.
Personal: Recieved a JD (1979), MPA (Taxation) (1977) and BBA (Accounting) (1975) from the University of Texas.

KATZ, Marvin M
Mayer, Brown, Rowe & Maw, Houston
713 546 0513
mkatz@mayerbrownrowe.com
Recommended in Real Estate
Specialization: Real estate, estate planning, probate, corporate.
Prof. Memberships: Admitted in Texas, 1958. US District Court for the Southern District of Texas, 1959. US Court of Appeals for the Fifth Circuit, 1961. US Supreme Court, 1972.
Career: Joined *Mayer, Brown, Rowe & Maw* as partner, 1989. *De Lange, Hudspeth, Pitman & Katz*, Houston, 1959-89. United States Air Force, 1955-57.
Personal: Born 12 May 1935. University of Texas School of Law, LLB with honors, 1959; Order of the Coif; Article Editor, 'Texas Law Review'. Texas A&M University, BBA, 1954. Speaks Spanish.

KELLER, Mary
York, Keller & Field, Austin Null
Recommended in Insurance

KELLEY, Jay
Vinson & Elkins LLP, Houston
713 758 4838
jkelley@velaw.com
Recommended in Energy, Projects
Specialization: Commercial practice, with an emphasis on project development and finance in the energy sector, particularly LNG and power.
Prof. Memberships: Member: State Bar of Texas, New York State Bar Association, International Bar Association, and College of the State Bar of Texas.
Career: Lecturer: International Practice Conference on Infrastructure Development in Emerging Markets, South Texas College of Law; Houston Bar Association; 8th Annual Advanced International Law Institute. Admitted to practice law in Texas (1985) and New York (1995).
Personal: Graduated from The University of Texas, BBA (Accounting) in 1981, and the University of Houston, JD summa cum laude in 1985.

KELLY, Mark
Vinson & Elkins LLP, Houston
713 758 4592
mkelly@velaw.com
Recommended in Corporate/M&A
Specialization: Corporate financing law, mergers and acquisitions law, and securities offerings law.
Career: Admitted to Texas Bar in 1981. Came to the firm in 1981 and was admitted to the partnership in January 1989.
Personal: Graduated from Texas A&M University, BBA in 1978, and Southern Methodist University, JD in 1981.

KEYES, David
Vinson & Elkins LLP, Houston
713 758 2418
dkeyes@velaw.com
Recommended in Banking & Finance
Specialization: Structured, secured and commercial finance; Uniform Commercial Code; Bank-payments systems. Clients include large banks, corporations and clearing-house organizations.
Prof. Memberships: ABA, State Bar of Texas, Houston Bar Association (Fellow in each). Vice Chairman of State Bar Business Law Section Legal Opinion Committee.
Career: Admitted to Texas Bar in 1968. Joined the firm in 1969 and admitted to partner in 1975.
Publications: Articles on legal opinions, investment property collateral, and conflicts of law.
Personal: Graduated from Princeton University, 1965 and The University of Texas Law School with high honors, 1968.

KIRKLAND, David
Baker Botts LLP, Houston
713 229 1234
Recommended in Corporate/M&A

KNULL, William H III
Mayer, Brown, Rowe & Maw, Houston
713 546 0528
wknull@mayerbrownrowe.com
Recommended in Litigation
Specialization: Extensive experience in transnational disputes involving oil and gas, mergers and acquisitions, contracts, corporate, lending practices; UNCITRAL arbitrations, governance, AAA, ICC and NASD. Lead counsel in multi-billion dollar disputes in Middle Eastern, Central Asian and Chinese oil and gas projects.
Prof. Memberships: LCIA. Advisory Board, Institute of Transnational Arbitration. Member, Chartered Institute of Arbitrators. Fellow, Center for International Legal Studies.
Career: Joined *Mayer, Brown, Rowe & Maw*, Houston, 1986; partner 1987. *Sullivan & Cromwell*, New York, 1977-86. US Navy, 1970-74.
Publications: 'Betting the Farm on International Arbitration: Is it Time to Offer an Appeal Option?' 11 Am. Rev. Int'l. Arb. 531 (2002). 'Uncertainty in the Courts: Split in U.S. Appellate Courts on Expanded Judicial Review by Agreement of Parties' presented at Barriers to Free Movement of Civil Justice, CILS, Salzburg, Austria, November 2001. 'Arbitrating Oil and Gas Disputes Involving CIS Parties', Moscow, October 2000. 'Practical Lessons from Arbitrating Claims from Foreign Investments in Hydrocarbon Projects: Turkmenistan', Moscow, October 2000.
Personal: Born 14 April 1948. University of Virginia, JD, 1977; Order of the Coif; Virginia Law Review, Member, 1975-77; Notes Editor, 1976-77. Yale University, BA, magna cum laude, 1970; Departmental Honors in Political Science.

KREBS, Arno
Fulbright & Jaworski LLP, Houston
713 651 5522
akrebs@fulbright.com
Recommended in Insurance
Specialization: Extracontractual liability and insurance coverage.
Prof. Memberships: Listed in a leading US publication. Member of the Houston, Dallas and American Bar Associations, State Bar of Texas, International Association of Defense Counsel and the American Board of Trial Advocates.
Career: Admitted to Texas Bar (1967). Admitted to the United States Court of Appeals for the Fifth and Eleventh Circuits. Partner in *Fulbright & Jaworski LLP*'s Houston office.
Personal: Received a BA (1964) from Texas A&M University and an LLB (1967) from the University of Texas.

KREBS, Stephen
Baker Botts LLP, Houston
713 229 1234
Recommended in Projects

KRUSE, Layne
Fulbright & Jaworski LLP, Houston
713 651 5194
lkruse@fulbright.com
Recommended in Antitrust
Specialization: Antitrust, Marketing & Trade Regulation; Securities Litigation; International Litigation; Intellectual Property Litigation; Class Actions & Government Investigations.
Prof. Memberships: Member of the Litigation and Antitrust Sections of the ABA; Chair, Ethics & Professional Responsibility Committee, ABA Antitrust Section; Former Chair of Exemption & Immunities Committee, ABA Antitrust Section; Served as Chair of the Antitrust and Business Litigation Section of the Texas Bar (1992-93).
Career: Partner since 1986. Former judicial clerk, Chief Judge John Brown, US court of Appeals, Fifth Circuit. He practices in the area of business litigation and arbitration, with an emphasis on antitrust and securities litigation, international disputes, and other business problems. Co-chair of Firm Antitrust, Marketing & Trade Regulation Practice Group.
Personal: Graduated from Yale Law School in 1977. Received MSc from the London School of Economics (1974) and a BA from Texas A&M University (1973).

TEXAS LEADERS

KUTZSCHBACH, George
Fulbright & Jaworski LLP, Houston
713 651 3702
gkutzschbach@fulbright.com
Recommended in Energy
Specialization: Energy.
Prof. Memberships: Houston and American Bar Associations and the State Bar of Texas.
Career: He is a partner in the firm's Houston office and Co-Chairman of the firm's Energy Practice Group. He focuses his practice on domestic and international transactions related to the exploration, acquisition, disposition, development and financing of (and joint venture, operational, transportation and marketing activities concerning) oil, gas, petrochemical and energy properties, pipelines, plants, refineries and other energy assets and companies.
Personal: He received a BBA in 1969 and a JD in 1972 from The University of Texas at Austin.

LAFUZE, William L
Vinson & Elkins LLP, Houston
713 758 2595
blafuze@velaw.com
Recommended in Intellectual Property
Specialization: Practices in most areas of intellectual property law, with emphasis on electronics, oilfield equipment, and computer-related litigation.
Prof. Memberships: Member: Patent Public Advisory Committee, United States Patent and Trademark Office. Vice Chair: American Bar Association, Section of Intellectual Property Law. Former President: American Intellectual Property Law Association.
Career: Admitted to practice: Texas, 1973. Joined *Vinson & Elkins*, 1973; admitted to partnership, 1980.
Personal: The University of Texas, BS, 1969; Southern Methodist University, MS in Applied Science, 1971; The University of Texas School of Law, JD, 1973.

LAWLESS, Mark
Nickens, Lawless & Flack LLP, Austin
512 472 3067
Recommended in Insurance

LONDA, Jeffrey
Ogletree, Deakins, Nash, Smoak & Stewart, PC, Houston 713 655 0855
Recommended in Employment

MARSTON, Edgar
Bracewell & Patterson LLP, Houston
713 221 1315
emarston@bracepatt.com
Recommended in Corporate/M&A
Specialization: Representative transactions include asset acquisitions, business combinations and divestitures, securities offerings and contests for corporate control. Has represented clients in various industries, including oil and gas, cement production, computer manufacturing, telecommunications, biotech, heating and air conditioning manufacturing and retail sales businesses. Has served as counsel to special committees of boards of directors and controlling stockholders in public companies.
Career: Taking a hiatus from the firm, served eight years as director, executive vice president and general counsel for a major United States cement and concrete producer.
Personal: LLB, The University of Texas School of Law, 1964; BA, Brown University, 1961.

MARTIN, Brian
Thompson, Coe, Cousins & Irons, LLP, Houston 713 403 8210
Recommended in Insurance

MARTIN, Christopher W
Martin, Disiere, Jefferson & Wisdom LLP, Houston 713 632 1700
martin@mdjwlaw.com
Recommended in Insurance
Specialization: Specializes in the evaluation and handling of insurance matters and disputes involving questions of coverage, industry practices, claims handling, underwriting, legal exposure, inter-insurer disputes, and other legal issues of interest to insurers conducting business in Texas. He has been named two years running in leading legal publications in Texas. As a lawyer, he represents parties in civil litigation and appeals involving insurance claims and coverage disputes in state and federal courts across Texas. He frequently serves as a mediator of complex insurance claims and insurance lawsuits. He is also retained regularly to serve as an expert consultant in insurance disputes. Also has extensive experience in coverage disputes and litigation arising out of general liability, property and casualty, life and health, excess and umbrella, surplus lines, and workers-compensation policies. Has served as the Adjunct Professor of Insurance Law at the University of Houston Law Center for the past seven years.
Prof. Memberships: Is Board Certified in Consumer Law, the specialization covering Insurance Law, by the Texas Board of Legal Specialization.
Career: Is a founding partner of *Martin, Disiere, Jefferson & Wisdom, LLP*, where he heads the firm insurance coverage litigation practice. Before forming this Texas litigation boutique, he was a partner with the international law firm of *Bracewell & Patterson, LLP*. He is a graduate of Baylor University and the Baylor University School of Law.
Publications: Is the author of two legal treatises: The Lawyer's Guide to Texas Insurance Code, Article 21.21 (Lexis Legal Publishing 3rd Ed., 1998) and Texas Practice Guide: Insurance Litigation (West Publishing 2001). He is also the author of numerous articles written for CLE seminars, professional publications and educational institutions. He is also the editor of The Journal of Texas Insurance Law, a quarterly publication of the State Bar of Texas.

MARTIN, Ernest
Haynes and Boone, LLP, Dallas
214 651 5641
ernest.martin@haynesboone.com
Recommended in Insurance
Specialization: Represents company policyholders and specializes in handling complex insurance coverage matters involving first and third party policies, including, but not limited to, environmental, directors and officers; liability, securities and general liability coverage claims, and bad faith claims.
Career: Partner and Chair of the Insurance Coverage Practice Group; Co-Founder and Past-Chairman of the Texas Insurance Law Section of the State Bar of Texas and 2003 Chair of the Tort and Insurance Section of the Dallas Bar Association. He is also an Adjunct Professor in the area of Insurance Law at the SMU School of Law and has co-chaired the University of Texas Insurance Law Symposium (2000-02). He is a frequent author and speaker, both locally and nationally, on insurance-related issues.

MASLANKA, Michael
Godwin Gruber, Dallas 214 939 4400
Recommended in Employment

MASSAD, Stephen
Baker Botts LLP, Houston
713 229 1234
Recommended in Corporate/M&A

MAUEL, John
Baker & McKenzie, Houston
713 427 5000
john.g.mauel@bakernet.com
Recommended in Projects
Specialization: Practice involves domestic and international energy projects, oil and gas transactions, and project finance; including the development, financing, acquisition and sale of electric power projects, oil and gas reserves, pipelines, processing plants, LNG receiving and regasification terminals, and LNG tankers.
Prof. Memberships: State Bar of Texas, American Bar Association, Houston Bar Association.
Career: Admitted to practice law in Texas in 1986. Partner with *Baker & McKenzie* since joining the firm in 2001.
Publications: Regular author and presenter on energy projects.
Personal: Received his BA (cum laude) from Harvard University in 1983 and his JD from Notre Dame University in 1986.

MCCOMBS, David
Haynes and Boone, LLP, Dallas
972 739 8636
david.mccombs@haynesboone.com
Recommended in Intellectual Property
Specialization: Practice includes all aspects of intellectual property law, with emphasis on patent procurement, patent litigation, and licensing in the electronics, software, and telecommunications fields. He specializes in architecting patent portfolios for companies with the end goal of monetizing patents through licensing or litigation. He has drafted key patents for both large and small companies and have negotiated numerous multi-million dollar licenses and settlements for patent owners. He has litigated several complex patent infringement suits, handling technical aspects of cases in cooperation with lead trial counsel.

MCCONNELL, Mike
Winstead Sechrest & Minick, Dallas
817 420 8214
mmcconnell@winstead.com
Recommended in Insolvency
Specialization: Shareholder Bankruptcy Section. He represents clients across all aspects of reorganization and bankruptcy related litigation. Represents secured and unsecured creditors in business restructurings, the formulation of pre-packaged Chapter 11 Plans of Reorganization, and Chapter 11 Debtor and Chapter 11 Official Unsecured Creditor Committee representation. Advises Boards of Directors on liability and fiduciary responsibility issues.
Prof. Memberships: National Conference of Bankruptcy Judges, National Foundation of American Inns of Court.
Career: Admitted State Bar of Texas and former US Bankruptcy Judge for the Northern District of Texas.
Personal: Received JD The University of Texas School of Law 1975, and Loyola University 1969.

MCCORMACK, William
Hughes & Luce LLP, Dallas
214 939 5500
Recommended in Corporate/M&A

MCKOOL, Mike
McKool Smith, Dallas 214 978 4000
Recommended in Litigation

MCNEIL, Barry
Haynes and Boone, LLP, Dallas
214 651 5580
barry.mcneil@haynesboone.com
Recommended in Antitrust
Specialization: Has over 30 years of experience as a trial lawyer, first with the Antitrust Division of the Department of Justice and now in private practice. He has defended companies and senior officers before juries throughout the country in class actions and in civil and criminal fraud cases. He was recently ranked as one of the 15 top litigators in the trial bar by a leading publication. In The National

Law Journal's 'Biggest Defense Verdict of 1999', he led the successful defense of a national healthcare provider, winning a 'slam-dunk defense verdict' (NLJ, May 22, 2000).

MCNIEL, Ferguson
Vinson & Elkins LLP, Houston
713 758 3882
fmcniel@velaw.com
Recommended in Litigation

Specialization: Represents clients in various types of litigation. Practice concentrates on professional malpractice, toxic tort, product liability and construction claims. Certified in civil trial law and personal injury trial law by Texas Board of Legal Specialization.
Prof. Memberships: Member: International Bar Association; American Board of Trial Advocates; International Association of Defense Counsel; American Bar Association; Texas Association of Defense Counsel; Defense Research Institute; Houston Bar Association. Fellow: Texas Bar Foundation; Houston Bar Foundation.
Career: Admitted to practice: Texas, 1980. Joined *Vinson & Elkins*, 1980; admitted to partnership, 1990.
Personal: University of Arkansas, BSBA, 1977; University of Arkansas, JD, 1980.

MEDLOCK, Bryan
Sidley Austin Brown & Wood, Dallas
214 981 3300
Recommended in Intellectual Property

MELO, Thomas
Bracewell & Patterson LLP, Houston
713 221 1425 tmelo@bracepatt.com
Recommended in Employment

Specialization: Represents management in litigation and counseling concerning employment discrimination, wrongful discharge, equal employment opportunity, occupational safety and health, employee benefits disputes, union-management relations, wage and hour matters, executive employment contracts and other issues which concern the employment relationship. Experienced litigator in both state and federal court, as well as in arbitration and administration.
Prof. Memberships: Serves as the statewide treasurer of the Texas Association of Business. Honored as a fellow in the College of Labor and Employment Lawyers.
Personal: JD, University of Virginia School of Law, 1977; BBA, University of Georgia, 1974.

MERWIN, Bruce
Haynes and Boone LLP, Houston
713 547 2116
bruce.merwin@haynesboone.com
Recommended in Construction

Specialization: Has 25 years of experience working on all types of complex real estate transactions, with a particular emphasis on construction-related transactions. Recent transactions include representation of: developer in structuring and documenting land acquisition, financing, construction and leasing of a multi-building medical complex in The Woodlands, Texas; architects in negotiating and drafting agreements with respect to the Houston football/rodeo stadium complex and the Houston basketball arena and related parking garage; owners, developers, architects and contractors in drafting and negotiating over 50 architect's agreements and construction contracts annually; developers and several major tenants occupying multiple floors of office buildings and build-to-suit office/warehouse projects; borrowers in all types of real estate financing, including conduit loans an defeasance transactions; sellers and purchasers of apartment and shopping center portfolio transactions; and land development lender on more than 200 loans and sales of participation interests.

MEYERS III, Robert L
Jones Day, Dallas 214 969 4829
rlmeyers@jonesday.com
Recommended in Construction

Specialization: Design and construction transactions and dispute resolution. Represents all parties to the design construction process across the US and worldwide. Numerous landmark projects include Dallas Market Center, Embarcadero Redevelopment/San Francisco, and JP Morgan World Headquarters/NYC.
Prof. Memberships: Charter member and past-chairman of the ABA Construction Litigation Committee, founding member and past-chairman of both the Texas Bar and Dallas Bar Construction Law Sections, currently serving as vice-chairman Texas Center for Legal Ethics & Professionalism, Board of Trustees for Center for American & International Law, and charter fellow and current president of the American College of Construction Lawyers. Continued support of SMU Law School includes chairing the Alumni Council Development Committee and membership on the Dean's Council for Excellence and the Executive Board, received the Distinguished Alumni Award in 1995.
Publications: Author of numerous articles. Frequent speaker for such outstanding programs as the Practising Law Institute National Construction Law Seminar, the Construction Litigation Superconference and numerous state and local bar presentations on construction law topics.

MICCICHE, Daniel
Akin Gump Strauss Hauer & Feld LLP, Dallas 214 969 2800
Recommended in Tax

MILES, Robin J
Bracewell & Patterson LLP, Houston
713 221 1319
rmiles@bracepatt.com
Recommended in Banking & Finance

Specialization: Extensive experience in representing lenders or borrowers in most every commercial finance transaction, including syndicated secured and unsecured loans, maritime financings, trade financings, asset and accounts securitizations, structured financings, lease financings, project and acquisition financings, credit enhancement of bond financings, private debt placements, restructuring of problem credits, senior debt financings, subordinated debt offerings, leveraged buyouts, recapitalizations and various hedge arrangements. Serves foreign and US money center banks as agent and lender in syndicated commercial loans, including secured and unsecured lines of credit.
Personal: JD, The University of Kansas School of Law, 1986. BS, University of Colorado, 1978.

MILLS, Jerry
Baker Botts LLP, Dallas 214 953 6500
Recommended in Communications, Intellectual Property

MOORE, Charles A
LeBoeuf, Lamb, Greene & MacRae, LLP, Houston 713 287 2086
cmoore@llgm.com
Recommended in Energy

Specialization: An internationally recognized authority in the field of energy industry regulation. He has held a number of high level government positions in this field. In private practice, he has been involved in numerous international and domestic transactions in the energy sector.
Prof. Memberships: American Bar Association (Litigation Section); Energy Bar Association; Maritime Law Association of the United States.
Career: Joined *LeBoeuf* in 2002. Chariman, Energy and Converging Industries, *Akin, Gump, Strauss, Hauer & Feld, LLP*; General Counsel, US Federal Energy Regulatory Commission (1981-83).
Personal: University of Houston (JD magna cum laude) 1975; University of Houston (BA) 1972.

NEWSOME, Jonathan Kent
Fulbright & Jaworski LLP, Houston
713 651 3659
kent@fulbright.com
Recommended in Real Estate

Specialization: Commercial real estate, real estate development, hospital acquisitions and development, entertainment law, general business law, and internet related transactions.
Prof. Memberships: Member of the Houston and American Bar Associations and the State Bar of Texas. Fellow of the Houston Bar Foundation and member of the American College of Real Estate Lawyers. Voting member of the National Academy of Recording Arts and Sciences.
Career: Admitted to practice law in Texas in 1985. Joined the firm in 1985, is a partner in *Fulbright & Jaworski LLP*'s Houston office.
Personal: Received a BA, cum laude, in 1982 from Wake Forest University and a JD in 1985 from Vanderbilt University.

NIEBRUEGGE, Michael E
Mayer, Brown, Rowe & Maw, Houston
713 561 0507
mniebruegge@mayerbrownrowe.com
Recommended in Banking & Finance

Specialization: Represents lenders and arrangers in negotiating and documenting secured lending and securitization agreements with corporations, general partnerships, limited partnerships, individuals, and trusts engaged in energy, mining, transportation and manufacturing. Represents creditors in negotiating and documenting debt restructurings; disputes with other creditors and debtors. Represents oil and gas producers in a variety of onshore matters. Represents corporations engaged principally in service businesses and extractive businesses on employment contracts; real property acquisitions; general corporate matters.
Prof. Memberships: State Bar of Texas. Texas Association of Bank Counsel. Admitted in Texas, 1981. Illinois, 1977. US District Court for the Southern District of Texas, 1988. US District Court for the Northern District of Illinois, 1977.
Career: Joined *Mayer, Brown, Rowe & Maw*, 1982; became partner, 1984. Partner-in-charge of Houston office, 1995 to date. Formerly with Gulf Coast Royalty Co., Vice President and General Counsel, Houston, 1981-82. *Mayer, Brown, Rowe & Maw,* Chicago, 1977-81. Northwestern University, Lecturer in Business Law, Chicago, 1979-80.
Personal: Born 21 April 1952. Cornell University, JD, 1977; note and comment editor, Cornell Law Review. Harvard College, AB, cum laude, 1974.

NONDORF, Kurt
Jackson Walker LLP, Dallas
214 953 6000
Recommended in Real Estate

NORRIS, John
Howrey Simon Arnold & White, Houston
713 787 1400
Recommended in Intellectual Property

O'LEARY, Michael
Andrews & Kurth LLP, Houston
713 220 4200
moleary@akllp.com
Recommended in Corporate/M&A

Specialization: Practice includes expertise in all aspects of corporate transactions including representation of public and private companies and investment in banking firms; formation of partnerships and joint ventures; public offerings and private placements of equity and debt; publicly traded limited partnerships;

spin-offs; mergers, acquisitions and dispositions (by tender offer, exchange offer and otherwise) of corporations, divisions of corporations and other entities; redemptions and exchanges of preferred equity and debt; advising clients on changes of control and strategic alliances; structuring 'going private' transactions; defensive techniques; director fiduciary duties; advising special board committees; restructurings; liquidisations; project financings (including partnership and limited partnership financings); and international joint ventures and alliances. Has particular experience in energy and oilfield service companies, pipeline transportation, staff leasings, royalty trusts and forest products companies.
Prof. Memberships: Houston Bar Association.
Career: Admitted to the State Bar of Texas in 1980.
Personal: Graduated from the University of Alabama (BS, Finance, cum laude, 1977) and received law degree from the University of Houston Law Center (JD with honors, 1980).

OLIVER, Rufus
Baker Botts LLP, Dallas 214 953 6500
Recommended in Antitrust

OSTERBERG, Edward
Vinson & Elkins LLP, Houston
713 758 2192
eosterberg@velaw.com
Recommended in Tax
Specialization: Federal income taxation with emphasis on international transactions, mergers and acquisitions, and partnerships and joint ventures.
Career: Admitted to Texas Bar in 1966. Came to the firm in 1967 and was admitted to the partnership in January 1974.
Personal: Graduated from Northwestern University, BA in 1963 and JD cum laude in 1966, and Southern Methodist University, LLM in Taxation in 1972.

OXFORD, Terrell
Susman Godfrey LLP, Dallas
214 754 1900
Recommended in Antitrust

PARKER, David
Fulbright & Jaworski LLP, Austin
512 536 3055
dparker@fulbright.com
Recommended in Intellectual Property
Specialization: Litigation, prosecution, licensing, and biotechnology.
Prof. Memberships: Member of the American Bar Association, the American Intellectual Property Law Association, the Austin Intellectual Property Law Association, the Travis County Bar Association and the Association of the University Technology Managers.
Career: Admitted to the United States Court of Appeals for the Federal circuit, the United States Supreme Court, and the United States Patent and Trademark Office.
Personal: Received a BA (1976) from the University of Texas, a PhD in Molecular Pharmacology and Genetic Engineering (1981) from Baylor College of Medicine and a JD (1986) from The University of Texas.

PARTRIDGE, Scott
Baker Botts LLP, Houston
713 229 1234
Recommended in Intellectual Property

PATTON, David
Locke Liddell & Sapp LLP, Houston
713 226 1254
dpatton@lockeliddell.com
Recommended in Energy
Specialization: For over 25 years he has concentrated his practice on oil and gas issues. Has represented clients in the acquisition and disposition of oil and gas properties, the negotiation and preparation of agreements relating to the ownership and operation of oil and gas interests, including operating agreements, drilling contracts, exploration and seismic agreements, marketing agreements, processing agreements and surface use agreements. He has advised clients on a daily basis concerning the practical implications of oil and gas law upon their on-going business affairs. His representative clients include Ocean Energy, Dynegy, Black Stone Minerals Company, Energen, El Paso, Entergy, Amerada Hess, JP Morgan Chase Bank and Bank One.
Prof. Memberships: State Bar of Texas; Houston Bar Association; Federal Bar Association (Board of Directors South Texas Region); Rocky Mountain Mineral Law Foundation (Chairman Regional Planning Committee 2001 and 2002).
Career: Admitted to State Bar of Texas 1977; Practiced with *Locke Liddell & Sapp LLP* entire career, named partner in 1982.
Personal: JD University of Houston 1977. BA University of Texas 1973

PEDEN, David
Porter & Hedges, LLP, Houston
713 226 0600
Recommended in Construction

PEREZ, Alfredo R
Weil, Gotshal & Manges LLP, Houston
713 546 5040
alfredo.perez@weil.com
Recommended in Insolvency
Specialization: Is a partner in the Business Finance and Restructuring Department of *Weil, Gotshal & Manges LLP*. Heads the Business Finance and Restructuring Practice in the firm's Houston office. Has practiced in the areas of business reorganizations, debtors' and creditors' rights and insolvency since 1980. Concentrates his practice in the representation of chapter 11 debtors and other diverse claimants, including secured creditors and committees in all aspects of corporate restructurings, formal bankruptcy proceedings and out-of-court workouts. Has represented numerous acquirors and potential acquirors of assets from bankruptcy estates and companies in financial distress. Has also represented statutory and ad hoc bondholder committees, agent banks in syndicated credits, secured and unsecured creditors in many industry sectors including energy, hi-tech, transportation, real estate, telecommunications, and power, and litigants in adversary proceedings involving alleged preferences, fraudulent conveyances and other avoidance claims.
Prof. Memberships: Is admitted to all Federal District Courts in Texas and the Fifth and First Circuit Courts of Appeal. Is a member of the StateBar of Texas, the American Bankruptcy Institute and the American and Housten Bar Association. Is past Chair of the Bankruptcy Section of the Houston Bar Association and past president of the Insolvency Working Group of the Union Internationale des Advocats. Is also a member of the Southern District of Texas Complex Chapter 11 Advisory Committee.
Personal: Graduated with a BA degree in Chemistry from Haverford College and a JD from The University of Chicago Law School.

PETERSON, Pete
Cox & Smith Incorporated, San Antonio
210 554 5500
Recommended in Intellectual Property

PHELAN, Robin
Haynes and Boone, LLP, Dallas
214 651 5612
robin.phelan@haynesboone.com
Recommended in Insolvency
Specialization: His practice is exclusively devoted to insolvency, reorganization and related areas, including extensive litigation in the bankruptcy court and other federal courts. He is a frequent speaker on panels and programs throughout the United States and internationally regarding developments in bankruptcy and insolvency law and is the author of numerous publications, several relating to tax, governmental and environmental claims. He is a contributor to several major treatises on bankruptcy and has testified before both the Congressional Bankruptcy Review Commission and the United States Congress on insolvency matters. He has recently participated in a program sponsored by the United States Department of State and the United Nations to develop model cross border insolvency provisions and participated in a White House program to improve the United States bankruptcy system.

PINKERTON, Glenn
Vinson & Elkins LLP, Houston
713 758 2701
gpinkerton@velaw.com
Recommended in Projects
Specialization: Member of the firm's Private Equity Practice Group, Project Finance and Development Practice Group, and International Practice Group. Has extensive experience in mergers and acquisitions, project development and finance, and international transactions.
Career: Admitted to Texas Bar, 1986. Came to the firm, 1986 and was admitted to the partnership, January 1995.
Personal: Graduated from The University of Texas at Austin, BBA in 1981, and Columbia University, JD in 1986.

PIRKEY, Louis
Fulbright & Jaworski LLP, Austin
512 536 3001
lpirkey@fulbright.com
Recommended in Intellectual Property
Specialization: Trademark litigation and counseling, unfair competition law.
Prof. Memberships: Past President of the American Intellectual Property Law Association, past Chairman of the Intellectual Property Law Section of the State Bar of Texas, and was the charter President of the Austin Intellectual Property Law Association.
Career: Represented clients in over 300 trademark and unfair competition litigations in federal district and appellate courts across the country.
Personal: Received a BSChE (1960) from the University of Texas at Austin and a JD, with honors, (1964) from The George Washington University.

PODVIN JR, F John
Bracewell & Patterson LLP, Dallas
214 758 1083
jpodvin@bracepatt.com
Recommended in Communications
Specialization: Assists financial institutions and other entities to develop new products and services, including electronic commerce and banking services, internet services and other information technology. Works with clients implementing and interpreting information privacy and security laws. Advises financial institutions on state and federal banking laws, regulations, supervisory agencies, mergers and acquisitions and litigation.
Career: Served as an attorney at the Office of the Comptroller of the Currency, where he counseled the comptroller, staff, bankers and bank counsel on the interpretation and enforcement of federal banking laws.
Personal: JD, University of Wisconsin Law School, 1991; BA, Economics, Georgetown University, 1988.

POWELL, Charles
Haynes and Boone LLP, Houston
713 547 2052
charles.powell@haynesboone.com
Recommended in Communications

Specialization: Head of the firm's Technology Practice in Houston and handles venture capital, securities offerings, mergers and acquisitions, and representation of technology companies including telecom companies and enterprises deploying technology in the energy industry. He was lead counsel in the following matters: strategic investor in $23 million investment in a wireless company; VC investor in $10 million telecom preferred stock investment; $30 million venture capital investment in two telecom equipment manufacturers; energy service e-commerce company in its $60,000,000 merger with an online well service and product procurement company; NYSE seismic products manufacturer in $60,000,000 preferred stock placement; energy company in $100 million preferred stock placement and $1.2 billion restructuring of offshore deepwater business.

POWERS, Werner
Haynes and Boone, LLP, Dallas
214 651 5581
werner.powers@haynesboone.com
Recommended in Insurance

Specialization: Has over twenty-five years of experience representing a broad spectrum of clients in complex litigation matters. A 'plaintiff's lawyer'; for corporate America, he has devoted substantially all of his practice to insurance coverage, insurance torts, securities, RICO, and large contract disputes.

RAFTE, Alan
Bracewell & Patterson LLP, Houston
713 221 1411
arafte@bracepatt.com
Recommended in Energy

Specialization: Handles a wide array of commercial transactions involving energy industries such as electric power, oil and gas exploration and production and gas and liquids pipeline and facilities. Has represented clients such as project sponsors, equity investors and credit providers in transactions that have included acquisitions and divestitures of a variety of assets and companies, structured and commercial finance and project development and project finance. Recognized by 'Project Finance' magazine with 'Deal of the Year' honors for innovative work representing a power generation industry client.
Personal: JD, Emory University School of Law, 1979; BA, Syracuse University, 1976.

RAMAN, William
Thompson & Knight LLP, Austin
512 469 6132
william.raman@tklaw.com
Recommended in Intellectual Property

Specialization: Intellectual property, including litigation and counseling on patent, copyright, trademark, trade dress, dilution and unfair competition matters, with an emphasis on trademark, trade dress, dilution, and unfair competition.
Prof. Memberships: State Bar of Texas. American Bar Association. American Intellectual Property Law Association. Austin Intellectual Property Law Association; President (1995). Travis County Bar Association. State Bar of Texas, Intellectual Property Law Section.International Trademark Association: United States Legislation Committee (1992-95); Issues and Policy Committee (1996-98); Meetings Committee (1998-2000); Alternative Dispute Resolution Committee (2000-present).
Career: Associated with *T&K*: 2000. JD University of Texas School of Law, 1977. BS, with honors, Mechanical Engineering, The University of Texas, 1974.
Publications: Publishes and speaks frequently on trademark-related topics.

RAY, Hugh M
Andrews & Kurth LLP, Houston
713 220 4164
hray@akllp.com
Recommended in Insolvency

Specialization: He heads the national bankruptcy practice of *Andrews & Kurth*. Past Chair, Business Bankruptcy Committee of the American Bar Association's Business Law Section. He has represented the Agent Bank and Bank Syndicate in In re William Herbert Hunt, Nelson Bunker Hunt Trust Estate, et al; the Institutional Lenders for In re Storage Technology; the Institutional Creditors of In re Continental Airlines, Inc (both cases); the Unsecured Creditors'; Committee of Flagstar Corporation (Denny's); the Trustee for the Bank of New England Corporation; the Unsecured Creditors' Committees of In re First Republic Bank Corporation; Encompass Services; Rubus Realty (Furr's Supermarkets); Drypers Corporation; Doskocil (Wilson Foods); the Debtor in Friede Goldman Halter, Inc.; the Debtor in Physicians Resource Group; the ad hoc Bondholder's Committee of American Rice, Inc; and the Insurance Company Lenders of In re Braniff Airlines, Inc. He has also represented the Bank Lenders for Appletree Markets and In re CompuAdd Corporation and the Unsecured Creditors' Committee and Petitioning Creditors for In re First City Bancorporation of Texas. He also represented the bondholders in the CalFed and GlenFed restructurings.
Prof. Memberships: Past Member, Standing Committee on Judicial Selections Tenure and Compensation of the American Bar Association; Board Certified, Business Bankruptcy Specialist, Texas Board of Legal Specialization and the American Board of Bankruptcy Certification; Elected, American College of Bankruptcy; Selected, Best Lawyers in America; Elected Member, American Law Institute Member, Consultative Group for Redraft of Article 9 of the Uniform Commercial Code; Member, Consultative Group, Transnational law project; Past Chair, Bankruptcy Committee, State Bar of Texas 1986-89; Past Program Director, Advanced Business Bankruptcy Institute, State Bar of Texas.
Career: Started with *Andrews & Kurth* as an associate in 1968, has been a partner with the firm since 1977.
Publications: He is a co-author of 'Bankruptcy Investing' and is a co-author of 'Texas Practice Guide - Creditors' Rights' Vols. 1 and 2 (West Publishing - 2002).
Personal: Received BA (1965) and LLB (1967) from Vanderbilt University.

REASONER, Harry
Vinson & Elkins LLP, Houston
713 758 2358
hreasoner@velaw.com
Recommended in Antitrust, Litigation

Specialization: Principal practice is complex civil litigation. Served as lead trial counsel in litigation and arbitration involving antitrust, securities, insurance, contract and tort claims.
Prof. Memberships: Fellow: American College of Trial Lawyers; International Academy of Trial Lawyers; International Society of Barristers; American Law Institute; American Board of Trial Advocates.
Career: Admitted to practice: Texas, 1962; District of Columbia, 1974; New York, 1980. Joined *Vinson & Elkins*, 1963; admitted to partnership, 1970.
Personal: Rice University, BA, 1960; The University of Texas Law School, JD, 1962.

REDDEN, Joe
Beck, Redden & Secrest, Houston
713 951 3700
Recommended in Litigation

RICHARD, Molly
Thompson & Knight LLP, Dallas
214 969 1677
molly.richard@tklaw.com
Recommended in Intellectual Property

Specialization: Representation of clients extensively in trademark clearance and registration worldwide, copyright protection and advice, and litigation in trademark and copyright matters. Listed in top US legal publication 2003-04 (Intellectual Property Law).
Prof. Memberships: State Bar of Texas. Admitted to practice before the United States District Courts for the Northern, Southern, and Western Districts of Texas. State Bar of Texas; Intellectual Property Law Section (Chair 2002-03; Vice-Chair 2000-01; Secretary 1999-2000; Chair, Professionalism Committee 1997; Council 1993-94; Past Chair, Trademark Committee). American Bar Association; Young Lawyers Division (Past Vice-Chair, Computer Law and Copyright Law Committees). Dallas Bar Association; Intellectual Property Section (Past Chair). Dallas/Fort Worth Intellectual Property Law Association. Dallas Association of Young Lawyers (Director 1985-87; President 1990). Texas Young Lawyers Association (Director 1990-92).
Career: Associated with *Thompson & Knight* since 2002. JD, Southern Methodist University School of Law, 1981. BA Austin College, 1977.
Publications: Numerous publications on trademark and copyright law and related topics.

ROBERTS, Harry
Thompson & Knight LLP, Dallas
214 969 1616
harry.roberts@tklaw.com
Recommended in Real Estate

Specialization: Permanent and construction loan work for institutional lenders, purchase and sale of commercial real estate for institutional and private investors, development of real property involving the assembly of land and zoning and construction issues, complex real estate transactions involving exchanges, lease-backs and development agreements, leasing of office building and other commercial space, loan servicing including modification agreements and assumption agreements, management agreements, reciprocal and other easements, local counsel opinions and counseling, loan workouts, foreclosure, and usury analysis. Recommended in real estate law and banking law (secured transactions) by a leading US legal publication.
Prof. Memberships: State Bar of Texas. American College of Real Estate Lawyers.par State Bar of Texas; Council of Real Estate, Probate, and Trust Law Section (1978-85), Chairman (1984-85); Title Insurance Committee (1978-), Chairman (1978-84); Lawyers' Opinion Letter Committee (1982-); Real Estate Specialization Committee (1977-85); Partnership Committee (1977-82).par Chairman, Dallas Bar Association; Real Estate Section (1981). College of the State Bar of Texas. Fellow, American Bar Foundation. Texas Bar Foundation. Dallas Bar Foundation. Visiting Scholar, The University of Texas Law School. State Board of Insurance; Advisory Committee on Title Insurance (1987-91). Vice President and Director, Texas Academy of Real Estate, Probate, and Trust Lawyers (1988-90). Texas College of Real Estate Attorneys (1990-); Vice Chair and Director (1990-93). Chairman, Texas Mortgage Lending Institute (1990-91).
Career: Associated with *Thompson & Knight* since 1963. Bachelor of Laws, Harvard Law School, 1963. BBA., Accounting, Southern Methodist University, 1960.
Publications: Publishes and speaks frequently on topics related to real estate and real estate lending.

TEXAS LEADERS

ROSENBERG, Gregg
Gregg M Rosenberg & Associates, Houston 713 960 8300
Recommended in Employment

SALCH, Steven
Fulbright & Jaworski LLP, Houston
713 651 5433
ssalch@fulbright.com
Recommended in Tax
Specialization: Tax controversy, state and federal tax planning, multi-national tax and business law, mediation, arbitration, expert witness, administrative agency determinations and rulemaking legislation, antiboycott compliance, foreign asset controls, and export administration.
Prof. Memberships: Listed in a leading American publication. Past Chair, Section of Taxation, Amercian Bar Association. Fifth Circuit Regent, American College of Tax Counsel. Member of the American Law Institute, the International Fiscal Association, the American Bar Foundation, the Southwestern Legal Foundation and the Houston Bar Foundation.
Career: Admitted to Texas Bar (1968). Partner in the Houston office of *Fulbright & Jaworski* since 1975.
Personal: Received a BBA in Accounting (1965) and a JD (1968) from Southern Methodist University.

SCHOENBRUN, Larry
Gardere Wynne Sewell LLP, Dallas
214 999 4703
lschoenbrun@gardere.com
Recommended in Corporate/M&A
Specialization: With more than 30 years of experience as a corporate and securities practitioner, has served as the coordinator of legal activities for a number of large and medium-sized corporations. He has represented corporations in their initial public offerings and other matters, including corporate reorganizations, reincorporations, roll-ups and structuring of employee benefit plans. Has also represented underwriters in public offerings, buyers and sellers in various corporate acquisitions and dispositions and venture capitalists in their investments. He has served as counsel for special committees of boards of directors in dealing with affiliate transactions and conflict situations and for audit committees in dealing with various corporate governance issues.
Prof. Memberships: Member, Dallas Bar Association; Member, American Bar Association; Former Chairman, Securities Committee of the Council of the Business Law Section of the State Bar of Texas; Former Chairman, Texas Business Law Foundation; Former Chairman, Council of the Business Law Section of the State Bar of Texas.
Career: Former Managing Partner, *Gardere Wynne Sewell LLP.*
Publications: Is a frequent speaker on corporate and securities matters and on corporate governance issues.
Personal: Former Chairman, North Texas-Oklahoma Regional Board of Directors of the Anti-Defamation League; Former President, Community Homes for Adults, Inc.; Director and Vice President, Jewish Federation of Greater Dallas; Former Chairman, Foundation of the Jewish Federation of Greater Dallas; Former Director, United Way of Metropolitan Dallas; former member, Dallas Citizen's Council; former Director, Texas General Counsels Forum; Director, Temple Shalom.

SEALS, Paul
Akin Gump Strauss Hauer & Feld LLP, Austin 512 499 6200
Recommended in Environment

SELINGER, Jerry
Jenkens & Gilchrist, Dallas
214 855 4500
Recommended in Intellectual Property

SHANK, Mark
Hughes & Luce LLP, Dallas
214 939 5500
Recommended in Employment

SHEEDER, Robert
Jenkens & Gilchrist, Dallas
214 855 4500
Recommended in Employment

SHEINFELD, Myron
Akin Gump Strauss Hauer & Feld, LLP, Houston 713 220 5800
Recommended in Insolvency

SLUSSER, William C
Slusser & Frost LLP, Houston
713 860 3300
slusser@slusserfrost.com
Recommended in Intellectual Property
Specialization: Extensive jury trial experience in patent, antitrust, ERISA, general business and products liability cases. Typically, he and his firm are the attorneys in charge in complex jury trials.
Prof. Memberships: American College of Trial Lawyers; American Law Institute; Best Lawyers in America; State Bar of Texas; ABA; American and Houston Intellectual Property Lawyers Associations.
Career: Admitted Texas Bar, 1973. *Baker Botts* (1973-99) including Executive Committee and head of the Trial Department; *Slusser & Frost, LLP* (1999 to present).
Personal: JD, with honors, University of Texas School of Law, 1972. Bachelor of Science in Electrical Engineering, University of Texas-Arlington, 1970.

SMITH, James
Beirne, Maynard & Parsons, L.L.P., Houston 713 623 0887
Recommended in Environment

SOSLAND, Martin
Weil, Gotshal & Manges LLP, Dallas
214 746 7730
martin.sosland@weil.com
Recommended in Insolvency
Specialization: Since joining the firm when the Dallas Office opened in 1987, concentrated in the area of business reorganizations, debtor and creditors' rights, and refinancings and acquisitions of troubled companies. Was involved in the firm's representation of The Western Company of North America, Zale Corporation, MCorp, Edison Brothers Stores, Inc., and PennCorp Financial Group, Inc. and led the Firm's representation of US ONE Communications Corp. and Heartland Wireless Communications in their cases under chapter 11 of the Bankruptcy Code. Led the firm's representation of the statutory creditors' committee for Diagnostic Health Systems, Inc. and has been involved in the representation of statutory creditors' committees for First Republicbank Corporation, Texas American Bancshares, National Gypsum Company and New Valley Corporation. Has been involved in the firm's representation of aircraft lessors in a number of restructurings including TWA and Viscount Airlines, Inc. and led the firm's representation of a major aircraft lessor in the chapter 11 case of Express One International, Inc. Also involved in the firm's representation of PennCorp Financial Group, Inc. in its acquisition of Southwestern Life Insurance Company from ICH Corporation and led the Firm's representation of the largest creditor of FFSC, Inc., which acquired that company pursuant to its chapter 11 plan of reorganization. Has led the firm's representation of major financial institutions in a number of cases including Harbor Financial Group, First-Plus Financial Group, Atlantic International Mortgage and Genesis Physicians Practice Association.
Prof. Memberships: Member of the Dallas and American Bar Associations and the American Bankruptcy Institute.
Personal: He received his BA from Rice University and his JD with honors from the University of Texas at Austin School of Law.

STEWART, Dan
Vinson & Elkins LLP, Dallas
214 215 4046
dstewart@velaw.com
Recommended in Insolvency
Specialization: Practice spans all aspects of debtor/creditor relationships. Major creditor representations include agent banks, bank groups, and creditor committee representations in connection with bankruptcy proceedings for major corporations. Served as lead counsel for Borrowers in some of the largest workouts and reorganizations in Texas for over 25 years. Served as Bankruptcy Trustee in hundreds of Chapter 7 and Chapter 11 cases under the Bankruptcy Act and Code.
Prof. Memberships: Dallas Bar Association.
Career: Admitted to Texas Bar, 1972. Came to the firm as a partner, 1999.
Personal: Graduated from Brown University, BA (1969), and Duke University School of Law, JD (1972).

STEWART, Robert
Baker Botts LLP, Austin 512 322 2500
Recommended in Environment

STILL, Charles
Fulbright & Jaworski LLP, Houston
713 651 5270
cstill@fulbright.com
Recommended in Corporate/M&A
Specialization: Corporate and securities laws
Career: Partner in *Fulbright & Jaworski LLP*'s Houston office. His areas of practice include corporate governance and finance and securities law, mergers and acquisitions, and other corporate specialty areas including the Foreign Corrupt Practices Act and general corporate legal compliance programs. He is a well known adviser to directors and boards of directors in connection with securities and corporate matters, including takeover matters and takeover defense matters and other important corporate governance contexts and has represented audit and special committees of boards and others in internal investigations.
Personal: He received a BBA in Accounting from Texas Tech University in 1965 and a JD, with honors, from the University of Texas in 1968.

STROUBE, Rey
Akin Gump Strauss Hauer & Feld, LLP, Houston 713 220 5800
Recommended in Insolvency

STRUBECK, Lou
Fulbright & Jaworski LLP, San Antonio
214 855 8040
lstrubeck@fulbright.com
Recommended in Insolvency
Specialization: Bankruptcy law and creditors rights law, creditor representation, creditors rights, debtor representation, institutional lenders, and reorganization.
Prof. Memberships: Member of the American Bankruptcy Institute, the Dallas and American Bar Associations, the State Bar of Texas, the Fee Dispute and Judiciary Subcommittee of the Dallas Bar Association and the Dallas and Tarrant County Bankruptcy Bar Associations.
Career: Admitted to Texas Bar (1983). Partner in the Dallas office of *Fulbright & Jaworski LLP* since 1992. Former panel bankruptcy trustee in the Northern District of Texas.
Personal: Graduated from the College of Charleston with a BA in 1980 and received a JD from Temple University in 1983.

SUSMAN, Stephen
Susman Godfrey LLP, Houston
713 651 9366
Recommended in Antitrust, Litigation

SUTHERLAND, Mike
Winstead Sechrest & Minick, Dallas
817 420 8216
msutherland@winstead.com
Recommended in Insolvency

Specialization: Shareholder Bankruptcy Section. He has experience representing clients in bankruptcy and insolvency cases. His practice includes representation in the areas of debtors, committees, and secured creditors in Chapters 7, 9 and 11. Client services include bankruptcy, business reorganization, workouts, and business litigation.
Prof. Memberships: United States District Courts for the Northern, Eastern, Western and Southern Districts of Texas, United States Court of Appeals for the Fifth Circuit, and United States Supreme Court.
Career: Admitted State Bar of Texas.
Personal: Received JD The University of Texas School of Law in 1981 and BA summa cum laude Abilene Christian University in 1976.

SWANSON, Joel
Baker Botts LLP, Houston
713 229 1234
Recommended in Corporate/M&A

SZALKOWSKI, Charles
Baker Botts LLP, Houston
713 229 1234
Recommended in Communications, Corporate/M&A

TAYLOR, Lyndon C
Skadden, Arps, Slate, Meagher & Flom LLP & Affiliates, Houston 713 655 5110
ltaylor@skadden.com
Recommended in Energy, Projects

Specialization: Head of *Skadden's* Houston office energy practice. Concentrates on domestic and international project finance, with emphasis on the development and financing of electric power plants and other energy infrastructure projects. Has represented project developers, commercial lenders, investment banks, construction companies, fuel suppliers, utility companies, and equity investors. Also represents clients in energy-related corporate matters, including a number of complex natural gas and petroleum asset and securities acquisition transactions.
Career: JD, University of Oklahoma College of Law, 1984 (With Honors, Order of the Coif, Earl Appleton Brown Award for Oil & Gas Law); BS, Industrial Engineering, Oklahoma State University, 1981.

TEMPLIN, Donald
Haynes and Boone, LLP, Dallas
214 651 5590
don.templin@haynesboone.com
Recommended in Intellectual Property

Specialization: Has over 25 years experience as a trial lawyer in business disputes and is a member of the American Board of Trial Advocates. He is the head of the firm's Business Litigation section and practices in the Intellectual Property Litigation Group, handling patent, trademark and copyright litigation. He is also a senior member of the firm's First Amendment and media defense practice.

TERRELL, Irvin
Baker Botts LLP, Houston
713 229 1234
Recommended in Litigation

THOMPSON, Dahl
Andrews & Kurth LLP, Houston
713 220 4376
dahlthompson@akllp.com
Recommended in Projects

Specialization: Extensive experience representing project developers, financial institutions and equity investors in domestic and international project finance transactions, with particular emphasis on electrical power plants and other energy infrastructure projects. His representation has included all aspects of the structuring, development, financing, acquisition and sell-down of such projects, including the negotiation and drafting of joint venture agreements, shareholder and partnership agreements, power sales contracts, tolling agreements, construction contracts, water supply and fuel supply agreements, gas and electricity interconnection agreements, operation and maintenance agreements, long term service agreements, credit agreements, security agreements, equity subscription agreements, guaranties, letters of credit, complex funds flow agreements and stock and asset purchase and sale agreements.
Prof. Memberships: State Bar of Texas, 1990.
Personal: Received JD from Columbia University in 1990 and was named Harlan Fiske Stone Scholar. Received BS (summa cum laude) from Utah State University in 1987.

THOMPSON, Jay
Thompson, Coe, Cousins & Irons, LLP, Austin 512 708 8200
Recommended in Insurance

THURBER, Mark
Andrews & Kurth LLP, Houston
713 220 4200
markthurber@akllp.com
Recommended in Energy, Projects

Specialization: Partner in the business transactions section of *Andrews & Kurth LLP*. Experience includes work on behalf of power and energy developers, has represented a variety of financial institutions, including lenders, investment banks and other capital providers and arrangers, in connection with financing domestic and foreign power and other infrastructure projects and acquisitions; has led a comprehensive range of oil and gas transactions, international joint venture arrangements and indigenous hydrocarbon concessions.
Prof. Memberships: State Bar of Texas; Japan America Society of Houston (board and past president).
Personal: Brigham Young University (BS with high honors, 1980); Brigham Young University (MBA, 1981); Columbia University (JD, 1989), articles editor, 'Columbia Business Law Review'.

TUCKER, Eliot
Mandell & Wright, Houston
713 228 1521
Recommended in Employment

TURNER, Robert
Jones Day, Dallas 214 969 2984
rwturner@jonesday.com
Recommended in Intellectual Property

Specialization: Worked in private practice of intellectual property law since 1965, with primary emphasis in the area of patent litigation. Lead trial counsel in numerous complex patent, trade secret, trademark and copyright matters for a number of Fortune 500 companies. Listed in the intellectual property section of a leading American legal publication. Former Judicial Law Clerk.
Prof. Memberships: Chairman of the Intellectual Property Section of the State Bar of Texas, 1999-2000. Member of the ABA, the State Bar of Texas (Intellectual Property Law and, Litigation, Sections), the Dallas Bar Association, and the Dallas-Ft. Worth Intellectual Property Law Association. An adjunct professor of law at The University of Texas School of Law and is on the faculty of the Patent Resources Group in Washington, DC.

UNDERKOFLER, Paul
Goins, Underkofler, Crawford & Langdon LLP, Dallas 214 969 5454
Paulu@gucl.com
Recommended in Construction

Specialization: Consultation with owner/developers, prime contractors, program managers, subcontractors and vendors relating to the avoidance of disputes and to the formation, termination and enforcement of contracts for construction of commercial, industrial and public projects. Representation in the dispute resolution process, including mediation, arbitration and litigation of claims in state and federal courts. Engaged for the perfection, enforcement and removal of statutory and constitutional mechanic's liens and priority contests against other liens and security interests. Selected as mediator and arbitrator (both sole and panel member) of nearly 100 construction controversies.
Prof. Memberships: Member of the Construction, ADR and Litigation Sections of the State Bar of Texas, a Fellow of the State Bar Foundation and a member of the College of the State Bar of Texas. Member of the Construction Industry Forum and the Public Contract Section of the American Bar Association. Member of the Litigation Section and the Construction Section (Chairman, 1989) of the Dallas Bar Association.
Career: A founding partner of his firm in 1977. Admitted to the State Bar of Texas (1961), the American Bar Association and the Dallas Bar Association. Admitted to practice before the Northern, Eastern and Western Districts of Texas, the 5th and 11th Circuits and the US Court of Federal Claims.
Personal: Educated at the University of Notre Dame (AB 1958) and the Law School of the University of Virginia (LLB 1961). Peer-evaluation as one of the best construction lawyers in the Dallas area, as reported in 'D' Magazine (May, 2001).

UNGER, Timothy
Andrews & Kurth LLP, Houston
713 220 4200
tunger@akllp.com
Recommended in Energy, Projects

Specialization: Representation of a variety of corporate and institutional clients. In recent years practice has focused primarily on cogeneration and independent power projects, as well as oil and gas industry financings.
Prof. Memberships: The State Bar of Texas, 1974.
Career: Partner with *Andrews & Kurth*, practising in the Business Section. Has been with the firm since 1974, and has represented a variety of corporate and institutional clients.
Personal: Received undergraduate degree from the University of Notre Dame (AB, magna cum laude, 1969) and law degree from the Univesity of Texas (JD, with honors, 1974). During law school was a member of the Texas Law Review and Order of the Coif.

VAN FLEET, Allan
Vinson & Elkins LLP, Houston
713 758 2006
avanfleet@velaw.com
Recommended in Antitrust

Specialization: Co-chair of *Vinson & Elkins'* Antitrust Practice Group; practice also includes complex commercial and technical litigation and legal ethics.
Prof. Memberships: Delegate: House of Delegates, Antitrust Law Section, and American Bar Association. Council Member: State Bar of Texas, International Law Section. US Delegate and Rapporteur: Free Trade Area of the Americas Working Group on Competition Law and Policy. Past President, Texas-Mexico Bar Association.
Career: Admitted to practice: Texas, 1978. Joined *Vinson & Elkins*, 1977; admitted to partnership, 1984.
Personal: Rice University, BA summa cum laude, 1976; Columbia University School of Law, JD (first in class), 1977.

TEXAS LEADERS

VOGEL, Peter
Gardere Wynne Sewell LLP, Dallas
214 999 4422
pvogel@gardere.com
Recommended in Communications
Specialization: For the past 24 years he combined his Masters in Computer Science and past experience as a programmer, systems analyst, and management consultant with effective legal skills. Is often appointed as an Arbitrator, Court Ordered Mediator, and Special Master in Internet and computer technology litigation. Has also devoted a substantial amount of time and energy serving government agencies and non-profit organizations by addressing their computer and Internet issues.
Prof. Memberships: Chair, Texas Supreme Court Judicial Committee on Information Technology. Vice Chair, Dallas Bar Foundation. Member, Texas Task Force for the Uniform Electronic Transaction Act (UETA).
Career: Co-chair, Gardere's Internet and Computer Technology Practice; former member, Board of Directors, State Bar of Texas; Past President, Dallas Bar Association (1994); founding Chair, State Bar of Texas, Computer Section; former Chair, State Bar of Texas, Minimum Continuing Legal Education Committee (MCLE); Former Chair, Annual Practical Computer Seminars; Adjunct Professor - the Law of the Internet, SMU School of Law.
Publications: 'Due Diligence and Don't Be Sorry - 7 Absolute Rules of Computer Contracts' www.watchIT.com, January 2002. 'Internet, e-Evidence and Privacy Issues for CIOs', CIO Forum, Society of Information Management, April 2002, Dallas. 'Security and e-Evidence', Information Systems Security Association, February 2002, Tulsa. 'Service Level Contracts and e-Law', Internet Based Claims Processing, International Quality & Productivity Center, July 2001, Chicago. 'Legal Concerns for B2B and e-Alliances', e-Partnerships & Alliances, International Quality & Productivity Center, January 2001, Orlando. 'Service Level Agreements Workshop', Government Technology Conference, February 2001, Austin. 'e-Intellectual Property and the Internet', 6th Annual World of Awards Conference, March 2001, Dallas. 'Electronic Evidence: Discovery and Admission, Annual Advanced Civil Trial Course, State Bar of Texas, August, September, October, 2001, Houston, San Antonio, Dallas.
Personal: Chair, Grants Committee, Board of Directors of the Dallas Bar Foundation; Member, Board of Directors, Family Gateway.

WALLENSTEIN, Jim
Jenkens & Gilchrist, Dallas
214 855 4500
Recommended in Real Estate

WEINER, Sandford
Vinson & Elkins LLP, Houston
713 758 2558
sweiner@velaw.com
Recommended in Real Estate
Specialization: Principal areas of practice are commercial law, real estate law, and structured finance law.
Prof. Memberships: Member: Board of Governors (President), American College of Real Estate Law; Anglo-American Real Property Institute; Houston Real Estate Lawyers Council; Texas College of Real Estate Attorneys.
Career: Admitted to Texas Bar, 1971. Joined *Vinson & Elkins*, 1971 and was admitted to the partnership, January 1978.
Personal: Graduated from The University of Texas, BA in 1968, and Harvard University, JD in 1971.

WEST, Glenn D
Weil, Gotshal & Manges LLP, Dallas
214 746 7780
glenn.west@weil.com
Recommended in Banking & Finance, Corporate/M&A
Specialization: Has practiced law for over 20 years. Is the Managing Partner of the Dallas office and a member of the firm's 13 person Management Committee. Practice concentrates on private equity, mergers and acquisitions and corporate finance for domestic and international clients. Has led public and private acquisition and corporate finance transactions for the following clients, among others: Carlyle Management Group, Hicks, Muse, Tate & Furst Incorporated, American Airlines, Greyhound Lines, Inc., Six Flags, Inc., Home Interiors & Gifts, Inc., Cooperative Computing, Inc., Viasystems Group, Inc., LIN Television Corporation, International Seed Holdings, LP, Generation Partners, NextMedia Group, Thomas Weisel Capital Partners and Brazos Equity Partners. Also represents Southwest Sports Group, which owns the Texas Rangers Baseball Club and the Dallas Stars Hockey Club; and he also led the project finance for the new American Airlines Center in Dallas. Is one of the lead lawyers assisting Enron Corporation in its reorganization process.
Prof. Memberships: New York, Texas and District of Columbias Bars.

WHEAT, David
Thompson & Knight LLP, Dallas
(214) 969-1468
david.wheat@tklaw.com
Recommended in Tax
Specialization: Client counseling and representation in transactional consultations, document preparation, and preparation of tax opinions on federal and state tax implications of business transactions, including corporate mergers and acquisitions as well as formation and operation of partnerships and limited liability companies; compliance, administrative, and judicial litigation in federal and state tax matters. Listed as one of the Best Lawyers Under 40 and Best Lawyers in Dallas - 2001, by D magazine. Also recommended in tax law in the 2001-02 and 2003-04 editions of a legal publication.
Prof. Memberships: Admitted State Bar of Texas. State Bar of Louisiana. Licensed to practice before the United States Tax Court, the United States Court of Federal Claims, the Fifth Circuit Court of Appeals, and the United States Supreme Court. American Bar Association; Taxation Section, Chair-Elect of ABA Corporate Tax Committee, 2001-02; Vice-Chair 2000-01; Chairman of Subcommittee on Taxable Distributions, 1997-2000. State Bar of Texas; Taxation Section, Chairman of the Corporate Tax Committee, 1997-98; Council Member, 1999-2001; Treasurer, 2001-02. College of the State Bar of Texas. Dallas Bar Association; Taxation Section; Council Member, 2000-01; Treasurer, 2001; Chair 2002 Fellow, Dallas Bar Foundation. State Bar of Louisiana; Taxation Section.
Career: Associated with *Thompson & Knight* since 1989. Master of Laws, Taxation, New York University School of Law, 1989; Graduate Editor, Tax Law Review; Wallace Scholar. JD, Louisiana State University Paul M Herbert Law Center, 1988; Order of the Coif; Chancellor's List; Louisiana Law Review. BS, with honors, Louisiana State University, 1985; Beta Gamma Sigma.
Publications: Frequent speaker and publisher on tax-related topics.

WILLIAMSON, Deborah
Cox & Smith Incorporated, San Antonio
210 554 5275
dwilliamson@coxsmith.com
Recommended in Insolvency
Specialization: Has been with the law firm *Cox & Smith Incorporated* since 1982. She is a shareholder and the Department Leader for the Bankruptcy Department and is Board Certified by the Texas Board of Legal Specialization in Business Bankruptcy Law and by the American Bankruptcy Board of Certification in Business Bankruptcy Law. She advises clients on all aspects of business bankruptcy, including pre-bankruptcy strategic planning, fraudulent conveyances, institutional and corporate acquisitions, financial institutions and lending, and complex issues in real estate and commercial transactions. Representation has included the committees in AgriBioTech, Inc., American Rice Inc., and Al Copeland Enterprises; the debtors in NeoStar, Inc. and Solo Serve Corp.; and the Chapter 11 Trustees in living.com and Empire Funding Corp.
Prof. Memberships: Past President of the American Bankruptcy Institute; Former Executive Editor of the ABI Journal; Author of Bench Notes Column, ABI Journal; Vice President - Business for the Bankruptcy Section of the State Bar of Texas; Chair Texas Board of Legal Specialization (Bankruptcy); Chair of the Bankruptcy Subcommittee, Federal Courts Committee of San Antonio Bar Association; Director of the American Board of Certification; Former Vice President of the San Antonio Bankruptcy Bar Association; Former Chair of the Bankruptcy Local Rules Committee for the Western District of Texas; Fellow of the American Bankruptcy College, the Texas Bar Foundation and the San Antonio Bar Foundation and a Member of the American Inns of Court.
Career: Has testified before the United States Senate Judiciary Committee, Subcommittee on Administrative Oversight and the Courts and was selected as an Outstanding National Bankruptcy Attorney in 1998. Is a frequent speaker on bankruptcy related topics including the attorney client privilege, successor liability, spousal liability and the tracing of assets, oil and gas, single asset cases, involuntary bankruptcies, effects of a failed chapter 11, pre-bankruptcy waivers, recent judicial and legislative developments, plan confirmation and pre-bankruptcy issues, executory contracts and intellectual property.
Personal: Education: JD Cum Laude, 1981, University Of Houston Law Center. Order of the Coif; Order of the Barons; Director, Board of Advocates; Phi Delta Phi. BA - Political Science, 1977, University of Texas at El Paso.

WILSON, Randall
Susman Godfrey LLP, Houston
713 651 9366
Recommended in Litigation

WILSON, Robert
Haynes and Boone, LLP, Dallas
214 651 5601
robert.wilson@haynesboone.com
Recommended in Real Estate
Specialization: Has more than 30 years of experience in business transactions. In the past year, he has completed transactions involving: representation of agent/lender in multi-jurisdiction real estate loan workout; representation of REIT subsidiary in pre-packaged bankruptcy; representation of pension fund in acquisition of 15 warehouses located in multiple states; representation of tenant in relocation of headquarters to Dallas in lease of 100,000 square feet of downtown office space; representation of agent/lender in financing of 16 luxury hotels located in seven states owned by REIT; representation of investor in acquisition of eight assisted living facilities located in four states; representation of investor in acquisition of publicly traded bonds secured by real estate; representation of developer in acquisition and con-

struction of world distribution warehouse; representation of foreign investor in acquisition of downtown San Francisco office building.

WORTLEY, Michael
Vinson & Elkins LLP, Dallas
214 220 7732
mwortley@velaw.com
Recommended in Corporate/M&A
Specialization: Primary area of practice is corporate and securities law. Experience in the telecommunications, oil and gas, REITs, manufacturing, healthcare, biotechnology, and high technology industries. Clients include issuers, underwriters, and investors in public and private securities transactions.
Prof. Memberships: American Bar Association and Dallas Bar Association.
Career: Admitted to Texas Bar, 1978. Came to the firm as a partner, 1995.
Personal: Graduated from Southern Methodist University, BA with highest honors, 1970, the University of North Carolina at Chapel Hill, Masters of Regional Planning, 1973, and Southern Methodist University, JD with honors, 1978.

WULFE, Scott
Vinson & Elkins LLP, Houston
713 758 2750
swulfe@velaw.com
Recommended in Corporate/M&A
Specialization: Corporate financing law, mergers and acquisitions law, and securities offerings law.
Career: Admitted to Texas Bar in 1983. Came to the firm in 1983 and was admitted to the partnership in January 1991.
Personal: Graduated from The University of Texas, BA in 1979 and JD in 1983.

YEATES, Marie
Vinson & Elkins LLP, Houston
713 758 4576
myeates@velaw.com
Recommended in Litigation
Specialization: Chairs *Vinson & Elkins*' appellate practice; practice concentrates on matters relating to appeals in civil cases. Certified in civil appellate law by Texas Board of Legal Specialization.
Prof. Memberships: Member: American Academy of Appellate Lawyers.
Career: Admitted to practice: Louisiana, 1980; Texas, 1982. Joined *Vinson & Elkins*, 1981; admitted to partnership, 1988.
Personal: Louisiana State University, BS, summa cum laude, 1977; Louisiana State University School of Law, JD, 1980 (first in class), (Editor in Chief, 'Louisiana Law Review').

YORK, Larry
York, Keller & Field, Austin Null
Recommended in Insurance

YOUNG, William
Vinson & Elkins LLP, Dallas
214 220 7994
byoung@velaw.com
Recommended in Banking & Finance
Specialization: Represents US and international private investment funds, commercial banks and corporations in private debt and equity transactions, including syndicated credits, asset based loans, real estate finance and mezzanine debt and equity investments. Significant emphasis is on international financings, and particularly, the financing of Japanese distressed debt and real estate portfolios. In 2001 and 2002 represented a key participant in over 20 international financing transactions exceeding $2 billion.
Prof. Memberships: Section on Business Law, American Bar Association, International Law Section, and Dallas Bar Association.
Career: Admitted to Texas Bar in 1985. Came to the firm as partner in 1998.

YUNGBLUT, Stephen
Jenkens & Gilchrist, Dallas
214 855 4500
Recommended in Construction

UTAH

CORPORATE/M&A

CONTENTS: Corporate/M&A p.684; Employment: Mainly Plaintiff p.685; Mainly Defendant p.686; Litigation: General Commercial p.686; Real Estate p.688; Individuals' profiles p.690.

UTAH'S TOP THREE
1. Stoel Rives
2. Parsons Behle & Latimer
2. Snell & Wilmer

Ranking based on Chambers' research within the state.

All quotes in the text are from interviews with clients and competitors.

OVERVIEW: Stoel Rives, a regional law firm with 49 attorneys in Utah, scored well in *Chambers'* research. An excellent team of lawyers with particular strengths in real estate and corporate law placed this firm above the rest. Market sources singled out real estate attorneys Thomas Ellison and Ervin Holmes as leading lights in the department, while the efforts of Brian Lloyd and Ron Moffitt have pushed the firm into the top band of our corporate rankings. The firm also houses star litigator David Jordan.

Well-established **Parsons Behle & Latimer**, in joint second place, is widely recognized for its labor and employment, and litigation practice groups. Observers cited Francis Wikstrom and Ray Etcheverry as top litigators in the market, while Shawn Ferrin was highly rated in real estate for his resort development work.

Snell & Wilmer is a Phoenix-based firm that fields 360 attorneys in six offices throughout five western states. Interviewees noted its strength in litigation, corporate and real estate matters. The firm is respected as one of the best business litigation firms in Utah, and Alan Sullivan was singled out as a top trial lawyer.

CORPORATE/M&A

UTAH
Leading firms (Corporate/M&A)

1. **STOEL RIVES LLP** Salt Lake City
2. **DORSEY & WHITNEY LLP** Salt Lake City
   JONES WALDO HOLBROOK Salt Lake City
   PARR WADDOUPS BROWN GEE Salt Lake City
   WILSON SONSINI GOODRICH Salt Lake City
3. **BALLARD SPAHR ANDREWS** Salt Lake City
   HOLLAND & HART LLP Salt Lake City
   SNELL & WILMER LLP Salt Lake City
4. **HOLME ROBERTS & OWEN LLP** Salt Lake City
   PARSONS BEHLE & LATIMER PC Salt Lake City

Leading individuals (Corporate/M&A)

1. POELMAN Ronald *Jones Waldo Holbrook*, Salt Lake City
   TAYLOR Nolan *Dorsey & Whitney LLP*, Salt Lake City
2. ANDERSON Chris *Snell & Wilmer LLP*, Salt Lake City
   LLOYD Brian *Stoel Rives LLP*, Salt Lake City
   LOVELESS Scott *Parr Waddoups Brown*, Salt Lake City
   O'CONNOR Robert *Wilson Sonsini*, Salt Lake City
3. MOFFITT Ronald *Stoel Rives LLP*, Salt Lake City
   RUDD David *Ballard Spahr Andrews*, Salt Lake City
   TAYLOR Tom *Holme Roberts & Owen*, Salt Lake City
4. ANGERBAUER David *Holland & Hart*, Salt Lake City
   HANSEN Gordon *Parsons Behle & Latimer*, Salt Lake City
   LINDLEY Greg *Holland & Hart LLP*, Salt Lake City
   LITTLE David *Holme Roberts & Owen*, Salt Lake City
   WILSON Randon *Jones Waldo Holbrook*, Salt Lake City

Firms and individuals are listed alphabetically in each band.

Stoel Rives LLP

The Firm: The firm was unanimously recommended by rivals for having a *"large, deep and strong"* corporate practice with a *"first-rate team of lawyers."* The group's focus is on corporate securities and finance work. An envied client roster includes two of Utah's largest corporations: Huntsman Packaging and Huntsman Chemical.
The Lawyers: The firm's standout attorney is **Brian Lloyd**, who won plaudits from peers for his *"outstanding"* securities work. Seen to be gaining stature in the market, Lloyd maintains a generalist practice focusing on corporate and securities work with a particular specialty in venture capital financing. His impressive résumé includes the representation of venture capital firms in a number of transactions, and activity for corporate clients in acquisitions and joint venture agreements. *"Top transactional lawyer"* **Ronald Moffitt** was recommended to researchers for his expertise in *"huge dollar amount"* M&A deals. As former general counsel to Huntsman Packaging, Moffitt brings substantial *"business know-how"* to the negotiating table. Much of his practice is devoted to national and international M&A transactions.
The Clients: Huntsman Chemical; Huntsman Packaging; SkyWest Airlines; Intermountain Health Care and PacifiCorp.

Dorsey & Whitney LLP

The Firm: Commentators agree that this global firm can *"draw on broad resources."* Although the Salt Lake office houses only eight attorneys, the firm boasts 750 attorneys worldwide. Widely recommended for its transactional capacities, the group here commands strength in M&A, IP and capital markets.
The Lawyers: Spearheading the team, **Nolan Taylor** was consistently recommended as an *"accomplished"* corporate lawyer with an edge over competitors for complex securities work. Clients appreciate his *"conscientious"* approach and *"good bedside manner."* His work in capital markets and M&A centers on the representation of buyers and sellers of private and public companies. He advised Nu Skin Asia Pacific in connection with its IPO in the US and Japan, and Mity-Lite on its flotation. He also represents numerous venture capital funds such as vSpring Capital and Peterson Capital in private equity investments.
The Clients: Source One Services; HealthRider; Inkleys; Trebor and Monroc.

Jones Waldo Holbrook & McDonough PC

The Firm: The firm gained high marks from interviewees for its concentration of *"highly skilled lawyers."* The 15-strong corporate team was widely recommended for its broad coverage of the market. A niche in the representation of hi-tech companies complements its general corporate practice.
The Lawyers: Front runner **Ronald Poelman** was said by market sources to be a *"key name on every client's list."* He combines experience in hi-tech matters with a *"committed and honest"* approach, making him an *"ideal choice"* for the representation of new and emerging companies. Poelman advised Bonneville International in the $170 million acquisition of 15 radio stations from Simmons Media Group, and acted for Agilix Labs in a $1.5 million preferred stock investment and strategic alliance with Franklin Covey. Corporate group leader **Randon Wilson** was praised as *"the agriculture cooperative guy;"* his national M&A practice focuses extensively on their representation. Noted by peers to *"love what he does,"* Wilson acts for sugar beet, potato and sugar cane growers, among others.
The Clients: Scottish Power; Albertson's; Wells Fargo; Salt Lake Tribune; Document Control Systems; FutureSmart; System Connection; Amirsys; IBC Technologies and emerging companies in new technology sectors.

CORPORATE/M&A — UTAH

Parr Waddoups Brown Gee & Loveless
The Firm: The firm is consistently recognized by peers and clients for its sophisticated corporate work. Specialties include M&A, airplane finance, tax & estate planning and securities.
The Lawyers: Market sources referred to **Scott Loveless** as *"the top M&A guy in town."* This *"levelheaded"* attorney is said to possess *"an excellent business, as well as legal, mind."* His recent representations include the $155 million sale of a public company.
The Clients: SkyWest Airlines; Franklin Covey; Kinross Gold; Workers Compensation Fund; The Boyer Company and Huntsman Corporation.

Wilson Sonsini Goodrich & Rosati
The Firm: This national firm, headquartered in Palo Alto CA, is a relatively new entry to the Utah market. The firm is a traditional heavyweight in venture capital and with technology and emerging industry companies. Market sources praised the Salt Lake City office for its provision of *"first-rate service backed by extensive resources."*
The Lawyers: Managing partner of the Salt Lake City office **Robert O'Connor** was repeatedly endorsed by peers as *"the go-to guy for IPOs."* Clients praised him as *"accessible and easy to work with."* His practice focuses on emerging companies with a heavy emphasis on software and IT firms. O'Connor advised on the flotations of both Altiris and Overstock.com.
The Clients: NPS Pharmaceuticals; Huntsman Biotechnology and Merit Medical Systems.

Ballard Spahr Andrews & Ingersoll LLP
see firm details p.769
The Firm: Recommended by market sources for its *"great reputation in bond financing,"* this firm has over 450 lawyers in seven offices located in five Mid-Atlantic States as well as Colorado and Utah.
The Lawyers: Market sources endorsed **David Rudd** for his *"international experience"* and expertise in corporate securities. His practice encompasses M&A, securities, energy project finance and general corporate matters. He has experience representing US companies in their acquisition of both foreign and domestic companies, and is well known in the market for his extensive work in Latin America.
The Clients: Flying J; 1-800 Contacts; Nature's Sunshine Products; Nu Skin Enterprises; Wasatch Venture Funds and Kennecott Utah Copper.

Holland & Hart LLP
see firm details p.819
The Firm: The firm's corporate practice was lauded for its *"depth of expertise"* and sizable stable of strong attorneys. The Salt Lake City office focuses on representing start-up companies in the biotech, software and telecom arenas. The group covers all aspects of M&A, private equity transactions and corporate securities.
The Lawyers: Head of the corporate group **David Angerbauer** (see p.690) has established a solid *"all-round"* corporate practice with an emphasis on securities work. He acted as US securities corporate and antitrust counsel for Franco-Nevada Mining in its acquisition by Newmont Mining, which had also bought Normandy Mining. **Greg Lindley** (see p.690) was also noted for his comprehensive knowledge of securities law.
The Clients: First National of America; TheraDoc; Phonex Broadband and IKANO Communications.

Snell & Wilmer LLP
The Firm: Firmwide, Snell Wilmer boasts 360 attorneys in six offices throughout the western US. Interviewees recommended the Salt Lake City practice for its solid corporate work and strength in securities and M&A.
The Lawyers: Winning respect from market sources, **Chris Anderson** was praised as a *"great lawyer and individual."* Peers cited Anderson's experience in venture capital transactions for emerging companies.
The Clients: Evans & Sutherland Computer; Albertson's; Bank of Utah; Voicestream Wireless and 3M. Fortune 500 companies, emerging businesses and individual entrepreneurs are also clients.

Holme Roberts & Owen LLP
The Firm: Headquartered in Denver, this regional firm was felt to owe much of its reputation in the area to the strong individual profiles of Tom Taylor and David Little. The practice covers M&A, debt financing, real estate and general business ownership transfers.
The Lawyers: A recent addition to the firm, **Tom Taylor** was commended by peers as a *"diligent corporate attorney"* who specializes in M&A, private equity and venture capital. Clients called him a *"top-notch advocate,"* and praised his *"fair"* approach and sense of humor. Market sources also recommend **David Little** as a *"smart and thorough"* attorney who has a busy practice in securities and corporate compliance.
The Clients: Qwest; Huntsman Chemical and Intermountain Power Agency.

Parsons Behle & Latimer PC
The Firm: One of the oldest and best-known law firms in the region, this firm was recommended as *"a name in the corporate transactional field."*
The Lawyers: Market sources identified **Gordon Hansen** as a *"strong transactional corporate and tax lawyer."* Hansen's experience includes M&A, financings, corporate reorganizations and federal income tax matters.
The Clients: Canopy Group; Sarcos; First Community Bank; Kennecott; AT&T and Wal-Mart.

EMPLOYMENT & LABOR LAW — MAINLY PLAINTIFF

UTAH
Leading firms
(Employment: Mainly Plaintiff)
1. HOOLE & KING *Salt Lake City*
   STRINDBERG & SCHOLNICK *Salt Lake City*
2. WILDE & ASSOCIATES *Midvale*

Firms are listed alphabetically in each band.

Hoole & King
The Firm: This small firm was cited by employers and employees as *"one of the top choices for referrals in Utah."* **Roger Hoole**, described as *"a tiger on employment litigation cases,"* and his small team were warmly praised for their expertise in Title VII cases, sexual harassment and sex and race discrimination claims and some preventative work.

Strindberg & Scholnick
The Firm: *"A famous name for the weighty cases,"* **Erik Strindberg** enjoys recognition by the market for his extensive experience and successful track record on employment matters. After nearly ten years practicing in a small Utah firm, Strindberg founded his own firm in 2002 with partner Lauren Scholnick. Devoted almost exclusively to representing employees, the two-partner practice was described as *"one of the busiest in town."*

UTAH — EMPLOYMENT & LABOR LAW

UTAH
Leading individuals
(Employment: Mainly Plaintiff)

1 HOOLE Roger *Hoole & King*, Salt Lake City
  STRINDBERG Erik *Strindberg & Scholnick*, Salt Lake City
2 WILDE Robert *Wilde & Associates*, Midvale

Individuals are listed alphabetically in each band.

EMPLOYMENT & LABOR LAW — MAINLY DEFENDANT

UTAH
Leading firms
(Employment: Mainly Defendant)

1 JONES WALDO HOLBROOK Salt Lake City
  RAY, QUINNEY & NEBEKER PC Salt Lake City
2 HOLME ROBERTS & OWEN LLP Salt Lake City
  JANOVE BAAR ASSOCIATES Salt Lake City
  PARSONS BEHLE & LATIMER PC Salt Lake City

Leading individuals
(Employment: Mainly Defendant)

1 SMITH Janet *Ray, Quinney*, Salt Lake City
2 BAAR Lois *Janove Baar Associates*, Salt Lake City
  DUNNING Elizabeth *Holme Roberts*, Salt Lake City
  O'BRIEN Michael *Jones Waldo Holbrook*, Salt Lake City

Firms and individuals are listed alphabetically in each band.

Wilde & Associates
The Firm: *"First-tier"* **Robert Wilde** was warmly rated by employers and employees in Utah as *"a high-profile lawyer doing effective work."* Supported by two associates, Wilde has acted in major employment litigation cases for plaintiffs across the state. Although the firm mainly represents employees, it also occasionally advises small companies. Regarded as one of the best niche practices of its size, the firm is said to be *"excellent for wrongful discrimination cases and constitutional torts."*

Jones Waldo Holbrook & McDonough PC
The Firm: The employment department here earns unanimous peer endorsement as *"a deep practice led by experienced lawyers."* Its extensive resources and long tradition of handling employment litigation places the large team among the best regarded in the field. The firm acts for clients in the financial, retail and manufacturing sectors. Famed practitioner **Michael O'Brien** was identified to researchers as *"the firm's best asset."* Boasting long experience in the field, O'Brien focuses on individual employment rights, employee benefits, wage and hour issues and counseling. He recently participated in an employment audit of a national retail company with over 100,000 employees.

Ray, Quinney & Nebeker PC
The Firm: Commentators in the market agree that this Salt Lake City firm is *"a major player in the employment law sphere."* The group's workload is divided between preventative counseling and employment litigation matters. Niche strengths include Title VII actions, ADA, ADEA and wrongful termination claims. Much of the firm's profile lies with **Janet Hugie Smith**, who was described by contemporaries as *"an exceptional litigator on all aspects of the law."* Said to be *"practicing longer than anyone else in Utah,"* this *"wonderful lawyer"* has undertaken major cases before the Utah Supreme Court.

Holme Roberts & Owen LLP
The Firm: Well known for its litigation prowess, the firm has successfully expanded beyond its Denver base to become a *"serious competitor"* in the Rocky Mountain region. The Salt Lake City employment group enjoys an excellent reputation in the state, largely thanks to the presence of **Elizabeth Dunning**. A *"prolific practitioner,"* Dunning commands almost 25 years' experience in employment law. One rival commented: *"She is good at everything she does - from litigation to arbitration."* Interviewees noted in particular her experience in discrimination and wrongful termination suits, in which she acts on behalf of healthcare and manufacturing clients. Dunning also has niche expertise in educational institutions cases. In the past year, she represented an education institution in a disability discrimination case and defended a Utah employer against sexual harassment claims before a federal court.

Janove Baar Associates
The Firm: A boutique firm with a respected niche practice representing employers. Founded in 2001, the firm gained peer approval for *"playing a major role despite its small size."* With years of experience in the field, the team primarily stands out for *"litigating employment cases with superb results."* A well-known name for management training work, it also provides arbitration, mediation and counseling advice. Although occasionally acting on the plaintiff side, the team primarily represents small and mid-sized companies across a range of industries. Former partner at Parsons, Behle & Latimer, **Lois Baar** was acclaimed by interviewees as a *"brilliant trial lawyer"* and gained plaudits for her *"consistently successful career."*

Parsons Behle & Latimer PC
The Firm: Adjudged *"a long-established practice,"* this firm's strength lies in its concentration of quality attorneys. Eighteen lawyers offer a wide range of expertise in employment litigation and preventative counseling as well as in OSHA and MSHA matters. Operating in support of the corporate and litigation practice, the group is visible advising on a large number of discrimination and wrongful discharge claims. While the emphasis is on employer representation, the practice, led by David Anderson, also undertakes a significant amount of work for employees. The firm obtained a dismissal of age discrimination charges brought against a store chain before the Utah Labor Commission. It also successfully defended Sprint against claims of sexual harassment, retaliation, promissory and constructive discharge. Kennecott Utah Copper, Barrick Gold and the Management & Training Corporation are clients.

LITIGATION — GENERAL COMMERCIAL

Bendinger, Crockett Peterson & Casey
The Firm: This 15-attorney litigation boutique enjoys a *"top-flight"* market reputation for complex commercial litigation. High-profile work in the $100 million range sets it apart from local competitors. Attorneys here also have considerable litigation experience defending the Big Five accounting firms in securities litigation. The firm was counsel to the State of Utah in litigation against the major tobacco companies, and represented the Discover Bank credit card in a major jury verdict case against Visa.

The Lawyers: Gary Bendinger (see p.690) earned widespread praise as the *"top guy in town*

LITIGATION — UTAH

UTAH
Leading firms
(Litigation: General Commercial)

1
- BENDINGER, CROCKETT PETERSON — Salt Lake City
- BURBIDGE & MITCHELL — Salt Lake City
- RAY, QUINNEY & NEBEKER PC — Salt Lake City
- SNELL & WILMER LLP — Salt Lake City

2
- PARSONS BEHLE & LATIMER PC — Salt Lake City

3
- BERMAN, GAUFIN, TOMSIC, SAVAGE — Salt Lake City
- HOLME ROBERTS & OWEN LLP — Salt Lake City
- PARR WADDOUPS BROWN GEE — Salt Lake City
- STOEL RIVES LLP — Salt Lake City
- VAN COTT, BAGLEY, CORNWALL — Salt Lake City

4
- FABIAN & CLENDENIN — Salt Lake City

Leading individuals
(Litigation: General Commercial)

1
- BENDINGER Gary — *Bendinger, Crockett*, Salt Lake City
- BURBIDGE Richard — *Burbidge & Mitchell*, Salt Lake City
- JARDINE James — *Ray, Quinney & Nebeker*, Salt Lake City
- SULLIVAN Alan — *Snell & Wilmer LLP*, Salt Lake City

2
- CAMPBELL Robert — *Van Cott, Bagley*, Salt Lake City
- WIKSTROM Francis — *Parsons Behle*, Salt Lake City

3
- ETCHEVERRY Raymond — *Parsons Behle*, Salt Lake City
- GREENWOOD David — *Van Cott, Bagley*, Salt Lake City
- HALEY George — *Holme Roberts & Owen*, Salt Lake City
- JORDAN David — *Stoel Rives LLP*, Salt Lake City

4
- BERMAN Daniel — *Berman, Gaufin, Tomsic*, Salt Lake City
- BILLINGS Peter — *Fabian & Clendenin*, Salt Lake City
- CLARK Robert — *Parr Waddoups Brown*, Salt Lake City
- WADDOUPS Clark — *Parr Waddoups Brown*, Salt Lake City

Firms and individuals are listed alphabetically in each band.

---

defending major accounting firms." His practice focuses on complex, commercial litigation in such areas as antitrust and securities. Known for his *"tough, aggressive"* style, Bendinger was recommended for his *"thoroughness"* and the *"excellent results"* he achieves in complex cases. He recently acted as lead counsel on a dispute between two competing newspapers regarding an option to acquire The Salt Lake Tribune.

The Clients: Arthur Andersen; KPMG; Ernst & Young; Deloitte & Touche; AT&T; Bonneville International; Bridgestone/Firestone; Comdata; Delta Air Lines; E Excel International; Huntsman Packaging; GECC; Intermountain Health Care; I-Link; Katy Industries; TCI Telecommunications and Union Pacific Railroad.

Burbidge & Mitchell
The Firm: Described by interviewees as a *"small shop with a big reputation,"* this five-attorney litigation boutique earned high marks for its work in complex commercial disputes. Areas of emphasis include securities fraud, antitrust, banking and real estate matters.

The Lawyers: *"Creative"* attorney **Dick Burbidge** earned high praise for his excellence in commercial litigation matters. *"Wonderful in the courtroom,"* Burbidge was applauded for his experience and *"street smarts."* Peers agreed that his effective style is complemented by his reputation for trustworthiness. He recently won a $20 million verdict in a patent suit as plaintiffs' counsel for a Utah company.

The Clients: The firm acts for large and small businesses, national and local concerns and prominent individuals.

Ray, Quinney & Nebeker PC
The Firm: One of the oldest and largest law firms in Utah and the Intermountain West region. The firm has over 80 attorneys in its principal office in Salt Lake City. Interviewees commended the firm as a good, local full-service practice with particular strength in business litigation. Products liability, employment and IP litigation are core areas of focus.

The Lawyers: The practice's standout attorney is **Jim Jardine**, who was recommended to researchers as *"one of the key litigators in town."* Clients referred to him as an *"excellent strategist"* who manages complex commercial litigation with ease. This *"superb"* lawyer, peers said, is a *"pleasure to work with, and against."* His practice covers antitrust, securities, commercial and IP litigation. Jardine is currently acting in high-profile litigation over the ownership of The Salt Lake Tribune newspaper. Other notable work includes the representation of a Wall Street investment firm in an investigation by the State of Utah of the firm's investment practices.

The Clients: Wells Fargo; CR England & Sons; OC Tanner; Utah Transit Authority and Marriott International.

Snell & Wilmer LLP
The Firm: Market sources agree that the 40-lawyer Salt Lake City practice of this large regional firm is *"one of the top business litigation firms in the area."* Niche strength exists in relation to products liability litigation.

The Lawyers: Distinguished for both his *"thorough preparation"* and *"analytical mind,"* **Alan Sullivan** commands extensive experience representing healthcare providers, corporate clients and academic institutions. He appears in front of federal and state courts on a broad range of matters, and is said to possess *"enormous credibility with judges and lawyers."* Recent highlights include a dispute between AT&T and The Salt Lake Tribune Publishing Company regarding the sale of a subsidiary, and the defense of insurance company State Farm in a class action suit.

The Clients: Evans & Sutherland Computer; Albertson's; Bank of Utah; Voicestream Wireless and 3M.

Parsons Behle & Latimer PC
The Firm: This 120-year-old firm boasts one of the largest and broadest litigation departments in the area. The group has a heavy emphasis on representing clients in the mining and natural resources industries in matters such as environmental, mining and toxic tort litigation.

The Lawyers: Francis Wikstrom and **Raymond Etcheverry** were recommended as *"the two top attorneys at the firm,"* having followed in the footsteps of legendary litigator Gordon Roberts. Wikstrom was warmly commended as an *"energetic, experienced and effective"* practitioner. His general commercial litigation practice is particularly developed in the areas of IP and insurance coverage litigation and toxic tort defense. He is currently working on a number of patent cases and recently settled a very large toxic tort matter. Etcheverry also received consistent recognition as an excellent litigator with broad range of experience.

The Clients: Baker Hughes; American Express; AT&T; Bank One; Barrick Gold; BSD Medical; El Paso; Delta Air Lines; Duke Energy; Kennecott Utah Copper; Lodestar Energy; Merrill Lynch; Petro Source; Salomon Smith Barney; Sarcos; Utah Associated Municipal Power and Wal-Mart.

Berman, Gaufin, Tomsic, Savage & Campbell
The Firm: Specializing in complex litigation and trial practice, this 12-lawyer business litigation firm owes much of its reputation in the market to name partner Daniel Berman.

The Lawyers: Viewed as a *"tough competitor,"* **Daniel Berman** employs a *"hard-nosed"* litigation style in commercial disputes and antitrust litigation. Highlights of his practice include obtaining a $90 million present value benefits award for PacifiCorp in a long-running coal contract dispute.

Holme Roberts & Owen LLP
The Firm: Headquartered in Denver, this 50-attorney firm has a strong focus on corporate representation of clients in the natural resources, hi-tech and communications industries.

The Lawyers: George Haley was singled out as a *"polished courtroom performer."* His commercial litigation experience includes extensive class action work as well as high-end securities cases for both plaintiffs and defendants. Haley recently secured a $110 million counterclaim for Questar Corporation after obtaining a dismissal of plaintiffs' claims.

The Clients: Coors Brewing Co; Burlington Resources; Citibank Private Bank; Hanifen, HealthONE; Intermountain Power Agency; Merrill Lynch; Paige Sports Entertainment; Qwest; US Olympic Committee and UnitedGlobalCom.

UTAH — LITIGATION

Parr Waddoups Brown Gee & Loveless
The Firm: This comprehensive business and litigation firm has 25 attorneys handling commercial disputes and corporate litigation. Attorneys here have experience advising on a range of claims related to securities, IP, antitrust, construction, products liability and environmental law.
The Lawyers: The most senior litigator at the firm, **Clark Waddoups** maintains a varied practice encompassing alternative dispute resolution, securities and IP litigation. Rivals endorse him as *"experienced, thorough and intelligent."* Waddoups defended Kinross Gold in a securities class action suit brought by stockholders. Said to be *"effective at organizing complex facts and getting to the heart of the matter,"* **Robert Clark** received client and peer praise for his commercial litigation practice and niche expertise in class actions and securities litigation.
The Clients: The firm acts for local and national companies and clients in such industries as manufacturing, broadcasting, banking and finance, automotive, oil and gas, and real estate.

Stoel Rives LLP
The Firm: A large regional law firm with 49 lawyers in its Salt Lake City branch. Much of the litigation group's profile rests with David Jordan.
The Lawyers: *"Smart and talented"* **David Jordan** was recommended to researchers for his litigation abilities and *"high IQ."* He has represented businesses and individuals in a wide variety of civil matters, including employment, IP, environmental, mining and securities cases.
The Clients: Chevron USA; Delta Air Lines; Huntsman Chemical; Interwest Mining; Johnson & Johnson; KeyBank National Association; Maverik Country Stores; Mrs Fields Cookies and Wasatch Oil & Gas.

Van Cott, Bagley, Cornwall & McCarthy
The Firm: This *"old, established "* Utah firm has offices in Salt Lake City, Ogden, and Park City. A 20-litigator general commercial trial practice has experience handling major government contract cases.
The Lawyers: Recommended to researchers as an *"indefatigable fighter who gets good results,"* **Robert Campbell** handles a range of antitrust, securities and commercial fraud cases, partnership disputes and commercial real property litigation. Campbell recovered a $7.1 million judgment involving punitive damages in a major commercial fraud real property matter, and represented a large international trucking company in a fraud case. **David Greenwood**, chair of the firm's litigation section, was endorsed by peers as a *"sound ethical lawyer."* Greenwood has represented clients in most types of complex civil litigation matters including mass condemnation, construction and arbitration.
The Clients: Deer Valley Resort; Delta Air Lines; Chevron; Citicorp; Huntsman Chemical; Intermountain Health Care; Lockheed Martin; 3M; NationsBank USA; New York Life; United Communications Group and Utah Association of Municipal Power Systems (UAMPS).

Fabian & Clendenin
The Firm: This full-service Utah firm has a 30-strong litigation department focusing primarily on business litigation. Areas covered include antitrust, insurance litigation and IP.
The Lawyers: Lauded as an *"able trial attorney,"* **Peter Billings** specializes in bankruptcy, professional malpractice and antitrust law. He was particularly commended for his skill in insolvency proceedings. Recent work includes representing Steiner Corporation in an antitrust class action case.
The Clients: JR Simplot Company; 7-Eleven; IBM; Qwest; The Campbell Soup Company; Chase Manhattan Bank and Ford.

REAL ESTATE

UTAH
Leading firms (Real Estate)

1. PARR WADDOUPS BROWN GEE *Salt Lake City*
   STOEL RIVES LLP *Salt Lake City*
2. JONES WALDO HOLBROOK *Salt Lake City*
3. KIRTON & MCCONKIE *Salt Lake City*
   PARSONS BEHLE & LATIMER PC *Salt Lake City*
   VAN COTT, BAGLEY, CORNWALL *Salt Lake City*
4. BALLARD SPAHR ANDREWS *Salt Lake City*
   FABIAN & CLENDENIN *Salt Lake City*
   RAY, QUINNEY & NEBEKER PC *Salt Lake City*
   SNELL & WILMER LLP *Salt Lake City*

Firms are listed alphabetically in each band.

Parr Waddoups Brown Gee & Loveless
The Firm: According to market sources, the firm's real estate practice handles many of the state's top-end real estate deals, and is doing *"great work for major developers."* The group handles a range of general real estate matters with a focus on zoning issues and the representation of contractors in disputes, land use planning and leasing transactions.
The Lawyers: **Charles Maak** is regarded by commentators as *"the dean of real estate law in Utah."* Sources describe him as *"thorough, meticulous and reasonable in negotiation,"* with a forceful yet *"honest"* style. He has represented many big lenders and developers in transactions involving shopping centers, office buildings, warehouse properties and condominiums. *"Superb real estate litigator,"* **Bruce Maak** concentrates on title insurance litigation, representing title insurers and their insured. Peers praise him as a *"hard negotiator with a broad range of experience."* **David Gee** was widely endorsed as a *"top real estate attorney"* who is *"always willing to make the deal work well for both sides."* He represents a number of developers and has niche expertise in federal taxation of real estate transactions and municipal finance. Gee recently acted for developers in a $400 million retail office project, and in 12 strip mall shopping center projects.
The Clients: The Boyer Company; The Rouse Companies; DAKCS Software Systems; Sun Life Assurance Company; Wal-Mart and the University of Utah.

Stoel Rives LLP
The Firm: Market sources were unanimous in rating this *"one of the top real estate law firms in Utah."* It focuses on land use issues, acquisitions, financing, and large-scale community and resort development. Its planning and zoning work was particularly praised.
The Lawyers: Peers and clients consistently praised **Thomas Ellison**. His experience in zoning and land use planning is particularly admired, with some interviewees dubbing him *"the leader in this practice area, and a great attorney overall."* His core work includes development, land use approvals and financing. Two current projects include Deer Crest, a ski resort in Deer Valley, and Promontory, a golf resort community. According to peers, **Ervin Holmes** has *"great integrity,"* which makes him *"the type of person clients respect."* Clients themselves praise Holmes' *"thorough and knowledgeable"* approach. He acts in real estate transactions, leasing, title work and financing, and recently assisted a large convenience store chain in buying out all Circle K retail outlets in Utah.
The Clients: Geneva Rock Products and Maverik Country Stores are also clients.

Jones Waldo Holbrook & McDonough PC
The Firm: The real estate team at this full-service law firm wins high praise from clients and peers. It acts in a range of real estate financing and management matters, and has niches in representing anchor tenants in shopping center acquisitions, and in multi-family housing. It recently helped

REAL ESTATE | UTAH

UTAH
Leading individuals (Real Estate)

[1]
- ELLISON Thomas *Stoel Rives LLP,* Salt Lake City
- GEE David *Parr Waddoups Brown Gee,* Salt Lake City
- MAAK Charles *Parr Waddoups Brown Gee,* Salt Lake City
- MORRILL Denis *Kirton & McConkie,* Salt Lake City

[2]
- BERGGREN Thomas *Jones Waldo,* Salt Lake City
- COOK Rand *Van Cott, Bagley, Cornwall,* Salt Lake City
- HELLEWELL Read *Kirton & McConkie,* Salt Lake City
- MAAK Bruce *Parr Waddoups Brown Gee,* Salt Lake City
- MOORE Larry *Ray, Quinney & Nebeker,* Salt Lake City

[3]
- BANKS Diane *Fabian & Clendenin,* Salt Lake City
- FERRIN Shawn *Parsons Behle & Latimer,* Salt Lake City
- HOLMES Ervin *Stoel Rives LLP,* Salt Lake City
- JONES Cary *Snell & Wilmer LLP,* Salt Lake City
- ROWE Keven *Jones Waldo Holbrook,* Salt Lake City
- WILLIAMS Gregory *Van Cott, Bagley,* Salt Lake City

Individuals are listed alphabetically in each band.

acquire 15 sites for big box retailers and represented a public company in negotiating a deal for an office development.

The Lawyers: Thomas Berggren chairs the firm's real estate practice group, and is active in real estate purchases and sales, leasing and financing. Sources describe him as *"responsive to clients' needs, scholarly and detail-oriented."* He recently advised on the acquisition of two distribution centers, valued at $800,000 and $1.2 million, and assisted with the sale of a $10 million office building. **Keven Rowe** gained high marks from observers for his work on behalf of Wells Fargo. His practice is focused on commercial real estate and real estate finance.

The Clients: Albertson's and Target Corporation are also clients.

Kirton & McConkie

The Firm: The firm gains high marks from observers for its work on behalf of The Church of Jesus Christ of Latter-day Saints. It offers a wide range of services covering everything from residential to major commercial developments. Typical work includes purchases and sales, project development and financing.

The Lawyers: "Leading player" **Denis Morrill** was said by peers to be *"dependable and highly expert."* He handles large-scale transactions for buyers and sellers, and is involved in planning and zoning matters and work with lenders. Another strong member of the team, **Read Hellewell** was recommended by sources for *"getting the job done instead of arguing about irrelevant things."* His practice is focused on commercial lending, leasing and the development and operation of condominium and timeshare projects.

The Clients: Along with The Church of Jesus Christ of Latter-day Saints, the firm acts for: Associated Food Stores; Boston Mutual Life Insurance; Farm Management Company; Craig Gasser & Associates; Harmon City; Ralph L Wadsworth Construction; Utah Industrial Depot and Zions Securities Corporation.

Parsons Behle & Latimer PC

The Firm: This is one of the oldest and largest firms in Utah. It is considered by some to be *"up there with the best of them in public land development."*

The Lawyers: Shawn Ferrin has a name as a *"talented lawyer with a breadth of experience in resort development."* Much of his work involves the acquisition, development and financing of ski resorts.

The Clients: Amsource Realty; Wolf Creek Properties; Nationwide Life Insurance; Allstate and Jackson National Life Insurance.

Van Cott, Bagley, Cornwall & McCarthy

The Firm: This long-established player in the real estate market maintains its principal practice in Salt Lake City. The team acts on a range of deals, but received particular endorsement for its work in secured financing.

The Lawyers: Rand Cook won high praise from peers and clients alike. Peers envy his *"volume of institutional clients"* and experience of *"big dollar real estate mortgage loans,"* while clients admire his *"attention to detail."* He represents lenders, developers, landlords and tenants, and is active in resort development. Recent work includes the foreclosure and resale of a major hotel. Another recognized member of the team is **Gregory Williams**, who possesses a *"well-rounded, quality practice."*

The Clients: The firm's clients include ski resorts, pension funds, real estate developers and management companies, banks and savings institutions, healthcare companies, sand and gravel operations and insurance companies.

Ballard Spahr Andrews & Ingersoll LLP
see firm details p.769

The Firm: This firm wins respect from market sources for its *"overall strength and top-rank clientele."* It is active in a broad range of traditional real estate work, including development, purchases and sales, and zoning.

The Lawyers: The real estate group includes Steve Peterson, Harry McCoy II and Thomas Bennett.

Fabian & Clendenin

The Firm: This prominent firm boasts a real estate group of six. Its broad expertise includes representing lenders, developers, owners, landlords and tenants in a range of real property transactions, many of them involving complex financing. It has assisted a developer in a 2200-acre master-planned community with two golf courses and in 3000 housing and commercial units.

The Lawyers: Commentators agree that *"patient, dogged and careful"* **Diane Banks** stands out from this team. She is said to be picking up the baton from the esteemed George Melling. The team recently assisted a group of beet growers in acquiring and financing a processing plant.

The Clients: 7-Eleven; Sun Pacific Farming; National Food Processors Association; GE and Wasatch Constructors.

Ray, Quinney & Nebeker PC

The Firm: This is one of the largest firms in the state. Its real estate department handles transactions and related litigation, and receives strong support from the firm's other departments.

The Lawyers: Much of the credit for the high profile of the firm's real estate practice rests with **Larry Moore**. Sources praise both his *"expertise and major deal experience."* He represents ski resorts, grocery store chains and real estate developers, among others.

The Clients: Bank of America; Brian Head Ski Resort; CIGNA Investments; Smith's Food & Drug Centers; Solitude Ski Corporation; University of Utah; Washington Mutual and Wells Fargo.

Snell & Wilmer LLP

The Firm: The firm draws on the strength and resources of six offices throughout the western US. Interviewees noted that it has acted in a wealth of large real estate transactions. These include representing a joint venture of two rock promoters in the development of an amphitheater concert venue.

The Lawyers: Cary Jones was endorsed as *"a deal-maker."* He represented the buyer in the largest acquisition in Utah for the commuter rail project, and handled all the hotel acquisitions connected with Park City Mountain Resort.

The Clients: Individuals, developers, financial institutions, and national and international firms are clients.

UTAH

Leaders in Utah

ANDERSON, Chris
Snell & Wilmer LLP, Salt Lake City
801 257 1900
Recommended in Corporate/M&A

ANGERBAUER, David
Holland & Hart LLP, Salt Lake City
801 595 7808
dangerbauer@hollandhart.com
Recommended in Corporate/M&A
Specialization: Partner practicing in securities, venture capital, technology, and M&A. Represents a wide range of clients, including start-ups, emerging growth businesses, and public companies (United States and foreign). Has counseled both issuers and underwriters in more than two billion dollars of public and private equity and debt offerings, including US and international financings. Significant experience working with regional and national investment banking and venture capital firms in connection with venture capital financing, initial public offerings, secondary offerings, mergers, and acquisitions.
Prof. Memberships: Business Law Section, Utah State Bar (President, 1993-94); Utah Chapter, National Association of Stock Plan Professionals (President, 1993-96); MountainWest Venture Group (Chairman, 2001-present; Vice Chairman, 1999-2000; President,1997-98; Vice President, 1995-96), Securities Section and Business Law Section, Utah State Bar, Section of Business Law, American Bar Association.
Career: Admitted to the Utah Bar (1986).
Personal: Received a JD from the University of Utah (1986, Order of the Coif, William H Leary Scholar), an MBA (1986, Gertrude T Peterson Scholarship) and a BA from the University of Utah (Finance, 1982).

BAAR, Lois
Janove Baar Associates, Salt Lake City
801 530 0404
Recommended in Employment

BANKS, Diane
Fabian & Clendenin, Salt Lake City 801 531 8900
Recommended in Real Estate

BENDINGER, Gary F
Bendinger, Crockett Peterson & Casey, Salt Lake City 801 533 8383
gfb@bcpclaw.com
Recommended in Litigation
Specialization: Practices in complex commercial litigation in federal courts throughout the United States. His experience involves securities, antitrust and intellectual property litigation involving claims for hundreds of millions of dollars.
Prof. Memberships: Is a Fellow in the American College of Trial Lawyers and has been consistently recognized by the a leading publication in the area of Commercial Litigation. Is a member of the State Bar of Utah, the American Bar Association, and has been admitted to practice before the United States Supreme Court, The United States Court of Appeals for the Ninth and Tenth Circuits and numerous federal and state courts.
Career: Started his career by representing plaintiffs in federal antitrust litigation and has since represented both plaintiffs and defendants in complex commercial litigation involving important issues and claims for substantial monetary damages. Has tried successfully numerous cases to jury verdict. Was recently recognized by Utah Business as one of the most feared litigators in the State of Utah.

BERGGREN, Thomas
Jones Waldo Holbrook & McDonough PC, Salt Lake City 801 521 3200
Recommended in Real Estate

BERMAN, Daniel
Berman, Gaufin, Tomsic, Savage & Campbell, Salt Lake City 801 328 2200
Recommended in Litigation

BILLINGS, Peter
Fabian & Clendenin, Salt Lake City
801 531 8900
Recommended in Litigation

BURBIDGE, Richard
Burbidge & Mitchell, Salt Lake City
803 355 6677
Recommended in Litigation

CAMPBELL, Robert
Van Cott, Bagley, Cornwall & McCarthy, Salt Lake City 801 532 3333
Recommended in Litigation

CLARK, Robert
Parr Waddoups Brown Gee & Loveless, Salt Lake City 801 532 7840
Recommended in Litigation

COOK, Rand
Van Cott, Bagley, Cornwall & McCarthy, Salt Lake City 801 532 3333
Recommended in Real Estate

DUNNING, Elizabeth
Holme Roberts & Owen LLP, Salt Lake City 801 521 5800
Recommended in Employment

ELLISON, Thomas
Stoel Rives LLP, Salt Lake City
801 328 3131
Recommended in Real Estate

ETCHEVERRY, Raymond
Parsons Behle & Latimer PC, Salt Lake City 801 532 1234
Recommended in Litigation

FERRIN, Shawn
Parsons Behle & Latimer PC, Salt Lake City 801 532 1234
Recommended in Real Estate

GEE, David
Parr Waddoups Brown Gee & Loveless, Salt Lake City 801 532 7840
Recommended in Real Estate

GREENWOOD, David
Van Cott, Bagley, Cornwall & McCarthy, Salt Lake City 801 532 3333
Recommended in Litigation

HALEY, George
Holme Roberts & Owen LLP, Salt Lake City 801 521 5800
Recommended in Litigation

HANSEN, Gordon
Parsons Behle & Latimer PC, Salt Lake City 801 532 1234
Recommended in Corporate/M&A

HELLEWELL, Read
Kirton & McConkie, Salt Lake City
801 328 3600
Recommended in Real Estate

HOLMES, Ervin
Stoel Rives LLP, Salt Lake City
801 328 3131
Recommended in Real Estate

HOOLE, Roger
Hoole & King, Salt Lake City
801 272 7556
Recommended in Employment

JARDINE, James
Ray, Quinney & Nebeker PC, Salt Lake City 801 532 1500
Recommended in Litigation

JONES, Cary
Snell & Wilmer LLP, Salt Lake City
801 257 1900
Recommended in Real Estate

JORDAN, David
Stoel Rives LLP, Salt Lake City
801 328 3131
Recommended in Litigation

LINDLEY, Greg
Holland & Hart LLP, Salt Lake City
801 595 7829
glindley@hollandhart.com
Recommended in Corporate/M&A
Specialization: Partner who focuses his practice on securities law, mergers and acquisitions, and franchise law. Has worked on numerous public and private offerings of securities for a wide variety of clients, including medical diagnostic and equipment companies, real estate syndicators, and internet companies. Represents public companies in the compliance work required by the Securities and Exchange Act of 1934, including the preparation of Forms 10-K, 10-Q, and 8-K and proxy statements, and the Sarbanes-Oxley Act. Has represented both buyers and sellers in many mergers and acquisitions in a variety of industries, including food manufacture and distribution, banking, printing and publishing, insurance, mine drill bit manufacturing and servicing, and medical diagnostics. Has also represented franchisors in the restaurant, fixed-based airport service centers, and home security businesses in the preparation of franchise agreements and offering circulars. Has counseled many companies with organizational, executive compensation, and fundraising issues.
Prof. Memberships: Utah State Bar, State Bar of Texas.
Career: Admitted to the Texas (1983) and Utah (1988) Bar.
Personal: Received a JD from Duke University (1983), and an MBA (1981) and a BS (Biology, 1978) from Utah State University.

LITTLE, David
Holme Roberts & Owen LLP, Salt Lake City 801 521 5800
Recommended in Corporate/M&A

LLOYD, Brian
Stoel Rives LLP, Salt Lake City
801 328 3131
Recommended in Corporate/M&A

LOVELESS, Scott
Parr Waddoups Brown Gee & Loveless, Salt Lake City 801 532 7840
Recommended in Corporate/M&A

MAAK, Bruce
Parr Waddoups Brown Gee & Loveless, Salt Lake City 801 532 7840
Recommended in Real Estate

MAAK, Charles
Parr Waddoups Brown Gee & Loveless, Salt Lake City 801 532 7840
Recommended in Real Estate

MOFFITT, Ronald
Stoel Rives LLP, Salt Lake City
801 328 3131
Recommended in Corporate/M&A

MOORE, Larry
Ray, Quinney & Nebeker PC, Salt Lake City 801 532 1500
Recommended in Real Estate

MORRILL, Denis
Kirton & McConkie, Salt Lake City
801 328 3600
Recommended in Real Estate

O'BRIEN, Michael
Jones Waldo Holbrook & McDonough PC, Salt Lake City 801 521 3200
Recommended in Employment

O'CONNOR, Robert
Wilson Sonsini Goodrich & Rosati, Salt Lake City 801 993 6400
Recommended in Corporate/M&A

POELMAN, Ronald
Jones Waldo Holbrook & McDonough PC, Salt Lake City 801 521 3200
Recommended in Corporate/M&A

ROWE, Keven
Jones Waldo Holbrook & McDonough PC, Salt Lake City 801 521 3200
Recommended in Real Estate

RUDD, David
Ballard Spahr Andrews & Ingersoll LLP, Salt Lake City 801 531 3000
Recommended in Corporate/M&A

SMITH, Janet
Ray, Quinney & Nebeker PC, Salt Lake City 801 532 1500
Recommended in Employment

STRINDBERG, Erik
Strindberg & Scholnick, Salt Lake City 801 359 4169
Recommended in Employment

SULLIVAN, Alan
Snell & Wilmer LLP, Salt Lake City 801 257 1900
Recommended in Litigation

TAYLOR, Nolan
Dorsey & Whitney LLP, Salt Lake City 801 933 7360
Recommended in Corporate/M&A

TAYLOR, Tom
Holme Roberts & Owen LLP, Salt Lake City 801 521 5800
Recommended in Corporate/M&A

WADDOUPS, Clark
Parr Waddoups Brown Gee & Loveless, Salt Lake City 801 532 7840
Recommended in Litigation

WIKSTROM, Francis
Parsons Behle & Latimer PC, Salt Lake City 801 532 1234
Recommended in Litigation

WILDE, Robert
Wilde & Associates, Midvale 801 255 4774
Recommended in Employment

WILLIAMS, Gregory
Van Cott, Bagley, Cornwall & McCarthy, Salt Lake City 801 532 3333
Recommended in Real Estate

WILSON, Randon
Jones Waldo Holbrook & McDonough PC, Salt Lake City 801 521 3200
Recommended in Corporate/M&A

VERMONT

CORPORATE/M&A

CONTENTS: Corporate/M&A p.94; Employment Mainly Plaintiff p.95; Mainly Defendant p.95; Insolvency p.96; Litigation: General Commercial p97; Real Estate p.99; Individuals' Profiles p.99.

VERMONT'S TOP FOUR
1. Downs Rachlin Martin
1. Gravel and Shea
2. Paul, Frank & Collins
3. Dinse, Knapp & McAndrew

Ranking based on Chambers' research within the state.

All quotes in the text are from interviews with clients and competitors.

OVERVIEW: Vermont's largest law firm **Downs Rachlin Martin** houses more than 50 attorneys in its four statewide offices. Rivals and clients alike commended the firm's breadth of expertise and its ability to attract top-tier clients. The labor and employment group is the largest in the state, while recent corporate work has included the large-scale acquisition of assets in over 20 states on behalf of Crown Castle USA. Concord Group Insurance and Otis Elevator Company are also clients.

Gravel and Shea, in joint first place, is another of the state's larger firms, comprising 23 attorneys based in Burlington. The firm has an impressive standing in the commercial arena, borne out by its consistently high ranking across a broad range of practice groups. Champlain Oil Company and IBM are typical of the firm's high-caliber client base.

In second place, **Paul, Frank & Collins** has 25 attorneys in a Burlington office and an additional base in Plattsburgh, NY. The firm is particularly admired for its corporate law and litigation prowess. Clients valued the high-quality, practical transactional experience of these attorneys. The firm serves a US and Canadian client base, attracting such high-profile names as Ben & Jerry's and Unilever.

Founded in 1917, **Dinse, Knapp & McAndrew**, ranked third, is one of the oldest firms in the state. Its 21 attorneys also practice from offices in Burlington and Plattsburgh. According to market sources, this firm possesses a particularly impressive litigation department, and has a strong reputation for general commercial disputes and insurance defense. The firm counts Middlebury College and The University of Vermont on its client roster.

CORPORATE/M&A

VERMONT
Leading firms (Corporate/M&A)

1. **DOWNS RACHLIN MARTIN PLLC** Burlington
1. **GRAVEL AND SHEA** Burlington
1. **PAUL, FRANK & COLLINS PC** Burlington
2. **DINSE, KNAPP & MCANDREW PC** Burlington
3. **EGGLESTON & CRAMER LTD** Burlington

Leading individuals (Corporate/M&A)

1. **FRYE** Michael *Paul, Frank & Collins PC*, Burlington
   KNAPP Spencer *Dinse, Knapp*, Burlington
   MCCONAUGHY Stewart *Gravel and Shea*, Burlington
   ODE Paul *Downs Rachlin Martin PLLC*, Burlington
2. **BOE** Kathleen *Eggleston & Cramer Ltd*, Burlington
   ERLY Peter *Gravel and Shea*, Burlington
   HAEFNER Gail *Paul, Frank & Collins PC*, Burlington
   MARTIN Allen *Downs Rachlin Martin PLLC*, Burlington
3. **EGGLESTON** Jon *Eggleston & Cramer Ltd*, Burlington
   MONTGOMERY Margaret *Gravel and Shea*, Burlington
   PORT Alan *Paul, Frank & Collins PC*, Burlington

Firms and individuals are listed alphabetically in each band.

Downs Rachlin Martin PLLC

The Firm: The state's largest law firm with over 50 attorneys, it is home to a *"corporate department that has horsepower."* Clients describe its lawyers as *"quality advisers, all of whom have impressive levels of experience in dealing with commercial transactions."* The acquisitions and development team assisted Crown Castle USA in acquiring nearly 10,000 assets located in more than 20 states, and worked on the development of databases for internal use in managing the assets.

The Lawyers: *"Top-notch"* **Paul Ode** attracts praise from peers as a *"careful and thoughtful problem solver,"* while clients singled him out as having *"an exceptional legal and business mind."* Head of the M&A practice, **Allen Martin** has impressed clients with his *"tremendous grasp of the commercial objectives."*

The Clients: Crown Castle USA; Brattleboro Retreat; EHV-Weidmann Industries; Fletcher Allen Health Care; Marlboro College and Vermont Gas Systems.

Gravel and Shea

The Firm: One of the state's *"movers and shakers,"* the firm has a strong commercial focus, fielding a team that advises on general corporate matters as well as financing, structuring, acquisitions, sales, tax and trust work. Peers describe these lawyers as *"energetic, highly professional and skilled."* Clients further recommend the firm for *"hiring the best people who develop trusted relationships,"* while pointing out that *"the solutions provided are, quite simply, consistently spot on."* Highlights include the representation of the purchasers of a local ski resort, and advice given to a publisher on the purchase of another publisher.

The Lawyers: *"Excellent and truly outstanding corporate lawyer"* **Stewart McConaughy** garners an array of plaudits as a lawyer *"able to craft a deal that takes into account the client's needs."* Clients are attracted to his *"business judgment and firm grasp over all practice areas."* Observers also praised **Peter Erly** for his *"keen understanding of the law,"* and the *"impressive"* **Margaret Montgomery**.

The Clients: Merchants Bank; Champlain Oil Company; IBM; The Burlington Free Press and The Rutland Herald.

Paul, Frank & Collins PC

The Firm: A *"first-class law firm."* The corporate team is well-established in the local market. Clients impressed upon researchers that *"its service and advice have always been outstanding"* and while *"cost-effective, the quality of work is comparable with the best of the big city firms."* The firm provides a comprehensive corporate practice and has a respected insurance practice of which the clients are typically Fortune 500 companies. The team also handles company immigration work for clients such as Bell Helicopter. In the transactional sphere, the firm advised Bond Auto Parts in the acquisition of another auto parts distributor.

The Lawyers: **Michael Frye** heads the corporate practice and *"enjoys a good reputation in town,"* in particular for his M&A and reorganization work. Clients described him as *"one of the sharpest business people around."* **Gail Haefner** is part of the core corporate team and an *"efficient and prompt attorney."* One of **Alan Port**'s primary areas of concentration involves advising clients in the captive and traditional insurance industries. He is recommended for his *"succinct advice"* and *"strong negotiation skills."*

The Clients: Unilever; Ben & Jerry's; Tubbs

EMPLOYMENT & LABOR LAW

VERMONT

Snowshoes; Bond Auto Parts; AN Deringer and Bell Helicopter.

Dinse, Knapp & McAndrew PC

The Firm: Clients described the corporate group's lawyers as *"all of high intellectual caliber, unpretentious and very likable."* They highlighted *"the firm's genuine concern for tailoring its services to meet the clients' needs."* The firm provides a full range of advice to clients in the construction, financial services, telecom, hi-tech, manufacturing, transportation, real estate and service industries. Examples include advising Middlebury College on a bond refinancing and representing The Vermont Teddy Bear Company in a $10.5 million cash tender offer. The firm has also been involved in the large sale of part of a college based in the state.

The Lawyers: *"Outstanding"* **Spencer Knapp** has recently been appointed acting general counsel for Fletcher Allen Health Care. He is respected for his corporate work, particularly for healthcare, nonprofit and tax-exempt organizations. Peers commended him as an *"imaginative lawyer,"* while clients refered to his *"smart and prudent"* approach to cases.

The Clients: Leading clients include The Vermont Teddy Bear Company.

Eggleston & Cramer Ltd

The Firm: The corporate team provides advice on a range of legal issues to both established businesses and new ventures. The team advises on corporate planning, business purchases and sales, securities law, antitrust and trade regulation and tax-related matters. Market commentators endorsed its attorneys as *"well-qualified lawyers and fantastic business consultants."* Clients commended the team's responsiveness and its understanding of issues that affect the healthcare industry.

The Lawyers: *"One of the best lawyers in the state,"* **Kathleen Boe** undertakes general corporate work, acquisitions and financings. She also has a niche in advising nonprofit corporations. Clients described her as *"a bright and experienced attorney."* **Jon Eggleston** also received recommendation, which particularly highlighted his expertise in tax matters.

The Clients: Porter Medical Center; Central Vermont Medical Center; Northeastern Vermont Regional Hospital and Vermont Association of Hospitals and Health Systems.

EMPLOYMENT & LABOR LAW

MAINLY PLAINTIFF

VERMONT
Leading firms
(Employment: Mainly Plaintiff)

1
- COLLINS, MCMAHON & HARRIS PLLC *Burlington*
- HOFF, CURTIS, PACHT, CASSIDY, FRAME *Burlington*

2
- BLACKWOOD ASSOCIATES PC *Burlington*
- LANGROCK SPERRY & WOOL LLP *Burlington*
- MELLO & KLESCH LLP *South Burlington*

3
- EDWIN L HOBSON PC *Burlington*

Leading individuals
(Employment: Mainly Plaintiff)

1
- CASSIDY Richard *Hoff, Curtis, Pacht, Burlington*

2
- BLACKWOOD Eileen *Blackwood Associates, Burlington*
- COLLINS John *Collins, McMahon & Harris, Burlington*
- MELLO Robert *Mello & Klesch LLP, South Burlington*

3
- HARRIS Michael *Collins, McMahon & Harris, Burlington*
- HOBSON Edwin *Edwin L Hobson PC, Burlington*

Firms and individuals are listed alphabetically in each band.

Collins, McMahon & Harris PLLC

The Firm: This five-attorney Burlington firm received market recommendation for its *"reasonable and highly competent"* plaintiff employment attorneys. The work undertaken encompasses discrimination, harassment, breach of contract, implied contract and handbook disputes, and violation of state and federal medical leave acts. Overtime disputes and violation of wage and hour laws are also prominent in the caseload.

The Lawyers: *"Smart and aggressive"* **John Collins** impresses defendant attorneys as one who is *"not afraid to try a case."* He successfully represented a client in an overtime and false imprisonment claim against Wal-Mart. **Michael Harris** is typical of the firm's attorneys who *"care for their clients and take the employment field seriously."*

Hoff, Curtis, Pacht, Cassidy, Frame, Somers & Katims PC

The Firm: The ten-lawyer firm has offices in Burlington and Portland, ME. It combines expertise in defendants and plaintiff employment practices with extensive knowledge of labor relations matters. Client feedback praises the team as *"impressive, professional and personable at the same time."*

The Lawyers: *"Dedicated, hard-working and knowledgeable"* **Richard Cassidy**'s employment litigation practice centers on the representation of individuals and labor unions. His specialty is higher education-related matters; for instance, he has advised the Vermont State Colleges Faculty Federation, AFL-CIO Local 3180 on labor matters. He has also represented doctors and other healthcare professionals, such as in achieving a several million-dollar settlement for a doctor in a Qui Tam case against a local hospital. Clients described him as *"absolutely excellent"* and commented on his *"skilful negotiations."*

The Clients: United Professions of Vermont AFT; Teamsters Local 597 and Vermont State Colleges Faculty Federation, AFL-CIO Local 3180.

Blackwood Associates PC

The Firm: This two-lawyer Burlington firm was founded by **Eileen Blackwood** in 1992. The *"talented and dedicated"* Blackwood represents both plaintiffs and defendants within the employment law arena, in a practice that also incorporates areas such as special education law. She attracts market recommendation for her *"superb mediation skills"* and her plaintiffs' work. Peers praised her as *"smart and diligent"* and commented on her *"excellent judgment"* and *"good perception of people in the real world."* Examples of recent settlements for plaintiffs include a sexual harassment case, a sexual orientation discrimination case and a disability discrimination case.

Langrock Sperry & Wool LLP

The Firm: This firm is one of the largest in Vermont with 24 lawyers and offices in both Burlington and Middlebury. The firm's employment practice includes labor relations as well as both plaintiffs' and defendants' works with the plaintiffs' side holding the higher profile. A *"capable team"* undertakes a range of employment matters, including discrimination, harassment, disability, leave and overtime issues, wrongful termination and the negotiation and review of employment agreements.

Mello & Klesch LLP

The Firm: This three-lawyer statewide civil and administrative litigation firm is based in South Burlington. The group advises on labor matters, such as in the representation of police unions, although the majority of its employment caseload is on behalf of individuals against their current or former employers. Examples of recent work include handling disability discrimination, whistle-blower wrongful termination, sexual harrassment and ERISA matters and a claim alleging breach of the FMLA. The team has also resolved a significant wage and hour claim filed in federal court.

The Lawyers: *"Cordial and calm"* **Robert Mello** received strong recommendation from his peers as an *"effective, thorough and persuasive"* attorney. Clients rated him as someone who *"knows how to make his point and how to win a case."*

VERMONT

EMPLOYMENT & LABOR LAW

Edwin L Hobson PC
The Firm: Burlington-based **Edwin Hobson** practices primarily plaintiffs' employment and civil rights litigation. Although he does a modest amount of handbook work, the bulk of his employment practice is statutory plaintiffs' matters, which include discrimination claims and whistle-blower cases. Examples of recent work include a tenure case, which is due to go before the Vermont Labor Relations Board and a whistle-blower case before the Department of Labor. Interviewees singled him out as *"a tough lawyer,"* who is *"always well-apprised of cutting-edge developments in the law."* Clients lauded him as *"an extremely honest, open and honorable individual."*

EMPLOYMENT & LABOR LAW — MAINLY DEFENDANT

VERMONT
Leading firms
(Employment: Mainly Defendant)
1. DOWNS RACHLIN MARTIN *Brattleboro, Burlington*
   GRAVEL AND SHEA *Burlington*
2. DINSE, KNAPP & MCANDREW PC *Burlington*
   PAUL, FRANK & COLLINS PC *Burlington*

Leading individuals
(Employment: Mainly Defendant)
1. BRIGGS Heather *Gravel and Shea, Burlington*
   GRANT Elizabeth *Paul, Frank & Collins PC, Burlington*
   MCANDREW Karen *Dinse, Knapp, Burlington*
   SABALIS Patricia *Downs Rachlin Martin, Burlington*
2. MCKEARIN Robert *Dinse, Knapp, Burlington*
   ROBB Peter *Downs Rachlin Martin PLLC, Brattleboro*

Firms and individuals are listed alphabetically in each band.

Downs Rachlin Martin PLLC
The Firm: The labor and employment group at this firm is the largest in Vermont and represents employers in all aspects of employment law. Clients reported that *"their work has always been excellent."* Highlights of the past year include the successful representation of the employer hospital in Dulude v Fletcher Allen Health Care.
The Lawyers: Patricia Sabalis *"really knows her field and she assesses cases realistically."* Clients praised her as *"well informed, pro-active and sharp."* Head of employment **Peter Robb** conducts his national labor and employment practice from the Brattleboro office. *"Responsive, bright and practical,"* clients also pointed out that *"his experience and negotiation skills render him a fantastic lawyer and an invaluable aid."*
The Clients: Otis Elevator Company; Dominion Resources Services; Entergy; IBM and Fletcher Allen Health Care.

Gravel and Shea
The Firm: The *"top rank"* employment and labor relations group represents management in all aspects of the employment relationship, and occasionally represents plaintiffs. Recent highlights include successfully defending a wrongful discharge claim brought by a manager at Geiger of Austria.
The Lawyers: *"Extremely personable,"* **Heather Briggs** is described by rivals as a *"no-nonsense lawyer, who understands the finer issues."* Clients applauded her as *"highly professional and competent."* Briggs is supported in complex trial work by general commercial litigator, Robert Hemley.
The Clients: Leading clients include Merchants Bank and Geiger of Austria.

Dinse, Knapp & McAndrew PC
The Firm: Based in one of the oldest firms in Vermont, the employment law group assists employers and human resource professionals in both counseling and litgation matters. Clients extol the firm as *"without a doubt one of the best multi-purpose law firms."* Work examples include the prosecution of a violation of a covenant not to compete in the hi-tech industry and the representation of The University of Vermont in a reverse discrimination case.
The Lawyers: Observers recommended *"tough trial lawyer"* **Karen McAndrew** as an attorney *"familiar with college culture and the unique problems facing universities."* Active at both federal and state level, she has recently obtained summary judgment for Ryder Truck in a discrimination claim. McAndrew also represented Middlebury College in a number of faculty tenure cases. Head of employment **Robert McKearin** is *"an impressive litigator,"* while interviewees also recommended him as *"easy to work with."*
The Clients: Verizon; The University of Vermont; Middlebury College and Ryder Truck.

Paul, Frank & Collins PC
The Firm: A *"leading competitor,"* the employment group represents employers in litigation and alternative dispute resolution matters, as well as providing general employment counseling. The team has assisted Ben & Jerry's in the employment aspects of its acquisition by Unilever. Clients reported that they were *"impressed by the firm's reputation within the Vermont community – particularly in the higher education field."* These attorneys *"grasped issues quickly, advised accurately, and were conceptually and intellectually gifted."*
The Lawyers: Head of the employment group, **Elizabeth Grant** was described by clients as *"thoughtful, calm and measured"* and noted that *"she was always willing and available 24 hours a day, every single day of the week."* Further client feedback highlighted her *"advanced understanding of the law's role in enacting organizational change."*
The Clients: Ben & Jerry's; Unilever; Green Mountain Coffee Roasters and Gap.

LITIGATION — GENERAL COMMERCIAL

Dinse, Knapp & McAndrew PC
The Firm: One of the oldest firms in the state, with 21 lawyers and offices in Burlington and in Plattsburgh, NY. Market feedback highlights the firm's *"particularly impressive lawyers"* and its *"strong litigation department."* Attorneys impress with their *"good work in insurance defense and general commercial litigation."* Recent cases include acting for a major bank in trust litigation. In the construction arena, the group represented Weeks Marine in the successful mediation of a dispute with the City of Burlington.
The Lawyers: Rivals noted that the *"trustworthy"* head of the litigation group **Karen McAndrew** has *"all the materials involved to make a first-class litigator,"* agreeing that *"you cannot push her around at all."* Clients described her as *"an extremely sharp and responsive litigator – an absolute pleasure to deal with."* She has recently acted for a local business in a Medicaid billing claim by the federal government. **Ritchie Berger** is a *"tenacious examiner of details,"* while clients were keen to impress upon researchers that *"he is a real tiger in defense work and the kind of man that leaves absolutely no stone unturned."* Interviewees perceived that *"judges and juries really like* **John Monahan**" and that *"he accomplishes what*

LITIGATION — VERMONT

VERMONT
Leading firms
(Litigation: General Commercial)

1
- DINSE, KNAPP & MCANDREW PC *Burlington*
- DOWNS RACHLIN MARTIN PLLC *Burlington*
- GRAVEL AND SHEA *Burlington*
- PAUL, FRANK & COLLINS PC *Burlington*

2
- SHEEHEY FURLONG & BEHM PC *Burlington*

3
- CLEARY SHAHI ASSOCIATES PC *Rutland*
- EGGLESTON & CRAMER LTD *Burlington*
- O'NEILL KELLNER & GREEN PC *Burlington*

Leading individuals
(Litigation: General Commercial)

1
- HEMLEY Robert *Gravel and Shea, Burlington*

2
- MCANDREW Karen *Dinse, Knapp, Burlington*
- RACHLIN Robert *Downs Rachlin Martin, Burlington*
- SARTORE John *Paul, Frank & Collins PC, Burlington*

3
- BEHM Jeffrey *Sheehey Furlong & Behm PC, Burlington*
- BERGER Ritchie *Dinse, Knapp & McAndrew, Burlington*
- CLEARY David *Cleary Shahi Associates PC, Rutland*
- HEATH Marc *Downs Rachlin Martin PLLC, Burlington*
- KLINE Scot *Eggleston & Cramer Ltd, Burlington*
- O'NEILL Robert *Gravel and Shea, Burlington*

4
- BENNETT Crocker *Paul, Frank & Collins, Burlington*
- MONAHAN John *Dinse, Knapp & McAndrew, Burlington*
- O'NEILL Jerome *O' Neill Kellner & Green, Burlington*

Firms and individuals are listed alphabetically in each band.

---

attorneys. Rivals praised the litigation team as *"experienced litigators, especially at trial level,"* while clients were impressed by *"their great reputation in the corporate world"* and professed themselves *"more than satisfied with the service provided by the firm."* Recent highlights include the successful defense of a bank in a Vermont federal court antitrust trial, and the successful challenge of the constitutionality of a Vermont tax statute on behalf of a group of lobbyists.

The Lawyers: *"Naturally talented"* **Robert Hemley** receives strong market recommendation for the *"broad variety of commercial litigation"* he undertakes, particularly his First Amendment work. Commentators describe him as *"hardworking – he has a great grasp of all types of cases and he gets the job done."* Clients agree that he is *"an excellent attorney who impressed us with his thorough preparation and commanding presence in the courtroom."* **Robert O'Neill** was singled out by clients as *"a brilliant thinker and a talented litigator."*

The Clients: The firm's typical clients include banks, lobbyist groups and groups of insurance trade associations.

Paul, Frank & Collins PC

The Firm: One of the largest firms in Vermont with 25 attorneys in its office in Burlington and one in Plattsburgh, NY. Rivals described the team as *"one of the best litigation groups in Vermont"* and clients praised its *"expert handling of complex litigation matters."* These attorneys have recently had a patent infringement and a trademark infringement case in federal courts in both Vermont and New York.

The Lawyers: Head of the litigation group **John Sartore** was described by rivals as an *"extremely capable, tough and effective"* litigator. His recent cases include protection of trade secrets and antitrust matters. *"Bright"* **Crocker Bennett**'s primary area of concentration is in medical malpractice, while he is equally adept in all manner of business disputes. Peers said that *"he knows his subject matter well"* and applauded his *"fast uptake."* Clients described him as *"a wonderful trial attorney who particularly excels at depositions."*

The Clients: Leading clients include financial institutions, educational establishments and various hospitals and medical practice groups.

Sheehey Furlong & Behm PC

The Firm: A ten-attorney firm based in Burlington. Peers applauded the commercial litigation group as *"a leading competitor."* Examples of the team's work include acting for a prominent Vermont electrical utility in such matters as property damage cases and insurance coverage. It also represented Brueggers in contract actions and franchise litigation. Pending appeal, the firm had a successful outcome in the trial of Howard Opera House Associates v Urban Outfitters.

The Lawyers: **Jeffrey Behm** receives strong market feedback as *"a primary litigator,"* highlighting his *"commercial and governmental investigation defense work"* and his success in attracting a substantial client base. His caseload has included acting for a large pharmaceutical wholesaler in antitrust litigation.

The Clients: Green Mountain Power; Mount Mansfield Television Corporation; Burlington Drug Company; Brueggers; Merchants Bank and Chittenden Bank.

Cleary Shahi Associates PC

The Firm: A five-attorney firm based in Rutland, it is principally active in the defense arena, although it does undertake some plaintiffs' work. Specialties include medical malpractice, professional liability, ski area liability and insurance coverage. The team is often picked as mediators for construction and professional liability claims. Commentators praised the firm as *"a good statewide practice."* Recent success includes member Kaveh Shahi's representation of AIU in the 2002 Supreme Court ruling Northshire Communications, Inc v AIU Insurance Company.

The Lawyers: **David Cleary** is recognized as *"a high-energy litigator"* and *"a strong opponent."* Clients described this *"real-life Perry Mason"* as *"having an absolutely amazing mind – a real workhorse with a larger than life personality"* and *"a dynamic presence in the courtroom."*

The Clients: American International Group of Insurance Companies and Vermont Ski Areas Association.

Eggleston & Cramer Ltd

The Firm: A 15-lawyer firm based in Burlington. Clients endorsed the litigation group for its *"practical and business-oriented attorneys."* The team achieved recent success at trial level in the representation of the bank in the lender liability trial of the case Merchants Bank v Vescio.

The Lawyers: Clients highlighted *"bright"* **Scot Kline** and his *"ability to write briefs as erudite and intellectual as anyone in a top ten US firm."* Other commentators claimed that *"he has a fair amount of tax expertise"* and that he is *"responsive, thoughtful and willing to consult."*

The Clients: Leading names include Banknorth, Chittenden Bank and KeyBank National Association.

O' Neill Kellner & Green PC

The Firm: Boutique three-partner litigation practice based in Burlington. This is a *"leading litigation firm,"* which handles a volume of plaintiffs' personal injury work. Examples of its recent commercial work include acting for a UK company in a products liability matter. The team has also defended a bank in loan disputes and repre-

---

he needs to while retaining a high level of civility."

The Clients: Leading clients include banks, insurance carriers and ski resorts.

Downs Rachlin Martin PLLC

The Firm: This is Vermont's largest law firm with over 50 attorneys practising out of four offices around the state and one in New Hampshire. Peers commended its *"high-quality lawyers with whom it would be an honour to litigate with,"* while clients reported: *"The service provided is always timely and comprehensive."* Highlights include insurance coverage cases as well as the representation of both owners and contractors in a variety of commercial and industrial disputes.

The Lawyers: Interviewees recognized **Robert Rachlin** as *"extremely smart"* and *"a worthy adversary."* Litigation chair **Marc Heath**, whose specialty is construction law, is described by clients as *"an absolutely tenacious and diligent litigator"* who is *"clearly out to win."*

The Clients: Leading names include Concord Group Insurance, Vermont Mutual Insurance and Scott Construction.

Gravel and Shea

The Firm: Based in Burlington, this is one of Vermont's oldest and larger law firms fielding 23

sented both creditors and borrowers in lender liability and bankruptcy litigation.

The Lawyers: Although **Jerome O'Neill** is better known for his prowess in the personal injury sector, he was praised by interviewees as an *"experienced and effective commercial litigator."*

The Clients: Acts for regional, national and international corporates and financial institutions.

REAL ESTATE

VERMONT
Leading firms (Real Estate)

[1]
- DOWNS RACHLIN MARTIN PLLC *Burlington*
- GRAVEL AND SHEA *Burlington*
- LANGROCK SPERRY & WOOL LLP *Burlington*

[2]
- DINSE, KNAPP & MCANDREW PC *Burlington*
- PAUL, FRANK & COLLINS PC *Burlington*

[3]
- EGGLESTON & CRAMER LTD *Burlington*
- LISMAN, WEBSTER, KIRKPATRICK *Burlington*
- LITTLE, CICCHETTI & CONARD PC *Burlington*

Leading individuals (Real Estate)

[1]
- MURPHY Liam *Langrock Sperry & Wool*, Burlington
- RUSHFORD Robert *Gravel and Shea*, Burlington
- SCHROEDER William *Downs Rachlin Martin*, Burlington

[2]
- CONARD David *Little, Cicchetti & Conard*, Burlington
- KRONK Catherine *Paul, Frank & Collins PC*, Burlington
- LEBOWITZ Molly *Dinse, Knapp & McAndrew*, Burlington

[3]
- LISMAN Carl *Lisman, Webster, Kirkpatrick*, Burlington
- WHEELWRIGHT Neil *Eggleston & Cramer*, Burlington

Up-and-coming individuals
- FARKAS Michelle *Gravel and Shea*, Burlington
- KNUDSEN Eric *Langrock Sperry & Wool*, Burlington

Firms and individuals are listed alphabetically in each band.

Downs Rachlin Martin PLLC
The Firm: *"One of the top firms for real estate,"* according to *Chambers'* interviewees. The firm's real estate practice concentrates mainly on representing developers and businesses, including advising on the regulatory process, title work and commercial real estate lending. It is also involved in landlord and tenant matters, construction contracts and low income housing tax credit projects. The team has recently assisted in the development of a village numbering approximately 500 units at the base of one of Vermont's major ski areas.

The Lawyers: *"Solutions-oriented"* **William Schroeder** is a prominent player in the real estate team. Peers described him as *"a bright and capable attorney who is always a pleasure to deal with."* Clients endorsed him as *"an outstanding real estate lawyer, well versed in both environmental and real estate matters – he is simply preeminent in his field."*

The Clients: Leading names include Hannaford Brothers.

Gravel and Shea
The Firm: The firm's commercial real estate practice won plaudits from rivals and clients alike as a *"top-notch"* operation. The team advises commercial clients on such staples as the acquisition, financing and development of properties. The practice also specializes in permit work, which includes helping clients present and appeal development applications. An example of recent work is the representation of a Sprint affiliate in obtaining permits for a wireless network in Vermont. Clients were particularly impressed by the *"excellent all-round service"* provided by the team and endorsed the firm's size: *"It is large enough to be able to offer specialist advice in all practice areas."*

The Lawyers: **Robert Rushford** advises developers of shopping centers and of single-family and multi-family projects. He attracts praise from clients as *"a first-rate, quick-witted real estate lawyer,"* while rivals *"have a high regard for his professionalism."* Clients singled out associate **Michelle Farkas** for her *"comprehensive knowledge."*

The Clients: Leading names include Snyder Company and a Sprint affiliate.

Langrock Sperry & Wool LLP
The Firm: The commercial real estate practice covers such areas as transactions and title work, financing, development, permitting and leasing. The group is also active in the development of condominium communities, and represents many homeowner associations. Clients recommended the group as *"certainly one of the best in the market."* It has advised telecom companies in the locating, siting and obtaining of cell site permits.

The Lawyers: Commentators pointed to the *"intellectual"* **Liam Murphy**'s *"reputation for knowing the details behind real estate concepts."* Among his highlights of the past year, Murphy has been involved in the financing and development aspects of the $130 million Winooski Community Development downtown redevelopment project. **Eric Knudsen** was also brought to researchers' attention, with one interviewee describing him as *"the best lawyer under 40 I have ever worked with in this state."*

The Clients: Redstone; Davis Development Group; WIZN and Winooski Community Development.

Dinse, Knapp & McAndrew PC
The Firm: According to competitors this is *"a leading real estate practice."* The real estate group assists clients including developers, financiers and investors in the acquisition, development, sale and financing of real estate. Examples of such work include projects such as retail shopping centers, institutional campuses and mixed residential/recreational/commercial developments. Clients commented on the *"top-flight lawyers"* and wanted to impress upon researchers that the firm *"is genuinely concerned with providing the best possible service to its clients and not simply with making its business profitable."*

The Lawyers: **Molly Lebowitz** plays a prominent part in the real estate team and is particularly recommended by rivals for her representation of financial institutions in real estate transactions and mortgage-related matters. Clients praised her as *"an intelligent transactional and real estate specialist – someone whose advice can always be trusted."*

The Clients: Leading clients include The University of Vermont and Middlebury College.

Paul, Frank & Collins PC
The Firm: This *"talented real estate team"* handles substantial transactions for purchasers and sellers, involving financing, project development, permitting, zoning and planning. Attorneys also negotiate and draft commercial leases for both landlords and tenants. Clients reported that the firm *"provides a service so satisfying that there is no need to go elsewhere."*

The Lawyers: Market commentators cited head of department **Catherine Kronk** as *"tenacious, a great transactional lawyer"* and *"a true asset to a company seeking sound legal advice."*

The Clients: Leading names include Banknorth and Casella Waste Systems.

Eggleston & Cramer Ltd
The Firm: The real estate practice represents lenders, sellers and purchasers in all areas of real estate transactions from acquisition and finance to development and leasing. Attorneys also negotiate and draft commercial leases, and advise on the obtaining of permits. Interviewees were keen to praise the team's advice as *"detailed and focused."*

The Lawyers: Peers endorsed **Neil Wheelwright** as a *"smart and thorough real estate lawyer."*

The Clients: Leading clients include CENTURY 21 Jack Associates, Chicago Title Insurance and University Wholesalers.

Lisman, Webster, Kirkpatrick & Leckerling PC
The Firm: *"One of the top firms in general, not just real estate."* The real estate team represents both borrowers and lenders in commercial transactions, and numbers commercial and real estate developers among its clients. Attorneys also rep-

resent owners' associations and advise clients on timeshare issues. Commercial leasework is also a staple of the practice, as is regulatory work for development projects.
The Lawyers: Senior partner **Carl Lisman** was described by rivals as " *one of the deans of the real estate bar.*" He was singled out for his knowledge of condominium communities and timeshare matters.
The Clients: The firm's typical clients include owners' associations and commercial borrowers and lenders.

Little, Cicchetti & Conard PC
The Firm: The five-lawyer Burlington practice advises on real estate matters as part of a broader commercial practice. A busy residential real estate practice is combined with a respected commercial development and loan transactional group. In the commercial arena, the team has represented Merchants Bank and Chittenden Bank in loan transactions involving real estate and real estate development. Clients commended the firm for *"its superior level of personal attention, commitment and cost-effectiveness."*
The Lawyers: David Conard *"understands the complexities of difficult real estate transactions."* Interviewees also described him as *"outgoing, incredibly helpful and a lawyer who interacts brilliantly with his clients."*
The Clients: Bowl New England; Merchants Bank; Chittenden Bank and First American Title Insurance Company.

Leaders in Vermont

BEHM, Jeffrey
Sheehey Furlong & Behm PC, Burlington
802 864 9891
Recommended in Litigation

BENNETT, Crocker
Paul, Frank & Collins, PC, Burlington
802 658 2311
Recommended in Litigation

BERGER, Ritchie
Dinse, Knapp & McAndrew PC, Burlington 802 864 5751
Recommended in Litigation

BLACKWOOD, Eileen
Blackwood Associates PC, Burlington
802 863 2517
Recommended in Employment

BOE, Kathleen
Eggleston & Cramer, Ltd, Burlington
802 864 0880
Recommended in Corporate/M&A

BRIGGS, Heather
Gravel and Shea, Burlington
802 658 0220
Recommended in Employment

CASSIDY, Richard
Hoff, Curtis, Pacht, Cassidy, Frame, Somers & Katims PC, Burlington
802 864 4531
Recommended in Employment

CLEARY, David
Cleary Shahi Associates, A Professional Corporation, Rutland 802 775 8800
Recommended in Litigation

COLLINS, John
Collins, McMahon & Harris PLLC, Burlington 802 862 3524
Recommended in Employment

CONARD, David
Little, Cicchetti & Conard PC, Burlington
802 862 6511
Recommended in Real Estate

EGGLESTON, Jon
Eggleston & Cramer, Ltd, Burlington
802 864 0880
Recommended in Corporate/M&A

ERLY, Peter
Gravel and Shea, Burlington
802 658 0220
Recommended in Corporate/M&A

FARKAS, Michelle
Gravel and Shea, Burlington
802 658 0220
Recommended in Real Estate

FRYE, Michael
Paul, Frank & Collins, PC, Burlington
802 658 2311
Recommended in Corporate/M&A

GRANT, Elizabeth
Paul, Frank & Collins, PC, Burlington
802 658 2311
Recommended in Employment

HAEFNER, Gail
Paul, Frank & Collins, PC, Burlington
802 658 2311
Recommended in Corporate/M&A

HARRIS, Michael
Collins, McMahon & Harris PLLC, Burlington 802 862 3524
Recommended in Employment

HEATH, Marc
Downs Rachlin Martin PLLC, Burlington
802 863 2375
Recommended in Litigation

HEMLEY, Robert
Gravel and Shea, Burlington
802 658 0220
Recommended in Litigation

HOBSON, Edwin
Edwin L Hobson PC, Burlington
802 863 2000
Recommended in Employment

KLINE, Scot
Eggleston & Cramer, Ltd, Burlington
802 864 0880
Recommended in Litigation

KNAPP, Spencer
Dinse, Knapp & McAndrew PC, Burlington 802 864 5751
Recommended in Corporate/M&A

KNUDSEN, Eric
Langrock Sperry & Wool, LLP, Burlington
802 864 0217
Recommended in Real Estate

KRONK, Catherine
Paul, Frank & Collins, PC, Burlington
802 658 2311
Recommended in Real Estate

LEBOWITZ, Molly
Dinse, Knapp & McAndrew PC, Burlington 802 864 5751
Recommended in Real Estate

LISMAN, Carl
Lisman, Webster, Kirkpatrick & Leckerling, P.C., Burlington
802 864 5756
Recommended in Real Estate

MARTIN, Allen
Downs Rachlin Martin PLLC, Burlington
802 863 2375
Recommended in Corporate/M&A

MCANDREW, Karen
Dinse, Knapp & McAndrew PC, Burlington 802 864 5751
Recommended in Employment, Litigation

MCCONAUGHY, Stewart
Gravel and Shea, Burlington
802 658 0220
Recommended in Corporate/M&A

MCKEARIN, Robert
Dinse, Knapp & McAndrew PC, Burlington 802 864 5751
Recommended in Employment

MELLO, Robert
Mello & Klesch LLP, South Burlington
802 862 3200
Recommended in Employment

MONAHAN, John
Dinse, Knapp & McAndrew PC, Burlington 802 864 5751
Recommended in Litigation

MONTGOMERY, Margaret
Gravel and Shea, Burlington
802 658 0220
Recommended in Corporate/M&A

MURPHY, Liam
Langrock Sperry & Wool, LLP, Burlington
802 864 0217
Recommended in Real Estate

ODE, Paul
Downs Rachlin Martin PLLC, Burlington
802 863 2375
Recommended in Corporate/M&A

O'NEILL, Jerome
O' Neill Crawford & Green PC, Burlington
802 865 4700
Recommended in Litigation

O'NEILL, Robert
Gravel and Shea, Burlington
802 658 0220
Recommended in Litigation

PORT, Alan
Paul, Frank & Collins, PC, Burlington
802 658 2311
Recommended in Corporate/M&A

RACHLIN, Robert
Downs Rachlin Martin PLLC, Burlington
802 863 2375
Recommended in Litigation

ROBB, Peter
Downs Rachlin Martin PLLC, Brattleboro
802 258 3070
Recommended in Employment

RUSHFORD, Robert
Gravel and Shea, Burlington
802 658 0220
Recommended in Real Estate

SABALIS, Patricia
Downs Rachlin Martin PLLC, Burlington
802 863 2375
Recommended in Employment

SARTORE, John
Paul, Frank & Collins, PC, Burlington
802 658 2311
Recommended in Litigation

SCHROEDER, William
Downs Rachlin Martin PLLC, Burlington
802 863 2375
Recommended in Real Estate

WHEELWRIGHT, Neil
Eggleston & Cramer, Ltd, Burlington
802 864 0880
Recommended in Real Estate

VIRGINIA

CONSTRUCTION

CONTENTS: Construction p.698; Corporate/M&A p.699; Employment: Mainly Plaintiff p.701; Mainly Defendant p.701; Litigation: General Commercial p.702; Real Estate p.703; Individuals' Profiles p.704.

VIRGINIA'S TOP THREE
1. Hunton & Williams
2. McGuireWoods
3. Troutman Sanders

Ranking based on Chambers' research within the state.

All quotes in the text are from interviews with clients and competitors.

OVERVIEW: Top-ranked Richmond giant **Hunton & Williams** boasts a truly national practice and closely follows the organizational model of larger Wall Street firms. The firm also possesses noteworthy international expertise and has an ability to coordinate transactions across its offices in London, Brussels, Bangkok and Hong Kong. The Richmond office forms the base of the firm's national corporate practice, which is well known for traditional strength in M&A. Market sources also note the firm's developing securitization and capital markets practice, amply demonstrated by its work on Kraft's $8.68 billion IPO in 2001. Locally, its profile is ensured by the presence of Allen Goolsby, the acknowledged dean of Virginia corporate law. The firm's classic litigation practice, featuring top attorney Thomas Slater, is said to be capable of any type of representation. Additionally, a first-tier employment practice benefits from the legal savvy of leading lawyer Hill Wellford.

In second place, **McGuireWoods**, a large national law firm with considerable operations outside Virginia, enjoys a significant local profile, due in part to its institutional ties to some of the major corporations in the state. The firm's litigation practice includes former state Attorney General Bill Broaddus. However, it is the firm's national products liability practice that truly distinguishes it. Here, it is especially noted for its representation of auto industry clients in major cases. The corporate team also acts for a number of Fortune 500 companies as well as many of Virginia's largest corporations. An expert in energy sector transactions, Leslie Grandis is highly visible in the market, acting for such clients as Dominion Resources and Virginia Electric & Power Company.

Headquartered in Atlanta, **Troutman Sanders** merged with the deep-rooted Richmond firm Mays & Valentine in January 2001 to form a widely respected regional practice. Here, the firm, ranked third, wins general commendation for its concentration of outstanding attorneys. Litigator Jim Roberts in particular was lauded as a model for the profession. Banking, insurance and regulatory work are staples of the firm's statewide trial practice. The corporate group, featuring Jay Johnston, is found regularly acting for companies in the energy, financial and insurance sectors, and is the leading midmarket practice in the state.

CONSTRUCTION

VIRGINIA
Leading firms (Construction)
1. WATT, TIEDER, HOFFAR & FITZGERALD *McLean*
2. VENABLE LLP *Vienna*
   WICKWIRE GAVIN *Vienna*
3. SMITH PACHTER MCWHORTER & ALLEN *Vienna*

Leading individuals (Construction)
1. HOFFAR Julian *Watt, Tieder, Hoffar & Fitzgerald,* McLean
   LANE David *Venable LLP,* Vienna
   TIEDER John *Watt, Tieder, Hoffar & Fitzgerald,* McLean
   WRIGHT Murray *Wright Robinson Osthimer,* Richmond
2. BAKER Lewis *Watt, Tieder, Hoffar & Fitzgerald,* McLean
   FITZGERALD Robert *Watt, Tieder, Hoffar,* McLean
   LOULAKIS Michael *Wickwire Gavin,* Vienna
   WATT Robert *Watt, Tieder, Hoffar & Fitzgerald,* McLean
3. COX Robert *Watt, Tieder, Hoffar & Fitzgerald,* McLean
   LALLE Wayne *Venable LLP,* Vienna
   MCWHORTER Val *Smith Pachter McWhorter,* Vienna
   WICKWIRE Jon *Wickwire Gavin,* Vienna

Firms and individuals are listed alphabetically in each band.

Watt, Tieder, Hoffar & Fitzgerald LLP

The Firm: This nationwide firm operates from offices in California and DC as well as its headquarters in McLean, Virginia. A full range of construction matters is handled by the team, which has a focus on contentious work. Clients predominantly fall into two categories: large contractors and sureties. Interviewees frequently endorsed this team as *"the finest in the region, with an incredible array of talent."*

The Lawyers: Market sources described **Julian Hoffar** as a *"practical and knowledgeable"* attorney. His construction expertise encompasses the preparation and negotiation of contracts and the litigation of construction disputes. **John Tieder** is an experienced attorney who has recently acted on several high-profile mediations and arbitrations. Peers recognized that *"he undertakes a host of projects for many high-end international contractors"* active in Asia and Africa. He has also advised owners and general contractors on power projects and sports arenas in the US. Clients respect **Lewis Baker** as *"an excellent litigator."* He has represented contractors on the San Roque Dam in the Philippines, and advised on a delay claim relating to the Advanced Mixed Waste Treatment Plant in Idaho. His prominent clients include Washington Group International, formerly Morrison Knudsen. The *"pre-eminent"* **Bob Fitzgerald** has secured a following among general contractors. Interviewees spoke of his expertise on tunnel-related matters, such as his advice to Peter Kiewit Sons', Kenny Construction and Atkinson Construction on litigation arising from the Outfall Tunnel in Boston. He also advised Perini Corporation, Skanska and others on issues concerning the New York City Water Tunnel. **Bob Watt** was widely respected for his surety work and his experience before construction arbitration panels and federal and state courts across the US. **Bob Cox**'s clients include owners, contractors, suppliers and sureties on both public and private projects.

The Clients: Bechtel and Obayashi are additional clients.

Venable LLP

The Firm: This large full-service Maryland firm has a substantial presence in Vienna, Virginia with five partners and three associates dedicated to construction matters. The team represents a wide range of clients including owners, developers, public and private contractors, and lenders. Projects arising from industrial, office, retail and residential developments feature in the workload.

The Lawyers: Competitors respect **David Lane**'s *"consistent success and high level of integrity."* Acting for a host of prestigious clients, he has represented the media organization Gannett Company in a court litigation with a construction contractor, and acted for Raytheon in a multimillion dollar Dutch arbitration with Hollandse Constructie Groep (HCG) on the expansion of a facility in The Netherlands. **Wayne Lalle** was commended to researchers for his litigation on behalf of contractors and public owners.

The Clients: Zachry Construction; Washington Group International; Dynalectric Company and The Shaw Group.

CORPORATE/M&A

VIRGINIA

Wickwire Gavin
The Firm: Founded in 1974, this boutique has always been highly regarded for its work in construction law and government contracts. Market sources portrayed the firm as *"effective advisers who are capable of taking a case from the cradle to the grave."* Over 30 attorneys operate from four offices in Los Angeles, Madison, WI and the headquarters in Vienna.
The Lawyers: Mike Loulakis was viewed by his rivals as *"a class act."* He is active both in non-contentious work such as contract preparation and contentious work. Respected for his representation of design builders, he is on the board of directors of the Design-Build Institute of America (DBIA). Firm founder **Jon Wickwire** was described *"a dean of the bar."* Much of his work focuses on the preparation of construction policies and procedures for Fortune 500 corporations. He has acted as an expert witness on the central artery tunnel project in Boston, and has represented the Metropolitan Washington Airport Authority in connection with contractor claims.
The Clients: Conoco; Intel; The Industrial Company (TIC); Baker Concrete Construction and Consolidated Edison.

Smith Pachter McWhorter & Allen
The Firm: This firm has 17 lawyers working exclusively on construction law and government contracts. A majority of work is undertaken for owners, general contractors and subcontractors. Market observers endorsed the practice as *"a true boutique with a high degree of expertise."*
The Lawyers: Val McWhorter is carrying on the fine work of Richard Smith, who now acts in an of counsel capacity. Interviewees recognized McWhorter as a skilled practitioner in the field. He frequently represents contractors in complex claims arising under federal, state and local government contracts as well as contracts between private parties.
The Clients: Bechtel and Washington Group International are clients.

Other Notable Practitioners
Murray Wright, founder member of Richmond firm Wright Robinson Osthimer & Tatum, was consistently cited as *"without doubt one of the most notable names in Virginia representing architects and engineers."* He has acted as defense counsel in litigation, mediation and alternative dispute resolution proceedings.

CORPORATE/M&A

VIRGINIA
Leading firms (Corporate/M&A)
1. HUNTON & WILLIAMS *Richmond*
   MCGUIREWOODS LLP *Richmond*
2. TROUTMAN SANDERS LLP *Richmond*
   WILLIAMS MULLEN *Richmond*
3. KAUFMAN & CANOLES *Norfolk*
   WILLCOX & SAVAGE *Norfolk*
4. COOLEY GODWARD LLP *Reston*
   HALE AND DORR *Reston*
   LECLAIR RYAN *Richmond*
   SHAW PITTMAN LLP *McLean*

Leading individuals (Corporate/M&A)
1. BURRUS Robert *McGuireWoods LLP,* Richmond
   GOOLSBY Allen *Hunton & Williams,* Richmond
   GRANDIS Leslie *McGuireWoods LLP,* Richmond
   JOHNSTON Jay *Troutman Sanders LLP,* Richmond
   MOORE Thurston *Hunton & Williams,* Richmond
   RAINEY Gordon *Hunton & Williams,* Richmond
2. MASTRACCO Vincent *Kaufman & Canoles,* Norfolk
   SMITH Julious *Williams Mullen,* Richmond
   SYLVESTER David *Hale and Dorr,* Reston
   VAUGHAN Porter *Hunton & Williams,* Richmond
3. BUCKLEY Kevin *Hunton & Williams,* Richmond
   THOMPSON Gary *Hunton & Williams,* Richmond

Firms and individuals are listed alphabetically in each band.

Hunton & Williams
The Firm: This international practice provides a *"truly quality product"* from its base in Richmond. Peers observe that the firm has the depth and expertise to provide a *"strong team of capable attorneys"* on any type of matter. While clearly skilled in traditional corporate governance and M&A advice, the practice has developed in line with the needs of its clients. Experience in securities and asset securitization has allowed the firm to retain long-standing local and national clients, against the competition of Wall Street firms. The firm continues to benefit from the afterglow of its representation of Kraft in its 2001 $8.68 billion IPO, the second largest in US history. The team has also represented Bank of America on home equity securitizations of $10 billion, advised Ginnie Mae on the issuance of securities totaling over $21 billion. A long-term focus on the energy industry has seen the firm involved in substantial work for coal, gas and electricity companies, in conjunction with its Dallas office. Other areas of emphasis include the food and consumer industries and REITs.
The Lawyers: Allen Goolsby is widely viewed by peers as the *"dean"* of the Virginia corporate bar, and has drafted several statutes of state corporation law. His national practice incorporates traditional industries such as manufacturing and chemicals. **Thurston Moore** was described as an *"extremely talented corporate lawyer."* Although managing partner of the firm, peers were impressed with his continued commitment to active practice. He undertakes corporate and securities work in the private equity and real estate spheres. Chairman of the firm, **Gordon Rainey** is an *"extraordinarily* knowledgeable*"* lawyer. He has particular expertise in financial services, and acts for healthcare institutions in M&A work. **Porter Vaughan** maintains a traditional counseling practice, oversees operations at the firm, and acts for clients in the capital markets and M&A arenas. Clients view him as a safe pair of hands with *"trusted judgment."* **Kevin Buckley** is cohead of the firm's asset securitization group. He focuses on mortgage and asset-backed securitizations and other structured financings. Clients describe his as a *"clear, creative thinker"* with a *"calming presence"* in the meeting room. He recently represented the US Department of Veterans Affairs in designing a vendee loan securitization program. **Gary Thompson** was also revealed as a key figure in the practice; he focuses on M&A, tender offers, securities offerings and corporate governance.
The Clients: Dana Corporation; DTE Energy Services; Ginnie Mae; Kraft; Owens & Minor; Philip Morris; SunTrust; Tredegar Corporation; TXU; Verizon; Wells Fargo; Wolseley and WS Atkins.

McGuireWoods LLP
The Firm: Headquartered in Richmond, this is the largest law firm in the state, and fields *"excellent people,"* according to interviewees. Its corporate group is sustained by ongoing general representation to a host of Fortune 500 companies, alongside its strong ties to local corporates. The energy industry is a core focus of the group, particularly through its relationship with Dominion Resources. Recent work for Dominion includes a $250 million 6-month credit agreement for its Cove Point acquisition. It also acted for Virginia Electric & Power Company in a $1.6 billion medium-term note program, and for CSX in on a registered public offering of $400 million in senior notes. The team has also represented Circuit City Stores in its spin-off of CarMax.
The Lawyers: Robert Burrus is chairman of the firm and a *"senior statesman"* of the corporate bar.

VIRGINIA

CORPORATE/M&A

Interviewees agree that he has long-standing relationships with a *"wonderful clientele of public corporations."* He is experienced in energy and transportation matters, and is typically involved with debt financing issues. Described by clients as *"an expert in his field,"* **Leslie Grandis** is said to be particularly experienced in dealing with companies in growth or acquisition phases. His practice is weighted toward M&A, representing both buyers and sellers. He has advised Dominion Resources on a number of recent acquisitions, including the $2.3 billion purchase of Louis Dreyfus Natural Gas.

The Clients: Dominion Resources; CSX Corporation; Circuit City Stores and Consolidated Natural Gas Company.

Troutman Sanders LLP
The Firm: This national firm merged with Virginia practice Mays & Valentine in January 2001, consolidating offices around the state. The large team in Richmond has a primarily mid-Atlantic public company practice, while the client base of other offices leans more toward private businesses. The firm is frequently found undertaking special committee work, and is heavily involved in the energy industry. It also acts for financial institutions, banks and their affiliates, and handles regulatory and corporate work for insurance companies.

The Lawyers: A popular choice for referrals, **Jay Johnston** is *"as good as anyone around."* Sources recommend his corporate governance work, and he is also active in securities and M&A. They agree that he is a *"great lawyer"* with *"good judgment,"* and *"totally reliable."* He has been counsel for the underwriters in the sale by Dominion Resources and its subsidiaries of over $6 billion of debt/equity securities since 1998.

The Clients: National, regional and local businesses, both public and private, are clients.

Williams Mullen
The Firm: A smaller general service firm with five offices in Virginia has *"grown substantially,"* according to observers, and has secured a reputation for high-quality corporate work. Competitors respect its strong regional presence, deeming it a *"worthy competitor."* The group acts for about 12 NYSE-listed companies and a number of private interests. Attorneys have recently worked on a $100 million securities issuance for financial institutions, and the $350 million tender offer and asset sale of the Richmond, Fredericksburg and Potomac Railroad. The group also represented Metro Information Services in its $215 million merger with Keane.

The Lawyers: Endorsed as a *"prominent lawyer,"* **Julious Smith** has a traditional business practice, with particular expertise in representing private companies. Managing partner of the firm, he has experience acting in the financial and insurance sector, and for service-based companies.

The Clients: DTE Energy Services; Hilb, Rogal & Hamilton Company; LandAmerica Financial Group; Media General; Universal Corporation; Eastern Virginia Bankshares; First National Corporation; Grayson Bankshares.; Guaranty Financial Corporation and Solomon Alliance Group.

Kaufman & Canoles
The Firm: This Virginia firm can draw upon the support of offices around the state. The corporate group based in Norfolk has carved out a reputation among peers as the *"go-to firm in that part of the state."* Peers also spoke of its *"high-quality"* practice, which is the result of attracting *"talented lawyers."*

The Lawyers: **Vincent Mastracco** is *"a well-known and effective attorney,"* agree interviewees. Picked out as a *"good negotiator with a strong business sense,"* he focuses on securities law, corporate finance, and IPOs. He has recently advised companies marketing products using advanced technologies that were developed in federally-funded research labs.

The Clients: The firm advises public and private companies, both regional and national. It has also attracted international companies to its client base.

Willcox & Savage
The Firm: This full-service firm of 65 lawyers has two offices in the Hampton Roads area; interviewees perceived the firm to be a *"major force"* in the Norfolk market. Under the leadership of managing partner Thomas Johnson, it provides *"quality service"* and is respected for its *"strong business ties"* to the local community. M&A, joint venture agreements, securities issues and corporate governance are the key areas covered by the practice. It is also respected for its work in related areas such as tax planning.

The Clients: Alongside a base of regional and national corporates, the group also advises US subsidiaries of foreign-owned companies, particularly Scandinavian corporations, in areas such as international tax planning.

Cooley Godward LLP
The Firm: The Reston office of this California firm was opened to compete in the northern Virginia technology market. The group undertakes corporate work for hi-tech companies and financial institutions in growth areas and emerging technology markets. Venture capital work accounts for a significant portion of the practice, and the team has worked closely with start-up companies in successive rounds of financing.

The Lawyers: Fielding attorneys of the caliber of Mike Lincoln and Mark Spato, this firm is said to provide *"wonderful service."*

The Clients: The bulk of the client base comprises hi-tech ventures in the local market, and financial institutions and venture capitalists seeking investment opportunities.

Hale and Dorr
The Firm: The Reston office of this highly respected Boston firm opened in 2000 to access the mid-Atlantic technology market. Sources singled out its efforts in venture capital financing and M&A as proof that it *"has established a strong corporate practice in the region."*

The Lawyers: According to interviewees, **David Sylvester** is *"a delight to work with."* He acts for public and private corporate technology clients in the venture capital, IP, technology licensing and securities areas. Judged to be a *"skilled"* attorney in the technology market, he represents both hi-tech companies and venture capital funds

The Clients: The firm serves hi-tech companies and financiers in the local market.

LeClair Ryan
The Firm: This Richmond-based firm was established as a securities and venture capital boutique to serve entrepreneurs and venture capitalists on financings and M&A. Interviewees respect the firm as a *"successful player"* in this area.

The Lawyers: Name partners Gary LeClair and Dennis Ryan act for several NASDAQ companies and two NYSE-listed companies in all aspects of their business operations.

Shaw Pittman LLP
The Firm: Located in Tysons Corner, this DC firm has established a presence representing high-growth technology companies. A multidisciplinary team, which features Jack Lewis and Steven Meltzer, works with start-up clients on all aspects of corporate, financing and licensing matters. The firm has been involved in a large number of ventures in both healthcare and IT, and has worked on a number of venture capital financings. The team recently represented Landmark Systems in its $59 million cash sale to Allen Systems Group.

The Clients: Software; e-commerce; IT and telecoms growth companies; healthcare companies and venture capital investors.

EMPLOYMENT & LABOR LAW

VIRGINIA

EMPLOYMENT & LABOR LAW — MAINLY PLAINTIFF

VIRGINIA
Leading firms
(Employment: Mainly Plaintiff)
1. CHARLSON BREDEHOFT *Reston*
2. BUTLER, WILLIAMS, PANTELE *Richmond*

Leading individuals
(Employment: Mainly Plaintiff)
1. BREDEHOFT Elaine Charlson *Charlson*, Reston
2. BUTLER Harris *Butler, Williams, Pantele*, Richmond
3. LEVIT Jay *Levit, Mann, Halligan & Warren*, Richmond
   SIMONSEN David *Sole Practitioner*, Richmond

Firms and individuals are listed alphabetically in each band.

Charlson Bredehoft
The Firm: This small group focuses on representing individuals in employment discrimination and civil rights disputes. The group also has experience representing corporates such as Advent Group and Alcatel Data Networks. It has a busy civil litigation practice in both federal and state courts, primarily in northern Virginia and DC. Employment discrimination, civil rights matters, medical malpractice and general tort litigation constitute a majority of the practice.
The Lawyers: Elaine Charlson Bredehoft was nominated by interviewees for being *"as good as any employment lawyer across the country."* Focused on employment law and medical malpractice, she has an *"aggressive approach"* in court.

Butler, Williams, Pantele & Skilling
The Firm: *"A key player"* according to interviewees, this group maintains a selective plaintiffs' practice and regularly handles discrimination, sexual harassment, employee benefit and workplace safety disputes. It also provides advice and counsel on related preventative measures.
The Lawyers: The key name mentioned by market sources is **Harris Butler**. He has handled individual and class action employment-related claims, appearing before both state and federal courts, in combination with his work on tort litigation and personal injury matters.

Other Notable Practitioners
Jay Levit of Levit, Mann, Halligan & Warren was recommended to researchers as *"an seasoned attorney."* Based in Richmond, he focuses on labor and employment law, employee benefits, business litigation and personal injury matters. Sole practitioner **David Simonsen** was particularly recommended for his talent in *"arguing a point before the jury."* His practice encompasses all employment-related matters, including discrimination law, wage and hour issues and family medical leave.

EMPLOYMENT & LABOR LAW — MAINLY DEFENDANT

VIRGINIA
Leading firms
(Employment: Mainly Defendant)
1. HUNTON & WILLIAMS *Richmond*
   WILLIAMS MULLEN *Richmond*
2. MCGUIREWOODS LLP *Richmond*
3. TROUTMAN SANDERS LLP *Richmond*

Leading individuals
(Employment: Mainly Defendant)
1. MEATH James *Williams Mullen*, Richmond
   WELLFORD Hill *Hunton & Williams*, Richmond
2. ROBERTSON Gregory *Hunton & Williams*, Richmond
   WEBB Eugene *Troutman Sanders LLP*, Richmond
3. YOUNGER Carter *McGuireWoods LLP*, Richmond

Firms and individuals are listed alphabetically in each band.

Hunton & Williams
The Firm: Rivals endorsed this firm as *"the strongest of the competition."* Its employment litigation practice is particularly known for defending employers in class actions and discrimination claims resulting from company closures and workforce reductions. The group also consists of a large compliance practice experienced in dealing with federal audits and equal opportunity investigations. Attorneys here are thought to have *"represented every type of labor and employment case you can get."* A sizable practice in union negotiations and collective bargaining is complemented by general labor law representation and management training projects.
The Lawyers: The key name mentioned by peers was **Hill Wellford**. A *"savvy legal strategist,"* he is said to *"look at every conceivable point of view."* He holds extensive trial experience in large-scale discrimination cases and has recently defended a fair labor standards class action relating to overtime compensation. Also recommended by peers was **Gregory Robertson**. *"A significant player,"* he focuses on traditional labor law, including union and management relations and related litigation. He recently represented a Fortune 500 company in a non-compete case relating to several executives leaving the firm for a competitor. He also has experience with labor matters in the coal, textile and tobacco industries.
The Clients: Bunzel; HealthSouth Corporation; Dimon International; UPS; Volvo; Philip Morris; Mead Westvaco and Honeywell.

Williams Mullen
The Firm: Described by peers as *"a substantial practice,"* it is respected for its strong labor focus. The team represents employers facing unionization and those dealing with unions on a daily basis. For example, the group negotiated a labor agreement with an international union on behalf of a multinational. Collective bargaining agreements and unfair labor practice claims also feature in the workload. The firm is additionally recognized among sources for its *"aggressive"* employment litigation practice, which incorporates the defense of discrimination claims, wrongful discharge and emotional distress. Completing its full-service provisions, the group provides training in human resources issues and advice on employee benefits.
The Lawyers: Interviewees dubbed **James Meath** *"a classic labor relations lawyer."* Described as *"friendly but tough,"* he focuses on traditional labor law such as contracts negotiations, union avoidance, strikes and lockouts. He has negotiated with the United Steelworkers, which was trying to organize the workplace of his steel manufacturing client. He has also worked extensively in labor and international trade issues, particularly in South America.
The Clients: International Paper; Media General; Universal Corporation and American Standard Companies.

McGuireWoods LLP
The Firm: *"A regionally focused firm with a significant practice,"* according to peers. Drawing on the firm's reputation for *"trial prowess,"* the group is respected for its handling of employment-related litigation. The energy, chemical and pulp and paper industries are key sector clients, and the group has defended a paper manufacturer in a race discrimination class action. There is also a focus on union matters and labor law with attorneys counseling on employee relations, union campaigns and contract negotiations. The group is distinguished by its ability to attract international work, and advises both US and international companies that are expanding globally.

VIRGINIA — LITIGATION

The Lawyers: Respected as a *"tough litigator,"* **Carter Younger** has recently defended a paper manufacturer in a class action concerning employees rights to severance pay after the company was sold. His other specialties include drafting affirmative action plans for compliance and audits relating to government contracts.
The Clients: Siemens; DuPont; Dominion Resources and Bank of America.

Troutman Sanders LLP
The Firm: Following the merger of Virginia practice Mays & Valentine with Troutman Sanders, the Richmond team can now draw on the resources of a national firm, and has secured representation of matters outside of the state. For example, it represented a cigarette paper manufacturer in North Carolina in a collective bargaining agreement. Discrimination, wage and hour and breaches of contract claims form part of the workload. The group also advises clients on workplace issues, such as human resources policies, incentive pay systems and union avoidance strategies.

The Lawyers: Clients describe **Eugene Webb** as *"skilled and knowledgeable."* Expert in employment litigation, he regularly represents companies against claims on race and disability discrimination and sexual harassment claims. He also offers expertise in union-management relations and other labor law matters.
The Clients: Swedish Match North America, Infinity Technologies and Cadmus Communications are clients.

LITIGATION — GENERAL COMMERCIAL

VIRGINIA
Leading firms
(Litigation: General Commercial)

1. **HUNTON & WILLIAMS** Richmond
   MCGUIREWOODS LLP Richmond
2. **TROUTMAN SANDERS LLP** Richmond
3. **KAUFMAN & CANOLES** Norfolk
   WILLCOX & SAVAGE Norfolk
4. **CHRISTIAN & BARTON LLP** Richmond
   HIRSCHLER, FLEISCHER, WEINBERG Richmond
   WILLIAMS MULLEN Richmond

Leading individuals
(Litigation: General Commercial)

1. **ALLEN Everette** *Allen & Allen,* Richmond
   BROADDUS William *McGuireWoods LLP,* Richmond
   ROBERTS James *Troutman Sanders LLP,* Richmond
   SLATER Thomas *Hunton & Williams,* Richmond
   SMITH Michael *Christian & Barton LLP,* Richmond
2. **FARNHAM James** *Hunton & Williams,* Richmond
   KING William *McGuireWoods LLP,* Richmond
   PAGE Rosewell *McGuireWoods LLP,* Richmond
   POFF William *Woods, Rogers & Hazlegrove,* Roanoke
   SHUMADINE Conrad *Willcox & Savage,* Norfolk
   SIMS Hunter *Kaufman & Canoles,* Norfolk
   STILLMAN Gregory *Hunton & Williams,* Norfolk
   WHITTEMORE Anne Marie *McGuireWoods,* Richmond
   WITTHOEFFT Charles *Hirschler, Fleischer,* Richmond

Firms and individuals are listed alphabetically in each band.

Hunton & Williams
The Firm: Interviewees spoke of a *"nationally recognized"* litigation practice of *"extremely competent lawyers"* headquartered in Richmond. Competitors concede that such is the size of this group, *"they have the depth to handle any kind of commercial case."* Regarded as a *"classic"* litigation practice, its general commercial litigators undertake complex tort, antitrust, environmental and IP disputes.

The Lawyers: *"Top-notch"* **Thomas Slater** is best known for his antitrust expertise. He also litigates matters arising from national trade regulation, IP and patent disputes. He has extensive experience on a national level in price-fixing cases, and recently was lead counsel on such issues for a major paper manufacturer. The *"terrific"* **Jim Farnham** is renowned for his work in corporate and commercial litigation, such as securities and M&A disputes and business torts. He has been active recently in the financial services industry for a range of institutions, including plaintiffs and defendants in disputed IPOs. Managing partner of the Norfolk office, **Greg Stillman** is a *"wonderful commercial litigator,"* according to clients. Experienced in government contract litigation, he has lately been occupied with patent, IP and business torts.
The Clients: The firm attracts clients from the manufacturing, retail and financial services sector on both a national and international level.

McGuireWoods LLP
The Firm: This is a major Virginia-based law firm with *"excellent commercial trial lawyers."* Sources also pointed to a *"host of talented junior litigators around the big names."* The firm's products liability subgroup has a recognized expertise in representing Fortune 100 companies in national cases, and regularly represents leading auto manufacturers around the country. Historically strong in insurance, the firm is also commended for its antitrust expertise.

The Lawyers: Sources singled out **Bill Broaddus**, a former Attorney General of Virginia, for his *"outstanding reputation"* gained in private practice. He is active in environmental disputes, land use, and government regulation and securities disputes. He recently acted for a client in a suit brought under the CWA. **Bill King** has a national reputation for products liability litigation. He predominantly acts for two clients in the automotive, and science and technology industries, and has recently been involved in the high-profile lead paint litigation. **Rosewell Page** is a *"preeminent trial lawyer"* with a national practice. He has represented several auto manufacturers in products liability litigation. His activities include some healthcare and malpractice litigation, and he has also established litigation management systems for a number of product manufacturers. Observers reported that **Anne Marie Whittemore** displays *"superb litigious skills."* She has a trial and appellate practice that includes corporate, antitrust, securities and constitutional litigation matters.
The Clients: The firm has long-standing ties major Virginia corporations in the utilities, railroad and automobile industries. Ford, GM, Smithfield Foods and CSX Transportation are clients.

Troutman Sanders LLP
The Firm: Researchers were informed about the excellent statewide and local trial practice here that forms a key part of this full-service firm. Attorneys regularly represent the firm's major banking clients in a variety of cases, including suits brought against large debtors. The team also has an active regulatory practice in the electricity, gas and telecom industries. Close ties to the Virginia insurance industry, has been a fruitful source of work; attorneys have defended claims and advised on regulatory matters.
The Lawyers: **James Roberts** won accolades across the market, and is *"generally recognized as the top litigator in the state."* Competitors claim that he is a *"benchmark"* for the local bar and *"a tribute to the profession."* He recently represented a major accounting firm that had audited a corporation subsequently investigated by the SEC.
The Clients: The firm represents several railroad companies and large retailers in employment litigation, while clients are also drawn from firm's healthcare practice.

LITIGATION

VIRGINIA

Kaufman & Canoles
The Firm: Portrayed by sources as a *"strong"* practice based in an *"excellent commercial firm."* The litigation group is active in tort and insurance defense, IP, securities and antitrust matters. Products liability is a key strand in the firm's workload. The team is also respected for its work in alternative dispute resolution and mediation.
The Lawyers: **Hunter Sims** was singled out to researchers as a *"bright and honorable lawyer."* He acts for clients in antitrust and securities litigation, legal malpractice and libel matters.
The Clients: The firm acts for national and regional clients from the manufacturing, retail and construction industries.

Willcox & Savage
The Firm: This full-service Virginia law firm has two offices located in the Hampton Roads area. Its practice attracts work on a national level including products liability defense and bankruptcies.
The Lawyers: According to peers, **Conrad Shumadine** is *"one of the preeminent trial lawyers in Virginia."* He has experience in antitrust and banking litigation and is well regarded for his media cases including libel and First Amendment issues. He has acted for a local broadcasting company attempting to dissolve a limited liability company in which it had an investment.
The Clients: Local newspapers, national broadcasting companies, and other media holding companies are clients.

Christian & Barton LLP
The Firm: A smaller, full-service firm acting for emerging and established businesses in the Mid-Atlantic and Southeast regions. Its 20 lawyer litigation practice in the Richmond office is active in insurance coverage claims, securities disputes and products liability matters.
The Lawyers: Chair of the litigation practice **Michael Smith** has a broad scope of activity incorporating securities, healthcare, products liability and insurance defense. Sources commended him as *"good on his feet"* and *"well prepared for complex trials,"* they agreed that he is a *"big name"* in the state for complex commercial cases.
The Clients: Fortune 500 and private companies, drawn from the banking, communications, health care and transport industries, are clients.

Hirschler, Fleischer, Weinberg, Cox & Allen PC
The Firm: This full-service firm based in Richmond has a 23-trial lawyer team that focuses on securities, products liability, bankruptcy and construction litigation. The firm's excellent real estate practice ensures some land use and related litigation, too.
The Lawyers: Deemed a *"terrific litigator"* by interviewees, **Charles Witthoefft** handles contracts disputes and RICO and real estate related litigation, mostly within Virginia. A *"levelheaded"* presence, he recently represented a major insurance company in a dispute with local agents.
The Clients: Insurance companies, construction companies and real estate developers are clients.

Williams Mullen
The Firm: A Virginia firm with a network of offices around the state. The practice is structured by specialties and is active across a range of areas including insurance, products liability, banking, and bankruptcy litigation, mainly acting for creditors. In the utility industry, the firm represented Virginia's largest independent producer of electric power in a contract dispute with the state's largest utility. The firm has advised a manufacturer of recreational vehicles in products liability litigation, and acted for one of Virginia's largest banks in multimillion dollar environmental litigation.
The Lawyers: While no single individual stood out, researchers were impressed by the number of different litigators recommended at the firm. **Samuel Hixon** is a key member of this *"talented team."*
The Clients: National financial institutions and corporates, utilities and insurance companies are clients.

Other Notable Practitioners
Researchers were impressed with the level of endorsement for **Buddy Allen** of Allen & Allen Everette PC as a *"remarkably talented litigator."* His reputation as a *"tough, tenacious and aggressive"* attorney makes him a *"lawyer of choice in Richmond."* **Bill Poff** of Woods Rogers & Hazlegrove PLC is *"long recognized as the dean of the Roanoke bar."* His broad experience includes construction and labor work. Recent activity includes securitization, antitrust and class action litigation.

REAL ESTATE

VIRGINIA
Leading firms (Real Estate)

1
- HIRSCHLER, FLEISCHER, WEINBERG *Richmond*
- HUNTON & WILLIAMS *Richmond*
- MCGUIREWOODS LLP *Richmond*

2 TROUTMAN SANDERS LLP *Richmond*

Leading individuals (Real Estate)

1 WALSH William *Hunton & Williams, Richmond*

2
- BAGLEY Phillip *Troutman Sanders LLP, Richmond*
- WEINBERG Jay *Hirschler, Fleischer, Fredericksburg*

3
- AXSELLE Ralph *Williams Mullen, Richmond*
- LITTLE Nancy *McGuireWoods LLP, Richmond*

Firms and individuals are listed alphabetically in each band.

Hirschler, Fleischer, Weinberg, Cox & Allen PC
The Firm: This assertive group was recommended by clients offering service *"that can't be faulted."* A mid-sized, full-service firm, it is heavily weighted toward its real estate practice. Attorneys here advise on all areas of related law, and are dominant in supplying zoning and land use counsel. The group recently represented a client in the extension of a planned community and also negotiated permission for the development of an assisted-living facility for the elderly. Other subspecialties of the team include planned unit communities, multi-family leasing, mortgages and real estate tax.
The Lawyers: **Jay Weinberg** was described by peers as *"the dean of land use and zoning lawyers in Richmond."* He is noted for his expertise in zoning, variances, special use permits and subdivisions. He advised on Virginia Union University's rezoning of land for institutional use, and recently negotiated on behalf of Orient Express Hotels permission to expand its Keswick Hall development by 75 new resort units. Weinberg also covers some transactional real estate work, mostly acquisitions and dispositions of apartments and shopping centers.
The Clients: Wal-Mart; KFC; Ukrop's Supermarkets and HH Hunt.

Hunton & Williams
The Firm: One of the *"traditional competitors on the scene,"* according to rivals. The firm covers the gamut of real estate-related law, focusing on transactions, land use and development issues. It has expertise in financial matters, including problem loans, and assists foreign investors with managing and selling real estate in the US. It recently represented a national restaurant company in the lease-based financing of 160 restaurants.
The Lawyers: Sources described **William Walsh** as a *"good negotiator and straight-talking lawyer."*

VIRGINIA   REAL ESTATE

He is the head of the real estate group and specializes in commercial transactions. Described as *"self-effacing,"* he focuses on strategic planning, land development and financings. Walsh recently represented a public university in creating a private-sector structure to finance, construct and operate student housing units.
The Clients: Real estate investment companies, shopping center developers, real estate developers and large corporations with real estate needs are clients.

McGuireWoods LLP
The Firm: Interviewees singled out this firm for its *"real estate connections and political muscle."* It offers a varied practice that covers affordable housing developments and corporate transactions, public/private partnerships and leasings. An environmental practice supports the group, and the firm recently extended the life of a major landfill in Richmond. Attorneys represented Dominion Power in its acquisition of the Millstone Nuclear Power Plant in Connecticut, and assisted in the development of a 400,000 sq ft shopping center in Richmond.

The Lawyers: This group was recommended for its *"collection of fine lawyers"*. However **Nancy Little** was consistently cited by peers for her *"specialist expertise"* in synthetic leases, and sale and leasebacks. She has recently been working on nontraditional off-balance sheet financing for core corporate assets, such as headquarters and aircraft, and is also respected for her work in municipal financings and public/private partnerships.
The Clients: Capital One; Faison Associates; Dominion Virginia Power; Liberty Trust; City of Richmond; Wal-Mart and Arlington County.

Troutman Sanders LLP
The Firm: This group is the result of a merger between Virginia-based Mays & Valentine and Troutman Sanders in January 2001. The small group based in Richmond was recommended by peers as able to *"attract national companies who are moving to the area."* Amid its broad practice, the team specializes in multi-family financing and general commercial real estate, including development, financing and leasing.

The Lawyers: Phillip Bagley has *"a large practice in commercial transactional real estate law,"* according to peers. Financing takes up the majority of his time, particularly for shopping center developments. He also advises on the purchase, development and financing of office buildings. Land use and zoning makeup a smaller amount of his practice. Bagley has recently represented the lender in financing a $100 million regional shopping center in northern Virginia. He has also represented the developer of a $125 million, 750,000 sq ft shopping center in Richmond.
The Clients: Taubman Company, Teachers Insurance and Annuity Association of America and Wachovia Bank are clients.

Other Notable Practitioners
Ralph (Bill) Axselle of Williams Mullen is described by peers as an *"excellent lobbyist and zoning lawyer."* Chair of the firm's governmental affairs section, he focuses on land use, zoning, regulatory and administrative law.

Leaders in Virginia

ALLEN, Everette
Allen & Allen Attorneys at Law, PC, Richmond 804 545 1500
Recommended in Litigation

AXSELLE, Ralph
Williams Mullen, Richmond
804 643 1991
Recommended in Real Estate

BAGLEY, Phillip
Troutman Sanders LLP, Richmond
804 697 1200
Recommended in Real Estate

BAKER, Lewis
Watt, Tieder, Hoffar & Fitzgerald, L.L.P., McLean 703 749 1000
Recommended in Construction

BREDEHOFT, Elaine Charlson
Charlson Bredehoft, Reston
703 318 6800
Recommended in Employment

BROADDUS, William
McGuireWoods LLP, Richmond
804 775 1000
Recommended in Litigation

BUCKLEY, Kevin
Hunton & Williams, Richmond
804 788 8200
Recommended in Corporate/M&A

BURRUS, Robert
McGuireWoods LLP, Richmond
804 775 1000
Recommended in Corporate/M&A

BUTLER, Harris
Butler, Williams, Pantele & Skilling, Richmond 804 648 4848
Recommended in Employment

COX, Robert
Watt, Tieder, Hoffar & Fitzgerald, L.L.P., McLean 703 749 1000
Recommended in Construction

FARNHAM, James
Hunton & Williams, Richmond
804 788 8200
Recommended in Litigation

FITZGERALD, Robert
Watt, Tieder, Hoffar & Fitzgerald, L.L.P., McLean 703 749 1000
Recommended in Construction

GOOLSBY, Allen
Hunton & Williams, Richmond
804 788 8200
Recommended in Corporate/M&A

GRANDIS, Leslie
McGuireWoods LLP, Richmond
804 775 1000
Recommended in Corporate/M&A

HOFFAR, Julian
Watt, Tieder, Hoffar & Fitzgerald, L.L.P., McLean 703 749 1000
Recommended in Construction

JOHNSTON, Jay
Troutman Sanders LLP, Richmond
804 697 1200
Recommended in Corporate/M&A

KING, William
McGuireWoods LLP, Richmond
804 775 1000
Recommended in Litigation

LALLE, Wayne
Venable LLP, Vienna 703 760 1600
Recommended in Construction

LANE, David
Venable LLP, Vienna 703 760 1600
Recommended in Construction

LEVIT, Jay
Levit, Mann, Halligan & Warren, Richmond 804 355 7766
Recommended in Employment

LITTLE, Nancy
McGuireWoods LLP, Richmond
804 775 1000
Recommended in Real Estate

LOULAKIS, Michael
Wickwire Gavin, Vienna 703 790 8750
Recommended in Construction

MASTRACCO, Vincent
Kaufman & Canoles, Norfolk
757 624 3000
Recommended in Corporate/M&A

MCWHORTER, Val
Smith Pachter McWhorter & Allen, Vienna 703 847 6300
Recommended in Construction

MEATH, James
Williams Mullen, Richmond
804 643 1991
Recommended in Employment

MOORE, Thurston
Hunton & Williams, Richmond
804 788 8200
Recommended in Corporate/M&A

PAGE, Rosewell
McGuireWoods LLP, Richmond
804 775 1000
Recommended in Litigation

POFF, William
Woods, Rogers & Hazlegrove, P.L.C., Roanoke
540 983 7600; 800 552 4529
Recommended in Litigation

RAINEY, Gordon
Hunton & Williams, Richmond
804 788 8200
Recommended in Corporate/M&A

ROBERTS, James
Troutman Sanders LLP, Richmond
804 697 1200
Recommended in Litigation

ROBERTSON, Gregory
Hunton & Williams, Richmond
804 788 8200
Recommended in Employment

SHUMADINE, Conrad
Willcox & Savage, Norfolk
757 628 5500
Recommended in Litigation

SIMONSEN, David
David Simonsen Jnr - Sole Practitioner, Richmond 804 285 1337
Recommended in Employment

SIMS, Hunter
Kaufman & Canoles, Norfolk
757 624 3000
Recommended in Litigation

SLATER, Thomas
Hunton & Williams, Richmond
804 788 8200
Recommended in Litigation

SMITH, Michael
Christian & Barton, L.L.P., Richmond
804 697 4100
Recommended in Litigation

SMITH, Julious
Williams Mullen, Richmond
804 643 1991
Recommended in Corporate/M&A

STILLMAN, Gregory
Hunton & Williams, Norfolk
757 640 5300
Recommended in Litigation

SYLVESTER, David
Hale and Dorr, Reston 703 654 7000
Recommended in Corporate/M&A

THOMPSON, Gary
Hunton & Williams, Richmond
804 788 8200
Recommended in Corporate/M&A

TIEDER, John
Watt, Tieder, Hoffar & Fitzgerald, L.L.P., McLean 703 749 1000
Recommended in Construction

VAUGHAN, Porter
Hunton & Williams, Richmond
804 788 8200
Recommended in Corporate/M&A

WALSH, William
Hunton & Williams, Richmond
804 788 8200
Recommended in Real Estate

WATT, Robert
Watt, Tieder, Hoffar & Fitzgerald, L.L.P., McLean 703 749 1000
Recommended in Construction

WEBB, Eugene
Troutman Sanders LLP, Richmond
804 697 1200
Recommended in Employment

WEINBERG, Jay
Hirschler, Fleischer, Weinberg, Cox & Allen A Professional Corporation, Fredericksburg 540 372 3515
Recommended in Real Estate

WELLFORD, Hill
Hunton & Williams, Richmond
804 788 8200
Recommended in Employment

WHITTEMORE, Anne Marie
McGuireWoods LLP, Richmond
804 775 1000
Recommended in Litigation

WICKWIRE, Jon
Wickwire Gavin, Vienna 703 790 8750
Recommended in Construction

WITTHOEFFT, Charles
Hirschler, Fleischer, Weinberg, Cox & Allen A Professional Corporation, Richmond 804 771 9500
Recommended in Litigation

WRIGHT, Murray
Wright Robinson Osthimer & Tatum, Richmond 804 783 1100
Recommended in Construction

YOUNGER, Carter
McGuireWoods LLP, Richmond
804 775 1000
Recommended in Employment

WASHINGTON

CORPORATE/M&A

CONTENTS: Corporate/M&A p.706; Employment: Mainly Plaintiff p.707; Mainly Defendant p.708; Litigation: General Commercial p.709; Real Estate p.710; Individuals' Profiles p.712.

WASHINGTON'S TOP THREE
1. Perkins Coie
2. Davis Wright Tremaine
3. Preston Gates & Ellis

Ranking based on Chambers' research within the state.

All quotes in the text are from interviews with clients and competitors.

OVERVIEW: Top-ranking **Perkins Coie** fares well across the board, and the firm's breadth of work is one of its key selling points. A top-tier corporate practice attracts the biggest clients in the state, and is particularly noted for its corporate finance work. The firm also has one of the largest employment groups in Washington; much of its expertise in this area is rooted to its work representing Boeing. The respected litigation practice has a strong commercial slant, too. Here, the relationship with Boeing has produced a niche in aviation and aerospace issues. The firm's real estate practice represents clients across a range of industries and benefits from considerable strength in tax and financing matters. Stewart Landefeld, chair of the corporate finance practice, is widely respected, as is William Green, an expert in corporate real estate. Clients include Amazon.com and the University of Washington.

Second-ranked **Davis Wright Tremaine** has made a name for itself in corporate finance and business advice. It is particularly active in venture capital matters, and corporate lawyer Joseph Weinstein is well known for his M&A work. The firm is also admired for its litigation capacities, which have been boosted recently by the addition of specialists from the Seed Law Group. A respected employment group, chaired by litigator Michael Reiss, has earned a reputation for a proactive and preventative approach to employment disputes. Clients include Bank of America and Starbucks.

Preston Gates & Ellis, in third place, is widely associated with marquee client Microsoft. Bill Gates' father is one of the founders of this firm, and the association with Microsoft has engendered a strong reputation for the firm's litigation practice in relation to IP and hi-tech issues. The corporate practice here, featuring Kent Carlson, is active in emerging growth markets. A real estate department, including new recruit Scott Osbourne, represents a number of high-profile clients on major property transactions. Clients include T-Mobile and the State of Alaska.

CORPORATE/M&A

WASHINGTON
Leading firms (Corporate/M&A)
1. **PERKINS COIE LLP** Seattle
2. **DAVIS WRIGHT TREMAINE LLP** Seattle
   PRESTON GATES & ELLIS LLP Seattle
3. **LANE POWELL SPEARS LUBERSKY LLP** Seattle
4. **FOSTER PEPPER & SHEFELMAN PLLC** Seattle

Leading individuals (Corporate/M&A)
1. **CARLSON** Kent *Preston Gates & Ellis LLP,* Seattle
   MORGAN Michael *Lane Powell Spears,* Seattle
   WEINSTEIN Joseph *Davis Wright Tremaine,* Seattle
2. **DWYER** Michael *Lane Powell Spears Lubersky,* Seattle
   GITTINGER Wayne *Lane Powell Spears Lubersky,* Seattle
   LANDEFELD Stewart *Perkins Coie LLP,* Seattle

Firms and individuals are listed alphabetically in each band.

Perkins Coie LLP

The Firm: This *"outstanding firm"* provides general corporate counseling on public offerings, M&A, venture capital investments, joint ventures and strategic alliances. The firm is thought to have a *"solid business practice,"* which particularly excels in corporate finance matters, and has been described to researchers as the *"volume leader"* for corporate work in the state. Attorneys represent a broad range of clients, with particular concentration in the biotech, software and telecom sectors. The past year has seen an increased demand for financing work, particularly in relation to existing company portfolios. A rise in private sector M&A and the creation of strategic alliances has also helped to ensure that the group has been in demand despite a relatively soft market. Practitioners have been repeatedly commended for their *"extremely thorough"* approach, and for the outstanding technical quality of their work.

The Lawyers: Chair of the corporate finance practice **Stewart Landefeld** is a highly respected attorney whose practice encompasses private company M&A, public offerings and IPOs, venture capital, alternative equity investments, and an increasing amount of public company work. Landefeld was recently involved in the IPO for Quinton Cardiology Systems, and advised upon the $6.5 billion exchange offer for AT&T Wireless Services.

The Clients: Amazon.com; Weyerhaeuser; Expedia; AT&T Wireless Services; ZymoGenetics; Puget Sound Energy; EDEN Bioscience; Quinton Cardiology Systems; Atlas Venture and Northwest Venture Associates.

Davis Wright Tremaine LLP
see firm details p.787

The Firm: This firm's *"fine reputation"* for corporate finance and general business advice extends throughout the Northwest. A team of *"highly capable"* lawyers undertakes a range of commercial and corporate work for all industry groups, and is exceptionally well regarded for its banking work. The group has been particularly active in venture capital financing, and has shown strength in dealing with LLC transactions and partnership formations. Private investment partnership work features heavily in the firm's workload, with a large proportion undertaken by its Seattle and Portland offices. Representation of hedge funds is proving a growth area for the firm, recently resulting in lateral hiring within the corporate finance department in order to meet increasing demand. Commentators consistently remark that the firm's size has not affected the quality of its service; clients praise Davis Wright Tremaine as *"a large firm that conducts itself like a mid-sized firm,"* observing that *"they treat us as though we were their only client."* Although the firm is more than equipped to handle big deals, midmarket transactions appear to be its forte. Nevertheless, the firm's stature as a player in international corporate matters has been augmented by work for clients such as the global service provider, Tenzing Communications.

The Lawyers: **Joseph Weinstein** (see p.713) received strong market commendation as a *"talented"* and *"highly esteemed"* member of the M&A group. His varied experience in corporate matters includes representing the owners in the sale of the basketball team, the Vancouver Grizzlies, and advising upon M&A issues relating to the food industries.

The Clients: Lanoga; RB Rubber Products; Tenzing Communications and Pacific Crest Securities.

CORPORATE/M&A

WASHINGTON

Preston Gates & Ellis LLP
The Firm: The firm provides a full range of corporate legal services, although particular strength was felt to exist in public and private M&A, private equity transactions and cross-border work with Canadian companies. The group is especially active in emerging growth markets, representing issuers in preferred stock financings and advising clients on exploiting venture capital opportunities. Practitioners often appear on high-profile matters; notable work includes counseling Microsoft in the transfer of its stake in Expedia to USA Networks. The firm has also advised on the $500,000 purchase of bonds and warrants for common stock issues by Korea Telecom and the acquisitions of PowerTel and Aerial Communications by VoiceStream Wireless. Interviewees particularly praised the group's hardworking ethic, noting practitioners' willingness to *"jump into the fray at a moment's notice"* and *"work 24/7"* on large transactions.
The Lawyers: **Kent Carlson**, former chair of the business law section of the Washington State Bar Association, has long been considered *"the hit of the corporate practice."* His practice encompasses M&A, complex strategic relationships, financings and reorganizations. He acted in the sale of Optiva Corporation to Philips Holdings USA.
The Clients: Microsoft; T-Mobile; Flow International; Western Wireless and Labor Ready.

Lane Powell Spears Lubersky LLP
The Firm: Clients and peers describe the firm's broad corporate practice as both *"excellent"* and *"responsive."* An overarching business department incorporates a variety of industry focus groups, including banking, financial services, M&A, corporate finance and securities, emerging companies, venture investment and international business. Practitioners have a loyal following among industries from the Pacific Northwest. Although more frequently seen acting for small to mid-sized companies, the firm's regular representation of Nordstrom demonstrates its capacity to undertake large corporate deals. The firm represented DataChannel in its acquisition by Netegrity, acted for Northwest Biotherapeutics in its recent IPO, and advised ImageX.com on a PIPE (private investment in public equity) financing of common stock.
The Lawyers: **Michael Morgan** was described as a *"fabulous"* attorney skilled at *"moving along"* M&A and corporate finance transactions. Much of his practice involves providing general corporate advice to publicly and privately held companies. Morgan recently represented Highwire in its sale to Galileo International, and Enchanted Parks in its sale to Six Flags. Comanaging partner **Michael Dwyer** was recommended as an *"excellent"* corporate attorney. His *"easy manner"* and *"responsive attitude"* make him a favorite of local clients. Interviewees endorse **Wayne Gittinger** for his ability to *"resolve issues fairly in transactions"* in a way that *"leaves both parties feeling good about the outcome."*
The Clients: Nordstrom; Northwest Biotherapeutics; ImageX.com; Highwire; DataChannel; Fluent Communications; Vincor International; Primal Inc and Corus Pharma.

Foster Pepper & Shefelman PLLC
The Firm: A noted presence in the Northwest, the firm's business group advises on emerging company and venture capital work, M&A and reorganizations, corporate finance and securities. A strategic alliance with DC-based Akin Gump Strauss Hauer & Feld is felt to have significantly expanded the practice's coverage and corporate capabilities. This 22-strong group of *"fine lawyers"* provides general business counseling to publicly traded corporations, closely held businesses and individuals. The firm has particular experience in corporate finance matters, and is often associated with long-standing client Washington Mutual. Individual practitioners focus on sports-related matters, and the firm notably represented Football Northwest, a Paul Allen company, in its acquisition of the Seattle Seahawks.
The Lawyers: **Allen Israel** cochairs the mergers, acquisitions and reorganizations practice group from the Seattle office.
The Clients: Paul Allen; Football Northwest; First & Goal; the Washington State Investment Board and Costco Companies.

EMPLOYMENT & LABOR LAW

MAINLY PLAINTIFF

WASHINGTON
Leading firms
(Employment: Mainly Plaintiff)
[1] **FRANK ROSEN FREED ROBERTS LLP** Seattle
MACDONALD, HOAGUE & BAYLESS Seattle
RINEHART ROBBLEE HANNAH Seattle

Firms are listed alphabetically in each band.

Frank Rosen Freed Roberts LLP
The Firm: This *"effective"* five-partner practice specializes in representing individual employees and labor unions throughout the state. On the union side, work undertaken includes representation in grievance and arbitration processes, collective bargaining and providing training and litigation. The greater part of the practice consists of individual representation, and practitioners have diverse experience counseling employees on individual claims and strategies for negotiating with management. The firm represents employees in all employment matters apart from workers' compensation issues. The group recently represented the Amalgamated Transit Union, Local 587, at state Supreme Court level in its successful challenge to the constitutional validity of a King County transit tax initiative.
The Lawyers: Felt to be *"one of the best"* plaintiffs attorneys in the state, **Jon Rosen** is widely respected for courtroom successes such as a notable win in the Sellsted v Washington Mutual Savings Bank age discrimination case. Rosen acts primarily for individual employees, although a significant proportion of his practice also entails counseling and representing trade unions.
The Clients: Amalgamated Transit Union; American Federation of Teachers and Washington State Council of County and City Employees.

MacDonald, Hoague & Bayless
The Firm: The firm was warmly recommended as a *"professional and knowledgeable"* outfit, staffed by *"straight-talking"* attorneys with deep experience in the area. Members represent public and private sector unions and individual employees in all areas of labor and employment law, particularly before state and federal courts and administrative agencies. Much of the group's work overlaps with a well-developed civil rights practice. The firm is known for successfully obtaining an injunction barring physically invasive searches of female prisoners by male guards in the landmark Jordan v Gardner case.
The Lawyers: *"Effective"* **Kay Frank** is considered the *"lead lawyer"* of the practice. Peers and rivals admire her *"unflagging dedication"* to employment and civil liberties cases. Her practice centers largely around discrimination and sexual harassment issues. On the civil rights side, Frank is well known for bringing a class action against the Washington Corrections Center for Women in connection with the healthcare received by prisoners.
The Clients: Practitioners advise both public and private sector unions and individual employees on all aspects of labor and employment law.

Rinehart Robblee Hannah
The Firm: Acting exclusively for labor unions, this nine-lawyer group has built up a loyal following among local labor associations. The firm's

WASHINGTON — EMPLOYMENT & LABOR LAW

WASHINGTON
Leading individuals
(Employment: Mainly Plaintiff)

1
- **ARDITI Abraham** Sole Practitioner, Seattle
- **FLETCHER Kelby** Peterson, Young, Putra, Seattle
- **FRANK Katrin** MacDonald, Hoague & Bayless, Seattle
- **HANNAH David** Rinehart Robblee Hannah, Seattle
- **LONNQUIST Judith** Sole Practitioner, Seattle
- **RINEHART John** Rinehart Robblee Hannah, Seattle
- **ROSEN Jon** Frank Rosen Freed Roberts LLP, Seattle

Individuals are listed alphabetically in each band.

historic commitment to the area is felt to give it a competitive edge; practitioners were particularly commended for their *"comprehensive"* knowledge of the development and application of labor law. Typical work includes counseling unions on their negotiations with management on behalf of individual members, providing advocacy in defending and contesting union decisions, and representing labor unions as employers. The firm was involved in the Aztech Electric Co case, in which it successfully challenged a labor practice that denied opportunities to union members and organizers.

The Lawyers: **David Hannah** was recognized as a *"trustworthy"* labor lawyer with the ability to see *"the big picture."* *"Exceptional"* attorney **John Rinehart** is widely respected as *"a trusted counsel to the labor movement."* His practice focuses primarily on labor arbitration matters.

The Clients: The firm advises the International Association of Machinists and Aerospace Workers and the United Food and Commercial Workers Union (Washington), as well as construction trade worker, electrical, carpentry and operating engineer unions.

Other Notable Practitioners

Considered by some to be the *"dean of the plaintiffs' bar,"* sole practitioner **Abraham Arditi** (see p.712) was praised as a *"zealous advocate"* who *"will do anything for his clients."* This *"careful and meticulous"* attorney handles a range of sex, race, age and national origin discrimination suits. He has recently been involved in public policy discharge and reasonable accommodation cases. Also recommended for her advocacy skills, **Judith Lonnquist** is said to be *"charming but deadly"* in litigation. Peers agree she *"gets results"* in discrimination cases, commenting that *"don't want to be against her without a cast-iron defense."* **Kelby Fletcher** of Peterson, Young, Putra, Fletcher, Zeder, Massong & Knopp is well known for representing individuals on the plaintiffs' side. Described as *"the model of what a good lawyer should be,"* Fletcher broke new ground by persuading the court to recognize sexual dysphoria as a disability under Washington state law.

EMPLOYMENT & LABOR LAW — MAINLY DEFENDANT

WASHINGTON
Leading firms
(Employment: Mainly Defendant)

1
- **DAVIS WRIGHT TREMAINE LLP** Seattle
- **PERKINS COIE LLP** Seattle

2
- **RIDDELL WILLIAMS PS** Seattle
- **SEBRIS BUSTO** Bellevue

Leading individuals
(Employment: Mainly Defendant)

1
- **JONES Karen** Riddell Williams PS, Seattle
- **LEMLY Tom** Davis Wright Tremaine LLP, Seattle
- **PERISHO Russell** Perkins Coie LLP, Seattle

2
- **ASLIN John** Perkins Coie LLP, Seattle
- **BUSTO Mark** Sebris Busto, Bellevue
- **CAIRNS Carolyn** Stokes Lawrence, PS, Seattle
- **HUTCHESON Mark** Davis Wright Tremaine, Seattle
- **PRESTON Anne** Garvey, Schubert & Barer, Seattle
- **REISS Mike** Davis Wright Tremaine LLP, Seattle
- **SEBRIS Robert** Sebris Busto, Bellevue

Firms and individuals are listed alphabetically in each band.

Davis Wright Tremaine LLP
see firm details p.787

The Firm: This firm is thought to have an *"excellent"* and *"well-organized"* labor and employment group comprising a *"number of highly capable and well-respected lawyers."*

The team advises on labor/management relations, litigation, pensions and insurance matters. Additional practitioners in the Seattle office contribute specialized immigration and ERISA expertise. The firm emphasizes a proactive and preventative approach to employment disputes, and makes a broad range of products, seminars and training opportunities available to employers.

The Lawyers: Chair of the firm's employment litigation practice, **Michael Reiss** (see p.713) maintains a varied workload that encompasses mediation and litigation of discrimination suits, wrongful discharge cases and wage and hour class actions.

A former regional attorney to the EEOC, Reiss acted as cocounsel for Boeing in a nationwide employment class action, and served as court-appointed special master in a nationwide Title VII race discrimination class action. **Tom Lemly** (see p.713) receives widespread praise for his broad experience in employment matters. Rivals describe him as a *"tough opponent"* with a *"careful and impressive"* courtroom style. Robert Blackstone handles executive employment, non-competition and trade secrets issues in addition to his traditional labor law and management relations practice. This *"effective"* attorney has shown particular aptitude in dealing with politically sensitive employment issues. Blackstone was involved in negotiating labor contracts for AT&T Broadband in multiple locations in California. His colleague, **Mark Hutcheson** (see p.713), practices traditional management labor law and has particular expertise in representing the healthcare and maritime industries.

The Clients: The group has a number of long-standing clients, and frequently advises employers from the healthcare, retail, technology and media and communications industries. Clients include: American Red Cross; Bank of America; The Seattle Times; University of Puget Sound; Boeing and Home Depot.

Perkins Coie LLP

The Firm: Reported to have *"one of the largest and deepest"* employment practices in the state, the firm is felt to do a *"top-notch job"* on labor and employment matters. A *"blue-ribbon"* department grew from the firm's historical representation of Boeing, and subsequently developed expertise in a wide variety of class action matters. The firm focuses exclusively on employers' defense work, for both public and private clients. Although a significant proportion of the group's work has been for forest parks and Pacific maritime interests, it has recently attracted a number of clients from the technology and telecom sectors. The past year has seen a rise in traditional labor law matters, and the group has been active on a steady influx of wage and hour class actions and disability discrimination claims. The firm offers seminar training for employers and runs a monthly 'breakfast briefing' series to inform clients about emerging employment law issues and to promote a preventative approach to employment problems.

The Lawyers: **John Aslin,** is widely thought to be a *"standout"* litigator with specific expertise in equal opportunities matters. Described as *"fair-minded"* and *"scrupulously honest,"* Aslin has been involved in the EEOC v Alaska Airlines age discrimination class action, and in discrimination litigation relating to Thurston v First Interstate Bank. Another *"preeminent"*

EMPLOYMENT & LABOR LAW

WASHINGTON

practitioner at the firm, **Russell Perisho**, has been described to *Chambers'* researchers as a *"dynamite"* employment trial lawyer. Perisho's practice incorporates acting for businesses and public agencies in disability discrimination, general employment and labor relations matters.

The Clients: Boeing; Amazon.com; Starbucks; Seattle Mariners; Seattle Sonics; IBM; City of Bellevue; University of Washington and King County.

Riddell Williams PS

The Firm: This highly respected eight-attorney practice provides a broad range of employment-related services to employers, including management training, annual seminars and regular employment law updates. The firm also offers counseling on labor/management relations and has a well-developed alternative dispute resolution practice to address employment-related grievances. Practitioners have experience of defending employers in a variety of courts and administrative agencies, and notably represented a hospital in a landmark appeal that resulted in changes to the state's Employment Security Department's regulations.

The Lawyers: Peers recommend **Karen Jones** as an *"absolutely terrific"* attorney, *"deeply committed"* to the field. Her practice ranges from harassment and trade secrets misappropriation claims to management and employee training programs. Jones is well known as a speaker on employment issues. She was once appointed by the Washington Supreme Court to assist in developing pattern jury instructions to be used in employment cases tried in the Washington courts.

The Clients: The group represents United Airlines, Allstate, Pizza Hut and other regional and national private and public employers.

Sebris Busto

The Firm: Interviewees report that this Bellevue labor and employment boutique *"stands out for the quality of its lawyers."* Nine lawyers act exclusively for management on litigation and arbitration proceedings and provide them with strategic advice and day-to-day employment counseling. The firm also carries out investigations on behalf of clients and third parties and undertakes a significant amount of referred cases. The firm has a diverse mix of public and private sector clients, and has particular expertise in representing municipalities and healthcare clients in a range of employment law issues.

The Lawyers: Managing partner **Mark Busto** (see p.712) received widespread commendation as a *"bright and capable litigator,"* with extensive experience of labor and employment law matters. Busto serves on the executive committee of the labor and employment law section of the Washington State Bar Association and has been cocounsel in the protracted Drinkwitz v Alliant Techsystems litigation. He was also recently involved in obtaining a summary judgment in a retaliation case brought against contractor Lease Crutcher Lewis.

His partner **Robert Sebris** (see p.713) was reported to have *"an edge"* in traditional labor law matters. Sebris has significant expertise in collective bargaining, negotiation and general counseling matters. He speaks frequently and writes widely on a variety of employment and labor law issues at the Washington State Bar.

The Clients: The firm acts exclusively for the management of public and private companies and for a large number of healthcare clients, public sector organizations and local municipalities.

Other Notable Practitioners

Carolyn Cairns of Stokes Lawrence has consistently been recognized as an able general employment practitioner, whose broad and successful practice includes employee relations counseling, litigation and training matters. She has been trial attorney and supervisory trial attorney for the EEOC, past president of the Federal Bar Association of the Western District of Washington, and chair of the employment law section of the Washington State Trial Lawyers Association. **Anne Preston** of Garvey Schubert & Barer was also recommended for her practical and responsive approach to clients. She undertakes a mix of management training, general counseling and litigation work on behalf of employers.

LITIGATION

GENERAL COMMERCIAL

WASHINGTON
Leading firms
(Litigation: General Commercial)

1. **BYRNES & KELLER** Seattle
2. **DAVIS WRIGHT TREMAINE LLP** Seattle
   LANE POWELL SPEARS LUBERSKY LLP Seattle
3. **CORR CRONIN LLP** Seattle
   PERKINS COIE LLP Seattle
   PRESTON GATES & ELLIS LLP Seattle

Leading individuals
(Litigation: General Commercial)

1. **BYRNES Peter** *Byrnes & Keller*, Seattle
2. **KELLER Brad** *Byrnes & Keller*, Seattle
3. **CORR Kelly** *Corr Cronin LLP*, Seattle

Firms and individuals are listed alphabetically in each band.

Byrnes & Keller

The Firm: Since the firm's inception in 1984, Byrnes & Keller has rapidly acquired an outstanding reputation for its trial practice, and has subsequently become one of the undisputed leaders for litigation matters in the Pacific Northwest. The boutique has a distinct commercial bias, although attorneys undertake a broad scope of work ranging from defense and prosecution in complex commercial disputes to personal injury matters. Accomplishments include defending local law firms against professional liability claims and serving as special counsel to the Washington State Commission on Judicial Conduct. Practitioners were reported to display particular *"flair"* for securities cases and professional and products liability suits. The firm has been involved in a number of high-profile cases entailing the defense of pharmaceutical manufacturers against class action suits, and has handled some of the first US fetal alcohol syndrome products liability cases. With a reputation as a responsive firm that charges reasonable rates, clients agree: *"It is hard to find a small firm with as high a caliber of lawyers as Byrnes & Keller."*

The Lawyers: *"Top-notch"* **Peter Byrnes** is highly sought after in complex litigation matters. His experience as lead counsel in high-profile cases such as the 'Exxon Valdez' oil spill has secured his status among peers and clients as *"the man we call when we're in trouble."* His partner, **Brad Keller**, was also recognized as an outstanding attorney with an aggressive courtroom style. Keller's *"personable rapport"* with clients makes him a frequent recipient of referrals and repeat custom. He has represented Boeing and Honeywell in toxic fumes suits, and has acted on numerous liability, securities and RICO cases.

The Clients: Honeywell; Boeing; Abbott Laboratories; American National Insurance Company; Kimberly-Clark; Washington State Commission on Judicial Conduct and RJ Reynolds.

Davis Wright Tremaine LLP

see firm details p.787

The Firm: This *"well-respected"* firm boasts a large and comprehensive litigation practice, equipped to handle a wide variety of contentious matters. It litigates on commercial, antitrust and healthcare matters and represents defendants in personal injury cases. The litigation group is perhaps best known for its representation of institutional clients

WASHINGTON

LITIGATION

in the banking, media and real estate sectors. However, the recent addition of IP and litigation specialists from the Seed Law Group has significantly boosted the firm's patent, trademark and trade secrets capabilities. Within the Washington market, the group still receives kudos for its successful representation of the plaintiffs in the 'Exxon Valdez' oil spill, which resulted in the largest punitive damages verdict ever assessed by a jury.
The Lawyers: Ladd Leavens heads the Seattle litigation practice.
The Clients: Bank of America; Microsoft; Starbucks and The Seattle Times.

Lane Powell Spears Lubersky LLP
The Firm: Market commentators routinely recommend the firm as *"strong at all levels"* from mediation and arbitration to trial and appeal matters. A large commercial litigation team handles disputes ranging from securities and commercial contracts suits to IP and internet matters. A small but highly regarded appellate unit has experience defending industries in nearly every sector at the highest levels of litigation, and deals with all contested matters apart from criminal and family work. A large proportion of the group's workload consists of employment, IP, maritime and pollution cases. Much of the practice's work originates in the Northwest, although the appellate practice has developed its international reach by undertaking work emerging from the firm's international and London practice groups, which rely heavily upon institutional ties to large UK insurers. Recent cases include a win for First American Title Insurance against the Washington State Department of Revenue in a landmark case concerning the taxation of insurance premiums. Another favorable verdict was achieved for Wal-Mart in a suit concerning the application of 'shopkeeper's privilege' and the admissibility of reputation testimony.
The Clients: Nordstrom; Cutter & Buck; Chevron Texaco; Wal-Mart and First American.

Corr Cronin LLP
The Firm: This relatively new litigation boutique comprises *"good, no-nonsense lawyers"* with both the ability and the enthusiasm to deal with large, complicated litigation issues. The bulk of the firm's workload relates to commercial disputes varying from employment and personal injury to products liability and IP matters. The firm has earned a solid reputation for class action defense work, and recently defended the State of Washington in suits arising from multiple placements of young people in foster care. Practitioners act for both multinationals and local businesses, but are known to be particularly experienced in high-stakes commercial litigation for corporations with interests in the Northwest. The extensive experience of the firm's litigators and its boutique status have proved to be a potent mix, which has attracted some of the most complex cases and high-profile clients in the State of Washington. Among the new clients are several from the oil and gas industry, following its successful representation of ExxonMobil in a $1.3 billion tax assessment dispute with the State of Alaska concerning the valuation of oil produced by the company in the state over a seven-year period.
The Lawyers: Peers commend **Kelly Corr** for his ability to obtain favorable results in large, complex court cases. Corr has extensive experience in high-profile civil and criminal litigation matters, and was selected as lead trial counsel for Nirvana LLC in its dispute with Courtney Love over her representation of Kurt Cobain's estate and the release of additional Nirvana music.
The Clients: Nirvana LLC; Alaska Airlines; ExxonMobil; Alamo Rent A Car and National Car Rental.

Perkins Coie LLP
The Firm: This well-respected litigation practice maintains a strong commercial slant but undertakes all manner of contentious cases ranging from antitrust and IP suits to criminal and personal injury cases. A substantial niche in aviation and aerospace matters has grown up around the firm's long-standing ties with Boeing, who the group continues to advise in the capacity of worldwide products liability counsel. Practitioners deal increasingly with class action suits in the biotech and e-commerce industries. The firm's size and local prominence attracts a variety of high-profile cases for a client base of private and public companies, Fortune 500 companies and national government associations. Highlights include the successful alternative dispute resolution settlement of a large antitrust and trade secrets dispute, involvement in a landmark trial regarding insurance coverage for environmental costs, and the defense of an investment banking firm against a shareholder class action proceeding from a merger fairness opinion.
The Lawyers: The litigation practice group is chaired by Thomas Boeder.
The Clients: Boeing; Puget Sound Energy; Weyerhaeuser; Louisiana-Pacific; GlaxoSmithKline; Mallinckrodt; Amazon.com and Yahoo!

Preston Gates & Ellis LLP
The Firm: A historical association with Microsoft has engendered a particularly strong reputation for IP and general commercial litigation on behalf of hi-tech organizations. The practice emphasizes business and commercial litigation, although a noteworthy municipal finance department generates an increasing amount of public sector litigation for the group. An extremely varied department is divided according to practice group, covering areas as disparate as health, antitrust, election and environmental law and class actions. The firm enjoys a similarly diverse client base, and has gained widespread respect for the breadth of the litigation matters it undertakes. The practitioners have been described as trustworthy, high-quality attorneys whose *"word is their bond."* The firm represented the State of Alaska in the 1989 'Exxon Valdez' oil spill litigation, which resulted in a $1 billion settlement for the state, defended a Fortune 100 company in a class action monopolization claim, and negotiated a settlement of a natural resource damage claim brought against a Seattle regional sewer and waste water authority by the NOAA (National Oceanic and Atmospheric Administration).
The Lawyers: Karl Quackenbush chairs the litigation practice group.
The Clients: Microsoft; Aketon Technologies; Voicestream Wireless; CallVision; State of Alaska; City of Bellingham; Harley-Davidson and The Raymond Corporation.

REAL ESTATE

Foster Pepper & Shefelman PLLC
The Firm: This *"exceptionally fine"* real estate and land use practice offers a comprehensive range of services to a varied clientele. The team applies a multidisciplinary approach to real estate issues, drawing on strengths in the related areas of real estate litigation, public and private projects and bankruptcy/creditors' rights. The practice has a Northwest and multi-state focus, with particular emphasis on regional development projects. The group receives strong market recommendation for its visibility on large public projects such as the new Seattle Seahawks Stadium, the runway project for the Port of Seattle and the 'Experience Music Project.' Peers frequently remark on the team's breadth and depth, while clients value its *"balance,"* commenting that the practice is *"big enough to meet our needs, but not so big that we get lost."*
The Lawyers: **Michael Kuntz** has been described as the firm's strongest lawyer, known for his responsive and analytical approach to problem solving. His real estate and real estate finance practice focuses on the representation of commercial and residential developers and development interests. Also

REAL ESTATE — WASHINGTON

WASHINGTON
Leading firms (Real Estate)

1 FOSTER PEPPER & SHEFELMAN PLLC *Seattle*
PRESTON GATES & ELLIS LLP *Seattle*
2 ALSTON, COURTNAGE & BASSETTI LLP *Seattle*
BUCK & GORDON LLP *Seattle*
3 PERKINS COIE LLP *Seattle*
4 PHILLIPS MCCULLOUGH WILSON HILL *Seattle*
STOEL RIVES LLP *Seattle*

WASHINGTON
Leading individuals (Real Estate)

1 OSBOURNE Scott *Preston Gates & Ellis LLP, Seattle*
2 COURTNAGE Michael *Alston, Courtnage, Seattle*
GREEN William *Perkins Coie LLP, Seattle*
KUNTZ Michael *Foster Pepper & Shefelman, Seattle*
SKINNER Shannon *Preston Gates & Ellis LLP, Seattle*
3 BLOCK William *Buck & Gordon LLP, Seattle*
DIAL Ellen *Perkins Coie LLP, Seattle*
FLUHRER Gary *Foster Pepper & Shefelman, Seattle*
MCCULLOUGH Jack *Phillips McCullough, Seattle*
NUEGEBAUER Robert *Preston Gates & Ellis, Seattle*
ROCKWELL David *Stoel Rives LLP, Seattle*
THOMAS Cynthia *Real Property Law Group, Seattle*

Firms and individuals are listed alphabetically in each band.

outstanding is **Gary Fluhrer**, who was recognized by peers as a *"bright"* and *"straightforward"* attorney. Fluhrer is thought to particularly excel in corporate real estate matters. His practice encompasses real estate development, leasing, financing, and general corporate work for local and multi-state projects.
The Clients: Costco Companies; Washington Mutual; Washington State Investment Board; Wright Runstad & Company; Corporate Property Investors; developers of the Nike Town/Planet Hollywood project; Amazon.com; Safeway; Seattle Sheraton Hotel and Seattle University.

Preston Gates & Ellis LLP
The Firm: The firm's real estate practice has represented a number of high-profile clients such as Microsoft, and is felt to have developed greatly under the guidance of senior attorney, John Gose. The group focuses on transactional matters, often working in interdisciplinary teams comprising attorneys from the corporate, environmental and land use, and municipal finance departments. Members advise on all facets of acquisition, sale, development, leasing, financing and construction transactions. In addition, the firm and its wholly-owned corporation, Washington Administrative Services, offer extensive foreclosure services. Past cases include acting for a microchip manufacturing company in the acquisition of a 91-acre semiconductor facility in Puyallup, Washington, and advising a public development authority on the acquisition of property in downtown Seattle for the development of a public sculpture park. The firm also counseled a life insurance company in relation to a $160 million loan on a Seattle office tower and handled a workout on a stalled condominium construction project in Seattle.
The Lawyers: A recent addition to the real estate group, **Scott Osbourne** was thought to be *"one of the best technical real estate lawyers in the state."* Osbourne frequently advises on high-profile projects; he represented the purchaser of an oil refinery and 120 retail gas station outlets, and a lender consortium in a $225 million financing of an electrical cogeneration plant. **Shannon Skinner** is reported to be a *"tremendously good real estate lawyer"* with notable experience of representing lenders in real estate financings. Rated by interviewees as a *"bright and responsive"* attorney, **Robert Nuegebauer** focuses on commercial real estate transactions, financings and complex leasing arrangements.
The Clients: Dividend Housing Corporation; Merrill Gardens; Simon Property Group and The Newland Group.

Alston, Courtnage & Bassetti LLP
The Firm: This *"small but sophisticated"* six-attorney practice focuses entirely on transactional real estate work, but collaborates with other firms for land use and litigation matters. The firm's *"collegial atmosphere"* and partner-led service has not hindered either the firm's reputation or its development of a national practice. Practitioners advise a varied base of institutional clients on sales and acquisitions, company formation and development financings. The firm undertakes real estate financing and transactions for GE Capital and Bank of America, and recently acted in the leasing and sale of Microsoft's Lakeridge project.
The Lawyers: **Michael Courtnage** is felt to be the *"anchor of the firm."* This talented attorney undertakes general corporate and real estate matters for both US and foreign clients, with a particularly strong following in the seafood industry.
The Clients: Bank of America; GE Capital; SAFECO; Freddie Mac; Fannie Mae; Metzler North America; high net-worth individuals and local, national and overseas clients.

Buck & Gordon LLP
The Firm: Widely recognized as the *"preeminent"* real estate and land use boutique, the firm enjoys local renown for quality work and a large proportion of *"high-caliber"* practitioners. Traditionally, the practice has emphasized land use and environmental issues, and its reputation remains strongest in these areas. However, the group is equipped to handle all aspects of real estate law, and routinely provides advice on municipal law, zoning matters, mediation, litigation and arbitration on large projects and real estate transactions. A diverse client base ranges from builders and developers to local government bodies and citizens' groups. The firm recently resolved a land use case involving alleged illegal construction by a wealthy individual. Additionally, the group advised on the implementation of a community relations program and successfully negotiated the repeal of a stop-work order.
The Lawyers: This *"congenial"* group of attorneys has a strong and active presence in the community. **Bill Block** (see p.712) is well known in the real estate bar for his extensive writing and speaking on real estate, construction and municipal law matters. He has broad experience in all facets of real estate transactions and is active in arbitrations proceeding from property disputes.
The Clients: Amazon.com; Haggen; University of Washington; Washington Capital Management; McDonald's; City of Bellevue; Starbucks and Washington State Baseball Stadium Public Facilities District.

Perkins Coie LLP
The Firm: A ten-partner practice provides comprehensive real estate services, benefiting from firm-wide strength in tax and finance on large commercial transactions. Areas of emphasis include the acquisition and disposition of commercial properties, project development, financing, leasing, workouts and restructuring. The firm represents a range of industries, with a growing proportion of clients in the hi-tech and biotech sectors. Interviewees singled out the group for its extensive leasing capabilities. Practitioners frequently appear for Washington landlords, tenants and retail centers in negotiations of master leases for industrial and commercial projects. Representative transactions include advising a major financial services corporation in the sale of its $500 million shopping center portfolio. The firm also advised an equity investor in the development of a new office tower as part of the expansion of downtown Seattle's Convention Center.
The Lawyers: **William Green** was recommended to researchers as a *"bright and business-minded"* attorney focusing on commercial real estate work for large corporate clients. He has notably represented Intel in the acquisition and development of a research and development campus in DuPont, Washington and counsels various hi-tech companies in built-to-suit lease transactions. His partner, **Ellen Conedera Dial** has particular experience in relation to industrial and environmentally sensitive properties. She advises a large number of landlords and tenants in her leasing practice. She has represented a purchaser in the acquisition of office properties in excess of $200 million.
The Clients: Amazon.com; Barclay's Realty and Management Co; Birmingham Steel; Boeing; University of Washington; Haggen/Top Foods; Puget Sound Energy; SAFECO; Seattle Mariners and Wells Fargo.

WASHINGTON LEADERS

Phillips McCullough Wilson Hill & Fikso
The Firm: Still a relative newcomer to the Washington market, this real estate boutique has developed a strong local reputation for land use matters. Seven attorneys handle a range of financing, leasing, development and acquisition transactions. The firm provides litigation services in connection with land use matters, although it does not undertake bankruptcy-related work or commercial litigation cases. The firm represents Quadrant (Weyerhaeuser's real estate development arm) in all its real estate matters, and has historically advised the Fred Hutchinson Cancer Research Center on permitting and land use issues.
The Lawyers: *"Talented"* **Jack McCullough** (see p.713) was recognized for his long experience in land use and zoning issues. McCullough has represented a number of Seattle office developers and acts as primary outside counsel to Wal-Mart on real estate matters.
The Clients: Wal-Mart; Quadrant; Seattle School District; Fred Hutchinson Cancer Research Center; Weyerhaeuser; AT&T Wireless; Seattle Housing Authority; Bedford Property Investors and Unico Properties.

Stoel Rives LLP
The Firm: The firm has a number of practice groups that handle the varied needs of its commercial clientele, such as a construction and design practice group, an environmental and natural resources group and a land use and land use litigation group. Combined, these represent a wide-ranging real estate practice, advising on all aspects of property-related sales, acquisitions, development, financings, entity formation and leasing transactions. The team successfully represented Fluke Capital in obtaining a shoreline permit for a hotel in Bellevue, despite challenges made at the Washington Court of Appeals and Washington Supreme Court.
The Lawyers: Peers praise **David Rockwell** as a *"tremendously good"* real estate lawyer with a *"lively and inquisitive"* manner. His practice has a commercial real estate bias, and he is felt to possess broad experience in financing, sales and exchanges, leasing and condominium-related work.
The Clients: The group acts for a varied base of local, national and overseas clients.

Other Notable Practitioners
Cynthia Thomas, of the Real Property Law Group, was consistently recommended for her transactional real estate practice encompassing property acquisition, development, sales, leasing and finance. She designed a real estate excise tax structure for a $140 million reorganization and leveraged buyout of segments of a major real estate development company.

Leaders in Washington

ARDITI, Abraham A
Abraham A Arditi, Seattle
206 623 1593
aarditi@qwest.net
Recommended in Employment
Specialization: Represents individual employees in claims against employers, including claims of discrimination, retaliation, wrongful discharge, breach of contract, discharge in violation of public policy and violation of civil rights.
Prof. Memberships: Washington State Bar Association, Washington Employment Lawyers Association.
Career: Admitted to practice in Washington and Western District of Washington in 1972, Ninth Circuit in 1975 and US Supreme Court in 1985. Co-recipient of Charles A Goldmark Distinguished Service Award from Legal Foundation of Washington in 1990. Recipient of Federal Bar Association Outstanding Service Award in 1988.
Personal: Received a BA from Yale University in 1967 and a JD and MA from Yale University in 1972.

ASLIN, John
Perkins Coie LLP, Seattle 206 583 8888
Recommended in Employment

BLOCK, William
Buck & Gordon LLP, Seattle
206 382 9540
wblock@buckgordon.com
Recommended in Real Estate
Specialization: Represents substantial national and regional builder-developers, construction companies, commercial real estate owners of office, retail and warehouse properties, property management firms, public authorities, syndicators, banks and municipalities in all facets of real estate transactions, including acquisition, financing, construction, sales, and leasing. Lectures on real estate, construction, and municipal law for the state and county bar associations and for private education providers. Each year, chairs the Annual Advanced Conference on Real Estate Leases and the Annual Advanced Conference on Commercial Real Estate Purchases and Sales for Law Seminars International. Serves as both arbitrator and mediator through the American Arbitration Association and by private contract. Was recently named one Washington's top lawyers by a leading peer review.
Prof. Memberships: King County Bar Association, Washington State Bar Association, American Arbitration Association, District of Columbia Bar (inactive status).
Personal: Urban Enterprise Center; Port Jobs; Seattle Center Advisory Board; Seattle Low-Income Housing Levy; Former Chairman of the Board, Seattle Housing Authority; Former President, AIDS Housing of Washington.

BUSTO, Mark
Sebris Busto, Bellevue 425 450 9600
mbusto@sebrisbusto.com
Recommended in Employment
Specialization: Labor and employment law (management/defense).
Prof. Memberships: Washington State Bar Association (Secretary/Treasurer, Labor and Employment Law Section); King County Bar Association.
Career: Field Rep./organizer, California State Employees Association (1975-79); Employee Rels. Consultant, State of California (1979); Associate, Foster, Pepper & Riviera (1983-85); Partner, Schweppe, Krug & Tausend (1985-90); Of Counsel, Davis Wright Tremaine (1990-92); Shareholder, Sebris Busto, P.S. (1992 - present); King County Personnel Board, Member (1992-94), Chair (1994-96); University of Washington Faculty Hearing Officer (2001-present); 'Best Lawyers in Seattle' and was listed in a leading American publication.
Personal: Occidental College, BA with honors, cum laude (1974); University of Southern California Law Center, JD (1983); Northwest Aids Foundation, Board Member (1986-92); Board Chair, Forest Ridge School of the Sacred Heart (2000 - present); Married, 3 children.

BYRNES, Peter
Byrnes & Keller, Seattle
206 622 2000
Recommended in Litigation

CAIRNS, Carolyn
Stokes Lawrence, PS, Seattle
206 626 6000
Recommended in Employment

CARLSON, Kent
Preston Gates & Ellis LLP, Seattle
206 623 7580
Recommended in Corporate/M&A

CORR, Kelly
Corr Cronin LLP, Seattle
206 625 8600
Recommended in Litigation

COURTNAGE, Michael
Alston, Courtnage & Bassetti LLP, Seattle
206 623 7600
Recommended in Real Estate

DIAL, Ellen
Perkins Coie LLP, Seattle 206 583 8888
Recommended in Real Estate

DWYER, Michael
Lane Powell Spears Lubersky LLP,
Seattle 206 223 7000
Recommended in Corporate/M&A

FLETCHER, Kelby
Peterson, Young, Putra, Fletcher, Zeder, Massong & Knopp, Seattle
206 624 6800
Recommended in Employment

FLUHRER, Gary
Foster Pepper & Shefelman PLLC,
Seattle 206 447 4400
Recommended in Real Estate

FRANK, Katrin
MacDonald, Hoague & Bayless, Seattle
206 622 1604
Recommended in Employment

GITTINGER, Wayne
Lane Powell Spears Lubersky LLP,
Seattle 206 223 7000
Recommended in Corporate/M&A

GREEN, William
Perkins Coie LLP, Seattle
206 583 8888
Recommended in Real Estate

HANNAH, David
Rinehart Robblee Hannah, Seattle
206 467 6700
Recommended in Employment

WASHINGTON

LEADERS

HUTCHESON, Mark
Davis Wright Tremaine LLP, Seattle
206 628 7678
markhutcheson@dwt.com
Recommended in Employment
Specialization: Partner in employment/labor law department. Focuses on employment law, including labor relations counseling and extensive experience representing employers in collective bargaining. Has negotiated agreements on behalf of employers engaged in a number of industries throughout the West Coast, Alaska and Hawawii.
Prof. Memberships: Washington State Bar Association; Fellow, College of Labor and Employment Lawyers.
Career: Firm Chairman (1994-present) and former Managing Partner (1989-1994). Joined *DWT* in 1968 and became a partner in 1973.
Publications: Co-Author, 'Employer's Guide to Strike Planning and Prevention', (Practicing Law Institute, 1985).
Personal: JD, University of Washington, 1967. BA, University of Puget Sound, 1964.

JONES, Karen
Riddell Williams PS, Seattle
206 624 3600
Recommended in Employment

KELLER, Brad
Byrnes & Keller, Seattle 206 622 2000
Recommended in Litigation

KUNTZ, Michael
Foster Pepper & Shefelman PLLC,
Seattle 206 447 4400
Recommended in Real Estate

LANDEFELD, Stewart
Perkins Coie LLP, Seattle 206 583 8888
Recommended in Corporate/M&A

LEMLY, Tom
Davis Wright Tremaine LLP, Seattle
206 628 7716
tomlemly@dwt.com
Recommended in Employment
Specialization: Partner, employment/labor law. Experience includes employment litigation and counseling in most employment law matters, including discrimination, wrongful discharge, enforcement of non-competition agreements and related contracts. Clients include Bank of America, Farmers Insurance Group, Microsoft Corp., FlightSafety-Boeing International.
Prof. Memberships: Fellow, American College of Trial Lawyers. Chair, Association of Washington Business Human Resources Council. Member, Executive Committee, Washington Association of Business.
Career: Admitted Washington State Bar (1973). Joined firm, 1973; became partner, 1979.
Publications: Editor, 'Washington, Alaska, California and Oregon Employment Law Deskbooks'. Principal Contributor,

'Employment Discrimination Law'.
Personal: JD, with honors, North Carolina Law School, 1973. BA, Duke University, 1970.

LONNQUIST, Judith
Law Offices of Judith A Lonnquist,
Seattle 206 622 2086
Recommended in Employment

MCCULLOUGH, Jack
McCullough Hill Fikso Kretschmer
Smith, Seattle 206 448 1818
jack@mhfks.com
Recommended in Real Estate
Specialization: Focuses his practice on real estate development and finance, with a particular emphasis on land use permitting, zoning entitlements and environmental matters. He typically acts on behalf of property owners, developers, users and other parties seeking to develop real estate.
Prof. Memberships: Memberships have included ABA; Urban Land Institute; American Planning Association; ICSC; Downtown Seattle Association; Greater Seattle Chamber of Commerce.
Career: Has practiced for over 20 years in real estate and land use law in the Pacific Northwest. He was previously a partner at *Heller Ehrman White & McAuliffe*. Graduated from Harvard Law School (JD 1982) and Harvard College (AB 1978).

MORGAN, Michael
Lane Powell Spears Lubersky LLP,
Seattle 206 223 7000
Recommended in Corporate/M&A

NUEGEBAUER, Robert
Preston Gates & Ellis LLP, Seattle
206 623 7580
Recommended in Real Estate

OSBOURNE, Scott
Preston Gates & Ellis LLP, Seattle
206 623 7580
Recommended in Real Estate

PERISHO, Russell
Perkins Coie LLP, Seattle 206 583 8888
Recommended in Employment

PRESTON, Anne
Garvey, Schubert & Barer, Seattle
206 464 3939
Recommended in Employment

REISS, Mike
Davis Wright Tremaine LLP, Seattle
206 628 7750
mikereiss@dwt.com
Recommended in Employment
Specialization: Partner, employment/labor law. Experience includes litigating cases on behalf of large/small employers throughout the West Coast. Served as lead counsel in state/nationwide race discrimination, sex discrimination and wage/hour class actions. Also served as court-appointed Special Master in nationwide Title VII

race discrimination class action.
Prof. Memberships: Washington State Bar. California Bar. American Employment Law Council. National Employment Law Institute.
Career: Law Professor, University of Southern California Law Center (1968-79). Program Director, National Institute for Trial Advocacy (1975-present). Joined as partner, 1986.
Publications: Principal Contributor, Lindemann & Grossman, 'Employment Discrimination Law'.
Personal: JD, Yale, 1968. BA, with high honors, Harvard, 1965.

RINEHART, John
Rinehart Robblee Hannah, Seattle
206 467 6700
Recommended in Employment

ROCKWELL, David
Stoel Rives LLP, Seattle 206 624 0900
Recommended in Real Estate

ROSEN, Jon
Frank Rosen Freed Roberts LLP, Seattle
206 682 6711
Recommended in Employment

SEBRIS, Robert
Sebris Busto, Bellevue 425 450 0300
rsebris@sebrisbusto.com
Recommended in Employment
Specialization: He practices exclusively in labor and employment law, representing employers. Emphasis areas for his practice include collective bargaining, arbitration, representation cases, discrimination law, wage and hour matters, wrongful discharge cases, and other employment matters.
Prof. Memberships: American Bar Association (ABA), Labor & Employment Law Section, Committee on Employee Rights & Responsibilities. American Health Lawyers Association. Society of Human Resource Management (SHRM). Washington State Bar Association, Labor & Employment Law Section. District of Columbia Bar Association (inactive). King County Bar Association, Labor & Employment Law Section.
Career: Shareholder, Sebris Busto, PS (1992 to present), Bellevue, WA. Partner, *Davis Wright Tremaine* (1985-92), Seattle & Bellevue, WA. Associate, *Davis, Wright, Todd, Reise & Jones* (1980 to 1985), Seattle, WA. Labor/Employee Relations Manager, US Treasury Dept./BFGO (1975-80), Washington, DC Labor Relations Specialist, US Dept. Labor/LMSA (1972-75), Washington, DC Labor Relations Specialist, Onondaga County (Syracuse), NY, (IPA) (September 1973- March 1974).
Publications: Practising Law Institute, Employer's Guide to Stike Planning and Prevention (1985), Project Leader & Co-Author. Commerce Clearing House, Labor Law Journal, 'Bargaining Unit Determina-

tion Case Trends of the NLRB', (June 1986), Co-Author. Numerous trade association speeches and training programs.
Personal: Cornell University, School of Industrial Relations, BS-IL&R (1972). George Washington University, National Law Center, JD (1978). Expert Witness, US Senate, Committee on Labor & Human Resources, TEAM, Amendments to NLRA, (February 1997), Washington, D.C. Chair, University of Washington Law School, Labor & Employment Emphasis Certificate Program, (1996-97). Board of Trustees, Bellevue Community College Foundation (1988-95), President (1995). Chair, King County Bar Association, Labor & Employment Law Section (1993). Pacific Coast Labor Law Conference & Committee (1983-93), Chair (1992). All-Ivy League Soccer (Hon. Mention 1969). Eagle Scout (BSA 1963). Coach Youth Sports - Soccer, Basketball, Baseball (1992-2002).

SKINNER, Shannon
Preston Gates & Ellis LLP, Seattle
206 623 7580
Recommended in Real Estate

THOMAS, Cynthia
Real Property Law Group PLLC, Seattle
206 625 1717
Recommended in Real Estate

WEINSTEIN, Joseph
Davis Wright Tremaine LLP, Seattle
206 628 7791
joeweinstein@dwt.com
Recommended in Corporate/M&A
Specialization: Partner, corporate finance department. Experience includes representing owners in the sale of National Basketball Association team; representing Tyson Foods, Inc in multi-state sale of seafood division; representing Japanese lease companies in structure sale of 25 Boeing aircraft; handling the purchase and finance of a major fish processing company.
Prof. Memberships: Maritime Law Association of the US.
Career: Admitted to Washington State Bar (1981). Joined *DWT* 1986; became partner, 1991.
Publications: Frequent speaker on topics concerning lawyer ethics, representation of clients in international transactions and investment in the maritime industry.
Personal: JD, University of Washington, 1981. BA, Unversity of Washington, 1978.

WEST VIRGINIA

CORPORATE/M&A

CONTENTS: Corporate/M&A p.714; Employment: Mainly Plaintiff p.716; Mainly Defendant p.716; Litigation: General Commercial p.718; Real Estate p.719; Individuals' Profiles p.721.

WEST VIRGINIA'S TOP FOUR
1. Jackson Kelly
2. Steptoe & Johnson
3. Bowles Rice McDavid Graff & Love
4. Spilman Thomas & Battle

Ranking based on Chambers' research within the state.

All quotes in the text are from interviews with clients and competitors.

OVERVIEW: Founded in 1822, top-ranked **Jackson Kelly** is the oldest firm in the state as well as one of the largest. With seven offices in West Virginia, the firm advises clients on the full range of business-related issues. Chambers' research identified corporate, litigation and real estate law as areas of strength. Louis Southworth is a top tax attorney, while Dennis Broglio boasts long experience in commercial real estate. The firm's clients include national and international corporations, many of them drawn from the coal and chemical industries. Key clients include Alliance Coal, Dow Chemical and BB&T.

Steptoe & Johnson, in second place, is another contender for the accolade of largest firm in the state, comprising some 150 attorneys distributed among offices in Clarksburg, Charleston, Morgantown, Martinsburg, and Wheeling. Market sources report that labor and employment is the fastest growing practice in this full-service firm. Chief executive Robert Steptoe is a noted labor defense attorney and department chair David Morrison has a first-rate reputation. The firm was also commended for the strength of its real estate department. Clients include American Electric Power and Consolidation Coal Company.

Bowles Rice McDavid Graff & Love, in third place, boasts nearly 100 attorneys throughout its six offices in West Virginia, Kentucky and Virginia. West Virginia locations include Charleston, Martinsburg, Morgantown and Parkersburg. A full-service firm, it represents corporate clients including Peabody Coal company and Monsanto. Peers endorsed attorneys here for their expertise in litigation and real estate, and particularly commended its respected niche in mineral law.

Well-established West Virginia firm **Spilman Thomas & Battle** earns praise for its dedication to corporate clients. Headquartered in Charleston, the practice also operates from offices in Parkersburg, Morgantown and Weirton. This fast-growing practice was noted in the market for its recent recruitment efforts and a young, dynamic management team. Litigation is a strong suit for the firm, particularly in relation to medical monitoring cases. A varied list of national and international clients includes DuPont and Pechiney.

CORPORATE/M&A

WEST VIRGINIA
Leading firms (Corporate/M&A)
1. **JACKSON KELLY PLLC** Charleston
2. **BOWLES RICE MCDAVID GRAFF & LOVE** Charleston
   STEPTOE & JOHNSON PLLC Clarksburg
3. **SPILMAN THOMAS & BATTLE PLLC** Charleston
4. **GOODWIN & GOODWIN LLP** Charleston
   HUDDLESTON, BOLEN, BEATTY Huntington
   ROBINSON & MCELWEE PLLC Charleston
5. **KAY CASTO & CHANEY PLLC** Charleston
   PHILLIPS GARDILL KAISER & ALTMEYER Wheeling

Leading individuals (Corporate/M&A)
1. **HEYWOOD Thomas** Bowles Rice McDavid, Charleston
   LUKENS John Spilman Thomas & Battle, Charleston
   SOUTHWORTH Louis Jackson Kelly PLLC, Charleston
2. **BOOKER William** Kay Casto & Chaney PLLC, Charleston
   CAPPELLANTI Ellen Jackson Kelly PLLC, Charleston
   DEEM Patrick Steptoe & Johnson PLLC, Clarksburg
   DUNBAR Charles Jackson Kelly PLLC, Charleston
   FERRETTI David Spilman Thomas & Battle, Charleston
   GARDILL James Phillips Gardill Kaiser, Wheeling
   MURRAY Thomas Huddleston, Bolen, Beatty, Huntington
3. **ALBERT Michael** Jackson Kelly PLLC, Charleston
   FERGUSON Mark Sprouse & Ferguson, Charleston
   KING Evans Steptoe & Johnson PLLC, Clarksburg
   LORENSEN Charles George & Lorensen, Charleston

Firms and individuals are listed alphabetically in each band.

Jackson Kelly PLLC
see firm details p.821

The Firm: Traditionally regarded as *"the state's premier law practice,"* This firm is the oldest and among the largest in West Virginia. It also boasts offices in offices in Kentucky and Colorado. Interviewees note the firm's commercial client base and particular strength in mineral transactions. Jackson Kelly boasts a number of specialists with *"remarkable legal talent across the various practice groups,"* making them well-equipped to provide *"comprehensive"* advice on corporate matters.

The Lawyers: Best known for his tax work, **Louis Southworth** (see p.722) sits as the chairman of the executive committee in addition to his general corporate, M&A, federal tax trusts and estates practice. He enjoys a statewide reputation, and sits easily *"at the top of the profession."* His recent work includes a large timber transaction, and the reorganization of a coal company. **Ellen Cappellanti** enjoys a fine reputation for bankruptcy work; interviewees stressed her *"keen sense of commercial law."* She recently represented a large ski resort and other entities in the creation of common ownership communities, and has been involved in numerous timber transactions. *"The banking lawyer"* **Charles Dunbar** (see p.721) plays an active role in bank formations for clients both in and out of state. Said to possess *"a wide range of experience in corporate matters,"* Dunbar recently completed a multimillion acquisition of a composite materials manufacturer for an aerospace industry client. **Michael Albert** (see p.721) handles both transactional and regulatory work, and is recognized by peers for his *"outstanding"* work on public utilities matters. He is currently working on the RWE/Thames acquisition of American Water Works Company's common stock and acted for Allegheny Power in its acquisition of Mountaineer Gas.

The Clients: Dow Chemical; Pittston Coal; AEI Resources; Alliance Coal and McDonald's.

Bowles Rice McDavid Graff & Love PLLC

The Firm: A *"long-standing institutional firm"* with offices across West Virginia, Virginia and Kentucky. Attorneys here command *"considerable expertise and experience"* and enjoy a steady diet of general corporate work within the firm's broad, commercially-focused practice. The corporate client base includes energy, distribution, chemical and coal companies as well as banks and insurance companies. The firm's success has been supported by the *"classic rainmaker"* F Thomas Graff who, while less visible on transactional work, continues to attract big-name clients to the practice.

The Lawyers: The *"star"* of the practice, **Thomas Heywood** supplements a robust corporate practice with involvement in public-private ventures, including an ongoing $164 million dollar project, and the opening of the state's first public/private funded park. He is also currently involved with one of the first projects in the state to make use of the

CORPORATE/M&A

WEST VIRGINIA

new tax increment financing technique (TIF). The project is a $244 million pubic/private urban redevelopment of downtown Morgantown, which will create a mixed-use development of student housing and commercial space. The project is entitled 'The Square at Falling Run.' This *"well-connected"* attorney is also thought to enjoy a high profile within the bar and in the wider community.

The Clients: United Bankshares; McJunkin; Peabody Coal Company; MetLife and Monsanto.

Steptoe & Johnson PLLC

The Firm: Recommended for its *"tremendous depth and breadth,"* this *"old, established"* firm has six offices throughout the state. The business practice group has grown substantially in the last five years through heavy recruitment from government and in-house practices.

The Lawyers: Department chair **Patrick Deem** ranks as *"one of the top business lawyers in the state."* He is visible representing major local banks on cororate transactions and serving as West Virginia counsel to out-of-state banks establishing and extending their presence in the state. Over the last year he has represented the franchisee in the sale of fifty restaurants of the Hardees restaurant chain. The transaction was in excess of $25 million, and took place over the three states of West Virginia, Ohio and Pennsylvania.

"Bright and thorough" **Evans King** acts in the areas of M&A and commercial banking. His recent workload has consisted primarily of acquisitions and loan documentation on behalf of a major client in the newpaper industry.

The Clients: Bank One; American Electric Power; AIG; Bell Mining; Ogden Newspapers; Zurich-America Insurance and Huntingdon National Bank.

Spilman Thomas & Battle PLLC

The Firm: Smaller than its competitors, the firm is seen to have *"sharpened its aggressive edge"* and boosted its profile by the recent recruitment of eight corporate lawyers. This *"re-emerging"* practice now boasts a well-respected corporate department stocked with *"good business-minded lawyers."*

The Lawyers: John Lukens has come out of retirement to work for Spilman Thomas & Battle, after twenty years at rival, Jackson Kelly. Interviewees recognized him as one of the *"premier banking and corporate lawyers within the state."* He recently acted for Weirton Steel on securities and corporate governance issues, which included advising on the corporation's code of ethics and Sarbanes-Oxley compliance.

Clients report him to be *"excellent, extremely experienced and able."*

Peers hold **David Ferretti** in high esteem for his expertise in transactional matters. He is currently involved in several venture capital transactions, both on behalf of investors and IT and biotech start-ups obtaining angel and venture capital funding. He also advises on the sale and purchase of healthcare companies and reviews and drafts business contracts for corporate clients.

The Clients: DuPont, Pechiney, West Virginia Economic Development Authority are also clients.

Goodwin & Goodwin LLP

The Firm: This broad-based practice was said to be sufficiently large to *"cover all the bases"* and yet still provide the *"personal client service"* of a small firm. A general corporate practice encompasses securities, financings, public offerings, bond work, tax and private placement. Peers commended the group's particular skill in municipal finance, bonds and tax work, and felt it to be *"the main competition in that area."* Attorneys also coordinate local work for out-of-state firms. *"They come with the highest recommendation,"* asserts a client, adding that *"the whole firm is outstanding."*

The Clients: The Asbestos and Insulation Company; Chase Securities; Columbia Gas Transmission; CSX and Delaware North companies.

Huddleston, Bolen, Beatty, Porter & Copen LLP

The Firm: This *"old-line"* West Virginia firm offers full-service capacities, focusing largely on loan workouts and foreclosures, commercial lending and fundraising for projects and acquisitions. Located in the two largest cities in the state and with another office in neighboring Kentucky, the firm commands a considerable regional presence. Commentators perceived a bias toward mineral and railroad work, noting the firm's reputation as firmly based in those areas. Historically, the firm developed in tandem with the creation of the railroads and its client base still comprises many transportation companies.

The Lawyers: *"Talented"* **Thomas Murray** was endorsed by peers for is broad expertise in banking and corporate law.

The Clients: CSX Transportation; Western Pocahontas Properties; Appalachian Power; The Ohio River Company; Champion Industries and Merrill Lynch Credit.

Robinson & McElwee PLLC

The Firm: This *"sophisticated West Virginia practice"* was observed to have weathered *"numerous changes"* throughout its history. It nevertheless maintains a niche in public utility and environmental work and is oriented toward the West Virginia business community. Attorneys are active on regulatory work relating to electric utilities and are involved in the drafting of legislation. They also represent banks in corporate transactions.

The Clients: American Electric Power; Marathon Ashland Petroleum; Columbia Gas; Columbia Natural Resources; KMart; Charleston Newspapers and Nationwide.

Kay Casto & Chaney PLLC

The Firm: The corporate practice was thought to possess some *"strong business lawyers"* with noteworthy experience in the field. Attorneys handle contract reviews, leasing work and agreement preparation, and provide general advice to corporate clients.

The Lawyers: William Booker attracted comment as an *"exceptionally talented corporate attorney"* involved in bankruptcy, business litigation, transactional work, general business and banking matters, and in defense of financial institutions. This *"straight-shooting"* practitioner recently completed a workout for Bank One West Virginia, involving a claim for over $1.7 million, which was recovered in full. He additionally advised Huntingdon National Bank in connection with a $1.5 million bankruptcy claim and two loan workouts involving more that $1 million.

The Clients: Ford Motor Credit Company, CUNA Mutul and BB&T are also clients.

Phillips Gardill Kaiser & Altmeyer

The Firm: Based in Wheeling, this smaller firm has a corporate focus on clients in the southern part of the state. It is widely recommended for its strength in securities matters. Peers also noted the group's banking work, in particular its representation of WesBanco.

The Lawyers: A *"top-notch"* attorney with a niche in securities, **James Gardill** has earned a strong reputation in banking and commercial transactions.

The Clients: The firm is most visible in its work on behalf of banking client, WesBanco.

Other Notable Practitioners

In Charleston, **Mark Ferguson** of Sprouse & Ferguson is seen as a *"well-regarded tax attorney with an up-and-coming client base."* Peers regularly refer M&A and bankruptcy work to **Charles Lorensen** of George & Lorensen, also in Charleston. Commentators recommend him as a *"true tax lawyer"* with an *"excellent reputation."*

WEST VIRGINIA
EMPLOYMENT & LABOR LAW

EMPLOYMENT & LABOR LAW — MAINLY PLAINTIFF

WEST VIRGINIA
Leading firms
(Employment: Mainly Plaintiff)

1. ALLAN N KARLIN *Morgantown*
   CRANDALL PYLES HAVILAND *Charleston*
2. DONNELLY & CARBONE *Charleston*
   HAMMER FERRETTI & SCHIAVONI *Martinsburg*

Leading individuals
(Employment: Mainly Plaintiff)

1. HAVILAND James *Crandall Pyles Haviland*, Charleston
   KARLIN Allan *Allan N. Karlin*, Morgantown
2. CASSIDY Patrick *Cassidy Myers Cogan*, Wheeling
   DONNELLY Charles *Donnelly & Carbone*, Charleston
   RANSON Michael *Ranson Law Offices*, Charleston
3. BAYLESS Kathryn *The Bayless Law Firm*, Princeton
   HAMMER David *Hammer Ferretti*, Martinsburg
   SCHIAVONI Robert *Hammer Ferretti*, Martinsburg

Up-and-coming individuals
FLORIO Michael *Sole Practitioner*, Clarksburg

Firms and individuals are listed alphabetically in each band.

Allan N Karlin
The Firm: This small Morgantown plaintiffs' firm numbers three attorneys, all of whom practice in the labor and employment area with a small amount of personal injury matters. The firm focuses on primarily employee discrimination, wrongful discharge and sexual harassment cases.
The Lawyers: Identified as the *"preeminent plaintiffs' lawyer in West Virginia,"* **Allan Karlin** was praised for his *"tenacity, aggression, and creativity."* Well respected by the defense bar as an *"excellent trial lawyer,"* Karlin recently served as plaintiffs' counsel in a number of wrongful discharge cases.

Crandall Pyles Haviland & Turner
The Firm: This small firm has offices in Charleston, Logan and Lewisburg. Matters handled include employment discrimination, disability and workers' compensation, immigration matters, environmental issues, and complex personal injury and wrongful death. The labor and employment practice concentrates on employee representation in both state and federal courts and before administrative agencies.
The Lawyers: **James Haviland** is respected in the market for his labor work, but practices in the areas of pensions and benefits, ERISA, and employment litigation. The team enjoys the ongoing support of founding partner Grant Crandall, who also serves as general counsel to the United Mine Workers. His labor work has earned him respect among peers, who dubbed him *"excellent."*

Donnelly & Carbone
The Firm: A four-attorney plaintiff practice based in Charleston with an emphasis on labor and employment issues. Sources commend the firm's *"skilled and ethical lawyers,"* and acknowledge their reputation in the area of union representation.
The Lawyers: *"Knowledgeable and experienced"* **Charles Donnelly** is well known for labor work and union representation. He is active in pensions and benefits, collection of wages, mediation, arbitration and ADR. Much of this work is on behalf of federal and state courts and the postal service.

Hammer Ferretti & Schiavoni
The Firm: *"Clearly one of the top plaintiffs' firms",* the firm divides its practice equally between employment law and medical malpractice. Employment cases have included race, disability, gender and age discrimination cases. Practitioners are active in the field of litigation particularly in relation to wage and hour claims and overtime pay cases. Interviewees praise attorneys as *"diligent, forthright and creative."*
The Lawyers: **David Hammer** was noted for his success in employment law, particularly in relation to class action cases. Recent casework includes plaintiff representation in disability discrimination suits, and class actions concerning wage payment collection. He recently recovered $6.8 million for 2,300 employees in a wage class action. His colleague **Robert Schiavoni** was also distinguished for his success in employment class action cases.

Other Notable Practitioners
"Bright and knowledgeable" **Patrick Cassidy** of Cassidy Myers Cogan Voegelin & Tennant was admired for his union and employee representation and counsel on workers' compensation issues. Interviewees singled out **Michael Ranson** at Ranson Law Offices as *"one of the leading plaintiffs' lawyers in Charleston."* His practice encompasses both labor and employment law and personal injury litigation. Market sources commended him as an *"aggressive trial lawyer."* Up-and-coming sole practitioner **Michael Florio** was praised as a *"hard-working and creative"* plaintiffs' lawyer. This *"high-energy"* attorney devotes a substantial proportion of his practice to labor and employment matters. *"Bright and capable"* **Kathryn Reed Bayless** of The Bayless Law Firm maintains a mixed practice in employment and labor, education and personal injury law. Although recommended primarily as a plaintiffs' lawyer, Bayless also undertakes work for employers. She recently settled a disability discrimination case against a hospital, following its refusal to grant an employee leave on grounds of depression.

EMPLOYMENT & LABOR LAW — MAINLY DEFENDANT

WEST VIRGINIA
Leading firms
(Employment: Mainly Defendant)

1. STEPTOE & JOHNSON PLLC *Clarksburg*
2. BOWLES RICE MCDAVID GRAFF *Charleston*
   JACKSON KELLY PLLC *Charleston*
   SPILMAN THOMAS & BATTLE PLLC *Charleston*
3. DINSMORE & SHOHL LLP *Charleston*
   JENKINS FENSTERMAKER PLLC *Huntington*
   ROBINSON & MCELWEE PLLC *Charleston*

Firms are listed alphabetically in each band.

Steptoe & Johnson PLLC
The Firm: A 40-strong group of *"excellent"* labor and employment attorneys benefits from the firm's extensive resources and institutional client base. Interviewees report that the practice has been expanding rapidly, particularly within the ERISA field, following a recent recruitment drive. The practice is known for its *"interdisciplinary"* approach to employment matters. Attorneys advise on issues ranging from union relations, discrimination and employment contracts to promotion, discharge and conduct issues. Dedicated subgroups deal with employee benefits, occupational diseases, occupational and coal mine safety issues, and toxic tort claims. Clients particularly praised their OSHA and workers' compensation work. Market opinion considered attorneys here to be *"the people with the broadest knowledge at hand."*
The Lawyers: Clarksburg-based chief executive **Robert Steptoe** divides his time equally between management duties and legal practice. Regarded by peers as a *"top-tier"* traditional labor defense attorney, Steptoe also handles employment counseling and litigation. He maintains strong ties to clients in the ski resort, aerospace, natural gas and newspaper industries and is seen to be handling increasing amounts of arbitration and mediation work on labor and employment issues. He has been heavily involved in the

EMPLOYMENT & LABOR LAW

WEST VIRGINIA

WEST VIRGINIA
Leading individuals
(Employment: Mainly Defendant)

1
- BROWN Ricklin *Bowles Rice McDavid Graff,* Charleston
- KRIEGER Thomas *Jenkins Fenstermaker,* Huntington
- MORRISON David *Steptoe & Johnson,* Clarksburg
- ROLES Forrest *Dinsmore & Shohl LLP,* Charleston
- STEPTOE Robert *Steptoe & Johnson PLLC,* Clarksburg
- WOLFE Roger *Jackson Kelly PLLC,* Charleston

2
- COKELY Bryan *Steptoe & Johnson PLLC,* Charleston
- LEDBETTER Cheryl *Jackson Kelly PLLC,* Charleston
- PRICE Joseph *Robinson & McElwee PLLC,* Charleston
- WOODY Charles *Spilman Thomas & Battle,* Charleston

Individuals are listed alphabetically in each band.

negotiation of labor agreements around the country and has tried cases involving age, gender, race and disability discrimination, wage and hour claims and retaliatory discharge. Department chair **David Morrison** enjoys a *"first-rate reputation"* among peers as an *"extremely ethical and competent"* lawyer. He recently handled a breach of contract case for Ogden Newspapers, and age discrimination and workers' compensation cases for Eastern Associated Coal Corporation. He has also worked on a number of in-house investigations in the healthcare, natural gas and coal industries and regularly advises on employee training issues. Praised by peers as a *"formidable defense lawyer,"* **Bryan Cokely** concentrates primarily on employment litigation. Recent cases have included several discharge suits, sexual harassment, race, disability and age discrimination, defamation, breaches of contract and whistle-blower cases.

The Clients: Columbia Gas Transmission; Eastern Associated Coal; Huntington Bancshares; Stonewall Jackson Memorial Hospital; Ogden Newspapers; Consolidation Coal Company; Peabody Coal Company; Dominion Energy; Columbia Gas Transmission; Adidas; American Electric Power; HCA and Chubb Insurance.

Bowles Rice McDavid Graff & Love PLLC
The Firm: The employment department of this large, full-service firm covers all aspects of labor and employment law. The practice is devoted entirely to employer representation and emphasizes preventative counseling. Litigation experience extends to trials and appeals in the state and federal courts and hearings before administrative agencies. Matters covered include wrongful discharge cases, defamation, workers compensation, discrimination and harassment claims, ERISA, unfair labor practices, OSHA and documentation drafting. Rivals envy the group's *"diverse clientele and impressive book of business."*

The Lawyers: Defense attorney **Ricklin Brown** is highly esteemed for his *"ability, style and excellent results."* His recent caseload has included a number of sexual harassment and hostile work environment claims, in addition to several race and age discrimination cases. He regularly advises manufacturers, contractors, financial institutions and media clients on a range of employment and labor matters.

The Clients: Prudential Insurance; Prudential Securities; NGK Spark Plugs; Chicago Tube & Iron Company and Adecco.

Jackson Kelly PLLC
see firm details p.821

The Firm: Considered *"one of the preeminent firms in the state,"* the full-service firm is committed to serving the employment needs of its large base of corporate and business clients. Employment and labor attorneys across the firm's seven West Virginia offices offer comprehensive advice on the gamut of employment law matters, and work closely with the firm's dedicated workers compensation unit. Interviewees recommend the firm for its strength in employment defense, much of which is handled by attorneys in the firm's litigation department.

The Lawyers: Litigator **Roger Wolfe** (see p.722) attracts commendation for his work in employment defense. His expertise encompasses discrimination, wrongful discharge and general worker contracts with some traditional labor law involving union agreements and contract negotiation. Particularly recommended for his *"skill in written analysis,"* Wolfe recently completed union contract negotiations for a large West Virginia hospital. **Cheryl Ledbetter** (see p.721) is described as an *"experienced and skilled litigator"* with a concentration on sexual harassment, discrimination and wrongful discharge cases. She also advises clients on employee discipline and termination issues and recently handled several wrongful discharge cases where employees have alleged their dismissals were due to the filing of workers' compensation claims.

The Clients: Dow Chemical; Wal-Mart; Wheeling-Pittsburgh Steel and Mountaineer Park Race Track and Gaming Resort.

Spilman Thomas & Battle PLLC
The Firm: This old-line West Virginia firm boasts an 11-strong employment section, described by interviewees as a *"considerable presence"* in the market. Peers particularly complimented the practice's *"impressive client list"* and *"aggressive marketing"* strategies. The *"A-rated"* labor and employment team is the fastest growing department in the firm. It handles a range of matters, including traditional labor work, union organizing, employment litigation and general employment counseling. The firm recently obtained a favorable result for a television station in a counter suit brought by an anchorman, and acted for a coal company on an age discrimination/wrongful discharge suit.

The Lawyers: Head of the litigation department, **Charles Woody** was noted for his depth of experience in representing coal industry employers. He devotes about half of his litigation-based practice to labor and employment matters, and possesses expertise in unfair labor practice procedure, wrongful discharge cases, age, sex and race discrimination and union organization issues. His counseling work has involved drafting labor and employment provisions and restrictive covenants for contracts and transaction documentation.

The Clients: DuPont; Lucent Technologies, Triana Energy, Charleston Area Medical Center, GE Specialty Chemicals, Pechiney Rolled Products and Weirton Steel.

Dinsmore & Shohl LLP
The Firm: This multi-state firm opened a Charleston office a year ago and has since welcomed five attorneys, including three partners and two associates, from Heenan Althen & Roles, to form its Charleston labor and employment practice group. The team enjoys an outstanding reputation in the field, and was recommended for strength in coal company representation and traditional labor law.

The Lawyers: Named by clients as *"the dean of labor law,"* **Forrest Roles** was identified as *"one of the leading lawyers in the state"* for traditional labor law matters. He represents employers on union-related certification issues and also undertakes mediation and arbitration. He recently acted on a number of wrongful discharge cases.

Jenkins Fenstermaker PLLC
The Firm: Praised by clients for *"across the board quality,"* this regional full-service Huntington firm represents corporate and business clients in traditional labor law and union work, counseling, arbitration, workers' compensation and employment-related administrative litigation. The employment and labor department also provides advisory services to clients in areas including collective bargaining negotiations, opposing union-organizing campaigns, sexual harassment, discrimination and wage and hour claims. Attorneys are experienced in drafting documentation for labor agreements, contracts, severance agreements and advise in the implementation of workforce reductions.

The Lawyers: Practice head, **Thomas Krieger** earned widespread commendation for his focus on traditional labor law. Much of his work involves contract negotiation and collective bargaining issues. He also handles grievance

WEST VIRGINIA

LITIGATION

arbitration and representation for the NLRB. He successfully advised clients on maintaining their non-union status and has defended a number of employment claims before the West Virginia Human Rights Commission and the EEOC.
The Clients: Special Metals Corporation; ACF Industries; Cabell Huntington Hospital; Steel of West Virginia and American National Rubber Company.

Robinson & McElwee PLLC
The Firm: This mid-sized firm has five attorneys focusing exclusively on labor and employment issues. A *"classic"* employment practice covers a broad spectrum of matters ranging from NLRB work to discrimination, workers' compensation claims and unemployment compensation.
The Lawyers: Market sources singled out **Joseph Price** as the firm's most experienced labor and employment attorney. His practice emphasizes National Labor Relations, labor arbitrations and collective bargaining negotiations. He is currently involved in an arbitration for Bayer CropScience (formerly Aventis CropScience) and also has some significant pending discrimination cases for AT&T.
The Clients: American Electric Power; Allegheny Power; Columbia Natural Resources and Georgia-Pacific.

LITIGATION — GENERAL COMMERCIAL

WEST VIRGINIA
Leading firms
(Litigation: General Commercial)

1
- BOWLES RICE MCDAVID GRAFF *Charleston*
- JACKSON KELLY PLLC *Charleston*
- SPILMAN THOMAS & BATTLE PLLC *Charleston*

2
- FARMER, CLINE & ARNOLD PLLC *Charleston*
- STEPTOE & JOHNSON PLLC *Clarksburg*

3
- ALLEN GUTHRIE & MCHUGH *Charleston*

Leading individuals
(Litigation: General Commercial)

1
- FARMER Stephen *Farmer, Cline & Arnold*, Charleston
- TINNEY John *The Tinney Law Firm*, Charleston

2
- EMCH A L *Jackson Kelly PLLC*, Charleston
- JERNIGAN Henry *Dinsmore & Shohl*, Charleston
- LOVE Charles *Bowles Rice McDavid Graff*, Charleston

3
- BAILEY Benjamin *Bailey & Glasser LLP*, Charleston
- GEORGE Shawn *George & Lorensen*, Charleston
- GOODWIN Thomas *Goodwin & Goodwin*, Charleston
- LUSK Neva *Spilman Thomas & Battle*, Charleston
- MCHUGH Thomas *Allen Guthrie & McHugh*, Charleston
- STOWERS Gerard *Bowles Rice McDavid*, Charleston
- THOMAS David *Allen Guthrie & McHugh*, Charleston

Firms and individuals are listed alphabetically in each band.

Bowles Rice McDavid Graff & Love PLLC
The Firm: One of the larger full-service firms in West Virginia, possessing four offices across the state as well as one each in Kentucky and Virginia. The litigation practice focuses on all types of business and banking defense. Peers approved of the quality of attorneys here, describing their *"significant commercial litigation expertise"* and *"professional"* approach to complex cases.
The Lawyers: Practice chair **Charles Love** has a reputation among peers as an *"excellent trial lawyer with a statewide following."* Interviewees praised general commercial litigator **Gerald Stowers** as an attorney who *"really works a case,"* and is *"willing to get his hands dirty."* In recent years, Stowers has handled a large amount of work for companies concerning contracts with departing employees, trade secrets and other termination issues.
The Clients: Bridgestone/Firestone; Royal & SunAlliance; McJunkin; Acordia; United National Bank and Monsanto Chemical.

Jackson Kelly PLLC
see firm details p.821
The Firm: Acclaimed by clients *"one of the best firms in the state,"* Jackson & Kelly boasts a large Charleston-based litigation practice with between ten and 15 attorneys focusing on business and commercial litigation. This *"established"* firm possesses a diverse client base and a number of *"talented"* defense litigators who have *"experience across a range of areas."*
The Lawyers: Peers recommended chief executive **A L Emch** (see p.721) as a *"preeminent lawyer in the state,"* he has an ability to *"turn his hand to any type of case."* While more involved in firm management, Emch still undertakes a substantial share of products liability and mass tort litigation, with a predominant emphasis on defense work. Presently he is acting for a coal company and its parent in a mass consolidation suit, against 150 plaintiffs alleging nuisance due to dust, noise and light. They seek compensatory damages of over $10 million in addition to punitive damages. He is also involved as liaison counsel in products liability litigation pending before a West Virginia mass litigation judge, representing one of 20 defendants against 350 plaintiffs who claim loss of hearing from exposure to the defendant's heavy equipment. In addition he is presently lead and liaison counsel for the firm in representing several coal, timber and land-holding companies in mass consolidation litigation brought by more than 3000 plaintiffs alleging contribution to flooding and liability for hundreds of millions of dollars.
The Clients: Alliance Coal, Shell Oil and Coastal Coal are clients.

Spilman Thomas & Battle PLLC
The Firm: A *"major presence"* in West Virginia, this mid-sized firm was noted for its recent recruitment and expansion efforts and young *"dynamic"* management team. The group predominantly handles corporate defense but also undertakes some commercial plaintiff work. Practitioners have noteworthy experience in medical monitoring litigation; clients praised their *"considerable background in commercial and business affairs"* and *"aggressive"* litigation style.
The Lawyers: **Neva Lusk** concentrates the areas of medical monitoring, toxic tort, and products liability as well as business litigation work for manufacturers of pesticides, solvents, firearms, and medical devices. Recent matters include a medical device defense and toxic tort suits. Peers described her as *"a very attentive lawyer"* who is able to establish a *"good rapport with the jury."* Clients praised her *"good practical judgment"* and found her to be *"bright and responsive."* She recently defeated class certification sought by local residents and employees of a creosote tie-treatment facility. Lusk serves as lead counsel for corporate clients and as liaison counsel in federal and state courts in multiple plaintiff products liability matters.
The Clients: Weirton Steel; DuPont; Beazer East; Koppers Industries and VISX.

Farmer, Cline & Arnold PLLC
see firm details p.793
The Firm: This smaller boutique practice comprises ten lawyers acting in both plaintiff and defense litigation. Involved in a broad variety of cases, members regularly defend corporate clients in products liability, coal litigation, environmental matters, drug suits and asbestos and tobacco matters. Plaintiffs' work consists mainly of products liability, personal injury and medical malpractice claims. Peers describe this as an up-and-coming practice with a *"hard-hitting"* reputation.
The Lawyers: **Stephen Farmer** splits his practice between commercial litigation and products liability, acting for both plaintiffs and defendants. *"A pure trial lawyer,"* he recently obtained a $3 million victory on behalf of a coal company. Farmer also represented ExxonMobil in a mass asbestos case brought by 3,000 plaintiffs. Interviewees noted he was *"as good a lawyer as there is."*
The Clients: ExxonMobil; Horizon Resources; Wyeth; Johnson & Johnson and GlaxoSmithKline.

LITIGATION

WEST VIRGINIA

Steptoe & Johnson PLLC
The Firm: This large full-service firm handles defense work for a national base of corporate clients. *"Aggressive and growing,"* the firm is seen to be in a hiring mode and is expected to expand more in coming years. A combined environmental energy and commercial litigation group undertakes numerous suits on behalf of coal, and oil and gas industry clients. Recent cases include representing Columbia Gas Transmission in successfully opposing a development above a gas transmission line. The firm has seen an increase in IP litigation, primarily with pharmaceutical issues, and often linked with antitrust considerations. Interviewees place the firm *"close to the top tier,"* and praise its attorneys as *"professional and responsive."*
The Clients: Consolidated Coal; Peabody Coal Company; and Dominion Transmission are clients.

Allen Guthrie & McHugh
The Firm: Formed in 1981, this is a small litigation boutique acting for both defendants and corporate and individual plaintiffs in commercial, civil and complex criminal litigation. Commentators endorsed the practice for its *"ethical, hardworking lawyers"* with *"stellar individual reputations."* The firm has also proved itself a platform for advancement, with one of the founders, Robert King, being appointed to the bench.
The Lawyers: Former chief justice of the West Virginia Supreme Court of Appeals, **Thomas McHugh** was credited with *"an impeccable reputation"* and noteworthy skill in mediation work. Managing partner **David Thomas** is widely regarded as a *"top-shelf trial lawyer,"* and possibly *"the future of the firm."*
The Clients: Advanta Mortgage; City of Charleston and Dow Chemical.

Other Notable Practitioners
Currently in the process of expanding his new Charleston litigation boutique, The Tinney Law Firm, **John Tinney** is recognized as *"a premier lawyer and litigator."* Acting primarily as defense counsel, Tinney has recently been involved in products liability, pharmaceutical, defective design and unfair trade practice cases. His clients include GM, International Paper and Ernst & Young. Cordial v Ernst & Young twice successfully defended two partners and one senior manager of the accountancy firm against $94 million worth of claims of professional malpractice, gross negligence and negligence. He also represented Koppers Industries, Beazer East and CSX Transportation in products liability/toxic tort case, Appel et al v Koppers Industries. **Henry Jernigan** is developing the West Virginia office of Dinsmore & Shohl LLP, which opened in January 2002 in Charleston. In addition to representing four of the major energy companies in the state, he has been involved in several products liability and pharmaceutical cases. He is currently defending Purdue Pharma in cases pending across the US regarding the marketing of its pain medication OxyContin. Other clients include Eaglehawk Carbon, Peabody Energy, FMC and USX. Interviewees regard him as *"an excellent old-school attorney."* **Benjamin Bailey** at plaintiff/defendant firm Bailey and Glasser LLP enjoys a good reputation among peers as a *"type-A trial lawyer."* **Shawn George** is the litigation partner of the two-man firm George & Lorensen, in Charleston. Recognized as *"effective in commercial litigation,"* George has a practice that is much respected by the market commentators.
Thomas Goodwin, of Goodwin & Goodwin LLP, handles an even balance of transactional corporate work and complex litigation. His expertise ranges from major contract disputes to products liability, general commercial work and appellate work. His clients include Energy Corporation of America. Interviewees described him as *"highly skilled attorney."*

REAL ESTATE

WEST VIRGINIA
Leading firms (Real Estate)

1. BOWLES RICE MCDAVID GRAFF *Charleston*
   JACKSON KELLY PLLC *Charleston*
   STEPTOE & JOHNSON PLLC *Clarksburg*
2. SPILMAN THOMAS & BATTLE PLLC *Charleston*
3. HUDDLESTON, BOLEN, BEATTY *Huntington*
   REEDER & SHUMAN *Morgantown*
   ROBINSON & MCELWEE PLLC *Charleston*

Firms are listed alphabetically in each band.

Bowles Rice McDavid Graff & Love PLLC
The Firm: The ten-partner real estate group here is closely linked with the firm's energy and natural resources practices and attracts comment for its strength in coal, oil, gas, timber and mineral real estate work. Its kudos in the field are such that peers observed the team has *"legendary expertise on the mineral side."* The practice advises developers, banks, lenders and title insurance companies throughout West Virginia.
The Lawyers: Interviewees endorsed **Thomas Lane** for his *"excellent"* reputation in coal and oil and gas work, particularly commending him as an *"effective mineral real estate lawyer."* **Carl Andrews** specializes in commercial real estate, working in the areas of coal, oil and gas, timber and residential real estate and zoning. He recently completed a large refinancing for a commercial limited partnership and is advising on title work for a mall in southern West Virginia. Interviewees regard him as a *"preeminent"* real estate lawyer, who is well known for his transactional skill. Based in the Morgantown office, **Robert Dinsmore** focuses predominantly on mineral work for regional coal companies, but also represents commercial enterprises and homeowners in property acquisitions. He is currently advising on the development of a coal mine. Peers praise him for being *"knowledgeable and easy to work with."*
The Clients: Consolidated Coal Companies; Peabody Coal Company; United Bank; Mingo County Redevelopment Authority and Lawyers Title Corporation.

Jackson Kelly PLLC
see firm details p.821
The Firm: The size and *"extensive"* resources of this large full-service firm fosters a high level of specialization in its practice groups. Located within the broader business group, the real estate practice covers the gamut of commercial property matters, including land acquisition and development, planning and zoning and industrial and mining law. Interviewees noted the firm's activity in different markets within the state.
The Lawyers: The *"excellent"* **Dennis Broglio** (see p.721) boasts long experience of commercial real estate and title matters. In the Morgantown office, **Eric London** (see p.722) was recognized for both his *"responsive"* attitude and *"keen intellect."* He recently advised a wharf developer in $1 million investments in a combined hotel, condominium, conference center and marina complex. **Robert Fluharty** (see p.721) heads the real estate practice in Charleston. Peers remarked upon his *"bailiwick in mineral property"* and deep expertise in title law and mortgage lending work. He is currently acting on a financing for a large power-generating utilities company that involves title work for 20 sites. The real estate section is bolstered by the continued presence of Harvey Siler, who is now of counsel. Recognized for his *"outstanding commercial experience,"* Siler remains a valuable resource to the team.
The Clients: BB&T; Chico Enterprises; Centra Bank and Platinum Properties.

Steptoe & Johnson PLLC
The Firm: Clients report that this large, full-service practice offers the *"personalized service of a small firm,"* while rivals envy the group's

WEST VIRGINIA

REAL ESTATE

WEST VIRGINIA
Leading individuals (Real Estate)

[1]
- **ANDREWS Carl** Bowles Rice McDavid Graff, Charleston
- **BROGLIO Dennis** Jackson Kelly PLLC, Charleston
- **DEEM Patrick** Steptoe & Johnson PLLC, Clarksburg
- **LANE Thomas** Bowles Rice McDavid Graff, Charleston

[2]
- **HAMMOND David** Spilman Thomas & Battle, Charleston
- **LONDON Eric** Jackson Kelly PLLC, Morgantown
- **OFSA Joyce** Spilman Thomas & Battle, Charleston
- **SHUMAN Stephen** Reeder & Shuman, Morgantown

[3]
- **DINSMORE Robert** Bowles Rice McDavid, Charleston
- **FLUHARTY Robert** Jackson Kelly PLLC, Charleston
- **FRISK Fred** Sole Practitioner, Charleston
- **GILPIN Thomas** Huddleston, Bolen, Beatty, Huntington
- **MCELWEE Douglas** Robinson & McElwee, Charleston
- **O'CONNOR Otis** Steptoe & Johnson PLLC, Charleston
- **PILL Richard** Pill & Pill, Martinsburg
- **PLYBON Christopher** Huddleston, Bolen, Huntington

Individuals are listed alphabetically in each band.

"sheer manpower" and "deep knowledge base." The 30-attorney team practices from five offices across the state, advising on all aspects of real estate law from residential mortgage work and commercial loans to mineral projects and local development work. The firm assembles interdisciplinary groups to handle large projects, and enjoys special referral relationships with many commercial banks and title insurance companies. Major work includes a shopping center development and a number of coal site sales.

The Lawyers: Chair of the business department **Patrick Deem** is a commercial lawyer with *"excellent strength in real estate matters."* He is credited with establishing a loyal base of title insurance companies and mortgage lenders, and was recommended for his expert handling of the real estate aspects of larger commercial transactions. He recently acted on the sale of coal reserves in West Virginia to public company, Penn Virginia Resource Partners. **Otis O'Connor** commands a wealth of experience in real estate law and is highly regarded for his niche in real estate financing for both residential and commercial properties. Typical work includes the financing of new restaurants and companies and compiling title reports for lenders.

The Clients: Huntington National Bank; Huntington Mortgage Company; Chicago Title Insurance; Allied Homes Mortgage Capital Corporation, Carteret Mortgage; Consolidation Coal Company; Dominion Resources; Bank One, First American Title Insurance; Fidelity National Title Insurance; Drilling Appalachian Corporation and Marin Docks.

Spilman Thomas & Battle PLLC
The Firm: This well-established firm is said to have grown significantly in the past few years. The real estate department handles residential, commercial, refinancing, mineral transactional and condemnation work, illustrating its generalist approach. The practice is linked to the commercial/corporate activity of the firm, and so encompasses the creation of business entities, bankruptcies, and loan work as well as the representation of local, state and out-of-state lenders. Staffed with *"competent and professional"* attorneys, the group also advises on urban renewal and redevelopment.

The Lawyers: Head of the corporate department **Joyce Ofsa** was admired by peers for her *"toughness."* She recently acted in several transactions connected with coal properties, involving title examinations and mineral abstraction. Ofsa also undertakes financing work in connection with mineral, commercial and industrial transactions. **David Hammond** was acknowledged as a *"strong player"* with a *"standout"* reputation. Clients particularly appreciated his thoroughness in transactions, remarking that *"he leaves no stone unturned."* Recent matters include serving as title counsel to a national retailer opening sites in West Virginia, and acting for a bank that was financing the purchase of several media outlets in the state.

The Clients: United Bank; First American Title Insurance; Wells Fargo and Bankers Trust.

Huddleston, Bolen, Beatty, Porter & Copen LLP
The Firm: Located in the west of the state along the border with Kentucky and Ohio, this mid-sized firm enjoys a strong regional reputation. The group is known for its long-standing ties to railroad clients, but also acts for local lenders and developers in an array of commercial real estate transactions and financings. Real estate transactions linked to coal, oil and gas properties are a growing area for the firm, and practitioners are increasingly involved in the use of combined public and private funds to finance commercial and industrial projects. One client asserted: *"Every time I deal with them, it's a good experience."*

The Lawyers: Corporate lawyer **Thomas Gilpin** maintains a mixed practice, encompassing the varied fields of commercial, healthcare and real estate law. Active in minerals, he recently counseled Western Pocahontas Properties on its $45.6 million acquisition of a 25% interest in coalfields. **Christopher Plybon** enjoys a statewide reputation as a *"fine real estate lawyer."* Peers particularly drew researchers' attention to his expertise in financing matters. He recently represented a local public transport authority in the joint creation with a private developer of a transport facility and entertainment complex.

The Clients: Western Pocahontas Properties; Bank One; Tri-State Transit Authority and Huntington Municipal Development Authority.

Reeder & Shuman
The Firm: A *"collegial"* seven-attorney firm, based in Morgantown. The group maintains a strong profile in the region for real estate matters, in which interviewees claim it gives larger rivals a *"run for their money."*

The Lawyers: *"The heart of the firm"* **Stephen Shuman** was commended by interviewees for his extensive knowledge of real estate law. One client commented that *"anything he does is excellent."* Most of his practice is dedicated to coal, oil and gas real estate work, although he is also involved in residential and commercial real estate work. Peers commend him as a *"tough and thorough lawyer."* His son Robert Shuman is tipped to continue the family's niche in real estate law, and ranks in *Chambers'* tables as up-and-coming.

Robinson & McElwee PLLC
The Firm: Celebrating its 20th anniversary, this mid-sized firm commands a *"stellar reputation"* for environmental and mineral work. The real estate group advises clients on natural resources and mineral transactions, shopping center developments and title work from within the firm's commercial practice.

The Lawyers: Commercial real estate practitioner **Douglas McElwee** garners praise for his focus on mineral transactions. He recently represented Pittston Coal in the sale of assets to Amvest Minerals and has been involved in a number of shopping center developments and timber financing work.

The Clients: American Electric Power; FMC; RAG American Coal and Farm Credit of the Virginias.

Other Notable Practitioners
Sole practitioner **Fred Frisk** was described as *"just the tops"* for residential real estate matters. He also undertakes some commercial real estate work.

Richard Pill of Pill & Pill was also endorsed for residential real estate work. Active in the state's eastern region, Pill handles commercial transactions in addition to a volume of residential foreclosures. His clients include Centra Bank and Countrywide Home Loans.

Leaders in West Virginia

ALBERT, Michael
Jackson Kelly PLLC, Charleston
304 340 1287
malbert@jacksonkelly.com
Recommended in Corporate/M&A
Specialization: Administrative, business and commercial, corporate, insurance regulation, public utilities, securities, transportation law.
Prof. Memberships: American Bar Association; WV Bar Association; WV State Bar; WVU Alumni Association; Kanawha County Bar Association.
Career: Charleston Regional Chamber of Commerce (Board of Directors); National Institute for Chemical Studies (Chairman of the Board, Board of Directors and Executive Committee; Chairman, Development Committee); and the Kanawha County Public Library (Board of Directors); Listed in a leading American legal publication.
Personal: BS from West Virginia University, JD from the West Virginia University School of Law.

ANDREWS, Carl
Bowles Rice McDavid Graff & Love PLLC, Charleston 304 347 1100
Recommended in Real Estate

BAILEY, Benjamin
Bailey & Glasser LLP, Charleston
304 345 6555
Recommended in Litigation

BAYLESS, Kathryn Reed
The Bayless Law Firm, Princeton
304 487 8707
Recommended in Employment

BOOKER, William
Kay Casto & Chaney PLLC, Charleston
304 345 8900
Recommended in Corporate/M&A

BROGLIO, Dennis
Jackson Kelly PLLC, Charleston
304 340 1322
dbroglio@jacksonkelly.com
Recommended in Real Estate
Specialization: Real estate/property law; Business and Commercial Practice Group.
Prof. Memberships: West Virginia State Bar, Kanawha County Bar Association, California State Bar Association, New York State Bar Association.
Personal: JD, West Virginia University; BSCE, University of Notre Dame.

BROWN, Ricklin
Bowles Rice McDavid Graff & Love PLLC, Charleston 304 347 1100
Recommended in Employment

CAPPELLANTI, Ellen
Jackson Kelly PLLC, Charleston
304 340 1277
ecappellanti@jacksonkelly.com
Recommended in Corporate/M&A
Specialization: Bankruptcy, real estate development, business and commercial.
Prof. Memberships: Dean's Development Council, WVU College of Law; American Bar Association; WV State Bar; Kanawha County Bar Association; Master, The Judge John A Field, Jr. Inn of Court; Commercial Law League; Judicial Conference of the United States Court of Appeals for Fourth Circuit; West Virginia Law Institute.
Career: Listed in a leading American legal publication (bankruptcy law).
Personal: JD, West Virginia University; BA, West Virginia University.

CASSIDY, Patrick
Cassidy Myers Cogan Voegelin & Tennant, Wheeling 304 232 8100
Recommended in Employment

COKELY, Bryan
Steptoe & Johnson PLLC, Charleston
304 353 8000
Recommended in Employment

DEEM, Patrick
Steptoe & Johnson PLLC, Clarksburg
304 624 8377
Recommended in Corporate/M&A, Real Estate

DINSMORE, Robert
Bowles Rice McDavid Graff & Love PLLC, Charleston 304 347 1100
Recommended in Real Estate

DONNELLY, Charles
Donnelly & Carbone, Charleston
304 342 3650
Recommended in Employment

DUNBAR, Charles
Jackson Kelly PLLC, Charleston
304 340 1196
cdunbar@jacksonkelly.com
Recommended in Corporate/M&A
Specialization: Banking, business and commercial, contracts, insurance, international, commercial litigation, corporate, securities, technology and computer law.
Prof. Memberships: American Bar Association, Section on Corporations; Banking and Business Law, Section on International Law; West Virginia State Bar; Kanawha County Bar.
Career: Listed in a leading American legal publication (banking law).
Publications: Interest, Inducements and the IRS, Compliance with Regulations Q and D in the New Competitive Landscape, 'American Banking Association Bank Compliance Magazine', 2001.
Personal: JD, West Virginia University; CPA; BS, West Virginia University.

EMCH, A L
Jackson Kelly PLLC, Charleston
304 340 1172
aemch@jacksonkelly.com
Recommended in Litigation
Specialization: Admiralty, alternative dispute resolution, aviation, class actions, contracts, insurance, mediation, personal injury litigation, product liability, toxic and mass tort litigation.
Prof. Memberships: Fellow, American College of Trial Lawyers; American Board of Trial Advocates; International Association of Defense Counsel; Fellow, American Bar Foundation; par West Virginia Bar Foundation, Inc.; Mediator, US District Courts, Northern and Southern Districts of West Virginia, state courts; Defense Trial Counsel of West Virginia, Fourth Circuit Judicial Conference.
Career: WV Air National Guard, Pilot, Lt. Col. Retired; United States Air Force; Listed in a leading American legal publication.
Personal: JD University of Virginia, AB West Virginia University.

FARMER, Stephen
Farmer, Cline & Arnold, Charleston
304 346 5990
Recommended in Litigation

FERGUSON, Mark
Sprouse & Ferguson, Charleston
304 342 9100
Recommended in Corporate/M&A

FERRETTI, David
Spilman Thomas & Battle, PLLC, Charleston 304 340 3800
Recommended in Corporate/M&A

FLORIO, Michael
Michael J Florio, Clarksburg TBA
Recommended in Employment

FLUHARTY, Robert
Jackson Kelly PLLC, Charleston
304 340 1174
rfluharty@jacksonkelly.com
Recommended in Real Estate
Specialization: Business and commercial law, commercial and mineral real estate law, natural resources recovery, transportation and sales.
Prof. Memberships: West Virginia State Bar; West Virginia Bar Association; Kanawha County Bar Association; American Bar Association; Eastern Mineral Law Foundation, Trustee.
Personal: LLM, Cambridge University (England); JD, Rutgers University; BA, Washington & Lee University.

FRISK, Fred
Fred M Frisk Jr - Sole Practitioner, Charleston 304 344 3858
Recommended in Real Estate

GARDILL, James
Phillips Gardill Kaiser & Altmeyer, Wheeling 304 232 6810
Recommended in Corporate/M&A

GEORGE, Shawn
George & Lorensen, Charleston
304 343 5555
Recommended in Litigation

GILPIN, Thomas
Huddleston, Bolen, Beatty, Porter & Copen, LLP, Huntington 304 529 6181
Recommended in Real Estate

GOODWIN, Thomas
Goodwin & Goodwin, LLP, Charleston
304 346 7000
Recommended in Litigation

HAMMER, David
Hammer Ferretti & Schiavoni, Martinsburg 304 364 8505
Recommended in Employment

HAMMOND, David
Spilman Thomas & Battle, PLLC, Charleston 304 340 3800
Recommended in Real Estate

HAVILAND, James
Crandall Pyles Haviland & Turner, Charleston 304 345 3080
Recommended in Employment

HEYWOOD, Thomas
Bowles Rice McDavid Graff & Love PLLC, Charleston 304 347 1100
Recommended in Corporate/M&A

JERNIGAN JR, Henry
Dinsmore & Shohl LLP, Charleston Null
Recommended in Litigation

KARLIN, Allan
Allan N. Karlin, Morgantown
304 296 8266
Recommended in Employment

KING JR, Evans
Steptoe & Johnson PLLC, Clarksburg
304 624 8377
Recommended in Corporate/M&A

KRIEGER, Thomas
Jenkins Fenstermaker, PLLC, Huntington
304 523 2100
Recommended in Employment

LANE, Thomas
Bowles Rice McDavid Graff & Love PLLC, Charleston 304 347 1100
Recommended in Real Estate

LEDBETTER, Cheryl
Jackson Kelly PLLC, Charleston
304 340 1107
cledbetter@jacksonkelly.com
Recommended in Employment
Specialization: Employment discrimination with an emphasis on sexual harassment law.
Prof. Memberships: Kanawha County

WEST VIRGINIA LEADERS

Bar; West Virginia Bar Association; American Bar Association (Labor Section).
Personal: JD, Washington & Lee University; BA, University of Arkansas.

LONDON, Eric
Jackson Kelly PLLC, Morgantown
304 284 4109
elondon@jacksonkelly.com
Recommended in Real Estate
Specialization: Banking, business/commercial, contracts, landlord/tenant, leasing, real estate/property law, trusts/estates.
Prof. Memberships: West Virginia State Bar Association; Monongalia County Bar Association.
Career: Frequent speaker on banking, business and related topics.
Personal: JD, University of Pittsburgh School of Law; BS, Pennsylvania State University.

LORENSEN, Charles
George & Lorensen, Charleston
304 343 5555
Recommended in Corporate/M&A

LOVE, Charles
Bowles Rice McDavid Graff & Love PLLC, Charleston 304 347 1100
Recommended in Litigation

LUKENS, John
Spilman Thomas & Battle, PLLC, Charleston 304 340 3800
Recommended in Corporate/M&A

LUSK, Neva
Spilman Thomas & Battle, PLLC, Charleston 304 340 3800
Recommended in Litigation

MCELWEE, Douglas
Robinson & McElwee PLLC, Charleston
304 344 5800
Recommended in Real Estate

MCHUGH, Thomas
Allen Guthrie & McHugh, Charleston
304 345 7250
Recommended in Litigation

MORRISON, David
Steptoe & Johnson PLLC, Clarksburg
304 624 8377
Recommended in Employment

MURRAY, Thomas
Huddleston, Bolen, Beatty, Porter & Copen, LLP, Huntington 304 529 6181
Recommended in Corporate/M&A

O'CONNOR, Otis
Steptoe & Johnson PLLC, Charleston
304 353 8000
Recommended in Real Estate

OFSA, Joyce
Spilman Thomas & Battle, PLLC, Charleston 304 340 3800
Recommended in Real Estate

PILL, Richard
Pill & Pill, Martinsburg
304 263 4971
Recommended in Real Estate

PLYBON, Christopher
Huddleston, Bolen, Beatty, Porter & Copen, LLP, Huntington 304 529 6181
Recommended in Real Estate

PRICE, Joseph
Robinson & McElwee PLLC, Charleston
304 344 5800
Recommended in Employment

RANSON, Michael
Ranson Law Offices, Charleston
304 345 1990
Recommended in Employment

ROLES, Forrest
Dinsmore & Shohl LLP, Charleston Null
Recommended in Employment

SCHIAVONI, Robert
Hammer Ferretti & Schiavoni, Martinsburg 304 364 8505
Recommended in Employment

SHUMAN, Stephen
Reeder & Shuman, Morgantown
304 292 8488
Recommended in Real Estate

SOUTHWORTH II, Louis S
Jackson Kelly PLLC, Charleston
304 340 1231
lsouthworth@jacksonkelly.com
Recommended in Corporate/M&A
Specialization: Administrative, legislative services, business/commercial, mergers/acquisitions, business planning, securities, corporate, taxation, leases, trusts/estates.
Prof. Memberships: American Bar Association; West Virginia Bar Association; Kanawha County Bar Association; American College of Tax Counsel, Fellow; West Virginia Tax Institute; University of Charleston, Trustee Emeritus; CAMC Foundation, Trustee; Highland Hospital Foundation, Trustee; Clay Foundation, Board Member; par West Virginia Bar Foundation, Fellow.
Career: Listed in a leading American legal publication (corporate law and tax law).
Personal: LLM, New York University; JD, West Virginia University; AB, Marshall University.

STEPTOE, Robert
Steptoe & Johnson PLLC, Clarksburg
304 624 8377
Recommended in Employment

STOWERS, Gerard
Bowles Rice McDavid Graff & Love PLLC, Charleston 304 347 1100
Recommended in Litigation

THOMAS, David
Allen Guthrie & McHugh, Charleston
304 345 7250
Recommended in Litigation

TINNEY, John
The Tinney Law Firm, Charleston
304 720 3310
Recommended in Litigation

WOLFE, Roger
Jackson Kelly PLLC, Charleston
304 340 1105
rwolfe@jacksonkelly.com
Recommended in Employment
Specialization: Discrimination, labor and employment, unemployment compensation, litigation, union, organizational campaigns, collective bargaining, class actions, statistics, public sector employment law, alternative dispute resolution.
Career: Listed in a leading American legal publication (labor and employment law); Frequent lecturer on various employment law topics; Adjunct Professor of Employment Law for West Virginia University.
Personal: JD, West Virginia University; AB, West Virginia University.

WOODY, Charles
Spilman Thomas & Battle, PLLC, Charleston 304 340 3800
Recommended in Employment

WISCONSIN

CORPORATE/M&A

CONTENTS: Corporate/M&A p.723; Employment: Mainly Plaintiff p.724; Mainly Defendant p.725; Litigation: General Commercial p726; Real Estate p.727; Individuals' Profiles p.729.

WISCONSIN'S TOP THREE
1. Foley & Lardner
2. Quarles & Brady
3. Michael Best & Friedrich

Ranking based on Chambers' research within the state.

All quotes in the text are from interviews with clients and competitors.

OVERVIEW: In a close contest, **Foley & Lardner** topped the *Chambers'* rankings by the narrowest of margins. Like Quarles & Brady, the firm is respected for the breadth of its coverage in commercial law. The corporate client base here is diverse and includes such well-known names as Kimberly-Clark and Goldman Sachs. Alongside M&A and securities expertise, the firm is skilled in related areas such as international tax planning. Tom Shriner, described as a brilliant legal thinker and strategist, stands out from a deep team of respected litigators. Attorneys here are active in multimillion dollar products liability disputes as well as securities litigation. Home to the largest real estate practice in the state, the firm advises developers and investors on a broad range of projects. It assisted, for example, The Milwaukee Brewers baseball team in the $400 million development of Miller Park stadium.

Quarles & Brady, in second place, was recommended for its strength in depth across the board. In corporate matters, in addition to its broad commercial expertise locally, the firm is active on international transactions; it advised Wisconsin electrical equipment manufacturer Electronic Theater Controls on its expansion into Germany. Clients remarked on the firm's well-rounded approach to litigation, which allows attorneys to advise clients on cases across a number of practice areas. The team has acted for Mitsui and Microsoft in two antitrust actions, and is also highly respected for its sizable presence in the employment law market. In addition, the firm runs an integrated real estate practice that pools together attorneys in Wisconsin, Illinois, Arizona and Florida.

Market observers applauded **Michael Best & Friedrich**'s success in attracting an entrepreneurial client base that ensures the firm is a natural choice for private equity houses and venture capitalists. Tod Linstroth and the team, said to inspire tremendous client loyalty, impress with their IP and technology law expertise. The team advised Seattle Systems on the $700 million sale of a subsidiary to Mattel. Researchers were impressed with the level of recommendation for the firm's alternative dispute resolution proficiency as well as for its work in construction claims and employment-related litigation. The firm also possesses the largest employment department in the state, fielding over 50 attorneys who are considered to be both talented lawyers and great business developers.

CORPORATE/M&A

WISCONSIN
Leading firms (Corporate/M&A)
1. FOLEY & LARDNER *Milwaukee*
   QUARLES & BRADY LLP *Milwaukee*
2. GODFREY & KAHN SC *Milwaukee*
   MICHAEL BEST & FRIEDRICH LLP *Milwaukee*
   REINHART, BOERNER, VAN DEUREN, *Milwaukee*

Leading individuals (Corporate/M&A)
1. LINSTROTH Tod *Michael Best & Friedrich*, Madison
   SOMMERHAUSER Peter *Godfrey & Kahn*, Milwaukee
2. GARMER Ben *Foley & Lardner*, Milwaukee
   SKINDRUD Michael *LaFollette Godfrey & Kahn*, Madison
   ZILAVY Thomas *DeWitt Ross & Stevens SC*, Madison
3. BARTELL Jeff *Quarles & Brady LLP*, Madison
   BÖER Ralf-Reinhard *Foley & Lardner*, Milwaukee
   ERNE David *Reinhart, Boerner, Van Deuren*, Milwaukee
   KRINGEL Jerry *Michael Best & Friedrich LLP*, Milwaukee
   ROBISON John *Quarles & Brady LLP*, Madison

Firms and individuals are listed alphabetically in each band.

Foley & Lardner

The Firm: The firm's diverse client base has kept it *"buoyant,"* despite adverse market conditions. Market sources recognize it is the *"preeminent player"* in the Midwest in the areas of banking, industrial products, telecommunications, real estate and consumer products.

The Lawyers: Lauded as a *"terrific lawyer,"* **Ben Garmer** advises public and private companies on acquisitions, financings and takeover defense. Straddling the firm's business law and transactional securities teams, Garmer is visible in the market representing CSFB, Merrill Lynch and Goldman Sachs. **Ralf-Reinhard Böer** was warmly recommended as *"a fine and prominent international lawyer."* Böer serves as general counsel for numerous European clients, and is special counsel to several Scandinavian clients with regard to their worldwide acquisitions, joint ventures and licensing activities.

The Clients: Johnson Controls; WPS Resources; Kimberly-Clark; Goldman Sachs; Merrill Lynch; CSFB and several Fortune 500 companies.

Quarles & Brady LLP

The Firm: Interviewees offered glowing recommendation for this firm, particularly noting its *"strength in depth."* A number of individuals within the corporate practice were recognized for broad expertise in M&A, securities and corporate governance. This active practice is seen to be busy on significant transactions across a range of sectors.

The Lawyers: Market sources endorse **Jeff Bartell** as a *"securitization expert."* A former state commissioner of securities and a member of the state regulation of Securities Committee, he has been deeply involved in the drafting of legislation aimed at providing standardized securitization models. Commentators also singled out *"fine attorney"* **John Robison** as *"one of Quarles & Brady's best."* His expertise includes representing clients in the dairy, retail, manufacturing and healthcare sectors. He recently advised Wisconsin electrical equipment manufacturer Electronic Theater Controls on its expansion into Germany.

The Clients: Dairy cooperatives, physician groups and manufacturing, retail, service sector and Fortune 500 companies feature on its client roster.

Godfrey & Kahn SC

The Firm: The firm's pursuit of a full-service model has earned it a good share of some of the larger M&A deals, particularly within Milwaukee. Attorneys were described as *"younger, more aggressive, hands-on types"* who *"can handle major transactions without relying too heavily on the firm's senior figures."*

The Lawyers: The *"extraordinarily bright"* **Peter Sommerhauser** is recognized as *"one of the stalwarts"* of the practice. He has built up an *"enviable"* profile in Wisconsin, advising clients in the retail, manufacturing and service sectors. He continues to advise Kohl's Department Stores on business and transactional matters. Based in Madison, **Michael Skindrud** was described to researchers as *"a highly ethical and first-rate lawyer."* His practice covers M&A, private equity and debt financings and strategic partnering on behalf of healthcare and technology clients.

The Clients: Kohl's Department Store; Appleton Papers and other leading retail, service and manufacturing companies.

WISCONSIN
EMPLOYMENT & LABOR LAW

Michael Best & Friedrich LLP
The Firm: Frequently associated with its entrepreneurial client base, the firm has a wealth of experience advising early and late start-ups, venture capitalists and private equity houses and their portfolio companies. Members have been particularly active in Madison on financing work for start-ups associated with the university. The firm is seen to inspire *"tremendous client loyalty,"* and is steadily expanding its scope as clients grow and begin to engage in out-of-state transactions.
The Lawyers: With a background in real estate law, **Tod Linstroth** enjoys a *"terrific"* reputation as a highly respected corporate lawyer whose *"extraordinarily busy"* practice is driven predominantly by his transactional abilities. He has a strong technology focus and advises on IP based transactions for numerous clients associated with Madison University. He advised Seattle Systems on the $700 million sale of one of its subsidiaries to Mattel, and frequently represents high-profile entrepreneurs and life science companies. **Jerry Kringel** was consistently recommended for his broad experience in tax and corporate law. He advises a varied portfolio of clients ranging from family-owned businesses and SMEs to much larger corporates, and is currently acting on several major manufacturing transactions.
The Clients: Seattle Systems; Berbee; Promega Corporation; Ultratech; Newell Industries; biotech, medical and life science companies and individual entrepreneurs.

Reinhart, Boerner, Van Deuren, Norris & Rieselbach SC
The Firm: This *"extremely respected"* full-service firm is increasingly visible acting on significant commercial transactions within the state. The practice's 12 securities lawyers are noted for their efficiency in structuring, locating, negotiating and closing financing transactions.
The Lawyers: David Erne elicited widespread praise as a talented finance and creditors' rights attorney. He sits as a member of the American College of Bankruptcy, a professional association and has been involved in a number of high-profile bankruptcy cases.
The Clients: Emmber Foods; Resolute Systems; Allen-Edmonds; Sargento Cheese; Riley Construction; GIC Management; Ruud Lighting and SkilTech of Madison.

Other Notable Practitioners
Deemed *"one of Wisconsin's finest"* by fellow practitioners, **Tom Zilavy** of DeWitt Ross & Stevens SC was highlighted for his reputation among local and Midwestern financial institutions. Zilavy acts as counsel to several financial institutions on regulatory matters, secured lending and trust department operations, and regularly represents a large charitable foundation client before the IRS.

EMPLOYMENT & LABOR LAW — MAINLY PLAINTIFF

WISCONSIN
Leading firms (Employment: Mainly Plaintiff)
1. **FOX & FOX** Madison
2. **FIRST, BLONDIS, ALBRECHT** Milwaukee
   SHNEIDMAN, HAWKS & EHLKE Madison
3. **LAWTON & CATES SC** Madison
   PERRY, SHAPIRO, QUINDEL, SAKS, Milwaukee

Leading individuals (Employment: Mainly Plaintiff)
1. **FOX Michael** Fox & Fox, Madison
2. **FIRST Curry** First, Blondis, Albrecht, Milwaukee
   HAWKS Tim Shneidman, Hawks & Ehlke, Madison
3. **KELLY Walter** Sole Practitioner, Milwaukee
   SCHNEIDMAN Dan Shneidman, Hawks, Milwaukee

Firms and individuals are listed alphabetically in each band.

Fox & Fox
The Firm: This five-partner Madison-based law firm primarily represents plaintiffs in personal injury and civil law suits. Sources regarded this firm as home to Wisconsin's *"smartest and toughest negotiators and litigators."* Attorneys here possess an *"outstanding trial record"* and boast superb research capabilities; they have secured some of the largest settlements and jury awards in the state.
The Lawyers: One of Wisconsin's best-known lawyers is **Mike Fox**, who is respected by peers for his *"tremendous jury appeal."* Over the years, he has scored a number of landmark victories such as Huebschen v Wisconsin Department of Health and Social Services – a female on male harassment case, as well as Title VII victories endorsing the concept of the altered and hostile working environment.

First, Blondis, Albrecht & Novotnak
The Firm: This small, six-attorney firm specializes in employment and civil rights claims from the US Supreme Court to federal, state and local trial courts. Interviewees recognized the *"good depth of experience"* in the team, which advises on harassment, discrimination, workforce reduction in force and ADA-related matters.
The Lawyers: The *"extremely capable"* **Curry First** advises on employment and labor law and general civil rights litigation. Peers endorsed him as an *"especially doughty opponent."*

Shneidman, Hawks & Ehlke
The Firm: Comprises 15 labor and employment attorneys pursuing workers' compensation, civil rights and other general practice matters.
The Lawyers: Many commentators expressed their high regard for attorney **Tim Hawks**, who primarily represents unions. A superb negotiator, his depth of legal knowledge is widely respected. *"Elder statesman"* **Dan Schneidman** impresses as *"a fiery and effective advocate."*

Lawton & Cates SC
The Firm: Based in Madison, this firm of 20 attorneys acts for labor unions and individuals with civil rights and discriminatory complaints and in related litigation. Peers reported that the firm has *"notched up many multimillion dollar successes;"* among them is the first million dollar personal injury verdict in Dane County. The firm is also recommended for its work representing US citizens in Mexico, and Mexican citizens living in the US.
The Lawyers: Bruce Davey acts on employment litigation, civil rights and discrimination matters for public sector employees and private clients. Trilingual **Victor Arellano** advises on immigration and employment issues.
The Clients: Wisconsin State Employees Union; private clients and Mexican citizens and other individuals involved in Mexican affairs.

Perry, Shapiro, Quindel, Saks, Charlton & Lerner
The Firm: Interviewees commended this *"talented and experienced"* firm of five employment attorneys.
The Lawyers: Katherine Charlton and **Barbara Quindel** are key members of the group, which advises on discrimination claims and contract negotiations, particularly following reorganizations and employee separation.

Other Notable Practitioners
Sole practitioner **Walter Kelly** has carved out an admirable reputation for *"pursuing his cases with incredible diligence."* He made a name for himself by scoring some significant victories over governmental agencies.

EMPLOYMENT & LABOR LAW — WISCONSIN

MAINLY DEFENDANT

WISCONSIN
Leading firms
(Employment: Mainly Defendant)

1
- MICHAEL BEST & FRIEDRICH LLP *Milwaukee*
- QUARLES & BRADY LLP *Milwaukee*

2
- FOLEY & LARDNER *Madison*
- LINDNER & MARSACK SC *Milwaukee*

3
- DAVIS & KUELTHAU SC *Milwaukee*
- MELLI, WALKER, PEASE & RUHLY SC *Madison*

Leading individuals
(Employment: Mainly Defendant)

1
- AUEN Michael *Foley & Lardner*, Madison
- KERN David *Quarles & Brady LLP*, Milwaukee
- SCRIVNER Tom *Michael Best & Friedrich LLP*, Milwaukee

2
- DUFFY Robert *Quarles & Brady LLP*, Milwaukee
- LEICHTLING Ely *Quarles & Brady LLP*, Milwaukee
- MARSACK Gary *Lindner & Marsack SC*, Milwaukee

3
- BOBBER Bernard *Foley & Lardner*, Milwaukee
- CRONE Tom *Melli, Walker, Pease & Ruhly SC*, Madison
- CROYSDALE David *Michael Best & Friedrich*, Milwaukee
- JASPAN Stanley *Foley & Lardner*, Milwaukee
- LYNCH Larry *Foley & Lardner*, Milwaukee
- NINNEMAN Mary *Quarles & Brady LLP*, Milwaukee

Firms and individuals are listed alphabetically in each band.

Michael Best & Friedrich LLP

The Firm: Possesses the largest employment division in the state with over 50 attorneys. The firm's client base is growing swiftly, not least in the retail and wholesale sectors, and the reputation of the firm is such that peers respect its ability to attract stand-alone work. Attorneys here were recommended to researchers as *"talented labor lawyers, who are all great business developers."*

The Lawyers: Sources pointed to the *"truly outstanding"* **Tom Scrivner**'s practice, which encompasses elements of labor and employment counseling and litigation. He has recently been involved in complex NLRB arbitrations relating to subcontracting within unionized organizations. Another Michael Best *"big gun"* is **Dave Croysdale**, who is a labor relations specialist, active on behalf of a number of newspaper, food retail and manufacturing clients. He has represented defense facilities maintenance organizations on union-related issues and defended claims brought before the Armed Services Board of Appeal. The group can draw on the support of Tom Obenberger, head of the employment group and managing partner John Sapp.

The Clients: Pfizer; Warner-Lambert; governmental agencies and major retail, wholesale, manufacturing and service sector companies. The firm advised on employment issues arising from Unilever's acquisition of Bestfoods in 2000. It also handled all the labour agreements in ProSource Distribution Services' coast-to-coast acquisitions.

Quarles & Brady LLP

The Firm: A major presence across Wisconsin for employment matters. Clients endorsed this *"incredibly accessible and responsive"* firm, which has 37 full-time members. Attorneys address a full range of issues including discrimination, affirmative action programs, wage and hour issues and wrongful discharge. A significant percentage of the work involves corporate reorganizations and related workforce reductions, including representing overseas companies with interests in the US.

The Lawyers: Sources proclaimed that **Dave Kern** is *"a man of high integrity and a good legal analyst."* His expertise lies in traditional labor matters such as union relations and strikes as well as a range of discrimination issues for healthcare, manufacturing and banking clients. He advised Brady Corporation on issues relating to its reorganization, and has handled discrimination and collective bargaining work for GE Medical Systems. One client believed that Kern *"dispenses such tailored advice that he deserves a seat at board level."* The *"terrific litigator"* **Bob Duffy** is involved in civil rights, union-related issues and discrimination litigation. He recently acted for Prairie Du Chien Memorial Hospital and successfully obtained the dismissal of defamation and wrongful discharge claims. Interviewees commended **Ely Leichtling**'s *"brightness and his ability to assimilate the salient points of any case swiftly."* His expertise includes age, gender and race discrimination claims as well as FMLA-related matters. The *"highly responsive"* **Mary Pat Ninneman** counsels on employment policies; she specializes in wrongful discharge, defamation, and discrimination litigation. She successfully overturned a recent $25 million employee compensatory decision.

The Clients: M&I Bank; Miller Brewing; Apogent Technologies; Aurora Health Care; WS Packaging Group and UPS Milwaukee Transport Services.

Foley & Lardner

The Firm: With 15 labor and employment attorneys based in Milwaukee and seven in Madison, this firm boasts expertise ranging from pure labor, collective bargaining, trade secrets and corporate strategy to discrimination litigation. Observers agree that the firm has proved *"extremely attractive"* to small and medium-sized enterprises. The team is active at both federal and state level, and before agencies such as the NLRB, EEOC, OSHA and the US Department of Labor.

The Lawyers: Peers say the *"most visible"* attorney here is **Michael Auen**. A *"highly competent trial attorney"* and an accomplished negotiator, he has represented a diversified private sector client base in labor negotiations, union-organizing efforts, discrimination claims and restrictive covenants. **Bernard (Bud) Bobber**'s employment practice features discrimination defense, wage and hour claims and trade secret matters. He was described to researchers as a *"hugely intelligent attorney who has had considerable successes."* **Larry Lynch** is *"one of the state's best analysts,"* active in wage and hour claims, OSHA and a variety of discrimination litigation. Managing partner **Stan Jaspan** also represents employers in collective bargaining, compensation negotiations and general policy issues.

The Clients: Johnson Controls; utilities and manufacturing, distribution and retail clients.

Lindner & Marsack SC

The Firm: One of Wisconsin's boutique firms specializing in labor and employment matters. The Milwaukee office is home to 17 attorneys practising 50% traditional labor, 40% employment and 10% workers' compensation matters. The firm's core client base is made up of SMEs, particularly manufacturing and retail concerns, and Lindner & Marsack's size and structure makes it ideally suited to address this band.

The Lawyers: President and senior stockholder of the firm is **Gary Marsack**, described as being *"as good a labor lawyer as there is in the state."* Marsack is a traditional labor lawyer who devotes the majority of his time to counseling, collective bargaining and contract administration matters. He has been a key adviser to numerous venture capital groups and major accounting firms, assisting their clients in the employment law aspects of M&A, consolidations and downsizing. As a result of his expertise in this area, he has co-authored the respected book Management's Guide to Mergers and Acquisitions.

The Clients: Harnischfeger Corporation; Newall Industries; Mercury Marine; Fortune Brands; Masterlock and retailers, manufacturers and emerging hi-tech concerns.

Davis & Kuelthau SC

The Firm: The 32 labor attorneys here have a slight bias toward public sector employment matters, but also display a depth of experience in corporate labor relations. The group is particularly endorsed for its representation of municipalities.

The Lawyers: Dennis Rader is a key member of the team. In public sector work, their advice on

WISCONSIN — LITIGATION

employment issues covers school law, student discipline, due processes and free speech. Much of the work has been EEOC-related. The team has also advised major corporates and SMEs on discrimination litigation and wage and hour claims.
The Clients: Public sector clients include nonprofit entities, school districts and municipalities. Private sector clients range from major corporates to SMEs.

Melli, Walker, Pease & Ruhly SC
The Firm: Of the firm's 14 attorneys, nine practice labor and employment law in all sectors, particularly for schools and construction and manufacturing companies. Commentators respect the group as *"tough litigators,"* with many agreeing that *"whenever an employer wants a fight, they'd be the guys I'd be inclined to recommend."*
The Lawyers: **Tom Crone** advises on employment discrimination, civil rights and wrongful discharge claims before administrative agencies, and in state and federal courts.
The Clients: Associated Builders & Contractors of Wisconsin; primarily nonunion companies, especially contractors, building and construction firms. The firm represented Town & Country Electric before the US Supreme Court on union issues.

LITIGATION — GENERAL COMMERCIAL

WISCONSIN
Leading firms
(Litigation: General Commercial)

1. **FOLEY & LARDNER** Milwaukee
2. **HELLER EHRMAN WHITE** Madison
   MICHAEL BEST & FRIEDRICH LLP Milwaukee
   QUARLES & BRADY LLP Milwaukee
   REINHART, BOERNER, VAN DEUREN Milwaukee
3. **GODFREY & KAHN SC** Milwaukee
   STAFFORD ROSENBAUM LLP Madison

Leading individuals
(Litigation: General Commercial)

1. **HANSEN Scott** Reinhart, Boerner, Milwaukee
   SHRINER Tom Foley & Lardner, Milwaukee
   SKILTON John Heller Ehrman White, Madison
2. **BOWEN Michael** Foley & Lardner, Milwaukee
   BUSCH John Michael Best & Friedrich LLP, Milwaukee
   BUTLER Brian Stafford Rosenbaum LLP, Madison
3. **CHRISTIANSEN John** Foley & Lardner, Milwaukee
   MCSWEENEY Maurice Foley & Lardner, Milwaukee
   PARSONS Stuart Quarles & Brady LLP, Milwaukee
   SENNETT Nancy Foley & Lardner, Milwaukee

Firms and individuals are listed alphabetically in each band.

Foley & Lardner
The Firm: The preeminent litigation firm of the Midwest, Foley & Lardner boasts an *"enviable"* list of highly esteemed business litigators, and sets the standard in terms of successful multimillion dollar front-page cases. The large team here handles all types of commercial litigation, including products liability, toxic torts, securities, IP, antitrust and bankruptcy.
The Lawyers: Lauded as a *"brilliant legal thinker and strategist,"* **Tom Shriner** concentrates on commercial and public law. He represents corporate clients in both state and federal courts and earns praise for his expertise in appellate work. **Michael Bowen** was nominated as an *"incredibly sharp"* attorney with *"tremendous expertise"* in antitrust and trade regulation matters. Bowen has particular strength in relation to distribution issues, billing and lender liability, and the enforcement and termination of agreements. Bowen is best known for his co-authorship of the Wisconsin Fair Dealership Law (1988) and for his successful prosecution of Zenith Electronics under this very law a decade later. Interviewees recommended *"bright and able"* **John Christiansen** for his long experience of litigating distribution cases on behalf of suppliers, distributors and dealers. **Nancy Sennett** is credited with founding and developing the firm's securities litigation practice. Her workload covers all aspects of commercial and business litigation but has a focus on securities litigation, in which she represents corporations, boards of directors, broker-dealers, investment advisers and individuals. She represented broker-dealer defendants in the Orange County bankruptcy litigation and in the SEC's 'yield burning' enforcement action. National chair of the firm's litigation department, **Maurice (Marc) McSweeney** focuses on a wide variety of commercial litigation and counseling, including antitrust, dealer and distributor disputes, malpractice, securities and takeover matters.
The Clients: The firm represents major electronic, medical, retail and media companies, and a large concentration of suppliers and distributors in all aspects of commercial litigation.

Heller Ehrman White & McAuliffe LLP
The Firm: This Californian firm opened a Madison office in 2001, becoming the first out-of-state law firm to move into Wisconsin. Since then, the firm has recruited heavily in the area and has established itself as a player in the Wisconsin market. The litigation group benefits from the firm's full-service resources and is highly recommended for its IP litigation practice. It attracts a steady volume of patent, software licensing, trade secrets, copyright and trademark cases. The firm also has a niche practice dedicated to Native American affairs.
The Lawyers: Deemed a *"truly excellent litigator"* by peers, **John Skilton** is best known for his concentration on patent litigation. However, this *"accomplished"* attorney also has wide experience of managing complex commercial, antitrust, distribution, products liability and constitutional cases. He has litigated matters in state and federal courts around the country and also has significant experience in Europe.
The Clients: Microsoft; VISA; National Guardian Life Insurance; Wisconsin Alumni Research Foundation; Excalibur Technologies; Avista Corporation and various biotech, pharmaceutical, genetics and proteomics companies.

Michael Best & Friedrich LLP
The Firm: Although well known locally as a pioneer of alternative dispute resolution, the firm also boasts a renowned and comprehensive litigation division of over 50 attorneys. The practice acts for a wide range of clients, but strong links with unionized industries make it a popular choice for construction claims and employment-related litigation. The firm's Madison branch is closely associated with technology clients and undertakes a large share of finance and securities litigation on behalf of local start-ups.
The Lawyers: Researchers were told that **John Busch** maintains a busy general litigation practice and is *"deeply respected within the state."* He recently acted in a major personal injury case against a scaffolding manufacturing firm, and successfully defended a Fortune 500 company against regulatory challenges brought by the State of Wisconsin. Recommended by peers as a *"creative brainstormer,"* Busch has particular expertise in the evaluation of securities claims.
The Clients: American Appraisal Associates; Ameritech; Fiserv; GE Marquette Medical Systems; Harley-Davidson; HK Systems; Promega and TruServ.

Quarles & Brady LLP
The Firm: The practice is known for its *"flexible"* organizational structure, which allows attorneys to advise a portfolio of clients across a range of practice areas. Clients appreciate this *"well-rounded"* approach to business counseling and litigation, and note that many of the firm's experienced litigators are also fine transactional attorneys.

LITIGATION

WISCONSIN

The Lawyers: W Stuart Parsons has an *"impressive history"* of successful cases to his name. His business litigation practice focuses upon antitrust, securities and lender liability issues. He recently defended Mitsui and Microsoft in two antitrust actions, and acted for Kohler Plumbing in federal securities litigation and a dissenters' rights proceeding. Parsons is also active in the public sector; he is representing Milwaukee Public Schools in a class action on behalf of 16,000 special needs children.
The Clients: Harley-Davidson; Wisconsin Energy Corporation; Harnischfeger Industries; Firstar and DuPont.

Reinhart, Boerner, Van Deuren, Norris & Rieselbach SC
The Firm: Litigation is a core practice area for this firm, and a large department of over 40 attorneys advises on all aspects of business litigation. This *"strong and visible"* team received widespread endorsement for its breadth and scope of practice. Attorneys represent clients in administrative proceedings, arbitrations and alternative dispute resolutions as well as in trial and appellate courts throughout the country.
The Lawyers: Department chair **Scott Hansen** was recognized by interviewees as *"one of the strongest litigators in the state."* Hansen has an impressive resumé of successful cases in the fields of antitrust, commercial contract, patent, wrongful termination and environmental litigation. He is also a prolific speaker and writer on litigation matters and has helped draft some Wisconsin state laws.
The Clients: Harley-Davidson; International Paper; Blommer Chocolate; Criticare Systems; Weigel Broadcasting, Bayer; Associated Bank; Jason Incorporated; Alpine Lace Brands; Milwaukee County and City of Milwaukee.

Godfrey & Kahn SC
The Firm: Although lacking the high-profile individual names of its major rivals, a sizable litigation team here benefits from the firm's general strength in securities, banking and finance. Matters covered include trade regulation cases, distribution disputes and IP litigation. Members also have significant experience in ADR and international arbitration. A recent highlight is the firm's successful representation of the Wisconsin Patients Compensation Fund in upholding a breach of fiduciary duty verdict in the Wisconsin Court of Appeals.
The Lawyers: Howard Pollack and Bill Levit are contact partners for the firm's litigation practice.

The Clients: Manpower; George Fischer Foundry Systems; Pillar Corporation; Rexnord Industries and Beer Capitol Distributing.

Stafford Rosenbaum LLP
The Firm: This 31-attorney firm has 16 litigators practicing from offices in Madison and Sun Prairie. Interviewees report that this smaller practice is ideally suited to advising SMEs, and the firm has acquired a *"great reputation."*
The Lawyers: *"Distinguished"* managing partner **Brian Butler** (see p.729) was singled out as the firm's key litigator. His considerable experience encompasses antitrust, lender liability, contract disputes, defamation, insurance coverage, civil rights and patent cases. Butler represented a defendant in a suit brought by a large healthcare management software provider claiming misappropriation of trade secrets. He also acted for and represented a group of fast food franchisees in a dispute with the franchiser over its establishment of competing restaurants.
The Clients: American Suzuki Motor; Dana Corporation; General Beverage Sales Co.; Joseph Brewing; LF George and Huber the Wisconsin Wholesale Beer Distributors Association.

REAL ESTATE

WISCONSIN
Leading firms (Real Estate)

1. FOLEY & LARDNER *Milwaukee*
   QUARLES & BRADY LLP *Milwaukee*
2. GODFREY & KAHN SC *Milwaukee*
   MICHAEL BEST & FRIEDRICH LLP *Milwaukee*
   REINHART, BOERNER, VAN DEUREN, *Milwaukee*
3. HORTON LAW OFFICES *Madison*
   WHYTE HIRSCHBOECK DUDEK SC *Madison*

Leading individuals (Real Estate)

1. HATCH Michael *Foley & Lardner*, Milwaukee
   JOST Lawrence *Quarles & Brady LLP*, Milwaukee
2. BLOCK Bruce *Reinhart, Boerner, Van Deuren*, Milwaukee
   CHERNOF Steve *Godfrey & Kahn SC*, Milwaukee
3. DALTON Larry *Whyte Hirschboeck*, Milwaukee
   DANIELS John *Quarles & Brady LLP*, Milwaukee
   HORTON William *Horton Law Offices*, Madison
   LEVIN Jim *Michael Best & Friedrich LLP*, Milwaukee
   ROTH George *Whyte Hirschboeck Dudek SC*, Milwaukee

Firms and individuals are listed alphabetically in each band.

Foley & Lardner
The Firm: Boasting the largest real estate group in the state, the firm acts for a plethora of development projects and multi-family and industrial properties, and advises investment trusts in mortgage securitization transactions. Members have experience advising on government-backed projects involving tax-driven financings and environmental matters. Commentators note the firm's strength in building strong and lasting relationships; it is adept in *"making great friendships with everyone, from ranchers to real estate financiers."* In the past year, the practice has been particularly active on multi-family and office developments. The firm also has a strong following among sports clients. It recently represented The Milwaukee Brewers baseball team in connection with the $400 million development of Miller Park stadium.
The Lawyers: Practice head **Mick Hatch** is a *"distinguished name, within a distinguished firm."* Peers acknowledge his depth of experience in real estate development, financing and restructuring matters. His expertise in the field extends to advising on public/private partnerships, brownfield and urban redevelopment, historic rehabilitation and REIT formation and investment. He has acted as lead counsel on some of Wisconsin's largest real estate transactions, including Milwaukee Center, East Point Commons, and the purchase and sale of the Firstar Center. He is well known outside Wisconsin too for his strong relationships with governmental agencies.
The Clients: Johnson Controls; Harley Davidson; The Milwaukee Brewers; The Green Bay Packers and the State of Wisconsin.

Quarles & Brady LLP
The Firm: An integrated national real estate practice, spread across the firm's offices in Wisconsin, Illinois, Arizona and Florida, serves a predominantly commercial clientele. Interviewees name the firm as an attractive choice for the acquisition, sale and development of commercial properties, and for real estate financing and leasing issues pertaining to pension funds and insurance companies.
The Lawyers: Researchers were told that **Larry Jost** is a *"deal-maker, not a deal-breaker."* Jost represents mortgage lenders and real estate developers, focusing primarily on commercial real estate development and industrial warehouse deals. He represented key client WISPARK in the sale of its 1600-acre Pabst Farms Development. Jost's *"copilot"* in the real estate department is **John Daniels**, who is widely known for his position as national president of the American College of Real Estate Lawyers.

WISCONSIN REAL ESTATE

The Clients: Wisconsin Electric Power Company, leading pension funds and insurance companies and Fortune 500 companies.

Godfrey & Kahn SC

The Firm: A large real estate team is able to advise clients on a full gamut of matters, ranging from purchases, sales and financings to construction, land use and environmental issues. Practitioners interact with local and state governments in connection with zoning, land use and government assistance programs. The firm has recently been involved in a number of transactions involving the renovation and rehabilitation of listed buildings.

The Lawyers: *"Top-class"* **Steve Chernof**'s (see p.729) forte is in major commercial developments, particularly office complexes. Notable recent work includes advising on the rehabilitiation of famous Milwaukee landmark, the old Marshall Fields Building. His reputation for sophisticated tax-driven transactions extends beyond the state.

The Clients: The firm represents REITs, pension funds, owners, developers, contractors, construction managers and other participants in real estate acquisition, development and financing transactions.

Michael Best & Friedrich LLP

The Firm: Commended as a team of *"go-getting business developers,"* the firm's real estate practice earns respect for its *"entrepreneurial"* approach to real estate projects. The group has extensive experience representing developers, landlords, tenants, lenders and financiers in an array of transactional property matters. Particular strength exists in relation to multi-family and mixed-use developments.

The Lawyers: Esteemed as a *"man of great integrity and repute,"* **Jim Levin** boasts a distinguished career, advising on intricate public financing issues and real estate taxation. He has developed strong relationships with government and muncipal bodies and has been active in a number of development projects in downtown Milwaukee.

The Clients: Major construction companies, contractors, finance and leasing companies, developers, owners and lenders.

Reinhart, Boerner, Van Deuren, Norris & Rieselbach SC

The Firm: Operating from offices in Milwaukee, Madison and Denver, the firm's real estate practice attracts particular praise for its highly developed knowledge of the public sector. The practice's structure encourages specialization, and the firm's attorneys are able to advise a broad client base across a wide range of real estate issues. Clients appreciate the *"high-quality, cost-effective service"* on offer here.

The Lawyers: Praised as a *"first-rate attorney in every respect,"* **Bruce Block** commands long-standing experience in the field in both the commercial and public sectors. His practice focuses on land use and zoning matters, private finance initiatives and complex tax incremental funding cases. He represents the property interests of many large institutions such as Northwestern Mutual Life Insurance, and regularly acts for regional and national developers.

The Clients: Lenders, investors, syndication firms, contractors, pension funds, hospitals, schools and other public sector clients.

Horton Law Offices

The Firm: This smaller Madison firm specializes primarily in transactional work, with particular focus on single-purpose entities. Practitioners regularly dispense advice to insurance and pension funds in relation to their real estate investments.

The Lawyers: The firm owes much of its profile to the outstanding individual reputation of **William Pharis Horton**, said by some to be *"the most technically able lawyer in the state."* This *"extremely knowledgeable"* practitioner undertakes licensing regulatory work and title insurance defense cases. He acts for a loyal base of local clients, which includes real estate brokerages, insurance companies, condominium associations and commercial and residential developers.

Whyte Hirschboeck Dudek SC

The Firm: This *"highly reputable"* firm handles purchases, sales and tax-deferred exchanges, leasehold arrangements for office, commercial and industrial space and zoning and land use planning in connection with real estate development and construction. Researchers were told that the real estate practice is the *"centerpiece"* of this full-service firm.

The Lawyers: **Larry Dalton** and **George Roth** were commended to researchers as *"hard-working attorneys with outstanding reputations."* Dalton's practice is geared toward representing clients in the negotiation, drafting and completion of transactions involving the acquisition, disposition and financing of commercial, industrial and residential properties. Roth is experienced in land development, construction, purchase and sales, workouts and the operational aspects of real estate businesses.

The Clients: The firm represents a cross-section of purchasers, sellers, tenants, landlords, municipalities, developers, contractors and lenders.

Leaders in Wisconsin

AUEN, Michael
Foley & Lardner, Madison 608 257 5035
Recommended in Employment

BARTELL, Jeff
Quarles & Brady LLP, Madison
608 251 5000
Recommended in Corporate/M&A

BLOCK, Bruce
Reinhart, Boerner, Van Deuren, Norris & Rieselbach, SC, Milwaukee
414 298 1000
Recommended in Real Estate

BOBBER, Bernard
Foley & Lardner, Milwaukee
414 271 2400
Recommended in Employment

BOER, Ralf
Foley & Lardner, Milwaukee
414 271 2400
Recommended in Corporate/M&A

BOWEN, Michael
Foley & Lardner, Milwaukee
414 271 2400
Recommended in Litigation

BUSCH, John
Michael Best & Friedrich LLP, Milwaukee
414 271 6560
Recommended in Litigation

BUTLER, Brian
Stafford Rosenbaum LLP, Madison
608 259 2609
bbutler@staffordlaw.com
Recommended in Litigation
Specialization: Dealership disputes; representation of plaintiffs in legal malpractice litigation; mediation of disputes.
Prof. Memberships: American College of Trial Lawyers. American, Wisconsin, and Dane County Bar Associations.
Career: For 35 years, he has represented clients in litigation. His experience encompasses anti-trust, dealership, lender liability, intracorporate disputes, defamation, legal malpractice, building construction, patent infringement, civil rights, and business torts.
Publications: Co-author of 'The Wisconsin Fair Dealership Law,' a treatise published by the State Bar of Wisconsin, and 'Protection of Multi-Line Dealers by State Relationship Laws,' published in the 'Franchise Law Journal.'
Personal: JD, Northwestern Law School, 1968; AB, Dartmouth College, 1965. Has lectured on litigation topics for the State Bar of Wisconsin, the University of Wisconsin Law School, and business groups. He is a Master in the James E Doyle Chapter of the American Inns of Court. He served as his law firm's managing partner, is a former member of the Dane County Board of Supervisors and the Regional Planning Commission, and serves as a big brother in Big Brothers and Sisters of Dane County.

CHERNOF, Steve
Godfrey & Kahn, SC, Milwaukee
414 273 3500
schernof@gklaw.com
Recommended in Real Estate
Specialization: Member of the Real Estate Practice Group in the Milwaukee office. His practice encompasses both sophisticated real estate and corporate matteres. He regularly represents a variety of developers, institutional lenders, real estate brokerage companies, and others in the real estate field on a wide variety of matters, including developers and others engaged in the subsidized and tax credit housing market.
Personal: Graduated with honors from the University of Wisconsin Law School and is a member of the Order of the Coif, a national honorary legal society. He was articles editor of the 'Wisconsin Law Review' in 1968 and law clerk to the Honorable Myron L Gordon of the US District Court for the Eastern District of Wisconsin, 1968-69. His undergraduate degree in political science is also from the University of Wisconsin. He is a past President of the Milwaukee Jewish Frederation, a past Chairman of the Board of Directors of the Milwaukee Urban League, and a past President of the Milwaukee Jewish Council. He is also active in various other civic and philanthropic organizations.

CHRISTIANSEN, John
Foley & Lardner, Milwaukee 414 271 2400
Recommended in Litigation

CRONE, Tom
Melli, Walker, Pease & Ruhly, S.C., Madison 608 257 4812
Recommended in Employment

CROYSDALE, David
Michael Best & Friedrich LLP, Milwaukee
414 271 6560
Recommended in Employment

DALTON, Larry
Whyte Hirschboeck Dudek S.C., Milwaukee 414 273 2100
Recommended in Real Estate

DANIELS, John
Quarles & Brady LLP, Milwaukee
414 277 5000
Recommended in Real Estate

DUFFY, Robert
Quarles & Brady LLP, Milwaukee
414 277 5000
Recommended in Employment

ERNE, David
Reinhart, Boerner, Van Deuren, Norris & Rieselbach, SC, Milwaukee
414 298 1000
Recommended in Corporate/M&A

FIRST, Curry
First, Blondis, Albrecht & Novotnak, Milwaukee 414 271 1972
Recommended in Employment

FOX, Michael
Fox & Fox, Madison 608 258 9588
Recommended in Employment

GARMER, Ben
Foley & Lardner, Milwaukee 414 271 2400
Recommended in Corporate/M&A

HANSEN, Scott W
Reinhart, Boerner, Van Deuren, Norris & Rieselbach, SC, Milwaukee
414 298 1000
Recommended in Litigation

HATCH, Michael
Foley & Lardner, Milwaukee
414 271 2400
Recommended in Real Estate

HAWKS, Tim
Shneidman, Hawks & Ehlke, Madison 608 257 0400
Recommended in Employment

HORTON, Pharis
Horton Law Offices, Madison
608 231 3220
Recommended in Real Estate

JASPAN, Stanley
Foley & Lardner, Milwaukee
414 271 2400
Recommended in Employment

JOST, Lawrence
Quarles & Brady LLP, Milwaukee
414 277 5000
Recommended in Real Estate

KELLY, Walter
Walter F Kelly - Sole Practitioner, Milwaukee 414 271 2400
Recommended in Employment

KERN, David
Quarles & Brady LLP, Milwaukee
414 277 5000
Recommended in Employment

KRINGEL, Jerry
Michael Best & Friedrich LLP, Milwaukee
414 271 6560
Recommended in Corporate/M&A

LEICHTLING, Ely
Quarles & Brady LLP, Milwaukee
414 277 5000
Recommended in Employment

LEVIN, Jim
Michael Best & Friedrich LLP, Milwaukee
414 271 6560
Recommended in Real Estate

LINSTROTH, Tod
Michael Best & Friedrich LLP, Madison
608 257 3501
Recommended in Corporate/M&A

LYNCH, Larry
Foley & Lardner, Milwaukee
414 271 2400
Recommended in Employment

MARSACK, Gary
Lindner & Marsack, S.C., Milwaukee
414 273 3910
Recommended in Employment

MCSWEENEY, Maurice
Foley & Lardner, Milwaukee
414 271 2400
Recommended in Litigation

NINNEMAN, Mary Pat
Quarles & Brady LLP, Milwaukee
414 277 5000
Recommended in Employment

PARSONS, Stuart
Quarles & Brady LLP, Milwaukee
414 277 5000
Recommended in Litigation

ROBISON, John
Quarles & Brady LLP, Madison
608 251 5000
Recommended in Corporate/M&A

ROTH, George
Whyte Hirschboeck Dudek S.C., Milwaukee 414 273 2100
Recommended in Real Estate

SCHNEIDMAN, Dan
Schneidman, Hawks & Ehlke SC, Milwaukee 608 257 0400
Recommended in Employment

SCRIVNER, Tom
Michael Best & Friedrich LLP, Milwaukee
414 271 6560
Recommended in Employment

SENNET, Nancy
Foley & Lardner, Milwaukee
414 271 2400
Recommended in Litigation

SHRINER, Tom
Foley & Lardner, Milwaukee
414 271 2400
Recommended in Litigation

SKILTON, John
Heller Ehrman White & McAuliffe LLP, Madison 680 663 7460
Recommended in Litigation

SKINDRUD, Michael
LaFollette Godfrey & Kahn, SC, Madison
608 257 3911
Recommended in Corporate/M&A

SOMMERHAUSER, Peter
Godfrey & Kahn, SC, Milwaukee
414 273 3500
Recommended in Corporate/M&A

ZILAVY, Thomas
DeWitt Ross & Stevens SC, Madison
608 255 8891
Recommended in Corporate/M&A

WYOMING

CORPORATE/M&A

CONTENTS: Corporate/M&A p.730; Employment: Mainly Plaintiff p.731; Mainly Defendant p.731; Litigation: General Commercial p.732; Real Estate p.733; Individuals' Profiles p.734.

WYOMING'S TOP TWO
1. Williams, Porter, Day & Neville
2. Holland & Hart

Ranking based on Chambers' research within the state.

All quotes in the text are from interviews with clients and competitors.

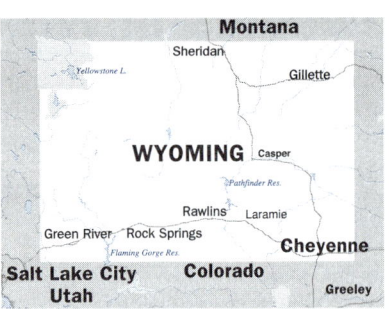

OVERVIEW: Based in Casper, **Williams, Porter, Day & Neville** comes in first in Wyoming as the market leader in the real estate, employment and litigation fields. This well-established firm houses one of the top attorneys in the state, Barry Williams, who was unanimously praised by peers for both his real estate practice and his work on behalf of First American Title Insurance. Other top-tier partners include employment defense lawyer Scott Ortiz, who is said to have a great presence, and litigator Richard Day, who was commended for his expertise in mineral law.

In second place, but ranked in all four practice areas is regional firm **Holland & Hart**, headquartered in Denver. Its Jackson and Cheyenne offices in Wyoming are widely respected by market sources. Representing many large natural resource companies in the state, the firm features leading litigator Don Schultz and real estate gem John Gallinger. Corporate lawyers Jim Belcher and Teresa Buffington are also highlighted, as is outstanding employment defense attorney Brad Cave.

CORPORATE/M&A

WYOMING
Leading firms (Corporate/M&A)

1. BROWN, DREW & MASSEY LLP *Casper*
   DRAY, THOMSON & DYEKMAN PC *Cheyenne*
   THOMAS N LONG *Cheyenne*
2. HIRST & APPLEGATE PC *Cheyenne*
   HOLLAND & HART LLP *Cheyenne*

Leading individuals (Corporate/M&A)

1. LONG Thomas *Thomas N. Long, Cheyenne*
2. BELCHER James *Holland & Hart LLP, Cheyenne*
   DYEKMAN Gregory *Dray, Thomson, Cheyenne*
   MCCALL Donn *Brown, Drew & Massey LLP, Casper*
3. BARBE Kenneth *Brown, Drew & Massey LLP, Casper*
   BUFFINGTON Teresa *Holland & Hart LLP, Cheyenne*
   COTTAM Dale *Hirst & Applegate PC, Cheyenne*
   DRAY Perry *Dray, Thomson & Dyekman PC, Cheyenne*
   METZKE John *Hirst & Applegate PC, Cheyenne*
   REED Randall *Dray, Thomson & Dyekman, Cheyenne*

Firms and individuals are listed alphabetically in each band.

Brown, Drew & Massey LLP
The Firm: One of Wyoming's largest firms, this *"well-respected"* practice was highly recommended for its ability to handle large and complex commercial transactions. The group advises a number of international clients in the formation of a variety of business structures under Wyoming's favorable company law.
The Lawyers: Market sources referred to **Donn McCall** as a *"wizard"* at asset-based finance and lending law. He was also named as a top attorney for representation of creditors in bankruptcy matters. McCall routinely advises on multi-state financings within the $20-200 million range. **Kenneth Barbe** also received general endorsement as *"one of the firm's top business transactions lawyers."* His broad-based practice has a heavy emphasis on representing real estate developers in commercial transactions.
The Clients: Wells Fargo Wyoming; JPMorgan Chase Bank; Nations Bank; Citibank; The CIT Group Sales Financing and Albertsons.

Dray, Thomson & Dyekman PC
The Firm: This seven-attorney firm received praise from interviewees for its involvement in *"big business deals."* Its general civil practice boasts strength in both business and real estate law.
The Lawyers: *"Bright and able"* attorney **Gregory Dyekman** was applauded by peers and clients for his *"sound business judgment."* His diverse practice encompasses much commercial litigation, banking, lending, real estate, estate planning and probate matters. Dyekman has participated in several commercial lending transactions in connection with construction projects. A senior figure within the practice, **Perry Dray** was noted for his role as corporate counsel to several large companies. His practice entails healthcare regulatory issues, business formation and commercial litigation. Another esteemed member of the team, **Randall Reed** received recommendations from peers for his commercial law practice.
The Clients: Key Bank, USA; Motion Picture Association of America; Union Pacific Railroad; Sierra Trading Post; Anheuser-Busch Companies; Alberta Energy Company; Basin Electric Power Cooperative; Coca-Cola and Kennedy-Western University.

Thomas N. Long
The Firm: Boutique firm of three dominated by preeminent corporate attorney Tom Long.
The Lawyers: Referred to as *"the best business lawyer in Wyoming,"* **Tom Long** was rated by peers as *"the foremost tax practitioner"* in the state. Said to practice *"at the highest level of the profession,"* this *"accomplished"* lawyer offers sophisticated legal advice on tax and corporate matters. His practice includes estate and business planning, trusts and wills, with a specialty in gift, estate and business transaction tax. He notably represented the seller in the sale of an $8 million ranch and acted for a newspaper company in a $13 million merger transaction.
The Clients: American National Bank of Cheyenne (Trust Division); L Liquor Inc.; Cheyenne Radiology Group; Montgomery Broadcasting LLC; Citicorp Investment Bank Ltd; Wyoming Government Investment Fund; Warren Ranch Company and Wyoming Department of Revenue and Taxation.

Hirst & Applegate PC
The Firm: This 11-attorney Cheyenne firm boasts niches in limited liability company formation and transfers and continuances. Attorneys possess particular experience in advising corporate clients in regard to energy-related assets.
The Lawyers: **Dale Cottam** was recommended to researchers for his corporate representation and business planning work. He provided Wyoming state law analysis and legal work for the multimillion dollar Rocky Mountain Pipeline acquisition of a crude oil pipeline.
Interviewees praised **John Metzke** for his *"attention to detail"* and expertise in estate planning. This *"bright and effective"* practitioner regularly advises on corporate formation, estate administration, living trusts and retirement planning.
The Clients: Cycomm International, Rocky Mountain Pipeline System and Denali Ventures.

Holland & Hart LLP
see firm details p.819
The Firm: The Wyoming branches of this large regional firm earned recognition for their strength in natural resources and corporate law. Known to represent many of the major US mining and oil and gas companies, the practice derives support from the firm's extensive network of offices across the Midwest.

EMPLOYMENT & LABOR LAW — WYOMING

The Lawyers: A *"man of many talents,"* **Jim Belcher** (see p.734) combines expertise in corporate and real estate law in counseling clients on company formation, organization and operation. Recommended to researchers as *"excellent in oil and gas law,"* **Teresa Buffington** (see p.734) is well known for her representation of natural resource companies in real estate acquisition and development. Her areas of practice include business transactions, real estate, construction contracts, commercial finance and corporate law.

The Clients: The firm acts for a number of international corporations in establishing US operations and advises Fortune 500 companies on a variety of business matters.

EMPLOYMENT & LABOR LAW — MAINLY PLAINTIFF

WYOMING
Leading firms
(Employment: Mainly Plaintiff)
1. **MARK W GIFFORD** Casper
2. **MARY ELIZABETH GALVAN** Laramie
   PATRICK E HACKER Cheyenne
3. **LAW OFFICE OF BRUCE T MOATS** Cheyenne
   YONKEE & TONER LLP Sheridan

Leading individuals
(Employment: Mainly Plaintiff)
1. **GIFFORD Mark** Mark W. Gifford, Casper
2. **GALVAN Mary** Mary Elizabeth Galvan, Laramie
   HACKER Patrick Patrick E Hacker, Cheyenne
3. **DAVIS Michael** Yonkee & Toner LLP, Sheridan
   EVANS David Hickey, Mackey, Evans & Walker, Cheyenne
   MOATS Bruce Law Office of Bruce T Moats, Cheyenne

Firms and individuals are listed alphabetically in each band.

Mark W. Gifford
The Firm: Market sources cited **Mark Gifford** as having *"the best reputation for employment law in the state."* He received unanimous endorsement for his plaintiffs' employment practice. Described as an *"effective attorney with good jury demeanor,"* Gifford recently represented the employee in Capshaw v WERCS, where he won a $220,000 wrongful termination claim currently on appeal. Experience in civil rights employment discrimination cases, oil and gas contracts disputes, personal injury and mediation rounds out his practice.

Mary Elizabeth Galvan
The Firm: Interviewees described top plaintiffs' employment lawyer, **Mary Elizabeth Galvan**, as a *"very strong advocate for clients"* and *"a formidable foe."* A *"bulldog in court,"* Galvan represents both employees and employers in civil rights and breach of contract cases. Her work of late has included a lawsuit against a town regarding qualified immunity, and the issue of homosexual rights in employment.

Patrick E Hacker
The Firm: Peers endorsed **Patrick Hacker** for his work as counsel for Wyoming's education system. He represents teachers across the state in their employment issues. Hacker was praised as an *"excellent attorney with a strong reputation."*

Law Office of Bruce T Moats
The Firm: Market sources pointed to **Bruce Moats**' skills in advising on First Amendment issues. His *"great reputation"* has secured him the referrals of his peers for plaintiffs' employment issues.

Yonkee & Toner LLP
The Firm: Interviewees singled out this firm for its broad-based labor and employment practice. **Michael Davis** has a strong profile for his work on both defendants' and plaintiffs' cases, one of the few true generalists in the state. Civil rights and discrimination litigation are core areas for this respected boutique.

Other Notable Practitioners
Known as a traditional labor lawyer, **David Evans** of Hickey, Mackey, Evans & Walker represents many of the labor unions in Wyoming including: Carpenters Union; Plumbers and Pipefitters Union; Labors Union; Operating Engineer Union; International Union of Police Associations and firefighters in two cities;. Boasting a varied practice, Evans specializes in labor and employment law, commercial law, bankruptcy and school law.

EMPLOYMENT & LABOR LAW — MAINLY DEFENDANT

WYOMING
Leading firms
(Employment: Mainly Defendant)
1. **WILLIAMS, PORTER, DAY & NEVILLE PC** Casper
2. **DAVIS & CANNON** Cheyenne
   SCHWARTZ, BON, WALKER & STUDER LLP Casper
   YONKEE & TONER LLP Sheridan
3. **HOLLAND & HART LLP** Cheyenne
   MURANE & BOSTWICK LLC Casper

Firms are listed alphabetically in each band.

Williams, Porter, Day & Neville PC
The Firm: This 15-attorney firm is one of the largest in Wyoming. Clients reported that the highly respected firm has *"many strong members."*
The Lawyers: Leader of the pack **Scott Ortiz** was said by market observers to be *"an excellent litigator,"* with a great presence before the jury. The majority of Ortiz's work includes labor and employment matters, federal discrimination claims and professional malpractice defense. He successfully represented Orken in a wrongful termination case and upheld labor terminations brought to arbitration.
The Clients: Sinclair Oil; PacifiCorp; municipalities and corporate defendants.

Davis & Cannon
The Firm: The firm gained high marks from observers for its work on behalf of a *"healthy list of employer clients."* Discrimination litigation, wage and hour matters and labor law issues all feature on the agenda here.
The Lawyers: Market sources recommended *"top-notch"* **Kate Fox** for her work representing both plaintiffs and defendants. Much of her general civil litigation practice entails employment and water law.
The Clients: First Interstate Bank of Commerce; Life Care Centers of America; Memorial Hospital of Sheridan County and Marion Merrell Dow.

Schwartz, Bon, Walker & Studer LLC
The Firm: Market sources described the firm as a *"highly skilled player"* in the labor and employment arena.
The Lawyers: Interviewees endorsed **Judith Studer** as someone to whom they refer clients. A *"talented attorney,"* her broad practice entails discrimination litigation and civil rights law as well as advice on insurance disputes.
The Clients: The firm advises insurance companies, shopping centers, and banks, among others.

Yonkee & Toner LLP
The Firm: Six-attorney trial law firm recommended for employment law on the strength of its leading light, Michael Davis.

WYOMING

LITIGATION

WYOMING
Leading individuals
(Employment: Mainly Defendant)

1
- ORTIZ Scott *Williams, Porter, Day & Neville PC*, Casper

2
- DAVIS Michael *Yonkee & Toner LLP*, Sheridan
- FOX Kate *Davis & Cannon*, Cheyenne
- STUDER Judith *Schwartz, Bon, Walker*, Casper

3
- CAVE Bradley *Holland & Hart LLP*, Cheyenne
- SHUMATE Roger *Murane & Bostwick LLC*, Casper

Individuals are listed alphabetically in each band.

The Lawyers: Competitors portrayed **Michael Davis** as a *"very bright attorney,"* who has secured *"good victories on both the plaintiff and defense sides."* His practice encompasses race, gender and age discrimination, wrongful dismissal and civil rights litigation. Although many of his competitors act for both the plaintiff and the defendant, Davis is the only attorney to be included in both areas in *Chambers' USA*.

The Clients: Both corporate defendants and individual plaintiffs.

Holland & Hart LLP
see firm details p.819

The Firm: This regional law firm is characterized by its wealth of natural resources clients. Much of the firm's profile in this sector lies with Brad Cave.

The Lawyers: Peers referred to the *"strong reputation"* of **Brad Cave** (see p.735), whose practice focuses on employment law and litigation. He represents employers in discrimination, harassment, wrongful discharge and defamation issues, and wage and hour disputes. He recently represented a mining company in the successful defense of a lawsuit brought by the EEOC on behalf of an employee. Cave has also secured successful jury verdicts on behalf of mining, oil and gas companies.

The Clients: Represents employers only in the healthcare, mining, oil and gas and retail industries.

Murane & Bostwick LLC

The Firm: This eight-lawyer firm was cited by competitors to be a *"well-respected player in the market."* Its employment law activities of late have included discrimination litigation, termination of contracts and workers compensation claims. The attorneys were recommended to researchers for their trial skills.

The Lawyers: Clients and peers alike singled out **Roger Shumate** for his employment defense work. His varied workload includes personal injury and insurance litigation as well as workers' compensation and discrimination litigation. He has also been active in wrongful termination actions and civil rights cases.

The Clients: Oil field service and rental companies, trucking companies, hospitals, city government, county government, individuals and local businesses.

LITIGATION

GENERAL COMMERCIAL

WYOMING
Leading firms
(Litigation: General Commercial)

1
- HICKEY, MACKEY, EVANS & WALKER *Cheyenne*
- WILLIAMS, PORTER, DAY & NEVILLE PC *Casper*

2
- HIRST & APPLEGATE PC *Cheyenne*
- HOLLAND & HART LLP *Cheyenne*
- MASON & MASON PC *Pinedale*
- YONKEE & TONER LLP *Sheridan*

3
- LATHROP & RUTLEDGE *Cheyenne*
- SCHWARTZ, BON, WALKER & STUDER LLC *Casper*

Leading individuals
(Litigation: General Commercial)

1
- DAY Richard *Williams, Porter, Day & Neville PC*, Casper
- HICKEY Paul *Hickey, Mackey, Evans & Walker*, Cheyenne
- MASON Gerald *Mason & Mason PC*, Pinedale
- TONER Tom *Yonkee & Toner LLP*, Sheridan

2
- GIFFORD Mark *Mark W. Gifford*, Casper
- NICHOLAS Thomas *Hirst & Applegate PC*, Cheyenne
- SCHULTZ Donald *Holland & Hart LLP*, Cheyenne

3
- RUTLEDGE Kent *Lathrop & Rutledge*, Cheyenne
- WALKER Cameron *Schwartz, Bon, Walker*, Casper

Firms and individuals are listed alphabetically in each band.

Hickey, Mackey, Evans & Walker

The Firm: An eight-lawyer general civil practice with an emphasis on business and administrative law. The firm is highly recommended for its litigation expertise and boasts trial victories at all federal court levels.

The Lawyers: Star litigator **Paul Hickey** received widespread praise for his *"top of the line"* practice. Recommended by peers as a *"skilled orator"* with a *"great legal mind,"* Hickey maintains an active trial practice, heavily focused on the representation of public utilities and natural resources companies. This *"hard-working"* attorney has experience of litigating transfer of water rights, abandonment of water rights and preferential rights cases. He recently represented PacifiCorp in a coal case where the judge ruled in the company's favor for summary judgment. Hickey is also well known as one of the attorneys involved in litigating the constitutionality of methods of determining governmental funding for public schools.

The Clients: Kinder Morgan; PacifiCorp and Laramie County School District #1.

Williams, Porter, Day & Neville PC

The Firm: This 15-attorney Casper firm maintains a widely respected civil litigation practice, highly visible on trial work in the state and federal courts. Competitors named it as one of the top litigation firms in the area, particularly citing the group's outstanding work in insurance defense and school administration litigation.

The Lawyers: Market sources placed **Richard Day** in the *"top tier"* of the state's leading litigators. Commended as *"excellent in oil and gas law,"* Day specializes in mineral law and corporate defense litigation. Other areas of expertise include insurance defense, tax litigation and malpractice defense in the accounting and legal sectors.

The Clients: PacifiCorp; True Industries; Marathon Oil Co.; Devon Energy; Sinclair Oil and Natrona County School District #1.

Hirst & Applegate PC

The Firm: This 11-lawyer Cheyenne firm is highly thought of for its skill in trial work. Litigation figures prominently among the firm's core practice areas. The group successfully represented an employer in the Wyoming Supreme Court in upholding a summary judgment in a wrongful termination suit.

The Lawyers: Widely admired for his insurance defense work, **Thomas Nicholas** rates as one of the field's most eminent practitioners. Peers commended his considerable experience in federal court cases. His broad-based practice incorporates insurance defense, environmental litigation, civil rights claims and administrative hearings and appeals.

The Clients: American Insurance Group; Interstate Insurance Group; Transamerica Insurance Group (TIG); Aetna Life & Casualty; Royal Insurance; Nationwide Mutual Insurance; Scottsdale Insurance and Ranger Insurance.

Holland & Hart LLP
see firm details p.819

The Firm: The Wyoming branch of this large regional law firm earns plaudits for its prowess in natural resource litigation. The firm represents major coal producers in the region and has extensive experience in oil and gas litigation.

The Lawyers: Hailed by interviewees as the *"preeminent oil and gas litigator,"* **Don Schultz**

LITIGATION

WYOMING

(see p.735) enjoys an excellent market reputation as a *"bright and able"* attorney. He acts exclusively on energy litigation and boasts particular expertise in natural gas royalties and defense of pipeline companies.

The Clients: The firm acts for a large concentration of energy, coal and oil and gas companies such as Triton Coal, ChevronTexaco and ExxonMobil.

Mason & Mason PC

The Firm: This father and son outfit has a high profile in the market for general commercial litigation.

The Lawyers: Peers described **Gerald Mason** as *"one of the best trial lawyers in Wyoming."* His busy commercial litigation practice has a heavy emphasis on mineral and real estate litigation. This *"go-to"* attorney possesses a noted niche in contracts and covenants disputes.

The Clients: Clients include several homeowner associations and a local school district.

Yonkee & Toner LLP

The Firm: The firm is synonymous in the market with its leading litigator Tom Toner, recommended to researchers as a *"top legal mind."* The six-attorney practice is active in civil litigation in state and federal courts.

The Lawyers: Unanimously hailed by peers as an outstanding litigator, **Tom Toner** was said to be well respected by the judiciary. His *"impressive intellect"* and *"charming Boy Scout quality"* enable him to *"obtain excellent results for clients"* in civil trials. His varied practice is deemed particularly strong in relation to natural resources litigation.

The Clients: State Farm; Met Life; Ohio Hospital Insurance Company and Lexington Insurance Company.

Lathrop & Rutledge

see firm details p.837

The Firm: Interviewees recommended the seven-lawyer firm for its experience in general civil trial matters and appellate cases in both state and federal courts. Areas of practice include insurance defense, commercial, real estate and construction litigation.

The Lawyers: *"First-rate trial attorney"* **Kent Rutledge** attracted praise as a skilled and hard-working practitioner. His varied workload encompasses professional liability, insurance defense, products liability, construction, commercial and toxic tort litigation.

The Clients: Omaha Property & Casualty Insurance; underwriters at Lloyd's; Continental General Insurance; Underwriters Indemnity; CIGNA Insurance Group; Infinity Insurance; Titan Insurance and underwriters at Lloyd's.

Schwartz, Bon, Walker & Studer LLC

The Firm: Based in Casper, the seven-lawyer firm owes much of its market profile to the litigation skills and outstanding individual reputation of Cameron Walker. This general civil and trial practice has particular specialty in representing insurance clients at state and federal court level.

The Lawyers: *"Top notch"* litigator **Cameron Walker** is best known for his expertise in insurance defense and personal injury litigation. Other areas of practice include commercial litigation, products liability and oil and gas litigation.

The Clients: Equitable; St. Paul; Great West Insurance Co; Wyoming Self-Insurance Fund and ITT Hartford Insurance Company.

Other Notable Practitioners

Acknowledged as a top employment lawyer in the state, **Mark Gifford** also attracts praise for his general litigation abilities. Market sources commended his work on behalf of plaintiffs in employment and personal injury cases. Gifford also undertakes complex commercial cases and oil and gas litigation as well as an increasing volume of mediation proceedings.

REAL ESTATE

WYOMING
Leading firms (Real Estate)

1 WILLIAMS, PORTER, DAY & NEVILLE PC *Casper*

2 HOLLAND & HART LLP *Jackson*
MULLIKIN, LARSON & SWIFT *Jackson*
YONKEE & TONER LLP *Sheridan*

3 BROWN, DREW & MASSEY LLP *Casper*
DAVIS & CANNON *Sheridan*
DRAY, THOMSON & DYEKMAN PC *Cheyenne*
JORGENSON LAW OFFICE *Jackson*
MACPHERSON KELLY & THOMPSON *Rawlins*
PHIBBS & RESOR PC *Jackson*

Firms are listed alphabetically in each band.

Williams, Porter, Day & Neville PC

The Firm: This *"absolutely first-rate"* practice earned praise from clients and peers alike. It secures its top band position off the back of the highly rated transactional abilities of Barry Williams.

The Lawyers: Consistently lauded by market commentators, **Barry Williams** was said to be *"one of the top lawyers in the state."* Widely recognized for his expertise in title issues, Williams regularly advises First American Title Insurance in matters throughout the state. He also acts as Wyoming counsel to the lenders in synthetic lease transactions and represents development companies in closing numerous SBA 504 commercial loans.

The Clients: PacifiCorp; First American Title Insurance; Frontier Certified Development Company; Baker Hughes Cos. and Casper Area Economic Development Alliance.

Holland & Hart LLP

see firm details p.819

The Firm: Headquartered in Denver, this large regional firm receives high marks for its national client base and expansive resources.

The Lawyers: **John Gallinger** enjoys an excellent market reputation for his representation of high-end clients in large real estate transactions. Recent work includes representation of a buyer in a $40 million residential real estate purchase. He also acted for the buyer in purchasing a $100 million ranch and obtaining conservation easements.

The Clients: The firm represents owners, property companies and realtors and undertakes some real estate work for Sotheby's.

Mullikin, Larson & Swift

The Firm: This six-lawyer firm draws upon the experience of senior partners in providing *"top-notch"* real estate advice.

The Lawyers: Acclaimed a *"guru in land use planning,"* **David Larson** earns plaudits for his ability to *"make deals happen."* He is particularly recognized for his niche in land use law relating to zoning and project permitting. **Phelps Swift** also rates highly as a *"deeply experienced"* real estate lawyer. Specialties include real estate finance, land use planning and real estate development.

The Clients: Jackson State Bank; Teton County School District; Teton Pines Resort; retailers and resort developers.

Yonkee & Toner LLP

The Firm: This six-attorney firm earned recognition for the work of leading attorney Tom Toner.

The Lawyers: *"Cerebral"* **Tom Toner** was praised by commentators as *"one of the best attorneys in the state."* Said to do *"a bit of everything"* his real estate practice includes oil and gas, natural resources and water rights.

The Clients: State Farm; Met Life; Wyeth Laboratories; Utica Mutual Insurance Company;

WYOMING — REAL ESTATE

WYOMING
Leading individuals (Real Estate)

1
- **WILLIAMS Barry** *Williams, Porter, Day*, Casper

2
- **DYEKMAN Gregory** *Dray, Thomson*, Cheyenne
- **GALLINGER John** *Holland & Hart LLP*, Jackson
- **LARSON David** *Mullikin, Larson & Swift*, Jackson
- **TONER Tom** *Yonkee & Toner LLP*, Sheridan

3
- **BARBE Kenneth** *Brown, Drew & Massey LLP*, Casper
- **DAVIS Richard** *Davis & Cannon*, Sheridan
- **JORGENSON Larry** *Jorgenson Law Office*, Jackson
- **MACPHERSON John** *MacPherson Kelly*, Rawlins
- **PHIBBS Henry** *Phibbs & Resor PC*, Jackson
- **RICHARD Andrea** *Rothgerber Johnson*, Cheyenne
- **SWIFT Phelps** *Mullikin, Larson & Swift*, Jackson

Individuals are listed alphabetically in each band.

Sheridan County School Districts 1, 2 and 3; Memorial Hospital of Sheridan County and West Park Hospital.

Brown, Drew & Massey LLP
The Firm: This *"well-established"* firm handles a steady volume of work on behalf of local oil and gas companies and real estate developers. Much of the firm's reputation in the market lies with leading attorney Kenneth Barbe.
The Lawyers: Endorsed for his real estate and corporate work, **Kenneth Barbe** maintains a diverse transactional practice, encompassing general real estate work, corporation law, limited liability companies and partnerships. He has a loyal following of real estate developer clients in and around Casper.
The Clients: The firm represents Albertson's and several local real estate developers.

Davis & Cannon
The Firm: Operating from offices in Sheridan and Cheyenne, this nine-attorney firm is a popular choice in the state for real estate referrals.
The Lawyers: Managing partner **Richard Davis** enjoys a particularly strong following in the northern part of the state. This *"excellent and experienced"* attorney also boasts related expertise in probate, estate planning, trusts and business planning.
The Clients: First Interstate Bank of Commerce; Memorial Hospital of Sheridan County; Sheridan County School District No.2; Wyoming Sawmills; Decker Coal; Black Butte Coal; Town of Dayton; Padlock Ranch; Kearney Lake Land & Reservoir and Lower Clear Creek Irrigation District.

Dray, Thomson & Dyekman PC
The Firm: This Cheyenne firm has a high profile in the market for zoning matters such as annexation. The real estate practice also benefits from the firm's general expertise in business and commercial banking work.
The Lawyers: Roundly praised as *"honest and good to work with,"* **Gregory Dyekman** has a mixed practice, encompassing commercial lending transactions, annexation matters and representation of creditors in bankruptcy court.
The Clients: The practice represents real estate developers, municipal government bodies, lenders and individuals.

Jorgenson Law Office
The Firm: **Larry Jorgenson**'s one-man shop received solid market endorsement. Recommended as a *"great all-around attorney"* Jorgenson specializes in commercial real estate transactions, litigation and land use matters. He acts for financial institutions, developers and private individuals and receives a steady stream of referral work from colleagues throughout Wyoming.

MacPherson Kelly & Thompson
The Firm: This five-lawyer Rawlins firm boasts a specialty in representing agricultural ranches.
The Lawyers: Consistently recommended by market sources, **John MacPherson** represents buyers and sellers of ranches throughout Wyoming and Colorado.
The Clients: Silver Spur Land and Cattle; Weber Ranch Co.; Carbon County; State of Wyoming; Overland Trail Cattle Company.

Phibbs & Resor PC
The Firm: This small practice is recommended for the work of Henry Phibbs.
The Lawyers: Peers praised **Henry Phibbs** for his *"extensive real estate involvement"* and representation of *"significant landowners"* in the area. He represents buyers and sellers in the acquisition and sale of real estate property in the $400,000 to $10 million range.
The Clients: The practice acts for both owners and developers in a range of real estate matters.

Other Notable Practitioners
Trial lawyer **Andrea Richard** (see p.735) of Rothgerber Johnson & Lyons LLP is visible in the market litigating real estate brokerage issues. This *"bright"* attorney represents a wide variety of clients including the Wyoming Association of Realtors, developers and construction managers.

Leaders in Wyoming

BARBE, Kenneth
Brown, Drew & Massey, LLP, Casper
307 234 1000 800 877 6755
Recommended in Corporate/M&A, Real Estate

BELCHER, James
Holland & Hart LLP, Cheyenne
307 778 4200
jbelcher@hollandhart.com
Recommended in Corporate/M&A
Specialization: Partner practicing in all areas of financial and corporate business matters. Works with corporations, limited partnerships and limited liability companies in formation, merger, continuance into Wyoming, and transfer from Wyoming to another jurisdiction. Has also assisted clients with securities matters. Assists clients with energy development and transmission, including wind energy projects, natural gas gathering and pipelines, and electrical transmission, including project development and finance, right of way acquisition and condemnation and related advice. In his financial and corporate practice, has assisted both borrowers and lenders with UCC, real estate, mortgage, and loan documentation, and has extensive experience in issuing opinions for business and secured transactions.
Prof. Memberships: Wyoming Bar Association, Business Law Section (Past Chairman), Wyoming Bar Foundation (Director and Vice President).
Career: Admitted to the Wyoming (1988) and Colorado (1989) Bar. Commercial Finance (1972-85); Attorney (1988-present).
Publications: Editor, 'The Wyoming Law of Mortgages' (2d ed. 1993).
Personal: Received a JD from the University of Wyoming (1988, With Honors) and a BS from the University of Colorado (1972).

BUFFINGTON, Teresa
Holland & Hart LLP, Cheyenne
307 778 4237
tbuffington@hollandhart.com
Recommended in Corporate/M&A
Specialization: A partner practicing in all areas of commercial transactions throughout the state of Wyoming, including real estate, business, finance, and construction. Her practice includes acquisitions and sales, development projects, contract preparation and negotiation, energy project transactions, rights of way for pipelines and other utilities, commercial financing, entity formation and continuation, design, engineering and construction projects, transactional due diligence, and legal opinions. Has assisted clients in a variety of industries, projects, and businesses, including electrical, natural gas, coal, trona, and construction.
Prof. Memberships: Laramie County Bar Association, Wyoming Bar Association, Colorado Bar Association, American Bar Association.
Career: Admitted to the Colorado (1985) and Wyoming Bar (1991). Administrative partner of *Holland & Hart*'s Cheyenne Office. Formerly Manager of Firm's Business Entities and Transactions Practice Group.
Personal: Received a JD from the University of Colorado (1985) and a BA from Ohio University (1977, With Highest Honors).

WYOMING

CAVE, Bradley
Holland & Hart LLP, Cheyenne
307 778 4210
bcave@hollandhart.com
Recommended in Employment
Specialization: A partner practicing employment law and litigation, he represents employers in matters involving discrimination, harassment, wage and hour disputes, defamation, wrongful discharge, breach of contract and employment-related torts. Also advises employers on issues related to employee handbooks and personnel policies, compliance with federal and state statutes and regulations and employee investigations, discipline and termination. Regularly conducts training sessions for employers, managers and supervisors in areas such as investigations, discipline and termination, harassment, discrimination, disability accommodation and supervisory responsibilities.
Prof. Memberships: American Bar Association, Wyoming Bar Association, Colorado Bar Association, Wyoming Association of Defense Trial Counsel, Defense Research Institute, Society of Human Resource Management.
Career: Admitted to the Colorado (1988) and Wyoming (1991) Bar. Editor of the Wyoming Employment Law Letter.
Personal: Received a JD from George Washington University (1988, With Honors) and a BS from the University of Wyoming (1985).

COTTAM, Dale
Hirst & Applegate, PC, Cheyenne
307 632 0541
Recommended in Corporate/M&A

DAVIS, Michael
Yonkee & Toner LLP, Sheridan
307 674 7451
Recommended in Employment

DAVIS, Richard
Davis & Cannon, Sheridan
307 672 7491
Recommended in Real Estate

DAY, Richard
Williams, Porter, Day & Neville, P.C., Casper 307 265 0700
Recommended in Litigation

DRAY, Perry
Dray, Thomson & Dyekman, PC, Cheyenne 307 634 8891
Recommended in Corporate/M&A

DYEKMAN, Gregory
Dray, Thomson & Dyekman, PC, Cheyenne 307 634 8891
Recommended in Corporate/M&A, Real Estate

EVANS, David
Hickey, Mackey, Evans & Walker, Cheyenne 307 634 1525
Recommended in Employment

FOX, Kate
Davis & Cannon, Cheyenne
307 643 3210
Recommended in Employment

GALLINGER, John
Holland & Hart LLP, Jackson
307 739 9741
Recommended in Real Estate

GALVAN, Mary Elizabeth
Mary Elizabeth Galvan, Laramie
307 745 7091
Recommended in Employment

GIFFORD, Mark
Mark W. Gifford, Casper
307 265 3265
Recommended in Employment, Litigation

HACKER, Patrick
Patrick E Hacker, Cheyenne
307 778 8844
Recommended in Employment

HICKEY, Paul
Hickey, Mackey, Evans & Walker, Cheyenne 307 634 1525
Recommended in Litigation

JORGENSON, Larry
Jorgenson Law Office, Jackson
307 733 6021
Recommended in Real Estate

LARSON, David
Mullikin, Larson & Swift, Jackson
307 733 3923
Recommended in Real Estate

LONG, Thomas
Thomas N. Long, Cheyenne
307 635 0413
Recommended in Corporate/M&A

MACPHERSON, John
MacPherson Kelly & Thompson, Rawlins
307 324 2713
Recommended in Real Estate

MASON, Gerald
Mason & Mason PC, Pinedale
307 367 2134
Recommended in Litigation

MCCALL, Donn
Brown, Drew & Massey, LLP, Casper
307 234 1000 800 877 6755
Recommended in Corporate/M&A

METZKE, John
Hirst & Applegate, PC, Cheyenne
307 632 0541
Recommended in Corporate/M&A

MOATS, Bruce
Law Office of Bruce T Moats, Cheyenne
307 778 8844
Recommended in Employment

NICHOLAS, Thomas
Hirst & Applegate, PC, Cheyenne
307 632 0541
Recommended in Litigation

ORTIZ, Scott
Williams, Porter, Day & Neville, P.C., Casper 307 265 0700
Recommended in Employment

PHIBBS, Henry
Phibbs & Resor P.C., Jackson
307 733 5004
Recommended in Real Estate

REED, Randall
Dray, Thomson & Dyekman, PC, Cheyenne 307 634 8891
Recommended in Corporate/M&A

RICHARD, Andrea Leah
Rothgerber Johnson & Lyons LLP, Cheyenne 307 638 6262
arichard@rothgerber.com
Recommended in Real Estate
Specialization: A partner with the firm since 1999, she successfully represents clients in conjunction with business-related claims, including real estate, construction, and employment matters.
Prof. Memberships: Laramie County Bar Association, Wyoming State Bar, and American Bar Association
Career: Admitted 1991 to practice before Wyoming District Courts, the Wyoming Supreme Court, US Bankruptcy Court for the District of Wyoming, the US District Court for the District of Wyoming, and the United States Court of Appeals, Tenth Circuit.
Personal: Received a JD from the University of Wyoming in 1991 and a BA from the University of Kansas in 1988.

RUTLEDGE, Kent
Lathrop & Rutledge, Cheyenne
307 632 0554
Recommended in Litigation

SCHULTZ, Donald I
Holland & Hart LLP, Cheyenne
307 778 4217
dschultz@hollandhart.com
Recommended in Litigation
Specialization: A partner practicing in commercial litigation, primarily in the oil and gas and construction industries. Serves as court-appointed Liaison Counsel to coordinate among hundreds of defendants in nearly 100 MDL-consolidated gas measurement and gas valuation lawsuits. Has jury trial and appellate experience in gas measurement disputes, gas contract pricing and take-or-pay disputes, JOA disputes, and gas balancing claims. Represents owners in litigation of construction disputes involving pipelines, gas plants, refineries, coal mines, trona mines, and resort properties.
Prof. Memberships: American Bar Association, Forum of the Construction Industry, Wyoming Bar Association, Defense Lawyers Association of Wyoming.
Career: Admitted to the Colorado (1982) and Wyoming (1985) Bar.
Personal: Received a JD from Harvard University (1982) and a BA from the University of Wyoming (1979).

SHUMATE, Roger
Murane & Bostwick, L.L.C., Casper
307 234 9345
Recommended in Employment

STUDER, Judith
Schwartz, Bon, Walker & Studer, LLC, Casper 307 235 6681
Recommended in Employment

SWIFT, Phelps
Mullikin, Larson & Swift, Jackson
307 733 3923
Recommended in Real Estate

TONER, Tom
Yonkee & Toner LLP, Sheridan
307 674 7451
Recommended in Litigation, Real Estate

WALKER, Cameron
Schwartz, Bon, Walker & Studer, LLC, Casper 307 235 6681
Recommended in Litigation

WILLIAMS, Barry
Williams, Porter, Day & Neville, P.C., Casper 307 265 0700
Recommended in Real Estate

FORTUNE 500 LAWYERS

**CHAMBERS
USA
2003–2004**

FORTUNE 500

3M Company
John J Ursu, *Senior Vice President,*
Legal Affairs & General Counsel
3M Centre, Building 220-14W-07, St Paul MN
55144-1000
Tel: 651 733 1110
Fax: 612 773 9973
Email: jjursu@mmm.com
Website: www.3m.com

Abbott Laboratories Limited
David Wardell, *Divisional Vice President,*
International Legal Operations
Department 323/AP6D, 100 Abbott Park Road,
Abbott Park IL 60064-3500
Tel: 847 937 6100
Fax: 847 938 6277
Website: www.abbott.com

Adams Resources & Energy Inc
Richard B Abshire, *Vice President Finance*
& Chief Financial Officer
4400 Post Oak Parkway, Suite 2700,
Houston TX 77027
Tel: 713 881 3600
Fax: 713 881 3408

Adelphia Communications Corporation
Randell D Fisher, *Vice President, General*
Counsel & Corporate Secretary
1 North Main Street, Coudersport PA 16915-1141
Tel: 814 274 9830
Fax: 814 274 8631
Website: www.adelphia.net

Administaff Inc
John H Spurgin II, *Vice President Legal, General*
Counsel & Secretary,
19001 Crescent Springs Drive, Kingwood TX 77339
Tel: 281 348 3251
Fax: 281 348 2859
Email: John_Spurgin@administaff.com
Website: www.administaff.com

Advanced Micro Devices Inc
Thomas M McCoy, *Senior Vice President,*
General Counsel & Secretary
1 AMD Place, Sunnyvale CA 94088-3453
Tel: 408 732 2400
Fax: 408 774 7399
Website: www.amd.com

AdvancePCS Inc
Susan S de Mars, *Senior Vice*
President & General Counsel
5215 North O'Connor Boulevard, Suite 1600, Irving
TX 75039
Tel: 469 420 6000
Fax: 972 830 6168
Website: www.advparadigm.com

AES Corporation
William R Luraschi, *Senior Vice President,*
General Counsel & Secretary
Corporate Office, 1001 North 19th Street, Arlington
VA 22209
Tel: 703 522 1315
Fax: 703 528 4510
Website: www.aesc.com

Aetna Inc
L Edward Shaw Jr, *Executive Vice President &*
General Counsel
151 Farmington Avenue, Hartford CT 06156
Tel: 860 273 0123
Fax: 860 273 1732
Website: www.aetna.com

AFLAC Inc
Joey Laudermilk, *Executive Vice President;*
General Counsel & Corporate Secretary
1932 Wynnton Road, Columbus GA 31999-0001
Tel: 706 323 3431
Fax: 706 324 6330
Website: www.aflac.com

Agilent Technologies Inc
D Craig Nordlund, *Senior Vice President,*
General Counsel & Secretary
395 Page Mill Road, PO Box 10395,
Palo Alto CA 94306-0870
Tel: 650 857 1501
Fax: 650 857 7299
Website: www.agilent-tech.com

Air Products & Chemicals Inc
W Douglas Brown, *Vice President,*
General Counsel & Secretary
7201 Hamilton Boulevard, Allentown
PA 18195-1501
Tel: 610 481 7351
Fax: 610 706 8161
Email: brownwd@apci.com
Website: www.airproducts.com

Airborne Inc
David C Anderson, *Senior Vice President,*
General Counsel & Secretary
3101 Western Avenue, PO Box 662,
Seattle WA 98111-0662
Tel: 206 285 4600
Fax: 206 281 1444
Website: www.airborne.com

AK Steel Holding Corporation
David C Horn, *Vice President & General Counsel*
703 Curtis Street, Middletown OH 45043-0001
Tel: 513 425 2690
Fax: 513 425 5607
Email: david.horn@aksteel.com
Website: www.aksteel.com

Albertson's Inc
John R Sims, *Executive Vice President*
& General Counsel
250 Parkcenter Boulevard, PO Box 20,
Boise ID 83726
Tel: 208 395 6200
Fax: 208 385 6110
Website: www.albertsons.com

Alcoa Inc
Lawrence R Purtell, *Executive Vice Presiden*
& General Counsel
390 Park Avenue, New York NY 10022
Tel: 212 836 2652
Fax: 212 836 2809
Email: lawrence.purtell@alcoa.com
Website: www.alcoa.com

Allegheny Energy
Thomas K Henderson, *Vice President*
& General Counsel
10435 Downsville Pike, Hagerstown
MD 21740-1766
Tel: 301 790 3400
Fax: 301 790 6085
Website: www.alleghenyenergy.com

Allied Waste Industries Inc
Steven M Helm, *Vice President, Legal*
Corporate Counsel & Corporate Secretary
15880 North Greenway, Hayden Loop, Suite 100,
Scottsdale AZ 85260
Tel: 480 627 2700
Fax: 480 627 2701
Website: www.alliedwaste.com

Allmerica Financial
J Kendall Huber, *Vice President*
& General Counsel
440 Lincoln Street, Worcester MA 01653
Tel: 508 855 1000
Fax: 508 856 9526
Website: www.allmerica.com

The Allstate Insurance Company
Michael McCabe, *Senior Vice President*
& General Counsel
2775 Sanders Road, Suite F7, Northbrook
IL 60062-6127
Tel: 847 402 6363
Fax: 847 402 5670
Email: mmc01@allstate.com
Website: www.allstate.com

ALLTEL Corporation
Francis X Frantz, *Executive Vice President,*
External Affairs, General Counsel & Secretary
One Allied Drive, Little Rock AR 72202
Tel: 501 905 8000
Fax: 501 905 0962
Website: www.alltel.com

Amazon.com Inc
Michelle Wilson, *Senior Vice President, Human*
Resources, General Counsel
& Corporate Secretary
1200 12th Avenue South, (PO Box 81226, Seattle,
WA 98108-1226), Seattle WA 98144-2734
Tel: 206 266 1000
Fax: 206 266 4206
Website: www.amazon.com

Amerada Hess Corporation
J Barclay Collins, *Executive Vice President*
& General Counsel
1185 Avenue of the Americas, New York
NY 10036-2601
Tel: 212 997 8500
Fax: 212 536 8390
Website: www.hess.com

Ameren Corporation
Stephen R Sullivan, *General Counsel*
1901 Chouteau Avenue, St Louis MO 63103
Tel: 314 621 3222
Fax: 314 554 3801
Website: www.ameren.com

American Axle & Manufacturing Holdings Inc
Richard G Raymond, *General Counsel*
1840 Holbrook Avenue, Detroit MI 48212-3488
Tel: 313 974 2000
Fax: 313 974 3090
Website: www.aam.com

American Electric Power Company (AEP)
Jeffrey D Cross, *Senior Vice President*
& General Counsel
1 Riverside Plaza, Columbus OH 43215-2373
Tel: 614 716 1580
Fax: 614 716 1560
Email: jdcross@aep.com
Website: www.aep.com

American Express Company
Louise M Parent, *Executive Vice President*
& General Counsel
American Express Tower, 200 Vesey Street, New York
NY 10285-4900
Tel: 212 974 2000
Fax: 212 640 0131
Email: louise.parent@aexp.com
Website: www.americanexpress.com

FORTUNE 500

American Family Insurance Group
James F Eldridge, Executive Vice President, Corporate Legal & Secretary
6000 American Parkway, Madison WI 53783
Tel: 608 249 2111
Fax: 608 243 4921
Website: www.amfam.com

American Financial Group
James E Evans, Senior Vice President & General Counsel
One East Fourth Street, Suite 919, Cincinnati OH 45202
Tel: 513 579 2121
Fax: 513 579 2113
Website: www.amfnl.com

American International Group Inc (AIG)
Ernest Patrikis, Senior Vice President & General Counsel
70 Pine Street, New York NY 10270
Tel: 212 770 5427
Fax: 212 425 2175
Email: ernest.patrikis@aig.com
Website: www.aig.com

American Standard
Paul McGrath, Senior Vice President, General Counsel and Secretary
1 Centennial Avenue, PO Box 6820, Piscataway NJ 08855-6820
Tel: 732 980 6057
Fax: 732 980 3340
Website: www.americanstandard.com

AmerisourceBergen Corporation
William D Sprague, Vice President, General Counsel & Secretary
1300 Morris Drive, Suite 100, Chesterbrook PA 19087-5594
Tel: 610 727 7000
Fax: 610 727 3600
Website: www.amerisourcebergen.net

Ames Department Stores Inc
David H Lissy, Senior Vice President, General Counsel & Secretary
2418 Main Street, Rocky Hill CT 06067-2598
Tel: 860 257 2000
Fax: 860 257 2168
Website: www.AmesStores.com

Amgen Inc
Steven Odre, Senior Vice President, General Counsel & Secretary
1 Amgen Centre Drive, Mail Stop 38-5-A, Thousand Oaks CA 91320-1799
Tel: 805 447 1000
Fax: 805 447 1010
Email: sodre@amgen.com
Website: www.amgen.com

AMR Corporation
Anne H McNamara, General Counsel
4333 Amon Carter Boulevard, Fort Worth TX 76155
Tel: 817 963 1234
Fax: 817 963 2523
Website: www.amrcorp.com

AmSouth Bancorp
Steve Yodder, General Counsel
AmSouth-Sonat Tower, 1900 Fifth Avenue North 35203, PO Box 11007, Birmingham AL 35203
Tel: 205 326 5120
Fax: 205 583 4497
Email: 10312,1342@Compuserv.com
Website: www.amsouth.com

Anadarko Petroleum Corporation
J Stephen Martin, Vice President & General Counsel
1201 Lake Robbins Drive, The Woodlands TX 77380
Tel: 832 636 1000
Website: www.anadarko.com

Anheuser-Busch Companies Inc
Stephen K Lambright, Group Vice President & General Counsel
One Busch Place 202-9, St Louis MO 63118-1852
Tel: 314 577 2000
Fax: 314 577 2900
Email: stephen.lambright@anheuser-busch.com;stephenlambright@anheuserbusch.com
Website: www.anheuser-busch.com

Anixter International Inc
James E Knox, Senior Vice President, Law & Secretary
4711 Golf Road, Skokie IL 60076-1278
Tel: 847 677 2600
Fax: 847 677 8557
Website: www.anixter.com

Anthem Inc
David R Frick, Executive Vice President, Chief Legal & Administrative Officer
120 Monument Circle, Indianapolis IN 46204
Tel: 317 488 6000
Fax: 317 488 6891
Email: david.frick@anthem.com
Website: www.anthem-inc.com

AOL Time Warner Inc
Paul Cappuccio, Executive Vice President, General Counsel & Secretary
75 Rockefeller Plaza, 28th Floor, New York NY 10019
Tel: 212 484 7980
Fax: 212 258 3172
Website: www.timewarner.com

Aon Corporation
Raymond Skilling, Executive Vice President & Chief Counsel
Corporate Headquarters, Aon Center, 200 East Randolph Street, Chicago IL 60601
Tel: 312 381 1000
Website: www.aon.com

Apple Computer Inc
Nancy Heinen, Senior Vice President, General Counsel & Secretary
1 Infinite Loop, Cupertino CA 95014-2084
Tel: 408 996 1010
Fax: 408 974 8530
Email: heinen@apple.com
Website: www.apple.com

Applied Materials Inc
Joseph J Sweeney, Group Vice President, Legal Affairs and Intellectual Property & Corporate Secretary
2881 Scott Boulevard, Mail Stop 2064, Santa Clara CA 95050
Tel: 408 748 5420
Fax: 408 563 4635
Website: www.appliedmaterials.com

Aquila Inc
Leslie J Parrette Jr, Senior Vice President, General Counsel & Corporate Secretary
Corporate Office, 20 West 9th Street, Kansas City MO 64105
Tel: 816 421 6600
Fax: 816 467 9732
Website: www.aquila.com

ARAMARK Corporation
Bart J Colli, ESq Executive Vice President, General Counsel & Secretary
The Aramark Tower, 1101 Market Street, 31st Floor, Philadelphia PA 19107
Tel: 215 238 6846
Fax: 215 238 3333
Email: colli-bart@ARAMARK.com
Website: www.aramark.com

Archer Daniels Midland Company (ADM)
David J Smith, Senior Vice President, General Counsel & Secretary
4666 Faries Parkway, PO Box 1470, Decatur IL 62525-1820
Tel: 217 424 5200
Fax: 217 424 6196
Website: www.admworld.com

Armstrong Holdings Inc
John N Rigas, Senior Vice President, Secretary and General Counsel
2500 Columbia Avenue, PO Box 3001, Lancaster PA 17604-3001
Tel: 717 396 2577
Fax: 717 396 6133
Email: jnrigas@armstrong.com
Website: www.armstrong.com

Arrow Electronics Incorporated
Robert Klatell, Executive Vice President & General Counsel
25 Hub Drive, Melville NY 11747
Tel: 516 391 1300
Fax: 516 391 1683
Website: www.arrow.com

ArvinMeritor Inc
Vernon G Baker II, Senior Vice President & General Counsel
2135 West Maple Road, Troy MI 48084-7186
Tel: 248 435 0786
Fax: 248 435 2184
Website: www.arvinmeritor.com

Ashland Incorporated
David L Hausrath, Vice President & General Counsel
Corporate Headquarters, 50 East RiverCenter Boulevard, PO Box 391, Covington KY 41012-0391
Tel: 859 815 3333
Fax: 859 815 5053
Website: www.ashland.com

AT&T Corporation
James W Cicconi, Executive Vice President, Law and Government Affairs & General Counsel
295 North Maple Avenue, Basking Ridge NJ 07920
Tel: 908 221 2000
Fax: 908 221 2528
Website: www.att.com

Automatic Data Processing Incorporated
James Benson, General Counsel, Vice President of Corporate Legal & Secretary to the Board
One ADP Boulevard, Roseland NJ 07068-1728
Tel: 973 994 5000
Fax: 973 974 5495
Website: www.adp.com

AutoNation Inc
Jonathan P Ferrando, Senior Vice President, General Counsel & Secretary
110 South East 6th Street, Fort Lauderdale FL 33301
Tel: 954 769 6000
Fax: 954 769 6537

FORTUNE 500

AutoZone Inc
Harry L Goldsmith, Senior Vice President, General Counsel & Secretary
123 South Front Street, Memphis TN 38103
Tel: 901 495 6500
Fax: 901 495 8300
Website: www.autozone.com

Avaya Inc
Pamela Craven, Senior Vice President, General Counsel & Secretary
211 Mount Airy Road, Basking Ridge NJ 07920
Tel: 908 953 6000
Fax: 908 953 7609
Website: www.avaya.com

Avery Dennison Corporation
Robert Van Schoonenberg, Vice President & General Counsel
150 North Orange Grove Boulevard, Pasadena CA 91103-3534
Tel: 626 304 2000
Fax: 626 792 7312
Website: www.averydennison.com

Avista Corporation
David J Meyer, Senior Vice President & General Counsel
1411 East Mission Avenue, Spokane WA 99202-2600
Tel: 509 489 0500
Fax: 509 495 8851
Website: www.avistacorp.com

Avnet Incorporated
David R Birk, Senior Vice President, General Counsel & Secretary
2211 South 47th Street, Phoenix AZ 85034
Tel: 480 643 2000
Fax: 480 643 7240
Website: www.avnet.com

Avon Products Inc
Donna Edbril, Vice President
1251 Avenue of the Americas, New York NY 10020
Tel: 212 282 7247
Fax: 212 282 6672
Email: donna.edbril@avon.com
Website: www.avon.com

Baker Hughes Incorporated
Alan R Crain, Vice President & General Counsel
Corporate Headquarters, 3900 Essex Lane, Suite 1200, Houston TX 77027-5177
Tel: 713 439 8718
Fax: 713 439 8699
Email: alan.crain@bakerhughes.com
Website: www.bakerhughes.com

Ball Corporation
Donald C Lewis, Vice President, Assistant Corporate Secretary & General Counsel
10 Longs Peak Drive, Broomfield CO 80021-2510
Tel: 303 460 2236
Fax: 303 460 2691
Email: dlewis@ball.com
Website: www.ball.com

Bank of America Corporation
Paul J Polking, Executive Vice President & General Counsel
Bank of America Corporate Center, 100 North Tryon Street, Charlotte NC 28255
Tel: 704 386 5724
Fax: 704 370 3515
Email: paul.polking@bankofamerica.com
Website: www.bankofamerica.com

The Bank of New York Company Inc
J Michael Shepherd, Executive Vice President, General Counsel & Secretary
1 Wall Street, New York NY 10286-0001
Tel: 212 635 1643
Fax: 212 635 1070
Email: mshepherd@bankofny.com
Website: www.bankofny.com

Bank One Corp
Christine A Edwards, Executive Vice President, Chief Legal Officer & Secretary
1 Bank One Plaza, Two South Dearborn Street, Mail Suite IL 1-0276, 9th Floor Chicago IL 60670
Tel: 312 732 4000
Fax: 312 732 3366
Website: www.bankone.com

Barnes & Noble Inc
Larry Zilavy, Chief Financial Officer
122 Fifth Avenue, New York NY 10011-5605
Tel: 212 633 3300
Fax: 212 675 0413
Website: www.barnesandnobleinc.com

Baxter International Inc
Thomas Sabatino, Senior Vice President & General Counsel
1 Baxter Parkway, Deerfield IL 60015-4633
Tel: 847 948 2000
Fax: 847 948 2450
Email: tom_sabatino@baxter.com
Website: www.baxter.com

BB & T Corporation
Jerone Herring, General Counsel
200 West Second Street, Winston-Salem NC 28359-1489
Tel: 336 733 2000
Fax: 336 733 2009
Website: www.bbandt.com

The Bear Stearns Companies Inc
Mark E Lehman, Executive Vice President, Senior Managing Director & General Counsel
Legal Department, 383 Madison Avenue, 6th Floor, New York NY 10179
Tel: 212 272 2000
Fax: 212 272 6594
Website: www.bearstearns.com

Becton Dickinson & Company
Bridget M Healy, Vice President, Secretary & General Counsel
1 Becton Drive, Franklin Lakes NJ 07417-1880
Tel: 201 847 6800
Fax: 201 847 6475
Website: www.bd.com

BellSouth Corporation
Charles R Morgan, Executive Vice President & General Counsel
1155 Peachtree Street North East, Suite 2002, Atlanta GA 30309-3610
Tel: 404 249 2000
Fax: 404 249 5948
Website: www.bellsouth.com

Berkshire Hathaway Inc
Marc D Hamburg, Vice President, Chief Finance Officer & Treasurer
1440 Kiewit Plaza, Omaha NE 68131
Tel: 402 346 1400
Fax: 402 346 3575
Email: berkshire@berkshirehathaway.com
Website: www.berkshirehathway.com

Best Buy Co Inc
Joseph Joyce, Senior Vice President & General Counsel
PO Box 9312, Minneapolis MN 55440-9312
Website: www.bestbuy.com

Bethlehem Steel Corporation
William H Graham, Senior Vice President, General Counsel & Secretary
Martin Tower, 1170 Eighth Avenue, Bethlehem PA 18016-7699
Tel: 610 694 2424
Fax: 610 694 6920
Website: www.bethsteel.com

Big Lots Inc
Charles W Haubiel, Vice President, General Counsel & Secretary
300 Phillipi Road, Columbus OH 43228-0512
Tel: 614 278 6800
Fax: 614 279 6676
Website: www.cnstores.com

BJ's Wholesale Club Inc
Sarah M Gallivan, Vice President, General Counsel & Secretary
One Mercer Road, Natick MA 01760
Tel: 508 651 7400
Fax: 508 651 6114
Website: www.bjswholesale.com

The Black & Decker Corporation
Charles E Fenton, Senior Vice President & General Counsel
701 East Joppa Road, Towson MD 21286
Tel: 410 716 3900
Fax: 410 716 2933
Website: www.blackanddecker.com

The Boeing Company
Douglas G Bain, Senior Vice President & Chief Legal Counsel
Boeing World Headquarters, 100 North Riverside Plaza, Chicago IL 60606-2609
Tel: 312 544 2000
Fax: 312 544 2082
Website: www.boeing.com

Boise Cascade Corporation
John W Holleran, Senior Vice President, Human Resources & General Counsel
1111 West Jefferson Street, PO Box 50, Boise ID 83728-0001
Tel: 208 384 6161
Fax: 208 384 7189
Website: www.bc.com

Borders Group Inc
Thomas D Carney, Vice President, General Counsel & Secretary
100 Phoenix Drive, Ann Arbor MI 48108-2202
Tel: 734 913 1100
Fax: 734 477 1965
Website: www.bordersgroupinc.com

Bristol-Myers Squibb Company
John L McGoldrick, Executive Vice President & General Counsel
World Headquarters, 345 Park Avenue, New York NY 10154-0037
Tel: 212 546 4000
Fax: 212 546 9562
Website: www.bms.com

FORTUNE 500

Brunswick Corporation
Marshall I Smith, Vice President Secretary
& General Counsel
1 North Field Court, Lake Forest IL 60045-4811
Tel: 847 735 4700
Fax: 847 735 4765
Website: www.brunswick.com

Burlington Northern Santa Fe Corporation (BNSF)
Jeffrey Moreland, Executive Vice President, Law, Government Affairs and Corporate Secretary
2650 Lou Menk Drive, Second Floor,
Fort Worth TX 76131-2830
Tel: 817 333 2000
Fax: 817 352 7111
Website: www.bnsf.com

Burlington Resources Inc
Frederick J Plaeger II, Vice President
& General Counsel
5051 Westheimer, Suite 1400, Houston
TX 77056-5686
Tel: 713 624 9500
Fax: 713 624 9645
Website: www.br-inc.com

Cablevision Systems Corporation
Robert S Lemle, Vice Chairman,
General Counsel & Secretary
One Media Crossways, Woodbury NY 11797-2062
Website: www.cablevision.com

Calpine Corporation
Lisa Bodensteiner, Vice President
& General Counsel
50 West San Fernando Street, San José CA 95113
Tel: 408 995 5115
Fax: 408 995 0505
Website: www.calpine.com

Campbell Soup Company
Ellen Oran Kaden, Senior Vice President, Law
& Government Affairs
Campbell Place, Camden NJ 08103-1799
Tel: 856 342 4800
Fax: 856 342 5216
Email: ellen_kaden@campbellsoup.com
Website: www.campbellsoup.com

Capital One Financial
John G Finneran, Senior Vice President,
General Counsel & Corporate Secretary
2980 Fairview Park Drive, Suite 1300, Falls Church
VA 22042-4255
Tel: 703 205 1000
Fax: 703 205 1755
Website: www.capitalone.com

Cardinal Health Inc
Paul Williams, Executive Vice President
& Chief Legal Officer
7000 Cardinal Place, Dublin OH 43017
Tel: 614 757 7768
Fax: 614 757 6948
Email: paul.williams@cardinal.com
Website: www.cardinal-health.com

Caremark RX
Edward L Hardin, General Counsel
3000 Galleria Tower, Birmingham AL 35244
Tel: 205 733 8996
Fax: 205 733 9780
Website: www.caremarkrx.com

Caterpillar Inc
James B Buda, Vice President,
General Counsel & Secretary
100 North East Adams Street, Peoria IL 61629-7310
Tel: 309 675 1000
Fax: 309 675 1182
Website: www.caterpillar.com

CDW Computer Centers Inc
Christine A Leahy, Vice President,
General Counsel & Corporate Secretary
200 North Milwaukee Avenue, Vernon Hills IL 60061
Tel: 847 465 6000
Fax: 847 465 6800
Website: www.cdw.com

Cendant Corporation
James E Buckman, Vice Chairman,
General Counsel & Assistant Secretary
9 West 57th Street, 37th Floor, New York NY 10019
Tel: 212 413 1800
Fax: 212 413 1918
Website: www.cendant.com

Cenex Harvest States Cooperatives
David Kastelic, General Counsel
5500 Cenex Drive, Inver Grove Heights MN 55077
Tel: 651 451 5151
Fax: 651 306 6431
Website: www.cenexharveststates.com

Centex Corporation
Raymond G Smerge, Executive Vice President
& Chief Legal Officer
2728 North Hardwood, PO Box 19000-75219, Dallas
TX 75201-0001
Tel: 214 981 5000
Fax: 214 981 6859
Website: www.centex.com

CH Robinson Worldwide Inc (CHRW)
Owen P Gleason, General Counsel
8100 Mitchell Road, Suite 200, Eden Prairie MN 55344-2231
Tel: 952 937 8500
Fax: 952 937 6714
Website: www.chrobinson.com

Charles Schwab Corporation
Hardy Callcott, Senior Vice President
& General Counsel
101 Montgomery Street, San Francisco CA 94104
Tel: 415 627 7000
Fax: 415 636 5241
Website: www.schwab.com

Charter Communications Inc
Curt Shaw, Senior Vice President,
General Counsel & Secretary
Corporate Headquarters, 12405 Powerscourt Drive,
St Louis MO 63131-3660
Tel: 314 965 0555
Fax: 314 965 9745
Website: www.chartercom.com

ChevronTexaco Corporation
Charles A James, Vice President
& General Counsel
6001 Bollinger Canyon Road, San Ramon CA 94583
Tel: 925 842 3232
Fax: 925 842 7084
Email: cjae@chevrontexaco.com
Website: www.ChevronTexaco.com

The Chubb Corporation
Joanne L Bober, Senior Vice President
& General Counsel
15 Mountain View Road, PO Box 1615, Warren
NJ 07061-1615
Tel: 908 903 2000
Fax: 908 903 3607
Website: www.chubb.com

CIGNA Corporation
Judith E Soltz, Executive Vice President
& General Counsel
1601 Chestnut Street, Mail Stop OL55E, Two Liberty
Plaza, Philadelphia PA 19192
Fax: 215 761 5519
Website: www.cigna.com

Cinergy Corporation
Marc E Manly, Executive Vice President
& Chief Legal Officer
Atrium II, 25th Floor, Cincinnati OH 45202
Tel: 513 287 3200
Website: www.cinergy.com

Circuit City Group
W Stephen Cannon, General Counsel
9950 Mayland Drive, Richmond VA 23233
Tel: 804 527 4000
Fax: 804 527 4194
Website: www.circuitcity.com

Cisco Systems Inc
Mark W Chandler, Vice President, Legal Services
& General Counsel
300 East Tasman Drive, Mail Stop SJC10/5/3,
San José CA 95134
Tel: 408 527 0238
Fax: 408 525 4757
Email: machandl@cisco.com
Website: www.cisco.com

Citigroup
Stephanie Mudick, Co-General Counsel
399 Park Avenue, 8th floor, Zone 14,
New York NY 10043
Tel: 212 559 1000
Fax: 212 793 3946
Website: www.citi.com

Citigroup Inc
Joan Guggenheimer, Co-General Counsel
399 Park Avenue, New York NY 10043
Tel: 212 559 1000
Fax: 212 793 3946
Website: www.citigroup.com

Clear Channel Communications
Kenneth E Wyker, Senior Vice President,
General Counsel & Secretary
Corporate Headquarters, 200 East Basse Road,
San Antonio TX 78209
Tel: 210 822 2828
Fax: 210 832 3428
Email: kenwyker@clearchannel.com
Website: www.clearchannel.com

Clorox Co
Pete D Bewley, Senior Vice President,
General Counsel & Secretary
1221 Broadway, Oakland CA 94612-1888
Tel: 510 271 7000
Fax: 510 832 1463
Website: www.clorox.com

FORTUNE 500

CMS Energy Corporation
Belina Foxworth, General Counsel
Fairlane Plaza South, Suite 1100, 330
Town Center Drive, Dearborn MI 48126
Tel: 313 436 9200
Fax: 313 436 9225
Website: www.cmsenergy.com

CNF Inc
Eberhard G H Schmoller, Senior Vice President,
General Counsel & Secretary
3240 Hillview Avenue, Palo Alto CA 94304-1201
Tel: 650 494 2900
Fax: 650 494 8372
Email: CNFCorp@cnf.com
Website: www.cnf.com

Coca-Cola Company
Deval L Patrick, Executive Vice President,
General Counsel & Corporate Secretary
1 Coca-Cola Plaza North West, NAT2414,
Atlanta GA 30313
Tel: 404 676 1947
Fax: 404 515 4609
Website: www.cocacola.com

Coca-Cola Enterprises Inc
John R Parker, Vice President
& Senior Vice President
2500 Windy Ridge Parkway, Atlanta GA 30339
Tel: 770 989 3000
Fax: 770 989 3784
Website: www.cokecce.com

Colgate-Palmolive Company
Andrew D Hendry, Senior Vice President,
General Counsel & Company Secretary
300 Park Avenue, New York NY 10022-7499
Tel: 212 310 2239
Fax: 212 310 3754
Email: andrew_hendry@colpal.com
Website: www.colgate.com

Comcast Corporation
Arthur R Block, Senior Vice President,
General Counsel & Secretary
1500 Market Street, Philadelphia PA 19102-2148
Tel: 215 981 7564
Fax: 215 981 7794
Email: ablock@comcast.com
Website: www.comcast.com

Comdisco Holding Company Inc
Robert Lackey, Senior Vice President,
Chief Legal Officer & Secretary
6111 North River Road, Rosemont IL 60018
Tel: 847 698 3000
Fax: 847 518 5440
Website: www.comdisco.com

Comerica Incorporated
George W Madison, Executive Vice President,
General Counsel & Corporate Secretary
Comerica Tower at Detroit Center, 500 Woodward
Avenue, MC 3391, Detroit MI 48226
Tel: 313 222 7937
Fax: 313 961 8624
Email: gwmadison@comerica.com
Website: www.comerica.com

Computer Associates International Inc (CA)
Steven M Woghin, Senior Vice President
& General Counsel
1 Computer Associates Plaza, Islandia NY 11749
Tel: 631 342 6000
Fax: 631 342 4866
Email: steven.wogin@cai.com
Website: www.cai.com

Computer Sciences Corporation (CSC)
Hayward D Fisk, Vice President,
General Counsel & Secretary
2100 East Grand Avenue, El Segundo
CA 90245-5098
Tel: 310 615 0311
Fax: 310 322 9768
Website: www.csc.com

ConAgra Foods Inc
David Hefflinger, General Counsel
1 ConAgra Drive, Omaha NE 68102-5001
Tel: 402 595 4000
Fax: 402 341 3070
Website: www.conagra.com

ConocoPhillips Inc
Rick A Harrington, Senior Vice President,
Legal & General Counsel
600 North Dairy Ashford, Houston TX 77079-1175
Tel: 281 293 1085
Fax: 281 293 1054
Website: www.conocophillips.com

Conseco Inc
David K Herzog, Executive Vice President,
Secretary & General Counsel
11825 North Pennsylvania Street, PO Box 1911,
Carmel IN 46032-4555
Tel: 317 817 6100
Fax: 317 817 2726
Website: www.conseco.com

Consolidated Edison Inc
Charles E McTiernan Jr, General Counsel
4 Irving Place, Room 1810-S, New York
NY 10003-3598
Tel: 212 460 2432
Fax: 212 674 7329
Website: www.conedison.com

Constellation Energy Group
Kathleen Chagnon, Vice President, General
Counsel & Secretary
39 West Lexington Street, PO Box 1642,
Baltimore MD 21201
Tel: 410 234 5000
Fax: 410 234 5220
Website: www.constellationgroup.com

Continental Airlines Inc
Jennifer L Vogel, Vice President
& General Counsel
Legal Department, 1600 Smith Street, Houston
TX 77002
Tel: 713 324 5131
Fax: 713 324 5161
Email: corpcomm@coair.com
Website: www.continental.com

Cooper Industries Ltd
Diane K Schumacher, Senior Vice President,
General Counsel & Secretary
600 Travis Street, Suite 5800, Houston
TX 77002-1001
Tel: 713 209 8400
Fax: 713 209 8995
Email: info@cooperindustries.com
Website: www.cooperindustries.com

Cooper Tire & Rubber
Richard D Teeple, Vice President,
General Counsel & Secretary
701 Lima Avenue, Findlay OH 45840, PO Box 550,
Findlay OH 45839-0550
Tel: 419 424 4318
Fax: 419 420 6052
Website: www.coopertire.com

Corning Incorporated
William D Eggers, Senior Vice President
& General Counsel
One Riverfront Plaza, MP-HQ-E2-10,
Corning NY 14831-0001
Tel: 607 974 9000
Fax: 607 974 8091
Email: eggerswd@corning.com
Website: www.corning.com

Costco Wholesale Corporation
Joel Benoliel, Senior Vice President, Legal and
Administration & Chief Legal Officer
999 Lake Drive, Issaquah WA 98027
Tel: 425 313 8193
Fax: 425 313 8162
Email: jbenoliel@costco.com
Website: www.costco.com

Costco Wholesale Corporation
Richard Olin, Vice President & General Counsel
999 Lake Drive, Issaquah WA 98027
Tel: 425 313 8100
Fax: 425 313 8103
Website: www.costco.com

Countrywide Financial Corporation
Sandor E Samuels, Senior Managing Director,
Chief Legal Officer & Secretary
4500 Park Granada Boulevard, Calabasas
CA 91302-1613
Tel: 818 225 3000
Fax: 818 225 4051
Website: www.countrywide.com

Coventry Health Care Inc
Thomas C Zielinski, Senior Vice President
& General Counsel
6705 Rockledge Drive, Suite 100,
Bethesda MD 20817
Tel: 301 581 0600
Fax: 301 493 0752
Website: www.cvty.com

Cox Communications Inc
James A Hatcher, Senior Vice President,
Legal and Regulatory Affairs
1400 Lake Hearn Drive North East,
Atlanta GA 30319-1464
Tel: 404 843 5000
Fax: 404 843 5845
Website: www.cox.com

Crown Cork & Seal Company Inc
William T Gallagher, Senior Vice President,
Secretary & General Counsel
1 Crown Way, Philadelphia PA 19154-4599
Tel: 215 698 5383
Fax: 215 698 6061
Email: wgallagh@crowncork.com
Website: www.crowncork.com

CSX Transportation Inc
Ellen M Fitzsimmons, Chief Legal Officer, Senior
Vice President, Law & General Counsel
500 Water Street, Speed Code J-150,
Jacksonville FL 32202
Tel: 904 359 3100
Website: www.csx.com

Cummins Inc
Marya Rose, Vice President,
General Counsel & Corporate Secretary
500 Jackson Street, Columbus OH 47202
Tel: 812 377 5000
Fax: 812 377 3334
Website: www.cummins.com

FORTUNE 500

CVS Corporation
Zenon Lankousky, Head of Legal
One CVS Drive, Woonsocket RI 02895
Tel: 401 765 1500
Fax: 401 765 7887
Email: zplankousky@cvs.com
Website: www.cvs.com

Dana Corporation
Michael L DeBacker, Vice President, General Counsel & Secretary
PO Box 1000, Toledo OH 43697
Tel: 419 535 4647
Fax: 419 535 4544
Email: Mike.DeBacker@Dana.com
Website: www.dana.com

Danaher Corporation
Patrick W Allender, Executive Vice President, Chief Financial Officer & Secretary
2099 Pennsylvania Avenue North West, Washington, DC DC 20006
Website: www.danaher.com

Darden Restaurants
Paula Shives, Senior Vice President, General Counsel & Secretary
5900 Lake Ellenor Drive, Orlando FL 32809-4634
Tel: 407 245 4000
Fax: 407 245 5114
Website: www.darden.com

Dean Foods Company
Michelle P Goolsby, Executive Vice President, Chief Administrative Officer, General Counsel & Corporate Secretary
2515 McKinney Avenue, Suite 1200, Dallas TX 75201
Tel: 214 303 3400
Fax: 214 303 3499
Website: www.deanfoods.com

Deere & Company
James R Jenkins, Senior Vice President & General Counsel
One John Deere Place, Moline IL 61265-8098
Tel: 309 765 4675
Fax: 309 765 4735
Email: jenkinsjamesr@johndeere.com
Website: www.deere.com

Dell Computer Corporation
Thomas B Green, Senior Vice President & Secretary, Law and Administration
1 Dell Way, Round Rock TX 78682-2244
Tel: 512 338 4400
Fax: 512 728 7100
Website: www.dell.com

Delphi Corporation
Logan G Robinson, Vice President & General Counsel
5725 Delphi Drive, Troy MI 48098-2815
Tel: 248 813 2537
Fax: 248 813 3251
Email: logan.robinson@delphi.com
Website: www.delphiauto.com

Delta Air Lines Inc
Robert S Harkey, Senior Vice President, General Counsel & Secretary
Hartsfield Atlanta International Airport, 1030 Delta Boulevard, Atlanta GA 30320-6001
Tel: 404 715 2600
Fax: 404 715 5042
Website: www.delta.com

Devon Energy Corporation
Duke R Ligon, Senior Vice President & General Counsel
20 North Broadway, Suite 1400, Oklahoma City OK 73102-8260
Tel: 405 552 4604
Fax: 405 552 4648
Email: duke.ligon@dvn.com
Website: www.devonenergy.com

Dillard's Inc
Paul J Schroeder Jr, Vice President & General Counsel
1600 Cantrell Road, Little Rock AR 72201-1110
Tel: 501 376 5200
Fax: 501 399 7831
Website: www.dillards.com

Dole Food Company Inc
C Michael Carter , Vice President, General Counsel & Corporate Secretary
One Dole Drive, Westlake Village CA 91362
Tel: 818 879 6600
Fax: 818 879 6754
Website: www.dole.com

Dollar General Corporation
Susan S Lanigan , Vice President, General Counsel, Corporate Secretary
100 Mission Ridge, Goodlettsville TN 37072
Tel: 615 855 4000
Fax: 615 855 5252
Website: www.dollargeneral.com

Dominion Resources Inc
James Stutts, General Counsel
901 East Byrd Street, Suite 1700,Richmond VA 23219-6111
Tel: 804 775 5700
Fax: 804 819 2205
Website: www.dom.com

Dover Corporation
Joseph W Schmidt , Vice President, General Counsel & Secretary
280 Park Avenue, New York NY 10017-1292
Tel: 212 922 1640
Fax: 212 953 4326
Email: jws@dovercorp.com
Website: www.dovercorporation.com

Dow Chemical Company
Richard L Manetta, Corporate Vice President & General Counsel
2030 Dow Center, Midland MI 48674
Tel: 989 636 1000
Fax: 989 636 1830
Website: www.dow.com

DR Horton
David Morice, Vice President & General Counsel
1901 Ascension Boulevard, Suite 100, Arlington TX 76006-6521
Tel: 817 856 8200
Fax: 817 856 8249
Website: www.drhorton.com

DTE Energy Company
Bruce Peterson, Senior Vice President & General Counsel
2000 Second Avenue, Detroit MI 48226-1279
Tel: 313 235 4000
Fax: 313 235 0223
Website: www.dteenergy.com

Duke Energy Corporation
Richard W Blackburn, Executive Vice President, General Counsel & Chief Administrative Officer
526 South Church Street, Charlotte NC 28201-1802
Tel: 704 382 0711
Fax: 704 382 7705
Email: rwblackb@duke-energy.com
Website: www.duke-energy.com

Dynegy Inc
Kenneth E Randolph, Executive Vice President, General Counsel & Secretary
1000 Louisiana Street, Suite 5800, Houston TX 77002-5050
Tel: 713 507 6816
Fax: 713 507 6808
Email: kera@dynegy.com
Website: www.dynegy.com

Eastman Chemical Company
Theresa K Lee, Senior Vice President, General Counsel & Secretary
PO Box 511, Kingsport TN 37662
Tel: 423 229 2000
Fax: 423 229 1351
Website: www.eastman.com

Eastman Kodak Company
Gary P Van Graafeiland, Senior Vice President & General Counsel
343 State Street, Rochester NY 14650-0218
Tel: 585 724 9549
Fax: 585 724 9549
Website: www.kodak.com

Eaton Corporation
J Robert Horst, General Counsel
Eaton Center, 1111 Superior Avenue, Cleveland OH 44114-2584
Tel: 216 523 5000
Fax: 216 523 4787
Website: www.eaton.com

EchoStar Communications Corporation
David K Moskowitz, Executive Vice President, General Counsel & Secretary
5701 South Santa Fe Drive, Littleton CO 80120
Tel: 303 723 1040
Fax: 303 723 1699
Email: david.moskowitz@echostar.com
Website: www.echostar.com

Edison International
Bryant C Danner, Executive Vice President & General Counsel
2244 Walnut Grove Avenue, PO Box 999, Rosemead CA 91770
Tel: 626 302 1212
Fax: 626 302 4815
Website: www.edison.com

El duPont de Nemours and Company Inc
Stacey J Mobley, Senior Vice President, Chief Administrative Officer & General Counsel
1007 Market Street, Room D-7038, Wilmington DE 19898
Tel: 302 774 8051
Fax: 302 773 4679
Email: stacey.j.mobley@usa.dupont.com
Website: www.dupont.com

El Paso Corporation
Peggy A Heeg, Executive Vice President & General Counsel
1001 Louisiana Street, Houston TX 77002
Tel: 713 420 2600
Fax: 713 420 6030
Website: www.epenergy.com

Electronic Data Systems Corporation (EDS)
D Gilbert Friedlander, Senior Vice President, General Counsel & Corporate Secretary
5400 Legacy Drive, Plano TX 75024
Tel: 972 604 6000
Fax: 972 605 5610
Email: Gil.Friedlander@eds.com
Website: www.eds.com

Eli Lilly & Company
James T Burns, Assistant General Counsel
Lilly Corporate Center, Indianapolis IN 46285-0001
Tel: 317 276 2000
Fax: 317 276 6221
Email: jburns@lilly.com
Website: www.lilly.com

EMC Corporation
Paul T Dacier, Senior Vice President & General Counsel
171 South Street, Hopkinton MA 01748
Tel: 508 435 1000
Fax: 508 497 6915
Email: dacier_paul@emc.com
Website: www.emc.com

Emcor Group
Sheldon I Cammaker, Executive Vice President, Secretary & General Counsel
301 Merritt Seven, Norwalk CT 06851
Tel: 203 849 7800
Fax: 203 849 7900
Website: www.emcorgroup.com

Emerson Electric Company
Wayne Withers, Senior Vice President, General Counsel & Secretary
8000 West Florissant Avenue, PO Box 4100, St Louis MO 63136-8506
Tel: 314 553 2000
Fax: 314 553 3205
Email: wayne.withers@emerson.com
Website: www.emersonelectric.com / www.gotoemerson.com

Encompass Services Corporation
Gray H Muzzy, Senior Vice President, Secretary & General Counsel
3 Greenway Plaza, Suite 2000, Houston TX 77046
Tel: 713 860 0100
Fax: 713 626 4766
Website: www.encompserv.com

Energy East Corporation
Kenneth M Jasinski, Executive Vice President & Chief Financial Officer
PO Box 3200, Ithaca NY 14852-3200
Tel: 607 347 2561
Fax: 607 762 4345
Website: www.energyeast.com

Engelhard Corporation
Arthur Dornbusch II, Vice President, General Counsel & Secretary
101 Wood Avenue, Iselin NJ 08830-0370
Tel: 732 205 6000
Fax: 732 632 9253
Website: www.engelhard.com

Enron Corp
Robert H Walls Jr, Executive Vice President & General Counsel
General Counsel, 1400 Smith Street, Houston TX 77002-7361
Tel: 713 345 5416
Fax: 713 646 6227
Email: rob.walls@enron.com
Website: www.enron.com

Entergy Corporation
Michael G Thompson, Executive Vice President, General Counsel & Secretary
Legal Department, 639 Loyola Avenue, New Orleans LA 70161
Tel: 504 576 4214
Fax: 504 576 4150
Email: webmaster@entergy.com
Website: www.entergy.com

Enterprise Products Partners LP
Richard H Bachmann, Executive Vice President, Chief Legal Officer & Secretary
2727 North Loop West, PO Box 4324, Houston TX 77210
Tel: 713 880 6500
Fax: 713 880 6668
Website: www.epplp.com

Equity Office Properties Trust
Stanley M Stevens, Executive Vice President, Chief Legal Counsel & Secretary
Two North Riverside Plaza, 22nd Floor, Chicago IL 60606
Tel: 312 466 3300
Fax: 312 930 4486
Website: www.equityoffice.com

Estée Lauder Companies Inc
Paul E Konney, Senior Vice President General Counsel & Secretary
767 Fifth Avenue, 42nd Floor, New York NY 10153
Tel: 212 572 4200
Fax: 212 572 3989
Website: www.elcompanies.com

Exelon Corporation
Randall E Mehrberg, Executive Vice President & General Counsel
10 South Dearborn Street, 37th Floor, Post Office Box A-3005, Chicago IL 60690-3005
Tel: 312 394 7398
Fax: 312 394 2900
Website: www.exeloncorp.com

Express Scripts Inc
Thomas M Boudreau, Senior Vice President & General Counsel
13900 Riverport Drive, Maryland Heights MO 63043-4827
Tel: 314 770 1666
Fax: 314 702 7037
Website: www.express-scripts.com

Exxon Mobil Corporation (Law Department)
Charles W Matthews Jr, Vice President & General Counsel
5959 Las Colinas Boulevard, Irving TX 75039
Tel: 972 444 1000
Fax: 972 444 1456
Website: www.exxon.mobil.com

Family Dollar Stores Inc
George R Mahoney, Executive Vice President, General Counsel & Secretary
10401 Old Monroe Road, Charlotte NC 28201-1017
Tel: 704 847 6961
Fax: 704 847 0189
Website: www.familydollar.com

Fannie Mae
Anne Kappler, Senior Vice President & General Counsel
3900 Wisconsin Avenue North West, Washington, DC DC 20016-2892
Tel: 202 752 4850
Fax: 202 752 3868
Website: www.fanniemae.com

Farmland Industries Inc
Bob Schuller, Vice President, General Counsel & Corporate Secretary
12200 North Ambassador Drive, Kansas City MO 64163
Tel: 816 459 6000
Fax: 816 713 6464
Website: www.farmland.com

Federal-Mogul Corp
James Zamoyski, General Counsel
26555 Northwestern Hwy, Southfield MI 48034
Tel: 248 354 7700
Fax: 248 354 8950
Website: www.Federal-Mogul.com

Federated Department Stores Inc
Thomas G Cody, Executive Vice President, Legal and Human Resources
7 West Seventh Street, Cincinnati OH 45202
Tel: 513 579 7000
Fax: 513 579 7555
Website: www.federated-fds.com

FedEx Corporation
Kenneth R Masterson, Executive Vice President, General Counsel & Secretary
942 Shady Grove Road, Memphis TN 38120
Tel: 901 369 3600
Fax: 901 818 7590
Email: webmaster@fedex.com
Website: www.fedex.com

Fidelity National Financial Inc
Peter T Sadowski, Executive Vice President & General Counsel
4050 Calle Real, Santa Barbara CA 93110
Tel: 805 696 7000
Fax: 805 696 7814
Website: www.fnf.com

Fifth Third Bancorp
Paul L Reynolds, General Counsel
38 Fountain Square Plaza, Mail Drop 10AT76, Cincinnati OH 45263
Tel: 513 579 4370
Fax: 513 534 6757
Email: Paul.Reynolds@53.com
Website: www.53.com

First American Corporation
Craig I DeRoy, Executive Vice President & General Counsel
1 First American Way, Santa Ana CA 92707-5913
Tel: 714 800 3000
Fax: 714 800 3151
Website: www.firstam.com

First Data Corporation
Michael T Whealy, Executive Vice President, General Counsel & Chief Administrative Officer
10825 Old Mill Road, M 10, Omaha NE 68154
Tel: 402 222 5237
Fax: 402 222 5256
Email: mike.whealy@firstdatacorp.com
Website: www.firstdatacorp.com

FirstEnergy Corporation
Leila Vespoli, Senior Vice President & General Counsel
76 South Main Street, Akron OH 44308-1890
Tel: 330 384 5100
Fax: 330 384 3866
Website: www.firstenergycorp.com

FORTUNE 500

FleetBoston Financial Corporation
Gary A Spiess, Executive Vice President, General Counsel & Secretary
Legal Department, 100 Federal Street, Boston MA 02110
Tel: 617 434 2200
Fax: 617 434 6525
Website: www.fleetboston.com

Fleming Companies Inc
Carlos M Hernandez, Senior Vice President, General Counsel & Secretary
1945 Lakepointe Drive, Box 299013, Lewisville TX 75057
Tel: 972 906 8000
Fax: 972 906 7810
Website: www.fleming.com

Fluor Corporation
Lawrence N Fisher, Senior Vice President, Law & Secretary
One Enterprise Drive, Aliso Viejo CA 92656-2606
Tel: 949 349 2000
Fax: 949 349 5271
Website: www.fluor.com

Foot Locker Inc
Gary M Bahler, Senior Vice President & General Counsel
112 West 34th Street, New York NY 10120
Tel: 212 720 3700
Fax: 212 720 4397
Website: www.venator.com

Ford Motor Company
Dennis E Ross, Vice-President & General Counsel
World Headquarters, One American Road, Dearborn MI 48126-2798
Tel: 313 322 7453
Fax: 313 248 7450
Email: dross9@ford.com
Website: www.ford.com

Fortune Brands Inc
Mark Roche, General Counsel
300 Tower Parkway, Lincolnshire IL 60069-3640
Tel: 847 484 4400
Fax: 847 478 0073
Email: generalinquiries@fortunebrands.com
Website: www.fortunebrands.com

Foster Wheeler Corporation
Thomas R O'Brien, Senior Vice President, Corporate Affairs & General Counsel
Perryville Corporate Park, PO Box 4000, Clinton NJ 08809-4000
Tel: 908 730 4000
Fax: 908 730 5300
Website: www.fwc.com

FPL Group
Dennis P Coyle, General Counsel
700 Universe Boulevard, PO Box 14000, Juno Beach FL 33408-0420
Tel: 561 694 4000
Fax: 561 694 4620
Email: dennis_coyle@fpl.com
Website: www.fplgroup.com

Freddie Mac
Maud Mater, Executive Vice President, General Counsel & Secretary
8200 Jones Branch Drive, McLean VA 22102
Tel: 703 903 2800
Fax: 703 903 2544
Website: www.freddiemac.com

Gannett Co Inc
Thomas L Chapple, Senior Vice President, General Counsel & Secretary
7950 Jones Branch Drive, McLean VA 22107
Tel: 703 854 6000
Fax: 703 854 2031
Email: tchapple@gci1.gannett.com;tchapple@gcil.gannett.com
Website: www.gannett.com

The Gap Inc
Lauri M Shanahan, Senior Vice President & General Counsel
2 Folsom Street, San Francisco CA 94105
Tel: 650 952 4400
Fax: 650 874 7828
Website: www.gap.com

Gateway Inc
Javade Chaudhri, Senior Vice President & General Counsel
14303 Gateway Place, Poway CA 92064
Tel: 858 848 3401
Fax: 858 848 3402
Website: www.gateway.com

General Dynamics Corporation
David A Savner, Senior Vice President & General Counsel
3190 Fairview Park Drive, Falls Church VA 22042-4523
Tel: 703 876 3010
Fax: 703 876 3554
Website: www.gendyn.com

General Electric Company
Benjamin W Heineman Jr, Senior Vice President, General Counsel & Secretary
3135 Easton Turnpike, Fairfield CT 06431
Tel: 203 373 2492
Fax: 203 373 3922
Website: www.ge.com

General Mills Inc
Siri S Marshall, Senior Vice President, Corporate Affairs, General Counsel & Secretary
PO Box 1113, Minneapolis, MN 55440, 1 General Mills Boulevard, Minneapolis MN 55426
Tel: 763 764 7230
Fax: 763 764 3302
Website: www.generalmills.com

General Motors Corporation
Thomas A Gottschalk, Executive Vice President, Public Policy and Law & General Counsel
300 Renaissance Center, 428-C25 D-81, Detroit MI 48265-3000
Tel: 313 667 3406
Fax: 313 667 3188
Email: t.gottschalk@gm.com
Website: www.gm.com

Genuine Parts Company (GPC)
Scott Smith, Vice President & Corporate Counsel
2999 Circle 75 Parkway, Atlanta GA 30339-3073
Tel: 770 953 1700
Fax: 770 956 2211
Email: webmaster@genpt.com
Website: www.genpt.com

Georgia-Pacific Corporation
James F Kelley, Executive Vice President & General Counsel
133 Peachtree Street North East, PO Box 105605, Atlanta GA 30303-1847
Tel: 404 652 4000
Fax: 404 584 1470
Website: www.gp.com

Gevity HR Inc
Gregory M Nichols, General Counsel
600 301 Boulevard West, Suite 202, Bradenton FL 34205
Tel: 941 748 4540
Fax: 941 741 4333
Website: www.gevityhr.com

The Gillette Company
Richard K Willard, Senior Vice President, Legal & General Counsel
Legal Department, Prudential Tower Building, 48th Floor, Boston MA 02199
Tel: 617 421 7606
Fax: 617 421 7874
Email: richard_willard@gillette.com
Website: www.gillette.com

Golden West Financial Corp
Michael Roster, General Counsel
1901 Harrison Street, Oakland CA 94612-3588
Tel: 510 446 3420
Fax: 510 446 4259

Goldman Sachs Group Inc
Gregory K Palm, Executive Vice President & General Counsel
Law Department, One New York Plaza, 37th Floor, New York NY 10004
Email: gregory.palm@gs.com
Fax: 212 482 3966
Website: www.gs.com

Goodrich Corporation
Terrence G Linnert Esq, Senior Vice President, Human Resources and Administration, General Counsel & Secretary
Four Coliseum Centre, 2730 West Tyvola Street, Charlotte NC 28217-4578
Tel: 704 423 7000
Fax: 704 423 7100
Website: www.goodrich.com

The Goodyear Tire & Rubber Company
C Thomas Harvie, Senior Vice President, General Counsel & Secretary
1144 East Market Street, Akron OH 44316-0001
Tel: 330 796 2408
Fax: 330 796 7891
Email: tom_harvie@goodyear.com
Website: www.goodyear.com

Graybar Electric Company Inc
Thomas F Dowd, Vice President, General Counsel & Secretary
34 North Meramec Avenue, St Louis MO 63105
Tel: 314 512 9200
Fax: 314 512 9453
Website: www.graybar.com

Group 1 Automotive Inc
Beth Sibley, Manager, Legal Services
950 Echo Lane, Suite 100, Houston TX 77024
Tel: 713 647 5763
Fax: 713 647 5868
Email: bsibley@Group1Auto.com
Website: www.group1auto.com

Guardian Life Insurance Company of America
John Peluso, Vice President & General Counsel
7 Hanover Square, New York NY 10004-2616
Tel: 212 598 8000
Fax: 212 919 2170
Website: www.glic.com

Harley-Davidson Inc
Gail A Lione, Vice President,
General Counsel & Secretary
3700 West Juneau Avenue, Milwaukee
WI 53201-0653
Tel: 414 342 4680
Fax: 414 343 4990
Email: gail_lione@harley-davidson.com
Website: www.harley-davidson.com

Harrah's Entertainment
Stephen H Brammell, Senior Vice President
& General Counsel
PO Box 98905, Las Vegas NV 89193
Tel: 702 407 6000
Fax: 702 579 6418
Website: www.harrahs.com

Hartford Life
Christine Hayer Repasy, Senior Vice President
& General Counsel
200 Hopemeadow Street, Simsbury CT 06089
Tel: 860 843 3125
Fax: 860 843 8665
Website: www.thehartford.com

HCA Inc
Robert A Waterman, Senior Vice President
& General Counsel
1 Park Plaza, Nashville TN 37203
Tel: 615 344 9551
Fax: 615 344 1531
Email: bob.waterman@columbia.net
Website: www.hcahealthcare.com

Health Net Inc
B Curtis Westen, General Counsel
21600 Oxnard Street, Woodland Hills CA 91367
Tel: 818 676 6000
Fax: 818 676 8591
Website: www.health.net

HEALTHSOUTH Corporation
William W Horton, Executive Vice President
& Corporate Counsel
1 HealthSouth Parkway, Birmingham AL 35243
Tel: 205 967 7116
Fax: 205 969 4719
Website: www.healthsouth.com

Hershey Foods Corporation
Burton H Snyder, Senior Vice President
International, General Counsel & Secretary
100 Crystal A Drive, PO Box 810, Hershey
PA 17033-0810
Tel: 717 534 7912
Fax: 717 534 7156
Website: www.hersheys.com

Hewlett-Packard Company
Ann O Baskins, Senior Vice President,
General Counsel & Secretary
3000 Hanover Street, Mail Stop 20BQ, Palo Alto
CA 94304-1112
Tel: 650 857 1501
Fax: 650 857 5518
Website: www.hp.com

Hilton Hotels Corporation
Madeleine Kleiner, Executive Vice President
& General Counsel
9336 Civic Center Drive, Beverly Hills CA 90210
Tel: 310 278 4321
Fax: 310 205 7678
Website: www.hilton.com

HJ Heinz Company
Laura Stein, General Counsel
& Senior Vice President
600 Grant Street, Pittsburgh PA 15219-2857
Tel: 412 456 5700
Fax: 412 456 5795
Email: laura.stein@hjheinz.com
Website: www.heinz.com

The Home Depot Inc
Frank L Fernandez, Executive Vice President,
Secretary & General Counsel
2455 Paces Ferry Road North West, Atlanta GA
30339-4024
Tel: 770 433 8211
Fax: 770 384 5552
Website: www.homedepot.com

Honeywell International Inc
Peter M Kreindler, General Counsel
101 Columbia Road, Morristown, NJ 07960, PO Box
2245, Morristown NJ 07962-2245
Tel: 973 455 5513
Fax: 973 455 4217
Email: peter.kreindler@honeywell.com
Website: www.honeywell.com

Hormel Foods Corporation
Mahlon C Schneider, Senior Vice President,
External Affairs & General Counsel
1 Hormel Place, Austin MN 55912-3680
Tel: 507 437 5611
Fax: 507 437 5489
Website: www.hormel.com

Host Marriott Corporation
Elizabeth Abdoo, Vice President
& General Counsel
10400 Fernwood Road, Bethesda MD 20817
Tel: 301 380 9000
Fax: 301 380 8413
Website: www.hostmarriott.com

Household International
Kenneth Robin, Executive Vice President
& General Counsel
2700 Sanders Road, Prospect Heights IL 60070
Tel: 847 564 5000
Fax: 847 205 7452
Website: www.household.com

Humana Inc
Art Hipwell, Senior Vice President
& General Counsel
The Humana Buiding, 500 West Main Street,
Louisville KY 40202-1438
Tel: 502 580 1000
Fax: 502 580 4188
Website: www.humana.com

Idacorp Inc
Robert W Stahman, General Counsel
1221 West Idaho Street, Boise ID 83702-5627
Tel: 208 388 2200
Fax: 208 388 6955
Website: www.idacorpinc.com

IKON Office Solutions, Inc.
Don H Liu, Senior Vice President,
General Counsel & Secretary
70 Valley Stream Parkway, Malvern PA 19355-0989
Tel: 610 296 8000
Fax: 610 408 7264
Website: www.ikon.com

Illinois Tool Works Inc
Stewart S Hudnut, Senior Vice President,
General Counsel & Secretary
Legal Department, 3600 West Lake Avenue,
Glenview IL 60025
Tel: 847 657 4074
Fax: 847 657 4392
Email: shudnut@itw.com
Website: www.itw.com

Ingram Micro Inc
James E Anderson Jr, Senior Vice President,
Secretary & General Counsel
1600 East St Andrew Place, Santa Ana CA 92705
Tel: 714 566 1000
Fax: 714 566 7900
Website: www.ingrammicro.com/corp

Intel Corporation
F Thomas Dunlap, Vice President, Secretary
& General Counsel
2200 Mission College Boulevard, Santa Clara
CA 95052-8119
Tel: 408 765 8080
Fax: 408 765 1859
Email: tom.dunlap@intel.com
Website: www.intel.com

International Business Machines Corporation (IBM)
Lawrence R Ricciardi, Senior Vice President
& General Counsel
New Orchard Road, Armonk NY 10504
Tel: 914 499 1900
Fax: 914 499 6252
Email: lrr@us.ibm.com
Website: www.ibm.com

International Paper Company
James P Melican, Executive Vice President,
Legal & External Affairs
International Paper Plaza, 400 Atlantic Street,
Stamford CT 06921
Tel: 203 541 8000
Fax: 203 541 8200
Website: www.internationalpaper.com

Interpublic Group of Companies Inc
Nicholas Camera, Senior Vice President,
General Counsel & Secretary
1271 Avenue of the Americas, New York
NY 10020-1449
Tel: 212 399 8000
Fax: 212 399 8280
Email: ncamera@interpublic.com
Website: www.interpublic.com

Interstate Bakeries Corporation
Kent B Magill, Vice President,
General Counsel& Secretary
12 East Armour Boulevard, Kansas City
MO 64111-1202
Tel: 816 502 4000
Fax: 816 502 4126
Website: www.irin.com/ibc

ITT Industries Inc
Vincent Maffeo, Senior Vice President
& General Counsel
4 West Red Oak Lane, White Plains NY 10604
Tel: 914 641 2000
Fax: 914 696 2950
Website: www.ittind.com

Jabil Circuit
Robert L Paver, General Counsel & Secretary
10560 Ninth Street North, St Petersburg FL 33716
Tel: 727 577 9749
Fax: 727 579 8529
Website: www.jabil.com

FORTUNE 500

Jacobs Engineering Group Inc
William C Markley III, Vice President, General Counsel & Secretary
PO Box 7084, Pasadena, CA 91109-7084, 1111 South Arroyo Parkway, Pasadena CA 91105-3063
Tel: 626 578 3500
Fax: 626 578 6916
Website: www.jacobs.com

JC Penney Company Inc
Charles R Lotter, Executive Vice President, Secretary & General Counsel
6501 Legacy Drive, Plano TX 75024-3698
Tel: 972 431 1000
Fax: 972 431 1362
Website: www.jcpenney.net

JDS Uniphase Corporation
Michael C Phillips, Senior Vice-President, Business Development & General Counsel
1768 Automation Parkway, San José CA 95931
Tel: 408 546 5000
Fax: 408 954 0813
Website: www.jdsuniphase.com

Jefferson-Pilot Corporation
John D Hopkins, Executive Vice President & General Counsel
100 North Greene Street, Greensboro NC 27401
Tel: 336 691 3308
Fax: 336 691 3639
Email: john.hopkins@Jpfinancial.com
Website: www.jpfinancial.com

John Hancock Financial Services Inc
Wayne A Budd, Executive Vice President & General Counsel
John Hancock Place, PO Box 111, Boston MA 02117-0011
Tel: 617 572 6000
Fax: 617 572 9799
Website: www.johnhancock.com

Johnson & Johnson
Roger Fine, Corporate Vice President & General Counsel
1 Johnson & Johnson Plaza, New Brunswick NJ 08933-0001
Tel: 732 524 2440
Fax: 732 524 3039
Website: www.jnj.com

Jones Apparel Group Inc
Ira M Dansky, Secretary & General Counsel
1411 Broadway, New York NY 10018
Tel: 212 642 3860
Fax: 212 536 9584
Website: www.jny.com

JP Morgan Chase
William H McDavid, General Counsel
270 Park Avenue, 8th Floor, New York NY 10017
Tel: 212 270 2611
Fax: 212 270 4288
Email: william.mcdavid@chase.com
Website: www.jpmorganchase.com

KB Home
Barton P Pachino, Senior Vice President & General Counsel
10990 Wilshire Boulevard, Los Angeles CA 90024-4341
Tel: 310 231 4000
Fax: 310 231 4222
Website: www.kbhome.com

Kellogg Company
Janet Langford Kelly, Executive Vice President, Corporate Development and Administration, General Counsel & Secretary
1 Kellogg Square, PO Box 3599, Battle Creek MI 49016-3599
Tel: 269 961 2181
Fax: 269 961 6598
Email: janet.kelly@kellogg.com
Website: www.kelloggs.com

Kelly Services Inc
George M Reardon, Senior Vice President, General Counsel & Secretary
999 West Big Beaver Road, Troy MI 48084-4782
Tel: 248 362 4444
Fax: 248 813 3990
Email: kelly_first@kellyservices.com
Website: www.kellyservices.com

Kerr-McGee Corporation
Gregory F Pilcher, Senior Vice President, General Counsel & Corporate Secretary
Kerr-McGee Center, 123 Robert S Kerr Avenue, Oklahoma City OK 73102
Tel: 405 270 1313
Fax: 405 270 3029
Website: www.kerr-mcgee.com

KeyCorp
Thomas C Stevens, Vice Chairman, Chief Administrative Officer & Secretary
127 Public Square, Cleveland OH 44114-1306
Tel: 216 689 6300
Fax: 216 689 7827
Email: thomas_stevens@keybank.com
Website: www.keybank.com

KeySpan Corporation
Steven L Zelkowitz, General Counsel
One Metrotech Center, Brooklyn NY 11201-3851
Tel: 718 403 2000
Fax: 718 488 1782
Website: www.keyspanenergy.com

Kimberly-Clark Corporation
O George Everbach, Senior Vice President - Law and Government Affairs
351 Phelps Drive, Irving TX 75038
Tel: 972 281 1200
Fax: 972 281 1490
Website: www.kimberly-clark.com

Kindred Healthcare Inc
M Suzanne Riedman, Senior Vice President & General Counsel
Corporate Headquarters, 680 South Fourth Street, Louisville KY 40202-2412
Tel: 502 596 7300
Fax: 502 596 4075
Website: www.kindredhealthcare.com/

Kmart Corporation
Janet G Kelley, Executive Vice President & General Counsel
3100 West Big Beaver Road, Troy MI 48084-3004
Tel: 248 643 1000
Fax: 248 463 5636
Website: www.kmart.com/www.bluelight.com

The Kroger Company
Paul W Heldman, Senior Vice President, General Counsel & Secretary
1014 Vine Street, Cincinnati OH 45202-1100
Tel: 513 762 4000
Fax: 513 762 4935
Email: pheldman@kroger.com
Website: www.kroger.com

Kohl's Corporation
Sigrid E Dynek, Vice President & General Counsel
N56 W17000 Ridgewood Drive, Menomonee Falls WI 53051-5660
Tel: 262 703 7000
Fax: 262 703 6143
Website: www.kohls.com

Lear Corporation
Joseph McCarthy, Secretary & General Counsel
21557 Telegraph Road, Southfield MI 48086
Tel: 248 746 1500
Fax: 248 447 1722
Website: www.lear.com

Leggett & Platt Incorporated
Ernest C Jett Jr, Vice President, General Counsel & Secretary
No 1 Leggett Road, Carthage MO 64836-0757
Tel: 417 358 8131
Fax: 417 358 8449
Website: www.leggett.com

Lehman Brothers Holdings Inc
Thomas A Russo, Vice Chairman & Chief Legal Officer
399 Park Avenue, 15th floor, New York NY 10022
Tel: 212 526 0858
Fax: 201 524 4349
Website: www.lehman.com

Lennar Corporation
David B McCain, Vice President, General Counsel and Secretary
700 North West 107th Avenue, Miami FL 33172-3154
Tel: 305 229 6400
Fax: 305 229 6453
Website: www.lennar.com

Lennox International Inc
Carl E Edwards Jr, Executive Vice President, General Counsel & Secretary
2140 Lake Park Boulevard, Richardson TX 75080
Tel: 972 497 5000
Fax: 972 497 5299
Website: www.lennoxinternational.com

Levi Strauss & Co
Albert Moreno, Senior Vice President & General Counsel
1155 Battery Street, San Francisco CA 94111
Tel: 415 501 6000
Fax: 415 501 3939
Website: www.levistrauss.com

Lexmark International Inc
Vincent J Cole, Vice President, General Counsel & Secretary
1 Lexmark Centre Drive, 740 West New Circle Road, Lexington KY 40550
Tel: 859 232 2000
Fax: 859 232 2403
Website: www.lexmark.com

Liberty Mutual Insurance Group
Christopher C Mansfield, Senior Vice President and General Counsel
175 Berkeley Street, Boston MA 02117
Tel: 617 357 9500
Fax: 617 350 7648
Website: www.libertymutual.com

Limited Brands
Samuel P Fried, Senior Vice President, General Counsel & Secretary
3 Limited Parkway, PO Box 16000, Columbus OH 43230
Tel: 614 415 7000
Fax: 614 415 7440
Website: www.limited.com

FORTUNE 500

Lincoln National Corporation
John Steinkamp, General Counsel
200 East Berry Street, Fort Wayne IN 46802-2706
Tel: 219 455 2000
Fax: 219 455 2301
Website: www.lfg.com

Liz Claiborne Inc
Roberta S Karp, Vice President & General Counsel
1441 Broadway, New York NY 10018
Tel: 212 354 4900
Fax: 212 626 3416
Website: www.lizclaiborne.com

Lockheed Martin Corporation
Frank H Menaker, Senior Vice President & General Counsel
6801 Rockledge Drive, Bethesda MD 20817-1877
Tel: 301 897 6000
Fax: 301 897 6791
Website: www.lockheedmartin.com

Loews Corporation
Gary Garson, Senior Vice President, General Counsel & Corporate Secretary
667 Madison Avenue, New York NY 10021-8087
Tel: 212 545 2000
Fax: 212 935 6801
Website: www.loews.com

Longs Drug Stores Corporation
Orlo D Jones, Senior Vice President, Properties, General Counsel & Secretary
141 North Civic Drive, PO Box 5222, Walnut Creek CA 94596-1222
Tel: 925 937 1170
Fax: 925 210 6886
Website: www.longs.com

Lowe's Companies Inc
Stephen Hellrung, Senior Vice President, General Counsel & Secretary
1605 Curtis Bridge Road, North Wilkesboro NC 28697
Tel: 336 658 4000
Fax: 336 658 5446
Website: www.lowes.com

Lucent Technologies Inc
Richard J Rawson, Senior Vice President, General Counsel & Secretary
Corporate Headquarters, 600 Mountain Avenue, Murray Hill NJ 07974 0636
Tel: 908 528 8503
Fax: 908 508 2576
Email: execoffice@lucent.com
Website: www.lucent.com

Lyondell Chemical Company
Kerry Galvin, Senior Vice President, General Counsel & Secretary
1221 McKinney Street, Suite 700, Houston TX 77010
Tel: 713 652 7200
Fax: 713 309 2074
Website: www.lyondell.com

Manpower Inc
Mark Toth, Vice President & Chief Legal Officer
5301 North Ironwood Road, Milwaukee WI 53217
Tel: 414 961 1000
Fax: 414 961 7081
Website: www.manpower.com

Marathon Oil Company
Dan D Sandman, Vice Chief Chair & Legal Administrative Officer
600 Grant Street, Pittsburgh PA 15219-4776
Tel: 412 433 1121
Fax: 412 433 4818
Website: www.marathon.com

Marriott International Inc
Joseph Ryan, Executive Vice President & General Counsel
Law Department, 1 Marriott Drive, Washington, DC DC 20058
Tel: 301 380 9555
Fax: 301 380 6727
Email: joe.ryan@marriott.com

Marsh & McLennan Companies Inc (MMC)
William L Rosoff, Senior Vice President & General Counsel
Legal Department, 1166 Avenue of the Americas, New York NY 10036-2774
Tel: 212 345 5000
Fax: 212 345 5627
Website: www.mmc.com

Masco Corporation
John R Leekley, Senior Vice President & General Counsel
21001 Van Born Road, Taylor MI 48180-1340
Tel: 313 729 6340
Fax: 313 792 4107
Email: john_leekley@mascohq.com
Website: www.masco.com

Massachusetts Mutual Life Insurance
Lawrence V Burkett Jr, Executive Vice President & General Counsel
1295 State Street, Springfield MA 01111-0002
Tel: 413 744 8411
Fax: 413 744 6005
Website: www.massmutual.com

Mattel Inc
Robert Normile, Senior Vice President, General Counsel & Secretary
333 Continental Boulevard, El Segundo CA 90245-5012
Tel: 310 252 2000
Fax: 310 252 2180
Website: www.mattel.com

Maxtor Corporation
Glenn H Stevens, Senior Vice President, General Counsel & Secretary
500 McCarthy Boulevard, Milpitas CA 95035
Tel: 408 894 5000
Fax: 408 952 3600
Website: www.maxtor.com

May Department Stores Company
Alan Charlson, Senior Vice President & General Counsel
611 Olive Street, St Louis MO 63101
Tel: 314 342 6300
Fax: 314 342 3066
Website: www.maycompany.com

Maytag Corporation
Roger K Scholten, Senior Vice President & General Counsel
403 West 4th Street North, PO Box 39, Newton IA 50208-0039
Tel: 641 792 7000
Fax: 641 787 8376
Website: www.maytagcorp.com

MBNA America Bank NA
Louis J Freeh, Senior Vice Chairman & General Counsel
1100 North King Street, Wilmington DE 19884
Tel: 302 453 9930
Fax: 302 432 1494
Website: www.mbnainternational.com

McDonald's Corporation
Gloria Santona, General Counsel
COB Building, Oak Brook IL 60523
Tel: 630 623 3000
Fax: 630 623 8005
Website: www.mcdonalds.com

McGraw-Hill Companies Inc
Kenneth M Vittor, Executive Vice President & General Counsel
1221 Avenue of the Americas, New York NY 10020-1095
Tel: 212 512 2564
Fax: 212 512 4827
Email: kvittor@mcgraw-hill.com
Website: www.mcgraw-hill.com

McKesson Corporation
Ivan D Meyerson, Senior Vice President, General Counsel & Secretary
Corporate Headquarters, One Post Street, San Francisco CA 94104
Tel: 415 983 8300
Fax: 415 983 7160
Website: www.mckesson.com

MeadWestvaco Corporation
Wendell L Willkie, Senior Vice President & General Counsel
One High Ridge Park, Stamford CT 06905-1322
Tel: 203 461 7400
Website: www.meadwestvaco.com

Medtronic
David Jones Scott, Senior Vice President, General Counsel & Secretary
710 Medtronic Parkway North East, Minneapolis MN 55432-5604
Tel: 612 514 4000
Fax: 612 574 4879
Website: www.medtronic.com

Mellon Financial Corporation
Michael Bleier, General Counsel
One Mellon Center, 500 Grant Street, Pittsburgh PA 15258-0001
Tel: 412 234 5000
Fax: 412 234 6283
Website: www.mellon.com

Merck & Co Inc
Kenneth C Frazier, Senior Vice-President & General Counsel
1 Merck Drive, Mail Code: WS2A-57, PO Box 100, Whitehouse Station NJ 08889-0100
Tel: 908 423 1000
Fax: 908 735 1253
Website: www.merck.com

Merrill Lynch & Co Inc
Rosemary T Berkery, Executive Vice President & General Counsel
Global Headquarters, 4 World Financial Center, 250 Vesey Street, New York NY 10281-1312
Tel: 212 449 1000
Fax: 212 236 4384
Email: iweb@exchange.ml.com
Website: www.ml.com

Metropolitan Life Insurance Company (MetLife)
Gary A Beller, Senior Executive, Vice President & General Counsel
One Madison Avenue, New York NY 10010-3690
Tel: 212 578 5899
Fax: 212 578 3916
Email: info@metlife.com
Website: www.metlife.com

FORTUNE 500

MGM MIRAGE
Gary Jacobs, Executive Vice President, General Counsel & Secretary
3600 Las Vegas Boulevard South, Las Vegas NV 89109
Tel: 702 693 7129
Fax: 702 693 7628
Website: www.mgmmirage.com

Micron Technology Inc
Roderic W Lewis, Vice President of Legal Affairs; General Counsel & Corporate Secretary
8000 South Federal Way, Mail Stop 507, Boise ID 83707-0006
Tel: 650 638 5846
Fax: 208 368 4435
Website: www.micron.com

Microsoft Corporation
Bradford L Smith, Senior Vice President & General Counsel
One Microsoft Way, Redmond WA 98052-6399
Tel: 425 882 8080
Fax: 425 936 7329
Website: www.microsoft.com

Mirant Corporation
Douglas L Miller, Senior Vice President & General Counsel
Corporate Headquarters, 1155 Perimeter Center West, Atlanta GA 30338
Tel: 678 579 7000
Fax: 678 579 5754
Email: information@mirant.com
Website: www.mirant.com

Mohawk Industries Inc
Salvatore J Perillo, General Counsel
160 South Industrial Boulevard, Calhoun GA 30701
Tel: 706 629 7721
Fax: 706 602 0278
Website: www.mohawkind.com

Monsanto Company
Charles W Burson, Executive Vice President, General Counsel & Secretary
800 North Lindbergh Boulevard, St Louis MO 63167-0001
Tel: 314 694 8418
Fax: 341 694 6399
Email: charles.w.burson@monsanto.com
Website: www.monsanto.com

Morgan Stanley
Donald G Kempf Jr, Executive Vice President, Chief Legal Officer & Secretary
1585 Broadway, 39th Floor, New York NY 10036
Tel: 212 761 6321
Fax: 212 761 0331
Website: www.morganstanley.com

Motorola Inc
A Peter Lawson, Executive Vice President, General Counsel & Secretary
1303 East Algonquin Road, Schaumburg IL 60196-1079
Tel: 847 576 5012
Fax: 847 576 6301
Website: www.motorola.com

Murphy Oil Corporation
Steven A Cosse, Senior Vice President & General Counsel
200 Peach Street, PO Box 7000, El Dorado AR 71731-7000
Tel: 870 862 6411
Fax: 870 864 6373
Email: murphyoil@murphyoilcorp.com
Website: www.murphyoilcorp.com

The Mutual of Omaha Companies
Thomas J McCusker, Executive Vice President & General Counsel
Mutual of Omaha Plaza, Omaha NE 68175
Tel: 402 351 3003
Fax: 402 351 2000
Website: www.mutualofomaha.com

Nash Finch Company
Kathleen McDermott, Senior Vice President & General Counsel
7600 France AvenueSouth, Edina MN 55435
Tel: 952 832 0534
Fax: 952 844 1234
Website: www.nashfinch.com

National City Corporation
David L Zoeller, Executive Vice President, General Counsel & Secretary
1900 East 9th Street, Cleveland OH 44114-3484
Tel: 216 575 2000
Fax: 216 575 2353
Website: www.national-city.com

Nationwide Financial Services Inc
Patricia R Hatler, Senior Vice President, General Counsel & Corporate Secretary
One Nationwide Plaza, Columbus OH 43215-2220
Tel: 614 249 7111
Fax: 614 249 7705
Website: www.nationwidefinancial.com

Navistar International Corporation
Robert A Boardman, Senior Vice President & General Counsel
4201 Windfield Road, Warenville IL 60555
Tel: 630 753 5000
Fax: 630 753 5217
Website: www.navistar.com

NCR Corporation
Jon Hoak, General Counsel
1700 South Patterson Boulevard, Dayton OH 45479
Tel: 937 445 5000
Fax: 937 445 1682
Website: www.ncr.com

New York Life Insurance Company
Sheila K Davidson, Senior Vice President & General Counsel
51 Madison Avenue, New York NY 10010-1603
Tel: 212 576 7000
Fax: 212 576 8145
Website: www.newyorklife.com

New York Times Company
Solomon Watson, Senior Vice President & General Counsel
229 West 43rd Street, New York NY 10036-3959
Tel: 212 556 1234
Fax: 212 556 4011
Website: www.nytco.com

Newell Rubbermaid Inc
Dale L Matschullat, Vice President & General Counsel
6833 Stalter Drive, Suite 101, Rockford IL 61108
Tel: 815 381 8110
Fax: 815 381 8160
Website: www.newellco.com

Nextel Communications Inc
Leonard J Kennedy, Senior Vice President & General Counsel
2001 Edmund Halley Drive, Reston VA 20191
Tel: 703 433 4000
Fax: 703 433 4343
Website: www.nextel.com

Nike Inc
Lindsay D Stewart, Vice President, Law and Corporate Affairs & Assistant Secretary
1 Bowerman Drive, Beaverton OR 97005-6453
Tel: 503 671 6453
Fax: 503 671 6300
Website: www.nike.com

NiSource Inc
Peter V Fazio Jr, Executive Vice President & General Counsel
801 East 86th Avenue, Merrillville IN 46410-6272
Tel: 219 853 5200
Fax: 219 647 5589
Website: www.nisource.com

Nordstrom Inc
David L Mackie, Vice President, Real Estate & Corporate Secretary
17000 7th Avenue, Suite 1000, Seattle WA 98101-1742
Tel: 206 303 4410
Fax: 206 303 4419
Email: dave.mackie@nordstrom.com
Website: www.nordstrom.com

Norfolk Southern Corporation
Henry Light, Vice President, Law
Three Commercial Place, Box 227, Norfolk VA 23510
Tel: 757 629 2600
Fax: 757 629 2344
Website: www.nscorp.com

Northeast Utilities
Gregory B Butler, Vice President, General Counsel & Secretary
107 Seldon Street, Berlin, CT 06037-1616, PO Box 270, Hartford CT 06037
Tel: 860 665 5000
Fax: 860 665 5504
Website: www.nu.com

Northern Trust Corporation
Kelly R Welsh, Executive Vice President & General Counsel
50 South LaSalle Street, Chicago IL 60675
Tel: 312 630 6000
Fax: 312 630 1596
Website: www.ntrs.com

Northrop Grumman Corporation
W Burks Terry, Vice President & General Counsel
1840 Century Park East, Los Angeles CA 90067-2199
Tel: 310 553 6262
Fax: 310 553 2076
Website: www.northgrum.com

Northwest Airlines Inc
Michael Miller, Vice President Law & Secretary
2700 Lone Oak Parkway, Eagan MN 55121
Tel: 612 726 2111
Fax: 612 727 7795
Website: www.nwa.com

Northwestern Corp
Alan D Dietrich, Vice President, Legal Administration & General Counsel
Corporate Headquarters, 125 South Dakota Avenue, Sioux Falls SD 57104-6403
Tel: 605 978 2908
Fax: 605 978 2910
Email: nor.mail@northwestern.com
Website: www.northwestern.com

FORTUNE 500

Northwestern Mutual
Robert J Berdan, Vice President,
General Counsel & Secretary
720 East Wisconsin Avenue, Milwaukee
WI 53202-4797
Tel: 414 271 1444
Fax: 414 665 5792
Website: www.northwesternmutual.com

NStar
Douglas S Horan, Senior Vice President; Strategy,
Law & Policy, Secretary/Clerk & General Counsel
800 Boylston Street, Boston MA 02199-2599
Tel: 617 424 2000
Fax: 617 424 4032
Website: www.nstaronline.com

NTL Incorporated
Richard J Lubasch, General Counsel
110 East 59th Street, 26th Floor, New York NY 10022
Tel: 212 906 8440
Fax: 212 752 1157
Website: www.ntl.com

Nucor Corporation
Terry Lisenby, Executive Vice President, Chief
Financial Officer & Treasurer
2100 Rexford Road, Charlotte NC 28211-3484
Tel: 704 366 7000
Fax: 704 362 4208
Website: www.nucor.com

Office Depot Inc
David C Fannin, Executive Vice President
& General Counsel
2200 Old Germantown Road, Delray Beach
FL 33445
Tel: 407 278 4800
Fax: 561 438 4001
Website: www.officedepot.com

OfficeMax Inc
Ross Pollock, Executive Vice President,
General Counsel & Secretary
3605 Warrensville Centre Road, Shaker Heights
OH 44122-5203
Tel: 216 921 6900
Fax: 216 491 4040
Website: www.officemax.com

OGE Energy Corporation
Peter D Clark, General Counsel
PO Box 321, Oklahoma City, OK 73101-0321, 321
North Harvey, Oklahoma City OK 73101
Tel: 405 553 3000
Fax: 405 553 3290
Email: Webmaster@oge.com
Website: www.oge.com

Omnicom Group
Barry J Wagner, Secretary & General Counsel
437 Madison Avenue, New York NY 10022-7001
Tel: 212 415 3700
Fax: 212 415 3470
Email: barry_wagner@omnicomny.com
Website: www.omnicomgroup.com

ONEOK Inc
John A Gaberino Jr, General Counsel
100 West Fifth Street, PO Box 871, Tulsa OK 74103
Tel: 918 588 7906
Fax: 918 588 7971
Email: jgaberino@oneok.com
Website: www.oneok.com

Oracle Corporation
Daniel Cooperman, Senior Vice President,
General Counsel
and Corporate Secretary
500 Oracle Parkway, Mail Stop 5op7, Redwood
Shores CA 94062
Tel: 650 506 5500
Fax: 650 633 1813
Email: daniel.cooperman@oracle.com
Website: www.oracle.com

Owens & Minor Inc
Drew St J Carneal, Senior vice President
& Corporate General Counsel
4800 Cox Road, Glen Allen VA 23060-6292
Tel: 804 747 9794
Fax: 804 270 7281
Website: www.owens-minor.com

Owens Corning
Maura J Abeln-Smith, Senior Vice President &
General Counsel
Toledo World Headquarters, 1 Owens Corning
Parkway, 3rd Floor, Toledo OH 43659
Tel: 419 248 8000
Fax: 419 248 5337
Website: www.owenscorning.com

Owens-Illinois Inc
Thomas L Young, Executive Vice President,
Administration & General Counsel
1 SeaGate, Toledo OH 43666
Tel: 419 247 5000
Fax: 419 247 2226
Website: www.o-i.com

Oxford Health Plans Inc
Daniel N Gregoire, Executive Vice President
& General Counsel
48 Munro Turnpike, Trumbull CT 06611
Tel: 203 459 6000
Fax: 203 459 6464
Website: www.oxhp.com

PACCAR Inc
G Glen Morie, Vice President & General Counsel
PACCAR Building, 777 106th Avenue North East,
PO Box 1518, Bellevue WA 98004
Tel: 425 468 7400
Fax: 425 828 8882
Website: www.paccar.com

Pacific Life Insurance Company
David R Carmichael, Senior Vice President
& General Counsel
700 Newport Center Drive, Newport Beach
CA 92660-6307
Tel: 949 219 3011
Fax: 949 219 3706
Email: dcarmichael@pacificlife.com
Website: www.pacificlife.com

PacifiCare Health Systems Inc
Joseph Konowiecki, Senior Executive Vice
President & General Counsel
5995 Plaza Drive, Mailstop CY20-552, Cyprus
CA 90630
Tel: 714 825 5200
Website: www.pacificare.com

Park Place Entertainment Corporation
Bernard DeLury, Senior Vice President
& Chief Legal Officer
3930 Howard Hughes Parkway, Las Vegas NV 89109
Tel: 702 699 5000
Fax: 702 699 5202
Website: www.parkplace.com

Parker Hannifin Corporation
Thomas Piroino, Vice President,
General Counsel & Secretary
6035 Parkland Boulevard, Cleveland
OH 44112-1290
Tel: 216 896 3000
Fax: 216 896 4000
Website: www.parker.com

Pathmark Stores Inc
Mark A Strassler, Senior Vice President,
General Counsel & Secretary
200 Milik Street, Carteret NJ 07008
Tel: 732 499 3000
Fax: 732 499 3072
Website: www.pathmark.com

PepsiCo Inc
David R Andrews, Senior Vice President
& General Counsel
700 Anderson Hill Road, Purchase NY 10577-1444
Tel: 914 253 2000
Fax: 914 253 2070
Website: www.pepsico.com

The Pepsi Bottling Group Inc
Pamela McGuire, Senior Vice President,
General Counsel & Secretary
One Pepsi Way, Sommers, New York NY 10589
Tel: 914 767 7982
Fax: 914 767 1161
Email: pamela.mcguire@pepsi.com
Website: www.pbg.com

Performance Food Group Company
Roger L Boeve, Executive Vice President
& Chief Financial Officer
12500 West Creek Parkway, Richmond VA 23238
Tel: 804 484 7700
Fax: 804 484 7701
Website: www.pfgc.com

Peter Kiewit Sons' Inc
Tobin A Schropp, Senior Vice President
& General Counsel
Kiewit Plaza, Omaha NE 68131
Tel: 402 342 2052
Fax: 402 271 2830
Website: www.kiewit.com

Pfizer Inc
Jeffery B Kindler, Senior Vice President
& General Counsel
235 East 42nd Street, New York NY 10017
Tel: 212 573 2323
Fax: 212 573 7851
Website: www.pfizer.com

PG & E Corporation
Bruce R Worthington, Senior Vice President
& General Counsel
One Market Street, Spear Tower, Suite 2400,
San Francisco CA 94105
Tel: 415 267 7133
Fax: 415 267 7257
Email: bruce.worthington@pge-corp.com
Website: www.pgecorp.com

Pharmacia Corporation
Richard Collier, Senior Vice President
& General Counsel
100 Route 206 North, Peapack NJ 07977
Tel: 908 901 8000
Fax: 908 901 7700
Email: webmaster.int@am.pnu.com
Website: www.pnu.com

FORTUNE 500

Phelps Dodge Corporation
S David Colton, Senior Vice President
& General Counsel
One North Central Avenue, Phoenix AZ 85004-3014
Tel: 602 366 8100
Fax: 602 234 8050
Website: www.phelpsdodge.com

Philip Morris Companies Inc
Charles R Wall, Senior Vice President
& General Counsel
120 Park Avenue, New York NY 10017
Tel: 917 663 3302
Fax: 917 663 2167
Website: www.philipmorris.com

Pinnacle West Capital Corporation
Nancy C Loftin, Vice President, Chief Legal
Counsel & Secretary
400 East Van Buren Street, Suite 800, Phoenix
AZ 85004
Tel: 602 379 2500
Fax: 602 250 2430
Website: www.pinnaclewest.com

Pitney Bowes Inc
Sara E Moss, Senior Vice President
& General Counsel
One Elmscroft Road, MSC 6407, Stamford
CT 06926-0700
Tel: 203 356 5000
Fax: 203 351 6835
Website: www.pitneybowes.com

Plains All American Pipeline LP
Tim Moore, Vice President & General Counsel
333 Clay Street, Suite 2900, Houston TX 77002-4648
Tel: 713 646 4100
Fax: 713 646 4147
Website: www.paalp.com

The PNC Financial Services Group Inc
Helen Pudlin, Manager & General Counsel
One PNC Plaza, 249 Fifth Avenue, Pittsburgh
PA 15222-2707
Tel: 412 767 8257
Fax: 412 768 2875
Website: www.pncbank.com

PPG Industries Inc
James Diggs, Senior Vice President
& General Counsel
One PPG Place, Pittsburgh PA 15272-0001
Tel: 412 434 2935
Fax: 412 434 2134
Email: charlier@ppg.com
Website: www.ppg.com

PPL Corporation
Robert J Grey, Senior Vice President,
General Counsel & Secretary
Corporate Headquarters, 2 North 9th Street,
Allentown PA 18101-1179
Tel: 610 774 5587
Fax: 610 774 4455
Email: rjgrey@papl.com
Website: www.pplweb.com

Praxair Inc
David H Chaifetz, Vice President,
General Counsel & Secretary
Legal Department, 39 Old Ridgebury Road,
Danbury CT 06810-5113
Tel: 203 837 2060
Fax: 203 837 2515
Website: www.praxair.com

Premcor Inc
Michael D Gayda , Senior Vice President
& Corporate Counsel
1700 East Putnam Avenue, Suite 500, Old Greenwich
CT 06870
Tel: 203 698 7500
Fax: 203 698 7940
Email: michael.gayda@premcor.com
Website: www.premcor.com

Principal Financial Group Inc
Karen E Shaff, Senior Vice President
& General Counsel
711 High Street, Des Moines IA 50392
Tel: 515 247 5111
Fax: 515 246 5475
Website: www.principal.com

The Procter & Gamble Company (P&G)
James J Johnson, Chief Legal Officer
One Procter & Gamble Plaza, Cincinnati
OH 45202-3393
Tel: 513 983 1100
Fax: 513 983 4381
Website: www.pg.com

Progress Energy
William D Johnson, Executive Vice President
& General Counsel
411 Fayetteville Street, PO Box 1551, Raleigh
NC 27602
Tel: 919 546 6111
Fax: 919 546 3805
Website: www.cplc.com

The Progressive Corporation
Chuck Jarrett, Chief Legal Officer
6300 Wilson Mills Road, Mayfield Village
OH 44143-2182
Tel: 440 461 5000
Fax: 440 603 4420
Website: www.progressive.com

Providian Financial Corporation
Ellen Richey, General Counsel
201 Mission Street, San Francisco CA 94105
Tel: 415 543 0404
Fax: 415 278 6028
Website: www.providian.com

Prudential Insurance Company
John Liftin, Senior Vice President
& General Counsel
751 Broad Street, Newark NJ 07102-3777
Tel: 973 802 6000
Fax: 973 802 3876
Website: www.prudential.com

Public Service Enterprises Group Incorporated (PSEG)
Edwin Selover, Executive Vice President
& General Counsel
80 Park Plaza, Newark NJ 07101
Tel: 973 430 7000
Fax: 973 623 5389
Website: www.pseg.com

Publix Super Markets Inc
John Attaway, General Counsel
PO Box 407, Lakeland FL 33802-0407
Tel: 863 688 1188
Fax: 863 284 5532
Website: www.publix.com

Puget Sound Energy
Stephen A McKeon , Senior Vice President -
Finance and Legal, Chief Financial Officer
411 108th Avenue North East, Bellevue WA 98004
Tel: 425 454 6363
Fax: 425 462 3444
Website: www.pse.com

Pulte Homes Inc
John R Stoller, Senior Vice President,
General Counsel & Secretary
100 Bloomfield Hills Parkway, Suite 200, Bloomfield
Hills MI 48304-2946
Tel: 248 647 2750
Fax: 248 433 4598
Website: www.pulte.com

Quantum Corporation
Shawn D Hall, Vice President & General Counsel
501 Sycomore Drive, Milpitas CA 95035
Tel: 408 894 4000
Fax: 408 894 3218
Website: www.quantum.com

Quest Diagnostics Incorporated
Michael E Prevoznik , Corporate Vice President,
Legal and Compliance & General Counsel
1 Malcolm Avenue, Teterboro NJ 07608
Tel: 201 393 5000
Fax: 201 462 4715
Website: www.questdiagnostics.com

Qwest Communications International Inc
Richard Baer, Senior Vice President
& General Counsel
1801 California Street, 38th Floor, Denver
CO 80202
Website: www.qwest.com

RadioShack Corporation
Mark C Hill, General Counsel
100 Throckmorton Street, Suite 1800, Fort Worth
TX 76102-2819
Tel: 817 415 3700
Fax: 817 415 2647
Website: www.radioshackcorporation.com

Raytheon Company
Neal E Minahan, Senior Vice President
& General Counsel
141 Spring Street, Lexington MA 02421-7860
Tel: 781 862 6600
Fax: 781 860 2172
Email: corpcom@raytheon.com
Website: www.raytheon.com

Regions Financial Corporation
Samuel E Upchurch Jr, Executive Vice President
General Counsel & Secretary
417 North 20th Street, Birmingham AL 35203-3203
Tel: 205 944 1300
Fax: 205 326 7756
Website: www.regionsbank.com

Reliant Resources Inc
Hugh Rice Kelly, Executive Vice President,
General Counsel & Corporate Secretary
1111 Louisiana Street, Houston TX 77002
Tel: 713 497 3000
Fax: 713 207 0215
Website: www.reliant.com

Rite Aid Corporation
Robert Sari, Senior Vice President,
General Counsel & Secretary
30 Hunter Lane, Camp Hill PA 17011
Tel: 717 761 2633
Fax: 717 975 5871
Website: www.riteaid.com

FORTUNE 500

RJ Reynolds Tobacco Holdings Inc
Charles Blixt, Executive Vice President & General Counsel
401 North Main Street, Winston-Salem
NC 27102-2866
Tel: 336 741 5500
Fax: 336 741 4238
Website: www.rjrt.com

Rockwell Automation Corporation
William J Calise, Senior Vice President, General Counsel & Secretary
777 East Wisconsin Avenue, Suite 1400, Milwaukee WI 53202
Tel: 414 212 5355
Fax: 414 212 5357
Email: wjcarlise@corp.rockwell.com
Website: www.rockwell.com

Rohm & Haas Company
Robert Lonergan, Vice President & General Counsel
100 Independence Mall West, Philadelphia PA 19106-2399
Tel: 215 592 3000
Fax: 215 592 3377
Website: www.rohmhaas.com

Roundy's Inc
Darren W Karst, Executive Vice President & Chief Financial Officer
23000 Roundy Drive, Pewaukee WI 53072
Tel: 262 953 7999
Fax: 262 953 6580
Website: www.roundys.com

RR Donnelley & Sons Company
Monica M Fohrman, Senior Vice President, General Counsel & Corporate Secretary
77 West Wacker Drive, Chicago IL 60601-1696
Tel: 312 326 8000
Fax: 312 326 8543
Website: www.rrdonnelley.com

Ryder System Inc
Vicki A O'Meara, Executive Vice President & General Counsel
3600 North West 82nd Avenue, Miami FL 33166-6623
Tel: 305 500 3726
Fax: 305 500 3198
Website: www.ryder.com

SAFECO Corporation
James W Ruddy, General Counsel
SAFECO Plaza, 4333 Brooklyn Avenue North East, Seattle WA 98185-0001
Tel: 206 545 5000
Fax: 206 545 5995
Website: www.safeco.com

Safeway Inc
Robert A Gordon, Senior Vice President & General Counsel
5918 Stoneridge Mall Road, Pleasanton CA 94588-3229
Tel: 925 467 3000
Fax: 925 467 3321
Email: robert.gordon@safeway.com
Website: www.safeway.com

Saks Incorporated
Brian J Martin, Executive Vice President of Law & General Counsel
750 Lakeshore Parkway, Birmingham AL 35211
Tel: 205 940 4000
Fax: 205 940 4987
Website: www.saksincorporated.com

Sanmina-SCI Corporation
Michael Sullivan, Vice President & General Counsel
2700 North 1st Street, San José CA 95134
Tel: 408 964 3500
Fax: 408 964 3636
Email: info@sanmina.com
Website: www.sanmina.com

Sara Lee Corporation
Roderick Palmore, Senior Vice President, General Counsel & Corporate Secretary
3 First National Plaza, Chicago IL 60602
Tel: 312 726 2600
Fax: 312 345 5706
Website: www.saralee.com

SBC Communications Inc
James D Ellis, Senior Executive Vice President & General Counsel
175 East Houston Street, San Antonio TX 78205-2233
Tel: 210 351 3300
Fax: 210 351 2298
Website: www.sbc.com

SCANA Corp
H Tom Arthur, Senior Vice President, General Counsel & Assistant Secretary
1426 Main Street, Columbia SC 29218-0001
Tel: 803 748 3000
Fax: 803 217 8119
Website: www.scana.com

Schering-Plough Corporation
Joseph C Connors, Executive Vice President & General Counsel
Legal Department, 2000 Galloping Hill Road, Kenilworth NJ 07033-0530
Tel: 908 298 4000
Fax: 908 298 1960
Website: www.sch-plough.com

Science Applications International Corporation (SAIC)
Douglas E Scott, Senior Vice President & General Counsel
10260 Campus Point Drive, San Diego CA 92121
Tel: 858 546 6000
Fax: 858 546 6800
Website: www.saic.com

Sealed Air Corporation
H Katherine White, General Counsel & Secretary
Park 80 East, Saddle Brook NJ 07663-5291
Tel: 201 791 7600
Fax: 201 703 4205
Website: www.sealedaircorp.com

Sears Roebuck & Co
Anastasia D Kelly, Executive Senior Vice President & General Counsel
3333 Beverly Road, B6-210B, Hoffman Estates IL 60179
Tel: 847 286 2500
Fax: 847 286 2471
Website: www.sears.com

Sempra Energy
John R Light, Executive Vice President & General Counsel
101 Ash Street, San Diego CA 92101-3017
Tel: 619 696 2000
Fax: 619 696 4463
Website: www.sempra.com

The ServiceMaster Company
Jim Kaput, Senior Vice President & General Counsel
3250 Lacey Road, Suite 600, Downers Grove IL 60515
Tel: 630 663 2000
Fax: 630 663 2001
Website: www.svm.com

The Sherwin-Williams Company
Louis E Stellato, Vice President, General Counsel & Secretary
101 Prospect Avenue North West, Cleveland OH 44115-1075
Tel: 216 566 2200
Fax: 216 566 2947
Email: lestellato@sherwin.com
Website: www.sherwin-williams.com

ShopKo Stores Inc
Steven R Andrews, Senior Vice President & General Counsel
700 Pilgrim Way, Green Bay WI 54304-5263
Tel: 920 429 2211
Fax: 920 429 7401
Email: sandrews@shopko.com
Website: www.shopko.com

Sierra Pacific Resources
C Stanley Hunterton, Senior Vice President, General Counsel & Secretary
Nevada Power, 6226 West Sahara Avenue, Las Vegas NV 89146
Website: www.sierrapacific.com

SLM Corporation
Marianne M Keler, Executive Vice President & General Counsel
11600 Sallie Mae Drive, Reston VA 20193
Tel: 703 810 3000
Fax: 703 810 7053
Website: www.salliemae.com

Smith International Inc
Neal S Sutton, Senior Vice President, Administration, General Counsel, & Secretary
16740 Hardy Street, Houston TX 77032
Tel: 281 443 3370
Fax: 281 233 5259
Website: www.smith.com

Smithfield Foods Inc
Michael H Cole, Secreaty & Assistant General Counsel
200 Commerce Street, Smithfield VA 23430
Tel: 757 365 3000
Fax: 757 365 3017
Email: information@smithfieldfoods.com.
Website: www.Smithfieldfoods.Com

Smurfit-Stone Container Corporation (SSCC)
Craig A Hunt, Vice Presiden, Secretary & General Counsel
8182 Maryland Avenue, Clayton MO 63105
Tel: 314 746 1100
Website: www.smurfit-stone.net

Solectron Corporation
Robert Aeschliman, General Counsel
847 Gibraltar Drive, Milpitas CA 95035-6328
Tel: 408 957 8500
Fax: 408 957 2717
Email: robertaeschliman@ca.slr.com
Website: www.solectron.com

FORTUNE 500

Sonic Automotive Inc
Stephen K Coss, Vice President & General Counsel
6415 Idlewild Road, Suite 109, Charlotte NC 28212
Tel: 704 566 2400
Fax: 704 927 3412
Email: webmaster@sonicautomotive.com
Website: www.sonicautomotive.com

The Southern Company
Steven Wakefield, Vice President & Senior Counsel
270 Peachtree Street North West, Atlanta GA 30303
Tel: 404 506 5000
Fax: 404 506 0455
Email: swakefi@southernco.com
Website: www.southernco.com

SouthTrust Corporation
John Buchanan, General Counsel
420 North 20th Street, Birmingham AL 35203-3204
Tel: 205 254 5000
Fax: 205 254 6697
Website: www.southtrust.com

Southwest Airlines
Deborah Ackerman, General Counsel
2702 Love Field Drive, PO Box 36611, Dallas TX 75235-1611
Tel: 214 792 4000
Fax: 214 792 5151
Website: www.southwest.com

Spartan Stores Inc
David M Staples, Executive Vice President & Chief Financial Officer
850 76th Street South West, PO Box 8700, Grand Rapids MI 49518-8700
Tel: 616 878 2000
Fax: 616 878 8802
Website: www.spartanstores.com

Sprint Corporation
Richard Devlin, Executive Vice President, General Counsel & External Affairs
KSOPHFO410-4A203, 6200 Sprint Parkway, Overland Park KS 66251
Tel: 913 794 1435
Fax: 913 794 1436
Email: richard.devlin@mail.sprint.com
Website: www.sprint.com

SPX Corporation
Christopher J Kearney, Vice President, Secretary & General Counsel
13515 Ballantyne Corporate Place, Charlotte NC 28277
Website: www.spx.com

St Paul Companies Inc
John A MacColl, Vice Chairman & General Counsel
5801 Smith Avenue, Baltimore MD 21209-3693
Tel: 410 205 3000
Email: john.maccoll@stpaul.com
Website: www.stpaul.com

Staples Inc
Jack VanWoerkom, General Counsel & Secretary
500 Staples Drive, Framingham MA 01702
Tel: 508 253 5000
Fax: 508 253 8989
Website: www.staples.com

Starwood Hotels and Resorts Worldwide Inc
Kenneth S Siegel, Executive Vice President, General Counsel & Secretary
1111 Westchester Avenue, White Plains NY 10604
Tel: 914 640 8235
Fax: 914 640 8260
Website: www.starwood.com

State Farm Insurance Companies
Kim M Brunner, Executive Vice President and General Counsel
1 State Farm Plaza, Bloomington IL 61710-0001
Tel: 309 766 2311
Fax: 309 766 3621
Website: www.statefarm.com

State Street Corporation
Maureen Scannell Bateman, Executive Vice President, General Counsel & Corporate Secretary
225 Franklin Street, PO Box 351, Boston MA 02110
Tel: 617 786 3000
Fax: 617 664 4747
Website: www.statestreet.com

Steelcase
Jon D Botsford, Senior Vice President, Secretary & Chief Legal Officer
901 44th Street, Grand Rapids MI 49508
Tel: 616 247 2710
Fax: 616 475 2270
Website: www.steelcase.com

Sun Microsystems Inc
John D Croll, Senior Vice President, General Counsel & Secretary
4120 Network Circle, Mailstop: USCA12-201, Santa Clara CA 95054
Website: www.sun.com

Sunoco Inc
Michael S Kuritzkes, Vice President & General Counsel
1801 Market Street, Ten Penn Center, Philadelphia PA 19103-1699
Tel: 215 977 3000
Fax: 215 977 3409
Website: www.sunocoinc.com

SunTrust Banks Inc
Raymond D Fortin, Senior Vice President & General Counsel & Secretary
SunTrust Plaza, 303 Peachtree Street North East, Atlanta GA 30308
Tel: 404 588 7711
Fax: 404 332 3875
Website: www.suntrust.com

Supervalu Inc
Stephen P Kilgriff, Vice President, Legal
11840 Valley View Road, Eden Prairie MN 55344
Tel: 952 828 4000
Fax: 952 828 8998
Website: www.supervalu.com

Sysco Corporation
Michael C Nichols, Vice President & General Counsel
1390 Enclave Parkway, Houston TX 77077-2099
Tel: 281 584 1390
Fax: 281 584 2510
Email: nichols.michael@corp.sysco.com
Website: www.syscosmart.com

Target Corporation
James T Hale, Executive Vice President, General Counsel & Corporate Secretary
Legal Department, 1000 Nicollet Mall, TPS 3155, Minneapolis MN 55403
Tel: 612 304 6073
Fax: 612 696 3731
Email: jim.hale@target.com
Website: www.target.com

Teachers Insurance and Annuity Association-College Retirement Equities Fund (TIAA-CREF)
Charles H Stamm, Executive Vice President & General Counsel
730 Third Avenue, New York NY 10017-3206
Tel: 212 490 9000
Fax: 212 916 4840
Website: www.tiaa-cref.org

Tech Data Corporation
David R Vetter, Corporate Vice President & General Counsel
5350 Tech Data Drive, Mailstop C1-7, Clearwater FL 33760
Tel: 727 539 7429
Fax: 727 539 7803
Website: www.techdata.com

Temple-Inland Inc
J Bradley Johnston, General Counsel
1300 South Mopac Expressway, Austin, TX 78746, PO Box 40, Austin TX 78767
Tel: 512 434 8053
Fax: 812 434 8051
Email: brad.johnston@templeinland.com
Website: www.templeinland.com

Tenet Healthcare Corporation
Christi R Sulzbach, Chief Corporate Officer & General Counsel
3820 State Street, Santa Barbara CA 93105
Tel: 805 563 7011
Fax: 805 563 6857
Email: christi.sulzbach@tenethealth.com
Website: www.tenethealth.com

Tenneco Automotive Inc
Timothy R Donovan, Senior Vice President & General Counsel
500 North Field Drive, Lake Forest IL 60045
Tel: 847 482 5000
Fax: 847 482 5942
Website: www.tenneco-automotive.com

Tesoro Petroleum Corporation
James C Reed Jr, Executive Vice President, General Counsel & Secretary
300 Concord Plaza Drive, San Antonio TX 78216-6999
Tel: 210 828 8484
Fax: 210 283 2045
Email: webmaster@tesoropetroleum.com.
Website: www.tesoropetroleum.com

Texas Instruments Incorporated
Joseph F Hubach, Senior Vice President, Secretary & General Counsel
7839 Churchill Way, MS 3999, Dallas TX 75251
Tel: 972 917 5452
Fax: 214 480 5061
Website: www.ti.com

Textron Inc
Terrence O'Donnell, Executive Vice President & General Counsel
40 Westminster Street, Providence RI 02903-2596
Tel: 401 457 2555
Fax: 401 457 2418
Email: todonnell@textron.com
Website: www.textron.com

Thrivent Financial for Lutherans
Woodrow E Eno, Senior Vice President,
General Counsel & Secretary
625 Fourth Avenue South, Minneapolis
MN 55414-1665
Tel: 612 340 5183
Fax: 612 340 4285
Email: woody.eno@thrivent.com
Website: www.thrivent.com

The TJX Companies Inc
Jay H Meltzer, Senior Vice President,
General Counsel & Secretary
Legal Department, 770 Cochituate Road,
Framingham MA 01701
Tel: 508 390 1000
Fax: 508 390 2457
Website: www.tjx.com

Toys "R" Us Inc
Christopher K Kay, Executive Vice President,
General Counsel & Corporate Secretary
461 From Road, Paramus NJ 07652-3524
Tel: 201 262 7800
Fax: 201 262 8112
Website: www.toysrus.com

TransMontaigne Inc
Erik B Carlson , Senior Vice President
& General Counsel
2750 Republic Plaza, 370 17th Street, Denver
CO 80202
Tel: 303 626 8200
Fax: 303 626 8228
Website: www.transmontaigne.com

Tribune Company
Crane H Kenney, Senior Vice President, General
Counsel & Secretary
435 North Michigan Avenue, Chicago IL 60611-4001
Tel: 312 222 9100
Fax: 312 222 1573
Website: www.tribune.com

TXU Corporation
Peter B Tinkham, General Counsel & Secretary
Energy Plaza, 1601 Bryan Street, 33rd Floor, Dallas
TX 75201-3411
Tel: 214 812 4600
Fax: 214 812 7077
Website: www.txu.com

Tyson Foods Inc
Les R Baledge, Executive Vice President
& General Counsel
2210 West Oaklawn Drive, Springdale AR 72762
Tel: 479 290 4000
Fax: 479 290 4061
Website: www.tyson.com

UAL Corporation
Francesca M Maher, General Counsel
1200 East Algonquin Road, Elk Grove Township
IL 60007-0919
Tel: 847 700 4000
Fax: 847 700 4081
Website: www.united.com

Union Pacific Corporation
Carl von Bernuth, General Counsel
1416 Dodge Street, Room 1230, Omaha NE 68179
Tel: 402 271 6304
Fax: 402 271 6633
Website: www.up.com

Union Planters Corporation
Jim Houre, General Counsel
7130 Goodlett Farms Parkway, Memphis TN 38018
Tel: 901 580 6000
Fax: 901 580 2396
Website: www.unionplanters.com

Unisys Corporation
Nancy S Sundheim, Vice President, General
Counsel & Secretary
Unisys Way, Blue Bell PA 19424-0001
Tel: 215 986 4011
Fax: 215 986 2312
Website: www.unisys.com

United Auto Group Inc (UAG)
Robert Kurnick Jr, Executive Vice President,
General Counsel & Secretary
2555 Telegraph Road, Bloomfield Hills
MI 48302-0954
Tel: 248 648 2500
Fax: 248 648 2155
Website: www.uag.com

United Parcel Service Inc (UPS)
Joseph Moderow, Senior Vice President of Legal
& Public Affairs
55 Glenlake Parkway North East, Atlanta GA 30328
Tel: 404 828 6000
Fax: 404 828 6562
Website: www.ups.com

United Services Automobile Association (USAA)
Bradford Rich, General Counsel & Secretary
9800 Fredericksburg Road, USAA Building, San
Antonio TX 78288
Tel: 210 498 2211
Fax: 210 498 9940
Website: www.usaa.com

United Stationers Inc
Deidra D Gold, Senior Vice President,
General Counsel & Secretary
2200 East Golf Road, Des Plaines IL 60016-1267
Tel: 847 699 5000
Fax: 847 699 0891
Website: www.unitedstationers.com

United Technologies Corporation
William H Trachsel, Senior Vice President,
General Counsel & Secretary
1 Financial Plaza, Hartford CT 06101
Tel: 860 728 7845
Fax: 860 728 7862
Website: www.utc.com

UnitedHealth Group Incorporated
David J Lubben, General Counsel & Secretary
UnitedHealth Group Center, 9900 Bren Road East,
Minnetonka MN 55343
Tel: 952 936 1300
Fax: 952 936 0044
Website: www.unitedhealthcare.com

Unocal Corporation
Charles O Strathman, Vice President
& Chief Legal Officer
2141 Rosecrans Avenue, Suite 4000, El Segundo
CA 90245
Tel: 310 726 7600
Fax: 310 726 7819
Website: www.unocal.com

UNUMProvident
F Dean Copeland, Executive Vice President
&General Counsel
One Fountain Square, Suite 756, Chattanooga
TN 37402-1330
Tel: 423 755 1011
Fax: 423 770 4455
Website: www.unumprovident.com

US Airways Inc
Michelle V Bryan, Executive Vice President,
Corporate Affairs & General Counsel
Crystal Park Four, 8th floor, Arlington VA 22227
Tel: 703 872 7000
Fax: 703 872 5307
Website: www.usairways.com

US Bancorp
Lee Mitau, Executive Vice President,
General Counsel & Secretary
US Bank Place, 601 Second Avenue South,
Minneapolis MN 55402-4302
Tel: 612 973 0069
Fax: 612 303 0898
Website: www.usbank.com

USA Interactive Inc
Julius Genachowski, Executive
Vice President & General Counsel
152 West 57th Street, 43rd Floor, New York
NY 10019
Tel: 212 314 7330
Fax: 212 314 7329
Website: www.usainteractive.com

USG Corporation
Stanley L Ferguson, Senior Vice President
& General Counsel
125 South Franklin Street, (PO Box 6721, Chicago,
IL 60680-6721), Chicago IL 60606-4678
Tel: 312 606 4000
Fax: 312 606 4093
Website: www.usg.com

Valero Energy Corporation
Gregory C King, Executive Vice President
& General Counsel
One Valero Place, San Antonio, TX 78212-3186,
PO Box 500, San Antonio TX 78292-0500
Tel: 210 370 2000
Fax: 210 370 2646
Website: www.valero.com

Verizon Communications Incorporated
William P Barr, Executive Vice President
& General Counsel
1095 Avenue of the Americas, 39th Floor, New York
NY 10036
Tel: 212 395 2121
Fax: 212 597 2587
Website: www.verizon.com

VF Corporation
Candace S Cummings, General Counsel
105 Corporate Center Boulevard, Greensboro
NC 27408
Tel: 336 424 6000
Fax: 336 424 7696
Website: www.vfc.co

Viacom Inc
Michael D Fricklas, Executive Vice President,
General Counsel & Secretary
1515 Broadway, 51st Floor, New York NY 10036-5794
Tel: 212 258 6070
Fax: 212 258 6099
Email: michael.fricklas@viacom.com
Website: www.viacom.com

FORTUNE 500

Visteon Corporation
Stacy Fox, Senior Vice President,
General Counsel and Secretary
290 Town Centre Drive, 10th Floor, Dearborn MI 48126
Tel: 313 755 2760
Fax: 313 755 2762
Website: www.visteon.com

Wachovia Corporation
Mark C Treanor, General Counsel
Wachovia Centre, 301 South College Street,
Charlotte NC 28288-0630
Tel: 704 374 6161
Fax: 704 374 3425
Website: www.wachovia.com

Walgreen Co
Allan Resnick, Divisional Vice President, Law
200 Wilmot Road, Deerfield IL 60015
Tel: 847 914 3570
Fax: 847 914 2825
Website: www.walgreens.com

Wal-Mart Stores Inc
Thomas D Hyde, Executive Vice President,
Legal and Corporate Affairs & Secretary
702 South West Eighth Street, Mailstop 0105,
Bentonville AR 72716
Tel: 479 273 4000
Fax: 479 273 1917
Website: www.walmartstores.com

The Walt Disney Company
Louis M Meisinger, Executive
Vice President & General Counsel
500 South Buena Vista Street, Burbank CA 91521-0922
Tel: 818 560 1000
Fax: 818 238 0404
Website: www.disney.com

Washington Mutual Inc
Fay Chapman, Senior Executive
Vice President & General Counsel
1201 Third Avenue, Seattle WA 98101 **Tel:** 206 461 2000
Fax: 206 461 5739
Website: www.wamu.com

Waste Management Inc
David P Steiner, Senior Vice President, General Counsel & Corporate Secretary
1001 Fannin Street, First City Tower, Suite 4000, Houston TX 77002
Tel: 713 512 6200
Fax: 713 512 6299
Website: www.wm.com

WellPoint Health Networks
Thomas C Geiser, Executive Vice
President & General Counsel
1 WellPoint Way, Thousand Oaks CA 91362
Tel: 805 557 6655
Fax: 805 557 6872
Website: www.wellpoint.com

Wells Fargo & Company
Stanley S Stroup, Executive Vice President
& General Counsel
420 Montgomery Street, San Francisco CA 94163
Tel: 415 396 6019
Fax: 415 975 7819
Website: www.wellsfargo.com

WESCO International Inc
Stephen A Van Oss, Vice President,
Chief Financial Officer
Commerce Court, Suite 700, Four Station Square, Pittsburgh PA 15219
Tel: 412 454 2200
Fax: 412 454 2505
Website: www.wescodist.com

Western Gas Resources Inc
John C Walter, Executive Vice President,
General Counsel, & Secretary
12200 North Pecos Street, Denver CO 80234-3439
Tel: 303 452 5603
Fax: 303 252 6150
Website: www.westerngas.com

Weyerhaeuser Company
Robert A Dowdy, Vice President
& General Counsel
33663 Weyerhaeuser Way South, Federal Way WA 98003
Tel: 253 924 5025
Fax: 253 924 3253
Website: www.weyerhaeuser.com

The Williams Companies Inc
William G Von Glahn, Senior Vice President
& General Counsel
1 Williams Center, Tulsa OK 74172-0000
Tel: 918 573 2000
Fax: 918 573 5942
Email: bill.vonglahn@williams.com
Website: www.williams.com

Winn-Dixie Stores Inc
Larry Appel, Senior Vice President
& General Counsel
5050 Edgewood Court, Jacksonville FL 32254
Tel: 904 370 7007
Fax: 904 783 5651
Email: larryappel@Winn-Dixie.com
Website: www.winn-dixie.com

Wisconsin Energy Corporation
Larry Salustro, Senior Vice President
& General Counsel
231 West Michigan Street, Milwaukee WI 53290
Tel: 414 221 2345
Fax: 414 221 2554
Website: www.wisconsinenergy.com

WorldCom Inc
Michael H Salsbury, Executive Vice
President & General Counsel
1133 19th Street North West, Washington, DC 20036
Tel: 703 341 4448
Website: www.wcom.com

WW Grainger Inc
John L Howard, Senior Vice President
& General Counsel
100 Grainger Parkway, Lake Forest IL 60045-5201
Tel: 847 535 4341
Fax: 847 535 4585
Email: howard.j.x@grainger.com
Website: www.grainger.com

Wyeth
Louis L Hoynes Jr, Executive
Vice President & General Counsel
Five Giralda Farms, Madison NJ 07940
Tel: 973 660 6040
Fax: 973 660 7050
Email: hoynesl@wyeth.com
Website: www.wyeth.com

Xcel Energy Inc
Gary R Johnson, Vice President
& General Counsel
800 Nicolet Mall, Minneapolis MN 55402-2023
Tel: 612 330 5500
Fax: 612 330 2900
Website: www.xcelenergy.com

Xerox Corporation
Christina Clayton, Vice President
& General Counsel
800 Long Ridge Road, Stamford CT 06904
Tel: 203 968 3000
Fax: 203 968 3430
Website: www.xerox.com

Yellow Corporation
Daniel J Churay, Senior Vice President,
General Counsel & Secretary
10990 Roe Avenue, Overland Park, KS 66207,
PO Box 7563, Overland Park KS 66207-0563
Tel: 913 696 6171
Fax: 913 696 6116
Website: www.yellowcorp.com

York International Corporation
Jane Davis, Vice President,
General Counsel & Secretary
PO Box 1592, York, PA 17405-1592, 631
South Richland Avenue, York PA 17403
Tel: 717 771 7890
Fax: 717 771 7381
Website: www.york.com

Yum! Brands Inc
Christian L Campbell, Senior Vice President,
General Counsel & Secretary
1441 Gardiner Lane, Louisville KY 40213
Tel: 502 874 8300
Fax: 502 874 8790
Website: www.yum.com

A-Z OF LEADING LAWYERS

**CHAMBERS
USA
2003–2004**

AHMAD, ZAVITSANOS & ANAIPAKOS, P.C.

THE FIRM

Partners: Joseph Ahmad, John Zavitsanos, Demetrios Anaipakos

Number of partners: 3
Number of other lawyers: 4

HEAD OFFICE

TEXAS
One Houston Center, Suite 3460, 1221 Mckinney Street, **Houston** TX 77010
Tel: 713 655 1101 **Fax:** 713 655 0062

FIRM OVERVIEW: Ahmad, Zavitsanos & Anaipakos, P.C., was founded in 1993 as a litigation boutique firm. The name partners have tried over 100 cases to verdict in state and federal courts in a variety of areas, including oil and gas disputes, employment issues, business torts, and commercial disputes. The firm prides itself in the use of innovative trial techniques. It serves individual clients and Business Clients throughout Texas.

CLIENTS: The firm's clients include AAA Life Insurance Company; Advanced Technologies, Inc.; American Automobile Association; Buison, Inc.; Chung's Food, Inc.; Genuine Parts Company; Hines Interests Limited Partnership; Mercedes-Benz USA; Mi-jack Products, Inc.; Milnot Co.; Rap-a-Lot Records; Residential Warranty Corp.; Southern Farm Bureau Casualty Insurance Co.; Sygenta Crop Protection, Inc.; Technical Star Consulting, Inc.; Texas Farm Bureau Mutual Insurance Co.; Urban Publishing Co.; Wireless Retail, Inc.; Zeneca, Inc.

MAIN AREAS OF PRACTICE: Civil trial law, employment law, class actions and commercial litigation.

LEADING LAW FIRMS

AKERMAN SENTERFITT

THE FIRM

Chairman & CEO: J Thomas Cardwell

FIRM OVERVIEW: With more than 360 attorneys in eight offices, Akerman Senterfitt is the largest law firm exclusively in the State of Florida. This statewide presence allows the firm's attorneys to represent the interests of their in-state, national and international clients anywhere in Florida.

MAIN AREAS OF PRACTICE:

Corporate: Akerman Senterfitt has the largest corporate practice in Florida with more than 100 attorneys. In the past several years the firm has managed billions of dollars worth of transactions. The firm regularly represents domestic and foreign public companies, including nearly half of the largest public companies in Florida. Akerman Senterfitt also represents financial institutions, private equity and venture capital funds, and the companies in which they invest, as well as individual entrepreneurs. Its primary areas of focus are mergers and acquisitions, securities, taxation, public finance, banking and lending and employee benefits.

Environmental: Representing both the private and public sectors, Akerman Senterfitt's environmental attorneys have substantial experience in representing a wide variety of businesses, governmental entities, and other organizations. The firm handles such matters as federal, state, and local regulatory compliance and permitting, managing environmental risks and conducting due diligence investigations, managing the assessment and remediation of contaminated property, defending enforcement actions, and prosecuting or defending civil actions to recover cleanup costs or environmental damages to property.

Government: Few facets of life are not touched by the institutions of government and the people who constitute its bodies. The firm's clients, by virtue of their size or the broad public impact of the projects they undertake, are no exception. In order to represent their interests, Akerman Senterfitt has built a large and effective government practice. The firm has points of entry into almost every governmental or quasi-governmental body in Florida, and into many agencies in Washington as well. The firm is as effective in its lobbying and dialog with these agencies as it is in its administrative proceedings or litigation against them.

International: As Florida's role in international trade and finance expands, Akerman Senterfitt has developed a multilingual, multicultural, cross-disciplinary international practice. The firm's goal is to assist US clients to grow their international business activities and to assist foreign clients to establish businesses and flourish in the United States. The international practice group includes attorneys from all the firm's offices and from every major practice group, including corporate and securities, banking, tax, immigration, admiralty, aviation, intellectual property, real estate, and litigation.

Intellectual Property: Akerman Senterfitt's intellectual property practice is the largest and most broadly experienced in Florida. The firm's IP lawyers are engineers and scientists from many rapidly developing fields of industry such as fuel cells, biomedical devices, semiconductor materials and software. This knowledge base helps the firm's lawyers to create broader patents, draft better contracts, develop more profitable licenses, and litigate more effectively. The firm represents clients across the globe including many Fortune 500 firms and major research universities.

Litigation: The firm has the largest litigation department in Florida, which is chaired by the former Chief Judge of the United States District Court for the Southern District of Florida, Edward B Davis. The former Chief Judge of the United States Court of Appeals for the Eleventh Circuit, Joseph Hatchett, heads the Appellate Practice Group. The experience of the firm's litigators ranges from small disputes to complex lawsuits such as securities, class action, antitrust, trademark and copyright litigation.

Real Estate: Akerman Senterfitt has more than 60 lawyers who focus on the needs of clients in the real estate industry. This represents one of the largest full service real estate practices in Florida. The firm provides comprehensive representation through changing business cycles at all levels of activity. The firm manages the legal aspects of large land deals and construction projects, assists developers in meeting tough environmental regulations, and advises on all aspects of transactional work, including workouts and restructurings. The firm's focus areas include land use and entitlements, debt and equity finance, income property, and the acquisition and development of projects within all real estate asset classes.

Trusts, Estates & Family Law: Akerman Senterfitt has carefully built a broadly experienced and highly respected trusts, estates, and family law practice. Not only does the firm administer and litigate personal legal matters, it has crafted some of the laws that govern these affairs. The firm's statewide presence allows it to manage the legal issues of families and their businesses regardless of venue. And while some firms segregate the attorneys in this area into separate groups, the firm believes in the cross-pollination of ideas that results from maintaining one cohesive practice. The firm's planners understand litigation and can design agreements that minimize the possibility of future legal actions.

CLIENTS: Akerman Senterfitt provides a full range of legal services, with experienced attorneys in each area to serve its diverse client base. The firm has served its clients since 1920 and now represents nearly half of the largest public companies in Florida, as well as private companies, government entitites, education establishments and high net worth individuals.

US OFFICES

FLORIDA

2650 North Military Trail, Suite 240
Boca Raton, FL 33431-7391
Tel: 561 912 9008 Fax: 561 998 0028
Website: www.akerman.com

Las Olas Centre II, 350 East Las Olas Boulevard, Suite 1600
Fort Lauderdale, FL 33301-2229
Tel: 954 463 2700 Fax: 954 463 2224

50 North Laura Street, Suite 2500
Jacksonville, FL 32202-3646
Tel: 904 798 3700 Fax: 904 798 3730

One Southeast Third Avenue, 28th Floor
Miami, FL 33131-1714
Tel: 305 374 5600 Fax: 305 374 5095

Citrus Center, 17th Floor, 255 South Orange Avenue
Orlando, FL 32801-3483
Tel: 407 843 7860 Fax: 407 843 6610

301 South Bronough, Suite 200
Tallahassee, FL 32301-1707
Tel: 850 222 3471 Fax: 850 222 8628

Wachovia Center, 100 South Ashley Drive, Suite 1500
Tampa, FL 33602-5311
Tel: 813 223 7333 Fax: 813 223 2837

Esperante Building, 222 Lakeview Avenue, Suite 400
West Palm Beach, FL 33401-6183
Tel: 561 653 5000 Fax: 561 659 6313

LEADING LAW FIRMS

AKIN GUMP STRAUSS HAUER & FELD LLP

THE FIRM

Chairman: R Bruce McLean

Number of partners: 273

FIRM OVERVIEW: Recognized for its sophisticated clients and capabilities as well as its outstanding team of professionals, Akin Gump Strauss Hauer & Feld is one of the world's largest law firms, with 16 offices and nearly 1,000 lawyers in more than 50 practice disciplines. Steadfast client service and visionary leadership are key factors in this first generation law firm's swift rise to the top of the profession.

MAIN AREAS OF PRACTICE:
Corporate & Securities: The firm advises on mergers and acquisitions, corporate finance, international transactions, investment fund management and restructuring, and provides sophisticated counsel on US and international tax and governance issues.
Financial Restructuring: The firm represents committees of bondholders, noteholders, institutional investors and trade creditors, including the official creditors' committee in the WorldCom bankruptcy.
Health: The firm advises on key industry issues, including Medicare and Medicaid reimbursement litigation and counseling, HIPAA compliance, and antitrust planning and litigation.
Intellectual Property: The firm provides counsel on patent prosecution and litigation, trademark, copyright, trade secret and unfair competition matters.
Labor & Employment: The firm advises management in both traditional matters, such as collective bargaining and discrimination lawsuits, and emerging issues, including class action wage-hour and EEO litigation and restructuring labor contracts in bankruptcy.
Litigation: The firm represents clients in civil and criminal matters in state and federal trial and appellate courts. A 2002 survey of the Fortune 250 ranked Akin Gump among corporate America's five most frequently relied upon firms for significant litigation matters.
Project & Infrastructure Development: The firm provides fully integrated project development services, including environmental, land use, project structuring and finance, construction, energy, water and transportation.
Public Law & Policy: The firm has one of the world's most sophisticated and diverse US and international public law and policy practices, representing corporations, individuals, nonprofits, foreign governments, and coalitions and trade associations.
Real Estate: The firm maintains full-service real estate capabilities and handles the full range of US and international transactions.

INTERNATIONAL WORK: The firm is recognized for its Russia/CIS practice, which is comprised of two former ambassadors to the Russian Federation and top-ranking former US government officials with significant experience in the region. In 2003 the firm launched three of its core practices - investment funds, financial restructuring and emerging markets - to London, adding significant staff and resources there.

HEAD OFFICES

TEXAS
1700 Pacific Avenue, Suite 4100, **Dallas**, 75201-4675
Tel: 214 969 2800 **Fax:** 214 969 4343
Email: dallasinfo@akingump.com
Website: www.akingump.com

DISTRICT OF COLUMBIA
Robert S Strauss Building, 1333 New Hampshire Avenue, NW, **Washington**, 20036-1564
Tel: 202 887 4000 **Fax:** 202 887 4288
Email: washdcinfo@akingump.com

BRANCH OFFICES

CALIFORNIA
2029 Century Park East, Suite 2400, **Los Angeles**, 90067-3012
Tel: 310 229 1000 **Fax:** 310 229 1001

COLORADO
1675 Broadway, Suite 2300, **Denver**, 80202-4623
Tel: 303 825 7000 **Fax:** 303 825 7005

NEW YORK
590 Madison Avenue, **New York**, 10022-2524
Tel: 212 872 1000 **Fax:** 212 872 1002

PENNSYLVANIA
One Commerce Square, 2005 Market Street, Suite 2200, **Philadelphia**, 19103-7013
Tel: 215 965 1200 **Fax:** 215 965 1210

TEXAS
300 West 6th Street, Suite 2100, **Austin**, 78701-2916
Tel: 512 499 6200 **Fax:** 512 499 6290

1900 Pennzoil Place – South Tower, 711 Louisiana Street, **Houston**, 77002-2720
Tel: 713 220 5800 **Fax:** 713 236 0822

300 Convent Street, Suite 1500, **San Antonio**, 78205-3732
Tel: 210 281 7000 **Fax:** 210 224 2035

VIRGINIA
1676 International Drive - Penthouse, **McLean**, 22102-4832
Tel: 703 891 7500 **Fax:** 703 891 7501

INTERNATIONAL OFFICES:

The firm also has offices in Brussels, Riyadh (Affiliate Office), London and Moscow.

CONTACTS

Corporate & Securities	Rick L Burdick (Washington)
Financial Restructuring	H Rey Stroube III (London)
Health Industry	David H Eisenstat (Washington)
Intellectual Property	Ronald L Panitch (Philadelphia)
Labor & Employment	Richard L Wyatt Jr (Washington)
Litigation	David R McAtee (Dallas)
Project & Infrastructure Development	Jeffrey L Stanfield (Washington)
Public Law & Policy	Joel Jankowsky (Washington)
Real Estate	Carl B Lee (Dallas)

LEADING LAW FIRMS

ALSCHULER GROSSMAN STEIN & KAHAN LLP

THE FIRM

Managing Partner: Dana N Levitt

Number of partners: 52
Number of other lawyers: 50

FIRM OVERVIEW: Founded in 1952, Alschuler Grossman Stein & Kahan LLP enjoys a national reputation for vigorous and creative advocacy in complex business and entertainment litigation and business transactions. This select group of diverse professionals is committed to finding practical solutions that produce tangible and cost-effective results for clients. The firm's hands-on commitment to the practice of law sets Alschuler Grossman Stein & Kahan LLP apart from many other leading law firms. The firm's involvement in and knowledge of the business, judicial, political, and cultural characteristics unique to its hometown of Los Angeles is unparalleled. The scope of the firm's practice has led it to establish relationships with leading law firms throughout the world through its founding membership in the Association of Commercial Lawyers International. These relationships give the firm the access necessary to represent clients' interests effectively in out-of-state and foreign jurisdictions.

CLIENTS: The firm's clientele includes domestic and multinational *Fortune* 500 companies, emerging companies, and individuals in diverse areas of business and the entertainment industry.

INTERNATIONAL WORK: Alschuler Grossman Stein & Kahan LLP represents domestic and international clients in all aspects of international business, trade, and investment. It advises clients about such matters as litigation (including patent and intellectual property litigation), foreign and domestic regulatory compliance, investigations, product distribution, licensing, franchising, and contractual issues. The firm is a founding member of the Association of Commercial Lawyers International. Its Greater China Practice Group has particular experience representing US clients in Greater China and representing Chinese clients in the United States; several of the firm's lawyers are fluent in Chinese.

HEAD OFFICE

CALIFORNIA
The Water Garden, 1620 26th Street, Fourth Floor, North Tower,
Santa Monica, CA 90404-4060
Tel: 310 907 1000 **Fax:** 310 907 2000
Email: info@agsk.com
Website: www.agsk.com

CONTACTS

Business Litigation	Marshall B Grossman
Corporate Transactions	Robert L Kahan
Entertainment Litigation	Stanton 'Larry' Stein
Financial Institutions	William S Small
Franchise	Susan Grueneberg
Insolvency	Henry S David
Insurance/Reinsurance	Bruce A Friedman
Intellectual Property	Jeffrey C Briggs
Professional Liability Defense	Bruce A Friedman
Real Estate	James D Richman
Securities Litigation	Michael A Sherman
Taxation	Marilyn Barrett

LEADING LAW FIRMS

ALTHEIMER & GRAY

THE FIRM

Managing Partner: Jeffrey N Smith
Chairman: Gery Chico
Number of partners: 132
Number of other lawyers: 229

HEAD OFFICE

ILLINOIS
10 South Wacker Drive, **Chicago** IL 60606
Tel: 312 715 4000 **Fax:** 312 715 4800
Website: www.altheimer.com

BRANCH OFFICES

CALIFORNIA
1 Bush Street, Suite 1200, **San Francisco** CA 94104
Tel: 415 262 8600 **Fax:** 415 262 8601

ILLINOIS
600 Second Street, **Springfield** IL 62704
Tel: 217 789 1040 **Fax:** 217 789 1077

INTERNATIONAL OFFICES
Altheimer & Gray has offices in Prague, Warsaw, Kyiv, Istanbul, Bratislava, Bucharest, Shanghai, London and Paris and an affiliated office in Budapest

FIRM OVERVIEW: Established in Chicago in 1915, Altheimer & Gray has more than 360 attorneys in 13 offices in Chicago, Springfield, San Francisco, Prague, Warsaw, Kyiv, Istanbul, Bratislava, Bucharest, Shanghai, London, Paris and Budapest. It serves corporate and business clients, providing cross-border and domestic legal advice primarily in the US, Europe and China.

MAIN AREAS OF PRACTICE:

Corporate, Corporate Finance & Securities: The firm has handled a large number of investment, financing, privatisation, joint venture and real estate development transactions in established and emerging markets. The firm has established a substantial practice in private equity and management-led investment groups, acting as lead counsel in hundreds of successful transactions. Work also includes follow-on investments and add-on acquisitions. In recent years, the firm has handled global securities issues and complex financings representing a wide range of clients in Rule 144A and registered offerings. The firm has become increasingly involved in takeovers involving public companies and representing special committees.

Private Equity & Venture Capital: The firm represents global private equity, venture capital and mezzanine investors and has acted as lead counsel in hundreds of investments, mergers, acquisitions, dispositions and mezzanine financings. It provides legal solutions during all phases of the investment cycle, involving all levels of the capital structure, particularly equity and subordinated debt.

Banking & Finance: The firm represents major financial institutions and multilateral financial institutions in connection with secured and unsecured credit facilities, securitisations, and global securities offerings of high-yield and other debt. The firm has particular experience in developing such structures in emerging market economies.

Insurance: The firm advises on all aspects of insurance law for corporate and insurance industry clients. Matters handled range from drafting insurance contracts, reinsurance audits and a broad range of insurance litigation and arbitration cases for US and other insurers and reinsurers, as well as major national and international insurance brokers. The firm advises on the insurance laws and markets of western, central and eastern Europe and China, and has experience with ministries and insurers in these areas.

Bankruptcy, Workout & Insolvency: The firm combines new loan documentation with workout and bankruptcy and represents institutional investors, unsecured creditors, creditors' committees and business debtors.

Intellectual Property & IT: The firm provides comprehensive litigation, patent, trademark, copyright, technology and trade secrets services and advises on the development of worldwide intellectual property strategy.

Internet & Hi-tech: The firm advises on e-commerce strategies, M&A, start-ups, venture investing, government incentives and site acquisitions.

Litigation: The firm handles civil and criminal matters and international arbitrations. It is able to field cross-jurisdictional teams of lawyers to handle complex arbitrations involving the laws of multiple jurisdictions. The firm focuses primarily in litigation involving intellectual property and patent law, labor and employment, white collar criminal defense, antitrust, insurance, real estate, construction, hotel, and civil rights representation.

Real Estate: The firm has experience in structuring complex commercial and financial transactions throughout the world. It advises financial investors, developers, property managers, architects, construction companies, hotel owners and developers and others in connection with a wide variety of real estate projects ranging from industrial to retail to hotels to commercial office buildings and mixed use facilities. The firm represents major multinational corporations who have outsourced all of their global real estate legal work.

Tax: The firm helps to design business structures and advises on the international, federal, state and local tax implications of various alternatives. It also litigates in all the administrative tribunals, federal and state courts. The firm's attorneys have arranged teams of lawyers across Europe and in Canada, Mexico, the Caribbean, South Africa, India, Thailand, Korea, Japan, Australia, New Zealand, Singapore, Indonesia, Chile and Venezuela.

Hedge Funds: The firm's practice involves private equity, securities and tax lawyers focusing on the unique and changing needs of hedge fund clients - from fund organization, structuring and formation, tax planning, capital raising, tracking issues, fiduciary issues and overall securities compliance and investment, structured or otherwise.

Corporate Governance, Risk & Crisis Management: The firm represents boards and audit, compensation and governance committees seeking to meet good governance standards. It identifies and assesses core business, financial, legal, reputational, regulatory and other risks, helping clients avoid and control these risks, including in crisis situations.

CLIENTS: The firm's clients include multinational aeronautical, telecommunications, tobacco, engineering, food distribution and processing, fertilizer and chemical, high technology and petroleum companies; American and European banks, investment houses and public and private equity investment funds; real estate investment trusts, real estate companies, hotel companies, national retailers and pension advisors; individual entrepreneurs, portfolio companies and publicly and family-owned businesses engaged in a wide range of manufacturing and service businesses.

INTERNATIONAL WORK: The international practice group consists of lawyers with experience in finance and banking, acquisitions, securities, antitrust, real estate, tax, litigation and arbitration, patents, licensing and intellectual property and insurance. As well as advising clients on inward and outward bound business and financial transactions, the firm serves clients involved in foreign investment in the US; direct US investment abroad; the licensing of technology abroad; international joint ventures; Eurocurrency/Eurodollar financing transactions; international arbitration; international taxation; complex financings; international real estate transactions and construction projects and international acquisitions and divestitures. The firm is particularly involved in the developing markets of central, eastern and southern Europe. Unlike most international firms in the region, it decided to staff its foreign offices predominantly with prominent local lawyers, who work closely with US lawyers experienced in cross-border transactions.

LEADING LAW FIRMS

ANDREWS & KURTH LLP

THE FIRM

Managing Partner: Howard Ayers

Number of partners: 152
Number of other lawyers: 375

AREAS OF PRACTICE:
Litigation	24%
Business Transactions	22%
Corporate & Securities	19%
Bankruptcy	15%
Public Law	7%
Tax	4%
Environmental	3%
Energy	3%
Labor & Employment	2%
Intellectual Property	1%

FIRM OVERVIEW: A prominent participant in the early commercial development of the Southwest region of the US, Andrews & Kurth today is a nationally ranked and recognized firm that handles the vital interests of established companies and emerging businesses around the globe. Founded in 1902, the firm is organized into 24 practice areas, utilizing experience and notable strengths to form the best team for each client. The result is the consistent delivery of efficient, effective and valuable legal services. Andrews & Kurth enjoys an international presence, providing legal services worldwide from offices in major corporate and government centers on two continents.

MAIN AREAS OF PRACTICE:

Corporate & Securities: The firm represents businesses of all sizes, entity types and in various stages of development, including newly formed or existing private and public corporations, partnerships, limited liability companies, master limited partnerships, financial institutions, REITs and joint ventures. The corporate practice is especially active in energy, oil, timber, coal, mining and other natural resource industries, energy services, commodities trading, petrochemical, electronics, outsourced services, healthcare, telecommunications and computer (hardware and software) services industry segments in recent years.

Business Transactions: Lawyers in this practice counsel to a far-ranging client base, with specific emphasis on transactional matters related to energy, banking, public and private financing and real estate. These involve work in project and structured finance, syndicated lending, leasing, swaps and loan workouts, restructuring and in the real estate area, acquisition and development and the financing of a wide array of commercial, industrial and public projects. In addition, the firm's work includes representation to all aspects of the energy industry.

Litigation: With trial lawyers in Houston, Dallas, New York, Austin, Washington, DC and Los Angeles, the firm offers coast to coast experience in jury and bench trials in state and federal courts and other tribunals. The majority of the firm's lawyers concentrate on general corporate and business litigation, handling a variety of complex cases for companies in virtually every industry.

HEAD OFFICE

TEXAS
600 Travis, Suite 4200, **Houston**, TX 77002
Tel: 713 220 4200   **Fax:** 713 220 4285
E-mail: webmaster@akllp.com
Website: www.akllp.com / www.aktechlaw.com

BRANCH OFFICES

TEXAS
111 Congress Ave., Suite 1700, **Austin**, Texas 78701
Tel: 512 320 9200   **Fax:** 512 320 9292

1717 Main Street, Suite 3700, **Dallas**, Texas 75201
Tel: 214 659-4400   **Fax:** 214 659 4401

Waterway Plaza Two, 10001 Woodloch Forest Drive, Suite 200
The Woodlands, Texas 77380
Tel: 713 220 4801   **Fax:** 713 220 4815

CALIFORNIA
601 South Figueroa, Suite 1725, **Los Angeles**, California 90017
Tel: 213 896 3100   **Fax:** 213 896 3137

NEW YORK
805 Third Avenue, **New York**, New York 10022
Tel: 212 850 2800   **Fax:** 212 850 2929

WASHINGTON
1701 Pennsylvania Avenue, N.W., Suite 300, **Washington, DC** 20006-5805
Tel: 202 662 2700   **Fax:** 202 662 2739

INTERNATIONAL OFFICES

The firm also has an office in London, England.

CONTACTS

Corporate & Securities	Michael O'Leary
Business Transactions	Thomas J Perich
Litigation	A Ross Rommel, Jr
Bankruptcy	Hugh M Ray

Bankruptcy: The firm offers a sophisticated insolvency practice, representing clients nationwide in large, complex bankruptcies under both Chapter 11 and Chapter 7. Currently, Andrews & Kurth ranks among the country's seven largest bankruptcy practices. The firm enjoys a large, diverse client base, representing debtors, creditors, trustees, creditors' committees, and institutional lenders. Bankruptcy issues are handled out of all the firm's offices. Firm lawyers also handle a significant volume of out of court restructurings and workouts, and Houston and New York lawyers handle the regulatory aspects of financial institution insolvency work.

ARNOLD & PORTER

THE FIRM

Chairman: Michael N Sohn
Managing Partner: James J Sandman

Number of partners worldwide: 243
Number of other lawyers worldwide: 480

AREAS OF PRACTICE
Litigation	50%
Regulatory	25%
Transactional	25%

FIRM OVERVIEW: Arnold & Porter is a full service, international firm responsive to the needs of clients in a highly competitive and litigious marketplace. With offices in Washington, DC, Northern Virginia, New York, Los Angeles, Century City, Denver, and London, and over 700 lawyers worldwide, Arnold & Porter has a distinct perspective on the pivotal relationship between government and business. The firm offers clients a unique window on the legal, policy, and political processes affecting almost every aspect of the international economy. The firm's lawyers collectively have experience in a broad range of legal practice. Arnold & Porter maintains substantial litigation, transactional, and regulatory practices, as well as those involving many contemporary areas of law.

MAIN AREAS OF PRACTICE:

Litigation: More than half of the 700 lawyers are actively engaged in litigation in the federal and state courts, as well as in both national and international arbitrations. In addition to serving in all traditional litigation roles, the firm frequently serves as 'national co-ordinating counsel' for its clients, defending related cases across the country through networks of local counsel. Arnold & Porter's litigation practice is distinguished by its proficiency at assembling versatile teams of litigators to advance complex client interests. Each team is individually fashioned, taking into account the attorney's knowledge of the area in dispute and general litigation experience. When it is in the best interests of the client, the team may include litigators from more than one of the firm's offices.

Regulatory: Long known for its regulatory expertise, Arnold & Porter is especially well known for its award-winning, international antitrust practice, which includes many former high-ranking government officials. The firm's transatlantic team advises clients involved in national and international transactions or who have national or European competition issues before the FTC, DOJ, and the EC Commission.

Transactional: Arnold & Porter also handles hundreds of major transactions each year with clients ranging from large multinational corporations to regional companies to rising small-cap companies to start-ups and entrepreneurs. They come from many industries and include companies headquartered in North and South America, Europe, Africa, Asia, and Australia. In every case, Arnold & Porter focuses on the client's business objectives and on achieving their goals in the transaction. For many relatively routine transactions, the firm works hard to maximize value by closing quickly and cost effectively. But the firm also takes pride in its success in structuring complicated and novel transactions.

HEAD OFFICE

DISTRICT OF COLUMBIA
555 Twelfth Street, NW, **Washington** DC 20004-1206
Tel: 202 942 5000 **Fax:** 202 942-5999
Website: www.arnoldporter.com

BRANCH OFFICES

NEW YORK
399 Park Avenue, 34th Floor, **New York** NY 10022-4690
Tel: 212 715 1000 **Fax:** 212 715 1399

CALIFORNIA
777 South Figueroa Street, 44th Floor, **Los Angeles** CA 90017-5844
Tel: 213 243 4000 **Fax:** 213 243 4199

1900 Avenue of the Stars, 17th Floor, **Los Angeles** CA 90067-4408
Tel: 310 552 2500 **Fax:** 310 552 1191

VIRGINIA
1600 Tysons Boulevard, Suite 900, **McLean** VA 22102-4865
Tel: 703 720 7000 **Fax:** 703 720 7399

COLORADO
370 Seventeenth Street, Suite 4500, **Denver** CO 80202-1370
Tel: 303 863 1000 **Fax:** 303 832 0428

INTERNATIONAL OFFICES

The firm also has an office in London.

CONTACTS

Antitrust/Competition	Bill Baer
Bankruptcy	Daniel Lewis
Consumer Product Safety	Eric Rubel
Corporate & Securities	Steven Kaplan
Derivatives	Dan Waldman
Employee Benefits	Edward Bintz
Environmental	Thomas Milch
Financial Services	Patrick Doyle
Food, Drug & Medical Devices	William Vodra
Government Contracts	Joseph West
Intellectual Property & Technology	David Apatoff
	Joel Freed
Life Sciences/Biotech	Rick Johnson
Litigation	Robert Weiner
National Security Law & Policy	Jeffrey Smith
Outsourcing	George Kimball
Privacy	John Bentivoglio
Private Equity	John Fitzgerald
Product Liability	Robert Weiner
	Ellen Reisman
Project Finance	Ken Langan
Public Policy & Legislative	Jeffrey Smith
Real Estate	George Covucci
Sports Industry	John Kronstadt
Tax & Estates	Richard Hubbard
Telecommunications	Norman Sinel
White Collar Crime	Robert Litt

ARNOLD & PORTER

LEADING LAW FIRMS

ASTIGARRAGA DAVIS

THE FIRM

Contact: José I Astigarraga

AREAS OF PRACTICE:
Litigation & Arbitration 100%

HEAD OFFICE

FLORIDA
701 Brickell Avenue, 16th Floor, **Miami** FL 33131
Tel: 305 372 8282   **Fax:** 305 372 8202
Email: jia@astidavis.com
Website: www.astidavis.com

FIRM OVERVIEW: Astigarraga Davis is a boutique litigation and arbitration firm. With a broad range of experience, its lawyers prosecute and defend a wide variety of commercial litigation and business tort cases. Serving primarily multinational corporate clients, the firm's principal areas of practice are international litigation and arbitration; financial services litigation including bankruptcy; prosecution of commercial fraud including asset recovery; defense of consumer class actions; and intellectual property litigation.

MAIN AREAS OF PRACTICE:

Litigation & Arbitration: Representing primarily North American and European multinational companies, Astigarraga Davis both prosecutes and defends cases in federal and state courts involving international business disputes. Using its extensive international experience, multilingual capabilities, multicultural background, and broad network of contacts in the region, the firm also oversees and directs substantial business litigation pending in Latin American courts.

The firm has a leading international arbitration practice handling cases before the major international arbitral institutions. The firm's lawyers are active in arbitration and litigation initiatives. José Astigarraga, for example, was one of eight delegates appointed by the United States Government to advise the NAFTA Commission on international arbitration and dispute resolution. He is a member of the American Arbitration Association's International Rules Advisory Committee, is a founder of the Latin American Users' Council of the London Court of International Arbitration, and has lectured extensively on international litigation and arbitration including to the negotiators of the Free Trade Agreement of the Americas.

Financial Services Litigation, including Bankruptcy: Astigarraga Davis has extensive litigation experience representing lenders, creditors, banks and other financial institutions in disputes in the United States and abroad. The firm represents financial institutions in state and federal court litigation in investor disputes, securities issues, and loan enforcement. The firm's lawyers handle much creditors' rights litigation including such pre-judgment creditors' remedies as replevin, garnishment, attachment and injunctions.

As well, the firm represents lenders and creditors domestically in bankruptcy courts in Florida and other states, and internationally in Latin America, including in multijurisdictional insolvencies. Founding shareholder Greg Grossman has extensive bankruptcy experience, having handled cases in a number of domestic bankruptcy courts in a diverse array of cases. José Astigarraga has served as consultant to the World Bank on Latin American insolvency law issues and has handled international insolvency cases for both bank and non-bank clients.

Commercial Fraud & Asset Recovery: The firm's work includes a strong practice in fraud prosecution and asset recovery. Working with its network of lawyers and contacts, the firm has pursued fraudsters in a variety of jurisdictions to recover fraudulently obtained assets. The firm devises fraud prevention and contingency response plans for corporate clients and advises audit committees on such issues. Name partner Edward H Davis, Jr is a member of the Certified Fraud Examiners' Association and has lectured extensively on fraud prevention and recovery.

Defense of Consumer Class Actions: Astigarraga Davis has experienced class action litigators, including founding shareholder Edward Mullins who has defended numerous class actions in state and federal courts. He has defended financial institutions and insurance companies in claims involving the Truth-in-Lending Act, the Florida Unfair Trade Practices Act, Florida's usury statute, and claims derived from various consumer insurance statutes. The firm's expertise in arbitration has benefited the class action defense practice, including in litigation over whether arbitration clauses in consumer contracts are unconscionable and unenforceable.

Intellectual Property: The firm has extensive experience in intellectual property, with capabilities including trademark, trade secret, internet, e-commerce, and media law disputes. Founding shareholder Edward Mullins, a former chair of the Florida Bar Media and Communications Law Committee, has represented newspapers, magazines, radio and television stations, and television networks in numerous lawsuits involving libel, slander, invasion of privacy, outrage, tortious interference with advantageous relationships, trademark infringement, copyright infringement and other publication disputes. The firm's deep knowledge allows it to represent its corporate clients in domain name disputes, intellectual property infringement claims based on the internet, and similar publication claims.

CLIENTS: Astigarraga Davis' clients include multinational companies, global banks, Fortune 500 corporations and government entities.

ASTIGARRAGA DAVIS

LEADING LAW FIRMS

BAKER & McKENZIE

THE FIRM

Chairman of the Executive Committee: Christine Lagarde
US Managing Partner: John Conroy

Number of North American partners: 155
Number of other lawyers in North America: 388
Number of partners worldwide: 623
Number of other lawyers worldwide: 2640

FIRM OVERVIEW: Baker & McKenzie is a truly global law firm committed to providing superior service to its clients. Since its foundation over 50 years ago, the firm has established teams of prominent and highly experienced attorneys who are knowledgeable in both domestic and international law. By leveraging its unrivaled network of over 60 offices in 35 countries, Baker & McKenzie is able to offer integrated cross-border service to multinational and domestic clients across the full spectrum of commercial law.

MAIN AREAS OF PRACTICE:
Banking, Finance & Major Projects: Practitioners represent clients in all aspects of financing and capital market transactions, including debt restructuring and insolvency, as well as in a variety of areas relevant to major projects, where practitioners have particular experience in industries such as power, oil and gas, telecommunications, transportation, water, environmental, and renewable resources.
Corporate & Securities: Practitioners serve clients in a broad spectrum of corporate and securities matters in the US and abroad, including mergers and acquisitions, US and global securities, venture capital and private equity, corporate investigations/Foreign Corrupt Practices Act, SEC and regulatory matters, independent counsel, and corporate litigation.
Compensation & Employment Law: Practitioners handle the entire range of corporate labor and employment law issues, inclusive of counseling and litigation, executive compensation and employee benefits, business immigration and executive transfers, and global equity services.
Information Technology/Communications/E-commerce: Practitioners offer a wide array of legal services relating to complex IT licensing, e-commerce, privacy, and media and entertainment, representing major public companies, leading trade associations, government agencies, and other businesses and entrepreneurs around the world.
Intellectual Property: Practitioners provide a wide range of services involving patents, copyrights, and trademarks, including counseling and litigation in the US and abroad.
International: Multicultural practitioners provide specialized assistance in a broad spectrum of cross-border and general commercial law issues to US companies operating abroad, as well as to foreign companies operating in the United States.
Litigation (& Antitrust): Attorneys provide a full range of dispute resolution and litigation services, acting as trial and appellate counsel in state and federal courts and provide representation before tribunals, mediation panels, administrative agencies, and grand juries.
Tax: Consistently regarded as one of the premier international tax practices, attorneys provide a wide range of services, concentrating in the areas of tax planning, transfer pricing, mergers and acquisitions, global tax minimization, private banking, fringe benefits and employment taxation, state and local, e-tax, and litigation.

CLIENTS: Baker & McKenzie provides exceptional service to domestic and international clients in almost every industry and sector by forming dedicated multidisciplinary teams that share their clients' interests. The firm's extensive client list includes multinational and domestic entities, a great many of whom engage the firm on a multijurisdictional basis. Clients include major corporations, financial institutions, and other business organizations, as well as governments and multilateral agencies.

INTERNATIONAL WORK: From its inception, Baker & McKenzie has recognized the importance of maintaining a global perspective in all its client services. The firm is a pioneer in understanding that global clients are best served by locally experienced, yet internationally qualified lawyers who are intimately familiar with the legal and business practices of their country and region. Baker & McKenzie has created its multinational culture through internal strategy and growth, which ensures outstanding firm-wide identity and camaraderie that forges strong personal relationships among its attorneys and reflects the firm's belief that the best cross-border service comes from lawyers who know each other and practice law with each other on a daily basis.

HEAD OFFICE

ILLINOIS
One Prudential Plaza, 130 East Randolph Dr., **Chicago**, IL 60601
Tel: 312 861 8000 **Fax:** 312 861 2899
Email: info@bakernet.com
Website: www.bakernet.com

BRANCH OFFICES

TEXAS
2300 Trammell Crow Center, 2001 Ross Avenue, **Dallas**, TX 75201
Tel: 214 978 3000 **Fax:** 214 978 3099
Email: mark.d.taylor@bakernet.com

Chevron Tower, 1301 McKinney St., Ste 3300, **Houston**, TX 77010
Tel: 713 427 5000 **Fax:** 713 427 5099
Email: j.richard.hammett@bakernet.com

FLORIDA
1200 Brickell Avenue, 19th Floor, **Miami**, FL 33131
Tel: 305 789 8900 **Fax:** 305 789 8953
Email: donald.hayden@bakernet.com

NEW YORK
805 Third Avenue, **New York**, NY 10022
Tel: 212 751 5700 **Fax:** 212 759 9133
Email: gerald.j.hayes@bakernet.com

CALIFORNIA
660 Hansen Way, **Palo Alto**, CA 94304
Tel: 650 856 2400 **Fax:** 650 856 9299
Email: peter.j.engstrom@bakernet.com

101 West Broadway, 12th Floor, **San Diego**, CA 92101
Tel: 619 236 1441 **Fax:** 619 236 0429
Email: charles.h.dick@bakernet.com

Two Embarcadero Center, 24th Floor, **San Francisco**, CA 94111
Tel: 415 576 3000 **Fax:** 415 576 3099
Email: peter.j.engstrom@bakernet.com

DISTRICT OF COLUMBIA
815 Connecticut Avenue, NW, **Washington, DC** 20006
Tel: 202 452 7000 **Fax:** 202 452 7074
Email: thomas.j.egan@bakernet.com

INTERNATIONAL OFFICES

Baker & McKenzie has over 50 offices in 34 countries outside of the United States.

LEADING LAW FIRMS

BALCH & BINGHAM LLP

THE FIRM

Managing Partner & Chairman, Executive Committee: James F Hughey, Jr

Number of partners: 103
Number of other lawyers: 69

AREAS OF PRACTICE:
Litigation	.30%
Financial Services & Transactions	19%
Utility, Legislative & Regulatory	18%
Corporate, Tax & Finance	17%
Labor & Employment	9%
Environmental & Natural Resources	7%

FIRM OVERVIEW: Founded in 1922, Balch & Bingham LLP is one of the largest law firms in Alabama with offices in Birmingham, Montgomery, and Huntsville, Alabama, Gulfport and Jackson, Mississippi, and Washington, DC. Balch & Bingham LLP serves a diverse group of clients in business and litigation matters.

MAIN AREAS OF PRACTICE:

Litigation: Attorneys in this group handle trial and appellate practice before federal and state courts, administrative agencies and arbitration panels. The litigation attorneys handle cases in the areas of antitrust, professional liability, consumer finance, insurance, personal injury and property damage, securities, accounting, construction, products liability, intellectual property and trade secrets, computers and technology, First Amendment and media. This group supports the litigation needs of the firm's other practice groups, including banking, healthcare, ERISA and managed care litigation, environmental, labor and commercial disputes.

Financial Services & Transactions: The firm represents financial institutions in bank and bank holding formations, mergers and acquisitions, establishing branches, interstate banking, and compliance with state and federal regulatory matters. In the area of commercial real estate, developers, owners and mortgage lenders are represented in the many aspects of project development. The firm has played a major role in significant real estate projects throughout the State of Alabama. The firm's Bankruptcy Practice is devoted to creditors' rights, debt restructuring, workouts, debt collection and bankruptcy.

Utility, Legislative & Regulatory: The Utility, Legislative and Regulatory Practice handles legal issues associated with every energy option. In addition to being active in the field of utility regulation and rate making, these attorneys handle contract work, including drafting, negotiation and administration and have particular expertise with contracts relating to the purchase, sale and transportation of coal, natural gas and other energy resources. Attorneys are also actively involved in the drafting and evaluating of proposed federal and state legislation and regulations.

Corporate, Tax & Finance: The firm's Corporate and Securities Practice provides business planning and counseling services to corporations, partnerships and individuals, including structuring and restructuring business organizations and preparing agreements for corporate and partnership governance, shareholder and partnership relationships and employment arrangements. The firm assists clients with public and private securities offerings, corporate transactions and finance, project finance, intellectual property, and antitrust matters. This group also includes attorneys practicing in the following areas: (1) general taxation, including tax planning and representation in complex business transactions involving publicly traded and closely held corporations, general and limited partnerships, joint ventures, proprietorships, and charitable and other tax-exempt organizations, tax litigation, and representation before the Internal Revenue Service and state and local administrative bodies; (2) estate planning and administra-

HEAD OFFICE

ALABAMA
1710 Sixth Avenue North, **Birmingham**, AL 35203
Tel: 205 251 8100 **Fax:** 205 226 8798
Email: nyardley@balch.com
Website: www.balch.com

BRANCH OFFICES

ALABAMA
2 Dexter Avenue, **Montgomery**, AL 36104
Tel: 334 834 6500 **Fax:** 334 269 3115

655 Gallatin Street, **Huntsville**, AL 35801
Tel: 256 551 0171 **Fax:** 256 512 0119

DISTRICT OF COLUMBIA
1275 Pennsylvania Avenue, N.W., **Washington, DC**, 20004
Tel: 202 347 6000 **Fax:** 202 347 6001

MISSISSIPPI
1310 Twenty Fifth Avenue, **Gulfport**, MS 39501
Tel: 228 864 9900 **Fax:** 228 864 8221

401 East Capitol Street, Suite 200, **Jackson**, MS 39201
Tel: 212 751 5700 **Fax:** 212 759 9133

CONTACTS

Litigation	Alan T Rogers
Financial Services & Transactions	H Hampton Boles
Utility, Legislative & Regulatory	DH McCrary
	M Stanford Blanton
Labor & Employment	Charles B Paterson
Environmental & Natural Resources	William H Satterfield

tion, including preparation of wills and trusts and counseling and representation in gift and estate tax matters; and (3) governmental and public authority finance, in which area the firm's attorneys serve as bond counsel, underwriter's counsel and issuer's counsel in tax-exempt and taxable financing on behalf of the State of Alabama, agencies and departments of the State, municipalities and counties and numerous public authorities, boards and corporations at the State and local levels.

Labor & Employment: Attorneys in this group advise clients on employment and labor issues and represent clients in administrative proceedings, elections, arbitrations, and jury and non-jury trials in state and federal forums. Development of effective employment policies, testing and other employee selection procedures, employee manuals, and programs to control drug and alcohol abuse are among the services offered. Industries served by the firm's labor and employment attorneys include utility, construction, manufacturing, retail, banking and financial organizations as well as municipalities, school boards and universities.

Environmental & Natural Resources: The Environmental and Natural Resources Group provides representation and counseling on environmental and natural resource issues to clients ranging from individuals and small businesses to large corporations. Attorneys are actively engaged in state and federal legislation processes and the related administrative rulemaking proceedings. Using their knowledge of the laws, regulations and political climate, the attorneys provide direction on compliance issues, applications for environmental permits, and the appeal and litigation defense of state and federal environmental issues.

INTERNATIONAL WORK: The firm has assisted its clients from time to time in transactions in foreign countries.

LEADING LAW FIRMS

BALLARD SPAHR ANDREWS & INGERSOLL, LLP

THE FIRM

Chairman: Arthur Makadon

Number of partners: 195
Number of other lawyers: 450

FIRM OVERVIEW: Ballard Spahr Andrews & Ingersoll, LLP was founded in 1886. Throughout its history, the firm has been committed to excellence in the practice of law. It has grown to be one of the 100 largest law firms in the country, with over 450 lawyers and seven offices located throughout the mid-Atlantic corridor and the western United States. As a large, multi-office, multi-regional law firm, Ballard Spahr is able to combine a national scope of practice with strong local market knowledge to represent companies, individuals, and other entities in virtually every state and around the world.

MAIN AREAS OF PRACTICE:

Business & Finance: The firm's Business and Finance Department has a regional, national, and international practice involving public and private companies and nonprofit organizations. Their clients are engaged with wide-ranging and dynamic technology, manufacturing, and service functions; pharmaceutical, energy, telecommunications, and software manufacturing companies; financial institutions; investment companies; sports and other franchises; public utilities; and hospitals and health services. They also represent issuers, underwriters, lenders, and venture capitalists in equity and debt financing for companies large and small, private and public. The firm's business and finance lawyers serve their clients on a national basis in mergers, acquisitions, and other complex transactions and provide legal counseling and compliance for investment companies and advisors, banks, broker/dealers, consumer finance companies, credit card issuers, and public companies and their boards of directors.

Financial Planning & Management: Ballard Spahr's Financial Planning and Management Department includes lawyers in the Tax Group, Employee Benefits Group, and Family Wealth Management Group. The firm's tax practice involves sophisticated tax planning and handling tax disputes at all levels of government – federal, state, local, and international. The Employee Benefits Group provides clients with legal advice regarding the full range of qualified and nonqualified plans. The Family Wealth Management Group provides a comprehensive range of estate planning services to individuals of means.

Litigation: The Litigation Department represents a wide range of local, national, and international clients, including large and small companies in the public, private, and nonprofit sectors. They handle all types of complex litigation and regularly represent clients in local, state, and federal courts, at both the trial and appellate levels, as well as other forums throughout the country.

Public Finance: Ballard Spahr has a nationally recognized practice in the field of public finance and federal tax matters relating to the issuance of municipal bonds. The firm has consistently been ranked as one of the leading bond and underwriter counsel firms in the country. The firm's public finance lawyers serve as bond counsel, underwriter's counsel, trustee's counsel, and borrower's counsel for state and local governments and authorities throughout the United States, and have a wide range of experience in many areas of law, including municipal, tax, securities, real estate, housing, environmental, public utilities, energy, health care, education, banking, administrative, and corporate.

Real Estate: The firm's real estate lawyers provide cutting-edge representation for national and regional clients, including corporate, institutional, entrepreneurial, and public clients in acquisition, development, financing, leasing and sales, and other flagship transactions. In order to serve their clients effectively, the department is organized into discrete service groups: acquisitions and dispositions; complex development; construction; finance; hotel/resort/timeshare and workouts; housing; leasing; valuation; workouts; and zoning and land use.

HEAD OFFICE

PENNSYLVANIA
1735 Market Street, 51st Floor **Philadelphia**, PA 19130-7599
Tel: 215 665 8500 Fax: 215 864 8999
Email: lawyers@ballardspahr.com Website: www.ballardspahr.com

BRANCH OFFICES

COLORADO
1225 17th Street, Suite 2300, **Denver**, CO 80202-5596
Tel: 303 292 2400 Fax: 303 296 3956

DELAWARE
919 N. Market Street, 17th Floor, **Wilmington**, DE 19807
Tel: 302 252 4465 Fax: 302 252 4466

DISTRICT OF COLUMBIA
601 13th Street, NW, Suite 1000 South, **Washington**, DC 20005-3807
Tel: 202 661 2200 Fax: 202 661 2299

MARYLAND
300 East Lombard Street, 18th Floor, **Baltimore**, MD 21202-3268
Tel: 410 528 5600 Fax: 410 528 5650

NEW JERSEY
Plaza 1000-Suite 500, Main Street, **Voorhees**, NJ 08043-4636
Tel: 856 761 3400 Fax: 856 761 1020

UTAH
One Utah Center, Suite 600, 201 South Main Street, **Salt Lake City**, UT 84111-2221
Tel: 801 531 3000 Fax: 801 531 3001

CONTACTS

Bankruptcy	William A Slaughter
Business & Finance	William H Rheiner
Construction	Lynn R Axelroth
Consumer Financial Services	Alan S Kaplinsky
Eminent Domain/Condemnation	S David Brandt, George J Kroculick
Employee Benefits	John M Bernard
Energy & Project Finance	C Baird Brown, Charles S Henck
Environmental	David G Mandelbaum
Family Wealth Management	Benjamin R Neilson
Financial Planning & Management	Frederic L Ballard Jr
Franchise & Distribution	Benjamin A Levin
Government Enforcement/White Collar Crime	Eric W Sitarchuk
Health Care	Jennifer L Bragg
Housing	Steven P Berman
Intellectual Property	Jamie B Bischoff
Investment Management	William H Rheiner
Labor & Employment	John B Langel
Land Use	Michael Sklaroff
Litigation	Charisse R Lillie
Mergers & Acquisitions	Richard J Braemer
Public Finance	Blake K Wade
Real Estate	Michael Sklaroff
Real Estate Development	Richard R Goldberg
Real Estate Finance	Beverly J Quail, Fred Wolf III
Real Estate Investment Trusts	James J Hanks Jr
Real Estate Leasing	David L Pollack
Resorts & Hotels	Harry E McCoy II
Securities	Justin P Klein
Securitization	Lisa M Sloan
Tax	Wayne R Strasbaugh
Technology & Emerging Companies	Raymond D Agran
Telecommunications	Jerold G Oldroyd
Transactional Finance	Carl H Fridy
Valuation	Philip B Korb

LEADING LAW FIRMS

BEIRNE, MAYNARD & PARSONS, L.L.P.

THE FIRM

Managing Partner: Martin D Beirne

Number of partners: 30
Number of other lawyers: 72 (include of counsels as well as associates)

AREAS OF PRACTICE:
Civil Trials, Appellate & Arbitration 100%

FIRM OVERVIEW: Founded in 1987, with eight lawyers, Beirne, Maynard & Parsons, L.L.P. has become a nationally significant force in civil trial and appellate work. The firm is now the largest firm in Texas dedicated solely to litigation. Beirne, Maynard & Parsons has pursued a growth path based on both general litigation and industry specialization. As specialists, the firm has developed one of the nation's leading life sciences and pharmaceutical litigation practices, along with prestigious national practice teams serving the energy and transportation industries. As generalists, the firm continues to serve a diverse range of Fortune 500 companies locally, nationally, and internationally. Because the firm specializes in winning trials, all its lawyers are trained to practice in court, which, in turn, has enabled Beirne, Maynard & Parsons to attract attorneys who might not otherwise obtain courtroom experience working at larger firms. The firm's arbitration specialists have vast experience before national and international tribunals. The Arbitration/Alternative Dispute Resolution Group (AADR) has successfully resolved disputes through mediation, national and international arbitration and other resolution forums. Beirne, Maynard & Parsons understands that going to court may not always be in the client's best interest. There are many avenues for dispute resolution. As such, the firm's trial lawyers are also trained to recognize when matters are best resolved through other mechanisms.

MAIN AREAS OF PRACTICE: Civil Trials, Appellate and Arbitration: As one of the nation's leading litigation firms, Beirne, Maynard & Parsons is distinguished for both breadth and depth. As civil trial generalists, Beirne, Maynard & Parsons represents hundreds of diverse corporations and other clients. Cases have ranged from product liability defense to anti-counterfeiting to a legation on behalf of sovereign states. The firm's biomedical litigation specialty is supported by a network of MDs, PhD pathologists, and 25 nurse paralegals. In addition to energy and transportation, the firm continues its significant practices in aviation, intellectual property, coverage and mass tort litigation and computer sciences. Because Texas is a plaintiff-friendly jurisdiction, Fortune 500 companies throughout the country have retained the firm when they are sued in the state. Additionally, Beirne, Maynard & Parsons' trial practice also includes substantial work in courtrooms and arbitration panels throughout the United States and globally.

CLIENTS: As generalists, the firm's client list includes AIG Companies; Chevron Chemical Company; Fireman's Fund Insurance Companies; Lloyd's of London; Marriott Corporation; Pratt & Whitney of Canada, Inc; The Travelers Insurance Companies; and United Technologies Corporation. The firm's fabled transportation client list includes: American Suzuki Motor Corporation; Associated Aviation Underwriters; Aviation Office of America; The Cessna Aircraft Company; Freightliner, LLC; Hyundai North America; Mercedes-Benz Truck Company; Mitsubishi Motor Sales of American, Inc; Subaru of America, Inc; Toyota Motor Sales, USA, Inc; Union Tank Car Company; and Volvo North American Corporation. The list also includes the People's Republic of China and the Republic of Estonia. Energy clients include Air Liquide Corporation; BP Amoco; Chevron Phillips; Schlumberger Technology Corporation and Brazos Electric Power Cooperative, Inc. In Life Sciences, Pfizer Inc is a major client; Beirne, Maynard & Parsons represents Pfizer in major litigation matters. Among other leading life science clients: Tanox, a biopharmaceutical company with expertise in allergy, asthma and immunological diseases; Enchira, a leader in breast cancer research; and Baylor College of Medicine, an internationally respected medical institution.

INTERNATIONAL WORK: Beirne, Maynard & Parson's work in overseas jurisdictions belies perceptions that only larger firms can handle matters outside the United States. The firm has represented numerous Fortune 500 companies in foreign disputes. In addition, the firm has been retained by sovereign nations like the People's Republic of China and the Republic of Estonia to litigate on their behalf. In one major case, Beirne, Maynard & Parsons represented the Republic of Estonia in a bilateral investment treaty issue. The Arbitration of the case was conducted under the auspices of the International Center for the Settlement of Investment Disputes (ICSID). The case was arbitrated in Switzerland, the UK and Washington, DC, with a final decision rendered on behalf of the Republic of Estonia.

HEAD OFFICE

TEXAS
Wells Fargo Tower, 25th floor, 1300 Post Oak Boulevard,
Houston, TX, 77056
Tel: 713 623 0887 **Fax:** 713 960 1527
Email: info@bmpllp.com
Website: www.bmpllp.com

BRANCH OFFICES

TEXAS
1700 Pacific Avenue, 44th floor, **Dallas**, TX 75201
Tel: 214 237 4300 **Fax:** 214 237 4340

CONTACTS

General Litigation/Commercial	Jeffrey R Parsons
	Roger L McCleary
	Martin D Beirne
Life Sciences & Pharmaceutical	Jack Urquhart
	Thomas Sartwelle
Transportation	Martin D Beirne
Energy/Utilities	Edward J Murphy
	Sawnie A McEntire
Telecommunications	Joseph S Cohen
Intellectual Property	William Norvell
	James Smith
Toxic Tort/Environmental	James Smith
	Timothy Hogan
Aviation	William L Maynard
Appellate	Jeffrey Nobles
	Terry Adams
Product Liability	Sawnie A McEntire
	William L Maynard
	Roger L McCleary
Coverage/Reinsurance Bad Faith	Jay W Brown
	David A Clark
	Roger L McCleary
	Marcy Rothman

LEADING LAW FIRMS

BEVERIDGE & DIAMOND, P.C.

THE FIRM

Managing Director: Robert Brager

Number of Directors: 29
Number of other lawyers: 50

FIRM OVERVIEW: Since opening in 1974, Beveridge & Diamond, P.C. has focused on environmental law and litigation. In court, in negotiations, and before government agencies, Beveridge & Diamond resolves complex problems and disputes, particularly in the environmental area, keeping in mind its clients' business goals.

MAIN AREAS OF PRACTICE:

Environmental: Beveridge & Diamond's practice encompasses all areas of environmental law, and the firm's long history and experience allow it to successfully handle the most significant and complicated environmental matters. Beveridge & Diamond represents domestic and international clients on environmental issues related to air, surface water and groundwater, solid and hazardous wastes, product use, stewardship and recycling, environmental reporting and disclosure, and compliance with the wide array of federal and state environmental laws and regulations. The firm also represents clients across the country with regard to environmentally contaminated properties, including 'brownfields' projects, and in negotiations with buyers, sellers, developers, and insurers of these properties. In addition, Beveridge & Diamond provides strategic advice to clients with regard to their environmental management systems, and has assisted clients with their environmental due diligence efforts in the United States and across the world.

Environmental Litigation & ADR: The firm's environmental litigation and alternative dispute resolution practice challenges agency actions in administrative, trial and appellate proceedings, defends against government enforcement actions and citizen suits, and represents clients in cases brought under the federal 'Superfund' law, other federal or state statutes, or common law with regard to the extent of remediation necessary to protect the environment and who should pay for the rememdiation. The firm litigates numerous other environmental cases in state and federal courts across the country, including takings and related land use matters.

Civil & White Collar Litigation: Beveridge & Diamond's civil litigation practice is accomplished in defending against toxic tort, product liability, and mass tort claims, and includes a strong commercial litigation component. The firm's appellate practice safeguards clients' rights after trial, and its litigators have pursued or defended against countless appeals in the United States Supreme Court, every federal circuit court of appeals, and state appellate courts around the country. In the white collar criminal area, the firm has extensive experience in assisting its clients in responding to ever increasing criminal enforcement efforts aimed at corporate entities and individual officers, directors, and employees. Its white collar attorneys have a unique environmental criminal practice, combining their experience on criminal matters with the firm's renowned reputation in environmental law to provide comprehensive and effective defenses.

Project Development: Major private project developments in the United States generally require one or more federal, state, or local permits or approvals under statutes protecting endangered species, wetlands, and other environmentally sensitive areas. The firm assists its clients with successful development strategies that are comprehensive, timely, and responsive to project needs and environmental regulatory requirements.

HEAD OFFICE

DISTRICT OF COLUMBIA
Suite 700, 1350 I Street, NW, **Washington, DC** 20005-3311
Tel: 202 789 6000 **Fax:** 202 789 6190
Email: contact.bd@bdlaw.com
Website: www.bdlaw.com

BRANCH OFFICES

CALIFORNIA
Suite 1800, 456 Montgomery Street, **San Francisco**, CA 94104-1251
Tel: 415 262 4000 **Fax:** 415 262 4040

31st Floor, 555 West Fifth Street, **Los Angeles**, CA 90013-1018
Tel: 213 996 8350 **Fax:** 213 996 8304

MARYLAND
Suite 2210, 201 North Charles Street, **Baltimore**, MD 21201-4150
Tel: 410 230 3850 **Fax:** 410 230 3868

NEW JERSEY
Beveridge & Diamond, 26 Franklin Street, **Tenafly**, NJ 07670-2515
Tel: 201 568 2797 **Fax:** 201 568 9570

NEW YORK
15th Floor, 477 Madison Avenue, **New York**, NY 10022-5802
Tel: 212 702 5400 **Fax:** 212 702 5450

CONTACTS

Environmental/Environmental Litigation	Donald J Patterson, Jr
Litigation	John N Hanson
Project Development	Jennifer L Hernandez

CLIENTS: Beveridge & Diamond represents domestic and international resource and energy companies, manufacturers, chemical companies, makers of pesticides, biotechnology companies, producers of raw materials, transportation companies, high-tech component makers, food and consumer products companies, financial institutions, trade associations, and real estate developers.

INTERNATIONAL WORK: As clients pursue international trade and investment opportunities, the firm has continued to expand its international environmental practice in order to help companies identify, understand, and comply with the expanding body of international, national, and sub-national environmental law in countries and regions throughout the world. The firm regularly advises clients on a wide range of matters arising under multilateral environmental agreements, the environmental aspects of multilateral trade and investment agreements, and significant environmental regulatory and policy developments across the globe.

LEADING LAW FIRMS

BILZIN SUMBERG BAENA PRICE & AXELROD LLP

THE FIRM

Managing Partner: John C Sumberg

Number of partners: 34
Number of other lawyers: 36

AREAS OF PRACTICE:
Real Estate	28%
Insolvency	22%
Litigation	17%
Land Use, Local Government & Environmental Law	16%
Corporate & Securities	14%
Tax & Estate Planning	3%

HEAD OFFICE

FLORIDA
200 South Biscayne Boulevard, Suite 2500, **Miami**, FL 33131
Tel: 305 374 7580 Fax: 305 374 7593
Email: info@bilzin.com
Website: www.bilzin.com

CONTACTS
Real Estate	John C Sumberg
Corporate & Securities	Alan D Axelrod
Insolvency	Scott L Baena
Land Use	Stanley B Price
Litigation	Alvin D Lodish
Tax & Estate Planning	Richard M Goldstein

FIRM OVERVIEW: Bilzin Sumberg Baena Price & Axelrod LLP is a full service law firm with 70 attorneys. The firm has extensive experience in the areas of commercial real estate, corporate and securities, restructuring and bankruptcy, land use/zoning and governmental law, civil litigation and dispute resolution, and tax, trusts and estates. The attorneys in the firm combine legal expertise with business insight and innovative solutions in handling complex matters and transactions and assisting clients in achieving their objectives.

MAIN AREAS OF PRACTICE:

Real Estate: The Real Estate Department provides legal counsel in all facets of commercial real estate transactions, from the routine to the highly complex, including development and redevelopment of real estate projects, the purchase and sale of commercial real estate assets, leasing, condominium law, and related governmental and regulatory issues. The firm also counsels clients in highly specialized real estate transactions such as redeveloping properties into telcom/internet facilities.

Corporate & Securities: The attorneys in the Corporate and Securities Department combine legal expertise with business acumen in assisting both public and private companies and entrepreneurs with organizing, structuring, operating, financing and growing their businesses and accomplishing their goals. The Department regularly represents clients in complex transactions related to the structuring of business, joint venture and strategic relationships; corporate governance matters including shareholder arrangements and board of directors and audit committee representations; public and private offerings including Regulation D, Rule 144A and Regulation S offerings; mergers and acquisitions including leveraged buyouts; federal and state securities law compliance and reporting obligations; venture capital and debt financing including lines of credit, asset based and cash flow financing, subordinate and mezzanine financing, securitizations, repurchase, swap and hedging arrangements and equipment lease financing; employment and non-competition arrangements and executive compensation; and licensing.

Insolvency: The Restructuring and Bankruptcy Department has extensive experience with routine and complex in-court and out-of-court reorganizations, workouts, assignments for the benefit of creditors and bankruptcy litigation. The firm represents all constituencies in chapter 7 and 11 cases. It currently serves as counsel to asbestos committees of WR Grace and US Gypsum, the liquidating trustees of Crown Vantage, ContiFinancial and Southern Pacific Financial, the Celotex Property Damage Claims Facility, and, Heilig-Meyers (a debtor) as special litigation counsel.

Land Use, Local Government & Environmental: The Land Use Department has extensive experience in local governmental practice, including Growth Management Act issues, the expanding area of landowner relief, procurements by public agencies and the administration of government contracts. The Department frequently facilitates co-operative efforts of public agencies and private organizations in Miami-Dade and Broward Counties on projects of major economic, civic and cultural significance. Additionally, the Department counsels clients in environmental matters including remediation activities, civil liability, risk management and claims by and against others.

Litigation: The Litigation Department has vast experience litigating complex cases before all federal and state trial and appellate courts, as well as federal and state administrative bodies. The Department's expertise includes class actions, products liability, construction, business disputes, business torts, real estate disputes, condemnation, and insurance litigation. Recent representations resulted in the defeat of class certification in a major homeowner class action on behalf of a developer; a favorable settlement for a foreign corporation with the Government of Honduras; the resolution of a complex dispute between a major hotel against its management company; and the prosecution and settlement of fraudulent conveyance actions in the WR Grace bankruptcy for $1 billion. The firm represents clients before the Department of Justice, the Securities & Exchange Commission, the Federal Aviation Administration, the FDIC and the Department of Transportation.

Tax & Estate Planning: The Tax Department provides sophisticated tax counseling, including tax planning, tax litigation, estate planning, probate administration and the representation of non-resident aliens and foreign business organizations in their US activities and the representation of US citizens and domestic business organizations in business conducted abroad.

CLIENTS: The firm's clients include BAC Florida Bank, Coldwell Banker, Constructa, Inc., GE Capital Realty Group, Inc., Gibraltar Bank, Goodwill Industries, Inc., GPA-I. LP (Developers of SouthCom Headquarters), Heilig-Meyers, Lehman Brothers Holdings, Inc., Lennar Corporation, LNR Property Corporation, MDM Brickell (JW Marriott Miami), Mellon United National Bank, Merck & Co., National Beverage Corporation, Skyline Equities Realty, Swerdlow Real Estate Group, Total Health Choice, Inc., Trade Station Group, Inc. and Westbrook Partners, as well as numerous official creditors committees and liquidating trustees.

LEADING LAW FIRMS

BODMAN, LONGLEY & DAHLING LLP

THE FIRM

Chairman, Executive Committee: Larry R Shulman

Number of partners: 68
Number of other lawyers: 51

AREAS OF PRACTICE:
Banking	27%
Litigation	17%
Individual Clients	13%
Business/Corporate	9%
Real Property	8%
Debtor-Creditor Rights & Bankruptcy	6%
Labor & Employment	6%
Tax	4%
Intellectual Property	3%
Environmental	3%
Municipal Law & Finance	2%
Construction	2%

HEAD OFFICE

MICHIGAN
34th Floor, 100 Renaissance Center, **Detroit**, MI 48243
Tel: 313 259 7777 **Fax:** 313 393 7579
Email: info@bodmanlongley.com
Website: www.bodmanlongley.com

BRANCH OFFICES

MICHIGAN
Suite 300, 110 Miller, **Ann Arbor**, MI 48104
Tel: 734 761 3780 **Fax:** 734 940 2494
Email: info@bodmanlongley.com

229 Court Street, PO Box 405, **Cheboygan**, MI 49721
Tel: 231 627 4351 **Fax:** 231 627 2802
Email: info@bodmanlongley.com

Suite 500, 201 West Big Beaver Rd., **Troy**, MI 48084
Tel: 248 743 6000 **Fax:** 248 743 6002
Email: info@bodmanlongley.com

CONTACTS
Banking	Kathleen O'Callaghan Hickey
Litigation	Robert G Brower
Business/Corporate	Terrence B Larkin
Real Property	David W Hipp
Individual Clients	David P Larsen
Debtor-Creditor Rights & Bankruptcy	Robert J Diehl, Jr.
Labor & Employment	John C Cashen
Intellectual Property	Susan M Kornfield
Municipal Law & Finance	Jerold Lax
Environmental	Fredrick J Dindoffer
Construction	Harvey W Berman
Tax	Christopher J Dine

FIRM OVERVIEW: Founded in 1927, Bodman, Longley & Dahling LLP offers a full range of business law services. Its 119 attorneys practice in four offices located in Detroit, Oakland County, Ann Arbor and Northern Michigan. Bodman, Longley & Dahling LLP's Banking Practice Group is one of the most experienced in the United States. In 1933, it incorporated Manufacturers Bank and became its general counsel. Forty years later, it established the bank's holding company, which merged with Comerica Incorporated in 1992. The firm continues to represent Comerica, and is counsel or special counsel to more than 90 other financial institutions in Michigan and across the nation. Services to financial institution clients include representation in all aspects of Michigan, national and international lending transactions; in workouts, in state and federal regulatory matters, in debt restructurings and bankruptcy proceedings; in their roles as corporate trustees under bond indentures and other debt issues, including industrial revenue and other tax exempt bonds; in multi-bank credits (both as agent and as participant bank); and in the preparation, administration and enforcement of domestic and international letters of credit.

CLIENTS: Representative financial institution clients include: Comerica Incorporated; Standard Federal Bank, N.A.; National City Bank of Michigan/Illinois; The Huntington National Bank; Franklin Bank, N.A.; Federal National Mortgage Association (Fannie Mae); Bombardier Capital. Representative non-financial institution clients include: The Archdiocese of Detroit; Blue Cross and Blue Shield of Michigan; Booth Newspapers, Inc.; CSX Transportation, Inc.; City of Detroit; The Detroit Lions, Inc.; Ford Estates; City of Grosse Pointe Park; Lear Corp.; Michigan Insurance Commissioner; Charles Stewart Mott Foundation; National Association of Investors Corporation; National Automotive Parts Association; Norfolk Southern Corporation; Pacific Mutual Life Insurance Company; PanEnergy Corp.; Pulte Homes of Michigan; St. John Health System; Sisters of Mercy; State Farm Insurance Companies; Sun America Insurance Company; University of Detroit-Mercy; Viacom Outdoor Group; Wayne County; Jervis B. Webb Company.

INTERNATIONAL WORK: Bodman Longley represents numerous international clients with business interests in Michigan and elsewhere within the United States. Representative International clients include: Daimler-Chrysler; Allied Irish Banks, PLC; Blue Circle America, Inc.; Techform Products, Ltd.

BODMAN, LONGLEY & DAHLING LLP

LEADING LAW FIRMS

BRACEWELL & PATTERSON L.L.P.

THE FIRM

Managing Partner: Patrick C Oxford

Number of partners: 155
Number of other lawyers: 202

FIRM OVERVIEW: Bracewell & Patterson maintains 11 offices in Texas; Virginia; Washington, DC; London and Kazakhstan. It is one of Texas' largest firms with 357 attorneys. Founded in 1945 in Houston, Bracewell & Patterson has enjoyed steady growth and expansion by responding to the needs of clients and fostering a culture of collaboration among firm members. The firm has 50 practice areas and a balanced offering of business, litigation and government policy-related legal services.

MAIN AREAS OF PRACTICE

Energy: With its roots in Houston, an international energy center, a key Bracewell strength is its energy practice. The firm literally grew up with the industry and, throughout its history, has represented energy companies in matters ranging from finance to litigation to labor and employment. Its client portfolio includes national and international companies and encompasses oil and gas, power, liquefied natural gas and alternative energy.

Finance: In 2002, the firm's finance work in the power generation industry was recognized by *Project Finance* magazine with 'Deal of the Year' honors. Bracewell also ranked as one of the top 10 project finance legal advisors in North America in that magazine's annual league tables.

Corporate & Securities: Beyond energy and finance, Bracewell has been lauded for its corporate and securities representation. Firm partners are regularly recognized among the 'Best Lawyers in America' and recently *Board of Directors* magazine named the firm as one of the five best to do business with in Houston.

Intellectual Property: In intellectual property law, the firm ranks among the top 10% of US firms in the number of patents issued in 2001. Partners in this practice have been recognized for the value of the patents they have filed and for being among the state's top lawyers in representing leading-edge technology.

Banking: Bracewell's banking practice took off in 1973, launched by a partner who served as Comptroller of the Currency under two Presidents. Since then, the firm has built a team that last year participated in 13 merger and acquisition deals and was recently ranked by *Bank Director* magazine as one of the 10 most active bank legal advisers in the country.

Labor & Employment: The firm has one of the largest labor and employment practices in the Southwest with more than 60 lawyers, many of whom are board certified specialists. Five have been named fellows by the prestigious College of Labor & Employment Lawyers.

Trial: Bracewell's trial practice includes more than 100 attorneys experienced in arguing before Texas courts and federal district courts in commercial and complex tort contingency cases.

Other: The firm has equally strong assets across the balance of its practice areas including bankruptcy, environmental, tax, real estate, government relations and strategy, regulated and restructured industries and school and public law.

HEAD OFFICE

TEXAS
711 Louisiana, Ste. 2900, **Houston**, TX 77002
Tel: 713 223 2900 **Fax:** 713 221 1212
Website: www.bracepatt.com

BRANCH OFFICES

Austin, Texas; Corpus Christi, Texas; Dallas; Fort Worth, Texas; Northern Virginia; San Antonio, Texas; Washington, DC

INTERNATIONAL OFFICES

Kazakhstan and London

CONTACTS

Bankruptcy	Trey A Wood III
Business & Technology	Thomas W Adkins, Gail Papermaster
Corporate & Securities	William D Gutermuth
Environmental	Luis M Nido
Financial Services	William T Luedke IV
Government Relations & Strategy	Gene E Godley
Intellectual Property	Andrew J Dillon, Ben D Tobor
Labor & Employment	Thomas M Melo, J Tullos Wells
Public Law	Jeffrey J Horner
Real Estate, Energy & Finance	Mark C Evans
Regulated & Restructured Industries	Charles H Shoneman
Tax & Wealth Management	Roger D Aksamit
Trial	J Clifford Gunter III

CLIENTS: Firm clients include numerous Fortune 500 and 1000 companies in a diverse array of industries as well as government and public entities, both national and international.

INTERNATIONAL WORK: Bracewell & Patterson provides counsel to companies, private investors, financial institutions and foreign governments. Its overseas locations include London and Kazakhstan. The firm advises businesses in Europe, Latin America and Central Asia on ways to build and solidify investments in the United States and helps US companies evaluate and launch new ventures abroad.

BROWN & BAIN, P.A.

THE FIRM

Managing Partner: Joseph E Mais
Senior Partner: C Randall Bain

Number of partners: 33
Number of other lawyers: 32

HEAD OFFICE

ARIZONA
2901 North Central Avenue, Suite 2000, **Phoenix**, AZ 85001-2788
Tel: 602 351 8000 **Fax:** 602 648 7000
Email: info@brownbain.com
Website: www.brownbain.com

FIRM OVERVIEW: Brown & Bain was founded in 1960 by the late Jack Brown, who was lauded as the "Dean of the High Tech Bar" for his leading role in the formative years of technology-related litigation. Along with Randy Bain, who continues to practice, Jack built a national practice of outstanding reputation. Although its core practice continues to be complex intellectual property and commercial litigation, the firm offers a wide range of other services in corporate, transactional and regulatory matters. The firm is based in Arizona, but many of its attorneys are licensed elsewhere, from New York to California and in many states in between.

MAIN AREAS OF PRACTICE:

Intellectual Property: Intellectual property litigation, especially matters involving semiconductors and other computer-related technology, continues to be a major focus of Brown & Bain's practice. The firm handles major patent cases nationwide for leading technology companies such as Intel, Cypress Semiconductor and Maxim Integrated Products. In 1998, Randy Bain and the firm won a unanimous decision in the US Supreme Court in Pfaff v. Wells Electronics, which adopted the firm's suggestion to revise the test for the 'on-sale bar' to patenting. The firm regularly litigates and tries trade secret cases involving complex technology and related legal issues, including the 'inevitable disclosure' of trade secrets by recently departed employees. Trademark and copyright registration, litigation and advice are other mainstays of the firm's practice. The firm likewise maintains an active practice licensing intellectual property, negotiating joint development agreements and litigating disputes over technology-related contracts.

Antitrust, Unfair Trade Practices, Securities, Professional Liability & Appellate Practice: In the field of antitrust, the firm has long represented clients in investigations by federal and state antitrust authorities and has both brought and defended many private antitrust actions. For example, the firm represented Intel Corporation in monopolization claims brought by Advanced Micro Devices and Cyrix Corp. The firm regularly conducts antitrust training programs for its clients, and handles many matters involving allegations of unfair trade practices such as deceptive advertising claims. Brown & Bain has extensive experience in securities litigation and regularly represents clients in NASD arbitrations as well. In recent years, the firm has developed special expertise representing clients in government investigations and commercial litigation alleging violations of professional standards or rules of professional responsibility. For example, it has successfully defended several major accounting firms in civil and regulatory actions alleging malpractice. In addition, Brown & Bain has an extensive appellate practice spanning the field of civil litigation, including many cases in which the firm has been specially retained to overturn large adverse verdicts or argue issues of first impression.

Other Commercial Litigation & Advice: The firm's litigation expertise extends to a wide array of other matters, including class actions in both state and federal courts. Its product liability practice is extensive and combines the firm's nationally recognized litigation and dispute resolution skills with substantive familiarity with products ranging from computer chips to automobile tires to composite piping materials. Brown & Bain attorneys have also served as plaintiff's and defense counsel in construction-related disputes ranging from claims for leaking roofs to complex lawsuits involving large construction projects, performance bonds and insurance issues. The firm's government relations practice assists clients by monitoring legislative and executive branch activities, lobbying for and against legislation, facilitating meetings between clients and government officials, and participating in bid protests. Firm lawyers have served as elected officials, legislative staff, or government attorneys at all levels of government. In the field of labor and employment, Brown & Bain represents corporations in employment discrimination and wrongful termination actions, wage and hour matters, internal and government investigations, cases involving restrictive covenants and a variety of labor relations matters. Brown & Bain is well-known for its support of open government and First Amendment rights, and its media law practice has earned a national reputation. In addition to defending libel actions, Brown & Bain advises numerous media reporters and publishers in their efforts to obtain access to meetings, records and judicial proceedings. The firm assists its media clients in general litigation, antitrust issues, and various corporate transactions. Brown & Bain maintains a longstanding relationship with several Indian nations, advising them on issues involving land ownership, mineral development, water rights and gaming. The firm's litigation practice also encompasses environmental, administrative and utilities law.

Corporate & Real Estate: Brown & Bain's corporate and transactional practice includes banking and finance, bankruptcy, e-commerce and internet law, health care, labor and employment, mergers and acquisitions, securities, tax and commercial law matters. The firm's high technology client base presents many opportunities to prepare and negotiate licensing and technology transfer agreements and other complex transactions. Brown & Bain represents real estate clients with local, national and international interests. Its practice encompasses the acquisition, sale, and tax-free exchange of developed and undeveloped properties; development, entitlement and construction of residential, retail, industrial, hotel and office projects; secured and unsecured financing for lenders and borrowers; and leasing transactions on behalf of both landlords and tenants. The firm also advises on related issues such as subcontractor relationships, mechanic's liens, title insurance, water rights, adverse possession, environmental concerns, bonding and zoning.

CLIENTS: The firm's clients include America West Airlines, Applied Materials, Best Western International, Cemex, Cendant, Citibank, Citizens Communications, the Colorado River Indian Tribes, Comerica Bank, Cypress Semiconductor, Deloitte & Touche, Engle Homes, GAF, Goodyear Tire & Rubber, Honeywell, IBM, Intel, Maxim Integrated Products, Merrill Lynch, Microchip Technology, Morgan Stanley Dean Witter, the Navajo Nation, Newmont Mining, Phelps Dodge, PricewaterhouseCoopers, San Diego Gas & Electric Company, United Technologies, Vitesse Semiconductor, and Wells Fargo Bank.

INTERNATIONAL WORK: Brown & Bain prosecutes, defends, and maintains the trademark portfolio of the world's largest hotel chain, Best Western International, in 166 countries. Brown & Bain's work in the international arena includes copyrights, trademarks, domain names and unfair competition matters.

LEADING LAW FIRMS

BROWN RAYSMAN MILLSTEIN FELDER & STEINER LLP

THE FIRM

Managing Partners: Peter Brown, Richard Raysman and Julian Millstein
Number of partners: 79
Number of other lawyers: 145

FIRM OVERVIEW: Brown Raysman Millstein Felder & Steiner LLP is a full-service law firm and a leader in the areas of information technology, outsourcing, media and communications, e-commerce, intellectual property, life sciences, corporate and securities law, commercial finance, tax, real estate finance and leasing, banking and financial services, commercial and intellectual property litigation, antitrust, employment law, creditors' rights and bankruptcy and trusts and estates.

MAIN AREAS OF PRACTICE:

IT & Outsourcing: Brown Raysman is a recognized leader in information technology and outsourcing, with a premier clientele that includes many industry leaders. Many of the firm's attorneys have degrees in computer science or hands-on experience in the IT industry as systems analysts or programmers. Partners in the group have published several treatises and hundreds of articles in the areas of computer law, intellectual property and e-commerce.

Media & Communications: The firm offers a wide range of business and litigation services within the television, film, cable, on-line media, music, print publishing, music publishing, communications (including wireless, wireline, ILEC, CLEC, cellular, paging and Internet) and advertising industries.

E-Commerce: The firm's attorneys are steeped in the constantly-evolving business models, rapidly emerging technologies and ever changing legal environments of the global e-commerce marketplace. Its partners authored one of the earliest treatises on doing business on the Internet and contributed to one of the first European treatises on the subject.

Intellectual Property: Brown Raysman offers unparalleled services in the global clearance, acquisition, maintenance and enforcement of patents, trademarks, service marks, copyrights, trade secrets and related intellectual property such as Internet domain names. In particular, Brown Raysman has a premier high-technology and life sciences patent prosecution and litigation practice.

Corporate & Commercial Finance: The firm regularly represents issuers, underwriters, placement agents and selling shareholders in private placements, initial and secondary public offerings of debt and equity securities and other capital-raising transactions. It advises its public company clients on federal and state securities laws, as well as stock exchange and NASD requirements, and assists them in preparing SEC reports and other regulatory filings. In addition, the firm counsels its clients on cutting-edge corporate governance and shareholder-relations issues. The firm also has wide ranging expertise in commercial lending, asset-based lending, single investor and leveraged equipment finance, project and structured finance and securitization transactions.

Private Equity & Fund Formation: The firm advises funds and other private equity investors in their portfolio investments, from the term sheet through due diligence and closing, and in connection with the management of their assets. The firm is experienced in organizing both domestic and offshore private equity funds.

Mergers & Acquisitions: The firm structures, negotiates and closes complex domestic and cross-border mergers, acquisitions and strategic alliances for a broad range of public and private companies.

Real Estate Finance, Development & Leasing: Brown Raysman represents clients in all aspects of sophisticated real estate transactions nationwide, including financings, loan workouts and enforcements and loan portfolio purchases and sales. In recent years, the firm's real estate attorneys have closed billions of dollars in loans for financial institutions including investment banks, commercial banks, insurance companies and pension funds. The firm is retained on a regular basis to represent a broad range of domestic and foreign clients in the acquisition, development, disposition and leasing of commercial, office, hotel, multifamily and industrial properties nationwide. It is a national leader in representing owners and tenants in complex leasing transactions.

HEAD OFFICE

NEW YORK
900 Third Avenue, **New York**, NY 10022
Tel: 212 895 2000 **Fax:** 212 895 2900
Email: info@brownraysman.com
Website: www.brownraysman.com

BRANCH OFFICES

CALIFORNIA
1880 Century Park East, Suite 711, **Los Angeles**, CA 90067
Tel: 310 712 8300 **Fax:** 310 712 8383

CONNECTICUT
Cityplace II, 185 Asylum Street, **Hartford**, CT 06103
Tel: 860 275 6400 **Fax:** 860 275 6410

NEW JERSEY
163 Madison Avenue, PO Box 1989, **Morristown**, NJ 07962-1989
Tel: 973 775 8900 **Fax:** 973 775 8901

INTERNATIONAL OFFICES

The firm also has an office in Toronto, Canada, through an exclusive affiliation with Mann & Gahtan LLP.

Litigation & Arbitration: Brown Raysman's litigation and arbitration practice encompasses all of the firm's practice areas, particularly intellectual property, high technology and the Internet, securities (including NASD and NYSE arbitrations), contracts, employment, banking, bankruptcy, real estate, construction, antitrust and finance.

Antitrust & Trade Regulation: The firm is retained on a regular basis to represent clients in a broad range of transactions and litigation raising antitrust, unfair competition and consumer protection issues, particularly related to the technology and communications industries.

Employment & Labor: Represents companies on a full range of employment matters, including employment litigation and jury trials, benefits and ERISA issues and employment contracts. It has a proven track record of successfully representing Fortune 100 and smaller companies in connection with virtually every type of labor and employment controversy, and has counseled senior management on the most sensitive and complex employee relations topics.

Bankruptcy & Creditors' Rights: The firm regularly represents a broad range of debtors, creditors and other stakeholders in a wide range of business restructuring and insolvency matters, including bankruptcy cases, creditors' rights, litigations and out of court restructurings.

CLIENTS: Brown Raysman has a wide range of domestic and international clientele, including multinational media conglomerates and telecommunications companies, software developers, application providers and other high-tech industry companies, insurance companies, banks, investment firms, energy companies and pharmaceutical companies.

INTERNATIONAL WORK: The firm routinely represents its international clients in complex technology, corporate, real estate and commercial transactions, including cross-border M&A and the establishment of joint ventures and other strategic relationships. As one of the first law firms to practice technology law, many companies throughout the world turn to Brown Raysman for its keen understanding of the development, protection, commercialization and procurement of computer software and hardware. The firm has many associations in Europe, Israel and Japan, as well as a cross-border practice with its Canadian affiliate office. The firm's Canadian partners, affiliated through an exclusive association with the firm of Mann & Gahtan LLP and based in Toronto, position the firm to provide its clients with a broad range of Canadian legal services similar to those provided by the firm in the US. The firm's Canadian partners are recognized worldwide as leaders in technology and intellectual property law.

BUTZEL LONG

THE FIRM

Chairman & CEO: Richard E Rassel
President: Philip J Kessler
Chief Marketing Officer: Joseph J Melnick

Number of partners: 109
Number of other lawyers: 95

AREAS OF PRACTICE:
Litigation 35%
Corporate/Tax/Real Estate/Wealth Planning 35%
Labor/Employment/Benefits/Immigration 30%

FIRM OVERVIEW: The firm is one of Michigan's leading law firms, with over 200 lawyers and eight offices in Michigan and Florida. Since its founding in 1854, the firm has played a prominent role in the development of Detroit as a research, industrial and manufacturing center. The firm strives to be on the cutting edge of significant trends and developments in the business world including advanced technology and manufacturing, e-commerce, internet law, and global operations and transactions. The firm's approach is to provide a personalized attorney-client relationship based on a recognition of and responsiveness to each client's unique concerns and requirements. It seeks a clear understanding of the business needs of each client through industry-focused research, knowledge management and partnering relationships. A distinguishing advantage of the firm is a commitment to providing 'value added' counseling and advice to its clients. It is dedicated to providing full value for every dollar invested in legal services. Fees and billing mechanisms are structured to fit each client's situation. The firm's clients can expect superlative service and uncompromising work quality delivered in a cost-effective manner.

MAIN AREAS OF PRACTICE:
Litigation: Litigation remains one of the firm's core practice strengths throughout its 150 year history. Several areas of concentration provide representation throughout the United States. The firm continues its tradition of landmark, precedent setting matters in several areas of the law. The practice consists of skilled attorneys who by expertise and experience specialize in finding solutions for disputes arising out of business transactions and operations. The range of business matters successfully handled by this practice is as broad as business itself.
Corporate/Tax/Real Estate/Wealth Planning: The firm has a reputation as leader on all types of transaction and compliance issues. The firm maintains a depth of experience in all areas of corporate advice and counsel.
Labor/Employment/Benefits/Immigration: The firm is the established leader in all areas of workforce issues. Clients from around the globe are advised on all aspects of employment concerns.

INTERNATIONAL WORK: The firm has broad experience in all manner of international issues. A cross-disciplinary Global Trade and Transactions Group represents client interests throughout the world. The firm has developed a thriving Global Automotive Practice. The firm's lawyers serve as key advisors to automotive companies from Canada, the UK, Germany, other European suppliers, Japan and Korea. Special focus on developing economies of China and Mexico. Recently formed China Alliance to provide on the ground capabilities in Shanghai and Beijing. A founding member of Lex Mundi, a firm shareholder is the past Chair of the organization. Firm shareholder named by British Consulate as Honorary Consul for Michigan.

HEAD OFFICE

MICHIGAN
150 West Jefferson, Suite 900, **Detroit**, MI 48226
Tel: 313 225 7000 **Fax:** 313 225 7080
E-mail: info@butzel.com
Website: www.butzel.com

BRANCH OFFICES

FLORIDA
1200 North Federal Highway, Suite 420, **Boca Raton**, FL 33432
Tel: 561 368 2151 **Fax:** 561 368 4668

801 Laurel Oak Drive, Suite 705, **Naples**, FL 34108
Tel: 239 597 4500 **Fax:** 239 597 5623

11382 Prosperity Farms Road, Suite 227,
Palm Beach Gardens, FL 33410
Tel: 561 625 4442 **Fax:** 561 625 6901

MICHIGAN
350 S. Main Street, Suite 300, **Ann Arbor**, MI 48104
Tel: 734 995 3110 **Fax:** 734 995 1777

100 Bloomfield Hills Parkway, Suite 200, **Bloomfield Hills**, MI 48304
Tel: 248 258 1616 **Fax:** 248 258 1439

25 West 8th Street, Suite 200, **Holland**, MI 49423
Tel: 616 396 8860 **Fax:** 616 396 1771

110 West Michigan Avenue, Suite 1100, **Lansing**, MI 48933
Tel: 517 372 6622 **Fax:** 517 372 6672

LEADING LAW FIRMS

CADWALADER, WICKERSHAM & TAFT

THE FIRM

Managing Partner: Robert O Link Jr
Number of partners worldwide: 94
Number of other lawyers worldwide: 417

FIRM OVERVIEW: Established in New York in 1792, Cadwalader, Wickersham & Taft, a premier international law firm with over 500 attorneys in four offices, offers legal advice in banking, corporate finance, environmental, global public affairs, healthcare, insolvency, insurance and reinsurance, litigation, mergers and acquisitions, private client, project finance, real estate, securitization, structured finance, and tax matters.

MAIN AREAS OF PRACTICE:

Banking & Project Finance: This department advises in all aspects of banking and finance, including commercial lending, special bank regulatory needs, mortgage banking, and domestic and cross-border leasing. An expanding projects group handles all aspects of project finance, infrastructure, equipment and trade finance, privatization, and energy trading transactions in more than 50 jurisdictions worldwide.

Capital Markets: This pre-eminent practice includes traditional fixed-income and equity capital markets, structured finance, synthetic products, hybrid products, and derivatives. In recognition of the firm's excellence in securitization, Cadwalader was named 'Best Law Firm for North America' for 2001 by *International Securitisation Report* and perennially ranks at or near the top of annual rankings in issuer and underwriter representations in both commercial mortgage-backed and asset-backed securitization transactions. The firm also has a broad asset-backed commercial paper practice counseling sponsors and placement agents regarding asset-backed commercial paper conduits.

Corporate/Mergers & Acquisitions: Representing issuers, purchasers and underwriters of securities in the domestic and foreign public and private capital markets, the firm's corporate attorneys participate in the full range of securities transactions, including initial public offerings, exchange and secondary offerings, private placements and workouts of senior and subordinated debt, convertible debt and equity securities, venture capital and start-up financing and commercial paper in the US and Eurodollar markets. Lawyers in the firm have represented US and multinational clients in many of the most complex and noteworthy mergers, acquisitions, recapitalizations, spin-offs, and split-offs in recent years.

Financial Restructuring: Recently honored by *Legal Business* as 'Restructuring Team of the Year,' and possessing significant cross-border expertise, this department represents secured and unsecured lenders, bondholders, creditors' committees, borrowers, asset purchasers, and other entities involved in financial restructuring transactions or reorganization cases. The firm's attorneys have been at the forefront of many of the largest and most complex recent US and international insolvencies and routinely advise clients with interests in Europe, Asia, Latin America, and Africa.

Healthcare/Not-for-Profit: Cadwalader is a leader in healthcare law, with considerable resources and talented practitioners in the diverse areas affecting the industry - corporate governance, corporate finance, government regulation, Medicare and Medicaid, insolvency and restructuring, labor relations, litigation, risk management, securities, capital markets, and tax.

Litigation: Cadwalader's renowned litigators handle significant disputes for a broad spectrum of financial institutions, major commercial, industrial and service corporations, and high net worth individuals in state and federal courts throughout the US and in England, as well as proceedings before administrative and regulatory agencies and international tribunals. The practice focuses on business, corporate and securities litigation; derivatives, complex financial products and commodities; employment; environmental and 'toxic tort' liability; insurance and reinsurance; international litigation; real estate; trade regulation and antitrust; and business fraud.

Private Client: Providing effective and creative personal, financial, charitable, and tax planning to individual clients and closely-held family companies, this department places particular emphasis on the preservation of wealth and the minimization of wealth transfer and income taxation.

Real Estate: This premier practice handles transactions throughout the US and the world, including financings, acquisitions, sales and exchanges, development, construction, joint ventures, real estate investment funds, loan syndications, management, leasing, workouts, land use, government-assisted projects, and environmental matters. Real estate finance is of particular importance - the firm's lawyers pioneered many of the legal structures for securitized products that are now the standard worldwide - and the department is an industry leader in single asset/single borrower commercial mortgage securitizations.

Tax: While playing a crucial role in the firm's leading securitization, mergers and acquisitions, insolvency, structured products, and corporate finance practices, this sophisticated and diverse department also pioneers innovative tax structures that drive complex, tax-advantaged transactions, many of which involve cross-border components. Following the firm's groundbreaking work to develop the US federal regime for taxing asset-backed securities, Cadwalader remains a leader in formulating tax-advantaged securitization vehicles. The firm maintains a significant tax controversy practice for US and non-US corporations and financial institutions.

INTERNATIONAL WORK: With strategically placed offices in New York, Charlotte, Washington, DC and London, Cadwalader is superbly positioned to offer top-flight legal services to internationally-based clients conducting transactions all over the world. The firm has built a strong and diverse international practice that can dispatch the most demanding, time-critical and resource-intensive transactions across a wide range of complementary practice areas. Fully integrated into the firm's Wall Street practice, Cadwalader's London office provides a powerful presence in Europe and serves clients interested in capitalizing on the European markets, as well as those seeking US-style investment banking services and access to American capital.

CLIENTS: The firm provides prestigious financial institutions, corporations, government entities, charitable and healthcare organizations, and private clients with innovative solutions to key legal and financial issues.

HEAD OFFICE

NEW YORK
100 Maiden Lane, **New York**, NY 10038, USA
Tel: 212 504 6000   **Fax:** 212 504 6666
Email: cwtinfo@cwt.com
Website: www.cadwalader.com

BRANCH OFFICES

DISTRICT OF COLUMBIA
1201 F Street, NW, **Washington**, DC 20004
Tel: 202 862 2200   **Fax:** 202 862 2400

NORTH CAROLINA
227 West Trade Street, **Charlotte**, NC 28202
Tel: 704 348 5100   **Fax:** 704 348 5200

INTERNATIONAL OFFICE

The firm also has an office in the United Kingdom

LEADING LAW FIRMS

CANTERBURY, STUBER, ELDER, GOOCH & SURRATT

THE FIRM

Managing Committee: Joe F Canterbury, Jr
W Kyle Gooch
David G Surratt

Number of partners: 8
Number of other lawyers: 7

AREAS OF PRACTICE:
Construction 65%
Labor & Employment. 15%
Corporate & Real Estate 10%
Personal Injury 10%

HEAD OFFICE

TEXAS
Occidental Tower, 5005 LBJ Freeway, Suite 1000, **Dallas**, TX 75244
Tel: 972 239 7493 **Fax:** 972 490 7739
Email: jcanterbury@canterburylaw.com
Website: www.canterburylaw.com

FIRM OVERVIEW: The firm has an emphasis on construction law and labor and employment law related to the construction industry. The firm's practice has expanded into the areas of real estate, corporate, public construction law, personal injury law and insurance law; however, the mainstay is the construction industry. Three members of the firm are also active in arbitration and mediation of construction disputes.

MAIN AREAS OF PRACTICE:
Construction: The firm has expertise and extensive experience in the construction industry. Members of the firm have represented developers, owners, contractors, subcontractors and suppliers in construction disputes and other legal problems of construction and development, including commercial, industrial, highway, power plant and pipeline projects.
Labor & Employment: The firm represents employers in labor and employment matters. Specifically, the firm handles defense of discrimination and other claims arising under the State and Federal Equal Employment Opportunity law, Occupational Safety and Health Act, and the National Labor Relations Act. The firm has extensive experience in advising clients regarding union-related matters, personnel situations, harassment situations and wage and hour claims. It will review and prepare, where appropriate, personnel manuals and handbooks on behalf of clients.
Corporate/Real Estate: The firm provides corporate services in entity organization and corporate reorganizations such as mergers and conversions by analyzing innovative business solutions that serve the firm's clients' best interest. The firm represents sellers and purchasers of asset and stock purchase transactions. The firm serves as counselors and negotiators for developers, buyers, sellers, landlords and tenants in office and industrial properties. The firm counsels borrowers in construction financing and analyzes a wide variety of construction issues for commercial developments.
Personal Injury: The firm actively represents its corporate clients and employees of its clients in the defense and prosecution of claims arising out of trucking accidents, products liability and workplace injuries. The firm has defended and continues to defend claims relating to asbestos exposure, construction site injuries and claims of building defects.

CLIENTS: Clients include Independent Electrical Contractors Association; Balcke-Dürr, Inc.; Centex Construction Co.; Charter Builders; Clark Contractors, Inc.; Dee Brown Masonry, Inc.; DFW Airport; douglas e. barnhart, inc.; Driver Pipeline Company; Federal Reserve Bank of Dallas; Gilbane Building Company; GLF Construction Corporation; Granite Construction Co.; Hensel-Phelps Construction; Independent Electrical Contractors Association; JPI Companies; L.H. Lacy Company; Linbeck Construction; Lloyd Plyler Construction, Inc.; Manhattan Construction; Marek Companies; Mills Electrical Contractors, Inc.; Sundt Corporation; Morgan Buildings; Pepper-Lawson Construction; Prudential Insurance Company; Roy Anderson Corporation; Sunmount Corp.; Tellepsen Builders, L.P.; S&B Constructors and Engineers; Carter & Burgess, Inc.; Zachry Construction Company.

Canterbury
Stuber,
Elder,
Gooch &
Surratt

LEADING LAW FIRMS

CARTER LEDYARD & MILBURN LLP

THE FIRM

Managing Partner: Judith A Lockhart

Number of partners: 48
Number of other lawyers: 70

FIRM OVERVIEW: Founded in 1854, Carter Ledyard & Milburn LLP is a full service law firm serving corporations, financial institutions, government agencies and individuals. The Corporate Practice focuses on international mergers and acquisitions, joint ventures, IPOs and other public offerings, private equity, asset management and investment funds, antitrust, telecommunications and other government regulation. The Litigation and Arbitration Practice concentrates on commercial, securities, employment, environmental, intellectual property, criminal defense, maritime, insurance defense and reinsurance disputes. Other practice areas include intellectual property, bankruptcy and reorganization, real estate, trusts and estates, corporate investigations, employment, tax, employee benefits, tax exempt organizations and immigration.

HEAD OFFICE

NEW YORK
Two Wall Street, **New York** NY 10005
Tel: 212 732 3200 **Fax:** 212 732 3232
Email: info@clm.com
Website: www.clm.com

BRANCH OFFICES

DISTRICT OF COLUMBIA
1401 Eye Street, NW, Suite 300, **Washington** DC 20005
Tel: 202 898 1515 **Fax:** 202 898 1521

NEW YORK
570 Lexington Avenue, 41st Floor, **New York** NY 10022
Tel: 212 371 2720 **Fax:** 212 371 4234

MAIN AREAS OF PRACTICE:

Corporate/M&A/Securities: Mergers and acquisitions, joint ventures and strategic alliances, public and private securities offerings, venture capital and private equity investments, bank lending, securitizations, antitrust, telecommunications, broker-dealer and other regulatory compliance and investigations.

Litigation/Arbitration: Complex litigations, arbitrations and alternative dispute resolution proceedings to resolve commercial contract, securities, employment, environmental, intellectual property, insurance defense, reinsurance, criminal, first amendment and construction disputes.

Investment Management: Advice on the formation, registration, operation and regulation of exchange-traded funds, mutual funds, unit investment trusts, hedge funds, private equity funds, investment advisors, broker-dealers and other financial institutions.

Media & Technology: Representing technology-based business in media, e-commerce, telecommunications, software and biotechnology industries based in the US and overseas in financing, mergers and acquisitions, licensing transactions and general representation. The firm has helped more than 50 Israeli technology clients start and develop operations in the US.

Telecommunications: Representing television cable and radio broadcasters, programming companies, telephone system operators and telecom equipment manufacturers in all regulatory and licensing matters, mergers and acquisitions, carriage and distribution agreements and related litigation.

Real Estate: Representing property owners, lenders, tenants and government agencies in commercial and residential property sales, leases, financings, and development contracts.

Intellectual Property: Advice on protecting and commercialising technology and intellectual property assets. Filing and prosecution of patents, trademarks, copyrights and domain names, protection of trade secrets, software and technology licensing, e-commerce contracts and handling of litigation and administrative proceedings.

Maritime/Shipping: Ship finance transactions, charter parties, cross-border leasing, regulatory advice, environmental advice, bankruptcy and workouts, attachments and arrests, insurance coverage and claims, capital markets transactions, maritime litigation and arbitration.

Personal Representation: Representing US and offshore individuals in all aspects of their personal affairs requiring legal counsel, including estate and income tax planning and structuring, will and trust instrument drafting and estate administration, real estate, criminal defense and immigration work.

Bankruptcy/Reorganization: Representing creditors, debtors and asset acquirers in Chapter 11 and other bankruptcy cases and in non-bankruptcy workouts and enforcement actions. Environmental: Environmental regulatory advice, litigation and administrative proceedings, land use planning, environmental impact assessment and disclosure, compliance and environmental audits.

Employment: Counseling concerning employment and immigration laws, regulations and claims. Litigation and arbitration of employment termination, discrimination, harassment and employee non-competition, confidentiality and trade secret claims.

Tax/Employee Benefits: Tax planning advice, transaction structuring advice, and IRS representation. Planning, documentation, IRS qualification and regulation of employee benefit and incentive plans, executive compensation plans, stock option plans, and other benefits.

CLIENTS: Clients also include American Stock Exchange, Bank of New York, Bank Polska Kasa Opieki SA, Barclays Global Advisors, Bristol-Myers Squibb, Danisco A/S, Electrolux AB, Goldman Sachs, Globus-Gateway Tours Ltd., JP Morgan Chase, Kaneka Ltd., Kreditanstalt fur Wiederaufbau, Liberty Media, MGM Networks Latin America, Mitsui Marine, Paxson Communications, Placer Dome Inc., Trinity Biotech plc, Tullett & Tokyo Liberty plc, Union Bank of Switzerland and Warsteiner Brauerei.

INTERNATIONAL WORK: Recent cross-border transactions include representing Orient-Express Hotels Ltd. (Bermuda) in its IPO and NYSE listing; United Business Media plc (UK) in the US acquisitions of CMP Media Inc., Audits & Surveys Worldwide Inc., Strategic Marketing Corporation and Allison-Fisher International Inc. and the sales of Visual Communications Group and United Advertising Publications; Cultor Corporation (Finland) in its acquisition of the food science group of Pfizer Inc. and in its merger with Danisco A/S (Denmark); Magic Software Enterprises Ltd. (Israel) in its IPO, NASDAQ listing, follow-on public equity offerings and acquisitions; Sea Containers Ltd. (Bermuda) in its joint venture with GE Capital (US) to form shipping container lessor GE SeaCo SRL (Barbados); Bowater Incorporated (US) in its acquisition of Alliance Forest Products Inc. (Canada); SeraNova Inc. (US) in its merger with Silverline Technologies Ltd. (India); Garban plc (UK) and Intercapital plc (UK) in their merger to create Garban-Intercapital plc (now ICAP plc); ICAP plc (UK) in its acquisitions of APB Energy, Inc. and First Brokers Securities, Inc.; Avnet, Inc. (US) in its acquisitions of Eurotronics B.V. (Holland) and the computer solutions division of JBA Holdings plc (UK) and the sale of its Allied Electronics unit to Electrocomponents plc (UK); and Pengrowth Energy Trust (Canada) in its acquisition of Calpine Corporation and in its U.S. public securities offering and New York Stock Exchange Listing.

LEADING LAW FIRMS

CHADBOURNE & PARKE LLP

THE FIRM

Managing Partner: Charles K O'Neill

Number of partners: 108
Number of other lawyers: 257

FIRM OVERVIEW: Founded in 1902, Chadbourne & Parke LLP has evolved into an international law firm with eight offices in key markets around the world. The firm provides an array of legal services, both in the United States and internationally. The firm's diversity of practices enables attorneys from different practices to work together to meet its clients' full range of legal needs.

MAIN AREAS OF PRACTICE: Chadbourne provides a diverse portfolio of legal services, including mergers and acquisitions, securities, project finance, corporate finance, energy, telecommunications, commercial and products liability litigation, intellectual property, antitrust, domestic and international tax, reinsurance and insurance, environmental, real estate, bankruptcy and financial restructuring, employment law and ERISA, trusts and estates and government contract matters.

CLIENTS: The firm's clients include leading international and US corporations, financial institutions, trade associations and foundations, start-up businesses, partnerships and individuals.

INTERNATIONAL WORK: With its global network of approximately 370 attorneys, the firm is positioned to analyze market, institutional and regulatory trends as they evolve, and offer its clients a full range of legal services on virtually all matters affecting them. In addition to its European work, the firm has established substantial practices in the Commonwealth of Independent States (CIS), Central Asia and Latin America. The firm's knowledge and experience is enhanced through its long-term working relationships with law firms in other key markets around the world.

HEAD OFFICE

NEW YORK

30 Rockefeller Center, New York, NY 10112

Office Profile: As the hub of Chadbourne's international network of offices, the New York office draws on the expertise of its other offices, both within and outside the United States, to represent clients both nationally and internationally.
Main Areas of Practice: Attorneys in the New York office represent all of the firm's practice areas, including bankruptcy and financial restructuring, corporate, employment, intellectual property, commercial and products liability litigation, project finance, reinsurance and insurance, real estate, tax, and trusts and estates.

BRANCH OFFICES

CALIFORNIA

350 South Grand Avenue, Suite 3300, Los Angeles, CA 90071

Number of lawyers 7

Office Profile: Chadbourne attorneys in Los Angeles represent clients on a range of matters and litigation both national and international in scope.
Main Areas of Practice: Attorneys in the Los Angeles office specialize in complex business litigation, involving commercial and securities fraud and government contract matters; products liability counseling and litigation; and reinsurance/insurance.

HEAD OFFICE

NEW YORK
30 Rockefeller Plaza, **New York**, NY 10112
Tel: 212 408 5100 Fax: 212 541 5369
Website: www.chadbourne.com

BRANCH OFFICES

CALIFORNIA
350 South Grand Avenue, Suite 3300, **Los Angeles**, CA 90071
Tel: 213 892 1000   Fax: 213 622 9865

DISTRICT OF COLUMBIA
1200 New Hampshire Avenue, NW, **Washington**, DC 20036
Tel: 202 974 5600   Fax: 202 974 5602

TEXAS
1100 Louisiana Street, **Houston**, TX 77002
Tel: 713 571 5900   Fax: 713 571 5970

INTERNATIONAL OFFICES

The firm also has offices in Beijing, China; Moscow, Russian Federation; London, United Kingdom; and Tashkent, Uzbekistan

DISTRICT OF COLUMBIA

1200 New Hampshire Avenue, NW, Washington, DC 20036

Number of lawyers: 61

Office Profile: Attorneys in the Washington office handle a wide variety of sophisticated international and domestic transactions, as well as complex litigation.
Main Areas of Practice: Attorneys in the Washington office represent the firm's project finance and energy, corporate, reinsurance/insurance, tax, environmental law and lobbying practices.

TEXAS

1100 Louisiana Street, Houston, TX 77002

Number of lawyers: 5

Office Profile: Lawyers in the Houston office advise clients on all aspects of energy transactions, including acquisitions and divestitures, general corporate transactions, restructurings and refinancings, project development and bank and capital markets financings. The Houston office is also one of the hubs of Chadbourne's liquefied natural gas (LNG) and natural gas practice, with special expertise in the structuring, development and financing of production, pipeline and marine transportation and receiving facilities, and commodity sale, purchase, storage and transportation arrangements.
Main Areas of Practice: Attorneys in the Houston office focus primarily on corporate, project finance, energy and oil and gas matters.

CHADBOURNE & PARKE LLP

LEADING LAW FIRMS

CLEARY GOTTLIEB STEEN & HAMILTON

THE FIRM

Managing Partner: Peter Karasz

Number of partners worldwide: 152
Number of lawyers worldwide: 729

FIRM OVERVIEW: Cleary Gottlieb is a leading international law firm widely recognized for its expertise in finance and mergers and acquisitions and for its tax, regulatory and litigation practice. The firm represents corporations, banks and other financial institutions engaged in US and international business. The firm also represents sovereign governments and international organizations, as well as individuals, trusts and nonprofit institutions. For more than 50 years, clients have relied on the firm for its vast legal expertise, quick responsiveness and business acumen, all of which combined provide unparalleled value. The firm's New York and Washington offices were established in 1946 and approximately two-thirds of the firm's lawyers practice in the United States. Recent accolades include Competition/Antitrust International Law Firm of the Year in *Chambers Global 2002-2003*; Number two in Worldwide Mergers & Acquisitions in *Thomson Financial* (January 2002); Number one in Latin American M&A in *Thomson Financial* (July 2002); Number one advisor to the underwriters in worldwide IPOs by US issuers in *Thomson Financial* (July 2002); Landmark Deal of the Year in *Corporate Finance* (May 2002); Latin American Telecoms and Latin American Transport Project Finance Deals of the Year in *Project Finance* (March 2002); Innovative Financing of the Year in *Real Estate Investment and Finance* (April 2002).

MAIN AREAS OF PRACTICE: Antitrust and competition; banking and financial institutions; corporate governance; derivatives and structured products; employee benefits and ERISA; environmental; global capital markets; individual clients and charitable organizations; intellectual property and technology; international trade; Latin America; litigation and arbitration; mergers, acquisitions and joint ventures; project development and infrastructure; real estate; restructuring; sovereigns; tax; white collar defense.

BRANCH OFFICES

NEW YORK
One Liberty Plaza, New York, NY 10006

Office Profile: The New York office handles corporate, securities and structured finance matters; mergers, acquisitions and joint ventures; litigation; banking and financial institutions; bankruptcy and insolvency; representation of sovereign governments in financial matters; taxation; employee benefits; real estate; and work for individual clients and charitable organizations. Clients range from the top investment banking firms and corporate entities to sovereign governments throughout Latin America and high net worth individuals. The New York office has more than 350 lawyers.

HEAD OFFICE

NEW YORK
One Liberty Plaza, **New York**, NY 10006
Tel: 212 225 2000 **Fax:** 212 225 3999
Website: www.clearygottlieb.com

BRANCH OFFICES

DISTRICT OF COLUMBIA
2000 Washington Avenue, NW, **Washington**, DC 20006
Tel: 202 974 1500 **Fax:** 202 974 1999

INTERNATIONAL OFFICES

EUROPE: Brussels, Frankfurt, London, Moscow, Paris, Milan and Rome.
ASIA: Hong Kong and Tokyo.

WASHINGTON
2000 Washington Avenue, NW, Washington, DC 20006

Office Profile: The Washington office focuses on banking and financial institutions regulation; corporate and securities law; environmental, public and administrative law; structured finance; litigation; antitrust and international trade; taxation; and legislative counseling. The office serves as the focal point for the firm's US regulatory practice and, in particular, its counsel on corporate governance issues. Clients range from government loan agencies to Fortune 500 corporations. More than 80 lawyers work in the Washington office.

CLEARY GOTTLIEB STEEN & HAMILTON

CLIFFORD CHANCE US LLP

THE FIRM

Regional Managing Partner: John Carroll
Deputy Regional Managing Partner: David Taub
Number of partners: 123
Number of other lawyers: 539

HEAD OFFICE

NEW YORK
200 Park Avenue, **New York**, NY 10166 0153
Tel: 212 878 8000 Fax: 212 878 8375
Email: info@cliffordchance.com
Website: www.cliffordchance.com

BRANCH OFFICES

CALIFORNIA
601 South Figueroa Street, **Los Angeles**, CA 90017 5704
Tel: 213 312 9400 Fax: 213 312 9401

Five Palo Alto Square, 3000 El Camino Real, **Palo Alto**, CA 94306 2121
Tel: 650 858 4300 Fax: 650 858 4399

3811 Valley Centre Drive, **San Diego**, CA 92130 3318
Tel: 858 720 3500 Fax: 858 720 3501

One Market, Steuart Tower, **San Francisco**, CA 94105 1420
Tel: 415 778 4700 Fax: 415 778 4701

DISTRICT OF COLUMBIA
2001 K Street NW, **Washington**, DC 20006 1001
Tel: 202 912 5000 Fax: 202 912 6000

CONTACTS

M&A & Private Equity	Steve Hobbs
Capital Markets	Bob King
Financial Products	Steve Kolyer
Banking & Restructuring	Bob Finley
	Margot Schonholtz
Litigation	Jim Benedict
Real Estate	Alan Gosule
Tax & ERISA	David Moldenhauer

FIRM OVERVIEW: US and global organizations increasingly require the highest quality US legal capability coupled with seamless international advice. Clifford Chance offers a comprehensive and nationally recognized US practice, backed by top-ranked practices in 32 of the world's major financial and business centers. Through a single, worldwide partnership and a client-focused approach, the firm delivers consistent, commercially-oriented advice wherever its clients do business.

In the US, Clifford Chance's practice is equally dedicated to complex corporate and financial transactions and high-stakes dispute resolution. At 451 lawyers, Clifford Chance's New York office is its largest in the US (and ranks among the largest of any New York firm). The firm also has nearly 100 lawyers in Washington, DC. In 2002, Clifford Chance established a major presence in California, opening offices in San Francisco, Los Angeles, San Diego and Palo Alto.

Clifford Chance's clients include leading Wall Street and international financial institutions and US and international corporations, as well as governments and multilateral agencies. Nearly one half of the *Fortune* 500 call on the firm.

MAIN AREAS OF PRACTICE:

M&A & Private Equity: Clifford Chance has a long history of acting in landmark US and cross-border transactions. The firm represents publicly and privately held buyers and sellers, joint venture partners, venture capitalists, fund sponsors and financial advisors. Clifford Chance's M&A capability is complemented by its internationally recognized practice in US and EU merger clearance. The firm also offers investment fund specialists, as well as tax, ERISA and regulatory specialists, who work together to advise leading private equity groups. In addition, Clifford Chance has an interdisciplinary practice in corporate technology, bringing commercial and intellectual property expertise to the structuring of complex IT-driven ventures.

Capital Markets: Clifford Chance leverages its industry and product knowledge to raise capital in the most strategic way for each client. The firm has a track record of successful domestic and cross-border transactions on behalf of a wide range of issuers and virtually every Wall Street underwriter. Product coverage includes: IPOs, secondary equity, ADRs, private placements, preferred equity, equity-linked products, REITs, debt and high yield offerings.

Financial Products: Clifford Chance has a leading position as advisor to issuers and investment banks in the securitization and derivatives markets. The firm's team has been at the forefront of developing and issuing hybrid and synthetic products and transactions, including, among others, specialized derivatives and SEC-registered cross-border securitizations. This experience has led the group to advise regulators rating and responding to CBO, CLO, bank solvency and other specialized regulatory matters.

Banking & Restructuring: The firm's financial restructuring and insolvency practice advises lenders and companies on transactions involving financially distressed situations. In addition, sophisticated lenders and borrowers call on the firm for acquisition finance, asset finance, bank lending, securities and financial regulation and leasing advice. The firm's top-ranked projects team represents lenders, sponsors and developers, particularly in the oil and gas, telecom and petrochemical sectors.

Litigation: Clifford Chance offers a preeminent litigation practice, helping clients resolve complex disputes in a manner that promotes their business objectives and develop compliance programs to assist in minimizing future risks. With the addition of its West Coast offices, the firm has the largest, most experienced team of securities litigators in the US, combined with a preeminent white collar capability. Its top-rated antitrust practice, which includes several former high-level federal antitrust officials, is involved in many of the most significant antitrust and fair trade cases before the courts today. The firm's intellectual property team litigates bet-the-company patent disputes on behalf of leaders in the biotechnology, pharmaceutical, chemical and IT sectors, as well as providing copyright and trademark expertise. The firm also has strength in employment, insurance/reinsurance, media and arbitration.

Real Estate: Clifford Chance helps clients execute real estate dispositions, acquisitions, leasing transactions and development arrangements. The firm offers sophisticated real estate finance expertise and is a leader in private equity real estate investment funds.

Tax & ERISA: The tax group provides advice on US and international taxation, covering financing, investment, corporate and commercial transactions, the design of tax-efficient structured deals, and advice on tax disputes and transfer pricing. The firm offers an in-depth understanding of US rules, combined with the knowledge of international tax systems and how the systems interlink. It also provides ERISA and executive compensation advice.

COOPER & SCULLY, P.C.

THE FIRM

Managing & Senior Partner: R Brent Cooper

Number of partners: 19
Number of other lawyers: 36

AREAS OF PRACTICE:
Professional Liability	40%
Healthcare & Medical Malpractice	20%
Appellate	15%
Insurance Coverage	15%
Bad Faith	10%
Construction	5%
Employment	5%
Governmental Entities	5%
Products Liablity	5%

HEAD OFFICE

TEXAS
900 Jackson Street, Suite 900, **Dallas**, TX 75202
Tel: 214 712 9500   **Fax:** 214 712 9450
Email: bcooper@cooperscully.com
Website: www.cooperscully.com

BRANCH OFFICES

TEXAS
2700 Chase Tower, 600 Travis Street, **Houston**, TX 77002
Tel: 713 236 6800   **Fax:** 713 236 6880
Email: jraley@cooperscully.com

200 N Travis, Suite 500, PO Box 1235, **Sherman**, TX 75090
Tel: 903 813 3900   **Fax:** 903 868 1919
Email: cgoosen@cooperscully.com

FIRM OVERVIEW: Cooper & Scully, P.C. is recognized as one of the leading firms in Texas for the handling of complex litigation. The firm is known for its expertise and ability in trial and appellate work. Areas of litigation practice include insurance coverage, professional liability, bad faith, products liability, representation of governmental entities, construction, employment, and health care and medical malpractice. Cooper & Scully P.C. is engaged in the representation of clients on a statewide basis and has the staffing and resources that permit it to pursue aggressively all types of cases, from the most complicated to the most basic.

MAIN AREAS OF PRACTICE:

Appellate Practice: The firm has a statewide reputation for the handling of appeals in both state and federal courts, and as a result, receives referral appeals from numerous attorneys throughout the state. The Appellate Section is involved in the drafting of final pleadings and common jury charges, and in the handling of post-trial motions. The Appellate Section has been involved in a number of landmark cases in Texas jurisprudence, involving both Texas procedure as well as Texas substantive law.

Insurance Coverage: The firm has extensive knowledge and expertise in the analysis of insurance coverage matters. The firm represents both insurers and insureds in disputes over the coverage afforded by various policies. Additionally, the firm is among a relatively small number of firms who have the expertise to represent reinsurers.

Professional Liability: The firm has represented many professionals in both legal malpractice, agents, errors and omissions, and other professional errors and omissions. The services provided to many professionals include representation before the respective licensing boards as well as in the courtroom.

Bad Faith: The firm has been at the forefront in the development of Texas law in the area of bad faith. The firm has attorneys who have tried numerous bad faith cases to successful results. The firm's attorneys have the knowledge and expertise to analyze and evaluate the exposure presented by these cases, in addition to providing advice to its insurance clients on steps that can be taken to minimize such risks.

Products Liability: The firm represents manufacturers directly and others through their insurance carriers. The firm provides representation and advice to various manufacturers on issues of design defects, warnings, and negligence in the manufacture of the particular product. The clients represented include designers and manufacturers of medical equipment and pharmaceutical products, as well as manufacturers of other products.

Governmental Entities: The firm has represented cities, police and fire departments, school districts, and other diverse governmental entities throughout the state in both state and federal courts. These cases run the gamut from all types of civil rights suits to employment cases to zoning.

Construction: The firm provides a variety of services to its construction clients. These include the drafting and interpretation of contract documents, as well as contract negotiations. Included in these services is the analysis of risk presented by certain projects and drafting of contract provisions to minimize risk to the client. The firm is also well experienced in construction personal injury litigation, litigation involving contract claims, and construction defect litigation.

Employment: The firm also handles employment work.

Healthcare & Medical Malpractice: The firm has an extensive practice in the representation of physicians, hospitals, and other healthcare providers. The firm's attorneys have substantial experience and expertise in the trial of medical negligence cases. In addition, the firm provides advice to individual healthcare providers, as well as institutional healthcare providers. The firm also represents individuals and entities before state and federal agencies. The firm provides representation in administrative areas such as peer review and credentialing process. The firm also provides representation to insurers and healthcare providers in all aspects involving managed healthcare.

CLIENTS: Acceleration National Insurance Company; AIAC; AIGRM; AIU North America (Texas), Inc.; American Bankers Insurance Group; American Continental Insurance Company; American Contractors Insurance Group; American International Group; American Physicians Insurance Exchange; Ameristar Insurance Services, Inc.; Argonaut Insurance Company; Associated International Insurance Company; Chubb Group of Insurance Companies; Cigna Property & Casualty Company; CNA Insurance Company; Commercial Underwriters Insurance Company; Crawford & Company; Farmers Insurance Group of Companies; Foremost Insurance Company; Fortress Insurance Company; General Accident Fire & Life Assurance Company; General Reinsurance Corporation; General Star Management Company; Great American Insurance Companies; Interstate Insurance Companies; Joint Underwriters Association; Kemper National Insurance Companies; Medical Claims Management Group; The Medical Protective Company; NAMC Insurance Company, Inc.; National Union Fire Insurance Company; Northwestern National Life Insurance Company; Occidental Fire & Casualty Company; Old American County Mutual Fire Insurance Co.; Providian Insurance Company; Republic Insurance Company; RISC, Inc.; Risk Enterprise Management Limited; St. Paul Insurance Company; State Farm Insurance Company; Texas Medical Liability Insurance Company; Texas Medical Liability Trust; The Travelers Companies; TML-Texas Municipal League; TML-Intergovernmental Risk Pool; Transamerica Insurance Company; Trinity Universal Insurance Company; U.S. Risk, Inc.; Underwriters Adjustment Company, Inc.; Underwriters of Lloyds, London; United Fire and Casualty Company; USAA Property & Casualty Insurance; Zurich-American Insurance Company.

LEADING LAW FIRMS

CORRERO FISHMAN HAYGOOD PHELPS WALMSLEY & CASTEIX, LLP

THE FIRM

Number of partners: 8
Number of other lawyers: 10

HEAD OFFICE

LOUISIANA
201 St Charles Avenue, 46th Floor, **New Orleans**, LA 70170-4600
Tel: 504 586 5252   **Fax:** 504 586 5250
Website: www.cfhlaw.com

FIRM OVERVIEW: Correro Fishman Haygood Phelps Walmsley & Casteix, LLP, was founded in the mid-1990's by leading business and litigation lawyers from three of the largest law firms in Louisiana. Their corporate lawyers have been repeatedly recognized in national and regional publications as among the best. They regularly represent public and private companies in a variety of corporate and securities matters. They also have an extensive general business law practice that focuses on real estate, commercial transactions, commercial finance, banking, bank regulation and general contractual matters. The firm has a higher percentage of its New Orleans lawyers listed in a leading American publication than any other firm. Four of the firm's partners are former chairmen of the Corporate and Business Law Section of the Louisiana State Bar Association. Three partners have served on the Planning Committee of the Tulane Corporate Law Institute and one partner teaches Corporate Finance at Louisiana State University's Law School and Securities Regulation at Tulane University Law School. The firm's litigators have handled some of the most challenging and interesting business litigation in their region, including representing SMG, the world's largest facilities manager, in a challenge by the New Orleans Saints of its lease of the Louisiana Superdome; IBM, in multi-district patent litigation; Manpower Inc., in the defense of class action claims arising out of the Kaiser plant explosion; The Times-Picayune and The Associated Press, in access issues arising out of the trial of former Louisiana Governor Edwin Edwards; and the State of Louisiana, in actions to collect tens of millions of dollars of disputed taxes.

MAIN AREAS OF PRACTICE:

Corporate, Securities & Corporate Finance: The firm regularly represents public and private companies in corporate and securities matters, such as public and private offerings, mergers and acquisitions, periodic reporting and general SEC compliance.

Banking: The firm is a leader among law firms representing financial institutions in Louisiana. For two years in a row they were ranked No. 1 in the Southwest by *The Merger Strategy Report* and Shushunoff Information Services in the handling of legal work associated with acquisitions of financial institutions. The firm's lawyers have been involved in at least 50 of these transactions. They also routinely counsel clients regarding regulatory compliance and reorganizations, and have handled branch purchases and sales, commercial financing transactions, and secured transactions. Their banking clients include AmSouth Bank, Coastal Commerce Bank, First Bank & Trust, First Community Bank, First Guaranty Bank, Gulf Coast Bank, IBERIABANK, Liberty Bank, MidSouth Bank, Omni Bank, Resource Bank, and Whitney National Bank.

Mergers & Acquisitions: The firm's corporate lawyers handle mergers and acquisitions of private as well as public companies involving both negotiated and unsolicited acquisitions, going-private transactions, and acquisitions of minority interest. Lawyers in the firm have been involved in some of the largest M&A transactions in Louisiana.

Real Estate: They handle all aspects of commercial real estate transactions, including commercial and industrial leasing, acquisitions, financings, developments and large tract opportunities. They are also experienced in transactions involving historic and low-income housing tax credits. They routinely advise clients on all aspects of real estate leasing, and often represent landlords and tenants in lease negotiations, incuding major league sports leases by clients with the NFL New Orleans Saints and the NBA New Orleans Hornets.

Litigation: The firm's litigators regularly represent: The Times-Picayune Publishing Corporation in libel, defamation and invasion-of-privacy cases and public record and access disputes, as well as Associated Press and Capital City Press in various access disputes. They also represent defendants in class action litigation, including mass tort and securities litigation; litigation in contract disputes of various kinds, including options, purchase agreements and leases; clients in products liability and tort actions in federal and state courts throughout Louisiana and elsewhere relating to the oil industry and the various large industrial facilities located in this region; plaintiffs and defendants in securities litigation and arbitration, including broker-dealer disputes and public company disclosure; clients involved in arbitrated disputes, including proceedings administered by the American Arbitration Association, National Association of Securites Dealers, and the New York Stock Exchange; and the State of Louisiana in corporate income and franchise tax matters, including obtaining a $26 million jury verdict awarding taxes, interest and penalties, that is believed to be the largest jury award of its kind in Louisiana history.

CLIENTS: Some clients that have entrusted legal matters to the firm are: Amedisys, Inc, Amsouth Bank, ASCO plc, Associated Press, Bayou Steel Inc, Capitol City Press, Community Coffee Company, FBT Investments, Inc, First Bank and Trust, First Guaranty Bank, Great Lakes Chemical Corporation, Hibernia Southcoast Capital, Inc, Historic Restoration, Inc, IBERIABANK Corporation, IBM Corporation, The Laitram Corporation, Louisiana Companies, Midsouth Bankcorp Inc, Offshore Logistics, Inc, Pennington Medical Foundation, Petroleum Helicopters, Inc, Resource Bankshares, Inc, Sanderson Farms, Inc, SMG, Times-Picayune Publishing Corporation, TL James & Company, Inc, Tulane University, US Unwired Inc, Whitney National Bank, and Wyndham International, Inc.

LEADING LAW FIRMS

COVINGTON & BURLING

THE FIRM

Managing Partner: Stuart Stock
Vice Chairman: Philip K Howard

Number of partners worldwide: 161
Number of other lawyers worldwide: 384

FIRM OVERVIEW: Covington & Burling is an 80 year-old international firm representing approximately half of the Fortune 500 companies throughout the world on their most significant transactional, regulatory, public policy and litigation matters. The firm has particular expertise in technology and intellectual property matters in the IT and life science sectors and has great experience in dealing with virtually every government and agency that is involved in the regulation of international commerce, including the European Commission and the WTO. The firm has long been one of the premier regulatory, legislative and competition firms in the United States, and its longstanding advisory relationships with most of the major industries has permitted its attorneys to gain significant expertise and insight into the strategic issues and technologies facing industry worldwide. With a vibrant corporate presence in New York, the expansion of its corporate practice in London, and a Silicon Valley office in San Francisco, the firm has coupled its substantive industry expertise with expanded M&A, private equity, commercial law, securities and financial experience. As a consequence, Covington & Burling has been at the forefront of major transactions in the technology, software, life science and biotechnology areas. Its corporate group has, for example, handled four of the largest software company acquisitions in the world, and the London group has handled major English and cross-border transactions in England, several countries in the EU and Eastern Europe. Its competition lawyers have handled several of the last major mergers, including ExxonMobil. Its international trade lawyers, headed by Stuart Eizenstat, former US ambassador to the EU, have been deeply involved in recent WTO issues.

CLIENTS: Representative clients include AstraZeneca, Bacardi, Bank of America, Benetton, Calpine Corporation, Computer Associates, Electronic Arts, Eli Lilly, ExxonMobil, Federal Home Loan, GE Capital, GlaxoSmithKline, Johnson & Johnson, Medarex, Merck, Microsoft, Monsanto, National Football League, National Geographic, National Hockey League, Newsweek, Proctor & Gamble, Qualcomm, Scherling Plough, The Business Software Alliance, UBS Warburg, Warner-Lambert.

INTERNATIONAL WORK: The firm represents Microsoft and the Business Software Alliance on policy, electronic commerce and software copyright enforcement matters in the EU, and it supervises enforcement programs in some 40 countries in Western and Eastern Europe, Africa and the Middle East from its European offices. It has particular expertise in cross-border corporate transactions in a diverse range of industry sectors, benefiting from the broad range of nationalities represented amongst its transactional lawyers. The firm also has one of Europe's pre-eminent life sciences and pharmaceutical practices, in which it provides pan-European corporate, public policy and regulatory advice to many of the world's major pharmaceutical companies.

HEAD OFFICE

DISTRICT OF COLUMBIA
1201 Pennsylvania Avenue NW, **Washington** DC 20004-2401
Tel: 202 662 6000 **Fax:** 202 662 6291
Email: sstock@cov.com
Website: www.cov.com

OTHER OFFICES

CALIFORNIA
One Front Street, **San Francisco** CA 94111
Tel: 415 591 6000 **Fax:** 415 591 6091
Email: jsnipes@cov.com

NEW YORK
1330 Avenue Of The Americas, **New York** NY10019
Tel: 212 841 1056 **Fax:** 212 841 1010
Email: phoward@cov.com

INTERNATIONAL OFFICES

The firm also has offices in London and Brussels.

CONTACTS

Antitrust	Jim Atwood
Corporate, Tax & Benefits	Scott Smith
International Trade	Stuart Eizenstat, Peter Flannagan
Life Sciences	Richard Kingham
Litigation	Bobby Burchfield, William Phillips
Technology, Media & Communications	Jonathan Blake

LEADING LAW FIRMS

DAVIS WRIGHT TREMAINE LLP

THE FIRM

Firmwide Managing Partner: Richard D Ellingsen
Chairman: Mark A Hutcheson

Number of partners: 225
Number of other lawyers: 181

AREAS OF PRACTICE:
Litigation (covers all areas of law) 41%
Business Transactions/Tax/Corporate Finance/
Commercial Transactions 27%
Real Property/Environment & Natural Resources 14%
Communications, Media Law & First Amendment 12%
Employment/Employee Benefits/Immigration 12%
Healthcare 11%
Intellectual Property 6%

FIRM OVERVIEW: Davis Wright Tremaine LLP is one of the nation's largest full service law firms with over 400 attorneys in 10 offices across the US and in Shanghai, China.

MAIN AREAS OF PRACTICE:

Business Transactions/Tax/Corporate Finance/Commercial Transactions: DWT has a significant general corporate and transactional practice representing every type of client. The firm's experience in M&A and commercial finance is extensive. The robust Financial Institutions Industry Practice represents banks and financial institutions in the US and foreign financial institutions doing business in the US.

Communications, Media Law & First Amendment: A leader in media and First Amendment law for decades, clients include many of the nation's most recognized print and online publishers, producers of news and entertainment programs, and national publishers and broadcasters. Telecommunications clients include international telephony carriers and online networks.

Employment/Employee Benefits/Immigration: The firm provides all services: human resources counseling, regulatory advice, labor/management relations, employee benefits plans, and complex litigation. Many immigration lawyers are bilingual.

Healthcare: The firm has an unparalleled depth and breadth of expertise in virtually every aspect of healthcare law. The firm was a pioneer in advising on the impact of technology on the healthcare industry.

Intellectual Property: DWT's fastest growing practice, the Intellectual Property Group offers the full range of services - from traditional copyright, trademark, trade secret and patent issues to the developing law of the internet and computers, with licensing and litigation experience in all areas.

Litigation: Over 70 lawyers concentrate their practices in litigation, some focusing almost exclusively in media, antitrust, securities, employment and environmental litigation. The practice embraces virtually every subject matter.

Real Property/Environmental and Natural Resources: The Real Estate and Land Use Group coordinates with the Environmental and Natural Resources Law and Energy Industry Groups to address the complexities of purchasing, owning, developing and using real estate.

CLIENTS: adidas America, Inc., AT&T Wireless, Bank of America, N.A., Bank of Tokyo, Ltd., The Boeing Company, British Petroleum, CBS, Equilon Enterprises LLC, Ford Motor Credit Co., GE Capital Services, Holland-America Lines, Intel Corporation, Los Angeles Times, Microsoft Corp., Mitsubishi International, Royal Bank of Canada, Shell Oil Company, Starbucks Coffee Co., Sony Pictures Entertainment, Toshiba America, Turner Broadcasting/CNN.

HEAD OFFICE

WASHINGTON
1501 Fourth Avenue, Suite 2600, **Seattle** 98101
Tel: 206 622 3150 Fax: 206 628 7699
Email: info@dwt.com
Website: www.dwt.com

BRANCH OFFICES

CALIFORNIA
865 South Figueroa Street, Suite 2400, **Los Angeles** 90017
Tel: 213 633 6800

One Embarcadero Center, Suite 600, **San Francisco** 94111
Tel: 415 276 6500

DISTRICT OF COLUMBIA
1500 K Street NW, Suite 450, **Washington, DC** 20005
Tel: 202 508 6600

NEW YORK
1740 Broadway, **New York** 10019
Tel: 212 489 8230

OREGON
1300 SW Fifth Avenue, Suite 2300, **Portland** 97201
Tel: 503 241 2300

CONTACTS

Business Tax ....Martin Morfeld
Business Transactions/Corporate Finance ....Greg Adams
....Keith Baldwin, Dave Baca
China Practice ....Norm Page
Communications/Media ....Victor Kovner, Dan Waggoner
Credit Recovery & Bankruptcy ....Ragan Powers
Employee Benefits ....Anne Northrup/Jim Ambrose
Employment/Labor Law ....Mary Drobka
Energy ....Steve Greenwald
Environmental Law & Natural Resources ....Rick Glick
....Lynn Manolopoulos
Finance & Commercial Transactions ....Norm Page, Bill Miller
Health Law ....Susan Duffy, Peter Grant, Keith Korenchuk
Intellectual Property ....Bruce Kaser, Allie Nicholson
International ....Rich Rawson
Litigation ....Martin Fineman, Ladd Leavens
Real Property ....Tom Goeltz
Telecommunications ....Mark Trinchero
Trusts & Estates ....Jim Flaggert

INTERNATIONAL WORK: The firm provides services to international businesses, particularly in the Pacific Rim and Canada. In 1994, DWT became the first US law firm licensed to practice in Shanghai. The International Group represents clients establishing subsidiaries, forming international joint ventures and investing in the US and in international financing, development/financing for energy infrastructure, international trade, maritime law, international tax, technology transfers, immigration, transnational litigation, and other related matters. The firm is a member of Lex Mundi, the world's leading association of law firms in 155 countries, states and provinces, and of the Pacific Rim Advisory Council, an alliance of 30 law firms that serve major international companies across the Pacific Rim.

LEADING LAW FIRMS

DEBEVOISE & PLIMPTON

THE FIRM

Presiding Partner: Martin Frederic Evans

Number of partners: 124
Number of partners in US offices: 106
Number of other lawyers: 416
Number of other lawyers in US offices: 338

FIRM OVERVIEW: Debevoise & Plimpton, an international law firm, was founded in 1931. The firm offers a diverse range of sophisticated legal services in corporate, international, litigation, tax, and trust and estates law to businesses and individuals. Debevoise & Plimpton offices are located in New York, Washington, DC, London, Paris, Frankfurt, Moscow, Hong Kong and Shanghai.

MAIN AREAS OF PRACTICE:

Corporate: The Corporate Department is the firm's largest practice group. The department's work spans the full range of general corporate, transactional and regulatory representations in the United States, and throughout the world, including internationally top-ranked mergers and acquisitions and private equity fund work. Major corporate practice areas cover mergers and acquisitions; private equity; capital markets; project, equipment and acquisition finance; real estate; insurance industry; investment management; media and technology; bankruptcy and workouts; derivatives and structured finance.

Litigation: The Litigation Department handles a broad range of complex matters in federal and state courts nationwide, and before agencies, arbitrators and panels worldwide. Mary Jo White, the former US Attorney for the Southern District of New York, heads the litigation practice and the firm's litigators include seven former Assistant US Attorneys, a former General Counsel of the Securities and Exchange Commission, a former Director of the Federal Trade Commission's Bureau of Competition and other lawyers with distinguished records of public service. Areas of concentration include antitrust; bankruptcy; general commercial litigation; international arbitration; insurance industry disputes; intellectual property and media; products liability; securities litigation and enforcement proceedings; and white collar crime.

Tax: The Tax Department is an essential component of the firm's worldwide transactional practice, working closely with the firm's corporate lawyers in structuring transactions. The department also focuses on tax planning and advice for business entities, high net worth individuals and exempt organizations and includes an active executive compensation and employee benefits practice.

Trusts & Estates: The firm has a diverse and highly sophisticated Trusts and Estates practice that combines a significant tax orientation with frequent interdisciplinary projects involving the litigation and corporate areas.

US REPRESENTATIONS:

Corporate Representations: Recent corporate representations include Zurich Scudder Investments in its US$2.5 billion sale to Deutsche Bank; Provident Mutual Life Insurance Co. in connection with its $1.56 billion acquisition by Nationwide Financial Services; Sithe Energies Inc. in the $1.69 billion sale of its Sithe New England Holdings LLC unit to Exelon Generation Co. LLC; Westfield America Trust in the $5.3 billion acquisition of Rodamco North America, B.V.; AXA Financial Inc. in the $11.5 billion sale of its Donaldson, Lufkin & Jenrette, Inc. subsidiary to Credit Suisse First Boston; Reliance Group Holdings as debtor and the creditors committees for Laidlaw, Inc. and Global Telesystems, Inc. in three of the top bankruptcies in 2001.

Litigation Representations: Recent litigation representations include Global Crossing, in over 60 securities class actions, governmental investigations

HEAD OFFICE

NEW YORK
919 Third Avenue, **New York** NY 10022
Tel: 212 909 6000 **Fax:** 212 909 6836
Email: mailbox@debevoise.com
Website: www.debevoise.com

BRANCH OFFICES

DISTRICT OF COLUMBIA
555 13th Street, NW, **Washington** DC 20004
Tel: 202 383 8000 **Fax:** 202 383 8118
Email: mailbox@debevoise.com

INTERNATIONAL OFFICES

Debevoise & Plimpton has offices in London, Paris, Frankfurt, Hong Kong, Moscow and Shanghai.

CONTACTS

Corporate	Meredith M Brown
Mergers & Acquisitions	Paul S Bird
Private Equity	Woodrow W Campbell, Jr
Insurance Industry	Wolcott B Dunham, Jr
Capital Markets	Michael W Blair
Litigation	Mary Jo White
Securities	Ralph C Ferrara
Products Liability	Roger E Podesta
Intellectual Property/Internet	Bruce P Keller
International Arbitration	David W Rivkin
White Collar	Mary Jo White
Tax	Bruce D Haims
Trusts & Estates	Theodore A Kurz

and Congressional hearings; American Airlines, to defend the company in all litigation arising from the September 11 attacks; National Football League against the NFL Players' Association and Coors Brewing to protect the NFL's exclusive right to license its trademark to corporate sponsors; Pizza Hut and its parent, Yum Restaurants International (formerly Tricon Restaurants International) in international franchise disputes; Gap Inc. in connection with an infringement action brought by design company Charles Anderson; Owens Corning, in asbestos litigation; and Rosie O'Donnell in a contract dispute with Gruner + Jahr.

INTERNATIONAL REPRESENTATIONS: Pernod-Ricard in its successful US$8 billion joint bid with Diageo for Seagram's wine and spirits business; Clayton, Dubilier & Rice in its £616 million acquisition of Brake Bros plc; Dentsu Inc. in Publicis Group S.A.'s $3 billion acquisition of Bcom3 Group Inc; General Electric in various international disputes; CME in an arbitration against the Czech State.

BRANCH OFFICES

WASHINGTON, DC

555 13th Street, NW, Washington DC 20004

Managing Partner: Ralph C Ferrara

Office Profile: The Washington, DC office which has 24 lawyers, provides client services in corporate securities regulation and enforcement, white collar criminal practice and commercial litigation, corporate regulatory and transaction work for industrial and financial institutions and international telecommunications and intellectual property matters.

LEADING LAW FIRMS

DECHERT LLP

THE FIRM

Chairman: Barton J Winokur

Number of partners: 225
Number of other lawyers: 519

Website: www.dechert.com

FIRM OVERVIEW: Dechert LLP is an international law firm offering a full range of legal services to business, government, and individual clients worldwide.

MAIN AREAS OF PRACTICE: Corporate finance, mergers and acquisitions, private equity, business and technology, complex litigation, mass torts and product liability, financial services, finance and real estate, tax.

Corporate Finance: The firm represents issuers, sponsors, investors, underwriters, and placement agents in all types of public and private issuances of debt and equity securities.

Mergers & Acquisitions: The firm's internationally recognized M&A group represents buyers, sellers, and advisers in planning, negotiating, and executing a full range of public and private transactions.

Private Equity: The firm's dedicated private equity team focuses on fund formation and capital raising, funds' investment activities, and portfolio company transactions.

Business & Technology: The firm provides strategic transactional and intellectual property legal services to life sciences, IT, and other technology companies in all stages of growth.

Complex Litigation: A national litigation team represents clients in sophisticated antitrust, securities, corporate governance, and white collar litigation. The firm also has well-established employment, commercial, environmental, and health care litigation practices.

Mass Torts & Product Liability: The firm's nationally recognized mass tort and product liability defense team represents consumer goods, chemical, and pharmaceutical companies in complex class actions and multi-district litigation.

Financial Services: The services of one of the country's largest financial services practice include formation and operation of open- and closed-end investment companies as well as private, hedge, and offshore funds; mutual funds representation; regulation and compliance; and broker-dealer issues.

Finance & Real Estate: Lawyers handle mortgage finance, mezzanine lending, and synthetic and sale-leaseback financing for lenders, institutional owners, and investors as well as asset-backed securitizations and other structured finance transactions for issuers, sellers, and others.

Tax: Tax lawyers advise on M&As, restructurings, real estate transactions, and investment management activities. The practice also includes employee benefits/executive compensation and private client legal services and one of the largest state tax practices in the US.

CLIENTS: The firm's clients include many of the world's largest financial services companies and financial institutions; *Fortune* 500 pharmaceutical, manufacturing, and technology companies; domestic and international private equity funds and portfolio companies; hospitals and health care systems; major tax-exempt organizations; and municipal and national governments.

INTERNATIONAL WORK: With more than 740 lawyers in 14 offices in the US and Europe, Dechert has the resources to deliver seamless, sophisticated legal services to clients worldwide.

USA OFFICES

CALIFORNIA
Newport Beach, 4675 MacArthur Court, Suite 1400
Newport Beach, CA 92660-8842
Tel: 949 442 6000 **Fax:** 949 442 6010

One Maritime Plaza, Suite 1510, **San Francisco**, CA 94111-3404
Tel: 415 262 4500 **Fax:** 415 262 4555

CONNECTICUT
90 State House Square, **Hartford**, CT 06103-3702
Tel: 860 524 3999 **Fax:** 860 524 3930

DISTRICT OF COLUMBIA
1775 I Street, NW, **Washington**, DC 20006-2401
Tel: 202 261 3300 **Fax:** 202 261 3333

MASSACHUSETTS
200 Clarendon Street, 27th Floor, **Boston**, MA 02116-5021
Tel: 617 728 7100 **Fax:** 617 426 6567

NEW JERSEY
Princeton Pike Corporate Center, 997 Lenox Drive, Building 3, Suite 210, **Lawrenceville**, NJ 08648-5218
Tel: 609 620 3200 **Fax:** 609 620 3259

NEW YORK
30 Rockefeller Plaza, **New York**, NY 10112-2200
Tel: 212 698 3500 **Fax:** 212 698 3599

PENNSYLVANIA
Thirty North Third Street, **Harrisburg**, PA 17101-1603
Tel: 717 237 2000 **Fax:** 717 237 2040

4000 Bell Atlantic Tower, 1717 Arch Street, **Philadelphia**, PA 19103-2793
Tel: 215 994 4000 **Fax:** 215 994 2222

INTERNATIONAL OFFICES

The firm also has offices in Brussels, Frankfurt, London, Luxembourg, and Paris. For further details on these offices, please visit the firm's website.

CONTACTS

Corporate Finance	Carmen J Romano
Mergers & Acquisitions	William G Lawlor
Private Equity	G Daniel O'Donnell
Business & Technology	James A Lebovitz, Glenn A Gundersen
Complex Litigation	Robert C Heim
Mass Torts & Product Liability	Sean P Wajert
Financial Services	Robert W Helm
Finance & Real Estate	John J Gillies Jr, Richard D Jones, Malcolm S Dorris
Tax	Thomas E Doran

LEADING LAW FIRMS

DEWEY BALLANTINE LLP

THE FIRM

Managing Partner: Everett L Jassy
Administrative Partner: Richard Shutran

Number of partners worldwide: 155
Number of other lawyers worldwide: 392

AREAS OF PRACTICE:
Corporate	19%
Litigation	15%
Project Financing & Leasing	13%
Real Estate & Investment Management	11%
Tax & Private Clients	10%
Mergers & Acquisitions	10%
International Trade	8%
Capital Markets	7%
Bankruptcy	5%
Energy & Communications	2%

FIRM OVERVIEW: Founded in 1909, Dewey Ballantine LLP is an international law firm that combines an active financial transactional practice with expertise in trade, legislative and international issues, and complex litigation and dispute resolution. Lawyers at the firm are fluent in Afrikaans, Arabic, Armenian, Bengali, Chinese (Cantonese and Mandarin), Czech, Dutch, Egyptian Arabic, English, Estonian, Finnish, French, French Creole, German, Greek, Hebrew, Hindi, Hungarian, Italian, Japanese, Kanneda, Korean, Modern Standard Arabic, Native Czech, Polish, Portuguese, Romanian, Russian, Sanskrit, Slovak, Spanish, Swedish, Tamil, Turkish, Ukrainian, Urdu and Yiddish.

MAIN AREAS OF PRACTICE: Antitrust and trade regulation; arbitration and alternative dispute resolution; banking and financial institutions litigation; bankruptcy litigation; capital markets; compensation and benefits; corporate reorganization and bankruptcy; debt finance; derivatives; emerging markets; employment law; energy and communications; environmental health and safety; insurance; insurance/reinsurance litigation; intellectual property and technology; international legislative reform; international trade; internet; investment management; Latin America; leasing; legislative; litigation; mergers and acquisitions; oil and gas; private clients; private equity; products liability/mass torts litigation; project finance; real estate; securities, M&A and corporate governance litigation; structured finance; tax; tax controversy; tax exempt financing; tax litigation; taxation for corporate acquisitions and reorganizations; taxation of financial products; taxation of international transactions; technology; telecommunications and mass media; venture capital; white collar crime and corporate internal investigations.

CLIENTS: The firm represents multinationals, financiers, banks, pension funds, multilateral institutions, developers, charitable foundations, estates, individuals and governments worldwide. Corporate clients come from many industries including banking, healthcare, insurance, energy and utilities, media, consumer and industrial goods, technology, telecommunications, and transportation.

INTERNATIONAL WORK: Recent international transactions include: advising Burns Philp & Co. Ltd. on its US$2.2bn unsolicited bid for Goodman Fiedler Limited, and its US$110m acquisition of the Latin America industrial bakery ingredients business of Kraft Foods International, Inc.; counseling Cathay Financial Holding Co., Ltd. on its US$3.5bn acquisition of United World Chinese Commercial Bank; representing American Electric Power in the US$2bn sale of SEEBOARD Group plc, to London Electricity Group plc; advising Sony Corporation of America on the US$435m acquisition of InterTrust Technologies Corporation by Sony and Koninklijke Philips Electronics N.V.; representing Associated British Foods plc in the US$361m acquisition of Mazola and related brands from Unilever plc; advising The Walt Disney Company on a US$4.5bn Euro Commercial Paper Programme; representing American Honda Finance Corporation on the creation of a US$4bn Euro Medium-Term Note Programme; representing the lenders, with BNP Paribas as lead arranger, on a $236 million financing in Mexico; representing the lenders, with BNP Paribas, Citibank N.A. and Export Development Canada as joint lead arrangers, on the $563.1m financing of the La Rosita Power Project in Baja California, Mexico, which was named Latin America Power Deal of the Year by Project Finance Magazine; representing joint bookrunners and lead managers JPMorgan and Morgan Stanley in The National Bank of Kuwait's US$450m Eurobond issue; representing UK and Polish quoted PKN ORLEN regarding the €140m acquisition of 494 German filling stations from BP plc. Private Equity: representing Coller Capital Limited in the formation of its US$2.5 billion secondaries fund, Coller International Partners IV.

HEAD OFFICE

NEW YORK
1301 Avenue of the Americas, **New York** NY 10019-6092
Tel: 212 259 8000   Fax: 212 259 6333
Email: ejassy@deweyballantine.com
Website: www.deweyballantine.com

BRANCH OFFICES

CALIFORNIA
333 South Grand Avenue, Suite 2600, **Los Angeles** CA 90071-1530
Tel: 213 621 6000   Fax: 213 621 6100
Email: pwalker@deweyballantine.com

2300 Geng Road, **Palo Alto** CA 94303-3323
Tel: 650 845 7000   Fax: 650 845 7333
Email: jelacqua@deweyballantine.com

DISTRICT OF COLUMBIA
1775 Pennsylvania Avenue, NW, **Washington** DC 20006-4605
Tel: 202 862 1000   Fax: 202 862 1093
Email: awolff@deweyballantine.com

TEXAS
816 Congress Avenue, Suite 1900, **Austin** TX 78701-2478
Tel: 512 226 0300   Fax: 512 226 0333
Email: kkudlac@deweyballantine.com

700 Louisiana, Suite 1900, **Houston** TX 77002-2725
Tel: 713 445 1500   Fax: 713 445 1533
Email: agover@deweyballantine.com

INTERNATIONAL OFFICES

Dewey Ballantine LLP also has offices in London, Warsaw, Budapest, Prague and Frankfurt.

LEADING LAW FIRMS

DRUMMOND WOODSUM & MACMAHON

THE FIRM

Managing Partner: Jerrol A Crouter

Number of shareholders: 29
Number of associates and consultants: 11

HEAD OFFICE

MAINE
245 Commercial Street, PO Box 9781, **Portland**, ME 04104-5081
Tel: 207 772 1941
Email: info@dwmlaw.com
Websites: www.dwmlaw.com; www.SchoolLaw.com

CONTACTS

Business Services	Michael E High
Indian Services Group	Gregory Sample
Public Sector Group	Harry R Pringle
Trial Services	Melissa Hewey

FIRM OVERVIEW: Founded in 1965, Drummond Woodsum & MacMahon is one of Maine's largest and most well respected law firms. The firm's attorneys have earned a reputation for providing high quality counsel to clients across a wide spectrum of legal practice areas. Drummond Woodsum & MacMahon's philosophy of quality, responsiveness and efficiency in the delivery of legal services to firm clients has led to the development of some of the best lawyers in the United States. The reputation of the firm's attorneys was recently recognized nationally when, in 2001 and 2002, firm member Robert E. Hirshon became the first Maine lawyer in nearly 100 years to serve as President of the American Bar Association.

MAIN AREAS OF PRACTICE

Public Sector Group: The firm offers expertise in municipal and school law in areas including labor relations, employment matters, special education, finance, construction, employee benefits and litigation, and has litigated numerous precedent-setting cases on behalf of public sector clients. The school practice is widely recognized as pre-eminent in Maine and the school law website is nationally known.

Employment Services: The employment group consists of attorneys and highly skilled consultants who defend both private and public sector employers' interests. The practice includes substantial litigation in federal and state courts along with an active practice before all relevant federal and state agencies including the National Labor Relations Board, the Equal Employment Opportunity Commission, the Maine Labor Relations Board, the Maine Human Rights Commission, and other administrative bodies.

Business Services: The business group handles a full range of corporate and securities matters, advising clients on acquisitions and mergers, corporate tax planning and financing, multi-state financings, venture capital and private placements, and international trade. Attorneys in the firm are approved 'Red Book' bond counsel and have extensive experience in public utility law, franchising, executive compensation, foreign investment regulation, bankruptcy and securities matters, and other areas of corporate and business law.

Trial Services: The firm is involved in every type of civil litigation in federal and state courts and administrative agencies including the United States Supreme Court. Recent cases fall into a broad range of areas including business and commercial litigation, employment, securities, intellectual property, antitrust, real estate and land, construction disputes, and product liability.

Indian Law: The Indian practice provides legal services to Native American tribes in the United States in areas including litigation in tribal, federal and state courts, transactions by and with tribal businesses, economic development strategies, tribal employment law and personnel management, developing tribal laws and governmental processes, Indian housing, federal contracting, and tribal gaming.

CLIENTS: Clients include Fortune 500 and private corporations, insurance companies, commercial banks and institutions, public utilities, municipalities, private and public schools, and Native American Tribes throughout the US, Canada, and Great Britain.

INTERNATIONAL WORK: The firm is the only Maine law firm to be a member of Meritas, a worldwide organization that offers high-quality legal services through a closely integrated, yet independent, group of full-service law firms which provides clients a single local contact for obtaining reliable legal services throughout the country and around the world. Membership in Meritas is by invitation only and requires firms to adhere to rigorous quality standards and a stringent code of ethics.

DRUMMOND
WOODSUM &
MACMAHON
Attorneys at Law

LEADING LAW FIRMS

EIMER STAHL KLEVORN & SOLBERG

THE FIRM

Managing Partner: Nathan P Eimer

Number of partners: 6
Number of other attorneys: 18

HEAD OFFICE

ILLINOIS
224 S. Michigan Avenue, Suite 1100, **Chicago**, IL 60604
Tel: 312 660 7600 **Fax:** 312 692 1718
Website: www.eimerstahl.com

CONTACTS

Antitrust/Commercial Litigation ....Nathan P Eimer, Andrew G Klevorn
Energy/Commercial Litigation ....David M Stahl

FIRM OVERVIEW: Founded in July 2000, Eimer Stahl Klevorn & Solberg engages in complex litigation throughout the United States. It also has substantial experience with respect to the antitrust aspects of proposed transactions. The firm is dedicated to providing top quality legal services in a cost-effective manner. With a commitment to client service and advanced technology, the firm partners with clients to obtain creative solutions to complex legal problems. The firm is proud to serve as trial counsel to some of the country's foremost corporations.

MAIN AREAS OF PRACTICE: The firm concentrates on complex litigation across a variety of subject areas, including antitrust, environmental, commercial, securities, energy, unfair competition, product liability, toxic torts, construction, and regulatory affairs. The firm has particular expertise relating to the defense of class action lawsuits, as well as claims brought under the Sarbanes-Oxley Act. Some of the leading matters on which the firm has recently worked include government investigations and private suits relating to energy prices, defense of class action claims alleging injuries arising from the use of fuel additives, multimillion dollar breach of contract claims in the paper and cement industries, and defense of price-fixing claims in the chemical, dairy and paper industries. The firm also advises clients with respect to obtaining government clearance of proposed mergers and acquisitions. This involves working with antitrust agencies and competition authorities regarding assessment of the competitive effects of contemplated transactions. Members of the firm have provided advice regarding these matters across a wide variety of industries, including consumer goods, paper, chemicals, commercial printing, cosmetics, telecommunications, crop nutrients and fertilizers, foodstuffs, and automotive parts.

CLIENTS: The firm serves clients across a wide array of industries, including CITGO Petroleum, Kimberly-Clark, Dow Chemical, Exelon, Land O' Lakes Dairy, Corn Products International, Praxair, The Williams Companies, and Holcim Inc. Superior client service is a hallmark of the firm's operating philosophy and principles.

FARMER, CLINE & ARNOLD PLLC

THE FIRM

Managing Partner: Stephen B Farmer

Number of lawyers: 9

AREAS OF PRACTICE:
Commercial Litigation 40%
Products Liability Litigation 40%
Miscellaneous Litigation 20%

FIRM OVERVIEW: The firm was established in 1996 by Stephen B Farmer, Robert D Cline and James S Arnold, all experienced litigators. The firm provides representation for many businesses, including coal and energy companies, pharmaceutical companies, law firms and small businesses.

MAIN AREAS OF PRACTICE:
Commercial Litigation: The firm represents clients in all aspects of commercial litigation. These matters include large-scale and long-running cases, as well as specialist expertise in key niche areas such as coal-related transactions and employment issues.
Products Liability Litigation: The firm has experience in both the prosecution and defense of products liability actions. Specific areas include prescription drugs, asbestos, tobacco, dietary supplements and defective design cases.
Miscellaneous Litigation: The firm is often retained to represent clients in special instances on important specific projects. These include malpractice, securities litigation and employer's rights.

CLIENTS: The firm's clients include *Fortune* 500 companies engaged in energy, healthcare, pharmaceutical, tobacco and coal. The firm also represents small companies in the banking, automobile, retail and healthcare sectors. The firm also provides counsel to professional organizations including large law firms and physician groups.

HEAD OFFICE

WEST VIRGINIA
7 Players Club Drive, **Charleston**, WV 25311
Tel: 304 346 5990

Postal Address: Post Office Box 3842, **Charleston**, WV 25338

CONTACTS
Commercial Litigation . . . . .Stephen B Farmer
Products Liability Litigation . . . . .Stephen B Farmer
Miscellaneous Litigation . . . . .Stephen B Farmer

LEADING LAW FIRMS

FINN DIXON & HERLING LLP

THE FIRM

Founding Partners: Harold B Finn III
Brett W Dixon (also Managing Partner)
Michael J Herling

Number of partners: 12
Number of other lawyers: 13

FIRM OVERVIEW: With 25 attorneys, Finn Dixon & Herling LLP provides a broad spectrum of legal services to the business and financial community. The firm's clients are located throughout the United States, many of whom have international operations. The firm recently opened a small office in New Haven, Connecticut. Since its founding in 1987, Finn Dixon has focused on issues affecting businesses and business transactions. The firm strives to provide the highest level of customer service and practical, solution-oriented advice, grounded on a thorough understanding of each client's business. The firm has developed a litigation capability that support's the firm's core client base and serves other clients involved in commercial litigation matters.

MAIN AREAS OF PRACTICE:

BUSINESS: Finn Dixon's business practice is focused on eight key areas:
Mergers & Acquisitions/Private Equity: Represents buyers, sellers and investors in various transactions, including mergers and other business combinations, leveraged buy-outs and recapitalizations, growth capital investments, 'roll up' transactions, proxy contests, stock swaps and public company mergers.
Venture Capital/Emerging Companies: Represents venture capital firms in both early-stage and growth capital investments and in the formation, organization and operation of venture capital funds.
Investment Management: Represents domestic and offshore investment partnerships and trusts, common and collective trust funds, investment advisers, commodity trading advisers and commodity pool operators and registered broker-dealers. Investment advisory clients include a number of nationally-renowned firms that manage billions of dollars in assets as well as smaller state-registered entities. Also represents sources of private equity and money managers in their investments in domestic and offshore funds, including hedge funds and other alternative investment vehicles.
Banking & Lending: Advises banks and other financial institutions on all aspects of lending transactions. Also assists such clients on various regulatory issues, including with respect to general compliance as well as acquisitions and dispositions of banks and bank holding companies and the establishment by out of state banks of branch offices or other operations in Connecticut.
Securities: Advises clients regarding federal and state securities laws that affect public offerings and private placements by both publicly-held companies and privately-owned businesses, annual reports and proxy statements and the organization of, and offerings by, private investment companies.

HEAD OFFICE
CONNECTICUT
One Landmark Square, Suite 1400 **Stamford**, CT 06901 2689
Tel: 203 325 5000 **Fax:** 203 348 5777
Website: www.fdh.com

BRANCH OFFICES
CONNECTICUT
31 Whitney Avenue, 2nd Floor
New Haven, CT 06510
Tel: 203 848 6488 **Fax:** 203 848 6490

Public Finance: Represents underwriters and trustees in municipal bond issuances and municipalities in general finance or specialized project finance matters.
Tax: Finn Dixon offers tax expertise, including structuring and other advice to its transactional clients as well as advice in connection with federal and state taxation of the ongoing activities of its corporate, partnership and limited liability clients.
General Business Representation: Finn Dixon helps many clients address a wide variety of operational and strategic issues on a continuous basis, including consultation on choice of entity, protection and coordination of the rights of owners, commercial real estate transactions, employment matters, including executive compensation, severance arrangements, stock options and employee benefits, financings, licensing and strategic alliance and joint venture arrangements and compliance with regulatory requirements.
LITIGATION: Finn Dixon's litigation practice encompasses civil litigation in state and federal courts, appellate advocacy, arbitration and other forms of alternative dispute resolution and proceedings before administrative agencies. The firm's practice also includes bankruptcy and workouts and employment law.

CLIENTS: Finn Dixon's clients include a wide array of commercial entities, from substantial private equity and venture capital groups, middle market public and private corporations, and banks and financial institutions to risk-taking entrepreneurs and start-up ventures.

FITZPATRICK, CELLA, HARPER & SCINTO

THE FIRM

Managing Partner: Dominick A Conde

Number of partners: 58
Number of other lawyers: 108

AREAS OF PRACTICE:
Intellectual Property 100%

HEAD OFFICE
NEW YORK
30 Rockefeller Plaza, **New York** NY 10112
Tel: 212 218 2100   **Fax:** 212 218 2200
Website: www.fitzpatrickcella.com

BRANCH OFFICES
CALIFORNIA
650 Town Center Drive, Suite 1600, **Costa Mesa** CA 92626
Tel: 714 540 8700   **Fax:** 714 540 9823

DISTRICT OF COLUMBIA
1900 K Street, NW, **Washington** DC 20006
Tel: 202 530 1010   **Fax:** 202 530 1055

FIRM OVERVIEW: Founded in 1971, Fitzpatrick, Cella, Harper & Scinto has grown to over 160 attorneys specializing in intellectual property law. The firm's practice covers the spectrum of intellectual property services, including applying for protection, litigation, appeals, interferences, alternative dispute resolution, licensing, opinions, corporate transactions and due diligence. The firm provides these services to clients from virtually every industry, including pharmaceuticals, chemicals, automotive, energy, biotechnology, medical products, consumer products, computers, electronics, transportation, telecommunications, financial services, food products, and e-commerce. As new technologies emerge, the firm is at the forefront in developing strategies for its clients' intellectual property protection. 90 percent of the firm's attorneys hold scientific degrees and most have substantial industry experience in various fields of technology including chemistry, biotechnology, pharmaceuticals, electronics, physics, software, computers and the mechanical arts.

MAIN AREAS OF PRACTICE: Patent, trademark, copyright, trade secret, unfair competition, computer law, licensing, antitrust and international trade law. Trials and appeals in Federal and State courts and administrative agencies.

Patent & Trademark Litigation: The firm is involved in all aspects of litigation with respect to patents, trademarks, counterfeiting, trade secrets, unfair competition, international trade, and copyrights, including trials and appeals, and proceedings before the International Trade Commission. In 2002, the firm's clients prevailed in several major intellectual property litigations. The firm successfully defended AstraZeneca patents against validity challenges to its US$5 billion per year Prilosec® product; successfully defended a multi-billion dollar infringement claim and received an award of over US$32 million in attorneys fees for client Bristol-Myers Squibb; and successfully enforced and defended patents and trademarks in several jury and bench trials for clients including Bausch & Lomb, Becton-Dickinson, IBM, Novartis, and Takeda Chemical Industries.

Patent & Trademark Prosecution: The firm has an extensive practice in the prosecution of patent and trademark applications, trademark oppositions and cancellations, due diligence studies, patent and trademark opinions, technology transfers and licensing. In addition, the firm is experienced in specialized and sophisticated areas such as patent interference procedures and prosecuting applications under the Patent Cooperation Treaty. The firm has prosecuted over 15,000 patents to issuance in the past 10 years, and is responsible for obtaining more than 1,900 patents in 2002 alone.

INTERNATIONAL WORK: The firm's clients include some of the world's largest multinational corporations in the United States, Asia, Europe, Australia and South America. The firm counsels clients on global intellectual property strategies, coordinates international litigation strategies and works closely with co-counsel throughout the world. The firm also conducts worldwide filing for patent, trademark and copyright protection and maintains worldwide trademark portfolios.

CLIENTS: Fitzpatrick, Cella represents the world's technology and business leaders - including AstraZeneca, Bausch & Lomb, Bristol-Myers Squibb, Canon, Conde Nast, Hughes Network Systems, IBM, Merck, Novartis, Pfizer, Pharmacia, Prudential, Salomon Smith Barney and Takeda Chemical Industries, as well as smaller corporations and Universities from the United States and abroad.

LEADING LAW FIRMS

FRIED, FRANK, HARRIS, SHRIVER & JACOBSON

THE FIRM

Co-Managing Partners: Valerie Ford Jacob, Paul M Reinstein
Senior Partner: Arthur Fleischer, Jr

Number of partners in US offices: 135
Number of other lawyers in US offices: 425

AREAS OF PRACTICE:

Corporate	49%
Litigation	26%
Bankruptcy & Restructuring	7%
Real Estate	5%
Tax	5%
Antitrust	3%
Benefits & Compensation	2%
Intellectual Property & Technology	2%
Trusts & Estates	1%

HEAD OFFICE

NEW YORK
One New York Plaza, **New York**, NY 10004
Tel: 212 859 8000 **Fax:** 212 859 4000
Website: www.friedfrank.com

BRANCH OFFICES

DISTRICT OF COLUMBIA
1001 Pennsylvania Avenue, NW, **Washington, DC** 20004
Tel: 202 639 7000 **Fax:** 202 639 7003

LOS ANGELES
350 South Grand Avenue, **Los Angeles** CA 90071
Tel: 213 473 2000 **Fax:** 213 473 2222

FIRM OVERVIEW: Fried Frank is an international law firm with approximately 560 attorneys located in New York, Washington, DC, Los Angeles, London and Paris. The firm's rich and distinguished traditions date back before the beginning of the 20th century, and the firm continues to provide innovative and imaginative solutions to business and legal problems in the 21st.

MAIN AREAS OF PRACTICE:
CORPORATE:

Mergers & Acquisitions, including Private Equity: Fried Frank concentrates on novel and complex transactions that bring to bear sophisticated merger and acquisition, financing and tax capabilities. These deals include acquisition transactions, domestic and international, in which the firm represents both principals and global investment banks, and private equity transactions, in which it represents leading firms in leveraged buyouts and other investments. Recent representations: AEA Investors Inc. in the investment by HSBC Holdings plc in a new private equity fund formed by AEA; Datek Online Holdings Corp. in its acquisition by Ameritrade Holding Corp.; Goldman, Sachs & Co. and Banc of America Securities LLC, financial advisors and dealer managers for The Limited Inc. in an exchange offer for the 16% of Intimate Brands, Inc. The Limited did not already own; GS Capital Partners LP and other affiliates of Goldman Sachs in their acquisition of Berry Plastics Corporation; GS Capital Partners-led investor group in their acquisition of National Golf Properties; Metro-Goldwyn-Mayer Inc. in the acquisition of its 20% interest in the Bravo cable television network by the National Broadcasting Company, Inc.; Pegaso Telecomunicaciones SA de CV in its acquisition by Telefónica Móviles SA, the cellular unit of Telefónica, SA; Pepsi-Gemex SA in its acquisition by Pepsi Bottling Group Inc.; Procter & Gamble Company in the combination of its Jif/Crisco business with JM Smucker Company in a Morris Trust transaction; Rouse Company in its joint acquisition with Westfield America Trust and Simon Property Company of Rodamco North America NV; Wm. Wrigley Jr. Co. in its proposed acquisition of Hershey Foods Co.; and Goldman Sachs as financial advisor in various transactions: to BCE Inc. in the repurchase of the 20% interest in Bell Canada that BCE had sold to SBC Communications Inc.; to Golden State Bancorp in connection with its acquisition by Citigroup; to Hercules Inc. in the proposed sale of Hercules' BetzDearborn water treatment division to GE Specialty Materials, a unit of the General Electric Company; to State Street Corp. in its acquisition of the securities lending and record-keeping business of Deutsche Bank AG; and to Vivendi Universal Entertainment in its acquisition of the entertainment assets of USA Networks, Inc.

Capital Markets, including Banking & Finance & Structured Finance: The firm has a major presence in the capital markets, representing many *Fortune* 500 companies, as well as Wall Street's best-known underwriters, in a wide variety of public and private debt and equity offerings in the United States and abroad. The firm also works on complex financings and novel structured finance and securitization transactions. Recent representations: Merrill Lynch & Co., Goldman, Sachs & Co., JPMorgan Chase & Co., Banc of America Securities LLC and Salomon Smith Barney Inc. as underwriters or initial purchasers in many equity and debt (including high yield) offerings, such as Goldman Sachs, Merrill Lynch and Salomon Smith Barney, co-lead underwriters, for the IPO of Platinum Underwriters Holding, Ltd., which was formed by The St. Paul Companies, Inc. as a Bermuda reinsurer; Merck & Co., Inc. in its spinoff and IPO of Medco Health Solutions Inc. (postponed); Millennium Chemicals Inc. and its subsidiary Millennium America Inc. in a follow-on Rule 144A debt offering to be followed by an exchange offer; Procter & Gamble Company in various debt offerings; Rouse Company in its issuance of common stock; Grupo Televisa SA in the first issuance of 30-year senior notes by a Mexican corporation; Diversified Global Securities Limited as issuer and Société Générale as initial purchaser of a collateralized debt obligation secured by a portfolio including other CDOs, structured finance securities and synthetic securities; and Gardena Holding AG in a senior subordinated mezzanine financing for its leveraged buyout transaction sponsored by Industri Kapital AG.

Corporate Counseling & Governance: Fried Frank provides a wide range of corporate counseling and corporate governance advice to clients on everyday matters and in special situations. The firm acts as regular outside general counsel to many companies, as well as regular US counsel to a number of non-US companies, particularly those with securities traded on US stock exchanges.

Litigation & Securities Regulation, Compliance & Enforcement: In addition to focusing on general commercial litigation, Fried Frank's Litigation Department handles securities and shareholder litigation, in which the firm defends class actions and other litigation, including derivative actions, relating to allegations of securities fraud, as well as litigation involving takeovers and proxy fights resulting from merger and acquisition transactions. For disputes best resolved outside the courtroom, Fried Frank's litigators are also experienced in domestic and international arbitration and alternative dispute resolution. Fried Frank's Securities Regulation, Compliance and Enforcement Practice has an international reputation in representing corporations and individuals before state and federal regulatory bodies. The practice involves crisis management and crafting creative solutions to

LEADING LAW FIRMS

FRIED, FRANK, HARRIS, SHRIVER & JACOBSON

unprecedented problems. In a related area, the white collar Criminal Defense and Civil Litigation Team, led by some of the country's best former prosecutors, tackles a wide range of cases, including insider trading, securities fraud and RICO matters. The Internal Investigation, Compliance and Monitoring Practice conducts internal investigations for companies, boards of directors and audit committees involving allegations of misconduct or other improprieties. In addition, the firm has one of the country's leading practices in defense of parties accused of violating the Civil False Claims Act, including many of the most complex and unusual cases brought under its unique qui tam enforcement mechanism. The Government Contracts Practice represents clients doing business with US government agencies, as well as with state and local entities. Recent representations: Merck & Co. Inc. in several domestic and international commercial disputes; the New York Stock Exchange in a United States Securities and Exchange Commission investigation of alleged regulatory deficiencies and other governmental inquiries and related civil suits; Lloyd's of London in an investigation by the United States Attorney and in a variety of litigations and other disputes between Lloyd's and its US Names; ARCO Chemical (now Lyondell Chemical Company) in connection with a breach-of-fiduciary-duty litigation; Delta & Pine Land Company in a series of litigations relating to its aborted merger with Monsanto Company; Tracinda Corp. in its federal securities lawsuit relating to DaimlerBenz AG's acquisition of Chrysler Corp.; and TRW Inc. in a False Claims Act proceeding brought by the United States alleging accounting irregularities in connection with billings under the company's government contracts.

Bankruptcy & Restructuring: Fried Frank's Bankruptcy and Restructuring Practice represents both debtors and creditors, along with other interested parties, in formal bankruptcies as well as out-of-court restructurings of financially troubled companies. The firm recently represented the Official Committee of Bondholders in a Chapter 11 restructuring of NTL Inc.; the ad hoc committee of bondholders in a financial restructuring agreement for Telewest Communications, plc; and ANC Rental Corporation in its Chapter 11 restructuring.

Real Estate: Fried Frank's leading Real Estate Practice, representing developers, owners, institutional investors, tenants and lenders, encompasses a broad range of transactions involving every type of property. The firm recently represented Brookfield Financial Properties in its acquisition of Lehman Brothers' 51% interest in Three World Financial Center in New York City; Condé Nast Publications, as tenant, in its lease at Four Times Square in New York City; and RFR Realty LLC in its acquisition of the Seagram Building, also in New York City.

Tax: Fried Frank's tax lawyers have a primarily transactional focus, working on matters involving major public and private corporations and partnerships. They counsel clients in the many US and international tax aspects of mergers and acquisitions, as well as in private equity, capital markets and real estate transactions and in bankruptcy and restructuring matters, as well as in the area of tax controversies.

Antitrust: Fried Frank's antitrust attorneys provide clients with a full range of leading-edge representation, counseling and litigation services in transactions involving competition law in the United States and abroad. The group has been involved in several of the highest-profile matters in recent times, including Microsoft Corp. in its settlement with the United States Department of Justice following its three-year antitrust case and Northrop Grumman Corporation's contested takeover of Newport News Shipping Inc.

Benefits & Compensation: In the area of executive compensation and employee benefits, Fried Frank's attorneys have a transactional focus, working with companies of all types and individuals on matters ranging from stock options to retirement plans, which are frequently the issues that can make or break a transaction.

Intellectual Property & Technology: Fried Frank's IP and Technology Practice, which includes the firm's Electronic Commerce Practice, offers a full range of services associated with technology-related or content-oriented business activities and transactions, including patents, trademarks, copyrights, trade secrets, advertising and unfair competition, as well as acquisition, divestiture, development, exploitation, procurement, alliance, outsourcing and similar agreements.

Trusts & Estates: Fried Frank's trusts and estates attorneys advise US and non-US individuals and families with substantial wealth in a wide variety of personal planning matters and estate administration.

OTHER PRACTICES:

Environmental: Fried Frank's Environmental Practice represents companies in Superfund and other civil and criminal enforcement proceedings, as well as in a broad range of private environmental litigation. A significant component of the practice involves the environmental aspect of corporate and bankruptcy transactions. The firm also represents clients before federal and state environmental agencies and counsels clients on compliance programs, environmental audits and site remediation.

Insurance: Fried Frank's Insurance Practice provides legal services to all segments of the industry, including corporate transactions, demutualizations, mutual holding company reorganizations, insurance regulation and government investigations. The firm represented the Massachusetts Division of Insurance in connection with Liberty Mutual Group's reorganization into a mutual holding company structure, the largest to date of a mutual property and casualty insurer.

International Trade: Fried Frank's International Trade Practice responds to the growing strategic needs of international and multinational corporations for legal services, including strategic consulting, international negotiation, transnational government procurement, the protection of intellectual property, advice on foreign investment restrictions, dispute resolution, arbitration and ADR.

CLIENTS: AEA Investors, American Express, ANC Rental, Aquila, Banc of America Securities, Bear Stearns, BellSouth, Brookfield Financial Properties, Chevron, CS First Boston, Delta & Pine Land, Deutsche Bank, Dial, Dow Jones, El Paso, First Union Securities, Fluor Daniel, Forstmann Little, GE Capital, General Semiconductor, Goldman Sachs, GPU, Humana, Invensys, JPMorgan Chase, Lazard Frères, Lloyd's of London, Merck, Merrill Lynch, Microsoft, MGM, Morgan Stanley, Northrop Grumman, NYSE, Procter & Gamble, Rouse, Salomon Smith Barney, Sara Lee, Shamrock Holdings, Televisa, TIAA, Tishman Speyer Properties, Tracinda, UBS PaineWebber, Urenco, White Consolidated Industries, Wm. Wrigley Jr. Company.

INTERNATIONAL WORK: Fried Frank has an established international practice with a concentration in cross-border mergers and acquisitions and joint ventures; private equity investments; US registered and Rule 144A securities offerings; non-US debt and equity offerings, including high yield debt; commercial financing transactions; structured and securitized financings; establishment of leveraged buyout funds; international trade and investment; and tax. Lawyers in the firm's London office practice US law. Lawyers in the firm's Paris office practice US and French law. Also, in April 2000, Fried Frank and Canada's largest law firm, McCarthy Tétrault LLP, formalized a 20 year working relationship by creating the McCarthy/Fried Frank Alliance, a collaboration on individual matters, primarily cross-border corporate transactions, by the two law firms, which remain entirely independent.

LEADING LAW FIRMS

FROST BROWN TODD LLC

THE FIRM

Managing Partners: Richard J Erickson, C Edward Glasscock

Number of partners: 185
Number of lawyers: 182

FIRM OVERVIEW: Frost Brown Todd LLC, one of the largest law firms in the Central United States, offers responsive, sophisticated legal services at nationally competitive rates. Created by the merger of two premier law firms on November 1, 2000, Frost Brown Todd is backed by the service of over 800 professionals, drawing from the foundations of legacy law firms with more than a century of service to clients. The firm meets the diverse legal challenges of local, regional and international business in over 40 different practice areas.

MAIN AREAS OF PRACTICE:

Business & Corporate: Over 70 attorneys provide a full range of transactional, regulatory and other advisory services to the firm's regional, national and multinational business clients. The firm handles mergers and acquisitions, public companies and securities, tax, emerging business and venture capital, international, e-business and technology, employee benefits and executive compensation, health law, financial institutions, investment management, public finance and government.

Commercial Transactions/Real Estate: The firm offers significant experience in the areas of commercial finance, financial restructuring and real estate, including financial institution regulation, equipment leasing, asset securitization, land use, economic development incentives and shopping centers/retail development.

Environmental: With one of the largest and most diverse environmental practices in the region, the firm helps clients navigate through federal, state and local environmental regulations, and assists clients in creating solutions that achieve their business objectives, avoid disputes and minimize transactional costs.

Intellectual Property: From litigation to licensing, from prosecution to unfair competition, the firm is ready to serve its clients in developing, obtaining, protecting and enforcing creative assets. After handling intellectual property litigation throughout the US for a variety of *Fortune* 500 clients, the firm was named one of the top ten patent litigation firms in the US by *Managing Intellectual Property Magazine*.

Labor & Employment: Over 40 attorneys handle labor and employment issues, such as collective bargaining, employment discrimination, sexual harassment, OSHA inspections, workers' compensation, arbitration, alternative dispute resolution, wage and hour, common law employment claims and immigration.

Litigation: The firm counsels and represents a variety of clients, and has extensive experience in complex litigation, multi-party cases and class actions. The firm also has experience in the following areas: antitrust, appellate practice, banking/commercial, catastrophic loss, construction, surety and real estate, drug and medical device, fire and explosion, First Amendment, franchise and distribution, government enforcement and compliance, insurance coverage, fraud and bad faith, personal injury and tort defense, product liability, securities and professional liability, toxic tort/chemical exposure, trucking and commercial transportation and unfair competition.

Personal Planning & Family Business: The firm counsels individuals in the areas of wealth preservation and wealth transfer matters involving estate, income tax, retirement, charitable and business succession planning. Closely held businesses are served in all tax matters, ranging from choice of business structure and operational issues to the transfer, sale or liquidation of the business.

HEAD OFFICES

KENTUCKY
400 West Market Street, 32nd Floor, **Louisville** KY 40202-3363
Tel: 502 589 5400 **Fax:** 502 581 1087
Email: info@fbtlaw.com **Website:** www.frostbrowntodd.com

OHIO
2200 PNC Center, 201 East Fifth Street, **Cincinnati** OH 45202-4182
Tel: 513 651 6800 **Fax:** 513 651 6981

BRANCH OFFICES

INDIANA
120 West Spring Street, Suite 400, **New Albany** IN 47150-3655
Tel: 812 948 2800 **Fax:** 812 948 7994

KENTUCKY
2700 Lexington Financial Center, **Lexington** KY 40507-1749
Tel: 859 231 0000 **Fax:** 859 231 0011

OHIO
One Columbus, Suite 1000, 10 West Broad Street,
Columbus OH 43215-3467
Tel: 614 464 1211 **Fax:** 614 464 1737

300 North Main Street, Suite 200, **Middletown** OH 45042-1919
Tel: 513 422 2001 **Fax:** 513 422 3010

TENNESSEE
424 Church Street, Suite 1600, **Nashville** TN 37219-2308
Tel: 615 251 5550 **Fax:** 615 251 5551

CONTACTS

Business & Corporate	R James Straus
Commercial Trans/Real Estate	E Richard Oberschmidt
Environmental	Paul W Casper Jr
Intellectual Property	Steven J Goldstein
Intellectual Property Litigation	Arthur S Beeman, David E Schmit
International	Joseph J Dehner, Jay Middleton Tannon
Labor & Employment	Robert A Dimling, D Patton Pelfrey
Litigation	Winston E Miller
Personal Planning & Family Business	Patricia D Laub

International: Frost Brown Todd provides a wide range of legal services required by international businesses as they expand into the US and by US businesses as they market and operate abroad. The firm handles various international transactions, including direct investments, mergers and acquisitions, joint ventures, licensing, trade law compliance, as well as international commercial dispute resolution. The group's international practice concentrates on corporate, commercial, tax, intellectual property, labor and immigration law, as well as litigation and arbitration services. The firm recently received an Export Achievement Award from the US Department of Commerce in recognition of its involvement with export focused organizations.

LEADING LAW FIRMS

FULBRIGHT & JAWORSKI LLP

THE FIRM

Managing Partner: Steven B Pfeiffer

Number of partners: 319
Number of other lawyers: 519

FIRM OVERVIEW: Founded in 1919, Fulbright & Jaworski LLP is a full-service law firm equipped to meet the legal needs of clients wherever those needs may arise, whether locally, nationally or internationally. As one of the largest law firms in the United States, Fulbright & Jaworski has approximately 750 attorneys in 11 offices in the United States, Europe and Asia.

MAIN AREAS OF PRACTICE

Arbitration & ADR: Fulbright & Jaworski's Arbitration and ADR practice group moves easily between traditional litigation, arbitration and ADR. More recently, the firm was ranked by its peers as one of five highly recommended national law firms in the US for dispute resolution in the *Global Counsel 2002 Dispute Resolution Handbook* published by Practical Law Company, and is the only Texas-based firm included in the overall national law firm rankings.

Bankruptcy: Fulbright & Jaworski's Bankruptcy, Reorganization and Creditors' Rights Department represents creditors and debtors in restructure, refinance and insolvency litigation, including bankruptcy. It has substantial experience in restructure and refinance negotiations and documentation and in insolvency litigation, particularly valuation litigation.

Corporate: Fulbright & Jaworski's Business and Financial practice is national and international in scope. The Corporate, Securities and Transactions Department includes in its client base some of the world's largest business and financial institutions, as well as many middle market and emerging companies.

Energy: Fulbright & Jaworski is recognized as a premier energy firm with a diversified practice that serves the needs of the global energy industry. With over 50 years of experience in energy matters. The firm's attorneys are regularly involved in both international and domestic energy matters and are highly skilled in energy transactions, regulatory matters and dispute resolution.

Healthcare: Fulbright & Jaworski represents large and small healthcare providers across the nation, from nationally renowned hospital centers, including the Texas Medical Center, which its attorneys were instrumental in establishing, to community health clinics. For more than 50 years, Fulbright & Jaworski has represented healthcare clients in a wide range of issues, including tax matters, federal compliance issues and commercial and professional malpractice claims.

Information Technology: Fulbright & Jaworski's Information Technology practice group serves both types of IT clients: companies that are starting up and businesses that are large, well-established leaders in their respective fields. To accommodate the very different needs of these two extremes, the firm's Information Technology practice group is both broad and diverse, extending to virtually ever segment of the IT arena.

Intellectual Property & Technology: Fulbright & Jaworski's Intellectual Property and Technology Department encompasses one of the largest concentrations of intellectual property attorneys in the country. The firm's experienced team of attorneys, patent agents and technical advisors helps clients obtain and protect intellectual property rights in the United States and around the world. The breadth of the firm's services is extensive as it: counsels clients about copyrights, patents, trade secrets and trademarks; practices before government agencies to secure those rights; handles arbitration, mediation and other litigation alternatives; negotiates licenses to maximize the value of such property; handles technology transfers, manufacturing and supply agreements, research and development agreements, and start up agreements; handles intellectual property audits and due diligence, either separately or as part of mergers and acquisitions.

HEAD OFFICE

TEXAS
1301 McKinney, Suite 5100, **Houston**, TX 77010-3095
Tel: 713 651 5151 **Fax:** 713 651 5246
Email: info@fulbright.com
Website: www.fulbright.com

BRANCH OFFICES

NEW YORK
666 Fifth Avenue, **New York**, NY 10103-3198
Tel: 212 318 3000 **Fax:** 212 318 3400
Email: info@fulbright.com

DISTRICT OF COLUMBIA
801 Pennsylvania Avenue, NW, Market Square, **Washington, DC** 20004-2623
Tel: 202 662 0200 **Fax:** 202 662 4643
Email: info@fulbright.com

CALIFORNIA
865 South Figueroa, Twenty-Ninth Floor, **Los Angeles**, CA 90017-2571
Tel: 213 892 9200 **Fax:** 213 680 4518
Email: info@fulbright.com

MINNESOTA
225 South Sixth Street, Suite 4850, **Minneapolis**, MN 55402-4320
Tel: 612 321 2800 **Fax:** 612 321 9600
Email: info@fulbright.com

TEXAS
600 Congress Avenue, Suite 2400, **Austin**, TX 78701-3271
Tel: 512 474 5201 **Fax:** 512 536 4598
Email: info@fulbright.com

2200 Ross Avenue, Suite 2800, **Dallas**, TX 75201-2748
Tel: 214 855 8000 **Fax:** 214 855 8200
Email: info@fulbright.com

300 Convent Street, Suite 2200, **San Antonio**, TX 78205-3792
Tel: 210 224 5575 **Fax:** 210 270 7205
Email: info@fulbright.com

CONTACTS

Arbitration & ADR	Mark Baker, John Bowman
Bankruptcy	Evelyn H Biery
Corporate	Mike Conlon, Paul Jacobs
Energy & Real Property	Michael P Irvin, Jeff Dykes
Healthcare	Jerry Bell
Intellectual Property & Technology	Paul Krieger
International	Steven B Pfeiffer
Labor & Employment Law	John Harper
Litigation	Stephen Dillard
Technology & Emerging Companies	John Boehm
	Poe Leggette, Robert Gray
	Merrill Kraines, George Kutzschbach

Labor & Employment Law: Fulbright & Jaworski's Labor and Employment Department provides extensive services that range from counseling companies relative to the increasing number of state, federal, and local laws regulating employment to representation in state and federal jury and non-jury trials and before administrative agencies.

Litigation: Fulbright & Jaworski's Litigation Department emphasizes a hands-on philosophy tailored to a client's specific needs, covering the widest possible range of legal matters from local litigation to the most complex international disputes. Attorneys frequently author legal treatises and law

LEADING LAW FIRMS

FULBRIGHT & JAWORSKI LLP cont'd

review articles, participate in continuing legal education programs sponsored by national, state and local organizations and serve as elected leaders of the local, state and American Bar Associations.

Technology & Emerging Companies: Fulbright & Jaworski has a long history of representing start-up companies and mature companies alike. The TEC Department is an innovative portal for the firm's emerging-company and technology clients to access a wide spectrum of experience, including corporate finance, tax, securities compliance, real estate, labor and employment, intellectual property and technology, information technology and e-commerce, product liability and class actions, and general litigation.

INTERNATIONAL WORK: Fulbright & Jaworski's international lawyers have counseled and represented US and non-US businesses with regard to their international activities in almost every part of the world. The firm's International Department comprises more than 70 attorneys from its US, European (London and Munich) and Asian (Hong Kong) offices and has considerable experience in the wide array of business and legal issues involved in cross-border financial, commercial and investment transactions. Its international clients represent a broad cross-sector of industry groups, including energy, manufacturing, mining, information and communications technologies, telecommunications, banking and financial services and insurance. To meet the diversity of clients' needs, Fulbright & Jaworski's international attorneys are drawn from throughout the firm's departments and work closely with attorneys in all areas of practice. Many of the firm's international lawyers are multilingual, have lived and worked outside of the United States and are intimately familiar with different legal and business cultures. As a complement to its own capabilities, the firm has developed an extensive network of relationships with law firms throughout the world that provide expert assistance with respect to various 'host' nation legal issues that arise in international investments, transactions and disputes.

International Offices: Fulbright and Jaworski LLP has offices in Hong Kong, London and Munich.

Languages: Afrikaans, Arabic, Bengali, Cantonese, Chinese, Croatian, Dutch, French, German, Hebrew, Hindu, Italian, Japanese, Korean, Mandarin Chinese, Polish, Portuguese, Romanian, Russian, Spanish, Tagalog, Taiwanese, Urdu, Vietnamese and Yugoslavian.

BRANCH OFFICES

NEW YORK

666 Fifth Avenue, New York, NY 10103-3198
Partner in charge: William Bush
Number of lawyers: 110
Office Profile: Formed over 65 years ago, the New York office serves a broad client base including large publicly-held corporations, investment banking and brokerage firms, venture capital and leveraged buyout firms, investment funds, private equity and institutional investors, life science, high-technology and other emerging growth companies, privately-held companies, partnerships, individuals, estates and charitable organizations and foundations.

WASHINGTON, DC

801 Pennsylvania Avenue, NW, Market Square, Washington, DC 20004-2623
Partner in charge: Steven B Pfeiffer
Number of lawyers: 86
Office Profile: Since its founding in 1927, Fulbright & Jaworski's Washington, DC office has grown from a few lawyers providing federal agency representation in support of the firm's practice, to a full-service office of more than 80 lawyers handling litigation, business and regulatory matters for a national and international clientele.

CALIFORNIA

865 South Figueroa, Twenty-Ninth Floor, Los Angeles, CA 90017-2571
Partner in charge: Harry Hathaway
Number of lawyers: 60
Office Profile: Fulbright & Jaworski's growing Los Angeles office is full-service, with a diverse litigation and sophisticated business practice that includes: appellate; corporate, securities and transactions; banking and business; bankruptcy, reorganization and creditors' rights; environmental; healthcare; intellectual property and technology; international; labor and employment law; litigation; public finance; real estate; tax; trusts and estates; venture capital.

MINNESOTA

225 South Sixth Street, Suite 4850, Minneapolis, MN 55402-4320
Partner in charge: Chaz De La Garza
Number of lawyers: 12
Office Profile: The Minneapolis office of Fulbright & Jaworski opened in February 2000 as a result of joining forces with members of the former intellectual property specialty firm of Arnold White & Durkee. In October 2001, the office doubled in size when the practice group from Larkin, Hoffman, Daly and Lindgren, Ltd joined the firm. This office's strength in helping multinational businesses protect their intellectual capital globally continues to grow, and its presence in the Twin Cities broadens its ability to serve clients in the Midwest. In providing the most thorough representation, the attorneys in Fulbright & Jaworski's Minneapolis office team with lawyers in the firm's Austin office to provide clients with a full range of intellectual property litigation and counseling services.

TEXAS

600 Congress Avenue, Suite 2400, Austin, TX 78701-3271
Partner in charge: Pike Powers
Number of lawyers: 84
Office Profile: Opened in January 1978, Fulbright & Jaworski's Austin Office is a full-service presence with more than 85 lawyers. In 2000 alone it added more than 35 patent, trademark and technology attorneys and scientific advisors in Austin, many of whom joined the firm from the IP specialty firm Arnold, White & Durkee, and several of whom have served as senior in-house counsel. Integrating that in-house experience with the firm's practice reflects Fulbright & Jaworski's commitment to deliver prompt and practical solutions to its clients.

2200 Ross Avenue, Suite 2800, Dallas, TX 75201-2748
Partner in charge: Lawrence Kalinec
Number of lawyers: 77
Office Profile: Fulbright & Jaworski's Dallas office opened in 1981 by merging with the bond firm of Dumas, Huguenin, Boothman & Morrow. For several years, the firm's Dallas attorneys focused on municipal finance transactions, then expanded to a full-service office to include: appellate; bankruptcy, reorganization and creditors' rights; corporate, securities, and transactions; healthcare; intellectual property and technology; international; labor and employment law; litigation; public finance; real estate; tax.

300 Convent Street, Suite 2200, San Antonio, TX 78205-3792
Partner in charge: Philip J Pfeiffer
Number of lawyers: 55
Office Profile: Fulbright & Jaworski opened its San Antonio office in 1980, which has since grown to a full-service office with more than 50 attorneys to include: appellate; bankruptcy, reorganization and creditors' rights; corporate, securities and transactions; environmental; healthcare; labor and employment law; litigation; public finance; real estate; tax and employee benefits; trusts and estates.

LEADING LAW FIRMS

GARDERE WYNNE SEWELL LLP

THE FIRM

Managing Partner: Stephen D Good

Number of partners: 161
Number of other lawyers: 128

AREAS OF PRACTICE:
Trial	28%
Corporate	22%
Financial Services	19%
Labor & Employment	9%
Environmental	8%
Tax	8%
Intellectual Property	6%

FIRM OVERVIEW: Gardere is one of the preeminent full-service law firms in the Southwest. With approximately 290 lawyers and over 35 practice areas to serve its clients, Gardere is strong and diverse, combining the comprehensive resources of a large firm with an interdisciplinary approach to providing clients with effective counsel, in terms of time, cost, and results. This approach creates a professional service environment in which attorneys experienced in specific areas of law and particular industries are available to provide effective, timely counsel according to specific client needs. The firm provides solutions to complicated legal matters and achieve its client's goals - Gardere's primary objective.

MAIN AREAS OF PRACTICE

Corporate: Counsels companies on strategic planning, outsourcing and a full range of issues involving business operations. Attorneys are recognized for their aggressive approach to finding meaningful solutions for the companies they represent, and not only provide general counsel but specialized expertise in areas such as investment partnerships, major business transactions, partnership interests, public and private offerings, start-up ventures, and venture capital.

Environmental: Covers a breadth of issues including high-stakes complex litigation involving multiple parties, regulatory rulemaking, transactions and compliance assistance for ongoing operations. This national practice includes team members from diverse backgrounds including federal and state environmental agencies, the judiciary, Fortune 500 companies and academia.

Financial Services: Serves both public and private as well as regulated and unregulated entities and institutions in a variety of issues including regulatory matters, financing transactions, development transactions and restructurings. Attorneys have experience with virtually every form of commercial financing, both secured and unsecured, and handle transactions involving all types of assets, including real estate, mineral interests, inventory, accounts receivable, factoring and various forms of intangible properties. Attorneys are particularly experienced in the special issues involved in the financing and operation of hotels and resorts, ships, and energy assets, such as drilling rigs and production platforms.

Intellectual Property: Focuses on patent, trademark, copyright, trade secret and unfair competition law and the antitrust aspects of intellectual property law, with significant expertise in trademark and patent prosecution, licensing, IPO's, and related litigation. Clients range between individual inventors, artists and authors, universities and large multinational corporations.

Labor & Employment: Provides counsel and representation for employers in decision making and litigation involving the National Labor Relations Act, the Fair Labor Standards Act, and individual and class action employment discrimination matters. This includes wrongful discharge claims, such as workers compensation retaliation, negligent hiring or retention, implied contract, acquisition-related, and those pendant to employment claims (libel, slander, infliction of emotional distress, fraud); Executive Order 11246 affirmative action plans and audits; Occupational Safety and Health Act matters; government contractor employment issues; and immigration and naturalization matters.

Tax: Consists of several practice specialties including federal income taxation, state and local taxation, international taxation, estate planning and administration, employee benefits and executive compensation.

Trial: Focuses on trials in United States District Courts and all State courts, and appellate matters in both federal and state courts of appeals and the US Supreme Court and representation before various state, national and international arbitration boards. Practice areas within the section include admiralty, antitrust, appellate, aviation litigation, class action, computer technology, construction, environmental/toxic tort, government contracts, medical malpractice, securities, and tort defense/insurance litigation.

INTERNATIONAL WORK: Provides a comprehensive range of legal services to both Mexican and foreign clients. The office of Gardere, Arena y Robles, S.C. (GAR) in Mexico City is a civil partnership formed by Mexican and US attorneys. GAR has developed a special focus on: assisting Mexican and foreign clients in acquisitions, joint ventures, and other investments; the development of infrastructure projects with the Mexican government and private sector entities involving the privatization or operations of public assets, e.g., tollroads, potable water and water treatment facilities, airports, seaports, drilling contracts and electrical energy projects; and representing clients generally in the energy, manufacturing, technology, telecommunications, financial and environmental sectors.

HEAD OFFICE

TEXAS
3000 Thanksgiving Tower, 1601 Elm Street, **Dallas**, TX 75201-4761
Tel: 214 999 3000   **Fax:** 214 999 4667
Website: www.gardere.com

BRANCH OFFICES

TEXAS
3000 One American Center, 600 Congress Avenue, **Austin**, TX 78701-2978
Tel: 512 542 7000   **Fax:** 512 542 7100

1000 Louisiana, Suite 3400, **Houston**, Texas 77002-5007
Tel: 713 276 5500   **Fax:** 713 276 5555

DISTRICT OF COLUMBIA
1667 K Street, NW, Suite 450, **Washington, DC** 20006-1649
Tel: 202 659 3560   **Fax:** 202 659 3565

INTERNATIONAL OFFICES

Gardere, Arena y Robles, S.C. is based in **Lomas de Chapultepec**, Mexico.

CONTACTS

Corporate	NL Stevens
Environmental	Richard Faulk
Financial Services	Clifford Risman
Intellectual Property	Sanford Warren
Labor & Employment	Ronald Gaswirth
Tax	Suzan Fenner
Trial	Curtis Frisbie, Jr

LEADING LAW FIRMS

GIBBS & BRUNS, LLP

THE FIRM

Managing Partner: Robin C Gibbs

Number of partners: 13
Number of other lawyers: 10

AREAS OF PRACTICE:
Commercial Litigation 90%
Appellate 10%

HEAD OFFICE

TEXAS
Gibbs & Bruns, LLP, 1100 Louisiana, Suite 5300, **Houston**, TX 77002
Tel: 713 650 8805 **Fax:** 713 750 0903

CONTACTS

Commercial Litigation ....Robin C Gibbs
Appellate ....Jeffrey C Alexander
....Jennifer H Greer

FIRM OVERVIEW: Gibbs & Bruns, LLP engages exclusively in a commercial litigation practice in Texas, throughout the United States and in various courts and tribunals outside the United States. The firm practices in a broad range of business-related complex litigation, and has been involved in much of the major litigation in the region since the firm's inception in 1983. The firm prides itself on its ability to handle difficult and novel legal problems and routinely represents plaintiffs and defendants in significant contract, securities, trade secret, intellectual property, patent, insurance, class action, antitrust, lender liability, oil and gas, director liability, copyright, and partnership disputes.

MAIN AREAS OF PRACTICE:
Commercial Litigation: The firm represents plaintiffs and defendants in a wide variety of litigation matters. In recent years the firm has obtained jury verdicts in cases for corporate Plaintiffs totaling nearly $500 million. During this same period the firm has obtained for corporate defendants '0' damages verdicts in cases where the evidence presented exposure of over $1.2 billion. Gibbs & Bruns was recently named one of the 10 best litigation firms in the United States by International Commercial Litigation magazine. The Howard C Bloom Company, an attorney search firm, also ranked Gibbs & Bruns first in the state of Texas in its most recent evaluation of the academic credentials of Texas law firms, with the highest numerical rating ever awarded.
Appellate: The firm's appellate attorneys prosecute and defend appeals in a variety of jurisdictions and at all levels of the appellate process, including the Supreme Court of the United States. Gibbs & Bruns' appellate work arises from litigation work performed by the firm as well as cases in which other counsel has handled the case in the lower courts.

CLIENTS: The firm's clients include many of the world's largest industrial companies, banks, brokerage firms and professional firms. Representative clients are El Paso Energy, Merrill Lynch Investment Managers, Franklin Templeton Funds, Fidelity Management & Research, The M.W. Kellogg Company, the outside directors of Enron Corporation, UBS Painewebber, Hermann Hospital, John J. Moores (owner of the San Diego Padres), Pennzoil Company, Preussag AG, Saipem SpA, Zachry Construction Corporation and Panhandle Eastern Transmission Corp.

INTERNATIONAL WORK: The firm practices in a wide variety of international courts and tribunals. Recently, the firm has handled litigation in the courts of the United Kingdom and arbitration panels in the United Kingdom and Kuala Lampur. The firm is also frequently called upon to handle multi-jurisdictional litigation that involves simultaneous proceedings in the United States and other countries. Recently, the firm has handled such litigation involved disputes addressed jointly by the courts of the United States and the courts of Norway and the United Kingdom.

LEADING LAW FIRMS

GILLESPIE, ROZEN & WATSKY, PC

THE FIRM

Number of partners: 3

FIRM OVERVIEW: This firm represents labor organizations and individual plaintiffs in employment matters. Gillespie, Rozen & Watsky attorneys have extensive trial, arbitration, mediation, appellate and office experience concerning the laws of breach of contract, age discrimination, sex discrimination, sexual harassment, disability discrimination, tortious interference with contract, defamation and wrongful discharge. In addition, the firm handles a full range of union representation, including matters under the National Labor Relations Act, the Railway Labor Act and Labor Arbitrations. All three partners and the Of Counsel attorney are Board Certified in Labor and Employment Law.

HEAD OFFICE

TEXAS
3402 Oak Grove Avenue, Suite 200, **Dallas** TX 75204
Tel: 214 720 2009 **Fax:** 214 720 2291
Website: www.lawyers.com/grwlaw

GOINS, UNDERKOFLER, CRAWFORD & LANGDON, LLP

THE FIRM

Number of partners: 17
Number of other lawyers: 3

HEAD OFFICE

TEXAS
1201 Elm Street, Suite 4800, **Dallas** TX 75270
Tel: 214 969 5454 **Fax:** 214 969 5902
Email: gucl@gucl.com

FIRM OVERVIEW: Since its founding in 1977, Goins, Underkofler, Crawford & Langdon has grown steadily in practice areas as clients' needs have dictated. The firm believes that the growth derives from its client-oriented approach of responsiveness, effectiveness and sensitivity to the cost of providing legal services. The attorneys are intent upon being positive, practical problem-solvers working with clients to resolve broad business challenges at hand. Many of the attorneys are recognized authorities in their fields, serving as authors of professional articles, seminar lectures and officers or directors of professional organizations within their practice areas. The firm's attorneys are, above all, committed to providing the highest quality legal services through attentive, aggressive and innovative application of the law to situations its clients encounter in today's changing business environment. Communication with clients on current developments in the law is effected through written bulletins and client seminars as well as through close personal contacts. The attorneys' breadth of expertise and depth of knowledge within their practice areas equip the firm to respond within time and budget constraints.

MAIN AREAS OF PRACTICE:

General Business & Commercial Law: The firm is engaged primarily in a general business and commercial law practice. While all members of the firm may concentrate their practice in one or more areas, they are first and foremost business lawyers who assist their clients in their commercial business activities, including the formation and operation of corporations, partnerships and other business entities, the interrelationship between their clients and other businesses and government agencies and the resolution of business controversies through mediation, arbitration and litigation.

Business Litigation: The firm counsels clients extensively on measures to avoid litigation. However, when necessary the firm's attorneys aggressively represent clients before state and federal courts, arbitration panels and administrative agencies. The firm frequently defends corporations in contract, construction, real estate, insurance coverage and other commercial matters. The firm's litigation experience includes, federal and state anti-trust and general corporate matters, securities, business takeovers, intellectual property, state and federal constitutional issues, plaintiff's personal injury matters, including medical malpractice.

Commercial Construction Law: Several attorneys in the firm are regularly engaged in all phases of commercial and residential construction law. The activities include counseling developers, owners, contractors, construction managers, subcontractors, design professionals, material fabricators and suppliers on such matters as construction financing, contract negotiation, drafting of contract documents, public bid protests and disputes, strategy with regard to potential disputes, contract interpretation and compliance, project close-out and settlement, achievement of minority participation goals, delay and impact claim development and presentation, defense of claims, compliance with bond and lien statutes, contract terminations for default and for convenience, contractor substitutions, and labor-management relations. The firm also regularly represents parties to construction disputes and their sureties in all aspects of dispute resolution. Some of the firm's attorneys have acted as court-appointed masters to find and determine facts in complex construction cases. Others have been selected by construction litigants to arbitrate or mediate their disputes prior to or in lieu of trial.

Taxation: The firm's Tax Practice encompasses all phases of tax planning, including mergers and acquisitions, reorganizations, divestitures, venture capital financing, real estate acquisitions, transactional planning for partnerships, trusts and estates and individuals. The firm's tax lawyers work closely with other practice areas concerning the tax implications of transactions, and to develop tax strategies that maximize the preservation of assets and the client's bottom line.

Employment & Labor Relations: The firm's Labor Practice includes the following issues and areas: collective bargaining, National Labor Relations Board proceedings, grievances, arbitration, rejection of the Texas Workers Compensation Act, representation of management in proceedings before federal and state regulatory agencies, equal employment and health and safety matters. Its attorneys represent management before the state and federal agencies level during the investigatory phase of discrimination complaints based on race, sex, age, national origin and religion. The firm also represents management in litigation on these issues if the need arises. Its labor lawyers counsel non-unionized employers in maintaining open shop work environments. The firm has also been involved in the preparation of company personnel and policy manuals, the obtaining of injunctions to prohibit unfair labor practices and trial of wrongful termination issues.

Insurance: The firm handles commercial coverage and 'bad faith' claims for insurers and corporate clients, as well as referrals from other attorneys. The firm has an active insurance defense practice as well, taking referrals at the defense of policy holders from several carriers.

Real Estate: The firm represents a number of significant real estate developers, syndicators, owners and entrepreneurs in the Dallas/Fort Worth Metroplex in connection with the preparation of syndication documents and offering memoranda, representation of clients from the contracting stage through closing, preparation of partnership agreements and organization of other business entities in connection with the development and ownership of real property, negotiation and documentation of loan transactions, negotiation and preparation of leases, representation of clients in general landlord/tenant matters, and representation of clients with respect to environmental matters.

Franchising & Intellectual Property: The firm represents and counsels major franchisors as well as clients exploring franchising as a means of distributing products or services. This representation includes assistance in the preparation of a franchise program, drafting of offering circulars and agreements, registration of the documentation, assistance with an ongoing compliance program.

Banking: The firm represents state, national and foreign commercial banks in such areas as negotiation and preparation of loan documentation for new credit facilities, extensions and restructuring of debts by financially distressed debtors.

CLIENTS: The firm's clients include publicly-held NYSE corporations, privately-held businesses and emerging entrepreneurial firms that embrace an array of industries and present a broad range of legal needs. The firm's clients are involved in a variety of industries, including commercial and residential construction, insurance, banking, real estate development, franchising, equipment leasing, manufacturing and distribution.

INTERNATIONAL WORK: The firm has regularly engaged, and has been engaged by, counsel in Canada and Mexico for consultation and representation with respect to legal matters in North America.

LEADING LAW FIRMS

GOODWIN PROCTER LLP

THE FIRM

Chairman & Managing Partner: Regina M Pisa
Partners nationwide: 160
Total attorneys: 505

FIRM OVERVIEW: Goodwin Procter LLP is one of the nation's leading law firms, with a team of 500 attorneys and offices in Boston, New York, New Jersey and Washington, DC. The firm develops innovative solutions to complex legal problems and couples practical advice with proactive strategic counsel. The firm provides legal services nationwide to Fortune 500 and other companies in matters involving corporate/transactional work, complex litigation, real estate, financial services and intellectual property. Goodwin Procter understands that people are its most important asset. Consequently, the firm devotes considerable resources to recruiting, training and retaining its lawyers and staff. The firm hires talented, motivated people committed to a culture based on teamwork. Goodwin Procter has long been committed to establishing a diverse workplace reflective of today's society. The firm is one of only a handful of comparably sized law firms in the United States to have a woman acting as managing partner. A number of the firm's partners serve or have served as leaders of minority law associations, and Goodwin Procter is a founding member of a group known nationally for helping law firms recruit and retain minority lawyers. The firm believes strongly in its obligations as a corporate citizen and is dedicated to community service. Through its longstanding and extensive pro bono program, the firm strongly encourages its legal staff to assist those unable to afford legal representation.

MAIN AREAS OF PRACTICE: Work includes corporate, litigation, real estate, financial services, intellectual property, tax, ERISA and employee benefits, labor and employment, environmental, and estate planning.
Corporate: The Corporate Practice - the firm's largest - offers a multidisciplinary approach and strong industry focus, combined with a formidable tax capability. Goodwin Procter consistently ranks among the nation's leaders in financial services and REIT transactions, and its Private Equity and Intellectual Property Practices are among the firm's fastest-growing areas.
Litigation: The firm's Litigation Practice assists clients in complex, contested matters around the country. Its attorneys provide counsel on litigation avoidance and control, risk management and dispute resolution, and its work includes appearing before state and federal courts - including matters at the appellate level. A number of litigators have served as Assistant United States Attorneys, and two federal district court judges are former partners of the firm.

CLIENTS: Goodwin Procter maintains a diverse client base, with clients ranging from entrepreneurial start-ups to established multinationals. The firm's clients present complex issues and expect cost-effective results to be delivered under tight deadlines. Client service begins with knowing the client, knowing their business and knowing their competitors. With this information, the firm's attorneys are able to leverage their specialized skills and expertise to deliver responsive, knowledgeable and practical legal advice. The firm maximizes its practice efficiency by focusing on effective use of technology and knowledge management.

HEAD OFFICE

MASSACHUSETTS
Exchange Place, **Boston**, MA 02109
Tel: 617 570 1000 **Fax:** 617 523 1231
Email: rpisa@goodwinprocter.com
Website: www.goodwinprocter.com

BRANCH OFFICES

DISTRICT OF COLUMBIA
1717 Pennsylvania Avenue, **Washington, DC** 20006
Tel: 202 974 1000 **Fax:** 202 331 9330
Email: jbuckley@goodwinprocter.com

NEW JERSEY
Seven Becker Farm Road, **Roseland**, NJ 07068
Tel: 973 992 1990 **Fax:** 973 992 4643
Email: mhildebrand@goodwinprocter.com

NEW YORK
599 Lexington Avenue, **New York**, NY 10022
Tel: 212 813 8800 **Fax:** 212 355 3333
Email: rinsolia@goodwinprocter.com

CONTACTS

Boston...Regina M Pisa
Roseland...Mary Hildebrand
New York..Robert Insolia
Washington, DC..Jeremiah Buckley

GOODWIN
PROCTER

LEADING LAW FIRMS

GRAY CARY WARE & FREIDENRICH LLP

THE FIRM

CEO: Terry O'Malley
Chair, Global Steering Committee: Henry Lesser
Managing Partner, Transactions: Howard Clowes
Managing Partner, Litigation: Marcie Mihaila
Managing Partner, Operations: Bob Shuman
Number of partners: 161
Number of other lawyers: 250

FIRM OVERVIEW: Gray Cary Ware & Freidenrich LLP (Gray Cary) is a national law firm that represents a full spectrum of business enterprises and individuals, including emerging growth and technology companies. With more than 410 attorneys practicing in Palo Alto, San Diego, San Francisco, Austin, Sacramento, Seattle and Washington, DC, the firm is organized into distinct practice areas based on specific industries and complimentary areas of law. It provides expertise, responsiveness and cost-effective solutions in order to meet the needs of each client. Members work as business counselors to the client's management team, providing practical, innovative solutions.

MAIN AREAS OF PRACTICE:

Corporate & Securities: The firm advises in the negotiation of joint ventures (including due diligence on potential partners, country risk and business issues), acquiring and selling foreign companies and other business entities, legal issues relating to foreign acquisitions of US entities (including US report requirements), structuring international channels of distribution, corporate governance, drafting outbound and inbound sales and service agreements, agency agreements and representation agreements.

M&A: The firm advises on the structuring and implementation of a broad range of domestic and cross-border M&A transactions, including both public and private company acquisitions.

Intellectual Property: Gray Cary provides a full spectrum of intellectual property legal services for a wide variety of industries. The firm's attorneys counsel clients on the development, acquisition, protection and exploitation of proprietary technology as well as the development, manufacturing and distribution of products. Additionally, the firm offers a full range of business and litigation services related to intellectual property, including privacy, licensing, patent, trademark, trade secret and copyright.

Litigation: Gray Cary's trial attorneys are experienced in every aspect of litigation, including case management of multiparty cases to trial and appeal of high exposure lawsuits. The firm's litigators have attained a national reputation for the high quality of their legal services, extensive trial experience and ability to deliver practical, economical legal solutions to business disputes.

Real Estate: Gray Cary provides a broad range of real estate, land use and environmental services through the firm's Real Estate Services Group. The group is experienced in advising a wide variety of property owners and developers, including partnerships, private and public companies, individuals, and public agencies. The firm serves clients in the real estate, construction, high technology, life sciences, retail, manufacturing, telecommunications, healthcare, financial services, professional services and hospitality industries, as well as landowners, tenants and citizens groups.

Employment & Employee Benefits: Gray Cary represents and advises employers on all aspects of employee relations and employee benefits. The firm's employment and labor attorneys understand the numerous complex laws governing the employer-employee relationship. The firm helps clients plan their employee relations strategies in order to comply with the law in a cost-effective, productive manner to avoid potential liability.

HEAD OFFICE

CALIFORNIA
400 Hamilton Avenue, **Palo Alto**, CA 94301-1833
Tel: 650 833 2000 Fax: 650 833 2001
Email: info@graycary.com
Website: www.graycary.com

BRANCH OFFICES

CALIFORNIA
1755 Embarcadero Road, **Palo Alto**, CA 94303-3340
Tel: 650 833 2000 Fax: 650 320 7401

400 Capitol Mall, Suite 2400, **Sacramento**, CA 95814-4428
Tel: 916 930 3200 Fax: 916 930 3201

4365 Executive Drive, Suite 1100, **San Diego**, CA 92121-2133
Tel: 858 677 1400 Fax: 858 677 1401

401 B Street, Suite 2000, **San Diego**, CA 92101-4240
Tel: 619 699 2700 Fax: 619 699 2701

153 Townsend Street, Suite 800, **San Francisco**, CA 94107-1907
Tel: 415 836 2500 Fax: 415 836 2501

DISTRICT OF COLUMBIA
1625 Massachusetts Avenue, NW, Suite 300,
Washington, DC 20036-2247
Tel: 202 238 7700 Fax: 202 238 7701

TEXAS
1221 S Mopac Expressway, Suite 400, **Austin**, TX 78746-6875
Tel: 512 457 7000 Fax: 512 457 7001

WASHINGTON
701 Fifth Avenue, Suite 7000, **Seattle**, WA 98104-7044
Tel: 206 839 4800 Fax: 206 839 4801

Tax & Trusts: Gray Cary's Tax Group serves the legal tax needs of multinational corporations, closely held businesses, venture funds and high net worth individuals concerning all aspects of US and international tax planning, administrative tax appeals and tax litigation. The firm has a significant track record of helping its clients develop and implement tax strategies that provide a bottom line advantage, as well as prevailing in tax audits and appeals. The firm is also often called upon to review and analyze complex tax plans proposed and implemented by its clients' consultants and accountants. Gray Cary is known for being result focused, creative and efficient, and for packaging its tax advice in easily, understandable communications.

CLIENTS: Gray Cary's clients include public and private companies, ranging from start-ups to Fortune 500 corporations. The firm's clients do business in a variety of domestic and international markets, and they operate in major industry sectors, including software, hardware, life sciences, healthcare, telecommunications, manufacturing, retail, media and e-commerce, real estate and construction, semiconductor and nanotechnology. Gray Cary also represents service providers, investment banking and financial institutions, venture capital firms, entrepreneurs and high net worth individuals.

INTERNATIONAL WORK: Gray Cary provides a wide variety of services to international clients in the areas of corporate, M&A, licensing agreements, patents, trademarks, copyrights, employee benefits and employment law, international regulatory compliance, international trade regulation, export controls and customs, tax and estate planning, real estate and litigation.

LEADING LAW FIRMS

GREENBERG GLUSKER FIELDS CLAMAN MACHTINGER & KINSELLA

THE FIRM

Managing Partner: Norman H Levine

Senior Partners: Arthur Greenberg, Bertram Fields, Stephen Claman, Sidney Machtinger and Dale Kinsella

Number of partners: 55
Number of other lawyers: 46

FIRM OVERVIEW: Greenberg Glusker is one of California's leading business and entertainment law firms. The firm provides the highest quality legal services and strategic business advice to companies and individuals.

MAIN AREAS OF PRACTICE:

Business & Tax: The firm's Business and Tax Department provides securities, tax, mergers/acquisition and general business advice to a broad range of companies (both publicly-held and privately-owned), entrepreneurs and high net worth individuals whose business operations span a variety of industries, including technology, entertainment services, health and fitness and manufacturing. The department employs a service-oriented, interdisciplinary team approach to its clients' business needs, with a view toward developing an in-depth understanding and appreciation of the types of issues and problems that are likely to arise.

Commercial Transactions & Restructurings: The firm's national practice includes handling complex debtor/creditor issues, financing and loan transactions, disputes among creditors, enforcement of creditors' rights, business bankruptcies, restructurings, assignments for the benefit of creditors and acquisitions of assets from troubled companies.

Entertainment: The firm's Entertainment Department is best known for its representation of talent such as actors, writers, directors and producers in the motion picture and television business. The firm negotiates talent agreements and contracts for the financing, development and production of motion pictures. Representation of talent extends beyond simply negotiating employment contracts; members of the firm interact with artists, agents and other representatives to help its clients achieve career goals and to assist in personal and business transactions.

Environmental: The firm's Environmental Department focuses on cost recovery litigation involving contaminated properties, environmental liabilities in real estate transactions, brownfields and environmental redevelopment and regulatory counseling. The firm's pioneering recovery theories and strategies and successful use of alternative dispute resolution techniques allows it to achieve cost-effective solutions in environmental litigation.

Intellectual Property & Technology: With its sophisticated clientele and wide ranging network of contacts, the firm plays a pivotal role as intellectual property lawyers in the converging worlds of entertainment, technology and business.

Labor & Employment: The firm's Labor and Employment Department provides a complete array of services designed to keep its clients informed about and in compliance with laws governing the workplace. To minimize client exposure to costly litigation and administrative claims, the firm provides training and counseling on a variety of topics, including sexual harassment, discipline, termination and privacy in the workplace. The department prepares employee handbooks, contracts and other employment documents. The department also actively litigates employment disputes of all kinds in all forums.

Land Use: The firm's unique land use and administrative law expertise is an essential element of the services provided to its prestigious roster of real estate and business clients. The firm assists clients in cities and counties across the state on a wide range of entitlements, including general plans, specific plans, subdivisions, variances, CEQA compliance, conditional use permits, zone changes, site plan reviews, development agreements, initiatives and referenda, encompassing the full spectrum of discretionary local planning decisions. When necessary, the firm has successfully defended the hard won entitlements against legal challenge and has also successfully challenged overreaching governmental regulations.

Litigation: The firm's Litigation Department is the largest single department at the firm. On any given day, the firm's litigators can be found in state and federal trial and appellate courts, bankruptcy court and various arbitration tribunals, handling high level litigation, including entertainment, real estate, corporate, intellectual property, employment, environmental and probate matters.

Probate & Estate Planning: The firm's estate planning services range from development of a basic estate plan, to complex arrangements for the transmission of family wealth to younger generations. The firm also provides comprehensive probate and trust administration and litigation services. In addition, it devises planned giving and other services for numerous charities, including hospitals, educational institutions, community organizations and private foundations.

Real Estate: Real estate is an important part of the California economy, and has been a focus of the firm's practice since its inception. Greenberg Glusker is considered one of California's premier real estate law firms. The firm has helped its clients develop and operate office buildings, shopping centers, residential sub-divisions, apartments, hotels, golf courses, mixed-use and redevelopment projects and multimillion dollar luxury homes all over the west coast.

CLIENTS: The firm is well known for its representation of high profile entertainment companies and talent, as well as major players in real estate. Businesses and individuals appreciate the firm's multidisciplinary approach as it reduces the costs, both opportunity and financial, of using more than one law firm.

INTERNATIONAL WORK: The firm's intellectual property, entertainment and commercial transactions clients span the globe. The firm also advises international companies on US law. Greenberg Glusker is the Los Angeles member of the World Law Group, which is comprised of 40 different law firms with over 6,800 lawyers in 30 countries around the world.

HEAD OFFICE

CALIFORNIA
1900 Avenue of the Stars, 21st Floor, **Los Angeles**, CA 90067
Tel: 310 553 3610 **Fax:** 310 553 0687
Email: info@ggfirm.com
Website: www.ggfirm.com

CONTACTS

Business & Tax	Ron Fujikawa
Commercial Transactions & Restructurings	Karl Block
Entertainment	Robert Marshall
Environmental	David Cranston
Intellectual Property & technology	Miriam Claire Beezy
Labor & Employment	Ann Kane Smith
Land Use	Dale Goldsmith
Litigation	Charles Shephard
Probate & Estate Planning	Robert Bennett
Real Estate	Dennis Ellman

LEADING LAW FIRMS

GREENBERG TAURIG, LLP

THE FIRM

Chief Executive Officer: Cesar L Alvarez
Number of partners: 396
Number of other lawyers: 504

FIRM OVERVIEW: Greenberg Traurig, LLP is a US-based, international, full-service business law firm. Its lawyers bring a business perspective to every transaction and matter. Founded in 1967 with three attorneys, Greenberg Traurig has evolved into a premier law firm, with more than 900 attorneys and lobbyists in 20 offices. The firm represents clients around the world in their business communities and courthouses – as well as in the capitals of government, finance, technology and entertainment. It assists international clients seeking access to the US, and also US and foreign clients doing business in other countries.

MAIN AREAS OF PRACTICE:

Corporate & Securities: Greenberg Traurig helps its clients with the legal and business aspects of organizing, operating, financing and expanding their businesses. It routinely handle complex mergers, acquisitions and business combinations, divestitures, corporate restructurings and bankruptcy reorganizations, private equity and venture capital financings, leveraged buyouts, IPOs and underwritten securities offerings, project financings, securitizations, going-private transactions, credit enhancement transactions, broker-dealer and investment company advisory matters, derivatives transactions and syndicated lending transactions.

Litigation: Greenberg Traurig has been at the center of some of the most pivotal cases of recent times, from tobacco and securities class actions to the landmark George W Bush for President trial court proceedings and appeal. With more than 200 seasoned lawyers, the firm has extensive experience in cases involving class actions, products liability, securities regulation, insurance coverage disputes, commercial and construction contracts, government contracts, partnership disputes, white collar criminal defense and intellectual property issues.

Real Estate: Greenberg Traurig's representation and counsel spans the entire range of local, national and international real estate transactions affecting commercial, residential, retail and industrial properties, including: acquisitions; traditional and securitized financing; planning and development; hotels; condominium and cooperative offerings; leasing; sale/leaseback transactions; tax free exchanges; and foreclosures, litigation and restructurings.

Tax, Trusts & Estates: Greenberg Traurig's tax attorneys help clients develop and implement tax strategies to maximize returns and minimize taxes anywhere in the world. The firm's wealth preservation attorneys assist high net worth individuals, families and closely held businesses grow family assets through planning. It has developed tax saving techniques and designed innovative wealth preservation programs to facilitate the transfer of family wealth to future generations at significant tax savings.

Intellectual Property: Multinational companies know that patents, trademarks, copyrights and trade secrets are among their most valuable assets. Greenberg Traurig's Intellectual Property Department offers full-service protection for the intellectual property of clients in all technologies, from biotechnology, pharmaceuticals, medical devices and chemistry to mechanical, electronics and computer software and e-commerce.

Government: Greenberg Traurig has a team of preeminent and politically connected professionals who represent corporations and governmental entities before the legislative and executive branches in federal, state and local governments. The firm's team includes former elected officials, top aides and policy officials for members of the US House and Senate and various state legislatures and local government bodies.

Environmental: Major companies in a variety of industry segments, as well as municipalities, turn to Greenberg Traurig for assistance and counsel on

US OFFICES

The firm has offices in Atlanta, Boca Raton, Boston, Chicago, Denver, Fort Lauderdale, Los Angeles, Miami, New Jersey, New York, Orlando, Philadelphia, Phoenix, Tallahassee, Tysons Corner, Washington, DC, West Palm Beach, Wilmington

INTERNATIONAL OFFICES

The firm also has offices in Zurich in Switzerland and Amsterdam in The Netherlands. For further details of all offices please see firm's website: www.gtlaw.com

their most challenging environmental problems. The firm has unparalleled experience dealing with difficult environmental issues such as development of wetland and coastal zones, endangered species and water use.

Reorganization, Bankruptcy & Restructuring: Greenberg Traurig's Practice is one of the largest and most active in the nation. As part of an integrated national network of professionals who focus their practice on all aspects of reorganizations, bankruptcies, restructurings, workouts and buyouts, the firm's attorneys are able to respond quickly to complex troubled situations arising anywhere and in any industry.

Employment: The firm is aware that companies today require labor and employment attorneys who will provide advice and counseling on all aspects of the employment relationship; handle matters involving union avoidance and organizational work; formulate strategies to anticipate problems; keep them informed of new developments in the law; assist in drafting policies and procedures; and defend the company against discrimination charges at the agency level and in court. Greenberg Traurig delivers these services at all levels of the administrative and litigation process.

Entertainment: With offices in the center of the entertainment industry, Greenberg Traurig has a preeminent, full-service entertainment practice. Its entertainment team focuses on the music, motion picture, television, live stage and cable industries, including the convergence of new technologies, digital delivery systems and the role of advertising and sponsor-driven financing models. We have access to key players in the entertainment industry and provide clients with the pragmatic counsel needed in today's multi-disciplined, multimedia entertainment marketplace.

Health: Greenberg Traurig's Health Business Group provides legal services to a diverse group of healthcare businesses and organizations, including for-profit and not for profit hospitals, long term care and sub-acute providers, health maintenance organizations, provider networks, physicians and physician groups, employer and provider trade organizations, dietary supplement and pharmaceutical companies, assisted living companies, clinical laboratories, biotech companies and medical device manufacturers.

Immigration: Members of the US Immigration Law Department are experienced in all aspects of corporate immigration law, particularly multinational non-immigrant visa and permanent residency work. The attorneys understand the immigration process in all its complexity. They represent clients in such industries as finance, tourism, insurance, electronics, healthcare, shipping and pharmaceuticals with their immigration needs.

Public Finance: Members of Greenberg Traurig's Public Finance Department have extensive experience in serving the needs of state and local issuers and underwriters in all areas of public finance. The firm has broad experience in all forms of tax-exempt financing. For the past several years, the firm has been among the top bond counsel firms in the US, according to the ranking criteria developed by Securities Data Co. and The Bond Buyer, a municipal finance publication.

CLIENTS: The firm represents a diverse client base, including public/private companies, financial institutions, governmental entities and entrepreneurs.

GRIFFITH & NIXON, P.C.

THE FIRM

Managing Partner: Scott Griffith
Senior Partner: Scott Griffith

Number of partners: 4
Number of other lawyers: 8

AREAS OF PRACTICE:

Construction Law	70%
Business Litigation	10%
Insurance Defense	10%
Real Estate	5%
Corporate & Partnership Law	5%

HEAD OFFICE

TEXAS
One Lincoln Centre, 5400 LBJ Freeway, Suite 1025
Dallas, TX 75240
Tel: 972 386 8988 Fax: 972 386 8985
Website: www.griffithnixon.com

CONTACTS

Construction Law	Scott Griffith
Business Litigation	Scott Griffith
Insurance Defense	Scott Griffith
Real Estate	Kimberly Davison
Corporate & Partnership Law	Kimberly Davison

FIRM OVERVIEW: Griffith & Nixon, P.C. is a client oriented law firm, which provides a full range of services in the areas of commercial litigation, business law, construction law, insurance defense, real estate and corporate transactions.

MAIN AREAS OF PRACTICE:

Construction Law: Griffith & Nixon, P.C. provides legal representation in all areas of construction law. The firm can assist clients in the drafting and review of all types of construction contracts. Experience includes all types of prime contracts such as, lump sum, construction management agreements, costs plus a fee and design build. In addition, the firm is familiar with all types of subcontracts and purchase orders. It is familiar with all AIA documents and AGC documents, as well as independent forms. Griffith & Nixon, P.C. also provides full representation with respect to the preparation and filing of a mechanic's liens and bond claims. Experience includes all types of projects, including state, federal, private, commercial, industrial, and heavy highway work. Griffith & Nixon, P.C. has vast experience in all types of construction litigation, including arbitrations, state and federal court litigation. The firm also has extensive experience with respect to alternative dispute resolutions. It has prosecuted and defended all types of construction claims such as wrongful termination, delay claims, defective plans and specifications, changed conditions, acceleration and inefficiency. In addition, Griffith & Nixon, P.C. has a vast network of professional consultants and expert witnesses specializing in every area of construction.

Business Litigation: Griffith & Nixon, P.C. provides representation in all forms of business litigation. This representation includes collection matters, shareholder disputes, breach of contract, tortious interference, employment disputes and disputes with public agencies. The firm also provides representation with respect to insurance coverage and related disputes. It has extensive experience in state and federal courts, as well as alternative dispute resolution methods, such as arbitration and mediation.

Insurance Defense: Griffith & Nixon, P.C. provides insurance defense representation to many clients in connection with construction and business litigation matters. The firm has substantial experience in personal injury insurance defense in connection with construction related accidents and premises liability. Experience includes representation of many sureties in connection with defending against bond claims and bad faith claims. Griffith & Nixon, P.C. has provided insurance defense services for clients such as CNA, Fidelity & Deposit Company of Maryland, Maryland Casualty, St. Paul Fire & Marine Insurance Company, Zurich American, American Safety Casualty Insurance Company, Royal & Sun Alliance Insurance Company.

Real Estate: Griffith & Nixon, P.C. provides full representation with respect to all types of real estate transactions including commercial, industrial, farm and ranch and residential. The firm can assist clients with all aspects of real estate transactions including preparation or review of contracts for sale, deeds, surveys, property restrictions and convenants, title commitments, surveys, and related documentation. Griffith & Nixon, P.C. also provides representation with respect to all related financial transactions, including negotiations with lenders, drafting and review of deeds of trust and promissory notes. In addition to real estate transactions, Griffith & Nixon, P.C. can provide clients with representation in connection with lease negotiations, drafting and review of lease agreements, and all related transactions including, commercial, retail and ground leases. In addition, the firm has a vast network with consultants and professionals in the real estate field, including environmental engineers, appraisers, surveyors, title companies, and lenders.

Corporate & Partnership Law: Griffith & Nixon, P.C. provides representation with respect to business entity formation, modifications and maintenance of corporate documents. The firm can provide assistance in the selection and formation of all types of business entities, including corporations (Subchapter S and Subchapter C, limited liability companies, limited partnerships, non-profit corporation and professional corporations). It can also provide all types of counseling with respect to a range of business needs including overall strategy, employment matters, insurance needs, finances, safety issues, risk prevention, and other areas. Griffith & Nixon, P.C. also has substantial experience in representing purchasers and sellers in connection with all types of mergers and acquisitions. Griffith & Nixon, P.C. can prepare or review employee handbooks, safety programs, insurance programs, and insurance coverage issues. Griffith & Nixon, P.C. can also provide assistance with respect to the drafting or review of employment contracts, including non-compete and confidentiality agreements. Griffith & Nixon, P.C. can also prepare or revise shareholder agreements, annual and special meeting minutes and provide assistance with annual updates of required corporate documentation.

CLIENTS: Representative clients include Abstract Construction Co., AIG Insurance Company, AIGTS Environmental Claims, Alpha Testing, Inc., CNA Insurance, D.P.I.C., Driver Pipeline Co., Inc., Fidelity and Deposit Insurance Co. of Maryland, Great American Insurance Companies, Heartland Claims Service, Jordan Paving Corp., Knoebel Construction, Inc., Leigh Engineering Inc., Meridian Commercial Inc., Mt. Hawley Insurance Company, Naylor Commercial Interiors, Inc., Otis Elevators, Inc., Pacific Builders, Inc., Patton Contractors, Inc., Phoenix Commercial, RAS Builders, Inc., The Ridgemont Co., Scott & Reid General Contractors, Inc., Southwest Construction Services, Spring Valley Construction Company, Univesco, Inc., The Venetian Hotel & Casino, W. B. Kibler Construction Co., Inc., Whiting–Turner Contracting Co., Westdale Asset Management, Ltd., Wright Commercial Contracting, Inc.

LEADING LAW FIRMS

HALE LANE PEEK DENNISON AND HOWARD

THE FIRM

Managing Shareholder: Kristin B McMillan

Number of shareholders: 29
Number of other lawyers: 19

FIRM OVERVIEW: Hale Lane was founded over 30 years ago by Edward Everett Hale (1929-93) upon a core real property and litigation practice in Reno, Nevada. Over the years the firm has developed into a leading full service firm with offices in Reno, Las Vegas, and Carson City, Nevada. The firm's practice spans areas such as energy and utility law, environmental law, healthcare law and securities law, in addition to its long-standing real estate, lending and financial, corporate, tax and estate planning, bankruptcy and litigation practices. Experience, expertise and results are the building blocks of success that make Hale Lane one of Nevada's premier law firms.

MAIN AREAS OF PRACTICE:

Bankruptcy & Insolvency Group: The firm's Bankruptcy and Insolvency Group employs its combined experience of over 35 years in creating cost-effective solutions for its clients in insolvency planning, bankruptcy cases, asset protection planning, workouts, reorganizations, and asset purchases from bankruptcy estates. The group places a strong emphasis on secured and unsecured creditor representation for committees of creditors, institutional, and individual creditors and pre-petition and post-petition lenders and purchasers. With Nevada's growing emphasis on entity formations, the group also participates and assists in major bankruptcy filings for entities whose headquarters are located out of the state.

Business Ventures Group: The firm's Business Ventures Group offers a full range of general and specialized corporate services to individuals and entities, is heavily involved in mergers and acquisitions, and represents companies and individuals in a wide array of public and private securities transactions. Its tax practice encompasses individual, corporate, and business tax planning and consultation. The group's healthcare practice includes the formation and representation of independent practice associations and other models of provider delivery systems, as well as representation of providers, physicians, and nurses. The Business Ventures Group has continued its role as Nevada counsel to EchoStar Communications Corporation (owner of the DISH Network satellite television system) in connection with EchoStar's multibillion dollar bid to purchase Hughes Electronics and its DirectTV network. The group has also recently worked with a leading international financial concern to implement two multibillion dollar financial transactions structured around entities formed under Nevada's business trust statutes.

Estate Planning Group: The firm's Estate Planning Group assists its clients in setting lifetime personal and financial goals as early as possible to maximize their lifetime benefits and to effectively distribute their assets to their heirs after death. The lawyers in this group have a depth of experience and knowledge in the technical strategies to facilitate asset management, to preserve wealth, and to effectively distribute wealth to the next generation.

Litigation Group: The firm's Litigation Group is composed of experienced practitioners who have represented clients before all state and federal courts. In addition to traditional litigation practice, the firm's lawyers have extensive experience before sophisticated arbitration, complex settlement conferences, private mediation and administrative hearings before commissions and committees who are experts in their fields. The firm's Litigation Group has been in the forefront of high-profile litigation such as the Venetian Casino Resort construction litigation in Las Vegas, multimillion dollar construction litigation in northern Nevada, the multimillion dollar litigation between Summa Corporation and Echo Bay Mining over mining claims in Nevada, the historic litigation over the Transcontinental Railroad on behalf of the University of California and Stanford University, election law challenges in US Senate campaigns, First Amendment issues in downtown redevelopment in Las Vegas, multimillion dollar condemnation litigation in northern Nevada, among many other such matters.

Real Property & Finance Group: The firm's Real Property and Finance Group has provided for over 30 years the highest quality legal representation and forward-thinking advice to real estate developers, purchasers, sellers, borrowers, lenders, title companies, and owners in a service delivery mode based on hard work, efficient and cost-effective case management, and thorough attention to detail and the clients' objectives. The combined experience of the lawyers in the Real Property and Finance Group exceeds that of any other firm in the state.

Regulatory & Administrative Law Group: The firm's Regulatory and Administrative Law Group counsels clients faced with unique problems when trying to navigate through regulatory and licensing issues with state and local government boards and commissions. In particular, this group has participated in many high profile administrative, judicial, and legislative proceedings relating to energy, telecommunications, and water issues, and practices extensively before the Public Utilities Commission of Nevada. In addition to its widespread experience in utilities law matters, the Regulatory and Administrative Law Group provides legal representation in the areas of transportation, land use, local government franchises, and redevelopment.

CLIENTS: Clients of Hale Lane include business organizations from lenders, developers, title companies and publicly traded companies to entrepreneurs and closely-held corporations, healthcare organizations, telecommunications, energy and water companies, hotel casinos and gaming manufacturers and suppliers. The firm also represents many individuals with regard to estate planning, tax issues and other personal matters.

HEAD OFFICE

NEVADA
100 West Liberty Street, Tenth Floor, **Reno**, NV 89501
Tel: 775 327 3000   **Fax:** 775 786 6179
Email: info@halelane.com
Website: www.halelane.com

BRANCH OFFICES

NEVADA
2300 West Sahara Avenue, Eighth Floor, Box 8, **Las Vegas**, NV 89102
Tel: 702 222 2500   **Fax:** 702 365 6940

777 East William Street, Suite 200, **Carson City**, NV 89701
Tel: 775 684 6000   **Fax:** 775 684 6001

CONTACTS

Bankruptcy & Insolvency Group	Timothy A Lukas
Business Ventures Group	David A Garcia
Estate Planning Group	Matthew E Woodhead
Litigation Group	Jeremy J Nork
Real Property & Finance Group	Karen D Dennison
Regulatory & Administrative Law Group	Kristin B McMillan

HANCOCK ROTHERT & BUNSHOFT LLP

THE FIRM

Chairman: Ray L Wong

Number of partners: 40
Number of other lawyers: 66

FIRM OVERVIEW: Hancock Rothert & Bunshoft has more than 50 years' experience representing US and international clients in litigation and transactional matters. Equally adept in negotiations or in the courtroom, the firm excels at applying advocacy skills to advance its clients' business and litigation interests to their advantage. Based in California, the firm has an extraordinary track record in the state, federal and appellate courts.

MAIN AREAS OF PRACTICE: The firm emphasizes business litigation; construction litigation; labor and employment litigation and counseling; insurance coverage litigation; products liability and professional liability litigation; real estate litigation and transactional work; and technology-related litigation and counseling. Additionally, the firm is known for its appellate work in state and federal courts, having appeared as counsel on more than 140 published decisions.

Business Litigation: The firm handles a wide range of contract disputes and business tort claims for clients, including breach of contract, unfair business practice claims, class actions, consumer fraud, directors and officers liability, antitrust, real estate, RICO, technology-related litigation and trade secrets.

Insurance: The firm counsels and represents both insurers and others in coverage disputes arising from asbestos, health hazard, the environment and technology. The firm also has experience in subrogation, reinsurance, bad faith, and professional indemnity matters. Additionally, the firm has expertise in the drafting and negotiation of insurance policies – particularly, with respect to technology and other rapidly evolving areas of the economy.

Products Liability: The firm has extensive products liability experience, particularly in the automotive, sports and exercise equipment, water craft, child equipment and toy industries. It specializes in coordinating the nationwide defense of class actions for insurers, distributors and manufacturers. The firm also assists clients with recalls when necessary and in negotiations with the US Consumer Product Safety Commission.

Professional Liability: The firm represents the following professionals and their insurers in all business liability claims: architects and engineers, contractors, real estate brokers and agents, corporate directors and officers, insurance brokers, lawyers and law firms, entertainment industry professionals and organizations, employers, and sports agents.

Sports & Recreation: The firm pioneered much of the sports and recreation practice in California, and continues to represent a wide variety of recreational interests, including ski resort owners and operators, golf course owners and operators, professional sports teams and the facilities they own or use, the makers of sporting goods and equipment, and the owners and operators of other recreational businesses, such as tour companies.

HEAD OFFICE

CALIFORNIA
San Francisco, Four Embarcadero Center, **San Francisco**, CA 94111
Tel: 415 981 5550 **Fax:** 415 955 2599
Email: info@hrblaw.com
Website: www.hrblaw.com

BRANCH OFFICES

CALIFORNIA
515 S. Figueroa St., 17th Floor, **Los Angeles**, CA 90071
Tel: 213 623 7777 **Fax:** 213 623 5405

The Lighthouse Center, 850 N. Lake Blvd, Ste 15
PO Box 7199, **Tahoe City**, CA 96145
Tel: 530 583 7767 **Fax:** 530 581 3215

INTERNATIONAL OFFICES

The firm also has an office in London.

CLIENTS: The firm represents a wide variety of US and international clients, from small businesses to *Fortune* 500 firms, including US and London-based insurers. Clients receive superior service through personal contact, the latest technology and the firm's client dedicated intranet.

INTERNATIONAL WORK: The firm handles a variety of work for international clients, particularly in the fields of insurance, construction, real estate, products liability and sports and recreation. Additionally, it has relationships with lawyers around the globe through ALFA International, an invitation-only affiliation of top law firms worldwide. Languages spoken by those at the firm include: Cantonese, Farsi, French, German, Mandarin, and Spanish.

LEADING LAW FIRMS

HARE, WYNN, NEWELL & NEWTON

THE FIRM

Managing Partner: Leon Ashford
Senior Partners: Neal C Newell, Alex W Newton

Number of partners: 12
Number of other lawyers: 6

HEAD OFFICE

ALABAMA
The Historic Massey Building, 2025 Third Avenue North, Suite 800
Birmingham, AL 35203
Tel: 205 328 5330 **Fax:** 205 324 2165
Website: www.hwnn.com

BRANCH OFFICES

ARKANSAS
Metropolitan National Plaza, 4220 N. Rodney Parham Rd., Suite 250
Little Rock, AR 72212
Tel: 501 219 0077 **Fax:** 501 219 2277

FIRM OVERVIEW: Hare, Wynn, Newell & Newton is the oldest existing plaintiff's firm in the State of Alabama. In 1991, the firm entered its second century of practice. The firm's philosophy is based upon a dedication to protecting and preserving the dignity and rights of all individuals. Representing the rights of all citizens with the same degree of service previously available only to the corporate community, the firm stands today as an enduring testament to the original vision and ideals of its founder in providing quality representation for individuals and businesses requiring our services.

MAIN AREAS OF PRACTICE:

Aviation: Hare, Wynn, Newell & Newton's aviation practice is national in scope. The firm has handled aviation cases which have occurred throughout the US, Canada, Mexico and South America. The firm has represented catastrophically injured clients and wrongful death victims of aviation disasters for over 50 years. Hare, Wynn, Newell & Newton has actively engaged in all areas of aviation relative to personal injuries and wrongful death which include: litigation against the major airlines, military, general aviation, the US government and all major aircraft manufacturers. The firm is actively involved in many facets of aviation including operating the firm jet throughout the United States on a weekly basis.

Commercial Litigation: Cases that the firm has been involved in include sales persons' claims for commissions, breach of contract and other related employment disputes. The firm has also represented small businesses in claims that have involved the misappropriation of trade secrets, including claims for computer piracy. The firm has also been involved in numerous fraud actions were businesses or individuals have been cheated. The firm has represented numerous businesses that were sold defective and outdated batteries, as well as small gas station owners against major oil companies.

The Consumer Protection/Consumer Fraud: The firm prosecutes cases across a broad spectrum of consumer protection and consumer fraud law. These cases are brought under specific statutes or through common law causes of action such as misrepresentation, suppression or deceit.

Environmental: The environmental litigation practice focuses on the representation of clients who have been harmed in person or property by exposure to environmentally hazardous substances. The types of cases the firm handles include chemical exposures of workers and members of the general public. The environmental practice encompasses litigation concerning water and land contamination by chemical companies and other third parties. Litigation in the environmental arena includes representation of individual claimants and large numbers of people through class actions.

Personal Injury: The firm represents individuals who have suffered personal injury as a result of the negligence or willful misconduct of others in any number of situations to include motor vehicle accidents, tractor-trailer collisions, construction related accidents, aviation disasters, medical malpractice, as well as other situations resulting in significant personal injury to individuals.

Product Liability: Several noteworthy and groundbreaking products liability cases, both in state and out of state, have been handled by Hare Wynn lawyers. The firm's lawyers maintain active participation in the best known information sharing legal groups, both in state and through the national trial lawyers organization, which helps us provide our clients with the latest developments in technology and the law as it applies to these cases.

Securities Fraud: Hare, Wynn, Newell & Newton lawyers have represented dozens of victims of unethical and improper investing, whereby monies were negligently or fraudulently invested by unscrupulous agents. Many of the firm's clients have suffered significant losses to their retirement and other investment accounts due to unauthorized trading by stockbrokers and brokerage firms. Many cases have involved claims where a stockbroker invested in stocks and securities that were not authorized by the client or were stocks that maintained at a risk level which exceeded the risk tolerance allowed by the investment objectives set forth by the client in the brokerage agreement. Other cases have involved instances of insider trading, whereby a broker invests monies based on information he obtained illegally. Other cases have involved investments whereby a broker invested a large percentage of his client's monies in an effort to manipulate the price of a stock for his own personal gain.

Hare Wynn Newell & Newton LLP

HARRISON, KEMP & JONES, LLP

THE FIRM

Managing Partner: J Randall Jones

Number of partners: 5
Number of other lawyers: 7

HEAD OFFICE

NEVADA
3800 Howard Hughes Parkway, Seventeenth Floor,
Las Vegas, NV 89109
Tel: 702 385 6000
Email: hkj@hkj-law.com

FIRM OVERVIEW: Founding partners, Will Kemp, Kirk Harrison and J Randall Jones, founded Harrison, Kemp & Jones, LLP in 1993 to provide superior civil litigation representation.

MAIN AREAS OF PRACTICE: Maintaining a highly diversified practice, Harrison, Kemp & Jones, LLP, handles all types of complex commercial litigation, and personal injury actions for both plaintiffs and defendants. The firm was a pioneer in Nevada's construction defect litigation, having successfully tried the first major homeowner versus developer class actions in the state to verdict. As innovators in multi-district product defect litigation and other mass torts, the firm has prosecuted hundreds of breast implant, pedicle bone screw, diet drug and other claims, and Harrison, Kemp & Jones, LLP, has been instrumental in making the tobacco industry accountable to smokers. The firm's practice also includes defense work for prominent Las Vegas resorts, developers, contractors, insurance companies, and municipalities. The firm practices in all venues from mediation, to trial and through all levels of the appellate court system, including the United States Supreme Court.

LEADING LAW FIRMS

HAYNES AND BOONE, LLP

THE FIRM

Managing Partner: Robert Wilson
Co-Founding Partner: Michael Boone

Number of partners: 173
Number of other lawyers: 252

AREAS OF PRACTICE:
Business Litigation	17%
Corporate	14%
Bankruptcy & Reorganization	8%
Labor, Employment & Immigration	7%
Intellectual Property & Technology Transactions	7%
Financial Transactions	6%
White Collar Defense & Antitrust	6%
Real Estate	6%
Business Planning & Tax	4%
Appellate	4%

FIRM OVERVIEW: Haynes and Boone is one of the largest and fastest growing corporate law firms in the US. The firm believes that the world of business belongs to companies keen to compete, quick to adapt, eager to listen and learn and resolved to continually challenge themselves. It measures itself by the same standards. Haynes and Boone's teamwork culture, willingness to change quickly to meet the demands of the marketplace and drive to be the best have been the key factors behind its success. The firm has grown from a handful of lawyers in 1970 to more than 425 lawyers today, adding more than 25 practice specialties, expanding to nine offices and becoming a national leader in the use of technology to deliver legal services. The firm delivers value to its clients by using a collaborative effort to help them achieve their business objectives. Haynes and Boone lawyers are innovative problem solvers, creative strategists and trusted advisors.

MAIN AREAS OF PRACTICE: These include business litigation; corporate; banking and reorganization; labor, employment and immigration; intellectual property and technology transactions; financial transactions; white collar defense and antitrust; real estate; business planning and tax; appellate.

CLIENTS: Haynes and Boone serves a diverse group of clients in a wide array of domestic and global business transactions and litigation matters worldwide. The firm's client base reflects virtually every business industry and includes more than 100 Fortune 500 companies, many major foreign companies and large financial institutions.

INTERNATIONAL WORK: Haynes and Boone has long served its clients' global business activities by building cross-border practice capabilities, strategically adding international legal expertise and establishing working relationships with leading law firms throughout the world. Haynes and Boone lawyers are fluent in 12 foreign languages. The firm's Mexico City office, opened in 1994, has grown to be one of the three largest US-based law firms in Mexico, with both Mexican and US qualified attorneys who are fully bilingual and bi-cultural, with extensive contacts within the Mexican business community. During 2002, Haynes and Boone's global reach included more than 100 foreign countries, assisting clients in cross-border matters ranging from acquisitions and financings to dispute resolution.

HEAD OFFICE

TEXAS
901 Main St., Suite 3100, **Dallas**, TX 75202
Tel: 214 651 5000 **Fax:** 214 651 5940
Email: strockw@haynesboone.com
Website: www.haynesboone.com

BRANCH OFFICES

DISTRICT OF COLUMBIA
555 11th Street N.W., Suite 650, **Washington**, DC 20004
Tel: 202 654 4500 Fax: 202 654 4501
Email: mcginnie@haynesboone.com

TEXAS
600 Congress Ave., Suite 1600, **Austin**, TX 78701
Tel: 512 867 8400 **Fax:** 512 867 8470
Email: kingj@haynesboone.com

7501 North Capital of Texas Highway, Bldg. A, Suite 130
Austin, TX 78731
Tel: 512 692 8300 **Fax:** 512 692 8370
Email: kingj@haynesboone.com

201 Main St., Suite 2200, **Fort Worth**, TX 76102
Tel: 817 347 6600 **Fax:** 817 347 665
Email: barnardb@hanesboone.com

1000 Louisiana St., Suite 4300, **Houston**, TX 77002
Tel: 713 547 2000 **Fax:** 713 547 2600
Email: broughtk@haynesboone.com

2505 N. Plano Road, Suite 4000, **Richardson**, TX 75082
Tel: 972 739 6900 **Fax:** 972 680 7551
Email: boeingw@haynesboone.com

112 East Pecan St., Suite 1600, **San Antonio**, TX 78205
Tel: 210 978 7000 **Fax:** 210 978 7450
Email: jeffersl@haynesboone.com

INTERNATIONAL OFFICES

The firm also has an office in Mexico City, Mexico.

CONTACTS

Business Litigation	Don Templin
Corporate	Greg Samuel
Bankruptcy & Reorganization	Judy Elkin
Labor, Employment & Immigration	Jonathan Wilson
Intellectual Property & Technology Transactions	Jeff Becker
Financial Transactions	Judy Elkin
White Collar Defense & Antitrust	Stacy Brainin
Real Estate	Ann Saegert
Business Planning & Tax	Ken Bezozo
Appellate	Stacy Brainin

LEADING LAW FIRMS

HEALY & BAILLIE, LLP

THE FIRM

Executive Committee: John D Kimball, Jack A Greenbaum, LeRoy Lambert

Number of partners: 16
Number of other lawyers: 17

FIRM OVERVIEW: Founded in 1948, Healy & Baillie, LLP is an international law firm known around the world for its expertise in all aspects of maritime law. The firm's practice extends, however, to general commercial litigation and arbitration, transactional deals from simple ship mortgages to real estate to public offerings, insurance and reinsurance disputes of all kinds, and bankruptcies of all sizes. Members of the firm have authored the leading texts on maritime law, Time Charters and Voyage Charters and the foremost law school case book. They are editors of maritime treatises and professional journals, teach maritime law at two law schools, are officers and former officers of national and international maritime professional associations, have served as advisors to governmental and United Nations organizations, and have testified as experts on US maritime law in foreign courts and arbitrations. The firm's attorneys include: one naval architect, one merchant marine officer, one former Coast Guard investigating officer, a US Naval Academy graduate and Navy Commander, Navy deck officers, a past commissioner of pilots for the Port of New York and New Jersey, and a present member of the Connecticut Pilot Commission. Languages include Greek, Norwegian, Mandarin, Cantonese, German, French, Japanese and Spanish.

MAIN AREAS OF PRACTICE: Maritime, commercial litigation and arbitration, transactional, insurance and reinsurance, bankruptcy.

CLIENTS: Marine and transportation insurers (P&I, Hull, Cargo, Liability), shipowners, vessel operators, vessel managers, charterers, NVOCC's, shippers, banks, trading companies, reinsurers, foreign governments and agencies.

INTERNATIONAL WORK: Maritime casualties (APL China, Barge Texas, Amphion, Achille Lauro hijacking, Atllantic Empress/Aegean Captain and Seiryu/Stena Freighter collisions, Marine Electric sinking, Amoco Cadiz and Torrey Canyon pollution incidents); hundreds of maritime arbitrations; over two hundred personal injury jury trials; Norwegian Guarantee Institute v Hambros Bank, Lexmar, Premier Tankers, and Westbond litigations; US Lines, Hellenic Lines, Regency Lines, Premier Cruise Lines and Millenium bankruptcies. Through its offices in Hong Kong, Connecticut, and New Jersey, the firm maintains contacts with its clients there and is able to serve their needs locally as well as in New York.

HEAD OFFICE

NEW YORK
29 Broadway, **New York**, NY 100006
Tel: 212 943 3980 **Fax:** 212 425 0131
Email: reception@healy.com
Website: www.healy.com

BRANCH OFFICES

CONNECTICUT
The Lock Building, 20 Marshall Street, Suite 104, **South Norwalk**, CT 06854
Tel: 203 354 1360 **Fax:** 203 354 1363

NEW JERSEY
374 Millburn Avenue, **Millburn**, NJ 07041
Tel: 973 912 8955 **Fax:** 973 912 9767

INTERNATIONAL OFFICES

The firm also has an office in Hong Kong.

HEALY & BAILLIE, LLP

LEADING LAW FIRMS

HELMSING, LEACH, HERLONG, NEWMAN & ROUSE, PC

THE FIRM

Managing Partner: James B Newman
Senior Partner: Frederick G Helmsing
Number of partners: 10
Number of other lawyers: 3

AREAS OF PRACTICE:
Commercial Litigation	60%
Banking & Finance	20%
M&A	20%

HEAD OFFICE

ALABAMA
150 Government Street, Suite 2000, **Mobile**, AL 36602
Tel: 251 432 5521 **Fax:** 251 432 0633
Website: www.helmsinglaw.com

CONTACTS

Banking & Financing	Robert H Rouse
Litigation/White Collar Criminal Practice	Frederick G Helmsing
M&A	Robert H Rouse

FIRM OVERVIEW: The firm was founded in 1976 when successful partners of large firms joined forces to create a firm that could offer a diverse array of legal services with enthusiasm, expertise, and confidence. As a full service firm of medium size, Helmsing, Leach, Herlong, Newman & Rouse, PC combines the characteristics of smaller firms' vigor and personality with the quality and efficiency attributed to larger groups. Since 1976, the firm has been dedicated to providing quality legal services to business, professionals, families and individuals.

MAIN AREAS OF PRACTICE:

Banking & Finance: The firm is routinely involved in all phases of banking and financial transactions as counsel for both borrowers and lenders. Its representation of banks, other financial institutions and borrowers includes negotiating and structuring loans, analyzing loan terms and conditions, and developing and drafting loan documents and agreements.

Bankruptcy: The firm has engaged in the active practice of all creditors' rights, workouts and insolvency litigation. This practice group offers a comprehensive array of services regarding the protection and enforcement of creditors' interests in bankruptcy and non-bankruptcy workouts. The firm has extensive experience in representing asset-based lenders and financial service institutions, including local, regional and national banks. The firm also has significant experience involving representation of bankruptcy trustees, examiners and other fiduciaries. The firm represents both creditors and corporate debtors faced with the numerous issues that accompany business' insolvencies.

Business & Corporate Matters: The firm regularly performs the functions involved in modern corporate law. It creates, maintains, reorganizes, liquidates and dissolves corporations, partnerships, limited liability companies, joint ventures, and professional corporations and associations. The firm has significant experience in the resolution and litigation of business and corporate disputes. It administers corporate acquisitions and mergers, and works out corporate structural changes among stockholders, partners, and other business owners.

Taxation & Tax Planning: Several of the firm's lawyers have received advanced training in taxation. The firm regularly advises its clients on individual and corporate tax matters spanning the total spectrum of State and Federal taxation.

White Collar Criminal Defense: The firm has broad experience in white collar criminal practice, including tax crimes, fraud, health fraud, RICO, antitrust, bank and credit charges, embezzlement and other economic crimes. The firm provides representation for those undergoing criminal investigation by the Internal Revenue Service and other governmental agencies, as well as grand jury investigation. The firm handles the case in every phase of investigation, trial and appellate proceedings.

Litigation: The firm conducts a substantial Litigation Practice. It has tried major cases in all surrounding State and Federal courts and has handled appeals to the highest levels of the State and Federal judicial systems. The firm is known for successfully handling complicated and significant cases and disputes. The firm has extensive experience in virtually all types of business litigation, whether involving breach of contract, tortious conduct, equitable or extraordinary remedies, or statutory relief.

Eminent Domain & Condemnation: For more than 20 years the firm has specialized in the practice of eminent domain law. It represents landowners and condemning agencies throughout the State of Alabama in a wide variety of takings, both direct and inverse, at the local, state, and federal level and administrative, trial and appellate proceedings.

Product Liability: The firm has extensive and significant experience in representing manufacturers, component part suppliers, distributors, and individuals in product liability cases. Products the firm has defended include aircraft, aviation equipment, aircraft engines, helicopters, automobiles, automobile parts, seatbelts, boats, marine products, chainsaws, household appliances, power tools, drugs, pharmaceutical products, medical devices and equipment, surgical supplies, tires, motor homes, water heaters, papermaking machinery, wire rope and other steel products and heavy machinery and engines. The firm has also represented manufacturers and distributors of chemicals and other products and toxic tort cases and class actions. Recently, a team of its lawyers successfully represented Kumho Tire Company in the United States Supreme Court landmark decision clarifying that the trial court's gatekeeping duty under Federal Rule of Evidence 702 applies to all experts and not just scientific experts (Kumho Tire Co. v Carmichael), 119 S.CT.1167 (1999).

Real Estate Law: The firm has a broad Real Estate Practice, representing clients engaged in all areas of the real estate industry. Its clients include residential and commercial buyers and sellers, shopping center owners and tenants, apartment complex and condominium owners and developers, brokerage companies, residential and commercial contractors, real estate investment trusts, title companies, and banks and other financial institutions who lend money secured by real estate.

Government Relations: The firm has full scale capability in handling matters arising from the regulation of business affairs by the government at all levels. Such activities include the regulation of pharmaceutical products, the environment, healthcare facilities, public utilities, zoning and matters involving the licensure of businesses, professions and contractors.

Health Law: The firm maintains an active Health Law Section dedicated to serving the healthcare community in administrative, regulatory and compliance matters. The firm has represented clients' interests in matters involving Medicare, Medicaid, HCFA, the United State Department of Justice and the Alabama Attorney General's office, in successfully defending clients accused of Medicare and Medicaid fraud and abuse.

Employment Law: The firm is engaged, primarily by employers, in employment-related transactions and disputes. The firm's attorneys assist its business clients in dealing with a wide range of employment matters, including employment contracts, arbitration agreements, day-to-day employment issues with the goal of avoiding or minimizing conflicts, and responses to EEOC or other complaints. The firm also has an extensive Litigation Practice in this area of law.

LEADING LAW FIRMS

HENDRICK, PHILLIPS, SALZMAN & FLATT, P.C.

THE FIRM

Managing Partner: William D Flatt, Esq
Senior Partner: David R Hendrick, Esq

Number of partners: 5
Number of other lawyers: 7

HEAD OFFICE

GEORGIA
230 Peachtree Street, N.W. Suite 1800 **Atlanta**, GA 30303
Tel: 404 522 1410 **Fax:** 404 522 9545
Email: drh@hpsf-law.com
Website: www.hpsslaw.com

CONTACTS

Construction ....David R Hendrick

FIRM OVERVIEW: Hendrick, Phillips, Salzman & Flatt has earned a national reputation for providing sophisticated legal services and counseling to businesses involved in the construction industry for over 20 years. Its practice concentrates on the unique and specialized legal needs of such businesses spanning all phases of construction law and construction related legal transactions and involving public, private and 'privatized' construction projects. Additionally, Hendrick, Phillips, Salzman & Flatt offers the full range of legal and business planning services necessary for the successful formation, operation and guidance of construction and related businesses. The firm is dedicated to providing legal services on the basis of a complete understanding of each client's objectives and operations in order to provide efficient, experienced, and personalized service. The firm stresses proper advance counseling with our clients to avoid or minimize their legal and business risks. Its emphasis is on counseling and pursuit of preventive measures and dispute avoidance techniques, seeking to avoid disruptive and costly disputes and to resolve those disputes which do arise in a 'business' rather than 'litigation' context. However, attorneys of the firm are thoroughly familiar with and experienced in all forms of dispute resolution including administrative and judicial litigation in federal and state forums at all levels, as well as alternative dispute resolution procedures such as mediation and arbitration. The firm's attorneys are regularly involved in the prosecution or defense of client interests in large, complex construction disputes in many different jurisdictions and they have tried many cases before national arbitration and administrative panels and courts at all levels and in many different jurisdictions.

MAIN AREAS OF PRACTICE: The principal area of practice is construction law.

CLIENTS: The firm's commitment to and recognition by the construction industry is demonstrated by the broad diversified client base that it maintains throughout the United States. Firm clients include national, regional and local contractors, construction managers, subcontractors, and vendors, as well as public and private owners, developers, design professionals, insurance and surety companies, and international, national and regional trade associations serving the construction industry. The firm has established professional relationships with clients of all sizes and descriptions. Most of its clients are associated with the construction and development business and include public and private owners, developers, contractors, design professionals, manufacturers and suppliers. The firm is counsel to the National Roofing Contractors Association and the National Roofing Legal Resource Center, has served as consel to American Subcontractors Association, and is counsel to various state and local contractor and specialty contractor trade associations, including the Associated Builders & Contractors of Georgia, Inc.; Georgia Mechanical Contractors Association, Georgia Lathing and Plastering Contractors Association, Inc., Georgia Concrete and Products Association, Mechanical Industries Council, Roofing & Sheet Metal Contractors Association of Georgia, Montana Roofing Contractors Association and Master Roofing Contractors Association of Atlanta. The following is a representative listing of some of the companies the firm has recently represented or currently represents in construction matters: RMC Allied Readymix Inc.; Anning-Johnson Company; Arcadis Geraghty & Miller; Archer Western Contractors, Ltd.; Anne Arundel County Public Schools; Bechtel Corporation; Beers/Skanska Construction Company, Inc.; Centex Construction Company; Dudley Barrett Construction Company; E.I. Dupont de Nemours & Co.; Ellis Don Construction Ltd.; Fairgreen Capital, Inc./Northside Realty; Fischbach and Moore, Inc.; Grinnell Fire Protection Systems Company; J.A. Jones Construction Co., Inc.; Juneau Construction Company, LLC; Keene Construction of Central Florida, Inc.; Kemron Environmental Services, Inc.; Lockwood Greene Engineers, Inc.; Metric Constructors, Inc.; Mirant Corporation; Morris-Shea Bridge Company, Inc.; Nissan Motor Manufacturing Corporation; RMC Industries Corporation; John W. Rooker Construction Company, Inc.; Samsung Electronics; Siemens Energy and Automation, Inc.; United States Fidelity & Guaranty Company; and Yokogawa Corporation of America.

LEADING LAW FIRMS

HOGAN & HARTSON LLP

THE FIRM

Chairman: J Warren Gorrell, Jr

Number of partners: 396
Number of other lawyers: 487

FIRM OVERVIEW: Founded in 1904, Hogan & Hartson LLP is the oldest and the largest major law firm based in Washington, DC. Today, it has more than 900 lawyers serving clients in a practice that cuts across virtually all legal disciplines. In addition to its Washington, DC office, which provides a natural base for the firm's national and international practice, the firm has European offices in Berlin, Brussels, London, Paris, Budapest, Prague, Warsaw, Moscow; Asian offices in Beijing and Tokyo; and US offices in New York, Baltimore, Northern Virginia, Miami, Los Angeles, Denver, Boulder, and Colorado Springs.

MAIN AREAS OF PRACTICE: More than 40% of Hogan & Hartson's lawyers handle corporate, securities, financial, intellectual property, tax, and other transactions throughout the world. Approximately a quarter litigate commercial and other disputes before state, federal and international tribunals, and engage in domestic and international arbitration. About 30% of the lawyers in the firm practice in areas of government regulation and policy, where decisions made in Washington, Brussels and other world capitals affect the competitive position and strategies of organizations around the globe.

INTERNATIONAL WORK: The firm's Berlin, Brussels, London, Paris, Budapest, Prague, Warsaw, and Moscow offices provide Hogan & Hartson with a strong presence and capability throughout Europe. The firm works extensively on European business transactions, and on European Union law and regulation, and assists European entities doing business in the United States. In Asia, where the firm has offices in Beijing and Tokyo, Hogan & Hartson has a long history of representing both Asian clients, as well as Western clients doing business throughout the region. In Beijing, the resident lawyers and legal professionals represent local and multinational clients in cross-border mergers and acquisitions, joint ventures and other investments, financings, infrastructure development and company restructurings; government regulatory matters, with a significant focus on international trade; and intellectual property. The firm's practice in Tokyo focuses principally on patent and intellectual property matters, corporate and securities, and legal issues associated with doing business in Japan. In the Middle East and Africa, attorneys in the firm's US and European offices represent clients in a wide range of projects and matters, as well as Middle Eastern and African clients doing business in the United States and Europe. The firm also has extensive experience assisting clients with matters involving Central and South America and the Caribbean, particularly in the areas of project and international finance, mergers and acquisitions, joint ventures and other investments, and international trade.

CLIENTS: Hogan & Hartson's clients range from start-up ventures to large multinational corporations in industries such as information technology; healthcare; biotechnology; pharmaceuticals; medical devices; education; food and agriculture; communications (satellite, common carrier, broadcast, and cable); energy; environmental; government procurement; real estate; and transportation and infrastructure. In addition, the firm represents private equity, venture capital and investment banking firms, financial institutions, nonprofit associations, quasi-governmental organizations, and foreign governments.

HEAD OFFICE

WASHINGTON, DC
555 Thirteenth Street, N.W., **Washington, DC** 20004
Tel: 202 637 5600   **Fax:** 202 637 5910
Website: www.hhlaw.com

BRANCH OFFICES

NEW YORK
875 Third Avenue, **New York**, NY 10022
Tel: 212 918 3000   **Fax:** 212 918 3100

885 Third Avenue, **New York**, NY 10022
Tel: 212 918 6000   **Fax:** 212 918 6100

551 Fifth Avenue, **New York**, NY 10176
Tel: 212 661 6500   **Fax:** 212 697 6686

MARYLAND
111 South Calvert Street, **Baltimore**, MD 21202
Tel: 410 659 2700   **Fax:** 410 539 6981

VIRGINIA
8300 Greensboro Drive, **McLean**, VA 22102
Tel: 703 610 6100   **Fax:** 703 610 6200

FLORIDA
Barclays Financial Center, 1111 Brickell Avenue, **Miami**, Florida 33131
Tel: 305 459 6500   **Fax:** 305 459 6550

CALIFORNIA
2049 Century Park East, **Los Angeles**, CA 90067
Tel: 310 551 6655   **Fax:** 310 551 0364

Biltmore Tower, 500 South Grand Avenue, **Los Angeles**, California 90071
Tel: 213 337 6700   **Fax:** 213 337 6701

COLORADO
1470 Walnut Street, **Boulder**, CO 80302
Tel: 720 406 5300   **Fax:** 720 406 5301

Two North Cascade Avenue, **Colorado Springs**, CO 80903
Tel: 719 448 5900   **Fax:** 719 448 5922

One Tabor Center, **Denver**, Colorado 80202
Tel: 303 899 7300   **Fax:** 303 899 7333

CONTACTS

Business & Finance .... James J Rosenhauer
Government Regulation .... Richard S Rodin
Intellectual Property .... James J Rosenhauer
Litigation .... Austin S Mittler

LEADING LAW FIRMS

HOLLAND & HART LLP

THE FIRM

Managing Partner: Edward H Flitton III
Senior Partner: Anne J Castle (Chair, Management Committee)

Number of partners: 143
Number of other lawyers: 127

Email: info@hollandhart.com
Website: www.hollandhart.com

FIRM OVERVIEW: Since its inception in 1947, Holland & Hart has grown to more than 260 lawyers in 12 offices in Colorado, Wyoming, Idaho, Montana, New Mexico, Utah, and the District of Columbia. The firm offers a full range of integrated legal solutions to companies of all sizes, from emerging businesses to *Fortune* 500 corporations located throughout the country and internationally. The firm is focused on the issues facing clients who have business interests in the Mountain West. Holland & Hart is the only law firm based in the Rocky Mountain Region to make a leading American legal publication's list of the top 200 firms in the United States.

MAIN AREAS OF PRACTICE: The firm handles appellate; bankruptcy; broadband transactions; business transactions and litigation; construction and real estate transactions and litigation; corporate finance; credit finance and lending; emerging growth and venture capital; employee benefits; energy; environment and resources; intellectual property protection and litigation; international; labor and employment; mining; oil and gas; project development and finance; taxes and estates; technology transfer; torts and insurance; water.

CLIENTS: The firm represents business entities of all sizes, including more than 100 of the *Fortune* 500 companies. Holland & Hart serves clients in a wide variety of industries, including aerospace, agriculture, airlines, biotechnology, construction, energy, financial, healthcare, hospitality, manufacturing, mining, oil and gas, real estate, resorts and recreation, retail, services, technology, telecommunications and broadband, and water rights and quality, among others.

INTERNATIONAL WORK: The firm has been involved in a broad range of transactions in most Latin American, Pacific Rim and European countries. These transactions have included mergers, project finance transactions, venture capital investments, mezzanine financings, telecommunications (including telephony, internet services and cable television), power generation and distribution projects, private placements, license or concession acquisitions, privatizations, environmental matters and capital markets transactions.

HEAD OFFICE

COLORADO
Suite 3200, 555 Seventeenth Street, **Denver**, CO 80202
Tel: 303 295 8000 **Fax:** 303 295 8261

BRANCH OFFICES

COLORADO
Suite 104, 600 East Main Street, **Aspen**, CO 81611
Tel: 970 925 3476 **Fax:** 970 925 9367

Suite 500, 1050 Walnut Street, **Boulder**, CO 80302
Tel: 303 473 2700 **Fax:** 303 473 2720

Suite 1000, 90 South Cascade Avenue, **Colorado Springs**, CO 80903
Tel: 719 475 7730 **Fax:** 719 634 2461

Suite 400, 8390 East Crescent Parkway, **Greenwood Village**, CO 80111
Tel: 303 290 1600 **Fax:** 303 290 1606

DISTRICT OF COLUMBIA
Suite 230, 801 Pennsylvania Avenue, NW, **Washington**, DC 20004
Tel: 202 347 9272 **Fax:** 202 347 1684

IDAHO
Suite 1400, 101 South Capitol Blvd., **Boise**, ID 83702
Tel: 208 342 5000 **Fax:** 208 343 8869

MONTANA
Suite 1500, 401 North 31st Street, **Billings**, MT 59101
Tel: 406 252 2166 **Fax:** 406 252 1669

NEW MEXICO
Suite 1, 110 North Guadalupe, **Santa Fe**, NM 87501
Tel: 505 954 7298 **Fax:** 505 983 6043

UTAH
Suite 2000, 60 East South Temple, **Salt Lake City**, UT 84111
Tel: 801 595 7800 **Fax:** 801 364 9124

WYOMING
Suite 450, 2515 Warren Avenue, **Cheyenne**, WY 82001
Tel: 307 778 4200 **Fax:** 307 778 8175

Suite 200, 25 South Willow Street, **Jackson Hole**, WY 83001
Tel: 307 739 9741 **Fax:** 307 739 9744

CONTACTS

Appellate	Joseph Halpern
Bankruptcy	Risa Wolf-Smith
Broadband Transactions	Stephen Villano
Business Transactions	Chris Groll
Coal	Patrick Day
Commercial Litigation	Christopher Toll
Construction & Real Estate Litigation	Daniel Frost
Emerging Growth & Venture Capital	Betty Arkell
Employee Benefits	Jane Francis
Energy	Robert Pomeroy
Environment & Resources	Brad Berge
Financial	Elizabeth Carney
Indian Law	Douglas Nash
Intellectual Property Litigation	Donald Degnan
Intellectual Property Protection	Scott Havlick
International	Kevin Johnson
Labor & Employment	Jude Biggs
Mining	Jean Feriancek
Oil & Gas	Donald Schultz
Project Development & Finance	Mark Safty
Real Estate Transactions	Elizabeth Sharrer
Securities	Mark Levy
Taxes & Estates	John Wilson
Technology Transfer	Kevin Crandell
Torts & Insurance	Joe Teig
Water	Chris Thorne

LEADING LAW FIRMS

HOLLAND & KNIGHT LLP

THE FIRM

Managing Partner: Robert R Feagin, III

Number of partners: 746
Number of other lawyers: 527

AREAS OF PRACTICE:
Litigation	42%
Corporate	32%
Real Estate & Public Land Use	18%
Public Law	8%

FIRM OVERVIEW: Holland & Knight is a commercial law firm with more than 1250 lawyers in 32 offices throughout the world.

In the United States, offices are located in Annapolis, Maryland; Atlanta, Georgia; Bethesda, Maryland; Boston, Massachusetts; Bradenton, Florida; Chicago, Illinois; Ft. Lauderdale, Florida; Jacksonville, Florida; Lakeland, Florida; Los Angeles, California; Miami, Florida; New York, New York; McLean, Virginia; Oakbrook Terrace, Illinois; Orlando, Florida; Portland, Oregon; Providence, Rhode Island; San Antonio, Texas; San Francisco, California; Seattle, Washington; St Petersburg, Florida; Tallahassee, Florida; Tampa, Florida; Washington, DC and West Palm Beach, Florida.

Internationally, offices are located in Helsinki, Finland; Mexico City, Mexico; Rio de Janeiro, Brazil; São Paulo, Brazil; and Tokyo, Japan, with representative offices in Caracas, Venezuela and Tel Aviv, Israel.

Holland & Knight is among the 15 largest firms worldwide, providing representation in all major areas of law. The firm's multi-office, one firm structure enables it to provide efficient legal advice to local and international clients.

Holland & Knight LLP is a limited liability partnership registered under Florida law. In Illinois, attorneys practice as Holland & Knight LLC, an Illinois limited liability company.

HEAD OFFICE

NEW YORK
195 Broadway, 24th Floor, **New York**, NY 10007
Tel: 212 513 3200
Email: whonan@hklaw.com
Website: www.hklaw.com

JACKSON KELLY PLLC

THE FIRM

Chief Executive Officer: AL Emch
Assistant Managing Member: Michael D Foster

Number of members: 88
Number of other lawyers: 58

HEAD OFFICE

WEST VIRGINIA
1600 Laidley Tower, PO Box 553, **Charleston**, WV 25322
Tel: 304 340 1000   **Fax:** 304 340 1033
Website: www.jacksonkelly.com

BRANCH OFFICES

The firm also has offices in Morgantown, WV; Fairmont, WV; New Martinsville, WV; Martinsburg, WV; Parkersburg, WV; Wheeling, WV; Denver, CO; Lexington, KY; Washington, DC.

FIRM OVERVIEW: Historically synonymous with the practice of law, Jackson Kelly PLLC is the oldest and largest law firm in West Virginia, tracing its roots back to the early 1800s. Combining diversity, specialization and commitment to excellence, Jackson Kelly PLLC consists of nearly 150 lawyers. While the majority of the firm's lawyers are located in Charleston, West Virginia, the firm has lawyers resident in a number of offices strategically positioned in nine other locations to provide optimum client support. Although meeting the legal needs of myriad corporate and individual clients effectively and efficiently is of paramount concern, the firm maintains a strong tradition of public involvement through charitable generosity and participation in the arts and education. The tradition that has become the trademark of one of West Virginia's most prestigious law firms is perhaps exemplified in these areas of support, a dedication that complements the legal services performed for employers, business and commercially-oriented clients.

MAIN AREAS OF PRACTICE:

Business & Commercial: The firm offers services that range from general corporate law and public and private financing to more specialized areas such as the formation of bank holding companies. Businesses of all sizes seek the firm's advice, from companies planning multimillion dollar mergers and acquisitions to small, family-owned businesses planning to incorporate.

Employee Benefits: In an effort to assist with the development and administration of the firm's clients' employee benefits plans, Jackson Kelly established the Employee Benefits Group. The focus of this group includes non-qualified and qualified plan design, consultation and administration.

Energy & Natural Resources: Jackson Kelly is a national leader in all aspects of the law relating to the extraction of Federal, Native American, state, and private natural resources and the industries associated with the development, processing, refining, transportation, and marketing of those resources, including: coal, oil, natural gas, coalbed methane, metals, hard rock, synfuels, aggregates, timber, and other minerals, as well as alternate energy, electricity, and power marketing.

Environmental: The firm provides assistance in obtaining permits and approvals, and in defending both private and governmental environmental claims in numerous areas. Firm lawyers are nationally known as experts in the handling of claims involving hazardous waste disposal.

Federal & Workers' Compensation: A management-oriented firm, Jackson Kelly provides the nation's largest defense practice against claims arising under the Federal Black Lung Act. The firm also has one of the most extensive defense practices under the Kentucky Workers' Compensation Act and the largest defense practice in West Virginia.

Government Contracts: An important part of Jackson Kelly's service to its clients is to help government prime contractors and subcontractors meet applicable statutory and regulatory requirements in various procurement environments through a number of menus, including compliance audits and training. The firm also assists clients in initiating and defending both private and governmental contract claims, disputes and protests.

Health Law: The Health Law Group's specialized experience and expertise assists healthcare organizations in meeting the challenges offered by today's environment of keen economic competition, strict government regulation, and new business relationships.

Immigration: This practice covers all aspects of legal representation relating to immigration and naturalization, including temporary and permanent immigration visa petitions, visa application and processing abroad, and exclusion and deportation proceedings. The practice also encompasses internal reviews of company compliance with employment-related immigration rules and representations in any civil proceedings that may result from enforcement of such rules.

Intellectual Property: Services involve legal counseling regarding the various aspects of broadcasting, copyrights, patents, trademarks, or other matters concerning the many facets of intellectual property and technology law.

International Law: Whether clients are buying or selling goods internationally or considering the establishment of operations in a foreign country or the United States, Jackson Kelly's International Law Group can help.

Labor & Employment: An employer-oriented firm, Jackson Kelly is dedicated to representing management's interests in all types of employment-related matters at both the state and federal levels.

Legislative Services: In addition to considerable experience in legislative drafting, Jackson Kelly lawyers render lobbying services to clients by regularly advising about the impact of pending legislation, preparing position statements, preparing legislative amendments, and testifying at or preparing witnesses for committee appearances. Included in this field of expertise are lawyers who have served in the West Virginia Legislature or as clerks of major committees of the West Virginia Legislature and in Kentucky as members of various state commissions and study committees.

Litigation: The firm offers its clients experienced representation from advice, planning and litigation avoidance or mitigation to case development and trial representation including jury trials and, if necessary, appellate advocacy.

Medical Professional Liability: This MPL Practice Group provides aggressive representation of hospitals, physicians and other healthcare providers. Through thorough medical and legal research, the firm's goal is to identify issues and problems and come to an early evaluation of the best defense strategy for a given case. The MPL Practice Group also offers advice and counsel on risk management, confidentiality and medical records issues.

Occupational Safety & Health: Jackson Kelly's Safety and Health practice group provides a broad spectrum of services to the firm's clients, emphasizing MSHA, OSHA, and DOT.

Taxes, Estates & Trusts: Clients, which include lawyers outside the firm, accountants, fiduciaries and other professionals, are advised with regard to tax planning, purchases and sales of business interests, corporate mergers, and personal estate planning.

CLIENTS: Clients include manufacturing, natural resources, business and commercial, trade associations, medical, retail, transportation, government contractions, utilities, local, state and federal agencies.

JENNER & BLOCK, LLC

THE FIRM

Managing Partner: Robert L Graham
Chairman: Jerold S Solovy

Number of partners: 160
Number of other lawyers: 230

HEAD OFFICE

ILLINOIS
1 IBM Plaza, **Chicago** 60611
Tel: 312 222 9350 **Fax:** 312 527 0484
Website: www.jenner.com

BRANCH OFFICES

DISTRICT OF COLUMBIA
Suite 1200 South, 601 Thirteenth Street, NW, **Washington, DC** 20005
Tel: 202 639 6000 **Fax:** 202 639 6066

TEXAS
3150 Bank One Center, 1717 Main Street, **Dallas** 75201
Tel: 214 746 5700 **Fax:** 214 746 5757

FIRM OVERVIEW: Jenner & Block is an international, full service law firm of nearly 400 attorneys offering significant experience in virtually every area of the law. Founded in Chicago in 1914, the firm delivers excellent business advice and counsel and secures victories for its clients from the trial level through the United States Supreme Court.

MAIN AREAS OF PRACTICE:

Business Transaction: Jenner & Block has a substantial Business Transaction practice, with experienced groups focusing on corporate and commercial transactions including mergers and acquisitions, corporate governance, securities, corporate and commercial finance, tax, real estate, environmental, insurance, commercial law, technology and intellectual property, bankruptcy and reorganization, benefits, employment, labor and executive compensation, government, healthcare and associations. The firm's lawyers have authored books and treatises in many of these areas, most recently on such topics as director and officer liability, securities, environmental law, insurance coverage, intellectual property and the Uniform Commercial Code. Jenner & Block handles transactional work for a wide range of large public corporations as well as privately held businesses, financial institutions, prominent trade associations, nonprofit organizations, new ventures, and individuals. The firm's lawyers represent many international and domestic clients in connection with mergers and acquisitions, joint ventures, strategic alliances and dispositions of businesses, and regularly advise clients in connection with public and private securities offerings and financings.

Litigation: Jenner & Block has one of the most prominent and successful litigation practices in the country. The firm's more than 250 litigators have won impressive victories in a broad range of complex and challenging civil and criminal cases before federal, state and administrative courts. Jenner & Block regularly represents clients before the United States Supreme Court, in all of the 13 United States Circuit Courts of Appeals, and in federal district courts and state courts nationwide. The quality and competence of the firm's trial lawyers is well known. Among them are two partners who are former United States Attorneys, many former Assistant US Attorneys, two former Chairs of the ABA Litigation Section, and numerous leaders of national, state and local bar associations. Currently, 11 partners in the firm are Fellows of the American College of Trial Lawyers, the country's most prestigious trial group. Many of the firm's trial lawyers clerked for judges in the federal and state systems, including a dozen who clerked for one or more United States Supreme Court Justices. In addition, several former partners now serve as federal judges, maintaining a remarkable history of judicial service by members of the firm.

Public Service: Public service is part of the fabric of Jenner & Block. Throughout its history, the firm has served as a national leader in pro bono advocacy and continues to run one of the strongest and largest public service programs in the nation. The firm's lawyers contribute more than 5% of their billable hours annually to pro bono work. Last year its attorneys logged more than 46,000 pro bono hours firmwide, with an average of nearly 90 hours per lawyer. Of the nation's largest law firms, Jenner & Block is continually ranked among the very top in pro bono work by *American Lawyer* magazine.

CLIENTS: Jenner & Block's clients range from large, international conglomerates to individuals and family-owned businesses and include industrial, commercial, research and development, technology, telecommunications and utility companies, as well as financial and service enterprises. In the public sector, the firm represents a variety of state and local governmental entities.

LEADING LAW FIRMS

JONES DAY

THE FIRM

Managing Partner: Stephen J Brogan
Number of partners worldwide: 555
Number of other lawyers worldwide: 1505
Website: www.jonesday.com

AREAS OF PRACTICE:
Litigation	48%
Business Practice	39%
Tax	7%
Government Regulation	6%

FIRM OVERVIEW: Founded in 1893, Jones Day is one of the world's largest law firms. It has US offices in Atlanta, Chicago, Cleveland, Columbus, Dallas, Houston, Irvine, Los Angeles, Menlo Park, New York, Pittsburgh and Washington DC, seven offices in Europe and eight in Asia. The firm advises more than half the *Fortune* 500 companies as well as a wide variety of other entities. In 2002 Jones Day was selected Litigation Department of the Year by a leading legal publication, International Litigation Firm of the Year by Chambers and Partners, was ranked number one for a number of deals completed worldwide by Thomson Financial, and was ranked first for client service by the BTI Consulting Group.

CLIENTS: In addition to representing a large number of its United States-based clients in international matters, Jones Day represents many major companies based in Europe, the Middle East, Asia and Latin America.

INTERNATIONAL WORK: The firm's international practice is significant and growing. Jones Day maintains a significant presence in the principal legal and regulatory capitals of the world. In Europe, more than 400 lawyers are based in Brussels, Frankfurt, London, Madrid, Milan, Munich and Paris. In Asia, more than 125 lawyers are based in Hong Kong, Shanghai, Singapore, Sydney, Taipei and Tokyo. In Mumbai and New Delhi, Jones Day has an associate relationship with Pathak & Associates. The firm's international practice focuses primarily on mergers and acquisitions, joint ventures and other investment transactions; securities and finance matters; tax, labour, environmental, competition and other significant regulatory matters; and international litigation and arbitration. The firm's international practice balances US lawyers posted outside the United States and foreign lawyers experienced in representing US-based clients. The firm's lawyers are licensed in most significant jurisdictions in Europe and Asia and are fluent in virtually all principal languages relevant to international business.

US OFFICES

IRVINE
3 Park Plaza, Suite 1100, Irvine CA 92614-8502

Office Profile: Jones Day's Irvine office is located in the center of Southern California's Technology Coast. The office provides legal services to both emerging and established companies responding to today's accelerated business environment. These services involve focused legal teams active in litigation and intellectual property.

LOS ANGELES
555 West Fifth Street, Suite 4600, Los Angeles CA 90013-1025

Office Profile: Jones Day's Los Angeles office represents many of California's major corporations, institutions, and emerging companies. The office has a dominating litigation practice and is home to the Firm's strong health care practice and a burgeoning technology and intellectual property practice.

US OFFICE CONTACTS

CALIFORNIA
3 Park Plaza, Suite 1100, **Irvine** CA 92614-8502
Tel: 949 851 3939 **Fax:** 949 553 7539
Email: counsel@jonesday.com

555 West Fifth Street, Suite 4600, **Los Angeles** CA 90013-1025
Tel: 213 489 3939 **Fax:** 213 243 2539
Email: counsel@jonesday.com

2882 Sand Hill Rd, Suite 240, **Menlo Park** CA 94025
Tel: 650 739 3939 **Fax:** 650 739 3900
Email: counsel@jonesday.com

DISTRICT OF COLUMBIA
51 Louisiana Avenue, NW, **Washington** DC 20001-2113
Tel: 202 879 3939 **Fax:** 202 626 1700
Email: counsel@jonesday.com

GEORGIA
3500 SunTrust Plaza, 303 Peachtree Street, NE, **Atlanta** GA 30308-3242
Tel: 404 521 3939 **Fax:** 404 581 8330
Email: counsel@jonesday.com

ILLINOIS
77 West Wacker, **Chicago** IL 60601-1692
Tel: 312 782 3939 **Fax:** 312 782 8585
Email: counsel@jonesday.com

OHIO
North Point, 901 Lakeside Avenue, **Cleveland** OH 44114-1190
Tel: 216 586 3939 **Fax:** 216 579 0212
Email: counsel@jonesday.com

41 South High Street, Suite 1900, **Columbus** OH 43215-6113
Tel: 614 469 3939 **Fax:** 614 461 4198
Email: counsel@jonesday.com

NEW YORK
222 East 41st Street, **New York** NY 10017-6702
Tel: 212 326 3939 **Fax:** 212 755 7306
Email: counsel@jonesday.com

PENNSYLVANIA
One Mellon Bank Center, 31st Floor, 500 Grant Street,
Pittsburgh PA 15219-2502
Tel: 412 391 3939 **Fax:** 412 394 7959
Email: counsel@jonesday.com

TEXAS
2727 North Harwood Street, **Dallas** TX 75201-1515
Tel: 214 220 3939 **Fax:** 214 969 5100
Email: counsel@jonesday.com

Chase Tower, Suite 6500, 600 Travis Street, **Houston** TX 77002-3008
Tel: 832 239 3939 **Fax:** 832 239 3600
Email: counsel@jonesday.com

JONES DAY cont'd

MENLO PARK
2882 Sand Hill Rd, Suite 240, Menlo Park CA 94025

Office Profile: The Menlo Park office enables the firm's technology practice to provide high quality legal services for Silicon Valley entrepreneurial and venture capital clients and also provides localized capacity for new and existing public companies focused on emerging technology.

WASHINGTON, DC
51 Louisiana Avenue, NW, Washington DC 20001-2113

Office Profile: Jones Day established its Washington office in 1946. Today, over 250 lawyers practicing in the business practice, government regulation, litigation, and tax areas are housed in a historic office building across the street from the US Capitol.

ATLANTA
3500 SunTrust Plaza, 303 Peachtree Street, NE, Atlanta GA 30308-3242

Office Profile: Jones Day Atlanta, opened in 1989, is composed of more than 130 lawyers. The diverse business law practice addresses the legal needs of capital users and capital providers under the leadership of experienced corporate and real estate practitioners. The office has substantial litigation, tax, finance, and banking practices.

CHICAGO
77 West Wacker, Chicago IL 60601-1692

Office Profile: Jones Day's Chicago office opened in 1987. With more than 160 lawyers, the office provides a full range of legal services for clients ranging from *Fortune* 500 companies to privately held and emerging companies and international concerns. Chicago lawyers handle a wide variety of US and international business transactions as well as litigation.

CLEVELAND
North Point, 901 Lakeside Avenue, Cleveland OH 44114-1190

Office Profile: Jones Day Cleveland, the firm's original office, opened in 1893. Today, the Cleveland office encompasses over 280 lawyers who provide legal services in business transactions, government regulation, litigation, and tax to a diverse group of clients based throughout the United States and around the world.

COLUMBUS
41 South High Street, Suite 1900, Columbus OH 43215-6113

Office Profile: Opened in 1980, Jones Day Columbus today has more than 90 lawyers and provides a full range of legal services to public and private businesses and individuals located or having legal needs in Central Ohio and around the country.

NEW YORK
222 East 41st Street, New York NY 10017-6702

Office Profile: Opened in 1986, the New York office has grown to more than 220 lawyers, ranking it among the largest New York offices of any non-New York-based national firm. Jones Day New York plays a leading role in the firm's capital markets and international activities.

PITTSBURGH
One Mellon Bank Center, 31st Floor, 500 Grant Street, Pittsburgh PA 15219-2502

Office Profile: Jones Day opened its Pittsburgh office in January 1989 as the firm's 14th office. It has more than 50 lawyers who provide legal service in five principal areas of practice: business practice and transactions, real estate, environmental, litigation, and labor and employment law.

DALLAS
2727 North Harwood Street, Dallas TX 75201-1515

Office Profile: Jones Day's Dallas office consists of over 180 lawyers. The office represents a wide variety of corporate clients engaged in the banking, financial services, investment, technology, electronic commerce, software services, oil and gas, energy, health care, real estate, construction, manufacturing, consumer products, and retail industries.

HOUSTON
Chase Tower, Suite 6500, 600 Travis Street, Houston TX 77002-3008

Office Profile: Opened on January 1, 2001, the office has more than 30 lawyers who provide legal services in three principal areas of practice: business transactions, litigation, and energy regulation. Jones Day's Houston office is also the worldwide headquarters of the firm's Energy Specialized Industry Practice, which brings the best of the firm's practice resources and extensive industry experience to the representation of energy clients.

LEADING LAW FIRMS

JONES, FOSTER, JOHNSTON & STUBBS, P.A.

THE FIRM

Managing Partner: Sidney A Stubbs

Number of partners worldwide: 19
Number of other lawyers worldwide: 8

HEAD OFFICE

FLORIDA
505 South Flagler Drive, Suite 1100
West Palm Beach, FL 33401
Tel: 561 659 3000 **Fax:** 561 832 1454
Website: www.jones-foster.com

CONTACTS

Litigation:	Sidney A Stubbs, Scott G Hawkins
Agriculture:	John B McCracken
Real Estate Development:	Larry B Alexander
Private Client Services:	Thornton M Henry
Financial Institutions:	Peter S Holton
Employment:	Margaret L Cooper
Employee Benefits:	David E Bowers
Eminent Domain:	H Adams Weaver
Product Liability Defense:	Steven J Rothman
Probate Litigation:	Peter A Sachs

FIRM OVERVIEW: Since its founding in the early 1900's, Jones, Foster, Johnston & Stubbs, P.A. has maintained a strong reputation for superb and innovative trial work and high ethical standards. The firm's attentive and dedicated staff is qualified to handle most legal needs as they combine experience with leading-edge technology to consistently deliver a quality work product in an efficient and cost-effective manner.

MAIN AREAS OF PRACTICE:

Commercial Litigation Group: Jones Foster's experience, creative thinking and its use of state of the art technology have helped to build the long-standing reputation of the firm's innovative and resourceful trial team. The firm represents clients in a broad spectrum of complex litigation ranging from financial and land-use disputes to technology issues, corporate governance, partnerships and fiduciary disputes.

Agriculture Practice Group: Second only to tourism, agriculture is big business in Florida, representing over $54 billion per year in revenue and 30% of the state's jobs. Few law firms in the state can offer similar depth and breadth of services to the agricultural industry. Jones Foster has represented a wide variety of individuals and companies in the citrus, sugar cane, dairy, and nursery industries since 1909 and has handled a myriad of issues including: product markets issues, management of agriculture cooperatives and environmental practices.

Commercial Real Estate Development Practice Group: For more than 75 years, Jones Foster has provided developers and owners of office buildings, retail centers, and industrial properties the full range of legal representation they require. Jones Foster understands Florida's commercial real estate industry and its requirements of legal counsel.

Private Client Services Group: Jones Foster assists a diverse group of families and individuals throughout the nation in a wide variety of estate planning and wealth preservation matters. Each client receives personalized attention and care in the planning and administration of their estate to reflect individual wishes while providing for maximum tax and other savings. The firm's overriding goal is to conserve the assets of its clients as they pass from one generation to the next.

Financial Institutions Practice Group: Jones Foster represents a variety of financial institutions in the preparation and negotiation of loan and financing documents, in troubled debt restructurings and in litigation and bankruptcy matters. Whether a Florida-based community bank, a large regional bank doing business in Florida, or a money-center bank, each client receives a highly focused level of attention to its matter.

Employment Practice Group: Jones Foster represents management of a wide array of businesses in all types of employment-related matters, including complicated issues involving pension and profit sharing plans, ERISA plans, non-qualified deferred compensation plans, health plans and estate planning for employee benefits. Whether a closely held business, an emerging regional corporation, or a Fortune 500 company doing business in Florida, each client receives a highly personalized level of attention to its matter.

Eminent Domain Practice Group: For decades, Florida has been among the fastest growing states in the country, and that growth is projected to continue. Government, through its power of eminent domain (condemnation), often takes private property to support this growth. Roads, water and sewage systems and drainage systems, and other public facilities are constructed to support the hundreds of thousands of people who move to Florida each year. Jones, Foster has effectively represented private property owners adversely affected by the eminent domain process for over 30 years.

Residential Real Estate Development Practice Group: Jones, Foster has been representing real estate developers for over 75 years and understands the industry and its requirements. The firm offers developers and owners of residential real estate projects full-service legal representation and a high level of commitment as the firm partners with them to understand the needs and objectives of their development projects throughout the state.

Product Liability Defense Group: For over 30 years, Jones Foster has defended the integrity of products designed, manufactured and distributed by some of the country's most well-known companies. The firm maintains the highest ethical and professional standards while vigorously opposing, at every level, the all too frequent efforts to expand the discovery process to abusive proportions. It is dedicated to the defense of its clients' products and the protection of trade secret and proprietary materials.

JONES FOSTER JOHNSTON & STUBBS, P.A.
Attorneys and Counselors

LEADING LAW FIRMS

JONES WALKER WAECHTER POITEVENT CARRÈRE & DENÈGRE, LLP

THE FIRM

Managing Partner & Chairman of Executive Committee: William H Hines

Number of partners: 113
Number of other lawyers: 108

FIRM OVERVIEW: Jones Walker is one of the largest full-service firms in the Gulf South, with over 220 attorneys located in offices in Baton Rouge, Houston, Lafayette, Miami, New Orleans, and Washington, DC. Major companies, money center financial institutions, and worldwide insurers routinely call on Jones Walker to handle matters of regional, national and international scope. Jones Walker continually strives to balance the traditional one on one relationship of attorney and client with the demands of today's increasingly complex legal problems that often require the attention of a team of attorneys. By building strong, personal relationships with our clients, Jones Walker focuses on getting the best result in the most efficient manner.

MAIN AREAS OF PRACTICE: Corporate and securities, general business and energy, healthcare litigation, estates and tax, labor and employment, litigation, maritime, government relations, intellectual property, and environmental and toxic tort.

INTERNATIONAL WORK: The firm's International Practice Group attorneys have significant experience in the foreign investment, corporate, commercial, financial, tax, and administrative laws and regulations relevant to the global operations of firm clients, and have lived and studied around the world, thus bringing a unique cultural perspective to the practice. The International Practice Group draws on the specialized expertise of attorneys throughout the firm's various practice areas. The firm has elected not to be part of an international law firm exchange. Instead, with our correspondent network of foreign lawyers specializing in the specific practice areas implicated in the global projects of our clients, it is capable of handling complex transactions involving diverse areas of law, in a cross-border environment. Its attorneys have assisted clients in all forms of international transactions, including in connection with: joint ventures; international capital markets (including issuers and underwriters on debt and equity offerings); project finance (including developers, borrowers, lenders and the World Bank); M&A; real estate; energy; maritime; telecommunications; international tax, tax compliance and planning; intellectual property; healthcare; antitrust and unfair trade practices; export controls; government regulation; environmental; labor and employment; and arbitration and dispute resolution. The firm conducts business in Spanish, Portuguese, French, Italian, German, and Turkish, and has handled transactions in some 30 countries in Latin America, Europe, Asia, and Africa.

CLIENTS: Banking and finance; communications and technology; energy and mining; healthcare; maritime; media/advertising; manufacturing/industrial; public sector; transportation; wholesale/retail/service industries.

HEAD OFFICE

LOUISIANA
201 St Charles Avenue, **New Orleans** LA 70170-5100
Tel: 504 582 8000 **Fax:** 504 582 8583
Email: info@joneswalker.com
Website: www.joneswalker.com

BRANCH OFFICES

DISTRICT OF COLUMBIA
499 South Capitol Street, SW, Suite 600, **Washington**, DC 20003-4013
Tel: 202 203 1000 **Fax:** 202 203 0000

FLORIDA
601 Brickell Key Drive, Suite 500, **Miami** FL 33131
Tel: 305 679 5700 **Fax:** 305 679 5710

LOUISIANA
8555 United Plaza Boulevard, **Baton Rouge** LA 70809-7000
Tel: 225 248 2000 **Fax:** 225 248 2010

500 Dover Boulevard, Suite 120, **Lafayette** LA 70503-5269
Tel: 337 406 5610 **Fax:** 337 406 5620

TEXAS
10001 Woodloch Forest Drive, Suite 350, The Woodlands, TX 77380 **Houston**
Tel: 281 296 5900 **Fax:** 281 296 5910

CONTACTS

Corporate & Securities	Curtis R Hearn
Environmental & Toxic Tort	Michael A Chernekoff
Estates & Tax	Rudolph R Ramelli
General Business & Energy	William H Hines
Government Relations	R Christian Johnsen
Healthcare Litigation	Stewart E Niles Jr
Intellectual Property	Thomas K Potter III
International	William H Hines
Labor & Employment	Mark Adams
Litigation	R Patrick Vance
Maritime	Glenn G Goodier

KATTEN MUCHIN ZAVIS ROSENMAN

THE FIRM

Managing Partner: Vincent AF Sergi
Number of partners: +250
Number of other lawyers: +370

FIRM OVERVIEW: Katten Muchin Zavis Rosenman (www.kmzr.com) offers integrated, full-service legal capabilities in the nation's largest centers of business, government and technology: New York City; Los Angeles; Chicago; Washington, DC; Charlotte, North Carolina; Palo Alto, California; Newark, New Jersey. The firm's more than 600 attorneys in 60 practice areas are business advisors and advocates for a wide range of public and private companies, from entrepreneurial, emerging-growth and middle-market firms to global *Fortune* 100 companies, as well as government entities and not-for-profit organizations. To meet the needs of the firm's increasingly global clientele, it maintains important affiliations with leading international firms.

MAIN AREAS OF PRACTICE:

Corporate: KMZ Rosenman's Corporate Department is comprised of teams of corporate and securities attorneys, as well as lawyers from other disciplines, such as tax, employee benefits, intellectual property and labor. Corporate services include: counseling and providing legal solutions on the structure, formation, funding and operation of business entities; structuring project-specific financings and public and private debt and equity offerings; providing merger and acquisition counsel; conducting due diligence investigations; providing counsel on partnerships and joint ventures; and structuring joint ventures and other multi-party contracts.

Customs & International Trade: KMZ Rosenman has one of the largest Customs and International Trade practices in the US, with 13 attorneys and two paralegals, who are licensed customs brokers. Its attorneys have extensive experience, both in government and private practice, concerning customs and international trade issues. In particular, the practice includes former senior US Customs Service attorneys who served at Customs Headquarters in Washington, DC, as well as regional offices.

Entertainment: The firm's Entertainment Practice conducts a general business practice for clients engaged in all areas of entertainment, communications, new media, hi-tech and related fields, including motion pictures, television, internet, merchandising, licensing, technology, book and e-book publishing, music, stage productions, interactive games and entertainment and communication systems, film finance, banking and related areas, labor relations, executive employment agreements and estate planning and advises and counsels clients on copyright and trademark regulation and protection of intellectual property in all media worldwide.

Intellectual Property: The Intellectual Property Practice provides the legal advice and representation necessary to enable businesses to take advantage of and protect their patents, trademarks, copyrights, service marks and trade secrets, including confidential information such as customer lists and client files and computer software.

Litigation: KMZ Rosenman's trial lawyers are adept at achieving the business objectives of the firm's predominantly large corporate clients in substantial and significant cases. The firm's attorneys practice in federal and state courts across the nation, at the trial and appellate level, before arbitration tribunals and administrative law judges, as well as in specialty courts, such as the US Tax Court and the US Court of International Trade.

Mergers & Acquisitions: The Mergers and Acquisitions Practice is involved in all aspects of public and private mergers, acquisitions and divestitures. In the public arena, the firm has an active takeover practice where it has represented both targets and bidders in major hostile takeovers and has substantial experience in defensive planning for clients through implementation of anti-takeover devices and other defensive actions. The group also serves as counsel to investment bankers, financial institutions and special committees of boards of directors.

Private Equity & Emerging Growth Companies: The firm's Private Equity Practice provides equity funds and growth companies with leading capabilities in key areas of transactional representation, including equity and mezzanine fund formation. The group represents leading private equity funds throughout the US, with a practice that spans the representation of early-stage venture investors to traditional LBO sponsors. In addition, this practice group is regularly engaged by start-up companies, emerging growth companies and mature businesses in a wide variety of industries, including both conventional and hi-tech businesses. Along with general corporate counseling and acquisition work, KMZ Rosenman attorneys provide services to emerging growth companies that include negotiating and structuring investments from private equity sources, from start-up rounds, late-stage financings through IPO and beyond.

Real Estate: KMZ Rosenman has one of the most extensive national real estate practices in the US. The firm's real estate lawyers practice full time in real estate, including the related areas of environmental law, REITs, property tax and income taxation of real estate owners, foreign investment and international real estate transactions, and whose experience extends to virtually every area of real estate law.

Securities: The Securities Practice represents both publicly and privately held companies on a wide range of securities matters ranging from IPOs to private placements, proxy battles, mergers and acquisitions and asset securitization transactions. The group provides a variety of services relating to ongoing securities compliance, including insider trading policies, proxy statements and solicitations, and customary 34 Act reporting. Other ongoing securities-related matters handled range from managing relationships with analysts, market makers and the press to other general legal and business issues.

Technology & New Media: Attorneys in KMZ Rosenman's Technology and New Media practice counsel some of the nation's top hi-tech companies and e-businesses in such areas as antitrust, patent and trademark audit and protection, brand extension licensing, intangibles leveraging, content acquisition and exploitation, litigation, and technology licensing and distribution.

HEAD OFFICE

ILLINOIS
525 W Monroe, Suite 1600, **Chicago**, IL 60661-3693
Tel: 312 902 5200 **Fax:** 312 902 1061
Website: www.kmzr.com

BRANCH OFFICES

CALIFORNIA
2029 Century Park East, Suite 2600, **Los Angeles**, CA 90067-3012
Tel: 310 788 4400 **Fax:** 310 788 4471

260 Sheridan Avenue, Suite 450, **Palo Alto**, CA 94306-2047
Tel: 650 330 3652 **Fax:** 650 321 4746

NEW JERSEY
One Gateway Center, **Newark**, NJ 07102-5397
Tel: 973 645 0572 **Fax:** 973 645 0573

NEW YORK
575 Madison Avenue, **New York**, NY 10022-2585
Tel: 212 940 8800 **Fax:** 212 940 8776

NORTH CAROLINA
401 South Tryon Street, Suite 2600, **Charlotte**, NC 28202-1935
Tel: 704 444 2000 **Fax:** 704 444 2050

WASHINGTON
1025 Thomas Jefferson St., N.W., East Lobby: Suite 700, **Washington, DC** 20007-5201
Tel: 202 625 3500 **Fax:** 202 298 7570

LEADING LAW FIRMS

KELLY HAGLUND GARNSEY + KAHN LLC

THE FIRM

Senior Member Contact: Walter W Garnsey, Jr

Number of members: 9
Number of other lawyers: 3

AREAS OF PRACTICE:
Family Law	.42%
Commercial Litigation	.34%
Employment Law	.8%
Environmental Law	.6%
Special Counsel to Governmental Entities	.6%
Civil Rights Law	.4%

HEAD OFFICE

COLORADO
1441 Eighteenth Street, 300 Blake Street Building, **Denver** 80202
Tel: 303 296 9412   **Fax:** 303 293 8705
Email: webmaster@khgk.com
Website: www.khgk.com

CONTACTS

Commercial Litigation	Walter W Garnsey, Jr
Family Law	Terrance R Kelly
Employment Law	James W Hubbell
Civil Rights Law	Federico C Alvarez
Environmental Law	Lori Potter
Special Counsel to Governmental Entities	David R Fine

FIRM OVERVIEW: Founded in 1972, Kelly Haglund Garnsey + Kahn LLC is primarily a litigation firm. Its attorneys specialize in complex commercial litigation, family law, environmental law, and civil rights and employment law, and serve as special counsel to governmental entities. With 12 experienced lawyers, the firm offers its clients the sophistication of big-firm practice and the responsiveness and cost-effective service of a small firm. Staffing practices ensure that highly skilled and seasoned professionals are involved in every project. Its attorneys bring a hands-on approach to client problems. On average, each firm member has more than 20 years experience, and each paralegal more than 12. Seven of the firm's nine members are listed among the top Colorado attorneys in a leading legal publication. The firm's attorneys have received widespread recognition from their peers and the community as a whole. Its attorneys are energetically involved with the Colorado Bar Association and local and specialty bar associations. They lecture and publish on legal issues and serve actively on community and non-profit boards. Integral to the firm's legal practice is its commitment to community service.

MAIN AREAS OF PRACTICE:

Commercial Litigation: The firm's attorneys try cases in several specialized areas of commercial litigation. Their courtroom experience includes state and federal trial and appellate courts in Colorado and elsewhere. Specific litigation sub-specialities include: banking and financial institutions law; bankruptcy; constitutional law; construction law; contract law; business entity law (eg, the law of corporations, limited liability companies and partnerships), including officer and director defense; election law; health law; insurance law; intellectual property law; media law; professional liability law; real estate and housing law; securities law; statutory attorney's fee recovery law; and telecommunications law.

Family Law: The firm specializes in complex family law matters, including interstate and international cases. The nature of the work requires evidentiary valuation of globally-located assets, analyses of cross-jurisdiction conflict of laws and choice of law issues, resolution of issues raised by offshore trusts, and Hague Convention work concerning international custody disputes. The lawyers include a former general jurisdiction trial court judge whose tenure included presiding in family law cases.

Employment Law: The firm represents employers and employees in employment matters including: claims for breach of express and implied contracts; race, gender, age, and disability discrimination (e.g., federal claims under Title VII, the Americans with Disabilities Act (ADA), the Age Discrimination in Employment Act (ADEA) and state claims under the Colorado Civil Rights Act); covenant not to compete and trade secret disputes; and negotiating employment and severance agreements.

Civil Rights Law: The firm represents plaintiffs and defendants in civil rights issues including First Amendment and §§ 1981 and 1983 claims, SLAPP (Strategic Lawsuit Against Public Participation) defense, and housing discrimination claims.

Environmental Law: The firm represents businesses, governmental entities, and individuals in the various environmental and public land matters encountered in the Rocky Mountain West. Its attorneys have substantial experience in state and federal court and before administrative agencies in environmental matters including: public land management law; access, rights-of-way and transportation issues; water resources, mining, endangered species and wildlife law; and land use, hazardous waste, citizen's suits/enforcement, open records, access to information, and open meetings matters.

Special Counsel to Governmental Entities: The firm represents cities, towns, counties, quasi-governmental authorities, Indian tribes, special districts and similar entities in matters relating to federal Indian law, employment, land use, environment, civil rights, fair housing, and utility franchises.

CLIENTS: The firm's clients are a wide range of public and private businesses, individuals, governmental entities and non-profit organizations.

INTERNATIONAL WORK: Languages spoken: English and Spanish.

KELLY | HAGLUND | GARNSEY + KAHN LLC
ATTORNEYS AT LAW

LEADING LAW FIRMS

KING & SPALDING LLP

THE FIRM

Chairman: Walter W Driver, Jr
Managing Partner, New York: Mark Zvonkovic
Managing Partner, Texas: Randolph C Coley
Managing Partner, District of Columbia: J Sedwick Sollers

Number of partners: 217
Number of other lawyers: 494

FIRM OVERVIEW: Established in 1885, the firm has offices in Atlanta, Houston, London, New York and Washington, DC. Since its inception, King & Spalding has provided high caliber legal counsel to clients in the United States and abroad. With over 700 attorneys, King & Spalding currently represents more than 250 public companies in over 48 practice areas.

MAIN AREAS OF PRACTICE:

Financial Transactions: The practice group provides legal services for domestic and non-US banks and other financial institutions. It handles all aspects of credit-facilities and financial products, including traditional secured and unsecured credit facilities, asset-based financing, venture and mezzanine arrangements, trade credits, swaps and derivatives.

Corporate Finance: The firm serves as counsel to issuers and underwriters/placement agents in over 185 public/Rule 144A offerings having an aggregate market value of over $38 billion. The firm represents issuers, underwriters, investors, and other corporate finance participants, as well as providing continuing corporate advice to public and private companies.

Energy: The firm's energy attorneys have been involved in transactions throughout the world related to energy and natural resources, including domestic and international exploration, production, processing, transportation, storage and sale of hydrocarbons; electric power project development, marketing and finance; minerals and mining transactions and dispute resolution. King & Spalding's experience includes developing project structures as well as the drafting and negotiating of project agreements, contracts and documentation.

Intellectual Property: The firm's IP lawyers concentrate on acquiring, creating, licensing, protecting and litigating intellectual property rights, both domestically and internationally. The group advises clients on trademarks, patents, copyrights, marketing, competition and antitrust issues, joint ventures, mergers and acquisitions and other related matters in a wide range of industries, including computer software, telecommunications and biotechnology.

International: The firm's international transactions group advises clients in cross-border mergers and acquisitions, trade and customs, e-commerce, energy, Islamic finance and investment, intellectual property, international trademarks, structured finance and international arbitration and mediation. The firm has undertaken extensive work in Latin America, East Asia, and the Middle East, as well as with foreign companies investing in the United States.

Litigation & Arbitration: The firm provides litigation services in the areas of antitrust, appellate, class action, commercial litigation product liability, shareholder and securities litigation, trade and customs and toxic tort. The firm also has a substantial international arbitration practice.

M&A: Ranking among the top 10 US law firms, measured by announced M&A transaction dollar volume, and among the top 20 US law firms, measured by the number of announced transactions, the firm's experience spans a wide range of industries.

Real Estate: The firm's real estate practice includes acquisition, development, financing and leasing of commercial real estate primarily for nationally recognized developers and non-US institutional and private investors, including lenders in asset portfolio transactions, securitization and creation of real estate investment trusts.

Tax: The firm works with clients on the planning and execution of business transactions of all sizes and types arising in domestic and cross-border settings, including acquisitions, disposition, joint ventures and financing transactions. Advice covers the full range of federal income tax issues, with extensive experience in the corporate partnership and international practice areas.

Technology: The firm takes an integrated and multidisciplined approach to technology-related matters. Clients range from Fortune 50 multinational corporations to single proprietor inventors.

CLIENTS: 3M Company, The Coca-Cola Company, ChevronTexaco, Credit Suisse First Boston, Delta Air Lines, Inc., Dow Chemical Company, ExxonMobil Corporation, General Electric Company, The Home Depot, Inc., Jefferson-Pilot Corporation, Lehman Brothers, Lend Lease Real Estate Investments, Inc., Lockheed Martin Corporation, Sprint Corporation, Sun Trust Banks, Inc., General Motors Corp., Georgia-Pacific Corporation, Turner Broadcasting System, United Parcel Services, Inc.

HEAD OFFICE

GEORGIA
191 Peachtree Street, **Atlanta**, GA 30303-1763
Tel: 404 572 4600   Fax: 404 572 5100
Email: kingspalding@kslaw.com
Website: www.kslaw.com

BRANCH OFFICES

DISTRICT OF COLUMBIA
1730 Pennsylvania Avenue, N.W., **Washington, DC** 200006-4706
Tel: 202 737 0500   Fax: 202 626 3737
Email: kingspalding@kslaw.com

NEW YORK
1185 Avenue of the Americas, **New York**, NY 10036-4003
Tel: 212 556 2100   Fax: 212 556 2222
Email: kingspalding@kslaw.com

TEXAS
1100 Louisiana, Suite 4000, **Houston**, TX 77002-5213
Tel: 713 751 3200   Fax: 713 751 3290
Email: kingspalding@kslaw.com

INTERNATIONAL OFFICES

The firm has an associated office in London

CONTACTS

Financial Transactions	Margaret O'Neil
Corporate Finance	John Kelley
Energy	Philip Weems
Intellectual Property	Bruce Baber
International	John Cogan, Jr
Litigation & Arbitration	Doak Bishop
M&A	John Capers
Real Estate	Eileen Brumback
Tax	Robert Woodward
Technology	Steven de Groot

LEADING LAW FIRMS

KIRKLAND & ELLIS

THE FIRM

Number of partners: 359
Number of other lawyers: 36

BRANCH OFFICES

ILLINOIS
Aon Center, 200 East Randolph Drive, **Chicago** IL 60601-6636
Tel: 312 861 2000 Fax: 312 861 2200
Email: jack.levin@kirkland.com

CALIFORNIA
777 S. Figueroa Street, **Los Angeles** CA 90017-5800
Tel: 213 680 8400 Fax: 213 680 8500
Email: jdavidson@kirkland.com

333 Bush Street, **San Francisco** CA 94104-2806
Tel: 415 439 1400 Fax: 415 439 1500
Email: sjohnson@kirkland.com

DISTRICT OF COLUMBIA
655 Fifteenth Street NW, **Washington** DC 20005-5793
Tel: 202 879 5000 Fax: 202 879 5200
Email: tyannucci@kirkland.com

NEW YORK
Citigroup Center, 153 East 53rd Street, **New York** NY 10022-4611
Tel: 212 446 4800 Fax: 212 446 4900
Email: kradke@kirkland.com

FIRM OVERVIEW: Founded nearly 100 years ago, Kirkland & Ellis, one of America's premier law firms, has handled complicated transactional, tax, restructuring, workout and bankruptcy, intellectual property, litigation and counselling matters for major US and international clients. Today, Kirkland & Ellis continues to work with a base of long-standing clients engaged in varied industries such as hi-tech, manufacturing, computers, transportation, private equity capital, oil and gas, healthcare, real estate, chemicals, food products, finance, insurance, advertising, and accounting. On the transactional side, Kirkland is known for its ability to negotiate and close highly sophisticated transactions, representing venture capital investors and public and private companies in merger and acquisition, securities, spin-off and split-off, and private equity transactions. The firm has a premier private equity practice, having represented private investment funds, the private equity groups at several major money center banks and other participants in this industry for over 25 years.

MAIN AREAS OF PRACTICE:

Tax: The firm's practice provides its clients with the most creative tax planning available in a responsive and cost-efficient manner. The firm's tax practice has developed a strong international reputation for providing sophisticated tax counseling on both US, foreign and state tax issues, and effectively representing its clients in tax disputes worldwide. Kirkland's tax practice can be divided broadly into two areas: (1) tax planning in connection with mergers, acquisitions, buyouts, restructurings, financings, executive compensation plans, and other sophisticated transactions; and (2) contested tax matters in connection with challenges by the Internal Revenue Service and by foreign and state tax authorities. Kirkland's goal in both types of matters is the same: to achieve the best possible tax results in the most efficient manner.

Restructuring: The firm's restructuring, insolvency, workout and bankruptcy group provides a broad range of business advisory and crisis management skills with extensive experience in US and international insolvency matters to navigate clients through the turmoil of situations involving financially troubled companies. The group has earned a distinguished national and international reputation for providing outstanding legal advice and judgment to all constituencies in situations where companies face impending insolvency. The firm acts for a varied range of national and international clients: debtors; financial institutions; secured creditors; lessors; unsecured creditors; investors; and committees in complex corporate restructuring, workout and bankruptcy planning, negotiation and litigation.

Intellectual Property: Kirkland & Ellis represents some of the world's leading technology companies and brings its expertise to all areas of intellectual property, including biotechnology, semiconductor processing, telecommunications, and internet and e-commerce technology. With a dedicated practice dating from 1925, the firm has been at the forefront of IP developments throughout the 20th century. Kirkland & Ellis has adopted and adapted to the internet and e-commerce, and its 175 intellectual property lawyers understand fully the intricacies, implications, legal issues and arguments surrounding today's and tomorrow's communication and emerging technologies.

Litigation & Arbitration: Kirkland has earned a stellar reputation as trial lawyers (not just 'litigators') by successfully defending companies with business-threatening lawsuits and class actions in diverse legal areas such as commercial, intellectual property, product liability, insurance coverage, environmental, employment, securities law, mass torts, and antitrust issues, handling the trial, appellate, and US Supreme Court phases. This trial-ready reputation has been the impetus for favorable and prompt results for clients through settlements as well as through the various Alternative Dispute Resolution mechanisms (ADRs) employed whenever practicable and desired by the client.

INTERNATIONAL WORK: During the last five years, Kirkland's private equity practice has represented more than 50 different clients in hundreds of leveraged acquisitions and other types of transactions and has been principal counsel in over US$70 billion in fund formations. In the M&A and securities area, Kirkland has recently represented clients ranging from some of the world's largest corporations to major banks and investment banks in some of the world's largest and most complex M&A transactions and securities offerings. Kirkland & Ellis bases its commitment to client service on developing an intimate knowledge of each client's needs and objectives. The firm seeks long-term, partnering relationships with clients, to the end of providing the best total solution to the client's multidisciplined and industry-specific legal service needs. The firm's goal is to be an instrumental part of each client's success. Lawyers at Kirkland & Ellis are fluent in English, Chinese, French, German, Greek, Hebrew, Hindi, Italian, Japanese, Korean, Russian and Spanish.

KLEE, TUCHIN, BOGDANOFF & STERN LLP

THE FIRM

Co-Managing Partners: Lee R Bogdanoff, Michael L Tuchin

Number of partners: 8
Number of other lawyers: 7

HEAD OFFICE

CALIFORNIA
1880 Century Park East, Suite 200, **Los Angeles**, CA 90067-1698
Tel: 310 407 4000 **Fax:** 310 407 9090
Website: www.ktbslaw.com

FIRM OVERVIEW: Klee Tuchin Bogdanoff & Stern is a national, boutique law firm that specializes in business reorganizations, corporate insolvency, commercial litigation, bankruptcy-related asset acquisitions, bankruptcy litigation and appellate advocacy, and expert witness services in the bankruptcy field. KTB&S represents debtors, creditors, equity holders, committees, trustees, landlords, potential acquirers of assets, and other parties with interests in financially distressed businesses. KTB&S also provides expert witness services on matters of bankruptcy law. The members of KTB&S have decades of experience practicing in this unique area of law, and are actively involved in teaching and providing expert witness consultation and testimony in this field. KTB&S lawyers are headquartered in Los Angeles, California, but regularly handle matters and appear in bankruptcy proceedings throughout the United States. KTB&S is widely recognized as a national leader in its field.

CLIENTS: Since KTB&S was established in June 1999, the firm has attracted a notable list of clients. The nature and diversity of these representations illustrate the breadth and depth of KTB&S' expertise in all aspects of bankruptcy and insolvency practice. The firm's non-confidential representations include the following, which are listed by client categories:

DEBTORS: Anacomp, Inc.: document storage and information retrieval technology company; successfully confirmed prepackaged chapter 11 plan in 57 days. Crescent Jewelers: jewelry retailer; successful out-of-court restructuring. Custom Food Products: processor of custom and value added meat products; successful confirmation of plan of reorganization financed by Fleet Capital Corporation, junior capital provided by Simon/Triton Partners I, LLC. Fountain View, Inc. and Affiliates: skilled nursing facilities, assisted living facilities, pharmacy and therapy businesses; chapter 11 debtors presently undergoing reorganization. Frederick's of Hollywood and Affiliates: retailers of innovative specialty apparel; chapter 11 debtors presently undergoing reorganization. Guidance Software: Software development company; successful chapter 11 restructuring and voluntary dismissal. Incomnet, Inc.: reseller of long distance telephone services; successful development, proposal and confirmation of a chapter 11 plan of reorganization in eight months. Matthews Studio Equipment Group, Hollywood Rental Co. LLC, FourStar Inc., Matthews Studio Sales, Inc. (a/k/a Olesen) and related entities: major sellers, lessors, and outsourcers of production equipment for the entertainment industry, including theatrical, motion picture and television production; currently chapter 11 debtors. Outsource International And Affiliates: temporary employment services; successfully preserved operations for purposes of an orderly chapter 11 sale. Pacific Gateway Exchange, Inc., International Exchange Communications, Inc., Onyx Networks, Inc. and Affiliates: international wholesaler of telecommunications services, retail long distance reseller, and internet/co-location services provider; coordinated sale of assets and negotiation of chapter 11 liquidating plan. Prime Matrix Wireless Communications: retail reseller of cellular communications capacity; successfully coordinated orderly sale of the company.

BONDHOLDERS & OTHER CREDITORS: Adelphia Communications Corporation Unsecured Creditors' Committee: KTB&S presently serves as special counsel to the official unsecured creditors' committee in this case, investigating potential claims relating to approximately $13 billion in secured and unsecured debt. Ameriserve: represented one of the largest unsecured creditors in the chapter 11 case of Ameriserve. First Alliance Mortgage Company Official Unsecured Creditors' Committee: represent official committee of unsecured creditors in chapter 11 case of major sub-prime residential real estate lender. ICO Global Communications: represented bondholder group in ICO Global Communications chapter 11 case, comprised of Magten Asset Management Corp., Oaktree Capital Management, Cerberus Capital Management, LLC, Aristeia Capital LLC, Mackay Shields Financial Corporation. Iridium Official Unsecured Creditors' Committee: represented official committee of unsecured creditors in chapter 11 cases of the Iridium companies, a failed satellite enterprise involving over $3 billion in debt; KTB&S served as special litigation counsel to investigate and prosecute claims against Iridium's lenders; successfully negotiated a settlement for unsecured creditors in excess of $50 million. Maxicare Official Unsecured Creditors' Committee: represent official committee of unsecured creditors in chapter 11 case of major health maintenance organization. Paramount Studios/Viacom: major creditor in the Kmart, Carmike, Edwards Cinemas, General Cinemas and United Artists Theater bankruptcies; creditor and purchaser in Weststar (Mann Theaters) chapter 11 cases. Prandium, Inc.: represent an informal group of bondholders holding a majority of approximately $120 million (principal plus interest) in outstanding bonds in connection with pre-packaged chapter 11 restructuring; company engaged in the operation of restaurants in the full-service and fast-casual industry segments. ZiLOG, Inc.: represent an informal group of secured bondholders holding approximately $157 million of $280 million in outstanding bonds in connection with prepackaged chapter 11 restructuring; company designs, manufactures and markets semiconductor micro devices.

EQUITY HOLDERS: 203 North LaSalle Street Limited Partnership and Related Entities: represented investors under chapter 11 reorganization plan on remand from the United States Supreme Court in the case of 203 North LaSalle Street Partnership; subsequent plan successfully confirmed. Einstein/Noah Bagel Corporation: represented Gerald K. Smith, Trustee for the Boston Chicken Plan Trust, in the chapter 11 case filed by Einstein/Noah Bagel Corporation and Einstein/Noah Bagel Partners, L.P. Transpacific Enterprises, Inc.: represent the Joint Administrators of Ansett Holdings, Ltd., the sole shareholder of Transpacific Enterpises, Inc., a full service airline support company. Pittsburgh Penguins: represented a significant shareholder in the Pittsburgh Penguins hockey team, in connection with the chapter 11 case of that team.

ACQUIRERS AND OTHERS: The Century Trust: purchaser of real estate assets in chapter 11 case of Trancas Town Ltd. Crusader Entertainment: acquirer of intellectual properties out of the Red Fern bankruptcy. GAP / Old Navy: purchaser in the Loehman's, Service Merchandise, Lauriat's, Crowley's, Steinbachs, and Caldor chapter 11 cases. The Lusk Company: landlord in numerous chapter 11 cases. Paramount Pictures and Affiliates: creditor and purchaser of the Mann Theatre chain. Starwood Ceruzzi LLC and Vornado Realty LLC: purchaser in Hechingers chapter 11 case.

LEADING LAW FIRMS

KRAMER LEVIN NAFTALIS & FRANKEL LLP

THE FIRM

Managing Partner: Paul S Pearlman

Number of partners: 85
Number of other lawyers: 194

HEAD OFFICE

NEW YORK
919 Third Avenue, **New York**, NY 10022
Tel: 212 715 9100 **Fax:** 212 715 8000
Website: www.kramerlevin.com

CONTACTS

Corporate	Scott S Rosenblum
Creditors' Rights & Bankruptcy	Kenneth H Eckstein
Employee Benefits	Michael J Nassau
Employment & Labor	Kevin B Leblang
Environmental	Richard G Leland
Individual Clients	John C Novogrod
Intellectual Property & Technology	Nicholas L Coch
Land Use	Samuel H Lindenbaum
Litigation	Gary P Naftalis
Paris Office	Alexander Marquardt
Real Estate	Jay A Neveloff
Tax	Howard J Rothman

FIRM OVERVIEW: Kramer Levin Naftalis & Frankel LLP is a world-class, full-service law firm with offices in New York and Paris. It also has a long standing affiliation with the Studio Santa Maria firm in Italy and a new alliance with UK-based Berwin Leighton Paisner. The firm's strong focus on client service has helped it to build long-term relationships with major corporations, institutions and individuals who look to it for innovative and practical solutions. Kramer Levin's counsel has guided entrepreneurs and growing businesses across a range of industries to fully realize their goals. As a leading practitioner in its fields, Kramer Levin applies its broad expertise and experience to help its clients get the results they need. With more than 280 attorneys in 20-plus practice areas, Kramer Levin has the deep knowledge and expertise to provide a full range of innovative legal solutions. As the firm grows, it continues to draw on the qualities that have fueled its earliest successes: a single-minded commitment to excellence, an entrepreneurial spirit and a dynamic yet practical approach to achieving superior results for its clients.

MAIN AREAS OF PRACTICE:

Corporate: Handles virtually every type of complex corporate and securities transaction from public offerings and private placements to mergers, acquisitions, dispositions and joint ventures, while also providing the full range of general corporate law services from contract preparation to strategic counseling. The department regularly represents companies large and small, domestic and foreign, public and private, mature and entrepreneurial in cutting-edge as well as conventional transactions.

Creditors' Rights & Bankruptcy: The Creditors' Rights and Bankruptcy practice, one of the nation's foremost, has played a central role in many of the country's largest and most complex reorganizations. Working closely with the firm's other departments, this diverse practice includes representation of creditors' committees, debtors, banks, bondholders, trade creditors, landlords, investors, debtor-in-possession lenders and acquirors as well as investors in the purchase and sale of securities and assets of troubled companies.

Intellectual Property & Technology Law: Handles all aspects of intellectual property law - patents, trademarks, copyrights, trade secrets, technology transfer, unfair competition and false advertising, Internet and new media. Attorneys in this full-service department provide litigation, prosecution and registration, counseling and transactional services to their clients to help them acquire, value, maintain, protect and exploit all forms of intellectual property.

Litigation: From the its start in 1968, Kramer Levin has specialized in the litigation of high-profile, high-stakes commercial cases. The firm's White Collar Criminal Defense and SEC Regulatory group is one of the nation's most prominent. The Litigation Department is chaired by Gary P. Naftalis, one of the country's leading trial lawyers, and numbers over 60 lawyers. Litigation Department attorneys work in virtually every area of commercial litigation. Such expertise spans the following practice areas: antitrust; appellate and constitutional litigation; bankruptcy litigation; commercial litigation; employment and labor; ERISA litigation; insurance litigation; international dispute resolution; real estate litigation; securities and shareholder litigation; trademark, copyright and white collar criminal defense.

Real Estate: The Real Estate Department's attorneys have extensive experience analyzing and applying all the relevant law—real estate, corporate, environmental, land use, restructuring and tax—to deliver creative, cost-effective and practical legal and business solutions. The department has the size, knowledge, experience and dedication to assist on the full array of real property matters including office, residential, industrial, hotel and retail property development, acquisitions and sales; financings and refinancings; workouts and restructuring transactions for lenders, borrowers, and equity participants; retail and office and industrial leasing; joint ventures; structured finance sales/leasebacks; the conversion of new and existing commercial and residential properties to condominium and cooperatives uses; and zoning.

CLIENTS: Kramer Levin has played key roles in developing entrepreneurial successes in industries as diverse as fashion and cosmetics, telecommunications, and financial services. Today, many of Kramer Levin's clients are Fortune 500 companies that continue to look to the firm for creative solutions for their rapidly changing needs.

INTERNATIONAL WORK: Through its Paris office, Kramer Levin offers clients the benefits of a full-service legal practice based in Europe. The firm's Paris-based attorneys assist domestic and foreign clients with a wide variety of corporate matters, including mergers and acquisitions, corporate securities and finance, banking law, structured financings and securitizations, reorganizations and bankruptcies, complex real estate matters, employment law, and foreign investment. The firm also represents clients in all types of business litigation before French courts and in international arbitrations. Moreover, working with long-standing affiliate, Studio Santa Maria, with offices in Milan and Rome, the firm regularly advises Italian-based clients regarding their activities in the United States, and counsels U.S. and other clients investing or doing business in Italy. Kramer Levin's new alliance with UK-based Berwin Leighton Paisner, further strengthens its ability to provide truly superior global representation. The UK-based alliance focuses on cross-border corporate and finance matters, and on some of the firm's other highly regarded practice areas including: real estate, litigation, intellectual property and technology, bankruptcy and tax.

KUMMER KAEMPFER BONNER & RENSHAW

THE FIRM

Managing Partner: Michael J Bonner

Number of partners: 13
Number of other lawyers: 20

AREAS OF PRACTICE:
Corporate/Real Estate/Transactional/SEC & Gaming 37%
Commercial/Complex Litigation 37%
Governmental Affairs/Zoning/Land Use/Licensing 26%

HEAD OFFICE

NEVADA
3800 Howard Hughes Parkway, Seventh Floor, **Las Vegas**, NV 89109-0907
Tel: 702 792 7000   **Fax:** 702 796 7181
Email: info@kkbr.com
Website: www.kkbr.com

FIRM OVERVIEW: The firm is a prominent force in the dynamic and fast-growing Las Vegas Metropolitan and Southern Nevada region. It serves a diverse group of local, regional, national and international clients, including business organizations, institutions, private individuals and non-profit organizations. Founded in 1994, the law firm of Kummer Kaempfer Bonner & Renshaw was originally the Las Vegas office of another long-established statewide firm. The firm's attorneys include a former United States Congressman, a former general counsel of one of southern Nevada's largest and most successful real estate developers, and a former Deputy Secretary of State, Nevada Securities Division. Firm attorneys are active members of committees of the State Bar of Nevada, participate in the drafting of new business legislation, and are sought after as lecturers on local, regional and national legal topics.

MAIN AREAS OF PRACTICE:

Corporate/Real Estate/Transactional/Securities & Gaming: KKB&R's attorneys are recognized to be among the best corporate and transactional lawyers in Nevada and have participated in a broad range of complex business transactions including merger and acquisition matters. The firm has the premier Nevada-based practice in federal and state securities law representation and has handled initial public offerings, private and public debt and equity securities offerings, development stage and venture capital financings and a broad range of corporate and business entity counseling and representation for issuers, underwriters, lenders and investors. KKB&R has represented owners, developers, tenants and financiers in a multitude of real estate transactional and financing matters and has significant experience in drafting and negotiating agreements for a variety of clients, projects and industries. The firm counsels clients on personal and entity tax issues in a broad range of business matters. KKB&R has represented clients in all aspects of Nevada's gaming regulatory matters including license and disciplinary proceedings.

Commercial/Complex Litigation: KKB&R's trial and appellate attorneys have reputations for litigation excellence. Litigation areas include professional responsibility litigation (including attorney and accountant liability), alternative dispute resolution, employment litigation, business disputes, administrative and regulatory matters, construction litigation, general insurance litigation (including coverage issues), securities litigation, real estate litigation, and receivership.

Governmental Relations, Zoning, Land Use & Licensing: KKB&R is the leading law firm in the Las Vegas Metropolitan area representing developers and other businesses before governmental bodies on licensing, planning, zoning, and building matters. The firm's legislative affairs team provides select clients with legislative representation before the Nevada State Legislature. The firm also has affiliate relationships in Washington, DC for federal legislative and administrative representation.

Meritas: KKB&R is the Las Vegas, Nevada member firm of Meritas, an international affiliation of business law firms. Meritas is a worldwide alliance consisting of 4885 lawyers in 183 business law firms located in 61 countries around the world, each working together to provide clients the best of both worlds: a local legal partner with deep international resources. The alliance has a 12-year record of successful co-operation, offering clients the ability to access high quality legal service worldwide supported by a common technology platform. Membership is by invitation only and firms are subject to a rigorous selection and ongoing monitoring process. (www.meritas.org)

CLIENTS: Clients include Astoria Homes; Boyd Gaming Corporation; Camco, Inc; Chelsea Property Group; Exxon-Mobil Corporation; Herbst Gaming, Inc; Inamed Corporation; Kinder Morgan Energy Partners, LP; Lamar Advertising; Marnell Corrao Associates, Inc; Marshall Management Company; Molasky Companies; Monarch Casino & Resorts, Inc; Nevada Development Authority; Pulte Homes; Reading International, Inc; Republic Services of Southern Nevada; USA Capital, Inc.

LAMBERTH, CIFELLI, STOKES & STOUT, P.A.

THE FIRM

Managing & Senior Partner: J Michael Lamberth

Number of partners: 8
Number of other lawyers: 6

AREAS OF PRACTICE:

Corporate Reorganization & Bankruptcy	82%
Business & Commercial Litigation	7%
Commercial Real Estate	5%
Domestic Relations	3%
Corporate & General Business	3%

HEAD OFFICE

GEORGIA
Atlanta Financial Center, 3343 Peachtree Road, NE, East Tower
Suite 550, **Atlanta**, GA 30326-1022
Tel: 404 262 7373 **Fax:** 404 262 9911
Email: cls@lcsslaw.com
Website: www.lcsslaw.com

CONTACTS

Corporate Reorganization & Bankruptcy	J Michael Lamberth
Domestic Relations	Gary D Stokes
Corporate & General Business	Carter L Stout
Business & Commercial Litigation	Stuart F Clayton
Commercial Real Estate	Carter L Stout

FIRM OVERVIEW: Lamberth, Cifelli, Stokes & Stout, P.A., a professional association organized in 1972, is engaged in a general civil practice, with emphasis and concentrations in the areas of creditors' rights, bankruptcy and insolvency law, business reorganization, general business, commercial real estate, and trial and appellate practice.

MAIN AREAS OF PRACTICE:

Corporate Reorganization & Bankruptcy: Within the framework of its creditor/debtor law and bankruptcy practice, the firm has substantial experience in the representation of trustees, state court receivers, Chapter 11 debtors, creditors' committees, and other fiduciaries in business bankruptcy cases. Members of the firm have served as Chapter 11 and Chapter 7 Trustees and state court receivers.

Domestic Relations: The firm represents clients in all domestic matters, such as divorce and separation proceedings, custody and support contests, and negotiation of prenuptial agreements.

Corporate & General Business: The firm's business practice provides quality and cost effective business and legal advice to privately held businesses focusing on improving profitability by increasing revenues, lowering expenses, effectively managing risk and legal administration. The firm assists in all aspects of a privately held business including: choosing the appropriate legal entity and capital structure, employer-employee relations, business succession planning, purchase or sale of a business, protecting intellectual property, negotiating and drafting general agreements with suppliers, customers, and landlords, and legal administration.

Business & Commercial Litigation: The firm regularly represents clients in a wide variety of litigation matters involving commercial disputes in federal and state trial and appellate courts throughout Georgia.

Commercial Real Estate: The firm has a substantial transactional practice in commercial real estate matters, such as the purchase and sale of real property, drafting of contracts and leases, foreclosure of real property, and documentation of real estate transactions. The firm is an agent for Lawyers Title Insurance Corporation.

CLIENTS: The firm's clients include troubled businesses engaged in non-judicial workouts, Chapter 11 debtors-in-possession, Chapter 7 and 11 trustees, creditors' committees, secured and unsecured creditors, and equity interests in significant business bankruptcies, state and federal court receivers, and other fiduciaries. Clients also include small businesses and parties to commercial, business and domestic litigation. The firm served as primary debtor counsel to Hays Microcomputer Products, Inc, First American Health Care, Inc., World Access, Inc., Tennessee Chemical Company, and Colorocs, Inc., represented the Chapter 11 trustee in All American of Ashburn, Inc., RDM Sports Group, Inc., and Brown Transport, Inc., and represented committees in WWG Industries, Inc., Lewis Carpet Mills, Inc., and Southmark, Inc.

LEADING LAW FIRMS

LATHAM & WATKINS LLP

THE FIRM

Managing Partner: Robert M Dell
Number of partners worldwide: 428
Number of other lawyers worldwide: 1123

Website: www.lw.com
Email: webmaster@lw.com

FIRM OVERVIEW: Named 'International Law Firm of the Year' at the Chambers Global Awards in 2002, Latham & Watkins has grown to more than 1500 lawyers in 21 offices, including Brussels, Frankfurt, Hamburg, London, Milan, Moscow, Paris, Hong Kong, Singapore and Tokyo. Latham is divided into five departments: Corporate; Environment, Land & Resources; Finance & Real Estate; Litigation; and Tax, with lawyers also working interdepartmentally in practice groups, such as insolvency and project finance. From its very beginnings in Los Angeles in 1934, Latham's founders instilled an ethic of hard work, commitment and quality that flourishes today and has nurtured the firm's dramatic growth from a 42-lawyer Los Angeles firm in 1969 into one of the world's premier business law firms. Today, the firm is one of the 15 largest law firms in the world.

MAIN AREAS OF PRACTICE:

Antitrust & Competition: Latham's practice is comprehensive in discipline – from mergers and acquisitions to litigation, dominance investigations, cartel enforcement, counseling, joint ventures and criminal grand jury matters. Latham lawyers have analyzed antitrust issues in nearly every aspect of business for hundreds of clients ranging from technology start-ups to *Fortune* 50 corporations. The firm's lawyers regularly conduct antitrust audits, prepare antitrust compliance programs and provide day-to-day counseling advice on distribution matters, pricing, intellectual property licensing strategies, joint venture formation and every other significant antitrust issue.

Capital Markets & Finance: Latham & Watkins has been involved in equity and debt financings for companies in the US, Asia, Europe and Latin America. The firm has served as legal counsel in public and private offerings totaling billions of dollars in a number of currencies. Latham lawyers represent underwriters, borrowers and issuers in high yield and senior debt deals that have financed a wide variety of transactions, including management buyouts, strategic acquisitions, leveraged recapitalisations, refinancings and capital expansion projects. The firm also provides strategic legal counsel to emerging and later-stage companies in the technology industry – as well as investment banks, venture capital firms and other entities that service such companies.

Energy: Latham's Energy Industry Practice Group focuses on the regulation of the energy industry and its markets for the firm's clients involved in electric generation and transmission, gas transportation, electric and gas marketing, and investment and commercial banking. The group handles regulatory policy and legislative matters on behalf of electric and gas utilities, producers and power marketers. Latham lawyers have negotiated and drafted innovative gas and electric interconnection and power purchase/sale and tolling agreements and have a solid background in project development. The firm's attorneys have been involved in the development and implementation of market rules and governance structures in most of the new electric markets throughout the country.

Environment, Land & Resources: Latham & Watkins has one of the preeminent environmental, land and resources practices in the United States, possessing experience in all aspects of environmental, energy, land and resources law, including counseling, administrative proceedings, litigation, enforcement, and legislative matters relating to all of the major environmental laws. The firm's attorneys provide advice and representation in environmental matters ranging from permitting, compliance, agency rule-making and legislation, to enforcement actions and litigation under all of the major environmental statutes. These clients represent a broad range of industries, including power producers, chemicals, electronics, motor vehicles, aerospace, pharmaceuticals, forest products, healthcare, oil, waste management and disposal, alternative energy, printing and others.

Intellectual Property & Technology: Latham represents individual and corporate clients in transactions and disputes involving trademarks, copyrights, patents, domain names, counterfeiting, rights of privacy, trade secrets, internet liability, unfair competition and false advertising claims, as well as publicity and multimedia rights. The firm's transactional experience includes the registration, licensing, sale, acquisition and secured financing of complex intellectual property rights. Latham lawyers also have significant expertise in network security, including protecting companies' assets on the web, preventing the online theft of intellectual property and responding to hacker intrusion and other cybercrimes.

Litigation & Arbitration: Latham & Watkins has been recognized by the largest and most sophisticated corporations in the United States as one of

US OFFICES

CALIFORNIA
633 West Fifth Street, Suite 4000, **Los Angeles**, CA 90071-2007
Tel: 213 485 1234   **Fax:** 213 891 8763

650 Town Center Drive, 20th Floor, **Costa Mesa**, CA 92626-1925
Tel: 714 540 1235   **Fax:** 714 755 8290

135 Commonwealth Drive, **Menlo Park**, CA 94025-1105
Tel: 650 328 4600   **Fax:** 650 463 2600

701 B Street, Suite 2100, **San Diego**, CA 92101-8197
Tel: 619 236 1234   **Fax:** 619 696 7419

505 Montgomery Street, Suite 1900, **San Francisco**, CA 94111-2562
Tel: 415 391 0600   **Fax:** 415 395 8095

ILLINOIS
Sears Tower, Suite 5800, 233 South Wacker Drive, **Chicago**, IL 60606-6401
Tel: 312 876 7700   **Fax:** 312 993 9767

MASSACHUSETTS
Riverside Centre, 275 Grove Street, 4th Floor, Newton, **Boston**, MA 02466
Tel: 617 663 5700   **Fax:** 617 663 5319

NEW JERSEY
One Newark Center, 16th Floor, **Newark**, NJ 07101-3174
Tel: 973 639 1234   **Fax:** 973 639 7298

NEW YORK
885 Third Avenue, Suite 1000, **New York**, NY 10022-4802
Tel: 212 906 1200   **Fax:** 212 751 4864

VIRGINIA
11400 Commerce Park Drive, Suite 200, **Reston**, VA 20191-1549
Tel: 703 390 0900   **Fax:** 703 390 0901

WASHINGTON
555 Eleventh Street, NW, Suite 1000, **Washington**, DC 20004-1304
Tel: 202 637 2200   **Fax:** 202 637 2201

INTERNATIONAL OFFICES

The firm also has offices in Belgium, France, Germany, Hong Kong, Italy, Japan, Russia, Singapore and the United Kingdom.

LEADING LAW FIRMS

LATHAM & WATKINS LLP cont'd

the best litigation practices, offering outstanding expertise and service in a multitude of substantive fields around the world. With over 400 litigators, broken into several interdisciplinary practice groups, Latham has a sizable team of trial lawyers with the depth, breadth and geographic proximity necessary to handle any matter efficiently and effectively.

Mergers & Acquisitions: Latham advises clients on all phases of M&A, including crafting anti-takeover strategies, responding to acquisition offers, arranging public and private financing and cross-border transactions. Latham handled over $122 billion in mergers and acquisitions in 2001, representing principal entities or financial advisors in both public and private transactions. In 2002, Latham acted on some of the largest deals in the world, including Amgen's $16 billion biotech acquisition of Immunex and The Carlyle Group and Welsh, Carson's $7.05 billion buyout of QwestDex. The firm combines US, UK, German and French corporate and finance law expertise in Europe and offers US, UK, Hong Kong and Japanese qualified lawyers in its Asian offices. The firm also has Italian, Russian, Spanish and Scandinavian M&A experience.

Project Finance: Latham has handled the development and financing of large infrastructure projects in the US, Middle East, Africa, Asia and Latin America. The firm's internationally recognized practice represents project lenders and developers in all phases of project development. In the past year, Latham advised the lenders on the $1.8 billion trio of Genholdings I, LLC projects in the US, sponsored by National Energy group, and acted for the lenders on the $400 million Conectiv Bethlehem energy project in the US. Latham is advising both the Renminbi and US dollar lenders on the Nanhai petrochemical complex in China, one of the largest Sino-foreign projects in history with a required investment of $4 billion. Latham attorneys are experienced in dealing with the variety of legal issues that arise in project financings, including matters of energy and environmental law, corporate and public finance, tax, banking and real estate law.

Real Estate: Latham has been involved in numerous landmark real estate developments across the US. Latham lawyers assist in the purchase and sale of all types of real estate, from unimproved land to fully improved and occupied projects. Latham lawyers advise institutional investors, project developers and companies on all areas of construction and real estate law. Work has included structuring complex transactions and providing representation with regard to acquisitions, dispositions, project and construction financings, securitisation, restructurings and recapitalisations, joint ventures and real estate syndications for projects of all types.

Restructuring/Insolvency: Latham offers a full range of services in bankruptcy proceedings, workouts and restructurings, both pre and post-petition. The firm has represented creditors' committees, major secured and unsecured creditors, and debtors in a wide range of bankruptcy proceedings in the US, Asia and Europe. Internationally recognized partners lead teams throughout Latham's global network, working on some of the largest bankruptcies in history, including advising creditors in the current Enron and WorldCom bankruptcies. In addition to the firm's traditional bankruptcy practice, Latham has played significant roles in many major pre-packaged bankruptcies.

Securities & Professional Liability: Latham has one of the most comprehensive securities litigation defense practices in the nation, representing clients in class action securities fraud matters, derivative litigation, insider trading cases, SEC investigations and enforcement proceedings, stock exchange investigations and battles for corporate control. Collectively, Latham attorneys in this group have handled more than 1000 such cases in the last decade alone. The firm's attorneys manage all aspects of the defense in securities investigations, enforcement proceedings and litigation, for clients such as *Fortune* 500 companies, Wall Street securities and underwriting firms, and major accounting firms.

Tax: Latham counsels a wide array of businesses and individuals with respect to federal, state, local and international tax issues. The firm's business clients include corporations, limited liability companies, partnerships, REITs and other pass-through entities, and financial institutions, such as banks, insurance companies, LBO and venture capital firms and financial advisory firms. The firm's Controversy Practice includes audits, administrative appeals and judicial proceedings in federal and state trial courts and appellate courts. The Department's members possess a thorough knowledge of IRS litigation policy and practice. Latham attorneys in the US, UK, France and Germany can handle tax issues in all phases of M&A, disposition, financing and restructuring activities. The attorneys have experience in all major types of direct investment into the US and have developed a wide variety of innovative structures for investing in US businesses and real estate.

Telecommunications: Latham is a global leader in all aspects of communications law, including telecommunications, mobile services, such as cellular telephone and personal communications service; satellites; mass media technologies, such as radio and television broadcasting as well as cable television; information services; multimedia; and emerging technologies. The firm has advised clients on investment opportunities and regulatory reform in countries throughout the world. Recently, the firm advised Lockheed Martin Global Telecommunications (LMGT) in the privatization of Intelsat, estimated at US$6 billion. LMGT is the largest shareholder of the new company. Latham also advised the lead arrangers in the EURO 1.1 billion financing for ONO, Spain's largest integrated broadband services provider.

White Collar Defense: Latham & Watkins has one of the largest teams of white collar/business crime specialists with vast experience conducting high stakes internal investigations, defending against enforcement actions and representing clients in a broad array of criminal and parallel civil trials. The attorneys bring a wealth of knowledge and insight into the inner workings of government investigative, regulatory and prosecutive agencies. Having conducted hundreds of investigations both inside and outside of government, the members of the White Collar Practice Group are particularly skilled at devising and conducting internal investigations to assist clients in defending against enforcement matters and/or criminal prosecutions. The group has handled numerous enterprise-threatening criminal and quasi-criminal matters involving a wide array of substantive areas including antitrust, securities fraud, healthcare fraud, tax and financial fraud, bribery (both US and international), government procurement fraud, computer fraud and environmental crimes, just to name a few.

LEADING LAW FIRMS

LATHROP & RUTLEDGE

THE FIRM

Managing Partner: J Kent Rutledge
Senior Partner: Carl L Lathrop

Number of partners: 4
Number of other lawyers: 2

AREAS OF PRACTICE:
Professional Litigation	40%
Commercial Litigation	30%
Other Litigation	10%
Employment Law	10%
Business Law	5%
Wills, Trusts & Estates	5%

HEAD OFFICE

WYOMING
1920 Thomes Avenue, Suite 500, PO Box 4068, **Cheyenne**, WY 82003
Tel: 307 632 0554 **Fax:** 307 635 4502
Email: mail@lathropandrutledge.com

CONTACTS
All Areas .... J Kent Rutledge

FIRM OVERVIEW: Lathrop & Rutledge, PC is the successor to Lathrop & Lathrop, which was established in 1958. The firm is engaged in the general civil practice of law. Most of the firm's practice is devoted to litigation in all state and federal courts in Wyoming. The firm is listed in numerous legal directories and both the firm's managing and senior partners have been recognised by a leading legal publication.

MAIN AREAS OF PRACTICE:
Litigation: The firm handles a wide variety of litigation and administrative proceedings in all of the state courts and in the federal courts in Wyoming. The firm has represented clients in matters involving commercial disputes (for example, The City of Cheyenne, Board of Public Utilities v The Polo Ranch Company, et al); corporate disputes, including issues of corporate governance (including Safecard Services Inc., v Peter Halmos et al.); insurance coverage disputes and bad faith claims (including Sinclair Oil Corporation v Republic Insurance Company); professional negligence and/or licensing claims against physicians, hospitals, chiropractors, architects and engineers; defense and prosecution of personal injury claims, including oil field accidents, automobile and truck collisions, construction accidents, and toxic tort claims; defense and prosecution of wrongful termination, discrimination and other employment claims; and bankruptcy. Members of the firm also have substantial experience in alternative dispute resolutions, including mediation and arbitration.
Business Law: The firm has established and provided on-going legal services as general counsel for corporations, limited liability companies, partnerships, and limited partnerships.
Employment Law: The firm provides advice to its business clients concerning employment matters, and has represented clients in administrative hearings as well as litigation concerning employment matters.
Wills, Trusts & Estates: The firm drafts wills and trusts and represents clients in the probate and administration of estates.

CLIENTS: The firm is general counsel for: Cheyenne Medical Specialists, P.C.; Cheyenne Newspapers, Inc.; Emergency Medical Physicians, P.C.; Wyoming Hospital Association; National Intercollegiate Rodeo Association. Insurance clients of the firm include: Amica Mutual Insurance Company; CIGNA Cos. (P&C Group); The Cincinnati Insurance Companies; Continental General Ins. Co.; CUMIS Insurance Society, Inc.; The GAINSCO Companies; Health Care Indemnity Inc.; Infinity Insurance Company; The Doctors' Company; National Chiropractic Mutual Insurance Co.; OHIC Insurance Company; Omaha Property & Casualty; Republic Ins. Co.; Underwriters Indemnity Co.; United States Life Insurance Company; and Zurich Insurance.

INTERNATIONAL WORK: The firm has provided legal services in litigation matters as well as business matters for foreign clients.

LEADING LAW FIRMS

LEBOEUF, LAMB, GREENE & MACRAE, L.L.P.

THE FIRM

Co-Chairmen: Steven H Davis, Peter R O'Flinn
Number of partners: 224
Number of other lawyers: 496

FIRM OVERVIEW: LeBoeuf, Lamb, Greene & MacRae, L.L.P. has lawyers practicing in 14 US offices and in 10 other cities acround the globe. Well known as one of the preeminent legal services providers to the insurance/financial services and energy and utilities industries, the firm has built upon these strengths to gain prominence in corporate, litigation, bankruptcy, international, environmental, taxation, information technology/intellectual property and real estate practice.

MAIN AREAS OF PRACTICE:

Insurance: LeBoeuf has been widely recognized as a leading legal advisor to the insurance industry for the past four decades. Its practice covers every segment of the insurance industry, with an impressive depth of resources and experience. This depth has enabled the firm to develop strong working relationships with major insurers, brokers, investment bankers, commercial bankers, regulators, legislators, actuaries and other service providers to the insurance industry.

Energy: LeBoeuf represents energy and utility suppliers in all aspects of their business. More than 100 LeBoeuf attorneys devote the bulk of their time to providing services that touch upon the energy, telecommunications and water industries, making LeBoeuf a recognized leader in the energy and utilities legal practice worldwide.

Corporate: LeBoeuf's corporate practice consists primarily of mergers and acquisitions, public and private securities offerings, private equity and venture capital transactions, securitizations, derivatives and investment management.

Litigation: Litigation is one of the firm's largest practice groups, with more than 150 litigators worldwide. Clients most often call upon the firm to litigate matters that are complex, high-profile and time sensitive. LeBoeuf regularly appears before courts of original and appellate jurisdiction throughout the world on the local, state/provincial and national levels, sometimes in multijurisdictional disputes. It prosecutes and defends civil claims, and defends against criminal allegations.

Bankruptcy & Restructuring: LeBoeuf has one of the largest and most accomplished bankruptcy and restructuring practices in the United States. With more than 20 highly experienced lawyers practicing in the area on a full-time basis, the firm offers top-quality service in this specialized field of law.

Technology & Intellectual Property: LeBoeuf combines its expertise in intellectual property law with a multidisciplinary approach and multinational coverage to devise creative and efficient methods of acquiring, protecting and exploiting intellectual property rights on a global basis. For nearly 20 years, LeBoeuf attorneys have provided legal advice to technology clients.

Tax: LeBoeuf's tax practice is broad-based, reflecting the diversified nature of the firm's practice and experience in many subspecialty areas. The firm counsels clients on a variety of sophisticated tax issues.

Executive Compensation, Employee Benefits & ERISA: LeBoeuf has developed a comprehensive practice in employee benefits and executive compensation, reaching a clientele with the same broad scope and range as that of the firm as a whole.

Environmental, Health & Safety: LeBoeuf has developed a substantial environmental, health and safety (EHS) practice to counsel regulated business operations and support merger, acquisition and divestiture strategies.

Telecommunications: Since the 1970s, LeBoeuf has been engaged in representing clients in the telecommunications field. While the firm's practice in this area is centered in its Washington, DC office, its telecommunications work is truly national and international in character, often crossing borders and oceans as its clients expand and their legal needs grow, to combine its telecommunications expertise with local insight in numerous markets.

Real Estate, Trusts & Estates: LeBoeuf also has significant real estate and trusts and tax practices.

HEAD OFFICE

NEW YORK
125 West 55th Street, **New York**, NY 10019
Tel: 212 424 8000 **Fax:** 212 424 8500
Email: info@llgm.com **Website:** www.llgm.com

BRANCH OFFICES

NEW YORK
One Commerce Plaza, Suite 2020, 99 Washington Avenue
Albany, NY 12210-2820
Tel: 518 626 9000 **Fax:** 518 626 9010

MASSACHUSETTS
260 Franklin Street, **Boston**, MA 02110-3173
Tel: 617 439 9500 **Fax:** 617 439 0341

COLORADO
633 Seventeenth Street, Suite 2000, **Denver**, CO 80202
Tel: 303 291 2600 **Fax:** 303 297 0422

PENNSYLVANIA
200 North Third Street, Suite 300, P.O. Box 12105
Harrisburg, PA 17108-2105
Tel: 717 232 8199 **Fax:** 717 232 8720

CONNECTICUT
Goodwin Square, 225 Asylum Street, 13th Floor, **Hartford**, CT 06103
Tel: 860 293 3500 **Fax:** 860 293 3555

TEXAS
1000 Louisiana, **Houston**, TX 77002
Tel: 713 287 2000 **Fax:** 713 287 2100

FLORIDA
50 North Laura Street, Suite 2800, **Jacksonville**, FL 32202-3650
Tel: 904 354 8000 **Fax:** 904 353 1673

CALIFORNIA
725 South Figueroa Street, Suite 3100, **Los Angeles**, CA 90017-5404
Tel: 213 955 7300 **Fax:** 213 955 7399

NEW JERSEY
One Riverfront Plaza, **Newark**, NJ 07102-5490
Tel: 973 643 8000 **Fax:** 973 643 6111

PENNSYLVANIA
One Gateway Center, 420 Fort Duquesne Boulevard, Suite 1600
Pittsburgh, PA 15222-1437
Tel: 412 594 2300 **Fax:** 412 594 5237

UTAH
1000 Kearns Building, 136 South Main Street, **Salt Lake City**, UT 84101
Tel: 801 320 6700 **Fax:** 801 359 8256

CALIFORNIA
One Embarcadero Center, **San Francisco**, CA 94111-3619
Tel: 415 951 1100 **Fax:** 415 951 1180

DISTRICT OF COLUMBIA
1875 Connecticut Ave., N.W., Suite 1200, **Washington, DC** 20009-5728
Tel: 202 986 8000 **Fax:** 202 986 8102

INTERNATIONAL OFFICES

The firm also has offices in Almaty, Beijing, Bishkek, Brussels, Johannesburgh, London, Moscow, Paris, Riyadh and Tashkent.

LePATNER & ASSOCIATES LLP

THE FIRM

Managing Partner: Barry B LePatner

Number of partners: 5
Number of other lawyers: 4
Number of design consultants: 2

AREAS OF PRACTICE:
Commercial Litigation & Claims Representation 35%
Construction Contracts 35%
Business Advisory Services 30%

HEAD OFFICE
NEW YORK
101 East 52nd Street, 21st Floor, **New York**, NY 10022
Tel: 212 935 4400 **Fax:** 212 935 4404
Email: blepatner@lepatner.com
Website: www.lepatner.com

CONTACTS
Contracts & Business Advisory Services . . . . .Barry B LePatner

FIRM OVERVIEW: Founded by Barry LePatner in 1980, LePatner & Associates LLP is widely recognized as one of the nation's leading law firms providing business and legal advice affecting the real estate, design and construction industries. On behalf of its many corporate and institutional and commercial real estate clients, the firm provides sophisticated project planning, state of the art contracts and respected advisory services at all levels of today's complex real estate projects.

MAIN AREAS OF PRACTICE:
Construction Contracts: For more than 20 years, the firm has been instrumental in protecting owners' capital investments from pre-construction to lease negotiations and through post-construction claims handling. Seamlessly coordinated construction agreements are specifically tailored to address the business imperatives of each project. The firm's dedicated contract law team provides negotiation services including due diligence of all team members, structuring agreements, contract negotiation with project teams, insurance and bonding compliance and coordination of design/construction scheduling. In the area of coordinated construction contracts, the firm has outstanding expertise.
Business Advisory Services: The firm offers business advisory and consulting services for the design and construction industry from site selection, due diligence and selection of the construction team, project management, applicability of industry laws, regulations and codes, through claims management and handling of warranty issues.
Commercial Litigation & Claims: The firm is widely recognised for its expertise in litigation and arbitration, dispute resolution alternatives, claims analysis and negotiation and claims avoidance strategies.

CLIENTS: The firm's clients represent a spectrum of major commercial and residential property owners, corporations, institutions of higher education, and real estate developers, and includes: Starwood Resorts and Hotels, the Government of Spain, Thirteen.wnet, United Nations Mission in Kosovo, Rosewood Hotels and Resorts, Barnard College, DaimlerChrysler, the Osborn Retirement Community, Asprey Ltd.

INTERNATIONAL WORK: The firm has advised international corporations and foreign government entities operating within the US with regard to their construction projects. In addition to protecting their construction investment, LePatner & Associates guides these clients through the complex maze of government building codes and regulations.

LEADING LAW FIRMS

LEVINE, BLASZAK, BLOCK & BOOTHBY, LLP

THE FIRM

Senior Partner: Henry D Levine

Number of partners: 11
Number of other lawyers: 6

AREAS OF PRACTICE:
Telecom/IT Procurement	60%
Telecom/IT Workouts & Dispute Resolution	20%
Telecom/IT Regulation	20%

HEAD OFFICE
DISTRICT OF COLUMBIA
2001 L Street NW, Suite 900, **Washington, DC** 20036
Tel: 202 857 2550 **Fax:** 202 223 0833
Website: www.lb3law.com

FIRM OVERVIEW: Founded in 1993, Levine, Blaszak, Block & Boothby, LLP (LB3) specializes in communications and technology law, with particular emphasis on the representation of large users, information technology companies, and companies built on new technologies. Its clients include more than 50% of the Fortune 100. LB3 has unparalleled experience in negotiating custom network service agreements, network outsourcings, and related transactions on behalf of large users. In partnership with its consulting affiliate, TechCaliber, LLP, the firm provides its clients with the legal and financial expertise they need to secure leading edge telecom contracts. The firm is also the principal representative of large end users and IT companies before the FCC and other regulators, and before courts and arbitrators when their relationships with communications providers break down. LB3 also advises clients in connection with e-commerce/internet agreements, software licenses, and telecom related acquisitions and securities offerings.

MAIN AREAS OF PRACTICE:

Custom Network Service Agreements: LB3 specializes in the negotiation of custom network service agreements and other complex telecommunications transactions. Such agreements typically involve an array of voice and data services, and may include satellite, internet and network management services as well. The purchase/lease of complex equipment and wireless services may be folded in or negotiated separately. LB3 lawyers pioneered these agreements, and today assist clients in the development of telecom procurement strategies; assist in vendor selection; and negotiate the required contracts.

Network Outsourcing/Managed Network Services: Over the past decade, network service arrangements have evolved to encompass sophisticated management services and the purchase of customer equipment, software licenses and the hiring of customer personnel as part of an agreement under which the customer outsources telecommunications operations and/or management to a third party. LB3 has represented purchasers in many of the largest and most sophisticated telecom outsourcings.

Internet & E-commerce: The firm develops creative and durable frameworks that minimize risk and scale to meet clients' evolving workforces, network topologies, and application platforms. LB3 lawyers have negotiated agreements for internet access, internet protocol multicasting, Virtual Private Networks (VPNs), and voice-over-internet services to support client business requirements. LB3 attorneys have also structured e-commerce transactions ranging from web hosting to application hosting, content management, remote application maintenance, streaming media, co-branding and global portal development. In connection with web services, the firm negotiates software agreements covering applicatons development, implementation and maintenance.

Carrier Purchasers & New Entrants: Carriers have turned to the firm for advice on carrier-to-carrier transport, Indefeasible Rights of Use, and dark fibre agreements. The firm also represents new carriers in negotiating (and arbitrating) interconnection agreements, and provides counsel on regulatory matters, entry strategy, certifications, and communications-related securities issues.

Corporate & IPO Support: The firm frequently works with securities counsel on the telecommunications regulatory or industry-specific portions of SEC filings and prospectuses.

Communications Policy & Regulation: LB3 keeps large users informed of regulatory and legal developments that affect their service acquisition strategies, and represents them in policy proceedings before regulatory and legislative bodies. The firm is known for its ability to penetrate the complex issues spawned by changes in the telecom law and regulations; the growth of competition; the emergence of new technologies; the convergence of IT and communications; and the rise of the internet. The policy debates confronting the information technology industry often raise issues for which there is no precedent. In these areas, the firm has helped to write, not just interpret, the law. The issues in which LB3 has been involved include usage-based charges for internet services; efforts to regulate the internet; competitive deployment of broadband services, cable equipment, wireless internet services; and US digital television standards.

Contract Workouts: Disputes are inevitable, and the firm is a leader in the representation of purchasers in disputes arising out of the terms or termination of their telecom agreements. The firm has been involved in the amicable (or not so amicable) resolution of scores of disputes involving service levels; shortfall penalties; and billing.

FCC Complaints & Litigation: The Communications Act prohibits 'unjust and unreasonable practices' by carriers. The firm's lawyers have broad and deep expertise with claims and complaint proceedings before courts, state regulators and the FCC. The firm's lawyers have also assisted parties and counsel when communications issues arise in areas such as the interpretation of contracts and tariffs; service cost and reliability; and billing disputes, and have served as expert witnesses on such issues in a variety of settings.

CLIENTS: The firm's international clients include General Motors, IBM, DuPont, Merrill Lynch, Pearson, Inc., and the New Zealand Dairy Board.

INTERNATIONAL WORK: The firm has helped a number of the world's largest multinational corporations negotiate contracts to purchase telecommunications and related services on a regional or global basis with reasonable uniformity of terms, appropriate accountability for performance, and due regard for the special regulatory, technical and business challenges posed by these transactions.

LOWENSTEIN SANDLER PC

THE FIRM

Managing Partner: Michael L Rodburg

Number of partners: 63
Number of other lawyers: 127

HEAD OFFICE

NEW JERSEY
Lowenstein Sandler PC, 65 Livingston Avenue, **Roseland** NJ 07068
Tel: 973 597 2500 **Fax:** 973 597 2400
Website: www.lowenstein.com

FIRM OVERVIEW: Lowenstein Sandler, a nationally recognized law firm, has 190 attorneys who provide a full range of legal services to the corporate, financial, industrial and governmental communities. Lowenstein Sandler offers the sophistication and depth of a national law firm, with the personal attention of a smaller firm. The firm's clients range from Fortune 500 corporations to small public and privately held companies. Given the breadth of the firm's practice areas and the collective experience of its attorneys, Lowenstein Sandler can effectively marshal the resources and talent necessary to assist clients with a variety of sophisticated business and legal issues. The firm has a long history of inclusion in a leading legal publication and was recently ranked among New Jersey's top firms in connection with attorney listings. The firm is recognized in a diverse spectrum of legal practices, including bankruptcy, business litigation, corporate, environmental, tax, real estate, and trusts and estates, and has even been ranked number one among New Jersey law firms with the greatest number of corporate and tax attorneys listed. Furthermore, Lowenstein Sandler has been ranked highly (both nationally and at state level) for its pro bono initiatives by, among others, the *New Jersey Law Journal*. It was also recently awarded high rankings for use of technology in a survey carried out by *AmLaw Tech*. Lowenstein Sandler's recent achievements include: the writing of the definitive guides to New Jersey corporate, employment and environmental laws; two of the firm's directors led the teams responsible for drafting the New Jersey Business Corporation Act and the New Jersey Banking Act; two of the firm's directors founded and co-chaired the New Jersey State Bar Association's Securities Litigation & Regulatory Enforcement Committee; several of the firm's directors have been recognized by various publications as leaders in their chosen areas of practice.

Lowenstein Sandler's subsidiary, Issues Management, is consistently ranked as one of the top lawyer-lobbying consulting firms in New Jersey. Issues Management was created to find solutions to complex business problems that fall outside the traditional realm of legal services. Issues Management provides counseling and advocacy to corporate clients in areas ranging from lobbying and regulatory work to communications and marketing. The principals of Issues Management draw on their extensive public policy, legal and governmental backgrounds to bring clients a unique synthesis of talents.

MAIN AREAS OF PRACTICE:

CORPORATE LAW:

Corporate representation has been the primary focus of the firm since its inception. The firm has extensive experience in corporate counseling and transactional work, as well as business reorganizations. The firm's corporate attorneys, through their experience and in-depth knowledge, seek to find creative solutions that allow clients to meet their business objectives. The firm provides a full range of services to corporate clients in connection with: organization and structuring of business entities; initial public offerings and subsequent offerings; general business counseling; mergers and acquisitions; financing transactions; investment management; bankruptcy, reorganization and creditors' rights. Lowenstein Sandler also provides a full range of tax services to the business community, as well as tax and estate planning for individuals.

Representative Corporate Practice Areas: Asset-based lending; banking and financial services; bankruptcy, financial reorganization and creditors' rights; closely held business services; corporate finance; employment law; estate planning and administration; employee benefits and executive compensation; intellectual property; investment management; mergers and acquisitions; mortgage banking; real estate; tax law; technology.

LITIGATION:

The firm's litigation practice represents clients in all stages of litigation (both trial and appellate) in both state and federal courts, as well as before administrative and governmental agencies. Lowenstein Sandler is often chosen by out of state clients embroiled in complex litigation in New Jersey. The skill and experience required in serving this diverse group has helped the firm to establish a sophisticated and national litigation practice. As a result, Lowenstein Sandler has successfully developed several prominent, nationally recognized niche practices in areas such as environmental litigation and toxic tort defense, insurance coverage litigation, securities litigation and white collar criminal defense.

Representative Litigation Practice Areas: Administrative agency litigation; alternative dispute resolution; antitrust and trade regulation; broker-dealer regulation; construction; employment litigation; environmental; insurance coverage; intellectual property litigation; products liability defense; securities; toxic tort; white collar criminal defense.

MARTIN, DISIERE, JEFFERSON & WISDOM LLP

THE FIRM

Senior Partner: Christopher W Martin
Managing Partner: David D Disiere

Number of partners: 7
Number of other lawyers: 17

AREAS OF PRACTICE
Insurance Coverage & Litigation 70%
Appellate 10%
Employment & Labor 10%
Commercial Litigation 10%

FIRM OVERVIEW: Martin, Disiere, Jefferson and Wisdom LLP is a Texas litigation boutique that specializes in first-party insurance lawsuits in Texas, with an emphasis on those suits alleging extra-contractual causes of action or complex coverage claims. The vast majority of the suits the firm handles involve personal or commercial lines insurance claims. The firm also has extensive experience in handling disputes and lawsuits arising out of commercial and professional liability policies including environmental and products coverage issues, primary and excess disputes, and defense/indemnity coverage questions. The firm also has considerable familiarity in defending lawsuits arising out of homeowner policies with particular expertise in SIU claims (including arson, alleged theft) as well as foundation claims allegedly caused by subsurface plumbing leaks. The firm also has extensive experience in UM/UIM value disputes and auto property claims. The firm regularly handles liability disputes arising out of auto, homeowner, commercial and professional policies including Stowers disputes. Additionally, the firm represents life and health insurers in lawsuits arising out of life, major medical, and medicare supplement sales practices, underwriting, and claims. Over the past decade, the firm's lawyers have literally reshaped and redefined the parameters of Texas Insurance Law. The firm handles a wide range of lawsuits from large class-action insurance lawsuits to multi-party coverage disputes, from value dispute auto cases to property loss homeowner claims, and from problematic life insurance claims to pre-existing health claims. For some insurers, the firm also defends third-party claims against their insureds. These third party liability cases usually involve fatalities, mass torts, severe personal injuries, or other catastrophe damage claims. The firm also has considerable expertise in representing employers in a wide variety of employment and labor disputes. In addition to defending labor and employment disputes and lawsuits, the law firm provides advice and consultation to employers on a wide variety of topics including drug testing, hiring and termination practices, RIFs, OSHA investigations and employment training and compliance. The partner in charge of the firm's Labor and Employment Practice, Jack Wisdom, is Board Certified in Labor and Employment Law by the Texas Board of Legal Specialization.

HEAD OFFICE

TEXAS
808 Travis, Suite 1800, **Houston** TX 77002
Tel: 713 632 1700 **Fax:** 713 222 0101
Email: martin@mdjwlaw.com
Website: www.mdjwlaw.com

BRANCH OFFICES

TEXAS
The Littlefield Building, 106 East Sixth Street, Suite 900,
Austin, TX 78701
Tel: 512 322 5757 **Fax:** 512 322 5707
Email: farrell@mdjwlaw.com

CONTACTS

Insurance Coverage & Litigation ....Christopher Martin
Employment Law ....Jack Wisdom
Appellate ....Levon Hovnatanian
Commercial Litigation ....Dale Jefferson

MAIN AREAS OF PRACTICE:

Insurance Coverage & Litigation: The firm is one of the premier first-party coverage and insurance litigation firms in Texas and its lawyers handle coverage matters, extra-contractual suits, and declaratory judgment actions in Texas and in multiple jurisdictions across the country.
Appellate: The firm routinely handles appeals before the Texas Supreme Court, the intermediate appellate courts of Texas, and the Fifth Circuit Court of Appeals.
Employment & Labor: The firm has particular expertise in advising and defending employers in claims alleging discrimination, wrongful discharge, harassment, affirmative action, privacy violations, non-competition agreements, wage and hour disputes, OSHA compliance, Title VII violations, and ADEA compliance.
Commercial Litigation: The firm represents a host of public and private companies in litigation involving business torts, partnership disputes, real estate transactions, First Amendment violations, fiduciary duty claims, and indemnity obligations.

CLIENTS: The firm's clients consist of a wide array of businesses and corporations including some of the largest property, casualty, life and health insurers in the world.

LEADING LAW FIRMS

MAYER, BROWN, ROWE & MAW

THE FIRM

Chairman: Tyrone C Fahner
Managing Partner: Debora de Hoyos
Number of partners in US offices: 338
Number of other lawyers in US offices: 652

AREAS OF PRACTICE:
Litigation & Arbitration	32%
Finance, Banking & Insurance	22%
Corporate & Securities	21%
Tax	9%
Oil, Gas & Real Estate	8%
Antitrust	7%
Other	1%

FIRM OVERVIEW: Mayer, Brown, Rowe & Maw is the sixth largest law firm in the United States and is among the 10 largest law firms in the world - the result of the February 1, 2002, combination between US-based Mayer, Brown & Platt and UK-based Rowe & Maw. Mayer, Brown & Platt was founded in Chicago in 1881 and Rowe & Maw in London in 1895. The combination capped a year of expansion for the firm: since January 2001, the firm had merged with the Paris firm, Lambert & Lee, and the Frankfurt firm, Gaedertz, and had opened a new office in Palo Alto and a trade office in Shanghai. The firm has more than 1,300 lawyers practicing in 13 offices worldwide.

MAIN AREAS OF PRACTICE: The firm handles appellate and litigation, finance, structured bank finance, corporate and M&A, outsourcing, asset securitizations, capital markets and securities, fund management and financial services regulation, commodities and derivatives, international arbitration, global trade.

CLIENTS: Mayer, Brown, Rowe & Maw's newly combined strengths now give the firm strong client bases on both sides of the Atlantic. The legacy US firm serves 65 of the *Fortune* 100 companies and one out of every three US banks, while legacy UK ranked ninth in both the *Financial Times* Stock Exchange 100 Index principal advisors survey and its most-used law firm survey. Firm clients include Abbott Laboratories, Banc One, Bank of America, BASF, Bertelsmann, Brunswick Corporation, Deutsche Bank, Dow Chemical, EMI, General Electric, ICI, Morgan Stanley, Nestlé, Pfizer, Starwood Hotels & Resorts, State Farm Insurance Companies and Unilever.

INTERNATIONAL WORK:

Mega Telecom Contract: Advised Unilever on a €1 billion contract – one of the biggest commercial contracts in UK telecoms history – with British Telecom to manage and develop Unilever's entire global communications infrastructure.
Nestlé Acquisition: Represented Nestlé Holdings, Inc. in its $2.6 billion purchase of all assets of Chef America Inc., the owner of Hot Pockets, Lean Pockets and Croissant Pockets brands of frozen hand-held sandwiches
UK Pop Idol: Represented EMI Recorded Music in one of the UK's biggest record deals with UK pop sensation Robbie Williams. The innovative agreement has EMI involved not only in Mr Williams's recording activities but his touring, publishing and merchandising as well.
DoD Contract Suit: Representing 19 oil companies (including seven of the top 10) in a lawsuit against the US Department of Defense, seeking a combined $2.5 billion for alleged underpayment in military jet fuel contracts during the 1980s and 1990s. The suit alleges that the DoD used illegal pricing methods, which resulted in underpayment of as much as 10 percent between 1985 and 1996.

HEAD OFFICE

ILLINOIS
190 South LaSalle Street, **Chicago**, IL 60603-3441
Tel: 312 782 0600 **Fax:** 312 701 7711
Email: info@mayerbrown.com
Website: www.mayerbrown.com

BRANCH OFFICES

CALIFORNIA
350 South Grand Avenue, 25th Floor, **Los Angeles**, CA 90071-1503
Tel: 213 229 9500 **Fax:** 213 625 0248

555 College Street, **Palo Alto**, CA 94306
Tel: 650 331 2000 **Fax:** 650 331 2060

DISTRICT OF COLUMBIA
1909 K Street, NW, **Washington**, DC 20006-1101
Tel: 202 263 3000 **Fax:** 202 263 3300

NEW YORK
1675 Broadway, **New York**, NY 10019-5820
Tel: 212 506 2500 **Fax:** 212 262 1910

NORTH CAROLINA
214 North Tryon Street, Suite 2400, **Charlotte**, NC 28202
Tel: 704 444 3500 **Fax:** 704 377 2044

TEXAS
700 Louisiana Street, Suite 3600, **Houston**, TX 77002-2730
Tel: 713 221 1651 **Fax:** 713 224 0248

INTERNATIONAL OFFICES

The firm also has offices in Belgium, France, Germany and the United Kingdom, two associated offices in China and an independent correspondent firm in Mexico

Labor Law Headline: Represented Chevron Texaco in its Supreme Court victory in which the Court ruled unanimously in a highly publicized case against a worker with a liver condition who sought to continue employment in a Chevron Texaco refinery where exposure to toxins could further endanger his health.
Capital Merger: Represented ProLogis regarding the distribution of its shares owned by Security Capital as a portion of the merger consideration in Security Capital's merger with GE Capital. Aggregate deal size was $5.5 billion.
Securitization First: Represented Banco do Brasil in the first international securitization by a Brazilian bank. The transaction securitized all of the bank's rights to receive current and future dollar-denominated payments relating to 'payment orders' from US banks. It was selected by Emerging Markets Investor Magazine as the securitization deal of the year.
Fourth Largest REIT: Represented Archstone Communities Trust in its stock-for-stock merger with Charles E Smith Residential Realty. The deal had a transaction value of $3.6 billion, making it the fourth largest REIT in the United States based on total capitalization.
Luxury Apparel: Represented Donna Karan International, Inc., in its merger with LVMH Moet Hennessy-Louis Vuitton.
Largest Online Brokerage: Represented Ameritrade Holding Corporation in its merger agreement with Datek Online Holdings Corp. in an all-stock transaction valued at $1.28 billion – upon closing, the largest online brokerage measured by equity trades per day.
Global Antitrust: Represented BASF Corporation in antitrust work in the US, the UK, the Netherlands, Germany, France and Spain.

LEADING LAW FIRMS

McAFEE & TAFT

THE FIRM

Managing Partner: John N Hermes

Number of partners: 57
Number of other lawyers: 47

AREAS OF PRACTICE:
Business Law	20%
Tax, Estate Planning & Benefits	18%
Litigation	15%
Securities	14%
Labor & Employment	12%
Intellectual Property	10%
Aircraft	6%
Health Care	5%

HEAD OFFICE

OKLAHOMA
Two Leadership Square, 10th Floor, 211 North Robinson **Oklahoma City**, OK 73102-7103
Tel: 405 235 9621 **Fax:** 405 235 0439
Website: www.mcafeetaft.com

CONTACTS
Aircraft	Frank Polk
Business Law	J Michael Nordin
Health Care	Elizabeth Tyrrell
Intellectual Property	Anthony Rahhal
Labor & Employment	Sam Fulkerson
Litigation	Joseph Bocock
Securities	Bruce Crum
Tax, Estate Planning & Benefits	Dee Replogle

MAIN AREAS OF PRACTICE:

Aviation: The firm represents local, national and international clients of all sizes on aviation matters, including documentation of an aircraft transaction and aircraft title and registration matters and aircraft title insurance. Because the Federal Aviation Administration is located in Oklahoma City, the firm also assists clients in various aspects of closing aircraft transactions, including searches of the FAA records, acting as escrow agent, conducting closings, and issuing closing and post-closing opinions. The firm also advises clients on related matters, including fractional aircraft transactions, regulations affecting the operation of private and corporate aircraft and structuring transactions to comply with FAA regulations (including the use of trusts).

Business Law: The firm is experienced in all aspects of business transactions in various industries, including acquisitions and mergers, joint ventures and commercial contracts. The firm represents borrowers and creditors in all types of financings and workouts. They represent clients in the acquisition, development, leasing, financing and sale of all types of real estate projects, including office buildings, apartment projects, shopping centers and hotels. They advise clients on the formation, governance and day-to-day operation of corporations, limited partnerships, limited liability companies and other business entities. They advise clients with respect to all aspects of oil, gas and other mineral transactions and operations.

Health Care: The firm is involved in counseling hospitals, hospital systems, physicians, physician groups and other healthcare institutions and facilities with respect to managed care contracting, facilities development or expansion, peer review, medical staff issues, medical-legal-ethical issues and affiliation strategies. In regulatory healthcare practice, the firm routinely counsels and advises clients on the fraud and abuse, Stark, tax and antitrust implications related to joint venture arrangements, investment and ownership arrangements, development of outpatient and ancillary facilities, physician practice mergers and acquisitions, corporate affiliations and physician compensation relationships.

Intellectual Property: The firm represents individual and corporate clients in transactions and disputes involving trademarks, copyrights, patents, domain names, counterfeiting, rights of privacy, trade secrets, internet liability, unfair competition and false advertising claims, as well as publicity and multimedia rights. The firm's transactional experience includes the registration, licensing, sale and acquisition of complex intellectual property rights. The intellectual dispute practice includes trials, appeals and alternate dispute resolution proceedings.

Labor & Employment: The firm represents management in all areas of employment-related law. Its labor practice includes representation of both private sector and public entities in drafting and negotiating labor agreements, resolving labor disputes through arbitration and defending unfair labor practice charges before regulatory agencies. The practice includes design and implementation of preventive workplace practices (e.g., policies, procedures, programs and training), ensuring compliance with state and federal requirements, representation of management before state and federal administrative agencies and litigation of employment claims in state and federal courts. The firm is actively involved in designing workplace arbitration agreements and arbitration of employment-related cases.

Litigation: The firm has represented clients in all types of commercial disputes, including litigation and arbitration involving banking, corporations, partnerships and other business entities, franchises, healthcare, insurance, municipal bonds, divorce, oil and gas, products liability, real estate, securities, tax, trusts, telecommunications, trademarks and patents. They pride themselves in learning the details of their clients' business to provide advice before, during and after disputes.

Securities: The firm advises clients on mergers and acquisitions of private and public entities, public and private offerings of securities, tender offers and other forms of financing involving enterprises engaged in energy, insurance, commercial and mortgage banking, telecommunications, real estate, retailing and technology.

Tax, Estate Planning & Benefits: The firm has long been a leader in providing complex tax advice to the business community and individuals. They provide advice and assistance in connection with all forms of estate and tax planning, including commercial and private transactions, mergers and acquisitions, oil and gas operations, real estate transactions, deferred compensation arrangements, gift and estate planning, post-mortem planning, foreign transactions and state and local tax issues.

CLIENTS: The firm's clients are engaged in aviation, banking, construction, employment, energy, wholesale food distribution, franchising, healthcare, insurance, real estate, services, telecommunications, transportation and a wide range of manufacturing. The firm also represents non-profit organizations including universities and foundations, entrepreneurs and individuals.

MCANDREWS, HELD & MALLOY, LTD.

THE FIRM

Founding Partners: George P McAndrews, John J Held, Timothy J Malloy
Senior Partner: George P McAndrews

Number of lawyers: 73

HEAD OFFICE

ILLINOIS
500 West Madison Street, **Chicago**, Illinois 60661
Tel: 312 775 8000 **Fax:** 312 775 8100
Website: www.mhmlaw.com

FIRM OVERVIEW: McAndrews, Held & Malloy is one of the nation's pre-eminent legal resources for intellectual property and technology matters. The firm's attorneys serve as counsel of choice for companies and institutions ranging from major multinationals and start-ups to world-class colleges and universities. The firm's reputation, founded upon an unparalleled record of litigation successes before juries, as well as in bench trials and ADR proceedings, encompasses a full range of legal services. The firm's attorneys are known for their clear and effective communication skills, expertise and training in engineering and science, their passion for technology law, their command of winning business strategy and their tenaciousness – both inside and outside of the courtroom.

MAIN AREAS OF PRACTICE:
Litigation (Patent, Trademark, Copyright, Antitrust, Trade Secret, Unfair Competition & Other Technology): Includes the firm's primary practice in all areas of intellectual property and complex technology litigation, including jury and bench trials, appeals, practice before the International Trade Commission, as well as ADR proceedings. The firm is strategically located so that its nationwide litigation practice measures up with its coast to coast clientele.
Patent & Trademark Procurement & Portfolio Management: Includes the prosecution of patents (ranging from simple mechanical devices to complex electrical systems) and trademarks, obtaining and maintaining intellectual property assets, and management of overall corporate or institutional holdings.
Patent Interferences: Includes all aspects of these complex, highly specialized proceedings, including pre-interference investigation and patent prosecution.
Trademark Oppositions & Cancellations: Includes all contested administrative proceedings before the Trademark Trial and Appeal Board.
International Practice: Includes all aspects of international intellectual property litigation, foreign prosecution, global transactions, licensing, appeals of patents and trademarks in other jurisdictions, and all issues related to foreign patents.
Intellectual Property/Technology Opinions & Investigations: Includes highly specialized strategic investigations, counsel and opinion analysis.
Due Diligence & M&A Support: Includes merger and acquisition counsel and support involving due diligence processes, investigations regarding asset quality and potential infringements.
Technology Licensing & Joint Ventures: Includes counsel regarding a wide variety of revenue-generating opportunities related to intellectual property holdings.
Technology Transfers & Donations: Includes the donation of intellectual property assets as charitable gifts.

CLIENTS: The firm's clients represent a diverse group of domestic and international clients covering a broad range of technology and proprietary rights. Clients include many leading companies in such diverse industrial and commercial fields as chemical, mechanical, and electrical manufacture, processing and use; such as, cell biology, angioplasty catheters, kidney dialysis equipment, medical imaging, pharmaceuticals, petrochemicals, digital cellular telephony, electronic games, computer memories and other hardware, software, satellite communications, fuel cells, power sources, industrial equipment (from paving equipment through mining equipment through papermaking machinery), printing equipment, sporting goods equipment (such as basketballs, softballs, golf balls and golf clubs), giftware, heating and air-conditioning, measurement instruments, appliances, furniture, aviation, avionics, transportation, confections and foodstuffs, and financial instruments.

McDERMOTT, WILL & EMERY

THE FIRM

Managing Partner: Larry Gerber
Number of partners: 528
Number of other lawyers: 423

FIRM OVERVIEW: McDermott, Will & Emery is an international law firm with more than 925 lawyers in three European and eight US offices. The firm represents a wide range of industrial, financial and commercial enterprises, both publicly and privately held, and is experienced in representing clients before government agencies and committees.

INTERNATIONAL EXPERIENCE: Firm lawyers have been involved in cross-border matters on every continent and in virtually every sector of business. International matters include cross-border mergers and acquisitions; joint ventures; financings; corporate restructuring and reorganizations; the structuring of distributorship, licensing and agency arrangements; the negotiation of commercial contracts; compliance with investment laws; privatization; cross-border tax planning; international litigation and dispute resolution; public law; enviromental; real estate; banking; anti-competition; e-business and intellectual property, acquisitions, dispositions and financings. The firm has represented clients from more than 60 countries, advising on matters in more than 60 countries.

MAIN INTERNATIONAL AREAS OF PRACTICE:
Practice areas include agribusiness; alcohol beverages and products; antitrust and competition; biotech and life sciences; bankruptcy; construction; corporate; responsibility; e-business; employee benefits and pensions; energy; environmental; executive compensation; finance and banking; financial products; food and beverage; health; hospitality; insurance; intellectual property; international; labor and employment; legislative and government relations; mergers and acquisitions; OSHA; pharmaceutical; private clients; product liability and regulation; real estate; securities; sports and entertainment; taxation; technology; telecommunications; transportation; trial; utilities; venture capital/private equity; white collar crime.
Antitrust & Competition: The practice is comprised of approximately 50 lawyers, many of whom have prior government experience with the European Commission, Federal Trade Commission, the Antitrust Division of the Department of Justice or the office of a State Attorney General.
Bankruptcy: The firm represents debtors, trustees and various creditor and equality constituencies on a regular basis, including banks, bondholders, trade creditors, credit corporations and acquirers.
Biotech & Life Sciences: The firm's biotech lawyers have advanced scientific degrees and practical experience as research biologists, biochemist, chemical engineers, pharmaceutical research scientists and regulatory managers. Services include IP, corporate and corporate finance, product regulation and reimbursement, OSHA, environmental, health regulatory, mass tort and products liability, securities, executive compensation, labor/employment, tax, international trade and governmental relations.
Environmental: The practice includes lawyers with substantial governmental and private experience. The firm represents clients in the practical and legal aspects of environmental compliance and liability. Experience includes hazardous wastes, toxic substances, pollution, solid waste, land reclamation, land development, wetlands regulation, storage tank regulation, OSHA, right to know laws and environmental impact statements.
Finance & Banking: The firm has an integrated finance and banking team of more than 70 lawyers, with recognized experience in all areas of US, UK and international corporate finance.
Labor, Employment & OSHA: The practice has considerable experience in all employment-related matters. Its lawyers advise on wrongful and unfair dismissal, executive severance, confidentiality and restrictive covenants,

HEAD OFFICE

ILLINOIS
227 West Monroe Street, **Chicago** IL 60606-5096, USA
Tel: 312 372 2000 Fax: 312 984 7700

Website: www.mwe.com

BRANCH OFFICES

CALIFORNIA
18191 Von Karman Avenue, Suite 1100, **Irvine** CA 92612-0187
Tel: 949 851 0633 Fax: 949 851 9348

2049 Century Park East, 34th Floor, **Los Angeles** CA 90067-3208
Tel: 310 277 4110 Fax: 310 277 4730

3150 Porter Drive, **Palo Alto** CA 94304-1212
Tel: 650 813 5000 Fax: 650 813 5100

DISTRICT OF COLUMBIA
600 13th Street NW, **Washington DC** 20005-3096
Tel: 202 756 8000 Fax: 202 756 8087

FLORIDA
201 South Biscayne Boulevard, **Miami** FL 33131-4336
Tel: 305 358 3500 Fax: 305 347 6500

MASSACHUSSETTS
28 State Street, **Boston** MA 02109-1775
Tel: 617 535 4000 Fax: 617 535 3800

NEW YORK
50 Rockefeller Plaza, **New York** NY 10020-1605
Tel: 212 547 5400 Fax: 212 547 5444

INTERNATIONAL OFFICES

The firm also has offices in Düsseldorf, London and Munich.

breaches of fiduciary duty, fraud by employees, sex/race/disability discrimination, early retirement programs, development of employee manuals, wage-hour compliance, workers' compensation, substance abuse programs, drug testing, equal pay, Working Time Regulations, union recognition and works councils, TUPE, employment aspects of acquisitions and OSHA.
Intellectual Property: The firm's IP lawyers hold degrees in a wide variety of technical and scientific fields and are uniquely capable of handling matters in virtually every technical or scientific discipline. The firm advises on every aspect of IP law. Among these services, the firm's IP practice is renowned for its trial and appellate experience. The IP practice includes client counseling, procurement, and licensing in the patent, trademark, trade dress, copyright, trade secret, entertainment and computer law areas. The firm's IP lawyers undertake all forms of IP litigation and have assisted clients with oppositions in the European Patent Office and the Community Trade Mark Office.
M&A: The firm advises on the purchase, sale and merger of businesses. The firm handles takeovers, acquisitions and disposals, MBOs and MBIs, LBOs and LBIs and reorganisations and restructurings.
White Collar Crime: Many of the lawyers in the firm's white collar crime practice group have served as senior federal prosecutors, including 16 former prosecutors from US Attorney's Offices and the US Department of Justice. The firm has extensive practical experience in a variety of white collar criminal matters, including healthcare, securities, environmental, tax, antitrust, government contracting, commodities and the Foreign Corrupt Practices Act.

LEADING LAW FIRMS

MCGLINCHEY STAFFORD

THE FIRM

Managing Partner: Rodolfo J Aguilar, Jr
Number of partners: 81
Number of other lawyers: 80

AREAS OF PRACTICE:

Commercial Litigation:	31%
Insurance Defense:	19%
Corporate:	14%
Labor & Employment:	9%
Health Care:	6%
Real Estate:	6%
Admiralty:	3%
Public Law:	3%
Collection/Repossession:	2%
Estate/Trust/Probate:	2%
Government/Municipal (other than bond work):	2%
Bankruptcy:	1%
IP:	1%
Tax:	1%

FIRM OVERVIEW: McGlinchey Stafford was founded in New Orleans in 1974 and has grown into one of the largest law firms in the southeastern region of the United States. Attorneys throughout each of the firm's offices work together to maintain a full service commercial and defense practice in various areas of the law and to provide competent, cost-effective service to their clients.

MAIN AREAS OF PRACTICE:

Commercial Litigation: Represents domestic and international business interests; manufacturers; distributors; banks; antitrust and trade regulation laws; pricing and product distribution; dealer terminations; unfair competition; deceptive acts and practices; advertising; patent abuse; franchising; complex multi-district and class action litigation; RICO; Department of Justice and FTC investigations.

Insurance Defense: In-depth understanding of insurance industry; interpreting wide range of insurance policies; high risk, complex insurance and reinsurance coverage issues, bad faith claims, class actions, environmental and toxic torts, product and professional liability, maritime, aviation and medical malpractice.

Corporate: Formation and maintenance of corporations, LLCs, partnerships; business associations; corporate governance; shareholder rights; mergers, acquisitions and divestitures; asset sales and purchases; franchisors and franchisees; regulatory requirements; franchise offering circulars; franchise agreements; commercial law; contracts; purchase and sales agreements; financing documents; employment matters.

Labor & Employment: International reputation representing union and non-union companies in the labor and employment arena. Attorneys advise executives on how to manage their businesses in a variety of ways, all of which culminate in the objective of building successful and constructive employee relations.

Healthcare: One of the largest and most diverse healthcare practices in the South. Represents physicians, hospitals, clinics, HMOs, PPOs, allied healthcare professionals, pharmaceutical device manufacturers and their insurers; general business and compliance matters; licensing; loss control; risk management; acquisitions; joint ventures; financings and reinvestments; certifications and reimbursements; medical staff issues; self-insurance arrangements; draft, monitor and lobby legislation.

Real Estate: Acquisitions and sales; bankruptcy; laws regulating the workplace (including labor practices); uniform commercial code; Americans With Disabilities Act; specialized environmental and zoning laws; structuring of leveraged leases; acquisitions and leveraged buyout financings; letters of credit and other credit enhancement vehicles. Projects include industrial plants and warehouses; multi-family housing; merchant power and cogeneration plants; multi-tenant office buildings and apartment complexes; river boat and other gaming projects; hotel development, including historic tax credit projects; golf course developments; planned unit developments; wireless networks; national restaurant chains; condominium conversions and residential developments; low income housing developments. The firm has its own title insurance agency MACSTAM Title Company, LLC.

CLIENTS: National and international manufacturers, suppliers, service companies, banks, financial services providers, insurance companies, healthcare providers and other individual and business interests.

INTERNATIONAL WORK: The firm is a member of the International Lawyers Network, an association of high quality, full service law firms with more than 4000 lawyers worldwide. The Network provides clients with easily accessible legal services in 59 countries on six continents. Firm member David Willenzik serves on the Governing Board.

HEAD OFFICE

LOUISIANA
643 Magazine Street, **New Orleans**, LA 70130
Tel: 504 586 1200 **Fax:** 504 596 2800
Email: info@mcglinchey.com
Website: www.mcglinchey.com

BRANCH OFFICES

TEXAS
1001 McKinney, Suite 1500, **Houston**, TX 77002
Tel: 713 520 1900 **Fax:** 713 520 1025

LOUISIANA
One American Place, 9th Floor, 301 Main Street, **Baton Rouge**, LA 70825
Tel: 225 383 9000 **Fax:** 225 343 3076

1811 Tower Drive, Suite A, **Monroe**, LA 71201
Tel: 318 651 0807 **Fax:** 318 651 0809

MISSISSIPPI
SkyTel Centre South, Suite 1100, 200 South Lamar Street, **Jackson**, MS 39201
Tel: 601 960 8400 **Fax:** 601 960 8406

OHIO
Three Commerce Park Square, 23230 Chagrin Blvd., Suite 700, **Cleveland**, OH 44122
Tel: 216 378 9905 **Fax:** 216 378 9910

CONTACTS

Commercial Litigation	David S Willenzik
Insurance Defense	Henri Wolbrette III
Corporate	David S Willenzik
Labor & Employment	E Fredrick Preis, Jr
Health Care	Donna Guinn Klein
Real Estate	R Keith Colvin

MCGLINCHEY STAFFORD PLLC

LEADING LAW FIRMS

MCKEE NELSON LLP

THE FIRM

Senior Partners: William S McKee, William F Nelson

Number of partners: 36
Number of other lawyers: 84

FIRM OVERVIEW: McKee Nelson LLP, an independent law firm allied with Ernst & Young LLP, was founded on 1 November 1999 with the objective of becoming the first US law firm to access the knowledge, infrastructure and resources of an international professional services firm. The firm's lawyers are experienced in serving the tax litigation, transactional structuring and capital markets needs of multinational companies. This experience is enhanced by efficient access to the talent, methodology and technology offered through the firm's alliance with Ernst & Young. The result is a law firm that is positioned to help companies conduct business throughout the world.

HEAD OFFICE

DISTRICT OF COLUMBIA
1919 M Street NW, Suite 800, **Washington** DC 20036
Tel: 202 775 1880 **Fax:** 202 775 8586
Email: info@mckeenelson.com
Website: www.mckeenelson.com

BRANCH OFFICES

NEW YORK
5 Times Square, 35th Floor, **New York** NY 10036
Tel: 917 777 4200 **Fax:** 917 777 4299
Email: info@mckeenelson.com

MAIN AREAS OF PRACTICE:

Corporate/Securities, Finance & Mergers & Acquisitions: This practice handles a diverse range of sophisticated public and private transactions - in the United States and internationally. The group advises clients on complex and sensitive corporate governance issues, and handles a broad array of corporate, real estate and project financing transactions. These range from short-term working capital facilities to cash and risk management techniques to longer term capital asset purchasing vehicles to mergers and acquisitions financings. The group represents borrowers, commercial banks, institutional investors and investment banks in all phases of the structuring, negotiation, documentation, underwriting, issuance, placement and syndication of senior and subordinated, secured and unsecured, corporate financings. It also represents numerous companies, developers, sponsors, investors and lenders in complex real estate and project financing transactions. In addition, the lawyers in the practice group have represented acquirers, targets, investors, advisors, shareholders, employees, investment banks and lenders in numerous acquisition and disposition transactions. They also work closely with the tax planning practice to structure and negotiate taxable and nontaxable transactions.

Securitisation & Structured Finance: This practice is experienced in handling domestic and cross-border offerings and private placements of mortgage-backed and asset-backed securities through US and offshore issuing vehicles. The asset categories range from the esoteric to the mature. The assets have been both prime and subprime, performing and non-performing, guaranteed and conventional. Members of the group have a long history with on and off-balance sheet warehouse financings, repurchase arrangements and other financing transactions, whole loan sales and sales of other assets, servicing transfers and other servicing-related matters, loan participations, originations, workouts, and defeasance transactions. They have structured a broad range of transactions, fixed and revolving, including REMICs, FASITs, owner trusts, grantor trusts, master trusts and commercial paper vehicles, using virtually every cash flow structure and every form of credit enhancement. Members of the group have represented every major Wall Street investment bank as underwriter or placement agent, and have represented most of the major federal agency guarantors and sponsors as well as originators, conduits, servicers, portfolio buyers and sellers of securitised assets in domestic and international structured finance transactions. Clients have also included banks and thrifts in securitisation transactions, and REITS in tax, financing and other matters.

Tax Litigation: This practice represents US and foreign taxpayers in large and legally significant federal tax cases. The firm offers clients the combination of technical tax expertise and tax litigation experience to respond effectively to any federal tax challenge - from IRS audits, appeals, and competent authority matters, to the most complex trial and appellate litigation.

The lawyers of the tax litigation practice are tax lawyers as well as veteran trial and appellate lawyers with considerable insight into government behaviour. The group includes a former IRS Chief Counsel, former IRS and US Treasury Department officials, and former IRS and Justice Department tax litigators.

Tax Planning: This practice helps businesses strategise and structure complex transactions in ways that minimise their tax burden. Transactions often involve multinationals doing business in multiple jurisdictions, regions and countries, where tax implications can be significant. The key areas of focus include partnerships, joint ventures, asset securitisations, complex financings, mergers, acquisitions and dispositions. Most deals are economically complex and require significant structuring, so the practice makes cross-disciplinary solutions a top priority. This approach offers clients seamless co-ordination of tax and structural advice from veteran lawyers who are recognised leaders in their field. The firm's founding partners, Bill McKee and Will Nelson, co-authored the leading treatises on partnership taxation and the structuring and drafting of partnership agreements. Nelson is a former Chief Counsel of the IRS, and McKee was the Tax Legislative Counsel at the US Treasury Department.

INTERNATIONAL WORK: McKee Nelson is internationally allied to serve the legal requirements of companies doing business in multiple markets. The firm provides leadership in tax litigation, tax planning and many aspects of capital markets law, including structured finance, securitisation, corporate/securities transactions, and mergers and acquisitions. In addition, the Ernst & Young alliance provides clients with access to Ernst & Young's vast accounting, business, tax, financial and analytical resources - plus the law firms allied or affiliated with Ernst & Young in more than 65 countries.

CLIENTS: McKee Nelson represents some of the world's largest corporations. The firm's clients are generally *Fortune* 500 companies, including nine of the *Fortune* 16, from a diverse range of business sectors. Clients include US firms engaged in foreign business activities, as well as foreign-based firms operating within the United States.

LEADING LAW FIRMS

MCLANE GRAF RAULERSON & MIDDLETON, PA

THE FIRM

Managing Partner: Linda C Connell
Senior Partner: Jack B Middleton

Number of partners: 32
Number of other lawyers: 44

AREAS OF PRACTICE:
Corporate	30%
Commercial Litigation	25%
Real Estate	11%
Environmental	11%

FIRM OVERVIEW: Located in New Hampshire, McLane, Graf, Raulerson & Middleton is the state's largest full service law firm. 75 attorneys and more than 25 legal assistants advise a wide range of domestic and international corporate clients with their legal needs in the greater New England area. The firm counts amongst its attorneys Fellows of the American Colleges of Trial Lawyers, Real Estate Lawyers, and Trust and Estates Counsel. Members have drafted legislation, including the Business Corporation and Limited Liability Company Acts of New Hampshire, and are the authors of the State of New Hampshire's Environmental Law Handbook. Attorneys are licensed in Arizona, California, Connecticut, Georgia, Maine, Massachusetts, Missouri, Nebraska, New Jersey, New York, Pennsylvania, Rhode Island, and Washington, DC.

HEAD OFFICE

NEW HAMPSHIRE
City Hall Plaza, 900 Elm Street, **Manchester**, NH 03101
Tel: 603 625 6464 **Fax:** 603 625 5650
Email: law@mclane.com
Website: www.mclane.com

BRANCH OFFICES

NEW HAMPSHIRE
Bicentennial Square, 15 North Main Street, **Concord**, NH 03301
Tel: 603 226 0400 **Fax:** 603 224 8180

400 Amherst Street, **Nashua**, NH 03063
Tel: 603 595 9700 **Fax:** 603 578 5127

10 Pleasant Street, **Portsmouth**, NH 03801
Tel: 603 436 2818 **Fax:** 603 436 5672

CONTACTS

Corporate	Richard A Samuels
Commercial Litigation	Bruce W Felmly
Real Estate	Peter B Rotch
Environmental	Gregory H Smith

MAIN AREAS OF PRACTICE:

Corporate: The firm's Corporate Department advises clients on merger and acquisition transactions and securities matters, including public and private offerings of equity securities, as well as entity formation, governance, commercial matters and all aspects of corporate finance. The department has industry focus areas in the energy, utilities, telecommunications, manufacturing, high tech, financial services and banking. Recent transaction includes the representation of a publicly traded energy company in connection with the sale of their interests in the Seabrook Nuclear Power Plant, representing 17% of an $800 million transaction.

Commercial Litigation: The firm's Litigation Department possesses trial experience in all of the New England courts, covering a wide range of cases including: computer software antitrust litigation; disputes over development of software for international businesses; reinsurance contract disputes over asbestos claims; patent infringement litigation; environmental insurance coverage disputes; securities arbitration and litigation; product liability; trademark opposition proceedings; and trade secret and non-competition agreement litigation. Recent cases include: Carpet One v Mercator Software, which involved claims by the firm's client, one of the World's largest floor covering retail organizations, relating to complex software design and purchase. The litigation proceeded simultaneously in the federal district court in Connecticut as well as in the Missouri state courts and was settled at the end of the third week of trial on a confidential basis successfully for the firm's client; and WPI Decisionkey, Inc. v Volvo Truck Parts, Inc., which involved a dispute concerning a contract for custom developed software which was settled after considerable discovery in the US and in Sweden.

Real Estate: The firm's Real Estate Practice advises clients on general commercial and construction financing, land use matters, leasing, and other aspects of real estate and business ownership. The firm recently obtained on behalf of a client all the necessary permits for a highly efficient electric generating station for the production of competitive-cost power, which included representation regarding the acquisition of all real estate for the site, easements for the transmission lines and all the environmental and regulatory work for the new 16-mile, interstate gas transmission pipeline.

CLIENTS: Abbott Laboratories; Algonquin Power Fund; BAUER Nike Hockey U.S.A., Inc.; NEXIQ Technologies, Inc; Hitchiner Manufacturing Co., Inc.; Hyundai Motor Company; Microsoft Corporation; Moran Towing and Transportation, Synagro Technologies, Inc; and Verizon, NH.

LEADING LAW FIRMS

MCTURNAN & TURNER

THE FIRM

Managing Partner: Wayne C Turner
Senior Partner: Lee B McTurnan

Number of partners: 5
Number of other lawyers: 7

AREAS OF PRACTICE:
Business Litigation 100%

HEAD OFFICE

INDIANA
2400 Market Tower, 10 West Market Street, **Indianapolis**, IN 46204
Tel: 317 464 8181 **Fax:** 317 464 8131
Website: www.mtlitig.com

FIRM OVERVIEW: McTurnan & Turner concentrates in relatively complex business litigation. The firm's goal is to provide the high quality of representation expected from the largest firms with the responsive and efficient services that distinguish the best small firms. The firm has assembled a group of unusually talented lawyers who work closely with the client or corporate counsel to plan and implement strategies throughout pre-trial and trial proceedings. In 2003 three new lawyers (all having completed judicial clerkships) will join the firm.

MAIN AREAS OF PRACTICE: The firm's lawyers have litigated issues concerning:
Corporate Securities/Governance: Fraud or misstatements in sales of securities or financial statements; shareholder derivative claims; breaches of fiduciary duties of directors, officers and employees and of corporate governance provisions; tender offers/takeover.
Class Actions: Representing defendants in alleged class actions related to securities laws, equal employment opportunity laws (race, sex and age), consumer fraud, product liability, and federal and state taxation.
Employment/Discrimination Matters: Race, sex and age discrimination; employment contracts; covenants not to compete.
Professional Responsibility: Defending professionals such as accountants, lawyers and securities broker-dealers against claims of negligence or misconduct.
Competition/Regulation: Restraints of trade, antitrust; regulation of utilities (telephone, electric, natural gas).
Contracts: Sales of goods, equipment, or services; insurance; franchises; commissions; guarantees; leases; construction.
Business Torts: Product liability; consumer fraud; lender liability; trade secrets; unfair competition; environmental liability; tortious interference.
First Amendment: Defamation; protection of free speech and press; third-party discovery from media; newsgatherers' rights and privileges; access to public records and proceedings.
Reported Cases: Some reported cases handled by the firm include: Midwest Gas Services, Inc., et al. v Indiana Gas Co., Inc. and ProLiance Energy, LLC, _ F.3d _ (7th Cir. Feb. 2003) (affirming dismissal of multiple Sherman Act claims); United States Gypsum Inc. v Indiana Gas Co., Inc., ProLiance Energy LLC, et al., 735 N.E.2d 790 (Ind. 2000) (opinion affirming ruling by the Indiana Utility Regulatory Commission that client ProLiance Energy LLC, a natural gas marketer, is not a public utility subject to state regulation); Indianapolis Newspapers v Indiana State Lottery Comm'n and James F. Maguire, 739 N.E.2d 144 (Ind.Ct.App. 2000) (reversing trial court's decision that would have eliminated client Indianapolis Newspapers' statutory right to recover attorneys' fees if it substantially prevails on the merits of its claim for public access to Lottery sales records); Adams v Indiana Bell Telephone Co., Inc. and Ameritech Services, Inc., 2 F. Supp. 2d 1077-1134 (S.D. Ind. 1998) (summary judgment in favor of client Ameritech Services, Inc. against class and individual claims of age and pension discrimination in downsizing; affirmed as to pension claims and reversed as to age claims, 231 F.3d 414 (7th Cir. 2000)); Indiana Wholesale Wine & Liquor Co., Inc. v State of Indiana ex rel. Indiana Alcoholic Beverage Commission, 695 N.E.2d 99-108 (Ind. 1998) (opinion upholding client Indiana Wholesale's liquor distribution permits on statutory ground; Court of Appeals had ruled for Indiana Wholesale on U.S. constitutional Commerce Clause and 21st Amendment bases, 662 N.E.2d 950-970 (Ind.App. 1996)); In re WTHR-TV and McGraw-Hill Broadcasting Company, Inc. d/b/a WRTV-6; State of Indiana v Krista M. Cline, 693 N.E.2d 1-16 (Ind. 1998) (Indiana Supreme Court's opinion of first impression on Indiana third-party discovery and access to television out-takes); IPALCO Enterprises, Inc. v PSI Resources, Inc., 148 F.R.D. 604-608 (S.D. Ind. 1993) (discovery/privilege issues in merger/tender-offer dispute).

CLIENTS: The firm's corporate clients include SBC Communications, Inc.; PricewaterhouseCoopers LLP; Prudential Securities Incorporated; ProLiance Energy LLC; CitiFinancial; DaimlerChrysler Corp.; Salomon Smith Barney, Inc.; Western Newspaper Publishing Co.; and McGraw-Hill Broadcasting Co., Inc. (WRTV-6). The firm is regularly employed by corporate counsel or through other law firms to represent corporate or individual clients in substantial, non-recurring litigation matters.

INTERNATIONAL WORK: The firm has represented a number of non-US clients in litigation within the United States. These clients include: Onkyo Japan; Shell International BV; Langen Packaging, Inc.; Molins PLC; Autoliv; Euribrid, Inc.; Sleeman Breweries, Inc; and Tagsys Q.

LEADING LAW FIRMS

MILLER NASH LLP

THE FIRM

Managing Partner, Portland, Oregon: Thomas C Sand
Partner in Charge, Vancouver, Washington: Stephen W Horenstein
Partner in Charge, Seattle, Washington: Donald K Franklin

Number of partners: 76
Number of other attorneys: 69

AREAS OF PRACTICE:

Business Law	40%
Litigation	24%
Administrative Law	16%
Labor, Employment & Employee Benefits	11%
Estate Planning, Trusts & Charitable Organizations	6%
Intellectual Property	3%

HEAD OFFICE

OREGON
3400 U.S. Bancorp Tower, 111 S.W. Fifth Avenue, **Portland**, OR 97204
Tel: 503 224 5858 **Fax:** 503 224 0155
Email: clientservices@millernash.com
Website: www.millernash.com

BRANCH OFFICES

WASHINGTON
4400 Two Union Square, 601 Union Street, **Seattle**, WA 98101-2352
Tel: 206 622 8484 **Fax:** 206 622 7485

500 East Broadway, Suite 400, Post Office Box 694, **Vancouver**, WA 98660-3324
Tel: 360 699 4771 **Fax:** 360 694 6413

FIRM OVERVIEW: Miller Nash LLP serves clients in the Pacific Northwest and around the world from its offices in Portland, Oregon, and Seattle and Vancouver, Washington. The firm offers comprehensive, creative, and innovative service through its ever-expanding local, national, and international network of resources. Miller Nash LLP serves a wide range of leading businesses, nonprofit organizations, public entities, and individuals.

MAIN AREAS OF PRACTICE:
Administrative Law: The firm's administrative law practice includes environmental and natural resources; education and public institutions; public policy and government; and native American tribes and organizations.
Affordable Housing: Each year, the firm hosts one of the West Coast's largest seminars on developing affordable housing.
Banking & Financial Institutions: The firm has a long history of bank representation in the Pacific Northwest.
Business Law: Miller Nash provides business legal services to a wide range of industries. Practice includes affordable housing; banking and financial institutions; creditors' rights; emerging business and technology; energy and communications; health care; insolvency, reorganization, and bankruptcy; international trade; land use; public finance; real estate; and tax.
Health Care: The firm represents numerous hospitals and health care organizations.
Labor & Employment: The firm holds annual labor and employment seminars for employers that are attended by representatives of more than 250 companies and organizations.
Land Use: The Pacific Northwest has some of the nation's most progressive zoning laws. Miller Nash is the only law firm with a full-time land use planner on staff.
Litigation, Arbitration, & Mediation: Miller Nash has one of the Pacific Northwest's largest litigation departments. Practice includes appellate practice; construction litigation; creditors' rights; securities, corporate and shareholder disputes; international and national litigation, arbitration and mediation; construction defect litigation; product defect litigation; and business litigation.

CLIENTS: Representative clients include Alcoa; China Ocean Shipping (Group) Company; Cingular Wireless; City of Portland; First American Title Insurance Co. of Oregon; Fred Meyer, Inc.; Gardenburger, Inc.; GlaxoSmithKline; Hyundai Motor America; InSport International, Inc.; Johnson & Johnson; Kalispel Tribe of Indians; Louisiana-Pacific Corp.; McMorgan & Company; Merck & Co., Inc.; Merrill Lynch; Northwest Hospital & Medical Center; Oregon Community Foundation; Oregon Public Broadcasting; Pacific Seafood Group; Paine Webber Inc.; Phillips 66; Portland Community College; Portland Public Schools; Potlatch Corp.; Providence Health System; R.B. Pamplin Corporation; Rentrak Corp.; Rockmore International; Salomon Smith Barney; Seattle University; Southwest Washington Medical Center; Sprint Spectrum, LP; The London Mutual Steam-Ship Owners' Mutual Insurance Association Ltd.; University of Portland; U.S. Bancorp; Wacker Siltronic Corp.; Wells Fargo Securities LLC; West Coast Bancorp; Western States Petroleum Association; Widmer Brothers Brewing Co.; Williams Communications, Inc.; WinCo Foods, Inc.

INTERNATIONAL WORK: The firm's international practice includes arbitrations before the dispute resolution ICC, Stockholm Chamber of Commerce, London Court of Arbitration, CIETAC, AAA, and other international arbitration institutions; litigation in US courts involving transnational issues; and confirmation and enforcement of foreign arbitral awards under the New York Convention in state and federal courts. Miller Nash is a member of the Employment Law Alliance, a network of labor and employment lawyers offering experienced lawyers around the globe.

LEADING LAW FIRMS

MONTELEONE & McCRORY, LLP

THE FIRM

Managing Partner: Michael F Minchella

Senior Partners: Patrick J Duffy, Michael F Minchella, William J Ingalsbe, Thomas P McGuire, Philip C Putnam

Number of partners: 12
Number of other lawyers: 11

AREAS OF PRACTICE:
Business & Commercial Litigation	75%
Company & Commercial	15%
Estate Planning	10%

HEAD OFFICE

CALIFORNIA
725 South Figueroa Street, Suite 3750, **Los Angeles**, CA 90017
Tel: 213 612 9900   **Fax:** 213 612 9930
Email: montmcc@mmlawyers.com
Website: www.mmlawyers.com

BRANCH OFFICES

CALIFORNIA
450 West Fourth Street, Suite 130, **Santa Ana**, CA 92701
Tel: 714 565 3170   **Fax:** 714 565 3184

CONTACTS
Litigation	Michael F Minchella
	Patrick J Duffy
	William J Ingalsbe (Santa Ana)
Estate Planning & Taxation	Philip C Putnam
Business	Thomas P McGuire

FIRM OVERVIEW: Monteleone & McCrory, LLP is a full-service law firm that handles commercial and business litigation, with a national reputation in the construction industry. Monteleone & McCrory, LLP is headquartered in downtown Los Angeles, California and also maintains offices in Orange County (Santa Ana), California. Each office's legal staff offers a full range of legal expertise in its fields of practice with an emphasis on quick, effective response to the needs of its clients. The firm currently numbers 23 attorneys with varying degrees of experience of up to 35 years or more. Its close-knit environment utilizes that experience through routine contact among members and associates. Communication with clients is also of utmost importance to maximize the effective use of all resources. Major decisions affecting tactics or economics of each case, including the scope of discovery efforts and assignment of tasks to lawyers, are routinely shared with the client. Many of Monteleone & McCrory's clients establish long-term relationships with one or more of the firm's partners and rely on them for particular expertise concerning that client's activities. Because the firm's size and style of business permits it, Monteleone & McCrory, LLP encourages clients to become acquainted with all of its lawyers and to deal directly with anyone with whom they are comfortable. The firm also encourages all of its lawyers to become familiar with each client to the fullest extent possible in order to offer assistance whenever a client feels it is urgent. Thus, Monteleone & McCrory, LLP endorses clients' interests in the security of ongoing and readily accessible legal counsel, no matter what the size or complexity of their affairs may be.

MAIN AREAS OF PRACTICE:

Business & Commercial Litigation: Approximately 60% of the firm's business involves construction industry matters. The firm acts as the sole legal representative for many of its clients and thus is experienced in all legal aspects of that industry as well as the general business community. The firm has successfully handled virtually every type of public and private construction dispute. These include large and complex cases involving the construction of dams, bridges, freeways, subways, tunnels, treatment plants, pipelines, street improvements, commercial and highrise buildings and housing tracts, and smaller cases ranging from collection matters to labor disputes. The firm has extensive experience with claims, bid protests, mechanic's liens and stop notices, subcontractor substitutions, prevailing wage disputes, contractor license problems, OSHA violations, collective bargaining disputes, bond and indemnity claims, professional liability, insurance coverage disputes, and construction defects and accidents. During the past 30 years, the firm has been involved in a variety of landmark projects, including, for example, the Los Angeles MetroRail; Staples Center; BART system in the San Francisco area; the Washington, DC subway system (WMATA); the Transamerican Headquarters Building in San Francisco; the Interstate 5/Columbia River Bridge in Portland, Oregon; the John Day Dam; the Chicago Deep Tunnels Project; the Bradley International Terminal at the Los Angeles International Airport; the San Onofre Nuclear Generating System; the Eisenhower Medical Center in Palm Desert; the Imperial Medical Center Complex in Teheran, Iran; the Phoenix Drain Tunnels; many state highway and water projects, especially those involving California Department of Transportation and Department of Water Resources. The firm also handles general business and tort litigation. These have included large and complex cases, which have been litigated in both state and federal courts, including Miller actions. Typically, however, the firm's general trial practice involves business disputes arising from dealership and sales agreements, employment, unfair competition, trade secrets and real estate and lease agreements. Monteleone & McCrory's attorneys have experience in many areas of civil litigation, including partnership disputes, federal and state securities violations, corporate litigation (including minority shareholder suits) and environmental and toxic waste matters.

Estate Planning: The firm handles both business and personal tax planning, personal estate planning, wills, trusts, conservatorships, probate and trust administration. In the area of business tax, it handles revenue ruling requests, administrative tax hearings and other tax litigation.

Company & Commercial: Monteleone & McCrory, LLP also practices in the general area of corporate transactional law. Its work includes organization, reorganization and acquisition of businesses ranging in size from small proprietorships to publicly-traded corporations.

CLIENTS: Engineering and building contractors, engineers, architects, real property developers, material vendors, equipment manufacturers, commercial businesses and individuals.

LEADING LAW FIRMS

MORGAN & FINNEGAN, LLP

THE FIRM

Number of partners: 44
Number of other lawyers: 49

AREAS OF PRACTICE:
Intellectual Property 100%

HEAD OFFICE

NEW YORK
345 Park Avenue, **New York**, NY 10154-0053
Tel: 212 758 4800 **Fax:** 212 751 6849
Website: www.morganfinnegan.com

BRANCH OFFICES

DISTRICT OF COLUMBIA
1775 Eye Street, NW, Suite 400, **Washington**, DC 20006
Tel: 202 857 7887 **Fax:** 202 857 7929

FIRM OVERVIEW: Morgan & Finnegan is one of the largest and most experienced law firms specializing in securing, protecting and litigating intellectual property rights. For more than a century, the firm has represented a wide variety of clients in all aspects of intellectual property law including patents, trademarks, copyrights, trade secrets, unfair competition and antitrust matters. Morgan & Finnegan has compiled a distinguished record in patent and other complex intellectual property litigation. Several of the patent cases litigated by the firm have achieved landmark status. In fact, two inventions based on patents prosecuted by Morgan & Finnegan attorneys, one for a portable computer navigational system and the other for synthetic diamonds, are part of the permanent collection of the Smithsonian Institution in Washington. The firm also has received a certificate of recognition from the Television Academy of Arts & Sciences for its contribution to a client's prime time Emmys®. The award was for outstanding achievement in engineering for the development of a new lighting system. Today, in an era of increasingly complex science and technology, the necessity for protecting innovation is more important than ever. As boundaries expand, and as new industries grow, the vision of the firm's founders is reflected in the high standards of service and value that the firm provides and in the spectrum of clients that it represents.

MAIN AREAS OF PRACTICE: The firm has more than 100 partners, counsel, associates and PhD scientific advisors in six primary practice groups. These are: biotechnology; chemicals and pharmaceuticals; computers and electronics; e-commerce and financial systems; medical and mechanical; and trademark, copyright and unfair competition. All the attorneys are devoted entirely to intellectual property and related unfair competition and antitrust matters.

INTERNATIONAL WORK: Morgan & Finnegan is at the forefront of international intellectual property developments. The firm's expertise enables it to understand more precisely the problems and concerns of Asian and European companies doing business both in the United States and abroad, and brings benefits to its multinational clients. The firm is a proud sponsor of the official intellectual property website of the Supreme Court of China.

MORRISON & FOERSTER LLP

THE FIRM

Chair of the Firm: Keith C Wetmore
Managing Partners for Operations: Laurie S Hane, Frederick Z Lodge, Pamela J Reed

Number of partners worldwide: 299
Number of US partners: 275
Number of other lawyers worldwide: 678
Number of other US lawyers: 606

FIRM OVERVIEW: Morrison & Foerster is a widely recognized international law firm with approximately 1000 lawyers in 18 offices. Morrison & Foerster combines technology and other leading industry expertise with a global full service legal practice in key financial and technology centers around the world. The firm is experienced in domestic and international corporate and corporate finance, securities and capital markets, US antitrust competition, banking and finance law. The firm's employment, litigation and arbitration, and tax practices are widely regarded as amongst the pre-eminent practices in their respective fields.

MAIN AREAS OF PRACTICE: Bankruptcy and restructuring, corporate, finance and infrastructure, financial services, intellectual property, investment management, labor and employment, land use and environmental, litigation and dispute resolution, real estate, tax and technology transactions.
Corporate: The firm's Corporate Group represents some of the most dynamic companies in the world and can provide a full range of corporate finance advice, including venture financing, public offerings, strategic alliances, technology transactions, and mergers and acquisitions.
Litigation: The firm's Litigation Department includes some of the top trial and appellate lawyers in the United States, as well as leading practitioners in the areas of antitrust, securities, financial services, criminal defense, environmental and patent litigation.
Intellectual Property: The firm has one of the largest intellectual property practices of any general practice firm, including over 50 patent and trademark lawyers.
Employment: The firm's Employment Law Group represents companies in their most difficult labor law matters.
Tax: The firm's Tax Department contains the country's leading state and local tax practice, as well as providing federal and international tax advice.

INTERNATIONAL WORK: The firm has offices in key business centers around the world including London, Brussels, Hong Kong, Beijing, Singapore and Tokyo, as well as a strategic alliance with Alvarez Prado, Cabanellas & Kelly in Buenos Aires, Argentina.

HEAD OFFICE

CALIFORNIA
425 Market Street, **San Francisco**, CA 94105 2482
Tel: 415 268 7000   **Fax:** 415 268 7522
Email: info@mofo.com
Website: www.mofo.com

BRANCH OFFICES

CALIFORNIA
755 Page Mill Road, **Palo Alto**, CA 94304-1018
Tel: 650 813 5600   **Fax:** 650 494 0792

101 Ygnacio Valley Road, Suite 450, **Walnut Creek**, CA 94596-4095
Tel: 925 295 3300   **Fax:** 925 946 9912

400 Capitol Mall, Suite 2600, **Sacramento**, CA 95814
Tel: 916 448 3200   **Fax:** 916 448 3222

555 West Fifth Street, Suite 3500, **Los Angeles**, CA 90013-1024
Tel: 213 892 5200   **Fax:** 213 892 5454

19900 MacArthur Boulevard, Twelfth Floor, **Irvine**, CA 92612
Tel: 949 251 7500   **Fax:** 949 251 0900

1925 Century Park East, Suite 2200, **Los Angeles**, CA 90067-2701
Tel: 310 203 4000   **Fax:** 310 203 4040

3811 Valley Centre Drive, Suite 500, **San Diego**, CA 92130-2332
Tel: 858 720 5100   **Fax:** 858 720 5125

COLORADO
5200 Republic Plaza, 370 Seventeenth Street, **Denver**, CO 80202-5638
Tel: 303 592 1500   **Fax:** 303 592 1510

DISTRICT OF COLUMBIA
2000 Pennsylvania Avenue, NW, Suite 5500,
Washington, DC 20006 1888
Tel: 202 887 1500   **Fax:** 202 887 0763

NEW YORK
1290 Avenue of the Americas, **New York**, NY 10104-0050
Tel: 212 468 8000   **Fax:** 212 468 7900

VIRGINIA
1650 Tysons Boulevard, Suite 300, **McLean**, VA 22102
Tel: 703 760 7700   **Fax:** 703 760 7777

CONTACTS

Business	Robert S Townsend
Labor	Raymond L Wheeler
Litigation	Lori A Schechter
Tax	Paul H Frankel
	Steve L Feldman

Lawyers for the global economy℠

MOYE, O'BRIEN, O'ROURKE, PICKERT & MARTIN, LLP

THE FIRM

Managing Partner: James E Moye
Senior Partners: James E Moye
Stephen W Pickert
Gregory S Martin

Number of partners: 5
Number of other lawyers: 8

AREAS OF PRACTICE:
Construction Litigation 85%
Labor & Employment 10%
Commercial Litigation 5%

HEAD OFFICE
FLORIDA
800 South Orlando Avenue, **Maitland** FL 32751
Tel: 407 622 5250 **Fax:** 407 622 5440
Email: moopm@earthlink.net

AFFILIATE OFFICE
ILLINOIS
O'Rourke, Hogan, Fowler & Dwyer
10 South LaSalle Street, Suite 2900, **Chicago** IL 60603
Tel: 312 739 3500 **Fax:** 312 739 3535

FIRM OVERVIEW: Established in 1989, Moye, O'Brien, O'Rourke, Pickert & Martin, LLP dedicates its practice to the representation of national and international clients within the construction industry. The firm has dedicated itself to the prompt, efficient, and economic delivery of such legal services. The firm's philosophy is to provide aggressive, high quality legal services at a fair rate, while always striving to extricate its clients from unavoidable controversies at the earliest practicable, most economical and beneficial juncture.

MAIN AREAS OF PRACTICE
Construction Litigation: The firm represents clients, including national and multinational general contractors, owners, design professionals and other construction-related entities, from contract preparation, review and negotiation through ultimate dispute resolution including litigation, arbitration and other alternative resolution procedures.
Labor & Employment: The firm has a wide range of experience in representing clients in all phases of labor and employment law, including union and trade dealings and employment practices and disputes.
Commercial Litigation: The firm represents clients in a variety of contract and tort disputes between corporate entities.

CLIENTS: The firm has represented clients throughout the United States of America, the Caribbean basin, Central America, and Canada. A representative listing of clients includes: Archer-Western Contractors, Ltd.; Arden Villas University, Ltd.; Balfour Beatty, Inc.; Balfour Beatty Construction, Inc.; Balfour Beatty Rail Systems, Inc.; Centex Homes; The City of Hollywood; Hazen and Sawyer, P.C.; Peter Kiewit Sons', Inc.; Leggett & Platt, Inc.; Loews Corporation; MACTEC Engineering & Consulting, Inc.; Marta Track Constructors; Metroplex Corporation; Odebrecht Construction, Inc.; PCL Civil Constructors, Inc.; PCL Construction Services, Inc.; Parsons Transportation Group; Professional Services Industries, Inc.; QORE Property Sciences; Universal City Development Partners, Ltd; Universal Studios Florida; Universal Technical Institute; Walsh Group, Inc.; ZOM Companies.

INTERNATIONAL WORK: The firm advises international companies operating within the US. The firm also advises US companies on their foreign activities.

MURPHY SHENEMAN JULIAN & ROGERS

THE FIRM

Chairman: Patrick A Murphy
Managing Partners: Cecily A Dumas
Gary B Rosenbaum

Number of partners: 22
Number of associates: 18
Number of counsel: 7

HEAD OFFICE

CALIFORNIA

101 California Street, Suite 3900, **San Francisco**, CA 94111
Tel: 415 398 4700 **Fax:** 415 421 7879
Email: msjr@msjr.com
Website: www.msjr.com

BRANCH OFFICES

CALIFORNIA

2049 Century Park East, Suite 2100, **Los Angeles**, CA 90067
Tel: 310 788-3700 **Fax:** 310 788 3777

FIRM OVERVIEW: Founded in 1978, Murphy Sheneman Julian & Rogers maintains a specialized practice in finance, creditors' remedies, insolvency and restructuring, business litigation, and real estate finance. Because the firm specializes solely in these areas, it can provide practical, focused, and cost-effective advice to business entities dealing with financially troubled customers or clients, or addressing their own financial issues. Many of the matters in which the firm becomes involved require the services of several of the practice groups and many of the firm's attorneys practice in more than one group.

MAIN AREAS OF PRACTICE

The Creditors' Remedies Group: Represents creditors and creditor groups in all aspects of commercial bankruptcy cases and out-of-court restructurings. The firm has represented official creditors' committees in major Chapter 11 cases and has also represented creditors as members of the official committees. The lawyers in the Creditors' Remedies Group regularly represent lenders to companies in hi-tech industries, as well as manufacturers of technology and equipment that have extended credit to distributors, resellers, or end users. These representations require a practical understanding of the interplay among bankruptcy law, commercial law, and intellectual property law.

The Restructuring Group: Represents financially troubled business enterprises in out-of-court workouts and in reorganization cases under the Bankruptcy Code. Clients of the firm's Restructuring Group have included major public corporations, publicly held partnerships, and other business entities, as well as bankruptcy trustees, Chapter 11 examiners, and assignees for the benefit of creditors. The firm has represented workout and Chapter 11 debtors in virtually every business sector and the firm's attorneys are expert in drafting, negotiating, and obtaining confirmation of reorganization plans.

The Finance Group: Serves lenders, lessors, and investors in structuring and documenting a broad range of finance and equity transactions. While the firm's Finance Group ordinarily represents lenders who provide asset-based and cash-flow loans, it also provides advice in connection with equity investments, venture lending and leasing, and other equity and warrant-supported financing products. The firm also represents manufacturers of computer equipment and software that extend credit to distributors and resellers of their products.

The Business Litigation Group: Represents a wide range of clients in commercial and business litigation matters. Although the firm has particular expertise in bankruptcy court litigation, it maintains a major part of its practice in state and federal courts. The firm has achieved excellent results in business tort cases, insurance defense, and complex contracts litigation. The Business Litigation Group also serves clients in disputes arising in debtor-creditor relationships, including enforcement of creditors' rights, litigation related to secured transactions, and the defense of lender liability, truth-in-lending, and securities fraud claims.

The Real Estate Group: Maintains a local and national real estate law practice, including California issues such as seller disclosure, the one-form-of-action rule, judicial foreclosure, and foreclosure of mixed real and personal property collateral. The firm's real property practice includes the structuring and negotiation commercial acquisitions and dispositions, seller and third party financing, and construction lending and highly sophisticated lending transactions.

LEADING LAW FIRMS

NELSON MULLINS RILEY & SCARBOROUGH, LLP

THE FIRM

Managing Partner: David E Dukes
Senior Partner: Ed Mullins

Number of partners: 172
Number of other lawyers: 147

AREAS OF PRACTICE:
Corporate Finance	30%
Business Litigation	15%
Mass Tort Litigation	15%
Pharmaceuticals & Medical Devices	13%
Health Care	12%
Labor & Employment	10%
Government Relations	5%

FIRM OVERVIEW: Founded in South Carolina in 1897 and located in Georgia, North Carolina and South Carolina, Nelson Mullins has more than 35 diversified practice areas 319 attorneys in eight offices. The firm represents a wide variety of clients that range in size from start-up technology companies to Fortune 500 corporations.

MAIN AREAS OF PRACTICE:

Mass Tort Litigation: Firm attorneys are equipped to handle or coordinate the defense of mass torts claims on an individual, regional or national basis. Firm attorneys serve as national trial and coordinating counsel for major US companies.

Business Litigation: Attorneys in this group provide counsel throughout the nation in the areas of business, securities and financial fraud, business torts, antitrust matters, lender liability claims, contract disputes, and many others.

Corporate Finance: Firm attorneys handle a broad range of securities, finance and regulatory matters for clients ranging from development stage private companies to large publicly held companies in a wide range of industries.

Health Care: This group of attorneys is capable of providing a comprehensive array of client services. They have experience providing services to health care clients in corporate transactions, regulatory and governmental affairs, litigation, finance, and tax.

Government Relations: This group's attorneys have extensive experience with a wide range of clients in many areas of lobbying and legislative analysis.

Labor & Employment: This diverse group of lawyers defends companies in all facets of labor and employment disputes.

Pharmaceuticals & Medical Devices: Firm attorneys have detailed knowledge in many areas of science and technology in order to effectively handle claims regarding the firm's clients' products and services. The attorneys have experience with mass torts and multi-district litigation, requiring coordination with attorneys from across the country.

CLIENTS: The firm's clients include major manufacturers, Fortune 500 companies, commercial banks, financial institutions, public utilities, venture capital and private equity firms, industrial and service corporations, partnerships, profit and non-profit organizations, government and government agencies, entrepreneurs and individuals.

INTERNATIONAL WORK: Nelson Mullins has an International Team headquartered in Atlanta and an affiliation with the European law firm Graf von Westphalen Bappert & Modest with offices in Germany, Austria and Belgium.

HEAD OFFICE

SOUTH CAROLINA
Keenan Building, Third Floor, 1330 Lady Street, **Columbia**, SC 29201-3332
Tel: 803 799 2000   **Fax:** 803 256 7500
Website: www.nmrs.com

BRANCH OFFICES

GEORGIA
First Union Plaza, Suite 1400, 999 Peachtree Street, NE, **Atlanta**, GA 30309-3964
Tel: 404 817 6000   **Fax:** 404 817 6050

NORTH CAROLINA
Bank of America Corporate Center, Suite 2400, 100 North Tryon Street **Charlotte**, NC 28202-4021
Tel: 704 417 3000   **Fax:** 704 377 4814

Highwoods Tower One at Highwoods Office Center, 3200 Beechleaf Court, 9th Floor, **Raleigh**, NC 27604

1381 Old Mill Circle, Suite 308, **Winston-Salem**, NC 27103

SOUTH CAROLINA
Liberty Center, Suite 600, 151 Meeting Street, **Charleston**, SC 29401-2239
Tel: 843 853 5200 Fax: 843 722 8700

Poinsett Plaza, Suite 900, 104 South Main Street, **Greenville**, SC 29601-2122
Tel: 864 250 2300   **Fax:** 864 232 2925

Founders Centre, Suite 301, 2411 North Oak Street, **Myrtle Beach**, SC 29577-3165
Tel: 843 448 3500   **Fax:** 843 448 3437

CONTACTS

Business Litgation	Stephen Morrison
Corporate Finance	Glenn Sturm
Government Relations	Edward E Poliakoff
Health Care	Stanley S Jones
Labour & Employment	Kenneth E Young
Mass Tort Litigation	R Bruce Shaw
Pharmaceuticals & Medical Devices	David E Dukes

LEADING LAW FIRMS

NIXON PEABODY LLP

THE FIRM

Co-managing Partners: Nestor M Nicholas, Harry P Trueheart, III

Number of lawyers: 614

FIRM OVERVIEW: Nixon Peabody attorneys practice in virtually all areas of business. They provide comprehensive legal services at every level for major US and international companies including private and publicly-owned businesses, organizations, and individuals. A fully integrated organizational structure provides clients with access to all of the firm's services through any Nixon Peabody office.

MAIN AREAS OF PRACTICE

Business: The firm serves a broad range of business clients, from entrepreneurs to multi-national corporations, regarding securities, finance, mergers and acquisitions, tax, international trade and many other matters.

Energy & Environment: The firm, with an in-house staff of engineers and scientists, is well practiced in such matters as large-scale infrastructure projects, environmental clean-up and recovery facilities.

Financial Services & Specialty Finance: Services include: private equity, venture capital, corporate trust, credit, leasing and other aspects of business finance.

Health Services: Service to health care providers including: corporate, regulatory, licensing and certificates of need, reimbursement counseling, development and financing of capital projects, strategic planning, graduate medical education and residency training accreditation matters, physician/hospital and medical staff issues, patient care issues, physician practice issues and managed care contracting.

Private Clients: Services including income, estate and gift tax planning and compliance, financial planning, estate administration, retirement planning and asset protection.

Public Finance: Nixon Peabody has one of the largest public finance practices in the US, regularly ranked among the 10 most active bond and underwriter counsels nationally in dollar value of bonds issued. The firm's experience extends from the financing of arenas and stadiums to power generation facilities and housing projects.

Technology & Intellectual Property: The firm is adept in helping businesses protect their innovations, bring concepts to market, and exploit the value of their brands and inventions.

Bankruptcy: Nixon Peabody is skilled in addressing a wide spectrum of insolvency issues, from debt restructuring and negotiating reorganization plans to asset liquidation.

Business Litigation: More than a third of the firm's attorneys litigate a wide array of business matters concerning: antitrust, government investigations, international disputes, professional relations, real estate, and securities.

Insurance: The firm provides comprehensive services to the insurance industry with an emphasis on corporate, regulatory, litigation and pre-litigation strategic counseling. The group tries coverage disputes throughout the US in all major industries, including pharmaceuticals, manufacturing, financial services, energy, construction, and maritime, and provides counsel on a host of insurance-related matters.

Labor & Employment: Experience includes counsel to large corporations, partnerships, and entrepreneurs regarding public and private employment matters, as well as multi-plaintiff and class action litigation.

Products Liability: Nixon Peabody attorneys have repeatedly proven their abilities in high stakes cases involving products liability and complex tort litigation across many industries.

US OFFICES

CALIFORNIA
2040 Main Street, Suite 850, **Irvine**, CA 92614-7218
Tel: 949 475 6900
Website: www.nixonpeabody.com

Two Embarcadero Center, **San Francisco**, CA 94111-3996
Tel: 415 984 8200

CONNECTICUT
185 Asylum Street, **Hartford** CT 06103
Tel: 860 275 6820

DISTRICT OF COLUMBIA
401 9th Street, N.W., Ste. 900 **Washington, DC** 200004-2128
Tel: 202 585 8000

MASSACHUSETTS
101 Federal Street, **Boston**, MA 02110-1832
Tel: 617 345 1000

NEW HAMPSHIRE
889 Elm Street, **Manchester**, NH 03101
Tel: 603 628 4000

NEW YORK
30 South Pearl Street, **Albany**, NY 12207
Tel: 518 427 2650

1600 Main Place Tower, **Buffalo**, NY 14202
Tel: 716 853 8100

437 Madison Avenue, **New York**, NY 10022
Tel: 212 940 30000

1300 Clinton Square, **Rochester**, NY 14604-1792
Tel: 585 263 1000

Long Island, 990 Stewart Avenue, **Garden City**, NY 11530
Tel: 516 832 7500

RHODE ISLAND
One Citizens Plaza, **Providence**, RI 02903
Tel: 401 454 1000

VIRGINIA
8180 Greensboro Drive, Ste. 800, **McLean**, VA 22102
Tel: 703 770 9300

Affordable Housing: With years of government and private sector experience, the firm assists clients in the numerous legal aspects of building, managing, buying, and selling federally assisted housing.

Real Estate: The firm serves developers, landlords, tenants, lenders, and others concerning a variety of commercial, industrial and multi-family real estate projects.

Syndication: The firm's syndication attorneys have more than 30 years of experience in matters involving equity investing for housing and other forms of real estate.

INTERNATIONAL WORK: Nixon Peabody clients include international banks and multinational and foreign-based corporations in a wide range of industries. The firm acts as general counsel to large industrial corporations, banks, media companies, developers, leasing companies, and public utilities. Its experience also includes handling major international transactions. Languages include Afrikaans, Chinese, Danish, Dutch, French, German, Italian, Norwegian, Portuguese, Russian, Spanish and Swedish.

LEADING LAW FIRMS

ORRICK, HERRINGTON & SUTCLIFFE LLP

THE FIRM

Chairman & Chief Executive Officer: Ralph H Baxter, Jr.
Chief Operating Officer: Douglas Benson
Number of partners: 231
Number of other lawyers: 410

AREAS OF PRACTICE:
Public Finance	17%
Corporate	15%
Litigation	14%
Structured Finance	11%
Intellectual Property	10%
Private Finance	9%
Employment Law	7%
Global Energy, Communications & Infrastructure	7%
Real Estate	6%
Tax	2%
Compensation & Benefits	2%

FIRM OVERVIEW: Orrick's lawyers are located in 11 cities around the world: New York, San Francisco, Silicon Valley, Washington, DC, Los Angeles, Sacramento, Seattle, Orange County, London, Tokyo and Paris. Orrick is a market leader in structured, project, and public finance. The firm is also known for its expertise in complex commercial litigation, intellectual property, and corporate law.

MAIN AREAS OF PRACTICE:
CORPORATE
Corporate: Orrick's corporate practice covers a wide range of areas, from banking and commercial finance to market regulation, mergers and acquisitions, public and private offerings, emerging companies, and venture capital financings.
Real Estate: The firm's real estate group serves the US and Asia, and its practice includes the full range of real estate issues faced in large real estate investments, developments, and other projects.
Compensation & Benefits: Orrick's compensation and benefits attorneys partner with individuals, corporations, and institutions to create and implement the best available pay and benefit packages.
Tax: The firm's tax practice includes corporate tax, employee benefits, personal estates, public finance tax, and tax litigation.

ADVOCACY
Litigation: Orrick's national litigation practice encompasses virtually every business-related issue encountered today-intellectual property, securities, antitrust, distribution and trade regulation, product liability, environmental, tax, and white collar criminal defense.
Employment: Orrick's employment lawyers handle all varieties of employment litigation, wrongful discharge claims, EEO affirmative action compliance, and general employment matters.
Intellectual Property: The firm's national IP team has extensive experience in virtually every aspect of intellectual property law, including patent, copyright, and trademark infringement, unfair competition, and trade secret actions. They also advise clients in licensing, litigation avoidance, due diligence, and other matters across the complete spectrum of intellectual property issues.

FINANCE
Public Finance: The firm's public finance practice is the largest and most diverse in the US. The firm ranks first in the country in the volume of financings for which it serves as bond counsel and as underwriters counsel.
Structured Finance: Orrick's structured finance attorneys have had significant experience in the development of the asset securitization market in the US and abroad.

HEAD OFFICE
CALIFORNIA
Old Federal Reserve Bank Building, 400 Sansome Street,
San Francisco, CA 94111-3143
Tel: 415 392 1122 **Fax:** 415 773 5759
Email: info@orrick.com

BRANCH OFFICES
CALIFORNIA
777 South Figueroa Street, Suite 3200, **Los Angeles**, CA 90017-5855
Tel: 213 629 2020 **Fax:** 213 612 2499

4 Park Plaza, Suite 1600, Irvine, **Orange County**, CA 92614-2558
Tel: 949 567 6700 **Fax:** 949 567 6710

400 Capitol Mall, Suite 3000, **Sacramento**, CA 95814-4497
Tel: 916 447 9200 **Fax:** 916 329 4900

1000 Marsh Road, **Menlo Park**, CA 94025-1021
Tel: 650 614 7400 **Fax:** 650 614 7401

DISTRICT OF COLUMBIA
Washington Harbour, 3050 K Street, N.W.,
Washington, DC 20007-5135
Tel: 202 339 8400 **Fax:** 202 339 8500

NEW YORK
666 Fifth Avenue, **New York**, NY 10103-0001
Tel: 212 506 5000 **Fax:** 212 506 5151

WASHINGTON
719 Second Avenue, Suite 900, **Seattle**, WA 98104-7097
Tel: 206 839 4300 **Fax:** 206 839 4301

INTERNATIONAL OFFICES
The firm also has offices in France, Japan, and the United Kingdom.

Global Energy, Communications & Infrastructure: Orrick's global energy, communications and infrastructure attorneys work collaboratively on projects throughout the world, including power plants, telecommunications facilities, industrial plants, waste disposal and resource recovery facilities, pipelines, toll roads, and other infrastructure projects.
Private Finance: The firm's private finance practice has broad expertise in virtually every area of commercial finance, including secured and unsecured lending, project and infrastructure finance, leasing and asset-based financing, aircraft finance, institutional private placements, letters of credit, swaps and other hedging mechanisms, asset-backed commercial paper financings, workouts, bankruptcy, and bank regulatory issues.

CLIENTS: Orrick's clients include major commercial and investment banks, industrial and financial corporations, technology companies, developers, and public and governmental entities.

INTERNATIONAL WORK: Orrick is one of the world's leading securitization and structured finance firms. The firm's securitization group is active in Japan, Korea, Hong Kong, Indonesia, Malaysia, and Thailand. Orrick's project finance and infrastructure experience is extensive, and boasts projects throughout Latin America, Asia, and Europe. The firm also has one of the leading emerging market financial sector reform and corporate debt restructuring practices, and is currently increasing its high-profile work in the technology and telecommunications sectors.

LEADING LAW FIRMS

PACHULSKI, STANG, ZIEHL, YOUNG, JONES & WEINTRAUB P.C.

THE FIRM

Management Committee: Richard M Pachulski, Dean A Ziehl, Ira D Kharasch, William P Weintraub, Laura Davis Jones, Robert J Feinstein

Number of partners: 28
Number of other lawyers: 47

FIRM OVERVIEW: Pachulski, Stang, Ziehl, Young, Jones & Weintraub P.C. was founded in 1983, and has developed into one of the largest insolvency practices in the US. With over 70 attorneys in four offices, the firm's attorneys concentrate on business reorganizations (workouts, restructurings and chapter 11), bankruptcy and insolvency matters, commercial and real estate transactions, general commercial law and business litigation. Because the core of the firm's practice involves debtor-creditor relations and sophisticated financial restructurings, all of the firm's senior attorneys have broad and deep experience in business reorganization, bankruptcy and insolvency matters.

MAIN AREAS OF PRACTICE:

Business Reorganization & Workouts: The firm has a nationally recognized bankruptcy practice that is one of the largest in the country. The firm represents all of the major constituencies in bankruptcy proceedings and out of court workouts, including debtors, creditors' committees, equity committees, trustees, secured and major unsecured creditors, bondholders, asset purchasers and third-party plan proponents.

Litigation: The firm represents both plaintiffs and defendants in general commercial and business litigation, as well as banking, bankruptcy and insurance litigation. The prosecution and defense of litigation in bankruptcy court is a particular strength and the firm's litigators are well versed in bankruptcy jurisdictional disputes. The firm's national insolvency practice frequently requires client representation in fraudulent conveyance, preference and other bankruptcy-related litigation.

Corporate & Transactional: The firm's transactions practice features expertise over a broad spectrum, including real estate purchase and sales, development and commercial leasing; financing and workouts; sales of companies or their assets. The firm's transactional attorneys are uniquely qualified to handle the problems and issues associated with representing clients in complex bankruptcy transactions.

High Technology/Telecommunications: The firm has considerable experience with the special issues facing high technology/telecommunications debtors and sophisticated acquirers of high technology/telecommunications companies, including Covad Communications Group, Inacom Corp., Northpoint Communications, Peregrine Systems Inc., Tie Communications Inc. and UniSil Corporation.

Retail & Restaurant Chains: The firm's combination of insolvency, real estate and commercial financial expertise enables members of the firm to represent a wide range of interests arising from the insolvency of large restaurant chains and retail outlets, including B.U.M. International Inc., C&R Clothiers Inc., Fedco Inc., The Boston Store, Sizzler International Inc. and Specialty Restaurants Corporation.

Insurance & Reinsurance: The firm's extensive involvement with restructuring in the insurance industry has given its lawyers recognized expertise in handling insurance and reinsurance disputes. Members of the firm have represented receivers, reinsurers, policyholders and other creditors in some of the largest insurance and reinsurance insolvencies in the world, including First Capital Holdings, Corp., First Executive Corporation (Executive Life Insurance Company), Superior National, Transit, Mission, Fremont and Kwelm.

HEAD OFFICE

CALIFORNIA
10100 Santa Monica Boulevard, Suite 1100, **Los Angeles**, CA 90067
Tel: 310 277 6910   **Fax:** 310 201 0760
Email: dziehl@pszyj.com
Website: www.pszyj.com

BRANCH OFFICES

CALIFORNIA
3 Embarcadero, Suite 1020, **San Francisco**, CA 94111
Tel: 415 263 7000   **Fax:** 415 263 7010

DELAWARE
919 North Market Street, Suite 1600, **Wilmington**, DE 19801
Tel: 302 652 4100   **Fax:** 302 652 4400

NEW YORK
461 Fifth Avenue, 25th Floor, **New York**, NY 10017-6234
Tel: 212 561 7700   **Fax:** 212 561 7777

Entertainment Insolvency: The firm has played prominent roles in some of the nation's largest production and distribution company chapter 11 cases, as well as high profile entertainers, including United Artists, Loews Cinemas, General Cinemas, Mann Theaters, 21st Century Film Group, Quintex Entertainment and entertainers Toni Braxton, Ronald Isley and Johnny Gill.

CLIENTS: The firm acts or has acted as bankruptcy counsel to many large public and private corporations, including AgriBioTech Inc., American Rice Inc., AmeriServe Food Distributors Inc., Breed Technologies Inc., F&C Corp., Federal-Mogul Inc., Gencor Inc., Harnischfeger Industries Inc., HomePlace Stores Inc., Imperial Hotels Corporation, LogoAthletics Inc., MVP.com, PG&E Corporation, RBX Corporation, Sunbelt Nursery Group Inc., Trans World Airlines, TreeSweet Juice Company, Tri Valley Growers, Webvan Group (Homegrocer.com), W.R. Grace & Co. and Zenith Electronics. The firm has also served as counsel to court-appointed committees of creditors or other interest groups in the chapter 11 cases of America West Airlines Inc., Cirrus, Fruit of the Loom, FundAmerica, Guy F. Atkinson Company, Home Fed Corp., Lynx Golf Inc., Orange County, Pannell Kerr Forster, Pioneer Take-Out Corp., and Sun World International Inc. Other clients represented by the firm in litigation, transactions or as creditors or other parties in interest in bankruptcy cases include Chicago Title, DSL Transportation, Farmers Commonwealth Insurance Co., Gilda Marx Incorporated, Heller Financial Inc., Hilton Hotels, Imperial Hotels Inc., National Broadcasting Company Inc., PaineWebber Funding Inc., Safeway Corporation, The Hahn Company and Xerox Corporation.

INTERNATIONAL WORK: The firm has substantial expertise in international or cross-border insolvency cases. A member of the firm, Arnold Quittner, is a frequent lecturer and internationally recognized expert in this area. He is joined in this practice by Jeremy Richards, a graduate of both Oxford and Harvard Law School, and a founding member of the British-American Bar Association. Both have published articles on cross-border insolvency issues. Among other matters, Mr Quittner acted as chief counsel in the first and largest concurrent reorganization case in Japan and the United States (Maruko Inc. in the Tokyo District Court and US Bankruptcy Court), and represented Bramalea Inc. in parallel Canadian-American reorganization proceedings. The firm also represents Bell Canada in the dual Canadian-American reorganization proceedings of Teleglobe Inc.

PAUL, HASTINGS, JANOFSKY & WALKER LLP

THE FIRM

Chair of the Firm: Seth M Zachary
Managing Partner: Greg M Nitzkowski

Number of partners: 206
Number of other lawyers: 595

Email: info@paulhastings.com
Website: www.paulhastings.com

US OFFICES

CALIFORNIA
695 Town Center Drive, **Costa Mesa**, CA 92626
Tel: 714 668 6200   **Fax:** 714 979 1921

515 South Flower Street, **Los Angeles**, CA 90071
Tel: 213 683 6000   **Fax:** 213 627 0705

55 Second Street, **San Francisco**, CA 94105
Tel: 415 856 7000   **Fax:** 415 856 7100

CONNECTICUT
1055 Washington Boulevard, **Stamford**, CT 06901
Tel: 203 961 7400   **Fax:** 203 359 3031

DISTRICT OF COLUMBIA
1299 Pennsylvania Avenue, NW, **Washington**, DC 20004
Tel: 202 508 9500   **Fax:** 202 508 9700

GEORGIA
24th Floor, 600 Peachtree Street, NE, **Atlanta**, GA 30308
Tel: 404 815 2400   **Fax:** 404 815 2424

NEW YORK
75 East 55th Street, **New York**, NY 10022
Tel: 212 318 6000   **Fax:** 212 319 4090

INTERNATIONAL OFFICES

The firm also has offices in Beijing, Hong Kong, London and Tokyo.

FIRM OVERVIEW: Founded in 1951, Paul Hastings currently conducts its global law practice through an international network of offices that links the world's leading financial centers. The firm has more than 800 lawyers in 11 offices, including Beijing, Hong Kong, London and Tokyo, and is considered one of the top law firms in the world. The firm's position as a leading international law firm is built on its ability to draw upon the resources of its globally integrated practice areas that are organized into five departments: Corporate, Real Estate, Tax, Litigation and Employment Law. The firm provides legal advice and services to *Fortune* 500 and *Forbes International* 500 companies, as well as smaller and emerging business enterprises.

MAIN AREAS OF PRACTICE:

Corporate: With a mix of US, UK, Hong Kong, PRC and Japanese qualified lawyers, Paul Hastings provides a full range of advice in international and cross-border corporate transactions. The firm advises on a wide range of transactions under the laws of several jurisdictions and provides in-depth experience in many world markets, including all parts of Europe, Asia and Africa. The firm's lawyers have advised investment, commercial and development banks, investment advisors, investors and issuers in connection with commercial finance transactions, equity and debt offerings, secured financings and international corporate restructurings and workout transactions, venture capital transactions, and project and acquisition finance around the world.

Litigation: The firm handles litigation and arbitration proceedings and government investigations involving entities based abroad, ranging from antitrust to breach-of-contract cases, including handling international trade and commercial disputes, intellectual property issues, international litigation and arbitration, handling discovery in an international context, and its attorneys are knowledgeable on the Hague Conventions on Service of Judicial Documents and Evidence Taking, and other conventions and treaties imposing limitations on discovery by foreign countries.

Employment Law: The firm has counseled its international clients with respect to traditional labor law, equal employment opportunity laws, wrongful discharge, sexual harassment, employee benefits matters and other employment related issues. The firm's experience in identifying and understanding cultural differences is invaluable in its representation of international clients in this area. As the volume of cross-border acquisitions increases, its insights into the employment laws and customs of non-US jurisdictions are welcomed by its US and non-US based clients alike.

Real Estate: The firm's Real Estate Practice is among the largest and most experienced of any US law firm and is internationally recognized for its excellence, having been named 'International Real Estate Law Firm of the Year' by *Chambers Global - The World's Leading Lawyers 2002-2003* audited by the British Market Research Bureau. 37 partners oversee a practice of nearly 160 lawyers in 11 offices whose cumulative experience extends to the lending, acquisition, leasing and investment management of real estate assets on a national and international scale. The firm has been at the forefront of the introduction of international standards and practices to the acquisition, financing and workout of non-performing secured and unsecured real estate and corporate loans and assets.

Tax: The firm's International Tax Practice is spearheaded by a motivated group of dynamic practitioners whose expertise and interests extend well beyond the concepts of international tax planning. Their practice covers mergers and acquisitions, capital market offerings, investment and joint venture structuring, leasing, structured and project finance, and financial product planning and structuring, as well as tax controversy and tax litigation matters.

LEADING LAW FIRMS

PAUL, WEISS, RIFKIND, WHARTON & GARRISON LLP

THE FIRM

Managing Partner: Alfred D Youngwood

Number of partners: 105
Number of other lawyers: 547

FIRM OVERVIEW: Paul, Weiss, Rifkind, Wharton & Garrison LLP is a globally orientated, full-service firm of approximately 500 attorneys, with offices in New York, Washington, London, Paris, Tokyo, Hong Kong and Beijing. From its New York City base, the firm is engaged in a diverse and highly dynamic international practice serving clients throughout the United States, Canada, Latin America, Europe and Asia. The firm's core practice is concentrated in the areas of litigation and corporate law, including mergers and acquisitions and public and private financing. The firm is equally recognized for its activities and experience in real estate, intellectual property, communications, technology, new media and the internet, entertainment, employee benefits and executive compensation, personal representation, antitrust, environmental regulation, tax and bankruptcy and corporate reorganization.

HEAD OFFICE

NEW YORK
1285 Avenue of the Americas, **New York**, NY 10019-6064
Tel: 212 373 3000 **Fax:** 212 757 3990
Email: mailbox@paulweiss.com
Website: www.paulweiss.com

BRANCH OFFICES

DISTRICT OF COLUMBIA
1615 L Street, NW, Suite 1300, **Washington** DC 20036-5694
Tel: 202 223 7300 **Fax:** 202 223 7420

PECKAR & ABRAMSON, P.C.

THE FIRM

Managing Partner: Robert S Peckar

Number of partners: 24
Number of other lawyers: 33

FIRM OVERVIEW: Peckar & Abramson has achieved national recognition for its successes in the representation of members of the construction industry, both domestically and internationally. The firm combines its unique problem-solving expertise and litigation/arbitration experience with its substantial experience counseling clients regarding the management of transactional risks inherent in the industry. Having represented clients in every category of construction, Peckar & Abramson has successfully resolved disputes at all levels of complexity arising from a wide range of construction projects, from moderately sized projects to mega-projects in both the public and private sectors. The firm has particular expertise in projects such as airports, government buildings, highways and bridges, power generation facilities, environmental clean-ups, sports arenas, manufacturing facilities, hotels and other hospitality industry projects and residential communities. In addition to and complementing its construction industry practice, the firm offers the full services of its employment and labor law group, as well as its business and real estate transactional practice. Peckar & Abramson serves the needs of its clients from its offices in New York, New Jersey, Florida and California and offers its international clients the benefits of its relationship with allied international firms through its membership in the International Construction Law Alliance.

CLIENTS: The firm focuses its practice on the representation of construction managers and contractors throughout the US, Asia, the Middle East, the Caribbean, Latin America and Europe. Additionally, the firm represents owners, design professionals and other construction industry participants.

HEAD OFFICE

NEW YORK
546 Fifth Avenue, 17th Floor, **New York**, NY 10036
Tel: 212 382 0909   **Fax:** 212 382 3456
Email: rpeckar@pecklaw.com
Website: www.pecklaw.com

BRANCH OFFICES

CALIFORNIA
555 West 5th Street, Suite 3000, **Los Angeles**, CA 90013
Tel: 213 489 9220   **Fax:** 213 489 9215

250 Montgomery Street, 16th Floor, **San Francisco**, CA 94104
Tel: 415 8371968   **Fax:** 415 837 1320

FLORIDA
One Southeast Third Avenue, Suite 3050, **Miami**, FL 33131
Tel: 305 358 2600   **Fax:** 305 375 0328

Fort Lauderdale
Tel: 954 969 0101   **Fax:** 954 696 0328

NEW JERSEY
70 Grand Avenue, **River Edge**, NJ 07661
Tel: 201 343 3434   **Fax:** 201 343 6306

NEW YORK
546 Fifth Avenue, 17th floor, **New York**, NY 10036
Tel: 212 382 0909   **Fax:** 212 382 3456

LEADING LAW FIRMS

PHELPS DUNBAR

THE FIRM

Managing Partner: Richard N Dicharry

Number of partners: 93

FIRM OVERVIEW: Founded in 1853 in New Orleans, Phelps Dunbar is one of the oldest law firms in continuous practice in the South. The firm is a progressive and diverse partnership, with a practice that is international in scope. It now has offices in New Orleans and Baton Rouge, Louisiana; Jackson, Tupelo, and Gulfport, Mississippi; Houston, Texas; Tampa, Florida; and London, England. Through the firm's network of regional offices, clients have access to more than 220 attorneys representing an extensive range of talent and experience. No matter how intricate a client's legal needs, the firm's professional depth and experience offer accessible, cost-effective, and reliable service. The firm continually refocuses our major practice areas to serve the changing needs of our client community. Attorneys in all practice areas work together to provide a broad base of legal services to institutions and individuals. Phelps Dunbar handles virtually every type of civil case in federal and state courts across the region. The firm was recognized in 2002 for its efforts in diversity by receiving the Defense Research Institute (DRI) National Diversity Award and for being ranked first in the nation in percentage of African-American lawyers by the Minority Law Journal.

CLIENTS: Clients include public and private companies, financial institutions, insurance companies, health care systems, educational institutions, partnerships, estates, governmental agencies and individuals.

US OFFICE CONTACTS

TAMPA
100 South Ashley Drive, Suite 1900, Tampa, FL 33602-5311

Office Profile: Phelps Dunbar recently extended its legal services from Texas to Florida by opening its eighth office in Tampa on April 1, 2001. The Tampa office handles admiralty and tort litigation, business, commercial litigation, insurance, and labor and employment matters, practice areas that are aligned with Florida's business community.

BATON ROUGE
City Plaza, 445 North Boulevard, Suite 701, Baton Rouge, LA 70802-5707

Office Profile: The firm's Baton Rouge office was the first regional office of Phelps Dunbar, opening in 1984. The office has experienced steady growth since its opening. With over 30 attorneys, the Baton Rouge office has become one of the largest law offices in the state capital. Our attorneys support clients with a full-service litigation and business practice, as well as counseling on employment, regulatory, environmental and intellectual property matters.

GULFPORT
NorthCourt One, 2304 1th Street, Suite 300, Gulfort, MS 39501

Office Profile: Phelps Dunbar opened its seventh office on December 1, 2000, in Gulfport, Mississippi. The Gulfport office handles business litigation, construction, real estate, financing, products liability, insurance litigation, and environmental litigation and the Gulfport office draws upon attorneys in its New Orleans and other Mississippi offices as the nature of a legal project might require.

HEAD OFFICE

LOUISIANA
Canal Place
365 Canal Street, Suite 2000, **New Orleans**, LA 70130-6534
Tel: 504 566 1311 **Fax:** 504 568 9130
Email: info@phelps.com
Website: www.phelpsdunbar.com

BRANCH OFFICES

FLORIDA
100 South Ashley Drive, Suite 1900, **Tampa**, FL 33602-5311
Tel: 813 472 7550 **Fax:** 813 472 7570

LOUISIANA
City Plaza, 445 North Boulevard, Suite 701, **Baton Rouge**, LA 70802-5707
Tel: 225 346 0285 **Fax:** 225 381 9197

MISSISSIPPI
NorthCourt One, 2304 19th Street, Suite 300, **Gulfport**, MS 39501
Tel: 228 679 1130 **Fax:** 228 679 1131

SkyTel Centre, 200 South Lamar Street, Suite 500, **Jackson**, MS 38201
Tel: 601 352 2300 **Fax:** 601 360 9777

One Mississippi Plaza, 201 S. Spring Street, Seventh Floor, **Tupelo**, MS 38804
Tel: 662 842 7907 **Fax:** 662 842 3873

TEXAS
3040 Post Oak Boulevard, Suite 900, **Houston**, TX 77056
Tel: 713 626 1386 **Fax:** 713 626 1388

JACKSON
SkyTel Centre, 200 South Lamar Street, Suite 500, Jackson, MS 38201

Office Profile: The Jackson office opened in 1986 as a result of a merger with a firm of young attorneys who had previously been with major Jackson firms. Now, with more than fifty attorneys, the Jackson office provides full-service litigation and traditional business practice for a diverse clientele.

TUPELO
One Mississippi Plaza, 201 S. Spring Street, Seventh Floor, Tupelo, MS 38804

Office Profile: Phelps Dunbar is the only law firm with substantial offices in Tupelo, Jackson, and Gulfport Mississippi. The offices coordinate projects for many clients with legal business throughout the state. As the center of the firm's thriving healthcare practice, the Tupelo office employs attorneys well-versed in the subtleties of this constantly evolving field of law. Our health law attorneys represent hospitals, physicians, managed care organizations and other health care providers throughout the Southeast as counsel on corporate, tax and health law matters. In addition, it maintains a business and a litigation practice.

HOUSTON
3040 Post Oak Boulevard, Suite 900, Houston, TX 77056

Office Profile: With a foundation in the strength and tradition of a law firm over a century old, the firm's Houston office is a young and aggressive group. Opened in 1990, our Houston office has 18 attorneys with extensive trial and appellate experience supplemented by excellent academic and professional back-grounds. Consistent practice standards ensure the delivery of high quality legal services.

LEADING LAW FIRMS

PIERCE ATWOOD

THE FIRM

Managing Partner: Bruce A Coggeshall
Senior Partner: Ralph I Lancaster, Jr

Number of partners: 72
Number of other lawyers: 44

HEAD OFFICE

MAINE
One Monument Square, **Portland**, ME 04101
Tel: 207 791 1100 **Fax:** 207 791 1350
Email: info@pierceatwood.com
Website: www.pierceatwood.com

BRANCH OFFICES

MAINE
77 Winthrop Street, **Augusta**, ME 04330
Tel: 207 623 6311 **Fax:** 207 623 9367

MASSACHUSETTS
Six Harris Street, **Newburyport**, MA 01950
Tel: 978 465 9599 **Fax:** 978 465 9945

NEW HAMPSHIRE
One New Hampshire Avenue, Suite 350, **Portsmouth**, NH 03801
Tel: 603 433 6300 **Fax:** 603 433 6372

FIRM OVERVIEW: Pierce Atwood is the leading full-service commercial law firm north of Boston, and is recognized nationally and internationally in selected areas of expertise. Its non-metro location enhances the value of its services. Clients range from regional and local enterprises, utilities, financiers, middle-market companies and entrepreneurs to national and multinational corporations and foreign governments. Pierce Atwood Consulting provides governmental relations, economic development, and diversity consulting services.

MAIN AREAS OF PRACTICE:
Corporate Commercial: Known for sophistication in all types of complex transactions and leadership in creative public policy solutions to business and economic problems. The firm has premier practices in banking and consumer financial services, bankruptcy, public finance and real estate.
Intellectual Property & Technology: Provides the entire spectrum of services, with particular expertise in biotechnology (patent prosecution, licensing, and litigation), engineering patent prosecution, trademarks, and entertainment.
Litigation: Members include the two most recent Chief Justices of the Maine Supreme Judicial Court, a former Independent Counsel, and a past President and four Fellows of the American College of Trial Lawyers. Practices before state and federal courts and administrative agencies nationwide in matters as diverse as commercial, energy, white collar, products liability, ERISA, and insurance coverage disputes.
Environmental: Beginning in 1970 and now with 15 lawyers devoted exclusively to environmental issues, the practice addresses all major federal, state, and local laws, including land use, wastewater discharge, air emissions, solid waste, hazardous waste, chemical disclosure, wetlands, endangered species, and all other natural resources law.
Energy & Utilities: The firm has built a national and international reputation serving domestic utilities, deregulated enterprises such as major merchant plants, and foreign emerging economies' need for energy market expertise. Clients are regional, national (utilities, independent project developers, lenders and investors in over 20 states), and international, including foreign governments and international financial institutions.
Tax: The federal, state, and local practice is highly regarded for its expertise in government relations and public policy, and helping to create economic incentives for businesses facing real estate, business and equipment, sales, and income tax issues. Expertise covers corporate structuring, M&A and other transactions, business planning, succession and estate planning, and IRS controversies.
Employment: The group seeks to build management expertise through counseling and training in all relevant areas. Specialty practices include benefits, immigration, FLSA, OSHA. Extensive experience with state and federal trial, appellate, administrative and ADR proceedings, and with the NLRA and RLA (bargaining, arbitrations, board proceedings, organizing and labor disputes).

CLIENTS: Include American Skiing Co., Anthem, Casella, Central Maine Power Company, Charles River Laboratories, Chittenden Bank, Enterasys, FPLE Seabrook, Fairchild Semiconductor, General Electric, J.D. Irving, Ltd., IDEXX, KeyBank N.A., MBNA, Maine Medical Center, McCormick, Poland Spring, State of California, Tom's of Maine, UNUMProvident, USAID, Verizon, World Bank, Wright Express.

INTERNATIONAL WORK: Encompasses multilateral transactions; cross-border financings; enterprise restructuring; energy and environmental law; EU compliance; regulatory reform and compliance; competition; privatization; litigation; and arbitration. Attorneys have worked in 50 countries. The firm manages patent and trademark portfolios spanning 90 countries. Languages include Bulgarian, French, German, Macedonian, Mandarin Chinese, Norwegian, Russian, Spanish, Swedish, Telugu, Thai.

LEADING LAW FIRMS

PILLSBURY WINTHROP

THE FIRM

Chair: Mary Cranston
Vice Chair: John Pritchard
Managing Partner: Marina Park

Number of partners in US offices: 276
Number of other lawyers in US offices: 462

AREAS OF PRACTICE:
Capital Markets & Finance	30%
Technology/Intellectual Property	24%
Litigation	22%
Global Energy	14%
Other	10%

FIRM OVERVIEW: Formed in 2001 by the merger of Pillsbury Madison & Sutro LLP and Winthrop, Stimson, Putnam & Roberts, the firm's experience spans three centuries and several continents. With offices in major capital finance and technology centers throughout the world, and using a team-based client service model, the firm counsels clients on all aspects of global business, technology transactions, intellectual property protection, energy and high value litigation.

MAIN AREAS OF PRACTICE:

Capital Markets & Finance: The firm provides counsel in all areas of capital markets and finance, centered on sophisticated capital formation strategies, mergers and acquisitions and structured financial solutions. It comprises one of the largest bankruptcy and creditors' rights groups in the country.

Technology/Intellectual Property: The firm's understanding of both the law and the unique industry segments makes the firm's legal services unique and invaluable in dealing with this ever changing landscape. Pillsbury Winthrop attorneys have been involved in more than 300 significant intellectual property litigation cases tried in US courts over the last ten years. The firm's IP practice ranks among the top three in the US.

Litigation: With over 250 trial lawyers, Pillsbury Winthrop has the depth and experience to handle an extensive range of complex litigation. The firm's litigators have resolved many high-profile cases in forums throughout the United States and around the world.

Global Energy: The firm is recognized as an international law firm at the center of all sectors of the energy and utility industry. The firm's energy and utilities industry practice is interdisciplinary, encompassing every practice area required by broad client base in this industry, and advises oil and gas producers, transporters, distributors and managers, electric and gas utilities, utility holding companies and affiliates, independent power producers, and underwriters, lenders and investors.

CLIENTS: The firm represents a broad spectrum of industries, including biotech, education, energy, financial institutions and professional services, food services, life sciences, manufacturing, retail, technology and telecommunications.

INTERNATIONAL WORK: A strong emphasis on corporate and finance matters, the firm also represents clients in Europe, Asia and Australia in matters involving global energy, technology, intellectual property, real estate, insolvency and employment law. The firm provides on the spot advice and assistance for a wide variety of matters, including support for litigation and other forms of dispute resolution. International clients include banking and financial institutions, insurance companies, trading companies, manufacturing, shipping, government entities, oil and gas industry and utilities.

HEAD OFFICES

CALIFORNIA
50 Fremont Street, **San Francisco**, CA 94105
Tel: 415 983 1000 **Fax:** 415 983 1200

NEW YORK
One Battery Park Plaza, **New York**, NY 10004
Tel: 212 858 1000 **Fax:** 212 858 1500
Email: info@pillsburywinthrop.com
Website: www.pillsburywinthrop.com

BRANCH OFFICES

CALIFORNIA
10100 Santa Monica Boulevard, Suite 2300, **Los Angeles**, CA 90067
Tel: 310 203 1100 **Fax:** 310 286 6672

725 South Figueroa Street, Suite 2800, **Los Angeles**, CA 90017
Tel: 213 488 7100 **Fax:** 213 629 1033

650 Town Center Drive, 7th Floor, **Costa Mesa**, CA 92626
Tel: 714 436 6800 **Fax:** 714 436 2800

400 Capitol Mall, Suite 1700, **Sacramento**, CA 95814
Tel: 916 329 4700 **Fax:** 916 441 3583

SBC Building, 101 West Broadway, Suite 1800, **San Diego**, CA 92101
Tel: 619 234 5000 **Fax:** 619 236 1995

11682 El Camino Real, Suite 200, **San Diego**, CA 92130
Tel: 858 509 4000 **Fax:** 858 509 4010

2550 Hanover Street, **Palo Alto**, CA 94304
Tel: 650 233 4500 **Fax:** 650 233 4545

CONNECTICUT
Financial Centre, 695 East Main Street, PO Box 6760,
Stamford, CT 06904
Tel: 203 348 2300 **Fax:** 203 965 8226

TEXAS
2 Houston Center, 909 Fannin, 22nd Floor, **Houston**, TX 77010
Tel: 713 425 7300 **Fax:** 713 425 7373

VIRGINIA
1600 Tysons Boulevard, **McLean**, VA 22102
Tel: 703 905 2000 **Fax:** 703 905 2500

DISTRICT OF COLUMBIA
1133 Connecticut Avenue, NW, **Washington, DC** 20036
Tel: 202 775 9800 **Fax:** 202 833 8491

INTERNATIONAL OFFICES

Pillsbury Winthrop has international offices in London, Singapore, Sydney and Tokyo.

CONTACTS

Capital Markets & Finance	Rodney Peck
Technology/Intellectual Property	William Abrams
Litigation	Sarah Flanagan
Global Energy	David Falck

LEADING LAW FIRMS

PIPER RUDNICK LLP

THE FIRM

Managing Partners: Francis B Burch Jr, Lee I Miller
Chief Operating Officer: Jeffrey F Liss
Number of partners worldwide: 396
Number of other lawyers worldwide: 459

AREAS OF PRACTICE:
Litigation	32%
Real Estate	16%
Corporate & Securities	12%
Banking, Finance & Business Reorganisation	9%
Intellectual Property, IT, E-commerce & Privacy	7%
Venture Capital	6%
Franchise & Distribution	5%
Environmental	3%
Other	10%

FIRM OVERVIEW: Piper Rudnick is a business law firm of approximately 900 lawyers with offices in Baltimore, Chicago, Dallas, Edison, Las Vegas, Los Angeles, New York, Philadelphia, Reston, Tampa and Washington. Main areas of practice:

Business & Technology: Includes corporate and securities, corporate governance, business tax, franchise and distribution, intellectual property, information technology, biosciences, IPOs, taxation, mergers and acquisitions, and other major transactions for companies of all sizes.

Real Estate: Comprises one of the largest and most diverse practices in the US, covering every aspect of commercial, retail, industrial and residential property transactions, finance, project finance and securities.

Litigation: Includes a white collar group led by a former Watergate prosecutor, and national product liability, securities, labor and commercial litigation practices.

Government Affairs: Includes the nationally-known federal affairs and legislation group formerly with Verner Liipfert Bernhard McPherson and Hand; a government controversies practice headed by the former general counsel of a leading telecommunications company; and prominent regulatory practices in government contracts, environmental, e-commerce and privacy, tax legislation, antitrust and communications.

International Commerce & Litigation: Includes international dispute resolution and public international law, and is supplemented by the firm's strategic alliance with The Cohen Group, an international strategic business consulting firm headed by former US Secretary of Defense, William S Cohen.

MAIN AREAS OF PRACTICE:

Intellectual Property: The firm's intellectual property and information technology practice includes 20 lawyers who are admitted to practice before the United States Patent and Trademark Office. The firm is responsible for over 25,000 active patents and trademarks in more than 150 countries.

E-commerce & Privacy: The firm's e-commerce practice represents entities ranging from large, international corporations to start-up ventures in transactions ranging from complex e-commerce development initiatives to routine matters, including Web hosting and development agreements, and Web linking and partnering agreements, domain name registration, disputes and transfers, hacking and unsolicited commercial e-mail.

Franchise & Distribution: The firm has represented more than 160 companies in international franchising and distribution matters. A substantial number are headquartered in Europe, Canada, Latin America, the Middle East and Japan, and represent a wide variety of industries.

Project Finance: The project finance practice includes a strong outbound international component, with experience in projects in more than 30 countries, in Europe, Central and South America, the Middle East and Africa, and Asia.

HEAD OFFICE

ILLINOIS
Piper Rudnick, an Illinois General Partnership, 203 North LaSalle Street, Suite 1800, **Chicago** IL 60601-1293
Tel: 312 368 4000 **Fax:** 312 236 7516
Email: info@piperrudnick.com
Website: www.piperrudnick.com

BRANCH OFFICES

CALIFORNIA
Piper Rudnick LLP, 1999 Avenue of the Stars, Suite 400, **Los Angeles** CA 90067 6022
Tel: 310 595 3000 **Fax:** 310 595 3300

DISTRICT OF COLUMBIA
Piper Rudnick LLP, 1200 Nineteenth Street, NW, **Washington**, DC 20036-2412
Tel: 202 861 3900 **Fax:** 202 223 2085

Piper Rudnick LLP, 901 Fifteenth Street, NW, **Washington**, DC 20005-2301
Tel: 202 371 6000 **Fax:** 202 371 6279

FLORIDA
Piper Rudnick LLP, 101 East Kennedy Boulevard, Suite 2000, **Tampa** FL
Tel: 813 229 2111 **Fax:** 813 229 1447

MARYLAND
Piper Rudnick LLP, 6225 Smith Avenue, **Baltimore** MD 21209-3600
Tel: 410 580 3000 **Fax:** 410 580 3001

NEVADA
Piper Rudnick LLP, 3960 Howard Hughes Parkway, **Las Vegas** NV 89109
Tel: 702 737 3433 **Fax:** 702 737 1612

NEW JERSEY
Piper Rudnick LLP, a New Jersey Limited Liability Partnership (Robert A. Assuncao, Managing Partner), 379 Thornhill Street, Eighth Floor, **Edison**, NJ 08837- 2226
Tel: 732 590 1850 **Fax:** 732 590 1860

NEW YORK
Piper Rudnick LLP, 1251 Avenue of the Americas, **New York** NY 10020-1104
Tel: +1 212 835 6000 **Fax:** +1 212 835 6001

PENNSYVANIA
Piper Rudnick LLP, 3400 Two Logan Square, 18th and Arch Streets, **Philadelphia** PA 19103-2762
Tel: 215 656 3300 **Fax:** 215 656 3301

TEXAS
Piper Rudnick LLP, 1717 Main Street, Suite 4600, **Dallas** TX 75201-4605
Tel: 214 743 4500 **Fax:** 214 743 4545

VIRGINIA
Piper Rudnick LLP, 1775 Wiehle Avenue, Suite 400, **Reston** VA 20190
Tel: 703 773 4000 **Fax:** 703 773 5000

INTERNATIONAL WORK: Piper Rudnick's international team of over 150 lawyers represents clients in all types of international issues, including litigation, arbitration and dispute resolution, commercial transactions related to business conducted in countries around the world, government regulation of commerce and international trade in the US, Europe, the Middle East, Latin America and Asia, and counseling on public policy issues in the US and in numerous foreign countries in Europe, the Middle East, Latin America and Asia.

LEADING LAW FIRMS

QUATTLEBAUM, GROOMS, TULL & BURROW PLLC

THE FIRM

Number of partners: 7
Number of other lawyers: 7

HEAD OFFICE
111 Center Street, Suite 1900 **Little Rock**, Arkansas 72201
Tel: 501 379 1700 **Fax:** 501 379 1701
Website: www.qgtb.com

CONTACTS
Banking & Finance	Patrick A Burrow
Commercial Property	Timothy W Grooms
Environmental	Al Eckert
Litigation	Steven W Quattlebaum
	John E Tull III
	J Leon Holmes
	Kristine G Baker
	EB (Chip) Chiles, IV

FIRM OVERVIEW: Quattlebaum, Grooms, Tull & Burrow PLLC provides a full range of business-related legal services. The firm represents individuals, sole proprietorships, partnerships, limited liability companies, corporations, and government organizations. Its practice encompasses a wide variety of transactions, litigation, regulatory work, and estate planning.

MAIN AREAS OF PRACTICE

Corporate & Commercial: The firm has extensive experience in litigating complex business and commercial cases, including class actions. It has been involved in numerous matters involving multiple parties and claims pending in multiple jurisdictions. These cases have included antitrust litigation, business and commercial disputes, construction disputes, securities disputes, franchise disputes, employment discrimination and related disputes, real estate litigation, toxic tort claims, products liability claims, professional malpractice claims, libel and First Amendment claims, constitutional law claims, and insurance coverage litigation. The firm has represented corporate and individual clients, as both plaintiffs and defendants. It also has extensive litigation experience in trial and appellate courts on both the state and federal levels.

Banking & Finance: The firm has extensive experience in a wide range of banking issues for state and national banks and bank holding companies, including bank formation, holding company formation, loan transactions, representation of the bank as creditor, as well as regulatory and compliance issues involving the FDIC, the OCC, and the Federal Reserve Board. It is frequently called upon to prepare loan documentation and provide legal opinions in the areas of usury, enforceability of security interests, and choice of law issues. The firm has advised clients on issues involving financing for public and private entities. It has acted as bond counsel and trustee counsel in Arkansas Development Finance Authority bond issues. The firm has counseled issuers in numerous corporate securities offerings, including initial and secondary capital offerings for financial institutions, offerings for bank holding companies, and restricted offerings pursuant to Regulation D. Frequently in connection with securities offerings, the firm is called upon to offer professional advice on ancillary issues in securities offerings, such as taxation, real estate, banking and environmental issues.

Real Estate: The firm represents, among others, developers, lenders, investment banks, pension funds, domestic investors and major corporations in connection with real estate-related transactions involving the purchase, sale, construction, financing, development, management and operation of commercial, industrial and residential projects throughout Arkansas and the United States; the public and private offering of various types of real estate securities; securitized lending transactions; leasing on behalf of landlords and major tenants; real estate litigation; and debt restructuring transactions on behalf of lenders and borrowers.

CLIENTS: Arkansas Community Bankers; Arkansas Press Association; Arkansas REALTORS® Association; BASF Corporation; Building & Utility Contractors, Inc.; Entergy Corporation; Koppers Industries, Inc.; Simmons First National Bank; Uniroyal, Inc.; Wal-Mart Stores, Inc.; Multi-Purpose Civic Center Facility Board for Pulaski County (Alltel Arena); Mercedes-Benz USA, Inc.; Moses Tucker Real Estate, Inc.; Reliant Energy/ARKLA; Salomon Smith Barney, Inc.; Schering-Plough Corp.; Vulcan Materials Company; and Waste Management, Inc.

QUINN EMANUEL URQUHART OLIVER & HEDGES, LLP

THE FIRM

Managing Partner: John B Quinn

Number of partners: 57
Number of other lawyers: 128

FIRM OVERVIEW: Quinn Emanuel is a 185-lawyer business litigation firm - the largest in the United States devoted solely to business litigation. The firm's lawyers have tried over 819 cases and won 92.2%. When representing defendants, the firm's trial experience allows it to achieve better settlements or defense verdicts. When representing plaintiffs, the firm's lawyers have garnered over $1.5 billion in judgments and settlements.

MAIN AREAS OF PRACTICE: Business litigation in the areas of intellectual property (patent, copyright, trademark and trade secrets litigation); international and domestic arbitration; unfair competition; antitrust and trade regulation litigation; employment and employee movement litigation; securities litigation; entertainment litigation; real estate development and construction litigation; banking and financial institution litigation; government contracts litigation and counseling; insurance coverage; healthcare; internet and new media litigation; white collar criminal litigation; corporate governance and internal investigations.

CLIENTS: The firm's clients include Academy of Motion Picture Arts and Sciences, AOL Time Warner, Avery Dennison Corporation, Bank of America, CBS, Inc., Computer Sciences Corporation, Credit Suisse First Boston, The Walt Disney Company, Leland Stanford University, Columbia University, Newscorp, Viacom, DIRECTV, Earthlink, eBay, Inc., FOX, Inc., General Electric Co., General Motors Corporation, Goldman, Sachs & Co., HBO, Hitachi, IBM Corporation, Johnson & Johnson, Lockheed Martin Corporation, Los Angeles Times, Mattel, Inc., Northrop Grumman Corporation, Oracle Corporation, Seiko Instruments, Sony Electronics, Nike, Inc., Toyota Motor Sales, U.S.A., Inc.

INTERNATIONAL WORK: The firm has advised international companies operating within the US, and also advised US companies on their overseas activities. In addition, the firm's lawyers have arbitrated cases under rules of the London Court of International Arbitration, the International Chamber of commerce, and the American Arbitration Association, UNCITRAL, ICSID, and arbitration statutes of various countries, in New York, Los Angeles, London, Paris, Stockholm, Bermuda, Montreal and Lima involving companies from England, Germany, Greece, Peru, Sweden, the United Kingdom, Russia and Venezuela. Each year the firm sponsors an international arbitration conference attended by advocates and arbitrators from around the world. The firm's lawyers are familiar with, and in some cases helped draft, international and domestic arbitration codes.

HEAD OFFICE

CALIFORNIA
865 South Figueroa Street, 10th Floor, **Los Angeles**, CA 90017-2543
Tel: 213 624 7707 **Fax:** 213 624 0643
Email: johnquinn@quinnemanuel.com
Website: www.quinnemanuel.com

BRANCH OFFICES

CALIFORNIA
555 Twin Dolphin Drive, Suite 560, **Redwood Shores**, CA 94065-2139
Tel: 650 620 4500 **Fax:** 650 620 4555
Email: charlesverhoeven@quinnemanuel.com

201 Sansome Street, 6th Floor, **San Francisco**, CA 94104-2303
Tel: 415 986 5700 **Fax:** 415 986 5707
Email: charlesverhoeven@quinnemanuel.com

45-025 Manitou Drive, Suite 8, **Indian Wells**, CA 92210-9068
Tel: 760 345 4757 **Fax:** 760 345 2414
Email: hwh@quinnemanuel.com

4445 Eastgate Mall, Suite 200, **San Diego**, CA 92121-1979
Tel: 858 812 3107 **Fax:** 858 812 3336
Email: mxd@quinnemanuel.com

NEW YORK
805 Third Avenue, 11th Floor, **New York**, NY 10022-7534
Tel: 212 702 8100 **Fax:** 212 702 8200
Email: andreapollack@quinnemanuel.com

CONTACTS

Los Angeles	John B Quinn
	A William Urquhart
	Fred G Bennett
New York	Andrea Pollack
San Francisco/Silicon Valley	Charles K Verhoeven
San Diego	Mitch Danzig
Indian Wells	Harold W Hopp

LEADING LAW FIRMS

ROPES & GRAY

THE FIRM

Managing Partner: Douglass N Ellis Jr
Executive Director: Michael S Karlson

Number of partners: 146
Number of lawyers: 336

AREAS OF PRACTICE:
Corporate	48%
Litigation	16%
Intellectual Property	12%
Tax & Benefits	10%
Private Client Group	6%
Labor & Employment	3%
Bankruptcy & Creditors' Rights	2%
International	2%

HEAD OFFICE
MASSACHUSETTS
One International Place, **Boston** MA 02110-2624
Tel: 617 951 7000 **Fax:** 617 951 7050
Website: www.ropesgray.com

BRANCH OFFICES
CALIFORNIA
One California Street, Suite 2200, **San Francisco** CA 94111-5423
Tel: 415 315 6300 **Fax:** 415 315 6350

DISTRICT OF COLUMBIA
1301 K Street, NW, Suite 800 East, **Washington** DC 20005-7008
Tel: 202 626 3900 **Fax:** 202 626 3961

1900 K Street, NW, Suite 750, **Washington** DC 20006-1163
Tel: 202 626 3900 **Fax:** 202 626 3961

NEW YORK
885 Third Avenue, Suite 3200, **New York** NY 10022-4834
Tel: 212 497 3600 **Fax:** 212 497 3650

CONTACTS
Corporate	David C Chapin
Litigation	Roscoe Trimmier Jr
Intellectual Property	Edward G Black
Tax & Benefits	Susan A Johnston
Private Client Group	Robert N Shapiro
Labor & Employment	Nelson G Ross
Bankruptcy & Creditors' Rights	William F McCarthy
International	Ivor Cary Armistead III

FIRM OVERVIEW: Based on a foundation of over 135 years of dedication to building strong client relationships, Ropes & Gray represents interests across a broad spectrum of industries in corporate law and litigation matters. In addition, the firm offers counsel on labor and employment issues, tax and benefits, creditors' rights, and private client services. Clients range in size from large to small companies and include financial institutions, government agencies, hospitals and healthcare organizations, colleges and universities, and families and individuals. Over 530 lawyers strive to provide the highest quality legal advice available. The firm combines superior talent with a supportive environment where nothing gets in the way of solving their clients' problems.

MAIN AREAS OF PRACTICE:

Corporate: The Corporate Practice is Ropes & Gray's largest practice area and includes practices in: debt financing, government relations and regulatory, healthcare, intellectual property and rights management, investment management, life sciences, private equity, public finance, real estate, securities and public companies, sports law, technology company, and venture capital.

Litigation: The firm's litigators practice in the following areas: alternative dispute resolution, antitrust, bankruptcy, commercial and business, environmental, government contracts, government enforcement, healthcare, insurance, intellectual property and technology litigation, investigative services, labor and employment, and securities and corporate.

Intellectual Property: The Intellectual Property Practice consists of intellectual property and rights management, and intellectual property and technology litigation. From acquisitions, licensing and transaction support to resolving and assessing disputes, Ropes & Gray provides intellectual property services to clients in diverse industries.

Tax and Benefits: The core of Ropes & Gray's Tax Practice consists of transaction-related tax planning for investors and business entities. The firm also has one of the largest employee benefits practices in the United States and was the first major US law firm to add actuaries and benefits consultants to their staff.

Private Client Group: The Private Client Group at Ropes & Gray is one of the largest practices of its kind in the United States. The practice is focused primarily on three areas: estate and gift planning, estate settlement, and trust services, including investment management of trust assets. The group's lawyers are supported by more than 40 professionals including trust administrators, tax preparers, probate accountants, financial planners, philanthropic advisers, and trusts and estates paralegals.

Labor & Employment: The Labor and Employment Practice focuses on employment law and labor law, with its attorneys dedicated to helping clients avoid and solve workplace problems. The attorneys represent both private and public sector clients.

Bankruptcy & Creditors' Rights: Ropes & Gray lawyers have extensive experience representing clients in bankruptcy cases and distressed situations throughout the United States. Their lawyers maintain a practical focus and combine backgrounds in both commercial litigation and transactional practice to provide clients with advice founded on experience. The firm also has substantial experience in contentious litigation, inside and outside of the insolvency context, designed to protect clients' interests.

International: The International Practice at Ropes & Gray reaches across all areas of the firm's practice including: antitrust/competition law, corporate transactions, financing and securities, foreign corrupt practices act, insolvency, intellectual property licensing and rights management, investment management, life sciences, litigation and commercial arbitration, and tax planning.

INTERNATIONAL WORK: With their roots in Boston, a major US port city, Ropes & Gray's practice has always had significant international components. Over the years their international business expertise has grown and developed, allowing them to provide their domestic and foreign clients with legal support for the full array of their international needs. To support their International Practice, the firm maintains a conference center in London and has corresponding relationships with local firms throughout the world.

ROSS & COHEN, LLP

THE FIRM

Managing & Senior Partners: Allen Ross
Frederick Cohen

Number of partners: 9
Number of other lawyers: 10

AREAS OF PRACTICE:
Construction Industry Services 80%
Real Estate Services 20%

HEAD OFFICE
NEW YORK
711 Third Avenue, **New York**, NY 10017
Tel: 212 370 1200 **Fax:** 212 370 0334
Email: law@rosscohen.com
Website: www.rosscohen.com

FIRM OVERVIEW: Established in 1978 by Allen Ross and Frederick Cohen, Ross & Cohen, LLP enjoys and unparalleled reputation for personal service and technical expertise in the highly specialized world of construction and real estate law. Ross & Cohen, LLP retains some of the most experienced and technically proficient specialists in these areas of law. The firm is committed to finding the most appropriate and cost-effective solutions to its clients' legal problems and provide advice and counsel that enables them to achieve their business objectives.

MAIN AREAS OF PRACTICE:
Construction Industry Services: The construction-related legal services Ross & Cohen, LLP provides encompass the complete life cycle of a project, from the earliest planning stage to occupancy and beyond including project advice; planning and counseling; construction lending; contract negotiation; preparation and review for all types of construction and development ventures; suretyship and guarantees; prosecution and defense of claims related to breach of contract, defective work, payment, delay and mechanics' liens; administrative law hearings; bid contracts and construction-related labor law matters. The additional areas of Ross & Cohen, LLP's practice related to construction of special interest to its clients are mediation and arbitration and compliance audits.

Real Estate Services: The real estate services Ross & Cohen, LLP provides to its clients are the transactional services they need to support real estate activities in both commercial and residential setting. The firm's attorneys are experts in acquisition and sales; commercial and retail leasing; construction financing and real estate secured loan transactions; workout, restructuring and foreclosure; representing co-operative corporations; and real estate taxation and tax certiorari proceedings.

CLIENTS: Ross & Cohen, LLP serves a diverse group of clients including publicly-held corporations, developers, landlords, property managers, general contractors, subcontractors, material and equipment suppliers, design and construction professionals, financial institutions, governmental agencies and municipalities on a broad range of construction and real estate issues. The firm regularly represents clients involved in such diverse projects as hotels, healthcare facilities, shopping centers, warehouses, manufacturing plants, mixed-use development, office buildings, restaurants, co-operative and condominium residences and a whole range of public projects including building and civil construction.

LEADING LAW FIRMS

SCHWARTZ, COOPER, GREENBERGER & KRAUSS, CHARTERED

THE FIRM

Managing Partner: Robert Dunn Glick
Administrative Partner: Ronald B Grais

Number of partners: 35
Number of other lawyers: 35

FIRM OVERVIEW: Established over 50 years ago, SCG&K is one of Chicago's most well respected law firms. The firm offers an extensive range of commercial legal services to both US and international clients.

MAIN AREAS OF PRACTICE: The firm handles banking and finance, real estate, corporate, bankruptcy, litigation, taxation and estate planning and technology and intellectual property law.

Banking & Finance: The firm's Banking and Finance Practice Group represents banks, insurance companies, savings and loan associations and financial institutions in all types of public and private financings.

Real Estate: The firm has a prominent national Commercial Real Estate Practice and represents owners, developers, investors and financial institutions in all types of real estate transactions. The attorneys in the Real Estate Practice Group have extensive experience in real estate finance, real estate development, commercial leasing, acquisitions and dispositions, structured finance, construction law and land use and zoning.

Corporate: The firm is a pre-eminent provider of business law services to middle market companies and to banks and private equity funds and institutions. The firm's practice extends to employment and ERISA law, energy development, environmental law and regulation, franchise and distribution law, mergers and acquisitions, private equity and venture capital transactions, securities law compliance and private placements.

Bankruptcy: The firm has a nationally known Bankruptcy and Insolvency Practice encompassing every aspect of insolvency and bankruptcy, including the representation of secured and unsecured creditors, creditors' committees, purchasers of insolvent companies, trustees and assignees for the benefit of creditors.

Litigation: The firm's trial and appellate attorneys have extensive experience in complex business litigation in state and Federal courts throughout the United States. The firm represents clients of all sizes across a broad spectrum of the economy and in different industries. Areas of practice in litigation include antitrust, business torts and unfair competition, construction disputes, contracts and commercial disputes, corporate governance litigation, criminal defense work, financial institutions, including lender liability, fraud, RICO litigation and numerous other areas.

HEAD OFFICE

180 North LaSalle Street, Suite 2700, **Chicago**, IL 60601
Tel: 312 346 1300 **Fax:** 312 782 8416
Website: www.scgk.com

CONTACTS

Banking & Finance	Martin W Salzman
Real Estate	Michael S Kurtzon
Corporate	Bernard A Schlifke
	Jay S Berlinsky
Bankruptcy	Malcolm M Gaynor
Litigation & Dispute Resolution	Richard M Schultz
Taxation & Estate Planning	Steven W Swibel
Technology & Intellectual Property Law	Edward S Weil

Taxation & Estate Planning: SCG&K represents clients in all facets of Federal and state taxation including tax planning for businesses and individuals and counsels clients on estate planning and wealth management.

Technology & Intellectual Property Law: The firm provides legal services to technology companies as well as manufacturers and service businesses that use and license technology. The firm represents numerous technology-based businesses, including software companies, IT consultancy firms and internet-based businesses. Firm attorneys have substantial experience in structuring and negotiating software licenses, consulting agreements, trademark and patent license agreements and other agreements, including joint ventures in transactions involving complex cross-licensing of intellectual property rights.

CLIENTS: The firm's clients include Bank One, NA; Eltek, LLC; Equity Residential Properties Trust; Fifield Corporation; ING Realty Partners; LaSalle Bank National Association; Lante Corporation; Mesirow Stein; MB Financial, Inc.; PPM America, Inc.; RTC Commercial Asset Trust; SBC Corporation; Siemens Corporation; Transco Inc.; Wickes Lumber Company.

LEADING LAW FIRMS

SHAWE & ROSENTHAL, LLP

THE FIRM

Managing Partners: Stephen D Shawe /Bruce S Harrison
Partner: J Michael McGuire

Number of partners: 10
Number of other lawyers: 5

HEAD OFFICE

MARYLAND
20 S. Charles Street, 11th Floor, **Baltimore**, MD 21201
Tel: 410 752 1040 **Fax:** 410 752 8861
Website: www.shawe.com

FIRM OVERVIEW: One of the first law firms in the country devoted exclusively to the representation of management in labor and employment matters, Shawe & Rosenthal was founded in 1947 by Earle K Shawe. Shawe & Rosenthal's practice involves both traditional labor and employment law matters, including claims brought under the Civil Rights Act, Age Discrimination in Employment Act, and the Americans with Disabilities Act. The firm defends claims involving employment discrimination, wrongful termination, defamation, ERISA, wage and hour, and occupational safety and health matters. It represents management in NLRB hearings, representation campaigns and collective bargaining negotiations. The firm provides advice and assistance in the formulation of covenants not to compete and trade secret protection commitments, and is active in litigation associated with disputes over restrictive covenants and trade secrets. The firm also provides advice and counsel in the creation of affirmation action plans and compliance with OFCCP regulations. From its inception in 1947, Shawe & Rosenthal decided to remain small (15 labor attorneys), select and centralized rather than expand into regional offices. This philosophy has contributed to a professional excellence that has attracted clients from across the nation. The firm has for decades represented many Fortune 500 companies, including some of the country's largest manufacturing, public utility, retail, health care and insurance concerns. Over the past three years the firm has handled two labor cases in the United States Supreme Court (Allentown Mack v. NLRB, 118 S.Ct. 818 (1998) and Kolstad v. American Dental Association, 527 U.S. 526 (1999)). Shawe & Rosenthal is a compact well managed organization, and is therefore able to provide clients with uniform and consistent advice, greater efficiencies in rendering services, and greater capabilities in providing short and long-term strategic planning. All of the firm's clients are represented in their general business affairs by other law firms, indeed some of the largest law firms in the country. Many of these other law firms have their own labor law sections. The firm's clients have, nonetheless, continued to turn to Shawe & Rosenthal for advice and counsel in the labor and employment field because of the firm's specialized knowledge and experience, and capability to provide advice quickly and efficiently. Members of the firm have written many publications in the employment field, including the 'Employment Law Deskbook' (1989) and two chapters in 'NLRA Law & Practice' (1991), both published by Mathew Bender. The firm also wrote the 'Maryland and Federal Employment Law Manual' (2001), published by the American Chamber of Commerce Publishers.

MAIN AREAS OF PRACTICE: Labor management relations; employment discrimination; human resources advice and counsel; employment tort and contract litigation; covenants not-to-compete litigation; intellectual property and trade secret litigation; wage and hour laws (FLSA, Portal to Portal Act); Occupational Safety and Health Acts (OSHA); Affirmative Action Programs (AAPs); Family and Medical Leave Act (FMLA); Workers' Adjustment and Retraining Act (WARN); Employee Benefits/ERISA; employment agreements; employment handbooks, policies, and procedures; appellate litigation; class actions.

CLIENTS: The firm has been for many years labor and employment counsel to such large companies as Black & Decker Corp., Bethlehem Steel Corporation, GEICO, Huffy Corporation, McDonald's Corporation, The May Department Stores Co., The Federal Reserve Bank of Richmond, Joseph A. Bank Clothiers and National Railroad Passenger Corporation (AMTRAK).
International Clients: Bermuda Hotel Association. For more than 20 years, Stephen Shawe served as chief spokesman for the Association in its collective bargaining negotiations with the union representing the Island's 3000 hotel employees. When Bermuda passed legislation requiring interest arbitration to resolve unresolved collective bargaining negotiations, Stephen presented the hotel employers' position at interest arbitration hearings in Hamilton, Bermuda.

LEADING LAW FIRMS

SHEARMAN & STERLING

THE FIRM

Senior Partner: David Heleniak
Managing Partner: Robert Treuhold

Number of partners worldwide: 220
Number of other lawyers worldwide: 844

FIRM OVERVIEW: Founded in 1873, Shearman & Sterling is a leading corporate law firm with more than 1,000 lawyers and 18 offices in the major financial and commercial centers of the world. As a full-service law firm, the firm's practice comprises approximately 20 major areas of corporate, commercial and business law, with particular strengths in mergers and acquisitions, capital markets, litigation and arbitration, executive compensation and employee benefits, antitrust and other essential industry sectors. The firm has established several industry-specific multidisciplinary teams, including financial services, media and entertainment, energy, healthcare and technology.

MAIN AREAS OF PRACTICE: Antitrust/competition law, bank finance, bankruptcy and reorganization, broker-dealer regulatory, capital markets, environmental, executive compensation and employee benefits, intellectual property, international arbitration, international trade and government relations, investment funds and asset management, litigation, mergers and acquisitions, outsourcing, private client, privatization, project development and finance, property, securitization and derivatives and tax.

CLIENTS: As a major player in the international arena, Shearman & Sterling represents many of the world's leading corporations, financial institutions, emerging growth companies, governments and state-owned enterprises and advises them on a wide range of legal matters. Approximately half of Shearman & Sterling clients are non-US entities.

INTERNATIONAL WORK: As a leading global law firm, Shearman & Sterling has an integrated network of 18 offices in major financial centers in North America, Europe, Asia and the Middle East, each of which has an extensive portfolio of international representations. The firm is one of the few genuinely integrated global firms, and practices English, French, German and US law. More than one-third of Shearman & Sterling's attorneys practice outside of the United States. The firm's attorneys are fluent in over 30 languages.

HEAD OFFICE

NEW YORK
599 Lexington Avenue, **New York**, NY 10022-6069
Tel: 212 848 4000 **Fax:** 212 848 7179
Email: rtreuhold@shearman
Website: www.shearman.com

BRANCH OFFICES

CALIFORNIA
1080 Marsh Road, **Menlo Park**, CA 94025-1022
Tel: 650 838 3600 **Fax:** 650 838 3699
Email: jwilson@shearman.com

555 California Street, Suite 2000, **San Francisco**, CA 94104-1522
Tel: 415 616 1100 **Fax** 415 616 1199
Email: jwilson@shear man.com

DISTRICT OF COLUMBIA
801 Pennsylvania Avenue, N.W., **Washington, DC** 20004-2604
Tel: 202 508 8000 **Fax:** 202 508 8100
Email: tmartin@shearman.com

INTERNATIONAL OFFICES

The firm also has offices in: Belgium, Canada, China, France, Germany, Hong Kong, Italy, Japan, Singapore, the United Arab Emirates and the United Kingdom. For futher details on these branches, please visit the firm's website at www.shearman.com.

SHEEHAN PHINNEY BASS + GREEN

THE FIRM

Managing Partner: William J Donovan

Number of partners: 39
Number of associates: 7
Number of counsel: 8

AREAS OF PRACTICE:
Corporate & Finance	45%
Litigation	37%
Real Estate/Environmental	7%
Trusts & Estates	6%
Labor & ERISA	5%

HEAD OFFICE

NEW HAMPSHIRE
1000 Elm Street, PO Box 3701, **Manchester**, NH 03105-3701
Tel: 603 668 0300 **Fax:** 603 627 8121
Website: www.sheenan.com

BRANCH OFFICES

MASSACHUSETTS
260 Franklin Street, **Boston**, MA 02110
Tel: 616 897 5600 **Fax:** 617 439 9363

NEW HAMPSHIRE
142 North Main Street, **Concord**, NH 03301
Tel: 603 223 2020 **Fax:** 603 224 8899

CONTACTS
Corporate Finance	Michael J Drooff
Corporate	Alan L Reische
Healthcare	Stephen E Weyl
Labor	James P Reidy
Litigation	James Q Shirley
Real Estate	Susan A Manchester
Banking	Kenneth A Viscarello

FIRM OVERVIEW: Sheehan Phinney Bass + Green has been serving clients throughout New England for over 50 years. While the firm's core clients remain businesses, institutions and municipalities based in New England, the firm also regularly represents the interests of national and international concerns throughout the region and the United States. Sheehan Phinney is known for professional excellence, practical counsel, and commitment to both its clients and the communities it serves. To enhance the services provided to its clients, the firm has expanded beyond its offices in Manchester and Concord by opening an office in the heart of Boston's financial district, and establishing a presence in New Hampshire's technology-rich Upper Valley. The firm's geographic expansion springs from the regional growth and diversity of its clients and their needs, including access to major capital and international markets. These service-oriented developments complement the firm's expansion of its government relations and tax advisory services through its affiliates, the Sheehan Phinney Capitol Group and Sheehan Phinney Tax Group. The firm is a member of Lex Mundi, an international network of law firms.

MAIN AREAS OF PRACTICE:

Corporate: Includes banking, bankruptcy, tax and securities law. The firm has particular expertise in mergers and acquisitions, corporate finance, healthcare, real estate, and labor law as well as corporate governance. Areas of practice also include tax matters, public and private securities, bankruptcy and insolvency, business formation, education, intellectual property and technology, import/export control and trust and estate planning.

Litigation: The firm's business litigation practice is one of the most well respected in Northern New England. Its personal injury litigation practice includes representation of both plaintiffs and defendants. Recent outcomes include: successfully defended multimillion dollar claim for commissions in arbitration resulting in award only for those commissions we conceded were due; obtained dismissal, which was affirmed on appeal, of claim that company acquiring another company by merger must register with the Bureau of Securities Regulation under State's Anti-Takeover Act before consummating merger; successfully defended attempts to enjoin $18 Million merger transaction and then successfully defended claims against directors of merging corporations of breaching fiduciary duties to dissenting stockholders, obtaining award of attorney's fees against plaintiffs in excess of $400,000, served as lead class action counsel for class of 15,000 taxpayers seeking refunds of interest and dividends tax in violation of US Commerce Clause and successfully represented minority stockholder in enjoining squeeze out by majority stockholder.

Banking & Finance: In addition to its frequent representation of borrowers and lenders in numerous transactions, the firm has served as counsel in more than a billion dollars of tax-exempt financings in New Hampshire and Massachusetts over the past 18 months. The firm's clients in public finance transactions include New Hampshire's largest issuer of tax-exempt bonds, as well as borrowers, underwriters and corporate trustees.

Labor: Increasing governmental regulation of the workplace and ever-expanding rights of employees have made "preventive law" the soundest method for avoiding significant liability in employment law. Legal services in this area include: developing effective anti-discrimination policies, proper employee screening and verifying procedures, wage and salary administration strategies (FLSA), executive employment agreements, employee handbooks and policies, noncompetition and nondisclosure covenants, employment applications and performance evaluation policies, severance agreements, early retirement programs, reduction in force procedures, substance abuse policies, workplace privacy policies, workplace violence prevention or response plans, leave of absence programs (including FMLA, maternity, military and jury duty), and personnel file record-keeping procedures.

Real Estate: The firm works with clients in all areas of commercial real estate financing and construction matters, advising and representing developers, lenders and users of commercial properties: office buildings, shopping centers, condominiums, affordable housing projects, corporate headquarters and airports. Representation includes negotiation of purchase, construction and financing documentation (including IRC Section 42 financing), appearance before land use boards and registration of condominiums with State Department of Justice (Consumer Protection Division). Agent for major title insurance companies.

CLIENTS: The firm's clients represent a diverse range of industries including: healthcare, education, manufacturing, insurance, import/export, technology, communications, banking and finance, not-for-profit, pension and mutual funds, government relations, religious institutions, commercial lending and public finance.

LEADING LAW FIRMS

SHOOK, HARDY & BACON

THE FIRM

Managing Partner: John F Murphy (also Chairman)

Number of partners & counsel: 263
Number of attorneys: 600

FIRM OVERVIEW: International law firm Shook, Hardy & Bacon L.L.P. (SHB) possesses a litigation legacy spanning more than a century. Established in Kansas City in 1889, the firm today has 600 attorneys and 2,250 employees worldwide. SHB's efficiencies and innovations have evolved over time, yet the foundational beliefs in working for the client's best interest have remained, and are reflective by the firms representation of many of the nation's major corporations included in *Fortune*'s elite top 100. Clients are served from offices strategically located in Geneva, Houston, Kansas City, London, Miami, New Orleans, Overland Park, San Francisco, Tampa and Washington, DC. SHB's culture and values focus on the firms collective and collaborative strengths within practice areas and our people. This strength creates a strong global stance which serves clients around the world.

MAIN AREAS OF PRACTICE:

Litigation: The litigation legacy of Shook, Hardy & Bacon (SHB) spans more than a century, being the firm of choice for corporations facing high-stakes litigation. SHB attorneys are nationally noted and have tried cases to verdict or to judgment in virtually every substantive area and business segment including: antitrust, corporate finance, employee benefits, employment litigation and policy, environmental, ERISA, healthcare, intellectual property, products liability, public policy, securities litigation and tax. Many litigation cases also involve class actions, where SHB attorneys are at the forefront in efforts to reform the class action device and its application. Shook, Hardy & Bacon has played a key role in developing potential revisions to federal and state court class action rules, including developing legislation to curtail the increasingly common abuses of the class action device. In recent years, SHB attorneys have also filed amicus briefs on behalf of organizations involved in high-profile appeals that raise significant class action-related policy questions.

Corporate Finance & Banking: Attorneys in SHB's Corporate Finance and Banking Section concentrate their practices in mergers and acquisitions, joint ventures, strategic alliances, securities matters, private equity and financing transactions, commercial finance and banking and the general representation of publicly-held and private entities. Corporate finance attorneys are experienced in all aspects of corporate transactions, including private placements, mergers, acquisitions and divestitures, joint ventures, distributorships, public offerings, tender offers, venture capital financing, equity and debt restructuring, project finance, workouts, corporate governance and general corporate law. SHB's banking and commercial law attorneys counsel local, national and international financial institutions and corporate borrowers on loan transactions and regulatory issues and are nationally recognized experts in various areas of commercial law.

HEAD OFFICE

MISSOURI
One Kansas City Place, 1200 Main Street
Kansas City, MO 64105-2118
Tel: 816 474 6550 **Fax:** 816 421 5547

BRANCH OFFICES

CALIFORNIA
333 Bush Street, Suite 600
San Fransisco, CA 94104-2828
Tel: 415 544 1900 **Fax:** 415 391 0281

DISTRICT OF COLUMBIA
Hamilton Square, 600 14th Street, NW, Suite 800
Washington, DC, 20005-2004
Tel: 202 783 8400 **Fax:** 202 783 4211

FLORIDA
Miami Center, Suite 2400, 201 South Biscayne Boulevard
Miami, FL 33131-4332
Tel: 305 358 5171 **Fax:** 305 358 7470

100 North Tampa Street, Suite 2900
Tampa, FL 33602-5810
Tel: 813 202 7100 **Fax:** 813 221 8837

LOUISIANA
LL&E Tower, 909 Poydras, Suite 1100
New Orleans, LA 70112-4017
Tel: 504 310 4088 **Fax:** 504 522 5771

KANSAS
84 Corporate Woods, 10801 Mastin, Suite 1000
Overland Park, KS 66210-1671
Tel: 913 451 6060 **Fax:** 913 451 8879

TEXAS
JP Morgan/Chase Tower, 600 Travis Street, Suite 1600
Houston, TX 77002-2911
Tel: 713 227 8008 **Fax:** 713 227 9508

CONTACTS

Missouri	John F Murphy
California	Shannon L Spangler
Kansas	Justin J Johl
Louisiana	Howard Shapiro
Miami	Kenneth J Reilly
Tampa	Daniel F Molony
Texas	K B Battaglini
Washington	Keith T Borman

SIDLEY AUSTIN BROWN & WOOD

THE FIRM

Chairman of Executive Committee: Thomas A Cole
Chairman of the Management Committee: Charles W Douglas
Vice-Chairman of Management Committee: Thomas R Smith, Jr

Number of partners: 535
Number of other lawyers: 1011

AREAS OF PRACTICE:
Commercial/Business Litigation	24%
Corporate Transactions/Contracts	21%
Securitization & Banking	20%
Real Estate	6%
Taxation/International	5%
Intellectual Property	5%
Funds	3%
Environmental/Energy/Natural Resources	3%
Employment/Labor/Benefits	3%
Product/Professional Liability	2%
Government	2%
Public Finance	1%
Healthcare	1%
Probate/Trusts & Estates	1%
Private Clients	1%
Other	2%

US OFFICES

CALIFORNIA
555 West Fifth Street, **Los Angeles**, CA 90013
Tel: 213 896 6000 **Fax:** 213 896 6600

555 California Street, Suite 5000, **San Francisco**, CA 94104-1715
Tel: 415 772 1200 **Fax:** 415 397 4621

DISTRICT OF COLUMBIA
1501 K Street, NW, **Washington**, DC 20005
Tel: 202 736 8000 **Fax:** 202 736 8711

ILLINOIS
Bank One Plaza, 10 South Dearborn Street, **Chicago**, IL 60603
Tel: 312 853 7000 **Fax:** 312 853 7036

NEW YORK
787 Seventh Avenue, **New York**, NY 10019
Tel: 212 839 5300 **Fax:** 212 839 5599

TEXAS
717 N Harwood, Suite 3400, **Dallas**, TX 75201
Tel: 214 981 3300 **Fax:** 214 981 3400

INTERNATIONAL OFFICES

The firm also has offices in Beijing, Hong Kong, Shanghai, Singapore, Switzerland, Tokyo and the United Kingdom

FIRM OVERVIEW: Sidley Austin Brown & Wood is one of the world's largest full service law firms. With more than 1500 lawyers practicing on three continents (North America, Europe and Asia), the firm provides a broad range of integrated services to meet the needs of both large and small businesses as well as governments, institutions, associations, foundations, professional firms and individuals. The firm was recently named the 'Number One law firm in the US' for overall client service by *BTI Consulting* in its annual survey of how large corporate law departments rate their outside law firms. According to BTI, general counsel from *Fortune* 1000 companies interviewed recognized excellence in 'every aspect of Sidley Austin's client service and delivery, specifically noting the firm's dedication to helping clients and to understanding clients' business-specific issues and goals'.

MAIN AREAS OF PRACTICE: Sidley Austin Brown & Wood has a major corporate and financial transactions practice with significant activity in all areas, including mergers and acquisitions, spin-offs, capital markets, divestitures and joint ventures as well as all types of financings, including public offerings, project financings, asset securitizations and bank lending transactions.

CLIENTS: The firm's clients include individuals, entrepreneurs and executives, industrial and service corporations; venture capital/private equity firms; partnerships; investment banks; commercial banks; public utilities; non-profit organizations; mutual funds; insurance and other financial services companies; and government agencies.

INTERNATIONAL WORK: The firm handles work in Arabic, Bahasa (Indonesia), Chinese (Cantonese, Mandarin, Shanghainese), Danish, Efik (African), Finnish, French, German, Greek, Hebrew, Hindi, Hungarian, Italian, Japanese, Latvian, Lithuanian, Malay, Norwegian, Portuguese, Russian, Sanskrit, Serbian, Spanish, Swedish, Tagalog, Taiwanese, Tamil, Telugu, Yoruba (African).

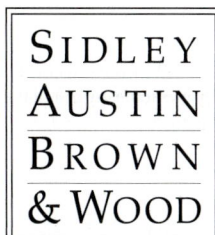

LEADING LAW FIRMS

SKADDEN, ARPS, SLATE, MEAGHER & FLOM LLP & AFFILIATES

THE FIRM

Executive Partner: Robert C Sheehan
Senior Partner: Joseph H Flom

Number of US partners: 324
Number of other US lawyers: 1308

FIRM OVERVIEW: With approximately 1800 attorneys in 23 offices, Skadden, Arps, Slate, Meagher & Flom LLP and affiliates is one of the largest law firms in the world. The firm provides a wide array of legal services globally to the corporate, financial, industrial and governmental communities.

MAIN AREAS OF PRACTICE
Corporate/M&A: Skadden has consistently ranked first among law firms in the US for handling the greatest number of the largest M&A transactions announced annually, and has been involved in many of the largest transactions ever. The firm's clients range from start-ups and middle market companies, to the cream of the *Fortune* 250. Transactions include recapitalizations and restructurings, including spin-offs, divestitures and other techniques for maximizing value for the client.
Corporate Restructuring: The firm's corporate restructuring group serves corporations and their principal creditors and investors by providing 'upper margin,' value-added legal solutions to troubled company merger and acquisition, financial and restructuring situations. The firm has advised on some of the most widely publicized corporate restructurings recently announced or pending, including several of the largest Chapter 11 cases in US history. The firm also has a substantial practice in advising clients on non-judicial restructurings.
Litigation: Skadden represents clients in federal and state trial and appellate courts nationwide, and has developed a premier securities class action defense practice. The firm's work on antitrust matters includes counseling and litigating for clients in connection with mergers, acquisitions and joint ventures. The firm assists clients in resolving disputes without litigation by using various alternative dispute resolution procedures, including arbitration, mediation, conciliation, and mini-trials, and has represented US and non-US clients in arbitrations under all major rules systems and before every major arbitral institution worldwide.
Banking & Finance: Skadden advises underwriters, issuers and purchasers in public and private financings. It advises on all types of debt and equity instruments; structured finance; public finance; lease and project financings; commodities; futures and derivative products. The firm's clients include investment companies; advisors and broker-dealers; and private investment funds.
Industry-related Practices: The firm has a number of industry-related practice areas, namely banking and financial services, communications, energy, environmental, healthcare, information technology, insurance, real estate and utilities.

CLIENTS: The firm represents a broad spectrum of clients, from small high-technology start-up companies to nearly half of the *Fortune* 250 industrial and service corporations in the US.

HEAD OFFICE

NEW YORK
Four Times Square, **New York**, NY 10036
Tel: 212 735 3000 **Fax:** 212 735 2000
Website: www.skadden.com

BRANCH OFFICES

CALIFORNIA
300 South Grand Avenue, **Los Angeles**, CA 90071
Tel: 213 687 5000 **Fax:** 213 687 5600

525 University Avenue, Suite 1100, **Palo Alto**, CA 94301
Tel: 650 470 4500 **Fax:** 650 470 4570

Four Embarcadero Center, **San Francisco**, CA 94111
Tel: 415 984 6400 **Fax:** 415 984 2698

DELAWARE
One Rodney Square, PO Box 636, **Wilmington**, DE 19899
Tel: 302 651 3000 **Fax:** 302 651 3001

DISTRICT OF COLUMBIA
1440 New York Avenue, NW, **Washington, DC** 20005
Tel: 202 371 7000 **Fax:** 202 393 5760

ILLINOIS
333 West Wacker Drive, **Chicago**, IL 60606
Tel: 312 407 0700 **Fax:** 312 407 0411

MASSACHUSETTS
One Beacon Street, **Boston**, MA 02108
Tel: 617 573 4800 **Fax:** 617 573 4822

NEW JERSEY
One Newark Center, **Newark**, NJ 07102
Tel: 973 639 6800 **Fax:** 973 639 6858

TEXAS
1600 Smith Street, Suite 4400, **Houston**, TX 77002
Tel: 713 655 5100 **Fax:** 713 655 5200

VIRGINIA
11911 Freedom Drive, Suite 550, **Reston**, VA 20190
Tel: 703 796 2345 **Fax:** 703 796 2344

INTERNATIONAL WORK: Skadden's offices in Beijing, Brussels, Frankfurt, Hong Kong, London, Moscow, Paris, Singapore, Sydney, Tokyo, Toronto and Vienna, in addition to substantial practices in Latin America, the Middle East and Africa, enable the firm to offer clients an integrated cross-border service. Main practices overseas include corporate transactions such as mergers and acquisitions, privatizations, joint ventures, project financing, international trade matters, litigation, capital markets, and banking and finance transactions.

LEADING LAW FIRMS

SLUSSER & FROST, LLP

THE FIRM

Senior Partner: William C Slusser

Number of partners: 4
Number of other lawyers: 2

AREAS OF PRACTICE:
Intellectual Property Litigation	70%
Commercial Litigation	20%
Appellate	10%

HEAD OFFICE

TEXAS
4890 Three Allen Center, 333 Clay Street, **Houston**, Texas 77002
Tel: 713 860 3300 **Fax:** 713 860 3333
Email: slusser@slusserfrost.com
Website: slusserfrost.com

CONTACTS

Intellectual Property Litigation	William C Slusser
Commercial Litigation	William C Slusser
Appellate	Claudia Wilson Frost

FIRM OVERVIEW: The firm has distinguished itself in jury trials of complex cases, typically, but not exclusively, intellectual property cases. The firm was founded in January 1999 by William C Slusser, former head of the trial department of the Houston Office of Baker Botts, LLP, and Claudia Wilson Frost, founder and former head of the appellate section of the Houston Office of Baker Botts. The firm was joined by Michael E Wilson, who practiced complex litigation and intellectual property law as a former partner at Baker Botts; Jayme Partridge, who formerly practiced intellectual property law and complex litigation at Baker Botts before managing intellectual property litigation at ExxonMobil; Laura F Jones, who formerly practiced complex litigation, antitrust, and intellectual property law at Baker Botts; and Keith Jaasma, who practiced complex litigation, antitrust, and intellectual property law at Baker Botts. The firm focuses on intellectual property litigation and commercial litigation for both plaintiffs and defendants at trial and on appeal. Clients of the firm range from individuals to multibillion dollar corporations. In addition to their intellectual property experience, the firm's attorneys have litigated matters involving business torts, energy, environmental, antitrust, ERISA, professional liability, and products liability, enabling them to handle virtually any variation of complex commercial litigation. The firm's attorneys have been involved in litigation in Texas, California, Delaware, Illinois, Louisiana, Michigan, New York, and Virginia.

MAIN AREAS OF PRACTICE:

Intellectual Property Litigation: The firm's intellectual property cases, in which it has represented both plaintiffs and defendants, have ranged from actions brought on behalf of individual patent holders to actions between multibillion dollar corporations. Attorneys of the firm have been involved in patent litigation involving polyolefin production, offshore pipelines, deepwater platform technology, petroleum and natural gas well drilling, petroleum and natural gas well fracturing, motor oil additives, factory automation, computer networks, knee surgery, eye surgery, and a pharmaceutical license agreement. Mr. Slusser has litigated a significant trademark case and affirmed the judgment on appeal, and also served as an arbitrator in a complex patent licensing and infringement dispute. Mr Slusser, Mr Wilson, and Ms Partridge have degrees in Electrical Engineering, Chemical Engineering, and Mechanical Engineering, respectively. Mr Wilson and Ms Partridge are licensed to practice before the United States Patent and Trademark Office.

Commercial Litigation: The firm also handles complex commercial litigation, and the firm's lawyers have been involved in antitrust litigation, ERISA litigation, shareholder derivative suits, complex oil and gas litigation, and class actions. The firm also has experience in arbitrating complex commercial cases.

Appellate: In addition to handling appeals arising out of cases they have litigated on the trial level, the firm's lawyers have handled numerous appeals of cases originally handled by other firms on the trial level, involving products liability claims, complex commercial disputes, oil and gas matters, professional negligence, and copyright infringement. The firm's lawyers have also provided assistance with pre- and post-trial motion practice, including preparation and argument of jury charges. The firm's lawyers have practiced before the Texas Supreme Court and Courts of Appeals, and the United States Court of Appeals for the Federal Circuit, Fifth Circuit, Ninth Circuit, Tenth Circuit, and DC Circuit.

CLIENTS: The firm's attorneys have serviced clients in the following industries: petroleum exploration and production, chemicals, plastics, oilfield services, retailing, cable television, telecommunications, pharmaceuticals, law, software development, transportation, higher education, and consumer products. Representative clients include: Shell Oil Company, Shell Chemical Company, BJ Services Company, ExxonMobil Corporation, the Gillette Company, Basell North America Inc, Marathon Oil Company, and Equistar Chemicals, L.P. The firm has also represented small companies and individuals in patent infringement and commercial disputes.

SMITH, ANDERSON, BLOUNT, DORSETT, MITCHELL & JERNIGAN, LLP

THE FIRM

Managing Partner: John L Jernigan

Number of partners: 48
Number of other lawyers: 41

HEAD OFFICE

NORTH CAROLINA
2500 First Union Capitol Center, **Raleigh**, NC 27601
Tel: 919 821 1220 **Fax:** 919 821 6800
Website: www.smithlaw.com

CONTACTS

Commercial	C Steven Mason
Corporate/Securities	Gerald F Roach
Litigation	Samuel G Thompson
Regulatory	Julian D Bobbitt, Jr

FIRM OVERVIEW: Since the firm's founding in 1912, it has grown to be the largest law firm in Raleigh and the Research Triangle region of North Carolina, and one of the largest in the state. The firm provides a full range of legal services and is dedicated to the principles of professionalism, excellence, and service to its clients and the community. The firm values long-term relationships with its clients and is constantly working to meet their changing needs. The firm represents clients at every level of the judicial system, including the state and federal trial and appellate courts. It also appears regularly before state and federal agencies and in other forums to advance the interests of its clients and is experienced in all forms of alternative dispute resolution.

MAIN AREAS OF PRACTICE:

Commercial Transactions: The firm has been a leader in assisting North Carolina businesses and individuals with commercial transactions, and has the legal and business skills needed for dynamic businesses today, including bank and other private finance, access to capital markets, mergers and acquisitions, environmental compliance, commercial real estate, bankruptcy, and international transactions. The firm has significant experience in secured and unsecured bank lending, joint ventures and strategic alliances, venture and mezzanine investments, leveraged buyouts and acquisition financing, letters of credit, mergers and acquisitions, commercial paper, derivatives, workouts and reorganizations, commercial real estate, environmental compliance, conduit financing, securitizations and other asset-based financings, divestitures, licensing, international trade and transactions, and franchising.

Contract Disputes & Commercial Litigation: The firm's Commercial Litigation Practice Group has substantial trial experience, and is adept at handling complex, document-intensive cases. The firm offers expertise in all forms of alternative dispute resolution. Some members of the commercial litigation practice group are certified mediators or arbitrators. The commercial litigation practice group includes members of the American College of Trial Lawyers, the International Society of Barristers, the International Association of Defense Counsel, the American Board of Trial Advocates, the American Judicature Society, and the Judicial Conference of the Fourth Circuit Court of Appeals. The firm has extensive experience in counseling and representing clients in banking litigation, disputes between buyers and sellers of goods and services, commercial real estate disputes, and insurance disputes.

Insurance Law & Regulation: The firm's insurance law and regulation group has substantial experience representing domestic and foreign insurers, HMOs, and other insurance industry participants in a broad range of matters, including formation, licensing, transactional, compliance and general counsel matters. The firm often represents clients before the North Carolina Department of Insurance and other regulatory agencies. Areas of extensive experience include formations and company licensing, financial, market conduct and other examinations, mergers, acquisitions and other changes of control, surplus lines issues, policy and contract drafting and analysis, reinsurance treaties and assumption reinsurance, form and rate filings and approvals, regulatory compliance, administrative proceedings, coverage questions, Holding Company Act filings and approvals, agent licensing and appointment, service area expansions, and general and corporate advice.

Health Care Law: The firm's health care practice provides business and regulatory counsel to a wide variety of health care clients across the Southeast, from physicians and physician organizations to other providers to informatics companies and e-health entities. Primary services and typical transactions include antitrust, business/contract disputes, certificate of need, covenants not to compete, employment agreements, HIPAA and other federal and state confidentiality and privacy laws, fraud and abuse, including Stark, health care financing, licensing board issues, managed care, medical staff issues, medicare compliance, mergers and acquisitions/joint ventures, negotiations with insurers, physician organizations, PSOs and insurance, and quality assurance.

Medical Malpractice Defense: The firm's medical malpractice group defends physicians, hospitals, and other health care providers with a philosophy that combines an aggressive and efficient approach to litigation with an in-depth understanding of relevant medical issues. It is experienced in assisting health care providers through every stage of malpractice actions, including prelitigation claims, discovery, depositions, trial, and appellate advocacy. The firm has represented health care providers insured by most of the medical malpractice insurance companies currently operating in North Carolina.

Securities & Growth Companies: The firm's securities and growth companies practice group focuses on the special needs of fast-moving public and growth companies, blending its primary role as outside corporate counsel with its transactional experience in venture and public financing and mergers and acquisitions. The firm provides a full range of general corporate securities, corporate finance, mergers and acquisitions, contracting, venture capital, and intellectual property advice to clients ranging from start-ups to established public companies, many in technology fields. Most recently, the firm has communicated with clients and developed materials to help public companies deal with the effects of the Sarbanes-Oxley Act and 10-K and proxy requirements in light of numerous new regulatory changes.

CLIENTS: The firm's clients include some of the largest financial institutions, insurance companies, public utilities, retailers, manufacturing, pharmaceutical, and biotechnology companies in its region and the nation, as well as emerging growth and technology companies. The firm also represents smaller businesses and individuals, as well as trade and professional associations and their members.

INTERNATIONAL WORK: The firm represents several international companies that have ongoing business interests in its market, including companies based in the United Kingdom, Japan, Germany, and Israel.

LEADING LAW FIRMS

SMITH HULSEY & BUSEY

THE FIRM

Chairman: Stephen D Busey
Managing Partner: William E Kuntz

HEAD OFFICE

FLORIDA
225 Water Street, Suite 1800 **Jacksonville**, FL 32202
Tel: 904 359 7700 **Fax:** 904 359 7708
Website: www.smithhulsey.com

CONTACTS

Business & Finance	M Richard Lewis Jr
Environmental	Tim E Sleeth
Health Care	M Richard Lewis Jr
Litigation & Insolvency	Stephen D Busey
Real Estate & Land Use	Harry M Wilson III

FIRM OVERVIEW: Smith Hulsey & Busey is a full service Florida business law firm which began as Lamson & Smith in 1936. The firm has a proven track record of sound counsel, innovative problem solving and successful dispute resolution. The firm's clients with national and international operations have provided the firm regular experience in major transactions and dispute resolution throughout the world. The firm offers the very best legal services with an efficiency not typical in larger firms.

MAIN AREAS OF PRACTICE:

Business and Finance: The firm advises clients in mergers and acquisitions; venture capital investments; initial public offerings; public offerings, periodic reporting and SEC compliance for publicly held companies; regulation of broker-dealers, investment advisors, and mutual funds; and partnership and other syndication transactions. In addition, the firm's public finance group has extensive experience representing clients in every aspect of tax-exempt public financing transactions, including bond counsel, disclosure counsel, underwriter's counsel, bank counsel, trustee's counsel and borrower's counsel.

Environmental: Florida has a strong commitment to the protection of the natural environment. As a result, the firm has developed a comprehensive environmental law practice, assisting its clients with compliance, permitting and clean up issues as well as development of business plans to economically manage environmental obligations. The firm has special expertise in identifying and enforcing insurance coverage rights for environmental problems. The Environmental Group also assists our Real Estate and Land Use Group with environmental problems of real property owners and managers.

Health Care: The firm has one of the largest and most diverse health care practice groups in Florida. The firm represents hospitals and health systems, academic medical centers, continuing care retirement communities, home health care providers, skilled nursing facilities, clinical laboratories, medical technology companies, managed care companies, IDOs, PHOs, physician group practices and individual physicians throughout Florida. The firm's health care practice includes formation of health care entities, strategic alliances of health care providers, mergers and acquisitions, joint ventures, reimbursement, Medicare, Medicaid, regulatory matters, fraud and abuse, licensing, certificates of need, risk management, and labor relations. Attorneys in the Health Care Group have expertise in the many areas that affect health industry clients, including antitrust, insurance regulation, tax exemption, and financing. Additionally, members of the Health Care Group work closely with legislators and other officials from the State of Florida, as well as the Agency for Health Care Administration, to help shape state health care legislation, rules and regulations.

Insolvency: The firm has represented debtors, creditors, committees, trustees and examiners in major business reorganizations throughout the United States. The firm has represented a number of New York Stock Exchange companies as debtors in successful reorganization proceedings in Florida. The firm counsels financially troubled companies outside of bankruptcy proceedings regarding their restructuring alternatives, and fiduciary and governance issues. The firm has special expertise in health care insolvencies. The firm also is experienced in assignments for the benefit of creditors and bankruptcy liquidations.

Litigation: The firm's lawyers try complex commercial disputes, class actions, mass torts and catastrophic injury cases before juries in state and federal courts throughout Florida. The firm tries high exposure cases on a regular basis. Although the firm is experienced and successful in taking complex litigation through trial, the firm's goal is to resolve disputes short of the risk or expense of trial. The firm's reputation for trying cases, and the results it has achieved, help facilitate early resolution of disputes.

Real Estate & Land Use: The firm's real estate and land use attorneys represent developers, investors, lenders, and business users in the acquisition, development, financing, sale, and leasing of real estate throughout the Southeast. The firm is experienced in planning the structure of and negotiating complex real estate transactions, as well as the legal analysis and documentation. The firm's expertise includes condominium and time-sharing forms of ownership, real estate syndication, taxation of real estate, zoning, and the regulation of land use.

Other Practices: For further practice area detail, including the firm's tax, intellectual property, labor, estate planning and governmental affairs practices, and information regarding the firm's lawyers, please refer to their website: www.smithhulsey.com.

LEADING LAW FIRMS

SONNENSCHEIN NATH & ROSENTHAL

THE FIRM

Chairman: Duane C Quaini
Number of partners: 278
Number of other lawyers: 322

FIRM OVERVIEW: With 600 attorneys in nine US offices and a history of engagements involving client matters throughout Europe, Asia and Latin America, Sonnenschein serves many of the world's largest and best known businesses, nonprofits and individuals.

MAIN AREAS OF PRACTICE:

Antitrust, Franchising & Distribution: Counsels on antitrust, distribution, licensing, franchise and dealer law, marketing, franchisee relations, supplier arrangements; litigates antitrust, franchising, distribution matters.

Bankruptcy & Restructuring: Handles bankruptcy, restructuring for official unsecured creditor, equity committees, Chapter 11 debtors/debtors-in-possession, insurers, indenture trustees, asset acquirers, secured creditors.

Biotech/Life Sciences: Counsels in scientific environment; backgrounds: genetics, organic chemistry, biochemistry, molecular, cellular biology.

Communications, Information Technology & Media: Counsels major cable television, broadcasting companies, telecommunication services providers; advises on global telecommunications services arrangements, information technology, information services outsourcing, contracting, compliance.

Corporate & Securities/Corporate Governance: Provides value-added, solution-oriented advice, services in mergers, acquisitions; joint ventures, strategic alliances; technology investment, licensing; complex outsourcing arrangements; public, private securities offerings; private equity transactions; commercial financing; securities law compliance; corporate control, takeover defense; corporate governance matters.

Employee Benefits & Executive Compensation: Negotiates executive agreements, strategies for change-in-control compensation, equity plans. Counsels in development, management of tax-qualified retirement plans, deferred compensation, welfare plans, HIPAA; class action defense of ERISA fiduciary, benefit claims.

Environmental/Energy: Counsels on avoiding/minimizing environmental liability; litigates in government, private party suits, including before applicable regulatory bodies; negotiates innovative alternative agreements; develops plans for managing environmental liability, facilitating new project, product development, structuring, supporting environmental management programs; develops energy policy, legislation; counsels energy clients.

Government Contracts: Advises, litigates disputes involving contract performance, bid protests, civil, criminal False Claims Act investigations, actions between prime and subcontractors; advises, litigates matters involving construction projects with public agencies; develops strategies to maximize opportunities for new contracts, retention of existing business.

Healthcare: Provides legal solutions for challenges facing businesses in changing healthcare industry with extensive experience in all aspects of healthcare law, including joint ventures, mergers, acquisitions, e-health, managed care transactions, healthcare financing, Medicare/Medicaid reimbursement.

Insurance: Counsels in crisis management, complex commercial litigation; provides legal solutions, including in major class actions, constitutional cases, coverage disputes, employment, regulatory, compliance matters.

Intellectual Property & Technology: Counsels, litigates on development, use, protection of intellectual property; represents clients in application for, prosecution of patent, trademark rights; technical expertise in electronic, computer, telecommunications disciplines, aerospace, mechanical design, engineering arts, chemistry, pharmaceutical science, biotech.

International Trade & Import/Export Regulation: Counsels on laws governing movement of goods, technology across national borders. Advises on trade policy matters, customs regulation, export controls, enforcement, penalties, boycotts, sanctions, embargoes, import relief investigations, including anti-dumping, countervailing duty scope determinations, unfair trade practices; develops export, import management systems, internal controls.

Labor & Employment: Counsels on compliance issues, including training, internal investigations; representation in all forums, including single employee litigation, arbitrations, administrative investigations, class actions, corporate transactions including mergers, acquisitions, downsizings.

Litigation & Business Regulation: Provides full range of nationally recognized commercial litigation services, including class action defense, insurance, white collar crime, product liability, intellectual property, technology, real estate, construction, financial transactions, securities, antitrust, franchising, distribution, government contracts, federal regulation.

Public Law & Policy Strategies: Concentrates on issues, strategies important to clients with matters before Congress, Executive Branch, national policymakers, state, local legislators, regulators; assists in direct advocacy, budget, appropriations, grassroots communications, crisis management, coalition development, marketing, partnership development, international government relations.

Real Estate: Sophisticated multi-state acquisitions, dispositions; construction, permanent, mezzanine financing; equity investment; commercial, multifamily development; leasing; affordable housing; hotels, hospitality.

Taxation: Structures, advises on highly complex corporate acquisitions, dispositions involving US and non-US entities, financing techniques (including cross-border financings), general US and non-US planning for USMNCs, partnerships, other joint ventures, real estate, foreign transactions; experienced in exempt organizations, tax controversies, including tax litigation.

Trusts & Estates: Counsels individuals, families with substantial wealth with tax, estate planning; advises on trust and estate-related litigation issues; handles administration of estates, trusts, fiduciary accountings.

US OFFICES

CALIFORNIA
601 South Figueroa Street, Suite 1500, **Los Angeles** CA 90017
Tel: 213 623 9300 **Fax:** 213 623 9924

685 Market Street, 6th Floor, **San Francisco** CA 94105
Tel: 415 882 5000 **Fax:** 415 543 5472
Website: www.sonnenschein.com

DISTRICT OF COLUMBIA
1301 K Street NW, Suite 600, East Tower, **Washington** DC 20005
Tel: 202 408 6400 **Fax:** 202 408 6399

FLORIDA
Phillips Point, West Tower, 777 South Flagler Drive, Suite 1102, **West Palm Beach** FL 33401
Tel: 561 833 2410 **Fax:** 561 833 8387

ILLINOIS
8000 Sears Tower, 233 South Wacker Drive, **Chicago** IL 60606-6404
Tel: 312 876 8000 **Fax:** 312 876 7934

MISSOURI
4520 Main Street, Suite 1100, **Kansas City** MO 64111
Tel: 816 460 2400 **Fax:** 816 531 7545

One Metropolitan Square, Suite 3000, **St Louis** MO 63102
Tel: 314 241 1800 **Fax:** 314 259 5959

NEW JERSEY
820 Morris Turnpike, **Short Hills** NJ 07078
Tel: 973 564 6480 **Fax:** 973 564 6493

NEW YORK
1221 Avenue of the Americas, **New York** NY 10020
Tel: 212 768 6700 **Fax:** 212 768 6800

STARNES & ATCHISON LLP

THE FIRM

Managing Partner: W Michael Atchison

Number of partners: 23
Number of other attorneys: 25

FIRM OVERVIEW: Founded in 1975, Starnes & Atchison LLP has always been a firm devoted exclusively to litigation. Today, Starnes & Atchison LLP is made up of over 40 attorneys and continues to be committed to a civil litigation practice. The firm's distinguished list of clients includes physicians, attorneys, architects, accountants and other professionals, as well as corporations, hospitals, long-term care facilities, nursing homes and insurance companies. Starnes & Atchison LLP has its main office in Birmingham, with a second office in Mobile. The firm handles litigation matters throughout Alabama and serves as lead counsel in a number of cases pending around the United States. The attorneys who make up Starnes & Atchison LLP are recognized as ranking among the most experienced trial lawyers in the state - three of the firm's partners are Fellows of the American College of Trial Lawyers, five of its partners are members of the American Board of Trial Advocates and four of its attorneys are listed in the Best Lawyers in America. Starnes & Atchison LLP is a young and energetic firm which holds a respected position in the legal community. The firm places emphasis on continuing legal education through weekly in-house programs. In addition, the firm maintains substantial legal and medical libraries and utilizes state of the art computer technology so as to provide clients with excellent resources and professional legal expertise.

CLIENTS:

Corporations & Institutions: Primeamerica; AT&T Universal Card Services; National Bank of Commerce; Citigroup, Inc.; Bancorp South, Inc.; G.E. Capital, Inc.; Alabama National Bancorporation; Verizon; International Paper; Murphy Oil; Capital One; Caremark RX, Inc.; American Mining, Co.; National Service Industries; Murphy Oil USA, Inc.; Lowes; Drummond Company, Inc.; Allen-Bradley Company; American Arbitration Association; American Honda; Apache Products Company; Auburn University; Automatic Data Processing, Inc.; Babcock-Wilcox, Inc.; Business Council of Alabama; Coats Company; Crown Central Petroleum Corporation; Crum & Forster Corp.; East Penn Manufacturing Company; First Community Bank of the South; GTE; GTE Mobilnet; Harbert International Corp.; Hennessy Company; Highland Bank; Jasper Corp.; Mercedes Benz of North America, Inc.; Murray, Inc.; Owens-Illinois, Inc.; Rheem Manufacturing Company; Synthes (USA); W.R. Grace Company; Waste Management, Inc.; Home Depot; Marubeni Corp.
Medical: ProNational Inc; ProAssurance Inc; American Health Insurance Company; Brookwood Medical Center, Inc.; Glaxo Wellcome, Inc.; HealthPartners of Alabama, Inc.; Hoffman-LaRoche, Inc.; Med Partners, Inc.; Medical Care International; Mobile Infirmary Medical Center; Medical Assurance, Inc.; Podiatry Insurance Company of America; St. Vincent's Hospital; University of Alabama at Birmingham; University of Alabama Health Services Foundation; Tenet Health Systems; Woodcrest Service, Inc.; Ascension Health Care.

HEAD OFFICE

ALABAMA
100 Brookwood Place, 7th Floor, P.O. Box 598512, **Birmingham**, AL 35259
Tel: 205 868 6000 **Fax:** 205 868 6099
Website: www.starneslaw.com

BRANCH OFFICES

ALABAMA
Riverview Plaza, Suite 1106, 63 S. Royal Street, **Mobile**, AL 36602
Tel: 251 433 6049

Insurance: Protective, Inc.; Alabama Municipal Insurance, Corp.; Liberty Mutual; Markel Insurance Co.; Aetna Insurance Company; Allstate Insurance Company; American National Insurance Company; American Heritage Insurance Company; Associated Aviation Underwriters; Attorneys Insurance Mutual; Attorneys Liability Assurance Society; Chubb Group Insurance; CNA Insurance Company; Commercial Union Insurance Company; Employers Mutual Companies; Farmers Insurance Company; Fidelity and Deposit Company of Maryland; The Fidelity and Casualty Company of New York; First Colonial Insurance Company; General Accident Insurance Company; Great American Insurance Company; Hartford Insurance Company; Home Insurance Company; International Fidelity Insurance Company; J. C. Penney Life Insurance Company; Mutual of Omaha; Old Republic Insurance Company; Peerless Insurance Company; Reliance Insurance Company; Republic Insurance Company; Safeco Insurance Company; St. Paul Fire and Marine Insurance Company; State Farm Insurance Company; AI Transport Insurance Company; Travelers Insurance Company; Universal Adjusters, Inc.; Western Surety Company; Zurich Insurance Company.

LEADING LAW FIRMS

STEIN, RAY & HARRIS

THE FIRM

Managing Partners: Steven GM Stein
Stephen E Ray
Robert J Harris

Number of partners: 6
Number of other lawyers: 12

AREAS OF PRACTICE:
Construction Litigation 75%
Construction Transactions 15%
Commercial Litigation 10%

HEAD OFFICE

ILLINOIS
222 West Adams Street, Suite 1800, **Chicago**, IL 60606
Tel: 312 641 3700 **Fax:** 312 641 3701
Website: www.steinrayharris.com

CONTACTS

Construction Litigation ....Steven GM Stein
Construction Transactions ....Stephen E Ray
Commercial Litigation ....Robert J Harris

FIRM OVERVIEW: Stein, Ray & Harris' (SRH) practice is devoted largely to the resolution of construction disputes and legal management of construction projects, including contract negotiation and transactional work. SRH is the largest such specialized firm in the Midwest and one of the nation's largest firms concentrating in the construction industry. SRH also has a growing commercial litigation practice and currently represents a number of Fortune 500 clients in various commercial disputes. Stein, Ray & Harris partner Steven GM Stein is the Editor-in-Chief of the nation's leading treatise on Construction Law, *Stein, Construction Law*. First published in 1986 and supplemented annually, this four-volume treatise is cited authoritatively by the courts. Mr. Stein is also the Editor-in-Chief of the American Institute of Architect's Legal Citator and of the *Construction Law Digest*.

MAIN AREAS OF PRACTICE:

Construction Litigation: SRH's litigation experience in construction disputes is vast and includes delay and disruption claims, differing site condition disputes, construction and design defect claims, environmental risks, insurance coverage disputes, labor issues, enforcement of intellectual property rights involving design, process engineering and output requirement disputes, change order disputes, lost productivity and sequence claims, worker injury suits, lien issues in many different jurisdictions, bid protests, and numerous other claims that frequently arise in the construction industry.

Construction Transactions: SRH lawyers represent clients in a wide range of transactional work relating to the construction industry. SRH has represented several nationally prominent owners, contractors and design firms in negotiating design and construction contracts on numerous multi-million dollar projects.

Commercial Litigation: SRH's commercial litigation practice has involved representation of clients in the areas of intellectual property law, business torts, breach of sophisticated commercial contracts, employment law including executive employee disputes, real estate litigation, defamation litigation, and other business and commercial disputes.

Multijurisdictional Practice: Stein, Ray & Harris' clients often select SRH for representation on high stakes matters instead of the client's usual counsel. Some of these representative cases include: Defense of a top five EPC firm against a $70M claim for delay and lost profit damages by the owner of a semiconductor chip manufacturing facility in Idaho; defense of a top 10 engineering firm against a $60M error and omission claim with respect to a deep tunnel project in Wisconsin; prosecution of a $50M claim for a top 20 contractor against surety for completion costs in Michigan; defense of a top five EPC firm against a $40M claim for consequential damages, including lost profits for failure to design and construct a synthetic caffeine plant in Wisconsin to meet output requirements; defense of a top five EPC firm against a $30M claim for consequential damages arising from Department of Energy research and development project; defense of a top 20 engineering firm against a $20M claim for breach of contract action alleging rights in government remediation contracts associated with a project in South Dakota; defense of a top 100 engineering firm against a $20M personal injury claim arising from the collapse of structural steel at the new Chicago Post Office in Illinois; defense of $18M in claims against a top 50 A/E firm involving a famous football stadium in Indiana; prosecution of a $15M claim for recovery of liquidated damages arising from delayed completion of a distillery in Toronto, Canada for a top 5 EPC firm; defense of a top 25 A/E firm against a $15M structural engineering error and omission claim with respect to Comiskey Park in Chicago, Illinois; prosecution of $9M claim for additional compensation against urban transit authority for a major contractor in Illinois ; represented a top 50 contractor in Texas against a $8M claim for lost profits associated with a Southeast Asian LNG project; represented a top 20 contractor in Florida for a $7M claim for damages arising from improper design of a motor speedway grandstand; and defended a top five A/E firm in Oregon against a $3M error and omission claim arising from structural steel design for a printing plant.

CLIENTS: The firm's clients include many of the nation's largest construction firms, engineering/procurement/construction ("EPC") companies, design/builders, design firms, owners and developers. Numerous SRH clients are listed among ENR's 'Top 500' list of design firms or the 'Top 400' list of contractors.

Contractors: Bovis Lend Lease (9); Gilbane Building (13); Hunt Construction Group (24); The Walsh Group (26); Clark Construction (35); Chicago Bridge & Iron (36); McShane (97); Power Contracting (117); Graycor (123).

EPC & Design/Build: Bechtel (2); Jacobs Engineering (3); AECOM (4); Fluor Corp. (5); Earth Tech (6); Parsons (7); CH2M Hill (8); Black & Veatch (12); MWH (14).

Design only firms: HOK (30); RTKL (65); Ellerbe Beckett (75); A. Epstein & Sons (77); Thornton Tomasetti (144); OWP&P (201); H.W. Lochner (311); Crawford, Murphy, Tilly (315); Ambitech (397); Lohan Caprile Goettsch (470).

Owners: University of Chicago, Pepsi Bottling Company, Pizza Hut, Mesirow Stein Real Estate, Bovis Lend Lease Real Estate Investments, Pep Boys, AIMCO.

STUTMAN, TREISTER & GLATT PROFESSIONAL CORPORATION

THE FIRM

Chairman of the Executive Committee: Robert A Greenfield

Number of partners: 18
Number of counsel: 9
Number of associates: 7

HEAD OFFICE

CALIFORNIA
3699 Wilshire Boulevard, Suite 900, **Los Angeles**, CA 90010
Tel: 213 251 5100 **Fax:** 213 251 5288
Email: info@stutman.com
Website: www.stutman.com

FIRM OVERVIEW: Stutman, Treister & Glatt Professional Corporation is a pre-eminent law firm in the practice of reorganization, bankruptcy, and insolvency law. The firm has long been known as a creative innovator in its field, focusing primarily on creating viable business reorganizations. The firm has successfully concluded some of the most complex and difficult out-of-court restructurings, prepackaged and pre-negotiated Chapter 11 plans and Chapter 11 reorganizations, and related purchases and sales of assets and businesses.

MAIN AREAS OF PRACTICE: Since 1948, the law firm has focused particularly on the representation of (i) financially troubled business organizations; (ii) creditors' and equity holders' committees; (iii) sellers and buyers of troubled companies; (iv) bondholders and bondholders committees and (v) significant secured and unsecured creditors.

CLIENTS: ST&G's national practice is highlighted by the cases in which the firm has been actively involved. The firm's debtor representations include Applied Magnetics Corporation, Barney's Inc., Barry's Jewelers, Inc., Broadband Sports.com, Bumble Bee Seafoods, Inc., Carter Hawley Hale Stores, Inc., Clark Retail Enterprises, Inc., County of Orange, Daewoo Motor America, Inc., Diva Systems Corporation, Edwards Theatres Circuit, Inc., El Camino Resources, Ltd., Graham & James LLP, Hechingers (equity), Home Fed Corporation, Huntsman Corporation, Itel Corporation, Kenetech Windpower, Inc., Krause Furniture, Inc., Lamonts Apparel, Inc., Leasing Solutions, Inc., Lyon & Lyon LLP, Maxicare, MTP Grand Place Tower, a Maguire Company, NBI, Public Service Co. of New Hampshire, The Regent Las Vegas (The Resort ofSummerlin), Restaurant Enterprises Group, Inc., Southern California Edison Company, Standard Brands Paint Co., Storage Technology Corporation, Store of Knowledge, Inc., Thrifty Oil Co., Toy Time.com, Inc., Westmoreland Coal Company and Wickes Companies, Inc. ST&G's present and former creditor and strategic investor clients include Apollo Advisors, LP, BP America, Inc., Catholic Healthcare West (in MedPartners chapter 11 case), Converse, Inc., Fidelity Investments, FINOVA, First American Title Insurance Co., General Cinemas, Home Savings of America, Litton Industries, Leucadia National Corporation, Metro-Goldwyn-Mayer Studios, Inc., Paramount Pictures Corporation,Pennzoil CO., Sony Corporation of America (and its affiliates), Tri-Star Pictures, United Airlines, Inc., U.S. Airways, Inc., and Viacom, Inc. The firm also represents creditors and creditor's committees in chapter 11 cases and out-of-court restructurings, including formal and informal committees; such representations have been in connection with the restructurings of Aladdin Gaming LLC, Bally's Grand, Inc., Charter Medical Corporation, Consolidated Freightways, Inc., Enron Corp., Global Crossing, Golden Ocean Group, Limited, JP Stevens, Orion Pictures Corporation, Papercraft Corporation, PRIMESTAR, Inc., and Resorts International, Inc. In addition to the firm's success in nationally significant cases, it has, throughout its history, maintained a strong presence in the rehabilitation of smaller closely-held business enterprises, including family businesses, real estate partnerships and entertainment entities.

INTERNATIONAL WORK: The firm has represented either foreign debtors, or the foreign representative appointed, in connection with foreign insolvency proceedings where the foreign debtors or the foreign representative required relief from a United States plenary court to dismiss a lawsuit on the grounds of comity or lack of jurisdiction, or from a United States Bankruptcy Court under the ancillary proceeding provisions of section 304 of the United States Bankruptcy Code to enjoin the enforcement of remedies against assets located in the United States or the continuation of litigation. Clients assisted include a large debtor in possession in reorganization proceedings in Mexico, as well as Canadian, German and Italian foreign representatives.

LEADING LAW FIRMS

SULLIVAN & CROMWELL LLP

THE FIRM

Chairman: H Rodgin Cohen

Number of partners worldwide: 152
Number of other lawyers worldwide: 577

FIRM OVERVIEW: Founded in 1879, Sullivan & Cromwell comprises more than 700 lawyers conducting a global practice through a network of 12 offices on four continents. The firm's organisation as a single, unified partnership worldwide, combined with its reliance primarily on internally generated growth, has contributed to its reputation for providing consistently high quality legal services.

MAIN AREAS OF PRACTICE:
Capital Markets: Each year, Sullivan & Cromwell advises principals or their financial advisors in hundreds of securities transactions by a variety of issuers: large and first-time, US and international, commercial and governmental. The firm is a leader in SEC-registered and exempt offerings by both US and non-US issuers and is known for innovative work on the largest and most complex offerings worldwide.
Litigation: Sullivan & Cromwell's litigation group regularly represents industrial corporations, financial institutions and individual clients before state and federal courts throughout the US. Anti-trust, EC competition and international commercial arbitration matters comprise a significant component of the overall litigation practice.
M&A: Sullivan & Cromwell has advised on some of the largest US mergers and acquisitions as well as on cross-border and domestic transactions in major domestic markets in Europe and Asia.
Financial Institutions: The firm's financial institutions practice encompasses M&A, the development of new products and services, regulatory matters, credit activities and litigation and enforcement matters for US and international banks, insurance companies and investment management firms.
E-business & Technology: Sullivan & Cromwell has established itself as a major player in advising e-business and technology enterprises, at all stages of their development and growth. Its e-business and technology group focuses on the strategic opportunities and issues that challenge clients in this sector.
Estates and Personal: The firm has an extremely active national and international private clients practice. The scope of services provided includes estate planning, tax planning, litigation, the creation and administration of small businesses, charitable activities and a broad range of personal matters.
Real Estate: The firm advises on the purchase, sale, construction, financing, and securitisation of real estate assets worldwide. Clients include investors, developers, lenders and investment bankers.
Project Finance: Sullivan & Cromwell is counsel to sponsors of, and lenders to, world-class projects in developed and emerging markets. The practice is well diversified by industry, including oil and gas, mining, infrastructure development, telecommunications and power.
Tax: The firm's tax group plays a leading role in structuring new, tax-advantaged financial instruments and complex M&A transactions, and represents prominent industrial and commercial enterprises worldwide in both US and cross-border tax matters.

HEAD OFFICE

NEW YORK
125 Broad Street, **New York** NY 10004-2498
Tel: 212 558 4000 **Fax:** 212 558 3588
Email: osbornc@sullcrom.com
Website: www.sullcrom.com

BRANCH OFFICES

CALIFORNIA
1888 Century Park East, **Los Angeles** CA 90067-1725
Tel: 310 712 6600 **Fax:** 310 712 8800
Email: sacksr@sullcrom.com

1870 Embarcadero Road, **Palo Alto** CA 94303-3308
Tel: 650 461 5600 **Fax:** 650 461 5700
Email: millersc@sullcrom.com

DISTRICT OF COLUMBIA
1701 Pennsylvania Avenue, NW, **Washington** DC 20006-5805
Tel: 202 956 7500 **Fax:** 202 293 6330
Email: craftr@sullcrom.com

INTERNATIONAL OFFICES

London, Paris, Frankfurt am Main, Tokyo, Hong Kong, Beijing, Melbourne, Sydney

CLIENTS: Sullivan & Cromwell advises many of the world's most demanding clients, in many cases based on relationships that extend over decades. Geographically, approximately half of the firm's clients are US-based; non-US clients come from Canada, Europe, Asia, Australasia, Latin America, Africa and the Middle East. The firm provides legal advice and services to industrial and commercial clients; financial institutions, including commercial banks, insurance companies, investment banks and investment companies; governments and governmental bodies; individuals; and estates and trusts.

INTERNATIONAL WORK: Sullivan & Cromwell has long played a leading role in global privatisation transactions; the expanding access by non-US enterprises to US capital markets; cross-border mergers and acquisitions; the integration of financial services; cross-border litigation and cross-border competition law matters; the evolution of the e-business and technology industry; and project and structured finance for developed and emerging markets.

SULLIVAN & CROMWELL LLP

LEADING LAW FIRMS

SUTHERLAND ASBILL & BRENNAN LLP

THE FIRM

Managing Partner: James L Henderson, III (Atlanta, GA)
Administrative Partner: W Mark Smith (Washington, DC)
Number of partners: 133
Number of associates: 166
Total number of attorneys: 351

HEAD OFFICES

GEORGIA
999 Peachtree Street, NE **Atlanta**, GA 30309-3996
Tel: 404 853 8000 **Fax:** 404 853 8806
Email: info@sablaw.com
Website: www.sablaw.com

DISTRICT OF COLUMBIA
1275 Pennsylvania Avenue, NW, **Washington, DC** 20004-2415
Tel: 202 383 0100 **Fax:** 202 637 3593

Sutherland Asbill & Brennan LLP also has offices in Austin, Houston, New York and Tallahassee. For more details please visit the website.

FIRM OVERVIEW: Sutherland Asbill & Brennan LLP is a national law firm known for solving challenging business problems and resolving unique legal issues for many of the nation's largest corporations, as well as emerging and smaller, established companies. Sutherland was founded in 1924. Throughout its history, the firm has served clients across America. It has grown to become a firm of more than 350 lawyers handling matters in every part of the world. The firm consistently attracts lawyers who have the skills and perspective to address issues of national significance in virtually every area of practice. Six major practice areas - corporate, energy, intellectual property, litigation, real estate and tax - provide the framework that contains an extensive range of specialty areas, allowing its lawyers to serve a diverse client base that includes a number of Fortune 500 companies.

MAIN AREAS OF WORK

Corporate: The firm's corporate practice encompasses the full range of legal services required by corporations and other business entities. The practice includes representation of public and private companies in their general commercial affairs, public and private buyers and sellers in acquisitions and dispositions of business, lenders and borrowers in corporate finance transactions, and issuers and underwriters and broker-dealers in securities law matters, including initial and secondary public offerings of debt and equity securities and enforcement matters. In addition, the firm's lawyers have extensive experience working with mutual funds and other investment companies, including insurance company separate accounts and business development companies. The firm counsels investment advisors, including those affiliated with investment companies and those affiliated with non-investment company institutional and individual clients; companies in or facing financial distress; companies undertaking financial restructurings; issuers, underwriters and financial institutions in tax-exempt and taxable bond issues; financial institutions in regulatory and transactional matters; and federal government sponsored enterprises. The firm also represents companies and financial institutions in a variety of structured finance transactions designed to accomplish specific investment, tax, liquidity and balance sheet management goals.

Energy: Sutherland has a highly active energy regulatory, transaction, finance, and litigation practice at the state, federal and international levels. Matters handled by the group embrace virtually all aspects of the natural gas, electric power and petroleum industries. The firm's lawyers have been at the forefront of the developing regulatory issues surrounding the energy industries, both at the policy stage and in the implementation phases. The firm has also developed extensive experience analyzing and assisting clients in taking advantage of business opportunities involving natural gas, electricity, cogeneration and petroleum products.

Intellectual Property: Sutherland has an extensive intellectual property practice. The firm represents a broad mix of clients - emerging technology start-ups, small and mid-sized companies and Fortune 500 and other public companies - in all areas including patents, trademarks, service marks, copyrights, trade secrets and unfair competition. The firm handles intellectual property matters in a number of technical fields including biotechnology, pharmaceuticals, computers, chemical technology, telecommunications, software and minerals. A significant number of Sutherland's intellectual property lawyers hold specialized or advanced degrees in biology, chemical engineering, computer engineering, mechanical engineering, microbiology, immunology, molecular genetics and other scientific disciplines, and many are registered to practice before the United States Patent and Trademark Office.

Litigation: Litigation is a major part of the firm's practice. Approximately one third of its 350 lawyers practice in this area and have tried and/or argued cases in the US Supreme Court, all thirteen circuits of the United States Court of Appeals, the Court of Federal Claims, the Tax Court and many other federal district and state trial and appellate courts. The firm also has extensive experience in arbitrations and mediations as well as in administrative proceedings and hearings before various federal and state agencies. The areas of concentration within our litigation group include general commercial and civil litigation; antitrust, trade regulation and consumer protection; construction and procurement litigation; criminal investigations and litigation; education; employment and ERISA; environmental; health care; insurance; intellectual property; international trade disputes; motor vehicle franchise law; professional liability litigation; securities litigation; tax litigation; telecommunications; and timber.

Real Estate: The firm's real estate practice is national in scope; handling real estate matters in virtually every state and in all major real estate markets. The broad range of experience of the firm's real estate lawyers enables it to provide this continuity. The lawyers in the real estate group have the ability to manage dispute resolutions, to provide creditors' rights and bankruptcy advice and representation, to advise on regulatory issues, and to identify and resolve tax questions, thus saving the expense and inefficiency of engaging different legal counsel for each of a client's separate business and legal problems. The areas of focus for the firm's real estate practice include acquisition and development; real estate finance and equity formation; pension fund investments; commercial leasing; hospitality industry; international transactions; natural resources; foreclosure, bankruptcy and workouts; mergers and acquisitions; partnerships and partnership taxation; and environmental issues.

Tax: The firm serves as tax counsel to a number of major corporations and medium-sized and small corporations and their shareholders, as well as cooperatives, partnerships, joint ventures, tax-exempt organizations, trusts, estates and individuals. By virtue of the size of the tax practice and its varied client base, we have an active practice in almost every area of taxation, including corporate taxation, employee benefits and executive compensation, taxation of financial products, timber taxation, international taxation, partnership taxation, state and local tax, tax accounting, tax legislation, federal tax litigation, business and estate planning and tax-exempt organizations.

LEADING LAW FIRMS

THELEN REID & PRIEST LLP

THE FIRM

Chairman: Richard N Gary
Vice-Chairman: Thomas J Igoe, Jr

Number of partners: 198
Number of other lawyers: 230

FIRM OVERVIEW: Thelen Reid & Priest LLP represents clients in all aspects of corporate law, domestically and internationally, including corporate finance, litigation and dispute resolution, project development and finance, regulatory services, intellectual property, construction and government contract, and government affairs and regulatory services.

MAIN AREAS OF PRACTICE:

Business & Finance: The firm's business and finance practice provides legal representation and counseling in a wide range of domestic and international corporate and commercial finance transactions. The practice focuses on capital markets transactions, mergers and acquisitions and general corporate representation, as well as matters involving US regulation of utilities, securities law compliance, general contract matters, partnerships, creditors' rights and patent, copyright and trademark prosecution and counseling.

Commercial Litigation: The firm's commercial litigation team provides representation in the following areas: antitrust and trade regulation, banking, bankruptcy, contracts, entertainment, insurance coverage and regulation, intellectual property, product liability, toxic tort and asbestos, and securities litigation. Thelen Reid has been in the forefront of international arbitration law and practice and has pioneered efforts to develop faster, more economical mechanisms for resolving commercial disputes outside of traditional litigation.

Construction & Government Contracts: Thelen Reid's construction practice is one of the leading practices of its kind in the United States. Its lawyers work with clients from the initiation of projects and preparation of contract documents through dispute resolution, including negotiation, mediation, arbitration and trial. The firm's construction attorneys have worked on all types of projects, ranging from individual buildings through some of the largest infrastructure projects in the world.

Government Affairs: The firm's government affairs team represents clients – from such industries as defense, transportation, aviation and agriculture – on complex and sophisticated issues before the US Congress and the executive branch.

Labor & Employment: Thelen Reid's labor attorneys have extensive experience in virtually all aspects of workplace law and serve clients in a broad range of industries. The labor practice represents management in matters related to workplace torts, traditional labor issues, employment law aspects of business transactions, facility closings and reductions in force, fair labor standards/wage and hour interpretations, occupational safety and health, employee benefits, and business immigration.

Project & Asset Finance: Thelen Reid's project and asset finance attorneys have represented clients in the development and acquisition of energy and infrastructure projects throughout the US and in more than sixty foreign countries, and have closed more than $20 billion of energy project acquisitions and financings in recent years. The firm has been rated in the top group of US project finance law firms by The American Lawyer, Privatization International and Euromoney.

Real Estate: The Thelen Reid real estate practice has significant experience in all fields of real estate practice, including: institutional representation; entrepreneurial transactions; lending, leasing, hotel, resort, convention and leisure industry property; foreign investments; tax counseling; workout and restructuring; litigation, and regulatory, environmental and land use matters.

HEAD OFFICES

NEW YORK
875 Third Avenue, 10th Floor, **New York**, NY 10022
Tel: 212 603 2000   **Fax:** 212 603 2001
Website: www.thelenreid.com

CALIFORNIA
101 Second Street, Suite 1800, **San Francisco**, CA 94105
Tel: 415 371 1200   **Fax:** 415 371 1211

BRANCH OFFICES

CALIFORNIA
333 South Hope Street, **Los Angeles**, CA 90071
Tel: 213 576 8000   **Fax:** 213 576 8080

333 West Santa Clara Street, **San Jose**, CA 94127
Tel: 408 292 5800   **Fax:** 408 287 8040

DISTRICT OF COLUMBIA
Market Square, 701 Pennsylvania Avenue, NW
Washington, DC 20004-2625
Tel: 202 508 4000   **Fax:** 202 508 4321

NEW JERSEY
65 Madison Avenue, Suite 100, **Morristown**, NJ 07960
Tel: 973 644 3400   **Fax:** 973 644 3159

CONTACTS

Business & Finance	Burton K Haimes
Commercial Litigation	Wynne S Carvill
	Jonathan D Siegfried
Construction & Government Contracts	Stephen V O'Neal
Government Affairs	William A Kirk, Jr
Labor & Employment	Charles S Birenbaum
Project & Asset Finance	Deborah A DeMasi
	Mark P Weitzel
Real Estate	Richard J Kane
Tax & Employee Benefits	John M Mooney

Tax & Employee Benefits: Thelen Reid provides business and individual clients with a full-range of tax planning, administrative and litigation services. The firm represents clients on matters related to: corporate taxation, partnerships and limited liability companies, and taxation of financial instruments. The practice's clients include foreign corporations from over 40 countries and US-based multinational corporations and institutional investors.

INTERNATIONAL WORK: For over 70 years, Thelen Reid has represented clients around the world in all of their international endeavors. Thelen Reid actively participates in over 40 international associations and is a sponsoring firm of the Institute of the Americas. Many of the firm's attorneys are active in Chambers of Commerce involving Latin American, European and Far East countries, as well as in various international committees of the American and International Bar Associations and the United States Council for International Business. Languages: Bahasa Melayu, Chinese-Cantonese, Chinese-Mandarin, French, German, Greek, Hebrew, Hindi, Italian, Japanese, Korean, Lithuanian, Malagasy, Polish, Portuguese, Punjabi, Russian, Spanish, Swedish, Tagalog and Vietnamese.

LEADING LAW FIRMS

THOMPSON & KNIGHT LLP

THE FIRM

Managing Partner: Peter J Riley
Number of attorneys: 361

FIRM OVERVIEW: Thompson & Knight is a full service law firm with an emphasis on all aspects of the energy industry and on complex litigation. In these and every Thompson & Knight practice area, the firm's attorneys have achieved a reputation for both integrity and skill in helping clients achieve their goals. Since 1887, Thompson & Knight attorneys have advised clients on opportunities, in disputes, and in responding to changes - always striving to meet or surpass client expectations.

MAIN AREAS OF PRACTICE:

Corporate & Securities: The firm represents a diverse range of public and private corporations, partnerships, limited liability companies, and other business entities. Clients include insurance companies, financial institutions, investment advisors, and investment banking firms - with Thompson & Knight often serving as outside general counsel.

Corporate Reorganization & Creditors' Rights: The firm plays a leading role in corporate reorganizations, in and out of court, and in bankruptcy proceedings of all types throughout the country. The firm represents trade creditors, lien claimants, and both creditor and debtor companies, large and small, in all aspects of bankruptcy litigation, including preference, avoidance, fraudulent transfer, as well as trustee claims against officers and directors, and often serves as special litigation counsel in extremely complex cases.

Energy: For more than 80 years, the firm has counseled oil, gas, and energy industry clients. The firm has represented clients in transactions or in resolving disputes in more than 50 countries. The firm's energy clients compose a 'who's who' of the industry, including large integrated oil and gas companies, independents, host government oil and gas companies, large utilities, private power plant projects, energy industry service giants, refineries, petrochemical companies, financial institutions, and multinational drilling contractors and construction companies.

Environmental: The firm's environmental practice includes air quality, water quality, solid and hazardous waste, energy recovery, toxic substances, hazardous materials, underground storage, risk assessment, and community right-to-know. The firm's environmental attorneys play a key role in many types of transactions and litigation.

Finance: The firm's attorneys negotiate and document all types of domestic and international private debt and commercial finance transactions. Clients include banks, insurance companies, pension fund managers, savings and loan associations, factoring companies, and other lenders located around the world. The firm also represents borrowers in many US and multinational industries.

Government Relations & Public Policy: Thompson & Knight attorneys counsel clients in government-related and public policy matters. The firm assists clients in negotiating with governmental and quasi-governmental entities, and represent clients' interests in regulatory, legislative, administrative rulemaking, and licensure matters.

Intellectual Property: The firm counsels clients of all sizes in virtually every industry in the development, valuation, licensing, and protection of intellectual property assets. The firm's counsel to hi-tech, telecommunications, media, and sports and entertainment clients guides their planning and decision-making in advertising, First Amendment protections, franchising, employment agreements, technology transfer and licensing, asset valuation, taxation, finance, including initial public offerings, mergers, and acquisitions.

Labor & Employment: The firm counsels employers in all aspects of the employment relationship. The firm's lawyers have broad experience in labor and employment law, and extensive trial, hearing, arbitration, and appellate experience in employment-related disputes. In addition, employee-benefits tax lawyers regularly assist in employment-related cases that involve issues under ERISA.

Real Estate: The firm's real estate practice involves billions of dollars in real property and assets, providing counsel to developers, buyers and sellers, landlords, and tenants of retail, office, and industrial properties throughout the US and abroad. The firm has been involved in structuring, documenting, and syndicating financing of properties including facilities used for research, retail, distribution, microelectronics manufacture, and suburban corporate and other business offices.

Tax, Benefits & Estate Planning: Thompson & Knight attorneys offer comprehensive personal and business planning advice to its clients. The firm's tax attorneys maintain the highest level of expertise possible. Several of the firm's tax attorneys are licensed to practice in states other than Texas and, through the firm's Interlaw affiliation, the firm can access tax lawyers throughout the world.

Technology: Thompson & Knight's Technology Practice Group serves the complex legal needs of technology-based businesses and institutions. The firm represents emerging companies, *Fortune* 500 industrials, multinationals, venture capital funds, hi-tech incubators, and academic and commercial research institutions in such diverse areas as aerospace, computer hardware and software, biogenetics, semiconductors, electronics, telecommunications, power generation, pollution control, and waste treatment.

Trial & Appellate: Litigation clients include household-name companies in every industry, from airlines to chemical companies, the entertainment industry, and every conceivable type of case. For over 110 years, Thompson & Knight has been engaged in an extensive and challenging trial practice in state and federal courts in Texas, across the Southwest, and throughout the US. In recent decades, its Trial Practice has spread to international venues and expanded to include arbitration, mediation, and other forms of alternative dispute resolution.

CLIENTS: The firm's clients include businesses in every industry and of every size from *Fortune* 500 companies to new ventures just beginning.

INTERNATIONAL WORK: Thompson & Knight's international experience and presence allows the firm to keep pace with the growth of its clients' businesses and the opening of new markets and global opportunities. The firm has served clients in 118 of the world's 191 nations, and its membership in Interlaw gives its clients access to more than 4500 attorneys in more than 116 business centers worldwide.

HEAD OFFICE

TEXAS
1700 Pacific Avenue, Suite 3300, **Dallas**, TX 75201
Tel: 214 969 1700 **Fax:** 214 969 1751
Website: www.tklaw.com

BRANCH OFFICES

TEXAS
98 San Jacinto Boulevard, Suite 1200, **Austin**, TX 78701
Tel: 512 469 6100 **Fax:** 512 469 6180

Burnett Plaza, Suite 1600, 801 Cherry Street, Unit 1,
Fort Worth, TX 76102-6881
Tel: 817 347 1700 **Fax:** 817 347 1799

333 Clay Street, Suite 3300, **Houston**, TX 77002
Tel: 713 654 8111 **Fax:** 713 654 1871

INTERNATIONAL OFFICES

The firm also has offices in Algiers, Algeria; Monterrey, Mexico; and Paris, France.

LEADING LAW FIRMS

THOMPSON HINE LLP

THE FIRM

Managing Partner: David J Hooker

Number of partners: 166
Number of other lawyers: 205

FIRM OVERVIEW: Established in 1911, Thompson Hine is among the largest business law firms in the United States. For the last two years, the firm has been named one of the best corporate law firms in American in an annual survey of 32,000 corporate directors conducted by Corporate Board Member Magazine. Thompson Hine attorneys serve more than 3,000 corporate clients nationwide and across the globe, including Ford, Toyota, Goodrich, Goodyear, The Hartford, Nationwide, KeyCorp, Lexis-Nexis, Limited Brands, Newell Rubbermaid, Parker Hannifin, PolyOne, Procter & Gamble, Sherwin-Williams, Time Warner, Toro, Verizon, Victoria's Secret and Whirlpool.

MAIN AREAS OF PRACTICE:

Admiralty & Maritime: Represents more than 200 carriers and shippers before state and federal courts and agencies.
Bankruptcy: Represents lenders, creditors' committees, debtors and other parties in finance transactions, workouts and bankruptcy matters.
Biotech: Represents emerging and established biotechnology companies on matters ranging from financing to joint ventures to intellectual property.
Business Litigation: Represents clients in a wide variety of business litigation - from corporate control contests and insurance disputes, to class actions, securities fraud, and tax controversies.
Business Regulation & Government Affairs: Represents clients before state, federal and local agencies, including DOT, ITC, CPSC, Federal Reserve Board, FDIC, FCC, FAA, FHA, FDA, FRA, FERC, PUCO, STB among others.
Commercial, Antitrust & White Collar Crime: Represents clients in trade restraint price discrimination, franchising and distribution, trade secrets, false advertising, fraud, etc.
Commercial & Public Finance: Handle commercial finance transactions, public finance, asset securitizations and general bank regulatory law.
Construction: Represents owners, design professionals, construction managers, contractors and sureties. Serves in the role of project counsel for billions of dollars of construction at sites across the US.
Corporate Transactions & Securities: Represents both emerging and established businesses in their most important business transactions, from start-up through IPOs, joint ventures, mergers, acquisitions and beyond.
Customs & International Trade: Advises domestic and foreign clients on a broad range of federal laws and programs affecting imports and exports.
e-Business & Emerging Technologies: Helps businesses realize the opportunities and manage the risks of electronic and technological commerce.
Employee Benefits & Executive Compensation: Advises clients regarding benefit plans, ERISA issues, controversies with the IRS, DOL, PBGC and other agencies; incentive and equity-based compensation arrangements, ESOPs, etc.
Energy & Utilities: Advises traditional and new business entities participating in the evolving energy markets at state and federal levels.
Environmental: Advises clients on the environmental aspects on their business transactions, crafting methods of allocating risk and counseling them on their compliance obligations under local, federal and state laws.
Heathcare: Represents physician groups, hospitals, clinical laboratories, diagnostic service providers, pharmaceutical manufacturers, medical device manufacturers and health insurance providers.

HEAD OFFICE

OHIO
3900 Key Center, 127 Public Square, **Cleveland** OH 44114-1291
Tel: +1 216 566 5500 **Fax:** +1 216 566 5800
Email: info@ThompsonHine.com

BRANCH OFFICES

DISTRICT OF COLUMBIA
1920 N Street, NW, Suite 800, **Washington** DC 20036-1600
Tel: +1 202 331 8800 **Fax:** +1 202 331 8330
Email: info@ThompsonHine.com

NEW YORK
One Chase Manhattan Plaza, 58th Floor, **New York** NY 10005-1401
Tel: +1 212 344 5680 **Fax:** +1 212 809 6890
Email: info@ThompsonHine.com

OHIO
312 Walnut Street, 14th Floor, **Cincinnati** OH 45202-4089
Tel: +1 513 352 6700 **Fax:** +1 513 241 4771
Email: info@ThompsonHine.com

10 West Broad Street, **Columbus** OH 43215-3435
Tel: +1 614 469 3200 **Fax:** +1 614 469 3361
Email: info@ThompsonHine.com

2000 Courthouse Plaza, NE PO Box 8801, **Dayton** OH 45401-8801
Tel: +1 937 443 6600 **Fax:** +1 937 443 6635
Email: info@ThompsonHine.com

Intellectual Property: Assists clients with patents, trademarks, copyrights, trade secrets, computer software, internet-related issues, and IP litigation.
International: The firm advises US clients on matters in all regions of the world, as well as foreign clients with interests in the US.
Labor & Employment: Represents clients in employment litigation, workers' compensation, immigration, collective bargaining, proceedings before the Department of Labor, OSHA, EEOC, NLRB and various state agencies.
Personal & Succession Planning: Assists clients in the management and transmission of wealth, the succession of businesses and other personal and family concerns.
Private Companies: Offers a wide range of business, tax and succession planning services to owners and venture capitalists in the US and abroad.
Product Liability: The firm has handled thousands of product liability matters involving mechanical, chemical, electrical, medical, aerospace, automotive and other products.
Product Safety: Represents companies before the Consumer Product Safety Commission; advise on recalls and safety standards.
Real Estate: Represents clients in real estate development, corporate real estate, zoning and land use; real estate investment and financing, and REITs.
Tax: Advises clients in business transactions and financings, tax controversy litigation, legislative and regulatory activities, international taxation, state and local taxation and foundation and exempt organization matters.

VINSON & ELKINS

THE FIRM

Managing Partner: Joseph C Dilg

Number of partners worldwide: 322
Number of other lawyers worldwide: 544

FIRM OVERVIEW: For nearly a century, lawyers at Vinson & Elkins have provided outstanding legal representation for clients whose needs are as diverse as the entities they represent. From their established roots in Texas, the firm has become a trusted advisor to its clients around the world. With more than 866 lawyers in nine offices around the globe, Vinson & Elkins is one of the world's largest international law firms.

MAIN AREAS OF PRACTICE: As a global law firm recognized for its leading international practice, lawyers at Vinson & Elkins have represented clients in almost every country in the world. With broad experience in transactions spanning multiple jurisdictions, cultures and languages, Vinson & Elkins' lawyers have extensive knowledge of the international business environment and the experience to recognize and resolve the legal issues that arise in multinational transactions. The firm effectively guides its clients through a wide range of transactions, including mergers and acquisitions, joint ventures and strategic alliances, public and private offerings of securities in the developed and emerging capital markets, as well as development and financing a variety of projects. Since Vinson & Elkins was founded, it has attracted an outstanding and diverse group of attorneys as well as an international client list, including some of the most innovative public and private companies, financial institutions, entrepreneurs, governments and governmental organizations around the world. Vinson & Elkins lawyers also know the importance of seeking proper protection against adverse developments and have handled many high stakes international disputes. The firm's international dispute resolution team engages in international arbitration under all leading institutional rules as well as international civil litigation in US courts and in other jurisdictions. The firm's lawyers work with their clients to develop effective solutions to the complex problems and unique challenges of international business.

CLIENTS: The firm's clients include the governments of sovereign nations and North American states, as well as public and private companies from around the world, domestic and international financial institutions, cities and municipalities, new enterprises, joint ventures, project companies and individuals.

INTERNATIONAL WORK: The firm handles work in Arabic, Bahasa, Cantonese, Chinese, Dutch, French, German, Greek, Gujurati, Hebrew, Hindi, Indonesian, Italian, Malay, Mandarin, Polish, Portuguese, Punjabi, Russian, Slovenian, Spanish, Taiwanese and Urdu.

HEAD OFFICE

TEXAS
2300 First City Tower, 1001 Fannin, **Houston** TX 77002-6760
Tel: 713 758 2222 **Fax:** 713 758 2346
Website: www.velaw.com

BRANCH OFFICES

DISTRICT OF COLUMBIA
The Willard Office Building, 1455 Pennsylvania Avenue NW, **Washington** DC 20004-1008
Tel: 202 639 6500   **Fax:** 202 639 6604

NEW YORK
666 Fifth Ave., 26th Floor, **New York** NY 101031-0040
Tel: 917 206 8000   **Fax:** 917 206 8100

TEXAS
The Terrace 7, 2801 Via Fortuna, Suite 100, **Austin** TX 78746-7568
Tel: 512 495 8400   **Fax:** 512 495 8612

3700 Trammell Crow Center, 2001 Ross Avenue, **Dallas** TX 75201-2975
Tel: 214 220 7700   **Fax:** 214 220 7716

INTERNATIONAL OFFICES

The firm also has offices in Beijing, China; Moscow, Russia; Singapore; and London, United Kingdom.

LEADING LAW FIRMS

WACHTELL, LIPTON, ROSEN & KATZ

THE FIRM

Managing Partner: Richard D Katcher

Number of partners worldwide: 77
Number of other lawyers worldwide: 123

HEAD OFFICE

NEW YORK
51 West 52nd Street, **New York**, NY 10019
Tel: 212 403 1000 **Fax:** 212 403 2000
Email: info@wlrk.com
Website: www.wlrk.com

FIRM OVERVIEW: Founded in 1967, Wachtell, Lipton, Rosen & Katz is one of the most prominent business law firms in the US. The firm specializes in merger and acquisition transactions, sensitive litigation matters, advice on corporate governance and related matters, and corporate restructurings. Comprising 200 lawyers, the leanly staffed firm handles demanding, high profile transactions and advisory matters on an extremely personalized basis. The relatively concentrated nature of the practice, together with and in addition to the absence of repetitive, standardized transactions, means that the firm's lawyers each have a broad range of skills and experience. Clients include industrial firms, financial institutions, securities firms, healthcare providers, technology companies and news and information systems companies, including a number of *Fortune 500* companies.

MAIN AREAS OF PRACTICE:

Corporate: The firm has handled some of the largest and most complex US and international transactions. It advises on a range of corporate matters including mergers and acquisitions, public offerings, financial products, and financing transactions. Wachtell, Lipton, Rosen & Katz also counsels companies, and their boards of directors, on difficult and sensitive corporate disclosure, governance and policy issues, and is serving as counsel to the New York Stock Exchange, Inc. in connection with the revision of the New York Stock Exchange, Inc.'s listing standards and other matters.

Litigation: Wachtell, Lipton, Rosen & Katz handles a wide variety of high profile, complex litigation for major corporations and leading financial institutions. Work undertaken includes precedent-setting securities and corporate governance litigation, and libel and First Amendment cases. The firm has been involved in landmark corporate governance litigation cases in Delaware, including the Household, Revlon, Macmillan, Interco, Time Warner and Paramount cases. The firm is representing Silverstein Properties, Inc., the 99-year lessee of the World Trade Center, in connection with the September 11, 2001 collapse of the Twin Towers and in the redevelopment of the World Trade Center. The firm represented IBP, Inc. in its successful litigation with Tyson Foods, Inc., which resulted in forcing Tyson Foods, Inc. to complete its acquisition of IBP, Inc. On behalf of Philip Morris Companies Inc., the firm took the leading role in negotiating the tobacco settlements with all of the States, and has obtained unanimous decisions from seven separate appellate courts affirming dismissals of claims brought by third-party payors of medical expenses and foreign governments, as well as a district court decision dismissing the US Government's claims for healthcare reimbursement. The firm represents insurance companies and defendants faced with asbestos and other mass tort liabilities. The firm has defended major securities firms, financial institutions, retailers, software manufacturers, healthcare providers, news and information systems companies and a variety of other companies in various enforcement proceedings and class actions, in which the claims may substantially exceed US$1.0 billion.

Bankruptcy & Creditors' Rights: The firm's bankruptcy and creditors' rights practice represents buyers, investors, lenders and creditors in national and multinational bankruptcy cases and out-of-court debt restructurings. Its lawyers regularly work with the firm's corporate group in handling complicated acquisitions of businesses in financial distress, highly leveraged transactions and major transactions involving significant creditors' rights issues. Recent restructuring work has included representing multiple parties in Kmart Corporation's bankruptcy, including the largest holder of bank debt and bond debt; representing the creditors of The FINOVA Group, Inc. and PSINet Inc.; and representing bank and bondholder groups in the restructurings of Rand McNally & Company, Allegheny Energy, Inc., Pacific Gas and Electric Company, Budget Rent-a-Car, World Kitchen, National Century Financial Enterprises, Sunbeam Corporation, Winstar Communications, Inc., 360networks Corporation, Fruit of the Loom, Inc., Regal Cinemas, Inc. and many other companies. The group's lawyers also have significant expertise in asbestos matters and in the defense of bankruptcy-related litigation, such as fraudulent transfer litigation and litigation against control persons of bankrupt entities.

Antitrust: Wachtell, Lipton, Rosen & Katz's antitrust practice focuses on mergers and acquisitions, government investigations, international antitrust, and banking antitrust issues. Wachtell, Lipton, Rosen & Katz analyzes transactions to determine whether they raise antitrust issues, develops strategies to address those issues, and represents clients before the United States Department of Justice, the United States Federal Trade Commission, the Board of Governors of the Federal Reserve System, state attorneys general, and in antitrust litigation challenging transactions. Wachtell, Lipton, Rosen & Katz is active on matters involving foreign antitrust enforcement authorities, frequently serving as worldwide lead antitrust counsel and participating with local counsel in proceedings and investigations in the European Union, Canada, Australia, Mexico and many other jurisdictions. Recent transactions handled by Wachtell, Lipton, Rosen & Katz that are or were subject to investigations by, and, where applicable, negotiation of consent decrees with, the antitrust authorities include AT&T Corp. in the sale of its cable broadband operations to Comcast Corporation, Phillips Petroleum Company in its merger with Conoco Inc., General Mills, Inc. in its acquisition of The Pillsbury Company from Diageo plc, Dreyer's Grand Ice Cream, Inc. in its acquisition by Nestlé S.A., Heller Financial, Inc. in its acquisition by General Electric Capital Corporation, Newmont Mining Corporation in its acquisitions of Normandy Mining Limited and Franco-Nevada Mining Corporation, and Cardinal Health, Inc. in its acquisition of Syncor International Corporation. In addition, Wachtell, Lipton, Rosen & Katz has represented the buyer or the seller in most of the largest bank mergers in US history.

Tax: The firm's tax practice focuses on United States and international tax matters, primarily in connection with structuring complex mergers and acquisitions transactions, as well as divestitures, restructurings, and spin-offs. The firm's tax group also reviews the tax implications of structuring complicated financial instruments.

Employment & Benefits: The firm's executive compensation and employee benefits practice focuses primarily on compensation and benefit issues in connection with mergers and acquisitions and other corporate transactions, and for executive officers of major corporations and financial institutions.

Real Estate: Wachtell, Lipton, Rosen & Katz's real estate group focuses on strategic real estate transactions, including mergers and acquisitions of REITs and other real estate companies, strategic joint ventures, major development projects, structuring real estate opportunity funds, acquisitions and dispositions of significant assets or portfolios, innovative capital markets transactions, and restructurings. Among other matters, Wachtell, Lipton, Rosen & Katz currently is representing the Silverstein Properties group, the 99-year lessee of the World Trade Center, in connection with the redevel-

WACHTELL, LIPTON, ROSEN & KATZ

opment of the World Trade Center, and Taubman Centers, Inc. in connection with Simon Property Group's unsolicited offer. Wachtell, Lipton, Rosen & Katz has been involved in real estate merger and acquisition transactions involving Security Capital Group, Lend Lease Corporation Limited, Taubman Centers, Inc., AvalonBay Communities, Inc., New Plan Excel Realty Trust, Inc., First Union Real Estate Equity and Mortgage Investments and Boston Properties, Inc., among others; in Tishman Speyer Properties L.P.'s acquisition and recapitalization of the Chrysler Building and other properties; in significant hotel and resort developments for Universal Studios, Inc. and others; and in the formation of the Apollo and PaineWebber real estate opportunity funds, and various transactions for Lazard's real estate opportunity funds.

INTERNATIONAL WORK: Wachtell, Lipton, Rosen & Katz recently represented or currently is representing AT&T Corp. (AT&T Broadband & Internet Services) in its US$72.0 billion transaction with Comcast Corporation and the split-up of the US$9.0 billion Time Warner Entertainment Co., LP partnership; Phillips Petroleum Company in its US$35.0 billion combination with Conoco Inc. and its US$9.4 billion acquisition of Tosco Corporation; Household International, Inc. in its US$14.2 billion transaction with HSBC Holdings plc; USA Networks, Inc. in its US$11.7 billion joint venture with Vivendi Universal; Philip Morris Companies Inc. in its US$5.6 billion sale of Miller Brewing Co. to South African Breweries plc; Newmont Mining Corporation in its US$4.4 billion acquisitions of Normandy Mining Limited of Australia and Franco-Nevada Mining Corporation Limited of Canada; Jefferson Smurfit Group plc in its US$3.5 billion acquisition by Madison Dearborn Partners, L.L.C.; Publicis Groupe S.A. in its US$3.3 billion transaction with Bcom3Group, Inc.; Wal-Mart Stores, Inc. in its US$1.9 billion acquisition of The Seiyu, Ltd. and its bid for Safeway PLC; Dreyer's Grand Ice Cream, Inc. in its US$2.5 billion acquisition of Nestlé S.A.'s United States ice cream business; Taubman Centers in responding to the US$1.1 billion hostile tender offer by Simon Property Group; Security Capital Group Incorporated in its US$1.8 billion acquisition of Storage USA, Inc. and its US$5.5 billion acquisition by General Electric Capital Corporation; Golden State Bancorp Inc. in its US$5.9 billion acquisition by Citigroup, Inc.; Trigon Healthcare, Inc. in its US$4.0 billion transaction with Anthem, Inc.; First Virginia Banks Inc. in its US$3.4 billion merger with BB&T Corporation; Hercules Incorporated (BetzDearborn water treatment business) in its US$1.8 billion acquisition by General Electric Capital Company (GE Specialty Materials); Cardinal Health, Inc. in its US$206.0 million acquisition of Boron, LePore & Associates, Inc. and in its US$802.0 million acquisition of Syncor International Corporation; Goodrich Corporation in its US$1.5 billion acquisition of TRW Aeronautics Systems; Allied Irish Banks, plc in the US$3.1 billion sale of Allfirst Financial Inc. to M&T Bank Corporation; State Street Bank & Trust Corp. in its US$1.5 billion acquisition of Deutsche Bank AG's worldwide custody business; Unocal Corporation in its US$456 million acquisition of Pure Resources Inc.; and HotJobs.com, Ltd. in its US$436.0 million acquisition by Yahoo! Inc. In addition, corporate work handled recently includes representing VoiceStream Wireless Corporation in its US$55.0 billion transaction with Deutsche Telekom AG; American International Group Inc. in its US$24.6 billion acquisition of American General Corp.; Wachovia Corp. in its US$13.6 billion transaction with First Union Corp.; General Mills, Inc. in its US$10.5 billion acquisition of The Pillsbury Company; AT&T Wireless Services, Inc. (wholly owned subsidiary of AT&T Corp.) in the US$9.8 billion investment by NTT DoCoMo Inc.; FleetBoston Financial Corporation in its US$7.0 billion merger with Summit Bancorp; Valero Energy Corp. in its US$6.2 billion acquisition of Ultramar Diamond Shamrock Corp.; IBP, Inc. in its US$6.0 billion transaction with Tyson Foods, Inc.; Heller Financial Inc. in its US$6.0 billion transaction with General Electric Capital Corp.; Litton Industries Inc. in its US$5.2 billion transaction with Northrop Grumman Corporation; Kellogg Company in its US$4.5 billion acquisition of Keebler Foods Company; Westvaco Corp. in its US$3.0 billion transaction with Mead Corp.; and The Furukawa Electric Co., Ltd. in its US$2.3 billion acquisition of Lucent Technologies Inc.'s optical fibre business. The firm also represented The Reader's Digest Association, Inc. in its recapitalization, and Pinault-Printemps-Redoute S.A. in its strategic investment in and acquisition of majority control of Gucci Group NV, including the settlement among Pinault-Printemps-Redoute S.A., Gucci Group NV and LVMH Moët Hennessy Louis Vuitton SA, as well as in a number of other group acquisitions, and dispositions, including its US$799.0 million sale of its office-supplies mail-order business to Staples Inc. In addition, the firm represented The National Basketball Association in connection with its joint venture with AOL Time Warner Inc., and Michael Jordan in his acquisition of an interest in the Washington Wizards and then his disposition of that interest in connection with his return to the National Basketball Association as a player. The firm represented Martha Stewart Living Omnimedia Inc. and FMC Technologies, Inc. in their initial public offerings; and AT&T Wireless Group in its US$18.8 billion spin-off to shareholders. The firm represents the New York Stock Exchange, Inc., including the Corporate Accountability and Listing Standards Committee of the Exchange, and in connection with revising the New York Stock Exchange, Inc.'s Listed Company Manual. The firm is representing a number of major corporations, such as Citigroup Inc., in connection with corporate governance and related matters, and has advised special committees of boards of directors, including PNC Financial Service Group Inc. and National Australia Bank, in connection with various corporate governance investigations and related matters.

LEADING LAW FIRMS

WALKER, BRYANT, TIPPS & MALONE

THE FIRM

Managing Partner: J Mark Tipps
Senior Partner: Robert J Walker

Number of lawyers: 12

AREAS OF PRACTICE:
Commercial Litigation	70%
Personal Injury/Professional Liability, Defense	20%
Personal Injury/Plaintiff	10%

FIRM OVERVIEW: Walker, Bryant, Tipps & Malone is a law firm located in Nashville, Tennessee, focusing exclusively on civil litigation. The principals at the firm formerly practiced with the civil litigation section of a much larger Nashville law firm and they have devoted their law careers to civil litigation and dispute resolution. WBTM represents individual, corporate, and institutional clients in Tennessee and throughout the Southeastern United States. Our attorneys regularly practice before federal and state courts in both jury and non-jury trials and at appellate levels. They have extensive experience in all forms of alternative dispute resolution, including arbitration and mediation. WBTM attorneys also represent clients in administrative matters before federal and state departments, agencies, boards, and commissions. The attorneys at WBTM concentrate their law practices in civil litigation and dispute resolution. Three of the firm's attorneys are Fellows in the American College of Trial Lawyers and are also listed in a leading American Publication as the top attorney's in America. WBTM attorneys have served as judicial clerks to federal district and appellate court judges and as counsel to congressional investigation committees. The firm was originally formed as Walker, Bryant & Tipps on January 1, 2000, by eight attorneys formerly associated with a large Nashville law firm. Those attorneys desired to continue their well-developed civil litigation practices in a smaller law firm, focusing exclusively on trial work. On May 1, 2002, the law firm became Walker, Bryant, Tipps & Malone when Gayle Malone, a senior partner in the litigation group of another prominent Nashville law firm, joined the firm. WBTM has grown from the initial eight attorneys to twelve and has assembled an outstanding staff of support personnel. WBTM has earned a reputation as a quality litigation boutique, whose attorneys hold their clients' interest paramount while providing efficient and effective representation.

MAIN AREAS OF PRACTICE:
Commercial Litigtion: The firm's commercial litigation includes defense of class action suits in securities, private and public corporate governance, product liability, and other commercial matters.
Dispute Resolution: Two of the firm's partners are Rule 31 listed Civil Mediators.

CLIENTS: The firm's clients include commercial banks, insurance and other financial institutions, venture capital and private equity firms, industrial and service corporations, partnerships and myriad of business clients in the fields of healthcare, prison management, accounting and other services industries.

INTERNATIONAL WORK: The firm has represented a number of international companies engaged in civil litigation in the United States.

HEAD OFFICE

TENNESSEE
2300 One Nashville Place, 150 Fourth Avenue, North
Nashville, TN 37219
Tel: 615 313 6000   **Fax:** 615 313 6001
Email: info@walkerbryant.com

CONTACTS

Dispute Resolution	Gayle Malone, John Bryant
Financial Institutions/Insurance	Mark Tipps, Joe Welborn
Personal Injury/Defense	John Bryant, Steve Anderson
Personal Injury/Plaintiff	Gayle Malone, Joe Welborn
Product Liability	Gayle Malone, Clisby Barrow
Securities & Corporate Governance	Bob Walker, John Hayworth

WALLACK SOMERS & HAAS P.C.

THE FIRM

Senior Partners: Barry Z Wallack
George W Somers
Karl P Haas

Number of partners: 4
Number of other lawyers: 3

AREAS OF PRACTICE:
Commercial Real Estate Development	40%
Municipal Redevelopment	25%
Commercial Leasing	15%
Commercial Real Estate Lending	15%
Commercial Real Estate Litigation	5%

HEAD OFFICE

INDIANA
One Indiana Square, Suite 1500, **Indianapolis**, IN 46204
Tel: 317 231 9000 **Fax:** 317 231 9900

CONTACTS

Commercial Real Estate Development	George W Somers
Municipal Redevelopment	Karl P Haas
Commercial Leasing	Barry Z Wallack
Commercial Real Estate Lending	Barry Z Wallack
Commercial Real Estate Litigation	Michael S Wallack

FIRM OVERVIEW: Wallack Somers & Haas, P.C. is an Indianapolis, Indiana-based boutique law firm concentrating its practice in all aspects of commercial real estate development, leasing, and financing. Comprised of experienced and innovative attorneys, the firm provides legal advice to local, regional and national clients.

MAIN AREAS OF PRACTICE:

Commercial Real Estate Development: The firm's attorneys have extensive experience in assisting commercial real estate developers in achieving their goals, including the development and redevelopment of shopping malls, retail centers, business campuses, industrial facilities, hotels, sports centers, office buildings and multi-family housing.

Municipal Redevelopment: The firm has an established municipal redevelopment practice, focusing on the unique requirements of urban and suburban mixed, public/private redevelopment projects.

Commercial Leasing: The firm represents both landlords and tenants in office, retail and industrial leasing.

Commercial Real Estate Lending: The firm represents local and national borrowers and lenders for construction and permanent lending, tax credit transactions, mezzanine financing, syndications and securitized lending.

Commercial Real Estate Litigation: The firm acts as counsel to clients in a limited array of commercial real estate disputes, including landlord-tenant disputes and mechanic's liens.

CLIENTS: The firm's clients include commercial banks, insurance and other financial institutions, developers, landlords, tenants, non-profit organizations, municipal entities and individual entrepreneurs and investors.

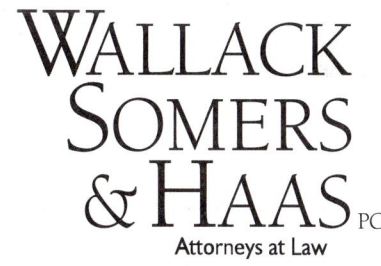

WATSON, FARLEY & WILLIAMS

THE FIRM

Chairman: Christopher Preston
Managing Partner: Michael Greville
New York Office Head: Alfred Yudes

Number of partners worldwide: 56
Number of other lawyers worldwide: 220

FIRM OVERVIEW: Opened in 1990, the New York office originally serviced ship finance, tax and litigation markets, but quickly expanded to include asset finance and leasing, bank finance and corporate and securities work. The firm's presence in New York acknowledges the significance of New York and US federal law to international financial and corporate transactions and the significance of New York as a global business centre. The New York office advises on US federal law and New York law. The firm works aggressively to find innovative, quality answers to meet the rapidly changing needs of clients. By using its resource of international lawyers, the firm can deliver global solutions. Particular expertise include: asset finance and leasing; ship finance, shipping, oil and gas; litigation and arbitration; bank finance and regulation; corporate, mergers and acquisitions and capital markets; bankruptcy and workouts; and taxation.

HEAD OFFICE

NEW YORK
380 Madison Avenue, **New York** NY 10017
Tel: 212 922 2200 **Fax:** 212 922 1512
Email: ayudes@wfw.com
Website: www.wfw.com

INTERNATIONAL OFFICES

The firm also has offices in Paris, Piraeus, Rome, Singapore, Bangkok and London.

MAIN AREAS OF PRACTICE:

Asset Finance & Leasing: Watson, Farley & Williams has a substantial international equipment finance and leasing practice. Specialists have extensive experience with aircraft, satellites, vessels, rail equipment, real estate and power generation facilities and other industrial equipment. The practice complements our international ship finance practice. In addition to straightforward secured asset-based financings, the firm has successfully developed and completed innovative transactions involving domestic and cross-border tax leasing, off-balance sheet 'synthetic' leasing, securitization, credit enhancement, Eximbank and European ECA guaranteed financing, political risk insurance and the restructuring of transactions under the US bankruptcy laws.

Ship Finance, Shipping & Oil & Gas: Watson, Farley & Williams has one of the largest shipping practices in the world. The firm acts for owners seeking finance and for banks and other financial institutions providing it. The firm advises on all legal aspects of the shipping business in all our offices. Watson, Farley & Williams' experience encompasses newbuilding and secondhand ship acquisitions and financings, cross border leasing, bareboat charters, operating leases and other off-balance sheet financings, credit enhancement structures, syndication and securitization and advice on environmental laws and all major ship registries.

Litigation & Arbitration: The litigation group handles all varieties of commercial litigation in US and UK courts and before all major international arbitration in tribunals. The firm's litigators are admitted to practice before all state and federal courts in New York and have appeared in courts and tribunals throughout the country. Several have been appointed as commercial arbitrators in recognition of their expertise in matters relating to international finance and trade, transportation, insurance, securities and EC law. In New York, the firm advises shipping and energy clients on US environmental laws, including the Oil Pollution Act 1990.

Bankruptcy & Workouts: The bankruptcy and workout practice in New York has developed in conjunction with the firm's general asset finance practice with particular expertise in shipping, aviation, offshore drilling and other cross-border transactions. The firm represents various banking interests as secured creditors in Chapter 11 bankruptcy proceedings. The firm's lawyers have represented secured creditors (including creditors committees) and major trade creditors in every major shipping related bankruptcy in the US, recently including Global Ocean, Golden Ocean, Commodore Cruises and Hvide. The firm represent secured and unsecured creditors in major cases involving US bankruptcy proceedings and has also represented creditors in tandem with its London, Paris and Singapore partners in cross-border administration proceedings, such as those in the Maxwell/Macmillian/Berlitz matters.

Taxation: The tax specialists both advise clients directly and work closely with the firm's banking, asset finance, shipping and corporate teams. The firm has particular expertise in the US taxation of international financings and corporate transactions. The firm represents taxpayers in controversies with the Internal Revenue Service and state and local taxing authorities. The firm's international offices and contacts allow us to address the worldwide tax issues that arise in cross border financings and other international business transactions. Watson, Farley & Williams' tax lawyers are frequently involved in developing tax efficient structures for their clients.

LEADING LAW FIRMS

WEIL, GOTSHAL & MANGES LLP

THE FIRM

Chairman: Stephen J Dannhauser
Number of partners worldwide: 285
Number of other lawyers worldwide: 790

AREAS OF PRACTICE:
Corporate	22%
International Finance	22%
Litigation	20%
Corporate Restructuring & Insolvency	10%
IP, Technology & Communications	8%
Telecommunications	8%
Taxation	5%
Property Transactions & Finance	3%
Corporate Governance	1%
Trusts & Estates	1%

FIRM OVERVIEW: Weil, Gotshal & Manges is an international law firm of over 1,000 attorneys, including approximately 285 partners. The lawyers in the firm's practice groups (which include anti-trust, banking and finance, capital markets, corporate, corporate governance, corporate restructuring and insolvency, e-commerce, litigation, IP, technology, property transactions and finance, structured finance, tax, trade regulatory and trusts and estates) work together to provide full-service legal advice to clients in sectors as diverse as energy, structured finance and the hi-tech industries.

MAIN AREAS OF PRACTICE:

Corporate: The corporate department is the firm's largest, with lawyers in the US, across Europe and in Asia. The department advises international financial institutions and corporate clients in complex public and private mergers and acquisitions, private equity deals, strategic alliances and other commercial transactions.

Finance: The firm advises on a wide range of financing activities and has particular interest and expertise in acquisition finance, asset-based finance, debt restructuring and insolvency, debt and equity capital markets, derivatives, high yield debt, project finance, securitization, structured finance and telecom and multi-media financing. In these areas, the firm is recognized as a market leader in the handling of complex and innovative finance transactions under both US and European Law.

Litigation: The firm's litigation practice advises international clients on all major areas of the law and has extensive experience in all aspects of dispute resolution. It advises clients in jury trials and appeals, as well as arbitration and alternative dispute forums.

Corporate Restructuring & Insolvency: The firm has one of the largest, most broadly based bankruptcy and business reorganization practices in the US. It includes attorneys in New York, Houston, Dallas, Miami and London. The department has been involved in virtually all major chapter 11 reorganization cases in the US and in major national and international out-of-court debt restructuring.

IP, Technology & Communications: The firm has a leading intellectual property and technology practice and advises a number of the world's major technology, media and telecommunications companies. It also acts for investors in technology, media and communications entities. The practice handles patent infringement, outsourcing transactions, strategic alliances, cross-border mergers and acquisitions, investments and IPOs. The firm advises on the protection and exploitation of IP and on a wide range of e-commerce matters including data protection.

HEAD OFFICE

NEW YORK
767 Fifth Avenue, **New York** NY 10153, USA
Tel: 212 310 8000 **Fax:** 212 310 8007
Website: www.weil.com

BRANCH OFFICES

CALIFORNIA
201 Redwood Shores Parkway, Silicon Valley, **Redwood Shores** CA 94065
Tel: 650 802 3000 **Fax:** 650 802 3100

DISTRICT OF COLUMBIA
1501 K Street NW, Suite 100, **Washington** DC 20005
Tel: 202 682 7000 **Fax:** 202 857 0940

FLORIDA
701 Brickell Avenue, Suite 2100, **Miami** FL 33131
Tel: 305 577 3100 **Fax:** 305 374 7159

MASSACHUSSETS
101 Federal Street, **Boston** MA 02110
Tel: 617 772 8300 **Fax:** 617 772 8333

TEXAS
8911 Capital of Texas Highway, Suite 4140, **Austin** TX 78759
Tel: 512 349 1930 **Fax:** 512 527 0798

100 Crescent Court, Suite 1300, **Dallas** TX 75201-6950
Tel: 214 746 7700 **Fax:** 214 746 7777

700 Louisiana, Suite 1600, **Houston** TX 77002
Tel: 713 546 5000 **Fax:** 713 244 9511

INTERNATIONAL OFFICES

The firm also has offices Brussels, Budapest, Frankfurt, London, Paris, Prague, Singapore and Warsaw.

It has expertise in regulatory telecoms matters.

Taxation: The tax department provides advice on international and domestic taxation, covering many different economic sectors. The department works closely with the firm's other departments to find innovative solutions to problems that present various and competing multi-disciplinary considerations.

Property Transactions & Finance: The firm's property transactions and finance practice handles complex real estate transactions (including finance, securitizations, development, leasing, sales, acquisitions and debt restructurings) across the US and Europe. It also advises clients on real estate M&A transactions and transactions involving real estate investment trusts.

CLIENTS: The firm advises a broad and diverse group of clients including many of the largest and most prominent corporations and government agencies around the globe and leading financial institutions.

INTERNATIONAL WORK: The firm developed a network of offices across the United States in the 1960s and 70s to cater for the expansion of its client base. Weil, Gotshal was one of the first international law firms to establish a major presence in Central Europe. The firm now has established offices in Brussels, Budapest, Frankfurt, London, Prague and Warsaw.

LEADING LAW FIRMS

WILLIAMS & ANDERSON LLP

THE FIRM

Senior Partners: W Jackson Williams, Philip S Anderson

Number of partners: 10
Number of other lawyers: 9

AREAS OF PRACTICE:
Litigation	30%
Securities & Municipal Finance	30%
Banking	20%
Corporate & M&A	10%
Media Law	10%

HEAD OFFICE

ARKANSAS
Twenty-Second Floor, 111 Center Street, **Little Rock**, AR 72201
Tel: 501 372 0800 **Fax:** 501 376 6453
Website: www.williamsanderson.com

CONTACTS
Corporate & M&A	W Jackson Williams
Banking	Paul W Hoover
Securities/Municipal Finance	David F Menz
Litigation	Peter G Kumpe
Media Law	Philip S Anderson

FIRM OVERVIEW: Founded on December 1, 1988 by six Little Rock lawyers, Williams & Anderson LLP is a premier corporate and commercial law firm in Arkansas, offering expertise in municipal finance, banking and corporate law, litigation and media law. The firm's partners include a past President of the American Bar Association and a current board member and officer of the National Association of Bond Lawyers.

MAIN AREAS OF PRACTICE:
Corporate: The firm represents a broad range of clients in matters of corporate finance, mergers and acquisitions, new and joint ventures, and business organization and governance.
Banking: The firm is general counsel to the largest Arkansas-based bank and represents clients on a regional basis in commercial transactions and credit facilities.
Securities/Municipal Finance: The firm has a particular expertise in municipal and public finance, with vast experience and a regional presence in facilities and improvement bonds, student loans, housing, and water districts. The firm has regularly represented the University of Arkansas system, the Arkansas Development Finance Authority, and the Arkansas Student Loan Authority in public debt offerings. The firm structured legislation to use Arkansas's share of proceeds from tobacco litigation to finance a number of healthcare initiatives. The firm represents public and private clients in securities offerings and regulatory matters.
Litigation: The firm has an established, active and sophisticated litigation practice involving commercial matters, corporate, business and partnership disputes, franchising and distribution, antitrust and trade regulation, construction, creditor's rights, First Amendment and employment. The litigation group has a particular niche in complex, high stakes litigation and serves both as trial and appellate counsel. The firm regularly serves as special appellate counsel in significant cases.
Media Law: The firm is primary counsel to a regional newspaper and cable television company and has developed an expertise in media and publishing law over 25 years. The firm has long served national clients in media and access matters in Arkansas and is counsel to Arkansas's state-wide daily newspaper and numerous additional media clients throughout the region.

CLIENTS: Include commercial banks and national financial institutions, state, municipal and local issuers of public debt, real estate development companies, newspapers and other media, manufacturing, retail, service and distribution companies, holding companies, governments and government agencies, church-affiliated and nonprofit organizations, entrepreneurs, individuals, trusts, and universities.

WILLIAMS & ANDERSON
REGISTERED LIMITED LIABILITY PARTNERSHIP

WILLIAMS & CONNOLLY LLP

THE FIRM

Firm Management (Executive Committee):
Brendan V Sullivan, Jr., John K Villa, Kevin T Baine, Robert B Barnett, Bruce R Genderson

Number of partners: 82
Number of total lawyers: 187

HEAD OFFICE

DISTRICT OF COLUMBIA
725 Twelfth Street, **Washington**, DC 20005
Tel: 202 434 5000 **Fax:** 202 434 5029
Website: www.wc.com

CONTACTS

Civil & Criminal Litigation	Brendan V Sullivan, Jr
	John K Villa
	Kevin T Baine
	Robert B Barnett
	Bruce R Genderson

FIRM OVERVIEW: Williams & Connolly LLP is a firm of almost 200 lawyers located in Washington, DC. Founded in the late 1940s by one of America's greatest trial lawyers, Edward Bennett Williams (1920-1988), Williams & Connolly specializes in, and relishes complex and difficult cases and is nationally recognized as a premier trial and appellate litigation firm. Williams & Connolly also offers well-established corporate, banking, sports and tax practices. In a short period of time, the firm has grown from a few lawyers engaged principally in high profile criminal defense work to an institution that is regularly involved in challenging legal matters of local, regional, national, and international concern. The firm is often retained for complex or novel matters where the stakes are high. It is known for its experienced and talented trial lawyers with the skills and determination not simply to discover and settle, but to take the case to trial. Because adversaries recognize that Williams & Connolly will not hesitate to try the case, the firm can achieve successful settlements when that is in the client's best interest. The firm's lawyers appear in a broad array of judicial and non-judicial fora: federal and state trial courts, appellate courts throughout the country including the United States Supreme Court, Congressional committees, administrative agencies, arbitration panels and other alternative dispute resolution fora, and university and other private bodies. Williams & Connolly is proud of its reputation for integrity, excellence, and hard work, values passed on to the firm by its founder. A number of the firm's lawyers have national reputations as trial lawyers, counselors, or experts in specific legal fields; many have distinguished themselves in public service. Williams & Connolly selects its associates from the top echelons of the best law schools and teaches them to furnish legal representation and counsel of the highest order.

CLIENTS: The defense of individuals in highly publicized controversies continues to be a major part of the firm's practice. Representative cases include Brendan Sullivan's representation of Oliver North; Vince Fuller and Greg Craig's representation of John Hinckley; Craig's representation of the parental rights of Juan Miguel Gonzalez in the Elian Gonzalez custody case; and David Kendall's representation of President and Mrs Clinton. As the firm's reputation has grown, more and more of the country's major institutions have retained Williams & Connolly. The Washington Post, General Electric Co., AOL Time Warner Inc., Twentieth Century Fox Film Corp., Southeast Toyota Distributors, GTE Corp., Wyeth (formerly American Home Products Corp.), Georgetown University, and Bayer Corporation have all been advised by Williams & Connolly in recent years. Although the firm remains, first and foremost, a litigation firm, it has added a tax and business capacity that enables the firm to handle a broad range of non-litigation problems, – from the negotiation of book contracts for media celebrities and political figures, such as Bob Woodward, Karen Hughes and William Bennett, to promotional affiliations for sports stars, such as Grant Hill, Tim Duncan, and Chamique Holdsclaw, to documentation of mammoth financial and securities transactions for Southeast Toyota and others.

MAIN AREAS OF PRACTICE: Administrative law, antitrust, appellate, arbitration, business, transactions and tax, criminal defense, employment and labor, federal programs and national defense, first amendment and media, general civil litigation, health care and medical products, intellectual property, international disputes, plaintiffs' litigation, product liability, torts and medicine, professional liability defense, real estate, securities and financial services litigation, sports, and trusts and estates.

LEADING LAW FIRMS

WILLKIE FARR & GALLAGHER

THE FIRM

Chairman, Executive Committee: Jack H Nusbaum
Co-Chairman: Myron Trepper
Partners in US offices: 106
Number of other lawyers in US: 300

FIRM OVERVIEW: Established in New York City in 1888, the firm comprises 123 partners and 417 other lawyers in offices in New York, Washington, DC, Paris, London, Milan, Rome, Frankfurt, and Brussels. The firm's international practice has expanded and its lawyers regularly handle international transactions. The firm represents financial buyers of businesses requiring M&A, private equity and related advice on business operations in multiple jurisdictions throughout the world.

MAIN AREAS OF PRACTICE: Corporate and financial services, insurance, litigation, real estate, business reorganization and restructuring, telecommunications, tax, intellectual property, trusts and estates, international trade, government relations, environmental, executive compensation and employee benefits, other.

Corporate & Financial Services: The firm's Corporate and Financial Services Department offers corporations and financial institutions broad expertise in all types of commercial transactions and regulatory matters. Its extensive corporate practice includes mergers and acquisitions, private equity/venture capital, investment management, public finance, insurance, broker-dealer regulation, private placement and banking, institutional lending, structured finance, and 144A offerings. The firm is a national leader in the area of public offerings in the United States and abroad of all types of equity securities by both US and foreign issuers, and is internationally renowned for its handling of complex, cross-border M&A transactions.

Litigation: The firm represents clients in every type of forum, including federal and state court actions, government regulatory and administrative proceedings, and arbitration, mediation and other alternative dispute resolution proceedings. It is well known for its expertise in all of the major areas of business and corporate litigation, including securities and transactional litigation, class-action lawsuits, battles for corporate control, antitrust issues, white collar crime, First Amendment and media litigation, accountants' and other professional liability actions, insurance brokerage and coverage actions, environmental litigation, and employee benefits and employment litigation.

Business Reorganization & Restructuring: The firm represents debtors, lenders, secured and unsecured creditors, creditors' and shareholders' committees, shareholders, governmental units, investment advisors, investors, landlords and tenants, and entities seeking investment opportunities in chapter 11 cases. The practice also includes deal structuring with respect to potential insolvency and bankruptcy issues.

Real Estate: The firm is regularly involved in major domestic and international real estate transactions, including REIT mergers and debt and equity offerings, pooled and stand-alone securitized financings, development projects, commercial leases, sales and acquisitions, construction and permanent financings, restructurings, joint ventures, private placements of domestic and foreign real estate funds, and real estate aspects of corporate and bankruptcy transactions. It has significant experience in all aspects of the real estate capital markets and all property types, including retail, office, healthcare, lodging and gaming, storage, and residential.

CLIENTS: The firm represents a roster of significant corporate clients on a wide variety of legal matters across many borders.

HEAD OFFICE

NEW YORK
787 Seventh Ave, **New York** NY 10019-6099
Tel: 212 728 8000 **Fax:** 212 728 8111
Website: www.willkie.com

BRANCH OFFICES

WASHINGTON
1875 K Street, NW, **Washington DC** 20006-1238
Tel: 202 303 1000 **Fax:** 202 303 2000

INTERNATIONAL OFFICES

The firm also has offices in Washington, DC, Paris, London, Milan, Rome, Frankfurt and Brussels.

CONTACTS

Business Reorganization & Restructuring	Myron Trepper
Corporate & Financial Services	Jack Nusbaum
Environmental	Carolyn Conkling
Executive Compensation & Employee Benefits	Stephen Lindo
Government Relations	Russell L Smith
Insurance	John D'Alimonte
Intellectual Property	William Ried
International Trade	William H Barringer
Litigation	Richard Posen
Real Estate	Eugene Pinover
Tax	Richard L Reinhold
Telecommunications	Philip L. Verveer, Bruce Kraus
Trusts & Estates	David J McCabe

INTERNATIONAL WORK:

M&A: The firm buys and sells companies in cross-Atlantic and intra-European cross-border transactions. The firm represents a large number of issuers and underwriters in relation to debt and equity offerings in the United States.

International Trade: The firm advises many foreign manufacturers and foreign governmental bodies on issues arising from regulations governing the importation of goods from the United States.

Business & Finance: The firm handles matters such as corporate law, private equity, litigation, securitisation/structured finance, taxation, environmental and international trade.

Telecommunications & IT/Internet Media: The firm has advised on all types of related transactions and issues in telecommunications, information technology and outsourcing, e-commerce, media and entertainment.

WILMER, CUTLER & PICKERING

THE FIRM

Managing Partner: William J Perlstein

Number of partners: 143
Number of other lawyers: 360

FIRM OVERVIEW: Wilmer, Cutler & Pickering opened its doors in Washington, DC, in 1962, with 19 lawyers. Today the firm has more than 500 lawyers, with offices in Washington, New York, Baltimore, Northern Virginia, London, Brussels, and Berlin. The firm has a broad international regulatory, corporate, and litigation practice, with particular focus on the United States, Western Europe, and Latin America.

MAIN AREAS OF PRACTICE:
Regulatory: Within the firm's Regulatory Section, the Antitrust and Competition practice includes counseling; clearance of mergers and acquisitions in the United States, the European Union (EU), and throughout the world; representation in grand jury and other investigations; and private and government litigation in the courts and before the Federal Trade Commission (FTC). The International Aviation, Defense, and Aerospace practice involves advising clients in the aviation and defense industries on a wide range of regulatory, legislative, and enforcement matters before US and foreign governments, and representing them in international negotiations and transactions. The Communications and Electronic Commerce practice provides counseling on business and regulatory issues and advises and represents clients on matters before the Federal Communications Commission, the EU, and their countries' national regulatory agencies. The Financial Institutions practice includes representation of banks, thrift institutions, and other financial service providers on both a domestic and international basis. The Trade practice includes counseling clients who wish to influence trade negotiations, use trade agreements to improve their export market access or cope with US export control regulations, as well as participating in trade proceedings, such as antidumping and countervailing duty proceedings, before government bodies in the United States and Europe.
Business Transactions: Within WCP's Business Transactions Section, the Corporate practice covers a wide range of matters including national and international business and securities transactions, mergers and acquisitions (both friendly and contested), formation of joint ventures and investment funds, equity and debt financings, restructurings and recapitalizations, proxy contests and takeover defense matters. This group also encompasses the firm's Latin American practice, Bankruptcy and Workout practice, and Patent practice. The Tax practice involves advising clients on sophisticated tax matters ranging from transfer pricing to ERISA and also assists the Corporate practice in all aspects of transactional tax planning, including mergers and acquisitions, partnership structuring, international transactions, and bankruptcies.
Securities: The Securities Section represents clients in enforcement and administrative proceedings before the SEC, the NYSE, the NASD, and other agencies, and provides regulatory advice to the securities and financial industry. The Securities practice also handles private civil litigation, internal corporate investigations, and white collar criminal work. Within the Securities Section, the Investment Management practice furnishes legal services to domestic and international banks, hedge funds, investment companies, and investment advisers in capital markets around the world. The Capital Markets/Broker-Dealer practice provides regulatory and compliance advice on a variety of complex issues relating to the trading, sale, and underwriting of equities, fixed income securities, options, and derivatives.

HEAD OFFICE

DISTRICT OF COLUMBIA
2445 M Street, N.W. **Washington, DC** 20037-1420
Tel: 202 663 6300 **Fax:** 202 663 6363
Email: law@wilmer.com
Website: www.wilmer.com

BRANCH OFFICES

MARYLAND
100 Light Street, **Baltimore**, MD 21202
Tel: 410 986 2800 **Fax:** 410 986 2828

NEW YORK
399 Park Avenue, **New York**, NY 10022
Tel: 212 230 8800 **Fax:** 212 230 8888

VIRGINIA
1600 Tysons Boulevard, Tenth Floor, **Tysons Corner**, VA 22102
Tel: 703 251 9700 **Fax:** 703 251 9797

INTERNATIONAL OFFICES

The firm also has offices in Berlin, Brussels and London.

CONTACTS

Regulatory	William T Lake
Business Transactions	Robert F Hoyt
Securities	Harry J Weiss
Litigation	Roger M Witten

Litigation: WCP's Litigation Section represents clients in complex civil and criminal litigation throughout the United States, and internationally, in matters that routinely involve multi-faceted legal and public policy dimensions. This practice consists of three principal areas: the Civil Litigation Trial and Appellate practice, which involves litigation in federal and state courts throughout the country; the Criminal and Investigative practice, which defends both companies and individuals being investigated or prosecuted by federal or state law enforcement authorities; and the International Arbitration and Litigation practice, which includes one of the world's leading international commercial arbitration practices and representation of global and foreign companies sued in the United States in both private commercial actions and litigation with a governmental dimension.

CLIENTS: The firm's lawyers provide the highest quality legal services to corporations, financial institutions, governmental entities, and individuals.

INTERNATIONAL WORKS: Virtually from its start in 1962, WCP lawyers have had a significant role in helping clients understand and shape the legal and policy terrain, initially in Washington and thereafter in Europe. WCP practices before courts, legislatures, regulatory agencies, and multinational institutions based in the United States and Europe. As the businesses of its clients have become global in nature, the firm has expanded its corporate, litigation, and regulatory practices through growth and diversification in the United States and Europe. With lawyers based in Washington, as well as three major European capitals, including Brussels -- the regulatory center of the European Union -- WCP is particularly well suited to represent US and multinational corporations in complex business transactions, regulatory matters, litigation, and other dispute resolution and trade controversies.

LEADING LAW FIRMS

WINSTEAD SECHREST & MINICK P.C.

THE FIRM

Chairman, CEO: W Mike Baggett

Number of partners in US: 175
Number of other lawyers in US: 152
Number of partners in Mexico: 1
Number of other lawyers in Mexico: 9

Website: www.winstead.com

FIRM OVERVIEW: Winstead Sechrest & Minick P.C. has grown steadily since it was founded as a 20 attorney practice in Dallas in 1973. The firm's initial period of growth was organic, but in the last few years it has expanded by merging with small firms that specialize in its traditional strengths of real estate and corporate law. In 2001, the firm bucked the industry-wide trend for downsizing by acquiring three Texas boutique firms in the space of five months, and now employs more than 330 attorneys in seven locations across the US and Mexico. The political consulting practice of Winstead Sechrest & Minick P.C., Winstead Consulting Group LLC, provides local, state and federal government relations and strategic services throughout the United States, Mexico, Canada, and countries worldwide.

MAIN AREAS OF PRACTICE:

Banking & Credit Transactions: The firm advises regional, national, and international financial institutions, financial services companies, and other lending organizations in virtually all aspects of their business activities. Attorneys represent and counsel lenders, agents, participants, and borrowers in single-lender and syndicated credit facilities of all types and complexities. Winstead also represents the firm's corporate clients in establishing and maintaining credit facilities. Attorneys have extensive experience in restructurings of troubled credits, debtor-in-possession financing, post-confirmation financing, and other workout matters. The firm regularly advises financial services clients who seek counsel on mergers and acquisitions, the development of new products and services, regulatory matters, enforcement actions, litigation, and other financial service problems.

Business Restructuring/Bankruptcy: Winstead's Business Restructuring/Bankruptcy Practice is one of the largest in Texas and the southwestern United States. This cross-sectional practice involves not only the traditional bankruptcy practice, but also attorneys from banking, corporate, securities, tax, real estate and other areas, who all have extensive experience in both operational and financial restructurings. The practice is national in scope and focuses on non-judicial workouts and restructures, as well as the traditional bankruptcy court process. This unique focus, combined with the substantial experience of the firm's Business Restructuring Practice, provides clients with the ability to analyze all of the possible options in a workout, from the inception. The practice covers representation of debtors, creditors, committees, and other parties in interest in all aspects of financial restructurings, including out-of-court restructurings, pre-bankruptcy negotiation and strategy, the bankruptcy process itself, and all types of litigation arising out of, or related to, bankruptcy and insolvency matters. Given their broad diversity of experience, Winstead's business restructuring professionals are able to provide a keen understanding of the business goals, of all interested parties, to any transaction, along with the ability to craft solutions that will achieve those goals in a manner that is consistent with the client's goals and expectations.

Corporate & Taxation: Winstead attorneys are experienced in corporate finance, securities regulation and tax matters related to federal, state, and local governments, insurance regulation, asset securitization, and investment management. Attorneys also provide specialized counsel and insight with respect to the successful operation of both public and private businesses. The firm represents clients in connection with the offering and sale of public and private equity, public and private debt, mortgage and asset-backed securities, and tax-exempt public bond issuances. Winstead provides counsel to both mature and start-up businesses with respect to corporate governance, public and private financing, mergers, acquisitions and divestitures, antitrust issues, shareholder disputes and agreements, adoption of employee incentive and stock option plans, implementation of anti-takeover defenses, non-competition agreements, and protection and exploitation of intellectual property and other proprietary information.

Government Relations: Winstead operates a local, state, federal and international government relations practice supported by Winstead Consulting Group LLC, the firm's wholly owned, political consulting subsidiary. Attorneys and consultants represent a wide range of corporate clients, associations and large public entities before all levels of government. Winstead's government relations practice is managed out of the Washington, DC office and focuses on federal and national government relations. Each of the firm's Texas offices handles state and local government matters working with the Governor's office, Texas Legislature and state agencies as well as municipal governments. Winstead's Mexico City office concentrates on local and national government issues for Mexican and American clients. The firm

US OFFICES

DISTRICT OF COLUMBIA
Metropolitan Square, 1450 G Street NW, Suite 810, **Washington**, DC 20005
Tel: 202 572 8000 **Fax:** 202 572 8001

TEXAS
100 Congress Avenue, Suite 800, **Austin**, TX 78701
Tel: 512 474 4330 **Fax:** 512 370 2850

5400 Renaissance Tower, 1201 Elm Street, **Dallas** TX 75270
Tel: 214 745 5400 **Fax:** 214 745 5390

2100 McKinney Avenue, Suite 1501, **Dallas**, TX 75201
Tel: 214 745 5400 **Fax:** 214 745 5883

777 Main Street, Suite 1100, **Fort Worth**, TX 76102
Tel: 817 420 8200 **Fax:** 817 420 8201

2400 Bank One Center, 910 Travis Street, **Houston**, TX 77002
Tel: 713 650 8400 **Fax:** 713 650 2400

600 Town Center One, 1450 Lake Robbins Drive, **The Woodlands**, TX 77380
Tel: 281 681 5900 **Fax:** 281 681 5901

INTERNATIONAL OFFICES

The firm also has an office, Winstead y Rivera S.C., in Mexico City.

CONTACTS

Banking & Credit	Michael W Hilliard
Bankruptcy	R Michael Farquhar
Corporate	Thomas W Hughes
Government Relations	Mark L Cushing
Intellectual Property	Kelly K Kordzik
Labor & Employment	Dan C Dargene
Litigation	Jay J Madrid
Real Estate	T Andrew Dow

WINSTEAD SECHREST & MINICK P.C.

also has a significant practice in the NAFTA arena, representing major clients from Mexico, Texas and Canada. Attorneys' and consultants' expertise includes, but is not limited to, condemning authority in condemnation litigation matters, healthcare, energy, telecommunications, financial institutions, transportation including public-private partnerships, government procurement and contracting, sports authorities and facilities, international trade, high technology, land use, environment and natural resources, public finance and real estate.

Intellectual Property: The firm's IP lawyers seek to identify, exploit, and protect a client's intellectual property by a wide variety of techniques, beginning with the protection of trade secrets and know-how, to the preparation and prosecution of patents, copyrights, trademarks, to the negotiation of related technology agreements and licenses, to the enforcement and/or defense of such rights, in all forums, ie mediation, arbitration, various state and US District/Appellate Courts, and the International Trade Commission. Clients are drawn from diverse sciences and technologies, ranging from oilfield, display signage, highway safety, and medical devices to the emerging area of nanotechnology.

Labor & Employment: Winstead represents employers across the spectrum of the employment relationship. The firm's representation includes traditional union-management disputes before labor arbitrators and administrative law judges, as well as the needs of management in the multi-faceted and complex area of employees' individual rights. Attorneys provide comprehensive advice to employers faced with restrictions on the exercise of their business judgment in dealing with employees, and counsel employers so they may act in a manner that is lawful, yet consistent with their business objectives. Winstead also offers advice and training programs aimed at preventing employment-related complaints and lawsuits. The Labor and Employment Group has substantial experience defending all forms of workplace litigation, including defense of claims under virtually every federal and state fair employment practices statute, governmental entities against whistleblower claims, substantive and procedural due process claims, and other state and federal constitutional and statutory claims unique to the public employment sector. Winstead's employment litigators are also experienced in the defense of labor arbitrations, administrative proceedings before state and federal agencies, and all forms of alternate dispute resolution.

Litigation: When it is reasonably possible and consistent with the firm's clients' objectives, Winstead initially strives to resolve a dispute without resorting to litigation. In this regard, negotiation, arbitration, and mediation are viable alternatives. When litigation is unavoidable, however, the firm provides analysis, advice, and representation that enables its clients to properly evaluate, manage, and control the risks, costs, and uncertainties associated with litigation. Attorneys enforce or defend clients' rights wherever disputes arise, in Texas or elsewhere, and whether in court (state or federal) or an arbitration organization. From massive class actions for publicly traded entities to simple commercial disputes for small businesses, Winstead represents clients from numerous industries in a wide variety of cases, and in many different venues.

Real Estate: Winstead's Real Estate Group includes over 60 full time real estate attorneys and more than 20 paralegals. The depth and breadth of Winstead's real estate expertise gives its clients access to real estate professionals with experience in virtually every type of real estate and every transaction structure, anywhere in the US and in any stage of the real estate cycle. For example, Winstead has successfully represented Fortune 500 retailers in the rapid roll-out of new retail concepts during periods of economic expansion. Yet at the same time, Winstead enjoys, as a result of the significant size of its Real Estate Group, a national reputation in the field of real estate restructuring. Winstead's client list includes many of the largest and most active real estate development companies, institutional investors, mortgage lenders and loan servicers in the United States, as well as individual investors and entrepreneurs. The firm's attorneys achieve desired results across the full real estate spectrum, including the development of all property types in mixed use configurations and common ownership structures, acquisition and disposition of all property types, zoning and land use, construction, environmental, corporate facilities management, development and private investment, real estate finance (including new construction, mezzanine, portfolio, and CMBS debt and structured leases), loan servicing, restructuring and workouts, REITs and REMICs, sports and public facilities, taxation issues (from TIF districts to 1031 exchanges), leasing and asset management, portfolio acquisitions and dispositions, and institutional equity and mortgage investments.

INTERNATIONAL WORK: Group attorneys have experience in over 30 foreign jurisdictions and have represented US and foreign clients engaged in international business throughout the world and in a variety of industries. The firm opened an office in Mexico City in 1993, Winstead y Rivera S.C., which enables it to provide clients with a cross-border team approach to international transactions in Mexico and Latin America. The firm is a member of both The Interlex Group and The Bridge Group, which are associations of leading law firms serving international clients.

LEADING LAW FIRMS

WINSTON & STRAWN

THE FIRM

Managing Partner: James M Neis
Senior Partner: James R Thompson (Chairman)
Paul Hensel (Administrative Partner)

Number of partners in US: 361
Number of other lawyers in US: 425

FIRM OVERVIEW: Founded in 1853. One of the oldest and largest US law firms with more than 850 attorneys in Chicago; New York; Washington, DC; Los Angeles; Paris, France; and Geneva, Switzerland.

MAIN AREAS OF PRACTICE:

Litigation: Winston & Strawn's litigators are consistently entrusted with some of corporate America's highest stakes litigation. They have tried major jury trials in virtually every federal district in the United States, and have appeared before the United States Supreme Court and the US Courts of Appeals. Their work involves antitrust; construction, technology, and other contractual disputes; corporate internal investigations and white collar criminal defense; product liability; patent/trademark/copyright infringement; securities; international litigation and arbitration; environmental; employment and ERISA; professional liability; tax controversy; and unfair competition and trade regulation.

Corporate & Financial: The Corporate and Financial Practice Group provides a range of transaction-related legal services to enterprises of all types and sizes. Corporate attorneys advise on mergers and acquisitions, securities transactions and regulation, corporate governance, commercial lending, private equity, information technology, leasing, asset securitization, project finance, public finance, financial services regulatory, and bankruptcy, workout, and financial restructuring.

Labor & Employment Relations: The firm counsels major employers and a variety of closely held business enterprises on labor and employment relations programs and policies, as well as employment, labor, and ERISA litigation in state and federal courts throughout the country. It also represents clients before federal, state, and local administrative agencies, including the EEOC and the NLRB.

Real Estate: Real estate attorneys counsel all types of sophisticated real estate market participants in the acquisition, financing, sale, development, and leasing of commercial, industrial, and multifamily properties.

Intellectual Property: IP lawyers provide general IP counseling; litigation throughout the United States and before the US Patent and Trademark Office and the Federal Circuit Court of Appeals; management of trademark, patent, and copyright portfolios; and patent, trademark, and copyright prosecution and licensing.

Tax: The Tax Practice assists in virtually every area of corporate tax law, from planning through audit as well as appeals and litigation. Its transactional attorneys are known for innovation in domestic and cross-border structured finance transactions, particularly in leasing and asset securitization. Tax controversy attorneys represent clients in judicial and administrative proceedings at both the state and federal levels.

Governmental Relations & Regulatory Affairs: Led by former four-term Illinois governor James R Thompson, this group includes attorneys and advisors who have held major positions with national trade associations, congressional committees, and congressional leaders. Work includes legislative and regulatory representation, counseling and bill analysis, congressional lobbying, executive branch advocacy on policy questions, legislative drafting, and preparation and presentation of congressional testimony.

HEAD OFFICE

ILLINOIS
35 West Wacker Drive, **Chicago** IL 60601
Tel: 312 558 5600 **Fax:** 312 558 5700
Email: info@winston.com
Website: www.winston.com

BRANCH OFFICES

CALIFORNIA
333 South Grand Avenue, **Los Angeles** CA 90071
Tel: 213 615 1700 **Fax:** 213 615 1750

DISTRICT OF COLUMBIA
1400 L Street, N.W., **Washington, DC** 20005
Tel: 202 371 5700 **Fax:** 202 371 5950

NEW YORK
200 Park Avenue, **New York** NY 10166
Tel: 212 294 6700 **Fax:** 212 294 4700

CONTACTS

Litigation	Dan K Webb
Corporate & Financial	John L MacCarthy
Labor & Employment Relations	Columbus R Gangemi, Jr
Real Estate	Christopher D Murtaugh
Intellectual Property	Stephen P Durchslag
Tax	Robert F Denvir
Governmental Relations & Regulatory Affairs	James R Thompson
Energy	Nicholas S Reynolds
Environmental	Jennifer T Nijman
	William Hall
Employee Benefits & Executive Compensation	Michael S Melbinger
Healthcare	Thomas L Mills
Contracts	David C Romm
Maritime & Admiralty	Constantine G Papavizas
Trusts & Estates	Christine A Albright

Energy: This department ranks among the largest in the nation, representing entities engaged in all aspects of the energy industry, including production, transmission, and distribution of electricity and natural gas.

Environmental: This practice encompasses all aspects of environmental law including litigation matters, corporate transactions, and regulatory issues. The Paris practice includes regulatory, transactional, and litigation aspects of environmental law of the European Community.

Employee Benefits & Executive Compensation: The firm advises on issues regarding compensation of employees and the planning and administration of employee benefits. It also assists in the design and drafting of all forms of executive compensation plans.

CLIENTS: Significant relationships with companies including Abbott Laboratories, American Airlines, Bank One, N.A., Barr Laboratories, Deutsche Bank AG, Exelon Corporation, Gateway, Inc., Lear Corporation, McDonald's Corporation, Microsoft Corporation, Morgan Stanley, Motorola, Inc., PPG Industries, Philip Morris Companies, Inc., Salomon Smith Barney, and Smurfit-Stone Container.

INTERNATIONAL WORK: Clients include ALSTOM S.A., Altadis, S.A., Bank Audi Group, Cap Gemini S.A., Credit Suisee First Boston, EuroDisney, S.C.A., Export-Import Bank of the United States, Formosa Plastics Group, Iberdola S.A., Luxottica Group S.p.A., Maritech, Ltd., Overseas Private Investment Corporation, PPG Industries, Inc., Rhodia, Rolaco Group, Telefónica, S.A., Terra Networks, S.A., and Vivendi S.A.

LEADING LAW FIRMS

WOLF, BLOCK, SCHORR AND SOLIS-COHEN LLP

THE FIRM

Chairman: Mark L Alderman

Number of partners: 138
Number of other lawyers: 139

FIRM OVERVIEW: Founded in 1903, WolfBlock is one of Philadelphia's largest law firms. With seven offices in Pennsylvania, New York, New Jersey and Delaware, the firm provides a range of commercial and private legal services to clients in the US and abroad. The firm has more than 275 lawyers working in 18 practice groups. These groups include business litigation, communications, complex liability/surety/fidelity, corporate/securities, employee benefits, employment services, environmental law, family law, financial services, government assisted/affordable housing, health law, intellectual property/information technology, private client services, real estate, real estate structured finance, tax law, utility regulation, and securitization. Complementing the firm's legal offerings are its ancillary services provided through The Wolf Institute, a division of WolfBlock, and WolfBlock Government Relations, a wholly owned subsidiary. Employee management and executive training courses are offered at The Wolf Institute. WolfBlock Government Relations is dedicated to promoting effective government relations and lobbying services for clients.

MAIN AREAS OF PRACTICE:

Business Litigation: The firm's Business Litigation Practice covers a range of commercial disputes, including virtually every substantive area, such as: securities, antitrust, construction, malpractice, civil RICO, products liability, trademark and copyright infringement, and real estate, and First Amendment and defamation law. The firm is frequently called upon to represent many of the largest companies in both the United States and throughout the world.

Corporate/Securities: The firm has a large, diversified Corporate/Securities Practice Group. Its lawyers are noted for their work in the fields of securities, mergers and acquisitions, venture capital, and emerging business enterprises and represent public and private companies at all stages of development, including family businesses that have been firm clients for decades; start-up and emerging businesses in e-commerce, biotechnology, and other developing areas of commerce; clients going public; clients that are public; and public companies going private.

Complex Liability/Surety/Fidelity: The Complex Liability/Surety/Fidelity Group represents clients in numerous jurisdictions, including almost every major US city, and most US states, as well as Brazil, Puerto Rico, and Chile. The group has wide-ranging experience in a number of areas including: construction, directors and officers liability, errors and omissions liability, bad faith, subrogation, quia timet, indemnification, exoneration, reinsurance, bankruptcy, and policy coverage.

Real Estate: The Real Estate Group's practice is national in scope and encompasses the full range of real estate-related transactions. The group works closely with other firm lawyers skilled in other areas – including securities, tax, and environmental law – on multidisciplinary teams as needed to serve individual client segments or industries.

HEAD OFFICE

PENNSYLVANIA
1650 Arch Street, 22nd Floor, **Philadelphia**, PA 19103
Tel: 215 977 2000 **Fax:** 215 977 2334

BRANCH OFFICES

DELAWARE
Wilmington Trust Center, 1100 N. Market Street, Suite 1001, **Wilmington**, DE 19801
Tel: 302 777 5860 **Fax:** 302 777 5863

NEW JERSEY
1940 Route 70 East, Suite 200, **Cherry Hill**, NJ 08003
Tel: 856 424 8200 **Fax:** 856 424 4446

744 Broad Street, Suite 1515, **Newark**, NJ 07102
Tel: 973 824 7723 **Fax:** 973 424 5740

NEW YORK
250 Park Avenue, **New York**, NY 10177
Tel: 212 986 1116 **Fax:** 212 986 0604

PENNSYLVANIA
Three Penn Court, 325 Swede Street, **Norristown**, PA 19404
Tel: 610 272 5555 **Fax:** 610 272 6976

212 Locust Street, Suite 300, **Harrisburg**, PA 17101
Tel: 717 237 7160 **Fax:** 717 237 7161

CONTACTS

Business Litigation	Jerome Shestack
Communications	Stuart Shorenstein
Complex Liability, Surety Fidelity	Ian Strogatz
Corporate/Securities	David Gitlin
Employee Benefits	Warren Fusfeld
Employment Services	James Redeker
Environmental Law	Kenneth Warren
Private Client Services	Clifford Schlesinger
Family Law	Lynne Gold-Bikin
Financial Services	Bruce Lesser
Government Assisted/Affordable Housing	Bernard Lee
Health Law	Paula Sanders
Intellectual Property & Information Technology	Robert Zielinski
Real Estate Practice Group	Herman Fala
Real Estate Structured Finance Group	Abby Wenzel
Securitization Practice Group	Keith Krasney
Tax Law	Thomas Gallagher
Utility Regulation	Daniel Clearfield

CLIENTS: The firm's clients include large national and international corporations in nearly every industry: banking, financial and insurance institutions, REITs, real estate developers, public utilities, venture capital and private equity investors, healthcare organizations, government entities, technology and biotechnology companies and non-profit organizations.

LEADING LAW FIRMS

WOMBLE CARLYLE SANDRIDGE & RICE PLLC

THE FIRM

Managing Member: Keith W Vaughan

Number of partners: 197
Number of other lawyers: 243

FIRM OVERVIEW: Womble Carlyle Sandridge & Rice, PLLC, which traces its history to 1876, is one of the largest law firms in the Southeast and mid-Atlantic, with 430 lawyers in nine offices from Atlanta to Washington, DC. Womble Carlyle is a full-service business law firm providing legal advice to a wide spectrum of regional, national and international clients in sectors that include financial services, manufacturing, transportation, telecommunications, energy, health care, life sciences, government, education and technology.

MAIN AREAS OF PRACTICE:

Capital Markets: The firm provides legal services – including regulatory compliance and the structuring, negotiating and closing of capital markets transactions – to participants in the capital markets, including capital providers (such as commercial banks, investment banks and investment funds), entities accessing the capital markets to obtain capital (from startups to *Fortune* 500 companies) and intermediaries acting in the capital markets to mitigate risk related to movement in the values of currencies, commodities, equities and interest rate indices.

Corporate & Securities: Lawyers in the Corporate and Securities Practice provide representation in the areas of general corporate law, mergers and acquisitions, venture capital, securities offerings and securities regulation, fiduciary obligations and rights of directors and officers, partnership and limited liability company formation and syndication and business contract negotiations.

Tax: The firm provides creative tax planning and advice on mergers and acquisitions, corporate reorganizations, real estate development, tax controversies before the Internal Revenue Service and state taxing authorities, and tax-sensitive and tax-enhanced financings.

Antitrust, Trade Practices & Commerce: Members of this practice group regularly counsel clients and litigate cases involving federal and state antitrust laws, unfair and deceptive trade practices, business torts, advertising laws and regulations, unfair competition laws and trade libel.

Intellectual Property: Representation includes all aspects of domestic and foreign intellectual property law, including patent investigations and analyses, procurement of US and foreign patents and general client counseling regarding license agreements, corporate-sponsored research contracts, development agreements, technology transfer agreements and software protection.

Litigation & Arbitration: The firm has a litigation practice of national scope, encompassing business litigation; intellectual property litigation; environmental and toxic tort litigation; insurance, governmental and tort litigation; and product liability litigation. Attorneys have handled matters from trials of national class actions, to coordination of litigation nationally, to defense of clients in mediation and arbitration in many states throughout the country, including potentially high verdict jurisdictions.

Employee Benefits: Lawyers in this group provide all facets of employee benefits representation, including design, drafting and implementation of tax-qualified retirement and welfare benefit plans, non-qualified retirement arrangements, and executive compensation programs. The group also counsels clients regarding ERISA compliance and related federal and state legislation affecting employee benefit programs.

Government Relations: Womble Carlyle bridges the gap between law practice and public policy by delivering expert advice and assistance in dealing effectively with all levels and branches of government – local, state and federal. Members of this group combine years of on-the-job experience in government with legal training and the resources of an established law firm to engage the legislative and regulatory system expertly and persistently.

HEAD OFFICE

NORTH CAROLINA
One West Fourth Street, **Winston-Salem**, NC 27101
Tel: 336 721 3600 **Fax:** 336 721 3660
Email: kmoser@wcsr.com
Website: www.wcsr.com

BRANCH OFFICES

The firm has branch offices in Atlanta, Georgia; Charlotte, Durham, Greensboro and Raleigh in North Carolina; Greenville, South Carolina; Tysons Corner, Virginia; and Washington, DC. Please see firm's website for further details.

CONTACTS

Bankruptcy & Creditors Rights	William B Sullivan
Business Litigation	Timothy G Barber
Capital Markets	James E Lilly
Corporate & Securities	Jeffrey C Howland
Employee Benefits	Michael D Gunter
Environmental	R Howard Grubbs
Government Relations	Burley B Mitchell, Jr
Insurance, Governmental & Tort Litigation	Reid C Adams, Jr
Labor & Employment	Charles A Edwards
Product Liability Litigation	Keith A Clinard
Real Estate Development	Bobby D Hinson
Tax	Howard N Solodky
Technology & Commerce	Mark N Poovey
Trust & Estates	George A Ragland

Labor & Employment: The firm represents management in every aspect of the employer-employee relationship, including employment-related litigation before federal and state courts, agencies and arbitration panels, as well as providing advice on how to avoid litigation and minimize legal liabilities.

CLIENTS: Representative clients include: ALLTEL Carolina, Inc.; American International Group, Inc.; Armstrong World Industries, Inc.; BB&T Corporation; Bank of America; Centex Homes; Clarus Corporation; Collins & Aikman Floorcoverings, Inc.; GlaxoSmithKline; Innogenetics, N.V.; IntelliNet Corporation; J.A. Jones Construction Company; LifeStyle Furnishings International, Ltd.; Lowes Companies, Inc.; Medigital, Inc.; Novartis Pharmaceuticals Corporation; Parkdale Mills, Inc.; R.J. Reynolds Tobacco Company; Remington Arms Corporation, Inc.; Salem College; Sealy Corp.; Technology Ventures, LLC; Thomas Built Buses, Inc.; Thomasville Furniture Industries, Inc.; The Travelers; Unicomp, Inc.; Universal Tax Systems, Inc.; UnumProvident Corporation; Wachovia Bank, National Association; and Wake Forest University.

INTERNATIONAL WORK: The firm's lawyers advise on business acquisitions, joint ventures, the protection and licensing of intellectual property, commercial leasing, sales and distribution arrangements, US export controls, customs and immigration in the context of inbound and outbound international transactions and operations. The firm defends the interests of its clients, including patent and trademark rights, in dispute resolution involving litigation, mediation and international arbitration throughout the world.

LEADING LAW FIRMS

YOUNG CONAWAY STARGATT & TAYLOR, LLP

THE FIRM

Chairman: James L Patton, Jr
Administrative Partner: Richard A Levine
Number of partners: 47
Number of other lawyers: 36

AREAS OF PRACTICE:
Bankruptcy	30%
Corporate Litigation & Transactions	17%
Personal Injury & Workers Compensation	16%
Employment Law	9%
Real Estate	9%
Taxation & Estate Planning	8%
Commercial Transactions & Banking	4%
Environmental Law	3%
Intellectual Property Litigation	3%
General Commercial Litigation	1%

HEAD OFFICE
DELAWARE
1000 West Street, The Brandywine Building, 17th Floor, **Wilmington**, DE 19801
Tel: 302 571 6600 **Fax:** 302 571 1253
Website: www.ycst.com

BRANCH OFFICES
DELAWARE
110 West Pine Street, **Georgetown**, DE 19947
Tel: 302 856 3571 **Fax:** 302 856 9338

CONTACTS
Bankruptcy	James L Patton, Jr
Corporate Litigation & Transactions	William D Johnston
Real Estate	Eugene A DiPrinzio
Intellectual Property Litigation	Josy W Ingersoll
Employment Law	Sheldon N Sandler
Taxation & Estate Planning	Joseph M Nicholson
General Commercial Litigation	Janet Z Charlton
Personal Injury & Workers' Compensation	Ben T Castle
Environmental Law	Anthony G Flynn
Commercial Transactions & Banking	Richard A Levine

FIRM OVERVIEW: Founded in 1959, Young Conaway Stargatt & Taylor, LLP has enjoyed over 40 years as one of Delaware's largest, most prestigious and multifaceted law firms. The firm's attorneys have experience in a variety of practice areas and deliver successful outcomes in Delaware's state and federal courts, as well as courts across the country. Young Conaway also appears frequently before state and federal agencies and actively participates in vital issues pending before its state legislature.

MAIN AREAS OF PRACTICE:

Bankruptcy: The firm's Bankruptcy Group is the largest in Delaware and plays a major role in virtually every significant bankruptcy in this district. The Group routinely represents debtors, creditor committees, and shareholder groups in this jurisdiction and around the country. It provides a full array of services including out-of-court workouts, debt restructurings and pre-planned bankruptcies. This Group is often referred to as Delaware's leading bankruptcy experts by the media.

Corporate Litigation & Transactions: The firm's Corporate Group, one of the most experienced corporate litigation and counseling teams in the country, provides advice to corporations, stockholders and other law firms locally, nationally and throughout the world. The practice ranges from structuring corporation transactions to litigating takeover battles and shareholder suits. The team includes members of the Council of the Corporation Law Section of the Delaware State Bar Association, which drafts amendments to the Delaware General Corporation Law.

Real Estate: The firm offers a full range of services required for commercial development and financing for interstate and intrastate projects, including acquisitions, sales, financing for banks or businesses, leasing, zoning and land use projects such as shopping centers, office buildings, residential developments, and communications towers.

Intellectual Property Litigation: The firm's intellectual property attorneys represent national corporate clients and local businesses in the litigation of intellectual property disputes, including issues of trade secrets, trademarks, copyrights, patent infringement and unfair competition, and they serve on a variety of committees to assist in developing the practices and procedures employed by their court systems.

Employment Law: The Employment Law Group is the largest in Delaware and provides legal services to private and public employers in every area of employment law, including discrimination and sexual harassment claims, wrongful discharge lawsuits, union issues, workforce reductions, immigration.

Taxation & Estate Planning: The firm's Taxation Group is engaged in federal and state tax planning for businesses and individuals. The Group advises major corporations and their owners in Delaware on matters of entity formation, shareholder agreements, business organization, sales and acquisitions, employee benefits, pension plans and more. The estate planning attorneys represent individuals in the creation of trusts, wills for inter-generational asset management and financial planning.

General Commercial Litigation: The firm's Commercial Litigation Team brings all of the firm's commercial and litigation experience to bear on the business developments and problems faced by its clients, from contract or licensing disputes to complex transactional problems.

Personal Injury & Workers' Compensation: The firm's personal injury litigators are recognized as some of the most experienced and skilled trial attorneys in the state. The litigators handle an array of personal injury matters including automobile and construction accident litigation, medical negligence, product liability and premises liability actions, complex tort litigation and workers' compensation, and consistently obtain substantial verdicts and settlements.

Environmental Law: The firm provides counsel on regulatory compliance matters and representation in administrative agency proceedings and in public and private party litigation. From compliance law to permits to environmental audits, the firm offers assistance in all areas of environmental law.

Commercial Transactions & Banking: The firm's Commercial Group provides a broad range of legal advice to businesses in the Delaware Valley as well as to national and international businesses using Delaware business entities.

CLIENTS: Litigation clients range from national and international corporations (some doing business as Delaware business entities), to businesses throughout the Delaware Valley (including state and local governments, school districts, banks, developers, professional practices) and individuals (primarily in the medical negligence and personal injury areas). The firm's transactional practice has the same mix of clients and provides estate and tax planning for individuals.

OTHER RECOMMENDED LAWYERS

CHAMBERS
USA
2003–2004

OTHER RECOMMENDED FIRMS

ABATO, RUBENSTEIN AND ABATO, PA (Maryland)
809 Gleneagles Court, Baltimore, MD 21286
Tel: 410 321 0990

ABRAHAM A ARDITI (Washington)
600 University Street, Suite 2100, Seattle, WA 98101-4185
Tel: 206 623 1593 **Fax:** 206 676 7575

ABRAHAMS KASLOW & CASSMAN LLP (Nebraska)
8712 West Dodge Road, Suite 300, Omaha, NE 68114
Tel: 402 392 1250 **Fax:** 402 392 0816

ABRAHAMSON VORACHEK & MIKVA (Illinois)
120 North La Salle Street, Suite 1050, Chicago, IL 60602
Tel: 312 263 2698 **Fax:** 312 419 6770

ACKLEY, KOPECKY & KINGERY (Iowa)
500 Higley Building, 118 3rd Avenue Sout East, PO Box 75062, Cedar Rapids, IA 52401-5062
Tel: 319 364 2463

ADAMS & JONES CHARTERED (Kansas)
600 Market Centre, 155 North Market, PO Box 1034, Wichita, KS 67201-1034
Tel: 316 265 8591 **Fax:** 316 265 9719

ADAMS AND REESE LLP (Louisiana)
4500 One Shell Square, New Orleans, LA 70139
Tel: 504 581 3234 **Fax:** 504 566 0210

ADELMAN GETTLEMAN MERENS BERISH & CARTER (Illinois)
53 West Jackson Boulevard, Suite 1050, Chicago, IL 60604
Tel: 312 435 1050 **Fax:** 312 435 1059

ADELMAN LAVINE GOLD & LEVIN (Pennsylvania)
Suite 1900, Two Penn Center Plaza, Philadelphia, PA 19102-1799
Tel: 215 568 7515

ADLER POLLOCK & SHEEHAN P.C. (Rhode Island)
2300 Financial Plaza, Providence, RI 02903
Tel: 401 274 7200 **Fax:** 401 751 0604

AHLERS & COONEY, PC (Iowa)
100 Court Avenue, Suite 600, Des Moines, IA 50309
Tel: 515 243 7611 **Fax:** 515 243 2149

ALBERTINI, SINGLETON, GENDLER & DARBY LLP (Maryland)
3201 North Charles Street, Baltimore, MD 21218
Tel: 410 243 9400 **Fax:** 410 241 9599

ALLAN N. KARLIN (West Virginia)
174 Chancery Row, Morgantown, WV 26505
Tel: 304 296 8266 **Fax:** 304 296 8640

ALLEN & ALLEN ATTORNEYS AT LAW, PC (Virginia)
The Federal Reserbe Bank Building, 701 East Byrd Street, PO Box 610, Richmond, VA 23218-0610
Tel: 804 545 1500 **Fax:** 804 545 1501

ALLEN & OVERY (New York)
1221 Avenue of the Americas, NY 10020
Tel: 212 610 6300 **Fax:** 212 610 6399

ALLEN GUTHRIE & MCHUGH (West Virginia)
1300 Bank One Center, PO Box 3394, Charleston, WV 25333
Tel: 304 345 7250

ALLEN, MATKINS, LECK, GAMBLE & MALLORY LLP (California)
515 South Figueroa Street, Los Angeles, CA 90071-3398
Tel: 213 622 5555 **Fax:** 213 620 8816

ALLEN, NORTON & BLUE, P.A. (Florida)
Third Floor, 121 Majorca Avenue, Suite 300, Coral Gables, FL 33134
Tel: 305 445 7801 **Fax:** 305 442 1578

ALLISON, MACKENZIE, RUSSELL, PAVLAKIS, WRIGHT & FAGAN, LTD (Nevada)
402 North Division Street, Carson City, NV 89702
Tel: 775 687 0202 **Fax:** 775 882 7918

ALSTON & BIRD LLP (Georgia)
One Atlantic Center, 1201 West Peachtree Street, Atlanta, GA 30309-3424
Tel: 404 881 7000 **Fax:** 404 881 7777

ALSTON COURTNAGE BASSETTI (Washington)
1000 Second Avenue, Suite 3900, Seattle, WA 98104
Tel: 206 623 7600 **Fax:** 206 623 1752

ALSTON HUNT FLOYD & ING ATTORNEYS AT LAW, A LAW CORPORATION (Hawaii)
Pacific Tower, 18th Floor, 1001 Bishop Street, Honolulu, HI 96813
Tel: 808 524 1800 **Fax:** 808 524 4591

AMBURGEY & RUBIN PC (Oregon)
Riverplace Office Building, 1750 SW Harbor Way, Suite 450, Portland, OR 97201-0104
Tel: 503 221 0309 **Fax:** 503 242 2457

AMLONG & AMLONG (Florida)
Second Floor, 500 Northeast Fourth Street, Fort Lauderdale, Fl 33301
Tel: 954 462 1983 **Fax:** 954 523 3192

ANDERSON & BOTTRELL (North Dakota)
3100 Thirteenth Avenue, South West, Suite 202, PO Box 10247, Fargo, ND 58106-0247
Tel: 701 235 3300

ANDERSON & KREIGER (Massachusetts)
43 Thorndike Street, Cambridge, MA 02141
Tel: 617 252 6575

ANDERSON KILL & OLICK (New York)
1251 Avenue of the Americas, New York, NY 10020
Tel: 212 278 1000 **Fax:** 212 278 1733

ANTHONY OSTLUND & BAER (Minnesota)
90 South Seventh Street, Suite 3600, Minneapolis, MN 55402
Tel: 612 349 6969 **Fax:** 612 349 6996

ARENT FOX (District of Columbia)
1050 Connecticut Avenue NW, Washington, DC, DC 20036
Tel: 202 857 6000 **Fax:** 202 857 6395

ARMSTRONG ALLEN, PLLC (Tennessee)
Brinkley Plaza, Suite 700, 80 Monroe Avenue, Memphis, TN 38103
Tel: 901 523 8211 **Fax:** 901 524 4936

If you can't find a firm here, see full profiles (pages 759-907)

OTHER RECOMMENDED FIRMS

ARMSTRONG HIRSCH JACKOWAY TYERMAN & WERTHEIMER (California)
Suite 1800, 1888 Century Park East, Century City, Los Angeles, CA 90067
Tel: 310 553 0305 **Fax:** 310 553 5036

ARMSTRONG TEASDALE SCHLAFLY & DAVIS (Missouri)
One Metropolitan Square, Suite 2600, St Louis, MO 63102-2740
Tel: 314 621 5070 **Fax:** 314 621 5065

ARNALL GOLDEN GREGORY LLP (Georgia)
2800 One Atlantic Center, 1201 West Peachtree Street, Atlanta, GA 30309
Tel: 404 873 8500 **Fax:** 404 873 8501

ARNOLD & KADJAN (Illinois)
Suite 300, 19 W Jackson Boulevard, Chicago, IL 60604 3957
Tel: 312 236 0415

ARTER & HADDEN LLP (Ohio)
1100 Huntingdon Building, 925 Euclid Avenue, Cleveland, OH 44115-1475
Tel: 216 696 1100 **Fax:** 216 696 2645

ASHBURN & MASON, PC (Alaska)
1130 West 6th Avenue, Suite 100, Anchorage, AK 99501
Tel: 907 276 4331 **Fax:** 907 277 8235

ASHBY & GEDDES (Delaware)
222 Delaware Avenue, 17th Floor, PO Box 1150, Wilmington, DE 19899
Tel: 302 654 1888 **Fax:** 302 654 2067

ASHER, GITTLER, GREENFIELD, COHEN & D'ALBA (Illinois)
125 South Wacker Drive, Suite 1100, Chicago, IL 60606
Tel: 312 263 1500 **Fax:** 312 263 1520

ASHFORD & WRISTON (Hawaii)
Alii Place, Suite 1400, 1099 Alakea Street, Honolulu, HI 96810
Tel: 808 539 0400 **Fax:** 808 533 4945

ATER WYNNE LLP (Oregon)
222 SW Columbia Street, Suite 1800, Portland, OR 97201
Tel: 503 226 1191 **Fax:** 503 226 0079

ATKINSON, CONWAY & GAGNON (Alaska)
420 L Street, Suite 500, Anchorage, AK 99501-1989
Tel: 907 276 1700

AUGUST & KULUNAS (Florida)
250 Australian Avenue South, Suite 1100, West Palm Beach, FL 33401
Tel: 561 835 9600 **Fax:** 561 835 9602

AUSLEY & MCMULLEN (Florida)
Washington Square Building, 227 South Calhoun Street, PO Box 391, Tallahassee, FL 32302
Tel: 850 224 9115 **Fax:** 850 222 7560

AVANT & FALCON (Louisiana)
429 Government Street, Baton Rouge, LA 70802 -6114
Tel: 225 387 4462

AXINN VELTROP & HARKRIDER LLP (New York)
1370 Avenue of Americas, New York, NY 10019-6708
Tel: 212 728 2200 **Fax:** 212 728 2201

BAACH ROBINSON & LEWIS (District of Columbia)
One Thomas Circle, NW, Suite 200, Washington, DC, DC 20005-5803
Tel: 202 833 8900 **Fax:** 202 466 5738

BABST, CALLAND, CLEMENTS AND ZOMNIR, A PROFESSIONAL CORPORATION (Pennsylvania)
Two Gateway Center, Pittsburgh, PA 15222
Tel: 412 394 5400 **Fax:** 412 394 6576

BACKUS MEYER SOLOMON ROOD & BRANCH LLP (New Hampshire)
116 Lowell Street, P.O. Box 516, Manchester, NH 03105-0516
Tel: 603 668 7272 **Fax:** 603 668 0730

BAILEY & GLASSER LLP (West Virginia)
227 Capitol Street, Charleston, WV 25301
Tel: 304 345 6555 **Fax:** 304 342 1110

BAIRD, HOLM, MCEACHEN, PEDERSEN, HAMANN & STRASHEIM LLP (Nebraska)
1500 Woodmen Tower, Omaha, NE 68102
Tel: 402 344 0500 **Fax:** 402 344 0588

BAKER & DANIELS (Indiana)
300 North Meridian Street, Suite 2700, Indianapolis, IN 46204-1782
Tel: 317 237 0300 **Fax:** 317 237 1000

BAKER & HOSTETLER LLP (District of Columbia)
Washington Square, Suite 1100, 1050 Conneticut Ave, Washington, DC, DC 20036-5304
Tel: 202 861 1621 **Fax:** 202 861 1783

BAKER BOTTS LLP (Texas)
One Shell Plaza, 910 Louisiana, Houston, TX 77002-4995
Tel: 713 229 1234 **Fax:** 713 229 1522

BAKER, DONELSON, BEARMAN & CALDWELL (Tennessee)
20th Floor, First Tennessee Building, 165 Madison, Memphis, TN 38103
Tel: 901 526 2000 **Fax:** 901 577 2303

BALL JANIK LLP (Oregon)
One Main Place, 101 SW Main Street, Suite 1100, Portland, OR 97204
Tel: 503 228 2525 **Fax:** 503 295 1058

BANGS, MCCULLEN, BUTLER, FOYE & SIMMONS, LLP (South Dakota)
818 St Joseph Street, PO Box 2670, Rapid City, SD 57709
Tel: 605 343 1040 **Fax:** 605 343 1503

BANKSTON, GRONNING, O'HARA, SEDOR, MILLS & HEAPHEY, PC (Alaska)
550 West 7th Avenue, Suite 1800, Anchorage, AK 99501
Tel: 907 276 1711 **Fax:** 907 279 5358

BANNER & WITCOFF, LTD (District of Columbia)
1001 G Street NW, Washington, DC, DC 20001
Tel: 202 508 9100 **Fax:** 202 508 9299

BAPTISTE & WILDER (District of Columbia)
1150 Connecticut Avenue NW, Suite 500, Washington, DC 20036
Tel: 202 223 0723 **Fax:** 202 223 9677

OTHER RECOMMENDED FIRMS

BARACK FERRAZZANO KIRSCHBAUM PERLMAN & NAGELBERG (Illinois)
333 West Wacker, Suite 2700, Chicago, IL 60606-1227
Tel: 312 984 3100 **Fax:** 312 984 3150

BARGER & WOLEN (California)
515 South Flower Street, 34th Floor, Los Angeles, CA 90071
Tel: 213 680 2800

BARIA FYKE HAWKINS & STRACENER (Mississippi)
Spengler Thomas Building, 129B South President Street, Jackson, Ms 39201
Tel: 601 969 9692 **Fax:** 601 914 3580

BARLOW & WILCOX PA (New Mexico)
201 Third Street North West, Suite 1130, Albuquerque, NM 87102
Tel: 505 248 1300 **Fax:** 505 248 1100

BARNES & THORNBURG (District of Columbia)
1401 Eye Street North West, Suite 500, Washington, DC, DC 20005
Tel: 202 289 1313 **Fax:** 202 289 1330

BARNETT, BOLT, KIRKWOOD & LONG (Florida)
601 Bayshore Bouldevard, Suite 700, Tampa, FL 33601
Tel: 813 253 2020 **Fax:** 813 251 6711

BARRAN LIEBMAN (Oregon)
601 SW Second Avenue, Suite 2300, Portland, OR 97204
Tel: 503 228 0500 **Fax:** 503 274 1212

BARRETT, JOHNSTON & PARSLEY (Tennessee)
217 Second Avenue North, Nashville, TN 37201-1601
Tel: 615 244 2202 **Fax:** 615 252 3798

BARRIS, SOTT, DENN & DRIKER, PLLC (Michigan)
211 West Fort Street, Fifteenth Floor, Detroit, MI 48226-3281
Tel: 313 965 9725 **Fax:** 313 965 5398

BARTLIT BECK HERMAN PALENCHAR & SCOTT (Illinois)
Courthouse Place, 54 West Hubbard Street, Chicago, IL 60610
Tel: 312 494 4400 **Fax:** 312 494 4440

BASS, BERRY & SIMS PLC (Tennessee)
315 Deaderick Street, Suite 2700, Nashville, TN 37238
Tel: 615 742 6200 **Fax:** 615 742 6293

BASSFORD, LOCKHART, TRUESDELL & BRIGGS, P.A. (Minnesota)
3550 Multifoods Tower, Minneapolis, MN 55402
Tel: 612 333 3000 **Fax:** 612 333 8829

BASTIANELLI, BROWN & KELLEY (District of Columbia)
1133 Twenty First Street, North West Suite 500, Washington, DC, DC 20036
Tel: 202 293 8815 **Fax:** 202 293 7994

BATES & CAREY (Illinois)
333 West Wacker Drive, Suite 900, Chicago, IL 60606
Tel: 312 762 3100 **Fax:** 312 762 3200

BEASLEY, ALLEN, CROW, METHVIN, PORTIS & MILES, PC (Alabama)
218 Commerce Street, PO Box 4160, Montgomery, AL 36104
Tel: 334 269 2343 **Fax:** 334 954 7555

BECK & ELDERGILL, PC (Connecticut)
447 Center Street, Manchester, CT 06040
Tel: 860 646 5606 **Fax:** 860 646 0054

BECK, REDDEN & SECREST (Texas)
One Houston Center, 1221 McKinney Street, Suite 4500, Houston, TX 77010-2010
Tel: 713 951 3700 **Fax:** 713 951 3720

BECKER & POLIAKOFF, P.A. (Florida)
Emerald Lake Corporate Park, 3111 Stirling Road, Fort Lauderdale, FL 33310
Tel: 954 987 7550 **Fax:** 954 985 4176

BECKMAN LAWSON, LLP (Indiana)
800 Standard Federal Plaza, Fort Wayne, IN 46802
Tel: 219 422 0800 **Fax:** 219 420 1013

BEDELL, DITTMAR, DEVAULT, PILLANS & COXE (Florida)
The Bedell Building, 101 East Adams Street, Jacksonville, FL 32202
Tel: 904 353 0211 **Fax:** 904 353 9307

BEDRAVA & LYMAN (Illinois)
1301 W. 22nd Street, Suite 914, Oak Brook, IL 60523-2018
Tel: 630 575 0020 **Fax:** 630 575 0999

BELIN LAMSON MCCORMICK ZUMBACH FLYNN, PC (Iowa)
The Financial Center, 666 Walnut Street, Suite 2000, Des Moines, IA 50309
Tel: 515 243 7100 **Fax:** 515 244 7818

BELL DAVIS & PITT (North Carolina)
Century Plaza, Suite 600, 100 Noth Cherry Street, Winston-Salem, NC 27101
Tel: 336 722 3700 **Fax:** 336 722 3700

BELL, BOYD & LLOYD (Illinois)
Three First National Plaza,, Suite 3300, 70 West Madison Street, Chicago, IL 60602-4027
Tel: 312 372 1121 **Fax:** 312 372 2098

BENDINGER, CROCKETT PETERSON & CASEY (Utah)
170 South Main Street, Suite 400, Salt Lake City, UT 84101
Tel: 801 533 8383 **Fax:** 801 531 1486

BENESCH, FRIEDLANDER, COPLAN & ARONOFF LLP (Ohio)
2300 BP Tower, 200 Public Square, Cleveland, OH 44114
Tel: 216 363 4500 **Fax:** 216 363 4588

BENETAR BERNSTEIN SCHAIR & STEIN (New York)
330 Madison Avenue, 39th Floor, New York, NY 10017
Tel: 212 697 4433 **Fax:** 212 697 3510

BENEZRA & CULVER (Colorado)
141 Union Boulevard, Suite 260, Lakewood, CO 80228
Tel: 303 716 0254 **Fax:** 303 716 0327

BERENBAUM, WEINSHIENK & EASON (Colorado)
370 Seventeenth Street, Republic Plaza, Suite 2600, Denver, CO 80202
Tel: 303 825 0800 **Fax:** 303 629 7610

OTHER RECOMMENDED FIRMS

BERENSTEIN, MOORE, BERENSTEIN, HEFFERNAN & MOELLER (Iowa)
300 Firstarbank Building, 501 Pierce Street, PO Box 3207, Sioux City, IA 51102
Tel: 712 252 0020

BERGER & MONTAGUE (Pennsylvania)
1622 Locust Street, Philadelphia, PA 19103
Tel: 215 875 3000

BERGER SINGERMAN (Florida)
215 South Monroe Street, Suite 705, Tallahassee, FL 32301
Tel: 850 561 3010 Fax: 850 561 3013

BERKES CRANE ROBINSON & SEAL, LLP (California)
515 South Figueroa Street, Suite 1500, Los Angeles, CA 90071
Tel: 213 955 1150 Fax: 213 955 1155

BERKOWITZ LEFKOVITS ISOM & KUSHNER (Alabama)
South Trust Tower, 420 20th Street North, Suite 1600, Birmingham, AL 35203-0480
Tel: 205 328 0480 Fax: 205 322 8007

BERKOWITZ, STANTON, BRANDT, WILLIAMS & SHAW (Missouri)
Two Emanuel Cleaver II Boulevard, Suite 500, Kansas City, MO 64112
Tel: 816 561 7007 Fax: 816 561 1888

BERMAN & SIMMONS (Maine)
85 Exchange Street, Portland, ME 04101
Tel: 207 774 5277

BERMAN, GAUFIN, TOMSIC, SAVAGE & CAMPBELL (Utah)
50 South Main Street, Suite 1250, Salt Lake City, UT 84144
Tel: 801 328 2200 Fax: 801 531 9926

BERMAN, PALEY, GOLDSTEIN & KANNRY (New York)
500 Fifth Avenue, New York, NY 10110
Tel: 212 354 9600 Fax: 212 354 9873

BERNSTEIN, SHUR, SAWYER & NELSON, PA (Maine)
100 Middle Street, PO Box 9729, Portland, ME 04104
Tel: 207 774 1200 Fax: 207 774 1327

BETZER ROYBAL & EISENBERG PC (New Mexico)
4900 Lang Avenue North East, Suite 202, Albuquerque, NM 87109-4303
Tel: 505 797 0105 Fax: 505 797 0170

BIESER, GREER, & LANDIS LLP (Ohio)
400 National City Center, 6 North Main Street, Dayton, OH 45402-1908
Tel: 937 223 3277 Fax: 937 223 6339

BINGHAM MCCUTCHEN LLP (Massachusetts)
150 Federal Street, Boston, MA 02110
Tel: 617 951 8000 Fax: 617 951 8736

BINGHAM MCHALE LLP (Indiana)
2700 Market Tower, 10 West Market Street, Indianapolis, IN 46204
Tel: 317 635 8900 Fax: 317 236 9907

BIOFF, FINUCANE, COFFEY, HOLLAND & HOSLER LLP (Missouri)
Suite 400 The Stilwell Building, 104 West Ninth Street, Kansas City, MO 64105-1718
Tel: 816 842 8770 Fax: 816 842 8767

BIRCH, HORTON, BITTNER & CHEROT (Alaska)
1127 West 7th Avenue, Anchorage, AK 99501
Tel: 907 276 1550 Fax: 907 276 3680

BLACKWELL SANDERS PEPER MARTIN LLP (Missouri)
Two Pershing Square, Suite 110, 2300 Main Street, Kansas City, MO 64141-6777
Tel: 816 983 8000 Fax: 816 983 8080

BLACKWOOD ASSOCIATES PC (Vermont)
90 Main Street, Burlington, VT 05401
Tel: 802 863 2517 Fax: 802 863 0262

BLANK ROME COMISKY & MCCAULEY LLP (Pennsylvania)
One Logan Square, Philadelphia, PA 19103-6998
Tel: 215 569 5500 Fax: 215 569 5555

BLECHER & COLLINS (California)
611 West Sixth Street, 20th Floor, Los Angeles, CA 90017
Tel: 213 622 4222

BLISH & CAVANAGH, LLP (Rhode Island)
Commerce Center, 30 Exchange Terrace, Providence, RI 02903
Tel: 401 831 8900 Fax: 401 751 7542

BOIES, SCHILLER & FLEXNER LLP (New York)
80 Business Park Drive, Suite 110, Armonk, New York, NY 10504-1710
Tel: 914 749 8200 Fax: 914 273 9810

BONDURANT, MIXSON & ELMORE, LLP (Georgia)
1201 West Peachtree Street NW, Suite 3900, Atlanta, GA 30309
Tel: 404 881 4100 Fax: 404 881 4111

BOONE, KARLBERG PC (Montana)
201 West Main Street, Suite 300, PO Box 9199, Missoula, MT 59807-9199
Tel: 406 543 6646 Fax: 406 549 6804

BOOSE CASEY CIKLIN LUBITZ MARTENS MCBANE & O'CONNELL (Florida)
Northbridge Tower 1, Nineteenth Floor, 515 North Flagler Drive, West Palm Beach, FL 33401
Tel: 561 832 5900 Fax: 561 833 4209

BORNN & SURLS (California)
330 Washington Boulevard, Suite 400, Marina Del Rey, CA 90292
Tel: 310 577 8712 Fax: 310 577 8613

BOSE MCKINNEY & EVANS LLP (Indiana)
2700 First Indiana Plaza, 135 North Pennsylvania Street, Indianapolis, IN 46204
Tel: 317 684 5000 Fax: 317 684 5173

BOULT, CUMMINGS, CONNERS & BERRY, PLC (Tennessee)
414 Union Street, Suite 1600, PO Box 198062, Nashville, TN 37219
Tel: 615 244 2582 Fax: 615 252 6380 852980

OTHER RECOMMENDED FIRMS

BOWDITCH & DEWEY LLP (Massachusetts)
311 Main Street, PO Box 15156, Worcester, MA 01615-0156
Tel: 508 791 3511 **Fax:** 508 756 7636

BOWEN RILEY WARNOCK & JACOBSON (Tennessee)
1906 Wet End Avenue, Nashville, TN 37203
Tel: 615 320 3700 **Fax:** 615 320 3737

BOWLES RICE MCDAVID GRAFF & LOVE PLLC (West Virginia)
600 Quarrier Street, PO Box 1386, Charleston, WV 25325-1386
Tel: 304 347 1100 **Fax:** 304 343 2867

BOYCE, PASHBY & WELK (South Dakota)
101 North Phillips Avenue, Suite 600, PO Box 5015, Sioux Falls, SD 57117-5015
Tel: 605 336 2424 **Fax:** 605 334 0618

BRADLEY & RILEY, PC (Iowa)
2007 First Avenue SE, PO Box 2804, Cedar Rapids, IA 52406
Tel: 319 363 0101 **Fax:** 319 363 9824

BRADLEY ARANT ROSE & WHITE LLP (Alabama)
200 Clinton Avenue West, Suite 900, Huntsville, AL 35801-4900
Tel: 256 517 5100 **Fax:** 256 517 5200

BRADSHAW, FOWLER, PROCTOR & FAIRGRAVE, PC (Iowa)
801 Grand Avenue, Suite 3700, Des Moines, IA 50309
Tel: 515 243 4191 **Fax:** 515 246 5808

BRANSTETTER, KILGORE, STRANCH & JENNINGS (Tennessee)
227 Second Avenue North, Fourth Floor, Nashville, TN37201-1631
Tel: 615 254 8801 **Fax:** 615 255 5419

BRAUER, BUESCHER, GOLDHAMMER, KELMAN & ECKERT (Colorado)
1563 Gaylord Street, Denver, CO 80206
Tel: 303 333 7751 **Fax:** 303 333 7758

BREAZEALE, SACHSE & WILSON, L.L.P. (Louisiana)
Twenty-Third Floor, One American Place, PO Box 3197, Baton Rouge, LA 70821
Tel: 225 387 4000 **Fax:** 225 381 8029

BREDHOFF & KAISER (District of Columbia)
805 Fifteenth Street, N.W, Washington, DC, DC 20005-2207
Tel: 202 842 2600 **Fax:** 202 842 1888

BRENSKE & CHRISTENSEN (Nevada)
630 South Third Street, Las Vegas, NV 89101
Tel: 702 385 3300

BRICKER & ECKLER LLP (Ohio)
100 South Third Street, Columbus, OH 43215
Tel: 614 227 2300 **Fax:** 614 227 2390

BRIDGER-RILEY & ASSOCIATES, PC (Oklahoma)
Suite 306, 7030 South Yale Avenue, Tulsa, OK 74137
Tel: 918 494 6699

BRIGGS AND MORGAN, PROFESSIONAL ASSOCIATION (Minnesota)
2400 IDS Center, 80 South Eighth Street, Minneapolis, MN 55402
Tel: 612 334 8400 **Fax:** 612 334 8650

BRINKS HOFER GILSON & LIONE (Illinois)
NBC Tower, 455 North Cityfront Plaza Drive, Suite 3600, Chicago, IL 60611-5599
Tel: 312 321 4200 **Fax:** 312 321 4299

BROAD AND CASSEL (Florida)
Miami Center, Suite 3000, 201 South Biscayne Boulevard, Miami, FL 33131
Tel: 305 373 9435 **Fax:** 305 995 6406

BROBECK, PHLEGER & HARRISON LLP (California)
One Market Plaza, Spear Street Tower, San Francisco, CA 94105
Tel: 415 442 0900 **Fax:** 415 442 1010

BRONSTEIN, CARLSON, GLEIM & SMITH, PA (Florida)
Suite 1100, 150 Second Avenue North, St Petersburg, FL 33701
Tel: 727 898 6688 **Fax:** 727 989 8811

BROOKS, PIERCE, MCLENDON, HUMPHREY & LEONARD, L.L.P. (North Carolina)
2000 Renaissance Plaza, 230 North Elm Street (27401), Greensboro, NC 27420
Tel: 336 373 8850 **Fax:** 336 378 1001

BROOM, JOHNSON & CLARKSON (Nebraska)
1722 St Mary's Avenue, Omaha, NE 68102
Tel: 402 346 8323 **Fax:** 402 346 5426

BROWN CLARK CHRISTOPHER & DEMAY, PA (Florida)
1819 Main Street, Suite 1100, Sarasota, FL 34236-5999
Tel: 941 957 3800 **Fax:** 941 957 3888

BROWN LAW FIRM, PC (Montana)
315 North 24th Street, PO Drawer 849, Billings, MT 59101
Tel: 406 248 2611 **Fax:** 406 248 3128

BROWN MCCARROLL, LLP (Texas)
111 Congress Avenue, Suite 1400, Austin, TX 78701-4043
Tel: 512 472 5456 **Fax:** 512 479 1101

BROWN RUDNICK BERLACK ISRAELS (Massachusetts)
One Financial Center and, 745 Atlantic Avenue, Boston, MA 02111
Tel: 617 856 8200 **Fax:** 617 856 8201

BROWN, DREW & MASSEY, LLP (Wyoming)
Ohio Oil Building, Suite 200, 159 North Wolcott Street, Casper, WY 82601
Tel: 307 234 1000 800 877 6755 **Fax:** 307 265 8025

BROWN, WINICK, GRAVES, GROSS, BASKERVILLE AND SCHOENEBAUM PLC (Iowa)
666 Grand Avenue, Suite 2000, Des Moines, IA 50309
Tel: 515 242 2400 **Fax:** 515 283 0231

BROWNING & PEIFER (New Mexico)
20 First Plaza Center North West, Suite 725, Albuquerque, NM 87102 -3347
Tel: 505 247 4800

BROWNSTEIN HYATT & FARBER, PC (Colorado)
410 Seventeenth Street, Twenty-Second Floor, Denver, CO 80202-4437
Tel: 303 223 1100 **Fax:** 303 223 1111

OTHER RECOMMENDED FIRMS

BRUDER GENTILE & MARCOUX LLP
(District of Columbia)
1100 New York Avenue North West, Suite 510 East, Washington, DC, DC 20005-3934
Tel: 202 783 1350 **Fax:** 202 737 9117

BRUNINI, GRANTHAM, GROWER & HEWES, PLLC
(Mississippi)
1400 Trustmark Building, 248 East Capitol Street, Jackson, MS 39205
Tel: 601 948 3101 **Fax:** 601 960 6902

BRYAN CAVE LLP (Missouri)
One Metropolitan Square, 211 North Broadway, Suite 3600, St Louis, MO 63102-2750
Tel: 314 259 2000 **Fax:** 314 259 2020

BUCHANAN INGERSOLL (Pennsylvania)
1 Oxford Centre, 20th Floor, 301 Grant Street, Pittsburgh, PA 15219-1410
Tel: 412 562 8800 **Fax:** 412 562 1041

BUCK & GORDON LLP (Washington)
902 Waterfront Place, 1011 Western Avenue, Seattle, WA 98104-1097
Tel: 206 382 9540 **Fax:** 206 626 0675

BUCKINGHAM DOOLITTLE & BURROUGHS (Ohio)
191 West Nationwide Boulevard, Suite 300, P.O. Box 151120, Columbus, OH 43215-8120
Tel: 614 221 8448

BUCKLEY & KLEIN (Georgia)
Atlantic Center Plaza, 1180 West Peachtree Street, Suite 1100, Atlanta, GA 30309
Tel: 404 781 1100 **Fax:** 404 420 5961

BUIST, MOORE, SMYTHE & MCGEE, P.A.
(South Carolina)
Five Exchange Street, PO Box 999, Charleston, SC 29402
Tel: 843 722 3400

BULLARD SMITH JERNSTEDT WILSON (Oregon)
1000 SW Broadway, Suite 1900, Portland, OR 97205
Tel: 503 248 1134 **Fax:** 503 224 8851

BULLIVANT HOUSER BAILEY PC (Oregon)
300 Pioneer Tower, 888 SW Fifth Avenue, Portland, OR 97204
Tel: 503 228 6351 **Fax:** 503 295 0915

BURBIDGE & MITCHELL (Utah)
139 East South Temple, Suite 2001, Salt Lake City, UT 84111
Tel: 803 355 6677 **Fax:** 801 355 2341

BURCH, PORTER & JOHNSON (Tennessee)
130 North Court Avenue, Memphis, TN 38103
Tel: 731 524 5000 **Fax:** 731 524 5024

BURKE & PARSONS (New York)
1114 Avenue of Americas, 34th Floor, New York, NY 10036-7743
Tel: 212 354 3800 **Fax:** 212 221 1432

BURKHALTER & ASSOCIATES (Tennessee)
P.O. Box 2777, 111 South Central Avenue, Knoxville, TN 37901
Tel: 423 524 4974 **Fax:** 423 524 0172

BURNETTE & LECLAIR P.A (South Carolina)
2322 Devine Street, Columbia, SC 29205
Tel: 803 251 0202 **Fax:** 803 251 0222

BURNETTE, DOBSON & HARDEMAN (Tennessee)
713 Cherry Street, Chattanooga, TN 37402
Tel: 423 266 2121 **Fax:** 423 266 3324

BURR & FORMAN LLP (Alabama)
Southtrust Tower, 420 North Twentieth Street, Suite 3100, Birmingham, AL 35203
Tel: 205 251 3000 **Fax:** 205 458 5100

BURR, PEASE & KURTZ, PC (Alaska)
810 N Street, Anchorage, AK 99501
Tel: 907 276 6100 **Fax:** 907 258 2530

BUSH ROSS GARDNER WARREN & RUDY, PA (Florida)
220 South Franklin Street, P.O. Box 3913, Tampa, FL 33602-5330
Tel: 813 224 9255 **Fax:** 813 223 9620

BUSSE & HUNT (Oregon)
521 American Bank Building, 621 SW Morrison Street, Portland, OR 97205
Tel: 503 248 0504 **Fax:** 503 248 2131

BUTLER & HARRIS (Texas)
3223 Smith Street, Suite 308, Houston, TX 77006
Tel: 713 526 5677 **Fax:** 713 526 5691

BUTLER RUBIN SALTARELLI & BOYD (Illinois)
70 West Madison, Suite 1800, Chicago, IL 60602
Tel: 312 444 9660 **Fax:** 312 444 9287

BUTLER, SNOW, O'MARA, STEVENS & CANNADA, PLLC (Mississippi)
17th Floor, AmSouth Plaza, 210 East Capitol Street, Jackson, MS 39225
Tel: 601 948 5711 **Fax:** 601 949 4555

BUTLER, WILLIAMS, PANTELE & SKILLING (Virginia)
1309 East Cary Street, Second Floor, Richmond, VA 23219
Tel: 804 648 4848 **Fax:** 804 648 6814

BUTLER, WOOTEN, FRYHOFER, DAUGHTERY & SULLIVAN, LLP (Georgia)
1500 Second Avenue, PO Box 2766, Columbus, GA 31902
Tel: 706 322 1990 **Fax:** 706 323 2962

BYAM & HOARTY (Nebraska)
317 American National Building, 8990 West Dodge Road, Omaha, NE 68114
Tel: 402 397 0303 **Fax:** 402 397 5004

BYRNES & KELLER (Washington)
1000 Second Avenue, 38th Floor, Seattle, WA 98104
Tel: 206 622 2000 **Fax:** 206 622 2522

CABANISS, JOHNSTON, GARDNER, DUMAS & O'NEAL
(Alabama)
2001 Park Place North, Suite 700, Birmingham, AL 35203
Tel: 205 716 5200 **Fax:** 205 716 5389

OTHER RECOMMENDED FIRMS

CADES SCHUTTE FLEMING & WRIGHT (Hawaii)
Cades Schutte Fleming & Wright Building, 1000 Bishop Street, Suite 1200, PO Box 939, Honolulu, HI 96808
Tel: 808 521 9200 **Fax:** 808 521 9210

CADWELL SANFORD DEIBERT & GARRY LLP (South Dakota)
120 North Phillips Avenue, P.O. Box 1157, Sioux Falls, SD 57101-1157
Tel: 605 336 0828 **Fax:** 605 336 6036

CAESAR, RIVISE, BERNSTEIN, COHEN & POKOTILOW LTD (Pennsylvania)
1635 Market Street, 12th Floor, Philadelphia, PA 19103-2212
Tel: 215 567 2010 **Fax:** 215 751 1142

CAHILL GORDON & REINDEL (New York)
80 Pine Street, New York, NY 10005-1702
Tel: 212 701 3900 **Fax:** 212 269 5420

CALFEE, HALTER & GRISWOLD LLP (Ohio)
1400 McDonald Investment Center, 800 Superior Avenue, Cleveland, OH 44114
Tel: 216 622 8200 **Fax:** 216 241 0816

CAMPBELL & WILLIAMS (Nevada)
1409 Bank of America Plaza, 300 South Fourth Street, Las Vegas, NV 89101
Tel: 702 382 5222 **Fax:** 702 382 0540

CAPLIN & DRYSDALE (District of Columbia)
One Thomas Circle NW, Suite 1100, Washington, DC, DC 20005-5802
Tel: 202 862 5000 **Fax:** 202 429 3301

CARL R GOLD (SOLE PRACTITIONER) (Maryland)
402 West Pennsylvania Avenue, Baltimore, MD 21204-4228
Tel: 410 337 5545

CARLOCK COPELAND SEMLER & STAIR, LLP (Georgia)
2600 Marquis Two Tower, 285 Peachtree Center Avenue, Atlanta, GA 30303
Tel: 404 522 8220 **Fax:** 404 523 2345

CARLSMITH BALL (District of Columbia)
700 14th Street, NW, 9th Floor, DC 20005
Tel: 202 508 1025 **Fax:** 202 508 1026

CARLTON FIELDS (Florida)
One Harbour Place, 777 South Harbour Island Boulevard, Tampa, FL 33601
Tel: 813 223 7000 **Fax:** 813 229 4133

CARMODY & TORRANCE LLP (Connecticut)
50 Leavenworth Street, PO Box 1110, Waterbury, CT 06721
Tel: 203 573 1200 **Fax:** 203 575 2600

CARPENTER & CHAVEZ LTD (New Mexico)
1600 University Boulevard N.E, Suite A, Albuquerque, NM 87102 1724
Tel: 505 243 1336 **Fax:** 505 243 1339

CARPENTER & KLATSKIN (Colorado)
1500 Denver Club Building, Denver, CO 80202
Tel: 303 534 6315

CARPENTER, BENNETT & MORRISSEY (New Jersey)
Three Gateway Center, 17th Floor, 100 Mulberry Street, Newark, NJ 07102
Tel: 973 622 7711 New York City: 212 943 6530 **Fax:** 973 622 5314

CARR, TABB, POPE & FREEMAN, LLP (Georgia)
10 North Parkway Square, Atlanta, GA 30327
Tel: 404 442 9000 **Fax:** 404 442 9700

CARRINGTON, COLEMAN, SLOMAN & BLUMENTHAL, LLP (Texas)
200 Crescent Court, Suite 1500, Dallas, TX 75201
Tel: 214 855 3000 **Fax:** 214 855 1333

CARRUTHERS & ROTH (North Carolina)
235 North Edgeworth Street, P.O.Box 540, Greensboro, NC 27402
Tel: 336 273 8651 **Fax:** 336 273 7885

CARVER, DARDEN, KORETZKY, TESSIER, FINN, BLOSSMAN & AREAUX L.L.C (Louisiana)
1100 Poydras Street, Suite 2700, New Orleans, LA 70163
Tel: 504 585 3800 **Fax:** 504 585 3801

CASE BIGELOW & LOMBARDI A LAW CORPORATION (Hawaii)
2600 Pacific Guardian Center, Mauka Tower, 737 Bishop Street, Honolulu, HI 96813
Tel: 808 547 5400 **Fax:** 808 523 1888

CASPER & DE TOLEDO LLC (Connecticut)
111 Summer Street, Stamford, CT 06905
Tel: 203 325 8600 **Fax:** 203 323 5970

CASSIDY MYERS COGAN VOEGELIN & TENNANT (West Virginia)
The First State Capitol, 1413 E Off Street, Wheeling, WV 26003-3582
Tel: 304 232 8100

CHAMBERLAIN, HRDLICKA, WHITE, WILLIAMS & MARTIN (Texas)
1200 Smith Street, Suite 1400, Houston, TX 77002
Tel: 713 658 1818; 800 342 5829 **Fax:** 713 658 2553

CHAPMAN AND CUTLER (Illinois)
111 West Monroe Street, Chicago, IL 60603-4080
Tel: 312 845 3000 **Fax:** 312 701 2361

CHARLSON BREDEHOFT (Virginia)
11260 Roger Bacon Drive, Suite 201, Reston, VA 20190
Tel: 703 318 6800 **Fax:** 703 318 6808

CHESTER, WILLCOX & SAXBE LLP (Ohio)
17 South High Street, Suite 900, Columbus, OH 43215
Tel: 614 221 4000 **Fax:** 614 221 4012

CHISENHALL, NESTRUD & JULIAN, PA (Arkansas)
400 West Capitol, Suite 2840, Little Rock, AR 72201
Tel: 501 372 5800 **Fax:** 501 372 4941

CHOATE HALL & STEWART (Massachusetts)
Exchange Place, 53 State Street, Boston, MA 02109-2891
Tel: 617 248 5000 **Fax:** 617 248 4000

CHONIN & SHER (Florida)
95 Merrick Way, Suite 100, Miami, FL 33134
Tel: 305 443 5125 **Fax:** 305 444 9524

OTHER RECOMMENDED FIRMS

CHRISTENSEN, MOORE, COCKRELL, CUMMINGS & AXELBERG PC (Montana)
Two Medicine Building, 160 Heritage Way, PO Box 7370, Kalispell, MT 59904-0370
Tel: 406 751 6000 **Fax:** 406 756 6522

CHRISTIAN & BARTON, L.L.P. (Virginia)
909 East Main Street, Suite 1200, Richmond, VA 23219
Tel: 804 697 4100 **Fax:** 804 697 4112

CHRISTIAN & SMALL LLP (Alabama)
Financial Center, 505 North Twentieth Street, Suite 1800, Birmingham, AL 35203-2607
Tel: 205 795 6588 **Fax:** 205 328 7234

CHRISTIAN, SAMSON, JONES & CHISHOLM, PLLC (Montana)
310 West Spruce, P.O.Box 8479, Missoula, MT 59807
Tel: 406 721 7772 **Fax:** 406 721 7776

CHRISTIE, PARKER & HALE, LLP (California)
350 West Colorado Boulevard, Suite 500, Pasadena, CA 91105
Tel: 626 795 9900 **Fax:** 626 577 8800

CICHANOWICZ, CALLAN, KEANE, VENGROW & TEXTOR LLP (New York)
61 Broadway, 30th Floor, Suite 3000, New York, NY 10006-2802
Tel: 212 344 7042 **Fax:** 212 344 7285

CLAPP PETERSON & STOWERS LLC (Alaska)
711 H Street, Suite 620, Anchorage, AK 99501-3442
Tel: 907 272 9272 **Fax:** 907 272 9586

CLARK HILL PLC (Michigan)
500 Woodward Avenue, Suite 3500, Detroit, MI 48226
Tel: 313 965 8300 **Fax:** 313 965 8252

CLARK, ATCHESON & REISERT (New York)
535 Fifth Avenue, New York, NY 10017
Tel: 212 297 0257 **Fax:** 212 297 0316

CLEARY SHAHI ASSOCIATES, A PROFESSIONAL CORPORATION (Vermont)
110 Merchants Row, Suite 7, PO Box 6740, Rutland, VT 05702-6740
Tel: 802 775 8800 **Fax:** 802 775 8809

CLIFFORD LAW OFFICES (Illinois)
120 North LaSalle Street, 31st Floor, Chicago, Il 60602
Tel: 312 899 9090 **Fax:** 312 251 1160

CLINE, WILLIAMS, WRIGHT, JOHNSON & OLDFATHER LLP (Nebraska)
1900 US Bank Building, 233 South 13th Street, Lincoln, NE 68508
Tel: 402 474 6900 **Fax:** 402 474 5393

COATS ROSE YALE RYMAN LEE (Texas)
800 First City Tower, 1001 Fannin, Houston, TX 77002-6707
Tel: 713 651 0111 **Fax:** 713 651 0222

COBLENTZ, PATCH, DUFFY & BASS LLP (California)
222 Kearny Street, Seventh Floor, San Francisco, CA 94108
Tel: 415 391 4800 **Fax:** 415 989 1663

COFFMAN, COLEMAN, ANDREWS & GROGAN (Florida)
2065 Herschel Street, PO Box 40089, Jacksonville, FL 32203
Tel: 904 389 5161 **Fax:** 904 387 9340

COHEN & GRIGSBY, PC (Pennsylvania)
11 Stanwix Street, 15th Floor, Pittsburgh, PA 15222
Tel: 800 394 4904 **Fax:** 412 209 0672

COHEN WEISS & SIMON (New York)
330 West 42nd Street, New York, NY 10036
Tel: 212 563 4100 **Fax:** 212 695 5436

COHEN, MILSTEIN, HAUSFELD & TOLL, PLLC (District of Columbia)
1100 New York Avenue, NW, Suite 500, West Tower, Washington, DC, DC 20005
Tel: 202 408 4600 **Fax:** 202 408 4699

COHN KHOURY MADOFF & WHITESELL (Massachusetts)
101 Arch Street, Boston, MA 02110
Tel: 617 951 2505 **Fax:** 617 951 0679

COKINOS, BOSIEN AND YOUNG (Texas)
2919 Allen Parkway, Suite 1500, Houston, TX 77019
Tel: 713 535 5500 **Fax:** 713 535 5533

COLE, SCHOTZ, MEISEL, FORMAN & LEONARD, P.A., A PROFESSIONAL CORPORATION (New Jersey)
Court Plaza North, 25 Main Street, Hackensack, NJ 07602
Tel: 201 489 3000 **Fax:** 201 489 1536

COLLIER, JACOB & MILLS (New Jersey)
Corporate Park III, Third Floor, 580 Howard Avenue, Somerset, NJ 08873
Tel: 732 560 7100

COLLINS, MCMAHON & HARRIS PLLC (Vermont)
PO Box 1623, Burlington, VT 05402-1623
Tel: 802 862 3524 **Fax:** 802 862 1794

COLLISON & BECHTOLD (Colorado)
1756 Gilpin Street, Denver, CO 80218
Tel: 303 388 4551

COLSON HICKS EIDSON (Florida)
255 Aragon Avenue, Miami, FL 33131-5008
Tel: 305 476 7400 **Fax:** 305 476 7444

COMITER & SINGER (Florida)
3801 PGA Boulevard, Suite 802, Palm Beach Gardens, FL 33410
Tel: 561 626 4742 **Fax:** 561 626 4742

COMMERCIAL LAW GROUP (Oklahoma)
2725 Oklahoma Tower, 210 Park Avenue, Oklahoma City, OK 73102-5643
Tel: 405 232 3001

CONLEY, ROSE & TAYON (Texas)
The Chase Building, 700 Lavaca, Suite 800, Austin, TX 78701-3102
Tel: 512 476 1400 **Fax:** 512 703 1250

CONLIN & ASSOCIATES (Iowa)
Plaza 5, 300 Walnut, Des Moines, IA 50309
Tel: 515 282 3333

OTHER RECOMMENDED FIRMS

CONMY FESTE LTD (North Dakota)
200 Wells Fargo Center, 406 Main Avenue, PO Box 2686, Fargo, ND 58108-2686
Tel: 701 293 9911 **Fax:** 701 293 3133

CONNER & WINTERS, A PROFESSIONAL CORPORATION (Oklahoma)
3700 First Place Tower, 15 East 5th Street, Tulsa, OK 74103-4344
Tel: 918 586 5711 **Fax:** 918 586 8982

CONNOLLY, O'MALLEY, LILLIS, HANSEN & OLSON LLP (Iowa)
317 Sixth Avenue, Suite 300, Bank of America Building, Des Moines, IA 50309
Tel: 515 234 81 57

CONRAD O'BRIEN GELLMAN & ROHN (Pennsylvania)
1515 Market Street, Sixteenth Floor, Philadelphia, PA 19102
Tel: 215 864 9600 **Fax:** 215 864 9620

CONSOLE LAW OFFICES (Pennsylvania)
1528 Walnut Street, Suite 600, Philadelphia, PA 19103-2756
Tel: 215 545 7676

CONSTANGY, BROOKS & SMITH, LLC (Georgia)
Suite 2400, 230 Peachtree Street North West, Atlanta, GA 30303-1557
Tel: 404 525 8622 **Fax:** 404 525 6955

CONWAY & MROWIEC (Illinois)
300 South Wacker Drive, Suite 601, Chicago, IL 60606
Tel: 312 692 1700 **Fax:** 312 692 1701

COOK & MOLAN (New Hampshire)
100 Hall Street, P.O. Box 1465, Concord, NH 03302-1465
Tel: 603 225 3323 **Fax:** 603 225 8930

COOK, LITTLE, ROSENBLATT & MASON PLLC (New Hampshire)
The Center of New Hampshire, 650 Elm Street, Manchester, NH 03101
Tel: 603 621 7100 **Fax:** 603 621 7111

COOLEY GODWARD LLP (California)
5 Palo Alto Square, 3000 El Camino Real, Palo Alto, CA 94306-2155
Tel: 650 843 5000 **Fax:** 650 857 0663

CORR CRONIN LLP (Washington)
1001 Fourth Avenue, Suite 3900, Seattle, WA 98154
Tel: 206 625 8600 **Fax:** 206 625 0900

COSHO, HUMPHREY, GREENER & WELSH, PA (Idaho)
The Carnegie Building, 815 West Washington, Boise, ID 83702
Tel: 208 344 7811 **Fax:** 208 338 3290

COSTELLO PORTER HILL HEISTERKAMP BUSHNELL & CARPENTER LLP (South Dakota)
200 Security Building, 704 St Joseph Street, PO Box 290, Rapid City, SD 57709
Tel: 605 343 2410 **Fax:** 605 343 4262

COTCHETT, PITRE, SIMON & MCCARTHY (California)
San Francisco Airport Office Center, 840 Malcolm Road, Suite 200, Burlingame, CA 94010
Tel: 650 697 6000 **Fax:** 650 697 0577

COUDERT BROTHERS (New York)
The Grace Building, 1114 Avenue of the Americas, New York, NY 10036-7703
Tel: 212 626 4400 **Fax:** 212 626 4120

COX & SMITH INCORPORATED (Texas)
112 East Pecan Street, Suite 1800, San Antonio, TX 78205
Tel: 210 554 5500 **Fax:** 210 226 8395

COX CASTLE & NICHOLSON LLP (California)
2049 Century Park East, 28th Floor, Los Angeles, CA 90067
Tel: 310 277 4222 **Fax:** 310 277 7889

COZEN O'CONNOR (Pennsylvania)
1900 Market Street, Philadelphia, PA 19103
Tel: 215 665 2000 **Fax:** 215 665 2013

CRAFT & CRAFT, A PROFESSIONAL LAW CORPORATION (Louisiana)
2310 Perkins Road, Baton Rouge, LA 70808
Tel: 225 344 6090

CRANDALL PYLES HAVILAND & TURNER (West Virginia)
122 Capitol Street, Suite 300, P.O. Box 3465, Charleston, WV 25301
Tel: 304 345 3080

CRAVATH, SWAINE & MOORE (New York)
Worldwide Plaza, 825 Eighth Avenue, New York, NY 10019-7475
Tel: 212 474 1000 **Fax:** 212 474 3700

CRISPIN & ASSOCIATES (Oregon)
280 Plaza West, 9600 SW Oak Street, Portland, OR 97223-6585
Tel: 503 293 5770 **Fax:** 503 293 5766

CROKER, HUCK, KASHER, DEWITT, ANDERSON & GONDERINGER, PC (Nebraska)
Suite 1250 Commercial Federal Tower, 2120 South 72nd Street, Omaha, NE 68124
Tel: 402 391 6777 **Fax:** 402 390 9221

CROMER & MABRY (South Carolina)
1225 Pickens Street, P.O. Box 11675, Columbia, SC 11675
Tel: 803 799 9530 **Fax:** 803 799 9533

CRONIN, FRIED, SEKIYA, KEKINA & FAIRBANKS ATTORNEYS AT LAW (Hawaii)
1900 Davies Pacific Center, 841 Bishop Street, Honolulu, HI 96813-3908
Tel: 808 524 1433 **Fax:** 808 536 2073

CROSS, GUNTER, WITHERSPOON & GALCHUS, PC (Arkansas)
500 President Clinton Avenue, Suite 200, Little Rock, AR 7220172203
Tel: 501 371 9999 **Fax:** 501 371 0035

CROWE & DUNLEVY (Oklahoma)
1800 Mid-America Tower, 20 North Broadway, Oklahoma City, OK 73102
Tel: 405 235 7700 **Fax:** 405 239 6651

CROWELL & MORING LLP (District of Columbia)
C&M International Ltd, 1001 Pennsylvania Avenue North West, Washington, DC, DC 20004-2595
Tel: 202 624 2500 **Fax:** 202 628 5116

If you can't find a firm here, see full profiles (pages 759-907)

OTHER RECOMMENDED FIRMS

CROWLEY, HAUGHEY, HANSON, TOOLE & DIETRICH, P.L.L.P. (Montana)
500 Transwestern II, 490 North 31st Street, Billings, MT 59103
Tel: 406 252 3441 **Fax:** 406 259 4159

CUMMINGS & LOCKWOOD (Connecticut)
4 Stamford Plaza, Stamford, CT 06904-0120
Tel: 203 327 1700 **Fax:** 203 351 4534

CUNNINGHAM, BOUNDS, YANCE, CROWDER & BROWN, LLC (Alabama)
1601 Dauphin Street, PO Box 66705, Mobile, AL 36660
Tel: 251 471 6191 **Fax:** 251 479 1031

CURTIS, MALLET-PREVOST & GILIOLI (New York)
101 Park Avenue, NY 10178-0061
Tel: 212 696 6165 **Fax:** 212 697 1559

CUTLER & DONAHOE LLP (South Dakota)
100 North Phillips Avenue, 9th Floor, Sioux Falls, SD 57104-6725
Tel: 605 335 4950 **Fax:** 605 335 4961

D'ANCONA & PFLAUM LLC (Illinois)
111 East Wacker Drive, Suite 2800, Chicago, IL 60601
Tel: 312 602 2000 **Fax:** 312 602 3000

DANIEL MARKS (Nevada)
302 East Carson, Suite 702, Las Vegas, NV 89101
Tel: 702 386 9600

DANN PECAR NEWMAN & KLEIMAN, PC (Indiana)
One American Square, Suite 2300, Indianapolis, IN 46282
Tel: 317 632 3232 **Fax:** 317 632 2962

DAVENPORT, EVANS, HURWITZ & SMITH LLP (South Dakota)
513 South Main Avenue, PO Box 1030, Sioux Falls, SD 57101
Tel: 605 336 2880 **Fax:** 605 335 3639

DAVID R. ARENDALL - SOLE PRACTITIONER (Alabama)
950 Financial Centre, 505 North 20th Street, Birmingham, AL 35203
Tel: 205 252 1550 **Fax:** 205 252 1556

DAVID SIMONS - SOLE PRACTITIONER (Hawaii)
Penthouse One, Ocean View Center, 707 Richards St, Honolulu, HI 96813
Tel: 808 536 3255 **Fax:** 808 524 5593

DAVID SIMONSEN JNR - SOLE PRACTITIONER (Virginia)
1600 Forest Avenue, Richmond, VA 23229-5007
Tel: 804 285 1337 **Fax:** 804 285 1350

DAVIS & BOGHIGIAN, PC (New Hampshire)
221 Main Street, Suite 301, P.O. Box 525, Nashua, NH 03061-0525
Tel: 603 595 0210 **Fax:** 603 595 9049

DAVIS & CANNON (Wyoming)
40 South Main Street, PO Box 728, Sheridan, WY 82801
Tel: 307 672 7491 **Fax:** 307 672 8955

DAVIS & CERIANI (Colorado)
1350 17th Street, Denver, CO 80202
Tel: 303 534 9000 **Fax:** 303 534 4618

DAVIS & KUELTHAU, S.C. (Wisconsin)
111 East Kilbourn Avenue, Suite 1400, Milwaukee, WI 53202
Tel: 414 276 0200 **Fax:** 414 276 9369

DAVIS GRAHAM & STUBBS LLP (Colorado)
1550 Seventeenth Street, Suite 500, Denver, CO 80202
Tel: 303 892 9400 **Fax:** 303 893 1379

DAVIS POLK & WARDWELL (New York)
450 Lexington Avenue, New York, NY 10017
Tel: 212 450 4000 **Fax:** 212 450 3800

DAVIS, BROWN, KOEHN, SHORS & ROBERTS, PC (Iowa)
The Financial Center, 666 Walnut Street, Suite 2500, Des Moines, IA 50309
Tel: 515 288 2500 **Fax:** 515 243 0654

DAY CASEBEER MADRID & BATCHELDER LLP (California)
20300 Stevens Creek Boulevard, Suite 400, Cupertino, CA 95014
Tel: 408 255 3255 **Fax:** 408 873 0220 / 408 255 3254

DAY, BERRY & HOWARD LLP (Connecticut)
CityPlace I, Hartford, CT 06103-3499
Tel: 860 275 0100 **Fax:** 860 275 0343

DEAN, MEAD, EGERTON, BLOODWORTH, CAPOUANO & BOZARTH PA (Florida)
800 North Magnolia Avenue, Suite 1500, Orlando, FL 32803
Tel: 407 841 1200 **Fax:** 407 423 1831

DEANER, DEANER, SCANN, MALAN & LARSEN (Nevada)
720 South Fourth Street, Suite 300, Las Vegas, NV 89101
Tel: 702 382 6911 **Fax:** 702 366 0854

DENISE J KNECHT & ASSOCIATES CO (Ohio)
75 Public Square, Suite 1300, Cleveland, OH 44113
Tel: 216 621 4882 **Fax:** 216 621 9640

DEORCHIS & PARTNERS, LLP (New York)
61 Broadway, 26th Floor, New York, NY 10006
Tel: 212 344 4700 **Fax:** 212 422 5299

DEPEW AND GILLEN LLC (Kansas)
151 North Main, Suite 800, Wichita, KS 67202-1409
Tel: 316 262 4000 **Fax:** 316 265 3819

DERRICK & BRIGGS LLP (Oklahoma)
Bank One Center, 20th Floor, 100 North Broadway Avenue, Oklahoma City, OK 73102
Tel: 405 235 1900 **Fax:** 405 235 1995

DEVINE MILLINET & BRANCH PA (New Hampshire)
PO Box 719, 111 Amherst Street, Manchester, NH 03105-0719
Tel: 603 669 1000 **Fax:** 603 669 8547

DEWITT ROSS & STEVENS SC (Wisconsin)
2 East Mifflin Street, Suite 600, Madison, WI 53703
Tel: 608 255 8891 **Fax:** 608 252 9243

DICKINSON WRIGHT PLLC (Michigan)
500 Woodward, Suite 4000, Detroit, MI 48226-3425
Tel: 313 223 3500 **Fax:** 313 223 3598

OTHER RECOMMENDED FIRMS

DICKINSON, MACKAMAN, TYLER & HAGEN, P.C. (Iowa)
Suite 1600 Hub Tower, 699 Walnut Street, Des Moines, IA 50309
Tel: 515 244 2600 **Fax:** 515 246 4550

DICKSTEIN SHAPIRO MORIN & OSHINSKY LLP (District of Columbia)
2101 L Street NW, Washington, DC, DC 20037-1526
Tel: 202 785 9700 **Fax:** 202 887 0689

DILWORTH PAXSON LLP (Pennsylvania)
3200 Mellon Bank Center, 1735 Market Street, Philadelphia, PA 19103
Tel: 215 575 7000 **Fax:** 215 575 7200

DINSE, KNAPP & MCANDREW PC (Vermont)
PO Box 988, 209 Battery Street, Burlington, VT 05402-0988
Tel: 802 864 5751 **Fax:** 802 862 6409

DINSMORE & SHOHL LLP (Ohio)
1900 Chemed Center, 255 East Fifth Street, Cincinnati, OH 45202
Tel: 513 977 8200 **Fax:** 513 977 8141

DKE LAW OFFICE (Missouri)
2345 Grand Boulevard, Suite 2110, Kansas City, MO 64108
Tel: 816 842 1515

DODSON, PARKER, DINKINS & BEHM (Tennessee)
Realtors Building, Suite 400, 306 Gay Street, Nashville, TN 37201-1115
Tel: 615 254 2291

DOERNER, SAUNDERS, DANIEL & ANDERSON, LLP (Oklahoma)
320 South Boston Avenue, Suite 500, Tulsa, OK 74103
Tel: 918 582 1211 **Fax:** 918 591 5360

DOFFERMYRE, SHIELDS, CANFIELD, KNOWLES & DEVINE (Georgia)
1355 Peachtree Street 1600, Atlanta, GA 30309 - 3269
Tel: 404 881 8900 **Fax:** 404 881 3007

DOLLINGER & DOLLINGER (New Jersey)
Mack-Cali Centre II, One Mack Centre Drive, Paramus, NJ 07652 3906
Tel: 201 599 8400 **Fax:** 201 599 8405

DONATI & ASSOCIATES (Tennessee)
1545 Union Avenue, Memphis, TN 38104-3726
Tel: 901 465 9511

DONNELLY & CARBONE (West Virginia)
3rd Floor, 113 Goff Mountain Road, Charleston, WV 25313
Tel: 304 342 3650

DORSEY & WHITNEY LLP (Minnesota)
50 South Sixth Street, Minneapolis, MN 55402-1498
Tel: 612 340 2600 **Fax:** 612 340 2868

DOVER DIXON HORNE (Arkansas)
425 West Capitol, Suite 3700, Little Rock, AR 72201
Tel: 501 375 9151 **Fax:** 501 375 6484

DOWD & DOWD (Nebraska)
1905 Harney Street, Omaha, NE 68102
Tel: 402 341 1020

DOWD, BLOCH & BENNETT (Illinois)
19th Floor, 8 South Michigan Avenue, Chicago, IL 60603 3320
Tel: 312 372 1361 **Fax:** 312 372 6599

DOWNS RACHLIN MARTIN PLLC (Vermont)
90 Prospect Street, PO Box 99, St Johnsbury, VT 05819
Tel: 802 748 8324 **Fax:** 802 748 4394

DRAY, THOMSON & DYEKMAN, PC (Wyoming)
204 East 22nd Street, Cheyenne, WY 82001
Tel: 307 634 8891 **Fax:** 307 634 8902

DRINKER BIDDLE & REATH LLP (Pennsylvania)
One Logan Square, 18th & Cherry Streets, Philadelphia, PA 19103
Tel: 215 988 2700 **Fax:** 215 988 2757

DUANE MORRIS LLP (Pennsylvania)
One Liberty Place, 1650 Market Street, Philadelphia, PA 19103-7396
Tel: 215 979 1000 **Fax:** 215 979 1020

DUFFY & SWEENEY, LTD (Rhode Island)
One Turks Head Place, Suite 1200, Providence, RI 02903
Tel: 401 455 0700 **Fax:** 401 455 0701

DUGGAN SHADWICK & DOERR (Kansas)
11040 Oakmont Park, Overland Park, KS 66210
Tel: 913 498 3536 **Fax:** 913 498 3538

DUNN CARNEY ALLEN HIGGINS & TONGUE LLP (Oregon)
Pacific First Federal Building, 851 SW Sixth Avenue, Suite 1500, Portland, OR 97204
Tel: 503 224 6440 **Fax:** 503 224 7324

DURANT, NICHOLS, HOUSTON HODSON & CORTESE-COSTA PC (Connecticut)
1057 Broad Street, Bridgeport, CT 06601-0351
Tel: 203 366 3438 **Fax:** 203 384 0317

DURKOVICH SALAZAR & SULLIVAN (New Mexico)
412 Eleventh Street North West, Albuquerque, NM 87102
Tel: 505 247 2367 **Fax:** 505 242 8678

DURRELL LAW GROUP, PC (Alaska)
1400 West Benson Boulevard, Suite 370, Anchorage, AK 99503
Tel: 907 258 3224 **Fax:** 907 258 3229

DUVIN, CAHN & HUTTON (Ohio)
Erieview Tower, 20th Floor, 1301 East Ninth Street, Cleveland, OH 44114
Tel: 216 696 7600 **Fax:** 216 696 2038

DWYER & COLLORA (Massachusetts)
600 Atlantic Avenue, Boston, MA 02210-2211
Tel: 617 371 1006 **Fax:** 617 371 1037

DWYER SCHRAFF MEYER JOSSEM & BUSHNELL (Hawaii)
1800 Pioneer Plaza, 900 Fort Street Mall, Honolulu, HI 96813
Tel: 808 524 8000 **Fax:** 808 537 4667

DYKEMA GOSSETT PLLC (District of Columbia)
Third Floor West, Franklin Square, 1300 I Street North West, Washington, DC, DC 20005
Tel: 202 522 8600 **Fax:** 202 906 8669

If you can't find a firm here, see full profiles (pages 759-907)

OTHER RECOMMENDED FIRMS

EATON PEABODY (Maine)
Fleet Center-Exchange Street, PO Box 1210, Bangor, ME 04402-1210
Tel: 207 947 0111 **Fax:** 207 942 3040

EAVES BARDACKE BAUGH KIERST & KIERNAN PA (New Mexico)
6400 Uptown Boulevard North East, Suite 110 - West (87110), PO Box 35670, Albuquerque, NM 87176
Tel: 505 888 4300 **Fax:** 505 883 4406

EDDY & JONES (Oklahoma)
Suite 615, 228 Robert S. Kerr, Oklahoma City, OK 73102
Tel: 405 239 2524 **Fax:** 405 239 2665

EDELSTEIN & PAYNE (North Carolina)
315 E Jones St, PO Box 28186, Raleigh, NC 27611
Tel: 919 828 1456

EDWARDS & ANGELL, LLP (Massachusetts)
101 Federal Street, Boston, MA 02110
Tel: 617 439 4444 **Fax:** 617 439 4170

EDWARDS FRICKLE HALVERSON & ANNER-HUGHES (Montana)
1601 Lewis Avenue, Suite206, PO Box 20039, Billings, MT 59104
Tel: 406 256 8155 **Fax:** 406 256 8159

EDWIN L HOBSON PC (Vermont)
289 College Street, Burlington, VT 05401
Tel: 802 863 2000

EGAN, LEV & SIWICA (Florida)
231 East Colonial Drive, PO Box 2231, Orlando, FL 32806
Tel: 407 422 1400 **Fax:** 407 422 3658

EGGLESTON & CRAMER, LTD (Vermont)
150 South Champlain Street, PO Box 1489, Burlington, VT 05402
Tel: 802 864 0880 **Fax:** 802 864 0328

EISENBERG & BOGAS (Michigan)
Suite 145, 33 Bloomfield Hills Parkway, Bloomfield Hills, MI 48304
Tel: 248 258 6080 **Fax:** 248 258 9212

ELAM & BURKE, PA (Idaho)
Key Financial Center, 702 West Idaho Street, Boise, ID 83701
Tel: 208 343 5454 **Fax:** 208 384 5844

ELARBEE, THOMPSON, SAPP & WILSON, LLP (Georgia)
800 International Tower, 229 Peachtree Street NE, Atlanta, GA 30303
Tel: 404 659 6700 **Fax:** 404 222 9718

ELDERKIN & PIRNIE PLC (Iowa)
115 First Avenue South East, PO Box 1968, Cedar Rapids, IA 52406
Tel: 319 362 2137 **Fax:** 319 362 1640

ELDRIDGE COOPER STEICHEN & LEACH PLLC (Oklahoma)
Suite 200, 110 West Seventh Street, Tulsa, OK 74119
Tel: 918 388 5555 **Fax:** 918 388 5654

ELLIOT PISHKO MORGAN (North Carolina)
426 Old Salem Road, P.O. Box 20545, Winston-Salem, NC 27101-5283
Tel: 336 724 2828 **Fax:** 336 724 3335

ELLISON SCHNEIDER & HARRISON (California)
2015 H Street, Sacramento, CA 95814-3109
Tel: 916 447 2166

ELLMAN, BURKE, HOFFMAN & JOHNSON (California)
One Ecker Building, Suite 200, Ecker and Stevenson Streets, San Francisco, CA 94105
Tel: 415 777 2727

ELLZEY & BROOKS LLC (South Carolina)
1901 Main Street, Suite 1400, Columbia, SC 29201
Tel: 803 255 0000 **Fax:** 803 255 020

ELZI PRINGLE & GURR (Colorado)
950 Seventeenth Street, Suite 1875, Denver, CO 80202
Tel: 303 623 9111 **Fax:** 303 623 9191

EPSTEIN BECKER & GREEN PC (New York)
250 Park Avenue, New York, NY 10177-0077
Tel: 212 351 4500 **Fax:** 212 661 0989

ERICKSON & SEDERSTROM, PC (Nebraska)
Regency Westpointe, 10330 Regency Parkway Drive, Suite 100, Omaha, NE 68114
Tel: 402 397 2200 **Fax:** 402 390 7137

EUBANKS, WELCH, BAKER & SCHULZE (Arkansas)
The Riley Building, 630 West Third Street, Little Rock, AR 72203-3685
Tel: 501 537 1000 **Fax:** 501 537 1001

EVANS AND CLESI, PLC (Louisiana)
336 Lafayette Street, Suite 200, New Orleans, LA 70130
Tel: 504 523 8523

FABIAN & CLENDENIN (Utah)
215 South State Street, 12th Floor, PO Box 510210, Salt Lake City, UT 84111
Tel: 801 531 8900 **Fax:** 801 596 2814

FABYANSKE, WESTRA & HART PA (Minnesota)
920 Second Avenue, Suite 110, Minneapolis, MN 55402
Tel: 612 338 0115 **Fax:** 612 338 3857

FAEGRE & BENSON LLP (Minnesota)
2200 Wells Fargo Center, 90 South Seventh Street, Minneapolis, MN 55402-3901
Tel: 612 766 7000 **Fax:** 612 766 1600

FARELLA BRAUN & MARTEL LLP (California)
Thirtieth Floor, Russ Building, 235 Montgomery Street, San Francisco, CA 94104
Tel: 415 954 4400 **Fax:** 415 954 4480

FARR & TARANTO (District of Columbia)
Suite 800, 1220 19th Street, NW, Washington, DC, DC 20036-2435
Tel: 202 775 0184 **Fax:** 202 223 8679

FARUKI GILLIAM & IRELAND PLL (Ohio)
500 Courthouse Plaza, SW, 10 North Ludlow Street, Dayton, OH 45402
Tel: 937 227 3700 **Fax:** 937 227 3717

FAULKNER, MUSKOVITZ & PHILLIPS, LLP (Ohio)
820 West Superior Avenue, Suite 900, Cleveland, OH 44113
Tel: 216 781 3600 **Fax:** 216 781 8839

OTHER RECOMMENDED FIRMS

FAY, SHARPE, FAGAN, MINNICH & McKEE, LLP (Ohio)
1100 Superior Avenue, Seventh Floor, Cleveland, OH 44114
Tel: 216 861 5582 **Fax:** 216 241 1666

FELDMAN & ORLANSKY (Alaska)
500 L Street, Suite 400, Anchorage, AK 99501
Tel: 907 272 3538 **Fax:** 907 274 0819

FELHABER, LARSON, FENLON & VOGT, PC (Minnesota)
601 2nd Avenue South, Suite 4200, Minneapolis, MN 55402
Tel: 612 339 6321 **Fax:** 612 338 0535

FELLERS, SNIDER, BLANKENSHIP, BAILEY & TIPPENS, A PROFESSIONAL CORPORATION (Oklahoma)
Bank One Tower, 100 North Broadway, Suite 1700, Oklahoma City, OK 73102-8820
Tel: 405 232 0621 **Fax:** 405 232 9659

FENNEMORE CRAIG (Arizona)
3003 North Central Avenue, Suite 2600, Phoenix, AZ 85012-2913
Tel: 602 916 5000 **Fax:** 602 916 5999

FENWICK & WEST (California)
Two Palo Alto Square, Palo Alto, CA 94306
Tel: 650 494 0600 **Fax:** 650 494 1417

FERGUSON STEIN CHAMBERS WALLAAS ADKINS GRESHAM & SUMTER (North Carolina)
741 Kenilworth Avenue, Suite 300, Charlotte, NC 28204-2828
Tel: 704 375 8461

FERNANDEZ FRIEDMAN GROSSMAN & KOHN PLLC (Kentucky)
2400 National City Tower, 101 South Fifth Street, Louisville, KY 40202
Tel: 502 589 1001 **Fax:** 502 589 7333

FERRELL SCHULTZ CARTER ZUMPANO & FERTEL PA (Florida)
201 South Biscayne Bolevard, 34th Floor Miami Center, Miami, FL 33131 4325
Tel: 305 371 8585 **Fax:** 305 371 5732

FILLENWARTH, DENNERLINE, GROTH & TOWE (Indiana)
1213 North Arlington Avenue, Suite 204, Indianapolis, IN 46219
Tel: 317 353 9363 **Fax:** 317 351 7232

FINCH BETTMANN MAKS & HOGUE P.C (South Dakota)
304 Main Street, P.O.Box 2934, Rapid City, SD 57709-2934
Tel: 605 348 6547 **Fax:** 605 348 9086

FINE KAPLAN & BLACK (Pennsylvania)
Twenty Third Floor, 1845 Walnut Street, Philadelphia, PA 19103
Tel: 215 567 6565

FINLEY, ALT, SMITH, SCHARNBERG, CRAIG, HILMES & GAFFNEY PC (Iowa)
Equitable Building, 4th Floor, 604 Locust Street, Des Moines, IA 50309-3705
Tel: 515 288 0145 **Fax:** 515 288 2724

FINNEGAN HENDERSON FARABOW GARRETT & DUNNER LLP (District of Columbia)
Suite 700, 1300 I Street, Washington, DC, DC 20005-3315
Tel: 202 408 4000 **Fax:** 202 408 4400

FIRST, BLONDIS, ALBRECHT & NOVOTNAK (Wisconsin)
158 North Broadway Street, Sixth Floor, Milwaukee, WI 53202
Tel: 414 271 1972 **Fax:** 414 271 1511

FISH & NEAVE (New York)
1251 Avenue of the Americas, New York, NY 10020
Tel: 212 596 9000 **Fax:** 212 596 9090

FISH & RICHARDSON (New York)
45 Rockefeller Plaza, Suite 2800, New York, NY 10111
Tel: 212 765 5070 **Fax:** 212 258 2291

FISHER & PHILLIPS LLP (Georgia)
1500 Resurgens Plaza, 945 East Paces Ferry Road, Atlanta, GA 30326
Tel: 404 231 1400 **Fax:** 404 240 4249

FISK & FIELDER (Texas)
2710 Stemmons Fwy # 400, Dallas, TX 75207-2210
Tel: 214 638 3744 **Fax:** 214 638 5105

FITZPATRICK & ASSOCIATES (District of Columbia)
Universal Building North, 1875 Connecticut Avenue, NW, Suite 1140, Washington, DC, DC 20009-5728
Tel: 202 588 5300 **Fax:** 202 588 5023

FLECK, MATHER & STRUTZ, LTD. (North Dakota)
Sixth Floor, Norwest Bank Building, 400 East Broadway, Bismarck, ND 58502
Tel: 701 223 6585 **Fax:** 701 222 4853

FLEESON, GOOING, COULSON & KITCH, LLC (Kansas)
125 North Market Street, Suite 1600, PO Box 997, Wichita, KS 67201
Tel: 316 267 7361 **Fax:** 316 267 1754

FLYGARE SCHWARZ & CLOSSON PLLC (New Hampshire)
11 Court Street, P.O.Box 439, Exeter, NH 03833
Tel: 603 778 7300 **Fax:** 603 778 7373

FLYNN, GASKINS & BENNETT (Minnesota)
2900 Metropolitan Center, Minneapolis, MN 55402
Tel: 612 333 9500 **Fax:** 612 333 9579

FOGARTY, COHEN, SELBY & NEMIROFF LLC (Connecticut)
88 Field Point Road, Greenwich, CT 06836-2508
Tel: 203 661 1000

FOGEL, FELDMAN, OSTROV, RINGLER & KLEVENS (California)
1620 26th Street, Suite 100 South, Santa Monica, CA 90404-4040
Tel: 310 453 6711 **Fax:** 310 828 2191

FOLEY HOAG LLP (Massachusetts)
155 Seaport Boulevard, Boston, MA 02210-2600
Tel: 617 832 1000 **Fax:** 617 832 7000

OTHER RECOMMENDED FIRMS

FORD & HARRISON LLP (Georgia)
600 Peachtree at the Circle Building, 1275 Peachtree Street, N.E., Atlanta, GA 30309
Tel: 404 888 3800 **Fax:** 404 888 3863

FORD WHITE & NASSEN (Texas)
1100 Highland Park Place, 4514 Cole Avenue, Dallas, TX 75205
Tel: 214 523 5100 **Fax:** 214 521 4601

FORMAN PERRY WATKINS KRUTZ & TARDY, PLLC (Mississippi)
Twelfth Floor, One Jackson Place, Jackson, MS 39225
Tel: 601 960 8600 **Fax:** 601 960 8613

FOSTER JOHNSON MCDONALD LUCERO KOINIS LLP (New Mexico)
40 First Plaza, NW, Suite 735, Albuquerque, NM 87102
Tel: 505 243 3000 **Fax:** 505 243 4323

FOSTER PEPPER & SHEFELMAN PLLC (Washington)
34th Floor, 1111 Third Avenue, Seattle, WA 98101
Tel: 206 447 4400 **Fax:** 206 447 9700

FOULSTON SIEFKIN LLP (Kansas)
Bank of America Center, 100 North Broadway, Suite 700, Wichita, KS 67202
Tel: 316 267 6371 **Fax:** 316 267 6345

FOWLER WHITE BOGGS BANKER (Florida)
Suite 1700, 501 East Kennedy Boulevard, PO Box 1438, Tampa, FL 33601
Tel: 813 228 7411 **Fax:** 813 229 8313

FOX & FOX (Wisconsin)
44 East Mifflin Street, Suite 403, Madison, WI 53703
Tel: 608 258 9588 **Fax:** 608 258 9105

FOX ROTHSCHILD O'BRIEN & FRANKEL LLP (Pennsylvania)
2000 Market Street, Tenth Floor, Philadelphia, PA 19103-3291
Tel: 215 299 2000 **Fax:** 215 299 2150

FRANCZEK SULLIVAN (Illinois)
300 South Wacker Drive, Suite 3400, Chicago, IL 60606
Tel: 312 986 0300 **Fax:** 312 986 9192

FRANK ROSEN FREED ROBERTS LLP (Washington)
1200 Hoge Building, 705 Second Avenue, Seattle, WA 98104
Tel: 206 682 6711 **Fax:** 206 682 0401

FRANTZ WARD LLP (Ohio)
55 Public Square Boulevard, Nineteenth Floor, Cleveland, OH 44113-1999
Tel: 216 515 1660 **Fax:** 216 515 1650

FRASER STRYKER LAW FIRM (Nebraska)
500 Energy Plaza, 409 South 17th Street, Omaha, NE 68102
Tel: 402 341 6000 **Fax:** 402 341 8290

FRED M FRISK JR - SOLE PRACTITIONER (West Virginia)
511 Central Avenue, Suite 400, Charleston, WV 25302
Tel: 304 344 3858

FREDRIKSON & BYRON, PA (Minnesota)
1100 International Centre, 900 Second Avenue South, Minneapolis, MN 55402
Tel: 612 347 7000 **Fax:** 612 347 7077

FREEBORN & PETERS (Illinois)
311 South Wacker Drive, Suite 3000, Chicago, IL 60606
Tel: 312 360 6000 **Fax:** 312 360 6520

FREEDMAN BOYD DANIELS HOLLANDER GOLDBERG & CLINE PA (New Mexico)
20 First Plaza, Suite 700, Albuquerque, NM 87102
Tel: 505 842 9960 **Fax:** 505 842 0761

FREEHILL HOGAN & MAHAR LLP (New York)
80 Pine Street, New York, NY 10005
Tel: 212 425 1900 **Fax:** 212 425 1901

FREEMAN, FREEMAN & SALZMAN (Illinois)
401 North Michigan Avenue, Suite 3200, Chicago, IL 60611-4207
Tel: 312 222 5100 **Fax:** 312 822 0870

FREILICH, LEITNER & CARLISLE (Missouri)
1150 One Main Plaza, 4435 Main Street, Kansas City, MO 64111-7727
Tel: 816 561 4414 **Fax:** 816 561 7931

FREKING & BETZ (Ohio)
215 East Ninth Street, Fifth Floor, Cincinnati, OH 45202
Tel: 513 721 1975 **Fax:** 513 651 2570

FRESHFIELDS BRUCKHAUS DERINGER (New York)
520 Madison Avenue, 34th Floor, NY 10022
Tel: 212 277 4000 **Fax:** 212 277 4001

FRIDAY, ELDREDGE & CLARK (Arkansas)
2000 Regions Center, 400 West Capitol Avenue, Little Rock, AR 72201
Tel: 501 376 2011 **Fax:** 501 376 2147

FRIEDMAN, RUBIN & WHITE (Alaska)
1227 West Ninth Avenue, 2nd Floor, Anchorage, AK 99501
Tel: 907 258 0704 **Fax:** 907 278 6449

FRILOT, PARTRIDGE, KOHNKE & CLEMENTS LC (Louisiana)
1100 Poydras Street, Suite 3600, New Orleans, LA 70163
Tel: 504 599 8000 **Fax:** 504 599 8100

FRUTH, JAMISON & ELSASS (Minnesota)
4705 IDS Center, 80 South Eighth Street, Minneapolis, MN 55402
Tel: 612 344 9700 **Fax:** 612 344 9705

FULLENKAMP, DOYLE & JOBEUN (Nebraska)
11440 West Center Road, Omaha, NE 68144
Tel: 402 334 0700 **Fax:** 402 334 0815

GABLE & GOTWALS, A PROFESSIONAL CORPORATION (Oklahoma)
1100 Oneok Plaza, 100 West Fifth Street, Tulsa, OK 74103
Tel: 918 595 4800 **Fax:** 918 595 4990

GAINES PANSING & HOGAN (Nebraska)
200 Regency One Building, 10050 Regency Circle, Omaha, NE 68114
Tel: 402 397 5500 **Fax:** 402 397 4853

OTHER RECOMMENDED FIRMS

GAINSBURGH, BENJAMIN, DAVID, MEUNIER & WARSHAUER (Louisiana)
2800 Energy Centre, 1100 Poydras, New Orleans, LA 70163-2800
Tel: 504 522 2304 **Fax:** 504 528 9973

GALLAGHER & KENNEDY, PA (Arizona)
2575 East Camelback Road, Phoenix, AZ 85016-9225
Tel: 602 530 8000 **Fax:** 602 530 8500

GALLAGHER, CALLAHAN AND GARTRELL, PA (New Hampshire)
214 North Main Street, PO Box 1415, Concord, NH 03302
Tel: 800 528 1181 **Fax:** 603 224 7588

GALLEGOS LAW FIRM PC (New Mexico)
460 St Michael's Drive, Building 300, Santa Fe, NM 87505
Tel: 505 983 6686 **Fax:** 505 986 0741

GALLOP, JOHNSON & NEUMAN, L.C. (Missouri)
Interco Corporate Tower, 101 S. Hanley, St Louis, MO 63105
Tel: 314 615 6000800 330 6635 **Fax:** 314 615 6001

GANG TYRE RAMER & BROWN (California)
132 South Rodeo Drive, Beverly Hills, CA 90212
Tel: 310 777 4800 **Fax:** 310 777 4801

GARDNER CARTON & DOUGLAS (District of Columbia)
1301 K Street NW, Suite 900 East, Washington, DC, DC 20005
Tel: 202 408 7100 **Fax:** 202 289 1504

GARLINGTON, LOHN & ROBINSON, PLLP (Montana)
199 West Pine Street, PO Box 7909, Missoula, MT 59807
Tel: 406 523 2500 **Fax:** 406 523 2595

GARRISON, LEVIN-EPSTEIN CHIMES & RICHARDSON PC (Connecticut)
405 Orange Street, New Haven, CT 06511
Tel: 203 777 4425 **Fax:** 203 776 3965

GARVEY, SCHUBERT & BARER (Oregon)
Eleventh Floor, 121 SW Morrison Street, Portland, OR 97204
Tel: 503 228 3939 **Fax:** 503 226 0259

GATHRIGHT & HARDY (Kentucky)
PNC Plaza, Suite 2450, 500 West Jefferson Street, Louisville, KY 40202
Tel: 502 569 2030 **Fax:** 502 569 2040

GELBER, GELBER, INGERSOLL & KLEVANSKY A LAW CORPORATION (Hawaii)
Topa Financial Center, 745 Fort Street, Suite 1400, West Tower, Honolulu, HI 96813-3823
Tel: 808 524 0155 **Fax:** 808 531 6963

GENOVA, BURNS & VERNOIA (New Jersey)
Eisenhower Plaza II, 354 Eisenhower Parkway, Livingston, NJ 07039
Tel: 973 533 0777 **Fax:** 973 533 1112

GENOVESE JOBLOVE & BATTISTA P.A. (Florida)
Bank of America Tower International Place, 100 Southeast Second Street, Thirty Sixth Floor, Miami, FL 33131
Tel: 305 349 2300 **Fax:** 305 349 2310

GEORGE & LORENSEN (West Virginia)
1526 Kanawhwa Boulevard E, Charleston, WV 25311-2413
Tel: 304 343 5555 **Fax:** 304 342 2513

GEORGE S. COBYN JR, PLLC (Oklahoma)
Two Leadership Square, 211 North Robinson, Suite 1120, Oklahoma City, OK 73102
Tel: 405 239 7055 **Fax:** 405 239 2436

GIBBS, GIDEN, LOCHER & TURNER (California)
2029 Century Park East, 34th Floor, Los Angeles, CA 90067-3039
Tel: 310 552 3400 **Fax:** 310 552 0805

GIBSON, DUNN & CRUTCHER LLP (California)
333 South Grand Avenue, Los Angeles, CA 90071-3197
Tel: 213 229 7000 **Fax:** 213 229 7520

GIGNILLIAT, SAVITZ & BETTIS LLP (South Carolina)
900 Elmwood Avenue, Suite 100, Columbia, SC 29201
Tel: 803 799 9311 **Fax:** 803 254 6951

GILBERT HEINTZ & RANDOLPH (District of Columbia)
1350 l Street North West, Suite 200, Washington, DC, DC 20005-3324
Tel: 202 772 2200 **Fax:** 202 772 3333

GILKEY & STEPHENSON PA (New Mexico)
500 Marquette North West, Suite 505, Post Office Drawer 25566, Albuquerque, NM 87125
Tel: 505 242 4466 **Fax:** 505 242 3145

GILMARTIN, POSTER & SHAFTO (New York)
One William Street, New York, NY 10004
Tel: 212 425 3220 **Fax:** 212 425 3130

GIORDANO HALLERAN & CIESLA PC (New Jersey)
125 Half Mile Road, PO Box 190, Middletown, NJ 07748
Tel: 732 714 3900 **Fax:** 732 224 6599

GIVENS PURSLEY LLP (Idaho)
Park Place, 277 North 6th Street, Suite 200, Boise, ID 83701
Tel: 208 388 1200 **Fax:** 208 388 1300

GLANKLER BROWN, PLLC (Tennessee)
Suite 1700, One Commerce Square, Memphis, TN 38103
Tel: 901 525 1322 **Fax:** 901 525 2389

GLENN MILLS & FISHER (North Carolina)
Suite 709 South Bank Building, 400 West Main Street, P.O.Drawer 3865, Durham, NC 27702-3865
Tel: 919 683 2135

GLENN RASMUSSEN FOGARTY & HOOKER (Florida)
100 South Ashley Drive, Suite 1300, Tampa, FL 33601 3333
Tel: 813 229 3333 **Fax:** 813 229 5946

GLICKMAN & HUGHES LLP (Texas)
First City Tower, 1001 Fannin Street, Suite 1460, Houston, TX 77002
Tel: 713 658 1122 **Fax:** 713 658 0925

GODFREY & KAHN, SC (Wisconsin)
780 North Water Street, Milwaukee, WI 53202
Tel: 414 273 3500 **Fax:** 414 273 5198

OTHER RECOMMENDED FIRMS

GODWIN GRUBER (Texas)
Renaissance Tower, 1201 Elm Street, Suite 1700, Dallas, TX 75270
Tel: 214 939 4400 **Fax:** 214 760 7332

GOETZ FITZPATRICK MOST & BRUCKMAN LLP (New York)
One Penn Plaza, New York, NY 10119
Tel: 212 695 8100 **Fax:** 212 629 4013

GOETZ, GALLICK, BALDWIN & DOLAN PC (Montana)
35 North Grand Avenue, PO Box 6580, Bozeman, MT 59771-6580
Tel: 406 587 0618 **Fax:** 406 587 5144

GOLD SCHWARTZ & COMPANY (Ohio)
1500 Leader Building, Cleveland, OH 44114-1498
Tel: 216 696 6122

GOLDBERG, KOHN, BELL, BLACK, ROSENBLOOM & MORITZ, LTD (Illinois)
55 East Monroe Street, Suite 3700, Chicago, IL 60603
Tel: 312 201 4000 **Fax:** 312 332 2196

GÛMEZ & PETITTI (Arizona)
2525 East Camelback Road, Suite 860, Phoenix, AZ 85016
Tel: 602 957 8686 **Fax:** 602 956 9854

GOODELL, STRATTON, EDMONDS & PALMER, LLP (Kansas)
515 South Kansas Avenue, Topeka, KS 66603-3999
Tel: 785 233 0593 **Fax:** 785 233 8870

GOODIN MACBRIDE SQUERI RITCHIE & DAY LLP (California)
Suite 900, 505 Sansome Street, San Francisco, CA 94111
Tel: 415 392 7900

GOODMAN & ZUCHLEWSKI LLP (New York)
500 Fifth Avenue, Suite 5100, New York, NY 10110-5197
Tel: 212 869 1940 **Fax:** 212 768 3020

GOODSILL ANDERSON QUINN & STIFEL (Hawaii)
Alii Place, Suite 1800, 1099 Alakea Street, Honolulu, HI 96813
Tel: 808 547 5600 **Fax:** 808 547 5880

GOODWIN & GOODWIN, LLP (West Virginia)
300 Summers Street, Suite 1500, PO Box 2107, Charleston, WV 25328-2107
Tel: 304 346 7000 **Fax:** 304 344 9692

GOOLD PATTERSON DEVORE ALES & ROADHOUSE (Nevada)
4496 South Pecos Road, Las Vegas, NV 89121
Tel: 702 436 2600 **Fax:** 702 436 2650

GORDON & GLICKSON (Illinois)
444 North Michigan Ave, Suite 3600, Chicago, IL 60611-3903
Tel: 312 321 7660 **Fax:** 312 321 9324

GORDON & SILVER, LTD (Nevada)
Ninth Floor, 3960 Howard Hughes Parkway, Las Vegas, NV 89109
Tel: 702 796 5555 **Fax:** 702 369 2666

GORDON, ARATA, MCCOLLAM, DUPLANTIS & EAGAN LLP (Louisiana)
201 St Charles Avenue, Suite 4000, New Orleans, LA 70170-4000
Tel: 504 582 1111 **Fax:** 504 582 1121

GORDON, FEINBLATT, ROTHMAN, HOFFBERGER & HOLLANDER, LLC (Maryland)
The Garrett Building, 233 East Redwood Street, Baltimore, MD 21202
Tel: 410 576 4000 **Fax:** 410 576 4246

GORDON, SILBERMAN, WIGGINS & CHILDS (Alabama)
1400 South Trust Tower, Birmingham, AL 35203-3213
Tel: 205 328 0640 **Fax:** 205 254 1500

GORSUCH KIRGIS LLP (Colorado)
Tower 1, Suite 1000, 1515 Arapahoe Street, Denver, CO 80202
Tel: 303 376 5000 **Fax:** 303 376 5001

GOUGH, SHANAHAN, JOHNSON & WATERMAN (Montana)
33 South Last Chance Gulch, PO Box 1715, Helena, MT 59601-1715
Tel: 406 442 8560 **Fax:** 406 442 8783

GOULSTON & STORRS (Massachusetts)
400 Atlantic Avenue, Boston, MA 02110
Tel: 617 482 1776 **Fax:** 617 574 4112

GRANT & EISENHOFER PA (Delaware)
1220 North Market Street, Suite 500, Wilmington, DE 19801
Tel: 302 622 7000 **Fax:** 302 622 7100

GRAVEL AND SHEA (Vermont)
Corporate Plaza, 76 St Paul Street, PO Box 369, Burlington, VT 05402-0369
Tel: 802 658 0220 **Fax:** 802 658 1456

GRAY, HARRIS & ROBINSON, PA (Florida)
301 East Pine Street, Suite 1400, Orlando, FL 32802
Tel: 407 843 8880 **Fax:** 407 244 5690

GRAY, PLANT, MOOTY, MOOTY & BENNETT, PA (Minnesota)
3400 City Center, 33 South Sixth Street, Minneapolis, MN 55402
Tel: 612 343 2800 **Fax:** 612 333 0066

GREEN LUCAS SAVITS & MAROSE (New Jersey)
111 Northfield Avenue, Suite 312, West Orange, NJ 07052
Tel: 973 736 4949

GREEN, GREEN, ADAMS, PALMER & CRAIG (Michigan)
900 Victors Way, Suite 240, Ann Arbor, MI 48108
Tel: 734 665 4036

GREENBAUM, ROWE, SMITH, RAVIN, DAVIS AND HIMMEL LLP (New Jersey)
Metro Corporate Campus I, PO Box 5600, Woodbridge, NJ 07095
Tel: 732 549 5600 **Fax:** 732 549 1881

GREENBERG DAUBER EPSTEIN & TUCKER (New Jersey)
Suite 600, One Gateway Center, Newark, NJ 07102-5311
Tel: 973 643 3700

OTHER RECOMMENDED FIRMS

GREENE ESPEL PLLP (Minnesota)
200 South Sixth Street, Suite 1200, Minneapolis, MN 55402-1415
Tel: 612 373 0830 **Fax:** 612 373 0929

GREENE, BROILLET, TAYLOR, WHEELER & PANISH (California)
100 Wilshire Boulevard, 21st Floor, Santa Monica, CA 90401-1162
Tel: 310 576 1200 **Fax:** 310 576 1220

GREENEBAUM DOLL & MCDONALD PLLC (Kentucky)
3300 National City Tower, Louisville, KY 40202
Tel: 502 589 4200 **Fax:** 502 587 3695

GREENSTEIN DELORME & LUCHS (District of Columbia)
1620 L Street Northwest, Suite 900, Washington, DC, DC 20036-5605
Tel: 202 452 1400 **Fax:** 202 452 1410

GREGG M CORWIN & ASSOCIATES LAW OFFICE, PC (Minnesota)
508 East Parkdale Plaza Building, Minneapolis, MN 55416-1534
Tel: 952 544 7774 **Fax:** 952 544 7151

GREGG M ROSENBERG & ASSOCIATES (Texas)
11 Greenway Plaza, Suite 2810, Houston, TX 77046
Tel: 713 960 8300 **Fax:** 713 621 6670

GREGORY BLEDSOE & ASSOCIATES (Oklahoma)
1717 S Cheyenne Avenue, Tulsa, OK 74119-4611
Tel: 918 599 8123

GREGORY P. JOSEPH LAW OFFICES LLC (New York)
805 Third Avenue, 31st Floor, New York, NY 10022
Tel: 212 407 1200 **Fax:** 212 407 1280

GRIFFIN COCHRANE & MARSHALL (Georgia)
127 Peachtree Street, North East, 14th Floor, Atlanta, GA 30303 1810
Tel: 404 523 2000 **Fax:** 404 523 9655

GRONEK & LATHAM (Florida)
390 North Orange Avenue, Suite 600, P.O.Box 3353, Orlando, FL 32602
Tel: 407 481 5800 **Fax:** 407 481 5801

GROSS & WELCH, P.C. (Nebraska)
800 Commercial Federal Tower, 2120 South 72nd Street, Omaha, NE 68124
Tel: 402 392 1500 **Fax:** 402 392 1538

GROSSBERG YOCHELSON FOX & BEYDA (District of Columbia)
2000 L Street North West, Suite 675, Washington, DC, DC 20036-4907
Tel: 202 296 9696 **Fax:** 202 296 7777

GROTTA, GLASSMAN & HOFFMAN (New Jersey)
75 Livingston Avenue, Roseland, NJ 07068
Tel: 973 992 4800

GUESS & RUDD PC (Alaska)
510 L Street, Suite 700, Anchorage, AK 99501
Tel: 907 793 2200 **Fax:** 907 793 2299

GUNDERSON DETTMER STOUGH VILLENEUVE FRANKLIN & HACHIGIAN (California)
155 Constitution Drive, Menlo Park, CA 94025
Tel: 650 321 2400 **Fax:** 650 321 2800

GUNDERSON, PALMER, GOODSELL & NELSON LLP (South Dakota)
440 Mount Rushmore Road, 3rd and 4th Floors, Rapid City, SD 57709
Tel: 605 342 1078 **Fax:** 605 342 9503

GUNHUS, GRINNELL, KLINGER, SWENSON & GUY, LTD. (North Dakota)
514 Gate City Building, PO Box 2783, Fargo, ND 58108
Tel: 701 235 2506 **Fax:** 701 235 9862

GUNSTER, YOAKLEY & STEWART PA (Florida)
Phillips Point, Suite 500 East, 777 South Flagler Drive, West Palm Beach, FL 33401
Tel: 561 655 1980 **Fax:** 561 655 5677

GURLEY DRAMIS (Florida)
535 South Palm Avenue, Sarasota, FL 34236
Tel: 941 365 4501 **Fax:** 941 365 2916

HADSELL & STORMER (California)
128 North Fair Oaks Avenue, Marine Building, Suite 204, Pasadena, CA 91103-3614
Tel: 818 585 9600 **Fax:** 818 577 7079

HAHN LOESER & PARKS LLP (Ohio)
3300 BP Tower, 200 Public Square, Cleveland, OH 44114
Tel: 216 621 0150 **Fax:** 216 241 2824

HALE AND DORR (Massachusetts)
60 State Street, Boston, MA 02109-1803
Tel: 617 526 6000 **Fax:** 617 526 5000

HALL & EVANS, LLC (Colorado)
Suite 1700, 1200 Seventeenth Street, Denver, CO 80202
Tel: 303 628 3300 **Fax:** 303 628 3368

HALL DICKLER KENT GOLDSTEIN & WOOD LLP (New York)
909 Third Avenue, 27th Floor, New York, NY 10022
Tel: 212 339 5400 **Fax:** 212 935 3121

HALL, ESTILL, HARDWICK, GABLE, GOLDEN & NELSON, PC (Oklahoma)
320 South Boston Avenue, Suite 400, Tulsa, OK 74103
Tel: 918 594 0400 **Fax:** 918 594 0505

HALL, FARLEY, OBERRECHT & BLANTON, PA (Idaho)
Key Financial Center, 702 West Idaho Street, Suite 700, Boise, ID 83701
Tel: 208 395 8500 **Fax:** 208 395 8585

HAMMER FERRETTI & SCHIAVONI (West Virginia)
408 West King Street, Martinsburg, WV 25401-3204
Tel: 304 364 8505

HAMMONS & ASSOCIATES (Oklahoma)
325 Dean A. McGee, Oklahoma City, OK 73102
Tel: 405 235 6100 **Fax:** 405 235 6111

HANEY, WOLOSON & MULLINS (Nevada)
301 East Clark Avenue, Suite 700, Las Vegas, NV 89101
Tel: 702 474 7557 **Fax:** 702 474 7009

OTHER RECOMMENDED FIRMS

HANGLEY, ARONCHICK, SEGAL & PUDLIN
(Pennsylvania)
One Logan Square, 18th and Cherry Streets, Philadelphia, PA 19103-6933
Tel: 215 568 6200 **Fax:** 215 568 0300

HANIFY & KING (Massachusetts)
21st Floor, One Beacon Street, Boston, MA 02108-3107
Tel: 617 423 0400 **Fax:** 617 423 0498

HANKINS & HICKS (Arkansas)
800 West Fourth Street, PO Box 5670, Little Rock, AR 72119
Tel: 501 371 9226 **Fax:** 501 371 0204

HARALSON, MILLER, PITT & MCANALLY (Arizona)
One South Church Avenue, Suite 900, Tucson, AZ 85701-1620
Tel: 520 792 3836

HARDING SCHULTZ & DOWNS (Nebraska)
800 Lincoln Square, 121 South 13th Street, P.O. Box 82028, Lincoln, NE 68501-2028
Tel: 402 434 3000 **Fax:** 402 434 3030

HARKINS CUNNINGHAM (Pennsylvania)
2800 One Commerce Square, Philadelphia, PA 19103 7042
Tel: 215 851 6701

HARRILL & SUTTER PLLC (Arkansas)
310 Natural Resources Drive, Little Rock, AR 72205
Tel: 501 224 1050 **Fax:** 501 223 9136

HARRIS, WILTSHIRE & GRANNIS LLP
(District of Columbia)
1200 Eighteenth Street NW, Suite 1200, Washington, DC, DC 20036-2560
Tel: 202 730 1300 **Fax:** 202 730 1301

HARRISON & MOBERLY LLP (Indiana)
135 North Pennsylvania Street, Suite 2100, Indianapolis, IN 46204
Tel: 317 639 4511 **Fax:** 317 639 9565

HARTIG RHODES HOGE & LEKISCH PC (Alaska)
717 K Street, Anchorage, AK 99501
Tel: 907 276 1592 **Fax:** 907 277 4352

HARTZOG CONGER CASON & NEVILLE, PC (Oklahoma)
1600 Bank of Oklahoma Plaza, 201 Robert S Kerr, Oklahoma City, OK 73102
Tel: 405 235 7000 **Fax:** 405 235 7329

HARVEY & FRANK (Maine)
Two City Center, PO Box 126, Portland, ME 04112-0126
Tel: 207 775 1300

HARWELL HOWARD HYNE GABBERT & MANNER, P.C.
(Tennessee)
315 Deaderick Street, Suite 1800, Nashville, TN 37238
Tel: 615 256 0500 **Fax:** 615 251 1057

HASKIN LAUTER & LARUE (Indiana)
850 Fort Wayne Avenue, Indianapolis, IN 46204-1239
Tel: 317 955 9500 **Fax:** 317 955 2570

HATCHER, STUBBS, LAND, HOLLIS & ROTHSCHILD, LLP (Georgia)
The Corporate Center, Suite 500, Columbus, GA 31902
Tel: 706 324 0201 **Fax:** 706 322 7747

HAWLEY TROXELL ENNIS & HAWLEY LLP (Idaho)
877 Main Street, Suite 1000, PO Box 1617, Boise, ID 83702
Tel: 208 344 6000 **Fax:** 208 342 3829

HAYNSWORTH BALDWIN JOHNSON & GREAVES LLC
(South Carolina)
918 South Pleasantburg Drive, PO Box 10888, Greenville, SC 29603
Tel: 864 271 7410 **Fax:** 864 241 1861

HAYNSWORTH SINKLER BOYD PA (South Carolina)
160 East Bay Street, PO Box 340, Charleston, SC 29402-0340
Tel: 843 722 3366 **Fax:** 843 722 2266

HEARD & HOWARD (Montana)
219 North Fourth Street, Columbus, MT 59019
Tel: 406 322 4429

HEATH, DAVIS & MCCALLA (Texas)
200 Perry-Brooks Building, 720 Brazous Street, Austin, TX 78701
Tel: 512 478 5671 **Fax:** 512 476 1451

HELLER EHRMAN WHITE & MCAULIFFE LLP
(California)
333 Bush Street, San Francisco, CA 94104-2878
Tel: 415 772 6000 **Fax:** 415 772 6268

HELMS MULLISS & WICKER PLLC (North Carolina)
201 North Tryon Street, PO Box 31247, Charlotte, NC 28202
Tel: 704 343 2000 **Fax:** 704 343 2300

HENDERSON DAILY WITHROW & DEVOE (Indiana)
One Indiana Square, Suite 2600, Indianapolis, IN 46204-2071
Tel: 317 639 4121 **Fax:** 317 639 0191

HENNIGAN, BENNETT & DORMAN (California)
601 South Figueroa Street, Suite 3300, Los Angeles, CA 90017
Tel: 213 694 1200 **Fax:** 213 694 1234

HENSON & EFRON (Minnesota)
220 South Sixth Street, Suite 1800, Minneapolis, MN 55402-4503
Tel: 612 339 2500 **Fax:** 612 339 6364

HERMAN, HERMAN, KATZ & COTLAR LLP (Louisiana)
820 O'Keefe Avenue, New Orleans, LA 70113-1116
Tel: 504 581 4892 **Fax:** 504 561 6024

HICKEY, MACKEY, EVANS & WALKER (Wyoming)
1800 Carey Avenue, Suite 700, P.O. Drawer 467, Cheyenne, WY 82003
Tel: 307 634 1525 **Fax:** 307 638 7335

HILL & ROBBINS (Colorado)
1441 18th Street, 100 Blake Street Building, Denver, CO 80202
Tel: 303 296 8100 **Fax:** 303 296 2388

HILL RIVKINS & HAYDEN LLP (New York)
45 Broadway, New York, NY 10006
Tel: 212 669 0600 **Fax:** 212 669 0698

OTHER RECOMMENDED FIRMS

HILL, WARD & HENDERSON, PA (Florida)
101 East Kennedy Boulevard, Suite 3700, PO Box 2231, Tampa, FL 33601
Tel: 813 221 3900 **Fax:** 813 221 2900

HINCKLEY, ALLEN & SNYDER LLP (Massachusetts)
28 State Street, 29th Floor, Boston, MA 02109 1775
Tel: 617 345 9000 **Fax:** 617 345 9020

HINKLE ELKOURI LAW FIRM LLC (Kansas)
Suite 2000 Epic Center, 301 North Main Street, Wichita, KS 67202
Tel: 316 267 2000 **Fax:** 316 264 1518

HINKLE HENSLEY SHANOR & MARTIN LLP (New Mexico)
400 Pen Plaza, Suite 700, Roswell, NM 88202
Tel: 505 622 6510 **Fax:** 505 623 9332

HIRSCHLER, FLEISCHER, WEINBERG, COX & ALLEN A PROFESSIONAL CORPORATION (Virginia)
The Federal Reserve Bank Building, 701 East Byrd Street, Richmond, VA 23218
Tel: 804 771 9500 **Fax:** 804 644 0957

HIRST & APPLEGATE, PC (Wyoming)
1720 Carey Avenue, Suite 200, PO Box 1083, Cheyenne, WY 82003-1083
Tel: 307 632 0541 **Fax:** 307 632 4999

HITE, FANNING & HONEYMAN LLP (Kansas)
200 West Douglas Avenue, Suite 600, Wichita, KS 67202-3089
Tel: 316 265 7741 **Fax:** 316 267 7803

HOEVET, SNYDER & BOISE PC (Oregon)
1000 SW Broadway, Suite 1500, Portland, OR 97205
Tel: 503 228 0497 **Fax:** 503 228 7112

HOFF, CURTIS, PACHT, CASSIDY, FRAME, SOMERS & KATIMS PC (Vermont)
100 Main Street, P.O. Box 1124, Burlington, VT 05402 1124
Tel: 802 864 4531

HOFFMAN REILLY POZNER & WILLIAMSON (Colorado)
511 Sixteenth Street, Suite 700, Denver, CO 80202
Tel: 303 893 6100 **Fax:** 303 893 6110

HOLME ROBERTS & OWEN LLP (Colorado)
1700 Lincoln Street, Suite 4100, Denver, CO 80203-4541
Tel: 303 861 7000 **Fax:** 303 866 0200

HOLT NEY ZATCOFF & WASSERMAN, LLP (Georgia)
100 Galleria Parkway, Suite 600, Atlanta, GA 30339
Tel: 770 956 9600 **Fax:** 770 956 1490

HONIGMAN MILLER SCHWARTZ AND COHN (Michigan)
2290 First National Building, 660 Woodward Avenue, Detroit, MI 48226-3583
Tel: 313 465 7000 **Fax:** 313 465 8000

HOOLE & KING (Utah)
4276 South Highland Drive, Salt Lake City, UT 84124
Tel: 801 272 7556 **Fax:** 801 272 7557

HOPPING, GREEN & SAMS PA (Florida)
123 South Calhoun Street, Tallahassee, FL 32301
Tel: 850 222 7500 **Fax:** 850 224 8551

HORN & PAYNE (Mississippi)
P.O. Box 1725, 2603 Brookwood, Jackson, MS 39215-1725
Tel: 601 373 0170

HORTON LAW OFFICES (Wisconsin)
222 North Midvale Boulevard, Suite Seven, Madison, WI 53705
Tel: 608 231 3220 **Fax:** 608 231 3720

HOWARD, RICE, NEMEROVSKI, CANADY, FALK & RABKIN (California)
Three Embarcadero Center, 7th Floor, San Francisco, CA 94111-4065
Tel: 415 434 1600 **Fax:** 415 217 5910

HOWREY SIMON ARNOLD & WHITE (District of Columbia)
1299 Pennsylvania Avenue, NW, Washington, DC, DC 20004-2402
Tel: 202 783 0800 **Fax:** 202 383 6610

HOYT & BLEWETT (Montana)
501 Second Avenue North, PO Box 2807, Great Falls, MT 59403
Tel: 406 761 1960 **Fax:** 406 761 7186

HUDDLESTON, BOLEN, BEATTY, PORTER & COPEN, LLP (West Virginia)
611 Third Avenue, PO Box 2185, Huntington, WV 25722
Tel: 304 529 6181 **Fax:** 304 522 4312

HUGHES & LUCE LLP (Texas)
1717 Main Street, Suite 2800, Dallas, TX 75201
Tel: 214 939 5500 **Fax:** 214 939 6100

HUGHES HUBBARD & REED LLP (New York)
One Battery Park Plaza, New York, NY 10004-1482
Tel: 212 837 6000 **Fax:** 212 422 4726

HUGHES THORSNESS POWELL HUDDLESTON & BAUMAN LLC (Alaska)
550 West Seventh Avenue, Suite 1100, Anchorage, AK 99501
Tel: 907 274 7522 **Fax:** 907 263 8320

HUGHES, KELLNER, SULLIVAN & ALKE (Montana)
40 West Lawrence, P.O. Box 1166, Helena, MT 59624
Tel: 406 442 3690 **Fax:** 406 449 4849

HUMMEL, COAN, MILLER & SAGE (Kentucky)
Seventeenth Floor, 239 South Fifth Street, Louisville, KY 40202-3213
Tel: 502 585 3545 **Fax:** 502 585 3548

HUNT LAW FIRM (Arkansas)
320 West Harding Avenue, Pine Bluff, AR 71601
Tel: 870 535 4967 **Fax:** 870 535 4967

HUNT, ORTMANN, BLASCO, PALFFY & ROSSELL INC (California)
301 North Lake Avenue, Suite 700, Pasedena, CA 91101
Tel: 626 440 5200 **Fax:** 626 796 0107

HUNTER, MACLEAN, EXLEY & DUNN, PC (Georgia)
200 East Saint Julian Street, PO Box 9848, Savannah, GA 31412
Tel: 912 236 0261 **Fax:** 912 236 4936

OTHER RECOMMENDED FIRMS

HUNTON & WILLIAMS (Virginia)
Riverfront Plaza, East Tower, 951 East Byrd Street, Richmond, VA 23219-4074
Tel: 804 788 8200 **Fax:** 804 788 8218

HURLEY TOEVS STYLES HAMBLIN & PANTER PA (New Mexico)
4155 Montgomery Boulevard NE, Albuquerque, NM 87109
Tel: 505 888 1188 **Fax:** 505 888 9215

HURWITZ & SAGARIN LLC (Connecticut)
PO Box 112, Milford, CT 06460
Tel: 203 877 8000 **Fax:** 203 878 9800

HUSCH & EPPENBERGER, LLC (Missouri)
1200 Main, Suite 1700, Kansas City, MO 63105
Tel: 816 421 4800 **Fax:** 816 421 0596

HYATT & STUBBLEFIELD, PC (Georgia)
225 Peachtree Street North East, 1200 Center South Tower, Atlanta, GA 30303
Tel: 404 659 6600 **Fax:** 404 658 1725

ICE MILLER (Indiana)
One American Square, Box 82001, Indianapolis, IN 46282
Tel: 317 236 2100 **Fax:** 317 236 2219

IRELL & MANELLA LLP (California)
1800 Avenue of the Stars, Suite 900, Los Angeles, CA 90067-4276
Tel: 310 277 1010 **Fax:** 310 203 7199

ISAACSON, ROSENBAUM, WOODS & LEVY, PC (Colorado)
633 17th Street, Suite 2200, Denver, CO 80202
Tel: 303 292 5656 **Fax:** 303 292 3152

IVINS, PHILLIPS & BARKER (District of Columbia)
1700 Pennsylvania Ave NW, Suite 600, Washington, DC, DC 20006
Tel: 202 393 7600 **Fax:** 202 393 7601

JACKSON LEWIS (New York)
One North Broadway, White Plains, NY 10601
Tel: 914 328 0404 **Fax:** 914 328 1882

JACKSON WALKER LLP (Texas)
901 Main Street, Suite 6000, Dallas, TX 75202-3797
Tel: 214 953 6000 **Fax:** 214 953 5822

JACOBS, CHASE, FRICK, KLEINKOPF & KELLEY (Colorado)
1050 17th Street, Suite 1500, Denver, CO 80265
Tel: 303 685 4800 **Fax:** 303 685 4869

JACOBS, GRUDBERG, BELT & DOW PC (Connecticut)
350 Orange Street, New Haven, CT 06503
Tel: 203 772 3100

JAFFE, RAITT, HEUER & WEISS, PC (Michigan)
One Woodward Avenue, Suite 2400, Detroit, MI 48226
Tel: 313 961 8380 **Fax:** 313 961 8358

JAMES MCCOLLUM - SOLE PRACTITIONER (Alaska)
550 West 7th Avenue, Suite 1940, Anchorage, AK 99501
Tel: 907 770 7773

JANOVE BAAR ASSOCIATES (Utah)
9 Exchange Place, Suite 1112, Salt Lake City, UT 84111
Tel: 801 530 0404 **Fax:** 801 530 0428

JENKENS & GILCHRIST (Texas)
1445 Ross Avenue, Suite 3200, Dallas, TX 75202-2799
Tel: 214 855 4500 **Fax:** 214 855 4300

JENKINS FENSTERMAKER, PLLC (West Virginia)
401 Eleventh Street, 1100 Coal Exchange Building, PO Box 2688, Huntington, WV 25726-2688
Tel: 304 523 2100 **Fax:** 304 523 2347

JENNINGS & SIGMOND (Pennsylvania)
The Penn Mutual Towers, 16th Floor, 510 Walnut Street, Philadelphia, PA 19106-3683
Tel: 215 351 0624 **Fax:** 215 922 3524

JENNINGS, STROUSS & SALMON, PLC (Arizona)
One Renaissance Square, Two North Central Avenue, Phoenix, AZ 85004-2385
Tel: 602 262 5911 **Fax:** 602 253 3255

JENSEN BAIRD GARDNER & HENRY (Maine)
Ten Free Street, PO Box 4510, Portland, ME 04112
Tel: 207 775 7271 **Fax:** 207 775 7935

JERMAIN, DUNNAGAN & OWENS PC (Alaska)
3000 A Street, Suite 300, Anchorage, AK 99503
Tel: 907 563 8844 **Fax:** 907 563 7322

JOHN D SAXON - SOLE PRACTITIONER (Alabama)
2119 3rd Avenue North, Birmingham, AL 35203-3314
Tel: 205 324 0223 **Fax:** 205 323 1583

JOHN WALKER - SOLE PRACTITIONER (Arkansas)
1723 South Broadway, Little Rock, AR 72206-1220
Tel: 501 374 3758 **Fax:** 501 374 4187

JOHNSON & WEBBERT, LLP (Maine)
160 Capitol street, Augusta, ME 04332-0079
Tel: 207 623 5110 **Fax:** 207 622 4160

JOHNSON, BLAKELY, POPE, BOKOR, RUPPEL & BURNS, PA (Florida)
911 Chestnut Street, PO Box 1368, Clearwater, FL 33756
Tel: 727 461 1818 **Fax:** 727 441 8617

JOHNSTON BARTON PROCTOR & POWELL LLP (Alabama)
2900 AmSouth/Harbert Plaza, 1901 Sixth Avenue North, Birmingham, AL 35203-2618
Tel: 205 458 9400 **Fax:** 205 458 9500

JONES VARGAS (Nevada)
3773 Howard Hughes Parkway, Third Floor South, Las Vegas, NV 89109
Tel: 702 734 2220 **Fax:** 702 737 7705

OTHER RECOMMENDED FIRMS

JONES WALDO HOLBROOK & MCDONOUGH PC (Utah)
1500 Wells Fargo Plaza, 170 South Main Street, Salt Lake City, UT 84101
Tel: 801 521 3200 **Fax:** 801 328 0537

JORGENSON LAW OFFICE (Wyoming)
242 East Broadway, Jackson, WY 83001
Tel: 307 733 6021 **Fax:** 307 734 7402

JUBELIRER, PASS & INTRIERI (Pennsylvania)
219 Ford Pitt Boulevard, Pittsburgh, PA 15222-1505
Tel: 412 281 3850

JULIUS & SIMPSON LLP (South Dakota)
731 St. Joseph Street, Suite 230, Rapid City, SD 57701
Tel: 605 716 1000 **Fax:** 605 716 1078

KAHN KLEINMAN (Ohio)
2600 Erieview Tower, 1301 East Ninth Street, Cleveland, OH 44114-1824
Tel: 216 696 3311 **Fax:** 216 623 4912

KAHN, SMITH & COLLINS, PA (Maryland)
201 North Charles Street, 10th Floor, Baltimore, MD 21201
Tel: 410 244 1010 **Fax:** 410 244 8001

KALIJARVI, CHUZI & NEWMAN PC (District of Columbia)
1730 K Street, NW, Suite 1011, Washington, DC, DC 20006
Tel: 202 331 9260 **Fax:** 202 872 9562

KAMER ZUCKER & ABBOTT (Nevada)
3000 West Charleston Boulevard, Suite 3, Las Vegas, NV 89102
Tel: 702 259 8640 **Fax:** 702 259 8646

KANTROW, SPAHT, WEAVER & BLITZER (Louisiana)
Suite 300, City Plaza, 445 North Boulevard, PO Box 2997, Baton Rouge, LA 70821-2997
Tel: 225 383 4703 **Fax:** 225 343 0630

KAPLAN, BREWER, MAXEY & HARALSON (Arkansas)
415 Main Street, Little Rock, AR 72201
Tel: 501 372 0400 **Fax:** 501 376 3612

KAPLAN, STRANGIS & KAPLAN (Minnesota)
5500 Wells Fargo Center, Minneapolis, MN 55402
Tel: 612 375 1138 **Fax:** 612 375 1143

KARAGANIS, WHITE & MAGEL (Illinois)
414 North Orleans Street, Suite 810, Chicago, IL 60610
Tel: 312 836 1177 **Fax:** 312 836 9083

KASOWITZ BENSON TORRES & FRIEDMAN (New York)
1633 Broadway, New York, NY 10019
Tel: 212 506 1700 **Fax:** 212 506 1800

KATZ RANDALL WEINBERG & RICHMOND (Illinois)
333 West Wacker Drive, Suite 1800, Chicago, IL 60606
Tel: 312 807 3800 **Fax:** 312 807 3903

KATZ, KUTTER, HAIGLER, ALDERMAN, BRYANT & YON, PA (Florida)
106 East College Avenue, 12th Floor, Tallahassee, FL 3230132302-1877
Tel: 850 224 9634 **Fax:** 850 222 0103

KAUFMAN & CANOLES (Virginia)
One Commercial Place, PO Box 3037, Norfolk, VA 23514
Tel: 757 624 3000 **Fax:** 757 624 3169

KAY CASTO & CHANEY PLLC (West Virginia)
1600 Bank One Center, PO Box 2031, Charleston, WV 25327
Tel: 304 345 8900 **Fax:** 304 345 8909

KAYE SCHOLER LLP (New York)
425 Park Avenue, New York, NY 10022-3598
Tel: 212 836 8000 **Fax:** 212 836 8689

KEAN, MILLER, HAWTHORNE, D'ARMOND, MCCOWAN & JARMAN, LLP (Louisiana)
One American Place, 301 Main Street, 22nd Floor, Baton Rouge, LA 70821
Tel: 225 387 0999 **Fax:** 225 388 9133

KEATING, MUETHING & KLEKAMP, P.L.L. (Ohio)
1400 Provident Tower, One East Fourth Street, Cincinnati, OH 45202
Tel: 513 579 6400 **Fax:** 513 579 6457

KEGLER, BROWN, HILL & RITTER (Ohio)
Capitol Square, Suite 1800, 65 East State Street, Columbus, OH 43215-4294
Tel: 614 462 5400 **Fax:** 614 464 2634

KEKER & VAN NEST LLP (California)
710 Sansome Street, San Francisco, CA 94111
Tel: 415 391 5400 **Fax:** 415 397 7188

KELEHER & MCLEOD, PA (New Mexico)
201 Third Street NW, Twelfth Floor, Albuquerque, NM 87103
Tel: 505 346 4646 **Fax:** 505 346 1370

KELLOGG, HUBER, HANSEN, TODD & EVANS PLLC (District of Columbia)
1615 M Street North West, Suite 400, Washington, DC, DC 20036
Tel: 202 326 7900 **Fax:** 202 326 7999

KELLY & BERENS P.A. (Minnesota)
Suite 3720 IDS Center, 80 South Eighth Street, Minneapolis, MN 55402
Tel: 612 349 6171 **Fax:** 612 349 6416

KELLY & MCKEE (Florida)
1718 East Seventh Avenue, Suite 301, Tampa, FL 33605
Tel: 813 248 6400

KENNEDY COVINGTON LOBDELL & HICKMAN, L.L.P. (North Carolina)
Bank of America Corporate Center, 42nd Floor, Charlotte, NC 28202
Tel: 704 331 7400 **Fax:** 704 331 7598

KENNY NACHWALTER SEYMOUR ARNOLD CRITCHLOW & SPECTOR (Florida)
1100 Miami Center, 201 South Biscayne Boulevard, Miami, FL 33131
Tel: 305 373 1000 **Fax:** 305 372 1861

KENYON & KENYON (District of Columbia)
1500 K Street North West, Suite 700, Washington, DC, DC 20005-1257
Tel: 202 220 4200 **Fax:** 202 220 4201

KERR RUSSELL & WEBER (Michigan)
Detroit Center, 500 Woodward Avenue, Suite 2500, Detroit, MI 48226-3427
Tel: 313 961 0200 **Fax:** 313 961 0388

OTHER RECOMMENDED FIRMS

KEVIN C. EFROYMSON (Nevada)
2915 West Charleston Boulevard, Las Vegas, NV 89101

KIENBAUM OPPERWALL HARDY & PELTON (Michigan)
325 South Old Woodward Avenue, Birmingham, MI 48009
Tel: 248 645 0000 **Fax:** 248 645 1385

KIESEWETTER WISE (Tennessee)
3725 Champion Hills Drive, Suite 300, Memphis, TN 32125
Tel: 901 795 6695 **Fax:** 901 795 1646

KILLMER & LANE (Colorado)
1543 Champa Street, Suite 400, Denver, CO 80202
Tel: 303 571 1000 **Fax:** 303 571 1001

KILLWORTH, GOTTMAN, HAGAN & SCHAEFF LLP (Ohio)
One Dayton Centre, One South Main Street, Suite 500, Dayton, OH 45402-2023
Tel: 937 223 2050 **Fax:** 937 223 0724

KILPATRICK STOCKTON LLP (Georgia)
1100 Peachtree Street North East, Suite 2800, Atlanta, GA 30309-4530
Tel: 404 815 6500 **Fax:** 404 815 6555

KING & BALLOW (Tennessee)
1100 Union Street Plaza, 315 Union Street, Nashville, TN 37201
Tel: 615 259 3456 **Fax:** 615 254 7907

KING & GREISEN (Colorado)
1670 York Street, Denver, CO 80206
Tel: 303 298 9878 **Fax:** 303 298 9879

KING HERSHEY, A PROFESSIONAL CORPORATION (Missouri)
2345 Grand Boulevard, Suite 2100, Kansas City, MO 64108
Tel: 816 842 3636 **Fax:** 816 842 2414

KING, BLACKWELL & DOWNS (Florida)
25 East Pine Street, Orlando, FL 32802-1631
Tel: 407 422 2472 **Fax:** 407 648 0161

KINGSMILL RIESS L.L.C (Louisiana)
201 St. Charles Avenue, Suite 3300, New Orleans, LA 70170
Tel: 504 581 3300

KIRK & CHANEY (Oklahoma)
101 Park Avenue, Suite 800, Oklahoma City, OK 73102
Tel: 405 235 1333

KIRKPATRICK & LOCKHART LLP (Pennsylvania)
Henry W. Oliver Building, 535 Smithfield Street, Pittsburgh, PA 15222-2312
Tel: 412 355 6500 **Fax:** 412 355 6501

KIRSCHNER & LEGLER (Florida)
300-A Wharfside Way, Jacksonville, FL 32207
Tel: 904 346 3200

KIRTON & MCCONKIE (Utah)
1800 Eagle Gate Tower, 60 East South Temple, Salt Lake City, UT 84111
Tel: 801 328 3600 **Fax:** 801 321 4893

KLEHR HARRISON HARVEY BRANZBERG & ELLERS LLP (Pennsylvania)
260 South Broad Street, Philadelphia, PA 19102-5003
Tel: 215 568 6060 **Fax:** 215 568 6603

KLETT ROONEY LIEBER & SCHORLING (Pennsylvania)
One Oxford Centre, Pittsburgh, PA 15219
Tel: 412 392 2000 **Fax:** 412 392 2128

KLUGER, PERETZ, KAPLAN & BERLIN P.L. (Florida)
Miami Center, Seventeenth Floor, 201 South Biscayne Boulevard, Miami, FL 33131
Tel: 305 379 9000 **Fax:** 305 379 3428

KNOBBE MARTENS OLSON & BEAR (California)
2040 Main Street, 14th Floor, Irvine, CA 92614
Tel: 949 760 0404 **Fax:** 949 760 9502

KOBAYASHI, SUGITA & GODA (Hawaii)
999 Bishop Street, Suite 2600, Honolulu, HI 96813
Tel: 808 539 8700 **Fax:** 808 539 8799

KOHN SWIFT & GRAF (Pennsylvania)
One South Broad Street, Suite 2100, Philadelphia, PA 19107 3389
Tel: 215 238 1700

KOHN, SHANDS, ELBERT, GIANOULAKIS & GILJUM, LLP (Missouri)
One US Bank Plaza, Suite 2410, St Louis, MO 63101
Tel: 314 241 3963 **Fax:** 314 241 2509

KOLLMAN & SAUCIER PA (Maryland)
Sun Life Building, 8th Floor, 20 South Charles Street, Baltimore, MD 21201-3225
Tel: 410 727 4300 **Fax:** 410 727 4391

KOZYAK TROPIN & THROCKMORTON (Florida)
2800 First Union Financial Center, 200 Biscayne Boulevard, Miami, FL 33131
Tel: 305 372 1800 **Fax:** 305 372 3508

KRAMON & GRAHAM, PA (Maryland)
One South Street, Suite 2600, Baltimore, MD 21202-3201
Tel: 410 752 6030 **Fax:** 410 539 1269

KRASOW, GARLICK & HADLEY LLC (Connecticut)
One State Street, Hartford, CT 06103
Tel: 860 549 7100

KREHBIEL BANNERMAN & WILLIAMS PA (New Mexico)
6400 Uptown Boulevard North East, Suite 200 - West, Albuquerque, NM 87110
Tel: 505 837 1900 **Fax:** 505 837 1800

KRIEG DEVAULT LLP (Indiana)
One Indiana Square, Suite 2800, Indianapolis, IN 46204
Tel: 317 636 4341 **Fax:** 317 636 1507

KRONISH LIEB WEINER & HELLMAN LLP (New York)
1114 Avenue of the Americas, New York, NY 10036-7798
Tel: 212 479 6000 **Fax:** 212 479 6275

OTHER RECOMMENDED FIRMS

KROVATIN & ASSOCIATES LLC (New Jersey)
744 Broad Street, Suite 1903, Newark, NJ 07102
Tel: 973 424 9777

KUTAK ROCK LLP (Nebraska)
The Omaha Building, 1650 Farnam Street, Omaha, NE 68102-2186
Tel: 402 346 6000 **Fax:** 402 346 1148

LAMSON, DUGAN & MURRAY, LLP (Nebraska)
Lamson, Dugan & Murray Building, 10306 Regency Parkway Drive, Omaha, NE 68114
Tel: 402 397 7300 **Fax:** 402 397 7824

LANDYE BENNETT BLUMSTEIN LLP (Oregon)
3500 Wells Fargo Center, 1300 SW Fifth Avenue, Portland, OR 97201
Tel: 503 224 4100 **Fax:** 503 224 4133

LANE & WATERMAN (Iowa)
220 North Main Street, Suite 600, Davenport, IA 52801
Tel: 563 324 3246 **Fax:** 563 324 1616

LANE POWELL SPEARS LUBERSKY LLP (Washington)
1420 Fifth Avenue, Suite 4100, Seattle, WA 98101-2338
Tel: 206 223 7000 **Fax:** 206 223 7107

LANER, MUCHIN, DOMBROW, BECKER, LEVIN, TOMINBERG (Illinois)
515 North State Suite, Suite 2800, Chicago, IL 60610
Tel: 312 467 9800 **Fax:** 312 467 9479

LANGERMAN LAW OFFICES (Arizona)
350 East Virginia Avenue, Suite 100, Phoenix, AZ 85004
Tel: 602 240 5525 **Fax:** 602 230 8180

LANGROCK SPERRY & WOOL, LLP (Vermont)
111 South Pleasant Street, P.O. Drawer 351, Middlebury, VT 05753
Tel: 802 388 6356 **Fax:** 802 388 6149

LATHROP & GAGE LC (Missouri)
2345 Grand Boulevard, Suite 2800, Kansas City, MO 64108
Tel: 816 292 2000 **Fax:** 816 292 2001

LAVEY & BURNETT (Arkansas)
904 West 2nd Street, Little Rock, AR 72201
Tel: 501 376 2269 **Fax:** 501 372 1134

LAW CHAMBERS NICHOLAS CRITELLI PC (Iowa)
317 Sixth Avenue, Suite 950, Des Moines, IA 50309-4128
Tel: 515 243 3122 **Fax:** 515 243 2932

LAW OFFICE OF ALICE W. BALLARD (Pennsylvania)
255 South Fifteenth Street, Suite 1700, Philadelphia, PA 19103-6996
Tel: 215 893 9708 **Fax:** 215 893 9997

LAW OFFICE OF BRUCE T MOATS (Wyoming)
2515 Pioneer Avenue, Cheyenne, WY 82001
Tel: 307 778 8844 **Fax:** 307 638 1227

LAW OFFICE OF R. BRUCE MACMURDO LLC (Louisiana)
341 Charles Street, Baton Rouge, LA 70802
Tel: 255 344 1333

LAW OFFICE OF THOMAS S. NEUBERGER P.A. (Delaware)
Suite 302, 2 East Seventh Street, Wilmington, DE 19801-3707
Tel: 302 655 0582

LAW OFFICES OF ARCHIBALD J. THOMAS, III (Florida)
1301 Riverplace Boulevard, Suite 1640, Jacksonville, FL 32207
Tel: 904 396 2322 **Fax:** 904 398 3271

LAW OFFICES OF CAROLINE MITCHELL (Pennsylvania)
Gulf Tower, 707 Grant Street, Suite 1730, Pittsburgh, PA 15219-1913
Tel: 412 232 3131 **Fax:** 412 471 3689

LAW OFFICES OF JONATHAN H. (JASON) WARNER, PA (Florida)
9400 South Dadeland Boulevard, Suite 600, Miami, FL 33156
Tel: 305 670 0007 **Fax:** 305 670 0005

LAW OFFICES OF JUDITH A LONNQUIST (Washington)
1218 3rd Avenue, Suite 1500, Seattle, WA 98101
Tel: 206 622 2086 **Fax:** 206 233 9165

LAW OFFICES OF THOMAS CLAY (Kentucky)
239 South Fifth Street, Suite 2000, Louisville, KY 40202
Tel: 502 561 2005

LAW OFFICES OF WILLIAM H BOOTH (California)
1500 Newell Avenue, 5th Floor, Walnut Creek, CA 94596
Tel: 925 296 2460 **Fax:** 925 296 2464

LAWLER METZGER & MILKMAN (District of Columbia)
1909 K Street North West, Suite 820, Washington, DC, DC 20006
Tel: 202 777 7700 **Fax:** 202 777 7763

LAWTON & CATES, S.C. (Wisconsin)
10 East Doty Street, Suite 400, Madison, WI 53701
Tel: 608 282 6200 **Fax:** 608 282 6252

LAXALT & NOMURA (Nevada)
Bank of America Plaza, 50 West Liberty Street, Suite 700, Reno, NV 89501
Tel: 775 322 1170

LEAGRE CHANDLER & MILLARD LLP (Indiana)
1400 First Indiana Plaza, 135 North Pennsylvania Street, Indianapolis, IN 46204-2489
Tel: 317 808 3000 **Fax:** 317 808 3100

LEATHERWOOD WALKER TODD & MANN, P.C. (South Carolina)
100 East Coffee Street, PO Box 87, Greenville, SC 29602
Tel: 864 242 6440 **Fax:** 864 240 2477

LEBAU & NEUWORTH, LLC (Maryland)
606 Baltimore Avenue, Suite 201, Baltimore, MD 21204
Tel: 410 296 3030 **Fax:** 410 296 8660

LECLAIR RYAN (Virginia)
707 East Main Street, 11th Floor, Richmond, VA 23219
Tel: 804 783 2003 **Fax:** 804 783 2294

LEE HOLEN LAW OFFICE (Alaska)
441 West 5th Avenue, Suite 400, Anchorage, AK 99501
Tel: 907 278 0298 **Fax:** 907 278 0247

OTHER RECOMMENDED FIRMS

LEFF, HAUPERT, TRAW & WILLMAN LLP (Iowa)
222 South Linn Street, PO Box 2447, Iowa City, IA 52244 2447
Tel: 319 338 7551 **Fax:** 319 338 6902

LEHR MIDDLEBROOKS PRICE & PROCTOR (Alabama)
2021 Third Avenue North, Suite 300, Birmingham, AL 35203
Tel: 205 326 3002 **Fax:** 205 326 3008

LEIBY TAYLOR STEARNS LINKHORST & ROBERTS, PA (Florida)
1390 North University Drive, Fort Lauderdale, FL 33322
Tel: 954 382 9199 **Fax:** 954 382 9063

LEITMAN, SIEGAL & PAYNE, PC (Alabama)
The Land Title Building, 600 North 20th Street, Suite 400, Birmingham, AL 35203
Tel: 205 251 5900 **Fax:** 205 323 2098

LEMLE & KELLEHER, LLP (Louisiana)
21st Floor, Pan-American Life Center, 601 Poydras Street, New Orleans, LA 70130
Tel: 504 586 1241 **Fax:** 504 584 9142

LEONARD & ASSOCIATES PC (Oklahoma)
120 N Robinson Avenue, Oklahoma City, OK 73102
Tel: 405 239 3800

LEONARD, STREET AND DEINARD, PROFESSIONAL ASSOCIATION (Minnesota)
Suite 2300, 150 South Fifth Street, Minneapolis, MN 55402
Tel: 612 335 1500 **Fax:** 612 335 1657

LESESNE & CONNETTE (North Carolina)
101 Elizabeth Avenue, Suite 1-D, Charlotte, NC 28204-2234
Tel: 704 372 5700

LEVINE SULLIVAN & KOCH LLP (District of Columbia)
1050 Seventeenth Street N.W., Suite 800, Washington, DC, DC 20036
Tel: 202 508 1100 **Fax:** 202 861 9888

LEVIT, MANN, HALLIGAN & WARREN (Virginia)
Hamilton Place, Suite 100, 1301 North Hamilton Street, Richmond, VA 23230-3959
Tel: 804 355 7766 **Fax:** 804 355 8752

LEVY PHILLIPS & KONIGSBERG LLP (New York)
520 Madison Avenue, New York, NY, New York, NY 10022
Tel: 212 605 6200 **Fax:** 212 605 6290

LEVY RAM OLSON & ROSSI (California)
639 Front Street, 4th Floor, San Francisco, CA 94111
Tel: 415 433 4949 **Fax:** 415 433 7311

LEWIS AND ROCA (Arizona)
40 North Central Avenue, Phoenix, AZ 85004-4429
Tel: 602 262 5311 **Fax:** 602 262 5747

LEWIS, LONGMAN & WALKER PA (Florida)
1700 Palm Beach Lakes Boulevard, Suite 1000, West Palm Beach, FL 33401
Tel: 561 640 0820 **Fax:** 561 640 8202

LEWIS, RICE & FINGERSH (Missouri)
1010 Walnut, Suite 500, Kansas City, MO 64106
Tel: 816 421 2500 **Fax:** 816 472 2500

LEYDIG, VOIT & MAYER, LTD (Illinois)
Two Prudential Plaza, 180 North Stetson Avenue, Suite 4900, Chicago, IL 60601-6780
Tel: 312 616 5600 **Fax:** 312 616 5700

LIDDLE & ROBINSON, LLP (New York)
685 Third Avenue, New York, NY 10017
Tel: 212 687 8500 **Fax:** 212 687 1505

LIGHTFOOT, FRANKLIN & WHITE, LLC (Alabama)
The Clark Building, 400 20th Street North, Birmingham, AL 35203
Tel: 205 581 0700 **Fax:** 205 581 0799

LILES, GAVIN, COSTANTINO & MURPHY (Florida)
One Enterprise Center, Suite 1500, 225 Water Street, Jacksonville, FL 32202
Tel: 904 634 1100 **Fax:** 904 634 1234

LINDA S MENSCH PC - SOLE PRACTITIONER (Illinois)
200 South Michigan Avenue, Suite 1240, Chicago, IL 60604
Tel: 312 922 2910

LINDNER & MARSACK, S.C. (Wisconsin)
411 East Wisconsin Avenue, Suite 1000, Milwaukee, WI 53202
Tel: 414 273 3910 **Fax:** 414 273 0522

LINDQUIST & VENNUM PLLP (Minnesota)
4200 IDS Center, 80 South 8th Street, Minneapolis, MN 55402
Tel: 612 371 3211 **Fax:** 612 371 3207

LINNELL CHOATE & WEBBER LLP (Maine)
83 Pleasant Street, Auburn, ME 04210
Tel: 207 784 4563 **Fax:** 207 784 1981

LINOWES AND BLOCHER LLP (Maryland)
1010 Wayne Avenue, Suite 1000, Silver Spring, MD 20910
Tel: 301 588 8580 **Fax:** 301 495 9044

LIONEL SAWYER & COLLINS (Nevada)
1700 Bank of America Plaza, 300 South Fourth Street, Las Vegas, NV 89101
Tel: 702 383 8888 **Fax:** 702 383 8845

LISKOW & LEWIS, PLC (Louisiana)
One Shell Square, 701 Poydras Street, Suite 5000, New Orleans, LA 70139-5099
Tel: 504 581 7979 **Fax:** 504 556 4108

LISMAN, WEBSTER, KIRKPATRICK & LECKERLING, P.C. (Vermont)
84 Pine Street, PO Box 728, Burlington, VT 05402
Tel: 802 864 5756 **Fax:** 802 864 3629

LITCHFORD & CHRISTOPHER (Florida)
Bank of America Center, 390 North Orange Avenue, PO Box 1549, Orlando, FL 32802
Tel: 407 841 0325 **Fax:** 407 841 0325

LITTLE, CICCHETTI & CONARD PC (Vermont)
117 St Paul Street, Burlington, VT 05402
Tel: 802 862 6511 **Fax:** 802 862 5645

LITTLER MENDELSON PC (California)
650 California Street, 20th Floor, San Francisco, CA 94108-2693
Tel: 415 433 1940 **Fax:** 415 399 8490

OTHER RECOMMENDED FIRMS

LIVINGSTON ADLER PULDA MEIKELJOHN & KELLY PC (Connecticut)
557 Prospect Avenue, Hartford, CT 06105
Tel: 860 233 9821 **Fax:** 860 232 7818

LOCKE LIDDELL & SAPP LLP (Texas)
2200 Ross Avenue, Suite 2200, Dallas, TX 75201-6776
Tel: 214 740 8000 **Fax:** 214 740 8800

LOEB & LOEB LLP (California)
10100 Santa Monica Boulevard, Suite 2200, Los Angeles, CA 90067-4164
Tel: 310 282 2000 **Fax:** 310 282 2200

LOHF, SHAIMAN, JACOBS & HYMAN (Colorado)
950 South Cherry Street, Suite 900, Denver, CO 80246
Tel: 303 753 9000

LOMMEN, NELSON, COLE & STAGEBERG, P.A. (Minnesota)
1800 IDS Center, 80 South 8th Street, Minneapolis, MN 55402
Tel: 612 339 8131 **Fax:** 612 339 8064

LONG, BURNER, PARKS & DELARGY (Texas)
515 Congress Avenue, Suite 1500, PO Box 2212, Austin, TX 78768-2212
Tel: 512 474 1587 **Fax:** 512 322 0301

LORD, BISSELL & BROOK (California)
300 S. Grand, Suite 800, Los Angeles, CA 90071-3200
Tel: 213 485 1500

LOTTNER RUBIN FISHMAN BROWN & SAUL, PC (Colorado)
633 Seventeenth Street, Suite 2700, Denver, CO 80202-3635
Tel: 303 292 1200 **Fax:** 303 292 1300

LOVELLS (New York)
900 Third Avenue, 16th Floor, NY 10022
Tel: 212 909 0600 **Fax:** 212 909 0666

LOWE GRAY STEELE & DARKO LLP (Indiana)
Bank One Tower, 111 Monument Circle, Suite 4600, Indianapolis, IN 46244-0924
Tel: 317 236 8020 **Fax:** 317 236 6472

LOWNDES DROSDICK DOSTER KANTOR & REED, PA (Florida)
215 North Eola Drive, Orlando, FL 32801
Tel: 407 843 4600 **Fax:** 407 843 4444

LUEDERS, ROBERTSON, KONZEN & FITZHENRY (Illinois)
1939 Delmar Avenue, Granite City, IL 62040
Tel: 618 876 8500 **Fax:** 618 876 4534

LUM DANZIS DRASCO & POSITAN (New Jersey)
103 Eisenhower Parkway, Roseland, NJ 07068-1049
Tel: 973 403 9000

LYONS & ELLSWORTH LTD (Nevada)
512 South Eighth Street, Las Vegas, NV 89101
Tel: 702 432 8655 **Fax:** 702 432 8715

MACDONALD, HOAGUE & BAYLESS (Washington)
Hoge Building, 15th Floor, 705 Second Avenue, Seattle, WA 98104 1745
Tel: 206 622 1604 **Fax:** 206 343 3961

MACEY MACEY & SWANSON (Indiana)
445 North Pennsylvania Street, Suite 404, Indianapolis, IN 46204
Tel: 317 637 2345 **Fax:** 317 637 2369

MACPHERSON KELLY & THOMPSON (Wyoming)
616 West Buffalo, PO Box 999, Rawlins, WY 82301
Tel: 307 324 2713 **Fax:** 307 324 7348

MADISON HARBOUR MROZ & BRENNAN PA (New Mexico)
Suite 1600 Albuquerque Plaza, 201 Third Street North West, PO Box 25467, Albuquerque, NM 87102
Tel: 505 242 2177 **Fax:** 505 242 7184

MANATT, PHELPS & PHILLIPS, LLP (California)
11355 West Olymoic Boulevard, Los Angeles, CA 90064
Tel: 310 312 4000 **Fax:** 310 312 4224

MANCINI WELCH & GEIGER LLP (Hawaii)
The Kahului Building, 33 Lono Avenue, Suite 470, Kahului, HI 96732-1681
Tel: 808 871 8351 **Fax:** 808 871 0732

MANDELL & WRIGHT (Texas)
JPMorgan Chase Building, 712 Main, Suite 1600, Houston, TX 77002-3297
Tel: 713 228 1521 **Fax:** 713 228 0321

MANKO, GOLD, KATCHER & FOX LLP (Pennsylvania)
401 City Avenue, Suite 500, Bala Clynwyd, PA 19004
Tel: 484 430 5700 **Fax:** 484 430 5711

MANNING FULTON & SKINNER (North Carolina)
P.O. Box 20389, Raleigh, NC 27619-0389
Tel: 919 787 8880

MARC GURSKY - SOLE PRACTITIONER (Rhode Island)
18 Imperial Place suite 1-D, Providence, RI 02903
Tel: 401 454 7400

MARING WILLIAMS LAW OFFICE PC (North Dakota)
1220 Main Avenue, Suite 105, PO Box 2103, Fargo, ND 58107-2103
Tel: 701 241 4141 **Fax:** 701 235 2268

MARISCAL, WEEKS, MCINTYRE & FRIEDLANDER, PA (Arizona)
2901 North Central Avenue, Suite 200, Phoenix, AZ 85012
Tel: 602 285 5000 **Fax:** 602 285 5100

MARK W. GIFFORD (Wyoming)
243 South Park Street, P.O. Box 2508, Casper, WY 82602
Tel: 307 265 3265 **Fax:** 307 265 3266

MARKOWITZ & RICHMAN (Pennsylvania)
1100 North American Building, Philadelphia, PA 19107
Tel: 215 875 3100 **Fax:** 215 790 0668

MARKOWITZ, HERBOLD, GLADE & MEHLHAF PC (Oregon)
3000 Pacwest Center, 1211 South West Fifth Avenue, Portland, OR 97204-3730
Tel: 503 295 3085 **Fax:** 503 323 9105

If you can't find a firm here, see full profiles (pages 759-907)

OTHER RECOMMENDED FIRMS

MARR HIPP JONES AND PEPPER (Hawaii)
Pauahi Tower, 1001 Bishop Street, Suite 1550, Honolulu, HI 96813
Tel: 808 536 4900 **Fax:** 808 536 6700

MARSHALL HILL CASSAS & DE LIPKAU (Nevada)
Suite 300, Holcomb Professional Center, 333 Holcomb Avenue, PO Box 2790, Reno, NV 89505-2790
Tel: 775 323 1601 **Fax:** 775 348 7250

MARSHALL, GERSTEIN & BORUN (Illinois)
6300 Sears Tower, 233 South Wacker Drive, Chicago, IL 60606-6402
Tel: 312 474 6300 **Fax:** 312 474 0448

MARTIN & CHURCHILL CHARTERED (Kansas)
500 North Market Street, Wichita, KS 67214-3590
Tel: 316 263 3200 **Fax:** 316 263 6298

MARTIN, PRINGLE, OLIVER, WALLACE & BAUER, L.L.P. (Kansas)
100 North Broadway, Suite 500, Wichita, KS 67202
Tel: 316 265 9311 **Fax:** 316 265 2955

MARTZELL & BICKFORD, APC (Louisiana)
338 Lafayette Street, New Orleans, LA 70130-3244
Tel: 504 581 9065 **Fax:** 504 581 7635

MARY ELIZABETH GALVAN (Wyoming)
165 North 5th Street, Laramie, WY 82072
Tel: 307 745 7091

MASLON EDELMAN BORMAN & BRAND, LLP (Minnesota)
3300 Wells Fargo Center, 90 South Seventh Street, Minneapolis, MN 55402
Tel: 612 672 8200 **Fax:** 612 672 8397

MASON & MASON PC (Wyoming)
Box 785, Pinedale, WY 82941
Tel: 307 367 2134

MATKOV SALZMAN MADOFF & GUNN (Illinois)
55 East Monroe Street, Suite 2900, Chicago, IL 60603-5709
Tel: 312 332 0777 **Fax:** 312 332 6130

MAUK & BURGOYNE (Idaho)
515 South Sixth Street, PO Box 1743, Boise, ID 83701 1743
Tel: 208 345 2654 **Fax:** 208 345 3319

MAUPIN TAYLOR & ELLIS, P.A. (North Carolina)
Highwoods Tower One, Suite 500, 3200 Beechleaf Court, Raleigh, NC 27604
Tel: 919 981 4000 **Fax:** 919 981 4300

MAXEY WANN (Mississippi)
Deposit Guaranty Plaza, Suite 1900, P.O.Box 3977, 210 East Capitol Street, Jackson, MS 39201-2301
Tel: 601 355 8855 **Fax:** 601 355 8881

MAY, ADAM, GERDES & THOMPSON, L.L.P. (South Dakota)
503 South Pierre Street, PO Box 160, Pierre, SD 57501
Tel: 605 224 8803 **Fax:** 605 224 6289

MAYNARD, COOPER & GALE PC (Alabama)
Harbert Plaza, 1901 Sixth Avenue North, Suite 2400, Birmingham, AL 35203
Tel: 205 254 1000 **Fax:** 205 254 1999

MAZUR CARP RUBIN (New York)
2 Park Avenue, New York, NY 10016
Tel: 212 686 7700 **Fax:** 212 532 1425

MCCARTER & ENGLISH (New Jersey)
Four Gateway Center, 100 Mulberry Street, Newark, NJ 07102-0652
Tel: 973 622 4444 **Fax:** 973 624 7070

MCCORRISTON MILLER MUKAI MACKINNON LLP (Hawaii)
Five Waterfront Plaza, 4th Floor, 500 Ala Moana Boulevard, Honolulu, HI 96803-2800
Tel: 808 529 7300 **Fax:** 808 524 8293

MCCULLOUGH HILL FIKSO KRETSCHMER SMITH (Washington)
2025 First Avenue, Suite 1130, Seattle, WA 98121
Tel: 206 448 1818 **Fax:** 206 448 3444

MCCULLOUGH, WAREHEMAN & LABUNKER (Kansas)
1507 Topeka Boulevard, Topeka, KS 66601
Tel: 785 233 2323

MCDADE FOGLER MAINES LLP (Texas)
Two Houston Center, 909 Fannin, Suite 1200, Houston, TX 77010-1006
Tel: 713 654 4300 **Fax:** 713 654 4343

MCDONALD CARANO WILSON MCCUNE BERGIN FRANKOVICH & HICKS LLP (Nevada)
241 Ridge Street, Reno, NV 89501
Tel: 775 788 2000 **Fax:** 775 788 2020

MCGINN & CARPENTER PA (New Mexico)
420 Central South West, Suite 200, Albuquerque, NM 87102
Tel: 505 843 6161 **Fax:** 505 242 8227

MCGRATH, NORTH, MULLIN & KRATZ, PC (Nebraska)
One Central Park Plaza, Suite 1400, Omaha, NE 68102
Tel: 402 341 3070 **Fax:** 402 341 0216

MCGUINN, HILLSMAN & PALEFSKY (California)
535 Pacific Avenue, San Francisco, CA 94133
Tel: 415 421 9292 **Fax:** 415 403 0202

MCGUIREWOODS LLP (Virginia)
One James Center, 901 East Cary Street, Richmond, VA 23219-4030
Tel: 804 775 1000 **Fax:** 804 775 1061

MCKENNA LONG & ALDRIDGE (District of Columbia)
1900 K Street North West, Washington, DC, DC 20006
Tel: 202 496 7500 **Fax:** 202 496 7756

MCKINNEY & STRINGER, A PROFESSIONAL CORPORATION (Oklahoma)
Corporate Tower, 101 North Robinson, Oklahoma City, OK 73102
Tel: 405 239 6444 **Fax:** 405 239 7902

OTHER RECOMMENDED FIRMS

MCKOOL SMITH (Texas)
300 Crescent Court, Suite 1500, Dallas, TX 75201
Tel: 214 978 4000 **Fax:** 214 978 4044

MCLAUGHLIN & MCCAFFREY, LLP (Ohio)
Eaton Center, 1111 Superior Avenue East, Suite 1350, Cleveland, OH 44114-3198
Tel: 216 623 0900 **Fax:** 216 623 0935

MCMAHON, DEGULIS, HOFFMAN & LOMBARDI LLP (Ohio)
The Caxton Building, Suite 650, Cleveland, OH 44115-1126
Tel: 216 621 1312 **Fax:** 216 621 0577

MCMANUS, SCHOR, ASMAR & DARDEN (District of Columbia)
1301 Conneticut Avenue North West, Suite 600, Washington, DC, DC 20036
Tel: 202 296 9260 **Fax:** 202 659 3732

MCMORAN & O'CONNOR (New Jersey)
Fourth Floor, 766 Shrewsbury Avenue, Tinton Falls, NJ 07724
Tel: 732 758 8181

MCNAIR LAW FIRM PA (South Carolina)
1301 Gervais Street, PO Box 11390, Columbia, SC 29211
Tel: 803 799 9800 **Fax:** 803 799 9804

MCNAIR, LARSON & CARLSON LTD (North Dakota)
PO Box 2189, Fargo, ND 58108
Tel: 701 293 9190

MCNAMARA & MARTINEZ LLP (Colorado)
1640 East Eighteenth Avenue, Denver, CO 80218
Tel: 303 333 8700 **Fax:** 303 331 6967

MCNAMARA & MCNAMARA (Ohio)
Suite 1250, 88 East Broad Street, Columbus, OH 43215-3558
Tel: 614 228 6131 **Fax:** 614 228 6126

MCTEAGUE, HIGBEE, CASE, COHEN, WHITNEY & TOKER, PA (Maine)
4 Union Park, Topsham, ME 04086
Tel: 207 725 5581 **Fax:** 207 725 1090

MEARDON, SUEPPEL & DOWNER (Iowa)
122 South Linn Street, Iowa City, IA 52240
Tel: 319 338 9222 **Fax:** 319 338 7250

MECKLER, BULGER & TILSON (Illinois)
8200 Sears Tower, 233 S Wacker Drive, Chicago, IL 60606 6306
Tel: 312 474 7900 **Fax:** 312 474 7898

MEELHEIM, WILKINSON & MEELHEIM (Alabama)
2013 2nd Avenue North, Birmingham, AL 35203
Tel: 205 252 2500 **Fax:** 205 252 5838

MEITES, MULDER, BURGER & MOLLICA (Illinois)
Suite 1410, 208 S Lasalle Street, Chicago, IL 60604 1102
Tel: 312 263 0272 **Fax:** 312 263 2942

MELLI, WALKER, PEASE & RUHLY, S.C. (Wisconsin)
Suite 900, Ten East Doty, PO Box 1664, Madison, WI 53701
Tel: 608 257 4812 **Fax:** 608 258 7470

MELLO & KLESCH LLP (Vermont)
1795 Williston Road, South Burlington, VT 05403
Tel: 802 862 3200 **Fax:** 802 862 8384

MELVA HARMON - SOLE PRACTITIONER (Arkansas)
Stephens Building, 111 Center Street, Little Rock, AR 72201
Tel: 501 372 1133 **Fax:** 501 688 8477

MENDES & MOUNT, LLP (New York)
750 Seventh Avenue, New York, NY 10019-6829
Tel: 212 261 8000 **Fax:** 212 261 8750

MESSERMAN & MESSERMAN CO, LPA (Ohio)
4100 Key Tower, 127 Public Square, Cleveland, OH 44114
Tel: 216 574 9990 **Fax:** 216 574 9596

MESSING, RUDAVSKY & WELIKY PC (Massachusetts)
44 School Street, Boston, MA 02108
Tel: 617 742 0004

MEULEMAN & MILLER, LLP (Idaho)
960 Broadway Avenue, Suite 400, Boise, ID 83701
Tel: 208 342 6066 **Fax:** 208 336 9712

MEYER CAPEL (Illinois)
Athenaeum Building, 306 West Church Street, Champaign, IL 61826-6750
Tel: 217 352 1800 **Fax:** 217 352 9294

MEYER, HENDRICKS & BIVENS (Arizona)
3003 North Central Avenue, Suite 1200, Phoenix, AZ 85012-2915
Tel: 602 604 2200 **Fax:** 602 263 5333

MICHAEL BEST & FRIEDRICH LLP (Wisconsin)
100 East Wisconsin Avenue, Suite 330, Milwaukee, WI 53202-4108
Tel: 414 271 6560 **Fax:** 414 277 0656

MICHAEL J FLORIO (West Virginia)
333 East Main Street, Clarksburg, WV 26302
Tel: TBA

MIDDLETON REUTLINGER, P.S.C. (Kentucky)
2500 Brown and Williamson Tower, Louisville, KY 40202
Tel: 502 584 1135 **Fax:** 502 561 0442

MILBANK, TWEED, HADLEY & MCCLOY (New York)
1 Chase Manhattan Plaza, 47th Floor, New York, NY 10005
Tel: 212 530 5000 **Fax:** 212 530 5219

MILBERG WEISS BERSHAD HYNES & LERACH LLP (New York)
One Pennsylvania Plaza, New York, NY 10119-0165
Tel: 212 594 5300 **Fax:** 212 868 1229

MILES & STOCKBRIDGE PC (Maryland)
10 Light Street, Baltimore, MD 21202-1487
Tel: 410 727 6464 **Fax:** 410 385 3700

MILLER & CHEVALIER (District of Columbia)
655 Fifteenth Street North West, Suite 900, Washington, DC, DC 20005-5701
Tel: 202 626 5800 **Fax:** 202 628 0858

OTHER RECOMMENDED FIRMS

MILLER & MARTIN LLP (Tennessee)
1200 One Nashville Place, 150 Fourth Avenue North, Nashville, TN 37219
Tel: 615 244 9270 **Fax:** 615 256 8197

MILLER O'BRIEN (Minnesota)
One Financial Plaza, Suite 2400, Minneapolis, MN 55402
Tel: 612 333 5831 **Fax:** 612 342 2613

MILLER, BALIS & O'NEIL, PC (District of Columbia)
1140 Nineteenth Street NW, Suite 700, Washington, DC, DC 20036
Tel: 202 296 2960 **Fax:** 202 296 0166

MILLER, CANFIELD, PADDOCK AND STONE PLC (Michigan)
150 West Jefferson, Detroit, MI 48226-4415
Tel: 313 963 6420 **Fax:** 313 496 7500

MILLER, MORTON, CAILLAT & NEVIS (California)
50 West San Fernando, Suite 1300, San Jose, CA 95113-2413
Tel: 408 292 1765 **Fax:** 408 292 4484

MILLER, STRATVERT & TORGERSON, PA (New Mexico)
500 Marquette Avenue, NW, Suite 1100, Albuquerque, NM 87125
Tel: 505 842 1950 **Fax:** 505 243 4408

MILLISOR & NOBIL (Ohio)
9150 South Hills Boulevard, Suite 300, Cleveland, OH 44147-3599
Tel: 440 838 8000 **Fax:** 440 838 8805

MINER, BARNHILL & GALLAND (Illinois)
14 West Erie Street, Chicago, IL 60610
Tel: 312 751 1170 **Fax:** 312 751 1170

MINTZ LEVIN COHN FERRIS GLOVSKY AND POPEO PC (Massachusetts)
One Financial Center, Boston, MA 02111
Tel: 617 542 6000 **Fax:** 617 542 2241

MIRO WEINER & KRAMER, PC (Michigan)
38500 Woodward Avenue, Suite 100, PO Box 908, Bloomfield Hills, MI 48303-0908
Tel: 248 646 2400 **Fax:** 248 646 2681

MITCHELL HURST JACOBS & DICK (Indiana)
152 E Washington Street, Indianapolis, IN 46204
Tel: 317 633 7680 **Fax:** 317 633 7687

MITCHELL WILLIAMS SELIG GATES WOODYARD, PLLC (Arkansas)
425 West Capitol Avenue, Suite 1800, Little Rock, AR 72201-3525
Tel: 501 688 8800 **Fax:** 501 688 8807

MOCK, SCHWABE, WALDO, ELDER, REEVES & BRYANT (Oklahoma)
Fourteenth Floor, Two Leadership Square, 211 North Robinson Avenue, Oklahoma City, OK 73102
Tel: 405 235 1110 **Fax:** 405 235 0333

MODRALL, SPERLING, ROEHL, HARRIS & SISK, PA (New Mexico)
500 Fourth Street, NW, Bank of America Centre, Suite 1000, Albuquerque, NM 87103
Tel: 505 848 1800 **Fax:** 505 848 1889

MOEHRKE, MACKIE & SHEA, P.C. (Massachusetts)
137 Newbury Street, Boston, MA 02116
Tel: 617 266 5700 **Fax:** 617 266 5237

MOFFATT THOMAS BARRETT ROCK & FIELDS (Idaho)
101 South Capitol Boulevard, 10th Floor, PO Box 829, Boise, ID 83701
Tel: 208 345 2000 **Fax:** 208 385 5384

MONTGOMERY, MCCRACKEN, WALKER & RHOADS, LLP (Pennsylvania)
123 South Broad Street, Philadelphia, PA 19109
Tel: 215 772 1500 **Fax:** 215 772 7620

MOON, MOSS, MCGILL & SHAPIRO (Maine)
Ten Free Street, PO Box 7250, Portland, ME 04112-7250
Tel: 207 775 6001 **Fax:** 207 775 6407

MOORE & VAN ALLEN PLLC (South Carolina)
40 Calhoun Street, Suite 300, Charleston, SC 29401
Tel: 843 579 7000 **Fax:** 843 579 7099

MORGAN BROWN AND JOY LLP (Massachusetts)
One Boston Place, Boston, MA 02108-4472
Tel: 617 523 6666 **Fax:** 617 367 3125

MORGAN, LEWIS & BOCKIUS LLP (Pennsylvania)
1701 Market Street, Philadelphia, PA 19103-2921
Tel: 215 963 5000 **Fax:** 215 963 5299

MORRIS PICKERING & SANNER (Nevada)
900 Bank of America Plaza, 300 South Fourth Street, Las Vegas, NV 89101
Tel: 702 474 9400 **Fax:** 702 474 9422

MORRIS, JAMES, HITCHENS & WILLIAMS, LLP (Delaware)
222 Delaware Avenue, PO Box 2306, Wilmington, DE 19899-2306
Tel: 302 888 6800 **Fax:** 302 571 1750

MORRIS, LAING, EVANS, BROCK & KENNEDY, CHARTERED (Kansas)
Fourth Floor, 200 West Douglas, Wichita, KS 67202
Tel: 316 262 2671 **Fax:** 316 262 6226; 262 5991

MORRIS, MANNING & MARTIN, LLP (Georgia)
1600 Atlanta Financial Center, 3343 Peachtree Road North East, Atlanta, GA 30326
Tel: 404 233 7000 **Fax:** 404 504 5444

MORRIS, NICHOLS, ARSHT & TUNNELL (Delaware)
1201 North Market Street, PO Box 1347, Wilmington, DE 19899-1347
Tel: 302 658 9200 **Fax:** 302 658 3989

MOULTON, BELLINGHAM, LONGO & MATHER, PC (Montana)
Suite 1900 Sheraton Plaza, 27 North 27th Street, Billings, MT 59103
Tel: 406 248 7731 **Fax:** 406 248 7889

MOYER & BERGMAN, PLC (Iowa)
2720 First Avenue, N.E., Cedar Rapids, IA 52406
Tel: 319 366 7331 **Fax:** 319 366 3668

MR JERRY HIATT - SOLE PRACTITIONER (Hawaii)
65-1279 Kawaihae Road, Suite 204, Honolulu, HI 96825
Tel: 808 885 3400 **Fax:** 808 885 6765

OTHER RECOMMENDED FIRMS

MS SUSAN ICHINOSE - SOLE PRACTITIONER (Hawaii)
701 Bishop Street, 1st Floor, Honolulu, HI 96813
Tel: 808 585 0333

MUCH SHELIST FREED DENENBERG AMENT & RUBENSTEIN, PC (Illinois)
200 North La Salle Street, Suite 2100, Chicago, IL 60601
Tel: 312 346 3100 **Fax:** 312 621 1750

MULLER MINTZ (Florida)
First Union Financial Boulevard, 200 Suth Biscayne Boulevard, Miami, FL 33131
Tel: 305 358 5500 **Fax:** 305 379 3802

MULLIKIN, LARSON & SWIFT (Wyoming)
Suite 200, 155 East Pearl Street, P.O. Box 4099, Jackson, WY 83001
Tel: 307 733 3923 **Fax:** 307 733 3947

MUNGER, TOLLES & OLSON (California)
355 South Grand Avenue, 35th Floor, Los Angeles, CA 90071-1560
Tel: 213 683 9100 **Fax:** 213 687 3702

MURANE & BOSTWICK, L.L.C. (Wyoming)
201 North Wolcott, Casper, WY 82601
Tel: 307 234 9345 **Fax:** 307 237 5110

MURPHY & SHAFFER (Maryland)
36 South Charles Street, Suite 1400, Baltimore, MD 21201-3109
Tel: 410 783 7000 **Fax:** 410 783 8823

MURPHY, GOLDAMMER & PRENDERGAST (South Dakota)
101 North Phillips Avenue, Suite 604, P.O. Box 5015, Sioux Falls, SD 57117-5015
Tel: 605 331 2975 **Fax:** 605 331 6473

MURTAGH & CAHILL (Pennsylvania)
110 Swinderman Road, Wexford, PA 15090
Tel: 412 935 7555

MURTHA CULLINA LLP (Connecticut)
CityPlace I, 29th Floor, 185 Asylum Street, Hartford, CT 06103
Tel: 860 240 6000 **Fax:** 860 240 6150

MYERS OLIVER & PRICE (New Mexico)
1401 Central North West, Albuquerque, NM 87104
Tel: 505 247 9080 **Fax:** 505 247

NAGIN GALLOP FIGUERDO (Florida)
3225 Aviation Avenue, Suite 301, Coconut Grove, FL 33133
Tel: 305 854 5353 **Fax:** 305 854 5351

NAKAMURA, QUINN & WALLS (Alabama)
Suite 300, Landmark Center, 2100 First Avenue North, Birmingham, AL 35203-4226
Tel: 205 323 8504 **Fax:** 205 323 1102

NEAL GERBER & EISENBERG (Illinois)
Two North La Salle Street, Suite 2200, Chicago, IL 60602
Tel: 312 269 8000 **Fax:** 312 269 1747

NEEDLE & ROSENBERG (Georgia)
The Candler Building, 127 Peachtree Street, North East, Atlanta, GA 30303-1811
Tel: 404 688 0700 **Fax:** 404 688 9880

NEXSEN PRUET JACOBS & POLLARD, LLC (South Carolina)
1441 Main Street, 15th Floor, P.O. Drawer 2426, Columbia, SC 29202
Tel: 803 771 8900 **Fax:** 803 253 8277

NICHOLS KASTER & ANDERSON PLLP (Minnesota)
4644 IDS Center, 80 South 8th Street, Minneapolis, MN 55402-2113
Tel: 612 338 1919 **Fax:** 612 338 4878

NICKENS, LAWLESS & FLACK LLP (Texas)
327 Congress Avenue, Suite 490, Austin, TX 78701
Tel: 512 472 3067

NICOLETTI HORNIG CAMPISE SWEENEY & PAIGE (New York)
Wall Street Plaza, 88 Pine Street, New York, New York, NY 10005-1801
Tel: 212 220 3830 **Fax:** 212 220 3780

NILLES, HANSEN & DAVIES, LTD. (North Dakota)
1800 Radisson Tower, PO Box 2626, Fargo, ND 58108
Tel: 701 237 5544 **Fax:** 701 280 0762

NING LILLY & JONES (Hawaii)
Suite 700 Ocean View Center, 707 Richards Street, PO Box 3439, Honolulu, HI 96801
Tel: 808 528 1100 **Fax:** 808 531 2415

NIRO, SCAVONE, HALLER & NIRO (Illinois)
181 West Madison, Suite 4600, Chicago, IL 60602-4515
Tel: 312 236 0733 **Fax:** 312 236 3137

NOEDING & MOODY PC (New Mexico)
San Mateo Corporate Center, 4300 San Mateo Boulevard North East, Suite B260, Albuquerque, NM 87110
Tel: 505 878 0515 **Fax:** 505 878 0398

NORMAN, HANSON & DETROY, LLC (Maine)
Fifth Floor, 415 Congress Street, PO Box 4600, Portland, ME 04112
Tel: 207 774 7000 **Fax:** 207 775 0806

NOURSE & BOWLES LLP (New York)
One Exchange Plaza at 55 Broadway, New York, NY 10006
Tel: 212 952 6200 **Fax:** 212 952 0345

NUNGESSER & HILL (New Hampshire)
56 State Route 25, Meredith, NH 03253
Tel: 603 279 8182 **Fax:** 603 279 3096

NUTTER, MCCLENNEN & FISH, LLP (Massachusetts)
One International Place, Boston, MA 02110-2699
Tel: 617 439 2000 **Fax:** 617 973 9748

NYEMASTER, GOODE, VOIGTS, WEST, HANSELL & O'BRIEN, PC (Iowa)
700 Walnut, Suite 1600, Des Moines, IA 50309
Tel: 515 283 3100 **Fax:** 515 283 3108

OTHER RECOMMENDED FIRMS

O' NEILL CRAWFORD & GREEN PC (Vermont)
159 Bank Street, PO Box 5359, Burlington, VT 05402-5359
Tel: 802 865 4700

OBERMAYER, REBMANN, MAXWELL & HIPPEL LLP (Pennsylvania)
One Penn Center, 19th Floor, 1617 John F. Kennedy Boulevard, Philadelphia, PA 19103-1895
Tel: 215 665 3000 **Fax:** 215 665 3165

O'BRIEN & GREVE PC (Iowa)
2322 East Kimberly Road, Davenport, IA 52807
Tel: 563 355 6060 **Fax:** 563 355 6666

O'DONNELL & SHAEFFER (California)
633 West Fifth Street, Suite 1700, Los Angeles, CA 90071
Tel: 213 532 2000 **Fax:** 213 532 2020

OERTEL, HOFFMAN, FERNANDEZ & COLE PA (Florida)
301 South Bronough Street, Fifth Floor, PO Box 1110, Tallahassee, FL 32301-1110
Tel: 850 521 0700 **Fax:** 850 521 0720

OGDEN NEWELL & WELCH (Kentucky)
1700 Citizens Plaza, 500 West Jefferson Street, Louisville, KY 40202
Tel: 502 582 1601 **Fax:** 502 581 9564

OGG, CORDES, MURPHY & IGNELZI (Pennsylvania)
245 Fort Pitt Boulevard, Pittsburgh, PA 15222-1511
Tel: 412 471 8500 **Fax:** 412 471 8503

OGLETREE, DEAKINS, NASH, SMOAK & STEWART, PC (South Carolina)
The Ogletree Building, 300 North Main Street, Greenville, SC 29601
Tel: 864 271 1300 **Fax:** 864 235 8806

OHNSTAD TWICHELL PC (North Dakota)
901 Thirteenth Avenue East, Second Floor, PO Box 458, Fargo, ND 58078
Tel: 701 282 3249 **Fax:** 701 282 0825

O'KEEFE ASHENDEN LYONS & WARD (Illinois)
30 North LaSalle, Suite 4100, Chicago, IL 60602
Tel: 312 621 0400 **Fax:** 312 621 0297

OLDFATHER & MORRIS (Kentucky)
1330 South Third Street, Louisville, KY 40208
Tel: 502 637 7200 **Fax:** 502 637 3999

OLSON BURNS LEE PC (North Dakota)
PO box 1180, Minot, ND 58702
Tel: 701 839 1740

O'MELVENY & MYERS LLP (California)
400 South Hope Street, Los Angeles, CA 90071-2899
Tel: 213 430 6000 **Fax:** 213 430 6407

OPPENHEIMER WOLFF & DONNELLY LLP (California)
2029 Century Park East, Suite 3800, Los Angeles, CA 90067
Tel: 310 788 5000 **Fax:** 310 277 1297

ORLOFF, LOWENBACH, STIFELMAN & SIEGEL (New Jersey)
101 Eisenhower Parkway, Roseland, NJ 07068
Tel: 973 622 6200 **Fax:** 973 622 3073

ORR & RENO, PA (New Hampshire)
One Eagle Square, PO Box 3550, Concord, NH 03302
Tel: 603 224 2381 **Fax:** 603 224 2318

OSBORN MALEDON, PA (Arizona)
2929 North Central Avenue, Suite 2100, Phoenix, AZ 85012
Tel: 602 640 9000 **Fax:** 602 640 9050

OSHIMA, CHUN, FONG & CHUNG (Hawaii)
Davies Pacific Center, Fourth Floor, 841 Bishop Street, Honolulu, HI 96813
Tel: 808 528 4200 **Fax:** 808 531 8466

OTTEN, JOHNSON, ROBINSON, NEFF & RAGONETTI, PC (Colorado)
950 Seventeenth Street, 16th Floor, Denver, CO 80202
Tel: 303 825 8400 **Fax:** 303 825 6525

OTTERBOURG, STEINDLER, HOUSTON & ROSEN (New York)
230 Park Avenue, New York, NY 10169
Tel: 212 661 9100 **Fax:** 212 682 6104

OUTTEN & GOLDEN LLP (New York)
1740 Broadway, 25th Floor, New York, NY 10019
Tel: 212 245 1000 **Fax:** 212 977 4005

OWENS & TURNER, PC (Alaska)
1500 West 33rd Avenue, Suite 200, Anchorage, AK 99503-3502
Tel: 907 276 3963 **Fax:** 907 277 3695

OXFELD COHEN (New Jersey)
50 Commerce Street, Newark, NJ 07102
Tel: 973 642 0161 **Fax:** 973 802 1055

PACKMAN, NEUWAHL & ROSENBERG (Florida)
1500 San Remo Avenue, Suite 125, Coral Gables, FL 33146
Tel: 305 665 3311 **Fax:** 305 665 1244

PALMER & DODGE (Massachusetts)
11 Huntington Avenue At Prudential Center, Boston, MA 02199 7613
Tel: 617 239 0100 **Fax:** 617 227 4420

PAPPAS METCALF JENKS AND MILLER (Florida)
200 West Forsyth, Suite 1400, Jacksonville, FL 32202
Tel: 904 353 1980 **Fax:** 904 353 5217

PARKER, HUDSON, RAINER & DOBBS LLP (Georgia)
1500 Marquis Two Tower, 285 Peachtree Center Avenue North East, Atlanta, GA 30303
Tel: 404 523 5300 **Fax:** 404 522 8409

PARKER, POE, ADAMS & BERNSTEIN LLP (North Carolina)
Three First Union Center, 401 South Tryon Street, Suite 3000, Charlotte, NC 28202
Tel: 704 372 9000 **Fax:** 704 334 4706

PARKS, CHESIN, WALBERT & MILLER (Georgia)
26th Floor, 75 Fourteenth Street, Atlanta, GA 30309
Tel: 404 873 8000 **Fax:** 404 873 8050

PARR WADDOUPS BROWN GEE & LOVELESS (Utah)
Suite 1300, 185 South State Street, Salt Lake City, UT 84111
Tel: 801 532 7840 **Fax:** 801 532 7750

OTHER RECOMMENDED FIRMS

PARSONS BEHLE & LATIMER PC (Utah)
One Utah Center, 201 South Main Street, Suite 1800, Salt Lake City, UT 84145
Tel: 801 532 1234 **Fax:** 801 536 6111

PARTRIDGE SNOW & HAHN LLP (Rhode Island)
180 South Main Street, Providence, RI 02903
Tel: 401 861 8200 **Fax:** 401 861 8210

PAT NELSON-SOLE PRACTITIONER (Georgia)
PO Box 109, Athens, GA 30603
Tel: 706 549 5598

PATRICIA A FELCH - ATTORNEY AT LAW (Illinois)
1510 Main Street, Evanston, IL 60202-1617
Tel: 847 475 8085 **Fax:** 847 475 8094

PATRICIA E ANDREWS - SOLE PRACTITIONER (Rhode Island)
170 Westminster Street, Providence, RI 02903
Tel: 401 421 0966

PATRICK E HACKER (Wyoming)
5198 Hoy Road, Cheyenne, WY 82009
Tel: 307 778 8844

PATRICK N. CHAPIN (Nevada)
2920 North Green Valley Parkway, Suite 421, Henderson, NV 89014
Tel: 702 433 8780

PATTERSON HARKAVY & LAWRENCE (North Carolina)
200 West Morgan Street, P.O. Box 27927, Raleigh, NC 27601
Tel: 919 755 1812

PATTISHALL, MCAULIFFE, NEWBURY, HILLIARD & GERALDSON (Illinois)
311 South Wacker Drive, Suite 5000, Chicago, IL 60606
Tel: 312 554 8000 **Fax:** 312 554 8015

PAUL A. BECK & ASSOCIATES (Pennsylvania)
Suite 100, 157 McFarland Road, Pittsburgh, PA 15216
Tel: 412 343 9700 **Fax:** 412 343 5787

PAUL, FRANK & COLLINS, PC (Vermont)
One Church Street, PO Box 1307, Burlington, VT 05402
Tel: 802 658 2311 **Fax:** 802 658 0042

PAUL, JOHNSON, PARK & NILES, ATTORNEYS AT LAW, A LAW CORPORATION (Hawaii)
Pacific Tower, Suite 1300, 1001 Bishop Street, Honolulu, HI 96813
Tel: 808 524 1212 **Fax:** 808 528 1654

PAUSTIAN & EVANS (Nevada)
300 South Fourth Street, Suite 710, Las Vegas, NV 89101
Tel: 702 382 6440 **Fax:** 702 384 9102

PEARCE & DURICK (North Dakota)
314 East Thayer Avenue, PO Box 400, Bismarck, ND 58502
Tel: 701 223 2890 **Fax:** 701 223 7865

PEARSON CHRISTENSEN LLP (North Dakota)
24 North Fourth Street, PO Box 5758, Grand Forks, ND 58201
Tel: 701 775 0521 **Fax:** 701 775 0524

PEMBERTON, SORLIE, RUFER & KERSHNER, PLLP (Minnesota)
Law Office Building, 110 North Mill Street, P.O. Box 866, Fergus Falls, MN 56538-0866
Tel: 218 736 5493 **Fax:** 218 736 3950

PENNIE & EDMONDS LLP (New York)
1155 Avenue of the Americas, New York, NY 10036-2711
Tel: 212 790 9090 **Fax:** 212 869 8864

PENNINGTON, MOORE, WILKINSON, BELL & DUNBAR, PA (Florida)
215 South Monroe Street, Second Floor, Tallahassee, FL 32301
Tel: 850 222 3533 **Fax:** 850 222 2126

PENNY NATHAN KAHAN & ASSOCIATES (Illinois)
Suite 1660, 208 South Lasalle St, Chicago, IL 60604-1103
Tel: 312 855 1660 **Fax:** 312 855 1431

PEPE & HAZARD LLP (Connecticut)
Goodwin Square, Hartford, CT 06103
Tel: 860 522 5175 **Fax:** 860 522 2796

PEPPER HAMILTON LLP (Pennsylvania)
3000 Two Logan Square, 18th and Arch Streets, Philadelphia, PA 19103-2799
Tel: 215 981 4000 **Fax:** 215 981 4750

PERKINS COIE LLP (Washington)
1201 Third Avenue, Seattle, WA 98101-3099
Tel: 206 583 8888 **Fax:** 206 583 8500

PERKINS SMITH & COHEN LLP (Massachusetts)
1 Beacon Street, Boston, MA 02108-3106
Tel: 617 854 4000 **Fax:** 617 854 4040

PERKINS, THOMPSON, HINCKLEY & KEDDY, P.A. (Maine)
One Canal Plaza, PO Box 426, Portland, ME 04112
Tel: 207 774 2635 **Fax:** 207 871 8026

PERRY, SHAPIRO, QUINDEL, SAKS, CHARLTON & LERNER (Wisconsin)
823 North Cass Street, Milwaukee, WI 53203-3405
Tel: 414 272 7400 **Fax:** 414 272 7450

PETERSON, YOUNG, PUTRA, FLETCHER, ZEDER, MASSONG & KNOPP (Washington)
1501 Fourth Avenue, Seattle, WA 98101-1609
Tel: 206 624 6800 **Fax:** 206 682 1415

PETRUCCELLI MARTIN & HADDOW LLP (Maine)
50 Monument Square, PO Box 17555, Portland, ME 04112-8555
Tel: 207 775 0200 **Fax:** 207 775 2360

PETTIETTE, ARMAND, DUNKELMAN, WOODLEY, BYRD & CROMWELL L.L.P. (Louisiana)
509 Market Street, Suite 200, PO Box 1786, Shreveport, LA 71101
Tel: 318 221 1800

PHIBBS & RESOR P.C. (Wyoming)
PO Box 1028, 330 East Snow King Avenue, Jackson, WY 83001
Tel: 307 733 5004

OTHER RECOMMENDED FIRMS

PHILLIPS GARDILL KAISER & ALTMEYER (West Virginia)
61 Fourteenth Street, Wheeling, WV 26003
Tel: 304 232 6810

PHILLIPS MCFALL MCCAFFREY MCVAY & MURRAH, P.C. (Oklahoma)
One Leadership Square, 12th Floor, 211 North Robinson, Oklahoma City, OK 73102
Tel: 405 235 4100 **Fax:** 405 235 4133

PILL & PILL (West Virginia)
1444 Edwin Miller Boulevard, Martinsburg, WV 25401
Tel: 304 263 4971 **Fax:** 304 267 5840

PIRCHER, NICHOLS & MEEKS (California)
1925 Century Park East, 17th Floor, Los Angeles, CA 90067
Tel: 310 201 8900 **Fax:** 310 201 8922

PITNEY, HARDIN, KIPP & SZUCH LLP (New Jersey)
Park Avenue at Morris County, PO Box 1945, Morristown, NJ 07962
Tel: 973 966 6300 New York City: 212 687 6000 **Fax:** 642014 973 966 1550

PITT DOWTY MCGEHEE & MIRER (Michigan)
Washington Square Plaza, 306 South Washington, Sixth Floor, Royal Oak, MI 48067
Tel: 248 398 9800 **Fax:** 248 398 9804

PODHURST, ORSECK, JOSEFSBERG, EATON, MEADOW, OLIN & PERWIN (Florida)
Suite 800 City National Bank Building, 25 West Flagler Street, Miami, FL 33130-1780
Tel: 305 358 2800 **Fax:** 305 358 2382

POLSINELLI SHALTON & WELTE, A PROFESSIONAL CORPORATION (Missouri)
700 West 47th Street, Suite 1000, Kansas City, MO 64112
Tel: 816 753 1000 **Fax:** 816 753 1536

POORE, ROTH & ROBINSON, P.C. (Montana)
1341 Harrison Avenue, PO Box 2000, Butte, MT 59702
Tel: 406 497 1200 **Fax:** 406 782 0043

PORTER & HEDGES, LLP (Texas)
Bank of America Center, 700 Louisiana Street, 35th Floor, Houston, TX 7700277210-4744
Tel: 713 226 0600 **Fax:** 713 228 1331

PORTER WRIGHT MORRIS & ARTHUR (District of Columbia)
1667 K Street NW, Suite 1100, Washington, DC, DC 20006-1605
Tel: 202 778 3000 **Fax:** 202 778 3063

POSTNER & RUBIN (New York)
17 Battery Place, New York, NY 10004
Tel: 212 269 2510 **Fax:** 212 425 0968

POTTER ANDERSON & CORROON LLP (Delaware)
Hercules Plaza, 1313 North Market Street, Wilmington, DE 19899-0951
Tel: 302 984 6000 **Fax:** 302 658 1192

POWELL, GOLDSTEIN, FRAZER & MURPHY LLP (District of Columbia)
1001 Pennsylvania Avenue North West, Sixth Floor, Washington, DC, DC 20004
Tel: 202 347 0066 **Fax:** 202 624 7222

POYNER & SPRUILL L.L.P. (North Carolina)
3600 Glenwood Avenue, PO Box 10096, Raleigh, NC 27605
Tel: 919 783 6400 **Fax:** 919 783 1075

PRESTON GATES & ELLIS LLP (Washington)
701 Fifth Avenue, Suite 5000, Seattle, WA 98104-7078
Tel: 206 623 7580 **Fax:** 206 623 7022

PRETI, FLAHERTY, BELIVEAU, PACHIOS & HALEY, LLC (Maine)
One City Center, PO Box 9546, Portland, ME 04112
Tel: 207 791 3000 **Fax:** 207 791 3111

PRIDDY, EISENBERG, MILLER & MEADE (Kentucky)
802 Republic Building, 429 West Muhammad Ali Boulevard, Louisville, KY 40202
Tel: 502 569 2888

PROSKAUER ROSE LLP (New York)
1585 Broadway, New York, NY 10036-8299
Tel: 212 969 3000 **Fax:** 212 969 2900

PYLE ROME LICHTEN & EHRENBERG (Massachusetts)
18 Tremont Street, suite 500, Boston, MA 02108
Tel: 617 367 7200 **Fax:** 617 367 4820

QUARLES & BRADY LLP (Wisconsin)
411 East Wisconsin Avenue, Suite 2040, Milwaukee, WI 53202
Tel: 414 277 5000 **Fax:** 414 271 3552

RALSTON POPE & DIEHL LLC (Kansas)
2913 Southwest Maupin Lane, Topeka, KS 66614-4139
Tel: 785 273 8002 **Fax:** 785 273 0744

RAMSAY, BRIDGFORTH, HARRELSON & STARLING LLP (Arkansas)
Eleventh Floor, Simmons First National Building, 501 Main Street, Post Office Box 8509, Pine Bluff, AR 71611-8509
Tel: 870 535 9000 **Fax:** 870 535 8544

RANDALL G. WELLS (Louisiana)
6541 Sheffield Avenue, Baton Rouge, LA 70806
Tel: 225 928 5157

RANSON LAW OFFICES (West Virginia)
Bank One Center, Charleston, WV 25301
Tel: 304 345 1990

RAPAPORT & RAPAPORT (Massachusetts)
One Bowdoin Square, Boston, MA 02114-2925
Tel: 617 747 7600 **Fax:** 617 747 7601

RATNER & PRESTIA (Pennsylvania)
Suite 301, One Westlakes Berwyn, PO Box 980, Valley Forge, PA 19482
Tel: 610 993 4204 **Fax:** 610 407 0701

OTHER RECOMMENDED FIRMS

RAVICH MEYER KIRKMAN MCGRATH & NAUN PC (Minnesota)
4545 IDS Center, 80 South Eighth Street, Minneapolis, MN 55404
Tel: 612 332 8511 **Fax:** 612 332 8302

RAY, QUINNEY & NEBEKER PC (Utah)
79 South Main Street, Suite 400, Salt Lake City, UT 84145
Tel: 801 532 1500 **Fax:** 801 532 7543

RAYNES, MCCARTY, BINDER, ROSS & MUNDY (Pennsylvania)
1845 Walnut Street, 20th Floor, Philadelphia, PA 19103
Tel: 215 568 6190 **Fax:** 215 988 0618

REAL PROPERTY LAW GROUP PLLC (Washington)
1218 Third Avenue, Suite 1900, Seattle, WA 98101
Tel: 206 625 1717 **Fax:** 206 374 2782

REBEIN BANGERTER PA (Kansas)
810 West Frontview, Dodge City, KS 67801
Tel: 620 227 8126

REBEN, BENJAMIN & MARCH (Maine)
97 India Street, Portland, ME 04112-4248
Tel: 207 874 4771 **Fax:** 207 772 6402

REBOUL, MACMURRAY, HEWITT, MAYNARD & KRISTOL (New York)
45 Rockefeller Plaza, New York, NY 10111
Tel: 212 841 5700 **Fax:** 212 841 5725

REED SMITH LLP (Pennsylvania)
435 Sixth Avenue, Pittsburgh, PA 1521915230-2009
Tel: 412 288 3131 **Fax:** 412 288 3063

REED WEITKAMP SCHELL & VICE PLLC (Kentucky)
500 West Jefferson, Suite 2400, Louisville, KY 40202
Tel: 502 589 1000 **Fax:** 502 562 2200

REEDER & SHUMAN (West Virginia)
PO Box 842, Morgantown, WV 26507
Tel: 304 292 8488

REINHART, BOERNER, VAN DEUREN, NORRIS & RIESELBACH, SC (Wisconsin)
1000 North Water Street, PO Box 514000, Milwaukee, WI 53203
Tel: 414 298 1000 **Fax:** 414 298 8097

REITMAN PARSONNET PC (New Jersey)
744 Broad Street, Suite 1807, Newark, NJ 07102
Tel: 973 642 0885 **Fax:** 973 642 0946

RICCOLO & BAKER PC (Iowa)
APAC Building, Suite 1140, 425 Second Street South East, Cedar Rapids, IA 52401
Tel: 319 365 9200

RICHARD R. WIER, JR., P.A. (Delaware)
1220 Market Street, Suite 600, Wilmington, DE 19801
Tel: 302 888 3222 **Fax:** 302 888 3225

RICHARD S. SEGERBLOM (Nevada)
704 South 9th Street, Las Vegas, NV 89101
Tel: 702 388 9600

RICHARDS LAYTON & FINGER (Delaware)
One Rodney Place, PO Box 551, Wilmington, DE 19899-1328
Tel: 302 658 6541 **Fax:** 302 658 6548

RICHMAN GREER WEIL BRUMBAUGH MIRABITO & CHRISTENSEN (Florida)
Miami Center, Tenth Floor, 201 Biscayne Boulevard, Miami, FL 33131
Tel: 305 373 4000 **Fax:** 305 373 4099

RIDDELL WILLIAMS PS (Washington)
1001 Fourth Avenue Plaza, Suite 4500, Seattle, WA 98154
Tel: 206 624 3600 **Fax:** 206 389 1708

RIDER, BENNETT, EGAN & ARUNDEL, LLP (Minnesota)
333 South Seventh Street, Suite 2000, Minneapolis, MN 55402
Tel: 612 340 7951 **Fax:** 612 340 7900

RIEGELS CAMPOS & KENYON (California)
2500 Venture Oaks Way, Suite 220, Sacramento, CA 95833
Tel: 916 779 7114 **Fax:** 916 779 7120

RIKER, DANZIG, SCHERER, HYLAND & PERRETTI LLP (New Jersey)
Headquarters Plaza, One Speedwell Avenue, Morristown, NJ 07962
Tel: 973 538 0800 **Fax:** 973 538 1984

RINEHART ROBBLEE HANNAH (Washington)
1620 Metropolitan Park Building, 1100 Olive Way, Seattle, WA 98101
Tel: 206 467 6700 **Fax:** 206 467 7589

ROBEIN URANN & LURYE A PROFESSIONAL LAW CORPORATION (Louisiana)
2540 Severn Avenue, Suite 400, PO Box 6768, Metairie, LA 70009-6768
Tel: 504 885 9994

ROBERT E PANOFF PA (Florida)
Suite 106, 9400 South Dadeland Boulevard, Miami, FL 33156
Tel: 305 670 6547 **Fax:** 305 670 6548

ROBERT M. KNIGHT (Montana)
526 East Front Street, PO Box 8899, Missoula, MT 59807-8899
Tel: 406 721 5440 **Fax:** 406 721 8644

ROBERT WEISBERG - SOLE PRACTITIONER (Florida)
1450 Madruga Avenue, Suite 209, Coral Gables, FL 33146
Tel: 305 666 6095

ROBERTS & HOLLAND LLP (New York)
Worldwide Plaza, 825 Eighth Avenue, New York, NY 10019-7416
Tel: 212 903 8700 **Fax:** 212 974 3059

ROBINS KAPLAN MILLER & CIRESI (Minnesota)
2800 LaSalle Plaza, 800 LaSalle Avenue, Minneapolis, MN 55402
Tel: 612 349 8500 **Fax:** 612 339 4181

ROBINSON & COLE LLP (Connecticut)
280 Trumbull Street, Hartford, CT 06103
Tel: 860 275 8200 **Fax:** 860 275 8299

ROBINSON & MCELWEE PLLC (West Virginia)
600 United Center, 500 Virginia Street East, Charleston, WV 25326
Tel: 304 344 5800 **Fax:** 304 344 9566

If you can't find a firm here, see full profiles (pages 759-907)

OTHER RECOMMENDED FIRMS

ROBINSON, BRADSHAW & HINSON, P.A. (North Carolina)
101 North Tryon Street, Suite 1900, Charlotte, NC 28246
Tel: 704 377 2536 **Fax:** 704 378 4000

ROBISON, BELAUSTEGUI, SHARP & LOW (Nevada)
71 Washington Street, Reno, NV 89503
Tel: 775 329 3151 **Fax:** 775 329 7941

RODEY, DICKASON, SLOAN, AKIN & ROBB, PA (New Mexico)
201 Third Street North West, Suite 2200, Albuquerque, NM 87102
Tel: 505 765 5900 **Fax:** 505 768 7395

RODGERS, POWERS & SCHWARTZ (Massachusetts)
30 Federal Street, Boston, MA 02110
Tel: 617 482 7771 **Fax:** 617 338 1923

ROETZEL & ANDRESS, A LEGAL PROFESSIONAL ASSOCIATION (Ohio)
222 South Main Street, Akron, OH 44308
Tel: 330 376 2700 **Fax:** 330 376 4577

ROGER K DOOLITTLE & RICHARD REHFELT (Mississippi)
Briarwood One Building, Suite 500, 460 Briarwood Drive, Jackson, MS 39206-3057
Tel: + 601 957 9777

ROGERS & HARDIN (Georgia)
229 Peachtree Street, 2700 International Tower, Atlanta, GA 30303-1601
Tel: 404 522 4700 **Fax:** 404 525 2224

ROGERS, TOWERS, BAILEY, JONES & GAY, PA (Florida)
1301 Riverplace Boulevard, Suite 1500, Jacksonville, FL 32207
Tel: 904 398 3911 **Fax:** 904 396 0663

ROLLER & ALLENSWORTH (Texas)
620 Congress Avenue, Austin, TX 78701 -3229
Tel: 512 708 1250 **Fax:** 512 708 0519

RONEY & LABINGER (Rhode Island)
344 Wickenden Street, Providence, RI 02903
Tel: 401 421 9794 **Fax:** 491 421 0132

ROSE LAW FIRM (Arkansas)
120 East Fourth Street, Little Rock, AR 72201-2893
Tel: 501 375 9131 **Fax:** 501 375 1309

ROSEMAN & KAZMIERSKI (Colorado)
1120 Lincoln Street, Suite 1607, Denver, CO 80203
Tel: 303 839 1771

ROSENTHAL, MONHAIT, GROSS & GODDESS, PA (Delaware)
919 Market Street, Suite 1401, Wilmington, DE 19899-1070
Tel: 302 656 4433 **Fax:** 302 658 7567

ROSS & HARDIES (Illinois)
Suite 2500, 150 North Michigan Avenue, Chicago, IL 60601
Tel: 312 558 1000 **Fax:** 312 750 8600

ROTHGERBER JOHNSON & LYONS LLP (Colorado)
One Tabor Center, 1200 17th Street, Suite 3000, Denver, CO 80202
Tel: 303 623 9000 **Fax:** 303 623 9222

ROTHMAN GORDON P.C (Pennsylvania)
Grant Building, Third Floor, Pittsburgh, PA 15219 2203
Tel: 412 338 1100 **Fax:** 412 281 7304

ROTHSTEIN, ROSENFELDT DOLIN & PANCIER (Florida)
300 Las Olas Place, 300 South East 2nd Street, Suite 860, Fort Lauderdale, FL 33301
Tel: 954 522 3456 **Fax:** 954 527 8663

ROUSE HENDRICKS GERMAN MAY PC (Missouri)
One Petticoat Lane Building, 1010 Walnut Street, Suite 400, Kansas City, MO 64106
Tel: 816 471 7700 **Fax:** 816 471 2221

RUBY & SCHOFIELD (California)
60 South Market Street, Suite 1500, San JosÈ, CA 95113
Tel: 408 998 8500 **Fax:** 408 998 8503

RUDDY, BRADLEY, KOLKHORST & REGES (Alaska)
PO Box 34338, Juneau, AK 99803
Tel: 907 789 0047 **Fax:** 907 789 0783

RUDEN, MCCLOSKY, SMITH, SCHUSTER & RUSSELL, PA (Florida)
200 East Broward Boulevard, PO Box 1900, Fort Lauderdale, FL 33302
Tel: 954 764 6660 **Fax:** 954 764 4996

RUDMAN & WINCHELL LLC (Maine)
84 Harlow Street, PO Box 1401, Bangor, ME 04402
Tel: 207 947 4501 **Fax:** 207 941 9715

RUDY, EXELROD & ZIEFF, LLP (California)
351 California Street, Suite 700, San Francisco, CA 94104
Tel: 415 434 9800 **Fax:** 415 434 0513

RUSHTON, STAKELY, JOHNSTON & GARRETT (Alabama)
184 Commerce Street, Montgomery, AL 36104
Tel: 334 834 8480 **Fax:** 334 262 6277

RUSING & LOPEZ, PLLC (Arizona)
6262 North Swan Road, Suite 200, Tucson, AZ 85718
Tel: 520 792 4800 **Fax:** 520 529 4262

RYAN & WHALEY (Oklahoma)
900 Robinson Renaissance, 119 North Robinson Avenue, Oklahoma City, OK 73102
Tel: 405 239 6040

SACKS MONTGOMERY (New York)
800 Third Avenue, New York, NY 10022
Tel: 212 355 4660 **Fax:** 212 593 7297

SAIBER SCHLESINGER SATZ & GOLDSTEIN, LLC (New Jersey)
One Gateway Center, Thirteenth Floor, Newark, NJ 07102-5311
Tel: 973 622 3333 **Fax:** 973 622 3349

OTHER RECOMMENDED FIRMS

SALES, TILLMAN & WALLBAUM (Kentucky)
1900 Waterfront Plaza, 325 Main Street, Louisville, KY 40202
Tel: 502 589 5600 **Fax:** 502 814 5500

SANTORO, DRIGGS, WALCH, KEARNEY, JOHNSON & THOMPSON (Nevada)
3773 Howard Hughes Parkway, Suite 290N, Las Vegas, NV 89109
Tel: 702 791 0308 **Fax:** 702 791 1912

SAUL EWING LLP (Pennsylvania)
Centre Square West, 1500 Market Street, 38th Floor, Philadelphia, PA 19102-2186
Tel: 215 972 7777 **Fax:** 215 972 7725

SAVAGE & SAVAGE (Rhode Island)
156 Airport Road, Warwick, RI 02889
Tel: 401 732 9500 **Fax:** 401 732 0166

SCHELL BRAY AYCOCK ABEL & LIVINGSTON PLLC (North Carolina)
Suite 1500 Renaissance Plaza, 230 North Elm Street, Greensboro, NC 27401
Tel: 336 370 8800 **Fax:** 336 370 8830

SCHIFF HARDIN & WAITE (Illinois)
6600 Sears Tower, 233 South Wacker Drive, Chicago, IL 60606-6473
Tel: 312 258 5500 **Fax:** 312 258 5600

SCHLEIER, JELLISON & SCHLEIER (Arizona)
3101 North Central Avenue, Suite 800, Phoenix, AZ 85012
Tel: 602 277 0157 **Fax:** 602 230 9250

SCHNADER HARRISON SEGAL & LEWIS LLP (Pennsylvania)
1600 Market Street, Suite 3600, Philadelphia, PA 19103-7286
Tel: 215 751 2000 **Fax:** 215 751 2205

SCHOTTENSTEIN, ZOX & DUNN (Ohio)
The Huntington Center, 41 South High Street, Columbus, OH 43215-6106
Tel: 614 462 2700 **Fax:** 614 462 5135

SCHRECK BRIGNONE (Nevada)
300 South Fourth Street, Suite 1200, Las Vegas, NV 89101
Tel: 702 382 2101 **Fax:** 702 382 8135

SCHULER MESSERSMITH DALY & LANSDOWNE (New Mexico)
4300 San Mateo North East, Suite B380, Albuquerque, NM 87110
Tel: 505 872 0800 **Fax:** 505 872 0900

SCHULTE ROTH & ZABEL LLP (New York)
919 Third Avenue, New York, NY 10022
Tel: 212 756 2000 **Fax:** 212 593 5955

SCHWABE, WILLIAMSON & WYATT, PC (Oregon)
Suites 1600-1900 Pacwest Center, 1211 SW Fifth Avenue, Portland, OR 97204
Tel: 503 222 9981 **Fax:** 503 796 2900

SCHWARTZ, BON, WALKER & STUDER, LLC (Wyoming)
141 South Center, Suite 505, Casper, WY 82601
Tel: 307 235 6681 **Fax:** 307 234 5099

SCHWARZWALD & MCNAIR (Ohio)
616 Penton Media Building, 1300 East Ninth Street, Cleveland, OH 44114-1503
Tel: 216 566 1600 **Fax:** 216 566 1814

SCROGGINS & WILLIAMSON (Georgia)
1500 The Candler Building, 127 Peachtree Street North East, Atlanta, GA 30303
Tel: 404 893 3880 **Fax:** 404 893 3886

SEARCY DENNEY SCAROLA BARNHART & SHIPLEY, PA (Florida)
2139 Palm Beach Lakes Boulevard, PO Drawer 3626, West Palm Beach, FL 33402 3626
Tel: 561 686 6300 **Fax:** 561 478 0754

SEBRIS BUSTO (Washington)
14205 SE 36th Street, Suite 325, Bellevue, WA 98006
Tel: 425 454 4233 **Fax:** 425 453 9005

SEGAL ROITMAN & COLEMAN (Massachusetts)
11 Beacon Street, suite 500, Boston, MA 02108
Tel: 617 742 0208 **Fax:** 617 742 2187

SEGAL, STEWART, CUTLER, LINDAY, JANES & BERRY (Kentucky)
1400 B Waterfront Plaza, 325 West Main Street, Louisville, KY 40202-4251
Tel: 502 568 5600 **Fax:** 502 581 1437

SENN LEWIS & VISCIANO (Colorado)
1801 California Street, Suite 4300, Denver, CO 80205
Tel: 303 298 1122

SERKLAND LAW FIRM, PC (North Dakota)
10 Roberts Street, PO Box 6017, Fargo, ND 58108
Tel: 701 232 8957 **Fax:** 701 237 4049

SEWARD & KISSEL (New York)
One Battery Park Plaza, New York, NY 10004
Tel: 212 574 1200 **Fax:** 212 480 8421

SEYFARTH SHAW (Illinois)
55 East Monroe Street, Suite 4200, Chicago, IL 60603-5803
Tel: 312 346 8000 **Fax:** 312 269 8869

SHAFT, REIS & SHAFT LTD (North Dakota)
Gate City Federal Building, P.O. Box 5116, Grand Forks, ND 58206-5116
Tel: 701 772 8156 **Fax:** 701 772 9564

SHANNON, GRACEY, RATLIFF & MILLER LLP (Texas)
777 Main Street, #3800, Fort Worth, TX 76102
Tel: 817 336 9333 **Fax:** 817 336 3735

SHAPIRO FUSSELL WEDGE SMOTHERMAN MARTIN & PRICE, LLP (Georgia)
One Midtown Plaza, Suite 1200, 1360 Peachtree Street, Atlanta, GA 30309-3214
Tel: 404 870 2200 **Fax:** 404 870 2222

SHAW PITTMAN (District of Columbia)
2300 North Street North West, Washington, DC, DC 20037
Tel: 202 663 8000 **Fax:** 202 663 8007

OTHER RECOMMENDED FIRMS

SHEA & GARDNER (District of Columbia)
1800 Massachusetts Avenue. N.W., Suite 800, Washington, DC, DC 20036
Tel: 202 828 2000 **Fax:** 202 828 2195

SHEEHEY FURLONG & BEHM PC (Vermont)
Gateway Square, 30 Main Street, Burlington, VT 05402
Tel: 802 864 9891 **Fax:** 802 864 6815

SHEMIN LAW FIRM (Arkansas)
214 West Dickson Street, Fayetteville, AR 72701-5221
Tel: 479 973 4442 **Fax:** 479 973 4443

SHEPPARD, MULLIN, RICHTER & HAMPTON LLP (California)
333 South Hope Street, 48th Floor, Los Angeles, CA 90071
Tel: 213 620 1780 **Fax:** 213 620 1398

SHER GARNER CAHILL RICHTER KLEIN MCALISTER & HILBERT, LLC (Louisiana)
909 Poydras Street, Twenty Eight Floor, New Orleans, LA 70112-1033
Tel: 504 299 2100 **Fax:** 504 299 2300

SHERARD & ROE (Tennessee)
Suite 2000, 424 Church Street, Nashville, TN 37219

SHERIN AND LODGEN (Massachusetts)
100 Summer Street, Boston, MA 02110
Tel: 617 646 2225

SHERMAN & HOWARD LLC (Colorado)
633 Seventeenth Street, Suite 3000, Denver, CO 80202
Tel: 303 297 2900 **Fax:** 303 298 0940

SHERRARD & ROE, PLC (Tennessee)
SunTrust Center, 20th Floor, 424 Church Street, Suite 2000, Nashville, TN 37219
Tel: 615 742 4200 **Fax:** 615 742 4539

SHIPMAN & GOODWIN LLP (Connecticut)
One American Row, Hartford, CT 06103
Tel: 860 251 5000 **Fax:** 860 251 5099

SHNEIDMAN, HAWKS & EHLKE (Wisconsin)
2175 Hampton, PO Box 2155, Madison, WI 53701-2155
Tel: 608 257 0400 **Fax:** 608 256 0236

SHUGHART THOMSON & KILROY PC (Missouri)
Twelve Wyandotte Plaza, 120 West 12th Street, Kansas City, MO 63105
Tel: 816 421 3355 **Fax:** 816 374 0509

SHULMAN, ROGERS, GANDAL, PORDY & ECKER, PA (Maryland)
11921 Rockville Pike, Third Floor, Rockville, MD 20852
Tel: 301 230 5200 **Fax:** 301 230 2891

SHUMAKER, LOOP & KENDRICK LLP (Ohio)
North Courthouse Square, 1000 Jackson, Toledo, OH 43624
Tel: 419 241 9000 **Fax:** 419 241 6894

SHUMAKER, LOOP & KENDRICK, LLP (Florida)
Suite 2800, 101 East Kennedy Boulevard, Tampa, FL 33602
Tel: 813 229 7600 **Fax:** 813 229 1660

SHUTTLEWORTH & INGERSOLL PLC (Iowa)
115 Third Street South East, Suite 500, PO Box 2107, Cedar Rapids, IA 52406
Tel: 319 365 9461 **Fax:** 319 365 8443

SHUTTS & BOWEN (Florida)
1500 Miami Centre, 201 South Biscayne Boulevard, Miami, FL 33131
Tel: 305 358 6300 **Fax:** 305 381 9982

SIEGEL, O'CONNOR, ZANGARI, O'DONNELL & BECK PC (Connecticut)
150 Trumbell Street, Hartford, CT 06103
Tel: 860 727 8900 **Fax:** 860 527 5131

SIEGFRIED, RIVERA, LERNER, DE LA TORRE & SOBEL, PA (Florida)
Suite 1102, 201 Alhambra Circle, Miami, FL 33134
Tel: 305 442 3334 **Fax:** 305 443 3292

SILLS CUMMIS RADIN TISCHMAN EPSTEIN & GROSS, A PROFESSIONAL CORPORATION (New Jersey)
One Riverfront Plaza, Newark, NJ 07102
Tel: 973 643 7000 **Fax:** 973 643 6500

SILVER GOLUB & TEITELL LLP (Connecticut)
184 Atlantic Street, Stamford, CT 06904
Tel: 203 325 4491 **Fax:** 203 325 3769

SIMMONS PERRINE ALBRIGHT & ELLWOOD P.L.C. (Iowa)
115 Third Street S.E., Suite 1200, Cedar Rapids, IA 52401
Tel: 319 366 7641 **Fax:** 319 366 1917

SIMPSON THACHER & BARTLETT (New York)
425 Lexington Avenue, New York, NY 10017
Tel: 212 455 2000 **Fax:** 212 455 2502

SIROTE & PERMUTT PC (Alabama)
2311 Highland Avenue South, PO Box 55727, Birmingham, AL 35205
Tel: 205 930 5100 **Fax:** 205 930 5101

SIVE PAGET & RIESEL PC (New York)
460 Park Avenue, New York, NY 10022
Tel: 212 421 2150

SMITH & KOTCHKA LTD (Nevada)
317 South Sixth Street, Las Vegas, NV 89101
Tel: 702 382 1707 **Fax:** 702 382 9370

SMITH & MCELWAIN (Iowa)
505 Fifth, Suite 530, PO Box 1194, Sioux City, IA 51102
Tel: 712 255 8094 **Fax:** 712 255 3825

SMITH & SMITH (Kentucky)
200 South Fifth Street, Louisville, KY 40202
Tel: 502 587 0761 **Fax:** 502 589 5345

SMITH JAMES ROWLETT & COHEN (North Carolina)
101 Soute Elm Street, Suite 310, P.O.Box 990, Greensboro, NC 27402
Tel: 336 274 2992

OTHER RECOMMENDED FIRMS

SMITH MACKINNON PA (Florida)
Suite 800 Citrus Center
(Orange Co.), 255 South Orange Avenue, Orlando, FL 32801
Tel: 407 843 7300 Fax: 407 843 2448

SMITH MOORE, LLP (North Carolina)
300 North Greene Street, First Union Tower, Suite 1400, Greensboro, NC 27420
Tel: 336 378 5200 Fax: 336 378 5400

SMITH MULLIN (New Jersey)
240 Claremont Avenue, Montclair, NJ 07042
Tel: 973 783 7607 Fax: 973 783 9894

SMITH PACHTER MCWHORTER & ALLEN (Virginia)
8000 Towers Crescent Drive, Suite 900, Vienna, va 22182
Tel: 703 847 6300 Fax: 703 847 6312

SMITH, CURRIE & HANCOCK LLP (Georgia)
2600 Harris Tower-Peachtree Center, 233 Peachtree Street, N.E., Atlanta, GA 30303
Tel: 404 521 3800 Fax: 404 688 0671

SMITH, GAMBRELL & RUSSELL, LLP (Georgia)
Suite 3100, Promenade II, 1230 Peachtree Street North East, Atlanta, GA 30309
Tel: 404 815 3500 Fax: 404 815 3509

SNELL & WILMER LLP (Arizona)
One Arizona Center, Phoenix, AZ 85004-2202
Tel: 602 382 6000 Fax: 602 382 6070

SOMMER BARNARD ACKERSON ATTORNEYS, PC (Indiana)
111 Monument Circle #4000, PO Box 44363, Indianapolis, IN 46204-5198
Tel: 317 630 4000 Fax: 317 236 9802

SOMMERS, SCHWARTZ, SILVER & SCHWARTZ PC (Michigan)
2000 Town Center, Suite 900, Southfield, MI 48075
Tel: 248 355 0300 Fax: 248 746 4001

SOWELL GRAY STEPP & LAFFITTE LLC (South Carolina)
1310 Gadsden Street, Columbia, SC 29201
Tel: 803 929 1400 Fax: 803 929 0300

SPATER GITTES & SCHULTE (Ohio)
723 Oak Street, Columbus, OH 43205
Tel: 614 222 4735 Fax: 614 221 9655

SPEAR, WILDERMAN, BORISH, ENDY, SPEAR & RUNCKEL (New Jersey)
36 Tanner Street, Haddonfield, NJ 08033
Tel: 856 428 5255

SPECTOR GADON & ROSEN, PC (Pennsylvania)
Seven Penn Center, 1635 Market Street, 7th Floor, Philadelphia, PA 19103
Tel: 215 241 8888 Fax: 215 241 8844

SPENCER FANE BRITT & BROWNE LLP (Missouri)
1000 Walnut Street, Suite 1400, Kansas City, MO 64106
Tel: 816 474 8100 Fax: 816 474 3216

SPERLING & SLATER (Illinois)
55 West Monroe Street, Suite 3300, Chicago, IL 60603-5010
Tel: 312 641 3200 Fax: 312 641 6492

SPIEHT BELL MCCURDY & NEWELL CO, LPA (Ohio)
2000 Huntington Building, 925 Euclid Avenue, Cleveland, OH 44115-1496
Tel: 216 696 4700 Fax: 216 696 2706

SPILMAN THOMAS & BATTLE, PLLC (West Virginia)
Spilman Center, 300 Kanawha Boulevard, East, Charleston, WV 25321
Tel: 304 340 3800 Fax: 304 340 3801

SPINK BUTLER CLAPP (Idaho)
PO Box 639, Boise, ID 83701
Tel: 208 388 1000 Fax: 208 388 1001

SPRADLING, ALPERN & GUM, L.L.P. (Oklahoma)
101 Park Avenue, Suite 700, Oklahoma City, OK 73102-7283
Tel: 405 272 0211 Fax: 405 236 0992

SPRAGUE & SPRAGUE (Pennsylvania)
The Wellington Building, Suite 400, 135 South Nineteenth Street, Philadelphia, PA 19103
Tel: 215 561 7681

SPRENGER & LANG, PLLC (District of Columbia)
1614 Twentieth Street, NW, Washington, DC, DC 20009
Tel: 202 265 8010 Fax: 202 332 6652

SPRIGGS & HOLLINGSWORTH (District of Columbia)
1350 I Street North West, Washington, DC, DC 20005
Tel: 202 898 5800 Fax: 202 682 1639

SPROUSE & FERGUSON (West Virginia)
Suite 100, 608 Virginia Street E, Charleston, WV 25301-2139
Tel: 304 342 9100 Fax: 304 342 9119

SQUIRE, SANDERS & DEMPSEY L.L.P (Ohio)
4900 Key Tower, 127 Public Square, Cleveland, OH 44114-1304
Tel: 216 479 8500 Fax: 216 479 8780

STAFFORD ROSENBAUM LLP (Wisconsin)
3 South Pinckney Street, Suite 1000, PO Box 1784, Madison, WI 53701
Tel: 608 256 0226 Fax: 608 259 2600

STANFORD FAGAN & GIOLITO (Georgia)
1401 Peachtree Street NE, Suite 238, Atlanta, GA 30309-3000
Tel: 404 897 1000 Fax: 404 897 1990

STANLEY & SCHADT (Alaska)
2909 Arctic Boulevard, Number 103, Anchorage, AK 99503
Tel: 907 376 4979 Fax: 907 562 0989

STANTON HUGHES DIANA CERRA MARIANI & MARGELLO (New Jersey)
10 Madison Avenue, Suite 402, Morristown, NJ 07960
Tel: 973 656 1600 Fax: 973 656 1600

STARK & GORDON (Michigan)
1020 Greene Street, Ann Arbor, MI 48109-1444
Tel: 248 542 3784

OTHER RECOMMENDED FIRMS

STATMAN HARRIS SIEGEL & EYRICH (Ohio)
2900 Chemed Center, 225 East Fifth Street, Cincinnati, OH 45202-2912
Tel: 513 621 2666 **Fax:** 513 241 8111

STEARNS WEAVER MILLER WEISSLER ALHADEFF & SITTERSON, P.A. (Florida)
Suite 2200 Museum Tower, 150 West Flagler Street, Miami, FL 33130
Tel: 305 789 3200 **Fax:** 305 789 3395

STEEG AND O'CONNOR LLC (Louisiana)
201 St Charles Avenue, Suite 3201, New Orleans, LA 70170
Tel: 504 582 1199 **Fax:** 504 582 1240

STEEL HECTOR & DAVIS LLP ()
200 South Biscayne Boulevard, SUITE 4000, FL 33131-2398
Tel: 305 577 7000 **Fax:** 305 577 7001

STEIN VOLINSKY & CALLAGHAN PA (New Hampshire)
One Barberry Lane, P.O.Box 2159, Concord, NH 03302-2159
Tel: 603 228 1109 **Fax:** 603 228 5326

STEINER DARLING & HUTCHINSON (Colorado)
303 E. 17th Avenue, Suite 850, Denver, CO 80203
Tel: 303 837 2380 **Fax:** 303 837 1968

STEPHEN BRISCHETTO - SOLE PRACTITIONER (Oregon)
520 SW Yamhill St, Suite 500, Portland, OR 97204
Tel: 503 223 5814 **Fax:** 503 228 1317

STEPHEN RAKUSIN PA (Florida)
1 East Broward Boulevard, Suite 1111, Fort Lauderdale, FL 33301-1843
Tel: 954 356 0496 **Fax:** 954 356 0416

STEPTOE & JOHNSON LLP (District of Columbia)
1330 Connecticut Avenue, NW, Washington, DC, DC 20036
Tel: 202 429 3000 **Fax:** 202 429 3902

STEPTOE & JOHNSON PLLC (West Virginia)
Bank One Center, Sixth Floor, P.O.Box 2190, Clarksburg, WV 26302-2190
Tel: 304 624 8377 **Fax:** 304 624 8384

STERNE KESSLER GOLDSTEIN & FOX (District of Columbia)
1100 New York Avenue N.W, Washington, DC, DC 20005
Tel: 202 371 2600 **Fax:** 202 371 2540

STEVEN NOVICK - SOLE PRACTITIONER (Oklahoma)
1717 South Cheyenne Avenue, Tulsa, OK 74119
Tel: 918 582 4441 **Fax:** 918 582 7830

STEVENS & LEE A PROFESSIONAL CORPORATION (Pennsylvania)
111 North Sixth Street, Reading, PA 19603-0679
Tel: 610 478 2000 **Fax:** 610 376 5610

STEWART ESTES & DONNELL (Tennessee)
Sun Trust Center, Suite 1401, 424 Church Street, Nashville, TN 37219-2392
Tel: 615 244 6538 **Fax:** 615 256 8386

STICHTER, RIEDEL, BLAIN & PROSSER (Florida)
110 East Madison Street, Suite 200, Tampa, FL 33602-4700
Tel: 813 229 0144 **Fax:** 813 229 1811

STINSON MORRISON HECKER LLP (Missouri)
2600 Grand Avenue, Kansas City, MO 64108
Tel: 816 691 2600 **Fax:** 816 474 4208

STITES & HARBISON PLLC (Kentucky)
400 West Market Street, Suite 1800, Louisville, KY 40202
Tel: 502 587 3400 **Fax:** 502 587 6391

STOEL RIVES LLP (Oregon)
900 SW Fifth Avenue, Suite 2600, Portland, OR 97204
Tel: 503 224 3380 **Fax:** 503 220 2480

STOKES BARTHOLOMEW EVANS & PETREE, P.A. (Tennessee)
SunTrust Center, 424 Church Street, Suite 2800, Nashville, TN 37219
Tel: 615 259 1450 **Fax:** 615 259 1470

STOKES LAWRENCE, PS (Washington)
800 Fifth Avenue, Suite 4000, Seattle, WA 98104-3179
Tel: 206 626 6000 **Fax:** 206 464 1496

STOLL STOLL BERNE LOKTING & SHLACHTER (Oregon)
209 Southwest Oak Street, Portland, OR 97204
Tel: 503 227 1600 **Fax:** 503 227 6840

STOLL, KEENON & PARK, LLP (Kentucky)
300 W. Vine Street, Suite 2100, Lexington, KY 40507
Tel: 859 231 3000 **Fax:** 859 253 1093; 859 253 1027

STONE PIGMAN WALTHER WITTMANN LLC (Louisiana)
546 Carondelet Street, New Orleans, LA 70130
Tel: 504 581 3200 **Fax:** 504 581 3361

STOWELL & FRIEDMAN (Illinois)
Suite 1400, 321 S Plymouth Court, Chicago, IL 60604-3912
Tel: 312 431 0888 **Fax:** 312 431 0228

STRASBURGER & PRICE LLP (Texas)
4300 NationsBank Plaza, 901 Main Street, Dallas, TX 75202
Tel: 214 651 4300 **Fax:** 214 651 4330

STRECKER & ASSOCIATES (Oklahoma)
2150 Mid-Continent Tower, 401 South Boston Avenue, Tulsa, OK 74103-4009
Tel: 918 582 1716 **Fax:** 918 582 1734

STRINDBERG & SCHOLNICK (Utah)
39 Exchange Place, Suite 60, Salt Lake City, UT 84111
Tel: 801 359 4169 **Fax:** 801 359 4313

STROOCK & STROOCK & LAVAN LLP (New York)
180 Maiden Lane, New York, NY 10038-4982
Tel: 212 806 5400 **Fax:** 212 806 6000

SUGARMAN & SUSSKIND (Florida)
2801 Ponce de Leon Boulevard, Suite 1640, Coral Gables, FL 33134
Tel: 305 529 2801 **Fax:** 305 447 8115

SUGARMAN, ROGERS, BARSHAK & COHEN, PC (Massachusetts)
101 Merrimac Street, Boston, MA 02114-4737
Tel: 617 227 3030

OTHER RECOMMENDED FIRMS

SULLIVAN & WORCESTER (Massachusetts)
One Post Office Square, Boston, MA 02109
Tel: 617 338 2800 **Fax:** 617 338 2880

SULLOWAY & HOLLIS, PLLC (New Hampshire)
9 Capitol Street, PO Box 1256, Concord, NH 03302
Tel: 603 224 2341 **Fax:** 603 224 2557; 226 2404; 226 2405; 228 0787

SUSAN K EGGUM, PC (Oregon)
621 SW Alder Street, Suite 600, Portland, OR 97205
Tel: 503 228 9607 **Fax:** 503 228 5790

SUSMAN GODFREY LLP (Texas)
Suite 5100, 1000 Louisiana Street, Houston, TX 77002-5096
Tel: 713 651 9366 **Fax:** 713 654 6666

SUSMAN, DUFFY & SEGALOFF P.C. (Connecticut)
55 Whitney Avenue, Sixth Floor, New Haven, CT 06510
Tel: 203 624 9830 **Fax:** 203 782 2889

SUTIN, THAYER & BROWNE (New Mexico)
Two Park Square, Suite 1000, 6565 Americas Parkway, N.E. (87110), Albuquerque, NM 87103
Tel: 505 883 2500 **Fax:** 505 888 6565

SWIDLER BERLIN SHEREFF FRIEDMAN LLP (District of Columbia)
3000 K Street North West, Suite 300, Washington, DC, DC 20007-5116
Tel: 202 424 7500 **Fax:** 202 424 7643

TAFT, STETTINIUS & HOLLISTER LLP (Ohio)
1800 Firstar Tower, 425 Walnut Street, Cincinnati, OH 45202
Tel: 513 381 2838 **Fax:** 513 381 0205

TAKAHASHI MASUI & VASCONCELLOS (Hawaii)
547 Halekauwila Street, Suite 206, Honolulu, HI 96813-5029
Tel: 808 526 3003

TAROLLI, SUNDHEIM, COVELL, TUMMINO & SZABO LLP (Ohio)
1111 Leader Building, 526 Superior Avenue, Cleveland, OH 44114
Tel: 216 621 2234 **Fax:** 216 621 4072

TAYLOR, COVINGTON & SMITH PA (Mississippi)
315 Tombigbee Street, PO Box 3509, Jackson, MI 39207-3509
Tel: 601 969 7817 **Fax:** 601 969 7826

TAYLOR, PORTER, BROOKS & PHILLIPS, LLP (Louisiana)
Bank One Centre, 8th Floor, 451 Florida Street, Baton Rouge, LA 70821
Tel: 225 387 3221 **Fax:** 225 346 8049

TESCHER GUTTER CHAVES JOSEPHER RUBIN RUFFIN & FORMAN PA (Florida)
Boca Corporate Center, 2101 Corporate Boulevard, Suite 107, Boca RatÛn, FL 33431-7343
Tel: 561 998 7847 **Fax:** 561 998 2642

TESTA, HURWITZ & THIBEAULT LLP (Massachusetts)
125 High Street, Boston, MA 02110
Tel: 617 248 7000 **Fax:** 617 248 7100

THACHER PROFFITT & WOOD (New York)
11 West 42nd Street, New York, NY 10036
Tel: 212 789 1200 **Fax:** 212 789 3500

THE BAYARD FIRM (Delaware)
222 Delaware Avenue, Suite 900, Wilmington, DE 19899
Tel: 302 655 5000 **Fax:** 302 658 6395

THE BAYLESS LAW FIRM (West Virginia)
1607 West Main Street, Princeton, WV 24740
Tel: 304 487 8707

THE JAMES LAW FIRM PC (Iowa)
630 Equitable Building, 604 Locust Street, Des Moines, IA 50309
Tel: 515 246 8484 **Fax:** 515 246 8767

THE KULLMAN FIRM A PROFESSIONAL LAW CORPORATION (Louisiana)
1600 Energy Centre, 1100 Poydras Street, PO Box 60118, New Orleans, LA 70160
Tel: 504 596 4105 **Fax:** 504 598 0004

THE LAW OFFICE OF CHRIS KEY (New Mexico)
500 Tijeras North West, Albuquerque, NM 87102
Tel: 505 242 9097 **Fax:** 505 843 7129

THE LAW OFFICE OF MARK J. SVONKIN P.C. (Connecticut)
18 North Main Street, West Hartford, CT 06107
Tel: 860 521 2811

THE LAW OFFICE OF WILLIAM E. SNEAD (New Mexico)
201 12th Street Noth West, Albuquerque, NM 87102
Tel: 505 842 8177 **Fax:** 505 842 8079

THE LAW OFFICES OF KATHLEEN CAHILL, LLC

THE LAW OFFICES OF KATHLEEN CAHILL, LLC (Maryland)
15 East Chesapeake Avenue, Baltimore, MD 21286
Tel: 410 321 6171

THE LAW OFFICES OF STEPHEN GODOFF (Maryland)
14 West Madison Street, Baltimore, MD 21201
Tel: 410 539 0717 **Fax:** 410 539 1906

THE LINESCH FIRM (Florida)
700 Bee Pond Road, Palm Harbor, FL 34683-1401
Tel: 727 786 0000 **Fax:** 727 786 0974

THE LOUTHIAN LAW FIRM PA (South Carolina)
The Marlboro Building, Suite 300, 1116 Blanding Street, P.O.Box 1299, Columbia, SC 29202
Tel: 803 454 1200 **Fax:** 803 256 6033

THE MEYERS LAW FIRM LC (Missouri)
222 West Gregory, Suite 340, Kansas City, MO 64114
Tel: 816 444 8500 **Fax:** 816 444 8508

THE POPHAM LAW FIRM PC (Missouri)
323 West 8th Street, Suite 200, Kansas City, MO 64105
Tel: 816 221 2288 **Fax:** 816 221 3999

OTHER RECOMMENDED FIRMS

THE TINNEY LAW FIRM (West Virginia)
Fourteenth Floor, 707 Virginia Street, Charleston, WV 25301
Tel: 304 720-3310

THOMAS J GAGLIARDO (SOLE PRACTITIONER) (Maryland)
8701 Georgia Avenue, Suite 500, Silver Spring, MD 20910-3723
Tel: 301 589 1900 **Fax:** 301 589 1985

THOMAS KAYDEN HORTSTEMEYER & RISLEY LLP (Georgia)
100 Galleria Parkway North West, Suite 1750, Atlanta, GA 30339
Tel: 770 933 9500 **Fax:** 770 951 0933

THOMAS N. LONG (Wyoming)
American National Bank Building, Suite 406, Cheyenne, WY 82003-0087
Tel: 307 635 0413 **Fax:** 307 635 0710

THOMPSON COBURN (Missouri)
One Mercantile Center, St Louis, MO 63101
Tel: 314 552 6000 **Fax:** 314 552 7000

THOMPSON, COE, COUSINS & IRONS, LLP (Texas)
200 Crescent Court, Eleventh Floor, Dallas, TX 75201
Tel: 214 871 8200 **Fax:** 214 871 8209

THOMPSON, ROLLINS, SCHWARTZ & BOROWSKI (Georgia)
750 Commerce Drive #100, Decatur, GA 30030
Tel: 404 377 7717 **Fax:** 404 377 5119

THOMPSON, SIZEMORE & GONZALEZ (Florida)
501 East.Kennedy Boulevard, Suite 1400, PO Box 639, Tampa, FL 33602
Tel: 813 273 0050 **Fax:** 813 273 0072

THORP REED & ARMSTRONG (Pennsylvania)
One Oxford Centre, Fourteenth Floor, Pittsburgh, PA 15219-1425
Tel: 412 394 7711

TIMOTHY S KELLEY - SOLE PRACTITIONER (Illinois)
55 East Washington Street, Suite 1441, Chicago, IL 60602
Tel: 312 641 3560 **Fax:** 312 641 3163

TINDALL BENNETT & SHOUP PC (Alaska)
508 West 2nd Avenue, Third Floor, Anchorage, AK 99501
Tel: 907 278 8533 **Fax:** 907 278 8536

TINKLER & BENNETT (New Mexico)
309 Johnson Street, Santa Fe, NM 87501
Tel: 505 986 0269 **Fax:** 505 982 6698

TOBIAS KRAUS & TORCHIA (Ohio)
414 Walnut Street, Suite 911, Cincinnati, OH 45202
Tel: 513 241 8137 **Fax:** 513 241 7863

TODD & WELD (Massachusetts)
28 State Street, Boston, MA 02109
Tel: 617 720 2626 **Fax:** 617 227 5777

TOM RILEY LAW FIRM PLC (Iowa)
4040 First Avenue North East, PO Box 998, Cedar Rapids, IA 52406-0998
Tel: 319 363 4040 **Fax:** 319 363 9789

TONKON TORP LLP (Oregon)
1600 Pioneer Tower, 888 SW Fifth Avenue, Portland, OR 97204
Tel: 503 221 1440 **Fax:** 503 274 8779

TORKILDSON, KATZ, FONSECA, JAFFE, MOORE & HETHERINGTON ATTORNEYS AT LAW, A LAW CORPORATION (Hawaii)
Amfac Building, 15th Floor, 700 Bishop Street, Honolulu, HI 96813
Tel: 808 523 6000 **Fax:** 808 523 6001

TOWNSEND AND TOWNSEND AND CREW LLP (California)
Two Embarcadero Center, Eighth Floor, San Francisco, CA 94111-3834
Tel: 415 576 0200 **Fax:** 415 576 0300

TRENAM, KEMKER, SCHARF, BARKIN, FRYE, O'NEILL & MULLIS PA (Florida)
2700 Bank of America Plaza, 101 East Kennedy Boulevard, Tampa, FL 33602
Tel: 813 223 7474 **Fax:** 813 229 6553

TRIPLETT, WOOLF & GARRETSON LLC (Kansas)
2959 North Rock Road, Suite 300, Wichita, KS 67226
Tel: 316 630 8100 **Fax:** 316 630 8101

TROUTMAN SANDERS LLP (District of Columbia)
401 Ninth Street North West, Suite 1000, Washington, DC, DC 20004-2134
Tel: 202 274 2950 **Fax:** 202 274 2994

TRUHLAR & TRUHLAR (Colorado)
1901 West Littleton Boulevard, Littleton, CO 80120
Tel: 303 794 2404

TSCHIDER & SMITH (North Dakota)
Professional Building, Suite 200, 418 East Rosser Avenue, Bismarck, ND 58501
Tel: 701 258 4000 **Fax:** 701 258 4001

TYLER COOPER & ALCORN LLP (Connecticut)
205 Church Street, PO Box 1936, New Haven, CT 06509
Tel: 203 784 8200 **Fax:** 203 789 2133

UGRIN, ALEXANDER, ZADICK & HIGGINS, PC (Montana)
2 Railroad Square, PO Box 1746, Great Falls, MT 59403
Tel: 406 771 0007 **Fax:** 406 452 9360

ULMER & BERNE LLP (Ohio)
Ninth Floor, Penton Media Building, 1300 East Ninth Street, Suite 900, Cleveland, OH 44114
Tel: 216 621 8400 **Fax:** 216 621 7488

UPTON AND HATFIELD, L.L.P. (New Hampshire)
10 Centre Street, PO Box 1090, Concord, NH 03302
Tel: 603 224 7791 **Fax:** 603 224 0320

VAN COTT, BAGLEY, CORNWALL & MCCARTHY (Utah)
50 South Main Street, Suite 1600, PO Box 45340, Salt Lake City, UT 84145
Tel: 801 532 3333 **Fax:** 801 534 0058

VAN HOY REUTLINGER ADAMS & DUNN (North Carolina)
737 East Boulevard, Charlotte, NC 28203
Tel: 704 375 6022 **Fax:** 704 375 6024

OTHER RECOMMENDED FIRMS

VAN NESS FELDMAN (District of Columbia)
Seventh Floor, 1050 Thomas Jefferson Street NW, Washington, DC, DC 20007
Tel: 202 298 1800 **Fax:** 202 338 2416

VARNUM, RIDDERING, SCHMIDT & HOWLETT LLP (Michigan)
Bridgewater Place, PO Box 352, Grand Rapids, MI 49501
Tel: 616 336 6000 **Fax:** 616 336 7000

VAUGHAN & MURPHY (Georgia)
233 Peachtree Street North East, Suite 700, Harris Tower, Atlanta, GA 30303
Tel: 404 577 6550 **Fax:** 404 577 0060

VEDDER, PRICE, KAUFMAN & KAMMHOLZ (Illinois)
222 North LaSalle Street, Chicago, IL 60601
Tel: 312 609 7500 **Fax:** 312 609 5005

VENABLE LLP (Maryland)
1800 Mercantitle Bank & Trust Building, 2 Hopkins Plaza, Baltimore, MD 21201
Tel: 410 244 7400 **Fax:** 410 244 7742

VENTURE LAW GROUP (California)
2775 Sand Hill Road, Menlo Park, CA 94025
Tel: 650 854 4488 **Fax:** 650 233 8386

VERCRUYSSE METZ & MURRAY (Michigan)
31780 Telegraph Road, Suite 200, Bingham Farms, MI 48226-3602
Tel: 248 540 8019 **Fax:** 248 540 8059

VERRILL & DANA, LLP (Maine)
One Portland Square, Portland, ME 04112
Tel: 207 774 4000 **Fax:** 207 774 7499

VLADECK, WALDMAN, ELIAS & ENGELHARD, P.C. (New York)
1501 Broadway, Suite 800, New York, NY 10036-5560
Tel: 212 403 7300

VOGEL, WEIR, HUNKE & MCCORMICK, LTD. (North Dakota)
502 First Avenue North, PO Box 1389, Fargo, ND 58107
Tel: 701 237 6983 **Fax:** 701 237 0847

VORYS, SATER, SEYMOUR AND PEASE LLP (Ohio)
52 East Gay Street, PO Box 1008, Columbus, OH 43216-1008
Tel: 614 464 6400 **Fax:** 614 464 6350

WADLEIGH, STARR & PETERS PLLC (New Hampshire)
95 Market Street, Manchester, NH 03101
Tel: 603 669 4140 **Fax:** 603 669 6018

WADSWORTH, DAVIS & WADSWORTH, PA (Florida)
203 North Gadsden Street, Suite One, PO Box 10529, Tallahassee, FL 32302-2529
Tel: 850 224 9037 **Fax:** 850 561 6119

WAIDE & ASSOCIATES (Mississippi)
P.O.Box 1357, 332 North Spring Street, Tupelo, MS 38802-1357
Tel: 662 842 7324 **Fax:** 601 842 8056

WALDER, HAYDEN & BROGEN P.A. (New Jersey)
5 Becker Farm Road, P.O. Box 901, Roseland, NJ 07068
Tel: 973 992 5300

WALLER LANSDEN DORTCH & DAVIS (Tennessee)
Nashville City Center, 511 Union Street, Suite 2100, Nashville, TN 37219
Tel: 615 244 6380 **Fax:** 615 244 6804

WALTER F KELLY - SOLE PRACTITIONER (Wisconsin)
158 North Broadway, Suite 600, Milwaukee, WI 53202-5367
Tel: 414 271 2400 **Fax:** 414 271 1511

WARD AND SMITH, P.A. (North Carolina)
1001 College Court, PO Box 867, New Bern, NC 28563
Tel: 252 672 5400 **Fax:** 252 672 5477

WARNER NORCROSS & JUDD LLP (Michigan)
900 Old Kent Building, 111 Lyon Street North West, Grand Rapids, MI 49503
Tel: 616 752 2000 **Fax:** 616 752 2500

WARREN & SINKLER (South Carolina)
Suite 340, 171 Church Street, PO Box 1254, Charleston, SC 29402
Tel: 843 577 0660 **Fax:** 843 577 6843

WATANABE ING KAWASHIMA & KOMEIJI (Hawaii)
First Hawaiian Center, 999 Bishop Street, 23rd Floor, Honolulu, HI 96813
Tel: 808 544 8300 **Fax:** 808 544 8399

WATKINS & EAGER PLLC (Mississippi)
The Emporium Building, Suite 300, 400 East Capitol Street, Jackson, MS 39205
Tel: 601 948 6470 **Fax:** 601 354 3623

WATKINS LUDLAM WINTER & STENNIS PA (Mississippi)
633 North State Street, PO Box 427, Jackson, MS 39205
Tel: 601 949 4900 **Fax:** 601 949 4804

WATT, TIEDER, HOFFAR & FITZGERALD, L.L.P. (Virginia)
7929 Westpark Drive, Suite 400, McLean, VA 22102
Tel: 703 749 1000 **Fax:** 703 893 8029

WEBB ZIESENHEIM LOGSDON ORKIN & HANSON, PC (Pennsylvania)
700 Koppers Bldg, 436 Seventh Ave, Pittsburgh, PA 15219-1818
Tel: 412 471 8815 **Fax:** 412 471 4094

WEINBERG, WHEELER, HUDGINS, GUNN & DIAL, LLC (Georgia)
999 Peachtree Street, North East, Suite 2700, Atlanta, GA 30309
Tel: 404 876 2700 **Fax:** 404 875 9433

WEISSMANN, WOLFF, BERGMAN, COLEMAN, SILVERMAN & HOLMES, LLP (California)
Suite 900, 9665 Wilshire Boulevard, Beverly Hills, CA 90212-2345
Tel: 310 858 7888 **Fax:** 310 550 7191

WELBAUM, GUERNSEY, HINGSTON, GREENLEAF & GREGORY LLP. (Florida)
Penthouse Suite, 901 Ponce de Leon Boulevard, Miami, FL 33134-3009
Tel: 305 441 8900 **Fax:** 305 441 2255

If you can't find a firm here, see full profiles (pages 759-907)

OTHER RECOMMENDED FIRMS

WESTON BENSHOOF ROCHEFORT RUBALCAVA MACCUISH LLP (California)
333 South Hope Street, 16th Floor, Los Angeles, CA 90071
Tel: 213 576 1000

WHATLEY DRAKE, LLC (Alabama)
2323 2nd Avenue North, Birmingham, AL 35203
Tel: 205 328 9576 **Fax:** 205 328 9669

WHITE & CASE LLP (New York)
1155 Avenue of the Americas, New York, NY 10036-2787
Tel: 212 819 8200 **Fax:** 212 354 8113

WHITE GOSS BOWERS MARCH SCHULTE & WEISENFELS, A PROFFESIONAL CORPARATION (Missouri)
4510 Belleview Avenue, Suite 300, Kansas City, MO 64111
Tel: 816 753 9200 **Fax:** 816 753 9201

WHITEFORD, TAYLOR & PRESTON LLP (Maryland)
7 Saint Paul Street, Baltimore, MD 21202
Tel: 410 347 8700 **Fax:** 410 752 7092

WHITEMAN, OSTERMAN & HANNA (New York)
One Commerce Plaza, Albany, NY 12260
Tel: 518 487 7600 **Fax:** 518 487 7777

WHITFIELD & EDDY, PLC (Iowa)
317 6th Avenue, Suite 1200, Locust at 6th, Des Moines, IA 50309
Tel: 515 288 6041 **Fax:** 515 246 1474

WHITING HAGG & HAGG (South Dakota)
601 W. Boulevard, P.O. Box 8008, Rapid City, SD 57709-8008
Tel: 605 348 1125 **Fax:** 605 348 9744

WHYTE HIRSCHBOECK DUDEK S.C. (Wisconsin)
One East Main Street, Suite 300, Madison, WI 53703
Tel: 608 258 7138 **Fax:** 608 258 7138

WHYTE HIRSCHBOECK DUDEK S.C. (Wisconsin)
111 E. Wisconsin Avenue, Suite 2100, Milwaukee, WI 53202
Tel: 414 273 2100 **Fax:** 414 223 5000

WICKWIRE GAVIN (Virginia)
8100 Boone Boulevard, Suite 700, Vienna, VA 22182
Tel: 703 790 8750

WIGGIN & DANA (Connecticut)
One Century Tower, New Haven, CT 06508
Tel: 203 498 4400 **Fax:** 203 782 2889

WIGGIN & NOURIE (New Hampshire)
20 Market Street, PO Box 808, Manchester, NH 03105-0808
Tel: 603 669 2211 **Fax:** 603 623 8442

WILDE & ASSOCIATES (Utah)
935E South Union Ave, Midvale, UT 84047-2393
Tel: 801 255 4774 **Fax:** 801 255 4846

WILEY REIN & FIELDING LLP (District of Columbia)
1776 K Street North West, 10th Floor, Washington, DC, DC 20006
Tel: 202 719 7000 **Fax:** 202 719 7049

WILLCOX & SAVAGE (Virginia)
One Commercial Place, Suite 1800, Norfolk, VA 23510
Tel: 757 628 5500 **Fax:** 757 628 5566

WILLIAM D PRESTON (Florida)
2937 Kerry Forest Parkway, Suite B-1, Tallahassee, FL 32309-6825
Tel: 850 668 4986 **Fax:** 850 668 6345

WILLIAM H. REINHARDT JR, PLC (Louisiana)
3421 North Causeway Boulevard, Suite 802, PO Box 7782, Metairie, LA 70002
Tel: 504 832 9984 **Fax:** 504 832 9988

WILLIAM JASON GROVES - SOLE PRACTITIONER (South Dakota)
909m St. Joseph Street, 3rd Floor, P.O.Box 8417, Rapid City, SD 57709
Tel: 605 341 4747

WILLIAMS MULLEN (Virginia)
Two James Center, 1021 East Cary Street, Richmond, VA 23218
Tel: 804 643 1991 **Fax:** 804 783 6507

WILLIAMS, PORTER, DAY & NEVILLE, P.C. (Wyoming)
159 North Wolcott Street, Suite 400, Casper, WY 82602
Tel: 307 265 0700 **Fax:** 307 266 2306

WILLIG, WILLIAMS & DAVIDSON (Pennsylvania)
24th Floor, 1845 Walnut Street, Philadelphia, PA 19103
Tel: 215 656 3600 **Fax:** 215 561 5135

WILSON SONSINI GOODRICH & ROSATI (California)
650 Page Mill Road, Palo Alto, CA 94304-1050
Tel: 650 493 9300 **Fax:** 650 493 6811

WILSON, ELSER, MOSKOWITZ, EDELMAN & DICKER LLP (New York)
150 East 42nd Street, New York, NY 10017-5639
Tel: 212 490 3000 **Fax:** 212 490 3038

WINER & BENNETT LLP (New Hampshire)
111 Concord Street, P.O.Box 488, Nashua, NH 03061-0488
Tel: 603 882 5157 **Fax:** 603 882 2694

WINFREE LAW OFFICE (Alaska)
301 Cushman Street, Suite 200, Fairbanks, AK 99701
Tel: 907 451 6500

WINN & ALEXANDER LLP (California)
820 Bay Avenue, Suite 109, Capitola, CA 95010
Tel: 831 479 3490 **Fax:** 831 447 0949

WINTHROP & WEINSTINE, A PROFESSIONAL ASSOCIATION (Minnesota)
3000 Dain Rauscher Plaza, 60 South Sixth Street, Minneapolis, MN 55402
Tel: 612 347 0700 **Fax:** 612 347 0600

WINTHROP & WEINSTINE, A PROFESSIONAL ASSOCIATION (Minnesota)
3200 Minnesota World Trade Center, 30 East Seventh Street, St Paul, MN 55101
Tel: 651 290 8400 **Fax:** 651 292 9347

OTHER RECOMMENDED FIRMS

WISE CARTER CHILD & CARAWAY, PROFESSIONAL ASSOCIATION (Mississippi)
401 East Capitol Street, Suite 600, PO Box 651, Jackson, MS 39205
Tel: 601 968 5500 **Fax:** 601 968 5519

WOLD JOHNSON PC (North Dakota)
400 Gate City Building, P.O.Box 1680, Fargo, ND 58107
Tel: 701 235 5515 **Fax:** 701 232 2585

WOLF TAYLOR & MCCALEB (New Mexico)
4163 Montgomery Boulevard NE, Albuquerque, NM 87109
Tel: 505 888 6600 **Fax:** 505 888 6640

WONG FLEMING (New Jersey)
821 Alexander Road, Suite 150, P.O.Box 3663, Princeton, NJ 08543-3663
Tel: 609 951 9520

WOOD, HERRON & EVANS, LLP (Ohio)
2700 Carew Tower, Cincinnati, OH 45202
Tel: 513 241 2324 **Fax:** 513 421 7269

WOODBURN AND WEDGE (Nevada)
6100 Neil Road, Suite 500, Reno, NV 89511
Tel: 775 688 3000 **Fax:** 775 688 3088

WOODCOCK WASHBURN (Pennsylvania)
One Liberty Place, Forty Sixth Floor, Philadelphia, PA 19103
Tel: 215 568 3100 **Fax:** 215 568 3439

WOODEN & MCLAUGHLIN LLP (Indiana)
1600 Capital Center South, 201 North Illinois Street, Indianapolis, IN 46204
Tel: 317 639 6151 **Fax:** 317 639 6444

WOODS, FULLER, SHULTZ & SMITH PC (South Dakota)
300 South Phillips Avenue, Suite 300, PO Box 5027, Sioux Falls, SD 57117
Tel: 605 336 3890 **Fax:** 605 339 3357

WOODS, ROGERS & HAZLEGROVE, P.L.C. (Virginia)
First Union Tower, Suite 1400, 10 South Jefferson Street, Roanoke, VA 24038
Tel: 540 983 7600; 800 552 4529 **Fax:** 540 983 7711

WORD & BODARGUS (New Mexico)
500 Tijeras North West, Albuquerque, NM 87102
Tel: 505 842 1905 **Fax:** 505 843 7129

WORDEN, THANE & HAINES, P.C. (Montana)
Suite 600, 111 N. Higgins, Missoula, MT 59806
Tel: 406 721 3400 **Fax:** 406 721 6985

WRIGHT ROBINSON OSTHIMER & TATUM (Virginia)
411 East Franklin Street, Suite 400, Richmond, VA 23219
Tel: 804 783 1100 **Fax:** 804 783 1138

WRIGHT, LINDSEY & JENNINGS LLP (Arkansas)
200 West Capitol Avenue, Suite 2200, Little Rock, AR 72201-3699
Tel: 501 371 0808 **Fax:** 501 376 9442

WYATT, TARRANT & COMBS LLP (Kentucky)
PNC Plaza, Louisville, KY 40202
Tel: 502 589 5235 **Fax:** 502 589 0309

WYCHE, BURGESS, FREEMAN & PARHAM, PA (South Carolina)
44 East Camperdown Way, PO Box 728, Greenville, SC 29602
Tel: 864 242 8200 **Fax:** 864 235 8900

YONKEE & TONER LLP (Wyoming)
319 West Dow Street, PO Box 6288, Sheridan, WY 82801
Tel: 307 674 7451 **Fax:** 307 672 6250

YORK, KELLER & FIELD (Texas)
1265 Frost Bank Plaza, 816 Congress Avenue, Austin, TX 78701

YOUNG, CLEMENT, RIVERS & TISDALE, LLP (South Carolina)
28 Broad Street, PO Box 993, Charleston, SC 29402
Tel: 843 577 4000 **Fax:** 843 724 6600

YOUNG, SOMMER, WARD, RITZENBERG, WOOLEY, BAKER & MOORE LLC (New York)
5 Palisades Drive, Executive Woods, Albany, NY 12205
Tel: 518 438 9907 **Fax:** 518 438 9914

ZEIGER & CARPENTER LLP (Ohio)
1600 Huntington Center, 41 South High Street, Columbus, OH 43215
Tel: 614 365 4100 **Fax:** 614 365 9145

ZETLIN & DE CHIARA (New York)
801 Second Avenue, New York, NY 10017
Tel: 212 682 6800 **Fax:** 212 682 6861

ZEVNIK HORTON LLP (California)
333 South Grand Avenue, 21st Floor, Los Angeles, CA 90071
Tel: 213 437 5207 **Fax:** 213 437 5222

ZIFFREN BRITTENHAM BRANCA FISCHER GILBERT-LURIE & STIFFELMAN LLP (California)
1801 Century Park West, Los Angeles, CA 90067-6406
Tel: 310 552 3388 **Fax:** 310 553 7068

ZIMNEY, FOSTER, JOHNSON, DITTUS & FLATEN, CHARTERED (North Dakota)
Bremer Financial Center, Suite 200, 3100 Sooouth Columbia Road, PO Box 13417, Grand Forks, ND 58208 3417
Tel: 701 772 8111 **Fax:** 701 772 7328

ZINOBER & MCCREA, P.A. (Florida)
Southtrust Plaza, 201 East Kennedy Boulevard Suite 800, PO Box 1378, Tampa, FL 33602
Tel: 813 224 9004 **Fax:** 813 223 4881

ZUCKERMAN SPAEDER LLP (Florida)
Miami Center, 201 Biscayne Boulevard, Suite 900, Miami, FL 33131
Tel: 305 358 5000 **Fax:** 305 579 9749

ZUGER KIRMIS & SMITH (North Dakota)
316 North Fifth Street, PO Box 1695, Bismarck, ND 58502
Tel: 701 223 2711 **Fax:** 701 223 7387; 701 223 9619

FIRM INDEX

**CHAMBERS
USA
2003–2004**

INDEX TO THE LEADING FIRMS

A

Abato, Rubenstein and Abato, PA (Maryland)
Profile: p 910
Table: p 328

Abrahams Kaslow & Cassman LLP (Nebraska)
Profile: p 910
Table: p 400

Abrahamson Vorachek & Mikva (Illinois)
Profile: p 910
Table: p 235

Ackley, Kopecky & Kingery (Iowa)
Profile: p 910
Table: p 290

Adams & Jones Chartered (Kansas)
Profile: p 910
Table: p 297

Adams and Reese LLP (Louisiana)
Profile: p 910
Table: p 308, 311, 313

Adelman Lavine Gold & Levin (Pennsylvania)
Profile: p 910
Table: p 607

Adler Pollock & Sheehan P.C. (Rhode Island)
Profile: p 910
Table: p 621, 622

Ahlers & Cooney, PC (Iowa)
Profile: p 910
Table: p 286, 288, 289

Ahmad, Zavitsanos & Anaipakos, PC (Texas)
Profile: p 759
Table: p 651

Akerman Senterfitt (Florida)
Profile: p 760
Table: p 151, 152, 155, 158, 161, 164, 167, 169

Akin Gump Strauss Hauer & Feld LLP (District of Columbia)
Profile: p 761
Table: p 53, 112, 119, 127, 471, 488, 608, 611, 651, 653, 655, 657, 658

Albertini, Singleton, Gendler & Darby LLP (Maryland)
Profile: p 910
Table: p 328

Allan N Karlin (West Virginia)
Profile: p 910
Table: p 716

Allen Guthrie & McHugh (West Virginia)
Profile: p 910
Table: p 718

Allen, Matkins, Leck, Gamble & Mallory LLP (california)
Profile: p 910
Table: p 56

Allen, Norton & Blue, P.A. (Florida)
Profile: p 910
Table: p 158

Allen & Overy (London)
Profile: p 910
Table: p 451

Allison, MacKenzie, Russell, Pavlakis, Wright & Fagan, Ltd (Nevada)
Profile: p 910
Table: p 410

Alschuler Grossman Stein & Kahan LLP (California)
Profile: p 762
Table: p 50

Alston Hunt Floyd & Ing Attorneys At Law, A Law Corporation (Hawaii)
Profile: p 910
Table: p 214, 215

Alston & Bird LLP (Georgia)
Profile: p 910
Table: p 181, 183, 184, 186, 189, 191, 192, 193, 195, 197, 199, 201

Alston Courtnage & Bassetti LLP (Washington)
Profile: p 910
Table: p 711

Altheimer & Gray (Illinois)
Profile: p 763
Table: p 249

Amlong & Amlong (Florida)
Profile: p 910
Table: p 157

Anderson & Kreiger (Massachusetts)
Profile: p 910
Table: p 344

Anderson Kill & Olick (New York)
Profile: p 910
Table: p 476

Andrews & Kurth LLP (Texas)
Profile: p 764
Table: p 114, 645, 646, 649, 653, 657, 664, 665

Anthony Ostlund & Baer (Minnesota)
Profile: p 910
Table: p 372

Arent Fox (District of Columbia)
Profile: p 910
Table: p 127

Armstrong Allen, PLLC (Tennessee)
Profile: p 910
Table: p 640

Armstrong Hirsch Jackoway Tyerman & Wertheimer (California)
Profile: p 911
Table: p 53

Armstrong Teasdale Schlafly & Davis (Missouri)
Profile: p 911
Table: p 385, 387, 389

Arnold & Porter (District of Columbia)
Profile: p 765
Table: p 75, 103, 107, 117, 119, 122, 127, 468

Arter & Hadden LLP (Ohio)
Profile: p 911
Table: p 568

Ashburn & Mason, PC (Alaska)
Profile: p 911
Table: p 12, 13

Ashby & Geddes (Delaware)
Profile: p 911
Table: p 97

Asher, Gittler, Greenfield, Cohen & D'Alba (Illinois)
Profile: p 911
Table: p 235

Ashford & Wriston (Hawaii)
Profile: p 911
Table: p 216

Astigarraga Davis (Florida)
Profile: p 766
Table: p 165

Ater Wynne LLP (Oregon)
Profile: p 911
Table: p 587, 590

Atkinson, Conway & Gagnon (Alaska)
Profile: p 911
Table: p 12, 13

August & Kulunas (Florida)
Profile: p 911
Table: p 169

Avant & Falcon (Louisiana)
Profile: p 911
Table: p 310

B

Baach Robinson & Lewis (District of Columbia)
Profile: p 911
Table: p 120

Babst, Calland, Clements and Zomnir, A Professional Corporation (Pennsylvania)
Profile: p 911
Table: p 604

Backus Meyer Solomon Rood & Branch LLP (New Hampshire)
Profile: p 911
Table: p 417

Baird, Holm, McEachen, Pedersen, Hamann & Strasheim LLP (Nebraska)
Profile: p 911
Table: p 400, 402, 403, 404

Baker & Daniels (Indiana)
Profile: p 911
Table: p 277, 279, 280, 281

Baker & Hostetler LLP (District of Columbia)
Profile: p 911
Table: p 125, 559, 562, 564, 566, 568, 569, 571

Baker, Donelson, Bearman & Caldwell (Tennessee)
Profile: p 911
Table: p 378, 381, 635, 639, 640

Baker Botts LLP (Texas)
Profile: p 911
Table: p 114, 122, 478, 481, 644, 645, 646, 649, 651, 653, 655, 657, 660, 662, 664, 665, 667

Baker & McKenzie (Illinois)
Profile: p 767
Table: p 58, 129, 169, 229, 251, 443

Balch & Bingham (Alabama)
Profile: p 768
Table: p 1, 4, 6, 380

Ballard Spahr Andrews & Ingersoll LLP (Pennsylvania)
Profile: p 769
Table: p 81, 331, 426, 597, 599, 602, 604, 611, 613, 684, 688

Ball Janik LLP (Oregon)
Profile: p 911
Table: p 592

Bangs, McCullen, Butler, Foye & Simmons, LLP (South Dakota)
Profile: p 911
Table: p 632

Banner & Witcoff, Ltd (District of Columbia)
Profile: p 911
Table: p 121

Baptiste & Wilder (District of Columbia)
Profile: p 911
Table: p 112

Barack Ferrazzano Kirschbaum Perlman & Nagelberg (Illinois)
Profile: p 912
Table: p 249

Barger & Wolen (California)
Profile: p 912
Table: p 46

Barnes & Thornburg (District of Columbia)
Profile: p 912
Table: p 277, 279, 280, 281

Barnett, Bolt, Kirkwood & Long (Florida)
Profile: p 912
Table: p 169

Barran Liebman (Oregon)
Profile: p 912
Table: p 589

Barrett, Johnston & Parsley (Tennessee)
Profile: p 912
Table: p 636

Barris, Sott, Denn & Driker, PLLC (Michigan)
Profile: p 912
Table: p 363

Bartlit Beck Herman Palenchar & Scott (Illinois)
Profile: p 912
Table: p 79, 245

Bass, Berry & Sims PLC (Tennessee)
Profile: p 912
Table: p 635, 637, 639, 640

Bassford, Lockhart, Truesdell & Briggs, P.A. (Minnesota)
Profile: p 912
Table: p 372

Bastianelli, Brown & Kelley (District of Columbia)
Profile: p 912
Table: p 110

Beasley, Allen, Crow, Methvin, Portis & Miles, PC (Alabama)
Profile: p 912
Table: p 4

Beck, Redden & Secrest (Texas)
Profile: p 912
Table: p 662

Becker & Poliakoff, P.A. (Florida)
Profile: p 912
Table: p 153

Bedell, Dittmar, DeVault, Pillans & Coxe (Florida)
Profile: p 912
Table: p 164

FIRMS INDEX

Bedrava & Lyman (Illinois)
Profile: p 912
Table: p 231

Beirne, Maynard & Parsons, L.L.P. (Texas)
Profile: p 770
Table: p 655

Belin Lamson McCormick Zumbach Flynn, PC (Iowa)
Profile: p 912
Table: p 286, 288, 289, 290

Bell, Boyd & Lloyd (Illinois)
Profile: p 912
Table: p 231, 249

Bendinger, Crockett Peterson & Casey (Utah)
Profile: p 912
Table: p 687

Benesch, Friedlander, Coplan & Aronoff LLP (Ohio)
Profile: p 912
Table: p 560, 571

Benetar Bernstein Schair & Stein (New York)
Profile: p 912
Table: p 466

Berenbaum, Weinshienk & Eason (Colorado)
Profile: p 912
Table: p 77

Berger & Montague (Pennsylvania)
Profile: p 913
Table: p 595

Berger Singerman (Florida)
Profile: p 913
Table: p 161

Berkowitz Stanton Brandt Williams & Shaw LLP (Missouri)
Profile: p 913
Table: p 389

Berkowitz Lefkovits Isom & Kushner (Alabama)
Profile: p 913
Table: p 1, 6

Berman & Simmons (Maine)
Profile: p 913
Table: p 320, 322

Berman, Gaufin, Tomsic, Savage & Campbell (Utah)
Profile: p 913
Table: p 687

Berman, Paley, Goldstein & Kannry (New York)
Profile: p 913
Table: p 458

Bernstein, Shur, Sawyer & Nelson, PA (Maine)
Profile: p 913
Table: p 322, 323

Beveridge & Diamond PC (District of Columbia)
Profile: p 771
Table: p 117

Bilzin Sumberg Dunn Baena Price & Axelrod LLP (Florida)
Profile: p 772
Table: p 167

Bingham McCutchen LLP (Massachusetts)
Profile: p 913
Table: p 29, 36, 42, 50, 91, 127, 336, 338, 339, 342, 348, 353, 471

Bingham McHale LLP (Indiana)
Profile: p 913
Table: p 280, 281

Bioff, Finucane, Coffey, Holland & Hosler LLP (Missouri)
Profile: p 913
Table: p 387

Birch, Horton, Bittner & Cherot (Alaska)
Profile: p 913
Table: p 9

Blackwell Sanders Peper Martin LLP (Missouri)
Profile: p 913
Table: p 294, 385, 387, 389, 391, 400, 402, 403, 404

Blackwood Associates PC (Vermont)
Profile: p 913
Table: p 693

Blank Rome LLP (Pennsylvania)
Profile: p 913
Table: p 597, 599, 602, 607, 611, 613

Blecher & Collins (California)
Profile: p 913
Table: p 29, 50

Blish & Cavanagh, LLP (Rhode Island)
Profile: p 913
Table: p 621

Bodman, Longley & Dahling LLP (Michigan)
Profile: p 773
Table: p 360

Boies, Schiller & Flexner LLP (New York)
Profile: p 913
Table: p 103, 106, 440, 481

Bondurant, Mixson & Elmore, LLP (Georgia)
Profile: p 913
Table: p 181, 188, 197

Boone, Karlberg PC (Montana)
Profile: p 913
Table: p 396

Boose Casey Ciklin Lubitz Martens McBane & O'Connell (Florida)
Profile: p 913
Table: p 153

Born & Surls (California)
Profile: p 913
Table: p 39

Bose McKinney & Evans LLP (Indiana)
Profile: p 913
Table: p 279, 280, 281

Boult, Cummings, Conners & Berry, PLC (Tennessee)
Profile: p 913
Table: p 635, 637, 639, 640

Bowditch & Dewey LLP (Massachusetts)
Profile: p 914
Table: p 344

Bowen Riley Warnock & Jacobson, PLC (Tennessee)
Profile: p 914
Table: p 639

Bowles Rice McDavid Graff & Love PLLC (West Virginia)
Profile: p 914
Table: p 714, 716, 718, 719

Boyce, Pashby & Welk (South Dakota)
Profile: p 914
Table: p 631, 632

Bracewell & Patterson LLP (Texas)
Profile: p 774
Table: p 645, 646, 649, 651, 653, 655, 660, 664, 665

Bradley & Riley, PC (Iowa)
Profile: p 914
Table: p 286, 288, 290

Bradley Arant Rose & White LLP (Alabama)
Profile: p 914
Table: p 1, 3, 4, 6, 381

Bradshaw, Fowler, Proctor & Fairgrave, PC (Iowa)
Profile: p 914
Table: p 286, 289, 290

Branstetter, Kilgore, Stranch & Jennings (Tennessee)
Profile: p 914
Table: p 636

Brauer, Buescher, Goldhammer, Kelman & Eckert (Colorado)
Profile: p 914
Table: p 77

Breazeale, Sachse & Wilson, LLP (Louisiana)
Profile: p 914
Table: p 311

Bredhoff & Kaiser (District of Columbia)
Profile: p 914
Table: p 112

Bricker & Eckler LLP (Ohio)
Profile: p 914
Table: p 560, 566, 571

Bridger-Riley & Associates, PC (Oklahoma)
Profile: p 914
Table: p 581

Briggs and Morgan, Professional Association (Minnesota)
Profile: p 914
Table: p 368, 371, 372, 374

Brinks Hofer Gilson & Lione (Illinois)
Profile: p 914
Table: p 244

Brooks, Pierce, McLendon, Humphrey & Leonard, L.L.P. (North Carolina)
Profile: p 914
Table: p 545, 548, 549

Broom, Johnson Clarkson & Lanphier (Nebraska)
Profile: p 914
Table: p 401

Brown & Bain, P.A. (Arizona)
Profile: p 775
Table: p 19

Brown, Drew & Massey, LLP (Wyoming)
Profile: p 914
Table: p 730, 733

Brown, Winick, Graves, Gross, Baskerville and Schoenebaum PLC (Iowa)
Profile: p 914
Table: p 286

Browning & Peifer (New Mexico)
Profile: p 914
Table: p 435

Brown Law Firm, PC (Montana)
Profile: p 914
Table: p 396

Brown McCarroll, LLP (Texas)
Profile: p 914
Table: p 655

Brown Raysman Millstein Felder & Steiner LLP (New York)
Profile: p 776
Table: p 456

Brown Rudnick Berlack Israels (Massachusetts)
Profile: p 914
Table: p 91, 351, 471

Brownstein Hyatt & Farber, PC (Colorado)
Profile: p 914
Table: p 75, 78, 81

Brunini, Grantham, Grower & Hewes, PLLC (Mississippi)
Profile: p 915
Table: p 378, 381, 382

Bryan Cave LLP (Missouri)
Profile: p 915
Table: p 1, 9, 16, 18, 20, 23, 28, 75, 87, 94, 102, 150, 180, 212, 223, 277, 294, 300, 307, 319, 327, 336, 360, 378, 385, 387, 389, 400, 406, 415, 424, 433, 439, 492, 544, 554, 558, 587, 595, 624, 630, 635, 643, 684, 692, 698, 706, 714, 723

Buchanan Ingersoll (Pennsylvania)
Profile: p 915
Table: p 599, 602, 608, 611

Buck & Gordon LLP (Washington)
Profile: p 915
Table: p 711

Buckingham Doolittle & Burroughs (Ohio)
Profile: p 915
Table: p 560

Buckley & Klein, LLP (Georgia)
Profile: p 915
Table: p 188

Buist, Moore, Smythe & McGee, P.A. (South Carolina)
Profile: p 915
Table: p 626, 627

Bullard Smith Jernstedt Wilson (Oregon)
Profile: p 915
Table: p 589

Bullivant Houser Bailey PC (Oregon)
Profile: p 915
Table: p 590

Burbidge & Mitchell (Utah)
Profile: p 915
Table: p 687

Burch, Porter & Johnson (Tennessee)
Profile: p 915
Table: p 640

Burke & Parsons (New York)
Profile: p 915
Table: p 496

Burkhalter & Associates (Tennessee)
Profile: p 915
Table: p 636

Burr & Forman LLP (Alabama)
Profile: p 915
Table: p 1, 3, 6

Burr, Pease & Kurtz, PC (Alaska)
Profile: p 915
Table: p 12

Busse & Hunt (Oregon)
Profile: p 915
Table: p 588

Butler & Harris (Texas)
Profile: p 915
Table: p 651

Butler, Williams, Pantele & Skilling (Virginia)
Profile: p 915
Table: p 701

FIRMS INDEX

Butler, Snow, O'Mara, Stevens & Cannada, PLLC (Mississippi)
Profile: p 915
Table: p 378, 381, 382

Butler Rubin Saltarelli & Boyd (Illinois)
Profile: p 915
Table: p 242

Butzel Long (Michigan)
Profile: p 777
Table: p 361, 362, 363, 364

Byam & Hoarty (Nebraska)
Profile: p 915
Table: p 401

Byrnes & Keller (Washington)
Profile: p 915
Table: p 709

C

Cabaniss, Johnston, Gardner, Dumas & O'Neal (Alabama)
Profile: p 915
Table: p 3

Cades Schutte Fleming & Wright (Hawaii)
Profile: p 916
Table: p 212, 214, 215, 216

Cadwalader, Wickersham & Taft LLP (New York)
Profile: p 778
Table: p 451, 453, 459, 471, 476, 481, 492, 544

Cadwell Sanford Deibert & Garry LLP (South Dakota)
Profile: p 916
Table: p 632

Caesar, Rivise, Bernstein, Cohen & Pokotilow Ltd (Pennsylvania)
Profile: p 916
Table: p 608

Cahill Gordon & Reindel (New York)
Profile: p 916
Table: p 447, 481, 485

Calfee, Halter & Griswold LLP (Ohio)
Profile: p 916
Table: p 559, 562, 568

Campbell & Williams (Nevada)
Profile: p 916
Table: p 409

Canterbury, Stuber, Elder, Gooch & Surratt, PC (Texas)
Profile: p 779
Table: p 648

Caplin & Drysdale (District of Columbia)
Profile: p 916
Table: p 129

Carlsmith Ball (Distrito Federal)
Profile: p 916
Table: p 212, 215, 216

Carlton Fields (Florida)
Profile: p 916
Table: p 151, 153, 161, 164, 167, 169

Carpenter, Bennett & Morrissey (New Jersey)
Profile: p 916
Table: p 426

Carrington, Coleman, Sloman & Blumenthal, LLP (Texas)
Profile: p 916
Table: p 644, 662

Carruthers & Roth PA (North Carolina)
Profile: p 916
Table: p 544

Carter Ledyard & Milburn LLP (New York)
Profile: p 780
Table: p 468, 496

Carver Darden Koretzky Tessier Finn Blossman & Areaux LLC (Louisiana)
Profile: p 916
Table: p 307

Case Bigelow & Lombardi A Law Corporation (Hawaii)
Profile: p 916
Table: p 212

Chadbourne & Parke LLP (New York)
Profile: p 781
Table: p 114, 126, 490

Chamberlain, Hrdlicka, White, Williams & Martin (Texas)
Profile: p 916
Table: p 201

Chapman and Cutler (Illinois)
Profile: p 916
Table: p 226

Charlson Bredehoft (Virginia)
Profile: p 916
Table: p 701

Choate Hall & Stewart (Massachusetts)
Profile: p 916
Table: p 336, 348

Christensen, Moore, Cockrell, Cummings & Axelberg PC (Montana)
Profile: p 917
Table: p 396

Christian & Small LLP (Alabama)
Profile: p 917
Table: p 4

Christian & Barton LLP (Virginia)
Profile: p 917
Table: p 702

Christian, Samson, Jones & Chisholm, PLLC (Montana)
Profile: p 917
Table: p 394

Christie, Parker & Hale, LLP (California)
Profile: p 917
Table: p 47

Chonin & Sher (Florida)
Profile: p 916
Table: p 157

Cichanowicz, Callan, Keane, Vengrow & Textor LLP (New York)
Profile: p 917
Table: p 496

Clapp Peterson & Stowers LLC (Alaska)
Profile: p 917
Table: p 10

Clark, Atcheson & Reisert (New York)
Profile: p 917
Table: p 496

Cleary Shahi Associates, A Professional Corporation (Vermont)
Profile: p 917
Table: p 695

Cleary Gottlieb Steen & Hamilton (New York)
Profile: p 782
Table: p 103, 443, 445, 447, 451, 453, 459, 471, 481, 492, 498

Clifford Chance LLP (London)
Profile: p 783
Table: p 50, 103, 440, 476, 478, 481, 485

Cline, Williams, Wright, Johnson & Oldfather LLP (Nebraska)
Profile: p 917
Table: p 400, 403

Coats Rose Yale Ryman Lee (Texas)
Profile: p 917
Table: p 648

Coblentz, Patch, Duffy & Bass LLP (California)
Profile: p 917
Table: p 56

Coffman, Coleman, Andrews & Grogan (Florida)
Profile: p 917
Table: p 158

Cohen & Grigsby, PC (Pennsylvania)
Profile: p 917
Table: p 599, 602

Cohen Weiss & Simon (New York)
Profile: p 917
Table: p 466

Cohn Khoury Madoff & Whitesell LLP (Massachusetts)
Profile: p 917
Table: p 346

Cokinos, Bosien and Young (Texas)
Profile: p 917
Table: p 648

Cole, Schotz, Meisel, Forman & Leonard, P.A. (New Jersey)
Profile: p 917
Table: p 429

Collier, Jacob & Mills (New Jersey)
Profile: p 917
Table: p 426

Collins, McMahon & Harris PLLC (Vermont)
Profile: p 917
Table: p 693

Collison & Bechtold (Colorado)
Profile: p 917
Table: p 77

Colson Hicks Eidson (Florida)
Profile: p 917
Table: p 164

Commercial Law Group (Oklahoma)
Profile: p 917
Table: p 580

Conley, Rose & Tayon (Texas)
Profile: p 917
Table: p 660

Conmy Feste Ltd (North Dakota)
Profile: p 918
Table: p 554, 556

Conner & Winters, PC (Oklahoma)
Profile: p 918
Table: p 580, 582

Connolly, O'Malley, Lillis, Hansen & Olson LLP (Iowa)
Profile: p 918
Table: p 290

Conrad O'Brien Gellman & Rohn PC (Pennsylvania)
Profile: p 918
Table: p 611

Constangy, Brooks & Smith, LLC (Georgia)
Profile: p 918
Table: p 3, 189, 387, 548

Conway & Mrowiec (Illinois)
Profile: p 918
Table: p 231

Cook & Molan (New Hampshire)
Profile: p 918
Table: p 417

Cook, Little, Rosenblatt & Manson PLLC (New Hampshire)
Profile: p 918
Table: p 415

Cooley Godward LLP (California)
Profile: p 918
Table: p 32, 34, 37, 58, 75, 699

Cooper & Scully, PC (Texas)
Profile: p 784
Table: p 658

Corr Cronin LLP (Washington)
Profile: p 918
Table: p 709

Correro Fishman Haygood Phelps Walmsley & Casteix LLP (Louisiana)
Profile: p 785
Table: p 308

Cosho, Humphrey, Greener & Welsh, PA (Idaho)
Profile: p 918
Table: p 220

Costello Porter Hill Heisterkamp Bushnell & Carpenter LLP (South Dakota)
Profile: p 918
Table: p 632

Cotchett, Pitre, Simon & McCarthy (California)
Profile: p 918
Table: p 50

Coudert Brothers (New York)
Profile: p 918
Table: p 485

Covington & Burling (District of Columbia)
Profile: p 786
Table: p 107, 117, 120, 122

Cox & Smith Incorporated (Texas)
Profile: p 918
Table: p 657

Cox Castle & Nicholson LLP (California)
Profile: p 918
Table: p 36, 56

Cozen O'Connor (Pennsylvania)
Profile: p 918
Table: p 607

Crandall Pyles Haviland & Turner (West Virginia)
Profile: p 915
Table: p 716

Cravath, Swaine & Moore (New York)
Profile: p 918
Table: p 440, 445, 447, 453, 459, 468, 481, 498

Crispin & Associates (Oregon)
Profile: p 918
Table: p 588

Croker, Huck, Kasher, DeWitt, Anderson & Gonderinger, PC (Nebraska)
Profile: p 918
Table: p 404

FIRMS INDEX

Cronin, Fried, Sekiya, Kekina & Fairbanks Attorneys At Law (Hawaii)
Profile: p 918
Table: p 215

Cross, Gunter, Witherspoon & Galchus, PC (Arkansas)
Profile: p 918
Table: p 24

Crowe & Dunlevy (Oklahoma)
Profile: p 918
Table: p 580, 582, 583, 584

Crowell & Moring LLP (District of Columbia)
Profile: p 918
Table: p 103, 114

Crowley, Haughey, Hanson, Toole & Dietrich, PLLP (Montana)
Profile: p 919
Table: p 394, 395, 396, 397

Cummings & Lockwood (Connecticut)
Profile: p 919
Table: p 87, 88, 90

Cunningham, Bounds, Yance, Crowder & Brown, LLC (Alabama)
Profile: p 919
Table: p 4

Curtis, Mallet-Prevost & Gilioli (Undefined)
Profile: p 919
Table: p 481

Cutler & Donahoe LLP (South Dakota)
Profile: p 919
Table: p 632

D

D'Ancona & Pflaum LLC (Illinois)
Profile: p 919
Table: p 249

Dann Pecar Newman & Kleiman, PC (Indiana)
Profile: p 919
Table: p 281

Davenport, Evans, Hurwitz & Smith LLP (South Dakota)
Profile: p 919
Table: p 630, 631, 632

Davis & Boghigian, PC (New Hampshire)
Profile: p 919
Table: p 420

Davis & Cannon (Wyoming)
Profile: p 919
Table: p 731, 733

Davis & Kuelthau, S.C. (Wisconsin)
Profile: p 919
Table: p 725

Davis, Brown, Koehn, Shors & Roberts, PC (Iowa)
Profile: p 919
Table: p 286, 288, 290

Davis Graham & Stubbs LLP (Colorado)
Profile: p 919
Table: p 75, 78, 79

Davis Polk & Wardwell (New York)
Profile: p 919
Table: p 32, 440, 445, 447, 451, 459, 468, 471, 481, 487, 488, 490, 498

Davis Wright Tremaine LLP (Washington)
Profile: p 787
Table: p 9, 11, 13, 41, 53, 485, 587, 590, 706, 708, 709

Day, Berry & Howard LLP (Connecticut)
Profile: p 919
Table: p 87, 88, 90, 91

Day Casebeer Madrid & Batchelder LLP (California)
Profile: p 919
Table: p 47

Dean, Mead, Egerton, Bloodworth, Capouano & Bozarth PA (Florida)
Profile: p 919
Table: p 167, 169

Deaner, Deaner, Scann, Malan & Larsen (Nevada)
Profile: p 919
Table: p 410

Debevoise & Plimpton (New York)
Profile: p 788
Table: p 440, 443, 459, 471, 476, 481, 485, 487, 488, 492, 498

Dechert (London)
Profile: p 789
Table: p 91, 595, 599, 602, 604, 611, 613

DeOrchis & Partners, LLP (New York)
Profile: p 919
Table: p 496

Depew and Gillen LLC (Kansas)
Profile: p 919
Table: p 295

Devine Millimet & Branch PA (New Hampshire)
Profile: p 919
Table: p 415, 417, 418, 420

Dewey Ballantine LLP (New York)
Profile: p 790
Table: p 56, 114, 453, 468, 476, 490

Dickinson, Mackaman, Tyler & Hagen, P.C. (Iowa)
Profile: p 920
Table: p 288, 290

Dickinson Wright PLLC (Michigan)
Profile: p 919
Table: p 361, 362, 363, 364

Dickstein Shapiro Morin & Oshinsky LLP (District of Columbia)
Profile: p 920
Table: p 114, 120

Dilworth Paxson LLP (Pennsylvania)
Profile: p 920
Table: p 607

Dinse, Knapp & McAndrew PC (Vermont)
Profile: p 920
Table: p 692, 694, 695, 696

Dinsmore & Shohl LLP (Ohio)
Profile: p 920
Table: p 302, 562, 564, 566, 568, 716

DKE Law Office (Missouri)
Profile: p 920
Table: p 387

Dodson, Parker, Dinkins & Behm (Tennessee)
Profile: p 920
Table: p 636

Doerner, Saunders, Daniel & Anderson, LLP (Oklahoma)
Profile: p 920
Table: p 582

Doffermyre, Shields, Canfield, Knowles & Devine (Georgia)
Profile: p 920
Table: p 197

Dollinger & Dollinger (New Jersey)
Profile: p 920
Table: p 429

Donati & Associates (Tennessee)
Profile: p 920
Table: p 636

Donnelly & Carbone (West Virginia)
Profile: p 920
Table: p 716

Dorsey & Whitney LLP (Minnesota)
Profile: p 920
Table: p 9, 12, 13, 368, 371, 372, 374, 394, 396, 555, 684

Dover Dixon Horne (Arkansas)
Profile: p 920
Table: p 26

Dowd & Dowd (Nebraska)
Profile: p 920
Table: p 401

Dowd, Bloch & Bennett (Illinois)
Profile: p 920
Table: p 235

Downs Rachlin Martin PLLC (Vermont)
Profile: p 920
Table: p 692, 694, 695, 696

Dray, Thomson & Dyekman, PC (Wyoming)
Profile: p 920
Table: p 730, 733

Drinker Biddle & Reath LLP (Pennsylvania)
Profile: p 920
Table: p 424, 428, 429, 595, 597, 599, 604, 608, 613

Drummond Woodsum & MacMahon (Maine)
Profile: p 791
Table: p 319, 321, 323

Duane Morris LLP (Pennsylvania)
Profile: p 920
Table: p 595, 597, 599, 607, 608

Duffy & Sweeney, Ltd (Rhode Island)
Profile: p 920
Table: p 621

Dunn Carney Allen Higgins & Tongue LLP (Oregon)
Profile: p 920
Table: p 592

Durant, Nichols, Houston Hodson & Cortese-Costa PC (Connecticut)
Profile: p 920
Table: p 88

Duvin, Cahn & Hutton (Ohio)
Profile: p 920
Table: p 564

Dykema Gossett PLLC (District of Columbia)
Profile: p 920
Table: p 361, 362, 363, 364

E

Eaton Peabody (Maine)
Profile: p 921
Table: p 319, 321

Eaves Bardacke Baugh Kierst & Kiernan PA (New Mexico)
Profile: p 921
Table: p 435

Eddy & Jones (Oklahoma)
Profile: p 921
Table: p 581

Edwards Frickle Halverson & Anner-Hughes (Montana)
Profile: p 921
Table: p 395

Edwards & Angell, LLP (Massachusetts)
Profile: p 921
Table: p 338, 476, 620, 621, 622

Edwin L Hobson PC (Vermont)
Profile: p 921
Table: p 693

Egan, Lev & Siwica (Florida)
Profile: p 921
Table: p 157

Eimer Stahl Klevorn & Solberg (Illinois)
Profile: p 792
Table: p 224

Eisenberg & Bogas (Michigan)
Profile: p 921
Table: p 362

Elam & Burke, PA (Idaho)
Profile: p 921
Table: p 220

Elarbee, Thompson, Sapp & Wilson, LLP (Georgia)
Profile: p 921
Table: p 189

Elderkin & Pirnie PLC (Iowa)
Profile: p 921
Table: p 289

Elliot Pishko Morgan (North Carolina)
Profile: p 921
Table: p 547

Ellman, Burke, Hoffman & Johnson (California)
Profile: p 921
Table: p 56

Ellzey & Brooks LLC (South Carolina)
Profile: p 921
Table: p 625

Epstein Becker & Green PC (New York)
Profile: p 921
Table: p 466

Erickson & Sederstrom, PC (Nebraska)
Profile: p 921
Table: p 400, 403

Eubanks, Welch, Baker & Schulze (Arkansas)
Profile: p 921
Table: p 24

F

Fabian & Clendenin (Utah)
Profile: p 921
Table: p 687, 688

Fabyanske, Westra & Hart PA (Minnesota)
Profile: p 921
Table: p 374

Faegre & Benson LLP (Minnesota)
Profile: p 921
Table: p 75, 78, 79, 81, 368, 371, 372, 374

Farella Braun & Martel LLP (California)
Profile: p 921
Table: p 36, 50

Farmer, Cline & Arnold PLLC (West Virginia)
Profile: p 793
Table: p 718

FIRMS INDEX

Faulkner, Muskovitz & Phillips, LLP (Ohio)
Profile: p 921
Table: p 564

Fay, Sharpe, Fagan, Minnich & McKee, LLP (Ohio)
Profile: p 922
Table: p 568

Feldman & Orlansky (Alaska)
Profile: p 922
Table: p 12

Felhaber, Larson, Fenlon & Vogt, PC (Minnesota)
Profile: p 922
Table: p 371, 374

Fellers, Snider, Blankenship, Bailey & Tippens, A Professional Corporation (Oklahoma)
Profile: p 922
Table: p 583

Fennemore Craig (Arizona)
Profile: p 922
Table: p 16, 18, 19, 20

Fenwick & West (California)
Profile: p 922
Table: p 34, 47, 58

Ferguson Stein Chambers Wallaas Adkins Gresham & Sumter (North Carolina)
Profile: p 922
Table: p 547

Ferrell Schultz Carter Zumpano & Fertel PA (Florida)
Profile: p 922
Table: p 161

Fillenwarth, Dennerline, Groth & Towe (Indiana)
Profile: p 922
Table: p 278

Finch Bettmann Maks & Hogue P.C (South Dakota)
Profile: p 922
Table: p 631

Fine Kaplan & Black (Pennsylvania)
Profile: p 922
Table: p 595

Finley, Alt, Smith, Scharnberg, Craig, Hilmes & Gaffney PC (Iowa)
Profile: p 922
Table: p 289

Finn Dixon & Herling LLP (Connecticut)
Profile: p 794
Table: p 87

Finnegan Henderson Farabow Garrett & Dunner LLP (District of Columbia)
Profile: p 922
Table: p 47, 121, 195

First, Blondis, Albrecht & Novotnak (Wisconsin)
Profile: p 922
Table: p 724

Fish & Richardson (New York)
Profile: p 922
Table: p 348, 478

Fisher & Phillips LLP (Georgia)
Profile: p 922
Table: p 158, 189, 311

Fish & Neave (New York)
Profile: p 922
Table: p 47, 478

Fisk & Fielder (Texas)
Profile: p 922
Table: p 648

Fitzpatrick, Cella, Harper & Scinto (New York)
Profile: p 795
Table: p 478

Fleeson, Gooing, Coulson & Kitch, LLC (Kansas)
Profile: p 922
Table: p 297

Flygare Schwarz & Closson PLLC (New Hampshire)
Profile: p 922
Table: p 417

Flynn, Gaskins & Bennett (Minnesota)
Profile: p 922
Table: p 371

Fogel, Feldman, Ostrov, Ringler & Klevens (California)
Profile: p 922
Table: p 50

Foley Hoag LLP (Massachusetts)
Profile: p 922
Table: p 336, 338, 339, 342, 344, 346, 348, 353

Foley & Lardner (Wisconsin)
Profile: p 155, 158, 167, 238, 723, 725, 726, 727

Ford & Harrison LLP (Georgia)
Profile: p 923
Table: p 158, 189, 637

Ford White & Nassen (Texas)
Profile: p 923
Table: p 648

Forman Perry Watkins Krutz & Tardy, PLLC (Mississippi)
Profile: p 923
Table: p 381

Foster Pepper & Shefelman PLLC (Washington)
Profile: p 923
Table: p 12, 706, 711

Foulston Siefkin LLP (Kansas)
Profile: p 923
Table: p 294, 295, 296

Fowler White Boggs Banker (Florida)
Profile: p 923
Table: p 158, 164

Fox & Fox (Wisconsin)
Profile: p 923
Table: p 724

Fox Rothschild O'Brien & Frankel LLP (Pennsylvania)
Profile: p 923
Table: p 604

Franczek Sullivan (Illinois)
Profile: p 923
Table: p 236

Frank Rosen Freed Roberts LLP (Washington)
Profile: p 923
Table: p 707

Frantz Ward LLP (Ohio)
Profile: p 923
Table: p 560, 564

Fraser Stryker Law Firm (Nebraska)
Profile: p 923
Table: p 400, 402, 403, 404

Fredrikson & Byron, PA (Minnesota)
Profile: p 923
Table: p 368, 372, 374

Freeborn & Peters (Illinois)
Profile: p 923
Table: p 247

Freedman Boyd Daniels Hollander Goldberg & Cline PA (New Mexico)
Profile: p 923
Table: p 435

Freehill Hogan & Mahar LLP (New York)
Profile: p 923
Table: p 496

Freshfields Bruckhaus Deringer (London)
Profile: p 923
Table: p 443, 490

Friday, Eldredge & Clark (Arkansas)
Profile: p 923
Table: p 23, 24, 25

Fried, Frank, Harris, Shriver & Jacobson (New York)
Profile: p 796
Table: p 103, 440, 453, 459, 471, 476, 487, 492, 498

Friedman, Rubin & White (Alaska)
Profile: p 923
Table: p 12

Frilot, Partridge, Kohnke & Clements LC (Louisiana)
Profile: p 923
Table: p 313

Frost Brown Todd LLC (Kentucky)
Profile: p 798
Table: p 300, 302, 303, 304, 559, 560, 562, 564, 568

Fulbright & Jaworski LLP (Texas)
Profile: p 799
Table: p 114, 644, 646, 649, 651, 653, 655, 657, 658, 660, 662, 665, 667

Fullenkamp, Doyle & Jobeun (Nebraska)
Profile: p 923
Table: p 404

G

Gable & Gotwals, A Professional Corporation (Oklahoma)
Profile: p 923
Table: p 583

Gaines Pansing & Hogan (Nebraska)
Profile: p 923
Table: p 404

Gainsburgh, Benjamin, David, Meunier & Warshauer (Louisiana)
Profile: p 924
Table: p 313

Gallagher & Kennedy, PA (Arizona)
Profile: p 924
Table: p 20

Gallagher, Callahan and Gartrell, PA (New Hampshire)
Profile: p 924
Table: p 417, 418, 420

Gallop, Johnson & Neuman, L.C. (Missouri)
Profile: p 924
Table: p 389

Gang Tyre Ramer & Brown (California)
Profile: p 924
Table: p 53

Gardere Wynne Sewell LLP (Texas)
Profile: p 801
Table: p 657, 665

Garlington, Lohn & Robinson, PLLP (Montana)
Profile: p 924
Table: p 394, 395, 396, 397

Garrison, Levin-Epstein Chimes & Richardson PC (Connecticut)
Profile: p 924
Table: p 88

Gelber, Gelber, Ingersoll & Klevansky A Law Corporation (Hawaii)
Profile: p 924
Table: p 212

Genova, Burns & Vernoia (New Jersey)
Profile: p 924
Table: p 426

Genovese Joblove & Battista P.A. (Florida)
Profile: p 924
Table: p 161

Gibbons, Del Deo, Dolan, Griffinger & Vecchione (New Jersey)
Profile: p 924
Table: p 428

Gibbs & Bruns, LLP (Texas)
Profile: p 802
Table: p 662

Gibbs, Giden, Locher & Turner (California)
Profile: p 924
Table: p 36

Gibson, Dunn & Crutcher LLP (California)
Profile: p 924
Table: p 29, 30, 32, 37, 39, 42, 50, 56, 58, 103, 111, 112, 117, 122, 485

Gignilliat, Savitz & Bettis LLP (South Carolina)
Profile: p 924
Table: p 625

Gilbert Heintz & Randolph (District of Columbia)
Profile: p 924
Table: p 120

Gilkey & Stephenson PA (New Mexico)
Profile: p 924
Table: p 434

Gillespie, Rozen & Watsky, PC (Texas)
Profile: p 803
Table: p 651

Gilmartin, Poster & Shafto (New York)
Profile: p 924
Table: p 496

Givens Pursley LLP (Idaho)
Profile: p 924
Table: p 221

Glankler Brown, PLLC (Tennessee)
Profile: p 924
Table: p 640

Glenn Rasmussen Fogarty & Hooker (Florida)
Profile: p 924
Table: p 161

Glickman & Hughes LLP (Texas)
Profile: p 924
Table: p 651

Godfrey & Kahn, SC (Wisconsin)
Profile: p 924
Table: p 723, 726, 727

Goetz, Gallick, Baldwin & Dolan PC (Montana)
Profile: p 925
Table: p 395, 396

FIRMS INDEX

Goetz Fitzpatrick Most & Bruckman LLP (New York)
Profile: p 925
Table: p 458

Goins, Underkofler, Crawford & Langdon LLP (Texas)
Profile: p 804
Table: p 648

Goldberg, Kohn, Bell, Black, Rosenbloom & Moritz, Ltd (Illinois)
Profile: p 925
Table: p 226, 240, 249

Gómez & Petitti PC (Arizona)
Profile: p 925
Table: p 17

Goodin MacBride Squeri Ritchie & Day LLP (California)
Profile: p 925
Table: p 41

Goodman & Zuchlewski LLP (New York)
Profile: p 925
Table: p 466

Goodsill Anderson Quinn & Stifel (Hawaii)
Profile: p 925
Table: p 212, 215, 216

Goodwin & Goodwin, LLP (West Virginia)
Profile: p 925
Table: p 714

Goodwin Procter LLP (Massachusetts)
Profile: p 805
Table: p 338, 339, 342, 344, 346, 348, 350, 351, 353

Goold Patterson DeVore Ales & Roadhouse (Nevada)
Profile: p 925
Table: p 410

Gordon & Silver, Ltd (Nevada)
Profile: p 925
Table: p 410

Gordon, Arata, McCollam, Duplantis & Eagan LLP (Louisiana)
Profile: p 925
Table: p 313

Gordon, Feinblatt, Rothman, Hoffberger & Hollander, LLC (Maryland)
Profile: p 925
Table: p 329, 331

Gordon, Silberman, Wiggins & Childs (Alabama)
Profile: p 925
Table: p 2

Gough, Shanahan, Johnson & Waterman (Montana)
Profile: p 925
Table: p 395, 396

Goulston & Storrs (Massachusetts)
Profile: p 925
Table: p 344, 348, 351

Grant & Eisenhofer PA (Delaware)
Profile: p 925
Table: p 97

Gravel and Shea (Vermont)
Profile: p 925
Table: p 692, 694, 695, 696

Gray, Harris & Robinson, PA (Florida)
Profile: p 925
Table: p 153

Gray, Plant, Mooty, Mooty & Bennett, PA (Minnesota)
Profile: p 925
Table: p 368, 371, 372, 374

Gray Cary Ware & Freidenrich LLP (California)
Profile: p 806
Table: p 34

Green Lucas Savits & Marose (New Jersey)
Profile: p 925
Table: p 426

Greenbaum, Rowe, Smith, Ravin, Davis & Himmel LLP (New Jersey)
Profile: p 925
Table: p 424, 428, 429

Greenberg Dauber Epstein & Tucker (New Jersey)
Profile: p 925
Table: p 428

Greenberg Glusker Fields Claman Machtinger & Kinsella LLP (California)
Profile: p 807
Table: p 53

Greenberg Traurig LLP (Florida)
Profile: p 808
Table: p 1, 9, 16, 23, 28, 75, 87, 94, 102, 150, 155, 160, 161, 164, 167, 169, 180, 219, 223, 277, 286, 294, 300, 307, 319, 327, 336, 360, 368, 378, 394, 400, 404, 415, 424, 433, 439, 544, 554, 558, 580, 587, 595, 620, 624, 630, 635, 643, 692, 698, 706, 714, 723, 730

Greene, Broillet, Taylor, Wheeler & Panish (California)
Profile: p 926
Table: p 50

Greenebaum Doll & McDonald PLLC (Kentucky)
Profile: p 926
Table: p 300, 302, 303, 304

Gregg M Corwin & Associates Law Office, PC (Minnesota)
Profile: p 926
Table: p 370

Gregg M Rosenberg & Associates (Texas)
Profile: p 926
Table: p 651

Griffin Cochrane & Marshall (Georgia)
Profile: p 926
Table: p 184

Griffith & Nixon, P.C. (Texas)
Profile: p 809
Table: p 648

Gronek & Latham (Florida)
Profile: p 926
Table: p 161

Grotta, Glassman & Hoffman (New Jersey)
Profile: p 926
Table: p 426

Guess & Rudd PC (Alaska)
Profile: p 926
Table: p 12

Gunderson Dettmer Stough Villeneuve Franklin & Hachigian (California)
Profile: p 926
Table: p 34

Gunderson, Palmer, Goodsell & Nelson LLP (South Dakota)
Profile: p 926
Table: p 630, 632

Gunhus, Grinnell, Klinger, Swenson & Guy, Ltd. (North Dakota)
Profile: p 926
Table: p 555

Gunster, Yoakley & Stewart PA (Florida)
Profile: p 926
Table: p 152, 160

H

Hadsell & Stormer (California)
Profile: p 926
Table: p 39

Hahn Loeser & Parks LLP (Ohio)
Profile: p 926
Table: p 560

Hale and Dorr (Massachusetts)
Profile: p 926
Table: p 336, 339, 342, 344, 346, 348, 350, 351, 353, 424, 456, 699

Hale Lane Peek Dennison and Howard (Nevada)
Profile: p 810
Table: p 406, 409, 410

Hall, Estill, Hardwick, Gable, Golden & Nelson, PC (Oklahoma)
Profile: p 926
Table: p 582

Hall, Farley, Oberrecht & Blanton, PA (Idaho)
Profile: p 926
Table: p 220

Hall Dickler Kent Goldstein & Wood LLP (New York)
Profile: p 926
Table: p 247

Hammer Ferretti & Schiavoni (West Virginia)
Profile: p 926
Table: p 716

Hammons & Associates (Oklahoma)
Profile: p 926
Table: p 581

Hancock Rothert & Bunshft LLP (California)
Profile: p 811
Table: p 46

Hangley Aronchick Segal & Pudlin (Pennsylvania)
Profile: p 927
Table: p 607, 611

Hanify & King (Massachusetts)
Profile: p 927
Table: p 346

Hankins & Hicks (Arkansas)
Profile: p 927
Table: p 26

Haralson, Miller, Pitt & McAnally (Arizona)
Profile: p 927
Table: p 19

Harding Schultz & Downs (Nebraska)
Profile: p 927
Table: p 402

Hare, Wynn, Newell & Newton LLP (Alabama)
Profile: p 812
Table: p 4

Harrill & Sutter PLLC (Arkansas)
Profile: p 927
Table: p 24

Harrison, Kemp & Jones, LLP (Nevada)
Profile: p 813
Table: p 409

Harris, Wiltshire & Grannis LLP (District of Columbia)
Profile: p 927
Table: p 107

Hartig Rhodes Hoge & Lekisch PC (Alaska)
Profile: p 927
Table: p 12

Hartzog Conger Cason & Neville, PC (Oklahoma)
Profile: p 927
Table: p 580, 583

Harvey & Frank (Maine)
Profile: p 927
Table: p 322

Harwell Howard Hyne Gabbert & Manner, P.C. (Tennessee)
Profile: p 927
Table: p 635, 639

Haskin Lauter & LaRue (Indiana)
Profile: p 927
Table: p 278

Hawley Troxell Ennis & Hawley LLP (Idaho)
Profile: p 927
Table: p 219, 220, 221

Haynes and Boone, LLP (Texas)
Profile: p 814
Table: p 644, 646, 649, 651, 655, 657, 658, 660, 662, 665

Haynsworth Baldwin Johnson & Greaves LLC (South Carolina)
Profile: p 927
Table: p 625

Haynsworth Sinkler Boyd PA (South Carolina)
Profile: p 927
Table: p 624, 626, 627

Healy & Baillie LLP (New York)
Profile: p 815
Table: p 496

Heard & Howard (Montana)
Profile: p 927
Table: p 397

Heiman, Aber, Goldlust & Baker (Delaware)
Table: p 95

Heller Ehrman White & McAuliffe LLP (California)
Profile: p 927
Table: p 29, 39, 46, 50, 726

Helmsing, Leach, Herlong, Newman & Rouse, PC (Alabama)
Profile: p 816
Table: p 4

Helms Mulliss & Wicker PLLC (North Carolina)
Profile: p 927
Table: p 544, 545, 549, 550

Henderson Daily Withrow & DeVoe (Indiana)
Profile: p 927
Table: p 277

Hendrick Phillips Salzman & Flatt PC (Georgia)
Profile: p 817
Table: p 184

Hennigan, Bennett & Dorman (California)
Profile: p 927
Table: p 50

FIRMS INDEX

Henson & Efron (Minnesota)
Profile: p 927
Table: p 368

Herman, Herman, Katz & Cotlar LLP (Louisiana)
Profile: p 927
Table: p 313

Hickey, Mackey, Evans & Walker (Wyoming)
Profile: p 927
Table: p 732

Hill & Robbins PC (Colorado)
Profile: p 927
Table: p 79

Hill, Ward & Henderson, PA (Florida)
Profile: p 928
Table: p 164

Hill Rivkins & Hayden LLP (New York)
Profile: p 927
Table: p 496

Hinckley, Allen & Snyder LLP (Massachusetts)
Profile: p 928
Table: p 415, 620, 621, 622

Hinkle Hensley Shanor & Martin LLP (New Mexico)
Profile: p 928
Table: p 435

Hinkle Elkouri Law Firm LLC (Kansas)
Profile: p 928
Table: p 297

Hirschler, Fleischer, Weinberg, Cox & Allen A Professional Corporation (Virginia)
Profile: p 928
Table: p 702, 703

Hirst & Applegate, PC (Wyoming)
Profile: p 928
Table: p 730, 732

Hite, Fanning & Honeyman LLP (Kansas)
Profile: p 928
Table: p 296

Hoff, Curtis, Pacht, Cassidy, Frame, Somers & Katims PC (Vermont)
Profile: p 928
Table: p 693

Hoffman Reilly Pozner & Williamson (Colorado)
Profile: p 928
Table: p 79

Hogan & Hartson LLP (District of Columbia)
Profile: p 818
Table: p 75, 78, 103, 107, 111, 120, 122, 127, 327, 330, 485

Holland & Hart LLP (Colorado)
Profile: p 819
Table: p 75, 78, 79, 220, 394, 395, 684, 730, 731, 732, 733

Holland & Knight LLP (New York)
Profile: p 820
Table: p 127, 151, 152, 153, 155, 160, 161, 164, 167, 169, 247, 496, 621, 622

Holme Roberts & Owen LLP (Colorado)
Profile: p 928
Table: p 75, 78, 79, 81, 684, 686, 687

Holt Ney Zatcoff & Wasserman, LLP (Georgia)
Profile: p 928
Table: p 199

Honigman Miller Schwartz and Cohn (Michigan)
Profile: p 928
Table: p 361, 363, 364

Hoole & King (Utah)
Profile: p 928
Table: p 685

Hopping, Green & Sams PA (Florida)
Profile: p 928
Table: p 160

Horn & Payne (Mississippi)
Profile: p 928
Table: p 379

Horton Law Offices (Wisconsin)
Profile: p 928
Table: p 727

Howard, Rice, Nemerovski, Canady, Falk & Rabkin (California)
Profile: p 928
Table: p 44

Howrey Simon Arnold & White (District of Columbia)
Profile: p 928
Table: p 29, 46, 103, 120, 121, 660

Hoyt & Blewett (Montana)
Profile: p 928
Table: p 395, 396

Huddleston, Bolen, Beatty, Porter & Copen, LLP (West Virginia)
Profile: p 928
Table: p 714, 719

Hughes, Kellner, Sullivan & Alke (Montana)
Profile: p 928
Table: p 395

Hughes Hubbard & Reed LLP (New York)
Profile: p 928
Table: p 106

Hughes & Luce LLP (Texas)
Profile: p 928
Table: p 649, 667

Hughes Thorsness Powell Huddleston & Bauman LLC (Alaska)
Profile: p 928
Table: p 9

Hunt, Ortmann, Blasco, Palffy & Rossell Inc (California)
Profile: p 928
Table: p 36

Hunter, Maclean, Exley & Dunn, PC (Georgia)
Profile: p 928
Table: p 192

Hunton & Williams (Virginia)
Profile: p 929
Table: p 114, 117, 126, 151, 152, 164, 699, 701, 702, 703

Hurley Toevs Styles Hamblin & Panter PA (New Mexico)
Profile: p 929
Table: p 437

Husch & Eppenberger, LLC (Missouri)
Profile: p 929
Table: p 296, 385, 389

I

Ice Miller (Indiana)
Profile: p 929
Table: p 277, 279, 280, 281

Irell & Manella LLP (California)
Profile: p 929
Table: p 47, 58

Isaacson, Rosenbaum, Woods & Levy, PC (Colorado)
Profile: p 929
Table: p 81

Ivins, Phillips & Barker (District of Columbia)
Profile: p 929
Table: p 129

J

Jackson Kelly PLLC (West Virginia)
Profile: p 821
Table: p 714, 716, 718, 719

Jackson Lewis (New York)
Profile: p 929
Table: p 88, 158, 189, 342, 466, 602

Jackson Walker LLP (Texas)
Profile: p 929
Table: p 665

Jacobs, Chase, Frick, Kleinkopf & Kelley (Colorado)
Profile: p 929
Table: p 79, 81

Jaffe, Raitt, Heuer & Weiss, PC (Michigan)
Profile: p 929
Table: p 364

Janove Baar Associates (Utah)
Profile: p 929
Table: p 686

Jenkens & Gilchrist (Texas)
Profile: p 929
Table: p 110, 646, 648, 651, 660, 665

Jenkins Fenstermaker, PLLC (West Virginia)
Profile: p 929
Table: p 716

Jenner & Block (Illinois)
Profile: p 822
Table: p 125, 229, 239, 240, 245, 247

Jennings, Strouss & Salmon, PLC (Arizona)
Profile: p 929
Table: p 16

Jensen Baird Gardner & Henry (Maine)
Profile: p 929
Table: p 323

Jermain, Dunnagan & Owens PC (Alaska)
Profile: p 929
Table: p 10

Johnson, Blakely, Pope, Bokor, Ruppel & Burns, PA (Florida)
Profile: p 929
Table: p 169

Johnston Barton Proctor & Powell LLP (Alabama)
Profile: p 929
Table: p 3

Jones, Foster, Johnston & Stubbs, P.A. (Florida)
Profile: p 825
Table: p 164

Jones Walker Waechter Poitevent Carrère & Denègre, LLP (Louisiana)
Profile: p 826
Table: p 308, 311, 313, 314

Jones Day (Ohio)
Profile: p 823
Table: p 103, 112, 114, 238, 245, 471, 478, 559, 562, 564, 568, 569, 571, 604, 648, 660

Jones Vargas (Nevada)
Profile: p 929
Table: p 406, 409, 410

Jones Waldo Holbrook & McDonough PC (Utah)
Profile: p 930
Table: p 684, 686, 688

Jorgenson Law Office (Wyoming)
Profile: p 930
Table: p 733

Jubelirer, Pass & Intrieri (Pennsylvania)
Profile: p 930
Table: p 601

K

Kahn Kleinman (Ohio)
Profile: p 930
Table: p 571

Kahn, Smith & Collins, PA (Maryland)
Profile: p 930
Table: p 328

Kalijarvi, Chuzi & Newman PC (District of Columbia)
Profile: p 930
Table: p 112

Kamer Zucker & Abbott (Nevada)
Profile: p 930
Table: p 408

Kantrow, Spaht, Weaver & Blitzer (Louisiana)
Profile: p 930
Table: p 308

Kaplan, Strangis & Kaplan (Minnesota)
Profile: p 930
Table: p 368

Karaganis, White & Magel (Illinois)
Profile: p 930
Table: p 239

Kasowitz Benson Torres & Friedman (New York)
Profile: p 930
Table: p 471

Katten Muchin Zavis Rosenman (Illinois)
Profile: p 827
Table: p 226, 232, 249, 492

Katz, Kutter, Haigler, Alderman, Bryant & Yon, PA (Florida)
Profile: p 930
Table: p 164

Katz Randall Weinberg & Richmond (Illinois)
Profile: p 930
Table: p 249

Kaufman & Canoles (Virginia)
Profile: p 930
Table: p 699, 702

Kay Casto & Chaney PLLC (West Virginia)
Profile: p 930
Table: p 714

Kaye Scholer LLP (New York)
Profile: p 930
Table: p 240, 456, 466

Kean, Miller, Hawthorne, D'Armond, McCowan & Jarman, LLP (Louisiana)
Profile: p 930
Table: p 307, 308, 311, 313

Keating, Muething & Klekamp, P.L.L. (Ohio)
Profile: p 930
Table: p 562

Kegler, Brown, Hill & Ritter (Ohio)
Profile: p 930
Table: p 560

FIRMS INDEX

Keker & Van Nest LLP (California)
Profile: p 930
Table: p 47, 50

Keleher & McLeod, PA (New Mexico)
Profile: p 930
Table: p 433, 435, 437

Kellogg, Huber, Hansen, Todd & Evans PLLC (District of Columbia)
Profile: p 930
Table: p 107

Kelly & Berens P.A. (Minnesota)
Profile: p 930
Table: p 372

Kelly & McKee (Florida)
Profile: p 930
Table: p 157

Kelly Haglund Garnsey + Kahn (Colorado)
Profile: p 828
Table: p 79

Kennedy Covington Lobdell & Hickman, L.L.P. (North Carolina)
Profile: p 930
Table: p 544, 545, 549, 550

Kenny Nachwalter Seymour Arnold Critchlow & Spector (Florida)
Profile: p 930
Table: p 151, 164

Kenyon & Kenyon (District of Columbia)
Profile: p 930
Table: p 478

Kienbaum Opperwall Hardy & Pelton (Michigan)
Profile: p 931
Table: p 362

Kiesewetter Wise Kaplan Schwimmer & Prather, PLC (Tennessee)
Profile: p 931
Table: p 637

Killmer & Lane (Colorado)
Profile: p 931
Table: p 77

Killworth, Gottman, Hagan & Schaeff LLP (Ohio)
Profile: p 931
Table: p 568

Kilpatrick Stockton LLP (Georgia)
Profile: p 931
Table: p 181, 183, 184, 186, 189, 192, 193, 195, 197, 199, 201, 545, 549, 550

King Hershey, A Professional Corporation (Missouri)
Profile: p 931
Table: p 391

King & Ballow (Tennessee)
Profile: p 931
Table: p 637

King & Greisen (Colorado)
Profile: p 931
Table: p 77

King, Blackwell & Downs PA (Florida)
Profile: p 931
Table: p 164

King & Spalding LLP (Georgia)
Profile: p 829
Table: p 181, 183, 184, 186, 189, 191, 192, 193, 195, 197, 199, 201, 653, 664

Kirk & Chaney (Oklahoma)
Profile: p 931
Table: p 583

Kirkland & Ellis (Illinois)
Profile: p 830
Table: p 47, 122, 125, 224, 226, 229, 232, 240, 242, 244, 245, 249, 251, 478, 481, 487, 488

Kirkpatrick & Lockhart LLP (Pennsylvania)
Profile: p 931
Table: p 599, 602, 604, 608, 611

Kirschner & Legler (Florida)
Profile: p 931
Table: p 155

Kirton & McConkie (Utah)
Profile: p 931
Table: p 688

Klee, Tuchin, Bogdanoff & Stern (California)
Profile: p 831
Table: p 44

Klett Rooney Lieber & Schorling (Pennsylvania)
Profile: p 931
Table: p 597, 602, 604, 607

Kluger, Peretz, Kaplan & Berlin P.L. (Florida)
Profile: p 931
Table: p 161

Knobbe Martens Olson & Bear (California)
Profile: p 931
Table: p 47

Kohn Swift & Graf (Pennsylvania)
Profile: p 931
Table: p 595

Kohn, Shands, Elbert, Gianoulakis & Giljum, LLP (Missouri)
Profile: p 931
Table: p 389

Kozyak Tropin & Throckmorton (Florida)
Profile: p 931
Table: p 161, 164

Kramer Levin Naftalis & Frankel LLP (New York)
Profile: p 832
Table: p 471, 481, 492

Kramon & Graham, PA (Maryland)
Profile: p 931
Table: p 330

Krieg DeVault LLP (Indiana)
Profile: p 931
Table: p 277, 280, 281

Kummer Kaempfer Bonner & Renshaw (Nevada)
Profile: p 833
Table: p 406, 409, 410

Kutak Rock LLP (Nebraska)
Profile: p 932
Table: p 23, 26

L

Lamberth, Cifelli, Stokes & Stout, PA (Georgia)
Profile: p 834
Table: p 193

Lamson, Dugan & Murray, LLP (Nebraska)
Profile: p 932
Table: p 403

Lane & Waterman (Iowa)
Profile: p 932
Table: p 286, 289, 290

Lane Powell Spears Lubersky LLP (Washington)
Profile: p 932
Table: p 706, 709

Laner, Muchin, Dombrow, Becker, Levin, Tominberg (Illinois)
Profile: p 932
Table: p 236

Langerman Law Offices (Arizona)
Profile: p 932
Table: p 17

Langrock Sperry & Wool, LLP (Vermont)
Profile: p 932
Table: p 693, 696

Latham & Watkins LLP (California)
Profile: p 835
Table: p 29, 30, 32, 34, 37, 39, 41, 44, 46, 50, 55, 56, 58, 107, 111, 114, 117, 126, 226, 232, 240, 251, 447, 471, 487, 490, 492

Lathrop & Rutledge (Wyoming)
Profile: p 837
Table: p 732

Lathrop & Gage LC (Missouri)
Profile: p 932
Table: p 294, 296, 297, 385, 389, 391

Lavey & Burnett (Arkansas)
Profile: p 932
Table: p 24

Law Office of Bruce T Moats (Wyoming)
Profile: p 932
Table: p 731

Law Offices of Thomas Clay (Kentucky)
Profile: p 932
Table: p 301

Lawler Metzger & Milkman LLC (District of Columbia)
Profile: p 932
Table: p 107

Lawton & Cates, S.C. (Wisconsin)
Profile: p 932
Table: p 724

Laxalt & Nomura (Nevada)
Profile: p 932
Table: p 409

Leagre Chandler & Millard LLP (Indiana)
Profile: p 932
Table: p 277

Leatherwood Walker Todd & Mann, P.C. (South Carolina)
Profile: p 932
Table: p 626, 627

Lebau & Neuworth, LLC (Maryland)
Profile: p 932
Table: p 328

LeBoeuf, Lamb, Greene & MacRae, LLP (New York)
Profile: p 838
Table: p 114, 167, 468, 476

LeClair Ryan (Virginia)
Profile: p 932
Table: p 699

Lehr Middlebrooks Price & Proctor (Alabama)
Profile: p 933
Table: p 3

Leiby Taylor Stearns Linkhorst & Roberts, PA (Florida)
Profile: p 933
Table: p 153

Leitman, Siegal & Payne, PC (Alabama)
Profile: p 933
Table: p 6

Lemle & Kelleher, LLP (Louisiana)
Profile: p 933
Table: p 314

Leonard & Associates PC (Oklahoma)
Profile: p 933
Table: p 581

Leonard, Street and Deinard Professional Association (Minnesota)
Profile: p 933
Table: p 368, 371, 372, 374

LePatner & Associates LLP (New York)
Profile: p 839
Table: p 458

Lesesne & Connette (North Carolina)
Profile: p 933
Table: p 547

Levine, Blaszak, Block & Boothby LLP (District of Columbia)
Profile: p 840
Table: p 107

Levine Sullivan & Koch LLP (District of Columbia)
Profile: p 933
Table: p 125

Levy, Ram & Olson (California)
Profile: p 933
Table: p 53

Lewis, Longman & Walker PA (Florida)
Profile: p 933
Table: p 160

Lewis, Rice & Fingersh (Missouri)
Profile: p 933
Table: p 385, 389, 391

Lewis and Roca (Arizona)
Profile: p 933
Table: p 16, 18, 19, 20

Leydig, Voit & Mayer, Ltd (Illinois)
Profile: p 933
Table: p 244

Lightfoot, Franklin & White, LLC (Alabama)
Profile: p 933
Table: p 4

Lindner & Marsack, S.C. (Wisconsin)
Profile: p 933
Table: p 725

Lindquist & Vennum PLLP (Minnesota)
Profile: p 933
Table: p 368, 372, 374

Linowes and Blocher LLP (Maryland)
Profile: p 933
Table: p 331

Lionel Sawyer & Collins (Nevada)
Profile: p 933
Table: p 406, 408, 409, 410

Liskow & Lewis, PLC (Louisiana)
Profile: p 933
Table: p 307, 308, 313, 314

Lisman, Webster, Kirkpatrick & Leckerling, P.C. (Vermont)
Profile: p 933
Table: p 696

Little, Cicchetti & Conard PC (Vermont)
Profile: p 933
Table: p 696

Littler Mendelson PC (California)
Profile: p 933
Table: p 39, 236, 602, 651

FIRMS INDEX

Livingston Adler Pulda Meikeljohn & Kelly PC (Connecticut)
Profile: p 934
Table: p 88

Locke Liddell & Sapp LLP (Texas)
Profile: p 934
Table: p 646, 653, 665, 667

Lommen, Nelson, Cole & Stageberg, P.A. (Minnesota)
Profile: p 934
Table: p 368, 372

Lord, Bissell & Brook (California)
Profile: p 934
Table: p 242

Lovells (London)
Profile: p 934
Table: p 242

Lowe Gray Steele & Darko LLP (Indiana)
Profile: p 934
Table: p 278

Lowenstein Sandler PC (New Jersey)
Profile: p 841
Table: p 424, 428, 429

Lowndes Drosdick Doster Kantor & Reed, PA (Florida)
Profile: p 934
Table: p 167

Lueders, Robertson, Konzen & Fitzhenry (Illinois)
Profile: p 934
Table: p 238

Lum Danzis Drasco & Positan (New Jersey)
Profile: p 934
Table: p 426

Keith M Lyons (Nevada)
Profile: p 934
Table: p 407

M

MacDonald, Hoague & Bayless (Washington)
Profile: p 934
Table: p 707

Macey Macey & Swanson (Indiana)
Profile: p 934
Table: p 278

MacPherson Kelly & Thompson (Wyoming)
Profile: p 934
Table: p 733

Madison Harbour Mroz & Brennan PA (New Mexico)
Profile: p 934
Table: p 435

Manatt, Phelps & Phillips, LLP (California)
Profile: p 934
Table: p 53

Mancini Welch & Geiger LLP (Hawaii)
Profile: p 934
Table: p 216

Mandell & Wright (Texas)
Profile: p 934
Table: p 651

Manko, Gold, Katcher & Fox LLP (Pennsylvania)
Profile: p 934
Table: p 604

Manning Fulton & Skinner (North Carolina)
Profile: p 934
Table: p 550

Mariscal, Weeks, McIntyre & Friedlander, PA (Arizona)
Profile: p 934
Table: p 20

Mark W. Gifford (Wyoming)
Profile: p 934
Table: p 731

Markowitz & Richman (Pennsylvania)
Profile: p 934
Table: p 601

Markowitz, Herbold, Glade & Mehlhaf PC (Oregon)
Profile: p 934
Table: p 590

Marr Hipp Jones and Pepper (Hawaii)
Profile: p 935
Table: p 214

Marshall, Gerstein & Borun (Illinois)
Profile: p 935
Table: p 244

Marshall Hill Cassas & De Lipkau (Nevada)
Profile: p 935
Table: p 406

Martin & Churchill Chartered (Kansas)
Profile: p 935
Table: p 295

Martin, Disiere, Jefferson & Wisdom LLP (Texas)
Profile: p 842
Table: p 658

Martin, Pringle, Oliver, Wallace & Bauer, L.L.P. (Kansas)
Profile: p 935
Table: p 295

Mary Elizabeth Galvan (Wyoming)
Profile: p 935
Table: p 731

Maslon Edelman Borman & Brand, LLP (Minnesota)
Profile: p 935
Table: p 372

Mason & Mason PC (Wyoming)
Profile: p 935
Table: p 732

Matkov Salzman Madoff & Gunn (Illinois)
Profile: p 935
Table: p 236

Mauk & Burgoyne (Idaho)
Profile: p 935
Table: p 219

Maupin Taylor & Ellis, P.A. (North Carolina)
Profile: p 935
Table: p 548

Maxey Wann (Mississippi)
Profile: p 935
Table: p 379

May, Adam, Gerdes & Thompson, L.L.P. (South Dakota)
Profile: p 935
Table: p 632

Mayer, Brown, Rowe & Maw (Illinois)
Profile: p 843
Table: p 56, 107, 122, 127, 224, 226, 229, 232, 236, 238, 239, 240, 242, 244, 245, 249, 251, 445, 451, 453, 645, 662, 665

Maynard, Cooper & Gale PC (Alabama)
Profile: p 935
Table: p 1, 3, 4, 6

Mazur, Carp & Rubin PC (New York)
Profile: p 935
Table: p 458

McAfee & Taft, PC (Oklahoma)
Profile: p 844
Table: p 580, 582, 583, 584

McAndrews, Held & Malloy, Ltd (Illinois)
Profile: p 845
Table: p 244

McCarter & English, LLP (New Jersey)
Profile: p 935
Table: p 424, 428

McCorriston Miller Mukai MacKinnon LLP (Hawaii)
Profile: p 935
Table: p 215, 216

McCullough, Wareheman & Labunker (Kansas)
Profile: p 935
Table: p 295

McCullough Hill Fikso Kretschmer Smith (Washington)
Profile: p 935
Table: p 711

McDade Fogler Maines LLP (Texas)
Profile: p 935
Table: p 662

McDermott, Will & Emery (Illinois)
Profile: p 846
Table: p 47, 58, 121, 129, 226, 232, 245, 251, 344

McDonald Carano Wilson McCune Bergin Frankovich & Hicks LLP (Nevada)
Profile: p 935
Table: p 409, 410

McGlinchey Stafford (Louisiana)
Profile: p 847
Table: p 307, 308, 311, 314, 378

McGrath, North, Mullin & Kratz, PC (Nebraska)
Profile: p 935
Table: p 400, 402, 403, 404

McGuinn, Hillsman & Palefsky (California)
Profile: p 935
Table: p 39

McGuireWoods LLP (Virginia)
Profile: p 935
Table: p 699, 701, 702, 703

McKee Nelson LLP (District of Columbia)
Profile: p 848
Table: p 129, 453

McKenna Long & Aldridge (District of Columbia)
Profile: p 935
Table: p 117, 186, 191, 192, 193, 199

McKinney & Stringer, A Professional Corporation (Oklahoma)
Profile: p 935
Table: p 580, 582, 583

McKool Smith (Texas)
Profile: p 936
Table: p 660

McLane, Graf, Raulerson & Middleton PA (New Hampshire)
Profile: p 849
Table: p 415, 417, 418, 420

McMahon, DeGulis, Hoffman & Lombardi LLP (Ohio)
Profile: p 936
Table: p 566

McManus Schor Asmar & Darden, LLP (District of Columbia)
Profile: p 936
Table: p 110

McNair Law Firm PA (South Carolina)
Profile: p 936
Table: p 624, 626, 627

McNamara & Martinez LLP (Colorado)
Profile: p 936
Table: p 77

McTeague, Higbee, Case, Cohen, Whitney & Toker, PA (Maine)
Profile: p 936
Table: p 320

McTurnan & Turner (Indiana)
Profile: p 850
Table: p 280

Meckler, Bulger & Tilson (Illinois)
Profile: p 936
Table: p 236

Meelheim, Wilkinson & Meelheim (Alabama)
Profile: p 936
Table: p 2

Meites, Mulder, Burger & Mollica (Illinois)
Profile: p 936
Table: p 235

Melli, Walker, Pease & Ruhly, S.C. (Wisconsin)
Profile: p 936
Table: p 725

Mello & Klesch LLP (Vermont)
Profile: p 936
Table: p 693

Mendes & Mount, LLP (New York)
Profile: p 936
Table: p 476

Messing, Rudavsky & Weliky PC (Massachusetts)
Profile: p 936
Table: p 341

Meuleman & Miller, LLP (Idaho)
Profile: p 936
Table: p 221

Meyer, Hendricks & Bivens (Arizona)
Profile: p 936
Table: p 19

Meyer Capel, a Professional Corporation (Illinois)
Profile: p 936
Table: p 229

Michael Best & Friedrich LLP (Wisconsin)
Profile: p 936
Table: p 723, 725, 726, 727

Middleton Reutlinger, P.S.C. (Kentucky)
Profile: p 936
Table: p 303

Milbank, Tweed, Hadley & McCloy (New York)
Profile: p 936
Table: p 32, 41, 44, 55, 445, 456, 471, 490

FIRMS INDEX

Milberg Weiss Bershad Hynes & Lerach LLP (New York)
Profile: p 936
Table: p 50, 481

Miles & Stockbridge PC (Maryland)
Profile: p 936
Table: p 327, 329

Miller & Martin LLP (Tennessee)
Profile: p 937
Table: p 637

Miller, Canfield, Paddock and Stone PLC (Michigan)
Profile: p 937
Table: p 360, 361, 362, 363, 364

Eggleston & Cramer, Ltd (Vermont)
Profile: p 921
Table: p 692, 695, 696

Miller, Stratvert & Torgerson, PA (New Mexico)
Profile: p 937
Table: p 435

Miller & Chevalier (District of Columbia)
Profile: p 936
Table: p 129

Miller Nash LLP (Oregon)
Profile: p 851
Table: p 587, 589, 590

Miller-O'Brien, PLLP (Minnesota)
Profile: p 937
Table: p 370

Millisor Co, LPA (Ohio)
Profile: p 937
Table: p 564

Miner, Barnhill & Galland (Illinois)
Profile: p 937
Table: p 235

Mintz Levin Cohn Ferris Glovsky and Popeo PC (Massachusetts)
Profile: p 937
Table: p 107, 339, 342, 344, 346, 348, 351

Miro Weiner & Kramer, PC (Michigan)
Profile: p 937
Table: p 364

Mitchell Williams Selig Gates Woodyard, PLLC (Arkansas)
Profile: p 937
Table: p 24, 25, 26

Mock, Schwabe, Waldo, Elder, Reeves & Bryant (Oklahoma)
Profile: p 937
Table: p 584

Modrall, Sperling, Roehl, Harris & Sisk, PA (New Mexico)
Profile: p 937
Table: p 433, 435, 437

Moehrke, Mackie & Shea, P.C. (Massachusetts)
Profile: p 937
Table: p 344

Moffatt Thomas Barrett Rock & Fields (Idaho)
Profile: p 937
Table: p 220

Monteleone & McCrory, LLP (California)
Profile: p 852
Table: p 36

Montgomery, McCracken, Walker & Rhoads, LLP (Pennsylvania)
Profile: p 937
Table: p 595, 604, 611

Moon, Moss, McGill & Shapiro (Maine)
Profile: p 937
Table: p 321

Moore & Van Allen PLLC (South Carolina)
Profile: p 937
Table: p 544, 545, 549, 550

Morgan Brown and Joy LLP (Massachusetts)
Profile: p 937
Table: p 342

Morgan & Finnegan (New York)
Profile: p 853
Table: p 478

Morgan, Lewis & Bockius LLP (Pennsylvania)
Profile: p 937, 914
Table: p 39, 55, 103, 112, 114, 117, 158, 424, 466, 471, 595, 597, 599, 602, 604, 607, 611, 613

Morris, James, Hitchens & Williams, LLP (Delaware)
Profile: p 937
Table: p 95, 99

Morris, Laing, Evans, Brock & Kennedy, Chartered (Kansas)
Profile: p 937
Table: p 295, 297

Morris, Nichols, Arsht & Tunnell (Delaware)
Profile: p 937
Table: p 94, 96, 97

Morrison & Foerster LLP (California)
Profile: p 854
Table: p 29, 30, 34, 39, 41, 42, 47, 50, 56, 58, 107, 456

Morris Pickering & Sanner (Nevada)
Profile: p 937
Table: p 409

Moulton, Bellingham, Longo & Mather, PC (Montana)
Profile: p 937
Table: p 397

Moye, O'Brien, O'Rourke, Pickert & Martin, LLP (Florida)
Profile: p 855
Table: p 153

Moyer & Bergman, PLC (Iowa)
Profile: p 937
Table: p 286, 288, 290

Much Shelist Freed Denenberg Ament & Rubenstein, PC (Illinois)
Profile: p 938
Table: p 231

Muller Mintz (Florida)
Profile: p 938
Table: p 158

Mullikin, Larson & Swift (Wyoming)
Profile: p 938
Table: p 733

Munger, Tolles & Olson (California)
Profile: p 938
Table: p 46, 50

Murane & Bostwick, L.L.C. (Wyoming)
Profile: p 938
Table: p 731

Murphy Sheneman Julian & Rogers (California)
Profile: p 856
Table: p 44

Murtha Cullina LLP (Connecticut)
Profile: p 938
Table: p 90

Myers Oliver & Price (New Mexico)
Profile: p 938
Table: p 437

Nakamura, Quinn & Walls (Alabama)
Profile: p 938
Table: p 2

Neal Gerber & Eisenberg (Illinois)
Profile: p 938
Table: p 249

Needle & Rosenberg (Georgia)
Profile: p 938
Table: p 195

Nelson Mullins Riley & Scarborough, LLP (South Carolina)
Profile: p 857
Table: p 624, 625, 626

Nexsen Pruet Jacobs & Pollard, LLC (South Carolina)
Profile: p 938
Table: p 624, 625, 626, 627

Nichols Kaster & Anderson PLLP (Minnesota)
Profile: p 938
Table: p 370

Nicoletti Hornig Campise Sweeney & Paige (New York)
Profile: p 938
Table: p 496

Nilles, Hansen & Davies, Ltd. (North Dakota)
Profile: p 938
Table: p 555, 556

Ning Lilly & Jones (Hawaii)
Profile: p 938
Table: p 213

Nixon Peabody LLP (New York)
Profile: p 858
Table: p 415, 468

Noeding & Moody PC (New Mexico)
Profile: p 938
Table: p 434

Norman, Hanson & DeTroy, LLC (Maine)
Profile: p 938
Table: p 322

Nourse & Bowles LLP (New York)
Profile: p 938
Table: p 496

Nungesser & Hill (New Hampshire)
Profile: p 938
Table: p 420

Nutter, McClennen & Fish, LLP (Massachusetts)
Profile: p 938
Table: p 336, 344, 351

Nyemaster, Goode, Voigts, West, Hansell & O'Brien, PC (Iowa)
Profile: p 938
Table: p 286, 288, 289, 290

O' Neill Kellner & Green PC (Vermont)
Profile: p 939
Table: p 695

O'Donnell & Shaeffer (California)
Profile: p 939
Table: p 50

Oertel, Hoffman, Fernandez & Cole PA (Florida)
Profile: p 939
Table: p 160

Ogden Newell & Welch (Kentucky)
Profile: p 939
Table: p 300, 303

Ogletree, Deakins, Nash, Smoak & Stewart, PC (South Carolina)
Profile: p 939
Table: p 3, 112, 189, 279, 548, 625

Ohnstad Twichell PC (North Dakota)
Profile: p 939
Table: p 556

O'Keefe Ashenden Lyons & Ward (Illinois)
Profile: p 939
Table: p 229

O'Melveny & Myers LLP (California)
Profile: p 939
Table: p 29, 30, 37, 39, 44, 46, 50, 53, 56, 58, 103, 466, 485

Oppenheimer Wolff & Donnelly LLP (California)
Profile: p 939
Table: p 368, 372, 374

Orr & Reno, PA (New Hampshire)
Profile: p 939
Table: p 415, 418

Orrick, Herrington & Sutcliffe (California)
Profile: p 859
Table: p 30, 39, 41, 55, 56, 58, 453, 466, 490

Osborn Maledon, PA (Arizona)
Profile: p 939
Table: p 16, 19

Oshima, Chun, Fong & Chung (Hawaii)
Profile: p 939
Table: p 216

Otten, Johnson, Robinson, Neff & Ragonetti, PC (Colorado)
Profile: p 939
Table: p 81

Otterbourg, Steindler, Houston & Rosen (New York)
Profile: p 939
Table: p 471

Outten & Golden LLP (New York)
Profile: p 939
Table: p 466

Owens & Turner, PC (Alaska)
Profile: p 939
Table: p 11

Oxfeld Cohen (New Jersey)
Profile: p 939
Table: p 426

P

Pachulski, Stang, Ziehl, Young, Jones & Weintraub P.C. (California)
Profile: p 860
Table: p 44, 96

Packman, Neuwahl & Rosenberg (Florida)
Profile: p 939
Table: p 169

Palmer & Dodge (Massachusetts)
Profile: p 939
Table: p 336, 339, 342

Parker, Poe, Adams & Bernstein LLP (North Carolina)
Profile: p 939
Table: p 549, 550

FIRMS INDEX

Parker, Hudson, Rainer & Dobbs LLP (Georgia)
Profile: p 939
Table: p 186, 193

Parks, Chesin, Walbert & Miller (Georgia)
Profile: p 939
Table: p 188

Parr Waddoups Brown Gee & Loveless (Utah)
Profile: p 939
Table: p 684, 687, 688

Parsons Behle & Latimer PC (Utah)
Profile: p 940
Table: p 684, 686, 687, 688

Partridge Snow & Hahn LLP (Rhode Island)
Profile: p 940
Table: p 621

Patrick E Hacker (Wyoming)
Profile: p 940
Table: p 731

Patterson Harkavy & Lawrence (North Carolina)
Profile: p 940
Table: p 547

Pattishall, McAuliffe, Newbury, Hilliard & Geraldson (Illinois)
Profile: p 940
Table: p 244

Paul, Frank & Collins, PC (Vermont)
Profile: p 940
Table: p 692, 694, 695, 696

Paul, Johnson, Park & Niles, Attorneys At Law, A Law Corporation (Hawaii)
Profile: p 940
Table: p 215

Paul, Hastings, Janofsky & Walker LLP (California)
Profile: p 861
Table: p 39, 56, 112, 189, 492

Paul, Weiss, Rifkind, Wharton & Garrison LLP (New York)
Profile: p 862
Table: p 107, 471, 481, 485, 492, 498

Pearson Christensen LLP (North Dakota)
Profile: p 940
Table: p 554, 555

Peckar & Abramson, P.C. (New York)
Profile: p 863
Table: p 153, 458

Pemberton, Sorlie, Rufer & Kershner, PLLP (Minnesota)
Profile: p 940
Table: p 370

Pennie & Edmonds LLP (New York)
Profile: p 940
Table: p 478

Pennington, Moore, Wilkinson, Bell & Dunbar, PA (Florida)
Profile: p 940
Table: p 164

Pepper Hamilton LLP (Pennsylvania)
Profile: p 940
Table: p 595, 599, 602, 607, 611

Perkins, Thompson, Hinckley & Keddy, P.A. (Maine)
Profile: p 940
Table: p 323

Perkins Coie LLP (Washington)
Profile: p 940
Table: p 11, 12, 587, 590, 592, 706, 708, 709, 711

Perkins Smith & Cohen LLP (Massachusetts)
Profile: p 940
Table: p 341

Perry, Shapiro, Quindel, Saks, Charlton & Lerner (Wisconsin)
Profile: p 940
Table: p 724

Phelps Dunbar LLP (Louisiana)
Profile: p 864
Table: p 307, 308, 311, 313, 314, 378, 380, 381

Phibbs & Resor P.C. (Wyoming)
Profile: p 940
Table: p 733

Phillips Gardill Kaiser & Altmeyer (West Virginia)
Profile: p 941
Table: p 714

Phillips McFall McCaffrey McVay & Murrah, P.C. (Oklahoma)
Profile: p 941
Table: p 584

Pierce Atwood (Maine)
Profile: p 865
Table: p 319, 321, 322, 323

Pillsbury Winthrop LLP (New York)
Profile: p 866
Table: p 30, 34, 42, 56, 58

Piper Rudnick LLP (Illinois)
Profile: p 867
Table: p 110, 127, 231, 238, 240, 242, 249, 327, 329, 330, 331, 351, 408

Pircher, Nichols & Meeks (California)
Profile: p 941
Table: p 56

Pitney, Hardin, Kipp & Szuch LLP (New Jersey)
Profile: p 941
Table: p 424, 426, 428, 429

Pitt Dowty McGehee & Mirer (Michigan)
Profile: p 941
Table: p 362

Podhurst, Orseck, Josefsberg, Eaton, Meadow, Olin & Perwin (Florida)
Profile: p 941
Table: p 164

Polsinelli Shalton & Welte, A Professional Corporation (Missouri)
Profile: p 941
Table: p 294, 297, 385, 389, 391

Poore, Roth & Robinson, P.C. (Montana)
Profile: p 941
Table: p 396

Porter & Hedges, LLP (Texas)
Profile: p 941
Table: p 648

Porter Wright Morris & Arthur (District of Columbia)
Profile: p 941
Table: p 559, 562, 566, 571

Postner & Rubin (New York)
Profile: p 941
Table: p 458

Potter Anderson & Corroon LLP (Delaware)
Profile: p 941
Table: p 94, 95, 96, 97

Powell, Goldstein, Frazer & Murphy LLP (District of Columbia)
Profile: p 941
Table: p 183, 186, 193, 195, 197, 199, 201

Poyner & Spruill L.L.P. (North Carolina)
Profile: p 941
Table: p 550

Preston Gates & Ellis LLP (Washington)
Profile: p 941
Table: p 9, 11, 107, 592, 706, 709, 711

Preti, Flaherty, Beliveau, Pachios & Haley, LLC (Maine)
Profile: p 941
Table: p 322

Priddy, Eisenberg, Miller & Meade (Kentucky)
Profile: p 941
Table: p 301

Proskauer Rose LLP (New York)
Profile: p 941
Table: p 466, 485, 492

Pyle Rome Lichten & Ehrenberg (Massachusetts)
Profile: p 941
Table: p 341

Q

Quarles & Brady LLP (Wisconsin)
Profile: p 941
Table: p 16, 18, 19, 20, 723, 725, 726, 727

Quattlebaum, Grooms, Tull & Burrow PLLC (Arkansas)
Profile: p 868
Table: p 25, 26

Quinn Emanuel Urquhart Oliver & Hedges, LLP (California)
Profile: p 869
Table: p 50

R

Ralston Pope & Diehl LLC (Kansas)
Profile: p 941
Table: p 295

Ratner & Prestia (Pennsylvania)
Profile: p 941
Table: p 608

Ravich Meyer Kirkman McGrath & Naun PC (Minnesota)
Profile: p 942
Table: p 374

Ray, Quinney & Nebeker PC (Utah)
Profile: p 942
Table: p 686, 687, 688

Reben, Benjamin & March (Maine)
Profile: p 942
Table: p 320

Reboul, MacMurray, Hewitt, Maynard & Kristol (New York)
Profile: p 942
Table: p 488

Reeder & Shuman (West Virginia)
Profile: p 942
Table: p 719

Reed Smith LLP (Pennsylvania)
Profile: p 942
Table: p 595, 597, 599, 602, 604, 607, 608, 611

Reinhart, Boerner, Van Deuren, Norris & Rieselbach, SC (Wisconsin)
Profile: p 942
Table: p 723, 726, 727

Reitman Parsonnet PC (New Jersey)
Profile: p 942
Table: p 426

Richards Layton & Finger (Delaware)
Profile: p 942
Table: p 94, 96, 97, 99

Richman Greer Weil Brumbaugh Mirabito & Christensen (Florida)
Profile: p 942
Table: p 164

Riddell Williams PS (Washington)
Profile: p 942
Table: p 708

Rider, Bennett, Egan & Arundel, LLP (Minnesota)
Profile: p 942
Table: p 368, 371, 374

Riegels Campos & Kenyon (California)
Profile: p 942
Table: p 53

Riker, Danzig, Scherer, Hyland & Perretti LLP (New Jersey)
Profile: p 942
Table: p 428, 429

Rinehart Robblee Hannah (Washington)
Profile: p 942
Table: p 707

Robein Urann & Lurye A Professional Law Corporation (Louisiana)
Profile: p 942
Table: p 310

Robert M. Knight (Montana)
Profile: p 942
Table: p 397

Roberts & Holland LLP (New York)
Profile: p 942
Table: p 498

Robins Kaplan Miller & Ciresi (Minnesota)
Profile: p 942
Table: p 371, 372

Robinson & Cole LLP (Connecticut)
Profile: p 942
Table: p 87, 90, 91

Robinson & McElwee PLLC (West Virginia)
Profile: p 942
Table: p 714, 716, 719

Robinson, Bradshaw & Hinson, P.A. (North Carolina)
Profile: p 943
Table: p 544, 545, 549, 550

Robison, Belaustegui, Sharp & Low (Nevada)
Profile: p 943
Table: p 409

Rodey, Dickason, Sloan, Akin & Robb, PA (New Mexico)
Profile: p 943
Table: p 433, 434, 435, 437

Rodgers, Powers & Schwartz (Massachusetts)
Profile: p 943
Table: p 341

FIRMS INDEX

Roetzel & Andress, PA (Ohio)
Profile: p 943
Table: p 566

Roger K Doolittle & Richard Rehfelt (Mississippi)
Profile: p 943
Table: p 379

Rogers & Hardin (Georgia)
Profile: p 943
Table: p 181, 186, 189, 197

Rogers, Towers, Bailey, Jones & Gay, PA (Florida)
Profile: p 943
Table: p 167

Roller & Allensworth (Texas)
Profile: p 943
Table: p 648

Roney & Labinger (Rhode Island)
Profile: p 943
Table: p 620

Ropes & Gray (Massachusetts)
Profile: p 870
Table: p 336, 338, 339, 342, 346, 348, 350, 353

Rose Law Firm (Arkansas)
Profile: p 943
Table: p 24, 25

Roseman & Kazmierski (Colorado)
Profile: p 943
Table: p 77

Rosenthal, Monhait, Gross & Goddess, PA (Delaware)
Profile: p 943
Table: p 97

Ross & Cohen, LLP (New York)
Profile: p 871
Table: p 458

Ross & Hardies (Illinois)
Profile: p 943
Table: p 236, 239, 247

Rothgerber Johnson & Lyons LLP (Colorado)
Profile: p 943
Table: p 79

Rothman Gordon PC (Pennsylvania)
Profile: p 943
Table: p 601

Rothstein, Rosenfeldt Dolin & Pancier (Florida)
Profile: p 943
Table: p 157

Rouse Hendricks German May PC (Missouri)
Profile: p 943
Table: p 389

Ruden, McClosky, Smith, Schuster & Russell, PA (Florida)
Profile: p 943
Table: p 167

Rudman & Winchell LLC (Maine)
Profile: p 943
Table: p 321

Rudy, Exelrod & Zieff, LLP (California)
Profile: p 943
Table: p 39

Rushton, Stakely, Johnston & Garrett (Alabama)
Profile: p 943
Table: p 4

Rusing & Lopez, PLLC (Arizona)
Profile: p 943
Table: p 19

S

Sacks Montgomery (New York)
Profile: p 943
Table: p 458

Jennings Sigmond (Pennsylvania)
Profile: p 929
Table: p 426

Sales, Tillman & Wallbaum (Kentucky)
Profile: p 944
Table: p 301

Santoro, Driggs, Walch, Kearney, Johnson & Thompson (Nevada)
Profile: p 944
Table: p 410

Saul Ewing LLP (Pennsylvania)
Profile: p 944
Table: p 96, 99, 331, 604, 613

Savage & Savage (Rhode Island)
Profile: p 944
Table: p 620

Schell Bray Aycock Abel & Livingston PLLC (North Carolina)
Profile: p 944
Table: p 545

Schiff Hardin & Waite (Illinois)
Profile: p 944
Table: p 229, 231, 232, 236, 238, 239, 242

Schleier, Jellison & Schleier (Arizona)
Profile: p 944
Table: p 17

Schnader Harrison Segal & Lewis LLP (Pennsylvania)
Profile: p 944
Table: p 595, 604, 611, 613

Schottenstein, Zox & Dunn (Ohio)
Profile: p 944
Table: p 560, 571

Schreck Brignone (Nevada)
Profile: p 944
Table: p 406, 408, 410

Schulte Roth & Zabel LLP (New York)
Profile: p 944
Table: p 488

Schwabe, Williamson & Wyatt, PC (Oregon)
Profile: p 944
Table: p 590, 592

Schwartz, Bon, Walker & Studer, LLC (Wyoming)
Profile: p 944
Table: p 731, 732

Schwartz, Cooper, Greenberger & Krauss, Chartered (Illinois)
Profile: p 872
Table: p 249

Schwarzwald & McNair (Ohio)
Profile: p 944
Table: p 564

Sebris Busto (Washington)
Profile: p 944
Table: p 708

Segal, Stewart, Cutler, Linday, Janes & Berry (Kentucky)
Profile: p 944
Table: p 301

Segal Roitman & Coleman (Massachusetts)
Profile: p 944
Table: p 341

Serkland Law Firm, PC (North Dakota)
Profile: p 944
Table: p 554, 555

Seward & Kissel (New York)
Profile: p 944
Table: p 496

Seyfarth Shaw (Illinois)
Profile: p 944
Table: p 39, 112, 236, 342

Shapiro Fussell Wedge Smotherman Martin & Price, LLP (Georgia)
Profile: p 944
Table: p 184

Shawe & Rosenthal LLP (Maryland)
Profile: p 873
Table: p 329

Shaw Pittman (District of Columbia)
Profile: p 944
Table: p 107, 111, 127, 456, 699

Shea & Gardner (District of Columbia)
Profile: p 945
Table: p 122

Shearman & Sterling (New York)
Profile: p 874
Table: p 103, 440, 443, 445, 447, 451, 459, 471, 481, 490, 492, 498

Sheehan Phinney Bass + Green PC (New Hampshire)
Profile: p 875
Table: p 415, 417, 418, 420

Sheehey Furlong & Behm PC (Vermont)
Profile: p 945
Table: p 695

Sheppard, Mullin, Richter & Hampton LLP (California)
Profile: p 945
Table: p 30, 39, 44, 56

Sher Garner Cahill Richter Klein McAlister & Hilbert, LLC (Louisiana)
Profile: p 945
Table: p 308, 314

Sherman & Howard LLC (Colorado)
Profile: p 945
Table: p 75, 78, 81

Sherrard & Roe PLC (Tennessee)
Profile: p 945
Table: p 635, 639

Shipman & Goodwin LLP (Connecticut)
Profile: p 945
Table: p 88, 90, 91

Shneidman, Hawks & Ehlke (Wisconsin)
Profile: p 945
Table: p 724

Shook, Hardy & Bacon LLP (Missouri)
Profile: p 876
Table: p 164, 294, 296, 385, 387, 389

Shughart Thomson & Kilroy PC (Missouri)
Profile: p 945
Table: p 294, 296, 385, 389

Shulman, Rogers, Gandal, Pordy & Ecker, PA (Maryland)
Profile: p 945
Table: p 331

Shumaker, Loop & Kendrick LLP (Ohio)
Profile: p 945
Table: p 566

Shuttleworth & Ingersoll PLC (Iowa)
Profile: p 945
Table: p 286, 288, 289, 290

Shutts & Bowen LLP (Florida)
Profile: p 945
Table: p 152, 155, 167

Sidley Austin Brown & Wood (Illinois)
Profile: p 877
Table: p 44, 107, 114, 117, 122, 224, 226, 229, 232, 236, 238, 239, 240, 242, 244, 245, 247, 249, 251, 447, 453, 468, 660

Siegel, O'Connor, Zangari, O'Donnell & Beck PC (Connecticut)
Profile: p 945
Table: p 88

Siegfried, Rivera, Lerner, De La Torre & Sobel, PA (Florida)
Profile: p 945
Table: p 153

Sills Cummis Radin Tischman Epstein & Gross, PA (New Jersey)
Profile: p 945
Table: p 424, 428, 429

Simmons Perrine Albright & Ellwood P.L.C. (Iowa)
Profile: p 945
Table: p 288, 290

Simpson Thacher & Bartlett (New York)
Profile: p 945
Table: p 32, 440, 443, 445, 447, 453, 459, 468, 471, 476, 481, 487, 488, 490, 492, 498

Sirote & Permutt PC (Alabama)
Profile: p 945
Table: p 1

Sive Paget & Riesel PC (New York)
Profile: p 945
Table: p 468

Skadden, Arps, Slate, Meagher & Flom LLP & Affiliates (New York)
Profile: p 878
Table: p 32, 34, 37, 44, 47, 94, 96, 97, 107, 114, 129, 226, 232, 240, 245, 251, 339, 440, 443, 445, 447, 451, 453, 456, 459, 468, 471, 476, 481, 490, 492, 498, 653, 664

Slusser & Frost LLP (Texas)
Profile: p 879
Table: p 660

Smith & Smith (Kentucky)
Profile: p 945
Table: p 302

Smith Hulsey & Busey (Florida)
Profile: p 881
Table: p 161

Smith James Rowlett & Cohen (North Carolina)
Profile: p 945
Table: p 547

Smith Pachter McWhorter & Allen (Virginia)
Profile: p 946
Table: p 698

Smith & Kotchka Ltd (Nevada)
Profile: p 945
Table: p 408

FIRMS INDEX

Smith, Anderson, Blount, Dorsett, Mitchell & Jernigan, L.L.P. (North Carolina)
Profile: p 880
Table: p 545, 549, 550

Smith, Currie & Hancock LLP (Georgia)
Profile: p 946
Table: p 184

Smith, Gambrell & Russell, LLP (Georgia)
Profile: p 946
Table: p 183, 184, 195

Smith Moore, LLP (North Carolina)
Profile: p 946
Table: p 549, 550

Smith Mullin (New Jersey)
Profile: p 946
Table: p 426

Snell & Wilmer LLP (Arizona)
Profile: p 946
Table: p 1, 9, 16, 18, 19, 20, 23, 28, 75, 87, 94, 102, 150, 180, 212, 219, 223, 277, 286, 294, 300, 307, 319, 327, 336, 360, 378, 394, 400, 406, 424, 433, 439, 544, 554, 558, 580, 587, 595, 620, 624, 630, 635, 643, 684, 687, 688, 692, 698, 706, 714, 723, 730

Sommer Barnard Ackerson Attorneys, PC (Indiana)
Profile: p 946
Table: p 277, 280, 281

Sonnenschein Nath & Rosenthal (Illinois)
Profile: p 882
Table: p 46, 224, 229, 232, 239, 240, 247, 249, 385, 389

Spear, Wilderman, Borish, Endy, Spear & Runckel (New Jersey)
Profile: p 946
Table: p 601

Spencer Fane Britt & Browne LLP (Missouri)
Profile: p 946
Table: p 294, 296, 385, 387, 389

Spilman Thomas & Battle, PLLC (West Virginia)
Profile: p 946
Table: p 714, 716, 718, 719

Spink Butler Clapp (Idaho)
Profile: p 946
Table: p 221

Spradling, Alpern & Gum, L.L.P. (Oklahoma)
Profile: p 946
Table: p 584

Sprenger & Lang, PLLC (District of Columbia)
Profile: p 946
Table: p 112, 370

Squire, Sanders & Dempsey LLP (Ohio)
Profile: p 946
Table: p 16, 20, 559, 560, 562, 564, 566, 569, 571

Stafford Rosenbaum LLP (Wisconsin)
Profile: p 946
Table: p 726

Stanford Fagan & Giolito (Georgia)
Profile: p 946
Table: p 188

Stanley & Schadt (Alaska)
Profile: p 946
Table: p 13

Stanton Hughes Diana Cerra Mariani & Margello (New Jersey)
Profile: p 946
Table: p 426

Stark & Gordon (Michigan)
Profile: p 946
Table: p 362

Starnes & Atchison LLP (Alabama)
Profile: p 883
Table: p 4

Statman, Harris, Siegel & Eyrich, LLC (Ohio)
Profile: p 947
Table: p 559

Stearns Weaver Miller Weissler Alhadeff & Sitterson, P.A. (Florida)
Profile: p 947
Table: p 161, 167

Steeg and O'Connor LLC (Louisiana)
Profile: p 947
Table: p 314

Steel Hector & Davis LLP (London)
Profile: p 947
Table: p 155, 164, 169

Stein Volinsky & Callaghan PA (New Hampshire)
Profile: p 947
Table: p 417

Stein, Ray & Harris (Illinois)
Profile: p 884
Table: p 231

Steiner, Darling & Hutchinson LLP (Colorado)
Profile: p 947
Table: p 81

Stephen Rakusin PA (Florida)
Profile: p 947
Table: p 153

Steptoe & Johnson LLP (District of Columbia)
Profile: p 947
Table: p 18, 114, 120, 129

Steptoe & Johnson PLLC (West Virginia)
Profile: p 947
Table: p 714, 716, 718, 719

Sterne Kessler Goldstein & Fox (District of Columbia)
Profile: p 947
Table: p 121

Stevens & Lee A Professional Corporation (Pennsylvania)
Profile: p 947
Table: p 607

Stewart Estes & Donnell (Tennessee)
Profile: p 947
Table: p 636

Stichter, Riedel, Blain & Prosser (Florida)
Profile: p 947
Table: p 161

Stinson Morrison Hecker LLP (Missouri)
Profile: p 947
Table: p 294, 296, 297, 385, 389, 391

Stites & Harbison PLLC (Kentucky)
Profile: p 947
Table: p 300, 303, 304

Stoel Rives LLP (Oregon)
Profile: p 947
Table: p 219, 220, 221, 587, 589, 590, 592, 684, 687, 688, 711

Stokes Bartholomew Evans & Petree, P.A. (Tennessee)
Profile: p 947
Table: p 640

Stoll, Keenon & Park, LLP (Kentucky)
Profile: p 947
Table: p 300, 302, 303

Stoll Stoll Berne Lokting & Shlachter (Oregon)
Profile: p 947
Table: p 590

Stone Pigman Walther Wittmann L.L.C. (Louisiana)
Profile: p 947
Table: p 308, 313, 314

Stowell & Friedman (Illinois)
Profile: p 947
Table: p 235

Strasburger & Price LLP (Texas)
Profile: p 947
Table: p 658

Strecker & Associates (Oklahoma)
Profile: p 947
Table: p 582

Strindberg & Scholnick (Utah)
Profile: p 947
Table: p 685

Stroock & Stroock & Lavan LLP (New York)
Profile: p 947
Table: p 451, 471, 476, 492

Stutman, Treister & Glatt Professional Corporation (California)
Profile: p 885
Table: p 44

Sugarman & Susskind (Florida)
Profile: p 947
Table: p 157

Sullivan & Cromwell LLP (New York)
Profile: p 886
Table: p 32, 440, 443, 445, 447, 451, 459, 466, 468, 476, 481, 490, 492, 498

Sullivan & Worcester (Massachusetts)
Profile: p 948
Table: p 353

Sulloway & Hollis, PLLC (New Hampshire)
Profile: p 948
Table: p 417, 418, 420

Susman, Duffy & Segaloff P.C. (Connecticut)
Profile: p 948
Table: p 91

Susman Godfrey LLP (Texas)
Profile: p 948
Table: p 644, 662

Sutherland Asbill & Brennan LLP (District of Columbia)
Profile: p 887
Table: p 129, 184, 186, 191, 195, 197, 199, 201

Sutin, Thayer & Browne (New Mexico)
Profile: p 948
Table: p 433

Swidler Berlin Shereff Friedman LLP (District of Columbia)
Profile: p 948
Table: p 107, 117, 119

T

Taft, Stettinius & Hollister LLP (Ohio)
Profile: p 948
Table: p 559, 562, 564, 566

Tarolli, Sundheim, Covell, Tummino & Szabo LLP (Ohio)
Profile: p 948
Table: p 568

Taylor, Covington & Smith PA (Mississippi)
Profile: p 948
Table: p 382

Taylor, Porter, Brooks & Phillips, LLP (Louisiana)
Profile: p 948
Table: p 308, 311

Tescher Gutter Chaves Josepher Rubin Ruffin & Forman PA (Florida)
Profile: p 948
Table: p 169

Testa, Hurwitz & Thibeault LLP (Massachusetts)
Profile: p 948
Table: p 339, 342, 350, 353

Thacher Proffitt & Wood (New York)
Profile: p 948
Table: p 453

The Louthian Law Firm PA (South Carolina)
Profile: p 948
Table: p 625

The Meyers Law Firm LC (Missouri)
Profile: p 948
Table: p 387

The Popham Law Firm PC (Missouri)
Profile: p 948
Table: p 387

The Kullman Firm A Professional Law Corporation (Louisiana)
Profile: p 948
Table: p 311, 380

Thelen Reid & Priest LLP (California)
Profile: p 888
Table: p 36, 55, 110, 443, 458, 468

Thomas Kayden Hortstemeyer & Risley LLP (Georgia)
Profile: p 949
Table: p 195

Thomas N. Long (Wyoming)
Profile: p 949
Table: p 730

Thompson, Coe, Cousins & Irons, LLP (Texas)
Profile: p 949
Table: p 658

FIRMS INDEX

Thompson, Sizemore & Gonzalez (Florida)
Profile: p 949
Table: p 158

Thompson Coburn (Missouri)
Profile: p 949
Table: p 385, 387, 389

Thompson Hine LLP (Ohio)
Profile: p 890
Table: p 559, 560, 562, 566, 568, 569, 571

Thompson & Knight LLP (Texas)
Profile: p 889
Table: p 644, 646, 655, 657, 660, 665, 667

Thorp Reed & Armstrong (Pennsylvania)
Profile: p 949
Table: p 611

Tindall Bennett & Shoup PC (Alaska)
Profile: p 949
Table: p 10

Tinkler & Bennett (New Mexico)
Profile: p 949
Table: p 434

Tobias Kraus & Torchia (Ohio)
Profile: p 949
Table: p 564

Todd & Weld LLP (Massachusetts)
Profile: p 949
Table: p 348

Tonkon Torp LLP (Oregon)
Profile: p 949
Table: p 587

Torkildson, Katz, Fonseca, Jaffe, Moore & Hetherington Attorneys At Law, A Law Corporation (Hawaii)
Profile: p 949
Table: p 214

Townsend and Townsend and Crew LLP (California)
Profile: p 949
Table: p 47

Trenam, Kemker, Scharf, Barkin, Frye, O'Neill & Mullis PA (Florida)
Profile: p 949
Table: p 151, 155, 169

Triplett, Woolf & Garretson LLC (Kansas)
Profile: p 949
Table: p 297

Troutman Sanders LLP (District of Columbia)
Profile: p 949
Table: p 114, 181, 183, 186, 189, 191, 192, 193, 195, 197, 199, 699, 701, 702, 703

Truhlar & Truhlar (Colorado)
Profile: p 949
Table: p 77

U

Ugrin, Alexander, Zadick & Higgins, PC (Montana)
Profile: p 949
Table: p 395

Ulmer & Berne LLP (Ohio)
Profile: p 949
Table: p 560, 564

Upton and Hatfield, L.L.P. (New Hampshire)
Profile: p 949
Table: p 420

V

Van Hoy Reutlinger Adams & Dunn (North Carolina)
Profile: p 949
Table: p 548

Van Cott, Bagley, Cornwall & McCarthy (Utah)
Profile: p 949
Table: p 687, 688

Van Ness Feldman (District of Columbia)
Profile: p 950
Table: p 114

Vaughan & Murphy (Georgia)
Profile: p 950
Table: p 181

Vedder, Price, Kaufman & Kammholz (Illinois)
Profile: p 950
Table: p 226, 236

Venable LLP (Maryland)
Profile: p 950
Table: p 117, 127, 327, 329, 330, 331, 698

Venture Law Group (California)
Profile: p 950
Table: p 34

Vercruysse Metz & Murray (Michigan)
Profile: p 950
Table: p 362

Verrill & Dana, LLP (Maine)
Profile: p 950
Table: p 319, 322, 323

Vinson & Elkins LLP (Texas)
Profile: p 891
Table: p 114, 644, 645, 646, 649, 651, 653, 655, 657, 658, 660, 662, 664, 665, 667

Vladeck, Waldman, Elias & Engelhard, P.C. (New York)
Profile: p 950
Table: p 466

Vogel, Weir, Hunke & McCormick, Ltd. (North Dakota)
Profile: p 950
Table: p 554, 555, 556

Vorys, Sater, Seymour & Pease LLP (Ohio)
Profile: p 950
Table: p 559, 562, 566, 569, 571

W

Wachtell, Lipton, Rosen & Katz (New York)
Profile: p 892
Table: p 440, 459, 471, 481, 492, 498

Wadleigh, Starr & Peters P.L.L.C. (New Hampshire)
Profile: p 950
Table: p 418, 420

Waide & Associates (Mississippi)
Profile: p 950
Table: p 379

Walder, Hayden & Brogen P.A. (New Jersey)
Profile: p 950
Table: p 428

Walker, Bryant, Tipps & Malone (Tennessee)
Profile: p 894
Table: p 639

Wallack Somers & Haas PC (Indiana)
Profile: p 895
Table: p 281

Waller Lansden Dortch & Davis (Tennessee)
Profile: p 950
Table: p 635, 637, 639, 640

Warner Norcross & Judd LLP (Michigan)
Profile: p 950
Table: p 360, 361

Watanabe Ing Kawashima & Komeiji (Hawaii)
Profile: p 950
Table: p 214, 215

Watkins & Eager PLLC (Mississippi)
Profile: p 950
Table: p 378, 380, 381

Watkins Ludlam Winter & Stennis PA (Mississippi)
Profile: p 950
Table: p 378, 382

Watson, Farley & Williams (London)
Profile: p 896
Table: p 496

Watt, Tieder, Hoffar & Fitzgerald, L.L.P. (Virginia)
Profile: p 950
Table: p 36, 698

Webb Ziesenheim Logsdon Orkin & Hanson, PC (Pennsylvania)
Profile: p 950
Table: p 608

Weil, Gotshal & Manges LLP (New York)
Profile: p 897
Table: p 47, 339, 440, 445, 447, 453, 456, 459, 471, 478, 481, 485, 487, 488, 492, 498, 649, 657

Weinberg, Wheeler, Hudgins, Gunn & Dial, LLC (Georgia)
Profile: p 950
Table: p 184

Weissmann, Wolff, Bergman, Coleman, Silverman & Holmes, LLP (California)
Profile: p 950
Table: p 53

Welbaum, Guernsey, Hingston, Greenleaf & Gregory LLP. (Florida)
Profile: p 950
Table: p 153

Weston Benshoof Rochefort Rubalcava MacCuish LLP (California)
Profile: p 951
Table: p 42

Whatley Drake, LLC (Alabama)
Profile: p 951
Table: p 2

White Goss Bowers March Schulte & Weisenfels, A Professional Corporation (Missouri)
Profile: p 951
Table: p 391

White & Case LLP (New York)
Profile: p 951
Table: p 41, 106, 126, 152, 155, 160, 169, 443, 445, 490

Whiteford, Taylor & Preston LLP (Maryland)
Profile: p 951
Table: p 329, 331

Whiteman, Osterman & Hanna (New York)
Profile: p 951
Table: p 468

Whitfield & Eddy, PLC (Iowa)
Profile: p 951
Table: p 288, 289

Whyte Hirschboeck Dudek S.C. (Wisconsin)
Profile: p 951
Table: p 727

Wickwire Gavin (Virginia)
Profile: p 951
Table: p 698

Wiggin & Nourie (New Hampshire)
Profile: p 951
Table: p 418

Wiggin & Dana LLP (Connecticut)
Profile: p 951
Table: p 88, 90, 91

Wilde & Associates (Utah)
Profile: p 951
Table: p 685

Wiley Rein & Fielding LLP (District of Columbia)
Profile: p 951
Table: p 107, 120

Willcox & Savage (Virginia)
Profile: p 951
Table: p 699, 702

Williams & Anderson LLP (Arkansas)
Profile: p 898
Table: p 25

Williams & Connolly LLP (District of Columbia)
Profile: p 899
Table: p 122, 125

Williams Mullen (Virginia)
Profile: p 951
Table: p 699, 701, 702

Williams, Porter, Day & Neville, P.C. (Wyoming)
Profile: p 951
Table: p 731, 732, 733

Willig, Williams & Davidson (Pennsylvania)
Profile: p 951
Table: p 601

Willkie Farr & Gallagher (New York)
Profile: p 900
Table: p 107, 456, 459, 471, 481, 492

Wilmer, Cutler & Pickering (District of Columbia)
Profile: p 901
Table: p 103, 106, 107, 111, 119, 122, 331

Wilson, Elser, Moskowitz, Edelman & Dicker LLP (New York)
Profile: p 951
Table: p 476

Wilson Sonsini Goodrich & Rosati (California)
Profile: p 951
Table: p 32, 34, 37, 39, 50, 684

Winer & Bennett LLP (New Hampshire)
Profile: p 951
Table: p 420

Winfree Law Office (Alaska)
Profile: p 951
Table: p 10

Winn & Alexander LLP (California)
Profile: p 951
Table: p 53

FIRMS INDEX

Winstead Sechrest & Minick (Texas)
Profile: p 902
Table: p 657, 665

Winston & Strawn (Illinois)
Profile: p 904
Table: p 224, 226, 232, 236, 239, 245, 247, 249, 251

Winthrop & Weinstine, A Professional Association (Minnesota)
Profile: p 951, 951
Table: p 372, 374

Wise Carter Child & Caraway, Professional Association (Mississippi)
Profile: p 952
Table: p 378

Wolf, Block, Schorr and Solis-Cohen LLP (Pennsylvania)
Profile: p 905
Table: p 597, 599, 604, 607, 613

Womble Carlyle Sandridge & Rice PLLC (North Carolina)
Profile: p 906
Table: p 544, 545, 548, 549, 550

Wood, Herron & Evans, LLP (Ohio)
Profile: p 952
Table: p 568

Woodburn and Wedge (Nevada)
Profile: p 952
Table: p 406

Woodcock Washburn (Pennsylvania)
Profile: p 952
Table: p 608

Woods, Fuller, Shultz & Smith PC (South Dakota)
Profile: p 952
Table: p 630, 631, 632

Worden, Thane & Haines, PC (Montana)
Profile: p 952
Table: p 395, 397

Wright, Lindsey & Jennings LLP (Arkansas)
Profile: p 952
Table: p 23, 24, 25, 26

Wyatt, Tarrant & Combs LLP (Kentucky)
Profile: p 952
Table: p 300, 302, 303, 304

Wyche, Burgess, Freeman & Parham, PA (South Carolina)
Profile: p 952
Table: p 624, 626

Y

Yonkee & Toner LLP (Wyoming)
Profile: p 952
Table: p 731, 732, 733

York, Keller & Field (Texas)
Profile: p 952
Table: p 658

Young, Clement, Rivers & Tisdale, LLP (South Carolina)
Profile: p 952
Table: p 626

Young, Sommer, Ward, Ritzenberg, Wooley, Baker & Moore LLC (New York)
Profile: p 952
Table: p 468

Young Conaway Stargatt & Taylor, LLP (Delaware)
Profile: p 907
Table: p 94, 95, 96, 97, 99

Z

Zeiger & Carpenter LLP (Ohio)
Profile: p 952
Table: p 569

Zetlin & De Chiara (New York)
Profile: p 952
Table: p 458

Ziffren Brittenham Branca Fischer Gilbert-Lurie & Stiffelman LLP (California)
Profile: p 952
Table: p 53

Zimney, Foster, Johnson, Dittus & Flaten, Chartered (North Dakota)
Profile: p 952
Table: p 554

Zinober & McCrea, P.A. (Florida)
Profile: p 952
Table: p 158

Zuckerman Spaeder LLP (Florida)
Profile: p 952
Table:

LEADING LAWYERS INDEX

CHAMBERS
USA
2003–2004

INDEX TO THE LEADING LAWYERS

A

Aaron, Roger S (New York)
Profile: p.503

Abaunza, Donald R
(Louisiana)
Profile: p.316
Litigation **Band 2**
Table: p.313

Abel, Sally (California)
Profile: p.60
Intellectual Property **Band 3**
Table: p.48

Abell, Nancy (California)
Profile: p.60
Employment **Band 2**
Table: p.40

Abelson, Barry M
(Pennsylvania)
Profile: p.615
Corporate/M&A **Band 1**
Table: p.599

Abelson, Ned (Massachusetts)
Profile: p.354
Environment **Band 3**
Table: p.344

Aber, Gary (Delaware)
Profile: p.99
Employment **Band 3**
Table: p.95

Abernathy, Thomas (Georgia)
Profile: p.202
Construction **Band 1**
Table: p.184

Abrahamson, Vicki (Illinois)
Profile: p.253
Employment **Band 2**
Table: p.235

Abrams, Floyd (New York)
Profile: p.503
Media & Entertainment **Band 1**
Table: p.485

Abrams, Harold E (Georgia)
Profile: p.202
Tax **Band 4**
Table: p.201

Abrams, Jeffrey (Indiana)
Profile: p.283
Real Estate **Band 4**
Table: p.282

Abrams, Kevin (Delaware)
Profile: p.99
Litigation **Band 4**
Table: p.98

Abrams, Lee N (Illinois)
Profile: p.253
Antitrust **Band 1**
Table: p.224

Abrams, Marc (New York)
Profile: p.503
Insolvency **Band 2**
Table: p.472

Acker, Lawrence G
(District of Columbia)
Profile: p.131
Energy **Band 2**
Table: p.115

Adamo, Kenneth R (Ohio)
Profile: p.573
Intellectual Property **Band 1**
Table: p.568

Adams, Alfred (North Carolina)
Profile: p.552
Real Estate **Band 1**
Table: p.551

Adams, Deborah (Ohio)
Profile: p.573
Employment **Band 4**
Table: p.565

Adams, Garth (Iowa)
Profile: p.292
Corporate/M&A **Band 2**
Table: p.286

Adams, Helen (Iowa)
Profile: p.292
Employment **Band 2**
Table: p.288

Adams, Katherine (New York)
Profile: p.503
Environment **Band 2**
Table: p.469

Adams, Mark (Louisiana)
Profile: p.316
Employment **Band 3**
Table: p.311

Adams, Stephen (Kansas)
Profile: p.299
Corporate/M&A **Band 1**
Table: p.294

Adams Jr, Alfred (Georgia)
Profile: p.92,202
Real Estate **Band 2**
Table: p.199

Addison, James W (Georgia)
Profile: p.202
Real Estate **Band 3**
Table: p.199

Adelman, Howard (Illinois)
Profile: p.253
Insolvency **Band 3**
Table: p.241

Adler, Arthur S (New York)
Profile: p.503
Real Estate **Band 3**
Table: p.493

Adler, Gregg (Connecticut)
Profile: p.92
Employment **Band 2**
Table: p.88

Adler, Howard
(District of Columbia)
Profile: p.131
Corporate/M&A **Band 2**
Table: p.111

Adler, Sheldon S (New York)
Profile: p.503
Energy **Band 3**
Table: p.468

Ahearn, Dale (Kentucky)
Profile: p.305
Real Estate **Band 2**
Table: p.304

Ahmad, Joseph (Texas)
Profile: p.668
Employment **Band 2**
Table: p.651

Aichele, Stephen S.
(Pennsylvania)
Profile: p.615
Real Estate **Band 2**
Table: p.613

Aiello, Anthony (Illinois)
Profile: p.253
Real Estate **Band 4**
Table: p.249

Aiello, John (New Jersey)
Profile: p.430
Corporate/M&A **Band 3**
Table: p.425

Aizenstein, Neal (Illinois)
Profile: p.253
Corporate/M&A **Band 4**
Table: p.233

Aksen, Gerald (New York)
Profile: p.503
Arbitration **Band 1**
Table: p.443

Albergotti, Robert (Texas)
Profile: p.668
Insolvency **Band 1**
Table: p.657

Albert, Michael (West Virginia)
Profile: p.721
Corporate/M&A **Band 3**
Table: p.714

Albrecht, Thomas (Illinois)
Profile: p.253
Banking & Finance **Band 2**
Table: p.226

Alden, Steven M (New York)
Profile: p.503
Real Estate **Band 4**
Table: p.493

Aldock, John
(District of Columbia)
Profile: p.131
Litigation **Band 2**
Table: p.123

Aldridge, John (Georgia)
Profile: p.202
Real Estate **Band 3**
Table: p.199

Ale, John (Texas)
Profile: p.668
Energy **Band 3**
Table: p.653
Projects **Band 2**
Table: p.664

Alegria, David (Kansas)
Profile: p.299
Employment **Band 1**
Table: p.295

Alessandra, Nan (Louisiana)
Profile: p.316
Employment **Band 4**
Table: p.311

Alexander, Bruce (Florida)
Profile: p.171
Construction **Band 1**
Table: p.154

Alexander, Frederick H
(Delaware)
Profile: p.99
Corporate/M&A **Band 1**
Table: p.94

Alexander, James (Alabama)
Profile: p.7
Employment **Band 1**
Table: p.3

Alexander, Judith (California)
Profile: p.60
Media & Entertainment **Band 4**
Table: p.53

Alexander, Miles (Georgia)
Profile: p.202
Intellectual Property **Band 1**
Table: p.195

Alexander, Troy (New York)
Profile: p.503
Projects **Band 3**
Table: p.491

Alfred, Richard
(Massachusetts)
Profile: p.354
Employment **Band 1**
Table: p.342

Alhadeff, Richard (Florida)
Profile: p.171
Real Estate **Band 2**
Table: p.167

Alito, Rosemary (New Jersey)
Profile: p.430
Employment **Band 2**
Table: p.427

Allen, Andrew (Alabama)
Profile: p.7
Employment **Band 4**

Table: p.2

Allen, Everette (Virginia)
Profile: p.704
Litigation **Band 1**
Table: p.702

Allen, Pinney L (Georgia)
Profile: p.202
Tax **Band 3**
Table: p.201

Allen, Randall (Georgia)
Profile: p.202
Antitrust **Band 4**
Table: p.181

Allensworth, William (Texas)
Profile: p.668
Construction **Band 2**
Table: p.648

Allerhand, Joseph (New York)
Profile: p.503
Litigation **Band 5**
Table: p.481

Alley, John-Edward (Florida)
Profile: p.171
Employment **Band 1**
Table: p.158

Allison, Christopher (Texas)
Profile: p.668
Tax **Band 3**
Table: p.667

Alstater, Lynn (Pennsylvania)
Profile: p.615
Intellectual Property **Band 3**
Table: p.609

Alston, Paul (Hawaii)
Profile: p.218
Litigation **Band 2**
Table: p.215

Alvarez, Fred (California)
Profile: p.60
Employment **Band 3**
Table: p.40

Alvarez, Victor M (Florida)
Profile: p.171
Banking & Finance **Band 2**
Table: p.152

Amandes, Christopher
(Texas)
Profile: p.668
Environment **Band 2**
Table: p.655

Amburgey, Larry (Oregon)
Profile: p.593
Employment **Band 3**
Table: p.589

Amdur, Martin (New York)
Profile: p.503
Tax **Band 4**
Table: p.499

Amend, James M (Illinois)
Profile: p.253
Intellectual Property **Band 2**
Table: p.244

Amlong, William (Florida)
Profile: p.171
Employment **Band 3**
Table: p.157

Andersen, Richard E
(New York)
Profile: p.504
Tax **Band 4**
Table: p.499

Andersen, Steven (Idaho)
Profile: p.222
Litigation **Band 3**
Table: p.221

Anderson, Chris (Utah)
Profile: p.690
Corporate/M&A **Band 2**
Table: p.684

Anderson, Eugene (New York)
Profile: p.504
Insurance **Band 1**
Table: p.477

Anderson, Reuben
(Mississippi)
Profile: p.383
Litigation **Band 2**
Table: p.381

Anderson, Robert (South Dakota)
Profile: p.633
Litigation **Band 2**
Table: p.632

Andeweg, Robert (Iowa)
Profile: p.292,292
Real Estate **Band 4**
Table: p.291

Andrews, Carl (West Virginia)
Profile: p.721
Real Estate **Band 1**
Table: p.720

Andrews, Patricia (Rhode Island)
Profile: p.623
Employment **Band 1**
Table: p.621

Andrews, William (Florida)
Profile: p.171
Employment **Band 3**
Table: p.158

Andril, David
(District of Columbia)
Profile: p.131
Energy **Band 3**
Table: p.115

Angelo, Percy L (Illinois)
Profile: p.253
Environment **Band 1**
Table: p.239

Angerbauer, David (Utah)
Profile: p.690
Corporate/M&A **Band 4**
Table: p.684

Anglehart, Donald
(Massachusetts)
Profile: p.354
Environment **Band 3**
Table: p.344

Anthony, Joseph (Minnesota)
Profile: p.376
Litigation **Band 1**
Table: p.372

Appelbaum, Jeffrey (Ohio)
Profile: p.573
Construction **Band 1**
Table: p.560

Appicelli, Frank (Connecticut)
Profile: p.92
Real Estate **Band 3**
Table: p.91

Aquila, Francis J (New York)
Profile: p.504

Arditi, Abraham A
(Washington)
Profile: p.712
Employment **Band 1**
Table: p.708

Arendall, David R (Alabama)
Profile: p.7
Employment **Band 4**
Table: p.2

Armistead III, Ivor Cary
(Massachusetts)
Profile: p.354
Antitrust **Band 2**
Table: p.337

Armstrong, Stephen
(Pennsylvania)
Profile: p.615

www.ChambersandPartners.com 975

LEADING LAWYERS INDEX

Antitrust **Band 3**
Table: p.596

Arnholz, John
(District of Columbia)
Profile: p.132
Capital Markets **Band 4**
Table: p.453

Arnold, Dennis (California)
Profile: p.60
Real Estate **Band 5**
Table: p.56

Arnold, Scott (Georgia)
Profile: p.202
Real Estate **Band 2**
Table: p.199

Aro, Edwin (Colorado)
Profile: p.83
Employment **Band 3**
Table: p.78

Aronson, Clifford H
(New York)
Profile: p.504
Antitrust **Band 5**
Table: p.441

Aronson, Daniel H (Florida)
Profile: p.171
Corporate/M&A **Band 3**
Table: p.156

Aronson, Seth (California)
Profile: p.60
Litigation **Band 3**
Table: p.50

Aronson, Virginia (Illinois)
Profile: p.254
Real Estate **Band 2**
Table: p.249

Aronzon, Paul S (California)
Profile: p.60
Insolvency **Band 1**
Table: p.44

Arquit, Kevin J (New York)
Profile: p.504
Antitrust **Band 1**
Table: p.441

Aschleman, James A
(Indiana)
Profile: p.283
Corporate/M&A **Band 1**
Table: p.277

Ash, James (Missouri)
Profile: p.392
Corporate/M&A **Band 2**
Table: p.386

Ashburn, Mark (Alaska)
Profile: p.14
Litigation **Band 2**
Table: p.13

Ashby, Kimberly (Florida)
Profile: p.171
Construction **Band 3**
Table: p.154

Ashby, Lawrence (Delaware)
Profile: p.99
Litigation **Band 2**
Table: p.98

Ashe, Lawrence (Georgia)
Profile: p.202
Employment **Band 1**
Table: p.189

Asher, Steven (Pennsylvania)
Profile: p.615
Antitrust **Band 3**
Table: p.596

Asher Jr, William B
(Massachusetts)
Profile: p.354
Corporate/M&A **Band 1**
Table: p.340

Ashford, Leon (Alabama)
Profile: p.7
Litigation **Band 2**
Table: p.4

Askew, Anthony (Georgia)
Profile: p.202
Intellectual Property **Band 2**
Table: p.195

Aslin, John (Washington)
Profile: p.712
Employment **Band 2**
Table: p.708

Asmar, Mark (Connecticut)
Profile: p.92
Real Estate **Band 2**
Table: p.91

Asmus, David (Texas)
Profile: p.668
Energy **Band 1**
Table: p.653
Projects **Band 1**
Table: p.664

Asofsky, Paul (Texas)
Profile: p.668
Tax **Band 3**
Table: p.667

Asselin, Thomas (Georgia)
Profile: p.202
Construction **Band 4**
Table: p.184

Astigarraga, José I (Florida)
Profile: p.171
Litigation **Band 2**
Table: p.165

Atchison, W Michael
(Alabama)
Profile: p.7
Litigation **Band 3**
Table: p.4

Atkins, Peter Allan (New York)
Profile: p.504
Corporate/M&A **Band 1**
Table: p.460

Attridge, Byron (Georgia)
Profile: p.202
Litigation **Band 2**
Table: p.198

Auen, Michael (Wisconsin)
Profile: p.729
Employment **Band 1**
Table: p.725

Auerbach, Reed (New York)
Profile: p.504
Capital Markets **Band 2**
Table: p.453

Aughtry, David D (Georgia)
Profile: p.202
Tax **Band 1**
Table: p.201

August, Jerald (Florida)
Profile: p.171
Tax **Band 2**
Table: p.170

Austin, Jesse (Georgia)
Profile: p.202
Insolvency **Band 2**
Table: p.193

Avila, Alcides (Florida)
Profile: p.171
Banking & Finance **Band 2**
Table: p.152

Awner, Jonathan L (Florida)
Profile: p.171
Corporate/M&A **Band 2**
Table: p.156

Axelroth, Lynn (Pennsylvania)
Profile: p.615
Real Estate **Band 5**
Table: p.613

Axinn, Stephen (New York)
Profile: p.504
Antitrust **Band 3**
Table: p.441

Axselle, Ralph (Virginia)
Profile: p.704
Real Estate **Band 3**
Table: p.703

Ayres, Jeffrey (Maryland)
Profile: p.332
Employment **Band 2**
Table: p.329

Azoff, Elliot (Ohio)
Profile: p.573
Employment **Band 3**
Table: p.565

B

Baach, Martin
(District of Columbia)
Profile: p.132
Insurance **Band 3**
Table: p.120

Baar, Lois (Utah)
Profile: p.690
Employment **Band 2**
Table: p.686

Babbe, David B (California)
Profile: p.60
Insurance **Band 3**
Table: p.46

Babcock, Kathleen (Kansas)
Profile: p.299
Employment **Band 2**
Table: p.296

Baber, Bruce (Georgia)
Profile: p.203
Intellectual Property **Band 2**
Table: p.195

Babson, Marshall
(District of Columbia)
Profile: p.132
Employment **Band 3**
Table: p.112

Babst III, Chester
(Pennsylvania)
Profile: p.615
Environment **Band 1**
Table: p.604

Baca, David C (Oregon)
Profile: p.593
Corporate/M&A **Band 4**
Table: p.587

Bach, Robert (Colorado)
Profile: p.83
Real Estate **Band 3**
Table: p.81

Backman, John (Nebraska)
Profile: p.405
Real Estate **Band 2**
Table: p.404

Backus, Marcia (Texas)
Profile: p.669
Energy **Band 4**
Table: p.653

Baecher, John (New York)
Profile: p.504
Projects **Band 3**
Table: p.491

Baechtold, Robert (New York)
Profile: p.504
Intellectual Property **Band 1**
Table: p.479

Baena, Scott (Florida)
Profile: p.172
Insolvency **Band 2**
Table: p.162

Baer, Bill (District of Columbia)
Profile: p.132
Antitrust **Band 1**

Table: p.103

Bagley, Phillip (Virginia)
Profile: p.704,704
Real Estate **Band 2**
Table: p.703

Baier, Kelly (Iowa)
Profile: p.292
Employment **Band 2**
Table: p.288

Bailey, Benjamin (West Virginia)
Profile: p.721
Litigation **Band 3**
Table: p.718

Bailey, Burck (Oklahoma)
Profile: p.585
Litigation **Band 1**
Table: p.583

Baine, Kevin T
(District of Columbia)
Profile: p.132
Media & Entertainment **Band 1**
Table: p.125

Baird, Peter (Arizona)
Profile: p.21
Litigation **Band 1**
Table: p.19

Baker, D J (Jan) (New York)
Profile: p.504
Insolvency **Band 2**
Table: p.472

Baker, David (Ohio)
Profile: p.573
Real Estate **Band 2**
Table: p.572

Baker, Lewis (Virginia)
Profile: p.704
Construction **Band 2**
Table: p.698

Baker, Tyler A (Texas)
Profile: p.669
Antitrust **Band 3**
Table: p.644

Baker Jr, William T
(New York)
Profile: p.505
Energy **Band 1**
Table: p.468

Baldwin III, Garza (North Carolina)
Profile: p.552
Corporate/M&A **Band 2**
Table: p.546

Balis, Stanley
(District of Columbia)
Profile: p.132
Energy **Band 3**
Table: p.115

Ball, Corinne (New York)
Profile: p.505
Insolvency **Band 2**
Table: p.472

Ball, Robert (Oregon)
Profile: p.593
Real Estate **Band 2**
Table: p.592

Ballantine, John (Kentucky)
Profile: p.305
Litigation **Band 3**
Table: p.303

Ballard, Alice (Pennsylvania)
Profile: p.615
Employment **Band 1**
Table: p.601

Ballard, Brian (Idaho)
Profile: p.222
Real Estate **Band 2**
Table: p.222

Ballati, Deborah (California)
Profile: p.60
Construction **Band 2**
Table: p.36

Balotti, Frank (Delaware)
Profile: p.99
Corporate/M&A **Band 2**
Table: p.94
Litigation **Band 2**
Table: p.98

Bankoff, Joseph (Georgia)
Profile: p.203
Intellectual Property **Band 3**
Table: p.195

Banks, Diane (Utah)
Profile: p.690,704
Real Estate **Band 3**
Table: p.689

Bankston, William M
(Alaska)
Profile: p.14
Litigation **Band 3**
Table: p.13

Banoff, Sheldon (Illinois)
Profile: p.253,254
Tax **Band 4**
Table: p.252

Baptista, Robert C Jr
(Illinois)
Profile: p.254
Banking & Finance **Band 1**
Table: p.226

Baptiste, Robert
(District of Columbia)
Profile: p.132
Employment **Band 3**
Table: p.112

Barad, Edward N (Colorado)
Profile: p.83
Real Estate **Band 2**
Table: p.81

Barbe, J Kenneth (Wyoming)
Profile: p.734
Corporate/M&A **Band 3**
Table: p.730
Real Estate **Band 3**
Table: p.734

Barber, Timothy
(North Carolina)
Profile: p.552
Litigation **Band 3**
Table: p.549

Barbour, David (Texas)
Profile: p.669
Banking & Finance **Band 3**
Table: p.645

Barbour, Larry (Texas)
Profile: p.669
Banking & Finance **Band 2**
Table: p.645

Barbuti, Thomas (Maryland)
Profile: p.332,332
Real Estate **Band 4**
Table: p.331

Bardacke, Paul (New Mexico)
Profile: p.438
Litigation **Band 3**
Table: p.435

Barfield II, Lee (Tennessee)
Profile: p.641
Litigation **Band 2**
Table: p.639

Barker, Christopher
(Massachusetts)
Profile: p.354
Real Estate **Band 3**
Table: p.351

Barker, Scott (Colorado)
Profile: p.83
Litigation **Band 4**
Table: p.79

LEADING LAWYERS INDEX

Barkett, John (Florida)
Profile: p.172
Environment **Band 4**
Table: p.160

Barksdale, David A (Nevada)
Profile: p.412
Real Estate **Band 3**
Table: p.411

Barlow, Richard (New Mexico)
Profile: p.438
Corporate/M&A **Band 2**
Table: p.433

Barmeyer, Patricia (Georgia)
Profile: p.203
Environment **Band 1**
Table: p.192

Barnard, Thomas (Ohio)
Profile: p.573
Employment **Band 1**
Table: p.565

Barnett, Bonnie
(Pennsylvania)
Profile: p.615
Environment **Band 1**
Table: p.604

Barnett, Leslie (Florida)
Profile: p.172
Tax **Band 3**
Table: p.170

Baronsky, Kenneth
(California)
Profile: p.60
Capital Markets **Band 3**
Table: p.32

Barr, Lynne (Massachusetts)
Profile: p.354
Banking & Finance **Band 2**
Table: p.338

Barr, Michael R (California)
Profile: p.60
Environment **Band 2**
Table: p.43

Barran, Paula (Oregon)
Profile: p.593
Employment **Band 1**
Table: p.589

Barrett, Gayle (Oklahoma)
Profile: p.585
Employment **Band 3**
Table: p.582

Barrett, George (Tennessee)
Profile: p.641
Employment **Band 1**
Table: p.637

Barrett, Patrick (Nebraska)
Profile: p.405
Employment **Band 1**
Table: p.402

Barrier, Christopher
(Arkansas)
Profile: p.27
Real Estate **Band 1**
Table: p.26

Barrow, Peter (Illinois)
Profile: p.254
Banking & Finance **Band 4**
Table: p.226

Barshak, Edward
(Massachusetts)
Profile: p.354
Litigation **Band 3**
Table: p.349

Bartel II, Paul W (New York)
Profile: p.505
Antitrust **Band 4**
Table: p.441

Bartell, Jeff (Wisconsin)
Profile: p.729
Corporate/M&A **Band 3**
Table: p.723

Bartine, William (Iowa)
Profile: p.292
Real Estate **Band 1**
Table: p.291

Bartlit Jr., Fred (Colorado)
Profile: p.83
Litigation **Band 4**
Table: p.79

Bartner, Douglas (New York)
Profile: p.505
Insolvency **Band 2**
Table: p.472

Barton, Bernard (Florida)
Profile: p.172
Tax **Band 2**
Table: p.170

Bason Jr, George R
(New York)
Profile: p.505
Private Equity **Band 1**
Table: p.487

Bass Jr, Ross (Mississippi)
Profile: p.383
Litigation **Band 2**
Table: p.381

Bassett, Peter (Georgia)
Profile: p.203
Litigation **Band 3**
Table: p.198

Bastianelli, Adrian
(District of Columbia)
Profile: p.132
Construction **Band 2**
Table: p.110

Bateman, Randall (Oregon)
Profile: p.593
Real Estate **Band 4**
Table: p.592

Bates, Bob (Arizona)
Profile: p.21
Real Estate **Band 3**
Table: p.20

Bates, Jeffrey
(Massachusetts)
Profile: p.354
Environment **Band 2**
Table: p.344

Bates, Robert (Illinois)
Profile: p.254
Insurance **Band 3**
Table: p.242

Batson, Neal (Georgia)
Profile: p.203
Insolvency ✪
Table: p.193

Batty, Jerome (Rhode Island)
Profile: p.623
Real Estate **Band 2**
Table: p.622

Bauman, Todd (Oregon)
Profile: p.593
Corporate/M&A **Band 3**
Table: p.587

Baumgarten, Jon
(District of Columbia)
Profile: p.132
Intellectual Property **Band 3**
Table: p.122

Baxley, Bill (Georgia)
Profile: p.203
Corporate/M&A **Band 2**
Table: p.187

Baxter, Michael St Patrick
(District of Columbia)
Profile: p.132
Insolvency **Band 3**
Table: p.119

Bayless, Kathryn Reed
(West Virginia)
Profile: p.721

Employment **Band 3**
Table: p.716

Bayt, Phillip L (Indiana)
Profile: p.283
Real Estate **Band 2**
Table: p.282

Beall, George (Maryland)
Profile: p.332
Litigation **Band 2**
Table: p.330

Beane, Jerry (Texas)
Profile: p.669
Antitrust **Band 3**
Table: p.644

Beard, RT (Arkansas)
Profile: p.27
Litigation **Band 3**
Table: p.25

Beasley, Jere (Alabama)
Profile: p.7
Litigation **Band 3**
Table: p.4

Beattie, Richard (New York)
Profile: p.505
Private Equity **Band 1**
Table: p.487

Beaudrot Jr, Charles R
(Georgia)
Profile: p.202,203
Tax **Band 4**
Table: p.201

Beavers, Charles (Alabama)
Profile: p.7
Real Estate **Band 2**
Table: p.6

Beck, David (Texas)
Profile: p.669
Litigation **Band 1**
Table: p.663

Beck, Joseph (Georgia)
Profile: p.203
Intellectual Property **Band 3**
Table: p.195

Beck, Paul (Pennsylvania)
Profile: p.615
Intellectual Property **Band 2**
Table: p.609

Beck, Philip (Illinois)
Profile: p.254
Litigation **Band 2**
Table: p.245

Beck, Philip (Georgia)
Profile: p.203
Construction **Band 5**
Table: p.184

Becker, Wendy (Kentucky)
Profile: p.305
Employment **Band 3**
Table: p.302

Beckham Jr, Charles (Texas)
Profile: p.669
Insolvency **Band 3**
Table: p.657

Bedree, Melvin (Ohio)
Profile: p.573
Banking & Finance **Band 1**
Table: p.559

Beeman, Arthur (Kentucky)
Profile: p.305
Litigation **Band 3**
Table: p.303

Beeson, Christopher (Idaho)
Profile: p.222
Real Estate **Band 1**
Table: p.222

Behm, Jeffrey (Vermont)
Profile: p.697
Litigation **Band 3**
Table: p.695

Behm, Margaret (Tennessee)
Profile: p.641
Employment **Band 1**
Table: p.637

Behnia, Hatef (California)
Profile: p.60
Tax **Band 2**
Table: p.58

Belcher, James (Wyoming)
Profile: p.734
Corporate/M&A **Band 2**
Table: p.730

Bell, Stephen (Illinois)
Profile: p.254
Real Estate **Band 4**
Table: p.249

Bell, Thomas (New York)
Profile: p.505
Private Equity **Band 1**
Table: p.489

Bell Jr, Albert (North Carolina)
Profile: p.552
Employment **Band 3**
Table: p.548

Bellah Maguire, Jennifer
(California)
Profile: p.60
Capital Markets **Band 3**
Table: p.32

Beller, Daniel (New York)
Profile: p.505
Litigation **Band 5**
Table: p.481

Bello, Kenneth
(Massachusetts)
Profile: p.354
Employment **Band 3**
Table: p.342

Belt, David (Connecticut)
Profile: p.92
Litigation **Band 4**
Table: p.90

Belzer, Irvin (Missouri)
Profile: p.392
Litigation **Band 1**
Table: p.389

Ben-Ami, Leora (New York)
Profile: p.505
Intellectual Property **Band 4**
Table: p.479

Bender, Jeanne Matthews
(Montana)
Profile: p.398
Employment **Band 1**
Table: p.395

Bendicksen, Perry
(New Mexico)
Profile: p.438
Corporate/M&A **Band 3**
Table: p.433

Bendinger, Gary F (Utah)
Profile: p.690
Litigation **Band 1**
Table: p.687

Benedict, James (New York)
Profile: p.505
Litigation **Band 5**
Table: p.481

Benham III, Paul B
(Arkansas)
Profile: p.27
Corporate/M&A **Band 1**
Table: p.23

Benjamin, Alan (California)
Profile: p.60
Banking & Finance **Band 4**
Table: p.30

Bennett, Barry (Illinois)
Profile: p.254
Employment **Band 3**

Table: p.235

Bennett, David (Oregon)
Profile: p.593,593
Real Estate **Band 3**
Table: p.592

Bennett, Fred G (California)
Profile: p.60
Construction **Band 3**
Table: p.36

Bennett, Mary
(District of Columbia)
Profile: p.132
Tax **Band 4**
Table: p.130

Bennett, Robert
(District of Columbia)
Profile: p.132
Litigation **Band 3**
Table: p.123

Bennett II, Crocker (Vermont)
Profile: p.697
Litigation **Band 4**
Table: p.695

Benoit, Wilfred
(Massachusetts)
Profile: p.354
Employment **Band 3**
Table: p.342

Benvenutti, Peter J
(California)
Profile: p.60
Insolvency **Band 4**
Table: p.44

Berchild, John (California)
Profile: p.60
Banking & Finance **Band 4**
Table: p.30

Berenter, Steven (Idaho)
Profile: p.222
Employment **Band 2**
Table: p.220

Berg, Eric L (New York)
Profile: p.505
Banking & Finance **Band 3**
Table: p.445

Berger, Lawrence
(Pennsylvania)
Profile: p.615
Banking & Finance **Band 3**
Table: p.598

Berger, Ritchie (Vermont)
Profile: p.697
Litigation **Band 3**
Table: p.695

Bergère, Timothy
(Pennsylvania)
Profile: p.615
Environment **Band 4**
Table: p.604

Berggren, Thomas (Utah)
Profile: p.690
Real Estate **Band 2**
Table: p.689

Berghoff, John C Jr (Illinois)
Profile: p.254
Environment **Band 3**
Table: p.239

Bergin, Leo (Nevada)
Profile: p.412,412
Real Estate **Band 3**
Table: p.411

Bergtraum, Howard
(New York)
Profile: p.505
Private Equity **Band 3**
Table: p.489

Berkman, Jerome
(Connecticut)
Profile: p.92
Real Estate **Band 3**

B

LEADING LAWYERS INDEX

Table: p.91

Berkowitz, Alan (Pennsylvania)
Profile: p.615
Employment **Band 4**
Table: p.602

Berlin, Howard (Florida)
Profile: p.
Insolvency **Band 3**
Table: p.162

Berman, Daniel L (Utah)
Profile: p.690
Litigation **Band 4**
Table: p.687

Berne, Gary (Oregon)
Profile: p.593
Litigation **Band 4**
Table: p.590

Berner, Frederic (District of Columbia)
Profile: p.132
Energy **Band 5**
Table: p.115

Bernick, Carol (Oregon)
Profile: p.593
Employment **Band 4**
Table: p.589

Bernick, David M (Illinois)
Profile: p.254
Litigation **Band 1**
Table: p.245

Bernstein, Alan (Pennsylvania)
Profile: p.615
Intellectual Property **Band 2**
Table: p.609

Bernstein, Bruce (Illinois)
Profile: p.254
Banking & Finance **Band 1**
Table: p.226
Insolvency **Band 2**
Table: p.241

Bernstein, Donald S (New York)
Profile: p.505
Insolvency **Band 1**
Table: p.472

Bernstein, Michael (New York)
Profile: p.505
Employment **Band 3**
Table: p.467

Berry, Andrew (New Jersey)
Profile: p.430
Litigation **Band 1**
Table: p.428

Berry IV, Dewees (Tennessee)
Profile: p.641
Real Estate **Band 3**
Table: p.640

Bertelsen, Mark (California)
Profile: p.61

Beshar, Sarah (New York)
Profile: p.505
Capital Markets **Band 4**
Table: p.448

Bessette-Smith, Suzanne (Illinois)
Profile: p.254
Real Estate **U**
Table: p.249

Betzer, Stan (New Mexico)
Profile: p.438
Corporate/M&A **Band 3**
Table: p.433

Bevan, William (Pennsylvania)
Profile: p.615
Employment **Band 1**
Table: p.602

Beyda, Richard (District of Columbia)
Profile: p.132
Real Estate **Band 3**
Table: p.127

Bialkin, Kenneth J (New York)
Profile: p.505
Corporate/M&A **Band 2**
Table: p.460

Bick, John (New York)
Profile: p.505
Private Equity **Band 3**
Table: p.487

Bieke, James (District of Columbia)
Profile: p.132
Environment **Band 5**
Table: p.117

Bienenstock, Martin (New York)
Profile: p.505
Insolvency **Band 1**
Table: p.472

Bilger, Bruce (Texas)
Profile: p.669
Energy **Band 1**
Table: p.653
Projects **Band 1**
Table: p.664

Billings Jr., Peter W. (Utah)
Profile: p.690
Litigation **Band 4**
Table: p.687

Bilzin, Brian (Florida)
Profile: p.172
Real Estate **Band 1**
Table: p.167

Binnig, Christian F (Illinois)
Profile: p.254
Communications **Band 2**
Table: p.229

Birnbaum, Sheila L (New York)
Profile: p.506
Litigation **Band 4**
Table: p.481

Biron, Thomas (Pennsylvania)
Profile: p.615
Insolvency **Band 3**
Table: p.607

Bishop, Doak (Texas)
Profile: p.669
Energy **Band 3**
Table: p.653

Bishop III, George W (Tennessee)
Profile: p.641
Corporate/M&A **Band 2**
Table: p.635

Bithell, Walter (Idaho)
Profile: p.222
Litigation **Band 1**
Table: p.221

Black, Allen (Pennsylvania)
Profile: p.615
Litigation **Band 3**
Table: p.611

Black, Bruce (Colorado)
Profile: p.83
Litigation **Band 2**
Table: p.79

Black, Kathryn (Alaska)
Profile: p.14
Corporate/M&A **Band 2**
Table: p.9

Black Jr, Lewis S (Delaware)
Profile: p.99
Corporate/M&A **Band 2**
Table: p.94

Blackstock, Jerry (Georgia)
Profile: p.203

Intellectual Property **Band 2**
Table: p.195

Blackwood, Eileen (Vermont)
Profile: p.697
Employment **Band 2**
Table: p.693

Blair, Andrew (Colorado)
Profile: p.83
Corporate/M&A **Band 3**
Table: p.75

Blake, Jonathan D (District of Columbia)
Profile: p.132
Communications **Band 2**
Table: p.107

Blake Jr., Joseph (South Carolina)
Profile: p.628
Corporate/M&A **Band 2**
Table: p.624

Bland, Doug (Texas)
Profile: p.669
Energy **Band 4**
Table: p.653
Projects **Band 2**
Table: p.664

Blashek, Robert D (California)
Profile: p.61
Tax **Band 3**
Table: p.58

Blassberg, Franci J (New York)
Profile: p.506
Private Equity **Band 2**
Table: p.487

Blaszak, James (District of Columbia)
Profile: p.133
Communications **Band 5**
Table: p.107

Blattner, David (Massachusetts)
Profile: p.354
Tax **Band 1**
Table: p.353

Bleakley, Peter (District of Columbia)
Profile: p.133
Litigation **Band 3**
Table: p.123

Blecher, Maxwell (California)
Profile: p.61
Antitrust **Band 3**
Table: p.29
Litigation **Band 2**
Table: p.50

Blechman, Bill (Florida)
Profile: p.172
Antitrust **Band 2**
Table: p.151

Bleck, Daniel (Massachusetts)
Profile: p.354
Insolvency **U**
Table: p.346

Bledsoe, Gregory (Oklahoma)
Profile: p.585
Employment **Band 1**
Table: p.581

Blessing, Peter H (New York)
Profile: p.506
Tax **Band 2**
Table: p.499

Blewett III, Alexander (Montana)
Profile: p.398
Employment **Band 1**
Table: p.395
Litigation **Band 2**
Table: p.396

Block, Bruce (Wisconsin)
Profile: p.729

Real Estate **Band 2**
Table: p.727

Block, Dennis (New York)
Profile: p.506
Litigation **Band 4**
Table: p.481

Block, William (Washington)
Profile: p.712
Real Estate **Band 3**
Table: p.711

Bloom, Herschel (Georgia)
Profile: p.203
Tax **Band 2**
Table: p.201

Bloom, Jerry (California)
Profile: p.61
Energy **Band 1**
Table: p.41

Bloom, Mark D (Florida)
Profile: p.172
Insolvency **Band 1**
Table: p.162

Bloom, Michael (Pennsylvania)
Profile: p.615
Insolvency **Band 2**
Table: p.607

Blue, James (Florida)
Profile: p.172
Employment **Band 3**
Table: p.158

Blume, Fred (Pennsylvania)
Profile: p.615
Corporate/M&A **Band 4**
Table: p.599

Blumenthal, William (District of Columbia)
Profile: p.133
Antitrust **Band 5**
Table: p.103

Blumkin, Linda R (New York)
Profile: p.506
Antitrust **Band 4**
Table: p.441

Boast, Molly S (New York)
Profile: p.506
Antitrust **Band 4**
Table: p.441

Bobber, Bernard (Wisconsin)
Profile: p.729
Employment **Band 3**
Table: p.725

Bochner, Steven (California)
Profile: p.61
Communications **Band 4**
Table: p.34

Boe, Kathleen M. (Vermont)
Profile: p.697
Corporate/M&A **Band 2**
Table: p.692

Boe, Tim (Arkansas)
Profile: p.27
Employment **Band 1**
Table: p.24

Boeglin, Daniel L (Indiana)
Profile: p.283
Corporate/M&A **Band 3**
Table: p.277

Boehrer, Charles (Illinois)
Profile: p.254
Banking & Finance **Band 3**
Table: p.226

Böer, Ralf-Reinhard (Wisconsin)
Profile: p.729
Corporate/M&A **Band 3**
Table: p.723

Bogas, Kathleen (Michigan)
Profile: p.366

Employment **Band 2**
Table: p.362

Bogdanoff, Lee R (California)
Profile: p.61
Insolvency **Band 4**
Table: p.44

Bogdanow, Alan (Texas)
Profile: p.669
Corporate/M&A **Band 4**
Table: p.649

Bogen, Andy (California)
Profile: p.61
Corporate/M&A **Band 1**
Table: p.37

Bogue, Stevenson (Nebraska)
Profile: p.405
Employment **Band 3**
Table: p.402

Bohm, Richard D (New York)
Profile: p.506
Private Equity **Band 4**
Table: p.487

Boice, William (Georgia)
Profile: p.203
Employment **Band 2**
Table: p.189
Litigation **Band 3**
Table: p.198

Boies, David (New York)
Profile: p.507
Antitrust **Band 2**
Table: p.441
Litigation **Band 1**
Table: p.481

Boisseau, Richard (Georgia)
Profile: p.203
Employment **Band 2**
Table: p.189

Bokor, Bruce (Florida)
Profile: p.171,172
Tax **Band 1**
Table: p.170

Boldt, Michael H (Indiana)
Profile: p.283
Employment **Band 2**
Table: p.279

Boles, Hampton (Alabama)
Profile: p.7
Real Estate **Band 1**
Table: p.6

Bolstein, Joel (Pennsylvania)
Profile: p.615
Environment **Band 3**
Table: p.604

Bolt, Robert (Florida)
Profile: p.172
Tax **Band 3**
Table: p.170

Bomse, Stephen (California)
Profile: p.61
Antitrust **Band 3**
Table: p.29

Bond, Thomas (Texas)
Profile: p.669
Insurance **Band 1**
Table: p.659

Bondurant, Emmet (Georgia)
Profile: p.203
Antitrust **Band 1**
Table: p.181
Employment **Band 2**
Table: p.188
Litigation **Band 1**
Table: p.198

Bonner, Michael J (Nevada)
Profile: p.412
Corporate/M&A **Band 2**
Table: p.406

Booker, Daniel I

LEADING LAWYERS INDEX

(Pennsylvania)
Profile: p.615
Antitrust**Band** 3
Table: p.596

Booker, William (West Virginia)
Profile: p.721
Corporate/M&A**Band** 2
Table: p.714

Boone, Michael (Texas)
Profile: p.669
Corporate/M&A**Band** 2
Table: p.649

Boone Jr., Sidney (South Carolina)
Profile: p.628,628
Real Estate**Band** 1
Table: p.628

Booth, Brian (Oregon)
Profile: p.593
Corporate/M&A**Band** 2
Table: p.587

Booth, William (California)
Profile: p.61
Energy**Band** 3
Table: p.41

Boothby, Colleen (District of Columbia)
Profile: p.133
Communications**Band** 4
Table: p.107

Borden, Mark (Massachusetts)
Profile: p.354
Corporate/M&A**Band** 1
Table: p.340

Borders, Sarah (Georgia)
Profile: p.203
Insolvency**Band** 4
Table: p.193

Borders, Thomas (Illinois)
Profile: p.255
Tax**Band** 4
Table: p.252

Borish, Warren (Pennsylvania)
Profile: p.615
Employment**Band** 3
Table: p.601

Born, S R (Indiana)
Profile: p.283
Employment**Band** 1
Table: p.279

Bornn, Nancy (California)
Profile: p.61
Employment**Band** 2
Table: p.39

Borowitz, Peter L (New York)
Profile: p.507
Insolvency**Band** 4
Table: p.472

Bossert, Terry (Pennsylvania)
Profile: p.615
Environment**Band** 4
Table: p.604

Bostelman, John T (New York)
Profile: p.507
Capital Markets**Band** 4
Table: p.448

Boston, Robert (Tennessee)
Profile: p.641
Employment**Band** 1
Table: p.637

Botica, Matthew (Illinois)
Profile: p.255
Insolvency**Band** 3
Table: p.241

Bottrell, Lowell (North Dakota)
Profile: p.557
Corporate/M&A**Band** 3
Table: p.554

Bouknight, Lon (District of Columbia)
Profile: p.133
Energy**Band** 1
Table: p.115

Boulden, Michael (Texas)
Profile: p.669
Real Estate**Band** 4
Table: p.665

Boulet, Virginia (Louisiana)
Profile: p.316
Corporate/M&A**Band** 4
Table: p.309

Bowe Jr, James F (District of Columbia)
Profile: p.133
Energy**Band** 3
Table: p.115

Bowen, Michael (Wisconsin)
Profile: p.729
Litigation**Band** 2
Table: p.726

Bowen, Stephen S (Illinois)
Profile: p.253,255
Tax**Band** 1
Table: p.252

Bowers, James (Missouri)
Profile: p.392
Real Estate**Band** 3
Table: p.391

Bowie, Scott (New York)
Profile: p.507
Private Equity**Band** 4
Table: p.489

Bowman, John (Texas)
Profile: p.669
Energy**Band** 3
Table: p.653

Bowman, William (District of Columbia)
Profile: p.133
Insurance**Band** 2
Table: p.120
Litigation**Band** 3
Table: p.123

Boxer, Leonard (New York)
Profile: p.507
Real Estate**Band** 1
Table: p.493

Boyajian, Victor (New Jersey)
Profile: p.430
Corporate/M&A**Band** 1
Table: p.425

Boyd, Paul (Idaho)
Profile: p.222
Corporate/M&A**Band** 1
Table: p.219

Boyd, William (South Carolina)
Profile: p.628
Corporate/M&A**Band** 2
Table: p.624
Real Estate**Band** 2
Table: p.628

Bozarth, Stephen (Florida)
Profile: p.172
Real Estate**Band** 3
Table: p.167

Brach, Richard (New York)
Profile: p.507
Projects**Band** 3
Table: p.491

Bradford, Darryl (Illinois)
Profile: p.255
Communications**Band** 1
Table: p.229

Bradford, Donald E (Louisiana)
Profile: p.316
Real Estate**Band** 2
Table: p.314

Bradley, Craig (Kentucky)
Profile: p.305
Corporate/M&A**Band** 2
Table: p.300

Bradley, Michael (Georgia)
Profile: p.203
Energy**Band** 1
Table: p.191

Bradley, William H (Georgia)
Profile: p.203
Tax**Band** 4
Table: p.201

Bradshaw, Penni Pearson (North Carolina)
Profile: p.552
Employment**Band** 2
Table: p.548

Brady, Francis (Connecticut)
Profile: p.92
Litigation**Band** 1
Table: p.90

Brady, Robert S (Delaware)
Profile: p.99
Insolvency**Band** 4
Table: p.96

Braemer, Richard (Pennsylvania)
Profile: p.615
Corporate/M&A**Band** 4
Table: p.599

Brakke, Jon (North Dakota)
Profile: p.557
Corporate/M&A**Band** 1
Table: p.554

Bramlett, Jeffrey (Georgia)
Profile: p.204
Employment**Band** 2
Table: p.188

Bramnick, James (Florida)
Profile: p.172
Employment**Band** 4
Table: p.158

Brandes, Lawrence (New York)
Profile: p.507
Litigation**Band** 5
Table: p.481

Brandow, John M (New York)
Profile: p.507
Capital Markets**Band** 2
Table: p.451

Brann, Richard (Texas)
Profile: p.670
Employment**Band** 1
Table: p.652

Brannan, William (New York)
Profile: p.507
Tax**Band** 4
Table: p.499

Brauer, Walter (Colorado)
Profile: p.83
Employment**Band** 2
Table: p.77

Braun, Stephen (Tennessee)
Profile: p.641
Corporate/M&A**Band** 3
Table: p.635

Bray, John (District of Columbia)
Profile: p.133
Litigation**Band** 2
Table: p.123

Breay, James (Michigan)
Profile: p.366
Banking & Finance**Band** 1
Table: p.360

Bredehoft, Elaine Charlson (Virginia)
Profile: p.704
Employment**Band** 1

Breslow, Stephanie (New York)
Profile: p.507
Private Equity**Band** 3
Table: p.489

Brewer Jr., Wilburn (South Carolina)
Profile: p.628
Litigation**Band** 1
Table: p.626

Brewster, William (Georgia)
Profile: p.204
Intellectual Property**Band** 5
Table: p.195

Brian, Brad (California)
Profile: p.61
Litigation**Band** 2
Table: p.50

Bridge, Catherine (Indiana)
Profile: p.283
Corporate/M&A**Band** 2
Table: p.277

Bridger-Riley, Kay (Oklahoma)
Profile: p.585
Employment**Band** 2
Table: p.581

Bridges, Andrew (California)
Profile: p.61
Intellectual Property**Band** 4
Table: p.48

Briggs, Heather (Vermont)
Profile: p.697
Employment**Band** 1
Table: p.694

Bright Jr, William (Connecticut)
Profile: p.92
Litigation**Band** 3
Table: p.90

Brignone, Andrew (Nevada)
Profile: p.412
Employment**Band** 1
Table: p.408

Brinkley, Robert (North Carolina)
Profile: p.552
Real Estate**Band** 2
Table: p.551

Brinkman, David (Ohio)
Profile: p.573
Intellectual Property**Band** 2
Table: p.568

Brischetto, Stephen (Oregon)
Profile: p.593
Employment**Band** 1
Table: p.588

Bristow, Daryl (Texas)
Profile: p.670
Litigation**Band** 2
Table: p.663

Brittain, Max (Illinois)
Profile: p.255
Employment**Band** 4
Table: p.236

Bro, Ruth Hill (Illinois)
Profile: p.255
Communications**Band** 4
Table: p.229

Broaddus, William (Virginia)
Profile: p.704
Litigation**Band** 1
Table: p.702

Broglio, Dennis (West Virginia)
Profile: p.721
Real Estate**Band** 1
Table: p.720

Bromberg, Steve (Michigan)
Profile: p.366

Real Estate**Band** 1
Table: p.365

Bronstein, Joel (Florida)
Profile: p.171,172
Tax**Band** 3
Table: p.170

Brooks, Robert (Rhode Island)
Profile: p.623
Employment**Band** 1
Table: p.621

Broom, Bob (Nebraska)
Profile: p.405
Employment**Band** 1
Table: p.401

Brooman, David (Pennsylvania)
Profile: p.615
Environment**Band** 2
Table: p.604

Brose, Steve (District of Columbia)
Profile: p.133
Energy**Band** 3
Table: p.115

Brosnahan, James (California)
Profile: p.61
Litigation**Band** 1
Table: p.50

Broth, Mark (New Hampshire)
Profile: p.421
Employment**Band** 1
Table: p.417

Brountas, Paul (Massachusetts)
Profile: p.354
Corporate/M&A**Band** 2
Table: p.340

Brown, Barbara (District of Columbia)
Profile: p.133
Employment**Band** 1
Table: p.112

Brown, Bowman (Florida)
Profile: p.172
Banking & Finance**Band** 1
Table: p.152
Corporate/M&A**Band** 4
Table: p.156

Brown, Daryl (Florida)
Profile: p.172
Construction**Band** 3
Table: p.154

Brown, David H (Texas)
Profile: p.670
Insurance**Band** 4
Table: p.659

Brown, Dickson (New York)
Profile: p.507
Tax**Band** 2
Table: p.499

Brown, Donald J (Iowa)
Profile: p.292
Corporate/M&A**Band** 4
Table: p.286

Brown, Donald W (California)
Profile: p.
Insurance**Band** 1
Table: p.46

Brown, Duane (New Mexico)
Profile: p.438
Corporate/M&A**Band** 4
Table: p.433

Brown, James (Florida)
Profile: p.172
Employment**Band** 3
Table: p.158

Brown, James (Pennsylvania)
Profile: p.615
Employment**Band** 3
Table: p.602

www.ChambersandPartners.com

LEADING LAWYERS INDEX

Brown, Jeff (Indiana)
Profile: p.283
Corporate/M&A Band 2
Table: p.277

Brown, John (Massachusetts)
Profile: p.355
Tax Band 1
Table: p.353

Brown, Kim (Tennessee)
Profile: p.641
Real Estate Band 1
Table: p.640

Brown, Meredith M (New York)
Profile: p.507

Brown, Reagan (Texas)
Profile: p.670
Insurance Band 1
Table: p.659

Brown, Ricklin (West Virginia)
Profile: p.721
Employment Band 1
Table: p.717

Brown, Robert (Colorado)
Profile: p.83
Real Estate Band 1
Table: p.81

Brown, Stephen (Alabama)
Profile: p.7
Employment Band 4
Table: p.3

Brown, Stephen (Pennsylvania)
Profile: p.615
Antitrust Band 3
Table: p.596

Brown, Stephen Ross (Montana)
Profile: p.398
Corporate/M&A Band 2
Table: p.394

Browne, Graham (New Mexico)
Profile: p.438
Corporate/M&A Band 3
Table: p.433

Brownell, William (District of Columbia)
Profile: p.133
Environment Band 4
Table: p.117

Browning, James (New Mexico)
Profile: p.438
Litigation Band 4
Table: p.435

Brownstein, Andrew R (New York)
Profile: p.507
Corporate/M&A Band 3
Table: p.460

Brubaker, Robert (Ohio)
Profile: p.573
Environment Band 2
Table: p.567

Brunell, Richard (Massachusetts)
Profile: p.355
Antitrust Band 2
Table: p.337

Brunner, Thomas (District of Columbia)
Profile: p.134
Insurance Band 3
Table: p.120

Bruns, Phil (Texas)
Profile: p.670
Litigation Band 3
Table: p.663

Bryan, Karen (California)
Profile: p.61
Tax Band 2
Table: p.58

Buchanan, John (District of Columbia)
Profile: p.134
Insurance Band 3
Table: p.120

Buchanan, Paul (Oregon)
Profile: p.593
Employment Band 2
Table: p.589

Buchanan Jr., Robert (Massachusetts)
Profile: p.355
Antitrust Band 2
Table: p.337

Buchenroth, Stephen (Ohio)
Profile: p.573
Real Estate Band 1
Table: p.572

Buchholtz, David (New Mexico)
Profile: p.438
Corporate/M&A Band 1
Table: p.433

Buchsbaum, Peter (New Jersey)
Profile: p.430
Real Estate Band 3
Table: p.429

Buck, Gurdon (Connecticut)
Profile: p.92
Real Estate Band 2
Table: p.91

Buck, Peter (North Carolina)
Profile: p.552
Banking & Finance Band 2
Table: p.544
Corporate/M&A Band 1
Table: p.546

Buckler, Robert H (Georgia)
Profile: p.204
Employment Band 3
Table: p.189

Buckley, Christopher (District of Columbia)
Profile: p.134
Environment Band 5
Table: p.117

Buckley, Edward (Georgia)
Profile: p.204
Employment Band 1
Table: p.188

Buckley, Kevin (Virginia)
Profile: p.704
Corporate/M&A Band 3
Table: p.699

Buckley, Martin (Colorado)
Profile: p.83
Employment Band 2
Table: p.77

Buckley, Mert (Kansas)
Profile: p.299
Real Estate Band 4
Table: p.298

Buckley, Michael (Nevada)
Profile: p.412
Corporate/M&A Band 3
Table: p.406
Real Estate Band 1
Table: p.411

Budofsky, Daniel (New York)
Profile: p.507
Capital Markets Band 3
Table: p.451

Bueide, Daniel (North Dakota)
Profile: p.557,557
Real Estate Band 3
Table: p.557

Buente, David (District of Columbia)
Profile: p.134
Environment Band 1
Table: p.117

Buffington, Teresa (Wyoming)
Profile: p.735
Corporate/M&A Band 3
Table: p.730
Corporate/M&A Band 3
Table: p.730

Buford, C Douglas (Arkansas)
Profile: p.27
Corporate/M&A Band 1
Table: p.23

Buoncristiani, David (California)
Profile: p.61
Construction Band 2
Table: p.36

Burbidge, Richard D (Utah)
Profile: p.690
Litigation Band 1
Table: p.687

Burch Jr, Francis B (Maryland)
Profile: p.332
Litigation Band 2
Table: p.330

Buresh, James (New York)
Profile: p.507
Banking & Finance Band 4
Table: p.445

Burger, Peter (New Hampshire)
Profile: p.421
Corporate/M&A Band 4
Table: p.415

Burgoyne, Grant (Idaho)
Profile: p.222
Employment Band 1
Table: p.219

Burke, Arthur J (New York)
Profile: p.507
Antitrust Band 5
Table: p.441

Burke, Carl (Idaho)
Profile: p.222
Litigation Band 2
Table: p.221

Burke, David (Florida)
Profile: p.172
Tax Band 3
Table: p.170

Burke, Ray (New York)
Profile: p.507
Shipping Band 1
Table: p.496

Burke, Steven (New Hampshire)
Profile: p.421
Corporate/M&A Band 4
Table: p.415

Burke, Ted (New York)
Profile: p.508
Projects Band 3
Table: p.491

Burke, Thomas (California)
Profile: p.61
Media & Entertainment Band 4
Table: p.53

Burkhalter, David (Tennessee)
Profile: p.641
Employment Band 2
Table: p.637

Burling, James (Massachusetts)
Profile: p.355
Antitrust Band 2
Table: p.337

Burner, Burnie (Texas)
Profile: p.670
Insurance Band 4
Table: p.659

Burnett, John (Arkansas)
Profile: p.27
Employment Band 3
Table: p.24

Burnette, Harry (Tennessee)
Profile: p.641
Employment Band 2
Table: p.637

Burnette, Malissa (South Carolina)
Profile: p.628
Employment Band 1
Table: p.625

Burns, David (Texas)
Profile: p.670
Banking & Finance Band 3
Table: p.645

Burrell, Lizabeth (New York)
Profile: p.508
Shipping Band 3
Table: p.496

Burrus, Robert (Virginia)
Profile: p.704
Corporate/M&A Band 1
Table: p.699

Burt, Donald (Nebraska)
Profile: p.405
Corporate/M&A Band 2
Table: p.400

Burt, Laurie (Massachusetts)
Profile: p.355
Environment Band 1
Table: p.344

Busch, John (Wisconsin)
Profile: p.729
Litigation Band 2
Table: p.726

Busch, William (Minnesota)
Profile: p.376
Corporate/M&A Band 3
Table: p.369

Buser, James (Nebraska)
Profile: p.405
Real Estate U
Table: p.404

Busey, Roxane (Illinois)
Profile: p.255
Antitrust Band 4
Table: p.224

Busey, Stephen (Florida)
Profile: p.172
Insolvency Band 1
Table: p.162

Bussard, Donald A (Delaware)
Profile: p.100
Corporate/M&A Band 1
Table: p.94

Busse, Richard (Oregon)
Profile: p.593
Employment Band 1
Table: p.588

Busto, Mark (Washington)
Profile: p.712
Employment Band 2
Table: p.708

Butler, Brian (Wisconsin)
Profile: p.729
Litigation Band 2
Table: p.726

Butler, Harris (Virginia)
Profile: p.704
Employment Band 2
Table: p.701

Butler, James (Georgia)
Profile: p.204
Litigation Band 3
Table: p.198

Butler, James (Georgia)
Profile: p.204
Construction Band 5
Table: p.184

Butler, Patrick (Louisiana)
Profile: p.316
Corporate/M&A Band 5
Table: p.309

Butler Jr, John Wm (Jack) (Illinois)
Profile: p.255
Insolvency Band 1
Table: p.241

Butt, Layne (Nevada)
Profile: p.412
Real Estate Band 3
Table: p.411

Byowitz, Michael H (New York)
Profile: p.508
Antitrust Band 3
Table: p.441

Byrne, Richard (Pennsylvania)
Profile: p.615
Intellectual Property Band 2
Table: p.609

Byrnes, Peter (Washington)
Profile: p.712
Litigation Band 1
Table: p.709

C

Cacciabeve, Charles (Florida)
Profile: p.172
Construction Band 3
Table: p.154

Cagle, Molly (Texas)
Profile: p.670
Environment Band 2
Table: p.655

Cahill, Kathleen (Maryland)
Profile: p.333
Employment Band 2
Table: p.328

Cahoon, Susan (Georgia)
Profile: p.204
Litigation Band 3
Table: p.198

Cairns, Carolyn (Washington)
Profile: p.712
Employment Band 2
Table: p.708

Calland, Dean (Pennsylvania)
Profile: p.615
Environment Band 1
Table: p.604

Calof, Lawrence (California)
Profile: p.61
Corporate/M&A Band 4
Table: p.37

Calvin, Charles (Colorado)
Profile: p.83
Real Estate Band 4
Table: p.81

Camahort, Steve (California)
Profile: p.61
Communications Band 5
Table: p.34

Campbell, Charles (Georgia)
Profile: p.204
Insolvency Band 1
Table: p.193

Campbell, Craig (North Dakota)
Profile: p.557
Litigation Band 3
Table: p.556

LEADING LAWYERS INDEX

Campbell, Dave (Indiana)
Profile: p.283
Litigation **Band 2**
Table: p.280

Campbell, Donald (Nevada)
Profile: p.412
Litigation **Band 1**
Table: p.409

Campbell, Lawrence
(Michigan)
Profile: p.366
Litigation **Band 2**
Table: p.364

Campbell, William (Oregon)
Profile: p.593
Corporate/M&A **Band 4**
Table: p.587

Campbell II, L Webb
(Tennessee)
Profile: p.641
Litigation **Band 2**
Table: p.639

Campbell Jr, John (Louisiana)
Profile: p.316
Corporate/M&A **Band 4**
Table: p.309

Campbell Jr, Robert S (Utah)
Profile: p.690
Litigation **Band 2**
Table: p.687

Campbell Jr, Woodrow W
(New York)
Profile: p.508
Private Equity **Band 1**
Table: p.489

Campbell Jr., Boyd (North Carolina)
Profile: p.552
Banking & Finance **Band 3**
Table: p.544

Campion, Thomas
(New Jersey)
Profile: p.430
Litigation **Band 1**
Table: p.428

Cane, Paul (California)
Profile: p.61
Employment **Band 3**
Table: p.40

Canellos, Peter C (New York)
Profile: p.508
Tax **Band 1**
Table: p.499

Cannada, Barry (Mississippi)
Profile: p.383
Corporate/M&A **Band 1**
Table: p.378

Cannada, Don (Mississippi)
Profile: p.383
Real Estate **Band 1**
Table: p.382

Cannon, Kinder (Florida)
Profile: p.172
Corporate/M&A **Band 4**
Table: p.156

Canterbury, Jr, Joe (Texas)
Profile: p.670
Construction **Band 1**
Table: p.648

Cantlin, Richard (Oregon)
Profile: p.593
Real Estate **Band 2**
Table: p.592

Cappellanti, Ellen (West Virginia)
Profile: p.721
Corporate/M&A **Band 2**
Table: p.714

Cardwell, J Thomas (Florida)
Profile: p.173

Banking & Finance **Band 3**
Table: p.152
Litigation **Band 3**
Table: p.165

Carey, Stevens (California)
Profile: p.62
Real Estate **Band 5**
Table: p.56

Cargile, Ann Peldo
(Tennessee)
Profile: p.641
Real Estate **Band 3**
Table: p.640

Carlino, James (Indiana)
Profile: p.283
Real Estate **Band 4**
Table: p.282

Carlotti, Stephen (Rhode Island)
Profile: p.623
Corporate/M&A **Band 1**
Table: p.620

Carlson, Bruce (North Dakota)
Profile: p.557
Litigation **Band 1**
Table: p.556

Carlson, James (Ohio)
Profile: p.573
Corporate/M&A **Band 2**
Table: p.562

Carlson, Kent (Washington)
Profile: p.712
Corporate/M&A **Band 1**
Table: p.706

Carlson, Walter (Illinois)
Profile: p.255
Litigation **Band 5**
Table: p.245

Carmagnola, Domenick (New Jersey)
Profile: p.430
Employment **Band 1**
Table: p.427

Carpenter, Bill (New Mexico)
Profile: p.438
Litigation **Band 2**
Table: p.435

Carpenter, David (Illinois)
Profile: p.255
Communications **Band 1**
Table: p.229

Carpenter, Edward (South Dakota)
Profile: p.633
Litigation **Band 3**
Table: p.632

Carpenter, Willis (Colorado)
Profile: p.83
Real Estate **Band 2**
Table: p.81

Carr, Stephen (Massachusetts)
Profile: p.355
Corporate/M&A **Band 3**
Table: p.340

Carr, William (Missouri)
Profile: p.392
Real Estate **Band 1**
Table: p.391

Carrell, Richard (Texas)
Profile: p.670
Antitrust **Band 2**
Table: p.644

Carroll, Frank (Iowa)
Profile: p.292
Corporate/M&A **Band 3**
Table: p.286

Carroll, James (Pennsylvania)
Profile: p.615
Employment **Band 3**
Table: p.601

Carron, Reid (Minnesota)
Profile: p.376
Employment **Band 1**
Table: p.371

Carruthers, Thomas Neely
(Alabama)
Profile: p.7
Corporate/M&A **Band 1**
Table: p.1

Carson, Van (Ohio)
Profile: p.574
Environment **Band 2**
Table: p.567

Carssow, Tim (Georgia)
Profile: p.204
Real Estate **Band 2**
Table: p.199

Carter, Francis (Florida)
Profile: p.173
Insolvency **Band 2**
Table: p.162

Carter, James H (New York)
Profile: p.508
Arbitration **Band 1**
Table: p.443

Cary, George
(District of Columbia)
Profile: p.134,508
Antitrust **Band 2**
Table: p.103

Cary, William (North Carolina)
Profile: p.552
Employment **Band 1**
Table: p.548

Case, Daniel H (Hawaii)
Profile: p.218
Corporate/M&A **Band 1**
Table: p.212

Case, James H (Hawaii)
Profile: p.218
Corporate/M&A **Band 3**
Table: p.212

Case, Stephen H (New York)
Profile: p.508
Insolvency **Band 2**
Table: p.472

Casey, David (Massachusetts)
Profile: p.355
Employment **Band 1**
Table: p.342

Casey, Michael (Florida)
Profile: p.173
Employment **Band 2**
Table: p.158

Cashdan, Jeff (Georgia)
Profile: p.204
Antitrust **Band 5**
Table: p.181

Cass, George (Pennsylvania)
Profile: p.615
Insolvency **Band 3**
Table: p.607

Cassidy, Bart (Pennsylvania)
Profile: p.615
Environment **U**
Table: p.604

Cassidy, Patrick (West Virginia)
Profile: p.721
Employment **Band 2**
Table: p.716

Cassidy, Richard (Vermont)
Profile: p.697
Employment **Band 1**
Table: p.693

Cassis, Charlie (Kentucky)
Profile: p.305
Litigation **Band 3**
Table: p.303

Castaldo, Neil
(New Hampshire)
Profile: p.422
Corporate/M&A **Band 3**
Table: p.415

Castel, Kevin (New York)
Profile: p.508
Litigation **Band 4**
Table: p.481

Cates, C. Thomas
(Tennessee)
Profile: p.641
Real Estate **Band 2**
Table: p.640

Cathcart, David (California)
Profile: p.62
Employment **Band 1**
Table: p.40

Cathcart, Patrick (California)
Profile: p.62
Insurance **Band 2**
Table: p.46

Catron, Stephen (Kentucky)
Profile: p.305
Corporate/M&A **Band 3**
Table: p.300

Caulkins, Charles (Florida)
Profile: p.173
Employment **Band 3**
Table: p.158

Cavanagh Jr, Joseph V.
(Rhode Island)
Profile: p.623
Litigation **Band 1**
Table: p.622

Cave, Bradley (Wyoming)
Profile: p.735
Employment **Band 3**
Table: p.732

Caverly, Joseph (Louisiana)
Profile: p.316
Corporate/M&A **Band 2**
Table: p.309

Cawley, Douglas (Texas)
Profile: p.670
Intellectual Property **Band 4**
Table: p.661

Cendali, Dale (New York)
Profile: p.508
Media & Entertainment **Band 4**
Table: p.485

Ceriani, Gary (Colorado)
Profile: p.83
Litigation **Band 2**
Table: p.79

Chadakoff, Richard
(New York)
Profile: p.508
Real Estate **Band 3**
Table: p.493

Chadsey, Phillip (Oregon)
Profile: p.593
Litigation **Band 4**
Table: p.590

Chaffetz, Peter (New York)
Profile: p.508
Insurance **Band 4**
Table: p.477

Champoux, David (Maine)
Profile: p.325
Corporate/M&A **Band 3**
Table: p.319

Chandler, Harry (Idaho)
Profile: p.222
Employment **Band 2**
Table: p.220

Chandler, John (Georgia)
Profile: p.204
Litigation **Band 2**
Table: p.198

Chang, Leo (New York)
Profile: p.508
Shipping **Band 2**
Table: p.496

Chapin, Patrick (Nevada)
Profile: p.412
Employment **Band 2**
Table: p.407

Charles, David (Iowa)
Profile: p.292
Litigation **Band 2**
Table: p.290

Chase, Jeffrey (Colorado)
Profile: p.83
Litigation **Band 1**
Table: p.79

Chatham, Henry (Mississippi)
Profile: p.383
Corporate/M&A **Band 2**
Table: p.378

Chatilovicz, Peter
(District of Columbia)
Profile: p.134
Employment **Band 2**
Table: p.112

Cheatham, Richard R
(Georgia)
Profile: p.204
Banking & Finance **Band 1**
Table: p.183

Cheatwood, Roy C
(Louisiana)
Profile: p.316
Litigation **Band 2**
Table: p.313

Checov, Martin S (California)
Profile: p.62
Insurance **Band 3**
Table: p.46

Cheek III, James (Tennessee)
Profile: p.641
Corporate/M&A **Band 1**
Table: p.635

Chefitz, Joel (Illinois)
Profile: p.255
Antitrust **Band 3**
Table: p.224

Chehi, Mark S (Delaware)
Profile: p.100
Insolvency **Band 4**
Table: p.96

Chepiga, Michael J
(New York)
Profile: p.508
Litigation **Band 3**
Table: p.481

Chernof, Steve (Wisconsin)
Profile: p.729
Real Estate **Band 2**
Table: p.727

Chesler, Evan (New York)
Profile: p.509
Antitrust **Band 4**
Table: p.441
Litigation **Band 5**
Table: p.481

Chico, Gery (Illinois)
Profile: p.255
Real Estate **Band 4**
Table: p.249

Child, Ralph (Massachusetts)
Profile: p.355
Environment **Band 1**
Table: p.344

Childs, Robert (Alabama)
Profile: p.7
Employment **Band 3**
Table: p.2

Chilton, Fred (California)
Profile: p.62

LEADING LAWYERS INDEX

Tax **Band 3**
Table: p.58

Chinn, Adam D (New York)
Profile: p.509
Tax **Band 4**
Table: p.499

Chisholm, David (Montana)
Profile: p.398
Corporate/M&A **Band 1**
Table: p.394

Choi, Paul (Illinois)
Profile: p.255
Corporate/M&A **Band 4**
Table: p.233

Chonin, Neil (Florida)
Profile: p.173
Employment **Band 1**
Table: p.157

Chriss, Timothy (Maryland)
Profile: p.333
Real Estate **Band 4**
Table: p.331

Christensen, Dana (Montana)
Profile: p.398
Litigation **Band 1**
Table: p.396

Christensen, Douglas (North Dakota)
Profile: p.557
Corporate/M&A **Band 2**
Table: p.554

Christian, Tom (Alabama)
Profile: p.7
Litigation **Band 3**
Table: p.4

Christiansen, John (Wisconsin)
Profile: p.729
Litigation **Band 3**
Table: p.726

Christy, Angela (Minnesota)
Profile: p.376
Real Estate **Band 2**
Table: p.374

Chu, Morgan (California)
Profile: p.62
Intellectual Property ✪
Table: p.48

Chun, Deborah (Hawaii)
Profile: p.218,218
Real Estate **Band 2**
Table: p.217

Chun, Nelson N S (Hawaii)
Profile: p.218
Corporate/M&A **Band 2**
Table: p.212

Churchill, Stanley (Kansas)
Profile: p.299
Employment **Band 3**
Table: p.296

Chuzi, George (District of Columbia)
Profile: p.134
Employment **Band 2**
Table: p.112

Cicero, Jr, Frank (Illinois)
Profile: p.255
Litigation **Band 3**
Table: p.245

Cifelli, James (Georgia)
Profile: p.204
Insolvency **Band 3**
Table: p.193

Circo, Carl J (Missouri)
Profile: p.299
Real Estate **Band 1**
Table: p.298

Ciresi, Michael V. (Minnesota)
Profile: p.376
Litigation **Band 1**
Table: p.372

Citron, Diane (New York)
Profile: p.509
Capital Markets **Band 3**
Table: p.453

Civins, Jeff (Texas)
Profile: p.670
Environment **Band 1**
Table: p.655

Clair, John (California)
Profile: p.62
Tax **Band 1**
Table: p.58

Clark, Anthony W (Delaware)
Profile: p.100
Insolvency **Band 4**
Table: p.96

Clark, James (New York)
Profile: p.509
Capital Markets **Band 4**
Table: p.448

Clark, James (Illinois)
Profile: p.255
Banking & Finance **Band 1**
Table: p.226

Clark, John (California)
Profile: p.62
Construction **Band 1**
Table: p.36

Clark, Merlyn (Idaho)
Profile: p.222
Litigation **Band 2**
Table: p.221

Clark, Peter (New York)
Profile: p.509
Shipping **Band 4**
Table: p.496

Clark, Reginald J (Georgia)
Profile: p.204
Tax **Band 4**
Table: p.201

Clark, Robert (Utah)
Profile: p.690
Litigation **Band 4**
Table: p.687

Clark, William H (Pennsylvania)
Profile: p.615
Corporate/M&A **Band 1**
Table: p.599

Clark Jr, Jude (Kentucky)
Profile: p.305
Real Estate **Band 3**
Table: p.304

Claverie, Philip deV. (Louisiana)
Profile: p.316
Banking & Finance **Band 1**
Table: p.307
Real Estate **Band 1**
Table: p.314

Clay, Stephens (Georgia)
Profile: p.204
Litigation **Band 3**
Table: p.198

Clay, Thomas (Kentucky)
Profile: p.305
Employment **Band 1**
Table: p.301

Cleary, David L (Vermont)
Profile: p.697
Litigation **Band 3**
Table: p.695

Cleary, Richard (Kentucky)
Profile: p.305
Employment **Band 1**
Table: p.302

Clees, Joseph (Arizona)
Profile: p.21
Employment **Band 2**
Table: p.18

Clement, Rodney (Mississippi)
Profile: p.383
Real Estate **Band 1**
Table: p.382

Clemow, Brian (Connecticut)
Profile: p.92
Employment **Band 2**
Table: p.89

Cleveland, Christopher (Minnesota)
Profile: p.376
Corporate/M&A **Band 2**
Table: p.369

Cleveland III, William (South Carolina)
Profile: p.628
Litigation **Band 3**
Table: p.626

Clifford, Robert (Illinois)
Profile: p.255
Litigation **Band 5**
Table: p.245

Climan, Richard (California)
Profile: p.62
Communications **Band 2**
Table: p.34
Corporate/M&A **Band 4**
Table: p.37

Clineburg, William (Georgia)
Profile: p.204
Employment **Band 4**
Table: p.189

Cloherty, Thomas (Connecticut)
Profile: p.92
Employment **Band 3**
Table: p.89

Coalson, John L (Georgia)
Profile: p.204
Tax **Band 1**
Table: p.201

Coan, Marvin (Kentucky)
Profile: p.305
Employment **Band 2**
Table: p.301

Coats, William M (Texas)
Profile: p.670
Construction **Band 2**
Table: p.648

Coben, Jerome L (California)
Profile: p.62
Corporate/M&A **Band 2**
Table: p.37

Cochran, Eric L (New York)
Profile: p.509
Corporate/M&A **U**
Table: p.460

Cockrum, James (Kentucky)
Profile: p.305
Employment **Band 3**
Table: p.302

Cogan, Kevin J (Ohio)
Profile: p.574
Litigation **Band 3**
Table: p.570

Cogan, Jr, John (Texas)
Profile: p.670
Energy **Band 1**
Table: p.653
Projects **Band 1**
Table: p.664

Coglianese, Matthew (Florida)
Profile: p.173
Environment **Band 3**
Table: p.160

Cogut, Charles (New York)
Profile: p.509
Corporate/M&A **Band 1**
Table: p.460
Private Equity **Band 1**
Table: p.487

Cohen, Arnold Shep (New Jersey)
Profile: p.430
Employment **Band 2**
Table: p.426

Cohen, Ben (New York)
Profile: p.509
Tax **Band 3**
Table: p.499

Cohen, Bret A. (Massachusetts)
Profile: p.355
Employment **U**
Table: p.342

Cohen, Charles (Pennsylvania)
Profile: p.615
Corporate/M&A **Band 3**
Table: p.599

Cohen, Ezra H (Georgia)
Profile: p.204
Insolvency **Band 4**
Table: p.193

Cohen, George (District of Columbia)
Profile: p.134
Employment **Band 1**
Table: p.112

Cohen, H Rodgin (New York)
Profile: p.509
Banking & Finance **Band 1**
Table: p.445

Cohen, Jerold (Georgia)
Profile: p.204
Tax **Band 1**
Table: p.201

Cohen, Jon (Arizona)
Profile: p.21
Corporate/M&A **Band 2**
Table: p.16

Cohen, Jules (Florida)
Profile: p.173
Insolvency **Band 2**
Table: p.162

Cohen, Michael Marks (New York)
Profile: p.509
Shipping **Band 3**
Table: p.496

Cohen, Nancy (California)
Profile: p.62
Insurance **Band 3**
Table: p.46

Cohen, R Scott (Texas)
Profile: p.671
Corporate/M&A **Band 4**
Table: p.649

Cohen, Richard (Arizona)
Profile: p.21
Employment **Band 3**
Table: p.18

Cohen, Stanley (Pennsylvania)
Profile: p.615
Intellectual Property **Band 2**
Table: p.609

Cohen, Steven (New Jersey)
Profile: p.430
Corporate/M&A **Band 3**
Table: p.425

Cohen, Steven (New Hampshire)
Profile: p.422
Corporate/M&A **Band 2**
Table: p.415

Cohn, Daniel (Massachusetts)
Profile: p.355
Insolvency **Band 1**
Table: p.346

Coil, James (Georgia)
Profile: p.205
Employment **Band 3**
Table: p.189

Cokely, Bryan (West Virginia)
Profile: p.721
Employment **Band 2**
Table: p.717

Cokinos, Greg (Texas)
Profile: p.671
Construction **Band 3**
Table: p.648

Colacino, Antonio (Iowa)
Profile: p.292
Real Estate **Band 2**
Table: p.291

Cole, Chase (Tennessee)
Profile: p.641
Corporate/M&A **Band 1**
Table: p.635

Cole, Howard (Nevada)
Profile: p.412
Employment **Band 2**
Table: p.408

Cole, Terry (Florida)
Profile: p.173
Environment **Band 4**
Table: p.160

Cole, Thomas (Illinois)
Profile: p.255
Corporate/M&A **Band 1**
Table: p.233

Cole III, Kenneth M (Maine)
Profile: p.325
Real Estate **Band 2**
Table: p.324

Coleman, Aubrey (Georgia)
Profile: p.205
Construction **Band 4**
Table: p.184

Coleman, James (Texas)
Profile: p.671
Litigation **Band 3**
Table: p.663

Coleman, John (Alabama)
Profile: p.7
Employment **Band 3**
Table: p.3

Coleman, Lynn R (District of Columbia)
Profile: p.134
Energy **Band 4**
Table: p.115

Coleman, Patrick (Florida)
Profile: p.173
Employment **Band 2**
Table: p.158

Coleman, Thomas (California)
Profile: p.62
Banking & Finance **Band 4**
Table: p.30

Colen, Frederick (Pennsylvania)
Profile: p.615
Intellectual Property **Band 2**
Table: p.609

Collier, Philip (Kentucky)
Profile: p.305
Litigation **Band 2**
Table: p.303

Collings, Robert (Pennsylvania)
Profile: p.615
Environment **Band 3**
Table: p.604

LEADING LAWYERS INDEX

Collins, E Michael (Massachusetts)
Profile: p.355
Private Equity **Band 3**
Table: p.350

Collins, John (Vermont)
Profile: p.697
Employment **Band 2**
Table: p.693

Collins, Joseph P (New York)
Profile: p.509
Capital Markets **Band 3**
Table: p.451

Collins, Kevin (Iowa)
Profile: p.292
Litigation **Band 2**
Table: p.290

Collins, Mark (Delaware)
Profile: p.100
Insolvency **Band 2**
Table: p.96

Collins, Wayne Dale (New York)
Profile: p.
Antitrust **Band 2**
Table: p.441

Collison, Madeline (Colorado)
Profile: p.83
Employment **Band 3**
Table: p.77

Colson, Dean (Florida)
Profile: p.173
Litigation **Band 2**
Table: p.165

Colton, Neal (Pennsylvania)
Profile: p.615
Insolvency **Band 2**
Table: p.607

Colvin, Keith (Louisiana)
Profile: p.316
Real Estate **Band 2**
Table: p.314

Comiter, Richard (Florida)
Profile: p.171,173
Tax **Band 2**
Table: p.170

Compton, Charles (California)
Profile: p.62
Antitrust **Band 4**
Table: p.29

Conard, David (Vermont)
Profile: p.697,697
Real Estate **Band 2**
Table: p.696

Condon, Creighton (New York)
Profile: p.509
Corporate/M&A **Band 4**
Table: p.460

Conlin, Roxanne (Iowa)
Profile: p.292
Employment **Band 1**
Table: p.288

Conlon, Michael (Texas)
Profile: p.671
Corporate/M&A **Band 2**
Table: p.649

Conlon, William (Illinois)
Profile: p.255
Litigation **Band 4**
Table: p.245

Connelly, Vincent J (Illinois)
Profile: p.256
Litigation **Band 2**
Table: p.245

Conner, Stewart (Kentucky)
Profile: p.305
Corporate/M&A **Band 1**
Table: p.300

Connette III, Edward (North Carolina)
Profile: p.552
Employment **Band 2**
Table: p.547

Connolly, Dennis (Georgia)
Profile: p.205
Insolvency **Band 2**
Table: p.193

Connolly, Walter (Michigan)
Profile: p.366
Employment **Band 3**
Table: p.363

Connor, Terence (Florida)
Profile: p.173
Employment **Band 1**
Table: p.158

Connors, Eugene (Pennsylvania)
Profile: p.615
Employment **Band 3**
Table: p.602

Conrad, Albert H (Georgia)
Profile: p.205
Banking & Finance **Band 3**
Table: p.183

Conrad, David (Ohio)
Profile: p.574
Real Estate **Band 2**
Table: p.572

Conrad Jr, Winthrop B (New York)
Profile: p.509
Capital Markets **Band 4**
Table: p.448

Console , Stephen (Pennsylvania)
Profile: p.615
Employment **Band 1**
Table: p.601

Contratto, Dana (District of Columbia)
Profile: p.134
Energy **Band 4**
Table: p.115

Conway, Michael (Illinois)
Profile: p.256
Media & Entertainment **Band 3**
Table: p.247

Conway, Susan (Texas)
Profile: p.671
Insurance **Band 3**
Table: p.659

Conway, Tim (Illinois)
Profile: p.256
Construction **Band 3**
Table: p.231

Coogan, Peter (Massachusetts)
Profile: p.355
Banking & Finance **Band 2**
Table: p.338

Cook, Bryson (Maryland)
Profile: p.333
Corporate/M&A **Band 2**
Table: p.327

Cook, James G (New Hampshire)
Profile: p.422
Corporate/M&A **Band 2**
Table: p.415

Cook, Jay (Minnesota)
Profile: p.376
Real Estate **Band 1**
Table: p.374

Cook, Philip C (Georgia)
Profile: p.205
Tax **Band 2**
Table: p.201

Cook, Rand (Utah)
Profile: p.690

Real Estate **Band 2**
Table: p.689

Cooke, Susan (Massachusetts)
Profile: p.355
Environment **Band 1**
Table: p.344

Coolman Amlong, Karen (Florida)
Profile: p.173
Employment **Band 3**
Table: p.157

Cooney, James (North Carolina)
Profile: p.552
Litigation **Band 3**
Table: p.549

Cooper, Jim (New York)
Profile: p.509
Banking & Finance **Band 1**
Table: p.445

Cooper, John H (Alabama)
Profile: p.7
Corporate/M&A **Band 3**
Table: p.1

Cooper, R Brent (Texas)
Profile: p.671
Insurance **Band 1**
Table: p.659

Cooper, Robert (California)
Profile: p.62
Antitrust **Band 1**
Table: p.29
Litigation **Band 2**
Table: p.50

Corash, Michèle B (California)
Profile: p.62
Environment **Band 2**
Table: p.43

Corbyn, George (Oklahoma)
Profile: p.585
Litigation **Band 1**
Table: p.583

Cordes, Samuel (Pennsylvania)
Profile: p.615
Employment **Band 3**
Table: p.601

Corgan, Brian (Georgia)
Profile: p.205
Construction **Band 5**
Table: p.184

Corr, Kelly (Washington)
Profile: p.712
Litigation **Band 3**
Table: p.709

Corrente, Robert (Rhode Island)
Profile: p.623
Litigation **Band 1**
Table: p.622

Correro, Anthony (Louisiana)
Profile: p.316
Corporate/M&A **Band 1**
Table: p.309

Corso, Ann Fortenberry (Mississippi)
Profile: p.383
Real Estate **Band 3**
Table: p.382

Cortesio, John (Iowa)
Profile: p.292
Corporate/M&A **Band 3**
Table: p.286

Corwin, Gregg (Minnesota)
Profile: p.376
Employment **Band 2**
Table: p.370

Costley, Kevin (Minnesota)
Profile: p.376

Corporate/M&A **Band 3**
Table: p.369

Cotchett, Joseph (California)
Profile: p.63
Litigation **Band 2**
Table: p.50

Cottam, Dale (Wyoming)
Profile: p.735
Corporate/M&A **Band 3**
Table: p.730

Cotter, James (New York)
Profile: p.509
Energy **Band 3**
Table: p.468

Coukos, Steven (Massachusetts)
Profile: p.355
Banking & Finance **Band 3**
Table: p.338

Court, Leonard (Oklahoma)
Profile: p.585
Employment **Band 1**
Table: p.582

Courtnage, Michael S (Washington)
Profile: p.712
Real Estate **Band 2**
Table: p.711

Couser, Richard B. (New Hampshire)
Profile: p.422
Litigation **Band 3**
Table: p.419

Coutroulis, Chris (Florida)
Profile: p.173
Antitrust **Band 3**
Table: p.151

Covey, Tyson J (Illinois)
Profile: p.256
Communications **Band 2**
Table: p.229

Covington , George C (North Carolina)
Profile: p.552
Litigation **Band 3**
Table: p.549

Covington, Peter J (North Carolina)
Profile: p.552
Litigation **Band 1**
Table: p.549

Cowan, Cameron (District of Columbia)
Profile: p.134
Capital Markets **Band 1**
Table: p.453

Cowan, J Donald (North Carolina)
Profile: p.552
Litigation **Band 1**
Table: p.549

Cowart, Richard (Tennessee)
Profile: p.641
Corporate/M&A **Band 3**
Table: p.635

Cox, Randy (Montana)
Profile: p.398
Litigation **Band 2**
Table: p.396

Cox, Robert (Virginia)
Profile: p.704
Construction **Band 3**
Table: p.698

Crabb, Joseph (Arizona)
Profile: p.21
Corporate/M&A **Band 3**
Table: p.16

Craft, Jill (Louisiana)
Profile: p.316
Employment **Band 3**

Table: p.310

Crane, Steven (California)
Profile: p.63
Insurance **Band 4**
Table: p.46

Crangle, Mary (New Jersey)
Profile: p.430
Employment **Band 2**
Table: p.426

Crass, Kevin (Arkansas)
Profile: p.27
Litigation **Band 2**
Table: p.25

Craven, George W (Illinois)
Profile: p.256
Tax **Band 4**
Table: p.252

Creel, Thomas (New York)
Profile: p.509
Intellectual Property **Band 4**
Table: p.479

Crement, Anthony (Illinois)
Profile: p.256
Employment **Band 4**
Table: p.236

Cremin, Pat (Oklahoma)
Profile: p.585
Employment **Band 1**
Table: p.582

Crisafi, Frank A (Georgia)
Profile: p.202,205
Tax **Band 4**
Table: p.201

Crispin, Craig (Oregon)
Profile: p.593
Employment **Band 3**
Table: p.588

Crist, Paul (Ohio)
Profile: p.574
Litigation **Band 3**
Table: p.570

Critelli Jr, Nicholas (Iowa)
Profile: p.292
Litigation **Band 2**
Table: p.290

Crochet, Vicki (Louisiana)
Profile: p.317
Employment **Band 4**
Table: p.311

Cromer, Lewis (South Carolina)
Profile: p.628
Employment **Band 1**
Table: p.625

Cromwell, David (Louisiana)
Profile: p.317
Banking & Finance **Band 2**
Table: p.307

Cronan IV, Charles J (Kentucky)
Profile: p.305
Litigation **Band 1**
Table: p.303

Crone, Tom (Wisconsin)
Profile: p.729
Employment **Band 3**
Table: p.725

Crosby, Douglas (Nevada)
Profile: p.413
Corporate/M&A **Band 2**
Table: p.406

Crow, William (Oregon)
Profile: p.593
Litigation **Band 2**
Table: p.590

Crowe, Austin (Oregon)
Profile: p.593
Litigation **Band 4**
Table: p.590

LEADING LAWYERS INDEX

Croysdale, David (Wisconsin)
Profile: p.729
Employment **Band 3**
Table: p.725

Crumbaugh, David G (Illinois)
Profile: p.256
Banking & Finance **Band 1**
Table: p.226

Crutcher Jr, Pepper
(Mississippi)
Profile: p.383
Employment **Band 3**
Table: p.380

Crystal, Jules (Illinois)
Profile: p.256
Employment **Band 4**
Table: p.236

Cubell, Howard
(Massachusetts)
Profile: p.355
Tax **Band 1**
Table: p.353

Cuff, Terence (California)
Profile: p.63
Tax **Band 2**
Table: p.58

Culbertson, Robert
(District of Columbia)
Profile: p.131,134
Tax **Band 4**
Table: p.130

Culhane, James (Colorado)
Profile: p.83
Real Estate **Band 4**
Table: p.81

Culhane, Thomas (Nebraska)
Profile: p.405
Litigation **Band 2**
Table: p.403

Cullen, Gary P (Illinois)
Profile: p.256
Corporate/M&A **Band 4**
Table: p.233

Culley, Peter (Maine)
Profile: p.325
Litigation **Band 3**
Table: p.322

Culotta, Ken (Texas)
Profile: p.671
Energy **Band 2**
Table: p.653

Culver, John (Colorado)
Profile: p.83
Employment **U**
Table: p.77

Cunningham, Dan (New York)
Profile: p.509
Capital Markets **Band 1**
Table: p.451

Cunningham, Robert
(Alabama)
Profile: p.7
Litigation **Band 2**
Table: p.4

Cupps, David (Ohio)
Profile: p.574
Litigation **Band 3**
Table: p.570

Curley, Michael (New York)
Profile: p.509
Employment **Band 2**
Table: p.467

Currie, John Withers (South Carolina)
Profile: p.628
Corporate/M&A **Band 1**
Table: p.624

Currie, Michael (Ohio)
Profile: p.574
Construction **Band 2**

Curtin, John (Jack)
(Massachusetts)
Profile: p.355
Antitrust **Band 1**
Table: p.337
Litigation **Band 3**
Table: p.349

Curtin, Lawrence (Florida)
Profile: p.173
Environment **Band 4**
Table: p.160

Curtin, Neal (Massachusetts)
Profile: p.355
Banking & Finance **Band 1**
Table: p.338

Curtis, J Vaughan (Georgia)
Profile: p.205
Corporate/M&A **Band 4**
Table: p.187

Curtis, Patricia (Nevada)
Profile: p.412,413
Real Estate **Band 3**
Table: p.411

Curtis, Susan M (New York)
Profile: p.509
Capital Markets **Band 2**
Table: p.453

Curzon, Thomas H (Arizona)
Profile: p.21
Corporate/M&A **Band 2**
Table: p.16

Cutler, Kenneth (Minnesota)
Profile: p.376
Corporate/M&A **Band 1**
Table: p.369

Cutler, Richard A (South Dakota)
Profile: p.633,633
Corporate/M&A **Band 2**
Table: p.630
Real Estate **Band 1**
Table: p.633

Cutler Jr, Irwin (Kentucky)
Profile: p.305
Employment **Band 2**
Table: p.301

Cyphert, Michael (Ohio)
Profile: p.574
Environment **Band 3**
Table: p.567

D

Dagenais, Don F (Missouri)
Profile: p.392
Real Estate **Band 4**
Table: p.391

Dagenhart, Larry (North Carolina)
Profile: p.552
Corporate/M&A **Band 2**
Table: p.546

Dahlk, Thomas (Nebraska)
Profile: p.405
Litigation **Band 3**
Table: p.403

D'Alba, Joel (Illinois)
Profile: p.256
Employment **Band 3**
Table: p.235

Dale, James (Idaho)
Profile: p.222
Employment **Band 2**
Table: p.220

Daley, Paul (Massachusetts)
Profile: p.355
Insolvency **Band 1**
Table: p.346

Dallas, Bruce (California)
Profile: p.63
Capital Markets **Band 1**
Table: p.32

Dalton, John (Georgia)
Profile: p.205
Litigation **Band 1**
Table: p.198

Dalton, Larry (Wisconsin)
Profile: p.729
Real Estate **Band 3**
Table: p.727

Daly, Lawrence (Montana)
Profile: p.398
Litigation **Band 2**
Table: p.396

Damgaard, Roger (South Dakota)
Profile: p.633
Corporate/M&A **Band 2**
Table: p.630

Damon, Lisa (Massachusetts)
Profile: p.355
Employment **Band 2**
Table: p.342

Danenbarger, Wright
(New Hampshire)
Profile: p.422
Litigation **Band 2**
Table: p.419

Daniel, Aubrey
(District of Columbia)
Profile: p.134
Litigation **Band 2**
Table: p.123

Daniel, Thomas M (Alaska)
Profile: p.14
Employment **Band 1**
Table: p.11

Daniels Jr, John W
(Wisconsin)
Profile: p.729
Real Estate **Band 3**
Table: p.727

D'Aquila, Barbara Jean
(Minnesota)
Profile: p.376
Employment **Band 1**
Table: p.371

D'Armond, William
(Louisiana)
Profile: p.317
Employment **Band 2**
Table: p.311

Dash, James (Illinois)
Profile: p.256
Construction **Band 3**
Table: p.231

Dauchot, Luke (Ohio)
Profile: p.574
Intellectual Property **Band 2**
Table: p.568

Davenport, David
(Massachusetts)
Profile: p.354,355
Tax **Band 3**
Table: p.353

Davenport, Kirk A (New York)
Profile: p.510
Capital Markets **Band 2**
Table: p.448

Davidson, Barry (Florida)
Profile: p.173
Litigation **Band 3**
Table: p.165

Davidson, Gordon (California)
Profile: p.63
Communications **Band 1**
Table: p.34
Corporate/M&A **Band 4**
Table: p.37

Davidson, Joshua (Texas)
Profile: p.671
Corporate/M&A **Band 3**
Table: p.649

Davies, Scott (Minnesota)
Profile: p.376
Employment **Band 2**
Table: p.371

Davis, Alan (New Jersey)
Profile: p.430
Corporate/M&A **Band 3**
Table: p.425

Davis, Alan (Pennsylvania)
Profile: p.615
Litigation **Band 1**
Table: p.611

Davis, Alvin (Florida)
Profile: p.173
Litigation **Band 3**
Table: p.165

Davis, Ames (Tennessee)
Profile: p.641
Litigation **Band 3**
Table: p.639

Davis, Christopher
(Massachusetts)
Profile: p.355
Environment **Band 1**
Table: p.344

Davis, Doreen (Pennsylvania)
Profile: p.615
Employment **Band 3**
Table: p.602

Davis, Fred (New York)
Profile: p.510
Litigation **Band 5**
Table: p.481

Davis, Gardner (Florida)
Profile: p.173
Corporate/M&A **Band 3**
Table: p.156

Davis, Gary (Oklahoma)
Profile: p.585
Litigation **Band 3**
Table: p.583

Davis, James
(District of Columbia)
Profile: p.134
Intellectual Property **Band 2**
Table: p.122

Davis, Jefferson
(New Hampshire)
Profile: p.421,422
Real Estate **Band 1**
Table: p.420

Davis, Jeffrey J (North Carolina)
Profile: p.552
Litigation **Band 3**
Table: p.549

Davis, Mark (Mississippi)
Profile: p.383
Real Estate **Band 2**
Table: p.382

Davis, Michael
(Massachusetts)
Profile: p.354,355
Tax **Band 2**
Table: p.353

Davis, Michael (Wyoming)
Profile: p.735
Employment **Band 3**
Table: p.731
Employment **Band 2**
Table: p.732

Davis, Oscar (Arkansas)
Profile: p.27
Employment **Band 2**
Table: p.24

Davis, Platt (Texas)
Profile: p.671
Energy **Band 4**
Table: p.653

Davis, Richard (Wyoming)
Profile: p.734,735
Real Estate **Band 3**
Table: p.734

Davis, Scott J (Illinois)
Profile: p.256
Corporate/M&A **Band 2**
Table: p.233

Davis, Steven H (New York)
Profile: p.510
Energy **Band 3**
Table: p.468

Davis, Will (Texas)
Profile: p.671
Insurance **Band 4**
Table: p.659

Davis, William (North Carolina)
Profile: p.552
Litigation **Band 1**
Table: p.549

Davis II, William Allison
(North Carolina)
Profile: p.552
Corporate/M&A **Band 2**
Table: p.546

Davis Jones, Laura
(Delaware)
Profile: p.100
Insolvency **Band 3**
Table: p.96

Dawahare, Debra (Kentucky)
Profile: p.305
Employment **Band 3**
Table: p.302

Dawes, Paul (California)
Profile: p.63
Litigation **Band 3**
Table: p.50

Dawson, Jon S (Alaska)
Profile: p.14
Corporate/M&A **Band 2**
Table: p.9

Dawson, Stephen E
(Michigan)
Profile: p.366
Real Estate **Band 2**
Table: p.365

Day, Lloyd (Rusty) (California)
Profile: p.63
Intellectual Property **Band 2**
Table: p.48

Day, Michael (California)
Profile: p.63
Energy **Band 4**
Table: p.41

Day, Richard (Wyoming)
Profile: p.735
Litigation **Band 1**
Table: p.732

De Meules, James H
(California)
Profile: p.63
Banking & Finance **Band 1**
Table: p.30

De Sear, Edward (New York)
Profile: p.510
Capital Markets **Band 1**
Table: p.453

De Toledo, Victoria
(Connecticut)
Profile: p.92
Employment **Band 2**
Table: p.88

Deakins, Homer (Georgia)
Profile: p.205
Employment **Band 3**

LEADING LAWYERS INDEX

Table: p.189

Deaner, Charles (Nevada)
Profile: p.413
Real Estate Band 2
Table: p.411

Dee, Frank (New Jersey)
Profile: p.430
Employment Band 1
Table: p.427

Deem, Patrick D. (West Virginia)
Profile: p.721
Corporate/M&A Band 2
Table: p.714
Real Estate Band 1
Table: p.720

Deeny, Ray (Colorado)
Profile: p.83
Employment Band 2
Table: p.78

Degnan, Peter (Georgia)
Profile: p.205
Energy Band 3
Table: p.191

DeHihns III, Lee (Georgia)
Profile: p.205
Environment Band 1
Table: p.192

del Calvo, Jorge (California)
Profile: p.63
Communications Band 2
Table: p.34

Delaney, John (New York)
Profile: p.510
Communications Band 3
Table: p.456

Delikat, Michael (New York)
Profile: p.510
Employment Band 3
Table: p.467

Dellinger, Walter
(District of Columbia)
Profile: p.134
Litigation Band 1
Table: p.123

DeLucia, Richard (New York)
Profile: p.510
Intellectual Property Band 4
Table: p.479

Denger, Michael
(District of Columbia)
Profile: p.134
Antitrust Band 5
Table: p.103

DeNinno, David (Pennsylvania)
Profile: p.615
Corporate/M&A Band 3
Table: p.599

Dennard, H Lane (Georgia)
Profile: p.205
Employment Band 4
Table: p.189

Dennerline, Frederick
(Indiana)
Profile: p.283
Employment Band 2
Table: p.279

Dennison, Karen D (Nevada)
Profile: p.413
Real Estate Band 1
Table: p.411

DeOrchis, Vincent M (New York)
Profile: p.510
Shipping Band 4
Table: p.496

DePrez, Anne (Indiana)
Profile: p.283
Litigation Band 3
Table: p.280

Derrick, Gary (Oklahoma)
Profile: p.585
Corporate/M&A Band 3
Table: p.580

DeSantis, Victor
(District of Columbia)
Profile: p.134
Projects Band 1
Table: p.126

Desmarais, John M
(New York)
Profile: p.510
Intellectual Property Band 5
Table: p.479

Despins, Luc (New York)
Profile: p.510
Insolvency Band 1
Table: p.472

DeTroy, Peter (Maine)
Profile: p.325
Litigation Band 2
Table: p.322

Dettmann, David (Iowa)
Profile: p.292,292
Real Estate Band 2
Table: p.291

Dettmer, Scott (California)
Profile: p.63
Communications Band 3
Table: p.34

Detzel, Lauren (Florida)
Profile: p.173
Tax Band 3
Table: p.170

DeVault, John (Florida)
Profile: p.173
Litigation Band 1
Table: p.165

DeWald, Scott (Arizona)
Profile: p.21
Corporate/M&A Band 3
Table: p.16

Dezzani, David J (Hawaii)
Profile: p.218
Litigation Band 2
Table: p.215

Dial, David (Georgia)
Profile: p.205
Construction Band 4
Table: p.184

Dial, Ellen (Washington)
Profile: p.712
Real Estate Band 3
Table: p.711

DiAngelo, Christopher
(New York)
Profile: p.510
Capital Markets Band 3
Table: p.453

DiBlasi, Gandolfo V
(New York)
Profile: p.510
Litigation Band 2
Table: p.481

Dichter, Mark (Pennsylvania)
Profile: p.615
Employment Band 2
Table: p.602

Dickinson, John (Florida)
Profile: p.173
Employment Band 2
Table: p.158

Dickos, George (Pennsylvania)
Profile: p.615
Intellectual Property Band 3
Table: p.609

Diehl, Mary Grace (Georgia)
Profile: p.205
Insolvency Band 2
Table: p.193

Dietz, Wallace (Tennessee)
Profile: p.641
Litigation Band 3
Table: p.639

DiGiovanni, Nick (Illinois)
Profile: p.257
Insurance Band 3
Table: p.242

DiGiovanni, Pete (Missouri)
Profile: p.392
Real Estate Band 3
Table: p.391

Dilg, Joe (Texas)
Profile: p.671
Corporate/M&A Band 3
Table: p.649
Energy Band 2
Table: p.653

Dillon, Andrew J (Texas)
Profile: p.671
Intellectual Property Band 4
Table: p.661

Dimon, Samuel (New York)
Profile: p.511
Tax Band 1
Table: p.499

Dingel, Allyn (Idaho)
Profile: p.222
Litigation Band 2
Table: p.221

Dinkins, Carol (Texas)
Profile: p.671
Environment Band 3
Table: p.655

Dinsmore, Robert (West Virginia)
Profile: p.721
Real Estate Band 3
Table: p.720

Dinwiddie, Thomas (Indiana)
Profile: p.283,283
Real Estate Band 4
Table: p.282

DiPrinzio, Eugene A
(Delaware)
Profile: p.99,100
Real Estate Band 2
Table: p.99

Divola, Julie (California)
Profile: p.63
Tax Band 2
Table: p.58

Dobbs, C Edward (Georgia)
Profile: p.205
Banking & Finance Band 4
Table: p.183
Insolvency Band 1
Table: p.193

Dockery, Michael (Montana)
Profile: p.398
Real Estate Band 1
Table: p.397

Docksey, Ross (Illinois)
Profile: p.257
Communications Band 4
Table: p.229

Dodson, Gerald (California)
Profile: p.63
Intellectual Property Band 4
Table: p.48

Doerr, Brian (Kansas)
Profile: p.299
Real Estate Band u
Table: p.298

Doetsch, Douglas A (Illinois)
Profile: p.257
Banking & Finance Band 3
Table: p.226

Dokos, Daniel S (New York)
Profile: p.511

Banking & Finance Band 3
Table: p.445

Dolin, Mitchell F
(District of Columbia)
Profile: p.134
Insurance Band 2
Table: p.120

Dolin, Susan (Florida)
Profile: p.173
Employment Band 3
Table: p.157

Doliner, Nathaniel (Florida)
Profile: p.173
Corporate/M&A Band 4
Table: p.156
Tax Band 3
Table: p.170

Dollinger, Martin (New Jersey)
Profile: p.430,430
Real Estate Band 1
Table: p.429

Dolson, Scott (Kentucky)
Profile: p.305
Corporate/M&A Band 3
Table: p.300

Donadio, Donald (North Carolina)
Profile: p.552
Real Estate Band 3
Table: p.551

Donati, Donald (Tennessee)
Profile: p.641
Employment Band 2
Table: p.637

Donnelly, Charles (West Virginia)
Profile: p.721
Employment Band 2
Table: p.716

Donnelly, Paul (Missouri)
Profile: p.392
Employment Band 4
Table: p.388

Donohue, Daniel (South Dakota)
Profile: p.633,633
Real Estate Band 1
Table: p.633

Donohue, John (Pennsylvania)
Profile: p.615
Intellectual Property Band 2
Table: p.609

Donohue, Michael (Iowa)
Profile: p.292
Corporate/M&A Band 3
Table: p.286

Donovan, Donald Francis
(New York)
Profile: p.511
Arbitration Band 1
Table: p.443

Donovan, John
(Massachusetts)
Profile: p.355
Litigation Band 3
Table: p.349

Donovan, Richard (Arkansas)
Profile: p.27
Litigation Band 3
Table: p.25

Doolittle, Roger (Mississippi)
Profile: p.383
Employment Band 2
Table: p.379

Doran, James (Illinois)
Profile: p.257
Banking & Finance Band 4
Table: p.226

Doran, Scott (Ohio)
Profile: p.574

Environment Band 3
Table: p.567

Dorris, William (Georgia)
Profile: p.205
Construction Band 5
Table: p.184

Dorsey, Rufus Thomas
(Georgia)
Profile: p.205
Insolvency Band 4
Table: p.193

Dorton, David (North Carolina)
Profile: p.552,552
Real Estate Band 3
Table: p.551

Douglas, Charles (Illinois)
Profile: p.257
Litigation Band 5
Table: p.245

Douglas, James M (New York)
Profile: p.511
Banking & Finance Band 2
Table: p.445

Douglas, John L (Georgia)
Profile: p.205
Banking & Finance Band 1
Table: p.183

Douglas, Peter R (New York)
Profile: p.511

Douglas, Robert J (Iowa)
Profile: p.292
Real Estate Band 3
Table: p.291

Dover, Darrell (Arkansas)
Profile: p.27
Real Estate Band 1
Table: p.26

Dow, Melvin (Texas)
Profile: p.671
Real Estate Band 2
Table: p.665

Dow, Robert M Jr (Illinois)
Profile: p.257
Communications Band 3
Table: p.229

Dow, T Andrew (Texas)
Profile: p.672
Real Estate Band 4
Table: p.665

Dowd, Tom (Nebraska)
Profile: p.405
Employment Band 1
Table: p.401

Dowdy, Craig (Georgia)
Profile: p.205
Energy Band 2
Table: p.191

Downer, Robert (Iowa)
Profile: p.292,292
Real Estate Band 4
Table: p.291

Downs, Clark Evans
(District of Columbia)
Profile: p.134
Energy Band 2
Table: p.115

Dowsley, Felix (Tennessee)
Profile: p.641
Real Estate Band 2
Table: p.640

Doyle, William (Connecticut)
Profile: p.92
Litigation Band 2
Table: p.90

Doyle Jr., John (North Carolina)
Profile: p.552
Employment Band 1
Table: p.548

LEADING LAWYERS INDEX

Drake, Jack (Alabama)
Profile: p.7
Employment Band 4
Table: p.2

Dranoff, David (Illinois)
Profile: p.257
Banking & Finance Band 3
Table: p.226

Dray, Perry (Wyoming)
Profile: p.735
Corporate/M&A Band 3
Table: p.730

Drew, Mark L (Alabama)
Profile: p.7
Corporate/M&A Band 3
Table: p.1

Driggs, Jay Douglas (Nevada)
Profile: p.412,413
Real Estate Band 4
Table: p.411

Driker, Eugene (Michigan)
Profile: p.366
Litigation Band 1
Table: p.364

Drinkwater, Robert (Mississippi)
Profile: p.383
Corporate/M&A Band 1
Table: p.378

Drinkwater, Wayne (Mississippi)
Profile: p.383
Litigation Band 1
Table: p.381

Dryden, William (Idaho)
Profile: p.222
Litigation Band 2
Table: p.221

DuBose, Charles (North Carolina)
Profile: p.552
Real Estate Band 3
Table: p.551

Duffell, David (Rhode Island)
Profile: p.623
Corporate/M&A Band 2
Table: p.620

Duffy, Pamela S (California)
Profile: p.63
Real Estate Band 4
Table: p.56

Duffy, Robert (Rhode Island)
Profile: p.623
Litigation Band 2
Table: p.622

Duffy, Robert H (Wisconsin)
Profile: p.729
Employment Band 2
Table: p.725

Dukes, David E (South Carolina)
Profile: p.628
Litigation Band 2
Table: p.626

Dulcich, Thomas (Oregon)
Profile: p.593
Litigation Band 4
Table: p.590

Dunbar, Charles (West Virginia)
Profile: p.721
Corporate/M&A Band 2
Table: p.714

Duncan III, Brooke (Louisiana)
Profile: p.317
Employment Band 4
Table: p.311

Dunham, Edward Wood (Connecticut)
Profile: p.92
Litigation Band 4
Table: p.90

Dunham Jr, Wolcott B (New York)
Profile: p.511
Insurance ✪
Table: p.477

Dunlay, Jon (Texas)
Profile: p.672
Real Estate Band 4
Table: p.665

Dunlop, Fred (Texas)
Profile: p.672
Real Estate Band 4
Table: p.665

Dunn, William B (Michigan)
Profile: p.366
Real Estate Band 2
Table: p.365

Dunn Jr, J Thomas (North Carolina)
Profile: p.552
Banking & Finance Band 3
Table: p.544

Dunner, Donald (District of Columbia)
Profile: p.134
Intellectual Property Band 1
Table: p.122

Dunning, Elizabeth (Utah)
Profile: p.690
Employment Band 2
Table: p.686

Durant, Terry (Connecticut)
Profile: p.92
Employment Band 2
Table: p.89

Durchslag, Stephen (Illinois)
Profile: p.257
Media & Entertainment Band 2
Table: p.247

Durick, Patrick (North Dakota)
Profile: p.557
Litigation Band 3
Table: p.556

Durkin, Thomas M (Illinois)
Profile: p.257
Litigation Band 4
Table: p.245

Durkovich, Stephen (New Mexico)
Profile: p.438
Litigation Band 4
Table: p.435

Durrell , Brian (Alaska)
Profile: p.14
Corporate/M&A Band 1
Table: p.9

Dutton, Diana (Texas)
Profile: p.672
Environment Band 3
Table: p.655

Duvin, Robert (Ohio)
Profile: p.574
Employment Band 1
Table: p.565

Dworetzky, Joseph (Pennsylvania)
Profile: p.616
Insolvency Band 1
Table: p.607

Dwyer, Jeffry (District of Columbia)
Profile: p.135
Real Estate Band 4
Table: p.127

Dwyer, Michael (Washington)
Profile: p.712

Corporate/M&A Band 2
Table: p.706

Dye, Alexander M (New York)
Profile: p.511
Insurance Band 1
Table: p.477

Dye, Scott (Nebraska)
Profile: p.405
Real Estate Band 2
Table: p.404

Dyekman, Gregory C (Wyoming)
Profile: p.735
Corporate/M&A Band 2
Table: p.730
Real Estate Band 2
Table: p.734

E

Earthman, Douglas (Tennessee)
Profile: p.641
Real Estate Band 3
Table: p.640

Eastham, John (New Mexico)
Profile: p.438
Employment Band 2
Table: p.435

Eastment, Thomas (District of Columbia)
Profile: p.135
Energy Band 2
Table: p.115

Easton, Richard L (Delaware)
Profile: p.100
Corporate/M&A Band 3
Table: p.94

Eatman, Louis P (California)
Profile: p.63
Real Estate Band 3
Table: p.56

Ebby, Stuart (Pennsylvania)
Profile: p.616
Real Estate Band 3
Table: p.613

Ebert, Kim (Indiana)
Profile: p.283
Employment Band 1
Table: p.279

Eckstein, Kenneth (New York)
Profile: p.511
Insolvency Band 4
Table: p.472

Eckstein, Paul F (Arizona)
Profile: p.21
Litigation Band 1
Table: p.19

Eddy, Rand (Oklahoma)
Profile: p.585
Employment Band 1
Table: p.581

Edelman, Marty (New York)
Profile: p.511
Real Estate Band 1
Table: p.493

Edwards, A Clifford (Montana)
Profile: p.398
Employment Band 1
Table: p.395
Litigation Band 2
Table: p.396

Edwards, Charles (Illinois)
Profile: p.258
Real Estate Band 1
Table: p.249

Edwards, Mark (Pennsylvania)
Profile: p.616
Antitrust Band 2
Table: p.596

Edwards, Michael (Alabama)
Profile: p.7
Litigation Band 2
Table: p.4

Efflandt, Charles (Kansas)
Profile: p.299
Litigation Band 2
Table: p.297

Efron, Stanley (Minnesota)
Profile: p.376
Corporate/M&A Band 2
Table: p.369

Efroymson, Kevin (Nevada)
Profile: p.413
Employment Band 3
Table: p.408

Egan, Dennis (Missouri)
Profile: p.392
Employment Band 1
Table: p.387

Egan, James (District of Columbia)
Profile: p.135
Antitrust Band 5
Table: p.103

Egan, Joseph (Florida)
Profile: p.173
Employment Band 3
Table: p.157

Egan, Michael (Georgia)
Profile: p.205
Corporate/M&A Band 1
Table: p.187

Egerton, Charles (Florida)
Profile: p.173
Tax Band 1
Table: p.170

Eggert, Russell R (Illinois)
Profile: p.258
Environment Band 2
Table: p.239

Eggleston, Jon R. (Vermont)
Profile: p.697
Corporate/M&A Band 3
Table: p.692

Eggum, Susan (Oregon)
Profile: p.593
Employment Band 3
Table: p.588

Ehrenberg, Peter H (New Jersey)
Profile: p.431
Corporate/M&A Band 1
Table: p.425

Ehrlich, Kenneth (Massachusetts)
Profile: p.355
Banking & Finance Band 3
Table: p.338

Eidson, Mike (Florida)
Profile: p.173
Litigation Band 4
Table: p.165

Eimer, Nathan P (Illinois)
Profile: p.258
Antitrust Band 2
Table: p.224

Einhorn, David M (New York)
Profile: p.512
Tax Band 4
Table: p.499

Eisenberg, David (New York)
Profile: p.512
Capital Markets Band 3
Table: p.453

Eisenberg, Theodore (New Jersey)
Profile: p.431
Employment Band 3
Table: p.427

Edwards, Michael — *see above*

Eisenstat, Larry (District of Columbia)
Profile: p.135
Energy Band 5
Table: p.115

Eisner, Rebecca (Illinois)
Profile: p.258
Communications Band 4
Table: p.229

Ek, Dale (New Mexico)
Profile: p.438
Real Estate Band 3
Table: p.437

Elam, Theodore M. (Oklahoma)
Profile: p.585
Corporate/M&A Band 2
Table: p.580

Elberger, Ronald (Indiana)
Profile: p.283
Litigation Band 2
Table: p.280

Elder, James (Oklahoma)
Profile: p.585,586
Real Estate Band 2
Table: p.585

Eldergill, Kathleen (Connecticut)
Profile: p.92
Employment Band 2
Table: p.88

Elfman, Eric (Massachusetts)
Profile: p.355
Tax Band 3
Table: p.353

Elgison, Martin (Georgia)
Profile: p.205
Intellectual Property Band 4
Table: p.195

Ellingson, Mae Nan (Montana)
Profile: p.398
Corporate/M&A Band 1
Table: p.394

Elliot, Robert (North Carolina)
Profile: p.552
Employment Band 1
Table: p.547

Ellis, Barnes (Oregon)
Profile: p.593
Litigation Band 1
Table: p.590

Ellison, Christopher (California)
Profile: p.63
Energy Band 3
Table: p.41

Ellison, Thomas (Utah)
Profile: p.690
Real Estate Band 1
Table: p.689

Ellman, Howard (California)
Profile: p.63
Real Estate Band 4
Table: p.56

Ellsworth, Carolyn (Nevada)
Profile: p.413
Employment Band 2
Table: p.407

Elrod, Eugene (District of Columbia)
Profile: p.135
Energy Band 2
Table: p.115

Emch, A L (West Virginia)
Profile: p.721
Litigation Band 2
Table: p.718

Emerson, Carter W (Illinois)
Profile: p.258

---

986   KEY TO RANKINGS: ✪ = STAR INDIVIDUAL   U = UP AND COMING   CHAMBERS USA 2003-2004

LEADING LAWYERS INDEX

Corporate/M&A **Band 3**
Table: p.233

Emerson, Dan (Indiana)
Profile: p.283
Employment **Band 3**
Table: p.279

Emmerich, Adam O (New York)
Profile: p.512

Engel, David (Massachusetts)
Profile: p.356
Corporate/M&A **Band 3**
Table: p.340

Engel, John
(District of Columbia)
Profile: p.135
Real Estate **Band 4**
Table: p.127

England, Kathleen (Nevada)
Profile: p.413
Employment **Band 1**
Table: p.407

English, Stephen (Oregon)
Profile: p.593
Litigation **Band 3**
Table: p.590

Epstein, Alan (Pennsylvania)
Profile: p.616
Employment **Band 1**
Table: p.601

Epstein, Gary
(District of Columbia)
Profile: p.135
Communications **Band 2**
Table: p.107

Epstein, Gary (Florida)
Profile: p.173
Corporate/M&A **Band 3**
Table: p.156

Epstein, Michael (New York)
Profile: p.512
Communications **Band 3**
Table: p.456

Epstien, Jay
(District of Columbia)
Profile: p.135
Real Estate **Band 1**
Table: p.127

Erickson, David (Iowa)
Profile: p.292
Real Estate **Band 2**
Table: p.291

Erickson, David (Kansas)
Profile: p.299
Litigation **Band 3**
Table: p.297

Erly, Peter (Vermont)
Profile: p.697
Corporate/M&A **Band 2**
Table: p.692

Erne, David A (Wisconsin)
Profile: p.729
Corporate/M&A **Band 3**
Table: p.723

Ernst, Andrew (Georgia)
Profile: p.205
Environment **Band 3**
Table: p.192

Erwin, Greg (Texas)
Profile: p.672
Real Estate **Band 4**
Table: p.665

Erwin, James (Maine)
Profile: p.325
Employment **Band 3**
Table: p.321

Erwin, Martin (North Carolina)
Profile: p.552
Employment **Band 3**

Table: p.548

Eschels, Philip (Kentucky)
Profile: p.305
Employment **Band 3**
Table: p.302

Essig, Leonard (Missouri)
Profile: p.392
Corporate/M&A **Band 3**
Table: p.386

Estes Jr., Reid (Tennessee)
Profile: p.641
Employment **Band 2**
Table: p.637

Estes, III, John N
(District of Columbia)
Profile: p.135
Energy **Band 5**
Table: p.115

Estridge, Larry D. (South Carolina)
Profile: p.628,629
Real Estate **Band 1**
Table: p.628

Etcheverry, Raymond J (Utah)
Profile: p.690
Litigation **Band 3**
Table: p.687

Ettinger, John R (New York)
Profile: p.512
Private Equity **Band 3**
Table: p.487

Eurich, Gregory (Colorado)
Profile: p.83
Employment **Band 2**
Table: p.78

Evanich, Kevin R (Illinois)
Profile: p.258
Corporate/M&A **Band 3**
Table: p.233

Evans, David (Wyoming)
Profile: p.735
Employment **Band 3**
Table: p.731

Evans, Ed (South Dakota)
Profile: p.633
Litigation **Band 2**
Table: p.632

Evans, Mark (Texas)
Profile: p.672
Banking & Finance **Band 1**
Table: p.645
Projects **Band 2**
Table: p.664

Evans, Mark
(District of Columbia)
Profile: p.135
Communications **Band 5**
Table: p.107

Evans, Martin Frederic
(New York)
Profile: p.512
Antitrust **Band 4**
Table: p.441

Evans III, Robert (New York)
Profile: p.512
Capital Markets **Band 4**
Table: p.448

Everett, Carl (Pennsylvania)
Profile: p.616
Environment **Band 4**
Table: p.604

Everson, David (Missouri)
Profile: p.392
Litigation **Band 1**
Table: p.389

Ewing, Jim (Georgia)
Profile: p.205
Intellectual Property **Band 3**
Table: p.195

Exelrod, Alan (California)
Profile: p.63
Employment **Band 2**
Table: p.39

F

Fagan, Christopher (Ohio)
Profile: p.574
Intellectual Property **Band 2**
Table: p.568

Fagan, James (Georgia)
Profile: p.205
Employment **Band 3**
Table: p.188

Fagen, Leslie (New York)
Profile: p.512
Litigation **Band**
Table: p.481
Litigation **Band 5**
Table: p.481

Fagin, Allen (New York)
Profile: p.512
Employment **Band 1**
Table: p.467

Fahey, Richard (Ohio)
Profile: p.574
Environment **Band 3**
Table: p.567

Fahner, Tyrone C (Illinois)
Profile: p.258
Litigation **Band 2**
Table: p.245

Fair, George (Mississippi)
Profile: p.383
Corporate/M&A **Band 3**
Table: p.378

Fala, Herman (Pennsylvania)
Profile: p.616
Real Estate **Band 1**
Table: p.613

Falcon, Floyd (Louisiana)
Profile: p.317
Employment **Band 2**
Table: p.310

Fantaci, James (Louisiana)
Profile: p.317
Corporate/M&A **Band 5**
Table: p.309

Farabow, Ford
(District of Columbia)
Profile: p.135
Intellectual Property **Band 2**
Table: p.122

Farkas, Michelle (Vermont)
Profile: p.697
Real Estate **U**
Table: p.696

Farmer, Guy (Florida)
Profile: p.173
Employment **Band 3**
Table: p.158

Farmer, Stephen
(West Virginia)
Profile: p.721
Litigation **Band 1**
Table: p.718

Farnham, James (Virginia)
Profile: p.704
Litigation **Band 2**
Table: p.702

Farr, Thomas (North Carolina)
Profile: p.552
Employment **Band 2**
Table: p.548

Farrar, Stanley F (California)
Profile: p.63
Banking & Finance **Band 3**
Table: p.30

Farrell, Michael (Mississippi)
Profile: p.383

Employment **Band 2**
Table: p.380

Faruki, Charles (Ohio)
Profile: p.575
Litigation **Band 3**
Table: p.570

Fastow, Jay N (New York)
Profile: p.512
Antitrust **Band 5**
Table: p.441

Feagin, III, Robert R (Florida)
Profile: p.173
Litigation **Band 4**
Table: p.165

Feder, Philip (California)
Profile: p.64
Real Estate **Band 3**
Table: p.56

Feeney, Matthew (Arizona)
Profile: p.21
Corporate/M&A **Band 2**
Table: p.16

Feiger, Lynn (Colorado)
Profile: p.83
Employment **Band 3**
Table: p.77

Feinstein, Deborah
(District of Columbia)
Profile: p.135
Antitrust **Band 5**
Table: p.103

Feinstein, Fred I (Illinois)
Profile: p.258
Real Estate **Band 3**
Table: p.249

Feintuch, Richard D
(New York)
Profile: p.512
Insolvency **Band 2**
Table: p.472

Felch, Patricia (Illinois)
Profile: p.259
Media & Entertainment **Band 2**
Table: p.247

Feldman, Boris (California)
Profile: p.64
Litigation **Band 3**
Table: p.50

Feldman, Jeff (Alaska)
Profile: p.14
Litigation **Band 1**
Table: p.13

Feldman, Larry (California)
Profile: p.64
Litigation **Band 3**
Table: p.50

Feldman, Matthew
(New York)
Profile: p.512
Insolvency **U**
Table: p.472

Feldman, Robert (California)
Profile: p.64
Litigation **Band 2**
Table: p.50

Felix, H Thomas
(Pennsylvania)
Profile: p.616
Employment **Band 2**
Table: p.602

Felman, David (Florida)
Profile: p.173
Corporate/M&A **Band 3**
Table: p.156

Felmly, Bruce
(New Hampshire)
Profile: p.422
Litigation **Band 1**
Table: p.419

Feltenstein, Martha
(New York)
Profile: p.513
Real Estate **Band 4**
Table: p.493

Felton, W Raymond
(New Jersey)
Profile: p.431
Corporate/M&A **Band 3**
Table: p.425

Fenley, David (Missouri)
Profile: p.392
Real Estate **Band 2**
Table: p.391

Feo, Edwin (California)
Profile: p.64
Energy **Band 1**
Table: p.41
Projects **Band 1**
Table: p.55

Ferenbach, Cam (Nevada)
Profile: p.413
Employment **Band 2**
Table: p.408

Ferguson, Mark (West Virginia)
Profile: p.721
Corporate/M&A **Band 3**
Table: p.714

Ferrazzano, Dennis (Illinois)
Profile: p.259
Real Estate **Band 4**
Table: p.249

Ferrell, Charles (Minnesota)
Profile: p.376
Real Estate **Band 1**
Table: p.374

Ferretti, David (West Virginia)
Profile: p.721
Corporate/M&A **Band 2**
Table: p.714

Ferrin, Shawn (Utah)
Profile: p.690
Real Estate **Band 3**
Table: p.689

Ferris, Charles
(District of Columbia)
Profile: p.135
Communications **Band 4**
Table: p.107

Fetscher, Candace (Montana)
Profile: p.398
Employment **Band 1**
Table: p.395

Feuerstein, Howard (Oregon)
Profile: p.593
Real Estate **Band 3**
Table: p.592

Fey, Albert E (New York)
Profile: p.513
Intellectual Property **Band 2**
Table: p.479

Fickle, Stanley (Indiana)
Profile: p.283
Litigation **Band 2**
Table: p.280

Field, Andrea Bear
(District of Columbia)
Profile: p.135
Environment **Band 3**
Table: p.117

Field, Lawrence (Minnesota)
Profile: p.376
Litigation **Band 3**
Table: p.372

Fields, Bertram (California)
Profile: p.64
Media & Entertainment **Band 3**
Table: p.53

LEADING LAWYERS INDEX

Fields, Henry (California)
Profile: p.64
Banking & Finance Band 3
Table: p.30

Fields, Jack (Texas)
Profile: p.672
Real Estate Band 3
Table: p.665

Fields, Leslie (Colorado)
Profile: p.83
Real Estate Band 4
Table: p.81

Fifer, Sam (Illinois)
Profile: p.259
Media & Entertainment Band 2
Table: p.247

Figenshaw, Michael H (Iowa)
Profile: p.292
Litigation Band 1
Table: p.290

Filardi, Edward V (New York)
Profile: p.513
Intellectual Property Band 3
Table: p.479

Fileti, Thomas (California)
Profile: p.64
Real Estate Band 4
Table: p.56

Finch, Dennis (South Dakota)
Profile: p.633
Employment Band 1
Table: p.631

Finke, Robert F (Illinois)
Profile: p.259
Antitrust Band 3
Table: p.224

Finkelson, Allen (New York)
Profile: p.513
Corporate/M&A Band 1
Table: p.460

Finkelstein, Jesse (Delaware)
Profile: p.100
Litigation Band 2
Table: p.98

Finley, John (New York)
Profile: p.513

Finley, Joseph (Minnesota)
Profile: p.376
Real Estate Band 2
Table: p.374

Finley, Thomas A (Iowa)
Profile: p.292
Litigation Band 1
Table: p.290

Finn Braddock, Patricia (Texas)
Profile: p.672
Environment Band 2
Table: p.655

Finn III, Harold B (Connecticut)
Profile: p.93
Corporate/M&A Band 1
Table: p.87

Finucane, Brian (Missouri)
Profile: p.392
Employment Band 3
Table: p.388

Fiorentino, Mark H (Nevada)
Profile: p.413
Real Estate Band 4
Table: p.411

First, Curry (Wisconsin)
Profile: p.729
Employment Band 2
Table: p.724

Fischer, John (Pennsylvania)
Profile: p.616
Real Estate Band 5
Table: p.613

Fischer, Ronald (North Dakota)
Profile: p.557
Litigation Band 2
Table: p.556

Fish, Ronald (Maryland)
Profile: p.333
Real Estate Band 2
Table: p.331

Fisher, Morton (Maryland)
Profile: p.333
Real Estate Band 1
Table: p.331

Fisher, Robert (Missouri)
Profile: p.392
Corporate/M&A Band 1
Table: p.386

Fisher, Stewart (North Carolina)
Profile: p.553
Employment Band 3
Table: p.547

Fishman, David (Maryland)
Profile: p.333
Real Estate Band 1
Table: p.331

Fishman, Louis Y (Louisiana)
Profile: p.317
Corporate/M&A Band 4
Table: p.309

Fishman, Robert A (Massachusetts)
Profile: p.356
Real Estate Band 3
Table: p.351

Fisk, Hollye (Texas)
Profile: p.672
Construction Band 4
Table: p.648

Fiske, Robert (New York)
Profile: p.513
Litigation Band 1
Table: p.481

Fitzgerald, Anthony (Connecticut)
Profile: p.93
Litigation Band 1
Table: p.90

Fitzgerald, James (Nebraska)
Profile: p.405
Litigation Band 3
Table: p.403

Fitzgerald, John (Colorado)
Profile: p.83
Corporate/M&A Band 3
Table: p.75

Fitzgerald, Peter (District of Columbia)
Profile: p.135
Projects Band 2
Table: p.126

Fitzgerald, Randi (Florida)
Profile: p.173
Real Estate Band 3
Table: p.167

Fitzgerald, Robert (Missouri)
Profile: p.392
Corporate/M&A Band 3
Table: p.386

Fitzgerald, Robert (Virginia)
Profile: p.704
Construction Band 2
Table: p.698

Fitzgerald, Thomas (Illinois)
Profile: p.253,259
Tax Band 4
Table: p.252

Fitzpatrick, Robert (District of Columbia)
Profile: p.135
Employment Band 2
Table: p.112

Fjelstad, Eric B (Alaska)
Profile: p.14
Environment Band 2
Table: p.12

Flake, Richard (Texas)
Profile: p.672
Construction Band 4
Table: p.648

Flaum, Keith (California)
Profile: p.64
Communications Band 5
Table: p.34

Fleischaker, Jon (Kentucky)
Profile: p.305
Employment Band 3
Table: p.302

Fleischer Jr, Arthur (New York)
Profile: p.513
Corporate/M&A Band 2
Table: p.460

Fleming, JD (Georgia)
Profile: p.205
Intellectual Property Band 5
Table: p.195

Fleming, John H (Georgia)
Profile: p.206
Litigation Band 3
Table: p.198

Fleming, Joseph (Florida)
Profile: p.174
Employment Band 2
Table: p.158

Flesher, Gail (New York)
Profile: p.513
Environment Band 2
Table: p.469

Fletcher, Jennifer (Georgia)
Profile: p.206
Construction Band 1
Table: p.184

Fletcher, Kelby (Washington)
Profile: p.712
Employment Band 1
Table: p.708

Flexner, Donald (District of Columbia)
Profile: p.135
Antitrust Band
Table: p.103
Antitrust Band 3
Table: p.103

Flick II, Lawrence (Pennsylvania)
Profile: p.616
Banking & Finance Band 2
Table: p.598

Flinn, Patrick (Georgia)
Profile: p.206
Intellectual Property Band 2
Table: p.195

Flint, Henry (North Carolina)
Profile: p.553
Banking & Finance Band 2
Table: p.544
Corporate/M&A Band 2
Table: p.546

Flom, Joseph H (New York)
Profile: p.513

Florack, James A (New York)
Profile: p.513
Banking & Finance Band 4
Table: p.445

Florio, Michael J. (West Virginia)
Profile: p.721

Employment U
Table: p.716

Fluharty, Robert (West Virginia)
Profile: p.721
Real Estate Band 3
Table: p.720

Fluhrer, Gary (Washington)
Profile: p.712
Real Estate Band 3
Table: p.711

Flygare, Thomas (New Hampshire)
Profile: p.422
Employment Band 1
Table: p.417

Flynn, Christopher (Illinois)
Profile: p.259
Energy Band 3
Table: p.238

Fogarty, James (Connecticut)
Profile: p.93
Litigation Band 2
Table: p.90

Fogg, Blaine V (New York)
Profile: p.513
Corporate/M&A Band 3
Table: p.460

Foggan, Laura (District of Columbia)
Profile: p.135
Insurance Band 3
Table: p.120

Fogler, Murray (Texas)
Profile: p.672
Litigation Band 4
Table: p.663

Foley, Mark (Pennsylvania)
Profile: p.616
Employment U
Table: p.602

Foradas, Michael P (Illinois)
Profile: p.259
Insurance Band 2
Table: p.242

Forcade, Bill (Illinois)
Profile: p.259
Environment Band 3
Table: p.239

Ford, Jeffrey (Texas)
Profile: p.672
Construction Band 3
Table: p.648

Ford, Paul (New York)
Profile: p.513
Capital Markets Band 3
Table: p.448

Fore, John (California)
Profile: p.64
Capital Markets Band 2
Table: p.32

Forelle, John (New York)
Profile: p.513
Real Estate Band 3
Table: p.493

Forman, Harvey (Pennsylvania)
Profile: p.616
Banking & Finance Band 1
Table: p.598

Forrester, Paul J (Illinois)
Profile: p.259
Banking & Finance Band 2
Table: p.226

Forry, Robert H (Georgia)
Profile: p.206
Energy Band 2
Table: p.191

Fort, Jeffrey (Illinois)
Profile: p.260
Environment Band 2
Table: p.239

Forte, Joseph (New York)
Profile: p.513
Real Estate Band 4
Table: p.493

Fortino, Paul (Oregon)
Profile: p.593
Litigation Band 2
Table: p.590

Foster, John (North Dakota)
Profile: p.557
Corporate/M&A Band 1
Table: p.554

Foster, Murphy (Louisiana)
Profile: p.317
Employment Band 3
Table: p.311

Fowler, John (Nevada)
Profile: p.413
Corporate/M&A Band 1
Table: p.406

Fox, Kate (Wyoming)
Profile: p.735
Employment Band 2
Table: p.732

Fox, Michael (Wisconsin)
Profile: p.729
Employment Band 1
Table: p.724

Fox, Steven (Georgia)
Profile: p.206
Corporate/M&A Band 4
Table: p.187

Foye, Thomas H (South Dakota)
Profile: p.633
Real Estate Band 2
Table: p.633

Fraidin, Stephen (New York)
Profile: p.513
Private Equity Band 2
Table: p.487

Franczek, James (Illinois)
Profile: p.260
Employment Band 2
Table: p.236

Frank, Katrin E (Washington)
Profile: p.712
Employment Band 1
Table: p.708

Frank, Robert (Massachusetts)
Profile: p.356
Intellectual Property Band 2
Table: p.348

Frank, Robert (Maine)
Profile: p.325
Litigation Band 2
Table: p.322

Frankel, Roger (District of Columbia)
Profile: p.135
Insolvency Band 1
Table: p.119

Franklin, Samuel (Alabama)
Profile: p.7
Litigation Band 1
Table: p.4

Frankovich, John (Nevada)
Profile: p.412,413
Real Estate Band 4
Table: p.411

Franson, Marc (Illinois)
Profile: p.260
Banking & Finance Band 4
Table: p.226

LEADING LAWYERS INDEX

Frantz, Michael (Ohio)
Profile: p.575
Employment **Band 2**
Table: p.565

Frantze, David W (Missouri)
Profile: p.392
Real Estate **Band 2**
Table: p.391

Franzetti, Susan (Illinois)
Profile: p.260
Environment **Band 3**
Table: p.239

Fraser, Thomas S (Minnesota)
Profile: p.376
Litigation **Band 2**
Table: p.372

Frazier, Sydney (Alabama)
Profile: p.7
Employment **Band 3**
Table: p.3

Frederick, Barry (Alabama)
Profile: p.7
Employment **Band 4**
Table: p.3

Freed, Michael (Illinois)
Profile: p.260
Antitrust **Band 3**
Table: p.224

Freel, Mark (Rhode Island)
Profile: p.623
Litigation **Band 1**
Table: p.622

Freeland, Byron (Arkansas)
Profile: p.27
Employment **Band 3**
Table: p.24

Freeman, Lee (Illinois)
Profile: p.260
Antitrust **Band 3**
Table: p.224

Freeman, Louis (Illinois)
Profile: p.260
Tax **Band 1**
Table: p.252

Freeman, Robert (Nebraska)
Profile: p.405
Corporate/M&A **Band 1**
Table: p.400

Freier, Elliot (California)
Profile: p.64
Tax **Band 2**
Table: p.58

Freilich, Robert H. (Missouri)
Profile: p.392
Real Estate **Band 4**
Table: p.391

Freking, Randolph (Ohio)
Profile: p.575
Employment **Band 1**
Table: p.564

Fremuth, Michael
(District of Columbia)
Profile: p.135
Energy **Band 4**
Table: p.115

French, John D. (Minnesota)
Profile: p.376
Litigation **Band 1**
Table: p.372

Freyer, Dana H (New York)
Profile: p.513
Arbitration **Band 2**
Table: p.443

Fridy, Carl (Pennsylvania)
Profile: p.616
Banking & Finance **Band 2**
Table: p.598

Friedland, Paul (New York)
Profile: p.514

Arbitration **Band 2**
Table: p.443

Friedlander, Mark (Illinois)
Profile: p.260
Construction **Band 1**
Table: p.231

Friedli, Helen (Illinois)
Profile: p.260
Corporate/M&A **Band 5**
Table: p.233

Friedman, David (New York)
Profile: p.514
Insolvency **Band 3**
Table: p.472

Friedman, David (Kentucky)
Profile: p.305
Employment **Band 3**
Table: p.301

Friedman, Dennis G (Illinois)
Profile: p.260
Communications **Band 2**
Table: p.229

Friedman, Gary (Mississippi)
Profile: p.383
Employment **Band 1**
Table: p.380

Friedman, Gary M (New York)
Profile: p.514
Tax **Band 4**
Table: p.499

Friedman, Richard (Alaska)
Profile: p.14
Litigation **Band 1**
Table: p.13

Friedman, Steven (Ohio)
Profile: p.575
Construction **Band 4**
Table: p.560

Fries, Joseph
(District of Columbia)
Profile: p.135
Real Estate **Band 2**
Table: p.127

Frisk Jr., Fred (West Virginia)
Profile: p.721,721
Real Estate **Band 3**
Table: p.720

Fritton, Karl (Pennsylvania)
Profile: p.616
Employment **Band 1**
Table: p.602

Fromm O'Brien, Eva (Texas)
Profile: p.672
Environment **Band 3**
Table: p.655

Fruth, Terence (Minnesota)
Profile: p.376
Litigation **Band 3**
Table: p.372

Frye, Michael B (Vermont)
Profile: p.697
Corporate/M&A **Band 1**
Table: p.692

Fryer, Greg (Maine)
Profile: p.325
Corporate/M&A **Band 2**
Table: p.319

Fryer, William (Georgia)
Profile: p.206
Real Estate **Band 3**
Table: p.199

Fuguet, Howard
(Massachusetts)
Profile: p.356
Antitrust **Band 3**
Table: p.337

Fullenkamp, John (Nebraska)
Profile: p.405
Real Estate **Band 1**

Table: p.404

Fuller, Gary (Oklahoma)
Profile: p.586
Corporate/M&A **Band 2**
Table: p.580

Fuller, James (California)
Profile: p.64
Tax **Band 1**
Table: p.58

Fullmer, Mark (Louisiana)
Profile: p.317
Corporate/M&A **Band 2**
Table: p.309

Fulton, Charles (North Carolina)
Profile: p.553
Real Estate **Band 2**
Table: p.551

Fyke, Marcie (Mississippi)
Profile: p.383
Employment **Band 2**
Table: p.379

G

Gabay, Donald (New York)
Profile: p.514
Insurance **Band 2**
Table: p.477

Gabbert, Craig (Tennessee)
Profile: p.641
Litigation **Band 2**
Table: p.639

Gabrio, Gino L (Hawaii)
Profile: p.218
Real Estate **Band 4**
Table: p.217

Gagliardo, Thomas
(Maryland)
Profile: p.333
Employment **Band 3**
Table: p.328

Gagnon, Bruce E (Alaska)
Profile: p.14,14
Real Estate **Band 2**
Table: p.14

Gagnon, Craig (Minnesota)
Profile: p.376
Litigation **Band 2**
Table: p.372

Gaillard, Foster (South Carolina)
Profile: p.629
Real Estate **Band 2**
Table: p.628

Galardi, Gregg M (Delaware)
Profile: p.100
Insolvency **Band 2**
Table: p.96

Gall, John (Ohio)
Profile: p.575
Litigation **Band 3**
Table: p.570

Galland, George (Illinois)
Profile: p.260
Employment **Band 1**
Table: p.235

Gallegos, Jean (New Mexico)
Profile: p.438
Litigation **Band 3**
Table: p.435

Gallinger, John (Wyoming)
Profile: p.735
Real Estate **Band 2**
Table: p.734

Gallo, Barbara (Georgia)
Profile: p.206
Environment **Band 4**
Table: p.192

Gallo, Greg (California)
Profile: p.64
Communications **Band 2**
Table: p.34

Galloway, Robert (Mississippi)
Profile: p.383
Litigation **Band 3**
Table: p.381

Galvan, Mary Elizabeth
(Wyoming)
Profile: p.735
Employment **Band 2**
Table: p.731

Galvani, Paul (Massachusetts)
Profile: p.356
Environment **Band 2**
Table: p.344
Litigation **Band 3**
Table: p.349

Galvis, Sergio J (New York)
Profile: p.514
Projects **Band 4**
Table: p.491

Gamboli, Michael (Rhode Island)
Profile: p.623
Employment **Band 1**
Table: p.621

Gangemi, Columbus (Illinois)
Profile: p.260
Employment **Band 4**
Table: p.236

Ganske, Lyle (Ohio)
Profile: p.575
Corporate/M&A **Band 1**
Table: p.562

Garcia, David A (Nevada)
Profile: p.413
Corporate/M&A **Band 2**
Table: p.406

Gardill, James (West Virginia)
Profile: p.721
Corporate/M&A **Band 2**
Table: p.714

Gardin, Lynn (Minnesota)
Profile: p.376
Corporate/M&A **Band 3**
Table: p.369

Gardner, Russell H (Maryland)
Profile: p.333
Employment **Band 2**
Table: p.329

Gardner, Stephen (New York)
Profile: p.514
Tax **Band 4**
Table: p.499

Gardner, William (Alabama)
Profile: p.7
Employment **Band 1**
Table: p.3

Garfink, Roger (Maryland)
Profile: p.332,333
Real Estate **Band 3**
Table: p.331

Garfinkel, Barry (New York)
Profile: p.514
Arbitration **Band 2**
Table: p.443

Garmer, Ben (Wisconsin)
Profile: p.729
Corporate/M&A **Band 2**
Table: p.723

Garnsey, Jr, Walter W
(Colorado)
Profile: p.83
Litigation **Band 4**
Table: p.79

Garon, Philip S (Minnesota)
Profile: p.376
Corporate/M&A **Band 1**

Table: p.369

Garrett, Theodore
(District of Columbia)
Profile: p.135
Environment **Band 2**
Table: p.117

Garrett, Tim (Tennessee)
Profile: p.641
Employment **Band 2**
Table: p.637

Garrison, Joseph
(Connecticut)
Profile: p.93
Employment **Band 1**
Table: p.88

Garrity Jr., Vincent
(Pennsylvania)
Profile: p.616
Corporate/M&A **Band 2**
Table: p.599

Gart, Brian (Florida)
Profile: p.174
Insolvency **Band 3**
Table: p.162

Gartrell, Donald E.
(New Hampshire)
Profile: p.422
Real Estate **Band 2**
Table: p.420

Garwood, Thomas (Florida)
Profile: p.174
Employment **Band 2**
Table: p.158

Gates, Allan (Arkansas)
Profile: p.27
Litigation **Band 2**
Table: p.25

Gathright, Joe (Kentucky)
Profile: p.305,305
Real Estate **Band 3**
Table: p.304

Gause, John (Maine)
Profile: p.325
Employment **Band 3**
Table: p.320

Gavin, John (Illinois)
Profile: p.260
Insurance **Band 3**
Table: p.242

Gaynor, Kevin
(District of Columbia)
Profile: p.136
Environment **Band 4**
Table: p.117

Gearen, John J (Illinois)
Profile: p.260
Real Estate **Band 1**
Table: p.249

Geary, Sean (New York)
Profile: p.514
Banking & Finance **Band 3**
Table: p.445

Gee, David E. (Utah)
Profile: p.690
Real Estate **Band 1**
Table: p.689

Geiger, Glenn (New Jersey)
Profile: p.430,431
Real Estate **Band 4**
Table: p.429

Geiger, Richard S (Texas)
Profile: p.672
Insurance **Band 2**
Table: p.659

Gelber, Stephen M (Hawaii)
Profile: p.218
Corporate/M&A **Band 3**
Table: p.212

Geller, Kenneth S

G

LEADING LAWYERS INDEX

(District of Columbia)
Profile: p.136
Litigation Band 3
Table: p.123

Gellman, Nancy (Pennsylvania)
Profile: p.616
Litigation Band 3
Table: p.611

Gelston, Philip (New York)
Profile: p.514
Corporate/M&A Band 3
Table: p.460

Genberg, Ira (Georgia)
Profile: p.206
Construction Band 2
Table: p.184

Genova, Angelo (New Jersey)
Profile: p.431
Employment Band 2
Table: p.427

Genovese, John (Florida)
Profile: p.174
Insolvency Band 3
Table: p.162

Gentile, Carmen (District of Columbia)
Profile: p.136
Energy Band 5
Table: p.115

George, Shawn P (West Virginia)
Profile: p.721
Litigation Band 3
Table: p.718

German, Charles (Missouri)
Profile: p.392
Litigation Band 1
Table: p.389

Gerrard, Michael (New York)
Profile: p.514
Environment Band 1
Table: p.469

Gerson, Herb (Tennessee)
Profile: p.641
Employment Band 3
Table: p.637

Gerstein, Allen (Illinois)
Profile: p.261
Intellectual Property Band 3
Table: p.244

Gerstein, Mark D (Illinois)
Profile: p.261
Corporate/M&A Band 5
Table: p.233

Gerstell, Glenn (District of Columbia)
Profile: p.136
Communications Band 3
Table: p.107

Gewin, James (Alabama)
Profile: p.7
Litigation Band 1
Table: p.4

Gibbons, John (New Jersey)
Profile: p.431
Litigation Band 1
Table: p.428

Gibbs, Charles (Texas)
Profile: p.672
Insolvency Band 4
Table: p.657

Gibbs, Kenneth (California)
Profile: p.64
Construction Band 1
Table: p.36

Gibbs, Lawrence (District of Columbia)
Profile: p.136
Tax Band 4

Gibbs, Robin C (Texas)
Profile: p.672
Litigation Band 1
Table: p.663

Giblin, Pamela (Texas)
Profile: p.672
Environment Band 1
Table: p.655

Gidley, James (Oregon)
Profile: p.593
Litigation Band 4
Table: p.590

Gifford, Mark (Wyoming)
Profile: p.735
Employment Band 1
Table: p.731
Litigation Band 2
Table: p.732

Gilberg, David J (New York)
Profile: p.514
Capital Markets Band 2
Table: p.451

Gilbert, Leonard (Florida)
Profile: p.174
Insolvency Band 2
Table: p.162

Gilbert, Scott (District of Columbia)
Profile: p.136
Insurance Band 2
Table: p.120

Gilford, Steven R (Illinois)
Profile: p.261
Insurance Band 2
Table: p.242

Gilkey, Duane (New Mexico)
Profile: p.438
Employment Band 1
Table: p.435

Gillespie, Hal (Texas)
Profile: p.672
Employment Band 2
Table: p.651

Gillespie, Thomas (Texas)
Profile: p.672
Banking & Finance Band 4
Table: p.645

Gillies, John (Connecticut)
Profile: p.93
Real Estate Band 3
Table: p.91

Gilpin, Thomas (West Virginia)
Profile: p.721
Real Estate Band 3
Table: p.720

Gilson, Gary (Missouri)
Profile: p.392
Corporate/M&A Band 2
Table: p.386

Ginos, Geoffrey (New York)
Profile: p.514
Shipping Band 5
Table: p.496

Giolito, Robert (Georgia)
Profile: p.206
Employment Band 3
Table: p.188

Giotto, Thomas (Pennsylvania)
Profile: p.616
Employment Band 3
Table: p.602

Gittes, Franklin M (New York)
Profile: p.514
Corporate/M&A Band 5
Table: p.460

Gittes, Frederick (Ohio)
Profile: p.575
Employment Band 1

Gittinger, Wayne (Washington)
Profile: p.712
Corporate/M&A Band 2
Table: p.706

Gittler, Marvin (Illinois)
Profile: p.261
Employment Band 2
Table: p.235

Giunta, Joseph J (California)
Profile: p.64
Corporate/M&A Band 4
Table: p.37

Givens, Leonard (Michigan)
Profile: p.366
Employment Band 2
Table: p.363

Glad, Paul E B (California)
Profile: p.64
Insurance Band 3
Table: p.46

Glade, Peter (Oregon)
Profile: p.593
Litigation Band 4
Table: p.590

Glahn, Wilbur (New Hampshire)
Profile: p.422
Litigation Band 1
Table: p.419

Glasgow, Norman (District of Columbia)
Profile: p.136
Real Estate Band 4
Table: p.127

Glass, Adam W (New York)
Profile: p.514
Capital Markets Band 4
Table: p.453

Glasscock, Ed (Kentucky)
Profile: p.305
Corporate/M&A Band 1
Table: p.300

Glassman, Neil (Delaware)
Profile: p.100
Insolvency Band 5
Table: p.96

Glazer, Michael (Massachusetts)
Profile: p.356
Real Estate Band 2
Table: p.351

Glazer, Steven D (New York)
Profile: p.514
Intellectual Property Band 5
Table: p.479

Glenn, Robert (Florida)
Profile: p.174
Insolvency Band 2
Table: p.162

Glick, Anna (New York)
Profile: p.515
Capital Markets Band 4
Table: p.453

Glickman, Julius (Texas)
Profile: p.673
Employment Band 2
Table: p.651

Glickstein, David (Illinois)
Profile: p.261
Real Estate Band 2
Table: p.249

Glosband, Daniel (Massachusetts)
Profile: p.356
Insolvency Band 1
Table: p.346

Glover, Stephen

(District of Columbia)
Profile: p.136
Corporate/M&A Band 3
Table: p.111

Godfrey, Lee (Texas)
Profile: p.673
Antitrust Band 2
Table: p.644
Litigation Band 3
Table: p.663

Godfrey, Richard C (Illinois)
Profile: p.261
Litigation Band 3
Table: p.245

Godoff, Stephen (Maryland)
Profile: p.333
Employment Band 2
Table: p.328

Goering, Kevin (New York)
Profile: p.515
Media & Entertainment Band 5
Table: p.485

Goetz, James (Montana)
Profile: p.398
Employment Band 1
Table: p.395
Litigation Band 1
Table: p.396

Goetz, Peter (New York)
Profile: p.515
Construction Band 4
Table: p.458

Goetzinger, Patrick (South Dakota)
Profile: p.633
Corporate/M&A Band 3
Table: p.630
Real Estate Band 2
Table: p.633

Gold, Carl (Maryland)
Profile: p.333
Employment Band 3
Table: p.328

Gold, Marc (Pennsylvania)
Profile: p.616
Environment Band 2
Table: p.604

Gold, Michael (Illinois)
Profile: p.261
Banking & Finance Band 4
Table: p.226

Goldammer, Vance (South Dakota)
Profile: p.633
Corporate/M&A Band 1
Table: p.630

Goldberg, Catherine (New Mexico)
Profile: p.438
Real Estate Band 3
Table: p.437

Goldberg, Daniel (Massachusetts)
Profile: p.356
Antitrust Band 3
Table: p.337

Goldberg, Donald (Pennsylvania)
Profile: p.616
Litigation Band 3
Table: p.611

Goldberg, Fred (District of Columbia)
Profile: p.136
Tax Band 2
Table: p.130

Goldberg, Joseph (New Mexico)
Profile: p.438
Litigation Band 4
Table: p.435

Goldberg, Richard (Pennsylvania)
Profile: p.616
Real Estate Band 4
Table: p.613

Goldberg, Stephen (California)
Profile: p.64
Insurance Band 2
Table: p.46

Golden, Arthur F (New York)
Profile: p.515
Antitrust Band 3
Table: p.441

Golden, Daniel H (New York)
Profile: p.515
Insolvency Band 1
Table: p.472

Golden, Gerald (Illinois)
Profile: p.261
Employment Band 4
Table: p.236

Golden, Jonathan (Georgia)
Profile: p.206
Corporate/M&A Band 3
Table: p.187

Golden, Joseph (Michigan)
Profile: p.366
Employment Band 3
Table: p.362

Goldfein, Shepard (New York)
Profile: p.515
Antitrust Band 3
Table: p.441

Goldman, Melvin (California)
Profile: p.64
Antitrust Band 4
Table: p.29
Litigation Band 2
Table: p.50

Goldman, Michael (Illinois)
Profile: p.261
Insurance Band 3
Table: p.242

Goldman, Michael (Delaware)
Profile: p.100
Corporate/M&A Band 3
Table: p.94
Litigation Band 3
Table: p.98

Goldman, Mike (New York)
Profile: p.515
Banking & Finance Band 3
Table: p.445

Goldring, Stuart (New York)
Profile: p.515
Tax Band 3
Table: p.499

Goldschmidt, David J (New York)
Profile: p.515
Capital Markets Band 4
Table: p.448

Goldsmith, Willis J (District of Columbia)
Profile: p.136
Employment Band 3
Table: p.112

Goldstein, Andrew (Illinois)
Profile: p.261
Media & Entertainment Band 3
Table: p.247

Goldstein, Bruce (New Jersey)
Profile: p.431
Litigation Band 2
Table: p.428

Goldstein, Marc (New York)
Profile: p.515
Arbitration Band 3
Table: p.443

LEADING LAWYERS INDEX

Goldstein, Marcia (New York)
Profile: p.515
Insolvency Band 2
Table: p.472

Goldstein, Mark (Nevada)
Profile: p.413
Corporate/M&A Band 2
Table: p.406

Goldstein, Marvin (New York)
Profile: p.515
Capital Markets Band 4
Table: p.451

Goldstein, Michael (Florida)
Profile: p.174
Environment Band 4
Table: p.160

Golemon, Kinnan (Texas)
Profile: p.673
Environment Band 3
Table: p.655

Golub, David (Connecticut)
Profile: p.93
Employment Band 3
Table: p.88

Gómez, David F (Arizona)
Profile: p.21
Employment Band 1
Table: p.18

Gonzalez, Thomas (Florida)
Profile: p.174
Employment Band 1
Table: p.158

Gooch, Kyle (Texas)
Profile: p.673
Construction Band 1
Table: p.648

Good, Julian (Louisiana)
Profile: p.317
Real Estate Band 2
Table: p.314

Goodell, Gerald (Kansas)
Profile: p.299
Real Estate Band 3
Table: p.298

Goodheart, Lisa
(Massachusetts)
Profile: p.356
Environment Band 4
Table: p.344

Goodman, Harold
(Pennsylvania)
Profile: p.616
Employment Band 3
Table: p.601

Goodman, Janice (New York)
Profile: p.515
Employment Band 2
Table: p.466

Goodman, Louis A
(Massachusetts)
Profile: p.356
Corporate/M&A Band 4
Table: p.340

Goodman, Mark (Illinois)
Profile: p.261
Insurance Band 2
Table: p.242

Goodman, Ronald
(District of Columbia)
Profile: p.136
Arbitration Band 4
Table: p.106

Goodman, Stephen
(Pennsylvania)
Profile: p.616
Corporate/M&A Band 1
Table: p.599

Goodman, Stuart (Illinois)
Profile: p.261
Corporate/M&A Band 5

Table: p.233

Goodman, William
(Mississippi)
Profile: p.383
Litigation Band 2
Table: p.381

Goodsell, Verne
(South Dakota)
Profile: p.633
Litigation Band 3
Table: p.632

Goodwillie, Eugene
(New York)
Profile: p.515
Projects Band 4
Table: p.491

Goodwin, David B (California)
Profile: p.65
Insurance Band 1
Table: p.46

Goodwin, Michael
(District of Columbia)
Profile: p.136
Real Estate Band 3
Table: p.127

Goodwin, Thomas (West Virginia)
Profile: p.721
Litigation Band 3
Table: p.718

Goold, Barry (Nevada)
Profile: p.413
Real Estate Band 1
Table: p.411

Goolsby, Allen (Virginia)
Profile: p.704
Corporate/M&A Band 1
Table: p.699

Goolsby, George (Texas)
Profile: p.673
Energy Band 2
Table: p.653

Gordanier, Dean C
(Massachusetts)
Profile: p.354,356
Tax Band 1
Table: p.353

Gordon, David A (New York)
Profile: p.515
Projects Band 1
Table: p.491

Gordon, Deborah (Michigan)
Profile: p.366
Employment Band 1
Table: p.362

Gordon, George
(Pennsylvania)
Profile: p.616
Antitrust Band 2
Table: p.596

Gordon, Mark (Illinois)
Profile: p.261
Communications Band 3
Table: p.229

Gordon, Robert
(Massachusetts)
Profile: p.356
Employment Band 1
Table: p.342

Gordon, Steve (New York)
Profile: p.516
Tax Band 3
Table: p.499

Gorrell, Jr, J Warren
(New York)
Profile: p.516

Gorson, Matthew (Florida)
Profile: p.174
Real Estate Band 1
Table: p.167

Gotts, Ilene Knable
(New York)
Profile: p.516
Antitrust Band 3
Table: p.441

Gowland, Kimbal (Idaho)
Profile: p.222,222
Real Estate Band 3
Table: p.222

Goyne, Roderick (Texas)
Profile: p.673
Banking & Finance Band 1
Table: p.645

Goza, Kirk (Missouri)
Profile: p.392
Litigation Band 2
Table: p.389

Grady, Kevin (Georgia)
Profile: p.206
Antitrust Band 2
Table: p.181

Grady, Timothy (Ohio)
Profile: p.575
Banking & Finance Band 2
Table: p.559

Graev, Lawrence (New York)
Profile: p.516
Private Equity Band 4
Table: p.487

Gragg, Lawrence (Florida)
Profile: p.174
Tax Band 1
Table: p.170

Graham, Andrew (Maryland)
Profile: p.333
Litigation Band 1
Table: p.330

Graham, Bruce (Hawaii)
Profile: p.218
Real Estate Band 1
Table: p.217

Graham, Christopher
(Rhode Island)
Profile: p.623
Corporate/M&A Band 1
Table: p.620

Grammig, Robert (Florida)
Profile: p.174
Corporate/M&A Band 4
Table: p.156

Granda, John (Missouri)
Profile: p.392
Corporate/M&A Band 1
Table: p.386

Grandis, Leslie (Virginia)
Profile: p.704
Corporate/M&A Band 1
Table: p.699

Grant, Elizabeth (Vermont)
Profile: p.697
Employment Band 1
Table: p.694

Grant, Eugene (Oregon)
Profile: p.593
Real Estate Band 4
Table: p.592

Graves, Judson (Georgia)
Profile: p.206
Litigation Band 1
Table: p.198

Graves, Kathlyn (Arkansas)
Profile: p.27
Employment Band 1
Table: p.24

Gray, Robert (Texas)
Profile: p.673
Communications Band 1
Table: p.646

Greaney, William

(District of Columbia)
Profile: p.136
Insurance Band 3
Table: p.120

Greeley, Jack (Florida)
Profile: p.174
Banking & Finance Band 3
Table: p.152

Green, Douglas
(District of Columbia)
Profile: p.136
Energy Band 3
Table: p.115

Green, Jonathan (New York)
Profile: p.516
Projects Band 2
Table: p.491

Green, Jordan (Arizona)
Profile: p.21
Litigation Band 2
Table: p.19

Green, Josh (California)
Profile: p.65
Communications Band 3
Table: p.34

Green, Philip (Michigan)
Profile: p.366
Employment Band 3
Table: p.362

Green, Ronald (New York)
Profile: p.516
Employment Band 2
Table: p.467

Green, William (Florida)
Profile: p.174
Environment Band 4
Table: p.160

Green, William (Washington)
Profile: p.712
Real Estate Band 2
Table: p.711

Greenbaum, Jack A
(New York)
Profile: p.516
Shipping Band 5
Table: p.496

Greenberg, Melvin
(New Jersey)
Profile: p.431
Litigation Band 3
Table: p.428

Greene, Browne (California)
Profile: p.65
Litigation Band 3
Table: p.50

Greene, Kenneth (North Carolina)
Profile: p.553
Banking & Finance Band 1
Table: p.544

Greene, Kevin C (Georgia)
Profile: p.206
Energy Band 1
Table: p.191

Greene, Kimberly (Kentucky)
Profile: p.305
Employment Band 3
Table: p.302

Greener, Richard (Idaho)
Profile: p.222
Litigation Band 1
Table: p.221

Greenfield, Robert A
(California)
Profile: p.65
Insolvency Band 3
Table: p.44

Greenfield, Russell R
(South Dakota)
Profile: p.633,633

Real Estate Band 2
Table: p.633

Greenspan, Steve
(Connecticut)
Profile: p.93
Litigation Band 4
Table: p.90

Greenstein, Abraham
(District of Columbia)
Profile: p.136
Real Estate Band 4
Table: p.127

Greenwald, Steve (California)
Profile: p.65
Energy Band 4
Table: p.41

Greenwood, David (Utah)
Profile: p.690
Litigation Band 3
Table: p.687

Greer, Alan (Florida)
Profile: p.174
Litigation Band 3
Table: p.165

Greer, David (Ohio)
Profile: p.575
Litigation Band 3
Table: p.570

Gregory, Donald (Ohio)
Profile: p.575
Construction Band 2
Table: p.560

Greig, Brian (Texas)
Profile: p.673
Employment Band 2
Table: p.652

Greising, Robert (Indiana)
Profile: p.283
Corporate/M&A Band 4
Table: p.277

Gremillion, L Todd (Texas)
Profile: p.673
Energy Band 3
Table: p.653

Grenier, John B (Alabama)
Profile: p.7
Corporate/M&A Band 2
Table: p.1

Gresham, John
(North Carolina)
Profile: p.553
Employment Band 2
Table: p.547

Griffin, James (Missouri)
Profile: p.392
Litigation Band 1
Table: p.389

Griffin, John W (Georgia)
Profile: p.206
Real Estate Band 2
Table: p.199

Griffinger, Mike (New Jersey)
Profile: p.431
Litigation Band 1
Table: p.428

Griffith, Richard (Kentucky)
Profile: p.305
Employment Band 2
Table: p.302

Grimm, Terry (Illinois)
Profile: p.261
Litigation Band 5
Table: p.245

Grishman, David (Mississippi)
Profile: p.383
Corporate/M&A Band 3
Table: p.378

Groark Jr, Thomas

G

www.ChambersandPartners.com

991

LEADING LAWYERS INDEX

(Connecticut)
Profile: p.93
Litigation **Band 3**
Table: p.90

Grogan, Michael (Florida)
Profile: p.174
Employment **Band 3**
Table: p.158

Grooms, Timothy (Arkansas)
Profile: p.27
Real Estate **Band 1**
Table: p.26

Gross, Steven R (New York)
Profile: p.516
Insolvency **Band 3**
Table: p.472

Grossenburg, Bradley C (South Dakota)
Profile: p.633
Corporate/M&A **Band 3**
Table: p.630

Grosshandler, Seth (New York)
Profile: p.516
Capital Markets **Band 2**
Table: p.451

Grossman, Marshall (California)
Profile: p.65
Litigation **Band 1**
Table: p.50

Grossman, Paul (California)
Profile: p.65
Employment **Band 1**
Table: p.40

Grossman, Theodore (Ohio)
Profile: p.575
Litigation **Band 3**
Table: p.570

Grout, Robert (Georgia)
Profile: p.206
Corporate/M&A **Band 4**
Table: p.187

Grove, Barry (New York)
Profile: p.516
Construction **Band 1**
Table: p.458

Grover, Parry (Alaska)
Profile: p.14
Employment **Band 2**
Table: p.11

Groves, William Jason (South Dakota)
Profile: p.633
Employment **Band 2**
Table: p.631

Guariglia, Michael (New Jersey)
Profile: p.431
Corporate/M&A **Band 2**
Table: p.425

Guinasso, John (Oregon)
Profile: p.593
Real Estate **Band 4**
Table: p.592

Guinn, Guy (Ohio)
Profile: p.575
Banking & Finance **Band 2**
Table: p.559

Gundersen, Glenn (Pennsylvania)
Profile: p.616
Intellectual Property **Band 4**
Table: p.609

Gunderson, Bob (California)
Profile: p.65
Communications **Band 1**
Table: p.34

Gunn, Paul (Mississippi)
Profile: p.383

Real Estate **Band 3**
Table: p.382

Gunter, Clifford (Texas)
Profile: p.673
Energy **Band 4**
Table: p.653

Gunter, Russell (Arkansas)
Profile: p.27
Employment **Band 2**
Table: p.24

Gurley, David (Florida)
Profile: p.174
Construction **Band 3**
Table: p.154

Gurney, Scott (Ohio)
Profile: p.575
Construction **Band 4**
Table: p.560

Gursky, Marc (Rhode Island)
Profile: p.623
Employment **Band 1**
Table: p.621

Gutowski, Peter (New York)
Profile: p.517
Shipping **Band 4**
Table: p.496

Gutter, Marvin (Florida)
Profile: p.174
Tax **Band 3**
Table: p.170

Guynn, Randall (New York)
Profile: p.517
Banking & Finance **Band 4**
Table: p.445

H

Haarlow, John (Illinois)
Profile: p.261
Insurance **Band 3**
Table: p.242

Haas, Karl P (Indiana)
Profile: p.283
Real Estate **Band 3**
Table: p.282

Hacker, Patrick (Wyoming)
Profile: p.735
Employment **Band 2**
Table: p.731

Hackett, Bob (Arizona)
Profile: p.21
Corporate/M&A **Band 3**
Table: p.16

Hackett, Kevin (New York)
Profile: p.517
Real Estate **Band 3**
Table: p.493

Haden, Bill (Kentucky)
Profile: p.305
Real Estate **Band 2**
Table: p.304

Hadley, Joseph P (New York)
Profile: p.517
Projects **Band 5**
Table: p.491

Haefner, Gail (Vermont)
Profile: p.697
Corporate/M&A **Band 2**
Table: p.692

Hafets, Richard J (Maryland)
Profile: p.333
Employment **Band 1**
Table: p.329

Hafter, Jerome (Mississippi)
Profile: p.383
Corporate/M&A **Band 3**
Table: p.378

Hagelstration, John (Alabama)
Profile: p.7

Real Estate **Band 1**
Table: p.6

Hagen, Catherine (California)
Profile: p.65
Employment **Band 4**
Table: p.40

Hagen, Paul (District of Columbia)
Profile: p.136
Environment **Band 5**
Table: p.117

Hagg, Rexford (South Dakota)
Profile: p.633
Employment **Band 2**
Table: p.631

Hahn, Arthur (Illinois)
Profile: p.261
Corporate/M&A **Band 5**
Table: p.233

Haims, Bruce D (New York)
Profile: p.517
Tax **Band 4**
Table: p.499

Haines, Harry (Montana)
Profile: p.398,398
Real Estate **Band 2**
Table: p.397

Haley, George M. (Utah)
Profile: p.690
Litigation **Band 3**
Table: p.687

Haley, James F (New York)
Profile: p.517
Intellectual Property **Band 5**
Table: p.479

Haley, Joseph (Massachusetts)
Profile: p.356
Real Estate **Band 3**
Table: p.351

Hall, Bruce (New Mexico)
Profile: p.438
Litigation **Band 1**
Table: p.435

Hall, Helena (Alaska)
Profile: p.15
Employment **U**
Table: p.11

Hall, Richard (New York)
Profile: p.517

Hall Jr., Cary (South Carolina)
Profile: p.629
Corporate/M&A **Band 2**
Table: p.624

Halliday, Joseph W (New York)
Profile: p.517
Banking & Finance **Band 3**
Table: p.445

Halsey, Douglas (Florida)
Profile: p.174
Environment **Band 1**
Table: p.160

Halvey, John K (New York)
Profile: p.517
Communications **Band 1**
Table: p.456

Hamann, Lee (Nebraska)
Profile: p.405
Real Estate **Band 1**
Table: p.404

Hamel, Mark (Minnesota)
Profile: p.376
Real Estate **Band 1**
Table: p.374

Hamill, John (Illinois)
Profile: p.261
Communications **Band 2**
Table: p.229

Hamilton, Russell (Florida)
Profile: p.174

Employment **Band 2**
Table: p.158

Hamilton Jr, John (Massachusetts)
Profile: p.356
Real Estate **Band 2**
Table: p.351

Hamilton Moody, James (Texas)
Profile: p.673
Insurance **Band 3**
Table: p.659

Hamm, Leisa (Illinois)
Profile: p.261
Insurance **Band 3**
Table: p.242

Hammer, David (West Virginia)
Profile: p.722
Employment **Band 3**
Table: p.716

Hammes, Jeffrey C (Illinois)
Profile: p.261
Corporate/M&A **Band 5**
Table: p.233

Hammond, David (West Virginia)
Profile: p.722
Real Estate **Band 2**
Table: p.720

Hammond, Herbert (Texas)
Profile: p.673
Communications **Band 3**
Table: p.646

Hammons, Mark (Oklahoma)
Profile: p.586
Employment **Band 2**
Table: p.581

Handelsman, Lawrence (New York)
Profile: p.517
Insolvency **Band 3**
Table: p.472

Handman, Laura (New York)
Profile: p.517
Media & Entertainment **Band 3**
Table: p.485

Hangley, William (Pennsylvania)
Profile: p.616
Litigation **Band 1**
Table: p.611

Hankins, Stuart (Arkansas)
Profile: p.27
Real Estate **Band 3**
Table: p.26

Hanks, James (Maryland)
Profile: p.333
Corporate/M&A **Band 3**
Table: p.327

Hannah, David (Washington)
Profile: p.712
Employment **Band 1**
Table: p.708

Hanrahan, Marc P (New York)
Profile: p.517
Banking & Finance **Band 4**
Table: p.445

Hanschen, Peter (California)
Profile: p.65
Energy **Band 3**
Table: p.41

Hansell, Edgar (Iowa)
Profile: p.292
Corporate/M&A **Band 1**
Table: p.286

Hansen, Gordon (Utah)
Profile: p.690
Corporate/M&A **Band 4**
Table: p.684

Hansen, Scott W (Wisconsin)
Profile: p.729
Litigation **Band 1**
Table: p.726

Hanson, Jr, Karl B (Florida)
Profile: p.174
Real Estate **Band 4**
Table: p.167

Hanzlik, Paul (Illinois)
Profile: p.262
Energy **Band 1**
Table: p.238

Haraldson, Comet (South Dakota)
Profile: p.633
Employment **Band 2**
Table: p.631

Hardcastle, Jay (Tennessee)
Profile: p.641
Corporate/M&A **Band 3**
Table: p.635

Hardie, Thornton (Texas)
Profile: p.668,673
Tax **Band 3**
Table: p.667

Hardin, Edward (Georgia)
Profile: p.206
Corporate/M&A **Band 1**
Table: p.187

Hardin III, Harry S (Louisiana)
Profile: p.317
Litigation **Band 2**
Table: p.313

Harding, William (Nebraska)
Profile: p.405
Employment **Band 2**
Table: p.402

Hardy, Michael (Ohio)
Profile: p.575
Environment **Band 1**
Table: p.567

Hardymon, Glen (North Carolina)
Profile: p.553
Real Estate **Band 3**
Table: p.551

Hariton, David P (New York)
Profile: p.517
Tax **Band 1**
Table: p.499

Harkavy, Jonathan (North Carolina)
Profile: p.553
Employment **Band 1**
Table: p.547

Harkavy, Ronald (Tennessee)
Profile: p.641
Real Estate **Band 2**
Table: p.640

Harkins Jr., John (Pennsylvania)
Profile: p.616
Litigation **Band 2**
Table: p.611

Harmelin, Stephen J (Pennsylvania)
Profile: p.616
Corporate/M&A **Band 4**
Table: p.599

Harmon, Melva (Arkansas)
Profile: p.27
Employment **Band 2**
Table: p.24

Harms, David B (New York)
Profile: p.517
Capital Markets **Band 3**
Table: p.448

Harnden, Ronald (Kansas)
Profile: p.299
Real Estate **Band 3**

LEADING LAWYERS INDEX

Table: p.298

Haroz, Michael (Massachusetts)
Profile: p.356
Real Estate **Band 2**
Table: p.351

Harper, Conrad K (New York)
Profile: p.517

Harper, John (Texas)
Profile: p.673
Employment **Band 2**
Table: p.652

Harper, Robert (Pennsylvania)
Profile: p.616
Corporate/M&A **Band 4**
Table: p.599

Harrell, Michael P (New York)
Profile: p.518
Private Equity **Band 1**
Table: p.489

Harrigan, Kenneth (New Mexico)
Profile: p.438
Litigation **Band 1**
Table: p.435

Harrington, James (Illinois)
Profile: p.262
Environment **Band 3**
Table: p.239

Harrington, Michael (Texas)
Profile: p.673
Corporate/M&A **Band 4**
Table: p.649

Harris, Adam (New York)
Profile: p.518
Insolvency **U**
Table: p.472

Harris, Alan (California)
Profile: p.65
Construction **Band 1**
Table: p.36

Harris, Dale (Colorado)
Profile: p.84
Litigation **Band 3**
Table: p.79

Harris, David L (New Jersey)
Profile: p.431
Litigation **Band 2**
Table: p.428

Harris, James (Texas)
Profile: p.674
Environment **Band 3**
Table: p.655

Harris, L Douglas (New York)
Profile: p.518
Projects **Band 3**
Table: p.491

Harris, Larry D (District of Columbia)
Profile: p.136
Construction **Band 1**
Table: p.110

Harris, Margaret (Texas)
Profile: p.674
Employment **Band 2**
Table: p.651

Harris, Matthew (Tennessee)
Profile: p.641
Real Estate **Band 2**
Table: p.640

Harris, Michael (Vermont)
Profile: p.697
Employment **Band 3**
Table: p.693

Harris, Morton A (Georgia)
Profile: p.202,206
Tax **Band 4**
Table: p.201

Harris, Scott (District of Columbia)
Profile: p.136
Communications **Band 4**
Table: p.107

Harris, Steve (Georgia)
Profile: p.206
Antitrust **Band 3**
Table: p.181

Hartig, Lawrence (Alaska)
Profile: p.15
Environment **Band 3**
Table: p.12

Hartle Munsch, Martha (Pennsylvania)
Profile: p.616
Employment **Band 2**
Table: p.602

Hartmann, James (Oklahoma)
Profile: p.586
Real Estate **Band 3**
Table: p.585

Hartmann, Michael (Illinois)
Profile: p.262
Intellectual Property **Band 3**
Table: p.244

Hartnett, William (New York)
Profile: p.518
Capital Markets **Band 3**
Table: p.448

Hartstein, Barry (Illinois)
Profile: p.262
Employment **Band 2**
Table: p.236

Harty, Frank (Iowa)
Profile: p.292
Employment **Band 1**
Table: p.288

Harty, Ronan P (New York)
Profile: p.518
Antitrust **Band 2**
Table: p.441

Harvell, Michael (New Hampshire)
Profile: p.422
Litigation **Band 2**
Table: p.419

Harvey, Charles (Maine)
Profile: p.325
Litigation **Band 2**
Table: p.322

Harvey, Dean (Texas)
Profile: p.674
Communications **Band 3**
Table: p.646

Hasson Jr, James K (Georgia)
Profile: p.206
Tax **Band 3**
Table: p.201

Hastie, John (Oklahoma)
Profile: p.585,586
Real Estate **Band 1**
Table: p.585

Hatch, Michael (Wisconsin)
Profile: p.729
Real Estate **Band 1**
Table: p.727

Hatley, Joseph (Kansas)
Profile: p.299
Litigation **Band 3**
Table: p.297

Hattersley III, Thomas (Montana)
Profile: p.398
Employment **Band 2**
Table: p.395

Hauck, Terry (Oregon)
Profile: p.593
Real Estate **Band 4**
Table: p.592

Havel, Richard W (California)
Profile: p.65
Insolvency **Band 4**
Table: p.44

Haviland, James (West Virginia)
Profile: p.722
Employment **Band 1**
Table: p.716

Hawk, Barry E (New York)
Profile: p.518
Antitrust **Band 1**
Table: p.441

Hawkins, Barry (Connecticut)
Profile: p.93
Real Estate **Band 1**
Table: p.91

Hawkins, Holmes (Georgia)
Profile: p.206
Intellectual Property **Band 4**
Table: p.195

Hawkins, Michael (Ohio)
Profile: p.575
Employment **Band 3**
Table: p.565

Hawks, Tim (Wisconsin)
Profile: p.729
Employment **Band 2**
Table: p.724

Hawthorne, Bruce (Georgia)
Profile: p.206
Corporate/M&A **Band 1**
Table: p.187

Hayden, Joe (New Jersey)
Profile: p.431
Litigation **Band 2**
Table: p.428

Hayden, Raymond P (New York)
Profile: p.518
Shipping **Band 1**
Table: p.496

Hayes, David (California)
Profile: p.65
Intellectual Property **Band 2**
Table: p.48

Hayes, David (District of Columbia)
Profile: p.137
Environment **Band 1**
Table: p.117

Hayes, Robert (South Dakota)
Profile: p.633
Corporate/M&A **Band 1**
Table: p.630
Real Estate **Band 2**
Table: p.633

Hayes, William (Texas)
Profile: p.674
Banking & Finance **Band 1**
Table: p.645

Haynes, Greg (Kentucky)
Profile: p.305
Litigation **Band 1**
Table: p.303

Haynes, John (Tennessee)
Profile: p.641
Real Estate **Band 3**
Table: p.640

Haynes, Joseph B (Georgia)
Profile: p.206
Litigation **Band 3**
Table: p.198

Haynie, Barbara (Louisiana)
Profile: p.317
Employment **Band 3**
Table: p.310

Haynor, Charles R (Minnesota)
Profile: p.376

Real Estate **Band 2**
Table: p.374

Hazan, Scott (New York)
Profile: p.518
Insolvency **Band 5**
Table: p.472

Hazlett, Mark (Hawaii)
Profile: p.218
Real Estate **Band 4**
Table: p.217

Hazlett, Richard (North Carolina)
Profile: p.553
Banking & Finance **Band 2**
Table: p.544

Headley, Linda (Texas)
Profile: p.674
Employment **Band 3**
Table: p.652

Healy, Martin (Massachusetts)
Profile: p.356
Environment **Band 2**
Table: p.344

Heard, Keith (New York)
Profile: p.518
Shipping **Band 5**
Table: p.496

Heard, Richard (Montana)
Profile: p.398,398
Real Estate **Band 1**
Table: p.397

Heath, Marc (Vermont)
Profile: p.697
Litigation **Band 3**
Table: p.695

Heaven Jr., Lewis (Pete) (Kansas)
Profile: p.299
Real Estate **Band 1**
Table: p.298

Hedian, Victoria (Maryland)
Profile: p.333
Employment **Band 2**
Table: p.328

Hedican, Chris (Nebraska)
Profile: p.405
Employment **Band 3**
Table: p.402

Heeter, James (Missouri)
Profile: p.392
Corporate/M&A **Band 2**
Table: p.386

Hefflinger, David (Nebraska)
Profile: p.405
Corporate/M&A **Band 1**
Table: p.400

Heftler, Thomas E (New York)
Profile: p.518
Capital Markets **Band 3**
Table: p.451

Heidelberger, Brian (Illinois)
Profile: p.262
Media & Entertainment **U**
Table: p.247

Heidelberger, Louis (Pennsylvania)
Profile: p.616
Intellectual Property **Band 3**
Table: p.609

Heihre, Michael (Hawaii)
Profile: p.218
Litigation **Band 2**
Table: p.215

Heim, Robert (Pennsylvania)
Profile: p.616
Litigation **Band 1**
Table: p.611

Heinke, Rex (California)
Profile: p.65

Media & Entertainment **Band 2**
Table: p.53

Heintz, John (District of Columbia)
Profile: p.137
Insurance **Band 1**
Table: p.120

Heinzelman, Kris (New York)
Profile: p.518
Capital Markets **Band 2**
Table: p.448

Heist, Dale (Pennsylvania)
Profile: p.616
Intellectual Property **Band 3**
Table: p.609

Heitner, Kenneth H (New York)
Profile: p.518
Tax **Band 2**
Table: p.499

Hejmanowski, Paul (Nevada)
Profile: p.413
Litigation **Band 3**
Table: p.409

Held, Jerry (Alabama)
Profile: p.7
Real Estate **Band 4**
Table: p.6

Heleniak, David W (New York)
Profile: p.518

Helfand, Thomas (Texas)
Profile: p.674
Tax **Band 3**
Table: p.667

Heller, David (Illinois)
Profile: p.262
Insolvency **Band 2**
Table: p.241

Hellewell, Read (Utah)
Profile: p.690
Real Estate **Band 2**
Table: p.689

Helman, Robert A (Illinois)
Profile: p.262

Helmsing, Frederick G (Alabama)
Profile: p.7
Litigation **Band 3**
Table: p.4

Hemley, Robert (Vermont)
Profile: p.697
Litigation **Band 1**
Table: p.695

Hemminger, Pamela (California)
Profile: p.65
Employment **Band 4**
Table: p.40

Henderson, Richard (North Dakota)
Profile: p.557
Litigation **Band 3**
Table: p.556

Henderson, Scott (Arizona)
Profile: p.22
Real Estate **Band 2**
Table: p.20

Henderson, Jr, Donald B (New York)
Profile: p.518
Insurance **Band 3**
Table: p.477

Hendrick, David (Georgia)
Profile: p.207
Construction **Band 2**
Table: p.184

Henegan, John (Mississippi)
Profile: p.383
Litigation **Band 3**

LEADING LAWYERS INDEX

Table: p.381

Hengen, Nancy (New York)
Profile: p.518
Shipping **Band 1**
Table: p.496

Henkel, Kathryn (Texas)
Profile: p.668,674
Tax **Band 4**
Table: p.667

Henlein, Carl (Kentucky)
Profile: p.305
Litigation **Band 2**
Table: p.303

Hennessey, Gilbert
(Massachusetts)
Profile: p.356
Intellectual Property **Band 3**
Table: p.348

Hennessey, Robert
(Minnesota)
Profile: p.376
Litigation **Band 3**
Table: p.372

Hennig, Gene (Minnesota)
Profile: p.376
Corporate/M&A **Band 3**
Table: p.369

Hennigan, Mike (California)
Profile: p.65
Litigation **Band 3**
Table: p.50

Hensler, David
(District of Columbia)
Profile: p.137
Litigation **Band 2**
Table: p.123

Herlihy, Edward D (New York)
Profile: p.518
Corporate/M&A **Band 1**
Table: p.460

Herman, Russ M (Louisiana)
Profile: p.317
Litigation **Band 1**
Table: p.313

Herman, Sarah Andrews
(North Dakota)
Profile: p.557
Employment **Band 1**
Table: p.555

Hermes, John N (Oklahoma)
Profile: p.586
Litigation **Band 2**
Table: p.583

Hernandez, Jennifer
(California)
Profile: p.65
Environment **Band 4**
Table: p.43

Hersch, Dennis S (New York)
Profile: p.518

Heryford, Craig (Pennsylvania)
Profile: p.616
Banking & Finance **Band 3**
Table: p.598

Hester, Tracy (Texas)
Profile: p.674
Environment **Band 2**
Table: p.655

Hewey, Melissa (Maine)
Profile: p.325
Employment **Band 3**
Table: p.321

Hewitt, Henry (Oregon)
Profile: p.593
Corporate/M&A **Band**
Table: p.587
Corporate/M&A **Band 1**
Table: p.587

Hewitt, William J (New York)
Profile: p.518
Private Equity **Band 2**
Table: p.489

Heyman, Robert (New Mexico)
Profile: p.438
Corporate/M&A **Band 4**
Table: p.433

Heywood, Thomas (West Virginia)
Profile: p.722
Corporate/M&A **Band 1**
Table: p.714

Hiatt, Jerry (Hawaii)
Profile: p.218
Employment **Band 2**
Table: p.213

Hickey, Michael (South Dakota)
Profile: p.633
Litigation **Band 3**
Table: p.632

Hickey, Paul (Wyoming)
Profile: p.735
Litigation **Band 1**
Table: p.732

Hickey, Jr, PC, John T
(Illinois)
Profile: p.262
Litigation **Band 5**
Table: p.245

Hicks, Robert J (Indiana)
Profile: p.283
Corporate/M&A **Band 3**
Table: p.277

Higgins, Keith
(Massachusetts)
Profile: p.357
Corporate/M&A **Band 1**
Table: p.340

Higgins, Roger (Texas)
Profile: p.674
Insurance **Band 3**
Table: p.659

High, Michael E (Maine)
Profile: p.325
Corporate/M&A **Band 3**
Table: p.319

Hill, Donald (Kansas)
Profile: p.299
Employment **Band 4**
Table: p.296

Hill, Douglas P
(New Hampshire)
Profile: p.421,422
Real Estate **Band 4**
Table: p.420

Hill, Frank (Oklahoma)
Profile: p.585,586
Real Estate **Band 2**
Table: p.585

Hill, James (North Dakota)
Profile: p.557
Litigation **Band 1**
Table: p.556

Hill, Reginald (Tennessee)
Profile: p.641
Corporate/M&A **Band 2**
Table: p.635

Hill, Robert F (Colorado)
Profile: p.84
Litigation **Band 1**
Table: p.79

Hill, Thomas (Ohio)
Profile: p.575
Litigation **Band 2**
Table: p.570

Hill III, Benjamin (Florida)
Profile: p.174
Litigation **Band 1**

Table: p.165

Hill Jr, B Harvey (Georgia)
Profile: p.207
Banking & Finance **Band 2**
Table: p.183

Hill Noto, Margaret (Oregon)
Profile: p.593
Corporate/M&A **Band 3**
Table: p.587

Hilliard, David (Illinois)
Profile: p.262
Intellectual Property **Band 3**
Table: p.244

Hilliard, Russell
(New Hampshire)
Profile: p.422
Litigation **Band 1**
Table: p.419

Hilson, John (California)
Profile: p.
Banking & Finance **Band 3**
Table: p.30

Hilton, Paul (Colorado)
Profile: p.84
Corporate/M&A **Band 1**
Table: p.75

Himmel, Michael (New Jersey)
Profile: p.431
Litigation **Band 3**
Table: p.428

Hinchey, John (Georgia)
Profile: p.207
Construction **Band 2**
Table: p.184

Hinderks, Mark (Kansas)
Profile: p.299
Litigation **Band 2**
Table: p.297

Hines, Barry (Kentucky)
Profile: p.305
Real Estate **Band 2**
Table: p.304

Hingle, Charles (Montana)
Profile: p.398
Corporate/M&A **Band 2**
Table: p.394
Litigation **Band 2**
Table: p.396

Hinkle IV, Samuel (Kentucky)
Profile: p.305
Litigation **Band 3**
Table: p.303

Hinman Jr, William (California)
Profile: p.
Capital Markets **Band 2**
Table: p.32

Hintze, John (Iowa)
Profile: p.292
Corporate/M&A **Band 4**
Table: p.286

Hipp, Ken (Hawaii)
Profile: p.218
Employment **Band 2**
Table: p.214

Hirsch, Barry (California)
Profile: p.65
Media & Entertainment **Band 4**
Table: p.53

Hirschberg, William E
(New York)
Profile: p.518
Banking & Finance **Band 1**
Table: p.445

Hise, Daniel (Mississippi)
Profile: p.383
Corporate/M&A **Band 2**
Table: p.378

Hite, Richard (Kansas)
Profile: p.299

Litigation **Band 1**
Table: p.297

Hoarty, Tom (Nebraska)
Profile: p.405
Employment **Band 1**
Table: p.401

Hobbins, Robert (Minnesota)
Profile: p.376
Employment **Band 1**
Table: p.371

Hobel, Lawrence (California)
Profile: p.65
Insurance **Band 3**
Table: p.46

Hoberg, Tim (Ohio)
Profile: p.575
Corporate/M&A **Band 3**
Table: p.562

Hobson Jr., Edwin L.
(Vermont)
Profile: p.697
Employment **Band 3**
Table: p.693

Hockett, Christopher
(California)
Profile: p.65
Antitrust **Band 4**
Table: p.29

Hodes, Scott (Illinois)
Profile: p.262
Media & Entertainment **Band 1**
Table: p.247

Hodge Jr, Clifton (Mississippi)
Profile: p.383
Corporate/M&A **Band 2**
Table: p.378

Hodges Taylor, Laura
(Massachusetts)
Profile: p.357

Hofer, Roy (Illinois)
Profile: p.262
Intellectual Property **Band 1**
Table: p.244

Hoffar, Julian (Virginia)
Profile: p.704
Construction **Band 1**
Table: p.698

Hoffman, Jerome (Florida)
Profile: p.174
Antitrust **Band 3**
Table: p.151

Hoffmann, Christian (Arizona)
Profile: p.22
Corporate/M&A **Band 3**
Table: p.16

Hogan, Dennis (Nebraska)
Profile: p.405
Real Estate **Band 2**
Table: p.404

Hogfoss, Robert (Georgia)
Profile: p.207
Environment **Band 4**
Table: p.192

Hokanson, Jeffrey A (Indiana)
Profile: p.283
Litigation **Band 3**
Table: p.280

Holcomb, James M (Iowa)
Profile: p.292,293
Real Estate **Band 2**
Table: p.291

Holden Jr, Frederick D
(California)
Profile: p.
Insolvency **Band 4**
Table: p.44

Holen, Lee (Alaska)
Profile: p.15
Employment **Band 1**

Table: p.10

Holman, Michael (Ohio)
Profile: p.575
Construction **Band 2**
Table: p.560

Holmes, Ervin (Utah)
Profile: p.690
Real Estate **Band 3**
Table: p.689

Holmes, Whitney (Colorado)
Profile: p.84
Corporate/M&A **Band 2**
Table: p.75

Holt, Robert (Georgia)
Profile: p.207
Real Estate **Band 3**
Table: p.199

Holt III, Berry (Tennessee)
Profile: p.641
Corporate/M&A **Band 2**
Table: p.635

Homburger, Tom (Illinois)
Profile: p.262
Real Estate **Band 2**
Table: p.249

Honan III, William J
(New York)
Profile: p.518
Shipping **Band 2**
Table: p.496

Hood, James (New Hampshire)
Profile: p.422
Corporate/M&A **Band 3**
Table: p.415

Hooker, David J (Ohio)
Profile: p.575
Litigation **Band 2**
Table: p.570

Hoole, Roger (Utah)
Profile: p.690
Employment **Band 1**
Table: p.686

Hooper, Chester (New York)
Profile: p.518
Shipping **Band 2**
Table: p.496

Hope, Stephen D
(North Carolina)
Profile: p.553
Corporate/M&A **Band 2**
Table: p.546

Hopkinson, R Ronald
(New York)
Profile: p.519
Private Equity **Band 4**
Table: p.487

Hopping, Wade (Florida)
Profile: p.175
Environment **Band 2**
Table: p.160

Hopson, Edwin (Kentucky)
Profile: p.305
Employment **Band 1**
Table: p.302

Horder, Richard (Georgia)
Profile: p.207
Environment **Band 1**
Table: p.192

Horn, Dennis (Mississippi)
Profile: p.383
Employment **Band 2**
Table: p.379

Hornak, Mark (Pennsylvania)
Profile: p.616
Employment **Band 4**
Table: p.602

Hornreich, Michael (Florida)
Profile: p.175
Construction **Band 2**

LEADING LAWYERS INDEX

Table: p.154

Horowitz, Mitchell (Florida)
Profile: p.171,175
Tax **Band 3**
Table: p.170

Horowitz, Philip
(District of Columbia)
Profile: p.137
Real Estate **Band 3**
Table: p.127

Horowitz, Richard M
(New York)
Profile: p.519
Capital Markets **U**
Table: p.453

Horowitz, Steven (New York)
Profile: p.519
Real Estate **Band 3**
Table: p.493

Horstmann III, John
(Pennsylvania)
Profile: p.616
Banking & Finance **Band 3**
Table: p.598
Insolvency **Band 2**
Table: p.607

Horton, William Pharis
(Wisconsin)
Profile: p.729
Real Estate **Band 3**
Table: p.727

Houghton, Robert (Iowa)
Profile: p.293
Litigation **Band 2**
Table: p.290

Houlihan Jr, Robert
(Kentucky)
Profile: p.305
Litigation **Band 3**
Table: p.303

Houser, Douglas (Oregon)
Profile: p.594
Litigation **Band 2**
Table: p.590

Hovis, James W (North Carolina)
Profile: p.553
Banking & Finance **Band 1**
Table: p.544

Hubbard, Paul (North Dakota)
Profile: p.557,557
Real Estate **Band 1**
Table: p.557

Huber, John
(District of Columbia)
Profile: p.137
Corporate/M&A **Band 2**
Table: p.111

Huck, L Francis (New York)
Profile: p.519
Banking & Finance **Band 1**
Table: p.445

Huck, Robert (Nebraska)
Profile: p.405,405
Real Estate **Band 2**
Table: p.404

Hudanish, David (New York)
Profile: p.519
Communications **Band 2**
Table: p.456

Huddleston, Michael (Texas)
Profile: p.674
Insurance **Band 2**
Table: p.659

Hudson, Robert (Florida)
Profile: p.175
Tax **Band 1**
Table: p.170

Hudson Jr, Paul (Georgia)
Profile: p.207

Corporate/M&A **Band 4**
Table: p.187

Huffman, Fordham (Ohio)
Profile: p.575
Litigation **Band 3**
Table: p.570

Huffman, Gregory (Texas)
Profile: p.674
Antitrust **Band 3**
Table: p.644

Hughes, Frank (California)
Profile: p.66
Construction **Band 3**
Table: p.36

Hughes, Hunter (Georgia)
Profile: p.207
Employment **Band 1**
Table: p.189

Hughey Jr, James F
(Alabama)
Profile: p.7
Corporate/M&A **Band 1**
Table: p.1

Hughs, William (Georgia)
Profile: p.207
Construction **Band 5**
Table: p.184

Hull Jr., Gerald (New Jersey)
Profile: p.430,431
Real Estate **Band 1**
Table: p.429

Humes, Gary
(District of Columbia)
Profile: p.137
Real Estate **Band 3**
Table: p.127

Humke, Steven K (Indiana)
Profile: p.283
Corporate/M&A **Band 2**
Table: p.277

Humphreys, Hunter
(Tennessee)
Profile: p.641,641
Real Estate **Band 2**
Table: p.640

Humphreys, Ivan (California)
Profile: p.66
Tax **Band 3**
Table: p.58

Hungar, Thomas (District of Columbia)
Profile: p.137
Litigation **Band 3**
Table: p.123

Hunt, Eugene (Arkansas)
Profile: p.27
Employment **Band 3**
Table: p.24

Hunt, Gordon (California)
Profile: p.66
Construction **Band 4**
Table: p.36

Hunt, Kay Nord (Minnesota)
Profile: p.376
Litigation **Band 3**
Table: p.372

Hunt, Jeffrey (Missouri)
Profile: p.392
Litigation **Band 3**
Table: p.389

Hunt, Scott (Oregon)
Profile: p.594
Employment **Band 2**
Table: p.588

Hunter, Forrest (Georgia)
Profile: p.207
Employment **Band 4**
Table: p.189

Hunter, Jerry (Missouri)
Profile: p.392
Employment **Band 3**
Table: p.388

Hunter, Rob (Missouri)
Profile: p.392
Corporate/M&A **Band 3**
Table: p.386

Hurley, Patrick (New Mexico)
Profile: p.438
Real Estate **Band 2**
Table: p.437

Hursh, Lynn (Missouri)
Profile: p.392
Litigation **Band 2**
Table: p.389

Hurwitz, Andrew (Arizona)
Profile: p.22
Litigation **Band 2**
Table: p.19

Husband, John (Colorado)
Profile: p.84
Employment **Band 1**
Table: p.78

Hutcheson, Mark A
(Washington)
Profile: p.713
Employment **Band 2**
Table: p.708

Hyatt, Wayne (Georgia)
Profile: p.207
Real Estate **Band 3**
Table: p.199

Hyde, Kevin (Florida)
Profile: p.175
Employment **Band 2**
Table: p.158

Hylton, Hartwell (New York)
Profile: p.519
Banking & Finance **Band 2**
Table: p.445

Hyman, Alan (New York)
Profile: p.519
Insolvency **Band 4**
Table: p.472

Hyman, Milt (California)
Profile: p.66
Tax **Band 2**
Table: p.58

Hyman, Jr, Thomas (Georgia)
Profile: p.207
Corporate/M&A **Band 4**
Table: p.187

Hyne II, Ernest (Tennessee)
Profile: p.641
Corporate/M&A **Band 3**
Table: p.635

I

Ichinose, Susan (Hawaii)
Profile: p.218
Employment **Band 2**
Table: p.213

Ilvedson, Duane (North Dakota)
Profile: p.557
Litigation **Band 2**
Table: p.556

Immelt, Stephen (Maryland)
Profile: p.333
Litigation **Band 3**
Table: p.330

Imse, Peter (New Hampshire)
Profile: p.422
Real Estate **Band 2**
Table: p.420

Indoe, William F (New York)
Profile: p.519
Tax **Band 3**
Table: p.499

Ingram, Fred (Alabama)
Profile: p.7
Employment **Band 2**
Table: p.3

Ingram, John (New York)
Profile: p.519
Shipping **Band 5**
Table: p.496

Iredale, Nancy L (California)
Profile: p.66
Tax **Band 3**
Table: p.58

Isaacson, Laurence B (New York)
Profile: p.519
Capital Markets **Band 2**
Table: p.453

Isken, Donald (Delaware)
Profile: p.100
Real Estate **Band 2**
Table: p.99

Isom, Chervis (Alabama)
Profile: p.7
Real Estate **Band 4**
Table: p.6

Ison, Eric (Kentucky)
Profile: p.305
Litigation **Band 3**
Table: p.303

Ivanhoe, Robert (New York)
Profile: p.519
Real Estate **Band 4**
Table: p.493

J

Jacob, Cynthia (New Jersey)
Profile: p.431
Employment **Band 2**
Table: p.427

Jacobs, Michael A (California)
Profile: p.66
Intellectual Property **Band 2**
Table: p.48

Jacobs, Neil (Massachusetts)
Profile: p.357
Employment **Band 3**
Table: p.342

Jacobs, Paul (Colorado)
Profile: p.84
Real Estate **Band 4**
Table: p.81

Jacobs-Meadway, Roberta
(Pennsylvania)
Profile: p.616
Intellectual Property **Band 2**
Table: p.609

Jacobson, Kenneth (Illinois)
Profile: p.262
Real Estate **Band 4**
Table: p.249

Jacobson, Martin (New York)
Profile: p.519
Projects **Band 3**
Table: p.491

Jacobson, Ronald H (Illinois)
Profile: p.262
Banking & Finance **Band 3**
Table: p.226

Jaffe, Helene D (New York)
Profile: p.519
Antitrust **Band 3**
Table: p.441

Jaffe, Ira (Michigan)
Profile: p.366
Corporate/M&A **Band 2**
Table: p.361

Jaffe, Kenneth
(District of Columbia)
Profile: p.137
Energy **Band 5**

Table: p.115

Jaffe, Michael
(District of Columbia)
Profile: p.137
Construction **Band 3**
Table: p.110

Jaffe, Seth (Massachusetts)
Profile: p.357
Environment **Band 1**
Table: p.344

James, David (North Carolina)
Profile: p.553
Employment **Band 1**
Table: p.547

James , Dwight W (Iowa)
Profile: p.293
Litigation **Band 2**
Table: p.290

Jamieson, Michael (Florida)
Profile: p.175
Corporate/M&A **Band 4**
Table: p.156

Janik, Stephen (Oregon)
Profile: p.594
Real Estate **Band 1**
Table: p.592

Janke, Ron (Ohio)
Profile: p.576
Environment **Band 3**
Table: p.567

Janowitz, Robert (Missouri)
Profile: p.392
Employment **Band 4**
Table: p.388

Jansonius, John (Texas)
Profile: p.674
Employment **Band 3**
Table: p.652

Jardine, James S (Utah)
Profile: p.690
Litigation **Band 1**
Table: p.687

Jarin, Kenneth (Pennsylvania)
Profile: p.616
Employment **Band 4**
Table: p.602

Jarman, William (Louisiana)
Profile: p.317
Litigation **Band 2**
Table: p.313

Jaspan, Stanley S (Wisconsin)
Profile: p.729
Employment **Band 3**
Table: p.725

Javaras, George B (Illinois)
Profile: p.263
Tax **Band 1**
Table: p.252

Jeffress, William
(District of Columbia)
Profile: p.137
Litigation **Band 1**
Table: p.123

Jeffries, M Hill (Georgia)
Profile: p.207
Corporate/M&A **Band 2**
Table: p.187

Jenner, Jesse J (New York)
Profile: p.519
Intellectual Property **Band 2**
Table: p.479

Jennings, Jan (Tennessee)
Profile: p.641
Employment **Band 1**
Table: p.637

Jennings, Tom (Pennsylvania)
Profile: p.616
Employment **Band 2**
Table: p.601

LEADING LAWYERS INDEX

Jepson, Edward (Illinois)
Profile: p.263
Employment **Band 2**
Table: p.236

Jernigan, John L.
(North Carolina)
Profile: p.553
Corporate/M&A **Band 2**
Table: p.546

Jernigan Jr. Henry
(West Virginia)
Profile: p.722
Litigation **Band 2**
Table: p.718

Jernstedt, Kenneth (Oregon)
Profile: p.594
Employment **Band 3**
Table: p.589

Jewell, Robert V (Texas)
Profile: p.674
Communications **Band 2**
Table: p.646
Corporate/M&A **Band 1**
Table: p.649

Joffe, Bob (New York)
Profile: p.519
Antitrust **Band 1**
Table: p.441

Johnson, Christopher
(Arizona)
Profile: p.22
Corporate/M&A **Band 1**
Table: p.16

Johnson, Craig (California)
Profile: p.66
Communications **Band 1**
Table: p.34

Johnson, Daniel (California)
Profile: p.66
Intellectual Property **U**
Table: p.48

Johnson, Donald (Michigan)
Profile: p.366
Banking & Finance **Band 2**
Table: p.360

Johnson, Duncan (Rhode Island)
Profile: p.623
Corporate/M&A **Band 2**
Table: p.620

Johnson, Edward E (Iowa)
Profile: p.293
Corporate/M&A **Band 4**
Table: p.286

Johnson, Jim (Georgia)
Profile: p.207
Intellectual Property **Band 5**
Table: p.195

Johnson, Linda
(New Hampshire)
Profile: p.422
Employment **Band 2**
Table: p.417

Johnson, Philip (North Dakota)
Profile: p.557,557
Real Estate **Band 2**
Table: p.557

Johnson, Richard (Indiana)
Profile: p.283
Real Estate **Band 3**
Table: p.282

Johnson, Steven
(North Dakota)
Profile: p.557
Corporate/M&A **Band 3**
Table: p.554

Johnson, Thomas (Nebraska)
Profile: p.405
Litigation **Band 1**
Table: p.403

Johnson, Weyman (Georgia)
Profile: p.207
Employment **Band 3**
Table: p.189

Johnson Jr, John H (Georgia)
Profile: p.207
Environment **Band 2**
Table: p.192

Johnston, Jay (Virginia)
Profile: p.704
Corporate/M&A **Band 1**
Table: p.699

Johnston, M Elaine
(New York)
Profile: p.519
Antitrust **Band 5**
Table: p.441

Johnston, Mike (Georgia)
Profile: p.207
Employment **Band 2**
Table: p.189

Johnston, Thomas (Maine)
Profile: p.325
Employment **Band 2**
Table: p.321

Johnstone, Andrea
(New Hampshire)
Profile: p.422
Employment **Band 1**
Table: p.417

Jones, Cary (Utah)
Profile: p.690
Real Estate **Band 3**
Table: p.689

Jones, J Randall (Nevada)
Profile: p.413
Litigation **Band 2**
Table: p.409

Jones, John (Montana)
Profile: p.398,398
Real Estate **Band 2**
Table: p.397

Jones, Karen (Washington)
Profile: p.713
Employment **Band 1**
Table: p.708

Jones, Leslie Terry (Nevada)
Profile: p.413
Real Estate **Band 2**
Table: p.411

Jones, Richard (Pennsylvania)
Profile: p.616
Real Estate **Band 4**
Table: p.613

Jones, Rod (Florida)
Profile: p.175
Banking & Finance **Band 2**
Table: p.152

Jones, Walker (Mississippi)
Profile: p.383
Litigation **Band 3**
Table: p.381

Jordan, Carl (Texas)
Profile: p.675
Employment **Band 1**
Table: p.652

Jordan, David J (Utah)
Profile: p.690
Litigation **Band 3**
Table: p.687

Jordan, James B (Georgia)
Profile: p.207
Real Estate **Band 3**
Table: p.199

Jordan, Stephen
(Pennsylvania)
Profile: p.616
Employment **Band 3**
Table: p.601

Jorgenson, Larry (Wyoming)
Profile: p.734,735
Real Estate **Band 3**
Table: p.734

Jorgenson, Mary Ann (Ohio)
Profile: p.576
Corporate/M&A **Band 1**
Table: p.562

Josefsberg, Robert (Florida)
Profile: p.175
Litigation **Band 1**
Table: p.165

Joseph, Gregory P (New York)
Profile: p.519
Litigation **Band 3**
Table: p.481

Joseph, Robert (Illinois)
Profile: p.263
Antitrust **Band 4**
Table: p.224

Joseph III, Alfred (Kentucky)
Profile: p.305
Real Estate **Band 1**
Table: p.304

Josepher, Richard (Florida)
Profile: p.175
Tax **Band 3**
Table: p.170

Jossem, Jared (Hawaii)
Profile: p.218
Employment **Band 3**
Table: p.214

Jost, Lawrence J (Wisconsin)
Profile: p.729
Real Estate **Band 1**
Table: p.727

Joswick, David (Michigan)
Profile: p.366
Banking & Finance **Band 2**
Table: p.360
Corporate/M&A **Band 2**
Table: p.361

Joy, Robert (Massachusetts)
Profile: p.357
Employment **Band 2**
Table: p.342

K

Kaden, Lewis B (New York)
Profile: p.519
Corporate/M&A **Band 4**
Table: p.460

Kadlick, Richard F (New York)
Profile: p.519
Capital Markets **Band 3**
Table: p.453

Kadue, David (California)
Profile: p.66
Employment **Band 4**
Table: p.40

Kafin, Robert (New York)
Profile: p.520
Environment **Band 3**
Table: p.469

Kahn, Adam (Massachusetts)
Profile: p.357
Environment **U**
Table: p.344

Kahn, David
(District of Columbia)
Profile: p.137
Real Estate **Band 4**
Table: p.127

Kahn, Richard (New Jersey)
Profile: p.430,431
Real Estate **Band 3**
Table: p.429

Kaim, Henry (Texas)
Profile: p.675
Insolvency **Band 4**
Table: p.657

Kaiser, Gordon (Ohio)
Profile: p.576
Corporate/M&A **Band 2**
Table: p.562

Kalteyer, Ronald (Texas)
Profile: p.675
Tax **Band 1**
Table: p.667

Kamer, Gregory (Nevada)
Profile: p.413
Employment **Band 1**
Table: p.408

Kant, Bob (Arizona)
Profile: p.22
Corporate/M&A **Band 2**
Table: p.16

Kantor, Hal (Florida)
Profile: p.175
Real Estate **Band 3**
Table: p.167

Kantrow, Lee (Louisiana)
Profile: p.317
Corporate/M&A **Band 3**
Table: p.309

Kaplan, Cathy (New York)
Profile: p.520
Capital Markets **Band 3**
Table: p.453

Kaplan, Edward
(New Hampshire)
Profile: p.422
Employment **Band 2**
Table: p.417

Kaplan, Elliot (Minnesota)
Profile: p.376
Litigation **Band 2**
Table: p.372

Kaplan, Jonathan (Tennessee)
Profile: p.641
Employment **Band 2**
Table: p.637

Kaplan, Philip (Arkansas)
Profile: p.27
Litigation **Band 2**
Table: p.25

Kaplan, Samuel (Minnesota)
Profile: p.376
Corporate/M&A **Band 2**
Table: p.369

Karabell, David (New York)
Profile: p.520
Private Equity **Band 4**
Table: p.487

Karaganis, Joseph (Illinois)
Profile: p.263
Environment **Band 3**
Table: p.239

Karlin, Allan N. (West Virginia)
Profile: p.722
Employment **Band 1**
Table: p.716

Karotkin, Stephen (New York)
Profile: p.520
Insolvency **Band 4**
Table: p.472

Karp, Marvin (Ohio)
Profile: p.576
Litigation **Band 3**
Table: p.570

Kaslow, Howard (Nebraska)
Profile: p.405
Corporate/M&A **Band 1**
Table: p.400

Kass, Stephen (New York)
Profile: p.520
Environment **Band 4**
Table: p.469

Kaster, James (Minnesota)
Profile: p.376
Employment **Band 1**
Table: p.370

Katcher, Richard D
(New York)
Profile: p.520
Corporate/M&A **Band 1**
Table: p.460

Katelman, John (Nebraska)
Profile: p.405
Corporate/M&A **Band 1**
Table: p.400
Real Estate **Band 1**
Table: p.404

Katsh, Salem (New York)
Profile: p.520
Intellectual Property **Band 3**
Table: p.479

Kattan, Joseph
(District of Columbia)
Profile: p.137
Antitrust **Band 3**
Table: p.103

Katz, Alvin Charles (Illinois)
Profile: p.263
Real Estate **Band 4**
Table: p.249

Katz, David A (New York)
Profile: p.520

Katz, Lawrence (Arizona)
Profile: p.22
Employment **Band 1**
Table: p.18

Katz, Marvin M (Texas)
Profile: p.675
Real Estate **Band 2**
Table: p.665

Katz, Robert S. (Hawaii)
Profile: p.218
Employment **Band 1**
Table: p.214

Kaufman, Christopher (Kit)
(California)
Profile: p.66
Communications **Band 2**
Table: p.34
Corporate/M&A **Band 2**
Table: p.37

Kaufman, David (Mississippi)
Profile: p.383
Litigation **Band 3**
Table: p.381

Kaufman, Mark (Georgia)
Profile: p.207
Corporate/M&A **Band 3**
Table: p.187

Kaufman, Mark S (Georgia)
Profile: p.208
Insolvency **Band 3**
Table: p.193

Kauss, Andrew (Georgia)
Profile: p.208
Real Estate **Band 3**
Table: p.199

Kavaler, Thomas (New York)
Profile: p.520
Litigation **Band 5**
Table: p.481

Kawashima, James (Hawaii)
Profile: p.218
Employment **Band 3**
Table: p.214
Litigation **Band 3**
Table: p.215

Kawata, Yukako (New York)
Profile: p.520
Private Equity **Band 1**
Table: p.489

LEADING LAWYERS INDEX

Kayatta Jr., William (Maine)
Profile: p.325
Litigation **Band 1**
Table: p.322

Kayle, Bruce E (New York)
Profile: p.520
Tax **Band 2**
Table: p.499

Kazmarek, Edward (Georgia)
Profile: p.208
Environment **Band 3**
Table: p.192

Keane, Paul (New York)
Profile: p.520
Shipping **Band 5**
Table: p.496

Keating, Michael
(Massachusetts)
Profile: p.357
Litigation **Band 1**
Table: p.349

Kee, Conrad (Connecticut)
Profile: p.93
Employment **Band 4**
Table: p.89

Keeler, Dennis (Maine)
Profile: p.325
Real Estate **Band 3**
Table: p.324

Keene, Thomas (Alabama)
Profile: p.7
Litigation **Band 2**
Table: p.4

Keiner, Jeffrey (Florida)
Profile: p.175
Construction **Band 3**
Table: p.154

Keith, Calvin (Oregon)
Profile: p.594
Employment **Band 4**
Table: p.589

Keker, John (California)
Profile: p.66
Intellectual Property **Band 3**
Table: p.48
Litigation **Band 1**
Table: p.50

Keleher, William (New Mexico)
Profile: p.438
Real Estate **Band 3**
Table: p.437

Kelleher, Thomas (Georgia)
Profile: p.208
Construction **Band 1**
Table: p.184

Keller, Brad (Washington)
Profile: p.713
Litigation **Band 2**
Table: p.709

Keller, Bruce P (New York)
Profile: p.520
Media & Entertainment **Band 4**
Table: p.485

Keller, Don (California)
Profile: p.66
Communications **Band 5**
Table: p.34

Keller, Mary (Texas)
Profile: p.675
Insurance **Band 3**
Table: p.659

Keller, Stanley
(Massachusetts)
Profile: p.357
Corporate/M&A **Band 4**
Table: p.340

Kelley, David (Minnesota)
Profile: p.376
Real Estate **Band 1**
Table: p.374

Kelley, Jay (Texas)
Profile: p.675
Energy **Band 3**
Table: p.653
Projects **Band 2**
Table: p.664

Kelley, John (Georgia)
Profile: p.208
Corporate/M&A **Band 3**
Table: p.187

Kelley, Timothy (Illinois)
Profile: p.263
Media & Entertainment **Band 2**
Table: p.247

Kellner, Robert (Maryland)
Profile: p.333
Employment **Band 2**
Table: p.329

Kellogg, Michael
(District of Columbia)
Profile: p.137
Communications **Band 1**
Table: p.107

Kelly, Henry (Illinois)
Profile: p.263
Communications **Band 3**
Table: p.229

Kelly, Mark (Texas)
Profile: p.675
Corporate/M&A **Band 2**
Table: p.649

Kelly, Mark (Florida)
Profile: p.175
Employment **Band 3**
Table: p.157

Kelly, Thomas (New York)
Profile: p.520
Insurance **Band 3**
Table: p.477

Kelly, Timothy (Minnesota)
Profile: p.376
Litigation **Band 1**
Table: p.372

Kelly, Walter (Wisconsin)
Profile: p.729
Employment **Band 3**
Table: p.724

Kemp, Will (Nevada)
Profile: p.413
Litigation **Band 3**
Table: p.409

Kendall, David
(District of Columbia)
Profile: p.137
Litigation **Band 2**
Table: p.123
Media & Entertainment **Band 1**
Table: p.125

Kennedy, Dennis (Nevada)
Profile: p.413
Litigation **Band 1**
Table: p.409

Kennedy, Donald J (New York)
Profile: p.521
Shipping **Band 4**
Table: p.496

Kennedy, Elizabeth Gregg
(Iowa)
Profile: p.293
Employment **Band 2**
Table: p.288

Kennedy, Mike (California)
Profile: p.66
Communications **Band 3**
Table: p.34
Corporate/M&A **Band 3**
Table: p.37

Kennedy, Thomas H
(New York)
Profile: p.521
Corporate/M&A **Band 5**

Kenyon, Charity (California)
Profile: p.66
Media & Entertainment **Band 3**
Table: p.53

Kern, David B (Wisconsin)
Profile: p.729
Employment **Band 1**
Table: p.725

Kerr, Diane G (New York)
Profile: p.521

Kerr, John (New York)
Profile: p.521
Arbitration **Band 2**
Table: p.443

Kessler, Mark (Pennsylvania)
Profile: p.616
Corporate/M&A **Band 4**
Table: p.599

Kessler, Philip J (Michigan)
Profile: p.366
Litigation **Band 3**
Table: p.364

Ketchmark, Michael
(Missouri)
Profile: p.392
Employment **Band 2**
Table: p.387

Key, Chris (New Mexico)
Profile: p.438
Employment **Band 1**
Table: p.434

Keyes, David (Texas)
Profile: p.675
Banking & Finance **Band 2**
Table: p.645

Keyes, Jeffrey (Minnesota)
Profile: p.376
Litigation **Band 2**
Table: p.372

Keyser, Denise (New Jersey)
Profile: p.431
Employment **Band 3**
Table: p.427

Kidd, John (New York)
Profile: p.521
Intellectual Property **Band 2**
Table: p.479

Kiely, Bruce
(District of Columbia)
Profile: p.137
Energy **Band 5**
Table: p.115

Kienbaum, Thomas
(Michigan)
Profile: p.366
Employment **Band 1**
Table: p.363

Kiernan, John S (New York)
Profile: p.521
Litigation **Band 5**
Table: p.481

Kiessling, Rob (New York)
Profile: p.521
Banking & Finance **Band 1**
Table: p.445

Kiggans, Thomas (Louisiana)
Profile: p.317
Employment **Band 4**
Table: p.311

Kikoler, Stephen (Illinois)
Profile: p.263
Construction **Band 3**
Table: p.231

Kilb, Brian (California)
Profile: p.66
Banking & Finance **Band 2**
Table: p.30

Kilbane, Thomas (Ohio)
Profile: p.576
Litigation **Band 1**
Table: p.570

Kilberg, William
(District of Columbia)
Profile: p.137
Employment **Band 3**
Table: p.112

Kilgore III, Cada (Georgia)
Profile: p.208
Energy **Band 1**
Table: p.191

Killmer, Darold (Colorado)
Profile: p.84
Employment **Band 1**
Table: p.77

Killworth, Richard (Ohio)
Profile: p.576
Intellectual Property **Band 1**
Table: p.568

Kim, Gregory R (Hawaii)
Profile: p.218
Corporate/M&A **Band 1**
Table: p.212

Kim, Robert C (Nevada)
Profile: p.413
Corporate/M&A **Band 3**
Table: p.406

Kimball, John D (New York)
Profile: p.521
Shipping ○
Table: p.496

King, Bruce (Florida)
Profile: p.175
Construction **Band 2**
Table: p.154

King, David (Florida)
Profile: p.175
Litigation **Band 3**
Table: p.165

King, Diane (Colorado)
Profile: p.84
Employment **Band 2**
Table: p.77

King, G Roger (Ohio)
Profile: p.576
Employment **Band 4**
Table: p.565

King, Kenton (California)
Profile: p.66
Capital Markets **Band 2**
Table: p.32
Communications **Band 3**
Table: p.34
Corporate/M&A **Band 2**
Table: p.37

King, Richard (Missouri)
Profile: p.392
Real Estate **Band 4**
Table: p.391

King, William (Virginia)
Profile: p.704
Litigation **Band 2**
Table: p.702

King Jr, George S (South Carolina)
Profile: p.629
Corporate/M&A **Band 1**
Table: p.624

King Jr., Evans (West Virginia)
Profile: p.722
Corporate/M&A **Band 3**
Table: p.714

Kingery, Gregory D (Iowa)
Profile: p.293
Real Estate **Band 4**
Table: p.291

Kirby, Matthew T (California)
Profile: p.66

Banking & Finance **Band 2**
Table: p.30

Kirchhoefer, Gregg (Illinois)
Profile: p.263
Communications **Band 2**
Table: p.229

Kirk, James (Oklahoma)
Profile: p.586
Litigation **Band 2**
Table: p.583

Kirkham, Steven (Tennessee)
Profile: p.641
Real Estate **Band 3**
Table: p.640

Kirkland, David (Texas)
Profile: p.675
Corporate/M&A **Band 2**
Table: p.649

Kirmis, Lyle (North Dakota)
Profile: p.557
Litigation **Band 2**
Table: p.556

Kirsch, Robert
(Massachusetts)
Profile: p.357
Environment **Band 2**
Table: p.344

Kirsch, William S (Illinois)
Profile: p.263
Corporate/M&A **Band 4**
Table: p.233

Kirschbaum, Howard (Illinois)
Profile: p.263
Real Estate **Band 4**
Table: p.249

Kirschner, Kenneth (Florida)
Profile: p.175
Corporate/M&A **Band 4**
Table: p.156

Kirwan, BJ (California)
Profile: p.66
Environment **Band 2**
Table: p.43

Kitchel, Chris (Oregon)
Profile: p.594
Employment **Band 3**
Table: p.589

Klaper, Martin J (Indiana)
Profile: p.284
Employment **Band 3**
Table: p.279

Klawiter, Donald
(District of Columbia)
Profile: p.137
Antitrust **Band 4**
Table: p.103

Kleban, Barry (Pennsylvania)
Profile: p.616
Insolvency **Band 3**
Table: p.607

Klee, Kenneth N (California)
Profile: p.66
Insolvency **Band 1**
Table: p.44

Klein, Daniel (Georgia)
Profile: p.208
Employment **Band 3**
Table: p.188

Klein, Frederick
(District of Columbia)
Profile: p.137
Real Estate **Band 2**
Table: p.127

Klein, Justin (Pennsylvania)
Profile: p.616
Corporate/M&A **Band 2**
Table: p.599

Klein, Linda B (New York)
Profile: p.521

K

997

LEADING LAWYERS INDEX

Capital Markets **Band 4**
Table: p.451

Klein, Michael
(District of Columbia)
Profile: p.137
Litigation **Band 3**
Table: p.123

Klein, Steven (Louisiana)
Profile: p.317
Corporate/M&A **Band 5**
Table: p.309

Kleinbard, Edward (New York)
Profile: p.521
Tax **Band 1**
Table: p.499

Klenk, James (Illinois)
Profile: p.263
Media & Entertainment **Band 2**
Table: p.247

Klepper, Martin
(District of Columbia)
Profile: p.138
Energy **Band 3**
Table: p.115
Projects **Band 2**
Table: p.126

Klett, Edwin L. (Pennsylvania)
Profile: p.616
Litigation **Band 3**
Table: p.611

Klevorn, Andrew (Illinois)
Profile: p.263
Antitrust **Band u**
Table: p.224

Klimko, Justin (Michigan)
Profile: p.366
Corporate/M&A **Band 2**
Table: p.361

Kline, Scot (Vermont)
Profile: p.697
Litigation **Band 3**
Table: p.695

Kling, Lou R (New York)
Profile: p.521
Corporate/M&A **Band 4**
Table: p.460

Klinger, Edward
(North Dakota)
Profile: p.557
Litigation **Band 2**
Table: p.556

Knapp, Spencer (Vermont)
Profile: p.697
Corporate/M&A **Band 1**
Table: p.692

Knauss, Charles
(District of Columbia)
Profile: p.138
Environment **Band 4**
Table: p.117

Knecht, Denise (Ohio)
Profile: p.576
Employment **Band 2**
Table: p.564

Knickrehm, Donald (Idaho)
Profile: p.222
Real Estate **Band 3**
Table: p.222

Knight, G Marcus
(South Carolina)
Profile: p.629
Corporate/M&A **Band 2**
Table: p.624

Knight, James T (New York)
Profile: p.521
Banking & Finance **Band 3**
Table: p.445

Knight, Robert (Montana)
Profile: p.398,398
Real Estate **Band 1**
Table: p.397

Knight Jr, Donald (Georgia)
Profile: p.208
Corporate/M&A **Band 4**
Table: p.187

Knipe, Quentin (Idaho)
Profile: p.222,222
Real Estate **Band 3**
Table: p.222

Knowles, Leo (Nebraska)
Profile: p.405
Litigation **Band 2**
Table: p.403

Knudsen, Eric (Vermont)
Profile: p.697
Real Estate **U**
Table: p.696

Knudson, David L (South Dakota)
Profile: p.633
Corporate/M&A **Band 1**
Table: p.630

Knudson, Kathryn L (Georgia)
Profile: p.208
Banking & Finance **Band 2**
Table: p.183

Knull, William H III (Texas)
Profile: p.675
Litigation **Band 4**
Table: p.663

Kobayashi Jr, Bert T (Hawaii)
Profile: p.218
Litigation **Band 2**
Table: p.215

Kociubes, Joseph
(Massachusetts)
Profile: p.357
Litigation **Band 2**
Table: p.349

Koenigsberg, Fred (New York)
Profile: p.521
Intellectual Property **Band 5**
Table: p.479

Kohl, Glen (California)
Profile: p.66
Tax **Band 1**
Table: p.58

Kohn, Alan (Missouri)
Profile: p.392
Litigation **Band 1**
Table: p.389

Kohn, Joseph (Pennsylvania)
Profile: p.617
Antitrust **Band 2**
Table: p.596

Kohn, Richard (Illinois)
Profile: p.264
Banking & Finance **Band 2**
Table: p.226

Kokoruda, Thomas (Missouri)
Profile: p.392
Litigation **Band 3**
Table: p.389

Kolb, Daniel (New York)
Profile: p.521
Litigation **Band 3**
Table: p.481

Komeiji, John T (Hawaii)
Profile: p.218
Litigation **Band 3**
Table: p.215

Koob, Charles E (New York)
Profile: p.521
Antitrust **Band 2**
Table: p.441
Litigation **Band 4**
Table: p.481

Koren, Ed (Florida)
Profile: p.175
Tax **Band 1**
Table: p.170

Korff, Phyllis G (New York)
Profile: p.521
Capital Markets **Band 4**
Table: p.448

Korman, Marty (California)
Profile: p.66
Communications **Band 4**
Table: p.34

Kornberg, Alan (New York)
Profile: p.521
Insolvency **Band 2**
Table: p.472

Kornreich, David (Florida)
Profile: p.175
Employment **Band 3**
Table: p.158

Kotchka, Malani (Nevada)
Profile: p.414
Employment **Band 2**
Table: p.408

Kovner, Victor (New York)
Profile: p.521
Media & Entertainment **Band 1**
Table: p.485

Kozak, John (Illinois)
Profile: p.264
Intellectual Property **Band 3**
Table: p.244

Kozyak, John W (Florida)
Profile: p.175
Insolvency **Band 1**
Table: p.162

Kraft, Barbara Simpson
(Alaska)
Profile: p.15
Corporate/M&A **Band 2**
Table: p.9

Kraftson, Daniel
(District of Columbia)
Profile: p.138
Construction **Band 2**
Table: p.110

Krambeck, James (Iowa)
Profile: p.293
Corporate/M&A **Band 1**
Table: p.286

Kramer, Jay (Arizona)
Profile: p.22
Real Estate **Band 2**
Table: p.20

Kramer, Morris J (New York)
Profile: p.522

Krapf, Robert (Delaware)
Profile: p.100
Real Estate **Band 1**
Table: p.99

Krasnow, Jordan
(Massachusetts)
Profile: p.357
Real Estate **Band 1**
Table: p.351

Krasow, Herbert (Connecticut)
Profile: p.93
Real Estate **Band 2**
Table: p.91

Kraus, Alan E (New Jersey)
Profile: p.431
Litigation **Band 3**
Table: p.428

Kraus, Bruce R (New York)
Profile: p.522
Communications **Band 3**
Table: p.456

Kravitt, Jason H P (New York)
Profile: p.522

Capital Markets **Band 1**
Table: p.453

Krebs, Arno (Texas)
Profile: p.675
Insurance **Band 4**
Table: p.659

Krebs, Stephen (Texas)
Profile: p.675
Projects **Band 2**
Table: p.664

Kreider, Gary (Ohio)
Profile: p.576
Corporate/M&A **Band 2**
Table: p.562

Kreiger, Arthur
(Massachusetts)
Profile: p.357
Environment **Band 4**
Table: p.344

Krieger, Thomas (West Virginia)
Profile: p.722
Employment **Band 1**
Table: p.717

Kringel, Jerry (Wisconsin)
Profile: p.729
Corporate/M&A **Band 3**
Table: p.723

Kristol, Daniel (Delaware)
Profile: p.99,100
Real Estate **Band 3**
Table: p.99

Kronk, Catherine (Vermont)
Profile: p.697
Real Estate **Band 2**
Table: p.696

Krouse Jr, George R
(New York)
Profile: p.522
Capital Markets **Band 4**
Table: p.448

Krovatin, Gerald (New Jersey)
Profile: p.431
Litigation **Band 2**
Table: p.428

Krueger, Herbert W (Illinois)
Profile: p.264
Real Estate **Band 4**
Table: p.249

Krupka, Robert G (California)
Profile: p.66
Intellectual Property **Band 2**
Table: p.48

Kruse, Layne (Texas)
Profile: p.675
Antitrust **Band 3**
Table: p.644

Kubicek, David W (Iowa)
Profile: p.293
Real Estate **Band 1**
Table: p.291

Kudenholdt, Stephen S
(New York)
Profile: p.522
Capital Markets **Band 4**
Table: p.453

Kummer, Thomas F (Nevada)
Profile: p.414
Litigation **Band 2**
Table: p.409

Kumpe, Peter (Arkansas)
Profile: p.27
Litigation **Band 3**
Table: p.25

Kuney, David
(District of Columbia)
Profile: p.138
Insolvency **Band 3**
Table: p.119

Kunkel, William (Illinois)
Profile: p.264
Corporate/M&A **Band 3**
Table: p.233

Kuntz, Michael (Washington)
Profile: p.713
Real Estate **Band 2**
Table: p.711

Kunz, C Thomas (New York)
Profile: p.522
Capital Markets **Band 1**
Table: p.453

Kunz, Donald (Michigan)
Profile: p.366
Corporate/M&A **Band 3**
Table: p.361

Kupec, Christopher C (North Carolina)
Profile: p.553
Banking & Finance **Band 2**
Table: p.544

Kurtzon, Michael S (Illinois)
Profile: p.264
Real Estate **Band 3**
Table: p.249

Kushner, Harold B (Alabama)
Profile: p.7
Corporate/M&A **Band 2**
Table: p.1

Kushner, Louis (Pennsylvania)
Profile: p.617
Employment **Band 1**
Table: p.601

Kutler, Marilyn (Pennsylvania)
Profile: p.617
Real Estate **Band 5**
Table: p.613

Kutzschbach, George (Texas)
Profile: p.676
Energy **Band 3**
Table: p.653

Kwasnick, Raymond
(Massachusetts)
Profile: p.357
Real Estate **Band 2**
Table: p.351

Kyper, James (Pennsylvania)
Profile: p.617
Intellectual Property **Band 4**
Table: p.609

L

La Suer, Gene (Iowa)
Profile: p.293
Employment **Band 2**
Table: p.288

Labate, Robert (Illinois)
Profile: p.264
Media & Entertainment **Band 2**
Table: p.247

Labinger, Lynette (Rhode Island)
Profile: p.623
Employment **Band 1**
Table: p.621

Lacy, Peyton (Alabama)
Profile: p.8
Employment **Band 3**
Table: p.3

Ladov, Donald (Pennsylvania)
Profile: p.617
Employment **Band 1**
Table: p.602

Lafferty, William (Delaware)
Profile: p.100
Litigation **Band 4**
Table: p.98

LaFuze, William L (Texas)
Profile: p.676
Intellectual Property **Band 1**

LEADING LAWYERS INDEX

Table: p.661

Laird, Michael (Oklahoma)
Profile: p.586
Real Estate Band 3
Table: p.585

Lake, William T
(District of Columbia)
Profile: p.138
Communications Band 3
Table: p.107

Lalle, Wayne (Virginia)
Profile: p.704
Construction Band 3
Table: p.698

Lamb, William S (New York)
Profile: p.522
Energy Band 2
Table: p.468

Lambert, LeRoy (New York)
Profile: p.522
Shipping Band 4
Table: p.496

Lamdin III, William (Montana)
Profile: p.398
Corporate/M&A Band 1
Table: p.394

Lamm, Carolyn
(District of Columbia)
Profile: p.138
Arbitration Band 2
Table: p.106

Lamson, William (Nebraska)
Profile: p.405
Litigation Band 1
Table: p.403

Landefeld, Stewart
(Washington)
Profile: p.713
Corporate/M&A Band 2
Table: p.706

Lane, David (Virginia)
Profile: p.704
Construction Band 1
Table: p.698

Lane, Robert (Pennsylvania)
Profile: p.617
Real Estate Band 3
Table: p.613

Lane, Thomas (West Virginia)
Profile: p.722
Real Estate Band 1
Table: p.720

Lang, Jane
(District of Columbia)
Profile: p.138
Employment Band 2
Table: p.112

Langan, J Andrew (Illinois)
Profile: p.264
Antitrust Band 2
Table: p.224

Langerman, Amy (Arizona)
Profile: p.22
Employment Band 2
Table: p.18

Langevin, Judith Bevis
(Minnesota)
Profile: p.376
Employment Band 3
Table: p.371

Lanier, Randolph (Alabama)
Profile: p.8
Real Estate Band 2
Table: p.6

Lansky, David (Arizona)
Profile: p.22
Real Estate Band 1
Table: p.20

Lapointe, Mary Jane
(Indiana)
Profile: p.284
Employment Band 2
Table: p.279

Lapowsky, Robert
(Pennsylvania)
Profile: p.617
Insolvency Band 3
Table: p.607

Lareau, Richard G.
(Minnesota)
Profile: p.376
Corporate/M&A Band 1
Table: p.369

LaRose, Edward (Florida)
Profile: p.175
Antitrust Band 3
Table: p.151

Larsen, Tracy (Michigan)
Profile: p.366
Corporate/M&A Band 3
Table: p.361

Larson, David (Wyoming)
Profile: p.734,735
Real Estate Band 2
Table: p.734

Larson, John (California)
Profile: p.
Corporate/M&A Band 4
Table: p.37

LaRue , Denise K (Indiana)
Profile: p.284
Employment Band 2
Table: p.279

Lascher, Alan (New York)
Profile: p.522
Real Estate Band 3
Table: p.493

Lassiter, Donnell (North Carolina)
Profile: p.553
Banking & Finance Band 2
Table: p.544

Latimer, Kenneth A (Illinois)
Profile: p.264
Banking & Finance Band 4
Table: p.226

Laupheimer, Ann Blair
(Pennsylvania)
Profile: p.617
Litigation Band 3
Table: p.611

Laurie, Ronald S (California)
Profile: p.67
Intellectual Property Band 3
Table: p.48

Laurie, Ty (Illinois)
Profile: p.264
Construction Band 3
Table: p.231

Lause, Michael (Missouri)
Profile: p.392
Corporate/M&A Band 2
Table: p.386

Lavey, Jack (Arkansas)
Profile: p.27
Employment Band 1
Table: p.24

Lawless, Mark (Texas)
Profile: p.676
Insurance Band 3
Table: p.659

Lawrence, Melinda (North Carolina)
Profile: p.553
Employment Band 3
Table: p.547

Lawson, Jack (Indiana)
Profile: p.283,284
Real Estate Band 4

Table: p.282

Laxalt, Bruce (Nevada)
Profile: p.414
Litigation Band 3
Table: p.409

Lazarow, Warren (California)
Profile: p.
Capital Markets Band 3
Table: p.32
Communications Band 5
Table: p.34

Leach, Donald (Ohio)
Profile: p.576
Construction Band 3
Table: p.560

Lebau, Steve (Maryland)
Profile: p.333
Employment Band 2
Table: p.328

Lebowitz, Molly (Vermont)
Profile: p.697
Real Estate Band 2
Table: p.696

Ledbetter, Cheryl
(West Virginia)
Profile: p.722
Employment Band 2
Table: p.717

Leddy, Bruce E (Maine)
Profile: p.325
Real Estate Band 3
Table: p.324

Leddy, Mark
(District of Columbia)
Profile: p.138,523
Antitrust Band 1
Table: p.103

Lederman, Alan (Florida)
Profile: p.171,175
Tax Band 1
Table: p.170

Lederman, Lawrence
(New York)
Profile: p.523

LeDuc, André (Illinois)
Profile: p.264
Tax Band 4
Table: p.252

Lee, Bill (Massachusetts)
Profile: p.357
Intellectual Property Band 1
Table: p.348

Lee, Carolyn Joy (New York)
Profile: p.523
Tax Band 4
Table: p.499

Lee, Jeffrey (Alabama)
Profile: p.8
Employment Band 3
Table: p.3

Lee, Stephen (Indiana)
Profile: p.284
Real Estate Band 3
Table: p.282

Lee, Steven J (New York)
Profile: p.523
Intellectual Property Band 5
Table: p.479

Lefeber, Peter (Connecticut)
Profile: p.93
Employment Band 4
Table: p.89

Leff, Philip (Iowa)
Profile: p.292,293
Real Estate Band 4
Table: p.291

Lefkowitz, Stephen
(New York)
Profile: p.523

Real Estate Band 2
Table: p.493

Legler, Mitchell (Florida)
Profile: p.175
Corporate/M&A Band 4
Table: p.156

Lehman, Steven (Montana)
Profile: p.398
Employment Band 2
Table: p.395

Leiby, Larry (Florida)
Profile: p.175
Construction ✪
Table: p.154

Leichtling, Ely A (Wisconsin)
Profile: p.729
Employment Band 2
Table: p.725

Leinwand, Robert (Oregon)
Profile: p.594
Employment Band u
Table: p.589

Leisner, Richard (Florida)
Profile: p.175
Corporate/M&A Band 3
Table: p.156

Lemein, Gregg D (Illinois)
Profile: p.253,264
Tax Band 3
Table: p.252

Lemly, Tom (Washington)
Profile: p.713
Employment Band 1
Table: p.708

Lenhard, Kirk (Nevada)
Profile: p.414
Litigation Band 1
Table: p.409

Lennon, Daniel
(District of Columbia)
Profile: p.138
Corporate/M&A Band 3
Table: p.111

Lents, Donald (Missouri)
Profile: p.392
Corporate/M&A Band 3
Table: p.386

Leon, Christopher (North Carolina)
Profile: p.553
Banking & Finance Band 3
Table: p.544

Leon, Michael
(Massachusetts)
Profile: p.357
Environment Band 4
Table: p.344

Leonard, Jana (Oklahoma)
Profile: p.586
Employment Band 2
Table: p.581

Leonard, Stephen
(Massachusetts)
Profile: p.357
Environment Band 2
Table: p.344

Leong , Donna Y L (Hawaii)
Profile: p.218
Real Estate Band 2
Table: p.217

Leong, Ron (Hawaii)
Profile: p.218
Employment Band 2
Table: p.214

LePatner, Barry (New York)
Profile: p.523
Construction Band 4
Table: p.458

Lerach, William (California)
Profile: p.67
Litigation Band 1
Table: p.50

Lerman, Bradley (Illinois)
Profile: p.264
Litigation Band 5
Table: p.245

Lerman, Cary (California)
Profile: p.67
Insurance Band 4
Table: p.46

Lerner, Jonathan J (New York)
Profile: p.523
Litigation Band 2
Table: p.481

Lerner, Stephen (Ohio)
Profile: p.576
Banking & Finance Band 2
Table: p.559

Lesesne Jr, Louis (North Carolina)
Profile: p.553
Employment Band 1
Table: p.547

Lesser, Bruce (Pennsylvania)
Profile: p.617
Banking & Finance Band 3
Table: p.598

Lesser, Henry (California)
Profile: p.67
Corporate/M&A Band 4
Table: p.37

Lesser, Steven (Florida)
Profile: p.175
Construction Band 3
Table: p.154

Lester, David (Kentucky)
Profile: p.305
Corporate/M&A Band 3
Table: p.300

Letzler, Kenneth
(District of Columbia)
Profile: p.138
Antitrust Band 5
Table: p.103

Leukart, Barbara (Ohio)
Profile: p.576
Employment Band 3
Table: p.565

Levi, Stuart D (New York)
Profile: p.523
Communications Band 3
Table: p.456

Levin, Barry (California)
Profile: p.67
Insurance Band 3
Table: p.46

Levin, Edward J (Maryland)
Profile: p.333
Real Estate Band 1
Table: p.331

Levin, Jack S (Illinois)
Profile: p.264
Corporate/M&A Band 1
Table: p.233
Tax Band 1
Table: p.252

Levin, Jim (Wisconsin)
Profile: p.729
Real Estate Band 3
Table: p.727

Levin, Peter (New York)
Profile: p.523
Banking & Finance Band 2
Table: p.445

Levine, Henry D
(District of Columbia)
Profile: p.138
Communications Band 4

LEADING LAWYERS INDEX

Table: p.107

Levine, Lee
(District of Columbia)
Profile: p.138
Media & Entertainment **Band 1**
Table: p.125

Levine, Richard A (Delaware)
Profile: p.99,100
Real Estate **Band 2**
Table: p.99

Levine, Richard E (Maryland)
Profile: p.333
Real Estate **Band 3**
Table: p.331

Levine, Ronald (Colorado)
Profile: p.84
Corporate/M&A **Band 1**
Table: p.75

Levit, Jay (Virginia)
Profile: p.704
Employment **Band 3**
Table: p.701

Levy, Mark (Colorado)
Profile: p.84
Corporate/M&A **Band 2**
Table: p.75

Lewin, John (Maryland)
Profile: p.333
Litigation **Band 2**
Table: p.330

Lewis, Daniel
(District of Columbia)
Profile: p.138
Insolvency **Band 1**
Table: p.119

Lewis, John (Ohio)
Profile: p.576
Employment **Band 4**
Table: p.565

Lewis, Sidney (Louisiana)
Profile: p.317
Employment **Band 4**
Table: p.311

Lewis, Terry (Florida)
Profile: p.175
Environment **Band 4**
Table: p.160

Lewis, William
(District of Columbia)
Profile: p.138
Environment **Band 3**
Table: p.117

Lewkow, Victor (New York)
Profile: p.523

Libbey, Keith A (Minnesota)
Profile: p.376
Corporate/M&A **Band 2**
Table: p.369

Libin, Jerome
(District of Columbia)
Profile: p.131,138
Tax **Band 2**
Table: p.130

Lichten, Harold
(Massachusetts)
Profile: p.357
Employment **Band 2**
Table: p.341

Liddle, Jeffrey (New York)
Profile: p.523
Employment **Band 2**
Table: p.466

Liddon, Rob (Tennessee)
Profile: p.641
Real Estate **Band 1**
Table: p.640

Liebenberg, Roberta
(Pennsylvania)
Profile: p.617

Antitrust **Band 2**
Table: p.596

Liebman, Richard (Oregon)
Profile: p.594
Employment **Band 1**
Table: p.589

Liebmann, Jeff S (New York)
Profile: p.523
Insurance **Band 1**
Table: p.477

Liggett, Luther (Ohio)
Profile: p.576
Construction **Band 4**
Table: p.560

Lightfoot, Warren (Alabama)
Profile: p.8
Litigation **Band 1**
Table: p.4

Lightsey, Wallace (South Carolina)
Profile: p.629
Litigation **Band 3**
Table: p.626

Liles, Rutledge (Florida)
Profile: p.175
Litigation **Band 3**
Table: p.165

Lillie, Charisse (Pennsylvania)
Profile: p.617
Employment **Band 3**
Table: p.602

Lillis, William (Iowa)
Profile: p.293
Real Estate **Band 2**
Table: p.291

Lindauer, Erik D (New York)
Profile: p.523
Banking & Finance **Band 2**
Table: p.445

Lindefjeld, Robert
(Pennsylvania)
Profile: p.617
Intellectual Property **U**
Table: p.609

Lindenbaum, Samuel H
(New York)
Profile: p.524
Real Estate **Band 1**
Table: p.493

Lindley, Greg (Utah)
Profile: p.690
Corporate/M&A **Band 4**
Table: p.684

Lindsey, David (New York)
Profile: p.524
Arbitration **Band 3**
Table: p.443

Linesch, David (Florida)
Profile: p.175
Employment **Band 1**
Table: p.157

Linfield, James (Colorado)
Profile: p.84
Corporate/M&A **Band 1**
Table: p.75

Linklater, Joe (Illinois)
Profile: p.265
Litigation **Band 5**
Table: p.245

Linstroth, Tod (Wisconsin)
Profile: p.729
Corporate/M&A **Band 1**
Table: p.723

Linton, John (South Carolina)
Profile: p.629
Litigation **Band 2**
Table: p.626

Lipman, Andy

(District of Columbia)
Profile: p.139
Communications **Band 3**
Table: p.107

Lipman, Frederick
(Pennsylvania)
Profile: p.617
Corporate/M&A **Band 4**
Table: p.599

Lips, Alan (Ohio)
Profile: p.576
Employment **Band 4**
Table: p.565

Lipsey, Charles
(District of Columbia)
Profile: p.139
Intellectual Property **Band 2**
Table: p.122

Lipson, Lawrence (New York)
Profile: p.524
Real Estate **Band 2**
Table: p.493

Lipton, Martin (New York)
Profile: p.524
Corporate/M&A ✪
Table: p.460

Lipton, Richard (Illinois)
Profile: p.253
Tax **Band 2**
Table: p.252

Lisher, Mary (Indiana)
Profile: p.284
Real Estate **Band 3**
Table: p.282

Lisicky, Joseph (Delaware)
Profile: p.100
Real Estate **Band 3**
Table: p.99

Lisker, Steven (Arizona)
Profile: p.22
Real Estate **Band 1**
Table: p.20

Lisman, Carl H. (Vermont)
Profile: p.697,697
Real Estate **Band 3**
Table: p.696

Litchford, Hal (Florida)
Profile: p.175
Antitrust **Band 3**
Table: p.151

Litt, Daniel
(District of Columbia)
Profile: p.139
Insolvency **Band 3**
Table: p.119

Little, David (Utah)
Profile: p.690
Corporate/M&A **Band 4**
Table: p.684

Little, Nancy (Virginia)
Profile: p.704,704
Real Estate **Band 3**
Table: p.703

Little Jr, Curtis
(New Hampshire)
Profile: p.422
Corporate/M&A **Band 2**
Table: p.415

Litwin, Stuart M (Illinois)
Profile: p.265
Banking & Finance **Band 3**
Table: p.226

Livingston, Daniel
(Connecticut)
Profile: p.93
Employment **Band 3**
Table: p.88

Livingston, Louis (Oregon)
Profile: p.594
Employment **Band 2**

Table: p.589

Livingston, Theodore A
(Illinois)
Profile: p.265
Communications **Band 1**
Table: p.229

Lloyd, Brian (Utah)
Profile: p.690
Corporate/M&A **Band 2**
Table: p.684

Lockett, Laurel (Florida)
Profile: p.175
Environment **Band 4**
Table: p.160

Loftis, James
(District of Columbia)
Profile: p.139
Antitrust **Band 3**
Table: p.103

Loftis Jr, W Randolph (North Carolina)
Profile: p.553
Employment **Band 1**
Table: p.548

Logan, Kenneth (New York)
Profile: p.524
Antitrust **Band 2**
Table: p.441

Logan III, Ben H (California)
Profile: p.67
Insolvency **Band 3**
Table: p.44

Lohr Jr, Walter (Maryland)
Profile: p.333
Corporate/M&A **Band 3**
Table: p.327

Lonardo, Joseph (District of Columbia)
Profile: p.139
Environment **Band 2**
Table: p.567

Londa, Jeffrey (Texas)
Profile: p.676
Employment **Band 3**
Table: p.652

London, Alan (Pennsylvania)
Profile: p.617
Banking & Finance **Band 3**
Table: p.598

London, Eric (West Virginia)
Profile: p.722
Real Estate **Band 2**
Table: p.720

London, Martin (New York)
Profile: p.524
Litigation **Band 2**
Table: p.481

Lonergan, Matthew
(Tennessee)
Profile: p.641
Employment **Band 3**
Table: p.637

Long, Clay (Georgia)
Profile: p.208
Corporate/M&A **Band 2**
Table: p.187

Long, Robert (California)
Profile: p.67
Litigation **Band 3**
Table: p.50

Long, Thomas (Wyoming)
Profile: p.735
Corporate/M&A **Band 1**
Table: p.730

Lonnquist, Judith
(Washington)
Profile: p.713
Employment **Band 1**
Table: p.708

Looman, James (Illinois)
Profile: p.265

Lopatka, Kenneth (Illinois)
Profile: p.265
Employment **Band 3**
Table: p.236

Lopes, James (California)
Profile: p.67
Insolvency **Band 4**
Table: p.44

Lord, Craig (Pennsylvania)
Profile: p.617
Real Estate **Band 3**
Table: p.613

Lorensen, Charles
(West Virginia)
Profile: p.722
Corporate/M&A **Band 3**
Table: p.714

Lotstein, James I
(Connecticut)
Profile: p.93
Corporate/M&A **Band 2**
Table: p.87

Lottner, Alan B (Colorado)
Profile: p.84
Real Estate **Band 3**
Table: p.81

Loulakis, Michael (Virginia)
Profile: p.704
Construction **Band 2**
Table: p.698

Loumiet, Carlos (Florida)
Profile: p.175
Banking & Finance **Band 2**
Table: p.152

Louthian Jr., Herbert W.
(South Carolina)
Profile: p.629
Employment **Band 1**
Table: p.625

Louthian Sr., Herbert W.
(South Carolina)
Profile: p.629
Employment **Band 1**
Table: p.625

Love III, Charles M (West Virginia)
Profile: p.722
Litigation **Band 2**
Table: p.718

Loveless, Scott (Utah)
Profile: p.690
Corporate/M&A **Band 2**
Table: p.684

Lowinger, Frederick C
(Illinois)
Profile: p.265
Corporate/M&A **Band 2**
Table: p.233

Lubin, Andrew (Connecticut)
Profile: p.93
Real Estate **Band 2**
Table: p.91

Lubin, Donald G (Illinois)
Profile: p.265
Corporate/M&A **Band 2**
Table: p.233

Lucas, Walter (New Jersey)
Profile: p.431
Employment **Band 1**
Table: p.426

Luce, Michael (South Dakota)
Profile: p.633
Litigation **Band 1**
Table: p.632

Lucero, Gene (California)
Profile: p.67
Environment **Band 3**
Table: p.43

LEADING LAWYERS INDEX

Ludwiszewski, Raymond
(District of Columbia)
Profile: p.139
Environment Band 4
Table: p.117

Luger, Andrew (Minnesota)
Profile: p.376
Litigation Band 3
Table: p.372

Lukens, John (West Virginia)
Profile: p.722
Corporate/M&A Band 1
Table: p.714

Lukey, Joan (Massachusetts)
Profile: p.357
Employment Band 2
Table: p.342
Litigation Band 2
Table: p.349

Lundberg, Andrew (California)
Profile: p.68
Insurance Band 4
Table: p.46

Lunin, Joseph (New Jersey)
Profile: p.431
Corporate/M&A Band 2
Table: p.425

Lunsford III, Rodgers
(Georgia)
Profile: p.208
Intellectual Property Band 4
Table: p.195

Lupo, Raphael
(District of Columbia)
Profile: p.139
Intellectual Property Band 2
Table: p.122

Lurey, Alfred (Georgia)
Profile: p.208
Insolvency Band 2
Table: p.193

Lurey, Michael (California)
Profile: p.68
Insolvency Band 2
Table: p.44

Lurie, Paul (Illinois)
Profile: p.265
Construction Band 1
Table: p.231

Lurye, William (Louisiana)
Profile: p.317
Employment Band 2
Table: p.310

Luscombe II, George A
(Illinois)
Profile: p.265
Tax Band 4
Table: p.252

Lusk, Neva (West Virginia)
Profile: p.722
Litigation Band 3
Table: p.718

Lustberg, Lawrence (New Jersey)
Profile: p.431
Litigation Band 1
Table: p.428

Lyle, George R. (Alaska)
Profile: p.15
Environment Band 3
Table: p.12

Lyman, Bill (Illinois)
Profile: p.265
Construction Band 2
Table: p.231

Lynch, James M (Illinois)
Profile: p.253,265
Tax Band 4
Table: p.252

Lynch, Larry (Wisconsin)
Profile: p.729
Employment Band 3
Table: p.725

Lynch, Patrick (California)
Profile: p.68
Antitrust Band 3
Table: p.29
Litigation Band 3
Table: p.50

Lyncheski, John
(Pennsylvania)
Profile: p.617
Employment Band 3
Table: p.602

Lyndrup, Peggy (Kentucky)
Profile: p.305
Corporate/M&A Band 2
Table: p.300

Lyon, Charles (Ohio)
Profile: p.576
Intellectual Property Band 1
Table: p.568

Lyons, Gregory
(Massachusetts)
Profile: p.357
Banking & Finance Band 3
Table: p.338

Lyons, James M (Colorado)
Profile: p.84
Litigation Band 1
Table: p.79

Lyons, Keith (Nevada)
Profile: p.414
Employment Band 2
Table: p.407

Lyons, Peter D (New York)
Profile: p.524
Corporate/M&A Band 4
Table: p.460

M

Maak, Bruce (Utah)
Profile: p.690
Real Estate Band 2
Table: p.689

Maak, Charles (Utah)
Profile: p.690
Real Estate Band 1
Table: p.689

Macbeth, Angus
(District of Columbia)
Profile: p.139
Environment Band 1
Table: p.117

MacBride, Owen (Illinois)
Profile: p.266
Communications Band 4
Table: p.229
Energy Band 2
Table: p.238

MacBride Jr, Thomas
(California)
Profile: p.68
Energy Band 4
Table: p.41

MacDonald, Alan (Kentucky)
Profile: p.305
Corporate/M&A Band 2
Table: p.300

MacDonald III, Ralph F
(Georgia)
Profile: p.208
Banking & Finance Band 4
Table: p.183

Mace, Damond (Ohio)
Profile: p.576
Litigation U
Table: p.570

Mace, James (Nevada)
Profile: p.414
Real Estate Band 3
Table: p.411

Macey, Barry (Indiana)
Profile: p.284
Employment Band 1
Table: p.279

MacGill, Robert (Indiana)
Profile: p.284
Litigation Band 2
Table: p.280

Machen, John (Maryland)
Profile: p.334
Real Estate Band 4
Table: p.331

Machlin, Barry N (Illinois)
Profile: p.266

Mack, Wayne (Pennsylvania)
Profile: p.617
Antitrust U
Table: p.596

Mackay, Douglas (Kansas)
Profile: p.299
Litigation Band 3
Table: p.297

MacKay 2nd, John R
(New Jersey)
Profile: p.431
Corporate/M&A Band 2
Table: p.425

MacKinnon, D Scott (Hawaii)
Profile: p.218
Real Estate Band 4
Table: p.217

MacLellan, Eleanor Holmes
(New Hampshire)
Profile: p.422
Employment Band 2
Table: p.417

Macmurdo, Bruce (Louisiana)
Profile: p.317
Employment Band 3
Table: p.310

MacMurray, John C (New York)
Profile: p.524
Private Equity Band 3
Table: p.489

MacPherson, John (Wyoming)
Profile: p.734,735
Real Estate Band 3
Table: p.734

Macpherson, Robert
(New York)
Profile: p.524
Construction Band 4
Table: p.458

Madden, John (New York)
Profile: p.524

Madison, William
(New Mexico)
Profile: p.438
Litigation Band 3
Table: p.435

Magee, John B
(District of Columbia)
Profile: p.139
Tax Band 3
Table: p.130

Magnuson, Roger
(Minnesota)
Profile: p.376
Litigation Band 2
Table: p.372

Mahony, Gael (Massachusetts)
Profile: p.357
Litigation Band 3
Table: p.349

Maledon, William (Arizona)
Profile: p.22
Litigation Band 1
Table: p.19

Malefatto, Alfred J (Florida)
Profile: p.175
Environment Band 4
Table: p.160

Maley, John (Indiana)
Profile: p.284
Litigation Band 2
Table: p.280

Malkin, Joseph (California)
Profile: p.68
Energy Band 2
Table: p.41

Mallory, Rick (California)
Profile: p.68
Real Estate Band 4
Table: p.56

Mallow, Matthew J
(New York)
Profile: p.524
Capital Markets Band 2
Table: p.448

Malloy, Timothy J (Illinois)
Profile: p.266
Intellectual Property Band 3
Table: p.244

Malone, Judith
(Massachusetts)
Profile: p.357
Employment Band 3
Table: p.342

Malone Jr., Ernest (Louisiana)
Profile: p.317
Employment Band 1
Table: p.311

Maloney, Marilyn (Louisiana)
Profile: p.317
Banking & Finance Band 1
Table: p.307
Real Estate Band 1
Table: p.314

Malt, Brad (Massachusetts)
Profile: p.357
Corporate/M&A Band 4
Table: p.340
Private Equity Band 2
Table: p.350

Maltz, Gerald (Arizona)
Profile: p.22
Litigation Band 2
Table: p.19

Manchester, Susan
(New Hampshire)
Profile: p.422
Real Estate Band 2
Table: p.420

Mancini, Paul (Hawaii)
Profile: p.218,218
Real Estate Band 4
Table: p.217

Mandelbaum, David
(Pennsylvania)
Profile: p.617
Environment Band 1
Table: p.604

Manko, Joe (Pennsylvania)
Profile: p.617
Environment Band 1
Table: p.604

Mann, Christopher L
(New York)
Profile: p.524
Projects Band 5
Table: p.491

Mann, Terry (Kansas)
Profile: p.299
Employment Band 3
Table: p.296

Manner, Mark (Tennessee)
Profile: p.641
Corporate/M&A Band 2
Table: p.635

Manning, John (Montana)
Profile: p.398
Corporate/M&A Band 1
Table: p.394

Mannino, Edward
(Pennsylvania)
Profile: p.617
Litigation Band 2
Table: p.611

Marcello III, Matthew T.
(Rhode Island)
Profile: p.623
Real Estate Band 2
Table: p.622

March, Aaron (Missouri)
Profile: p.392
Real Estate Band 3
Table: p.391

Marco, Frank J (Connecticut)
Profile: p.93
Corporate/M&A Band 2
Table: p.87

Mariani, Richard (New Jersey)
Profile: p.431
Employment Band 3
Table: p.427

Maring, David (North Dakota)
Profile: p.557
Litigation Band 1
Table: p.556

Marion, David H
(Pennsylvania)
Profile: p.617
Litigation Band 3
Table: p.611

Markowitz, David (Oregon)
Profile: p.594
Litigation Band 1
Table: p.590

Marks, Daniel (Nevada)
Profile: p.414
Employment Band 1
Table: p.407

Marr, Barry (Hawaii)
Profile: p.218
Employment Band 1
Table: p.214

Marsack, Gary (Wisconsin)
Profile: p.729
Employment Band 2
Table: p.725

Marsh, Gary (Georgia)
Profile: p.208
Insolvency Band 4
Table: p.193

Marshall, John (Pennsylvania)
Profile: p.617
Intellectual Property Band 4
Table: p.609

Marshall, John T (Georgia)
Profile: p.208
Antitrust Band 5
Table: p.181
Litigation Band 1
Table: p.198

Marston, Edgar (Texas)
Profile: p.676
Corporate/M&A Band 4
Table: p.649

Martens, Don (California)
Profile: p.68
Intellectual Property Band 2
Table: p.48

Martin, Allen (Vermont)
Profile: p.697

LEADING LAWYERS INDEX

Corporate/M&A Band 2
Table: p.692

Martin, Brian (Texas)
Profile: p.676
Insurance Band 2
Table: p.659

Martin, Christopher W
(Texas)
Profile: p.676
Insurance Band 1
Table: p.659

Martin, Chrys (Oregon)
Profile: p.594
Employment Band 4
Table: p.589

Martin, Ernest (Texas)
Profile: p.676
Insurance Band 1
Table: p.659

Martin, Keith
(District of Columbia)
Profile: p.139
Projects Band 3
Table: p.126

Martin, Renwick (New York)
Profile: p.524
Capital Markets Band 1
Table: p.453

Martin, Timothy (Kentucky)
Profile: p.305
Real Estate Band 1
Table: p.304

Martucci, William (Missouri)
Profile: p.392
Employment Band 1
Table: p.388

Martzell, Jack (Louisiana)
Profile: p.317
Litigation Band 1
Table: p.313

Marx, David (Illinois)
Profile: p.266
Antitrust Band 4
Table: p.224

Mascherin, Terri (Illinois)
Profile: p.266
Communications Band 2
Table: p.229

Maser, Joel (Florida)
Profile: p.176
Tax Band 2
Table: p.170

Maslanka, Michael (Texas)
Profile: p.676
Employment Band 3
Table: p.652

Mason, C Steven (North Carolina)
Profile: p.552,553
Real Estate Band 3
Table: p.551

Mason, David (Illinois)
Profile: p.266
Banking & Finance Band 4
Table: p.226

Mason, Gerald (Wyoming)
Profile: p.735
Litigation Band 1
Table: p.732

Mason, Richard G (New York)
Profile: p.524
Insolvency U
Table: p.472

Massad, Stephen A (Texas)
Profile: p.676
Corporate/M&A Band 1
Table: p.649

Massey, Ray (Missouri)
Profile: p.392

Litigation Band 2
Table: p.389

Massopust, Richard
(Minnesota)
Profile: p.376
Real Estate Band 2
Table: p.374

Mast, Greg (Arizona)
Profile: p.22
Real Estate Band 1
Table: p.20

Mastracco, Vincent (Virginia)
Profile: p.704
Corporate/M&A Band 2
Table: p.699

Masur, Daniel A
(District of Columbia)
Profile: p.139
Communications Band 3
Table: p.107

Matchett, Sam (Georgia)
Profile: p.208
Employment Band 4
Table: p.189

Mather, Barbara
(Pennsylvania)
Profile: p.617
Antitrust Band 2
Table: p.596
Litigation Band 1
Table: p.611

Mathias, Robert (Maryland)
Profile: p.334
Litigation Band 2
Table: p.330

Mathiason, Garry (California)
Profile: p.68
Employment Band 3
Table: p.40

Matis, Nina (Illinois)
Profile: p.266
Real Estate Band 1
Table: p.249

Matkins, Michael (California)
Profile: p.68
Real Estate Band 2
Table: p.56

Mattei, Andrew (New York)
Profile: p.524
Banking & Finance Band 4
Table: p.445

Matthews, Christopher
(Oregon)
Profile: p.594
Real Estate Band 4
Table: p.592

Matthews, Frank (Florida)
Profile: p.176
Environment Band 4
Table: p.160

Matthews, Philip (California)
Profile: p.68
Insurance Band 1
Table: p.46

Mattson, Lynn (Oklahoma)
Profile: p.586
Employment Band 2
Table: p.582

Mattson, Stephen J (Illinois)
Profile: p.266
Energy Band 1
Table: p.238

Mauel, John (Texas)
Profile: p.676
Projects U
Table: p.664

Mauk, Bill (Idaho)
Profile: p.222
Employment Band 2
Table: p.219

May, Bruce (Arizona)
Profile: p.22
Real Estate Band 2
Table: p.20

May, Gregory
(District of Columbia)
Profile: p.139
Tax Band 3
Table: p.130

May, James (Alabama)
Profile: p.8
Employment Band 3
Table: p.3

May, K. Rodney (Florida)
Profile: p.176
Insolvency Band 4
Table: p.162

Mayer, William
(Massachusetts)
Profile: p.357
Banking & Finance Band 1
Table: p.338

Mazo, Mark
(District of Columbia)
Profile: p.139
Corporate/M&A Band 3
Table: p.111

Mazur, Sayward (New York)
Profile: p.525
Construction Band 4
Table: p.458

McAndrew, Karen (Vermont)
Profile: p.697
Employment Band 1
Table: p.694
Litigation Band 2
Table: p.695

McAndrews, George P
(Illinois)
Profile: p.267
Intellectual Property Band 2
Table: p.244

McBride, David (Delaware)
Profile: p.100
Litigation Band 2
Table: p.98

McCall, Donn (Wyoming)
Profile: p.735
Corporate/M&A Band 2
Table: p.730

McCalla, Robert (Louisiana)
Profile: p.317
Employment Band 1
Table: p.311

McCareins, Mark (Illinois)
Profile: p.267
Antitrust Band 3
Table: p.224

McCartan, Patrick F (Ohio)
Profile: p.576
Litigation Band 1
Table: p.570

McCarthy, Michael
(Colorado)
Profile: p.84
Litigation Band 4
Table: p.79

McCarthy, William
(Massachusetts)
Profile: p.357
Insolvency Band 2
Table: p.346

McClellan, Roger (Kansas)
Profile: p.299
Employment U
Table: p.296

McClenahan, David
(Pennsylvania)
Profile: p.617
Litigation Band 2
Table: p.611

McClintock, Donald (Alaska)
Profile: p.15
Real Estate Band 1
Table: p.14

McCollam, John (Louisiana)
Profile: p.317
Litigation Band 2
Table: p.313

McCollum, James (Alaska)
Profile: p.14,15
Real Estate Band 2
Table: p.14

McCombs, David (Texas)
Profile: p.676
Intellectual Property Band 4
Table: p.661

McConaughy, Stewart
(Vermont)
Profile: p.697
Corporate/M&A Band 1
Table: p.692

McConnell, Karen (Arizona)
Profile: p.22
Corporate/M&A Band 2
Table: p.16

McConnell, Mike (Texas)
Profile: p.676
Insolvency Band 4
Table: p.657

McCormack, William (Texas)
Profile: p.676
Corporate/M&A Band 3
Table: p.649

McCormack, William F
(New York)
Profile: p.525
Private Equity Band 4
Table: p.489

McCormick, Mark (Iowa)
Profile: p.293
Litigation Band 2
Table: p.290

McCorriston, William C
(Hawaii)
Profile: p.218
Litigation Band 1
Table: p.215

McCrea, Richard (Florida)
Profile: p.176
Employment Band 3
Table: p.158

McCullough, Jack
(Washington)
Profile: p.712,713
Real Estate Band 3
Table: p.711

McCullough, Joe (Illinois)
Profile: p.267
Insurance Band 2
Table: p.242

McDaniels, William
(District of Columbia)
Profile: p.139
Litigation Band 3
Table: p.123

McDavid, Janet L
(District of Columbia)
Profile: p.139
Antitrust Band 2
Table: p.103

McDonald, John (Ohio)
Profile: p.577
Litigation Band 3
Table: p.570

McDonald, Randall (New Mexico)
Profile: p.438
Corporate/M&A Band 4
Table: p.433

McDonnell, Brendan (Oregon)
Profile: p.594
Corporate/M&A Band 4
Table: p.587

McDonough, Kathleen
(Delaware)
Profile: p.100
Employment Band 3
Table: p.96

McElhinny, Harold (California)
Profile: p.68
Intellectual Property Band 4
Table: p.48

McElwee, Douglas (West Virginia)
Profile: p.722
Real Estate Band 3
Table: p.720

McGee Jr, Emmett F
(Maryland)
Profile: p.334
Employment Band 2
Table: p.329

McGill, Linda (Maine)
Profile: p.325
Employment Band 1
Table: p.321

McGinn, Daniel (North Carolina)
Profile: p.553
Employment Band 1
Table: p.548

McGinn, Randi (New Mexico)
Profile: p.438
Litigation Band 2
Table: p.435

McGivaren Jnr, Crawford
(Alabama)
Profile: p.8
Litigation Band 3
Table: p.4

McGoey, William (Louisiana)
Profile: p.317
Employment Band 3
Table: p.310

McGough Jr, Thomas
(Pennsylvania)
Profile: p.617
Litigation Band 2
Table: p.611

McGrane, John
(District of Columbia)
Profile: p.140
Energy Band 5
Table: p.115

McGrath, Brian (Nebraska)
Profile: p.405
Employment Band 3
Table: p.402

McGuigan, Thomas (Florida)
Profile: p.176
Corporate/M&A Band 1
Table: p.156

McGuire, Frank (Maine)
Profile: p.325
Employment Band 3
Table: p.321

McGuire, J Michael
(Maryland)
Profile: p.334
Employment Band 3
Table: p.329

McHugh, Thomas (West Virginia)
Profile: p.722
Litigation Band 3
Table: p.718

McIsaac, Christopher
(District of Columbia)
Profile: p.140
Projects Band 3

LEADING LAWYERS INDEX

Table: p.126

McKay, Daniel G (Maine)
Profile: p.325
Corporate/M&A Band 3
Table: p.319

McKearin, Robert (Vermont)
Profile: p.697
Employment Band 2
Table: p.694

McKee, Bill
(District of Columbia)
Profile: p.140
Tax Band 2
Table: p.130

McKee, Robert (Florida)
Profile: p.176
Employment Band 2
Table: p.157

McKeithen, Malloy (North Carolina)
Profile: p.553
Banking & Finance Band 3
Table: p.544

McKeithen, Ward (North Carolina)
Profile: p.553
Litigation Band 1
Table: p.549

McKinney, Kenneth
(Oklahoma)
Profile: p.586
Litigation Band 2
Table: p.583

McKnight, Michael (South Dakota)
Profile: p.633
Employment Band 2
Table: p.631

McKool, Mike (Texas)
Profile: p.676
Litigation Band 4
Table: p.663

McLaughlin, Lawrence
(Michigan)
Profile: p.366
Real Estate Band 1
Table: p.365

McLaughlin, Mark T (Illinois)
Profile: p.267
Antitrust Band 3
Table: p.224

McLaughlin, Patrick (Ohio)
Profile: p.577
Litigation Band 4
Table: p.570

McLean, Michael
(Pennsylvania)
Profile: p.617
Corporate/M&A Band 3
Table: p.599

McLean, Ronald (North Dakota)
Profile: p.557
Litigation Band 1
Table: p.556

McLoughlin Jr, James P
(North Carolina)
Profile: p.553
Litigation Band 3
Table: p.549

McLucas, William
(District of Columbia)
Profile: p.140
Litigation Band 3
Table: p.123

McMahon, Michael (Ohio)
Profile: p.577
Environment Band 3
Table: p.567

McMahon, Terry (California)
Profile: p.68
Intellectual Property Band 1
Table: p.48

McMahon, Thomas (Illinois)
Profile: p.267
Environment Band 2
Table: p.239

McManus, Joseph
(District of Columbia)
Profile: p.140
Construction Band 3
Table: p.110

McMenamin, J Robert
(Illinois)
Profile: p.267
Banking & Finance Band 3
Table: p.226

McMichael, Lawrence
(Pennsylvania)
Profile: p.617
Insolvency Band 3
Table: p.607

McMillan II, L Richards
(Louisiana)
Profile: p.317
Corporate/M&A Band 1
Table: p.309

McMoran, Bruce (New Jersey)
Profile: p.431
Employment Band 1
Table: p.426

McNair, Eben (Ohio)
Profile: p.577
Employment Band 1
Table: p.564

McNamara, Neal
(Rhode Island)
Profile: p.623
Employment Band 1
Table: p.621

McNamara, Todd (Colorado)
Profile: p.84
Employment Band 2
Table: p.77

McNeil, Barry (Texas)
Profile: p.676
Antitrust Band 1
Table: p.644

McNeill, Thomas (Georgia)
Profile: p.208
Corporate/M&A Band 4
Table: p.187

McNichol Jr., William
(Pennsylvania)
Profile: p.617
Intellectual Property Band 3
Table: p.609

McNiel, Ferguson (Texas)
Profile: p.677
Litigation Band 4
Table: p.663

McSweeney, Maurice
(Wisconsin)
Profile: p.729
Litigation Band 3
Table: p.726

McTurnan, Lee B (Indiana)
Profile: p.284
Litigation Band 1
Table: p.280

McWhorter, Hobart
(Alabama)
Profile: p.8
Litigation Band 2
Table: p.4

McWhorter, Val (Virginia)
Profile: p.704
Construction Band 3
Table: p.698

Meade, Don (Kentucky)
Profile: p.305
Employment Band 2
Table: p.301

Meadows, Craig (Idaho)
Profile: p.222
Litigation Band 1
Table: p.221

Meadows, Stanley (Illinois)
Profile: p.267
Corporate/M&A Band 5
Table: p.233

Meath, James (Virginia)
Profile: p.704
Employment Band 1
Table: p.701

Mechanic, Jonathan
(New York)
Profile: p.525
Real Estate Band 1
Table: p.493

Medlock, Bryan (Texas)
Profile: p.677
Intellectual Property Band 1
Table: p.661

Medved, Joseph W (Missouri)
Profile: p.392
Corporate/M&A Band 3
Table: p.386

Meehan, Michael (Arizona)
Profile: p.22
Litigation Band 2
Table: p.19

Meelheim, Richard (Alabama)
Profile: p.8
Employment Band 4
Table: p.2

Mehlman, Mark (Illinois)
Profile: p.267
Real Estate Band 2
Table: p.249

Meiklejohn, D Stuart
(New York)
Profile: p.525
Antitrust Band 5
Table: p.441

Meir, Dennis (Georgia)
Profile: p.208
Insolvency Band 2
Table: p.193

Meites, Thomas (Illinois)
Profile: p.267
Employment Band 2
Table: p.235

Melamed, Doug
(District of Columbia)
Profile: p.140
Antitrust Band 2
Table: p.103

Mello, Robert (Vermont)
Profile: p.697
Employment Band 2
Table: p.693

Melo, Thomas (Texas)
Profile: p.677
Employment Band 2
Table: p.652

Melvin, Charles (North Carolina)
Profile: p.552,553
Real Estate Band 2
Table: p.551

Mendelsohn, David (Illinois)
Profile: p.267
Insurance Band 3
Table: p.242

Mendelson, Alan C
(California)
Profile: p.68
Communications Band 1

Table: p.34
Corporate/M&A Band 3
Table: p.37

Mendenhall, William
(Mississippi)
Profile: p.384
Corporate/M&A Band 3
Table: p.378

Menna, Gilbert
(Massachusetts)
Profile: p.357
Corporate/M&A Band 2
Table: p.340

Menotti, David
(District of Columbia)
Profile: p.140
Environment Band 5
Table: p.117

Mensch, Linda (Illinois)
Profile: p.267
Media & Entertainment Band 2
Table: p.247

Mensik, Michael (Illinois)
Profile: p.267
Communications Band 3
Table: p.229

Mentel, Michael (Ohio)
Profile: p.577
Environment Band 3
Table: p.567

Menzie, Edward (South Carolina)
Profile: p.629
Corporate/M&A Band 1
Table: p.624
Real Estate Band 1
Table: p.628

Merley, Dennis (Minnesota)
Profile: p.376
Employment Band 3
Table: p.371

Mermelstein, Joshua
(New York)
Profile: p.525
Real Estate Band 3
Table: p.493

Merriam, Dwight
(Connecticut)
Profile: p.93
Real Estate Band 1
Table: p.91

Merritt, Mark (North Carolina)
Profile: p.553
Litigation Band 2
Table: p.549

Mersol, Greg (Ohio)
Profile: p.577
Employment Band 2
Table: p.565

Merwin, Bruce (Texas)
Profile: p.677
Construction Band 4
Table: p.648

Messerman, Gerald (Ohio)
Profile: p.577
Litigation Band 1
Table: p.570

Messing, Ellen
(Massachusetts)
Profile: p.357
Employment Band 2
Table: p.341

Metcalf, Slade (New York)
Profile: p.525
Media & Entertainment Band 3
Table: p.485

Metzger, Richard
(District of Columbia)
Profile: p.140
Communications Band 2
Table: p.107

Metzke, John (Wyoming)
Profile: p.735
Corporate/M&A Band 3
Table: p.730

Meunier, Gerald E (Louisiana)
Profile: p.318
Litigation Band 1
Table: p.313

Meusey, Joseph K (Nebraska)
Profile: p.405
Litigation Band 2
Table: p.403

Meyer, George (Florida)
Profile: p.176
Construction Band 1
Table: p.154

Meyer, Jon (New Hampshire)
Profile: p.422
Employment Band 2
Table: p.417

Meyer, Michael (California)
Profile: p.68
Real Estate Band 2
Table: p.56

Meyers, Kent (Oklahoma)
Profile: p.586
Litigation Band 2
Table: p.583

Meyers, Martin (Missouri)
Profile: p.392
Employment Band 1
Table: p.387

Meyers, Michael (New York)
Profile: p.525
Projects Band 5
Table: p.491

Meyers III, Robert L (Texas)
Profile: p.677
Construction Band 3
Table: p.648

Meyerson, Lee (New York)
Profile: p.525
Corporate/M&A Band 5
Table: p.460

Micciche, Daniel (Texas)
Profile: p.677
Tax Band 4
Table: p.667

Middlebrooks, David
(Alabama)
Profile: p.8
Employment Band 2
Table: p.3

Middleton, Jack
(New Hampshire)
Profile: p.422
Litigation Band 1
Table: p.419

Mihlsten, George (California)
Profile: p.69
Real Estate Band 3
Table: p.56

Mikels, Rick (Massachusetts)
Profile: p.357
Insolvency Band 1
Table: p.346

Mikva, Mary (Illinois)
Profile: p.267
Employment Band 2
Table: p.235

Milam, Kenneth (Mississippi)
Profile: p.384
Employment Band 1
Table: p.380

Milch, Thomas
(District of Columbia)
Profile: p.140
Environment Band 2
Table: p.117

M

1003

LEADING LAWYERS INDEX

Miles, Robin J (Texas)
Profile: p.677
Banking & Finance Band 4
Table: p.645

Milkman, Ruth (District of Columbia)
Profile: p.140
Communications Band 5
Table: p.107

Millard, David (Indiana)
Profile: p.284
Corporate/M&A Band 4
Table: p.277

Millard, John A (New York)
Profile: p.525
Banking & Finance Band 4
Table: p.445
Projects Band 5
Table: p.491

Miller, Barry (Ohio)
Profile: p.577
Construction Band 2
Table: p.560

Miller, Bradley (Oregon)
Profile: p.594
Real Estate Band 3
Table: p.592

Miller, Charles (Missouri)
Profile: p.392
Real Estate Band 2
Table: p.391

Miller, Charles (North Dakota)
Profile: p.557
Litigation Band 3
Table: p.556

Miller, Charles E (Maine)
Profile: p.325
Real Estate Band 1
Table: p.324

Miller, Clifford (Hawaii)
Profile: p.218
Real Estate Band 3
Table: p.217

Miller, David (New York)
Profile: p.525
Tax Band 2
Table: p.499

Miller, David W (Indiana)
Profile: p.284
Employment Band 1
Table: p.279

Miller, Gale (Colorado)
Profile: p.85
Litigation Band 4
Table: p.79

Miller, Harlan (Georgia)
Profile: p.208
Employment Band 2
Table: p.188

Miller, Henry (Pennsylvania)
Profile: p.617
Real Estate Band 2
Table: p.613

Miller, Lee I (Illinois)
Profile: p.268
Real Estate Band 4
Table: p.249

Miller, Michelle (Massachusetts)
Profile: p.357
Antitrust Band 2
Table: p.337

Miller, Nicholas (Idaho)
Profile: p.222
Corporate/M&A Band 1
Table: p.219

Miller, Ranne (New Mexico)
Profile: p.438
Litigation Band 3
Table: p.435

Miller, Robert (Idaho)
Profile: p.222,222
Real Estate Band 2
Table: p.222

Miller, Roger (Nebraska)
Profile: p.405
Employment Band 2
Table: p.402

Miller, Winston (Kentucky)
Profile: p.305
Litigation Band 2
Table: p.303

Miller Jr, Ben R (Louisiana)
Profile: p.318
Corporate/M&A Band 5
Table: p.309

Milliman, Jim (Kentucky)
Profile: p.305
Litigation Band 3
Table: p.303

Millisor, Kenneth (Ohio)
Profile: p.577
Employment Band 2
Table: p.565

Mills, Jerry (Texas)
Profile: p.677
Communications Band 3
Table: p.646
Intellectual Property Band 2
Table: p.661

Mills, Osborne (Ohio)
Profile: p.577
Banking & Finance Band 2
Table: p.559

Mills, Phillip R (New York)
Profile: p.525

Millston, David (Ohio)
Profile: p.577
Employment Band 3
Table: p.565

Milmoe, J Gregory (New York)
Profile: p.525
Insolvency Band 5
Table: p.472

Minch, Roger (North Dakota)
Profile: p.557
Corporate/M&A Band 2
Table: p.554

Minchella, Michael F (California)
Profile: p.69
Construction Band 2
Table: p.36

Miraldi, Leslee (Ohio)
Profile: p.577
Banking & Finance Band 3
Table: p.559

Mirvis, Theodore N (New York)
Profile: p.526
Litigation Band 3
Table: p.481

Missner, David (Illinois)
Profile: p.268
Insolvency Band 3
Table: p.241

Mitchell, Caroline (Pennsylvania)
Profile: p.618
Employment Band 1
Table: p.601

Mitchell, David S (New York)
Profile: p.526
Capital Markets Band 2
Table: p.451

Mitchell, Marlee (Tennessee)
Profile: p.641
Corporate/M&A Band 3
Table: p.635

Mitchell, Marvin (Indiana)
Profile: p.284
Litigation Band 3
Table: p.280

Mitchell, Maurice (Arkansas)
Profile: p.27
Real Estate Band 2
Table: p.26

Mitchell, Micheal S (Louisiana)
Profile: p.318
Employment Band 4
Table: p.311

Mitchell, Stephen (Florida)
Profile: p.176
Real Estate Band 3
Table: p.167

Mixson, Dwight L (Alabama)
Profile: p.8
Real Estate Band 4
Table: p.6

Moats, Bruce (Wyoming)
Profile: p.735
Employment Band 3
Table: p.731

Moehrke, Anton (Massachusetts)
Profile: p.357
Environment Band 2
Table: p.344

Moeling, Walter G (Georgia)
Profile: p.208
Banking & Finance Band 1
Table: p.183

Moeller Jr., Armin J. (Mississippi)
Profile: p.384
Employment Band 3
Table: p.380

Moffitt, Ronald (Utah)
Profile: p.690
Corporate/M&A Band 3
Table: p.684

Molan, Richard (New Hampshire)
Profile: p.422
Employment Band 3
Table: p.417

Molavi, Kamyar (Georgia)
Profile: p.208
Construction Band 5
Table: p.184

Mollica, Paul (Illinois)
Profile: p.268
Employment Band 2
Table: p.235

Molo, Steven (Illinois)
Profile: p.268
Litigation Band 5
Table: p.245

Monaco, Daniel (Pennsylvania)
Profile: p.618
Intellectual Property Band 4
Table: p.609

Monahan Jr, John (Vermont)
Profile: p.697
Litigation Band 4
Table: p.695

Monk, Stephen (Alabama)
Profile: p.8
Real Estate Band 3
Table: p.6

Monroe, Bob (Missouri)
Profile: p.392
Corporate/M&A Band 2
Table: p.386

Monson, Patricia (North Dakota)
Profile: p.557

Employment Band 1
Table: p.555

Montague Jr. H Laddie (Pennsylvania)
Profile: p.618
Antitrust Band 3
Table: p.596

Montgomery, Margaret (Vermont)
Profile: p.697
Corporate/M&A Band 3
Table: p.692

Moon, Richard G. (Maine)
Profile: p.325
Employment Band 1
Table: p.321

Moore, Charles A (Texas)
Profile: p.677
Energy Band 4
Table: p.653

Moore, Charles L (New Mexico)
Profile: p.438
Corporate/M&A Band 1
Table: p.433

Moore, Dan (Iowa)
Profile: p.292,293
Real Estate Band 3
Table: p.291

Moore, George (New Hampshire)
Profile: p.422
Litigation Band 2
Table: p.419

Moore, Harold F (New York)
Profile: p.526
Projects Band 1
Table: p.491

Moore, Larry (Utah)
Profile: p.690
Real Estate Band 2
Table: p.689

Moore, Lynnwood (Oklahoma)
Profile: p.586
Corporate/M&A Band 3
Table: p.580

Moore, Michael (Arkansas)
Profile: p.27
Employment Band 2
Table: p.24

Moore, Robert (District of Columbia)
Profile: p.140
Tax Band 3
Table: p.130

Moore, Robert (California)
Profile: p.69
Insolvency Band 2
Table: p.44

Moore, Thurston (Virginia)
Profile: p.704
Corporate/M&A Band 1
Table: p.699

Moorman, Robert (Oregon)
Profile: p.594
Corporate/M&A Band 3
Table: p.587

Moorse, Charles (Minnesota)
Profile: p.376
Corporate/M&A Band 1
Table: p.369

Moran, Patrick G (Illinois)
Profile: p.268
Real Estate Band 2
Table: p.249

Morgan, Ann (Nevada)
Profile: p.414
Employment Band 3
Table: p.408

Morgan, Charles (New York)
Profile: p.526
Tax Band 2
Table: p.499

Morgan, Griffin (North Carolina)
Profile: p.553
Employment Band 2
Table: p.547

Morgan, Michael (Washington)
Profile: p.713
Corporate/M&A Band 1
Table: p.706

Morgan, Robert C (New York)
Profile: p.526
Intellectual Property Band 5
Table: p.479

Morison, Francis J (New York)
Profile: p.526
Capital Markets Band 2
Table: p.448

Morphy, James C (New York)
Profile: p.526
Corporate/M&A Band 3
Table: p.460

Morrill, Denis (Utah)
Profile: p.690
Real Estate Band 1
Table: p.689

Morris, Doug (Kentucky)
Profile: p.305
Employment Band 3
Table: p.301

Morris, Steve (Nevada)
Profile: p.414
Litigation Band 2
Table: p.409

Morrison, David (West Virginia)
Profile: p.722
Employment Band 1
Table: p.717

Morrison, Portia (Illinois)
Profile: p.268
Real Estate Band 3
Table: p.249

Morrison, Stephen G (South Carolina)
Profile: p.629
Litigation Band 1
Table: p.626

Morrison, Victoria (New Jersey)
Profile: p.431
Real Estate Band 2
Table: p.429

Morrow, James (Arizona)
Profile: p.22
Real Estate Band 3
Table: p.20

Morrow, John (Alabama)
Profile: p.8
Litigation Band 1
Table: p.4

Moscow, Cyril (Michigan)
Profile: p.366
Corporate/M&A Band 2
Table: p.361

Moser, Kenneth A (North Carolina)
Profile: p.553
Banking & Finance Band 2
Table: p.544

Moss, Edward (Florida)
Profile: p.176
Litigation Band 3
Table: p.165

LEADING LAWYERS INDEX

Moss, Gary (Nevada)
Profile: p.414
Employment Band 1
Table: p.408

Motenko, Neil
(Massachusetts)
Profile: p.357
Antitrust Band 1
Table: p.337

Mowe, Gregory (Oregon)
Profile: p.594
Litigation Band 4
Table: p.590

Moya, Bob (Arizona)
Profile: p.22
Corporate/M&A Band 2
Table: p.16

Moye, James E (Florida)
Profile: p.176
Construction Band 3
Table: p.154

Muchmore, Iris (Iowa)
Profile: p.293
Employment Band 2
Table: p.288

Muench, John E (Illinois)
Profile: p.268
Communications Band 3
Table: p.229

Mulaney, Charles (Illinois)
Profile: p.268
Corporate/M&A Band 1
Table: p.233

Muldoon, Robert
(Massachusetts)
Profile: p.357
Litigation Band 2
Table: p.349

Mullin, Neil (New Jersey)
Profile: p.431
Employment O
Table: p.426

Muncy, Dennis (Illinois)
Profile: p.268
Communications Band 2
Table: p.229

Munitz, Gerald (Illinois)
Profile: p.268
Insolvency Band 2
Table: p.241

Murphy, Charles (Georgia)
Profile: p.208
Antitrust Band 3
Table: p.181

Murphy, Harold
(Massachusetts)
Profile: p.357
Insolvency Band 2
Table: p.346

Murphy, Joseph (Illinois)
Profile: p.268
Communications Band 4
Table: p.229

Murphy, Liam (Vermont)
Profile: p.697
Real Estate Band 1
Table: p.696

Murphy, Patrick A (California)
Profile: p.69
Insolvency Band 2
Table: p.44

Murphy, William (Maryland)
Profile: p.334
Litigation Band 3
Table: p.330

Murray, Gregory (Illinois)
Profile: p.268

Murray, Thomas (West Virginia)
Profile: p.722
Corporate/M&A Band 2
Table: p.714

Murray, William
(Pennsylvania)
Profile: p.618
Intellectual Property Band 1
Table: p.609

Murtagh Jr., John
(Pennsylvania)
Profile: p.618
Employment Band 2
Table: p.601

Murtaugh, Christopher D
(Illinois)
Profile: p.268
Real Estate Band 4
Table: p.249

Musil, Gregory (Kansas)
Profile: p.299
Litigation Band 2
Table: p.297

Muskovitz, Susannah (Ohio)
Profile: p.577
Employment Band 3
Table: p.564

Musser, William (South Carolina)
Profile: p.629
Corporate/M&A Band 2
Table: p.624

Mutchnik, James (Illinois)
Profile: p.268
Antitrust Band u
Table: p.224

Muto, Fred (California)
Profile: p.69
Communications Band 5
Table: p.34

Myers, John (New Mexico)
Profile: p.438
Real Estate Band 2
Table: p.437

Myers, Marlee (Pennsylvania)
Profile: p.618
Corporate/M&A Band 3
Table: p.599

N

Nachbar, Kenneth (Delaware)
Profile: p.100
Litigation Band 3
Table: p.98

Nachwalter, Michael (Florida)
Profile: p.176
Litigation Band 1
Table: p.165

Nadel, Alan (Pennsylvania)
Profile: p.618
Intellectual Property Band 3
Table: p.609

Naeve, Clifford M
(District of Columbia)
Profile: p.141
Energy O
Table: p.115

Naftalis, Gary P (New York)
Profile: p.526
Litigation Band 3
Table: p.481

Nagelberg, Howard (Illinois)
Profile: p.269
Real Estate Band 3
Table: p.249

Nagin, Stephen (Florida)
Profile: p.176
Antitrust Band 3
Table: p.151

Nagle, James (Massachusetts)
Profile: p.357
Employment Band 2
Table: p.342

Nagle, Shannon Lowry
(Georgia)
Profile: p.208
Insolvency U
Table: p.193

Nakahata, John
(District of Columbia)
Profile: p.141
Communications Band 3
Table: p.107

Napolitano, Steven (Illinois)
Profile: p.269
Corporate/M&A U
Table: p.233

Nash, David (Ohio)
Profile: p.577
Environment Band 2
Table: p.567

Natale, Andrew (Ohio)
Profile: p.577
Construction Band 2
Table: p.560

Nathan, Charles (New York)
Profile: p.526
Corporate/M&A Band 5
Table: p.460

Nathan, Irvin
(District of Columbia)
Profile: p.141
Litigation Band 3
Table: p.123

Nathan Kahan, Penny
(Illinois)
Profile: p.269
Employment Band 3
Table: p.235

Natsis, Tony (California)
Profile: p.69
Real Estate Band 4
Table: p.56

Naugle, Louis (Pennsylvania)
Profile: p.618
Environment Band 2
Table: p.604

Neaher, Edward
(District of Columbia)
Profile: p.141
Projects Band 3
Table: p.126

Neal, Kathy (Oklahoma)
Profile: p.586
Employment Band 4
Table: p.582

Neckles, Peter J (New York)
Profile: p.527
Banking & Finance Band 3
Table: p.445

Needell, Benjamin F
(New York)
Profile: p.527
Real Estate Band 1
Table: p.493

Needle, Bill (Georgia)
Profile: p.208
Intellectual Property Band 1
Table: p.195

Neff, Daniel A (New York)
Profile: p.527
Corporate/M&A Band 4
Table: p.460

Neighbours, John T (Indiana)
Profile: p.284
Employment Band 3
Table: p.279

Nellis, Noel (California)
Profile: p.69
Real Estate Band 3
Table: p.56

Nelson, Carol Sue (Alabama)
Profile: p.8
Employment Band 3
Table: p.3

Nelson, Pat (Georgia)
Profile: p.208
Employment Band 2
Table: p.188

Nelson, Stephen (Iowa)
Profile: p.293
Real Estate Band 2
Table: p.291

Nelson, William F
(District of Columbia)
Profile: p.141
Tax Band 3
Table: p.130

Nesgos, Peter (New York)
Profile: p.527
Communications Band 3
Table: p.456

Ness, Andrew D
(District of Columbia)
Profile: p.141
Construction O
Table: p.110

Nestrud, Charles (Arkansas)
Profile: p.27
Litigation Band 3
Table: p.25

Neuberger, Thomas Stephen
(Delaware)
Profile: p.100
Employment Band 2
Table: p.95

Neuhaus, Joseph E
(New York)
Profile: p.527
Arbitration Band 3
Table: p.443

Neumann, Gordon (Iowa)
Profile: p.293
Corporate/M&A Band 3
Table: p.286

Neuner, Robert (New York)
Profile: p.527
Intellectual Property Band 3
Table: p.479
Litigation Band 5
Table: p.481

Neupert, John (Oregon)
Profile: p.594
Litigation Band 3
Table: p.590

Neveloff, Jay (New York)
Profile: p.527
Real Estate Band 4
Table: p.493

Neville, Jack (Oklahoma)
Profile: p.586
Litigation Band 3
Table: p.583

Newborn, Steve A
(District of Columbia)
Profile: p.141
Antitrust Band 2
Table: p.103

Newcom, Charles W
(Colorado)
Profile: p.85
Employment Band 4
Table: p.78

Newell, Francis Patrick
(Pennsylvania)
Profile: p.618
Antitrust Band 3
Table: p.596

Newell, Robert D (Oregon)
Profile: p.594
Litigation Band 4
Table: p.590

Newlin, William
(Pennsylvania)
Profile: p.618
Corporate/M&A Band 3
Table: p.599

Newman, Jeffrey (New Jersey)
Profile: p.430,431
Real Estate Band 2
Table: p.429

Newman, Jody
(Massachusetts)
Profile: p.357
Employment Band 3
Table: p.341

Newman, Lawrence W
(New York)
Profile: p.527
Arbitration Band 3
Table: p.443

Newman, Richard
(District of Columbia)
Profile: p.141
Real Estate Band 4
Table: p.127

Newman, Jr, John (Jack)
(Ohio)
Profile: p.577
Litigation Band 1
Table: p.570

Newsome, Jonathan Kent
(Texas)
Profile: p.677
Real Estate Band 4
Table: p.665

Newton, Trammell (Georgia)
Profile: p.208
Antitrust Band 5
Table: p.181

Ney, James M (Georgia)
Profile: p.208
Real Estate Band 3
Table: p.199

Nicely, Phil (Indiana)
Profile: p.284
Real Estate Band 3
Table: p.282

Nicholas, Thomas (Wyoming)
Profile: p.735
Litigation Band 2
Table: p.732

Nichols, Donald (Minnesota)
Profile: p.376
Employment Band 2
Table: p.370

Nichols, Phillip (California)
Profile: p.69
Real Estate Band 3
Table: p.56

Nicholson, Phillip R
(California)
Profile: p.69
Real Estate Band 3
Table: p.56

Nickel, Henry
(District of Columbia)
Profile: p.141
Environment Band 3
Table: p.117

Nicklin, Emily (Illinois)
Profile: p.269
Litigation Band 3
Table: p.245

Niebruegge, Michael E
(Texas)
Profile: p.677
Banking & Finance Band 2
Table: p.645

LEADING LAWYERS INDEX

Nijenhuis, Erika (New York)
Profile: p.527
Tax Band 2
Table: p.499

Nijman, Jennifer (Illinois)
Profile: p.269
Environment Band 4
Table: p.239

Nilson, George (Maryland)
Profile: p.334
Litigation Band 3
Table: p.330

Ning, Ke-Ching (Hawaii)
Profile: p.218
Employment Band 2
Table: p.213

Ninneman, Mary Pat (Wisconsin)
Profile: p.729
Employment Band 3
Table: p.725

Niro, Raymond (Illinois)
Profile: p.269
Intellectual Property Band 3
Table: p.244

Nix II, Robert Royal (Michigan)
Profile: p.366
Real Estate Band 3
Table: p.365

Nixon, Richard (Missouri)
Profile: p.392
Corporate/M&A Band 1
Table: p.386

Nocco, Frank (New York)
Profile: p.528
Capital Markets Band 3
Table: p.453

Nodine, Larry (Georgia)
Profile: p.209
Intellectual Property Band 2
Table: p.195

Noeding, Nicholas (New Mexico)
Profile: p.438
Employment Band 3
Table: p.435

Nolan, Tom (California)
Profile: p.69
Antitrust Band 4
Table: p.29

Nondorf, Kurt (Texas)
Profile: p.677
Real Estate Band 4
Table: p.665

Nonna, John M (New York)
Profile: p.528
Insurance Band 3
Table: p.477

Norris, John (Texas)
Profile: p.677
Intellectual Property Band 4
Table: p.661

North, John (Georgia)
Profile: p.209
Intellectual Property Band 5
Table: p.195

Northam, Patrick (Kentucky)
Profile: p.305
Corporate/M&A Band 3
Table: p.300

Norton, Bill (Tennessee)
Profile: p.641
Litigation Band 2
Table: p.639

Norton, Floyd (District of Columbia)
Profile: p.141
Energy Band 5
Table: p.115

Norton, Robert (Florida)
Profile: p.176
Employment Band 4
Table: p.158

Norton, Susan (Florida)
Profile: p.176
Employment Band 4
Table: p.158

Norwich, Donald (Minnesota)
Profile: p.376
Real Estate Band 2
Table: p.374

Nourse, David A (New York)
Profile: p.528
Shipping Band 2
Table: p.496

Nouss, James (Missouri)
Profile: p.393
Corporate/M&A Band 2
Table: p.386

Novacek, Stephen V (Nevada)
Profile: p.414
Real Estate Band 4
Table: p.411

Novak, Theodore (Illinois)
Profile: p.269
Real Estate Band 3
Table: p.249

Novick, Steven (Oklahoma)
Profile: p.586
Employment Band 2
Table: p.581

Novikoff, Harold S (New York)
Profile: p.528
Insolvency Band 1
Table: p.472

Nuechterlein, Mike (Florida)
Profile: p.176
Construction Band 2
Table: p.154

Nuegebauer, Robert (Washington)
Profile: p.713
Real Estate Band 3
Table: p.711

Nurkin, Sidney (Georgia)
Profile: p.209
Corporate/M&A Band 1
Table: p.187

Nusbaum, Jack H (New York)
Profile: p.528
Private Equity Band 3
Table: p.487

Nussbaum, Andrew J (New York)
Profile: p.528

Nussbaum, Bernard W (New York)
Profile: p.528
Litigation Band 2
Table: p.481

Nutt, Robert (Massachusetts)
Profile: p.357
Corporate/M&A Band 3
Table: p.340

Nyhan, Lawrence (Illinois)
Profile: p.269
Insolvency Band 2
Table: p.241

O

Oade, K Preston (Colorado)
Profile: p.85
Employment Band 2
Table: p.78

Oakes, Leslie (Georgia)
Profile: p.209
Environment Band 3
Table: p.192

Oakes, Royal (California)
Profile: p.69
Insurance Band 3
Table: p.46

Oakley, Mary Ann (Georgia)
Profile: p.209
Employment Band 3
Table: p.189

Oates, J Christopher (North Carolina)
Profile: p.553
Real Estate Band 3
Table: p.551

O'Brien, Clare (New York)
Profile: p.528
Corporate/M&A U
Table: p.460

O'Brien, Dorothy A (Iowa)
Profile: p.293
Employment Band 2
Table: p.288

O'Brien, George (Connecticut)
Profile: p.93
Employment Band 3
Table: p.89

O'Brien, Harry (California)
Profile: p.69
Construction Band 4
Table: p.36

O'Brien, Maurice (Minnesota)
Profile: p.376
Employment Band 1
Table: p.370

O'Brien, Michael (Utah)
Profile: p.690
Employment Band
Table: p.686
Employment Band 2
Table: p.686

O'Brien, Richard (Illinois)
Profile: p.269
Media & Entertainment Band 2
Table: p.247

O'Brien, William (Pennsylvania)
Profile: p.618
Litigation Band 1
Table: p.611

O'Bryan, Rory (Indiana)
Profile: p.283,284
Real Estate Band 3
Table: p.282

O'Connor, Otis (West Virginia)
Profile: p.722
Real Estate Band 3
Table: p.720

O'Connor, Robert (Utah)
Profile: p.690
Corporate/M&A Band 2
Table: p.684

O'Day, Stephen (Georgia)
Profile: p.209
Environment Band 4
Table: p.192

Ode, Paul (Vermont)
Profile: p.697
Corporate/M&A Band 1
Table: p.692

Odlaug, Bruce (Minnesota)
Profile: p.376
Real Estate Band 2
Table: p.374

O'Donnell, Earle (District of Columbia)
Profile: p.141
Energy Band 5
Table: p.115

O'Donnell, Pierce (California)
Profile: p.69
Litigation Band 2
Table: p.50

Odsen, Frederick (Alaska)
Profile: p.15
Corporate/M&A Band 2
Table: p.9

Oesting, David W (Alaska)
Profile: p.15
Litigation Band 3
Table: p.13

Oestreicher, Charles R (Maine)
Profile: p.325
Real Estate Band 3
Table: p.324

Offer, Stuart (California)
Profile: p.69
Tax Band 1
Table: p.58

O'Flaherty, Michael (Missouri)
Profile: p.393
Real Estate Band 1
Table: p.391

Ofsa, Joyce (West Virginia)
Profile: p.722
Real Estate Band 2
Table: p.720

Okun, Michael (North Carolina)
Profile: p.553
Employment Band 2
Table: p.547

Oland, Mark (Connecticut)
Profile: p.93
Real Estate Band 1
Table: p.91

O'Leary, Daniel (Oregon)
Profile: p.594
Litigation Band 3
Table: p.590

O'Leary, Michael (Texas)
Profile: p.677
Corporate/M&A Band 1
Table: p.649

Olian, Robert (Illinois)
Profile: p.269
Environment Band 2
Table: p.239

Oliver, David (Missouri)
Profile: p.393
Litigation Band 1
Table: p.389

Oliver III, Rufus W (Texas)
Profile: p.678
Antitrust Band 2
Table: p.644

Oliver Jr., Samuel (North Carolina)
Profile: p.553
Real Estate Band 1
Table: p.551

Olivier, Jeanne C (New York)
Profile: p.528
Projects Band 5
Table: p.491

Olson, Gary (California)
Profile: p.69
Corporate/M&A Band 4
Table: p.37

Olson, John (Florida)
Profile: p.176
Insolvency Band 3
Table: p.162

Olson, Karl (California)
Profile: p.69
Media & Entertainment Band 3
Table: p.53

Olson, Richard (North Dakota)
Profile: p.557
Corporate/M&A Band 1
Table: p.554

Olson, Ronald (California)
Profile: p.69
Litigation Band 2
Table: p.50

Olson, Stephen (Pennsylvania)
Profile: p.618
Employment Band 3
Table: p.602

Ominsky, Harris (Pennsylvania)
Profile: p.618
Real Estate Band 1
Table: p.613

O'Neal, Stephen V (California)
Profile: p.69
Construction Band 1
Table: p.36

O'Neal-Coble, Leslie (Florida)
Profile: p.176
Construction Band 1
Table: p.154

O'Neill, Albert (Florida)
Profile: p.176
Tax Band 2
Table: p.170

O'Neill, Brian D (District of Columbia)
Profile: p.141
Energy Band 2
Table: p.115

O'Neill, Jerome (Vermont)
Profile: p.697
Litigation Band 4
Table: p.695

O'Neill, Robert (Vermont)
Profile: p.697
Litigation Band 3
Table: p.695

Oosterhuis, Paul (District of Columbia)
Profile: p.142
Tax Band 1
Table: p.130

O'Reilly, Peter (Illinois)
Profile: p.269
Media & Entertainment Band 1
Table: p.247

Orloff, Larry (New Jersey)
Profile: p.431
Litigation Band 2
Table: p.428

Ortiz, Scott (Wyoming)
Profile: p.735
Employment Band 1
Table: p.732

Ortmann, Dale (California)
Profile: p.70
Construction Band 4
Table: p.36

Osborn, John W (New York)
Profile: p.528
Capital Markets Band 2
Table: p.451

Osborne, John (New York)
Profile: p.529
Shipping Band 1
Table: p.496

Osborne, Robert Stephen (Illinois)
Profile: p.269
Corporate/M&A Band 4
Table: p.233

Osbourne, Scott (Washington)
Profile: p.713
Real Estate Band 1
Table: p.711

LEADING LAWYERS INDEX

Oshinsky, Jerold (District of Columbia)
Profile: p.142
Insurance **Band 1**
Table: p.120

Osnos, David (District of Columbia)
Profile: p.142
Real Estate **Band 3**
Table: p.127

Osterberg, Edward (Texas)
Profile: p.678
Tax **Band 2**
Table: p.667

Ostrager, Barry (New York)
Profile: p.529
Insurance **Band 1**
Table: p.477
Litigation **Band 2**
Table: p.481

O'Sullivan, John (District of Columbia)
Profile: p.142
Energy **Band 5**
Table: p.115

Outten, Wayne (New York)
Profile: p.529
Employment **Band 1**
Table: p.466

Outwater, Lynn (Pennsylvania)
Profile: p.618
Employment **Band 4**
Table: p.602

Overman, Robert (Kansas)
Profile: p.299
Employment **Band 3**
Table: p.296

Oxfeld, Sanford (New Jersey)
Profile: p.431
Employment **Band 3**
Table: p.426

Oxford, Terrell (Texas)
Profile: p.678
Antitrust **Band 3**
Table: p.644

Ozier, William (Tennessee)
Profile: p.641
Employment **Band 1**
Table: p.637

P

Pace, Stanley Dan (Ohio)
Profile: p.577
Employment **Band 4**
Table: p.565

Pachulski, Isaac M (California)
Profile: p.70
Insolvency **Band 4**
Table: p.44

Pachulski, Richard M (California)
Profile: p.70
Insolvency **Band 2**
Table: p.44

Page, Rosewell (Virginia)
Profile: p.704
Litigation **Band 2**
Table: p.702

Page, Thomas (Oregon)
Profile: p.594
Real Estate **Band 2**
Table: p.592

Paget, David (New York)
Profile: p.529
Environment **Band 3**
Table: p.469

Painter, Robin (Massachusetts)
Profile: p.358
Private Equity **Band 1**
Table: p.350

Painter, William (Mississippi)
Profile: p.384
Corporate/M&A **Band 2**
Table: p.378

Paisley, Bonnie (New Mexico)
Profile: p.438
Corporate/M&A **Band 2**
Table: p.433

Pakenham, Tim (Georgia)
Profile: p.209
Real Estate **Band 2**
Table: p.199

Palefsky, Cliff (California)
Profile: p.70
Employment **Band 1**
Table: p.39

Palenchar, James (Colorado)
Profile: p.85
Corporate/M&A **Band 1**
Table: p.75

Palma, Laura (New York)
Profile: p.529
Capital Markets **Band 3**
Table: p.453

Palmer, Crisman (South Dakota)
Profile: p.633
Litigation **Band 1**
Table: p.632

Paltell, Eric (Maryland)
Profile: p.334
Employment **Band 3**
Table: p.329

Panitch, Ronald L (Pennsylvania)
Profile: p.618
Intellectual Property **Band 1**
Table: p.609

Panoff, Robert (Florida)
Profile: p.171,176
Tax **Band 1**
Table: p.170

Panovka, Robin (New York)
Profile: p.529
Real Estate **Band 4**
Table: p.493

Pantaleo, Peter (New York)
Profile: p.529
Insolvency **Band 3**
Table: p.472

Pappas, Lynn (Florida)
Profile: p.176
Real Estate **Band 4**
Table: p.167

Pappone, Michael (Massachusetts)
Profile: p.358
Insolvency **Band 2**
Table: p.346

Pardo Jr, James (Georgia)
Profile: p.209
Insolvency **Band 1**
Table: p.193

Paré, Jay (New York)
Profile: p.529
Shipping **Band 3**
Table: p.496

Parham Jr., James (South Carolina)
Profile: p.629
Litigation **Band 2**
Table: p.626

Pari, Joseph (District of Columbia)
Profile: p.131,142
Tax **Band 4**
Table: p.130

Paris, Zachary (Ohio)
Profile: p.577
Real Estate **Band 2**
Table: p.572

Parker, C Allen (New York)
Profile: p.529
Banking & Finance **Band 1**
Table: p.445

Parker, David (Texas)
Profile: p.678
Intellectual Property **Band 4**
Table: p.661

Parker, Douglas S (Alaska)
Profile: p.15
Employment **Band 2**
Table: p.11

Parker, James (New Mexico)
Profile: p.438
Corporate/M&A **Band 3**
Table: p.433

Parker, Richard G (District of Columbia)
Profile: p.142
Antitrust **Band 3**
Table: p.103

Parks, A Lee (Georgia)
Profile: p.209
Employment **Band 1**
Table: p.188

Parks, John R (Georgia)
Profile: p.209
Real Estate **Band 2**
Table: p.199

Parmley, Bruce (District of Columbia)
Profile: p.142
Real Estate **Band 4**
Table: p.127

Parsons, David (Illinois)
Profile: p.269
Employment **Band 4**
Table: p.236

Parsons, W Stuart (Wisconsin)
Profile: p.729
Litigation **Band 3**
Table: p.726

Partridge, Scott (Texas)
Profile: p.678
Intellectual Property **Band 3**
Table: p.661

Pashby, Gary (South Dakota)
Profile: p.633
Litigation **Band 3**
Table: p.632

Pasich, Kirk (California)
Profile: p.70
Insurance **Band 1**
Table: p.46

Pass Jr., Joseph (Pennsylvania)
Profile: p.618
Employment **Band 2**
Table: p.601

Passarelli, John (Nebraska)
Profile: p.405
Litigation **Band 3**
Table: p.403

Passman, Donald (California)
Profile: p.70
Media & Entertainment **Band 4**
Table: p.53

Patin, Douglas (District of Columbia)
Profile: p.142
Construction **Band 1**
Table: p.110

Patterson, Donna (District of Columbia)
Profile: p.142
Antitrust **Band 4**
Table: p.103

Patterson, Jeffrey (Nevada)
Profile: p.414
Real Estate **Band 3**
Table: p.411

Patterson, Robert S. (Tennessee)
Profile: p.641
Litigation **Band 3**
Table: p.639

Patterson, Tom (California)
Profile: p.70
Insolvency **Band 4**
Table: p.44

Patterson Jr., Robert (Maine)
Profile: p.325
Real Estate **Band 3**
Table: p.324

Patton, David (Texas)
Profile: p.678
Energy **Band 4**
Table: p.653

Patton, William (Massachusetts)
Profile: p.358
Antitrust **Band 2**
Table: p.337

Patton, Jr, James L (Delaware)
Profile: p.101
Insolvency **Band 1**
Table: p.96

Paul, James T (Hawaii)
Profile: p.218
Litigation **Band 3**
Table: p.215

Paustian, Kathleen (Nevada)
Profile: p.414
Employment **Band 3**
Table: p.408

Payne, Clare (Maine)
Profile: p.326
Employment **Band 2**
Table: p.321

Payne, M Travis (North Carolina)
Profile: p.553
Employment **Band 3**
Table: p.547

Payson, Robert (Delaware)
Profile: p.101
Litigation **Band 2**
Table: p.98

Pear, Charles (Hawaii)
Profile: p.218
Real Estate **Band 3**
Table: p.217

Pearlman, Samuel (Ohio)
Profile: p.577
Real Estate **Band 2**
Table: p.572

Pearlstein, Debra J (New York)
Profile: p.529
Antitrust **Band 4**
Table: p.441

Pearson, Jonathan (South Carolina)
Profile: p.629
Employment **Band 1**
Table: p.625

Pearson, Nick (New York)
Profile: p.529
Insurance **Band 4**
Table: p.477

Peaslee, James (New York)
Profile: p.529
Tax **Band 1**
Table: p.499

Peck, Rodney (California)
Profile: p.70
Banking & Finance **Band 3**
Table: p.30

Peckar, Robert S (New York)
Profile: p.529
Construction **Band 1**
Table: p.458

Peden, David (Texas)
Profile: p.678
Construction **Band 3**
Table: p.648

Peek, J Stephen (Nevada)
Profile: p.414
Litigation **Band 2**
Table: p.409

Peifer, Charles (New Mexico)
Profile: p.438
Litigation **Band 3**
Table: p.435

Pelfrey, Patton (Kentucky)
Profile: p.305
Employment **Band 1**
Table: p.302

Pemberton, Richard (Minnesota)
Profile: p.376
Employment **Band 2**
Table: p.370

Pence, Linda L (Indiana)
Profile: p.284
Litigation **Band 1**
Table: p.280

Pentelovitch, William (Minnesota)
Profile: p.376
Litigation **Band 1**
Table: p.372

Penzer, Michèle (New York)
Profile: p.529
Projects **Band 5**
Table: p.491

Pepe, Stephen P (California)
Profile: p.70
Employment **Band 4**
Table: p.40

Perez, Alfredo R (Texas)
Profile: p.678
Insolvency **Band 2**
Table: p.657

Perisho, Russell (Washington)
Profile: p.713
Employment **Band 1**
Table: p.708

Perlstein, William J (District of Columbia)
Profile: p.142
Insolvency **Band 1**
Table: p.119

Permut, Barry (Colorado)
Profile: p.85
Real Estate **Band 3**
Table: p.81

Pernick, Norman (Delaware)
Profile: p.101
Insolvency **Band 2**
Table: p.96

Perrin, Martha (Georgia)
Profile: p.209
Employment **Band 4**
Table: p.189

LEADING LAWYERS INDEX

Perry, Alan (Mississippi)
Profile: p.384
Litigation **Band 1**
Table: p.381

Persons, Oscar (Georgia)
Profile: p.209
Litigation **Band 2**
Table: p.198

Perwin, Scott (Florida)
Profile: p.176
Antitrust **Band 1**
Table: p.151

Petersen, John (Kansas)
Profile: p.299
Real Estate **Band 1**
Table: p.298

Petersen, Laurence
(Montana)
Profile: p.399
Corporate/M&A **Band 2**
Table: p.394

Peterson, Alan (Nebraska)
Profile: p.405
Litigation **Band 2**
Table: p.403

Peterson, Brad L (Illinois)
Profile: p.269
Communications **Band 2**
Table: p.229

Peterson, Karen (Nevada)
Profile: p.414
Real Estate **Band 4**
Table: p.411

Peterson, Ken (Kansas)
Profile: p.299
Employment **Band 2**
Table: p.295

Peterson, Pete (Texas)
Profile: p.678
Intellectual Property **Band 3**
Table: p.661

Peterson, Ron (Illinois)
Profile: p.270
Insolvency **Band 3**
Table: p.241

Petrikin, Ronald (Oklahoma)
Profile: p.586
Employment **Band 4**
Table: p.582

Petro, John (Ohio)
Profile: p.577
Construction **Band 3**
Table: p.560

Petruccelli, Gerald (Maine)
Profile: p.326
Litigation **Band 3**
Table: p.322

Pettibone, Jon (Arizona)
Profile: p.22
Employment **Band 3**
Table: p.18

Petumenos, Timothy J
(Alaska)
Profile: p.15
Employment **Band 2**
Table: p.10
Litigation **Band 2**
Table: p.13

Pfister, Thomas (California)
Profile: p.70
Employment **Band 3**
Table: p.40

Pharis, Michael (Louisiana)
Profile: p.318
Employment **Band 3**
Table: p.311

Phelan, Robin (Texas)
Profile: p.678
Insolvency **Band 1**
Table: p.657

Phibbs, Henry (Wyoming)
Profile: p.734,735
Real Estate **Band 3**
Table: p.734

Phillipp, James (California)
Profile: p.70
Tax **Band 3**
Table: p.58

Phillips, Carter
(District of Columbia)
Profile: p.142
Litigation **Band 1**
Table: p.123

Phillips, John (Missouri)
Profile: p.393
Employment **Band 2**
Table: p.388

Phillips, Lee (California)
Profile: p.70
Media & Entertainment **Band 2**
Table: p.53

Phillips, Stephen (Georgia)
Profile: p.
Construction **Band 5**
Table: p.184

Phillips IV, Barnet (New York)
Profile: p.530
Tax **Band 4**
Table: p.499

Phillips Jr, John (Tennessee)
Profile: p.641
Employment **Band 2**
Table: p.637

Pickens, Scott E (Illinois)
Profile: p.270
Banking & Finance **Band 4**
Table: p.226

Pickett, Andrew
(Massachusetts)
Profile: p.358
Employment **Band 3**
Table: p.342

Pickett, Donn (California)
Profile: p.70
Antitrust **Band 4**
Table: p.29

Pidgeon, Steve (Arizona)
Profile: p.22
Corporate/M&A **Band 1**
Table: p.16

Pierce, Morton A (New York)
Profile: p.530
Corporate/M&A **Band 4**
Table: p.460

Pierce, Patricia
(Pennsylvania)
Profile: p.618
Employment **Band 2**
Table: p.601

Pierce, Robert (Florida)
Profile: p.171,176
Tax **Band 3**
Table: p.170

Pierce, Rudolph
(Massachusetts)
Profile: p.358
Litigation **Band 3**
Table: p.349

Pill, Richard (West Virginia)
Profile: p.721,722
Real Estate **Band 3**
Table: p.720

Pinkerton, Glenn (Texas)
Profile: p.678
Projects **Band 2**
Table: p.664

Pinover, Eugene (New York)
Profile: p.530
Real Estate **Band 2**
Table: p.493

Pircher, Leo (California)
Profile: p.70
Real Estate **Band 5**
Table: p.56

Pirkey, Louis (Texas)
Profile: p.678
Intellectual Property **Band 1**
Table: p.661

Pisa, Regina (Massachusetts)
Profile: p.358
Banking & Finance **Band 2**
Table: p.338
Corporate/M&A **Band 3**
Table: p.340

Pisano, Vincent J (New York)
Profile: p.530
Capital Markets **Band 3**
Table: p.448

Pishko, David (North Carolina)
Profile: p.553
Employment **Band 2**
Table: p.547

Piskorski, Thomas (Illinois)
Profile: p.270
Employment **Band 4**
Table: p.236

Pitt, Michael (Michigan)
Profile: p.366
Employment **Band 1**
Table: p.362

Pittaro, Frederick
(Massachusetts)
Profile: p.358
Real Estate **Band 3**
Table: p.351

Placenti, Frank (Arizona)
Profile: p.22
Corporate/M&A **Band 2**
Table: p.16

Plambeck, Stephen (North Dakota)
Profile: p.557
Litigation **Band 3**
Table: p.556

Platt, L Steven (Illinois)
Profile: p.270
Employment **Band 2**
Table: p.235

Plevan, Bettina (New York)
Profile: p.530
Employment **Band 1**
Table: p.467

Plumb, Charles (Oklahoma)
Profile: p.586
Employment **Band 3**
Table: p.582

Plumridge, Richard
(Colorado)
Profile: p.85
Corporate/M&A **Band 2**
Table: p.75

Plybon, Christopher (West Virginia)
Profile: p.722
Real Estate **Band 3**
Table: p.720

Podhurst, Aaron (Florida)
Profile: p.176
Litigation **Band 2**
Table: p.165

Podvin Jr, F John (Texas)
Profile: p.678
Communications **Band 3**
Table: p.646

Poelman, Ronald (Utah)
Profile: p.691
Corporate/M&A **Band 1**
Table: p.684

Poff, William (Virginia)
Profile: p.704
Litigation **Band 2**
Table: p.702

Pogue, Mark (Rhode Island)
Profile: p.623
Litigation **Band 2**
Table: p.622

Pokempner, Joseph
(Maryland)
Profile: p.334
Employment **Band 2**
Table: p.329

Pokorski, Jody (Arizona)
Profile: p.21,22
Real Estate **Band 3**
Table: p.20

Pokotilow, Manny
(Pennsylvania)
Profile: p.618
Intellectual Property **Band 1**
Table: p.609

Polebaum, Mark
(Massachusetts)
Profile: p.358
Insolvency **Band 1**
Table: p.346

Pollack, Martin (New York)
Profile: p.530
Tax **Band 4**
Table: p.499

Pollak, Mark (Maryland)
Profile: p.332,334
Real Estate **Band 1**
Table: p.331

Polsinelli, James (Missouri)
Profile: p.393
Corporate/M&A **Band 1**
Table: p.386

Pomerantz, Alan J (New York)
Profile: p.530
Real Estate **Band 2**
Table: p.493

Pontone, Kathleen (Maryland)
Profile: p.334
Employment **Band 1**
Table: p.329

Pope, David (Georgia)
Profile: p.209
Environment **Band 4**
Table: p.192

Pope, Michael (Illinois)
Profile: p.270
Litigation **Band 5**
Table: p.245

Pope, Wallace (Florida)
Profile: p.176
Litigation **Band 4**
Table: p.165

Popeo, R. Robert
(Massachusetts)
Profile: p.358
Litigation **Band 1**
Table: p.349

Popofsky, Laurence
(California)
Profile: p.70
Antitrust **Band 3**
Table: p.29
Litigation **Band 3**
Table: p.50

Port, Alan D (Vermont)
Profile: p.697
Corporate/M&A **Band 3**
Table: p.692

Porter, David (Ohio)
Profile: p.577
Corporate/M&A **Band 1**
Table: p.562

Porter, Jeffrey
(Massachusetts)
Profile: p.358
Environment **Band 2**
Table: p.344

Porter, Stephen
(District of Columbia)
Profile: p.142
Real Estate **Band 3**
Table: p.127

Portnoy, Jeffrey (Hawaii)
Profile: p.218
Litigation **Band 1**
Table: p.215

Positan, Wayne (New Jersey)
Profile: p.431
Employment **Band 1**
Table: p.427

Poster, Robert (New York)
Profile: p.530
Shipping **Band 1**
Table: p.496

Postner, William (New York)
Profile: p.530
Construction **Band 2**
Table: p.458

Potenza, Joseph
(District of Columbia)
Profile: p.143
Intellectual Property **Band 3**
Table: p.122

Powell, Charles (Texas)
Profile: p.679
Communications **Band 2**
Table: p.646

Powell, David (Arkansas)
Profile: p.27
Litigation **Band 3**
Table: p.25

Powell, Fred (Alabama)
Profile: p.8
Real Estate **Band 1**
Table: p.6

Powell, Thomas O (Georgia)
Profile: p.209
Banking & Finance **Band 4**
Table: p.183

Powell III, Charles A
(Alabama)
Profile: p.8
Employment **Band 2**
Table: p.3

Powell Jr, David D (Colorado)
Profile: p.85
Employment **Band 3**
Table: p.78

Powers, John (Illinois)
Profile: p.270
Employment **Band 4**
Table: p.236

Powers, Kevin
(Massachusetts)
Profile: p.358
Employment **Band 3**
Table: p.341

Powers, Matthew D
(California)
Profile: p.70
Intellectual Property **Band 1**
Table: p.48

Powers, Tony (Georgia)
Profile: p.209
Antitrust **Band 2**
Table: p.181

Powers, Werner (Texas)
Profile: p.679
Insurance **Band 4**
Table: p.659

LEADING LAWYERS INDEX

Prather, Paul (Tennessee)
Profile: p.642
Employment **Band 2**
Table: p.637

Preis Jr, E Fredrick (Louisiana)
Profile: p.318
Employment **Band 2**
Table: p.311

Preovolos, Penelope A (California)
Profile: p.70
Antitrust **Band 4**
Table: p.29

Prestia, Paul (Pennsylvania)
Profile: p.618
Intellectual Property **Band 1**
Table: p.609

Preston, Anne (Washington)
Profile: p.713
Employment **Band 2**
Table: p.708

Preston, William D (Florida)
Profile: p.176
Environment **Band 3**
Table: p.160

Pretty, Laurence (California)
Profile: p.70
Intellectual Property **Band 2**
Table: p.48

Price, Charles (New Mexico)
Profile: p.438
Real Estate **Band 1**
Table: p.437

Price, Gene T (Alabama)
Profile: p.8
Corporate/M&A **Band 3**
Table: p.1

Price, Glenn (Kentucky)
Profile: p.305,306
Real Estate **Band 2**
Table: p.304

Price, Jim (Missouri)
Profile: p.393
Litigation **Band 3**
Table: p.389

Price, Joseph (West Virginia)
Profile: p.722
Employment **Band 2**
Table: p.717

Price, Stanley (Florida)
Profile: p.176
Real Estate **Band 2**
Table: p.167

Prichard, Allen (North Carolina)
Profile: p.553
Real Estate **Band 1**
Table: p.551

Priddy, Al (Kentucky)
Profile: p.306
Employment **Band 2**
Table: p.301

Priest, Jim (Oklahoma)
Profile: p.586
Employment **Band 4**
Table: p.582

Primavera, Carl (Pennsylvania)
Profile: p.618
Real Estate **Band 1**
Table: p.613

Prince, Alan (Georgia)
Profile: p.209
Corporate/M&A **U**
Table: p.187

Prince, Kenneth S (New York)
Profile: p.530
Antitrust **Band 4**
Table: p.441

Pringle, Harry (Maine)
Profile: p.326
Employment **Band 3**
Table: p.321

Proctor, David (Alabama)
Profile: p.8
Employment **Band 3**
Table: p.3

Proger, Phillip A (District of Columbia)
Profile: p.143
Antitrust **Band 2**
Table: p.103

Prowell, William (Iowa)
Profile: p.292,293
Real Estate **Band 4**
Table: p.291

Pruden III, Northfleet (North Carolina)
Profile: p.553
Corporate/M&A **Band 1**
Table: p.546

Pruellage, John (Missouri)
Profile: p.393
Corporate/M&A **Band 2**
Table: p.386

Pryor, Robert (North Carolina)
Profile: p.553
Banking & Finance **Band 3**
Table: p.544

Puleo, Frank (New York)
Profile: p.530
Banking & Finance **Band 3**
Table: p.445

Pyburn Jr, Keith M (Louisiana)
Profile: p.318
Employment **Band 3**
Table: p.311

Qasim, Imad I (Illinois)
Profile: p.270
Corporate/M&A **Band 3**
Table: p.233

Quail, Beverly (Colorado)
Profile: p.85
Real Estate **Band 4**
Table: p.81

Quale, John (District of Columbia)
Profile: p.143
Communications **Band 5**
Table: p.107

Quarles, John (District of Columbia)
Profile: p.143
Environment **Band 2**
Table: p.117

Quattlebaum, Marvin (South Carolina)
Profile: p.628,629
Real Estate **Band 2**
Table: p.628

Quattlebaum, Steven (Arkansas)
Profile: p.27
Litigation **Band 1**
Table: p.25

Quin, Whayne (District of Columbia)
Profile: p.143
Real Estate **Band 1**
Table: p.127

Quinn, John B (California)
Profile: p.70
Litigation **Band 3**
Table: p.50

Quinn, Linda C (New York)
Profile: p.531
Capital Markets **Band 1**
Table: p.448

Quinn, Michael (Alabama)
Profile: p.8
Employment **Band 1**
Table: p.2

Quinn, Yvonne S (New York)
Profile: p.531
Antitrust **Band 5**
Table: p.441

R

Raattama, Henry (Florida)
Profile: p.176
Tax **Band 1**
Table: p.170

Rabinowitz, Joel (California)
Profile: p.71
Tax **Band 3**
Table: p.58

Rachlin, Robert (Vermont)
Profile: p.697
Litigation **Band 2**
Table: p.695

Rackow, Julian (Pennsylvania)
Profile: p.618
Real Estate **Band 4**
Table: p.613

Radke, Kirk A (New York)
Profile: p.531
Private Equity **Band 3**
Table: p.487
Private Equity **Band 3**
Table: p.489

Radler, Barbara (Oregon)
Profile: p.594
Real Estate **Band 2**
Table: p.592

Rafte, Alan (Texas)
Profile: p.679
Energy **Band 4**
Table: p.653

Ragonetti, Thomas (Colorado)
Profile: p.85
Real Estate **Band 4**
Table: p.81

Raher, Patrick (District of Columbia)
Profile: p.143
Environment **Band 5**
Table: p.117

Rainey, Gordon (Virginia)
Profile: p.705
Corporate/M&A **Band 1**
Table: p.699

Rainey, Richard (North Carolina)
Profile: p.553
Employment **Band 3**
Table: p.548

Raisler, Kenneth M (New York)
Profile: p.531
Capital Markets **Band 1**
Table: p.451

Rakusin, Steve (Florida)
Profile: p.176
Construction **Band 1**
Table: p.154

Ralston, Eugene (Kansas)
Profile: p.299
Employment **Band 2**
Table: p.295

Raman, William (Texas)
Profile: p.679
Intellectual Property **Band 4**
Table: p.661

Ramer, Bruce (California)
Profile: p.71
Media & Entertainment **Band 1**
Table: p.53

Randall, Benjamin (Illinois)
Profile: p.270
Real Estate **Band 2**
Table: p.249

Ranson, Michael (West Virginia)
Profile: p.722
Employment **Band 2**
Table: p.716

Rapaport, David (Massachusetts)
Profile: p.358
Employment **Band 3**
Table: p.341

Raper, William (North Carolina)
Profile: p.553
Litigation **Band 1**
Table: p.549

Raskin, Debra (New York)
Profile: p.531
Employment **Band 3**
Table: p.466

Rasmussen, Robert (Florida)
Profile: p.176
Corporate/M&A **Band 2**
Table: p.156

Rassel, Richard E (Michigan)
Profile: p.366
Litigation **Band 3**
Table: p.364

Rathbun, Randy (Kansas)
Profile: p.299
Employment **Band 2**
Table: p.295

Ravich, Paul (Minnesota)
Profile: p.376
Real Estate **Band 2**
Table: p.374

Ravikoff, Ronald B (Florida)
Profile: p.176
Antitrust **Band 4**
Table: p.151

Rawson, Rachel (Ohio)
Profile: p.578
Banking & Finance **Band 2**
Table: p.559

Ray, Hugh M (Texas)
Profile: p.679
Insolvency **Band 4**
Table: p.657

Ray, Stephen E (Illinois)
Profile: p.270
Construction **Band 3**
Table: p.231

Reardon, Roy (New York)
Profile: p.531
Litigation **Band 1**
Table: p.481

Reasoner, Carroll J (Iowa)
Profile: p.293
Corporate/M&A **Band 3**
Table: p.286

Reasoner, Harry (Texas)
Profile: p.679
Antitrust **Band 1**
Table: p.644
Litigation **Band 1**
Table: p.663

Rebein, David (Kansas)
Profile: p.299
Litigation **Band 2**
Table: p.297

Reben, Howard (Maine)
Profile: p.326
Employment **Band 2**
Table: p.320

Reber, David J (Hawaii)
Profile: p.218
Corporate/M&A **Band 1**
Table: p.212

Reck, Joel (Massachusetts)
Profile: p.358
Real Estate **Band 3**
Table: p.351

Redden, Joe (Texas)
Profile: p.679
Litigation **Band 4**
Table: p.663

Redmond, Patricia (Florida)
Profile: p.176
Insolvency **Band 3**
Table: p.162

Reece, Joseph (Alaska)
Profile: p.14,15
Real Estate **Band 2**
Table: p.14

Reed, John (Kentucky)
Profile: p.306
Litigation **Band 2**
Table: p.303

Reed, Lucy (New York)
Profile: p.531
Arbitration **Band 2**
Table: p.443

Reed, Margery (Pennsylvania)
Profile: p.618
Banking & Finance **Band 3**
Table: p.598

Reed, Michael (Pennsylvania)
Profile: p.618
Insolvency **Band 3**
Table: p.607

Reed, Randall (Wyoming)
Profile: p.735
Corporate/M&A **Band 3**
Table: p.730

Reed, Steve (District of Columbia)
Profile: p.143
Energy **Band 4**
Table: p.115

Reed, William (Mississippi)
Profile: p.384
Litigation **Band 2**
Table: p.381

Reeder, Robert W (New York)
Profile: p.531
Capital Markets **Band 4**
Table: p.451

Reeves, Edward (Oregon)
Profile: p.594
Employment **Band 2**
Table: p.589

Reeves, James N (Alaska)
Profile: p.15
Environment **Band 2**
Table: p.12
Real Estate **Band 2**
Table: p.14
Real Estate **Band 2**
Table: p.14

Reeves, Susan (Alaska)
Profile: p.15
Environment **Band 1**
Table: p.12

Reges, Robert (Alaska)
Profile: p.15
Environment **Band 3**
Table: p.12

LEADING LAWYERS INDEX

Reich, Abraham (Pennsylvania)
Profile: p.618
Litigation **Band 3**
Table: p.611

Reich, Yaron Z (New York)
Profile: p.531
Tax **Band 4**
Table: p.499

Reidy, Daniel (Illinois)
Profile: p.270
Litigation **Band 2**
Table: p.245

Reidy, James (New Hampshire)
Profile: p.422
Employment **Band 1**
Table: p.417

Reilly, Daniel (Colorado)
Profile: p.85
Litigation **Band 3**
Table: p.79

Reilly, Gregory B (New Jersey)
Profile: p.432
Litigation **Band 3**
Table: p.428

Reinhardt Jr., William (Louisiana)
Profile: p.318
Employment **Band 4**
Table: p.310

Reinhart, Robert (Minnesota)
Profile: p.376
Employment **Band 1**
Table: p.371

Reinhold, Richard L (New York)
Profile: p.531
Tax **Band 3**
Table: p.499

Reische, Alan (New Hampshire)
Profile: p.423
Corporate/M&A **Band 1**
Table: p.415

Reisman, Stephen H (Florida)
Profile: p.176
Construction **Band 2**
Table: p.154

Reiss, Mike (Washington)
Profile: p.713
Employment **Band 2**
Table: p.708

Reiter, Glenn (New York)
Profile: p.531
Capital Markets **Band 4**
Table: p.448

Remele Jr, Lewis A (Minnesota)
Profile: p.376
Litigation **Band 1**
Table: p.372

Remington, Royce (Ohio)
Profile: p.578
Construction **Band 2**
Table: p.560

Renehan, Richard (Massachusetts)
Profile: p.358
Litigation **Band 1**
Table: p.349

Reno, Russell (Maryland)
Profile: p.332,334
Real Estate **Band 2**
Table: p.331

Reppert, Richard L (Ohio)
Profile: p.578
Real Estate **Band 2**
Table: p.572

Ressler, Alison (California)
Profile: p.71
Capital Markets **Band 2**
Table: p.32

Restivo Jr, James (Pennsylvania)
Profile: p.618
Litigation **Band 3**
Table: p.611

Reymond Jr, Leon J (Louisiana)
Profile: p.318
Banking & Finance **Band 3**
Table: p.307
Real Estate **Band 2**
Table: p.314

Rhodes, Tom (Georgia)
Profile: p.209
Antitrust **Band 3**
Table: p.181

Ricciardi, Mark (Nevada)
Profile: p.414
Employment **Band 1**
Table: p.408

Riccolo, John L (Iowa)
Profile: p.293
Litigation **Band 2**
Table: p.290

Rice, Stephen (Nevada)
Profile: p.414
Real Estate **Band 4**
Table: p.411

Rich, Bruce (New York)
Profile: p.531
Media & Entertainment **Band 5**
Table: p.485

Rich, Frederic C (New York)
Profile: p.531
Projects **Band 2**
Table: p.491

Richard, Andrea Leah (Wyoming)
Profile: p.734,735
Real Estate **Band**
Table: p.734
Real Estate **Band 3**
Table: p.734

Richard, Barry (Florida)
Profile: p.177
Litigation **Band 3**
Table: p.165

Richard, Molly (Texas)
Profile: p.679
Intellectual Property **Band 2**
Table: p.661

Richards, Charlie (Delaware)
Profile: p.101
Litigation **Band 3**
Table: p.98

Richards, Russell (Georgia)
Profile: p.209
Corporate/M&A **Band 2**
Table: p.187

Richardson, Joseph (Arizona)
Profile: p.22
Corporate/M&A **Band 1**
Table: p.16

Richardson, Todd (Nebraska)
Profile: p.405
Corporate/M&A **Band 2**
Table: p.400

Richman, Gerald (Florida)
Profile: p.177
Litigation **Band 3**
Table: p.165

Richman, Hershel (Pennsylvania)
Profile: p.618
Environment **Band 2**
Table: p.604

Richter, Peter (Oregon)
Profile: p.594
Litigation **Band 3**
Table: p.590

Riddell, Stephen (Georgia)
Profile: p.209
Employment **Band 4**
Table: p.189

Ridgley, Thomas (Ohio)
Profile: p.578
Litigation **Band 3**
Table: p.570

Ridley, Fred (Florida)
Profile: p.177
Real Estate **Band 4**
Table: p.167

Ridley, John (New Jersey)
Profile: p.432
Employment **Band 2**
Table: p.427

Riedel, Harley (Florida)
Profile: p.177
Insolvency **Band 5**
Table: p.162

Riedy, James (District of Columbia)
Profile: p.143
Tax **Band 4**
Table: p.130

Rieke, Robert (Nebraska)
Profile: p.405
Real Estate **Band 1**
Table: p.404

Riesel, Daniel (New York)
Profile: p.532
Environment **Band 3**
Table: p.469

Riggs, Richard (Oklahoma)
Profile: p.585,586
Real Estate **Band 3**
Table: p.585

Riley, Byron (Iowa)
Profile: p.293
Corporate/M&A **Band 4**
Table: p.286

Riley, Steven (Tennessee)
Profile: p.642
Litigation **Band 1**
Table: p.639

Riley, Tom (Iowa)
Profile: p.293
Employment **Band 3**
Table: p.288

Rill, James F (District of Columbia)
Profile: p.143
Antitrust **Band 2**
Table: p.103

Rinaldi, Joseph (Undefined)
Profile: p.
Corporate/M&A **Band 5**
Table: p.460

Rindy, Dean (North Dakota)
Profile: p.557,557
Real Estate **Band 3**
Table: p.557

Rinehart, John (Washington)
Profile: p.713
Employment **Band 1**
Table: p.708

Ringel, Dean (New York)
Profile: p.532
Media & Entertainment **Band 3**
Table: p.485

Rippie, Glenn (Illinois)
Profile: p.270
Energy **Band 1**
Table: p.238

Riter, Charles (South Dakota)
Profile: p.633,634
Real Estate **Band 2**
Table: p.633

Ritok, Joseph (Michigan)
Profile: p.366
Employment **Band 2**
Table: p.363

Ritt, Roger (Massachusetts)
Profile: p.358
Tax **Band 2**
Table: p.353

Rivkin, David W (New York)
Profile: p.532
Arbitration **Band 1**
Table: p.443

Robb, Peter (Vermont)
Profile: p.697
Employment **Band 2**
Table: p.694

Robein Jr., Louis (Louisiana)
Profile: p.318
Employment **Band 1**
Table: p.310

Roberts, Harry (Texas)
Profile: p.679
Real Estate **Band 4**
Table: p.665

Roberts, James (Virginia)
Profile: p.705
Litigation **Band 1**
Table: p.702

Roberts, John (District of Columbia)
Profile: p.144
Litigation **Band 1**
Table: p.123

Roberts, Richard (District of Columbia)
Profile: p.144
Energy **Band 5**
Table: p.115

Roberts, Thomas A (New York)
Profile: p.532
Private Equity **Band 4**
Table: p.487

Robertson, Ann (Alabama)
Profile: p.8
Employment **Band 3**
Table: p.2

Robertson, Eric (Illinois)
Profile: p.270
Energy **Band 3**
Table: p.238

Robertson, Gregory (Virginia)
Profile: p.705
Employment **Band 2**
Table: p.701

Robiner, Susan (Minnesota)
Profile: p.377
Employment **Band 3**
Table: p.371

Robins, Charles W (Massachusetts)
Profile: p.358
Private Equity **Band 3**
Table: p.350

Robinson, Bob (Arizona)
Profile: p.22
Real Estate **Band 2**
Table: p.20

Robinson, Donald C. (Montana)
Profile: p.399
Litigation **Band 1**
Table: p.396

Robinson, Frank (Colorado)
Profile: p.85
Real Estate **Band 1**
Table: p.81

Robinson, John (Florida)
Profile: p.177
Employment **Band 2**
Table: p.158

Robinson, Spencer (Arkansas)
Profile: p.27
Employment **Band 2**
Table: p.24

Robinson II, Russell M (North Carolina)
Profile: p.553
Corporate/M&A **Band 1**
Table: p.546

Robison, John (Wisconsin)
Profile: p.729
Corporate/M&A **Band 3**
Table: p.723

Robison, Kent (Nevada)
Profile: p.414
Litigation **Band 3**
Table: p.409

Robison, Reid (Oklahoma)
Profile: p.586
Litigation **Band 3**
Table: p.583

Robitzek, William (Maine)
Profile: p.326
Litigation **Band 3**
Table: p.322

Roby, Patrick M (Iowa)
Profile: p.293
Litigation **Band 1**
Table: p.290

Rocap, Donald E (Illinois)
Profile: p.270
Tax **Band 2**
Table: p.252

Rocap, James (District of Columbia)
Profile: p.144
Insurance **Band 3**
Table: p.120

Rocci, Stephen (Pennsylvania)
Profile: p.618
Intellectual Property **U**
Table: p.609

Rockwell, David (Washington)
Profile: p.712,713
Real Estate **Band 3**
Table: p.711

Rod, Jonathan (New York)
Profile: p.532
Projects **Band 4**
Table: p.491

Roddenberry, Stephen (Florida)
Profile: p.177
Corporate/M&A **Band 1**
Table: p.156

Rode, Helle (Oregon)
Profile: p.594
Employment **Band 4**
Table: p.589

Roe, Clifford (Ohio)
Profile: p.578
Corporate/M&A **Band 3**
Table: p.562

Rogers, CB (Georgia)
Profile: p.209
Antitrust **Band 5**
Table: p.181
Litigation **Band 1**
Table: p.198

LEADING LAWYERS INDEX

Rogers, Jr, Theodore O
(New York)
Profile: p.532
Employment **Band 1**
Table: p.467

Rohlf, Joan (Alaska)
Profile: p.15
Employment **Band 3**
Table: p.11

Rohrbach, Peter
(District of Columbia)
Profile: p.144
Communications **Band 2**
Table: p.107

Rokosz, Ronald (Illinois)
Profile: p.270
Banking & Finance **Band 2**
Table: p.226

Roles, Forrest (West Virginia)
Profile: p.722
Employment **Band 1**
Table: p.717

Rolfe, Ron (New York)
Profile: p.532
Antitrust **Band 4**
Table: p.441

Rolnick, Lawrence M
(New Jersey)
Profile: p.432
Litigation **Band 3**
Table: p.428

Rom, Rebecca (Minnesota)
Profile: p.377
Real Estate **Band 2**
Table: p.374

Rooney, John (Illinois)
Profile: p.270
Communications **Band 4**
Table: p.229

Ropski, Gary (Illinois)
Profile: p.270
Intellectual Property **Band 3**
Table: p.244

Rosati, Jack (Ohio)
Profile: p.578
Construction **Band 3**
Table: p.560

Rosati, Mario (California)
Profile: p.71
Communications **Band 5**
Table: p.34

Rosch, Tom (California)
Profile: p.71
Antitrust **Band 2**
Table: p.29

Roseman, Barry (Colorado)
Profile: p.85
Employment **Band 3**
Table: p.77

Rosen, Burt (New York)
Profile: p.532
Tax **Band 4**
Table: p.499

Rosen, Edward J (New York)
Profile: p.532
Capital Markets **Band 1**
Table: p.451

Rosen, J Philip (New York)
Profile: p.532
Real Estate **Band 4**
Table: p.493

Rosen, Jon (Washington)
Profile: p.713
Employment **Band 1**
Table: p.708

Rosen, Matthew A (New York)
Profile: p.533
Tax **Band 1**
Table: p.499

Rosen, Peter K (California)
Profile: p.71
Insurance **Band 4**
Table: p.46

Rosen, Richard (New York)
Profile: p.533
Litigation **Band 4**
Table: p.481

Rosen, Richard L
(District of Columbia)
Profile: p.144
Antitrust **Band 3**
Table: p.103

Rosenbaum, Robert
(Minnesota)
Profile: p.377
Corporate/M&A **Band 1**
Table: p.369

Rosenberg, Donald S
(Florida)
Profile: p.177
Construction **Band 3**
Table: p.154

Rosenberg, Gregg (Texas)
Profile: p.680
Employment **Band 1**
Table: p.651

Rosenberg, James (Maryland)
Profile: p.334
Employment **Band 3**
Table: p.328

Rosenberg, Marc S
(New York)
Profile: p.533
Capital Markets **Band 4**
Table: p.448

Rosenberg, Mark (New York)
Profile: p.533
Environment **Band 4**
Table: p.469

Rosenberg, Michael (Florida)
Profile: p.177
Tax **Band 1**
Table: p.170

Rosenberg, Robert
(New York)
Profile: p.533
Insolvency **Band 3**
Table: p.472

Rosenberg, Sumner (Georgia)
Profile: p.209
Intellectual Property **Band 4**
Table: p.195

Rosenberg, Thomas (Ohio)
Profile: p.578
Construction **Band 3**
Table: p.560

Rosenblatt, Paul (Georgia)
Profile: p.209
Insolvency **U**
Table: p.193

Rosenblatt, William W
(New York)
Profile: p.533
Insurance **Band 1**
Table: p.477

Rosenbloom, H David
(District of Columbia)
Profile: p.144
Tax **Band 1**
Table: p.130

Rosenbloom, Jim (Illinois)
Profile: p.270
Real Estate **Band 4**
Table: p.249

Rosenbloom, Lewis S
(Illinois)
Profile: p.270
Insolvency **Band 3**
Table: p.241

Rosenbloom, Robert
(Georgia)
Profile: p.209
Intellectual Property **Band 5**
Table: p.195

Rosenblum, Peter
(Massachusetts)
Profile: p.358
Corporate/M&A **Band 4**
Table: p.340

Rosenfeld, Robert (California)
Profile: p.71
Antitrust **Band 4**
Table: p.29

Rosenfeldt, Stuart (Florida)
Profile: p.177
Employment **Band 2**
Table: p.157

Rosenthal, Barry
(District of Columbia)
Profile: p.144
Real Estate **Band 3**
Table: p.127

Rosner, Douglas
(Massachusetts)
Profile: p.358
Insolvency **U**
Table: p.346

Rosner, Richard (Ohio)
Profile: p.578
Real Estate **Band 2**
Table: p.572

Ross, Allen (New York)
Profile: p.533
Construction **Band 3**
Table: p.458

Ross, David L (Florida)
Profile: p.177
Litigation **Band 4**
Table: p.165

Ross, Mickey (Georgia)
Profile: p.210
Antitrust **Band 2**
Table: p.181

Rossiter, Robert (Nebraska)
Profile: p.405
Employment **Band 1**
Table: p.402

Rossman, Vladimir R
(New York)
Profile: p.533
Banking & Finance **Band 2**
Table: p.445

Rosston, Richard (Alaska)
Profile: p.15
Corporate/M&A **Band 1**
Table: p.9

Rotch, Peter (New Hampshire)
Profile: p.423
Real Estate **Band 1**
Table: p.420

Roth, George (Wisconsin)
Profile: p.729
Real Estate **Band 3**
Table: p.727

Rothermel, Sarah
(Massachusetts)
Profile: p.358
Private Equity **Band 3**
Table: p.350

Rothstein, Scott (Florida)
Profile: p.177
Employment **Band 2**
Table: p.157

Rottenberg, Alan
(Massachusetts)
Profile: p.358
Real Estate **Band 2**
Table: p.351

Rotwitt, Jeffrey (Pennsylvania)
Profile: p.618
Real Estate **Band 4**
Table: p.613

Rounsaville, Keith (Florida)
Profile: p.177
Antitrust **Band 1**
Table: p.151

Roussel, Randy (Louisiana)
Profile: p.318
Banking & Finance **Band 3**
Table: p.307

Rovine, Arthur (New York)
Profile: p.533
Arbitration **Band 3**
Table: p.443

Rowe, Jack D (Missouri)
Profile: p.393
Employment **Band 4**
Table: p.388

Rowe, Keven (Utah)
Profile: p.691
Real Estate **Band 3**
Table: p.689

Rowe, Larry (Massachusetts)
Profile: p.358
Private Equity **Band 2**
Table: p.350

Rowe, Paul (New Jersey)
Profile: p.432
Litigation **Band 1**
Table: p.428

Rowen, Andrew S (New York)
Profile: p.533
Insurance **Band 3**
Table: p.477

Roy, Paul J N (Illinois)
Profile: p.271
Communications **Band 4**
Table: p.229

Rozmarin, George (Nebraska)
Profile: p.405
Employment **Band 1**
Table: p.402

Rubalcava, Sharon F
(California)
Profile: p.71
Environment **Band 3**
Table: p.43

Rubin, Blake D
(District of Columbia)
Profile: p.144
Real Estate **Band 4**
Table: p.127

Rubin, David (Rhode Island)
Profile: p.623
Real Estate **Band 1**
Table: p.622

Rubin, James (Illinois)
Profile: p.271
Insurance **Band 3**
Table: p.242

Rubin, Joel (Illinois)
Profile: p.271
Real Estate **Band 2**
Table: p.249

Rubin, Peter J (Maine)
Profile: p.326
Litigation **Band 3**
Table: p.322

Rubin, Robert (New York)
Profile: p.534
Construction **Band 2**
Table: p.458

Ruby, Allen (California)
Profile: p.71
Litigation **Band 3**
Table: p.50

Rudavsky, Dahlia
(Massachusetts)
Profile: p.358
Employment **Band 2**
Table: p.341

Rudd, David (Utah)
Profile: p.691
Corporate/M&A **Band 3**
Table: p.684

Rudman, Richard
(Massachusetts)
Profile: p.358
Real Estate **Band 2**
Table: p.351

Rudnick, Robert
(District of Columbia)
Profile: p.144
Tax **Band 4**
Table: p.130

Rudy, Mark (California)
Profile: p.71
Employment **Band 1**
Table: p.39

Ruegger, Philip (New York)
Profile: p.534
Private Equity **Band 2**
Table: p.487

Ruff, Randolph (Illinois)
Profile: p.271
Construction **Band 3**
Table: p.231

Rule, Charles F (Rick)
(District of Columbia)
Profile: p.144
Antitrust **Band 2**
Table: p.103

Rupe, Alan L (Kansas)
Profile: p.299
Employment **Band 1**
Table: p.296

Rusche, Mark C (Georgia)
Profile: p.210
Real Estate **Band 3**
Table: p.199

Rush, Jeffery (Ohio)
Profile: p.578
Banking & Finance **Band 1**
Table: p.559

Rushford, Robert (Vermont)
Profile: p.697
Real Estate **Band 1**
Table: p.696

Rusing, Michael J (Arizona)
Profile: p.22
Litigation **Band 3**
Table: p.19

Russ, Michael (Georgia)
Profile: p.210
Antitrust **Band 5**
Table: p.181
Litigation **Band 2**
Table: p.198

Russell, James (Illinois)
Profile: p.271
Environment **Band 4**
Table: p.239

Rutkowski, Larry (New York)
Profile: p.534
Shipping **Band 1**
Table: p.496

Rutledge, J Kent (Wyoming)
Profile: p.735
Litigation **Band 3**
Table: p.732

Rutter, David (Tennessee)
Profile: p.642
Real Estate **U**
Table: p.640

LEADING LAWYERS INDEX

Ruxin, Paul (Illinois)
Profile: p.271
Energy **Band 3**
Table: p.238

Ryan, Patrick (Oklahoma)
Profile: p.586
Litigation **Band 1**
Table: p.583

Ryan, Thomas (Illinois)
Profile: p.271
Antitrust **Band 1**
Table: p.224

Rydzel, James (Ohio)
Profile: p.578
Employment **Band 2**
Table: p.565

S

Sabalis, Patricia (Vermont)
Profile: p.697
Employment **Band 1**
Table: p.694

Sachs, John
(District of Columbia)
Profile: p.144
Projects **Band 2**
Table: p.126

Sacks, Stephen
(District of Columbia)
Profile: p.144
Litigation **Band 2**
Table: p.123

Sacripanti, Peter (New York)
Profile: p.534
Environment **Band 4**
Table: p.469

Sadler Jr, Luther (Florida)
Profile: p.177
Corporate/M&A **Band 3**
Table: p.156

Saeed, Faiza (New York)
Profile: p.534

Saffer, David (Kentucky)
Profile: p.306
Real Estate **Band 2**
Table: p.304

Sagarin, Daniel (Connecticut)
Profile: p.93
Litigation **Band 4**
Table: p.90

Sager, Kelli (California)
Profile: p.71
Media & Entertainment **Band 1**
Table: p.53

Saggese, Nicholas P
(California)
Profile: p.71
Capital Markets **Band 1**
Table: p.32
Corporate/M&A **Band 3**
Table: p.37

Saint-Antoine, Paul
(Pennsylvania)
Profile: p.618
Antitrust **U**
Table: p.596

Salazar, John (New Mexico)
Profile: p.438
Real Estate **Band 2**
Table: p.437

Salch, Steven (Texas)
Profile: p.680
Tax **Band 3**
Table: p.667

Salem, George
(District of Columbia)
Profile: p.145
Employment **Band 2**
Table: p.112

Sales, Kenneth (Kentucky)
Profile: p.306
Employment **Band 2**
Table: p.301

Salpeter, Alan N (Illinois)
Profile: p.271
Litigation **Band 3**
Table: p.245

Salter, Dean (Colorado)
Profile: p.85
Corporate/M&A **Band 1**
Table: p.75

Saltiel, David (Illinois)
Profile: p.271
Media & Entertainment **Band 1**
Table: p.247

Salvatore, Paul (New York)
Profile: p.534
Employment **Band 2**
Table: p.467

Salyers, Douglas D (Georgia)
Profile: p.210
Intellectual Property **Band 4**
Table: p.195

Salzman, Martin (Georgia)
Profile: p.210
Construction **Band 4**
Table: p.184

Samorajczyk, Stanley
(District of Columbia)
Profile: p.145

Sampson, Bill (Kansas)
Profile: p.299
Litigation **Band 1**
Table: p.297

Samuels, Leslie B (New York)
Profile: p.534
Tax **Band 3**
Table: p.499

Samuels, Richard
(New Hampshire)
Profile: p.423
Corporate/M&A **Band 1**
Table: p.415

Samuels, Stanley (Oregon)
Profile: p.594
Real Estate **Band 2**
Table: p.592

Samuels Jones, Karen
(Colorado)
Profile: p.85
Real Estate **Band 4**
Table: p.81

Samuelson, Jaki (Iowa)
Profile: p.293
Employment **Band 2**
Table: p.288

Sanders, David P (Illinois)
Profile: p.271
Media & Entertainment **Band 1**
Table: p.247

Sandler, Richard J (New York)
Profile: p.534
Capital Markets **Band 2**
Table: p.448

Sandler, Sheldon N
(Delaware)
Profile: p.101
Employment **Band 1**
Table: p.96

Sanford, Bruce
(District of Columbia)
Profile: p.145
Media & Entertainment **Band 1**
Table: p.125

Sanford, Steven (South Dakota)
Profile: p.634
Litigation **Band 1**
Table: p.632

Sanson, Paul (Connecticut)
Profile: p.93
Litigation **Band 4**
Table: p.90

Santi, Richard (Iowa)
Profile: p.293
Litigation **Band 1**
Table: p.290

Saper, Jeff (California)
Profile: p.72
Communications **Band 1**
Table: p.34
Corporate/M&A **Band 4**
Table: p.37

Sapp, Richard (Iowa)
Profile: p.293
Litigation **Band 2**
Table: p.290

Sartore, John T (Vermont)
Profile: p.697
Litigation **Band 2**
Table: p.695

Satriana, Dan (Colorado)
Profile: p.85
Employment **Band 4**
Table: p.78

Sattler, Bruce (Colorado)
Profile: p.85
Employment **Band 1**
Table: p.78

Saul, Gary (Florida)
Profile: p.177
Real Estate **Band 4**
Table: p.167

Saunders, Paul (New York)
Profile: p.534
Litigation **Band 5**
Table: p.481

Sauntry, June Ann (Georgia)
Profile: p.210
Antitrust **Band 4**
Table: p.181

Savage, Robert (Rhode Island)
Profile: p.623
Employment **Band 1**
Table: p.621

Savage, Stephen (Arizona)
Profile: p.22
Real Estate **Band 3**
Table: p.20

Savarise, Jeff (Kentucky)
Profile: p.306
Employment **Band 3**
Table: p.302

Sax, Paul (California)
Profile: p.72
Tax **Band 2**
Table: p.58

Saxbe, Charles Rockwell
(Ohio)
Profile: p.578
Litigation **Band 4**
Table: p.570

Saxon, John (Alabama)
Profile: p.8
Employment **Band 4**
Table: p.2

Sayler, Robert
(District of Columbia)
Profile: p.145
Insurance **Band 1**
Table: p.120
Litigation **✪**
Table: p.123

Scallen, Timothy (Minnesota)
Profile: p.377
Corporate/M&A **Band 2**
Table: p.369

Scanlon, Chris (Indiana)
Profile: p.284
Litigation **Band 1**
Table: p.280

Scarborough, Robert
(New York)
Profile: p.534
Tax **Band 2**
Table: p.499

Scavone, Arthur (New York)
Profile: p.534
Projects **Band 1**
Table: p.491

Schachter, Robert (New Jersey)
Profile: p.432
Real Estate **Band 3**
Table: p.429

Schadt, Gordon (Alaska)
Profile: p.14,15
Real Estate **Band 3**
Table: p.14

Schaefer, Lawrence
(Minnesota)
Profile: p.377
Employment **Band 1**
Table: p.370

Schaffer, Michael
(South Dakota)
Profile: p.
Litigation **Band 2**
Table: p.632

Schaffran, Andrew (New York)
Profile: p.534
Employment **Band 4**
Table: p.467

Schallhorn, Scott (Arkansas)
Profile: p.27
Real Estate **Band 3**
Table: p.26

Scharfstein, Joel (New York)
Profile: p.534
Tax **Band 3**
Table: p.499

Schechter, Mark
(District of Columbia)
Profile: p.145
Antitrust **Band 4**
Table: p.103

Scheler, Brad Eric (New York)
Profile: p.534
Insolvency **Band 2**
Table: p.472

Schell, J Michael (New York)
Profile: p.534

Schendel, William B (Alaska)
Profile: p.15
Employment **Band 1**
Table: p.10

Scher, Howard (Pennsylvania)
Profile: p.618
Litigation **Band 3**
Table: p.611

Scherman, William S
(District of Columbia)
Profile: p.145
Energy **Band 1**
Table: p.115

Schetman, Richard
(New York)
Profile: p.534
Capital Markets **Band 2**
Table: p.453

Scheu, William (Florida)
Profile: p.177
Real Estate **Band 4**
Table: p.167

Schiavoni, Robert (West Virginia)
Profile: p.722
Employment **Band 3**
Table: p.716

Schildkraut, Marc
(District of Columbia)
Profile: p.145
Antitrust **Band 4**
Table: p.103

Schiller, Eric (Illinois)
Profile: p.271
Real Estate **Band 4**
Table: p.249

Schiller, Jonathan
(District of Columbia)
Profile: p.145
Arbitration **Band 4**
Table: p.106

Schleier, Tod (Arizona)
Profile: p.22
Employment **Band 1**
Table: p.18

Schler, Michael (New York)
Profile: p.534
Tax **Band 1**
Table: p.499

Schloemer, Jeffrey (Ohio)
Profile: p.578
Banking & Finance **Band 1**
Table: p.559

Schlossman, William
(North Dakota)
Profile: p.557
Corporate/M&A **Band 3**
Table: p.554

Schmall, Deborah J
(California)
Profile: p.72
Environment **Band 4**
Table: p.43

Schnabl, Marco E (New York)
Profile: p.535
Arbitration **Band 3**
Table: p.443

Schneider, Jon
(Massachusetts)
Profile: p.358
Insolvency **Band 3**
Table: p.346

Schneider, Leslie
(District of Columbia)
Profile: p.145
Tax **Band 2**
Table: p.130

Schneider, Michael R
(Louisiana)
Profile: p.318
Real Estate **Band 2**
Table: p.314

Schneidman, Dan (Wisconsin)
Profile: p.729
Employment **Band 3**
Table: p.724

Schneidman, Edward J
(Illinois)
Profile: p.272
Corporate/M&A **Band 5**
Table: p.233

Schneidman, Leonard
(Massachusetts)
Profile: p.354,358
Tax **Band 3**
Table: p.353

Schoenberg, Clifford H
(New York)
Profile: p.535
Insurance **Band 4**
Table: p.477

LEADING LAWYERS INDEX

Schoenbrun, Larry (Texas)
Profile: p.680
Corporate/M&A **Band 4**
Table: p.649

Schonholtz, Margot
(New York)
Profile: p.535
Insolvency **Band 5**
Table: p.472

Schor, Laurence
(District of Columbia)
Profile: p.145
Construction **Band 2**
Table: p.110

Schorling, William H.
(Pennsylvania)
Profile: p.618
Insolvency **Band 2**
Table: p.607

Schraff, Christopher (Ohio)
Profile: p.578
Environment **Band 2**
Table: p.567

Schrag, Donald E. (Kansas)
Profile: p.299
Real Estate **Band 3**
Table: p.298

Schroeder, William (Vermont)
Profile: p.697
Real Estate **Band 1**
Table: p.696

Schuler, Alison (New Mexico)
Profile: p.438
Corporate/M&A **Band 4**
Table: p.433

Schulhofer, Ellen (Nevada)
Profile: p.414
Corporate/M&A **Band 2**
Table: p.406

Schull, E Gunner (Hawaii)
Profile: p.218
Corporate/M&A **Band 2**
Table: p.212

Schulman, Clifford (Florida)
Profile: p.177
Environment **Band 4**
Table: p.160

Schultz, Donald I (Wyoming)
Profile: p.735
Litigation **Band 2**
Table: p.732

Schulz, David (New York)
Profile: p.535
Media & Entertainment **Band 2**
Table: p.485

Schumacher, Kirk (Nevada)
Profile: p.414
Corporate/M&A **Band 2**
Table: p.406

Schumer, Robert B
(New York)
Profile: p.535
Corporate/M&A **Band 5**
Table: p.460

Schwab, Douglas (California)
Profile: p.72
Litigation **Band 3**
Table: p.50

Schwab, Stephen (Illinois)
Profile: p.272
Insurance **Band 1**
Table: p.242

Schwartz, Alan (Michigan)
Profile: p.366
Corporate/M&A **Band 3**
Table: p.361

Schwartz, Andrew
(Massachusetts)
Profile: p.358
Insolvency **Band 3**
Table: p.346

Schwartz, Daniel L
(Connecticut)
Profile: p.93
Employment **Band 4**
Table: p.89

Schwartz, David
(District of Columbia)
Profile: p.145
Energy **Band 5**
Table: p.115

Schwartz, Debra (Georgia)
Profile: p.210
Employment **Band 3**
Table: p.188

Schwartz, Donald (Illinois)
Profile: p.272
Banking & Finance **Band 2**
Table: p.226

Schwartz, Harvey
(Massachusetts)
Profile: p.358
Employment **Band 3**
Table: p.341

Schwartz, Herbert F
(New York)
Profile: p.535
Intellectual Property **Band 1**
Table: p.479

Schwartz, Jaimie Paul
(Maine)
Profile: p.326
Real Estate **Band 3**
Table: p.324

Schwartz, Jodi J (New York)
Profile: p.535
Tax **Band 2**
Table: p.499

Schwartz, Niki (Ohio)
Profile: p.578
Employment **Band 2**
Table: p.564
Litigation **Band 4**
Table: p.570

Schwartz, Paul
(Massachusetts)
Profile: p.358
Real Estate **Band 3**
Table: p.351

Schwartz , Robert C
(Georgia)
Profile: p.210
Banking & Finance **Band 3**
Table: p.183

Schwartz, Steven (New York)
Profile: p.535
Insurance **Band 4**
Table: p.477

Schwarz, James (Indiana)
Profile: p.284
Real Estate **Band 4**
Table: p.282

Schwed, Robert A (New York)
Profile: p.535
Private Equity **Band 4**
Table: p.489

Scimia, Joe (Indiana)
Profile: p.284
Real Estate **Band 3**
Table: p.282

Scott, Thane (Massachusetts)
Profile: p.358
Antitrust **Band 3**
Table: p.337

Scrivner, Tom (Wisconsin)
Profile: p.729
Employment **Band 1**
Table: p.725

Seabolt, Richard (California)
Profile: p.72
Insurance **Band 2**
Table: p.46

Seals, Paul (Texas)
Profile: p.680
Environment **Band 3**
Table: p.655

Searcy, Christian (Florida)
Profile: p.177
Litigation **Band 3**
Table: p.165

Seay, James (Florida)
Profile: p.177
Real Estate **Band 4**
Table: p.167

Sebris, Robert (Washington)
Profile: p.713
Employment **Band 2**
Table: p.708

Sederstrom, Charles
(Nebraska)
Profile: p.405
Corporate/M&A **Band 2**
Table: p.400

Segal, Earl
(District of Columbia)
Profile: p.145
Real Estate **Band 3**
Table: p.127

Segal, Herbert (Kentucky)
Profile: p.306
Employment **Band 2**
Table: p.301

Segerblom, Richard (Nevada)
Profile: p.414
Employment **Band 1**
Table: p.407

Seidel, Arthur (Pennsylvania)
Profile: p.618
Intellectual Property **Band 1**
Table: p.609

Seiffert, James (Kentucky)
Profile: p.306
Corporate/M&A **Band 3**
Table: p.300

Selber Silverstein, Laurie
(Delaware)
Profile: p.101
Insolvency **Band 3**
Table: p.96

Self, Shannon (Oklahoma)
Profile: p.586
Corporate/M&A **Band 2**
Table: p.580

Selig, John S (Arkansas)
Profile: p.27
Corporate/M&A **Band 1**
Table: p.23

Selinger, Jerry (Texas)
Profile: p.680
Intellectual Property **Band 4**
Table: p.661

Sellergren, David C
(Minnesota)
Profile: p.377
Real Estate **Band 2**
Table: p.374

Sellers, Joseph
(District of Columbia)
Profile: p.145
Employment **Band 3**
Table: p.112

Sellers, Lawrence (Florida)
Profile: p.178
Environment **Band 2**
Table: p.160

Selver, Paul (New York)
Profile: p.535
Real Estate **Band 2**
Table: p.493

Semple, Lloyd A (Michigan)
Profile: p.366
Corporate/M&A **Band 1**
Table: p.361

Seneker, Carl (Kim)
(California)
Profile: p.72
Real Estate **Band 3**
Table: p.56

Senn, Mark (Colorado)
Profile: p.85
Real Estate **Band 3**
Table: p.81

Sennett, Nancy (Wisconsin)
Profile: p.729
Litigation **Band 3**
Table: p.726

Sexton, Robert (Alabama)
Profile: p.8
Real Estate **Band 3**
Table: p.6

Seyfer, Greg (Iowa)
Profile: p.292,293
Real Estate **Band 3**
Table: p.291

Shachar, Avishai (New York)
Profile: p.535
Tax **Band 2**
Table: p.499

Shaft, Grant (North Dakota)
Profile: p.557,557
Real Estate **Band 2**
Table: p.557

Shalton, Lonnie (Missouri)
Profile: p.393
Real Estate **Band 2**
Table: p.391

Shanahan, Ward (Montana)
Profile: p.399
Litigation **Band 2**
Table: p.396

Shank, Mark (Texas)
Profile: p.680
Employment **Band 3**
Table: p.652

Shanks, Patricia L (California)
Profile: p.72
Environment **Band 4**
Table: p.43

Shannon, Brendan Linehan
(Delaware)
Profile: p.101
Insolvency **Band 5**
Table: p.96

Shapiro, Ben (Georgia)
Profile: p.210
Construction **Band 4**
Table: p.184

Shapiro, Howard (Louisiana)
Profile: p.318
Employment **Band 2**
Table: p.311

Shapiro, Jonathan (Maine)
Profile: p.326
Employment **Band 3**
Table: p.321

Shapiro, Raymond
(Pennsylvania)
Profile: p.618
Insolvency **Band 1**
Table: p.607

Shapley, Christopher
(Mississippi)
Profile: p.384
Litigation **Band 2**
Table: p.381

Sharf, Jesse (California)
Profile: p.72
Real Estate **Band 4**
Table: p.56

Sharp, F DeArmond (Nevada)
Profile: p.412,414
Real Estate **Band 2**
Table: p.411

Sharpe, Jeremy (Iowa)
Profile: p.293
Real Estate **Band 1**
Table: p.291

Sharpe, Kris (Minnesota)
Profile: p.377
Corporate/M&A **Band 1**
Table: p.369

Shaw, Gregory (New York)
Profile: p.535
Capital Markets **Band 2**
Table: p.453

Shawe , Stephen D
(Maryland)
Profile: p.334
Employment **Band 3**
Table: p.329

Shay, Stephen
(Massachusetts)
Profile: p.358
Tax **Band 2**
Table: p.353

Shea, James (Maryland)
Profile: p.334
Litigation **Band 2**
Table: p.330

Sheeder, Robert (Texas)
Profile: p.680
Employment **Band 2**
Table: p.652

Sheeran, Timothy (Ohio)
Profile: p.578
Employment **Band 4**
Table: p.565

Sheffield, Jeffrey T (Illinois)
Profile: p.272
Tax **Band 2**
Table: p.252

Sheinfeld, Myron (Texas)
Profile: p.680
Insolvency **Band 3**
Table: p.657

Shemin, Ken (Arkansas)
Profile: p.27
Litigation **Band 1**
Table: p.25

Shenker, Joseph C (New York)
Profile: p.535
Real Estate **Band 1**
Table: p.493

Shepherd, Kevin (Maryland)
Profile: p.332,334
Real Estate **Band 3**
Table: p.331

Shepherd, Thomas
(Mississippi)
Profile: p.384
Corporate/M&A **Band 2**
Table: p.378

Shepro, Richard Warren
(Illinois)
Profile: p.272
Corporate/M&A **Band 5**
Table: p.233

LEADING LAWYERS INDEX

Sher, Leopold (Louisiana)
Profile: p.318
Real Estate **Band 1**
Table: p.314

Sherck, Timothy C (Illinois)
Profile: p.272
Tax **Band 1**
Table: p.252

Sherk, Kenneth (Arizona)
Profile: p.22
Litigation **Band 3**
Table: p.19

Sherman, Morris (Minnesota)
Profile: p.377
Corporate/M&A **Band 1**
Table: p.369

Shiekman, Laurence
(Pennsylvania)
Profile: p.618
Antitrust **Band 3**
Table: p.596

Shields, Robert (Georgia)
Profile: p.210
Litigation **Band 3**
Table: p.198

Shilepsky, Nancy
(Massachusetts)
Profile: p.358
Employment **Band 1**
Table: p.341

Shim, Paul (New York)
Profile: p.535
Corporate/M&A **U**
Table: p.460

Shimshak, Stephen
(New York)
Profile: p.536
Insolvency **Band 5**
Table: p.472

Shockley, Steven C (Indiana)
Profile: p.284
Litigation **Band 3**
Table: p.280

Shoemaker Jr. James M.
(South Carolina)
Profile: p.629
Corporate/M&A **Band 2**
Table: p.624

Short, Barry (Missouri)
Profile: p.393
Litigation **Band 3**
Table: p.389

Shortlidge, Neil (Kansas)
Profile: p.299
Real Estate **Band 3**
Table: p.298

Shortz, Richard (California)
Profile: p.72
Projects **Band 2**
Table: p.55

Shoss, Cynthia R (New York)
Profile: p.536
Insurance **Band 3**
Table: p.477

Shoup, David H (Alaska)
Profile: p.15
Employment **Band 2**
Table: p.10

Shriner, Tom (Wisconsin)
Profile: p.729
Litigation **Band 1**
Table: p.726

Shugrue, John (Illinois)
Profile: p.272
Insurance **Band 3**
Table: p.242

Shuker, R. Scott (Florida)
Profile: p.178
Insolvency **Band 4**
Table: p.162

Shulman, Larry R (Michigan)
Profile: p.367
Banking & Finance **Band 2**
Table: p.360

Shulman, Lawrence
(Maryland)
Profile: p.334

Shulman, Robert
(District of Columbia)
Profile: p.145
Insurance **Band 2**
Table: p.120

Shulruff, Stuart (Illinois)
Profile: p.272
Banking & Finance **Band 4**
Table: p.226

Shultz, Jeff (South Dakota)
Profile: p.634
Employment **Band 2**
Table: p.631

Shumadine, Conrad (Virginia)
Profile: p.705
Litigation **Band 2**
Table: p.702

Shuman, Melvin
(Massachusetts)
Profile: p.358
Real Estate **Band 3**
Table: p.351

Shuman, Stephen
(West Virginia)
Profile: p.722
Real Estate **Band 2**
Table: p.720

Shumate, Roger (Wyoming)
Profile: p.735
Employment **Band 3**
Table: p.732

Shuter, Bruce (Pennsylvania)
Profile: p.618
Banking & Finance **Band 1**
Table: p.598

Shutran, Richard (New York)
Profile: p.536

Sicilian, James (Connecticut)
Profile: p.93
Litigation **Band 1**
Table: p.90

Sicular, David (New York)
Profile: p.536
Tax **Band 4**
Table: p.499

Siebert, Bernie (Colorado)
Profile: p.85
Employment **Band 4**
Table: p.78

Siegal, Bradley (Alabama)
Profile: p.8
Real Estate **Band 4**
Table: p.6

Siegal, Don (Alabama)
Profile: p.8
Real Estate **Band 4**
Table: p.6

Siegel, Bradd (Ohio)
Profile: p.578
Employment **Band 3**
Table: p.565

Siegel, Steven (Colorado)
Profile: p.85
Corporate/M&A **Band 2**
Table: p.75

Siegfried, Steven (Florida)
Profile: p.178
Construction **Band 1**
Table: p.154

Sigel, John (Massachusetts)
Profile: p.359
Insolvency **Band 2**
Table: p.346

Silberman, Alan (Illinois)
Profile: p.272
Antitrust **Band 3**
Table: p.224

Silberstein, Rebecca F
(New York)
Profile: p.536
Private Equity **U**
Table: p.489

Silbert, Earl
(District of Columbia)
Profile: p.145
Litigation **Band 3**
Table: p.123

Siler Jr, Thomas (Mississippi)
Profile: p.384
Employment **Band 1**
Table: p.380

Silver, Michael J (Maryland)
Profile: p.334
Corporate/M&A **Band 3**
Table: p.327

Silverman, Eric (New York)
Profile: p.536
Projects **Band 3**
Table: p.491

Silverman, Lawrence
(Florida)
Profile: p.178
Antitrust **Band 2**
Table: p.151

Silverman, Leslie N
(New York)
Profile: p.536
Capital Markets **Band 4**
Table: p.448

Silverman, Mark
(District of Columbia)
Profile: p.145
Tax **Band 3**
Table: p.130

Silvestri, Stephen (Maryland)
Profile: p.334
Employment **Band 1**
Table: p.329

Simkin, Steven (New York)
Profile: p.536
Real Estate **Band 2**
Table: p.493

Simmons, Sherwin (Florida)
Profile: p.178
Tax **Band 2**
Table: p.170

Simms, Marsha E (New York)
Profile: p.536
Banking & Finance **Band 4**
Table: p.445

Simon, Mark (Illinois)
Profile: p.273
Real Estate **Band 4**
Table: p.249

Simon, Michael (Oregon)
Profile: p.594
Litigation **Band 3**
Table: p.590

Simonoff, Howard (New Jersey)
Profile: p.432
Employment **Band 2**
Table: p.426

Simons, David (Hawaii)
Profile: p.218
Employment **Band 1**
Table: p.213

Simons, Laird (California)
Profile: p.72
Communications **Band 4**
Table: p.34

Simons, Susan Brunick
(South Dakota)
Profile: p.634
Employment **Band 1**
Table: p.631

Simonsen, David (Virginia)
Profile: p.705
Employment **Band 3**
Table: p.701

Simonson, James (Minnesota)
Profile: p.377
Litigation **Band 1**
Table: p.372

Simpson, Michael (South Dakota)
Profile: p.634
Employment **Band 2**
Table: p.631

Simpson, Patrick (Oregon)
Profile: p.594
Corporate/M&A **Band 3**
Table: p.587

Sims, Charles (New York)
Profile: p.536
Media & Entertainment **Band 4**
Table: p.485

Sims, Hunter (Virginia)
Profile: p.705
Litigation **Band 2**
Table: p.702

Sims, Joe (District of Columbia)
Profile: p.145
Antitrust **Band 1**
Table: p.103

Sims, Roger (Florida)
Profile: p.178
Environment **Band 4**
Table: p.160

Sinclair, Brad (North Dakota)
Profile: p.557
Corporate/M&A **Band 2**
Table: p.554

Singer, Alan (Pennsylvania)
Profile: p.618
Corporate/M&A **Band**
Table: p.599
Corporate/M&A **Band 4**
Table: p.599

Singer, Andrew (California)
Profile: p.72
Projects **Band 3**
Table: p.55
Projects **Band 3**
Table: p.491

Singer, Paul (Pennsylvania)
Profile: p.618
Insolvency **Band 1**
Table: p.607

Singer, Steven
(Massachusetts)
Profile: p.359
Corporate/M&A **Band 2**
Table: p.340

Singer, Stuart (Florida)
Profile: p.178
Antitrust **Band 4**
Table: p.151

Singerman, Paul (Florida)
Profile: p.178
Insolvency **Band 1**
Table: p.162

Singleton, John (Maryland)
Profile: p.334
Employment **Band 1**
Table: p.328

Siniscalco, Gary (California)
Profile: p.72
Employment **Band 2**
Table: p.40

Sink, Charles (California)
Profile: p.72
Construction **Band 1**
Table: p.36

Sinkfield, Richard H (Georgia)
Profile: p.210
Litigation **Band 1**
Table: p.198

Sirkin, Joel (Massachusetts)
Profile: p.359
Real Estate **Band 3**
Table: p.351

Sit, Po (New York)
Profile: p.536
Tax **Band u**
Table: p.499

Sitton, Larry (North Carolina)
Profile: p.553
Litigation **Band 2**
Table: p.549

Siwica, Richard (Florida)
Profile: p.178
Employment **Band 2**
Table: p.157

Skeffington, James (Rhode Island)
Profile: p.623
Corporate/M&A **Band 2**
Table: p.620

Skerritt, Daniel (Oregon)
Profile: p.594
Litigation **Band 4**
Table: p.590

Skilton, John (Wisconsin)
Profile: p.729
Litigation **Band 1**
Table: p.726

Skindrud, Michael
(Wisconsin)
Profile: p.729
Corporate/M&A **Band 2**
Table: p.723

Skinner, Shannon
(Washington)
Profile: p.713
Real Estate **Band 2**
Table: p.711

Skinner, William
(District of Columbia)
Profile: p.145
Insurance **Band 3**
Table: p.120

Sklar, Stanley P (Illinois)
Profile: p.273
Construction **Band 2**
Table: p.231

Sklaroff, Mike (Pennsylvania)
Profile: p.618
Real Estate **Band 1**
Table: p.613

Slater, Jim (Florida)
Profile: p.178
Real Estate **Band 4**
Table: p.167

Slater, Paul (Illinois)
Profile: p.273
Antitrust **Band 3**
Table: p.224

Slater, Thomas (Virginia)
Profile: p.705
Litigation **Band 1**
Table: p.702

Slonaker, Norman (New York)
Profile: p.536
Capital Markets **Band 3**
Table: p.448

LEADING LAWYERS INDEX

Slusky, Jerry (Nebraska)
Profile: p.405,405
Real Estate Band 2
Table: p.404

Slusser, William C (Texas)
Profile: p.680
Intellectual Property Band 3
Table: p.661

Small, Jeffrey (New York)
Profile: p.536
Capital Markets Band 2
Table: p.448

Smallwood, Mary (Florida)
Profile: p.178
Environment Band 3
Table: p.160

Smedinghoff, Thomas J
(Illinois)
Profile: p.273
Communications Band 3
Table: p.229

Smit, Robert (New York)
Profile: p.536
Arbitration Band 2
Table: p.443

Smith, Bradley Y (New York)
Profile: p.536
Banking & Finance Band 1
Table: p.445

Smith, Chris (New York)
Profile: p.536
Real Estate Band 3
Table: p.493

Smith, Edwin (Massachusetts)
Profile: p.359
Banking & Finance Band 2
Table: p.338

Smith, Felton (Alabama)
Profile: p.8
Real Estate Band 3
Table: p.6

Smith, George A (Tony)
(Georgia)
Profile: p.210
Construction Band 3
Table: p.184

Smith, Gregory (Nevada)
Profile: p.414
Employment Band 2
Table: p.408

Smith, Gregory C (California)
Profile: p.72
Communications Band 4
Table: p.34

Smith, James (Texas)
Profile: p.680
Environment Band 3
Table: p.655

Smith, James (Georgia)
Profile: p.210
Corporate/M&A Band 3
Table: p.187

Smith, Janet Hugie (Utah)
Profile: p.691
Employment Band 1
Table: p.686

Smith, Jeffrey (New York)
Profile: p.536
Environment Band 2
Table: p.469

Smith, Joel (Maryland)
Profile: p.334
Employment Band 2
Table: p.328

Smith, Julious (Virginia)
Profile: p.705
Corporate/M&A Band 2
Table: p.699

Smith, MacDonald (Iowa)
Profile: p.293
Employment Band 3
Table: p.288

Smith, Michael (Virginia)
Profile: p.705
Litigation Band 1
Table: p.702

Smith, Nancy Erika
(New Jersey)
Profile: p.432
Employment ⦿
Table: p.426

Smith, Nathan H (Maine)
Profile: p.326
Real Estate Band 2
Table: p.324

Smith, Neil (California)
Profile: p.72
Intellectual Property Band 4
Table: p.48

Smith, Norman (North Carolina)
Profile: p.553
Employment Band 3
Table: p.547

Smith, Paul
(District of Columbia)
Profile: p.145
Media & Entertainment Band 1
Table: p.125

Smith, Philip (Massachusetts)
Profile: p.359
Banking & Finance Band 2
Table: p.338

Smith, Sean (North Dakota)
Profile: p.557
Corporate/M&A Band 3
Table: p.554

Smith, Taylor (Mississippi)
Profile: p.384
Employment Band 1
Table: p.380

Smith, Tefft W (Illinois)
Profile: p.273
Antitrust Band 1
Table: p.224

Smith, Turner
(District of Columbia)
Profile: p.146
Environment Band 4
Table: p.117

Smith, William (Mississippi)
Profile: p.384
Real Estate Band 2
Table: p.382

Smith, Wm Randolph
(District of Columbia)
Profile: p.146
Antitrust Band 4
Table: p.103

Smith III, James Urey
(Kentucky)
Profile: p.306
Employment Band 2
Table: p.302

Smith Jr, Robert (Jay) W
(Maryland)
Profile: p.335
Corporate/M&A Band 1
Table: p.327

Smolen, Lee (Illinois)
Profile: p.273
Real Estate Band 3
Table: p.249

Smutny, Abby Cohen
(District of Columbia)
Profile: p.146
Arbitration Band 3
Table: p.106

Snead, William (New Mexico)
Profile: p.438
Litigation Band 4
Table: p.435

Snider, Lawrence K (Illinois)
Profile: p.273
Insolvency Band 3
Table: p.241

Snow, Ronald
(New Hampshire)
Profile: p.423
Litigation Band 2
Table: p.419

Snow, Stephen E
(Rhode Island)
Profile: p.623
Litigation Band 2
Table: p.622

Snow Jr, Tower C (California)
Profile: p.72
Litigation Band 3
Table: p.50

Snyder, Jack R (Indiana)
Profile: p.284
Corporate/M&A Band 2
Table: p.277

Snyder, Judy (Oregon)
Profile: p.594
Employment Band 2
Table: p.588

Snyder, Sheryl (Kentucky)
Profile: p.306
Litigation Band 3
Table: p.303

Snyder, Stephen (Minnesota)
Profile: p.377
Employment Band 2
Table: p.371

Snyder, W Henry
(Pennsylvania)
Profile: p.618
Corporate/M&A Band 4
Table: p.599

Sobel, Gerald (New York)
Profile: p.536
Intellectual Property Band 5
Table: p.479

Sohn, Michael N
(District of Columbia)
Profile: p.146
Antitrust Band 2
Table: p.103

Solada, Mary (Indiana)
Profile: p.284
Real Estate Band 3
Table: p.282

Sollner, Richard (Florida)
Profile: p.178
Real Estate Band 4
Table: p.167

Solomon, Andrew P
(New York)
Profile: p.536
Tax Band 2
Table: p.499

Solomon, Randall (Ohio)
Profile: p.578
Litigation Band 3
Table: p.570

Solovy, Jerold S (Illinois)
Profile: p.273
Litigation Band 5
Table: p.245

Solow, Michael (Illinois)
Profile: p.273
Insolvency Band 3
Table: p.241

Somers, George W (Indiana)
Profile: p.284
Real Estate Band 1
Table: p.282

Somerstein, Barry (Florida)
Profile: p.178
Real Estate Band 4
Table: p.167

Sommer, Dean (New York)
Profile: p.537
Environment Band 4
Table: p.469

Sommerhauser, Peter
(Wisconsin)
Profile: p.729
Corporate/M&A Band 1
Table: p.723

Sonnenfeld, Marc
(Pennsylvania)
Profile: p.618
Litigation Band 2
Table: p.611

Sonsini, Larry (California)
Profile: p.73
Capital Markets Band 1
Table: p.32
Communications ⦿
Table: p.34
Corporate/M&A Band 1
Table: p.37

Soriano, Robert (Florida)
Profile: p.178
Insolvency Band 1
Table: p.162

Sorin, David (New Jersey)
Profile: p.432
Corporate/M&A Band 1
Table: p.425

Sosland, Martin (Texas)
Profile: p.680
Insolvency Band 4
Table: p.657

Soussloff, Andrew D
(New York)
Profile: p.537
Capital Markets Band 4
Table: p.448

Southworth II, Louis S
(West Virginia)
Profile: p.722
Corporate/M&A Band 1
Table: p.714

Sowell, Thornwell
(South Carolina)
Profile: p.629
Litigation Band 3
Table: p.626

Spalding, William (Georgia)
Profile: p.210
Corporate/M&A Band 3
Table: p.187

Spangler, John (Georgia)
Profile: p.210
Construction Band 3
Table: p.184

Sparks III, Gilchrist
(Delaware)
Profile: p.101
Corporate/M&A Band 2
Table: p.94
Litigation Band 1
Table: p.98

Spatt, Robert E (New York)
Profile: p.537
Corporate/M&A Band 2
Table: p.460

Spear, Samuel (Pennsylvania)
Profile: p.618
Employment Band 3
Table: p.601

Spearman, Robert (North Carolina)
Profile: p.553
Litigation Band 3
Table: p.549

Spector, David (Illinois)
Profile: p.273
Insurance Band 1
Table: p.242

Spector, Phillip
(District of Columbia)
Profile: p.146,537
Communications Band 3
Table: p.107

Spector, Scott (California)
Profile: p.73
Communications Band 5
Table: p.34

Sperling, Allan G (New York)
Profile: p.537
Capital Markets Band 3
Table: p.448

Speth II, Charles
(South Carolina)
Profile: p.629
Employment Band 1
Table: p.625

Spielberg, David (California)
Profile: p.73
Projects Band 2
Table: p.55

Spier, Alan R (Connecticut)
Profile: p.93
Corporate/M&A Band 2
Table: p.87

Spink, Michael (Idaho)
Profile: p.222,222
Real Estate Band 2
Table: p.222

Spivey, John (Arkansas)
Profile: p.27
Real Estate Band 1
Table: p.26

Spradling, Scott (Oklahoma)
Profile: p.585,586
Real Estate Band 2
Table: p.585

Sprague, Richard
(Pennsylvania)
Profile: p.618
Litigation Band 2
Table: p.611

Spratling, Gary (California)
Profile: p.73
Antitrust Band 3
Table: p.29

Sprayregen, James H M
(Illinois)
Profile: p.273
Insolvency Band 1
Table: p.241

Sprenger, Paul (Minnesota)
Profile: p.377
Employment Band 2
Table: p.370

Spring, Gary (Ohio)
Profile: p.578
Employment Band 3
Table: p.565

Springer, Claudia
(Pennsylvania)
Profile: p.618
Insolvency Band 2
Table: p.607

Springer, Felix (Connecticut)
Profile: p.93
Employment Band 1
Table: p.89

LEADING LAWYERS INDEX

Stabler, Wendie (Delaware)
Profile: p.101
Real Estate **Band 3**
Table: p.99

Stack Jr, Stephen
(Pennsylvania)
Profile: p.618
Antitrust **Band 3**
Table: p.596

Stacy, David (Colorado)
Profile: p.85
Employment **Band 3**
Table: p.78

Staffaroni, Robert J
(New York)
Profile: p.537
Tax **Band 3**
Table: p.499

Stageberg, Roger
(Minnesota)
Profile: p.377
Corporate/M&A **Band 2**
Table: p.369

Stahl, Thomas (Missouri)
Profile: p.393
Corporate/M&A **Band 3**
Table: p.386

Stair, Kent (Georgia)
Profile: p.210
Construction **Band 5**
Table: p.184

Stallings, John (Kansas)
Profile: p.299
Real Estate **Band 2**
Table: p.298

Standish, Peter D (New York)
Profile: p.537
Antitrust **Band 2**
Table: p.441

Stanford, Douglas (Florida)
Profile: p.178
Real Estate **Band 4**
Table: p.167

Stanley, Douglas (Kansas)
Profile: p.299
Employment **Band 2**
Table: p.296

Stanley, Jim (Alaska)
Profile: p.14,15
Real Estate **Band 3**
Table: p.14

Stanton, Patrick (New Jersey)
Profile: p.432
Employment **Band 1**
Table: p.427

Stapleton, Benjamin F
(New York)
Profile: p.537
Corporate/M&A **Band 1**
Table: p.460

Stapleton, James
(Connecticut)
Profile: p.93
Litigation **Band 3**
Table: p.90

Starer, Brian (New York)
Profile: p.537
Shipping **Band 4**
Table: p.496

Stark, Stephen (Kansas)
Profile: p.299
Real Estate **Band 4**
Table: p.298

Starnes, Stancil (Alabama)
Profile: p.8
Litigation **Band 2**
Table: p.4

Starr, Judson
(District of Columbia)
Profile: p.146
Environment **Band 5**
Table: p.117

Starr, Kenneth W
(District of Columbia)
Profile: p.146
Litigation **Band 2**
Table: p.123

Statman, Alan (Ohio)
Profile: p.
Banking & Finance **Band 3**
Table: p.559

Stearns, Eugene (Florida)
Profile: p.178
Litigation **Band**
Table: p.165
Litigation **Band 2**
Table: p.165

Steeg, Robert M (Louisiana)
Profile: p.318
Real Estate **Band 1**
Table: p.314

Steel, Michael J (California)
Profile: p.73
Environment **Band 4**
Table: p.43

Stein, Grant (Georgia)
Profile: p.210
Insolvency **Band 3**
Table: p.193

Stein, Jeffrey (Georgia)
Profile: p.210
Corporate/M&A **Band 3**
Table: p.187

Stein, Joshua (New York)
Profile: p.538
Real Estate **Band 3**
Table: p.493

Stein, Steven GM (Illinois)
Profile: p.273
Construction **Band 1**
Table: p.231

Steinberg, Joseph LeVow
(New Jersey)
Profile: p.430,432
Real Estate **Band 4**
Table: p.429

Steinberg, Lewis (New York)
Profile: p.538
Tax **Band 1**
Table: p.499

Steinberg, Marty (Florida)
Profile: p.178
Litigation **Band 4**
Table: p.165

Steinberg, Michael
(District of Columbia)
Profile: p.146
Environment **Band 3**
Table: p.117

Steiner, Beat (Colorado)
Profile: p.86
Real Estate **Band 2**
Table: p.81

Stenmoe, Gregory
(Minnesota)
Profile: p.377
Employment **Band 2**
Table: p.371

Stephens, Kenneth (Oregon)
Profile: p.594
Corporate/M&A **Band 3**
Table: p.587

Stephenson, Alan (New York)
Profile: p.538
Corporate/M&A **Band 1**
Table: p.460

Stephenson, Barbara
(New Mexico)
Profile: p.438
Employment **Band 2**
Table: p.435

Stephenson, Mason (Georgia)
Profile: p.210
Real Estate **Band 1**
Table: p.199

Stepleton, Jim (Missouri)
Profile: p.393
Corporate/M&A **Band 3**
Table: p.386

Steptoe Jr, Robert M.
(West Virginia)
Profile: p.722
Employment **Band 1**
Table: p.717

Stern, Akiba (New York)
Profile: p.538
Communications **Band 3**
Table: p.456

Stern, Eric (Pennsylvania)
Profile: p.618
Real Estate **Band 4**
Table: p.613

Stern, Gary (Illinois)
Profile: p.274
Banking & Finance **Band 3**
Table: p.226

Stern, Joan (Pennsylvania)
Profile: p.618
Banking & Finance **Band 2**
Table: p.598

Sternberg, John (Colorado)
Profile: p.86
Real Estate **Band 2**
Table: p.81

Sterne, Robert
(District of Columbia)
Profile: p.146
Intellectual Property **Band 3**
Table: p.122

Sterner, Dan G (Indiana)
Profile: p.283,284
Real Estate **Band 4**
Table: p.282

Stetson, Roger (Iowa)
Profile: p.293
Litigation **Band 1**
Table: p.290

Steuber, David (California)
Profile: p.73
Insurance **Band 2**
Table: p.46

Stevens, Eric (Tennessee)
Profile: p.642
Employment **Band 3**
Table: p.637

Stever, Donald W (New York)
Profile: p.538
Environment **Band 2**
Table: p.469

Steverson, Randall (Hawaii)
Profile: p.218
Real Estate **Band 3**
Table: p.217

Stewart, Dan (Texas)
Profile: p.680
Insolvency **Band 2**
Table: p.657

Stewart , Michael
(Oklahoma)
Profile: p.586
Corporate/M&A **Band 1**
Table: p.580

Stewart, Robert (Texas)
Profile: p.680
Environment **Band 3**
Table: p.655

Stichter, Don (Florida)
Profile: p.178
Insolvency **Band 3**
Table: p.162

Still, Charles (Texas)
Profile: p.680
Corporate/M&A **Band 3**
Table: p.649

Stiller Rikleen, Lauren
(Massachusetts)
Profile: p.359
Environment **Band 3**
Table: p.344

Stillman, Gregory (Virginia)
Profile: p.705
Litigation **Band 2**
Table: p.702

Stillman, Nina (Illinois)
Profile: p.274
Employment **Band 3**
Table: p.236

Stinson, James (Illinois)
Profile: p.274
Insurance **Band 2**
Table: p.242

Stocks, Bruce (Colorado)
Profile: p.86
Corporate/M&A **Band 3**
Table: p.75

Stockton, David (Georgia)
Profile: p.210
Corporate/M&A **Band 4**
Table: p.187

Stokes, James (Georgia)
Profile: p.210
Environment **Band**
Table: p.192
Environment **Band 2**
Table: p.192

Stolkin, Ronald (Arizona)
Profile: p.22
Employment **Band 3**
Table: p.18

Stoll, Neal R (New York)
Profile: p.538
Antitrust **Band 4**
Table: p.441

Stoll, Richard
(District of Columbia)
Profile: p.146
Environment **Band 4**
Table: p.117

Stoll, Robert (Oregon)
Profile: p.594
Litigation **Band 2**
Table: p.590

Stone, Alan (Delaware)
Profile: p.101
Litigation **Band 4**
Table: p.98

Stone, Bruce (Florida)
Profile: p.178
Tax **Band 1**
Table: p.170

Stone, Jeffrey (Illinois)
Profile: p.274
Litigation **Band 4**
Table: p.245

Stormer, Dan (California)
Profile: p.73
Employment **Band 2**
Table: p.39

Stout, Mikel (Kansas)
Profile: p.299
Litigation **Band 1**
Table: p.297

Stover, Hayes (Pennsylvania)
Profile: p.618
Employment **Band 4**
Table: p.602

Stowers, Gerard
(West Virginia)
Profile: p.722
Litigation **Band 3**
Table: p.718

Strain, James A (Indiana)
Profile: p.284
Corporate/M&A **Band 1**
Table: p.277

Strain, Paul (Maryland)
Profile: p.335
Litigation **Band 3**
Table: p.330

Stranch III, James
(Tennessee)
Profile: p.642
Employment **Band 1**
Table: p.637

Strand, Peter (Illinois)
Profile: p.274
Media & Entertainment **Band 1**
Table: p.247

Strand, Robert (Hawaii)
Profile: p.218
Real Estate **Band 4**
Table: p.217

Strangis, Ralph (Minnesota)
Profile: p.377
Corporate/M&A **Band 1**
Table: p.369

Strasheim, Jerrold (Nebraska)
Profile: p.405
Corporate/M&A **Band 2**
Table: p.400

Stratton, David (Delaware)
Profile: p.101
Insolvency **Band 5**
Table: p.96

Strauch, John (Ohio)
Profile: p.579
Litigation **Band 1**
Table: p.570

Straus, James (Kentucky)
Profile: p.306
Corporate/M&A **Band 2**
Table: p.300

Strauss, Jesse (New Jersey)
Profile: p.432
Employment **Band 2**
Table: p.426

Strecker, David (Oklahoma)
Profile: p.586
Employment **Band 3**
Table: p.582

Streeter, Jon (California)
Profile: p.73
Intellectual Property **Band 3**
Table: p.48

Streff, Jr, William A (Illinois)
Profile: p.274
Intellectual Property **Band 2**
Table: p.244

Streit, Gary J (Iowa)
Profile: p.293
Corporate/M&A **Band 2**
Table: p.286

Striefsky, Linda (Ohio)
Profile: p.579
Real Estate **Band 2**
Table: p.572

Strindberg, Erik (Utah)
Profile: p.691
Employment **Band 1**
Table: p.686

Stringer, Martin (Oklahoma)
Profile: p.586
Corporate/M&A **Band 3**
Table: p.580

LEADING LAWYERS INDEX

Stringfellow, James S (New York)
Profile: p.538
Capital Markets U
Table: p.453

Stromfeld, Lary (New York)
Profile: p.538
Capital Markets Band 4
Table: p.451

Strong, Keith (Montana)
Profile: p.399
Litigation Band 1
Table: p.396

Stroube III, H Rey (Texas)
Profile: p.680
Insolvency Band 4
Table: p.657

Stroup, Robert (North Dakota)
Profile: p.557
Real Estate Band 1
Table: p.557

Strubeck, Lou (Texas)
Profile: p.680
Insolvency Band 4
Table: p.657

Stubbs, Sidney (Florida)
Profile: p.178
Litigation Band 2
Table: p.165

Stuckey, James (Louisiana)
Profile: p.318
Banking & Finance Band 2
Table: p.307

Studer, Judith (Wyoming)
Profile: p.735
Employment Band 2
Table: p.732

Stumo, Mary (Minnesota)
Profile: p.377
Employment Band 1
Table: p.371

Sturdivant, James (Oklahoma)
Profile: p.586
Litigation Band 3
Table: p.583

Stutts, Charles (Florida)
Profile: p.178
Banking & Finance Band 2
Table: p.152

Styles, Mark (New Mexico)
Profile: p.438
Real Estate Band 2
Table: p.437

Sudell, William (Delaware)
Profile: p.101
Insolvency Band 3
Table: p.96

Suflas, Steve (New Jersey)
Profile: p.432
Employment Band 1
Table: p.427

Sugarman, Robert (New York)
Profile: p.538
Media & Entertainment Band 5
Table: p.485

Sugarman, Robert (Florida)
Profile: p.178
Employment Band 1
Table: p.157

Sullivan, Alan (Utah)
Profile: p.691
Litigation Band 1
Table: p.687

Sullivan, Brendan V (District of Columbia)
Profile: p.146
Litigation
Table: p.123

Sullivan, John (Montana)
Profile: p.399
Employment Band 1
Table: p.395

Sullivan, Marcia (Illinois)
Profile: p.274
Real Estate Band 4
Table: p.249

Sullivan, Mary (Massachusetts)
Profile: p.359
Employment Band 2
Table: p.341

Sullivan, Robert J (New York)
Profile: p.539
Insurance Band 2
Table: p.477

Sullivan, Shaun (Connecticut)
Profile: p.93
Litigation Band 3
Table: p.90

Sullivan, Thomas (Illinois)
Profile: p.274
Litigation Band 5
Table: p.245

Sullivan, William (Illinois)
Profile: p.274
Employment Band 2
Table: p.236

Sumter, Geraldine (North Carolina)
Profile: p.553
Employment Band 2
Table: p.547

Sunshine, Steven C (District of Columbia)
Profile: p.146
Antitrust Band 4
Table: p.103

Suplee, Dennis (Pennsylvania)
Profile: p.618
Litigation Band
Table: p.611
Litigation Band 3
Table: p.611

Surkin, Elliot (Massachusetts)
Profile: p.359
Real Estate Band 3
Table: p.351

Susman, Stephen (Texas)
Profile: p.681
Antitrust Band 2
Table: p.644
Litigation Band 1
Table: p.663

Susskind, Howard (Florida)
Profile: p.178
Employment Band 3
Table: p.157

Sussman, Robert (District of Columbia)
Profile: p.146
Environment Band 4
Table: p.117

Sutherland, Mike (Texas)
Profile: p.681
Insolvency Band 4
Table: p.657

Sutter, Luther (Arkansas)
Profile: p.27
Employment Band 3
Table: p.24

Sutton, Jeffrey (Ohio)
Profile: p.579
Litigation Band 2
Table: p.570

Sutton, William (Arkansas)
Profile: p.27
Litigation Band 1
Table: p.25

Svonkin, Mark (Connecticut)
Profile: p.93
Real Estate Band 3
Table: p.91

Swaim, Hall (Massachusetts)
Profile: p.359
Insolvency Band 1
Table: p.346

Swain, Lawrence (Kansas)
Profile: p.299
Corporate/M&A Band 1
Table: p.294

Swanger, James R (Iowa)
Profile: p.293
Employment Band 2
Table: p.288

Swanson, Daniel (California)
Profile: p.73
Antitrust Band 4
Table: p.29

Swanson, Joel (Texas)
Profile: p.681
Corporate/M&A Band 1
Table: p.649

Sweeney, John (New York)
Profile: p.539
Intellectual Property Band 3
Table: p.479

Sweeney, Neal (Georgia)
Profile: p.210
Construction Band 3
Table: p.184

Swenson, C David (District of Columbia)
Profile: p.146
Tax Band 3
Table: p.130

Swenson, Erik (Georgia)
Profile: p.210
Energy Band 3
Table: p.191

Swhier, Claudia (Indiana)
Profile: p.284
Corporate/M&A Band 3
Table: p.277

Swider, David L (Indiana)
Profile: p.284
Employment Band 3
Table: p.279

Swift, Phelps (Wyoming)
Profile: p.734,735
Real Estate Band 3
Table: p.734

Swirsky, Sherry A. (Pennsylvania)
Profile: p.618
Antitrust Band 3
Table: p.596

Sykes, David (Pennsylvania)
Profile: p.618
Insolvency Band 1
Table: p.607

Sylvester, David (Virginia)
Profile: p.705
Corporate/M&A Band 2
Table: p.699

Symchych, Janice (Minnesota)
Profile: p.377
Litigation Band 3
Table: p.372

Symons, Howard J (District of Columbia)
Profile: p.146
Communications Band 2
Table: p.107

Szalkowski, Charles (Texas)
Profile: p.681
Communications Band 1
Table: p.646
Corporate/M&A Band 4
Table: p.649

T

Tabachnick, Gene (Pennsylvania)
Profile: p.618
Intellectual Property Band 2
Table: p.609

Taback, Gary A (Michigan)
Profile: p.367
Real Estate Band 3
Table: p.365

Tabak, Jeffrey E (New York)
Profile: p.539
Private Equity Band 2
Table: p.489

Takahashi, Herbert (Hawaii)
Profile: p.218
Employment Band 2
Table: p.213

Talley, Susan G (Louisiana)
Profile: p.318
Real Estate Band 1
Table: p.314

Tanenbaum, William (New York)
Profile: p.539
Communications Band 3
Table: p.456

Tannon, Jay Middleton (Kentucky)
Profile: p.306
Corporate/M&A Band 2
Table: p.300

Tanoury, Mark (California)
Profile: p.73
Communications Band 2
Table: p.34

Tarantino, John (Rhode Island)
Profile: p.623
Litigation Band 1
Table: p.622

Taranto, Richard (District of Columbia)
Profile: p.146
Litigation Band 2
Table: p.123

Tarolli, Thomas (Ohio)
Profile: p.579
Intellectual Property Band 1
Table: p.568

Tarullo, Michael (Ohio)
Profile: p.579
Construction Band 2
Table: p.560

Tarun, Robert (Illinois)
Profile: p.274
Litigation Band 3
Table: p.245

Tate, Joseph (Pennsylvania)
Profile: p.618
Antitrust Band 1
Table: p.596
Litigation Band 2
Table: p.611

Tate, Simmons (South Carolina)
Profile: p.629
Litigation Band 2
Table: p.626

Taylor, Daniel (North Carolina)
Profile: p.553
Litigation Band 3
Table: p.549

Taylor, Lyndon C (Texas)
Profile: p.681
Energy Band 3
Table: p.653
Projects Band 1
Table: p.664

Taylor, Nolan S. (Utah)
Profile: p.691
Corporate/M&A Band 1
Table: p.684

Taylor, Robert (California)
Profile: p.73
Antitrust Band 4
Table: p.29

Taylor, Roger (Georgia)
Profile: p.211
Intellectual Property Band 4
Table: p.195

Taylor, Ronald W (Maryland)
Profile: p.335
Employment Band 1
Table: p.329

Taylor, Tom (Utah)
Profile: p.691
Corporate/M&A Band 3
Table: p.684

Taylor, Willard B (New York)
Profile: p.539
Tax Band 2
Table: p.499

Teblum, Gary (Florida)
Profile: p.178
Corporate/M&A Band 4
Table: p.156

Tegeler, David W (Massachusetts)
Profile: p.359
Private Equity Band 1
Table: p.350

Tehan, John (New York)
Profile: p.539
Capital Markets Band 3
Table: p.448

Telegen, Arthur (Massachusetts)
Profile: p.359
Employment Band 2
Table: p.342

Temin, Michael (Pennsylvania)
Profile: p.618
Insolvency Band 3
Table: p.607

Templin, Donald (Texas)
Profile: p.681
Intellectual Property Band 4
Table: p.661

Tenev, Jovi (New York)
Profile: p.539
Shipping Band 2
Table: p.496

Teplin, Lawrence (California)
Profile: p.73
Construction Band 2
Table: p.36

Terr, Leonard (District of Columbia)
Profile: p.146
Tax Band 2
Table: p.130

Terrell, Irvin (Texas)
Profile: p.681
Litigation Band 3
Table: p.663

Tescher, Donald (Florida)
Profile: p.178
Tax Band 1
Table: p.170

www.ChambersandPartners.com 1017

LEADING LAWYERS INDEX

Tessier, Frank (Louisiana)
Profile: p.318
Banking & Finance **Band** 3
Table: p.307

Thane, Jeremy (Montana)
Profile: p.399
Employment **Band** 2
Table: p.395

Theiss, Paul W (Illinois)
Profile: p.274

Thiel, John (Minnesota)
Profile: p.377
Real Estate **Band** 1
Table: p.374

Thiem, Rebecca
(North Dakota)
Profile: p.557
Litigation **Band** 2
Table: p.556

Thimsen, Gary (South Dakota)
Profile: p.634
Litigation **Band** 1
Table: p.632

Thomas, Archibald (Florida)
Profile: p.178
Employment **Band** 2
Table: p.157

Thomas, Cynthia
(Washington)
Profile: p.712,713
Real Estate **Band** 3
Table: p.711

Thomas, Dale (Illinois)
Profile: p.274
Energy **Band** 4
Table: p.238

Thomas, David (West Virginia)
Profile: p.722
Litigation **Band**
Table: p.718
Litigation **Band** 3
Table: p.718

Thomas, Frederick B (Illinois)
Profile: p.274
Corporate/M&A **Band** 3
Table: p.233

Thomas, Michael
(North Dakota)
Profile: p.557
Corporate/M&A **Band** 2
Table: p.554

Thomasch, Roger (Colorado)
Profile: p.86
Litigation **Band** 3
Table: p.79

Thompson, Dahl (Texas)
Profile: p.681
Projects **U**
Table: p.664

Thompson, Gary (Virginia)
Profile: p.705
Corporate/M&A **Band** 3
Table: p.699

Thompson, Jay (Texas)
Profile: p.681
Insurance **Band** 3
Table: p.659

Thompson, John (Minnesota)
Profile: p.377
Employment **Band** 2
Table: p.371

Thompson, Ken (New Jersey)
Profile: p.432
Corporate/M&A **Band** 2
Table: p.425

Thompson, Robert (California)
Profile: p.73
Real Estate **Band** 4
Table: p.56

Thompson, Thomas M
(Pennsylvania)
Profile: p.619
Corporate/M&A **Band** 2
Table: p.599

Thompson, William J
(Georgia)
Profile: p.211
Real Estate **Band** 3
Table: p.199

Thomson, Parker (Florida)
Profile: p.178
Litigation **Band** 3
Table: p.165

Thornburgh, John R (Indiana)
Profile: p.284
Corporate/M&A **Band** 2
Table: p.277

Thornton, Charles (California)
Profile: p.73
Real Estate **Band** 5
Table: p.56

Thrapp, Richard J (Indiana)
Profile: p.284
Corporate/M&A **Band** 2
Table: p.277

Throckmorton, Charles
(Florida)
Profile: p.179
Insolvency **Band** 3
Table: p.162

Throckmorton, Rex (New Mexico)
Profile: p.438
Litigation **Band** 3
Table: p.435

Thrower, Randolph W
(Georgia)
Profile: p.211
Tax **Band** 4
Table: p.201

Thum, Robert (California)
Profile: p.73
Construction **Band** 2
Table: p.36

Thurber, Mark (Texas)
Profile: p.681
Energy **Band** 4
Table: p.653
Projects **Band** 2
Table: p.664

Thurston, Sally A (New York)
Profile: p.539
Tax **Band** u
Table: p.499

Thuston, W Lee (Alabama)
Profile: p.8
Corporate/M&A **Band** 2
Table: p.1

Tieder, John (Virginia)
Profile: p.705
Construction **Band** 1
Table: p.698

Tilghman Jr, Richard
(Maryland)
Profile: p.335
Corporate/M&A **Band** 2
Table: p.327

Tinkham, Thomas
(Minnesota)
Profile: p.377
Litigation **Band** 2
Table: p.372

Tinney, John (West Virginia)
Profile: p.722
Litigation **Band** 1
Table: p.718

Tinnin, Robert (New Mexico)
Profile: p.438
Employment **Band** 3
Table: p.435

Tipps, Maynard
(North Carolina)
Profile: p.553
Real Estate **Band** 2
Table: p.551

Tisdale Jr, Charles (Georgia)
Profile: p.211
Environment **Band** 2
Table: p.192

Tisdale Jr., Thomas S.
(South Carolina)
Profile: p.629
Litigation **Band** 2
Table: p.626

Tittle, Dave (Indiana)
Profile: p.284
Litigation **Band** 3
Table: p.280

Tobias, Paul (Ohio)
Profile: p.579
Employment **Band** 1
Table: p.564

Todd, Owen (Massachusetts)
Profile: p.359
Litigation **Band** 1
Table: p.349

Toder, Richard (New York)
Profile: p.540
Insolvency **Band** 2
Table: p.472

Todrys, Steven C (New York)
Profile: p.540
Tax **Band** 1
Table: p.499

Tohill, Jim (Mississippi)
Profile: p.384
Real Estate **Band** 1
Table: p.382

Tomlinson, PC, Stephen G
(Illinois)
Profile: p.275
Real Estate **Band** 4
Table: p.249

Toner, Tom (Wyoming)
Profile: p.735
Litigation **Band** 1
Table: p.732
Real Estate **Band** 2
Table: p.734

Tongue, Thomas (Oregon)
Profile: p.594
Litigation **Band** 2
Table: p.590

Tonsfeldt, Steve (California)
Profile: p.73
Communications **Band** 5
Table: p.34

Torchia, David (Ohio)
Profile: p.579
Employment **Band** 3
Table: p.564

Torchiana, William D
(New York)
Profile: p.540
Insurance **Band** 3
Table: p.477

Torgerson, Alan (New Mexico)
Profile: p.438
Litigation **Band** 4
Table: p.435

Torstrick, Brent
(North Carolina)
Profile: p.553
Real Estate **Band** 1
Table: p.551

Tortoriello, Robert (New York)
Profile: p.540
Banking & Finance **Band** 2
Table: p.445

Tosetti, Paul (California)
Profile: p.73
Corporate/M&A **Band** 1
Table: p.37

Tosi, Louis (Ohio)
Profile: p.579
Environment **Band** 2
Table: p.567

Toth, Bruce (Illinois)
Profile: p.275

Toulme, Nill (Georgia)
Profile: p.211
Environment **Band** 3
Table: p.192

Townsend, Christopher
(Illinois)
Profile: p.275
Energy **Band** 4
Table: p.238

Townsend, John M
(District of Columbia)
Profile: p.146
Arbitration **Band** 1
Table: p.106

Townsend, Robert (New York)
Profile: p.540
Corporate/M&A **U**
Table: p.460

Townsend, William (Florida)
Profile: p.179
Tax **Band** 1
Table: p.170

Tracy, David (Rhode Island)
Profile: p.623,623
Real Estate **Band** 2
Table: p.622

Trafford, Robert (Ohio)
Profile: p.579
Litigation **Band** 4
Table: p.570

Treece, John (Illinois)
Profile: p.275
Antitrust **Band** 3
Table: p.224

Trenkle, William (Kansas)
Profile: p.299
Corporate/M&A **Band** 1
Table: p.294

Trent, Tom (Tennessee)
Profile: p.642
Real Estate **Band** 1
Table: p.640

Trepper, Myron (New York)
Profile: p.540
Insolvency **Band** 1
Table: p.472

Trier, Dana L (New York)
Profile: p.540
Tax **Band** 1
Table: p.499

Tringali, Joseph (New York)
Profile: p.540
Antitrust **Band** 5
Table: p.441

Tripp, David (Missouri)
Profile: p.393
Litigation **Band** 3
Table: p.389

Tritt, Cheryl
(District of Columbia)
Profile: p.147
Communications **Band** 4
Table: p.107

Tropin, Harley (Florida)
Profile: p.179
Litigation **Band** 4
Table: p.165

Truax, Tim (California)
Profile: p.73
Construction **Band** 3
Table: p.36

Truhlar, Robert (Colorado)
Profile: p.86
Employment **Band** 1
Table: p.77

Truitt, Raymond (Maryland)
Profile: p.335
Real Estate **Band** 3
Table: p.331

Tuchin, Michael L (California)
Profile: p.73
Insolvency **Band** 3
Table: p.44

Tucker, Eliot (Texas)
Profile: p.681
Employment **Band** 1
Table: p.651

Tucker, Roy (Oregon)
Profile: p.594
Corporate/M&A **Band** 1
Table: p.587

Tucker, Stefan
(District of Columbia)
Profile: p.147
Real Estate **Band** 4
Table: p.127

Tucker, William
(New Hampshire)
Profile: p.421,423
Real Estate **Band** 2
Table: p.420

Turner, Robert (Texas)
Profile: p.681
Intellectual Property **Band** 3
Table: p.661

Turner, Wayne C (Indiana)
Profile: p.285
Litigation **Band** 2
Table: p.280

Tyler, Paul (Iowa)
Profile: p.293
Real Estate **Band** 3
Table: p.291

U

Ubinger Jr, John
(Pennsylvania)
Profile: p.619
Environment **Band** 3
Table: p.604

Ullman, Samuel (Florida)
Profile: p.179

Ulmer, Michael (Mississippi)
Profile: p.384
Litigation **Band** 2
Table: p.381

Ulwick, James (Maryland)
Profile: p.335
Litigation **Band** 2
Table: p.330

Underkofler, Paul (Texas)
Profile: p.681
Construction **Band** 3
Table: p.648

Unger, Timothy (Texas)
Profile: p.681
Energy **Band** 2
Table: p.653
Projects **Band** 1
Table: p.664

Upton II, Robert W
(New Hampshire)
Profile: p.421,423
Real Estate **Band** 3
Table: p.420

LEADING LAWYERS INDEX

Urda Kassis, Cynthia
(New York)
Profile: p.540
Projects **Band 4**
Table: p.491

Uris, Harvey R (New York)
Profile: p.540
Real Estate **Band 3**
Table: p.493

Utken, Greg (Indiana)
Profile: p.285
Employment **Band 3**
Table: p.279

V

Valentine, Debra A
(District of Columbia)
Profile: p.147
Antitrust **Band 5**
Table: p.103

Valukas, Anton (Illinois)
Profile: p.275
Litigation **Band 2**
Table: p.245

Van Dyke, Peter (Oklahoma)
Profile: p.586
Employment **Band 3**
Table: p.582

Van Dyke, Thomas (Missouri)
Profile: p.393
Corporate/M&A **Band 1**
Table: p.386

Van Fleet, Allan (Texas)
Profile: p.681
Antitrust **Band 3**
Table: p.644

Van Flein, Thomas V (Alaska)
Profile: p.15
Employment **Band 2**
Table: p.10

Van Hoy, Philip (North Carolina)
Profile: p.553
Employment **Band 1**
Table: p.548

Van Oot, Martha
(New Hampshire)
Profile: p.423
Litigation **Band 3**
Table: p.419

Van Winkle, Kenneth
(Arizona)
Profile: p.22
Real Estate **Band 2**
Table: p.20

Vance, Kim (Tennessee)
Profile: p.642
Employment **Band 3**
Table: p.637

VanCleave, Richard (Oregon)
Profile: p.594
Employment **Band 2**
Table: p.589

VanderBroek, Mark S
(Georgia)
Profile: p.211
Intellectual Property **Band 4**
Table: p.195

Vanyo, Bruce (California)
Profile: p.73
Litigation **Band 2**
Table: p.50

Vardaman, John
(District of Columbia)
Profile: p.147
Litigation **Band 1**
Table: p.123

Vardell, James (New York)
Profile: p.540
Banking & Finance **Band 2**
Table: p.445

Varner, Chilton (Georgia)
Profile: p.211
Litigation **Band 2**
Table: p.198

Varney, Christine
(District of Columbia)
Profile: p.147
Antitrust **Band 5**
Table: p.103

Vaughan, David (Georgia)
Profile: p.211
Antitrust **Band 4**
Table: p.181

Vaughan, Keith W
(North Carolina)
Profile: p.553
Litigation **Band 2**
Table: p.549

Vaughan, Porter (Virginia)
Profile: p.705
Corporate/M&A **Band 2**
Table: p.699

Vazquez-Bello, Clemente
(Florida)
Profile: p.179
Banking & Finance **Band 2**
Table: p.152

Vercruysse, Robert M
(Michigan)
Profile: p.367
Employment **Band 1**
Table: p.363

Vering III, John (Missouri)
Profile: p.393
Employment **Band 4**
Table: p.388

Verrilli, Donald
(District of Columbia)
Profile: p.147
Litigation **Band 2**
Table: p.123

Verveer, Philip L
(District of Columbia)
Profile: p.147
Communications **Band 1**
Table: p.107

Vetter, Jeff (California)
Profile: p.73
Communications **Band 5**
Table: p.34

Victor, A Paul (New York)
Profile: p.540
Antitrust **Band 3**
Table: p.441

Villa, John K
(District of Columbia)
Profile: p.147
Litigation **Band 2**
Table: p.123

Vincent, George (Ohio)
Profile: p.579
Corporate/M&A **Band 3**
Table: p.562

Vincenti, Mike (Kentucky)
Profile: p.306
Real Estate **Band 1**
Table: p.304

Vine, Stephen M (New York)
Profile: p.540
Private Equity **Band 2**
Table: p.489

Virtel, James (Missouri)
Profile: p.393
Litigation **Band 3**
Table: p.389

Visser, Kevin (Iowa)
Profile: p.293
Employment **Band 2**
Table: p.288

Vizcarrondo, Jr, Paul
(New York)
Profile: p.540
Litigation **Band 2**
Table: p.481

Vladeck, Anne (New York)
Profile: p.541
Employment **Band 3**
Table: p.466

Vladeck, Judith (New York)
Profile: p.541
Employment **Band 1**
Table: p.466

Vlahakis, Patricia A
(New York)
Profile: p.541
Corporate/M&A **Band 4**
Table: p.460

Voboril, Joseph (Oregon)
Profile: p.593,594
Real Estate **Band 4**
Table: p.592

Voge, William (New York)
Profile: p.541
Projects **Band 1**
Table: p.491

Vogel, Peter (Texas)
Profile: p.682
Communications **Band 3**
Table: p.646

Voigt, John (Tennessee)
Profile: p.642
Corporate/M&A **Band 3**
Table: p.635

Voigt, Richard (Connecticut)
Profile: p.93
Employment **Band 4**
Table: p.89

Voigts, Gene (Missouri)
Profile: p.393
Litigation **Band 1**
Table: p.389

Volinsky, Andru
(New Hampshire)
Profile: p.423
Employment **Band 1**
Table: p.417

Vollmann, Alan
(District of Columbia)
Profile: p.147
Real Estate **Band 4**
Table: p.127

Vollmer, Andrew
(District of Columbia)
Profile: p.148
Arbitration **Band 4**
Table: p.106

Von Ende, Carl H (Michigan)
Profile: p.367
Litigation **Band 3**
Table: p.364

Vyskocil, Mary Kay
(New York)
Profile: p.541
Insurance **Band 1**
Table: p.477

W

Wachsberger, Chaim
(New York)
Profile: p.541
Projects **Band 2**
Table: p.491

Wachtell, Herbert M
(New York)
Profile: p.541
Litigation **Band 1**
Table: p.481

Waddoups, Clark (Utah)
Profile: p.691
Litigation **Band 4**
Table: p.687

Wade, James A (Connecticut)
Profile: p.93
Litigation **Band 2**
Table: p.90

Wadlow, R Clark
(District of Columbia)
Profile: p.148
Communications **Band 5**
Table: p.107

Wadsworth, Murray (Florida)
Profile: p.179
Litigation **Band 4**
Table: p.165

Wagehoff Dale, Candy
(Idaho)
Profile: p.222
Employment **Band 1**
Table: p.220

Wagner, William (Montana)
Profile: p.399
Real Estate **Band 1**
Table: p.397

Waide, James (Mississippi)
Profile: p.384
Employment **Band 1**
Table: p.379

Waks, Jay (New York)
Profile: p.541
Employment **Band 1**
Table: p.467

Wakshlag, Stanley (Florida)
Profile: p.179
Litigation **Band 4**
Table: p.165

Walbolt, Sylvia (Florida)
Profile: p.179
Litigation **Band 4**
Table: p.165

Wald, Douglas
(District of Columbia)
Profile: p.148
Antitrust **Band 5**
Table: p.103

Walder, Justin (New Jersey)
Profile: p.432
Litigation **Band 2**
Table: p.428

Walker, Cameron (Wyoming)
Profile: p.735
Litigation **Band 3**
Table: p.732

Walker, John (New York)
Profile: p.541
Banking & Finance **Band 4**
Table: p.445

Walker, John (Arkansas)
Profile: p.27
Employment **Band 2**
Table: p.24

Walker, Paul (California)
Profile: p.74
Real Estate **Band 1**
Table: p.56

Walker, Robert (Tennessee)
Profile: p.642
Litigation **Band 1**
Table: p.639

Walker, William (Florida)
Profile: p.179
Real Estate **Band 3**
Table: p.167

Wall, Daniel (California)
Profile: p.74
Antitrust **Band 2**
Table: p.29

Wall, Robert (Illinois)
Profile: p.275
Corporate/M&A **Band 2**
Table: p.233

Wall, Steven (Pennsylvania)
Profile: p.619
Employment **Band 1**
Table: p.602

Wallack, Barry Z (Indiana)
Profile: p.285
Real Estate **Band 2**
Table: p.282

Wallenstein, Jim (Texas)
Profile: p.682
Real Estate **Band 1**
Table: p.665

Walsh, Peter (Delaware)
Profile: p.101
Litigation **Band 4**
Table: p.98

Walsh, Thomas (Missouri)
Profile: p.393
Litigation **Band 2**
Table: p.389

Walsh, William (Virginia)
Profile: p.704,705
Real Estate **Band 1**
Table: p.703

Walters, Stephen (Oregon)
Profile: p.594
Litigation **Band 4**
Table: p.590

Walton, Leigh (Tennessee)
Profile: p.642
Corporate/M&A **Band 1**
Table: p.635

Wander, Herb (Illinois)
Profile: p.275
Corporate/M&A **Band 1**
Table: p.233

Wann, Mark (Mississippi)
Profile: p.384
Employment **Band 3**
Table: p.379

Ward, Erica A
(District of Columbia)
Profile: p.148
Projects **Band 2**
Table: p.126

Ward, Larry (Missouri)
Profile: p.393
Litigation ✪
Table: p.389

Ward, Patrick (North Dakota)
Profile: p.557
Employment **Band 2**
Table: p.555

Ward, Richard
(Massachusetts)
Profile: p.359
Employment **Band 2**
Table: p.342

Ward Jr., Frank (North Carolina)
Profile: p.553
Employment **Band 3**
Table: p.548

Warden, John L (New York)
Profile: p.541
Antitrust **Band 3**
Table: p.441

Ware, Donald (Massachusetts)
Profile: p.359
Intellectual Property **Band 2**
Table: p.348

LEADING LAWYERS INDEX

Ware, Paul (Massachusetts)
Profile: p.359
Intellectual Property **Band 3**
Table: p.348

Warin, Roger
(District of Columbia)
Profile: p.148
Insurance **Band 1**
Table: p.120

Warnecke, Michael O
(Illinois)
Profile: p.275
Intellectual Property **Band 1**
Table: p.244

Warner, Jonathan (Florida)
Profile: p.171,179
Tax **Band 2**
Table: p.170

Warner, Michael (Illinois)
Profile: p.276
Employment **Band 1**
Table: p.236

Warner Jr, E Waide (New York)
Profile: p.541
Projects **Band 3**
Table: p.491

Warren, Jeffrey (Florida)
Profile: p.179
Insolvency **Band 3**
Table: p.162

Warren, Kenneth
(Pennsylvania)
Profile: p.619
Environment **Band 2**
Table: p.604

Warren III, John (South Carolina)
Profile: p.629
Corporate/M&A **Band 2**
Table: p.624
Real Estate **Band 2**
Table: p.628

Warshauer, David (Indiana)
Profile: p.285
Real Estate **Band 2**
Table: p.282

Washburne, Thomas
(Maryland)
Profile: p.335
Corporate/M&A **Band 3**
Table: p.327

Wasserman, Craig M
(New York)
Profile: p.541
Corporate/M&A **Band 3**
Table: p.460

Wasserman, Michael G
(Georgia)
Profile: p.202,211
Tax **Band 3**
Table: p.201

Waterman, Thomas D (Iowa)
Profile: p.293
Litigation **Band 2**
Table: p.290

Waterman III, Dana (Iowa)
Profile: p.293
Corporate/M&A **Band 2**
Table: p.286

Waterman Jr, Robert (Iowa)
Profile: p.293
Litigation **Band 1**
Table: p.290

Waters, Jennifer
(District of Columbia)
Profile: p.148
Energy **Band 4**
Table: p.115

Watkins, John (Jay) B
(Maryland)
Profile: p.335
Corporate/M&A **Band 3**
Table: p.327

Watt, Robert (Virginia)
Profile: p.705
Construction **Band 2**
Table: p.698

Waxman, Seth
(District of Columbia)
Profile: p.148
Litigation ✪
Table: p.123

Wayland, Eddie (Tennessee)
Profile: p.642
Employment **Band 1**
Table: p.637

Weathersby, Woods
(Tennessee)
Profile: p.641,642
Real Estate **Band 2**
Table: p.640

Webb, Dan (Illinois)
Profile: p.276
Litigation ✪
Table: p.245

Webb, Eugene (Virginia)
Profile: p.705
Employment **Band 2**
Table: p.701

Webb, Thompson (Maryland)
Profile: p.335
Corporate/M&A **Band 3**
Table: p.327

Webber, Rebecca (Maine)
Profile: p.326
Employment **Band 3**
Table: p.320

Webber, Walter E (Maine)
Profile: p.326
Real Estate **Band 1**
Table: p.324

Webbert, David (Maine)
Profile: p.326
Employment **Band 1**
Table: p.320

Weber, Robert (Ohio)
Profile: p.579
Litigation **Band 1**
Table: p.570

Weber, Victoria (Florida)
Profile: p.171,179

Webster, Robert (New York)
Profile: p.541
Banking & Finance **Band 2**
Table: p.445

Weems, Walter (Mississippi)
Profile: p.384
Corporate/M&A **Band 2**
Table: p.378

Weerasinghe, Rohan
(New York)
Profile: p.541
Capital Markets **Band 4**
Table: p.448

Wein, Howard (Pennsylvania)
Profile: p.619
Environment **Band 3**
Table: p.604

Weinberg, Jay (Virginia)
Profile: p.705
Real Estate **Band 2**
Table: p.703

Weinberger, Michael
(New York)
Profile: p.541
Real Estate **Band 4**
Table: p.493

Weiner, Michael L (New York)
Profile: p.542
Antitrust **Band 5**
Table: p.441

Weiner, Peter (California)
Profile: p.74
Environment **Band 3**
Table: p.43

Weiner, Sandford (Texas)
Profile: p.682
Real Estate **Band 2**
Table: p.665

Weinstein, Andrew (Florida)
Profile: p.179
Tax **Band 2**
Table: p.170

Weinstein, Joseph
(Washington)
Profile: p.713
Corporate/M&A **Band 1**
Table: p.706

Weinstein, Ken
(District of Columbia)
Profile: p.148
Environment **Band 5**
Table: p.117

Weinstine, Robert R
(Minnesota)
Profile: p.377
Litigation **Band 3**
Table: p.372

Weintraub, Lee (Florida)
Profile: p.179
Construction **Band 2**
Table: p.154

Weir, H Patrick (North Dakota)
Profile: p.557
Litigation **Band 3**
Table: p.556

Weirich, Geoff (Georgia)
Profile: p.211
Employment **Band 3**
Table: p.189

Weisberg, Robert (Florida)
Profile: p.179
Employment **Band 1**
Table: p.157

Weisburg, Henry (New York)
Profile: p.542
Arbitration **Band 3**
Table: p.443

Weisel, Sheldon
(District of Columbia)
Profile: p.148
Real Estate **Band 3**
Table: p.127

Weisfelner, Edward
(New York)
Profile: p.542
Insolvency **Band 4**
Table: p.472

Weiss, Christopher (Florida)
Profile: p.179
Construction **Band 2**
Table: p.154

Weiss, Gregory A (New York)
Profile: p.542
Banking & Finance **Band 4**
Table: p.445

Weiss, Jack (New York)
Profile: p.542
Media & Entertainment **Band 2**
Table: p.485

Weiss, Zeff (Indiana)
Profile: p.285
Real Estate **Band 1**
Table: p.282

Weissmann, Eric (California)
Profile: p.74
Media & Entertainment **Band 4**
Table: p.53

Weitzel, Mark P (California)
Profile: p.74
Projects **Band 3**
Table: p.55

Welbaum, Earl (Florida)
Profile: p.179
Construction **Band 1**
Table: p.154

Welch, Morgan (Arkansas)
Profile: p.27
Employment **Band 2**
Table: p.24

Welch, Scott (Mississippi)
Profile: p.384
Litigation **Band 3**
Table: p.381

Welch, Thomas (Hawaii)
Profile: p.218,218
Real Estate **Band 4**
Table: p.217

Welin, Peter (Ohio)
Profile: p.579
Construction **Band 2**
Table: p.560

Welk, Thomas (South Dakota)
Profile: p.634
Litigation **Band 2**
Table: p.632

Welke, William R (Illinois)
Profile: p.276
Tax **Band 3**
Table: p.252

Wellen, Robert
(District of Columbia)
Profile: p.148
Tax **Band 4**
Table: p.130

Wellford, Hill (Virginia)
Profile: p.705
Employment **Band 1**
Table: p.701

Wells, Della Wager (Georgia)
Profile: p.211
Energy **Band 3**
Table: p.191

Wells, Randall (Louisiana)
Profile: p.318
Employment **Band 4**
Table: p.310

Wenner, Adam
(District of Columbia)
Profile: p.148
Energy **Band 5**
Table: p.115

Werder, Richard (Ohio)
Profile: p.579
Litigation **Band 2**
Table: p.570

West, Glenn D (Texas)
Profile: p.682
Banking & Finance **Band 3**
Table: p.645
Corporate/M&A **Band 3**
Table: p.649

West, Joseph
(District of Columbia)
Profile: p.148
Construction **Band 1**
Table: p.110

West, M Holland (New York)
Profile: p.542
Capital Markets **Band 2**
Table: p.451

Wester, John (North Carolina)
Profile: p.553
Litigation **Band 1**
Table: p.549

Weston, Timothy
(Pennsylvania)
Profile: p.619
Environment **Band 1**
Table: p.604

Westra, James
(Massachusetts)
Profile: p.359
Corporate/M&A **Band 4**
Table: p.340

Westra, Mark (Minnesota)
Profile: p.377
Real Estate **Band 1**
Table: p.374

Wettach, Thomas
(Pennsylvania)
Profile: p.619
Intellectual Property **Band 3**
Table: p.609

Whalen, Thomas J (New York)
Profile: p.542
Shipping **Band 2**
Table: p.496

Whatley, Joe (Alabama)
Profile: p.8
Employment **Band 3**
Table: p.2

Wheat, David (Texas)
Profile: p.668,682
Tax **U**
Table: p.667

Wheat, James
(New Hampshire)
Profile: p.423
Litigation **Band 1**
Table: p.419

Wheaton, John (Minnesota)
Profile: p.377
Real Estate **Band**
Table: p.374
Real Estate **Band 1**
Table: p.374

Wheeler, Francis (Colorado)
Profile: p.86
Corporate/M&A **Band 2**
Table: p.75

Wheeler, Raymond
(California)
Profile: p.74
Employment **Band 4**
Table: p.40

Wheelwright, Neil (Vermont)
Profile: p.697
Real Estate **Band 3**
Table: p.696

Whistler, Philip A (Indiana)
Profile: p.285
Litigation **Band 1**
Table: p.280

Whitacre, Jack (Missouri)
Profile: p.393
Employment **Band 3**
Table: p.388

White, Benjamin T (Georgia)
Profile: p.211
Tax **Band 3**
Table: p.201

White, Jere (Alabama)
Profile: p.8
Litigation **Band 2**
Table: p.4

White, John (New York)
Profile: p.542
Capital Markets **Band 1**
Table: p.448

LEADING LAWYERS INDEX

White, Michael T. (Missouri)
Profile: p.393
Real Estate **Band 2**
Table: p.391

White, Robert J (California)
Profile: p.74
Insolvency **Band 2**
Table: p.44

White, W Christopher
(New York)
Profile: p.542
Real Estate **Band 4**
Table: p.493

White III, Fred B (New York)
Profile: p.542
Corporate/M&A **Band 5**
Table: p.460

Whittaker, Scott (Louisiana)
Profile: p.318
Corporate/M&A **Band 3**
Table: p.309

Whittemore, Anne Marie
(Virginia)
Profile: p.705
Litigation **Band 2**
Table: p.702

Whittemore, David (Nevada)
Profile: p.414
Real Estate **Band 3**
Table: p.411

Wiacek, Raymond
(District of Columbia)
Profile: p.131,148
Tax **Band 4**
Table: p.130

Wickwire, Jon (Virginia)
Profile: p.705
Construction **Band 3**
Table: p.698

Wiederrich, James
(South Dakota)
Profile: p.634
Corporate/M&A **Band 2**
Table: p.630

Wieman, Lawrence E
(New York)
Profile: p.542
Banking & Finance **Band 3**
Table: p.445

Wier Jr, Richard (Delaware)
Profile: p.101
Employment **Band 1**
Table: p.95

Wiggins, Robert (Alabama)
Profile: p.8
Employment **Band 2**
Table: p.2

Wight, Richard J (New York)
Profile: p.542
Banking & Finance **Band 4**
Table: p.445

Wikstrom, Francis M (Utah)
Profile: p.691
Litigation **Band 2**
Table: p.687

Wilbur, Brent A
(South Dakota)
Profile: p.634
Litigation **Band 3**
Table: p.632

Wilcox, Kirby (California)
Profile: p.74
Employment **Band 2**
Table: p.40

Wilde, Robert (Utah)
Profile: p.691
Employment **Band 2**
Table: p.686

Wildman, Bob (Indiana)
Profile: p.285
Corporate/M&A **Band 3**
Table: p.277

Wiley, Jay (Arizona)
Profile: p.22
Real Estate **Band 3**
Table: p.20

Wiley, Richard E
(District of Columbia)
Profile: p.148
Communications ✪
Table: p.107

Wilkinson, Cynthia (Alabama)
Profile: p.8
Employment **Band 4**
Table: p.2

Wilkinson, William (Ohio)
Profile: p.579
Litigation **Band 4**
Table: p.570

Willenzik, David S (Louisiana)
Profile: p.318
Banking & Finance **Band 1**
Table: p.307

Williams, Alaine
(Pennsylvania)
Profile: p.619
Employment **Band 3**
Table: p.601

Williams, Barry (Wyoming)
Profile: p.735
Real Estate **Band 1**
Table: p.734

Williams, David (Delaware)
Profile: p.101
Employment **Band 3**
Table: p.96

Williams, Douglas (Illinois)
Profile: p.276
Banking & Finance **Band 2**
Table: p.226

Williams, Gregory (Utah)
Profile: p.691
Real Estate **Band 3**
Table: p.689

Williams, Jim (North Carolina)
Profile: p.553
Litigation **Band 1**
Table: p.549

Williams, Lonnie (Arizona)
Profile: p.22
Employment **Band 2**
Table: p.18

Williams, William
(District of Columbia)
Profile: p.149
Energy **Band 3**
Table: p.115

Williams Jr, William J
(New York)
Profile: p.542
Capital Markets **Band 1**
Table: p.448

Williamson, Deborah (Texas)
Profile: p.682
Insolvency **Band 3**
Table: p.657

Williamson, Joel V (Illinois)
Profile: p.276
Tax **Band 1**
Table: p.252

Williamson, Robert (Georgia)
Profile: p.211
Insolvency **Band 4**
Table: p.193

Willig, Deborah (Pennsylvania)
Profile: p.619
Employment **Band 1**
Table: p.601

Willner, Keith
(District of Columbia)
Profile: p.149
Real Estate **Band 3**
Table: p.127

Willoughby, Barry (Delaware)
Profile: p.101
Employment **Band 2**
Table: p.96

Wilson, Michael (Florida)
Profile: p.179
Construction **Band 3**
Table: p.154

Wilson, Randall (Texas)
Profile: p.682
Litigation **Band 4**
Table: p.663

Wilson, Randon W. (Utah)
Profile: p.691
Corporate/M&A **Band 4**
Table: p.684

Wilson, Robert (Texas)
Profile: p.682
Real Estate **Band 2**
Table: p.665

Wilson, Stanford (Georgia)
Profile: p.211
Employment **Band 4**
Table: p.189

Wilson, Thomas (Nevada)
Profile: p.414
Litigation **Band 3**
Table: p.409

Winkler, Peter (Arizona)
Profile: p.22
Real Estate **Band 3**
Table: p.20

Winokur, Barton J
(Pennsylvania)
Profile: p.619
Corporate/M&A **Band 1**
Table: p.599

Winslow III, Edward
(North Carolina)
Profile: p.553
Corporate/M&A **Band 2**
Table: p.546

Wipperman, Robert
(New York)
Profile: p.542
Capital Markets **Band 2**
Table: p.453

Witherspoon, Carolyn B
(Arkansas)
Profile: p.27
Employment **Band 3**
Table: p.24

Witthoefft, Charles (Virginia)
Profile: p.705
Litigation **Band 2**
Table: p.702

Wittmann, Phillip A
(Louisiana)
Profile: p.318
Litigation **Band 1**
Table: p.313

Woelfling, Maxine
(Pennsylvania)
Profile: p.619
Environment **Band 3**
Table: p.604

Wogan, John D. (Louisiana)
Profile: p.318
Corporate/M&A **Band 4**
Table: p.309

Wojciechowski, Mark S
(New York)
Profile: p.542
Banking & Finance **Band 3**
Table: p.445

Wolf, Barry M (New York)
Profile: p.542
Private Equity **Band 2**
Table: p.489

Wolf, Jerome (Missouri)
Profile: p.393
Litigation **Band 3**
Table: p.389

Wolf, Larry (Maryland)
Profile: p.335
Employment **Band 2**
Table: p.329

Wolf, Wayne (New Mexico)
Profile: p.438
Litigation **Band 4**
Table: p.435

Wolfe, Gary (New York)
Profile: p.543
Shipping **Band 2**
Table: p.496

Wolfe, Richard (Louisiana)
Profile: p.318
Corporate/M&A **Band 3**
Table: p.309

Wolfe, Roger (West Virginia)
Profile: p.722
Employment **Band 1**
Table: p.717

Wolfe Jr, Donald (Delaware)
Profile: p.101
Litigation **Band 2**
Table: p.98

Wolff, Paul
(District of Columbia)
Profile: p.149
Litigation **Band 2**
Table: p.123

Wolfson, Mark (Florida)
Profile: p.179
Insolvency **Band 4**
Table: p.162

Wolitzer, Michael (New York)
Profile: p.543
Private Equity **Band 1**
Table: p.489

Wollman, Diana L (New York)
Profile: p.543
Tax **Band u**
Table: p.499

Woloson, Kenneth (Nevada)
Profile: p.414
Corporate/M&A **Band 2**
Table: p.406

Wolowitz, David
(New Hampshire)
Profile: p.423
Employment **Band 2**
Table: p.417

Wong, Linda (New Jersey)
Profile: p.432
Employment **Band 3**
Table: p.426

Wood, Lisa (Massachusetts)
Profile: p.359
Antitrust **Band 3**
Table: p.337

Wood, Robert (Tennessee)
Profile: p.642
Real Estate **Band 3**
Table: p.640

Woodward, Robert (Georgia)
Profile: p.211
Tax **Band 1**
Table: p.201

Woodworth, Stanley (Kansas)
Profile: p.299
Real Estate **Band 2**
Table: p.298

Woody, Charles (West Virginia)
Profile: p.722
Employment **Band 2**
Table: p.717

Wootton, Bob (Illinois)
Profile: p.276
Tax **Band 4**
Table: p.252

Word, Terry (New Mexico)
Profile: p.438
Litigation **Band 4**
Table: p.435

Worth, Diane (Kansas)
Profile: p.299
Employment **Band 4**
Table: p.296

Wortley, Michael (Texas)
Profile: p.683
Corporate/M&A **Band 1**
Table: p.649

Wovsaniker, Alan
(New Jersey)
Profile: p.432
Corporate/M&A **Band 2**
Table: p.425

Wren, Elizabeth
(North Carolina)
Profile: p.553
Corporate/M&A **Band 2**
Table: p.546

Wright, Doug (Colorado)
Profile: p.86
Corporate/M&A **Band 3**
Table: p.75

Wright, James (Maryland)
Profile: p.332,335
Real Estate **Band 3**
Table: p.331

Wright, Joyce (Arizona)
Profile: p.22
Real Estate **Band 3**
Table: p.20

Wright, Murray (Virginia)
Profile: p.705
Construction **Band 1**
Table: p.698

Wrobley, Ralph (Missouri)
Profile: p.393
Corporate/M&A **Band 1**
Table: p.386

Wulfe, Scott (Texas)
Profile: p.683
Corporate/M&A **Band 3**
Table: p.649

Wycoff, William
(Pennsylvania)
Profile: p.619
Litigation **Band 2**
Table: p.611

Wyld, Robert (Connecticut)
Profile: p.93
Litigation **Band 4**
Table: p.90

Wylie, Kenneth (Illinois)
Profile: p.276
Insurance **Band 3**
Table: p.242

Wyman Jr, Robert (California)
Profile: p.74
Environment **Band 1**
Table: p.43

Wymer, John (Georgia)
Profile: p.211
Employment **Band 1**
Table: p.189

Wyron, Richard
(District of Columbia)
Profile: p.149
Insolvency **Band 3**
Table: p.119

W

LEADING LAWYERS INDEX

Y

Yadley, Gregory (Florida)
Profile: p.179
Corporate/M&A Band 3
Table: p.156

Yance, Jim (Alabama)
Profile: p.8
Litigation Band 3
Table: p.4

Yannucci, Thomas D
(District of Columbia)
Profile: p.149
Litigation Band 1
Table: p.123
Media & Entertainment Band 1
Table: p.125

Yastrow, Joseph (Illinois)
Profile: p.276
Employment Band 3
Table: p.236

Yates, Jack (Missouri)
Profile: p.393
Employment Band 4
Table: p.388

Yde, Paul (District of Columbia)
Profile: p.149
Antitrust Band 5
Table: p.103

Yeager, Jay (Indiana)
Profile: p.285
Litigation Band 1
Table: p.280

Yeager, Robert (Pennsylvania)
Profile: p.619
Intellectual Property Band 2
Table: p.609

Yeates, Marie (Texas)
Profile: p.683
Litigation Band 4
Table: p.663

Yerkes, Kenneth J (Indiana)
Profile: p.285
Employment Band 2
Table: p.279

Yoder, Lowell (Illinois)
Profile: p.276
Tax Band 2
Table: p.252

Yoken, Stephen (Nevada)
Profile: p.414
Real Estate Band 4
Table: p.411

York, Larry (Texas)
Profile: p.683
Insurance Band 2
Table: p.659

Young, Cynthia (Kentucky)
Profile: p.306
Corporate/M&A Band 2
Table: p.300

Young, David (Ohio)
Profile: p.579
Litigation Band 2
Table: p.570

Young, Doug (California)
Profile: p.74
Litigation Band 3
Table: p.50

Young, Jeffrey (Maine)
Profile: p.326
Employment Band 2
Table: p.320

Young, Jeffrey (Georgia)
Profile: p.211
Intellectual Property Band 5
Table: p.195

Young, William (Texas)
Profile: p.683
Banking & Finance Band 3
Table: p.645

Young Jr, Rutledge
(South Carolina)
Profile: p.629
Litigation Band 2
Table: p.626

Younger, Carter (Virginia)
Profile: p.705
Employment Band 3
Table: p.701

Youngwood, Alfred D
(New York)
Profile: p.543
Tax Band 2
Table: p.499

Yund, George (Ohio)
Profile: p.579
Employment Band 4
Table: p.565

Yungblut, Stephen (Texas)
Profile: p.683
Construction Band 3
Table: p.648

Z

Zabel, Sheldon (Illinois)
Profile: p.276
Environment Band 1
Table: p.239

Zadick, Gary M (Montana)
Profile: p.399
Employment Band 1
Table: p.395

Zahler, Robert
(District of Columbia)
Profile: p.149
Communications Band 3
Table: p.107

Zaiger, Mark L (Iowa)
Profile: p.293
Employment Band 2
Table: p.288

Zakarian, Albert (Connecticut)
Profile: p.93
Employment Band 1
Table: p.89

Zandy, John C (Connecticut)
Profile: p.93
Employment Band 4
Table: p.89

Zarov, Herbert (Illinois)
Profile: p.276
Litigation Band 5
Table: p.245

Zeglovitch, Robert
(Minnesota)
Profile: p.377
Employment Band 2
Table: p.371

Zeiger, John (Ohio)
Profile: p.579
Litigation Band 2
Table: p.570

Zeilinger, John S (Nebraska)
Profile: p.405
Corporate/M&A Band 2
Table: p.400

Zelek, Eugene (Illinois)
Profile: p.276
Media & Entertainment Band 3
Table: p.247

Zetlin, Michael (New York)
Profile: p.543
Construction Band 3
Table: p.458

Ziffren, Kenneth (California)
Profile: p.74
Media & Entertainment Band 1
Table: p.53

Zilavy, Thomas (Wisconsin)
Profile: p.729
Corporate/M&A Band 2
Table: p.723

Zimbler, Jay (Illinois)
Profile: p.276
Tax Band 2
Table: p.252

Zimpritch, James B (Maine)
Profile: p.326
Corporate/M&A Band 1
Table: p.319

Zinober, Peter (Florida)
Profile: p.179
Employment Band 1
Table: p.158

Zirinsky, Bruce (New York)
Profile: p.543
Insolvency Band 3
Table: p.472

Zischke, Michael H
(California)
Profile: p.74
Environment Band 4
Table: p.41

Zonn, Sidney (Pennsylvania)
Profile: p.619
Employment Band 3
Table: p.602

Zovickian, Stephen
(California)
Profile: p.74
Construction Band 4
Table: p.36

Zuchlewski, Pearl (New York)
Profile: p.543
Employment Band 2
Table: p.466

Zucker, Carol (Nevada)
Profile: p.414
Employment Band 2
Table: p.408

Zucker, Jeffrey (Nevada)
Profile: p.414
Corporate/M&A Band 1
Table: p.406
Real Estate Band 1
Table: p.411

Zumbach, Steven E (Iowa)
Profile: p.293
Corporate/M&A Band 1
Table: p.286

Zussman, Richard A
(Michigan)
Profile: p.367
Real Estate Band 3
Table: p.365

Zweifach, Gerson
(District of Columbia)
Profile: p.149
Media & Entertainment Band 1
Table: p.125

WITHDRAWN